DIRECTORY
OF
AMERICAN
SCHOLARS

DIRECTORY OF AMERICAN SCHOLARS

NINTH EDITION

VOLUME **II**

ENGLISH, SPEECH, & DRAMA

Rita C. Velázquez, Editor

The Gale Group

DETROIT • SAN FRANCISCO • LONDON • BOSTON • WOODBRIDGE, CT

Rita C. Velázquez, Editor

Project Associates and Contributing Editors: Michelle
Eads, Amanda Quick

Contributing Staff: Mary Alampi, Caryn Anders, Katy Balcer, Anja
Barnard, Donna Batten, Donna Craft, Andrea DeJong, Sarah DeMar, Sheila Dow, Kim
Forster, William Harmer, Kelly Hill, LySandra Hill, Sonya Hill, Crystal Holombo, Theresa
MacFarlane, Christine Maurer, Matthew Miskelly, Jacqueline Mueckenheim, Erin Nagel,
Lynn Pearce, Terry Peck, Maureen Puhl, Donna Wood.

Contributors: Chapter House, IMPS; The Electronic
Scriptorium, Ltd.

Managing Editor: Keith Jones

Manager, Technical Support Services: Theresa Rocklin
Programmer/Analyst: Jim Edwards

Manufacturing Manager: Dorothy Maki
Senior Buyer: Wendy Blurton

Product Design Manager: Cindy Baldwin
Art Director: Eric Johnson
Graphic Artist: Gary Leach

CONTENTS

PREFACE

First published in 1942 under the auspices of the American Council of Learned Societies, The Directory of American Scholars remains the foremost biographical reference to American humanities scholars. With the ninth edition, The Gale Group is continuing the tradition.

The directory is arranged for convenient use in four subject volumes: Volume I: History; Volume II: English, Speech, and Drama; Volume III: Foreign Languages, Linguistics, and Philology; Volume IV: Philosophy, Religion, and Law. Each volume of biographical listings contains a geographic index. Volume V contains an alphabetical index, a discipline index, an institutional index and a cumulative geographic index of scholars listed in the first four volumes.

The ninth edition of the Directory of American Scholars profiles more than 24,000 United States and Canadian scholars currently active in teaching, research, and publishing. The names of entrants were obtained from a variety of sources, including former entrants, academic deans, or citations in professional journals. In most cases, nominees received a questionnaire to complete, and selection for inclusion was made based on the following criteria:

1. Achievement, by reason of experience and training, of a stature in scholarly work equivalent to that associated with the doctoral degree, coupled with current activity in such work;

or

2. Achievement as evidenced by publication of scholarly works;

or

3. Attainment of a position of substantial responsibility by reason of achievement as outlined in (1) and (2).

Enhancements to the ninth edition include an index volume, simplifying the search for a particular scholar or a particular group of scholars. Indexing by discipline is sorted by primary and secondary majors, in some cases including majors that are not traditionally considered as humanities. Those individuals involved in several fields are cross-referenced into appropriate volumes.

The ninth edition of The Directory of American Scholars is produced by fully automated methods. Limitations in the printing method have made it necessary to omit most diacritics.

Individual entries can include place and year of birth, *primary discipline(s), vital statistics, education, honorary degrees, past and present professional experience, concurrent positions, *membership in international, national and regional societies, honors and awards, *research interest, *publications, and mailing address. Elements preceded by an asterisk are limited as to the number of items included. If an entrant exceeded these limitations, the editors selected the most recent information. Biographies received in the offices of The Gale Group after the editorial deadline were included in an abbreviated manner.

The editors have made every effort to include material as accurately and completely as possible within the confines of format and scope. However, the publishers do not assume and hereby disclaim any liability to any party for any loss or damage caused by errors or omissions in the Directory of American Scholars, whether such errors or omissions result from negligence, accident, or any other cause.

Thanks are expressed to those who contributed information and submitted nominations for the new edition. Many societies provided membership lists for the research process and published announcements in their journals or newsletters, and their help is appreciated.

Comments and suggestions regarding any aspect of the ninth edition are invited and should be addressed to The Editors, Directory of American Scholars, The Gale Group, 27500 Drake Road, Farmington Hills, MI 48333-3535.

ADVISORS

David M. Fahey
Professor of History
Miami University
Miami, Ohio

Patricia Hardesty
Humanities Reference/Liaison Libraran
George Mason University
Fairfax, Virginia

Stephen Karetzky
Library Director, Associate Professor
Felician College
Lodi, New Jersey

ABBREVIATIONS

AAAS American Association for the Advancement of Science
AAUP American Association of University Professors
abnorm abnormal
acad academia, academic, academica, academie, academique, academy
accad accademia
acct account, accountant, accounting
acoust acoustical, accounstic(s)
adj adjunct, adjutant
actg acting
activ activities, activity
addn addition(s), additional
AID Agency for International Development
adjust adjust
admin administration, administrative
adminr administrator(s)
admis admissions
adv advisor(s), advisory
advan advance(d), advancement
advert advertisement, advertising
aerodyn aerodynamic(s)
aeronaut aeronautic(s), aeronautical
aesthet aesthetics
affil affiliate(s), affiliation
agr agricultural, agriculture
agt agent
AFB Air Force Base
AHA American Historical Association
akad akademi, akademia
Ala Alabama
Algem algemeen, algemen
allergol allergological, allergology
allgem allgemein, allgemeine, allgemeinen
Alta Alberta
Am America, Americain, American, Americana, Americano, Amerika, Amerikaansch, Amerikaner, Amerikanisch, Amerikansk
anal analysis, analytic, analytical
analog analogue
anat anatomic, anatomical, anatomy
ann annal(s)
anthrop anthropological, anthropology
anthropom anthropometric, anthropometrical, anthropometry
antiq antiquaire(s), antiquarian, antiquary(ies), antiquities
app appoint, appointed, appointment
appl applied
appln application
approx approximate, approximately
Apr April
apt apartment(s)

arbit arbitration
arch archiv, archiva, archive(s), archivio, archivo
archaeol archaeological, archaeology
archaol archaologie, archaologisch
archeol archeological, archeologie, archeologique, archeology
archit architectural, architecture
Arg Argentina, Argentine
Ariz Arizona
Ark Arkansas
asn association
asoc asociacion
assoc(s) associate(s), associated
asst assistant
Assyriol Assyriology
astrodyn astrodynamics
astron astronomical, astronomy
astronaut astronautical, astronautics
astronr astronomer
attend attendant, attending
atty attorney
audiol audiology
Aug August
auth author(s)
AV audiovisual
ave avenue

b born
BC British Columbia
bd board
behav behavior, behavioral, behaviour, behavioural
Bibl Biblical, Biblique
bibliog bibliografia, bibliographic, bibligraphical, bibliography(ies)
bibliogr bibliographer
bibliot biblioteca, bibliotec, bibliotek, bibliotheca,
bibliothek, bibliothequeca
biog biographical, biography
biol biological, biology
bk(s) books
bldg building
blvd boulevard
bol boletim, boletin
boll bollettino
bor borough
bot botanical, botany
br branch
Brit Britain, British
Bro(s) Brother(s)
bull bulletin
bur bureau

bus business
BWI British West Indies

c children
Calif California
Can Canada, Canadian, Canadien, Canadienne
cand candidate
cartog cartografic, cartographical, cartography
cartogra cartographer
Cath Catholic, Catholique
CBS Columbia Broadcasting System
cent central
Cent Am Central America
cert certificat, certificate, certified
chap chapter
chem chermical, chemistry
chg charge
chemn chairman
Cie Compagnie
cient cientifica, cientifico
class classical
clin(s) clinic(s)
Co Companies, Company, County
coauth coauth
co-dir co-director
co-ed co-editor
co-educ co-educational
col(s) colegio, college(s), collegiate
collab collaboration, collaborative, collaborating, collaborator
Colo Colorado
Comdr Commander
com commerce, commercial
commun communication(s)
comn(s) commission(s)
comnr commissioner
comp comparative, comparee
compos composition(s)
comput computer, computing
comt committee
conf conference
cong congress
Conn Connecticut
conserv conservacion, conservation, conservatoire, conservatory
consol consolidated, consolidation
const constitution, constitutional
construct construction
consult consultant, consulting
contemp contemporary
contrib contribute, contribution
contribur contributor

conv convention
coop cooperation, cooperative
coord coordinating, coordination
coordr coordinator
corresp corresponding
Corp Corporation
coun council, counsel, counseling
counr councillor, counselor
criminol criminology
Ct Court
ctr center
cult cultra, cultural, culturale, culture
cur curator
curric curriculum
cybernet cybernetics
CZ Canal Zone
Czeck Czechoslovakia

DC District of Columbia
Dec December
Del Delaware
deleg delegate, delegations
demog demographic, demography
demonstr demonstrator
dent dental, dentistry
dep deputy
dept department
Deut Deutsch, Deutschland
develop development
diag diagnosis, diagnostic
dialectol dialectology
dig digest
dipl diploma, diploma, diplomate, diplome
dir director(s), directory
    directory
Diss Abstr Dissertation Abstracts
dist district
distrib distributive
distribr distributors
div division, divorced
doc document, documentation
Dom Dominion
Dr Doctor, Drive
Drs Doctroandus

e east
ecol ecological, ecology
econ economic(s), economical, economy
ed edicion, edition, editor, editorial, edizione
educ education, educational
educr educator(s)
Egyptol Egyptology
elec electric, electrical, electricity
    electrical
elem elementary
emer emeriti, emeritus
encour encouragement
encycl encyclopedia
employ employment
Eng England
environ environment, environmental
EPDA Education Professions Development
Act
equip equipment
ERIC Educational Resources Information
Center
ESEA Elementary & Secondary Education
Act
espec especially
estab established, establishment
estud estudante, estudas, estudianet,
estudio(s), estudo(s)
ethnog ethnographical, ethnography
ethnol ethnological, ethnology
Europ European
eval evaluation
evangel evangelical
eve evening
exam examination
examr examiner

except exceptional
exec executive(s)
exeg exegesis(es), exegetic, exegetical,
exegetics
exhib exhibition(s)
exp experiment, experimental, experimentation
exped expedition(s)
explor exploration(s)
expos exposition
exten extension

fac faculties, faculty
facil facilities, facility
Feb February
fed federal
fedn federation
fel(s) fellow(s), fellowship(s)
filol filologia, filologico
filos filosofia, filosofico
Fla Florida
FLES Foreign Languages in the Elementary
Schools
for foreign
forsch forschung, forschungen
found foundation
Fr Francais(s), French
Ft Fort

Ga Georgia
gen general, generale
geneal genealogical, genealogy
genoot genootschap
geod geodesy, geodetic
geog geografia, geografico, geographer(s),
geographic,
geographie, geographical, geography
geogr geographer
geol geologic, geological, geology
geophys geophysical
Ger German, Germanic, Germanisch,
Germany
Ges gesellschaft
gov governing, governors
govt government
grad graduate
Gr Brit Great Britain
guid guidance
gym gymnasium

handbk(s) handbooks
Hawaii
Hisp Hispanic, Hispanico, Hispano
hist historie, historia, historial, historic,
historica,
historical, historique, historische, history
histol histology, histological
Hoshsch Hoshschule
hon honorable, honorary
hosp(s) hospital(s)
hq headquarters
HumRRO Human Resources Research
Office
hwy highway

Ill Illinois
illum illuminating, illumination
illus illustrate, illustration
illusr illustrator
imp imperial
improv improvement
Inc Incorporated
incl include, included, includes, including
Ind Indiana
indust(s) industrial, industry(ies)
infor information
inst institut, instritute(s), institution(s),
instituto
instnl institutional, institutionalized
instr instruction, instructor(s)

instruct instructional
int internacional, international,
internazionale
intel intelligence
introd introduction
invest investigacion, investiganda,
investigation,
investigative
investr investigator
ist istituto
Ital Italia, Italian, Italiana, Italiano, Italica,
Italien,
Italienisch, Italienne, Italy

J Journal
Jan January
jour journal, journalism
jr junior
jurisp jurisprudence
juv juvenile(s)

Kans Kansas
Koninki koninklijk
Ky Kentucky

La Louisiana
lab laboratorie, laboratorio, laboratorium,
laboratory(ies)
lang language(s)
lect lecture(s)
lectr lecturer
legis legislacion, legislatief, legislation,
legislative,
legislativo, legislature, legislazione
lett letter(s), lettera, letteraria, letterature,
lettere
lib liberal
libr libary(ies), librerio
librn librarian(s)
lic license, lecencia
ling linguistic(s), linguistica, linguistique
lit liteary, literatur, literatura, literature,
littera,
literature
Ltd Limited

m married
mach machine(s), machinery
mag magazine
Man Manitoba
Mar March
Mariol Mariological, Mariology
Mass Massachusetts
mat matematica, matematiche, matematico,
matematik
math mathematics, mathematical, mathematics, mathematik,
mathematique(s), mathematisch
Md Maryland
mech mechanical
med medical, medicine
Mediter Mediterranean
mem member, memoirs, memorial
ment mental, mentally
metrop metropolitan
Mex Mexican, Mexicano, Mexico
mfg manufacturing
mfr manufacture, manufacturer
mgr manager(s)
mgt management
Mich Michigan
mid middle
mil military
Minn Minnesota
Miss Mississippi
mitt mitteilung
mkt market, marketing
MLA Modern Language Association of
America
Mo Missouri

mod modern,moderna, moderne, moderno
monatsh monatsheft(e)
monatsschr monatsschrift
monogr monograph
Mont Montana
morphol morphologica, morphologie, morphology
mt mount, mountain(s)
munic municipal
mus museum(s)
musicol musicological, musicology

n north
nac nacional
NASA National Aeronautics & Space Administration
nat nationaal, national, nationale, nationalis, naturalized
NATO North Atlantic Treaty Organization
naz nazionale
NB New Brunswick
NC North Carolina
MCTE National Council of Teachers of English
NDak North Dakota
NDEA National Defense Education Act
NEA National Education Association
Nebr Nebraska
Ned Nederland, Nederlandsch
Nev Nevada
Neth Netherlands
Nfld Newfoundland
NH New Hampshire
NJ New Jersey
NMex New Mexico
no number
nonres nonresident
norm normal, normale
Norweg Norwegian
Nov November
NS Nova Scotia
NSW New South Wales
NT Northwest Territories
numis numismatic, numismatico, numismatique
NY New York
NZ New Zealand

occas occasional
occup occupation, occupational
Oct October
Ohio
OEEC Organization for European Economic Cooperation
off office, officer(s), official(s)
Okla Oklahoma
Ont Ontario
oper operation(s), operational, operative
ord ordnance
Ore Oregon
orgn organization, organizational
orient oriental, orientale, orientalist, orientalia
ornithol ornithological, ornithology

Pa Pennsylvania
Pac Pacific
paleontol paleontological, paleontology
PanAm Pan American
pedag pedagogia, pedagogic, pedagogical, pedagogico, pedagogoie, pedagogik, pedagogique, pedagogy
Pei Prince Edward Island
penol penological, penology
phenomenol phenomenological, phenomenologie, phenomenology
philol philologica, philological, philologie, philologisch, philology

philos philosophia, philosophic, philosophical, philosophie, philosophique, philosophisch, philosophical, philosohpy, philosozophia
photog photographic, photography
photogr photographer(s)
phys physical
pkwy parkway
pl place
polit politica, political, politicas, politico, politics, politek, politike, politique, politsch, politisk
polytech polytechnic
pop population
Pontif Pontifical
Port Portugal, Portuguese
postgrad postgraduate
PR Puerto Rico
pract practice
prehist prehistoric
prep preparation, preparatory
pres president
Presby Presbyterian
preserv preservation
prev prevention, preventive
prin principal(s)
prob problem(s)
probtn probation
proc proceding
prod production
prof professional, professor, professorial
prog program(s), programmed, programming
proj project, projective
prom promotion
prov province, provincial
psychiat psychiatria, psychiatric, psychiatrica, psychiatrie, psychiatrique, psychiatrisch, psychiatry
psychol psychological
pt point
pub pub, publique
publ publication(s), published, publisher(s), publishing
pvt private

qm quartermaster
quad quaderni
qual qualitative, quality
quart quarterly
Que Quebec

rd road
RD Rural Delivery, Rural Free Delivery Rural Free Delivery
rec record(s), recording
rech recherche
redevelop redevelopment
ref reference
regist register, registered, registration
registr registrar
rehabil rehabilitation
rel(s) relacion, relation(s), relative, relazione
relig religion, religious
rep representative
repub republic
req requirement(s)
res research, reserve
rev review, revised, revista, revue
rhet rhetoric, rhetorical
RI Rhode Island
Rt Right
Rte Route
Russ Russian
rwy railway

s south
SAfrica South Africa
SAm South America, South American

Sask Saskatchewan
SC South Carolina
Scand Scandinavian
sch(s) school(s)
scholar scholarship
sci science(s), scientia, scientific, scientifico, scientifique, scienza
SDak South Dakota
SEATO Southeast Asia Treaty Organization
sec secondary
sect section
secy secretary
sem seminaire, seminar, seminario, seminary
sen senator, sneatorial
Sept September
ser serial, series
serv service(s)
soc social, sociedad, sociedade, societa, societas, societate, societe, societet, society(ies)
soc sci social science(s)
sociol sociological, sociology
Span Spanish
spec special
sq square
sr senior
sister
St Saint, Street
sta station
statist statistical, statistics
Ste Sainte, Suite
struct structural, structure(s)
subcomt subcommittee
subj subject
substa substa
super superieur, superior, superiore
suppl supplement, supplementary
supt superintendent
supv supervising, supervision
supvr supervisor
supvry supervisory
surg surgical, surgery
surv survey
Swed Swedish
Switz Switzerland
symp symposium
syst system, systematic

tech technic(s), technica, technical, technicky, techniczny, techniek, technik, technika, technikum, technique, technisch
technol technologic, technological, technologicke, technologico, technologiczny, technologie, technologika, technologique, technologisch, technology
tecnol technologia, technologica, technologico
tel telegraph(s), telephone
temp temporary
Tenn Tennessee
Terr Terrace
teol teologia, teologico
Tex Texas
textbk textbook(s)
theol theological, theologie, theologique, theologisch, theology
theoret theoretic(al)
ther therapy
trans transactions
transp transportation
transl translation, translator(s)
treas treasurer, treasury
trop tropical
TV television
twp township

u und
UAR United Arab Republic
UK United Kingdom
UN United Nations
unemploy unemployment
UNESCO United Nations Educational, Scientific & Cultural Organization
UNICEF United Nations Children's Fund
univ(s) universidad, universite, university(ies)
UNRRA United Nations Relief & Rehabilitation Administration
UNRWA United Nations Relief & Works Agency
USA United States of America
US United States
USPHS United States Public Health Service
USSR Union of Soviet Socialist Republics
Utah

Va Virginia
var various
veg vegetable(s), vegetation
ver vereeniging, verein, vereingt, vereinigung
vet veteran, veterinarian, veterinary
VI Virgin Islands
vis visiting
voc vocational
vocab vocabulary
vol(s) volume(s), voluntary, volunteer(s)
vchmn vice chairman
vpres vice president
Vt Vermont

w west
Wash Washington
wetensch wetenschappelijk, wetenschappen
WHO World Health Organization
WI West Indies
wid widow, widowed, widower
Wis Wisconsin
wiss wissenschaft(en), wissenschaftliche(e)
WVa West Virginia
Wyo Wyoming

yearbk yearbook(s)
YMCA Young Men's Christian Association
YMHA Young Men's Hebrew Association
YWCA Young Women's Christian Association
YWHA Young Women's Hebrew Association

z zeitschrift

Biographies

A

AARSLEFF, HANS
PERSONAL Born 07/19/1925, Denmark **DISCIPLINE** ENGLISH **EDUCATION** Univ Copenhagen, BA, 45; Univ Minn, MA, 54, PhD, 60. **CAREER** From instr to assoc prof English, 56-72; prof, English, Princeton Univ, 72-98. **HONORS AND AWARDS** Jr fel coun humanities, Princeton Univ, 62; Am Coun Learned Soc fel, 64-65, 72-73; NEH fel, 75-76; fel Am Acad of Arts and Sci, 94; Howard T. Behrman Awd for Distinguished Achievement in the Hum, Princeton Univ, 94. **MEMBERSHIPS** Am Philos Soc; Royal Danish Acad of Sci and Lett; bd of eds, 79- , Bd of Dir, 81, J of the Hist of Ideas; Adv Bd, 88- , Hist of the Human Sci. **RESEARCH** History of doctrines about the nature and study of language and of the philosophy of language since the Renaissance; Locke; Leibniz; Condillac; Diderot; Herder; Breal. **SELECTED PUBLICATIONS** Auth, Descartes and Augustine on Genesis, Language and the Angels, in Leibniz and Adam, 93; auth, Locke's Influence, in Cambridge Companion to Locke, 94; auth, Language and Thought in the 17th and 18th Centuries, in Chicago Ling Soc, 96; auth, Herder's Cartesian Ursprung vs Condillac's Expressivist Essai, Philosophies and the Language Sciences: a Historical Perspective in honour of Lia Formigari, 96. **CONTACT ADDRESS** Dept of English, Princeton Univ, Princeton, NJ, 08544.

ABBOTT, ANTHONY S.
PERSONAL Born 01/07/1935, San Francisco, CA, m, 1960, 3 children **DISCIPLINE** ENGLISH **EDUCATION** Princeton Univ, AB, 57; Harvard Univ, PhD(English), 61. **CAREER** Instr English, Bates Col, 61-64; asst prof, 64-67, assoc prof, 67-80, PROF ENGLISH, DAVIDSON COL, 80- **MEMBERSHIPS** MLA; Soc Relig Higher Educ. **RESEARCH** Modern drama; history of English drama; American literature. **SELECTED PUBLICATIONS** Auth, Shaw and Christianity, Seabury, 56. **CONTACT ADDRESS** Dept of English, Davidson Col, Po Box 1719, Davidson, NC, 28036-1719.

ABBOTT, CRAIG STEPHENS
PERSONAL Born 11/23/1941, Washington, DC **DISCIPLINE** AMERICAN LITERATURE **EDUCATION** Tex A&M Univ, BA, 64, MA, 66; Univ Tex, Austin, PhD(English), 73. **CAREER** Asst prof, 73-78, assoc prof English, Northern Ill Univ, 78-85, prof, 85-, Assoc ed, Anal & Enumerative Bibliog, 77-98. **MEMBERSHIPS** Bibliog Soc Am; MLA; Soc Textual Scholar. **RESEARCH** Modern poetry; bibliography. **SELECTED PUBLICATIONS** Auth, Marianne Moore: A Descriptive Bibliography, Univ Pittsburgh, 77; Marianne Moore: A Reference Guide, G K Hall, 78, John Crowe Ransom, Whitston, 98; Co-auth, An Introduction to Bibliographical and Textual Studies, MLA, 85, 89, 98. **CONTACT ADDRESS** Dept of English, No Illinois Univ, 1425 W Lincoln Hwy, De Kalb, IL, 60115-2825. **EMAIL** cabbott@niu.edu

ABBOTT, H. PORTER
DISCIPLINE ENGLISH LITERATURE **EDUCATION** Univ Toronto, PhD, 66 **CAREER** PROF, UNIV CALIF, SANTA BARBARA. **SELECTED PUBLICATIONS** Auth, The Fiction of Samuel Beckett: Form and Effect, Univ California Press, 73; Diary Fiction: Writing as Action, Cornell Univ Press, 84; "Writing and Conversion: Conrad's Modernism Autobiography," Yale Jour of Criticism, 92; "Beginning Again: The Post-Narrative Art of Texts for Nothing and How It Is," The Cambridge Companion to Beckett, Cambridge, 93; "Character and Modernism: Reading Woolf Writing Woolf," New Lit Hist, 93; Beckett Writing Beckett: The Author in the Autograph, Cornell Univ Press, 96. **CONTACT ADDRESS** Dept of Eng, Univ Calif, Santa Barbara, CA, 93106-7150. **EMAIL** pabbott@humanitas.ucsb.edu

ABEL, RICHARD OWEN
PERSONAL Born 08/20/1941, Canton, OH, m, 1970 **DISCIPLINE** CINEMA STUDIES, COMPARATIVE LITERATURE **EDUCATION** Utah State Univ, BA, 63; Univ Southern Calif, MA, 65, PhD(comp lit), 70. **CAREER** Teaching asst comp lit, Univ Southern Calif, 65, teaching asst English, 65-66 & 66-67; instr English, 67-68; from instr to assoc prof, 68-80, prof English, Drake Univ, 80-, dir Cult Studies Prog, 90-93, dir Ctr for the Humanities, 96-99. **HONORS AND AWARDS** Theatre Library Asn Award for best book on recorded performance: for French Cinema: The First Wave, 1915-1929, 85; Jay Leyda Prize in Cinema Studies: for French Film Theory and Criticism, 89; Theatre Library Asn Award for best book on recorded performance: for The Cin Goes to Town: French Cinema, 1896-1914, 95; SCS Katherine Singer Kovacs Award for best essay in cinema studies, 1995-1997: for Path Goes to Town: French Films Create a Market for the Nickelodeon, 98; NEH Fel for Col Teachers, 83-83; ACLS Res Fel, 86; Nat Humanities Ctr Fel, 88-89; John Simon Guggenheim Memorial Fel, 93-93. **MEMBERSHIPS** MLA; Midwest MLA; Am Film Inst; Soc Cinema Studies. **RESEARCH** Developments in European poetry, 1900-1930; relationship between film and art, 1900-1930; recent theory and criticism of narrative film and prose fiction. **SELECTED PUBLICATIONS** Auth, French Cinema: The First Wave, 1915-1929, Princeton, 84; French Film Theory and Criticism, 1907-1939: A History/Anthology, 2 vols, Princeton, 88; The Cin Goes to Town: French Cinema, 1896-1914, Calif, 94; ed, Silent Film, In: Depth of Field, series, Rutgers, 96; author of numerous articles for journals and other collections. **CONTACT ADDRESS** Dept of English, Drake Univ, 2507 University Ave, Des Moines, IA, 50311-4505. **EMAIL** richard.abel@drake.edu

ABEL TRAVIS, MOLLY
DISCIPLINE TWENTIETH-CENTURY BRITISH AND AMERICAN LITERATURE **EDUCATION** Lamar Univ, BA, 72; Stephen F Austin State Univ, MA, 75; OH State Univ, PhD, 89. **CAREER** Instr, 89, Tulane Univ. **SELECTED PUBLICATIONS** Auth, Beloved and Middle Passage: Race, Narrative, and the Critic's Essentialism, Narrative 2.3, 94. **CONTACT ADDRESS** Dept of Eng, Tulane Univ, 6823 St Charles Ave, New Orleans, LA, 70118. **EMAIL** matravis@mailhost.tcs.tulane.edu

ABELMAN, ROBERT
DISCIPLINE BROADCASTING, MEDIA CRITICISM, PUBLIC RELATIONS **EDUCATION** MI State Univ, MA; Univ TX, PhD. **CAREER** Comm, Cleveland St Univ. **SELECTED PUBLICATIONS** Auth, Reclaiming the Wasteland: TV & Gifted Children, Hampton Press, 95; co-auth, Television and the Exceptional Child: A Forgotten Audience, Lawrence Erlbaum & Assoc, 92; Religious Television: Controversies and Conclusions, Ablex, 90. **CONTACT ADDRESS** Dept of Commun, Cleveland State Univ, 83 E 24th St, Cleveland, OH, 44115. **EMAIL** r.abelman@csuohio.edu

ABERNETHY, CECIL EMORY
PERSONAL Born 04/08/1908, Charleston, SC, m, 1940, 1 child **DISCIPLINE** ENGLISH **EDUCATION** Birmingham-Southern Col, AB, 30; Univ NC, Chapel Hill, AM, 35; Vanderbilt Univ, PhD, 40. **CAREER** Instr English, high sch, Ala, 31-35; teaching fel, Vanderbilt Univ, 35-37; instr English, Univ Ala, 37-38; from instr to prof, 39-76, emer prof English, Birmingham-Southern Col, 76-. **MEMBERSHIPS** English Asn Gt Brit; Renaissance Soc Am; AAUP. **CONTACT ADDRESS** Dept English, Sonoma State Univ, 1801 E Cotati Ave, Rohnert Park, CA, 94928-3609.

ABERNETHY, FRANCIS EDWARD
PERSONAL Born 12/03/1925, Altus, OK, m, 1948, 5 children **DISCIPLINE** ENGLISH **EDUCATION** Stephen F Austin State Col, BA, 49; La State Univ, MA, 51, PhD, 56. **CAREER** From asst prof to assoc prof English, Lamar State Col Tech, 56-65; PROF ENGLISH, STEPHEN F AUSTIN STATE UNIV, 65-, Lamar State Col Tech res grant, 59-63; resident grants res folklore, 59-68. **MEMBERSHIPS** Am Folklore Soc; SCent Renaissance Conf; SCent Mod Lang Asn; Asn Mex Cave Studies. **RESEARCH** Folklore; Renaissance drama; east Texas history. **SELECTED PUBLICATIONS** Auth, Social Protest Literature, 1485-1558, La State Univ, 62; Tales From the Big Thicket, Univ Tex, 66; J Frank Dobie, Steck-Vaughn Co, 67; The East Texas Communal Hunt, Publ Tex Folklore Soc, 71; ed & contribr, Observations and Reflections, Encino, 72; They Called It The War Effort, Oral Histories From WWII, Orange Tx, SW Hist Quart, Vol 0097, 94; State Lines, SW Hist Quart, Vol 0098, 94. **CONTACT ADDRESS** Dept of English, Stephen F Austin State Univ, Nacogdoches, TX, 75962.

ABINADER, ELMAZ
DISCIPLINE CREATIVE WRITING **EDUCATION** Univ Pittsburgh, BA, 74; Columbia Univ, MFA, 78; Univ Nebr, PhD, 85. **CAREER** Assoc prof; Mills Col, 93-. **RESEARCH** Creative writing; fiction and non-fiction. **SELECTED PUBLICATIONS** Auth, The Children of the Roojme, A Family's Journey from Lebanon, Madison, WI: Univ Wis Press, 97; The Children of the Roojme, A Family's Journey, NY: W.W. Norton & Co, 91; Looking for Our Lives, A Writer's Perspective on American Literature, Al Majal, 94; Beyond the Veil and Yemen can Wait, Metro, 93; Here, I'm an Arab; There, an American. The New York Times, 91; poetry, Anthologies: Reflections on a Gift of Watermelon Pickle, Eds Dunning and Lueders, NY: Scott Foresman, 94; Grape Leaves: A Century of Arab American Poetry, Salt Lake City: Univ Utah Press, 88; All My Grandmothers Could Sing, Lincoln, Nebr: Free Rein Press, 84; mag, Footworks: Paterson Lit Rev, Living with Opposition, Arabic Mus, Letters from Home, 94. **CONTACT ADDRESS** Dept of English, Mills Col, 5000 MacArthur Blvd, Oakland, CA, 94613-1301. **EMAIL** moses@mills.edu

ABRAHAM, JULIE L.
DISCIPLINE ENGLISH LANGUAGE AND LITERATURE **EDUCATION** Columbia Univ, PhD, 89. **CAREER** Assoc prof Eng/Women's Studies. **RESEARCH** Modern British literature; women's literature; feminist literary theory. **SELECTED PUBLICATIONS** Auth, Are Girls Necessary?: Lesbian Writing and Modern Histories. **CONTACT ADDRESS** English Dept, Emory Univ, 1380 Oxford Rd NE, Atlanta, GA, 30322-1950.

ABRAMS, MEYER HOWARD
PERSONAL Born 07/23/1912, Long Branch, NJ, m, 1937, 2 children **DISCIPLINE** ENGLISH LITERATURE **EDUCATION** Harvard Univ, AB, 34, AM, 37, PhD, 40. **CAREER** Instr, Harvard Univ, 38-42, res assoc, 42-45; from asst prof to prof English, 45-61, Whiton Prof, 61-73, Class of 1916 Prof, 73-83, prof emeritus, 83-, Cornell Univ; Rockefeller Found fel, 46-47; Ford Found fel, 53; Fulbright scholar, Royal Univ Malta & Cambridge Univ, 54; hon mem fac, Royal Univ Malta, 54-; Guggenheim fels, 58 & 60; Roache lectr, Ind Univ, 63; Alexander lectr, Univ Toronto, 64; adv ed, W W Norton & Co; mem, English Inst; mem, exec coun, MLA, 61-64; fel, Ctr Advan Studies Behav Sci, 67-68; Ewing lectr, Univ Calif, Los Angeles, 75; hon sr fel, Sch Critical Studies, Northwestern Univ, 76-; mem Founders Group, Nat Humanities Ctr, 76-; vis fel, All Souls Col, Oxford Univ, 77; Cecil & Ida Green lectr, Univ BC, 80. **HONORS AND AWARDS** Gauss Prize, 53; James Russell Lowell Prize, MLA, 72; LittD, Univ Rochester, 78, Northwest-

ern univ, 81 & Univ Chicago, 82; Am Acad award in Humanistic Stud, 84; Am Acad Inst Arts and Letters award, 90., LittD, Univ Rochester, 78, Northwestern Univ, 81 & Univ Chicago, 82. **MEMBERSHIPS** MLA; fel Am Philos Soc; fel Am Acad Arts & Sci; corresp fel, British Academy. **RESEARCH** History of literature; literary criticism; European romanticism. **SELECTED PUBLICATIONS** Auth, The Milk of Paradise, 34, 2nd ed, 70; Glossary of Literary Terms, Holt, Rinehart & Winston, 57, 7th ed, 98; ed, The Poetry of Pope, Holt, 58; auth, The Romantic Poets: Modern Essays in Criticism, Oxford Univ, 60; ed, The Norton Anthology of English Literature, 62, 7th ed, 99 & auth, Natural Supernaturalism: Tradition and revolution in Romantic literature, 71, Norton; Coauth & ed, Wordsworth: A Collection of Critical Essays, Prentice-Hall, 72; co-ed, Wordsworth's Prelude, 1799-1850, Norton, 78; auth, The Correspondent Breeze: Essays on English Romanticism, Norton, 84; auth, Doing Things with Texts: Essays in Criticism and Critical Theory, Norton, 89. **CONTACT ADDRESS** Dept of English, Cornell Univ, Ithaca, NY, 14853.

ABUDU, GABRIEL
DISCIPLINE LITERATURE **EDUCATION** Univ Ghana, BA; Temple Univ, PhD.. **RESEARCH** Twentieth-century Cuban poetry. **SELECTED PUBLICATIONS** Areas: Nancy Morejon. **CONTACT ADDRESS** York Col, Pennsylvania, 441 Country Club Road, York, PA, 17403.

ACHINSTEIN, SHARON
DISCIPLINE ENGLISH **EDUCATION** Princeton Univ, PhD. **CAREER** Prof, Northwestern Univ. **HONORS AND AWARDS** Milton Soc prize; CAS Outstanding Tchg Awd; McCormick Tchg Professorship. **RESEARCH** 17th-century literature and thought; social history; popular literature. **SELECTED PUBLICATIONS** Auth, Milton and The Revolutionary Reader, 94; essays on, Bacon; Milton; printing; women in politics; the plague. **CONTACT ADDRESS** Dept of English, Northwestern Univ, 1801 Hinman, Evanston, IL, 60208.

ACKER, PAUL
DISCIPLINE OLD AND MIDDLE ENGLISH LITERATURE **EDUCATION** Brown Univ, PhD. **CAREER** Eng Dept, St. Edward's Univ **SELECTED PUBLICATIONS** Auth, Revising Oral Theory: Formulaic Composition in Old English and Old Icelandic Verse, Garland, 98; Transl, The Saga of the People of Floi and Valla-Ljot's Saga in The Complete Sagas of Icelanders, Leifur Eriksson, 97. **CONTACT ADDRESS** St Edward's Univ, 3001 S Congress Ave, Austin, TX, 78704-6489.

ADAMS, BARRY BANFIELD
PERSONAL Born 08/31/1935, Boston, MA, m, 1962, 2 children **DISCIPLINE** ENGLISH **EDUCATION** Boston Col, BA, 57; Univ NC, MA, 59, PhD(English), 63. **CAREER** From instr to assoc prof, 63-75, chmn dept, 70-76, PROF ENGLISH, CORNELL UNIV, 75- **MEMBERSHIPS** MLA; Renaissance Soc Am. **RESEARCH** Middle and Renaissance English literature. **SELECTED PUBLICATIONS** Ed, John Bale's King Johan, Huntington Libr, 68; auth, The prudence of Prince Escalus, ELH, 3/68; The audiences of The Spanish Tragedy, J English & Ger Philol, 69; Orsino and the Spirit of Love (in Shakespeare's Twelfth Night), Shakespeare Quart, 78. **CONTACT ADDRESS** Dept of English, Cornell Univ, 252 Goldwin Smith Hall, Ithaca, NY, 14853-0001. **EMAIL** bba1@cornell.edu

ADAMS, CHARLES H.
DISCIPLINE AMERICAN LITERATURE **EDUCATION** Univ Va, PhD. **CAREER** English and Lit, Univ Ark. **HONORS AND AWARDS** Chair dept. **SELECTED PUBLICATIONS** Auth, 'By Sartain Laws': Cooper's Sea Fiction and The Red Rover, Studies Am Fiction, 88; Versions of Revision: Conflict and Community in the American Canon, Kenyon Rev, 91; History and the Literary Imagination in Hawthorne's 'Chiefly About War-Matters', English Studies, 93; Reading Ecologically: Language and Play in Bartram's Travels", Southern Quart, 94; The Guardian of the Law: Authority and Identity in James Fenimore Cooper, Penn State, 91. **CONTACT ADDRESS** Univ Ark, Fayetteville, AR, 72701.

ADAMS, DALE TALMADGE
PERSONAL Born 10/30/1937, Freeport, TX, m, 1960, 3 children **DISCIPLINE** ENGLISH **EDUCATION** NTex State Univ, BS, 60, BA, 64, MA, 65; Univ Tex, PhD, 76. **CAREER** Instr English, Lee Col, Tex, 65-. **MEMBERSHIPS** NCTE; Conf Col Compos & Commun; Two-Year Col English Asn-SW; Conf Col Teachers English; MLA. **RESEARCH** Film. **SELECTED PUBLICATIONS** Auth, Use of films in teaching composition, 10/75 & Not back to pedagogenic basics, 10/76, Col Compos & Commun. **CONTACT ADDRESS** Lee Col, 511 S Whiting St, Baytown, TX, 77520-4796. **EMAIL** dadams@lee.edu

ADAMS, ELSIE B.
PERSONAL Born 08/11/1932, Atoka, OK **DISCIPLINE** ENGLISH **EDUCATION** Univ Okla, BS, 53, MA, 59, PhD(English), 66. **CAREER** Instr English, Northeastern Okla A&M Jr Col, 53-54; teacher, high sch, Okla, 55-56; from asst prof to assoc prof English, Wis State Univ, Whitewater, 66-71; from asst prof to assoc prof, 71-77, PROF ENGLISH, SAN DIEGO STATE UNIV, 77-, ASSOC DEAN, COL ARTS & LETTS, 75- **RESEARCH** Bernard Shaw; female studies; Victorian literature. **SELECTED PUBLICATIONS** Auth, Bernard Shaws pre-Raphaelite drama, PMLA, 10/66; No exit: An explication of Kiplings A Wayside Comedy, English Lit Transition, 68; Gissings allegorical House of Cobwebs, Studies Short Fiction, spring 70; co-ed, Up Against the Wall, Mother ... On Womens Liberation, Glencoe, 71; auth, Israel Zangwill, Twayne, 71; Bernard Shaw and the Aesthetes, Ohio State Univ, 71; Feminism and Female Stereotypes in Shaw, Shaw Rev, 74; Shaw's Ladies, Shaw Rev, 80; Shaw, George Bernard and the Socialist Theatre, Eng Lit in Transition 1880-1920, Vol 0038, 95; Shaw, Bernard Theatrics, Selected Correspondence of Shaw, Bernard, English Lit in Transition 1880-1920, Vol 0039, 96; Shaw People Victoria to Churchill, Eng Lit in Transition 1880-1920, Vol 0040, 97. **CONTACT ADDRESS** Dept of English & Comp Lit, San Diego State Univ, San Diego, CA, 92102.

ADAMS, GEORGE ROY
PERSONAL Born 11/23/1928, Lime Springs, IA, m, 1959, 3 children **DISCIPLINE** ENGLISH, LINGUISTICS **EDUCATION** Univ Okla, BA, 52, PhD, 61. **CAREER** Instr English, Boston Univ, 61-63; asst prof, Harpur Col, State Univ NY Binghamton, 63-66; assoc prof, 66-76, prof English, Univ Wis, Whitewater, 76-. **MEMBERSHIPS** MLA; Mediaeval Acad Am. **RESEARCH** Medieval literary esthetic; medieval drama; history of the English language. **SELECTED PUBLICATIONS** Auth, Paul Goodman, Twayne; Chaucer's Shipman's Tale, Explicator, 66; coauth, Good and Bad Fridays and May 3 in Chaucer, English Lang Notes, 66; Chauntecleer's Paradise Lost and Regained, Mediaeval Studies, 67. **CONTACT ADDRESS** Dept of English, Univ of Wis, 800 W Main, Whitewater, WI, 53190-1790.

ADAMS, KATHERINE L.
DISCIPLINE INTERPERSONAL COMMUNICATION **EDUCATION** Univ UT, PhD. **CAREER** Instr, Grad coordr, Calif State Univ; assoc ed, Western J of Commun; assoc ed, Women's Stud in Commun. **SELECTED PUBLICATIONS** Auth, Aubrey Fisher's Interpersonal Communication: A Pragmatic Approach Textbook, 2nd ed; authored several instructor's manuals in interpersonal and small group communication. **CONTACT ADDRESS** California State Univ, Fresno, Fresno, CA, 93740.

ADAMS, KIMBERLY V.
DISCIPLINE 19TH-CENTURY BRITISH LITERATURE, BRITISH AND AMERICAN NOVEL, WOMEN'S STUDIES **EDUCATION** Harvard Univ, PhD. **CAREER** Instr, Rutgers, State Univ NJ, Camden Col of Arts and Sci. **HONORS AND AWARDS** Provost's Tchg Excellence Award, 93. **RESEARCH** Feminist symbol. **SELECTED PUBLICATIONS** Auth, Feminine Godhead, Feminist Symbol: The Madonna in the Work of Ludwig Feuerbach, Anna Jameson, Margaret Fuller, and George Eliot, J of Feminist Stud in Relig; The Madonna and Margaret Fuller, Women's Stud. **CONTACT ADDRESS** Rutgers, State Univ NJ, Camden Col of Arts and Sci, New Brunswick, NJ, 08903-2101. **EMAIL** schiavo@crab.rutgers.edu

ADAMS, MICHAEL F.
PERSONAL Born 03/25/1948, Montgomery, AL, m, 1969, 2 children **DISCIPLINE** COMMUNICATION **EDUCATION** Lipscomb Col, BA, 70; Ohio St Univ, MA, 71; PhD, 73. **CAREER** Pres & prof Polit Comm, Univ Ga, 97-; pres & prof Government, Centre Col, 89-97; vice-pres Univ Affairs & porf Polit Comm, Pepperdine Univ, 82-89; Staff, Gov Lamar Alexander, 80-82; Staff, Howard H Baker Jr, 75-79; asst prof Comm, Ohio St Univ, 73-75. **HONORS AND AWARDS** CASE Circle of Excellence Award, 96, 97; Knight Found Award for Ntl Pres Leadership, 96; Grand Gold Award from CASE, 87; CASE Ntl Alumni Prog Top Speaker; IABC Bronze Quill Award; NSPRA Award of Excellence; CASE Ntl Assembly Chair, 88; Ohio St Univ Fel, Highest Academic Honor; Grand Gold Public Relations for Persian Gulf Educ Day. **MEMBERSHIPS** Ntl Assoc Independent Col & Univ Chmn, 95-96; Amer Council Educ Finance Committee Chair, 97-98; Assoc of Presidents of Independent Col & Univ Board of Dir, 92-95; Ntl Collegiate Athletic Assoc Vice Chair, 95-96; S Assoc Col & Schools Exec Council, 94-; S Assoc Col & Schools Chair, 97-; Rhodes Scholar Selection Committee Ga St Chair, 97. **SELECTED PUBLICATIONS** Inspiration by Instruction, Atlanta Constitution, 98; The Inaugural Address of the 21st President, Univ Ga, 98; "The State of the University Address, Univ Ga, 98; The Advancement President in the Liberal Arts College, The Advancement President And the Academy: Profiles in Institutional Leadership, ACE, 97. **CONTACT ADDRESS** Dept of political Communications, Univ of Georgia, 570 Prince Ave, Athens, GA, 30601.

ADAMS, PERCY GUY
PERSONAL Born 12/16/1914, Beeville, TX **DISCIPLINE** ENGLISH **EDUCATION** Tex Col Arts & Indust, AB, 33; Univ Tex, AM, 37, PhD, 46. **CAREER** Tutor English, Univ Tex, 41-43; instr, Ohio State Univ, 46-48; from asst prof to prof, Univ Tenn, 48-66; prof, La State Univ, Baton Rouge, 66-70; PROF ENGLISH, UNIV TENN, KNOXVILLE, 70-, Fulbright lectr, Univs Aix-Marseille & Grenoble, France, 58-59; gen ed, Great travel books, Dover Publ, Inc, 65-; Nat Endowment Humanities sr fel, 76-77. **HONORS AND AWARDS** Chancelor's Scholar of the Year, Univ Tenn, Knoxville, 77. **MEMBERSHIPS** Comp Lit Asn; Soc Hist Discoveries; Soc Southern Lit; MLA; NCTE. **RESEARCH** Eighteenth century and comparative literature. **SELECTED PUBLICATIONS** Auth, Travelers and Travel Liars: 1660-1800, Univ Calif, 62; Historical importance of assonance to poets, PMLA, 73; Epic tradition and the novel, Southern Rev, 73; Faulkner and French literature, Proc Comp Lit Symp, 73; European Renaissance literature and the discovery of America, Comp Lit Studies, 76; Graces of Harmony: Alliteration, Assocance, and Consonance in Eighteenth-Century Poetry, Univ Ga, 77; Seventeenth- and Eighteenth-century travel literature: A survey of recent approaches, Tex Studies Lang & Lit, 78; The achievement of James Cook and his associates in perspective, In: Exploration in Alaska: Captain Cook Commemorative Lectures (1978), 80; Haunted Journeys, Desire and Transgression in European Travel Writings, Nineteenth Century Prose, Vol 0020, 93. **CONTACT ADDRESS** Dept of English, Univ of Tenn, Knoxville, TN, 37916.

ADAMS, RACHEL
DISCIPLINE 19TH- AND 20TH-CENTURY AMERICAN LITERATURE **EDUCATION** Univ Calif-Berkeley, BA, 90; Univ Mich, MA, 92; Univ Calif, Santa Barbara, PhD, 97. **CAREER** Prof. **HONORS AND AWARDS** Mng ed, Camera Obscura: Feminism, Culture, and Media Studies. **SELECTED PUBLICATIONS** Pub(s), Freakery: Cultural Spectacles of the Extraordinary Body; The Black Female Body; Mich Quart. **CONTACT ADDRESS** Dept of Eng, Columbia Col, New York, 2960 Broadway, New York, NY, 10027-6902.

ADAMS, STEPHEN J.
DISCIPLINE 19TH-CENTURY AMERICAN LITERATURE **EDUCATION** Univ Minn, PhD. **CAREER** Assoc prof, Univ Minn, Duluth. **SELECTED PUBLICATIONS** Auth Thoreau's Diet at Walden, Studies in the American Renaissance 1990, ed, Joel Myerson,UP Va, 90; The Genres of A Week on the Concord and Merrimack Rivers, Approaches to Teaching Thoreau, ed, Richard Schneider, MLA, 95; coauth, Revising Mythologies: The Composition of Thoreau's Major Works, UP Va, 88. **CONTACT ADDRESS** Dept of Eng, Univ Minn, Duluth, Duluth, MN, 55812-2496. **EMAIL** sadams@d.umn.edu

ADAMS, TIMOTHY D.
PERSONAL Born 12/11/1943, Monterey, CA, m, 1966, 1 child **DISCIPLINE** ENGLISH; AMERICAN LITERATURE **EDUCATION** Columbia, BS, 68; Texas, MA, 70; Emory Univ, PhD, 78. **CAREER** Instr, 72-75, Old Dominion Univ; asst prof, 79-81, Univ Ark; asst prof, 81-82, McMurry Col; asst prof, 82-84, assoc prof, 86-91; prof, 91- , W VA Univ. **MEMBERSHIPS** Mod Lang Asn **SELECTED PUBLICATIONS** Ed, Autobiography, Photography, and Narrative, Mod Fiction Stud, 94; auth, Life Writing and Light Writing: Photography in Autobiography, Mod Fiction Studies, 94; coed, Terms of Identity: Essays on the Theoretical Terminology of Lifewriting, a/b: Auto/Biography Stud, 95; Deafness and Deftness in CODA Autobiography: Ruth Sidransky's In Silence and Lou Ann Walkers A Loss for Words, Biog, 97; Running in the Family: Photography and Autobiography in the Memoirs of Michael and Christopher Ondaatje, Biog Creation, Presses Univ de Rennes, 97; Photography and Ventriloquy in Paul Austers The Invention of Solitude, True Relations: Essays on Autobiography and the Postmodern, Greenwood Press, 98; auth, Light Writing and Life Writing: Photography in Autobiography, Univ NC Press, 99. **CONTACT ADDRESS** English Dept, W Va Univ, PO Box 6296, Morgantown, WV, 26506-6296. **EMAIL** tadams@wvu.edu

ADAMS, TYRONE L.
DISCIPLINE COMMUNICATIONS **EDUCATION** St Petersburg Jr Coll, Assoc, 88; Univ Fla, BA, 90; Fla State Univ, MA, 92, PhD, 95. **CAREER** Asst Dir, Forensics, Fla State Univ, 90-93; Tchg Asssoc, Fla State Univ, 90-93; Fel, Fla State Univ, 93-95; Asst Prof, Univ Ark, 92-. **HONORS AND AWARDS** Chair, Speech Comm Major Assessment Comt; Ed, Am Comm Jour, 96-. **SELECTED PUBLICATIONS** Coauth, Empowerment as Simulatory Strategy in the 1992 Presidential Elections: The Bush Campaign Targets Minority Constituencies, Spectrum, 92; The Terror-rhetoric Genre: Exploring Aristotelian Foundations for Violence as Persuasive Text, Jour Comm studies, 94; The Emerging Role of the World-Wide-Web in Forensics: On Computer-mediated Research and Community Development, Forensic, 96; 'Follow the Yellow Brick Road:' Using Diffusion of Innovations Theory to Enrich Virtual Organizations in Cyberspace, S Comm Journal, 97; Making Sense of the 1994 Right-wing Revolution in the United States, Speaker & Gavel, 97. **CONTACT ADDRESS** Univ Ark- Monticello, BOX 3458, Monticello, AR, 71656. **EMAIL** ADAMS@UAMONT.EDU

ADAMSON, JOSEPH
DISCIPLINE ENGLISH LITERATURE **EDUCATION** Trent Univ, BA; Univ Toronto, MA, PhD. **RESEARCH** Literary the-

ory; Northrop Frye; comparative lit; American lit; mod lyric poetry. **SELECTED PUBLICATIONS** Auth, Melville, Shame, and the Evil Eye: A Psychoanalytic Reading, 97; auth, Northrop Frye: A Visionary Life, 93; auth, Wounded Fiction: Modern Poetry and Deconstruction, 88. **CONTACT ADDRESS** English Dept, McMaster Univ, 1280 Main St W, Hamilton, ON, L8S 4L9.

ADELMAN, JANET ANN
PERSONAL Born 01/28/1941, Mt. Kisco, NY **DISCIPLINE** ENGLISH LITERATURE **EDUCATION** Smith Col, BA, 62; Yale Univ, MA, 66, MPhil, 67, PhD(English), 69. **CAREER** Acting asst prof English, 68-70, asst prof, 70-72, assoc prof, 72-81, PROF ENGLISH, UNIV CALIF, BERKELEY, 81-. **HONORS AND AWARDS** Am Coun Learned Socs study fel, 76-77; Guggenheim Fel, 80-81. **MEMBERSHIPS** MLA; Shakespeare Asn Am; Interdisciplinary Member, San Francisco Psychoanalytic Inst. **RESEARCH** Shakespeare; English Renaissance narrative poetry; psychoanalytic criticism. **SELECTED PUBLICATIONS** Auth, Anger's my meat: Feeding, dependency, and aggression in Coriolanus, In: Shakespeare's Pattern of Excelling Nature, Univ Del, 78; Male Bonding in Shakespeare's Comedies, In: Shakespeare's Rough Magic: Renaissance Essays in Honor of C.L. Barber, Univ Del Press, 85; This Is and Is Not Cressid: The Characterization of Cressida, In: The (M)other Tongue: Essays in Feminist Psychoanalytic Interpretation, Cornell Univ Press, 85; Born of a Woman: Fantasies of Maternal Power in Macbeth, In: Cannibals, Witches, and Divorce: Estranging the Renaissance, Selected Papers from the English Inst, 85, 11th ed, The Johns Hopkins Univ Press, 87; Bed Tricks: On Marriage as the End of Comedy in All's Well That Ends Well and Measure for Measure, In: Shakespeare's Personality, Univ Calif Press, 89; She, Dying, Gave It Me: Dead Mothers and Dying Wives in Othello, In: Hebrew University Studies in Literature and the Arts: Essays in Honour of Ruth Nevo, 91; Suffocating Mothers: Fantasies of Maternal Origin in Shakespeare, Hamlet to the Tempest, Routledge, 92; Iago's Alter Ego: Race as Projection in Othello, Shakespeare Quart, 97; Making Defect Perfection: Shakespeare and the One-Sex Model, In: Enacting Gender on the English Renaissance Stage, Univ Ill Press, forthcoming 98. **CONTACT ADDRESS** Dept of English, Univ of California, Berkeley, 322 Wheeler Hall, Berkeley, CA, 94720-1030.

ADELMAN, MARA
DISCIPLINE COMMUNICATIONS **EDUCATION** UCLA, BA, 72; CA State Univ, San Diego, MA, 80; Univ WA, PhD, 86. **CAREER** Comm, Seattle Univ. **MEMBERSHIPS** Speech Commun Asn; Int Commun Asn; Int Network of Personal Relationship. **SELECTED PUBLICATIONS** Auth, Sustaining passion: Eroticism and safe-sex talk, Archives of Sexual Behavior, 21, 92; Play and incongruity: Framing safe-sex talk, Hea Commun, 3, 91; Social support and AIDS, J for AIDS and Publ Policy, 4, 90; Cross-cultural adjustment: A theoretical perspective and social support, Int J of Intercultural Relations, 12, 88; Healthy passions: Safe sex and play, AIDS: A communication perspective, Hillsdale, NJ: Lawrence Erlbaum Assoc(s), 92; Rituals of adversity and remembering: The role of possessions for persons and community living with AIDS, Advances in consumer research Vol 19, Provo, UT: Asn for Consumer Res, 91; coauth, The Fragile Community: Living Together with AIDS, Laawrence Erlbaum Assoc(s), Publishers; 97; Beyond language: Cross-cultural communication for English as a second language 2nd ed, Englewood Cliffs, NJ: Prentice-Hall, 93; Communicating social support, Newbury Park, CA: Sage, 87; Communication Practices in the Social Construction of Health in an AIDS Residence, J Hea Psychol, Vol 1, 3, 96; Formal intermediaries in the marriage market: A typology and review, J of Marriage and the Family, 54, 92; Mediated channels for mate seeking: A solution to involuntary singlehood, Critical Studies in Mass Communication, 8, 91; The pilgrim must embark: Creating and sustaining community in a residential facility for persons living with AIDS, Gp communication in context: Studies of natural gps, Hillsdale, NJ: Lawrence Erlbaum Assoc(s), 94; Market metaphors for meeting mates, Research in Consumer Behavior, Vol 6, London, England: JAI Press, 93; Building community life: Understanding individual, gp, and organizational processes, Handbook for assisted living, Chicago: Bonaventure House, 93; Beyond smiling: Social support and the service provider, Frontiers in service quality, Newbury Park, CA: Sage, 93; Two views on the consumption of mating and dating, Advances in consumer res, Vol 18, Provo, UT: Asn for Consumer Res, 91; video producer, Safe-sex talk, 88; video coproducer, The pilgrim must embark: Living in community, Annandale, VA: Speech Communication Association's Applied Communication Series, 91; rev(s), AIDS and the hospice community, Contemp Psychol, 38, 93; Life, liberty and the pursuit of health care: Multi- disciplinary perspectives on sustaining health in later life, Contemp Psychol, 37, 92. **CONTACT ADDRESS** Dept of Commun, Seattle Univ, 900 Broadway, Seattle, WA, 98122-4460. **EMAIL** mara@seattleu.edu

ADICKES, SANDRA
PERSONAL Born 07/14/1933, New York, NY, s, 3 children **DISCIPLINE** ENGLISH; AMERICAN LITERATURE **EDUCATION** Douglas Col, BA, 54; Hunter Col, MA, 64; New York Univ, PhD, 77 **CAREER** Teacher, NY Pubic High Schools, 60-72; asst prof, City Univ NY, 72-88; prof, Winona State Univ, 88-98 **MEMBERSHIPS** Modern Lang Assoc; Popular Culture Assoc **RESEARCH** American Women Political Writers and Activist **SELECTED PUBLICATIONS** Auth, To Be Young Was Very Heaven: Women in New York Before the First World War, 97; auth, Legends of Good Women (novel), 92; auth, The Social Quest, 91 **CONTACT ADDRESS** 579 W Seventh St., Winona, MN, 55987. **EMAIL** sadickes@eudoramail.com

ADICKS, RICHARD R.
PERSONAL Born 08/19/1932, Lake City, FL, m, 1959, 1 child **DISCIPLINE** ENGLISH **EDUCATION** Univ Fla, BAE, 54, MA, 59; Tulane Univ, PhD(English), 65. **CAREER** Teacher high schs, Fla, 56-58 & 59-61; instr English, Rollins Col, 61-63; asst prof, Ga Inst Technol, 65-68; from asst prof to assoc prof, 68-74, prof English, Univ Cent Fla, 74-; Fulbright lectr, Africa University, 97-98. **MEMBERSHIPS** Col English Asn; NCTE; MLA. **RESEARCH** Victorian literature; comparative literature. **SELECTED PUBLICATIONS** Auth, The sea-fight episode in Song of Myself, Walt Whitman Rev, 3/67; The Lily Maid and the Scarlet Sleeve, Univ Rev, 10/67; The unconsecrated Eucharist in Dubliners, Studies in Short Fiction, spring 68; Conrad and the politics of morality, Bull Asn Can Humanities, fall 72; coauth, Oviedo! Biography of a Town, private publ, 79 & 92; A Court for Owls, Pineapple Press, 89. **CONTACT ADDRESS** Dept of English, Univ of Central Florida, PO Box 161346, Orlando, FL, 32816-1346. **EMAIL** adicks@pegasus.cc.ucf.edu

ADISA, OPAL PALMER
PERSONAL Born 11/06/1954, Kingston, Jamaica, s, 3 children **DISCIPLINE** CARIBBEAN LITERATURE; ETHNIC LITERATURE **EDUCATION** Hunter Col, Univ of NY, BA, 75; San Francisco St Univ, MA, 81; San Francisco St Univ, MA, 86; Calif Univ, Berkeley, PhD, 92. **CAREER** Assoc prof & ch Ethnic Studies, Calif Col of Arts & Crafts, 93-; coordr, Lockwood, 97-; vis prof, Stanford Univ, 95; lctr, Holy Name's Col, 94; lctr, St Mary's Col, 93; instr, San Francisco St Univ, 87, 88, 90, 92, 93; lctr, San Francisco St Univ, 81-87; poet, Oakland Museum, 86-92; instr, City Col San Francisco, 80-84. **HONORS AND AWARDS** Creative Work Fund, 98-99; Intl Woman of Year Nominee, 96-97; Canute A Brodhurst Prize, 96; Writer-in-Residence, Headlands Center for Arts, 96; instr, Univ Calif Berkeley, 96; Caribbean Writer Summer Inst Recipient, Univ Miami, 95; Calif Col Tchg Develop Grant, 95; Daily News Prize, 95; Calif Col Tchg Develop Grant, 94; Literary Women Honoree, 94; PEN Oakland/Josephine Miles Lit Award, 92; Master Folk Artist, 91-92; Bay Area Woman Writer Award, 91; Affirmative Action Dissertation-Year Fel, 90-91; Phi Beta Kappa, 91; Grad Opportunity Fel, Univ Calif Berkeley, 88-90; Grad Minority Prog Grant, Univ Calif Berkeley, 87-88; Univ Calif Berkeley Feminist Inst & Gender Study Res Grant, 87; Pushcart Prize, 87. **MEMBERSHIPS** Assoc Caribbean Women Writers & Scholars; Calif Poets in Schools; Caribbean Assoc Feminist Res & Action; Ntl Assoc Ethnic Studies; Ntl Writers Union; Soc for Study of Multi-Ethnic Lit of US; Women's Intl League for Peach & Freedom; Northern Assoc of African Amer Storytellers. **SELECTED PUBLICATIONS** Until Judgement Comes, forthcoming; The Swelling of a Womb/the Forging of a Writer, in Caribbean Writer, 98; Lying in the Tall Grasses Eating Cane, in Zyzzyva, 98; It Begins With Tears, Heinemann Pr, 97. **CONTACT ADDRESS** Dept of Ethnic Studies Prog, California Col of Arts and Crafts, Oakland, PO Box 10625, Oakland, CA, 94618. **EMAIL** Opalpro@aol.com

ADLER, THOMAS PETER
PERSONAL Born 01/03/1943, Cleveland, OH, m, 1968, 2 children **DISCIPLINE** ENGLISH & AMERICAN LITERATURE **EDUCATION** Boston Col, AB, 64, AM, 66; Univ Ill, Urbana, PhD(English), 70. **CAREER** Asst prof, 70-75, from assoc prof to prof English, Purdue Univ, West Lafayette, 75-83, asst head dept, 80-83; assoc dean grad school, 84-88; assoc dean Lib Arts, 88-95; interim dean Lib Arts, 95-97; head English, 97-. **HONORS AND AWARDS** Phi Beta Kappa . **MEMBERSHIPS** AAUP; MLA; Cath Renascence Soc; Midwest MLA; O'Neill Society; Pinter Society. **RESEARCH** Modern British and American drama. **SELECTED PUBLICATIONS** Auth, Who's afraid of Virginia Woolf?: A long night's journey into day, Educ Theatre J, 3/73; Through a glass darkly: O'Neill's aesthetic theory as seen through his writer characters, Ariz Quart, Summer 76; The dialogue of incompletion: language in Tennessee Williams later plays, 77 & The search for God in the plays of Tennessee Williams, In: Tennessee Williams: A Collection of Critical Essays, 77, Prentice-Hall; Robert Anderson, Twayne, 78; From flux to fixity: Art and death in Pinter's No Man's Land, Ariz Quart, Autumn 79; Art or craft: Language in the plays of Albee's second decade, In: Edward Albee: Planned wilderness, Pan Am Univ Press, 80; The mirror as stage prop in modern drama, Comp Drama, Winter 80/81; A Critical History,Twayne-Macmillan, 94. **CONTACT ADDRESS** Dept of English, Purdue Univ, West Lafayette, IN, 47907-1356. **EMAIL** tadler@purdue.edu

ADOLPH, ROBERT
PERSONAL Born 02/15/1936, Cambridge, MA, m, 1958, 3 children **DISCIPLINE** ENGLISH **EDUCATION** Williams Col, BA, 57; Univ Mich, MA, 58; Harvard Univ, PhD(English), 64. **CAREER** From instr to asst prof English, Mass Inst Technol, 61-67; ASSOC PROF HUMANITIES & ENGLISH, YORK UNIV, 68-, Dir, Graduate Programme in Interdisciplinary Studies, 76-79, 82-83. **MEMBERSHIPS** MLA; Can Asn Univ Teachers; Can Asn Am Studies (treas, 71-73). **RESEARCH** Seventeenth century English literature; nineteenth and twentieth century prose fiction. **SELECTED PUBLICATIONS** Auth, The Rise of Modern Prose Style, Mass Inst Technol, 68; Reflections of a new Canadian professor, Can Dimension, 70; contribr, Mandeville Studies, Martinus Nijhoff, 76; auth, Does style mean anything anymore?, CEA Critic, 76, On the possibility of a history of prose style, Style, 82; Thinking Across the American Grain - Ideology, Intellect, and the New Pragmatism, Can Rev Am Stud, Vol 0023, 93. **CONTACT ADDRESS** Div of Humanities, York Univ, 4700 Keele St, Downsview, ON, M3J 1P3.

ADRIAN, DARYL B.
PERSONAL Born 09/24/1933, Hutchinson, KS, m, 1953, 3 children **DISCIPLINE** ENGLISH **EDUCATION** Tabor Col, AB, 55; KS State Tchrs Col, MA, 61; Univ MT, Columbia, PhD, 67. **CAREER** Educ therapist, Menninger Found, Topeka, KS, 57-63; lectr Eng, Washburn Univ, 62-63; instr, Univ MO, Columbia, 61-62 & 63-67; from asst prof to assoc prof Eng, 67-76, admin asst chmn dept, 69-76, Prof Eng, Ball State Univ, 76-, Chmn Dept, 76-85; Exec Dir, Nat Coun Relig & Pub Educ, 75-84. **HONORS AND AWARDS** 1988-97: Eleven Outstanding Fac Tchg Awards, Eng Dept, Honors Col, Blue Key, Golden Key, Mortar Board; Outstanding Fac Adv Awards, Eng Dept. **MEMBERSHIPS** MLA; Conf Christianity & Lit; Midwest Mod Lang Asn; John Steinbeck Soc Am; Milton Soc Am. **RESEARCH** Seventeenth and eighteenth century Brit lit, espec Milton; relig and lit; John Steinbeck; Medieval drama; John Donne's Holy Sonnets; Eng internships. **SELECTED PUBLICATIONS** Ed, John Bunyan's Pilgrim's Progress, Airmont, 69; auth, Humanities and the arts: non-fiction before 1900, In: Encounter With Books: A Guide to Reading, Intervarsity, 70; Steinbecks new image of American and Americans, Steinbeck Quart, fall 70; A comparative school curriculum and the study of religion, Relig Educ, 7-8/72. **CONTACT ADDRESS** Dept of Eng, Ball State Univ, 2000 W University, Muncie, IN, 47306-0002. **EMAIL** dadrian@gw.bsu.edu

AERS, DAVID
DISCIPLINE ENGLISH LITERATURE **EDUCATION** Univ York, PhD. **CAREER** Engl, Duke Univ. **RESEARCH** Late medieval and early mod lit, relig and cult in Engl. **SELECTED PUBLICATIONS** Auth, Piers Plowman and Christian Allegory, Arnold, 75; Chaucer, Langland and the Creative Imagination, Routledge, 80; Chaucer, Harvester, 83; , Community, Gender and Individual Identity, 1360-1430, Routledge, 88; ed, Medieval Literature: Criticism, Ideology, History, Harvester, 86; Culture and History, 1350-1600, Wayne State, 92. **CONTACT ADDRESS** Eng Dept, Duke Univ, Durham, NC, 27706.

AFIFI, WALID A.
DISCIPLINE INTERPERSONAL COMMUNICATION **EDUCATION** Univ Iowa, BA, 90; Univ Ariz, MA, 92; PhD, 96. **CAREER** Grad tchg asst/assoc, Univ Ariz, 90-95; asst prof, 96-. **HONORS AND AWARDS** Grad Col fel, Univ Ariz, 92; grad regist scholar Univ Ariz, 92-94; res trng fel, Univ Ariz, 95, Outstanding prof, Univ Del, 95. **MEMBERSHIPS** Mem, Speech Commun Assn, 90-; Intl Commun Assn, 90-; Intl Network on Personal Relationships, 91-; Intl Soce Stud Personal Relationships, 94-; Nat Coun on Family Rel(s), 94-. **SELECTED PUBLICATIONS** Co-auth, Media in Lebanon, Mass Media in the Middle East: A Comprehensive Reference Guide, Greenwood Publ Gp, 94; What Parents Don't Know: Taboo Topics and Topic Avoidance in Parent-Child Relationships, Parents, children, and Communication: Frontiers of Theory and Research, Lawrence Erlbaum, 95; Rethinking How to Measure Organizational Culture in the Hospital Setting: The Hospital Culture Scale, Evaluation and the Health Professions, 95; Some Things are Better Left Unsaid: Topic Avoidance in Family Relationships, Commun Quart, 95; Interpersonal Deception: XII Information Management Dimensions Underlying Deceptive and Truthful Messages, Commun Monogr(s), 96. **CONTACT ADDRESS** Dept of Commun, Univ Delaware, 162 Ctr Mall, Newark, DE, 19716.

AGGELER, GEOFFREY DONOVAN
PERSONAL Born 09/26/1939, Berkeley, CA, m, 1962, 3 children **DISCIPLINE** ENGLISH **EDUCATION** Univ CA, Davis, BA, 61, MA, 63, PhD, 66. **CAREER** Lectr Eng, CA State Polytech Col, 63-64; asst prof, Can Serv Col Royal Rds, 66-69; from asst prof to assoc prof, 69-75, Prof eng, Univ UT, 75. **HONORS AND AWARDS** Phi Beta Kappa (hon), 98. **MEMBERSHIPS** Marlowe Soc Am; Shakespear Asn Am; Asn Lit Scholars & Critics. **RESEARCH** Eng Renaissance drama; twentieth century Brit fiction; hist of ideas. **SELECTED PUBLICATIONS** Auth, Anthony Burgess: The Artist as Novelist, Univ AL, 79; Faust in the Labyrinth, Mod Fiction Studies, autumn 81; Ed, Critical Essays on Anthony burgess, G K Hall, 86; The Eschatological Crux in The Spanish Tragedy, JEGP, 7/87; Hamlet and the Stoic Sage, Hamlet Studies, summer 87; Confessions of Jimmy Ringo, Dutton, 87; Neostoicism and the En-

glish Protest Conscience, Renaissance and Reformation, summer 90; Good Pity in King lear, Neophilologus, 4/93; Ben Jonson's Justice Overdo and Joseph Hall's Good Magistrate, Engl Studies, 9/95; Nobler in the Mind: The Stoic-Skeptic Dialectic in English Renaissance tragedy, Assoc Univ Presses, 98. **CONTACT ADDRESS** Dept of Eng, Univ of UT, 3500 LNCO, Salt Lake City, UT, 84112-8916. **EMAIL** geoffrey.aggeler@m.cc.utah.edu

AHEARN, BARRY
PERSONAL Born 01/29/1950, Montague City, MA, m, 1983, 1 child **DISCIPLINE** ENGLISH **EDUCATION** Johns Hopkins Univ, PhD, 78; Johns Hopkins Univ, MA, 75; Trinity Col, BA, 73 **CAREER** Prof, Tulane Univ, 98-; assoc prof, Tulane Univ, 87-98; asst prof, Tulane Univ, 82-87; asst prof, Manhattan Col, 79-80 **MEMBERSHIPS** Mod Lang Assoc; Ezra Pound Soc; William Carlos Williams Soc **RESEARCH** Poetry; 20th century American Poetry; Textual Criticism; Autobiography **SELECTED PUBLICATIONS** "Pound/Cummings: The Correspondence of Ezra Pound and E.E. Cummings," Michigan Univ, 96; "William Carlos Williams and Alterity: The Early Poetry," Cambridge Univ, 94; Pound/Zukofsky: Selected Letters of Ezra Pound and Louis Zukofsky," New Directions, 87 **CONTACT ADDRESS** English Dept, Tulane Univ, New Orleans, LA, 70118. **EMAIL** ahearn@mailhost.tcs.tulane.edu

AHEARN, KERRY
DISCIPLINE SHORT STORY, CONTEMPORARY FICTION, AMERICAN LITERATURE **EDUCATION** Stanford Univ, BA, 67; Ohio Univ, MA, 68, PhD, 74. **CAREER** Engl, Oregon St Univ. **SELECTED PUBLICATIONS** Auth, 'Et In Arcadia Excrementum': Pastoral, Kitsch, and Philip Roth's The Great American Novel, Aethlon 94; Rural and Urban: Places in Oregon Literature, Ore Hum, 94. **CONTACT ADDRESS** Oregon State Univ, Corvallis, OR, 97331-4501. **EMAIL** kahearn@orst.edu

AIKEN, RALPH
DISCIPLINE ENGLISH **EDUCATION** Williams College, BA; MA; Duke Univ. **CAREER** Prof, Sweet Briar Col. **RESEARCH** Women and lit; Restoration and 18th century lit; and mod drama. **SELECTED PUBLICATIONS** Auth, articles on 19th century women novelists as well as Renaissance poetry. **CONTACT ADDRESS** Sweet Briar Col, Sweet Briar, VA, 24595.

AIKEN, SUSAN HARDY
PERSONAL Born 11/04/1943, Brooklyn, NY, m, 2 children **DISCIPLINE** ENGLISH **EDUCATION** Furman Univ, BA, 64, Duke Univ, MA, 66, PhD, 71. **CAREER** Instr Eng, Univ GA, 66-69; adj asst prof, State Univ NY, Stony Brook, 70-71; asst prof, Suffolk Community Col, 72-73; asst prof, 73-77, assoc prof, 78-89, prof eng, Univ AZ, 90, Univ Distinguised Prof, 98. **HONORS AND AWARDS** Ford Found fel, 64-65; Woodrow Wilson/Duke Univ fel, 65-66, Duke Univ fel, 69-70; Phi Beta Kappa, 71; Co-PI, NEH Curriculum Integration grant, Univ AZ, 84; Mortar Board Citation for Distinguished Acad Achievement, 85; Univ AZ Found Creative Tchg Award, 85; Women's Studies Advisory Coun Res Grant, 87, 90; Provost's Tchg Award, Univ AZ, 88; Burlington Northern Found Acad Excellence Award, 88; Steinfeld Found Res Grant, 89; Univ AZ Res Grant, 90; Guest lectr tour, Univ Copenhagen, Univ Aarhus and Univ Odense, Denmark, 91; Inaugural Scholarly Address, Karen Blixen Museet, Rungstedlund, Denmark, 91; NEH Interpretive Res Grant, 91-93; Univ Distinguished Prof, 98. **MEMBERSHIPS** MLA; Nat Women's Studies Asn. **RESEARCH** Nineteenth and Twentieth Century Brit and Am lit and cult; Isak Dinesen/Karen Blixen; Gender theory. **SELECTED PUBLICATIONS** Co-ed, Changing Our Minds: Feminist Transformations of Knowledge, SUNY Press, 88; Auth, Isak Dinesen and the Engendering of Narrative, Univ Chicago Press, 90; Dialogues/Dialogi: Literary and Cultural Exchanges Between (Ex)Soviet and American Women, Duke Univ Press, 94; Co-ed, Making Worlds: Gender, Metaphor, Materiality, Univ AZ Press, 98; Auth articles and bk chap on nineteenth- and twentieth-century lit, feminist theory, photography. **CONTACT ADDRESS** Dept of Eng, Univ of AZ, Tucson, AZ, 85721. **EMAIL** sha@u.arizona.edu

AKRIGG, GEORGE P.V.
PERSONAL Born 08/13/1913, Calgary, AB, Canada **DISCIPLINE** ENGLISH LITERATURE **EDUCATION** Univ BC, BA, 37, MA, 40; Univ Calif Berkeley, PhD, 44. **CAREER** Prof, 58-79, PROF EMER ENGLISH, UNIV BC, 79-. **MEMBERSHIPS** MLA. **SELECTED PUBLICATIONS** Auth, Jacobean Pageant or the Court of King James I, 62; auth, Shakespeare and the Earl of Southampton, 68; coauth, 1001 British Columbia Place Names, 69; coauth, British Columbia Chronicle 1778-1846, 75; coauth, British Columbia Chronicle 1847-1871, 77; coauth, British Columbia Place Names, 86; ed, Letters of King James VI & I, 84; ed, H.M.S. 'Virago' in the Pacific 1851-1955, 92. **CONTACT ADDRESS** 2575 Tolmie St, #8, Vancouver, BC, V6R 4M1.

ALAYA, FLAVIA M.
PERSONAL Born 05/16/1935, New Rochelle, NY, m, 1993, 3 children **DISCIPLINE** ENGLISH AND LITERATURE **EDUCATION** Barnard Col, Columbia Univ, BA, 56; Columbia Univ, MA, 60; Columbia Univ, PhD, 65. **CAREER** Instr, eng, Univ NC, 59-60; lectr, Barnard Col, 60-62; lectr, Hunter Col, 62-66; instr to asst prof, NY Univ, 66-71; assoc prof, 71-73, prof, 74-80, eng & comp lit & dir sch of Intercultural Studies, Ramapo Col; prof, lit & cultural hist, sch of soc sci, Ramapo Col, 80-. **HONORS AND AWARDS** Fulbright, 57-58; Guggenheim fel, 74-75; NEH, 85; Kress Found fel, 97; Dodge Found writing fel, 97. **MEMBERSHIPS** MLA; Northeast Victorian Studies Asn; Nat Trust for Hist Pres; Ital Amer Writers Asn. **RESEARCH** Nineteenth-twentieth century cultural history (Europe and America); Literature of national and cultural identity; Italy in Victorian literature; Eliz Barrett & Robert Browning; South African literature; Space and place; Historic preservation; History of Paterson, NJ; Women in literature; Women's autobiographies; Ital-Amer literature. **SELECTED PUBLICATIONS** auth, Jour Hist Ideas; auth, Victorian Poetry; articles, Browning Inst Studies; Ramapo papers; auth, William Sharp: Fiona Macleod: a Study in Later Victorian Cosmopolitanism, Harvard, 70; auth, Gaetano Federici: The Artist as Historian, Passaic County Hist Soc, 80; auth, Silk & Sandstone: the Story of Catholina Lambert and Hist Castle, Passaic County Hist Soc, 84. **CONTACT ADDRESS** School of Social Science, Ramapo Col, New Jersey, Mahwah, NJ, 07430. **EMAIL** falaya@ramapo.edu

ALBERTINI, VIRGIL
PERSONAL Born 04/01/1932, Frontenac, KS, m, 1960 **DISCIPLINE** ENGLISH **EDUCATION** Kans State Col, Pittsburg, BSEd, 53, MS, 60; Univ Tulsa, PhD, 74. **CAREER** Teacher, high schs, Kans, 54-60 & prep sch, Calif, 60-61; instr, 65-68, from asst prof to assoc prof English, 68-74, PROF ENGLISH, NORTHWEST MO STATE UNIV, 74- **HONORS AND AWARDS** English Dept Prof of the Year, 3 different years; Northwest's Turret Award Recipient for outstanding academic and athletic contributions, 95. **MEMBERSHIPS** NCTE; Cather Soc; ALAN; WLA. **RESEARCH** Nineteenth century American literature; Willa Cather; American literary naturalism; young adult literature. **SELECTED PUBLICATIONS** Auth, Towers in the Northwest, 1956-1980, Univ Wyo Press, 80; 35 articles in professional journals on American and British authors, 15 on Willa Cather. **CONTACT ADDRESS** 800 University Dr, Maryville, MO, 64468-6015. **EMAIL** lujack@acad.nwmissouri.edu

ALBRECHT, WILBUR T.
DISCIPLINE ROMANTIC POETS AND ESSAYISTS **EDUCATION** Brown Univ, BA, 60; Johns Hopkins Univ, MA, 61; Univ PA, 70. **CAREER** Instr, Drexel Univ, 64-67; prof, 67-. **RESEARCH** William Morris and the pre-Raphaelites. **SELECTED PUBLICATIONS** Publ, Profiles of the Monthly Rev, The Scots Rev, Eng Rev, The Lit Rev in Vol 1, Brit Lit Per. **CONTACT ADDRESS** Dept of Eng, Colgate Univ, 13 Oak Dr., Hamilton, NY, 13346.

ALBRIGHT, DANIEL
PERSONAL Born 10/29/1945, Chicago, IL, m, 1977, 1 child **DISCIPLINE** ENGLISH **EDUCATION** Rice Univ, BA, 67; Yale Univ, MPhil, 69, PhD, 70. **CAREER** Asst to full prof, Univ Va, 70-86; visiting prof, Univ Munich, 86-87; PROF OF ENGLISH, 87-, RICHARD L. TURNER PROF OF HUMANITIES, UNIV ROCHESTER, 95-. **HONORS AND AWARDS** Phi Beta Kappa, 66; NEH fel, 73; Guggenheim fel, 76. **MEMBERSHIPS** MLA. **RESEARCH** Modernism in music, literature, visual arts, and sciences. **SELECTED PUBLICATIONS** Auth, Quantum Poetics: Yeats, Pound, Eliot, and the Science of Modernism, Cambridge Univ Press, 97; Discrepancies Between Literary and Psychological Models of the Self, The Remembering Self: Construction and Accuracy in the Self-Narrative, Cambridge Univ Press, 94; Yeats and the Avant-garde, The Recorder, 94; Yeats and Science Fiction, Bullan: An Irish Studies J, 96; Beckett at the Bowling Alley, Contemporary Lit, 97; An Opera with No Acts: Four Saints in Three Acts, Southern Rev, 97; ed, W.B. Yeats: The Poems, J.M. Dent and Sons, 90 & 94. **CONTACT ADDRESS** Dept of English, Univ Rochester, 121 Van Voorlis Rd., Pittsford, NY, 14539.

ALEXANDER, DENNIS C.
DISCIPLINE COMMUNICATION STUDIES **EDUCATION** Ohio State Univ, PhD, 69. **CAREER** Assoc prof. **MEMBERSHIPS** Western States Commun Asn; Nat Commun Asn; Soc Study Symbolic Interaction. **SELECTED PUBLICATIONS** Auth, Communication as History and Evolution: Comparing Contextualism and Symbolic Interactionism, Context, 96. **CONTACT ADDRESS** Dept of Communication, Utah Univ, 100 S 1350 E, Salt Lake City, UT, 84112. **EMAIL** dennis.alexander@m.cc.utah.edu

ALEXANDER, DORIS M.
PERSONAL Born 12/14/1922, Newark, NJ, s **DISCIPLINE** ENGLISH **EDUCATION** Univ Mo, BA, 44; Univ Penn, MA, 46; NY Univ, PhD, 52. **CAREER** Dept ch, Rutgers Univ, CUNY, 56-62; Fulbright Prof, Univ Athens, Greece, 66-67; Vis Prof, Penn State Univ, 69. **HONORS AND AWARDS** Gregory Scholarship; Phi Beta Kappa; Univ Scholarship; Penfield Fellow, NY Univ, 46-47. **MEMBERSHIPS** Asn of Lit Schol & Critics; Eugene O'Niel Soc; Trustee, Dickens Soc. **RESEARCH** Creative process; O'Neil, Dickens, Tolstoy, R.L. Stevenson, Thomas Mann, E. Fitzgerald; theater history. **SELECTED PUBLICATIONS** Auth, The Tempering of O'Neill, Harcourt, Brace, 62; auth, Creating Characters with Charles Dickens, Penn State Press, 91; auth, Eugene O'Neill's Creative Struggle: The Decisive Decade 1924-1933, Penn State Press, 92; auth, Creating Literature Out of Life: The Making of Four Masterpieces, Penn State Press, 96. **CONTACT ADDRESS** San Trovaso 1116, Dorsoduro, Venice, ., 30123.

ALEXANDER, ESTELLA CONWILL
PERSONAL Born 01/19/1949, Louisville, Kentucky **DISCIPLINE** ENGLISH **EDUCATION** Univ of Louisville, BA 1975, MA 1976; Univ of IA, PhD 1984. **CAREER** Univ of Iowa, instructor/director of black poetry 1976-79; Grinnell Coll, asst prof 1979-80; KY State Univ, prof of English; poet, currently. **HONORS AND AWARDS** Recording Motion Grace Gospel Recordings 1983; KY Arts Council Grant 1986; Art Grant KY Foundation for Women 1986. **CONTACT ADDRESS** Dept of English, Hunter Col, CUNY, 695 Park Ave, New York, NY, 10021.

ALEXANDER, SANDRA CARLTON
PERSONAL Born 07/26/1947, Warsaw, NC, m, 1970, 2 children **DISCIPLINE** AMERICAN LITERATURE, RHETORIC **EDUCATION** NC A&T State Univ, BA, 69; Harvard Univ, MA, 70; Univ Pittsburgh, PhD(English), 76. **CAREER** Instr English, Coppin State Col, 73-74; from asst prof to prof, NC A&T State Univ, 74-. **HONORS AND AWARDS** NC Arts Coun Writers Fel, 92 **MEMBERSHIPS** Col Lang Asn. **RESEARCH** The life and works of Arna Bontemps; developing composition skills. **SELECTED PUBLICATIONS** Auth, Black Butterflies: Stories of the South in Transition, 94. **CONTACT ADDRESS** Dept of English, NC A&T State Univ, 1601 E Market St, Greensboro, NC, 27401-3209.

ALGEO, JOHN T.
PERSONAL Born 11/12/1930, St. Louis, MO, m, 1958, 2 children **DISCIPLINE** ENGLISH **EDUCATION** Univ of Miami, BEd, 55; Univ of Fla, MA, 57, PhD, 60. **CAREER** Instr, Fla State Univ, 59-61; asst prof , 61-66, assoc prof, 66-70, asst dean of the Grad School & dir of prog in Linguistics, 69-71, prof, Univ of Fla, 70-71; Prof, 71-88, Dir of prog in Linguistics, 74-79, Head, Dept of English, 75-79, Alumni Found Distinguished Prof of English, 88-94, Prof Emeritus, Univ of Ga, 94-; exchange prof, Univ of Erlangen, 85; Honorary Res Fel, Univ ClL London, Univ of London, 86-. **HONORS AND AWARDS** Phi Beta Kappa; Phi Kappa Phi; Fulbright Sr Res Scholar, Univ Col London, 86-87; Guggenheim Fel, 86-87; Univ of Ga Alumni Found Distinguished Prof, 88-94. **MEMBERSHIPS** Am Dialect Soc; Am Name Soc; Dictionary Soc of North Am; Int Asn of Univ Prof of English; Int Linguistic Asn; Int Phonetic Asn; Linguistic Soc of Am; MLA; Philological Soc. **RESEARCH** British-American linguistic differences; lexicography; neology; usage. **SELECTED PUBLICATIONS** Coauth, The Origins and Development of the English Language, Harcourt Brace Jovanovich, 93; auth, Fifty Years Among the New Words: A Dictionary of Neologisms 1941-1991, Cambridge UP, 91; Eigo no kigen to hattatsu, Bunkashobouhakubunsha, 91; British and American Biases in English Dictionaries, Cultures, Ideologies, and the Dictionary: Studies in Honor of Ladislav Zgusta, Niemeyer, 95; Having a Look at the Expanded Predicate, The Verb in Contemporary English: Theory and Description, Cambridge Univ Press, 95; Ther American Language and Its British Dialect, SECOL Rev, 95; American and British Words, Words: Proceedings of an Int Symposium, 96; Spanish Loanwords in English by 1900, Spanish Loanwords in the English Language: A Tendency towards Hegemony Reversal, Mouton de Gruyter, 96. **CONTACT ADDRESS** English Dept, Univ of Georgia, Athens, GA, 30602.

ALISKY, MARVIN HOWARD
PERSONAL Born 03/12/1923, Kansas City, MO, m, 1955, 2 children **DISCIPLINE** JOURNALISM, POLITICAL SCIENCE **EDUCATION** Univ TX, Austin, BA (liberal arts, political science & journalism combined), 46, MA (journalism), 47, PhD (political science, specifically Latin American politics), 53. **CAREER** NBC News correspondent in TX, 47, in Mexico, 48-49, Argentina-Uraguay, 49-50; asst prof journalism TV & govt, IN Univ, 53-57; assoc prof journalism and political science, AZ State Univ, 57-60; chmn, Mass Communications Dept, ASU, 57-65, prof political science, 60-90; founder, dir ASU Center for Latin American Studies, ASU, 65-72; Lect, US Information Agency, summers, Universities Mexico, Nicaragua, Costa Rica, Uraguay, Argentina, and Chile, 83-88; researcher, Latin Am Center in Beijing, China, 86, and in Soviet Union (Moscow and Leningrad) with World Media Asn, 89; once-a-month columnist, AZ Republic (Phoenix daily), 79-81, then with Phoenix Gazette, 81-83; nationally syndicated columnist on Latin Am, NCI syndicate 81-84. **HONORS AND AWARDS** Bd member (White House appointment), Fulbright Comm on Foreign Scholarships, 84-89; Envoy to UNESCO (4 month interim), 60; AZ-MEX Comm bd, 75-85; Town Hall fel, AZ Academy, 81-90. **MEMBERSHIPS** Life member, Sigma

Delta Chi (Soc of Professional Journalists); Am Political Science Asn; Western Political Science Asn; assoc member, Inter-Am Press Asn, 63-98; consultant, Liga de Municipios, State of Sonora, Mexico. **RESEARCH** Latin Am public life, govts, and mass media. **SELECTED PUBLICATIONS** Auth, Uruguay: Contemporary Survey, Praeger, 69; Political Forces in Latin America, Wadsworth Press, 70; Historical Dictionary of Peru, Scarecrow Press, 79; Latin America Media: Guidance and Sensorship, IA State Press, 81; co-auth with James Katz, Andres Ross, & Richard Latham, Arms Production in Developing Countries, Lexington Books, 84; co-auth with S H Surlin, W C Soderlung, Mass Media and the Caribbean, Gordon & Breach, 90; auth, Historical Dictionary of Mexico, Scarecrow Press, 81, 2nd ed, 99. **CONTACT ADDRESS** 44 W Palmdale, Tempe, AZ, 85282-2139.

ALLABACK, STEVE
DISCIPLINE AMERICAN LITERATURE **EDUCATION** Univ Wash, PhD, 66. **CAREER** PROF, ENG, UNIV CALIF, SANTA BARBARA. **RESEARCH** Writing of fiction. **SELECTED PUBLICATIONS** Auth, Alexander Solzhenitsyn, Warner, 79; Guide to the Journals of George and Anna Ticknor, Dartmouth Col Lib, 78. **CONTACT ADDRESS** Dept of Eng, Univ Calif, Santa Barbara, CA, 93106-7150. **EMAIL** steveall@humanitas.ucsb.edu

ALLEN, BRENDA J.
DISCIPLINE COMMUNCATION STUDIES **EDUCATION** Case Western Reserve Univ, BA; Howard Univ, MA, PhD. **CAREER** Assoc prof. **HONORS AND AWARDS** Tchr Recognition Awd. **MEMBERSHIPS** Black Student Asn. **RESEARCH** Organizational communication; computer mediated communication. **SELECTED PUBLICATIONS** Auth, Black womanhood and feminist standpoints, 98; Sapphire and Sappho: Allies in authenticity, 97; Gender and computer-mediated communication, 95; Diversity and organizational communication, Jour Applied Commun Res, 95; co-auth, Vocabularies of motives in a crisis of academic leadership: Hell hath no fury, 97. **CONTACT ADDRESS** Dept of Communication, Univ Colo Boulder, Boulder, CO, 80309. **EMAIL** Brenda.J.Allen@Colorado.edu

ALLEN, CHRIS
PERSONAL m, 2 children **DISCIPLINE** JOURNALISM AND BROADCASTING **EDUCATION** Iowa State Univ, BA, MA; Univ Mo, PhD, 96. **CAREER** Asst prof, Univ NDak, 87-92; instr, Univ Nebr, Omaha, 96-. **MEMBERSHIPS** Membership ch, Radio-TV Div, Asn for Educ in Jour and Mass Commun. **RESEARCH** Broadcast history. **SELECTED PUBLICATIONS** Published in Jour and Mass Commun Quart, Journ Educr, RTNDA Communicator and other publications. **CONTACT ADDRESS** Univ Nebr, Omaha, Omaha, NE, 68182. **EMAIL** cwallen@cwis.unomaha.edu

ALLEN, CRAIG MITCHELL
PERSONAL Born 02/06/1954, Portland, OR, m, 1990, 1 child **DISCIPLINE** MASS COMMUNICATION **EDUCATION** Linfield Col, BA, 76; Univ OR, MA, 77; OH Univ, PhD, 89. **CAREER** News dir, KAPP-TV, 78-80; news dir, KRDO, 81-82; asst news mgr, KMGH-TV, 82-84; news manager, KHQ-TV, 84-85. **HONORS AND AWARDS** Choice Award, 94; Sigma Delta Chi Award, 96; Canadian Embassy Teaching fel, 97. **MEMBERSHIPS** Radio-Television News Directors Asn; Int Commun Asn. **RESEARCH** International communication. **SELECTED PUBLICATIONS** Auth, Our First Television Candidate: Ike Over Stephenson, Journalism Quart, summer 88; Robert Montgomery Presents: Hollywood Debut in the Eisenhower White House, J of Broadcasting and Electronic Media, fall 91; Eisenhower's Congressional Defeat of 1956: Limitations of Television and the GOP, Presidential Studies Quart, spring 92; News Conference on TV: Ike-Age Politics Revisited, Journalism Quart, spring 93; Eisenhower and the Mass Media: Peace, Prosperity, and Prime Time TV, Univ NC Press, 93; When the News is You, US Dept of Interior, 94; Priorities of General Managers and News Directors in Anchor Hiring: Extending the Business-Journalism Dialectic to the Executive Suite, J of Media Economics, autumn 95; Exploring Newsroom Views About Consultants in Local TV: The Effect of Work Roles and Socialization, J of Broadcasting and Electronic Media, fall 96. **CONTACT ADDRESS** Stauffer Hall, Arizona State Univ, Tempe, Tempe, AZ, 85287-1305. **EMAIL** craig.allen@asu.edu

ALLEN, GILBERT BRUCE
PERSONAL Born 01/01/1951, Rockville Centre, NY, m, 1974 **DISCIPLINE** ENGLISH & AMERICAN POETRY **EDUCATION** Cornell Univ, BA, 72, MFA, 74, PhD(English & Am poetry), 77. **CAREER** Instr, Cornell Univ, 75-77; from asst prof to assoc prof, 77-89; prof English, Furman Univ, 89-; asst ed, Epoch, 72-77. **HONORS AND AWARDS** Amon Liner Award, 84; William Wordsworth Award, 89; Rainmaker Award, 90; David Ray Award, 94; Robert Penn Warren Award, 94, 95; Porter Fleming Award, 95; SC Fiction Proj Prize, 87, 89, 92, 98. **MEMBERSHIPS** South Atlantic Mod Lang Asn; NCTE; Poetry Soc of Am. **RESEARCH** Modern poetry; creative writing. **SELECTED PUBLICATIONS** Auth, Edward Thomas and Wilfred Owen: Sixty years after, Postscript, 83; Measuring the Mainstream, Southern Humanities Rev, 83; Heraclitean Dithering: The Criticism and Metacriticism of Stanley Fish, Furman Studies, 12/85; The Arc of a New Covenant: The Idea of the Reader in A.R. Ammon's poems, Pembroke Mag, 86; Canon Fodder: Models for Writers in an Especially Difficult Age, NMex Humanities Rev, 89; Millay and Modernism, Critical Essays on Edna St. Vincent Millay, 94; Dabney Stuart, Contemporary Poets, Dramatists, Essayists, and Novelists of the South, 94; Passionate Detachment in the Lyrics of Jeffer and Yeats, Robinson Jeffers and a Galaxy of Writers, 95; The Night the New Jesus Fell to Earth, Ga Rev, 95; In Everything: Poems 1972-1979, The Lotus Press, 82; Second Chances: Poems, Orchises Press, 91; Comandments at Eleven: Poems, Orchises Press, 94; co-ed, 45/96: The Ninety-Six Sampler of South Carolina Poetry, Ninety-Six Press, 94. **CONTACT ADDRESS** English Dept, Furman Univ, 3300 Poinsett Hwy, Greenville, SC, 29613-0438. **EMAIL** gil.allen@furman.edu

ALLEN, HARRIETTE LOUISE
PERSONAL Born 10/24/1943, Savannah, GA, d **DISCIPLINE** ENGLISH **EDUCATION** Fisk Univ, BA 1964; Univ of WI, MST 1972; George Peabody Coll for Tchrs Vanderbilt Univ, PhD English Educ 1980. **CAREER** S America Columbia, foreign exchange tchr of english 1964-65; Chicago Bd of Educ, spanish resource consult 1965-68; WI State Univ, asst proj dir tutorial prog 1970-72; Fisk Univ, poet-storyteller 1973-; Univ TN, poet-in-residence 1977-79; TN State Univ, asst prof of comm 1979-; State of TN, ambassador of letters 1979-. **HONORS AND AWARDS** 1st Black to receive Gov Spotlight Awd; 1st Black poet to be read into the Congressional Record; 1st poet to be pub in Attica Rebirth Newspaper of Attica Prison. **MEMBERSHIPS** Mem Alpha Kappa Alpha; Natl Theatre Assn; Black Theatre Assn SCETC; Natl Assn for Preservation & Perpetuation of Storytelling; Theta Alpha Phi Hon Forensic Frat; GA Soc of Poets; Natl Soc Pub Poets; Originator of Ballad Folk Theatre Art; star Jubas Jubilee Folktale Traveling Ensemble Co; 1st black storyteller at Natl Storytelling Fest Jonesboro TN. **SELECTED PUBLICATIONS** Auth, "Genesis & Jubas Folk Games". **CONTACT ADDRESS** State of Tennessee, #35 Legislative Plz, Nashville, TN, 37219.

ALLEN, M. AUSTIN
DISCIPLINE FILM **EDUCATION** Univ CA Berkley, BA; OH Univ, MA, PhD. **CAREER** Comm, Cleveland St Univ. **SELECTED PUBLICATIONS** Auth, Claiming open spaces. **CONTACT ADDRESS** Commun Dept, Cleveland State Univ, 83 E 24th St, Cleveland, OH, 44115. **EMAIL** m.allen@csuohio.edu

ALLEN, MYRIA
DISCIPLINE COMMUNICATIONS **EDUCATION** Univ Ky, BA, MA, PhD. **CAREER** Univ Ark **SELECTED PUBLICATIONS** Coauth, Broadcasting's silent majority: Departmental influence on perceptions and conflict, Journalism Quart, 88, Gender differences in perceptions of work: Limited access to decision-making power and supervisory support, Women's Studies Comm, 90; The impact of new technology on employees: A guide to consultants. Consultation, Int Jour, 90; A decade of organizational communication research: Journal articles 1980-1991, Comm Yearbook, 92; Communication and organizational commitment: Perceived organizational support as a mediating factor, Comm Quart, 92; Legimation endeavors: Impression management strategies used by an organization in crisis, Comm Monographs, 94; Communication variables shaping perceived organizational support, Western Jour Comm, 95; The relationship between communication, affect states, and voluntary turnover intentions, Southern Comm Jour, 96; Employee impression management strategy use when discussing their organization's public image. Jour Public Relations Res, 96; Total Quality Management, organizational commitment, perceived organizational support, and intraorganizational communication. Management Comm Quart, 97. **CONTACT ADDRESS** Univ Ark, Fayetteville, AR, 72701. **EMAIL** myria@comp.uark.edu

ALLEN, ORPHIA JANE
PERSONAL Born 09/14/1937, La Mesa, NM, 2 children **DISCIPLINE** WOMEN WRITERS **EDUCATION** NM State Univ, BA, 72, BA & MA, 74; Univ OK, PhD(English), 79. **CAREER** Instr, 76-79, asst prof, 79-86, assoc prof English, NM State Univ, 87-. **HONORS AND AWARDS** Publications Management received the Nat Coun of Teachers of English Best Collection in Technical and Scientific Communication Award, 95. **MEMBERSHIPS** MLA; Doris Lessing Soc. **RESEARCH** Rhetoric; technical and professional communication; women's studies, specifically 20th century women writers, women's autobiographical writing. **SELECTED PUBLICATIONS** Auth, The Function of the La Llorona Motif in Rudolfo Anaya's Bless Me Ultima, Latin Am Lit Rev, 77; Blake's Archetypal Criticism: The Canterbury Pilgrims, Genre, 78; Structure and Motif in Doris Lessing's A Man and Two Women, Mod Fiction Studies, 80; Interpreting The Sun Between Their Feet, Doris Lessing Newslett, 81; Interpreting Flavours of Exile, Doris Lessing Newslett, 7, 83; Barbara Pym: Writing a Life, Scarecrow Press, 94; co-ed, Publications Management: Essays for Professional Communicators, Baywood Press, 94. **CONTACT ADDRESS** PO Box 30001, Las Cruces, NM, 88003-8001. **EMAIL** oallen@nmsu.edu

ALLENTUCK, MARCIA EPSTEIN
PERSONAL Born 06/08/1928, Manhattan, NY, m, 1949, 1 child **DISCIPLINE** ENGLISH **EDUCATION** NY Univ, BA, 48; Columbia Univ, PhD, 64. **CAREER** Lectr English, Columbia Univ, 55-57 & Hunter Col, 57-59; from lectr to prof English, City Col NY, 59-88; prof Hist of Art, 74-88, prof emer, 88- , Grad Ctr, CUNY; Am Asn Univ Women Morrison fel, Huntington Libr, 58-59; Howard fel, Brown Univ, 66-67; Am Philos Soc res grant, 66-67; Huntington Libr fel, 68; Nat Transl Ctr fel, Univ Tex, 68-69; Chapelbrook Found fel, 70-71; sr res fel, Dumbarton Oaks, Harvard Univ, 72-73; sr res fel, Nat Endowment for Humanities, 73-74; vis fel, Wolfson Col, Oxford Univ, 74-; Brit Acad fel, Newberry Libr, 80; res fel, Schlesingen Libr, Radcliffe Col, Harvard Univ, 82; Swann res fel, 89-90. **HONORS AND AWARDS** Sussman Mem Medal, 46; hon MA, Oxon, 74. **MEMBERSHIPS** Fel Royal Soc of Arts London; Brit Soc Aesthet; MLA; Milton Soc Am; Augustan Reprint Soc. **RESEARCH** History of ideas; comparative literature; aesthetics. **SELECTED PUBLICATIONS** Auth, The works of Henry Needler, Augustan Reprint Soc, 61; Expression, aesthetic science and information theory, Proc Fifth Int Cong Aesthet, Amsterdam, 64; Fuseli and Lavater: Physiognomonical theory and the enlightenment, In: Studies on Voltaire and the Eighteenth Century, Lounz, 67; Isaac Balshevis Singer, Southern Ill Univ, 69; John Graham's System in modern art, Johns Hopkins Univ, 71; Fuseli and Herder, J Hist Ideas, 1/74. **CONTACT ADDRESS** 5 W 86th St Apt 12B, New York, NY, 10024.

ALLMAN, EILEEN JORGE
PERSONAL Born 06/22/1940, Mt. Vernon, NY, m, 1962, 1 child **DISCIPLINE** RENAISSANCE LITERATURE **EDUCATION** City Univ New York, BA, 61; Syracuse Univ, MA, 67, PhD, 73. **CAREER** Assoc prof, 70-98 Herbert H Lehman Col, CUNY **MEMBERSHIPS** MLA; Shakespeare Soc; Malone Soc. **RESEARCH** Jacobean tragedy; Shakespeare; Spenser. **SELECTED PUBLICATIONS** Auth, Player-King and Adversary: Two Faces of Play in Shakespeare, La St Univ Press, 81; auth, Jacobean Revenge Tragedy and the Politics of Virtue, Univ Delaware Press, 99. **CONTACT ADDRESS** 28 Frances Dr, Katonah, NY, 10536.

ALLMAN, WILLIAM ARTHUR
PERSONAL Born 06/10/1924, Tiffin, OH, m, 1950, 3 children **DISCIPLINE** THEATRE ARTS, SPEECH **EDUCATION** Heidelberg Col, BA, 49; Ohio Univ, MA, 51. **CAREER** Teacher & dir drama, High Sch, Ohio, 51-53; asst prof English & theatre arts, Ohio Northern Univ, 53-55; from asst prof to assoc prof speech & theatre, 55-77, dir drama, 55-81, prof speech & theatre, Baldwin-Wallace Col, 77-98. **HONORS AND AWARDS** Lifetime Achievement; Award from Cleveland Critics, 81; Grindstone (Person-of-the-Year) Award, in Berea, 83; Continuing Education Award from B-W Students, 87; Theatre Named in His Honor; Founder & Managing Dir of the Berea Summer Theatre, 57-96. **MEMBERSHIPS** Speech Commun Assn; Am Theatre Assn; Nat Theatre Conf; Theta Alpha Phi, Ohio Com Theatre Assoc, Ohio Theatre Alliance. **RESEARCH** Interpretative reading; theatre; films. **CONTACT ADDRESS** Dept of Speech, Baldwin-Wallace Col, 275 Eastland Rd, Berea, OH, 44017-2088. **EMAIL** biga7@aol.com

ALLMENDINGER, BLAKE
PERSONAL Born 04/02/1959, Lawton, OK, s **DISCIPLINE** ENGLISH **EDUCATION** Harvard Univ, AB, 81; Oxford Univ, MA, 83; Univ Pa, PhD, 89. **CAREER** Asst prof, 89-95, ASSOC PROF, UNIV CALIF, LOS ANGELES, 95-. **HONORS AND AWARDS** Ahmanson/Getty fel, 93-94. **RESEARCH** Lit, pop cult Am West **SELECTED PUBLICATIONS** Co-ed, Over the Edge: Remapping the American WEst, Univ Calif Press, 98; auth, Ten Most Wanted: The New Western Literature, Routledge, 98; auth, The Cowboy: Representations of Labor in an American Work Culture, Oxford Univ Press, 92. **CONTACT ADDRESS** Dept of English, Univ of California, Los Angeles, Box 90095-1930, Los Angeles, CA, 90095-1530. **EMAIL** allmendi@humnet.ucla.edu

ALSEN, EBERHARD
PERSONAL Born 10/26/1939, Nuremberg, Germany, m, 1986, 6 children **DISCIPLINE** AMERICAN LITERATURE **EDUCATION** Univ Bonn, Germany, BA, 62; Ind Univ, MA, 65, PhD, 67. **CAREER** Asst prof, 66-69, Univ Minn; assoc prof, prof, 69-98, SUNY, Cortland. **HONORS AND AWARDS** Fulbright Prof, 75-76, 81-82, Univ Tubingen; vis prof, 93-95, Univ Trier. **MEMBERSHIPS** MLA **RESEARCH** Contemporary Amer Fiction. **SELECTED PUBLICATIONS** Art, Toward the Living Sun: Richard Wright's Change of Heart from The Outsider to The Long Dream, CLA J 38.2, 94; auth, Romantic Postmodernism in American Fiction, Rodopi, 96; auth, Norman Mailer, Contemp Jew Amer Novelist, Greenwood, 97; art, Salinger's Franny, Short Story Criticism vol 28, Gale, 98; auth, Ernest J. Gaines, Toni Morrison, Contemp African-Amer Novelist, Greenwood, 98. **CONTACT ADDRESS** Dept of English, SUNY Cortland, Cortland, NY, 13045. **EMAIL** ebalsen@lightlink.com

ALTEGOER, DIANA B.
DISCIPLINE EARLY ENGLISH LITERATURE **EDUCATION** Vassar Col, BA, 84; Oxford Univ, MA, 87, PhD, 93.

CAREER Engl, Old Dominion Univ. **RESEARCH** Shakespeare, Renaissance non-dramatic literature. **SELECTED PUBLICATIONS** Areas: Baconian science and English Renaissance culture. **CONTACT ADDRESS** Old Dominion Univ, 4100 Powhatan Ave, BAL 442, Norfolk, VA, 23058. **EMAIL** DAltegoer@odu.edu

ALTER, JANE
PERSONAL Born 07/22/1938, Chicago, IL, d, 4 children **DISCIPLINE** ENGLISH **EDUCATION** Univ Chica, BA, 61; Trumen St Univ, MeD, 64; Texas Christ Univ, PhD, 70. **CAREER** Dir Pub Rel, Univ N Texas Heal Sci Cen, 78-80; Editor, TCU Press, 82-86; Dir, TCU Press, 87-. **HONORS AND AWARDS** Spur Awd Best West Novel; West Hert Wrangler Awds Nat Cowboy Hall of Fame; Texas Inst of Letters Best Juvenile. **MEMBERSHIPS** TX Inst Of Letters; West Writ of Am; Women Writ the West **RESEARCH** Women in the American west **SELECTED PUBLICATIONS** Sam Houston, Danbury, CT, Grolier Inc, 97; Rodeo! The Best Show on Dirt. Danbury, CT, Franklin Watts, 96; Meet Me at the Fair: County State and World Fairs and Expositions, Danbury CT, Franklin Watts, 97; Jessie, life Jessie Benton Fremont, NY Bantam, 95; Libbie, life Elizabeth Bacon Custer, NY Bantam, 94; Cherokee Rose, NY Bantam, 96; Callie Shaw, Stableboy, Austin TX, Eakin Pub, 96; Beauty Pagents: Tiaras, Roses and Runways, Danbury Ct, Franklin Watts, 97; Amusement Parks: Rollercoasters, Ferris Wheels and Cotton Candy, Danbury CT, Franklin Watts, 97; Wild West Shows: Rough Riders and Sure Shots, Danbury CT, Franklin Watts, 97. **CONTACT ADDRESS** TCU Press, Box 298300, Fort Worth, TX, 76129. **EMAIL** j.alter@tcu.edu

ALTMAN, CHARLES FREDERICK
PERSONAL Born 01/09/1945, De Ridder, LA, m, 1967 **DISCIPLINE** FRENCH LITERATURE; CINEMA **EDUCATION** Duke Univ, AB & MA, 66; Yale Univ, PhD, 71. **CAREER** Fulbright-Hayes fel and lectr, Am studies, Univ Paris X, Nanterre, 70-71; asst prof French and comp lit, Bryn Mawr Col, 71-74; asst prof French, 74-77; assoc prof French and comp lit, 77-82; assoc prof Film, French and Comp Lit, Univ Iowa, 82-86; prof French & Film, 86-; fel, Cornell Univ Soc for Hum, 74-75; dir, Paris Film Ctr, 80-81; vis prof, Univ Paris III-Censier, 80-81. **HONORS AND AWARDS** Russell B Nye Prize, Jour Pop Cult, 80; French nat. Decoration, Chevalier de L'Ordre des Palmes Academiques, 84; Soc for Cinema Studies prize, 84; French film critics award for best film book publ. in 1992, 92. **MEMBERSHIPS** MLA **RESEARCH** Narrative; 12th century Western culture; Film. **SELECTED PUBLICATIONS** Two types of opposition and the structure of Latin Saints' Lives, Medievalia et Humanistica New Series, 6: 1-11; Towards a historiography of American film, Cinema Jour, 16: 1-25 & Cinema Examined, Dutton, (in press); Psychoanalysis and Cinema: The imaginary discourse, Quart Rev of Film Studies, 2: 257-72; The medieval marquee: Church portal sculpture as publicity, Jour Pop Cult, 14: 37-46; Cinema/Sound, Yale French Studies, Vol 60, 80; Genre: The musical, Routledge & Kegan Paul, London and Boston 81; D W Griffith, Spec Issue Quart Rev of Film Studies, Vol 6, No 2; The American film musical, Ind Univ Press, 88; Sound Theory/Sound Practice, Routledge, 92; The State of Sound Studies, IRIS 27, 99; Film/Genre, Ind Univ Press, (in press). **CONTACT ADDRESS** Dept of Communication Studies, Univ of Iowa, Iowa City, IA, 52242-1528.

AMABILE, GEORGE
PERSONAL Born 05/29/1936, Jersey City, NJ **DISCIPLINE** ENGLISH **EDUCATION** Amherst Col, AB, 57; Univ Minn, MA, 61; Univ Conn, PhD, 69. **CAREER** Lectr to assoc prof, 63-86, PROF ENGLISH, UNIV MANITOBA, 87-. **HONORS AND AWARDS** Hunter Prize; Anna Von Helmholz Phelan Prize, Univ Minn, 61; Can Coun grants, 68, 81-82, 95-96; Can Authors Asn Nat Prize Poetry, 83. **MEMBERSHIPS** W Can Publ Asn; League Can Poets. **RESEARCH** Poetry. **SELECTED PUBLICATIONS** Auth, Blood Ties, 72; auth, Open Country, 76; auth, Flower and Song, 77; auth, Ideas of Shelter, 81; auth, The Presence of Fire, 82; auth, Four of a Kind 94; auth, Rumors of Paradise/Rumors of War, 95; co-founder & ed, The Far Point; ed, Northern Light; past ed, The Ivory Tower; past ed, The Penny Paper. **CONTACT ADDRESS** Dept of English, Univ of Manitoba, Winnipeg, MB, R3T 2N2.

AMASON, PATRICIA
DISCIPLINE INTERPERSONAL COMMUNICATION **EDUCATION** Univ Ark, BSE, 80; Univ Ky, MA, 83; Purdue Univ, PhD, 93. **CAREER** Comm Stu, Univ Ark **SELECTED PUBLICATIONS** Coauth, Popular, rejected, and supportive preadolescents: Social cognitive and communicative characteristics, Comm Yearbook, 87; Preadolescent support networks: Social-cognitive and communicative characteristics of natural "peer counselors", Jour Thought, 87. **CONTACT ADDRESS** Univ Ark, Fayetteville, AR, 72701.

AMATO, PHILIP P.
DISCIPLINE COMMUNICATION AND COMPUTER APPLICATIONS **EDUCATION** Emerson Col, BA, MA; MI State Univ, PhD. **CAREER** Com, Emerson Col. **SELECTED PUBLICATIONS** Auth, Organizational Patterns and Strategies in Speech Communication, Amato & Ecroyd, 75; Actuarial Mathematics of Finance, Satake, Amato and Gilligan, 94; A Summary of Statistical Inference, Satake, Amato and Hanssou, 94; Mathematical Reasoning: Sets, Logic and Probability, Satake and Amato, 97. **CONTACT ADDRESS** Emerson Col, 100 Beacon Street, Boston, MA, 02116-1596.

AMOS, MARK A.
DISCIPLINE LITERATURE **EDUCATION** Cornell Univ, AB, 81; Univ Miami, MA, 87; Duke Univ, PhD, 94. **CAREER** Grad instr, Univ of Miami, 85-86; asst, Univ Miami, 86-87; ed, Fuqua Sch Bus, 90; assoc coord, Duke Univ, 93; wrtg coord/instr, Duke Univ, 88-94; vis asst prof, Bates Col, 94-95; asst prof, 96-; ch, Curriculum Comm, 97-; ch, gen edu comm, 97; ch, core curriculum comm, 97; fac adv, 97-. **HONORS AND AWARDS** Tchg scholar, Univ of Miami, 85-87; outstanding tchg asst, Univ Miami, 87; master's thesis awaded distinstion, Univ Miami, 87; Univ travel fel(s), Univ Miami, 88-94; tchg fel, Am Assn Col(s) Jr, 91-92; res fel(s), Duke Univ, 92-94; curriculum wrtg grant, 97; res fel, 97-98; fel, 97-98. **RESEARCH** Medieval literature, history of English language, Renaissance literature, criticl theory. **SELECTED PUBLICATIONS** Rev, William Caxton and English Literary Culture, by N F Blake, Chaucer Yearbook 3, 96. **CONTACT ADDRESS** Dept of Eng, Wilkes Univ, 170 S Franklin St, Wilkes-Barre, PA, 18766. **EMAIL** amos@wilkes.edu

ANATOL, GISELLE L.
DISCIPLINE ENGLISH **EDUCATION** Yale Univ, BA, 92; Univ Pa, MA, 94, PhD, 98. **CAREER** Instr, Univ Pa, 93-97; asst prof, Univ Kans, 98-. **HONORS AND AWARDS** Andrew W. Mellon Dissertation Fel, 96-97; Irene Diamond Dissertation Fel, Leadership Alliance, 97-98. **MEMBERSHIPS** ALA; ASA; MLA; Asn of Carribean Women Writers and Scholars. **RESEARCH** Carribean and African-American literature. **SELECTED PUBLICATIONS** Auth, dis, Mother Countries, Motherlands, & Mother Love: Representations of Motherhood in 20th-Century Caribbean Women's Literature. **CONTACT ADDRESS** Dept of English, Univ of Kansas, 3114 Wescoe Hall, Lawrence, KS, 66045. **EMAIL** ganatol@falcon.cc.ukans.edu

ANDERSON, CAROLYN M.
PERSONAL Born 01/11/1939, Cleveland, OH, m, 1965, 2 children **DISCIPLINE** COMMUNICATION STUDIES **EDUCATION** Univ of Detroit, BA, 85; Wayne State Univ, MA, 88; Kent State Univ, PhD, 92. **CAREER** Adj prof, Univ of Detroit, 87-88; tchg fel, Kent State Univ, 88-91; vis asst prof, John Carroll Univ, 91-94; vis asst prof, Univ of Akron, 94-95; asst prof, Univ of Akron, 95- . **HONORS AND AWARDS** Kent State Grad Student Outstanding Tchg Award, 89/90; ICA Award Outstanding Grad Tchr, 89, 90. **MEMBERSHIPS** Nat Commun Asn; Central States Commun Asn. **RESEARCH** Hea Commun; Small Group Commun; Organizational Commun. **SELECTED PUBLICATIONS** Coauth, Nonverbal Behavior and rapport during nurse-practitioner-patient interviews, Mich Asn of Speech Commun Jour, 29, 94; Why employees speak to bosses and coworkers: Motives, gender, and organizational satisfaction, Jour of Bus Commun, 32, 95; Communication traits: A cross-generation investigation, Commun Res Reports, 13, 96; Argumentativeness and verbal aggressiveness, Jour of Social Behavior & Personality, 11; 96; The relationship between perceived understanding and self-disclosure in the sibling relationships, Commun Res Reports, 14, 97; Verbal aggression in sibling relationships, Commun Quarterly, 45, 97; Aggressive communication traits: How similar are young adults and their parents in argumentativeness, assertiveness, and verbal aggression, Western Jour of Commun, 61, 97; Reliability, separation of factors, and sex differences on the assertiveness-responsiveness measure: A Chinese sample, Commun Res Reports, 14, 97; Verbal aggression: A study of the relationship berween communication traits and feelings about a verbally aggressive television show, Commun Res Reports, 14, 97; The cognitive flexibility scale: Three validity studies, Commun Reports, 11, 98; Motives for communicating with family and friends: A Chinese Study, The Howard Jour of Commun, 9, 98. **CONTACT ADDRESS** Dept of Communication, Akron, OH, 44325-1003. **EMAIL** canders@uakron.edu

ANDERSON, CHRIS
DISCIPLINE CREATIVE NONFICTION, WRITING AND READING **EDUCATION** Gonzaga Univ Univ, BA, 77, MA, 79; Univ Wash, PhD, 83. **CAREER** Engl, Oregon St Univ. **SELECTED PUBLICATIONS** Auth, Style as Argument: Contemporary American Nonfiction. Southern Ill Univ Press, 87; Free/Style: A Direct Approach to Writing. Houghton-Mifflin, 92. Edge Effects: Notes from an Oregon Forest. Univ Iowa Press, 93; Coauth, Forest of Voices: Reading and Writing the Environment, Mayfield, 95. **CONTACT ADDRESS** Oregon State Univ, Corvallis, OR, 97331-4501. **EMAIL** canderson@orst.edu

ANDERSON, ERIC GARY
DISCIPLINE AMERICAN INDIAN LITERATURE **EDUCATION** Rutgers, PhD, 94. **CAREER** Engl, Okla St Univ. **MEMBERSHIPS** MLA; ASA; ALA; SCMLA; WLA; SAMLA; NEMLA. **RESEARCH** Late 19th early 20th century Am lit. **SELECTED PUBLICATIONS** Auth, Southwestern Dispositions: Migratory Encounters In Am Indian And Eurp-Am Lit, 98; Manifest Dentistry, or Teaching Oral Narrative in MCTEAGUE and Old Man Coyote, UP New England. **CONTACT ADDRESS** Oklahoma State Univ, 101 Whitehurst Hall, Stillwater, OK, 74078.

ANDERSON, FLOYD D.
DISCIPLINE COMMUNICATION STUDIES **EDUCATION** Idaho State Univ, BA; Univ Kans, MA; Univ Ill, PhD. **CAREER** Prof. **MEMBERSHIPS** Eastern Commun Asn. **RESEARCH** Postmodernist theories of rhetoric; feminist theories of language and rhetoric; orality and literacy. **SELECTED PUBLICATIONS** Auth, pubs on rhetorical theory and criticism. **CONTACT ADDRESS** Dept of Communication, State Univ NY Col Brockport, Brockport, NY, 14420. **EMAIL** fanderso@po.brockport.edu

ANDERSON, JUDITH HELENA
PERSONAL Born 04/21/1940, Worcester, MA, w, 1971 **DISCIPLINE** ENGLISH **EDUCATION** Radcliffe Coll, AB, 61; Yale Univ, MA, 62, PhD, 65. **CAREER** Instr, Cornell Univ, 64-66; asst prof, Cornell Univ, 66-72; vis lectr, Yale Univ, 73; asst prof, Univ Mich, 73-74; assoc prof, Ind Univ, 74-79; PROF, IND UNIV, 79-. **MEMBERSHIPS** Spenser Soc; Phi Beta Kappa; Renaisance Soc Am; Shakespeare Asn; Milton Soc; MLA; AAVP **RESEARCH** Renaissance literature & culture **SELECTED PUBLICATIONS** Auth, The Growth of a Personal Voice: "Piers Plowman" and "The Faerie Queene.", Yale Univ Press, 76; auth, Words that Matter: Linguistic Perception in Renaissance English, Stanford Univ Press, 96; co-edr, Spensers Life and the Subject of Biography, Univ Mass Press, 96. **CONTACT ADDRESS** English Dept, Indiana Univ, Bloomington, Bloomington, IN, 47405. **EMAIL** anders@indiana.edu

ANDERSON, LINDA
DISCIPLINE ENGLISH **EDUCATION** Univ Mn, PhD, 84 **CAREER** Assoc prof, Va Tech. **HONORS AND AWARDS** Col of Arts & Sci Cert of Teaching Excellence, 93-94 **MEMBERSHIPS** Shakespeare Soc of Amer; Int Shakespeare Soc; Renaissance Soc of Amer; SAMLA; SCMLA; SE Renaissance Conf. **RESEARCH** Shakespeare; renaissance lit; pop culture. **SELECTED PUBLICATIONS** Auth, Every Good Servant Does Not All Commands: Shakespeare's Servants and the Duty to Disobey, Upstart Crow, 92; art, What Movie Are We Watching Here: Cinematic Quotation in Recent Hollywood Films, Literature and Film in the Historical Dimension: Selected Papers from the Fifteenth Florida State University Conference on Literature and Film, Univ Press Fl, 94; auth, A Losing Office: Shakespeare's Use of Messengers, Upstart Crow, 97; art, Oh Dear Jesus It Is Female: Monster as Mother/Mother as Monster in Stephen King's It, Imagining the Worth: Stephen King and the Representation of Women, Greenwood Press, 98; auth, If Both My Sons Were on the Gallows, I Would Sign: Oppression of Children in Beaumont's The Knight of the Burning Pestle, Ilha do Desterro, Brazil, 98. **CONTACT ADDRESS** Dept of English, Va Tech, Blacksburg, VA, 24061-0112.

ANDERSON, STEVE
DISCIPLINE FILM **EDUCATION** Univ Miss, PhD. **CAREER** Comm Stu, Univ Ark. **HONORS AND AWARDS** Chair, eng dept; Ed, Technical Reader. **SELECTED PUBLICATIONS** Auth, American Expedition, Beloit Fiction Jour; Caesura, Beloit Fiction Jour; Skin, Beloit Fiction Jour; Forgiveness, Vietnam Generation; Strack, Perimeter Light. **CONTACT ADDRESS** Univ Ark Little Rock, 2801 S University Ave., Little Rock, AR, 72204-1099. **EMAIL** wsanderson@ualr.edu

ANDREAS, JAMES
DISCIPLINE ENGLISH LITERATURE **EDUCATION** Vanderbilt Univ, PhD, 73. **CAREER** Dept Eng, Clemson Univ **HONORS AND AWARDS** Ed, The Upstart Crow: A Shakespeare Jour; dir, Clemson Shakespeare Festival and SC Shakespeare Collaborative. **RESEARCH** Medieval and Renaissance literature. **SELECTED PUBLICATIONS** Auth, For O, the hobbyhorse is dead: Hamlet and the Death of Carnival, Renaissance Papers, SE Renaissance Conf, 97; Newe Science from Olde Bokes: A Bakhtinian Approach to the Summoner's Tale in Casebook on the Canterbury Tales, Macmillan, 97; Othello's African American Progeny in Materialist Shakespeare: A History, Verso Press, 95. **CONTACT ADDRESS** Clemson Univ, 611 Strode, Clemson, SC, 29634. **EMAIL** asjames@clemson.edu

ANDREWS, LARRY RAY
PERSONAL Born 08/09/1940, Greencastle, IN, m, 1961, 4 children **DISCIPLINE** ENGLISH; COMPARATIVE LITERATURE **EDUCATION** Ohio State Univ, BA, 62; Rutgers Univ, PhD(comp lit), 71. **CAREER** Instr English, Univ SC, 66-69; asst prof, 69-78, Assoc Prof English, Kent State Univ, 78-, Dean, Honors Col, 93-. **MEMBERSHIPS** Col Lang Asn. **RESEARCH** European romanticism; Russian-Western literary relations in 19th century; African American women's fiction. **SELECTED PUBLICATIONS** Auth, D V Venevitinov: A sketch of his life and works, Russ Lit Triquart, 74; Dostevskij and

Hugos Le Dernier Jour d'un Condamne, Comp Lit, 77; The Spatial Imagery of Oblomovism, Neophilologus, 88; Black Sisterhood in Gloria Naylor's Novels, CLAS, 89; Hugo's Gilliatt and Leskov's Golovan: Two Eccentric Folk-Epic Heroes, Comp Lit, 94. **CONTACT ADDRESS** Honors Col, Kent State Univ, PO Box 5190, Kent, OH, 44242-0001. **EMAIL** landrews@kent.edu

ANDRIA, MARCO
DISCIPLINE COMMUNCATION STUDIES **EDUCATION** Aston Univ, PhD. **CAREER** Asst prof. **SELECTED PUBLICATIONS** Co-auth, Face-to-Face: Interpersonal Communication in the Workplace, Prentice Hall, 94; Peter Gzowski: An Electric Life, ECW, 94; Music of Our Times: Eight Canadian Singer-Songwriters, Lorimer, 90. **CONTACT ADDRESS** Dept Communcation Studies, Athabasca Univ, 1 University Dr, Athabasca, AB, T9S 3A3. **EMAIL** marco@cs.athabascau.ca

ANDRUS, KAY L.
DISCIPLINE LEGAL RESEARCH **EDUCATION** Brigham Young Univ, BA, MLS, JD. **CAREER** Prof & dir, Law Libr; Creighton Univ, 90-; past assoc law lib dir, Northwestern Univ Sch Law; Reader Sevc(s) libn, asst prof, Southern Ill Univ; past sr ref libn, Southern Methodist Univ; past asst law lib dir, Okla City Univ. **SELECTED PUBLICATIONS** Pub(s) in, J Air Law and Commerce; Syllabus; Libr J & Southern Ill Univ Law J. **CONTACT ADDRESS** School of Law, Creighton Univ, 2500 California Plaza, Omaha, NE, 68178. **EMAIL** andrus@culaw.creighton.edu

ANGELOU, MAYA
PERSONAL Born 04/04/1928, St. Louis, MO, d **DISCIPLINE** LITERATURE, HISTORY **CAREER** Author, poet, playwright, stage and screen producer, director, actress, 1954-; Southern Christian Leadership Conference, coordinator, 1959-60; Arab Observer Egypt, associate editor, 1961-62; University of Ghana, asst administrator, 1963-66; African Review, editor, 1964-66; California State University, Wichita State University, visiting professor; WAKE FOREST UNIVERSITY, DEPARTMENT OF HUMANITIES, REYNOLDS PROFESSOR OF AMERICAN STUDIES, 1974-. **HONORS AND AWARDS** 32 Honorary Degrees; Pulitzer Prize Nomination, "Just Give Me A Cool Drink of Water 'fore I Diiie," 1972; Tony Award Nomination, "Look Away," 1975; Ladies Home Journal, one of the Women of the Year in Communications, 1976; Emmy Award Nomination, Performance, "Roots," 1977; Distingushed Woman of North Carolina, 1992; Essence Magazine, Woman of the Year, 1992; Horatio Alger Award, 1992; Women In Film, Crystal Award, 1992; American Academy of Achievement, Golden Plate Award, 1990; Horatio Alger Awards Dinner Chairman, 1993; National Society for the Prevention of Cruelty to Children, London, England, NSPCC Maya Angelou CPT and Family Centre, London, England, center dedication, June 20, 1991; NAACP, Image Award, Literary Work, Nonfiction, 1998. **MEMBERSHIPS** American Federation of Television & Radio Artists; board of trustees, American Film Institute, 1975-; Directors Guild; Actors' Equity; Women's Prison Assn. **SELECTED PUBLICATIONS** Author, works include: I Know Why the Caged Bird Sings, 1970; Just Give Me A Cool Drink of Water 'Fore I Die, 1971; Gather Together in My Name, 1974; Oh Pray My Wings Are Gonna Fit Me Well, 1975; Singin & Swingin & Getting Merry Like Christmas, 1976; And Still I Rise, 1978; The Heart of a Woman, 1981; Shaker, Why Don't You Sing? 1983; All God's Children Need Traveling Shoes, 1986; Mrs Flowers: A Moment of Friendship, 1986; Wouldn't Take Nothing for My Journey Now, Random, 1993; poems: Maya Angelou, 1986; Now Sheba Sings the Song, 1987; I Shall Not Be Moved, Random House, 1990; plays include: Cabraret for Freedom, 1960; The Least of These, 1966; Ajax, 1974; And Still I Rise, 1976; screenplays include: Georgia Georgia, 1972; All Day Long, 1974; PBS-TV Documentaries: "Who Cares About Kids" "Kindred Spirits," KERA-TV, Dallas, TX; "Rainbow In The Clouds," series, host, writer, WTVS-TV, Detroit, MI; "To The Contrary," Maryland Public Television; lecturer: Nancy Hanks Lecture, American Council for the Arts, 1990; contributing writer: "Brewster Place," mini-series, HARPO Productions; panelist: Institute for the Study of Human Systems, Zermatt, Switzerland, 1990; lyricist: "King Now," theatrical project, London, England; has appeared in numerous plays and TV productions as both an actress and singer; wrote and presented a poem for President Clinton's Swearing-In Ceremonies, 1993; Down in the Delta, director; named UNICEF National Ambassador, 1996. **CONTACT ADDRESS** Dept of Humanities, Wake Forest Univ, PO Box 7314, Winston-Salem, NC, 27109.

ANGYAL, ANDREW J.
PERSONAL Born 04/21/1946, Mineola, NY, m, 1971, 2 children **DISCIPLINE** ENGLISH & AMERICAN LITERATURE; ENVIRONMENTAL STUDIES **EDUCATION** Queens Col, NY, BA, 68; Yale Univ, MAR, 72; Duke Univ, PhD (English), 76. **CAREER** Instr English, New Haven Col, 69-70; master English & drama, South Kent Sch, 70-72; grad tutor English, Duke Univ, 74-76; prof English, Elon Col 76-, publ affairs officer US Environ Protection Agency, 72-74; partic polit sci, Duke fac fels in Commun Policy, 76; Fulbright lectr, Louis Kossuth Univ, Debrecen, Hungary, 86; Piedmont Independent Col Asn vis prof at Guilford Col, 88. **HONORS AND AWARDS** NY State Regents Grad Teaching Fel, 68; Tuition Scholar, Yale Univ, 68-70; Grad Tutorship, Duke Univ, 74-76; Grad Res Grant, Duke Univ, 75; Elon Col Fac Res Grants, 78-86; Weymouth House Writer-in-Residence, Southern Pines, NC, 80; Fulbright Lecturer in Am Lit (Hungary), 86; Fel in Eastern European Studies, Appalachian Humanities Prog, Appalachian State Univ, 90-91; Vassar Col Summer NEH Inst on The Environmental Imagination, 97. **MEMBERSHIPS** Soc for Study Southern Lit; Conf on Christianity & Lit; NAS; ALSC; PAC. **RESEARCH** American literature; textual and bibliographic studies; science and literature; natural history; environmental studies. **SELECTED PUBLICATIONS** Coauth, Some Early Frost Imitations of Poe, Poe Studies, 6/76; auth, Robert Frost's Poetry Before 1913: A Checklist, Proof 5: Yearbk Am Bibliog & Textual Studies, 5/77; Wallace Stevens' Sunday Morning as Secular Belief, Christianity & Lit, 10/79; Literary Politics and the Shaping of the Frost Poetic Canon, SC Rev, 4/80; Loren Eiseley, G K Hall, 83; Lewis Thomas, G K Hall, 89; Wendell Berry, Twayne, 95; From Swedenborg to William James: The Shaping of Frost's Religious Beliefs, Robert Frost Rev, Fall 94; The Complex Fate of Being an American: The African-American Essayist and the Quest for an Identity, CLA J, 9/93; Loren Eiseley's Immense Journey: The Making of a Literary Naturalist, The Lit of Sci. Univ Ga Press, 93. **CONTACT ADDRESS** Dept of English, Elon Col, Box 2245, Elon College, NC, 27244. **EMAIL** angyal@elon.edu

ANSPAUGH, KELLY C.
PERSONAL Born 03/12/1960, Lima, OH, s **DISCIPLINE** ENGLISH **EDUCATION** Univ Wis-Madison, PhD, 92 **CAREER** LECTR, OHIO STATE UNIV-LIMA, 92-. **RESEARCH** Modern British literature, the novel. **SELECTED PUBLICATIONS** Auth, "The Partially Purged: Beckett's 'The Calmative' as Anti-Comedy," Can Jour of Irish Studies, 96; auth, " 'When Lovely Wooman Stoops to Conk Him'": Virginia Woolf in Finnegans Wake," Joyce Studies Annual, 96; auth, "Getting Even with Uncle Ez: Wyndham Lewis's 'Doppelganger," Jour of Modern Lit, 95; auth, "'Faith, Hope, and - what was it?': Beckett Reading Joyce Reading Dante," Jour of Beckett Studies, 96; auth, "The Metempsychosis of Ajax: Leopold Bloom as Excremental Hero," Moderna Sprak, 96; auth, "'Delenda Est Bloomsbury': Wyndham Lewis Blasts Virginia Woolf," Wyndham Lewis Annual, 96; auth, "James Joyce, Wyndham Lewis, and the High Modern Grotesque," in Literature and the Grotesque, 95, Rodopi Press; auth, "Ulysses Upon Ajax: Joyce, Harington, and the Question of Cloacal Imperialism," South Atlantic Rev, 95; auth, "Repression or Suppression? Freud's Interpretation of the Dream of Irma's Injection," The Psychoanalytic Rev, 95; auth, "Dante on his Head: Conrad's Heart of Darkness," Conradiana, 95; auth, "Reading the Intertext in Jonathan Swift's 'A Panegyrick on the Dean," Essays in Lit, 95; auth, "Blasting the Bombardier: Another Look at Lewis, Joyce, and Woolf," Twentieth Century Lit, 94; auth, "How Butt Shot the Chamber Pot: Finnegans Wake II.3," James Joyce Quarterly, 94; auth, "Powers of Ordure: James Joyce and the Excremental Vision(s)," Mosaic, 94; auth, "'Three Mortal Hour¤ls: Female Gothic in Joyce's 'The Dead,'" Studies in Short Fiction, 94; auth, "Illustrating 'Mark Time's Finist Joke,'" Thalia: Studies in Lit Humor, 95; auth, "'Bung Goes the Enemay': Wyndham Lewis and the Uses of Disgust," Mattoid, 94; auth, "The Innocent Eye? E. W. Kemble's Illustrations to Adventures of Huckleberry Finn," American Literary Realism, 93. **CONTACT ADDRESS** 4240 Campus Dr, Lima, OH, 45804. **EMAIL** Anspaugh.2@osu.edu

ANTHES, SUSAN H.
PERSONAL Born 11/03/1944, Manitowac, WI, m, 1966, 2 children **DISCIPLINE** LIBRARY SCIENCE **EDUCATION** Univ Wis, BA, 66, MA, 67. **CAREER** Librn, Univ Wis Law Libry, 67-68; asst librn, Univ Miami, 68-71; asst librn, Pa State Univ, 71-81; asst librn, 71-91; librn, 81-91, assoc dir, 91-, Univ Colo Boulder. **MEMBERSHIPS** Am Libr Asn; Colo Libr Asn; Asn Col & Res Libr. **RESEARCH** Management in libraries; women in libraries. **SELECTED PUBLICATIONS** Coauth, art, The Collaborative Course: Innovative Teaching and Learning, 91; auth, art, A Potpourri of Practical Ideas from ACRL'S 6th National Conference: Administration, 92; coauth, art, Incorporating Information Literacy into the Core Curriculum, 92; auth, art, Outreach, Promotion and Bibliographic Instruction, 93; auth, art, Report on LAMA Preconference, 97. **CONTACT ADDRESS** 163 Gillaspie Dr, Boulder, CO, 80303. **EMAIL** anthes@spot.colorado.edu

ANTHONY, GERALDINE
PERSONAL Brooklyn, NY **DISCIPLINE** ENGLISH **EDUCATION** Mt St Vincent Univ, BA, 51; St John's Univ, MA, 56, PhD, 63. **CAREER** Tchr, Mt St Vincent Acad, 63-65; asst prof, 65-71, assoc prof, 71-77, prof, 77-87, chair, 83-86, PROF EMER ENGLISH, MT ST VINCENT UNIV 87-. **HONORS AND AWARDS** Fel Journalism, Wall St. J, 65; post-doc fel, Mod Drama, Columbia Univ, 69. **SELECTED PUBLICATIONS** Ed, Profiles in Canadian Drama, 77; ed, Canadian Theatre History, 80; ed, Canadian Theatre and Drama, 90-92. **CONTACT ADDRESS** Dept of English, Mount Saint Vincent Univ, 106 Shore Dr, Halifax, NS, B4A 2E1.

ANTUSH, JOHN V.
DISCIPLINE ENGLISH **EDUCATION** Gonzaga Univ, BA, 56, MA, 60; Stanford Univ, PhD, 67. **CAREER** Teaching fel, Stanford Univ, 61-63, from instr to prof, Fordham Univ, 64-; chemn of English dept, 85-88. **HONORS AND AWARDS** W. Wilson Fel Award, 63-64; Fordham Fac Fel, 67, 76, 89, 95; Fulbright Travel Award, 95. **SELECTED PUBLICATIONS** Auth, The New Puerto Rican in the Plays of Edward Gallardo, in SCAPR Newsletter 11, 90; The American Experience in Puerto Rican Drama/The Puerto Rican Experience in American Drama, in Sargasso: The Jour of Caribbean Studies 7, 91; Rene Marques' The Oxcart: Revolutionizing Drama of the Americans, in SCAPR Newsletter 12, 92; Roberto Rodriguez Suarez: Transcultural Catalyst of Puerto Rican Drama, in The J of Am Drama and Theatre 4, 92; Editing the Bilingual Text at Cross-Cultural Purposes, in TEXT: Transactions of the Soc for Textual Scholarship 6, 94; The Academic Politics and Commercial Possibilities of Publishing Puerto Rican Plays in New York, in Multicultural Rev, vol. 3, no. 2, 94; The Internal Third World Voice and Postcolonial Literature: Rene Marques's The Oxcart, in Staging Difference: Cultural Pluralism in Am Theatre and Drama, 95; ed, Simpson Street and Other Plays: by Edward Gallardo, 90; Recent Puerto Rican Theatre: Five Plays from New York, 91; Nuestro New York: An Anthology of Puerto Rican Plays, 94. **CONTACT ADDRESS** English Dept, Fordham Univ, Bronx, NY, 10458.

AOKI, ERIC
DISCIPLINE COMMUNICATION STUDIES **EDUCATION** Calif State Univ Fresno, BA, MA; Univ Wash, PhD. **CAREER** Prof. **RESEARCH** Intercultural communication; interpersonal communication; ethnography of communication. **SELECTED PUBLICATIONS** Auth, Passages of Guilt, Interrace Magazine. **CONTACT ADDRESS** Speech Communication Dept, Colorado State Univ, Fort Collins, CO, 80523. **EMAIL** akoi@vines.colostate.edu

APPEL, ALFRED, JR.
DISCIPLINE ENGLISH **EDUCATION** Columbia Univ, PhD. **CAREER** Dept Eng, Northwestern Univ **SELECTED PUBLICATIONS** Auth, Nabokov's Dark Cinema, 74; Signs of Life: a work on American photography and popular culture of the past five decades, 83; The Art of Celebration: The Expression of Joy in 20th Century Art, Literature, Photography and Music, Knopf, 92; rev ed, The Annotated Lolita. **CONTACT ADDRESS** Dept of English, Northwestern Univ, 1801 Hinman, Evanston, IL, 60208.

APPLEWHITE, JAMES W.
DISCIPLINE ENGLISH LITERATURE **EDUCATION** Duke Univ, PhD. **CAREER** Prof, Duke Univ. **SELECTED PUBLICATIONS** Auth, Wordswor Seas and Inland Journeys: Landscape and Consciousness fth to Roethke, Ga, 85; River Writing: An Eno Journal, Princeton, 88; Daytime and Starlight, LSU, 97; pubs on modern Am poetry; southern lit, and modernist and postmodernist aesthet poetry and visual art. **CONTACT ADDRESS** Eng Dept, Duke Univ, Durham, NC, 27706.

APPLEYARD, JOSEPH A.
PERSONAL Born 05/09/1931, Malden, MA **DISCIPLINE** ENGLISH **EDUCATION** Boston Col, AB, 53; Weston Col, PhL, 58; Harvard Uniy, PhD, 64; Faculteit SJ, Maastricht, Netherlands, STL, 67. **CAREER** From asst prof to assoc prof Eng, 67-91, prof eng, Boston Col, 91-, chmn dept, 79-, Dir, Col of Arts and Sci honors prog, 87-97, vpres, Univ mission and ministry, 98. **RESEARCH** Nineteenth and twentieth century Eng lit; lit criticism and theory. **SELECTED PUBLICATIONS** Auth, Coleridge's Philosophy of Literature, Harvard Univ, 65; Becoming a Reader, Cambridge Univ, 90. **CONTACT ADDRESS** Dept of Eng, Boston Col, 140 Commonwealth Ave, Chestnut Hill, MA, 02467-3800. **EMAIL** jospeh.appleyard@bc.edu

APSELOFF, MARILYN FAIN
PERSONAL Born 03/18/1934, Attleboro, MA, m, 1956, 4 children **DISCIPLINE** CHILDREN'S LITERATURE, AMERICAN LITERATURE **EDUCATION** Univ Cincinnati, BA, 56, MA, 57. **CAREER** From instr to prof Children's Lit, Kent State Univ, 68-. **HONORS AND AWARDS** Children's Lit Assoc Honor BK, 90 for Nonsense Lit for Children. **MEMBERSHIPS** MLA; Children's Lit Asn (pres-elect, 78-79). **RESEARCH** 20 th Century humorous books for children; whaling wives and children at sea. **SELECTED PUBLICATIONS** Auth, Virginia Hamilton: Ohio Explorer in the World of Imagination, State Libr Ohio, 78; Monograph, Virginia Hamilton: Ohio Explorer in the World of Imagination, State Libr Ohio, 78; Old Wine in New Bottles: Adult Poetry for Children, Children's Lit Educ, winter 79; Tom Thumb in Academia, The New Era, 5-6/81; They Wrote for Children Too, Greenwood, 89; Elizabeth George Speare, Twayne, 91; Nonsense Literature for Children with Celia C Anderson, Shoestring Press, 89. **CONTACT ADDRESS** Dept of English, Kent State Univ, PO Box 5190, Kent, OH, 44242-0001. **EMAIL** mapselof@kentvm.kent.edu

ARCANA, JUDITH
DISCIPLINE ENGLISH LITERATURE **EDUCATION** Northwestern Univ, BA; Univ Ill, MA; Univ Chicago, PhD. **CAREER** Lectr. **RESEARCH** Women's studies; improvisational theater performance; radical health care; magic and the old religion. **SELECTED PUBLICATIONS** Auth, Mamababy, 95; The Body of A Goddess, 95; My Father's Prostrate Gland, Sojourner, 94; The Book of Daniel, 94; Abortion is a Motherhood Issue, 94. **CONTACT ADDRESS** Union Inst, 440 E McMillan St., Cincinnati, OH, 45206-1925.

ARENBERG, NANCY
DISCIPLINE EPISTOLARY FICTION **EDUCATION** Grinnell Col, BA, 82; Univ Ill, MA, 89; Univ Ariz, PhD, 96. **CAREER** English and Lit, Univ Ark. **SELECTED PUBLICATIONS** Area: seventeenth- and eighteenth-century French literature. **CONTACT ADDRESS** Univ Ark, Fayetteville, AR, 72701.

ARLISS, LAURIE
DISCIPLINE COMMUNICATION STUDIES **EDUCATION** SUNY-Cortland Univ, BA, MA; SUNY Buffalo Univ, PhD. **CAREER** Assoc prof. **SELECTED PUBLICATIONS** Auth, pubs on gender and communication and family communication. **CONTACT ADDRESS** Dept of Speech Communication, Ithaca Col, 100 Job Hall, Ithaca, NY, 14850.

ARNASON, DAVID E.
DISCIPLINE ENGLISH LITERATURE **EDUCATION** Univ Manitoba, MA; Univ New Brunswick, PhD. **CAREER** Prof **HONORS AND AWARDS** Ed, Jour Can Fiction; ed, Macmillan Themes Can Lit; ed, Nineteenth Century Can Stories; ed, Turnstone Press. **SELECTED PUBLICATIONS** Auth, Marsh Burning; The Icelanders; Piece of Advice; The Circus Performer's Bar; The Happiest Man in the World; The Pagan Wall; Skragg; The New Icelanders; The Dragon and The Drygoods Princess; If Pigs Could Fly. **CONTACT ADDRESS** Dept of English, Manitoba Univ, Winnipeg, MB, R3T 2N2.

ARNER, ROBERT DAVID
PERSONAL Born 01/17/1943, Lehighton, PA, 2 children **DISCIPLINE** AMERICAN LITERATURE **EDUCATION** Kutztown State Col, BS, 64; PA State Univ, MA, 66, PhD(English), 70. **CAREER** From instr to asst prof English, Cent Mich Univ, 68-71; from asst prof to assoc prof, 71-75, PROF ENGLISH, UNIV CINCINNATI, 75-; Mem int bibliog comt, MLA, 68-; Fred Harris Daniels fel, Am Antiq Soc, 75; Henry E Huntington fel, Huntington Libr, 75; MEMLA/AAS fel, 91. **MEMBERSHIPS** MLA; SAMLA. **RESEARCH** Early American literature; 19th century American literature; American humor. **SELECTED PUBLICATIONS** Auth, Hawthorne and Jones Very: Two Dimensions of Satire in Egotism: Or, the Bosom Serpent, New England Quart, 6/69; Ebenezer Cooke's The Sot-Weed factor: The Structure of Satire, Southern Lit J, fall 71; Pastoral Patterns in William Bartram's Travels, Tenn Studies Lit, 73; Literature to 1800, Am Lit Scholarship, 74-77; Westover and the Wilderness: William Byrd's Images of Virginia, Southern Lit J, 75; Kate Chopin, La Studies, 75; The Romance of Roanoke: Virginia Dare and the Lost Colony in American Literature, 1585-1970, Southern Lit J, 78; James Thurber: An Introduction, Nat Endowment for Humanities Proj Ohio Cult, Ohio State Libr, 80; Dobson's Encyclopedia: The Publisher, Text, and Publication of America's First Britannica, Univ PA, 91; Historical Essay on Charles Brockden Brown's Alcuin and Stephen Calvert, Kent SUP, 86; Thomas Dobson's American Edition of the Encyclopedia Britannica, Voltaire Studies, no 315, 94; Thomas Dobson's Rolling Mill for Copper: A Note on the Publisher of the Encyclopedia, PMHB, 94. **CONTACT ADDRESS** Dept of English, Univ of Cincinnati, P O Box 210069, Cincinnati, OH, 45221-0069. **EMAIL** arnerrd@email.uc.edu

ARNESON, PAT
DISCIPLINE INTERPERSONAL COMMUNICATION **EDUCATION** OH Univ, PhD, 87. **CAREER** Prof, Univ Northern CO. **MEMBERSHIPS** CO Speech Commun Asn; Western States Commun Asn; Nat Commun Asn. **RESEARCH** Interpersonal commun; qualitative research methods. **SELECTED PUBLICATIONS** Auth, Sacred Dimensions of the shaman's web. Integrative Explorations, J of Cult and Consciousness, 4(1), 97; coauth, Interpersonal communication ethics and the limits of individualism, The Electronic J of Commun/La Rev Electronique de Commun, 6(4), 96; Educational Assessment as invitation for dialogue, J of the Asn for Commun Admin, 79, 97. **CONTACT ADDRESS** Univ Northern Colorado, Greeley, CO, 80639.

ARNETT, RONALD C.
PERSONAL Born 03/10/1952, Ft Wayne, IN, m, 1972, 2 children **DISCIPLINE** COMMUNICATION **EDUCATION** Manchester Col, BS, 74; Ohio Univ, MA, 75, PhD, 77; Bethany Col Seminary, MDiv, 83. **CAREER** Asst & Assoc Prof, St Cloud State Univ, 77-84; Adj Prof, Bethany Theol Seminary, 82-89; Ch, Assoc Prof, Marquette Univ, 84-87; Prof Commun Stud, VP/Dean Acad Aff, Manchester Col, 87-93; Ch & Prof, Dept of Commun, Duquesne Univ, 93-97; Ch & Prof, Aff Depts of Commun & Eng, Duquesne Univ, 97-. **HONORS AND AWARDS** Patron St for Saturday Col Commencement, Duquesne Univ, 77; Oustanding Alumnus & inductee into Interpersonal Commun Hall of Fame, 96. **MEMBERSHIPS** Int Commun Asn; Speech Commun Asn; Cent State Commun Asn; Speech Commun Asn of Pa (vp 77); Relig Speech Commun Asn; Cons on Peace Res, Educ, & Dev. **RESEARCH** Dialogue; communications ethics; philosophy of communications. **SELECTED PUBLICATIONS** Auth, Dwell in Peace: Applying Nonviolence to Everyday Relationships, Brethren Press, 80, 85; auth, Communication and Community: Implications of Martin Buber's Dialogue, S Ill Univ Press, 86; auth, Dialogue Education: Conversation About Ideas and Between Persons, S Ill Univ Press, 92, 97; co-ed, The Reach of Dialogue: Confirmation, Voice, and Community, Hampton Press, 94; co-auth, Communication Ethics in an Age of Diversity, Univ Ill Press, 96; co-auth, Dialogic Civility in a Cynical Age: Community, Hope, and Interpersonal Relationships, in press. **CONTACT ADDRESS** 9767 Griffith Rd, Wexford, PA, 15090. **EMAIL** arnett@duq2.cc.duq.edu

ARNEZ, NANCY L.
PERSONAL Born 07/06/1928, Baltimore, MD, d **DISCIPLINE** ENGLISH **EDUCATION** Morgan State Coll, AB 1949; Columbia Univ, MA 1954, EdD 1958; Harvard Univ, post doctoral 1962; Loyola Coll, 1965. **CAREER** Baltimore Pub Sch, English tchr 1949-58, dept head 1958-62; Morgan State Coll, dir student teaching 1962-66; Northeastern IL Univ, assoc prof/asst dir Cntr for Inner City Studies 1966-69, prof/dir Cntr for Inner City Studies 1969-74, co-founder, Cultural Linguistic, Follow Through Early Childhood CICS 1969-74; Howard Univ School of Educ, acting dean 1975, assoc dean 1974-, dept chairperson 1980-86, professor 1986-. **HONORS AND AWARDS** Assn of African History Serv Award 1972; Alpha Kappa Alpha Sor Serv Award 1971; Appointed Hon Citizen of Compton, CA 1972; Howard Univ distinguished faculty research awd 1983; 4th place in the international competition for Phi Delta Kappa's biennial awd for outstanding research 1985. **MEMBERSHIPS** Congress of African People 1968-70; Amer Assn of School Admin 1968-87; Black Child Devel Inst DC 1971-74; Assn of African Historians Chicago 1972; Assn of the Study of Afro-Amer Life & Hist 1972-77; mem African Heritage Studies Assn, bd of dir membership sec 1973-77; Natl Alliance of Black Sch Educators 1973-; Amer Assn of Sch Admin Resolutions Comm 1973-75; African Information Cntr Catalyst Chicago 1973-77; bd of dir DuSable Museum Chicago 1973-74; mem Black Women's Comm Devel Found DC 1974; Amer Assn of Coll Tchrs of Educ 1977; Natl Council of Negro Women 1977; mem Phi Delta Kappa Howard Univ Chap 1974-, editorial bd 1975-78; Journal of Negro Education, editorial bd 1975-80; AASA Professor, editorial bd 1981-84; NABSE Newsbrief, editor 1984-86;mem DC Alliance of Black School Educator 1984-, pres 1986-88. **SELECTED PUBLICATIONS** 180 publications. **CONTACT ADDRESS** Howard Univ, 2400 6th St, NW, Washington, DC, 20059.

ARNOLD, EDWIN P.
PERSONAL Born 07/09/1945, Brausa Falls, PA, m, 1968, 2 children **DISCIPLINE** HUMANITIES **EDUCATION** Geneva Col, BS, 67; Duquesne Univ, MA, 72; Univ Houston, EdD, 81. **CAREER** Dir, Tublic Sch, 67; assoc dir, Slippery Rock State Univ, 69-73; asst dir, Univ Houston, 74; chemn, Grove City Col, 75-. **MEMBERSHIPS** Am Band Masters Asn; DMEA; CBDNA; MENC. **CONTACT ADDRESS** Grove City Col, Grove City, PA, 16127.

ARNOLD TWINING, MARY
DISCIPLINE ENGLISH LITERATURE **EDUCATION** Ind Univ, PhD. **CAREER** Dept Eng, Clark Atlanta Univ **RESEARCH** African and African American traditional cultures and orature; Native American oral and written literature; Sea island folklore and folklife; African American science fiction writers; Southern literature. **SELECTED PUBLICATIONS** Co-ed, Sea Island Roots: African Presence in the Carolinas and Georgia. **CONTACT ADDRESS** Clark Atlanta Univ, 223 James P Brawley Dr, SW, Atlanta, GA, 30314.

ARONSON, ARNOLD
PERSONAL Born 03/08/1948, Morristown, NJ, m, 1988, 1 child **DISCIPLINE** PERFORMING ARTS **EDUCATION** Rutgers Univ, BA, 69; New York Univ, MA, 75, PhD, 77. **CAREER** From asst to assoc prof, Univ Va, 76-84; vis assoc prof, Cornell Univ, 84-85; vis assoc prof, Univ Del, 85-86; assoc prof, Univ Mich, 86-90; CUNY prof, Hunter Col, 90-91; prof, Columbia Univ. **HONORS AND AWARDS** Chemn, Univ Mich, 87-90; chemn, Hunter Col, 90-91, chemn, Columbia Univ, 91-98. **MEMBERSHIPS** Int Org of Scenographers, Theatre Archit, and Technicians; Am Soc for Theatre Res; US Inst for Theatre Tech. **RESEARCH** Theatre Hist. **SELECTED PUBLICATIONS** Auth, The History and Theory of Environmental Scenography, 81; auth, American Set Design, 85; auth, The Scenography of Chekhov's Plays, 99; auth, Theatre Technology and the Shifting Aesthetic, 97; auth, The History of Design for Dance, 97. **CONTACT ADDRESS** Div of Theatre, Columbia Univ, 2960 Broadway, 601 Dodge Hall-MC 1807, New York, NY, 10027. **EMAIL** apay@columbia.edu

ARTHUR, GWEN
PERSONAL Born 02/05/1953, Charleston, SC, m, 1991 **DISCIPLINE** COMMUNICATION; LIBRARY SERVICE **EDUCATION** Wesleyan Univ, BA, 75; Columbia Univ, MLS, 82; Univ Pa Philadelphia, 90. **CAREER** Co-ord to bibliogr, Temple Univ, 85-91; head, Bowling Green St Univ, 91-95; head, Trinity Col, 95-96; head, Trinity Col, 96- . **HONORS AND AWARDS** Cum laude, Wesleyan Univ; Beta Phi Mu, Columbia Univ. **MEMBERSHIPS** Amer Libr Assoc; Assoc of Col & Res Libr; Libr Admin & Mgmt Assoc; Ref & User Svc Assoc. **RESEARCH** Library personnel issues; electronic ref & collections; soc sci librarianship. **SELECTED PUBLICATIONS** Auth, Using Video for Reference Staff Training and Development: A Selective Bibliography, Ref Svc Rev, 92; 90's Alternatives for Library Staff Development, paper, Acad Libr Assoc Oh Annual Conf, 93; Customer Service Training in Academic Libraries, J of Acad Librarianship, 94; The Graying of Librarianship: Implications for Academic Library Managers, J of Acad Librarianship, 98. **CONTACT ADDRESS** 175 Brace Rd, West Hartford, CT, 06107-1812. **EMAIL** garthur@mail.trincoll.edu

ARTHUR, THOMAS H.
PERSONAL Born 01/04/1937, Chicago, IL, m, 1976, 4 children **DISCIPLINE** DRAMA **EDUCATION** Northwestern Univ, BS (general speech), 59; IN Univ, MA (theatre), 69, PhD (Am Studies), 73. **CAREER** Teaching asst in acting, directing, and oral interpretation, IN Univ, 65-68; adjunct lect in Theatre Hist, IL Wesleyan Univ, 72-73; asst prof, IL State Univ, 69-73; assoc prof, 73-80, prof, Center for Dance & Theatre, 85-86 & Dept of Commun Arts, 80-85, prof, School of Theatre & Dance, James Madison Univ, Harisonburg, VA, 86-. **HONORS AND AWARDS** Honorable mention, Russell B Nye Award, 81-82; selection of directorial work for the ACTF Southeast Regional Am Col Theatre Festival, Greensboro, NC, and Clemson, SC, 98; invited appearance of directing work, The Roadhouse Theatre for Contemporary Art, Erie, PA, 92; selection of producing work, ACTRF, Radford, VA, 92, and at ACTF Nat Festival at Kennedy Space Center; invitation/financing to write South African Theatre J Reviews ofm 92 Grahamstown Theatre Festival plays; James Madison Univ nomination for State Coun of Higher Ed in VA Outstanding Fac Award, 93, 95; US Information Agency Arts Am Consultant, Naples, Italy, Nov 95, Budapest, Hungary, March 94, Finland, Nov 89, and South Africa, June/July, 89; biography found in numerous publications. **MEMBERSHIPS** Am Soc for Theatre Res; Am Asn for Univ Prof; Asn for Theatre in Higher Ed; Black Theatre Network; Int Fed for Theatre Res; Nat Asn of Schools of Ed; Southeastern Theatre Conference; Speech Commun of Am; VA Theatre Asn. **SELECTED PUBLICATIONS** Auth, Review of Athol Fugard's My Children! My Africa! in Theatre J, May 90; Spaghetti Westerns and American Football: The Extraordinary Life of Actor Woody Strode, Encore Mag, May 90; Review of Method Acting: Three Generations of an American Acting Style by Steve Vineberg, Dramatics, Oct 91; Looking for My Relatives: The Political Implications of Family in Selected Works of Athol Fugard and August Wilson, SATJ, Sept 92; review of Deon Opperman's Women in the Wings at the 1992 Grahamstown Nat Theatre Festival, Theatre J, May 93; The 1994 Grahamstown Festival, co-auth by Michael D Arthur, South African Theatre J, Sept 94; review of David Edgar's Pentecost in Stages section of Theatre Insight, co-auth by Kathleen G Arthur, fall 96; the Heritage of Paul Reinhardt, Theatre Design and Technology, summer 98; Female Interpretations of Ibsen on Broadway, 1896-1947: Minnie Maddern Fiske, Alla Nazimova and Eva Le Galliene, Contemporary Approaches to Ibsen, Scandanavian Univ Press, fall 98; numerous other publications. **CONTACT ADDRESS** School of Theatre and Dance, James Madison Univ, Harrisonburg, VA, 22807. **EMAIL** arthurth@jmu.edu

ARZOOMANIAN, RALPH SARKIS
PERSONAL Born 01/23/1937, Providence, RI, m, 1957, 4 children **DISCIPLINE** DRAMA **EDUCATION** Boston Univ, BA, 61; Iowa Univ, MA, 63, PhD(drama), 65. **CAREER** Fel, Yale Univ, 65-66; instr theatre, Hunter Col, 66-71; asst prof, 71-80, assoc prof Speech & Theatre, Herbert H Lehman Col, 80-. **SELECTED PUBLICATIONS** Auth, The Coop (play), Prompt Theatre Mag, London, 6/68; Four Plays, Aranat Press; The Tack Room, published in Best American Short Plays, 92-93. **CONTACT ADDRESS** Dept of Speech & Theatre, Lehman Col, CUNY, 250 Bedford Park W, Bronx, NY, 10468-1527.

ASHBY, CLIFFORD
PERSONAL Born 06/11/1925, Effingham, IL, m, 1950, 2 children **DISCIPLINE** DRAMA **EDUCATION** State Univ IA, BA, 50; Univ HI, MA, 53; Stanford Univ, PhD, 63. **CAREER** Asst prof drama, Univ Pac, 53-54; instr, Univ FL, 54-57; asst prof, Univ NE, 61-63; assoc prof theatre, 63-67, res grant, 68, PROF THEATRE, TX TECH UNIV, 67-. **MEMBERSHIPS** Am Soc Theatre Res. **RESEARCH** Theatre history; popular theatre; playwriting. **SELECTED PUBLICATIONS** Auth, Theatrical Adventure on the Mississippi & Report on An Early Showboat Performance Around 1835, Theatre Hist Studies, vol 14, 94; Roofed Theatres of Classical Antiquity, with G. C. Izenour, Theatre Survey, vol 35, 94; Greek Tragic Theatre, with R. Rehm, Theatre Survey, vol 35, 94; The 3-Actor Rule & Applications to the Extant Tragedies and the Effect It Had Upon Acting and Production Practices During the Classic Period,

Theatre Res Int, vol 20, 95; The Context of Ancient Drama, with E. Csapo and W. J. Slater, Theatre Survey, vol 37, 96; Greek Tragedy on the American Stage, with K. V. Hartigan, Theatre Survey, vol 37, 96; Images of the Greek Theatre, with R. Green and E. Handley, Theatre Survey, vol 37, 96. **CONTACT ADDRESS** TX Tech Univ, Lubbock, TX, 79409.

ASHDOWN, PAUL GEORGE

PERSONAL New York, NY, m, 1975, 1 child **DISCIPLINE** JOURNALISM **EDUCATION** Univ Fla, BA, 66, MA, 69; Bowling Green St Univ, PhD, 75. **CAREER** United Press International, 69-70; inst, Univ Toledo, 71-75; asst prof, Western Ky Univ; PROF, UNIV TENNESSEE, 77-. **HONORS AND AWARDS** Fulbright-Hays Gra, 95; Fac Res Gran, 89; Outstanding Faculty Member, Univ Tenn Col of Commun, 83 & 92; Joseph Sbuttoni Key, 85; Faculty Res Award, 86; Univ Tenn Nat Alumni Assn Outstanding Teacher Award, 91; Univ Tenn Chancellor's Teacher-Scholar, 95-97; Robert Foster Cherry Award for Great Teachers, 98. **MEMBERSHIPS** Amer Jour Historians Assn; Soc of Professional Journalists. **RESEARCH** Journalism as literature; Journalism history. **SELECTED PUBLICATIONS** Coauth, Morbid Curiosity and the Mass Media: Proceedings of a Symposium, Gannett Found, 84; ed, James Agee: Selected Journalism, Univ Tenn, 85; WTVJ's War on Crime: Television's First Crusade, in 2nd Ann Communs Res Symposium, Univ Tenn, 79; Historical Perspectives of Mass Persuasion in Orientations Toward a Theory of Mass Persuasions, Bowling Green Univ, 81; A Profile of the Press in the Republic of Ireland in 4th Ann Communs Res Symposium, Univ Tenn, 81; Sherlock Holmes Makes a Dodge Commercial in Cats, Chocolate, Clowns & Other Amusing, Interesting and Useful Subjects Covered by Newsletters, Dembner Books, 82; Ireland in World Press Encycl, Facts on File 82; Paracelsus Paradigm: Reflections on the Journalism of Credulity, 6th Ann Communs Res Symposium, Univ Tenn, 83; James Agee's Magazine Journalism in 7th Ann Communs Res Symposium, Univ Tenn, 84; Freshmen Feel Anxiety, Hope, in Complete Reporter, Macmillan, 85; Assessment Tests in Journalism and Public Relations in Assessment of Student Outcomes in Higher Educ, Univ Tenn, 89; Seattle 1962: Seattle's World's Fair (Century 21 Exposition in Historical Dict of the World's Fairs and Expositions, 1851-1988, Greenwood, 90; James Agee & Ernest Hemingway in A Sourcebook of Amer Lit Jour: Representative Writers in an Emerging Genre, Greenwood, 92; Prophet from Highland Avenue: James Agee's Visionary Journalism in James Agee: Reconsideration, Univ Tenn, 92; Journalism and the Telepathic Planet in Journ & Journ Educ in a Free Society, Comenius Univ, 93 (also pub in Slovak); A Key to the Attic, foreword to Knoxville's Secret History, Scruffy City Pub, 95; James Agee in Encycl Americana, Grolier, 96; Ron Rosenbaum, Joan Didion & Samuel Lover in American Literary Journalists, 1945-95, Dict of Lit Biog, Bruccoli Clark Layman, 97 & 98; The Battle of Johnsonville in Tenn Encycl of History & Culture, Tenn Historical Soc, 98; T.S. Matthews & Thomas Willis White in Amer Nat Biog, Oxford, in press; That Delicate Flying Foot: South Florida as a Region and Metaphor in Regions & Regionalism in North America and Europe, Univ Bonn, in press; Joan Didion and Salvador, P.J. O'Rourke, & Hunter Thompson, in Dictionary of Political Communication, in press; Forget Being Trendy--Dullness is Editor's Fate: Newspapers Will Always Thrive with the Trivia of Everyday Life, Bulletin of Amer Soc of Newspaper Eds, Apr. 95; American Journeys and General Washington's Ghost, Vital Speeches of the Day, Nov 94; Glimpses of India, Tenn Alumnus, Summer 96; Spomin Zdravi in Prizadene, Vecer, Dec 14,96; Tovenarij in de Mediawereld, De Journalist, Apr 18, 97; Everything Changes in a Century, Ed & Pub, May 17, 97. **CONTACT ADDRESS** Sch of Journalism, Univ of Tennessee, 330 Communications Bldg, Knoxville, TN, 37996-0330. **EMAIL** pashdown@UTK.edu

ASHLEY, LEONARD R.N.

PERSONAL Born 12/05/1928, Miami, FL **DISCIPLINE** ENGLISH, LINGUISTICS **EDUCATION** McGill Univ, BA, 49, MA, 50; Princeton Univ, AM, 53, PhD, 56. **CAREER** Instr, 53-55, Univ Utah; instr, 55-56, Royal Can Air Force, London; 2nd asst to air hist, 56-58; instr, 58-61, Univ Rochester; from instr to assoc prof, 61-72, prof, 72-, prof emeritus, 95-, Brooklyn Col; res grants, Univ Utah, 55 & Univ Rochester, 60; lectr, 61-, New Sch Social Res; Brooklyn Col fac res grant, 68; contrib ed, Papertexts, Simon & Schuster & Washington Sq Press; consult, Harper & Row & Oxford Univ Press; exec bd, Amer Name Soc; ed bd, 65-, names reviewer, Bibliotheone d' Humanisme et Renaissance, Geneva; co-ed, 97, 99, Amer Soc of Geolinguistics. **HONORS AND AWARDS** Shakespeare Gold Medal, 49; hon, LHD, 98. **MEMBERSHIPS** MLA; Am Name Soc (pres, 79, 87); Int Conf Gen Semantics; NY Acad of Sci; Intl Linguistics Assn; Amer Soc of Geolinguistics, pres, 85, 91-. **RESEARCH** English drama; English language, especially onomastics and geolinguistics; English nondramatic literature. **SELECTED PUBLICATIONS** Auth, The Complete Book of Superstition, Prophecy, and Luck, Barricade Bks, 95; auth, The Complete Book of Magic and Witchcraft, Barricade Bks, 95; auth, The Complete Book of Devils and Demons, Barricade Bks, 96; auth, The Complete Book of Devil's Disciples, Barricade Bks, 96; auth, The Complete Book of Spells, Curses and Magical Recipes, Barricade Bks, 92; auth, The Complete Book of Vampires, Barricade Bks, 98; auth, The Complete Book of Ghosts and Poltergeists, 99; auth, George Alfred Henty and the Victorian Mind, Internet Scholar pub, 98; auth, Turkey: Names and Naming Practices, Internet Scholar pub, 98. **CONTACT ADDRESS** Dept of English, Brooklyn Col, CUNY, Brooklyn, NY, 11210.

ASKEW, TIMOTHY

DISCIPLINE ENGLISH LITERATURE **EDUCATION** Emory Univ, PhD. **CAREER** Dept Eng, Clark Atlanta Univ **RESEARCH** Early and 19th Century American literature, Southern literature, Autobiography, and Black Studies. **SELECTED PUBLICATIONS** Auth, Abbeville Road. **CONTACT ADDRESS** Clark Atlanta Univ, 223 James P Brawley Dr, SW, Atlanta, GA, 30314.

ASPIZ, HAROLD

PERSONAL Born 06/19/1921, St. Louis, MO, m, 1952, 1 child **DISCIPLINE** ENGLISH, AMERICAN LITERATURE **EDUCATION** Univ CA, Los Angeles, BA, 43, MA, 44, PhD(English), 49. **CAREER** Asst prof English, Lewis & Clark Col, 50-51; res technican & statistician, Div Hwy, State Bd Equalization, CA, 52-58; from asst prof to PROF ENGLISH, CA STATE UNIV, LONG BEACH, 58-, CA State Univ, Long Beach res fel, 65 & 81. **MEMBERSHIPS** MLA; Philol Asn Pac Coast; Melville Soc. **RESEARCH** Nineteenth century literature and popular culture; Walt Whitman; literary realism. **SELECTED PUBLICATIONS** Auth, An Early Feminist Tribute to Whitman, Am Lit, 11/79; The Lurch of the Torpedo-Fish: Electrical Concepts in Billy Budd, ESQ, 3rd Quarter, 80; Walt Whitman and the Body Beautiful, Univ IL Press, 80; Coming to Grips with 'Huckleberry Finn'--Essays on a Book, a Boy, and a Man, with T. Quirk, Am Lit, vol 66, 94; Whitman 'Poem of the Road,' Walt Whitman Quart Rev, vol 12, 95; Tom-Sawyers Games of Death, Studies in the Novel, vol 27, 95; Sentimental Twain, Clemens, Samuel in the Maze of Moral-Philosophy, with G. Camfield, Am Lit, vol 67, 95. **CONTACT ADDRESS** Dept of English, California State Univ, Long Beach, 6101 E Seventh St, Long Beach, CA, 90840.

ASTINGTON, JOHN H.

PERSONAL Born 01/20/1945, Stockport, England **DISCIPLINE** ENGLISH/DRAMA **EDUCATION** Univ Leeds, BA, 66; McMaster Univ, MA, 67; Univ Toronto, PhD, 74. **CAREER** Lectr, 71-75, asst prof, 75-78, ASSOC PROF ENGLISH, UNIV TORONTO, 78-. **HONORS AND AWARDS** Can Coun doctoral fel; Ont grad fel; SSHRCC res grants; Folger Libr fel (Washington, DC). **MEMBERSHIPS** Am Soc Theater Res; Shakespeare Asn Am; Int Shakespeare Asn; The Malone Soc. **SELECTED PUBLICATIONS** Ed, Modern Drama, 86-92; ed, The Development of Shakespeare's Theater, 92; drama rev, Univ Toronto Quart, 82-86. **CONTACT ADDRESS** Erindale Col, Univ of Toronto, 3359 Mississauga Rd N, Mississauga, ON, L5L 1C6.

ASTROFF, ROBERTA J.

PERSONAL Born 05/31/1953, New York, NY **DISCIPLINE** LIBRARY SCIENCE **EDUCATION** Univ Rochester, BA, 75; NY Univ, MA, 81; Univ Il Urbana-Champaign, PhD, 86; Ind Univ, MLS, 98. **CAREER** Asst prof Univ Wi Madison, 86-90; asst prof, Univ Pittsburgh, 90-97; librn, Penn St Univ, 98- . **MEMBERSHIPS** ALA; SALALM; ASIS. **RESEARCH** Humanities & new technologies; collection develop on the humanities; cultural stud; libr & int stud. **SELECTED PUBLICATIONS** Auth, Spanish Gold: Stereotypes, Ideology and the Construction of a U S Latino Market, Howard J of Commun, 89; The Politics and Political Economics of Language, Media Develop, 92; Advertising, Anthropology, and Cultural Brokers: A Research Report, in Global and Multi-National Advertising, Lawrence Erlbaum Assoc 94; Capital's Cultural Study, in Buy This Book, Routledge, 97; coauth, Cultural Identity, Civil Society, and Mass Communication in Catalonia, in Information Society and Civil Society: The Changing World Order, Purdue Univ Press, 94. **CONTACT ADDRESS** Arts & Humanities Libr, Pennsylvania State Univ, E502 Paterno Library, University Park, PA, 16802. **EMAIL** r4a@psulias.psu.edu

ATKIN, DAVID J.

DISCIPLINE TELECOMMUNICATIONS, MASS COMMUNICATION THEORY **EDUCATION** Univ CA, Berkley, AB; MI State Univ, MA, PhD. **CAREER** Internship dir; asst ch, Cleveland State Univ. **SELECTED PUBLICATIONS** Auth, Government Ambivalence Towards the Telephone Regulation: Using past as prologue in the videodialtone debate, Commun Law Jour, 1, 96; Local and long distance telephony, Commun Tech, Focal Press, 96; Assessing uses of the information superhighway for commun and consumer needs, Hong Kong Econ Jour, 94. **CONTACT ADDRESS** Commun Dept, Cleveland State Univ, 83 E 24th St, Cleveland, OH, 44115. **EMAIL** d.atkin@csuohio.edu

ATKINSON, COLIN B.

DISCIPLINE ENGLISH LANGUAGE; LITERATURE **EDUCATION** McGill, BEng; Sir George Williams, BA; Columbia, MA; NY Univ, PhD, 71. **CAREER** Assoc prof. **RESEARCH** Victorian period; women's studies; the drama. **SELECTED PUBLICATIONS** Pub (s), Sydney Owenson, Lady Morgan; Maria Edgeworth; attitudes to death in nineteeth-century American parlour songs; and the place of Thomas Bentley and Anne Wheathill in the devotional tradition of women in Renaissance England. **CONTACT ADDRESS** Dept of English Language and Literature, Univ of Windsor, 401 Sunset Ave, Windsor, ON, N9B 3P4. **EMAIL** p68@uwindsor.ca

ATKINSON, JAMES BLAKELY

PERSONAL Born 11/24/1934, Honolulu, HI, m, 1970, 1 child **DISCIPLINE** ENGLISH & COMPARATIVE LITERATURE **EDUCATION** Swarthmore Col, AB, 56; Columbia Univ, MA, 61, PhD(English & comp lit), 68. **CAREER** Asst prof English, Dartmouth Col, 66-73, fac fel, 71; ASST PROF ENGLISH, EARLHAM COL, 73-. **MEMBERSHIPS** MLA; Renaissance Soc Am; AAUP. **RESEARCH** Literature of the Renaissance in Europe and England; the novel. **SELECTED PUBLICATIONS** Transl, Mandrou Duby's A History of French Civilization, Random, 65; auth, Montaigne and Naivete, Romanic Rev, 73; Naivete and Modernity: The French Renaissance Battle for a Literary Vernacular, J Hist Ideas, 74; ed & translr, Machiavelli's The Prince, Bobbs-Merrill, 75; Changing Attitudes to Death, 19th-Century Parlor Songs as Consolation Literature, Can Rev of Am Studies, vol 23, 93; with Anne Wheathill, A 'Handfull of Holesome Through Homelie Hearbs' 1584, The First English Gentlewomans Prayer Book, Sixteenth Century J, vol 27, 96; Machiavellian Rhetoric-From the Counterreformation to Milton, with V. Kahn, Renaissance Quart, vol 50, 97. **CONTACT ADDRESS** 115 S 17th St, Richmond, IN, 47374.

ATKINSON, MICHAEL

PERSONAL Born 07/02/1942, Midland, TX **DISCIPLINE** LITERARY THEORY, ARCHETYPAL PSYCHOLOGY & LITERATURE **EDUCATION** Rice Univ, BA, 64; PA State Univ, MA, 67, PhD(English), 70. **CAREER** ASSOC PROF ENGLISH, UNIV CINCINNATI, 70-. **MEMBERSHIPS** MLA; AAUP; Midwest Mod Lang Asn; Popular Culture Asn. **RESEARCH** American renaissance; contemporary poetics. **SELECTED PUBLICATIONS** Auth, Collective Preconscious & Found Footage Film as an Inexhaustable Source of the Underground, Film Comment, Vol 29, 1993; Genuine B-Noir & Films of Director James B. Harris, Sight and Sound, Vol 3, 1993; Ousmane Sembene & The Film Director and African Cinema-We-Are-No-Longer-In-The-Era-of-Prophets, Film Comment, Vol 29, 1993; Between Worlds & Surrealists, Film and Hathaway, Henry 'Peter Ibbetson', Film Comment, Vol 29, 1993; The 'Tattooed Woman in Heavens Flower Shop', MI Quart Rev, Vol 32, 1993; Head Case & Arnaud Desplechin La 'Sentinelle', Film Comment, Vol 29, 1993; 'Airfield', Literary Rev, Vol 36, 1993; The 'Mask', wirh C. Russell, Sight and Sound, Vol 4, 1994; The Night Countries of the Brothers Quay & Film Directors, Film Comment, Vol 30, 1994; 'Highway Patrolman' , with A. Cox, Film Comment, Vol 30, 1994; 'Death and the Compass', Film Comment, Vol 30, 1994; Regulation of Science by Peer Review, Studies in Hist and Philos of Sciencs, Vol 25, 1994; Crossing ther Frontiers--with Everyone from Psychos to Scholars Hitting the Highway, Has the Road Movie Found New Wheels, Sight and Sound, Vol 4, 1994; The Faber Book of Movie Verse, with P. French and K. Wlaschin, Film Comment, Vol 30, 1994; The 'Paper', with R. Howard, Sight and Sound, Vol 4, 1994; A 'Perfect World', with C. Eastwood, Sight and Sound, Vol 4, 1994; Son of Apes & 'Planet of the Apes' Film Serials, Film Comment, Vol 31, 1995; Delirious Inventions--Why Have Comics and Cartoons from 'Popeye' Onwards So Often Been Translated into Live Action Movies, Sight and Sound, Vol 5, 1995; 'Jefferson in Paris', with J. Ivory, Sight and Sound, Vol 5, 1995; Earthly Creatures & Peter Jackson Horror Film "Heavenly Creatures', Film Comment, Vol 0031, 1995; The 'Specialist', with L. Llosa, Sight and Sound, Vol 5, 1995; 'Tommy Boy', with P. Segal, Sight and Sound, Vol 5, 1995; 'Beach Red' -, with C. Wilde, Film Comment, Vol 32, 1996; Naked Prey--The Cinema of Cornel Wilde, Introduction & Conclusions, Vol 32, 1996; 'Aeon Flux', Film Comment, Vol 32, 1996; Songs of Crushed Love--TheCinema of Stanley Kwan, Film Comment, Vol 32, 1996; 'No Blade of Grass', with C. Wilde, Film Comment, Vol 32, 1996; Best of 96 & Movies, Film Comment, Vol 33, 1997; 'Lumiere et Compagnie', with S. Moon, Film Comment, Vol 33, 1997. **CONTACT ADDRESS** Dept of English, Univ of Cincinnati, P O Box 210069, Cincinnati, OH, 45221-0069.

ATLAS, MARILYN JUDITH

DISCIPLINE ENGLISH **EDUCATION** Univ Ill, BS, 72; Univ Ill, AB, 73; Univ Ill, AM, 73; Mich State Univ, PhD, 79. **CAREER** Adv, Univ Ill, Col of Arts and Sciences, 72-74; grad asst, Mich State Univ, Dept of English, 74-78; instr and asst prof, Mich State Univ, Dept of Am Thought and Lang, 78-80; dir, Ohio Univ, Women's Studies, 80-82; asst prof, Ohio Univ, 80-84; vis prof, De La Salle Univ, Philippines, 85; assoc prof, Ohio Univ, 84-97. **HONORS AND AWARDS** Best Feminist Res Award, Women's Studies Program, Ohio Univ; Winner of the Excellence-in-Teaching Citation, Mich State Univ; Phi Beta Kappa; Phi Kappa Phi; Psi Chi; Kappa Delta Pi. **MEMBERSHIPS** Soc for the Study of Midwestern Lit; Am Culture Asn. **RESEARCH** Early Am lit; Am Renaissance; Am Modernism; contemporary lit; women's lit; ethnic lit; Jewish lit; literary hist; literary theory; canon formation. **SELECTED PUBLICATIONS** Auth, "Toni Morrison's Beloved and the Critics", in Midwestern Miscellany 18, 90; auth, "Tone and Technology in

Harriet Monroe's 'The Turbine'", in MidAmerica 22, 95; auth, "Cracked Psyches and Verba Putty: Geography and Integrity in Toni Morrison's Jazz", in Midwestern Miscellany 4, 96; auth, "The Roles of Chicago in the Careers of Ellen Van Volkenburg and Maurice Browne", in MidAmerica 23, 96. **CONTACT ADDRESS** Department of English, Ohio Univ, Athens, OH, 45701.

ATON, JAMES M.
PERSONAL Born 08/14/1949, Louisville, KY, s, 1 child **DISCIPLINE** ENGLISH **EDUCATION** Spring Hill Col, BA, 71; Univ of Ky, MA, 77; Ohio Univ, PhD, 81. **CAREER** PROF OF ENGLISH, SOUTHERN UTAH UNIV, 80-. **HONORS AND AWARDS** Distinguished Educator Awd, Southern Utah Univ; fulbright lectr, Indonesia, 89-90, China, 97-98. **MEMBERSHIPS** Am Soc of Environmental Hist; Utah State Historical Soc; Western Hist Asn. **RESEARCH** Environmental history of the Colorado plateau. **SELECTED PUBLICATIONS** Auth, John Wesley Powell, Dictionary of Lit Bio: Nineteenth-Century Western Am Writers Vol 186, Gale Res, 97; The River, The Ditch and The Volcano: Bluff, 1879-1884, Blue Mountain Shadows, 93; Us vs. Them: John Wesley Powell and Western Water Issues, Akademika, 90; Inventing: The Major, His Admirers and Cash Register Dams in the Colorado River Basin, SUSC Distinguished Fac Lectr, 88, reprinted by Five Quail Books, 94; An Interview With Barry Lopez, Western Am Lit, 86. **CONTACT ADDRESS** Dept of Lang and Lit, Southern Utah Univ, Cedar City, UT, 84720. **EMAIL** aton@suu.edu

ATTARDO, SALVATORE
DISCIPLINE LITERATURE **EDUCATION** Catholic Univ, Milan, PhD, 86; Purdue Univ, PhD, 91. **CAREER** Asst prof, Youngstown State Univ, 92-96, Assoc prof, Youngstown State Univ, 96-. **MEMBERSHIPS** Linguistics Soc Am; Int Pragmatics Asn; Speech Comm Asn; Int Soc Humor Studies; Col Eng Asn. **SELECTED PUBLICATIONS** Auth, Linguistic Theories of Humor, Mouton de Gruyter, 94; Introduction to Theoretical Linguistics: Course notes;York State Univ, Mimeo, 92; Humor, Handbook of Pragmatics, 96. **CONTACT ADDRESS** Youngstown State Univ, One University Plaza, Youngstown, OH, 44555. **EMAIL** sattardo@cc.ysu.edu

ATTEBERY, BRIAN
DISCIPLINE ENGLISH LITERATURE **EDUCATION** Brown Univ, PhD, 79. **CAREER** Prof. **RESEARCH** Fantasy and science fiction; folklore; American studies theory and methodology. **SELECTED PUBLICATIONS** Auth, The Fantasy Tradition in American Literature; Strategies of Fantasy; co-auth, The Norton Book of Science Fiction. **CONTACT ADDRESS** Dept of English and Philosophy, Idaho State Univ, Pocatello, ID, 83209. **EMAIL** attebria@isu.edu

ATTEBERY, JENNIFER
DISCIPLINE ENGLISH LITERATURE **EDUCATION** Ind Univ, PhD, 85. **CAREER** Prof. **RESEARCH** Swedish and Swedish-American culture and history. **SELECTED PUBLICATIONS** Auth, Building Idaho: An Architectural History; Building with Logs: Western Log Construction in Context. **CONTACT ADDRESS** Dept of English and Philosophy, Idaho State Univ, Pocatello, ID, 83209. **EMAIL** attejenn@isu.edu

ATTEBERY, LOUIE WAYNE
PERSONAL Born 08/14/1927, Weiser, ID, m, 1947, 2 children **DISCIPLINE** ENGLISH & AMERICAN LITERATURE, FOLKLORE **EDUCATION** Col ID, BA, 50; Univ Mont, MA, 51; Univ Denver, PhD, 61. **CAREER** Teacher English, Middleton High Sch, ID, 49-50, Payette High Sch, 51-52, Nyssa High Sch, Ore, 52-55 & East High Sch, Denver, 55-61, chmn dept, 61; from asst prof to assoc prof, 61-69, chmn dept, 68-73 & 76-78, PROF ENGLISH, COL OF ID, 69-, Prin lectr, Summer Inst Am Studies, 63-70, dir, 66-70; Bruern fel, Univ Leeds, 71-72; consult, EXPO 74. **MEMBERSHIPS** Western Lit Asn; Western Hist Asn; Am Folklore Soc. **RESEARCH** The epistemology of Western American literature; the cement truck urban belief tale; the Oregon cowboy: a continuing search for authenticity. **SELECTED PUBLICATIONS** Auth, Governor jokes, Southern Folklore Quart, 12/69; The American West and the Archetypal Orphan, Western Am Lit, fall 70; It was a DeSoto, J Am Folklore, 10-12/70; The Fiddle Tune: An American Artifact, Readings in Am Folklore, 79; Scottish Fantasy-Literature-A Critical Survey, with C. Manlove, Science Fiction Studies, Vol 24, 97. **CONTACT ADDRESS** Dept of English, Col of Idaho, Caldwell, ID, 83605.

ATTRIDGE, DEREK
DISCIPLINE ENGLISH LANGUAGE AND LITERATURE **EDUCATION** Natal Univ, BA; Cambridge Univ, BA; PhD. **CAREER** Dist vis prof English. **RESEARCH** British and Irish modernism; poetic form and performance; literary theory; South African writing. **SELECTED PUBLICATIONS** Auth, Poetic Rhythm: An Introduction, Cambridge, 95; auth, Peculiar Language: Literature as Difference from the Renaissance to James Joyce Cornell, 88; The Rhythms of English Poetry Longman, 82; Well-weighed Syllables: Elizabethan Verse in Classical Metres , Cambridge, 74; ed, Acts of Literature by Jacques Derrida, Routledge, 92; The Cambridge Companion to James Joyce, Cambridge, 90; co-ed, Writing South Africa: Literature, Apartheid, and Democracy, Cambridge, 98; Post-structuralist Joyce: Essays from the French, Cambridge, 84; The Linguistics of Writing: Arguments between Literature and Language, Routledge, 88; Post-structuralism and the Question of History, Cambridge, 87. **CONTACT ADDRESS** Dept of English, Rutgers Univ, 510 George St, Murray Hall, New Brunswick, NJ, 08901-1167.

ATWILL, WILLIAM D.
DISCIPLINE 19TH- AND 20TH-CENTURY AMERICAN LITERATURE **EDUCATION** Univ S Fla, BA; Fla Atlantic Univ, MA; Duke Univ, PhD. **CAREER** Assoc prof, Univ NC, Wilmington. **RESEARCH** Contemporary postmodern fiction and literary nonfiction from 1945 to the present. **SELECTED PUBLICATIONS** Auth, Fire and Power: The American Space Program as Postmodern Narrative, Univ Ga Press, 94. **CONTACT ADDRESS** Univ N. Carolina, Wilmington, Morton Hall, Wilmington, NC, 28403-3297. **EMAIL** atwillw@uncwil.edu

ATWOOD, MARGARET
PERSONAL Ottawa, ON, Canada **DISCIPLINE** AUTHOR/POET **EDUCATION** Victoria Col, Univ Toronto, BA, 61; Radcliffe Col, AM, 62. **CAREER** Lectr, English, Univ BC, 64-65; instr, Univ Alta, 69-70; asst prof, York Univ, 71-72; Writer-In-Residence, Univ Toronto, 72-73; MFA Hon Ch, Univ Alabama, 85; Berg Ch, New York Univ, 86; Writer-In-Residence, Macquarie Univ, Australia, 87; Writer-In-Residence, Trinity Univ, San Antonio, Tex, 89. **HONORS AND AWARDS** Gov Gen Award, 66, 86; Guggenheim Fel, 81; Companion Order Can, 81; Order Ont, 90; Trillium Award Excellence Ont, 94; Commonwealth Writers' Prize Can & Caribbean Region, 94; Chevalier dans l'Ordre des Arts et des Lettres, Govt France, 94; Sunday Times Award Literary Excellence, 94; DLitt, Trent Univ, 73; DLitt, Queen's Univ, 74; DLitt, Smith Col, MA, 82; DLitt, Univ Toronto, 83; DLitt, Univ Waterloo, 85; DLitt, Univ Guelph, 85; DLitt, Mount Holyoke Col, 85; DLitt, Univ Toronto, 87; DLitt, Univ de Montreal, 91; DLitt, Univ Leeds, 94. **MEMBERSHIPS** Writers' Union Can; PEN. **SELECTED PUBLICATIONS** Auth, The Circle Game, 64; auth, The Edible Woman, 69; auth, Surfacing, 72; auth, Lady Oracle, 76; auth, Life Before Man, 79; auth, Bodily Harm, 81; auth, The Handmaid's Tale, 85; auth, Cat's Eye, 88; auth, The Robber Bride, 93; auth, Alias Grace, 96. **CONTACT ADDRESS** McClelland & Stewart, 481 University Ave, Ste 900, Toronto, ON, M5G 2E9.

AUBREY, JAMES R.
PERSONAL Born 12/03/1945, Kittanning, PA, m, 1968, 2 children **DISCIPLINE** ENGLISH **EDUCATION** Univ Wash, PhD, 79. **CAREER** Prof, Metrop State Col Denver, 89- . **MEMBERSHIPS** MLA **RESEARCH** British literature. **SELECTED PUBLICATIONS** Auth, John Fowles: A Reference Companion, 91. **CONTACT ADDRESS** 2337 Ash St., Denver, CO, 80207. **EMAIL** aubreyj@mscd.edu

AUERBACH, JONATHON
PERSONAL Born 02/07/1954, Denver, CO, m, 1983, 1 child **DISCIPLINE** ENGLISH AND AMERICAN LITERATURE **EDUCATION** Univ Cal, Santa Cruz, BA, 76; Johns Hopkins Univ, MA, 78; PhD, 84. **CAREER** Prof, Univ Md, 84- . **HONORS AND AWARDS** Fulbright lectr, Portugal, 90; Huntington fel, 94. **RESEARCH** American literature and culture. **SELECTED PUBLICATIONS** Auth, Black Like Me, or How the Other Half Lives, Proceeedings of the 13th Conference of the Portuguese Association of Anglo-American Studies, 94; auth, 'The Nation Organized': Utopian Impotence in Edward Bellamy's Looking Backward, Am Lit Hist, 94; auth, 'Congested Mails': Buck and Jack's 'Call', Am Lit, 95; auth, Male Call: Becoming Jack London, 96. **CONTACT ADDRESS** English Dept, Univ of Maryland, College Park, MD, 20742. **EMAIL** ja44@umail.umd.edu

AUFDERHEIDE, PATRICIA
DISCIPLINE MASS COMMUNICATION **EDUCATION** Univ Minn, BA, MA, PhD. **CAREER** Assoc Prof, Am Univ. **HONORS AND AWARDS** John Simon Guggenheim Memorial Fel; Fulbright res fel, Brazil. **SELECTED PUBLICATIONS** Auth, Anwar Sadat; contrib auth, Seeing Through Movies; Watching Television: Voices of Dissent, theMedia; assoc ed, Black Film Rev; st ed, Am Film Mag; ed, Beyond PC: Toward a Politics of Understanding and Latin American Vision.. **CONTACT ADDRESS** American Univ, 4400 Massachusetts Ave, Washington, DC, 20016.

AUGUST, EUGENE R.
PERSONAL Born 10/19/1935, Jersey City, NJ, m, 1964, 2 children **DISCIPLINE** ENGLISH **EDUCATION** Rutgers Univ, AB, 58; Univ Conn, MA, 60; Univ Pittsburgh, PhD(English), 65. **CAREER** Asst English, Univ Conn, 58-60; from instr to asst prof, carnegie-Mellon Univ, 62-66; from asst prof to assoc prof, Univ Dayton, 66-74 vis assoc prof, Univ Hawaii, Manoa, 74-75; prof English, Univ Dayton, 76-, Nat Endowment for Humanities younger humanist fel, 73-74. **MEMBERSHIPS** NAS, ALSC, AMSA. **RESEARCH** Victorian literature; Divine Comeedies; Men's Studies. **SELECTED PUBLICATIONS** Auth, The Growth of the Windhover, PMLA, 10/67; ed, The Nigger Question & The Negro Question, 71, AMH Publ; Mill's Autobiography as Philosophic Commedia, Victorian Poetry, summer 73; Mill as Sage: The Essay on Bentham, PMLA, 1/74; auth, John Stuart Mill: A Mind at Large, Charles Scribner's Sons, 75; The Only Happy Ending: Divine Comedies in Western Literature, Bull Midwest; Modern Language Association, Vol 14, spring 81; Amours de Voyage and Matthew Arnold in Love, Victorian Newsletter, fall 81; The New Men's Studies, Libraries Unlim, 95. **CONTACT ADDRESS** Univ of Dayton, 300 College Park, Dayton, OH, 45469-1520. **EMAIL** august@checkor.hm.udayton.edu

AUKSI, PETER
PERSONAL Born 12/01/1942, Estonia, m, 1975 **DISCIPLINE** ENGLISH LITERATURE **EDUCATION** Univ Toronto, BA, 65; Oxford Univ, BA, 67, MA, 70; Harvard Univ, AM, 68, PhD(English lit), 71. **CAREER** Asst prof, 71-80, ASSOC PROF ENGLISH, UNIV WESTERN ONT, 80-. **RESEARCH** Reformation; rhetorical theory; aesthetic ideals. **SELECTED PUBLICATIONS** Auth, Wyclif's sermons and the plain style, Archiv f?r Reformations-geschichte, 75; Henry of Livonia and Balthasar Russow: The chronicler as literary artist, J Baltic Studies, 75; Milton's Sanctifi'd Bitternesse: Polemical technique in the early prose, Tex Studies Lit & Lang, 77; So rude and simple style: William Tyndale's polemical prose, J Medieval & Renaissance Studies, 78; Simplicity and silence: The influence of scripture on the aesthetic thought of the major reformers, J Religious Hist, 79; The Renaissance Bible-Scholarship, Sacrifice, and Subjectivity, with D. K. Shuger, Renaissance and Reformation, Vol 20, 96; English Humanist Books-Writers and Patrons, Manuscript and Print, 1475-1525, with D. R. Carlson, English Studies in Canada, Vol 22, 96. **CONTACT ADDRESS** Dept of English, Univ of Western Ont, London, ON, N6A 3K7.

AULT, C. THOMAS
PERSONAL Born 08/07/1936, Moline, IL, s **DISCIPLINE** THEATRE **EDUCATION** Univ Mich, BA, 65, MA, 67, PhD, 83. **CAREER** Lect, Univ Mich, 83-84; asst prof, Centenary Col La, 84-86; ASST PROF, UNIV PENN, 88-. **HONORS AND AWARDS** Merit Sabbatical, IUP, 96; ACTF, Meritorious Achsets; 7th Regional UCTA, best set, 85. **MEMBERSHIPS** Am Soc for Theatre Res; Asn Asian Perf; Soc Theatre Res (Eng.); Renaissance Soc N Am,; Am Asn Italian Stud. **RESEARCH** Theaters and theatrical machines. **SELECTED PUBLICATIONS** Auth, Scenes and Machines from the 18th Century: The Stagecraft of Jacopo Fabris and Citoyen Boullet, Theatre Libr, Asn, 86; auth, "The Queen's Cavern: A Sanskrit Theatre of Ancient Khalinga, Second Century B.C. India," Theatre Design & Tech, 96; auth, "Leone Battista Alberti on Theatre Architecture," Theatre Design & Tech, 97; auth, "Classical Humanist Drama in Transition: The First Phase of Renaissance Theatre in Ferrara," Theatre Ann, 98. **CONTACT ADDRESS** Dept of Theater, Univ of Pennsylvania, 206 Waller Hall, 401 S Eleventh St, Indiana, PA, 15701.

AUSTEN, ZELDA
DISCIPLINE VICTORIAN PERIOD, ENGLISH NOVEL **EDUCATION** SUNY, Stony Brook, PhD. **CAREER** Prof, Long Island Univ, C.W. Post Campus. **SELECTED PUBLICATIONS** Auth, Oliver Twist: A Divided View; Why Feminist Critics are Angry at George Eliot; The Ant and the Grasshopper: William Morris and Oscar Wilde in the Eighties; Factories and Fairy Palaces: The Response of Dickens and Other to the Industrial Revolution. **CONTACT ADDRESS** Long Island Univ, C.W. Post, Brookville, NY, 11548-1300.

AUSTIN, BOBBY WILLIAM
PERSONAL Born 12/29/1944, Bowling Green, KY, m **DISCIPLINE** LITERATURE **EDUCATION** Western Kentucky Univ, BA 1966; Fisk Univ, MA 1968; McMaster Univ, PhD 1972; Harvard Univ, Diploma 1986. **CAREER** Univ of DC, exec asst to the pres; Georgetown Univ, asst prof 1971-72; Dept of Soc Georgetown summer term, chmn 1972; The Urban League Review Natl Urban League, editor; UDC Bd Vis Team Creative Prod Black Amer Folklore NETA-WASH PBS, pol spec & spec asst; pres Austin & Assoc. **HONORS AND AWARDS** Kellogg Natl Fellow. **MEMBERSHIPS** Mem Natl Council for Accrdttn of Tchr Edn; mem Amer Soc Assn; Groves Conf on Marriage & the Family; Alpha Phi Alpha Frat; Natl Cong of Black Professionals; mem VOICE Inc; mem Alphi Phi Omega Natl Serv Fraternity; Peoples Congregational Church; Hannover Project, Germany; Academic Council on the UN Systems; Global Co-Operation for a Better World; UN Assn, DC Chapter **SELECTED PUBLICATIONS** Author of numerous publications; paper presented at the Assn for the Study of Afro-Amer Life & History New York, 1973; published Natl Black Opinion ACRA Inc 1977. **CONTACT ADDRESS** Austin & Associates, 6611 16th St NW, Washington, DC, 20012.

AUSTIN, GAYLE M.
DISCIPLINE THEATRE HISTORY **EDUCATION** CUNY, PhD. **CAREER** Instr, Hunter Col; instr, Univ SC; assoc prof,

Ga State Univ; exec dir, Southeast Playwrights Proj, 87-89. **SELECTED PUBLICATIONS** Auth, The Madwoman in the Spotlight: Plays of Maria Irene Fornes, in Making a Spectacle, Univ Mich Press, 89; The Exchange of Women and Male Homosocial Desire in Miller's 'Death of a Salesman' and Hellman's 'Another Part of the Forest,' in Feminist Rereadings of Modern American Drama, Fairleigh Dickinson UP, 89; Feminist Theories for Dramatic Criticism, Univ Mich Press, 90; Resisting the Birth Mark: Subverting Hawthorne in a Feminist Theory Play, in Upstaging Big Daddy: Directing Theater as if Gender and Race Matter, Univ Mich Press, 93. **CONTACT ADDRESS** Georgia State Univ, Atlanta, GA, 30303. **EMAIL** jougma@panther.gsu.edu

AUSTIN, LINDA
DISCIPLINE VICTORIAN STUDIES **EDUCATION** Rochester, PhD, 86. **CAREER** Engl, Okla St Univ. **SELECTED PUBLICATIONS** Auth, The Practical Ruskin: Economics and Audience in the Late Work, Johns Hopkins, 91. **CONTACT ADDRESS** Oklahoma State Univ, 101 Whitehurst Hall, Stillwater, OK, 74078.

AUSTIN, MICHAEL
DISCIPLINE ENGLISH **EDUCATION** Brigham Young Univ, BA, 90, MA, 92; Univ CA at Santa Barbara, PhD, 97. **CAREER** Asst prof, Shepherd Col, 97-; tchg assoc, Writing Prog, Univ CA at Santa Barbara, 97; tchg asst-instr, Univ CA,at Santa Barbara, 92-97; tchg assoc, Univ CA at Santa Barbara, 95; tchg asst, Brigham Young Univ, 90-92. **MEMBERSHIPS** MLA; Northeastern Soc for 18th-Century Stud; AAUP. **RESEARCH** Hist of criticism; hist of rhetoric; contemp critical theory, lit of the Bible. **SELECTED PUBLICATIONS** Auth, Saul and the Social Contract: Constructions of 1 Samuel 8-11 in Cowley's Davideis and Defoe's Jure Divino, Papers on Lang and Lit 32 4, 96; Marxist Criticism, textbk Chap, The Critical Experience, Dubuque, Iowa: Kendall/Hunt, 94; Saul Bellow and the Absent Woman Syndrome: Traces of India in Leaving the Yellow House, Saul Bellow J 11 2/12 1, 93-94; The Genesis of the Speaking Subject in Mr Sammler's Planet, Saul Bellow J 10 2, 92. **CONTACT ADDRESS** Dept of Eng and Mod Lang, Shepherd Col, Shepherdstown, WV, 25443. **EMAIL** maustin@shepherd.wvnet.edu

AUSTIN SMITH, BRENDA
DISCIPLINE ENGLISH LITERATURE **EDUCATION** Acadia Univ, BA; Victoria Univ, MA; Univ Manitoba, PhD. **CAREER** Asst prof **HONORS AND AWARDS** Ed, Can Dimension. **RESEARCH** Narration and rhetoric in fiction and film; representation of subjectivity in fiction and film; point of view; film and effect; 'women's' films; film theory; Henry James; critical theory. **SELECTED PUBLICATIONS** Auth, pubs on Patricia Rozema and Canadian film. **CONTACT ADDRESS** Dept of English, Manitoba Univ, Winnipeg, MB, R3T 2N2.

AUTER, PHILIP J.
DISCIPLINE COMMUNICATION **EDUCATION** Ga State Univ, BA, 85; Univ Ga, MA, 87; Univ Ky, PhD, 92. **CAREER** Asst prof. **RESEARCH** Uses and gratifications of television programming and computer services; computer mediated communication; parasocial interaction; effects of message production techniques on audience interaction, interest, involvement, and mood; history of television. **SELECTED PUBLICATIONS** Auth, A Fine Mess: A Look at the Effects of Colorization on Audience Interaction With a Comedy Program, 97; TV that talks back: An experimental validation of a parasocial interaction scale, 92; Analysis of the ratings for television comedy programs 1950-1959: The end of "Berlesque", 90; coauth, The challenge of developing online courses, 98; When characters speak directly to viewers: Breaking the fourth wall in entertainment television, 97; DuMont: The original fourth television network, 95; Buying from a friend: A content analysis of two teleshopping programs, 93. **CONTACT ADDRESS** W Florida Univ, 11000 Univ PKWY, Pensacola, FL, 32514. **EMAIL** pauter@uwf.edu

AVINS, CAROL JOAN
PERSONAL Born 05/09/1950, New York, NY **DISCIPLINE** RUSSIAN & COMPARATIVE LITERATURE **EDUCATION** Univ PA, BA, 70; Yale Univ, PhD(Slavic lang & lit), 74. **CAREER** Asst prof, 74-80, ASSOC PROF RUSSIAN LANG & LIT & COMP LIT, NORTHWESTERN UNIV, 80-. **MEMBERSHIPS** MLA; Am Asn Teachers Slavic & East Europ Lang; Am Asn Advan Slavic Studies; AAUP; Am Coun Teachers Russ. **RESEARCH** Twentieth century Russian literature; 20th century comparative literature. **SELECTED PUBLICATIONS** Auth, Border Crossings: The West and Russian Identity in Soviet Literature, 1917-1934, Univ CA Press; Kinship and Concealment in 'Red Cavalry' and Babel 1920 Diary, Slavic Rev, Vol 53, 94. **CONTACT ADDRESS** Dept of Slavic Lang & Lit, Northwestern Univ, Evanston, IL, 60201.

AVRAM, WESLEY D.
PERSONAL Born 03/21/1959, Detroit, MI **DISCIPLINE** RHETORICAL STUDIES **EDUCATION** Princeton Theolog Seminary, Mdiv, 84; Northwestern Univ, PhD, 94 **CAREER** Lctr Relig & Rhetoric, Col Chaplain, Bates Col, 90-96; Res Fel, Yale Univ Divinity School, 93-94; independent Scholar, Senior Pastor, First Presbyterian Church, 97- **HONORS AND AWARDS** Team Teaching Grant, Louisville Inst, 97; Summer Seminar Grant, Ntl Endowment Humanities, 95; Res Fel, Yale Univ Divinity School, 93; Presiden't Fel, Northwestern Univ, 85; Roberts Preaching Prize, Princeton Theolog Seminary, 83; Graduate Study Fel, Princeton Theolog Seminary, 84 **MEMBERSHIPS** Ntl Comm Assoc; Amer Acad Relig **RESEARCH** Philosophical Theology; Rhetorical Studies; Technology and Culture **SELECTED PUBLICATIONS** "Mother Teresa, Princess Di, and the Media," New Oxford Rev, 97; "On the Priority of 'Ethics' in Emmanuel Levinas," Jrnl Religious Ethics, 96; "Chaplaincy at the Present Moment," Still Small Voice, 92 **CONTACT ADDRESS** 816 Greenleaf Ave, Wilmette, IL, 60091. **EMAIL** wavram@unidial.com

AXELRAD, ARTHUR MARVIN
PERSONAL Born 08/26/1934, New York, NY **DISCIPLINE** ENGLISH LITERATURE **EDUCATION** Brooklyn Col, BA, 55; NY Univ, MA, 57, PhD, 62. **CAREER** Asst, Sch Com, NY Univ, 55-57; asst prof English, UT State Univ, 61-64; assoc prof, 64-72, PROF ENGLISH, CA STATE UNIV, LONG BEACH, 72-, Assoc ed in charge abstr, Seventeenth-Century News, 57-65; Woodrow Wilson rep, 68-; Danforth fel liaison officer, 68- **HONORS AND AWARDS** Founders' Day Distinguished Scholar Award, NY Univ, 63. **MEMBERSHIPS** Milton Soc Am; Int Arthurian Soc. **RESEARCH** English Renaissance, especially Milton; medieval, especially Arthurian literature. **SELECTED PUBLICATIONS** Co-ed, The Prose of John Milton, NY Univ, 67; contribr, Milton Encyclopedia, Univ WI; Cooper Leather-Stocking Novels-A Secular Reading, with G. Rans, Am Studies Int, Vol 31, 93; James Fenimore Cooper-Novelist of Manners, with D. Darnell, Am Studies Int, Vol 33, 95; William Town Cooper-Power and Persuasian on the Frontier of the Early American Republic, with A. Taylor, Am Studies Int, Vol 34, 96. **CONTACT ADDRESS** Dept of English, California State Univ, Fullerton, Fullerton, CA, 92634.

AXELROD, STEVEN GOULD
PERSONAL Born 05/15/1944, Los Angeles, CA, m, 1966, 1 child **DISCIPLINE** AMERICAN AND MODERN LITERATURE **EDUCATION** Univ Calif, Los Angeles, AB, 66, MA, 69, PhD, 72. **CAREER** Asst prof English, Univ Mo, St Louis, 72-73; vis assoc prof English, 78-79, Univ Colo, Boulder; asst prof, 73-78, prof English, 86-, dir Composition, 86-90,; chemn English dept, 92-96, Univ Calif, Riverside. **MEMBERSHIPS** MLA; PAMLA; CEA; Am Studies Assn; NCTE. **RESEARCH** American literature; Modern literature; poetry. **SELECTED PUBLICATIONS** Auth, Baudelaire and the poetry of Robert Lowell, Twentieth Century Lit, 10/71; art, Colonel Shaw in American poetry, Am Quart, 10/72; art, The Jewishness of Bellow's Henderson, Am Lit, 11/75; auth, Robert Lowell: Life and Art, Princeton Univ, 78; coauth, Robert Lowell: A Reference Guide, G K Hall, 82; auth, Sylvia Plath: The Wound & The cure of Words, Johns Hopkins UP, 90; auth, Critical Essays on William Carlos Williams, G K Hall, 95. **CONTACT ADDRESS** Dept of English, Univ of California, Riverside, 900 University Ave, Riverside, CA, 92521-0323. **EMAIL** steven.axelrod@ucr.edu

AXTON, WILLIAM F.
PERSONAL Born 09/24/1926, Louisville, KY, m, 1951, 3 children **DISCIPLINE** ENGLISH LITERATURE **EDUCATION** Yale Univ, AB, 48; Univ Louisville, MA, 51; Princeton Univ, PhD, 61. **CAREER** Instr English, Miami Univ, 52-53 & Brown Univ, 57-61; from asst prof to assoc prof, Univ KY, 61-67; assoc prof, 67-69, chmn dept, 71-74, PROF ENGLISH, UNIV LOUISVILLE, 69-, Assoc ed, Dickens Studies Ann, 68-; rev ed, Dickens Newslett, 69-71, prod ed, 75-; pres, Dickens Soc, 72. **MEMBERSHIPS** MLA; Victorian Soc; Dickens Soc; Victorian Soc Am; Browning Soc. **RESEARCH** Nineteenth century art and architecture; Dickens; Victorian aesthetics. **SELECTED PUBLICATIONS** Auth, Circle of Fire; Univ KY, 66; Keystone Structure in Dickens' Novels, Univ Toronto Quart, fall 67; Religious and Scientific Imagery in Bleak House, Nineteenth Century Fiction, 3/68; Great Expectations Once Again, Dickens Studies Ann, 72; Tobacco and Kentucky, Univ KY, 75; Dickens Now, In: Victorian Experience, OH Univ, 76; Victorian Landscape Painting, In: Nature and Victorian Imagination, Univ CA, 77; Robert B. Partlow, Jr., May 27, 1919 January 17, 1997-In Memoriam, Dickens Quart, Vol 14, 97. **CONTACT ADDRESS** Dept of English, Univ of Louisville, Louisville, KY, 40208.

AYCOCK, ROY E.
PERSONAL Born 04/11/1926, Greenville, SC **DISCIPLINE** ENGLISH **EDUCATION** Furman Univ, BA, 49; Univ NC, MA, 52, PhD, 60. **CAREER** Instr English, Auburn Univ, 52-54 & Ga Inst Technol, 54-57; assoc prof, 60-64, PROF ENGLISH, OLD DOMINION UNIV, 64-. **MEMBERSHIPS** MLA; Renaissance Soc Am; Shakespeare Asn Am. **RESEARCH** Shakespeare, Milton and Conne; 16th and 17th centuries; metaphysical poetry. **SELECTED PUBLICATIONS** Auth, Gray's-Inn Journal, Yearbk English Studies, 72; Shakespeare, Boito and Verdi, Musical Quart, 10/72; Dual Progression in Richard III, SAtlantic Bull; George Herbert and the Passion Week, Rivista Di Storia E Letteratura Religiosa, Vol 31, 95. **CONTACT ADDRESS** Dept of English, Old Dominion Univ, Norfolk, VA, 23508.

AYCOCK, WENDELL M.
DISCIPLINE ENGLISH AND COMPARATIVE LITERATURE **EDUCATION** Univ SC, PhD, 69. **CAREER** Prof, chp, dept Eng, TX Tech Univ, 90-97; bibliogr, Stud in Short Fiction. **HONORS AND AWARDS** Two Fulbright grants; NEH grant; Mellon grant. **RESEARCH** Short story. **SELECTED PUBLICATIONS** Ed or co-ed eighteen volumes coming from the Comparative Literature Symposium project at Texas Tech, produced 20th-Century Short Story Explication, New Ser, Vol II. **CONTACT ADDRESS** Texas Tech Univ, Lubbock, TX, 79409-5015. **EMAIL** W.Aycock@ttu.edu

B

BABB, GENIE
DISCIPLINE LITERATURE **EDUCATION** Brown Univ, PhD. **CAREER** Univ Alaska. **SELECTED PUBLICATIONS** Area: Two Old Women. **CONTACT ADDRESS** Univ Alaska Anchorage, 3211 Providence Dr., Anchorage, AK, 99508.

BABB, VALERIE M.
PERSONAL Born 05/06/1955, New York, New York **DISCIPLINE** ENGLISH **EDUCATION** Queens Coll, City Univ of New York, New York, NY, BA, 1977; State Univ of New York at Buffalo, Buffalo NY, MA, 1981, PhD, 1981. **CAREER** Georgetown Univ, Washington DC, asst prof, associate professor, professor, currently. **HONORS AND AWARDS** Award for Academic Excellence, Seek Program, City Univ of New York, 1985; MT. Zion United Methodist Church Award for "Black Georgetown Remembered: A Documentary Video," 1989. **SELECTED PUBLICATIONS** Book: Whiteness Visible: The Meaning of Whiteness in American Literature & Culture, NYU Press, 1998. **CONTACT ADDRESS** Dept of English, Georgetown Univ, PO Box Box 571131, Washington, DC, 20057-1131.

BABCOCK, WILLIAM
DISCIPLINE MASS COMMUNICATION STUDIES **EDUCATION** S Ill Univ, PhD. **CAREER** Assoc prof **HONORS AND AWARDS** Ed, Christian Sci Monitor. **SELECTED PUBLICATIONS** Co-auth, Three Major U.S. Newspapers' Content and President Kennedy's Press Conference Statements Regarding Space Exploration and Technology, Pres Studies Quarterly, 83; Reagan Inauguration, Hostages Release, or Both? Publications Time, Ownership, and Circulation Size as Factors in Daily Newspaper Editorial Decisions, Newspaper Res J, 82. **CONTACT ADDRESS** Mass Communication Dept, Univ of Minnesota, Twin Cities, 111 Murphy Hall, 206 Church St SE, Minneapolis, MN, 55455. **EMAIL** baco001@maroon.tc.umn.edu

BABIN, JAMES L.
DISCIPLINE AMERICAN LITERATURE **EDUCATION** Duke Univ, PhD, 70. **CAREER** Assoc prof, La State Univ, assoc ed, Henry James Rev, 79-. **RESEARCH** Voegelinian essays in American literature; 19th and 20th century religion and literature; the place of writers in American (modern) society. **SELECTED PUBLICATIONS** Auth, Melville's Billy Budd, in Explicator, 81; Captain Graveling in Melville's Billy Budd, in Explicator, 84; coed, The Nature of the Law and Related Writings, 91. **CONTACT ADDRESS** Dept of Eng, Louisiana State Univ, 212B Allen Hall, Baton Rouge, LA, 70803. **EMAIL** insandy@unix1.sncc.lsu.edu

BACH, REBECCA ANN
DISCIPLINE SHAKESPEARE AND EARLY MODERN ENGLISH LITERATURE **EDUCATION** Univ PA, PhD. **CAREER** Dept Eng, Univ Ala **SELECTED PUBLICATIONS** Articles, Studies Eng Lit 1500-1900, Medieval & Renaissance Drama Eng, and Race, Ethnicity and Power in the Renaissance. **CONTACT ADDRESS** Univ AL, 1400 University Blvd, Birmingham, AL, 35294-1150.

BACKSCHEIDER, PAULA R.
PERSONAL Born 03/31/1943, Brownsville, TN, m, 1964, 2 children **DISCIPLINE** ENGLISH LITERATURE **EDUCATION** Purdue Univ, PhD, 72. **CAREER** Asst prof, Rollins Coll; asst prof, assoc prof, prof, Univ Rochester; prof, Auburn Univ; Pepperell Philpot Eminent Scholar. **HONORS AND AWARDS** British Council Prize for best Book in the Humanities, 90; Guggenheim, NEH, ACLS, Inst for Advanced Studies Edinburgh. **MEMBERSHIPS** MLA; ASECS; SEASECS; NEASECS, AAUP. **RESEARCH** Eighteen-Century British Literature; Feminist Criticism; Biography. **SELECTED PUBLICATIONS** Auth, Daniel Defoe: His Life, 89; Spectacular Politics: Theatrical Power and Mass Culture in Early Modern England, 93; coauth, Popular Fiction by Women, 1660-1730: An Anthology, 96; ed, Selected Fiction and Drama of Eliza Haywood, 99. **CONTACT ADDRESS** English Dept, Auburn Univ, Auburn, AL, 36849. **EMAIL** pkrb@mail.auburn.edu

BAENDER, PAUL
PERSONAL Born 12/01/1926, Alameda, CA, m, 1957, 3 children **DISCIPLINE** AMERICAN LITERATURE **EDUCATION** Univ CA, Berkeley, AB, 49, MA, 52, PhD, 56. **CAREER** Instr English, Univ Chicago, 56-60; from asst prof to assoc prof, 60-68; PROF ENGLISH, UNIV IOWA, 68-. **MEMBERSHIPS** Midwest Mod Lang Asn. **RESEARCH** Nineteenth century American literature; Mark Twain; bibliography. **SELECTED PUBLICATIONS** Co-ed, Mark Twain's Roughing It, 72, ed, What is Man? and Other Philosophical Writings of Mark Twain, 73 & co-ed, Mark Twain's Adventures of Tom Sawyer, 80, Univ CA; Alias Macfarlane-Who in L was L, Resources fro Am Literary Study, Vol 19, 93. **CONTACT ADDRESS** Dept of English, Univ of IA, Iowa City, IA, 52242.

BAER, WILLIAM
DISCIPLINE ENGLISH LITERATURE **EDUCATION** Univ S Calif, MA; Johns Hopkins Univ, MA; NY Univ, MA; Univ SC, PhD. **CAREER** Fulbright prof, Portugal; prof. **HONORS AND AWARDS** T S Eliot prize in poetry; Jack Nicholson Screen Wrtg Award; Arts fel, NEH. **SELECTED PUBLICATIONS** Founding ed, and pub(s), The Formalist; auth, The Unfortunates Walcott. **CONTACT ADDRESS** Dept of Eng, Univ Evansville, 1800 Lincoln Ave, Evansville, IN, 47714. **EMAIL** wb4@evansville.edu

BAETZHOLD, HOWARD GEORGE
PERSONAL Born 01/01/1923, Buffalo, NY, m, 1950, 2 children **DISCIPLINE** ENGLISH **EDUCATION** Brown Univ, AB, 44, AM, 48; Univ WI, PhD(English & Am lit), 53. **CAREER** From asst dir to dir vet col, Brown Univ, 47-49, admis officer, 48-50; asst to the assoc dean, Col Lett & Sci, Univ WI, 51-53; from asst prof to assoc prof, 53-67, prof, 67-81, REBECCA CLIFTON READER PROF & HEAD DEPT ENGLISH, BUTLER UNIV, 81-, Univ IA & US Off Educ res grant for work on Iowa-CA Ed of Writings of Mark Twain, Univ CA, Berkeley, NY Pub Libr, Yale Univ, Princeton Univ & Univ VA, 65-66; Am Coun Learned Soc grant-in-aid, Univ CA, Berkeley, 67. **MEMBERSHIPS** MLA; Midwest Mod Lang Asn; Am Studies Asn; AAUP; Soc Study Midwestern Lit. **RESEARCH** Nineteenth century American literature, especially works of Mark Twain; 19th century Anglo-American literary relations; twentieth century American literature. **SELECTED PUBLICATIONS** Auth, Course of Composition of Mark Twain's A Connecticut Yankee, Am Lit, 5/61; What was the Model for Martin Chuzzlewit's Eden?, Dickensian, 9/59; Mark Twain and John Bull: The British Connection, IN Univ, 70; Found: Mark Twain's Lost Sweetheart, Am Lit, 11/72; Mark Twain on Scientific Investigation: Contemporary Allusions in Some Learned Fables for Good Old Boys and Girls, In: Literature and Ideas in America: Essays in Memory of Harry Hayden Clark, OH Univ, 75; Of Detectives and Their Derring-do: The Genesis of Mark Twain's The Stolen White Elephant, Studies Am Humor, 76; Our Famous Guest, Mark-Twain in Vienna, with C. Dolmetsch, Am Lit, Vol 66, 94. **CONTACT ADDRESS** Dept of English, Butler Univ, Indianapolis, IN, 46208.

BAGDIKIAN, BEN HAIG
PERSONAL Born 01/30/1920, Marash, Turkey, m, 1973, 2 children **DISCIPLINE** JOURNALISM **EDUCATION** Clark Univ, AB, 41. **CAREER** Corresp, Providence, RI J & Bull, 47-61; contrib ed, Sat Eve Post, 62-67; proj dir news media, Rand, 68-69; asst managing ed nat, Wash Post, 70-72; PROF JOUR, UNIV CA, BERKELEY, 77-, John Simon Guggenheim Found fel, 62. **HONORS AND AWARDS** LHD, Brown Univ, 61; LittD, Clark Univ, 63. **MEMBERSHIPS** Mellet Fund for Free & Responsible Press (pres, 66-76); Nat Prison Proj; Soc Sci Res Coun. **RESEARCH** Journalism; media structures; criminal justice. **SELECTED PUBLICATIONS** Ed, Man's Contracting World in an Expanding Universe, Brown Univ, 60; auth, In the Midst of Plenty, Beacon, 64; The Information Machines, Harper, 70; The Shame of the Prisons, Simon & Schuster, 72; The Effete Conspriacy, 72 & Caged, 76, Harper; The 'Media Monopoly" & Adapted From the Preface to the Recently Published 5th-Edition of the Book, Television Quart, Vol 28, 97. **CONTACT ADDRESS** 217 Gravatt Dr, Berkeley, CA, 94705.

BAHK, C.M.
DISCIPLINE COMMUNICATION **EDUCATION** Michigan State Univ, PhD, 94. **CAREER** Asst prof, Univ of Cincinnati, 95-. **HONORS AND AWARDS** Phillip K. Tompkins Award for Outstanding Research, SUNY at Albany. **MEMBERSHIPS** NCA, ICA, BEA. **RESEARCH** Mass media effects; intercultural interaction; health and environmental communication. **SELECTED PUBLICATIONS** Art, Descriptions of Sexual Content and Ratings of Movie Preference, Psychological Reports, 98; art, The Impact of Presence Versus Absence of Negative Consequences in Dramatic Portrayals of Alcohol Drinking, J of Alcohol and Drug Education, 97; auth, Interpersonal and Perceptions of Same-Sex and Opposite-Sex Friendships in the United States and Korea, Interpersonal Communication in Friend and Mate Relationships, SUNY Press, 93; coauth, The Relationship of Empathy to Comforting Behavior Following Film Exposure, Communication Research, 93. **CONTACT ADDRESS** Dept of Communication, Univ of Cincinnati, Univ of Cincinnati, Cincinnati, OH, 45221-0184. **EMAIL** bahkcm@uc.edu

BAILEY, RICHARD W.
PERSONAL Born 10/26/1939, Pontiac, MI, m, 1990, 1 child **DISCIPLINE** ENGLISH **EDUCATION** Dartmouth Col, AB, 61; Univ Conn, MA, 63; Univ Conn, PhD, 65 **CAREER** Prof, Univ Mich, 65- **HONORS AND AWARDS** U-M Press Book Award, 93, 98; Regents' Award Distinguished Public Service, 92; Distinguished Fac Achievement Award, 89 **MEMBERSHIPS** Amer Dialect Soc Pres, 87-89; MLA; NCTE; Linguistic Soc Amer **RESEARCH** English Language **SELECTED PUBLICATIONS** Images of English, 91; Nineteenth-Century English, 96 **CONTACT ADDRESS** English Dept, Univ Mich, Ann Arbor, MI, 48109-1003. **EMAIL** rwbailey@umich.edu

BAILEY, RICHARD WELD
PERSONAL Born 10/26/1939, Pontiac, MI, m, 1960, 2 children **DISCIPLINE** ENGLISH **EDUCATION** Dartmouth Col, AB, 61; Univ Conn, MA, 63, PhD(English), 66. **CAREER** From asst prof to assoc prof, 65-76, prof English, Univ Mich, Ann Arbor, 76-, fel, Inst Advan Study Humanities, Univ Edinburgh, 71; trustee, Washtenaw Community Col, 75-. **HONORS AND AWARDS** Rackham Fac Fel 67, 75; ACLS Grant for Computer-Oriented Res in the Humanities 68; Res Fel, Off of Res dmin, Univ Michigan 70; ACLS Grant-in-Aid Fel, Inst for Advanced Stud in the Humanities, Univ of Ediburg 71; Proj Dir, Early Mod English Dictionary Proj, supported by the Nat Endowment for the Humanities, 71-73, 75; Co-Proj Dir, Int Conf on the Semiotics of Art 78; Co-Proj Dir, Prog to Improve Student Writing, the Ford Found, 78-80; Proj Dir, Colloquium on English Lexicography, nat Endowment for the Humanitites, 85; Distinguished Fac Achievement Award, U-M, 89; Fel for Univ Teachers, Nat Endowment for the Humanitites, 91-92; Regent's Award for Distinguished Public Service, 92; U-M Press Book Award, 93. **MEMBERSHIPS** NCTE; MLA; Ling Soc Am; Asn Comput & Humanities; Am Dialect Soc; Dictionary Soc North Am. **RESEARCH** Stylistics; dialectology; computational lexicography; hist of English. **SELECTED PUBLICATIONS** Co-ed, English Stylistics: A Bibliography, Mass Inst Technol, 68; Statistics and Style, Am Elsevier, 69; Varieties of Present-Day English, Macmillan, 73; Michigan Early Modern English Materials, Xerox Univ Microfilms, 75; ed, Early Modern English, Georg Olms Verlag, 78; co-ed, The sign: Semiotics around the world, Mich Slavic Pub(s), 78; English as a World Language, Univ Mich Press, 82; ed, Computing in the Humanities, North-Holland, 82. Assoc Ed, The Oxford Companion to the English Language, Oxford and New York: Oxford Univ Press, 92; Auth, Nineteenth-Century English, Ann Arbor: Univ Mich Press, 96; Images of English: A Cultural History of the Language, Ann Arbor, Univ Mich Press 91, Cambridge Univ Press, 92. **CONTACT ADDRESS** Dept of English, Univ of Michigan, Ann Arbor, 505 S State St, Ann Arbor, MI, 48109-1003. **EMAIL** rwbailey@umich.edu

BAILEY, THOMAS CULLEN
PERSONAL Born 11/29/1940, m, 1962, 3 children **DISCIPLINE** ENGLISH & AMERICAN LITERATURE **EDUCATION** Oberlin Col, BA, 62; Univ MO, MA, 64; WA Univ, PhD(English), 74. **CAREER** Instr English, Westminster Col, 64-66; ASST PROF ENGLISH, WESTERN MI UNIV, 70-, Nat Endowment Humanities fel Am autobiog, Dartmouth Col, 75-76. **MEMBERSHIPS** MLA. **RESEARCH** Autobiography; John Clare's poems; Mark Twain. **SELECTED PUBLICATIONS** Auth, Ecotone, Wayfaring on the Margins, with F. Krall, Women's Studies-An Interdisciplinary J, Vol 25, 96. **CONTACT ADDRESS** Dept of English, Western Michigan Univ, Kalamazoo, MI, 49008.

BAILLIE, WILLIAM MAYAN
PERSONAL Born 11/04/1940, Boston, MA, m, 1962, 2 children **DISCIPLINE** ENGLISH LITERATURE **EDUCATION** Ball State Univ, AB, 62; Univ Chicago, MA, 64, PhD(English), 67. **CAREER** Asst prof English, OH State Univ, Columbus, 67-74; assoc prof, 74-80, PROF ENGLISH, BLOOMSBURG STATE COL, 80-. **MEMBERSHIPS** MLA; Shakespeare Asn Am. **RESEARCH** Elizabethan drama; bibliography. **SELECTED PUBLICATIONS** Auth, Authorship Attribution in Jacobean Dramatic Texts, Papers Int Conf Computers in Humanities, 74; Early Printed Books in Small Formats, Papers Bibliog Soc Am, 75; Henry VIII: A Jacobean Tragedy, Shakespeare Studies, 80; A Choice Ternary of English Plays, 82; Printing Bibles in the Interregnum-The 'Case of William Bentley' and a 'Short Answer', Vol 91, 97. **CONTACT ADDRESS** Dept of English, Bloomsburg Univ of Pennsylvania, 400 E 2nd St, Bloomsburg, PA, 17815-1399.

BAIRD, JOHN D.
PERSONAL Born 05/09/1941, Glasgow, Scotland **DISCIPLINE** ENGLISH LITERATURE **EDUCATION** St Andrews Univ, MA, 63; McMaster Univ, MA, 64; Princeton Univ, MA, 67, PhD, 70. **CAREER** Fac mem, 67-81, PROF ENGLISH LITERATURE, VICTORIA COL & UNIV TORONTO, 81-, dir grad stud, 85-89, assoc dean hum, sch grad stud, 92-95. **SELECTED PUBLICATIONS** Co-ed, The Poems of William Cowper, 80-95. **CONTACT ADDRESS** Victoria Col, Univ of Toronto, Toronto, ON, M5S 1K7.

BAKER, BEULAH PEARL
PERSONAL Baton Rouge, LA **DISCIPLINE** LITERATURE, HUMANITIES **EDUCATION** Spring Arbor Col, BA, 67; Mich State Univ, MA, 69, PhD, 76. **CAREER** Prof English lit, John Wesley Col, 69-79; prof English & chair dept English, Taylor Univ, 79-. **HONORS AND AWARDS** NEH grant; Teaching Excellence and Campus Leadership Award, 95. **MEMBERSHIPS** Conf Christianity & Lit; MLA; Col English Asn; MMLA. **RESEARCH** Modern and post-modern poetry, especially William Carlos Williams; African literature. **SELECTED PUBLICATIONS** Auth, reviews in CCL Journal. **CONTACT ADDRESS** Dept of English, Taylor Univ, 236 W Reade Ave, Upland, IN, 46989-1002. **EMAIL** BLBaker@TaylorU.edu

BAKER, C. EDWIN
PERSONAL Born 05/28/1947, Nashville, TN **DISCIPLINE** CONSTITUTIONAL LAW, LEGAL PHILOSOPHY, MASS MEDIA **EDUCATION** Stanford Univ, BA, 69; Yale Univ, JD, 72. **CAREER** Asst prof, Univ Toledo, 72-75; asst prof, Univ Ore, 75-79, assoc prof, 79-81 & prof, 81-82; Prof Law, Univ Pa, 82-, Fel, Harvard Univ, 74-75; vis prof law, Univ Tex, 80 & Univ Pa, 81-82; Staff Atty, ACLU, NY, 87-88; Fel, Shorentein Barone Ctr, Kennedy Sch Govt, Harvard, 92; vis prof, Cornell Univ, 93; Vis Lombard Prof, Kennedy Sch Govt, Harvard Univ, 93. **RESEARCH** Mass media; constitutional law. **SELECTED PUBLICATIONS** Auth, Human Liberty and Freedom of Speech, Oxford Univ 89; Advertising and a Democratic Press, Princeton, 94; author of numerous journal articles. **CONTACT ADDRESS** Law Sch, Univ of Pa, 3400 Chestnut St, Philadelphia, PA, 19104-6204. **EMAIL** ebaker@oyez.law.upenn.edu

BAKER, CHRISTOPHER P.
DISCIPLINE ENGLISH **EDUCATION** St. Lawrence Univ, BA, 68; Univ NC, Chapel Hill, MA, 79, PhD, 74. **CAREER** Inst to full prof, Lamar Univ, 76-94; head, langs/lit/drama, 94-98, PROF ENG, 98-, ARMSTRONG ATLANTIC STATE UNIV. **CONTACT ADDRESS** Armstrong Atlantic State Univ, 11935 Abercorn St., Savannah, GA, 31419. **EMAIL** chris_baker@mailgate.armstrong.edu

BAKER, DAVID ANTHONY
PERSONAL Born 12/27/1954, Bangor, ME, m, 1987, 1 child **DISCIPLINE** ENGLISH **EDUCATION** Cent Mo State Univ, BSE, 76, MA, 77; Univ Ut, PhD, 83. **CAREER** ED, KENYOU REV; CHR CREATIVE WRITING & PROF ENGLISH, DENISON UNIV; NEA fel; Oh Arts Coun fel. **HONORS AND AWARDS** Soc Midland Auth Book Award, Ohioana Poetry Award. **MEMBERSHIPS** AWD; MLA **RESEARCH** American poetry; Poetics. **SELECTED PUBLICATIONS** auth Laws of the Land, Ahsahta/Boise State Univ, 81; Haunts, Cleveland State Univ Poetry Ctr, 85; Sweet Home, Saturday Night, Ar, 91; After the Reunion, Ar, 94; Meter in English: A Critical Engagement, Ar, 96; The Truth about Small Towns, Univ Ar Press, 98. **CONTACT ADDRESS** Dept of English, Denison Univ, Granville, OH, 43023. **EMAIL** baker@denison.edu

BAKER, DELBERT WAYNE
PERSONAL Born 01/25/1953, Oakland, CA, m **DISCIPLINE** JOURNALISM **EDUCATION** Oakwood Coll, Huntsville, AL, BA (cum laude), 1975; Andrews Univ Seminary, Berrien Springs, MI, MDiv (with honors), 1978; Howard Univ, Washington, DC, PhD, 1992. **CAREER** Pastor in MI, VA, OH, 1975-85; Messsage Magazine, Hagerstown, MD, editor-in-chief, 1985-92; HOWARD UNIVERSITY, instructor, 1990-91; CONSULTANT, 1990-; LOMA LINDA UNIVERSTIY, ASSISTANT TO THE PRESIDENT, DIRECTOR OF DIVERSITY, ASSOCIATE PROFESSOR, 1992-. **HONORS AND AWARDS** Alumnus of the Year, Oakwood Coll, 1985; Editorial Journalism Awards, Editors Intl, 1988-90. **MEMBERSHIPS** Bd mem, San Mars Children's Home, 1986-89; bd mem, bd of dir, Oakwood Coll, 1985-; bd mem, Human Relations Council General Conference of Seventh-day Adventist Church, 1987-; Clergy's Black Caucus, 1985-; contributor video, Africa Continent of Explosive Growth, 1987; bd mem, Review & Herald Pub Assn, 1985-; board member, Loma Linda University; chairman, Diversity Advisory Committee. **SELECTED PUBLICATIONS** Author of four books: The Unknown Prophet, 1986; From Exile to Prime Minister, 1988; Profiles of Service, 1990; Communication and Change in Religious Organization, 1992. **CONTACT ADDRESS** Office of Diversity, Loma Linda Univ, Magan Hall, Rm 103, Loma Linda, CA, 92350.

BAKER, DENISE NOWAKOWSKI
PERSONAL Born 04/23/1946, Detroit, MI, m, 1970, 1 child **DISCIPLINE** ENGLISH **EDUCATION** Univ Mich, BA, 68; Univ Calif, Santa Barbara, MA, 70; Univ Va, PhD(English), 75. **CAREER** Asst prof to prof, Univ NC, Greensboro, 75-. **HONORS AND AWARDS** Fel, Southeastern Inst Medieval & Renaissance Studies, summer 78. **MEMBERSHIPS** Medieval Acad Am, MLA. **RESEARCH** Medieval literature; medieval mystics; Julian of Norwich; Langland's Piers Plowman. **SELECTED PUBLICATIONS** Auth, The Priesthood of Genius: A Study of the Medieval Tradition, Speculum, 4/76; From Plowing to Penitence: Piers Plowman and Fourteenth Century

Theology, Speculum, 10/80; Julian of Norwich's Showings: From Vision to Book, Princeton Univ Press, 94. **CONTACT ADDRESS** Dept of English, Univ N. Carolina McIver Bldg, 1000 Spring Garden, Greensboro, NC, 27402-0001. **EMAIL** bakerd@fagan.uncg.edu

BAKER, DONALD C.
PERSONAL Born 12/12/1928, Jonesboro, AR, m, 1952, 4 children **DISCIPLINE** ENGLISH MEDIEVAL LITERATURE **EDUCATION** AR State Col, AB, 49; Univ MS, MA, 50; Univ OK, PhD, 54. **CAREER** Instr English compos, Univ OK, 52-53 & Agr & Mech Col TX, 53-55; asst prof English lit, State Univ SD, 55-57; assoc prof, Univ MS, 57-62; assoc prof, 62-68, PROF ENGLISH, UNIV CO, BOULDER, 68- Fulbright lectr, Finland, 61-62. **MEMBERSHIPS** MLA; Mediaeval Acad Am; Renaissance Soc Am. **RESEARCH** Middle English; Old English; Renaissance literature. **SELECTED PUBLICATIONS** Auth, The Dreamer Again in Chaucer's Book of the Duchess, PMLA, 3/55; Gold Coins in Mediaeval English Literature, Speculum, 4/61; Gentilesse in the Clerk's Tale and the Wife of Bath's Tale, Studies Philol, 10/62; Chaucer 'Troilus and Crisyde', B. Windeatt, ed, English Lang Notes, Vol 33, 95; Chaucer and the Tradition of the Roman Antique, with B. F. Nolan, English Lang Notes, Vol 33, 95; Chaucer and His Readers, Imagining the Author in late Medieval England, with S. Lerer, English Lang Notes, Vol 34, 96; Women and Literature in Britain, 1150-1500, with C. Meale, English Lang Notes, Vol 33, 96; Punctuation and Its Dramatic Value in Shakespearean Drama, with A. G. White, English Lang Notes, Vol 34, 96; Thinking of Beowulf, with J. W. Earl, English Lang Notes, Vol 35, 97; Chaucer and the Politics of Discourse, with M. P. Grundin, English Lang Notes, Vol 35, 97. **CONTACT ADDRESS** Dept of English, Univ of CO, Boulder, CO, 80302.

BAKER, DONALD WHITELAW
PERSONAL Born 01/30/1923, Boston, MA, m, 1945, 2 children **DISCIPLINE** ENGLISH LITERATURE **EDUCATION** Brown Univ, AB, 47, AM, 49, PhD(English), 55. **CAREER** Instr English, Brown Univ, 48-52; from asst prof to prof English, 53-76, dir drama, 54-59, MILLIGAN PROF ENGLISH LIT & SHAKESPEARE, WABASH COL, 76-, POET IN RESIDENCE, 63-, Dir, New Writers Awards Prog, Great Lakes Col Asn, 76-. **MEMBERSHIPS** MLA; NCTE. **RESEARCH** English novel; modern fiction; creative writing. **SELECTED PUBLICATIONS** Auth, Three Poets, 7/67, Five Poets, 12/67 & The Poetry of James Dickey, 3/68, Poetry; Twelve Hawks, Sugar Creek Poetry Ser, 74; Topical Utopias, Radicalizing Humanism in 16th-Century England, Studies in English Literature 1500-1900, Vol 36, 96. **CONTACT ADDRESS** Dept of English Lit, Wabash Col, Crawfordsville, IN, 47933.

BAKER, HOUSTON A.
PERSONAL Born 03/22/1943, Louisville, KY, m, 1 child **DISCIPLINE** AFRICAN AMERICAN LITERATURE **EDUCATION** Howard Univ, BA, 65; Univ Cal at Los Angeles, MA, 66, PhD, 68. **CAREER** Instr, Howard Univ, 66; Instr, 68-69, Asst prof, 69-70, Yale; Assoc prof and mem of Ctr for Adv Studies, 70-73, prof, 73-74, Univ VA; Dir of Afro Amer studies 74-77, prof, 77-, Univ PA; Dir, Ctr for the Study of Black Lit and Culture, 87-. **HONORS AND AWARDS** Legion of Honor Chapel of the Four Chaplains (Philadelphia Commun Service Award), 81; Christian R. And Mary F. Lindback Found Award for Dist Teaching (Univ PA), 84; Alum Award for for Dist Achievement in Lit and the Humanities, Howard Univ, 85; Outstanding Alum Award of Howard Univ, 85; Dist Writer of the year, Mid Atlantic Writers Assoc, 86; Creative Scholarship Award College Lang Assoc of Amer for Afro Amer Poetics, 88; PA Governors Award for Excellence in the Humanities, 90; Fullbright 50th Anniv Dist Fel to Brazil, Council for Intl Exchange of Scholars, 96. **MEMBERSHIPS** English Inst Brd of Supervisors 89-91; MLA second vp 90-91, first vp 91-92, pres 92; School of Criticism and Theory, Cornell Univ, sr. Fel. **RESEARCH** Afro Amer Lit; Literary and cultural studies; Post Colonial studies; Psychoanalytic expressive cultural theory; Autobiography. **SELECTED PUBLICATIONS** Auth, Workings of the Spirit: A Poetics of Afro-American Women's Writing, 91; Black Studies, Rap and the Academy, 93; coed, Black British Cultural Studies: A Reader, 96. **CONTACT ADDRESS** Center for the Study of Black Literature and Cultu, Univ of Pennsylvania, 308 Walnut St., Philadelphia, PA, 19104-6136. **EMAIL** baker@dept.english.upenn.edu

BAKER, J. ROBERT
DISCIPLINE ENGLISH LITERATURE **EDUCATION** Univ Notre Dame, AB; MA; PhD. **CAREER** Prof, 94-, Fairleigh Dickinson Univ. **RESEARCH** Compos and lit; computer tech in the classroom; world lit; world novel; Southern lit; bible as lit. **SELECTED PUBLICATIONS** Coauth, CD-ROM hypertext on Malcolm X. **CONTACT ADDRESS** Fairleigh Dickinson Univ, 1000 River Rd, Teaneck, NJ, 07666. **EMAIL** jrb@fscvax.fairmont.wvnet.edu

BAKER, MOIRA
DISCIPLINE ENGLISH LITERATURE **EDUCATION** Col St Rose, BA magna cum laude, 73; Univ Notre Dame, MA, 76, PhD, 82. **CAREER** Rector. Lewis Hall, 78-82, adj asst prof, Univ Notre Dame, 82-86; asst to assoc prof, 86-97, prof Radford Univ, 97-. **HONORS AND AWARDS** Univ first-yr fel, Univ Notre Dame, 74; univ dissertation yr fel, Univ Notre Dame, 81; NOVUS Award, Conf for the Advan of Early Stud, 87; Omicron Delta Kappa, Nat Honor Soc, 89; fac prof and develop leave, Radford Univ, 97. **MEMBERSHIPS** Int Virginia Woolf Soc; Nat Coun of Tchr of Eng; Philol Asn of the Carolinas; South-Atlantic Mod Lang Asn; Southeastern Women's Stud Asn; South-Cent Renaissance Asn; VA Asn of Tchr of Eng. **SELECTED PUBLICATIONS** Auth, 'This Gift of Celestial Honey': A (W)rite of Passage to Renaissance Studies, Eric ED 295 214, 88; At Home in the Contra War, Notre Dame Mag 18.1, 89; 'The Dichotomiz'd Carriage of all our Sermons': Satiric Structure in the Sermons of Thomas Adams, Eng Renaissance Prose 3.1, 89; (En)Gendering Change: One Woman's Voice and the Traditional Canon, VA Eng Bull 40.2, 90; 'The Uncanny Stranger on Display': The Female Body in Sixteenth- and Seventeenth-Century Love Poetry, South-Atlantic Rev 56.2, 91; Mentoring as Teaching and Learning, ERIC ED 358 459, 93; Thomas Adams, in Dictionary of Literary Biography: British Prose Writers of the Early Seventeenth Century, Vol 151, ed Clayton D. Lein, Gale, 95; 'What is English?': Developing a Senior 'Capstone' Course for the English Major, ERIC ED 411 512, 97. **CONTACT ADDRESS** Radford Univ, Radford, VA, 24142. **EMAIL** mpbaker@runet.edu

BAKER, ROBERT SAMUEL
PERSONAL Born 09/30/1926, Weed, CA, 3 children **DISCIPLINE** ENGLISH **EDUCATION** Pac Univ, BA, 53; Univ Chicago, MA, 56. **CAREER** Instr, 57-60, ASST PROF HUMANITIES, OR COL EDUC, 60-, Fulbright teachers grant, Univ Trieste, 64-66. **MEMBERSHIPS** NCTE; MLA. **RESEARCH** Contemporary and comparative literature; translation theory. **SELECTED PUBLICATIONS** Auth, People Get Hooked, Commentary, 3/63; Italo Svevo and the Limits of Marriage, In: Essays on Italo Svevo, Univ Tulsa, 68; co-ed, The Wor(l)d on Wheels: Reading/Thinking/Writing About the Automobile in America, Allyn & Bacon, 72. **CONTACT ADDRESS** Dept of Humanities, Oregon Col of Educ, Monmouth, OR, 97361.

BAKER, ROBERT SAMUEL
PERSONAL Born 01/11/1940, St. Catharines, ON, Canada, m, 1968 **DISCIPLINE** ENGLISH LITERATURE **EDUCATION** Univ Western Ont, BA, 67, MA, 69; Univ IL, Urbana, PhD(English), 72. **CAREER** Instr English, Univ Western Ont, 68-69; asst prof, 72-77, ASSOC PROF ENGLISH, UNIV WI-MADISON, 77-. **HONORS AND AWARDS** Chancellorio Award for Excellence in Teaching, 81. **MEMBERSHIPS** MLA. **RESEARCH** Romantic and Victorian poetry; modern British literature; philosophy of history. **SELECTED PUBLICATIONS** Auth, Gabriel Nash's House of Strange Idols: Aestheticism in The Tragic Muse, Tex Studies Lit & Lang, spring 73; Sanctuary and Dungeon: The Imagery of Sentimentalism in Meredith's Diana of the Crossways, Tex Studies Lit & Lang, summer 76; Imagination and Literacy in Dicken's Our Mutual Friend, Criticism, winter 76; Faun and Satyr: Meredith's Theory of Comedy and The Egoist, Mosaic, 76; ; Romantic Onanism in Patrick White's The Vivisector, TX Studies Lit & Lang, summer 79; The Dark Historic Page: Social Satire and HIstoricism in the Novels of Aldovs Huxley, Univ WI Press, 82; Aldous Huxley, History and Science Betweeen the Wars, Clio-A J of Lit Hist and the Philos of Hist, Vol 25, 96; History and Periodization-Introduction, Clio-A J of Lit Hist and the Philos of Hist, Vol 26, 97. **CONTACT ADDRESS** Dept of English, Univ of WI, 600 North Park St, Madison, WI, 53706-1403.

BAKER, STUART EDDY
PERSONAL Born 08/13/1938, Albuquerque, NM **DISCIPLINE** DRAMATIC THEORY & CRITICISM **EDUCATION** New York Univ, BS, 62; City Univ New York, PhD(theatre), 77. **CAREER** Adj lectr theatre hist, Hunter Col, 72-75; asst prof, 77-82, ASSOC PROF THEATRE & DRAMA, FL STATE UNIV, 82-. **MEMBERSHIPS** Am Theatre Asn. **SELECTED PUBLICATIONS** Auth, Georges Feydeau and the Aesthetics of Farce, UMI Res Press, 81; Laughter in the Dark, The Plays of Alan Ayckbourn, with A. E. Kalson, Modern Drama, Vol 38, 95; Turrets and Tiring Houses on the Elizabethan Stage, Theatre Notebook, Vol 49, 95. **CONTACT ADDRESS** Sch of Theatre, Florida State Univ, 600 W College Ave, Tallahassee, FL, 32306-1096.

BAKER, TRACEY
DISCIPLINE RHETORIC AND COMPOSITION **EDUCATION** Purdue Univ, PhD, 84. **CAREER** Dept Eng, Univ Ala **SELECTED PUBLICATIONS** Coauth, Writing and Synthesis: A Multicultural Approach, HarperCollins, 93. **CONTACT ADDRESS** Univ AL, 1400 University Blvd, Birmingham, AL, 35294-1150.

BAKKER, BAREND H.
PERSONAL Born 09/12/1934, Hilversum, Netherlands **DISCIPLINE** LITERATURE **EDUCATION** Univ Toronto, BA, 56, MA, 58, PhD, 68. **CAREER** Lectr, Wilfrid Laurier Univ, 59-60; instr, Univ Toronto, 60-63; lectr, Ind Univ, 64-65; asst prof, 65-70, assoc prof, 70-75, dir, Zola Res Prog, 73-95, Prof French York Univ, 75-95 (RETIRED), Prin Investr & Sr Ed, The Zola Res Proj, 76-95; vis fel, Wolfson Col, Cambridge, 83; vis prof Waseda Univ (Tokyo), Aichi Univ (Nagoya), Univ Kyoto, 85; vis prof, Univ Calif Santa Barbara, 87. **HONORS AND AWARDS** Can Coun fel, 66-68, 72-73. **MEMBERSHIPS** MLA; Asn Profs Fre Univ & Cols Can; Societe litteraire des Amis d'Emile Zola. **RESEARCH** Emile Zola **SELECTED PUBLICATIONS** Auth, Naturalisme pas mort, Lettres inedites de Paul Alexis a Emile Zola 1871-1900, 71; ed, Emile Zola: Correspondence, vols 1-10, 78-95. **CONTACT ADDRESS** 12 De Vere Gardens, Toronto, ON, M5M 3E5.

BAKKER, JAN
PERSONAL Born 01/27/1936, New York, NY **DISCIPLINE** AMERICAN LITERATURE, TECHNICAL WRITING **EDUCATION** Univ VA, BA, 58, MA, 61; Univ TN, PhD (English), 75. **CAREER** Instr English, Clemson Univ, 60-62 & Memphis State Univ, 62-63; asst prof, Armstrong State Col, 67-68; lectr, Univ MD, 68-72; asst prof, 77-80, ASSOC PROF ENGLISH, UT STATE UNIV, 80-, UT State Univ fac res grant, 78; consult ed, Children's Literature; Fulbright vis prof, Univ Gadjah Mada, Indonesia, 80-81. **MEMBERSHIPS** MLA; Children's Lit Asn; Soc for Study Southern Lit; Am Studies Asn; Western Lit Asn. **RESEARCH** American literature; old south; children's literature. **SELECTED PUBLICATIONS** Auth, A List of the Juvenile Literature in the Hughes Public Library, Rugby, Tennessee, Children's Lit, 76; Time and Timelessness in Images of the Old South: Pastoral in John Pendleton Kennedy's Swallow Barn and Horse-Shoe Robinson, Tenn Studies in Lit, 79; Parallel Water Journeys into the American Eden in John Davis's The First Settlers of Virginia and F Scott Fitzgerald's The Great Gatsby, Early Am Lit, 81; Summer Reading at Woodlands: A Juvenile Library of the Old South, Children's Lit, 81; ... The Bold Atmosphere of Mrs Hentz' and Others: Fast food and Feminine Rebelliousness in Some Rmances of the Old South, J Popular Cult ; coauth, The Ruskin Experiment, Stonehill; Twist of Sentiment in Antebellum Southern Romance, Southern Literary J, Vol 26, 93. **CONTACT ADDRESS** Dept of English, UT State Univ, 3200 University Blvd, Logan, UT, 84322-3200.

BALAKIAN, PETER
DISCIPLINE AMERICAN POETRY, POETRY WRITING **EDUCATION** Bucknell Univ, BA, 73, Brown Univ, PhD, 80. **CAREER** Instr, PA Governor's Sch Arts; Bucknell Univ; prof, 80. **HONORS AND AWARDS** Acad Am Poets prize, 75; Yaddo fel, 80, 86, 88; Daniel Varoujan prize, New Eng Poetry Club, 87; NEA editing grants, Graham House Rev. **RESEARCH** Am poetry, genocide studies, peace studies, Armenian lit and cult. **SELECTED PUBLICATIONS** Auth, Father Fisheye, Sheep Meadow Press, 79; Sad Days of Light, Sheep Meadow Press, 83; Reply From Wilderness Island, Sheep Meadow Press, 88; Dyer's Thistle, Sheep Meadow Press, 96); (critical): Theodore Roethke's Far Fields(La State UP, 89; ed, Graham House Rev, Colgate UP. **CONTACT ADDRESS** Dept of Eng, Colgate Univ, 13 Oak Dr., Hamilton, NY, 13346.

BALDO, JONATHAN
DISCIPLINE ENGLISH **EDUCATION** SUNY at Buffalo, PhD. **CAREER** Assoc prof; taught at, SUNY, Buffalo & Univ FL. **RESEARCH** Contemp literary theory; soc hist. **SELECTED PUBLICATIONS** Publ on, Shakespeare, Shelley, Keats, Balzac, Kafka, Walter Benjamin, Garcia Marquez & Ingmar Bergman. **CONTACT ADDRESS** Dept of Eng, Univ of Rochester, 601 Elmwood Ave, Ste. 656, Rochester, NY, 14642. **EMAIL** urhomepage@cc.rochester.edu.

BALDWIN, ARMINTA TUCKER
PERSONAL Born 02/15/1939, West Union, WV, m, 1962, 1 child **DISCIPLINE** ENGLISH LITERATURE **EDUCATION** Glenville State Col, BA, 60; WVa Univ, MA, 62. **CAREER** Asst English, WVa Univ, 60-62; instr, Alderson-Broaddus Col, 62-66; assoc prof, 66-75, PROF ENGLISH & DEPT CHMN, WVA WESLEYAN COL, 75-, Teacher of humanities fed grant, 73 **HONORS AND AWARDS** Outstanding Young Women of WVa, 70; Community Council Outstanding Fac Award, 98. **MEMBERSHIPS** AAUP; NCTE; Nat Coun Publ Adv **RESEARCH** Women's literature. **SELECTED PUBLICATIONS** Auth, Keats & Shelley, WVEA Bulletin. **CONTACT ADDRESS** Dept of English, West Virginia Wesleyan Col, 59 College Ave, Buckhannon, WV, 26201-2699. **EMAIL** baldwin@wvwc.edu

BALDWIN, DEAN
PERSONAL Born 08/18/1942, Buffalo, NY, m, 1964, 2 children **DISCIPLINE** ENGLISH LITERATURE **EDUCATION** Capital Univ, BA, 64; Ohio State Univ, MA, 66; Ohio State Univ, PhD, 72. **CAREER** Central Missouri State Col, 66-67; Yankton Col, 67-69, 72-75; Penn State Erie, 75 -. **HONORS AND AWARDS** Coun of Fel Res Award; NWPCTE Distinguished Service Award; PCEA Outstanding Service Award. **MEMBERSHIPS** Pennsylvania Col English Asn; Asn of Literary Scholars and Critics; NCTE, Col English Asn; MLA. **RESEARCH** British short story; Shakespeare. **SELECTED PUBLICATIONS** Auth, "H.E. Bates", in Critical Survey of Long Fiction, Salem Press, 83; auth, "Atmosphere in the Short Stories of H.E. Bates", in Short Story Criticism, Gale Research, 93; auth, "The British Short Story in the 1950's", in The English Short Story: 1945-, 85; auth, H.E. Bates: A Literary Life, Selin-

sgrove: Susquehanna UP, 87; auth, V.S. Pritchett, Twayne, 87; auth, "Sylvia Townsend Warner", in An Encyclopedia of British Women Writers, Garland, 88; auth, Virginia Woolf: a Study of Short Fiction, Twayne, 89; coauth, H.E. Bates: A Literary Life, Selinsgrove: Susquehanna UP 87; auth, The Short Story in English: Britain and North America, Scarecrow Press, 94; auth, Introduction, in British Short Fiction Writers 1945-1980, Gale Research, 94; auth, "John Wain", in British Short Fiction Writers, Gale Research, 94; ed, British short Fiction Writers, 1945-1980, Gale Research, 94; auth, "H.E. Bates: the Poacher", in Recharting the Thirties, Susquehanny Press, 96; auth, Riverside Anthology of Short Fiction: Convention and Innovation, Houghton Mifflin, 97; coauth, Instructors Manual, Riverside Anthology of Short Fiction, Houghton Mifflin, 97; auth, "Sylvia Townsend Warner", in Women Writers of Great Britain and Europe, An Encyclopedia, Garland, 97. **CONTACT ADDRESS** The Behiend College, Pennsylvania State Univ, Erie, Station Rd., Erie, PA, 16563. **EMAIL** dxbll@psu.edu

BALDWIN, JOHN R.
DISCIPLINE COMMUNICATION; RELIGIOUS STUDIES **EDUCATION** Abilene Christian Univ, Masters, 91; Ariz State Univ, PhD, 94. **CAREER** Asst prof, Ill State Univ, 94-. **HONORS AND AWARDS** Ralph E. Cooley Award, top intercultural paper, nat conf of the Speech Commun Assn. **MEMBERSHIPS** Nat Commun Assn, Cent States Commun Assn, Int Network on Personal Rels, Soc for Int Educ, Training and Res. **RESEARCH** Intergroup/Intercultural commun; relationships; issues of tolerance. **SELECTED PUBLICATIONS** Co-auth, An African American communication perspective, Intercultural communication: A reader, Wadsworth, 7th ed, 140-147, 94; co-auth, Definitions of culture: Conceptualizations from five disciplines, Urban Studies Ctr, Ariz State Univ, 94; auth, Lost and Found: Ethics in intercultural/interethnic communication studies, Seeking understanding of communication, language and gender, CyberSpace, 94; co-auth, The layered perspective of cultural (in)tolerance(s): The roots of a multidisciplinary approach, Intercultural Communication Theory, Sage, 59-90, 95; Book review, Understudied relationships: Off the beaten track, ISSPR Bulletin: Official News Journal of the International Society for the Study of Personal Relationships, 16-18, 96; co-auth, An African American Communication Perspective, Intercultural communication: A reader, Wadsworth, 8th ed, 147-154, 97; co-auth, Family culture and relationship differences as a source of intercultural communication, Readings in cultural contexts, Mayfield, 335-344, 98; co-auth, Layers and holograms: A new look at prejudice, Communication of Prejudice, Sage, 57-84, 98; Auth, Tolerancee/intolerance: A historical and multi-disciplinary view of prejudice, Communication of Prejudice, Sage, 24-56, 98. **CONTACT ADDRESS** Dept of Commun, Illinois State Univ, Ill State Univ, PO Box 4480, Normal, IL, 61790-4480. **EMAIL** jrbaldw@ilstu.edu

BALES, KENT
PERSONAL Born 06/19/1936, Anthony, KS, m, 1958, 2 children **DISCIPLINE** ENGLISH **EDUCATION** Yale Univ, BA, 58; San Jose State Col, MA, 63; Univ CA, Berkeley, PhD, 67. **CAREER** Instr Eng, Menlo Sch & Col, 58-63; actg instr, Univ CA, Berkeley, 67; asst prof, 67-71, assoc prof, 71-82, prof eng, Univ MN, Minneapolis, 81, Ch, Eng Dept, Univ MN, 83-88, Vis Scholar, Inst Lit Sci, Budapest, 73-74 & 81; Fulbright lectr, Budapest, 80, res fel 88-89. **MEMBERSHIPS** MLA; Am Comp Lit Asn; Am Studies Asn; Midwest Mod Lang Asn. **RESEARCH** Am lit; lit and the other arts; comp studies in romanticism and the nineteenth century. **SELECTED PUBLICATIONS** Auth, The Blithedale Romance: Coverdale's mean and subversive egotism, Bucknell Rev, 73; The allegory and the radical romantic ethic of The Blithedale Romance, Am Lit, 74; Fishing the ambivalence, or, a reading of Trout Fishing in America, Western Humanities Rev, 75; Factors determining the translation of American Belles-Lettres into Hungarian, 1945-1973, Slavonic & E Europ Rev, 76; Hawthorne's prefaces and Romantic perspectivism, 77 & Sexual exploitation and the fall from natural virtue in Rappaccini's garden, 78, ESQ; O Henry, American Writers, suppl II, part I, Scribner's, 81; Pictures, Signs, and Stereotypes in Hawthorne's Meditations on the Origins of American Culture, In: The Origins and Originality of American Culture (Tibor Frank, ed), Akademiai Kiado, 84; From Emigre to Ethnic: Form, Subject, and Audience in Emigrant Hungarian Writing, In: The European Emigrant Experience in the USA (Walter Holbling and Reinhold Wagnleitner, ed), Gunter Narr Verlag, 92; Walt Whitman's Daughter, or Postcolonial Self-Transformation in the Fiction of Bharati Mukherjee, In: Daughters of Restlessness: Women's Literature at the End of the Millennium (Coelsch-Foisner, et al, ed), winter 98. **CONTACT ADDRESS** Dept of Eng, Univ of MN, 207 Church St S E, Minneapolis, MN, 55455-0156. **EMAIL** bales@tc.umn.edu

BALLSTADT, CARL P.A.
PERSONAL Born 12/28/1931, Sault Ste. Marie, ON, Canada **DISCIPLINE** ENGLISH **EDUCATION** Univ Western Ont, BA, 57, MA, 59; Univ London, PhD, 65. **CAREER** Tchr, Sault Ste Marie schs, 53-57, 59-60; fac mem, Univ Sask, 62-66; fac mem, Guelph Univ, 66-67; fac mem, 67-86, PROF ENGLISH, McMASTER UNIV, 86-. **MEMBERSHIPS** Bibliog Soc Can. **SELECTED PUBLICATIONS** Auth, The Search for English Canadian Literature, 75; auth, Catherine Parr Traill and Her Works, 83; coauth, Susanna Moodie: Letters of a Lifetime, 85; coauth, Letters of Love and Duty: The Correspondence of Susanna and John Moodie, 93; coauth, I Bless You In My Heart: Selected Correspondence of Catherine Parr Traill, 96; ed, Roughing it in the Bush (Susanna Moodie), 88; ed, Major John Richardson: A Selection of Reviews and Criticism, 72; co-ed, Forest and Other Gleanings: The Fugitive Writings of Catherine Parr Traill, 94; contribur, Dictionary Canadian Biography. **CONTACT ADDRESS** Dept of English, McMaster Univ, 1280 Main St W, Hamilton, ON, L8S 4L8.

BALSAMO, ANNE
DISCIPLINE MEDIA **EDUCATION** Univ Ill, Urbana-Champaign, PhD, 91. **CAREER** Assoc prof, dir, Grad Stud, Ga Inst of Technol. **RESEARCH** The development of new media genres. **SELECTED PUBLICATIONS** Auth, Technologies of the Gendered Body, Duke UP, 96. **CONTACT ADDRESS** Sch of Lit, Commun & Cult, Georgia Inst of Tech, Skiles Cla, Atlanta, GA, 30332. **EMAIL** anne.balsamo@lcc.gatech.edu

BALUTANSKY, KATHLEEN M.
PERSONAL Born 12/17/1954, Phaeton, Haiti, m, 1989, 1 child **DISCIPLINE** ENGLISH **EDUCATION** Goshen Col, BA, 76; Univ Notre Dame, MA, 78, PhD, 84. **CAREER** Asst Prof, Univ Va, 88-92; Assoc Prof, St Michael's Col, 92-. **HONORS AND AWARDS** Carter G Woodson Inst, Post-doctoral Fellow, 82-84; Ford Foundation, Post-doctoral Fellow, 91-92. **MEMBERSHIPS** Asn of Carib Women Writers & Sch; Asn of Carib Stud; Haitian StudAsn **RESEARCH** Caribbean lit; Caribbean women's fiction. **SELECTED PUBLICATIONS** Auth, Houses of the People and Houses of the Spirit,: An Interview with Marilene Phipps, Callaloo, 18.2, 419-26, 95; auth, Surviving Tokenism, Concerns, 2.2, 41-46, 95; auth, The Muse Speaks A New Tongue: New Perspectives on Language and Identity in Haitian American Women's Texts, MaComere, 1, 115-133, 98; co-ed, Representing Caribbean Creolization: Reflections on the Dynamics of Language and Literature, Univ Press of Fla, 98. **CONTACT ADDRESS** Dept of English, St Michael's Col, Colchester, VT, 05439. **EMAIL** kbalutansky@smcvt.edu

BAND, ARNOLD J.
PERSONAL Born 10/20/1929, Boston, MA, m, 1954, 2 children **DISCIPLINE** LITERATURE **EDUCATION** Harvard Univ, AB, 51, MA, 54, PhD(comp lit), 59; Hebrew Col, Boston, MHL, 51. **CAREER** Teaching fel humanities, Harvard Col, 54-58; asst Greek & Hebrew, Brandeis Univ, 58-59; from asst prof to assoc prof, 59-68, PROF HEBREW, UNIV CALIF, LOS ANGELES, 68-, Asst prof, Hebrew Col, Boston, 57-59; Am Philos Soc grant, 62; Am Coun Learned Soc-Cos Sci Res Coun joint grant, Mid East, 62; mem, Near Eastern Ctr, Univ Calif, Los Angeles, 62; Warburg fel, Hebrew Univ, Israel, 62; mem, Exam Comt Col Bd Hebrew Achievement Test, 63-68; fel, Inst Creative Arts, Univ CA, 66-67. **MEMBERSHIPS** MLA; Am Philol Asn: Nat Asn Prof Hebrew; Pen Club; Am Comp Lit Asn. **RESEARCH** Modern Hebrew literature; comedy. **SELECTED PUBLICATIONS** Auth, HaRe'i Bo'er Ba'esh, Ogdan, Jerusalem & Ogen, NY, 63; Notstalgia and Nightmare: A Study in the Fiction of S Y Agnon, Univ CA, Berkeley, 68; The Meaning of Yiddish, with B. Harshav, Modern Philol, Vol 91, 93. **CONTACT ADDRESS** Dept of Near Eastern Lang, Univ of CA, Los Angeles, CA, 90024.

BANERJEE, MARIA NEMCOVA
PERSONAL Born 11/22/1937, Prague, Czechoslovakia, m, 1961 **DISCIPLINE** RUSSIAN & COMPARATIVE LITERATURE **EDUCATION** Univ Paris, Baccalaureat, 55; Univ Montreal, MA, 57; Harvard Univ, PhD(Slavic), 62. **CAREER** Tutor Russ lit, Harvard Univ, 61-62; asst prof, Brown Univ, 62-64; from vis lectr to asst prof, 64-72, assoc prof, 72-79, PROF RUSS LIT, SMITH COL, 79-, Vis lectr, Wellesley Col, 63-64; Int Res & Exchanges Bd sr scholar, Int Russ Lit, Leningrad, 73-74. **MEMBERSHIPS** Am Asn Advan Slavic Studies; Czech Soc Arts & Sci Am. **RESEARCH** Nineteenth and 20th century Russian and European literatures, especially Dostoevsky and symbolism; Pushkin; Russian and European realism in the novel. **SELECTED PUBLICATIONS** Auth, Rozanov on Dostoevsky, Slavic East Europ J, winter 71; The Metamorphosis of an Icon, Female Studies, Vol IX, 75; Pushkin's The Bronze Horseman: An Agonistic Vision, Mod Lang Studies, 78; The Narrator and His Masks in Viacheslew Ivanov's Povest' o Suetomire Tsareviche, Can-Am Slavic Studies, 78; Vitezslov Nezval's Progue with Fingers of Rain: A Surrealistic Image, Slavic and East Europ J, 79; The American Revolver: An Essay on Dostoevsky's The Devils, Mod Fiction Studies, 81; Pavel Yavor and the Pathos of Exile, In: Far From You, Toronto, 81; Metapoesis-The Russian Tradition from Pushkin to Chekhov, with M. C. Finke, Russian Rev, Vol 55, 96. **CONTACT ADDRESS** Dept of Russ, Smith Col, Northampton, MA, 01061.

BANET-WEISER, SARAH
DISCIPLINE COMMUNICATION **EDUCATION** Univ CA, San Diego, BA, 89, MA, 90, PhD, 95. **CAREER** Lectr, Univ Southern CA, 97-98; lectr, UCLA, 94-96 & Univ CA, San Diego, 95-; postdoctoral res fel, Univ CA Hum Res Inst, 96-97. **RESEARCH** Feminist theory and politics; media studies; race and sexuality; contemp Am cult; nationalism; popular cult, qualitative methods. **SELECTED PUBLICATIONS** Auth, Crowning Identities: Performing Nationalism, Femininity, and Race in US Beauty Pageants, Univ Calif Press, 98; Fade to White: Racial Politics and the Troubled Reign of Vanessa Williams in Women Transforming Politics, NY UP, 97; Viva La Hispanidad: Constructions of National Identity, Femininity, and Ethnicity in Beauty Pageants, in Minority Discourses, Cultural Productions: Theories, Texts, and Contexts, Univ Calif Press, 98; Fade to White: Race, Nation and the Miss America Pageant, Ctr Feminist Res, Univ Southern Calif, 97 & Miss America/Miss Universe: Gender, Race and Nation in Televised Beauty Pageants, Int Commun Asn, 97, Montreal, Can; rev, Figures of Beauty, Figures of Nation: Global Contests of Femininity Amer Quart, Vol 50, 98. **CONTACT ADDRESS** Annenberg School for Commun, Univ of Southern California, University Park Campus, Los Angeles, CA, 90089. **EMAIL** sbanet@usc.edu

BANK, ROSEMARIE KATHERINE
PERSONAL Born 10/19/1942, Chicago, IL, m, 1970 **DISCIPLINE** THEATRE **EDUCATION** IN Univ, BA, 64; Univ IA, MA, 70, PhD(Theatre), 72. **CAREER** Instr theatre, Grinnell Col, IA, 70-71; asst prof, IL State Univ, 72-75; ASST PROF THEATRE, PURDUE UNIV, 76-80. **MEMBERSHIPS** Am Theatre Asn; Am Soc Theatre Res; Speech Commun Asn; AAUP. **RESEARCH** 19th century American theatre history and drama; melodrama; the frontier play, image of women. **SELECTED PUBLICATIONS** Auth, Melodrama as a Social Document: Social Factors in the American Frontier Play, Theatre Studies, No 22, 75-76; Strindgerg: Misogyny, Misanthropy, and Balance, Exchange, fall 76; ed, Theatre in Review, Educ Theatre J, 78-80; American Playwrights Since 1945, with P. C. Kolin, Theatre Survey, Vol 33, 92; Staging the Native, Making History in American Theater Culture, 1828-1838, Theatre J, Vol 45, 93; The History of World Theater, Vol 2, From the English Restoration to the Present, with F. H. Londre, Theatre Res Int, Vol 18, 93; 19th-Century American Women Theater Managers, with J. K. Curry, Theatre Survey, Vol 36, 95. **CONTACT ADDRESS** Rt 5, Lafayette, IN, 47905.

BANKOWSKY, RICHARD JAMES
PERSONAL Born 11/25/1928, Wallington, NJ, m, 1952, 3 children **DISCIPLINE** CREATIVE WRITING **EDUCATION** Yale Univ, BA, 52; Columbia Univ, MA, 54. **CAREER** From instr to assoc prof, 59-67, PROF ENGLISH, CALIF STATE UNIV, SACRAMENTO, 67-, Nat Inst Arts & Lett grant, 63; Rockefeller Found grant, 68 **RESEARCH** Writing novels **SELECTED PUBLICATIONS** Auth, A Glass Rose, 58, After Pentecost, 61, On a Dark Night, 64 & The Pale Criminals, 67, Random; The Barbarians at the Gates, Little, 72 **CONTACT ADDRESS** Dept of English, California State Univ, Sacramento, 6000 J St, Sacramento, CA, 95819-2694.

BANTA, MARTHA
PERSONAL Born 05/11/1928, Muncie, IN, s **DISCIPLINE** ENGLISH **EDUCATION** Indiana Univ, BA, 50, PhD, 64. **CAREER** Asst prof, Univ Calif, Santa Barbara, 64-70; assoc prof, 70-74, prof, 74-83, Univ Wash; prof, 83-98, Univ Calif Los Angeles. **HONORS AND AWARDS** Pres, Am Stud Asn; ed, PMLA; NEH fel; Guggenheim fel. **MEMBERSHIPS** MLA; Am Stud Asn. **RESEARCH** American literature and culture; art history. **SELECTED PUBLICATIONS** Ed and introd, Edith Wharton, The House of Mirth, Oxford, 94; auth, The Ghostly Gothic of Wharton's Everyday World, Am Lit Realism, 94; auth, The Three New Yorks: Topographical Narratives and Cultural Texts, Am Lit Hist, 95; auth, The Razor, The Pistol, and The Ideology of Race Etiquette, in Kartiganer, ed, Faulkner and Ideology: Essays from the Nineteenth Annual Yoknapatawpha Conference, Mississippi, 95; auth, The Excluded Seven: Practice of Omission/Aesthetics of Refusal, in McWhirter, ed, Henry James and the Construction of Authorship, Stanford, 95; auth, Strange Deserts: Hotels, Hospitals, Country Clubs, Prisons and the City of Brotherly Love, Henry James Rev, 96; auth, Being a Begonia in a Man's World, in, Rowe, ed, New Essays on The Education of Henry James, Cambridge, 96; auth, Men, Women, and the American Way, in The Cambridge Companion to Henry James, 97. **CONTACT ADDRESS** Dept of English, Univ of California, Los Angeles, Los Angeles, CA, 90095. **EMAIL** banta@ucla.edu

BAR, FRANCOIS
DISCIPLINE COMMUNICATIONS **CAREER** Sr res fel Berkeley Roundtable Int Econ (BRIE), Univ CA Berkeley; sr fel, San Diego Supercomput Ctr; asst prof, Standford Univ, present; dir net res, Stanford Comput IndusProj (SCIP), present. **HONORS AND AWARDS** Adv coun, CompuMentor; ed bd Comms & Strats, IDATE; adv comm, prog sci, tech, soc, Stanford Univ. **RESEARCH** Comp telecommun policy; economic, strategic and soc dimensions of computer networking, new media and the internet. **SELECTED PUBLICATIONS** Auth, Intelligent Manufacturing in the Global Information Economy in The Transition to a Global Economy: Challenges for United States and the World, 20th Century Fund, 95; Information Networks and Competitive Advantage: Issues for Government Policy and Corporate Strategy, Int Jour Tech Mgmt; coauth, From Welfare to Innovation: Toward a New Rationale for Universal Service, The Information Society, 98; Islands in the Bit-stream: Mapping the NII Interoperability Debate--BRIE Working Paper #79, UC-Berkeley, 95; Reseaux CAO-CFAO et Reseaux

Fournisseurs/Clients: Recherche sur la Mise en Place de l'Usine Integree, a partir d'une Etude Comparative France-Etats Unis dans l'Industrie Automobile, Rapport au Ministere de la Recherche, Universite de Paris-XIII, 93. **CONTACT ADDRESS** Stanford Univ, McClatchy Hall, Room 344, Stanford, CA, 94305. **EMAIL** fbar@leland.stanford.edu

BARASCH, FRANCES K.
PERSONAL Born 04/10/1928, New York, NY, m, 1952, 3 children **DISCIPLINE** ENGLISH **EDUCATION** Brooklyn Col, BA, 49; NY Univ, MA, 52, PhD(english), 64. **CAREER** Consultant, Choice, 66- ; rev, Shakespeare Bul, 92- . **HONORS AND AWARDS** NYU Grad Sch of Arts and Sci Alumni Certificate of Honor; NYU Alumni Federation Sesquicentennial Crystal Award, 82; NYU Alumni Meritorious Service Award, 83; Professional Staff Congress award, 93; AFT Women's Rights Committee Living the Legacy award, 98. **MEMBERSHIPS** Shakespeasre Asn of Am; Int Shakespeare Asn. **RESEARCH** Medieval and Renaissance literature and art; the grotesque; Commedia dell'Arte. **SELECTED PUBLICATIONS** Auth, Norwich Cathedral: The Bauchun Chapel Legend of the Accused Queen, in; The Early Drama, Art, and Music Rev, 93; auth, The Bayeux Painting and Shakespearean Improvisation, Shakespeare Bul, 93; auth, He's for a Iigge, or a Tale of Baudry: Sixteenth-Century Images of the Stage Jig, Shakespeare Bul, 95; auth, Castiliano Vulgo Revisited, Shakespeare Newsl, 96; auth, Language Immersion: A Progress Report, PSC Clarion, 98; auth, Shakespeare and the Italians, Shakespearean Int Yearbk, 99; auth, Theatrical Prints: Zany, Pantalone, and the Elizabethans, RuBriCa, 99. **CONTACT ADDRESS** Baruch Col, CUNY, Lexington Ave, New York, NY, 10010. **EMAIL** fbarasch@aol.com

BARBA, HARRY
PERSONAL Born 06/17/1922, Bristol, CT, m, 1965, 2 children **DISCIPLINE** ENGLISH, WRITING **EDUCATION** Bates Col, AB, 44; Harvard Univ, MA, 51; Univ Iowa, MFA, 60, PhD, 63. **CAREER** Instr, 47, Wilkes Col; instr, 47-49, Univ Conn, Hartford; instr, 59-63, Univ Iowa; from asst prof to assoc prof, 63-68, Skidmore Col, fac res fels, 65-67; prof & dir, 68-70, Marshall Univ; res & writing, 70-, Fulbright prof, 63-64, Damascus Univ; ed consult, Bantam Bks, Inc, 67 & Macmillan, 72; mem staff, Writers Conf; publ, Harian Press, NY & WVa; dir & consult, Spa Writers & Educ Conf, 67-73; Benedum res grant, Marshall Univ, 69; HEA grant, 69-70; residence fel, MacDowell Colony, 70; speaker & reader, NY State Coun on Arts, 71-76; dist vis lectr & consult writing comt, SUNY, Albany, 77-78. **MEMBERSHIPS** Auth League Am; MLA; Col English Assn; PEN Club; Poets & Writers. **RESEARCH** Creative and expository writing; interdisciplinary studies; the writing arts and American studies. **SELECTED PUBLICATIONS** Auth, For the Grape Season, Macmillan, 60; auth, Three by Harry Barba, 67; auth, How to Teach Writing, 69; auth, Teaching in Your Own Write, 70; auth, The Case for Socially Functional Education, 73; auth, One of A Kind--The Many Faces & Voices of America, 76; auth, The Day the World Went Sane, 79; auth, The Gospel According to Everyman, Harian, 81. **CONTACT ADDRESS** 47 Hyde Blvd, Ballston Spa, NY, 12020.

BARBER, MARGARET
DISCIPLINE COMPOSITION, ADVANCED COMPOSITION, SHAKESPEARE, WORLD LITERATURE, WOMEN IN **EDUCATION** TX Christian Univ, BA, 64, MA, 66, PhD, 77. **CAREER** Asst prof, Univ of Southern CO. **RESEARCH** Computer assisted compos; Shakespeare's Macbeth; women in early world lit; the novel; Lafcadio Hearn; ecofeminist theory. **SELECTED PUBLICATIONS** Publ on, artistic develop of Lafcadio Hearn. **CONTACT ADDRESS** Dept of Eng, Univ of Southern Colorado, 2200 Bonforte Blvd, Pueblo, CO, 81001-4901. **EMAIL** Barber@meteor.uscolo.edu

BARBERA, JACK VINCENT
PERSONAL Born 07/18/1945, Rockville Centre, NY **DISCIPLINE** CONTEMPORARY LITERATURE, FILM **EDUCATION** Univ Chicago, AB, 68, AM, 69, PhD, 76. **CAREER** Instr humanities, Roosevelt Univ, 74-75; asst prof English, 76-83, assoc prof English, 83-87, prof English, 87-, English, Univ Miss, 76-. **HONORS AND AWARDS** DeWitt Wallace/Readers Digest/MacDowell Colony Fel 81. **MEMBERSHIPS** MLA; Ed Bd 20th Century Lit. **RESEARCH** Modern poetry; film criticism; American literature. **SELECTED PUBLICATIONS** Ed Special Athol Fugard issue of Twentieth Century Literature, 93; Auth Introduction and Fugard as Director: An Interview with the Cast of Boesman and Lena, 20th Century Lit, 93; Entries on August Wilson, Ma Rainey's Black Bottom, Fences, and Two Trains Running, Identities and Issues in Literature, David Peck, ed, Salem Press, CA, 97; The Emotion of Multitude and David Rabe's Streamers, Am Drama, 97; MWP: John Crews, MS Writers Page; Fugard's Valley Song, The Nation, 96. **CONTACT ADDRESS** Dept English, Univ Ms, University, MS, 38677-9999.

BARBOUR, ALTON BRADFORD
PERSONAL Born 10/13/1933, San Diego, CA, m, 1996, 4 children **DISCIPLINE** COMMUNICATIONS **EDUCATION** Univ Northern Colo, BA, 56; Univ Denver, MA, 61, PhD, 68. **CAREER** Instr, 65, asst prof, 68, assoc prof, 73, prof, 77, chemn 80-98, Univ Denver. **HONORS AND AWARDS** Intellectual Freedom Award, Nat Council Tchrs English, 97; Hannah Weiner Distinguished Professional Serv Award, Am Soc Psychodrama and group Psychotherapy, 97., Trainer, Educ Practitioner Certification, 78, Am Board Examiners. **MEMBERSHIPS** Nat Commun Asn; Colo Lang Art Soc; Am Soc Psychodrama and Group Psychotherapy. **RESEARCH** Action methods in communication education. **SELECTED PUBLICATIONS** Auth, art, The Process of Becoming, 97; auth, art, The Train from Cheyenne: A Message from the Chair, 98; auth, art, A Rationale for Nonclinical Certification, 98; auth, art, On the Question of Professionalism: A Message from the Chair, 98; auth, art, Round Up the Usual Suspects: A Message from the Chair, 99. **CONTACT ADDRESS** Dept of Human Communications Studies, Univ of Denver, Denver, CO, 80208. **EMAIL** abarbour@dn.edu

BARBOUR, BRIAN MICHAEL
PERSONAL Born 07/26/1943, Lorain, OH, m, 1968, 3 children **DISCIPLINE** ENGLISH & AMERICAN LITERATURE **EDUCATION** Univ Notre Dame, BA, 65; Kent State Univ, MA, 66, PhD(English), 69. **CAREER** Asst prof, 69-74, assoc prof, 74-78, Prof English, Providence Col, 78-, Dir Am Studies, 81-85; chemn English, 86-88; dir Development of Western Civilization, 94; Ed, Providence Studies in Western Studies in Western Civilization, 95. **HONORS AND AWARDS** Vis Fel, St Edmund's Coll, Cambridge, 93-. **MEMBERSHIPS** Melville Soc Am; Fel of Catholic Scholars; Natl Assoc of Scholars; Assn of Literary Scholars & Critics. **RESEARCH** Am lit since 17th Century; 19th & 20th Century English Lit; Cambridge English; C S Lewis, Solzhenitsyn. **SELECTED PUBLICATIONS** Ed, American Transcendentalism: An Anthology of Criticism, Univ Notre Dame, 73; auth, The Great Gatsby, and the American Past, Southern Review, 73; Emerson's Poetic Prouse, Mod Lang Quart, 74; Poe and Tradition, Southern Lit J, 78; ed, Benjamin Franklin: A Collection of Critical Essays, Prentice-Hall, 78; Gaining Upon Certainty: Selected Literary Criticism of Rene Fortin, Providence College, 95; Lewis and Cambridge, Modern Philology, 98. **CONTACT ADDRESS** Dept of English, Providence Col, 549 River Ave, Providence, RI, 02918-0002. **EMAIL** bbarbour@providence.edu

BARBOUR, DOUGLAS F.
PERSONAL Born 03/21/1940, Winnipeg, MB, Canada **DISCIPLINE** ENGLISH LITERATURE **EDUCATION** Acadia Univ, BA, 62; Dalhousie Univ, MA, 64; Queen's Univ, PhD, 76. **CAREER** Asst prof, 69, assoc prof, 77, PROF ENGLISH, UNIV ALTA, 82-. **SELECTED PUBLICATIONS** Auth, Visible Visions, 84; Canadian Poetry Chronicle (1984), 85; Story for A Saskatchewan Night, 90; John Newlove and His Works, 92; Daphne Marlatt and her Works, 92; BP Nichol and His Works, 92; Michael Ondaatje, 93; coauth, The Pirates of Pen's Chance, 81; ed, The Story So Far, 78; Three Times Five 83; Richard Sommer: Selected and New Poems, 83; Beyond Tish, 91; co-ed, The Maple Laugh Forever, 81; Writing Right, 82; Tesseracts II, 87. **CONTACT ADDRESS** Dept of English, Univ of Alberta, Edmonton, AB, T6G 2E5. **EMAIL** doug.barbour@ualberta.ca

BARBOUR, PAULA LOUISE
PERSONAL Born 03/07/1949, Portland, ME, m, 1979 **DISCIPLINE** SEVENTEENTH CENTURY ENGLISH LITERATURE, WOMEN'S STUDIES **EDUCATION** Tufts Univ, BA, 71; Yale Univ, MA, 72, MPhil, 74, PhD(English), 75. **CAREER** ASST PROF ENGLISH, FLA STATE UNIV, 75-, Coordr, Woman's Studies Prog, Fla State Univ, 76-77 & 79-80; dir, Merit & Achievement Scholars Prog, 80-85; dir, Honors and Scholars Prog, FSU, 85-93; assistant in English, English Dept, FSU, 93-. **RESEARCH** Seventeenth-century English drama; women's studies (literature written before 1750). **CONTACT ADDRESS** Dept of English, Florida State Univ, Box 1580, Tallahassee, FL, 32306-1580. **EMAIL** pbarbour@english.fsu.edu

BARBOUR, RICHMOND
DISCIPLINE RENAISSANCE **EDUCATION** Stanford Univ Univ, BA, 70; Univ Calif, Berkley, PhD, 90. **CAREER** Engl, Oregon St Univ. **SELECTED PUBLICATIONS** Auth, The Elizabethan Jonson in Print,"Criticism, 92; 'When I Acted Young Antinous': Boy-Actors and the Erotics of Jonsonian Theater, PMLA, 95. **CONTACT ADDRESS** Oregon State Univ, Corvallis, OR, 97331-4501. **EMAIL** rbarbour@orst.edu

BARBUOR, ALTON
PERSONAL Born 10/13/1933, San Diego, CA, m, 1996, 4 children **DISCIPLINE** COMMUNICATIONS **EDUCATION** Univ Northern Colo, BA, 56; Univ Denver, MA, 61, PhD, 68. **CAREER** Instr, 65, asst prof, 68, assoc prof, 73, prof, 77, chemn 80-98, Univ Denver. **HONORS AND AWARDS** Intellectual Freedom Award, Nat Council Tchrs English, 97; Hannah Weiner Distinguished Professional Serv Award, Am Soc Psychodrama and group Psychotherapy, 97., Trainer, Educ Practitioner Certification, 78, Am Board Examiners. **MEMBERSHIPS** Nat Commun Asn; Colo Lang Art Soc; Am Soc Psychodrama and Group Psychotherapy. **RESEARCH** Action methods in communication education. **SELECTED PUBLICATIONS** Auth, art, The Process of Becoming, 97; auth, art, The Train from Cheyenne: A Message from the Chair, 98; auth, art, A Rationale for Nonclinical Certification, 98; auth, art, On the Question of Professionalism: A Message from the Chair, 98; auth, art, Round Up the Usual Suspects: A Message from the Chair, 99. **CONTACT ADDRESS** Dept of Human Communications Studies, Univ of Denver, Denver, CO, 80208. **EMAIL** abarbour@dn.edu

BARDEN, THOMAS E.
PERSONAL Born 08/05/1946, m, 3 children **DISCIPLINE** ENGLISH **EDUCATION** Univ Va, BA, 68, MA, 72, PhD, 75. **CAREER** US Army, 68-71; Grad Asst, Univ Va, 73-75; Acting Asst Prof, Univ Va, 75-76; Asst to Assoc to Prof, Univ Toledo, 75-91; Am Stud Prog Dir, Univ Toledo, 91-; Sr Fulbright Lecturer in Am Stud at Univ Swansea, UK, 93-94; Dir Grad Stud, Dept English, Univ Toledo, 97-. **HONORS AND AWARDS** Sr Fulbright Fellow, Univ Col in Swansea; Fellow, The David & Mary Eccles Ctr for Am Stud of the Brit Lib, 93; Univ Toledo Outstanding Fac Res Award, 92; Fac Res Fellow, Univ Toledo, 86, 91, 92; Summer Res Fellow, Va Ctr for Hum & Pub Policy, 90; Pi Upsilon Pi Chap of Omicron Delta Kappa. **MEMBERSHIPS** Gen Arts Advisory Panel; Traditional & Ethnic Arts Advisory Panel, Ohio Arts Council; Ohio Folklore Soc (VP 79-80, Pres 80-81); Hisp Commun Cultural Grp; Ohio Found on the Arts (bd of trustees), Arts & Sci Counc, (rep 94-96, secr, 80-82). **SELECTED PUBLICATIONS** Auth, Virginia Folk Legends, Univ Press of Va, 91; auth, John Millington Synge's In the Shadow of the Glen: A Study and Evaluation, Masterplots of Modern Drama, Salem Press, 815-19, 92; auth, The WPA Collection of Virginia Folk Legends, Va Calvacade, 41:3, 100-111, 92; auth, Some Old Virginia Analogs to Modern Urban Legends, Contemp Legend, 2, 155-164, 92; auth, Hines' Farm and the Rural Blues Scene in Northwest Ohio, 1950-1976, Living Blues, 30-37, 92; auth, entries in American Folklore: An Encyclopedia, Norton, 96; auth, Contemporary Legends of Am Soldiers in the Vietnam War, Fabula: J of Folktale Stud. 36, 4, 29-51, 95. **CONTACT ADDRESS** Dept of English, Univ Toledo, Toledo, OH, 43606.

BAREISS, WARREN J.
PERSONAL Born 11/08/1962, Pennsylvania, PA, m, 1990 **DISCIPLINE** MASS COMMUNICATION **EDUCATION** IN Univ, PhD, 96. **CAREER** Asst prof, South Dakota St Univ; asst prof, 96-98, Shorter Col. **MEMBERSHIPS** Intl Comm Asn **RESEARCH** Telemedicine; noncommercial media; community identity; radio drama history. **SELECTED PUBLICATIONS** Auth, The Life of Riley/Goodyear Playhouse/Original Amateur Hour, Encycl of TV, Fitzroy Dearborn, 97; auth, Suspense/Sustaining Prog, Hist Dist of Amer Radio, Greenwood Press, 97. **CONTACT ADDRESS** 20566 469th Ave., Brookings, SD, 57006. **EMAIL** wbareiss@cc.sdstate.edu

BARFIELD, RAYFORD
DISCIPLINE ENGLISH LITERATURE **EDUCATION** Univ Tenn, PhD, 69. **CAREER** Dept Eng, Clemson Univ **RESEARCH** Shakespeare, popular culture, and writing. **SELECTED PUBLICATIONS** Auth, Listening to Radio 1920-1950, Praeger, 96; coauth, Business Communications, Barron, 92. **CONTACT ADDRESS** Clemson Univ, 813 Strode, Clemson, SC, 29634. **EMAIL** brayfor@clemson.edu

BARGE, J. KEVIN
PERSONAL Born 08/08/1959, San Jose, CA, m, 1998 **DISCIPLINE** COMMUNICATIONS STUDIES **EDUCATION** Milliken Univ, BA, 81; Univ Kansas, MA, 85, PhD, 86. **CAREER** Assoc prof, Baylor Univ, 85-. **HONORS AND AWARDS** Baylor Univ Centennial Award; Outstanding Univ Prof, Baylor Univ, 92. **MEMBERSHIPS** Natl Commun Assn; Central States Commun Assn. **RESEARCH** Leadership in organizations; public dialogue. **SELECTED PUBLICATIONS** Auth, Leadership: Communications Skills for Organizations and Groups, 94; auth, "On Doing Appealing Work in Group Communication," Communication Studies, vol 45, 94; auth, "Putting Leadership Back to Work," Management Communication Quarterly, vol 8, 94; co-ed, Managing Group Life: Communicating in Decision-making Groups, 97. **CONTACT ADDRESS** Dept of Communication Studies, Castellaw Communications Center, Baylor Univ, 143 Castellaw, Waco, TX, 76798. **EMAIL** kevin_barge@baylor.edu

BARKER, THOMAS T.
DISCIPLINE ENGLISH LITERATURE **EDUCATION** Univ TX, Austin, PhD, 80. **CAREER** Assoc prof, TX Tech Univ. **RESEARCH** Computer documentation. **SELECTED PUBLICATIONS** Auth, Writing Software Documentation; ed, Perspectives on Software Documentation. **CONTACT ADDRESS** Texas Tech Univ, Lubbock, TX, 79409-5015. **EMAIL** TBarker@ttu.edu

BARKLEY, HEATHER S.
DISCIPLINE ENGLISH LITERATURE **EDUCATION** Yale Univ, PhD. **CAREER** Asst prof, TX Tech Univ. **RESEARCH** Anglo-Saxon lang and lit; the Old Irish Saga. **SELECTED PUBLICATIONS** Ed with the Yale Editions of the Papers of James Boswell. **CONTACT ADDRESS** Texas Tech Univ, Lubbock, TX, 79409-5015. **EMAIL** cbhsb@ttacs.ttu.edu

BARLOW, JUDITH ELLEN
PERSONAL Born 08/21/1946, Bronx, NY **DISCIPLINE** AMERICAN LITERATURE, MODERN DRAMA **EDUCATION** Cornell Univ, AB, 68; Univ Pa, AM, 70, PhD, 75. **CAREER** Instr, Univ PA, 71-72; lectr, 73-75, asst prof, 75-82, assoc prof eng, State Univ NY, Albany, 82-95, PROF, 95-, Adj prof women's studies, State Univ NY, Albany, 80-82, adj assoc prof, 82-; Assoc ed, Theatre Survey, 80. **HONORS AND AWARDS** Collins Fel, Univ Albany, SUNY, 97; Pres Award Excellence in Acade Service, Univ Albany, SUNY, 91; State of NY & UPP Excellence Award, 91; Pres Award for Excellence in Teaching, Univ Albany, SUNY, 83. **MEMBERSHIPS** MLA; Nat Women's Studies Asn; Eugene O'Neill Soc; Intl Women Playrights; assoc Theatre in Higher Edu. **RESEARCH** Am women playwrights; Eugene O'Neill. **SELECTED PUBLICATIONS** Auth, Semantic satiation and the semantic differential, Cornell J Social Rel, 10/66; coauth, Distinctive features in the pluralization rules of English speakers, Lang & Speech, 1-3/68; auth, Long Day's Journey into Night: From early notes to finished play, Mod Drama, 3/79; ed, Plays by American women: The early years, Avon, 81; auth, Plays by American Women 1930-1960, Applause Books, 94; Final Acts: The Creation of Three Late O'Neill Plays, Univ GA Press, 85; Plays by American Women 1900-1930, Applause Books, 85. **CONTACT ADDRESS** Eng Dept, State Univ, 1400 Washington Ave, Albany, NY, 12222-1000. **EMAIL** jebarlow@aol.com

BARNES, DANIEL RAMON
PERSONAL Born 05/16/1940, Fillmore, NY, m, 1963, 3 children **DISCIPLINE** AMERICAN LITERATURE, FOLKLORE **EDUCATION** St Bonaventure Univ, BA, 62; Univ KS, MA, 66; Univ KY, PhD(English), 70. **CAREER** From instr to asst prof, 68-73, ASSOC PROF ENGLISH, OH STATE UNIV, COLUMBUS, 73-, Consult, Smithsonian Inst Festival of Am Folklore, 71; ed, Motif: Int Newslett Res in Folklore & Lit, 81-. **MEMBERSHIPS** MLA; Am Folklore Soc; Asn Anthrop Study of Play; Int Soc Folk Narrative Res; Folklore Soc Britain. **RESEARCH** Nineteenth century American literature; folklore and literature; folklore and folklife. **SELECTED PUBLICATIONS** Auth, Ford and the Slaughtered Saints: A New Reading of The Good Soldier, Mod Fiction Studies, summer 68; Folktale Morphology and the Structure of Beowulf, Speculum, 4/70; Physical Fact and Folklore: Hawthorne's Egotism, or the Bosom Serpent, Am Lit, 3/71; The Bosom Serpent: A Legend in American Literature and Culture, J Am Folklore, 4/72; Toward the Establishment of Principles for the Study of Folklore and Lliterature, Southern Folklore Quart, 1/79; Telling it Slant: Emily Dickinson and the Proverb, Genre, summer 79; Joseph Chamberlain and the Challenge of Radicalism, with D. Watts, Welsh Hist Rev, Vol 17, 94; Neville Chamberlain-A Study in Failure, with P. Neville, Welsh Hist Rev, Vol 17, 94. **CONTACT ADDRESS** Dept of English, Ohio State Univ, 164 W 17th Ave, Columbus, OH, 43210-1326.

BARNES, JIM WEAVER
PERSONAL Born 12/22/1933, Summerfield, OK **DISCIPLINE** COMPARATIVE LITERATURE, CREATIVE WRITING **EDUCATION** Southeast Oklahoma State Univ, BA, 64; Univ Ark, Fayetteville, MA, 66, PhD, 72. **CAREER** Instr English, Northeastern Okla State Col, 65-68; prof comp lit, 70-, ed, The Chariton Review, Truman State Univ, 76-; Nat Endowment for the Arts creative writing fel, 78; Rockefeller Found Bellagio Fel, 90; Sr Fulbright to Switerland, 93-94; Akaademie Schloss Solitude Fel, 98. **HONORS AND AWARDS** Transl Prize Summons and Sign, Columbia Univ, 80; The Am Book Award, 98. **MEMBERSHIPS** Coord Coun of Lit Mags; MLA. **RESEARCH** Twentieth century fiction and poetry; creative writing. **SELECTED PUBLICATIONS** Auth, On Native Ground, University of Oklahoma Press, 97; auth, Paris, University of Illinois Press, 97. **CONTACT ADDRESS** Div of Lang & Lit, Northeast Missouri State Univ, 100 E Normal St, Kirksville, MO, 63501-4221. **EMAIL** jbarnes@truman.edu

BARNES, RICHARD G.
PERSONAL Born 11/05/1932, San Bernardino, CA, m, 1953, 9 children **DISCIPLINE** ENGLISH **EDUCATION** Pomona Col, BA, 54; Harvard Univ, AM, 59; Claremont Grad Sch, PhD, 60. **CAREER** Actg instr English, Univ Calif, Riverside, 58-59; from instr to prof, 61-98, Prof Emeritus English, Pomona Col, 98-. **HONORS AND AWARDS** Mellon fel poetry, 75. **MEMBERSHIPS** Medieval Asn Pac; Asn Lit Schol and Critics. **RESEARCH** Chaucer; medieval theatre; Sacramental theatre. **SELECTED PUBLICATIONS** Auth, John Cage, In: Richard Kostelanetz, Praeger, 70; The Complete Poems of R G Barnes, Grabhorn-Hoyem, 72; Episodes in Five Poetic Traditions, Chandler, 72; Thirty-One Views of San Bernardino (poem), Spectator, 75; ed, The Psalms, Arion, 77; Hungry Again The Next Day, 78 & Lyrical Ballads, 79, Barnes; A Lake on the Earth, Momentum, 82; auth, Few and Far Between, Asahta, 94. **CONTACT ADDRESS** Dept of English, Pomona Col, 333 N College Way, Claremont, CA, 91711-6319. **EMAIL** rbarnes@pomona.edu

BARNES, RONALD EDGAR
PERSONAL Born 03/12/1930, Minneapolis, MN, m, 1954 **DISCIPLINE** DRAMATIC LITERATURE **EDUCATION** Univ Minn, BA, 51; Stanford Univ, PhD(Drama), 63. **CAREER** From instr to asst prof Drama, Mills Col, 57-65; assoc prof, 56-69, prof Drama & chmn dept, Calif State Univ, San Bernardino, 70-88; retired, 97. **MEMBERSHIPS** US Inst Theatre Technol; CA Theatre Assn; Southern CA Theatre Assn. **RESEARCH** Dramatic analysis; theatre architecture. **SELECTED PUBLICATIONS** Auth, The Dramatic Comedy of William Somerset Maugham, Mouton, 68. **CONTACT ADDRESS** Dept of Drama, California State Univ, San Bernardino, 5500 University Pky, San Bernardino, CA, 92407-7500. **EMAIL** rbarnes@wiley.csusb.edu

BARNES, SUE
PERSONAL Born 04/26/1951, Trenton, NJ, m, 1997 **DISCIPLINE** COMMUNICATIONS **EDUCATION** Pratt Inst, BFA 73; NY Univ, MFA 75, PhD 95. **CAREER** Fordham Univ, digi med spec, assoc ch, asst prof, 96 to 98-; Marymont Manhattan College, adj prof, asst prof, 84-96; Fashion Inst Tech, SUNY, adj prof, 88-97, comp tchr, 90-94; Pratt Manhattan, vis inst, 88-90; Cen for the Media arts, inst, 84-88. **HONORS AND AWARDS** McGannon Gnt; Ames Gnt, 97&98; Best Paper Awd; SUNY Fac Gnt; Innovations Using Pagemaker winner. **MEMBERSHIPS** MEA; IEEECS; ACM; NJCA; NYSCA; ECA; NCA; ICA. **RESEARCH** Computer Mediated Communication; Visual Comm; Digital Comm; Comp and EDU ; Hist of Comp and Digital Media. **SELECTED PUBLICATIONS** Auth, Online Connections: Internet Interpersonal Relationships, Hampton Press, 99; Education and Technology: A cultural Faustian Bargain, Jour of Sci Tech Soc, 99; Developing a Concept of Self in Cyberspace Communities, in: The Emerging Cyberculture: Literacy, Paradigm and Paradox, eds, Stephanie Gibson and Ollie O. Oviedo, Hampton Press, 98; Ethical issues for a Virtual self, in: Law@Virtual Space, eds, Gary Gumbert and Susan Drucker, Hampton Press, 98; Are Computers Defining Our Culture? The NJ Jour of Comm, 98. **CONTACT ADDRESS** Dept of Comm and Media Studies, Fordham Univ, 441 E Fordham Rd, Bronx, NY, 10458. **EMAIL** barnes@murray.fordham.edu

BARNEY, STEPHEN ALLEN
PERSONAL Born 10/10/1942, Rocky Mount, NC, m, 1962, 2 children **DISCIPLINE** ENGLISH LITERATURE, MEDIEVAL STUDIES **EDUCATION** Univ Va, BA, 64; Harvard Univ, PhD(English), 69. **CAREER** From asst prof to assoc prof English, Yale Univ, 68-78; PROF ENGLISH, UNIV CA, IRVINE, 79-, Morse fel allegory, Yale Univ, 72-73; Am Coun Learned Soc fel Medieval Latin, 76; Nat Endowment Humanities fel Medieval Latin, 79-81; vis assoc prof English, Univ VA, 78. **HONORS AND AWARDS** Elliott Prize, Mediaeval Acad Am, 74. **MEMBERSHIPS** MLA; Mediaeval Acad Am; Early English Text Soc; New Chaucer Soc. **RESEARCH** Chaucer; Medieval Latin allegorical dictionaries; textual criticism. **SELECTED PUBLICATIONS** Auth, The Plowshare of the Tongue, Mediaeval Studies, 73; An Evaluation of the Pardoner's Tale, In: T-C Interpretations of the Pardoner's Tale, 73; Word-Hoard, Yale Univ, 77; Allegories of History, Allegories of Love, Archon Bks, 79; Chaucer's Troilus: Essays in Criticism, Archon Books, 80; Suddeness and Process in Chaucer, Chaucer Rev, 82; Visible Allegory, Harvard English Studies, 82; Ordo-Paginis, The 'Gloss' on 'Genesis 38', South Atlantic Quart, Vol 91, 92; The Life of Geoffrey Chaucer-A Critical Biography, with D. Pearsall, Notes and Queries, Vol 40, 93; Oxford Guides to Chaucer 'Troilus and Criseyde', with B. Windeatt, Notes and Queries, Vol 40, 93; Geoffrey Chaucer, with V. B Richmind, Speculum-A J of Medieval Studies, Vol 69, 94. **CONTACT ADDRESS** Univ CA Irvine, Irvine, CA, 92717.

BARNOUW, ERIK
PERSONAL Born 06/23/1908, The Hague, Netherlands, m, 1939, 3 children **DISCIPLINE** DRAMATIC ARTS **EDUCATION** Princeton Univ, AB, 29. **CAREER** Writer, dir & producer, 31-42; script ed, Nat Broadcasting Co, 42-44; consult, Secy War, 44; supvr ed unit, armed forces radio serv, US War Dept, 44-45; asst prof in charge courses in TV, radio & film, 46-53, ed, Ctr for Mass Commun, Univ Press, 49-72, from assoc prof to prof, 53-73, EMER PROF DRAMATIC ARTS, COLUMBIA UNIV, 73-, Consult, US Pub Health Serv, 48-51; Fulbright grant, India, 61-62; Guggenheim fel, 67; J D Rockefeller III Fund fel, Asia, 72; Woodrow Wilson fel, Smithsonian Inst, 76; film & TV specialist, Libr Cong, 77-78; chief, Motion Picture, Broadcasting and Recorded Sound Div, Libr Cong, 78-81. **HONORS AND AWARDS** Gavel Award, Am Bar Asn, 59; Bancroft Prize, Columbia Univ, 71; Preceptor Award, San Francisco State Col, 71; George Polk Award, Long Island Univ, 72; Silver Dragon Award, Cracow Film Festival, 72; Film Libr Quart Bk Award, 80. **MEMBERSHIPS** Auth League Am (secy, 49-53); Soc Am Historians; Soc Cinema Studies. **RESEARCH** Documentary film; television. **SELECTED PUBLICATIONS** Auth, A Tower in Babel, 66, The Golden Web, 68, The Image Empire, 70, Documentary: A History of the Non-Fiction Film, 74, Tube of Plenty: The Evolution of American Television, 75, The Sponsor: Notes on a Modern Potentate, 78, coauth, Indian Film, 2nd ed, 80 & auth, The Magician and the Cinema, 81, Oxford Univ; Televisionaries, with J. Robertson, Wide Angle-A Quart J of Film Hist Theory Criticism & Practice, Vol 16, 94; Dummerston Days & The Early Discussions at the Flaherty Barn, Wide Angle- A Quart J of Film Hist Theory Criticism & Practice, Vol 17, 95; Recollections & Participants of the Robert Flaherty Film Seminars Recall Seminar Events From the Past 40 Years, Wide Angle-A Quart J of Film Hist Theory Criticism & Practice, Vol 17, 95; Portrait Gallery & A Selection of Photographs and Edited Excerpts From Interviews with People Who Had Worked With Robert Flaherty, Wide Angle-A Quart J of Film Hist Theory Criticism and Practice, Vol 17, 95; Annals & Documents of the International Film Seminars, Inc. and Seminar History, Films Shown, Programmers, Discussion Leaders and Projectionists, Wide Angle-A Quart J of Film Hist Theory Criticism and Practice, Vol 17, 95; Bill Alexander & Chief Projectionist for the for the Flaherty Seminar, Wide Angle-A Quart J of Film Hist Theory Criticism and Practice, Vol 17, 95; The Flaherty, 4 Decades in the Cause of Independent Cinema-Prologue, Wide Angle-A Quart J of Film Hist Theory Criticism and Practice, Vol 17, 95; Etienne Gaspard Robertson, The Life of a Fantasmagore (French), with F. Levie, Wide Angle-A Quart J of Film Hist Theory Criticism and Practice, Vol 18, 96; Blacklisted, How FCC Commissioner Clifford Durr Earned His Place on the Cold Wars Roll of Honor & An Excerpt from 'Media Marathon, A 20th-Century Memoir', Television Quart, Vol 28, 96. **CONTACT ADDRESS** Columbia Univ, New York, NY, 10027.

BARNUM, CAROL
DISCIPLINE COMMUNICATION STUDIES **EDUCATION** Univ NC, BA; GA State Univ, MA, PhD. **CAREER** Prof tech commun, 79-. **MEMBERSHIPS** Soc Tech Commun. **SELECTED PUBLICATIONS** Auth, publ(s) on tech or prof commun. **CONTACT ADDRESS** Hum and Tech Commun Dept, Southern Polytech State Univ, S Marietta Pkwy, PO Box 1100, Marietta, GA, 30060.

BAROLSKY, PAUL
PERSONAL Born 07/13/1941, Paterson, NJ, m, 1966, 2 children **DISCIPLINE** ART HISTORY, LITERARY CRITICISM **EDUCATION** Middleburg Col, BA, 63; Harvard Univ, MA, 64, PhD(Art hist), 69. **CAREER** Asst prof, Cornell Univ, 68-69; ASSOC PROF ART HIST, UNIV VA, 69-. **RESEARCH** Italian Renaissance art; history of art criticism. **SELECTED PUBLICATIONS** Auth, Toward an Interpretation of One Pazzi Chapel, J One Soc Archit Historians, 73; Infinite Jest: Wit and Humor in Italian Renaissance Art, Univ MO Press, 78; Daniele da Volterra: A Catalogue Raisonne, Garland, 79; Walter Patev's Renaissance, VA Quart, 82; Cellini, Vasari, and the Marvels of Malady & Benvenuto Cellini 'Autobiography', Sixteenth Century J, Vol 24, 93; Andrea Del Castagno and His Patrons, with J. R. Spencer, Renaissance Quart, Vol 46, 93; The Painter Who Almost Became a Cheese & Paolo Ucello, VA Quart Rev, Vol 70, 94; Lord Byron, Strength-Romantic Writing and Commercial Society, with J. Christensen, VA Quart Rev, Vol 70, 94; Fables of Art, VA Quart Rev, Vol 71, 95; A Very Brief History of Art From Narcissus to Picasso, Classical J, Vol 90, 95; The Visionary Experience of Renaissance Art, Word & Image, Vol 11, 95; Johannes Vermeer, with A. K. Wheelock, VA Quart Rev, Vol 72, 96; Flesh and the Ideal-Winckelman and the Origins of Art History, with A. Potts, Classical J, Vol 91, 96; The Fable of Failure in Modern Art, VA Quart Rev, Vol 73, 97. **CONTACT ADDRESS** Dept of Art, Univ of VA, 102 Fayerweather, Charlottesville, VA, 22903.

BARON, DENNIS
PERSONAL Born 05/09/1944, New York, NY, m, 1979, 3 children **DISCIPLINE** ENGLISH **EDUCATION** Brandeis Univ, BA, 65; Columbia Univ, MA, 68; Univ Mich, PhD, 71. **CAREER** Assoc Prof to prof to dir to head, Univ Ill, 1984-. **HONORS AND AWARDS** NEH Fel, 89; Fulbright Fel, 78-79., PMLA Advisory Committee; MLA Delegate Assembly. **MEMBERSHIPS** MLA; NCTE; LSA; ADS. **RESEARCH** Literacy and technology; language legislation & linguistic rights; history of English language. **SELECTED PUBLICATIONS** Grammar and Good Taste: Reforming the American Language, 82; Grammar and Gender, 86; Declining Grammar and Other Essays on English Vocabulary, 89; The English-Only Question: An Official Language for Americans?, 90; Guide to Home Language Repair, 94. **CONTACT ADDRESS** Dept of English, Univ of Illinois, Urbana-Champaign, 608 S Wright St, Urbana, IL, 61801. **EMAIL** debaron@uiuc.edu

BARON, F. XAVIER
PERSONAL Born 07/19/1941, Springfield, MO, 3 children **DISCIPLINE** MEDIEVAL & ENGLISH LITERATURE **EDUCATION** Mo State Univ, BA, 63; Univ Iowa, MA, 65, PhD(-English), 69. **CAREER** Asst prof, 69-74, assoc prof English, Univ Wis, Milwaukee, 74-, exec dir, Milwaukee Humanities Prog, 78-79, consult, Ital-Am Hist Asn, Chicago Proj, 77-78. **HONORS AND AWARDS** Nat Endowment for Humanities younger humanist fel, 71-72. **MEMBERSHIPS** Int Arthurian Soc; MLA; Midwest Mod Lang Asn; Int Courtly Lit Soc (secytreas, 77-). **RESEARCH** Medieval Arthurian literature; Chaucer and Middle English literature; London in literature and art. **SELECTED PUBLICATIONS** Auth, Mother and Son in Sir Perceval of Galles, Papers Lang & lit, 72; Visual Presentation in Beroul's Tristan, 72 & Love in Chretien's Charrette: Reversed Values and Isolation, 73, Mod Lang Quart; coauth, Amour Courtois, The Medieval Ideal of Love: A Bibliography, Univ Louisville, 73; auth, Chaucer's Troilus and self-renunciation in love, Papers Lang & Lit, 74; Medieval Arthuri-

an Motifs in the Modernist Art and Poetry of David Jones, In: Studies in Medievalism IV: Medievalism in England, Boydell and Brewer, 92; Medieval Traditions in the English Renaissance: John Stow's Portrayal of London in 1603, In: Medieval and Renaissance Texts & Studies, Binghamton, NY, 94; Washington Irving, In: American Travel Writers, 1776-1864, Dictionary of Literary Biography, vol 183, Gale Res, 97; William Dean Howells, In: American Travel Writers, 1850-1915 ¤1920l, Dictionary of Literary Biography, vol 189, Gale Res, 98; auth, London 1066-1914: Literary Sources and Documents, 3 volumes, Helm Information, Ltd, 97. **CONTACT ADDRESS** Dept of English, Univ of Wis, PO Box 413, Milwaukee, WI, 53201-0413. **EMAIL** fxbaron@csd.uwm.edu

BARR, ALAN PHILIP
PERSONAL Born 11/25/1938, Brooklyn, NY, m, 1956, 2 children **DISCIPLINE** ENGLISH **EDUCATION** Mass Inst Technol, BA, 59; Univ Rochester, PhD, 63. **CAREER** From instr to asst prof English, Wayne State Univ, 63-68; from asst prof to assoc prof, 68-76, Prof English, Ind Univ Northwest, 76-. **RESEARCH** Victorian literature; modern drama. **SELECTED PUBLICATIONS** Auth, Diabolonian pundit: G B S as critic, Shaw Rev, 68; The paradise behind 1983, Eng Miscellany, 68; Cervantes' probing of reality & psychological realism in Don Quixote, Lit & Psychol, 68; Victorian Stage Pulpiteer: Bernard Shaw's Crusade, 73; ed, The Major Prose of Thomas Henry Huxley, Univ Ga Press, 97; ed and contribr, Thomas Henry Huxley's Place in Science and Letters: Centenary Essays, Univ Ga Press, 97; author of numerous journal articles. **CONTACT ADDRESS** Dept of English, Indiana Univ, Northwest, 3400 Broadway, Gary, IN, 46408-1101. **EMAIL** abarr@iunhaw1.iun.indiana.edu

BARR, JEANINE R.
PERSONAL Born 05/15/1941, Toledo, OH, m, 1981 **DISCIPLINE** SPEECH COMMUNICATON, RHETORIC AND PUBLIC ADDRESS, HEALTH COMMUN, INTERPERSONAL COMMUN **EDUCATION** OH Univ, BFA, 63; Mesme of OH, MA, 67; Univ MD, PhD, 94. **CAREER** Instr, SUNY, Albany; asst prof to assoc prof, York Col of PA, 70-. **HONORS AND AWARDS** NIH grant, summer 80. **MEMBERSHIPS** Nat Commun Asn; Pi Kappa Delta. **RESEARCH** Communication in recovery from addiction; forensics. **SELECTED PUBLICATIONS** Co-auth, Communication in Recovery; misc articles on addiction, recovery, and forensics. **CONTACT ADDRESS** York Col, Pennsylvania, 206D MAC Center, York, PA, 17403. **EMAIL** jbarr@eagle.ycp.edu

BARR, MARLEEN SANDRA
PERSONAL Born 03/01/1953, New York, NY **DISCIPLINE** WOMEN & LITERATURE **EDUCATION** State Univ NY Albany, BA, 74; Univ MI, MA, 75; State Univ NY Buffalo, PhD(-English), 79. **CAREER** ASST PROF ENGLISH, VA POLYTECH INST & STATE UNIV, 79-, Consult, Educ Testing Serv, 82 & Coun Wis Writers Annual Awards Competition, 82. **MEMBERSHIPS** MLA; Northeast Mod Lang Asn; Popular Cult Asn. **RESEARCH** Science fiction studies; contemporary American literature. **SELECTED PUBLICATIONS** Ed, Future Females: A Critical Anthology, Bowling Green Univ, Popular Press, 81; contribr, The Feminine Eye, 82, Frederick Ungar Co; auth, Science Fiction and the Fact of Women's Repressed Creativity, Extrapolation, spring 82; A Nerw Species-Gender and Science in Science-Fiction, with R. Roberts, Science-Fiction Studies, Vol 20, 93. **CONTACT ADDRESS** Dept English, Virginia Polytech Inst & State Univ, Blacksburg, VA, 24061.

BARRET, HAROLD
PERSONAL Born 03/20/1925, Heladsburg, CA, m, 1948, 4 children **DISCIPLINE** RHETORIC, SPEECH COMMUNICATION **EDUCATION** Univ Pac, BA, 49; MA, 52; Univ Ore, PhD 62. **CAREER** Teacher, Lodi High Sch, Lodi, CA; 50-54; instr, Compton Coll, 54-59; instr, Univ Ore, 59-61; asst prof, S Ore Univ, 61-63; prof, Calif State Univ, 63-92. **HONORS AND AWARDS** Outstanidng fac mem, Univ Ore, 63; outstanding prof, Univ Ore, 82. **MEMBERSHIPS** Nat Commun Asn; Western Speech Commun Asn; World Commun Asn. **RESEARCH** Rhetorical interaction; Narcissism and defensiveness, communication. **SELECTED PUBLICATIONS** Auth, Rhetoric and Civility, 91; Speaking, America, 93; Maintaining the Self, Communication, 98. **CONTACT ADDRESS** 33 S Modoc Ave, Medford, OR, 97504. **EMAIL** oldrhetor@aol.com

BARROS, CAROLYN
DISCIPLINE ENGLISH **EDUCATION** Univ TX at Arlington, BA, 76; TX Christian Univ, Med, 78; Univ TX at Dallas, PhD, 84. **CAREER** Assoc prof, Univ TX at Arlington, 96 & asst prof, 90 & 96; Dir, UTA Honors Prog, 95-; assoc dean, asst dean, asst to the dean, Col Liberal Arts, UTA, 77-90; dept ser, 95-96, ch, Hermann Lect Ser Comt; mem, Fac Search Comt, Rhetoric and Compos Div, Brit Lit Div & Grad Stud Comt; prior dept ser, interim dir, Freshman Engl; ch, Freshman Engl Comt, Hermann Lect Ser Comt, GTA Selection Comt & Comp Acquisition Comt; mem, Fac Search Comt, KA Porter Lect Ser, Fac Adv Comt, Res Enhancement Comt, Rhetoric and Compos Div, Brit Lit Div, Grad Stud Comt, Freshman Engl Comt & Travel Comt; lectr, Sigma Tau Delta Engl Honors Soc; Judge, Freshman Writing Contest; invited lect, Sigma Tau Delta, UTA, 94; Hermann Lecte Ser, UTA, 93; TCJC Cornerstone Prog, NEH Symp, Fort Worth, 91; Class Asn, Tulane Univ, New Orleans, 88; Conf Freshman Yr, Dallas, 87. **HONORS AND AWARDS** UTA Summer Stipend, $3,000, 96; Nat Collegiate Hon Coun Portz Grant, $500; NEH Summer Seminar Grant, 88; NEH Higher Educ Grant, $392,000, 85-87. **MEMBERSHIPS** Nat Collegiate Honors Coun; Great Plains Honors Coun; Cole Conf on Compos and Commun; Soc Lit, Science & Technol; MLA; S Cent MLA; Nat Coun Tchrs Eng; Conf Col Tchrs Eng. **RESEARCH** Rhetoric of Caroline Herschelis autobiography; autobiography of Gertrude Stein. **SELECTED PUBLICATIONS** Auth, Figura, Persona, Dynamis: Autobiography and Change, Biog 15 1, 92; Discourse Topics and the Problem of the Big Text and the Little Text, Readerly/Writerly Texts Vol 3, 95; The Literate Mind: Readers, 3 Vol(s), Dubuque, Kendal Hunt, 90; coauth, The Literate Mind, Second Edition, Dubuque, Kendal Hunt, 90. With Thomas E. Porter and Harry Reeder. **CONTACT ADDRESS** Dept of Eng, Univ of Texas at Arlington, 203 Carlisle Hall, PO Box 19035, Arlington, TX, 76019-0595. **EMAIL** CJAN@utarlg.uta.edu

BARROWS, FLOYD DELL
PERSONAL Born 12/05/1927, Ft Collins, CO, m, 1953, 2 children **DISCIPLINE** ENGLISH HISTORY **EDUCATION** Univ Calif, Los Angeles, BA, 56, PhD(English hist), 67. **CAREER** Teaching asst, Univ Calif, Los Angeles, 57-59; instr humanities, Northwest Mo State Col, 60-63; asst prof hist, 63-66; from instr to assoc prof, 66-78, prof humanities & asst chmn dept, Mich State Univ, 78-. **MEMBERSHIPS** AHA, Orgn Am Historians; Soc Hist Educ. **RESEARCH** Late Stuart and Hanoverian periods of English history; American history, Civil War period; war and peace: its influence on Western culture and the arts. **CONTACT ADDRESS** Dept Humanities, Michigan State Univ, East Lansing, MI, 48824.

BARRY, B. R.
PERSONAL Born 06/02/1949, London, England, m, 1984, 2 children **DISCIPLINE** VISUAL AND PERFORMING ARTS **EDUCATION** Univ London Goldsmith's, PhD, 82. **CAREER** Dept Visual Perf Arts, 7 yrs, Clark Univ; fac, 10 yrs, Radcliffe College; Chair, 10 yrs, Longy Sch of Music. **MEMBERSHIPS** SMT; NECMT. **RESEARCH** 19TH Century Music; Beethoven; Mahler. **SELECTED PUBLICATIONS** Auth, Inversional Symmetry in the Magic Flute, Opera J, 97; The Spider's Stratagem: The Motif of Masking, in, Don Giovanni, Opera J, 96; Recycling the End of the Leibquartett: Models Meaning and Propriety, in: Beethoven's Quarter in B-Flat Major Opus 130, J Musicology, 95. **CONTACT ADDRESS** Dept of Visual & Performing Arts, Clark Univ, 950 Main St, Worcester, MA, 01610. **EMAIL** agranquist@clarku.edu

BARRY, JACKSON GRANVILLE
PERSONAL Born 11/04/1926, Boston, MA, m, 1956, 1 child **DISCIPLINE** ENGLISH **EDUCATION** Yale Univ, BA, 50; Columbia Univ, MA, 51; Western Reserve Univ, MFA, 62, PhD(drama-aesthet), 63. **CAREER** Instr drama, DeCordova Mus, 53-56; instr, Smith Col, 58-61; asst prof humanities, Univ Miami, 63-64; asst prof drama, Villanova Univ, 64-67; assoc prof theatre arts, State Univ NY, Stony Brook, 67-70; assoc prof to PROF ENGLISH, UNIV MD, COLLEGE PARK, 70-, dir Graduate Studies, 79-84. **HONORS AND AWARDS** Ed bd, Am J of Semiotics. **MEMBERSHIPS** MLA;Medieval and Renaissance Drama Soc; Semiotic Soc Am; Linguistic Soc Am. **RESEARCH** Medieval and renaissance literature; semiotics and cognition. **SELECTED PUBLICATIONS** Auth, Dramatic Structure: The Shaping of Experience, Univ CA, 70; Art, Culture, and the Semiotics of Meaning, St Martin's, 98; articles in: Shakespeare Quart, Ed Theatre J, Language and Style, Ariel, Quart J Speech, Papers on Language and Literature, Am J Semiotics, Poetics Yoday, Interdisciplinary J Germanic Linguistics and Semiotic Analysis. **CONTACT ADDRESS** English Dept 8815, Univ MD, College Park, MD, 20742. **EMAIL** jb19@umail.umd.edu

BARRY, MICHAEL
DISCIPLINE AMERICAN LITERATURE **EDUCATION** Loyola Univ, BA; SUNY Buffalo, PhD. **CAREER** Instr, Turkey; People's Republic of China; asst prof, 94-. **RESEARCH** Relationship of ideology and aesthetics, literary components of liberation struggles. **SELECTED PUBLICATIONS** Pub(s), articles on Robert Penn Warren, John Steinbeck, and James Welch. **CONTACT ADDRESS** Dept of Eng, Univ Detrit Mercy, 4001 W McNichols Rd, PO BOX 19900, Detroit, MI, 48219-0900. **EMAIL** mbarry@libarts.udmercy.edu

BARSAM, RICHARD
PERSONAL Los Angeles **DISCIPLINE** FILM STUDIES **EDUCATION** Univ Southern Calif, PhD. **CAREER** Prof; Hunter Col, 94-; past consult, PBS for Films of Persuasion; Amer Film Inst/PBS for America in the Movies; CBS for Leni Riefenstahl & Camera Three prog; consult, Metropolitan Mus Art/J. Paul Getty Mus Proj for Art on Film and Video; Chancellor's staff as Univ dean for Fac and Res, CUNY, 84-88 & Univ dean Exec Search and Eval, 88-91; provost, Pratt Inst, 91-93. **HONORS AND AWARDS** Co-foundeer, baccalaureate and grad prog in Cinema Stud, Richmond Col-CUNY; organized, CUNY Film Fac. **MEMBERSHIPS** Past chem, CUNY Film Fac; exec coun, Soc for Cinema Stud; bd ed, Advisers Hist Amern Cinema; ed bo, Cinema J & adv panels, Nat Endowment for the Humanities; Nat Endowment for the Arts Panel for Support for Young Film Critics; dir, NEH Summer Sem for Cole Teachers in Nonfiction Film and the Realist Aesthet, 81. **SELECTED PUBLICATIONS** Auth, Nonfiction Film: A Critical History, Dutton, 73, rev and expanded ed, Ind UP, 92; The Vision of Robert Flaherty: The Artist as Myth and Filmmaker, IUP, 88; A Peaceable Kingdom: The Shaker Abecedarius, Viking, 78; In the Dark: A Primer for the Movies, Viking, 77; Filmguide to Triumph of the Will, IUP, 75; Nonfiction Film Theory and Criticism, Dutton, 75. **CONTACT ADDRESS** Dept of Film and Media Studies, Hunter Col, CUNY, 695 Park Ave, New York, NY, 10021.

BARSKY, ROBERT
DISCIPLINE ENGLISH LITERATURE **EDUCATION** Univ Brandeis; BA; McGill Univ, MA; PhD. **RESEARCH** Literary theory; legal studies; argumentation; discourse analysis; social discourse theory; sociocriticism; cross-cultural communication; Mikhail Bakhtin; 19th and 20th century literature; refugee studies. **SELECTED PUBLICATIONS** Auth, Arguing and Justifying, 98; Noam Chomsky: A Life of Dissent, MIT, 97; Introduction a la theorie litteraire, Quebec, 97; Constructing a Productive Other: Discourse Theory and the Convention Refugee Hearing, John Benjamins, 94; co-ed, Bakhtin and Otherness, 91. **CONTACT ADDRESS** Dept of English, Western Ontario Univ, London, ON, N6A 5B8.

BARTLETT, LEE
DISCIPLINE CREATIVE WRITING/POETRY AND AMERICAN LITERATURE **EDUCATION** Univ Calif, Davis, PhD, 79. **CAREER** Instr, Univ Nmex, 81-. **SELECTED PUBLICATIONS** Auth, Kenneth Rexroth and James Laughlin: Selected Letters; The Sun is But a Morning Star: Studies in West Coast Poetry and Poetics; William Everson: The Life of Brother Antoninus. **CONTACT ADDRESS** Univ NMex, Albuquerque, NM, 87131.

BARTON, MIKE ALAN
PERSONAL Born 09/30/1940, Wichita, KS, m, 1964, 1 child **DISCIPLINE** THEATRE HISTORY, DRAMATIC LITERATURE **EDUCATION** Kans State Teachers Col, BA, 61, MS, 66; Ind Univ, PhD(theatre hist), 71. **CAREER** Prof actor, New York City, 61-62; instr speech, Kans State Teachers Col, 65-66; instr theatre, Univ Omaha, 66-68; asst, Ind Univ, Bloomington, 68-71; prof Theatre, Drake Univ, 71-. **RESEARCH** Nineteenth century theatre history; film history. **SELECTED PUBLICATIONS** Auth, Silent films: High camp or genuine art, Advance, 11/72; Aline Bernstein, In: Notable American Women, Harvard Univ, 78. **CONTACT ADDRESS** Dept of Theatre Arts, Drake Univ, 2507 University Ave, Des Moines, IA, 50311-4505. **EMAIL** mike.barton@drake.edu

BARTOW, CHARLES L.
PERSONAL Born 11/03/1937, Somerville, NJ, m, 1964, 3 children **DISCIPLINE** SPEECH **EDUCATION** Mich State Univ, AB, 58; Princeton Theol Sem, BD, 63; Mich State Univ, MA, 64; NY Univ, PhD, 71. **CAREER** Asst prof, Princeton Theol Sem, 63-71; asst prof, Mansfield State Univ, 71-74; pastor, Presby Church of Deep Run, 74-80; assoc prof, San Francisco Theol Sem/Grad Theol Union, 80-84; prof, 84-91; prof, Princeton Theol Sem, 91- . **HONORS AND AWARDS** Honors graduate, Mich State Univ; 1980 Book of the Year Award, The Relig Speech Commun Asoc. **MEMBERSHIPS** Relig Speech Commun Asoc; Acad of Homiletics; Nat Commun Asoc; Societas Homiletica. **RESEARCH** Rhetorical and performance criticism in Scriptural hermeneutics and preaching; oral interpretation of poetry and Biblical literature; speech arts and liturgical praxis. **SELECTED PUBLICATIONS** Auth, Sermon Delivery, A Concise Encyclopedia of Preaching, 95; auth, Who Says the Song? Practical Hermeneutics as Humble Performance, Princeton Sem Bull, 96; auth, Just Now: Aimee Semple McPherson's Performance and Preaching of Jesus, J Commun and Relig, 97; auth, God's Human Speech: A Practical Theology of Proclamation, 97. **CONTACT ADDRESS** Princeton Theol Sem, 64 Mercer St, PO Box 821, Princeton, NJ, 08542-0803. **EMAIL** charles.bartow@ptsem.edu

BARUCH, ELAINE HOFFMAN
PERSONAL New York, NY, 1 child **DISCIPLINE** ENGLISH, WOMEN'S STUDIES **EDUCATION** Queens Col, NY, BA, 54; Radcliffe Col, MAT, 55; Columbia Univ, PhD(English, comp lit), 66. **CAREER** Lectr English, Queens Col, NY, 60-62 from instr to asst prof, 67-77, ASSOC PROF ENGLISH, YORK COL, NY, 78-, Gen ed, Women's Studies Ser, Everett/Edwards Cassette Curric, 74-. **MEMBERSHIPS** MLA. **RESEARCH** Seventeenth century. **SELECTED PUBLICATIONS** Auth, Theme and Counterthemes in Damon the Mower, Comp Lit, 74; Whatever Happened to Romantic Love?, Dissent, winter 77; Marvell's Nymph: A Study of Feminine Consciousness, Etudes Anglaises, summer 78; Women and Love: Some Dying Myths, In: Contemporary Methods of Literary Analysis & co-ed, Contemporary Methods of Literary Analysis, Bilingual Press; auth, The Feminine Bildungsroman: Education through Marriage, Mass v; Reviews, Poems and Short Pieces in

Louisville Courier-Jour, Dissent, Commentary & Pulp; Vested Interests-Cross-Dressing and Cultural Anxiety, with M. Garber, Partisan Rev, Vol 60, 93; Psychoanalysis and its Critics & A Discussion with Robert Michels Followed by a Question and Answer Session with the Audience, Partisan Rev, Vol 64, 97. **CONTACT ADDRESS** Dept of English, York Col, CUNY, Jamaica, NY, 11451.

BARUSHOK, JAMES WILLIAM
PERSONAL Born 02/26/1929, Chicago, IL, m, 1952, 3 children **DISCIPLINE** SPEECH **EDUCATION** Northwestern Univ, BA, 51, MA, 52; Mich State Univ, PhD(theatre), 66. **CAREER** Instr speech, Wright Jr Col, 54-56; from instr to assoc prof, Univ Maine, 56-68; CHMN DEPT SPEECH, NORTHEASTERN ILL UNIV, 68-, Maine fine arts rep, New Eng Ctr Continuing Educ, 66-68; Kellog Found fel, 81-82. **MEMBERSHIPS** Speech Commun Asn; Am Educ Theatre Asn; Am Acad Polit & Soc Sci. **RESEARCH** History of theatre; sociology of the community theatre; dramatic theory. **SELECTED PUBLICATIONS** auth, Lost prodigy: community theatre, Players, 9/69. **CONTACT ADDRESS** Dept of Speech, Northeastern Illinois Univ, 5500 N St Louis Ave, Chicago, IL, 60625-4625.

BASS, EBEN E.
PERSONAL Born 06/12/1924, Willimantic, CT, m, 1957 **DISCIPLINE** ENGLISH **EDUCATION** Univ CT, BA, 48, MA, 50; Univ Pittsburgh, PhD(English), 61. **CAREER** Asst instr English, OH State Univ, 54-56; from asst prof to prof, Geneva Col, 56-72, PROF ENGLISH & CHMN DEPT, SLIPPERY ROCK STATE COL, 72-. **MEMBERSHIPS** MLA; NCTE. **RESEARCH** Henry James and modern novel; English Romantic and Victorian writers. **SELECTED PUBLICATIONS** Auth, Dramatic scene and The Awkward Age, PMLA, 3/64; The Verbal Failure of Lord Jim, Col English, 3/65; The Fourth Element in Ode to the West Wind, Papers Lang & Lit, fall 67; The Languages of 'Losing Battles', Studies in Am Fiction, Vol 21, 93. **CONTACT ADDRESS** Dept of English, Slippery Rock State Col, Slippery Rock, PA, 16057.

BASSAN, MAURICE
PERSONAL Born 04/22/1929, New York, NY, m, 1960, 2 children **DISCIPLINE** AMERICAN LITERATURE **EDUCATION** New York Univ, BA, 51, MA, 52; Univ CA, Berkeley, PhD, 61. **CAREER** Instr English, Univ AZ, 58-60 & Univ NC, 61-63; from asst prof to assoc prof, 63-72, prof eng, San Francisco State Univ, 72, Lectr, Univ CA, Exten, Japan, 53-54; asst, Univ Calif, Berkeley, 55-58. **HONORS AND AWARDS** Fulbright lectr, Univ Valladolid, Spain, 67-68. **MEMBERSHIPS** MLA; Am Studies Asn; Hawthorne Soc; Stephen Crane Soc. **RESEARCH** Stephen Crane; late 19th century Am fiction; Am poetic traditions. **SELECTED PUBLICATIONS** Auth, Chaucer's Cursed Monk, Mediaeval Studies, 62; Flannery O'Connor's way, Renascence, 63; Some new perspectives on Stephen Crane's fiction, Studia Neophilologica, 63; ed, Stephen Crane's Maggie: Text and Context, Wadsworth, 66; Stephen Crane: A Collection of Critical Essays, Prentice-Hall, 67; auth, Hawthorne's Son, Ohio State Univ, 69; The True West Tales of Sam Shepard and Stephen Crane, American Literary Realism 28, 96. **CONTACT ADDRESS** Dept of Eng, San Francisco State Univ, 1600 Holloway Ave, San Francisco, CA, 94132-1740. **EMAIL** mbasson@sfsu.edu

BASSETT, CHARLES WALKER
PERSONAL Born 07/07/1932, Aberdeen, SD, m, 1956, 2 children **DISCIPLINE** AMERICAN LITERATURE & STUDIES **EDUCATION** Univ SDak, AB, 54, MA, 56; Univ Kans, PhD(English), 64. **CAREER** From instr to asst prof English, Univ Pa, 64-69; asst prof, 69-74, assoc prof, 74-80, prof English, Colby Col, 80-, chrm, dept of English, 87-89, Colby Col, dir AM studies, 71-96, Univ Pa fac res grant, 68; humanities grants, Colby Col, 78 & 79, Mellon grant, 79 & 83. **HONORS AND AWARDS** Mary C. Turpie Award, Am Stud Asn; Senior Class Teaching Award, 93, 97. **MEMBERSHIPS** Am Studies Asn; MLA. **RESEARCH** American fiction; American history. **SELECTED PUBLICATIONS** Auth, Katahdin, Wachusett, and Kilimanjaro: The symbolic mountains of Thoreau and Hemingway, Thoreau J, 4/71; O'Hara's roots (43 part ser), weekly in Pottsville Republican, Pa, 71-72; Undergraduate and graduate American studies programs in the US: A survey, Am Quart, 8/75; Naturalism revisited: The case of John O'Hara, Colby Libr Quart, 12/75; John O'Hara and The Noble Experiment: The use of alcohol in Appointment in Samarra, winter 78-79, John O'Hara: Irishman and American, 8/79 & O'Hara and history, 12/81, John O'Hara J; John O'Hara, In: Vol IX, Part 2, Dict of Literary Biography, 81. **CONTACT ADDRESS** Dept of English, Colby Col, 150 Mayflower Hill, Waterville, ME, 04901-4799. **EMAIL** cwbasset@colby.edu

BASSETT, JOHN E.
PERSONAL Born 05/12/1942, Washington, DC, m, 1964, 2 children **DISCIPLINE** ENGLISH **EDUCATION** Ohio Wesleyan Univ, BA 63, MA 66; Col of Rochester, PhD 70. **CAREER** Wayne State Univ, asst prof, assoc prof, 70-84; N Carolina State Univ, prof, Dept hd; Case Western Reserve Univ, prof, dean. **MEMBERSHIPS** MLA; SAMLA; SSSL; Phi Beta Kappa Assoc. **RESEARCH** American Lit; Faulkner; Twain; Sherwood Anderson. **SELECTED PUBLICATIONS** Auth, Wherefore This Southern Literature?, A Critical Tradition, 97; auth, Harlem in Review: The Critical Reaction to Black Amer Writers, 1920-1939, 1992; auth, A Heart of Ideality in My Realism, and other essays on Howells and Twain, 91; auth, Visions and Revisions, Essays on Faulkner, 89. **CONTACT ADDRESS** Dept of English, Case Western Reserve Univ, Cleveland, OH, 44106-7068. **EMAIL** jeb20@po.cwru.edu

BATE, WALTER JACKSON
PERSONAL Born 05/22/1918, Mankato, MN **DISCIPLINE** ENGLISH **EDUCATION** Harvard Univ, AB, 39, AM, 40, PhD, 42. **CAREER** From asst prof to prof English, 46-62, Lowell prof, 62-79, KINGSLEY PORTER UNIV PROF HUMANITIES, HARVARD UNIV, 79-. **HONORS AND AWARDS** Christian Gauss Prizes, 56, 64 & 70; Pulitzer Prize, 64 & 78; Nat Book Award, 78., LittD, IN Univ, 69, Merrimac Col, 70, Univ Chicago, 73; LHD, Boston Col, 71, Fordham Univ, 78. **MEMBERSHIPS** Am Acad Arts & Sci; Am Philos Soc. **RESEARCH** Eighteenth and 19th century English literature. **SELECTED PUBLICATIONS** Auth, Criticism: Major Texts, Harcourt, 52; Achievement of Samuel Johnson, Oxford Univ, 55; Prefaces to Criticism, Doubleday, 59; Yale Edition of Johnson, Vols 2-5, Yale Univ, 60-68; John Keats, Harvard Univ, 68; Coleridge, Macmillan, 68; The Burden of the Past and the English Poet, Harvard Univ, 70; Samuel Johnson, Harcourt, 77; Harry Tuchman Levin, July 18, 1912- May 29, 1994, Proceedings of the Am Philos Soc, Vol 140, 96; Notes From the Academy, Daedalus, Vol 126, 97. **CONTACT ADDRESS** Harvard Univ, 3 Warren House, Cambridge, MA, 02138.

BATES, BENJAMIN J.
PERSONAL Born 01/25/1954, Chillicothee, OH, s **DISCIPLINE** COMMUNICATIONS **EDUCATION** Pomona Col, BA, 76; Univ of Wis, Madison, MS, 78; Univ of Wis, Stevens Point, MA, 81; Univ of Mich, PhD, 86. **CAREER** Teaching/res asst, Univ of Wis, Madison, 76-78; grad asst, Univ of Wis, Stevens Point, 80-81; teaching/res asst, Univ of Mich, 81-85; instr, Rutgers Univ, 85-86; lectr, Univ of Calif, Santa Barbara, 86-88; visiting asst prof, Mich State Univ, 88-89; visiting lectr, The Chinese Univ of Hong Kong, 92-93; asst prof, Texas Tech Univ, 89-94; dir, Inst for Commun Res, 89-94; ASST PROF, 94-96, ASSOC PROF, 96-, UNIV OF TENN, KNOXVILLE. **HONORS AND AWARDS** Col of Commun Fac Res Award, Univ of Tenn, 95-96; Award for Acad Excellence, Univ of Wis, Stevens Point, 81; Grant, NEC Infor Industry Univ Fac Grant Prog, 89, 90, 91, 92, 93, & 94; Leo Burnet Scholar Award, Univ of Mich, 82; Fac Res Grant, Univ of Calif, Santa Barbara, 87; Fac Grant, Nat Cable Television Asn, 92; Fac Grant for 1995 Global Infor Infrastructure ComForum, 95; Fac Grant for IEC Commun Forum at Supercomm 98, IEC Infor Industry Fac Grant Prog, 98; Res Grant, Nat Asn of Broadcasters, 96; Fac Grant, Int Radio and Television Soc Found, 97. **RESEARCH** Telecom systems; economics; policy; new media systems. **SELECTED PUBLICATIONS** Coauth, The New World of Democratic Telecommunications: FidoNet as an Example of Horizontal Information Networks, Southwestern Mass Commun J, 93; coauth, Bypassing the Gateways: International News in the CNN WORLD REPORT, Commun Res Reports, 93; coauth, Political Distrust in Hong Kong: News Media Use and Political Beliefs Regarding the 1997 Transition, Asian J of Commun, 95; coauth, The Economic Basis for Radio Deregulation, J of Media Economics, forthcoming; coauth, Creating New Relations: The Internet in Central and Eastern Europe, Cyberimperialism: Global Relations in the New Electronic Frontier, Greenwood, forthcoming; auth, Concentration in Local Television Markets, J of Media Economics, 93; auth, Learning from the Evolution of Telecommunications in the Developed World, Telecommun and Development in China, Hampton Press, 97; auth, Valuation of Media Properties, Media Economics: A Reader, Lawrence Erlbaum Assocs, 93; auth, Introduction: Special Issue on the Economic Impact of the 1996 Telecommunications Act, J of Media Economics, 98; auth, Valuation of Media Properties, Media Economics: A Reader, Second Edition, Lawrence Erlbaum Assocs, forthcoming. **CONTACT ADDRESS** Dept of Broadcasting, College of Communications, Univ of Tennessee, 333 Communications, Knoxville, TN, 37996-0333. **EMAIL** bjbates@utk.edu

BATES, MILTON JAMES
PERSONAL Born 06/04/1945, Warrensburg, MO, m, 1972, 2 children **DISCIPLINE** ENGLISH LITERATURE **EDUCATION** St. Louis Univ, BA, 68; Univ of Calif, Berkeley, MA, 72, PhD, 77. **CAREER** Asst prof, Eng, Williams Col, 75-81; asst prof, Eng, Marquette Univ, 81-86; assoc prof, Marquette Univ, 86-90; PROF, MARQUETTE UNIV, 91-. **HONORS AND AWARDS** Am Coun of Learned Soc Fel, 80, 86; Nat Endowment for the Hum Summer Stipend, 85; Guggenheim Fel, 89. **MEMBERSHIPS** Wallace Stevens Soc. **RESEARCH** Wallace Stevens; William Faulkner; Vietnam War literature; American nature writing. **SELECTED PUBLICATIONS** auth, Wallace Stevens: A Mythology of Self, Univ of Calif Pr, 85; ed, Sur Plusieurs Beaux Subjects: Wallace Stevens' Commonplace Book, Stanford Univ Pr, 89; ed, Opus Posthumous, Alfred A. Knopf, 89; auth, The Wars We Took to Vietnam: Cultural Conflict and Storytelling, Univ of Calif Pr, 96. **CONTACT ADDRESS** Dept of English, Marquette Univ, PO Box 1881, Milwaukee, WI, 53201-1881. **EMAIL** Milton.Bates@marquette.edu

BATES, SCOTT
PERSONAL Born 06/13/1923, Evanston, IL, m, 1948, 4 children **DISCIPLINE** FRENCH, FILM **EDUCATION** Carleton Col, BA, 47; Univ WI, MA, 48, PhD(French), 54. **CAREER** Asst prof, 54-64, Prof French Lang & Lit, Univ of The South, 64-, Ed, Ecol Papers, 70-72. **MEMBERSHIPS** MLA. **RESEARCH** Modern French poetry; modern English and American poetry. **SELECTED PUBLICATIONS** Auth, Guillaume Apollinaire, Twayne, 67; ed, Poems of War Resistance, Grossman, 69; Petit glossaire des mots libres d'Apollinaire, Sewane, 75; The ABC of Radical Ecology, Highlander, 82; To Fix the Press & Efforts of the Hutchins-Commission to Define the Duties of a Free Press in the 1940's, Am Heritage, Vol 45, 94; 'Pizza', Sewanee Rev, Vol 103, 95; And Then There Was Usenet & The Beginnings of One of the Most Popular Features of Todays Internet, Am Heritage, Vol 46, 95; The Ancient-History of the Internet, Am Heritage, Vol 46, 95. **CONTACT ADDRESS** Dept of Lang & Lit, Univ of the South, Sewanee, TN, 37375.

BATTEIGER, RICHARD P.
DISCIPLINE EARLY BRITISH LITERATURE **EDUCATION** Univ Fla, PhD, 70. **CAREER** Engl, Okla St Univ. **HONORS AND AWARDS** Prog dir, Composition & Rhetoric. **SELECTED PUBLICATIONS** Area: whether direct instruction in grammar improves student writing. **CONTACT ADDRESS** Oklahoma State Univ, 101 Whitehurst Hall, Stillwater, OK, 74078.

BATTERSBY, JAMES L.
PERSONAL Born 08/24/1936, Pawtucket, RI, 1 child **DISCIPLINE** ENGLISH LITERATURE, CRITICAL THEORY **EDUCATION** Univ VT, BSEd, 61; Cornell Univ, MA, 62, PhD(English lit), 65. **CAREER** Asst prof English lit, Univ CA, Berkeley, 65-70; assoc prof, 70-82, PROF ENGLISH, OH STATE UNIV, 82-. **MEMBERSHIPS** MLA; Am Soc 18th Century Studies; Midwest Mod Lang Asn. **RESEARCH** Samuel Johnson; 18th century English literature; modern critical theory. **SELECTED PUBLICATIONS** Auth, Patterns of Significant Action in Samuel Johnson's Life of Addison, Genre, 1/69; Johnson and Shiels: Biographers of Addison, Studies English Lit, summer 69; Typical Folly: Evaluating Student Performance in Higher Education, Nat Coun Teachers English, 73; Elder Olson: Critic, Pluralist, and Humanist, Chicago Rev, winter 77; Coded Media and Genre: A Relation Reargued, Genre, fall 77; Rational Praise and Natural Lamentation: Johnson, Lycidas and Principles of Criticism, Assoc Univ Press, 80; The Strategy of Letters, with M. Hjort, Philos and Lit, Vol 18, 94; The Inescapability of Humanism, College English, Vol 58, 96. **CONTACT ADDRESS** Dept of English, Ohio State Univ, Columbus, OH, 43210.

BATTESTIN, MARTIN CAREY
PERSONAL Born 03/25/1930, New York, NY, m, 1952, 2 children **DISCIPLINE** ENGLISH LITERATURE **EDUCATION** Princeton Univ, BA, 52, PhD(English), 58. **CAREER** From instr to asst prof English, Wesleyan Univ, 56-61; from asst prof to prof, 61-75, WILLIAM R KENAN, JR PROF ENGLISH, UNIV VA, 75-, Am Coun Learned Soc fel, 60-61 & 67; Guggenheim fel, 64-65; adv ed, Eighteenth Century Studies & Studies in the Novel, 67-; vis prof, Rice Univ, 67-68; adv ed, Studies in English Lit, 68-; hon res fel, Univ Col, Univ London, 70-71; Sesquicentennial res fel, Univ VA, 70-71; Coun Humanities sr fel, Princeton Univ, 71; assoc Clare Hall, Cambridge Univ, 72; Am Coun Learned Socs fel, 72; Nat Endowment for Humanities fel, 75 & 79; mem, Ctr Advan Studies, Univ VA, 75-76. **MEMBERSHIPS** MLA; Acad Lit Studies; Am Soc 18th Century Studies; Int Asn Univ Prof English; Johnsonians. **RESEARCH** Eighteenth century literature and the arts: The British novel, especially Henry Fielding. **SELECTED PUBLICATIONS** Auth, The Moral Basis of Fielding's Art, Wesleyan Univ, 59; ed, Fielding's Joseph Andrews and Shamela, Houghton, 61; Fielding's Joseph Andrews, Clarendon & Wesleyan Univ, 67; auth, Henry Fielding, In: New Cambridge Bibliography of English Literature, Cambridge Univ, 71; co-ed, Fielding's Tom Jones, Clarendon & Wesleyan Univ, 74; auth, The Providence of Wit: Aspects of Form in Augustan Literature and the Arts, Clarendon, 74; A Sentimental Journey and the Syntax of Things, Augustan Worlds, Univ Leicester, 78; ed, Fielding's Amelia, Clarendon & Wesleyan Univ, 82; The Female Thermometer-18th-Century Culture and the Invention of the Uncanny, with T. Castle, Scriblerian and the Kit-Cats, Vol 29, 96; Uneasy Sensations-Smollett and the Body, with A. Douglas, Albion, Vol 28, 96; 'Mason and Dixon', with T. Pynchon, Sewanee Rev, Vol 105, 97. **CONTACT ADDRESS** Dept of English, Univ of VA, Charlottesville, VA, 22901.

BAUCOM, IAN
DISCIPLINE ENGLISH LITERATURE **EDUCATION** Duke Univ, PhD. **CAREER** Prof, Duke Univ. **RESEARCH** Twentieth century Brit Lit and Cult; African and Black Atlantic lit(s). **SELECTED PUBLICATIONS** Auth, publ(s) on colonial and postmodern nostalgia; theories of nationhood; postimperial melancholy in Research in African lit; mod fiction. **CONTACT ADDRESS** Eng Dept, Duke Univ, Durham, NC, 27706.

BAUER, OTTO FRANK
PERSONAL Born 12/01/1931, Elgin, IL, m, 1956, 2 children **DISCIPLINE** COMMUNICATION, SEMANTICS **EDUCATION** Northwestern Univ, BS, 53, MA, 55, PhD, 59. **CAREER** From instr to asst prof English, US Air Force Acad, 59-61; from instr to prof speech, 61-71, dir grad admis & fels, 65-69, asst dean grad sch, 67-69, asst vpres, 70-71, Bowling Green State Univ; vchancellor, Univ Wis, Parkside, 71-76, actg chancellor, 74-75, prof commun, 71-79; vchancellor acad affairs, 79-94, prof commun, 78-, vchancellor emeritus, 95, Univ Neb, Omaha; Midwest Forensic Asn res grant, 66-67; Am Coun Educ fel, Univ Calif, Berkeley, 69-70; spec asst to chancellor & vis prof commun arts, Univ Wis, Madison, 76-77. **MEMBERSHIPS** Am Forensic Asn; Speech Commun Asn. **RESEARCH** Semantics; debate; political campaigning. **SELECTED PUBLICATIONS** Auth, Fundamentals of Debate: Theory and Practice, Scott, 66; art, Student trust at Berkeley, Educ Rec, 71; art, Relational Abstracting and the Structural Differential, Research Designs in General Semantics, Gordon & Breach, 72; art, The Early Debates, Commun Asn Pac, 7/77; art, State Government Trust of Higher Education in Wisconsin, fall 79; auth, Lower Moments in Higher Education, Rockbrook Press, 97. **CONTACT ADDRESS** Dept of Communications, 6001 Dodge St, Omaha, NE, 68182-0002. **EMAIL** obauer@cwis.unomaha.edu

BAUERLEIN, MARK
DISCIPLINE ENGLISH LANGUAGE AND LITERATURE **EDUCATION** Univ Calif Los Angles, PhD, 88. **CAREER** Prof **RESEARCH** 19th-century American literature; critical theory. **SELECTED PUBLICATIONS** Auth, Literary Criticism: An Autopsy; The Pragmatic Mind: Explorations in the Psychology of Belief; Whitman and the American Idiom. **CONTACT ADDRESS** English Dept, Emory Univ, 1380 Oxford Rd NE, Atlanta, GA, 30322-1950.

BAULAND, PETER MAX
PERSONAL Born 12/19/1932, Ulm, Germany, m, 1961, 2 children **DISCIPLINE** ENGLISH, DRAMA, FILM **EDUCATION** Univ Pa, BA, 53, MA, 55, PhD, 64. **CAREER** Instr English, Lafayette Col, 57-58; from instr to asst prof, Drexel Inst, 59-64; asst prof, 64-69, chmn comp lit, 70-71, assoc prof English, Univ Mich, Ann Arbor, 69-, NEH fel, 69; Rackham res grant, 69, fac res fel, 77; Fulbright lectr & vis prof drama, Univ Munich, 71-72 & 79-80. **MEMBERSHIPS** Midwest Mod Lang Asn. **RESEARCH** Modern drama; film; comparative literature, especially German and English. **SELECTED PUBLICATIONS** Auth, The Hooded Eagle: Modern German Drama on the New York Stage, Syracuse Univ, 68; co-ed, The Tradition of the Theatre, Allyn & Bacon, 71; auth, chap, In: Modernes Amerikanisches Drama/Modern American Drama, Vandenhoeck & Ruprechet, for Univ Tubingen, Gottingen & Zurich, 73; transl, The judge's wife(novella), In: The Little Comedy and Other Stories, Ungar, 78; auth & transl, Gerhart Hauptmann's Before Daybreak: A Translation and an Introduction, Univ NC, 78. **CONTACT ADDRESS** Dept of English, Univ of Mich, 505 S State St, Ann Arbor, MI, 48109-1003. **EMAIL** pbauland@umich.edu

BAUMBACH, JONATHAN
PERSONAL Born 07/05/1933, New York, NY, m, 1968, 3 children **DISCIPLINE** ENGLISH, FILM STUDIES **EDUCATION** Brooklyn Col, AB, 55; Columbia Univ, MFA, 56; Stanford Univ, PhD(English & Am lit), 61. **CAREER** Asst prof English, Ohio State Univ, 61-64; dir writing, NY Univ, 64-66; assoc prof, 66-70, PROF ENGLISH, BROOKLYN COL, 71-, Mem bd dirs, Teachers & Writers Collaborative, 66-; vis prof English, Tufts Univ, 70-71; movie critic, Partisan Rev, 73-; Guggenheim fel, 78; vis prof creative writing, Univ Wash, Seattle, 78. **MEMBERSHIPS** Int PEN Club; Nat Soc Film Critics. **RESEARCH** American novel; cinema. **SELECTED PUBLICATIONS** Auth, The Landscape of Nightmare: Studies in Contemporary American Novel, NY Univ & Peter Owen, London, 65; A Man to Conjure With, Random & Gollanez, London, 65; What Comes Next, Harper, 68; Reruns (novel), 74, Babble (novel), 76 & co-ed, Statements II: New Fiction, 77, Fiction Collective/Braziller; Whats the Rumpus & The Characterization of American Fiction, ANQ-A Quart J of Short Articles, Notes, and Reviews, Vol 5, 92; 'Short Cuts', with R. Altman, Am Book Rev, Vol 16, 94; 'Juice', A Film by Oliver Stone, A Speculative Fiction Based on New Information Uncovered by the Filmaker, Film Comment, Vol 32, 96. **CONTACT ADDRESS** Brooklyn Col, CUNY, Brooklyn, NY, 11210.

BAUMLIN, JAMES S.
DISCIPLINE RENAISSANCE AND SEVENTEENTH-CENTURY LITERATURE **EDUCATION** Georgetown Univ, BA, 77; Brown Univ, PhD, 83. **CAREER** Southwest Tex State Univ **HONORS AND AWARDS** Nat Excellence Eng Award; SMSU Found Fac Achievement Award Outstanding Sch., Dir, Grad Studies eng. **SELECTED PUBLICATIONS** Auth, John Donne and the Rhetorics of Renaissance Discourse, Univ Miss Press, 91; Coed, Ethos: New Essays in Rhetorical and Critical Theory, SMU Press, 94. **CONTACT ADDRESS** Southwest MS State Univ, 901 S. National, Ste. 50, Springfield, MO, 65804-0094.

BAUMWOLL, DENNIS
PERSONAL Born 07/08/1932, New York, NY, m, 1956, 4 children **DISCIPLINE** ENGLISH **EDUCATION** Univ Okla, BA, 54, MA, 58, PhD(English), 64. **CAREER** Instr English, Boston Univ, 62-65; from instr to asst prof, 65-72, assoc prof, 72-79, PROF ENGLISH, BUCKNELL UNIV, 79-, Ed consult, Bucknell Rev, 65-; consult, Pa Dept Pub Instr, 67; coordr acad enrichment prog, US Penitentiary, Lewisburg, 67- **MEMBERSHIPS** MLA; Teachers of English to Speakers of Other Lang. **RESEARCH** The novel as genre; modern fiction; English as a second language. **SELECTED PUBLICATIONS** Coauth, Advanced Reading and Writing, Holt, 65, 2nd ed, 78. **CONTACT ADDRESS** Dept of English, Bucknell Univ, Lewisburg, PA, 17837-2029. **EMAIL** baumwoll@bucknell.edu

BAXTER-MOORE, NICK
DISCIPLINE COMMUNICATIONS **EDUCATION** Univ Manchester, BA; London Sch of Econ, MSc; Carleton Univ, PhD. **CAREER** Prof, Brock Univ. **RESEARCH** Nationalism and national identity; politics and popular culture/popular music; creation and dissemination of societal myth. **SELECTED PUBLICATIONS** Co-auth, Politics in Canada: Culture, Institutions, Behaviour and Public Policy, Prentice-Hall Can, 86; Studying Politics: An Introduction to Argument and Analysis, Copp Clark Longman, 94; auth, Ideology or Pragmatism?, The politics and management of the Mulroney government's privatization programme, Brit Jour Can Stud, 92. **CONTACT ADDRESS** Dept of Politics, Brock Univ, 500 Glenridge Ave, St. Catharines, ON, L2S 3A1.

BAY, LIBBY
PERSONAL Born 12/22/1932, New York, NY, m, 1995, 2 children **DISCIPLINE** ENGLISH **EDUCATION** Hunter Col, BA, 54; Univ Chicago, MA, 55. **CAREER** Lectr English, Brooklyn Col, 57-61 & Hunter Col, 61-65; Prof English. Rockland Commun Col, 65-93, Dept Chmn, 65-93, Chair, Humanities Div, 93-. **HONORS AND AWARDS** Penfield fel, NY Univ, 55-57; Chancellor's Award Excellence in Teaching, State Univ NY, 73; Nat Endowment for Humanities grant, proj dir interdisciplinary humanities, 74-75; Mellon fel, 80-81, 85-86; East/West Inst Fel, Spring 90; NCCCA Award for Most Outstanding Chair in NE, 93; Woman of the Year Award, Rockland AAWN, 98. **MEMBERSHIPS** NCTE; MLA; Asn Departments Teachers English; 4 C's; TYCA. **RESEARCH** Composition and rhetoric; contemporary American literature; modern adaptations of classical themes; women's literature. **SELECTED PUBLICATIONS** Auth, Towards uniformity in grading, 77 & Counterparting: Teaching through modern responses, 78, Eric; Save the tiger: Strategies for literature enrollment, Community Col Rev, 6/78; Peer Critiquing, Insight, 82; Honors programs in community colleges, NCCJ J, 77; Rerouting a Career, ADE, 93. **CONTACT ADDRESS** SUNY/Rockland Col, 145 College Rd, Suffern, NY, 10901-3611. **EMAIL** lbay@sunyrockland.edu

BAYLESS, OVID LYNDAL
PERSONAL Born 07/20/1931, Duncan, OK, m, 1953, 3 children **DISCIPLINE** SPEECH; COMMUNICATION **EDUCATION** Baylor Univ, BA, 53, MA, 59; Univ Denver, PhD(speech), 65. **CAREER** Instr, broadcasting workshop, Baylor Univ, 59; instr English, US Air Force Acad, 62-63, asst prof tech writing & speech, 65-67, assoc prof advan compos & speech, 67-74, deputy dir instr technol, 68-74; PROF SPEECH COMMUN & CHMN DEPT SPEECH COMMUN & DRAMATIC ARTS, ARK STATE UNIV, 74- **MEMBERSHIPS** Speech Commun Asn; Am Forensic Asn; Int Commun Asn; Broadcast Educ Asn. **RESEARCH** Group problem-solving; persuasion; broadcasting. **SELECTED PUBLICATIONS** Auth, The American forces Vietnam network, J Broadcasting, 69; The oral history program, 69 & Television as a demonstration tool, 69, Educ TV. **CONTACT ADDRESS** Arkansas State Univ, PO Drawer 396, State University, AR, 72467-0369.

BAYM, NINA
PERSONAL Born 06/14/1936, Princeton, NJ, m, 1958, 2 children **DISCIPLINE** ENGLISH **EDUCATION** Cornell Univ, BA, 57; Harvard Univ, MA, 58, PhD(English), 63. **CAREER** Asst English, Univ Calif, Berkeley, 62-63; from instr to assoc prof, 63-76, assoc head dept, 71-75, prof English, Univ Ill, Urbana, 72-, dir Sch Humanities, 76-87; Jubilee prof Lib Arts and Sciences, 87; Swanlund Endowd chmn, 97-; Cen for Adv Study prof, 97; Guggenheim fel, 75-76; Nat Endowment for Humanities fel, 82-83. **MEMBERSHIPS** MLA; Am Studies Asn; hon fel Am Asn Univ Women; Nathaniel Hawthorne Asn; Robert Frost Soc. **RESEARCH** American literature; American fiction women writers, gender issues, sociology of anthorship & canon-formation. **SELECTED PUBLICATIONS** Auth, Women in Cooper's Leatherstocking Tales, Am Quart, 71; The erotic motif in Herman Melville's Clarel, Tex Studies, 74; Revision and thematic change in The Portrait of a Lady, Mod Fiction Studies, 76; The Shape of Hawthorne's Career, 76 & Woman's Fiction: A Guide to Novels By and About Women in America 1820-1870, 78, Cornell Univ; Melville's quarrel with fiction, PMLA, 79; Melodramas of Beset Manhood: How theories of American fiction exclude women authors, Am Quart, 81; Nathaniel Hawthorne and his mother, Am Lit, 82. **CONTACT ADDRESS** Sch of Humanities, Univ of Illinois, Urbana-Champaign, 608 S Wright St, Urbana, IL, 61801-3613. **EMAIL** baymnina@uiuc.edu

BAZERMAN, CHARLES
DISCIPLINE ENGLISH LITERATURE **EDUCATION** Brandeis Univ, PhD, 71. **CAREER** PROF, ENG, UNIV CALIF, SANTA BARBARA. **RESEARCH** Rhetorical theory; rhetoric of science; academic writing; teaching of writing. **SELECTED PUBLICATIONS** Auth, Constructing Experience, South Ill Univ Press, 94; Shaping Written Knowledge: The Genre and Activity of the Experimental Article, Science, Univ Wis Press, 88; The Informed Writer, 5th Edition, Houghton Mifflin, 97; "Systems of Genre and the Enactment of Social Intentions," Genre and the New Rhetoric, 94; "Forums of Validation and Forms of Knowledge: The Magical Rhetoric of Otto von Guericke's Sulfur Globe," Configurations, 93; ed, "Rhetoric, Knowledge, and Society"; co-ed, "Landmark Essays in Writing Across the Curriculum." **CONTACT ADDRESS** Dept of Eng, Univ Calif, Santa Barbara, CA, 93106-7150. **EMAIL** bazerman@humanitas.ucsb.edu

BEALE, WALTER HENRY
PERSONAL Born 01/15/1945, Roseboro, NC, m, 1968, 1 child **DISCIPLINE** RHETORIC, ENGLISH LANGUAGE & LITERATURE **EDUCATION** Wake Forest Col, BA, 67; Univ MI, MA, 68, PhD, 71. **CAREER** Asst prof, 71-76, assoc prof English 76-86, prof English, 86-, Dean Col Arts Sci 90-, Univ NC, Greensboro, 76-. **MEMBERSHIPS** MLA; NCTE; Rhet Soc; Mediaeval Acad Am. **RESEARCH** Rhetorical theory and criticism; discourse theory; medieval literature. **SELECTED PUBLICATIONS** Auth, Walter Hilton and the concept of 'medlid lyf,' Am Benediction Rev, 75; Old and Middle English Poetry to 1500, Gale Res Co, 76; On rhetoric and poetry: John Donne's The Prohibition, Quart J Speech, 76; Rhetorical performating discourse: A new theory of epideictic, Philos & Rhet, 78; Rhetoric in the old English verse paragraph, Neuphilologische Mitteilungen, 79; Real Writing: Argumentation, Relflection, Information, & Stylistic Options, 82, Scott Foresman; A Pragmatic Theory of Discourse, S Il Press, 87. **CONTACT ADDRESS** Dept English, Univ N. Carolina, Greensboro, 105 Foust Bldg, Greensboro, NC, 27412. **EMAIL** WHBeale@HAMLET.uncg.edu

BEAN, BOBBY GENE
PERSONAL Born 01/15/1951, Houlka, MS, m, 1974 **DISCIPLINE** LIBRARY SCIENCE **EDUCATION** Southeast Missouri State University, BSE, 1974; Southern Illinois University, MSE, 1979, EDS, 1981; Lael University, EDD,1983; Atlanta University, MSLS, 1987; Interdenominational Theological Center, MDiv, 1989; Univ of Sarasota, EDD, candidate, 1998. **CAREER** Sikeston Public School, high school librarian assistant, 1972-73; East St Louis Public School, 6th grade teacher, 1974-82, junior high math teacher, 1982-83, junior high librarian, 1983-87; ATLANTA PUBLIC SCHOOL, JOHN HOPE ELEMENTARY, MEDIA SPECIALIST, 1988-; ATLANTA UNIVERSITY CENTER, RW WOODRUFF LIB, REF LIBRARIAN, 1988-; INTERDENOMINATIONAL THEOLOGY CENTER, INSTRUCTOR, 1992-. **HONORS AND AWARDS** American Biographical Institute, Research Board Advisor, 1990; Those Who Excel, School Media Service, Honorable Mention, 1987; ABI, Distinguished Leadership Award. **MEMBERSHIPS** ITC, Dean's List, 1988-89; United Negro College Fund Scholarship, 1989; Theta Phi, 1989; Atlanta University, Beta Phi Mu Library Science Honor Fraternity, 1987; American Library Assn; Georgia Library Assn; American Assn of School Librarians; Georgia Chaplain Assn. **CONTACT ADDRESS** Atlanta Public Schools, 112 Blvd NE, John Hope Elementary, Atlanta, GA, 30312.

BEASLEY, JERRY CARR
PERSONAL Born 09/15/1940, Nashville, TN, m, 1966, 2 children **DISCIPLINE** ENGLISH LITERATURE **EDUCATION** George Peabody Col, BA, 63; Univ KS, MA, 67; Northwestern Univ, PhD(English), 71. **CAREER** Asst prof, 69-74, assoc prof, 74-81, PROF ENGLISH, UNIV DE, 81-, ASSOC CHMN DEPT, 77-, Nat Endowment for Humanities summer grant, 77. **MEMBERSHIPS** MLA; Am Soc 18th Century Studies. **RESEARCH** English novel, 18th and 19th centuries. **SELECTED PUBLICATIONS** Auth, Fanny Burney and Jane Austen's Pride and Prejudice, English Miscellany, 73; English Fiction in the 1740's: Some Glances at the Major Minor Novels, Studies Novel, fall 73; The Role of Tom Pinch in Martin Chuzzlewit, Ariel, 74; co-ed, The Novel in England, 1700-1775, Garland Publ, 74-75; auth, Romance and the New Novels of Richardson, Fielding, and Smollett, Studies English Lit, summer 76; English Fiction, 1660-1800, Gale Res Co, 78; Portraits of a Monster: Robert Walpole and Early English Prose Fiction, Eighteenth Century Studies, summer 81; Novels of the 1740's, Univ GA Press, 82; The Intelligencer, with J. Woolley, Eighteenth-Century Studies, Vol 27, 94; Masquerade and Gender-Disguise and Female Identity in 18th-Century Fictions by Women, with C. Craftfairchild, Scriblerian and the Kit, Vol 27, 95. **CONTACT ADDRESS** Dept of English, Univ of DE, Newark, DE, 19711.

BEASLEY, VANESSA B.
DISCIPLINE RHETORICAL THEORY **EDUCATION** Univ Tex, PhD. **CAREER** Asst prof, Texsa A&M Univ. **SELECTED PUBLICATIONS** Publ in, Political Commun & The Encycl Of Television. **CONTACT ADDRESS** Dept of Speech Communication, Texas A&M Univ, College Station, TX, 77843-4234. **EMAIL** csnidow@tamu.edu

BEATIE, BRUCE A.
PERSONAL Born 03/04/1935, Oakland, CA, m, 1990 **DISCIPLINE** MEDIEVAL, FOLK, AND POPULAR LITERATURE **EDUCATION** Univ Calif, Berkeley, AB, 59; Univ Colo, MA, 60; Harvard Univ, PhD(comp lit), 67. **CAREER** Asst prof Ger, Univ Colo, 64-67, asst prof Ger & comp lit, 67-68; assoc prof, Univ Rochester, 68-70; chmn, Dept Mod Lang, 70-77, Prof Ger,Cleaveland State Univ, 77-88, Prof Comp & Medieval Studies, 89-. **HONORS AND AWARDS** Nat Endowment for Humanities younger scholar fel, 70. **MEMBERSHIPS** Midwest MLA; AAUP. **RESEARCH** Medieval comparative literature; popular and traditional narrative; folklore. **SELECTED PUBLICATIONS** Auth, Arthurian films and Arthurian texts: problems of reception and comprehension, Arthurian Interpretations, Spring 88; Arthur C. Clarke and the alien encounter: The background of Childhood's End, Extrapolation, Spring 89; E.E. Smith, In: Twentieth Century Science Fiction Writers, 3rd ed, St. James, 91; The broken quest: the Perceval romances of Chretien de Troyes and Eric Rohmer, In: The Arthurian Revival: Essays on Form, Tradition, and Transformation, Garland, 92; coauth, Reflected images in two Mexican poems of 1957: Piedra de sol by Octavio Paz and Misterios gozosos by Rosario Castellanos, Revista / Review Interamericana 26, 96; author of several other articles. **CONTACT ADDRESS** Dept of Mod Lang, Cleveland State Univ, 1983 E 24th St, Cleveland, OH, 44115-2440. **EMAIL** b.beatie@popmail.csuohio.edu

BEATTIE, THOMAS CHARLES
PERSONAL Born 02/07/1938, St. Johns, MI, m, 1962 **DISCIPLINE** ENGLISH LANGUAGE & LITERATURE **EDUCATION** MI State Univ, BA, 60; Univ PA, MA, 61; Univ MI Ann Arbor, PhD, 68. **CAREER** Tchg fel Eng, Univ MI, 63-68; asst prof, 68-76, assoc prof, 76-80, prof eng, & chmn dept, Hartwick Col, 78-93, assoc dean, Acad Affairs, 94. **MEMBERSHIPS** MLA; Col Eng Asn. **RESEARCH** Novel; Jane Austen; 18th century Eng lit; Toni Morrison. **SELECTED PUBLICATIONS** Writing Competency: A Handbook, 79; Moments of Meaning Dearly Achieved: Virginia Woolf's Sense of an Ending, Mod Fiction Studies, 86. **CONTACT ADDRESS** Office of Acad Affairs, Hartwick Col, Oneonta, NY, 13820-4020. **EMAIL** beattiet@hartwick.edu

BEATTY, MICHAEL
DISCIPLINE INTERPERSONAL AND ORGANIZATIONAL COMMUNICATION **EDUCATION** Univ MO, BS; Cent MO State Univ, MA; OH State Univ, PhD. **CAREER** Comm, Cleveland St Univ. **SELECTED PUBLICATIONS** Co-auth, Personality and Communication: Trait Perspectives, Hampton Press, 97; Trait Verbal Aggressiveness and the Appropriateness and Effectiveness of Fathers' Interaction Plans, Commun Quart, 96; auth, Thinking Quantitatively, An Integrated Approach to Communication Theory and Research, Hillsdale, NJ: Erlbaum, 96. **CONTACT ADDRESS** Commun Dept, Cleveland State Univ, 83 E 24th St, Cleveland, OH, 44115. **EMAIL** m.beatty@csuohio.edu

BEATY, FREDERICK L.
PERSONAL Born 10/22/1926, New Braunfels, TX, m, 1955, 2 children **DISCIPLINE** ENGLISH **EDUCATION** Univ TX, BA, 46; Harvard Univ, AM, 48, PhD, 52; Oxford Univ, BLitt, 50. **CAREER** Instr English, Cornell Univ, 54-55; from instr to assoc prof, 55-69, PROF ENGLISH, IN UNIV, BLOOMINGTON, 69-. **MEMBERSHIPS** MLA; Keats-Shelley Asn Am. **RESEARCH** Romantic period of English literature; Romantic writers and Romanticism. **SELECTED PUBLICATIONS** Ed, The Lloyd-Manning Letters, IN Univ, 57; auth, Byron and Story of Francesca de Rimini, PMLA, 60; Mrs Radcliffe's Fading Gleam, Philo Quart, 63; Harlequin Don Juan, J English & Ger Philol, 68; Byron on Malthus and population problem, Keats Shelley J, 69; Light From Heaven: Love in British Romantic Literature, Northern IL Univ, 71; Byron's Longbow and Strongbow, Studies English Lit, 72; Byron's Imitations of Juvenal and Persius, SIR, 76; Byron Heroines, with C. Franklin, Nineteenth-Century Lit, Vol 48, 93. **CONTACT ADDRESS** Dept of English, Indiana Univ, Bloomington, Bloomington, IN, 47401.

BEATY, JEROME
DISCIPLINE ENGLISH LANGUAGE AND LITERATURE **EDUCATION** Univ Ill, PhD, 56. **CAREER** Prof **RESEARCH** Victorian literature; poetics; the theory of the novel. **SELECTED PUBLICATIONS** Auth, Misreading Jane Eyre: A Postformalist Paradigm; coauth, Poetry: From Statement to Meaning; "Middlemarch" from Notebook to Novel; ed, Norton Introduction to the Short Novel; Norton Introduction to Fiction; Norton Introduction to Literature; New Worlds of Literature; Villette; Middlemarch. **CONTACT ADDRESS** English Dept, Emory Univ, 1380 Oxford Rd NE, Atlanta, GA, 30322-1950.

BEAVERS, MYRTLE B.
PERSONAL Born 04/21/1934, Page, OK, m, 1953, 3 children **DISCIPLINE** ENGLISH LITERATURE **EDUCATION** Okaloosa-Walton Community Col, AA, 72; Univ West FL, BA, 74, MA, 76; FL State Univ, PhD (English Lit), 94. **CAREER** Teacher, Ft. Walton Beach High School, 74-84; PROF, OKALOOSA-WALTON COMMUNITY COL, 84-, chair, Communications Dept, 94-97. **HONORS AND AWARDS** Bert and Ruth Davis Award for Outstanding Dissertation in British Literature for the Year 94-95. **RESEARCH** Thomas Hardy; Charles Dickens; 19th century British lit. **SELECTED PUBLICATIONS** Auth, book review of Baston Mountain Tales: Stories from a Cherokee Family by Glenn J. Twish, Greenfield Rev Press, 97, for the Am Indian Culture and Res Jour published by the Am Indian Studies Center of UCLA. **CONTACT ADDRESS** 712 Harbor Lane, Destin, FL, 32541-1806. **EMAIL** beaversm@owcc.net

BEBOUT, LINDA J.
DISCIPLINE ENGLISH LANGUAGE; LITERATURE **EDUCATION** Central, BA; San Francisco State Univ, MSc; Cornell, PhD, 77. **CAREER** Asst prof **RESEARCH** Teaching of second-language vocabulary and the usage of gender-related terms in popular culture, such as in song lyrics. **SELECTED PUBLICATIONS** Pub (s), usage of gender-related words in English; language; language disorders and cross cultural attitudes toward them & teaching and learning English as a Second Language. **CONTACT ADDRESS** Dept of English Language and Literature, Univ of Windsor, 401 Sunset Ave, Windsor, ON, N9B 3P4. **EMAIL** ljb@uwindsor.ca

BECKER, JOHN
DISCIPLINE ENGLISH LITERATURE **EDUCATION** Yale Univ, PhD. **CAREER** Fac, Fairleigh Dickinson Univ. **RESEARCH** Am lit, literary theory, and the Bible as lit. **SELECTED PUBLICATIONS** Auth, Hawthorne's Historical Allegory, Kennikat, 71; Worldview, The Literary Review, and Ethics and International Affairs in College English. **CONTACT ADDRESS** Fairleigh Dickinson Univ, 1000 River Rd, Teaneck, NJ, 07666.

BECKER, LLOYD GEORGE
PERSONAL Born 12/07/1942, Brooklyn, NY, m, 1995, 2 children **DISCIPLINE** AMERICAN LITERATURE & STUDIES **EDUCATION** Col William & Mary, AB, 64; State Univ NY Buffalo, MA, 68, PhD, 80. **CAREER** Instr, 67-69, asst prof, 69-73, assoc prof, 73-78, prof eng, Suffolk County Community Col, 78. **HONORS AND AWARDS** NEH Summer Res Grant, 92. **MEMBERSHIPS** Am Lit Asn; Asn Lit Scholars & Critics; Western Lit Asn; Ralph Waldo Emerson Soc; Mark Twain Circle; Jack London Soc. **RESEARCH** 19th Century Lit & Painting; Western Am Lit, esp. contemp fiction; Mythology. **SELECTED PUBLICATIONS** Auth, William Sidney Mount's Transparent Summer Morning, In: Paumanok Rising, Street Press, 80; Scenes of the Familiar, Emblems of the Eternal: Cultural Contexts of Shepherd Alonzo Mount, The Long Island Hist Jour, fall 90; Ken Nunn's Pomsra Queen, Western Am Lit, Aug. 94. **CONTACT ADDRESS** 533 College Rd, Selden, NY, 11784. **EMAIL** beckerl@sunysuffolk.edu

BECKMAN, RICHARD
PERSONAL Born 01/11/1932, New York, NY, m, 1952, 2 children **DISCIPLINE** ENGLISH LITERATURE **EDUCATION** Columbia Univ, BA, 53; Univ Rochester, MA, 54; Johns Hopkins Univ, PhD, 62. **CAREER** Instr English, Univ MD, 57-62; asst prof, 62-68, ASSOC PROF ENGLISH, TEMPLE UNIV, 68-. **MEMBERSHIPS** MLA. **RESEARCH** English Romantic and Victorian literature. **SELECTED PUBLICATIONS** Auth, A Character Typology for Hardy's Novels, ELH, 63; Panangelic Voices in 'Finnegan's Wake', J of Modern Lit, Vol 17, 91; Perils of Marriage in 'Finnegan's Wake', James Joyce Quart, Vol 33, 95. **CONTACT ADDRESS** Dept of English, Temple Univ, Philadelphia, PA, 19122.

BECKSON, KARL
PERSONAL Born 02/04/1926, New York, NY, m, 1957, 2 children **DISCIPLINE** ENGLISH **EDUCATION** Univ Az, BA, 49; Columbia Univ, MA, 52, PhD, 59. **CAREER** Lectr, Columbia Univ & Hunter Col, 56-69; instr English, Fairleigh Dickinson Univ, 60-61; from instr to assoc prof, 61-76, prof English, Brooklyn Col, 76-; lectr English in psychiat, Med Col, Cornell Univ, 80-95; ed bd English lit in transition, 81-. **HONORS AND AWARDS** Mellon fel, Clark Libr, UCLA, 78; NEH Fel, 89-90. **MEMBERSHIPS** MLA; Eighteen Nineties Soc London. **RESEARCH** Late 19th and 20th century British literature. **SELECTED PUBLICATIONS** Coauth, Literary Terms: A Dictionary, 61, 2nd ed, 75, 3rd ed, 89; & ed, Great Theories in Literary Criticism, 63, Farrar, Straus; Aesthetes & Decadents of the 1890's, Random, 66, 2nd ed, Acad Chicago, 81; Oscar Wilde: The Critical Heritage, Routledge & Kegan Paul, 70; co-ed, Max & Will: Max Beerbohm and William Rothenstein, Their Friendship and Letters, 1893-1945, Harvard Univ, 75; ed, Memoirs of Arthur Symons: Life and Art in the 1890's, Pa State, 77; auth, Henry Harland: His Life and Work, Eighteen Nineties Soc, London, 78; co-ed, Arthur Symons: A Life, Oxford, 87; Arthur Symons: Selected Letters, Macmillan, London, 89; co-auth Arthur Symons: A Bibliography, ELT Press, 90; London in the 1890's: A Cultural History, Norton, 93; Oscar Wilde Encyclo, AMS Press, 98. **CONTACT ADDRESS** Dept English, Brooklyn Col, CUNY, 2900 Bedford Ave, Brooklyn, NY, 11210-2889.

BECKWITH, SARAH
DISCIPLINE ENGLISH LITERATURE **EDUCATION** Univ London, PhD. **CAREER** Prof, Duke Univ. **RESEARCH** Middle Eng relig(s). **SELECTED PUBLICATIONS** Auth, Christ's Body: Identity, Religion and Society in Medieval English Writing, Routledge, 93; publ(s) on lit anchoritism, medieval theatre; sacramental cult. **CONTACT ADDRESS** Eng Dept, Duke Univ, Durham, NC, 27706.

BEDFORD, BONNIE C.
DISCIPLINE CONTEMPORARY DRAMA AND FICTION **EDUCATION** Waynesburg Col, BA; SUNY,Bighamton, MA, PhD. **CAREER** Tchg asst, SUNY; asst prof. **MEMBERSHIPS** Mem, Dramatists Guild; Author's League of Am; Assn Theatre in Higher Edu; Assoc Wrtg Prog; Nat Coun tThr(s) Eng; Delta Kappa Gamma. **SELECTED PUBLICATIONS** Auth, Sniper, play, produced at Wilkes Univ, and T. Schreiber Studio, NYC. **CONTACT ADDRESS** Dept of Eng, Wilkes Univ, 170 S Franklin St, Wilkes-Barre, PA, 18766. **EMAIL** bedford@wilkes1.wilkes.edu

BEDNARZ, JAMES P.
DISCIPLINE RENAISSANCE, SHAKESPEARE, CRITICAL THEORY **EDUCATION** Columbia Univ, PhD. **CAREER** Prof, Long Island Univ, C.W. Post Campus. **SELECTED PUBLICATIONS** Auth, Representing Jonson: Histriomastix and the Origin of the Poets' War; Ralegh in Spenser's Historical Allegory; Imitations of Spenser in A Midsummer Night's Dream; The Dual Nature of Paul Klee's Symbolic Language. **CONTACT ADDRESS** Long Island Univ, C.W. Post, Brookville, NY, 11548-1300.

BEENE, LYNNDIANNE
DISCIPLINE LANGUAGE AND RHETORIC, PROFESSIONAL WRITING, AND CONTEMPORARY FICTION **EDUCATION** Univ Kans, PhD. **CAREER** Instr, Univ NMex. **RESEARCH** Contemporary grammar models. **SELECTED PUBLICATIONS** Auth, The Riverside Handbook, 92. **CONTACT ADDRESS** Univ NMex, Albuquerque, NM, 87131.

BEER, BARRETT L.
PERSONAL Born 07/04/1936, Goshen, IN, m, 1965, 2 children **DISCIPLINE** ENGLISH HISTORY **EDUCATION** DePauw Univ, BA, 58; Univ Cincinnati, MA, 59; Northwestern Univ, PhD(hist), 65. **CAREER** Instr hist, Kent State Univ, 62-65; asst prof, Univ NM, 65-68, asst dean col art & sci, 66-68; assoc prof, 68-76, PROF HIST, KENT STATE UNIV, 76-, Res grants, Am Philos Soc, 66 & Univ NM, 66-68; vis assoc prof, Northwestern Univ, 69; res fel, Kent State Univ, 73 & 77. **MEMBERSHIPS** AHA; Conf Brit Studies. **RESEARCH** Early modern England. **SELECTED PUBLICATIONS** Auth, The Rise of John Dudley, Hist Today, 4/65; A Critique of the Protectorate, Huntington Libr Quart, 5/71; London and Rebellions of 1548-1549, J Brit Studies, 11/72; Northumberland: The Political Career of John Dudley, Duke of Northumberland, Kent State Univ, 73; co-ed, The Letters of William, Lord Paget of Beaudesert, 1547-1563, Camden Miscellany Vol XXV, Royal Hist Soc, London, 74; The Commoyson in Norfolk, 1549: A Narrative of Popular Rebellion in Sixteenth Century England, J Medieval & Renaissance Studies, spring 76; Hugh Latimer and the Lusty Knave of Kent: The Commonwealth Movement of 1549, Bull Inst Hist Res, 11/79; Rebellion and Riot: Popular Disorder in England during the Reign of Edward VI, Kent State Univ Press, 82; The Scottish Regency of the Earl of Albion-A Study in the Failure of Anglo-Scottish Relations, with D. Franklin, Albion, Vol 28, 96; Lordship and Community-The Lestrange Family and the Village of Hunstanton Norfolk in the First Half of thr 16th-Century, with C. Oestmann, Am Hist Rev, Vol 101, 96; The Ebbs and Flows of Fortune-The Life of Thomas Howard, 3rd Duke of Norfolk, with D. M. Head, Am Hist Rev, Vol 102, 97. **CONTACT ADDRESS** Kent State Univ, Kent, OH, 44242.

BEGIEBING, ROBERT J.
PERSONAL Born 11/18/1946, Adams, MA, m, 1968, 2 children **DISCIPLINE** ENGLISH **EDUCATION** Norwich Univ, BA, 68; Boston Col, MA, 70; Univ NH, PhD, 77. **CAREER** Instr, Univ Ky Extension Prog, 70-71; Tchng Asst, 72-76, Assoc & Asst Prof, 77-84, Full Prof, 84-, New Hampshire Col. **HONORS AND AWARDS** Who's Who Am Col & Univ; Dissertation Fellow, Univ NH, 76-77; Artist opportunity grant, NH Coun on the Arts, 93; Lila Wallace, Readers Dig Artist Fellow to the Am Antiquarian Soc, 96., Coord of Hum & Eng Language & Lit, NH Col, 94-96. **MEMBERSHIPS** MLA; AWP; Authors Guild. **RESEARCH** Nature writing; modern American & British literature. **SELECTED PUBLICATIONS** Auth, Acts of Regeneration: Allegory and Archetype in the Works of Norman Mailer, Univ Mo Press, 81; auth, Toward a New Synthesis: John Fowles, John Gardner, and Norman Mailer, Univ Rochester Press, 89; co-auth, The Literature of Nature: The British and American Traditions, Plexus Publishers, 90; auth, The Strange Death of Mistress Coffin, Algonquin Books, 91, 96. **CONTACT ADDRESS** Dept of English, New Hampshire Col, 2500 N River Rd, Manchester, NH, 03124. **EMAIL** rbegiebi@minerva.nhc.edu

BEGNAL, MICHAEL HENRY
PERSONAL Born 10/17/1939, Washington, DC, m, 1965, 2 children **DISCIPLINE** MODERN ENGLISH & COMPARATIVE LITERATURE **EDUCATION** Univ Conn, BA, 61; Pa State Univ, MA, 63; Univ Wash, PhD, 68. **CAREER** Instr English, Colgate Univ, 63-65; assoc prof, English & comp lit, 68-80, prof Eng & comp lit, 80-, PA State Univ; prof Am lit, Charles Univ Prague, 73-74 & 75-76. **RESEARCH** James Joyce; Irish literature; modern literature. **SELECTED PUBLICATIONS** Auth, Joseph Sheridan LeFanu, 71; auth, Narrator and Character in Finnegans Wake, Bucknell Univ, 74; co-ed & contribr, A Conceptual Guide to Finnegans Wake, Pa State Univ, 74; auth, On Miracle Ground: Essays on the Fiction of Lawrence Durrell, Buckness, 90. **CONTACT ADDRESS** Dept of English, Pennsylvania State Univ, Univ Park, 117 Burrowes Bldg, University Park, PA, 16802-6200. **EMAIL** mhb3@psu.edu

BEHDAD, ALI
PERSONAL Born 05/22/1961, Iran, m, 1996 **DISCIPLINE** LITERATURE **EDUCATION** Univ Calif Berkeley, BA, 83; Univ Mich, MA, PhD, 90. **CAREER** Asst prof, Univ Rochester, 90-93; assoc prof, UCLA, 93- . **HONORS AND AWARDS** Rockham Fel, Univ Mich, 89-90 **MEMBERSHIPS** MLA; MESA. **RESEARCH** US nationalism & immigration, postcolonial lit & theory **SELECTED PUBLICATIONS** Auth, Belated Travelers: Orientalism in the Age of Colonial Dissolution, Duke Univ Press, 94; Ins and Outs: Producing Delinquency at the Border, J of Chicano Stud, 98; Postcolonial Belatedness and Cultural Politics, Duke Univ Press, 98; global Disjunctures, Diasporic Differences, and the New World (Dis)Order, Blackwell, 98; Orientalist or Orienteur? Antoin Sevruguin and the Margin of Photography, Sackler Gallery Series, 99. **CONTACT ADDRESS** 3425 Inglewood Blvd, Los Angeles, CA, 90066. **EMAIL** behdad@humnet.ucla.edu

BEHRENDT, STEPHEN C.
PERSONAL Born 01/01/1947, Marinette, WI, m, 1969, 1 child **DISCIPLINE** ENGLISH LITERATURE **EDUCATION** Univ Wis, BA, 69, PhD(English), 74; Eastern Ky Univ, MA, 70. **CAREER** Vis asst prof English, Univ Minn, 75-77; instr English, Elizabethtown Col, 77-80; asst prof English, Univ Nebr, 80-, Am Philos Soc res grant, 78; Nat Endowment for Humanities summer sem, 79. **MEMBERSHIPS** MLA; Am Soc Eighteenth Century Studies; Midwest Mod Lang Asn. **RESEARCH** William Blake; English Romanticism, particularly Shelley; interrelations among the arts. **SELECTED PUBLICATIONS** Auth, Bright pilgrimage: William Blake's designs for L'Allegro and Il Penseroso, Milton Studies, 75; Blake's illustrations to Milton's Nativity Ode, Philol Quart, Winter 76; The polished artifact: Some observations on imitative criticism, Genre, Spring 77; The mental contest: Blake's Comus designs, Blake Studies, 78; The worst disease: Blake's Tiriel, Colby Libr Quart, 79; A Vocabulary of Lineaments: Blake and the Language of Art, Blake Studies (in press); The Exoteric Species: The Popular Idiom in Shelley's Poetry, Genre (in press); The Moment of Explosion: Blake and the Illustration of Milton, Univ Nebr Press, 83; A Step in the Dark, Mid-List Press, 96; Royal Mourning and Regency Culture: Elegies and Memorials of Princess Charlotte, Macmillan, 97; Romanticism, Radicalism, and the Press, Wayne State Univ Press, 97. **CONTACT ADDRESS** Dept of English, Univ of Nebraska, PO Box 880333, Lincoln, NE, 68588-0333. **EMAIL** sbehrend@unlinfo.unl.edu

BEIDLER, PETER GRANT
PERSONAL Born 03/13/1940, Bethlehem, PA, m, 1963, 4 children **DISCIPLINE** ENGLISH & AMERICAN LITERATURE, AMERICAN INDIAN STUDIES **EDUCATION** Earlham Col, BA, 62; Lehigh Univ, MA, 65, PhD(English), 68. **CAREER** From asst prof to prof, 68-78, Lucy G Moses Dist Prof English, Lehigh Univ, 78-; NEH fel anthrop, Univ AZ, 73-74. **HONORS AND AWARDS** CASE Nat Prof of the Year, 83; Lindback Teaching Award, 91, 94. **MEMBERSHIPS** MLA; Asn Study of Am Indian Lit. **RESEARCH** Chaucer; American Indian literature; Medieval literature. **SELECTED PUBLICATIONS** Auth, Fig Tree John, An Indian in Fact and Fiction, Univ AZ Press, 77; with Marion F Egge, The American Indian in Short Fiction: An Annotated Bibliography, Scarecrow Press, 79; John Gower's Literary Transformations in the Confessio Amantis, Univ Press Am, 82; Distinguished Teachers on Effective Teaching: Observations on Effective Teaching by College Professors Recognized by the Council for Advancment and Support of Education, Jossey-Bass, Pubs, 86; Ghosts, Demons, and Henry James: The Turn of the Screw at the Turn of the Century, Univ MO Press, 89; Writing Matters, McGraw-Hill, 90, Macmillan, 92; Henry James, The Turn of the Screw: Text and Five Contemporary Critical Essays, Bedford Books of St Martin's Press, 95; Geoffrey Chaucer, The Wife of Bath: Complete, Authoritative Text with Biographical and Historical Contexts, Critical History, and Essays from Five Contemporary Critical Perspectives, Bedford Books of St Martin's Press, 96; The Wife of Bath's Prologue and Tale: An Annotated Bibliography, with Elizabeth M. Biebel, Univ Toronto Press, 98; Masculinities in Chaucer, Boydell & Brewer, 98. **CONTACT ADDRESS** Dept English, Lehigh Univ, 35 Sayre Dr, Bethlehem, PA, 18015-3076. **EMAIL** pgb1@lehigh.edu

BEJA, MORRIS
PERSONAL Born 07/18/1935, New York, NY, m, 1957, 2 children **DISCIPLINE** ENGLISH **EDUCATION** City Col NY, BA, 57; Columbia Univ, MA, 58; Cornell Univ, PhD(English), 63 **CAREER** From instr to assoc prof, 61-71, PROF ENGLISH, OHIO STATE UNIV, 71-, chair, 83-94; Ohio State Univ res grants, 65, 68, 71, 75 & 78; Fulbright lectr Am lit, Univ Thessaloniki, 65-66; Develop Fund fac fel, 68; Fulbright vis prof English, Univ Col, Dublin, 72-73; Guggenheim fel, 72-73; co-ed, James Joyce Found Newslett, 77-. **HONORS AND AWARDS** Alumni Distinguished Teaching Award, 82 **MEMBERSHIPS** MLA; Am Comt Irish Studies; James Joyce Found; Virginia Woolf Soc **RESEARCH** Modern fiction, Anglo-Irish literature, film **SELECTED PUBLICATIONS** C0-ed, Samuel Beckett: Humanistic Perspectives, Ohio State Univ Press, 83; ed, Critical Essays on Virginia Woolf, G K Hall, 85; co-ed, James Joyce: The Centennial Symposium, Univ Ill Press, 86; co-ed, Coping with Joyce: Essays from the Copenhagen Symposium, Ohio State Univ Press, 89; auth, Joyce, The Artist Manque, and Indterminancy: A Lecture and an Essay, pamphlet, Princess Grace Irish Libr Lectr, Colin Smyth, 89; auth, James Joyce: A Literary Life, Ohio State Univ Press, Macmillan, London, Gill & Macmillan, Dublin, 92; ed, Perspectives on Orson Welles, G K Hall, 95; co-ed, Joyce in the Hibernian Metropolis: Essays, Ohio State Univ Press, 96; Virginia Woolf, Mrs Dalloway, Basil Blackwell, 96. **CONTACT ADDRESS** Dept of English, Ohio State Univ, 164 W 17th Ave, Columbus, OH, 43210-1326. **EMAIL** beja1@osu.edu

BEKENDORF, RAY R.
PERSONAL Born 05/04/1935, Saginaw, MI, m, 1979 **DISCIPLINE** RHETORICAL COMMUNICATION **EDUCATION** Univ MN, PhD, 86. **CAREER** Prof Speech Commun, 65-71, Chaffey Col, Alta Loma; adj asst prof, 68-71, Calif St Univ; prof, 71-, Southwestern Col, Chula Vista, CA; tchng assoc, 80-81, Univ Minn. **HONORS AND AWARDS** Alpha Psi Omega; Pi Kappa Delta; Phi Kappa Phi; Blue Key; Dean's List; NDEAS Grad fel, San Jose St Univ, 67; Who's Who Among Am Tchrs, 97. **MEMBERSHIPS** Nat Commun Asn; Western Commun Asn; Cent St Commun Asn; Int Commun Asn; Kenneth Burke Soc; Rhetoric Soc of Am; Int Soc for the Hist of Rhetoric; Int Churchill Soc. **RESEARCH** Classical rhetorical theory and contemporary rhetorical criticism. **SELECTED PUBLICATIONS** Ed bd, Communication Education, 76-82; ed advisor, J of the Am Forensic Asn, 77-79; ed bd, Moments in Rhetoric, Univ Minn Press, 75-77; NCA, recent res contrib & res panel chmn, Flowing Upward How the Basic Course Influences Theory, San Antonio, TX, 95; NCA res, chmn, Employing Burkeian Theory in the Construction of Social Reality, San Diego, CA, 96; NCA res, chmn, Burkeian Criticism and Its Utility Into the Investigation of Social Movements, Chicago, IL, 97; NCA, res, chmn, Burke and Clinton: Modern or Postmodern?, NY, 98. **CONTACT ADDRESS** Rhetoric and Communication Studies, Southwestern Col, Chula Vista, Chula Vista, CA, 92910.

BELASCO, SUSAN
PERSONAL Born 06/28/1950, Pittsburgh, PA **DISCIPLINE** ENGLISH **EDUCATION** Baylor Univ, BA, 72; Univ Leicester, MA, 82; Tex A&M Univ, PhD, 87. **CAREER** Instr, McLennan Commun Col, 76-87; asst prof, Allegheny Col, 87-92; assoc prof, Calif State Univ, 92-94; assoc prof, Univ Tulsa, 94-. **HONORS AND AWARDS** Rotary Found Graduate Fel for study abroad, 80-81. **MEMBERSHIPS** MLA; ALS; ALA; SHARP; Margaret Fuller Soc. **RESEARCH** Nineteenth century American literature and culture; rhetoric and composition. **SELECTED PUBLICATIONS** Auth, art, Basic Writer's and the Control of Our Environment, 91; auth, art, Summer on the Lakes: Margaret Fuller and the British, 91; auth, art, Workstation Technology: New Directions for the Teaching of Writing, 92; auth, art, Margaret Fuller in New York: Private Letters, Public Texts, 96; ed, intro, Ruth Hall, 96. **CONTACT ADDRESS** 440 S Gary Ave, Box 32, Tulsa, OK, 74104. **EMAIL** susan-belasco@utulsa.edu

BELL, BERNARD W.
DISCIPLINE ENGLISH **EDUCATION** Howard Univ, BA, 62, MA, 66; Univ MA, Amherst, PhD, 70. **CAREER** Teaching asst, Howard Univ, Washington, DC, 62-63; res asst, Prof Sterling Brown, summer 63; teacher, Calvin Coolidge High School, Washington, DC, 63-67; teaching asst, Univ MA, 67-68; teacher, Upward Bound Project, Univ MA, summer 68, 69, 71; lect/asst prof, Dept of English, Univ MA, Amherst, Sept 69- Feb 75; lect, Dept of Afro-Am Studies, Smith Col, Northampton, MA, Jan-June 73; vis prof, Dept of English, Clark Univ, Worcester, MA, Jan-June 72, Sept 73-Jan 74; lect, Inst of Afro-Am Culture, Univ IA, June 74; vis lect, Dept of English, Univ of Freiburg, West Germany, Sept 74-Aug 75; lect, Dept of English, Padagogische Hochschule, Freiburg, West Germany, 75; vis lect, Dept of English, Williams Col, Williamstown, MA, 79; Sr Fulbright Scholar, Univ of Coimbra, Portugal, 82-83; assoc prof, Dept of English, Univ MA, Amherst, 75-87; vis prof, Dept of Black Studies, Amherst Col, 88-89; prof, Dept of English, Univ MA, Amherst, 87-91; prof, Dept of English, PA State Univ, University Park, 91-; Sr Fulbright lect, Univ of Salamanca, Spain, Jan-June 96. **HONORS AND AWARDS** NDEA Fel, 65, 68-69; Phi Kappa Phi Honors, 69; NEH fel, 72-73; Col Lang Asn Creative Book Prize for The Afro-American Novel and Its Tradition, 89; Sr Fulbright-Hays Scholar: Univ of Coimbra, Portugal, Oct 82-July 83; Univ of Salamanca, Spain, Jan-June 96. **MEMBERSHIPS** Am Studies Asn, 88-; Multi-Ethnic Lit of the US Soc, 88-; Northeast Modern Lang Asn, 71-73; Modern Lang Asn, 71-78, 87-, delegate assembly, 95-97, exec comm div of Black Am lit and Culture, 95-; Col Lang Asn, 71-; Nat Coun of Teachers of English, 97. **RESEARCH** African Am studies; Am realism; modern British and Am novel; Jean Toomer; William Faulkner; Mark Twain; Vernacular Theory. **SELECTED PUBLICATIONS** Ed, Modern and Contemporary Afro-American Poetry, Allyn and Bacon, 74; auth, The Folk Roots of Contemporary Afro-American Poetry, Broadside Press, 74; The Afro-American Novel and Its Tradition, Univ MA Press, 87; guest ed, Clarence Major Special Issue, African Am Rev, 94; co-ed, Contemporary Literature in the African Diaspora, Univ of Salamanca, 97; co-ed, Call and Response: The African American Literary Tradition, Houghton Mifflin, 97; co-ed, W. E. B. DuBois on Race and Culture, Routledge, 97; more than 50 essays, articles, and reviews in such journals and periodicals as The MA Rev, Black World, The World and I, Commonwealth, College Lang Asn J, Phylon, Mark Twain J, MI Quart Rev, and Am Dialog. **CONTACT ADDRESS** Dept of English, Pennsylvania State Univ, 39 Burrowes, State College, PA, 16801. **EMAIL** bwb4@psu.edu

BELL, ILONA
DISCIPLINE ENGLISH **EDUCATION** Harvard Univ, BA, 69; Boston Col, PhD, 77. **CAREER** Prof. **RESEARCH** The poetry, politics, and practice of Elizabethan Courtship; renaissance women; Elizabeth I, John Donne. **SELECTED PUBLICATIONS** Auth,Elizabethan Women and the Poetry of Courtship, 98; Elizabeth I: A woman, and (if that be not enough) an unmarried Virgin; Polit Rhetoric, Power, and Renaissance Women, 95; What if it be a she, The Riddle of Donne's Curse, John Donne's desire of more: The Subject of Anne More Donne in His Poetry, 96; Under ye rage of a hott sonn & yr eyes: John Donne's Love Letters to Ann More, The Eagle and the Dove: Essays Reassessing John Donne, 86. **CONTACT ADDRESS** Dept of English, Williams Col, Stetson d-20, Williamstown, MA, 01267. **EMAIL** ibell@williams.edu

BELL, KIMBERLY
DISCIPLINE COMPOSITION **EDUCATION** Vanderbilt Univ, PhD, 72. **CAREER** Dept Eng, Clemson Univ **RESEARCH** Composition and writing. **SELECTED PUBLICATIONS** Auth, Resolving the Dichotomy Between Academic Discourse and Expressive Writing in High School and First-Year College Courses, Tenn Eng Jour, 97. **CONTACT ADDRESS** Clemson Univ, 507 Strode, Clemson, SC, 29634.

BELL, LINDA A.
DISCIPLINE FEMINIST THEORY, EXISTENTIALISM, ETHICS, CONTINENTAL PHILOSOPHY **EDUCATION** Emory Univ, PhD, 73. **CAREER** Prof, Ga State Univ. **SELECTED PUBLICATIONS** Auth, Visions of Women; Sartre's Ethics of Authenticity; Rethinking Ethics in the Midst of Violence: A Feminist Approach to Freedom. **CONTACT ADDRESS** Georgia State Univ, Atlanta, GA, 30303. **EMAIL** phllab@panther.gsu.edu

BELL, ROSEANN P.
PERSONAL Born 05/02/1945, Atlanta, GA, d **DISCIPLINE** ENGLISH **EDUCATION** Howard University, BA, 1966; Emory University, MA (cum laude), 1970, PhD (cum laude), 1974. **CAREER** US Civil Service Commission, typist, 1964-66; Atlanta Public School System, instructor, 1966-70; various/part-time teaching positions; freelance editor of education manuscripts, 1970-; Spelman College, asst professor, 1970-; Atlanta Voice Newspaper, columnist, 1971; Cornell University, Afro-American Studies Dept, asst professor; University of Mississippi, Dept of English, professor, currently. **HONORS AND AWARDS** Emory University, scholarship winner, 1968-70; Natl Institute of Humanities Fellowship, 1971-73; Natl Fellowships Fund Fellowship, Ford Foundation, 1973-74. **SELECTED PUBLICATIONS** Numerous articles. **CONTACT ADDRESS** Dept of English, Univ of Mississippi, University, MS, 38677-9701.

BELL, VEREEN M.
DISCIPLINE MODERN POETRY AND FICTION, CRITICAL THEORY **EDUCATION** Duke Univ, PhD. **CAREER** Instr, Vanderbilt Univ. **SELECTED PUBLICATIONS** Published books on Robert Lowell, Cormac McCarthy, and W. B. Yeats. **CONTACT ADDRESS** Vanderbilt Univ, Nashville, TN, 37203-1727.

BELL-METEREAU, REBECCA
DISCIPLINE FILM AND PROSE FICTION **EDUCATION** IN Univ, BA, MA, PhD. **CAREER** Southwest Tex State Univ **SELECTED PUBLICATIONS** Auth, Hollywood Androgyny; Writing With:(New Directions in Teaching, Learning, and Research); Essays in Women Worldwalkers: New Dimensions of Science Fiction and Fantasy; Cultural Conflicts in Contemporary Literature; Deciding Our Future: Technological Imperatives for Educations. **CONTACT ADDRESS** Southwest Texas State Univ, 601 University Dr, San Marcos, TX, 78666-4604.

BELLAMY, JOE DAVID
PERSONAL Born 12/29/1941, Cincinnati, OH, m, 1964, 2 children **DISCIPLINE** ENGLISH LITERATURE **EDUCATION** Antioch Col, BA, 64; Univ Iowa, MFA, 69. **CAREER** Asst col ed, Antioch col, 65-67; from instr to asst prof English, Mansfield State Col, 69-72; asst prof, 72-74, assoc prof, 74-80, PROF ENGLISH, ST LAWRENCE UNIV, 80-, Publ & ed, Fiction Int, 72-; Breadloaf scholar, Bridgeman Award, Middlebury Col, 73; dir, Ann Fiction Int-St Lawrence Univ Writer's Conf, 74-80; consult ed, Short Fiction Ser, Univ Ill Press, 74-; Nat Endowment Humanities grant, Brown Univ, 74. **HONORS AND AWARDS** Fels Award ed, Coord Coun Lit Mag, 76. **MEMBERSHIPS** MLA; Northeast Mod Lang Asn; AAUP; Coord Coun Lit Mag, (pres, 79-81). **RESEARCH** Formal innovation in contemporary fiction. **SELECTED PUBLICATIONS** Auth, 'Atomic Love', NAmer Rev, Vol 0278, 93; Literary Politics, Frohnmayer, 5 Sex Acts, Wild Thing, the Nea, and Me, Antioch Rev, Vol 0052, 94. **CONTACT ADDRESS** Dept of English, St Lawrence Univ, Canton, NY, 13617-1499.

BELLMAN, SAMUEL IRVING
PERSONAL Born 09/28/1926, El Paso, TX, m, 1952, 2 children **DISCIPLINE** ENGLISH **EDUCATION** Univ Tex, BA, 47; Wayne Univ, MA, 51; Ohio State Univ, PhD, 55. **CAREER** Teaching asst, Ohio State Univ, 53-54, asst instr, 54-55; instr English, Fresno State Col, 55-57; asst prof, Calif State Polytech Col, San Luis Obispo, 57-59; from asst prof to assoc prof, 59-66, PROF ENGLISH, CALIF STATE POLYTECH UNIV, POMONA, 66-, Vis exchange prof Am lit, Portsmouth Polytech, Eng, 75-76. **MEMBERSHIPS** Western Lit Asn. **RESEARCH** Modern Amer literature; poetics; literary criticism. **SELECTED PUBLICATIONS** Auth, Jackson,Shirley in A Study of the Short Fiction, Stud in Short Fiction, Vol 0031, 94; The Culture and Commerce of the Amer Short-Story, Modern Fiction Stud, Vol 0041, 95; Wharton, Edith Prisoners of Consciousness in A Study of Theme and Technique in the Tales, Stud in Short Fiction, Vol 0033, 96; 'Ethan Frome' in A Nightmare of Need, Stud in Short Fiction, Vol 0033, 96. **CONTACT ADDRESS** Dept of English, California State Polytech Univ, Pomona, CA, 91768.

BELLOW, SAUL
PERSONAL Born 06/10/1915, Lachine, PQ, Canada, m, 1974, 3 children **DISCIPLINE** WRITER **EDUCATION** Northwestern Univ, BS, 37; **HONORS AND AWARDS** Nobel Prize, 76; Pulitzer Prize; three National Book Awards. **SELECTED PUBLICATIONS** The Dangling Man, 44; The Victim, 47; Henderson the Rain King, 59; Herzog, 64; Humbolt's Gift, 74; auth, The Dean's December, 82; auth, More Die of Heartbreak, 87; auth, A Case of Love, 92; auth, The Acutal, 97. **CONTACT ADDRESS** Boston Univ, 754 Commonwealth Ave, Boston, MA, 02215.

BELTON, JOHN
DISCIPLINE ENGLISH LANGUAGE AND LITERATURE **EDUCATION** Columbia Univ, BA; Harvard Univ, MA; PhD. **CAREER** Prof **RESEARCH** Film theory; cultural studies. **SELECTED PUBLICATIONS** Auth, Widescreen Cinema; auth, America Cinema/American Culture. **CONTACT ADDRESS** Dept of English, Rutgers Univ, 510 George St, Murray Hall, New Brunswick, NJ, 08901-1167.

BEN ZVI, LINDA
DISCIPLINE ENGLISH LITERATURE **EDUCATION** Boston Univ, BA; NY Univ, MA, Univ Okla, PhD. **CAREER** Prof. **RESEARCH** Modern drama; women playwrights; women's studies. **SELECTED PUBLICATIONS** Auth, pubs on modern drama; works of Samuel Beckett. **CONTACT ADDRESS** Dept of English, Colorado State Univ, Fort Collins, CO, 80523. **EMAIL** lbenzvi@vines.colostate.edu

BENARDETE, JANE
PERSONAL Columbus, OH, m, 1961, 2 children **DISCIPLINE** ENGLISH & AMERICAN LITERATURE **EDUCATION** Radcliffe Col, AB, 52, AM, 54, PhD(Hist of Am civilization), 58. **CAREER** Instr hist & lit, Harvard Univ, 58-61; asst prof English, Northeastern Univ, 61-65; asst prof, 65-71, assoc prof, 71- , PROF ENGLISH, HUNTER COL, 82-, City Univ New York grants, 71 & 80. **MEMBERSHIPS** Am Studies Asn. **RESEARCH** American literature, especially 19th century. **SELECTED PUBLICATIONS** Ed, Crumbling Idols, Harvard Univ, 60; auth, Huckleberry Finn and the Nature of Fiction, Mass Rev, Spring 68; ed, American Realism, Putnam, 72; ed, Companions of Our Youth, Ungar, 80. **CONTACT ADDRESS** 31 W 12th St, New York, NY, 10011.

BENDER, CAROL
DISCIPLINE RHETORIC AND MODERN AMERICAN LITERATURE **EDUCATION** Mich State Univ, PhD. **CAREER** Assoc prof, coordr, writing prog, Alma Col. **HONORS AND AWARDS** Sears-Roebuck Tchg Excellence Award; Outstanding Fac Mem in Hum Award. **RESEARCH** Women's and African-American literature. **SELECTED PUBLICATIONS** Her articles have appeared in Lang and Style, Lang Arts J of Mich, Beyond Bindings and Boundaries and several Masterplots reference works. **CONTACT ADDRESS** Alma Col, Alma, MI, 48801.

BENDER, EILEEN TEPER
PERSONAL Born 12/01/1935, Madison, WI, m, 1956, 3 children **DISCIPLINE** AMERICAN LITERATURE, MODERN FICTION **EDUCATION** Northwestern Univ, BSJ, 56; Notre Dame Univ, PhD(English), 77. **CAREER** Assoc lectr English, Ind Univ, South Bend, 66-68, dir grant & spec proj, 76-78, asst chair Arts & Sci, 78-80, actg chair, 80; asst instr English, Yale Univ, 72-73; ASST PROF ENGLISH, NOTRE DAME UNIV, 80-, Mem adv bd, Danforth Found Grad Fel Prog, 78-81; mem, Ind Comt for Humanities, 78-; selection comt, Rhodes Scholar Prog, 79-; consult, Young Fel Sem, Carnegie Corp, 80; selection comt, Charlotte Newcombe Fel Prog, 81- **MEMBERSHIPS** Soc Values Higher Educ; MLA; Danforth Asn. **RESEARCH** Contemporary Amer novelists; modern English and Amer women writers; post contemporary narrative strategies. **SELECTED PUBLICATIONS** Auth, Hist As Womans Game, 'Bellefleur' As Texte De Jouissance, Soundings, Vol 0076, 93. **CONTACT ADDRESS** Indiana Univ, South Bend, S Bend, IN, 46615.

BENDER, NATHAN E.
DISCIPLINE ANTHROPOLOGY, LIBRARY SCIENCE **EDUCATION** Ohio State Univ, BA, 80; Univ Wash, MA, 83; Kent State Univ, MLS, 86. **CAREER** Princ Investigator/Dir, Piatt Park Archeol Proj, 84-85; libr Western Hist Collections, Univ Okla, 86-89; Head, spec collections, Mont State Univ Librs, 89-94; curator, head spec collections, WV Univ Librs, 94-97; curator, McCracker REs Libr, Buffalo Bill Hist Ctr, 97-. **CONTACT ADDRESS** McCracker Research Library, 720 Sheridan Ave, Cody, WY, 82414. **EMAIL** nbender@wavecom.net

BENDER, ROBERT M.
DISCIPLINE ENGLISH **EDUCATION** Univ Mich, PhD, 63. **CAREER** Prof; mem, Women Stud fac & dir, Special Degree Prog; adv bd, Univ Mo Inst Instruct technol. **HONORS AND AWARDS** Led the effort, Univ Mo comput-mediated writing into the classroom. **SELECTED PUBLICATIONS** Ed, The Sonnet, Simon & Schuster, 87; auth essays on, topics relating to Shakespeare, modern drama & women writers. **CONTACT ADDRESS** Dept of English, Univ of Missouri-Columbia, 309 University Hall, Columbia, MO, 65211.

BENDER, TODD K.
PERSONAL Born 01/08/1936, Stark County, OH, m, 1958, 2 children **DISCIPLINE** ENGLISH, CLASSICAL LANGUAGES **EDUCATION** Kenyon Col, BA, 58; Stanford Univ, PhD(class lang & English), 62. **CAREER** Instr English, Stanford Univ, 61-62; instr, Dartmouth Col, 62-63; asst prof, Univ Va, 63-65; assoc prof, 65-73, PROF ENGLISH, UNIV WIS, MADISON, 73-, Am Coun Learned Soc grant-in-aid, Oxford Univ, 63 & fel, Bibliot Nat, Paris, 65-66; Am Philos Soc grant, Paris, 69; vis prof, World Campus Prog, 73; Fulbright lectr, Univ Athens, Greece, 78-79. **MEMBERSHIPS** MLA. **RESEARCH** Nineteenth century English and European literature; Homeric Greek; computational linguistics. **SELECTED PUBLICATIONS** Auth, Conrad,Joseph and the Fictions of Skepticism, Anq--A Quart J of Short Articles Notes and Rev(s), Vol 0006, 93; Conrad Existentialism, Anq--A Quart J of Short Articles Notes and Rev(s), Vol 0006, 93; Hopkins in A Literary Biography, 19th-Century Lit, Vol 0049, 94; Representing Modernist Texts in Editing As Interpretation, Engl Lang Notes, Vol 0031, 94; The Invention of the West in Conrad, Joseph and the Double-Mapping of Europe and Empire, Clio--A J of Lit Hist and the Philos of Hist, Vol 0025, 96; Hopkins Against Hist, Clio--A J of Lite Hist and the Philos of Hist, Vol 0026, 97. **CONTACT ADDRESS** Dept of English, Univ of Wis, Madison, WI, 53706.

BENIGER, JAMES R.
PERSONAL m, 1984, 2 children **DISCIPLINE** COMMUNICATIONS AND SOCIOLOGY **EDUCATION** Harvard Univ, BA; Univ CA at Berkeley, MS, MA, PhD. **CAREER** Assoc prof, Univ Southern CA, 85-; res asst, Bureau Soc Sci Res, WA; lectr, UC-Berkeley; asst prof, Princeton Univ & vis assnt prof, Yale Univ. past consult, Off Technol Assessment, US Cong. **HONORS AND AWARDS** Asn Am Publ award; Phi Kappa Phi Fac Recognition Awd; NY Times Bk Rev, Notable Paperback Yr, 89; Nat Newspaper Fund fel. **MEMBERSHIPS** Past mem ed bd, Publ Opinion Quart, J Commun, Critical Stud in Mass Commun, Commun Theory & Knowledge; past assoce ed, Commun Res & auth, Far Afield; past bd, Overseers Gen Soc Survey, NORC, Univ Chicago & 2 yr elected terms, publ ch & sec-treas, Am Asn Publ Opinion Res. **SELECTED PUBLICATIONS** Auth, The Control Revolution: Technological and Economic Origins of the Information Society, Harvard UP, 86 & Trafficking in Drug Users: Professional Exchange Networks in the Control of Deviance, Cambridge UP, hardcover, 83 & paperback, 84; publ on, technol & soc change, mass media and publ opinion, popular cult & the arts. **CONTACT ADDRESS** Annenberg School for Commun, Univ of Southern California, University Park Campus, Los Angeles, CA, 90089.

BENIS, TOBY RUTH
DISCIPLINE BRITISH ROMANTICISM **EDUCATION** Columbia Univ, PhD. **CAREER** Eng Dept, St. Edward's Univ **SELECTED PUBLICATIONS** Auth, Epic, Sir James Mackintosh, Encyclopedia Romanticism, Garland, 92; Martha Ray's Face: Life During Wartime in Lyrical Ballads, Criticism, 97. **CONTACT ADDRESS** St Edward's Univ, 3001 S Congress Ave, Austin, TX, 78704-6489.

BENKE, ROBIN PAUL
PERSONAL Born 01/30/1953, Trinidad, West Indies, s **DISCIPLINE** LIBRARY SCIENCE **EDUCATION** Hampden-Sydney Col, BA, 75; Peabody Col, Vanderbilt Univ, MLS, 78. **CAREER** Reference librn, 78-88, dir of lib, 88- , Clinch Valley Col, Univ Va. **HONORS AND AWARDS** Clinch Valley Col Outstanding Service Award, 98; Univ Va Harrison Award, 98; Va Educ Media Asn Media Educator of the Year-Higher Educ, 96; Beta Phi Mu; Kappa Delta Pi. **MEMBERSHIPS** ALA; ACRL; AAUP; Va Lib Asn; Va Educ Media Asn. **RESEARCH** College librarianship; school media librarianship. **CONTACT ADDRESS** PO Box 1519, Wise, VA, 24293. **EMAIL** r_benke@clinch.edu

BENNETT, ALMA
DISCIPLINE ENGLISH LITERATURE **EDUCATION** Univ Tex, PhD, 91. **CAREER** Dept Eng, Clemson Univ **RESEARCH** Interdisciplinary humanities; 20th-century American & British literature. **SELECTED PUBLICATIONS** Auth, Mary Gordon, United States Authors Series, Twayne/Simon and Schuster, 96; Featured Event: Ethel Smyth and Argento/Woolf Recital and Freshwater, Virginia Woolf and the Arts: Selected Papers from the Sixth Annual Virginia Woolf Conference, Pace Univ Press, 97; Conversations with Mary Gordon, SC Rev, 95; Mary Gordon; American Writers Series, Scribner's, 96; Pound and the Malatestan Territory: A 1994 Update, Paideuma, 95; The Persistent Presence: Mathematical Language in Literature, Mathematical Connections, 94; coauth, A Selected Discography of Works by Ethel Smyth (1858-44) on Compact Disc, Virginia Woolf and the Arts: Selected Papers from the Sixth Annual Virginia Woolf Conference, Pace UP, 97. **CONTACT ADDRESS** Clemson Univ, 604 Strode, Clemson, SC, 29634. **EMAIL** balma@clemson.edu

BENNETT, BETTY T.
DISCIPLINE LITERATURE **EDUCATION** NY Univ, PhD. **CAREER** Prof, Am Univ. **HONORS AND AWARDS** . **RESEARCH** Romanticism. **SELECTED PUBLICATIONS** Auth, Mary Diana Dods: A Gentleman and a Scholar, co-ed, Mary Shelley Reader; ed, Letters of Mary Wollstonecroft Shelley. **CONTACT ADDRESS** American Univ, 4400 Massachusetts Ave, Washington, DC, 20016.

BENNETT, CARL D.
PERSONAL Born 07/22/1917, Waycross, GA, m, 1942, 3 children **DISCIPLINE** ENGLISH **EDUCATION** Emory Univ, BA, 40, MA, 44, PhD, 62. **CAREER** Instr English, WGA Col, 41-42; asst prof, Wesleyan Col, 44-47; assoc prof, 47-59; prof English, 59-82, chemn Afro-Asian Cultures, 63-67, chemn Hum & Fine Arts Div, 73-78, dist prof English, 82-88, Dist prof English Emer, 88- , St Andrews Presby Col; vis prof Mercer Univ, 48, Seinan Gakuin Univ, Japan, 80-81. **HONORS AND AWARDS** Fulbright-Hays grant, 64; NEH sem, 78. **MEMBERSHIPS** MLA; S Atlantic Mod Lang Asn; AAUP. **RESEARCH** American and English literature; Afro-American and non-Western literatures. **SELECTED PUBLICATIONS** Articles on ethics, on Booth Tarkington, Joseph Conrad, Thomas Hardy, Dorothy Richardson, Ruth Prawer Jhabvala, and Thomas Pynchon; a book of Joseph Conrad. **CONTACT ADDRESS** St Andrews Presbytarian Col, Laurinburg, NC, 28352. **EMAIL** bennettc@tartan.sapc.edu

BENNETT, JAMES RICHARD
PERSONAL Born 03/15/1932, Harrison, AR, m, 1951, 2 children **DISCIPLINE** ENGLISH LITERATURE, HUMANITIES **EDUCATION** Univ Ark, BA, 53, MA, 54; Stanford Univ, PhD(English, humanities), 61. **CAREER** From instr to asst prof English, Mont State Univ, 60-62; asst prof, Western Wash State Col, 62-65; from asst prof to assoc prof, 65-69, PROF ENGLISH, UNIV ARK, FAYETTEVILLE, 69-, CHMN HUMANITIES PROG, 75-, Co-ed, Style, 67-; Fulbright lectr, Yugoslavia, 68-69; mem deleg assembly, MLA, 78-80. **MEMBERSHIPS** NCTE; MLA; Rhetoric Soc Am; Am Civil Liberties Union. **RESEARCH** Nineteenth century literature; style; literature and film. **SELECTED PUBLICATIONS** Auth, After and Beyond New Criticism, Style, Vol 0026, 92; The Politics of Literary Theory, An Introduction to Marxist Criticism, Style, Vol 0027, 93; The Politics of Literary Theory, An Introduction to Marxist Criticism, Style, Vol 0027, 93; The New Criticism and the Corporate State, Cea Critic, Vol 0056, 94; Uncritical Theory in Postmodernism, Intellectuals, and the Gulf-War, Col Lit, Vol 0021, 94; Literature Versus Capitalism, the Criticism of Leavis,F.R., Southern Humanities Rev, Vol 0029, 95; Reading Theory, An Introduction to Lacan, Derrida, and Kristeva, Style, Vol 0029, 95; Reading Theory, An Introduction to Lacan, Derrida, and Kristeva, Style, Vol 0029, 95; Vision in the 'Holy Grail' in Tennyson Theistic Skepticism, Philolog Quart, Vol 0075, 96; Vision in the 'Holy Grail' in Tennyson Theistic Skepticism, Philolog Quart, Vol 0075, 96; Public Broadcasting in the United-States in A Bibliography of Criticism 2, J of Popular Film and Television, Vol 0024, 97; The Public Broadcasting Service in Censorship, Self Censorship,

and the Struggle For Independence, J of Popular Film and Television, Vol 0024, 97. **CONTACT ADDRESS** Dept of English, Univ of Ark, Fayetteville, AR, 72701-1202.

BENNETT, JOHN
PERSONAL Born 03/12/1920, Pittsfield, MA, m, 1960, 2 children **DISCIPLINE** ENGLISH & AMERICAN LITERATURE **EDUCATION** Oberlin Col, BA, 47; Univ wis, MA, 50, PhD, 56. **CAREER** Instr English, Ind Univ, 53-58; asst prof, Beloit Col, 58-59; from assoc prof to prof, Rockford Col, 59-68, chmn dept, 60-68; prof, 68-70, BERNARD H PENNINGS DISTINGUISHED PROF ENGLISH, ST NORBERT COL, 70-, POET-IN-RESIDENCE, 79-, Consult commun, Air War Col, Maxwell AFB, Ala, 51; ed, Beloit Poetry J, 58-72; mem fac adv comt, Ill Bd Higher Educ, 62-68. **HONORS AND AWARDS** Devins Mem Award, 70; Soc Midland Auth Poetry Award, 71 & 78. **MEMBERSHIPS** Melville Soc; Acad Am Poets. **RESEARCH** Herman Melville; modern poetry; creative writing. **SELECTED PUBLICATIONS** Auth, The Struck Leviathan, Univ Mo, 70; Griefs and Exultation, 70 & Knights and Squires, 72, St Norbert; Poems from a Christian enclave, Anglican Theol Rev, 76; Echoes From the Peaceable Kingdom, Eerdmans, 78; Seeds of Mustard, Seed of Tare, 79 & Fire in the Dust, 80, Houghton Col Press; Beyond the Compass Rose, Midwestern Writers Publ House, 82. **CONTACT ADDRESS** 526 Karen Lane, Green Bay, WI, 54301.

BENNETT, PAULA
PERSONAL Born 12/30/1936, Boston, MA, d, 2 children **DISCIPLINE** LITERATURE **EDUCATION** Columbia Univ, PhD, 70. **CAREER** Prof, 91-, Southern IL Univ. **HONORS AND AWARDS** NEH Amer Antiquarian Soc, 96-97; Phi Beta Kappa; Bunting Fel Radcliff Col, 96-97. **MEMBERSHIPS** MCA; NEMCA **RESEARCH** Emily Dickinson; 19th Cent Amer Womens Poetry. **SELECTED PUBLICATIONS** Art, Critical Clitoridectomy Female Sexual Imagery and Feminist Psychoanalytic Theory, Jour of Women I Culture and Soc, 93; auth, Family Plots Pride and Prejudice, in: Appr to Tchng Pride and Prejudice, 93; auth, Gender as Performance Shakespearean Ambiguity and the Lesbian Reader, in: Sex Prac Text Theory Lesbian Cultural Crit, 93; auth, Solitary Pleasures The Historical Literary and Artistic Discourses of Autoeroticism, Routledge, 95; auth, Lesbian Poetry in the United States 1890-1990 A Brief Overview, in: Gay and Lesbian Stud in Lit, 95; auth, Pomegranate Flowers: The Phantasmatic Productions of Late Nineteenth-Century Anglo-American Women Poets, and The Politics of Solitary Pleasures, in: Sol Pleasures the Hist Lit and Art Disc of Autoeroticism, 95; auth, Not Just Filler Not Just Sentimental Womens Poetry in American Victorian Periodicals 1860-1900, in: Period Lit in the Nineteenth Cent Amer, 95; auth, A Sheaf of Late Nineteenth Century American Women Poets, in: Tchrs Guide for the Heath Anth of Amer Lit, 98. **CONTACT ADDRESS** Southern Illin Univ, English Dept, Carbondale, IL, 62901. **EMAIL** pbernat@aol.com

BENOIT, RAYMOND
DISCIPLINE ROMANTICISM **EDUCATION** Univ OR, PhD. **CAREER** Eng Dept, St. Edward's Univ **SELECTED PUBLICATIONS** Auth, Single Nature's Double Name: The Collectedness of the Conflicting in British and American Romanticism, Mouton, 73; An Unpublished Note from Edwin Arlington Robinson to Stewart Beach, ANQ: Quart Jour Short Articles, Notes, & Rev, 93; Young Goodman Brown': The Second Time Around, The Nathaniel Hawthorne Rev, 93; The Existential Intuition of Flannery O'Connor in The Violent Bear it Away, Notes Comp Lit, 93; 'Moss-Picking': An Undergraduate Theme of Theodore Roethke, Eng Lang Notes, 96; Irving's 'The Legend of Sleepy Hollow', Explicator, 96; 'My Estrangement from Nature': An Undergraduate Theme of Theodore Roethke, ANQ: Quart Jour Short Articles, Notes, & Rev, 98. **CONTACT ADDRESS** St Edward's Univ, 3001 S Congress Ave, Austin, TX, 78704-6489.

BENOIT, WILLIAM L.
PERSONAL Born 03/17/1953, New Castle, IN, m, 1974, 1 child **DISCIPLINE** COMMUNICATION **EDUCATION** Ball State Univ, BS, 75; Central Mich Univ, MA, 76; Wayne State Univ, PhD, 75. **CAREER** Fac, Bowling State Green Univ; fac, Miami Univ; prof, Univ of Mo. **HONORS AND AWARDS** Outstanding Academic Book; Gold Chalk Graduate Teaching Award. **MEMBERSHIPS** Nat Commun Assoc; Int Commun Assoc; Am Forensic Assoc. **RESEARCH** Rhetorical theory & criticism; political communication, persuasion. **SELECTED PUBLICATIONS** Auth, Account, excuses, apologies: A theory of image restoration discourse, State Univ of NY Press, 95; co-auth, Candidates in conflict: Persuasive attack and defense in the 1992 presidential debates, University of Alabama Press, 96; co-auth, Effects of ideology and presidential debate watching on attitudes and knowledge, Argumentation & Advocacy, vol 34, 163-72, 98; auth, Merchants of Death: Persuasive defenses by the tobacco industry, Argument in a time of change: Definition, frameworks, and critiques, Speech Commun Assoc, 220-25, 98.co-auth, Campaign 96: A functional analysis of acclaiming, attacking, and defending, (in press). **CONTACT ADDRESS** Commun Dept, Univ Mo, 115 Switzler Hall, Columbia, MO, 65211. **EMAIL** comm4065@showme.missouri.edu

BENREMOUGA, KARIMA
DISCIPLINE COMMUNICATION STUDIES **EDUCATION** Univ Algiers, BA, 84; Univ Kans, MA, 87, PhD, 95. **CAREER** Asst prof, 95-. **RESEARCH** French language and culture; Arabic language and culture; Language methodology; Computer assisted language learning. **SELECTED PUBLICATIONS** Auth, Intoduction to Distance Learning, 97; The Grolier Multimedia Encyclopedia in the ESL Classroom, 96; Can't Say YES and Can't Say NO!, TESOL Jour, 97. **CONTACT ADDRESS** Div of Foreign Languages, Emporia State Univ, 1200 Commercial St, Emporia, KS, 66801-5087.

BENSELER, DAVID P.
DISCIPLINE LITERARY THEORY **EDUCATION** Western Wash Univ, BA, 64; Univ Ore, MA, PhD, 71. **CAREER** English, Case Western Reserve Univ. **HONORS AND AWARDS** Distinguished Grad Mod Langs, Western Wash Univ; Pro Lingua Award, 74; Publs Award, 85; Bundesverdienstkreuz, 85; Army Commendation Medal Outstanding Civilian Service, 88; CWRU Mortar Board's "Top Prof" award, 97., Chair, Dept Mod Lang & Literatures; Found Chair, interdepartmental Degree Prog, German Studies; Asst Chair, Dept Foreign Lang & Lit, Wash State Univ; Chair Dept German, Ohio State Univ; Ed, Mod Lang Jour, Distinguished Vis Prof For Lang US Military Acad, West Point, NY, NMex State Univ. **MEMBERSHIPS** Washington (State) Asn For Lang Tchrs; American Asn Tchrs German; Pacific Northwest Coun For Lang; Central States Conf Tchng For Lang; Joint Nat Comt on Lang; Nat Coun German Studies; Nat Fed Mod Lang Tchrs Asn. **SELECTED PUBLICATIONS** Auth The Dynamics of Language Program Direction (Heinle & Heinle, 1993) and Teaching German in America: Prolegomena to a History (Univ. of Wisconsin Press, 1988. **CONTACT ADDRESS** Case Western Reserve Univ, 10900 Euclid Ave, Cleveland, OH, 44106. **EMAIL** dpb5@po.cwru.edu

BENSMAN, MARVIN ROBERT
PERSONAL Born 09/18/1937, Two Rivers, WI, m, 1965, 2 children **DISCIPLINE** MASS COMMUNICATIONS, LAW **EDUCATION** Univ WI, Madison, BA, 60, MS, 64, PhD, 69; Memphis State Univ, JD, 81. **CAREER** Teacher speech, West High Sch, Green Bay, WI, 60-62 & North High Sch, Sheboygan, WI, 62-63; instr mass commun, Univ VT, 67-69; asst prof, 69-73, assoc prof Mass Commun, Memphis State Univ , 73-85; FULL PROF, UNIV OF MEMPHIS, 85-. **MEMBERSHIPS** Broadcast Educ Asn; Southern Speech Commun Asn; Radio Hist Soc Am. **RESEARCH** History of broadcasting; archival audio materials; survey research. **SELECTED PUBLICATIONS** Auth, WJAZ-Zenith Case and the Chaos of 1926, fall 70 & coauth, Broadcasting-film Academic Budgets 1971-1972, summer 71, J Broadcasting; co-ed, History of Radio-Television Collection, Arno, 71; coauth, Broadcasting-film Academic Budgets-Updated 1973-74, J Broadcasting, summer 74; Sources of Broadcast Audio Programming (microfiche), ERIC/RCS Clearinghouse, 75; contribr, Regulation of broadcasting by the Department of Commerce, 1921-1927, In: Source Book on History of Radio-Television, 75; Obtaining Old Radio Programs, J Popular Cult, 79; co-auth, Radio Themes Recognition Test, on long-term memory, with Dr Thomas Crook, Head, Center for Aging, Nat Institute of Mental Health, Bethesda, MD, 80; auth, Selected Legal Decisions of 1981, J of Broadcasting, Vol 26:2, spring 82; Broadcast Regulation: Selected Cases and Decisions, Univ Press of Am, DC, 1st ed, 83, 2nd ed, 85 (designated Best Seller by Univ Press); Victor H. Laughter: Radio Pioneer, Tn Speech Commun J, fall 85; The Differences Between Broadcast and Journalism Law, Feedback, Broadcast Education Asn, Vol 27:2, 85; Book of Days, sections on Radio and Television technology and regulation, Pierus Pubs, Ann Arbor, MI, 87; Broadcast/Cable Regulation, Univ Press of Am, DC, 90; The Preservation of Electronic Media Archives, forward of book, Re-runs On File: A Guide to Electronic Media Archives, Lawrence Erlbaum & Assoc, fall 91; Radio Broadcast Programming for Research and Teaching, J of Radio Studies, spring 93; Encyclopedia of Popular Culture, ed Frank Chorba, three articles on Broadcast Archives and Programming, Greenwood Press, forthcoming 98; Historical Dictionary of American Radio, ed Donald G. Godfrey and Frederic A. Leigh, ten articles on early radio regulation and personalities, Greenwood Press, forthcoming 98. **CONTACT ADDRESS** Dept Commun, Univ of Memphis, Campus box 5265, Memphis, TN, 38152-0001. **EMAIL** mbensman@memphis.edu

BENSON, JACKSON J.
PERSONAL Born 09/02/1930, San Francisco, CA, m, 1960, 2 children **DISCIPLINE** CONTEMPORARY AMERICAN LITERATURE **EDUCATION** Stanford Univ, AB, 52; San Francisco State Univ, MA, 56; Univ Southern Calif, PhD(English), 66. **CAREER** Assoc prof English, Orange Coast Col, 56-66; from asst prof to assoc prof, 66-72, PROF AM LIT, SAN DIEGO STATE UNIV, 72-, Consult, San Diego City Schs, 67-68; Nat Endowment for Humanities grant, 70; Am Philos Soc grant, 71; Nat Endowment for Humanities fel, 78-79. **MEMBERSHIPS** MLA; Am Stud Asn. **RESEARCH** Ernest Hemingway; John Steinbeck. **SELECTED PUBLICATIONS** Auth, Where the Old West Met the New--Stegner, Wallace 1909-1993, Montana-Mage of Western Hist, Vol 0043, 93; Stegner, Wallace 1909-1993/, Western Amer Literature, Vol 0028, 93; Finding A Voice of His Own in the Story of Stegner, Wallace Fiction, Western Amer Lit, Vol 0029, 94; A Friendship With Consequences in Frost,Robert and Stegner, Wallace, SDak Rev, Vol 0034, 96. **CONTACT ADDRESS** Dept of English, San Diego State Univ, San Diego, CA, 92182.

BENSON, LARRY DEAN
PERSONAL Born 06/20/1929, SD, m, 1951, 4 children **DISCIPLINE** ENGLISH **EDUCATION** Univ Calif, Berkeley, AB, 54, MA, 56, PhD, 59 Hon Degree: MA, Harvard Univ, 65. **CAREER** From instr to assoc prof, 59-69, PROF ENGLISH, HARVARD UNIV, 69-, Asst ed, Speculum, 66- **MEMBERSHIPS** Mediaeval Acad Am; Int Arthurian Soc. **RESEARCH** Old and middle English literature. **SELECTED PUBLICATIONS** Auth, Art and Tradition in Sir Gawain and the Green Knight, Rutgers Univ, 65; The literary character of Anglo-Saxon formulaic verse, PMLA, 10/66; The pagan coloring of Beowulf, In: Old English Poetry, Brown Univ, 67; The originality of Beowulf, In: The Interpretation of Narrative: Theory and Practice, Harvard Univ, 70; co-ed, The Literary Context of Chaucer's Fabliaux, 71 & ed, King Arthur's Death, The Middle English Alliterative Morte Arthure and Stanzaic Morte Arthur, 74, Bobbs; ed, The Learned and the Lewed, 75 & auth, Malory's Morte D'Arthur, 76, Harvard Univ; ed The Riverside Chaucer, 87. **CONTACT ADDRESS** Libr, Harvard Univ, 271 Widener Lib, Cambridge, MA, 02138-3800. **EMAIL** ldb@wjh.harvard.edu

BENSON, MORRIS
PERSONAL Born 12/01/1927, Bombay, India, w, 1 child **DISCIPLINE** ENGLISH LITERATURE **EDUCATION** Univ Bombay, BA, 47, MA, 49; Agra Univ, MA, 51, MC, 52; Syracuse Univ, PhD(English), 73. **CAREER** Chmn humanities, Nat Defence Acad, India, 49-53; sr lectr English, French & Ger & head dept English, Sch Mines, Agra Univ, 53-57; sr master English & French, Lister County Tech Sch, Eng, 57-58; lectr English, French & Ger, Univ Saarland, 58-60; prof English & Ger, Al-Tahrir Col, Univ Baghdad, 60-63; assoc prof English, Stephens Col, 63-64; head dept English, Dept Educ, Saudi Arabia, 64-65; sr lectr English & French, Medway Col Technol & Watford Col Technol, Eng, 65-67; prof, 67-76, DISTINGUISHED TEACHING PROF & PROF ENGLISH, STATE UNIV NY AGR & TECH COL, MORRISVILLE, 77- **MEMBERSHIPS** AAUP; MLA. **RESEARCH** Renaissance; 20th century post-Ibsenian existentialist literature; economic determinism and cultural change. **SELECTED PUBLICATIONS** Auth, The Champagne of Comedy, 47, A Critical Study of Galsworthy's Man of Property, 49 & How to Become a Master of English, 50, Browne Publ, Poona, India; Erring Othello, 71 & Renaissance Archetypes: the Long Shadows, 72, Coleman, London. **CONTACT ADDRESS** Div of Lib Arts, State Univ NY, Morrisville, NY, 13408.

BENSON, RICHARD LEE
PERSONAL Born 12/12/1930, Brawley, CA, m, 1958, 5 children **DISCIPLINE** DRAMA, SPEECH **EDUCATION** Univ Calif, Los Angeles, BA, 58; Univ Ill, Urbana, MA, 62, PhD(theatre), 68. **CAREER** From instr to asst prof drama, Beloit Col, 62-69; PROF SPEECH & THEATRE ARTS & CHMN DEPT, EASTERN KY UNIV, 69- **MEMBERSHIPS** Speech Commun Asn. **RESEARCH** Shakespearean promptbooks; Amer theatre history. **SELECTED PUBLICATIONS** Auth, A Trubute to Bowman, TCI, Vol 0027, 93. **CONTACT ADDRESS** Dept of Speech & Theatre Arts, Eastern Kentucky Univ, Richmond, KY, 40475.

BENSON, THOMAS W.
PERSONAL Born 01/25/1937, Abington, PA, m, 1960, 2 children **DISCIPLINE** SPEECH **EDUCATION** Hamilton Col, AB, 58; Cornell Univ, MA, 61, PhD, 66. **CAREER** 63-71, SUNY, Buffalo NY; 71-, Edwin Erle Sparks Prof of Rhetoric, 90-, Penn St Univ. **HONORS AND AWARDS** Eastern Comm Asn Scholar, 82-83; Robert A Kibler Mem Award, Speech Comm Asn, 83; Meritorious Svc Award, Eastern Comm Asn, 87; Dist Res Fel, Eastern Comm Asn, 98; Presidential Citation, Natl Comm Asn, 97; Douglas Ehninger Dist Rhetorical Scholar Award, Natl Comm Asn, 97; Dist Scholar Award, Natl Comm Asn, 97. **MEMBERSHIPS** Speech Comm Asn; Intl Comm Asn; Eastern Comm Asn; Rhetoric Soc of Amer; Speech Comm Asn of PA; Univ Film and Video Asn; Soc for Cinema Studies; Intl Soc for the History of Rhetoric. **RESEARCH** Rhetorical theory and criticism; political comm; media criticism. **SELECTED PUBLICATIONS** Ed, Landmark Essays on Rhetorical Criticism, Hermagoras Press, 93; coauth, The Freeing of Ticut Follies, Free Speech Yearbook 1992, Southern IL Univ Press, 93; coauth, Put Down the Camera and Pick up the Shovel An Interview with John Marshall, The Cinema of John Marshall, Academic Pub, 93; cuth, Beacons and Boundary Markers Landmarks in Rhetorical Criticism, Landmark Essays on Rhetorical Criticism, Hermagoras Press, 93; auth, Rhetorical Structure and Primate in Critical Questions Invention Creativity and the Criticism of Discourse and Media, St Martins, 94; auth, On the Margins of Technology, Technology Studies 1, 94; auth, The First E-Mail Election Electronic Networking and the Clinton Campaign, Bill Clinton on Stump State and Stage The Rhetorical Road to the White House, Univ of AR Press, 94; auth, Electronic Network Resources for Communication Scholars, Comm Ed, 94; auth, Longinus On the Sublime, Encycl of Rhet-

oric and Composition, Garland, 96; auth, Forward to Donn Abbott Rhetoric in the New World, Univ of SC Press, 96; auth, Desktop Demos New Communication Technologies and the Future of the Rhetorical Presidency, Beyond the Rhetorical Presidency, TX A&M Univ Press, 96; art, Computers Communication and Community, New Dimensions in Communication, Speech Comm Asn, 96; art, Rhetoric, Civility and Community Political Debate on Computer Bulletin Boards, Comm Quart 44,96; auth, ed, Rhetoric and political Culture in Nineteenth-Century America, MI St Univ Press, 97; auth, Looking for the Public in the Private American Lives UnAmerican Activities, Rhetoric and Public Affairs 1, 98; art, To Lend a Hand Gerald Ford Watergate and the White House Speechwriters, Rhetoric and Public Affairs, 98. **CONTACT ADDRESS** Pennsylvania State Univ, 227 Sparks Building, University Park, PA, 16802. **EMAIL** t3b@psu.edu

BENSTOCK, SHARI
PERSONAL Born 12/04/1944, San Diego, CA, s, 1 child **DISCIPLINE** ENGLISH **EDUCATION** Drake University, BA, 67, Drake University, MA, 70, Kent State University, PhD, 75. **CAREER** Inst, Dept English, Drake University, 70-72; teaching fel, Dept English, Kent State University, 72-74; admin asst to head, Dept of Polit Sci, 75-77, Admin Assoc, Med Schol Prog, Col Med, University IL at Urbana-Champaign; fel, Am Asn Univ Women, 81-82; associate prof English, Univ Tulsa, 82-86, dir, Tulsa Ctr for the Study of Women's Lit, 82-86; assoc prof, 86-87, prof, English and Women's Studies, Univ Miami, 88-, founding dir, Women's Studies Program, 87-90, chair, Dept English, 96-; Lamont Prof, Union Col, Spring 93. **HONORS AND AWARDS** Fel, Asn Univ Women, 81-82; Univ Ill, Res Bd, 81; Univ Tulsa Res Grants, 84, 85; Univ Miami Summer Res Grants, 88, 89, 95; Humanities Res Ctr, Univ Texas, Austin, 89; Rockefeller Found Fel, Bellagio Study Ctr, 90; Ball Brothers Fel, Ind Univ, 91; Donald C. Gallop Fel, Yale Univ, 91; NEH Sr Fel, 93-94; Phi Kappa Phi; Golden Key Honor Soc. **MEMBERSHIPS** Mod Lang Asn; Am Studies Asn; James Joyce Int Found; Int Comp Lit Asn; Am Asn Univ Women; MLA Women's Caucus; Edith Wharton Soc; Virginia Woolf Soc. **RESEARCH** Expatriate studies; gender studies; modernism; biography; autobiography. **SELECTED PUBLICATIONS** Coauth, Who's He When He's at Home: a James Joyce Directory, Univ Ill Press, 80; ed, Feminist Issues in Literary Scholarship, Ind Univ Press, 87; auth, Women of the Left Bank: Paris, 1900-1940, Univ Tex Press, 86; auth, Textualizing the Feminine: On the Limits of Genre, Univ Okla Press, 91; ed, Edith Wharton: The House of Mirth, St Martin's Press, 93; auth, No Gifts from Chance: A Biography of Edith Wharton, Charles Scribner's Sons, 94; co-ed, On Fashion, Rutgers Univ Press, 94; author of numerous articles and other publications. **CONTACT ADDRESS** Dept English, Univ Miami, Coral Gables, FL, 33124. **EMAIL** sbenstock@umiami.iv.miami.edu

BENTLEY, D. M. R.
PERSONAL Born 08/14/1947;, Kitale, Kenya, m, 1972 **DISCIPLINE** ENGLISH CANADIAN STUDIES **EDUCATION** Univ Victoria, BC, BA Hons, 69; Univ Paris, Sorbonne, Cert, 69; Dalhousie Univ, MA, 70; Univ London, PhD(English), 74; Carleton Univ, MA, 77. **CAREER** ASSOC PROF ENGLISH, UNIV WESTERN ONT, 78-, Co-ed, J Can Poetry: Stud, Documents, Rev, 77-; Soc Sci Humanities Res Coun Can fel, 81. **HONORS AND AWARDS** Monetary Award, Ont Arts Coun, 76. **MEMBERSHIPS** Asn Can Univ Teachers English; Fel Royal Soc Arts; Econ Res Coun, Eng. **RESEARCH** Victorian literature: Canadian literature; modern literature. **SELECTED PUBLICATIONS** Auth, The Borders of Nightmare in the Fiction of Richardson, John, Univ Toronto Quart, Vol 0063, 93; Parley,Peter and the Rossettis, Engl Lang Notes, Vol 0031, 93; the Wide Circle and Return, 'Tay John' and Vico, Dalhousie Rev, Vol 0073, 93; the 'Canadian Brothers Or the Prophecy Fulfilled in A Tale of the Late Amer War', Univ Toronto Quart, Vol 0063, 93; Scott,Duncan,Campbell and Maeterlinck,Maurice, Stud in Can Lit-Stud En Lit Can, Vol 0021, 96; The 'Last of England', the Literature of Emigration, and the Pathos of the Subject Brown, Ford, Maddox, Pre-Raphaelite Painting, J Pre Raphaelite Stud New Series, Vol 0005, 96; Roberts, Charles, G.D. and Campbell, William, Wilfred As Canadian Tour Guides 19th-Century Travel Writing, J Can Stud Revue D Etudes Canadiennes, Vol 0032, 97. **CONTACT ADDRESS** Dept of English, Univ Western Ont, London, ON, N6A 3K7.

BENTLEY, ERIC
PERSONAL Born 09/14/1916, England, m, 2 children **DISCIPLINE** DRAMA, COMPARATIVE LITERATURE **EDUCATION** Oxford Univ, BA, 38, BLitt, 39; Yale Univ, PhD, 41. **CAREER** Matthews prof dramatic lit, Columbia Univ, 54-69; CORNELL PROF THEATRE, STATE UNIV NY BUFFALO, 77-82, Guggenheim fel, 48-49 & 67-68; Charles Eliot Norton prof poetry, Harvard Univ, 60-61; ed, Works of Brecht, Grove Press, 60-67; Ford Found artist in residence, Berlin, 64-65. **HONORS AND AWARDS** Longview Award, 60; George Nathan Prize, 67; Obie, 78; inducted into the Theatre Hall of Fame, New York, 98., DFA, Univ Wis, 75; DLitt, Univ East Anglia, UK, 79. **MEMBERSHIPS** Fel Am Acad Arts & Sci; PEN Club; Am Acad of Arts and Letters; **RESEARCH** Literary record albums; poetry and songs. **SELECTED PUBLICATIONS** Auth, The Life of the Drama, 64; The Theatre of Commitment, 67; Theatre of War, 72; The Recantation, 72; Are You Now Or Have You Ever Been, 72; Rallying Cries, Three Plays, New Repub Bks, 77; Lord Alfred's Lover (play), Can Theatre ,Rev, 78; The Brecht Commentaries, Grove Press, 81; auth, The Kleist Variations, 81; auth, Monstrous Martyrdoms, 85; auth, Bentley on Brecht, 98. **CONTACT ADDRESS** 194 Riverside Dr, Ste 4E, New York, NY, 10025-7259.

BENTLEY, GERALD E., JR.
PERSONAL Born 08/23/1930, Chicago, IL **DISCIPLINE** LITERATURE **EDUCATION** Princeton Univ, BA, 52; Oxford Univ, BLitt, 54, DPhil, 56. **CAREER** Tchr, Univ Chicago, 56-60; fac mem to prof, Eng, Univ Toronto, 60-96, (RETIRED); tchr, Univ d'Alger (Algeria), 67-68; tchr, Univ Poona (India), 75-76; vis prof, Fudan Univ (China), 82-83, 88; vis prof, Univ Col, Swansea, 85; vis prof, Univ Hyderabad (India), 88; vis res prof, Princeton Univ, 92; vis res fel, Merton Col, Oxford, 93; vis res fel, Hatfield Col, Durham Univ, 96. **HONORS AND AWARDS** Guggenheim fel, 58-59; Can Coun fel, 63-64, 70-71, 77-78; SSHRC fel, 82-85, 91-94, 95-99; Harold White fel, Nat Libr Australia, 89; Fulbright lectr, 67-68, 75-76, 82-83; Connaught fel, 91-92; Rockefeller Found, Bellagio fel, 91; Jenkins Award Bibliog, 79; fel, Royal Soc Can, 86. **MEMBERSHIPS** MLA; Bibliog Soc; Oxford Bibliog Soc; Conf Ed Problems. **RESEARCH** 18th century literature; William Blake. **SELECTED PUBLICATIONS** Auth, The Early Engravings of Flaxman's Classical Designs, 64; auth, Blake Records, 69; auth, The Blake Collection of Mrs. Landon K. Thorne, 71; auth, William Blake: The Critical Heritage, 75; auth, A Bibliography of George Cumberland, 75; auth, Blake Books, 77; auth, Blake Records Supplement, 88; auth, Blake Studies in Japan, 94; auth, Blake Books Supplement, 95; ed, William Blake's Vala or the Four Zoas, 63; ed, Tiriel (Blake), 67; ed, America (Blake), 74; ed, Editing Eighteenth Century Novels, 75; ed, Europe (Blake), 75; ed, William Blake's Writings, 2 vols, 78; ed, William Blake's Writings in Conventional Typography, 84; ed, The Captive of the Castle of Sennaar (George Cumberland), 91. **CONTACT ADDRESS** 246 MacPherson Ave, Toronto, ON, M4V 1A2.

BENTMAN, RAYMOND
PERSONAL Born 07/09/1925, Philadelphia, PA, 2 children **DISCIPLINE** ENGLISH LITERATURE **EDUCATION** Kenyon Col, BA, 50; Univ Pa, MA, 51; Yale Univ, PhD , 61. **CAREER** Instr English, Univ Mich, 59-60 and Univ NC, 60-61; from instr to assoc prof, 61-70, PROF ENGLISH, TEMPLE UNIV, 70-, Am Philos Soc grant-in-aid, 68. **MEMBERSHIPS** MLA. **RESEARCH** Satire; 18th century British literature. **SELECTED PUBLICATIONS** Auth, Premodern and Postmodern Discourses, Vol 1, Enlightenment Crossings, Vol 2, Enlightenment Borders, Vol 3, Perilous Enlightenment, Scriblerian Kit Cats, Vol 0025, 92; Narrative Transvestism, Scriblerian Kit Cats, Vol 0025, 93. **CONTACT ADDRESS** Dept of English, Temple Univ, Philadelphia, PA, 19118.

BENTON, RICHARD PAUL
PERSONAL Born 08/24/1914, Everett, PA, m, 1941 **DISCIPLINE** ENGLISH **EDUCATION** Johns Hopkins Univ, BS, 52, MA, 53, PhD (aesthet of lit), 55. **CAREER** Draftsman-eng, Pa RR Co, 40-52; jr instr writing, Johns Hopkins Univ, 53-54; from instr to asst prof English, 55-71, ASSOC PROF ENGLISH, TRINITY COL, CONN, 71- **MEMBERSHIPS** NCTE; MLA; Int Soc Gen Semantics; Keats-Shelley Asn Am. **RESEARCH** British romantics; Victorians; Chinese literature. **SELECTED PUBLICATIONS** Auth, The German Face of Poe, Edgar, Allan--A Study of Literary References in his Works, Poe Stud Dark Romanticism, Vol 0028, 95; Poe the Cask of Amontillado--Its Cultural and Historical Backgrounds, Poe Stud Dark Romanticism, Vol 0029, 96. **CONTACT ADDRESS** Dept of English, Trinity Col, Hartford, CT, 06106.

BENTON, ROBERT MILTON
PERSONAL Born 07/06/1932, Braidwood, IL, m, 1956 **DISCIPLINE** ENGLISH **EDUCATION** Trinity Univ, BA, 54; Univ Colo, MA, 63, PhD (English), 67. **CAREER** Teaching assoc English, Univ Colo, 63-66, instr, 66-67; from asst prof to assoc prof, 67-77, PROF ENGLISH, CENT WASH UNIV, 77- **MEMBERSHIPS** MLA; John Steinbeck Soc Am; Pac Northwest Am Studies Asn; Western Lit Asn. **RESEARCH** Colonial American literature; environmental literature; John Steinbeck. **SELECTED PUBLICATIONS** Auth, A New Study Guide to Steinbeck Major Works, With Critical Explications, Western Am Lit, Vol 0029, 95; Steinbeck, John Fiction Revisited, Western Am Lit, Vol 0032, 97; Refuge--An Unnatural History of Family and Place, Western Am Lit, Vol 0028, 93; Parallel Expeditions--Darwin, Charles and the Art of Steinbeck, John, Western Am Lit, Vol 0032, 97; After the Grapes of Wrath--Essays on Steinbeck, John in Honor of Hayashi, Tetsumaro, Western Am Lit, Vol 0032, 97; The Steinbeck Question--New Essays in Criticism, Western Am Lit, Vol 0029, 95; Steinbeck, John--A Biography, Western Am Lit, Vol 0032, 97; American Nature Writing, 1994, Western Am Lit, Vol 0030, 95. **CONTACT ADDRESS** Dept of English, Central Washington Univ, Ellensburg, WA, 98926.

BERAN, CAROL L.
PERSONAL Born 01/29/1944, Brooklyn, NY, m, 1968, 2 children **DISCIPLINE** ENGLISH **EDUCATION** Susquehanna Univ, BA, 66; Johns Hopkins Univ, MAT, 67; Univ Calif, Berkeley, PhD, 77. **CAREER** Prof Eng, St Mary's Col, 77- . **HONORS AND AWARDS** Can Embassy St Fel Award, 91-92. **MEMBERSHIPS** Asn for Can Stud in the US; Western Soc Sci Asn; Margaret Atwood Soc; Margaret Laurence Soc; Soc for the Study of Narrative Lit. **RESEARCH** Canadian literature. **SELECTED PUBLICATIONS** Auth, Margaret Atwood's Life Before Man, ECW Press, 93; auth, The End of the World and Other Things, in Wilson, ed, Approaches to Teaching Atwood's The Handmaid's Tale; auth, The Studhorse Man: Translating the Boundaries of Text, Great Plains Q; auth, Intertexts of Margaret Atwood's Life Before Man, Am Rev of Can Stud; auth, Functional Ethnicity in Atwood's Life Before Man, Essays on Can Writing; auth, George, Leda, and a Poured Concrete Balcony: A Study of Three Aspects of the Evolution of Lady Oracle, Can Lit. **CONTACT ADDRESS** St Mary's Col, PO Box 4336, Moraga, CA, 94575-4336. **EMAIL** cberan@stmarys.ca.edu

BERETS, RALPH ADOLPH
PERSONAL Born 00/00/1939, Amersfoort, Netherlands, m, 1963, 3 children **DISCIPLINE** MODERN FICTION, FILM **EDUCATION** Univ Mich, BA & MA, 63, PhD(English), 69. **CAREER** Lectr Engineering English, Univ Mich, 69-70; Asst Prof Film, Kansas City Art Inst, 71-76; Asst Prof, 70-76, assoc prof English, Univ Mo Kansas City 76-, Chm English Dept 89-. **MEMBERSHIPS** MLA; Midwest Mod Lang Asn; ACA; Nat Coun, Teachers of English; Asn of Dept of English; Am Film Inst; Popular Culture Asn. **RESEARCH** Comparative literature; modern fiction; film; film and the law; ethics and the humanities; the literature of death and dying; from fiction into film; screenwriting; contemporary novel. **SELECTED PUBLICATIONS** Auth, The Magus: A Study in the Creation of a Personal Myth, Twentieth Century Lit, 4/73.; Van Eyck's The Just Judges in Camus' The Fall, Res Studies, 6/74; John Fowles, An Overview, Reader's Encycl of English Lit, 75; Repudiation and Reality Instruction in Saul Bellow's Fiction, Centennial Rev, Winter 76; Why Is There So Much Violence in Contemporary Films?, J of the Producers Guild of Am, 76; Saul Bellow, Contemporary Lit Criticism, Gale Research, X, 79; Changing Images of Justice in American Films, Legal Studies forum, XX, 96; From Real to Reel: The Depiction of Lawyers in Film, Legal Studies Forum, 97; Seeing the Holocaust Through Recent Films, publ on CD-ROM in the 1996 issue of ISSEI Journal, MIT Univ Press, 98; author of numerous other published articles. **CONTACT ADDRESS** Dept of English, Univ of Mo, 5100 Rockhill Rd., Kansas City, MO, 64110-2499. **EMAIL** rberets@umkc.edu

BERG, DAVID M.
DISCIPLINE INFLUENCE OF MASS COMMUNICATION ON CONTEMPORARY SOCIETY **EDUCATION** Minn, PhD, 63. **CAREER** Prof, Purdue Univ. **RESEARCH** The way in which media affect traditional forms of public communication such as political speaking. **SELECTED PUBLICATIONS** Auth, Rhetoric, reality, and mass media, Quart J of Speech, 72; coauth, Crisis management and the paradigm case, Rhetorical and Critical Approaches to Public Relations, Erlbaum, 92. **CONTACT ADDRESS** Dept of Commun, Purdue Univ, 1080 Schleman Hall, West Lafayette, IN, 47907-1080.

BERG, MAGGIE
DISCIPLINE ENGLISH LITERATURE **EDUCATION** Oxford Univ, DPhil. **CAREER** Dept Eng, Queen's Univ **RESEARCH** Victorian literature; literary theory; feminist theory. **SELECTED PUBLICATIONS** Auth, Jane Eyre: Portrait of a Life, G.K. Hall, 87; Wuthering Heights: The Writing in the Margin, G.K. Hall, 96; Escaping the Cave: Luce Irigaray and Her Feminist Critics, 88; Luce Irigaray and the 'Contradictions' of Poststructuralism and Feminism, J Women Cult Soc, 91. **CONTACT ADDRESS** English Dept, Queen's Univ, Kingston, ON, K7L N6. **EMAIL** bergm@qsilver.queensu.ca

BERGER, ARTHUR A.
PERSONAL Born 01/03/1933, Boston, MA, m, 1961, 2 children **DISCIPLINE** COMMUNICATIONS **EDUCATION** Univ of Mass, BA, 54; Univ of Iowa, MA, 56; Univ of Minn, PhD, 65. **CAREER** English and Am studies, 60-65; Fulbright lectr, Univ of Milan, 63-64; vis prof, Annenberg School for Commun, Univ of Southern Calif, 84-85; Prof, San Francisco State Univ, 65-. **HONORS AND AWARDS** Fulbright, 63-64. **RESEARCH** Communication; American culture; media criticism; cultural studies; popular culture; semiotics; humor. **SELECTED PUBLICATIONS** Auth, Blind Men & Elephants: Perspectives on Humor, Transaction, 95; Cultural Criticism: A Primer of Key Concepts, SAGE, 95; Essentials of Mass Communication Theory, SAGE, 95; Manufacturing Desire: Media, Popular Culture & Everyday Life, Transaction 96; The Genius of the Jewish Joke, Jason Aronson, 97; Bloom's Morning, Westview/Harper Collins, 97; The Art of Comedy Writing, Transaction 97; Postmortem for a Postmodernist, AltaMira, 97; The Postmodern Presence, AltaMira, 98. **CONTACT ADDRESS** Dept of Broadcast and Electronic Communication Arts, San Francisco State univ, San Francisco, CA, 94132. **EMAIL** aberger@sfsu.edu

BERGER, SIDNEY L.
PERSONAL Born 01/25/1936, New York, NY, m, 1963, 2 children **DISCIPLINE** THEATRE **EDUCATION** Brooklyn Col, BA, 57; Univ Ks, MA, 60, PhD, 64; **CAREER** Asst instr, Univ Ks, 58-63; asst prof to assoc prof, Mich St Univ, 64-69; prof, dir, Univ Houston, 69- . **HONORS AND AWARDS** All-Univ res grants, 67, 68; tour awards to Asia, Greenland, Iceland, Europe, Amer Theatre Assoc, Dept of Defense, 60, 63, 68, 72, 85; Nat Theatre Conf; Silver Award, Houston Int Film Festival, 89, 93; Outstanding Accomplishments in the Arts, 89, 93; Who's Who. **MEMBERSHIPS** Amer Theatre Assoc; Houston Coal for the Arts; Theatre & Film Prof Adv Bd, Univ Ks. **SELECTED PUBLICATIONS** Auth, Sweeney Todd, opera cues, 84; The Great Globe Itself, standpoints, 88; Contemporary American Theatre, standpoints, 89; coauth, The Theatre Team, 97; coed, The Playwright Versus the Director, Greenwood Press, 94;. **CONTACT ADDRESS** 4711 Imogene, Houston, TX, 77096.

BERGER, THOMAS LELAND
PERSONAL Born 03/26/1941, Oak Park, IL, 3 children **DISCIPLINE** ENGLISH LITERATURE, DRAMA **EDUCATION** Dartmouth Col, BA, 63; Duke Univ, MA, 67, PhD (English), 69. **CAREER** Instr English, Univ NC, Chapel Hill, 69-70; fel Macalester Col, 70-71; asst prof, 71-76, assoc prof, 76-80, PROF ENGLISH, ST LAWRENCE UNIV, 80-, Fac, Col Level Exam Prog, NY State Educ Dept. **MEMBERSHIPS** MLA; Shakespeare Asn Am; Renaissance Soc Am; Malone Soc. **RESEARCH** English Renaissance drama; bibliography and textual criticism. **SELECTED PUBLICATIONS** Auth, Casting Shakespeare Plays--London Actors and Their Roles, 1590-1642, Mod Lang Rev, Vol 0089, 94; Shakespeare Reread--The Texts in New Contexts, Renaissance Quart, Vol 0050, 97. **CONTACT ADDRESS** Dept of English, St Lawrence Univ, Canton, NY, 13617-1499.

BERGERON, DAVID M.
PERSONAL Born 02/08/1938, Alexandria, LA, m, 1966 **DISCIPLINE** ENGLISH **EDUCATION** La Col, BA, 60; Vanderbilt Univ, MA, 62, PhD, 64. **CAREER** Asst prof, Eng, Univ Louisville, 64-68; assoc prof, Eng, Univ New Orleans, 68-76; PROF, ENG, UNIV KANSAS, 76-. **HONORS AND AWARDS** Woodrow Wilson Fel, 60; ACLS Fel, 68-69; Folger Shakespeare Libr, summer Fel ACLS, Grant-in-Aid, 76. **MEMBERSHIPS** Shakespeare Asn of Am; Renaissance Soc Am; Mod Lang Asn. **RESEARCH** Shakespeare, Renaissance drama; British history (Stuarts). **SELECTED PUBLICATIONS** Auth, Shakespeare: A Study and Research Guide, 95; Reading and Writing in Shakespeare, 96; King James and Letters of Homoerotic Desire, 99. **CONTACT ADDRESS** Dept of English, Univ of Kansas, Lawrence, KS, 66045. **EMAIL** bergeron@kuhub.cc.ukans.edu

BERGGREN, PAULA S.
PERSONAL Born 07/10/1942, New York, NY, m, 1968 **DISCIPLINE** ENGLISH RENAISSANCE LITERATURE, ENGLISH POETRY & DRAMA, WORLD LITERATURE **EDUCATION** Barnard Col, AB, 63; Yale Univ, MA, 64, PhD(English), 67. **CAREER** Asst prof English, Yale Univ, 67-72; asst prof, 72-80, from assoc prof to prof English, Baruch Col, 81-86. **HONORS AND AWARDS** Recipient of Presidential Award for Distinguished Service, May 98; Nominated for Presidential Award for Distinguished Service, 97, 95; Inducted as Honorary Member, Golden Key National Honor Society, Fall, 96. **MEMBERSHIPS** MLA. **RESEARCH** Jacobean drama; female image in English and American literature. **SELECTED PUBLICATIONS** Auth, A lost soul: Work without hope, Awakening, Regionalism and Female Imagination, Spring 77; Womanish' mankind: Four Jacobean Heroines, Int J Women's Studies, 7/78 & 8/78; The wound in the thigh: The persistance of parody in Shakespeare's 1 Henry IV, Iowa English Bull, Fall 78; Spatial imagery in Webster's tragedies, Studies English Lit, Spring 80; The woman's part: Female sexuality as power in Shakespeare's plays, In: The Woman's Part: Feminist Criticism of Shakespeare, Univ Ill Press, 80; A prodigious thing: The Jacobean heroine in male disguise, Philol Quart (in prep); with the eds, Teaching with the Norton Anthology of World Masterpieces, Expanded Edition in One Volume, New York: W W Norton, 97. **CONTACT ADDRESS** Dept of English, Baruch Col, CUNY, 17 Lexington Ave, New York, NY, 10010-5518. **EMAIL** Paula-Berggren@baruch.cuny.edu

BERGMAN, DAVID L.
PERSONAL Born 03/13/1950, Fitchburg, MA, s **DISCIPLINE** ENGLISH **EDUCATION** Kenyon Col, AB, 72; Johns Hopkins Univ, MA, 74; PhD, 77. **CAREER** Prof, Towson Univ. **HONORS AND AWARDS** Gaiety Transfigured, Outstanding Book in the Field of Human Rights, Gustavus Myers Center for the Study of Human Rights, 92; Gaiety Transfigured, Oustanding Academic Book 1993, Choice, 93; 1996-97 Vice Versa Award for Excellence in the Gay and Lesbian Press, 1st place, Best Entertainment Feature for "Appreciation: Allen Ginsburg," 98. **MEMBERSHIPS** MLA **RESEARCH** American poetry; American gay literature. **SELECTED PUBLICATIONS** Ed, Men on Men 5: Best Gay Short Fiction, 94; ed, The Burning Library: Essays, 94; ed, Men on Men 6: Best New Gay Fiction, 96; auth, Heroic Measures, 98; ed, Men on Men 7: Best New Gay Fiction, 98. **CONTACT ADDRESS** English Dept., Towson Univ, Towson, MD, 21252. **EMAIL** dbergman@towson.edu

BERGMANN, FRANK
PERSONAL Born 01/20/1941, Markneukirchen, Germany, m, 4 children **DISCIPLINE** AMERICAN & COMPARATIVE LITERATURE **EDUCATION** Univ AR, MA, 66; Eberhard-Karls-Universitaet Tuebingen, GER, DPhil(Am lit), 69. **CAREER** Instr lang, KS Wesleyan Univ, 65-66; Wiss asst Am lit, Am Studies Dept at Tuebingen, WGer, 66-68 & Univ Frankfurt, WGer, 68-69; asst prof English & Ger, 69-73, chm div humanities, 73-76, assoc prof, 73-79, prof English & Ger, Utica Col, Syracuse Univ, 79-, assoc dean for humanities, 91-96, assoc dean for arts and sciences, 96-, acting dean of the fac, 98; mem, vis comt mod foreign lang & lit, Lehigh Univ, 74-78; member, fac ed comm, Syracuse Univ Press, 94-98; series ed, New York Classics reprints, Syracuse Univ Press, 86-; member, nat screening comm for Fulbright graduate study awards to Germany, 95-96. **HONORS AND AWARDS** Valedictorian, Ravensburg, 61; Fulbright scholarship to Hamilton Col, 61-62; Dr Phil, Magna Cum Laude, 69; Distinguished Teaching Award, Utica Col, 85; Clark Res Award, Utica Col, 94. **MEMBERSHIPS** AAHE; ALSC; Cooper Soc; Arthur Miller Soc; MLA; NYSHA. **RESEARCH** American literature 1861-1914; literature of upstate New York; fairy tales and literary fantasy. **SELECTED PUBLICATIONS** Auth, The Worthy Gentleman of Democracy: John William De Forest and the American Dream, Carl Winter Univ, Heidelberg, Ger, 71; Robert Grant, Twayne Publ, 82; ed and auth, Upstate Literature: Essays in Memory of Thomas F O'Donnell, Syracuse Univ Press, 85 (John Ben Snow manuscript prize; certificate of merit, Regional Conference of Hist Agencies, NY State). **CONTACT ADDRESS** Div Arts and Sciences, Utica Col of Syracuse Univ, 1600 Burrstone Rd, Utica, NY, 13502-4892. **EMAIL** fbergmann@utica.ucsu.edu

BERGMANN, LINDA S.
DISCIPLINE COMPOSITION, AMERICAN LITERATURE **EDUCATION** Oberlin Col, BA, 72; Univ Chicago, MA, 73, PhD, 83. **CAREER** Nonfiction ed, Chicago Rev, 78-80; ed consult, Deltak, Inc, Oak Brook, Ill, 79-80; instr/tutor/tchg asst, 75-89, Columbia Col Chicago, Loyola Univ Chicago, Ind Univ Northwest, Univ Chicago; asst prof, dir, writing, Hiram Col, 89-91; asst prof, dir, writing across curric, Ill Inst Technol, 91-96; assoc prof, dir, writing across curric, Univ Mo, Rolla, 96-; ed bd, ISLE: Interdisciplinary Stud in Lit and Environ; ed bd, J of Midwest MLA. **HONORS AND AWARDS** NEH summer sem, 90; Fac Serv Award, African Am Stud's Asn, Hiram Col, 91; Fac summer res grant, Ill Inst Technol, 92; Ethics Across Curric fel, Ill Inst Technol, 92; NEH summer stipend, 93; Booz-Allen & Hamilton Award for Excellence in Tchg and Serv, Ill Inst Technol, 95; Florence Howe Award, Women's Caucus for Mod Lang, 96. **MEMBERSHIPS** MLA; Midwest MLA; Soc for Lit and Sci; Asn for Stud of Lit and Environ; NCTE; Conf on Col Compos and Commun; Coun of Writing Prog Adminr; Women's Caucus for Mod Lang; Hist of Sci Soc; Soc for Critical Exchange. **RESEARCH** Elizabeth Agassiz. **SELECTED PUBLICATIONS** Auth, Academic Discourse and Academic Service: Composition vs. WAC in the Academy, ERIC Clearinghouse on Reading, Eng, and Commun Skills microfiche, Mar 94; Plagiarism in the Composition Classroom, in The Council Chronicle, NCTE, Vol 3, No 5, Je 94; Exploration and Discovery and Popular Science, in Bibliography of the Relations of Literature and Science, Configurations, Vols 1, 93, 2, 94, 3, 95; A Troubled Marriage of Discourses: Science Writing and Travel Narrative in Louis and Elizabeth Agassiz's A Journey in Brazil, J of Am Cult, 18, 95; Epic, Parody, and National Identity: George Washington in Nineteenth-Century American Humor, Stud in Am Humor, NS 3, No 2, 95; Funny Papers: Initiation and Subversion in First Year Writing, J of Tchg Writing 15.1, 96. **CONTACT ADDRESS** Dept of Eng, Univ Mo, Rolla, Rolla, MO, 65409. **EMAIL** bergmann@umr.edu

BERGSTROM, MARK
DISCIPLINE COMMUNICATION STUDIES **EDUCATION** Univ Okla, PhD, 95. **CAREER** Asst prof. **MEMBERSHIPS** Int Commun Asn; Northwest Commun Asn; Nat Commun Asn; Western Nat Commun Asn. **SELECTED PUBLICATIONS** Coauth, Cohort differences in interpersonal conflict: Implications for the older patient-younger care provider interaction, Health Commun, 96; The institutionalized elderly: Interactive implications of long-term care, Erlbaum, 96. **CONTACT ADDRESS** Dept of Communication, Utah Univ, 100 S 1350 E, Salt Lake City, UT, 84112. **EMAIL** Bergstrom@admin.comm.utah.edu

BERKELEY, DAVID SHELLEY
PERSONAL Pittsburgh, PA, m, 1943 **DISCIPLINE** ENGLISH LITERATURE **EDUCATION** Juniata Col, AB, 38; Harvard Univ, AM, 41, PhD , 49. **CAREER** From instr to assoc prof English, 48-60, chmn grad English studies, 69-76, PROF ENGLISH, OKLA STATE UNIV, 60-, Vis prof, Univ Okla, 65. **MEMBERSHIPS** MLA; SCent Mod Lang Asn; Milton Soc Am. **RESEARCH** Milton; Shakespeare; Restoration drama. **SELECTED PUBLICATIONS** Auth, Through the Telescope of Typology, What Adam Should Have Done, Milton Quart, Vol 0026, 92. **CONTACT ADDRESS** Dept of English, Oklahoma State Univ, Stillwater, OK, 74074.

BERKMAN, LEONARD
PERSONAL Born 07/21/1938, New York, NY, m, 1962, 2 children **DISCIPLINE** THEATRE, SPEECH **EDUCATION** Columbia Univ, BA, 60; Yale Univ, MFA, 63, DFA(Playwriting, Dramatic Lit & Criticism), 70. **CAREER** Instr English, Univ Tex, El Paso, 63-64; instr Playwriting, Univ Mass, 68-69; asst prof Theatre & Speech, 69-78, assoc prof Theatre, Smith Col, 78-83; prof, 83-94; Anne Hesseltine Hoyt prof of Theatre, 94. **HONORS AND AWARDS** Smith College Disting Teacher Award, 92; Charis Medal for Teaching, 94. **MEMBERSHIPS** Am Theatre Asn. **RESEARCH** Nineteenth and 20th century European drama; American drama; Afro-American and African drama; Latino and Latin American Drama; Canadian Drama; Australian Drama. **SELECTED PUBLICATIONS** Auth, Four books on rock, Mass Rev, Spring 71; Really, Now (play), Publ Broadcasting Syst, 71; Two Demon Plays, Can Broadcasting Corp, 73; Off-off-off Broadway, in Massachusetts, Magic Dust, Winter 78; Viola! Rape in Technicolor, Smith, 2/78; Jane Addams Mem Theatre, Chicago, 3/78; Til the Beatles reunite, WTTT, 3/79; Sleeping Through the End of the World: The Plays and Poems of Rochelle Owens, Parnaussus, Spring 82; I Won't Go See A Play Called A Parent's Worst Nightmare, NY Stage & Film Co, Poughkeepsie, NY, 95; Quits, NYU Experimental Theatre Wing, NYC, 98. **CONTACT ADDRESS** Dept Theatre, Smith Col, 98 Green St, Northampton, MA, 01063-0001. **EMAIL** lberkman@sophia.smith.edu

BERKOVE, LAWRENCE IVAN
PERSONAL Born 01/08/1930, Rochester, NY, m, 1967, 3 children **DISCIPLINE** ENGLISH & AMERICAN LITERATURE **EDUCATION** Univ Ill, AB, 51; Univ Minn, MA, 53; Univ Pa, PhD, 62. **CAREER** Asst instr, Univ Pa, 57-58 & 60-61; instr English, Skidmore Col, 58-60; instr, DePaul Univ, Pa, 61-62; from instr to asst prof English lit, Colo Col, 62-64; from asst prof to assoc prof English lit, 64-74, prof & am lit, Univ Mich, Dearborn, 74-. **HONORS AND AWARDS** Nat Endowment for Humanities proj develop grant, 75; consult, Nat Endowment for Humanities grant to Am Univ, 78-79; vis prof English & Am lit, Rikkyo Univ, Tokyo, Japan, 82-83; Pres, UM-Dearborn chap of AAUP, 94-97. **MEMBERSHIPS** MLA; Midwest Mod Lang Asn; Col English Asn; Am Studies Asn; AAUP. **RESEARCH** American literature of the nineteenth and early twentieth centuries; American studies; religious influences on literature; Am Assn of Univ Profs; MLA; Col English Assn. **SELECTED PUBLICATIONS** Auth, The poor players of Huckleberry Finn, Papers Mich Acad Sci, Arts & Lett, 68; Arms and the man: Ambrose Bierce's response to war, Mich Academician, winter 69; Henry James and Sir Walter Scott: A virtuous attachment?, Studies Scottish Lit, 80; The free man of color in The Grandissimes and works by Harris and Mark Twain, Southern Quart, summer 80; ed & introd, Ambrose Bierce: Skepticism and Dissent: Selected Journalism from 1898-1901, Ann Arbor: Delmas, 80; A strange adventure: The story behind a Bierce tale, Am Lit Realism, spring 81; The man with the burning pen: Ambrose Bierce as journalist, J Popular Culture, 81; The heart has its reasons: Ambrose Bierce's successful failure at Philosophy, In: Critical Essays on Ambrose Bierce, G K Hall, 82; Dan De Quille, The Sorceress of Attu, ed with intro Lawrence I Berkove, Dearborn, MI, Univ of Michigan-Dearborn, 94; Critical Essays on Kate Chopin, ed, Alice Hall Petry, NY, GK Hall, 96. **CONTACT ADDRESS** Dept of Humanities, Univ of Michigan, Dearborn, 4901 Evergreen Rd, Dearborn, MI, 48128-1491. **EMAIL** Iberkove@umich.edu

BERKOWITZ, GERALD MARTIN
PERSONAL Born 01/11/1942, New York, NY **DISCIPLINE** ENGLISH AND AMERICAN LITERATURE **EDUCATION** Columbia Univ, BA, 63, MA, 64; Ind Univ, MA, 67, PhD (English), 69. **CAREER** Instr, Univ Southern Calif, 67-69 & asst prof, 69-71; asst prof, 71-78, ASSOC PROF ENGLISH, NORTHERN ILL UNIV, 78- **RESEARCH** Contemporary British and American drama; Shakespeare; theatre and film. **SELECTED PUBLICATIONS** Auth, Realism and the American Dramatic Tradition, Mod Drama, Vol 0040, 97; Get the Guests, Psychoanalysis, Modern American Drama, and the Audience, Mod Drama, Vol 0038, 95; Staging Depth, Oneill, Eugene and the Politics of Psychological Discourse, Mod Drama, Vol 0039, 96. **CONTACT ADDRESS** Dept English, No Illinois Univ, 1425 W Lincoln Hwy, De Kalb, IL, 60115-2825.

BERLIN, NORMAND
PERSONAL Born 12/06/1931, New York, NY, m, 1956, 2 children **DISCIPLINE** ENGLISH **EDUCATION** NY Univ, BA, 53; Columbia Univ, MA, 56; Univ CA, Berkeley, PhD(-Eng), 64. **CAREER** From instr to asst prof Eng, McGill Univ, 61-65; from asst prof to assoc prof, 65-74, Prof Eng, Univ MA, AMHERST, 74-. **HONORS AND AWARDS** Distinguished Tchr Award, Univ MA, 76, Hum Res Fel, 89; Bronze Medal for Outstanding Work on O'Neil, 95. **RESEARCH** Shakespeare; Elizabethan and Jacobean drama; mod drama. **SELECTED PUBLICATIONS** Auth, The Base String: The Underworld in Elizabethan Drama, Fairleigh Dickinson Univ, 68; Thomas Sackville, Twayne, 74; The Secret Cause: A Discussion of Tragedy, Univ Mass Press, 81; Eugene O'Neill, Macmillan, London & Grove Press, 82; O'Neill's Shakespeare, Michigan, 93. **CONTACT ADDRESS** Dept of English, Univ of MA, Amherst, MA, 01002.

BERLIND, BRUCE
PERSONAL Born 07/17/1926, Brooklyn, NY, m, 1954, 5 children **DISCIPLINE** ENGLISH **EDUCATION** Princeton Univ, BA, 47; Johns Hopkins Univ, MA, 50, PhD , 58. **CAREER** From instr to assoc prof, 54-66, chmn dept, 67-72, prof, 66-80, CHARLES A DANA PROF ENGLISH AND CHMN DEPT, COLGATE UNIV, 80-, US Info Serv lectr, Ger, 63; vis assoc prof, Univ Rochester, 66; mem Hungarian PEN Transl Prog, Budapest, 77 and 79. **MEMBERSHIPS** MLA; AAUP; Poetry Soc Am. **RESEARCH** Contemporary American poetry; translation. **SELECTED PUBLICATIONS** Auth, Poetry and Politics, Am Poetry Rev, Vol 0022, 93; Meaning of Fragment, Fragment of Meaning, Poetry, Vol 0168, 96. **CONTACT ADDRESS** Dept of English, Colgate Univ, Hamilton, NY, 13346.

BERLINER, TODD
PERSONAL Born 12/11/1964, Los Angeles, CA, m, 1995, 1 child **DISCIPLINE** FILM STUDIES **EDUCATION** Univ of CA, Berkeley, PhD, 96, MA, 91, AB, 86 **CAREER** Asst Prof, 96-, Univ of NC **MEMBERSHIPS** Soc for Cinema Studies **RESEARCH** Am Film; Hollywood films of the 1970's **SELECTED PUBLICATIONS** Auth, Hollywood Movie Dialogue and the 'Real Realism' of John Cassavetes, Film Quarterly, vol. 52, no.3, 99 **CONTACT ADDRESS** Wilmington, NC, 28401. **EMAIL** berlinert@uncwil.edu

BERMAN, AVIS
PERSONAL Born 06/29/1949, Hartford, CT **DISCIPLINE** ENGLISH **EDUCATION** Bucknell Univ, BA (magna cum laude), English, 71; Rutgers Univ, MA, English literature, 74. **CAREER** Writer and art historian, 78-; oral historian, Archs of Amer Art, Mark Rothko Found, Estate of Stuart Davis, Pollock-Krasner House and Study Center, 80-90; guest lecturer, various universities and museums, 83-; dir, Archs of Amer Art, Oral History Program, 87-92; consult, New York Studio School of Drawing, Painting, and Sculpture, and the Pollock-Krasner House and Study Center, 91-93; consult, Addison Gallery of Amer Art, 91-96; consult, The Andy Warhol Gallery of Amer Art, 93-94; consult, Metropolitan Museum of Art Archs, 93-94; consult, Museum of Modern Art Arch, 96-97. **HONORS AND AWARDS** Res grants, John Sloan Memorial Found; Fellowship for Independent Study and Res, NEH; Grant-in-Aid, Amer Coun of Learned Societies; fellowships, Andrew W. Mellon; grant, Soc for the Preservation of Amer Modernists Publication **MEMBERSHIPS** Author's Guild; Natl Coalition of Independent Scholars; Intl Assn of Art Critics, Amer Section, bd of dirs, 93-98, membership chair, 94-98. **RESEARCH** American art, 1890-1950; museum history; women in the museum world; history of taste; James McNeill Whistler. **SELECTED PUBLICATIONS** Contrib, Addison Gallery of American Art: 65 Years, 96; auth, "Ursula von Rydingsvard," Dictionary of Women Artists, 97; contrib, Brassai: The Eyes of Paris, 98; "Remembering Leger, Champion of Nuts and Bolts," New York Times, 8 Feb, 98; "Ursula von Rydingsvard, Sculpts Metaphors in Wood," Smithsonian Magazine, May 98. **CONTACT ADDRESS** 425 W. End Ave., Rm. 5C, New York, NY, 10024.

BERNARD, KENNETH
PERSONAL Born 05/07/1930, Brooklyn, NY, m, 1952, 3 children **DISCIPLINE** ENGLISH **EDUCATION** City Col NY, BA, 53; Columbia Univ, MA, 56, PhD , 62. **CAREER** From instr to assoc prof, 59-71, PROF ENGLISH, LONG ISLAND UNIV, 71-, Guggenheim Found fel playwriting, 72-73; NY State Creative Artists Pub Serv Grant playwriting, 72-73; NY 73-74, consult, 74-75, grant fiction, 76; Rockefeller grant playwriting, 75; consult, Mass Arts and Humanities Found, 75, Wis Arts Bd, 75 and Md Arts Coun, 78; Nat Endowment for Arts grant fiction, 78; asst ed, Confrontation. **HONORS AND AWARDS** Arvon Poetry Prize, 80. **MEMBERSHIPS** PEN Club. **RESEARCH** Dramatic writing. **SELECTED PUBLICATIONS** Auth, Unbalancing Acts--Foundations or a Theater, Am Book Rev, Vol 0015, 93; Pinter the Homecoming, Explicator, Vol 0052, 94. **CONTACT ADDRESS** 788 Riverside Dr, New York, NY, 10032.

BERNE, STANLEY
PERSONAL Born 06/08/1923, New York, NY, m, 1952 **DISCIPLINE** ENGLISH **EDUCATION** Rutgers Univ, BS, 51; NY Univ, MA, 52. **CAREER** Asst prof, 63-67, assoc prof, 68-82, RES ASSOC PROF ENGLISH, CTR FOR ADVAN PROFESSIONAL STUDIES AND RES, EASTERN NMEX UNIV, 82-, Guest lectr, Univ of Americas, 65 and Univ SDak, 68; res grants, Eastern NMex Univ, 66-73; pres, Am-Can Publ Inc, 76-; co-producer, co-host, PBS TV Series, Future Writing Today, 80. **MEMBERSHIPS** Comt Small Mags, Eds & Publ; Rio Grande Writers Asn; Western Independent Publ. **RESEARCH** Contemporary novel and short story; aesthetics and criticism. **SELECTED PUBLICATIONS** Auth, Looking for a Lost House, Ploughshares, Vol 0020, 94. **CONTACT ADDRESS** Dept of English, Eastern New Mexico Univ, Portales, NM, 88130.

BERNSTEIN, CAROL L.
PERSONAL Born 02/09/1933, New York, NY, m, 1955, 4 children **DISCIPLINE** ENGLISH **EDUCATION** Swarthmore Col, BA, 54; Yale Univ, MA, 56, PhD(English), 61 **CAREER** Instr English, Hebrew Univ, Israel, 57-58; lectr, Albertus Magnus Col, 65; vis lectr English & Am lit Hebrew Univ, Israel, 65-66; lectr English, Univ Pa, 67-69, asst prof, 69-74; lectr, 74-76, assoc prof, 76-90, PROF ENGLISH, BRYN MAWR COL, 90-, PROF COMP LIT, 93-. **HONORS AND AWARDS** Phi Beta Kappa; Ford and Pew Found grants; NEH summer stipend; Fairbank Prof Humanitities, 92-97; Mary E Garrett Alumnae Prof English, 97-. **MEMBERSHIPS** MLA; ACLA **RESEARCH** Nineteenth and twentieth century literature; narrative theory; theories of the sublime; cultural memory. **SELECTED PUBLICATIONS** Auth, Precarious Enchantment: A Reading of Meredith's Poetry, Cath Univ Am Press, 79; The Celebration of Scandal: Toward the Sublime in Victorian Urban Fiction, Penn State Univ Press, 91. **CONTACT ADDRESS** Dept of English, Bryn Mawr Col, 101 N Merion Ave, Bryn Mawr, PA, 19010-2899. **EMAIL** cbernste@brynmawr.edu

BERNSTEIN, MATTHEW H.
PERSONAL Born 06/11/1958, New York, NY, m, 1980, 2 children **DISCIPLINE** FILM STUDIES **EDUCATION** Univ Wisc, Madison, BA, PhD; Columbia Univ, MFA. **CAREER** Lectr, 88-89, asst prof, 89-95, assoc prof, 95-, film stud, Emory Univ. **HONORS AND AWARDS** NEH fel, 89, res grant, 97-99; Emory Univ res grants, 90, 91, 93, 94. **MEMBERSHIPS** Soc for Cinema Stud; Univ Film and Video Asn. **RESEARCH** American film industry; classical Hollywood cinema; film comedy; Japanese film; post-war European film; documentary film; African-Americans and film. **SELECTED PUBLICATIONS** Auth, Robert and Me: Documentaphobia and Mixed Modes, Jour of Film and Video, 94; auth, Walter Wanger, Hollywood Independent, Calif, 94; auth, A Tale of Three Cities: The Banning of Scarlet Street, Cinema Jour, 95; auth, Nostalgia, Ambivalence, Irony: Song of the South and Race Relations in 1946 Atlanta, Film Hist, 96; co-ed, Visions of the East: Orientalism in Film, Rutgers, 97; auth, Walter Wanger, Adolph Zukor, in Garraty, ed, American National Biography, Oxford, 98; auth, Scratching Around in a Fit of Insanity: The Norman Film Manufacturing Company and the Race Film Business in the 1920s, Griffithiana, 98; auth, Model Criminals: Visual Style in Bonnie and Clyde, in Friedman, ed, Bonnie and Clyde, Cambridge, 99; auth, Floating Triumphantly: The American Critics on Titanic, in Studlar, ed, The Titanic Project, Rutgers, 99. **CONTACT ADDRESS** Dept of Film Studies, Emory Univ, Atlanta, GA, 30322. **EMAIL** mbernst@emory.edu

BERRY, BOYD MCCULLOCH
PERSONAL Born 05/29/1939, Chicago, IL, 2 children **DISCIPLINE** ENGLISH LITERATURE, RENAISSANCE **EDUCATION** Harvard Univ, BA, 61; Univ Mich, MA, 62, PhD (English), 66. **CAREER** Asst prof English, Ind Univ, 66-74; vis lectr, Ife Univ, Nigeria, 70-71; ASSOC PROF ENGLISH, VA COMMONWEALTH UNIV, 74- **MEMBERSHIPS** MLA; Milton Soc Am. **RESEARCH** John Milton; 16th and 17th century prose and poetry. **SELECTED PUBLICATIONS** Auth, Register of Sermons Preached at Pauls Cross, 1534-1642, Shakespeare Quart, Vol 0043, 92; Dismembered Rhetoric--English Recusant Writing, 1580-1603, Shakespeare Quart, Vol 0047, 96; Of the Manner in Which Askew, Anne Noised It, J Eng Ger Philol, Vol 0096, 97. **CONTACT ADDRESS** Dept of English, Va Commonwealth Univ, Richmond, VA, 23284.

BERRY, EDWARD I.
DISCIPLINE RENAISSANCE LITERATURE **EDUCATION** Wesleyan Col, BA; Univ Calif, Berkeley, MA, PhD. **CAREER** Prof. **HONORS AND AWARDS** Fulbright fel, 69-70. **RESEARCH** Shakespeare; Sidney. **SELECTED PUBLICATIONS** Auth, Patterns of Decay: Shakespeare's Early Histories, Va UP, 75; Shakespeare's Comic Rites, Cambridge UP, 84; Japanese translation, Univ Nagoya Press, 89; co-ed, True Rites and Maimed Rites, Univ Ill Press, 92; The Making of Sir Philip Sidney, U of Toronto P, 98. **CONTACT ADDRESS** Dept of English, Victoria Univ, PO Box 3070, Victoria, BC, V8W 3W1. **EMAIL** eberry@uvic.ca

BERRY, HERBERT
PERSONAL Born 05/09/1922, New York, NY, m, 1948, 4 children **DISCIPLINE** ENGLISH **EDUCATION** Furman Univ, BA, 47; Univ Nebr, MA, 48; Univ Colo, PhD (English), 53. **CAREER** Instr English, Univ Nebr, 50-51; asst prof, Univ Omaha, 51-55; assoc prof and head dept, Doane Col, 55-58; from asst prof to assoc prof, Univ Western Ont, 59-67; PROF ENGLISH UNIV, SASK, 67- **MEMBERSHIPS** MLA; Renaissance Soc Am. **RESEARCH** English literature of the 16th and 17th centuries. **SELECTED PUBLICATIONS** Auth, Shylock, Miles, Robert, and Events at the Theater, Shakespeare Quart, Vol 0044, 93; A London Plague Bill for 1592, Eng Lit Renaissance, Vol 0025, 95; Lewis Braces at the Red Lion, Theatre Notebook, Vol 0050, 96. **CONTACT ADDRESS** 1405 Ewart Ave, Saskatoon, SK, S7H 2K5.

BERRY, MARGARET
PERSONAL Greensboro, NC **DISCIPLINE** ENGLISH, SOUTH ASIAN STUDIES **EDUCATION** St Joseph Col, BA, 44; Cath Univ, Am, MA, 50; St Johns Univ, NY, PhD (English), 56; Univ Pa, MA, 68. **CAREER** From instr to assoc prof English, St Joseph Col, 54-65; ASSOC PROF ENGLISH, JOHN CARROLL UNIV, 65-, Ford Found Asian studies grant, 63-64; NDEA fel S Asia studies, 67-68; Danforth assoc, 72; vis res scholar, Univ Mysore, fall 73; vis lectr, Univ Madurai, fall 73; fac fel, John Carroll Univ, 73. **MEMBERSHIPS** Asn Asian Studies; AAUP. **RESEARCH** Literary criticism of the English Catholic revival; Indian fiction in English. **SELECTED PUBLICATIONS** Auth, Western Plainchant--A Handbook, Mus Times, Vol 0135, 94; Childe and Australia--Archaeology, Politics and Ideas, Australian Hist Stud, Vol 0027, 96; The Service Books of the Royal Abbey of Saint Denis--Images of Ritual and Music in the Middle Ages, J Theol Stud, Vol 0047, 96. **CONTACT ADDRESS** Dept of English, John Carroll Univ, 20700 N Park Blvd, Cleveland, OH, 44118.

BERRY, RALPH M.
PERSONAL Born 11/14/1947, Atlanta, GA, m, 1988 **DISCIPLINE** ENGLISH **EDUCATION** Furman Univ, BA, 70; Wesley Seminary at Am Univ, MTS, 74; Univ Iowa, MFA, 80, PhD, 85. **CAREER** Lectr, Univ de Tours (France), 85; Asst Prof, 86-91, Assoc Prof, Fla State Univ, 91-. **HONORS AND AWARDS** Fulbright Jr. Lectr, 85; Fiction Collective Award, 84; Honorable Mention Pushcart Prize, 91-92; Fla Individual Artist Grant, 88-89, 95-96. **MEMBERSHIPS** MLA; AWP; IAPL. **RESEARCH** 20th century literature; philosophy and literature. **SELECTED PUBLICATIONS** Auth, What Is a Narrative Convention?, Narrative, 95; In Which Henry James Strikes Bedrock, Philos & Lit, 97; Leonardo's Horse, 97. **CONTACT ADDRESS** English Dept, Florida State Univ, Tallahassee, FL, 32306-1036. **EMAIL** rberry@english.fsu.edu

BERST, CHARLES A.
PERSONAL Born 09/30/1932, Seattle, WA, m, 1962, 2 children **DISCIPLINE** ENGLISH **EDUCATION** Univ Wash, BA, 55, PhD, 65. **CAREER** Asst prof, Univ Alberta, 65-67; from asst to assoc prof, 67-81, prof, 81-94, prof emeritus, 94-, Univ Calif Los Angeles; chemn Col of Lett and Sci Fac, 77-81, vice chemn & chemn, Fac Senate, 87-89, UCLA. **HONORS AND AWARDS** Univ Wash, PhD (hon), 65; UCLA Distinguished Tchg Award, 87; UCLA Univ Service Award, 91. **MEMBERSHIPS** MLA. **RESEARCH** Bernard Shaw; modern drama; drama and religion **SELECTED PUBLICATIONS** Auth, Bernard Shaw and the Art of Drama, Univ Ill, 73; ed, Shaw and Religion, Penn State, 81; auth, As Kingfishers Catch Fire: The Saints and Poetics of Shaw and T.S. Eliot, in Dukore, ed, 1992: Shaw and the Last Hundred Years, Penn State, 94; auth, Pygmalion: Shaw's Spin on Myth and Cinderella, Twayne, 95; auth, Superman Theater: Gusts, Galumphs, and Grumps, in Laurence, Unpublished Shaw, Penn State, 96; auth, New Theatres for Old, in Innes, ed, The Cambridge Companion to Shaw, Cambridge, 98. **CONTACT ADDRESS** Dept of English, Univ of California, Los Angeles, Los Angeles, CA, 90095. **EMAIL** berst@humnet.ucla.edu

BERTELSEN, DALE A.
DISCIPLINE SPEECH COMMUNICATION **EDUCATION** Penn State Univ, MA, 85; PhD, 89. **CAREER** Asst prof, 88-93, assoc prof, 93-96, PROF, 96-, BLOOMSBURG UNIV; Emerging Scholar Award, 93, a nd Distinguished Serv Award, 96, from Kenneth Burke Soc; E L Hunt Scholar Award, 97; Distinguished tchg fel, 97, and Distinguished Serv Award, 98 from E Commun Asn. **MEMBERSHIPS** Nat Commun Asn; E Commun Asn; Speech Commun Asn of PA; Sppech Commun Asn of PR; Kenneth Burke Soc. **RESEARCH** Media criticism; Rhetorical criticism. **SELECTED PUBLICATIONS** Auth Media Form and Government: Democracy as an Archetypal Image in the Electronic Age, Commun Quart, 92; Kenneth Burke's Conception of Reality: The Process of Transformation and its Implic ations for Thetorical Criticism, Extensions of the Burkeian System, Univ Alabama Press, 93; Sophistry, Epistemology, and the Media Context, Philos and Rhetoric, 93; coauth Analyzing Media: Communication Technologies as Symbolic and Cognitive Systems, Guilford Publ, 96. **CONTACT ADDRESS** Dept of Commun Studies & Theatre Arts, Bloomsburg Univ of Pennsylvania, 400 E 2nd St, Bloomsburg, PA, 17815-1301. **EMAIL** dberte@planetx.bloomu.edu

BERTELSEN, LANCE
PERSONAL Born 10/24/1947, Inglewood, CA, d, 2 children **DISCIPLINE** ENGLISH LITERATURE, EIGHTEENTH CENTURY ENGLISH CULTURE **EDUCATION** Dartmouth Col, AB, 69; Univ WA, PhD(English), 79. **CAREER** Asst prof, 79-85, ASSOC PROF ENGLISH, UNIV TEX, AUSTIN, 86-, assoc chair, 94-97. **HONORS AND AWARDS** Fel, Nat Humanities center, 83; fel, Yale Center for British Art, 84; TX Inst of Letters O. Henry Award, 90; URI Fac Res assignment, 91; Frank C. Erwin Centennial Honors Prof, 94; Dean's Fel, 97. **MEMBERSHIPS** Am Soc 18th Century Studies; S Cent Am Soc 18th Century Studies. **RESEARCH** Fielding; WWII. **SELECTED PUBLICATIONS** Auth, Ireland, temple, and the Origins of the Drapier, Papers on Lang & Lit, 77; The Smollettian View of life, Novel, 78; David Garrick and English painting, 18th Century Studies, 78; Have at you all: Or, Bonnell Thornton's Journalism, Huntington Libr Quart, 81; New Information on a Brush for the Sign Painters, Eighteenth-Century Life, 7, 82; The Interior Structures of Hogarth's Marriage a la Mode, Art History, 6, 83; the Crab: An Unpublished Poem by Charles Churchill, Philol Quart, 63, 84; Jane Austen's Miniatures: Painting, Drawing, and the Novels, Modern lang Quart,

4, 84; The Nonsense Club: Literature and Popular Culture, 1749-1764, Oxford: Clarendon Press, 86; The Significance of the 1731 Revisions to The Fall of Mortimer, Restoration and Eighteenth-Century Theatre Res, 2nd ser, 2, winter 87; Icons on Two, J of Popular Culture, 22, spring 89; San Pietro and the Art of War, Southeast Rev, 74, 89; How Texas Won the Second World War, SE Rev, 76, 91; Journalism, Carnival, and Jubilate Agno, ELH, 59, 92; Committed by Justice Fielding, Eighteenth-Century Studies, 30, 97. **CONTACT ADDRESS** Dept English, Univ Texas, 0 Univ of TX, Austin, TX, 78712-1026. **EMAIL** lberte@uts.cc.utexas.edu

BERTHOFF, ANN EVANS
PERSONAL Born 02/13/1924, New York, NY, m, 1949, 2 children **DISCIPLINE** ENGLISH, LINGUISTICS **EDUCATION** Cornell Col, Iowa, AB, 45; Radcliffe Col, AM, 48. **CAREER** Instr English, Bradford Jr Col, 48-51, Bryn Mawr Col, 51-62 and Haverford Col, 63-65; lectr, Swarthmore Col, 65-67; assoc prof, 70-78, PROF ENGLISH, UNIV MASS, BOSTON, 78-, Mem, NCTE Comn on Compos, 78-81; consult, WNET/ Channel 13, 79- and Bread Loaf Sch English, 80; dir, Nat Endowment for Humanities Summer Sem, 80. **MEMBERSHIPS** NCTE; Conf Col Compos and Commun; Col English Asn; New England Col English Asn (pres, 77-78); MLA. **RESEARCH** English pedagogy; philosophy of language; Renaissance poetry. **SELECTED PUBLICATIONS** Auth, Problem Dissolving by Triadic Means, Coll Eng, Vol 0058, 96; Percy, Walker Castaway Essays, Sewanee Rev, Vol 0102, 94; Spiritual Sites of Composing--Introductory Remarks, Coll Compos Commun, Vol 0045, 94; Assigning Places--The Function of Introductory Composition as a Cultural Discourse, Coll Eng, Vol 0056, 94; Royce Mature Ethics, Rel Lit, Vol 0025, 93; Santayana, Pragmatism and the Spiritual Life, Rel Lit, Vol 0025, 93; Sign, Textuality, World, Rel Lit, Vol 0025, 93. **CONTACT ADDRESS** 14 Thoreau St, Concord, MA, 01742.

BERTHOFF, WARNER BEMENT
PERSONAL Born 01/22/1925, Oberlin, OH, m, 1949, 2 children **DISCIPLINE** ENGLISH **EDUCATION** Harvard Univ, BA, 47, MA, 49, PhD, 54. **CAREER** Tchng fel, 49-51, Harvard Univ; from asst prof to prof, 51-67, Bryn Mawr Col; prof Eng,67-90, Harvard Univ; Fulbright fel, vis prof, 57-58, Univ Catania; vis prof, Univ Warsaw, 63; vis prof, Univ Minn, 61; vis prof, Univ Calif, Berkeley, 62-63; Guggenheim fel, 68-69; sr fel, Soc for Human, 75-76, Cornell; Wilson Ctr fel, 84. **MEMBERSHIPS** Melville Soc. **SELECTED PUBLICATIONS** Auth, Literature and the Continuances of Virtue, Princeton Univ, 86; auth, Hart Crane: A Reintroduction, Minn, 89; auth, American Trajectories: Authors and Readings, 1790-1970, Penn St, 94. **CONTACT ADDRESS** Harvard Univ, Widener 446, Cambridge, MA, 02138.

BERTHOLD, DENNIS ALFRED
PERSONAL Born 10/29/1942, Los Angeles, CA, m, 3 children **DISCIPLINE** AMERICAN LITERATURE **EDUCATION** Univ CA, Riverside, BA, 64, MA, 66; Univ WI, Madison, PhD(English), 72. **CAREER** Instr English, Savannah State Col, 66-68; instr, Univ WI, Stevens Point, 71-72; asst prof, 72-75, assoc prof, 75-84, prof English, TX, A&M Univ, 84-. **HONORS AND AWARDS** Distinguished Teaching Award, Asn Former Students, TX A&M Univ, 77. **MEMBERSHIPS** MLA; S Cent Mod Lang Asn; Nathaniel Hawthorne Soc; Melville Soc. **RESEARCH** American lit and iconography; literature and the sea. **SELECTED PUBLICATIONS** Auth, Hawthorne, Ruskin, and the Gothic Revival: Transcendent Gothic in The Marble Faun, ESQ, 1/74; The Concept of Merit in Paradise Lost, Studies English Lit, winter 75; Anti-Idealism, In: Hawthorne's The Snow-Image, Ariz Quart, 82; A Transcendentalist Aesthetics of Imperfection, Am Transcendental Quart, 82; Charles Brockden Brown, Edgar Huntly, and the Origins of the American Picturesque, The William and Mary Quart, 41, 84; ed, with Kenneth M Price, Dear Brother Walt: The Letters of Thomas Jefferson Whitman, Kent, OH: Kent State Univ Press, 84; Desacralizing the American Gothic: An Iconographic Approach to Edgar Huntly, Studies in Am Fiction, 14, 86; Cape Horn Passages: Literary Conventions and Nautical Realities and Deeper Soundings: The Presence of Walden in Joshua Slocum's Sailing Alone Around the World, in Literature and Lore of the Sea, ed Patricia Ann Carlson, Amsterdam: RODOPI Press, 86; Hawthorne's American Travel Sketches and His Tour of 1832, with Alfred Weber and Beth L Lueck, Univ Press New England, 89; Melville and Dutch Genre Painting, in Savage Eye: Melville and the Visual Arts, ed Christopher Sten, Kent State Univ Press, 91; Durer At the Hostelry: Melville's Misogynist Iconography, Melville Soc Extracts, 95, 93; Prose Since 1960, in America and the Sea, ed Haskell Springer, Univ GA Press, 94; Melville, Garibaldi, and the Medusa's Revolution, Am Literary Hist, 9, 97. **CONTACT ADDRESS** Dept English, Texas A&M Univ, College Station, TX, 77843-4227. **EMAIL** d-berthold@tamu.edu

BERUBE, MICHAEL
DISCIPLINE HUMANITIES **EDUCATION** Univ Va, PhD, 89; **CAREER** Instr, 89-94, assoc prof, 94-95, prof, 96- , Dir, Ill Program for Res in Hum, 97- , Univ Ill, Urbana-Champaign. **SELECTED PUBLICATIONS** Auth, Marginal Forces/ Cultural Centers: Tolson, Pynchon, and the Politics of the Canon, Cornell, 92; auth, Public Access; Literary Theory and American Cultural Politics, Verson, 94; co-ed, Higher Education Under Fire: Politics, Economics, and the Crisis of the Humanities, Routledge, 95; auth, Life As We Know It: A Father, A Family, and an Exceptional Child, Pantheon, 96; auth, The Employment of English: Theory, Jobs, and the Future of Literary Study, NYU, 98. **CONTACT ADDRESS** Illinois Program for Research in the Humanities, 805 West Pennslyvania Ave, Urbana, IL, 61801. **EMAIL** m-berube@uiuc.edu

BEST, MICHAEL R.
DISCIPLINE RENAISSANCE DRAMA **EDUCATION** Univ Adelaide, BA, PhD. **CAREER** Prof; dept ch. **HONORS AND AWARDS** Co-ord ed, Internet Shakespeare Editions; Cmpt Software: Shakespeare's Life and Times, Intellimation: Santa Barbara, CA, 91; hypertext program for the Macintosh, Version 2.1, 92; version 3.0 for CD ROM, 94; Shakespeare dir, a program for blocking scenes from Shakespeare's plays, Intellimation: Santa Barbara, CA, 94. **RESEARCH** Shakespeare; electronic texts; computer-assisted learning. **SELECTED PUBLICATIONS** Co-ed, The Book of Secrets of Albertus Magnus, Clarendon, 73; auth, A Lost Glitter: Letters between South Australia and the Western Australian Goldfields, 1895-97, Wakefield Press, 86; Shakespeare I: Power and Justice, Open Lrng Inst BC, 85; Shakespeare II: Freedom and Restraint in Love (Text: Open Learning Institute of B.C., 1986)ed, Gervase Markham, The English Housewife, McGill-Queen's UP, 86; internet pub(s), Internet Shakespeare Editions, texts of 32 plays in original spelling; articles for EMLS and Text/ Technology. **CONTACT ADDRESS** Dept of English, Victoria Univ, PO Box 3070, Victoria, BC, V8W 3W1. **EMAIL** mbest1@uvic.ca

BETHEL, ELIZABETH RAUH
PERSONAL Born 08/27/1942, Grosse Pointe, MI **DISCIPLINE** SOCIOLOGY; COMMUNICATION **EDUCATION** Univ Oklahoma, PhD, 74. **CAREER** Lander Univ, prof, sociol, 74-; Univ Madras, Fulbright lectr, 90. **MEMBERSHIPS** ASA; SSS; NWU. **RESEARCH** African Am Culture; Southern US Culture; Global Ethnic Culture. **SELECTED PUBLICATIONS** Black Communities, in Neil Larry Schumsky, ed, American Cities and Suburbs: An Encyclopedia, Clio, pub 98; Journals and Voices: Mosaics of Community, in Documenting Cultural Diversity in the Resurgent American South, in: Margaret R Dittemore and Fred J Hay, eds, Am Lib Asn, 97; AIDS: Readings on a Global Crisis, Allyn and Bacon, 95; numerous other pub. **CONTACT ADDRESS** Dept Sociology, Lander Univ, Greenwood, SC, 29646. **EMAIL** ebethel@lander.edu

BETZ, PAUL F.
DISCIPLINE ENGLISH LITERATURE **EDUCATION** La Salle Col, BA; Cornell Univ, MA, PhD. **CAREER** Prof. **SELECTED PUBLICATIONS** Auth, British Romantic Art, 90; Pictures for a Revolution: Ten Contemporary Images, 92; Romantic Archaeologies, 95. **CONTACT ADDRESS** English Dept, Georgetown Univ, 37th and O St, Washington, DC, 20057.

BEVINGTON, DAVID M.
PERSONAL Born 05/13/1931, New York, NY, m, 1953, 4 children **DISCIPLINE** ENGLISH **EDUCATION** Harvard Univ, BA, 52, MA, 57, PhD 59. **CAREER** Instr Eng, Harvard Univ, 59-61; from asst prof to prof, Univ Va, 61-68; prof eng, Univ Chicago, 68-. Guggenheim fel, 64-65 & 81-82. **HONORS AND AWARDS** Phi Beta Kappa, bk prize, univ VA, 63; Guggenheim fel, 64-65;Quantrell tchg award, 79; sec guggenheim award, 81-82. **MEMBERSHIPS** MLA; Medieval Acad Am; Renaissance Soc Am; Shakespeare Asn Am; Malone Soc; Am academ arts sci; Am Pilos soc. **RESEARCH** Late medieval and Renaissance Eng Drama. **SELECTED PUBLICATIONS** Auth, From Mankin to Marlowe, Harvard Univ, 62; ed, Shakespeare's 1 Henry V1, Penguin, 67; Twentieth-Century Interpretations of Hamlet, Prentice-Hall, 68; auth, Tudor Drama and Politics, Harvard Univ, 68; ed, Medieval Drama, 75; Shakespeare, Pattern of Excelling Nature, 78; compiler, Bibliography of Shakespeare, 78; ed, The Complete Works of Shakespeare, 80,88,92,97; The Bantam Shakespeare, compl, 29 vols, Bantam, 88; ed, The Revels Student Series; ed, The Revels Series; ed, a new edition of Ben Jonson. **CONTACT ADDRESS** Dept of Eng, Univ of Chicago, 1010 E 59th St, Chicago, IL, 60637-1512. **EMAIL** bevi@midway.uchicago.edu

BIALOSTOSKY, DON
PERSONAL Born 05/11/1947, Portland, OR, m, 1966, 3 children **DISCIPLINE** ENGLISH **EDUCATION** Univ Chicago, AB, 69, MA, 73, PhD, 77. **CAREER** Lect, Univ Chicago, 73-75; vis instr, English, Univ UT, 75-77; asst prof, English, Univ WA, 77-83; assoc prof, English, 83-87, assoc prof, Comparative Lit, SUNY, Stony Brook, 87; prof English, Univ Toledo, 87-92, Distinguished Univ Prof of English, 92-93; PROF, ENGLISH, PA STATE UNIV, 93-, HEAD, DEPT OF ENGLISH, 95-. **HONORS AND AWARDS** Presidential Scholar, 65; Nat Merit Scholar, 65; Phi Bata Kappa, 68; Danforth fel, 69; R. S. Crane Award for writing on literary subjects, 74; NEH summer study grant, 78; ACLS grant for recent recipient of the PhD, 79; ACLS travel award, 85; Univ Toledo Summer Fac Res Award, 88, 89, 91; OH Bd of Regents Challenge grant in rhetorical theory (principal author), 89-95; Univ Toledo Outstanding Fac Res Award, 91; Univ Toledo Col of Arts & Sciences Exceptional Merit Award, 91; res and grad studies award for preparation of Rhetorical Traditions and British Romantic Literature, 93; EGO Award for Outstanding Teacher (shared with one other fac member), 94; Charles W. Kneupper Award for Outstanding Contrib to Rhetoric Soc Quart, shared with 3 others, 95; CIC Academic Leadership fel, 98-99. **MEMBERSHIPS** Modern Lang Asn; Asn for Depts of English; Nat Coun of Teachers of English; Conference on Col Composition and Communication; Soc for Critical Exchange; Soc for the Study of Narrative Lit; Rhetoric Soc of Am; Am Soc for the Hist of Rhetoric; Am Asn of Univ Profs. **RESEARCH** Hist and theory of rhetoric; literary theory; British Romantic poetry; William Wordsworth; Mikhail Bakhtin. **SELECTED PUBLICATIONS** Auth, Making Tales. The Poetics of Wordsworth's Narrative Experiments, Univ Chicago Press, 84; Wordsworth, Dialogics, and the Practice of Criticism, Cambridge Univ Press, 92; Bakhtin and the Future of Rhetorical Criticism: A Response to Halasek and Bernard-Donals, Rhetoric Soc Quart 22, 92, Landmark Essays on Bakhtin, Rhetoric, and Writing, ed Frank Farmer, Hermagoras Press, 98; Booth, Bakhtin, and the Culture of Criticism, Rhetoric and Pluralism: Legacies of Wayne Booth, Columbus OH State Univ Press, 95; Metaphors Critics Live By: Property, Names, and Colleagues in the Critical Archive, MN Rev, March 95; Antilogics, Dialogs, and Sophistic Social Psychology: Michael Billig's Reinvention of Bakhtin from Protagorean Rhetoric, Rhetoric, Pragmatism, Sophistry, ed Steven Mailloux, Cambridge Univ Press, 95; numerous other publications. **CONTACT ADDRESS** Dept of English, Pennsylvania State Univ, University Park, PA, 16802. **EMAIL** dhb1@psu.edu

BIBB, T. CLIFFORD
PERSONAL Born 10/29/1938, Montgomery, Alabama, s **DISCIPLINE** ENGLISH **EDUCATION** AL State Univ, BS 1960, MEd 1961; Northwestern Univ, PhD 1973. **CAREER** Rust Coll, chair English dept 1961-65; Daniel Payne Coll, chair English dept 1965-67; Miles Coll, English coord 1967-71; Northwestern Univ, English supr 1971-72; AL State Univ, chair advancement studies and dir four year plus curriculum prog. **HONORS AND AWARDS** Choir Dir/Singer in "The Long Walk Home", starring Whoopi Goldbert & Sissy Spacek. **MEMBERSHIPS** Dir upward prog Northwestern Univ 1972-73; commiss, composition NCTE 1973-76; sec Peterson-Bibb Lodge 762 1974-; fac adv Alpha Phi Alpha 1981-; exec comm NCTE 1983-88; exec sec & bd mem Central Montgomery Optimists 1984-86; desoto commiss State of AL 1986-95; National Council of Teachers of Eng, 1991-93; newsletter editor, AL Assn for Dev Ed, 1992-95; table leader (ETS), Ed Testing Service for APT/ENG, 1994-; Alabama State Council on The Arts, 1992-; NAT Council of Ed Opportunity Assn, 1992-; Natl Assn for Developmental Educ (NADE), pres-elect, 1997-98, pres, 1998-99. **CONTACT ADDRESS** Chair, Advancement Studies, Alabama State Univ, PO Box 234, Montgomery, AL, 36101-0271.

BICKNELL, JOHN W.
PERSONAL Born 01/22/1913, Mansfield, MA, m, 1936, 7 children **DISCIPLINE** ENGLISH **EDUCATION** Hamilton Col, BS, 35, MA, 36; Cornell Univ, PhD, 50. **CAREER** Instr English, St Lawrence Univ, 37-43; instr, Cornell Univ, 50-54; from assoc prof to prof, 54-78, chmn dept, 57-71, convener, Grad Prog English, 62-76, actg dean, Grad Sch, 67-69, EMER PROF ENGLISH, DREW UNIV, 78- **MEMBERSHIPS** MLA; Northeast Victorian Studies; Conf Brit Studies. **RESEARCH** Victorian literature; the history of intellectual history; Sir Leslie Stephen. **SELECTED PUBLICATIONS** Auth, Places of the Mind--The Life and Work of Thomson, James, Victorian Stud, Vol 0037, 94. **CONTACT ADDRESS** Dept of English, Drew Univ, Madison, NJ, 07940.

BIEGANOWSKI, RONALD
PERSONAL Born 05/23/1941, Milwaukee, WI **DISCIPLINE** ENGLISH, THEOLOGY **EDUCATION** St Louis Univ, BA, 65, MA, 66, PhL, 66; Jesuit Sch Theol, Berkeley, STM, 72; Fordham Univ, PhD (English), 77. **CAREER** Instr English, Marquette High Sch, Milwaukee, 66-69; ASST PROF ENGLISH, MARQUETTE UNIV, 76-, ASST CHMN, 80- **MEMBERSHIPS** MLA; Robert Frost Soc (treas, 78-). **RESEARCH** Robert Frost; modern American poetry; modern American fiction. **SELECTED PUBLICATIONS** Auth, Frost, Robert Star in a Stone Boat--A Grammar of Belief, Theol Stud, Vol 0057, 96. **CONTACT ADDRESS** Dept of English, Marquette Univ, Milwaukee, WI, 53233.

BIEN, GLORIA
PERSONAL Born 12/24/1940, Lanchow, China, m, 1979 **DISCIPLINE** LANGUAGE, LITERATURE **EDUCATION** Univ Calif, Berkeley, BA, 62, MA, 65; Univ Wash, Seattle, PhD, 75. **CAREER** Vis asst prof, 77-78, Indian Univ; asst prof, 74-80, Conn Col, N London CT; vis asst prof, 81-82, Univ Oregon; asst prof, 82-85, assoc prof, 85-, Colgate Univ. **RESEARCH** Chinese-French literary relations **CONTACT ADDRESS** Dept East Asian Lang & Lit, Colgate Univ, Hamilton, NY, 13346. **EMAIL** gbien@center.colgate.edu

BIEN, PETER ADOLPH
PERSONAL Born 05/28/1930, New York, NY, m, 1955, 3 children **DISCIPLINE** ENGLISH **EDUCATION** Haverford Col, BA, 52; Columbia Univ, MA, 57; PhD, 61. **CAREER** Lectr Eng, Columbia Univ, 59-60; from instr to prof, Dartmouth Col, 61-69, T & H Geisel Third Century prof hum, 74-79. Hon fel Greek, Univ Birmingham, 70-71 & 75; vis prof, Harvard Univ, 83. **HONORS AND AWARDS** E Harris Harbison Award, Danforth Found, 68. **MEMBERSHIPS** MLA; Mod Greek Studies Asn. **RESEARCH** Mod Brit and Greek lit. **SELECTED PUBLICATIONS** Transl, Nikos Kazantzakis, The Last Temptation of Christ, 60, Saint Francis, 62 & Report to Greco, 65, Simon & Schuster; auth, Nikos Kazantzakis, Columbia Univ, 72; Kazantzakis and the Linguistic Revolution in Greek literature, Princeton Univ, 72; transl, S Myrivilis, Life in the Tomb, Univ Press New England, 77; auth, Antithesis and Synthesis in the poetry of Yannis Ritsos, Kedros, Athens, 80; coauth, Demotic Greek II: O Iptamenos Thalamos, Univ Press New England, 82; auth, Three Generations of Greek Writers: Introductions to Cavafy, Kazantzakis, Ritsos, Efstathiadis, 83; auth, Kazantzakis: Politics of the Spirit, Princeton Univ, 89; Nikos Kazantkazis: Novelist, Duckworth, 89; coauth, God's Struggler: Religion in the Writings of Nikos Kazantzakis, Mercer Univ, 96. **CONTACT ADDRESS** Dept of English, Dartmouth Col, Hanover, NH, 03755. **EMAIL** peter.bien@dartmouth.edu

BIER, JESSE
PERSONAL Born 07/18/1925, Hoboken, NJ, m, 1950, 3 children **DISCIPLINE** ENGLISH **EDUCATION** Bucknell Univ, AB, 49; Princeton Univ, AM, 52, PhD (English), 56. **CAREER** Instr English lang and lit, Univ Colo, 52-55; from instr to assoc prof, 55-63, PROF ENGLISH, UNIV MONT, 63- Fulbright prof Am lit and civilization, Univs Lyon and Clermont, 57-58; vis lectr English, Bucknell Univ, 65-66; chair in Am lit, Univ Lausanne, 71-72; vis prof humanities, San Diego State Col, summer, 71; Can Govt study grant, 79. **HONORS AND AWARDS** Native Son Writer Award in Fiction, NJ State Teachers Asn, 65. **MEMBERSHIPS** Hon mem Mark Twain Soc; hon mem Am Humor Soc. **RESEARCH** American literature; creative writing; education. **SELECTED PUBLICATIONS** Auth, Enter Tainment and Exit Tainment--Literature and Sub Literature, Thalia Stud Lit Humor, Vol 0015, 95. **CONTACT ADDRESS** Wildcat Rd, Missoula, MT, 59801.

BIESECKER, BARBARA
PERSONAL Born 06/12/1959, Addington Heights, IL, s **DISCIPLINE** RHETORIC & COMMNICATION STUDIES **EDUCATION** Univ Pittsburgh, PhD, 89. **CAREER** Assoc prof, Univ Iowa, 91- . **MEMBERSHIPS** NCA **RESEARCH** Rhetorical theory and criticism, visual rhetorics, feminist theory and criticism **SELECTED PUBLICATIONS** co-auth with James P. McDaniel, The Irruptive Possibilities of the Other, The Encyclopedia of Rhetoric, 95; co-auth with Susan Biesecker, Gerald Mast, James McDaniel, A Genealogy of Oratory, The Encylopedia of Rhetoric, 95; auth, Addressing Postmodernity: Kenneth Burke, Rhetoric, and a Theory of Social Change, Studies in Rhetoric and Communication, 97; auth, Rhetoric and the 'New' Psychoanalysis: What's the Real Problem? or Framing the Problem of the Real, Quartelry Jour of Speech, 98; auth, Rhetorical Ventriloquism: Fantasy and/as National Identity, Proceedings of the Tenth SCA/AFA Conference on Argumentation, 98. **CONTACT ADDRESS** Rhetoric Dept, Univ Iowa, Iowa City, IA, 52240. **EMAIL** bbieseck@blue.weeg.uiowa.edu

BIESTER, JAMES
DISCIPLINE ENGLISH **EDUCATION** Stanford Univ, BA, 82; Columbia Univ, MA, 84,MPhil, 86, PhD, 90. **CAREER** Assoc prof; dir, grad prog(s). **RESEARCH** Early modern literature and culture; history of literary theory; history of rhetoric; modern poetry. **SELECTED PUBLICATIONS** Auth, Lyric Wonder: Rhetoric and Wit in Renaissance English Poetry, Cornell UP, 97; Admirable Wit: Deinotes and the Rise and Fall of Lyric Wonder, Rhetorica 14.3, 96; Nothing seene: Fear, Imagination, and Conscience in Fulke Greville's Caelica 100, Hellas 7.2, 96. **CONTACT ADDRESS** Dept of English, Loyola Univ, Chicago, 6525 N. Sheridan Rd., Chicago, IL, 60626. **EMAIL** jbieste@wpo.it.luc.edu

BING, JANET
DISCIPLINE ENGLISH, METHODS AND MATERIALS **EDUCATION** Coe Col, BA; Stanford Univ, MA; Univ Mass, PhD. **CAREER** Engl, Old Dominion Univ. **HONORS AND AWARDS** Rev, Nsf Proposals, 88; Conference Coorg, Lang Gender Interface: Theories & Methods Res & Tchg; Assoc ed, Women & Lang, 93; Assoc chair, Comt Status Women Linguistics, 94-95; Assoc ed, SECOL Rev, 95-. **RESEARCH** Phonology (syllable, tone, stress, intonation), Language and gender, Frame analysis, Kru languages. **SELECTED PUBLICATIONS** Auth, Talking Past Each Other about Sexual Harassment Discourse and Society, 97; Couth,The Question of Questions: Beyond Binary Thinking, in Rethinking Language; Coed, Gender Research: Theory and Practice, Victoria Bergvall, Longman, 94. **CONTACT ADDRESS** Old Dominion Univ, 4100 Powhatan Ave, BAL 423, Norfolk, VA, 23058. **EMAIL** JBing@odu.edu

BIRD, ROGER A.
PERSONAL Born 05/02/1938, Toronto, ON, Canada **DISCIPLINE** JOURNALISM **EDUCATION** Carleton Univ, BA, 61; Univ Minn, MA, 63, PhD, 69. **CAREER** Journ, vars publs, 65-68; asst prof Eng, Sir George Williams Univ, 68-74; ASSOC PROF JOURNALISM, CARLETON UNIV, 74-. **MEMBERSHIPS** Can Commun Asn; Asn Stud Can Radio & TV; Can Asn Journ; fel, Royal Can Geog Soc. **SELECTED PUBLICATIONS** Auth, The End of News, 97; ed, Documents of Canadian Broadcasting, 88; ed adv comt, Can Geog mag. **CONTACT ADDRESS** Journalism Dept., Carleton Univ, 1125 Colonel By Dr, Ottawa, ON, K1S 5B6.

BIRDSALL, ERIC
PERSONAL Born 06/28/1944, Glendale, CA, m, 1964, 1 child **DISCIPLINE** ENGLISH **EDUCATION** Johns Hopkins Univ, PhD, 76. **CAREER** Instr English, Salem Community Col, 74-75; instr, Penn State Univ, Shenango Valley, 75-76; assoc prof, Penn State Univ, Shenango Valley, 76-84; assoc prof, Penn State Univ, Shenango Valley, 84-87; prof English, Univ Akron, 87-; head, Dept of English, Univ Akron, 87-94. **HONORS AND AWARDS** Soc Res Grants, Am Philosophical Soc; award in the Humanities, Penn State Univ. **MEMBERSHIPS** Wordsworth-Coleridge Asn; North Am Soc for the Study of Romanticism. **RESEARCH** English and Am Romanticism; Wordsworth. **SELECTED PUBLICATIONS** Ed, Descriptive Sketches, Cornell Univ Press, 84; coauth, Writing on the Job: A Guide for Nurse Managers, Wiley, 86; auth, "Nature and Society in Descriptive Sketches", in Mod Philology 84, 86; auth, "Unmerited Contempt, Undeserved Praise: More on Wordsworth's Earliest Reviews", in The Wordsworth Circle 17, 86; auth, "Interpreting Henry James: Bogdanovich's Daisy Miller", in Literature/Film Quart 22, 94. **CONTACT ADDRESS** Department of English, Univ of Akron, Akron, OH, 44313. **EMAIL** ebirdsall@uakron.edu

BIRNBAUM, MILTON
PERSONAL Born 06/06/1919, Poland **DISCIPLINE** ENGLISH **EDUCATION** City Col NY, AB, 42; NY Univ, AM, 48, PhD(English), 56, D Lit, 96. **CAREER** Instr, 48-49, from asst prof to prof English, 50-73, chm dept, 62-73, Dean, Sch Arts & Sci, Am Int Col, 73-96, Retired, 96; Lectr, Univ Conn; prof, Holyoke Jr Col, 61-64; vis prof Shakespeare, St Hyacinth Col & Sem, 72-73. **MEMBERSHIPS** NAS; PBK; MLA; Jewish Acad Arts & Scis. **RESEARCH** British novel between the world wars; American romanticism; literature, philosophy and religion. **SELECTED PUBLICATIONS** Auth, The CEA Critic; Aldous Huxley's Quest for Values, Univ Tenn, 71; introd, An Encyclopedia of Pacifism, Garland Publ, 72; Professor Scylla & Professor Charybdis, 2/72 & Higher education, eh?, column, 72-75, Chronicle Higher Educ; The drift of College English in the last three years, Col English, 1/74; contribur, Aldous Huxley: A Collection of Critical Essays, Prentice-Hall, 74; Politics and character in point counter point, Studies in The Novel, winter 77; Ernest Hemingway read anew, Modern Age, summer 79; Are the Humanities Destined for Oblivion?, Mod Age, Spring 98.

BISHOP, ALLAN
DISCIPLINE ENGLISH LITERATURE **EDUCATION** Rhodes Univ, BA; Oxford Univ, MA, PhD. **RESEARCH** WWI literature; literature of peace and war; modern British novel. **SELECTED PUBLICATIONS** Ed, Joyce Cary, Selected Essays, 76; ed, Vera Brittain, Chronicle of Youth, 81; ed, Vera Brittain, Chronicle of Friendship, 86. **CONTACT ADDRESS** English Dept, McMaster Univ, 1280 Main St W, Hamilton, ON, L8S 4L9.

BISHOP, THOMAS G.
DISCIPLINE RENAISSANCE AND EARLY MODERN LITERATURE **EDUCATION** Univ Melbourne, BA; Yale Univ, PhD. **CAREER** English, Case Western Reserve Univ. **HONORS AND AWARDS** Dir, Baker-Nord Ctr Hum. **RESEARCH** Shakespeare; colonial & post-colonial lit. **SELECTED PUBLICATIONS** Auth, Shakespeare and the Theater of Wonder. **CONTACT ADDRESS** Case Western Reserve Univ, 10900 Euclid Ave, Cleveland, OH, 44106.

BITTENBENDER, J. CHRISTOPHER
DISCIPLINE TWENTIETH CENTURY, EIGHTEENTH CENTURY, AND MEDIEVAL BRITISH LITERATURE **EDUCATION** Univ St Andrews, PhD. **CAREER** Eastern Col **HONORS AND AWARDS** Ed, Janus, Running Press Book Publ. **SELECTED PUBLICATIONS** Areas: James Kelman, Robert Crawford, and Robert Burns. **CONTACT ADDRESS** Eastern Col, 1300 Eagle Rd, St. Davids, PA, 19087-3696.

BITTLE, WILLIAM GEORGE
PERSONAL Born 03/01/1943, Warren, OH, m, 1963, 2 children **DISCIPLINE** ENGLISH HISTORY **EDUCATION** E Stroudsburg State Col, BA, 70, MA, 71; Kent State Univ, PhD(hist), 75. **CAREER** ASST PROF HIST, KENT STATE UNIV, 75- **MEMBERSHIPS** AHA; Friend's Hist Asn; Conf Quaker Historians; Conf Brit Studies. **RESEARCH** Cromwellian England; English radical movements of the 17th century. **SELECTED PUBLICATIONS** Auth, The Battle of the Frogs and Fairfords Flies - Miracles and the Pulp Press During the English-Revolution, Am Hist Rev, Vol 0100, 95. **CONTACT ADDRESS** Dept of Hist, Kent State Univ, Canton, OH, 44720.

BITTRICH, LOUIS EDWARD
PERSONAL Born 11/04/1937, Omaha, NE, m, 1961, 2 children **DISCIPLINE** COMPARATIVE LITERATURE, THEATRE **EDUCATION** Gustavus Adolphus Col, BA, 59; Bowling Green State Univ, MA, 60; Univ NC, PhD (comp lit), 67; Southwest Texas State Univ, MA, 85. **CAREER** Instr English & dir theatre, Tex Lutheran Col, 60-62; instr English, Gustavus Adolphus Col, 62-63; asst prof, Winthrop Col, 65-66; asst prof, Gustavus Adolphus Col, 66-67; assoc prof, 67-79, prof English, 79-, chemn dept, 67-95, prof theatre, 95, chemn dept, Texas Lutheran Col; Exchange prof humanities, Winthrop Col, 65-66. **HONORS AND AWARDS** Ford Found fel, 65. **MEMBERSHIPS** MLA. **RESEARCH** Modern Roman elegies; contemporary mythology; Romantic poetry. **SELECTED PUBLICATIONS** Auth, Alchemy vindicated in our age, Cresset, 4/72. **CONTACT ADDRESS** Dept of Theatre, Texas Lutheran Univ, 1000 W Court St, Seguin, TX, 78155-5978. **EMAIL** bittrich@txlutheran.edu

BIZZELL, PATRICIA L.
PERSONAL Born 11/03/1948, Chicago, IL, m, 1977, 2 children **DISCIPLINE** ENGLISH LITERATURE **EDUCATION** Wellesley Col, BA, 70; Rutgers Univ, PhD, 75 **CAREER** Asst prof, Rutgers, 75-78; asst prof, Holy Cross, 78-81; assoc prof, Holy Cross,, 81-88; dir, Writing Programs, Holy Cross, 81-94; dir, College Honors Program, 94-98; prof, Holy Cross, 88- **HONORS AND AWARDS** Ntl Council Teachers of English Outstanding Book Award, 92 **MEMBERSHIPS** Modern Lang Assoc; Ntl Council Teachers English; Conf Col Composition and Comm; Amer Assoc Univ Professors; Speech Comm Assoc; Council Writing Program Admin; Rhetoric Soc Amer **RESEARCH** English Literature **SELECTED PUBLICATIONS** Coauth, The Bedford Bibliography for Teachers of Writing, St Martin, 96; coauth, Negotiating Difference: Readings in Multicultural American Rhetoric, St Martin, 95; auth, Academic Discourse and Critical Consciousness, Univ Pitt, 92 **CONTACT ADDRESS** English Dept, Holy Cross Col, Worcester, MA, 01610.

BJORK, ROBERT ERIC
PERSONAL Born 02/19/1949, Virgina, MN **DISCIPLINE** MEDIEVAL AND SCANDINAVIAN LITERATURE **EDUCATION** Pomona Col, BA, 71; Univ Calif, Los Angeles, MA, 75, PhD(English), 79. **CAREER** ADJ LECTR ENGLISH AND MED, UNIV CALIF, LOS ANGELES, 79-, Tech ed, J Community Health, 79-82; prin ed, Univ Calif, Los Angeles, Clinicl Scholars Prog, Sch Med, 80- **HONORS AND AWARDS** Elmer Friman Award, Health Sci Commun Asn, 82. **MEMBERSHIPS** MLA; Medieval Acad Am; Am Lit Transl Asn; Am Scand Found; Am Med Writers Asn. **RESEARCH** Old English poetry; modern Swedish literature; biomedical writing. **SELECTED PUBLICATIONS** Auth, Anglo-Saxon Litanies of the Saints, Albion, Vol 0024, 92; The Saxon 'Genesis' - An Edition of the West Saxon 'Genesis B' and the Old-Saxon Vatican 'Genesis,' Mich Ger Stud, Vol 0018, 92; Speech as Gift in 'Beowulf,' and Joining Methods of Style and Rhetorical Analysis With Medieval theories of Language, Speculum-J of Medieval Stud, Vol 0069, 94; A Grammar of Old-English, Vol 1 - Phonology, Speculum-J of Medieval Stud, Vol 0069, 94; A Sudden Liberating Thought, Scand Stud, Vol 0067, 95; Thorkelin,Grimur,Jonsson Preface to the First Edition of 'Beowulf,' 1815/, Scand Stud, Vol 0068, 96; In the Foreground - 'Beowulf,' Speculum-J of Medieval Stud, Vol 0071, 96; The Translators invisibility - A History of Translation, J of Eng and Ger Philol, Vol 0096, 97. **CONTACT ADDRESS** 18212 Nordhoff St, Northridge, CA, 91325.

BLACK, DANIEL
DISCIPLINE ENGLISH LITERATURE **EDUCATION** Temple Univ, PhD, 93. **CAREER** Joint fac Eng and African/African Am Studies. **RESEARCH** Black male studies and Africana Literary traditions. **SELECTED PUBLICATIONS** Auth, Dismantling Manhood, 96. **CONTACT ADDRESS** Clark Atlanta Univ, 223 James P Brawley Dr, SW, Atlanta, GA, 30314.

BLACK, EDWIN
PERSONAL Born 10/26/1929, Houston, TX, m, 1979 **DISCIPLINE** RHETORIC **EDUCATION** Univ Houston, BS, 51; Cornell Univ, MA, 53, PhD, 62. **CAREER** Instr/asst prof of English, Washington Univ, 56-61; vis prof, Univ Calif-Berkeley, 64; vis prof, Univ Minn, 67; vis prof, Calif State Univ, 69 & 72; vis prof, Univ Calif-Davis, 78 & 88; asst prof/prof of Speech, Univ Pittsburgh, 61-67; prof of commun arts, 67-94, PROF EMERITUS, UNIV WIS-MADISON, 94-. **HONORS AND AWARDS** Speech Commun Asn Book Award, 66; Speech Asn Monograph Award, 89. **MEMBERSHIPS** Nat Commun Asn. **RESEARCH** Rhetorical criticism. **SELECTED PUBLICATIONS** Auth, Rhetorical Questions: Studies of Public Discourse, Univ of Chicago Press, 92; Gettysburg and Silence, Quart J of Speech, 94; The Invention of Nixon, Beyond the Rhetorical Presidency, Tx A&M Univ Press, 96; The Aesthetics of Rhetoric, American Style, Rhetoric and Political Culture: Interpreting Am Public Discourse, Mich State Univ Press, 97; The Prospect of Rhetoric: Twenty-Five Years Later, Making and Unmaking the Prospects for Rhetoric, Lawrence Erlbaum Assocs Inc, 97. **CONTACT ADDRESS** 3326 Valley Creek Cr., Middleton, WI, 53526-1988. **EMAIL** e-black@msn.com

BLACK, LENDLEY C.
DISCIPLINE COMMUNICATION STUDIES **EDUCATION** Univ Tennessee, BA; Univ Conn, MA; Univ Kans, PhD. **CAREER** Prof, 82-. **SELECTED PUBLICATIONS** Auth, pubs on Russian theatre and drama; Michael Chekhov. **CONTACT ADDRESS** Div of Communcation and Theatre Arts, Emporia State Univ, 1200 Commercial St, Emporia, KS, 66801-5087. **EMAIL** blacklen@esumail.emporia.edu

BLACK, NANCY BREMILLER
PERSONAL Born 11/12/1941, Norristown, PA, m, 1964, 2 children **DISCIPLINE** ENGLISH; COMPARATIVE LITERATURE **EDUCATION** Vassar Col, BA, 63; Univ Pa, MA, 64; Columbia Univ, PhD(English), 71. **CAREER** Lectr English, City Col New York, 71-72; from instr to Assoc Prof, 72-95, PROF ENGLISH, BROOKLYN COL, 95-. **HONORS AND AWARDS** Shaughnessy scholar, 81-82. **MEMBERSHIPS** MLA; Mediaeval Acad Am. **RESEARCH** Medieval comparative literature. **SELECTED PUBLICATIONS** Co-ed, White on Red: Images of the American Indian, Kennikat, 76; ed and transl, The Perilious Cemetary, Garland, 94. **CONTACT ADDRESS** Dept of English, Brooklyn Col, CUNY, 2900 Bedford Ave, Brooklyn, NY, 11210-2813.

BLACK, STEPHEN AMES
PERSONAL Born 08/31/1935, Los Angeles, CA, m, 1980, 1 child **DISCIPLINE** AMERICAN LITERATURE **EDUCATION** Calif State Col, Los Angeles, BA, 60, MA, 61; Univ Wash, PhD(English), 64. **CAREER** Asst prof English, Monmouth Col, 64-66; asst prof, 66-69, assoc prof, 69-74, PROF ENGLISH, SIMON FRASER UNIV, 74-, Can Coun leave fel, 74-75; affil instr, Seattle Psychoanalytic Inst, 75- **MEMBERSHIPS** MLA. **RESEARCH** Psychoanalysis and literature; literary theory; American literature. **SELECTED PUBLICATIONS** Auth, Oneill Shakespeare, Am Lit, Vol 0066, 94. **CONTACT ADDRESS** Dept of English, Simon Fraser Univ, Burnaby, BC, V5A 1S6.

BLACK, STEVE
PERSONAL Born 12/12/1959, Huntsville, AL, m, 1980, 1 child **DISCIPLINE** LIBRARY SCIENCE **EDUCATION** Fla State, BA, 82; Univ Va, M.Ed, 87; SUNY, MLS, 93. **CAREER** Librn, Col Saint Rose, 95-. **RESEARCH** Economics of scholarly publications. **SELECTED PUBLICATIONS** Auth, art, Journal Collection Analysis at A Liberal Arts College, 97. **CONTACT ADDRESS** 10352 Duanesburg Rd, Quaker Street, NY, 12141. **EMAIL** blacks@rosnet.strose.edu

BLACKBURN, ALEXANDER
PERSONAL Born 09/06/1929, Durham, NC, m, 1975, 3 children **DISCIPLINE** ENGLISH **EDUCATION** Yale Univ, BA, 51; Univ North Carolina, MA, 56; Cambridge Univ, PhD, 63. **CAREER** Instr, Hampden-Sydney Col, 59-60; instr, Univ Penn, 63-65; lectr, Univ Maryland, Euro Div, 67-72; from asst prof to prof emer, Univ Colorado at Colorado Springs, 74-95. **HONORS AND AWARDS** Fac book awd, UCCS, 93; Chancellor's Awd, 94., Ed in chief, Writers' Forum, 74-95. **MEMBERSHIPS** RMMLA; Colo Auth League; PEN Ctr West; Writers Guild. **RESEARCH** Fiction. **SELECTED PUBLICATIONS** Auth, The Myth of the Picaro, 79; auth, The Cold War of Kitty Pentecost, 79; ed, The Interior Country: Stories of the Modern West, 87; auth, A Sunrise Brighter Still: The Visionary Novels of Frank Waters, 91; ed, Higher Elevations: Stories from the West, 93; auth, Suddenly a Mortal Splendor, 95. **CONTACT ADDRESS** 6030 Twin Rock Ct, Colorado Springs, CO, 80918.

BLACKBURN, THOMAS
PERSONAL Born 05/28/1932, m, 2 children **DISCIPLINE** ENGLISH **EDUCATION** Amherst Col, BA, 54; Oxford Univ, MA, 60; Stanford Univ, PhD, 63. **CAREER** Actg instr, Stanford Univ, 58-61; instr, Swarthmore Col, 61-63; vis lctr, Bryn Mawr Col, 68; asst prof, Swarthmore Col, 63-69; to assoc prof, 69-75; to chr Eng dept, 74-75; to dean 75-81; to prof 83-85; to dir undergrad wrtg assocs prog, 85-; to Centennial prof Engl, 92-. **HONORS AND AWARDS** Grant, Folger Shakespeare Inst, 88 and 90; ACLS Fellow, 65-66; NLA grant, Sloan Foundation, 87; res grants, Swarthmore Col, 93, 88-89, 81-82, 74-75, 70. **MEMBERSHIPS** MLA; Renaissance Soc Am; Milton Soc Am; Shakespeare Assoc Am; Nat Coun Tchrs Eng; Conf Col Comp Comm. **SELECTED PUBLICATIONS** Auth, Shakespeare in the Electronic Classroom, Shakespeare and the Classroom, 95; Lycidas: Eternity As Artifice, Milton Studies, 91; Carnal Rhetoric: Milton's Iconoclasm and the Poetics of Desire, Renaissance Quart, 97; The Ashland Shakespeare Festival, Shakespeare and the Classroom, 95; Shakespeare and the Changing Curriculum, Shakespeare and the Classroom, 93; John Milton in The Poetic Birth: Milton's Poems of 1645 by CWRD Moseley, and John Milton: Political Writings, Rev Engl Studies, 93. **CONTACT ADDRESS** Swarthmore Col, 500 College Ave, Swarthmore, PA, 19081-1397. **EMAIL** tblackb1@swarthmore.edu

BLACKEY, ROBERT ALAN
PERSONAL Born 12/17/1941, New York, NY, m **DISCIPLINE** ENGLISH HISTORY, HISTORY OF REVOLUTIONS, HISTORY EDUCATION **EDUCATION** City Col New York, BA, 63; NY Univ, MA, 64, PhD(hist), 68. **CAREER** Prof Hist, Calif State Univ, San Bernadino, 68-, Fel, William Andrews Clark Mem Libr, Univ Calif, Los Angeles, 69; chief reader, Col Bd Advan Placement Exam in Europ Hist, 77-80. **MEMBERSHIPS** AHA; Conf Brit Studies; Anglo-Am Asn. **RESEARCH** Eighteenth century English history. **SELECTED PUBLICATIONS** Auth, Fanon and Cabral: A Contrast in Theories of Revolution for Africa, J Mod African Studies, 6/74; coauth, Revolution and the Revolutionary Ideal, Schenkman, 76; auth, Modern Revolutions and Revolutionists: A Bibliography, ABC-Clio Bks, 76; A Politician in Ireland: The Lord Lieutenancy of the Earl of Halifax, 1761-63, Eire-Ireland, Winter, 79; Free at Last: Portuguese Colonies After Independence, African Studies Assoc Rev of Bks, 79; Beginning an Advanced Placement Course in European History, Col Entrance Exam Bd, 80; A Guide to the Skill of Essay Construction in History, Social Educ, 3/81; Revolution and Revolutionists: A Comprehensive Guide to the Literature, ABC-Clio Bks, 82. **CONTACT ADDRESS** Dept of History, California State Univ, San Bernardino, 5500 University Pky, San Bernardino, CA, 92407-7500. **EMAIL** rblackey@wiley.csusb.edu

BLACKMORE, ROBERT LONG
PERSONAL Born 09/13/1919, Akron, NY, m, 1941, 2 children **DISCIPLINE** ENGLISH **EDUCATION** Colgate Univ, BA, 41, MA, 61; Syracuse Univ, PhD(English), 65. **CAREER** From instr to assoc prof, 60-70, chmn dept, 72-75, actg dir humanities, 75, 77-78, provost & dean of fac, 79-80, prof English, 70-, prof emeritus, Colgate Univ; Dir, Colgate Univ Press, 64-; ed, Powys Newslett, 70- **MEMBERSHIPS** MLA. **RESEARCH** Nineteenth-century British literature; Georgian literature: creative writing. **SELECTED PUBLICATIONS** Auth, Introduction to Blackmore's Lorna Doone, Everyman's Libr, London, 66; Introduction to John Cowper Powys' Autobiography, Macdonald, London, 67; ed, Introduction to Blackmore's Springhaven, Everyman's Libr, 69; Advice to a Young Poet: Llewelyn Powys, Fairleigh Dickinson, 69; John Cowper Powys' An Englishman Upstate, Village, London, 74; auth, Powys to Knight, C Woolf, London, 82. **CONTACT ADDRESS** 21 University Ave, Hamilton, NY, 13346.

BLACKSTONE, MARY A.
PERSONAL Ellsworth, ME **DISCIPLINE** ENGLISH **EDUCATION** Univ Maine, BA, 71; Univ Brunswick, MA, 73, PhD, 78. **CAREER** Lectr, Univ Toronto, 79-81; asst prof, Washington & Jefferson Col, 81-82; coordr grad stud drama, Univ Alberta, 87-90; asst prof, 82-87, ASSOC PROF THEATRE, UNIV REGINA 90-, DEAN FINE ARTS 90-. **HONORS AND AWARDS** Maine/NB scholar, 69-70; REED post-doctoral fel, Univ Toronto. **MEMBERSHIPS** Can Asn Fine Arts Deans; Int Coun Fine Arts Deans; Am Soc Theatre Res; Int Shakespeare Asn. **SELECTED PUBLICATIONS** Auth, Robin Hood and the Friar, 81. **CONTACT ADDRESS** Faculty of Theatre Arts, Univ Regina, Regina, SK, S4S OA2. **EMAIL** mblackst@max.cc.uregina.ca

BLACKWELL, MARILYN JOHNS
PERSONAL Born 08/01/1948, Cincinnati, OH, m, 1980 **DISCIPLINE** SCANDINAVIAN LITERATURE, FILM **EDUCATION** Univ Wis, BA, 70; Univ Wash, MA, 73, PhD(Scand lit), 76. **CAREER** Lectr, Univ BC, 75-77; ASST PROF, UNIV VA, 77-, Mellon fac fel, Harvard Univ, 81-82. **MEMBERSHIPS** Soc Advan Scand Studies; MLA. **RESEARCH** Comparative literature. **SELECTED PUBLICATIONS** Auth, Dinesen,Isak - The Engendering of Narrative, Scand Stud, Vol 0065, 93; The Play and Mirrors - a Study of the Film Aesthetic of Bergman,Ingmar, Scand Stud, Vol 0066, 94; Swedish - a Comprehensive Grammar, Mod Lang J, Vol 0078, 94; Ideology and Specularity in Enquist, Per, Olov 'Tribadernas Natt,' Scand Stud, Vol 0067, 95; Strindberg Post-Inferno Plays, Scand Stud, Vol 0067, 95; Between Stage and Screen - Bergman,Ingmar Directs, Scand Stud, Vol 0068, 96; The Silence, in Bergman,Ingmar - Disruption and Disavowal in The Movement Beyond Gender, Scandinavica, Vol 0035, 96. **CONTACT ADDRESS** Dept Ger, Univ Va, Charlottesville, VA, 22903.

BLACKWOOD, ROY E.
PERSONAL Born 03/17/1944, Rochester, PA, m, 1980, 2 children **DISCIPLINE** COMMUNICATION **EDUCATION** US Marine Corps Commun Sch, 63-64; Univ AK, 67-68; Cleveland State Univ, BA, 72; Cornell Univ, MA, 75, PhD, 81. **CAREER** Commun Specialist, US Marine Corps, 63-67; manag ed, Polar Star, Univ AK, 67-68; reporter/photog, Daily News, Anchorage, AK, 68-69; freelance writer, 69-72; tchg asst, 72-73, news writer, 73-74, commun specialist, 74-78, Cornell Univ; commun specialist, Univ IL, 78-82; asst prof, 82-87, assoc prof, 87, Bemidji State Univ; foreign expert, journalism, Liaoning Univ, 88-89; assoc prof 89-91, prof, 91-, Bemidji State Univ; vis prof, Chulalongkorn Univ, 93-94; chair, Mass Commun, 97-. **HONORS AND AWARDS** Univ Merit Award, 84; Nat Tchg Award, 87; Study Tour Chinese Media, 87, US Academics; Fulbright Travel Grant, 90; Freedom Forum Sem, 91. **MEMBERSHIPS** Asn Educ Journalism and Mass Commun; Int Commun Asn; Canadian Commun Asn; Midwest Asn Canadian Studies. **RESEARCH** Treatment of US in Thai and Chinese press; treatment of US in Canadian editorial cartoons; international content of US and Canadian newsphotos; sex and race roles in newspaper photos. **SELECTED PUBLICATIONS** Auth, "The Content of News Photos: Roles Portrayed by Men and Women," Jour Quart, 83; "Using PC's As A Front-End Network to Produce A College Newspaper," Coll Media Rev, 86; "International News Photos in US and Canadian Papers," Jour Quart, 87; "Ronbo and the Peanut Farmer in Canadian Editorial Cartoons," Jour Quart, 89; "Great Walls: Barriers to Journalism Research in the People's Republic of China," Am Jour, 90. **CONTACT ADDRESS** Dept of Mass Communication, Bemidji State Univ, Bemidji, MN, 56601. **EMAIL** rblackwood@vax1.bemidji.msus.edu

BLAIR, JOHN
DISCIPLINE ENGLISH **EDUCATION** FL State Univ, BA, MA; Tulane Univ, PhD. **CAREER** Southwest Tex State Univ **SELECTED PUBLICATIONS** Auth, A Landscape of Darkness; Bright Angel. **CONTACT ADDRESS** Southwest Texas State Univ, 601 University Dr, San Marcos, TX, 78666-4604.

BLAISDELL, ROBERT EHLER
DISCIPLINE LITERATURE **EDUCATION** Univ Calif-Santa Barbara, BA, 81, MA, 84, PhD, 88. **CAREER** Tchg asst, 83-88, tchg assoc, 88, lectr, 88-92, Col Creative Stud & English Dept, Univ Cal-Santa Barbara; adj asst prof, Borough of Manhattan Comm Col, CUNY, 93-95; adj asst prof, Jersey City State Col, 96; asst prof, DeVry Inst, 96-97; substitute asst prof, 97-98, ASST PROF, 98- , KINGSBOROUGH COMM COL, CUNY. **HONORS AND AWARDS** Award for Innovative and Creative Teaching, DeVry Inst, 97. **RESEARCH** D H Lawrence; Leo Tolstoy. **SELECTED PUBLICATIONS** Rev, Janice Radway's A Feeling for Books, Am Book Rev, 98; rev, Martha C. Nussbaum's Cultivating Humanity, Am Book Rev, 98; auth, The Boy's Coach, Teaching and Learning: The Journal of Natural Inquiry, 98; Teaching Jamaica Kincaid's 'Putting Myself Together' College Teaching, 98; How Do You Know When You're in Love? , The Teachers & Writers Guide to William Carlos Williams, 98; My Antonia, Spectrum, 98; Hercules for Young Readers, Classical World, 98; Tolstoy, the Writing Teacher, Teaching and Learning Literature, 98; rev, Emmanuel Bove's A Winter's Journal, Am Book Rev, 99; auth, Sensational von Kleist: Using His Stories, Classics in the Classroom: Using Great Literature to Teach Writing, 99. **CONTACT ADDRESS** 401 W 118th St, No.33, New York, NY, 10027. **EMAIL** rblaisdell@kbcc.cuny.edu

BLAISE, CLARK L.
PERSONAL Born 04/10/1940, Fargo, ND **DISCIPLINE** CREATIVE WRITING **EDUCATION** Denison Univ, BA, 61, PhD(hon), 79; Univ Iowa, MFA, 64. **CAREER** Prof, Concordia Univ, 66-78; prof, York Univ, 78-80; prof, Skidmore Col, 80-81, 82-83; writer-in-residence, David Thompson Univ Ctr, 83; writer-in-residence, Emory Univ, 85; adj prof, Columbia Univ, 86; vis prof, 81-82, DIR, INTERNATIONAL WRITING PROG, UNIV IOWA, 90-. **HONORS AND AWARDS** Can Coun grants; Guggenheim fel, NEA grant. **MEMBERSHIPS** PEN. **SELECTED PUBLICATIONS** Auth, A North American Education, 73; auth, Tribal Justice, 74; auth, Lunar Attractions, 78; auth, Lusts, 83; auth, Resident Alien, 86; auth, Man and His World, 92; auth, I Had a Father, 93; coauth, Days and Nights in Calcutta, 77; coauth The Sorrow and the Terror, 97; co-ed, Here and Now, 77; co-ed, Best Canadian Stories, 78, 79, 80. **CONTACT ADDRESS** The Porcupine's Quill, 68 Main St, Erin, ON, N0B 1T0.

BLAKE, JAMES JOSEPH
PERSONAL Born 04/29/1939, New York, NY **DISCIPLINE** ENGLISH & IRISH LITERATURE **EDUCATION** Manhattan Col, BA, 62; NY Univ, MA, 64, PhD, 79 **CAREER** From instr to assoc prof, 65-78, PROF ENGLISH, NASSAU COMMUNITY COL, 78-, Sr bibliogr Irish Gaelic lit res, Celtic Lit Sect Head, MLA, 78-; broadcaster, Weekly hour prog in Spoken Irish, WFUV FM, Fordham Univ, 79-; adj prof, Irish lit, undergraduate, 88-95, graduate 91-95, NY Univ, Sch Arts and Science; adj lectr Irish-Gaelic, John Jay Col, 80-81; adj assoc prof mod Irish, Queens Col, 82; secy, Sub-Comt Irish Lang, Am Comt Irish Studies, 82-83. **HONORS AND AWARDS** Fulbright fel, Trinity Col, Dublin, Ireland, 69-70. **MEMBERSHIPS** MLA; Am Irish Studies; Exec comt Am Conf Irish Studies, 93-95; Exec comt, columbia Univ Seminar Irish Studies, 85-; Vpres, North Am Asn Celtic Lang Teachers, 98-99. **RESEARCH** William Butler Yeats; Irish Gaelic; Ireland's literary Renaissance in both English and Irish. **SELECTED PUBLICATIONS** Ed, Eire-Ireland: A Jour Irish Studies (quart), 86-90; Irish Lang ed, New Hibernia Rev (quart), 96-; consult ed, Jour Celtic Lang Learning (annual), 95-; auth, Irish in education and the media, Eire-Ireland, winter 94; Irish language cultural communities, Eire-Ireland, summer 95; The Irish language today: The enhanced public presence of Irish, New Hibernia Rev, summer 97; Beal Feirste (Belfast): An Irish language community, New Hibernia Rev, winter 98. **CONTACT ADDRESS** Nassau Comm Col, Garden City, NY, 11530-6793. **EMAIL** blakej@sunynassau.edu

BLAKE, RICHARD
PERSONAL Born 02/21/1939, New York, NY, s **DISCIPLINE** FILM STUDIES **EDUCATION** Fordham, MA, 65;

Northwestern, PhD, 72 **CAREER** Ed, 71-85, American Magazine; visiting prof, 85-87, Georgetown Univ; prof, 87-96, Le Moyne Coll; prof, 96-, Boston Coll. **HONORS AND AWARDS** Jesuit Chair, Georgetown, 85-86; Gasson Chair Boston Coll, 96-98. **MEMBERSHIPS** Soc for Cinema Studies **RESEARCH** Religious Imagination in Film **SELECTED PUBLICATIONS** Woody Auth, Allen Profane and Sacred, Scarecrow, 95; Redeemed in Blood, The Sacramental Universe of Martin Scorsese, in Journal of Popular Film & Television, Sring 96; Igmar Bergman's Post-Christian God: Silent, Absent and Female, Religion and the Arts, Spring 97; Frank Capra: It's a Dangerous Life, Boston College Magazine, Summer 98; Afterimage: Catholic Imagination in American Film, Loyola Press, 99. **CONTACT ADDRESS** Fine Arts Dept, Devlin Hall, Boston Col, Chestnut Hill, MA, 02467. **EMAIL** blaberi@bc.edu

BLAKE, ROBERT GRADY
PERSONAL Born 03/06/1934, Charlotte, NC, m, 1965, 2 children **DISCIPLINE** ENGLISH **EDUCATION** Harvard Univ, AB, 56; Duke Univ, MA, 59, PhD(English), 68. **CAREER** Asst prof English, Stetson Univ, 59-62; assoc prof, Morris Harvey Col, 64-68, acting chemn dept, 65-68; chemn dept, 68-77, William S Long Prof English, Elon Col, 68-, Lilly scholar, Duke Univ, 77-78. **MEMBERSHIPS** Phi Beta Kappa; Alpha Chi (honorary); Phi Kappa Phi (honorary); Sigma Tau Delta; Omicron Delta Kappa; Phi Theta Kappa. **RESEARCH** Periodicals of the 19th century; Victorian literature, especially poetry; 19th century poetry reviews. **SELECTED PUBLICATIONS** The Edinburgh Magazine, or Literary Miscellany, In: British Literary Magazines; Algernon Charles Swinburne, A E Housman, and Sociological Approaches to Poetry, In: Critical Survey of Poetry; Our Town, Masterplots II: Juvenile and Young Adults Supplement and The Jilting of Granny Weatherall; The Sire de Maledroit's Door, Masterplots II: Short Story Supplement; The Taming of the Shrew and Titus Andronicus, Masterplots: Twentieth Anniversary Revised Second Edition; Hershel Baker, Walter Jackson Bate, and Lionel Stevenson in Dictionary of Lit Bio; A C Swinburne, The St James Guide to Bio. **CONTACT ADDRESS** Dept of English, Elon Col, Elon College, NC, 27244. **EMAIL** blakeb@numen.elon.edu

BLANCH, ROBERT JAMES
PERSONAL Born 02/17/1938, Brooklyn, NY, m, 1961, 5 children **DISCIPLINE** MEDIEVAL LITERATURE **EDUCATION** Col Holy Cross, AB, 59; Northeastern Univ, MA, 61; State Univ NY, Buffalo, PhD(English), 67. **CAREER** Instr English, Northeastern Univ, 61-62; instr, Newman Prep Sch, Boston, 62-63; instr, State Univ NY, Buffalo, 63-66; asst prof, Canisius Col, 66-67; asst prof, Bentley Col Acct and Finance, 67-68; assoc prof, 68-78, PROF ENGLISH, NORTHEASTERN UNIV, 78-. **MEMBERSHIPS** MLA. **RESEARCH** The works of the Pearl Poet; Chaucer; courtly love literature. **SELECTED PUBLICATIONS** Auth, the Name and Fame of Gawain in 'Sir Gawain and the Green Knight,' Studia Neophilologica, Vol 0064, 92; 'Sir Gawain and the Green Knight' - a Dual-Language Version, Speculum-J of Medieval Stud, Vol 0068, 93; The Current State of 'Sir Gawain and the Green Knight' Criticism, Chaucer Rev, Vol 0027, 93; 'Sir Gawain and the Green Knight' and the Idea of Righteousness, J of Eng and Ger Philol, Vol 0093, 94. **CONTACT ADDRESS** Dept of English, Northeastern Univ, 360 Huntington Ave, Boston, MA, 02115-5000.

BLANCHARD, ROBERT O.
DISCIPLINE COMMUNICATIONS **EDUCATION** Northwestern Univ, BSJ, 55-57, MSJ, 57-58; Syracuse Univ, PhD, 66. **CAREER** Tchg asst, Northwestern Univ, 58-59; tchg asst, Syracuse Univ, 61-63; asst to the dean, Syracuse Univ, 63-64; asst prof, Am Univ, 65-66; ch, asst, assoc, full prof, Am Univ, 66-77; founting dean, prof, Am Univ, 77-78; dir, prof, PA tate Univ, 78-82; ch, dept prof, 82-92; prof, ch, 92-. **HONORS AND AWARDS** Curriculum consult, Southwestern, Xavier, Univ S Dakota, Evansville, Denison, Wichita State, St Michael's, Hofstra, S Ill, Linfield Col, Bradley, Univ Ariz, Ursinus Col, Bradley Univ, 86-; founding ed, Southwestern Mass Commun Jour, 85-88; columnist, The Marquise, 95-. **MEMBERSHIPS** Repr, Assn Commun Admin, 88-93; VP, 80-81, pres, 81-82, Am Assn Sch(s) and Dept(s) of Jour; Mem, Assn Commun Admin; Assn Edu in Jour and Mass Commun. **SELECTED PUBLICATIONS** Auth, Congress and the News Media, Hastings House, 74; Newspaper missed significant issues on city elections, council action, San Antonio Exprcss-Ncws, 97; The disintegration of professional integrity, Jour Edu, First Amendment Imperative, and the Changing Mctia Marketplacc, 97; co-auth, Mission Staternents, Outcomes, and the New Liberal Arts, Assessing Communicatwn, A Handbook for Media, Speech, and Theater L Erlbaum, 94; Beyond the Media Workshop, Fccdback, 94; Thoughts on Ehrlich's 'Newcomer: Fccdback, 94; The Undergraduate Communication, Colloquia: Theory Anyone? Fecdback, 94; Assessing media education in an integrated communication program, Media Edu Assessment Handbook, L Earlbaum, 97. **CONTACT ADDRESS** Dept of Commun, Trinity Univ, 715 Stadium Dr, San Antonio, TX, 78212.

BLANCHARD, SCOTT
DISCIPLINE SHAKESPEARE **EDUCATION** Columbia Univ, PhD. **CAREER** Engl, Col Misericordia **SELECTED PUBLICATIONS** Area: Renaissance satire. **CONTACT ADDRESS** Col Misericordia, 301 Lake St., Dallas, PA, 18612-1098. **EMAIL** sblancha@miseri.edu

BLANK, G. KIM
DISCIPLINE ENGLISH LITERATURE **EDUCATION** Univ Simon Fraser, BA; Univ Wales, MA; Univ Southampton, PhD. **CAREER** Prof; dir, Eng grad stud. **RESEARCH** Romantic poetry; critical approaches; professional writing; canonization. **SELECTED PUBLICATIONS** Auth, Wordsworth's Influence on Shelley: A Study of Poetic Authority, Macmillan, St. Martin's; Influence and Resistance in Nineteenth-Century English Poetry, Macmillan, St. Martin's; Wordsworth and Feeling: The Poetry of an Adult Child, Fairleigh Dickensen UP, Assoc UP; co-ed, The New Shelley: Later Twentieth-Century Views, Margot Louis, Macmillan, St. Martin's. **CONTACT ADDRESS** Dept of English, Victoria Univ, PO Box 3070, Victoria, BC, V8W 3W1. **EMAIL** gkblank@uvic.ca

BLASING, MUTLU KONUK
PERSONAL Born 06/27/1944, Istanbul, Turkey, m, 1965, 1 child **DISCIPLINE** ENGLISH **EDUCATION** Col of William and Mary, BA, 69; Brown Univ, PhD, 74. **CAREER** Lectr, Eng, Univ Mass, 74-76; asst prof, Eng, Pomona Col, 77-79; **HONORS AND AWARDS** Postdoctoral fel, U Mass, 74-76. **RESEARCH** American poetry; translation of poetry. **SELECTED PUBLICATIONS** Auth, The Art of Life, Texas, 77; auth, American Poetry, Yale, 87; auth, Politics and Form in Postmodern Poetry, Cambridge, 95. **CONTACT ADDRESS** English Dept, Brown Univ, PO Box 1852, Providence, RI, 02912. **EMAIL** mutlu_blasing@brown.edu

BLATT, STEPHEN J.
DISCIPLINE INTERPERSONAL COMMUNICATION **EDUCATION** Morehead State Univ, BA, 64; Ohio Univ, MA, 67; PhD, 70. **CAREER** Assoc prof, 71-. **RESEARCH** The use of small groups in classroom management strategies. **SELECTED PUBLICATIONS** Publ, Midwestern Edu Researcher, 95; Rev of Higher Edu, 96. **CONTACT ADDRESS** Dept of Commun, Univ Dayton, 300 Col Park, Dayton, OH, 75062. **EMAIL** Sblatt@Udayton.edu

BLAU, HERBERT
PERSONAL Born 05/03/1926, Brooklyn, NY, m, 1981, 4 children **DISCIPLINE** ENGLISH; COMPARATIVE LITERATURE **EDUCATION** NY Univ, BchE, 47; Stanford Univ, MA, 49, PhD, 54. **CAREER** From asst prof to prof, San Francisco State Univ, 50-65; co-found and co-dir, The Actor's Workshop of San Francisco, 52-65; co-dir, Repertory Theater of Lincoln Ctr, NY, 65-67; prof, City Univ of NY, 67-68; provost and dean, School of Theater and Dance, Calif Inst of the Arts, 68-71; found and artistic dir, KRAKEN theatre, 71-81; prof of the Arts and dir of Inter-Arts Prog, Oberlin Col, 72-74; dean, div of Arts and Hums, Univ of Md, 74-76; prof, Univ of Md, 76-78; prof, Univ of Wis, 78-84; disting. prof, Univ of Wis, 84- ; ed and adv bds, Performing Arts J, Discourse, Theater J, Assaph, World Encycl of Contemp Theatre, Mod Int Drama, Jour of Beckett Studies, Contemp Dramatists, The Drama Rev, Arts in Soc. **HONORS AND AWARDS** Ford Found fel, 59; President's Disting. Serv Award, 65; Guggenheim fels, 62, 77; Camargo Found fel, 84; George Nathan Award for Dramatic Criticism; Sen fel for Independant Study/Res, Nat Endowment for Hums, 84; Nat Endowment for Hums grant, 90; The Kenyon Rev prize for literary excellence, 93. **SELECTED PUBLICATIONS** Auth, The Impossible Theater: A Manifesto, 64; Blooded Thought: Occasions of Theater, 82; Take Up the Bodies: Theater at the Vanishing Point, 82; The Eye of Prey: Subversions of the Postmodern, 87; The Audience, 90; Universals of Performance; or, Amortizing Play, By Means of Performance: Intercult Studies of Theater and Ritual, ed R. Schechner and W. Appel, 90; The Oversight of Ceaseless Eyes, Around the Absurd: Essays on Modern and Postmodern Drama, ed E. Brater and R. Cohn, 91; Quaquaquaqua: The Babel of Beckett, The World of Beckett, ed J. Smith, Psychiatry and Humanities, vol 12, 91; The Surpassing Body, The Drama Rev 35.2, 91; Readymade Desire, Confronting Tennessee Williams? A Streetcar Named Desire: Essays in Critical Pluralism, ed P.C. Kolin, 92; Nothing in Itself: Complexions of Fashion, 92; The Prospect Before Us, Discourse 14.2, 92; Ideology, Performance, and the Illusions of Demystification, Crit Theory and Performance, ed J.G. Reinelt and J. Roach, 92; Spacing Out in the American Theater, The Kenyon Rev 14.2, 93; A Valediction: Chills and Fever, Mourning, and the Vanities of the Sublime, Performing Arts Jour 16.1, 94; Rhetorics of the Body: Do You Smell a Fault?, Cult Artifacts and the Production of Meaning: The Page, the Image and the Body, ed. M. Ezell and K. O'Brien O'Keefe, 94; Fantasia and Simulacra: Subtext of a Syllabus for the Arts in America, The Kenyon Rev 16.2, 94; Flat-Out Vision, Fugitive Images: From Photography to Video, ed P. Petro, 95; coed, Performance Issue(s): Happenings, Body, Spectacle, Discourse 14.2, 92. **CONTACT ADDRESS** Dept of English, Univ of Wisconsin, Milwaukee, PO Box 413, Milwaukee, WI, 53201.

BLAU, SHERIDAN
DISCIPLINE ENGLISH LITERATURE **EDUCATION** Brandeis Univ, PhD, 67. **CAREER** LECTR, ENG, UNIV CALIF, SANTA BARBARA. **RESEARCH** Seventeenth-century lit; Rhet and compos; Eng educ. **SELECTED PUBLICATIONS** Auth, numerous articles on Milton, Herbert, Renaissance thought, the development of literacy, the teaching of composition and literature, theory of the composing process. **CONTACT ADDRESS** Dept of Eng, Univ Calif, Santa Barbara, CA, 93106-7150. **EMAIL** blau@edstar.gse.ucsb.edu

BLAYDES, SOPHIA BOYATZIES
PERSONAL Born 10/16/1933, Rochester, NY, m, 1961, 2 children **DISCIPLINE** ENGLISH AND AMERICAN LITERATURE **EDUCATION** Univ Rochester, BA, 55; Ind Univ, Bloomington, MA, 58, PhD(English), 62. **CAREER** From instr to asst prof Am lit, Mich State Univ, 62-65; from asst prof to assoc prof English and Am lit, 66-77, PROF ENGLISH, WVA UNIV, 77-, Folger res fel, 81. **MEMBERSHIPS** Am Soc 18th Century Studies; MLA; English Inst; NCTE. **RESEARCH** Eighteenth-century poetry; Restoration and eighteenth-century drama; biography and autobiography. **SELECTED PUBLICATIONS** Auth, When Beauty Fires the Blood - Love and the Arts in the Age of Dryden, J of the Hist of Sexuality, Vol 0004, 93. **CONTACT ADDRESS** Dept of English, West Virginia Univ, PO Box 6296, Morgantown, WV, 26506-6296.

BLAZEK, RONALD DAVID
PERSONAL Born 06/13/1936, Chicago, IL, m, 1960, 2 children **DISCIPLINE** LIBRARY SCIENCE **EDUCATION** B.Ed. Chicago Teachers College, 58, M.Ed., Chicago Teachers College, 61, M.S.,Univ of Illinois, 65, PhD., Univ of Illinois, 71. **CAREER** Teacher-Librarian, Chicago Public School System, 58-64, Head Library Circulation Dept, Chicago Teachers College, 65-68, Asst Prof, Chicago State Univ, 68-71, Assoc Prof, Florida State Univ, 71-80, Prof, Florida State Univ, 81. **HONORS AND AWARDS** Oustanding Senior, Chicago Teachers College, Beta Phi Mu-National Hogan Fraternity, Univ of Illinois, Outstanding Academic Book Awards, Choice Magazine, 94, 95, Florida Assoc Travfour, Honor Roll, 36. **MEMBERSHIPS** American Library Association, Assoc for Library and Information, Sci Educ, Southeastern Library Assoc, Florida Library Assoc. **RESEARCH** Reference/Info Services, Bibliography , Library Hist **SELECTED PUBLICATIONS** United States Hist: A Selective Guide to Information Sources, 4th edition, with Anna H Perrault, Libraries Unlimited, 94; The Humanities: A Selective Guide to Information Sources, 4th edition, with Elizabeth Aversa, Libraries Unlimited, 94; The Humanities CD: An Electronic Guide to Information Sources, Libraries Unlimited, 95; Term Paper Resource Guide to 20th Century United States History, with Bob Muccigrosso and Theresa Maggio, Grenwood Press, 98; The Humanities: A Selective Guide to Information Sources, 5th edition, with Elizabeth Aversa, Libraries Unlimited, in process; Information Needs of the Rural Physician: A Descriptive Study, with Cheryl Dee, Medical Library Assoc Bulletin, 93; The Role of the School Library Media Specialist in a Literature-Based Reading Program, with Kay Bishop, School Media Quarterly, 94; The Nature of a Disscipline: A Bibliometric Study of Communication with Some Comparisons to Library Reference/Information Work, with Joan Dick, The Reference Librarian, 95, Transforming Library Services Through Action Research; with Anna Perrault, Florida Libraries, 97. **CONTACT ADDRESS** School of Library Science, Florida State Univ, Tallahassee, FL, 32306. **EMAIL** blazek@lis.fsu.edu

BLEDSOE, ROBERT TERRELL
PERSONAL Born 11/14/1944, Monticello, AR **DISCIPLINE** VICTORIAN LITERATURE **EDUCATION** Harvard Univ, BA, 66; Univ Kent, Canterbury, MA, 67; Princeton Univ, PhD, 71. **CAREER** Asst prof, 71-77, assoc prof English 77-91; prof English, 91-, Univ TX, El Paso, 77-. **MEMBERSHIPS** MLA; Res Soc for Victorian Per; Dickens Fel. **RESEARCH** 19th Century literature; 19th Century musical journalism. **SELECTED PUBLICATIONS** Auth, Sibi Constet: The goddess of Castlewood and the goddess of Walcote, Studies in Novel, summer 73; Pendennis and the power of sentimentality: A study of motherly love, Publ Mod Lang Asn Am, 10/76; Kubrick's Vanity Fair, Rocky Mountain Rev Lang & Lit, spring 77; Dickens and Chorley, Dickensian, fall 79; A reconsideration of the virgin of Villette, Women & Lit, 80; Vanity fair and singing, Studies in Novel, summer 81; Dickens and Opera, Dickens Stud Ann, 90; contrib Grove Dictionnary of Opera, 92; An Oxford Companion to Dickens,98; H F Charley: Victorian Journalist, Ashgate Press, 98. **CONTACT ADDRESS** Dept English, Univ Texas, 500 W University Ave, El Paso, TX, 79968-0001. **EMAIL** rbledsoe@utep.edu

BLEDSTEIN, ADRIEN
PERSONAL Born 03/04/1939, Los Angeles, CA, m, 1959, 2 children **DISCIPLINE** HISTORY; ENGLISH **EDUCATION** Univ California at Los Angeles, BA, 60; Teaching Certificate, 61. **CAREER** KAM Isiah Israel Congregation, Chicago, 30 years. **MEMBERSHIPS** SBL; Chicago Soc for Biblical Research **RESEARCH** Bible and ancient near Eastern lit. **SELECTED PUBLICATIONS** Auth, Was Eve Cursed (Or Did a Woman Write Genesis), Bible Review, 93; Are Women

Cursed in Genesis 3.16, A Feminist Companion to Genesis, 93; Binder, Trickster, Heel and Hairy-man: Re-reading Genesis 27 as a Trickster Tale Told by a Woman, A Feminist Companion to Genesis, 93; Is Judges a Woman's Satire of Men Who Play God, A Feminist Companion to Judges, 93; Female Companionships: If the Book of Ruth Were Written by a Woman, A Feminist Companion to Ruth, 93; Dr. Tamar, Bible Review, 95; Tamar and the Coat of Many Colours, A Feminist Companion to Samuel and Kings II, forthcoming. **CONTACT ADDRESS** 5459 S. Hyde Pk. Blvd., Chicago, IL, 60615-5801. **EMAIL** ajb@mcs.net

BLEETH, KENNETH ALAN
PERSONAL Born 03/12/1942, New York, NY **DISCIPLINE** MEDIEVAL LITERATURE **EDUCATION** Harvard Univ, AB, 63, AM, 65, PhD(English), 69. **CAREER** Asst prof, Boston Univ, 69-77; lectr, Univ Calif, Santa Barbara, 77-79; asst prof English, Conn Col, 79-83; from assoc prof to prof, 83-93; Nat Endowment for Humanities younger humanist fel, 73-74. **MEMBERSHIPS** MLA; Medieval Acad Am. **RESEARCH** Middle English poetry, especially Chaucer. **SELECTED PUBLICATIONS** Auth, Juliana, 647-652, Medium Aevum, 69; Narrator and landscape in the Commedia, Dante Studies, 70; The image of paradise in the Merchant's Tale, Harvard English Studies, 74; The rocks in the Franklin's tale of Ovid's Medea, Am Notes & Queries, 82; The Rocks and the Garden: The Limits of Illusion in Chaucer's Franklin's Tale, English Studies, 93. **CONTACT ADDRESS** Dept of English, Connecticut Col, 270 Mohegan Ave, New London, CT, 06320-4125. **EMAIL** kable@conncoll.edu

BLEICH, DAVID
DISCIPLINE ENGLISH **EDUCATION** NY Univ, PhD. **CAREER** Prof; Taught at, NY Univ, IN Univ & Simon Fraser Univ. **HONORS AND AWARDS** ACLS study fel, Res Ctr for Mental Hea NY Univ. **RESEARCH** Lang; lit; literacy; tchg; feminist critique of knowledge. **SELECTED PUBLICATIONS** Auth, Readings and Feelings, Subjective Criticism, Utopia: The Psychology of a Cultural Fantasy & The Double Perspective: Language, Literacy and Social Relations; ed, Writing With: New Directions in Collaborative Teaching, Learning, and Research, Collaboration and Change in the Academy; articles on, Morrison, Kafka, literary theory, teaching, curriculum, collaboration & academi c ideology. **CONTACT ADDRESS** Dept of Eng, Univ of Rochester, 601 Elmwood Ave, Ste. 656, Rochester, NY, 14642. **EMAIL** dblh@uhura.cc.rochester.edu

BLESSINGTON, FRANCIS CHARLES
PERSONAL Born 05/21/1942, Boston, MA, m, 2 children **DISCIPLINE** ENGLISH LITERATURE, CLASSICS **EDUCATION** Boston Col, AB, 63; Northeastern Univ, MA, 66; Brown Univ, PhD, 72, AM, 73. **CAREER** From instr to asst prof, 69-75, assoc prof English, prof English, 84-, Northeastern Univ, 75-. **MEMBERSHIPS** MLA. **RESEARCH** Milton; Renaissance English literature; classics. **SELECTED PUBLICATIONS** Auth, Euripides: The Bacchae and Aristophanes: The Frogs, Crofts Classics, 93; Review of The New Oxford Book of Seventeenth-Century Poetry, ed Alastair Fowler, The Scriblerian, 93; Review of Roger Pooley's English Prose of the Seventeenth Century: 1590-1700, The Scriblerian, 94. **CONTACT ADDRESS** Dept English, Northeastern Univ, Boston, MA, 02115.

BLEWETT, DAVID
DISCIPLINE ENGLISH LITERATURE **EDUCATION** Univ Manitoba, BA; MA; Univ Toronto, PhD. **RESEARCH** Eighteenth century English literature; literary illustration; Bloomsbury Group. **SELECTED PUBLICATIONS** Ed, Fielding's Amelia, 87; Ed, Jour Studies Eighteen Century Fiction. **CONTACT ADDRESS** English Dept, McMaster Univ, 1280 Main St W, Hamilton, ON, L8S 4L9.

BLISS, LEE
DISCIPLINE RENAISSANCE LITERATURE **EDUCATION** Univ Calif, Berkeley, PhD, 72. **CAREER** PROF, ENG, UNIV CALIF, SANTA BARBARA. **RESEARCH** Shakespearean and non-Shakespearean Renaissance drama; Modern drama. **SELECTED PUBLICATIONS** Auth, The World's Perspective: John Webster and the Jacobean Drama, Rutgers Univ, 83; Francis Beaumont, Twayne, 87; pub(s), articles on Shakespeare, Webster, Chapman, Beaumont, Fletcher, Renaissance dramatic genres, and sixteenth- and seventeenth-century retellings of the Griselda story. **CONTACT ADDRESS** Dept of Eng, Univ Calif, Santa Barbara, CA, 93106-7150. **EMAIL** lbliss@humanitas.ucsb.edu

BLISSETT, WILLIAM F.
PERSONAL Born 10/11/1921, East End, SK, Canada **DISCIPLINE** ENGLISH **EDUCATION** Univ BC, BA, 43; Univ Toronto, MA, 46, PhD, 50. **CAREER** Tchg asst, lect & instr, Univ Toronto, 46-50; assoc prof, 50-57, prof, Univ Sask, 57-60; prof & head Eng, Huron Col, 60-65; prof, 65-87, PROF EMER ENGLISH, UNIV TORONTO, 87-. **MEMBERSHIPS** Asn Can Univ Tchrs Eng; Can Fedn Hum, 80-84. **SELECTED PUBLICATIONS** Auth, The Long Conversation: A Memoir of David Jones, 81; ed, Reid MacCallum: Imitation and Design, 53; ed, Editing Illustrated Books, 80; ed, Craft and Tradition: Essays in Honour of William Blissett, 90; co-ed, The Spenser Encyclopedia, 90; ed, Univ Toronto Quart, 65-76 **CONTACT ADDRESS** Univ Col, Univ of Toronto, Toronto, ON, M5S 1A1.

BLOCH, CHANA
PERSONAL Born 03/15/1940, New York, NY, m, 1969, 2 children **DISCIPLINE** ENGLISH LITERATURE **EDUCATION** Cornell Univ, BA, 61; Brandeis Univ, MA, 63 & 65; Univ Calif, Berkeley, PhD, 75. **CAREER** Instr, Hebrew Univ, Jerusalem, 64-67; instr, 73-75, asst prof, 75-80, assoc prof, 81-87, chair Dept English, 86-89, PROF ENGLISH LIT, MILLS COL, 87-, W M KECK PROF ENGLISH, 96-99, dir, creative writing prog, 93-; Graves Award fel study & writing, Pomona Col, 76-77; NEH fel, 80. **HONORS AND AWARDS** Discovery Award (poetry), 74; Transl Award, Columbia Univ Transl Center, 78; Book of the Year Award, Conf on Christianity & Lit, 86; Writers Exchange Award, Poets & Writers, 88; Felix Pollak Prize, Poetry, 98. **MEMBERSHIPS** MLA; PSA; ALTA; ALSC. **RESEARCH** George Herbert; The Bible; The Song of Songs; contemporary poetry. **SELECTED PUBLICATIONS** Auth, Jacob Glatstein: The literary uses of Jewishness, Judaism, 65; Six days in June, Midstream, 67 & reprinted as American girl in the Holy City, in Under Fire, Norton, 68; transl, Yiddish poems by Glatstein, Sutzkever, Zeitlin, in A Treasury of Yiddish Poetry, 69; The riddle, Playboy, 70 & in A Friend of Kafka, 70; A Dress of Fire: Selected Poetry of Dahlia Ravikoritch, Menard Press, London, 76 & Sheep Meadow Press, 78; auth, Goerge Herbert and the Bible: A reading of love (III), English Lit Renaissance, fall 78; Spelling the word, in Too Rich to Clothe the Sunne, Pittsburgh Univ, 80; The Secrets of the Tribe (poems), Sheep Meadow Press, 81; Spelling the Word: George Herbert and the Bible, Univ Calif Press, 85; co-ed & transl, Selected Poems of Yehuda Amichai, Harper & Row, 86, rev ed, Univ Calif Press, 96; co-ed & transl, The Window: New & Selected Poems of Dahlia Ravikovitch, Sheep Meadow Press, 89; The Past Keeps Changing (poems), Sheep Meadow Press, 92; The Song of Songs: A New Translation with an Introduction and Commentary, Random House, 95; paperbk ed, Univ Calif Press, 98; Mrs Dumpty (poems), Univ Wis Press, 98. **CONTACT ADDRESS** Dept of English, Mills Col, 5000 MacArthur Blvd, Oakland, CA, 94613-1000. **EMAIL** chana@mills.edu

BLOCK, STEVEN
PERSONAL Born 11/05/1952, New York, NY, m, 1977, 7 children **DISCIPLINE** COMPOSITION THEORY **EDUCATION** Univ Pitts, PhD, 81. **CAREER** Asst Prof, 87-89, Northeastern IL Univ; Asst Prof, Assoc Prof, 89 to 95-, Univ New Mexico. **HONORS AND AWARDS** Teach Achiev Alumni Fac Awd; UNM Schl Awd. **MEMBERSHIPS** AMT; ACA. **RESEARCH** 20th Century Music and Music Theory; Free Jazz; Non-Western Music. **SELECTED PUBLICATIONS** Auth, Bemsha Swing: The Transformation of a Bebop Classic to Free Jazz, Music Theory Spectrum, 97; Vector Products and Intervallic Weighting, J Music Theory, 94; Organized Sound, Annual Rev of Jazz Studies, 93. **CONTACT ADDRESS** Dept of Music, Univ New Mexico, Albuquerque, NM, 87031. **EMAIL** sblock@unm.edu

BLOCKLEY, MARY EVA
PERSONAL Born 01/10/1956, Mt Vernon, IL **DISCIPLINE** EDUCATION **EDUCATION** Bryn Mawr Col, BA, 77; Yale Univ MA, 78, MPhil, 79, PhD, 84; **CAREER** Asst, Universite de Geneve, 81-82; instr English, Smith Col, 82-84; lectr, English, Yale Col, 84-85; asst prof, 85-92, assoc prof, 92- , English, Univ Texas Austin. **HONORS AND AWARDS** Fel, Yale Univ, 77-81; NEH Summer Stipend 87; NEH Fel, 89-90; Univ Texas Faculty Res Asst, 90, 96; URI Grant, 86. **MEMBERSHIPS** Ger Ling Asn; Int Soc Anglo-Saxonists; LSA; Mediaeval Acad Am; MLA. **RESEARCH** Old English syntax; history of the English language; English philology. **SELECTED PUBLICATIONS** Auth, Klaeber's Relineations of Beowulf and Verses Ending in Words Without Categorical Stress, Rev English Stud, 95; auth, Apposition and the Subjects of Clause-Initial Verbs, in Baker, ed, Words and Works, Univ Toronto, 98; auth, Caedmon's Conjunction: Caedmon's Hymn 71 Revisited, Speculum, 98; auth, Syntax Words from Beowulf to Wulfstan, 99; coauth, A Biography of the English Language, 3d ed, Harcourt, 2001. **CONTACT ADDRESS** Dept of English, Univ of Texas, Austin, Austin, TX, 78712-1164. **EMAIL** blockley@utxvms.utexas.edu

BLODGETT, EDWARD DICKINSON
PERSONAL Born 02/26/1935, Philadelphia, PA, m, 1960, 3 children **DISCIPLINE** MEDIAEVAL AND CANADIAN LITERATURE **EDUCATION** Amherst Col, AB, 56; Univ Minn, MA, 61; Rutgers Univ, PhD(comp lit), 69. **CAREER** Lectr French, Inst Am Univs, 61-62; instr English, Rutgers Univ, 63, instr gen lit, 65-66; instr classics, Douglass Col, 66; asst prof English & Romance lang, 66-70, assoc prof comp lit, 70-75, assoc chmn dept, 73-75; PROF COMP LIT/CHMN DEPT, UNIV ALTA, 75-. **HONORS AND AWARDS** Anna von Helmholtz Pehlan scholar creative writing, 60-61; Can Coun grant, 71-72. **MEMBERSHIPS** Can Comp Lit Assn (treas, 73-75); Mediaeval Acad Am; Can Asn Advan Neth Studies; Int Comp Lit Assn. **RESEARCH** Time in medieval literature; modern Canadian literature, modern English and American poetry. **SELECTED PUBLICATIONS** Auth, Sexualizing Power In Naturalism, Dreiser, Theodore and Grove, Frederick, Philip, Rev Intl Eng Lit, Vol 0026, 95; The Subject Of Violence, The 'Song Of Roland' And The Birth Of The State, Can Rev Comparative Lite-Rev Can Lit Comparee, Vol 0022, 95; Towards An Ethnic Style, Can Rev Comparative Lit-Rev Can Lit Comparee, Vol 0022, 95; Medieval Misogyny And The Invention Of Western Romantic Love, Can Rev Comparative Lit-Rev Can Lit Comparee, Vol 0020, 93. **CONTACT ADDRESS** Dept of Comp Lit, Univ of Alta, Edmonton, AB, T6G 2G2.

BLOOM, ABIGAIL BURNHAM
DISCIPLINE LITERATURE **EDUCATION** Boston Univ, BA, 73; Univ Mich, MA, 75; New York Univ, PhD, 89 **CAREER** Managing ed, Victorian Literature and Culture, 92-; adjunct instr, New School Univ, 96- **MEMBERSHIPS** MLA; NEMLA; MMLA; NVSA **RESEARCH** Victorian Literature **SELECTED PUBLICATIONS** Ed, "Nineteenth Century British Women Writers, Greenwood, forthcoming; "Anne Thackeray Ritchie," Cambridge Bibliography of English Literature, forthcoming; auth, "Portraits and Photographs of the Carlyles," "The Poetry of Jane Carlyle" and "Carlyle's Humor," The Carlyle Encyclopedia, forthcoming **CONTACT ADDRESS** 54 Riverside Dr., 15-D, New York, NY, 10024-6553. **EMAIL** abigail.bloom@nyu.edu

BLOOM, HAROLD
PERSONAL Born 07/11/1930, New York, NY, m, 1958, 2 children **DISCIPLINE** ENGLISH AND AMERICAN LITERATURE **EDUCATION** Cornell Univ, BA, 51; Yale Univ, PhD, 55. **CAREER** From instr to prof English, 55-74, William Clyde DeVane prof humanities, 74-77; PROF, HUMANITIES, YALE UNIV, 77-; lectr, Hebrew Univ, 59. **HONORS AND AWARDS** John Addison Porter Prize, 56; Morse fel, Yale Univ, 58-59; Guggenheim fel, 62-63; sr vis fel, Cornell Soc Humanities, 68-69; Melville Cane Award, Poetry Soc Am, 71; Morton Daunen Zabel Award, Am Acad Arts and Lett, 82., LittD, Boston Col, 73; LHD, Yeshiva Univ, 76. **MEMBERSHIPS** Am Acad Arts & Lett. **RESEARCH** English Romantic and Victorian poetry; theory of poetic influence, British and American poetry from the later 18th century to the present day. **SELECTED PUBLICATIONS** Auth, Operation Shylock--A Confession, NY Rev Bk(s), Vol 0040, 93; Bloom,Harold Interviewed By Wachtel,Eleanor, Queens Quart, Vol 0102, 95; Feminism As The Love Of Reading, Raritan Quarterly Rev. **CONTACT ADDRESS** Yale Univ, PO Box 208302, New Haven, CT, 06520-8302.

BLOOM, LYNN Z.
PERSONAL Born 01/11/1934, Ann Arbor, MI, m, 1958, 2 children **DISCIPLINE** ENGLISH **EDUCATION** Univ Mich, BA, 56, MA, 57, PhD, 63. **CAREER** Asst prof to assoc prof, Butler Univ, 70-74; assoc prof, Univ NM, 75-78; assoc prof, 76-83, dir writing, 78-83, Col Wm & Mary; prof, 82-90, dept head, 82-83, Va Commonwealth Univ; PROF ENGLISH, AETNA CHAIR WRITING, UNIV CONN, 88-. **HONORS AND AWARDS** Nat Counc Teachers Eng, 97-98; Aetna Chair of Writing, Univ Conn, 88-; U. S. Dept Ag, 96-99; NEH, 79-81, 84, 86-87. **MEMBERSHIPS** Phi Beta Kappa; Mod Lang Asn; Nat Counc Teachers. **RESEARCH** Creative nonfiction; composition studies; autobiography; essays; women writers. **SELECTED PUBLICATIONS** Auth, Composition Studies as a Creative ARt: Teaching, Writing, Scholarship, Administration, Utah State Univ Press, 98; co-ed, Composition in the 21st Century: Crisis and Change, S Ill Univ Press, 96; ed, Forbidden Family: A Wartime Memoir of the Philippines, 1941-45, Univ Wis Press, 89, 98; auth, Fact and Artifact: Writing Nonfiction, Harcourt, 85, reprint, Blair/Prentice Hall, 94; ed, The Essay Connection: Readings for Writers, Heath, 84, 88, 91, 95, Houghton Mifflin, 98; auth, The Essay Canon, Col Eng, March 99; auth, Subverting the Academic Masterplot, in Narration as Knowledge, Heinemann, 98. **CONTACT ADDRESS** Dept Eng, U-25, Univ Connecticut, Storrs, CT, 06268-1025. **EMAIL** Lbloom@uconnvm.uconn.edu

BLOOM, MELANIE
DISCIPLINE INTERCULTURAL COMMUNICATION, INTERPERSONAL COMMUNICATION **EDUCATION** OH Univ, PhD. **CAREER** Instr, ch, Acad Senate, CA State Univ. **RESEARCH** Cult differences in the learning styles of cultural groups represented at CSU Fresno. **SELECTED PUBLICATIONS** Auth, Sex Differences in Ethical Systems, Commun Quart, 90. **CONTACT ADDRESS** California State Univ, Fresno, Fresno, CA, 93740.

BLOOM, ROBERT
PERSONAL Born 05/28/1930, Brooklyn, NY, m, 1953, 3 children **DISCIPLINE** ENGLISH LITERATURE **EDUCATION** NY Univ, BA, 51; Columbia Univ, MA, 52; Univ Mich, PhD, 60. **CAREER** Instr English, Univ Mich, 58-60; from asst prof to assoc prof, 60-73, PROF ENGLISH, UNIV CALIF, BERKELEY, 73-, Bruern fel Am lit, Univ Leeds & Fulbright travel grant, Eng, 63-64; humanities res fel, Univ Calif, Berkeley, 67-68, humanities res prof, 79. **MEMBERSHIPS** MLA. **RESEARCH** Modern British and American literature; literary crit-

icism. **SELECTED PUBLICATIONS** Auth, Suppression and Facilitation Of Pragmatic Performance--Effects of Emotional Content on Discourse Following Right And Left Brain-Damage, Jour of Speech and Hearing Res, Vol 0036, 93; Flirting with the Postman, Queens Quart, Vol 0103, 96; Changes in Processing Adverbial Conjuncts Throughout Adulthood, Applied Psycholinguistics, Vol 0017, 96. **CONTACT ADDRESS** Dept of Eng, Univ of Calif, Berkeley, CA, 94720.

BLOTNER, JOSEPH LEO
PERSONAL Born 06/21/1923, Plainfield, NJ, m, 1946, 3 children **DISCIPLINE** ENGLISH **EDUCATION** Drew Univ, BA, 47; Northwestern Univ, MA, 47; Univ Pa, PhD, 51. **CAREER** Instr English, Univ Idaho, 53-55; from asst prof to assoc prof, Univ Va, 55-68; prof, Univ NC, Chapel Hill, 68-71; prof English, 72-93, PROF ENGLISH EMER, 93- , UNIV MICH, ANN ARBOR, 72-, Fulbright lectr Am lit, Univ Copenhagen, 58-59 & 63-64; Guggenheim fels, 64-65 & 67-68; William Faulkner lectr, Univ Miss, 77; res scholar, Rockefeller Bellagio Ctr, 79; vis prof, Trinity Col, 62, Univ Ariz, 82, & Univ Rome, 84; Off Fr Legion Hon, 97; Am Philos Soc fel; Am Coun Learned Soc fel; NEH fel. **MEMBERSHIPS** MLA; Am Lit Group; Soc Studies Southern Lit. **RESEARCH** Modern American and British literature; the novel. **SELECTED PUBLICATIONS** Auth, The Political Novel, Doubleday, 55; Fiction of J D Salinger, Univ Pittsburgh, 59; coauth, Faulkner in the University, 59 & auth, William Faulkner's Library: A Catalogue, 64, Univ Va; The Modern American Political Novel: 1900-1960, Univ Tex, 66; Faulkner: A Biography (2 vols), 74 & Selected Letters of William Faulkner, 77, Random; Uncollected Stories of William Faulkner, Random House, 79; coed William Faulkner: Novels 1930-1935, 85, Novels 1936-1940, 90, Novels 1942-1954, 94; auth Robert Penn Warren: A Biography , 97. **CONTACT ADDRESS** 108 Bedford Pl, Charlottesville, VA, 22903. **EMAIL** jblotner@aol.com

BLOUIN, LENORA
PERSONAL Born 07/07/1941, Seattle, WA, s **DISCIPLINE** LIBRARIAN-REFERENCE **EDUCATION** MA, 72; MLS, 74 **CAREER** Retired in 1996 after 23 years as professional librarian; Senior librarian, 88-98, San Jose Public Library. **MEMBERSHIPS** Natl Coalition of Independent Scholars; Modern Language Assoc. **RESEARCH** Bibliography **SELECTED PUBLICATIONS** Auth, The Independent Scholar, Some Further Comments on Library Research for Independent Scholars, summer 97; Puckerbrush Review, A Dose of Muses, summer/fall 97, Giving Away, winter/spring 98; The Independent Scholar, Independent Research on May Sarton, winter 97-98. **CONTACT ADDRESS** 4571 Madoc Way, San Jose, CA, 95130. **EMAIL** Blcknblu@ix.netcom.com

BLOUNT, MARCELLUS
DISCIPLINE AMERICAN AND AFRICAN-AMERICAN LITERARY AND CULTURAL STUDIES **EDUCATION** Williams Col, BA, 80; Yale Univ, PhD, 87. **CAREER** English and Lit, Columbia Univ **HONORS AND AWARDS** Stephen H. Tyng Grant, Res Fel Carter G. Woodson Inst; Vis Fel Wesleyan's Ctr Afro-Am Studies; Rockefeller Fel Ctr Study Black Lit & Cult. **SELECTED PUBLICATIONS** Coauth, In a Broken Tongue: Rediscovering African-American Poetry. **CONTACT ADDRESS** Columbia Univ, 2960 Broadway, New York, NY, 10027-6902.

BLUE, PHILIP Y.
PERSONAL Born 07/31/1956, Sanford, NC, s **DISCIPLINE** LIBRARY SCIENCE **EDUCATION** Univ NC, Chapel Hill, MS Library Sci, 89. **CAREER** SEN LAW LIBR, NY; State Supreme Ct Crim Branch Law Library, NY. **MEMBERSHIPS** ALA, ACRL. **RESEARCH** Law, legal hist, crim just. **SELECTED PUBLICATIONS** Rev, Library Journal **CONTACT ADDRESS** 11 Maiden Ln, #15-A, New York, NY. **EMAIL** pyblue@compuserve.com

BLUES, THOMAS
PERSONAL Born 06/16/1936, Detroit, MI, m, 1958, 2 children **DISCIPLINE** ENGLISH **EDUCATION** Univ Mich, BA, 58; Univ Iowa, MA, 60, PhD(English), 66. **CAREER** Asst prof, 65-70, ASSOC PROF ENGLISH, UNIV KY, 70-, Fulbright lectr, Univ Warsaw, 71-72. **MEMBERSHIPS** MLA; Am Studies Asn. **RESEARCH** American literature 1860 to present; Black literature. **SELECTED PUBLICATIONS** Auth, Norris,Frank--A Descriptive Bibliography, Quart Jour of Short Articles Notes and Rev(s), Vol 0008, 95. **CONTACT ADDRESS** Dept of English, Univ of Ky, 500 S Limestone St, Lexington, KY, 40506-0003.

BLUESTEIN, GENE
PERSONAL Born 05/01/1928, Bronx, NY, m, 1949, 4 children **DISCIPLINE** AMERICAN LITERATURE **EDUCATION** Brooklyn Col, BA, 50; Univ Minn, MA, 53, PhD(Am studies), 60. **CAREER** From instr to asst prof English, Mich State Univ, 59-63; from asst prof to assoc prof, 63-71, PROF ENGLISH, CALIF STATE UNIV, FRESNO, 71-, Carnegie Found fel, 57-58; James J Hill Family Found fel, 58; Calif State Cols & Univs fel, 67; Fulbright-Hays lectr, Helsinki Univ, 67-68. **MEMBERSHIPS** Philol Asn Pac Coast. **RESEARCH** American studies; folklore; American literature. **SELECTED PUBLICATIONS** Auth, The Strzegowa Ghetto--Holocaust Memorial Book Honoring The Victims Of Nazi Persecutions--The Way It Began, Yiddish, Vol 0010, 96. **CONTACT ADDRESS** Dept of English, Sch of Humanities Calif State Univ, Fresno, CA, 93710.

BLUMENTHAL, EILEEN
DISCIPLINE THEATER HISTORY AND CRITICISM **EDUCATION** Brown Univ, BA, MA; Yale, PhD. **CAREER** Instr, Rutgers, The State Univ NJ, Univ Col-Camden; consult, Nat Endowment for the Arts. **HONORS AND AWARDS** Woodrow Wilson fel, 68; Kent (Danforth) fel, 74; Guggenheim fel, 88; George Jean Nathan Award for Dramatic Criticism, 89; Asian Cult Coun grant, 90; Soc Sci Res Coun grant, 90; NEH fel, 92; Rockefeller Found Bellagio Residency, 93. **RESEARCH** The royal performing arts of Cambodia. **SELECTED PUBLICATIONS** Auth, Joseph Chaikin, Cambridge UP, 84. **CONTACT ADDRESS** Dept of Theater Arts, Rutgers, The State Univ of NJ, Mason Gross Sch of , 33 Livingston Ave, New Brunswick, NJ, 08901-1959. **EMAIL** msomvill@rci.rutgers.edu

BLYN, ROBIN
DISCIPLINE CONTEMPORARY FICTION **EDUCATION** Temple Univ, MA; Univ Wash, PhD. **CAREER** Instr, 97-. **RESEARCH** Influence of spectacle culture on the twentieth-century experiments in the novel. **SELECTED PUBLICATIONS** Auth, Memory Under Reconstruction: Beloved and the Fugitive Past, Ariz Quart; Freak Fictions: Kafka, Barnes and the Modern Spectacle. **CONTACT ADDRESS** Dept of Eng, Westfield State Col, 577 Western Ave., Westfield, MA, 01085.

BLYTHE, STUART
DISCIPLINE TEHNOLOGY AND WRITING **EDUCATION** Purdue Univ, BA, 86; Univ Ill, MA, 90; Purdue Univ, PhD, 97. **CAREER** Grad instr, Univ Ill, 87-89; Part-time instr, Purdue Univ, 89-92; Grad instr, Purdue Univ, 92-97; Asst prof, W Ky Univ, 97-. **HONORS AND AWARDS** Phi Beta Kappa, Nat Writing Ctrs Asn Dissertation Fell, 96; Purdue Research Found Summer Res Grant, 96; Excellence Tchg Bus Writing, 94-96; Golden Key Nat Honor Soc; Sigma Tau Delta. **MEMBERSHIPS** Nat Counc Tchs Eng; Conference Col Composition & Comm; Asn Tchs of Technical Writing; MLA; Nat Writing Ctrs Asn; Alliance Computers & Writing; Ky Coun of Tchs Eng. **RESEARCH** Professional writing with a particular focus on pedagogy. **SELECTED PUBLICATIONS** Auth, Toward Usable OWLs: Incorporating Usability Methods into Writing Center Research; Wiring the Center, Univ Utah Press; Technology in the Writing Center: Strategies for Implementation & Maintenance, Nat Writing Ctrs Asn, 98; Writing Centers + Networked Computers = ? Thinking About Computer Technology and Writing Center Practice, Writing Ctr Jour, 97; Coauth, A Discussion on Collaborative Design Methods for Collaborative Online Spaces Nat Writing Ctrs Asn. **CONTACT ADDRESS** Western Kentucky Univ, 1526 Big Red Way Street, Bowling Green, KY, 42101. **EMAIL** Stuart.Blythe@wku.edu

BOARDMAN, KATHY
DISCIPLINE ENGLISH AND AMERICAN LITERATURE **EDUCATION** Univ Nebr, BA, 69; Univ Wash, MA, 70; Univ Nebr, Lincoln, PhD, 92. **CAREER** Instr, dir, Core Writing prog, Univ Nev, Reno. **RESEARCH** Western American writers. **SELECTED PUBLICATIONS** His essays on autobiographical writing and western American writers have appeared in scholarly journals and special-interest newsletters. **CONTACT ADDRESS** Dept of Eng, Univ Nev, Reno, Reno, NV, 89557. **EMAIL** kab@unr.edu

BOCHIN, HAL WILLIAM
PERSONAL Born 02/23/1942, Cleveland, OH, m, 1975, 1 child **DISCIPLINE** SPEECH COMMUNICATION **EDUCATION** John Carroll Univ, BA, 64; Univ WI-Madison, MA, 67; IN Univ, Bloomington, PhD(speech), 70. **CAREER** Asst prof, 69-75, assoc prof, 75-77, PROF SPEECH COMMUN & DIR FORENSICS, CA STATE UNIV, FRESNO, 78-. **HONORS AND AWARDS** Meritorious Performance Awards, 88, 90; Outstanding Prof, 97. **MEMBERSHIPS** Am Forensics Asn; Nat Commun Asn. **RESEARCH** History of American public address; argumentation; rhetorical criticism. **SELECTED PUBLICATIONS** Auth, Caleb B Smith's opposition to the Mexican War, Ind Mag Hist, 6/73; Controlling Land Use: Issues & Evidence, Alan, 75; contribr, American broadcasting: A source book on the history of radio and TV, Hastings House, 75; coauth, The San Francisco simulation, Commun Educ, 3/77; auth, Law Enforcement: Issues & Evidence, Alan, 77; coauth, with Michael A. Weatherson, Hiram Johnson: A Bio-Bibliography, Greenwood Press, 88; auth, Richard Nixon: Rhetorical Strategist, Greenwood Press, 90; President Nixon's First Inaugural Address, in Halford Ryan, ed, The Inaugural Addresses of Twentieth Century American Presidents, Praeger, 93; Richard Milhous Nixon, in Halford Ryan, ed, U. S. Presidents as Orators, Greenwood Press, 95; coauth, with Michael A. Weatherson, Hiram Johnson: Political Revivalist, Univ Press of Am, 95; auth, Marcus Moziah Garvey, in Richard Leeman, ed, African-American Orators: A Bio-Critical Sourcebook, Greenwood, 96; President Clinton's First Inaugural Address, in Lloyd Rohler, ed, Great Speeches for Criticism and Analysis, Alistair Press, 97. **CONTACT ADDRESS** Dept of Commun, California State Univ, Fresno, 5201 N Maple, Fresno, CA, 93740-9739. **EMAIL** halb@csufresno.edu

BOCK, CAROL A.
DISCIPLINE 19TH-CENTURY BRITISH LITERATURE **EDUCATION** Univ Wis, Madison, PhD. **CAREER** Assoc prof, Univ Minn, Duluth. **SELECTED PUBLICATIONS** Auth, Charlotte Bronte and the Storyteller's Audience, Univ Iowa Press, 92. **CONTACT ADDRESS** Dept of Eng, Univ Minn, Duluth, Duluth, MN, 55812-2496.

BOCK, MARTIN F.
DISCIPLINE MODERN ENGLISH, IRISH AND AMERICAN LITERATURE **EDUCATION** Univ Wis, Madison, PhD. **CAREER** Assoc prof, Univ Minn, Duluth. **SELECTED PUBLICATIONS** Auth, Crossing the Shadow-line: The Literature of Estrangement,Ohio State UP, 89. **CONTACT ADDRESS** Dept of Eng, Univ Minn, Duluth, Duluth, MN, 55812-2496.

BODE, CARL
PERSONAL Born 03/14/1911, Milwaukee, WI, m, 1938, 3 children **DISCIPLINE** AMERICAN LITERATURE AND CULTURE **EDUCATION** Univ Chicago, PhB, 33; Northwestern Univ, AM, 38, PhD, 41. **CAREER** Teacher, Milwaukee Voc Sch, Wis, 33-37; asst prof English, Univ Calif, Los Angeles, 46-47; PROF ENGLISH, UNIV MD, COLLEGE PARK, 47-, Exec secy, Am Civilization Prog, Univ Md, College Park, 50-57; Ford Found fel, 52-53; Guggenheim Found fel, 54-55; cult attache, Am Embassy, London, 57-59; chmn, US Educ Comn UK, 57-59; deleg, Am Coun Learned Soc, 63-73; mem, Md Arts Coun, 71-79, chmn, 72-76, Md Comn for Humanities, 81-; vis prof, Calif Inst Technol, Claremont Cols, Northwestern Univ, Stanford Univ & Univ Wis. **MEMBERSHIPS** Mencken Soc (pres, 76); Am Studies Asn (pres, 52); Col English Asn; Thoreau Soc (pres, 60-61); Popular Cult Asn (vpres, 72-75, pres, 78-80). **RESEARCH** Mid-19th and mid-20th century American cultural history; New England transcendentalism; H L Mencken. **SELECTED PUBLICATIONS** Auth, Beyond, Around, Into-Ones-Own--Travel Lit as a Model for Lrng About the World, Poetica-Zeitschrift fur Sprach-und Literaturwissenschaft, Vol 0026, 94; The Limits of Interpretation, Poetica-Zeitschrift fur Sprach-und Literaturwissenschaft, Vol 0024, 92; Anglistik, Literature Studies and/or Cult-Stud, Anglia-Zeitschrift fur Eng Philol, Vol 0114, 96; The Prose Works of Shelley,Percy,Bysshe Vol-1, Zeitschrift fur Anglistik und Amerikanistik, Vol 0044, 96; The English Literature, Vol 1, Epochs And Forms, Vol 2, Zeitschrift fur Anglistik und Amerikanistik, Vol 0041, 93; Wordsworth and Coleridge--The Radical Years, Zeitschrift fur Anglistik und Amerikanistik, Vol 0042, 94; Anglistik, Lit Stud and/or Cult-Stud, Anglia-Zeitschrift fur Eng Philol, Vol 0114, 96; Shelley--, Zeitschrift fur Anglistik und Amerikanistik, Vol 0044, 96. **CONTACT ADDRESS** Dept of English, Univ of Md, College Park, MD, 20742.

BODE, ROBERT FRANCIS
PERSONAL Born 10/14/1944, Baltimore, MD **DISCIPLINE** ENGLISH LITERATURE **EDUCATION** Loyola Col, BS, 66; Univ SC, MA, 69; PhD, 70. **CAREER** Asst prof, 70-76, ASSOC PROF ENG, TENN TECHNOL UNIV, 76-. **MEMBERSHIPS** S Atlantic Mod Lang Asn; Southeastern Am Soc Eighteenth Cent Studies. **RESEARCH** Seventeenth century British drama; metaphysical poetry, Chaucer. **SELECTED PUBLICATIONS** Auth, A Back-To-The-Future--Formation Plus Back-Formation And The Etymology Of Contraption, Amer Speech, Vol 0068, 93. **CONTACT ADDRESS** Dept of English, Tenn Technol Univ, Cookeville, TN, 38501.

BODEN, JEAN
PERSONAL Born 11/05/1949, Paris, France, m, 1994, 1 child **DISCIPLINE** FILM & TELEVISION **EDUCATION** Birmingham S Col, BA, 73; Univ Ala, MA, 76; Fla State Univ, PhD, 83. **CAREER** Film dir, Hidden Fears, 1993; film producer, Seven Sundays, 95. **HONORS AND AWARDS** Gold Star, Brussels Festival; Telly Award. **MEMBERSHIPS** Dir Guild Am; Soc des Realisateurs De Films. **RESEARCH** Cinema **SELECTED PUBLICATIONS** Auth, Cinema: An Introduction, 98; auth, Essays on Chaplin, 85. **CONTACT ADDRESS** 2845 Thornhill Rd, Apt 121B, Birmingham, AL, 35213. **EMAIL** bodon@uab.edu

BODO, MURRAY
PERSONAL Born 06/10/1937, Gallup, NM, s **DISCIPLINE** ENGLISH **EDUCATION** St Anthony Novitiate, 55-56; profession of solemn vows, 56-60, BA, Duns Scotus Col, 59; ed for & ordination to the Priesthood, St Leonard Col, 60-64; Xavier Univ, MA, 67; Univ of Cincinnati, doctoral in English, 92-. **CAREER** Internship, St Boniface Parish, 64-65; English teacher, St Francis High School Seminary, 65-77; Provincial Board, Franciscan Province of St John the Baptist, 76-79; staff, Assisi Summer Pilgrimages, 76-88; prof, chair of English dept, dir of Young Friars, Duns Scotus Col, 77-79; instr, English, Chatfield Col, 87-92; ASST PROF OF ENGLISH, WERITER IN RESIDENCE, THOMAS MORE COL, 91-. **HONORS AND AWARDS** Cincinnati Editors' Award, 79; 3rd Prize for Poetry,

Catholic Press Asn, 84; Belly of the Whale Award, 91. **SELECTED PUBLICATIONS** Auth, Francisco, El Viaje y El Sueno, St Anthony Messenger Press, 94; auth, The Almond Tree Speaks, New and Selected Writings: 1974-94, St Anthony Messenger Press, 95; auth, The Way of St Francis, St Anthony Messenger Press, 95; auth, Tales of an Endishodi, Father Berard Haile and the Navajos 1900-1961, Univ of Nmex Press, 98; auth, The Poetic Line, Ceide, 98; auth, After the Earthquakes, The Paris Rev, 98; auth, How St Francis Teaches Us to Open Heaven, The Cord, 98; auth, On Hearing Gregorian Chant in the Abbey of Solesmes, Cistercian Studies Quart, 97; auth, St Clare Dies at Her Mirror, August 11, 1253, Tracks, 96; auth, Home Visit, Tracks, 94; The Earth Moves at Midnight, Tracks, 94; auth, Oscar Romero, Tracks, 94; auth, St Anthony in the Walnut Tree, Tracks, 94; auth, Transcribing the Life of The Little Priest, Provincial Chronicle, 98; auth, The Dalai Lama Visits Merton's Home, St Anthony Messenger, 97; auth, Followers of Francis: Fray Angelico Chaves, St Anthony Messenger, 96; coauth, The Basilica of St Francis, The Cord, 96; auth, A Retreat with Francis and Clare of Assisi, St Anthony Messenger Press, 96. **CONTACT ADDRESS** 1723 Pleasant St., Cincinnati, OH, 45210.

BODON, JEAN
PERSONAL Born 11/05/1949, Paris, France, m, 1994, 1 child **DISCIPLINE** FILM & TELEVISION **EDUCATION** Birmingham S Col, BA, 73; Univ Ala, MA, 76; Fla State Univ, PhD, 83. **CAREER** Film dir, Hidden Fears, 1993; film producer, Seven Sundays, 95. **HONORS AND AWARDS** Gold Star, Brussels Festival; Telly Award. **MEMBERSHIPS** Dir Guild Am; Soc des Realisateurs de Films. **RESEARCH** Cinema **SELECTED PUBLICATIONS** Auth, Cinema: An Introduction, 98; auth, Essays on Chaplin, 85. **CONTACT ADDRESS** 2845 Thornhill Rd, Apt 121B, Birmingham, AL, 35213. **EMAIL** bodon@uab.edu

BOGUS, DIANE ADAMZ
PERSONAL Born 01/22/1946, Chicago, IL, m, 1989 **DISCIPLINE** AMERICAN LITERATURE **EDUCATION** Stillman Coll Tuscaloosa AL, BA 1968; Syracuse Univ Syracuse NY, MA 1969; Miami Univ Oxford OH, PhD 1988; Univ of Hawaii, PhD, parapsychology, 1998. **CAREER** LA Southwest Coll, instructor 1976-81; Miami U, instructor 1981-84; WIM Publications, author 1971-, founder 1979-, publisher; California State University, Stanislaus Turlock, CA, professor of American literature, 1986-90; DeAnza College, Cupertino, CA, instructor, 1990-. **HONORS AND AWARDS** Honored by Art & Music Dept Trenton Public Lib 1983; works adapted into CA State Univ Archives 1982; nominated for Pulitzer Prize, Sapphire's Sampler 1982; nominated for Lambda Literary Award for The Chant of the Women of Magdalena; Black Writer's Award from Peninsula Book Club, 1992; Woman of Achievement Award, 1997. **MEMBERSHIPS** Mem Delta Sigma Theta Sorority 1965-; mem Nat Tchrs of Engl 1981-; mem Feminist Writer's Guild 1980-; mem COSMEP Independent Publishers 1975-; board member, Multicultural Publishers Exchange, 1989-92. **CONTACT ADDRESS** WIM Publications, PO Box 2087, Cupertino, CA, 95015.

BOLIN, JOHN SEELYE
PERSONAL Born 09/20/1943, Ft Bragg, NC, m, 1965, 1 child **DISCIPLINE** DRAMATIC LITERATURE, THEATRE HISTORY **EDUCATION** Kalamazoo Col, BA, 65; Univ MI, Ann Arbor, MA, 65, PhD, 70. **CAREER** Asst prof theatre, 70, prof eng & theatre ,Berea Col, 70, dir repertory theatre festival, 81-83, Assoc dean Gen Educ, 89-94, Dean Fac, 98-; Mellon Found, Berea Col, Sabbatical fel, 77-78. **HONORS AND AWARDS** Kellog Nat Fel, 83-86; Canadian Embassy, Fac Res Grant, 94-95. **MEMBERSHIPS** AAUP; William Morris Soc; Asn Canadian Studies in U S; Midwestern Asn canadian Studies; KY Hum Coun, bd mem,, Asn Am Col and Univ, 94-98. **RESEARCH** Theatre aesthetics; theatre hist; criticism of drama. **SELECTED PUBLICATIONS** Auth, var rev & articles on Canadian Theatre and drama. **CONTACT ADDRESS** Dept of Eng, Berea Col, 101 Chestnut St, Berea, KY, 40404-0003. **EMAIL** john_bolin@berea.edu

BOLING, BECKY
DISCIPLINE WOMEN WRITERS **EDUCATION** Northwestern State Univ, PhD. **CAREER** Literature, Carleton Col. **SELECTED PUBLICATIONS** Areas: Griselda Gambaro, Carlos Fuentes, Gabriel Garcia Marquez, Ana Lydia Vega, and Luisa Valenzuela. **CONTACT ADDRESS** Carleton Col, 100 S College St., Northfield, MN, 55057-4016.

BOLSTERLI, MARGARET JONES
PERSONAL Born 05/10/1931, Watson, AR, 2 children **DISCIPLINE** ENGLISH, CULTURAL HISTORY **EDUCATION** Univ Ark, BA, 53; Wash Univ, MA, 53; Univ Minn, PhD(English), 67. **CAREER** Asst prof English, Augsburg Col, 67-68; PROF ENGLISH, UNIV ARK, 68-, Nat Endowment Humanities Younger Humanist Award, 70-71; Ark Endowment Humanities grant, 80-81. **MEMBERSHIPS** MLA; SCent Mod Land Asn; Am Asn State & Local Hist. **RESEARCH** Nineteenth century Britain; the American south; women's studies. **SELECTED PUBLICATIONS** Auth, Porter,Katherine,Anne and Texas, Mod Fiction Stud, Vol 0038, 92; An Interview with Bolsterli,Margaret,Jones, Ark Hist Quart, Vol 0055, 96; Warren,Robert,Penn And The American Imagination--Mod Fiction Stud, Vol 0038, 92. **CONTACT ADDRESS** Dept of English, Univ of Ark, Fayetteville, AR, 72701.

BOLZ, BARBARA J.
DISCIPLINE COMMUNICATION **EDUCATION** Oakland Univ, BA; Wayne State Univ, MA, PhD. **CAREER** Prof, Univ Detroit Mercy, 89-. **HONORS AND AWARDS** Elizabeth Youngjohn Teaching awd, Wayne State Univ. **RESEARCH** Public speaking, public opinion, mass media, political campaign and organizational communication. **CONTACT ADDRESS** Dept of Communications, Univ of Detroit Mercy, 4001 W McNichols Rd, PO Box 19900, Detroit, MI, 48219-0900. **EMAIL** BOLZBY@udmercy.edu

BONENFANT, JOSEPH
PERSONAL Born 04/29/1934, St-Narcisse Champlain, PQ, Canada, m, 1960, 2 children **DISCIPLINE** LITERATURE **EDUCATION** Univ Laval, BA, 57; Univ Montreal, LLL, 59; Univ Paris, DrUniv, 66. **CAREER** Teacher French, Latin and Greek, Col Brebeuf, Montreal, 59-63; PROF FRENCH LIT, UNIV SHERBROOKE, 66-, Co-ed, Ellipse, Writers in Transl, 69-; Consult, Can Coun Arts, 71- and Humanities Res Coun Can, 72- **RESEARCH** French critics; le mouvement litteraire dans les Cantons de l' Est: 1925-1950; subventionne par le Conseil des Arts du Canada. **SELECTED PUBLICATIONS** Auth, The Pragmatic Approach to Poetry, Etudes Litteraires, Vol 0025, 92. **CONTACT ADDRESS** Dept of French Studies Fac of Arts, Univ of Sherbrooke, Sherbrooke, PQ, J1K 2R1.

BONNER, THOMAS
DISCIPLINE ENGLISH **CAREER** Xavier Univ, prof; Xavier Review Journal, editor. **HONORS AND AWARDS** Dist vis prof, USAF; Henry C McBay Fel; Bush Excell in Tchg Awd **MEMBERSHIPS** SO Cent Modern Lang Assoc, Pres. **RESEARCH** Southern lit and writers who have worked in New Orleans. **SELECTED PUBLICATIONS** Auth, William Faulkner: The William B. Wisdom Collection, 80; The Kate Chopin Companion, 88; editor of Above Ground, 93 and Immortelles, 95. **CONTACT ADDRESS** Dept of English, Xavier Univ, 25 West Park Place, New Orleans, LA, 70124.

BONNYMAN-STANLEY, ISABEL
DISCIPLINE ENGLISH **EDUCATION** BA, 77, MA, 82, East Tennessee State Univ; Univ Tennessee, PhD, 90. **CAREER** Assoc Prof, English, 83-, East Tennessee State Univ. **CONTACT ADDRESS** Dept of English, East Tennessee State Univ, Johnson City, TN, 37614. **EMAIL** stanleyi@etsu.edu

BONO, BARBARA JANE
PERSONAL Born 08/08/1948, Poughkeepsie, NY, m, 1970, 1 child **DISCIPLINE** ENGLISH LITERATURE, HISTORY OF IDEAS **EDUCATION** Fordham Univ, AB, 70; Brown Univ, PhD (English), 78. **CAREER** Instr, 75-78, ASST PROF ENGLISH, UNIV MICH, ANN ARBOR, 78- **MEMBERSHIPS** MLA; Renaissance Soc Am. **RESEARCH** Renaissance intellectual history; English and comparative literature; genre criticism. **SELECTED PUBLICATIONS** Auth, Medicine and Shakespeare in the English Renaissance, Lit Med, Vol 0012, 93; The Birth of Tragedy--Tragic Action in Julius Caesar, Engl Lit Renaissance, Vol 0024, 94 **CONTACT ADDRESS** Dept of English, Univ of Mich, Ann Arbor, MI, 48109.

BOOKER, JOHN T.
DISCIPLINE NINETEENTH-CENTURY LITERATURE **EDUCATION** Univ MN, PhD. **CAREER** Assoc prof, Univ KS. **RESEARCH** French novel **SELECTED PUBLICATIONS** Publ(s), on Stendhal, Balzac, Constant, Gide, and Mauriac. **CONTACT ADDRESS** Dept of French and Italian, Univ Kansas, Admin Building, Lawrence, KS, 66045.

BOOKER, M. KEITH
DISCIPLINE MODERN BRITISH AND IRISH LITERATURE **EDUCATION** Univ Fla, PhD. **CAREER** English and Lit, Univ Ark. **SELECTED PUBLICATIONS** Auth, Literature and Domination: Sex, Knowledge, and Power in Modern Fiction, Fla, 93; Vargas Llosa among the Postmodernists, Fla, 94; Flann O'Brien, Bakhtin, and Menippean Satire, Syracuse, 95; Joyce, Bakhtin, and the Literary Tradition: Toward a Comparative Cultural Poetics, Mich, 96;), A Practical Introduction to Literary Theory and Criticism, Longman, 96; : Colonial Power, Colonial Texts: India in the Modern British Novel, Mich, 97. **CONTACT ADDRESS** Univ Ark, Fayetteville, AR, 72701.

BOOS, FLORENCE SAUNDERS
PERSONAL Born 11/11/1943, Santa Barbara, CA, m, 1965, 1 child **DISCIPLINE** ENGLISH LITERATURE, WOMEN'S STUDIES **EDUCATION** Univ Mich, BA, 64; Harvard Univ, AM, 65; Univ Wis, PhD, 72. **CAREER** Instr English, Univ Sask, 70-71; asst prof, 73-77, assoc prof, 77-81, PROF ENGLISH, UNIV IOWA, 82-, Old Gold fel, Univ Iowa, 74 & 79, fac res grant, 75-76; bibliog, Women & Lit, 74-77, assoc ed, 75-80; Bunting fel, 80-81; Univ Iowa fac scholar, 81-84; Fulbright sr lectr, Univ Iceland, fall 85; NEH fel, Univ Iowa, summer 92. **HONORS AND AWARDS** Woodrow Wilson Nat fel, 64-65; Douglas Stuart fel, Queen's Univ, 66-67; Fac scholar award, Univ Iowa, 75, 90; Fac development assignment, Univ Iowa, 97. **MEMBERSHIPS** Midwest Victorian Studies Asn; MLA; Women's Caucus Mod Lang; Res Soc Victorian Periodicals; Hopkins Soc. **RESEARCH** Social and cultural history of Britain from the eighteenth century to the present; Victorian poetry. **SELECTED PUBLICATIONS** Auth, Catharine Macaulay's Letters on Education 1790: An Early Feminist Polemic, Univ Mich Papers Woman's Studies, No 2; The Poetry of Dante Gabriel Rossetti: A Critical and Source Study, Mouton, The Hague, 75, reprinted, in Nineteenth-Centruy Literature Criticism, Gale Res Co, 83; ed, Socialist Diary, Windhover Press, 81; The Juvenillia of William Morris, William Morris Soc, 82; ed, Bibliography of Women and Literature, 1975-80, 2 vol, Holmes and Meier, 88; ed & contrib, Socialism and the Literary Artistry of William Morris, Univ Mo Press, 90; The Design of William Morris's The Earthly Paradise, Edwin Mellen Press, 91; ed, & contrib, History and Community: Essays in Victorian Medievalism, Garland Publ, 92; guest ed, William Morris: 1896-1996, Victorian Poetry, winter 96; The Earthly Paradise by William Morris, vol I and II, Garland Publ, 98. **CONTACT ADDRESS** Dept of English, Univ of Iowa, 308 English Phil Bld, Iowa City, IA, 52242-1492. **EMAIL** florence-boos@uiowa.edu

BOOSE, LYNDA E.
DISCIPLINE ENGLISH LITERATURE **EDUCATION** UCLA, PhD. **CAREER** Prof, Dartmouth Col. **RESEARCH** Shakespearean drama; Renaissance and women's lit. **SELECTED PUBLICATIONS** Auth, The Priest, the Slanderer, the Historian, and the Feminist; Eng Lit Ren, 95; The Taming of the Shrew, Good Husbandry, and Enclosure in Re-Reading Shakespeare, Cornell UP, 94; The Getting of a Lawful Race: Racial Discourse in Early Modern England and the Unrepresentable Black Woman in Women, 'Race,' and Writing in the Early Modern Period, Routledge, 94; co-ed, Daughters and Fathers,. The Johns Hopkins UP, 88, rptd 93. **CONTACT ADDRESS** Dartmouth Col, 3529 N Main St, #207, Hanover, NH, 03755. **EMAIL** lynd.e.boose@dartmouth.edu

BOOTH, PHILIP
PERSONAL Born 10/08/1925, Hanover, NH, m, 1946, 3 children **DISCIPLINE** ENGLISH **EDUCATION** Dartmouth Col, AB, 48; Columbia Univ, AM, 49. **CAREER** Instr English, Bowdoin Col, 49-50; asst to dir admis, Dartmouth Col, 51-52, instr English, 53; from instr to asst prof, Wellesley Col, 54-61; assoc prof, 61-66, PROF ENGLISH, SYRACUSE UNIV, 66-, Guggenheim fel, 58-59 and 65; Rockefeller Found fel, 68; Nat Endowment for Arts fel, 80. **HONORS AND AWARDS** Hokin Prize, 55; Lamont Prize, 56; Saturday Rev poetry Award, 57; Phi Beta Kappa Poet, Columbia Univ, 62; co-recipient, Emily Clark Balch Prize, 64; Nat Inst Arts and Lett Award, 67; Theodore Roethke Prize, 70., DLitt, Colby Col, 68. **MEMBERSHIPS** PEN Club; Acad Am Poets. **RESEARCH** Contemporary poetry; poetry workshops; the novel. **SELECTED PUBLICATIONS** Auth, Writing it Down--Poetry, Vol 0171, 97; Rivers, Sam and the Rivbea Orchestra, Down Beat, Vol 0063, 96; Identification, Shenandoah, Vol 0047, 97; Seven States, Shenandoah, Vol 0046, 96; Three Awakenings in New England, New England Rev Middlebury Ser, Vol 0016, 94; A Dog Skin From Asthall, Intl J Osteoarchaeology, Vol 0006, 96; Sarasota Jazz Club--To Serve all Ages, Down Beat, Vol 0060, 93; Letter to the Poetry Editor, Gray-Flannel Poets, Concord, Mass, Oct 7, 1957, Chicago Rev, Vol 0042, 96; Key Views, Ga Rev, Vol 0049, 95; March Again, Poetry, Vol 0161, 93; Swinging at the Sandbox, Down Beat, Vol 0060, 93; Drew, Kenny--Father and Son on 2 Pianos, Down Beat, Vol 0060, 93; Ages, Poetry, Vol 0167, 95; Outlook, Poetry, Vol 0161, 93; Sentences, Am Poetry Rev, Vol 0023, 94; Half Life, Am Poetry Rev, Vol 0023, 94; Fog-Talk, Am Poetry Rev, Vol 0023, 94; Talk about Walking, Am Poetry Rev, Vol 0023, 94; Backcountry, Am Poetry Rev, Vol 0023, 94; Nov Sun, Poetry, Vol 0163, 93; Late Wakings, Ga Rev, Vol 0050, 96; Coming to, Poetry, Vol 0168, 96; Sixty Six, Am Poetry Rev, Vol 0023, 94. **CONTACT ADDRESS** Dept of Englis, Syracuse Univ, Syracuse, NY, 13210.

BOOTH, STEPHEN
PERSONAL Born 04/20/1933, New York, NY, m, 1959, 2 children **DISCIPLINE** ENGLISH, DRAMA, & VERSE **EDUCATION** Harvard Col, AB, 55; Cambridge Univ, Trinity Col, BA, 57, MA, 60; Harvard Univ, PhD(English), 64. **CAREER** From asst prof to assoc prof English, 62-74, prof English, Univ Calif, BerkeleY, 74-, Nat Endowment for Humanities fel, 68; Guggenheim fel, 70-71. **HONORS AND AWARDS** Marshall Scholar, Trinity College, Cambridge, 55-57; James Russell Lowell Prize for 1977, awarded 78 (for Shakespeare's Sonnets, ed with Commentary); Distinguished Teaching Award, Univ of Ca, Berkeley, 82; Doctor of Humane Letters, Georgetown Univ, May 91; OBE (Office of the British Empire), July 95. **MEMBERSHIPS** MLA; Shakespeare Asn Am. **RESEARCH** Aesthetics; Shakespeare. **SELECTED PUBLICATIONS** Auth, An Essay on Shakespeare's Sonnets, Yale Univ, 69; The Book Called Holinshead's Chronicles, Bk Club San Francisco, 69; On the value of Hamlet, In: Reinterpretations of Elizabethan Drama, Columbia Univ, 69; ed, Shakespeare's

Sonnets, Yale Univ, 77; auth, Shakespeare at Valley Forge, Shakespeare Quart, 27, 231-42, 76; Syntax as Rhetoric in Richard II, in Mosaic, x.3, 87-103, 77; Speculation on Doubling in Shakespeare's Plays, in Shakespeare: The Theatrical Dimension, ed P.C. McGuire and D.A. Samuelson, New York, 79; Henry IV, Part Two and the Aesthetics of Failure, in Shakespearte Plays, ed V.L. Lee, Dubuque, 80; Exit Pursued by a Gentleman Born, in Shakespeare's Art from a Comparative Perspective, ed W.M. Aycock, pp 51-66, Lubbock, 81; Milton's How soon hath time: A Colossus in a Cherrystone, ELH, 49, 449-67, with Jordan Flyer, 82; King Lear, Macbeth, Indefinition, & Tragedy, New Haven, 83; Poetic Richness: A Preliminary Audit, in Pacific Coast Philology, XIX, No 1-2, 68-78, 84; Twelfth Night, l.i: The Audience as Malvolio, in Shakespeare's Rough Magic: Renaissance Essays in Honor of C.L. Barber, ed Peter Erikson and Coppelia Kahn, pp. 149, Newark, Delaware, 85; The Shakespearean Actor as KamikazePilot, Shakespeare Quart, 36, 553-70, 85; The Function of Criticism at the Present Time and All Others, Shakespeare Quart, 41, 262-68, 90; Liking Julius Ceasar (pamphlet), Ashland, Oregon, 91; Close Readings Without Readings, in Shakespeare Reread: The Texts in New Contexts, ed Russ McDonald, pp 42-55, Ithaca: Cornell, 94; The Coherences of 1 Henry IV and of Hamlet, in Shakespeare set Free: Teaching Hamlet and 1 Henry IV, ed Peggy O'Brian, pp 32-46, New York: Washington Square Press, 95; Shakespeare's Language and the Language of Shakespeare's Time, Shakespeare Survey 50, 1-17, 98; A Long, Dull Poem by William Shakespeare, Shakespeare Studies, 25, 229-37, 98; Precious Nonsense: The Gettysburg Address, Ben Johnson's Epitaphs on His Children, and Twelfth Night, Berkeley, 98. **CONTACT ADDRESS** Dept of English, Univ of Calif, 322 Wheeler Hall, Berkeley, CA, 94720-1030.

BOOTH, WAYNE CLAYSON
PERSONAL Born 02/22/1921, American Fork, UT, m, 1946, 3 children **DISCIPLINE** ENGLISH LITERATURE **EDUCATION** Brigham Young Univ, AB, 44; Univ Chicago, AM, 47, PhD, 50. **CAREER** Instr, Univ Chicago, 47-50; asst prof English, Haverford Col, 50-53; prof and head dept, Earlham Col, 53-62; Pullman prof, 62-70, dean col, 64-69, chmn com ideas and methods, 73-75, DISTINGUISHED SERV PROF ENGLISH, UNIV CHICAGO, 70-, Fels, Ford fac, 52-53, Guggenheim, 56-57 and 69-70, Ind Univ, 62, Am Acad Arts and Sci, 72, Nat Endowment for Humanities, 75-76 and Rockefeller, 81-82; vis consult, US-SAfrica Leader Exchange Prog, 63; consult, Danforth Found, 63-69; mem bd trustees, Earlham Col, 65-75; co-ed, Critical Inquiry, 74- **HONORS AND AWARDS** Christian Gauss Award, Phi Beta Kappa, 62; David H Russell Award, NCTE, 66., LLD, Rockford Col, 65, St Ambrose Col, 71 and Univ NH, 77. **MEMBERSHIPS** MLA; NCTE; Conf Col Compos and Commun; AAUP; Acad Lit Studies. **RESEARCH** Theory of literary criticism; 18th century English literature; theory and practice of rhetoric. **SELECTED PUBLICATIONS** Auth, Science and the Demon-Haunted World--Response to Lewontin, Richard, NY Rev Bks, Vol 0044, 97; The Struggle to Tell the Story of the Struggle to Get the Story Told--How I Have Changed my Mind and Why, Narrative, Vol 0005, 97; Aristotle Rhetoric--An Art of Character Philos Lit, Vol 0019, 95; Where is the Authorial Audience in Biblical Narrative and in Other Authoritative Texts, Narrative, Vol 0004, 96; Straw Men and the Life of Criticism, Western Hum Rev, Vol 0051, 97. **CONTACT ADDRESS** Dept of English, Univ of Chicago, Chicago, IL, 60637.

BORCK, JIM SPRINGER
PERSONAL Born 08/16/1941, New Orleans, LA, m, 1977 **DISCIPLINE** ENGLISH LITERATURE **EDUCATION** Univ Fla, BA, 63, MA, 65; Univ Calif, Riverside, PhD (English), 69. **CAREER** Asst prof, 69-80, PROF ENGLISH, LA STATE UNIV, BATON ROUGE, 80- **MEMBERSHIPS** MLA; SCent Mod Lang Asn. **RESEARCH** Late 18th and early 19th century English literature. **SELECTED PUBLICATIONS** Auth, Composed in Tears, The Clarissa Proj, Stud Novel, Vol 0027, 95. **CONTACT ADDRESS** Dept of English, Louisiana State Univ, Baton Rouge, LA, 70803-0001.

BORDEN, DIANE M.
DISCIPLINE ENGLISH LITERATURE **EDUCATION** Lone Mountain Col, BA, 64; San Francisco State Univ, MA, 66; Univ CA, PhD, 71. **CAREER** Prof, Univ Pacific. **HONORS AND AWARDS** Graves Tchg Awd; UOP Spanos Tchg Awd. **SELECTED PUBLICATIONS** Auth, publ(s) on Bergman, De Sica, Bertolucci, Henry James, Wallace Stevens, Ezra Pound, Fassbinder, and Antonioni. **CONTACT ADDRESS** Eng Dept, Univ Pacific, Pacific Ave, PO Box 3601, Stockton, CA, 95211.

BORDEN, SANDRA L.
PERSONAL Born 11/07/1963, Argentina, m, 1986 **DISCIPLINE** MASS COMMUNICATION **EDUCATION** Univ of Mo, BJ, 85; Ohio State Univ, MA, 91; Indiana Univ, PhD, 97. **CAREER** Instr, Middle Tenn State Univ, 91-92; asst prof, Western Mich Univ, 96- . **HONORS AND AWARDS** Nom. for AEJMC Nafziger-White dissertation award. **MEMBERSHIPS** Asn for Educ in Jour & Mass Commun; Asn for Practical & Prof Ethics; Nat Commun Asn; Central States Commun Asn. **RESEARCH** Media ethics; Ethical discourse; Ethical decision making and organizational culture. **SELECTED PUBLICATIONS** Auth, Emphatic listening: The journalist's betrayal, Jour of Mass Media Ethics, 8 (4), 93; Gotcha! Deciding when sources are fair game, Jour of Mass Media Ethics, 10 (4), 96; Choice processes in a newspaper ethics case, Commun Monographs, 64, 97; Avoiding the pitfalls of case studies, Jour of Mass Media Ethics, 13 (1), 98; coauth, Deceiving sources, Journalism ethics: A reference handbook, eds E.D. Cohen and D. Elliott, 97; rev, Journalists and the community, Jour of Mass Media Ethics, 12 (3), 97. **CONTACT ADDRESS** Dept of Communication, Western Michigan Univ, 1201 Oliver St., Kalamazoo, MI, 49008. **EMAIL** sandra.borden@wmich.edu

BOREN, JAMES LEWIS
PERSONAL Born 03/19/1941, Phoenix, AZ, m, 1971 **DISCIPLINE** ENGLISH LITERATURE **EDUCATION** San Francisco State Univ, BA, 65, Univ of Iowa, MA, 67, PhD(English), 70. **CAREER** Asst prof, 70-76, assoc prof English, Univ Ore, 76-. **HONORS AND AWARDS** Ersted Award for Distinguished Teaching, Univ Ore, 77; Burlington Northern Foundation Faculty Achievement Award for Distinguished Teaching, Univ Ore, 87. **MEMBERSHIPS** Mediaeval Acad Am; Medieval Asn Pacific; New Chaucer Soc. **RESEARCH** Old English and middle English literature; Chaucer. **SELECTED PUBLICATIONS** Auth, Form and meaning in Cynewulf's Fates of the Apostles, Papers Lang & Lit, 69; Alysoun of Bath and the Vulgate Perfect Wife, Neuphilologische Mitteilungen, 75; The Design of the Old English Deor, In: Anglo-Saxon Poetry, Univ Notre Dame, 75; Narrative design in the alliterative Morte Arthure, Philol Quart, 77. **CONTACT ADDRESS** Dept of English, Univ of Oregon, Eugene, OR, 97403-1205.

BORIS, EDNA Z.
PERSONAL Born 02/25/1943, New York, NY, m, 1964, 1 child **DISCIPLINE** ENGLISH **EDUCATION** Hunter Col, BA, 64; Ind Univ, Bloomington, MA, 66, PhD, 74. **CAREER** Assoc instr Eng, IN Univ, 67-68; inst, Shippensburg State Col, 71-72; adj assoc prof, 74-79, asst prof eng, La Guardia Col, 79-, Dir, Words-Worth Assoc; Coordr, writing courses for ABLE prog, Adelphi Univ, 78-80. **MEMBERSHIPS** Board of Trustees Belle Zeller Scholarship Trust Fund; Shaksper electronic conference; Assoc ed Shakespeare and the Classroom; AAUP Comt on Prof Ethics; MLA; Shakespeare Asn; Scribes. **RESEARCH** Shakespeare; business writing; law and lit. **SELECTED PUBLICATIONS** Auth, Pairing of business communications and word processing classes, Am Bus Commun Asn Bull, 9/76; The Tudor Constitution and Shakespeare's two tetralogies, Col Lit, fall 77; Shakespeare's English Kings, The People and the Law, Assoc Univ, 78; The interview in a business writing course, Am Bus Commun Asn Bull, 7/78; A final memo, Am Bus Commun Asn Bull, 3/79; And now it's time to write, Nat Law J, 10/12/81; Co-auth Test your legal writing skills, Docket Call, Am Bar Asn, Spring 82; Classroom minutes: A valuable teacing device, In: Improving college & university teaching, Spring 83; Resumes, resumes, resumes, a student handout, The Bulletin, Dec 91; Teaching Shakespeare: Non-traditional research topics, The Shakespeare Newsletter, Fall 92; A student role in syllabus planning, Exercise exchange, Spring 94; Mastering bibliographic form through collaborative learning, Collaborative learning: a sourcebook for higher education, vol 2, Nat Center on Postsecondary Teaching, Learning, and Assessment, 94; Sentence structure and sentence sense, Perspectives: Teaching legal research and writing, Spring 96; CRASS Summer of 1995, Shakespeare and the classroom, Spring 96; To soliloquize or not to soliloquize, Q/W/E/R/T/Y, Arts, Litteratures & Civilisations du Monde Anglophone, Univ of Pau, France, Oct 96; Sentence sense: We, our, us problems, Perspectives: Teaching legal research and writing, Spring 97. **CONTACT ADDRESS** Dept of Eng, La Guardia Comm Col, 3110 Thomson Ave, Long Island City, NY, 11101-3071. **EMAIL** 104757.652@compuserve.com

BORSCH, FREDERICK HOUK
PERSONAL Born 09/13/1935, Chicago, IL, m, 1960, 3 children **DISCIPLINE** ENGLISH LITERATURE, THEOLOGY **EDUCATION** Princeton Univ, AB, 57; Oxford Univ, MA, 63; Univ Birmingham (UK), PhD, 66. **CAREER** Tutor, Queens Coll, Birmingham (UK), 63-66; assoc prof, Seabury-Western Theol Sem, 66-71; prof, General Theol Sem, 71-72; dean, prof, Church Div Sch of the Pacific, 72-81; dean of chapel, prof, Princeton Univ, 81-88. **MEMBERSHIPS** Am Acad Rel; Soc Bib Lit; Studiorum Novi Testamenti Soc; Phi Beta Kappa. **RESEARCH** New Testament theology and literature; early church history. **SELECTED PUBLICATIONS** Auth, The Son of Man in Myth and History, Westminster Press, 67; auth, The Christian and Gnostic Son of Man, SCM Press, 70; auth, God's Parable, Westminster Press, 77; auth, Introducing the Lessons of the Church Year, Seabury Press, 78; auth, Power in Weakness, Fortress Press, 83; ed, Anglicanism and the Bible, Morehouse-Barlow, 84; auth, Many Things in Parables, Fortress Press, 88; auth, Outrage and Hope, Trinity Press Int, 96. **CONTACT ADDRESS** Box 512164, Los Angeles, CA, 90051-0164. **EMAIL** bishop@ladiocese.org

BOSCAGLI, MAURIZIA
DISCIPLINE ENGLISH LITERATURE **EDUCATION** Brown Univ, PhD, 90. **CAREER** ASSOC PROF, ENG, UNIV CALIF, SANTA BARBARA. **RESEARCH** Gender stud and feminist theory; theories of subjectivity; Brit and Europe modernism; theories of mass cult. **SELECTED PUBLICATIONS** Auth, "A Moving Story: Masculine Tears and the Humanities of Televised Emotions," Discourse, 92-3; The Eye on the Flesh: Fashions of Masculinity in the Early Twentieth Century, Westview Press, 96; Translation of Toni Negri's Constituent Power, Univ Minn Press, 96; "The Squat, the Urn, the Tearoom, and the Designer Bathroom: Home to Class in Thatcher's England," Burning Down the House, Westview Press, 96; "Brushing Benjamin Against the Grain," Revising the Canon, Penn State, 96. **CONTACT ADDRESS** Dept of Eng, Univ Calif, Santa Barbara, CA, 93106-7150. **EMAIL** boscagli@humanitas.ucsb.edu

BOSMAJIAN, HAMIDA
DISCIPLINE ENGLISH **EDUCATION** Univ ID, BA; Univ CT, MA, PhD, 68. **CAREER** Eng, Seattle Univ. **MEMBERSHIPS** MLA, Children's Lit Asn. **SELECTED PUBLICATIONS** Auth, Psychoanalytic Criticism, The International Companion Encyclopedia of Children's Literature, NY: Routledge, 96; Memory and Desire In Sendak's Dear Mili, The Lion and the Unicorn, 19, 95; Mildred Taylor's Story of Cassie Logan: A Search for Law and Justice in a Racist Society, Children's Lit, 24, 96; The Anvil or the Crucible? Narrations of Youthful Experience in Nazi Germany, The Lion and the Unicorn, 13, 91. **CONTACT ADDRESS** Dept of Eng, Seattle Univ, 900 Broadway, Seattle, WA, 98122-4460. **EMAIL** bosmajian@seattleu.edu

BOSTDORFF, DENISE M.
PERSONAL Born 03/25/1959, Bowling Green, OH, m, 1987, 2 children **DISCIPLINE** COMMUNICATION **EDUCATION** Bowling Green State Univ, BA, 82; Univ Ill., MA, 83; Purdue Univ, PhD, 87. **CAREER** Vis asst prof, Purdue Univ, 87-88; from asst prof to assoc prof, Purdue Univ, 88-94; from asst prof to assoc prof, Col of Wooster, 94-. **HONORS AND AWARDS** B. Aubrey Fisher Outstanding Article Award, Western States Commun Asn, 92; W. Charles Redding Award for Excellence in Undergrad Tchg, Purdue Univ, 94; School of Liberal Arts Departmental Award for Educat. Excellence, Purdue Univ, 94. **MEMBERSHIPS** Nat Commun Asn, Ctr for the Study of the Presidency; Central States Commun Asn. **RESEARCH** Anal of polit rhet, particularly presidential rhet, also rhet pertaining to vice presidents and first ladies. **SELECTED PUBLICATIONS** Auth, The Presidency and the Rhetoric of Foreign Crisis, 94; Clinton's Characteristic Issue Management Style: Caution, Conciliation, and Conflict Avoidance in The Case of Gays in the Military, The Clinton Presidency: Issues, Images, & Communication Strategies, ed Robert E. Denton, Jr., and Rachel L. Holloway, 96; Hillary Rodham Clinton and Elizabeth Dole as Running Mates in the 1996 Campaign: Parallels in the Rhetorical Constraints of First Ladies and Vice Presidents, The 1996 Presidential Campaign: A Communication Perspective, ed Robert E. Denton, Jr., 98; coauth, Idealism and Pragmatism in American Foreign Policy Rhetoric: The Case of John F. Kennedy and Vietnam, Presidential Studies Quarterly 24, 94; Values Advocacy: Enhancing Organizational Images, Deflecting Public Criticism, and Grounding Future Arguments, Public Relations Review 20, 94; The Presidency and the Promotion of Domestic Crisis: John Kennedy's Management of the 1962 Steel Crisis, Presidential Studies Quarterly 27, 97. **CONTACT ADDRESS** Dept of Communication, Col of Wooster, 103 Wishart Hall, Wooster, OH, 44691. **EMAIL** dbostdorff@wooster.edu

BOSWELL, JACKSON CAMPBELL
PERSONAL Born 10/02/1934, Whiteville, NC, m, 1969 **DISCIPLINE** ENGLISH LITERATURE, AMERICAN STUDIES **EDUCATION** Univ NC, Chapel Hill, AB, 60, MA, 62; George Wash Univ, MPhil, 73, PhD, 74. **CAREER** Instr English, Col William & Mary, 62-63; Randolph-Macon Woman's Col, 63-65; asst prof, DC Teachers Col, 68-77; PROF ENGLISH, UNIV DC, 77-. **HONORS AND AWARDS** NEH Fel, Folger Shakespeare Libr, 78-79; Fulbright Fel, Brit Libr, Univ London, 81-82. **MEMBERSHIPS** Milton Soc Am; Col Lang Asn; Southeastern Renaissance Conf. **RESEARCH** Renaissance reputations of Chaucer, Dante, Petrarch, Cervantes and others; Am thought and culture; North Atlantic civilization. **SELECTED PUBLICATIONS** Contr, MLA International Bibliography, PMLA, 69-77; auth, Milton's Library, Garland, 75; auth, Register of Paul's Cross Sermons, Dovehouse, 89; auth, Sir Thomas More in the English Renaissance, MRTS, 94; auth, Dante's Fame in England, Delaware/AUP, 99. **CONTACT ADDRESS** Dept of English, Univ of DC, 4200 Connecticut N W, Washington, DC, 20008-1175. **EMAIL** jboswell@udc.edu

BOTAN, CARL H.
DISCIPLINE PUBLIC RELATIONS **EDUCATION** Wayne State, PhD, 85. **CAREER** Assoc prof, Purdue Univ. **SELECTED PUBLICATIONS** Auth, Communication Work and Electronic Surveillance; A Model for Predicting Panoptic Effects, Commun Monogr; International Public Relations: Critique and Reformation, Pub Rel Rev, 92; coauth, Public Relations Theory, Erlbaum, 90; Investigating Communication and Interpreting Communication, Prentice-Hall, 92; A Human Nature Approach to Image and Ethics in International Public Relations, Pub Rel Res, 93. **CONTACT ADDRESS** Dept of Commun, Purdue Univ, 1080 Schleman Hall, West Lafayette, IN, 47907-1080. **EMAIL** cbotan@sla.purdue.edu

BOUISSAC, PAUL A.
PERSONAL Born 11/17/1934, Perigueux, France DISCIPLINE HUMANITIES EDUCATION Sorbonne, LL, 56, DP, 70. CAREER Asst to assoc prof, 65-74, PROF, VICTORIA COL, UNIV TORONTO, 74-; fel, Netherlands Inst Advan Stud, 72-73. HONORS AND AWARDS John Simon Guggenheim Found, 73-74; Killam sr fel, 89-91. SELECTED PUBLICATIONS Auth, Les Demoiselles, 70; auth, La mesure des gestes, 73; auth, Circus and Culture, 76. CONTACT ADDRESS Victoria Col, Univ of Toronto, 73 Queens Park E, Toronto, ON, M5S 1K7.

BOURNE, LESLEY-ANNE
DISCIPLINE ENGLISH/CREATIVE WRITING EDUCATION York Univ, BA; Univ British Columbia, MFA, 89. CAREER Coord, Tchr Ctr, Senate Comm Enhancement, 90-92; LECTR CREATIVE WRITING, UNIV PRINCE EDWARD ISLAND 91-. HONORS AND AWARDS Bliss Carman Poetry Award, Banff Ctr Arts, 86; Air Can Award, Can Auth Asn, 94. MEMBERSHIPS League Can Poets. SELECTED PUBLICATIONS Auth, The Story of Pears, 90; auth, Skinny Girls, 93; auth, Field Day, 96. CONTACT ADDRESS Univ Prince Edward Island, 550 University Ave, Charlottetown, PE, C1A 4PS. EMAIL lbourne@upei.ca

BOUSON, J. BROOKS
DISCIPLINE ENGLISH EDUCATION Loyola Univ Chicago, PhD. CAREER Assoc prof. RESEARCH Modern British literature; psychoanalysis and literature; emotions and literature; trauma and narrative; women's literature; history of feminist criticism. SELECTED PUBLICATIONS Auth, Brutal Choreographies: Oppositional Strategies and Narrative Design in the Novels of Margaret Atwood, Amherst: Univ Mass Press, 93; The Empathic Reader: A Study of the Narcissistic Character and the Drama of the Self, Univ Mass Press, 89; A Feminist,Psychoanalytic Approach in a Women's College, Approaches to Teaching Margaret Atwood's The Handmaid's Tale, Modern Lang Asn, 96; Slipping Sideways into the Dreams of Women: The Female Dream Work of Power Feminism in Margaret Atwood's The Robber Bride, Lit 6, 95; The Politics of Empathy and Self in Christa Wolf's The Quest for Christa T, Mimetic Desire: Essays on Narcissism in German Literature from Romanticism to Post Modernism, Camden House, 95; Empathy and Self-Validation in Saul Bellow's Seize the Day, The Critical Response to Saul Bellow, Greenwood Press, 95. CONTACT ADDRESS Dept of English, Loyola Univ, Chicago, 6525 N. Sheridan Rd., Chicago, IL, 60626. EMAIL jbouson@luc.edu

BOWDEN, BETSY
DISCIPLINE MEDIEVAL LITERATURE, FOLKLORE EDUCATION UCLA, Berkeley, PhD. CAREER Ch, exec comt, Chaucer Div of MLA; instr, Rutgers, State Univ NJ, Camden Col of Arts and Sci. SELECTED PUBLICATIONS Auth, Performed Literature: Words and Music by Bob Dylan, Ind, 82; Chaucer Aloud: The Varieties of Textual Interpretation, Pa, 87; Listeners' Guide to Medieval English: A Discography, Garland, 88; ed, Eighteenth-Century Modernizations from the Canterbury Tales, Boydell & Brewer, 91. CONTACT ADDRESS Rutgers, State Univ NJ, Camden Col of Arts and Sci, New Brunswick, NJ, 08903-2101. EMAIL schiavo@crab.rutgers.edu

BOWEN, ROGER
PERSONAL Born 11/03/1942, Cardiff, Wales DISCIPLINE ENGLISH LITERATURE EDUCATION Cambridge Univ, BA, Hons, 65; Simon Fraser Univ, MA, 68; Harvard Univ, PhD(English), 72. CAREER Asst prof, 72-77, from assoc prof to prof English, Univ Ariz, 77-96. MEMBERSHIPS MLA; H G Wells Soc. RESEARCH Modern British poetry; modern British fiction; colonial & postcolonial lit. SELECTED PUBLICATIONS Auth, Confession and equilibrium: Robert Lowell's poetic development, Criticism, 69; A version of pastoral: E M Forster as country guardian, SAtlantic Quart, 76; Science, myth, and fiction in H G Wells's The Island of Dr Moreau, Studies Novel, 76; Philip Larkin's XX Poems: poet in transition, Iowa Rev, 77; Death, Failure, and survival in the poetry of Philip Larkin, Dalhousie Rev, 78; Native and exile: The poetry of Bernard Spencer, Malahat Rev, 1/79; The edge of a journey: Notes on Bernard Spencer, London Mag, 12/79 & 1/80; ed, Bernard Spencer: Collected Poems, Oxford Univ Press, 81; Orientalism and Empire in The Alexandria Quartet, Studies in the Literary Imagination, 91. CONTACT ADDRESS Dept of English, Univ of Arizona, 1 University of Az, PO Box 210067, Tucson, AZ, 85721-0001. EMAIL rbowen@u.arizona.edu

BOWERBANK, SYLVIA
DISCIPLINE ENGLISH LITERATURE EDUCATION McMaster Univ, BA, PhD; Simon Fraser, MA. RESEARCH 17th and 18th century English lit; cultural meaning of landscape literature; feminist theory and pedagogy; First-Nations writing; educational theory and the teaching of writing. CONTACT ADDRESS English Dept, McMaster Univ, 1280 Main St W, Hamilton, ON, L8S 4L9.

BOWERS, EDGAR
PERSONAL Born 03/02/1924, Rome, GA DISCIPLINE ENGLISH LITERATURE EDUCATION Univ NC, BA, 47; Stanford Univ, MA, 49, PhD(English), 53. CAREER Instr English, Duke Univ, 52-55; asst prof, Harpur Col, State Univ NY, 55-58; from asst prof to assoc prof, 58-67, PROF ENGLISH, UNIV CALIF, SANTA BARBARA, 67-, Sewanee Rev fel, 54; Guggenheim fels, 59 & 69. HONORS AND AWARDS Ingram Merrill Found, 74; Brandeis Creative Arts, 79. RESEARCH English, American and French lyric poetry and literary criticism. SELECTED PUBLICATIONS Auth, Hawthorne and the Extremes of Character, Sewanee Rev, Vol 0102, 94; John, poetry, vol 0161, 93. CONTACT ADDRESS 1502 Miramar Beach, Santa Barbara, CA, 93108.

BOWERS, JOHN M.
DISCIPLINE MEDIEVAL ENGLISH LITERATURE EDUCATION Duke Univ, BA, magna cum laude, 71; Univ Va, MA, 73; Oxford Univ, MPhil, 75; Univ Va, PhD, 78. CAREER Lectr, Univ Va, 78-80; asst prof, Hamilton Col, 80-82; asst prof, Princeton Univ, 84-87; assoc prof, 87-92, prof, 92-, chemn, Univ Nev, Las Vegas, 97-; referee and rev, Stud in the Age of Chaucer, Yearbk of Langland Stud, Envoi, Medium Aevum, Exemplaria: J of Theory in Medieval and Renaissance Stud. HONORS AND AWARDS Andrew W Mellon postdoctoral fel, Calif Inst of Technol, 82-84; NEH grant, 85; NEH summer stipend, Huntington Libr, 86; vis fac assoc, Calif Inst of Technol, 87; NEH fac develop inst, UNLV, 88; Outstanding Teacher, Univ Nev, Las Vegas, 89; Distinguished Tchr, Southern Nev Tchr of Eng, 90; Rita Deanin Abbey Tchr of the Yr Award, Univ Nev, Las Vegas, 90; NEH fel for Univ Tchr, 92-93; Outstanding Tchr of Eng, UNLV Alumni Asn, 95; NEH summer inst, Univ Colo, Boulder, 95; Tchr of the Yr Award, Consolidated Stud Univ Nev, 96; Phi Kappa Phi, UNLV, 97. MEMBERSHIPS Medieval Acad of Am; Early Eng Text Soc; MLA; Southeastern Medieval Asn; New Chaucer Soc; John Gower Soc; Philol Asn of the Pacific Coast; Medieval Asn of the Pacific. RESEARCH The relationship between sexuality and medieval literature. SELECTED PUBLICATIONS Auth, Ordeals, Privacy, and the Lais of Marie de France, J of Medieval and Renaissance Stud 24, 94; Mankind and the Political Interests of Bury St. Edmunds, AEstel 2, 94; The Politics of Pearl, Exemplaria: J of Theory in Medieval and Renaissance Stud 7, 95; Piers Plowman's William Langland: Editing the Text, Writing the Author's Life, Yearbk of Langland Stud 9, 95; Chaste Marriage: Fashion and Texts at the Court of Richard II, Pacific Coast Philol 30, 95; Pearl in its Royal Setting: Ricardian Poetry Revisited, Stud in the Age of Chaucer 17, 95. CONTACT ADDRESS Dept of Eng, Univ Nev, Las Vegas, 4505 Maryland Pky, Las Vegas, NV, 89154-5011. EMAIL bowers@nevada.edu

BOWERS, NEAL
PERSONAL Born 08/03/1948, Clarksville, TN, m, 1979 DISCIPLINE ENGLISH EDUCATION Autin Peay State Univ, BA, 70, MA, 71; Univ of Fla, PhD, 76. CAREER Asst prof of English, 77-83, assoc prof of English, 83-87, prof of English, 87-97, Distinguished Prof of Liberal Arts and Sci, Iowa State Univ, 97-. HONORS AND AWARDS First Place Master Columnist category, Iowa Newspaper Asn, 98; Frederick Bock Prize, 91, Union League Civic and Arts Poetry Prize, Poetry, 96; honorable mention, Yankee Magazine, 93; Nat Endowment for the Arts Poetry Fel, 89. MEMBERSHIPS Modern Poetry Asn; Assoc Writing Prog. RESEARCH Contemporary American Poetry. SELECTED PUBLICATIONS Auth, Words For the Taking: The Hunt for a Plagiarist, W.W. Norton, 97; No Secrets, Narration as Knowledge: Tales of the Teaching Life, Boynton/Cook (Heinemann), 97; Poised in the Galloping Moment: Maxine Kumin's Poetry, Telling the Barn Swallow: Poets on the Poetry of Maxine Kumin, Univ Press of New England, 97; Fear of Not Flying, The Sewanee Rev, 96; Bishop and Lowell: A Friendship and an Era, The Sewanee Rev, 96; Jeffers and Merwin: The World Beyond Words, Robinson Jeffers and a Galaxy of Writers, Univ of SC Press, 95; Working with Editors, Poet's Guide: How to Publish and Perform Your Work, Story Line Press, 95; Assembling Chapbooks and Books, Poet's Guide: How to Publish and Perform Your Work, Story Line Press, 95; A Loss For Words: Plagiarism and Silence, The Am Scholar, 94; Form as Substance in the Poetry of A.D. Hope, Shenandoah, 94; The Poetry Thief, 1994 Writer's Yearbook, 94; Foreword to Between Towns, Tx Tech Univ Press, 93. CONTACT ADDRESS English Dept, Iowa State Univ, 203 Ross Hall, Ames, IA, 50011. EMAIL nbowers@iastate.edu

BOWERS, PAUL
DISCIPLINE ENGLISH EDUCATION Univ Tulsa, BA; OK State Univ, M.A., PhD. CAREER English, Phillips Univ. RESEARCH Irish poetry and the writings of James Joyce. SELECTED PUBLICATIONS Auth, Taking Certain Measures, OK Best 97. CONTACT ADDRESS Dept of Eng, Phillips Univ, 100 S University Ave, PO Box 10, Enid, OK, 73701-6439. EMAIL paulbowers@hotmail.com

BOWMAN, LEONARD JOSEPH
PERSONAL Born 02/04/1941, Detroit, MI, m, 2 children DISCIPLINE RELIGION; LITERATURE EDUCATION Duns Scotus Col MI, BA 63; Univ Detroit, MA 67; Fordham Univ, PhD 73. CAREER Marycrest Intl Univ, prof 73-94, vpres acad dean 94-97; Col Notre Dame MD, vpres acd affs, 97-. MEMBERSHIPS AAUP RESEARCH Medieval Franciscan Spirituality; St. Bonaventure. SELECTED PUBLICATIONS Auth, A Retreat With St. Bonaventure, Element Books Ltd, 93. CONTACT ADDRESS Dept of Academic Affairs, Notre Dame Col, 4003 Roundtop Rd, Baltimore, MD, 21218. EMAIL lbowman@udm.edu

BOYD, BRIAN DAVID
PERSONAL Born 07/30/1952, Belfast, N Ireland, m, 1994, 3 children DISCIPLINE ENGLISH EDUCATION Canterbury Univ, BA, 73, MA, 74; Univ Toronto, PhD, 79. CAREER Post dr fel, 79-80, lectr, 80-85, sr lectr, 85-91, assoc prof, 91-98, prof, 98-, Univ Auckland; vis prof, 94-95, Univ De Nice. RESEARCH Nabokov; Shakespeare; narrative; evolutionary psychology; popper. CONTACT ADDRESS English Dept, Univ of Auckland, Private Bag 92019, Auckland, .. EMAIL b. boyd@auckland.ac.nz

BOYER, DALE KENNETH
PERSONAL Born 04/06/1936, Baker, OR, m, 1959, 3 children DISCIPLINE ENGLISH & AMERICAN LITERATURE EDUCATION Univ Ore, BA, 58, MA, 63; Univ Mo-Columbia, PhD(English), 69. CAREER Instr English, Univ Mo-Columbia, 63-68; from instr to assoc prof, 68-76, prof English, Boise State Univ, 76-, Co-ed, Ahsahta Press, Boise State Univ, 76-96. HONORS AND AWARDS Phi Beta Kappa, Univ Ore, 58. MEMBERSHIPS MLA; Western Lit Asn. RESEARCH Brit Romantic poetry and essay; 20th century Am and Brit poetry; Victorian poetry and essay. SELECTED PUBLICATIONS Ed, Winter Constellations, 77, Stealing The Children, 78, To the Natural World, 80, Agna Negra, 81, Ahsahta Press; auth, Ten poets: A review, Western Am Lit, Vol XV, 80; The Clock of Moss, 83; Deer in the Haystacks, 84; Flights of the Harves-mare, 85; Underground, 86; Men at Work, 89; Sycamore Oriole, 91; The One Right Touch, 92; Each Thing We Know Has Changed Because We Know It, 94; Prayers for the Dead Ventriloquist, 95; The Ahsahta Anthology: Poetry of the American West, 96. CONTACT ADDRESS Dept of English, Boise State Univ, 1910 University Dr, Boise, ID, 83725-0399.

BOYKIN, KEITH
PERSONAL Born 08/28/1965, St. Louis, MO, s DISCIPLINE LITERATURE EDUCATION Dartmouth Coll, AB, 1987; Harvard Univ, JD, 1992. CAREER White House, special asst to the President of the US, 1993-95; National Black Gay and Lesbian Leadership Forum, exec dir, 1995-98. HONORS AND AWARDS Gay Men of African Descent, Angel Award, 1998. SELECTED PUBLICATIONS One More River To Cross: Black & Gay in America, Doubleday, 1995; Respecting the Soul: Daily Reflections for Black Lesbians & Gays, 1998. CONTACT ADDRESS PO Box 73564, Washington, DC, 20056-3564.

BOYLE, FRANK
DISCIPLINE NEOCLASSICAL LITERATURE, ANGLO-IRISH LITERATURE EDUCATION Trinity Col, Dublin, PhD. CAREER Asst prof, Fordham Univ. SELECTED PUBLICATIONS Auth, This Necessary Work,A Modest Proposal, Press Endemique, 94. CONTACT ADDRESS Dept of Eng Lang and Lit, Fordham Univ, 113 W 60th St, New York, NY, 10023.

BOYLE, THOMAS CORAGHESSAN
PERSONAL Born 12/02/1948, m, 3 children DISCIPLINE ENGLISH HISTORY AND LITERATURE EDUCATION SUNY Potsdam, BA, 68; Univ Iowa, MFA, 74; Univ Iowa, PhD, 77. CAREER Dir, 78-90, founder of Creative Writing Prog, 78; asst prof, Eng, 78-82; assoc prof, Eng, 82-86, prof, Eng, 86, USC. HONORS AND AWARDS Coord Coun of Lit Mag Fiction Award, 77; Nat Endow for the Arts Grant, 77; St. Lawrence Award for Fiction, 80; Paris Rev, Aga Khan Prize for Fictin, 81; Nat Endow for the Arts Grant, 83; Paris Rev, John Train Humor Prize, 84; Commonwealth Club of Calif, Silver Medal for Lit, 86; Editors' Choice, NY Times Book Rev, 87; Guggenheim Fel, 88; PEN/Faulkner Award, 88; O'Henry Short Story Award, 88 and 89; Commonwealth Club of Calif Gold Medal for Lit, 88; Prix Passion publ prize, Fr, 89; PEN Ctr West Lit Prize, 89; Editors' Choice, NY Times Book Rev, 89; Doctor of Humane Letters hon degree, State Univ NY, 91; Howard D. Vursell Mem Award, Nat Acad of Arts and Letters, 93; Best Amer Stories, 97; Prix Medicis Etranger, Paris, 97. MEMBERSHIPS Mem, lit panel, Nat Endow for the Arts, 86-87. SELECTED PUBLICATIONS Auth, T. C. Boyle Stories, NY, Viking, 98; auth, Riven Rock, NY, Viking, 98; auth, The Tortilla Curtain, NY, Viking, 95; auth, Without A Hero, NY, Viking, 94; auth, The Road to Wellville, NY, Viking, 93; auth, East Is East, NY, Viking, 90; auth, If the River Was Whiskey, NY, Viking, 89; auth, World's End, NY, Viking, 87; auth, Greasy Lake, NY, Viking, 85; auth, Budding Prospects, NY, Viking, 84; auth, Water Music, Boston, Atlantic-Little, Brown, 82; auth, Descent of Man, Boston, Atlantic-Little, Brown, 79. CONTACT ADDRESS 136 E. 57th St., New York, NY, 10022.

BRACKELL, PAMELA
DISCIPLINE ENGLISH **EDUCATION** Catholic Univ Am, PhD, 94. **CAREER** Prof, Southern Nazarene Univ, 95-. **MEMBERSHIPS** South Central Modern Lang Asn; Asn Lit Scholars Critics; Nat Council Tchrs English. **RESEARCH** Victorian literature; Alice Meynell; William Morris; Julia Margaret Cameron. **SELECTED PUBLICATIONS** Auth, art, The Art Worker' Guild, 93; auth, intro, notes, The Table Turned or Nupkins Awakened, 94; auth, art, About Suffering They Were Never Wrong: Reflections on the Oklahoma Bombing, 95; auth, art, Scenes of Cultural Life: George Eliot and the Clergy, 95; auth, art, Fire and Ice: Clashing Visions of Iceland in the Travel Narratives of William Morris and Sir Richard Burton, 96. **CONTACT ADDRESS** Dept of English, Southern Nazarene Univ, 6729 NW 39th Expy, Bethany, OK, 73008. **EMAIL** pwiens@snu.edu

BRACKEN, JAMES K.
PERSONAL Born 03/16/1952, Toledo, OH, m, 1973, 4 children **DISCIPLINE** LIBRARY AND INFORMATION SERVICES **EDUCATION** Univ of Toledo, BA, 73, MA, 76; Univ of SC, ML, 79, PhD, 83. **CAREER** Reader Services Librn, Knox Col, 79-85; humanities bibliographer, asst prof, Purdue Univ, 85-88; Head of Second Floor Maim Libr Imfor Servies, Assoc Prof, The Ohio State Univ, 88-. **HONORS AND AWARDS** Ameritech Prize, 92, Outstanding Service Award, The Ohio State Univ, 95; OSU Office of Research Interdisciplinary Seed Grant, 93-94; U.S. Dept of Education Foreign Periodical Prog grant, 93-95. **RESEARCH** Bibliography; printing history. **SELECTED PUBLICATIONS** Auth, Literature, Humanities and the Library, Am Libr Asn, 93; Reference Works in British and American Literature, Libr Unlimited, 98; co-ed, The British Literary Book Trade 1700-1820 (Dictionary of Literary Biography Vol 154, Gale, 95; The British Literary Book Trade 1475-1700 (Dictionary of Literary Biography Vol 170), Gale, 96coauth, Telecommunications Research Resources: An Annotated Guide, Erlbaum, 95; Mass Communications Research Resources: An Annotated Guide, Erlbaum, 98. **CONTACT ADDRESS** Second Fl Main Libr Infor Services, The Ohio State Univ Libraries, 1858 Neil Ave Mall, Columbus, OH, 43210-1286. **EMAIL** bracken.1@osu.edu

BRACKEN, PAMELA
DISCIPLINE ENGLISH **EDUCATION** Catholic Univ Am, PhD, 94. **CAREER** Prof, Southern Nazarene Univ, 95-. **MEMBERSHIPS** South Central Modern Lang Asn; Asn Lit Scholars Critics; Nat Council Tchrs English. **RESEARCH** Victorian literature; Alice Meynell; William Morris; Julia Margaret Cameron. **SELECTED PUBLICATIONS** Auth, art, The Art Worker' Guild, 93; auth, intro, notes, The Table Turned or Nupkins Awakened, 94; auth, art, About Suffering They Were Never Wrong: Reflections on the Oklahoma Bombing, 95; auth, art, Scenes of Cultural Life: George Eliot and the Clergy, 95; auth, art, Fire and Ice: Clashing Visions of Iceland in the Travel Narratives of William Morris and Sir Richard Burton, 96. **CONTACT ADDRESS** Dept of English, Southern Nazarene Univ, 6729 NW 39th Expy, Bethany, OK, 73008. **EMAIL** pwiens@snu.edu

BRACY, WILLIAM
PERSONAL Born 03/25/1915, Rich Square, NC, m, 1962, 2 children **DISCIPLINE** ENGLISH **EDUCATION** Univ NC, Chapel Hill, AB, 36, MA, 39, PhD(English), 49. **CAREER** Asst, Univ NC, Chapel Hill, 39-42, part-time instr, 46-48, instr English, 48-49; asst prof, Univ Mo, Columbia, 49-54; asst ed humanities, Collier's Encycl, New York, 55-58; humanities ed & consult, Encycl Americana, 58-64; lectr English, City Col New York, 64-65; assoc prof, 65-68, acting chmn dept, 67-68, chmn, 69-71 & 77-80, PROF ENGLISH, BEAVER COL, 68-; Foyle res fel, Shakespeare Inst, Stratford-on-Avon, England, 53. **MEMBERSHIPS** MLA; Northeast Mod Lang Asn; Renaissance Soc Am; Shakespeare Asn Am. **RESEARCH** Shakespeare; Renaissance; English and modern drama. **SELECTED PUBLICATIONS** Auth, The Merry Wives of Windsor: the History and Transmission of Shakespeare's Text, Univ Mo, 52; Doctor Faustus ... Analysis with Critical Commentary, 65 & coauth, Early English Drama ... Middle Ages to the Early 17th Century, 66, Studies Master; articles for Collier's and Americana Encyclopedias; poetry. **CONTACT ADDRESS** Dept of English, Beaver Col, Glenside, PA, 19038.

BRADFORD, CLINTON W.
PERSONAL Born 11/05/1909, Grapevine, AR, w, 1946, 2 children **DISCIPLINE** SPEECH COMMUNICATION **EDUCATION** Univ Arkansas, BA, 38; State Univ Iowa, MA, 41; Louisiana State Univ, PhD, 51. **CAREER** Prof Speech Commun, Louisiana State Univ, 51-73. **RESEARCH** Researching and writing histories of Bradford family and Warbritton family. **SELECTED PUBLICATIONS** Auth, Ministry for Retired Persons, Reily Memorial Univ Church, 87. **CONTACT ADDRESS** 212 Amherst Ave, Baton Rouge, LA, 70808-4603.

BRADLEY, DORIS P.
DISCIPLINE SPEECH **EDUCATION** Univ Pittsburgh, PhD, CCC-SLP. **CAREER** Served as VP, Am Speech-Lang-Hearing Asn. **RESEARCH** Lang disorders; cleft palate; organic speech disorders. **SELECTED PUBLICATIONS** Publ articles & bk Chaps in her spec areas. **CONTACT ADDRESS** Dept of Speech and Hearing Sci(s), Univ of Southern MS, 2701 Hardy St, Hattiesburg, MS, 39406.

BRADLEY, RITAMARY
PERSONAL Born 01/30/1916, Stuart, IA **DISCIPLINE** ENGLISH LITERATURE **EDUCATION** Marygrove Col, PhB, 38; St Louis Univ, MA, 45, PhD(English), 53. **CAREER** Head dept English, Marycrest Col, 45-56; asst exec secy, Sister Formation Conf, 61-64, ed, Sister Formation Bull, 54-64; distinguished res fel, Univ Minn, 64-65; PROF ENGLISH, ST AMBROSE COL, 65-, Workshop philos in a tech cult, Cath Univ Am, 63; ed, 14th-Century English Mystics Newsletter, 75-; part-time fac mem, Inst Women Today, 77- **HONORS AND AWARDS** LLD, Marquette Univ, 60; LHD, Fordham Univ, 60. **MEMBERSHIPS** MLA; Mediaeval Acad Am; Relig Educ Asn; Nat Coalition Am Nuns. **RESEARCH** Women in literature; English medieval mystics; women in religious history. **SELECTED PUBLICATIONS** Auth, The Ways of the Spirit--Underhill, Relig & Lit, vol 0024, 92; Modern Guide to the Ancient Quest for the Holy--Underhill, Relig & Lit, vol 0024, 92; The Ways of the Spirit--Underhill, Relig & Lit, vol 0024, 92; Underhill, Evelyn--Artist of the Infinite Life--Greene, Relig & Lit, vol 0024, 92; The Saint and the City--Micheline-De-Pesaro Died, 1356, Franciscan Tertiary, J Medieval Studies, vol 0069, 94; From Virile Woman to Womanchrist--Studies In Medieval Religion And Literature, J Medieval Studies, vol 0071, 96; From Virile Woman to Womanchrist--Studies In Medieval Religion And Literature, J Medieval Sutdies, vol 0071, 96. **CONTACT ADDRESS** Dept of English, St Ambrose Col, 518 W Locust St, Davenport, IA, 52803-2898.

BRADY, LEO
PERSONAL Born 01/23/1917, Wheeling, WV, m, 1945, 8 children **DISCIPLINE** DRAMA **EDUCATION** Cath Univ Am, AB, 41, MA, 42. **CAREER** From assoc prof to PROF SPEECH & DRAMA, CATH UNIV AM, 46- **MEMBERSHIPS** Am Theatre Asn. **RESEARCH** Dramatic Criticism; history of drama; aesthetics. **SELECTED PUBLICATIONS** Auth, Horatio, Southerly, vol 0054, 94; Antidote, Southerly, vol 0056, 96; Solstice, Westerly, vol 0042, 97; Donegal, Southerly, vol 0053, 93. **CONTACT ADDRESS** Dept of Drama, Catholic Univ of America, Washington, DC, 20017.

BRADY, OWEN E.
PERSONAL Born 05/03/1946, Chicago, IL, m, 1971, 3 children **DISCIPLINE** DRAMATIC LITERATURE **EDUCATION** Ill Benedictine Col, BA, 68; Univ Notre Dame, MA, 70, PhD(English), 73. **CAREER** Instr English & humanities, Univ Notre Dame, 72-73; lectr English, Njala Univ Col, Univ Sierra Leone, WAfrica, 73-75; asst prof humanities, 75-81, assoc prof, 81-98, Dean Lib Studies, Clarkson Col, 82-94, Consult, Asn Depts English, summer, 80; res assoc, Inst Writing, Univ Iowa, 80-. **MEMBERSHIPS** NE MLA; Conf Col Compos & Commun. **RESEARCH** Performance criticism of drama; Shakespeare; Am drama; African Am Lit. **SELECTED PUBLICATIONS** Auth, Baraka's Experimental Death Unit # 1: Plan for (R)Evolution, Black Am Lit Forum, 75; Cult ritual and cultural conflict in LeRoi Jones' The Toilet, Educ Theatre J, 76; Wright's Lawd Today: The American dream festering in the sun, Col Lang Asn J, 78; LeRoi Jones' The Slave: A ritual of purgation, Black Lit in Rev, Obsidian, 78; Great Goodness of Life: Baraka's black bourgeoisie Blues, In: Imamu Amiri Baraka: A Collection of Critical Essays, Prentice-Hall, 78; contribr, Afro-American Literature: The Reconstruction of Instruction, MLA, 79; auth, Irony and sentiment: The delicate balance of the Guthrie Theater's 1979-80 Glass Menagerie, Tennessee Williams Newslett, 80; auth, Theodore Ward's Our Law: From the Slavery of Melodrama to the Freedom of Tragedy, Callaloo, 84; Blackness and the Unmanning of America in Dave Rabe's Streamers War, Literature, and the Arts, 97; 11 Theater Reviews in Theatre Journal, 79-95. **CONTACT ADDRESS** Ctr for Lib Studies, Clarkson Univ, Box 5750, Potsdam, NY, 13699-0000. **EMAIL** obrady@clvm.clarkson.edu

BRADY, ROBERT M.
DISCIPLINE INTERPERSONAL COMMUNICATION **EDUCATION** Univ Mich, PhD. **CAREER** Comm Stu, Univ Ark **HONORS AND AWARDS** Fulbright Cols Outstanding Adv Award., Vice-chair. **SELECTED PUBLICATIONS** Articles, Jour Business Comm; Comm Monographs; Western Jour Comm; Jour Language Soc Psychol; Soc Behavior Personality. **CONTACT ADDRESS** Univ Ark, Fayetteville, AR, 72701.

BRAENDLIN, BONNIE HOOVER
PERSONAL Born 03/03/1940, Dickinson, ND, m, 1968, 1 child **DISCIPLINE** MODERN BRITISH & AMERICAN MINORITY LITERATURE **EDUCATION** Augustana Col, BA, 62; Univ Pittsburgh, MA, 65; Fla State Univ, PhD(English lit), 78. **CAREER** Instr English, Calif Lutheran Col, 65-68; vis asst prof, 81-82, DIR FRESHMAN ENGLISH, FLA STATE UNIV, 82-, Ed newslett, Womens Caucus of SAtlantic Modern Lang Asn, 80-82. **MEMBERSHIPS** MLA; SAtlantic Modern Lang Asn; Soc Study of Multi-Ethnic Lit of the US; Col English Asn. **RESEARCH** The Bildungsroman; women's studies; modern novel. **SELECTED PUBLICATIONS** Auth, Noncanonical American Literature--Introduction, Cea Critic, vol 0055, 92. **CONTACT ADDRESS** Florida State Univ, 1915 Rhonda Dr, Tallahassee, FL, 32303.

BRAILOW, DAVID GREGORY
PERSONAL Born 10/31/1950, Penn Yan, NY, m, 1991, 1 child **DISCIPLINE** RENAISSANCE LITERATURE, BRITISH NOVEL **EDUCATION** Amherst Col, BA, 72; Univ Ore, MA, 76, PhD, 79. **CAREER** Vis asst prof, Wake Forest Univ, 79-82; from asst to assoc to prof Eng, 82-, John Peter Smith prof of Eng, McKendree Coll, 95-. **HONORS AND AWARDS** Sears Foundatin Award for Teaching Excellence and Campus Leadership, McKendree College, 89; NEH Summer Seminars and Institutes. **MEMBERSHIPS** Shakespeare Assn Am. **RESEARCH** Shakespeare in performance. **SELECTED PUBLICATIONS** Assoc ed, The Dictionary of British Literary Characters: The Eighteenth and Nineteenth Century Novel, Facts-on-File, 93; art, Twelfth Night Across the Continents: An Interview With Michael Pennington, Shakespeare Bulletin 14, 96; art, The Dream World of Richard II: Barbara Gaines Directs, Shakespeare Bulletin 14, 96; art, Authority and Interpretation: Hamlet at Shakespeare Repertory Theater, Essays in Theatre/Etudes theatrales, 98. **CONTACT ADDRESS** Humanities Div, McKendree Col, 701 College Rd, Lebanon, IL, 62254-1299. **EMAIL** dbrailow@atlas.mckendree.edu

BRAITHWAITE, DAWN O.
PERSONAL Born 01/13/1955, Chicago, IL, m, 1984 **DISCIPLINE** COMMUNICATION STUDIES **EDUCATION** Univ MN, Doctor of Philosophy, Speech-Communication, 88. **CAREER** Teaching assoc, 78-80, lect, dept commun, CA State Univ, Long Beach, 81-82; instr, div of the Humanities; Golden West Col, 79-82; lect, dept speech commun, CA State Univ, Fullerton, 80-82; instr, Univ MN, Continuing Ed for Women, 83-85; instr, Dept of Commun, The Col of St Catherine, 84; instr, Continuing Mangement Ed, Univ MN, 83-85; teaching assoc, dept of speech commun, 82-87, instr, dept speech & theatre, 85-87, asst prof, Univ MN, 88-89; dir graduate studies, dept commun studies, 89-92, asst prof, NM State Univ, 89-92; asst prof, dept commun studies, 92-96, affiliate fac member, Gerontology prog, 94-, interim dir, Gerontology prog, 96-97, assoc prof, dept of commun studies, 96-, AZ State Univ West; assoc prof, Dept Commun Studies, Univ NE-Lincoln, 98-, elected graduate fel, 98-, dir graduate studies, 99-2000. **HONORS AND AWARDS** Award of Excellence in Teaching by a Graduate Student, Int Commun Asn, 85; elected fac Commencement speaker, Univ MN, Morris, 86; elected First Vice Pres of Western States Commun Asn, 98, to become Pres, 2000. **MEMBERSHIPS** Nat Commun Asn; Western States Commun Asn; Central States Commun Asn; Int Network on Personal Relationships; Int Soc for the Study of Personal Relationships; Phi Kappa Phi Honor Soc. **RESEARCH** Communication strategies of people with disabilities; relational identity: communication and the development of stepfamilies; commun rituals; commun of social support. **SELECTED PUBLICATIONS** Co-auth, with D Labrecque, Responding to the Americans with Disabilities Act: Contributions of Interpersonal Communication Research and Training, J of Applied Commun, 22, 94; with L A Baxter, "I Do" Again: The Relational Dialectics of Renewing Marriage Vows, J of Social and Personal Relationships, 12, 95; auth, Ritualized Embarrassment at "Coed" Wedding and Baby Showers, Commun Reports, 8, 95; co-auth, A Binding Tie: Supportive Communication of Family Kinkeepers, J of Applied Commun Res, 24, 96; with C Cumber, A Study of Perceptions and Understanding of Multiculturalism, Howard J of Commun, 7, 96; auth, "I Am a Person First": Different Perspectives on the Communication of Persons with Disabilities, in E B Ray, ed, Case Studies in Communication and Disenfranchisement: Applications to Social Health Issues, Lawrence Erlbaum Assocs, Pubs, 96; Persons First: Expanding Communicative Choices by Persons with Disabilities, in E B Ray, ed, Case Studies in Communication and Disenfranchisement: Social Health Issues and Implications, Lawrence Erlbaum Assocs, Pubs, 96; co-auth, with A L Harper and C A Braithwaite, Here?: Strategies for Teaching About Cultural Diversity in Non-Diverse Regions, J of Professional Studies, 4, 97; co-auth, with C A Braithwaite, Understanding Communication of Persons with Disabilities as Cultural Communication, in L A Samovar and R Porter, eds, Intercultural Communication: A Reader, 8th ed, earlier versions in 4-7th eds, Wadsworth Pub, 97; numerous other publications and several new works in press. **CONTACT ADDRESS** Communication Studies Dept, Univ of Nebraska, Lincoln, 424 Oldfather Hall, Lincoln, NE, 68588-0329. **EMAIL** dbraithwaite@unl.edu

BRANCH, EDGAR MARQUESS
PERSONAL Born 03/21/1913, Chicago, IL, m, 1939, 3 children **DISCIPLINE** AMERICAN LITERATURE **EDUCATION** Beloit Col, AB, 34; Univ Chicago, AM, 38, Univ Iowa, PhD, 41. **CAREER** From instr to prof English, 41-64, chmn dept, 59-64, res prof, 64-78, EMER PROF ENGLISH & RES ASSOC AM LIT, MIAMI UNIV, 78-, Vis assoc prof, Univ Mo, 49; Nat Endowment for Humanities sr fel, 71-72, independent study, 76-77; Guggenheim Found Fel, 79. **HONORS AND AWARDS** Benjamin Harrison Medallion, Miami Univ, 78; Distinguished Serv Citation, Beloit Col, 79; Nancy Dasher Bk Award, Col English Asn, 80. **MEMBERSHIPS** Soc Studies Southern Lit; MLA; Am Studies Asn; Soc Study Midwestern Lit; Western Lit Asn. **RESEARCH** Mark Twain; 19th century American literature; James T Farrell. **SELECTED PUBLICATIONS** Auth, Bixby-Vs-Carroll, New Light on Clemens, Sam Early River Career, Mark Twain J, vol 0030, 92. **CONTACT ADDRESS** Dept of English, Miami Univ, Oxford, OH, 45056.

BRANDE, DAVID
DISCIPLINE ENGLISH LITERATURE **EDUCATION** Portland State Univ, BA, 85, MA, 88; Univ Wash, PhD, 95. **CAREER** Asst prof. **SELECTED PUBLICATIONS** Auth, The Business of Cyberpunk: Symbolic Economy and Ideology in William Gibson, Johns Hopkins Univ, 95; Making Yourself a Body without Organs: The Cartography of Pain in Kathy Acker's Don Quixote, 91. **CONTACT ADDRESS** Dept of Humanities, Illinois Inst of Tech, 3301 S Dearborn, Chicago, IL, 60616. **EMAIL** dbrande@charlie.cns.iit.edu

BRANDON, JAMES R.
PERSONAL Born 04/10/1927, St. Paul, MN, m, 1961, 1 child **DISCIPLINE** DRAMA **EDUCATION** Univ Wis, PhB, 48, MS, 49, PhD, 55. **CAREER** Instr drama & speech, Univ Conn, 50; asst cult attache, US Info Agency, Djakarta, 55-56, radio off, 56-57, Japanese lang off, Tokyo, 58-59, asst cult attache, 59-61; assoc prof drama, Mich State Univ, 61-67, prof theater, 67-68; PROF THEATER, UNIV HAWAII, 68-, Int Prog Mich State Univ-Ford Found res grant, Southeast Asia, 63-64; Fulbright Res Scholar grant, Japan, 66-68; Nat Endowment for Humanities sr fel, 71-72. **MEMBERSHIPS** Asia Soc; Japan Soc; Am Theatre Asn. **RESEARCH** Asian theatre. **SELECTED PUBLICATIONS** Auth, The Japanese Theater--From Shamanistic Ritual to Contemporary Plurality--Ortolani, Monumenta Nipponica, vol 0048, 93. **CONTACT ADDRESS** Dept of Drama & Theatre, Univ of Hawaii, 1770 E West Rd, Honolulu, HI, 96822-2317.

BRANDT, DIANA
PERSONAL Winkler, MB, Canada **DISCIPLINE** ENGLISH **EDUCATION** Can Mennonite Bible Col, BTh, 72; Univ Toronto, MA, 76; Univ Man, BA, 75, PhD, 93. **CAREER** Writer, 83-, lectr, asst prof, Eng, Univ Winnipeg, 86-95; WRITER IN RESIDENCE, 95-96, RES FEL, UNIV ALBERTA, 96-. **HONORS AND AWARDS** A.L. Wheeler Bk Prize, Univ Man, 75; Gerald Lampert Award, 87; Patrick Mary Plunkett Memorial Scholar, Univ Man, 89; McNally Robinson Award Man Bk of Year, 90; Nat Poetry Award, Can Authors' Asn, 95. **MEMBERSHIPS** Writers' Union Can; PEN; League Can Poets; Man Writers' Guild. **SELECTED PUBLICATIONS** Auth, questions I asked my mother, 87; auth, mother, not mother, 92; auth, Wild Mother Dancing: Maternal Narrative in Canadian Literature, 93; auth, Jersualem, beloved, 95; auth, Dancing Naked: Narrative Strategies for Writing Across Centuries, 96. **CONTACT ADDRESS** Dept of English, Univ Alta, Edmonton, AB, T6G 2E5.

BRANTLEY, JENNIFER
DISCIPLINE ENGLISH LITERATURE **EDUCATION** KS State Univ, MA; Univ NE Lincoln, PhD. **CAREER** Prof, Univ of WI. **RESEARCH** Women's lit; 20th century lit; poetry writing. **SELECTED PUBLICATIONS** Auth, pubs on Carson McCullers, Kate Chopin, and Anne Ellis. **CONTACT ADDRESS** Eng Dept., Univ Wisconsin, S 3rd St, PO Box 410, River Falls, WI, 54022-5001.

BRATER, ENOCH
PERSONAL Born 10/01/1944, New York, NY, m, 1973 **DISCIPLINE** ENGLISH & AMERICAN LITERATURE **EDUCATION** NY Univ, BA, 65; Harvard Univ, AM, 67, PhD(English), 71. **CAREER** Managing dir, Loeb Drama Ctr, Harvard Univ, 70-71; asst prof drama, Univ Pa, 71-75, coordr undergrad prog theater, 73-75; asst prof, 75-77, ASSOC PROF DRAMA, DEPT ENGLISH, UNIV MICH, 77-, DIR GRAD STUDIES, 82-, Fel, Univ Pa, 72; Am Philos Soc grant-in-aid, 73; ed, Mich Academician, Mich Acad Sci, Arts & Lett, 79-; dir summer prog in London, Univ Mich, 82- **MEMBERSHIPS** MLA; Northeast Mod Lang Asn; Samuel Beckett Soc (pres, 79-); Victorian Soc. **RESEARCH** Samuel Beckett; British drama, 20th century; American drama. **SELECTED PUBLICATIONS** Auth, American Clocks, Shepard, Sam Time Plays, Modern Drama, vol 0037, 94. **CONTACT ADDRESS** Dept of English, Univ Mich Ann, 505 S State St, Ann Arbor, MI, 48109-1045.

BRAUDY, LEO
PERSONAL Born 06/11/1941, Philadelphia, PA, m, 1974, 2 children **DISCIPLINE** LITERATURE **EDUCATION** Swarthmore Col, BA, 63; Yale Univ, MA, 64, PhD, 67. **CAREER** Danforth tchng fel, 65-66, instr, 66-68, Yale Univ; asst prof, 68-70, assoc prof, 70-73, prof, 73-76, Columbia Univ; fac, 72, 73, Bread Loaf Schl; vis instr, 73, 74, vis prof, 75, Yale Univ; prof, 74-77, 79-80, Univ Calif, Santa Barbara; prof, 76-83, Johns Hopkins Univ; prof, 83-85, 98-, Leo S. Bing prof, 85-, chmn, 83-86, 98-99, Univ So Calif. **RESEARCH** History of war, history of fame, 17th century English lit, film hist, theory & criticism, Amer popular cult. **CONTACT ADDRESS** Dept English, Univ of So California, Los Angeles, CA, 90089-0354. **EMAIL** braudy@mizar.usc.edu

BRAUN PASTERNACK, CAROL
DISCIPLINE ENGLISH LITERATURE **EDUCATION** UCLA, PhD, 83. **CAREER** ASSOC PROF, ENG, UNIV CALIF, SANTA BARBARA. **RESEARCH** Hist of Eng lang; Gender in the middle ages. **SELECTED PUBLICATIONS** Auth, Stylistic Disjunctions in The Dream of the Rood in Anglo-Saxon England, 84; Textuality in Old English Poetry, Cambridge Univ Press, 95; "Anonymous Polyphony and the Textuality of the Wanderer," Anglo-Saxon Eng, 91; co-ed, Vox intexta: Orality and Textuality in the Middle Ages, Univ Wis Press, 91. **CONTACT ADDRESS** Dept of Eng, Univ Calif, Santa Barbara, CA, 93106-7150. **EMAIL** cpaster@humanitas.ucsb.edu

BRAUNMULLER, A.P.
PERSONAL Born 11/25/1945, Plainfield, NJ **DISCIPLINE** ENGLISH LITERATURE **EDUCATION** Stanford Univ, BA, 67; Yale Univ, M Phil, 70, PhD (English), 71. **CAREER** Asst prof, Dept English, 71-76, assoc prof, Dept of English and Prog in Comparative Lit, 76-82, PROF, DEPT OF ENGLISH AND PROG OF COMPARATIVE LIT, 82-; vis prof, Univ Zurich, 90; Dean, Undergrad and Intercollege Curricular Development, 90-. **HONORS AND AWARDS** Nat Merit Scholarship, 63-67; NDEA Title IV Fel, 67-70; Eastman Fel, Yale Univ, 70-71; Folger Shakespeare Library Fel, summer 70, 73; NEH, Younger Humanist, summer 72; Regent's Fac Fel, summer 75; Harvey L. Eby Award for the Art of Teaching, UCLA, 80; Am Coun of Learned Socs Sr Fel, 85; Col of Letters and Science, UCLA, grant, 85; NEH-Folger Shakespeare Library Sr Fel, 88-89; Gold Shield Faculty Prize, UCLA, 94-96., Coun member, Malone Soc, 86-; VP, Renaissance English Text Soc, 90-; co-ed, Viator: Medieval and Renaissance Studies; ed bd, Shakespeare Quart, 89-; assoc general ed, New Cambridge Shakespeare, 89-; trustee, Shakespeare Asn of Am, 95-98; NEH Seminar Leader, Folger Shakespeare Library, 96; exec comm, Drama Div, Moden Lang Asn, 87-92; chair, exec comm, Drama Div, Modern Lang Asn, 91; ed bd, MA Studies in Early Modern Culture, 89-; exec comm, New Variorum Shakespeare Edition, Modern Lang Asn, 90-98. **MEMBERSHIPS** Modern Lang Asn; Shakespeare Asn of Am; Malone Soc; Renaissance Soc of Am; Renaissance English Text Soc. **RESEARCH** Early modern British and European drama; early modern European art and collecting; Nineteenth- and Twentieth-century British and European drama. **SELECTED PUBLICATIONS** Auth, The Captive Lady (anonymous drama, c. 1622) Malone Society Reprints, Oxford Univ Press, 82; George Peele, G. K. Hall, 83; A Seventeenth-Century Letter-Book: A Facsimile Edition of Folger MS. V.a. 321 with Transcription, Introduction, and Commentary, Univ of DE Press & Assoc Univ Presses, 83; Early Shakespearean Tragedy and Its Contemporary Context: Cause and Emotion in Titus Andronicus, Richard III, and The Rape of Lucrece, in M. Bradbury and D. J. Palmer, eds, Shakespearean Tragedy, Stratford-upon-Avon Studies, 20, Edward Arnold, 84; Comedy from Shakespeare to Sheridan: Change and Continuity in the English and European Tradition: Essays in Honor of Eugene M. Waith, ed and with intro by A. J. Braunmuller and J. C. Bulman, Univ DE Press & Assoc Univ Presses, 86; William Shakespeare, King John, Oxford English Texts, Oxford Univ Press, 89; 'Second Means': Agent and Accessory in Elizabethan Drama, in C. E. McGee and L. Magnusson, eds, Elizabethan Theatre XI, Meany, 90; 'To the Globe I Rowed': John Holles sees A Game at Chess, English Literary Renaissance, 20, 90; The Cambridge Companion to English Renaissance Drama, ed with Michael Hattaway, Cambridge Univ Press, 90; Natural Fictions: George Chapman's Major Tragedies, Univ DE Press & Assoc Univ Presses, 92; William Shakespeare, Macbeth, New Cambridge Shakespeare, Cambridge Univ Press, 97. **CONTACT ADDRESS** Dept of English, Univ of California, Los Angeles, Box 90095, Los Angeles, CA, 90095-1530. **EMAIL** barddoc@humnet.ucla.edu

BREDBECK, GREGORY W.
DISCIPLINE ENGLISH LITERATURE **EDUCATION** Ohio State Univ, BA; Univ Pa, PhD. **CAREER** PROF, ART HIST, UNIV CALIF, RIVERSIDE. **HONORS AND AWARDS** Outstanding Acad Bk, 91-92. **RESEARCH** English Renaissance studies; Modern and postmodern gay male writing. **SELECTED PUBLICATIONS** Auth, Sodomy and Interpretation: Marlowe to Milton, Cornell Univ Press, 91; Milton's Ganymede: Negotiations of Homoerotic Tradition in Paradise Regained, PMLA, 91. **CONTACT ADDRESS** Dept of Eng, Univ Calif, 1156 Hinderaker Hall, Riverside, CA, 92521-0209. **EMAIL** bredbeck@ucrac1.ucr.edu

BREDIN, MARIAN
DISCIPLINE COMMUNICATIONS **EDUCATION** Trent Univ, BA; Univ Leicester, MA; McGill Univ, PhD. **CAREER** Prof, Brock Univ. **RESEARCH** Cultural politics and cultural identity; minorities and media; aboriginal broadcasting in Canada; feminist cultural analysis. **SELECTED PUBLICATIONS** Auth, Histories of Appropriation: Territorial and Cultural Dispossessopm pf Aboriginal People in Canada, Appropriation and Re-Appropriation: the Return of Canadian Native Voices, Univ of Toronto, 97; Transforming Images: Communication Technologies and Cultural Identity in Nishnawbe- Aski, Cross-cultural Consumption, Routledge, 96; Ethnography and Communication: Approaches to Aboriginal Media, Can Jour Commun 18, 96. **CONTACT ADDRESS** Dept of Communications Studies, Brock Univ, 500 Glenridge Ave, St. Catharines, ON, L2S 3A1. **EMAIL** mbredin@spartan.ac.brocku.ca

BREEN, MARCUS
DISCIPLINE COMMUNICATION STUDIES **EDUCATION** Univ Queensland, BA; Australian Nat Univ, BLet; Victoria Univ Tech, PhD. **CAREER** Journalist, 81-90; fes fel, Ctr Int Res Communic, Info Techn, 90-94; consult, Dept State Dev, Victoria, Australia, 94- 96; ASST PROF, UNIV NC, CHAPEL HILL, 96-. **CONTACT ADDRESS** Dept of Communi Studies, Univ of No Carolina, Chapel Hill, 113 Bingham Hall, CB#3285, Chapel Hill, NC, 27599-3285. **EMAIL** mbreen@email.unc.edu

BREEN, MYLES P.
PERSONAL Born 06/06/1939, Ayr, Australia, m, 1969, 7 children **DISCIPLINE** MASS COMMUNICATION **EDUCATION** Wayne State Univ, PhD 69; Syracuse Univ MS 65; Univ Queensland Aus, BS 62. **CAREER** Charles Stuart Univ, prof 90-; Mitchell College, dean 84-90; N IL Univ, asst prof, assoc prof, prof, 69-84; Wayne State Univ, inst 66-68; Australian Broadcasting Co, broadcaster 62-65. **HONORS AND AWARDS** Select Leadershp Conf Co Univ; Ser Awd Soc Mot Pic & TV Eng; NIU tchg Awd. **MEMBERSHIPS** Aus & NZ Comm Assoc; Aus J Assoc; ICA; AAC; ARTS; JEA; NCA. **RESEARCH** Mass media; film stud; tv stud; intl cult mass media comm; instructional techno; comm theory. **SELECTED PUBLICATIONS** Journalism: Theory and Practice, ed, Sydney, Macleay Press, 98; Basic Filmmaking Notes, Minneapolis, Burgess, 81; Australian Programming, in: Encycl of TV, ed, H. Newcomb, Chicago, Fitzroy Dearborn, 97; Journalism Education and Modernity: A Respectable Paradigm, in, J. Tully, ed, Beyond 2000: Future Directions in Jour Education: Proceedings form the J EDU Annual Conf, Christchurch, U of Canterbury, 95; Tracking Research for Journalism Educators, coauth, Aus Jour Rev, 97; Has the Image of Australia on TV News Changed? Aus Stud in Jour, 96; Journalism and Constructive Learning: Trusting the Good Sense of our Students, AsiaPac Media EDU c, 96. **CONTACT ADDRESS** Dept of Communication, Charles Stuart Univ, 44 Osborne Av, Bathurst 2795. **EMAIL** mbreen@csu.edu.au

BREITROSE, HENRY S.
DISCIPLINE COMMUNICATIONS **EDUCATION** Univ WI, BA, 58; Northwestern Univ, MA 59; Stanford Univ, PhD, 66. **CAREER** Prof, 60, Stanford Univ. **HONORS AND AWARDS** NBC/BBC Europ Prod Unit, Thames TV; consult, Fr nat TV; consult, Nat Film Bd Can; consult, Asian Inst Broadcast Devel; consult, Corp Pub Broadcasting; found mem ed bd, Quart Rev Film Studies; found ed, Cambridge Studies Film; vpres CILECT, Int Assoc Film TV. **RESEARCH** Intellectual hist of the documentary idea. **SELECTED PUBLICATIONS** Auth, articles in film aesthetics/criticism and experimental attitude change and non-verbal commun in jour such as the Journal of Abnormal and Social Psychology and the Journal of Education Psychology. **CONTACT ADDRESS** Dept Commun, Stanford Univ, McClatchy Hall, Stanford, CA, 94305-2050. **EMAIL** hbreit@leland.stanford.edu

BRENNAN, ANNE DENISE
DISCIPLINE 20TH CENTURY AMERICAN AND BRITISH LITERATURE **EDUCATION** St. Louis Univ, PhD, 88. **CAREER** Engl, Col Mt. St. Vincent **HONORS AND AWARDS** Enright Award Tchg, 92; Higher Opportunity Prog Distinguished Serv Award, 94; Sr. Magdalen Horsting Spec Award-Sports Dept. CMSV, 96; Certificate Appreciation-Honors Track CMSV, 96; Honorary Student Life Staff mem, 98. **SELECTED PUBLICATIONS** Auth, Breaking the Ice: Some Highlights of the History of Humor. **CONTACT ADDRESS** Col of Mount Saint Vincent, 6301 Riverdale Ave, Riverdale, NY, 10471.

BRENNAN, ANTHONY
DISCIPLINE ENGLISH LITERATURE **EDUCATION** Oxford Univ, BA; McMaster Univ, MA, PhD. **RESEARCH** Shakespeare; modern British drama. **SELECTED PUBLICATIONS** Auth, Onstage/Offstage Worlds in Shakespeare's Plays, 89; auth, Shakespeare's Dramatic Structures, 86; auth, Henry V: A New Critical Introduction, 92. **CONTACT ADDRESS** English Dept, McMaster Univ, 1280 Main St W, Hamilton, ON, L8S 4L9.

BRENNAN, JOHN P.
PERSONAL Born 07/02/1942, Melrose, MA, m, 1966, 4 children **DISCIPLINE** ENGLISH **EDUCATION** Boston Col, BS, 63; Univ Calif, Davis, MA, 65, PhD, 67. **CAREER** Assoc English, Univ Calif, Davis, 66-67; asst prof, 67-86, ASSOC PROF, ENGLISH, IND UNIV-PURDUE UNIV, FT WAYNE, 86-, dir, Composition, 76-78, dir, Graduate Studies, 87-94. **HONORS AND AWARDS** IU summer fac fel, 69; IPFW summer fac fel, 76; NEH summer seminar, 78; Outstanding fac mem, Assisting Disabled Students, IPFW, 83-84; NEH summer inst, 90. **MEMBERSHIPS** AAUP; MLA; Mediaeval Acad Am; Sci Fiction Res Asn; NCTE. **RESEARCH** Chaucer; Old and Middle English literature; Greek and Latin classics; Folklore and traditional music; Science fiction. **SELECTED PUBLICATIONS** Coauth, Medieval manuscripts of Jerome Adversus Jovinianum, Manuscripta, 69; auth, Reflections on a gloss to the Prioress's tale from Jerome's Adversus Jovinianum, Studies Philol, 73; coauth, Anarchism and utopian tradition in The Dispossessed, in Writers of the 21st Century: Ursula K

Leguin, Taplinger Publ, 79; auth, Troilas and Criseyde, English Lang Notes, 79; The mechanical chicken: Psyche and society in The Space Merchants, Extrapolation, 84; Administering Truth, Papers in Comparative Studies, 85. **CONTACT ADDRESS** Dept of English & Ling, Indiana Univ-Purdue Univ, Fort Wayne, 2101 Coliseum Blvd E, Fort Wayne, IN, 46805-1499. **EMAIL** brennanj@ipfw.edu

BRENNAN, KIT
DISCIPLINE DRAMA **EDUCATION** MA, PhD, Queen's and the Univ Alberta. **CAREER** Assoc prof. **HONORS AND AWARDS** First prize, Can Nat Playwriting Competition, 94; Saskatchewan Writers' Guild lit award, 93; first prize, Dramatic GRAIN Competition, 92., Cooord, BFA Major in Playwriting. **SELECTED PUBLICATIONS** Auth, Tiger's Heart, Scirocco Drama, 96; Spring Planting, Nuage Editions, 98; ed, Going It Alone: Plays by Women for Solo Performers, Nuage Editions, 97. **CONTACT ADDRESS** Dept of Theatre, Concordia Univ, Montreal, 1455 de Maisonneuve W, Montreal, PQ, H3G 1M8.

BRENNAN, TIMOTHY ANDRES
DISCIPLINE ENGLISH LITERATURE **EDUCATION** Univ Wis, BA, 76; Columbia Univ, MA, 81, PhD, 87. **CAREER** Asst prof, Purdue Univ, 86-90; Vis asst prof, Univ Mich, 89-90; asst prof, 90-94; assoc prof, 94-. **HONORS AND AWARDS** Bunner Awd Am Lit, 81; Mary Brabyn Wackman Awd, 76. **MEMBERSHIPS** Tchr Democratic Culture; MLA; Am Studies Asn; Latin Am Studies Asn. **RESEARCH** Atlantic cultures; literature and culture of modern Britain; twentieth century literary and cultural theory; relations between literature, popular culture, and cultural policy. **SELECTED PUBLICATIONS** Auth, At Home in the World: Cosmopolitanism Now, Cambridge, 97; Salman Rushdie and the Third World: Myths of the Nation, Macmillan, 89; Salman Rushdie, Scribners, 97; Post-Iconoclasm (rev), 97; ed, The Writing of Black Britain, 90; Narratives of Colonial Resistance, 89. **CONTACT ADDRESS** Department of English, SUNY Stony Brook, Stony Brook, NY, 11794. **EMAIL** tbrennan@ccmail.sunysb.edu

BRENNAN WATTERS, KATHLEEN
PERSONAL Born 04/09/1957, Vancouver, BC, Canada **DISCIPLINE** DRAMA **EDUCATION** Queen's Univ, BA, 90; Univ Alta, MFA, 93. **CAREER** Actor/writer, 82-93; assoc prof, 93-98, PLAYWRITING COORDR, JOINT ENGLISH/THEATRE DEPT SPECIALIZATION, CONCORDIA UNIV. **SELECTED PUBLICATIONS** Coauth, Taking the Stage: Selections from Plays by Canadian Women, 94; Another Perfect Piece, 95; coauth/ed, Going It Alone: Plays by Women for Solo Performers, 97. **CONTACT ADDRESS** English Dept, Concordia Univ, Montreal, 7141 Sherbrooke St W, Montreal, PQ, H4B 1R6.

BRESLIN, PAUL
DISCIPLINE ENGLISH **EDUCATION** Univ Va, PhD. **CAREER** Prof, Northwestern Univ. **SELECTED PUBLICATIONS** Auth, The Psycho-Political Muse: American Poetry Since the Fifties, Chicago, 87; study of, Delmore Schwartz, Scribner's Am Writers series; essays & rev, about contemp poets. **CONTACT ADDRESS** Dept of English, Northwestern Univ, 1801 Hinman, Evanston, IL, 60208.

BRETT, SALLY A.
DISCIPLINE ENGLISH LITERATURE **EDUCATION** FL State Univ, PhD. **CAREER** Adj asst prof pract eng, Duke Univ. **SELECTED PUBLICATIONS** Auth, publ(s) in American Women Writers, Ungar. **CONTACT ADDRESS** Eng Dept, Duke Univ, Durham, NC, 27706.

BREWER, DANIEL
DISCIPLINE THE LITERATURE AND CULTURE OF THE ANCIEN REGIME AND ENLIGHTENMENT **EDUCATION** Johns Hopkins Univ, PhD. **CAREER** Instr, Univ Minn, Twin Cities. **RESEARCH** The reception and reinscription of Enlightenment in 19th- and 20th- century French literature, history, and philosophy. **SELECTED PUBLICATIONS** Auth, The Discourse of Enlightenment In Eighteenth-Century France, Cambridge, 93. **CONTACT ADDRESS** Univ Minn, Twin Cities, Minneapolis, MN, 55455.

BREWSTER, GLEN
DISCIPLINE ENGLISH **EDUCATION** Univ Tenn, BA, MA; Duke Univ, PhD, 94. **CAREER** Ex instr, Univ Tenn, Duke Univ, Auburn Univ, EC Univ. **HONORS AND AWARDS** John C.Hodges tchg excellence award, Univ Tenn, 94-95. **RESEARCH** Gender roles and refigurations in the poetry of William Blake. **SELECTED PUBLICATIONS** Publ, articles and rev(s), Nineteenth-Century Contexts, South Atlantic Rev, Proceedings of the Soc for the Interdisciplinary Study of Soc Imagery, NC Lit Rev, Southern Hum Rev, Am Studies Intl. **CONTACT ADDRESS** Dept of Engl, Westfield State Col, 577 Western Ave., Westfield, MA, 01085.

BREWTON, BUTLER E.
PERSONAL Born 02/07/1935, Spartanburg, SC, m **DISCIPLINE** ENGLISH **EDUCATION** Benedict, BA 1956; Montclair State, MA 1970; Rutgers, PhD 1978. **CAREER** Montclair State Coll, assoc prof, English, 1970-. **HONORS AND AWARDS** NDEA fellow SC State Coll 1965. **MEMBERSHIPS** Consultant, McGraw Hill Intl Press 1972; poet NJ State Council on the Arts 1970-76; speaker NCTE Kansas City 1978. **SELECTED PUBLICATIONS** Poems: Tramp, Lady of the Evening, 5 PM, Discovered, Pattern, Barren, Southbound, Idol, Yesterday Hangs, The Custodial Hour, Democracy, The Kiss, For A Reprieve, Peach Orchard, Full Measure, At the General Store, We Children, 1992; Grandpa's, 1992; Rafters, 1992; auth, A Diploma Must Mean What It's Supposed to Mean, New York Times 1986; auth, South and Border States, The Literary Guide to the US; auth, Richard Wright's Thematic Treatment of Women, ERIC; ed, Modern Century Encyclopedia. **CONTACT ADDRESS** English Dept, Montclair State Col, Upper Montclair, NJ, 07043.

BRIER, PETER A.
PERSONAL Born 03/05/1935, Vienna, Austria **DISCIPLINE** ENGLISH LITERATURE **EDUCATION** Yale Univ, BA, 56; Harvard Univ, MA, 58; Claremont Grad Sch & Occidental Col, PhD, 71. **CAREER** Instr English, Ark A&M State Col, 58-60; instr, Occidental Col, 65-68; from instr to asst prof, 69-75, assoc prof, 75-81, prof English, Calif State Univ, Los Angeles, 81-; Exchange prof, Maitre de Conf, Univ Clermont-Ferrand, 78-79. **MEMBERSHIPS** MLA; Philol Asn Pac Coast. **RESEARCH** English romantic writers; Charles Lamb; literary criticism. **SELECTED PUBLICATIONS** Auth, Acrostic to EB--an unpublished poem by Charles Lamb, English Lang Notes, 9/71; Dramatic characterization in the essays of Charles Lamb, Coranto, spring & summer 73; On teaching Coleridge, Pacific Coast Philol, 4/74; Reflections on Tintern Abbey, Wordsworth Circle, winter 74; Lamb, Dickens and the theatrical vision, Charles Lamb Bull, 4-7/75; The Ambulant mode: Pantomime and meaning in the prose of Charles Lamb, Huntington Libr Quart, 5/77; Caliban Reigns: Romantic theory and some contemporary fantasists, Denver Quart, spring 78; coauth (with Anthony Arthur), American Prose and Criticism, 1900-1950, A Guide to Information Sources, Vol 35, Gale Res Co, 81; Howard Mumford Jones and the Dynamics of Liberal Humanism, Univ Mo Press, 94. **CONTACT ADDRESS** Dept of English, California State Univ, Los Angeles, 5151 Rancho Castilla, Los Angeles, CA, 90032-4202. **EMAIL** pbrier@calstatela.edu

BRIGGS, JOHN
PERSONAL Born 01/08/1945, Detroit, MI, m, 1968 **DISCIPLINE** AESTHETICS AND PSYCHOLOGY, JOURNALISM **EDUCATION** Wesleyan Univ, college of Letters, Honors, BA, 68; NY Univ, MA, 72; The Union Inst, PhD, 81. **CAREER** English teacher, Patchogue High School, 68-71; Humanities fac, 73-87; adjunct fac, Brooklyn Col, 74; adjunct English dept fac, Mercy Col, 74-87; freelance sci writer, 81-; assoc prof , journalism coordr, WCSU, 87-95; prof, journalism coordr, WCSU, 95-; adjunct fac, Union Inst, 95-. **HONORS AND AWARDS** Listed in: Who's Who in the World; Who's Who in the East; Who's Who in Am Educ; Int Authors and Writers Who's Who; Contemporary Authors. **MEMBERSHIPS** Am Asn of Univ Profs; The National Writers' Union; The Sci and Medical Network; The Am Soc for Aesthetics. **RESEARCH** New science; aesthetics, creativity, war. **SELECTED PUBLICATIONS** Coauth, Looking Glass Universe, Simon and Schuster, 84; auth, Fire in the Crucible: The Alchemy of Creative Genius, St. Martin's Press, 88; coauth, Turbulent Mirror: an Illustrated Guide to Chaos Theory and the Science of Wholeness, Harper and Row, 89; coauth, Fractals: The Patterns of Chaos, Simon & Schuster, Touchstone, 92; auth, "Nuance, Metaphore and the Rhythm of the Mood Wave in Virginia Woolf", in Virginia Woolf Miscellanies: Proceedings of the First Annual Conference on Virginia Woolf, Pace Univ, 92; auth, "The Balm of Irony", in Voices on the Threshold of Tomorrow, Quest Books, 93; auth, "Dialogue between John Briggs and Morris Berman on the Possibility of Social Creativity and Its Attendant Dangers in Mass Society", in Troisiome Millionaire, 94; auth, "Exploring the Potentials of Creative Dialogue", ICIS Forum, 94; auth, "Chaos, Fractals, Aesthetics and the Environment", The Network, 94; auth, "Nuance and Omnivalence in the Creative Mind" in Advanced Development, A Journal of Adult Giftedness, 97. **CONTACT ADDRESS** Western Connecticut State Univ, White Street, Danbury, CT, 06810. **EMAIL** briggsjp@wcsu.ctstateu.edu

BRIGGS, JOHN C.
DISCIPLINE RENAISSANCE LITERATURE AND SHAKESPEARE **EDUCATION** Harvard Univ, BA; Univ Chicago, PhD. **CAREER** PROF, ART HIST, UNIV CALIF, RIVERSIDE. **HONORS AND AWARDS** Thomas J Wilson award, 88; fac tchg award, 95-96., Dir, Basic Wrtg Prog; Inland Area Wrtg Proj. **RESEARCH** Phenomenon of Shakespearean persuasion and the nature of catharsis; Study of Lincoln's rhetoric. **SELECTED PUBLICATIONS** Auth, Francis Bacon and the Rhetoric of Nature, Harvard Univ Press, 88; Edifying Violence: Peter Elbow and the Pedagogical Paradox, Jour of Adv Comp, 98. **CONTACT ADDRESS** Dept of Eng, Univ Calif, 1156 Hinderaker Hall, Riverside, CA, 92521-0209.

BRIGGS, JOHN P.
DISCIPLINE THE AESTHETICS OF THE NOVEL **EDUCATION** Wesleyan Univ, BA, 68; NY Univ, MA, 78, Union Inst, PhD, 81. **CAREER** Tchr, Patchogue High Sch, 68-71; Adj fac, Brooklyn Col, 74; Adj fac, Mercy Col, 74-87; Assoc prof, WCSU , 87-95; Prof, WCSU, 95-; Adj fac, Norwich Univ & Union Inst, 95. **SELECTED PUBLICATIONS** Auth Looking Glass Universe, Simon and Schuster, 84; Fire in the Crucible The Alchemy of Creative Genius, St Martin's Press, 88; ; Turbulent Mirror: An Illustrated Guide to Chaos Theory and the Science of Wholeness, Harper & Row, 89; Coauth, Metaphor, The Logic of Poetry, Rev ed, Pace Univ Press, 91; Fractals: The Patterns of Chaos, Simon & Schuster, Touchstone, 92. **CONTACT ADDRESS** Western Connecticut State Univ, 181 White Street, Danbury, CT, 28723. **EMAIL** briggsjp@wcsu.ctstateu.edu

BRIND'AMOUR, LUCIE
DISCIPLINE LATE MEDIEVAL AND 16TH CENTURY, AND QUEBEC LITERATURE **EDUCATION** Univ Montreal, PhD, 77. **CAREER** Assoc prof, La State Univ. **SELECTED PUBLICATIONS** Auth, Rhetorique et th?atralite, in Studi mediolatnini e volgari, 75-76; L'archeologie du signe, 83; La tradition de l'amour courtois, in A Comparative History of Literatures in European Languages, 88. **CONTACT ADDRESS** Dept of Fr Grad Stud, Louisiana State Univ, Baton Rouge, LA, 70803.

BRINK, JEANIE RENEE
PERSONAL Born 07/02/1942, Frankfort, IN, 2 children **DISCIPLINE** ENGLISH RENAISSANCE LITERATURE **EDUCATION** Northwestern Univ, BA, 64; Harvard Univ, MA, 66; Univ Wis, PhD(English), 72. **CAREER** ASSOC PROF ENGLISH, ARIZ STATE UNIV, 79-, Assoc ed, J Rocky Mountain Medieval & Renaissance Asn; dir, Ariz Ctr Medieval & Renaissance Studies. **HONORS AND AWARDS** Ariz State Univ Col Lib Arts Quality Teaching Award, 78. **MEMBERSHIPS** MLA; Rocky Mountain Conf British Studies; Rocky Mountain Medieval & Renaissance Soc. **RESEARCH** Biographical research on Sir John Davies; Utopian literature; Renaissance aesthetics. **SELECTED PUBLICATIONS** Auth, Documenting Spenser, Edmund, a New Life Record, Anq, Quart J Short Articles Notes and Rev(s), Vol 0007, 94; Dating Spenser Letter to Ralegh, Libr, Vol 0016, 94; Forms of Nationhood in the Elizabethan Writing of Engl, Anq--Quar J Short Articles Notes and Rev(s), Vol 0008, 95; Spenser Famous Flight in A Renaissance Idea of A Literary Career, 16th Century J, Vol 0026, 95; Spenser,Edmund Family in 2 Notes and a Query/, Notes and Queries, Vol 0044, 97. **CONTACT ADDRESS** Dept of English, Arizona State Univ, Tempe, Tempe, AZ, 85287.

BRISMAN, LESLIE
DISCIPLINE ENGLISH **EDUCATION** Columbia Col, AB, 65; Cornell Univ, MA, 65, PhD, 69. **CAREER** PROF ENGLISH, YALE UNIV, PRESENTLY **CONTACT ADDRESS** Dept of English, Yale Univ, New Haven, CT, 06520-8302. **EMAIL** leslie.brisman@yale.edu

BRKKILA, BETSY
DISCIPLINE ENGLISH **EDUCATION** UC, Berkeley, PhD. **CAREER** Prof, Northwestern Univ. **RESEARCH** 19th century American literature and culture. **SELECTED PUBLICATIONS** Auth, Walt Whitman Among the French: Poet and Myth, 80; Whitman the Political Poet, 89; The Wicked Sisters: Women Poets, Literary History. and Discord, 92; co-ed, Breaking Bounds: Whitman and American Cultural Studies; ed, Ezra Pound: The Contemporary Reviews, 94. **CONTACT ADDRESS** Dept of English, Northwestern Univ, 1801 Hinman, Evanston, IL, 60208.

BROADHEAD, GLENN J.
DISCIPLINE TECHNICAL WRITING, RHETORIC AND COMPOSITION **EDUCATION** Univ Calif, PhD, 73. **CAREER** Prog dir, Technical Writing; Assoc prof, Okla State Univ. **SELECTED PUBLICATIONS** Auth, Variables of Composition: Process and Product in a Business Setting. **CONTACT ADDRESS** Oklahoma State Univ, 101 Whitehurst Hall, Stillwater, OK, 74078.

BROCK, DEWEY HEYWARD
PERSONAL Born 06/02/1941, Greenville, SC, m, 1963, 3 children **DISCIPLINE** ENGLISH & AMERICAN LITERATURE **EDUCATION** Newberry Col, AB, 63; Univ KS, MA, 65, PhD(Eng), 69. **CAREER** From instr to asst prof Eng, 68-75, asst dean, col arts & sci, 69, assoc prof, 76-80, dir, Ctr Sci & Cult & Prog Cult Biomed, 77-79, Prof Eng & Life & Health Sci, Univ Of DE, 81-, Am Coun Learned Soc & Nat Sci Found fel, Summer Inst Humanistic Computation, 70; fac res grant, Univ DE, 71, 75 & 81; nat bd consults, Nat Endowment for the Hum, 77-83; gen ed, Studies in Sci & Cult, 79-; assoc ed, Lit & Med , 80-; Nat Sci Found & Nat Endowment for Hum Educ Proj, 80; Am Philos Soc fel, 81-82; vis prof, Univ Essex, England, 81-82. **MEMBERSHIPS** Council of Col(s) of Arts and Sci(s), Soc for Lit and Sci. **RESEARCH** Renaissance lit; lit and sci; Am lit. **SELECTED PUBLICATIONS** Coauth, Percy MacKaye: Community Drama and the Masque Tradition, Comp

Drama, 72; auth, The Portrait of Abbott Samson in Past and Present: Carlyle and Jocelin of Brakelond, Eng Miscellany, 72; coauth, Ben Jonson: A Quadricentennial Bibliography, 1947-1972, Scarecrow, 74; Graham Greene and the Structure of Salvation, Renascence, 74; auth, Durrenmatt's Der Besuch der alten Dame: The Stage and Screen Adaptations, Lit/Film Quart, 76; Mirrors of Man's Life: The Masques of Ben Jonson and social order, Artes Liberales, 76; ed Ben Jonson: Works 1616, Scholar, 76; A Ben Jonson Companion, Indiana, 83; The Doctor as Dramatic Hero, Perspectives in Bio and Med, 91. **CONTACT ADDRESS** Dept of English, Univ of DE, Newark, DE, 19711. **EMAIL** heyward.brock@mvs.udel.edu

BROCK, JAMES W.
PERSONAL Born 05/23/1919, Greensfork, IN, m, 1941, 3 children **DISCIPLINE** SPEECH **EDUCATION** Manchester Col, AB, 41; Northwestern Univ, MA, 42, PhD(theatre), 50. **CAREER** From instr to assoc prof speech, Albion Col, 45-55; asst prof commun skills, Mich State Univ, 55-56; asst prof speech, Univ Mich, 56-57; assoc prof, Fla State Univ, 57-58; from asst prof to assoc prof, 58-66, chmn dept, 66-69, prof, 66-80, EMER PROF THEATRE, CALIF STATE UNIV, NORTHRIDGE, 80-, Fac res grants, Calif State Univ, Northridge, 63-64, 65-68; Church Soc Col Work fel, 64-65. **MEMBERSHIPS** Nat Asn Arts & Humanities; Nat theatre Conf; Am theatre Asn. **RESEARCH** Elizabethan, religious and contemporary drama. **SELECTED PUBLICATIONS** Auth, Predation, Rationality, and Judicial Somnambulance, Univ Cincinnati Law Rev, Vol 0064, 96. **CONTACT ADDRESS** Dept of Law, Miami Univ, Oxford, OH, 45056.

BROCKMAN, WILLIAM
DISCIPLINE ENGLISH, LIBRARY SCIENCE **EDUCATION** Rutgers Univ, BA, 72, MLS, 77; Drew Univ, MA, 86. **CAREER** Ref librn, Rutgers Univ, 77; ref librn, Drew Univ, 77-89; ENG LIBRN, ASSOC PROF, UNIV ILL, URBANA-CHAMPAIGN, 89-. **CONTACT ADDRESS** Univ of Illinois, Urbana-Champaign, 1408 W Gregory Dr, Urbana, IL, 61801.

BROCKMANN, STEPHEN
DISCIPLINE EIGHTEENTH-CENTURY BRITISH LITERATURE **EDUCATION** Univ Wisc, PhD. **CAREER** Lit, Carnegie Mellon Univ **SELECTED PUBLICATIONS** Auth, Dancing on the Volcano: Essays on the Culture of the Weimar Republic, Camden House, 94; Revisiting Zero Hour 1945: The Emergence of Postwar German Culture, ed. Stephen Brockmann and Frank Trommler, Am Inst Contemporary German Studies, 96. **CONTACT ADDRESS** Carnegie Mellon Univ, 5000 Forbes Ave, Pittsburgh, PA, 15213.

BRODERICK, JOHN CARUTHERS
PERSONAL Born 09/06/1926, Memphis, TN, m, 1949, 2 children **DISCIPLINE** ENGLISH **EDUCATION** Southwestern at Memphis, AB, 48; Univ NC, MA, 49, PhD(English), 53. **CAREER** Instr English, Univ NC, 49-52; Univ Tex, 52-56, spec instr, 56-57; from asst prof to prof, Wake Forest Col, 57-65; specialist Am cult hist, 64-65, asst chief, 65-74, acting chief, 68, chief manuscript div, 75-79, ASST LIBRN RES SERV, LIBR CONG, 79-, Vis prof, Univ Va, 59; Am Coun Learned Soc grant-in-aid, 62-63; adj prof English, George Washington Univ, 64-; vis prof English, Univ NC, 68; mem adv bd, Resources for Am Lit Studies, 70-; Coun Libr Resources fel, 71; advisory comt, US Senate Hist off, 76-; mem, Nat Hist Publ & Records Comn, 78-; gen ed, the Journal of Henry D Thoreau, Princeton Univ, 81- **MEMBERSHIPS** MLA; Soc Am Archivists; Bibliog Soc Am; Am Antiquarian Soc. **RESEARCH** Literature of 19th century New England; Thoreau's essays on government and society; American literary and historical manuscripts. **SELECTED PUBLICATIONS** Auth, The Letters of Emerson, Ralph, Waldo, Vol 8, 1845-1859, 19th Century Prose, Vol 0020, 93; The Letters of Emerson, Ralph ,Waldo, Vol 7, 1807-1844, 19th Century Prose, Vol 0020, 93; The Nations Great Library in Putnam,Herbert and the Library of Congress, 1899-1939, Public Historian, Vol 0017, 95. **CONTACT ADDRESS** Manuscript Div Libr of Cong, Washington, DC, 20540.

BROGAN, JACQUELINE V.
DISCIPLINE 20TH-CENTURY AMERICAN, LANGUAGE THEORY **EDUCATION** Univ Texas, PhD. **CAREER** Instr, Univ Notre Dame. **HONORS AND AWARDS** NEH fel. **RESEARCH** The writing of poetry; the relations between poetry, politics, and ethics. **SELECTED PUBLICATIONS** Auth, Stevens and Simile: A Theory of Language; Part of the Climate: A Critical Anthology of American Cubist Poetry. **CONTACT ADDRESS** Univ Notre Dame, Notre Dame, IN, 46556.

BROKAW, JOHN W.
PERSONAL Born 09/17/1936, Phoenix, AZ, m, 1959, 2 children **DISCIPLINE** THEATRE, DRAMA **EDUCATION** Ariz State Univ, BA, 59; Univ Ariz, MA, 64; Ind Univ, PhD(theatre), 70. **CAREER** Teacher speech-drama, Phoenix High Schs, Ariz, 59-65; co-mgr, Ind Theatre Co, 66-68; from instr to asst prof, 68-74, from assoc prof Drama, Univ Tex, Austin, 74-88; consult, Oceana Publ Inc, 70-; Nat Endowment for Humanities fel, 73. **MEMBERSHIPS** Soc Theatre Res; Am Soc for Theatre Res. **RESEARCH** Anglo-American, Mexican and Chicano theatre, particularly in the 19th century. **SELECTED PUBLICATIONS** Ed, Thespis adorned, Tobin Found, 71; auth, A nineteenth century Mexican acting company--teatro de Iturbide: 1856-7, Latin Am Theatre Rev, 72; Wilson Barrett's papers: A theatrical legacy, Libr Chronicle, 74; Centro libre experimental de teatro y artistica, Educ Theatre J, 74; An inventory of gas lighting equipment in the Theatre Royal, Hull, 1877, Theatre Surv, 74; The repertory of a Mexican-American theatrical troupe: 1849-1924, Latin Am Theatre Rev, 74; A Mexican-American acting company: 1849-1924, 75 & Teatro Chicano: Some reflections, 77, Educ Theatre J; The London Stage, 1800-10, et, 88. **CONTACT ADDRESS** Dept of Drama, Univ of Texas, Austin, TX, 78712-1026. **EMAIL** gael@mail.utexas.edu

BROMMEL, BERNARD
PERSONAL Born 08/13/1930, Des Moines, IA, m, 1950, 6 children **DISCIPLINE** SPEECH, HISTORY **EDUCATION** IA Northern Univ, BA, 51; State Univ IA, MA, 55; IN Univ, PhD, 63; post doc, Family Inst, Northwestern univ, 83. **CAREER** Tchr, High Sch, IA, 51-54; Keokuk Sr High & Community Col, 54-59; assoc prof speech, IN State Univ, 59-67; prof & chmn dept, Univ ND, 67-71; prof speech, Northeastern IL Univ, 71-97, Mem bd dir, Eugene V Debs Found, 68-98; scholar in residence, Newberry Libr, 71-83; bd dir, Lakeview Mental Health Ctr & IL Labor Hist Soc, 71-91; priv psychotherapist, 80-98. **HONORS AND AWARDS** Best Biog Award, Soc Midland Authors, 79. **MEMBERSHIPS** Speech Commun Asn; Cent States Speech Commun Asn; Int Commun Asn; Soc Midland Authors (pres, 82-83). **RESEARCH** Hist; speech; commun; family commun. **SELECTED PUBLICATIONS** Auth, Pacifist Speechmaking of Eugene V Debs, Quart J Speech, 4/66; Debs' Cooperative Commonwealth Movement, Labor Hist, fall 71; coauth, Vocalic Communication in Persuasion, Quart J Speech, 10/72; Eugene V Debs: Spokesman for Labor & Socialism, 78; (with K Galvin), Family Communication: Cohesion and change, 5th ed, 99. **CONTACT ADDRESS** Dept of Speech, Northeastern Illinois Univ, 5500 N St Louis Ave, Chicago, IL, 60625-4625. **EMAIL** brnbrommel@aol.com

BROMWICH, DAVID
DISCIPLINE ENGLISH **EDUCATION** BA, 73, PhD, 77, Yale Univ. **CAREER** Instr, 77-78, Asst Prof, 78-83, Assoc Prof, 83-87, Mellon Prof, 87-88, Princeton Univ; Prof, 88-, Housum Prof, 95-, Yale Univ. **CONTACT ADDRESS** Dept of English, Yale Univ, New Haven, CT, 06520-8302.

BROOKS, A. RUSSELL
PERSONAL Born 05/19/1906, Montgomery, AL **DISCIPLINE** ENGLISH LITERATURE **EDUCATION** Morehouse Col, AB, 31; Univ Wis, AM, 34, PhD, 58. **CAREER** Instr English, Univ High Sch, Univ Atlanta, 32-33; prof & chmn, Agr & Tech Col NC, 34-44; prof, Morehouse Col, 46-60; PROF & HEAD DEPT, KY STATE COL, 60-72; RETIRED. **MEMBERSHIPS** MLA; NCTE; Col Lang Asn. **RESEARCH** James Boswell; Afro-American literature. **SELECTED PUBLICATIONS** Auth, A Tribute to Daniel,Maggie,Crowne, Cla J-Coll Lang Asn, Vol 0037, 94. **CONTACT ADDRESS** Kentucky State Univ, 415 College Park Dr, Frankfort, KY, 40601.

BROOKS, DWIGHT E.
PERSONAL Born 05/05/1955, Philadelphia, PA, m, 1991, 1 child **DISCIPLINE** COMMUNICATION STUDIES, MEDIA & CULTURAL STUDIES **EDUCATION** East Stoudsburg Univ, BA, 77; Ohio State Univ, MA, 79; Univ of Iowa, PhD, 91. **CAREER** Professional radio, commercial and non-commercial. **MEMBERSHIPS** Nat Commun Asn; Broadcast Ed Asn; Asn for Ed in Journalism & Mass Commun. **RESEARCH** Cultural studies; race, gender, & media; media programming; advertising & consumer culture. **SELECTED PUBLICATIONS** Auth, Magazine Advertising and Minorities, Hist of the Mass Media in the United States: An Encycl, Garland Pub, in press; auth, Black Magazines and National Advertising: An Historical Perspective, Hist of the Mass Media in the United States: An Encycl, Garland Pub, in press; auth, Space Traders, Media Criticism, and the Interpositional Communicative Strategy, Redings in Cultural Contexts, Mayfield Pub Co, 98; auth, Basic Cable Netowrk Programming, Broadcast/Cable Programming: Strategies and Practices, Wadsworth Pub, 96; auth, In Their Own Words: Advertisers' Construction of an African American Consumer Market, the World War II Era, The Howard J of Commun, 95; auth, Ebony and Our Consumer Culture, Afrian Am Forum, 95; coauth, Black Men in the Margins: Space Traders and the Interpositional Strategy Against B¤llacklash, Commun Studies, 96; couath, Research and Organizing Messages, Intro to Speech Commun, Waveland Press, 94. **CONTACT ADDRESS** Dept of Telecommunications, Henry W. Grady Col of Journalism & Mass Commun, Athens, GA, 30602-3018. **EMAIL** debrooks@arches.uga.edu

BROUGHTON, PANTHEA REID
PERSONAL Born 09/11/1940, Birmington, AL, m, 1976, 2 children **DISCIPLINE** AMERICAN LITERATURE, NOVEL **EDUCATION** Univ Ala, BA, 62, MA, 63, Univ NC, PhD(English), 71. **CAREER** Instr English, Univ Ala, 64-65, Montreat-Anderson Col, 65-66; from instr to asst prof, Va Polytech inst & State Univ, 67-74; vis asst prof, 74-75; assoc prof, 75-80, PROF ENGLISH, LA STATE UNIV, 80-, Sr Fulbright lectr, Portugal, 76; exec bd, Soc Study Southern Lit. **MEMBERSHIPS** MLA; Soc Study Southern Lit; Am Soc 18th Century Studies; South Cent Mod Lang Asn; Women's Caucus Mod Lang. **RESEARCH** Twentieth century novel; Faulkner; visual arts. **SELECTED PUBLICATIONS** Auth, The Flight of the Mind in Woolf,Virgina Art and Manic Depressive Illness, Engl Lit in Transition 1880-1920, Vol 0036, 93. **CONTACT ADDRESS** Dept of English, Louisiana State Univ, Baton Rouge, LA, 70803.

BROWN, ALANNA KATHLEEN
PERSONAL Born 03/07/1944, Austin, TX **DISCIPLINE** ENGLISH LITERATURE **EDUCATION** Univ Calif, Santa Barbara, BA, 66, MA, 68, PhD(English), 74. **CAREER** Asst prof, 73-78, assoc prof English & asst dean Lett & Sci, Mont State Univ, 78-83, Nat Endowment Humanities fel in residence, 75-76; Danforth Assoc, 75; act dir, Univ Honor's Prog, 82-85; from assoc prof to prof English, 78-95, 95-. **HONORS AND AWARDS** NEH Summer Stipend to work on Mourning Dove's Okanogan Sweat Hourse, 94; Outstanding Teacher, Col of Letters & Sci, 96. **MEMBERSHIPS** MLA; Western Literature Assoc. **RESEARCH** Victorian literature; Native American Literature & Victorian Literature. **SELECTED PUBLICATIONS** Auth, Rape, battering and abuse: Discussion in a safe classroom context, Plainswoman, 4/82; Mourning Dove Humishuma, Dictionary of Leterary Biography: Native American Writers of the United States, Vol 175, ed, Kenneth M Roemer, Detroit, Washington, DC, London: Bruccoli Clark Layman, 97. **CONTACT ADDRESS** Dept of English, Montana State Univ, Bozeman, MT, 59717-0001. **EMAIL** brown@english.montana.edu

BROWN, ARTHUR A.
PERSONAL Born 03/18/1955, New York, NY, m, 1985, 2 children **DISCIPLINE** ENGLISH **EDUCATION** Univ Calif, Berkeley, BA, 76; Univ N Mex, MA, 88; Univ Calif, Davis, PhD, 94. **CAREER** Asst prof, Univ Evansville, 95-. **HONORS AND AWARDS** Regents Fel, 92-93, Univ Calif, Davis. **MEMBERSHIPS** MLA **RESEARCH** American literature; narrative theory. **SELECTED PUBLICATIONS** Auth, art, Death and Telling in Poe's The Imp of the Rerverse, 94; auth, art, Benjy, the Reader, and Death: At the Fence in the Sound and the Fury, 95; auth, art, Literature and the Impossiblity of Death: Poe's Berenice, 96; auth, art, Henry James and Immortality: The Beast in the Jungle and Is There a Life After Death, 98; auth, art, Ghosts and the Nature of Death in Literature: Henry James Sir Edmund Orme, 98. **CONTACT ADDRESS** Dept of English, Univ of Evansville, 1800 Lincoln Ave, Evansville, IN, 47722. **EMAIL** ab48@evansville.edu

BROWN, CAROLE ANN
PERSONAL Born 05/26/1936, New York, NY, m, 1956, 2 children **DISCIPLINE** ENGLISH **EDUCATION** Univ Minn, BA, 56, MA, 61, PhD(English), 65. **CAREER** Teaching asst English, Univ Minn, 57-60, from instr to asst prof, 61-74, assoc prof, 74-80, PROF, HAMLINE UNIV, 80- **MEMBERSHIPS** MLA; NCTE; Conf Col Compos & Commun. **RESEARCH** Eighteenth century English literature; English Renaissance literature; modern novel. **SELECTED PUBLICATIONS** Auth, The art of the novel: Virginia Woolf's the Voyage Out, Virginia Woolf Quart, 77. **CONTACT ADDRESS** Dept of English, Hamline Univ, St Paul, MN, 55101.

BROWN, DAN
DISCIPLINE COMMUNICATION STUDIES **EDUCATION** Univ Mass, PhD, 82. **CAREER** Assoc prof, 84-. **SELECTED PUBLICATIONS** Auth, pubs on learning from media; effects of television on family values; entertainment features in children's educational television; content and uses of pornography; humor in mass media and college teaching; public communication about the causes of disease. **CONTACT ADDRESS** Dept of Communication, East Tennesee State Univ, PO Box 70717, Johnson City, TN, 37614-0717. **EMAIL** saucemaf@etsu.edu

BROWN, GEORGE HARDIN
DISCIPLINE ENGLISH **EDUCATION** BA, 55; PhL, 56; Univ St Louis Univ, MA, 59; Univ Innsbruck, BD, 63; Harvard Univ, PhD, 71. **CAREER** Prof, Stanford Univ. **RESEARCH** Old and Middle Eng philology; post-classical Latin, espec Anglo-Latin; Latin and Medieval vernacular paleography. **SELECTED PUBLICATIONS** Auth, Bede the Venerable, 87; The Dynamics of Literacy in Anglo-Saxon England in The 94 Toller Lecture, John Rylands Lib; Bede the Educator, Jarrow Lecture, 96. **CONTACT ADDRESS** Stanford Univ, Bldg 20, Main Quad, Stanford, CA, 94305.

BROWN, HARRY MATTHEW
PERSONAL Born 01/24/1921, Newark, OH, m, 1951, 4 children **DISCIPLINE** ENGLISH **EDUCATION** Malone Col, ThB, 45; Baldwin-Wallace Col, AB, 46; Western Reserve Univ, MA, 48, PhD(English), 55. **CAREER** Instr English, Baldwin-Wallace Col, 46-50; teaching fel, Western Reserve Univ, 50-53; asst prof, Shepherd Col, 53-56; from asst prof to assoc prof English, 56-63; intermediate instr, Calif State Polytech Col, 63-66;

dean humanities & soc sci, 68-78, prof English, Midwestern State Univ, 66-. **HONORS AND AWARDS** Minnie Stevens Piper Prof, 81. **MEMBERSHIPS** MLA; NCTE; Am Bus Commun Asn; Conf Col Teachers English. **RESEARCH** American literature; poetry; literature and religion. **SELECTED PUBLICATIONS** Coauth, Readings for College Writers, 2nd ed, Ronald, 67; Patterns in Poetry, Scott-Foresman, 68; A Workbook for Writers, 4th ed, Van Nostrand, 70; auth, Thought-Patterns for Composition, Prentice-Hall, 76; The Contemporary College Writer, 2nd, Van Nostrand, 77; coauth, Practical English Workbook, Van Nostrand, 78; auth, How to Write, Holt, 78; Business Report Writing, Van Nostrand, 80. **CONTACT ADDRESS** Dept of English, Midwestern State Univ, 3410 Taft Blvd, Wichita Falls, TX, 76308-2096.

BROWN, JAMES DALE
PERSONAL Born 04/28/1948, Spokane, WA **DISCIPLINE** AMERICAN LITERATURE, AUTOBIOGRAPHY **EDUCATION** Univ Wash, BA, 70, MA, 71; Univ Ore, PhD(English), 79. **CAREER** Instr English, Univ Ore, 79-80; RES & WRITING, 81-, Fiction ed, Northwest Rev, 78; chief ed, Northwest Rev Bks, 81. **MEMBERSHIPS** Am Studies Asn; Assoc Writing Prog; MLA; Philol Asn Pac Coast. **RESEARCH** American autobiography; American writers in Europe; Science fiction and fantasy. **SELECTED PUBLICATIONS** Auth, Henry Miller: From the Everglades to China, Northwest Rev, 78; coauth, Dict of Literary Biography: Americans in Paris, 1920-1939, Gale, 79; auth, Jay Martin's biogrpahy, Mod Fiction Studies, 79-80; coauth, Dict of Literary Biography Yearbook: 1980, 81, Dict of Literary Biography Yearbook: 1981, 82 & Documentary Encyl of Literature, 82, Gale; ed, The Anthology of Eugene Writers, Northwest Rev Bks, 82. **CONTACT ADDRESS** Box 2921, Eugene, OR, 97402.

BROWN, JARED
PERSONAL Born 12/03/1936, New York, NY, m, 1958, 2 children **DISCIPLINE** THEATER **EDUCATION** Ithaca Col, BA, 60; San Francisco St Col, MA, 62; Univ Minn, PhD, 67. **CAREER** Assoc prof, 65-78, prof, 79-89, acad dir, 79-80, Western Ill Univ; prof, dir, schl theatre arts, 89-, Ill Wesleyan Univ. **RESEARCH** Amer theatre history; dramatic theory. **CONTACT ADDRESS** Sch of Theatre Arts, Illinois Wesleyan Univ, PO Box 2900, Bloomington, IL, 61704-2900. **EMAIL** jbrown@titan.iwu.edu

BROWN, JESSIE LEMON
PERSONAL Born 05/15/1911, Columbia, SC, m **DISCIPLINE** ENGLISH **EDUCATION** Hampton Inst, BS, 34; Columbia Univ, MA, 45, EdD(English), 55. **CAREER** Teacher high sch, Va, 35-44; from instr to prof English, 44-70, dir spec proj upgrading & remediation, 65-70, dir div lang & lit, 67-70, OLD DOMINION PROF HUMANITIES & DIR FRESHMAN COMMUN CTR, HAMPTON INST, 70-, Consult teaching English, Va Sec Schs, 58-63. **HONORS AND AWARDS** Lindback Distinguished Teaching Award, 63-64. **MEMBERSHIPS** Col English Asn; Asn Higher Educ. **SELECTED PUBLICATIONS** Contribr, Communication in General Education, W C Brown, 60; auth, Identifying academic achievement, Va Teachers Asn Bull, 12/61; The road less traveled by--a message to college students, Negro Hist Bull, 3/64. **CONTACT ADDRESS** Dept of English, Hampton Inst, Hampton, VA, 23368.

BROWN, JOHN E.
PERSONAL Born 05/28/1939, Lawrence, KS, m, 1961, 1 child **DISCIPLINE** ENGLISH HISTORY **EDUCATION** Univ Kans, BA, 61; Stanford Univ, MA, 62, PhD(hist), 66. **CAREER** Instr hist, Stanford Univ, 65-67; asst prof, 67-72, assoc prof, 72-81, prof, 81-82, VPRES ACAD AFFAIRS & DEAN FAC, LEWIS & CLARK COL, 72-, Provost, Lewis & Clark Col, 79-82; PRES ELECT, COE COL, 82-. **RESEARCH** British business and the education of a gentleman in late Victorian England. **SELECTED PUBLICATIONS** The Goddess as Excellent Cow: Selling the Education of a Gentleman as a Prescription for Success in Late Victorian England, Albion, 70; The Sacred Center + the Peace-Pipe/, Parabola-Myth Tradition and the Search for Meaning, Vol. 21, 1996. **CONTACT ADDRESS** Off of Vpres for Acad Affairs, Lewis & Clark Col, Portland, OR, 97219.

BROWN, JOYCE COMPTON
PERSONAL Born 06/08/1942, Statesville, NC, m, 1962, 2 children **DISCIPLINE** AMERICAN LITERATURE **EDUCATION** Appalachian State Univ, BS, 63, MA, 65; Univ Southern Miss, PhD(Am lit), 71. **CAREER** Teacher English & French, Queen Anne's County Schs, Md, 64-66; from instr to asst prof, 66-75, ASSOC PROF ENGLISH, GARDNER WEBB COL, 75-. **MEMBERSHIPS** MLA. **RESEARCH** American fiction of 1930's and 1920's. **CONTACT ADDRESS** Box 856, Boiling Springs, NC, 28017.

BROWN, JULIA PREWITT
PERSONAL Born 02/10/1948, St. Louis, MO, m, 1978, 4 children **DISCIPLINE** ENGLISH LITERATURE **EDUCATION** Barnard Col, BA, 70; Columbia Univ, MA, 71, PhD(English), 75. **CAREER** Asst prof, 74-90, prof English, Boston Univ, 90-. **HONORS AND AWARDS** Mellon Grant, Harvard Univ, 79. **MEMBERSHIPS** MLA; ALSC. **RESEARCH** English novel; Victorian literature; late 19th century aestheticism in England. **SELECTED PUBLICATIONS** Auth, Jane Austen's Novels: Social Change and Literary Form, Harvard Univ; Reader's Guide to 19th Century Novel, Macmillan; Cosmopolitan Criticism: Oscar Wilde's Philosophy of Art, Virginia. **CONTACT ADDRESS** 236 Bay State Rd., Boston, MA, 02215-1403.

BROWN, LADY
DISCIPLINE COMPOSITION AND RHETORIC **EDUCATION** TX Tech Univ, PhD, 89. **CAREER** Lectr, dir, writing ctr, TX Tech Univ; exec bd, Alliance for Comput and Writing; ed bd, Writing Ctr J. **HONORS AND AWARDS** NWCA Outstanding Serv Award, 94, Outstanding fac mem, Mortar Bd and Omicron Delta Kappa, TX Tech Univ, 95. **MEMBERSHIPS** Pres, Nat Writing Ctr Asn.. **RESEARCH** Writing center theory and practice; computer-based writing instruction. **SELECTED PUBLICATIONS** Contrib biblir to the CCCC Bibliography of Composition and Rhetoric. **CONTACT ADDRESS** Texas Tech Univ, Lubbock, TX, 79409-5015. **EMAIL** L.Brown@ttu.edu

BROWN, LINDA BEATRICE
PERSONAL Born 03/14/1939, Akron, OH, m, 1985, 2 children **DISCIPLINE** ENGLISH LITERATURE, AFRICAN-AMERICAN LITERATURE, CREATIVE WRITING **EDUCATION** Bennett Col, BA, 61; Case Western Reserve, MA, 62; Union Inst, PhD, 80. **CAREER** Instr, Kent State Univ, 62-66; instr, Univ NC, Greensboro, 70-86; assoc prof, Guilford Col, 86-92; distinguished prof of Humanities, Bennett Col, 92-. **HONORS AND AWARDS** NC Coalition of the Arts Award for Best Novel by Minority Writers, 80; grant for summer in residence at Headlands, CA from NC Arts Coun, 94. **MEMBERSHIPS** NC Writers Network, bd member; HELUS. **RESEARCH** African-American history. **SELECTED PUBLICATIONS** Auth, Rainbow 'Roun Mah Shoulder, novel; Crossing Over Jordan, novel. **CONTACT ADDRESS** Bennett Col, 900 E Washington St, Greensboro, NC, 27401. **EMAIL** lbeatrice@aol.com

BROWN, LORRAINE ANNE
PERSONAL Born 04/03/1929, Grand Rapids, MI, m, 1951, 1 child **DISCIPLINE** ENGLISH, AMERICAN LITERATURE **EDUCATION** Univ Mich, BA, 52, MA, 61; Univ Md, PhD(Am lit), 68. **CAREER** Asst prof, 67-73, assoc prof, 74-80, PROF ENGLISH, GEORGE MASON UNIV, 80-; assoc dir, Fed Theatre Res Ctr, 76-78. **HONORS AND AWARDS** George Mason Univ res grant, 75; Nat Endowment for Humanities res grant, 76-78. **MEMBERSHIPS** MLA; SAtlantic Mod Lang Asn; Am Studies Asn; Am Theatre Asn; Women's Caucus Mod Lang Asn. **RESEARCH** Henrik Ibsen; Adrienne Kennedy; contemporary drama, American, English and continental. **SELECTED PUBLICATIONS** Auth, The characters are myself, Negro Educ Forum, fall 75; Swanhild and the Mermaid, Scand Studies, summer 75; coauth, FTP Scrapbook, New Repub Bks, 11/78; auth, Black Drama: Federal Theatre, Franklin (in press). **CONTACT ADDRESS** Dept of English, George Mason Univ, 4400 University Dr, Fairfax, VA, 22030-4444.

BROWN, MARION MARSH
PERSONAL Born 07/22/1908, Brownville, NE, m, 1937, 1 child **DISCIPLINE** ENGLISH **EDUCATION** Nebr State Teachers Col, Peru, AB, 27; Univ Nebr, MA, 31. **CAREER** Teacher English, High Sch, Auburn, Nebr, 27-29; Nebr Sch Agr, Curtis, Nebr, 29-31; high sch, Wayne, Nebr, 31-32; Franklin, 32-33; instr English & jour, Nebr State Teachers Col, Peru, 33-37; instr English, Univ Nebr, Omaha, 45-51, from asst prof to prof, 52-68; RETIRED. **HONORS AND AWARDS** Distinguished Serv Award, Nebr State Teachers Col, 79. **MEMBERSHIPS** Am Asn Univ Women; Nat League Am Pen Women. **RESEARCH** Semantics and linguistics; great Americans who make inspirational biographies for young people. **SELECTED PUBLICATIONS** Coauth, The Silent Storm, Abingdon, 63; auth, Stuart's Landing, Westminster, 68; coauth, Willa Cather: the Woman and her works, Scribner, 69; Marnie, Westminster, 71; auth, The Pauper Prince, Crescent, 73; The Brownville Story, Nebr State Hist Soc, 74; Only One Point of the Compass, Archer, 80; Homeward the Arrow's Flight, Abingdon, 80; Letters Home + Remarks on Reading of Personal Correspondence of Authors Deceased Father/, Harvard Libr Bull, Vol 4, 1993. **CONTACT ADDRESS** 2615 N 52nd St, Omaha, NE, 68104.

BROWN, PEARL LEBLANC
PERSONAL Born 06/28/1936, Youngsville, LA, m, 1960, 1 child **DISCIPLINE** ENGLISH **EDUCATION** Univ Southwestern La, BA, 57; Univ Ark, MA, 58, PhD(English), 65. **CAREER** Instr English, Univ Southwestern La, 58-60; asst prof, St Mary's Col, Minn, 63-66; asst prof, 66-72, ASSOC PROF ENGLISH, QUINNIPIAC COL, 72-. **RESEARCH** Romantic poetry, especially Keats. **CONTACT ADDRESS** Dept of English, Quinnipiac Col, 275 Mt Carmel Ave, Hamden, CT, 06518-1908.

BROWN, ROBERT D.
PERSONAL Born 07/01/1924, Whiting, IN **DISCIPLINE** ENGLISH **EDUCATION** Ind Univ, AB, 49, MA, 50, PhD(comp lit), 52. **CAREER** From instr to assoc prof English, Ore State Univ, 52-65; prof & chmn dept, 65-67, assoc acad dean, 67-68, acad dean, 68-70, PROF ENGLISH, WESTERN WASH STATE COL, 71-, Curric guide writer, Portland Curric Study, 60-61; lectr, sch visitor & grader, Advan Placement Coun 60-63. **MEMBERSHIPS** MLA; Am Comp Lit Asn; Mystery Writers Am. **RESEARCH** Anglo-French literary relations of the 19th century; modern poetry; fiction writing. **SELECTED PUBLICATIONS** Coauth, Exposition and Persuasion, Appleton, 55; The Bodley Head Press, Papers Bibliog Soc Am, 1st quarter 67; Writing Better Themes, Scott, 71; Go With the Flow, Ellery Queen's Mystery Mag, 79; Prime Suspect, Tower, 81. **CONTACT ADDRESS** Western Washington Univ, Bellingham, WA, 98225.

BROWN, ROBERT E.
PERSONAL Born 01/11/1945, New York, NY, d, 1 child **DISCIPLINE** ENGLISH; COMMUNICATIONS **EDUCATION** Univ Rochester, PhD, 66. **CAREER** Assoc prof, Salem State Col. **MEMBERSHIPS** Nat Commun Asn. **RESEARCH** Public Relations. **SELECTED PUBLICATIONS** Auth, Investor Relations Trends, Soc Sci Monitor, 1:2, 90; Senior Corporate Officer Perceptions About Communication, NY State Speech Jour, VII 1, 93; Congruence of Orientations Toward Public Relations: A Cross-Cultural Comparison of British and American Practicioners, World Commun Asn Jour, 22, 93; Communication Strategies of College Students: Winning a Public Relations Award, The Strategist, 97/98. **CONTACT ADDRESS** Dept of English, Salem State Col, 352 Lafayette Ave, Salem, MA, 01970. **EMAIL** D28man@aol.com

BROWN, RUSSELL MORTON
PERSONAL Born 12/02/1942, Elizabeth City, NC, m, 1964, 1 child **DISCIPLINE** ENGLISH **EDUCATION** Univ St Thomas, Houston, BA, 65; State Univ NY Binghamton, MA, 68, PhD(English), 72. **CAREER** Instr English, State Univ NY, Binghamton, 68-69; asst prof, Lakehead Univ, 69-77; ASSOC PROF ENGLISH, SCARBOROUGH COL, UNIV TORONTO, 77-, Ed, Lakehead Univ Rev, 72-75; co-ed, Descant, 78-. **MEMBERSHIPS** MLA. **RESEARCH** Canadian literature; Renaissance literature; literary criticism. **SELECTED PUBLICATIONS** Coauth, Magnus Eisengrim: The shadow of the trickster in the novels of Robertson Davies, Mod Fiction Studies, 76; auth, In search of lost causes: The Canadian novelist as mystery writer, Mosiac, 78; Critic, culture, text: Beyond thematics, Essays on Can Writing, 78; coauth, In place of Job: The emergence of the trickster figure in Canadian literature, J Commonwealth Lit, 79; auth, Atwood's sacred wells, Essays Can Writing, 80; Robert Kroetsch, Profiles Can Lit Ser, Dundern Press, 80; co-ed, An anthology of Canadian literature in English, Oxford Univ Press, 82. **CONTACT ADDRESS** Div of Humanities, Scarborough Col Univ of Toronto, West Hill, ON, MIC 1A4.

BROWN, RUTH CHRISTIANI
PERSONAL Born 11/18/1917, Sidney, MT, m, 1938, 3 children **DISCIPLINE** ENGLISH LITERATURE **EDUCATION** Univ Mont, Ba, 39; Univ Tex, El Paso, MA, 62; Ariz State Univ, PhD(English), 71. **CAREER** Lectr English, Ariz State Univ, 62-65; asst prof, 66-80, ASSOC PROF ENGLISH, CALIF STATE UNIV, SAN DIEGO, 80-. **MEMBERSHIPS** AAUP; MLA; NCTE. **RESEARCH** Nineteenth century British novel; modern British novel. **SELECTED PUBLICATIONS** Auth, The role of Densher in The Wings of the Dove, Mod Spraak, 71; A precursory vision, Poland, 12/72; Nostromo: Women opposing the world, the flesh, and the devil, In: Proc Int Contrad Conf, H Mursia, Milan, 74. **CONTACT ADDRESS** Dept of English, San Diego State Univ, San Diego, CA, 92115.

BROWN, STEPHEN JEFFRY
PERSONAL Born 03/30/1929, Moline, IL, m, 1969 **DISCIPLINE** ENGLISH LITERATURE **EDUCATION** Yale Univ, BA, 50, PhD(English), 59 Cambridge Univ, BA, 52. **CAREER** Instr English, Yale Univ, 57-60; asst prof, Swarthmore Col, 60-64; assoc prof, George Washington Univ, 64-68; assoc dean, 68-70, PROF ENGLISH, GEORGE MASON UNIV, 68-. **MEMBERSHIPS** MLA; Shakespeare Asn Am. **RESEARCH** English Renaissance drama and poetry; history, sociology and literature. **CONTACT ADDRESS** Dept of English, George Mason Univ, 4400 University Dr, Fairfax, VA, 22030.

BROWN, TERRY
DISCIPLINE ENGLISH LITERATURE **EDUCATION** VA Tech Univ, MA; Univ FL, PhD. **CAREER** Prof, Univ of WI. **SELECTED PUBLICATIONS** Auth, pubs on women's studies, Virginia Woolf, Kathy Acker; sexuality; classroom pedag. **CONTACT ADDRESS** Eng Dept, Univ Wisconsin, S 3rd St, PO Box 410, River Falls, WI, 54022-5001.

BROWN, THERESSA WILSON
PERSONAL Born 01/29/1904, Sewickley, PA, m, 1939 **DISCIPLINE** ENGLISH **EDUCATION** Oberlin Col, AB, 24; Univ Pittsburgh, AM, 29, PhD, 43. **CAREER** From instr to assoc prof English, Va State Col, 25-34; from instr to prof, Miner Teachers Col, 34-55; prof English & chmn div, DC

Teachers Col, 55-72; RETIRED. Vis prof English, Howard Univ, 69-77 & Washington Tech Inst, Washington, DC, 73-75. **MEMBERSHIPS** NCTE; MLA; Col English Asn; Conf Col Compos & Commun; Col Lang Asn. **RESEARCH** Biography as a literary type; Victorian biography; literary criticism. **SELECTED PUBLICATIONS** Auth, Froude and Carlyle, Univ Pittsburgh; The 'Mind Crime of August Saint' - Ariasmisson,A/, Am Bk Rev, Vol 16, 1994. **CONTACT ADDRESS** 1511 Michigan Ave, NE Washington, DC, 20017.

BROWN, THOMAS HOWARD
PERSONAL Born 01/03/1941, Granite Falls, MN, m, 1961, 3 children **DISCIPLINE** ENGLISH **EDUCATION** Western State Col, Colo, BA, 62; Ohio Univ, MA, 69; Univ Ga, PhD(English), 73. **CAREER** Teacher English, Minneapolis Pub Schs, 64-68; instr, Univ Ga, 72-73; ASST PROF ENGLISH, UNIV MISS, 74-. **MEMBERSHIPS** NCTE; SCent Mod Lang Asn; Col English Asn. **RESEARCH** Colonial American literature of the South; medicine in history. **SELECTED PUBLICATIONS** Auth, The quest of Dante Gabriel Rosetti in the Blessed Damozel, Victorian Poetry, 72; Noah Webster and the medical profession, J AMA, 10/13/75; An introduction to Go Down, Moses (monogr), Miss Libr Comn, 76; Flannery O'Connor's use of eye imagery in Wise Blood, SCent Bull, 77; co-ed, Dimensions; Essays for Composition, Winthrop, 79. **CONTACT ADDRESS** Univ of Miss, Box 994, University, MS, 38677.

BROWN-GUILLORY, ELIZABETH
PERSONAL Born 06/20/1954, Lake Charles, LA, m, 1983 **DISCIPLINE** ENGLISH **EDUCATION** University of Southwestern Louisiana, BA, English, 1975, MA, English, 1977; Florida State University, PhD, English, 1980. **CAREER** University of South Carolina, Spartanburg, assistant professor of English, 1980-82; Dillard University, assistant professor of English, 1982-88; University of Houston, professor of English, 1998-. **HONORS AND AWARDS** Sigma Tau Delta, Outstanding Professor, 1991; UH Council of Ethic Organization Award; Young Black Achievers of Houston Award; Louisiana state wide competition, First Place Playwriting Award, 1985; The City of New Orleans Playwriting Award, 1983; Florida State University, Research Fellowship, 1979; numerous grants and other awards. **MEMBERSHIPS** Southern Conference on Afro-American Studies, Inc; College Language Association; South Central Modern Language Association; Modern Language Association; International Women's Writing Guild; Amer Society for Theatre Research; Conference of College Teachers of English of Texas; Black Theater Network; Association for Theatre in Higher Education. **SELECTED PUBLICATIONS** Editor: Wines in the Wilderness: Plays by African-American Women from the Harlem Renaissance to the Present, 1990; Editor: omen of Color: Mother-Daughter Relationships in 20th Century Literature, 1996; Author: Their Place on the Stage: Black Women Playwrights in America, 1988; playwright: Mam Phyllis, Snapshots of Broken Dolls, 1987; Bayou Relics, 1983; numerous others. **CONTACT ADDRESS** Professor, English, University of Houston, 4800 Calhoun Rd, Houston, TX, 77204-3012.

BROWNE, DONALD R.
PERSONAL Born 03/13/1934, Detroit, MI, m, 1958, 3 children **DISCIPLINE** MASS COMMUNICATIONS **EDUCATION** Univ Mich, AB, 55, MA, 58, PhD(speech, polit sci), 61. **CAREER** Radio & TV off, US Inform Serv, 60-63; asst prof mass commun, Boston Univ, 63-65; speech, Purdue Univ, 65-66; assoc prof, 66-70, dir off int prog, 76-78, PROF RADIO & TV, UNIV MINN, MINNEAPOLIS, 70-; Off Int Prog res grant, Univ Minn, 67-68 & 70-, McMillan Fund travel grant, 70- & 72-; Fulbright-Hays vis prof, Am Univ Beirut, 73-74. **HONORS AND AWARDS** Outstanding Young Teacher Award, Cent States Speech Asn, 68. **MEMBERSHIPS** Broadcast Educ Asn; Int Commun Asn; Asn Educ in Jour; Int Inst Commun. **RESEARCH** International broadcasting; comparative broadcasting and national development. **SELECTED PUBLICATIONS** Auth, the BBC and the pirates, Jour Quart, spring 71; Citizen involvement in broadcasting, Pub Telecommun Rev, 10/73; The voices of Palestine, Middle East J, spring 75; Television and national stabilization, Jour Quart, winter 75; The voice of America, Jour Monogr, 2/76; Telecommunications, Mass-Media, and Democracy - The Battle for the Control of United-States Broadcasting, 1928-1935 - McChesney,RW/, Hist J Film Radio and Television, Vol 14, 1994; Sartre and the Media - Scriven,M/, Hist J of Film Radio and Television, Vol 14, 1994; Radio and Television in Cuba - The Pre-Castro Era - Salwen,MB/, Hist J Film Radio and Television, Vol 15, 1995; Signals in the Air - Native Broadcasting in America - Keith,MC/, Hist J Film Radio and Television, Vol 16, 1996; Vatican-Radio - Propagation by the Airwaves - Matelski,MJ/, Hist J Film Radio and Television, Vol 16, 1996; Media at War - Radios Challenge to the Newspapers, 1924-1939 - Jackaway,GL/, Hist J Film Radio and Television, Vol 16, 1996. **CONTACT ADDRESS** Dept of Speech, Univ of Minn, 9 Pleasant St S E, Minneapolis, MN, 55455-0194.

BROWNE, RAY B.
PERSONAL Born 01/15/1922, Millport, AL, m, 1952, 3 children **DISCIPLINE** ENGLISH **EDUCATION** Univ Ala, AB, 43; Columbia Univ, MA, 47; Univ Calif, Los Angeles, PhD, 56. **CAREER** Instr English, Univ Nebr, 47-50, Univ Md, 56-60; assoc prof, Purdue Univ, 60-67; PROF POPULAR CULT & ENGLISH, BOWLING GREEN STATE UNIV, 67-, CHMN DEPT, 80-, Exec secy, Popular Cult Hall of Fame; ed, J Popular Cult. **MEMBERSHIPS** MLA; Popular Cult Asn (secy-treas); Am Studies Asn; Am Folklore Soc. **SELECTED PUBLICATIONS** Auth, A Brand New Language - Commercial Influences in Literature and Culture - Friedman,M/, J Popular Cult, Vol 26, 1992; Propaganda - A Pluralistic Perspective - Smith,TJ/, J Popular Cult, Vol 26, 1992; Jung,C.G. and the Humanities - Toward a Hermeneutics of Culture - Barnaby,K, Dacierno,P/, J Popular Cult, Vol 26, 1992; Hideous Progenies, Dramatizations of 'Frankenstein' from the 19th-Century to the Present/, J Popular Cult, Vol 26, 1992; An Aesthetics of Junk Fiction - Roberts,TJ/, J Popular Cult, Vol 26, 1992; The Cognitive Revolution in Western Culture - Lepan,D/, J Popular Cult, Vol 26, 1992; The Work of Lamour,Louis - An Annotated-Bibliography and Guide - Hall,HW/, J Popular Cult, Vol 26, 1993; For Enquiring Minds - A Cultural-Study of Supermarket Tabloids - Bird,ES/, J Popular Cult, Vol 26, 1993; Western Rivermen, 1763-1861 - Ohio and Mississippi Boatmen and the Myth of the Alligator-Horse - Allen,M/, J Am Cult, Vol 16, 1993; America and the Daguerrotype - Wood,J/, J Am Cult, Vol 16, 1993; Mystic Chords of Memory - The Transformation of Tradition in American Culture - Kammen,M/, J American Cult, Vol 16, 1993; The Kentucky Encyclopedia - Kleber,JE/, J Am Cult, Vol 17, 1994; American Home Life, 1880-1930 - A Social-History of Spaces of Services - Foy,J, Schlereth,TJ/, J Am Cult, Vol 17, 1994; The Tragedy of Abundance - Myth Restoration in American Culture - Steffen,JO/, J Am Cult, Vol 17, 1994; Russian Eyes on American Literature - Chakovsky,S, Inge,MT/, J Am Cult, Vol 17, 1994; The Cultural-Geography of the United-States - Zelinsky,W/, J Am Cult, Vol 17, 1994; Acting Naturally - Twain,Mark in the Culture of Performance - Knoper,R/, J Am Cult, Vol 19, 1996; Roadside New-Jersey - Genovese,P/, J Am Cult, Vol 19, 1996; author of numerous other articles. **CONTACT ADDRESS** Dept of Popular Cult, Bowling Green State Univ, Bowling Green, OH, 43402.

BROWNE, WILLIAM FRANCIS
PERSONAL Born 12/26/1935, Pittsburgh, PA, m, 1961, 4 children **DISCIPLINE** VICTORIAN LITERATURE **EDUCATION** Long Island Univ, BA, 69, MA, 71; City Univ New York, PhD, 79. **CAREER** Adj lectr Am lit & compos, 71-73, instr, Eng & Am lit & compos, 73-79, asst prof eng & Am lit & compos,assoc prof, 82-96, prof, 96-, Brooklyn Col, 79. **MEMBERSHIPS** MLA. **RESEARCH** Victorian studies (Hardy, Gissing and Browning); Am studies (Melville, Twain, Wright and Browning). **SELECTED PUBLICATIONS** Auth, Gissing's Boinin Exile: spiritual distance between author and character, 4/79 & Gissing: The reluctant prophet, 4/80, Gissing Newslett; Two Kinds of Courage: Frederick Douglas and John Brown. **CONTACT ADDRESS** Dept Eng & Am Lit, Brooklyn Col, CUNY, 2901 Bedford Ave, Brooklyn, NY, 11210-2813. **EMAIL** wbrowne@catskill.net

BROWNING, JUDITH
DISCIPLINE RENAISSANCE LITERATURE, DRAMA, 19TH-20TH CENTURY WOMEN'S LITERATURE, COMPOS **EDUCATION** Northern AZ Univ, BS; Rutgers Univ, MA; Grad Theol Un, PhD. **CAREER** Assoc prof, assoc dean, Sch of Liberal Stud & Pub Aff, ed, Golden Gate Univ Fac News, Golden Gate Univ. **HONORS AND AWARDS** Outstanding Tchg Award, Golden Gate Univ, 96. **MEMBERSHIPS** MLA. **SELECTED PUBLICATIONS** Auth of articles on Milton, Renaissance lit, and tchg of lit. **CONTACT ADDRESS** Golden Gate Univ, San Francisco, CA, 94105-2968.

BROWNLEY, MARTINE WATSON
PERSONAL Born 07/27/1947, Spartanburg, SC **DISCIPLINE** ENGLISH LITERATURE **EDUCATION** Agnes Scott Col, BA, 69; Harvard Univ, AM, 71, PhD(English), 75. **CAREER** ASST PROF ENGLISH, EMORY UNIV, 75-, Fel Clarendon's hist, Am Asn Univ Women, 78-79. **HONORS AND AWARDS** Recognition Award, Am Asn Univ Women, 78. **MEMBERSHIPS** MLA; Am Soc 18th Century Studies; Southeastern Am Soc 18th Century Studies. **RESEARCH** 17th & 18th century British literary historiographers. **SELECTED PUBLICATIONS** Auth, Gibbon: The formation of mind and character, Daedalus, summer 76; Appearance and realty in Gibbon's history, J Hist Ideas, Oct-Dec 77; The narrator in Oroonoko, Essays Lit, fall 77; Defoe Politics, Parliament, Power, Kingship and 'Robinson Crusoe' - Schonhorn,M/, Studies in the Novel, Vol 25, 1993; The Reinvention of the World - English Writing, 1650-1750 - Chambers,D/, Albion, Vol 29, 1997; **CONTACT ADDRESS** Dept of English, Emory Univ, 1364 Clifton Rd N E, Atlanta, GA, 30322-0001.

BRUCCOLI, MATTHEW J.
PERSONAL Born 08/21/1931, New York, NY, m, 1957, 4 children **DISCIPLINE** ENGLISH **EDUCATION** Yale Univ, AB, 53; Univ Va, MA, 56, PhD, 61. **CAREER** Instr, 58-59, Sch Eng, Univ Va; asst instr, 60-61, from asst prof to prof, 61-69, Ohio St Univ; prof, 69-76, Jefferies Prof Eng, 76-, Univ SC; cir, Ctr Eds Am Auths, 69-76; gen ed, Pittsburgh Ser in Bibliog, Univ Pittsburgh, 67; series ed, Lost American Fiction, Southern Ill Univ Press, 72. **MEMBERSHIPS** Bibliog Soc Am; Bibliog Soc Univ Va Res. **RESEARCH** Fitzgerald; bibliography. **SELECTED PUBLICATIONS** Auth, F Scott Fitzgerald: A Life in Letters, Scribners, 94; auth, Fitzgerald and Hemingway: A Dangerous Friendship, Carroll & Graf, 94; coauth, Reader's Companion to F Scott Fitzgerald's Tender Is The Night, Columbia Univ, SC Press, 96; ed, Tender Is The Night, London Everyman, 96; ed, The Only Thing That Counts: The Ernest Hemingway-Maxwell Perkins Correspondence, Scribners, 96; co-ed, F Scott Fitzgerald on Authorship, Univ SC Press, 96; ed, Fie! Fie! Fi-Fi!, Columbia Univ SC Press, 96; auth, F Scott Fitzgerald Centenary Exhibition: The Matthew J and Arlyn Bruccoli Collection, The Thomas Cooper Library, Columbia Univ SC Press, 96; co-ed, American Expatriate Writers: Paris in the Twenties, Bruccoli Clark Layman/Gale, 97; ed, By Love Possessed, Carroll & Graff, 98; ed, The Bad and the Beautiful, Carbondale, S Ill Univ Press, 98; ed, The Rich Boy and Other Stories, Carbondale: S Ill Univ Press, 98; ed, Understanding Contemporary British Literature, 15 vols, Columbia Univ SC Press, 91-; ed, Facts on File Bibliography of American Fiction, 4 vols, NY Facts on File, 91-.94. **CONTACT ADDRESS** Dept of English, Univ South Carolina, Columbia, Columbia, SC, 29208. **EMAIL** Bruccolim@garnet.cla.sc.edu

BRUCE PRATT, MINNIE
DISCIPLINE ENGLISH LITERATURE **EDUCATION** Univ Ala, BA; Univ NC, PhD. **CAREER** Asst prof. **HONORS AND AWARDS** Gay and Lesbian Bk Awd, 91; Simpson Arnow Prize Poetry. **RESEARCH** Women's studies; intersections of race, class, and gender; Renaissance and seventeenth century literature. **SELECTED PUBLICATIONS** Auth, Rebellion: Essays 1980-1991, 91; Crime Against Nature, 90; Night Gives Us the Next Day, 88; Red String, 88; The Child Taken from the Mother, 88; Walking Song: Two, 88; My Mother's Question, 88. **CONTACT ADDRESS** Union Inst, 440 E McMillan St., Cincinnati, OH, 45206-1925. **EMAIL** mbpratt@aol.com

BRUDER, KURT A.
PERSONAL Born 09/15/1961, Battle Creek, MI, m, 1998, 1 child **DISCIPLINE** COMMUNICATIONS **EDUCATION** Michigan St univ, MA, 87; Univ of Texas, Austin, PhD, 94; Texas Tech Univ, MEd, 98. **CAREER** Asst prof, Texas Tech Univ, 94- . **HONORS AND AWARDS** Fulbright scholar award, 96-97. **MEMBERSHIPS** Natl Commun Assoc; Int Commun Assoc. **RESEARCH** The interdependence of communicative practice and psychological experience. **SELECTED PUBLICATIONS** Auth, Monastic Blessing: Deconstructing and Reconstructing the Self, Symbolic Interaction, 98; auth, A Pragmatic for Human-Divine Relationship: An Examination of the Monastic Blessing Sequence, in J of Pragmatics, 98. **CONTACT ADDRESS** Dept of Communications Studies, Texas Tech Univ, Box 43083, Lubbock, TX, 79409-3083. **EMAIL** qwbur@ttacs.ttu.edu

BRUFFEE, KENNETH ALLEN
PERSONAL Born 09/01/1934, Torrington, CT **DISCIPLINE** ENGLISH **EDUCATION** Wesleyan Univ, BA, 56; Northwestern Univ, MA, 57, PhD(English), 64. **CAREER** Instr English, Univ Va, 62-65, Columbia Univ, 65-66; from instr to assoc prof English, 66-75, dir, freshman writing prog, 70-74, chmn, MLA teaching writing div, 76, PROF ENGLISH, BROOKLYN COL, 76-, Fund Improv Post Sec Educ grant, 79-82. **MEMBERSHIPS** MLA; NCTE. **RESEARCH** Elegiac romance; modern fiction; collaborative learning. **SELECTED PUBLICATIONS** Auth, A Short Course in Writing, Winthrop, 2nd ed, 80; The way out: A critical survey of innovations in college teaching, Col English, 72; The Brooklyn plan: Attaining intellectual growth through peer group tutoring, 78, The structure of knowledge and the future of liberal education, 81 & The social justification of belief, 82, Lib Educ; CLTV: Collaborative learning television, Educ Commun & Technol J, 82; A Comment on Social Constructionism and Literacy Studies + Response to Sullivan,Patricia,A. Review of 'Collaborative Learning'/, Col English, Vol 58, 1996; Comment on Issue on Teaching Literature/, PMLA-Publ Mod Lang Asn Am, Vol 112, 1997. **CONTACT ADDRESS** Dept of English, Brooklyn Col, CUNY, 2901 Bedford Ave, Brooklyn, NY, 11210-2813.

BRUNER, M. LANE
PERSONAL Born 07/25/1958, Kansas City, MO, m, 1984 **DISCIPLINE** SPEECH COMMUNICATION/RHETORICAL AND CRITICAL THEORY **EDUCATION** CA State Univ, Northridge, BA, 91; Louisiana State Univ, MA, 93; Univ Washington, PhD, 97. **CAREER** Asst prof of communication, Babson Coll. **HONORS AND AWARDS** Wilma Grimes Memorial Teaching Award in Performance Studies, 94; MacFarlane Scholarship, Outstanding Humanities Graduate Student, 96. **MEMBERSHIPS** International Communication Assn; Natl Communication Assn; The Assn for the Study of Nationalities; Amer Soc for Hist of Rhetoric **RESEARCH** Rhetorical theory; collective identity construction and political memory; political theory; nationalism; critical theory. **SELECTED PUBLICATIONS** Auth, Producing Identities: Gender Problematization and Feminist Argumentation, Argumentation and Advocacy, Spring 96; Towards a Poststructural Rehetorical Critical Praxis: Foucault, Limit Work and Jenninger's Kristallnacht Address, Rhetorica, Spring 96; From Etnic of Nationalism to Strategic

Multiculturalism: Shifting Strategies of Remembrance in the Quebecois Secessionist Movement, Javnost, fall 97; Strategies of Remembrance in Pre-Unification West Germany, Quarterly Journal of Speech, 98. **CONTACT ADDRESS** History & Society Div, Babson Col, Babson Park, MA, 02157. **EMAIL** bruner@babson.edu

BRUNETTE, PETER
DISCIPLINE VISUAL ARTS **EDUCATION** Univ Wis, PhD. **CAREER** Prof. **RESEARCH** Literary theory; film theory and history; theories of visual representation. **SELECTED PUBLICATIONS** Auth, Deconstruction and the Visual Arts: Art, Media, Architecture, 94; Shoot the Piano Player, 93; Roberto Rosellini, 87; co-auth, Screen/Play: Derrida and Film Theory, 90. **CONTACT ADDRESS** Dept of Film and Media Studies, George Mason Univ, 4400 University Dr, Fairfax, VA, 22030.

BRUNING, STEPHEN D.
DISCIPLINE COMMUNICATION **EDUCATION** Ohio Univ, BSC, 87, MA, 88; Kent State Univ, PhD, 92. **CAREER** Assoc prof of commun, Ohio Univ; Tenure. **MEMBERSHIPS** NCA; AEJMC; ICA **RESEARCH** Public Relations. **SELECTED PUBLICATIONS** Coauth, Building Loyalty Through Community Relations, The Pub Rels Strategist, 3(2), 97; Community Relations and Loyalty: Toward a Relationship Theory of Public Relations, Bus Res Yearbook, 4, eds J. Biberman and A. Alkhafaji, 97; The Applicability of Interpersonal Relationship Dimensions to an Organizational Context: Toward a Theory of Relational Loyalty a Qualitative Approach, Acad of Managerial Communs Jour, 1, 97; Organizational-Public Relationships and Consumer Satisfaction: The Role of Relationships in the Satisfaction Mix, Commun Res Reports, 15(2), 98; Ten Guidelines for Effectively Managing the Organization-Public Relationship, Bus Res Yearbook, 5, eds J. Biberman and A. Alkhafaji, 98; Relationship Management in Public Relations: Dimensions of an Organization-Public Relationship, Public Relations Rev, 24, 98; The Media Audit: A Management Approach to Media Relations, Bus Res Yearbook, 5, eds J. Biberman and A. Alkhafaji, 98. **CONTACT ADDRESS** Dept of Communication, Capital Univ, 2199 E Main St, 118 Spielm, Columbus, OH, 43209-3913. **EMAIL** sbruning@capital.edu

BRUNS, GERALD L.
PERSONAL Born 04/10/1938, Minneapolis, MN, m, 1986, 4 children **DISCIPLINE** ENGLISH **EDUCATION** Marquette Univ, BA, 60, MA, 62; Univ of VA, PhD, 66. **CAREER** Asst Prof, 65-70, Ohio State Univ; Assoc Prof to Prof, 70-84, Univ of Iowa; Prof of Eng, William P. & Hazel B. White, 84-, Univ of Notre Dame. **HONORS AND AWARDS** Guggenheim Fellow; Fellow, Center for Advanced Stud, Hebrew Univ, Jerusalem; Fellow, Center for Advanced Stud in the Behavioral Sci, Stanford. **MEMBERSHIPS** MLA, APA, SPEP, Renaissance Soc Amer. **RESEARCH** Modern Drama; Henry James; Hermeneutics; Maurice Blanchot, Emmanuel Levians; 20th Century Poetics; Anglo-Irish Literature. **SELECTED PUBLICATIONS** Auth, Tragic Thoughts at the End of Philosophy: Language, Literature and Ethical Theory, Northwestern Univ Press, 99; Maurice Blanchot, The Refusal of Philosophy, Johns Hopkins Univ Press, 97; Hermeneutics Ancient and Modern, Yale Univ Press, 92; Inventions, Writing, Textuality and Understanding in Literary History, Yale Univ Press, 82; Modern Poetry and the Idea of Language, Yale Univ Press, 74. **CONTACT ADDRESS** Dept of English, Univ Notre Dame, Notre Dame, IN, 46556. **EMAIL** Gerald.L.Bruns.1@nd.edu

BRUNSDALE, MITZI MALLARIAN
PERSONAL Born 05/16/1939, Fargo, ND, m, 1961, 3 children **DISCIPLINE** ENGLISH, COMPARATIVE LITERATURE **EDUCATION** NDak State Univ, BS, 59, lMS, 61; Univ NDak, PhD(English), 76. **CAREER** Asst prof, 76-78, assoc prof English, Mayville State Col, 78-,prof, 83-, bk critic, Houston Post, Tex, 70-89; grant rev panelist, Nat Endowment for Humanities, 77-; chair, Humanities Coun, 80-, bk critic, The Armchair Detective, 96-, bk critic, Publishers Weekly, 96-. **RESEARCH** Early 20th century British literature; early 20th century European comparative literature; D H Lawrence. **SELECTED PUBLICATIONS** Auth, Lawrence and the Myth of Brynhild, Western Humanities Rev, autumn 77; The Effect of Mrs Rudolf Dircks' Translation of Schopenhauer's The Metaphysics of Love on D H Lawrence's Early Fiction, Rocky Mountain Rev Lang & Lit, spring 78; D H Lawrence and Raymond Otis: Brothers of Blood, NMex Humanities Rev, winter 78-79; The German Effect on D H Lawrence and his Works, 1885-1912, P L Verlag, Berne, 79; Alexander Solzhenitsy, In: The Encyclopedia of Short Fiction, 81, Boris Pasternak, In: The Encyclopedia of Short Fiction, 81 & D H Lawrence, In: A Critical Survey of Poetry (in prep), Salem Press; D H Lawrence's David: Drama as a Vehicle for Religious Prophecy, In: Themes in Drama V, Cambridge Univ Press, 82; Toward the Greater Day: Rilke, Lawrence, and Immortalilty, Comp Lit Sudies, 82; Sigrid Undset: Ch... of Norway, Oxford: Berg, 88; Dorothy L. Sayers: Solving the Mystery of Wickedness, Oxford: Berg, 90; James Joyce: The Short Fiction, NY: Twayne, 93; James Herriot, NY: Twayne, 96. **CONTACT ADDRESS** Mayville State Col, 330 3rd St NE, Mayville, ND, 58257-1299.

BRUNSON, MARTHA LUAN
PERSONAL Born 09/29/1931, Anna, IL, m, 1954, 4 children **DISCIPLINE** VICTORIAN & EIGHTEENTH CENTURY BRITISH LITERATURE **EDUCATION** Northwestern Univ, BSEd, 52; TX Tech Univ, MA, 58, PhD, 67. **CAREER** Tchr Eng & hist, Plainview Independent Sch Dist, TX, 53-56, Eng, Lubbock High Sch, 56-58; instr, Del Mar Col, 61-62, 64-65; from asst prof to assoc prof, 67-76, prof eng, Southwest TX State Univ, 76-, chmn dept, 72-83, assoc dean, Sch Lib Arts, 81-98, Pres, Asn Depts Eng 82. **MEMBERSHIPS** MLA; Col Eng Asn; NCTE. **RESEARCH** Thomas Hardy; Charles Dickens; Victorian women writers. **CONTACT ADDRESS** Dept of Eng, Southwest Texas State Univ, 601 Univ Dr, San Marcos, TX, 78666-4685. **EMAIL** mb14@swt.edu

BRUSTEIN, ROBERT
PERSONAL Born 04/21/1927, Brooklyn, NY **DISCIPLINE** ENGLISH **EDUCATION** Amherst Col, BA, 48; Columbia Univ, MA, 50, PhD, 57; Dr Art, Bard Col, 81. **CAREER** Instr English, Cornell Univ, 55-56; drama, Vassar Col, 56-57; lectr, Drama Sch, Columbia Univ, 57-58, from asst prof to prof English, 58-66; prof English & dean sch drama, 66-79, artistic dir, Yale Univ Repertory Theatre, 66-79; PROF ENGLISH, HARVARD UNIV, 79-, ART DIR, AM RES THEATRE, LOEB DRAMA CTR, 79-, Drama critic, New Repub, 59-; Guggenheim fel, 61-62; Ford Found grant, 64-65; mem panel, Theatre Div, Nat Endowment for Arts, 70-72; drama critic, The Observer, London, 72-73; monthly contribr, New York Times, 72-; trustee, Sarah Lawrence Col, 73- mem panel, Nat Endowment for the Humanities, 74-75 & 81. **HONORS AND AWARDS** George Jean Nathan Award, 62-63; George Polk Award in Theatre Criticism, 64; Jersey City J Award in Criticism, 65., DLitt, Lawrence Univ, 68 & Amherst Col, 72; LLD, Beloit Col, 74. **MEMBERSHIPS** MLA. **RESEARCH** Modern and classical drama; Elizabethan and Stuary drama. **SELECTED PUBLICATIONS** Auth, Madison Avenue villain, Partisan Rev, 62; Theatre of revolt, Atlantic Monthly, 64; Seasons of discontent, Simon & Schuster, 65; The Third Theatre, Knopf, 69; Revolution as Theatre: Notes on the New Radical Style, Liveright, 71; Cultural schizophrenia, New York Times Mag, 71; The Culture Watch: Essays on Theatre and Society, Knopf, 76; Can the show go on?, NY Times Mag, 77; Critical Movements, 80 & Making Scenes, 81, Ramdom House; Dumbocracy in America + Crypto-Maoist Roots of Political-Correctness/, Partisan Rev, Vol 60, 1993; The Theater of Guilt +/, New Theatre Quart, Vol 10, 1994; Cultural Politics and Coercive Philanthropy/, Partisan Rev, Vol 62, 1995; On Money + Money and the Theater/, Theater, Vol 27, 1996. **CONTACT ADDRESS** Loeb Drama Ctr, Warren House, Cambridge, MA, 02138-3800.

BRYDON, DIANA
PERSONAL Hamilton, ON, Canada **DISCIPLINE** ENGLISH **EDUCATION** Univ Toronto, BA, 72, MA, 73; Australian Nat Univ, PhD, 77. **CAREER** Asst prof, 79-87, assoc prof, 87-89, Univ BC; assoc prof, 89-92, PROF ENGLISH, UNIV GUELPH 92-. **HONORS AND AWARDS** George Drew Memorial Trust Fund Award; Distinguished Prof Tchr Award. **MEMBERSHIPS** Can Asn Commonwealth Lit & Lang Studs **SELECTED PUBLICATIONS** Ed, World Literature Written in English, 89-93; ed, Christina Stead, 87; ed, Decolonising Fictions, 93; ed, Writing on Trial: Timothy Findley's Famous Last Words, 95. **CONTACT ADDRESS** Dept of English, Univ Guelph, Guelph, ON, N1G 2W1. **EMAIL** dbrydon@uoguelph.ca

BRYSON, NORMAN
PERSONAL Born 08/04/1949, Glasgow, Scotland, m, 1988, 1 child **DISCIPLINE** LITERATURE **EDUCATION** Cambridge Univ, MA, 70, PhD, 77. **CAREER** Fel of King's Col, Cambrige Univ, 77-88; prof of visual and cultural studies, Univ of Rochester, 88-90; Prof of art hist, Harvard Univ, 90-. **HONORS AND AWARDS** Getty Res Fel, 98-99; Guggenheim Fel, 98-99. **RESEARCH** Modern art history and cultural studies. **SELECTED PUBLICATIONS** Auth, Word and Image: French Painting of the Ancien Resime, Cambridge Univ Press, 81; Tradition and Desire: From David to Delacroix, Cambridge Univ Press, 83; Vision and Painting: The Logic of the Gaze, Yale Univ Press, 84; Looking at the Overlooked: Four Essays on Still Life Painting, Harvard Univ Press, 91. **CONTACT ADDRESS** Dept of Fine Arts, Harvard Univ, 485 Broadway, Cambridge, MA, 02138. **EMAIL** bryson@fas.harvard.edu

BRYSON, RALPH J.
PERSONAL Born 09/10/1922, Cincinnati, OH, s **DISCIPLINE** ENGLISH **EDUCATION** Univ Cincinnati, BS 1947; Univ Cincinnati, MS 1950; OH State Univ, PhD 1953. **CAREER** So Univ, instr English 1949; Miles Coll, instr English 1949-50; AL State Univ, associate prof English 1953-62; prof & dept head 1962-75, chmn div of humanities 1975-77, prof of English 1977-; Univ of AL, adjunct prof 1987. **HONORS AND AWARDS** Dexter Ave King Memorial Baptist Church; Outstanding Journalistic Contributions & Achievement Kappa Alpha Psi; Outstanding Men of Yr & Montgomery; Cited Outstanding OH State Univ Graduate in They Came & They Conquered; Bryson Endowed Scholarships Established at University Cin'ti & Ohio State University, 1995; 56th Recipient of the Elder Watson Diggs Award, 72nd Grand Chapter elected grand historian, 73rd Grand Chapt, Kappa Alpha Psi, 1997. **MEMBERSHIPS** Pres Assn Coll English Tchrs AL; AL Council Tchrs English Exec Bd; Nat Council Tchrs English; Modern Language Assn; S Atlantic MLA; Coll Language Assn; Conf Coll Composition & Communication; Phi Delta Kappa; Lectr Author & Consult; Kappa Alpha Psi; Editor Column Books & Such; chmn Nat Achievement Commn; officer, mem Province Bd Dir; Am Bridge Assn; chmn exec bd & sectional vice pres, Montgomery Seminar Arts; bd of trustees, Museum Fine Arts Assn; Alabama Writers' Forum, bd of dirs. **CONTACT ADDRESS** English Dept, Alabama State Univ, 915 S Jackson St, Montgomery, AL, 36101-0271.

BUCCO, MARTIN
DISCIPLINE ENGLISH LITERATURE **EDUCATION** Highlands Univ, BA; Columbia Univ, MA, Univ Mo, PhD. **CAREER** Prof. **MEMBERSHIPS** Western Lit Asn. **RESEARCH** American literary realism; American criticism. **SELECTED PUBLICATIONS** Auth, pubs on Frank Waters, Wilbur, Daniel Steele, E.W. Howe, and Rene Wellek. **CONTACT ADDRESS** Dept of English, Colorado State Univ, Fort Collins, CO, 80523. **EMAIL** services@colostate.edu

BUCHANAN, RAYMOND W.
DISCIPLINE COMMUNICATION THEORY **EDUCATION** David Lipscomb Col, BA, 59; La State Univ, MA, 67, PhD, 70. **CAREER** Instr, Univ Ctr FL, 70-86; ch, 72-86; dir, Pepperdine's Florence, 89-91; prof, 86-. **HONORS AND AWARDS** Commun consult, high profile criminal trial FL v. Rolling, 93-94. **RESEARCH** Legal commun. **SELECTED PUBLICATIONS** Co-auth, Communication Strategies for Trial Attorneys. **CONTACT ADDRESS** Dept of Commun, Pepperdine Univ, 24255 Pacific Coast Hwy, Malibu, CA, 90263. **EMAIL** rbuchana@pepperdine.edu

BUCKALEW, RONALD EUGENE
PERSONAL Born 07/29/1935, Wilmington, DE, m, 1958, 2 children **DISCIPLINE** ENGLISH **EDUCATION** Col Wooster, BA, 57; Univ Ill, MA, 59, PhD, 64. **CAREER** Tchg asst, Univ IL, Urbana, 59-61, 62-63; asst prof Eng, 63-74, assoc prof eng, PA State Univ, 74-97, Germanistic Soc Am fel, univ Minister, 61-62; LSA post dr, fel, UCLA, 66; consult, Allyn & Bacon, Inc, 65-68; co-ed, Gen Ling, 70-74; fel, Inst Arts & Humanistic Studies, PA State Univ, 76-77; res grantee, Am Coun Learned Soc, 76-77, Am Philos Soc, 76-77 & 78-79 & Nat Endowment for Hum, 79; assoc mem, Clare Hall, Cambridge Univ, 77-78 & 80-81, life mem; spec adv, Dict Old Eng, Ctr Medieval Studies, Univ Toronto, 77-78. **MEMBERSHIPS** MLA; Ling Soc Am; Mediaeval Acad Am; Early Eng Text Soc; AAUP. **RESEARCH** Eng linguistics, espec historical; Old Eng lang and lit, espec Beowulf and Aelfric; Chaucer. **SELECTED PUBLICATIONS** Auth, A phonological analysis of present-day standard English, Gen Ling, fall 72; Night lessons on language, In: A Conceptual Guide to Finnegans Wake, Pa State Univ, 73; Beowulf, lines 1766-1767: Odde for seoddan?, Neuphilologische Mitteilungen, summer 74; Leland's Transcript of Aelfric's Glossary, Anglo-Saxon England, Cambridge Univ, 78; Nowell, Lambarde, and Leland: The significance of Lawrence Nowell's transcript of Aelfric's Grammar and Glossary, In: Anglo-Saxon Scholarship: The First Three Centuries, G K Hall, 82; Attempts to Equalize Sex References in American English, Strani Jezici, 85; Latin in Old England, Research, Penn State, 86; co found, assoc ed, Anglo-Saxon manuscripts in microfiche. **CONTACT ADDRESS** Dept of Eng, Pennsylvania State Univ, 116 Burrowes Bldg, University Park, PA, 16802-6200. **EMAIL** reb@psu.edu

BUCKLEY, JEROME HAMILTON
PERSONAL Born 08/30/1917, Toronto, ON, Canada, m, 1943, 3 children **DISCIPLINE** ENGLISH LITERATURE **EDUCATION** Univ Toronto, BA, 39; Harvard Univ, AM, 40, PhD, 42. **CAREER** From instr to prof English, Univ Wis, 42-54; vis assoc prof, Columbia Univ, 52-53, prof, 54-61; prof, 61-75, GURNEY PROF ENGLISH LIT, HARVARD UNIV, 75-, Guggenheim fel, 46-47 & 64; vis prof, Univ Colo, 60 & Univ Hawaii, 69; Huntington Libr fel, 78. **MEMBERSHIPS** MLA; Tennyson Soc; Int Asn Univ Professors English; Am Acad Arts & Sci; Acad Lit Studies. **RESEARCH** Romantic and Victorian literature; intellectual history; autobiography. **SELECTED PUBLICATIONS** Auth, The Victorian Temper, Harvard Univ, 51; Tennyson, the Growth of a Poet, Harvard Univ, 60; Poetry of the Victorian Period, Scott, 65; The Triumph of Time, Harvard Univ, 66; ed, The Pre-Raphaelites, Mod Libr, Random, 68; chap, In: The Victorian Poets, Harvard Univ, 68; auth, Season of Youth: Bildungsroman from Dickens to Golding, Harvard Univ, 74; Victorian Poets & Prose Writers, AHM, 77; High Victorian Culture - Morse,D/, Victorian Studies, Vol 37, 1993; The Victorians and Renaissance Italy - Fraser,H/, Albion, Vol 25, 1993; Tennyson and the Text, The Weaver Shuttle - Joseph,G/, Nineteenth-Century Lit, Vol 48, 1993; Annoying the Victorians - Kincaid,JR/, Nineteenth-Century Lit, Vol 50, 1995; Victorian Poetry - Poetry, Poetics, and Politics - Armstrong,I/, Albion, Vol 27, 1995. **CONTACT ADDRESS** Dept of English, Harvard Univ, Warren House 3, Cambridge, MA, 02138.

BUCKLEY, JOAN
DISCIPLINE ENGLISH LITERATURE **EDUCATION** St Olaf Col, BA; Univ Chicago, MA; Univ Iowa, PhD. **CAREER** Prof. **MEMBERSHIPS** MLA, MMLA, CCCC, Delta Kappa Gamma, Phi Delta Kappa, Phi Beta Kappa, NAHA. **SELECTED PUBLICATIONS** Auth, Han Ola og Han Per; More Han Ola og Han Per. **CONTACT ADDRESS** English Dept, Concordia Col, Minnesota, 901 8th St S, Moorhead, MN, 56562. **EMAIL** buckley@gloria.cord.edu

BUCKLEY, WILLIAM KERMIT
PERSONAL Born 11/14/1946, San Diego, CA, m, 1969, 1 child **DISCIPLINE** LITERARY CRITICISM, BRITISH LITERATURE **EDUCATION** Univ San Diego, BA, 69; San Diego State Univ, MA, 72, MA, 75; Miami Univ, PhD(English), 80. **CAREER** Instr Compos & Lit, San Diego State Univ, 71-72; instr, Reading Prog, Calif Community Cols, 72-74; instr & dir, Learning Skills, SDak State Univ, 74-75; asst prof Compos & Lit, Hanover Col, 79-82; prof Compos & Lit, Ind Univ Northwest, 82-, co-ed & co-founder, Recovering Lit, 72-. **HONORS AND AWARDS** Best Chapbook of Poetry, 97. **MEMBERSHIPS** MLA; Am Acad Poets. **RESEARCH** The life and works of Louis-Ferdinand Celine; the life and works of D H Lawrence. **SELECTED PUBLICATIONS** Auth, Alfred Tennyson's early poetry, Interpretations: Studies in Lang & Lit, Vol 12, 80; coauth, Louis-Ferdinand Celine: A Critical Bibliography (1932-1982), Garland Press, 85; Love and Hope, NY: Macmillan, 93. **CONTACT ADDRESS** English Dept, Indiana Univ, Northwest, 3400 Broadway, Gary, IN, 46408-1101. **EMAIL** wkbuckley@iun.1ind.eg.edu

BUCKNELL, BRAD
DISCIPLINE ENGLISH LITERATURE **EDUCATION** Univ Alberta, BA; MA; Univ Toronto, PhD. **CAREER** Asst prof **RESEARCH** Modernism; postmodernism; philosophy of aesthetics; philosophy of music; cultural studies; African American literature; twentieth century Irish literature; contemporary British literature; computers and writing. **SELECTED PUBLICATIONS** Auth, pubs on Pater, Wilde, Pound, Stein, Joyce, and musical and literary relations. **CONTACT ADDRESS** Dept of English, Manitoba Univ, Winnipeg, MB, R3T 2N2.

BUCKSTEAD, RICHARD C.
PERSONAL Born 03/17/1929, Viborg, SD, m, 1956, 4 children **DISCIPLINE** AMERICAN LITERATURE, ASIAN LITERATURE **EDUCATION** Yankton Col, BA, 50; Univ SDak, MA, 56; State Univ Iowa, PhD(English), 59. **CAREER** Instr English, Augustana Col, SDak, 57-58; asst prof, Southeast Mo State Col, 58-61; asst dean, 64-67, dir Asian studies, 71-73, asst prof to assoc prof, 61-80, prof English, St Olaf Col, 80-, Assoc Cols Midwest grant Asian studies, 67-68; vis prof, Chulalongkorn Univ Bangkok, 67-68. **MEMBERSHIPS** Asn Asian Studies. **RESEARCH** The novels of Yukio Mishima; Japanese prose; Chinese poetry. **SELECTED PUBLICATIONS** Auth, Kawabata and the Divided Self, China Printing, Taipei, 72; The meaning of symbol in Kawabata's Thousand Cranes, Tamkang Rev, Taipei, 11/72; The search for a symbol in Kawabata's Snow Country, 6/73 & The role of nature in Mishima's The Sound of Waves, 2/77, Asian Profile, Hong Kong; A conversation with a Master Luthier, The Strad, Kent, 5/77. **CONTACT ADDRESS** Dept of English, St Olaf Col, 1520 St Olaf Ave, Northfield, MN, 55057-1099. **EMAIL** buckster@stolaf.edu

BUDD, LOUIS JOHN
PERSONAL Born 08/26/1921, St. Louis, MO, m, 1945, 2 children **DISCIPLINE** ENGLISH **EDUCATION** Univ Mo, AB, 41, AM, 42; Univ Wis, PhD(English), 49. **CAREER** Instr English, Univ Mo, 42, 46; from instr to asst prof, Univ Ky, 49-52; from asst prof to assoc prof, 52-66, chmn dept, 73-79, PROF ENGLISH, DUKE UNIV, 66-, Guggenheim fel, 65-66; Fulbright-Hays lectr, Am Studies Res Ctr, Hyderabad, 67 & fall 72; managing ed, Am Lit, 79-; sr fel, Nat Endowment for Humanities, 79-80. **MEMBERSHIPS** MLA; SAtlantic MLA; Am Humor Studies Asn (pres, 79); Int Asn Univ Prof English. **RESEARCH** Mark Twain; realism and naturalism; American literary history, 1865-1920. **SELECTED PUBLICATIONS** Auth, Mark Twain, In: American Literary Scholarship, An Annual, Duke Univ, 78; ed, Critical Essays on Mark Twain, 82; Toward a New American Literary History, 80; Mark-Twain Letters, Vol 3 - 1869 - Fischer,V, Frank,MB, eds/, Miss Quart, Vol 46, 1993; The Sagebrush Bohemian - Mark-Twain in California - Lennon,N/, Miss Quart, Vol 46, 1993; Getting to be Mark-Twain - Steinbrink,J/, Miss Quart, Vol 46, 1993; Being a Boy Again, Autobiography and the American Boy Book - Jacobson,M/, Am Lit, Vol 67, 1995; Budd,Louis,J., A Personal Narrative + American Literature, Education, Academia/, Am Lit Realism 1870-1910, Vol 28, 1996; Twain,Mark on the Loose - A Comic Writer and the American Self - Michelson,B/, Am Lit, Vol 68, 1996; Listing of and Selections from Newspaper and Magazine Interviews with Clemens,Samuel,L. - A Supplement/, Am Lit Realism 1870-1910, Vol 28, 1996; Twain,Mark Letters - Volume 4, 1870-1871 - Fischer,V, Frank,MB, Salamo,L/, Miss Quart, Vol 49, 1996; Mark-Twain, Culture and Gender - Envisioning America through Europe - Stahl,JD/, Miss Quart, Vol 49, 1996; The Oxford Twain,Mark - Fishkin,SF/, Am Lit, Vol 69, 1997. **CONTACT ADDRESS** Dept of English, Duke Univ, 325 Allen Bldg, Durham, NC, 27706.

BUDICK, SANFORD
PERSONAL Born 07/05/1942, New York, NY, m, 1968, 3 children **DISCIPLINE** ENGLISH LITERATURE **EDUCATION** Harvard Univ, AB, 63; Yale Univ, MA, 64, PhD(English), 66. **CAREER** From instr to asst prof English, 66-72, assoc prof, 72-79, PROF ENGLISH, CORNELL UNIV, 79-, Vis sr lectr, Hebrew Univ Jerusalem, 70-71, assoc prof, 72-. **MEMBERSHIPS** MLA. **RESEARCH** Restoration poetry and theology; Augustan poetics; Milton. **SELECTED PUBLICATIONS** Auth, Dryden and the Abyss of Light: A Study of Religio Laici and The Hind and the Panther, 70 & Poetry of Civilization: Mythopoetic Displacement in the Verse of Milton, Dryden, Pope, and Johnson, 74, Yale Univ; Chiasmus and the Making of Literary Tradition, the Case of Wordsworth and the Days of Dryden and Pope/, English Lit Hist, Vol 60, 1993; The Experience of Literary-History + Literary-Criticism - Vulgar Versus Not-Vulgar/, New Lit Hist, Vol 25, 1994; Descartes Cogito, Kant Sublime, and Rembrandt Philosophers - Cultural Transmission as Occasion for Freedom/, Mod Lang Quart, Vol 58, 1997. **CONTACT ADDRESS** Dept Am Studies, Hebrew Univ, Jerusalem, ..

BUELL, FREDERICK HENDERSON
PERSONAL Born 11/17/1942, Bryn Mawr, PA, m, 1982, 2 children **DISCIPLINE** ENGLISH & AMERICAN LITERATURE **EDUCATION** Yale Univ, BA, 64; Cornell Univ, PhD, 69. **CAREER** From instr to asst prof, 69-74, assoc prof, 74-79, prof eng, Queens Col, 79. **HONORS AND AWARDS** NEA grant, 71; Yaddo Residency, 81; FIPSE grant, 87-90; New York Found for the Arts grant, 94; Excellence in Tchg Award, 96; ACLS grant, 97-98. **MEMBERSHIPS** MLA **RESEARCH** 20th Century Am lit; globalization and cult; Am environmental writing. **SELECTED PUBLICATIONS** Auth, W H Auden As a Social Poet, Cornell Univ, 73; Sylvia Plath's Traditionalism, boundary 2, 76; To be quiet in the hands of the Marvelous: The poetry of A R Ammons, Iowa Rev, 77; The Non-Literary Style of American Poetry, Cornell Rev, 79; National Culture and the New Global System, Johns Hopkins, 94; Post Nationalist Nationalism, Am Quart, 98. **CONTACT ADDRESS** Dept of Eng, Queens Col, CUNY, 6530 Kissena Blvd, Flushing, NY, 11367-1597. **EMAIL** buell@warwick.net

BUERKEL-ROTHFUSS, NANCY
PERSONAL Born 01/21/1951, Saginaw, MI, m, 1998, 1 child **DISCIPLINE** COMMUNICATIONS STUDIES **EDUCATION** Oakland Univ, BA, 73; Mich State Univ, MA, 75, PhD, 78. **CAREER** Asst prof, Univ Ky, 78-80; asst prof, 80-82, assoc prof, 82-86, full prof, 86- , Central Mich Univ. **HONORS AND AWARDS** Elected div chemn, Nat Commun Asn, 95-98 & 96-99. **MEMBERSHIPS** Nat Commun Asn; Int Commun Asn. **RESEARCH** Family communication; interpersonal communication; mass communication; instructional communication. **SELECTED PUBLICATIONS** Auth, Media, Sex and Adolescents; auth, Communication: Competencies and Contexts; auth, Understanding Family Communication. **CONTACT ADDRESS** Speech Communication & Drama Dept, Central Michigan Univ, 333 Moore Hall, Mt Pleasant, MI, 48859. **EMAIL** 34TXF2@cmich.edu

BUGGE, JOHN MICHAEL
PERSONAL Born 06/03/1941, Milwaukee, WI, m, 1966 **DISCIPLINE** MEDIEVAL ENGLISH LITERATURE **EDUCATION** Marquette Univ, BA, 63; Harvard Univ, MA, 66, PhD(-English), 70. **CAREER** Asst prof, 68-76, assoc prof English, Emory Univ, 76-, men screening comt, Harbison Award for Distinguished Teaching, Danforth Found, 71-72, Grad Fels for Women, 72-74; Nat Endowment for Humanities Young Humanist fel, 73-74; Professor Emory Univ, 96-. **MEMBERSHIPS** MLA; Mediaeval Acad Am. **RESEARCH** Concepts of virginity and female sexuality in Medieval literature; the Medieval English alliterative tradition; Chaucer. **SELECTED PUBLICATIONS** Auth, Damyan's Wanton Clyket and an Ironic New Twiste to the Merchant's Tale, Annuale Mediaevale, 73; Rhyme as Onomatopoeia in The Dry Salvages, Papers Lang & Lit, 74; Virginitas: An Essay in the History of a Medieval Ideal, Nijhoff, 75; The Virgin Phoenix, Mediaeval Studies, 76; Tell-Tale Context: Two Notes on Biblical Quotation in The Canterbury Tales, Am Notes and Queries, 76; The Arthurian Tradition: Essays in Convergence, 88. **CONTACT ADDRESS** Dept of English, Emory Univ, Atlanta, GA, 30322-0001. **EMAIL** engjmb@emory.edu

BUITENHUIS, PETER M.
PERSONAL Born 12/08/1925, London, England **DISCIPLINE** ENGLISH **EDUCATION** Jesus Col, Oxford, BA, 49, MA, 54; Yale Univ, PhD, 55. **CAREER** Instr, Univ Okla, 49-51; instr Am stud, Yale Univ, 54-59; asst to assoc prof, Univ Toronto, 59-66; vis prof, Univ Calif Berkeley, 66-67; prof, McGill Univ, 67-75; PROF EMER ENGLISH, SIMON FRASER UNIV, 75-. **HONORS AND AWARDS** Can Coun fel, 63-64; Am Coun Learned Soc fel, 72-73; SSHRC leave fel, 82-83, res grant, 91-94. **MEMBERSHIPS** Asn Can Stud; Can Asn Am Stud; Can Asn Univ Tchrs; Can Asn Chmn Eng. **SELECTED PUBLICATIONS** Auth, Hugh MacLennan, 68; auth, Viewpoints on Henry James' Portrait of a Lady, 68; ed, Selected Poems of E.J. Pratt, 69; ed, The Grasping Imagination: The American Writings of Henry James, 70; ed, The Restless Analyst: Essays by Henry James, 80; ed, The Great War of Words: British, American and Canadian Propaganda and Fiction 1914-1933, 87; co-ed, George Orwell: A Reassessment, 89; co-ed, The House of the Seven Gables: Severing Family and Colonial Ties, 91. **CONTACT ADDRESS** English Dept, Simon Fraser Univ, Burnaby, BC, V5A 1S6.

BUKALSKI, PETER J.
PERSONAL Born 06/05/1941, Milwaukee, WI, m, 1971, 2 children **DISCIPLINE** FILM **EDUCATION** Univ WI, Milwau, BA; Univ WI, Madis, MA; Univ Cal, Los Ang, MFA; Ohio State Univ, PhD. **CAREER** Franklin Col, asst prof, 66-70; Wright State Univ, Dir motion pic stud, 70-73; Ohio State Univ, teach assoc, 73-75; SO IL Univ, Carbondale, chr, cine photog, 75-79; Am Film Inst, dir edu serv, 79-83; School Fine Arts Comm, Dean, 84-89; SO IL Univ, prof theat and dance, 89-. **HONORS AND AWARDS** Numerous teaching awards **MEMBERSHIPS** Univ Film Video Asn; Soc for Cine Stud; Univ Film Video Found; Am Mus Instr Soc; Intl Double Reed Soc. **RESEARCH** Am film hist, 1927-1945; film edu; higher edu admin. **SELECTED PUBLICATIONS** Guide for Nontenured Faculty Members: Annual Evaluation, Promotion and Tenure, Atlanta GA, Univ Film and Video Asn, 93; How to Avoid Digging Your Own Grave or Is Your Dept a Target of Opportunity? UFVA Digest, 92; Oboe Making in the United States, A Laubin Inc, The Dble Reed, 90; Island of Saints and Souls, Southern Quarterly, 92; numerous articles, reviews. **CONTACT ADDRESS** Southern Illinois Univ, Dept Theater and Dance, Box 1777, Edwardsville, IL, 62026. **EMAIL** pbukals@siue.edu

BULGER, PEGGY A.
PERSONAL Born 12/13/1949, Albany, NY, m, 1979, 2 children **DISCIPLINE** FOLKLORE, FOLKLIFE **EDUCATION** Western KY, MA 75; Univ Penn, PhD 92. **CAREER** Bureau of Florida Folklife progs, admin, 75-89; Southern Arts Feder, Dir prog, sr prog off, 89-. **HONORS AND AWARDS** Wayland D Hand Prize; fel, Brit Coun For Exch; Emply of Prom Awd FL. **MEMBERSHIPS** Am Folklore Soc; North Am Folk Music Dance Allian. **RESEARCH** Southern culture and folk arts; celtic folklore. **SELECTED PUBLICATIONS** South Florida Folklife, with Tina Bucuvalas and Stetson Kennedy, Jackson, Univ Miss Press, 94; Musical roots of the South, ed, Atlanta GA, Southern Arts Fed, 92, several pub. **CONTACT ADDRESS** 1024 Viscount CT, Avondale Estates, GA, 30002. **EMAIL** pbulger@southarts.org

BULLARD, JOHN MOORE
PERSONAL Born 05/06/1932, Winston-Salem, NC **DISCIPLINE** BIBLICAL STUDIES; ENGLISH LANGUAGE AND LITERATURE **EDUCATION** AB, 53, AM, 55, UNC- Chapel Hill; Mdiv, 57, PhD, 62, Yale Univ. **CAREER** Asst in Instruction, Yale Univ, 57-62; Asst Prof, 61-65, Assoc Prof, 65-70, Albert C. Outler Prof, 70-, Chmn, Dept of Religion, 63-, Wofford Col. **HONORS AND AWARDS** James Graduate Fel at Yale, 57-62; Dana Fel, Emory Univ, 89-90. **MEMBERSHIPS** Amer Acad of Religion; Soc of Biblical Lit; South Carolina Acad of Religion; New Bach Soc; Moravian Music Fdn. **RESEARCH** The Hymn as Literary form from ancient Sumerians to the Hebrew Psalter and beyond. **CONTACT ADDRESS** Dept of Religion, Wofford Col, 429 N. Church St., Spartanburg, SC, 29303. **EMAIL** bullardjm@wofford.edu

BULLON-FERNANDEZ, MARIA
DISCIPLINE ENGLISH **EDUCATION** Univ Sevilla, BA, 89; Cornell Univ, PhD, 95. **CAREER** Eng, Seattle Univ. **MEMBERSHIPS** Medieval Acad Am; MLA; John Gower Soc; Soc Medieval Feminist Scholar; AEDEAN, Span Asn Anglo-North Am Stud; SELIM, Span Soc Medieval Engl Lang & Lit; ESSE, Europ Soc Stud Engl; New Chaucer Soc. **SELECTED PUBLICATIONS** Auth, Engendering Authority: Father and Daughter, State and Church in John Gower's Tale of Constance and Chaucer's Man of Law's Tale, in Revisioning Gower, 98; Confining the Daughter: Gower's 'Tale of Canace and Machaire' and the Polit of the Body, in Essays in Medieval Stud, 11, 94; Beyonde the water: Courtly and Religious Desire in Pearl, Stud in Philol, XCI 1, 94; Gower frente a las convenciones del amor cortes: el cuento de Rosiphelee y el papel social de la mujer en la Confessio Amantis, Actas del XV Congresó de AEDEAN, 91; La tentacion de Adan y Eva en la literatura inglesa de la Baja Edad Media: Caracterizacion alegorica, in ATLANTIS, 13 1-2, 91; collab, Caedmon y Beda: La traduccion del mensaje cristiano en la Inglaterra Anglosajona, Actas del XIV Congreso de AEDEAN, 90; rev, Estudio sobre Confessio Amantis de John Gower y su version castellana Confisyon del amante de Juan de Cuenca, Selim, 4, 95. **CONTACT ADDRESS** Dept of Eng, Seattle Univ, 900 Broadway, Seattle, WA, 98122-4460. **EMAIL** bullon@seattleu.edu

BUMP, JEROME FRANCIS ANTHONY
PERSONAL Born 06/13/1943, Pine River, MN, 2 children **DISCIPLINE** ENGLISH LITERATURE, COMPARATIVE STUDIES **EDUCATION** Univ Minn, Minneapolis, BA, 65; Univ Calif, Berkeley, MA, 66, PhD(English), 72 **CAREER** Asst prof, 70-76, assoc prof, 76-85, PROF ENGLISH, UNIV TEX, AUSTIN, 85-. **HONORS AND AWARDS** Nat Endowment for Humanities fel, 74. **MEMBERSHIPS** NCTE; Int

Hopkins Asn **RESEARCH** Emotional intelligence; creativity; Victorian literature. **SELECTED PUBLICATIONS** Auth, 1 bk, 1 ed, 35 articles, 9 chap, 2 ed letters, 1 bibliogr, 14 rev essays, 21 rev & 71 papers. **CONTACT ADDRESS** Dept of English, Univ of Tex, Austin, TX, 78712-1164. **EMAIL** bump@mail.utexas.edu

BUNGE, NANCY LIDDELL
PERSONAL Born 05/13/1942, La Crosse, WI **DISCIPLINE** AMERICAN LITERATURE, ENGLISH LITERATURE **EDUCATION** Radcliffe Col, AB, 64; Univ Chicago, MA, 66; Univ Wis-Madison, PhD, 70. **CAREER** From instr to asst prof Am lit, George Washington Univ, 68-73; from Asst Prof to Assoc Prof, 73-84, prof Am thought & lang, Mich State Univ, 84-. **HONORS AND AWARDS** Teacher-Scholar Award, Mich State Univ, 78; Sr Fulbright Lectr in Am Culture, Univ Vienna, 86-87. **MEMBERSHIPS** MLA; Midwest Mod Lang Asn. **RESEARCH** Writing. **SELECTED PUBLICATIONS** Interviewer & ed, Finding the Words: Conversations with Writers Who Teach, Swallow, 85; auth, Nathaniel Hawthorne: A Study of the Short Fiction, Twayne/Macmillan, 93. **CONTACT ADDRESS** Dept of Am Thought & Lang, Michigan State Univ, 229 Bessey Hall, East Lansing, MI, 48824-1033. **EMAIL** bunge@pilot.msu.edu

BURBICK, JOAN
DISCIPLINE AMERICAN LITERATURE **EDUCATION** Brandeis, PhD. **CAREER** Prof, Washington State Univ. **RESEARCH** Nationalism and gender in the American West. **SELECTED PUBLICATIONS** Auth, Thoreau's Alternative History: Changing Perspectives on Nature, Culture, and Language, 87 & Healing the Republic: The Language of Health and the Culture of Nationalism in Nineteenth Century America, 94. **CONTACT ADDRESS** Dept of English, Washington State Univ, 1 SE Stadium Way, PO Box 645020, Pullman, WA, 99164-5020. **EMAIL** burbick@wsu.edu

BURD, VAN AKIN
PERSONAL Born 04/19/1914, m, 1942, 1 child **DISCIPLINE** ENGLISH **EDUCATION** Univ Chicago, AB, 36; Stanford Univ, MA, 41; Univ Mich, PhD, 51. **CAREER** Teacher, pub schs, Mich, 36-40; teaching fel & jr instr English, Univ Mich, 46-51; prof, 51-74, chmn dept, 59-60, 61-63 & 65-68, res found fels, 55, 65, 68 & 73, prof, 73-79, DISTINGUISHED EMER PROF ENGLISH, STATE UNIV NY COL CORTLAND, 79-, Am Coun Learned Soc fel, 60-61, grant-in-aid, 68-69 & 78-79; Am Philos Soc grants-in-aid, 60, 68, 73 & 79; Delmus Found Venetian Studies grant-in-aid, 79. **MEMBERSHIPS** MLA; NCTE; Thoreau Soc; Turner Soc. **RESEARCH** Romantic and Victorian periods of English literature, especially John Ruskin. **SELECTED PUBLICATIONS** Ed, The Winnington Letters: The Correspondence of John Ruskin and M Bell, Harvard Univ, 69 & The Ruskin Family Letters, Cornell Univ, 73; auth, A new light on the writing of modern painters & Background to modern painters: The tradition and the Turner controversy, MLA Publ; Ruskin's quest for a theory of imagination, Mod Lang Quart; John Ruskin and Rose LaTouche, Oxford Univ, 79; Sharp,Frederick,James 1880-1957/, Bk Collector, Vol 44, 1995; Ruskin, Bembridge and Brantwood - The Growth of the Whitehouse-Collection - Dearden,JS/, Bk Collector, Vol 44, 1995. **CONTACT ADDRESS** Dept of English, State Univ of NY Col, Cortland, NY, 13045.

BURDE, EDGAR J.
PERSONAL Born 12/23/1930, New York, NY, m, 1963, 3 children **DISCIPLINE** ENGLISH **EDUCATION** Hobart Col, Geneva, NY, BA, 53; Univ of Edinburgh, Scotland, postgrad English studies, 55-56; Univ Calif, Berkeley, MA, 63; Claremont Grad Sch, Calif, PhD(English), 69. **CAREER** Instr English, Univ Mont, Missoula, 63-64; instr English, Whitman Col, 64-66; asst prof English, Claremont Men's Col, 69-70; from asst prof to assoc prof, 70-86, prof English, State Univ Ny Col Plattsburgh, 74-. **MEMBERSHIPS** MLA; ALSC. **RESEARCH** American literature. **SELECTED PUBLICATIONS** Auth, The Ambassadors and the Double Vision of Henry James, Essays in Literature, Spring 77; Mark Twain: The Writer as Pilot, PMLA, Oct 78; Slavery and the Boys: Tom Sawyer and the Germ of Huck Finn, Am Lit Realism, Fall 91. **CONTACT ADDRESS** Dept of English, State Univ NY, Plattsburgh, NY, 12901. **EMAIL** burdeej@splava.cc.plattsburgh.edu

BURGCHARDT, CARL
DISCIPLINE COMMUNICATION STUDIES **EDUCATION** Pa State Univ, BA; Univ Wis, MA, PhD. **CAREER** Prof. **RESEARCH** Public speaking; rhetorical criticism. **SELECTED PUBLICATIONS** Auth, Readings in Rhetorical Criticism; Discovering Rhetorical Imprints: La Follette, 'Iago' and the Melodramatic Scenario, Quarterly J Speech, 85; Two Faces of American Communism: Pamphlet Rhetoric of the Third Period and the Popular Front, Quarterly J Speech, 80. **CONTACT ADDRESS** Speech Communication Dept, Colorado State Univ, Fort Collins, CO, 80523. **EMAIL** cburgchardt@vines.colostate.edu

BURIAN, JARKA MARSANO
PERSONAL Born 03/10/1927, Passaic, NJ, m, 1951 **DISCIPLINE** DRAMATIC ART **EDUCATION** Rutgers Univ, BA, 49; Columbia Univ, MA, 50; Cornell Univ, PhD, 55. **CAREER** Instr English Cornell Univ, 54-55; from asst prof to assoc prof English, 55-63, chmn dept theatre, 71-74 & 77-78, prof, 63-93, prof emeritus, 93-, theater dept, SUNY Albany; vis assoc prof dramatic art, Univ Calif, Berkeley, 61-62; US State State Dept specialist's lect grant, Czechoslovakia, fall 65; Inter-Univ Comt Travel Grants res grant, Czechoslovakia, 68-69; Int Res & Exchange Bd res grant, Czechoslovakia, 74-75, Poland & Hungary 82; Czech Republic, 93-94; producer & artistic dir, Arena Summer Theatre, Albany, 59 & 63-64, 66-68 & 72-73; NEH fel, 74; Fulbright res award, 82, 88. **MEMBERSHIPS** US Inst Theatre Technol; Am Soc Theatre Res; AAUP. **RESEARCH** Comparative literature; play production. **SELECTED PUBLICATIONS** Auth, K H Hilar and the Early Twentieth Century Czech Theatre, Educ Thr J, 82; auth, Snoboda: Wagner, Wesleyan, 83; auth, Designing for the 90s, Cue Int, 89; auth, The Dark Era in Modern Czech Theatre: 1948-1950, Theatre Hist Stud, 95; auth, Two Women and Their Contribution to Contemporary Czech Scenography, Theatre Design and Technol, 96; auth, Laterna Magika as a Synthesis of Theatre and Film, Theatre Hist Stud, 97. **CONTACT ADDRESS** Dept of Theatre, SUNY, Albany, 1400 Washington Ave, Albany, NY, 12222.

BURKE, JOHN J.
PERSONAL Born 05/04/1942, Buffalo, NY, m, 1969, 4 children **DISCIPLINE** ENGLISH **EDUCATION** Boston Col, BA, 67; Northwestern Univ, MA, 68; UCLA, PhD, 74 **CAREER** Latin teacher, St Ignatius, Chicago; 68-69; teaching fel, UCLA, 69-73; asst prof, Univ Calif San Diego, 73-74; asst prof, Univ Ala, 74-79; assoc prof, Univ Ala, 79-85; prof English, Univ Ala, 85- **HONORS AND AWARDS** Morris L Mayer Award Outstanding Service to Students, 97; Teaching Excellence in Correspondence Courses, 95; Burlington Northern Faculty Achievement Award, 91; **MEMBERSHIPS** SEASECS; ECSSS; ASECS; SAMLA; MLA **RESEARCH** Johnson; Boswell; Shakespeare; Scott; Historiography **SELECTED PUBLICATIONS** Auth, "Boswell and the Text of Johnson's Logia," Age of Johnson, 98; auth, "Filling in the Blanks of Shakespeare's Biography," S Atlantic Rev, 95; co-ed, The Unknown Samuel Johnson, Univ Wis, 83 **CONTACT ADDRESS** Dept English, Univ Alabama, Box 870244, Tuscaloosa, AL, 35487-0244. **EMAIL** jburke@english.as.ua.edu

BURKMAN, KATHERINE H.
PERSONAL Born 06/13/1934, Chicago, IL, m, 1965, 2 children **DISCIPLINE** ENGLISH, THEATRE **EDUCATION** Radcliffe Col, AB, 55: Univ Chicago, MA & cert educ, 56; Ohio State Univ, PhD(theatre), 68. **CAREER** Teacher English, Columbia high sch, 57-59; teacher, Fieldston high sch, Riverdale, NY, 59-63; promotion writer textbooks, Harcourt, Brace & World, 63-64; teaching asst rhet, Univ Iowa, 64-65; instr English, Butler Univ, 65-66; asst prof comp lit, 68-77, ASSOC PROF ENGLISH, OHIO STATE UNIV, 77-, Dir, Nat Endowment for Humanities grant, 69-70, 71-72; dir, The Collection, 69-73. **MEMBERSHIPS** AAUP; Am Theatre Asn. **RESEARCH** Modern drama; uses of theatre in teaching literature. **SELECTED PUBLICATIONS** Auth, Pinter's A slight ache as ritual, Mod Drama, winter 68; The Dramatic World of Harold Pinter: It's Basis in Ritual, Ohio State Univ, 71; co-ed, Drama Through Performance, Houghton, 77; auth, Literature Through Performance, Ohio Univ, 78; Beckett 'Waiting for Godot'/, Theatre J, Vol 45, 1993; Pinter 'Old Times'/, Theatre J, Vol 46, 1994; Pinter,Harold - A Question of Timing - Regal,MS/, Mod Drama, Vol 39, 1996. **CONTACT ADDRESS** Dept of English, Ohio State Univ, Columbus, OH, 43210.

BURKS, DON M.
DISCIPLINE RHETORICAL THEORY, THE RELATIONSHIPS AMONG RHETORIC, PHILOSOPHY, AND LITERA **EDUCATION** Univ Wis, PhD, 62. **CAREER** Assoc prof, Purdue Univ. **RESEARCH** The works of Kenneth Burke, Henry Johnstone, and Wayne Booth. **SELECTED PUBLICATIONS** Auth, Rhetoric, Philosophy and Literature: An Exploration, 78; Dramatic Irony, Collaboration, and Kenneth Burke's Theory of Form, Pre/Text, 85; Kenneth Burke: The agro-Bohemian Marxoid, Commun Stud, 91; coauth, Rhetorical sensitivity and social interaction, Commun Monogr, 72. **CONTACT ADDRESS** Dept of Commun, Purdue Univ, 1080 Schleman Hall, West Lafayette, IN, 47907-1080.

BURLESON, BRANT R.
DISCIPLINE INTERPERSONAL COMMUNICATION **EDUCATION** Ill, PhD, 82. **CAREER** Prof, Purdue Univ. **RESEARCH** Social support; comforting; communication and emotion; philosophy of science. **SELECTED PUBLICATIONS** Auth, Comforting messages; Significance, approaches, and effects, Commun of Soc Support, 94; Thoughts about talk in romantic relationships; Similarity makes for attraction (and happiness, too), Commun Quart, 94; Personal relationships as a skilled accomplishment, Jour of Soc and Personal Relationships, 95; Men's and women's evaluations of communication skills in personal relationships: When sex differences make a difference-and when they don't, J of Soc and Personal Relationships, 96; The socialization of emotional support skills in childhood, Handbook of Soc Support and the Family, 96. **CONTACT ADDRESS** Dept of Commun, Purdue Univ, 1080 Schleman Hall, West Lafayette, IN, 47907-1080. **EMAIL** xwxf@vm.cc.purdue.edu

BURLIN, ROBERT B.
PERSONAL Born 10/07/1928, Cleveland, OH **DISCIPLINE** ENGLISH **EDUCATION** Yale Univ, BA, 50, PhD(English), 56. **CAREER** Instr English, Yale Col, 55-59, Morse fel, 59-60; from asst prof to assoc prof English, 60-69, chmn dept, 68-75, PROF ENGLISH, BRYN MAWR COL, 69-. **MEMBERSHIPS** MLA; Mediaeval Acad Am. **RESEARCH** Old and Middle English literature. **SELECTED PUBLICATIONS** Auth, The Old English Advent, Yale Univ, 68; ed, Old English Studies in Honour of John C Pope, Univ Toronto, 74; Chaucerian Fiction, Princeton Univ, 77; Truth and Textuality in Chaucer,Geoffrey Poetry - Kiser,LJ/, Speculum, Vol 68, 1993; Middle-English Romance - The Structure of Genre/, Chaucer Rev, Vol 30, 1995; **CONTACT ADDRESS** Dept of English, Bryn Mawr Col, Bryn Mawr, PA, 19010.

BURLING, WILLIAM J.
PERSONAL Born 01/27/1949, Ladysmith, WI, m, 1980, 2 children **DISCIPLINE** ENGLISH LITERATURE **EDUCATION** Univ of Wis, BS, 72, MA, 74; Penn State Univ, PhD, 85. **CAREER** Instr, Univ of Wis, 74-77; instr, Northern Ill Univ, 78-79; asst prof, Auburn Univ, 85-89; ASSOC PROF TO PROF, SOUTHWEST MO STATE UNIV, 89-. **HONORS AND AWARDS** SMSY Found Excellence in Res Award, 73. **MEMBERSHIPS** Am Soc of 18th Century Studies. **RESEARCH** English drama & theatre history, 1660-1843. **SELECTED PUBLICATIONS** Co-ed, The Plays of Colley Cibber, Fairleigh Dickinson Univ Press, 98; auth, Summer Theatre in London 1661-1820 and the Rise of the Little Haymarket Theatre, Fairleigh Dickinson Univ Press, 98; auth, A Checklist of New Plays and Entertainments on the London State 1700-1737, Fairleigh Dickinson Univ Press, 93; auth, A Preliminary Checklist and Finding Guide of the Correspondence of George Colman Jr, Bullt of Bibliog, 97; auth, British Plays 1697-1737: Premieres, Datings, Attributions, and publication Information, Studies in Bibliog, 89; auth, New Light on the Colley Cibber Canon: The Bulls and Bears and Damon and Phillida, Philolog Quart, 88; auth, Summer Theatre in London 1661-1694, Theatre Notebook XLII, 88; auth, A New Shadwell Letter, Modern Philol, 85; auth, Four More Lost Restoration Plays Found in Musical Sources, Music and Letters, 84; coauth, Theatrical Companies at the Little Haymarket Theatre 1720-1737, Essays in Theatre, 86. **CONTACT ADDRESS** Dept of English, Southwest Mo State Univ, 901 S National, Springfield, MO, 65804. **EMAIL** wjb692f@mail.smsu.edu

BURLINGAME, LORI
DISCIPLINE NATIVE AMERICAN LITERATURE **EDUCATION** PhD. **CAREER** E Mich Univ **HONORS AND AWARDS** FIPSE, 94-95. **SELECTED PUBLICATIONS** Auth, The Voice of the Serpent: An Interview with Leslie Marmon Silko, ." Bookpress: Newspaper Lity Arts, 93; Cultural Survival in Runner in the Sun, Univ Okla Press, 96. **CONTACT ADDRESS** Eastern Michigan Univ, Ypsilanti, MI, 48197. **EMAIL** Lori.Burlingame@online.emich.edu

BURNEKO, GUY
DISCIPLINE LITERATURE, PHILOSOPHY OF SCIENCE, EVOLUTION OF CONSCIOUSNESS **EDUCATION** Fordham Univ, BA; Univ AK, MA; Emory Univ, PhD. **CAREER** Assoc prof, dir, Grad Liberal Stud, Golden Gate Univ. **HONORS AND AWARDS** NEH fel, Claremont Grad Sch & Stanford Univ. **MEMBERSHIPS** Acad of Consciousness Stud, Princeton Univ. **SELECTED PUBLICATIONS** Auth of articles on intercultural and philosophical interpretation, philosophical hermeneutics, interdisciplinary and transdisciplinary educ, intuition and cult develop, and other topics. **CONTACT ADDRESS** Golden Gate Univ, San Francisco, CA, 94105-2968.

BURNER, DAVID B.
PERSONAL Born 05/10/1937, Cornwall, NY, m, 1958, 2 children **DISCIPLINE** HISTORY, LITERATURE **EDUCATION** AB Hamilton Col, 58; PhD Columbia Univ, 65. **CAREER** Colby Col, 62-63; Oakland Univ, 63-67; SUNY, Stony Brook, 67-. **HONORS AND AWARDS** Guggenheim Fellowship; NYS Excellence Award; Natl Hum Found. **MEMBERSHIPS** ASA; OAH; AHA. **RESEARCH** 20th century Am Poli. **SELECTED PUBLICATIONS** Making Peace with the 60s, Princeton Univ Press, 96; John F Kennedy and a New Generation, Little Brown, 89; Herbert Hoover: A Public Life, Alfred A Rucpt, 68; The Polotics of Provincialism: The Democratic Party in Transition, 1918-1932. **CONTACT ADDRESS** Dept Hist, State Univ of NY, Stony Brook, NY, 11794. **EMAIL** DBBurner@AOL.com

BURNETT, ANN K.
DISCIPLINE COMMUNICATION **EDUCATION** Colo Col, BA, 80; Univ of Northern Colo, MA, 81; Univ of Utah, PhD, 86. **CAREER** Teaching asst, Univ of Ariz and Univ of Northern Colo, 80-82; teaching asst, Univ of Utah, 83-88; asst prof,

Vanderbilt Univ, 86-88; assoc prof, Univ of Nebr, 88-97; assoc prof, North Dakota State Univ, 97-. **HONORS AND AWARDS** Recognition Award, UNL Parents' Asn/Teaching Coun, 90, 92, 94; Jaycee's Outstanding Young Professor Award, 92; Col of Arts and Scis Distinguished Teaching Award, 92; Walter Ulrich Award, 93; Al Johnson Award, Forensic Educator, 93; Chancellor's Award for Outstanding Service to Students, 94. **MEMBERSHIPS** Nat Commun Asn; Am Bar Asn; Am Forensic Asn; Delta Sigma Rho-Tau Kappa Alpha; Western Commun Asn; North Dakota Speech and Theatre Asn. **RESEARCH** Jury decision making and courtroom communication; group decision making process. **SELECTED PUBLICATIONS** Auth, The verdict is in: A study of jury decision making factors, moment of personal decision, and jury deliberations - from the jurors' point of view, in Commun Quart, 38, 90; From attitudinal inherency to permutation standards: A survey of judging philosophies from the 1988 National Debate Tournament, in Argumentation and Advocacy, 27, 91; Good people speaking well: Delta Sigma Rho-Tau Kappa Alpha, in Argumentation and Advocacy, 33, 96; Mock trials, Cause of action, and Civil action, manuscripts accepted for publ, in Magill's Legal Guide, 99; Jury decision-making processes in the O.J. Simpson criminal and civil trials, book chap in book on O.J. Simpson trials, 99; coauth, Analysis of forensics program administration: What will the 1990s bring?, in Nat Forensics J, 10, 92; Radio and world maintenance: A root metaphor analysis of the Grand Ole Opry, 1948-1958, in J of Radio Studies, 1, 92; The role of forensics when departments/ programs are targeted for elimination: A proposal to insure a 'call for support', in Nat Forensics J, 10, 93; Competitors' perceptions of questions in individual events rounds, in Nat Forensic J, 11, 93; Nonverbal involvement and sex: Effects on jury decision making, in J of Applied Commun, 22, 94; Coaching intercollegiate debate and raising a family: An analysis of perspectives from women in the trenches, in Nat Forensic J, 11, 94; The reason for decision in individual events: Its implementation and impact, in The Forensic Educator, 10, 95/96; The dark side of debate: The downfall of interpersonal relationships, in Speaker and Gavel, 35, 98. **CONTACT ADDRESS** Dept of Communication Studies, No Dakota State Univ, 321 Minard Hall, Fargo, ND, 58105. **EMAIL** aburnett@plains.nodak.edu

BURNHAM, MICHELLE
DISCIPLINE ENGLISH **EDUCATION** Trinity Col, BA, 84; SUNY, Buffalo, MS, 91, PhD, 94. **CAREER** Asst prof, Auburn Univ, 94-97; ASST PROF, SANTA CLARA UNIV, 97-. **CONTACT ADDRESS** Dept of English, Santa Clara Univ, Santa Clara, CA, 95053. **EMAIL** mburnham@scu.edu

BURRIS, SIDNEY
DISCIPLINE CONTEMPORARY POETRY **EDUCATION** Univ Va, PhD. **CAREER** English and Lit, Univ Ark. **HONORS AND AWARDS** Dir, Fulbright Col Honors Studies. **SELECTED PUBLICATIONS** Auth, The Riot of Gorgeousness: The Poetry and Prose of Marianne Moore, Rev, 88; The Return of Eliot and the Discovery of Auden, Sewanee Rev, 91; An Empire of Poetry, Southern Rev, 91; Auden's Generalizations, Shenandoah, 93; A Day at the Races, Utah, 89; The Poetry of Resistance: Seamus Heaney and the Pastoral Tradition, Ohio Univ Press, 90. **CONTACT ADDRESS** Univ Ark, Fayetteville, AR, 72701.

BURSK, CHRISTOPHER
PERSONAL Born 04/23/1943, Cambridge, MA, m, 1966, 3 children **DISCIPLINE** ENGLISH **EDUCATION** Boston Univ, PhD, 75; Warren Wilson Col, MFA, 87. **CAREER** Prof, Bucks County Community Col, 71-. **HONORS AND AWARDS** Guggenheim Fel; NEA Fel; PEW Fel. **SELECTED PUBLICATIONS** Auth, Cell Count, Tex Tech Univ Press; Auth, The One True Religion, Quart Rev. **CONTACT ADDRESS** Language and Literature Dept, Bucks County Comm Col, Swamp Rd, Newtown, PA, 18940.

BURT, SUSAN MEREDITH
PERSONAL Born 09/15/1951, Los Angeles, CA, m, 1976, 2 children **DISCIPLINE** ENGLISH **EDUCATION** Bryn Mawr Col, BA, 73; Univ Ill, Urbana, MA, 79, PhD, 86. **CAREER** Asst prof English, Univ Wisc, Oshkosh. **MEMBERSHIPS** Ling Soc of Am; Int Pragmatics Asn; TESOL. **RESEARCH** Intercultural conversation; code choice; language shift. **SELECTED PUBLICATIONS** Auth, Code Choice in Intercultural Conversation: Speech Accommodation Theory and Pragmatics, Pragmatics, 94; auth, Where Does Sociopragmatic Ambiguity Come From? Pragmatics and Lang Learning, 95; auth, Monolingual Children in a Bilingual Situation: Protest, Accommodation and Linguistic Creativity, Multilingua, 98. **CONTACT ADDRESS** Dept of English, Univ of Wisconsin, Oshkosh, 800 Algoma Blvd, Oshkosh, WI, 54901. **EMAIL** Burt@vaxa.cis.uwosh.edu

BURWELL, ROSE MARIE
PERSONAL Born 03/12/1934, 6 children **DISCIPLINE** MODERN FICTION, FILM **EDUCATION** Augustana Col, IL, BA, 59; Univ IA, MA, 66, PhD, 69. **CAREER** Asst prof, 70-81, assoc prof, 81-94, prof eng, Northern IL Univ, 94, Consult, Nat Endowment for Hum, 77; coordr, Ill Humanities Coun Proj, Sheridan State Correctional Ctr, 77-78 & Dwight State Correctional Ctr, 78; vis lectr, Univ Col, Oxford, 80 & 81. **HONORS AND AWARDS** Kennedy Lib Fel, 91, 92 & 94; Princeton Univ Friends of Lib Fel, 96 & 97; Andrew Mellon Fel, Univ Tex Austin, 93. **MEMBERSHIPS** MLA; AAUP. **RESEARCH** Eng novel. **SELECTED PUBLICATIONS** Auth, A chronological catalogue of D H Lawrence's reading, spec issue D H Lawrence Rev, fall 70; A chronological catalogue of D H Lawrence's reading: addenda, D H Lawrence Rev, spring 73; Joyce Carol Oates and an old master: A garden of earthly depths, Critique, summer 73; Schopenhauer, Hardy and Lawrence: Toward a new understanding of Sons and lovers, Western Humanities Rev, summer 74; The process of individuation as narrative structure: Joyce Carol Oates' Do With Me What You Will, Critique, fall 75; With Shuddering Fall: Joyce Carol Oates first novel, Can Lit, summer 77; Wonderland: Paradigm of the psycho-historical mode in comtemporary American literature, Mosaic, fall 81; D H Lawrence's Reading, In: A D H Lawrence Handbook, Univ Manchester Press, 82; Hemingway's Garden of Eden: Protecting the Masculine Text, TSLL, summer 93; New Pieces in the Posthumous Hemingway Puzzle, Princeton Univ Lib Chronicle, autumn 94; Hemingway: The Postwar Years, The Posthumous Novels, Cambridge Univ Press, 96. **CONTACT ADDRESS** Dept of Eng, No Illinois Univ, 1425 W Lincoln Hwy, De Kalb, IL, 60115-2825. **EMAIL** rmb39@interaccess.com

BUSBY, RUDOLPH E.
PERSONAL Born 11/01/1946, Beaumont, TX **DISCIPLINE** RHETORIC & COMMUNICATION THEORY, SPEECH COMMUNICATION **EDUCATION** Univ Houston, BA, 75, MA, 80, PhD, 83. **CAREER** Teaching asst, Univ Houston, 78-80; graduate teaching asst, Univ TX, 80; prof, San Francisco State Univ, 83-, campus coordinator, CA Pre-doctoral prof, 89-. **MEMBERSHIPS** Nat Commun Asn; Int Commun Asn. **RESEARCH** Rhetoric in cultural contexts. **SELECTED PUBLICATIONS** Auth, with R Majors, Basic Speech Communication: Principles and Practices, 89. **CONTACT ADDRESS** Dept of Commun Studies, San Francisco State Univ, 1600 Holloway Ave, San Francisco, CA, 94132-1722. **EMAIL** rbusby@sfsu.edu

BUSCH, FREDERICK MATTHEW
PERSONAL Born 08/01/1941, Brooklyn, NY, m, 1963, 2 children **DISCIPLINE** AMERICAN & MODERN LITERATURE **EDUCATION** Muhlenberg Col, AB, 62; Columbia Univ, MA, 67. **CAREER** Writer, NAm Precis Syndicate, Inc, 64-65; assoc ed, Sch Mgt Mag, 65-66; prof English, Colgate Univ, 66-, NEA, 70; Fairchild Prof of Lit, 86, dir, Prog Creative Writing, Univ Iowa, 78-79; panelist. **HONORS AND AWARDS** Guggenheim, 81; Ingram Merrill, 82; Award in Fiction, American Academy, 86; National Jewish Book Award-- Fiction, 86; Pen/ Malamud Award for Distinction in Short Fiction, 91. **MEMBERSHIPS** AAUP, Writers Guild, Authors Guild, Pen. **RESEARCH** Fiction writing; modern American fiction; 19th century British fiction. **SELECTED PUBLICATIONS** Auth, I Wanted a Year Without Fall, 71 & Breathing Trouble, 73, Calder & Boyars, London; Hawkes: A Guide to His Fictions, Syracuse Univ, 73; Manual Labor, 74 & Domestic Particulars, 76, New Directions; The Mutual Friend, Harper & Row, 78; Rounds, FSG, 79; Hardwater Country, Knopf, 79; Take This Man, FSG, 81; Invisible Mending, Godine, 84; Too Late American Boyhood Blues, 84; Sometimes I Live in the Country, Godine, 86; Absent Friends, Knopf, 89; War Babies, New Directions, 89; Closong Arguments, Ticknor and Fields, 91; Long Way from Home, Ticknor and Fields, 93; The Children in the Woods, Ticknor, 94; Girls, Harmony, 97; A Dangerous Profession, St. Martins, 98. **CONTACT ADDRESS** Dept of English, Colgate Univ, 13 Oak Dr, Hamilton, NY, 13346-1379.

BUSH JR, SARGENT
PERSONAL Born 09/22/1937, Flemington, NJ, m, 1960, 2 children **DISCIPLINE** HUMANITIES; ENGLISH **EDUCATION** Princeton Univ, AB, 59; Univ Iowa, MA, 64; PhD, 67. **CAREER** Wash & Lee Univ, Asst Prof, 67-71; Asst Prof, 71-73, Assoc Prof, 73-79, Prof, 79-, Ch, Dept Eng, 80-83, John Bascom Prof of Eng, 97-, Univ Wisc, Madison; Coll of Letters & Sci, Assoc Dean for Hum, 89-94. **HONORS AND AWARDS** Res fellow coop prog in the Hum, 69-70; ACLS, 74; Inst for res in the Hum, 78-79; Mass Hist Soc Fellow, 89-90; NEH Summer Stipends, 69, 86; Am Philos Soc Grants-in-Aid, 79, 97. **MEMBERSHIPS** Modern Lang Asn; Am Lit Asn; Asn for Documentary Editing; Cambridge Bibliographic Soc; Soc of Early Americanists; Am Stud Asn; Nathaniel Hawthorne Soc; Melville Soc; Thoreau Soc; SHARP. **RESEARCH** American literature, focus on 17th century Puritans. **SELECTED PUBLICATIONS** Auth, Epistolary Counseling in the Puritan Movement: The Examples of John Cotton, Puritanism: Transatlantic Perspectives on a Seventeenth Century Anglo-American Faith, Mass Hist Soc, 127-147, 93; auth, After Coming Over: John Cotton, Peter Bulkeley, and Learned Discourse in the Wilderness, Stud in the Lit Imagination, 27, 7-21, 94; auth, The Correspondence of John Cotton, Univ NC Press, 99. **CONTACT ADDRESS** Dept English, Univ Wisc, 600 N Park St, Madison, WI, 53706. **EMAIL** sbush@facstaff.wisc.edu

BUSHNELL, JACK
DISCIPLINE ENGLISH LITERATURE **EDUCATION** Univ Colo, BA; Rutgers Univ, MA; PhD. **CAREER** Fac. **RESEARCH** British romanticism; 19th century British literature and culture. **SELECTED PUBLICATIONS** Auth, Circus of the Wolves, William Morrow; Sky Dancer, William Morrow; articles on Romantic and Victorian literature. **CONTACT ADDRESS** Dept of English, Univ of Wisconsin, Eau Claire, Hibbard Hall 431, PO Box 4004, Eau Claire, WI, 54702-4004. **EMAIL** bushnejp@uwec.edu

BUTLER, GERALD JOSEPH
PERSONAL Born 02/24/1942, San Francisco, CA, m, 1964, 3 children **DISCIPLINE** ENGLISH LITERATURE **EDUCATION** Univ Calif, Berkeley, AB, 63; Univ Wash, MA, 65, Ph-D(English), 68. **CAREER** ASSOC PROF ENGLISH, SAN DIEGO STATE UNIV, 68-, Ed, Recovering Lit, 72-. **RESEARCH** Sex in literature; 19th century fiction; 20th century fiction. **SELECTED PUBLICATIONS** Auth, Recovering fiction, spring 72 & Arrows of desire, fall & winter, 74, Recovering Lit; Making Fielding Novels Speak for Law-and-Order + Reply to Richter,David,Henry/, Eighteenth Century-Theory and Interpretation, Vol 37, 1996. **CONTACT ADDRESS** PO Box 805, Alpine, CA, 92001.

BUTLER, J.
DISCIPLINE ENGLISH **EDUCATION** Yale Univ, BA, 78, MA, 82, M Phil, 82, PhD, 84; Heidelberg Univ, Cert Study, 78-79 **CAREER** Actg instr, 81 & 86, Yale Col; Prize tchg fel, 82-83, Yale Univ; vis instr & asst prof of Letters, 83-85, Andrew W Mellon Postdr fel, 85-86, Wesleyan Univ; asst prof philos, 86-89, George Wash Univ; assoc prof, Hum, 89-91, prof Hum, 91-94, Johns Hopkins Univ; prof of Rhet, 93-94, prof of rhetoric & compartive literature, 94-, chancellors prof, Univ Calif Berkeley. **HONORS AND AWARDS** Fac, Nat Endowment for Hum, 94 & 97; Donald M Kramer vis scholar Hum Brooklyn Col, 94; invited fac, Dartmouth School Criticism & Theory, 95; Hum res fel Univ Calif Berkeley, 96; invited fac C Europ Univ, 98; invited fac Univ Munich, 98; Guggenheim fel, 99. **MEMBERSHIPS** Amer Philos Asn; Mod Lang Asn; Engish Inst; Soc Critical Exchange; Int Gay & Lesbian Hum Rights Comn; Hum Res Inst. **RESEARCH** Feminist theory and sexuality studies; 19th and 20th Century continental philosophy; Philosophy and literature; Social and political thought. **SELECTED PUBLICATIONS** Auth, Bodies that Matter: On the Discursive Limits of Sex, Routledge, 93; Excitable Speech: A Politics of the Performative, Routledge, 97; The Psychic Life of Power: Theories in Subjection, Stanford Univ Press, 97; ed, Der Streit um Differenz: Feminismus und Postmoderne in der Gegenwart, Fischer Verlag, 93; auth, Feminist Contentions: A Philosophical Exchange, Routledge, 94; Diacritics, Critical Crossings, 94; Atopia, Stanford Univ Press; auth, Merely Cultural, Social Text, 97; Vocabularies of the Censor, Censorship and Silencing, Oxford Univ Press, 98; Sovereign Performatives in the Contemporary Scene of Utterance, Critical Inquiry, 97. **CONTACT ADDRESS** Dept of Rhetoric, Univ Calif Berkeley, 7408 Dwinelle Hall, Berkeley, CA, 94720-2670.

BUTLER, JAMES ALBERT
PERSONAL Born 05/18/1945, Pittsburgh, PA, m, 1967, 3 children **DISCIPLINE** ENGLISH & AMERICAN LITERATURE **EDUCATION** LaSalle Univ, BA, 67; Cornell Univ, MA, 70, PhD, 71. **CAREER** From asst prof to assoc prof, 71-78, prof English, LaSalle Univ, 78, from asst chmn to chmn dept English, 78-96; assoc ed, Four Quarters, 72-77 & 77-78; asst ed, The Cornell Wordsworth Series, 79-; assoc trustee, Wordsworth's Dove Cottage, 80-. **HONORS AND AWARDS** Amer Coun Learned Soc fel, 76-77; Lindback Award, Distinguished Teaching, 80; NEH Fel, 83-84. **MEMBERSHIPS** MLA; AAUP. **RESEARCH** Wordsworth; English Romantic period; contemporary poetry. **SELECTED PUBLICATIONS** Ed, The Ruined Cottage and The Pedlar, by William Wordsworth, in The Cornell Wordsworth Series, Cornell Univ, 78; Lyrical Ballads, by William Wordsworth, in The Cornell Wordsworth Series, Cornell Univ, 92; auth, The Duty to Withhold the Facts: Family and Scholars on Wordsworth's French Daughter, in Princeton Univ Libr Chronicle, Winter 96; Tourist or Native Son: Wordsworth's Homecomings of 1799-1800, in Nineteenth Century Lit, 6/96; writer and producer, Charles Willson Peale at Belfield, film, 96; auth, Stepping Stones to the Future, in Charles Lamb Bull, 1/97; William and Dorothy Wordsworth, "Emma", and a German Translation in the Alfoxden Notebook, in Studies in Romanticism, Summer 97; Travel Writing, in A Companion to Romanticism, Blackwell's, 97; The Cornell Wordsworth Series, Wordsworth Circle, Summer 97. **CONTACT ADDRESS** Dept of English, La Salle Univ, 1900 W Olney Ave, Philadelphia, PA, 19141-1199. **EMAIL** butler@lasalle.edu

BUTLER-EVANS, ELIOT
DISCIPLINE AFRICAN-AMERICAN LITERATURE **EDUCATION** Univ Calif, Santa Cruz, PhD, 87. **CAREER** ASSOC PROF, ENG, UNIV CALIF, SANTA BARBARA. **RESEARCH** Marxist cult theory, narr theory and soc semiotics, gender and sexuality. **SELECTED PUBLICATIONS** Auth, Race, Gender, and Desire: Narrative Strategies in the Fiction of Toni Cade Bambara, Toni Morrison, and Alice Walker, Temple

Univ Press, 89. **CONTACT ADDRESS** Dept of Eng, Univ Calif, Santa Barbara, CA, 93106-7150. **EMAIL** ebevans@humanitas.ucsb.edu

BUTTE, GEORGE
PERSONAL Born 05/29/1947, Tulsa, OK, m, 1993, 2 children **DISCIPLINE** ENGLISH LITERATURE **EDUCATION** Univ Ariz, BA, 67; Oxford Univ, BPhil, 70; Johns Hopkins Univ, PhD(English lit), 73. **CAREER** From instr to prof English, Bishop Col, 70-74; prof English, Colo Col, 74-. **MEMBERSHIPS** MLA. **RESEARCH** Nineteenth century British literature; film studies. **SELECTED PUBLICATIONS** Auth, numerous articles in SEL, Victorian Studies, Comparative Lit, The Hitchcock Annual, Studies in English Lit, and the Oxford Trollope Companion. **CONTACT ADDRESS** Dept of English, Colorado Col, 14 E Cache La Poudre, Colorado Springs, CO, 80903-3294.

BUTTERFIELD, BRUCE A.
DISCIPLINE ENGLISH **EDUCATION** Knox Col, BA; Univ IL, MA; PhD, 74. **CAREER** Fac, Plattsburgh State Univ of NY. **HONORS AND AWARDS** Chancellor's Awd Excellence Tchg, 90. **RESEARCH** 20th century Brit, Am and Canadian fiction. **SELECTED PUBLICATIONS** Auth, publs about Canadian fiction; ed, Plattsburgh Studies in Humanities series. **CONTACT ADDRESS** SUNY, Plattsburgh, 101 Broad St, Plattsburgh, NY, 12901-2681.

BUTTERS, RONALD R.
PERSONAL Born 02/12/1940, Cedar Rapids, IA, d, 3 children **DISCIPLINE** ENGLISH **EDUCATION** Univ Iowa, BA, 62; Univ Iowa, PhD, 67. **CAREER** Asst prof, Duke Univ, 67-74; assoc prof, Duke Univ, 74-89; prof, Duke Univ, 89-. **MEMBERSHIPS** Amer Dialect Soc; Dictionary Soc of NC; Int Asn Forensic Linguists; Law and Soc Asn; Ling Soc of Amer. **RESEARCH** Structure of mod English and present-day usage; sociolinguistics; lexicography; lang and law. **SELECTED PUBLICATIONS** Auth, Dialectology and Sociolinguistic Theory, 96; What Did Cary Grant Know About Going Gay' and When Did He Know it?: On the Development of the Popular Term gay Homosexual', 98; What Is About to Take Place Is a Murder: Construing the Racist Subtext in a Small-Town Virginia Courtroom; Grammar; Auntie(-man)/tanti in the Caribbean and North America, 97; The Divergence Controversy Revisited, 96; Historical and Contemporary Distribution of Double Modals in English, 96; Two Notes: the Origin of jaywalking, 95; Free Speech and Academic Freedom, 95; If the Wages of Sin Are for Death: The Semantics and Pragmatics of a Statutory Ambiguity, 93. **CONTACT ADDRESS** PO Box 90018, Durham, NC, 27708. **EMAIL** RonButters@aol.com

BUTTIGIEG, JOSEPH A.
DISCIPLINE MODERN BRITISH LITERATURE, LITERARY THEORY **EDUCATION** SUNY, Binghamton, PhD. **CAREER** Instr, Univ Notre Dame. **RESEARCH** The relationship between culture and politics; Antonio Gramsci. **SELECTED PUBLICATIONS** Auth, A Portrait of the Artist in Different Perspective; Antonio Gramsci's Triad: Culture, Politics, Intellectuals; ed, Criticism Without Boundaries. **CONTACT ADDRESS** Univ Notre Dame, Notre Dame, IN, 46556.

BUZZARD, KAREN S.
DISCIPLINE COMMUNICATION (INTERPERSONAL, GENDER, & MEDIA) **EDUCATION** Drury Col, BA, 71; Univ of Iowa, MA, 73; Univ of Wis, PhD, 85. **CAREER** ASSOC PROF, NORTHEASTERN UNIV, 85-. **HONORS AND AWARDS** Stephen H. Coltrin Award for Commun Excellence. **MEMBERSHIPS** Nat Commun Asn. **RESEARCH** Communication & gender; intimacy & communication; aging & communicating; communication & broadcast rating. **SELECTED PUBLICATIONS** Auth, Chains of Gold: Marketing the Ratings & Rating the Markets, 90; auth, Electronic Media Ratings: Turning Audiences into Dollars & Sense, 92; auth, Holding Pattern: When Intimacy Alludes Us in Adulthood; Foundations of Intimate Communication (book proposal). **CONTACT ADDRESS** 81 Golden Ave., Medford, MA, 02155. **EMAIL** kbuzzard@lynx.dac.neu.edu

BYARS, JACKIE L.
PERSONAL Born 01/05/1951, Harlingen, TX, m, 1983 **DISCIPLINE** FILM & TELEVISION STUDIES, AMERICAN CULTURE, WOMEN'S STUDIES **EDUCATION** Univ Tx at Austin, BA, 74, MA, 76, PhD, 83; Univ Calif School of Criticism & Theory, summer, 77; Inter-Univ Center for Film & Critical Studies, 80-81. **CAREER** Vis asst prof, 83-84, asst prof, Dept of Commun Arts, Univ Wis-Madison, 85-90; Andrew W. Mellon postdoctoral fel & lectr, Dept of the Hist of Art, Bryn Mawr Col, 84-85; asst prof, Dept of Radio-Television-Film, Tx Christian Univ, 90-91; vis asst prof, Dept of Commun, St. Mary's Col of Calif, 91-92; dir, women's studies prog, 94-97, CO-DIR, FILM STUDIES PROG, 95-, ASST PROF, DEPT OF COMMUN, WAYNE STATE UNIV, 92-. **MEMBERSHIPS** Soc for Cinema Studies; Union for Democratic Commun; Nat Commun Asn; Int Asn for Mass Commun Res. **RESEARCH** The representation of difference in mediated texts; the relation between corporate practices and screen representations; media fandom. **SELECTED PUBLICATIONS** Auth, All That Hollywood Allows: Re-reading Gender in 1950s Melodrama, Univ of NC Press & Routledge, 91; The Prime of Ms. Kim Novak: Struggling Over the Feminine in the Star Image, The Other 50s: Interrogating Midcentury Am Icons, Univ of Ill Press, 97; Feminism, Psychoanalysis, and Female-Oriented Melodramas of the 1950s, Multiple Voices in Feminist Film Theory and Criticism, Univ of Minn Press, 93; Gazes/Voices/Power: Expanding Psychoanalysis for Feminist Film and Television Theory, Female Spectators: Looking at Film and Television, Verso, 88; Reading Feminine Discourse: Prime-Time Television in the U.S., Commun, 87; coauth, Telefeminism: The Lifetime Cable Channel, Critical Studies in Mass Commun, forthcoming; Once in a Lifetime: Narrowcasting to Women, Camera Obscura, May-Sept-Jan, 94-95; Reading Difference: The Characters at Frank's Place, Women Making Meaning: The New Feminist Scholar in Commun, Routledge, 92. **CONTACT ADDRESS** Dept of Commun, Wayne State Univ, 585 Manoogian Hall, Detroit, MI, 48202.

BYERS, LORI
DISCIPLINE ORGANIZATIONAL COMMUNICATION **EDUCATION** PhD. **CAREER** Spalding Univ **SELECTED PUBLICATIONS** Auth chapter: Pearson and Nelson's text Understanding and Sharing: An Introduction to Speech Communication. **CONTACT ADDRESS** Spalding Univ, 851 S. Fourth St., Louisville, KY, 40203-2188.

BZDYL, DONALD
DISCIPLINE ENGLISH LITERATURE **EDUCATION** Univ Ill, PhD, 77. **CAREER** Dept Eng, Clemson Univ **RESEARCH** Medieval studies, historical linguistics, and business communication. **SELECTED PUBLICATIONS** Auth, Juliana: Cynewulf's Dispellar of Delusio, Cyenwulf: Basic Readings, Garland, 96. **CONTACT ADDRESS** Clemson Univ, 609 Strode, Clemson, SC, 29634. **EMAIL** bzdy609@clemson.edu

C

CABEZUT-ORTIZ, DELORES J.
PERSONAL Born 12/16/1948, Merced, CA, m, 1978, 2 children **DISCIPLINE** ENGLISH **EDUCATION** Merced Community Col, AA, 67; CA State Univ, Stanislaus, BA, 70, MA, 75. **CAREER** INSTR, MERCED COL, 76-, WRITING LAB COORDINATOR, 85-, HUMANITIES DIV CHAIR, 97-. **HONORS AND AWARDS** Outstanding Alumni at Merced Col., Weaver Elementary Board of Education, 86-. **MEMBERSHIPS** NEA; CTA; Merced County Arts Coun; Merced County Hist Soc. **RESEARCH** Local hist, specifically Hornitos and Indian Gulch, CA. **SELECTED PUBLICATIONS** Auth, Merced County: A Golden Harvest; Robert LeRoy Cooper: An Early Day Cattle Buyer; Merced Falls: An Early Industrial City. **CONTACT ADDRESS** 2465 McNamara Rd., Merced, CA, 95340. **EMAIL** dcortiz@elite.net

CAI, DEBORAH A.
PERSONAL Born 07/31/1961, MI, m, 1986, 3 children **DISCIPLINE** COMMUNICATION **EDUCATION** Trinity Evangelical Divimity School, MA, 91; MI State Univ, PhD, 94. **CAREER** Vis prof, MI State Univ, East Lansing, 94-95; asst prof, Univ MD, College Park, 95-. **MEMBERSHIPS** Nat Commun Asn; Int Commun Asn; Am Asn of Chinese Studies. **RESEARCH** Intercultural commun; persuasian; negotiation & conflict management. **SELECTED PUBLICATIONS** Ed, with W Donahue, Communicating and Connecting: The Functions of Human Communication, Harcourt Brace College Pubs, 96; co-auth, with E L Fink, Social Influence, in W Donohue and D A Cai, eds, Communicating and Connecting: The Functions of Human Communication, Harcourt Brace College Pubs, 96; co-auth with M I Bresnahan, Gender and Aggression in the Recognition of Interruption, Discourse Processes, 21 (2), 96; co-auth with A Williams, H Ota, H Giles, H D Pierson, C Gallois, SA-H Ng, T-S Lim, E B Ryan, L Somera, J Maher, J Harwood, Young People's Beliefs About Intergenerational Communication: An Initial Cross-Cultural Comparison, Communication Res, 24, 97; co-auth with J I Rodriguez, Adjusting to Cultural Differences: The Intercultural Adaptation Model, Intercultural Communication Studies, VI (2), 97; with W A Donahue, Determinants of Facework in Intercultural Negotiation, Asian J of Commun, 7 (1), 97; auth, Difficulties of Doing Survey Research Across Cultures, in J Martin, T Nakayama, & L Flores, eds, Readings in Cultural Contexts, Mayfield, 97; co-auth with H Giles & K Noels, Intergenerational Communication in the People's Republic of China; Perceptions of Older and Younger Adults and Their Link to Mental Health, J of Applied Commun Res, 26 (1), 98; co-auth with M S Kim and H C Shin, Cultural Influences on the Preferred Forms of Requesting and Re-Requesting, Communication Monographs, 98; co-auth with L Drake, Intercultural Business Negotiation: A Communication Perspective, in M E Roloff, ed, Communication Yearbook 21, 98; author and co-author of numerous other articles and publications including one in press. **CONTACT ADDRESS** Dept of Commun, Univ of Maryland, Col Park, 2110 Skinner Bldg, College Park, MD, 20742. **EMAIL** debcai@wam.umd.edu

CAILLER, BERNADETTE ANNE
PERSONAL Born 06/08/1941, Poitiers, France, w **DISCIPLINE** AFRICAN & CARIBBEAN LITERATURE **EDUCATION** Univ Poitiers, Lic es Lett, 61, Dipl d Etudes Superieures, 64; Univ Paris, Capes, 68; Cornell Univ, MA, 67, PhD(comp lit), 74. **CAREER** Asst prof, 74-79, Assoc Prof French, Univ Fla, 79- **MEMBERSHIPS** African Lit Assn; Conseil Int d'Etudes Francophones; African Stu Assn; Int Comp Lit Assn. **RESEARCH** Edouard Glissant; Negritude and post Negritude in relation to Emmanuel Levinas' philosophy; literature in a civil war context. **SELECTED PUBLICATIONS** Auth, Proposition poetique, Ine lecture de l'oeuvre d'Aime Cesaire, Naaman, 76, 2nd ed, Nouvelles du Sud, 94; authConquerants de la nuit nue: Edouard Glissant et l'H(h)istorie antillaise, Etudes Litteriares Francaises, vol 45, Gunter Narr Verlag, 88; co-ed, Toward Defining the African Aesthetic, Three Continents Press, 82; auth, If the Dead could only speak! Reflections on Texts by Niger, Hughes, an dFodeba, The Surreptious Speech: Presence Africaine and the Politics of Otherness, 1947-1987, Univ Chicago, 92; auth, Creolization versus Francophonie. Language, Identity and Culture in the Works of Edouard Glissant, L'Heritage de Caliban, 92; auth, The Impossible Ecstasy: an Analysis of Valentin Y. Mudimbe's Dechirures, Research in African Literatures, 93; auth, Hiterlerisme et enterprise coloniale 2: le cas Damas, French Cultural Studies, 94; auth, Si Marie-Madeleine se racontait:analyse d'une figure de Feux, Roman, Historie et Mythe dans l'oeuvre de Narguerite Yourcenar, SIEY, 95; auth, La transgression creatrice d'Andree Chedid: Nefertiti ou le reve d'Akhnaton, Les memoires d'un scribe, Litteratures autobiographiques de la Francophonie, C.E.L.F.A., 96; auth, Interface between Fiction and Autobiography: From Shaba 2 to Les Corps glorieux, Canad Jour of African Stu, Vol 30, No 3, 96. **CONTACT ADDRESS** Dept of Romance Lang and Lit, Univ Fla, PO Box 117405, Gainesville, FL, 32611-7405. **EMAIL** cailler@rll.ufl.edu

CALARCO, N. JOSEPH
PERSONAL Born 03/19/1938, New York, NY, m, 1964, 2 children **DISCIPLINE** DRAMA **EDUCATION** Columbia Univ, AB, 59, MA, 62; Univ Minn, PhD(theatre), 66. **CAREER** Asst prof dramatic art, Univ Calif, Berkeley, 66-68; asst prof, 68-71, assoc prof, 71-78, prof theater, Wayne State Univ, 78- ; Mem bd dir fine arts sect, Mich Acad Sci Arts & Letters, 70-73; judge, Prof Actg Auditions, Theatre Commun Group, 74-75; chmn, Am Bicentennial Playwriting Competition, 74-76. **MEMBERSHIPS** Am Theatre Asn; Am Asn Univ Prof; Nat Acad TV Arts & Sci; Soc Stage Dir & Choreographers. **RESEARCH** Directing; actor training; dramatic theory. **SELECTED PUBLICATIONS** Auth, Vision without compromise: Genet's The Screens, Drama Surv, spring 65; Tragedy as demonstration, Educ Theatre J, 10/66; Tragic Being: Apollo and Dionysus in Western Drama, Univ Minn, 68; contribr, Humanities and the Theatre, Am Theatre Asn, 73; auth, Production as criticism: Miller's The Crucible, Educ Theatre J, 10/77. **CONTACT ADDRESS** Univ Theatre, Wayne State Univ, 3225 Old Main St, Detroit, MI, 48202-1303. **EMAIL** joecalarco@aol.com

CALDER, ROBERT L.
PERSONAL Born 04/03/1941, Moose Jaw, SK, Canada **DISCIPLINE** ENGLISH **EDUCATION** Univ Sask, BA, 64, MA, 65; Univ Leeds, PhD, 70. **CAREER** Instr to assoc prof, 65-81, dept head, 79-81, PROF ENGLISH, UNIV SASKATCHEWAN, 81-, assoc dean fine arts & hum, 81-84. **HONORS AND AWARDS** Gov Gen Lit Award Non-fiction, 89. **SELECTED PUBLICATIONS** Auth, W. Somerset Maugham and the Quest for Freedom, 72; auth, Willie: The Life of W. Somerset Maugham, 89; coauth, Rider Pride: The Story of Canada's Best Loved Football Team, 85; co-ed, Time as a Human Resource, 91. **CONTACT ADDRESS** Dept of English, Univ of Saskatchewan, 9 Campus Dr, Saskatoon, SK, S7N 5A5.

CALDWELL, MARK
DISCIPLINE RENAISSANCE LITERATURE **EDUCATION** Harvard, PhD. **CAREER** Prof, Fordham Univ. **RESEARCH** Lit of AIDS, sci and lit. **SELECTED PUBLICATIONS** Auth, The Last Crusade: The War on Consumption, 1862-1954, Atheneum Press, 88; The Prose of Fulke Greville, Garland Press, 87. **CONTACT ADDRESS** Dept of Eng Lang and Lit, Fordham Univ, 113 W 60th St, New York, NY, 10023.

CALDWELL, MARK LEONARD
PERSONAL Born 03/14/1946, Troy, NY **DISCIPLINE** ENGLISH LITERATURE **EDUCATION** Fordham Univ, BA, 67; Cambridge Univ, BA, 69; Harvard Univ, PhD(English), 73. **CAREER** Prof English, Fordham Univ, 89. **MEMBERSHIPS** Authors Guild **RESEARCH** Literature of the English Renaissance, 1500-1660; science & literature, cultural studies. **SELECTED PUBLICATIONS** Auth, Sources and analogues of the Life of Sidney, Studies Philol, 7/77; Allegory: The Renaissance mode, ELH, winter 77; The Last Crusade: America's War on Consumption, 1862-1954, NY, Atheneum, 88; The Prose of Fulke Greville, Lord Brooke, NY, Garland, 87; A Short History of Rudeness, NY, Picador/St Martin's Press, 99, forthcoming. **CONTACT ADDRESS** Dept of English, Fordham Univ, 501 E Fordham Rd, Bronx, NY, 10458-5191.

CALENDRILLO, LINDA T.
DISCIPLINE ENGLISH COMPOSITION AND LANGUAGE EDUCATION St John's Univ, BA, 73; Purdue Univ, MA, 75, PhD, 88. CAREER Eng Dept, Eastern Ill Univ HONORS AND AWARDS Granted Fac Mini-Grant; EIU 93-94 Awarded Booth Library Fel, EIU, 94; EIU Fac Develop Mini-Grant, 94; EIU Col Arts & Hum Travel Grant NCTE, 95; EIU Fac Excellence Award Tchng, 95; EIU Disability Services Outstanding Assistance Recognition, 96; EIU Fac Achievement Award Tchng, Service, & Publ, 96. SELECTED PUBLICATIONS Coauth, Atomistic Versus Holistic Evaluation of Student Essays, Notes from the National Testing Network in Writing, 91; Margaret Atwood, Beacham Publ, 92; Playing with Character, Plot, Scene: Strategies To Help Students Write More Creative Fiction, Ill Eng Bull, 92; Rethinking the Externalization of the Arts of Memory, Jour Evolutionary Psychol, 92; Xeroxing, Memory Loss, and Research Papers: What Can Teachers Do to Encourage the Use of Memory and Why Should They Bother?, Ill Eng Bull, 94; Review Essay of Frederick Reynolds' Rhetorical Memory and Delivery, Rhetoric Rev, 94; Memory, Encyclopedia of Rhetoric, Garland, 95; Mental Imagery, Psychology, and Rhetoric: An Examination of Recurring Problems, JAEPL, 95-96; Review Essay of Roy Fox's Language, Media, and Mind, JAEPL, 95-96. CONTACT ADDRESS Eastern Illinois Univ, 600 Lincoln Ave, Charleston, IL, 61920-3099. EMAIL cfltc@eiu.edu

CALHOUN, RICHARD JAMES
PERSONAL Born 09/05/1926, Jackson, TN, m, 1954, 3 children DISCIPLINE ENGLISH EDUCATION George Peabody Col, BA, 48; Johns Hopkins Univ, MA, 50; Univ NC, PhD, 59. CAREER Jr instr, Johns Hopkins Univ, 48-50; instr English, Jacksonville State Col, 50-51; asst, Univ NC, 53-57; asst prof, Davidson Col, 58-61; from asst prof to prof, 61-69, ALUMNI PROF, CLEMSON UNIV, 69-, Duke Univ-Univ NC Coop Prog Humanities fel, 64-65; co-ed periodical, SC Rev, 73- HONORS AND AWARDS Fulbright-Hays lectr, Univ Ljubljana & Univ Sarajevo, 69-70; sr Fulbright lectr, Aarhus Univ & Odense Univ, Denmark, 75-76. MEMBERSHIPS MLA; SAtlantic Mod Lang Asn; Soc Study Southern Lit. RESEARCH Contemporary poetry; southern American literature; American literature. SELECTED PUBLICATIONS Auth, Simms--A Literary-Life, Resources For Amer Lit Stud, Vol 0022, 96. CONTACT ADDRESS Dept of English, Clemson Univ, Clemson, SC, 29631.

CALHOUN, THOMAS O.
PERSONAL Born 03/01/1940, Pittsburgh, PA, m, 1 child DISCIPLINE ENGLISH EDUCATION Princeton Univ, AB, 62; Univ Pittsburgh, MA, 63; Univ Mich, PhD(English), 67. CAREER Instr English & classical lit, Univ Mich, 63-67; ASST PROF ENGLISH & COMP LIT, UNIV DEL, 67-, Univ Mich fel, 67. MEMBERSHIPS MLA; Renaissance Soc Am; Milton Soc. RESEARCH Literature of the English Renaissance, 16th and 17th centuries; comparative literature; Petrarch. SELECTED PUBLICATIONS Auth, Paper and Printing in Jonson,Ben 'Sejanus', Papers Bibliog Soc Am, Vol 0087, 93; The 17th-Century--The Intellectual and Cultural-Context of English Literature, 1603-1700, Eng Lang Notes, Vol 0030, 93; The 1st and 2nd Dalhousie Manuscripts--Poems and Prose by Donne, John and Others--A Facsimile Edition, Eng Lang Notes, Vol 0030, 92. CONTACT ADDRESS Dept of English, Univ Del, Newark, DE, 19711.

CALLAHAN, JOHN FRANCIS
PERSONAL Born 12/31/1940, Meriden, CT, m, 1970, 1 child DISCIPLINE AMERICAN LITERATURE EDUCATION Univ Conn, BA, 63; Univ Ill, MA, 64, PhD(Am lit), 70. CAREER From instr to asst prof, 67-73, assoc prof, 73-80, PROF ENGLISH, LEWIS & CLARK COL, 80-, Nat Endowment for Humanities younger humanist fel, 73-74. MEMBERSHIPS MLA; Am Lit Group, MLA; Northwest Am Studies Asn. RESEARCH The American novel; Black literature and history; 20th century Irish literature and history. SELECTED PUBLICATIONS Auth, Mckay,Claude, A Black Poets Struggle for Identity, Contemp Lit, Vol 0034, 93; Frequencies of Memory--A Eulogy for Ellison, Ralph, Waldo March 1, 1914 April 16, 94, Callaloo, Vol 0018, 95; Stealing The Fire--The Art and Protest of Baldwin, James, Contemp Lit, Vol 0034, 93; Fitzgerald, F.Scott Evolving American-Dream--The Pursuit of Happiness in Gatsby, Tender Is The Night, And The Last Tycoon, Twentieth Century Lit, Vol 0042, 96. CONTACT ADDRESS Dept of English, Lewis & Clark Col, 0615 SW Palatine Hill Rd, Portland, OR, 97219-7879.

CAMARGO, MARTIN
DISCIPLINE MEDIEVAL ENGLISH LITERATURE, HISTORY OF ENGLISH, AND HISTORY OF RHETORIC EDUCATION Univ Ill, PhD, 78. CAREER Prof. HONORS AND AWARDS ACLS; Fulbright & Humboldt Found fel; Gold Chalk awd, 93. SELECTED PUBLICATIONS Auth, Middle English Verse Love Epistle, Niemeyer, 91 & Medieval Rhetorics of Prose Composition, Medieval& Renaissance Texts & Stud, 95. CONTACT ADDRESS Dept of English, Univ of Missouri-Columbia, 309 University Hall, Columbia, MO, 65211.

CAMERON, ELSPETH M.
PERSONAL Born 01/10/1943, Toronto, ON, Canada DISCIPLINE ENGLISH LITERATURE EDUCATION Univ BC, BA, 64; Univ NB, MA, 65; McGill Univ, PhD, 70. CAREER Prof, Eng, Concordia Univ, 70-77; coordr, Can Lit Lang, New Col, 80-90, PROF ENGLISH, UNIV TORONTO, 90-. MEMBERSHIPS Asn Can Stud; ACQL. SELECTED PUBLICATIONS Auth, Robertson Davies, 71; auth, Hugh MacLennan: A Writer's Life 81; ed, The Other Side of Hugh MacLennan: Selected Essays Old and New, 78; ed, Hugh MacLennan: 1982, 82; ed, Irving Layton: A Portrait, 85; ed, Robertson Davies: An Appreciation 91; ed, Earle Birney: A Life 94. CONTACT ADDRESS Dept of English, Univ Toronto, Univ Col, Toronto, ON, M5S 1A1. EMAIL cameron@chass.utoronto.ca

CAMERON, JOHN
PERSONAL Born 06/24/1930, Chicago, IL, d, 2 children DISCIPLINE ENGLISH EDUCATION Yale Univ, BA, 52, MA, 57, PhD, 63; Edinburgh Univ, dipl, 55. CAREER From instr to assoc prof, 58-70, prof English, Amherst Col, 70-. HONORS AND AWARDS MA, Amherst Col, 70. MEMBERSHIPS MLA; AAUP. RESEARCH Novel; film history and theory. CONTACT ADDRESS Dept of English, Amherst Col, Amherst, MA, 01002-5003. EMAIL jacameron@amherst.edu

CAMERON, SHARON
PERSONAL Born 02/15/1947, Cleveland, OH DISCIPLINE ENGLISH & AMERICAN LITERATURE EDUCATION Bennington Col, BA, 68; Brandeis Univ, MA, 69, PhD(English & Am lit), 73. CAREER Asst prof English, Boston Univ, 72-76 & Univ Calif, Santa Barbara, 77-78; assoc prof, 78-80, PROF ENGLISH, JOHNS HOPKINS UNIV, 81-, Fels, Nat Endow for Humanities, 79-80, Am Coun Learned Soc, 82 & Guggenheim, 82-83. MEMBERSHIPS MLA. RESEARCH American literature; lyric poetry; literary theory. SELECTED PUBLICATIONS Auth, The sense against calamity: Ideas of a self in three poems by Wallace Stevens, ELH, winter 76; A loaded gun: Dickinson and the dialectic of rage, PMLA, 5/78; Naming as history: Dickinson's poems of definition, Critical Inquiry, winter 78; Lyric Time: Dickinson and the Limits of Genre, 79 & The corporeal self: Allegories of our body, In: Melville and Hawthorne, Johns Hopkins Univ, 81; auth, The Way of Life by Abandonment: Emerson's Impersonal, Critical Inquiry, Fall 98; auth, Thinking of Henry James, Chicago, 89; auth, Choosing Not Choosing: Dickinson's Fascicles, Chicago, 92. CONTACT ADDRESS Dept of English, Johns Hopkins Univ, 3400 N Charles St, Baltimore, MD, 21218-2680.

CAMERON MUNRO, RUTH A.
DISCIPLINE ENGLISH LITERATURE EDUCATION Eastern Nazarene Col, BA; Boston Univ, MA, PhD. CAREER Eng Dept, Eastern Nazarene Col RESEARCH Gerard Manley Hopkins. SELECTED PUBLICATIONS Auth, Meditations on Advent, 91. CONTACT ADDRESS Eastern Nazarene Col, 23 East Elm Ave, Quincy, MA, 02170-2999.

CAMFIELD, GREGG
DISCIPLINE ENGLISH LITERATURE EDUCATION Brown Univ, MA, 80; Univ CA, 89. CAREER Asst prof, Univ Pacific. RESEARCH Am lit up to 1910; intellectual hist; lit humor; life and works of Mark Twain. SELECTED PUBLICATIONS Auth, Sentimental Twain: Samuel Clemens in the Maze of Moral Philosophy, 94. CONTACT ADDRESS Eng Dept, Univ Pacific, Pacific Ave, PO Box 3601, Stockton, CA, 95211.

CAMINALS-HEATH, ROSER
PERSONAL Born 06/30/1956, Barcelona, Spain, m, 1981 DISCIPLINE ENGLISH LITERATURE EDUCATION Univ Barcelona, Spain, PhD, 86. CAREER PROF OF SPANISH & CHR DEPT FOREIGN LANGUAGES, HOOD COL; Hodson fel. HONORS AND AWARDS 1st Prize Prose at Jocs Florals de la Diaspora, 98. MEMBERSHIPS Am Assoc Tchr Span & Port; Am Lit Transl Asn; Assoc Writers Prog. RESEARCH Creative writing; Literary translation; XIXth and XXth Century Spanish fiction. SELECTED PUBLICATIONS transl The House of Ulloa: An English translation of the novel Los Pazos de Ulloa, Univ Ga Press, 92; Once Remembered, Twice Lived, Peter Lang, 93; Un Segle de Prodigis, Columna Ed, Barcelona, 95; Les Herbes Secretes, Pages Ed, Lleida, 98. CONTACT ADDRESS Roser Caminals-Heath, 507 Elm St, Frederick, MD, 21701. EMAIL rheath@exiali.hood.edu

CAMINERO-SANTANGELO, BYRON
PERSONAL Born 06/24/1961, New York, NY, m, 1991 DISCIPLINE ENGLISH EDUCATION Claremont McKenna Col, BA, 84; Univ of Calif at Irvine, MA, 87, PhD, 93. CAREER Lectr, Irvine Valley Col, 93-94; lectr, Calif State Univ, 94-95; tchg asst/assoc, 85-92, lectr, Univ of Calif at Irvine, 94-95; asst prof, DePaul Univ, 95-97; ASST PROF, UNIV OF KANS, 97-. HONORS AND AWARDS General Res Funded New Fac Awd, Univ of Kans; Fac Development Seminar Grant, DePaul Univ; Fac Career Development Awd, Postdoctoral Tchg Awd, Univ of Calif at Irvine; Dissertation Fel, Univ of Calif at Irvine Dept of English Humanities. RESEARCH 20th-Century British Lit; African fiction; postcolonial fiction and the-

ory; critical theory. SELECTED PUBLICATIONS Auth, Neo-colonialsim and the Betrayal Plot in A Grain of Wheat: Ngugi wa Thiong'o's Re-Vision of Under Western Eyes, Res in African Lit, 98; Story-teller in the Body of a Seaman: Joseph Conrad and the Rise of the Professions, Conradiana, 97; Testing for Truth: Joseph Conrad and the Ideology of the Examination, cLIO, 94; A Moral Dilemma: Ethics in Tess of the D'Urbervilles, English Studies, 94; The Pump-House Gang, An Encycl of Am Lit of the Sea and the Great Lakes, forthcoming. CONTACT ADDRESS 805 Missouri St, Lawrence, KS, 66044. EMAIL bsantang@eagle.cc.ukans.edu

CAMINERO-SANTANGELO, MARTA
PERSONAL Born 12/19/1966, Quebec, PQ, Canada, m, 1991 DISCIPLINE ENGLISH EDUCATION Yale Univ, BA, 88; Univ Calif, MA, 91, PhD, 95. CAREER Asst prof English, De-Paul Univ, 95-97; ASST PROF ENGLISH, UNIV KANSAS, 97-. HONORS AND AWARDS Univ Kansas Provost's Fac Dev Grant; Ctr for Teach Excell Grant; Hall Ctr Teach Grant., Univ Calif, Irvine Chancellor's Fel; Pres Diss Fel; Dorothy and Donald Strauss Endowed Diss Fel. MEMBERSHIPS MELUS RESEARCH US Latinola lit, African-Am lit; US women's writing and feminist theory. SELECTED PUBLICATIONS Auth, "Multiple Personality and the Postmodern Subject: Theolrizing Agency," in Literature/Interpretation/Theolry, 96; "The Madwoman Can't Speak: Post-War Culture, Feminist Criticism, and Welty's 'June Recital,'" in Tulsa Studies in Women's Literature, 15.1,96; "Beyond Otherness: Negotiated Identities and Viramontes' 'The Cariboo Caf'"in Jour of the Short Story in Eng, 96; "Beyond Otherness: Negotiated Identities and Viramontes' 'The Cariboo Caf' in Women on the Edge: Ethnicity and Gender in Short Stories by Amican Women, 98; The Madwoman Can't Speak: Or Why Insanity Is Not Subversive, 98. CONTACT ADDRESS English Dept, Univ of Kansas, 3114 Wescoe Hall, Lawrence, KS, 66045. EMAIL camsan@eagle.cc.ukans.edu

CAMPBELL, C. JEAN
DISCIPLINE EARLY RENAISSANCE ART AND LITERATURE EDUCATION Johns Hopkins Univ, PhD, 92. CAREER Art, Emory Univ. SELECTED PUBLICATIONS Auth, The Game of Courting and the Art of the Commune of San Gimignano, 98. CONTACT ADDRESS Emory Univ, Atlanta, GA, 30322-1950.

CAMPBELL, ELIZABETH
DISCIPLINE NOVEL EDUCATION Univ Tenn, BA, 67; Univ Va, MA, 78; PhD, 83. CAREER Engl, Oregon St Univ. RESEARCH 19th-century Brit lit; George Eliot; Charles Dickens. SELECTED PUBLICATIONS Auth, Tess of the d'Urbervilles: Misfortune Is a Woman, Victorian Newsl, 89; Relative Truths: Teaching Middlemarch through Character: MLA approaches to Teaching 'Middlemarch', 90; Of Mothers and Merchants: Female Economics in Christina Rossetti's Goblin Market, Victorian Studies, 90; Minding the Wheel: Representations of Women's Time in Victorian Narrative, Rocky Mountain Rev Lang & Lit, 94; Great Expectations: Dickens and the Language of Fortune, Dickens Studies Annual, 95. CONTACT ADDRESS Oregon State Univ, Corvallis, OR, 97331-4501. EMAIL ecampbell@.orst.edu

CAMPBELL, FELICIA F.
DISCIPLINE ENVIRONMENTAL LITERATURE, AMERICAN AND ENGLISH LITERATURE EDUCATION Univ Wis, Madison, BS, 54, MS, 57; USIU, San Diego, PhD, 73. CAREER Tchg asst, Univ Wis, Madison, 55-57, 59-61; instr, Wis State Col, 57-59; instr, 62-67, dir compos, 65-69, 94-97, asst prof, 67-73; co-dir, Environ Stud, 73-74, assoc prof, 73-93, prof, Univ Nev, Las Vegas, 94-; ed, Popular Cult Rev, 91-; adv ed, J of Popular Cult, Bowling Green State Univ, 93-. HONORS AND AWARDS Phi Lambda Alpha, 85; Morris Tchg Award, 92. MEMBERSHIPS Pres, Nat Soc Prof, Univ Nev, Las Vegas, 74-75, 76; ch, Nev Governor's Comn on the Status of People, 75-77; exec dir, Far West Popular Cult Asn and Far West Am Cult Asn, 89-; pres, Popular Cult Asn, 93-95. SELECTED PUBLICATIONS Auth, Silver Screen, Shadow Play: The Tradition of the Wayang Kulit in The Year Of Living Dangerously, J of Popular Cult 28, No 1, 94; Frank Waters and Frank Bergon "Parallel Environmental Concerns", Stud in Frank Waters-X VI, 94; Nothing So Strange: The Atomic Scientist in Hilton and Waters, Stud in Frank Waters - XVII, 95; The Spell of the Sensuous in Frank Waters, Stud in Frank Waters - IX, 96. CONTACT ADDRESS Dept of Eng, Univ Nev, Las Vegas, 4505 Maryland Pky, PO Box 455011, Las Vegas, NV, 89154-5011. EMAIL raksha@nevada.edu

CAMPBELL, HILBERT HAYNES
PERSONAL Born 11/08/1934, Lookout, WV, m, 1959, 2 children DISCIPLINE ENGLISH AND AMERICAN LITERATURE EDUCATION Marshall Univ, BA, 58, MA, 60; Univ Ky, PhD(English), 66. CAREER Instr English, 59-60, 61-63, asst prof, Marshall Univ, 66-67; from asst prof to assoc prof, 67-77, actg dept head, 76-77, PROF ENGLISH, VA POLYTECH INST & STATE UNIV, 77-, ASSOC DEPT HEAD, 77-, Univ Ky Danforth fel, 63-66. MEMBERSHIPS MLA; S Atlantic Mod Lang Asn; Sherwood Anderson Soc; Women's Nat Bk Asn. RESEARCH Eighteenth century literature; twentieth

century American literature. **SELECTED PUBLICATIONS** Auth, The Shadow-People--Sologub, Foedor and Anderson, Sherwood Winesburg, Ohio, Stud in Short Fiction, Vol 0033, 96; Anderson, Sherwood And Wolfe, Thomas, Resources for Amer Lit Stud, Vol 0021, 95. **CONTACT ADDRESS** Dept of English, Va Polytech Inst & State Univ, 100 Virginia Tech, Blacksburg, VA, 24061-0002.

CAMPBELL, JACKSON JUSTICE
PERSONAL Born 01/09/1920, Nowata, OK **DISCIPLINE** ENGLISH **EDUCATION** Yale Univ, AB, 41; Univ Pa, AM, 46; Yale Univ, PhD, 50. **CAREER** Asst instr, Univ Pa, 45-46; from asst instr to instr, Yale Univ, 46-51; asst prof English, Univ Ill, 51-54; from asst prof to assoc prof, 54-64, Annan preceptor, Princeton Univ, 56-57; PROF ENGLISH, UNIV ILL, URBANA, 64- **MEMBERSHIPS** MLA; Mediaeval Acad Am; Early English Text Soc. **RESEARCH** Old English literature and language; Chaucer. **SELECTED PUBLICATIONS** Auth, The English Alliterative Tradition, Manuscripta, Vol 0036, 92. **CONTACT ADDRESS** Dept of English, Univ Ill, Urbana, IL, 61801.

CAMPBELL, JANE
PERSONAL Born 06/04/1934, Parry Sound, ON, Canada, m, 1965 **DISCIPLINE** ENGLISH **EDUCATION** Queen's, BA, 56; Oxford, Mlitt,59; Toronto, PhD, 65. **CAREER** From lectr to asst prof, 61-68, PROF ENGLISH, WILFRID LAURIER UNIV, 69-, Can Coun res grant, 70-71. **HONORS AND AWARDS** WLU Outstanding Tchr Awd, 86. **MEMBERSHIPS** Asn Can Univ Teachers English. **SELECTED PUBLICATIONS** Auth, Confecting Sugar: Narrative Theory and Practice in Antonia Byatt's Short Fiction; Everything: Gendered Transgression of Genre Boundaries in Sarah Ferguson's Autobiographies; Reaching Outwards: Versions of Reality in The Middle Ground; Both a Joke and a Victory: Humor as Narrative Strategy in Margaret Drabble's Fiction; The Hunger of the Imagination in A.S. Byatt's The Game. **CONTACT ADDRESS** Dept of English, Wilfrid Laurier Univ, 75 University Ave W, Waterloo, ON, N2L 3C5.

CAMPBELL, LEE
DISCIPLINE COMPOSITION, PROFESSIONAL WRITING, AND LINGUISTICS **EDUCATION** Ill State Univ, BA, 81, MA, 83; Purdue Univ, PhD, 90. **CAREER** Asst prof Eng, 95-, adv, Eng to speakers of other lang endorsement, 95-, web site mgr, dept Eng, 97-, ed, fac Handbk, Valdosta State Univ, 95-; asst prof Eng, Henderson State Univ, 92-95; Asst prof Eng, Marquette U niv, 90-92. **MEMBERSHIPS** Nat Coun of Tchr of Eng; Conf on Col Compos and Commun; Mod Lang Asn; S Atlantic Mod Lang Asn; Soc for Tech Commun; Southeastern Conf on Ling; Rhet Soc of Am; Phi Kappa Phi. **RESEARCH** Applied linguistic theory; argumentation and rhetorical theory. **SELECTED PUBLICATIONS** Auth, 'It is as if a green bough were laid across the page': Thoreau on Eloquence, in Rhet Soc Quart, 90; An Applied Relevance Theory of the Making and Understanding of Rhetorical Arguments, in Lang and Commun, 92; Argument,in Encycl of Eng Stud and Lang Arts, 95. **CONTACT ADDRESS** Dept of Eng, Valdosta State Univ, 1500 N. Patterson St, Valdosta, GA, 31698. **EMAIL** jlcampbe@valdosta.edu

CAMPBELL, SUEELLEN
DISCIPLINE ENGLISH LITERATURE **EDUCATION** Rice Univ, BA, Univ Va, MA, PhD. **CAREER** Prof. **SELECTED PUBLICATIONS** Auth, pubs on British Modernism; American environmental literature. **CONTACT ADDRESS** Dept of English, Colorado State Univ, Fort Collins, CO, 80523. **EMAIL** scampbell@vines.colostate.edu

CAMPOS, JAVIER F.
DISCIPLINE MODERN LANGUAGES AND LITERATURE **EDUCATION** Universidad de Concepcion, Pedagogia en Espanol; Univ MN, PhD **CAREER** Fac, Universidad de Concepcion, OH State Univ, CA State Univ Chico, and Marshall Univ; assoc prof, Fairfield Univ, current. **HONORS AND AWARDS** Letras de Oro, Univ Miami and Span govt, 91. **SELECTED PUBLICATIONS** Auth, Las Ultimas Fotografeas, 81; La Ciudad en Llamas, 86' Las Cartas Olvidadas del Astronauta, 92. **CONTACT ADDRESS** Fairfield Univ, 1073 N Benson Rd, Fairfield, CT, 06430.

CANARY, ROBERT HUGHES
PERSONAL Born 02/01/1939, Providence, RI, m, 1961, 2 children **DISCIPLINE** ENGLISH **EDUCATION** Denison Univ, BA, 60; Univ Chicago, MA, 62, PhD, 63. **CAREER** Asst prof English, San Diego Col, 63-66 & Grinnell Col, 66-68; assoc prof, Univ Hawaii, 68-70; assoc prof, 70-74, chmn, Div Humanities, 76-79, prof English, Univ Wis-Parkside, 74-, Chmn Div Humanities, 83-86, assoc ed, Catch Soc Am, 69-71; co-ed, Clio, J Lit Hist & Philos of Hist, 71-; assoc vice chanc 87-92; sec of fac, 93-98. **RESEARCH** American literature and popular culture; critical theory as applied to historiography; modern literature. **SELECTED PUBLICATIONS** The Cabell Scene, Revisionist, 77; co-ed, The Writing of History, Univ Wis, 78; auth, Robert Graves, Twayne, 80; auth, T.S. Eliot: The Poet and the Critics, Am Libr Asn Press, 82. **CONTACT ADDRESS** English Dept, Univ of Wisconsin, Parkside, Box 2000, Kenosha, WI, 53141-2000. **EMAIL** canary@vwp.edu

CANCEL, ROBERT
PERSONAL Born 07/16/1950, Brooklyn, NY, m, 1973, 2 children **DISCIPLINE** AFRICAN LITERATURE **EDUCATION** State Univ NY New Paltz, BS, 72; Univ Wis-Madison, MA, 77, PhD(African lang & lit), 81. **CAREER** Ed films, African Media Ctr, Mich State Univ, 78-80; ASST PROF AFRICAN & COMP LIT, DEPT LIT, UNIV CALIF, SAN DIEGO, 80- **MEMBERSHIPS** African Lit Asn; MLA. **RESEARCH** African oral narrative traditions, especially from the Tabwa people of Zambia; oral narrative traditions from the New World (Caribbean and the Americas); African and Caribbean written literatures in English, Spanish and Bantu languages **SELECTED PUBLICATIONS** Auth, Black-African Cinema, Res African Lit, Vol 0026, 95; Gordimer, Nadine Meets Ngugi-Wa-Thiongo--Text into Film in Oral-History, Res African Lit, Vol 0026, 95. **CONTACT ADDRESS** Dept of Lit D-007, Univ Calif, San Diego, La Jolla, CA, 92039.

CANDIDO, JOSEPH
DISCIPLINE RENAISSANCE LITERATURE **EDUCATION** Univ Va, PhD. **CAREER** English and Lit, Univ Ark. **HONORS AND AWARDS** Dir, Honors Studies English. **SELECTED PUBLICATIONS** Auth, Dining Out in Ephesus: Food in The Comedy of Errors, SEL, 90; 'Women and fooles break off your conference': Pope's Degradations and the Form of "King John, Shakespeare's Histories, 95; "Once More Into the Play: Beginning the Sequel in Shakespeare's Histories, Entering the Maze, 95; "Henry V": An Annotated Bibliography, Garland, 83; "King John": The Critical Tradition, Athlone, 96. **CONTACT ADDRESS** Univ Ark, Fayetteville, AR, 72701.

CANFIELD, JOHN DOUGLAS
PERSONAL Born 02/04/1941, Washington, DC, m, 1963, 3 children **DISCIPLINE** ENGLISH & AMERICAN LITERATURE **EDUCATION** Univ Notre Dame, AB, 63; Yale Univ, MAT, 64; Johns Hopkins Univ, MA, 66; Univ Fla, PhD, 69. **CAREER** Asst prof English, Univ Calif, Los Angeles, 69-74; assoc prof, 74-79, PROF ENGLISH, UNIV ARIZ, 79-94, REGENTS PROF, UNIV ARIZ, 94-. **HONORS AND AWARDS** NEH fel, summer 75; Folger Shakespeare Libr fel, summer 76; Clark Libr Mellon fel, summer 77; Five-Star fac award, Teaching, Univ Ariz, 84; Burlington Resources Found Fac Achievement Award, Teaching Excellence, Univ Ariz, 91; Leicester and Kathryn Sherril Creative Teaching Award, Univ Ariz, 93; CASE Ariz Prof of Year, 93. **MEMBERSHIPS** MLA; Am Soc Eighteenth Century Studies; Int Soc Eighteenth Century Studies; Group Early Mod Cult Studies. **RESEARCH** English literature, 750-1750; restoration drama; Faulkner. **SELECTED PUBLICATIONS** Auth, The unity of Boileau's Le Lutrin: The counter-effect of the mock-heroic, Philol Quart, 74; The jewel of great price: Mutability and constancy in Dryden's All For Love, ELH, 75; Nicholas Rowe and Christian Tragedy, Univ Fla, 77; The significance of the restoration rhymed heroic play, Eighteenth Century Studies, 79; Religious language and religious meaning in restoration comedy, Studies English Lit, 80; Faulkner's Grecian urn and Ike McCaslin's empty legacies, Ariz Quart, 80; The fate of the fall in Pope's essay on man, Eighteen Century: Theory & Interpretation, 82; ed, Sanctuary: A Collection of Critical Essays, Prentice-Hall, 82; The ideology of Restoration tragicomedy, ELH, 84; royalism's last dramatic stand: English political tragedy, 1679-89, Studies in Philol, 85; co-ed, Paul Hunter, Rhetorics of Order/Ordering Rhetorics in English Neoclassical Literature, Univ Del, 89; Word as Bond in English Literature from the Middle Ages to the Restoration, Univ Penn, 89; Don't touch me: Pope as Pharmakeus, in Approaches to Teaching Pope's Poetry, MLA, 93; co-ed, Cultural Readings of Restoration and Eighteenth-Century English Theater, Univ GA, 95; The critique of captialism and the retreat into art in Gay's Beggar's Opera and Fielding's Author's Farce, in Cutting Edges: Postmodern Studies in Eighteenth-Century Satire, Univ Tenn, 95; Tupping your rival's women: Citcuckolding as class warfare in Restoration comedy, Broken Boundaries: Women & Feminism in Restoration Drama, Univ Press of Ky, 96; The classic treatment of Don Juan in Tirso, Moliere, and Mozart: What cultural work does it perform?, Comparative Drama, 97; Tricksters and Estates: On the Ideology of Restoration Comedy, Univ Press Ky, 97; Kit Carson, John C Fremont, Minifest Destiny, and the Indians, or, Oliver North abets Lawrence of Arabia, Am Indian Culture and Res J, 98; Mother as other: The eruption of feminine desire in some late Restoration incest plays, The Eighteenth Century: Theory and Interpretation, 98. **CONTACT ADDRESS** Dept of English, Univ Ariz, Tucson, AZ, 85721-0001. **EMAIL** jdcanfie@u.arizon.edu

CANNON, GARLAND
PERSONAL Born 12/05/1924, Fort Worth, TX, m, 1947, 4 children **DISCIPLINE** ENGLISH **EDUCATION** Univ of Tex, BA, 47, PhD, 54; Stanford Univ, MA, 52 **CAREER** Instr, Univ of Hawaii, Honolulu, 49-52; instr, Univ of Tex, Austin, 52-54; instr, Univ of Mich, Ann Arbor, 54-55; asst prof, Univ of Calif, Berkeley, 55-56; acad dir, Am Univ Language Center, 56-57; asst prof, Univ of Fla, 57-58; visiting prof, Univ of PR, 58-59; asst prof, Columbia Univ, 59-62; dir, English language prog, Columbia Univ, 60-62; assoc prof, Northeastern Ill Univ, 62-63; assoc prof, Queens Col, CUNY, 63-66; ASSOC PROF, 66-68, PROF, 68-, TEXAS A&M UNIV; visiting prof, Univ of Mich, 70-71; visiting prof, Kuwait Univ, 79-81; visiting prof, Inst Teknologi Mara, 87; summer prof, Cambridge Univ, 80, Oxford Univ, 74, MIT, 69, Univ of Washington, 67. **HONORS AND AWARDS** Distinguished Achievement Award, Tex A&M Univ, 72; Indian Govt Grantee, 84; Am Philos Asn grantee, 64, 66, & 74; Linguistic Soc of Am/Am Council Learned Socs grantee, 84. **MEMBERSHIPS** MLA; Am Dialect Soc; Dictionary Soc of North Am; South Asian Lit Asn. **SELECTED PUBLICATIONS** Auth, Sir William Jones, Orientalist: A Bibliography, 52; coauth, German Loanwords in English, 94; auth, Oriental Jones: The Life and Mind of Sir William Jones, 90; auth, Japanese Loanwords in English, 96; auth, Historical Change and English Word-Formation, 87; coauth, Arabic Loanwords in English, 94; ed, The Letters of Sir William Jones, 70; auth, Objects of Enquiry: The Life and Influences of Sire William Jones, 95. **CONTACT ADDRESS** Dept of English, Texas A&M Univ, College Station, TX, 77843.

CANNON, KEITH
DISCIPLINE COMMUNICATIONS **EDUCATION** Clemson Univ, BA; Univ Fla, MAJC; Tex A&M Univ, PhD. **CAREER** Assoc prof. **SELECTED PUBLICATIONS** Auth and ed, USA Today; Houston Chronicle. **CONTACT ADDRESS** Commun Dept, Wingate Univ, Campus Box 3059, Wingate, NC, 28174. **EMAIL** kcannon@wingate.edu.

CANTOR, PAUL ARTHUR
PERSONAL Born 10/25/1945, Brooklyn, NY **DISCIPLINE** ENGLISH **EDUCATION** Harvard Univ, AB, 66, PhD(English), 71. **CAREER** Asst prof English, Harvard Univ, 71-77; assoc prof English, 77-85, prof English, Univ VA, 85-. **MEMBERSHIPS** ALSC; APSA; NAS. **RESEARCH** Renaissance literature, romantic literature. **SELECTED PUBLICATIONS** Auth, Shakespeare's Rome: Republic and Empire, Cornell Univ, 76; A Distorting Mirror: Shelley's The Cenci and Shakespearean Tragedy, In: Shakespeare: Aspects of Influence, Harvard Univ, 76; Shakespeare's The Tempest: The Wise Man as Hero, Shakespeare Quart, 80; Byron's Cain: A Romantic Version of the Fall, Kenyon Rev, 80; Prospero's Republic: The Politics of Shakespeare's The Tempest, In: Shakespeare as Political Thinker, Univ Dallas, 81; Friedrich Nietzsche: The Use and Abuse of Metaphor, In: Metaphor: Problems and Perspectives, Harvester Press, 82; Creature and Creator: Myth-making and English Romanticism, Cambridge Univ, 84; Shakespeare: Hamlet, Cambridge Univ, 89. **CONTACT ADDRESS** Dept English, Univ Virginia, 219 Bryan Hall, Charlottesville, VA, 22903. **EMAIL** pac2j@virginia.edu

CANTRELL, CAROL
DISCIPLINE ENGLISH LITERATURE **EDUCATION** Valparaiso Univ, BA; Northwestern Univ, PhD. **CAREER** Prof. **SELECTED PUBLICATIONS** Auth, pubs on Pound; feminist theory. **CONTACT ADDRESS** Dept of English, Colorado State Univ, Fort Collins, CO, 80523. **EMAIL** ccantrell@vines.colostate.edu

CANTRILL, JAMES G.
PERSONAL Born 11/06/1955, Seattle, WA, m, 1984 **DISCIPLINE** COMMUNICATION **EDUCATION** West Wash Univ, BA, 77; Humboldt State Univ, MA, 79; Univ of Ill, Urbana, PhD, 85. **CAREER** Iolani Sch, Hawaii, Fac member, Eng dept, 79-80; Parkland Community Col, Adjunct Fac, Champaign, Ill, 85; Univ of Ill-Urbana, visiting lecturer, Dir of Debate, 80-85; Emerson Col, Asst Prof, 85-86; Carroll Col, Gifted Stud Inst, Instructor, 85-86, Asst prof, 86-90; N Mich Univ, Outcomes Assessment Coord, 94-98; N Mich Univ, Prof, Commun & Perf Studs, 90-99. **HONORS AND AWARDS** Service Award, Carrol Col, 90; Adv of the Month Award, N Mich Univ, 91; Outstanding Fac Award, N Mich Univ, 92; Fac Merit Award, N Mich Univ, 91, 92, 93., Nat Recognition, Intercol Debate, 84, 85; Nat Discussion Contest, 84, 85. **MEMBERSHIPS** Nat Commun Assoc; Soc of Environ Journalists. **RESEARCH** Environ commun; relational commun. **SELECTED PUBLICATIONS** Co-auth, Communication and Interpersonal Influence, Handbook of Interpersonal Communication, Sage, 94; Co-ed, The Conference on Communication and Our Environment, N Mich Univ Printing Svcs, 93; co-auth, co-ed, The Symbolic Earth: Discourse and Our Creation of the Environment, Univ Press of Ky, 96; co-auth, Gold, Yellowstone, and the Search for a Rhetorical Identity, Green Culture: Rhetorical Analyses of Environmental Discourse, Univ of Wisc Press, 96; co-auth, Environmental Perception and the Beartooth Alliance: Socioeconomic Struggles at the Grassroots, Proceedings of the 1995 Conference on Communication and Our Environment, Univ of Tenn Press, 97; co-auth, Cognition and Romantic Relationships, Sage, (in press). **CONTACT ADDRESS** Commun & Perf Studs, No Michigan Univ, 1401 Presque Isle Av, Marquette, MI, 49855. **EMAIL** jcantril@nmu.edu

CAPPELLA, JOSEPH N.
PERSONAL Born 03/12/1947, Auburn, NY, m, 1947, 2 children **DISCIPLINE** COMMUNICATION **EDUCATION** LeMoyne Col, BS, 69; Mich State Univ, MS, PhD, 74. **CAREER** Univ of Wis, 74-90; Univ of Pa, 90-. **HONORS AND AWARDS** Fel, Int Commun Asn. **MEMBERSHIPS** Int Commun Asn; Soc for Experimental Social Psychology; Am Psychol Soc; Soc for Res in Child Development. **RESEARCH** Polit Commun; Persuasion and Attitudes; Nonverbal Commun.

SELECTED PUBLICATIONS Auth, Multivariate Techniques in Human Communication Research, 80; Sequence and Pattern in Communcative Behavior, 85; Spiral of Cynicism, 97. **CONTACT ADDRESS** Annenberg School of Communication, Univ of Pennsylvania, 3620 Walnut St, Philadelphia, PA, 19104-6220. **EMAIL** jcappella@POBox.Asc.Upenn.edu

CAPPS, JACK L.
PERSONAL Born 07/16/1926, Liberty, MO, m, 1953, 2 children **DISCIPLINE** ENGLISH **EDUCATION** US Mil Acad, BS, 48; Univ Pa, MA, 50, PhD, 63. **CAREER** From instr to assoc prof, 59-67, PROF ENGLISH & HEAD DEPT, US MIL ACAD, 67-88, Chm adv bd, Concordance of Works William Faulkner 70-92; vis prof Am lit, Am Univ Beirut, 71-72; gen ed, Faulkner Concordance Series, 35 v, Univ Microfilms Int, 77-90; vis prof, Royal Mil Acad, Sandhurst, 80-81. **HONORS AND AWARDS** Educational Award, John Brown Mem Asn, 77; Legion of Merit, 82; Brig Gen USA-ret, 88; Distinguished Service Medal, 88. **MEMBERSHIPS** AAUP; NCTE; MLA; Col Conf Compos & Commun. **RESEARCH** Nineteenth and 20th century American literature. **SELECTED PUBLICATIONS** Co-ed, Advanced Freshman English at West Point, Col Compos & Commun J, 5/63; auth, Emily Dickinson's Reading 1836-1886, Harvard, 66; co-ed, Benet's John Brown's Body, Holt, 68; Modern Education and the Military Academy, J Haile Selassie I Mil Acad, Ethiopia, 72; auth, Auxiliary Faulkner: Six New Volumes 1976-1977, Southern Lit J, fall 77; auth, Military Tradition, in, The Companion to Southern Literature, LSU, 99. **CONTACT ADDRESS** 210 Broadway, Hanover, PA, 17331-2501.

CAPPS, RANDALL
PERSONAL Born 10/23/1936, Peytonsburg, KY, m, 1961, 2 children **DISCIPLINE** SPEECH **EDUCATION** KY Wesleyan Col, BA, 57; Western KY Univ, MA, 61; Univ VA, EdD, 70. **CAREER** From Instr to Asst Prof English & Speech, 62-68, Assoc Prof, 68-73, Prof Commun, Western KY Univ, 73-79, 82-87, 94, Asst to the Pres, 79-82, Dept Head Commun & Broadcasting, 87-94, Actg Head Dept, 68-70, Head Dept Commun & Theatre, 70-79. **HONORS AND AWARDS** Univ Award Res, 78. **MEMBERSHIPS** Int Commun Asn; Comn Am Parliamentary Procedure; Nat Commun Asn. **RESEARCH** Public address; organizational communication; forensics. **SELECTED PUBLICATIONS** Auth, A History of Speech Education in Kentucky, Ky Asn Commun Arts, 72; The Rowan Story, Homestead, 76; Communication and Leadership, Sigma Nu Educ Found, 76; coauth, Speaking Out: Two Centuries of Kentucky Oratory, Hunter, 77; Fundamentals of Effective Speech Communication, Winthrop, 78; coauth, Communication for the Business and Professional Speaker, Macmillan, 81. **CONTACT ADDRESS** Dept of Commun, Western Kentucky Univ, 1 Big Red Way St, Bowling Green, KY, 42101-3576.

CAPTAIN, YVONNE
DISCIPLINE ROMANCE LANGUAGES; LITERATURE **EDUCATION** Pitzer Col, BA, 73, Stanford Univ, PhD, 84. **CAREER** Asst prof to assoc prof, George Washington Univ, 84- ; pres, Phi Beta Delta Honors Soc, 97-99. **HONORS AND AWARDS** Dorothy Danforth-Compton Dissertation Fel, 83; Fel, Sch of Criticism & Theory, 86; Post-Doctoral Fel, 87; Eulalia Bernard Award, 98; Maurice East Award, Outstanding Leadership, 98; Phi Beta Delta Recognition Award, 98. **MEMBERSHIPS** Phi Beta Delta Honors Soc for Int Scholars; Soc for Values in Higher Educ. **SELECTED PUBLICATIONS** Auth, The Culture of Fiction in the Works of Manuel Zapata Olivella, Univ of Mo Press, 93; El espiritu de la risa en el cuento de Ana Lydia Vega, Revista Iberoamericana, 93; Writing for the Future: Afro-Hispanicm in a Global, Critical Contest, Afro-Hispanic Rev, 94; The Poetics of the Quotidian in the Works of Nancy Morejon, in Singular Like a Bird, Howard Univ Press, 99; Manuel Zapata Olivella, in Encarta Africana, 99. **CONTACT ADDRESS** Dept of Romance Lang & Lit, George Washington Univ, Washington, DC, 20052. **EMAIL** ycaptain@gwu.edu; http://gwis2.circ.gwu.edu/üycaptain

CAPUTI, ANTHONY FRANCIS
PERSONAL Born 12/22/1924, Buffalo, NY, m, 1948, 4 children **DISCIPLINE** ENGLISH **EDUCATION** Univ Buffalo, BA, 49, MA, 51; Cornell Univ, PhD, 56. **CAREER** Asst prof, 50-51, Univ Buffalo; from instr to assoc prof, 53-73, prof, 67-73, Cornell Univ; Fulbright res fel, 64-65; Guggenheim fel, 64-65; fel, Villa I Tatti, 64-65; NEH fel, 71-72. **RESEARCH** English Renaissance literature; British and American drama; modern British and American literature. **SELECTED PUBLICATIONS** Auth, John Marston, Satirist, Cornell Univ, 61; auth, The Shallows Of Modern Serious Drama, Mod Drama, 61; art, Scenic Design in Measure for Measure, J English & Ger Philol, 61; art, Anthony and Cleopatra: Tragedy Without Terror, Shakespeare Quart, 65; auth, Norton Anthology of Modern Drama, Norton, 66; auth, Masterworks of World Drama (6 vols), Heath, 68; auth, Loving Evie, Harper, 74; auth, Buffo, The Genius of Vulgar Comedy, Wayne St, 78; auth, Storms and Son, Atheneum, 85. **CONTACT ADDRESS** Dept of English, Cornell Univ, Ithaca, NY, 14850. **EMAIL** Afc3@Cornell.edu

CARAFIOL, PETER
DISCIPLINE AMERICAN LITERATURE AND THEORY **EDUCATION** Amherst Col, BA, 70; Claremont Grad Sch, MA, 72, PhD, 75. **CAREER** Prof, 90-; grad comm. **HONORS AND AWARDS** John Simon Guggenheim Mem Found fel, 94; NEH fel, 87; Sr Fulbright prof, Regensburg, Ger, 82-3. **SELECTED PUBLICATIONS** Auth, The American Ideal: Literary History as a Worldly Activity, Oxford Univ Press, 91; Transcendent Reason, Fa State, 82; ed, The American Renaissance: New Dimensions, 83; publ, articles, Am Lit, Am Lit Hist, Col Eng, ESQ. **CONTACT ADDRESS** Dept of Eng, Portland State Univ, PO Box 751, Portland, OR, 97207-0751. **EMAIL** peter@nh1.nh.pdx.edu

CARAMELLO, CHARLES
PERSONAL Born 02/29/1948, Plymouth, MA, m, 1979, 1 child **DISCIPLINE** ENGLISH **EDUCATION** Wesleyan Univ, BA, 70; Univ Wis, Milwaukee, MA, 73, PhD, 78. **CAREER** Lectr, Univ Sorbonne, 75-76; vis fac, Wesleyan Univ, 82-83; asst prof to PROF ENGLISH, 78-, dir of grad stud, dept of Eng, 94-98, CHAIR ENG DEPT, 98-. **HONORS AND AWARDS** Res awards, Univ Md, 95, 86, 79; Andrew W. Mellon fel, Nat Humanities Ctr, 84-85; Andrew W. Mellon Postdoctoral fel Hum, Ctr for Human, Wesleyan Univ, 82-83; Frederick J. Hoffman Award, Univ Wis, 78,72; Winchester Fel, Wesleyan Univ, 70. **MEMBERSHIPS** Am Lit Asn; Autobio Soc; Henry James Soc; Mod Lang Asn, MLA Am Lit Section. **RESEARCH** Modernism and postmodernism; 20th century American literature, autobiography and biography. **SELECTED PUBLICATIONS** Auth, Performance in Postmodern Culture, 77; auth, Silverless Mirrors: Book, Self, and Postmodern American Fiction, 83; auth, Henry James, Gertrude Stein, and the Biographical Act, 96. **CONTACT ADDRESS** Dept of English, Univ of Maryland, 3101 Susquehanna Hall, College Park, MD, 20742. **EMAIL** cc5@umail.umd.edu

CARD, JAMES VAN DYCK
PERSONAL Born 04/14/1931, Montclair, NJ **DISCIPLINE** ENGLISH **EDUCATION** Rutgers Univ, BA, 53; Columbia Univ, MA, 57, PhD(James Joyce), 64. **CAREER** Lectr basic courses, Hunter Col, 61-62; instr, Washington & Jefferson Col, 63-64; vis asst prof 20th century Brit lit, Franklin & Marshall Col, 64-66; asst prof, 66-71, ASSOC PROF 20TH CENTURY BRIT LIT, OLD DOMINION COL, 71- **MEMBERSHIPS** MLA; Southern MLA. **RESEARCH** Twentieth century British literature. **SELECTED PUBLICATIONS** Auth, The Casablanca Man--The Cinema of Curtiz, Michael, Jour Pop Film and TV, Vol 0024, 96; Demille, Cecil, B. and American Culture--The Silent Era, Jour Pop Film and TV, Vol 0024, 96. **CONTACT ADDRESS** Dept of English, Old Dominion Univ, Norfolk, VA, 23508.

CARDACI, PAUL F.
DISCIPLINE ENGLISH LITERATURE **EDUCATION** Md Univ, BA, MA, PhD. **CAREER** Prof. **SELECTED PUBLICATIONS** Auth, Toward a Dialogical Method of Teaching, 85; Prose by Richare Lanham, 83; Trakl and Yevtushenki (rev), 80; The Seed of Revolt (rev), 77; His Life and Work (rev), 75; Dostoevsky's Underground as Symbol and Allusion, 74. **CONTACT ADDRESS** English Dept, Georgetown Univ, 37th and O St, Washington, DC, 20057.

CARDUCCI, ELEANOR
PERSONAL Born 12/05/1942, Mahoney City, PA, m, 1975, 1 child **DISCIPLINE** ENGLISH **EDUCATION** East Stroudsburg State Col, BS; Seton Hall Univ, MA; Rutgers Univ, PhD. **CAREER** Tchr, Dover Public Schools; assoc prof, English Educ, Centenary Col; Liberal Arts Coord, Sussex County Commun Col. **HONORS AND AWARDS** NJ Teaching and Leadership award; Sears Award for teaching excellence and leadership; leadership award, Nat Chair Acad; Kobat Award for teaching excellence. **MEMBERSHIPS** Natl Coun of Tchrs of English; Phi Delta Kappa. **CONTACT ADDRESS** Sussex County Community Col, College Hill, Newton, NJ, 07860.

CARDUCCI, JANE
DISCIPLINE ENGLISH RENAISSANCE LITERATURE **EDUCATION** Colo Col, BA, MA; Univ Nev, PhD. **CAREER** Prof. **RESEARCH** Shakespeare, composition and pedagogy. **SELECTED PUBLICATIONS** Contribu, Lit and Psychology, Lang and Lit, Cahiers Elisabethians. **CONTACT ADDRESS** Winona State Univ, PO Box 5838, Winona, MN, 55987-5838.

CAREY-WEBB, ALLEN
DISCIPLINE ENGLISH EDUCATION **EDUCATION** Swathmore Coll, BA, 79; Lewis and Clark Col, MA, 81; Univ Ore, MA, 88; PhD, 92. **CAREER** Tchr,West Linn High Sch, 80-86; Grad Tchg Asst, Univ Ore,86-91; Assoc prof, W Mich Univ, 92-. **HONORS AND AWARDS** Fac Res Grant, WMU, 93, 97; Hum Ctr Res Fel; Univ Ore Grad Student Res Awards, 89, 90. **MEMBERSHIPS** Asn Tchr Educators; M LA; Nat Coun Tch Engl; Mich Coun Tch Eng; Soc Crit Exchange. **SELECTED PUBLICATIONS** Auth, Teaching and Testimony: Rigoberta Mench and the North American Classroom, SUNY Press,96; co-ed, Interruptions: Border Testimony(ies) and Critical Discourse/s. **CONTACT ADDRESS** Kalamazoo, MI, 49008. **EMAIL** careywebb@wmich.edu

CARGAS, HARRY JAMES
PERSONAL Born 06/18/1932, Hamtramck, MI, m, 1957, 6 children **DISCIPLINE** WORLD & AMERICAN LITERATURE AND RELIGION **EDUCATION** Univ Mich, Ann Arbor, BA, 57, MA, 58; St Louis Univ, PhD(English), 68. **CAREER** Teacher English, St David's Sch, NY, 58-60 & Montclair Acad, NJ, 60-61; ed-in-chief, Cath Bk Reporter, New York, 61-62 & Queen's Work Mag, St Louis, Mo, 63-64; dir, Orientation English Foreign Students, St Louis Univ, 64-69; assoc prof & chmn dept, 69-80, PROF LIT, LANG & RELIG, WEBSTER COL, 80-, Mem bk rev prog, Mo Pub Radio, 75- **MEMBERSHIPS** PEN; Amnesty Int; Nat Inst on Holocaust. **RESEARCH** The Holocaust; contemporary world literature; process theology. **SELECTED PUBLICATIONS** Auth, Ace of Freedoms--Merton, Thomas Christ, Cithara-Essays Judeo-Christian Tradition, Vol 0033, 93. **CONTACT ADDRESS** Dept of English, Webster Col, 470 E Lockwood Ave, Saint Louis, MO, 63119-3194.

CARGILE, AARON C.
DISCIPLINE COMMUNICATION **EDUCATION** Univ Calif SB, PhD 96. **CAREER** Calif State Univ LB, asst prof, 96-. **MEMBERSHIPS** NCA; ICA. **RESEARCH** Intercultural/ Intergroup Communication **SELECTED PUBLICATIONS** Auth, Language Matters, in: L. Samovar, R. Porter, eds, Intercultural Comm: A Reader, Belmont CA; Wadsworth, in press; Meanings and Modes of Friendship: Verbal descriptions by Native Japanese, Howard Jour of Comm, in press; Language attitudes toward varieties of English: An Amer-Japanese context, coauth, Jour of Applied Comm Research, 98; rev, English with an Accent: Language ideology and discrimination in the US, Jour of Lang and Social Psychol, 98; Attitudes Toward Chinese-accented speech: An investigation in two contexts, Jour of Lang and Social Psychol, 97; auth, Understanding Language attitudes: Exploring listener affect and identity, coauth, Lang and Comm, 97; auth, Intercultural communication training: Review critique and a new theoretical framework, B. Burleson, ed, Comm Yearbook, Thousand Oaks CA, Sage, 96. **CONTACT ADDRESS** Dept of Communication Studies, California State Univ, Long Beach, 1250 N Bellflower Blvd, Long Beach, CA, 90840-0006. **EMAIL** acargile@csulb.edu

CARKEET, DAVID CORYDON
PERSONAL Born 11/15/1946, Sonora, CA, m, 1975, 2 children **DISCIPLINE** ENGLISH **EDUCATION** Univ Calif, Davis, Ba, 68; Univ Wis, MA, 70; Ind Univ, PhD(English), 73. **CAREER** From Asst Prof to Assoc Prof, 73-86, PROF ENGLISH, UNIV MO, ST LOUIS, 86-. **HONORS AND AWARDS** James D Phelan Award, San Francisco Found, 76; O Henry Award, Doubleday, 82. **RESEARCH** Fiction; English language. **SELECTED PUBLICATIONS** Auth, How critics write and how students write, Col English, 2/76; Old English correlatives: An exercise in internal syntactic reconstruction, Glossa, 76; Understanding syntactic errors in remedial writing, Col English, 3/77; Aspects of old English style, Lang and Style, 77; A new raising rule, Chicago Ling Soc, 77; The dialects in Huckleberry Finn, Am Lit, 11/79; Double negative, The Dial Press, 80; The source for the Arkansas gossips in Huckleberry Finn, Am Lit Realism, spring 81; The Greatest Slump of All Time, Harper and Row, 84; I Been There Before, Harper and Row, 85; The Full Catastrophe, Simon and Schuster, 90; The Error of Our Ways, Henry Holt, 97. **CONTACT ADDRESS** Dept of English, Univ of Missouri, St. Louis, 8001 Natural Bridge, St. Louis, MO, 63121-4499. **EMAIL** david_carkeet@umsl.edu

CARLSON, ERIC WALTER
PERSONAL Born 08/20/1910;, Sweden, m, 1938, 3 children **DISCIPLINE** ENGLISH LITERATURE **EDUCATION** Boston Univ, BS, 32, AM, 36, PhD(English), 47. **CAREER** Instr English, Portland Jr Col, 34-36, Boston Univ, 38-41 & Babson Inst, 41-42; from instr to prof, 42-79, EMER PROF ENGLISH, UNIV CONN, 79- **MEMBERSHIPS** MLA; AAUP; Poe Studies Asn (pres, 73-78). **RESEARCH** American literature, especially from 1800 to present: symbolic and cultural values in literary criticism; Poe, Emerson and Dickinson. **SELECTED PUBLICATIONS** Auth, Poe, Edgar Allan--His Life and Legacy, Quart Jour Short Articles Notes and Rev(s), Vol 0007, 94; Poe, Edgar A.--Mournful and Never-Ending Remembrance, Quart Jour Short Articles Notes and Rev(s), Vol 0007, 94; Poe Pym--Critical Explorations, Quart Jour Short Articles Notes and Rev(s), Vol 0007, 94; Poe, Edgar Allan--Critical Assessments, Quart Jour Short Articles Notes and Rev(s), Vol 0007, 94. **CONTACT ADDRESS** Dept of English, Univ Conn, Storrs, CT, 06268.

CARLSON, HARRY GILBERT
PERSONAL Born 09/27/1930, New York, NY, m, 1957 **DISCIPLINE** DRAMA & SPEECH **EDUCATION** Brooklyn Col, BA, 52; Ohio State Univ, MA, 55, PhD(theatre hist), 58. **CAREER** Instr drama & speech, Southwest Mo State Col, 57-59; asst prof, Valparaiso Univ, 59-61 & Northern Ill Univ, 61-64; assoc prof theatre & drama, Univ Ga, 64-66; assoc prof, 67-72, PROF THEATRE & DRAMA, QUEENS COL, 72-, PROF DANCE, 80-, Guggenheim Found fel, 66-67; City Univ NY Res Found grant, 70-71; mem theatre arts screening comt, Comt Int Exchange Persons, 68-71 & chmn, 71-72; Swedish Govt

Travel grant, 76. **HONORS AND AWARDS** Translation, Arur Lundkvist Found, Sweden, 76. **MEMBERSHIPS** Am Theatre Asn; Soc Advan Scand Studies; Am-Scand Found; Stringberg Soc. **RESEARCH** Scandinavian drama and theatre; theatre history; translation. **SELECTED PUBLICATIONS** Auth, Strindberg, August Letters, Scandinavian Stud, Vol 0065, 93. **CONTACT ADDRESS** Dept of Drama & Theatre, Queens Col, CUNY, 6530 Kissena Blvd, Flushing, NY, 11367.

CARLSON, JULIE
DISCIPLINE ENGLISH LITERATURE **EDUCATION** Univ Chicago, PhD, 85. **CAREER** ASSOC PROF, ENG, UNIV CALIF, SANTA BARBARA. **RESEARCH** British Romanticism; Drama theory. **SELECTED PUBLICATIONS** Auth, "Imposition of Form: Romantic Antitheatricalism and the Case Against Particular Women," ELH, 93; "Remorse for Jacobin Youth," Wordsworth Circle, 93; In the Theatre of Romanticism: Coleridge, Nationalism, Women, Cambridge Univ Press, 94; "Forever Young: Master Betty and the Queer Stage of Youth in English Romanticism," South Atlantic Quart, 96. **CONTACT ADDRESS** Dept of Eng, Univ Calif, Santa Barbara, CA, 93106-7150. **EMAIL** jcarlson@humanitas.ucsb.edu

CARLSON, KAY
PERSONAL Cambridge, ID, m **DISCIPLINE** LIBRARY SCIENCE **EDUCATION** E OR St, BS; IN Univ, MLS **CAREER** Lib Dir, pres, Northwest Col; Lib Dir, Dull Knife Mem Col; Asst Libr, Umatilla Co Lib Dist; Asst Llib, Treasure Valley Comnty Col **HONORS AND AWARDS** Clayton Shepard Awd **MEMBERSHIPS** Am Lib Asn; ACRL **RESEARCH** Online searching; bibliographic instruction **CONTACT ADDRESS** Powell, WY, 82435-9225. **EMAIL** carlsonk@mail.nwc.whecn.edu

CARLSON, MELVIN, JR.
PERSONAL Born 10/28/1942, Minot, ND, s **DISCIPLINE** ENGLISH LITERATURE/LIBRARY SCIENCE **EDUCATION** Olinet Nazarene Col, AB, 64; Univ of IL, MS, 66; Univ of MA, MA, 79; Columbia Univ, DLS, 89 **CAREER** Cataloger, 69-73, Univ of VT; Cataloger, 73-, Univ of MA **MEMBERSHIPS** Am Libr Sci **RESEARCH** Libr mgmt **CONTACT ADDRESS** PO Box 781, Amherst, MA, 01004-0781. **EMAIL** melvinc@library.umass.edu

CARLSON, THOMAS CLARK
PERSONAL Born 05/13/1944, Elizabeth, NJ, m, 1970, 1 child **DISCIPLINE** AMERICAN LITERATURE **EDUCATION** Bucknell Univ, AB, 66; Rutgers Univ, New Brunswick, MA, 70, PhD(English), 71. **CAREER** Asst prof, 70-80, ASSOC PROF ENGLISH, MEMPHIS STATE UNIV, 80-, Asst bibliogeed, Poe Studies Asn, 72- **MEMBERSHIPS** MLA; Poe Studies Asn; Melville Soc; AAUP. **RESEARCH** Colonial American literature; Melville; 19th century American theatre. **SELECTED PUBLICATIONS** Auth, Shifting Borders--East-European Poetries of the 1980s, Slavic and E Euro Jour, Vol 0038, 94; Shifting Borders--East-European Poetries of the 1980s, Slavic and E Euro Jour, Vol 0038, 94; Poe and His Times--The Artist and His Milieu, Miss Quart, Vol 0046, 93. **CONTACT ADDRESS** Dept of English, Memphis State Univ, 3706 Alumni St, Memphis, TN, 38152-0001.

CARMICHAEL, THOMAS
DISCIPLINE ENGLISH LITERATURE **EDUCATION** Guelph Univ, BA; Carleton Univ, MA; Univ Toronto, PhD. **RESEARCH** Literary theory; narrative and the political unconscious; postmodernism; cultural theory; American studies. **SELECTED PUBLICATIONS** Co-ed, Constructive Criticism: The Human Sciences in the Age of Theory, Toronto, 95. **CONTACT ADDRESS** Dept of English, Western Ontario Univ, London, ON, N6A 5B8.

CARMONA, VICENTE
DISCIPLINE 19TH AND 20TH CENTURY PENINSULAR LITERATURE **EDUCATION** UCLA, PhD, 95. **CAREER** Asst prof Span, undergrad adv, La State Univ. **RESEARCH** 19th and 20th century Peninsular literature; 20th century Latin American prose; literary theory. **SELECTED PUBLICATIONS** Auth, Federico Garcia Lorca: Dibujos, Ministerio de Cult, 86; El banquete del progreso en aquel Tiempo de silencio, Alba de Am, 95. **CONTACT ADDRESS** Dept of For Lang and Lit, Louisiana State Univ, 141 A Prescott Hall, Baton Rouge, LA, 70803. **EMAIL** Carmona@Homer.forlang.lsu.edu

CARNELL, CORBIN SCOTT
PERSONAL Born 07/07/1929, Ormond Beach, FL, m, 1951, 4 children **DISCIPLINE** ENGLISH **EDUCATION** Wheaton Col, BA, 52; Columbia Univ, MA, 53; Univ FL, PhD, 60. **CAREER** Instr Eng, Bethany Col, WVA, 53-56; tchg assoc, 58-60, asst prof, 60-68, assoc prof, 68-76, prof eng, Univ FL, 76, Danforth Found regional selection chmn, 65-69, mem nat adv coun, Danforth Assoc Prog, 67-70. **MEMBERSHIPS** MLA; Conf Christianity & Lit (vpres, 64-65, pres, 74-77); Am Acad Relig. **RESEARCH** Contemp Am and Brit lit; hist of ideas, espec interrelationships of lit, philos and theol; film studies. **SELECTED PUBLICATIONS** Auth, Why sentimentality is wrong, Eternity, 11/67; C S Lewis on Eros as a means of grace, In: Imagination and the Spirit, 71 & ed & auth introd to A Slow, Soft River: 7 Stories by Lawrence Dorr, 73 & Bright Shadow of Reality: C S Lewis and the Feeling Intellect, 74, Eerdmans; coauth, Body-love and the city: a closer look at Sunday Bloody Sunday, Christianity and Literature, summer 75; Film-Going on Religious Ritual, Catalyst, 5/76; The Meaning of Masculine and Feminine in the Work of C S Lewis, Modern British Literature, 77; Ransom in C S Lewis' Perelandra as hero in transformation, Studies in the Literary Imagination, fall 81. **CONTACT ADDRESS** Dept of Eng, Univ FL, PO Box 117310, Gainesville, FL, 32611-7310.

CARNEY, RAYMOND
PERSONAL Born 02/28/1947, Homestead, PA, m, 1972, 1 child **DISCIPLINE** AMERICAN LITERATURE, FILM **EDUCATION** Harvard Univ, BA, 69; Rutgers Univ, PhD(English), 78. **CAREER** ASST PROF LIT & FILM, MIDDLEBURY COL, 78- **RESEARCH** Contemporary American film; contemporary criticism; Henry James. **SELECTED PUBLICATIONS** Auth, Tune Up When Lights Are Low, Callaloo, Vol 0019, 96; Lester Leaps In, Callaloo, Vol 0019, 96; Three or Four Shades of Blues, Callaloo, Vol 0019, 96; In Primary Light, Lit Rev, Vol 0040, 97. **CONTACT ADDRESS** Dept of English, Middlebury Col, Middlebury, VT, 05753.

CARNOCHAN, WALTER BLISS
PERSONAL Born 12/20/1930, New York, NY **DISCIPLINE** ENGLISH LITERATURE **EDUCATION** Harvard Univ, AB, 53, AM, 57, PhD, 60. **CAREER** From instr to assoc prof, 60-73, chmn dept English, 71-73, vprovost & dean grad studies, 75-80, PROF ENGLISH, STANFORD UNIV, 73- **MEMBERSHIPS** MLA; Am Soc 18th Century Studies; AAUP. **RESEARCH** Eighteenth century. **SELECTED PUBLICATIONS** Auth, Johnson and Boswell--The Transit of Caledonia, Albion, Vol 0028, 96; The Case of Dorimants Elephant--Rare Book and Manuscript Libraries as Centers for Research and Teaching-Information, Interpretation, and the Archaeology of the Book, Harvard Library Bulletin, Vol 0004, 93. **CONTACT ADDRESS** Dept of English, Stanford Univ, Stanford, CA, 94305.

CARPENTER, CAROLE
DISCIPLINE HUMANITIES **EDUCATION** Dalhousie Univ, BA, 66; Univ Pa, MA, 68, PhD, 75. **CAREER** Dean's asst, Univ Pa, 66-69; lectr, 71-74, asst prof, 74-78, ASSOC PROF, UNIV YORK, 78-. **HONORS AND AWARDS** Award Excellence Tchr, Fac Arts, York Univ, 87; Writing award, Asn Can Studs, 93. **MEMBERSHIPS** Folklore Studs Asn Can; Am Folklore Soc; Hum Soc Sci Fedn Can. **SELECTED PUBLICATIONS** Auth, Many Voices: A Study of Folklore Activities and Their Role in Canadian Culture, 79; auth, Bibliography of Canadian Folklore in English, 81; auth, Explorations in Canadian Folklore, 85; auth, In Our Own Image: The Child, Canadian Culture and Our Future, 96; auth, Enlisting Children's Literature in the Goals of Multiculturalism in Mosaic 29, 96; ed, Bull Folklore Studs Asn Can. **CONTACT ADDRESS** Dept of Humanities, York Univ, 4700 Keele St, North York, ON, M3J 1P3. **EMAIL** carolec@yorku.ca

CARPENTER, CHARLES ALBERT
PERSONAL Born 06/08/1929, Hazleton, PA, m, 1950, 4 children **DISCIPLINE** ENGLISH, MODERN DRAMA **EDUCATION** Allegheny Col, BA, 51; Kent State Univ, MLS, 52; Cornell Univ, MA, 59, PhD(English), 63. **CAREER** From instr to asst prof English, Univ Del, 62-67; asst prof, 67-70, assoc prof, 70-81, PROF ENGLISH, STATE UNIV NY, BINGHAMTON, 81- **RESEARCH** Theatre of the absurd; international bibliography of modern drama. **SELECTED PUBLICATIONS** Auth, Modern Drama Studies--An Annual Bibliog, Mod Drama, Vol 0036, 93. **CONTACT ADDRESS** Dept of English, State Univ NY, Binghamton, NY, 13901.

CARPENTER, DELORES BIRD
PERSONAL Born 12/06/1942, Chattanooga, TN, d **DISCIPLINE** ENGLISH **EDUCATION** Boston Univ, BA, 67; Univ of Hartford, MA, 74; Univ of Mass, PhD, 78. **CAREER** Instr, Shrewsbury Jr High, 67-70; PROF, CAPE COD COMMUNITY COL, 77-. **HONORS AND AWARDS** Phi Beta Kappa, summa cum laude, Boston Univ; TA, Univ of Mass. **MEMBERSHIPS** Emily Dickinson Int Soc; Ralph Waldo Emerson Soc; Thoreau Soc. **SELECTED PUBLICATIONS** Ed, The Life of Lidian Jackson Emerson by Ellen Tucker Emerson, Twayne Pubs, 80; ed, The Selected Letters of Lidian Jackson Emerson, Univ of Mo Press, 87; ed, Land Ho!-1620 A Seaman's Story of the Mayflower, Her Construction, Her Navigation, and Her First Landfall, Mich State Univ Press, 97; auth, Lidian Emerson's Transcendental Bible, Studies in the Am Renaissance, Twayne Pubs, 80; auth, The Early Days of Cape Cod Community College, Cape Cod Community Col, 89; auth, Early Encounters: Native Americans and Europeans in New England from the Papers of W. Sears Nickerson, Mich State Univ Pres, 94 & 95. **CONTACT ADDRESS** 89 S. Sandwich Rd., Mashpee, MA, 02649.

CARPENTER, MARY
DISCIPLINE ENGLISH LITERATURE **EDUCATION** Brown Col, PhD. **CAREER** Dept Eng, Queen's Univ **RESEARCH** Victorian literature; literary theory; feminist, gender, and psychoanalytic theory; history of sexuality; women's writing. **SELECTED PUBLICATIONS** Auth, George Eliot and the Landscape of Time: Narrative Form and Protestant Apocalyptic History, Univ NC, 86; Representing Apocalypse: Sexual Politics and the Violence of Revelation, Univ Pa, 95; Female Grotesques: Ageism, Anti-feminism, and Feminists on the Faculty, Routlege, 96; The Trouble with Romola, Rutgers, 90; Masquerade, Oxford, 95; The Phallus, Garland, 96; 'Eat me, drink me, love me': The Consumable Female Body in Christina Rossetti's Goblin Market, 91. **CONTACT ADDRESS** English Dept, Queen's Univ, Kingston, ON, K7L 3N6.

CARPENTER, SCOTT
DISCIPLINE LITERATURE OF THE EIGHTEENTH AND NINETEENTH CENTURIES **EDUCATION** Univ Wisc, PhD. **CAREER** Literature, Carleton Col. **SELECTED PUBLICATIONS** Auth, Acts of Fiction: Resistance and Resolution from Sade to Baudelaire, Penn State Univ Press. **CONTACT ADDRESS** Carleton Col, 100 S College St., Northfield, MN, 55057-4016.

CARPENTER, WILLIAM MORTON
PERSONAL Born 10/31/1940, Cambridge, MA, s, 2 children **DISCIPLINE** ENGLISH & HUMANITIES **EDUCATION** Dartmouth Col, BA, 62; Univ Mn, PhD, 67. **CAREER** Asst prof English & Humanities, Univ Chicago, 67-73; mem fac Humanities, Col of the Atlantic, 73-, dean fac, 83-88. **HONORS AND AWARDS** Assoc Writing Prog, Poetry, 80; Samuel French Morse Prize 85; NEA Fel, 85. **MEMBERSHIPS** MLA. **RESEARCH** W B Yeats; modern poetry; creative writing. **SELECTED PUBLICATIONS** Auth, The Green Helmet poems and Yeats' myth of the Renaissance, Mod Philol, 8/69; The Hours of Morning, Univ Va, 81; Rain, Northeastern Univ, 85; Speaking Fire At Stones, Tilbury, 92; A Keeper of Sheep, Milkweed, 94. **CONTACT ADDRESS** Dept Humanities, Col of the Atlantic, 105 Eden St, Bar Harbor, ME, 04609-1198. **EMAIL** carpenter@acadia.net

CARPENTIER, MARTHA C.
DISCIPLINE ENGLISH LITERATURE **EDUCATION** Barnard Col, BA, 78; Columbia Univ, MA, 79; Fordham Univ, PhD, 88. **CAREER** Assoc prof, grad adv, Seton Hall Univ. **SELECTED PUBLICATIONS** Auth, Orestes in the Drawing Room: Aeschylean Parallels in T.S. Eliot' Family Reunion, 20th Century Lit, Vol. 3 No. 1, 89; Eleusinian Archetype and Ritual in 'Eumaeus' and 'Ithaca,' James Joyce Quart, Vol. 28, No 1, 90; Jane Ellen Harrison and the Ritual Theory, J of Ritual Stud Vol 8, No 1, 94; Susan Glaspell's Fiction: Fidelity as American Romance, 20th Century Lit Vol 40, No 1, 94; Why an old shoe?: Jacob's Room as l'Ecriture Feminine, Proc of the 4th Annual Virginia Woolf Conf, Pace UP, 95; Oedipal Conflict Through Mythical Allusion in T.S. Eliot's 'Sweeney Erect,' Yeats Eliot Rev Vol 14, No 3, 97. **CONTACT ADDRESS** Seton Hall Univ, South Orange, NJ. **EMAIL** carpenmr@shu.edu

CARR, ROBIN
DISCIPLINE ENGLISH LITERATURE **EDUCATION** Ill State Univ, PhD, BA, MA; Univ Ill, PhD. **CAREER** Assoc prof. **RESEARCH** Literature for children and adolescents; language arts; traditional oral storytelling and poetry for children. **SELECTED PUBLICATIONS** Auth, pubs on death and dying in children's books, dialect in books for children and adolescents, language arts. **CONTACT ADDRESS** Dept of English, Illinois State Univ, Normal, IL, 61761.

CARR, STEPHEN LEO
PERSONAL Born 11/09/1950, Brighton, MA, m, 1975, 2 children **DISCIPLINE** INTERDISCIPLINARY STUDIES, CRITICAL THEORY **EDUCATION** Williams Col, BA, 72; Univ Mich, MA, 73, PhD(English), 79. **CAREER** Vis instr, Carnegie-Mellon Univ, 77-79; asst prof English, 80-86, assoc prof, Univ Pittsburgh, 86-. **MEMBERSHIPS** MLA. **RESEARCH** Literature and the visual arts; literature and science. **SELECTED PUBLICATIONS** Auth, William Blake's print-making process in Jerusalem, J English Lit Hist, 80; Verbal-visual relationships: Zoffany's and Fuseli's illustrations of Macbeth, Art Hist, 80; The ideology of antithesis: science vs literature and the exemplary case of John Stuart Mill, Mod Lang Quart, 81; coauth, Seeing through Macbeth, Publ Mod Lang Asn, 81; auth, Visionary syntax: Non-tyrannical coherence and the style of Blake's visual art, 18th Century: Theory & Interpretation, 81; The rhetoric of argument in Berkeley's Siris, Univ Toronto Quart, 81. **CONTACT ADDRESS** Dept of English, Univ of Pittsburgh, 526 Cathedral/Learn, Pittsburgh, PA, 15260-2504. **EMAIL** SCARR+@pitt.edu

CARRIG, MARIA
DISCIPLINE ENGLISH **EDUCATION** Bryn Mawr Col, BA, 84; Yale Univ, MA, 88, PhD, 95. **CAREER** Asst prof. **RESEARCH** Shakespeare and Renaissance drama; commedia dell'arte; comic theory; origins of the novel; Renaissance phi-

losophy. **SELECTED PUBLICATIONS** Auth, Pregnant Meanings: Sexuality, Skepticism and the Uses of Comic Language in Measure for Measure, The Comic Turn, Univ Fla Press, 97. **CONTACT ADDRESS** Dept of English, Loyola Univ, Chicago, 6525 N. Sheridan Rd., Chicago, IL, 60626. **EMAIL** mcarrig@orion.it.luc.edu

CARRINGER, ROBERT L.
PERSONAL Born 05/12/1941, Knoxville, TN, m, 1968 **DISCIPLINE** FILM STUDIES, CULTURAL STUDIES, AMERICAN STUDIES **EDUCATION** Univ Tenn, AB, 62; Johns Hopkins Univ, MA, 64; Ind Univ, PhD, 70. **CAREER** PROF ENGLISH & FILM STUDIES, UNIV ILL, URBANA, 70-, fel, Fac Study Second Discipline (Cognitive psychol), 90-91; assoc, Center for Advan Studies, 83-84; NEH res ed grant, 86-87; Getty Scholar, 96-97. **HONORS AND AWARDS** Undergrad Instr Award, 79; Amoco Curric Develop Award, 80; Distinguished Prof Award, 85; Apple Computer Curric Innovation Award, 88. **MEMBERSHIPS** Soc Cinema Studies; Univ Film Asn; Film Div, Mod Lang Asn; Film Studies Sect, Midwest Mod Lang Asn. **RESEARCH** American film; American Literature. **SELECTED PUBLICATIONS** Auth, Circumscription of space and the form of Poe's Arthur Gordon Pym, PMLA, 5/74; Citizen Kane, The Great Gatsby, and some conventions of American narrative, Critical Inquiry, winter 75; Rosebud, dead or alive, PMLA, 3/76; coauth, Ernst Lubitsch, G K Hall, 78; auth, The Scripts of Citizen Kane, Critical Inquiry, fall 78, ed, The Jazz Singer, Univ Wis, 79; auth, Orson Wells and Gregg Toland, Critical Inquiry, summer 82; ed, Citizen Kane, Criterion Laserdisc 84, rev ed, 92; auth, The Making of Citizen Kane, Univ Calif, 85, rev ed, 96; ed, The Magnificent Ambersons, Criterion Laserdisc, 84, rev ed, 92; auth, The Magnificent Ambersons: A Reconstruction, Univ Calif, 93; Designing Los Angeles: Richard Sylbert, Wide Angle, 98; Hollywood's LA, Getty Res Inst, 99. **CONTACT ADDRESS** Dept of English, Univ of Ill, 608 S Wright St, Urbana, IL, 61801-3613. **EMAIL** fergus@uiuc.edu

CARRITHERS, GALE
DISCIPLINE ENGLISH RENAISSANCE, CULTURAL CRITICISM **EDUCATION** Yale, PhD, 60. **CAREER** Prof, former dept ch, La State Univ. **HONORS AND AWARDS** SUNY syst summer grants; Southern Reg Educ Bd, 86; Col of Arts and Sci summer grant; LSU Res Coun summer grants. **MEMBERSHIPS** Mem, MLA Comt on Careers, 80-84. **RESEARCH** Donne; Shakespeare. **SELECTED PUBLICATIONS** Auth, Donne at Sermons: A Christian Existential World, 72; City Comedy's Sardonic Hierarchy of Literacy, SEL, 89; Mumford, Tate, Eiseley: Watchers in the Night, 91; Eiseley and the Self as Search, Ariz Quart, 94; coauth, Milton and the Hermeneutic Journey, 94; Love, Power, Dust Royall, Gavelkinde, John Donne J, 95. **CONTACT ADDRESS** Dept of Eng, Louisiana State Univ, 229E Allen Hall, Baton Rouge, LA, 70803.

CARROLL, WILLIAM
PERSONAL Born 01/04/1936, Brooklyn, New York, m, 1966 **DISCIPLINE** ENGLISH **EDUCATION** Harvard Univ, Cambridge MA, 1964; Norfolk State Coll, Norfolk VA, BA 1965; Temple Univ, Philadelphia PA, MA 1967; Univ of North Carolina, Chapel Hill NC, PhD 1978. **CAREER** Norfolk State Univ, Norfolk VA, instructor 1967-73, asst prof 1974-77, assoc prof 1978-95, prof, 1995-. **HONORS AND AWARDS** Summer School Cooperative Scholarship, Harvard Univ, 1964; Teaching Fellowship, Univ of North Carolina, 1971. **MEMBERSHIPS** Mem Alpha Kappa Mu Natl Honor Society 1963-; mem Norfolk State Univ Alumni Assn 1965-; mem Coll Language Assn 1967-70, 1984-; mem Amer Assn of Univ Prof 1969-; vice pres Tidewater Fair Housing Inc 1969-70; mem Natl Council of Teachers of English 1975-86, 1988-; mem Sigma Tau Delta Intl Honor Society 1979-; mem NAACP 1982-; publicity dir Voter Registration 1982-84; mem United Council of Citizens & Civic Leagues 1982-; advisory board, Planned Parenthood of Southeastern Virginia, 1993; bd mem George Moses Horton Society; Middle Atlantic Writer's Assn, life mem, 1987-, vp, 1992-94. **SELECTED PUBLICATIONS** Co-author Rhetoric and Readings for Writing, 1981, Variations on Humankind: An Introduction to World Literature, 1990; author, "George Moses Horton," Dictionary of Literary Biography, 1986; contributor, Fifty More Southern Writers. **CONTACT ADDRESS** Professor, Norfolk State Univ, 2401 Corprew Ave, 205 Madison Communication Building, Norfolk, VA, 23504.

CARROLL, WILLIAM DENNIS
PERSONAL Born 08/25/1940, Sydney, Australia, m, 1968, 3 children **DISCIPLINE** DRAMA **EDUCATION** Univ Sydney, BA, 62, MA, 66; Univ Hawaii, MFA, 65; Northwestern Univ, PhD, 69. **CAREER** From Asst Prof to Assoc Prof, 69-82, PROF DRAMA, UNIV HAWAII, MANOA, 82-. **MEMBERSHIPS** Asn for Theatre in Higher Educ; Am Asn Australian Lit Studies. **RESEARCH** Australian and American theatre and drama; Finnish theatre. **SELECTED PUBLICATIONS** Ed, Kumu Kahua Plays, Univ Press Hawaii, 82; auth, Australian Contemporary Drama 1909-1982, Peter Lang, 85; David Mamet, In: Macmillan Modern Dramatists Series, Macmillan, 87; Australian Contemporary Drama, Currency Press, 2nd rev ed, 95; author of numerous articles, reviews, and book sections. **CONTACT ADDRESS** Dept Theatre & Dance, Univ Hawaii Manoa, 1770 E West Rd, Honolulu, HI, 96822-2453. **EMAIL** carroll@hawaii.edu

CARRUTHERS, VIRGINIA
DISCIPLINE LITERATURE **EDUCATION** Duke Univ, PhD. **CAREER** Assoc prof, Univ Baltimore. **RESEARCH** Australian literature and film; Shakespeare. **SELECTED PUBLICATIONS** Ed, CEAMAGazine, Middle Atlantic Gp; Assoc ed, Deus Loci: The Lawrence Durrell Jour. **CONTACT ADDRESS** Commun Dept, Univ Baltimore, 1420 N. Charles Street, Baltimore, MD, 21201.

CARSON, LUKE
DISCIPLINE 19TH; 20TH-CENTURY AMERICAN LITERATURE **EDUCATION** Univ McGill, BA; Univ Calif, LA, MA, PhD. **CAREER** Assoc prof; dir, Eng grad stud. **RESEARCH** Modern American poetry; critical theory; literary criticism. **SELECTED PUBLICATIONS** Auth, The Public Trust: Consumption and Depression in Gertrude Stein, Louis Zukofsky and Ezra Pound, Macmillan, 98; pub(s), articles, Sagetrieb, Mediations, Tex Stud in Lit and Lang. **CONTACT ADDRESS** Dept of English, Victoria Univ, PO Box 3070, Victoria, BC, V8W 3W1. **EMAIL** lcarson@uvic.ca

CARSON, MICHAEL
DISCIPLINE ENGLISH LITERATURE **EDUCATION** Ohio State Univ, PhD. **CAREER** Dept ch. **HONORS AND AWARDS** Poem, Words, nominated for the Pushcart Prize. **SELECTED PUBLICATIONS** Auth, Words, printed, Gulfstream; poems publ, Bitterroot, The Spoon River Anthology, The New Virginia Rev, The Beliot Jour, Anthology Of Hoosier Poets. **CONTACT ADDRESS** Dept of Eng, Univ Evansville, 1800 Lincoln Ave, Evansville, IN, 47714. **EMAIL** mc32@evansville.edu.

CARSON, WARREN JASON, JR.
PERSONAL Born 02/12/1953, Tryon, NC, s **DISCIPLINE** ENGLISH **EDUCATION** Univ of NC, AB 1974; Atlanta Univ, MA 1975; Univ of SC, Columbia, SC, PhD, 1990. **CAREER** Isothermal Community Coll, instructor 1975-76; Piedmont OIC, head of career prep div 1975-80; Rutledge Coll, dean for acad affairs 1980-84; Univ of SC at Spartanburg, prog dir, prof dept of English, 1984-. **HONORS AND AWARDS** Church And Comm Award 1984; Outstanding Teacher Award Piedmont OIC 1980; Outstanding Teacher Award Rutledge Clge 1982-83; Teacher of the Year, USC-Spartanburg, 1989; Amoco Outstanding Teacher Award, Univ of SC, 1989; Governor's Distinguished Professor, SC Commission on Higher Education, Governor's Office, 1989. **MEMBERSHIPS** Pres Polk Cty NAACP 1976-; chrmn Mayor's Adv Task Force 1980-83; pres Tryon Schls PTA 1980-81; member, Polk Co (NC) Board of County Commissioners, 1986-88; member, City Council, Tryon, NC, 1989-; member, Polk Co Dept of Social Services, 1986-94; mem, Polk County Child Protection Team, 1993-. **CONTACT ADDRESS** English, Univ of So Carolina, Spartanburg, 800 University Way, Spartanburg, SC, 29303.

CARTER, EVERETT
PERSONAL Born 04/28/1919, New York, NY, m, 1940, 2 children **DISCIPLINE** ENGLISH **EDUCATION** Univ Calif, Los Angeles, AB, 39, AM, 43, PhD, 47. **CAREER** Asst prof English, Claremont Col, 47-49 & Univ Calif, Berkeley, 49-57; assoc prof, 57-62, vchancellor, 59-62, spec asst to pres, 62-63, univ dean res, 63-66, PROF ENGLISH, UNIV CALIF, DAVIS, 62-, Guggenheim fels, 52-53, 61-62; lectr, Salzburg Sem, Austria, 53; Fulbright fel, Univ Copenhagen, 54-55; vis lectr, Harvard Univ, 57-58; Fulbright lectr, 61-62; lectr, Asian Ctr Am Studies Hyderabad, 65; Fulbright lectr, Univ Strasbourg, 67-68; dir ctr studies, Univ Calif at Univ Bordeaux, 70-72 & 78-80; resident fel, Rockefeller Cult Ctr, Bellagio, 77; lectr, Sapporo-Cool Sem Am Studies, 81. **HONORS AND AWARDS** Nonfiction Gold Medal, Commonwealth Club, Calif, 54. **MEMBERSHIPS** MLA; Am Soc Composers, Authors & Publ; Am Studies Asn. **RESEARCH** American literature, especially fiction. **SELECTED PUBLICATIONS** Auth, Wilson,Edmund Refights the Civil-War--The Revision of Tourgee, Albion Novels, Amer Lit Realism 1870-1910, Vol 0029, 97; Fragment, Tempo, Vol 0192, 95; Realists and Jews--American Fiction and Howells, William, Dean, Stud in Amer Fiction, Vol 0022, 94. **CONTACT ADDRESS** Univ Calif, 734 Hawthorn Lane, Davis, CA, 95616.

CARTER, LOCKE
DISCIPLINE RHETORIC AND COMPOSITION **EDUCATION** Univ TX, PhD, 97. **CAREER** Vis asst prof, TX Tech Univ; bd mem, Alliance for Comput and Writing; CEO, Daedalus Gp; sr ed, Labyrinth Publ. **HONORS AND AWARDS** Founder, Daedalus Gp, Inc. **RESEARCH** Theories of argumentation; hypertext. **SELECTED PUBLICATIONS** Auth, Daedalus Integrated Writing Environment, Composicion, McGraw-Hill; The Writer's Workshop, Addison-Wesley Longman. **CONTACT ADDRESS** Texas Tech Univ, Lubbock, TX, 79409-5015. **EMAIL** L.Carter@ttu.edu

CARTER, STEVEN RAY
PERSONAL Born 04/17/1942, Indianapolis, IN, m, 1976, 3 children **DISCIPLINE** ENGLISH **EDUCATION** Ohio State Univ, PhD 75, MA 67; Denison Univ, BA 64. **CAREER** Salem State Col, assoc prof, prof, 93 to 98-; Univ Puerto Rico, asst prof, assoc prof, prof, 82-94; Trenton State Col, ex prof, 91-92; Univ N C Wilmington, asst prof, 77-82; Univ Sassari Italy, Fulbright-Hays lectr, 76-77; Univ Akron, pt inst, 75-76; Ohio State Univ, tchg assoc, 72-75; Youngstown state Univ, inst, 68-70,72, 73. **HONORS AND AWARDS** Amer Bk Awd; Geo Hendrick Res Gnt; Fulbright-Hays Jr Lectr; 2 NEH; Ford Foun Gnt., Appeared in: Who's Who in the East; Contemporary Authors; The Writer's Directory. **MEMBERSHIPS** MLA **RESEARCH** African Amer Lit; contemp Amer lit; detective fiction; contemp sci-fi. **SELECTED PUBLICATIONS** Auth, James Jones, An American Orientalist Master, Univ IL Press, 98; Lorraine Hansberry, Amer Writers Supp, NY, Scribner's 97; Kathleen Collins, Woodie King Jr, Ted Shine, Richard Wesly and George C. Wolf, The Oxford Companion to African American Literature, eds, William L. Andrews, Frances Smith Foster and Trudier Harris, NY, Oxford Univ Press, 97; Adrienne Kennedy, The Oxford Companion to Women Writing in the US, eds, Cathy N. Davidson, Linda Wagner, NY, OUP, 95; Images of Men in Lorraine Hansberry's Writing, reprinted, Drama Criticism, Gale Research, Hansberry's Drama: Commitment Amid Complexity, Urbana IL, Univ IL Press, 91, pbk ed, New Amer Lib, NY, 93; Hansberry's Drama, reprinted, Black Literature Criticism, Gale Research, 93. **CONTACT ADDRESS** Dept of English, Salem State Col, Salem, MA, 01970.

CARTER-SANBORN, KRISTIN
DISCIPLINE ENGLISH **EDUCATION** Stanford Univ, BA, 87; UCLA, PhD, 95. **CAREER** Asst prof. **RESEARCH** Cultural studies; US Latin American Studies; women's studies; feminist theory. **SELECTED PUBLICATIONS** Auth, We Murder Who We Were: Jasmine and the Violence of Identity in Subjects and Citizens: Nation, Race, and Gender from Oroonoko to Anita Hill. **CONTACT ADDRESS** Dept of English, Williams Col, Oakley Center, Williamstown, MA, 01267. **EMAIL** kcarter@williams.edu

CARTWRIGHT, LISA
DISCIPLINE FILM AND MEDIA STUDIES, GENDER STUDIES, AND US CULTURAL STUDIES OF MEDICINE **EDUCATION** Yale Univ, PhD. **CAREER** Assoc prof; taught at, Yale Univ. **HONORS AND AWARDS** Chicago Hum Inst Rockefeller fel; Univ Chicago Pembroke Ctr for Tchg and Res on Women fel & Brown Univ Alumna, Whitney Mus Am Art Independent Study Prog. **RESEARCH** Modernist modes of visual representation in US med sci. **SELECTED PUBLICATIONS** Auth, Screening the Body: Tracing Medicine's Visual Culture; co-ed, The Visible Woman: Imaging Technologies, Inscribing Science; articles on, film modernism and sci, med imag ing and gender, media and commun technol(s) in health care & soc transformation through technol art and activism. **CONTACT ADDRESS** Dept of Eng, Univ of Rochester, 601 Elmwood Ave, Ste. 656, Rochester, NY, 14642. **EMAIL** lisac@troi.cc.rochester.edu

CARTWRIGHT, MARGUERITE DORSEY
PERSONAL Boston, MA, w **DISCIPLINE** COMMUNICATIONS **EDUCATION** Boston Univ, BS, MS; NY Univ, PhD 1948. **CAREER** Hunter Coll of the City Univ of NY, teacher, lecturer; communications, journalism other media; adv educ in foregin countries; Phelps Stokes Inst, rsch. **HONORS AND AWARDS** Phi Beta Kappa other scholarly hons & awds; Headliners Awd 1975; Highest Natl Awd of Women in Communications Inc; Awds from Ford Found, Links, various civic & professional groups; Amoris Alumna Pax Pope Paul VI; Knight Commander Order of African Redemption Rep of Liberia; Keys to Cities Wilmington Xenia Zurich; street name in Nigeria for serv to Univ of Nigeria; subj of various feature articles. **MEMBERSHIPS** Mem Provisional Council of Univ of Nigeria; served on various delegations & com; covered intl conf including Bandung Middle East African States African Peoples; state guest several Independence Celeb in Africa; mem Govs & Vice Pres Overseas Press Club of Amer bd mem Intl League for Human Rights & various civic orgns; mem UN Corres Assn; Women in Communications Inc; World Assn of Women Journalists & Writers other organs. **CONTACT ADDRESS** Phelps Stokes Inst, 10 East 87th St, New York, NY, 10028.

CARUTH, CATHY
DISCIPLINE ENGLISH LANGUAGE AND LITERATURE **EDUCATION** Yale Univ, PhD, 88. **CAREER** Prof Eng/Dir comp lit prog. **RESEARCH** English and German Romanticism; trauma theory; psychoanalytic theory. **SELECTED PUBLICATIONS** Auth, Unclaimed Experience: Trauma, Narrative and History; co-ed/intro, Critical Encounters: Reference and Responsibility in Deconstructive Writing; Trauma: Explorations in Memory; Empirical Truths and Critical Fictions: Locke Wordsworth, Kant, Freud. **CONTACT ADDRESS** English Dept, Emory Univ, 1380 Oxford Rd NE, Atlanta, GA, 30322-1950.

CARY, CECILE WILLIAMSON
PERSONAL Born 03/04/1938, Washington, DC, m, 1966, 3 children **DISCIPLINE** ENGLISH **EDUCATION** Macalester Col, BA, 59; Wash St. Louis Univ, MA, 64, PhD(English), 69. **CAREER** Instr English, Wayne State Univ, 64-67; from instr to asst prof, 67-72, assoc prof English, Wright State Univ, 72-. **HONORS AND AWARDS** Fulbright, 59-60. **MEMBERSHIPS** MLA. **RESEARCH** Renaissance English literature. **SELECTED PUBLICATIONS** Auth, Go break this lute: Music in Heywood's A Woman Killed with Kindness, Huntington Libr Quart, 74; Burlesque as a method of irony in Shakespeare's Troilus and All's Well, SMC, 75; It circumscribes us here: Hell in the Renaissance Stage, The Scenography of Hell, Kalamazoo: Med Institute Pub, 92. **CONTACT ADDRESS** Dept of English, Wright State Univ, 3640 Colonel Glenn, Dayton, OH, 45435-0002.

CASAGRANDE, PETER JOSEPH
PERSONAL Born 12/19/1938, Pen Argyl, PA, m, 1961, 5 children **DISCIPLINE** ENGLISH **EDUCATION** Gettysburg Col, BA, 60; Ind Univ, MA, 63, PhD(English), 67. **CAREER** Assoc chmn dept & chmn humanities, 71-72, dir, N Col, 72-73, dir honors, 73-75, from asst prof to ASSOC PROF ENGLISH, UNIV KANS, 67-, ASSOC DEAN, COL ARTS & SCI, 72-, Nat Endowment for Humanities fel, 73-74. **HONORS AND AWARDS** Outstanding Classroom Teacher Award, 73-74; Outstanding Educator, Mortar Bd, 76 & 81. **MEMBERSHIPS** MLA; Midwestern MLA. **RESEARCH** Novels and poems of Thomas Hardy; novels of George Eliot. **SELECTED PUBLICATIONS** Auth, Criticism In Focus-Hardy,Thomas, Univ Toronto Quart, Vol 0064, 94. **CONTACT ADDRESS** Dept of English, Univ Kans, Lawrence, KS, 66044.

CASAREGOLA, VINCENT
DISCIPLINE RHETORICAL THEORY **EDUCATION** Univ IA, PhD. **CAREER** Eng Dept, St. Edward's Univ **HONORS AND AWARDS** Ed, IA Jour Lit Studies. **SELECTED PUBLICATIONS** Coauth, Writing for Business and Industry, Univ Iowa, 89; Personal Authority Made Public; Personal Relationships and Audience Awareness, Readerly / Writerly Texts, 93; Technical Documentation and Technical Discourse, Technical Communication Frontiers: Explorations of an Emerging Discipline, 94; Personal Writing and Basic Writing: Some Reconsiderations, Readerly / Writerly Texts, 94; The Discourse of Values and the Literature of the Essay, Values and Public Life, Univ Press Am, 95; Winged Visions: Using Images of Aviation and Space Technology in Teaching the Literature and Popular Culture of Modern America, Community Col Huma Rev, 95. **CONTACT ADDRESS** St Edward's Univ, 3001 S Congress Ave, Austin, TX, 78704-6489.

CASE, ALISON
DISCIPLINE ENGLISH **EDUCATION** Oberlin, BA, 84; Cornell Univ, PhD, 91. **CAREER** Asst prof. **RESEARCH** Narrative in the 18th- and 19th-century British novel; Victorian women novelists; gender in Victorian poetry. **SELECTED PUBLICATIONS** Auth, Browning's 'Count Gismond': A Canvas for Projection; Tasting the Original Apple: Gender and the Struggle for Narrative Authority in Dracula; Gender and Narration in Aurora Leigh; Against Scott, the Anti-history of Dickens's Barnaby Rudge. **CONTACT ADDRESS** Dept of English, Williams Col, Stetson c-11, Williamstown, MA, 01267. **EMAIL** acase@williams.edu

CASEY, ELLEN MILLER
PERSONAL Born 12/07/1941, Evanston, IL, m, 1965, 3 children **DISCIPLINE** ENGLISH LITERATURE **EDUCATION** Loyola Univ Chicago, BS, 62; Univ Iowa, MA, 63; Univ Wis-Madison, PhD(English), 69. **CAREER** Instr English, Mt Mary Col, 65-66; asst prof, 69-74, assoc prof, 74-81, prof English, Univ Scranton, 81-, Nat endowment for Humanities younger humanist fel, 74-75; Danforth Assoc, 81-86. **MEMBERSHIPS** MLA; AAUP; Dickens Soc; Res Soc Victorian Periodicals. **RESEARCH** The English novel; Victorian literature; literature and society. **SELECTED PUBLICATIONS** Auth, Vicrorian Censorship: Not Wisely but Too Well, Proceedings of the Sixth Nat Convention of the Popular Culture, compiled by Michael T. Marsden, Bowling Green State Univ Popular Press, 76; The Victorian Age, Victorian Studies Bull 4.3: 3, Sept 80; Junior Honors Seminar, Nat Col Honors Soc Newsletter, 8, fall 80; That Specially Trying Mode of Publication: Dickens as Editor of the Weekly Serial, Victorian Periodicals Rev, fall 81; Other People's Prudery: Mary Elizabeth Braddon, Sexuality and Victorian Literature, ed Don Richard Cox, Tennessee Studies in Lit, vol 27: 72-82, Knoxville: Univ Tenn Press, 84; In the Pages of the Athenaeum: Fiction in 1883, VPR 18.2: 57-72, summer 85; The Honors Project at Scranton U, The Nat Honors Report 6.4: 15-16, winter 85; Weekly Reviews of Fiction: The Athenaeum vs. the Spectator and the Saturday Review, VPR 23.1: 8-12, spring 90; Saturday Review, The 1890's: An Encyclopedia of British Literature, Art, and Culture, ed G.A. Cevasco,pp 530-531, NY: Garland, 93; The Novel, The 1890's: An Encyclopedia of British Literature, Art, and Culture, ed G.A. Cevasco, pp 439-440, NY: Garland, 93; John Churton Collins (1848-1908), The 1890's: An Encyclopedia of British Literature, Art, and Culture, ed G. A. Cevasco, pp 117-118, NY: Garland, 93; Our Transatlantic Cousins: The Battle over American Analytoc Novels in the Athenaeum, Studies in American Fiction 21.2: 237-249, autumn 93; Anthony Hope (Sir Anthony Hope Hawkins), Late-Victorian and Edwardian British Novelists: First Series, ed George M. Johnson, Dictionary of Literary Biography, 153, Detroit, Washington, D.C., London: Gale Research Inc, 95, 127-137; Hecht's More Light! More Light!, The Explicator 54.2: 113-115, winter 96; Edging Women Out?: Fiction Reviews in the Athenaeum, 1860-1900, Victorian Studies 39.2: 151-171, winter 96. **CONTACT ADDRESS** Dept of English, Univ Scranton, 800 Linden St, Scranton, PA, 18510-4044. **EMAIL** caseye1@uofs.edu

CASEY, JOHN DUDLEY
PERSONAL Born 01/18/1939, Worcester, MA, m, 1982, 4 children **DISCIPLINE** HISTORY, LAW, AND LITERATURE **EDUCATION** Harvard Coll, BA; Harvard Law School, LLB; Univ of Iowa, MFA. **CAREER** Prof of English, Univ of Va, 72-92. **HONORS AND AWARDS** Nat Board Award for Fiction, 89. **MEMBERSHIPS** P.E.N. **SELECTED PUBLICATIONS** Auth, The Half-life of Happiness, 98; auth, Supper at the Black Pearl, 95; auth, Spartina, 89; auth, Testimony & Demeanor, 79; auth, An American Romance, 77. **CONTACT ADDRESS** Dept of English, Univ of Virginia, Bryant Hall, Charlottesville, VA, 22904.

CASEY, MICHAEL W.
PERSONAL Born 05/14/1954, Kennett, MO, m, 1 child **DISCIPLINE** COMMUNICATION; RHETORIC **EDUCATION** Abilene Christian Univ, BA 76, MA 79; Univ Pitts, MA 81, PhD 86. **CAREER** Univ Maine, asst prof, 84-86; Pepperdine Univ, assoc prof, prof, 87-. **HONORS AND AWARDS** Outstanding Young Man of America. **MEMBERSHIPS** NCA; RCA; DCHS. **RESEARCH** Rhetoric; Religious Communication; Hist of Pacifism. **SELECTED PUBLICATIONS** Auth, Saddlebags City Streets Cyberspace: A History of Preaching in the Churches of Christ, Abilene, Abilene Christian U Press, 95; auth, The Closing of Cordell Christian College: A Microcosm of American Intolerance during World War I, Chronicles of Oklahoma, 98; auth, Villains and Heroes of the Great Depression: The Evolution of Father Charles E. Coughlin's Fantasy Themes, coauth, Jour of Radio Stud, 97; auth, Church's of Christ and World War II Civilian Public Service: A Pacifist Remnant, in: Theron Schlabach and Richard Hughes, eds, Proclaim Peace: Christian Pacifism from Unexpected Qtrs, U of IL Press, 97; auth, Government Surveillance of the Churches of Christ in World War I: An Episode of Free Speech Suppression, Free Speech YR Book, 96; auth, Driving Out the Money Changers: Radio Priest Charles E. Coughlin's Rhetorical Vision, The Jour of Comm and Religion, 96. **CONTACT ADDRESS** Dept of Communication, Pepperdine Univ, 24255 Pacific Coast Hwy, Malibu, CA, 90263. **EMAIL** mcasey@pepperdine.edu

CASMIR, FRED L.
PERSONAL Born 12/30/1928, Berlin, Germany, m, 1986, 2 children **DISCIPLINE** SPEECH AND COMMUNICATION **EDUCATION** David Lipscomb Col, BA, 50; Ohio State Univ, MA, 55, PhD, 61. **CAREER** Part-time Fac, East Los Angeles Col, 73-74; Part-time Fac to Assoc Prof, San Fernando Valley State Col, 61-73; Instr to Prof Commun, 56-94, Distinguished Prof, Pepperdine Univ, 94-. **HONORS AND AWARDS** Outstanding Teacher, Pepperdine Univ, 73; Second-place winner, national papers contest, Nat Asn Educ Broadcasters, 81; Teacher of the Year, Alumni Asn, Pepperdine Univ, 85; PRSSA, Outstanding Fac Advisor, 86; Outstanding Sr Interculturalist, Soc Intercultural Educ, Training and Res, Int, 87; Assoc, Sears-Roebuck Found Grant and Assoc Project for Asian Studies, Fac Development, Pepperdine Univ, 90-91; Fel, Irvine Found Grant, 93; recipient of several research grants from Pepperdine University and others. **MEMBERSHIPS** Nat Commun Asn; Pi Kappa Delta; Ger Speech Asn; Int Commun Asn; World Commun Asn; Western Speech Commun Asn. **SELECTED PUBLICATIONS** Ed, Building communication theories: A sociocultural approach, Lawrence Erlbaum Assoc, 94; Communication in Eastern Europe: The role of history, culture and media in contemporary conflict, Lawrence Erlbaum Assoc, 95; auth, Foundations for the study of intercultural communication based on a third culture building model, Int J Intercultural Relations (in press); ed, Ethics in Intercultural and International Communication, Lawrence Erlbaum Assoc (in press); author and editor of numerous other articles and publications. **CONTACT ADDRESS** Seaver Col, Pepperdine Univ, 24255 Pacific Coast Hwy, Malibu, CA, 90263. **EMAIL** fcasmir@pepperdine.edu

CASS, MICHAEL MCCONNELL
PERSONAL Born 07/01/1941, Macon, GA, m, 1965, 2 children **DISCIPLINE** AMERICAN LITERATURE & HISTORY **EDUCATION** University of the South, BA, 63; Emory Univ, PhD(Am Studies), 71. **CAREER** From instr to asst prof, 69-76, from assoc prof to prof Interdisciplinary Studies, Mercer Univ, 76-84; chmn, Lamar Mem Lec Comm, 92. **MEMBERSHIPS** SAtlantic Mod Lang Assn; Soc for the Study of Southern Lit. **RESEARCH** Southern literature; southern culture. **SELECTED PUBLICATIONS** Auth, Charles C Jones Jr and the lost cause, Ga Hist Quart, Summer 71; The South Will Rise Again, Anniversary & October Poem (poems), Southern Rev, Autumn 74; foreword to Lewis P Simpson's The Dispossessed Garden: Pastoral and History in Southern Literature, 74 & to Walter L Sullivan's A Requiem for the Renaissance: The State of Fiction in the Modern South, 75, Univ Ga Press; Joshua & Coming Back to Poetry (poems), World Order, Summer 75; At Home in the Dark, The Fairest Lass in All Christendom & The Lonesome End (poems), Southern Rev, Spring 77; Georgia Preacher (poem), Christian Century, 10/4/78; Survivors (poem), Christianity & Lit, Winter 79; The Writer in the Postmodern South, Athens, 91; to Jack Temple Kirby, The Counter-Cultural South, Athens, 96. **CONTACT ADDRESS** Dept of English, Mercer Univ, 1400 Coleman Ave, Macon, GA, 31207-0003. **EMAIL** cass_mm@mercer.edu

CASSIDY, FREDERIC GOMES
PERSONAL Born 10/10/1907, Jamaica, WI, m, 1931, 4 children **DISCIPLINE** ENGLISH AND AMERICAN LANGUAGE **EDUCATION** Oberlin Col, AB, 30, Am, 32; Univ Mich, PhD, 38. **CAREER** Teaching fel English, Univ Mich, 34-35 & 36-38, instr, 38-39; lectr English lang, Univ Strasbourg, France, 35-36; from instr to assoc prof, 42-49, PROF ENGLISH, UNIV WIS-MADISON, 49-, Dir English Lang Surv, 48-, Res asst & ed, Early Mod English Dict, 31-35 & 36-37, Mid English Dict, 51; field worker, Ling Atlas of US & Can, Ohio & Wis, 39-41; Fulbright res scholar, 51-52 & 58-59; consult, Dialect Surv Brit Caribbean, 54-; first hon fel, Univ Col West Indies, 58-59; vis prof English lit, Stanford Univ, 63-64; consult, Funk & Wagnalls, 64-70; dir & ed, Dict Am Regional English, 65-. **HONORS AND AWARDS** Silver Musgrave Medal, Inst Jamaica, 62; Centenary Medal, 80. **MEMBERSHIPS** Ling Soc Am; Am Dialect Soc (pres, 55-57); MLA; Mediaeval Acad Am; Soc Caribbean Ling (pres, 72-76); Am Name Soc (pres, 80). **RESEARCH** Pidgin and Creole languages; English lexicography. **SELECTED PUBLICATIONS** Auth, Pigeons in Cahoots--Etymology of the Words Cahoots and Cahooter, Amer Speech, Vol 0068, 93; 50 Years Among the New Words--A Dictionary of Neologisms, 1941-1991, Lang, Vol 0069, 93; Short Note on Creole Orthography, Jour Pidgin and Creole Lang(s), Vol 0008, 93; Malcolm--An Essay on a Friend, Verbatim, Vol 0019, 93; Dialect Studies in Britain, Jour Intl Ling Assn, Vol 0046, 95; More on Jesus-H-Christ--American English Curse-Words, Amer Speech, Vol 0070, 95. **CONTACT ADDRESS** Univ Wis, 6123 Helen White Hall, Madison, WI, 53706.

CASSIS, AWNY F.
PERSONAL Born 08/23/1934, Tahta, Egypt **DISCIPLINE** ENGLISH LITERATURE **EDUCATION** Ain Shams Univ (Cairo), BA, 54, DPE, 55; Trinity Col, Univ Dublin, PhD, 60. **CAREER** Lectr, Tchrs Trng Col (Egypt), 61; lectr, fac arts, Ain Shams Univ, 64; asst prof to prof, 68-94, dean arts & sci, 80-85, PROF EMER ENGLISH, UNIV LETHBRIDGE, 95-. **RESEARCH** 20th century English literature; Graham Greene. **SELECTED PUBLICATIONS** Auth, The Twentieth Century English Novel: An Annotated Bibliography of Criticism, 77; auth, Graham Greene: An Annotated Bibliography of Criticism, 81; auth, Graham Greene, 94; auth, Graham Greene: Man of Paradox, 94. **CONTACT ADDRESS** Dept of English, Univ Lethbridge, 4401 University Dr, Lethbridge, AB, T1K 3M4.

CASSUTO, LENNY
DISCIPLINE PURITAN AND COLONIAL AMERICAN LITERATURE, AFRICAN-AMERICAN LITERATURE **EDUCATION** Harvard,PhD. **CAREER** Asst prof, Fordham Univ. **SELECTED PUBLICATIONS** Auth, The Seduction of American Religious Discourse in Foster's The Coquette, Mouton de Gruyter, 94. **CONTACT ADDRESS** Dept of Eng Lang and Lit, Fordham Univ, 113 W 60th St, New York, NY, 10023.

CASTAGNA, JOANN E.
DISCIPLINE ENGLISH **EDUCATION** East Conn, BA, 75; Univ Iowa, MA, 83, PhD, 89. **CAREER** Acad adv, PROF ASSOC, UNIV IOWA **MEMBERSHIPS** Am Antiquarian Soc **SELECTED PUBLICATIONS** Coauth, "Making Rape Romantic: A Study of Rosemary Rogers' 'Steve and Ginny' Novels" in Violence Against Women in Literature, Garland, 89; auth, bio entries on 19th and early 20th-century Am women writers in The Feminist Companion to Literature in English, Batsford/Yale, 90; auth, "Mary Daly," in The Oxford Companion to Women's Writing in the United States, Oxford Univ Press, 94; contr, Chronlogy of Women Worldwide, Gale Research, 97; auth, bio entries in the American National Biography series. **CONTACT ADDRESS** Ofc of Acad Prog, Univ of Iowa, 120 Schaeffer Hall, Iowa City, IA, 52242. **EMAIL** joann-castagna@uiowa.edu

CASTELLITTO, GEORGE P.
DISCIPLINE ENGLISH **EDUCATION** Fordham Univ, PhD, 84 **CAREER** Chair, Eng, 94-98, PROF ENG, FELICIAN COL, 98-. **CONTACT ADDRESS** 28 Elizabeth St, Dover, NJ, 07801-4475. **EMAIL** castellittog@iaet.felician.edu

CASTIGLIA, CHRISTOPHER
DISCIPLINE ENGLISH **EDUCATION** Amherst Col, BA; Columbia Univ, MA, PhD. **CAREER** Assoc prof. **RESEARCH** Antebellum American literature and culture; cultural Stud; gender Stud; Poststructuralist theory; popular culture. **SELECTED PUBLICATIONS** Auth, Bound and Determined:

Captivity, Culture-Crossing, and White Womanhood from Mary Rowlandson to Patty Hearst, Chicago, 96; Captives in History: Susanna Rowsom's Reuben and Rachel, Redefining the Polit Novel; Rebel Without a Closet, Engendering Men; In Praise of Extra-vagant Women: Catharine Sedgwick and the Captivity Romance, Legacy, 90. **CONTACT ADDRESS** Dept of English, Loyola Univ, Chicago, 6525 N. Sheridan Rd., Chicago, IL, 60626. **EMAIL** ccasti@luc.edu

CASTLE, TERRY
PERSONAL Born 10/18/1953, San Diego, CA **DISCIPLINE** ENGLISH **CAREER** Asst prof, English, 83-85, assoc prof, 85-87, PROF, STANFORD UNIV, 87-, WALTER A. HAAS PROF IN THE HUMANITIES, 98. **HONORS AND AWARDS** Guggenheim fel, 88-89; nominated for the Lambda Literary Award, 94 for The Apparitional Lesbian: Female Homosexuality and Modern Culture, Columbia Univ Press, 93, and selected as Breakthrough Book in Victorian Studies, Lingua Franca, Sept/Oct, 95, also Alternate Selection, Reader's Subscription Book Club, 94. **RESEARCH** 18th-20th century British lit; the hist of the novel; lit and sexuality; gay and lesbian lit. **SELECTED PUBLICATIONS** Auth, The Apparitional Lesbian: Female Homosexuality and Modern Culture, Columbia Univ Press, 93; Emma by Jane Austen, rev ed, with new intro, Oxford Univ Press, 95; In Praise of Brigitte Fassbaender, in Corinne Blackmer and Patricia J. Smith, eds, En Travesti: Women, Gender, Subversion, Opera, Columbia Univ Press, 95; The Female Thermometer: Eighteenth-Century Culture and the Invention of the Uncanny, Oxford Univ Press, 95, one of three books nominated for the PEN/Spielvogel-Diamonstein Award for the Art of the Essay, 96; Noel Coward and Radclyffe Hall: Kindred Spirits, Columbia Univ Press, 96; Women and Literary Criticism, in H. B. Nisbet and Claude Rawson, eds, The Cambridge History of Literary Criticism, Vol IV, Cambridge Univ Press, 97; The Mysteries of Udolpho by Ann Radcliffe, rev ed with new intro, Oxford Univ Press, 98; Masquerade, in International Encyclopedia of Dance, Univ CA Univ Press, forthcoming 98; Lesbian Aesthetics: A Historical View, in Michael Kelly, ed, Encyclopedia of Aesthetics, Oxford Univ Press, forthcoming; The Literature of Lesbianism: A Historical Anthology from Ariosto to Stonewall, Oxford Univ Press, in progress. **CONTACT ADDRESS** Dept of English, Stanford Univ, Stanford, CA, 94305-2087.

CASTRONOVO, DAVID
PERSONAL Born 10/30/1945, Brooklyn, NY **DISCIPLINE** ENGLISH AND COMPARATIVE LITERATURE **EDUCATION** Brooklyn Col, BA, 67; Columbia Univ, MA, 68, PhD, 75. **CAREER** Adjunct asst prof, Brooklyn Col, 72-76; adjunct asst prof, Pace, 76-78, asst prof, 79-86, assoc prof, 86-88, prof of English, Pace Univ, NY, 88-. **HONORS AND AWARDS** Fac fel, Columbia Univ, 67-71; New York Times Notable Book (Edmund Wilson), 85. **MEMBERSHIPS** PEN; MLA. **RESEARCH** 19th and 20th century lit; social hist; literary criticism. **SELECTED PUBLICATIONS** Auth, Edmund Wilson, Frederick Ungar, 84; Thornton Wilder, Frederick Ungar, 86; The English Gentleman, Frederick Ungar, 87; The American Gentleman, Continuum, 91; From the Uncollected Edmund Wilson, ed and introduced with Janet Groth, OH Univ Press, 95; Richard Yates: Am American Realist, with Steven Goldleaf, Twayne/Macmillan, 96; Edmund Wilson Revisited, Twayne/Macillan, 98. **CONTACT ADDRESS** Dept of English, Pace Univ, 1 Pace Plaza, New York, NY, 10038.

CATANO, JAMES
DISCIPLINE RHETORICAL AND CRITICAL THEORY, STYLISTICS **EDUCATION** Brown Univ, PhD, 80. **CAREER** Assoc prof, La State Univ. **HONORS AND AWARDS** Summer stipend, NEH, 83; grant, LSU CORE, 92. **RESEARCH** Gender theory; writing theory. **SELECTED PUBLICATIONS** Auth, Machines for the Garden, Writing Prog Admin, 83; Style and Stylistics, in Style, 85; Computer- Based Writing: Navigating the Fluid Text, in Col Compos and Commun, 85; Language, History, Style: Leo Spitzer and the Critical Tradition, 88; The Rhetoric of Masculinity: Origins, Institutions, and the Myth of the Self-Made Man, in Col Eng, 90; Stylistics, in Johns Hopkins Guide to Literary Criticism, 94. **CONTACT ADDRESS** Dept of Eng, Louisiana State Univ, 232C Allen Hall, Baton Rouge, LA, 70803. **EMAIL** catano@unix1.sncc.lsu.edu

CATLETT ANDERSON, CELIA
DISCIPLINE CHILDREN'S LITERATURE **EDUCATION** Univ CT, MA; Univ RI, PhD. **CAREER** Eng Dept, Eastern Conn State Univ **SELECTED PUBLICATIONS** Coauth, Nonsense Literature for Children: From Aesop to Seuss. **CONTACT ADDRESS** Eastern Connecticut State Univ, 83 Windham Street, Willimantic, CT, 06226. **EMAIL** ANDERSONC@ECSU.CTSTATEU.EDU

CATRON, LOUIS E.
PERSONAL Born 04/01/1932, Springfield, IL **DISCIPLINE** THEATRE, PLAYWRITING **EDUCATION** Millikin Univ, AB, 58; Southern Ill Univ, MA, 59, PhD(theatre), 66. **CAREER** Instr theatre & speech, Lincoln Col, 59-63; asst prof theatre, Ill State Univ, 64-65; assoc prof, 66-74, PROF THEATRE, COL WILLIAM & MARY, 74-, John Golden travel fel, 66; vis artist, Youngstown State Univ & Millikin Univ, 68. **MEMBERSHIPS** Am Theatre Asn; Speech Commun Asn. **RESEARCH** Theatre direction; history of the American theatre; history of war as depicted in fiction, especially dramatic literature. **SELECTED PUBLICATIONS** Auth, The Actions of Tigers, 66 & Lincoln at Springfield: January, 1859, 66, Southern Ill Univ; Centaur, Centaur! & The Rainbow Sign, 71, Col William & Mary; At a beetle's pace (play), 5/71, Where have all the lightning bugs gone (play), 11/71 & Touch the bluebird's song (play), 12/71, Dramatics; Where Have all the Lightning Bugs Gone, Touch the Bluebird's Song & At a Beetle's Pace (plays in book form), Samuel French, 72; The actions of tigers, One Act Publ Co, 73; auth, Writing, Producing, and Selling Your Play, Prentice Hall, 84; auth, The Director's Vision, Mayfield, 89; auth, Playwriting, Waveland Press, 90; auth, Overcoming Directorial Block About Blocking, Samuel French, 91; auth, The Elements of Playwriting, Macmillan, 93. **CONTACT ADDRESS** Dept of Theatre & Speech, Col of William and Mary, Williamsburg, VA, 23185. **EMAIL** lcatron@widomaker.com

CATT, STEPHEN E.
DISCIPLINE COMMUNICATION STUDIES **EDUCATION** Univ Ariz, BA, MA; Univ Ohio, PhD. **CAREER** Prof. **HONORS AND AWARDS** Lib Arts Sci Tchg Awd. **SELECTED PUBLICATIONS** Auth, Fundamentals of Management: A Framework for Excellence. **CONTACT ADDRESS** Div of Communcation and Theatre Arts, Emporia State Univ, 1200 Commercial St, Emporia, KS, 66801-5087. **EMAIL** cattstep@esumail.emporia.edu

CAUGHIE, PAMELA L.
DISCIPLINE ENGLISH **EDUCATION** Univ Va, PhD, 87. **CAREER** Assoc prof. **RESEARCH** The dynamics of responsibility. **SELECTED PUBLICATIONS** Auth, Virginia Woolf and Postmodernism: Literature in Quest and Question of Itself, Univ Ill Press, 91; articles, Let It Pass: Changing the Subject, Once Again, PMLA, 97; Passing as Pedagogy: Feminism in(to) Cultural Stud, in English Stud,Culture Stud, Univ Ill Press, 94; Making History, in Sandra M. Gilbert, Susan Gubar, and Feminist Literary History, Garland Publ, 93. **CONTACT ADDRESS** Dept of English, Loyola Univ, Chicago, 6525 N. Sheridan Rd., Chicago, IL, 60626. **EMAIL** pcaughi@orion.it.luc.edu

CAVANAGH, SHEILA T.
DISCIPLINE ENGLISH LANGUAGE AND LITERATURE **EDUCATION** Brown Univ, PhD, 88. **CAREER** Assoc prof **RESEARCH** Renaissance literature; Shakespeare; literary criticism; feminist theory. **SELECTED PUBLICATIONS** Auth, Wanton Eyes and Chaste Desires: Female Sexuality in The Faerie Queene. **CONTACT ADDRESS** English Dept, Emory Univ, 1380 Oxford Rd NE, Atlanta, GA, 30322-1950.

CAVANAUGH, WILLIAM CHARLES
PERSONAL Born 12/18/1932, Johnstown, PA, m, 1959, 3 children **DISCIPLINE** ENGLISH **EDUCATION** Univ Pittsburgh, AB, 54, MA, 59; Univ Wis, PhD(English), 66. **CAREER** Instr English, Loyola Univ, Ill, 61-65; from asst prof to assoc prof, 65-78, prof English, DePaul Univ, 78-, Ford Found humanities grant, 72. **HONORS AND AWARDS** Harte Crane Poetry prize, 76. **MEMBERSHIPS** MLA. **RESEARCH** Victorian and modern British literature; writing poetry; Thomas Hardy. **SELECTED PUBLICATIONS** Auth, Coriolanus and the ascent of F-6, Drama Critique, 61; Kite string youth (poem), Va Quart, Fall 68; Introduction to Poetry, W C Brown, 74; Killing Time (Poem), Hopewell Review, Indiana's Best Writers, 93; English Literature, Volume II; Study Guide, Collegiate Publishing Research, 93; California Cycles, (Poem), Hopewell Review, Indiana's Best Writers, 94. **CONTACT ADDRESS** DePaul Univ, 647 E Seminary St, Greencastle, IN, 46135-1736.

CAVE, RODERICK GEORGE
DISCIPLINE LIBRARY SCIENCE **EDUCATION** Loughborough, MA, 72; PhD, 79. **CAREER** Prof, lib sci, Univ of W Indies; PROF INFO STUD, NANYANG TECH UNIV. **MEMBERSHIPS** Am Antiquarian Soc **RESEARCH** Hist of printing in the W Indies **CONTACT ADDRESS** Dept of Info Stud, Nanyang Tech Univ, Singapore, ., 2263.

CECCARELLI, LEAH M.
DISCIPLINE COMMUNICATION STUDIES; RHETORIC **EDUCATION** Northwestern Univ, PhD, 95. **CAREER** Instr, Loyola Univ, 93-93; asst prof, Pa State Univ, 94-96; asst prof, Univ of Wash, 96- . **HONORS AND AWARDS** Gerald R. Miller Dissertation Award, Nat Commun Asn, 96. **MEMBERSHIPS** Nat Commun Asn; Rhet Soc of Am; Am Asn for the Rhet of Sci and Tech. **RESEARCH** Rhet of Sci; Pub Address, Rhet Criticism. **SELECTED PUBLICATIONS** Auth, A Masterpiece in a New Genre: The Rhetorical Negotiation of Two Audiences in Schroedinger's What is Life?, Tech Commun Quart, 3, 94; A Rhetoric of Interdisciplinary Scientific Discourse: Textual Criticism of Dobzhansky's Genetics and the Origin of Species, Social Epistemology 9, 95; The Ends of Rhetoric: Aesthetic, Political, Epistemic, in: Making and Unmaking the Prospects for Rhetoric, 97; Polysemy: Multiple Meanings in Rhetorical Criticism, Quart Jour of Speech, 84, 98; coauth, Introduction, spec issue: The Rhetoric of Science, Rhet Soc Quart, 26, 96; rev, Scott Montgomery, The Scientific Voice, in: Tech Commun Quart, 4, 96; Alan Gross and William Keith, eds Rhetorical Hermeneutics: Invention and Interpretation in the Age of Science, Rhet, 16, 97; Charles Alan Taylor, Defining Science: A Rhetoric or Demarcation, Quart Jour of Speech, 83, 97. **CONTACT ADDRESS** Dept of Speech Communication, Washington Univ, PO Box 353415, Seattle, WA, 98195-3415. **EMAIL** cecc@wwashington.edu

CEDERSTROM, LORELEI S.
PERSONAL Milwaukee, WI **DISCIPLINE** ENGLISH **EDUCATION** Valparaiso Univ, BA, 59; Carleton Univ, MA, 68; Univ Manitoba, PhD, 78. **CAREER** Lectr, Univ Man, 75-78; asst prof, 79-86, assoc prof, 87-94, PROF ENGLISH, BRANDON UNIV 94-. **MEMBERSHIPS** MLA; Can Asn Univ Tchrs. **SELECTED PUBLICATIONS** Auth, Fine Tuning the Feminine Psyche: Jungian Patterns in the Novels of Doris Lessing, 90; auth, Walt Whitman and the Imagists in Walt Whitman of Mickle Street: A Centennial Collection, 94; auth, The Great Mother in the Grapes of Wrath in Steinbeck & the Environment, 96. **CONTACT ADDRESS** Dept of English, Brandon Univ, Brandon, MB, R7A 6A9.

CEGALA, DONALD JOSEPH
PERSONAL Born 08/03/1946, Buffalo, NY, m, 1967, 1 child **DISCIPLINE** COMMUNICATION **EDUCATION** Univ Wis-Madison, BA, 68; Purdue Univ, Lafayette, MA, 69; Fla State Univ, PhD, 72. **CAREER** Instr commun, Fla State Univ, 71-72; assoc prof 73-83, prof, Ohio State Univ, 83-, Chairperson consensus comt, Nat Proj on Speech Commun Competencies Prekindergarten-12th Grade, 73-74. **MEMBERSHIPS** Nat Commun Asn, Int Commun Asn; Am Acad on Physician and Patient **RESEARCH** Doctor-patient communication; doctor and patient training in communication skills. **SELECTED PUBLICATIONS** Coath, A study of doctors' and patients' perceptions of information processing and communication competence during the medical interview, Health Commun, 7, 179-204, 95; coauth, Components of patients' and doctors' perceptions of communication competence during a primary care medical interview, Health Commun, 8, 1-28, 96; coauth, Provider-patient health communication research from a pateient-centered perspective, Health Commun, 9, 27-44, 97; auth, A Study of Doctors' and Patients' Patterns of Information Exchange and Relational Communication During a Primary Care Consultation: Implications for Communication Skills Training, Hour of Health Commun, 2, 169-194, 97. **CONTACT ADRESS** Dept of Commun, Ohio State Univ, 154 N Oval Hall, Columbus, OH, 43210-1330. **EMAIL** cegala.1@osu.edu

CELLA, CHARLES RONALD
PERSONAL Born 06/16/1939, Frankfort, KY, m, 1962, 3 children **DISCIPLINE** AMERICAN LITERATURE **EDUCATION** Transylvania Col, BA, 61; Univ Ky, MA, 62 PhD, 68. **CAREER** Instr English, Eastern Ky Univ, 63-64; asst prof, 68-71, assoc prof, 71-80, PROF ENGLISH, MURRAY STATE UNIV, 80- **MEMBERSHIPS** MLA; Am Studies Asn; Popular Cult Asn. **RESEARCH** American novel; theories of realism in fiction; literature and other arts. **SELECTED PUBLICATIONS** Auth, Mary Johnston, G K Hall & Co, 81. **CONTACT ADDRESS** Dept of English, Murray State Univ, 1 Murray St, Murray, KY, 42071-3310. **EMAIL** ron.cella@murraystate.edu

CERASANO, SUSAN P.
DISCIPLINE THEATER HISTORY, SHAKESPEARE, RENAISSANCE LITERATURE **EDUCATION** W Chester State Col, BA, 75; Univ MI, MA, PhD, 76, 81. **CAREER** Assoc prof, Colgate Univ. **HONORS AND AWARDS** Hon fel, Univ Keele, Staffordshire, England; NEH grants, 88-89, 83; ACLS grant, 90; Rackham fel, Univ MI, 79-81. **MEMBERSHIPS** Mem, Mus London, 89-; ed bd, Shakespeare Studies, 93-. **RESEARCH** Renaissance theater hist and drama. **SELECTED PUBLICATIONS** Auth, Edward Alleyn: Elizabethan Acor, Jacobean Gentleman Dulwich Picture Gallery, London, 94; Gloriana's Face: Women, Public and Private in the English Renaissance, Harvester/Simon and Schuster, 92; Borrowed Robes, Costume Prices and the Drawing of Titus Andronicus, Shakespeare Studies, 94; Tamburlaine and Edward Alleyn's Ring, Shakespeare Studies, 94; Philip Henslowe, Simon Forman, and the Theatrical Community of the 1590's, Shakespeare Quart, 93. **CONTACT ADDRESS** Dept of Eng, Colgate Univ, 13 Oak Dr., Hamilton, NY, 13346.

CERVO, NATHAN ANTHONY
PERSONAL Born 06/19/1930, New Haven, CT, m, 1964, 1 child **DISCIPLINE** ENGLISH LANGUAGE & LITERATURE **EDUCATION** Univ Conn, BA & MA, 54; Univ Toronto, PhD(English & philos), 59. **CAREER** Reader English, Univ Toronto, 56-57; instr, Boston Col, 58-59; asst prof, La State Univ, Baton Rouge, 60-61; from asst prof to assoc prof English & Dante, St Joseph Col, Conn, 61-66; asst prof English & Latin, Hartwick Col, 66-69; from assoc prof to prof, 70-77, PROF ENGLISH, FRANKLIN PIERCE COL, 77-, Fulbright res fel, Univ Florence, 59-60; fel, Yale Univ, 63-65. **MEMBERSHIPS** MLA. **RESEARCH** The pre-Raphaelites; the aesthetes; Tennyson and Browning. **SELECTED PUBLICATIONS** Auth,

Grey Riders of the Purple Sage, Explicator, Vol 0055, 97; Cool, I Faith and a Pans Face, the Social Unity of Shepherd and Flock in Browning Bishop Blougram Apology, Eng Lang Notes, Vol 0030, 93. **CONTACT ADDRESS** Dept of English Div of Humanities, Franklin Pierce Col, PO Box 60, Rindge, NH, 03461-0060.

CEVASCO, GEORGE ANTHONY
PERSONAL Born 09/22/1924, Brooklyn, NY, m, 1954, 2 children **DISCIPLINE** ENGLISH **EDUCATION** St John's Univ, NY, AB, 48; Columbia Univ, MA, 49. **CAREER** Instr English, Gannon Col, 51-52; from asst prof to assoc prof, Notre Dame Col, Staten Island, 52-55; asst dean, St John's Col, 65-69, asst prof, 55-71, ASSOC PROF ENGLISH, ST JOHN's UNIV, NY, 71-, Lectr, Fordham Univ, 54-67; consult, Choice, 65-; abstractor, Abstr English Studies. **HONORS AND AWARDS** DLitt, Univ London. **MEMBERSHIPS** MLA; Am Soc Aesthet; Soc Huysmans; fel Royal Soc Arts. **RESEARCH** Life and works of J-K Huysmans; American grammar; aestheticism and decadence in British literature, 1870-1890. **SELECTED PUBLICATIONS** Auth, Art and Christhood, the Aesthetics of Wilde, Oscar, Nineteenth Century Prose, Vol 0021, 94; Rituals of Dis-Integration, Romance and Madness in the Victorian Psychomythic Tale, Eng Lit In Transition 1880-1920, Vol 0037, 94; Wilde, Oscar Revalued, An Essay on New Materials and Methods of Research, Nineteenth Century Prose, Vol 0021, 94; The Voice of Rapture, a Symbolist System of Ecstatic Speech in Wilde, Oscar Salome, English Lit in Transition 1880-1920, Vol 0036, 93; Talk on the Wilde Side--Toward a Genealogy of a Discourse on Male Sexualities, Eng Lit in Transition 1880-1920, Vol 0037, 94; Delineating Decadence, the Influence of Huysmans, J.K. on Symons, Arthur, Nineteenth Century Prose, Vol 0023, 96; Hardy, Thomas and the Church, Cath Hist Rev, Vol 0083, 97; Wilde, Oscar, The Importance of Being Earnest and Other Plays, Eng Lit in Transition 1880-1920, Vol 0039, 96; Grim Phantasms--Fear in Poe Short-Fiction, Stud in Short Fiction, Vol 0031, 94; The Thief of Reason--Wilde, Oscar and Modern Ireland, Eng Lit in Transition 1880-1920, Vol 0040, 97; Webb, Beatrice--A Life, Eng Lit in Transition 1880-1920, Vol 0036, 93. **CONTACT ADDRESS** Dept of English, St John's Univ, Jamaica, NY, 11432.

CHACE, WILLIAM M.
DISCIPLINE ENGLISH LANGUAGE AND LITERATURE **EDUCATION** Univ Calif Berkeley, PhD, 68. **CAREER** Prof Eng/pres Emory Univ. **RESEARCH** Modern British and American literature. **SELECTED PUBLICATIONS** Auth, The Political Identities of Ezra Pound and T. S. Eliot; Lionel Trilling: Criticism and Politics; ed, Justice denied: The Black Man in White America; James Joyce: A Collection of Critical Essays. **CONTACT ADDRESS** English Dept, Emory Univ, 1380 Oxford Rd NE, Atlanta, GA, 30322-1950.

CHAFFEE, STEVEN H.
PERSONAL Born 08/21/1935 **DISCIPLINE** COMMUNICATIONS **EDUCATION** Univ Redlands, BA, 57; UCLA, MS, 62; Stanford Univ, PhD, 65. **CAREER** Dir Schl Jour Mass Comm, Univ WI Madison, 65-81; prof, Stanford Univ, 81-85; to chr 86-90; also to Janet M. Peck Prof Int Comm, 87. **HONORS AND AWARDS** Pres/fel, Int Comm Assn; dir, Inst Comm Res, 81-86. **RESEARCH** Mass media effects; polit commun; adolescent develop; health commun; international commun; interpersonal and family commun; media institutions; research methodology; commun as an academic field; cognitive theories of commun. **SELECTED PUBLICATIONS** Auth, Political Communication, 76; Television and Human Behavior, 78; Handbook of Communication Science, 87; Communication Concepts 1: Explication, 91; To See Ourselves: Comparing Traditional Chinese and American Cultural Values, 94; and The Beginnings of Communication Study in America, 97. **CONTACT ADDRESS** Dept Commun, Stanford Univ, 350 McClatchy Hall, Stanford, CA, 94305. **EMAIL** chaffee@leland.stanford.edu

CHAIKA, ELAINE
DISCIPLINE DEPARTMENT OF ENGLISH **EDUCATION** RI Col, B Ed, 60; Brown Univ, MAT; 65; Brown Univ, PhD, 72. **CAREER** Instr, Bryant Col, 65-66; instr, RI Sch of Design, 67-68; spec lectr Eng, 71, asst prof, 71-73, assoc prof, 74-78, prof Ling, Providence Coll, 79-; referee, Coll Commun and Compos; assoc, Brain and Behavior Sci; referee, J of Psycholinguistics, Psychiat Res, Bobbs-Merrill, Prentice-Hall, Holt, Rinehart, Winston, Chandler, Random House, St. Martin's Press, Newbury House. **HONORS AND AWARDS** Fel, NDEA, 68-70; Who's Who Among Am Tchr, 94; Outstanding Scholar Award, Am Asn of Univ Prof, 94; Fulbright fel, Norway, 94-95; sabbatical res, Brit's Nat Inst of Psychiat and Broadmoor Hosp, 96; consult linguist, SUNY Stony Brook Div of Psychiat Res; consult linguist, Oxford Univ/Dept of Psychiat. **MEMBERSHIPS** SUNY Stony Brook Div of Psychiat Res. **SELECTED PUBLICATIONS** Auth, Understanding Psychotic Speech: Beyond Freud and Chomsky, Chas. C. Thomas Publ, 90; Language: the Social Mirror, Heinle & Heinle, 94; On analysing schizophrenic speech: what model should we use?, in Speech and Language Disorders in Psychiatry, ed by A. Sims, Gaskell Press, 94. **CONTACT ADDRESS** Dept of Eng, Providence Col, EH 215, Providence, RI, 02918-0001. **EMAIL** echaika@sequent1.providence.edu

CHAKRAVORTY SPIVAK, GAYATRI
DISCIPLINE ENGLISH LITERATURE **EDUCATION** Univ Calcutta, BA, 59; Cornell Univ, MA, 62, PhD, 67. **CAREER** Instr, Brown Col; Univ Tex-Austin; Univ Calif-Santa Cruz; Jawaharlal Nehru Univ; Stanford Univ; Univ Brit Columbia; Goethe Univ, Frankfurt; Riyadh Univ; Emory Univ; Andrew W Mellon prof, Pittsburgh Univ; prof, 91-. **HONORS AND AWARDS** Fel, Nat Hum Inst; Ctr Hum, Wesleyan Col; Hum Res Ctr, Australian Nat Univ; Ctr Stud Soc Sci, Calcutta; Davis Ctr Hist Stud, Princeton; Rockefeller found, Bellagio; Kent fel; Guggenheim fel; distinguished fac fel, Tagore, Maharaja Sayajirao, Univ Baroda, India; transl prize, Sahitya Akademi, India, 97., Lect, Davie Memorial Lect, Cape Town; ed bd, Cultl Critique; New Formations; Diaspora; ARIEL; Re-thinking Marxism; Pub Cult; Parallax; Interventions; Year's Work in Critical & Cult Theory. **MEMBERSHIPS** Mem, Subaltern Studies Collective **RESEARCH** Works of Mahasweta Devi. **SELECTED PUBLICATIONS** Transl, Of Grammatology; Imaginary Maps and Breast. **CONTACT ADDRESS** Dept of Eng, Columbia Col, New York, 2960 Broadway, New York, NY, 10027-6902.

CHAMBERLIN, JOHN
DISCIPLINE PIERS PLOWMAN; ARTS OF DISCOURSE, ANCIENT; MODERN **EDUCATION** Haverford, BA; Toronto, MA, PhD. **CAREER** Asst Prof **SELECTED PUBLICATIONS** Auth, Increase and Multiply: Arts-of-Discourse Procedure in the Preaching of Donne, 76; What Makes Piers Plowman so hard to read?; The Rule of St. Benedict: The Abingdon Copy , 82; International Development Education in the English Classroom. **CONTACT ADDRESS** Wilfrid Laurier Univ, 75 University Ave W, Waterloo, ON, N2L 3C5. **EMAIL** jchamber@mach1.wlu.cas

CHAMBERS, ANTHONY HOOD
PERSONAL Born 07/01/1943, Pasadena, CA **DISCIPLINE** LITERATURE **EDUCATION** Pomona Col, BA, 65; Stanford Univ, MA, 68; Univ Mich, PhD, 74. **CAREER** Asst Prof, 71-75, Arizona St Univ; prof, 75-98, Wesleyan Univ; prof, 98-, Arizona St Univ. **RESEARCH** Japanese lit; lit translation **CONTACT ADDRESS** PO Box 870202, Tempe, AZ, 85287-9292. **EMAIL** anthony.chambers@asu.edu

CHAMETZKY, JULES
PERSONAL Born 05/24/1928, Brooklyn, NY, m, 1953, 3 children **DISCIPLINE** ENGLISH **EDUCATION** Brooklyn Col, BA, 50; Univ Minn, MA, 52, PhD(English lit), 58. **CAREER** Instr English, Univ Minn, 54-56; instr humanities, Boston Univ, 56-58; from vis lectr to assoc prof, 58-69, PROF ENGLISH, UNIV MASS, AMHERST, 69-, **HONORS AND AWARDS** Ed, Faulkner Studies, 53-54 & Mass Rev, 59-; Fulbright prof, Univ Tubingen, 62-63 & Univ Zagreb, 66-67; mem bd, dir, Coord Coun Lit Mag, 67-72; guest prof Am studies, Free Univ Berlin, 70-71, Freiburg, 76-77, Frankfurt Univ, 86, 92, Humboldt Univ, 94; Fulbright prof, Copenhagen, 98-99; Meius award for lifetime contribution to ethnic studies. **MEMBERSHIPS** MLA; Am Studies Asn; Asn Lit Mag Am(pres, 65-67). **RESEARCH** Jewish American literature; literature of immigration and ethnicity; American realism. **SELECTED PUBLICATIONS** Co-ed, Black & White in American Culture, Viking, 71; auth, Regional Literature and Ethnic Realities, Antioch Rev, Fall 71; From HUAC to Watergate: Eric Bentley's Are You Now, Performance 7, fall 73; James T Farrell's literary criticism, Twentieth Century Lit, 2/76; From the Ghetto: The Fiction of Abraham Cahan, Univ Mass, 77; auth, Our Decentralized Literature, Univ Mass, 86. **CONTACT ADDRESS** 244 Amity St, Amherst, MA, 01002.

CHAMPION, LARRY STEPHEN
PERSONAL Born 04/27/1932, Shelby, NC, m, 1956, 3 children **DISCIPLINE** LITERATURE **EDUCATION** Davidson Col, AB, 54; Univ Va, MA, 55; Univ NC, PhD, 61. **CAREER** Instr English, Davidson Col, 55-56 & Univ NC, 59-60; from instr to assoc prof, 60-68, from asst head dept to assoc head, 67-71, PROF ENGLISH, NC STATE UNIV, 68-, HEAD DEPT, 71-, Ed consult, Papers on Lang & **HONORS AND AWARDS** Outstanding Classroom Teacher Award, NC State Univ, 70. **MEMBERSHIPS** MLA; NCTE; Renaissance Soc Am; Southeastern Renaissance Conf(pres, 78); SAtlantic Asn Dept English (pres, 74-75). **RESEARCH** Elizabethan and Jacobean drama, especially Shakespeare and Jonson; seventeenth century poetry, especially Herbert and Milton. **SELECTED PUBLICATIONS** Auth, Shakespearean Subversions--The Trickster and the Play-Text, Eng Stud, Vol 0075, 94; Politics, Plague, and Shakespeare Theater--The Stuart Years, Eng Stud, Vol 0075, 94; Misrepresentations--Shakespeare and the Materialists, Eng Stud, Vol 0076, 95; The Politics of Tragicomedy--Shakespeare and After, Eng Stud, Vol 0074, 93; Motives of Woe, Shakespeare and Female Complaint--Critical Anthology, Eng Stud, Vol 0074, 93; Shakespeare Reshaped 1606-1623, Eng Stud, Vol 0076, 95; Biblical References in Shakespeare Comedies, Shakespeare Quart, Vol 0046, 95; Shakespeare Reshaped 1606-1623, Eng Stud, Vol 0076, 95; The Subjectivity Effect in Western Literary Tradition--Essays Toward the Release of Shakespeare Will, Eng Stud, Vol 0074, 93. **CONTACT ADDRESS** Dept of English, No Carolina State Univ, Raleigh, NC, 27607.

CHANDLER, ALICE
PERSONAL Born 05/29/1931, m, 1954, 2 children **DISCIPLINE** ENGLISH **EDUCATION** Barnard Col, Columbia Univ, AB, 51; Columbia Univ, MA, 53, PhD(English), 60. **CAREER** Instr English, Skidmore Col, 53-54; lectr, Barnard Col, Columbia Univ, 54-55 & Hunter Col, 56-57; from instr to assoc prof, City Col Ny, 61-73, prof, 73-79, provost & vpres acad affairs, 76-79; actg pres, 79-80, pres 80-96, PRES EMERITA, STATE UNIV NY, NEW PALTZ, 96-. **MEMBERSHIPS** MLA. **RESEARCH** Victorian literature; 19th century American literature; women novelists of the 19th century. **SELECTED PUBLICATIONS** Auth, The Prose Spectrum, Allyn & Bacon, 68; Tennyson's Maud and The Song of Songs, Victorian Poetry, 6/69; ed, The Theme of War, W C Brown, 69; auth, The Rationale of Rhetoric, 70 & coauth, The Rationale of the Essay, 71, Holt; auth, A Dream of Order: The Medieval Ideal in Nineteenth Century Literature, Univ Nebr, 70 & Routledge & Kegan Paul, 71; The visionary race: Poe's attitude toward his dreamers, In: New Approaches to Poe: A Symposium, 70; From Smollett to James, Univ Va, 81. **EMAIL** chandlerak@aol.com

CHANDLER, DANIEL ROSS
PERSONAL Born 07/22/1937, Wellston, OK **DISCIPLINE** SPEECH COMMUNICATION, RELIGION **EDUCATION** Univ Okla, BS, 59; Purdue Univ, MA, 65; Garrett Theol Sem, BD, 68; Ohio Univ, PhD(commun), 69. **CAREER** Asst prof speech, Cent Mich Univ, 69-70, State Univ NY, New Paltz, 70-71 & City Univ New York, 71-75; ASST PROF COMMUN, RUTGERS UNIV, NEW BRUNSWICK, 76-, Asst pastor, Peoples Church of Chicago, 65-66; mem denominational affairs comt, Community Church of New York, 72-, John Haynes Scholar comt, 72-; vis fel, Princeton Univ, 74-75, 77, 79-80; res fel, Yale Univ, 74-75, 77 & 78; Marland fel, Union Theol Sem Columbia Univ, 75-76; vis scholar, New Sch for Social Res, 76-77. **MEMBERSHIPS** Nat Coalition Against Censorship; Speech Commun Asn; Speech Commun Asn Eastern States; Relig Speech Commun Asn; Acad Freedom Clearinghouse. **RESEARCH** Liberal religious movement in America; communication of mass movements; history and philosophy of freedom of speech. **SELECTED PUBLICATIONS** Auth, The Dawn of Religious Pluralism--Voices From the Worlds-Parliament-Of-Religions, 1893, Rel Hum, Vol 0027, 93; A Celebration of Humanism and Freethought, Rel Hum, Vol 0029, 95; Crimes of Perception--An Encyclopedia of Heresies and Heretics, Rel Hum, Vol 0029, 95; The American Radical, Rel Hum, Vol 0029, 95; 50 Days of Solitude, Rel Hum, Vol 0029, 95; Blavatsky, Madame Baboon, Rel Hum, Vol 0029, 95; Solitude--A Philosophical Encounter, Rel Hum, Vol 0029, 95; The Secularization of the Academy, Rel Hum, Vol 0028, 94; A Nation of Victims--The Decay of te American Character, Rel Hum, Vol 0028, 94; Pilgrimage Of Hope--100-Years of Global Interfaith Dialog, Rel Hum, Vol 0027, 93; A Fire in the Mind--The Life of Campbell, Joseph, Rel Hum, Vol 0027, 93; The Minds Sky--Human Intelligence in a Cosmic Context, Rel Hum, Vol 0027, 93; Holy Fire, Rel Hum, 0029, 95; An Aristocracy of Everyone--The Politics of Education and the Future of Education, Rel Hum, Vol 0028, 94; Paine, Thomas--Apostle of Freedom, Rel Hum, Vol 0029, 95; A Brief-History of American Culture, Rel Hum, Vol 0029, 95; American Religious Humanism, Rel Hum, Vol 0030, 96; America Alternative Religions, Rel Hum, Vol 0029, 95; Mapping American Culture, Rel Hum, Vol 0029, 95; Dewey,John--An Intellectual Portrait, Rel Hum, Vol 0029, 95; Same-Sex Unions in Premodern Europe, Rel Hum, Vol 0029, 95; Selling God--American Religion in the Marketplace of Culture, Rel Hum, Vol 0028, 94; The Evolution of Progress--The End of Economic-Growth and the Beginnings of Human Transformation, Rel Hum, Vol 0028, 94; Visions Of A Better World, Rel Hum, Vol 0028, 94; The Lambda Directory of Religion and Spirituality--Sources of Spiritual Support for Gay Men and Lesbians, Rel Hum, Vol 0029, 95; Cosmos Crumbling--American Reform and the Religious Imagination, Rel Hum, Vol 0028, 94; The Worlds-Parliament-of-Religions --The East/West Encounter, Chicago, 1893, Rel Hum, Vol 0029, 95; One Nation Under God--Religion in Contemporary American Society, Rel Hum, Vol 0028, 94; Notes From a Wayfarer--The Autobiography of Thielicke, Helmut, Rel Hum, Vol 0029, 95. **CONTACT ADDRESS** Dept of Commun, Rutgers Univ, New Brunswick, NJ, 08903.

CHANG, BRIANKLE G.
PERSONAL Born 04/19/1954, Taipei, Taiwan **DISCIPLINE** COMMUNICATION **EDUCATION** Univ Il Champaign, PhD, 90 **CAREER** Asst prof, Univ Ma, 93- **MEMBERSHIPS** ICA **RESEARCH** Cultural stud; philos of commun; theory & criticism. **SELECTED PUBLICATIONS** Auth, Deconstructing Communication: Subject, Representation and Economies of Exchange, Univ Ma Press, 96 **CONTACT ADDRESS** Dept of Commun, Univ Ma, Machmer Hall 410, Amherst, MA, 01003. **EMAIL** bchang@comm.umass.edu

CHANG, JOSEPH S.
PERSONAL Born 09/01/1935, Honolulu, HI, m, 1961, 5 children **DISCIPLINE** ENGLISH **EDUCATION** St Mary's Col (Calif), BA, 56; Univ Wis, MA, 60, PhD(English), 65. **CAREER** Asst prof English, Tulane Univ, 64-66; asst prof, 66-71, ASSOC PROF ENGLISH, UNIV WIS-MILWAUKEE, 71-, Southeastern Inst Medieval & Renaissance Studies fel, 65. **RESEARCH** Shakespeare; Elizabethan drama; history of ideas in

the Renaissance. **SELECTED PUBLICATIONS** Auth, A Class-Based Approach to Word Alignment, Computational Ling, Vol 0023, 97. **CONTACT ADDRESS** 4224 N Ardmore Ave, Milwaukee, WI, 53211.

CHANG, TSAN-KUO
DISCIPLINE MASS COMMUNICATION STUDIES **EDUCATION** Nat Chengchi Univ, MA; Univ Tex Austin, PhD. **CAREER** Assoc prof **SELECTED PUBLICATIONS** Auth, The Press and China Policy: The Illusion of Sino-American Relations, 1950-1984, 93; co-auth, News as Social Knowledge in China: The Changing Worldview of Chinese National Media, J Commun, 94; Determinants of International News Coverage in the U.S. Media, Commun Res, 87. **CONTACT ADDRESS** Mass Communication Dept, Univ of Minnesota, Twin Cities, 111 Murphy Hall, 206 Church St SE, Minneapolis, MN, 55455. **EMAIL** chang003@tc.umn.edu

CHAPMAN, DAVID W.
PERSONAL Born 07/04/1954, Tulsa, OK, m, 1978, 2 children **DISCIPLINE** ENGLISH: RHETORIC AND COMPOSITION **EDUCATION** Univ Okla, BA, 76; Univ Tulsa, MA, 81; Texas Christian Univ, PhD, 85. **CAREER** Asst prof, Texas Tech Univ, 86-90; Assoc prof, Samford Univ, 90-95; prof, 95- ; dir, Writing Across the Curriculum, 90-95; assoc dean, Howard Col Arts & Sciences, 95- . **HONORS AND AWARDS** Phi Beta Kappa; Lichfield Poetry Award, 83; Boswell Prize, 92. **MEMBERSHIPS** NCTE; CCCC; ATAC; WPA; ACTE; ACETA. **RESEARCH** Literary nonficion; writing program administration; core curriculum; problem-based learning. **SELECTED PUBLICATIONS** Auth, Chapter, Encyclopedia of the Essay, 97; auth, Moral Essay, Encyclopedia of the Essay, 97; auth, George Orwell, Encyclopedia of the Essay, 97; auth, Problem-Based Learning and the Core Curriculum, PBL Insight, 98; WAC and the First-Yar Writing Course: Sellilng Ourselves Short, J Lang Learning Across the Disciplines, 98. **CONTACT ADDRESS** Samford Univ, Box 292260, Birmingham, AL, 35229-2260. **EMAIL** dwchapma@samford.edu

CHAPMAN, VIRGINIA
DISCIPLINE COMMUNICATION **EDUCATION** Ball State Univ, BS, MA; IN Univ, PhD. **CAREER** Prof, Anderson Univ, 82. **SELECTED PUBLICATIONS** Wrote a unit for the bk Beyond Boundaries--Sex and Gender Diversity. **CONTACT ADDRESS** Anderson Univ, Anderson, IN, 46012. **EMAIL** vchapman@anderson.edu

CHAPMAN, WAYNE
DISCIPLINE ENGLISH LITERATURE **EDUCATION** Wash State Univ, PhD, 88. **CAREER** Dept Eng, Clemson Univ **RESEARCH** Modern British and Anglo-Irish literature. **SELECTED PUBLICATIONS** Auth, L 's Dame Secretaire:' Alix Strachey, the Hogarth Press and Bloomsbury Pacifism, 1917-1960, Women in the Milieu of Leonard and Virginia Woolf: Peace, Politics, and Education, Pace Univ Press, 97; The Countess Cathleen Row of 1899 and the Revisions of 01 and 11, Yeats Annual, Macmillan, 95; coauth, Leonard and Virginia Woolf working together and the hitherto unpublished manuscript "InL ReNS" in Bloomsbury Heritage Series, Cecil Woolf, 97; co-ed, The Countess Cathleen: Manuscript Materials by WB Yeats in The Cornell Yeats, Cornell UP, 98. **CONTACT ADDRESS** Clemson Univ, Clemson, SC, 29634. **EMAIL** cwayne@clemson.edu

CHAPPELL, FRED DAVIS
PERSONAL Born 05/28/1936, Canton, NC, m, 1959, 1 child **DISCIPLINE** ENGLISH **EDUCATION** Duke Univ, BA, 61, MA, 64. **CAREER** From instr to assoc prof, 64-70, prof English, Univ NC, Greensboro, 70-; Rockefeller Found grant, 67-68. **HONORS AND AWARDS** Award in Lit, Nat Inst Arts & Letts, 68; Roanoke-Chowan Poetry Prize, 72, 75, 79, 80, 85, 89; Prix des Meilleur des Livres Etrangers, 72; Sir Walter Raleigh Prize, NC Hist Asn, 76; Oscar A Young Memorial Award, 80; North Carolina Award in Lit, 80; Zoe Kincaid Brockman Award, 81; Bollingen Prize on Poetry, 85; Endowed Chair: The Burlington Industries Professorship, Univ NC, 87; Ragin-Rubin Award, NC English Teachers Asn, 89; Thomas H Carter Essay Award, Shenendoah Magazine, 91; World Fantasy Award, Best Short Story, 92, 94; T S Eliot Prize, Ingersoll Found, 93; Aiken Taylor Award in Poetry, 96. **RESEARCH** Creative writing; 18th century literature; film. **SELECTED PUBLICATIONS** Auth, It is Time, Lord, Atheneum, 63; The Inkling, 65, Dagon, 68 & The Gaudy Place, 72, Harcourt; The World Between The Eyes, 71, River, 75 & Bloodfire, 78, LA State Univ Press; The Man Married Twice to Fire, Unicorn Press, 77; Awakening to Music, Briarpatch Press, 78; Wind Mountain, LA State Univ Press, 79; Earthsleep, LA State Univ Press, 80; Moments of Light, The New South Co, 80; Driftlake: A Leider Cycle, Mountain Press, 81; Midquest, LA State Univ Press, 81; Castle Tzingal, LA State Univ Press, 84;Source, LA State Univ Press, 85; I Am One of You Forever, LA State Univ Press, 85; The Fred Chappell Reader, St Martin's Press, 87; Brighten the Corner Where You Are, St Martin's Press, 89; First and Last Words, LA State Univ Press, 89; More Shapes Than One, St Martin's Press, 91; C: 100 Poems, LA State Univ Press, 93; Plow Naked: Selected Writings on Poetry, Univ MI Press, 93; Spring Garden: New and Selected Poems, LA State Univ Press, 95; Farewell, I'm Bound to Leave You, Picador USA, 96; Family Gathering, forthcoming. **CONTACT ADDRESS** Dept English, Univ N. Carolina, 1000 Spring Garden, Greensboro, NC, 27412-0001.

CHARI, V.K.
PERSONAL Born 11/28/1924, India, m, 1945, 2 children **DISCIPLINE** ENGLISH AND AMERICAN LITERATURE **EDUCATION** Banaras Hindu Univ, BA, 44, MA, 46, PhD(English), 50, dipl French, 65. **CAREER** Asst prof English, Govt Educ Serv, Madhya Pradesh, India, 50-62; reader, Banaras Hindu Univ, 62-66; assoc prof, 66-74, PROF ENGLISH, CARLETON UNIV, 74-, Fulbright fel, NY Univ, 59-60; vis prof, State Univ NY Col New Platz, 60-61; Can Coun res grant, 72-73; Can Coun res grant, 79-80. **RESEARCH** Literary theories in Sanskrit; modern and contemporary American and English poetry; Western and Indian literary aesthetics and criticism. **SELECTED PUBLICATIONS** Auth, Allen, Gay, Wilson, 1903-1995, Walt Whitman Quart Rev, Vol 0013, 95. **CONTACT ADDRESS** Dept of English, Carleton Univ, 1125 Colonel By Dr, Ottawa, ON, K1S 5B6.

CHARNEY, MARK
DISCIPLINE ENGLISH LITERATURE **EDUCATION** Tulane Univ, PhD, 87. **CAREER** Dept Eng, Clemson Univ **RESEARCH** Contemporary literature; film. **SELECTED PUBLICATIONS** Auth, Beauty in the Beast: Technological Reanimation in the Contemporary Horror Film in Trajectories of the Fantastic: Selected Essays from the Fourteenth International Conference on the Fantastic in the Arts, Greenwood, 97; It's a Cold World Out There: Redefining the Family in Contemporary American Film, Beyond the Stars 5: Themes and Ideologies in American Popular Film, Bowling Green State Univ Popular Press, 96. **CONTACT ADDRESS** Clemson Univ, 607 Strode, Clemson, SC, 29634. **EMAIL** cmark@clemson.edu

CHARNEY, MAURICE MYRON
PERSONAL Born 01/18/1929, Brooklyn, NY, m, 1954, 2 children **DISCIPLINE** ENGLISH **EDUCATION** Harvard Univ, AB, magna cum laude, 49; Princeton Univ, MA, 51, PhD(Eng), 52. **CAREER** Instr Eng, Hunter Col, 53-54; from instr to prof, 56-75, Distinguished Prof, Rutgers Univ, New Brunswick, 75-, Fulbright prof, Univ Bordeaux & Univ Nancy, 60-61; co-chmn, Am Civilization Sem, Columbia Univ, 77-79; vis prof, Concordia Univ, 81. **HONORS AND AWARDS** Medal of the City of Tours, 89; Pres, Acad of Lit Stud, 85-87; Pres, Shakespeare Asn of Am, 87-88. **MEMBERSHIPS** MLA; Malone Soc; Shakespeare Asn Am. **RESEARCH** Shakespeare and Elizabethan drama; hist and theory of the drama; theory of comedy. **SELECTED PUBLICATIONS** Auth, Shakespeare's Roman Plays, Harvard, 61; Shakespeare's Timon of Athens, New Am Libr, 65; Style in Hamlet, Princeton, 69; How to Read Shakespeare, McGraw, 71; coauth, The Language of Madwomen in Shakespeare and His Fellow Dramatists, Signs, 77; ed, Comedy: New Perspectives, NY Lit Forum, 78; auth, Comedy High and Low: An Introduction to the Experience of Comedy, Oxford Univ, 78; Sexual Fiction, Methven, 81; Joe Orton, Macmillian, 84; co-ed, The Psychoanalytic Study of Literature, Analytic Press, 85; ed, Classic Comedies, New AmLibrary, 85; ed, The Reader's Adviser, Vol 2, Bowker, 86; ed, Psychoanalytic Approaches to Literature and Film, Fairleigh Dickinson UnivPress, 87; Hamlet's Fictions, Routledge, 88; Titus Andronicus, Harvester, 90; All of Shakespeare, Columbia Univ, 93; ed, Julius Caesar, Applause Books, 96. **CONTACT ADDRESS** Dept of English, Rutgers Univ, 510 George St, New Brunswick, NJ, 08901-1167.

CHARTERS, ANN D.
PERSONAL Born 11/10/1936, Bridgeport, CT, m, 1959, 2 children **DISCIPLINE** AMERICAN LITERATURE **EDUCATION** Univ Calif, Berkeley, BA, 57; Colombia University, MA, 60, PhD, 65. **CAREER** Tchr, Colby Jr Col, 61-63; Tchr, Colombia Univ, 65-66; Tchr, NYC Comm Col, 67-70; Prof, Univ Conn, 74-; Fulbright Prof of Am Lit, Uppsala Univ, Sweden, 82-83; Brown Univ, Assoc Dean, Adjunct Prof, 89-90. **HONORS AND AWARDS** Phi Beta Kappa. **MEMBERSHIPS** MLA, Am Asn of Univ Women. **RESEARCH** Beat generation writers; the short story. **SELECTED PUBLICATIONS** Auth, Major Writers of Short Fiction, St. Martin's Press, 93; auth,The Story and Its Writer, St Martin's Press, 94; auth, The Kerouac Reader, Viking Penguin, 95; auth, Literature and Its Writers, Bedford Books, 97; auth, Grace Paley, Contemp Short Story Writers, Greenwood Press, 97; auth, Jack's Back, Gadfly, 97. **CONTACT ADDRESS** Eng Dept, Univ Conn, Box U-25, Storrs, CT, 06269.

CHASE HANKINS, JUNE
DISCIPLINE AFRICAN AMERICAN WOMEN NOVELISTS **EDUCATION** Univ AR, BA; TX A&M Univ, PhD. **CAREER** Southwest Tex State Univ **HONORS AND AWARDS** NEH Grant; Two NEH Summer Inst Grants. **SELECTED PUBLICATIONS** Auth, Janie's Place in the Academic Garden. **CONTACT ADDRESS** Southwest Texas State Univ, 601 University Dr, San Marcos, TX, 78666-4604.

CHAVKIN, ALLAN
DISCIPLINE MODERN COMIC FICTION **EDUCATION** Dickinson Col, BA; Univ IL, MA, PhD. **CAREER** Southwest Tex State Univ **SELECTED PUBLICATIONS** Auth, Bellow's Alternative to the Wasteland: Romantic Theme and Form in Herzog, Studies Novel, 79; Ivan Karamazov's Rebellion and Bellow's The Victim, Papers Lang & Lit, 80; The Imagination as the Alternative to Sutpen's Design, Ariz Quart, 81; Suffering and the Wilhelm Reich's Theory of Character-Armoring in Bellow's Seize the Day, Essays Lit, 82; The Hollywood Thread & The First Draft of Bellow's Seize the Day, Studies Novel, 82; Fathers and Sons: 'Papa' Hemingway and Saul Bellow, Papers Lang & Lit , 83; Humboldt's Gift and the Romantic Imagination, Philol Quart, 83; The Problem of Suffering in the Fiction of Saul Bellow, Comp Lit Studies, 84; Saul Bellow in the 1980's: A Collection of Critical Essays, Mich State Univ Press, 89; Wordsworth and Modern Literature , MLA, 86; English Romanticism and the Modern Novel, AMS Press, 93; Bellow's Dire Prophecy, Centennial Rev , 89; Conversations with John Gardner, Univ Press Miss, 90; Saul Bellow's Visionary Project, Greenwood Press, 95; Mr. Sammler's War of the Planets, Greenwood Press, 95; The Dean's December and Blake's The Ghost of Abel, Saul Bellow Jour, 95; Conversations with Louise Erdrich and Michael Dorris, Univ Press Miss, 95. **CONTACT ADDRESS** Southwest Texas State Univ, 601 University Dr, San Marcos, TX, 78666-4604.

CHAY, DEBORAH
DISCIPLINE ENGLISH LITERATURE **EDUCATION** Duke Univ, PhD, 92. **CAREER** Asst prof, Dartmouth Col. **RESEARCH** Eng and African lit; African Am Studies. **SELECTED PUBLICATIONS** Auth, Rereading Barbara Smith: Black Feminist Criticism and the Category of Experience, New Lit Hist, 93; Reconstructing Essentialism, Diacritics, 91. **CONTACT ADDRESS** Dartmouth Col, 3529 N Main St, #207, Hanover, NH, 03755. **EMAIL** deborah.chay@dartmouth.edu

CHEAH, PHENG
DISCIPLINE ENGLISH **EDUCATION** Cornell Univ, PhD. **CAREER** Assoc prof, Northwestern Univ. **RESEARCH** Postcolonial literature and theory of Asia and Anglophone Africa. **SELECTED PUBLICATIONS** Coauth, Thinking Through the Body of the Law, Allen and Unwin, 96 & NY Univ Press, 96; Cosmopolitics: Thinking and Feeling Beyond the Nation, Minnesota Univ Press, 97. **CONTACT ADDRESS** Dept of English, Northwestern Univ, 1801 Hinman, Evanston, IL, 60208.

CHELL, SAMUEL L.
DISCIPLINE ENGLISH LITERATURE AND COMPOSITION **EDUCATION** Augustana Col, BA; Univ Ill, MA; Univ Wisc, PhD. **CAREER** English, Carthage Col. **HONORS AND AWARDS** Grants: National Endowment for the Humanities and the University of Chicago Midwest Faculty Seminar. **SELECTED PUBLICATIONS** Auth, The Dynamic Self: Browning's Poetry of Duration, 84. **CONTACT ADDRESS** Carthage Col, 2001 Alford Dr., Kenosha, WI, 53140. **EMAIL** chells1@carthage.edu

CHEN, NI
DISCIPLINE COMMUNICATION **EDUCATION** OH Univ, PhD. **CAREER** Instr, Towson Univ. **RESEARCH** Chinese public rel(s). **SELECTED PUBLICATIONS** Coauthor of a scholarly bk about international public rel(s). **CONTACT ADDRESS** Towson Univ, Towson, MD, 21252-0001. **EMAIL** nchen@towson.edu

CHEN, SHIH-SHIN
PERSONAL Born 08/03/1957, Taiwan, m **DISCIPLINE** SPEECH COMMUNICATION, ORGANIZATIONAL ORGANIZATION **EDUCATION** Univ MD, College Park, PhD, 93. **CAREER** Assoc prof, Nat Taipei Col of Nursing. **HONORS AND AWARDS** ICA Convention,(Washington, DC), org comm div, top three paper, 93. **MEMBERSHIPS** ICA; NCA. **RESEARCH** Org culture; org comm. **SELECTED PUBLICATIONS** Co-auth, with E Fink, A Galileo Analysis of Organizational Climate, Human Communication Res, 21 (4), 95. **CONTACT ADDRESS** National Taipei Col of Nursing, 89, Nei-Chiang St, Wanhua, .. **EMAIL** shihshin@ntcn.ntcn.edu.tw

CHENEY, DONALD
PERSONAL Born 07/14/1932, Lowell, MA, m, 1956, 2 children **DISCIPLINE** ENGLISH, COMPARATIVE LITERATURE **EDUCATION** Yale Univ, BA, 54, MA, 57, PhD, 61. **CAREER** From instr to asst prof English, Yale Univ, 60-67; assoc prof, 67-75, PROF ENGLISH, UNIV MASS, AMHERST, 75-, Morse fel, Yale Univ, 64-65; corresp ed, Spenser Newslett, 70-78, ed, 74-78; co-ed, Spenser Encycl, 79- **MEMBERSHIPS** MLA; Renaissance Soc Am; Spenser Soc; Milton Soc Am; ACLA. **RESEARCH** Renaissance poetry and drama. **SELECTED PUBLICATIONS** Auth, Gazing on Secret Sights--Spenser, Classical Imitation, and the Decorum of Vision, Jour Eng and Ger Philol, Vol 0092, 93. **CONTACT ADDRESS** Dept of English, Univ of Mass, Amherst, MA, 01003-0002.

CHENEY, PATRICK
PERSONAL Born 07/24/1949, Great Falls, MI, m, 1974, 2 children **DISCIPLINE** ENGLISH **EDUCATION** Univ Mont, BA, 72; Univ Toronto, MA, 74, PhD, 79. **CAREER** Asst prof, 80-86, assoc prof,87-97, PROF ENG, COMP LIT, 97-, PA STATE UNIV. **HONORS AND AWARDS** Inst Arts, Hum Stud res fel, Pa State Univ, 87,95, 96, 97; Pa State Univ Fac Award, 95, 96, 97., Co-dir, The ARtist in an Age of Imperial Culture Careers in the Early Modern Period, summer inst, 98; co-dir, The Faerie Queene in the World, 1596-1996. Spenser among the Disciplines, Yale Univ, 96; chair, prog comt, Spenser at Kalamazoo, medieval inst, 97-99. **MEMBERSHIPS** Mod Lang Asn; Renaissance Soc Am; Int Spenser Soc; Marlowe Soc Am. **RESEARCH** 16th, 17th cent Br lit, esp Spenser, Marlow, Shakespeare. **SELECTED PUBLICATIONS** Auth, Marlowe's Counterfeit Profession: Ovid, Spenser, Counter-Nationhood, Univ Toronto Press, 97; auth, Spenser's Famous Flight: A Renaissance Idea of a Literary Career, Univ Toronto Press, 93; co-ed, Worldmaking Spenser: Explorations in the Early Modern Age, Univ Press Ky, 99; co-ed, Approaches to Teaching Shorter Elizabethan Poetry, Mod Lang Asn, 99; auth, Spenser's Pastorals: The Shepheardes Calendar and Colin Clouts Come Home Again, in The Cambridge Companion to Spenser, Cambridge Univ Press, forthcoming; auth, Recent Studies in Marlowe (1987- 1998), Eng Lit Renaissance; auth, Career Rivalry and the Writing of Counter-Nationhood: Ovid, Spenser, and Philomela in Marlowe's The Passionate Shepherd to His Love, ELH 65, 98; auth, Teaching Spenser's Marriage Poetry: Amoretti, Epithalamion, Prothelamion, in Approaches to Teaching Shorter Elizabethan Poetry, Mod Lang Asn, forthcoming; auth, Materials, in Approaches to Teaching Shorter Elizabethan Poetry, NY: Mod Lang Asn, forthcoming; introduction, Worldmaking Spenser: Explorations in the Early Modern Age, Univ Press Ky, forthcoming; auth, Thondring Word of Theatre: Marlowe, SPenser, and Renaissance ideas of a literary Career, in Marlowe, HIstory, and Sexuality: New Critical Essays on Christopher Malrowe, AMS Press, 98. **CONTACT ADDRESS** Dept of English, Pennsylvania State Univ, University Park, PA, 16802.

CHERCHI-USAI, PAOLO
DISCIPLINE ENGLISH **EDUCATION** Univ of Genoa, Italy, PhD. **CAREER** Adj prof & sr curator Motion Picture Dept, George Eastman House/Int Mus Photog and Film, Rochester, NY, taught at Int Sch for Film Restoration, Bologna. **HONORS AND AWARDS** Jean Vigo awd & Int al Film Guide awd., Cofounder, Domitor, Int Asn for the Develop Stud on Early Cinema. **MEMBERSHIPS** Co-dir, Silent Film Festival of Pordenone, Italy & bd directors, Int Fed Film Arch. **RESEARCH** Hist and aesthetics of film. **SELECTED PUBLICATIONS** Auth, Burning Passions: An Introduction to the Study of Silent Cinema, The Vitagraph Company of America 1897-1916; coauth, Silent Witnesses: Russian Films, 1908-1917; articles on, Lois Weber, early film pornography, pre-Technicolor techniques, Pastrone's hist epic Cabiria, Stanley Kubrick, film and archit, theory & methodology of film restoration; contribur, Sight & Sound, Film Hist, Iris & Hors Cadre; ed, Segnocinema, Griffithiana & J Film Preserv. **CONTACT ADDRESS** Dept of Eng, Univ of Rochester, 601 Elmwood Ave, Ste. 656, Rochester, NY, 14642. **EMAIL** usai@uhura.cc.rochester.edu

CHERNISS, MICHAEL DAVID
PERSONAL Born 04/07/1940, Los Angeles, CA **DISCIPLINE** ENGLISH **EDUCATION** Univ Calif, Berkeley, AB, 62, MA, 63, PhD(English), 66. **CAREER** From asst prof to assoc prof, 66-76, PROF ENGLISH, UNIV KANS, 76- **MEMBERSHIPS** MLA; Mediaeval Acad Am; New Chaucer Soc; Int Soc of Anglo-Saxonists **RESEARCH** Old and Middle English literature; continental medieval literature. **SELECTED PUBLICATIONS** Auth, Ingeld and Christ, Mouton, The Hague, 72; Boethian Apocalypse: Studies in Middle English Vision Poetry, Pilgrim Books, 97. **CONTACT ADDRESS** Dept of English, Univ of Kans, Lawrence, KS, 66045-0001.

CHERRY, CAROLINE LOCKETT
PERSONAL Born 06/16/1942, Washington, DC, m, 1968, 1 child **DISCIPLINE** ENGLISH LITERATURE **EDUCATION** Randolph-Macon Woman's Col, AB, 64; Univ NC, MA, 65, PhD(English Lit), 68. **CAREER** From asst prof to assoc prof, 68-78, prof English Lit, Eastern Col, PA, 78-, chmn Humanities Div, 72-; chmn English Dept, 88. **MEMBERSHIPS** MLA. **RESEARCH** Renaissance; literature, Milton; film studies. **SELECTED PUBLICATIONS** Coauth, Contemporary Composition, Prentice-Hall, 70; auth, The Most Unvaluedest Purchase: Women in the Plays of Thomas Middleton, Univ Salzburg, 73. **CONTACT ADDRESS** Dept of English, Eastern Col, 1300 Eagle Rd, St. Davids, PA, 19087-3696. **EMAIL** ccherry@eastern.edu

CHERRY, CHARLES L.
PERSONAL Born 07/30/1942, Baltimore, MD, m, 1968 **DISCIPLINE** ENGLISH LITERATURE, HISTORY OF PSYCHIATRY **EDUCATION** Loyola Col, Md, BA, 64; Univ NC, Chapel Hill, MA, 66, PhD(English), 68. **CAREER** Asst English, Univ NC, 65-68; asst prof, 68-77, dir honors prog, 72-77, assoc prof, 77-80, prof English, Villinova Univ, 80-; assoc acad vp, 79-94; chemn, English dept, 96-; Commun consult, fed govt & ins indust, 71-; Am Coun Educ fel & asst to pres of Univ Pa, 77-78; Cooper-Woods travel study grant, 77; Am Coun Educ fel, 77-78; Lilly Found fel hist of sci, 80; T Wistar Brown fel, Haverford Col, 82-83; A Quiet Haven: Quakers Moral Treatment and Asylum Reform, Fairleigh Dickinson Univ Press, 89. **MEMBERSHIPS** Nat Col Honors Coun; MLA; NCTE; Quaker Hist Soc. **RESEARCH** History of psychiatry; nineteenth century British literature; written communication. **SELECTED PUBLICATIONS** Auth, The apotheosis of desire: Dialectic and image in The French Revolution, Visions of the daughters of Albion, and the Preludium to America, Xavier Univ Studies, 7/69; William Blake and Mrs Grundy: Suppression of Visions of the daughters of Albion, Blake Newslett, 8/70; coauth, Contemporary Composition, Prentice-Hall, 70; One approach to a course in the methods of teaching composition, English Educ, 73; coauth, Write up the Ladder: A Communications Text, Goodyear, 76; auth, Friends Asylum, Morgan Hinchman, and moral insanity, Quaker Hist, spring 78; Scalpels and swords: The surgery of contingency planning, Educ Rec, fall 78; The southern retreat: Thomas Hodgkin and Archille-Louis Foville, Med Hist, London, 7/79. **CONTACT ADDRESS** Dept of English, Villanova Univ, 845 E Lancaster Ave, Villanova, PA, 19085. **EMAIL** ccherry@email.vill.edu

CHESEBRO, JAMES W.
PERSONAL Born 06/24/1944, Minneapolis, MN, s **DISCIPLINE** COMMUNICATION **EDUCATION** BA, Univ Minn, 66; MS, Ill State Univ, 67; PhD, Univ Minn, 72. **CAREER** Instr, Concordia Col, 67-69; assoc and asst prof, Temple Univ, 72-81; dir of educ svc, Nat Comm Asn, 89-92; prof, Dept Comm Arts and Sci, Queens Col, 81-89; prof, Dept of Comm, Indiana State Univ, 92-. **HONORS AND AWARDS** Distinguished Svc Award, Nat Comm Asn, 97; Distinguished Tchg and Res Fel, 98, 96; Eastern Hunt Award, 96, 89. **MEMBERSHIPS** Nat Comm Asn; Eastern Comm Asn. **RESEARCH** Study of all media systems as communication and cognitive systems. **SELECTED PUBLICATIONS** Auth, Analyzing Media: Communication Technologies as Symbolic and Cognitive Systems, NY, Guilford Publ Inc, 96; jour articles and book chap, Distinguishing Cultural Systems: Change as a Variable Explaining and Predicting Cross-cultural communication, 177-192, Communication and Identity Across Cultures, ed D. V. Tanno & A. Gonzalez, Intl and Intercultural Comm Annual, vol 21, Thousand Oaks, Calif, Sage Publ, 98; Change, Nation-States and the Centrality of a Communication Persepective, pp 215-225, Communication and Identity Across Cultures, ed D. V. Tanno & A. Gonzalez, Intl and Intercultural Comm Annual, vol 21, Thousand Oaks, Calif, Sage Publ, 98; Media as Symbolic and Cognitive Systems, pp 304-309, Communication: Views from the Helm for the 21st Century, ed J. S. Trent, Boston, Allyn and Bacon, 98; Introduction to the Candlelight March and Celebration of Diversity, Diversity: Celebration and Commitment, ed Sheron J. Dailey, Annandale, Va, Nat Comm Asn, 97; Ethical Communication and Sexual Orientation, Communication Ethics in an Age of Diversity, ed Josina M. Makau and Ronald C. Arnett, Urbana and Chicago, Univ Ill Press, 97; Communication Technologies as Cognitive Systems, Toward the Twenty-First Century: The Future of Speech Communication, ed Julia Wood and Richard Gregg, Cresskill, NJ, Hampton Press Inc, 95; Kenneth Burke and Jacques Derrida, Kenneth Burke and Contemporary Western Thought: A Rhetoric in Transition, ed Bernard L. Brock, Tuscaloosa, Ala, The Univ of Ala Press, Jun 95; Strategies for Increasing Achievement in Oral Communication, Educating Everybody's Children: Diverse Tchg Strategies for Diverse Learners, ed Robert W. Cole, Alexandria, Va, Asn for Supv and Curriculum Develop, 95. **CONTACT ADDRESS** 1307 South Center St., Terre Haute, IN, 47802-1119. **EMAIL** cmchese@ruby.indstate.edu

CHIKAGE, IMAI
PERSONAL Born 10/17/1961, Japan, s **DISCIPLINE** COMMUNICATION AND INTERPERSONAL COMMUNICATION **EDUCATION** Univ Okla, PhD, 97. **CAREER** Asst prof, Kansai Univ Intl Studies. **MEMBERSHIPS** NCA, ICA W SCA, Comm Asn Japan. **RESEARCH** Conversation analysis; Cross-cultural comparison. **SELECTED PUBLICATIONS** Social Interactants' Handling of Daily Misunderstanding: Close Examination of Actual Misunderstanding Cases, Kansai Univ Intl Studies, v12, 98; Recognition of Misunderstanding in Everyday Conversation, Human Comm Studies, vol 26, 98; Seeking the Mechanisms of Misunderstanding, Kansai Univ Intl Studies, v11, 97; Deconstructing and Reconstructing Misunderstanding, Human Comm Studies, v25, 97. **CONTACT ADDRESS** 1255 Toba, Sunplace 3, Akashi-city, ., 673-0003. **EMAIL** chiro@gold.ocn.ne.jp

CHILDERS, JOSEPH W.
DISCIPLINE ENGLISH LITERATURE **EDUCATION** Univ Ark, BA, MA; Columbia Univ, PhD. **CAREER** PROF, ART HIST, UNIV CALIF, RIVERSIDE. **HONORS AND AWARDS** Fel, Amer Coun of Learned Soc, 92., Assoc dir, UC Riverside's Ctr for Ideas and Soc, 96-97. **RESEARCH** Working-class and immigrant literature. **SELECTED PUBLICATIONS** Auth, Novel Possibilities: Fiction and the Formation of Early Victorian Culture, Univ Pa Press, 95; co-auth, The Columbia Dictionary of Modern Literary and Cultural Criticism, Columbia Univ Press, 95; Edwin Chadwick and the discursive formation of the Victorian working classes, Victorian Stud, 94; Class resistance and Victorian domesticity, Prose Stud, 94. **CONTACT ADDRESS** Dept of Eng, Univ Calif, 1156 Hinderaker Hall, Riverside, CA, 92521-0209.

CHING, MARVIN K.L.
DISCIPLINE LINGUISTIC PERSPECTIVES ON LITERATURE **EDUCATION** FL State Univ, PhD. **CAREER** Engl, Univ Neb. **SELECTED PUBLICATIONS** Ed, SECOL Rev. **CONTACT ADDRESS** Univ NE, NE.

CHINITZ, DAVID
PERSONAL Born 11/19/1962, Brooklyn, NY, m, 1991, 2 children **DISCIPLINE** ENGLISH **EDUCATION** Columbia Univ, PhD 93; Brown Univ, MSc 85; Amherst Col, BA 84. **CAREER** Loyola Univ, asst prof 93 to 98-. **HONORS AND AWARDS** NEH **MEMBERSHIPS** MLA; TS Eliot Soc; Langston Hughes Soc; E E Cummings Soc. **RESEARCH** Moderinst poetry; poetry and culture. **SELECTED PUBLICATIONS** Auth, A Jazz-Banjorine, Not a Lute: Eliot and Popular Music before The Waste Land, Ts Eliot and Music, ed, John Xiros Cooper, Garland, forthcoming; The Problem of Dullness: Eliot and the Lively Arts, 1921-1927, Time Present and Time Past: T. S. Eliot and Our Turning World, ed, Jewel Spears Brooker, Macmillan, forthcoming; Comedian of the Spirit: Kenneth Koch's Postmodern Pleasures, The New York Sch Poets, ed, Stephen Paul Miller and Terence Diggory, NPF, forthcoming; Inventions of the March Hare, By T. S. Eliot, rev, ANQ, 98; Rejuvenation through Joy: Langston Hughes, Primitivism, and Jazz, ALH, 97; Cumming's Challenge to Academic Standards, Spring, 96; Dance, Little Lady: Poets Flappers and the Gendering of Jazz, Modernism Gender and Culture, ed, Lisa Rado, Garland, 96. **CONTACT ADDRESS** Dept of English, Loyola Univ, 6525 N Sheridan Rd, Chicago, IL, 60626. **EMAIL** dchinit@luc.edu

CHINOY, HELEN KRICH
PERSONAL Born 09/25/1922, Newark, NJ, m, 1948, 2 children **DISCIPLINE** ENGLISH, THEATRE **EDUCATION** NY Univ, BA, 43, MA, 45; Columbia Univ, PhD, 63. **CAREER** Instr English, NY Univ, 44-45 & Queens Col, 45, 50 & Newark Col, Rutgers Univ, 46-48; instr English, 52-55, theatre, Smith Col, 56-60; lectr English, Univ Leicester, 63-64; from lectr to assoc prof, 65-71, chmn dept theatre & speech, 68-71, prof theatre, 75-97, PROF EMERITUS, SMITH COL, 97-; Assoc ed, Theatre Jour, Publ Am Theatre Asn; Nat Endowment for Humnities fel, 79-80. **HONORS AND AWARDS** Emmy Award, 89; Hoffman Eminent Scholar Chair in Theater, Fla State Univ, 90; Harold Clurman Prof, Hunter Col, 93. **MEMBERSHIPS** Nat Theatre Conf; fel Am Theatre Asn; Am Soc Theatre Res. **RESEARCH** History, theories and technicques of acting and directing; modern European and American drama and theater; Shakespearean staging, especially by modern directors. **SELECTED PUBLICATIONS** Coed, Actors on Acting, Crown, 49, rev ed, 70; coauth, Directors on Directing, Bobbs, 63; auth, The profession and the art: Directing 1860-1920, In: American Theatre: A Sum of its Parts, French, 71; Production and direction, In: Encycl Britannica; Reunion: A self portrait of the group theatre, Educ Theatre J, 12/76 & Am Theatre Asn, spring 77; Hallie Flanagan Davis, In: Notable American Women, Harvard Press, 80; auth, The Directory as Mythogog, Shakespeare Quarterly, Winter 76; coauth, Women in American Theatre, 81, 82, 87; auth, Art Versus Business: The Role of Women in American Theatre, The Drama Review, June 80; auth, The Poetics of Politics, Some Ntes on Style and Craft in the Theatre of the Thirties, Theatre J, Dec 83. **CONTACT ADDRESS** 230 Crescent St, Northampton, MA, 01060. **EMAIL** hchinoy@sophia.smith.edu

CHOW, KAREN
PERSONAL Born 06/20/1969, Weymouth, MA, s **DISCIPLINE** ENGLISH **EDUCATION** Univ of CA, Santa Barbara, PhD, 98, MA, 93; Univ of South CA, BS, 91 **CAREER** Asst Prof, 97-, Univ of CT **HONORS AND AWARDS** Summer Res Grant **MEMBERSHIPS** Mod Lang Asn; Am Studies Asn **RESEARCH** Am Lit **SELECTED PUBLICATIONS** Auth, Asian American Literature, Reference Guide to English and American Writers, St James Press, 96; Zora neale Hurston, Reference Guide to English and American Writers, St James Press, 96; Maxine Hong Kingston, Reference Guide to American Writers, Gale Research, Inc., 95; The Woman Warrior, Reference Guide to American Writers, Gale Research, Inc., 95 **CONTACT ADDRESS** Storrs, CT, 06219-1025. **EMAIL** kchow@uconnum.uconn.edu

CHRIST, CAROL TECLA
PERSONAL Born 05/21/1944, New York, NY **DISCIPLINE** ENGLISH **EDUCATION** Douglas Col, BA, 66; Yale Univ, MPhil, 69, PhD(English), 70. **CAREER** Asst prof, 70-76, ASSOC PROF ENGLISH, UNIV CALIF, BERKELEY, 76-, Nat Endowment for Humanities res, 77. **RESEARCH** Victorian studies; women's studies. **SELECTED PUBLICATIONS** Auth, Browning Corpses--The Theme and Representation of the Dead in His Poetry, Victorian Poetry, Vol 0033, 95; The American-University and Womens Studies--Anniversary Lecture, Tulsa Stud in Womens Lit, Vol 0016, 97. **CONTACT ADDRESS** Dept of English, Univ Calif, Berkeley, CA, 94720-0001.

CHRIST, WILLIAM G.
DISCIPLINE COMMUNICATION THEORY **EDUCATION** St Lawrence Univ, BA; Univ WI-Madison, MA; FL State Univ, PhD. **CAREER** Com, Trinity Univ. **RESEARCH** Audience analysis. **SELECTED PUBLICATIONS** Pub(s), children's stories. **CONTACT ADDRESS** Dept of Commun, Trinity Univ, 715 Stadium Dr, San Antonio, TX, 78212.

CHRISTIAN, BARBARA T.
PERSONAL Born 12/12/1943, St. Thomas, VI, d, 1 child **DISCIPLINE** BRITISH AND AMERICAN LITERATURE **EDUCATION** Columbia Univ, PhD, British and Amer contemporary literature, 70. **CAREER** Lecturer, SEEK program, City Coll NY, 65-71; lecturer, English Dept, 71-72, asst prof, 72-78, chair, 78-83, assoc prof, 78-86, full prof, 86-, African Amer Studies, Univ Calif Berkeley. **HONORS AND AWARDS** Melus Award for Contribution to Ethnic Studies and African Amer Studies Scholarship, 94; Louise Patterson Award for Best Black Faculty, Univ Calif Berkeley, 95; contribution to black literary arts, Gwendolyn Brooks Center, 95; Phi Beta Kappa Award for Distinguished Teaching, Northern California Chapter, 95; Amer Coun Learned Societies, 95-96; Fulbright, Center for Amer Studies, Ritsumeikan Univ, Summer Inst, 98. **MEMBERSHIPS** Modern Lang Assn; Toni Morrison Soc. **RESEARCH** African American literature; women's studies; multicultural studies. **SELECTED PUBLICATIONS** Ed, Norton Anthology of African American Literature, Contemporary Section, 96; auth, "Camouflaging Race and Gender," Representations, 96; coauth, Female Subjects in Black and White: Race, Psychoanalysis and Feminism, 97; auth, "Beloved: She's Ours," Narrative: Journal of the Society for the Study of Narrative Literature, Jan 97; auth, "Layered Rhythms: Toni Morrison and Virginia Woolf," in Reading Toni Morrison: Theoretical and Critical Approaches, 97. **CONTACT ADDRESS** Univ of California Berkeley, 660 Barrows Hall, Berkeley, CA, 94720. **EMAIL** bchristi@library.berkeley.edu

CHRISTIANS, CLIFFORD G.
PERSONAL Born 12/22/1939, Hull, IA, m, 1961, 3 children **DISCIPLINE** COMMUNICATIONS **EDUCATION** Univ of Ill-Urbana, PhD, 74. **CAREER** Res asst prof of commun, Univ of Ill-Urbana, 74-80; res assoc prof of commun, 80-87; res prof of commun, 87-; Dir, Inst of Commun Res, 87-. **HONORS AND AWARDS** Kappa Tau Alpha; Phi Kappa Phi; Univ of Ill Award for Excellence in Undergraduate Teach; Pew Evangelical Schol. **MEMBERSHIPS** Assoc for Educ in J & Mass Commun; Int Commun Assoc; Int Assoc for Mass Commun Res; Nat Commun Assoc. **RESEARCH** Media ethics; philosophy of technology; Jacques Ellul; communication theory. **SELECTED PUBLICATIONS** Co-auth, Media Ethics: Cases and Moral Reasoning, Longman Inc., 83, 2nd ed, 87, 3rd ed, 91, 4th ed, 95, 5th ed, 98; co-auth, Good News: A Social Ethics of the Press, Oxford Univ Press, 93; co-auth, Communication Ethics and Universal Values, The Ethics of Being Communications Context, Sage, chap 1, 3-23, 93; co-auth, Role of the Media Ethics Course in the Education of Journalists, J Educ, 49:3, 20-26, 94; auth, The Naturalistic Fallacy in Contemporary Interactionist-Interpretive Research, Studs in Symbolic Interaction, vol 19, 125-130, 95; auth, Review Essay: Current Trends in Media Ethics, Eur J of Commun, 10:4, 545-558, 95; auth, The Problem of Universals in Communication Ethics, Javnost: The Public, 2:2, 59-69, 95; auth, Propaganda and the Technological System, Public Opinion and the Communication of Consent, Guilford Pubs, 156-174, 95; auth, Communication Ethics as the Basis of Genuine Democracy, The Democratization of Communication, Univ of Wales Press, 75-91, 95; auth, Cultures of Silence and Technological Development, Responsible Communication: Ethical Issues in Business, Industry, and the Professions, Hampton Press, 267-283, 96; co-auth, The Status of Ethics Instruction in Communication Departments, Commun Educ, 45:3, 236-243, 7/96; auth, Social Responsibility: Ethics and New Technologies, Ethics in Human Communication, Waveland Press, 4th ed, 321-335, 96; auth, Common Ground and Future Hopes, Images that Injure: Pictorial Sterotypes in the Media, Praeger, 237-243, 261-262, 96; auth, The Common Good and Universal Values, Mixed News: The Public/Civic/Communitarian Journalism Debate, Lawrence Erlbuam, 18-33, 97; auth, Chronology: Contemporary Ethical Issues, Journalism Ethics: A Reference Handbook, ABC-CLIO, 97; auth, Social Ethics and Mass Media Practice, Communication Ethics in an Age of Diversity, Univ of Ill Press, 187-205, 97; auth, Technology and Triadic Theories of Meditation, Rethinking Media, Religion, and Culture, Sage, 65-82, 97; auth, Critical Issues in Communication Ethics, Communication: Views from the Helm for the Twenty-First Centuiry, Allyn & Bacon, 270-275, 98; auth, The Sacredness of Life, Media Development, 45:2, 3-7, 98; auth, The Politics of Recognition, Nat Media Ethics and Law Conf Book, Univ of Minn Silha Ctr, 139-159, 98; auth, Media Ethics and the Technological Society, J of Mass Media Ethics, 13:2, 98. **CONTACT ADDRESS** 1002 W William St, Champaign, IL, 61821. **EMAIL** cchrstns@uiuc.edu

CHRISTIANSON, PAUL
DISCIPLINE ENGLISH LANGUAGE AND LITERATURE **EDUCATION** St Olaf, BA, 55; State Univ Iowa, MA, 56; Wash Univ, PhD, 64. **CAREER** Mildred Foss Thompson prof. **SELECTED PUBLICATIONS** Auth, books on medieval cult and lit. **CONTACT ADDRESS** Dept of Eng, Col of Wooster, Wooster, OH, 44691.

CHRISTIANSON, SCOTT
DISCIPLINE 20TH-CENTURY AMERICAN AND BRITISH LITERATURE, LITERARY THEORY AND CRITICISM **EDUCATION** Harvard Univ, MA, 74; Augustana Col, BA, 77; Univ NE, MA, 78; Univ MN, PhD, 86. **CAREER** Tchg assoc, Univ MN, 80-86; asst prof, Moorhead State Univ, 86-87; undergrad adv cord, 89-91, gard recruitment and admis cord, 89-91, mem, grad fac, 90-, assoc prof, 93-, ch, peace and world Security Stud minor prog, 93-94, assoc ch, dept Eng, 93-94, actg ch, dept Eng, Radford Univ, 94. **HONORS AND AWARDS** Grant, Col Arts and Sci, 92-93, grant, Ctr for Acad Enrichment Prog, 92-93, fac prof develop Leave, 95, fac adv of best res MA thesis award, Radford Univ, 97. **RESEARCH** T. S. Eliot. **SELECTED PUBLICATIONS** Auth, Rev of Narrative Chance: Postmodern Discourse on Native American Indian Literatures, ed Gerald Vizenor, Western Am Lit 29.2, 94; Talkin' Trash and Kickin' Butt: Sue Grafton's Hardboiled Feminism, in Feminism in Women's Detective Fiction, ed Glenwood Irons, Univ Toronto Press, 95; Ella Constance Sykes, in Dictionary of Literary Biography 174: British Travel Writers, 1876-1909, eds. Barbara Brothers and Julia Gergits, Gale Res, 97; The Eternal Return of T. S. Eliot, rev of Mastery and Escape, by Jewel Spears Brooker, Yeats Eliot Rev 14.3, 97. **CONTACT ADDRESS** Radford Univ, Radford, VA, 24142. **EMAIL** schristi@runet.edu

CHRISTOPHER, GEORGIA B.
PERSONAL Barnesville, GA **DISCIPLINE** RENAISSANCE ENGLISH LITERATURE **EDUCATION** Anges Scott Col, BA, 55; Yale Univ, MAT, 57, PhD(English), 66. **CAREER** Teacher English, Needham Broughton High Sch, Raleigh, NC, 57-59; instr, Mercer Univ, 59-62; asst prof, Univ NC, Chapel Hill, 66-71; assoc prof, Westhampton Col, Univ Richmond, 71-78, actg chmn dept, 73, prof English, 78-81; ASSOC PROF, EMORY UNIV, 81-, Sr Folger fel, 75-76; Am Coun Learned Socs fel, 75-76. **MEMBERSHIPS** MLA; Milton Soc Am; SAtlantic Mod Lang Asn; Am Shakespeare Asn; Renaissance Soc Am. **RESEARCH** Milton; Renaissance; poetry and intellectual history. **SELECTED PUBLICATIONS** Auth, Subject and Macrosubject in l'Allegro and il Penseroso, Milton Stud, Vol 0028, 92. **CONTACT ADDRESS** Dept of English, Emory Univ, Atlanta, GA, 30322.

CHU, FELIX T.
PERSONAL Born 02/27/1949, Taipei, Taiwan, m, 1975, 1 child **DISCIPLINE** LIBRARY SCIENCE **EDUCATION** Univ Wi Madison, BA, 72; Univ Iowa, MA, 73, 74, BA, 81; Il St Univ, PhD, 93. **CAREER** Cataloger, Univ Nb Lincoln, 75-78; librn, Univ Iowa, 79-80; data proc anal, Nb Dept of Revenue, 81-84; asst to dir, W Il Univ, 88; librn co coord, W Il Univ, 88- . **MEMBERSHIPS** Amer Libr Assoc; Il Libr Assoc. **RESEARCH** Interdepartmental commun in the libr; commun between librns & patrons or outside agencies; lateral relations; org structures; leadership & change, access to libr materials. **SELECTED PUBLICATIONS** Auth, Collaboration in a loosely coupled system: Librarian-faculty relations in collection develop, Libr & Infor Sci Res, 95; The freezing of dynamic knowledge, Technicalities, 96; Framing reference encounters, RQ, 96; The librarian-faculty relations in collection develop, J of Acad Librarianship, 97; Another look at staffing the reference desk, Col & Res Libr News, 97. **CONTACT ADDRESS** Univ Library, W Il Univ, 1 University Cir, Macomb, IL, 61455-1390. **EMAIL** f-chu@wiu.edu

CHURCH, DAN M.
DISCIPLINE TWENTIETH-CENTURY THEATER AND FILM, TECHNOLOGY AND LANGUAGE ACQUISITION **EDUCATION** Wake Forest Col, BA, 61; Middlebury Col, MA, 62; Univ Wis, PhD, 68. **CAREER** Asst prof Fr, Antioch Col, 65-67; asst prof, 67-70; assoc prof, 70-; dir, Vanderbilt-in-Fr, 74-76; dir, Workshop on the Quest Authoring Syst, 86; dir, Mellon Regional fac develop sem, 86; dir, lang lab, Vanderbilt Univ, 88-96. **MEMBERSHIPS** Comput Assisted Lang Instr Consortium; chemn, Courseware Develop Spec Interest Gp. **SELECTED PUBLICATIONS** Auth, Interactive Audio for Foreign-Language Learning, Lit & Ling Comp, V, 2; AndrQ Barsacq, Gaston Baty, and Roger Planchon, Theatrical Directors: A Biographical Dictionary, Greenwood Press, 94; rev, GramDef French, CALICO J, 98. **CONTACT ADDRESS** Vanderbilt Univ, Nashville, TN, 37203-1727. **EMAIL** barrettt@ctrvax.vanderbilt.edu 3

CHURCHILL, ROBERT J.
DISCIPLINE 19TH-CENTURY BRITISH LITERATURE/VICTORIAN STUDIES **EDUCATION** Creighton Univ, BA, 66, MA, 70; Univ NE-Lincoln, PhD, 79. **CAREER** Asst prof, Creighton Univ, 80-; past instr, Univ NE-Lincoln. **SELECTED PUBLICATIONS** Written on, Carlyle, Tennyson, Browning, Victorian Mysticism, Joseph Conrad, Eastern Literature & 19th-Century Travel-Adventure Narratives. **CONTACT ADDRESS** Dept of Eng, Creighton Univ, 2500 CA Plaza, CA 311, Omaha, NE, 68178. **EMAIL** rchurch@creighton.edu

CIANCIO, RALPH ARMANDO
PERSONAL Born 12/01/1929, Pittsburgh, PA, m, 1959, 3 children **DISCIPLINE** ENGLISH **EDUCATION** Duquesne Univ, AB, 57; Pa State Univ MA, 58; Univ Pittsburgh, PhD(English), 64. **CAREER** From instr to asst prof English, Carnegie-Mellon Univ, 59-65; from asst prof to assoc prof, 65-75, PROF ENGLISH, SKIDMORE COL, 76-, CHMN DEPT, 80- **MEMBERSHIPS** MLA. **RESEARCH** American fiction; 20th century European novel. **SELECTED PUBLICATIONS** Auth, Richard Write, Eugene O'Neill, and The Beast in the skull, Modern Language Studies, Vol XXIII, No 3, Summer 98; auth, Laughing in Pain with Nathaniel West, Literature and the Grotesque, Rodophi Perspectives on Modern Literature, 15, 95; auth, Vico in Dixie, The Southern Literary Journal, Vol XXVI-II, No 1, Univ NC, Chapel Hill, Fall, 95. **CONTACT ADDRESS** Dept of Eng, Skidmore Col, 815 N Broadway, Saratoga Springs, NY, 12866-1698.

CIMA, GAY GIBSON
DISCIPLINE ENGLISH LITERATURE **EDUCATION** Univ Nebr, BA; Northwestern Univ, MA, Cornell Univ, PhD. **CAREER** Prof. **RESEARCH** History of American women as performance critics. **SELECTED PUBLICATIONS** Auth, Feminist Theatre; Performance Theory; Performing Women: Female Characters, Male Playwrights; Modern Stage, Cornell, 93. **CONTACT ADDRESS** English Dept, Georgetown Univ, 37th and O St, Washington, DC, 20057.

CIRILLO, ALBERT
DISCIPLINE LITERATURE **EDUCATION** Johns Hopkins Univ, PhD. **CAREER** Mellon fel, Harvard, 90-91; co-ed, Gender and Theatre Series for Routledge; several res fel(s), Canada. **SELECTED PUBLICATIONS** Auth, essays on and is an authority on the Working Women: Their Social Identity in Victorian Culture, 91; George Bernard Shaw and the Socialist Theatre, 94; essays on, theatre history and popular culture in Victorian and Edwardian Engl; 16th & 17th century poetry. **CONTACT ADDRESS** Dept of English, Northwestern Univ, 1801 Hinman, Evanston, IL, 60208.

CISAR, MARY
PERSONAL IL, m, 2 children **DISCIPLINE** EIGHTEENTH-CENTURY FRENCH LITERATURE **EDUCATION** Kalamazoo Col; Brown Univ, MA, PhD. **CAREER** French, St. Olaf Col. **SELECTED PUBLICATIONS** Area: Mennonite women's autobiography. **CONTACT ADDRESS** St Olaf Col, 1520 St Olaf Ave, Northfield, MN, 55057.

CLADER, LINDA
PERSONAL Born 02/11/1946, Evanston, IL, m, 1991 **DISCIPLINE** CLASSICAL PHILOLOGY; HOMILETICS **EDUCATION** Carleton Col, AB, 68; Harvard Univ, AM, 70, PhD, 73; Church Divinity School of Pacific, M Div, 88. **CAREER** Instr to full prof Classical languages, Carleton Col, 72-90; asst to assoc prof, homiletics, Church Divinity School Pacific, 91-. **HONORS AND AWARDS** Phi Beta Kappa, 68. **MEMBERSHIPS** AAR/SBL; Acad Homiletics **RESEARCH** Liturgical preaching; Myth; Homer. **SELECTED PUBLICATIONS** Auth, Preaching the Liturgical Narratives: The Easter Vigil and the Language of Myth, Worship, 98. **CONTACT ADDRESS** Church Divinity Sch of the Pacific, 2451 Ridge Rd, Berkeley, CA, 94709. **EMAIL** Lclader@cdsp.edu

CLAIR, ROBIN P.
DISCIPLINE COMMUNICATIONS **EDUCATION** Kent State U niv, PhD, 90. **CAREER** Assoc prof, Purdue Univ. **RESEARCH** Studies of socialization and sexual harassment; how aesthetic theory can be applied to studies of organizational life. **SELECTED PUBLICATIONS** Auth, The Use of Framing Devices to Sequester Organizational Narratives: Hegemony and Harassment, Commun Monogr, 93; The Political Nature of the Colloquialism, A Real Job: Implications for Organizational Socialization, Commun Monogr, 96. **CONTACT ADDRESS** Dept of Commun, Purdue Univ, 1080 Schleman Hall, West Lafayette, IN, 47907-1080. **EMAIL** rpclair@omni.cc.purdue.edu

CLANCY, JOSEPH P.
PERSONAL Born 03/08/1928, New York, NY, m, 1948, 5 children **DISCIPLINE** ENGLISH **EDUCATION** Fordham Univ, BA, MA, PhD. **CAREER** Instr, Fordham Col, 49-50; from asst prof to assoc prof, 50-65, PROF ENGLISH, MARYMOUNT MANHATTAN COL, 65-, CHMN DEPT, 50-, Am Philos Soc grant, 63 & 67; Nat Transl Ctr fel, 67. **MEMBERSHIPS** MLA. **RESEARCH** English drama to 1700; mediaeval Welsh poetry; 17th century English literature. **SELECTED PUBLICATIONS** Auth, In Transit, Poetry Wales, Vol 0032, 96; Deep North, Poetry Wales, Vol 0032, 96; Death Notices, Poetry Wales, Vol 0033, 97; Dail Glaswellt--Selection of Whitman,W alt Poems-Welsh, Walt Whitman Quart Rev, Vol 0013, 95; Capturing Poems--On Translating Poetry, Poetry Wales, Vol 0029, 94; Unselving--From the Poetry, Stand Mag, Vol 0038, 96. **CONTACT ADDRESS** Dept of English, Marymount Manhattan Col, New York, NY, 10021.

CLARESON, THOMAS DEAN
PERSONAL Born 08/26/1926, Austin, MN, m, 1954, 1 child **DISCIPLINE** ENGLISH **EDUCATION** Univ Minn, BA, 46; Ind Univ, MA, 49; Univ Pa, PhD(English), 56. **CAREER** Assoc prof, 55-67, PROF ENGLISH, COL WOOSTER, 67-,

Ed, Extrapolation, 59-; pres, Col English Asn Ohio, 71-72; consult ed reprint ser sci fiction mags & bks, Greenwood Press, 75-; exec comt, MLA Div Popular Cult, 76-80; delegate assembly, MLA, 82-84. **HONORS AND AWARDS** Pilgrim Award, Sci Fiction Res Asn, 77. **MEMBERSHIPS** MLA; Am Studies Asn; Sci Fiction Res Asn; Sci Fiction Writers Am. **SELECTED PUBLICATIONS** Auth, The Lost Worlds Romance--From Dawn Till Dusk, Extrapolation, Vol 0034, 93. **CONTACT ADDRESS** 2223 Friar Tuck, Wooster, OH, 44691.

CLARK, BASIL ALFRED
PERSONAL Born 07/19/1939, Prospect, ME, m, 1966, 2 children **DISCIPLINE** ENGLISH LITERATURE & LANGUAGE **EDUCATION** Bowdoin Col, AB, 60; Univ ME, MA, 69; OH State Univ, PhD, 75. **CAREER** From Asst Prof to Assoc Prof, 75-85, prof eng, Saginaw Valley State Univ, 85. **MEMBERSHIPS** MLA; NCTE. **RESEARCH** Medieval Brit lit. **SELECTED PUBLICATIONS** Heike Monogatari and Beowulf: A Comparative Study, Bull Shikoku Women's Univ 9.2, 90. **CONTACT ADDRESS** Saginaw Valley State Univ, 7400 Bay Rd, University Center, MI, 48710-0001. **EMAIL** baclark@svsu.edu

CLARK, BERTHA SMITH
PERSONAL Born 09/26/1943, Nashville, TN, m, 1973 **DISCIPLINE** SPEECH **EDUCATION** TN State Univ, BS (high distinction) 1964; George Peabody Clg for Tchrs, MA 1965; Natl Inst of Mental Hlth, Pre Doctoral Fellow 1978-80; Vanderbilt Univ, PhD 1982. **CAREER** Bill Wilkerson Hearing & Speech Center (BWHSC), head tchr OE #1 project 1965-70, speech pathologist 1965-78, 1980-87; TN State Univ, supvr of clinical practicum 1969-78, 1980-87; Mama Lere Parent Infant Home, Bill Wilkerson Hearing & Speech Center, parent-infant trainer 1982-86; Vanderbilt Univ, div of hearing and speech sciences, 1970-87, adjunct assistant professor, 1987-98; Middle TN State Univ, prof, currently. **HONORS AND AWARDS** Honors grad Haynes HS 1960, TN St Univ 1964; predoctoral flwshp Natl Inst of Mental Hlth 1978-80; Honors of TSHA, In Speech, Language Hearing Assn 1988; Office of Education Trainee, Office of Education 1964-65; Fellow, Southern Education Foundation 1964. **MEMBERSHIPS** Board of dir League for the Hearing Impaired 1973-87, The Childrens House (A Montessori Preschool) 1984-86; advsry Cmt Early Devel & Assistance Project Kennedy Cntr 1984-88; co-chrprsn mem YWCA 1985; mem Delta Sigma Theta Sorority, Inc 1962-; admin comm, vice pres for educ TN Speech and Hearing Assn 1985-87; chairperson Cochlear Implant Scholarship Comm, 1985-86; mem Compton Scholarship Comm Vanderbilt Univ 1985-86; bd of dirs Peabody Alumni 1986-89; board of directors Bill Wilkerson Center 1990-95; board of directors Effective Advocacy for Citizens with Handicaps 1991-92; board of directors CFAW, MTSU 1991-. **CONTACT ADDRESS** Dept of Speech & Theatre, Middle Tennessee State Univ, Communication Disorders, Murfreesboro, TN, 37132.

CLARK, DAVID L.
DISCIPLINE ENGLISH LITERATURE **EDUCATION** Univ Western Ontario, BA, MA, PhD. **RESEARCH** Romantic poetry and prose; Romantic critical theory; Schelling and Nietzsche; contemp philos; critical theory. **SELECTED PUBLICATIONS** Co-ed, Intersections, 96; co-ed, New Romanticisms, 95. **CONTACT ADDRESS** English Dept, McMaster Univ, 1280 Main St W, Hamilton, ON, L8S 4L9.

CLARK, DAVID RIDGLEY
PERSONAL Born 09/17/1920, Seymour, CT, m, 1948, 4 children **DISCIPLINE** ENGLISH **EDUCATION** Wesleyan Univ, BA, 47; Yale Univ, MA, 50, PhD, 55. **CAREER** Instr Eng, Mohawk Col, 47; tchg fel, IN Univ, 48-50; instr, Univ MA, 51-56; lectr, Smith Col, 56-57; from asst prof to assoc prof, 58-65, chmn dept, 75-76, Prof Eng, Univ MA, 65-85; Emer Prof, Univ MA, Amherst, 85-; Saxton fel, 57; Bollingen Found grant-in-aid, 57; Am Philos Soc grant, 57, 77, 83; Mod Lang Asn, 58; Fulbright lectr, Univ Iceland, 60-61 & Univ Col, Dublin, 65-66; Nat Endowment for Hum proj grant, 69, 78; vis prof Eng, Univ Victoria, BC, 71-72; vis fel, Wolfson Col, Univ Cambridge, 78; vis prof & chmn, St. Mary's Col, Notre Dame, IN, 85-87; vis prof Williams Col, 89,90. **MEMBERSHIPS** MLA, Am Conf Irish Stud. **RESEARCH** W B Yeats and the mod lit of Ireland; the poetry of Hart Crane; late 19th and 20th century lit. **SELECTED PUBLICATIONS** Coauth, A Curious Quire, poems, Univ Mass, 62,67; Auth, W B Yeats and the Theatre of Desolate Reality, Dolmen, Dublin, 65; Dry Tree, 66 & co-ed, A Tower of Polished Black Stones, 71, Dolmen, Dublin; ed, Twentieth Century Interpretations of Murder in the Cathedral, Prentice-Hall, 71-; co-ed, Druid Craft: The Writing of the Shadowy Waters, Univ Mass, 71 & Dolmen, Dublin, 72; auth, Lyric Resonance: Yeats, Frost, Crane, Cummings, and others, Univ Mass, 72; That Black Day, Dolmen, 80; ed, Critical Essays on Hart Crane, G K Hall, 82; auth, Yeats at Songs and Chorusus, Colin Smythe Ltd & Univ Mass, 83; coed, W B Yeats and the Writing of Sopholcles' King Oedipus, Am Philos Soc, Philadelphia, 89; ed, W B Yeats The Winding Stair Manuscript Materials, Cornell, 95. **CONTACT ADDRESS** 481 Holgerson Rd, Sequim, WA, 98382.

CLARK, EDWARD
PERSONAL Born 10/25/1923, Elyria, OH **DISCIPLINE** ENGLISH **EDUCATION** Miami Univ, AB, 49; Ind Univ, PhD(English), 55. **CAREER** Asst prof English, St Lawrence Univ, 55-61; assoc prof, 61-65, PROF ENGLISH, SUFFOLK UNIV, 65-, Fulbright lectr, Kiel Univ, 58-59. **MEMBERSHIPS** MLA; Col Lang Asn; AAUP. **RESEARCH** Leatherstocking tales of Fenimore Cooper; American and British novel; racial literature. **SELECTED PUBLICATIONS** Auth, Rosenberg, Sylvia, Strad, Vol 0105, 94; Under the Sign of the Bison--An Excerpt from the Book Tamrat-13 Days in the Sahara, New Eng Rev-Middlebury Series, Vol 0015, 93; Madoyan, Nikolai, Strad, Vol 0105, 94; Underneath Which Rivers Flow--The Islamic Garden as Archetype of Inner Quiet, Parabola-Myth Tradition and the Search for Meaning, Vol 0021, 96. **CONTACT ADDRESS** Dept of English, Suffolk Univ, Boston, MA, 02114.

CLARK, EDWARD DEPRIEST, SR.
PERSONAL Born 05/24/1930, Wilmington, North Carolina, d **DISCIPLINE** ENGLISH **EDUCATION** North Carolina A&T State University, Greensboro, NC, BS, 1948; New York University, New York, NY, MA, 1955; Syracuse University, Syracuse, NY, PhD, 1971. **CAREER** Union Point High School, Union Point, GA, English dept head, 1948-51; Greensboro High School, Greensboro, GA, English dept head, 1953-54; Emanuel County High School, Swainsboro, GA, English dept head, 1954-57; Albany State College, Albany, GA, asst prof, English, 1957-59; Southern University, Baton Rouge, LA, asst prof, English, 1960-61; Fayetteville State University, Fayetteville, NC, assoc prof, chairman, 1961-66, chairman, prof, English, 1971-75; North Carolina State University, Raleigh, NC, assoc prof, English, 1975-. **HONORS AND AWARDS** Outstanding Teacher Award, 1989, elected to Academy of Outstanding Teachers, 1989, North Carolina State University; Alumni Outstanding Teacher Award, North Carolina State University, 1989. **MEMBERSHIPS** Member, College Language Assn, 1961-; member, Modern Language Assn, 1961-; member, South Atlanta Modeern Language Assn, 1975-. **CONTACT ADDRESS** Professor, English, North Carolina State Univ, Raleigh, NC, 27602.

CLARK, GEORGE
DISCIPLINE ENGLISH LITERATURE **EDUCATION** Harvard Univ, PhD. **CAREER** Dept Eng, Queen's Univ **RESEARCH** Comparative studies in the early Middle Ages; characterization in early literature; representation of women in Old English and Norse-Icelandic literature. **SELECTED PUBLICATIONS** Auth, Beowulf, Twayne, 90; pubs on Beowulf, battle of Maldon, Old English poetry, Njals saga, the oral tradition, Robert Henryson, and Chaucer. **CONTACT ADDRESS** English Dept, Queen's Univ, Kingston, ON, K7L 3N6. **EMAIL** clarkg@post.queensu.ca

CLARK, GEORGE PEIRCE
PERSONAL Born 09/08/1915, Indianapolis, IN, m, 1946, 4 children **DISCIPLINE** ENGLISH AND AMERICAN LITERATURE **EDUCATION** Col Wooster, AB, 38; Yale Univ, PhD(English), 48. **CAREER** Asst prof English, Coe Col, 48-50; from asst prof to prof, Northern Ill Univ, 50-57; vis lectr, Univ Ill, 57-58; assoc prof, Mich State Univ, 59-60; cult affairs officer, US Info Agency, 60-67; prof & chmn dept, 67-81, EMER PROF ENGLISH, HANOVER COL, 81-, Ford fac fel, Harvard Univ, 53-54; Fulbright prof, Univ Mainz, 56-57. **MEMBERSHIPS** AAUP. **RESEARCH** Nineteenth-century American literature; Civil War history. **SELECTED PUBLICATIONS** Auth, Lakeside Toast, New Eng Rev-Middlebury Series, Vol 0016, 94; Mouthwash, New Eng Rev-Middlebury Series, Vol 0016, 94. **CONTACT ADDRESS** Hanover Col, PO Box 62, Hanover, IN, 47243.

CLARK, JAMES DRUMMOND
PERSONAL Born 03/01/1940, Lake Forest, IL, m, 1966, 1 child **DISCIPLINE** ENGLISH **EDUCATION** Colo Col, BA, 63; Univ Ariz, PhD, 67. **CAREER** Asst prof, 67-79, assoc prof Eng, Miami Univ, 79-. **MEMBERSHIPS** Malone Soc. **RESEARCH** Italian-English connections in early Elizabethan drama; Shakespearean comedy. **SELECTED PUBLICATIONS** Auth, The Bugbears: A Modernized Edition, Garland Publ, 79. **CONTACT ADDRESS** Dept of English, Miami Univ, 500 E High St, Oxford, OH, 45056-1602. **EMAIL** clarkjd@muohio.edu

CLARK, JUSTUS KENT
PERSONAL Born 09/29/1917, Blue Creek, UT, m, 1939, 3 children **DISCIPLINE** ENGLISH **EDUCATION** Brigham Young Univ, AB, 39; Stanford Univ, PhD, 50. **CAREER** Instr, Stanford Univ, 42-43, 46-47; from instr to assoc prof, 47-60, prof English, 60-86, PROF EMER, 86- , CALIF INST TECHNOL, 60- **RESEARCH** Eighteenth century English literature; 17th Century political history; Jonathan Swift; modern poetry. **SELECTED PUBLICATIONS** Auth, King's Agent, 58 & coauth, Dimensions in Drama, 64, Scribner; Goodwin Wharton (17th C biography), Oxford Univ Press, 85, Londo Sphere Press, 89. **CONTACT ADDRESS** Dept of English, California Inst of Tech, Pasadena, CA, 91125. **EMAIL** JKC@hss.caltech.edu

CLARK, L.D.
PERSONAL Born 10/22/1922, Gainesville, TX, m, 1951 **DISCIPLINE** ENGLISH **EDUCATION** Columbia Univ, BA, 53, MA, 54, PhD(English), 63. **CAREER** Instr English, Agr & Mech Col Tex, 54-55; from instr to assoc prof, 55-70, PROF ENGLISH, UNIV ARIZ, 70-, Vis prof, Univ Nice, 73-74; Nat Endowment for Humanities Text Materials fel, 78. **MEMBERSHIPS** MLA; D H Lawrence Soc. **RESEARCH** British literature of the 20th century, chiefly D H Lawrence. **SELECTED PUBLICATIONS** Auth, Gone Primitive--Savage Intellects, Modern Lives, D H Lawrence Rev, Vol 0023, 91; The Sense of an Ending in the Plumed Serpent, D H Lawrence Rev, Vol 0025, 94; The Risen Adam--Lawrence,D.H. Revistionist Typology, D H Lawrence Review, Vol 0024, 92. **CONTACT ADDRESS** Dept of English, Univ of Ariz, Tucson, AZ, 85721.

CLARK, MICHAEL
PERSONAL Born 01/16/1946, Upland, PA, m, 1974, 2 children **DISCIPLINE** AMERICAN LITERATURE, THE NOVEL **EDUCATION** Univ DE, BA, 69; Univ Akron, MA, 75; Univ WI-Madison, PhD, 81. **CAREER** Tchg asst Eng, Univ Akron, 74-75, Univ WI-Madison, 76-81; from Asst Prof to Assoc Prof, 81-92, prof eng, Widener Univ, 92. **MEMBERSHIPS** MLA; Melville Soc. **RESEARCH** Herman Melville; John Dos Passos. **SELECTED PUBLICATIONS** Auth, Dos Passo's Early Fiction, 1912-1938, Susquehanna Univ Press, 87; ed, Streets of Night, Susquehanna Press, 90; auth, Flannery O'Connor's A Good Man is Hard to Find: The Moment of Grace, English Lang Notes, 12/91; Bret Harte's The Outcasts of Poker Flat and the Donner Pass Tragedy, Short Story, Fall 93; Cultural Treasures of the Internet, Prentice Hall, 95, 2nd ed, 97; author numerous other articles. **CONTACT ADDRESS** Hum Dept, Widener Univ, 1 University Pl, Chester, PA, 19013-5792. **EMAIL** michael.clark@widener.edu

CLARK, PATRICIA
DISCIPLINE LIBRARY AND INFORMATION SERVICES **EDUCATION** Northern IL Univ, BA, 75, MA, 89; IL State Univ, MS 94. **CAREER** Library Clerk II, 80-84, Library Technical Asst II, 84-90, Founders Memorial Library, Northern IL Univ; Library Systems Coord, IL Library Computer Systems Office, Univ IL, 90-91; Reference Librarian, 91-92, acting head, General Information & Reference, 92, Reference Librarian, General Reference & Documents, 92-93, System Development Librarian/Asst prof, Milner Library, IL State Univ, 93-95; Microcomputer and Instructional Technology Systems Coordinator/Asst Prof, 95-98, ASSOC DIR, SYSTEMS/ASST PROF, PENROSE LIBRARY, UNIV DENVER, 98-. **MEMBERSHIPS** ALA; ACRL; LITA; RUSA; NCA. **RESEARCH** Technology management. **SELECTED PUBLICATIONS** Auth, New Age Section in Magazines for Libraries, 8th ed, Bill Katz, ed; Natural Language & Probabilistic Retrieval, LITA Newsletter, 16 (4), fall 95; A Systematic Approach to Computer Skills Traning for Library Staff, CO Libraries, 322 (3); Disciplinary Structures on the Internet, Library Trends, 45 (2); with K. Messas, A. Cowgill, L. Jones, and L. Catalucci, Staff Training and Development, ARL SPEC Kit 224, Washington, DC, Asn of Res Libraries, 97; Building Community Through Staff Development Initiatives, Haworth Press, Technical Services Quart, 15 (4), forthcoming 98; numerous other publications and presentations. **CONTACT ADDRESS** Univ of Denver, 2150 E. Evans Ave., Denver, CO, 80208-2007. **EMAIL** pclark@pasiphae.penlib.du.edu

CLARK, WILLIAM BEDFORD
PERSONAL Born 01/23/1947, Oklahoma City, OK, m, 1972, 2 children **DISCIPLINE** ENGLISH, AMERICAN LITERATURE **EDUCATION** Univ Okla, BA, 69; La State Univ, MA, 71, PhD(English), 73. **CAREER** Instr English, La State Univ, 72-73; asst prof, NC A&T State Univ, 74-77; asst prof, 77-80, ASSOC PROF ENGLISH, TEX A&M UNIV, 80-, Nat Endowment for Humanities fel Afro-Am studies, Yale Univ, 73-74. **MEMBERSHIPS** MLA; SCentral Mod Lang Asn; Soc Study Southern Lit; Nat Asn Interdisciplinary Ethnic Studies; Conf Christianity & Lit. **RESEARCH** Southern literature; literature of the West; race and the literary imagination. **SELECTED PUBLICATIONS** Auth, Pilgrim in the Ruins--A Life of Percy, Walker, Sewanee Rev, Vol 0101, 93; The House of Percy--Honor, Melancholy, and Imagination in a Southern Family, Sewanee Rev, Vol 0105, 97; The Literary Percys--Family History, Gender, and the Southern Imagination, Sewanee Rev, Vol 0105, 97; In the Shadow of His Smile--Warren Quarrel with Emerson, Sewanee Rev, Vol 0102, 94; Brooks, Cleanth and the Rise of Modern Criticism, Miss Quart, Vol 0050, 97; Souls Raised from the Dead, Sewanee Rev, Vol 0104, 96; Talking Animals, Medieval Latin Beast Poetry, 750-1150, Comp Lit Stud, Vol 0033, 96. **CONTACT ADDRESS** Dept of English, Tex A&M Univ Col, 1 Texas A and M Univ, College Station, TX, 77843.

CLARK SMITH, PAT
DISCIPLINE CREATIVE WRITING/POETRY, AMERICAN LITERATURE, AND WORLD LITERATURE **EDUCATION** Yale Univ, PhD, 70. **CAREER** Instr, Univ NMex, 70-. **SELECTED PUBLICATIONS** Auth, Changing Your Story, 91; coed, Western Literature in a World Context, 95. **CONTACT ADDRESS** Univ NMex, Albuquerque, NM, 87131.

CLARKE, BRUCE COOPER
PERSONAL Born 04/23/1950;, Munich, Germany, m, 1977 **DISCIPLINE** BRITISH ROMANTICISM **EDUCATION** Columbia Univ, BA, 74; State Univ NY, Buffalo, PhD(English), 80. **CAREER** Instr, La State Univ, 80-82; asst prof to prof English, Tex Tech Univ, 82-. **HONORS AND AWARDS** Butler Dissertation Fel, SUNY/Buffalo, 79-80; Am Coun of Learned Soc Grant-in Aid, Dora Marsden and Modern Letters, 85; State Organized Res Seed Grant, Modernist Individualism, 87; Am Coun of Learned Soc Travel Grant for Inter Meetings, D.H. Lawrence and the Egoist Group, 90; Gloria Lyerla Memorial Res Travel Grant, The Allegory of Thermodynamics, 95; Harry Ransom Humanities Res Ctr Fel, Univ Tex, The Allegory of Thermodynamics, 96; Proj Dir, Texas Tech Univ Fund 2005 Seed Grant, Center for the Interaction of the Arts and Sciences, 96. **MEMBERSHIPS** MLA. **RESEARCH** D H Lawrence studies; relations between British and German romanticism; psychological and philosophical approaches to literature. **SELECTED PUBLICATIONS** Auth, Miss Lonelyhearts and the Detached Consciousness, 12/75 & Imagination's Glory the One, the Sexual Body: Contexts for Dejection: An Ode, 9/77, Paunch; Wordsworth's Departed Sloans: Sublimation and Sublimity in Home at Grasmede, Studies in Romanticism, fall 80; auth multiple other essays; auth, The Body and the Text: Comparative Essays in Literature and Medicine, Tex Tech Univ Press, 90; Allegories of Writing: The Subject of Metamorphosis, State Univ of NY Press, 95; Dora Marsden and Early Modernism: Gender, Individualism, Science, Univ of Mich Press, 96. **CONTACT ADDRESS** Dept of English, Tex Tech Univ, Lubbock, TX, 79409-3091. **EMAIL** bruno@ttu.edu

CLARKE, GEORGE E.
PERSONAL Born 02/12/1960, Windsor, NS, Canada **DISCIPLINE** LITERATURE **EDUCATION** Univ Waterloo, BA, 84; Dalhousie Univ, MA, 89; Queen's Univ, PhD, 93. **CAREER** Columnist, The Daily News (Halifax), 88-89; writer-in-residence, St Mary's Univ, 90; writer-in-residence, Selkirk Col, 91; tchg asst, 91-93, asst adj prof, Queen's Univ, 94; ASST PROF ENGLISH & CANADIAN STUD, DUKE UNIV, 94-; COLUMNIST, HALIFAX HERALD LTD, 92-. **HONORS AND AWARDS** Ont Arts Coun grant, 89; Can Coun grant, 90. **MEMBERSHIPS** MLA; Writers Fedn NS; Writers Union Can; League Can Poets; Black Cultur Soc NS. **SELECTED PUBLICATIONS** ed, Fire on the Water: An Anthology of Black Nova Scotian Literature, 2 vols, 91, 92; ed, Eyeing the North Star: Directions in African-Canadian Literature, 97; co-ed, Border Lines: Contemporary Poems in English, 95. **CONTACT ADDRESS** Dept of English, Duke Univ, Box 90015, Durham, NC, 27708.

CLARKE, GEORGE ELLIOTT
DISCIPLINE ENGLISH LITERATURE **EDUCATION** Queen's Univ, PhD, 93. **CAREER** Prof, Duke Univ. **RESEARCH** New World African lit. **SELECTED PUBLICATIONS** Auth, Saltwater Spirituals and Deeper Blues, Pottersfield, 83; Whylah Falls, Polestar, 90; Lush Dreams, Blue Exile: Fugitive Poems 1978-1993, Pottersfield, 94; ed, Fire on the Water: An Anthology of Black Nova Scotian Writing, Pottersfield, 92; co-ed, Border Lines: Contemporary Poems in English, Copp-Clark, 95. **CONTACT ADDRESS** Eng Dept, Duke Univ, Durham, NC, 27706.

CLARKE, MICAEL
DISCIPLINE ENGLISH **EDUCATION** Univ Ill at Chicago Circle, AB, 74, MA, 76; Univ Ill at Urbana-Champaign, PhD, 83. **CAREER** Assoc prof; dir writing prog, 94-; fac coun, 90-;ch; fac status comt, 93-; exec comt, 95-. **RESEARCH** Theory of the Novel; Feminist Theory; Victorian Novel; William Thackekray; the Brontes. **SELECTED PUBLICATIONS** Auth, Thackeray and Women, Northern Ill UP, 95; Thackeray's Barry Lyndon: An Irony Against Misogynists, reprint from TSLL,87, in Nineteenth-Century Literature Criticism, Gale Res Inc, 94; A Mystery Solved: Ainsworth's Criminal Romances Censured in Fraser's by J Hamilton Reynolds, not Thackeray, Victorian Periodicals Rev 23, 90; William Thackeray's Fiction and Caroline Norton's Biography: Narrative Matrix of Feminist Legal Reform, Dickens Stud Annual 18, 89. **CONTACT ADDRESS** Dept of English, Loyola Univ, Chicago, 6525 N. Sheridan Rd., Chicago, IL, 60626. **EMAIL** mclarke1@wpo.it.luc.edu

CLAUSEN, CHRISTOPHER
DISCIPLINE ENGLISH **EDUCATION** Earlham Co, BA, 64; Univ Chicago, PhD, 65; queen's Univ, 72. **CAREER** Inst, Univ Hawaii, 65-66; asst prof, Concord col, 66-68; lectr, Univ Guelph, 73; asst prof, 73-79, asso prof, 79-84, prof, 84-85, Va Polytech Inst & State Univ; PROF, PA STATE UNIV, 85-. **CONTACT ADDRESS** Dept of English, Pennsylvania State Univ, University Park, PA, 16802-6200. **EMAIL** cqc1@psu.edu

CLAUSSEN, ERNEST NEAL
PERSONAL Born 08/15/1933, Petersburg, IL, m, 1961, 2 children **DISCIPLINE** SPEECH COMMUNICATION **EDUCATION** Ill State Univ, BS, 55; Southern Ill Univ, Carbondale, MA, 59, PhD(speech), 63. **CAREER** Instr speech & econ, Mendota High Sch, Ill, 55-56; asst prof speech, Colo State Col, 59-61; from asst prof to assoc prof, 63-71, assoc dean col lib arts & sci, 69-71, prof Speech, Bradley Univ, 71-. **HONORS AND AWARDS** The Harvard Award, 89; Sanford Award; 97 fror the Illinois Speech and Theatre Assoc. **MEMBERSHIPS** Speech Commun Asn; Rhetoric Soc Am. **RESEARCH** Rhetorical theory; rhetorical criticism; public communication. **SELECTED PUBLICATIONS** Auth, John Sharp Williams: Pacesetter for democratic keynoters, Southern Speech, 65; Hendrick B Wright and the nocturnal committee, Pa Mag Hist & Biog, 65; He kept us out of war: Martin H Glynn's keynote, Quart J Speech, 66; co-ed (with Karl R Wallace), John Lawson's Lectures Concerning Oratory, Southern Ill Univ Press, 72; Alben Barkley's rhetorical victory in 1948, Southern Speech Commun J, fall 79. **CONTACT ADDRESS** Dept of Speech Commun, Bradley Univ, 1501 W Bradley Ave, Peoria, IL, 61625-0002. **EMAIL** claussen@bradley.edu

CLAYDON, MARGARET
PERSONAL Born 07/19/1923, New York, NY **DISCIPLINE** ENGLISH LANGUAGE & LITERATURE **EDUCATION** Trinity Col, DC, AB, 45; Cath Univ Am, MA, 53, PhD, 59. **CAREER** From instr to asst prof 52-59, pres, 59-75, prof Eng, Trinity Col, DC, 75-; vis lectr, Notre Dame Col, Scotland, 58-59; mem bd trustees, Mid States Assn, 65-72; mem bd dir, Nat Coun Independent Cols & Univs, 71-; trustee, Emmanuel Col, Mass, 72-; postdoctoral res fel, Yale Univ; guest resident fel, Timothy Dwight Col, Yale Univ, 75-76. **HONORS AND AWARDS** LHD, Georgetown Univ, 67, 71 & Cath Univ of Am, 75. **MEMBERSHIPS** Nat Cath Educ Assn. **RESEARCH** Renaissance English literature; metaphysical poets; classical literature. **SELECTED PUBLICATIONS** Auth, Richard Crashaw's paraphrases of the Vexilla Regis, Stabat Mater, Adoro Te, Lauda Sion, Dies Irae, O Gloriosa Domina, Cath Univ Am, 59. **CONTACT ADDRESS** Trinity Col, 125 Michigan Ave NE, Washington, DC, 20017-1090.

CLAYTON, JAY
DISCIPLINE LITERARY THEORY, 19TH CENTURY, ROMANTICISM, CONTEMPORARY LITERATURE **EDUCATION** Univ Va, PhD. **CAREER** Instr, dir, grad stud, Vanderbilt Univ. **SELECTED PUBLICATIONS** Auth, Romantic Vision and the Novel, 87; Influence and Intertextuality in Literary History, 91; The Pleasures of Babel, 93. **CONTACT ADDRESS** Vanderbilt Univ, Nashville, TN, 37203-1727.

CLAYTON, JOHN J.
PERSONAL Born 01/05/1935, New York, NY, m, 1956, 3 children **DISCIPLINE** MODERN LITERATURE, HUMANITIES **EDUCATION** Columbia Univ, BA, 56; NY Univ, MA, 59; Ind Univ, PhD(English & Am lit), 66. **CAREER** Instr English, Univ Victoria, BC, 62-63; lectr, Univ Md European Div, 63-64; asst prof humanities, Boston Univ, 64-69; assoc prof, 69-73, PROF MOD LIT & CREATIVE WRITING, UNIV MASS, AMHERST, 73-, Nat Endowment for Humanities fel, 80. **RESEARCH** Modern fiction; creative writing. **SELECTED PUBLICATIONS** Auth, Night Talk, Va Quart Rev, Vol 0069, 93; Ghost Story, Sewanee Rev, Vol 0101, 93; Dance to the Old Worlds, Va Quart Rev, Vol 0071, 95. **CONTACT ADDRESS** Dept of English, Univ of Mass, Amherst, MA, 01002.

CLAYTON, TOM
PERSONAL Born 12/15/1932, New Ulm, MN, w, 1955, 4 children **DISCIPLINE** ENGLISH, CLASS & NEAR EASTERN STUDIES **EDUCATION** Univ Minn, BA, 54; Oxford Univ, DPhil, 60. **CAREER** Instr English, Yale Univ, 60-62; asst prof, Univ Calif, Los Angeles, 62-67, assoc prof, 67-68; assoc prof, 68-70, PROF ENGLISH, UNIV MINN, MINNEAPOLIS, 70-, PROF CLASS & NEAR EASTERN STUDIES, 80-, CHMN, CLASS CIVILIZATION PROG, 82-, MORSE-ALUMNI DISTINGUISHED TEACHING PROF ENGL & CLASSICAL STUDIES, 93-; Am Coun Learned Soc grant, 62-63; fel, Inst for Humanities, Univ Calif, 66-67; assoc, Danforth Assoc Prog, 72-77; Guggenheim fel, 78-79; Bush fel, Univ Minn, 85; NEH award, Div Res Tools, 88. **HONORS AND AWARDS** Rhodes Scholar, Minn and Wadham, 54; Distinguished Teaching Award, Col Lib Arts, Univ Minn, 71; Morse-Alumni Award, Outstanding contrib undergrad educ, Univ Minn 82. **MEMBERSHIPS** Asn of Am Rhodes Scholars; Asn Literary Scholars and Critics; Renaissance English Text Soc; Int Shakespeare Asn; Shakespeare Asn Am. **RESEARCH** Shakespeare; literary criticism; earlier 17th Century English literature. **SELECTED PUBLICATIONS** Ed & auth, The Shakespearean Addition in the Books of Sir Thomas Moore, Ctr Shakespeare Studies, 69; ed & auth, The Non-Dramatic Works of Sir John Suckling, Clarendon, 71; ed & auth, Cavalier Poets, Oxford Univ, 78; auth, Is this the promis'd end?, Revision in the role of the King himself, in The Division of the Kingdom, Clarendon, 83; The texts and publishing vicissitudes of Peter Nichol's Passion Play, in The Library, 87; ed & auth, The Hamlet First Published (Q1, 1603), Univ Del, 92; That's she that was myself: Not-so-famous last words and some ends of Othello, Shakespeare Survey, 94; So our virtues lie in the interpretation of the time: Shakespeare's Coriolanus and Coriolanus, and Some Questions of Value, Ben Johnson J, 94; Who has no children in Macbeth?, in Festschrift for Marvin Rosenbert, Univ Del, 98 (forthcoming); So quick bright things come to confusion, or what else was A Midsummer's Night Dream about?, in Festschrift for Jay L Halio, in prep. **CONTACT ADDRESS** Dept of English, Univ of Minn, 207 Church St SE, Minneapolis, MN, 55455-0134. **EMAIL** tsc@unm.edu

CLEARY, THOMAS R.
PERSONAL Born 05/23/1940, New York, NY, m, 1965, 3 children **DISCIPLINE** ENGLISH **EDUCATION** Queen's Col, CUNY, BA; Princeton Univ, MA, PhD. **CAREER** Instr English, Princeton Univ, 67-68; asst prof, 69-80, ASSOC PROF ENGLISH, UNIV VICTORIA, BC, 80-. **MEMBERSHIPS** MLA; Johnson Soc Northwest (secy, 73-74); Am Soc Eighteenth-Century Studies. **RESEARCH** Restoration and 18th-century literature; the novel; history of criticism. **SELECTED PUBLICATIONS** Auth, political biography of Fielding entitled Henry Fielding: Political Writer, Wilfrid Laurier UP, 84; Time, Literature and the Arts: Essays in Honor of Samuel L. Macey, Eng Lit Stud, no 61, 95. **CONTACT ADDRESS** Dept of English, Victoria Univ, PO Box 3070, Victoria, BC, V8W 3W1. **EMAIL** trcleary@uvic.ca

CLEGG, CYNDIA SUSAN
PERSONAL Born 11/28/1946, Long Beach, CA, m, 1977, 1 child **DISCIPLINE** ENGLISH LITERATURE **EDUCATION** Univ Calif, Los Angeles, PhD, 76. **CAREER** Dir compos, 76-84, prof, English, 84- , Pepperdine Univ. **HONORS AND AWARDS** Br Acad fel, 91, 99; Mellon fel, Huntington Library, 92. **MEMBERSHIPS** MLA; Shakespeare Assoc of Am; Renaissance Soc of Am; Pacific Ancient and Mod Lang Assoc. **RESEARCH** Press censorship in early modern England; Shakespeare; Elizabethan historiography. **SELECTED PUBLICATIONS** Auth, Critical Reading and Writing Across the Disciplines, Holt, Rinehart & Winston, 88; coauth, Students Writing Across the Disciplines, Holt, Rinehart & Winston, 91; auth, The 1586 Decrees for Order in Printing and the Practice of Censorship, Ben Jonson Jour, 95; auth, The Stationers' Company of London, 1557-1710, in Bracken, ed, The British Literary Book Trade, Bruccoli Clark Layman, 96; auth, Press Censorship in Elizabethan England, Cambridge, 97; auth, Ben Jonson and Censureship, Ben Jonson Jour, 97; auth, By the choise and invitation of al the realme: Richard II and Elizabethan Press Censorship, Shakespeare Quart, 97; auth, The Peacable and Prosperous Regiment of Blessed Queene: Elisabeth: A Facsimile from Holinshed's Chronicles, Huntington Lib, 98. **CONTACT ADDRESS** Dept of Humanities, Pepperdine Univ, 24255 Pacific Coast Hwy, Malibu, CA, 90263-4225. **EMAIL** cclegg@pepperdine.edu

CLEGHORN, CASSANDRA
DISCIPLINE ENGLISH **EDUCATION** Univ Calif, Santa Cruz, BA, 83; Yale Univ, PhD 95. **CAREER** Lectr & coordr, Williams Col Learning Technol Proj. **RESEARCH** American literature and cultural studies; theories of reading; contemporary poetry. **SELECTED PUBLICATIONS** Auth, Chivalric Sentimentalism: The Case of Dr Howe and Laura Bridgman, Sentimental and Men: Sentimentality and Masculinity in American Fiction and Culture. **CONTACT ADDRESS** Dept of English, Williams Col, Stetson 302, Williamstown, MA, 01267. **EMAIL** ccleghorn@williams.edu

CLENDENNING, JOHN
PERSONAL Born 10/12/1934, Huntington, WV, 2 children **DISCIPLINE** AMERICAN LITERATURE & CIVILIZATION **EDUCATION** Calif State Univ, Los Angeles, BA, 57; Univ Iowa, MA, 58, PhD, 62. **CAREER** From instr to PROF ENGLISH, CA STATE UNIV, NORTHRIDGE, 60-, INTERIM ASSOC DEAN, 97-98, chmn dept, 73-79; Am Coun Learned Soc study fel, 64-65 & fel, 68-69; Wesleyan Univ Ctr Advan Studies jr fel, 64-65; Guggenheim fel, 71-72; lectureship, Fulbright-Hays/Univ Athens, 77-78; mem delegate assembly, Mod Lang Asn, 78-80; pres, Stephen Crane Soc, 94-96. **HONORS AND AWARDS** Jerome Richfield Scholar, 96-97; Outstanding Prof, 96-97. **MEMBERSHIPS** MLA; Stephen Crane Soc. **RESEARCH** Philosophical themes in literature; American poetry. **SELECTED PUBLICATIONS** Auth, Cummings, comedy and criticism, Colo Quart, summer 63; Time, doubt and vision: Emerson and Eliot, Am Scholar, winter 66-67; Introd to Josiah Royce's The Feud of Oakfield Creek, 70; Letters of Josiah Royce, Univ Chicago, 70; The Life and Thought of Josiah Royce, Univ WI, 85; Stephen Crane and His Biographies, Am Lit Realism, 95. **CONTACT ADDRESS** Dept of English, California State Univ, Northridge, 18111 Nordhoff St, Northridge, CA, 91330-8200. **EMAIL** john.clendenning@csun.edu

CLOGAN, PAUL MAURICE
PERSONAL Born 07/09/1934, Boston, MA, 3 children **DISCIPLINE** ENGLISH, COMPARATIVE LITERATURE **EDUCATION** Boston Col, AB, 56, MA, 57; St Michael's Col, PhL, 58; Univ Ill, PhD, 61. **CAREER** From instr to asst prof English, Duke Univ, 61-65; assoc prof English & comp lit, Case Western Reserve Univ, 65-72; adj prof, Cleveland State Univ, 71-72; prof English, Univ N TX, 72-. **HONORS AND AWARDS** Duke Found grant, 62-63; Am Coun Learned Soc fels, 62-64 & 71-72; sr Fulbright-Hays res fels, Italy, 65-66, Scuola Vaticana di Paleografia e Diplomatica, 66-67 & France, 78; Fulbright-Hays res fel; vis lectr, Univ Pisa, 65; Am Philos Soc grants, 65-67 & 69-70; US/UK cult exchange vis lectr, Univ Keele, 66;

Bollingen Found & Prix de Rome fels, 66-67; fel, Am Acad Rome, 67; ed, Medievalia et Humanistica, 68-; mem steering comt, Asn Ctr Medieval & Renaissance Studies; Nat Endowment for Humanities fel, 70-71; vis mem, Inst Advan Study, NJ, 70 & 77; Univ N Tx; fac res grants, 72-75 & 80-81; vis lectr, Univ Tours, 78; MLA Mdeieval Exec Comt, 80-86; Deleg Assembly, 81-86; John Nicholas Brown Prize Comt, 81-83; Medieval Acad Am nominating comt, 75-76. **MEMBERSHIPS** MLA; Medieval Acad Am; Mod Humanities Res Asn; Ling Soc Am; Int Asn Univ Prof of English. **RESEARCH** Medieval literature and culture; history of the English language; literary theory. **SELECTED PUBLICATIONS** Auth, Chaucer and the Thebaid Scholia, Studies Philol, 64; Chaucer's use of the Thebaid, English Miscellany, 67; The medieval Achilleid, E J Brill, 68; The figural style and meaning of the second nun's prologue and tale, Medievalia et Humanistica, 72; coauth, Medieval hagiography and romance, 75; auth, Medieval poetics, 76, The narrative style and meaning of the man of law's tale, 77 & coauth, Transformation and continuity, 77, Cambridge Univ; Literary genres in a medieval textbook, Medievalia et Humanistica, 82; coauth Byzantine and Western Studies, 84; Fourteenth and Fifteenth Centuries, 86; The Early Renaissance, 87; Literary Theory, 88; Spectrum, 92; Columbian Qunicentenary, 92; Renaissance and Discovery, 93; Breaching the Boundaries, 94; Convergences, 94; Diversity, 95; Historical Inquiries, 97; Transitions, 98. **CONTACT ADDRESS** Univ of No Texas, PO Box 5074, Wayland, MA, 01778-6074. **EMAIL** pclogan@ibm.net

CLOUD, DANA L.
PERSONAL Born 05/09/1964, Waco, TX, 1 child **DISCIPLINE** COMMUNICATION STUDIES **EDUCATION** PA State Univ, BA (English & telecomm), 86; Univ IA, MA (Rhetorical Studies), 89, PhD (Rhetorical Studies), 92. **CAREER** Res fel, Univ IA, Iowa City, 87, 92, teaching asst, 88-91; asst prof, Univ TX, Austin, 93-; summer res award, Univ Res Inst, 94; ed bd member, Western J of Comm, 95-; Col Comm Jamail grant, 96; special res grant, Univ TX, 97; ed bd member, Women's Studies in Communication, 97-; assoc ed, Quart J of Speech, 97-. **HONORS AND AWARDS** Nichols-Ehninger Award in Rhetorical and Communication Theory, Speech Comm Asn, 94; B Aubrey Fisher Outstanding Article Award, Western States Comm Asn, 95; National Communication Asn Karl Wallace Memorial Award for Young Scholars in Rhetoric, 98; Dean's fel, Col Comm, Univ TX, spring 98. **SELECTED PUBLICATIONS** Auth, The Limits of Interpretation: Ambivalence and the Stereotype in Spenser: For Hire, Critical Studies in Mass Communication 9, 92; Materiality of Discourse as Oxymoron: A Challenge to Critical Rhetoric, Western J of Communication 58, 94; Hegemony of Concordance? The Rhetoric of Tokenism in Oprah Winfrey's Rags-to-Riches Biography, Critical Studies in Mass Comm 13, 96; Edwin Black, in Teresa Enos, ed, Encyclopedia of Rhetoric, 96; The Rhetoric of Family Values and the Public Sphere, Alta Conf on Argumantation Proceedings, Speech Commm Asn, 96; Capitalism, Concordance, and Conservatism: Rejoinder to Condit, Critical Studies in Mass Comm 13, 97; Control and Consolation in American Politcs and Culture: Rhetorics of Therapy, Sage Press, 98; Queer Theory and Family Values, Transformation, 98; The Rhetoric of Family Values: Scapegoating, Utopia, and the Privatization of Social Responsibility, Western J of Comm, 98; Of Pancake Queens and Mother Dreams: The Failed Rhetoric of Maternal Utopia in Films of the 1930's, in Mother Daughter Communication: Voices from the Professions, forthcoming; several other book chapters, and two publications currently under review. **CONTACT ADDRESS** Speech Communication, Univ of Texas, Austin, CMA 7 112 A1105, Austin, TX, 78712. **EMAIL** dcloud@mail.utexas.edu

CLOWERS, MARSHA L.
PERSONAL Born 04/25/1969, New Orleans, LA, s **DISCIPLINE** COMMUNICATION **EDUCATION** Arkansas State Univ, BS; Texas Tech, MA; Ohio Univ, PhD. **CAREER** Public Relations Agent, Senator M. Todd, 91; consult, Dept of Ed, Tx Tech Univ, 92; consult, Lubbock County Democratic Party, 92; Fordham Univ, 95-98; JOHN JAY COL OF CRIMINAL JUSTICE, 98-; ADJUNCT PROF, BEFORD HILLS CORRECTIONAL FACILITY, 98-. **HONORS AND AWARDS** First fac member appointed instr of the Fordham Freshman Symposium, 97; top four paper, Eastern Commun Asn convention, 97. **MEMBERSHIPS** NY State Commun Asn; Nat Commun Asn; Eastern Commun Asn. **RESEARCH** Health communication; criminology; incarcerated females. **SELECTED PUBLICATIONS** Coauth, Communication and Health, Commun and Health Outcomes, Hampton Press, 95; coauth, The Influences of Human Communication on Health Outcomes, Am Behavioral Sci, 94; coauth, An Examination of Communication Studies Department Curricula for Undergraduate Students and Areas of Growth in the Field, Tx Speech Commun J, 92; auth, Culture, Communication, and the Media: So What?, Iowa J of Commun, 97. **CONTACT ADDRESS** 284 City Island Ave., Bronx, NY, 10464.

CLUFF, RANDALL
PERSONAL Born 09/24/1951, Pheonix, AZ, m, 1979, 5 children **DISCIPLINE** ENGLISH **EDUCATION** Univ Tn, Knoxville, PhD, 97. **CAREER** Asst prof, chair, S Va Col, 97-. **MEMBERSHIPS** MLA; Melville Soc; SHARP. **RESEARCH** Melville; literary publishing history; American romanticism. **SELECTED PUBLICATIONS** Auth, John Greenleaf Whittier, Oliver Cowdrey, Amer Nat Biog, Oxford UP, 99; auth, Andrew Jackson and Gansevoort Melville: Did the Old Hero Hear the Young Orator?, Melville Soc Extracts, 99. **CONTACT ADDRESS** S Virginia Col, One College Hill Dr, Buena Vista, VA, 24416. **EMAIL** rcluff@southernvirginia.edu

CLUM, JOHN M.
DISCIPLINE ENGLISH LITERATURE **EDUCATION** Princeton Univ, PhD **CAREER** Prof, Duke Univ. **RESEARCH** Twentieth century Brit and Am drama. **SELECTED PUBLICATIONS** Auth, Acting Gay: Male Homosexuality in Modern Drama, Columbia, 92; co-ed, Displacing Homophobia: Essays in Gay Male Literature and Culture, Duke, 89. **CONTACT ADDRESS** Eng Dept, Duke Univ, Durham, NC, 27706.

COAD DYER, SAM
DISCIPLINE PUBLIC RELATIONS **EDUCATION** Univ TN, PhD, 91. **CAREER** Southwest Tex State Univ **SELECTED PUBLICATIONS** Areas: sale of electric corporations in New Zealand, the use of public opinion polls in news copy in Australia, and environmental monitoring strategies for public relations firms analysing media coverage of their clients. **CONTACT ADDRESS** Southwest MS State Univ, 901 S. National, Ste. 50, Springfield, MO, 65804-0094.

COAKLEY, JEAN ALEXANDER
PERSONAL Born 07/27/1930, Croton-on-Hudson, NY, m, 1973, 5 children **DISCIPLINE** BRITISH LITERATURE **EDUCATION** Miami Univ, Oxford, BA, 71; MA, 72, PhD(English), 82. **CAREER** ASST PROF ENGLISH, MIAMI UNIV, OXFORD, 82-, Ed, Charles F Kettering Found, 72-73, staff writer, 73-74. **RESEARCH** Restoration drama and political literature; Aphra Behn; 17th century British political history. **SELECTED PUBLICATIONS** Auth, The Public Prints--The Newspaper in Anglo-American Culture, 1665-1740, Historian, Vol 0057, 94. **CONTACT ADDRESS** Dept of English, Miami Univ, Oxford, OH, 45056.

COBB, JERRY
DISCIPLINE ENGLISH LITERATURE **EDUCATION** Gonzaga Univ, BA, 74; Univ WA, MA, 75, 81, Divinity Doctorate, 87. **CAREER** Instr, Seattle Univ. **MEMBERSHIPS** MLA; NCTE. **SELECTED PUBLICATIONS** Auth, The Ramsays as Dysfunctional Family in Woolf's To the Lighthouse. **CONTACT ADDRESS** Seattle Univ, Seattle, WA, 98122-4460. **EMAIL** jcobb@seattleu.edu

COBLEY, EVELYN M.
DISCIPLINE ENGLISH LITERATURE **EDUCATION** Univ Utah, BA; Univ Brit Col, MA, PhD. **CAREER** Prof **HONORS AND AWARDS** Raymond-Klibansky Bk Prize, Aid to Schol Publ Prog, 93-94; post-dr fel, SSHRC, 83-84; res fel, SSHRC, 95-98. **RESEARCH** Critical theory; comparative literature; cultural studies; 20th-century British and American fiction. **SELECTED PUBLICATIONS** Auth, Representing War: Form and Ideology in First World War Narratives; pub(s), articles in Contemp Lit, Semiotic Inquiry, Can Rev of Comparative Lit, Jour of Narrative Tech, Style, Mosaic, Eng Stud in Can, Can Lit. **CONTACT ADDRESS** Dept of English, Victoria Univ, PO Box 3070, Victoria, BC, V8W 3W1. **EMAIL** ecobley@uvic.ca

COBURN, WILLIAM LEON
DISCIPLINE EIGHTEENTH CENTURY BRITISH LITERATURE, RHETORIC **EDUCATION** Univ NMex, BA, 65; Univ Calif, Davis, MA, 68, PhD, 69. **CAREER** Instr, Davis, 66-69; instr, 69-, dir, undergrad stud, dir, freshman compos, Univ Nev, Las Vegas, 80-81, 85-91; state dir, 69-71, judge, NCTE Achievement Awards, 94; dir, Southern Nev Writing Proj, 85-90. **HONORS AND AWARDS** NEH summer sem grant, 78; Outstanding Eng Tchr Award, 83; Rita Dean Abbey Tchr of the Yr Award, 94. **RESEARCH** Imitation and modeling in the teaching of writing and standards in grading. **SELECTED PUBLICATIONS** Auth, Notes of a Freshman Freshman Composition Director, J of Coun of Writing Prog Adminr, Spg, 82. **CONTACT ADDRESS** Dept of Eng, Univ Nev, Las Vegas, 4505 Maryland Pky, PO Box 455011, Las Vegas, NV, 89154. **EMAIL** coburnw@nevada.edu

CODY, RICHARD JOHN
PERSONAL Born 01/05/1929, London, England, m, 1995, 2 children **DISCIPLINE** ENGLISH **EDUCATION** London Univ, BA, 52; Univ Minn, MA, 58, PhD, 61. **CAREER** From instr to asst prof English, Univ Minn, 60-63; assoc prof, 63-68, col librn, 70-74, chmn dept, 71-73, prof English, Amherst Col, 68-. **HONORS AND AWARDS** MA, Amherst Col, 68. **RESEARCH** Renaissance; modern literature. **SELECTED PUBLICATIONS** Auth, The Landscape of the Mind: Pastoralism and Platonic Theory in Tasso's Aminta and Shakespeare's Early Comedies, Clarendon, 69; ed & contribr, Newsletter of the Friends of the Amherst College Library, 72-97. **CONTACT ADDRESS** Dept of English, Amherst Col, Amherst, MA, 01002-5003.

COERS, DONALD V.
PERSONAL Born 06/02/1941, San Marcos, TX, m, 1966, 2 children **DISCIPLINE** ENGLISH **EDUCATION** Univ Tex at Austin, BA, 63, MA, 69; Tex A & M Univ, PhD, 74. **CAREER** Prof English, Sam Houston State Univ, 69-92; Coord of Grad Stud, 92-95; Assoc VP for Acad Affairs, 95-. **RESEARCH** John Steinbeck; Ebenezer Cook. **CONTACT ADDRESS** Academic Affairs, Sam Houston State Univ, Huntsville, TX, 77341. **EMAIL** coers@shsu.edu

COFFIN, TRISTRAM POTTER
PERSONAL Born 02/13/1922, San Marino, CA, m, 1944, 4 children **DISCIPLINE** ENGLISH **EDUCATION** Haverford Col, BS, 43; Univ Pa, AM, 47, PhD, 49. **CAREER** From instr to assoc prof English, Denison Univ, 49-58; assoc prof English & folklore, 58-64, vdean, Grad Sch Arts & Sci, 65-68, prof English, 64-84, PROF EMER ENGLISH AND FOLKLORE, UNIV PA, 84- . **HONORS AND AWARDS** Guggenheim fel, 53. **MEMBERSHIPS** MLA; Am Folklore Soc (secy-treas, 60-65, 2nd vpres, 67-); Folklore Soc England. **RESEARCH** Anglo-American ballad; folk literature; American Indian and Negro. **SELECTED PUBLICATIONS** Auth, Index to the Journal of American Folklore, Univ Tex Press, 58; co-ed Folklore in America, 67; auth, Uncertain Glory, 71; auth, The Old Ball Game, 71; The Book of Christmas Folklore, Seabury, 73; co-ed, Folklore from the Working Folk of America, Doubleday Anchor, 73; auth, The Female Hero, Seabury, 75; The British Traditional Ballad in North America, Am Folklore Soc, 77; The Proper Book of Sexual Folklore, Seabury, 78; coauth, The Parade of Heroes, Doubleday Ancho, 78; Great Game for a Girl, Exposition, 80; co-ed, Folklore of the American Holidays, Editions I & II. **CONTACT ADDRESS** PO Box 509, Wakefield, RI, 02880.

COGSWELL, FREDERICK W.
PERSONAL Born 11/08/1917, East Centreville, NB, Canada **DISCIPLINE** LITERATURE **EDUCATION** Univ NB, BA, 49, MA, 50; Edinburgh Univ (IODE Scholar), PhD, 52; St. Francis Univ, Hon LLD, 82; King's Univ, DCL, 85; Mt Allison Univ, LLD, 88. **CAREER** Ed, The Fiddlehead lit mag, 52-66; prof, 52-83, PROF EMER, UNIV NB, 83-; writer-in-residence, Scottish Arts Coun, 83-84. **HONORS AND AWARDS** Nuffield Fel, 59; Can Coun Sr Fel, 67; Order of Can, 81; Excellent Award, NB Govt, 95. **MEMBERSHIPS** League Can Poets; Asn Can Publs; Humanities Asn Can; NB Writers Fedn. **SELECTED PUBLICATIONS** Auth, A Long Apprenticeship: Collected Poems, 80; Selected Poems, 82; Pearls, 83; The Complete Poems of Emile Nelligan, 83; Charles GD Roberts and His Works, 83; ed, An Atlantic Anthology, vol 1 83, vol 2 84; Meditations, 86; An Edge to Life, 87; Charles Mair and his Works, 88; The Best Notes Merge, 88; Black and White Tapestry, 89; co-ed & co-transl, Unfinished Dreams: Contemporary Poetry of Acadie, 90; Watching an Eagle, 91; When the Right Light Shines, 92; In Praise of Old Music, 92; In My Own Growing, 93; As I See It, 95; The Trouble With Light, 96; Folds, 97. **CONTACT ADDRESS** 31 Island View Dr, Douglas, NB, E3A 7R7.

COHEN, ANDREW D.
PERSONAL Born 03/14/1944, Washington, DC, m, 1968, 2 children **DISCIPLINE** EDUCATION **EDUCATION** Harvard Univ, BA, 65; Stanford Univ, MA, 71; Stanford Univ, PhD, 73. **CAREER** Peace Corps volunteer, Bolivia, 65-67; Teaching Fel, Stanford Univ, 70-72; Coordr, English Placement Exam, UCLA, 72-75; Asst Prof, UCLA,72-75; Sr Lectr, Hebrew Univ Jerusalem, 75-79; Dir, Ctr Applied Ling, Hebrew Univ, 76-80; Academic Head, Dept English as a Foreign Lang, Hebrew Univ, 77-78; Assoc Prof Applied Ling, Hebrew Univ, 79-91; Vis Prof, UCLA, 80-81; Dir, Ctr Applied Ling Res, Hebrew Univ, 81-91; Fulbright Lectr and Researcher, Brazil, 86-87; Vis Scholar, Univ Hawaii, 96-97; Vis Scholar, Tel Aviv Univ, 97; Prof, Univ Minn. **HONORS AND AWARDS** Distinguished Scholar in Residence, Ga State Univ; Melton Fel, Johns Hopkins Univ; Bush Faculty Develop Program on Excellence in Teaching, Univ Minn; Distinguished Lectr Program, Temple Univ, Japan; Fulbright Researcher and Lectr, Brazil. **MEMBERSHIPS** TESOL; AAAL; MinneTESOL; ILTA; ACTFL; AERA. **RESEARCH** Bilingual and immersion education; language assessment; language learning and use strategies; speech acts; applied linguistic research methods. **SELECTED PUBLICATIONS** Auth, The Role of Instructors in Testing Summarizing Ability, A New Decade of Language Testing: Collaboration and Cooperation, TESOL, 93; coauth, The Production of Speech Acts by EFL Learners, TESOL Qrt, 27 (1), 93; auth, Assessing language ability in the classroom, 2nd ed, Newbury House/Heinle & Heinle, 94; ed, Focusing on Language and Language Processing: Beyond Test Scores, Language Testing, 11 (2), 94; auth, The Language Used to Perform Cognitive Operations During Full Immersion Math Tasks, Language Testing, 11 (2), 94; auth, Research Methodology in Second Language Acquisition, Erlbaum, 94; auth, SLA Theory and Pedagogy: Some Research Issues, Second Language Acquisition Theory and Pedagogy, Lawrence Erlbaum, 95; auth, In Which Language Do/Should Multilinguals Think?, Language, Culture and Curriculum, 8 (2), 95; auth, The Role of Language of Thought in Foreign Language Learning, Working Papers in Educational Linguistics, 11 (2); auth, Investigating the Production of Speech Act Sets, Speech Acts Across Cultures: Chal-

lenges to Communicate in a Second Language, Mouton de Gruyter, 96; auth, Developing the Ability to Perform Speech Acts, Second Language Acquisition, 18 (2), 96. **CONTACT ADDRESS** Dept of English as a Second Language, Univ of Minnesota, 320 16th Ave SE, Minneapolis, MN, 55455. **EMAIL** adcohen@tc.umn.edu

COHEN, EDWARD H.
PERSONAL Born 11/06/1941, Washington, DC, m, 1964, 2 children **DISCIPLINE** VICTORIAN STUDIES **EDUCATION** Univ Md, BA, 63; Univ Iowa, MA, 64; Univ NMex, PhD(English), 67. **CAREER** Asst prof English, 67-71, assoc prof, 71-79, PROF ENGLISH, ROLLINS COL, 79-, Am Philos Soc grant, 71 & 79; Arthur Vining Davis fel, 71-72; Henry E Huntington Libr fel, 72; Nat Endowment Humanities summer sem fel, 77; Am Coun on Educ fel in Acad Administration, 81-82. **HONORS AND AWARDS** Hugh F McKean Award, 80. **MEMBERSHIPS** MLA. **RESEARCH** Victorian studies. **SELECTED PUBLICATIONS** Auth, Ennui, an Uncollected Hospital Poem by Henley,W.E., Durham Univ Jour, Vol 0087, 95; Victorian Bibliography for 1993, Victorian Stud, Vol 0037, 94. **CONTACT ADDRESS** Dept of English, Rollins Col, 1000 Holt Ave, Winter Park, FL, 32789-4499.

COHEN, EILEEN Z.
PERSONAL Born 12/15/1932, Baltimore, MD **DISCIPLINE** ENGLISH LITERATURE **EDUCATION** Univ Md, BS, 53, MA, 58, PhD(English lit), 65. **CAREER** From instr to asst prof English, Temple Univ, 61-68; from asst prof to assoc prof English lit, 68-77, Prof English, St Joseph's Col, 77-. **MEMBERSHIPS** Conf Brit Studies; Northeast Mod Lang Asn; MLA; Renaissance Soc Am; NCTE. **RESEARCH** Renaissance drama; 17th century poetry and prose; American fiction. **SELECTED PUBLICATIONS** Auth, The old arcadia: A treatise on moderation, Rev Belge de Philol et d'Hist, 68; Sir Philip Sidney as Ambassador, Hist Mag, Protestant Episcopal Church, 6/69; The visible solemnity; ceremony and order in Shakespeare and Hooker, Tex Study Lit & Lang, summer 70; Alex in wonderland, or Portnoy's complaint, Twentieth Century Lit, 7/71; Henry James's Governess--again, Four Quarters, summer 74; The role of Cassio in Othello, English Studies, 4/76; Virtue is Bold! The Bed-trick and Characterization in All's Well That End's Well and Measure for Measure, Philos Quart, 6/86; and misc. poems. **CONTACT ADDRESS** Dept of English, St Joseph's Col, 5600 City Ave, Philadelphia, PA, 19131-1376. **EMAIL** ecohen@sjc.edu

COHEN, JOSEPH
PERSONAL Born 04/27/1926, Central City, KY, w, 3 children **DISCIPLINE** ENGLISH **EDUCATION** Vanderbilt Univ, BA, 49, MA, 51; Univ Tex, PhD(English), 55. **CAREER** Instr English, Univ Tex, 53-55; from instr to assoc prof, 55-75, asst dean, Col Arts & Sci, 57-58, assoc dean, 67-75, PROF ENGLISH, NEWCOMB COL, TULANE UNIV, 75-, Resident prof, Tulane-Newcomb jr yr in Gt Brit, 59-60, dir, 60-61; acad asst to dean, Newcomb Col, 61-67; assoc dir scholars & fels prog, Tulane Univ, 64-65, dir, 65-67, dir scholars prog, 67-68; contrib ed, J Higher Educ, 68-71; dir, Tulane Jewish Studies Prog, 81- **MEMBERSHIPS** MLA; Nat Col Honors Coun (pres, 70-71); SCent Mod Lang Asn; Asn Jewish Studies; Am Jewish Hist Soc. **RESEARCH** Contemporary literature, particularly British literature; 20th century war literature; Anglo-American Jewish literature. **SELECTED PUBLICATIONS** Auth, Vespers, So Hum Rev, Vol 0030, 96. **CONTACT ADDRESS** Tulane Univ, New Orleans, LA, 70118.

COHEN, MICHAEL MARTIN
PERSONAL Born 04/27/1943, Akron, OH, m, 1967, 2 children **DISCIPLINE** ENGLISH; LITERATURE **EDUCATION** Univ Ariz, AB, 65, MA, 67, PhD(English), 71. **CAREER** From instr to asst prof English, La State Univ, New Orleans, 70-76; from Asst Prof to Assoc Prof, 76-84, PROF ENGLISH, MURRAY STATE UNIV, 84-, Dept Chair, 94-98. **MEMBERSHIPS** MLA; SCent Mod Lang Asn; SAtlantic Mod Lang Asn; SCent Soc 18th Century Studies; Southeastern Atlantic Soc 18th Century Studies. **RESEARCH** Restoration and 18th century poetry, prose and drama; relationships between visual arts and literature. **SELECTED PUBLICATIONS** Auth, coauth, The Poem in Question, Harcourt Brace Jovanovich, 83; Engaging English Art, Alabama, 87; Hamlet in My Mind's Eye, Georgia, 89; Sisters: Relation and Rescue in Nineteenth-Century British Novels and Paintings, Fairleigh Dickinson, 95. **CONTACT ADDRESS** Dept of English, Murray State Univ, Murray, KY, 42071.

COHEN, MILTON
DISCIPLINE AMERICAN LITERATURE **EDUCATION** Syracuse Univ, PhD, 81. **CAREER** Assoc prof. **RESEARCH** 20th century American literature; modernist literature; painting and music. **SELECTED PUBLICATIONS** Auth, Fatal Symbiosis: Modernism and World War One, War Lit Arts, 96; The Futurist Exhibition of 1912: A Model of Prewar Modernism, Europ Studies Jour, 95; Fitzgerald's Third Regret: Intellectual Pretense and the Ghost of Edmund Wilson, Tex Studies Lit and Lang, 91; Subversive Pedagogies: Schoenberg's Theory of Harmony and Pound's A Few Don'ts by an Imagiste, Mosaic, 88; Poet and Painter: The Aesthetics of E.E. Cummings' Early Work, Wayne State Univ, 87. **CONTACT ADDRESS** Dept of Literature, Richardson, TX, 75083-0688. **EMAIL** mcohen@utdallas.edu

COHEN, RALPH ALAN
PERSONAL Born 09/07/1945, Columbia, SC, m, 1967, 3 children **DISCIPLINE** RENAISSANCE LITERATURE, FILM, SHAKESPEARE IN PERFORMANCE & TEACHING SHAKESP **EDUCATION** Dartmouth Col, AB, 67; Duke Univ, MA, 70, PhD, 73; Georgetown Univ, DHL (honorary), 98. **CAREER** Asst prof, 73-78, assoc prof, 78-84, prof, James Madison Univ, 84-, Dominion Fel, 90-91; Duke Univ Fel, 67-69, Danforth Tchg Fel, 70-71; NEH Folger Inst, Shakespeare's Text in Action, 87, Seminar leader, 3/93; Master tchr, NEH Seminar, A Time to Think about Shakespeare, 6/89, Center for Renaissance and Shakespearean Staging Inst, summer 95; Proj dir, VA Found for the Hum and Public Policy, Bringing Shakespeare Home, 6/92, proj dir, Women on the Page and Stage, 7/94. **HONORS AND AWARDS** Duke Dissertation Travel Award, 71; Va Found Grant, Film and the Polit Process, 75; JMU Summer Res Grant, 74, 77; JMU Admin Grant, 80; JMU Distinguished Tchg Award, 84; Madison Scholar, 86; State Coun Higher Educ in VA, Outstanding Fac award, 87; JMU Eminent Prof, 87. **MEMBERSHIPS** AAUP; Malone Soc; Southeastern Renaissance Conf; MLA; Shakespeare Asn; Shakespeare Theatre Asn Am. **SELECTED PUBLICATIONS** Auth, Reversal of gender in Rape of the Lock, SAtlantic Bull, 72; The function of setting in Eastward Ho, Renaissance Papers, 73; Reading and writing movie rev(s) in freshman Eng, Freshman Eng News, 75; The importance of setting in the revision of Every Man in His Humour, English Lit Renaissance, 78; Setting in Volpone, Renaissance Papers, 78; Misdirection in A Midsummer Night's Dream and Bartholomew Fair, Renaissance Papers, 82; Introduction to Shakespeare Quarterly, Edition on Teaching, summer 90; Lighting effects in Macbeth, Renaissance Papers, 94; Looking for cousin Ferdninand: folio stage directions in Taming of the Shrew, In: Textual Reformations (Laurie Maquire and Thomas Berger, ed), forthcoming; Staging comic divinity: the collision of high and low in Antony and Cleopatra, Shakespeare Bull, summer 95; Teaching the early comedies, Shakespeare's Sweet Thunder (Michael Collins, ed), Univ Del Press, 97; Original staging and the Shakespeare classroom, Teaching Shakespeare, MLA, 98. **CONTACT ADDRESS** Dept of Eng, James Madison Univ, 800 S Main St, Harrisonburg, VA, 22807-0002. **EMAIL** cohenra@jmu.edu

COHN, HENRY S.
PERSONAL Born 11/24/1945, Hartford, CT, m, 1971, 3 children **DISCIPLINE** LIBERAL ARTS **EDUCATION** Johns Hopkins, BA, 67. **CAREER** Asst state attorney general, Conn; Superior Court Judge, Hartford, Conn. **MEMBERSHIPS** Conn Bar Asn. **RESEARCH** Court history. **SELECTED PUBLICATIONS** Auth, Great Hartford Circus Fire, Yale, 91. **CONTACT ADDRESS** Superior Court, 75 Elm St., Hartford, CT, 06106. **EMAIL** 132main@house.com

COLBOURN, FRANK E.
PERSONAL Born 07/05/1926, New Haven, CT, 4 children **DISCIPLINE** DEBATE **EDUCATION** Boston Univ, BSBA, 48, LLB, 50; Brooklyn Law Sch, SJD (magna cum laude), 56. **CAREER** Asst to secy, Household Finance Corp, Chicago, 50-52; real estate exec, F W Woolworth Co, New York City, 52-60; assoc prof, 60-65, Prof Speech Pace Univ, 65-, Debate Coach, 60-92, Pres NYC Chapt AAUP (4 terms); Adj prof speech grad sch, C W Post Col, Long Island Univ, 64-78; dir, Long Island Debate Inst, 65-81; lectr speech, Mercer Sch Theol, 66-70; dir, Pace Speech Assocs, 67-70; lectr, NY State Police Acad, Albany, 77-78; debate coach, US Merchant Marine Acad, Kings Point, 78-82; pres, Colbourn Commun Consults, Inc, 80-; Cert Instr in Critical Thinking and mem advisory bd, Straus Thinking and Learning Ctr, NYC. **MEMBERSHIPS** Eastern Forensic Asn; Speech Commun Asn; Am Forensic Asn; DSR; TKA. **RESEARCH** Problems in negotiation; interviewing; communication theory. **SELECTED PUBLICATIONS** Auth, Legal aspects of negotiation of long term leases for chain stores in shopping centers, Brooklyn Law Rev, 4/62 & 12/62; The art of debate, 71 & How to judge a debate, 75 (records), Listening Libr. **CONTACT ADDRESS** Speech Comm Studies, Pace Univ, 1 Pace Plaza, New York, NY, 10038-1598.

COLBY, ROBERT ALAN
PERSONAL Born 04/15/1920, Chicago, IL, m, 1947 **DISCIPLINE** ENGLISH, LIBRARY SCIENCE **EDUCATION** Univ Chicago, BA, 41, MA, 42, PhD(English), 49; Columbia Univ, MS, 53. **CAREER** Instr English, DePaul Univ, 46-47; instr English & speech, Ill Inst Technol, 47-49; asst prof English, Lake Forest Col, 49-51; lectr, Hunter Col, 51-53; head lang lit & arts div, Libr, Queens Col, NY, 53-64; assoc prof libr sci, Southern Conn State Col, 64-66; assoc prof, 66-69, PROF LIBR SCI, QUEENS COL, NY, 69-, Asst ed, Wellesley Index to Victorian Periodicals, 77- Guggenheim fel, 78-79. **MEMBERSHIPS** MLA; Bibliog Soc Am; AAUP; Am Libr Asn; Asn Am Libr Schs; Victorian Soc Am. **RESEARCH** History of reading taste; history of books and printing; library history. **SELECTED PUBLICATIONS** Auth, Dickens and Thackeray, Punishment and Forgiveness, Nineteenth-Century Lit, Vol 0051, 96; Thackeray and Slavery, Nineteenth-Century Lit, Vol 0049, 94. **CONTACT ADDRESS** Grad Sch Libr Info Studies, Queens Col, CUNY, 6530 Kissena Blvd, New York, NY, 11367.

COLDIRON, ANNE E. B.
PERSONAL Greensboro, NC **DISCIPLINE** ENGLISH **EDUCATION** Univ Virginia, PhD, 96 **CAREER** Asst prof, 98-, Louisiana St Univ. **RESEARCH** Renaissance lit, poetics, comparative lit, Anglo-French lit relations, lit hist & theory. **CONTACT ADDRESS** English Dept, Louisiana State Univ, Baton Rouge, LA, 70803. **EMAIL** acoldiron@lsu.edu

COLDWELL, JOAN
PERSONAL Huddersfield, England **DISCIPLINE** ENGLISH **EDUCATION** Univ London, BA, 58, MA, 60; Harvard Univ, PhD, 67. **CAREER** Asst prof, 60-72, Univ Victoria; prof, 72-96, PROF EMER, McMASTER UNIV, 96-. **HONORS AND AWARDS** Tchr Award, McMaster Univ, 81-82; Tchr Award, Confed Univ Fac Asn, 89; Woman of Year, Hamilton, 89. **MEMBERSHIPS** Can Res Inst Advan Women; Int Asn Stud Anglo-Irish Lit. **SELECTED PUBLICATIONS** Auth, Charles Lamb on Shakespeare, 78; auth, The Collected Poems of Anne Wilkinson, 90; auth, The Tightrope Walker: Autobiographical Writings of Anne Wilkinson, 92. **CONTACT ADDRESS** Dept of English, McMaster Univ, Hamilton, ON, L8S 4L9. **EMAIL** coldwell@mcmail.cis.mcmaster.ca

COLE, DAVID WILLIAM
PERSONAL Born 02/16/1939, Worcester, MA, m, 1965, 2 children **DISCIPLINE** ENGLISH LITERATURE, COMPOSITION **EDUCATION** Oberlin Col, BA, 61; Syracuse Univ, MA, 63; Univ Wis-Madison, PhD(English), 70. **CAREER** Instr English, Univ Wis-Fox Valley, 65-66; from instr to asst prof, 68-73, assoc prof, 73-79, PROF ENGLISH, UNIV WIS CTR-BARABOO-SAUK COUNTY, 79-, Wis Higher Educ Aids Bd grant, 71. **RESEARCH** Victorian and Edwardian literature and culture; modern drama; modern rhetoric. **SELECTED PUBLICATIONS** Auth, Shakespeare the Taming of the Shrew, Explicator, Vol 0053, 95; Conrad Heart of Darkness, Explicator, Vol 0054, 95. **CONTACT ADDRESS** Dept of English, Univ of Wis Ctr-Baraboo-Sauk County, 1006 Connie Rd, Box 320, Baraboo, WI, 53913-1015.

COLE, HOWARD CHANDLER
PERSONAL Born 05/09/1934, Oak Park, IL, m, 1961, 2 children **DISCIPLINE** ENGLISH LITERATURE **EDUCATION** Wheaton Col, Ill, BA, 56; Yale Univ, MA, 61, PhD, 63. **CAREER** From instr to asst prof, 62-70, assoc prof Eng, Univ Ill, Urbana, 70-81, prof Eng, Univ Ill, Urbana 81-. **MEMBERSHIPS** MLA; Midwest Mod Lang Asn; Renaissance Soc Am. **RESEARCH** Elizabethan romantic comedy; Italian and French backgrounds of Shakespearean comedy. **SELECTED PUBLICATIONS** Auth, The Christian context of Measure for Measure, Jour Eng & Ger Philol, 7/65; A Quest of Inquirie: Some Contexts of Tudor Literature, Bobbs, 73; Dramatic interplay in the Decameron, Mod Lang Notes, 1/75; The moral vision of As You Like It, Col Lit, winter, 76; Bernardo Accolti's Virginia: The uniqueness of Unico Aretino, Renaissance Drama, 79; The All's Well Story from Boccaccio to Shakespeare, Univ Ill Press, 81. **CONTACT ADDRESS** Univ of Illinois, 608 S Wright St, Urbana, IL, 61801-3613.

COLE, JOHN Y., JR.
PERSONAL Born 07/30/1940, Ellensburg, WA, m, 1973 **DISCIPLINE** LIBRARIANSHIP **EDUCATION** Univ of Wash, BA, 62, MLS, 63; Johns Hopkins Univ, MLA, 66; George Washington Univ, PhD, 71. **CAREER** Libr of Congress, 66-; dir, Ctr for the Book, Libr of Congress, 77- . **MEMBERSHIPS** ALA, Am Stud Asn. **RESEARCH** History of books, reading, and libraries; history of the Library of Congress and its role in American culture and society. **SELECTED PUBLICATIONS** Auth, Jefferson's Legacy, 93; On These Walls, 95; The Library of Congress, 97. **CONTACT ADDRESS** Center for the Book, Library of Congress, Washington, DC, 20540. **EMAIL** jcole@loc.gov

COLE, MIKE
DISCIPLINE COMMUNICATIONS **EDUCATION** Ind Univ, PhD, 62. **CAREER** PROF, UNIV CALIF, SAN DIEGO. **RESEARCH** Elaboration of a mediational theory of mind. **SELECTED PUBLICATIONS** Co-auth, The Psychology of Literacy, Harvard, 81; auth, "A Conception of Culture for a Communication Theory of Mind," Intrapersonal Communication: Different Voices, Different Minds, Erlbaum, 94. **CONTACT ADDRESS** Dept of Commun, Univ Calif, San Diego, 9500 Gilman Dr, La Jolla, CA, 92093. **EMAIL** mcole@weber.ucsd.edu

COLEMAN, ARTHUR
DISCIPLINE AMERICAN LITERATURE **EDUCATION** NY Univ, PhD. **CAREER** Prof, Long Island Univ, C.W. Post Campus. **SELECTED PUBLICATIONS** Auth, Sinclair Lewis: The Early Years, Epic and Romance Criticism; Hemingway's 'The Spanish Earth;' The Americanization of H. G. Wells; Sociocultural Inferences from the Practice of Naming America's Major League Ball Parks; A Case in Point and Petals on a Wet Black Bough; coauth, Drama Criticism. **CONTACT ADDRESS** Long Island Univ, C.W. Post, Brookville, NY, 11548-1300.

COLEMAN, DANIEL
DISCIPLINE ENGLISH LITERATURE **EDUCATION** Campion Co, BA; Regina, BEd, MA; Univ Alberta, PhD. **RESEARCH** English-Canadian lit; lit of migration; critical theory. **SELECTED PUBLICATIONS** Auth, Masculine Migrations: Reading the Postcolonial Male in 'New Canadian' Narrative, 98. **CONTACT ADDRESS** English Dept, McMaster Univ, 1280 Main St W, Hamilton, ON, L8S 4L9.

COLEMAN, EDWIN LEON, II
PERSONAL Born 03/17/1932, El Dorado, Arkansas, m **DISCIPLINE** SPEECH **EDUCATION** City Coll of San Francisco, AA 1955; San Francisco State Univ, BA 1960, MA 1962; Univ of OR, PhD 1971. **CAREER** Melodyland Theatre, technician, 1960; Chico State Univ, Speech Dept, asst prof, 1963-66; Univ of OR Dept of English, dir, Folklore 1 Ethnic Program, currently; professional musician, currently. **HONORS AND AWARDS** Ford Fellow Educ Grant 1970; Danforth Assoc 1977-; Distinguished Black Faculty 1978; Outstanding Faculty Natl Mag OR Art Commission 1982; Frederick Douglass Scholarship Awd Natl Council of Black Studies 1986; University of Oregon, Charles S. Johnson Service Award; NAACP Lifetime Achievement Award. **MEMBERSHIPS** Bd Campus Interfaith Ministry 1975-; bd Sponsors Inc 1980-; bd Clergy & Laity Concerned 1980-; bd OR Arts Found 1981-84; pres OR Folklore Soc 1983-84; consul Natl Endowment for the Arts 1983-; Natl Humanities, faculty; mem Amer Folklore Soc; NAACP; Kappa Alpha Psi; Oregon Track Club; bd, Western States Arts Foundation. **CONTACT ADDRESS** Dept of English, Univ of Oregon, Eugene, OR, 97403.

COLEMAN, MARK
DISCIPLINE ENGLISH **EDUCATION** Harvard Univ, BA; Cornell Univ, PhD. **CAREER** Fac, Cornell Univ to Northwestern Univ; to GA Col; to SUNY Potsdam. **RESEARCH** Eng lit (Restoration and 18th century, Renaissance, Romanticism); lit and the visual arts; graphic and literary satire; writing instruction; computer pedag in writing and lit; hypermedia. **SELECTED PUBLICATIONS** Auth, recent publ(s) have been in the application of computing tech to the tchg of writing and lit. **CONTACT ADDRESS** SUNY Potsdam, 44 Pierrepont Ave, 248 Morey , Potsdam, NY, 13676. **EMAIL** scottja@potsdam

COLEMAN, ROBIN R.
PERSONAL Pittsburgh, PA, m, 1996 **DISCIPLINE** MASS COMMUNICATION **EDUCATION** Bowling Green State Univ, PhD, 96. **CAREER** Postdoctoral fel, Univ Pitts, 96-98; asst prof, NY Univ, 98- . **MEMBERSHIPS** Nat Commun Asn; Int Commun Asn. **RESEARCH** African Americans and mass media; reception study; media literacy. **SELECTED PUBLICATIONS** Auth African American Viewers and the Black Situation Comedy: Situating Racial Humor, Garland, 98. **CONTACT ADDRESS** 15 Washington Pl, 4J, New York, NY, 10003. **EMAIL** robin.coleman@nyu.edu

COLEMAN, WILLIAM S.E.
PERSONAL Born 06/07/1926, m, 2 children **DISCIPLINE** DRAMA **EDUCATION** Slippery Rock State Col, BS, 49; Pa State Univ, MA, 53; Univ Pittsburgh, PhD(Theatre Hist), 65. **CAREER** Instr high sch, Pa, 49-52; asst prof Theatre, Speech & English, Slippery Rock State Col, 53-55; assoc prof & head dept, Glenville State Col, 55-63; asst prof Theatre & Speech, State Univ NY Buffalo, 65-66; prof Theatre Arts, Drake Univ, 66-, chmn, WVa State Comt Re-study Speech Teacher Educ, 61-62; mem planning comt, WVa Centennial Showboat, 62-63; dir, Loving Knife, NY Stage Co, 65; Danforth Teacher study grant, 63 & 64; State Univ NY Found res grant; guest lectr univs, mus & soc, Gt Brit, Italy & WGer. **HONORS AND AWARDS** Certif of Merit Award, A Stranger to the Past, IMPA awards, 98; pres and founding mem Iowa Scriptwriters Alliance. **RESEARCH** London performances of The Merchant of Venice; William F Cody's performance career; American Indian Affairs. **SELECTED PUBLICATIONS** Auth, Found: An Author (play), The Playshop, 2/52; Planning for the Theatre, Univ Pittsburgh, 65; Post-restoration Shylocks prior to Macklin, Theatre Survey, 5/67; Buffalo Bill on stage, Players Mag, 12/71; coauth, Artand on an American campus, Oblique, 9/73; Buffalo Bill's Wild West (film script), 77 & Gods and Men in Ancient Greece (film script), 78, Perfection Form Co; William Shakespeare's King Lear, annotation, Perfection Forum, 97. **CONTACT ADDRESS** 2507 University Ave, Des Moines, IA, 50311-4505. **EMAIL** wc4781@acad.drake.edu

COLLETTE, CAROLYN PENNEY
PERSONAL Born 08/02/1945, Boston, MA, 2 children **DISCIPLINE** MEDIEVAL ENGLISH LITERATURE **EDUCATION** Mt Holyoke Col, AB, 67; Univ Mass, MA, 68, PhD, 71. **CAREER** From instr to asst prof English lit, 69-78, fac fel, 73-74, ASSOC PROF ENGLISH, MT HOLYOKE COL, 78-. **HONORS AND AWARDS** Phi Beta Kappa, 67; Phi Kappa Phi; 69; Woodrow Wilson Fel, 67; NEH Summer Stipend, 76; Prof of English Lang and Lit, Alumnae Found at Mount Holyoke, 93. **MEMBERSHIPS** MLA; William Morris Soc; New Chaucer Soc; Int Courtly Lit Soc, vice pres, 95-98, pres, 98-2001. **RESEARCH** Old and Middle English literature; Gothic revival in England, 1750-1870. **SELECTED PUBLICATIONS** Auth, Milton's Psalm translations; petition and praise, Eng Lit Renaissance, fall 72; Lord John Manners' Old Nobility, Am Notes & Queries, 3/75; A Closer Look at Seinte Cecile's Special Vision, spring 76 & Sense and sensibility in The Prioress' Tale, fall 80, Chaucer Rev; several articles and reviews in literary journals and publications between 80 and 92; auth, Common Ground: Personal Writing and Public Discourse, with Richard Johnson, NY: Harper Collins, 93; Criseyde's Honor, Integrity and Public Identity in Chaucer's Courtly Romance, in Literary Aspects of Courtly Culture, ed Maddox and Sturm-Maddox, Cambridge: D. S. Brewer, 94; 'Peyntyng with Gret Cost': Virginia as Image in the Physician's Tale, Chaucer Yearbook, 94; Chaucer's Discourse of Mariology, in Art and Context in Late Medieval English Narrative, ed Robert Edwards, by D. S. Brewer, 94; Some Aestetic Implications of Multiplication of Species, Avista, 9, 95; Heeding the Counsel of Prudence: A Context for the Melibee, The Chaucer Rev, 29, 95; Finding Common Ground: A Guide to Personal, Professional and Public Writing, with Richard Johnson, 2nd ed, NY: Addison Wesley Longman, 97; and several works in progress. **CONTACT ADDRESS** Dept of English, Mount Holyoke Col, 50 College St, South Hadley, MA, 01075-1461. **EMAIL** CCollett@MtHolyoke.edu

COLLEY, ANN C.
PERSONAL Born 01/09/1940, Bury, England, 1 child **DISCIPLINE** ENGLISH **EDUCATION** Unvi Chicago, PhD, 1983. **CAREER** Prof, Fisk Univ, 1969-82; State Univ Col NY at Buffalo, 85- . **HONORS AND AWARDS** Sr Fulbright fel, Warsaw, Poland, 95-96. **MEMBERSHIPS** MLA; Northeast Victorian Studies Asoc; Tennyson Soc; Am Studies Asoc. **RESEARCH** Victorian literature and culture; words and images. **SELECTED PUBLICATIONS** Auth, Robert Louis Stevenson and the Idea of Recollection, Victorian Lit and Cult, 97; auth, Writing Towards Home: The Landscape of Robert Louis Stevenson's A Child's Garden of Verses, Victorian Poetry, 97; auth, Ruskin and Turner's arrangements of Remberance', The Ruskin Gazette of the Ruskin Soc of London, 97; auth, Nostalgia and Recollection in Victorian Culture, 98; auth, Bodies and Mirrors: The Childhood Interiors of Ruskin, Pater, and Stevenson, Reading the Interior: Nineteenth Century Domestic Space, 99. **CONTACT ADDRESS** 332 Ashland Ave., Buffalo, NY, 14222. **EMAIL** colleyac@buffalostate.edu

COLLEY, NATHANIEL S.
PERSONAL Born 06/08/1956, Sacramento, CA, d **DISCIPLINE** THEATER **EDUCATION** University of Michigan, BA, 1977, Law School, JD, 1979; UC Davis, graduate study, anthropology. **CAREER** Colley-Lindsey & Colley, partner, 1980; Sextus Productions (entertainment), partner, 1974-; WCBN-FM Radio Station, general manager, 1979, program director, 1978, talk show host, 1976-78, disc jockey, 1974-76; PLAYWRIGHT, currently. **HONORS AND AWARDS** Natl Merit Scholarship Finalist, 1974. **MEMBERSHIPS** California Bar Assn, 1980; American Legion Boy's State CA, 1973; California Youth Senate, 1973; University of Michigan Assn of Black Communicators, 1974; vice pres, Sacramento NAACP Youth Council, 1973-74; natl bd dirs, NAACP 1972-75; Black Music Assn, 1979-. **SELECTED PUBLICATIONS** Playwright: "The Shoebox," Lorraine Hansberry Theatre; "A Sensitive Man,"; Moving Arts, LA Winner of 5 Dramalogue Awards; film: "The Abortion of Mary Williams,"; finalist "Showtime's Black Filmmaker Program," premiered on Showtime, 1998. **CONTACT ADDRESS** PO Box 741825, Los Angeles, CA, 90004.

COLLIE, KELSEY E.
PERSONAL Born 02/21/1935, Miami, FL, d **DISCIPLINE** DRAMA **EDUCATION** Hampton Inst, AB 1957; George Washington Univ, MFA 1970; Howard Univ, PhD, 1979. **CAREER** Library of Congress, accessioner & documents librarian 1960-70; Coll of Fine Arts Drama Dept, prof, asst dean 1976-79; Kelsey E Collie Playmakers Repertory Co, artistic dir 1976-; Diva Productions, artistic dir 1986-87; Howard Univ Children's Theatre, 1973-91; playwright; Kelsey E Collie Talent Assoc, talent mgr; Howard Univ, prof of drama 1973-. **HONORS AND AWARDS** Community Serv Award, Salisbury Cultural Arts Comm, 1978; Distinguished Serv Award, Univ Without Walls, 1980; Coalition of Professional Youth on the Move Award, 1981; appreciation award, Syphax School, Washington DC, 1989; director, Night of the Divas: Tribute to Marian Anderson, J F Kennedy Center, 1985; President's Award for play Black Images/Black Reflections, Dundalk International Maytime Festival, Ireland, 1977; Premiere Award for play Brother, Brother, Brother Mine, Dundalk International Maytime Festival, Ireland, 1979; Mainline to Stardom Award, 1996. **MEMBERSHIPS** Bd dir Pierce Warwick Adoption Serv 1973-89; mem Amer Community Theatre Assn 1977-87; Theatre Arts Productions Inc 1980-87; mem Artist-in-Educ Panel DC Commission on the Arts 1983-85; mem Amer Council on the Arts 1985-86; mem Black Theatre Network 1986-; artistic dir, Color Me Human Players, 1986-; pres, OPM Productions, 1991-93.

COLLIE, MICHAEL J.
PERSONAL Born 08/08/1929, Eastbourne, England **DISCIPLINE** ENGLISH/HISTORY OF SCIENCE **EDUCATION** St Catharine's Col, Cambridge Univ, MA, 56. **CAREER** Asst prof, Univ Man, 57; lectr, Univ Exeter, 61; assoc prof, Mt Allison Univ, 62; prof Eng, 65-90, dept ch, 67-69, dean grad stud, 69-73, PROF EMER, YORK UNIV, 90-. **MEMBERSHIPS** Int Asn Univ Profs Eng; Mod Hum Res Asn; Bibliog Soc; Bibliog Soc Am; Asn Can Univ Tchrs Eng (pres, 68-69); Can Bibliog Soc; Soc Hist Sci; Geol Soc Am; Geol Soc London; Edinburgh Bibliog Soc. **SELECTED PUBLICATIONS** Auth, George Borrow Eccentric, 82; auth, George Borrow: A Bibliographical Study, 84; auth, George Gissing: A Bibliographical Study, 85; auth, Henry Maudsley: Victorian Psychiatrist, 88; auth, Huxley at Work, 91; auth, Murchison in Moray: the Geologist on Home Ground, 95; auth, George Gordon: A Catalogue of His Scientific Correspondence, 96. **CONTACT ADDRESS** Winters Col, York Univ, North York, ON, M3J 1P3.

COLLIER, CHERYL A.
DISCIPLINE AMERICAN LITERATURE **EDUCATION** Univ Ga, PhD, 94. **CAREER** Dept Eng, Clemson Univ **RESEARCH** American literature. **SELECTED PUBLICATIONS** Auth, Biographical essays on Amy Tan and Maragaret Walker in The Cyclopedia of World Authors; Introduction essay, The Langston Hughes Rev (Fall 95 issue). **CONTACT ADDRESS** Clemson Univ, 312 Strode, Clemson, SC, 29634. **EMAIL** abramsc@clemson.edu

COLLIER, EUGENIA W.
PERSONAL Born 04/06/1928, Baltimore, MD, d **DISCIPLINE** LITERATURE **EDUCATION** Univ of MD, PhD 1976; Columbia Univ, MA 1950; Howard Univ, BA (magna cum laude) 1948. **CAREER** Balt Dept of Public Welfare, case worker 1950-55; Morgan State Univ, asst prof 1955-66; Comm Coll of Baltimore, prof 1966-74; So IL Univ, visiting prof 1970; Atlanta Univ, visiting prof 1974; Univ of MD, assoc prof 1974-77; Howard Univ, assoc prof 1977-87; Coppin State Coll, prof, 1987-92; Morgan State University, professor of English, 1992-96. **HONORS AND AWARDS** Gwendolyn Brooks Award for Fiction 1969; MAW, Creative Writing Award, 1984. **MEMBERSHIPS** National Conference on African-American Theater; National Council of Teachers of English; Middle Alantic Writers Association; College Language Association; African-American Writers' Guild; Arena Players, Baltimore, MD. **SELECTED PUBLICATIONS** Author: Breeder and Other Stories, 1994; co-editor, Afro-American Writing, w/Richard A Long. **EMAIL** ecollier@ix.netcom.com

COLLINS, CHRISTOPHER
PERSONAL Born 07/08/1936, Red Bank, NJ, m, 1968, 2 children **DISCIPLINE** POETIC THEORY, AMERICAN POETRY **EDUCATION** St Anselm's Col BA, 58; Univ Calif, Berkeley, MA, 59; Columbia Univ, PhD, 64. **CAREER** Asst prof English, Nassau Community Col, 63-65; from asst prof to assoc prof & chmn dept, Borough of Manhattan Community Col, 65-68; assoc prof, 68-91, prof, NY Univ, ch, colloquim on Psychoaesthetics, 79-83, assoc dir, poetics instT, 81-85, Vis Scholar, Gonville & Caius Col, Cambridge Univ, 70. **HONORS AND AWARDS** Woodrow Wilson Nat fel **MEMBERSHIPS** Conf Contemp Am Poetry; Northeastern Mod Lang Asn (secy, 78-79). **RESEARCH** Poetic theory; cognitive psychology and poetry; contemporary poetry. **SELECTED PUBLICATIONS** Auth, The Act of Poetry, Random, 70; The Uses of Observation: Correspondential Vision in the Writings of Emerson, Thoreau, and Whitman, Mouton, The Hague, 71; Figure, ground, and open field, NY Quart, winter 71; transl & auth, introd, The Daphnis and Chloe of Longus, Imprint Soc, 72; If your drink is bitter, be wine, Nation, 5/72; Notes on prosody, In: The Logic of Poetry, Monaco & Briggs, 74; auth, Reading the Written Image: Verval Play, Interpretation, and the Roots of Iconophobia, Penn State Press, 91; auth, The Petics of the Mind's Eye: Literature and the Psychology of Imagination. Univ Penn, 91; auth, Authority Figures: Metaphoes of Mastery from the Iliad to the Apocalypse, Rowman and Littlefield, 96. **CONTACT ADDRESS** Dept of English, NY Univ, 19 University Pl, New York, NY, 10003-4556. **EMAIL** cc3@is2.nyu.edu

COLLINS, DAN STEAD
PERSONAL Born 12/05/1919, Williamsport, PA, m, 1955 **DISCIPLINE** ENGLISH **EDUCATION** Univ Pa, BS, 41; Univ NC, MA, 51, PhD, 60. **CAREER** Instr English, Univ Tenn, 46-47; part-time instr, Univ NC, 49-52; from instr to asst prof, 53-73, ASSOC PROF ENGLISH, UNIV MASS, AMHERST, 73-, Managing ed, English Lit Renaissance, 72-74, ed, 75, 77. **MEMBERSHIPS** Col English Asn; MLA; Renaissance Soc Am. **RESEARCH** Milton. **SELECTED PUBLICATIONS** Auth, Spivack,Bernard 1911-1992, Eng Lit Renaissance, Vol 0023, 93. **CONTACT ADDRESS** Dept of English, Univ of Mass, Amherst, MA, 01003.

COLLINS, K.K.
PERSONAL Born 09/15/1947, Union City, TN, m, 1970, 1 child **DISCIPLINE** ENGLISH LANGUAGE AND LITERATURE **EDUCATION** Col William & Mary, AB, 69; Vanderbilt Univ, PhD(English), 76. **CAREER** Lectr, 76-77, asst prof, 77-82, ASSOC PROF ENGLISH, SOUTHERN ILL UNIV, CARBONDALE, 82- **HONORS AND AWARDS** Fel, Woodrow Wilson Diss, Nat Endowment Hum Summer, Mellon Sem; Sch of Criticism and Theory Sch; Am Philos Soc grant. **MEMBERSHIPS** MLA; Mod Humanities Res Asn; Dickens

Soc. **RESEARCH** Nineteenth-century English literature; literature and philosophy; literature and science. **SELECTED PUBLICATIONS** Auth, Lewes,G.H.--A Life, Nineteenth Century Prose, Vol 0020, 93; auth, Thomas Woolner and The Oxford and Cambridge Magazine, Notes and Quotes, 83; auth, The British and Foreign Rev, Brit Lit Mags, 84; coauth, Lewes at Colonus: An early Victorian view of translation from the Greek, mod Lang Rev, 87; auth, Reading George Eliot reading Lewes's obituaries, Mod Philol, 87. **CONTACT ADDRESS** Dept of English, Southern Ill Univ, Carbondale, IL, 62901-4300. **EMAIL** kkcoll@siu.edu

COLLINS, MARTHA
PERSONAL Born 11/25/1940, Omaha, NE **DISCIPLINE** POETRY, AMERICAN LITERATURE **EDUCATION** Stanford Univ, AB, 62; Univ Iowa, MA, 65, PhD(English), 71. **CAREER** Asst prof English, Northeast Mo State Col, 65-66; instr, 66-71, asst prof, 71-75, assoc prof to PROF ENGLISH, UNIV MASS, BOSTON, 75-; PROF CREATIVE WRITING, OBERLIN COL, 97-. **MEMBERSHIPS** Assoc Writing Prog. **RESEARCH** Poetry; American literature; women's studies. **SELECTED PUBLICATIONS** Auth, The center of consciousness on stage: Henry James Confidence, Studies Am Fiction, 75; The self-conscious poet: The case of William Collins, ELH, 75; The narrator, the satellites, and the lady: Point of view in The Portrait of a Lady, Studies Novel, 76; The contents of discontent: A preface to some poems by Peter Klappert, Agni Rev, 78; ed, Critical Essays on Louise Bogan, G K Hall, 84. **CONTACT ADDRESS** Dept of English, Univ of Massachusetts, 100 Morrissey Blvd, Boston, MA, 02125-3300.

COLLINS, MICHAEL J.
DISCIPLINE ENGLISH LITERATURE **EDUCATION** Fordham Univ, BA; Univ NY, MA, PhD. **CAREER** Prof. **RESEARCH** Shakespeare; British theatre since 1950; Anglo-Welsh poetry. **SELECTED PUBLICATIONS** Auth, pubs on Shakespeare, Anglo- Welsh poetry, and American literature; ed, Shakespeare's Sweet Thunder: Essays on the Early Comedies, Delaware, 97. **CONTACT ADDRESS** English Dept, Georgetown Univ, 37th and O St, Washington, DC, 20057.

COLLINS, ROBERT G.
PERSONAL Born 06/06/1926, Danbury, CT **DISCIPLINE** ENGLISH **EDUCATION** Miami Univ, Ohio, BA, 50, MA, 52; Univ Denver, PhD, 59. **CAREER** Ch grad Eng stud, Univ Man, 68-74; prof Eng, Univ Ottawa, 76-91; vis prof, Univ Kuwait, 94-97. **MEMBERSHIPS** MLA; Asn Can Univ Tchrs Eng; Bronte Soc; Kafka Soc Am; Conf Eds Learned J. **SELECTED PUBLICATIONS** Auth, Arch-Sinner: Branwell Bronte, 93; auth, E.J. Pratt, 88; auth, Tolerable Levels of Violence, 83; auth/comp, Critical Essays on John Cheever, 83. **CONTACT ADDRESS** 242 Elizabeth St, PO Box 522, Arnprior, ON, K7S 3T8.

COLLINS, THOMAS J.
PERSONAL Born 08/23/1936, London, ON, Canada, m, 1960, 3 children **DISCIPLINE** LITERATURE **EDUCATION** Univ Western Ont, BA, 59, MA, 61; Ind Univ, PhD, 65. **CAREER** PROF ENGLISH, UNIV WESTERN ONT, 65-, chmn, 74-82, dean arts, 82-86, vice pres acad & provost, 86-95. **HONORS AND AWARDS** Can Coun res grant, 74; Univ Western Ont acad develop fund grant, 82; SSHRC grants, 83-85, 87-89. **MEMBERSHIPS** MLA; Can Asn Univ Tchrs; Int Browning Soc; Comt Chmn Eng Ont; Can Asn Chmn Eng. **RESEARCH** Victorian literature and studies; Robert Browning. **SELECTED PUBLICATIONS** Auth, Robert Browning's Moral-Aesthetic Theory: 1833-55, 67; ed, Letters from the Brownings to the Tennysons, 71; ed, Letters of Robert Browning to the Rev J.D. Williams, 76; co-ed, Robert Browning: The Poems, 81; gen ed, Victorian Authors Manuscript Facsimile Series; co-compiler, A Concordance to the Poems of Robert Browning, 7 vols, 96; ed bd, Victorian Poetry, 74-; ed bd Victorian Stud, 79-; adv comt, Victorian Lit Cult, 91-. **CONTACT ADDRESS** English Dept, Univ of Western Ontario, London, ON, N6A 3K7.

COLLMER, ROBERT GEORGE
PERSONAL Born 11/28/1926, Guatemela City, Guatemala, m, 1948, 2 children **DISCIPLINE** ENGLISH **EDUCATION** Baylor Univ, BA, 48, MA, 49; Univ Pa, PhD(English), 53. **CAREER** Asst instr English, Univ Pa, 49-52; from assoc prof to prof, Hardin-Simmons Univ, 54-61; prof & dean col, Wayland Baptist Univ, 61-66; Fulbright prof English & Am lit, Nat Univ Paraguay, 66-67; prof English, Tex Tech Univ, 67-73, dir grad studies, 69-70, acting chmn dept English, 70; prof English & chmn dept, 73-79, DEAN GRAD STUDIES & RES, BAYLOR UNIV, 79-, Smith-Mundt prof English & Am lit, Inst Technol, Mex, 58-60; Southern Fel grant, 58. **HONORS AND AWARDS** Fulbright Sr Res Award, Univ Leiden, Neth, 82. **MEMBERSHIPS** MLA; Renaissance Soc Am; SCent MLA; SCent Renaissance Conf (pres, 70-71). **RESEARCH** English literature of late Renaissance; Anglo-Dutch literary relations; Anglo-Hispanic literary relations. **SELECTED PUBLICATIONS** Auth, Grotius,Hugo--The Religiousness of the States of Holland and Westfriesland 1613--Dutch, English, Jour Church and State, Vol 0039, 97; Bunyan and His England, 1628-88, Durham Univ Jour, Vol 0085, 93. **CONTACT ADDRESS** Baylor Univ, Waco, TX, 76798.

COLTRANE, ROBERT
PERSONAL Born 11/21/1938, Hampton, VA, m, 1972, 2 children **DISCIPLINE** ENGLISH **EDUCATION** VA Military Inst, BA, 61; Univ of VA, MA, 62; PA St Univ, Phd, 92 **CAREER** Instr, 65-68, Old Dominion Univ; Dir PR, 69-83, Lock Haven Univ; Asst Prof, 83-93, Assoc Prof, 93-, Lock Haven Univ **MEMBERSHIPS** Int Theodore Dreiser Soc **RESEARCH** 20th Cent Am Poetry **SELECTED PUBLICATIONS** Auth, The Crafting of Dreiser's Twelve Men, Papers on Language & Literature, S IL Univ, 91 **CONTACT ADDRESS** Lock Haven, PA, 17745. **EMAIL** rcoltran@eagle.lhup.edu

COLVERT, JAMES B.
PERSONAL Born 06/08/1921, Paris, TX, m, 1944, 2 children **DISCIPLINE** ENGLISH **EDUCATION** Henderson State Col, BA, 47; ETex State Univ, MA, 49; La State Univ, PhD(English), 53. **CAREER** From instr to asst prof English, Univ Tex, 53-57; asst prof, Univ Conn, 57-58; assoc prof, Univ Va, 59-68; head dept, 72-76, dir grad studies, 77-79, actg head dept, 79-80, PROF ENGLISH, UNIV GA, 68-. **RESEARCH** American literature. **SELECTED PUBLICATIONS** Auth, Day, Fred, Holland, Guiney, Louise, Imogen, and the Text of Crane,Stephen the Black Riders, Amer Lit Realism 1870-1910, Vol 0028, 96. **CONTACT ADDRESS** Dept of English, Univ of Ga, Athens, GA, 30601.

COLVIN, DANIEL LESTER
PERSONAL Born 03/10/1947, Amarillo, TX, m, 1969, 1 child **DISCIPLINE** ENGLISH LITERATURE **EDUCATION** Wheaton Col, BA, 69; Northwestern Univ, MA, 70, PhD(English), 76. **CAREER** Assoc prof, 72-80, assoc prof English, 80-86, prof English, Western Ill Univ, 86-. **HONORS AND AWARDS** NEH Inst, 95-96; NEH Summer Seminar, Univ of Mich, 77, Yale Univ, 88. **MEMBERSHIPS** MLA; Conf Christianity & Lit; AAUP; Shakespeare Asn of Am; Renaissance Soc of Am. **RESEARCH** Renaissance literary rhetoric; Christian literary criticism; theories of the pastoral; Shakespeare. **SELECTED PUBLICATIONS** Auth, The Renaissance, Western Ill Univ, 78; Milton's Comus and the Pattern of Human Temptation, Christianity & Lit, 78; Measure for Measure: A Study Guide and Teacher's Handbook, Folger Shakespeare Libr Inst, 96; Francesco Petrarch, Magill's Survey of World Lit, Salem, 92; The How-to Guide to Ad Libbing Shakespeare, The Fight Master: Journal of the Soc of Am Fight Directores XIII, 90; That Abler Soule: Donne and the Poetic of Knowledge, Res Publica Litterarum, 83. **CONTACT ADDRESS** Dept of English, Western Illinois Univ, 1 University Cir, Macomb, IL, 61455-1390. **EMAIL** DL-Colvin@wiu.edu

COLWELL, FREDERIC
DISCIPLINE ENGLISH LITERATURE **EDUCATION** Mich State Univ, PhD. **CAREER** Dept Eng, Queen's Univ **RESEARCH** Romantic poetry and art; psychoanalytic studies; Jungian psychology; travel literature of the 18th and 19th centuries; Richard Strauss. **SELECTED PUBLICATIONS** Auth, Rivermen: A Romantic Iconography of the River and the Source, McGill-Queen's Univ, 89; A Feast of Ashes, Oberon, 90; pubs on Romantic poetry and art. **CONTACT ADDRESS** English Dept, Queen's Univ, Kingston, ON, K7L 3N6.

COMENSOLI, VIVIANA
DISCIPLINE RENAISSANCE DRAMA **EDUCATION** Simon Fraser, BA, MA; British Columbia, PhD. **CAREER** Prof **SELECTED PUBLICATIONS** Auth, Household Business': Domestic Plays of Early Modern England, Univ Toronto, 96; Homophobia and the Regulation of Desire: A Psychoanalytic Reading of Marlowe's Edward II; Witchcraft and Domestic Tragedy in The Witch of Edmonton; Gender and Eloquence in Dekker's The Honest Whore, Part II. **CONTACT ADDRESS** Wilfrid Laurier Univ, 75 University Ave W, Waterloo, ON, N2L 3C5. **EMAIL** vcomenso@mach1.wlu.ca

COMFORT, JUANITA R.
DISCIPLINE COMPOSITION **EDUCATION** Old Dominion Univ, MA, BA; Ohio State Univ, PhD. **CAREER** Engl, Old Dominion Univ. **SELECTED PUBLICATIONS** Auth, A Rheotric of 'Cultural Negotiation': toward an Ethos of Empowerment for African American Women Graduate Students, in Rhetoric, Cult Studies & Literacy, Hillsdale, LEA, 95. **CONTACT ADDRESS** Old Dominion Univ, 4100 Powhatan Ave, BAL 205, Norfolk, VA, 23058. **EMAIL** JComfort@odu.edu

COMOR, EDWARD
DISCIPLINE POLITICAL ECONOMY OF COMMUNICATION AND CULTURE **EDUCATION** Univ Toronto; BA; Univ Leeds, MA; York Univ, PhD. **CAREER** Prof, Am Univ. **RESEARCH** United States foreign communication policy; The mediating role of free trade treaties and other international institutions; The political economic implications of global information infrastructure developments. **SELECTED PUBLICATIONS** Ed/contribur, The Global Political Economy of Communications, St. Martin's Press, 94, 96.. **CONTACT ADDRESS** American Univ, 4400 Massachusetts Ave, Washington, DC, 20016.

COMPRONE, JOSEPH JOHN
PERSONAL Born 03/11/1943, Lansdowne, PA, m, 1965, 1 child **DISCIPLINE** ENGLISH **EDUCATION** Springfield Col, BA, 65; Univ Mass, MA, 67, PhD(English), 70. **CAREER** Teaching asst English, Univ Mass, 66-69, asst dir freshman English, 68-69; asst prof English & coord compos, Univ Minn, Morris, 69-72; assoc prof English & dir freshman English, Univ Cincinnati, 72-76; prof English & dir compos, 76-81, DIR GRAD STUDIES ENGLISH, UNIV LOUISVILLE, 81-, Freshman English consult; consult & rev, St Martin's Press, Houghton Mifflin & W Norton, 74-78. **MEMBERSHIPS** NCTE; Conf Col Compos & Commun; AAUP; MLA; Writing Prog Adminr (treas, 76-78). **RESEARCH** Literary theory and modern literature; rhetoric and composition; film and pedagogy. **SELECTED PUBLICATIONS** Auth, Where Do We Go Next in Writing Across the Curriculum, Col Composition and Commun, Vol 0044, 93. **CONTACT ADDRESS** Dept of English, Univ of Louisville, Louisville, KY, 40208.

COMSTOCK, GEORGE ADOLPHE
PERSONAL Born 05/17/1932, Seattle, WA, d **DISCIPLINE** COMMUNICATIONS, SOCIAL PSYCHOLOGY **EDUCATION** Univ Wash, BA, 54; Stanford Univ, MA, 58, PhD(commun), 67. **CAREER** Asst prof jour, NY Univ, 67-68; social psychologist, Rand Corp, 68-70 & NIMH., 70-72; sr social psychologist, Rand Corp, 72-77; prof commun, S I Newhouse Sch Pub Commun, 77-79, S I NEWHOUSE CHAIR PUB COMMUN, SYRACUSE UNIV, 79- . **HONORS AND AWARDS** Sr sci adv, US Surgeon Gen Sci Adv Comt TV & Social Behavior, 70-72. **MEMBERSHIPS** Asn Educ Jour and Mass Commun; Am Asn Pub Opinion Res; Soc Psychol Study Social Issues. **RESEARCH** Behavioral effects of televised portrayals; influence of mass media on society. **SELECTED PUBLICATIONS** Co-ed, Media Content and Control, Vol I, Television and Social Learning, Vol II, Television and Adolescent Agressiveness, Vol III, Television in Day-to-day Life, Vol IV, Television's Effects: Further Explorations, Vol V, In: Television and Social Behavior, US Govt Printing Off, 72; coauth, Television and Human Behavior: The Research Horizon, Future and Present, & auth, Television and Human Behavior: The Key Studies, Rand Corp, 75; coauth, Television and Human Behavior, Columbia Univ, 78; auth, Television in America, Sage, 81; auth, Evolution of American Television, Sage, 89; auth, Television and the American Child, Academic, 91; auth, Television in the Lives of Americans, Academic, in press. **CONTACT ADDRESS** Pub Commun, Syracuse Univ, Syracuse, NY, 13210.

CONDON, WILLIAM
DISCIPLINE LITERATURE **EDUCATION** Brown, PhD. **CAREER** Assoc prof & dir, Washington State Univ. **HONORS AND AWARDS** Founding mem, Alliance for Comput and Writing. **MEMBERSHIPS** Past ch, Conf on Comput and Writing; mem, CCC Comt on Comput and Composition. **RESEARCH** How portfolios contribute to writing across the curriculum and on ways portfolios affect students' movement from one institution or school to another. **SELECTED PUBLICATIONS** Coauth, Portfolios in College Writing, 97 & Writing the Information Highway, 97. **CONTACT ADDRESS** Dept of English, Washington State Univ, 1 SE Stadium Way, PO Box 645020, Pullman, WA, 99164-5020. **EMAIL** bcondon@wsu.edu

CONGER, SYNDY MCMILLEN
PERSONAL Born 10/14/1942, Waterloo, IA, m, 1967 **DISCIPLINE** ENGLISH AND COMPARATIVE LITERATURE **EDUCATION** Univ Iowa, BA, 65, MA, 69, PhD(English), 76. **CAREER** Asst prof, 72-80, ASSOC PROF ENGLISH, WESTERN ILL UNIV, 80-. **MEMBERSHIPS** MLA; Am Soc Cinema Studies; Am Soc 18th Century Studies. **RESEARCH** Gothic literature; 18th century Anglo-German literary relations prose fiction. **SELECTED PUBLICATIONS** Auth, The Business of Common Life--Novels and Classical Economics Between Revolution and Reform, Jour Eng and Ger Philol, Vol 0095, 96; Women Travel Writers and the Language of Aesthetics, 1716-1818, Eighteenth-Century Stud, Vol 0030, 97; 18th-Century Sensibility and the Novel, the Senses in Social-Context, Studies in the Novel, Vol 0026, 94. **CONTACT ADDRESS** Dept of English, Western Illinois Univ, 1 University Cir, Macomb, IL, 61455-1390.

CONN, EARL LEWIS
PERSONAL Born 08/12/1927, Marion, IN, m, 1953, 6 children **DISCIPLINE** JOURNALISM **EDUCATION** Univ Ky, BA, 50; Ball State Univ, MS, 57; Ind Univ, Bloomington, DEd, 70. **CAREER** Staff writer, United Press, 50-51; wire ed, Chronicle-Tribune, Marion, Ind, 52-54; teacher jour & publ adv, Somerset High Sch, Ind, 54-57 & Richmond High Sch, 57-58; instr jour, Ball State Univ, 58-62; ed, Quaker Life, Friends United Meeting, 62-64; asst dir, Pub Info Serv, 64-65, from asst prof to assoc prof, 65-75, Prof Jour, 75-98, Dept Chair, 84-96, Dean, Col Of Commun, Infor, & Media, 96-98, Dean Emeritus, Ball State Univ, 98-. **HONORS AND AWARDS** Ind Jour Hall of Fame, 97; Ball State Jour Hall ot Fame, 97. **MEMBERSHIPS** Asn Educ in Jour; Oral Hist Asn; Soc Prof Journalists. **RESEARCH** Journalism history; media ethics; mass communications. **SELECTED PUBLICATIONS** Auth, Journalism 101 and the O.J. Trial, Ed & Publ, 11/11/95, and 5 Ind newspa-

pers; Commotion over Court Ordered Ad, Ed & Publ, 4/27/96; Julie Andrews: Doing What She Loves, The Saturday Evening Post, May/June 96; Posthumous Victory, Ed & Publ, 2/28/97; author of numerous other articles. **CONTACT ADDRESS** Dept of Jour, Ball State Univ, 2000 W University, Muncie, IN, 47306-0485. **EMAIL** 00elconn@bsu.edu

CONNOLLY, JULIAN WELCH
PERSONAL Born 10/19/1949, Newburyport, MA, m, 1991 **DISCIPLINE** LANGUAGES & LITERATURE **EDUCATION** Harvard Col, AB, 72; Harvard Univ, AM, 74, PhD(Slavic lang & lit), 77. **CAREER** Asst Prof Slavic Lang & Lit, Univ Va, 77- **MEMBERSHIPS** Am Asn Advan Slavic Studies; Am Asn Teachers Slavic & E Europ Lang; MLA. **RESEARCH** Symbolism; early Soviet prose; Nabokov. **SELECTED PUBLICATIONS** Auth, The role of duality in Sologub's Tvorimaja Legenda, Die Welt der Slaven, 74-75; A modernist's palette: Color in the prose fiction of Eugenij Zamjatin, Russ Lang J, 79; Bunin's Petlistye Ushi: The Deformation of a Byronic Rebel, Can-Am Slavic Studies, 80; Desire and renunciation: Buddhist elements in the prose of Ivan Bunin, Can Slavonic Papers, 81; The function of literary allusion in Nabokov's Despair, Slavic and East Europ J, 82; Ivan Bunin, G K Hall & Co, 82; Nabovov's Earl, Fiction: Patterns of Self and Other, Cambridge: Cambridge Univ Press, 92; Nabovov's "Invitation to a Beheading": A Critical Companion, Evanston: Northwestern Univ Press, 97. **CONTACT ADDRESS** Dept Slavic Lang & Lit, Univ Va, 109 Cabell Hall, Charlottesville, VA, 22903-3125. **EMAIL** jwc4w@virginia.edu

CONOLLY, LEONARD W.
PERSONAL Born 09/13/1941, Walsall, England **DISCIPLINE** ENGLISH/DRAMA **EDUCATION** Univ Wales, BA, 63, PhD, 70; McMaster Univ, MA, 64. **CAREER** Instr, Univ Sask, 65-67; asst prof, 70-74, assoc prof, 74-79, prof, Univ Alta, 79-81; prof drama & dept ch, 81-86, acting dean arts, 86-87, vice pres acad, 88-92, acting vice pres acad, Univ Guelph, 92-93; pres & vice chancellor, 94-97, PROF ENGLISH & FELLOW, CATHARINE PARR TRAILL COLLEGE, TRENT UNIV, 97-. **MEMBERSHIPS** Asn Can Theatre Res (pres, 77-79); Am Soc Theatre Res. **SELECTED PUBLICATIONS** Auth, The Censorship of English Drama 1737-1824, 76; coauth, English Canadian Theatre, 87; ed, Theatrical Touring and Founding in North America, 82; ed, Canadian Drama and the Critics, 87; co-ed, English Drama and Theatre 1800-1900, 78; co-ed, Nineteenth Century Theatre Research, 72-80; co-ed, Essays in Theatre, 82-89; co-ed, The Oxford Companion to Canadian Theatre, 89; co-ed, Bernard Shaw on Stage, 91; co-ed, The Encyclopedia of Post-Colonial Literatures in English, 94; gen ed, Selected Correspondence of Bernard Shaw; bd dir, World Encyclopedia of Contemporary Theatre (pres, 89-92). **CONTACT ADDRESS** Catharine Parr Traill Col, Trent Univ, Peterborough, ON. **EMAIL** lconolly@trentu.ca

CONRAD, BRYCE D.
DISCIPLINE AMERICAN LITERATURE **EDUCATION** Univ IA, PhD, 88. **CAREER** Assoc prof, TX Tech Univ; ed, William Carlos Williams Rev. **RESEARCH** Am modernism. **SELECTED PUBLICATIONS** Auth, Refiguring America: A Study of William Carlos Williams' In the American Grain. **CONTACT ADDRESS** Texas Tech Univ, Lubbock, TX, 79409-5015. **EMAIL** bryce@ttu.edu

CONRAD, CHARLES R.
DISCIPLINE ORGANIZATIONAL COMMUNICATION, RHETORICAL THEORY **EDUCATION** Univ Kansas, PhD. **CAREER** Prof, Texas A&M Univ. **HONORS AND AWARDS** Southern Commun Journal's Outstanding Article Awd; Distinguished Tchg Awd, Asn Former Stud at Texas A&M Univ. **SELECTED PUBLICATIONS** Auth, Strategic Organizational Communication; ed, The Ethical Nexus; assoc ed, Quart J Speech. **CONTACT ADDRESS** Dept of Speech Communication, Texas A&M Univ, College Station, TX, 77843-4234. **EMAIL** csnidow@tamu.edu

CONRAD, KATHRYN A.
PERSONAL Born 07/03/1968, Grand Rapids, MI **DISCIPLINE** ENGLISH **EDUCATION** Univ Mich, BA, 90; Univ Pa, MA, 93, PhD, 96. **CAREER** Post-doctoral lectr, 96-97, Univ Pa; asst prof, 97-, Univ Ks. **HONORS AND AWARDS** NEH Younger Scholars Award, 89; Jacob Javits Fel, 90; Nat Mellon Fel, 90-95; Dermot McGlinchey Award for pioneering work in Irish stud, Irish Amer Cultural Inst, 95., BA with honors & high distinction; Phi Beta Kappa. **MEMBERSHIPS** Modern Lang Assoc; Amer Conf for Irish Stud. **RESEARCH** Twentieth century Irish lit & culture; nationalism, sexuality, & gender. **SELECTED PUBLICATIONS** Coauth, Joyce and the Irish Body Politic: Sexuality and Colonization in Finnegans Wake, James Joyce Quart, 94; auth, Occupied Country: The Negotiation of Lesbianism in Irish Feminist Writing, Eire-Ireland, 96; coauth, Passing/Out: The Politics of Disclosure in Queer-Positive Pedagogy, Modern Lang Stud, 99; auth, Women Troubles, Queer Troubles: Gender, Sexuality, and the Politics of Selfhood in the Construction of the Northern Irish State, Reclaiming Gender: Transgressive Identities in Modern Ireland, St Martin's Press, 99. **CONTACT ADDRESS** Dept of English, Univ of Ks, 3116 Wescoe Hall, Lawrence, KS, 66044-2115. **EMAIL** kconrad@ukan.edu

COOGAN, DAVID
DISCIPLINE ENGLISH LITERATURE **EDUCATION** State Univ NY, PhD, 95. **CAREER** Instr. **SELECTED PUBLICATIONS** Auth, pubs in Computers and Composition. **CONTACT ADDRESS** Dept of Humanities, Illinois Inst of Tech, 3301 S Dearborn, Chicago, IL, 60616. **EMAIL** coogan@charlie.cns.iit.edu

COOK, ELEANOR
PERSONAL Toronto, ON, Canada **DISCIPLINE** ENGLISH **EDUCATION** Univ Toronto, BA, 54, PhD, 67. **CAREER** Lectr, Univ BC, 58-59; asst prof to assoc prof, 67-84, PROF VICTORIA COL, UNIV TORONTO 85-. **HONORS AND AWARDS** Jr fel, Can Asn Women, 54; A.S.P. Woodhouse Thesis Prize, 68; Connaught fel, 94; Guggenheim fel, 94; Killiam fel, 95. **MEMBERSHIPS** Royal Soc Can; Massey Col. **SELECTED PUBLICATIONS** Auth, Browning's Lyrics: An Exploration, 74; auth, Centre and Labyrinth: Essays in Honour of Northrop Frye, 83; auth, Poetry, Word-Play and Word-War in Wallace Stevens, 88. **CONTACT ADDRESS** Dept of English, Victoria Col, Univ Toronto, Toronto, ON, M5S 1K9.

COOK, JAMES WYATT
PERSONAL Born 09/08/1932, Hickman, KY, m, 1954, 3 children **DISCIPLINE** ENGLISH **EDUCATION** Wayne State Univ, BA, 54, PhD, 64; Univ Mich, MA, 55. **CAREER** From instr to assoc prof, 62-74, chmn dept, 71-77, Langbo Trustees' Prof English, Albion Col, 75-, Great Lakes Cols Asn grant, 64-66; Shell grant, 66; consult, Educ Methods Inc, 65-67 & Univ Mich Ctr Prog Instr Bus, 66-68; Carnegie Found & Great Lakes Cols grant, 67; pres, Validated Instr Assoc, 73-81; grad dean, Walden Univ, 75-77; Newberry fel, 77, 86, 89; Nat Endowment for Hum grant, 81; res assoc, Pontifical Inst Medieval Studies, Univ Toronto, 81-82. **MEMBERSHIPS** MLA; Mediaeval Soc Am; ASECS, Ren. Soc Am. **RESEARCH** Petrarch; Medieval language and literature; Chaucer. **SELECTED PUBLICATIONS** Auth, Augustinian neurosis and therapy of orthodoxy, Universitas, Wayne State Univ, spring 64; Poetry: Method and Meaning, Educ Methods, 68; Chaucer's Canterbury Art: Echoes and Reflections, Writer's Workshop, Calcutta, 76; Helping the hard to serve, Can Jour of Spec Educ, 76; That she was out of all charitee: Point, counterpoint in Chaucer's Wife of Bath's Tale, Chaucer Rev, 78; Toward making a new English verse canzoniere, Yale Ital Studies, 80; Petrarch's mirrors of love and hell, Ital Cult, 82; transl and ed, The Autobiography of Lorenzo Di Medici, MRTS, 94; Petrarch's Songbook, MRTS, 95; Florentine Drama for Convent and Festival, Univ Chicago, 96. **CONTACT ADDRESS** Dept of English, Albion Col, 611 E Porter St, Albion, MI, 49224-1831. **EMAIL** JCOOK@ALBION.EDU

COOK, SMALLEY MIKE
PERSONAL Born 03/10/1939, Chicago, IL **DISCIPLINE** THEATER **EDUCATION** Univ of Massachusetts, MA 1972; Union Grad Sch, PhD 1977. **CAREER** IMAGE ALLIANCE, WRITER/PRODUCER 1974-; UNIV OF IOWA, PROFESSOR OF DRAMS 1987-. **MEMBERSHIPS** Consultant Chicago Urban League 1973-; consultant Chicago Dept of Cultural Affairs 1983-; founder Dramatic Arts Repertory Ensemble for Youth 1986-. **SELECTED PUBLICATIONS** Writer-producer "Drums of the Night Gods," staged, Los Angeles Cultural Ctr 1981; Goodman Theatre Chicago 1983, Chicago Cultural Ctr 1983; writer-producer "The Fire and the Storm" Lindblom Park Dist Chicago 1986. **CONTACT ADDRESS** Drama, Univ of Iowa, 303 English-Philosophy Bldg, Iowa City, IA, 52242.

COOK, STEPHAN H.
DISCIPLINE ENGLISH **EDUCATION** Marquette Univ, PhD, 78. **CAREER** Instr, Marquette Univ, 73-75; lectr, Univ Calif, 78-80; prof, 96-. **HONORS AND AWARDS** Tchr yr, 86. **RESEARCH** Writing; art & lit; Eng romantic writers. **SELECTED PUBLICATIONS** Auth, Screenplaying: Seeing and Saying in Hart Crane, Santa Barbara Rev, 96; No Place for Paragraphs: The Correspondence Between Hart Crane and Waldo Frank, Whitston Press, 95; Purchasers of Heaven: Painting, Photography and Hart Crane, Iris Stud, 95; Peter Pan in Hell, Fac Dialogue, 87; Pulling Back the Water Ahead, Santa Barbara Rev, 93; Playing at the Father's Art, Santa Barbara Rev, 93; rev, Noah Ben Shea, The Word, Santa Barbara News Press, 95; Edward Brunner, Splendid Failure: Hart Crane & The Making of The Bridge, Christianity and Lit, 87; David Jasper, Coleridge as Poet and Religious Thinker, Christianity and Lit, 86. **CONTACT ADDRESS** Dept of Eng, Westmont Col, 955 La Paz Rd, Santa Barbara, CA, 93108-1099.

COOKE, THOMAS D.
DISCIPLINE MEDIEVAL LITERATURE AND FILM **EDUCATION** Univ Pittsburgh, PhD, 70. **CAREER** Prof. **RESEARCH** Comedy and tragedy with an emphasis on American movies. **SELECTED PUBLICATIONS** Pub on, Old French fabliaux, Chaucer and 14th century lit. **CONTACT ADDRESS** Dept of English, Univ of Missouri-Columbia, 309 University Hall, Columbia, MO, 65211.

COOKS, LEDA M.
PERSONAL Born 08/15/1965, Lakeland, FL **DISCIPLINE** COMMUNICATION **EDUCATION** Ohio Univ, PhD, 93. **CAREER** Asst prof, 93-, Univ Ma. **HONORS AND AWARDS** Fulbright Res/Lect fel, Panama, 97. **MEMBERSHIPS** Nat Comm Asn; Int Asn for Conflict Management; Latin Am Stud Asn; Eastern Comm Asn; Oral Hist Asn. **RESEARCH** Intercultural communication; int training and development; commun ed. **SELECTED PUBLICATIONS** Coauth, A Phenomenological Inquiry into the Relationship Between Perceived Coolness and Interpersonal Competence, Interpretive Approaches to Interpersonal Communication, SUNY Press, 94;coauth, The Dilema of Ethics in the Field of Mediation, Mediation Quart, 12, 94; coauth, Teaching Dispute Mediation from a Communication Perspective: Exploring the Practice and the Paradoxes, Focus on Legal Stud, 9 (2), Am Bar Asn, 94; coauth, Gender and Power, Gender, Power & Comm in Human Relationships, Lawrence Erlbaum Assocs, 95; auth, Putting Mediation in Context, Negotiation J, 11, 95; coauth, Northern Exposure's Sense of Place: Constructing and Marginalizing the Matriarchal Community, Women's Stud in Communication, 18 (2), 95; coauth, Giving Voice to Sexual Harassment: Dialogues in the Aftermath of the Hill-Thomas Hearings, The Lynching of Language, Univ IL Press, 96; auth, Warriors, Wampum, Gaming and Glitter: Foxwoods Casino and the Representation of Post Modern Native Identity, Readings in Cultural Contexts, Mayfield Pub, 98. **CONTACT ADDRESS** Dept of Communications, Univ of Massachusetts, 315 Machmer Hall, Amherst, MA, 01003. **EMAIL** Leda@comm.umass.edu

COOLEY, DENNIS O.
PERSONAL Born 08/27/1944, Estevan, SK, Canada **DISCIPLINE** LITERATURE **EDUCATION** Univ Sask, BEd, 66, BA, 67, MA, 68; Univ Rochester, PhD, 71. **CAREER** PROF, ST JOHN'S COL, UNIV MANITOBA, 73-. **SELECTED PUBLICATIONS** Auth, Leaving, 80; auth, Fielding, 83; auth, Bloody Jack, 84; auth, Soul Searching, 87; auth, The Vernacular Muse, 87; auth, Dedications, 88; auth, Goldfinger, 95; ed, Draft, 80; ed, RePlacing, 91; ed, Eli Mandel and His Works, 91; ed, Inscriptions: A Prairie Poetry Anthology, 92. **CONTACT ADDRESS** St. John's Col, Univ of Manitoba, Winnipeg, MB, R3T 2M5.

COOLEY, PETER JOHN
PERSONAL Born 11/19/1940, Detroit, MI, m, 1965, 3 children **DISCIPLINE** POETRY **EDUCATION** Shimer Col, BA, 62; Univ Chicago, MA, 64; Univ Iowa, PhD, 70. **CAREER** Assoc prof creative writing, Univ Wis, Green Bay, 70-75; prof creative writing, Tulane Univ, 75-, Poetry ed, NAm Rev, 70-. **MEMBERSHIPS** Poetry Soc Am; MLA; Assoc Writing Prog. **RESEARCH** Poetry writing. **SELECTED PUBLICATIONS** Auth, The Company of Strangers (poems), Univ Mo, 75; The Room Where Summer Ends (poems), Carnegie-Mellon Univ, 79; The Van Gogh Notebooks (poems); Sacred Conversations (poems). **CONTACT ADDRESS** Dept of English, Tulane Univ, 6823 St Charles Ave, New Orleans, LA, 70118-5698. **EMAIL** pjcooley@msn.com

COOLEY, THOMAS WINFIELD
PERSONAL Born 06/24/1942, Gaffney, SC, m, 1989, 1 child **DISCIPLINE** AMERICAN LITERATURE, AMERICAN STUDIES **EDUCATION** Duke Univ, BA, 64; Ind Univ, Bloomington, MA, 68, PhD(English), 70. **CAREER** Asst prof, 70-79, ASSOC PROF ENGLISH, OHIO STATE UNIV, 80-**HONORS AND AWARDS** NEH Research grants; U.S. State Dept "Participant", Australia, New Zealand, and Taiwan; Exec Comnr of Am Lit Section of MLA. **MEMBERSHIPS** MLA. **RESEARCH** American literature; autobiography; psychology of narrative; composition. **SELECTED PUBLICATIONS** Auth, Lincoln Steffens: American Innocent Abroad, Am Lit, 1/72; Educated Lives: The Rise of Modern Autobiography in America, Ohio State Univ Press, 76; The Norton Guide to Writing, W.W. Norton, 92; The Norton Sampler, W.W. Norton, 79, 5th ed, 97; The Norton Critical Edition of Adventures of Huckleberry Finn, W.W. Norton, 3rd ed, 98; Selected Letters of Sophia Hawthorne, Ohio State Univ Press (forthcoming); The Ivory Leg in the Ebony Cabinet: Madness, Race and Gender in the American Consciousness (submitted); author of articles and reviews in American literature. **CONTACT ADDRESS** Dept of English, Ohio State Univ, 164 W 17th Ave, Columbus, OH, 43210-1326. **EMAIL** Cooley.1@osu.edu

COOLIDGE, ARCHIBALD CARY, JR.
PERSONAL Born 06/09/1928, Oxford, England, m, 1951, 7 children **DISCIPLINE** ENGLISH **EDUCATION** Harvard Univ, BA, 51; Brown Univ, MA, 54, PhD, 56. **CAREER** Teacher, NY, 46-47; PROF, ENGLISH, UNIV OF IOWA, 74-. **HONORS AND AWARDS** Phi Beta Kappa. **RESEARCH** English novel; Greek drama; story form; English history. **SELECTED PUBLICATIONS** Auth, Beyond the Fatal Flaw: A Study of the Neglected Forms of Greek Drama, Moecepas Press, 80; auth, English Heroes and American Problems, 95; auth, Charles Dickens as Serial Novelist, Iowa State Univ Press, 67; auth, A Theory of Story, Moecepas Press, 89. **CONTACT ADDRESS** Dept of English, Univ of Iowa, Iowa City, IA, 52242.

COOLIDGE, JOHN STANHOPE
PERSONAL Born 07/26/1926, Laramie, WY, m, 1964, 2 children **DISCIPLINE** ENGLISH AND COMPARATIVE LITERATURE **EDUCATION** Harvard Univ, BA, 49, MA, 51, PhD(English), 57. **CAREER** Instr English, Swarthmore Col, 56-60; asst prof, 60-67, assoc prof, 67-80, PROF ENGLISH, UNIV CALIF, BERKELEY, 80-, Huntington Libr grant-in-aid, 64-65. **MEMBERSHIPS** MLA; Renaissance Soc Am; NCTE. **RESEARCH** Puritanism and the Bible; influence of classical on later literature. **SELECTED PUBLICATIONS** Auth, From Father to Son--Kinship, Conflict, and Continuity in Genesis, Cath Biblical Quart, Vol 0055, 93. **CONTACT ADDRESS** Dept of English, Univ of Calif, Berkeley, CA, 94720.

COOPER, JOHN REX
PERSONAL Born 05/14/1932, Edmonton, AB, Canada, m, 1965, 2 children **DISCIPLINE** ENGLISH LITERATURE **EDUCATION** State Univ NY, Albany, AB, 54; Yale Univ, MA, 57, PhD, 62. **CAREER** Instr English & humanities, 61-63, asst prof, 63-67, Univ Chicago; asst prof, 70-73, prof lit & hum, Portland State Univ, 73-, head, dept English, 81-88. **HONORS AND AWARDS** Kappa Phi Kappa **MEMBERSHIPS** AAUP **RESEARCH** Seventeenth century literature; Shakespeare; aesthetics. **SELECTED PUBLICATIONS** Auth, The Art of the Compleat Angler, Duke Univ, 68; art, Shylock's humanity, Shakespeare Quart, 69; auth, Intonation and Iambic Pentameter, PLL, papers on language & literature, 97. **CONTACT ADDRESS** Dept of English, Portland State Univ, PO Box 751, Portland, OR, 97207-0751.

COOPER, MARILYN MARIE
PERSONAL Born 07/19/1945, Detroit, MI **DISCIPLINE** LITERARY AND COMPOSITION THEORY **EDUCATION** Pa State Univ, BA, 67; Univ Mich, MA, 68; Univ Minn, PhD(English), 80. **CAREER** ASST PROF ENGLISH, UNIV SOUTHERN CALIF, 79-. **MEMBERSHIPS** MLA; Ling Soc Am; NCTE. **RESEARCH** Conversational behavior in contemporary drama; structure of expository texts; contemporary theory. **SELECTED PUBLICATIONS** Auth, Moments of Argument--Agonistic Inquiry and Confrontational Cooperation, Col Composition and Commun, Vol 0048, 97. **CONTACT ADDRESS** Dept of English, Univ of Southern Calif, Los Angeles, CA, 90007.

COOPER, VINCENT O'MAHONY
PERSONAL Born 12/03/1947, Basseterre, St. Kitts, m, 1975, 2 children **DISCIPLINE** LINGUISTICS, ENGLISH **EDUCATION** Univ Bordeaux, dipl, 67; Col VI, BA, 72; Princeton Univ, MA, 74, PhD, 79. **CAREER** Adj instr socioling, Hunter Col, City Univ New York, 76; Instr English, Col of the VI, 77-, from Asst Prof to Prof English/Ling, Univ VI, 79-. **HONORS AND AWARDS** ACLS Res Grant, 75; Fulbright Schol to Belize, 86; Martin Luther King-Rosa Parks, Cesar Chavez State Award for Outstanding Schol, Mich State Univ, 90; Cornel Univ Int Schol Award, 93; Cornell Univ Res Workshop Grant, Sept 18-20, 97. **RESEARCH** Sociolinguistics; Caribbean Creole languages; Caribbean literatures. **SELECTED PUBLICATIONS** Coauth, Three Islands (poetry), Univ VI, 87; Tremors (poetry), UVI, 89; auth, Mahogani and other poems, In: Kunapipi, Univ Haarhus Press, 93; The Poetry of Althea Romeo-Mark, In: Routledge Encyclopedia of Post Colonial Literatures, 94; Language and Gender in the Kalinago Amerindian Community of St. Croix, In: The Indigenous People of the Carribean, Univ Fl Press, 97; An Anthology of PanCarribean Poetry: With Selections in Translation from French, Spanish, and Dutch and Their Related Vernaculars, Harbrace Col Publ, 97 (in progress). **CONTACT ADDRESS** Dept of English, Univ of the Virgin Islands, 2 John Brewers Bay, St. Thomas, VI, 00802-9990. **EMAIL** vcooper@uvi.edu

COOPER, VIRGINIA W.
DISCIPLINE COMMUNICATIONS **EDUCATION** Univ Wash; PhD, 81. **CAREER** Dominion Univ. **MEMBERSHIPS** Speech Comm Asn; Int Comm Asn; World Comm Asn **SELECTED PUBLICATIONS** Auth, Participant and Observer Attribution of Affect in Interpersonal Communication: An Examination of Noncontent Verbal Behavior." Jour Nonverbal Behavior, 87; The Tactile Communication System: State of the Art and Research Perspectives, in Progress in Communication Sciences, Ablex Publ Corp, 88; The Measurement of Conflict Interaction Intensity: Observer and Participant Perceived Dimensions, Human Relations, 94; The Disguise of Self-Disclosure: The Relationship Ruse of a Soviet Spy, Jour Applied Com Res, 96. **CONTACT ADDRESS** Old Dominion Univ, 4100 Powhatan Ave, Norfolk, VA, 23508.

COPE, JACKSON IRVING
PERSONAL Born 09/01/1925, Muncie, IN **DISCIPLINE** ENGLISH **EDUCATION** Univ Ill, BA; Johns Hopkins Univ, PhD(English), 52. **CAREER** Instr English, Ohio State Univ, 52-54; asst prof, Washington Univ, 54-58; from assoc prof to prof, Rice Univ, 58-61; from assoc prof to prof, Johns Hopkins Univ, 62-72; LEO'S BING PROF ENGLISH, UNIV SOUTHERN CALIF, 72-, Guggenheim fel, 58-59; Am Coun Learned Soc fel, 63-64. **MEMBERSHIPS** MLA. **RESEARCH** Renaissance drama; contemporary fiction. **SELECTED PUBLICATIONS** Auth, Goldoni,Carlo--Theater-Italian, Mln-Mod Lang Notes, Vol 0108, 93. **CONTACT ADDRESS** Dept of English, Univ of Southern Calif, Los Angeles, CA, 90007.

COPE, KEVIN
DISCIPLINE RESTORATION & 18TH C. SATIRE, BIBLIOGRAPHY, ENLIGHTENMENT PHILOSOPHICA **EDUCATION** Harvard, PhD, 80. **CAREER** Prof, La State Univ. **RESEARCH** Early modern era; John Locke; enlightenment philosophical texts. **SELECTED PUBLICATIONS** Auth, A Roman Commonwealth of Knowledge: Fragments of Belief and the Disbelieving Power of Didactic, Stud in 18th-Century Cult, 90; Conversations Containing Truth: Dialogues with Berkeley's Lying God, Man and Nature/L'Homme et la Nature, 90; Gothic Novel as Social Contract: Locke, Shaftesbury, and Walpole and the Casual Annexation of the Supernatural, The Age of Johnson, 90; Criteria of Certainty: Truth and Judgement in the English Enlightenment, 90; ed, Enlightening Allegory: Theory, Practice, and Contexts of Allegory in the Late Seventeenth and Eighteenth Centuries, 91; Compendious Conversations: The Method of Dialogue in the Early Enlightenment, 92. **CONTACT ADDRESS** Dept of Eng, Louisiana State Univ, 210J Allen Hall, Baton Rouge, LA, 70803. **EMAIL** encope @lsuvm.sncc.lsu.edu

COPEK, PETER JOSEPH
PERSONAL Born 05/28/1945, Chicago, IL **DISCIPLINE** ENGLISH **EDUCATION** Loyola Univ, Chicago, BS, 67; Northwestern Univ, Chicago, MA, 69, PhD, 73. **CAREER** Asst prof, 72-77, assoc prof English, Ore State Univ, 77-; Dir, Ctr for the Humanities, 84-, fel, Rockefeller found, 75-76. **MEMBERSHIPS** MLA; Am Film Inst; Consortium for Humanities Ctrs and Inst. **RESEARCH** The English novel; literature and society; film. **CONTACT ADDRESS** Dept of English, Oregon State Univ, 238 Moreland Hall, Corvallis, OR, 97331-5302. **EMAIL** peter.copek@orst.edu

COPPEDGE, WALTER RALEIGH
PERSONAL Born 01/18/1930, Morelia, Mexico, m, 1958, 1 child **DISCIPLINE** ENGLISH **EDUCATION** Univ Miss, BA, 52; Oxford Univ, BLitt, 58; Memphis State Univ, MA, 63; Ind Univ, PhD(English), 67. **CAREER** Asst prof English, Ala Col, 57-60; headmaster, Lausanne Sch Girls, Tenn, 60-66; pres, Col Charleston, 66-68; asst vpres acad affairs, 68-71, PROF ENGLISH, VA COMMONWEALTH UNIV, 71-. **MEMBERSHIPS** Asn Am Rhodes Scholars; MLA. **SELECTED PUBLICATIONS** Auth, Mazursky Tempest, Something Rich, Something Strange, Lit-Film Quart, Vol 0021, 93. **CONTACT ADDRESS** 2014 Floyd Ave, Richmond, VA, 23220.

CORBETT, JANICE
DISCIPLINE ENGLISH LANGUAGE AND LITERATURE **EDUCATION** B.A. Eastern College, M.S.(Comm), PhD (Eng), Temple Univ **CAREER** Fac, Delaware Valley Col, 96-. **HONORS AND AWARDS** Fellow, Rome Sem Art and Ideology; NEH fellow, UCLA., Pub rel ed, staff writer, and dir. **RESEARCH** Eng wrting and compos. **SELECTED PUBLICATIONS** Auth, academic publ(s) in Perf Arts Jour, Tech Comms Jour, and JAISA. **CONTACT ADDRESS** Delaware Valley Col, 700 E Butler Ave, Doylestown, PA, 18901-2697. **EMAIL** CorbettJ@devalcol.edu

CORDELL, ROSEANNE M.
PERSONAL Born 07/06/1952, Fort Breckenridge, KY, m, 1973, 2 children **DISCIPLINE** LIBRARY SCIENCE- REFERENCE AND INSTRUCTION SERVICES **EDUCATION** IN Univ, South Bend, BS (Elementary Ed), 74, MS (Elementary Ed), 78; IN Univ, MLS (Library Science), 91. **CAREER** HEAD OF LIBRARY INSTRUCTION, IN UNIV, SOUTH BEND, 93-, HEAD OF REFERENCE SERVICES, 97-. **HONORS AND AWARDS** Teaching Excellence Recognition Award, IN Univ, 97. **MEMBERSHIPS** Am Library Asn; Asn of College & Res Librarians; IN Library Federation. **RESEARCH** Library reference services; library instruction; intellectual freedom. **SELECTED PUBLICATIONS** Auth, review of Nicholas Givotovsky's An Introduction to the Issues and Applications of Interactive Multimedia for Information Specialists, Special Libraries Asn, 94, in Academic Library Book Review, 10 (2), Feb 95; Current Issues in Intellectual Freedom, series of five articles for AIME News, Jan - May 95, reprinted in IN Media J 18 (2), winter 96; Enhancing Library Instruction for At-Risk Students with Multimedia Presentations, IN Libraries 14 (2), 95; Enhancing Library Instruction with Multimedia Presentations, in New Ways of Learning the Library & Beyond: Papers and Session Materials Presented at the Twenty-Third National LOEX Library Instruction Conference, Pierian Press, 96, reprinted from IN Libraries 14 (2), 95; Intellectual Freedom Issues, quart column, IN Media J, 95-98; Intellectual Freedom Issues, monthly column, AIME News, 95-98; with Nancy A. Wootton, Institutional Policy Issues for Providing Public Internet Access, RSR Reference Services rev 24 (1), 96; with Nancy Wootton Colborn, Moving from Subjective to Objective Assessments of Your Instruction Program, RSR Reference Services Rev 26 (3-4), fall/winter 98; Determination of Whether Indiana School Library Personnel Use the Results of an Intellectual Freedom Survey to Self-Censor, submitted for pub. **CONTACT ADDRESS** Schurz Library, Indiana Univ, South Bend, PO Box 7111, South Bend, IN, 46634. **EMAIL** rcordell@iusb.edu

CORE, GEORGE
PERSONAL Born 01/12/1939, Kansas City, MO, m, 1960, 4 children **DISCIPLINE** BRITISH AND AMERICAN LITERATURE **EDUCATION** Vanderbilt Univ, BA, 59, MA, 60; Univ NC, Chapel Hill, PhD(English), 71. **CAREER** Teaching asst, Univ NC, Chapel Hill, 65-66; instr English, Davidson Col, 66-68; asst prof English & sr ed, Univ Press, Univ Ga, 68-73; ED, SEWANEE REV & ASSOC PROF ENGLISH, UNIV OF THE SOUTH, 73-, Nat Endowment for Humanities Younger Humanist fel, 72-73, consult, 74- **MEMBERSHIPS** MLA; Soc Study South Lit (secy-treas, 73-76); SAtlantic Mod Lang Asn. **RESEARCH** Modern British and American fiction, especially Henry James; contemporary literary criticism; southern literary renaissance. **SELECTED PUBLICATIONS** Auth, Americans in London--Recent Theater Productions, Sewanee Rev, Vol 0102, 94; Lenten Anniversaries, Sewanee Rev, Vol 0102, 94; A Whiteness of the Bone, Sewanee Rev, Vol 0102, 94; As Far as Light Remains, Sewanee Rev, Vol 0102, 94; Words to Create a World, Sewanee Rev, Vol 0102, 94; Concrete Music, Sewanee Rev, Vol 0102, 94; Excursions in the Real World, Sewanee Rev, Vol 0103, 95; The Buried Houses, Sewanee Rev, Vol 0102, 94; Perrin,Noel Sampler, Sewanee Rev, Vol 0103, 95; Beckett Waiting For Godot, Sewanee Rev, Vol 0105, 97; The King My Fathers Wreck, Sewanee Rev, Vol 0103, 95; Flights in the Heavenlies, Sewanee Rev, Vol 0104, 96; Follow Me Home, Sewanee Rev, Vol 0104, 96; A Visit to Strangers, Sewanee Rev, Vol 0104, 96; With My Trousers Rolled, Sewanee Rev, Vol 0103, 95; Staying Put Making a Home in a Restless World, Sewanee Rev, Vol 0103, 95; The Afterlife and Other Stories, Sewanee Rev, Vol 0104, 96; American Quarterlies Today, Sewanee Rev, Vol 0103, 95; The Happiness of Getting it Down Right, Sewanee Rev, Vol 0104, 96; Trespassing, Sewanee Rev, Vol 0103, 95; Curriculum Vitae, Sewanee Rev, Vol 0103, 95; Dancing After Hours, Sewanee Rev, Vol 0104, 96; American-Catholic Arts And Fictions, Culture, Ideology, Aesthetics, Sewanee Rev, Vol 0101, 93; The New Princeton Handbook of Poetic Terms, Sewanee Rev, Vol 0102, 94; Exiles and Fugitives--The Letters of Maritain,Jacques and Maritain,Raissa, Tate,Allen and Gordon,Caroline, Sewanee Rev, Vol 0101, 93; Granville,Barker Waste, Sewanee Rev, Vol 0105, 97; Churchett Tom and Clem, Sewanee Rev, Vol 0105, 97; Hare Amys View, Sewanee Rev, Vol 0105, 97; Fatheralong, Sewanee Rev, Vol 0103, 95; The Class of 1848--From West-Point to Appomattox--Jackson,Stonewall, Mcclellan,George, and Their Brothers, Sewanee Rev, Vol 0103, 95; Complete Collected Essays, Sewanee Rev, Vol 0102, 94; Chekhov/Stoppard the Seagull, Sewanee Rev, Vol 0105, 97; Shakespeare Cymbeline, Sewanee Rev, Vol 0105, 97; The Cambridge Guide to Literature in English, Sewanee Rev, Vol 0102, 94; Adamson Grace Note, Sewanee Rev, Vol 0105, 97; Shakespeare Othello, Sewanee Rev, Vol 0105, 97; Whelan the Herbal Bed, Sewanee Rev, Vol 0105, 97; Shakespeare the Winters Tale, Sewanee Rev, Vol 0105, 97; Shakespeare The Life of Henry the Fifth, Sewanee Rev, Vol 0105, 97; Kyd the Spanish Tragedy, Sewanee Rev, Vol 0105, 97; Legacies, Sewanee Rev, Vol 0104, 96; Selected Stories, Sewanee Rev, Vol 0104, 96; Msumi Umabatha, the Zulu Macbeth, Sewanee Rev, Vol 0105, 97; Shakespeare in London--Dramatic Productions and Performances During July and August 1993, Sewanee Rev, Vol 0101, 93; A Writers Companion, Sewanee Rev, Vol 0103, 95; A Readers Guide to the 20th-Century Novel, Sewanee Rev, Vol 0103, 95; The New Companion to Literature in French, Sewanee Rev, Vol 0103, 95; Gray Life Support, Sewanee Rev, Vol 0105, 97. **CONTACT ADDRESS** Dept of English, Univ of the South, Sewanee, TN, 37375.

CORGAN, VERNA C.
DISCIPLINE COMMUNICATION ARTS **EDUCATION** Univ MN, BA, 84, MA, 86, PhD, 92. **CAREER** Assoc prof, Hamline Univ. **RESEARCH** Legal rhetoric. **SELECTED PUBLICATIONS** Publ in commun ethics and legal commun. **CONTACT ADDRESS** Hamline Univ, 1662 Drew Hall, St Paul, MN. **EMAIL** vcorgan@piper.hamline.edus

CORMAN, BRIAN
PERSONAL Born 02/23/1945, Chicago, IL, m, 1967, 1 child **DISCIPLINE** ENGLISH **EDUCATION** Univ Chicago, AB, 66, AM, 67, PhD(English), 71. **CAREER** Lectr, 70-71, asst prof, 71-76, ASSOC PROF ENGLISH, UNIV TORONTO, 76-, Can Coun leave fel, 75-76; Soc Sci & Humanities Res Counc Can fel, 81-82. **MEMBERSHIPS** Asn Can Univ Teachers English; MLA; Am Soc 18th Century Studies; Can Soc 18th Century Studies; Johnson Soc Cent Region. **RESEARCH** English drama 1660-1800; literary criticism; Jacobean drama. **SELECTED PUBLICATIONS** Auth, Vanbrugh,John--A Reference Guide, Scriblerian and the Kit-Cats, Vol 0028, 95; What is the Canon of English Drama, 1660-1737, Eighteenth-Century Stud, Vol 0026, 93; Without God or Reason--The Plays of Shadwell,Thomas and Secular Ethics in the Restoration, Scriblerian and the Kit-Cats, Vol 0027, 94; Shadwell,Thomas the Woman-Captain--A Critical Old-Spelling Edition, Scriblerian and the Kit-Cats, Vol 0027, 94; Devolving English Literature, Scriblerian and the Kit-Cats, Vol 0026, 94; The University in Ruins, Univ Toronto Quart, Vol 0066, 97. **CONTACT ADDRESS** Dept of English, Univ of Toronto, Mississauga, ON, L5L 1C6.

CORNELIA, MARIE E.
DISCIPLINE 16TH-CENTURY ENGLISH LITERATURE, ELIZABETHAN-JACOBEAN DRAMA **EDUCATION** Ford-

ham Univ, PhD. **CAREER** Evaluator, Mid States Asn; instr, dir, grad stud prog, Rutgers, State Univ NJ, Camden Col of Arts and Sci. **RESEARCH** Shakespeare, Donne, John Marston, Chaucer. **SELECTED PUBLICATIONS** Auth, The Function of the Masque in Jacobean Tragedy and Tragicomedy, Salzburg, 78. **CONTACT ADDRESS** Rutgers, State Univ NJ, Camden Col of Arts and Sci, New Brunswick, NJ, 08903-2101. **EMAIL** cornelia@camden.rutgers.edu

CORODIMAS, PETER
DISCIPLINE ENGLISH **EDUCATION** St Michaels Col, BA; John Carroll Univ, MA; OH State Univ, PhD, 71. **CAREER** Fac, Plattsburgh State Univ of NY. **RESEARCH** Contemp lit and creative writing. **SELECTED PUBLICATIONS** Auth, short stories in var magazines such as The Hudson Review, The New Yorker, and Redbook. **CONTACT ADDRESS** SUNY, Plattsburgh, 101 Broad St, Plattsburgh, NY, 12901-2681.

CORRIGAN, MAUREEN
DISCIPLINE ENGLISH LITERATURE **EDUCATION** Fordham Univ, BA; Univ Pa, MA, PhD. **CAREER** Prof. **RESEARCH** 19th century British literature; women's literature; popular culture; detective fiction; contemporary American literature; Anglo-Irish literature. **SELECTED PUBLICATIONS** Auth, The Androgynous Strain: Robert B. Parker and the Feminization of the Hard- Boiled From", Mystery Writers, 98; Ruskin, Chesterton, and Gill, Chesterton Rev, 82; A Search for Right Relationships: The Twentieth-Century Medievalism of Eric Gill, 81. **CONTACT ADDRESS** English Dept, Georgetown Univ, 37th and O St, Washington, DC, 20057.

COSGROVE, PETER
DISCIPLINE ENGLISH LITERATURE **EDUCATION** Columbia Univ, PhD, 89. **CAREER** Assoc prof, Dartmouth Col. **RESEARCH** Eng and Am lit. **SELECTED PUBLICATIONS** Auth, The Circulation of Genres in Gibbon's Decline and Fall of the Roman Empire, ELH, 96; Snapshots of the Absolute: Mediamachia in James Agee and Walker Evans's Let Us Now Praise Famous Men, Am Lit, 95; Undermining the Text: Edward Gibbon, Alexander Pope, and the Anti-Authenticating Footnote in Annotation and its Texts, Oxford UP, 91. **CONTACT ADDRESS** Dartmouth Col, 3529 N Main St, #207, Hanover, NH, 03755.

COSTA, RICHARD HAUER
PERSONAL Born 07/05/1921, Philadelphia, PA, m, 1950, 1 child **DISCIPLINE** ENGLISH **EDUCATION** West Chester State Col, BS, 43; Syracuse Univ, MA, 50; Purdue Univ, PhD(-English), 69. **CAREER** Asst prof English & jour, Utica Col, 61-68, assoc prof English, 68-70; assoc prof, 70-73, PROF ENGLISH, TEX A&M UNIV, 73-, Ed & publ, Quartet Mag, 68-78; exec-secy & prog chair, SCent Mod Lang Asn, 75-81; chair lit panel, Tex Com Arts, 81-83. **HONORS AND AWARDS** Distinguished teaching award, Asn Former Students, Tex A&M Univ, 76. **MEMBERSHIPS** MLA; SCent Mod Lang Asn. **RESEARCH** British and continental modern fiction; H G Wells and Malcolm Lowry; the short story. **SELECTED PUBLICATIONS** Auth, A Companion to the Characters in the Fiction and Drama of Maugham,W.Somerset, Eng Lit in Transition 1880-1920, Vol 0040, 97; The Rise and Fall of the Saturday-Globe, NY Hist, Vol 0074, 93. **CONTACT ADDRESS** Dept of English, Tex A&M Univ Col, Station, TX, 77843.

COSTANZO, WILLIAM VINCENT
PERSONAL Born 02/05/1945, Brooklyn, NY, m, 1973, 2 children **DISCIPLINE** ENGLISH, FILM **EDUCATION** Columbia Col, NY, AB, 67, Columbia Univ, MA, 68, PhD(English), 78. **CAREER** Asst prof, 70-78, assoc prof,78-84, prof English and film, Westchester Community Col, 84-, Nat Endowment for Humanities educ grant, 78-79; adj instr, Teachers Col, Columbia Univ, 80-. **HONORS AND AWARDS** NEH fel, 81; 10M Softwar Grant, 88; Fac Excellence Award, 90; NY State Chancellor's Award, 82. **MEMBERSHIPS** MLA; NCTE; Joseph Conrad Soc Am. **RESEARCH** Modern British literature; film studies; composition; SCS. **SELECTED PUBLICATIONS** Auth, The French Version of Finnegans Wake: Translation, Adaptation, Recreation, James Joyce Quart, winter, 71; I Found it at the Movies: A Cinematic Approach to Teaching Writing Skills, Insight, 77; The Duellists: Transposing Conrad's fiction into film, Joseph Conrad Today, 4/79; Conrad's Visit to America, Conradiana, winter 81; Polanski in Wessex: Filming Hardy's Tess of the d'Urbervilles, In: Literature/Film Quart, summer 81; Reading the Movies, 92; The Electronic Text, 89; Double Exposure, 84. **CONTACT ADDRESS** Dept of English, Westchester Comm Col, 75 Grasslands Rd, Valhalla, NY, 10595-1636. **EMAIL** wcostanzo@aol.com

COSTELLO, DONALD PAUL
PERSONAL Born 08/04/1931, Chicago, IL, m, 1952, 6 children **DISCIPLINE** AMERICAN STUDIES, DRAMA & FILM **EDUCATION** DePaul Univ, AB, 55; Univ Chicago, MA, 56, PhD, 62. **CAREER** Instr, Roosevelt Univ, 57-60 & Chicago City Jr Col, 58-59; from instr to assoc prof, 60-71, prof English, Univ Notre Dame, 71-, chmn Am studies & commun arts, 79-, soc relig higher educ fel, 64-65; consult, Educ Assoc, Inc for Proj Upward Bound, Wash, DC, 66-; consult/panelist, Nat Endowment for Humanities Lit & Fine Arts Panel, 77-. **MEMBERSHIPS** Soc Values Higher Educ; MLA. **RESEARCH** American literature; modern drama; cinema. **SELECTED PUBLICATIONS** Auth, The Language of The Catcher in the Rye, Am Speech, 10/59; art, Graham Greene and the Catholic Press, Renaissance, autumn 59; art, The Structure of the Turn of the Screw, Mod Lang Notes, 4/60; art, The Serpent's Eye: Shaw and the Cinema, Univ Notre Dame, 65; contribr, Black Man as Victim: The Drama of LeRoi Jones, Five Black Writers, New York Univ, 70; art, Counter-culture to Anti-culture: Woodstock, Easy Rider, and A Clockwork Orange, The Rev Polit, 10/72; art, Tennessee Williams' Fugitive Kind, Mod Drama, 5/72; art, Fellini's Road, Univ Notre Dame, 82. **CONTACT ADDRESS** Dept of English, Univ of Notre Dame, 356 Oshaugnessy Hall, Notre Dame, IN, 46556.

COTTER, JAMES FINN
PERSONAL Born 07/05/1929, Boston, MA, m, 1960, 3 children **DISCIPLINE** ENGLISH LITERATURE, PHILOSOPHY **EDUCATION** Boston Col, AB, 54, MA, 55; Fordham Univ, MA, 58, PhD(English), 63. **CAREER** From instr to asst prof English, Fordham Univ, 60-63; assoc prof, 63-68, prof English, Mt St Mary Col, NY, 68-; Fulbright-Hays lectr, Univ Oran, 70-71. **MEMBERSHIPS** MLA; Conf Christianity & Lit; Dante Soc. **RESEARCH** Dante; Renaissance poetry; Sir Philip Sidney; Gerard Manley Hopkins. **SELECTED PUBLICATIONS** Auth, Visions of Christ in Dante's Divine Comedy, Nemla Studies, 83-84; Hopkins: The Wreck of the Deutschland, 28, The Explicator, 85; Apocalyptic Imagery in Hopkins That Nature is a Heraclitean Fire and of the Comfort of the Resurrections, Victorian Poetry, 86; Look at it loom there! The Image of the Wave in Hopkins' The Wreck of the Deutschland, The Hopkins Quart, 87; Dante and Christ: The Pilgrim as Beatus Vir, The Italian Quart, 88; The Book Within the Book in Medieval Illumination, Florilegium 12, 93; The Song of Songs in The Wreck of the Deutschland in GM Hopkins and Critical Discourse, AMS Press, 94; Augustine's Confessions and The Wreck of the Deutschland in Saving Beauty: Further Studies in Hopkins, Garland, 95; The Divine Comedy and the First Psalm in Dante: Summa Medievalis, Stony Brook: Forum Italicum, 95. **CONTACT ADDRESS** 330 Powell Ave, Newburgh, NY, 12550-3412. **EMAIL** cotter@msmc.edu

COTTON, WILLIAM THEODORE
PERSONAL Born 07/14/1936, Manila, Philippines, m, 1959, 1 child **DISCIPLINE** ENGLISH LITERATURE **EDUCATION** Cornell Univ, BA, 58; Univ NMex, MA, 63, PhD(English), 74. **CAREER** Instr English, Univ NMex, 66-67; instr, 68-74, ASST PROF ENGLISH, LOYOLA UNIV OF THE SOUTH, 74- **MEMBERSHIPS** MLA. **RESEARCH** English Renaissance literature, especially romance-epic; utopian literature. **SELECTED PUBLICATIONS** Auth, The Given and the Made--Strategies of Poetic Redefinition, New Orleans Rev, Vol 0022, 96; The Breaking of Style--Hopkins, Heaney, Dove, Graham, New Orleans Rev, Vol 0022, 96. **CONTACT ADDRESS** Dept of English, Loyola Univ, New Orleans, 6363 St Charles Ave, New Orleans, LA, 70118-6195.

COULSON, J. PETER
PERSONAL Born 04/17/1933, Greenville, SC **DISCIPLINE** THEATRE, DRAMA **EDUCATION** Univ Ariz, BFA, 55, MA, 58; Univ Kans, PhD, 65. **CAREER** Dir theatre, McPherson Col, 58-62 & Ariz Western Col, 64-67; assoc prof theatre & drama & dir theatre, Wis State Univ, Eau Claire, 67-70; PROF THEATRE & DIR GRAD STUDIES, SOUTHWEST TEX STATE UNIV, 70-, Ed, Theatre Southwest, 77-80. **MEMBERSHIPS** Am Soc Theatre Res; Southwest Theatre Asn; Texas Educ Theatre Asn; Manuscript Soc. **RESEARCH** Theatre history-criticism; directing. **CONTACT ADDRESS** Dept of Theatre, Southwest Tex State Univ, 601 University Dr, San Marcos, TX, 78666-4685. **EMAIL** jc12@swt.edu

COUNCIL, NORMAN BRIGGS
PERSONAL Born 11/13/1936, Pensacola, FL, m, 1963, 2 children **DISCIPLINE** ENGLISH LITERATURE **EDUCATION** Univ of the South, BA, 58; Stanford Univ, MA, 64, PhD(English), 67. **CAREER** Instr English Lit, Univ Vt, 64-67; asst prof, Univ Calif, Santa Barbara, 67-76; chmn dept, 78-81, from assoc prof to prof English, Univ Utah, 76-93, dean, Col Humanities, 81-91, David P Gardner award, Univ Utah, 78-79. **MEMBERSHIPS** MLA. **RESEARCH** Shakespeare; Renaissance studies; Milton. **SELECTED PUBLICATIONS** Auth, Ben Jonson, Inigo Jones, and the transformation of Tudor Chivalry, J English Lit Hist, 47; Prince Hal: Mirror of success, Shakespeare Studies, 72; When Honour's at the Stake: Ideas of Honour in Shakespeare's Plays, Allen & Unwin, London, 73; O Dea Certe, Huntington Libr Quart, 76; L'Allegro Il Penseroso & the cycle of universal knowledge, Milton Studies, 76; Answering His Great Idean: The Fiction of Paradise Lost, Milton Studies, 96. **CONTACT ADDRESS** Col of Humanities, Univ of Utah, Orson Spencer Hall, Salt Lake City, UT, 84112-8916. **EMAIL** normanCouncil@u.cc.utah.edu

COUNTS, MICHAEL L.
DISCIPLINE THEATRE **EDUCATION** Pace Univ, BA; Hunter Col, MA; Grad Ctr CUNY, PhD. **CAREER** Asst prof & dir, Harlequin Theatre, Lyon Col. **RESEARCH** Acting; directing; theatre hist; theory and criticism. **SELECTED PUBLICATIONS** Auth, Coming Home: The Soldier's Return in Twentieth Century Drama, Peter Lang, NY, Bern, 88. **CONTACT ADDRESS** Dept of Theatre, Lyon Col, 300 Highland Rd, PO Box 2317, Batesville, AR, 72503.

COURAGE, RICHARD A.
PERSONAL Born 01/15/1946, Brooklyn, NY, m, 1969, 2 children **DISCIPLINE** ENGLISH **EDUCATION** Columbia Univ, PhD, 90 **CAREER** Assoc Prof English, Asst Chair English Dept, Westchester Community Coll, 90-. **HONORS AND AWARDS** State Univ NY Chancellor's Award for Exc; Nat Inst forStaff & Org Dev. **MEMBERSHIPS** Nat Coun Teachers Eng; Hudson Valley Writing Proj; Mod Lang Asn. **RESEARCH** Literacy, African-Am lit. **SELECTED PUBLICATIONS** Auth, Dangerous Narrative, in College Composition and Commun, Feb 96; auth, Interaction of Public and Private Liteacies, in College Composition and Commun, Dec 93; auth, Basic Writing: End of a Frontier, in J Teaching Writing, Fall/Winter 90; auth, James Baldwin's Go Tell It on the Mountain: Voices of a People, in CLA J, june 89. **CONTACT ADDRESS** Westchester Comm Col, Valhalla, NY, 10595.

COURT, FRANKLIN EDWARD
PERSONAL Born 11/26/1939, Youngstown, OH **DISCIPLINE** ENGLISH LITERATURE **EDUCATION** Youngstown State Univ, BA, 62; Univ Md, MA, 64; Kent State Univ, PhD(English), 69. **CAREER** Instr, Kent State Univ, 65-69; asst prof, 69-74, assoc prof, 74-80, PROF ENGLISH, NORTHERN ILL UNIV, 80-. **HONORS AND AWARDS** Huntington Libr Res Fel, 93; Folger Inst travel grant, 95. **MEMBERSHIPS** MLA; Midwest Mod Lang Asn; ACIS **RESEARCH** Victorian literature; celtic studies. **SELECTED PUBLICATIONS** Auth, Virtue sought as a hunter his sustenance: Pater's Amoral Aesthetic, J English Lit Hist, 74; Walter Pater: An Annotated Bibliography of Writings About Him, Northern Ill Univ Press, 80; Pater and His Early Critics, Univ Victoria ELS Monograph Series, 80; Tale of Two Cities: Dickens, Revolution, and the Other, Victorian Newsletter, Fall 91; Institutionalizing English Literature: The Culture and Politics of Literary Study, 1750-1900, Stanford Univ Press, 92; Jeremy Bentham's Wager, the Game of Reading, and Westron Wind, Mosaic: J for the Interdisciplinary Study of Lit, 12/97; The Early Impact of Scottish Literary Teaching in North America, In: The Scottish Invention of English Literature: Origins and Development of a University Discipline, Cambridge Univ Press, 98; Clark's The Wind and the Snow of Winter and Celtic Oisin, Studies in Short Fiction, Spring 98. **CONTACT ADDRESS** Dept of English, No Illinois Univ, 1425 W Lincoln Hwy, De Kalb, IL, 60115-2825. **EMAIL** fcourt@aol.com

COURTNEY, RICHARD
PERSONAL Born 06/04/1927, Newmarket, England, m, 1952, 2 children **DISCIPLINE** DRAMA, EDUCATION **EDUCATION** Univ Leeds, BA, 51, dipl educ, 52. **CAREER** Sr lectr drama, Trent Park Col, Inst Educ, Univ London, 58-67; assoc prof, Univ Victoria, BC, 68-71; prof, Univ Calgary, 71-74; PROF EDUC, ONT INST STUDIES IN EDUC, 74-, Ed, Discussions in Develop Drama, Univ Calgary, 71-74; chmn, Nat Inquiry into Arts & Educ in Can, 75-80; vis fel, Melbourne State Col, 79. **HONORS AND AWARDS** Queen's Silver Jubilee Medal, 77. **MEMBERSHIPS** Fel Royal Soc Arts; Can Conf Arts (pres, 73-76); Can Child & Youth Drama Asn (pres, 70-72); Am Soc Aesthetics; Am Theatre Asn. **RESEARCH** Developmental drama, the relationship of enactment to philosophy, ethnology, education, psychology and sociology. **SELECTED PUBLICATIONS** Auth, Tree,Beerbohm and Knight,G. Wilson--Reply to Pearce,Brian, New Theatre Quart, Vol 0013, 97. **CONTACT ADDRESS** Dept of Curric, Ontario Inst for Studies in Education, Toronto, ON, M5S 2L6.

COURTRIGHT, JOHN A.
PERSONAL Born 11/18/1948, m **DISCIPLINE** INTERPERSONAL COMMUNICATION **EDUCATION** Univ Iowa, BA, 71; MA, 73; PhD, 76. **CAREER** Res asst, Univ Iowa, 72-74; tchg asst, Univ Iowa, 74-76; instr, grad course in comp assisted statistical anal, Univ Iowa, 76; asst prof, Cleveland State Univ, 76-80; assoc prof, Cleveland State Univ, 80-85; asst dir, Comp Ctr, Cleveland State Univ, 83-86; prof, Cleveland State Univ, 85-86; prof, 86-; exec ed, Arts & Sci Newsletter, 92-96; ch, 86-. **HONORS AND AWARDS** Award, Speech Commun Assn, 91; grant, 95; grant, UNIDEL Found, 97., Assoc ed, mem, ed bd, Commun Res Rpt, 96-99; ed referee, Commun Rpt, 96; assoc ed, mem ed bd, Commun Quart, 96-99; Jour Commun, 96-99; Commun Edu, 96-99. **RESEARCH** Multimedia presentation; statistics and environmental design. **SELECTED PUBLICATIONS** Co-auth, Commun Research Methods. Glenview, Scott, Foresman, 84; Inertial Forces and the Implementation of a Socio-Technical Systems Approach: A Commun Study, Org Sci, 95; Thinking Rationally About Nonprobability, Jour of Broadcasting and Electronic Media, 96; Communicating Online: A Guide to the Internet, Mayfield Publ Co, 98; The Mayfield Quick Guide to the Internet: For Communincations Students, Mayfield Publ Co, 98. **CONTACT ADDRESS** Dept of Commun, Univ Delaware, 162 Ctr Mall, Newark, DE, 19716.

COURTS, PATRICK LAWRENCE
PERSONAL Born 04/28/1944, Chicago, IL, m, 1969, 1 child **DISCIPLINE** ENGLISH EDUCATION, AMERICAN LITERATURE **EDUCATION** Chicago State Col, BS, 66; Mich State Univ, MA, 68, PhD(English), 71. **CAREER** Teacher English, Chicago Bd Educ, 66-68; instr, Mich State Univ, 68-71; asst prof, 71-75, assoc prof, 75-80, PROF ENGLISH, STATE UNIV NY COL FREDONIA, 80- **MEMBERSHIPS** MLA; NCTE. **RESEARCH** Preparation of English Teachers for high school and college; teaching of composition and literature; subjective approaches to literature. **SELECTED PUBLICATIONS** Auth, Politicizing Literacy--Comment, Col Eng, Vol 0055, 93. **CONTACT ADDRESS** Dept of English, State Univ of NY Col, 1 Suny at Fredonia, Fredonia, NY, 14063-1143.

COUTENAY, LYNN
PERSONAL Born 07/08/1943, Nashville, TN, d, 2 children **DISCIPLINE** ENGLISH; HISTORY; ART HISTORY **EDUCATION** Vassar Coll, BA, 65; MA, PhD, 79, Univ of WI-Madison. **CAREER** Visiting lectr, University of WI-Madison; lectr, sr lectr, 84-96, asst prof, 96-, University of WI-Whitewata. **HONORS AND AWARDS** Fel in humanities, Newberry Library, 90-91; NEH Cooperative Project Grant, 91; Honorary Fel in Art hist, 94-97; elected Fel of the Soc of Antiquaries (members by invitation only), 95; Who's Who Among America's Teachers, Natl Honor Students' nomination, 96; University of WI System Fel: Inst for research in the humanities, 98-99 **MEMBERSHIPS** Soc of Antiquairies; ICMA; AVISTA; CAA; Vernacular Architecture Group; RAI; AIA (USA). **RESEARCH** Medieval Architecture; historic carpentry; Roman architecture; late medieval social and cultural hist; hist of technology. **SELECTED PUBLICATIONS** Auth, The Westminster Hall Roof: A New Archaeological Source, British Archaeological Association Journal, 90; Architectural Technology up to the Scientific Revolution: The Art and Structure of Large-scale Buildings, 93; Scale and Scantling: Technological Issues in large-scale Timberwork of the High Middle Ages, in Technology and Resource Use in Medieval Europe, Cathedrals, the Mills, and Mines, Dec 97; The Engineering of Gothic Cathedrals, Studies in the History of Civil Engineering, Dec 11, 1997. **CONTACT ADDRESS** 3100 Lake Mendota Dr., #504, Madison, WI, 53705. **EMAIL** hcourte@facstoff.wise.edu

COWAN, BAINARD
DISCIPLINE AMERICAN LITERATURE IN WORLD CONTEXT **EDUCATION** Yale, PhD, 75. **CAREER** Prof, La State Univ. **HONORS AND AWARDS** Newberry libr fel, 87-88; LEQSF Grant for Comp Lit, Inst and Colloquium, 92, 94, 96; NEH Higher Educ Grant, Comp Lit Inst, 94. **RESEARCH** World literatures and civilizations; science, technology, and literature. **SELECTED PUBLICATIONS** Auth, Exiled Waters: Moby Dick and the Crisis of Allegory, 82; America Between Two Myths: Moby Dick as Epic, The Epic Cosmos, 92; The Limits of Rationality: Oedipus the King, Class Texts and the Nature of Authority, 93; The Nomos of Deleuze and Guattari: Emergent Holism in A Thousand Plateaus, Ann of Scholar, 96; coed, Horizons in Theory and American Culture, LSU Press, 88; Theorizing American Literature: Hegel, the Sign, and History, 91. **CONTACT ADDRESS** Dept of Eng, Louisiana State Univ, 229D Allen Hall, Baton Rouge, LA, 70803. **EMAIL** encowa@lsuvm.sncc.lsu.edu

COWASJEE, SAROS
PERSONAL Born 07/12/1931, Secundrabad, India **DISCIPLINE** ENGLISH **EDUCATION** St John's Col (Agra, India), BA, 51; Agra Col, MA, 55; Univ Leeds, PhD, 60. **CAREER** Asst ed, Times of India Press (Bombay), 61-63; instr, 63, prof, 71-95, PROF EMER ENGLISH, UNIV REGINA, 95-; res assoc, Univ Calif Berkeley, 70-71; vis prof, Univ Aarhus (Denmark), 75. **HONORS AND AWARDS** N Tata scholar post-grad stud, Leeds Univ; Can Coun leave fels. **MEMBERSHIPS** Asn Can Univ Tchrs Eng; Can Asn Commonwealth Lit & Lang Stud; Authors Guild India; Writers Union Can; Zorastrian. **RESEARCH** Indian and Anglo-Indian literature **SELECTED PUBLICATIONS** Auth, Sean O'Casey: The Man Behind the Plays, 63; auth, O'Casey, 66; auth, 'Coolie': An Assessment, 76; auth, So Many Freedoms: A Study of the Major Fiction of Mulk Raj Anand, 77; auth, Studies in Indian and Anglo-Indian Fiction, 93; ed, Author to Critic: The Letters of Mulk Raj Anand, 73; ed, Mulk Raj Anand: A Check-list, 79; ed, Modern Indian Fiction, 81; ed, Modern Indian Short Stories, 82; ed, Stories From the Raj, 82; ed, More Stories From the Raj and After, 86; ed, When the British Left, 87; ed, The Raj and After, 87; ed, Women Writers of the Raj: Short Fiction, 90; ed, Orphans of the Storm: Stories on the Partition of India, 95; ed, The Best Short Stories of Flora Annie Steel, 95; ed, The Oxford Anthology of Raj Stories, 98; ed, Arnold Publ Literature of the Raj series, 84-. **CONTACT ADDRESS** English Dept, Univ of Regina, Regina, SK, S4S 0A2. **EMAIL** Saros.Cowasjee@uregina.ca

COWELL, PATTIE LEE
PERSONAL Born 03/10/1949, Auburn, WA **DISCIPLINE** ENGLISH **EDUCATION** Pacific Lutheran Univ, BA, 71; Univ Mass, MA, 73, PhD(English), 77. **CAREER** Teacher English, South Hadley High Sch, 72-74; teaching, Asst Rhetoric Prog, Univ Mass, 74-76; from instr to assoc prof, 77-86, Prof English, Colo State Univ, 86-, Chair, Women's Studies Interdisciplinary Program, 80-82, Admin Asst, Grad Sch, 82, Acting Dean, Grad Sch, 83-84, Acting Assoc Dean, Col of Arts, Humanities and Soc Sci, 86, Coordr of Grad Studies in English, 83-91; Ch, Dept of English, 91-; Ed Asst, Early Am Lit, 76; Field bibliographer in U.S. literature, MLA Int Bibliog, 82-98; Ed Board mem, Early Am Lit, 86-89; Advisory Board mem, Brown Univ Textbase of women Writers in English, 1350-1850, 89-. **HONORS AND AWARDS** Fac res Grant, Colo State Univ, 79; Dean's Award for Excellence, Col of Arts, Humanities and Soc Sci, CSU, 81; Dean's Schol Support Grant, CSU, 87; Professional Development Grant for Res Support, CSU, 89, 92, 95, 96; Cermak Award for Outstanding Graduate Advising, CSU, 91; Rockefeller Regional Schol, SW Inst for Res on Women, Univ Ariz, 91; Andrew W. Mellon Found Fel for research at the Library Company of Philadelphia, 96. **MEMBERSHIPS** MLA; NCTE; Women's Caucus Mod Lang; Rocky Mountain Mod Lang Asn. **RESEARCH** Early American literature; modern American fiction; cross-disciplinary perspectives on American culture. **SELECTED PUBLICATIONS** Auth, Introduction to Cotton Mather's Ornaments for the Daughters of Zion, Scholars' Facsimiles & Reprints, 78; Jane Colman Turell (1708-1735): Inclinations to poetry, 17th Century News, 78; Jane Colman Turell: A double birth, 13th Moon, 78; Women poets in pre-Revolutionary America, 1650-1735: A checklist, Bull Bibliog & Mag Notes, 79; seven entries, American Women Writers: A Critical Reference Guide (4 vols), Frederick Unger Publ, 79-82; Women Poets in Pre-Revolutionary America, 1650-1775, Whitston Publ Co, 81; Susanna Wright's verse epistle on the status of women in eighteenth-century America, Signs, 6: 795-800; Puritan women poets, In: A Companion to the Poetry of the Puritans, Pa State Univ Press, 85; co-ed, Critical Essays on Anne Bradstreet, G.K. Hall, 83; author of numerous articles, notes, and reviews. **CONTACT ADDRESS** Dept of English, Colorado State Univ, Fort Collins, CO, 80523-0001. **EMAIL** pcowell@vines.colostate.edu

COWGILL, KENT
DISCIPLINE LITERATURE **EDUCATION** Univ Nebr, MA, PhD. **CAREER** Prof. **RESEARCH** Chaucer, classical mythology, American literature. **SELECTED PUBLICATIONS** Auth, The Cranberry Trail: Misfits, Dreamers, and Drifters on the Heartland Road, 96. **CONTACT ADDRESS** Winona State Univ, PO Box 5838, Winona, MN, 55987-5838.

COX, DON RICHARD
PERSONAL Born 06/19/1943, Wichita, KS, m, 1976, 3 children **DISCIPLINE** VICTORIAN LITERATURE **EDUCATION** Wichita State Univ, BA, 66, MA, 68; Univ Mo, PhD(English), 75. **CAREER** Asst prof, 75-81, ASSOC PROF ENGLISH, UNIV TENN, 81-. **MEMBERSHIPS** MLA; SAtlantic Mod Lang Asn. **RESEARCH** Victorian novel. **SELECTED PUBLICATIONS** Auth, The Every-Saturday Page Proofs for the Mystery of Edwin Drood, Dickensian, Vol 0090, 94; Sexuality in Victorian Fiction, Journal of the History of Sexuality, Vol 0005, 94; Cant-You-See-A-Hint, The Mysterious 13th-Illustration to Edwin Drood, Dickensian, Vol 0092, 96; Mr-Grewgious-Experiences-A-New-Sensation--Dickens, Charles, Fildes, Luke--How Edwin Drood Was Illustrated, Dickensian, Vol 0093, 97; Child-Loving--The Erotic Child and Victorian Culture, Nineteenth-Century Lit, Vol 0048, 93. **CONTACT ADDRESS** Dept English, Univ Tenn, Knoxville, TN, 37996.

COX, E. SAM
PERSONAL Born 11/08/1947, Mountain Home, AK, m, 1967, 2 children **DISCIPLINE** COMMUNICATION **EDUCATION** Univ Ariz, PhD, 88. **CAREER** Asst, assoc prof, prof, comm, 85-, Central Mo St Univ. **HONORS AND AWARDS** Communicator Awards, ArlingtonTX, 98, hon men, PS Roadtrip - Electronic Field Trip #3. **MEMBERSHIPS** Natl Comm Assn; Amer Assn of Higher Ed. **RESEARCH** Technology & education; knowledge media; organizational communication. **SELECTED PUBLICATIONS** Auth, An Answer to The Call for Experimentation by the CEDA Assessment Conference: a Descriptive Study of a Peer-Judged Round, CEDA yearbk, 93; auth, A Reaction to Frank, and Horn and Underberg: An Assessment of Assessments, 20th Anniversary Assessment Conf Proc, Kendall/Hunt, 93; auth, The Officiated Approach to Return Tournament Debate to the Public Arena, Proc of Pi Kappa Delta Natl Develop Conf, 94; auth, The Need to Return Tournament Debate to the Public Arena, Pi Kappa Delta Natl Develop Conf, 94; coauth, Pi Kappa Delta as a Regulatory Agency for Competitive Debate: Toward Adapting and Adopting Officiated Debate, Pi Kappa Delta Natl Develop Conf, 95; coauth, The Value of Tournament Debating: An Analysis of Administrator's Views, Pi Kappa Delta Develop Conf, 95; auth, Toward Resolving the Debate Over Format: A Response to Panel Four, Pi Kappa Delta Develop Conf, 95; coauth, Pi Kappa Delta's Leadership Role in Competitive Debate: Toward Fairness, Civility and Accessibility, Forensic of Pi Kappa Delta, 80, 95; coauth, Valuing of Tournament Debate: Factors from Practitioners and Administrators, Forensic of Pi Kappa Delta, 80, 95; coauth, A Survey of the Entire CEDA Membership: Data for Decisions, J of Pragmatic Argumentation. **CONTACT ADDRESS** Central Missouri State Univ, Martin 136J, Warrensburg, MO, 64093. **EMAIL** cox@cmsu1.cmsu.edu

COX, JOHN D.
PERSONAL Born 08/09/1945, Red Oak, IA, m, 1968, 3 children **DISCIPLINE** ENGLISH LANGUAGE & LITERATURE **EDUCATION** Hope Col, BA, 67; Univ Chicago, MA, 68, PhD, 75. **CAREER** Asst prof English, Westmont Col, 73-75; asst prof English, Univ Victoria, BC, 75-78; Mellon fac fel English, Harvard Univ, Cambridge, 78-79; prof English, Hope Col, 96-. **HONORS AND AWARDS** NEH fellowship, 85-86; NEH Summer Stipend, 93; Pew Fellowship, 95-96. **MEMBERSHIPS** MLA; Shakespeare Assn Am; Medieval & Renaissance Drama Soc. **RESEARCH** English Renaissance drama and poetry. **SELECTED PUBLICATIONS** Auth, Shakespeare and the Dramaturgy of Power, Princeton UP, 89; A New History of Early English Drama, Columbia UP, 97. **CONTACT ADDRESS** Dept of English, Hope Col, Holland, MI, 49423-3698. **EMAIL** cox@hope.edu

COX, ROBERT
DISCIPLINE ENGLISH LITERATURE **EDUCATION** Northern AZ Univ, BA, 59; IN Univ, PhD, 65. **CAREER** Prof, Univ Pacific. **HONORS AND AWARDS** UOP Eberhardt Awd. **RESEARCH** Northern Europ lang(s); cult of the middle ages. **SELECTED PUBLICATIONS** Auth, pubs on Old English; Restoration drama; tchr educ. **CONTACT ADDRESS** Eng Dept, Univ Pacific, Pacific Ave, PO Box 3601, Stockton, CA, 95211.

COX, ROGER LINDSAY
PERSONAL Born 03/23/1931, Manson, IA, m, 1951, 4 children **DISCIPLINE** ENGLISH & COMPARATIVE LITERATURE **EDUCATION** Morningside Col, BA, 51; Univ Calif, Los Angeles, MA, 52; Columbia Univ, PhD, 61. **CAREER** Instr English, Bates Col, 58-61; from asst prof to assoc prof, DePauw Univ, 61-71; assoc prof, 71-75, PROF ENGLISH, UNIV DEL, 75-, vis prof, Jean-Moulin Univ, Lu¤yon, Fr, 93; Great Lakes Cols Asn award, 67-68; Am Coun Learned Soc fel, 67-68; Andrew Mellon fel, Univ Pittsburgh, 69-70. **RESEARCH** Tragedy; Comedys; Shakespeare; the novel. **SELECTED PUBLICATIONS** Auth, Hamlets Hamartia: Aristotle or St Paul?, Yale Rev, 66; Tragedy and the gospel narratives, Yale Rev, 68; Between Earth and Heaven: Shakespeare, Dostoevsky and the Meaning of Christian Tragedy, Holt, 69; The invented self: An essay on comedy, Soundings, summer 74; The structure of comedy, Thought, 3/75; Dostoevsky and the Ridiculous, Dostoevsky Studies, 80; Time and timelessness in Dostoevsky's fiction, Forum Int, fall 80; Stavrogin and Prince Hal, Canadian Slavonic Papers, 84; Kirillov, Stavrogin, and Suicide, Dostoevsky and the Human Condition after a Century, Greenwood Press, 86; Shakespeares Comic Changes: The Time-Lapse Metaphor as Plot Device, Univ Georgia Press, 91. **CONTACT ADDRESS** 404 Vassar Dr, Newark, DE, 19711. **EMAIL** ROGERLC@EROLS.COM

COX, SHELLY
PERSONAL Born 09/16/1948, Camden, NJ, s **DISCIPLINE** ENGLISH **EDUCATION** Univ of PA, BA, 70; Univ of Chicago, MA, 73; S IL Univ, MA, 81 **CAREER** Cataloger, 73-84, Librn, 85-, S IL Univ **MEMBERSHIPS** Am Libr Asn; Lawrence Durrell Soc **RESEARCH** Lawrence Durrell **SELECTED PUBLICATIONS** Auth, A Personal-Name Index to New Directions, Vol. 1-35. With a Historical Preface, Troy, NY, Whitston Publishing, 80 **CONTACT ADDRESS** Carbondale, IL, 62901-7248. **EMAIL** scox@lib.siv.edu

COX, STEPHEN D.
PERSONAL Born 01/12/1948, Niles, MI **DISCIPLINE** ENGLISH LITERATURE **EDUCATION** Univ Mich, BA, 72; Univ Calif, Los Angeles, MA, 73, PhD(English), 76 **CAREER** Lectr, 76-80, asst prof, 80-83, assoc prof, 83-92, PROF ENGLISH, DEPT LIT, UNIV CALIF, SAN DIEGO, 92-. **MEMBERSHIPS** Asn Literary Scholars & Critics; Am Soc for 18th Century Studies **RESEARCH** 18th century and romantic literature; Blake; classical liberalism; American religious history. **SELECTED PUBLICATIONS** Auth, The Stranger Within Thee: Concepts of the Self in Late Eighteenth Century Literature, Univ Pittsburgh Press, 80; Love and Logic: The Evolution of Blake's Thought, Univ Mich Press, 92; biogr intro, The God of the Machine, by Isabel Paterson, Transaction Publ, 93; Theory, Experience, and the American Religion, JETS, 93; The Two Liberalsims, Am Lit Hist, 94; The Devil's Reading List, Raritan, 96. **CONTACT ADDRESS** Dept of Lit 0306, Univ of Calif San Diego, 9500 Gilman Dr, La Jolla, CA, 92093-0306. **EMAIL** sdcox@ucsd.edu

COYLE, MICHAEL GORDON
DISCIPLINE LITERARY AND CRITICAL THEORY **EDUCATION** Miami Univ, BA, 78; Univ VA, MA, 81, PhD, 86. **CAREER** Assoc prof, Colgate Univ, 86. **HONORS AND AWARDS** Ford Found grant, 89; President's fel, Univ VA, 85-86; Lily Dabney fel, Univ London, 82. **RESEARCH** Modernist lit and cult Hist. **SELECTED PUBLICATIONS** Auth, Ezra Pound, Popular Genres, and the Discourse of Culture Col Park: Pa State UP, 95; A Present with Innumerable Pasts: Postmodernity and the Tracing of Modernist Origins, Rev, Univ Va P, 96; Ezra Pound, Am Lit Scholar, Duke UP, 96. **CONTACT ADDRESS** Dept of Eng, Colgate Univ, 13 Oak Drive, Hamilton, NY, 13346.

CRABTREE, CLARIE
DISCIPLINE AMERICAN LITERATURE **EDUCATION** Trinity Col, BA; Fordham Univ, MA; Wayne State Univ, PhD. **CAREER** Fulbright sr lectr, Romania, 94-95; assoc prof, 87-. **HONORS AND AWARDS** Dir, women's stud prog. **RESEARCH** William Faulkner. **SELECTED PUBLICATIONS** Pub(s), on Faulkner, and women writers sich as Erdrich, Hurston, and Toni Morrison. **CONTACT ADDRESS** Dept of Eng, Univ Detroit Mercy, 4001 W McNichols Rd, PO BOX 19900, Detroit, MI, 48219-0900. **EMAIL** CRABTREC@udmercy.edu

CRABTREE, ROBIN D.
PERSONAL Born 03/04/1960, CA **DISCIPLINE** COMMUNICATION **EDUCATION** Univ Minn, MA, 86, PhD, 92; Univ Cal, SB, BA, 82. **CAREER** Asst Prof, 93-, DCS, New Mexico State Univ; Asst Prof, 91-93, DePauw Univ; pub aff/host, 89-90, KUOM MN pub radio; grad teach Asst, 84-91, Univ Minn. **HONORS AND AWARDS** NM Dept Hlth Res Gnt; NMSU Res Gnt; LAS Con Awd; Pres Fac Gnt; BEA Harwood Diss Hon Men. **MEMBERSHIPS** ICA; NCA; WSCA; UDC. **RESEARCH** Intl Intercultural Communication, Development, Empowerment. **SELECTED PUBLICATIONS** Auth, Communication and social change: Applied communication theory in service learning, in: Voices of Strong Democracy: Service Learning and Comm Stud, eds, B O Murphy, D Droge, AAHE, 98; Mutual Empowerment in cross-cultural participatory development and service learning: Lessons in comm and social justice form projects in El Salvador and Nicaragua, J Applied Comm Res, 98; coauth, Communicating about emerging infectious diseases in the borderlands: Hantavirus education for rural border and migrant populations, in: Border Health: Res and Practice on the US-Mex Border, eds, J G Power, T Byrd, Thousand Oaks, Sage, 98; auth, Service learning and the liberal arts: Restructuring for integrated education, in: Restructuring for Integrative Edu: Multi Perspectives Multi Contexts, ed, TE Jennings, Westport CT, Bergin & Garvey, 97; coauth, Principles of Human Communication, Dubuque, Kendall/Hunt, 96. **CONTACT ADDRESS** Comm Studies, New Mexico State Univ, Box 30001, Las Cruces, NM, 88003-0001. **EMAIL** rcrabtre@nmsuvml.nmsu.edu

CRACROFT, RICHARD HOLTON
PERSONAL Born 06/28/1936, Salt Lake City, UT, m, 1959, 3 children **DISCIPLINE** AMERICAN LITERATURE **EDUCATION** Univ Utah, BA, 61, MA, 63; Univ Wis, PhD, 69. **CAREER** PROF ENGLISH, BRIGHAM YOUNG UNIV, 63-, CHMN DEPT, 75-80, DEAN, COL HUMANITIES, 81-86; Assoc ed, Dialogue: A J of Mormon Thought, 69-73; res ed, Western Am Lit, 73-. **MEMBERSHIPS** Western Am Lit Asn; Rocky Mountain Mod Lang Asn; NCTE; MLA. **RESEARCH** Western American literature; Mark Twain; Mormon literature. **SELECTED PUBLICATIONS** Auth, The Big Sky: A B Guthrie's use of historical sources, Western Am Lit, fall 71; The gentle blasphemer: Mark Twain, holy scripture and the Book of Mormon, Brigham Young Univ Studies, winter 71; A pebble in the pool: Organic unity in Thomas Wolfe's You Can't Go Home Again, Mod Fiction Studies, winter 72; co-ed, A Believing People: Literature of the Latter-day Saints, Brigham Young Univ, 74, 79; 22 Young Mormon Writers, Commun Workshop, 75; auth, Provo Patriotic Reader, Brigham Young Univ, 76; coauth, Voices from the past, 80. **CONTACT ADDRESS** Dept of English, Brigham Young Univ, 3146 Jkhb, Provo, UT, 84602-0002. **EMAIL** RHC@email.byu.edu

CRAFT, WILLIAM
DISCIPLINE LITERATURE OF THE RENAISSANCE AND REFORMATION **EDUCATION** Univ NC at Chapel Hill, MA, PhD. **CAREER** Newberry Libr Chicago fel; Amer Coun Educ fel; app 3-yr term, Undergrad dean. **SELECTED PUBLICATIONS** Auth, Labyrinth of Desire, 94. **CONTACT ADDRESS** Dept of English, Mount Saint Mary's Col, 16300 Old Emmitsburg Rd, Emmitsburg, MD, 21727-7799. **EMAIL** craft@msmary.edu

CRAIG, GEORGE ARMOUR
PERSONAL Born 11/15/1914, Cleveland, OH, m, 1939, 2 children **DISCIPLINE** ENGLISH LITERATURE **EDUCATION** Amherst Col, AB, 37; Harvard Univ AM, 38, PhD, 47. **CAREER** Instr English, Harvard Univ, 38-40; from instr to assoc prof, 40-55, prof, 55-80, KENAN PROF ENGLISH, AMHERST COL, 80-, Vis lectr, Harvard Univ, 55-56. **MEMBERSHIPS** MLA. **RESEARCH** Seventeenth century English philosophy and literature; 19th century prose fiction. **CONTACT ADDRESS** Dept of English, Amherst Col, Amherst, MA, 01002.

CRAIG, J. ROBERT
PERSONAL Born 12/21/1947, New Kensington, PA, m, 1971, 3 children **DISCIPLINE** COMMUNICATION **EDUCATION** Clarion State Col, BS, 69, MS, 71; Univ Mo, PhD, 81. **CAREER** Area Coordr, NWMSU, 74-80; chemn, 93-96, grad coordr, 85-, CMU. **HONORS AND AWARDS** Outstanding Young Men of Am, 84; Who's Who in Midwest Entertainment. **MEMBERSHIPS** BEA; FWest Pop Culture; IAFA; NEA. **RESEARCH** Elec Media Law; film; pop culture/children's TV. **SELECTED PUBLICATIONS** Coauth, article, The Devolution of Children's Television Programming: A Look at The Mighty Morphin Power Rangers, 97; auth, article, On Visual Tropes as Expressions of the Psyche in Roman Polanski's The Tenant, 98; auth, article, Reno v. American Civil Liberties Union: The First Amendment, Electronic Media, and the Internet Indecency Issue, 98; auth, article, Trapping Simians in the Scottish Highlands: A Viewer Reponds to the Hitchcock MacGuffin in Terry Gilliam's 12 Monkeys, 98; auth, article, Three Viewers Viewing: A Viewer-Response Symposium on Jacob's Ladder, 98. **CONTACT ADDRESS** Central Michigan Univ, 306 Moore Hall, Mount Pleasant, MI, 48859. **EMAIL** john.robert.craig@cmich.edu

CRAIG, ROBERT T.
PERSONAL Born 05/10/1947, Rochester, NY, m, 1979, 1 child **DISCIPLINE** COMMUNICATION **EDUCATION** Univ Wis-Madison, 69; Mich State Univ, MA, 70; PhD, 76. **CAREER** Asst prof, Pa State Univ, 76-79; asst prof, Univ Ill-Chicago, 79-81; asst/assoc prof, Temple Univ, 81-90; assoc prof, Univ Colo-Boulder, 90- . **MEMBERSHIPS** Nat Commun Asoc; Int Commun Asoc; Western States Commun Asoc. **RESEARCH** Communication theory; language and social interaction. **SELECTED PUBLICATIONS** Auth, with K. Tracy, Grounded Practical Theory: The Case of Intellectual Discussion, Commun Theory, 95; auth, Practical Theory: A Reply to Sandelands, J for the Theory of Soc Behav, 96; auth, Practical-Theoretical Argumentation, Argumentation, 96; auth with D.A. Carlone, Growth and Transformation of Communication Studies in U.S. Higher Education: Towards Reinterpretation, Commun Educ, 98. **CONTACT ADDRESS** Dept. of Communication, Univ of Colorado at Boulder, CB 270, Boulder, CO, 80309-0279. **EMAIL** robert.craig@colorado.edu

CRAIGE, BETTY JEAN
PERSONAL Born 05/20/1946, Chicago, IL **DISCIPLINE** LITERATURE **EDUCATION** Pomona Col, BA, 68; Univ Washington, MA, 70, PhD, 74. **CAREER** Instr to asst prof to assoc prof to prof, Univ Ga, 73- . **HONORS AND AWARDS** Honoratus Medal for Teaching, UGA Honors Prog, 87; Frederic W. Ness Book Award, 89; co-winner, Ga Author of the Year Award, 92; Univ Ga Alumni Soc Faculty Svc Award, 94., Dir, Center for Humanities & Arts, 93- ; Interim Head of Comparative Lit, 97-99. **MEMBERSHIPS** Modern Lang Assoc; Amer Comparative Lit Assoc. **RESEARCH** Holism **SELECTED PUBLICATIONS** Auth, Lorca's Poet in New York: The Fall into Consciousness, Univ Press Ky, 97; Literary Relativity, Bucknell Univ Press, 82; Reconnections: Dualism to Holism in Literary Study, Univ of Ga Press, 88; Laying the Ladder Down: The Emergence of Cultural Holism, Univ Ms Press, 92; America Patriotism in a Global Society, SUNY Press, 96. **CONTACT ADDRESS** Humanities Center, Univ Ga, Peabody Hall Room 1, Athens, GA, 30602. **EMAIL** BJCRAIGE@UGA.CC.UGA.EDU

CRAIN, PATRICIA
DISCIPLINE ENGLISH **EDUCATION** Bennington, BA, 70; Columbia Univ, MA, 89, PhD, 96. **CAREER** ASST PROF, ENG, PRINCETON UNIV **MEMBERSHIPS** Am Antiquarian Soc **SELECTED PUBLICATIONS** Auth, "The Story of A: Alphabetization and American Literature from the New England Primer to the Scarlet Letter," forthcoming. **CONTACT ADDRESS** Dept of Eng, Princeton Univ, McCosh 22, Princeton, NJ, 08544. **EMAIL** patcrain@princeton.edu

CRANE, JON
DISCIPLINE COMMUNICATION STUDIES **EDUCATION** Univ IL, PhD, 91. **CAREER** Assoc prof, Univ NC, Charlotte. **SELECTED PUBLICATIONS** Auth, Terror and everyday life: Singular moments in the hist of horror film, Sage, 94. **CONTACT ADDRESS** Univ N. Carolina, Charlotte, Charlotte, NC, 28223-0001.

CRANE, MILTON
PERSONAL Born 05/24/1917, Hartford, CT, m, 1940, 2 children **DISCIPLINE** ENGLISH AND AMERICAN LITERATURE **EDUCATION** Columbia Univ, AB, 37, AM, 38; Harvard Univ, AM, 41, PhD, 42. **CAREER** Instr English, Col William & Mary, 42-43 & Hunter Col, 44-47; asst prof, Univ Chicago, 47-52; res dir, US Dept State, 52-61, chief div res Brit Commonwealth, North & Cent Europe, 61-64; prof English lit, 64-76, EMER PROF ENGLISH, GEORGE WASHINGTON UNIV, 76-, Educ & res analyst, Off Strategic Serv, 43-45; assoc ed, Bantam Bk, Inc, 45-46; prof lectr, George Washington Univ, 55-61, 63. **MEMBERSHIPS** MLA; Shakespeare Asn Am. **RESEARCH** Shakespeare; George Bernard Shaw. **SELECTED PUBLICATIONS** Auth, They Hunt in Packs, Overland, Vol 0135, 94; Under the Bridge, Overland, Vol 0145, 96; A Dog Called Yesterday, Overland, Vol 0147, 97; How to Write the Perfect Suicide Note, Overland, Vol 0129, 92; The Race, Overland, Vol 0137, 94; Lullaby, Overland, Vol 0140, 95; The Ferryman, Meanjin, Vol 0054, 95. **CONTACT ADDRESS** Dept of English, George Washington Univ, 2023 G St NW, Washington, DC, 20006.

CRANE, SUSAN
DISCIPLINE ENGLISH LANGUAGE AND LITERATURE **EDUCATION** Univ Wisconsin, BA: Univ Calif Berkeley, MA; PhD. **CAREER** Prof **RESEARCH** Gender; cultural history; Medieval English and French literature. **SELECTED PUBLICATIONS** Auth, Insular Romance; auth, Gender and Romance in Chaucer's Canterbury Tales . **CONTACT ADDRESS** Dept of English, Rutgers Univ, 510 George St, Murray Hall, New Brunswick, NJ, 08901-1167.

CRAUN, EDWIN DAVID
PERSONAL Born 03/17/1945, Riverside, CA, m, 1967, 2 children **DISCIPLINE** MEDIEVAL & RENAISSANCE POETRY & PROSE, ENGLISH & LATIN **EDUCATION** Wheaton Col, Ill, BA, 67; Princeton Univ, PhD, 71. **CAREER** From Asst Prof to Prof, 71-95, asst dean col, 78-81, Henry S. Fox, Jr. Prof English, Washington & Lee Univ, 95-. **HONORS AND AWARDS** Wheaton Col Scholastic Honor Soc, 67; Woodrow Wilson Fel, 67-69; Fel, SEastern Inst Medieval and Renaissance Studies, Summer 76; NEH Summer Seminars Program, 83, 89; NEH Fel for Col Teachers, 86-87; Mednick Memorial Fel, Va Found for Independent Colleges, Summer 90; Phi Beta Kappa, 92. **MEMBERSHIPS** MLA; Southeastern Med Asn; Med Acad Am; New Chaucer Soc. **RESEARCH** Medieval and Renaissance narrative poetry. **SELECTED PUBLICATIONS** Auth, Inordinata Locutio: Blasphemy in Pastoral Literature, 1200-1500, Traditio 29, 83; Blaspheming Her "Awin God": Cressid's Lamentatioun in Henryson's Testament, Studies in Philol 82, 85; Verbum Nuncius es Rationis: Augustinian Sign Theory in Medieval Pastoral Discourse on Deviant Speech, Augustinian Studies 20, 89; Most Sacred Vertue She: Reading Book V Alongside Aristotle and Thomas Aquinas on Justice, In: Approaches to Teaching Spenser's Faerie Queene, Mod Lang Asn, 94; Lies, Slander, and Obscenity in Medieval English Literature: Pastoral Rhetoric and the Deviant Speaker, Cambridge Studies in Medieval Literature 33, Cambridge Univ Press, 97. **CONTACT ADDRESS** Dept of English, Washington & Lee Univ, Lexington, VA, 24450-2504. **EMAIL** craune@ulu.edu

CRAVEN, ALAN
DISCIPLINE ENGLISH **EDUCATION** Univ KS, AB, MA, PhD. **CAREER** Prof & dean, Col Fine Arts and Hum; 21 yrs dir, Div Engl, Classics, Philos & Commun; dean of the Col, 95-; taught at, Univ AR & Brandeis Univ. **RESEARCH** Bibl, renaissance lit, dramatic and non-dramatic; Shakespeare. **SELECTED PUBLICATIONS** Publ in, Engl Lang Notes, Papers of the Bibliog Soc of Amer, Stud in Bibliog, Shakespeare Quart. **CONTACT ADDRESS** Col of Fine Arts and Hum, Univ Texas at San Antonio, 6900 N Loop 1604 W, San Antonio, TX, 78249. **EMAIL** acraven@lonestar.utsa.edu

CRAWFORD, JERRY L.
PERSONAL Born 08/20/1934, Whittemore, IA, m, 1956, 3 children **DISCIPLINE** DRAMA **EDUCATION** Drake Univ, BFA, 56; Stanford Univ, MA, 57; Univ Iowa, PhD, 64. **CAREER** From instr to prof drama, 62-70, actg dean fac, 65-66, dean fac, 66-68, chmn dept speech & drama, 68-70, Prof Theatre Arts, 70-94, PROF EMER, 94- , UNIV NEV, LAS VEGAS, 70- ; Dir Lit Sem, Utah Shakespearean Fest. Cedar City, UT, 88- . **HONORS AND AWARDS** Best New Play Award, Southeastern Theatre Conf, 74; Gold Medallion, Am Oil Co, 77 & 80; Gov Nev Art Award, State Nev, 82. **MEMBERSHIPS** Assoc Theatre Higuer Ed; Col Fel Am Theatre, 91- ; Dramatists Guild, 81- . **RESEARCH** Theory, technique and practice of playwriting; contemporary dramatic literature; acting and directing in the contemporary theatre. **SELECTED PUBLICATIONS** Auth, The auction tomorrow, Southeastern Theatre Conf J, fall 74; coauth, The Actor: In Person and in Style, 75 & 94; auth, The auction tomorrow (play), Judy Bayley Summer Repertory Theatre, Las Vegas, 76, The Corner Theatre, Baltimore, 77, Univ Theatre, Calif State Univ, Fresno, 77, Stockton Calif, 78 & Hartman Theatre, Stanford, Conn, 80; The passing of Corky Brewster (play), Circle Repertory Co, New York, 2-3/77; Halftime at the Superbowl (play), Playwrights unit Actors Studio, New York, 1/77; Those were the days they gave babies away with half a pound of tea (play), Meadows Playhouse, Las Vegas, 4/78; The Last President (play), St Clements Theatre, NY, 79 & UNLV, 81; Dance for Rain, Redmen, That Was Number 99 (play), Dramatics Mag, 4/82; The Brothers Silence, UNLV, 97; **CONTACT ADDRESS** Dept of Theatre Arts, Univ of Nev, Las Vegas, NV, 89154.

CRAWSHAW, WILLIAM HENRY
DISCIPLINE GEORGIAN PERIODS OF BRITISH LITERATURE **EDUCATION** Univ FL, BA, 54; Univ Wales, MA, 59; Pa State Univ, PhD, 66. **CAREER** Prof, Colgate Univ, 63-. **RESEARCH** 18th century Brit lit. **SELECTED PUBLICATIONS** Publ, lit studies of US and Brit works in Studies, Burke & His Times, Conradiana, ESQ, DLB Mod Brit Playwrights, ANQ, Annual of Am Cult Studies; ed bd, Works of Joseph Conrad, Cambridge UP. **CONTACT ADDRESS** Dept of Eng, Colgate Univ, 13 Oak Drive, Hamilton, NY, 13346.

CREAN, SUSAN M.
PERSONAL Born 02/14/1945, Toronto, ON, Canada **DISCIPLINE** WRITING **EDUCATION** Univ Toronto, BA, 67, MA, 69; Ecole du Louvre, Dipl, 69-70. **CAREER** Arts & tchg positions, 66-85; MacLean Hunter Ch, dept creative writing, Univ BC, 89-90; ch, Writer's Union Can, 91-92. **SELECTED PUB-**

LICATIONS Auth, Who's Afraid of Canadian Culture?, 76; auth, Newsworthy: The Lives of Media Women, 84; auth, In the Name of the Fathers: The Story Behind Child Custody, 88; auth, Writing Along Gender Lines, in Language in Her Eye, 90; auth, Culture, Gender and Power, in Changing Focus, 91; auth, Taking the Missionary Position, in Racism in Canada, 91; auth, Grace Hartman, A Woman For Her Time, 95; coauth, Deux pays pour vivre: un plaidoyer, 80; coauth, Two Nations: An Essay on the Culture and Politics of Canada and Quebec in a World of American Pre-eminence, 82. **CONTACT ADDRESS** 1916 W 11th Ave, Vancouver, BC, V6J 2C6.

CREED, WALTER GENTRY
PERSONAL Born 12/30/1931, Philadelphia, PA, m, 1963, 2 children **DISCIPLINE** ENGLISH LITERATURE **EDUCATION** Univ Pa, BA, 60, MA, 61, PhD(English lit), 68. **CAREER** Instr English, Lafayette Col, 65-66, asst prof, 69; asst prof, 69-75, PROF ENGLISH, UNIV HAWAII, MANOA, 84-. **RESEARCH** Computers and writing; literature and science; critical theory. **SELECTED PUBLICATIONS** Auth, Pieces of the puzzle: The multiple-narrative structure of The Alexandria Quartet, Mosaic, winter 73; The whole pointless joke? Darley's search for truth in The Alexandria Quartet, Etudes Anglaises, 4-6/75; The Muse of Science and The Alexandria Quartet, Norwood Ed, 77; On reading Einstein, Four Quart, 1/79; Philosophy of science and theory of literary criticism: Some common problems, Philos Sci Asn, 1/80; The good soldier: Knowing and judging, English Lit Transition, 80; Is Einstein's work relevant to the study of literature?, In: After Einstein, Memphis State Univ Press, 81; Rene Wellek and Karl Popper on the Mode of Existence of Ideas in Literature and Science, J Hist Ideas, 49(1983); Writers Interact (software program). **CONTACT ADDRESS** Dept English, Univ Hawaii, 1733 Donaghho Rd, Honolulu, HI, 96822-2368. **EMAIL** creed@hawaii.edu

CREW, LOUIE
DISCIPLINE ENGLISH LITERATURE **EDUCATION** Baylor Univ, BA, 58; Auburn Univ, MA, 59; Univ of AL, PhD, 71. **CAREER** Assoc prof, Eng 94-; lectr, Acad Found, 92-94; assoc prof, Acad Found, 89-92; assoc prof, Claflin Col, 88-89; consult cmptr bus wrtg, Salme Ser, 87-88; lectr Eng, Chinese Univ Hong Kong, 84-87; vis for expert, Beijing 2d Inst For Langs, 83-84; assoc prof Eng, Univ WI, 79-84; assoc prof Eng, Ft Valley State Col, 73-79; prof Eng, Claflin Col, 71-73; acad dir, Exper Intl Living, 70-71; instr, Univ AL, 66-70; master Eng/Eng Hist, Penge Secon Mod Schl, 65-66; master Eng/Sacred Studies, Darlington Schl, 59-62. **RESEARCH** Computer software, lit, relig, gay/lesbian/bisexual issues. **SELECTED PUBLICATIONS** Auth, Loving Those on the Relig Right, Whosoever, 98; Let Us Now Praise Caustic Christians, More Light, 98; Autumn at Shum Shui Po, PBW, 97. Catherine Jordan's Prayer, Laughing Boy Rev, 97; Cruising, Stet Mag, 97; Death, Online Jour, 97; Ghost Houses, Switched/on Guenberg, 97; Gilded Nimbus, Vox Clamantis, 97; God, Bless Those Who Are Afraid, Prayers to Protest, 97; God's Flesh and Blood, Cz Mag, 97; I Believe in Fairies, The Exploding Chicken Fiasco, 97; In Old Milwaukee, Prairie Flame, 97; Lash Through History, Rave Review , 97; Let There Be, Ostraka, 97; Misdirections, Rave Review, 97; Mouths, Pif: Online Jour 97; Neighbor, Gruene Street, 97; Pansies, That's for Thoughts, Gruene Street, 97; Pound of Flesh, PBW, 97; Practical Joke, Pif: Online Journal, 97; Professional Calling Card Poems, Pif: Online Jour, 97; Rough Trade, Rag Shock 3: Bizarrotica, 97; Tenacity, or Woopiedoo for the Finale, Ostraka, 97; We Are Here, PBW, 97; With Morning Glories, Laughing Boy Review, 97; Deputy, Not 'Delegate', Vo, COVER, LET & QUERY, LET, Silent But Deadly, 94; ABCs of Gay Bashing, Voice of Integrity, 94; Hope About Homophobia, News Jersey January, 94; Gay Psalm from Fort Valley--Bound By Diversity, Sebastian, 94; Gay Psalm from Fort Valley, Literature Around the World, Kendall Hunt, , 94; Mace for the Child Molester, Feminist Parenting, Freedom, 94; Ancient Inhospitality, Hepcat's Revenge, 94; Cynic Gossips about Lutibelle, Making Waves, 94; Elbow Room, Hepcat's Revenge, 94; Ferryman's Epitaph, Caveat Lector, 94; Field Lullaby, Reach Magazine, 94; Grief Rehearsed, 94; I Wish I Was In, New Times, 94; One Easter Morning, Kaspah Raster, 94; Recalculating Words' Worth, RIF/T 2, 94; Sissy Be Nimble, Sissy Be Quick, RIF/T 2, 94; Terminal, Outlook, 94; This Strait Man, Backspace: An Alternative Queer Zine, 94; View from One Porn Booth, Minotaur, 94; Called Out, The Epistle, 94; Caveat Donor, Issues, 94; Clericalism in the Episcopal Church, Episcopal Voice, 94; Counting Down to Indianapolis, The Witness, 94; Cracks in the Wa. **CONTACT ADDRESS** Dept of Eng, Rutgers, State Univ of NJ, 350 Dr Martin Luther King Jr Blvd, Hill Hall, Newark, NJ, 07102-1801. **EMAIL** lcrew@newark.rutgers.edu

CREWE, JONATHAN V.
DISCIPLINE ENGLISH LITERATURE **EDUCATION** Univ Calif Berkeley, PhD, 80. **CAREER** Willard Prof drama and oratory; prof Eng and comp lit. **RESEARCH** Shakespearean and Renaissannce lit. **SELECTED PUBLICATIONS** Auth, Trials of Authorship: Anterior Forms and Poetic Reconstruction from Wyatt to Shakespeare, Univ Calif P, 90; Hidden Designs: The Critical Profession and Renaissance Literature, Methuen, 86; Unredeemed Rhetoric: Thomas Nashe and the Scandal of Authorship, Johns Hopkins UP, 82; Baby Killers, Differences, 95; In the Field of Dreams: Transvestism in Twelfth Night and The Crying Game, Representations, 95; Out of the Matrix: Shakespeare's Race-Writing, Yale Jour Crit, 95. **CONTACT ADDRESS** Dartmouth Col, 3529 N Main St, #207, Hanover, NH, 03755.

CREWS, FREDERICK
PERSONAL Born 02/20/1933, Philadelphia, PA, m, 1959, 2 children **DISCIPLINE** ENGLISH **EDUCATION** Yale, BA, 55; Princeton Univ, PhD, 58. **CAREER** Instr to prof, 58-94, Chr Grad Stud, 88-92, Dept Chr, 92-94, prof emer, 94-, Univ Cal Berkeley, 58-; Fulbright lectr Italy, 61-62; ACLS Study Fel, 65-66; Guggenheim Fel, 70-71; Gayley Lectr Univ Cal, 74-75; Ward-Phillips Lectr Univ Notre Dame, 74-75; Short Term Fel Princeton Univ, 78; Dorothy T. Burstein Lectr UCLA, 84; Distinguished Tchg Award, UCB, 85; Frederick Ives Carpenter vis lectr Univ Chicago, 85; John Dewey Lectr, 87-88; Nina Mae Kellogg Lectr Portland State Univ, 89; Fac Res Lectr UCB, 91-92. **HONORS AND AWARDS** Natl Coun Arts & Hum Essay Prize, 68; Spielvogel-Diamonstein PEN Award, 92. **MEMBERSHIPS** Mod Lang Asn; False Memory Syndrome Found **RESEARCH** Modern British literature; American literature; Psychological theory; Cultural criticism. **SELECTED PUBLICATIONS** Auth, The Random House Handbook, Random House, 92; The Critics Bear It Away: American Fiction and the Academy, Random House, 92; coauth,The Borzoi Handbook Handbook for Writers, Knopf, 93; ed, Anthology of American Literature, Macmillan, 93; auth, The Memory Wars: Freud's Legacy in Dispute, Granta Press, 97; ed, Unauthorized Freud: Doubters Confront a Legend, Viking Press, 98. **CONTACT ADDRESS** 636 Vincent Ave, Berkeley, CA, 94707-1524. **EMAIL** fredc@socrates.berkeley.edu

CROMPTON, LOUIS
PERSONAL Born 04/05/1925, Port Colborne, ON, Canada **DISCIPLINE** ENGLISH HISTORY **EDUCATION** Univ Toronto, BA, 47, MA, 48; Univ Chicago, AM, 50, PhD(English), 54. **CAREER** Lectr math, Univ BC, 48-49; lectr English, Univ Toronto, 53-55; from asst prof to assoc prof, 55-64, PROF ENGLISH, UNIV NEBR, 64-. **HONORS AND AWARDS** Christian Gauss Bk Award, Nat Phi Beta Kappa, 69. **MEMBERSHIPS** MLA; AAUP. **RESEARCH** Bernard Shaw; 19th century literature; homosexual history and literature. **SELECTED PUBLICATIONS** Auth, An Army of Lovers--Male Love and Military Prowess in Classical Greece --The Sacred Band of Thebes, Hist Today, Vol 0044, 94. **CONTACT ADDRESS** Dept of English, Univ of Nebr, Lincoln, NE, 68588.

CRONN-MILLS, DANIEL
PERSONAL Born 02/10/1964, Redwood Falls, MN, m, 1992, 1 child **DISCIPLINE** COMMUNICATION **EDUCATION** Univ Nebr, Lincoln, PhD, 95. **CAREER** Instr, Dept Speech Communication, Mankato State Univ, 92-95; asst prof, Mankato State Univ, 95-97; assoc prof, Mankato State Univ, 97-present. **HONORS AND AWARDS** Faculty Improvement Grant; Outstanding New Teacher of the Year, Central States Communication Asn; Arts and Humanities Res Mini-Grant; Mankato State Univ Found Special Projects Grant; nominated for Fac Appreciation Award, Mankato State Univ. **MEMBERSHIPS** Am Forensic Asn; Central States Commun Asn; Commun and Theatre Asn of Minn; Delta Sigma Rho-Tau Kappa Alpha; Mid-American Forensic League; Minn Collegiate Forensic Asn; Nat Federation Interscholastic Speech and Debate Asn; Nat Forensic Asn; Religious Speech Commun Asn; Soc for the Scientific Study of Religion; National Commun Asn; Twin City Forensic League; Valley Forensic League. **RESEARCH** Investigating rhetorical process of organized religion from an historical and contemporary perspective; primarily involving Jehovah's Witnesses. Investigating current pragmatic and theoretical concerns in intercollegiate forensics. **SELECTED PUBLICATIONS** Auth, Team exempt filing: A process for integration and workload reduction, in The Forensic Educator, 7, 93; auth, The interview fair: Maximizing opportunity and experience, in The Speech Communication Teacher, 7, 93; coauth, The role of forensics when departments/programs are targeted for elimination: A proposal to ensure a 'call for support' is heard, in Nat Forensic Journal, 11, 93; coauth, Competitor's perceptions of questions in individual events rounds, in Nat Forensic Journal, 11, 93; coauth, The 'reason for decision' in individual events: Its implications and impact, in The Forensic Educator, 10, 95; coauth, Multiple perspectives on hearing-impaired persons in competitive debate, in SpekerPoints, 96; coauth, Communication technology and individual events, in The Forensic Educator, 11, 96; coauth, The 'Unwritten rules' in oral interpretation: An assessment of current practices, in SpeakerPoints, 4(2), 97; coauth, Institutional circuit rider is the future of the DOF, in Southern Journal of Forensics, 2, 97; coauth, Book Review: Freedom of Speech in the Marketplace of Ideas, in Free Speech Yearbook, 97. **CONTACT ADDRESS** Mankato State Univ, MSU Box 89, PO Box 8400, Mankato, MN, 56002-8400. **EMAIL** daniel.cronn-mills@mankato.msus.edu

CROSLAND, ANDREW TATE
PERSONAL Born 08/17/1944, San Francisco, CA, m, 1968, 1 child **DISCIPLINE** ENGLISH, COMPUTER SCIENCE **EDUCATION** Belmont Abbey Col, AB, 66; George Peabody Col, MA, 68; Univ SC, PhD(English), 76. **CAREER** Teacher English, math & sci, York Sch Dist 1, 66-67; instr English, 68-73, asst prof, 73-78, assoc prof English, 78-84, asst vice chancellor for academic affairs, 84-91, prof English, Univ SC, Spartanburg, 85-; dir computer studies, 80-84. **MEMBERSHIPS** MLA; Asn Lit & Ling computing; Soc Study Southern Lit; Asn Comput Mach; Asn Comput in Humanities. **RESEARCH** American literature; research tools; computer applications in the humanites. **SELECTED PUBLICATIONS** Ed, A Concordance to F Scott Fitzgerald's The Great Gatsby, 75 & A Concordance to the Complete Poetry of Stephen Crane, 75, Gale Res; auth, Sleeping and Waking: The Literary Reputation of The Great Gatsby, 1927-1944, 75 & The Great Gatsby and the Secret Agent, 75, Fitzgerald/Hemingway Ann; The Concordance and the Study of the Novel, Asn Lit & Ling Computing Bull, 75; The Concordance as an Aid in the Historical Study of Style, Style, 77; Sources for Fitzgerald's The Curious Case of Benjamin Button, Fitzgerald/Hemingway Ann, 79; The New Computer Science, SIGCSE Bull, 82; Alica Walker's Nineteen Fifty-Five: Fiction and Fact, ELN, 96; The Text of Zora Neale Hurston: A Caution, CLAJ, 94. **CONTACT ADDRESS** Dept English, Univ S. Carolina, 800 University Way, Spartanburg, SC, 29303-4932. **EMAIL** acrosland@gw.uscs.edu

CROSMAN, ROBERT
PERSONAL Born 02/18/1940, Chicago, IL, d, 1 child **DISCIPLINE** ENGLISH LITERATURE **EDUCATION** Univ Calif Berkeley, BA, 63; Columbia Univ, MA, 65, PhD, 71. **CAREER** Asst prof, 69-73, Williams Col; vis asst prof, 75-76, Trinity Col; lectr, 77-79, Tuft's Univ; fellow, 80-81, Boston Univ; vis lectr, 81-82, Rice Univ; instr, 82, MIT; asst prof to assoc prof, 85-, Univ Ak Anchorage. **HONORS AND AWARDS** Phi Beta Kappa, 62; Explicator Award, 81., Nat Merit Scholar, 57-61; Harvard Nat Scholar, 57-61; W S Ferguson Hist Essay Prize, 59; Phi Beta Kappa, 62; Woodrow Wilson Fel, 63-64; Columbia President's fel, 65; Columbia Col Preceptorship, 66-68. **MEMBERSHIPS** MLA; Shakespeare Assoc of Amer. **RESEARCH** Shakespeare; reader response criticism; Milton. **SELECTED PUBLICATIONS** Auth, Reading Paradise Lost, Ind Univ Press, 80 **CONTACT ADDRESS** English Dept, Univ Ak Anchorage, Anchorage, AK, 99508.

CROSS, GILBERT B.
PERSONAL Born 05/02/1939, Manchester, England, m, 1965, 2 children **DISCIPLINE** ENGLISH LITERATURE **EDUCATION** Manchester Univ, BA, 61; Univ London, cert educ, 62; Univ Louisville, MA, 65; Univ MI, PhD, 71. **CAREER** Lectr Eng, Eastern KY Univ, 65-66; instr, 66-70, asst prof, 70-75, assoc prof, 75-80, Prof Eng, Eastern MI Univ, 80-, Am Philos Soc grant, 78; Am Coun Learned Socs grant-in-aid, 78. **HONORS AND AWARDS** Barnard Hewitt Award, 78. **MEMBERSHIPS** AAUP; Bronte Soc; Soc Theatre Res. **RESEARCH** Drama; Brontes; theatre. **SELECTED PUBLICATIONS** Coauth, Drury Lane Journal: Selections from the diaries of James Winston 1819-1827, Soc Theatre Res, 74; coauth (with A L Nelson), Aut Caesar, Aut Nullus: Edmund Kean's Articles of Agreement, 1825, 19th Century Theatre Res, autumn 74; auth, Next Week--East Lynne: Domestic Drama in Performance, Bucknell Univ Press, 77; coauth (with A L Nelson), A case of unassigned authorship: James Winston's Perseverance (1802), Educ Theatre J, 5/78; If These Be Truths, Farewell to Falsehoods: James Winston's Pedigree, Theatre Notebook, No 34, 80; auth, World Folktales: A Scribner Resource Collection, Scribner, 80; coauth, The Adelphi Theatre Calendar, Part I, 1806-1850, Greenwood, 90; coauth, The Adelphi Theatre Calendar, Part II, 1851-1900, Greenwood, 93. **CONTACT ADDRESS** Dept of Eng, Eastern Michigan Univ, 602M Pray Harrold, Ypsilanti, MI, 48197-2201. **EMAIL** Eng_Cross@online.emich.edu

CROSSLEY, ROBERT THOMAS
PERSONAL Born 12/20/1945, Philadelphia, PA, m, 1974, 1 child **DISCIPLINE** ENGLISH LITERATURE **EDUCATION** Rockhurst Col, CIAB, 67; Univ Va, MA, 68, PhD, 72. **CAREER** Asst prof, 72-78, assoc prof, 79-87, prof, 87-, chmn Eng, 96-, Univ Mass, Boston. **MEMBERSHIPS** MLA; Int Assn Fantastic in Arts; Sci Fiction Res Assn. **RESEARCH** British science fiction; Utopian literature; lit executor Olaf Stapledin. **SELECTED PUBLICATIONS** Auth, H G Wells, Starmont, 86; auth, Talking Across the World, N England, 87; auth, Olaf Stapledon: Speaking for the Future, Syracuse, 94; auth, An Olaf Stapledon Reader, Syracuse, 97. **CONTACT ADDRESS** English Dept, Univ of Massachusetts, Boston, 100 Morrissey Blvd, Boston, MA, 02125-3300. **EMAIL** crossley@umbsky.cc.umb.edu

CROWELL, DOUGLAS E.
DISCIPLINE ENGLISH LITERATURE **EDUCATION** SUNY, Buffalo, PhD, 81. **CAREER** Assoc prof, TX Tech Univ. **HONORS AND AWARDS** Short-story award, TX Inst Lett; NEA Creative Writing fel grant. **SELECTED PUBLICATIONS** Publ fiction in jour(s) including Crazyhorse, Epoch, Fiction Int, Miss Rev, and New Directions; his stories have been anthologized in New Stories from the South and South by Southwest. **CONTACT ADDRESS** Texas Tech Univ, Lubbock, TX, 79409-5015. **EMAIL** ykfdc@ttacs.ttu.edu

CROWL, SAMUEL
PERSONAL Born 10/09/1940, Toledo, OH, m, 1963, 2 children **DISCIPLINE** ENGLISH LITERATURE **EDUCATION** AB, Hamilton Coll, 62; PhD, IN Univ, 70. **CAREER** Trustee, Prof, Eng Lit, 92-; Dean, Univ Coll, OH Univ, 81-82; Prof, Eng, OH Univ, 80-92; Assoc Prof Eng, OH Univ, 75-80; Asst Prof Eng, OH Univ, 70-75; Lectruer, Eng, IN Univ-Indanapolis, 67-70; Teaching Assoc, IN Univ-Bloomington, 63-67. **HONORS AND AWARDS** Selected as a Univ Prof, 95-96; Selected as a Fellow of the Ping Inst for the Teaching of Hum, 93; Member of the Advisory Board for the MIT-NEH Shakespeare Interactive Video Project, 93-; Named Trustee Prof of Enf by the OH Univ Board of Trustees, 92; Elected to serve on the Hamilton Coll Alumni Council 91-94; 97-. **MEMBERSHIPS** Modern Lang Assoc; Shakespear Assoc of Amer; Elected Pres Assoc of Univ Coll Deans and Dir of Undergraduate Studies, 91-92; Who's Who In Amer; OH Univ Nominee CASE Prof of the Yr Award, 84; Elected to Mem in Phi Kappa Beta, 82; Elected a Fellow of the Royal Soc for the Arts, 76; Selected as a Univ Prof, 74-75. **RESEARCH** Shakespeare; Shakespeare on Film; Shakespeare on Stage. **SELECTED PUBLICATIONS** Shakespeare Observed; Studies in Performance on Stage and Screen, OH Univ Press, 92, 2nd printing, 93, 3rd, 95; Studies English Literature, 93; Academic Library Book Review, 94; Notes and Queries, 94; Etudes Anglaises, 94; Yearbook of English Studies, 95; Review of English Studies, 95; Shakespeare Newletter, 97. **CONTACT ADDRESS** Dept of Eng, Ohio Univ, Ellis Hall,Athens, OH, 45701.

CROWLEY, DAVID
DISCIPLINE COMMUNICATION STUDIES **EDUCATION** John Hopkins Univ, BA; Annenberg Univ, MA; McGill Univ, PhD. **CAREER** Assoc prof. **RESEARCH** Hist and theory of communications; communications and info policy; socio technical approaches to communication; public consultation; research design. **SELECTED PUBLICATIONS** Auth, Communications in History, Technology, Culture, Society, Longman, 91; art, Doing Things Electronically, Can Jour Commun, 94; auth, Distance Research in Communication, 95; auth, Introduction to the New Edition, Univ Toronto, 95; art, Communications in Canada-Enduring Themes, Emerging Issues, 94. **CONTACT ADDRESS** Dept Communications, McGill Univ, 845 Sherbrooke St, Montreal, PQ, H3A 2T5.

CROWLEY, J. DONALD
DISCIPLINE AMERICAN LITERATURE AND 20TH CENTURY AMERICAN POETRY **EDUCATION** Ohio State Univ, PhD, 64. **CAREER** Prof. **SELECTED PUBLICATIONS** Hist ed, Hawthorne's Major Tales and Sketches, Ohio St UP; ed, Robinson Crusoe, Oxford; co-ed, The Wings of the Dove, Norton; One Hundred Years of Huckleberry Finn, Mo UP & Critical Essays on Walker Percy, GK Hall; several yrs contribur, Hawthorne chap in Amer Lit Scholar. **CONTACT ADDRESS** Dept of English, Univ of Missouri-Columbia, 309 University Hall, Columbia, MO, 65211.

CROWLEY, JOHN W.
PERSONAL Born 12/27/1945, New Haven, CT, m, 1978, 3 children **DISCIPLINE** ENGLISH & AMERICAN LITERATURE **EDUCATION** Yale Univ, BA, 67; Ind Univ, MA, 69, PhD, 70. **CAREER** Asst prof, 70-74, assoc prof, 74-79, prof, 79-, eng, Syracuse Univ; dir grad studies, 86-89, chemn, 89-92, dir humanities doctoral prog, 85-88, 96-, Syracuse Univ. **HONORS AND AWARDS** Phi Beta Kappa, 66. **RESEARCH** American literature, 1850-1950. **SELECTED PUBLICATIONS** Auth, George Cabot Lodge, Twayne Publ, 76; auth, The Black Heart's Truth: The Early Career of W. D. Howells, Univ NC Press, 85; auth, The Mask of Fiction: Essays on W. D. Howells, Univ Mass Press, 89; auth, The White Logic: Alcoholism and Gender in American Modernist Fiction, Univ Mass Press, 94; ed, George Cabot Lodge: Selected Fiction and Verse, John Colet, 76; auth, Henry Adams, The Life of George Cabot Lodge, Scholars' Facsimiles & Reprints, 78; auth, The Haunted Dusk: American Supernatural Fiction, 1820-1920, Univ Ga Press, 82; auth, New Essays in Winesburg, Ohio, Cambridge Univ Press, 90; auth, Roger Austen, Genteel Pagan: The Double Life of Charles Warren Stoddard, Univ Mass Press, 91; auth, Charles Jackson, The Sunnier Side, Syracuse Univ Press, 95; auth, W. D. Howells, The Rise of Silas Lapham, Oxford Univ Press, 96; auth, Drunkard's Progress: Narratives of Addiction, Despair and Recovery, Johns Hopkins Univ Press, 99. **CONTACT ADDRESS** Dept. of English, Syracuse Univ, Syracuse, NY, 13244-1170.

CROWLEY, SUE MITCHELL
PERSONAL Born 10/31/1933, Columbus, OH, m, 1954, 2 children **DISCIPLINE** RELIGION AND LITERATURE **EDUCATION** St Mary's College Notre Dame, BA, cum laude 55; Ohio State Univ, MA, 68; Univ Iowa, PhD. **CAREER** Instr, lectr, Asst Dir, 72 to 84-, Univ Missouri; Instr, 82-84, Stephens College; lectr, Instr, 68-79, Univ Iowa; teacher, 67, Ursuline Acad. **HONORS AND AWARDS** Honors Teacher of the Year. **MEMBERSHIPS** AAR; MLA; Cen MO Colloquium on the Study of Religion. **RESEARCH** John Updike; Walker Percy; Robert Lowell; Toni Morrison. **SELECTED PUBLICATIONS** Coed, Critical Essays on Walker Percy, Boston, GK Hall, 89; auth, Tenderness detached from the source of tenderness, The Thanatos Syndrome: Walter Percy's Tribute to Flannery O'Connor, Walker Percy: Novelist and Philosopher, Jackson, Univ Mississippi Press, 91; coauth, Walker Percy's Grail, King Arthur Through the Ages, eds, Valerie M Lagorio, Mildred Leake Day, NY, and London, Garland Pub, 90. **CONTACT ADDRESS** 409 South Greenwood, Columbia, MO, 65203.

CROZIER, ALICE COOPER
PERSONAL Born 06/29/1934, New York, NY, m, 1968, 2 children **DISCIPLINE** AMERICAN LITERATURE **EDUCATION** Radcliffe Col, BA, 56; Harvard Univ, PhD, 64. **CAREER** Instr English, Smith Col, 61-66; asst prof, 66-72, assoc prof English, Rutgers Univ, New Brusnwick 72-, Am Asn Univ Women fel, 64-65; Nat Endowment for Humanities fel, 71-72. **RESEARCH** American literature. **SELECTED PUBLICATIONS** Auth, The Novels of Harriet Beecher Stowe, Oxford Univ, 69. **CONTACT ADDRESS** Dept of English, Rutgers Univ, PO Box 5454, New Brunswick, NJ, 08903. **EMAIL** acrozier@rci.rutgers.edu

CROZIER, LORNA
PERSONAL Born 05/24/1948, Swift Current, SK, Canada **DISCIPLINE** WRITING **EDUCATION** Univ Sask, BA, 69; Univ Alta, MA, 80. **CAREER** High sch Eng tchr, Sask, 72-77; creative writing tchr, Sask Summer Sch Arts, 77-81; dir comm, Dept Parks, Recreation & Culture, Govt Sask, 81-83; writer-in-residence, Regina Pub Libr, 84-85; instr, Banff Sch Fine Arts, 86-87; lectr, Univ Sask, 86-91; vis prof, 91-92, assoc prof, 92-96, PROF WRITING, UNIV VICTORIA, 96-; writer-in-residence, Univ Toronto, 89-90. **HONORS AND AWARDS** Sask Writers' Guild Poetry Award, 84, 87; Nat Radio Award, 87; Gov Gen Award Poetry, 92; Can Authors' Asn Award Poetry, 92; Pat Lowther Award, 92, 95; Nat Mag Award, Gold Medal Poetry, 95. **MEMBERSHIPS** Sask Writers' Guild; League Can Poets. **SELECTED PUBLICATIONS** Auth, Inside is the Sky, 76; auth, Crow's Black Joy, 78; auth, Humans and Other Beasts, 80; auth, The Weather, 83; auth, The Garden Going On Without Us, 85; auth, Angels of Silence, Angels of Flesh, 88; auth, Inventing the Hawk, 92; auth, Everything Arrives at the Light, 95; auth, A Saving Grace: The Collected Poems of Mrs. Bentley, 96; coauth, No Longer Two People, 79; co-ed, A Sudden Radiance, 87; co-ed, Breathing Fire, 95; co-ed, Alden Nowlan: Selected Poems, 96. **CONTACT ADDRESS** 1886 Cultra, Saanichton, BC, V8M 1L7.

CRUME, ALICE L.
DISCIPLINE COMMUNICATION STUDIES **EDUCATION** Carroll Col, BA; Univ Mont, MA; Bowling Green State Univ, PhD. **CAREER** Asst prof. **SELECTED PUBLICATIONS** Auth, Conflict Resolution Through Communication, Burgess, 96; Ethics in Mediation, 96. **CONTACT ADDRESS** Dept of Communication, State Univ NY Col Brockport, Brockport, NY, 14420. **EMAIL** acrume@po.brockport.edu

CRUMP, REBECCA
DISCIPLINE VICTORIAN POETRY, ROMANTIC POETRY, NINETEENTH-CENTURY BRITISH NOVEL **EDUCATION** Univ Tex, Austin, PhD, 70. **CAREER** Advis, undergrad prog, 96-, former assoc ch, codir, undergrad prog, dir, creative writing, prof, La State Univ. **HONORS AND AWARDS** ACLS summer grant, 72; NEH summer stipends, 74, 82; Guggenheim fel, 83-84; NEH senior fel, 87-88; LSU Found Distinguished Fac Award, 91; Col of Arts & Sci Nicholson Award, 96. **RESEARCH** Editing; bibliography. **SELECTED PUBLICATIONS** Auth, Christina Rossetti: A Reference Guide, 76; Charlotte and Emily Bronte, 1846-1915: A Reference Guide, 81; Charlotte and Emily Bronte, 1916-1954: A Reference Guide, 85; Charlotte and Emily Bronte, 1955-1983: A Reference Guide, 86; Order in Variety: Essays and Poems in Honor of Donald E. Stanford, 91; ed, Maude: Prose and Verse, Christina Rossetti, 76; The Complete Poems of Christina Rossetti: A Variorum Ed, 3 vols, 79-91. **CONTACT ADDRESS** Dept of Eng, Louisiana State Univ, 210B Allen Hall, Baton Rouge, LA, 70803.

CRUPI, CHARLES WILLIAM
PERSONAL Born 04/06/1939, Wadsworth, OH, m, 1960, 3 children **DISCIPLINE** ENGLISH **EDUCATION** Harvard Univ, AB, 61; Univ Calif, Berkeley, MA, 63; Princeton Univ, PhD(English), 67. **CAREER** From instr to asst prof English, Princeton Univ, 66-74; assoc prof to prof English, Albion Col, 74-, chmn dept, 78-97; vis prof, Drew Univ, 73 & Stockholm Univ, 81. **MEMBERSHIPS** MLA; Mencken Soc; Soc Am Baseball Res; ARBA; SICULA. **RESEARCH** Shakespeare; Renaissance drama. **SELECTED PUBLICATIONS** Auth or coauth (with R Aiuto) of 6 plays, including: Mencken and Sara (play), Baltimore, 81; Robert Greene, Boston, 84. **CONTACT ADDRESS** Dept of English, Albion Col, 611 E Porter St, Albion, MI, 49224-1831. **EMAIL** ccrupi@albion.edu

CULIK, HUGH
DISCIPLINE ENGLISH LITERATURE **EDUCATION** Univ Mich, BA, MA; Wayne State Univ, PhD. **CAREER** Dept ch; dir, Wrtg Across the Curric. **SELECTED PUBLICATIONS** Co-ed, Post Identity; pub(s), short fiction. **CONTACT ADDRESS** Dept of Eng, Univ Detroit Mercy, 4001 W McNichols Rd, PO BOX 19900, Detroit, MI, 48219-0900. **EMAIL** hugh@libarts.udmercy.edu

CULLER, ARTHUR DWIGHT
PERSONAL Born 07/25/1917, McPherson, KS, m, 1941, 2 children **DISCIPLINE** ENGLISH **EDUCATION** Oberlin Col, AB, 38; Yale Univ, PhD(English), 41. **CAREER** Instr English, Cornell Univ, 41-42; from instr to asst prof, Yale Univ, 46-55; assoc prof, Univ Ill, 55-58; prof English, 58-86, PROF EMERITUS, YALE UNIV, 86-, chmn dept, 71-75; Fulbright res fel, England, 50-51; Guggenheim fel, 61-62 & 75; mem, PMLA Adv Comt, 71-74; Nat Endowment for Humanities res fel, 79-80. **HONORS AND AWARDS** DLitt. Merrimack Col, 72; Am Acad Arts & Scis, 86; Phi Beta Kappa; Explicator Literary Fdn Award, 77. **MEMBERSHIPS** MLA. **RESEARCH** Victorian literature. **SELECTED PUBLICATIONS** Auth, Imperial Intellect, Yale Univ, 55; ed, Apologia Pro Vait Sua, 56 & Poetry and criticism of Matthew Arnold, 61, Houghton; auth, Imaginative Reason: The Poetry of Matthew Arnold, Yale, 66; The Poetry of Tennyson, Yale Univ, 77; auth, The Victorian Mirror of History, Yal, 86. **CONTACT ADDRESS** 80 Tokeneke Dr, North Haven, CT, 06518.

CULLINAN, BERNICE ELLINGER
PERSONAL Born 10/12/1926, Hamilton, OH, d, 2 children **DISCIPLINE** EDUCATION, SOCIOLOGY, PSYCHOLOGY **EDUCATION** Ohio State Univ, BSc, 48, MA, 51, PhD, 64. **CAREER** Elementary teacher, Ohio Public Schools, 46-59; instr, 59-64, asst prof, Ohio State Univ, 64-67; study dir, The Critical Reading Project, USOE, 64-67; prof, NYU, 67-97; EDITOR-IN-CHIEF, WORDSONG BOOKS, BOYDS MILLS PRESS, 90-. **HONORS AND AWARDS** Reading Hall of Fame, Int Reading Asn, 89; Arbuthnot Award, 89; Who's Who in Am Ed, 91; Jeremiah Ludington Award, 92; Citation for Outstanding Contribution to Literacy, Ind Univ, 95; Col of Education Hall of Fame, 95, Charlotte Huck Prof of Children's Lit, Ohio State Univ, 97; pres, Reading Hall of Fame, Int Reading Asn, 98. **MEMBERSHIPS** Chair, Selection Comm Ezra Jack Keats New Writer Award; editorial board, The New Advocate; advisor, IRA Teachers' Choices Project; Advisory Board, Ranger Rick Magazine; Board of Trustees, Highlights Found; Advisory Board, the Arthur Series, WGBH Boston Children's Programming. **RESEARCH** Childrens poems; literacy initiatives in the United States; development of children's responses to literature; young black children's language & reading competence. **SELECTED PUBLICATIONS** Auth, Let's Read About...Finding Books They'll Love to Read, Scholastic, 93; 75 Authors & Illustrators Everyone Should Know, Children's Book Coun, 94; coauth, Helping Your Child Learn to Read, U.S. Dept of Ed, 93; Three Voices: Invitation to Poetry Across the Curriculum, Stenhouse, 95; Language, Literacy, & the Child, Second Edition, Harcourt Brace, 97; Literature and the Child, Fourth Edition, Harcourt Brace, 98; ed, Fact and Fiction: Literature Across the Curriculum, Int Reading Asn, 93; Pen in Hand: Children Become Writers, Int Reading Asn, 93; Children's Voices: Talk in the Classroom, Int Reading Asn, 93; A Jar of Tiny Stars: Poems by NCTE Award-Winning Poets, Wordsong/NCTE, 96. **CONTACT ADDRESS** 10 E 40th St., New York, NY, 10016. **EMAIL** BerniceCullinan@Worldnet.att.net

CULROSS, JACK LEWIS
PERSONAL Born 06/04/1941, Rochester, NY, m, 1966, 2 children **DISCIPLINE** ENGLISH **EDUCATION** Spring Hill Col, BS, 63; La State Univ, Baton Rouge, MA, 66, PhD, 70. **CAREER** Instr English, La State Univ, 68-70; from Asst Prof to Assoc Prof, 70-80, Prof English, Eastern Ky Univ, 80-, Assoc Dean Undergrad Studies, 78-83, Dean Acad Support & Undergrad Studies, 83-. **RESEARCH** Victorian literature; literary criticism. **SELECTED PUBLICATIONS** Auth, Mary Barton: A Revaluation, Bull John Rylands Univ Libr Manchester 61, 78. **CONTACT ADDRESS** Office of the Dean, Undergrad Studies, Eastern Kentucky Univ, 521 Lancaster Ave, Richmond, KY, 40475-3102. **EMAIL** gsoculro@acs.eku.edu

CUMBERLAND, SHARON L.
DISCIPLINE ENGLISH LITERATURE **EDUCATION** Coe Col, BA; Drake Univ, MA; CUNY, Doctorate, 94. **CAREER** Instr, Seattle Univ. **MEMBERSHIPS** MLA; Soc for the Stud of Southern Lit; Popular Cult Asn; Acad of Am Poets; Poetry Soc of Am. **SELECTED PUBLICATIONS** Auth, Habit, What You Have, On Going In, Ploughshares, Apr, 94; The Rape of Sabine Women, Kalliope, 94; I Know I am Capable of Great Love, Laurel Rev, 94; Postulant, Smoke Offering, Ind Rev, Spg, 95; Before, Lipstick, Elberton Fling, Swing Alone, Westcoast, 95. **CONTACT ADDRESS** Seattle Univ, Seattle, WA, 98122-4460. **EMAIL** slc@seattleu.edu

CUMMINGS, PETER MARCH
PERSONAL Born 11/28/1941, Manchester, NH, m, 1965, 1 child **DISCIPLINE** ENGLISH LITERATURE **EDUCATION** Cornell Univ, BA, 63, Univ NC, Chapel Hill, MA, 64, PhD, 71. **CAREER** Lectr asst, Cornell Univ, 63-64; instr English Lit, Copenhagen Univ, 64-65; instr, Washington & Lee Univ, 68-69; asst prof, 70-76, assoc prof English, 76-82, PROF ENGLISH & COMP LIT, HOBART & WILLIAM SMITH COLS, 82-. **HONORS AND AWARDS** Mellon Found grant, 79. **MEMBERSHIPS** AAUP; MLA. **RESEARCH** Renaissance poetry and drama; literary criticism. **SELECTED PUBLICATIONS** Coauth, 24 American Poets, Gad Copenhagen, 66;

auth, Spenser's Amoretti as an allegory of love, Tex Studies Lang & Lit, 70; Northrop Frye and the necessary hybrid: Criticism as aesthetic humanism, In: The Quest for Imagination, Case Western Reserve Univ, 71; Bicycle story: Some theory and practice, Boston Phoenix, spring 74; Walt Whitman's Song of Myself and the History of the Future, Dansk Udsyn, 77; The Bicycle: History, Pyhsics, and Consciousness, Dansk Udsyn, 77; Bicycle Consciousness, Greenfield Rev Press, 79; Hearing in Hamlet: Poisoned Ears and the Psychopathology of Flawed Audition, Shakespeare Yearbook, 90; Violinmaking: An Alchemical Journal, Genre, 90; The Making of Meaning: Sex Words and Sex Acts in Shakespeare's Othello, The Gettysburg Rev, 90; The Alchemical Storm: Etymology, Wordplay, and New World Kairos in Shakespeare's The Tempest, The Upstart Crow, 92; Shakespeare's Bawdy Planet, The Sewanee Rev, 92; Learning to Read: The Heart of Liberal Arts Value, Liberal ed, 96; Verbal Energy in Shakespeare's Much Ado About Nothing, Shakespeare Yearbook, 97; Textuality and the Reader in Shakespeare's Non-Dramatic Poems, forthcoming in new journal, Shakespeare Studies, Moscow, 99; and auth of the following long poems: Hamlet at Sea, The Upstart Crow, 88; The Gasparo da Salo Viola, Notebook: A Little Magazine, 89; Shakespeare in Italy: Out of the Lost Years, Hobart and William Smith Cols, 89; Lear in the Country Near Dover, The Upstart Crow, 95; Kit on Will, The Upstart Crow, 97. **CONTACT ADDRESS** Dept of English, Hobart & William Smith Cols, 300 Pulteney St, Geneva, NY, 14456-3382.

CUMMINGS, SHERWOOD
PERSONAL Born 03/05/1916, Weehawken, NJ, m, 1939, 2 children **DISCIPLINE** ENGLISH **EDUCATION** Univ Ill, BS, 38; Univ Wis, MA, 46, PhD(English), 51. **CAREER** Asst English, Univ Wis, 46-48; from instr to prof, Univ SDak, 48-63; assoc prof, 63-65, prof, 65-80, EMER PROF AM LIT, CALIF STATE UNIV, FULLERTON, 80-, Vis prof, Univ Calif Berkeley, 60-61. **MEMBERSHIPS** MLA; Am Studies Asn; Am Lit Group. **RESEARCH** Mark Twain and science; American literature 1870-1910. **SELECTED PUBLICATIONS** Auth, Twain,Mark Letters, Vol 2, 1867-1868, Resources Amer Lit Stud, Vol 0021, 95. **CONTACT ADDRESS** California State Univ, Fullerton, Fullerton, CA, 92634.

CUMMINS, WALTER M.
PERSONAL Born 02/02/1936, Long Branch, NJ, m, 1981, 2 children **DISCIPLINE** ENGLISH **EDUCATION** Rutgers Univ, BA, 57; Univ Iowa, MA & MFA, 62, PhD(English), 65. **CAREER** Instr English, Univ Iowa, 62-65; from asst prof to assoc prof, 65-74, PROF ENGLISH, FAIRLEIGH DICKINSON UNIV, 74-; Ed-in-Chief, The Lit Rev, 84-. **HONORS AND AWARDS** NJ State Coun on the Arts Fel, 82. **MEMBERSHIPS** AAUP; Col English Asn. **SELECTED PUBLICATIONS** Auth, A Stranger to the Deed, 68 & Into Temptation, 68, Caravelle; co-ed, The Other Sides of Reality, Bryd & Fraser, 72; Witness (story collection), Samisdat, 75; Jantadeln and the reformation (story), Lit Rev, 77; Kaiser-fraser (story), West Branch, 81; Where we live (story collection), Kans Quart, 83; Shifting Borders: East European Poetry of the eighties (edited collection), FDU Press, 93. **CONTACT ADDRESS** Dept of English, Fairleigh Dickinson Univ, 285 Madison Ave, Madison, NJ, 07940-1099. **EMAIL** cummins@alpha.fdu.edu

CUNNINGHAM, FRANK ROBERT
PERSONAL Born 08/15/1937, Philadelphia, PA **DISCIPLINE** ENGLISH, DRAMA **EDUCATION** Villanova Univ, AB, 60, MA, 62; Lehigh Univ, PhD(English), 70. **CAREER** Instr English, Lehigh Univ, 66-68; asst prof, Franklin & Marshall Col, 68-69, Fordham Univ, 70-71 & Kans State Univ, 71-73; vis asst prof, San Jose State Univ, 73-76; Sen Fulbright lectr, Jagillonian Univ, Krakow, 76-77; ASSOC PROF ENGLISH, UNIV SDAK, 78-, vis fel, Princeton Univ, summer 81. **MEMBERSHIPS** MLA; Fulbright Alumni Asn; Eugene O'Neill Soc; Am Asn Advan Humanities. **RESEARCH** Modern drama; 20th century American literature; film. **SELECTED PUBLICATIONS** Auth, Songs of American Experience, The Vision of Oneill and Melville, Mod Drama, Vol 0036, 93; Conversations with Oneill,Eugene, Mod Drama, Vol 0036, 93; Oneill Shakespeare, Mod Drama, Vol 0039, 96. **CONTACT ADDRESS** Dept of English, Univ SDak, 414 E Clark St, Vermillion, SD, 57069-2390.

CUNNINGHAM, KAREN
PERSONAL Born 10/09/1946, Woonsocket, RI, m, 1971 **DISCIPLINE** ENGLISH **EDUCATION** Sacramento State Coll, BA, 69; San Francisco State Coll, MA, 72; Univ CA, Santa Barbara, PhD, 85. **CAREER** Lectr, 85-87, Univ CA; Asst Prof, 87-93, Florida State Univ; Visiting Prof, spring 93, Princeton Univ; Assoc Prof, 93-present, Florida State Univ. **HONORS AND AWARDS** Princeton Univ, Shelby Cullom Davis Ctr for Hist Research Fel, spring 93; Florida State Univ, Univ Teaching Award, 93-94; Dartmouth Coll, Sch of Criticism and Theory, Tuition Grant, summer 94; Florida State Univ, Teaching Incentive Program Award, fall 94; Comnr, Florida Commission on the Status of Women, 95-present; Florida State Univ, Committee on Faculty Sabbaticals, one semester sabbatical, full support, fall 95; Florida State Univ, Committee on Faculty Research and Creativity, research grant, summer 96. **MEMBERSHIPS** Amer Assoc of Univ Women; Marlowe Soc of Amer; Modern Language Assoc; Renaissance Soc of Amer; Shakespeare Assoc of Amer; Soc for the Study of Early Modern Women; South Atlantic Modern Language Assoc; Women's Caucus of th south Atlantic Modern Language Assoc. **RESEARCH** Shakespeare; renaissance drama; cultural studies; law and literature. **SELECTED PUBLICATIONS** auth, Journal of Medieval and Renaissance Studies, A Spanish Heart in an english Body': The Ralegh Treason Trial and the Poetics of Proof, fall 92; Exemplaria: A Journal of Theory in Medieval and Renaissance Studies, She Learns As She Lies': Work and the Exemplary Female in English Early Modern Education, spring 95; Renaissance Drama, Female Fiedelities on Trial: Proof in the Howard Attainder and Cymbeline, spring 96. **CONTACT ADDRESS** English Dept, Florida State Univ, 216 WJB, Tallahassee, FL, 32306. **EMAIL** kcunning@english.fsu.edu

CURLEY, MICHAEL JOSEPH
PERSONAL Born 12/23/1942, Hempstead, NY, 2 children **DISCIPLINE** MEDIEVAL LITERATURE, LATIN **EDUCATION** Fairfield Univ, BA, 64; Harvard Univ, MA, 65; Univ Chicago, PhD, 72. **CAREER** Prof Eng, dir Honors Prog, Univ Puget Sound, 71-; NEH fel classics, Univ Tex, Austin, 77-78; Am Coun Learned Soc fel Celtic, Harvard Univ, 79-80; Graves fel Celtic, Univ Wales, Aberystwyth, 82-83. **MEMBERSHIPS** Medieval Acad Am; Medieval Assn of Pac. **RESEARCH** Latin literature; palaeography; Celtic. **SELECTED PUBLICATIONS** Auth & trans, Maarie de France, Purgatory of Saint Patrick, Binghamton: Center for Medieval and Renaissance Texts, 93; auth, Geoffrey of Monmouth, New York: Macmillan, 94. **CONTACT ADDRESS** Honor's Program, Univ of Puget Sound, 1500 N Warner St, Tacoma, WA, 98416-0005. **EMAIL** curley@ups.edu

CURLEY, THOMAS MICHAEL
PERSONAL Born 05/22/1943, Waltham, MA, m, 1970, 3 children **DISCIPLINE** ENGLISH LITERATURE **EDUCATION** Boston Col, BS, 65; Harvard Univ, MA, 66, PhD(English), 70. **CAREER** Teaching asst English, Harvard Univ, 67-70; asst prof, Fordham Univ, 70-72; asst prof, 72-76, assoc prof, 76-81, PROF ENGLISH, BRIDGEWATER STATE COL, 81-, Harvard Univ Dexter Travelling fel, 69; Am Bar Found fel legal hist & Friends of London House Found grant, 78; Woodrow Wilson fac develop grant, 79; Nat Endowment for Humanities summer grant, 80 & fel, 81. **HONORS AND AWARDS** Bridgewater Distinguished Service Award, 79 & 81. **MEMBERSHIPS** MLA; Am Soc Eighteenth Century Studies; Northeast Mod Lang Asn. **RESEARCH** Eighteenth century English literature; travel literature; Anglo-American law and politics in literature. **SELECTED PUBLICATIONS** Auth, The Story of the Voyage--Sea-Narratives in 18th-Century England, Scriblerian and the Kit-Cats, Vol 0029, 96. **CONTACT ADDRESS** Dept of English, Bridgewater State Col, Bridgewater, MA, 02324.

CURRAN, SONIA TERRIE
DISCIPLINE DEPARTMENT OF ENGLISH **EDUCATION** Univ Wis, PhD. **CAREER** Instr, 66-69, tchg asst, Youngstown State Univ, 70-73; instr, Univ Wis Extension Div, 73, asst to assoc prof, 73-, chemn, dept Eng, Providence Col , 76-78 & 92-96; annual evaluator, New Eng Assn of Sch and Col. **RESEARCH** Literary history of the English language. **SELECTED PUBLICATIONS** Auth, The Word Made Flesh: The Christian Aesthetic in Dorothy L. Sayers The Man Born to be King, As Her Wimsey Took Her: Critical Essays on the Work of Dorothy L. Sayers, Kent State Univ Press, 79; The Cultural Context of Chaucer's Canterbury Tales, Approaches to Teaching Chaucer'sCanterbury Tales, ed. by Joseph Gibaldi, MLA, 80. **CONTACT ADDRESS** Dept of Eng, Providence Col, EH 215, Providence, RI, 02918-0001. **EMAIL** stcurran@providence.edu

CURRAN, STUART ALAN
PERSONAL Born 08/03/1940, Detroit, MI **DISCIPLINE** ENGLISH LITERATURE, ROMANTICISM **EDUCATION** Univ Mich, BA, 62, MA, 63; Harvard Univ, PhD(English), 67. **CAREER** From asst prof to assoc prof English, Univ Wis, Madison, 67-74; PROF ENGLISH, UNIV PA, 74-, Nat Endowment for Humanities jr fel Shelley, 70-71; John Simon Guggenheim Found fel, 73-74; ed, Keats-Shelley J, 80-93. **MEMBERSHIPS** MLA; Keats-Shelley Asn; Byron Soc; Int Asn Univ Prof English. **RESEARCH** English romanticism; Renaissance and romanticism; poetic genres. **SELECTED PUBLICATIONS** Auth, Shelley's CENCI: Scorpions Ringed with Fire, Princeton Univ, 70; ed, Le Bossu and Voltaire on the Epic, Scholars' Facsimiles, 70; co-ed, Blake's Sublime Allegory: Essays on The Four Zoas, Milton & Jerusalem, Univ Wis, 73; auth, Shelley's Annus Mirabilis: The Maturing of an Epic Vision, Huntington Libr, 75; auth, Poetic Form and British Romanticism, Oxford, 86; ed, The Poems of Charlotte Smith, Oxford, 93; ed, Cambridge Companion to British Romanticism, Cambridge, 93; co-ed, Shelley: Poet and Legislator of the World, Johns Hopkins, 96; ed, Mary Shelley, Valperga, Oxford, 97. **CONTACT ADDRESS** Dept of English, Univ Pa, 3340 Walnut St, Philadelphia, PA, 19104-6173. **EMAIL** curran@english.upenn.edu

CURRIE, WILLIAM W.
PERSONAL Born 09/24/1945, Midland, MI, s **DISCIPLINE** LIBRARY SCIENCE/ENGLISH **EDUCATION** Mich State Univ, BA, 68, MA, 76; W Mich Univ, MLS, 80 **CAREER** Librn Geol Survey Div, Mich Dept Nat Res, 77-78; Asst librn, 81-90, LIBRN, 90- , FIRELANDS COL-BOWLING GREEN STATE UNIV. **HONORS AND AWARDS** Beta Phi Mu; Librn Hon Soc, 80. **MEMBERSHIPS** Am Libr Asn; Asn Col & Res Libr; Acad Libr Asn Ohio. **RESEARCH** Indexing and abstracting; Collection development. **SELECTED PUBLICATIONS** Auth, Annotated List of the Publications of the Mich Geological Survey, 1838-1977: Indexed by Author, Mineral and County, Mich Dept Nat Res, 78; The Inventory Process at a Two-Year Branch Campus Library, Comm & Jr Col Libr, 84; Evaluation of the Collection of a Two-Year Branch Campus by Using Textbook Citations, Comm & Jr Col Libr, 89. **CONTACT ADDRESS** 216 Fremont Avenue, Huron, OH, 44839. **EMAIL** wcurrie@bgnet.bgsu.edu

CURRY, ELIZABETH REICHENBACH
PERSONAL Born 01/31/1934, Evanston, IL, m, 1958, 1 child **DISCIPLINE** ENGLISH **EDUCATION** Northwestern Univ, BA, 56; Univ Wis, PhD, 63. **CAREER** Instr English, Univ WI-Milwaukee, 63-65; asst prof, Alfred Univ, 65-69; from asst prof to assoc prof, 69-76, prof eng, Slippery Rock Univ, 76, coordr, Women's Studies Newslett, 77-81; chief Ginger Hill adv, 81. **HONORS AND AWARDS** Res Found grant, Alfred Univ, 67-68; Slippery Rock Univ Sch of Hum Fine Arts Pres Award, 76. **MEMBERSHIPS** Nat Orgn Women; Phi Beta Kappa. **RESEARCH** Women's studies; art hist of women; female studies in lit. **SELECTED PUBLICATIONS** Auth, Rex Warner on the Allegorical Novel, Power Politics and the Contemporary Scene; What Land is This?, book of poetry, SRU Press, 97; Internationally published poetry, in: Oxford Mag, Interim, Centennial Rev, Epicophany, Nexus, Gaia, Psychol Poetica, and others. **CONTACT ADDRESS** Slippery Rock Univ, SWC Bldg, Slippery Rock, PA, 16057-1326.

CURTIN, MICHAEL
DISCIPLINE COMMUNICATIONS **EDUCATION** Brown Univ, AB, 77; Univ of Wis-Madison, MA, 86, PhD, 90. **CAREER** ASST PROF, DEPT OF TELECOMMUNICATIONS, 90-97, DIR, CULTURAL STUDIES PROGRAM, 94-, ASSOC PROF, DEPT OF COMMUN & CULTURE, IND UNIV, 97-; visiting scholar, Chinese Univ of Hong Kong, 97-98; lectr, Dept of Commun Arts, Univ of Wis, 89-90; producer, Wis Public Television, 87-90; Tokyo correspondent, National Public Radio, 82-84; producer, Youth News, 81-82; acting news dir, KPFA-FM, 80; reporter, KPFA-FM, 78-80; magazine freelance writer, 78-84. **HONORS AND AWARDS** Corecipient, Research fund, City Univ of Hong Kong, 98; corecip, Multidisciplinary Ventures Fund, 96; corecip, Funding for collaborative multimedia project involving Cultural Studies and the Res Center for Lang and Semiotic Studies, 95; Course Development Grants, Ind Univ, 95; corecip, Inter-Programs Research and Projects Grant; Charline Wackman Award; Warren C. Price Award; Wisconsin Alumni Research Foundation Fellow, University of Wis; Kaltenborn Foundation Award; Corporation for Public Broadcasting, Public Radio Program Award, 82; Champion Media Award for Economic Understanding, 83; Gabriel Award, 82. **MEMBERSHIPS** Ed Board, J of Critical Media Sciences; reviewer, J of Monographs, J of Commun, J of Asian Pacific Commun, Am Hist Rev, Am ethnologist, Cambridge Univ Press, Duke Univ Press. **RESEARCH** Cultural studies, globalization of media, media history, political economy of the culture industries, social implications of new media technologies, documentary. **SELECTED PUBLICATIONS** Auth, Redeeming the Wasteland: Television Documentary and Cold War Politics, Rutgers Univ Press, 95; auth, Packaging Reality: The Influence of Fictional Forms on the Early Development of Television Documentary 1955-1965, Journalism Monographs, 93; co-ed, Making and Selling Culture, Wesleyan Univ Press, 96; coed, The Revolution Wasn't Televised: Sixties Television and Social Conflict, Routledge, 97; coauth, Images of Trust, Economies of Suspicion: Hong Kong Media after 1997, Hist J of Film, Radio, and Television, 98; auth, Transgressive Imagery on Transnational Television, Con-temporary, 98. 18, no.2 (1998) **CONTACT ADDRESS** Dept of Commun and Culture, Indiana Univ, Bloomington, 809 E 7th St, Bloomington, IN, 47405. **EMAIL** mcurtin@indiana.edu

CUSHMAN, STEPHEN B.
PERSONAL Born 12/17/1956, Norwalk, CT, m, 1982, 2 children **DISCIPLINE** ENGLISH AND AMERICAN LITERATURE **EDUCATION** Cornell Univ, BA, 78; Yale Univ, MA, 80, M Phil, 81, PhD, 82. **CAREER** Asst prof, Univ VA, 82-88, assoc prof, 88-94; prof, Univ VA, 94-. **HONORS AND AWARDS** Phi Beta Kappa, 77; fel, Am Coun of Learned Societies, 86-87; All-University Teaching Award, Univ VA, 92; Fulbright lect, Greece, 93; Mayo Distinguished Teaching Prof, 94-97; fel, Inst on Violence, Survival, and Culture, VA Found for the Humanities, 97. **MEMBERSHIPS** Modern Lang Asn; William Carlos Williams Soc. **RESEARCH** Am poetry; representations of the Civil War. **SELECTED PUBLICATIONS** Auth, William Carlos Williams and the Meanings of Measure, Yale, 85; Fictions of Form in American Poetry, Princeton, 93; Blue Pajamas (poems), LA State, 98; co-ed, Nation of Letters: A Concise Anthology of American Literature, 2 vols, Brandy-

wine, 98; Bloody Promenade: The Civil War in Words, Pictures, and Everyday Life, VA, forthcoming 99. **CONTACT ADDRESS** Dept of English Language and Literature, Univ of Virginia, Bryan Hall, Charlottesville, PA, 22903. **EMAIL** sbc9g@virginia.edu

D

D'AVANZO, MARIO L.
PERSONAL Born 11/11/1931, New Britain, CT, d, 2 children **DISCIPLINE** ENGLISH **EDUCATION** Dartmouth Col, AB, 53; Trinity Col, Conn, MA, 54; Brown Univ, PhD(English), 63. **CAREER** From instr to assoc prof English, Providence Col, 60-68; assoc prof, 68-73, prof English, Queen's Col, 73-. **MEMBERSHIPS** MLA. **RESEARCH** English romantic poetry; American literature. **SELECTED PUBLICATIONS** Auth, Keats's Metaphors for the Poetic Imagination, Duke Univ, 67; Keats's and Vergil's underworlds: Source and meaning in Book II of Endymion, Keats-Shelley J, winter 67; King Francis, Lucrezia, and the figurative language of Andrea del Sarto, Tex Studies Lang & Lit, winter 68; The literary sources of My Kinsman, Major Molineaux: Shakespeare, Coleridge, Milton, Studies Short Fiction, spring 73; Fortitude and nature in Thoreau's Cape Cod, Esquire, 74; The Literary Art of the Bible: A Commentary, Am Press, 88; Robert Frost and the Romantics, Am Univ Press, 91. **CONTACT ADDRESS** Dept of English, Queens Col, CUNY, 6530 Kissena Blvd, Flushing, NY, 11367-1597.

D'HEMECOURT, JULES
DISCIPLINE MASS COMMUNICATIONS **EDUCATION** Greenwich Univ, PhD, 91. **CAREER** Asst prof, La State Univ; atty; ling consult, MCI Telecommun. **SELECTED PUBLICATIONS** Auth, Breakfast TV, An Analysis of Morning Media, Ctr for Jour Stud, Gr Brit, 81; Feminization of Mass Communications in the Southern United States, Popular Cult Asn of the S; Am Cult Asn in the S, 90; Career Paths, Prof Communicator, Women in Commun mag, 94; coauth, Broadcast News English, 83. **CONTACT ADDRESS** The Manship Sch of Mass Commun, Louisiana State Univ, Baton Rouge, LA, 70803. **EMAIL** jdhemec@unix1.sncc.lsu.edu

DABNEY, ROSS H.
DISCIPLINE ENGLISH **EDUCATION** Princeton Univ, AB; Harvard, PhD. **CAREER** Chr and prof Eng, Sweet Briar Col. **HONORS AND AWARDS** Consult ed, Dickens Studies Annual. **RESEARCH** Research focus on parents and children in the Eng novel. **SELECTED PUBLICATIONS** Auth, Love and Property in the Novels of Dickens. **CONTACT ADDRESS** Sweet Briar Col, Sweet Briar, VA, 24595. **EMAIL** dabney@sbc.edu

DACE, TISH
PERSONAL Born 09/13/1941, Washington, DC, 2 children **DISCIPLINE** DRAMATIC LITERATURE & WRITING **EDUCATION** Sweet Briar Col, BA, 63; Kans State Univ, MA, 67, PhD(English lit), 71. **CAREER** Instr speech & drama, Kans State Univ, 61-71; asst prof speech & drama & bus mgr dept, 71-74, assoc prof speech & drama & chmn dept, John Jay Col Criminal Justice, 74-80, actg chmn dept, 78, chmn, 79-80; prof English & Drama & dean, Col of Arts & Sci; Univ Mass Dartmouth, 80-86; prof of English, 86-97; Chancelor Prof, 97-; Kans State Univ fac res award, 69-70; Folger Shakespeare Library Research Grant , 70; City Univ New York fac res awards, 72 & 73; asst ed, Shakespearean Res & Opportunities, 71-75; theatre critic, Soho Weekly News, 77-82, Other Stages, 78-82, The Villager, 82 & The Advocate, 82-. **HONORS AND AWARDS** New York Native, 83-89; UMD Scholar of the Year Award, 97. **MEMBERSHIPS** Am Soc Theatre Res; Theatre Libr Asn; British Theatre Inst: Am Theatre Critics Asn; Outer Critics Circle. **RESEARCH** Modern drama; contemporary British drama; contemporary American drama. **SELECTED PUBLICATIONS** Auth, LeRoi Jones: A Negerek Mozgalmanak Dramairoja, Nagyvilag, 12/70; LeRoi Jones (Imamu Amiri Baraka): A Checklist of Works by and About Him, Nether, London, 71; On Jean Genet and Martin Esslin or here absurdist, there absurdist, everywhere ..., Kans Quart, spring 71; coauth, The Theatre Student: Modern Theatre and Drama, Richards Rosen, 73; auth, LeRoi Jones/Amiri Baraka: From Muse to Malcolm to Mao, Village Voice, 8/77; contribr, Black American Writers, St Martin's, 78; Great Writers of the English Language, St Martin's, 79; Contemporary Dramatists, 82; Langston Hughes: the Contemproary Reviews, London, Cambridge University Press, 97. **CONTACT ADDRESS** Col of Arts & Sci, Southeastern Massachusetts Univ, 285 Old Westport Rd, North Dartmouth, MA, 02747-2300. **EMAIL** tdace@umassd.edu

DADDARIO, GINA
DISCIPLINE COMMUNICATOIN STUDIES **EDUCATION** Univ NC, BA, 76; Univ Md, MA, 82; Univ Mass, PhD, 88. **CAREER** Prof. **SELECTED PUBLICATIONS** Auth, Women's Sports and Spectacle: Gendered Coverage and the Olympic Games. **CONTACT ADDRESS** Dept of Communication, State Univ NY Cortland, PO Box 2000, Cortland, NY, 13045-0900. **EMAIL** Daddario@cortland.edu

DAHOOD, ROGER
PERSONAL Born 12/21/1942, New York, NY **DISCIPLINE** ENGLISH LITERATURE **EDUCATION** Colgate Univ, BA, 64; Stanford Univ, MA, 67, PhD, 70. **CAREER** Asst prof, 70-76, assoc prof, 76-85, prof eng, Univ AZ, 85. **MEMBERSHIPS** Int Arthurian Soc; Medieval Acad Am; Medieval Asn Pacific. **RESEARCH** Old and Middle Eng lit. **SELECTED PUBLICATIONS** Auth, Dubious readings in the French and Hale text of The Avowing of King Arthur, 71, A lexical puzzle in Ancrene Wisse, 78 & Four 13th century proverbs in MS Harley 47, 79, Notes & Queries; A Note on Beowulf, 1104-8a, Medium Aevum, 80; ed, The Avowing of King Arthur, 84; co-ed and transl, Ancrene Riwle: Introduction and part I, 84; Auth, Ancrene Wisse, the Katherine Group, and the Wohunge Group, In: Middle English Prose: A Critical Guide to Major Authors and Genres, 84; Four English Proverbs in the Hand of John Stow, Notes & Queries, 85; Design in Part I of Ancrene Riwle, Medium Aevum, 87; The Use of Coloured Initials and Other Division Maarkers in Early Versions of Ancrene Riwle, In: Medieval English Studies Presented to George Kane, 88; Variants of the Middle English Warning in William of Canterbury's Life of Becket, Parergon, 93; Hugh de Morville, William of Cantebury, and Anecdotal Evidence for English language History, Speculum 94; The Current State of Ancrene Wisse Group Studies, Medieval English Newsletter, 97. **CONTACT ADDRESS** Dept of Eng, Univ of AZ, Mod Lang(s) Bldg, Tucson, AZ, 85721-0001. **EMAIL** rdahood@u.arizona.edu

DAIGLE, LENNET
PERSONAL Born 01/28/1948, White Castle, LA, m, 3 children **DISCIPLINE** ENGLISH **EDUCATION** Univ Dallas TX, BA, 70; Univ SC Columbia, MA, 71; PhD, 76. **CAREER** Chmn & asst prof, 77-82, assoc prof, 82-84, Coastal Georgia Comm Col; Fulbright, assoc prof, 88-89, Tunghai Univ, Taiwan; chmn, assoc prof, 84-90 Georgia SW Col; dean, 95-, N Georgia Col & St Univ. **RESEARCH** Higher ed admin; composition theory, renaissance lit. **CONTACT ADDRESS** Sch of Arts and Letters, No Georgia Col and St Univ, Dahlonega, GA, 30597.

DAILEY, JOSEPH
DISCIPLINE ORGANIZATIONAL AND INTERPERSONAL COMMUNICATION **EDUCATION** Marquette Univ, MA; Univ Ill, PhD. **CAREER** Law, Caroll Col. **SELECTED PUBLICATIONS** Auth, The Reluctant Candidate: Dwight Eisenhower in 1951. **CONTACT ADDRESS** Carroll Col, Wisconsin, 100 N East Ave, Waukesha, WI, 53186.

DALE, HELEN
DISCIPLINE ENGLISH LITERATURE **EDUCATION** NY Univ, MA; Univ Wis Madison, PhD. **CAREER** Fac. **RESEARCH** Composition theory; collaborative writing; ethics of qualitative research; the links between theory and practice for student teachers; collaborative self-study as reform in teacher education; high school/university literacy partnerships. **SELECTED PUBLICATIONS** Auth, Co-authoring in the Classroom: Creating an Environment for Effective Collaboration. **CONTACT ADDRESS** Dept of English, Univ of Wisconsin, Eau Claire, Hibbard Hall 412, PO Box 4004, Eau Claire, WI, 54702-4004. **EMAIL** dalehn@uwec.edu

DALEY, GUILBERT ALFRED
PERSONAL Born 12/31/1923, Washington, DC, m **DISCIPLINE** SPEECH, THEATRE **EDUCATION** Catholic Univ of Amer, BA 1949, MA 1952; Univ of NC, LDA 1968; So IL Univ, PhD 1978. **CAREER** Shaw Univ, Raleigh NC, asst prof 1953-62; NC High School Drama Assoc, exec dir 1953-62; Intercollegiate Drama Assoc, exec dir 1956-60; IDA, pres 1960-62; The Crescent, natl editor 1978-79, 1981-; Coppin State Coll, prof & coord speech/theatre 1962-. **HONORS AND AWARDS** Carolina Playmakers Scholarship 1960; Teaching Fellow SIU Carbondale. **MEMBERSHIPS** Mem AAUP; Amer Theatre Assn; Coll Language Assn; Speech Assn of Amer; mem treas Gr Baltimore Arts Council 1966-69, pres 1969-71; pres, immediate past natl dir of educ, Distinguished Service Chap, Phi Beta Sigma; vice pres Baltimore Pan-Hellenic Council; pres Zeta Sigma Chap Phi Beta Sigma Frat Inc; pres Wm T Dorsey Educ Loan Fund 1984; founder, advisor, Delta, Delta Chap, Phi Beta Sigma Frat, Coppin State Coll, Baltimore MD; 100 Black Men of MD; pres, Baltimore Chap, Pan Hellenic Council; editor, The Crescent, 8 years; vp, African Amer Theatre, 1993. **CONTACT ADDRESS** Coordinator Speech Theatre, Coppin State Col, 2500 W North Ave, Baltimore, MD, 21216.

DALY, BRENDA O.
PERSONAL Born 06/27/1941, Hibbing, MN, d, 1 child **DISCIPLINE** ENGLISH **EDUCATION** Univ NDak, BA, 63; Mankato State Univ, MA; Univ Minn, PhD, 85. **CAREER** Dept Eng, Iowa St Univ **HONORS AND AWARDS** Ruud Scholarship, Univ Minn, 82; Doctoral Dissertation Fellow, Univ Minn, 83-84; Aff Schol, Ctr for Adv Feminist Stud, Univ Minn, 86-88, 93-94; Res Salary Support, Iowa State Univ, 88; Fac Improvement Grant, Iowa State Univ, 90; Course Dev Grant, Iowa State Univ, 91; Res Incentive Grant, Iowa State Col of LAS, 93; Fac Improvement Leave, Iowa State Univ, 93; Fulbright Fellow to Norway (declined), 95; Proj, Aware Grant, Iowa State Univ Ctr for Tchng Excellence, 96. **RESEARCH** American women's narratives; narrative theory; feminist theory; autobiographical criticism; pedagogy. **SELECTED PUBLICATIONS** Auth, Sexual Politics in Two Collections of Joyce Carol Oates's Short Fiction, Stud in Short Fic, 32, 83-93, 95; auth, Marriage as Emancipatory Metaphor: Women Wedded to Teaching and Writing in Joyce Carol Oates's Academic Fiction, Critique, 37:4, 270-88, 96; auth, Lavish Self-Divisions: The Novels of Joyce Carol Oates, Univ Press of Miss, 96; auth, Authoring a Life: A Woman's Survival in and Through Literary Studies, SUNY Press, 98; auth, Where is She Going, Where Are We Going, at Century's End? The Girl as Site of Cultural Conflict in Joyce Carol Oates's The Model, The Girl, St Martin's Press, 1-20, 98. **CONTACT ADDRESS** Dept of English, Iowa State Univ, 253 Ross Hall, Ames, IA, 50011.

DALY, ROBERT
PERSONAL Born 06/17/1943, Wayne County, OH, m, 1966, 2 children **DISCIPLINE** AMERICAN AND ENGLISH LITERATURE **EDUCATION** Univ Akron, BA, 65, MA, 67; Cornell Univ, PhD(English), 72. **CAREER** Instr English, Iowa State Univ, 67-69; asst prof, 73-77, assoc chmn dept, 80-81, ASSOC PROF ENGLISH, STATE UNIV NY, BUFFALO, 77-, Leverhulme fel England, The Leverhulme Trust, 72-73; consult & rev, Nat Endowment Humanities, Media Programs, 77-; Guggenheim fel, 79-80; vis prof, Cornell Univ, 80, & Chapman Col, 82. **HONORS AND AWARDS** Chancellor's Award for Excellence in Teaching, State Univ NY, 77. **MEMBERSHIPS** MLA. **RESEARCH** Early American literature; 17th-century English literature; modern American literature. **SELECTED PUBLICATIONS** Auth, The Fictive and the Imaginary, Charting Literary Anthropology, Comp Lit Stud, Vol 0032, 95; We Have Really No Country At All--Hawthorne Reoccupations of History, Arachne, Vol 0003, 96; Sinful Self, Saintly Self, the Puritan Experience of Poetry, Early Amer Lit, Vol 0029, 94. **CONTACT ADDRESS** 203 Callodine Ave, Amherst, NY, 14226.

DAMERON, JOHN LASLEY
PERSONAL Born 07/29/1925, Burlington, NC, m, 1949, 2 children **DISCIPLINE** ENGLISH **EDUCATION** Univ NC, BS, 50, MA, 52; Univ Tenn, PhD(English), 62. **CAREER** Instr English, Emory & Henry Col, 53-55 & Univ Tenn, 58-59 & 61-62; from asst prof to assoc prof, 62-72, PROF ENGLISH, MEMPHIS STATE UNIV, 72-, Nat Endowment Humanities grant, 67-68. **MEMBERSHIPS** MLA; Bibliog Soc Am; SAtlantic Mod Lang Asn; Cambridge Bibliog Soc; Poe Studies Asn (pres, 78-). **RESEARCH** Nineteenth century American and English literature; American authors, mid-19th century; bibliography of the criticism of Edgar Allan Poe. **SELECTED PUBLICATIONS** Auth, Melville and Scoresby on Whiteness--Moby-Dick by Melville,Herman and Scoresby,William Works on the Arctic and Whaling, Eng Stud, Vol 0074, 93; Poe Pym and Scoresby on Polar Cataracts, Resources for American Lit Stud, Vol 0021, 95; Simms, A Literary-Life, Miss Quart, Vol 0048, 95. **CONTACT ADDRESS** Dept of English, Memphis State Univ, Memphis, TN, 38152.

DAMES, NICHOLAS
DISCIPLINE ENGLISH LITERATURE **EDUCATION** Wash Univ, BA, 92; Harvard Univ, PhD, 98. **CAREER** Asst prof. **RESEARCH** Nineteenth-century British narrative and memory. **SELECTED PUBLICATIONS** Pub, on Charlotte Bronte. **CONTACT ADDRESS** Dept of Eng, Columbia Col, New York, 2960 Broadway, New York, NY, 10027-6902.

DAMICO, HELEN
DISCIPLINE OLD AND MIDDLE ENGLISH LITERATURE **EDUCATION** NY Univ, PhD, 80. **CAREER** Instr, Univ NMex, 81-. **SELECTED PUBLICATIONS** Ed, Medieval Scholarship: Biographical Studies on the Formation of a Discipline; Heroic Poetry in the Anglo-Saxon Period; New Readings on Women in Old English Literature. **CONTACT ADDRESS** Univ NMex, Albuquerque, NM, 87131.

DAMMERS, RICHARD HERMAN
PERSONAL Born 05/27/1943, Passaic, NJ, m, 1968, 1 child **DISCIPLINE** ENGLISH LITERATURE **EDUCATION** Holy Cross Col, Mass, 65; Univ Va, MA, 66; Univ Notre Dame, PhD(English), 71. **CAREER** Instr English, Holy Cross Col, Mass, 66-67; asst prof, 71-76, ASSOC PROF ENGLISH, ILL STATE UNIV, 76-, Folger Shakespeare Libr fel. **MEMBERSHIPS** Am Soc 18th Century Studies. **RESEARCH** Restoration drama; 18th century literature. **SELECTED PUBLICATIONS** Auth, A Checklist of New Plays and Entertainments on the London Stage, 1700-1737, Scriblerian and the Kit-Cats, Vol 0026, 93. **CONTACT ADDRESS** Dept of English, Illinois State Univ, Normal, IL, 61761.

DAMON-BACH, LUCINDA
DISCIPLINE ENGLISH **EDUCATION** Univ California-Berkeley, BA, 81; Middlebury Col, MA, 85; MA, 85, PhD, 95, SUNY (Buffalo). **CAREER** Preceptor, Harvard Univ, 91-97; Adjunct Prof, Boston Col, 97-98; Asst Prof, Salem State Col, 98-99. **CONTACT ADDRESS** English Dept, Salem State Col, 352 Lafayette St, Salem, MA, 01970. **EMAIL** lucinda.damonbach@salem.mass.edu

DAMROSCH, DAVID N.
PERSONAL Born 04/13/1953, Bar Harbor, ME, m, 1974, 3 children **DISCIPLINE** COMPARITIVE AND ENGLISH LITERATURE **EDUCATION** Yale Univ, BA, 75, PhD(comp lit), 80. **CAREER** Speechwriter & ed, Off Special Asst to the Pres for Health, White House, Washington, DC, 79; asst prof, 80-; prof comp lit, Columbia Univ, 87-. **MEMBERSHIPS** MLA; Am Comp Lit Asn. **RESEARCH** The novel; epic and romance; scripture. **SELECTED PUBLICATIONS** Auth, The Narrative Covenant, 87; We Scholars, 95; ed, The Longman Anthology of British Literature, 98. **CONTACT ADDRESS** Dept of English & Comp Lit, Columbia Univ, 2960 Broadway, New York, NY, 10027-6900. **EMAIL** dnd2@columbia.edu

DAMROSCH, LEO
PERSONAL Born 09/14/1941, Manila, Philippines, m, 1983, 4 children **DISCIPLINE** ENGLISH LITERATURE **EDUCATION** Yale Univ, BA, 63; Cambridge Univ, MA, 66; Princeton Univ, PhD, 68. **CAREER** Asst prof to full prof, Eng, Univ Va, 68-83; prof, Univ Md, 83-89; PROF, HARVARD UNIV, 89-. **RESEARCH** 18th century British and French literature **SELECTED PUBLICATIONS** Auth, Symbol and Truth in Blake's Myth, Princeton Univ Press, 80; auth, God's Plot and Man's Stories: Studies in the Fictional Imagination from Milton to Fielding, Univ Chicago Press, 85; auth, The Imaginative World of Alexander Pope, Univ Calif Press, 87; Fictions of Reality in the Age of Hume and Johnson, Univ Wis Press, 89; auth, The Sorrows of the Quaker Jesus: James Nayler and the Puritan Crackdown on the Free Spirit, Harvard Univ Press, 96. **CONTACT ADDRESS** Barker Center, Harvard Univ, 12 Quincy St, Cambridge, MA, 02138. **EMAIL** damrosch@fas.harvard.edu

DANCE, DARYL CUMBER
PERSONAL Born 01/17/1938, Richmond, VA, m **DISCIPLINE** ENGLISH **EDUCATION** VA State Coll, AB 1957, MA 1963; Univ of VA, PhD 1971. **CAREER** VA State Coll, asst prof of English 1962-72; VA Commonwealth Univ, asst prof of English 1972-78, assoc prof of English 1978-85; prof of English 1985-92; editorial advisor, Journal of West Indian Literature 1986-; University of California, Santa Barbara, visiting professor of African-American studies, 1986-87; University of Richmond, professor English dept, 1992-. **MEMBERSHIPS** Danforth Assoc 1964-; adv editor Black Amer Lit Forum 1978-. **SELECTED PUBLICATIONS** Auth, Shuckin' & Jivin', Folklore from Contemporary Black Americans, 1978; Fifty Caribbean Writers 1986; Long Gone The Mecklenburg Six & The Theme of Escape in Black Literature, 1987; New World Adams: Conversations with West Indian Writers, 1992; Honey, Hush! An Anthology of African American Women's Humor, 1998. **CONTACT ADDRESS** English, Univ of Richmond, Richmond, VA, 23173.

DANDRIDGE, RITA BERNICE
PERSONAL Richmond, VA **DISCIPLINE** ENGLISH AND AMERICAN LITERATURE **EDUCATION** Va Union Univ, BA, 61; Howard Univ, MA, 63, PhD(English), 70. **CAREER** Asst prof English lit, Morgan State Col, 64-71 & Univ Toledo, 71-74; assoc prof, 74-78, PROF ENGLISH, NORFOLK STATE COL, 78-. **MEMBERSHIPS** MLA; Col Lang Asn; Nat Coun Teachers English. **RESEARCH** Twentieth century Black literature, Black woman's novel and multi-ethnic literature. **SELECTED PUBLICATIONS** Auth, Bordering on the Body, the Racial Matrix of Modern Fiction and Culture, Amer Lit, Vol 0067, 95; Fragments of the Ark, African Amer Rev, Vol 0030, 96. **CONTACT ADDRESS** Dept of English, Norfolk State Col, 2401 Corprew Ave, Norfolk, VA, 23504-3993.

DANE, JOSEPH A.
PERSONAL Born 09/29/1947, Portland, ME **DISCIPLINE** MEDIEVAL LITERATURE **EDUCATION** Bowdoin Col, BA, 69; Tulane Univ, MA, 76; Columbia Univ, PhD(comp lit), 79. **CAREER** Asst prof classics, Univ SDak, 79-80; asst prof English, Bowdoin Col, 81-82; ASST PROF ENGLISH, UNIV SOUTHERN CALIF, 82-, Nat Endowment for Humanities fel, 80-81. **MEMBERSHIPS** MLA; Mediaeval Acad. **SELECTED PUBLICATIONS** Auth, On the Shadowy Existence of the Medieval Pricking Wheel, Scriptorium, Vol 0050, 96; The Notions of Text and Variant in the Prologue to Chaucer Legend of Good Women--Ms,Gg, Lines 127-38, Papers of the Bibliographical Society of America, Vol 0087, 93; Chaucer and the Fictions of Gender, Huntington Lib Quart, Vol 0056, 93; Queynte--Some Rime and Some Reason on a Chaucer Ian Pun, Jour Eng and Ger Phil, Vol 0095, 96; On Correctness--A Note on Some Press Variants in Thynne 1532 Edition of Chaucer, Lib, Vol 0017, 95; The Importance of Chaucer, Huntington Lib Quart, Vol 0056, 93; The Notion of Ring Composition in Classical and Medieval Studies--A Comment on Critical Method and Illusion, Neuphilologische Mitteilungen, Vol 0094, 93; Which-Is-The-Iustice-Which-Is-The-Theefe-Shakespeare--Variants of Transposition in the Text Of King Lear, Notes and Queries, Vol 0042, 95; On the Shadowy Existence of the Medieval Pricking Wheel, Scriptorium, Vol 0050, 96; What is a Text--Manuscripts, Literary Scholarship, Huntington Lib Quart, Vol 0058, 96; The Syntaxis-Recepta of Chaucer Prologue to the Millers Tale, Lines 3159-61, Eng Lang Notes, Vol 0031, 94; Bibliographical History Versus Bibliographical Evidence, the Plowmans Tale and Early Chaucer Editions, Bulletin John Rylands Univ Lib Manchester, Vol 0078, 96; Perfect Order and Perfected Order--The Evidence from Press-Variants of Early Seventeenth-Century Quartos, Papers Bibliog Soc Am, Vol 0090, 96; Who Is Buried in Chaucer Tomb--Prolegomena, Huntington Lib Quart, Vol 0057, 94. **CONTACT ADDRESS** Univ So Calif, LOS ANGELES, CA, 90007.

DANFORD, ROBERT E.
PERSONAL Born 01/18/1947, Kingsport, TN, m **DISCIPLINE** ENGLISH & LIBRARY SCIENCE **EDUCATION** ETSU, BS, 69; Univ Tn, MA, 71, MSLS, 73. **CAREER** Head of cataloging, 77-88, Washington & Lee Univ; librn, 88-96, Hartwich Col; libr dir, 96-, Widener Univ. **MEMBERSHIPS** ALA; ACRL; EDUCOM; CAUSES; ASIS. **RESEARCH** Inst organization; facilities mgmt & planning. **CONTACT ADDRESS** Wolfgram Mem, Widener Univ, Chester, PA, 19013. **EMAIL** robert.e.danford@widener.edu

DANIEL, HERSHEY
PERSONAL Born 02/12/1931, New York, NY, m, 1965, 2 children **DISCIPLINE** INTERDISCPLINARY STUDIES **EDUCATION** Cooper Union, BS, 53; Univ Tenn, PhD, 61. **CAREER** PROF, UNIV CINCINNATI, 62-. **HONORS AND AWARDS** Fulbright fel, 75 & 91; Tau Beta Pi teaching award, 70 & 72, 1st place, Cincinnati Eds Assn fiction writing, 75; Clinical Research Award, Amer Soc **MEMBERSHIPS** Int Soc for Systems Sciences; Amer Aging Assn; Amer Inst Chemical Engineers; Am Soc Bariatric Physicians. **RESEARCH** Aging, Evolving Systems, Living humans and Inanimate corporations and the universe. **SELECTED PUBLICATIONS** Ed, Chemical Engineering in Medicine and Biology, Plenum, 67; auth, In God We Trust, Vantage, 67; ed, Blood Oxygenation, Plenum, 70; auth, Everyday Science, Doubleday, 71; Transport Analysis, Plenum, 73; Lifespan and Factors Affecting It, CC Thomas, 74; A New Age-Scale for Humans, Lexington Books, 80; Must We Grow Old: From Pauling to Prigogine to Toynbee, Basal Books, 84; Diagnosing and Organizational Bureaucracy, Basal Books, 84; Entropy, Infinity, and God, Basal Books, 97. **CONTACT ADDRESS** 726 Lafayette Ave., Cincinnati, OH, 45220-1053.

DANIELL, BETH
DISCIPLINE ENGLISH LITERATURE **EDUCATION** Univ Tex, PhD, 86. **CAREER** Dept Eng, Clemson Univ **RESEARCH** Rhetoric, composition. **SELECTED PUBLICATIONS** Auth, Deena's Story: The Discourse of the Other, Jour Adv Comp, 96; A Communion of Friendship: Literacy, Orality, Voice, and Self Outside the Academy, Literacy Networks, 96; Composing (as) Power, College Comp and Comm, 94; Theory, Theory-Talk, and Composition, Writing Theory and Critical Theory, MLA, 94; coauth, Resisting Writing/Resisting Writing Teachers, The Subject is Writing, Boynton/Cook Heinemann, 93. **CONTACT ADDRESS** Clemson Univ, 608 Strode, Clemson, SC, 29634. **EMAIL** dbeth@clemson.edu

DANIELS, LEANNE
DISCIPLINE MEDIA AND SOCIETY, MEDIA MANAGEMENT, AND INTERNATIONAL NEWS AND COMMUNICATI **EDUCATION** Ind Univ, PhD, 94. **CAREER** Asst prof, La State Univ. **RESEARCH** Decision making in media organizations. **SELECTED PUBLICATIONS** Coauth, Public Opinion on Investigative Reporting in the 1980s, Jour Quart, 92. **CONTACT ADDRESS** The Manship Sch of Mass Commun, Louisiana State Univ, Baton Rouge, LA, 70803. **EMAIL** ldaniel@unix1.sncc.lsu.edu

DANIELS, RICHARD
DISCIPLINE CREATIVE WRITING **EDUCATION** Ohio State Univ, BA, 64, MA, 66, PhD, 72. **CAREER** Engl, Oregon St Univ. **RESEARCH** Mid and old Eng lit & lang. **SELECTED PUBLICATIONS** Auth, Uxor Noah: A Raven or a Dove, Chaucer Rev, 79; Yirmiyahu Yovel's Spinoza and other Heretics, Minn Rev, 91; Complaint, Fiction Int, 91; Larry's Song, Minn Rev, 93; Dream House, Kanasa Quart, 93. **CONTACT ADDRESS** Oregon State Univ, Corvallis, OR, 97331-4501. **EMAIL** rdaniels@orst.edu

DARBY, BARBARA
DISCIPLINE DRAMA, EIGHTEENTH-CENTURY LITERATURE **EDUCATION** Univ Lethbridge, AB, 88; Queen's Univ, MA, 89, PhD, 90-94. **CAREER** Asst prof, 98-99; part-time instr, 97-98; part-time instr, Mount Saint Vincent Univ, 95-97; adj asst prof, Queen's Univ, 94-95; tchg asst, Queen's Univ, 93-94; res asst, Queen's Univ, 91-92; tchg asst, Queen's Univ, 90-91; sessional instr, Univ Lethbridge, 89-90; tchg asst, Queen's Univ, 88-89; marking asst, Lethbridge Commun Col Learning Ctr, 88-89. **HONORS AND AWARDS** Postdoc fel, Soc Sci and Hum Res Coun of Can, 95-97; doc fel, Soc Sci and Hum Res Coun of Can, 90-94; Sir James Lougheed Grad award, Government of Alberta, 91-93; grad award, Queen's Univ, 88; gold medal, Univ Lethbridge Fac of Arts and Sci, 88; Louise B McKinney award, Government of Alberta, 97. **RESEARCH** Women writers, feminist theory, performance theory. **SELECTED PUBLICATIONS** Auth, Frances Burney, Dramatist: Gender, Performance, and the Late-Eighteenth-Century Stage, Univ Press of Ky, 97; Frances Burney's Dramatic Mothers, Eng Stud in Can, 97; "Tragedy, Feminism, and Frances Burney's Edwy and Elgiva," Jour of Dramatic Theory and Criticism, 97; "Bondage and Slavery in Eighteenth-Century Poetry by Women," Lumen 14, 95; Love, Chance, and the Arranged Marriage: Lady Mary Rewrites Marivaux, Restoration and Eighteenth-Century Theatre Research, 94. **CONTACT ADDRESS** Dept of Eng, Dalhousie Univ, Halifax, NS, B3H 3J5. **EMAIL** bdarby@is.dal.ca

DARSEY, JAMES
PERSONAL Born 01/11/1953, Sarasota, FL **DISCIPLINE** COMMUNICATION/RHETORIC STUDIES **EDUCATION** Fla State Univ, BA, 75; Purdue Univ, MA, 78; Univ Wisc, PhD, 85. **CAREER** Vis asst prof, Univ Iowa, 86-88; asst prof, Ohio State Univ, 88-95; asst prof, Northern Ill State Univ, 95-98; assoc prof, 98-. **HONORS AND AWARDS** Diamond Anniversary Book Award from Nat Commun Assoc, 98. **MEMBERSHIPS** Nat Commun Assoc; Central States Commun assoc; Modern Lang Assoc; Int Assoc for the Study of Argumentation. **RESEARCH** Radical rhetoric; political rhetoric; gay & lesbian rhetoric; hist of rhetorical theory; rhetorical-critical methods. **SELECTED PUBLICATIONS** Auth, Die Non: Gay Liberation and the Rhetoric of Pure Tolerance, Queer Words/Queer Images: Communication and the Construction of Homosexuality, NY Univ Press, 45-76, 94; Must We All be Rhetorical Theorists?: An Anti-Democratic Inquiry, Western J of Commun, vol 58, 164-181, 94; auth, Joe McCarthy's Fantastic Moment, Commun Monographs, vol 62, 65-86, 95; auth, The Prophetic Tradition and Radical Rhetoric in America, NY Univ Press, 97; auth, The Voice of Exile: W.E.B. DuBois and the Quest for Culture, Rhetoric and Community: Case Studies in Unity and Fragmentation, Univ of SC Press, 98. **CONTACT ADDRESS** Dept of Commun, No Illinois Univ, Watson Hall 210, DaKalb, IL, 060115. **EMAIL** jdarsey@niu.edu

DASH, IRENE GOLDEN
PERSONAL New York, NY, 2 children **DISCIPLINE** ENGLISH DRAMATIC LITERATURE, WOMEN'S STUDIES **EDUCATION** Beaver Col, BA; Columbia Univ, MA, PhD(English), 72. **CAREER** Lectr English, Queensborough Community Col, City Univ NY, 70-71; lectr, 72-74, ASST PROF ENGLISH, HUNTER COL, CITY UNIV NY, 74-, Int corresp, World Shakepeare Bibliog, 81. **MEMBERSHIPS** Shakespeare Asn Am; Am Soc 18th Century Studies; Am Name Soc; NCTE; Am Soc Theatre Res. **RESEARCH** Shakespeare's women. **SELECTED PUBLICATIONS** Auth, Single-Sex Retreats in 2 Early-Modern Dramas--Shakespeare,William and Cavendish, Margaret--Loves Labors Lost and the Convent of Pleasure, Shakespeare Quart, Vol 0047, 96. **CONTACT ADDRESS** 161 W 16th St, New York, NY, 10011.

DATES, JANNETTE LAKE
PERSONAL Baltimore, Maryland, m, 1960 **DISCIPLINE** COMMUNICATIONS **EDUCATION** Coppin State College, BS; The Johns Hopkins Univ, MEd; Univ of Maryland at College Park, PhD. **CAREER** Baltimore City Public School System, classroom demonstration teacher, 1958-63, televsion demonstration teacher, 1964-69; Morgan State Coll and Goucher College, instructor, 1970-72; Morgan State Univ, instructor, 1972-77, coordinator of television projects, 1973-80, asst prof, 1977-80; Howard Univ, asst prof, 1981-85, sequence coordinator, 1981-85; Coppin State College, associate prof, 1985-87, video production service dir, 1985-87; Howard Univ School of Communications, associate dean, 1987-92; Howard Univ, associate prof, 1990-; Howard Univ School of Communications, acting dean, 1993-96, dean, 1996-. **HONORS AND AWARDS** California State Univ at Dominquez Hills, Young, Gifted and Black Distinguished Resident Scholar, 1991; Freedom Forum Media Studies Center Fellowship, 1992; Gustavus Myer Award, co-editor, best book on human rights, 1990. **MEMBERSHIPS** Baltimore City Cable Television Commission, commissioner, 1979-81, education task force chairwoman, 1979-81; Baltimore Cable Access Corporation, pres, 1982-86, vice pres, 1986-88; Mayor's Cable Advisory Commission, education task force chairwoman, 1988-90, member, 1990-94. **SELECTED PUBLICATIONS** Co-author: Split Image: African Americans in the Mass Media, 1993; author: "African American TV Images Shaped By Others," Crisis magazine, December 1992; "Quantity, Not Quality, Suffices for Our TV Images," p 8, Sept 30-Oct 6, 1992; "This TV Season Will Be Blacker, But Will It Be Better?" September 13, 1992; reviewer: "A Review of the book Enlightened Racism," Journal of Broadcasting and Electronic Media, Fall 1993; "A Review of Said's Culture and Imperialism," Critical Studies in Mass Communications, Fall 1995. **CONTACT ADDRESS** Dean, School of Communications, Howard Univ, 525 Bryant St, NW, W2-203-G, Washington, VT, 20059. **EMAIL** jondates@aol.com

DAUGHERTY, TRACY
DISCIPLINE FICTION WRITING **EDUCATION** Southern Methodist Univ, BA, 76, MA, 83; Univ Houston, PhD, 85. **CAREER** Engl, Oregon St Univ. **SELECTED PUBLICATIONS** Auth, The Boy Orator, SMU Press, 88; Desire Provoked. Random House, 87; Low Rider, The New Yorker, 87; What Falls Away. W.W. Norton, 95; Almost Barcalona, Gettysburg Rev, 95; The Woman in the Oil Field. SMU Press, 95. **CONTACT ADDRESS** Oregon State Univ, Corvallis, OR, 97331-4501. **EMAIL** tdaugherty@orst.edu

DAUSE, CHARLES A.
DISCIPLINE COMMUNICATION STUDIES **EDUCATION** Muskingum Col, BA; Wayne State Univ, MA, PhD. **CAREER** Assoc dean, Liberal Arts; dir, Univ Adv and Acad Serv; assoc prof, Univ Detroit Mercy, 64-. **HONORS AND AWARDS** Developed & implemented, Acad Exploration Prog. **MEMBERSHIPS** Nat Acad Adv Asn. **RESEARCH** Public speaking, public opinion, mass media, political campaign and organizational communication. **SELECTED PUBLICATIONS** Coauth, Argumentation: Inquiry and Advocacy. **CONTACT ADDRESS** Dept of Communications, Univ of Detroit Mercy, 4001 W McNichols Rd, PO Box 19900, Detroit, MI, 48219-0900. **EMAIL** DAUSECA@udmercy.edu

DAVENPORT, GUY MATTISON
PERSONAL Born 11/23/1927, Anderson, SC **DISCIPLINE** ENGLISH **EDUCATION** Duke Univ AB, 48; Oxford Univ, BLitt, 50; Harvard Univ, PhD, 61. **CAREER** Instr English, Washington Univ, 52-55; tutor, Harvard Univ, 57-60; asst prof, Haverford Col, 60-63; prof English, 63-90, PROF EMER, 90-, UNIV KY, 63- ; McArthur fel, 90-95. **HONORS AND AWARDS** Zabel Prize, Am Acad Arts & Lett, 81. **MEMBERSHIPS** Am Poetry Soc; William Carlos Williams Soc. **RESEARCH** Post 1910 American and European literature; Greek, archaic period; 19th century American and English intellectual history. **SELECTED PUBLICATIONS** Auth, The Intelligence of Louis Agassiz, Beacon, 64; Da Vinci's Bicycle, Johns Hopkins, 75; Archilochos, Sappho, Alkman, Univ Calif, 80; Geography and the Imagination, 81 & Eclogues, 81, North Point; Herakleitos and Diogenes, 81 & The Mimes of Herondas, 81, Grey Fox; Tatlin!, Johns Hopkins, 82; Apples and Pears, N Point, 84; The Drummer of the 11th North Devonshire Fusiliers, N Point, 90; Thasos and Ohio, N Point, 85; Every Force Evolves a Form, N Point, 87; Cities on Hills, UMI Press, 83; The Jules Verne Steam Balloon, n Point, 87; A Balthus Notebook, Ecco, 89; A Table of Green Fields, New Directions, 93; Seven Greeks, New directions, 95; Charles Burchfields Seasons, Chameleon, 94; The Drawings of Paul Cadmus, Rizzoli, 96; The Cardiff Team, New Directions, 95; Objects on a Table, Counterpoint, 98. **CONTACT ADDRESS** 621 Sayre Ave, Lexington, KY, 40508.

DAVEY, FRANK W.
PERSONAL Born 04/19/1940, Vancouver, BC, Canada **DISCIPLINE** CANADIAN LITERATURE **EDUCATION** Univ BC, BA, 61, MA, 63; Univ S Calif, PhD, 68. **CAREER** Tchg asst, Univ BC, 61-63; lectr, Royal Roads Mil Col, 63-66; asst prof, 67-69, writer-in-residence, Sir George Williams Univ, 69-70; asst prof, 70-72, assoc prof, 72-80, prof English, York Univ, 80-90, dept ch, 85-90; CARL F. KLINCK PROF CANADIAN LITERATURE, UNIV WESTERN ONT, 90-. **HONORS AND AWARDS** Can Coun grants/fels, 66, 71-73, 74-75; Dept Nat Defence Arts Res grant, 65, 66, 68. **MEMBERSHIPS** Can Asn Univ Tchrs; Asn Can Col Univ Tchrs Eng; Asn Can Que Lit. **SELECTED PUBLICATIONS** Auth, The Arches, 80; auth, Louis Dudek and Raymond Souster, 81; auth, Capitalistic Affection!, 82; auth, Surviving the Paraphrase, 83; auth, Edward and Patricia, 84; auth, Margaret Atwood: A Feminist Poetics, 84; auth, The Louis Riel Organ and Piano Company, 85; auth, The Abbotsford Guide to India; auth, Reading Canadian Reading, 88; auth, Popular Narratives, 90; auth, Post-National Arguments: The Politics of the Anglophone-Canadian Novel since 1967, 93; auth, Reading 'KIM' Right, 93; auth, Canadian Literacy Power, 94; auth, Karla's Web, 94; auth, Cultural Mischief, 96. **CONTACT ADDRESS** English Dept, Univ of Western Ontario, London, ON, N6A 3K7. **EMAIL** fdavey@julian.uwo.ca

DAVID, ALFRED
PERSONAL Born 03/31/1929, Hamburg, Germany, m, 1968 **DISCIPLINE** ENGLISH **EDUCATION** Harvard Univ, AB, 51, AM, 54, PhD, 57. **CAREER** From instr to assoc prof, 58-68, PROF ENGLISH, IND UNIV, BLOOMINGTON, 68-, Sheldon traveling fel, 57-58; Guggenheim & Fulbright fels, 67-68. **MEMBERSHIPS** MLA; Medieval Acad Am; New Chaucer Soc. **RESEARCH** Chaucer; medieval literature; children's literature. **SELECTED PUBLICATIONS** Auth, The 18th-Century Hymn in England, Agenda, Vol 0033, 95; The Oxford Guides to Chaucer--The Shorter Poems, Mod Lang Rev, Vol 0092, 97. **CONTACT ADDRESS** Dept of English, Indiana Univ, Bloomington, Bloomington, IN, 47401.

DAVIDSON, ARNOLD E.
DISCIPLINE ENGLISH LITERATURE **EDUCATION** SUNY Binghamton, PhD, 77. **CAREER** Prof Can studies. **MEMBERSHIPS** MLA. **RESEARCH** Can and Brit fiction. **SELECTED PUBLICATIONS** Auth, Mordecai Richler, 83; Conrad's Endings, 84; JeanRhys, 85; Writing Against Silence: Joy Kogawa's Obasan, 93; CoyoteCountry: Fictions of the Canadian West,94; co-ed, The Art of Margaret Atwood, 81. **CONTACT ADDRESS** Eng Dept, Duke Univ, Durham, NC, 27706.

DAVIDSON, CATHY N.
DISCIPLINE ENGLISH **EDUCATION** Elmhurst, BA, 70; SUNY-Binghamton, MA, 73, PhD, 74 **CAREER** Assoc, prof, Eng, Mich State Univ; current, DEVARNEY PROF ENG, DUKE UNIV **MEMBERSHIPS** Am Antiquarian Soc **RESEARCH** Am Fict **SELECTED PUBLICATIONS** Co-ed, The Lost Tradition: Mothers and Daughters in Literature, 80; auth, The Experimental Fictions of Ambrose Bierce: Structuring the Ineffable, 84; auth, Revolution and the Word: The Rise of the Novel in America, 87; ed, Oxford University Press Early American Women Writers Series, editions of Charlotte Temple and Duloquita; Reading in the America: Literatures and Sonat Hastoz, Haphiers, 89 ; ed, with introd, Reading in America: Literature and Social History, Johns Hopkins Univ Press, 89 & 92; assoc ed, Columbia History of the American Name, 91; auth, The Book of Love: Writers and Their Love Letters, Pocket/Simon & Schuster, 92: Thirty-Six Views of Mt Fuji: On Finding Myself in Japan, Dutton-Signet, 93; co-ed, Oxford Companion to Women's Writing in the United States, Oxford Univ Press, 94; co-ed, Oxford Book of Women's Writing in the United States, 95; co-ed, Subjects and Citizens: Nation, Race and Gender from "Oroonoko" to Anita Hill, Duke Univ Press, 95. **CONTACT ADDRESS** Dept of English, Duke Univ, Durham, SC, 27706.

DAVIDSON, CLIFFORD OSCAR
PERSONAL Born 10/29/1932, Faribault, MN, m, 1954 **DISCIPLINE** ENGLISH **EDUCATION** St Cloud State Univ, BS, 54; Wayne State Univ, MA, 61, PhD, 66. **CAREER** Instr Eng, Wayne State Univ, 61-65; from Asst Prof to Prof Eng, 65-89, Prof Eng & Medieval Studies, Western MI Univ, 89-, Co-ed, Comp Drama, Western MI Univ, 67-98, bd mem, Medieval Inst, 69-74, 75-78, 88-91, 93-96 & chmn, 76-77, 94-95; exec ed, Early Drama, Art & Music, 76. **HONORS AND AWARDS** Fac res grant, 67, 92, 95; res fel, 71, 74, 75, 77, 79, 81, 83, 85, 87, 89; Distinguished Schol Award, Western MI Univ. **MEMBERSHIPS** Renaissance Soc Am; Medieval Acad Am; Malone Soc; Int Asn Univ Prof English; Int Soc for Study Medieval Drama; T.S. Eliot Soc; AAUP. **RESEARCH** Medieval and Renaissance drama; Eng lit of the late Middle Ages and Renaissance; iconography. **SELECTED PUBLICATIONS** Auth, On Tradition: Essays on the Use and Valuation of the Past, 92; ed, A Tretise of Miraclis Pleyinge, 93; The Iconography of Heaven, 94; Fools and Folly, 96; auth, Technology, Guilds, and Early English Drama, 97; coauth, Performing Medieval Music Drama, 98; auth, Baptism, the Three Enemies, and T.S. Eliot, Paul Watkins Publ. **CONTACT ADDRESS** The Medieval Inst, Western Michigan Univ, 1201 Oliver St, Kalamazoo, MI, 49008-3805. **EMAIL** davidson@wmich.edu

DAVIDSON, HARRIET
DISCIPLINE MODERN POETRY, CONTEMPORARY AMERICAN POETRY, THE CIRTICISM OF POETRY **EDUCATION** Univ Tex, Austin, BA, Vanderbilt MA, PhD. **CAREER** Dir, Women's Stud prog, Rutgers, The State Univ NJ, Univ Col-Camden. **RESEARCH** Twentieth century literature; critical theory. **SELECTED PUBLICATIONS** Auth, T.S. Eliot and Hermeneutics: Absence and Interpretation in "The Waste Land". **CONTACT ADDRESS** Dept of Lit in Eng, Rutgers, The State Univ NJ, Univ Col-Camden, New Brunswick, NJ, 08903. **EMAIL** hardav@rci.rutgers.edu

DAVIDSON, JOHN E.
PERSONAL Born 09/27/1960, Knoxville, TN **DISCIPLINE** FOREIGN LANGUAGES; LITERATURE **EDUCATION** Univ South, BA, 82; Univ Iowa, MA, 90; Cornell Univ, PhD, 93. **CAREER** Asst prof, USU, 93-. **HONORS AND AWARDS** Fulbright Scholar; NEH Summer Grant. **MEMBERSHIPS** AATG; MLA; GSA. **RESEARCH** Film; literature; cultural theory. **SELECTED PUBLICATIONS** Auth, art, Hegemony and Cinematic Strategy, 96; auth, art, In der Fuhrer's Face: Undermining Reflections in and on Winfried Bonengel's Beruf Neonazi, 97; auth, art, Overcoming the Germany's Past(s) in Film since the Wende, 97; auth, Deterritorializing the New German Cinema, 98; auth, art, Working for the Man, Whoever That May Be: The Vocation of Wolfgang Liebeneiner, 99. **CONTACT ADDRESS** Ohio State Univ, 314 Cunz Hall, Columbus, OH, 43210-1229. **EMAIL** davidson.92@osu.edu

DAVIDSON, ROBERTA
DISCIPLINE CREATIVE WRITING **EDUCATION** Sarah Lawrence Col, BA, 75; Princeton Univ, PhD, 86. **CAREER** Instr, Kenyon Col; reviewer, Tulas Stud in Woman Literature; Philosophy and Literature; asst prof-. **HONORS AND AWARDS** Co-founder, Whitman's Gender Stud Min. **RESEARCH** Medieval narratives of romance, spirituality and restriction. **SELECTED PUBLICATIONS** Auth, Cross-Dressing in Medieval Romance,Textual Bodies: Changing the Boundaries of Literary Representation, 97; I Have a Dream, PBS documentary.. **CONTACT ADDRESS** Dept of Eng, Whitman Col, 345 Boyer Ave, Walla Walla, WA, 99362-2038. **EMAIL** davidson@whitman.edu

DAVIES, GWENDOLYN
PERSONAL Born 02/12/1942, Halifax, NS, Canada **DISCIPLINE** ENGLISH **EDUCATION** Dalhousie Univ, BA, 63; Ont Col Educ, Univ Toronto Educ Cert, 64, 69; Univ Toronto, MA, 69; York Univ PhD, 80. **CAREER** Tchr, East York Col Inst, 63-67, 70-72; asst assoc, Centre d'etudes can, Univ Bordeaux, 74-75; asst to assoc prof, Mt Allison Univ, 76-88, assoc dir, Can studies, 80-81, dept head, 85-88; PROF ENGLISH, ACADIA UNIV, 88-, acting head, 91-92, head 94-; adj prof, Dalhousie Univ, 95-; W Stewart MacNutt Memorial Lectr, Univ NB, 92; vis prof Can stud, Univ London, 92-93; Dawson lectr, NS Tchrs Col, 95. **HONORS AND AWARDS** Acadia Asn Alumni Award Excellence Tchg, 92; Canada 125 Medal, 93. **MEMBERSHIPS** Asn Can Stud (bd mem, 85-87); Can Asn Chairs Eng, 86-89 (pres, 87-88); Can Inst Hist Microrepro, 90-93; Asn Can & Que Lit (vice-pres, 90-92); Bibliog Soc Can; Coun, Royal NS Hist Soc, 97-. **SELECTED PUBLICATIONS** Auth, The Mephibosheth Stepsure Letters by Thomas McCulloch, 90; auth, Studies in Maritime Literary History, 92; ed, Myth and Milieu, 93; co-ed, Canadian Poetry: From the Beginnings Through the First World War, 94; contribur, Dictionary of Canadian Biography/Dictionnaire biographique du Canada; adv bd, Routledge Encyclopedia of Post-Colonial Literatures, 88-92; adv bd, Newfoundland Studies, 94-99; adv bd, The Oxford Companion to Canadian Literature, 2nd ed, 95-97; ed bd, Canadian Literature, 96-. **CONTACT ADDRESS** English Dept, Acadia Univ, Wolfville, NS, B0P 1X0. **EMAIL** Gdavies@max.acadiau.ca

DAVIES, MORGAN
DISCIPLINE MEDIEVAL ENGLISH, WELSH, IRISH LANGUAGE, LITERATURE AND CULTURE **EDUCATION** Stanford, BA; Univ CA, MA, Cphil, PhD. **CAREER** Asst prof, Colgate Univ. **HONORS AND AWARDS** NEH Fel, Col Tchr(s), 95. **RESEARCH** Old Eng lit, old and middle Irish lit, middle Welsh lit. **SELECTED PUBLICATIONS** Auth, Dafydd Ap Gwilym and the Friars: The Poetics of Antimendicancy, Studia Celtica; Aed I'r Coed I Dorri Cof: Dafydd Ap Gwilym and the Metaphorics of Carpentry, Cambrian Medieval Celtic Studies. **CONTACT ADDRESS** Dept of Eng, Colgate Univ, 13 Oak Drive, Hamilton, NY, 13346.

DAVIS, CHARLES ROGER
PERSONAL Born 08/09/1943, Peoria, IL **DISCIPLINE** ENGLISH **EDUCATION** Yale Univ, BA, 65; Princeton Univ, MA, 69, PhD(English lang & lit), 73; Columbia Univ, MS, 72. **CAREER** NAm bibliogr, Univ Va Libr, 72-75; BIBLIOGR, SMITH COL LIBR, 75-, Corresp ed, Spenser Newslett, 75-79. **MEMBERSHIPS** MLA; Am Libr Asn; Renaissance Soc Am; Bibliogr Soc Eng; Bibliogr Soc Am. **RESEARCH** Renaissance poetry and prose; 18th century booktrade. **SELECTED PUBLICATIONS** Auth, The Poetics of Personification, Speculum-Jour Medieval Stud, Vol 0070, 95; King Arthurs Death--The Middle-English Stanzaic Morte Arthur and Alliterative Morte Arthur, Speculum-Jour Medieval Stud, Vol 0071, 96; Lancelot of the Laik and Sir Tristrem, Speculum-Jour Medieval Stud, Vol 0071, 96; The Shewings of Julian-Of-Norwich, Speculum-Jour Medieval Stud, Vol 0071, 96. **CONTACT ADDRESS** Library, Smith Col, Northampton, MA, 01060.

DAVIS, DALE W.
DISCIPLINE COMPARATIVE LITERATURE AND VICTORIAN LITERATURE **EDUCATION** Univ OK, PhD, 68. **CAREER** Assoc prof Eng, mem, grad fac, instr, Hum Stud, mem, Univ Honors Coun, dir, Bachelor of Gen Stud degree prog, TX Tech Univ. **RESEARCH** Interdisciplinary educ. **SELECTED PUBLICATIONS** Publ articles on Victorian lit, pedag, lit theory, and criticism, and co-auth a standard two-volume textbook on interdisciplinary hum--The Humanities in Western Culture (8th Edition). **CONTACT ADDRESS** Texas Tech Univ, Lubbock, TX, 79409-5015. **EMAIL** ditdd@ttacs.ttu.edu

DAVIS, JANET
DISCIPLINE RHETORIC, MASS COMMUNICATION, AND HEALTH COMMUNICATION **EDUCATION** Bristol Univ, Eng, BA; Univ NE, MA; Univ IA, PhD. **CAREER** Assoc prof, 94-, Truman State Univ. **HONORS AND AWARDS** First Class hon(s), Bristol Univ., Fac adv, Intl Film Club. **MEMBERSHIPS** Mem, Nat Commun Assn; Cent States Commun Assn; Amer Soc Hist of Rhetoric; Rhetoric Soc Am; Hon Soc Phi Kappa Phi. **SELECTED PUBLICATIONS** Pub(s), area of class rhetoric; articles, Encycl Rhetoric and Composition, Garland, 96. **CONTACT ADDRESS** Dept of Commun, Truman State Univ, 100 E Normal St, Kirksville, MO, 63501-4221. **EMAIL** FL06@Truman.edu

DAVIS, JED H.
PERSONAL Born 07/31/1921, Stillwater, MN, m, 1945, 3 children **DISCIPLINE** SPEECH; THEATRE **EDUCATION** Univ Minn, BA, 47, MA, 49, PhD, 58. **CAREER** Inst, 47-50, Asst prof, 50-53, Macalester Col; Asst Prof, Mich State Univ, 53-60; Vis Prof, Univ Minn, 66, 68; Vis Prof, Calif State Univ, Long Bch, 78; Asst Prof, 60-62, Assoc Prof, 62-65, Prof, Commun & Theatre, 65-86, Univ Kans; Prof Emeritus, Univ Kans, 87-. **HONORS AND AWARDS** AMOCO Gold Medallion, svc to ACTF Regional Festival, 73; Fellow of the Am Theatre Asn, 72; Photo Hangs in Portrait Gallery of Rarig Ctr, Univ Minn, 76; Kilty Kane, svc award, Kans Univ Theatre, 76; Kans Theatre Hall of Fame: Charter inductee, 80; Kans Univ Chancellor's Club Career Tchng Award, 85; Campton Bell Award, Am Asn of Theatre for Youth, 1987; Hon Fellow, Mid-Am Theatre Conf, 87; Dedicatory vol: Theatre for Young Audiences: Principles and Strategies for the Future; Medallion Awardee, Children's Theatre Found of Am, 98. **MEMBERSHIPS** Am Educ

Theatre Asn (Am Col Theatre Festival Ch & Cent Comte, pres, 72); Children's Theatre Conf (pres, 63-65); Winifred Ward Schol Prog (ch, subcmte on Inst Cert, 80-82); ASSITEJ; Assoc of Kans Theatre (pres, 74-75); Lawrence Arts Commission (secy 74-76); Children's Theatre Found; Univ & Col Theatre Asn; Col of Fellows of the Am Theatre (dean, 90-92). **RESEARCH** Children's theatre; technical theatre; child development; theatre hist; hist of theatre org & theatre honoraries. **SELECTED PUBLICATIONS** Co-auth, Children's Theatre: Play Production for the Child Audience, Harper & Bros, 60, 63, 65, 68; auth, Prospectus for Research in Children's Theatre, Educ Theatre J, vol 13, 4, 274-277, 12/61; compiler & ed, A Directory of Children's Theatres in the United States, Am Educ Theatre Asn, 68; auth, Theatre for Children, Encycl Americana, vol 26, 621, 73; co-auth, Theatre, Children, and Youth, Anchorage Press, 82, 87; ed, foreword, afterword, Theatre Education: Mandate for Tomorrow, Anchorage Press, 85; ed, American Theatre Fellows: The First Thirty Years, Col of Fellows of the Am Theatre, 95. **CONTACT ADDRESS** 2602 Louisiana, Lawrence, KS, 66046-4662.

DAVIS, JOHNETTA GARNER
PERSONAL Born 11/01/1939, Warrenton, VI **DISCIPLINE** SPEECH **EDUCATION** Tchrs Coll, BS 1961; George Washington U, MA 1969; Howard U, PhD 1976 **CAREER** UNIV OF MARYLAND, COLL PARK, OFFICE OF GRADUATE MINORITY EDUC, ASSOC DEAN, DIR, 1993-; Howard Univ, assoc dean, grad prof 1978-96, assoc prof, prof 1972-78; Amer Speech & Hearing Assn, asst sec for prog dev 1971-72; Federal City College, assistant professor, 1970-71; Teachers Coll, instructor 1969-71; Washington DC Public Schools, speech pathologist 1961-68. **HONORS AND AWARDS** Howard University, establishment of the Johnetta G Davis Award for Best Mentor of Graduate Students, 1993; Graduate Student Council, Administrator of the Year, 1992, Distinguished Service Awards, 1978-80, 1982, 1986, 1988, 1990; Outstanding faculty citation Students at DC Teachers Coll, 1971; Frederick Douglass Honor Soc Howard Univ Chap 1974; Outstanding Yng Women in Am 1976; Howard University, School of Communications, Outstanding Alumni Award, 1986; DC Teachers College, Outstanding Junior Faculty Award, 1971; US Office of Education, Fellowship, 1967; CCC-SP-L, Amer Speech-Language Hearing Assn, certificate, 1962. **MEMBERSHIPS** Potomac Chapter of Links Inc; American Speech-Language & Hearing Assn 1961-; DC Speech, Language and Hearing, 1963-; task force on intl grad educ Council of Grad Schs Task Force on Minority Education; board of directors Stoddard Bapt Home 1977-82; Sunday sch tchr Mt Sinai Bapt Ch 1977-82. **CONTACT ADDRESS** Office of Graduate Minority Education, 2122 Lee Bldg, College Park, MD, 20742-5121.

DAVIS, KATIE CAMPBELL
PERSONAL Born 09/11/1936, Lumber City, GA, m **DISCIPLINE** COMMUNICATIONS **EDUCATION** TN State Univ, BA 1957; TN State Univ, MA 1968; Univ IL, PhD 1974. **CAREER** Norfolk State Univ, prof, speech, English, theatre arts, currently; teacher various public school since 1951; communication consultant; spiritual, inspirational and motivational speaker. **HONORS AND AWARDS** National Consortium of Doctors' Perseverance Award, 1992. **MEMBERSHIPS** Mem Speech Comm Assn; mem NAACP; Alpha Kappa Alpha Sorority; American Association of University Women. **CONTACT ADDRESS** Speech Commun, Norfolk State Univ, 2401 Corprew Ave, Norfolk, VA, 23504.

DAVIS, KENNETH WALDRON
PERSONAL Born 06/15/1932, Holland, TX **DISCIPLINE** ENGLISH **EDUCATION** Tex Tech Col, BA, 54; Vanderbilt Univ, MA, 55, PhD, 63. **CAREER** From instr to assoc prof, 55-68, admin asst to dept head, 63, chmn sophomore English, 63-65, chmn grad studies, 65-69, PROF ENGLISH, TEX TECH UNIV, 68-. **MEMBERSHIPS** MLA; NCTE; SCent Mod Lang Asn. **RESEARCH** English novel; 19th century English literature; literature of the English Renaissance. **SELECTED PUBLICATIONS** Auth, Dancing with the Devil, Jour Pop Cult, Vol 0030, 96; Careless Weeds--6 Texas Novellas, West Amer Lit, Vol 0029, 95. **CONTACT ADDRESS** Dept of English, Tex Tech Univ, Lubbock, TX, 79409.

DAVIS, MARIANNA WHITE
PERSONAL Born 01/08/1929, Philadelphia, PA, w **DISCIPLINE** ENGLISH **EDUCATION** SC State College, BA English 1949; NY Univ, MA English 1953; Boston Univ, DEd English 1966. **CAREER** SC Pub Sch, tchr, 1949-51, 1955-56, 1986-96; SC State Coll, asst prof, 1956-64; Claflin Coll, prof, 1966-69; Voorhees Coll, vis prof, 1966-68; Boston Univ, vis prof, 1967; Univ of TN, vis prof, 1969; Benedict Coll, English prof & researcher, 1969-82; Upward Bound Tufts Univ; Denmark Tech Coll, acting pres, 1985-86; Davis & Assocs, pres, 1980-; Northeastern University, African-American Literature Teacher Training Project, co-director, 1992-94; Benedict College, special assistant to the president, 1996-. **HONORS AND AWARDS** SC State Coll Alumni Scholarship; Crusade Scholar doctoral studies 1964-66; Outstanding educator of Amer 1970-71; IBM-UNCF Fellowships post doctoral studies 1971 & 1974; Pi Lambda Theta Travel Scholarship for study in Soviet Union 1973; Outstanding Educ Award Kappa Alpha Psi Frat, Athens GA 1974; Contrib to Educ Award SC Comm Affairs 1976; Educators Roundtable Awd 1976; Outstanding Cit Awd Omega Psi Phi Frat 1977; Emory O Jackson Journalism Awd 1978 & 1996; Distinguished Research Award NAFEO 1980; Distinguished Faculty Awd Benedict Coll 1980; Distinguished Serv Award Columbia Urban League 1981; Distinguished Alumni Awd Boston Univ 1981; Distinguished Alumni Award SC State Coll 1981; Par Excellence Award in Educ Operation PUSH 1982; Outstanding Citizen Award, Cleveland, OH, 1984; Kappa Alpha Psi of SC Outstanding Black Woman Award 1987; Jacob Javits Fellowship Bd, Presidential Appointment, 1993; Governor's Award, Outstanding Achievement, 1995; contributed papers to Boston Univ (Mugar Memorial Library), 1989; exec producer, "The Struggle Continues," black history teleconf on PBS, 1986-. **MEMBERSHIPS** Bd dir Natl Council of Teachers of English 1958-80; co-founder & sec ABC Devel Corp 1972; chmn Conf on Coll Composition & Comm 1975-76; exec comm ADE Modern Language Assn 1976-79; commr SC Educational TV 1980-95; mem Public Broadcasting System Adv Bd 1981-83; Francis Burns United Methodist Ch; bd chm, Columbia Urban League Bd, 1981-82; Natl Council of Negro Women; YWCA; life mem NAACP; The Moles; coord, Coalition for Concerns of Blacks in Post Secondary Educ in SC; Alpha Kappa Alpha Sor; Order of Eastern Star; Chmn SC Intl Women's Yr Commission; founder VICOS Women's League for Comm Action; TISAWS; The Girl Friends, Inc; Civil Rights Comm Adv Bd 1985-; natl publicity chair, The Moles, 1988-92; bd of educ, S Carolina United Methodist Church 1988-96; board mem, board of visitors, Claflin Coll. **SELECTED PUBLICATIONS** Author of 18 books, numerous articles. **CONTACT ADDRESS** PO Box 3097, Columbia, SC, 29230.

DAVIS, MARIE
PERSONAL St. Catherine's, ON, Canada **DISCIPLINE** ENGLISH **EDUCATION** McMaster Univ, MA, 85. **CAREER** Lectr, Univ Western Ont, 91-96; asst ed, 90-92, ASSOC ED, CAN CHILDREN'S LIT, 92-. **HONORS AND AWARDS** Rotary Youth Leadership Award, 81; Pan-Hellenic Coun Tchr Award, Univ Western Ont, 93-94. **MEMBERSHIPS** ACCUTE; Children's Lit Asn; Can Soc Eighteenth-Century Studs. **SELECTED PUBLICATIONS** Auth, Walking on Revolving Walls: Coming of Age in Calgary, 90; auth, Susan Musgrave: An Interview with Paul Yee in CCL, 82, 96; auth, Parable or Parody: Tom King's Coyote Columbus Story in CCL, 83, 96. **CONTACT ADDRESS** Dept of English, Univ Guelph, Guelph, ON, N1G 2W1. **EMAIL** mdavis@bosshog.arts.uwo.ca

DAVIS, ROBERT LEIGH
DISCIPLINE ENGLISH AND EDUCATION **EDUCATION** Stanford Univ, BA, 78; MA, 81; Univ Calif Berkeley, PhD, 92. **CAREER** Eng tchr, Serra High Sch, San Mateo, Calif, 80-85; instr, Golden Gate Univ, San Francisco, Calif, 85-92; grad student instr, Univ Calif Berkeley, 85-92; asst prof eng, Wittenburg Univ, 92-. **HONORS AND AWARDS** BA with distinction, Stanford Univ, 78; fel, NEH Summer Sem for Secondary Sch Tchrs, Co Col, 84; Tchr of the Year, Serra High Sch, San Mateo, Calif, 85; Benjamin Putnam Kurtz Graduate Essay Prize, Univ Calif Berkeley, 89; highest distinction, comprehensive oral exam, Univ Calif Berkeley, 89; Omicron Delta Kappa Excellence in Tchr, Wittenburg Univ, 96; Southwest Oh Coun of Higher Educ Facult Excellence, 97. **SELECTED PUBLICATIONS** Auth, Whitman and the Romance of Medicine, Berkeley and Los Angeles, Univ Calif Press, 97; Articles, The Lunar Light of Student Writing: Portfolios and Literary Theory, Situating Portfolios: Four Perspectives, ed Kathleen Blake Yancy and Irwin Weiser, Provo, Ut State Univ Press, 97; Review Essay: Richard Selzer's Raising the Dead, Lit and Med, 13:2, fall, 94; America, Brought to Hospital: The Romance of Medicine and Democracy in Whitman's Civil War, The Wordsworth Cir, 24:2, winter, 94; Deconstruction and the Prophets of Literary Decline, The Chicago Tribune, Op-Ed, 29 March 94; The Art of the Suture: Richard Selzer and Medical Narrative, Lit and Med, 12:2, fall, 93; Whitman's Tympanum: A Reading of Drum-Taps, The Amer Transcendental Quart, 6:3, fall, 92; Medical Representation in Walt Whitman and William Carlos Williams, The Walt Whitman Quart Rev, 6:3, winter, 89; That Two-Handed Engine and the Consolation of Lycidas, Milton Quart, 20:2, May, 86. **CONTACT ADDRESS** Wittenberg Univ, 3388 Petre Rd., Springfield, OH, 45502.

DAVIS, RON
DISCIPLINE ENGLISH **EDUCATION** Mercer Univ, BA; Univ NC Chapel Hill, PhD, 75. **CAREER** Fac, Plattsburgh State Univ of NY. **RESEARCH** 19th century Eng lit; jour; the Bible. **SELECTED PUBLICATIONS** Auth, bk on American playwright Augustus Thomas; publ(s) about journalism. **CONTACT ADDRESS** SUNY, Plattsburgh, 101 Broad St, Plattsburgh, NY, 12901-2681.

DAVIS, SUSAN
DISCIPLINE COMMUNICATIONS **EDUCATION** Univ Pa, PhD, 83. **CAREER** ASSOC PROF, UNIV CALIF, SAN DIEGO. **RESEARCH** Processes of cult product and the polit uses of cult. **SELECTED PUBLICATIONS** Auth, "'Set Your Mood to Patriotic': History as Televised Special Event," Radical His Rev, 88; Parades and Power: Street Theatre in Nineteenth-Century Philadelphia, Univ Calif, 88; Spectacular Nature University of California, 95. **CONTACT ADDRESS** Dept of Commun, Univ Calif, San Diego, 9500 Gilman Dr, La Jolla, CA, 92093. **EMAIL** sdavis@weber.ucsd.edu

DAVIS, THADIOUS
DISCIPLINE 20TH CENTURY AMERICAN LITERATURE, AFRICAN-AMERICAN LITERATURE **EDUCATION** Boston Univ, PHD. **CAREER** Gertrude Conaway Vanderbilt Prof Eng, Vanderbilt Univ. **RESEARCH** Faulkner, Langston Hughes, Jessie Fauset, Carson McCullers. **SELECTED PUBLICATIONS** Auth, William Faulkner's "Negro" : Art and the Southern Context, 82; Nella Larsen, Novelist of the Harlem Renaissance: A Woman's Life Unveiled, 94; ed, Satire or Evasion: Black Perspectives on Huckleberry Finn, 92. **CONTACT ADDRESS** Vanderbilt Univ, Nashville, TN, 37203-1727. **EMAIL** hickmald@ctrvax.vanderbilt.edu

DAVIS, THOMAS M.
DISCIPLINE ENGLISH **EDUCATION** Kansas State Univ, BS, 57, MS, 59; Univ Missouri, PhD, 68. **CAREER** Prof & PROF EMER, ENG, KENT STATE UNIV **MEMBERSHIPS** Am Antiquarian Soc **SELECTED PUBLICATIONS** Ed, 14 by Emily Dickinson, 64; co-ed, College Reading and College Writing, 66 & 70; Edward Taylor's "Church Records" and Related Sermons, 81; Edward Taylor vs. Solomon Stoddard: The Nature of the Lord's Supper,81; ed, Edward Taylor's "Harmony of the Gospels," 82. **CONTACT ADDRESS** Dept of English, Kent State Univ, Kent, OH, 44242.

DAVIS, WENDELL EUGENE
PERSONAL Born 09/30/1934, Toledo, OH, m, 1962 **DISCIPLINE** ENGLISH LITERATURE **EDUCATION** Bowling Green State Univ, BA, 56, MA, 58; Western Reserve Univ, PhD, 62. **CAREER** Asst prof English, Thiel Col, 61-63; asst prof, 63-74, ASSOC PROF ENGLISH, PURDUE UNIV, WEST LAFAYETTE, 74-, Mem res & bibliog comt, conf English lit in transition, MLA, 66-69; Fulbright prof, Humboldt Univ, Freiburg, Ger, 69-70. **MEMBERSHIPS** Midwest Mod Lang Asn; MLA. **RESEARCH** The English novel; English literature 1880-1920; Victorian literature. **SELECTED PUBLICATIONS** Auth, Neglected Novelist of the 1890s, Batson,Henrietta,M--An Essay and Annotated Secondary Bibliography, Eng Lit in Transition 1880-1920, Vol 0040, 97; Hardy--The Margin of the Unexpressed, Eng Lit in Transition 1880-1920, Vol 0037, 94; Critical Essays on Hardy Poetry, Eng Lit in Transition 1880-1920, Vol 0039, 96; The Structures of Justice in the Secret Sharer, Conradiana, Vol 0027, 95; Letters of Hardy,Emma And Hardy,Florence, Eng Lit in Transition 1880-1920, Vol 0040, 97; Testamentary Acts--Browning, Tennyson, James, Hardy, Eng Lit in Transition 1880-1920, Vol 0036, 93; Thomas Hardy--Man of Wessex, Eng Lit in Transition 1880-1920, Vol 0038, 95. **CONTACT ADDRESS** Dept of English, Purdue Univ, West Lafayette, IN, 47906.

DAVIS, WILLIAM V.
PERSONAL Born 05/26/1940, Canton, OH, m, 1971, 1 child **DISCIPLINE** ENGLISH, RELIGION **EDUCATION** Ohio Univ, AB, 62, MA, 65, PhD(English), 67; Pittsburgh Theol Sem, MDiv, 65. **CAREER** Asst prof English, Ohio Univ, 67-78, Cent Conn State Col, 68-71, Tunxis Community Col, 71-72 & Univ Ill, Chicago Circle, 72-77; asst prof, 77-78, assoc prof, 78-79, PROF ENGLISH & WRITER IN RESIDENCE, BAYLOR UNIV, 79-, Sr Fulbright fel, Univ Vienna, Austria, 79-80. **HONORS AND AWARDS** Yale Series of Younger Poets Prize, 79. **MEMBERSHIPS** MLA; Poetry Soc Am; Assoc Writing Prog. **RESEARCH** Twentieth century English and American literature; creative writing; contemporary American poetry. **SELECTED PUBLICATIONS** Auth, Lowell,Robert and the Sublime, Amer Lit, Vol 0068, 96; Another Room, West Hum Rev, Vol 0046, 92; Stave Church, West Hum Rev, Vol 0046, 92; The Visit, Shenandoah, Vol 0043, 93; Summer Celestial, Shenandoah, Vol 0043, 93; To-Step-Lightly-Lightly-All-The-Way-Through-Your-Ruins, Wright,James Ohio Poems, Midwest Quart Jour Contemp Thought, Vol 0037, 96. **CONTACT ADDRESS** Dept of English, Baylor Univ, Waco, TX, 76703.

DAVISON, NEIL
DISCIPLINE MODERNIST LITERATURE **EDUCATION** Univ Md, BA, 82; Columbia Univ, MFA, 84; Univ Md, PhD, 93. **CAREER** Engl, Oregon St Univ. **RESEARCH** James Joyce; Irish Renaissance; Jewish Cultural Studies. **SELECTED PUBLICATIONS** Auth, Joyce's Matriculation Examination, James Joyce Quart, 93; Joyce's Homosocial Reckoning: Italo Svevo, Aesthetics and A Portrait of the Artist as a Young Man, Mod Lang Studies, 94; Inside the Sho'ah: Narrative, Documentation, and Schwarz-Bart's The Last of the Just, Clio, 95; James Joyce, Ulysses. And the Construction of Jewish Identity; Culture, Biography and The Jew in Modernist Europe. Cambridge Univ Press, 96, Paperback edition, Cambridge 98. **CONTACT ADDRESS** Oregon State Univ, Corvallis, OR, 97331-4501. **EMAIL** ndavison@orst.edu

DAWSON, ANTHONY BLANCHARD
PERSONAL Toronto, ON, Canada **DISCIPLINE** ENGLISH LITERATURE, DRAMA **EDUCATION** Concordia Univ, BA,

63; Harvard Univ, MA, 65, PhD(English), 69. **CAREER** Lectr English, Harvard Univ, 69-70; asst prof, 70-79, ASSOC PROF ENGLISH, UNIV BC, 70-. **MEMBERSHIPS** Shakespeare Asn Am; Asn Can Univ Teachers English. **RESEARCH** Shakespeare; Renaissance literature; Canadian literature. **SELECTED PUBLICATIONS** Auth, Much Ado About Nothing, Univ Toronto Quart, Vol 0064, 94; Gender and Play on the Shakespearean Stage, Boy Heroines and Female Pages, Essays in Theatre-Etudes Theatrales, Vol 0014, 96; Mistris-His-And-Haec, Representations of Frith,Moll--The Plays of Field,Nathan, Stud Eng Lit 1500-1900, Vol 0033, 93; Dangerous Familiars--Representations of Domestic Crime in England, 1550-1700, Shakespeare Quart, Vol 0048, 97. **CONTACT ADDRESS** Dept of English, Univ BC, Vancouver, BC, V6T 1W5.

DAWSON, WILLIAM
DISCIPLINE BRITISH ROMANTICISM **EDUCATION** Univ Mo, PhD, 84. **CAREER** Dir Undergrad Stud & Acad Adv. **HONORS AND AWARDS** Blue Chalk awd, 93. **RESEARCH** British romanticism. **SELECTED PUBLICATIONS** Publ on, British Romanticism, Shakespeare, Washington Irving & William Faulkner. **CONTACT ADDRESS** Dept of English, Univ of Missouri-Columbia, 309 University Hall, Columbia, MO, 65211.

DE CARO, FRANK
DISCIPLINE FOLKLORE, LOUISIANA CULTURES AND LITERATURE; NARRATIVE, PROVERBS **EDUCATION** Ind Univ, PhD, 73. **CAREER** Prof, La State Univ; chemn, La Gov's Comn on Folklife, 82-85; bd of dir, La Endowment for the Hum, 85-88; bk rev ed, Southern Folklore, 86-92; ed, La Folklore Miscellany, 90-94. **MEMBERSHIPS** Mem, Am Folklore Soc; La Folklore Soc. **RESEARCH** Folklore; Louisiana cultures and literature; narrative; proverbs. **SELECTED PUBLICATIONS** Auth, Folklife in Louisiana Photography: Images of Tradition, 90; Folklife and Louisiana Photography, Cult Vis, 91; Cultural Conservation: The Conference, J of Am Folklore, 91; The Three Great Lies: Riddles of Love and Death in a Postmodern Novel, Southern Folklore, 91; The Folktale Cat, 93; In This Folk-Lore Land: Race, Class, Identity, and Folklore Studies in Louisiana, J of Am Folklore, 96. **CONTACT ADDRESS** Dept of Eng, Louisiana State Univ, 223F Allen Hall, Baton Rouge, LA, 70803. **EMAIL** fdecaro@unix1.sncc.lsu.edu

DE GRAVE, KATHLEEN R.
DISCIPLINE ENGLISH LITERATURE **EDUCATION** University Wis Green Bay, BA; Univ Ark, MA; Univ Wis Madison, PhD. **CAREER** Assoc prof. **RESEARCH** American literature, 19th century women writers, 18th century British literature. **SELECTED PUBLICATIONS** Publ, Swindler, Spy, Rebel: The Confidence Woman in Nineteenth-Century America, 95; short stories, reviews, and articles on women's writing. **CONTACT ADDRESS** Dept of Eng, Pittsburg State Univ, 1701 S Broadway St, Pittsburg, KS, 66762. **EMAIL** kdegrave@pittstate.edu

DE GRAZIA, EDWARD
DISCIPLINE INTERNATIONAL TRANSACTIONS, COMMUNICATIONS LAW **EDUCATION** Univ Chicago, BA, 48; JD 51. **CAREER** Prof; **HONORS AND AWARDS** Dir, Georgetown Univ Prog Pretrial Diversion Accused Offenders to Community Mental Health Treatment Prog; Asso fel, Inst Policy Studies. **MEMBERSHIPS** Office Dir Gen UNESCO, 56-59; U.S. Dept State; U.S. Agency Int Devel; PEN Am Ctr. **RESEARCH** International transations; community law; first admenment legislation. **SELECTED PUBLICATIONS** Coath, Censorship Landmarks and Banned Films: Movies, Censors; First Amendment; auth, Girls Lean Back Everywhere: The Law of Obscenity and the Assault on Genius, Random House, 92. **CONTACT ADDRESS** Yeshiva Univ, 55 Fifth Ave, NY, NY, 10003-4301.

DE JONGH, JAMES LAURENCE
PERSONAL Born 09/23/1942, St Thomas, Virgin Islands of the United States, s **DISCIPLINE** ENGLISH **EDUCATION** Williams College, BA 1964; Yale Univ, MA 1967; New York Univ, PhD 1983. **CAREER** Rutgers Univ Newark, instructor 1969-70; The City Coll of the City Univ of New York (CUNY), prof 1970-; CUNY Inst for Research on the African Diapora in the Americas and the Caribean (IRADAC), interim dir, 1997-. **HONORS AND AWARDS** Fellow Center for Black Studies Univ of CA Santa Barbara 1981; Outstanding Achievement Awd The Black Action Council of the City Coll of New York 1982; Audelco Recognition Awd Outstanding Musical Creator 1984; Honorary Fellow Brookdale Ctr on Aging of Hunger Coll 1985; Natl Endowment for the Humanities Fellowship for College Teachers 1986; major plays and publications "Hail Hail the Gangs!" w/Carles Cleveland produced by NY Theatre Ensemble Inc 1976; "City Cool, A Ritual of Belonging," w/Carles Cleveland Random House 1978; "Do Lord Remember Me" Off-Broadway Premier Oct 10, 1982 produced by Wynn Handman The Amer Place Theater; "Play to Win, Jackie Robinson" w/ Carles Cleveland Natl school tour 1984-86. **MEMBERSHIPS** Mem The Dramatists Guild, Writers Guild of Amer East, Modern Language Assoc, Harlem Writers Guild, Zeta Psi Frat. **SELECTED PUBLICATIONS** Auth, Vicious Modernism: Black Harlem and the Literary Imagination, Cambridge Univ Press, 1990. **CONTACT ADDRESS** English Department, City Col, CUNY, IRADAC, Y-Bldg 307, New York, NY, 10031.

DE ORTEGO Y GASCA, FELIPE
PERSONAL Blue Island, IL **DISCIPLINE** COMMUNICATION STUDIES **EDUCATION** Univ Tex, BA, 59, MA, 66; Univ NMex, PhD, 71. **CAREER** Prof, 93-. **HONORS AND AWARDS** Distinguished Fac Awd, 97. **MEMBERSHIPS** Am Libr Asn; Tex Libr Asn; Nat Asn Bilingual Edu; Am Asn Higher Edu. **SELECTED PUBLICATIONS** Auth, pubs on British and American writers. **CONTACT ADDRESS** Sul Ros State Univ, 1866 Southern Lane, Decatur, GA, 30033-4097. **EMAIL** fortego@sulross.edu

DE SANTIS, CHRISTOPHER
DISCIPLINE AMERICAN AND AFRICAN-AMERICAN LITERATURE **EDUCATION** Lewis and Clark Col, BA, 89; Univ Wis-Madison, MA, 90; Univ Kans, PhD, 97. **CAREER** Ed, Langston Hughes and the Chicago Defender, Univ Ill Press, 95. **RESEARCH** Interdisciplinary study of the cultural myths engendered by social transformations of the post-Civil War era. **SELECTED PUBLICATIONS** Auth , Race, Politics, and Culture, Univ Ill Press, 95; bk rev(s), African Am Rev, The Langston Hughes Rev, The Southern Quart. **CONTACT ADDRESS** Dept of Engl, Westfield State Col, 577 Western Ave., Westfield, MA, 01085.

DE TORO, FERNANDO
DISCIPLINE ENGLISH LITERATURE **EDUCATION** Univ Carleton, BA; MA; Univ Montreal, PhD. **CAREER** Prof **RESEARCH** Colonial and post colonial literature; history of Latin American theatre; modern and post-modern fiction; architecture; theatre; philosophy; politics; post colonial theory; feminism; Latin American literature; literary theory; and structuralism and semiotics. **SELECTED PUBLICATIONS** Auth, pubs on colonial and post colonial poetry, fiction, feminism and literary theory. **CONTACT ADDRESS** Dept of English, Manitoba Univ, Winnipeg, MB, R3T 2N2.

DE VEAUX, ALEXIS
PERSONAL Born 09/24/1948, New York, NY **DISCIPLINE** LITERATURE **EDUCATION** Empire State College, BA, 1976; SUNY at Buffalo, MA, 1989, PhD, 1992. **CAREER** New Haven Board of Education, master artist, 1974-75; Sarah Lawrence College, adjunct lecturer, 1979-80; Norwich University, associate faculty, 1984-85; Wabash College, Owen Dutson visiting scholar, 1986-87; Essence Magazine, editor-at-large, 1978-90; SUNY AT BUFFALO, visiting assistant professor, 1991-92, ASST PROF, 1992-. **HONORS AND AWARDS** Drew Child Development Corp., Lorraine Hansberry Award, 1991; American Library Association, Coretta Scott King Award, 1981, 1988; MADRE, Humanitarian Award, 1984; Medgar Evers College, Fannie Lou Hamer Award, 1984; Lincoln University, Unity in Media Award, 1982, 1983; Brooklyn Museum, Art Books for Children Award, 1974, 1975; numerous others. **MEMBERSHIPS** Organization of Women Writers of Africa, Inc (OWWA). **SELECTED PUBLICATIONS** Author: An Enchanted Hair Tale, 1987, Don't Explain: A Song of Billie Holiday, 1980, Na-Ni, 1973, (all Harper & Row); Blue Heat, Poems, Diva Publishing, 1985; Spirits In The Street, Doubleday, 1973; writer: "Walking into Freedom with Nelson and Winnie Mandela," June 1990, "Forty Fine: A Writer Reflects on Turning Forty," Jan 1990, "Alice Walker: Rebel With A Cause," Sept 1989, (all Essence Magazine); numerous other poems, short stories and plays. **CONTACT ADDRESS** Dept Amer Studies, SUNY, Buffalo, 1010 Clemens Hall, Buffalo, NY, 14260.

DE VILLERS, JEAN-PIERRE
PERSONAL m **DISCIPLINE** MODERN LITERATURE **EDUCATION** Univ Colorado, PhD. **CAREER** Prof, Univ Windsor; Fulbright Scholar, Wesleyan Univ & Univ Colo at Boulder, 61-68; taught at, Univ Colo; Univ Notre Dame; US Air Force Lang Sch at Sacramento & Univ Calif. **HONORS AND AWARDS** Founder and ed, Stud on Futurism and the Avant-Garde. **RESEARCH** Futurist participation in the genesis of the Avant-Garde. **SELECTED PUBLICATIONS** Auth, Les drames de Roger Vitrac et le theatre d'avant-garde,Ann Arbor: Univ Microfilms, 67; Futurism And the Arts - Le Futurisme et les Arts - II e le Arti, Toronto and Buffalo: U of Toronto P, 75; FT Marinetti et le Premier Manifeste du Futurisme, U of Ottawa P, 86; Futurist Manifestoes / Manifestes Futuristes, U of Ottawa P, 98; Guns of Babylon Docudrama-novel, Toronto: Lugus Publ, 93; Le cas d'un marginal de genie: Alfred Jarry, Exile, Marginaux et parias dans les litteratures francophones, Toronto: Editions du Gref, 94; Con Marinetti e Boccioni a Dosso Casina, Simultaneita, Roma, Vol I, 97; Duchamp-Picabia et le Cubo-Futurisme. Penetration de l'Art Moderne aux Etats-Unis, Ligeia - Dossiers sur l'art, Paris, Centre National de la Recherche Scientifique, Oct 97-Juin 98; contrib, Dada in America, Edizioni De Luca, Roma: Dada, l'arte della negazione, 94; rev, Balla in Canada, Futurismo Oggi, 87 & Boccioni: Une retrospective, Ligeia - Dossiers sur l'Art, Paris: Centre National de la Recherche Scientifique, Oct 88-Mar 89. **CONTACT ADDRESS** Dept of French Language and Literature, Univ of Windsor, 401 Sunset Ave, Windsor, ON, N9B 3P4. **EMAIL** deville@uwindsor.ca

DEAGON, ANN FLEMING
PERSONAL Born 01/19/1930, Birmingham, AL, m, 1951, 2 children **DISCIPLINE** CLASSICS, CREATIVE WRITING **EDUCATION** Birmingham-Southern Col, BA, 50; Univ NC, MA, 51, PhD(Latin), 54. **CAREER** Asst prof classics, Furman Univ, 54-56; from asst prof to assoc prof, 56-75, prof Classics, Guilford Col, 75-92; Nat Endowment for Arts literary fel, 82. **MEMBERSHIPS** Am Philol Asn; Class Asn Midwest & S; Poetry Soc Am; Archaeological Inst Am. **SELECTED PUBLICATIONS** Auth, Poetics South, Blair, 74; Carbon 14, Univ Mass, 74; Indian Summer, Unicorn Press, 75; Women and Children First, Iron Mountain, 76; There is No Balm in Birmingham, Godine, 78; The Flood Story, Winthrop Col, 81; Habitats, Green River Press, 82; auth, The Diver's Tomb, St martins, 84; auth, The Polo Poems, Nebraska, 90. **CONTACT ADDRESS** 802 Woodbrook Dr, Greensboro, NC, 27410. **EMAIL** anndeacon@worldnet.att.net

DEAKINS, ROGER LEE
PERSONAL Born 12/04/1933, Decatur, IL, m, 1967, 3 children **DISCIPLINE** ENGLISH LITERATURE **EDUCATION** Univ Ill, BA, 56; Harvard Univ, MA, 58, PhD(English), 65. **CAREER** Instr English, Beloit Col, 61-65 & City Col New York, 65-68; asst prof, 68-72, ASSOC PROF ENGLISH, NY UNIV, 72- Am Coun Learned Soc fel, 72-73. **MEMBERSHIPS** Renaissance Soc Am; MLA. **RESEARCH** Renaissance literature; philosophy; history. **SELECTED PUBLICATIONS** Ed, Il Moro: Ellis Heywood's Dialogue in Memory of Thomas More, Harvard Univ, 72. **CONTACT ADDRESS** Dept of English, New York Univ, 19 University Pl, New York, NY, 10003-4556.

DEAN, DENNIS RICHARD
PERSONAL Born 05/29/1938, Belvidere, IL, m, 1968 **DISCIPLINE** ENGLISH, HISTORY OF SCIENCE **EDUCATION** Stanford Univ, AB, 60, AM, 62; Univ Wis-Madison, PhD(English), 68. **CAREER** Instr English, Kenosha Ctr, Univ Wis, 67-68; asst prof, 68-73, assoc prof English, 73-82, PROF ENGLISH & HUMANITIES, UNIV WIS-PARKSIDE, 82-, Fulbright award, Korea, 77; NSF grant, New Zealand, 82. **MEMBERSHIPS** AAUP; Hist Sci Soc; Keats-Shelley Asn. **RESEARCH** Literature and science; British romantics; history of science, especially geology. **SELECTED PUBLICATIONS** Auth, The San-Francisco Earthquake of 1906, Annals of Sci, Vol 0050, 93. **CONTACT ADDRESS** Humanities Div, Univ of Wis-Parkside, Kenosha, WI, 53140.

DEAN, JAMES S.
DISCIPLINE ENGLISH **EDUCATION** Birmingham Univ, PhD. **CAREER** Prof; taught in, NAm, SAm & Europe; done, oceanographic study, Mediter. **SELECTED PUBLICATIONS** Auth, The Art of Double Bass Playing, 73; Robert Greene: A Reference Guide, 84; Sailing A Square-Rigger, 95. **CONTACT ADDRESS** Dept of Eng, Univ of Wisconsin, Parkside, 900 Wood Rd, 272 Commun, PO Box 2000, Kenosha, WI, 53141-2000. **EMAIL** dean@uwp.edu

DEAN, JOAN FITZPATRICK
PERSONAL Born 12/24/1949, Dunkirk, NY **DISCIPLINE** ENGLISH **EDUCATION** Canisius Col, AB, 70; Purdue Univ, MA, 72, PhD(English), 75. **CAREER** Asst English, Purdue Univ, 70-74, grad instr, 74-75; asst prof, 75-81, ASSOC PROF ENGLISH, UNIV MO, KANSAS CITY, 81-. **MEMBERSHIPS** MLA. **RESEARCH** Contemporary drama; contemporary film; Renaissance literature. **SELECTED PUBLICATIONS** Auth, Barry,Sebastian the Steward of Christendom, Theatre Jour, Vol 0049, 97; Carr,Marina Portia Coughlan, Theatre Jour, Vol 0049, 97. **CONTACT ADDRESS** Dept of English, Univ of Mo, 5100 Rockhill Rd, Kansas City, MO, 64110-2499.

DEAN, MISAO A.
DISCIPLINE CANADIAN LITERATURE **EDUCATION** Carleton Univ, BA, MA; Queen's Univ, PhD. **CAREER** Assoc prof **RESEARCH** Canadian novel writing by women; gender stud; pop culture in Canada. **SELECTED PUBLICATIONS** Auth, A Different Point of View: Sara Jeannette Duncan, McGill-Queen's Press, 91; Practising Femininity: Domestic Realism and Gender in Early Canadian Fiction, Univ Toronto, 98. **CONTACT ADDRESS** Dept of English, Victoria Univ, PO Box 3070, Victoria, BC, V8W 3W1. **EMAIL** mdean@uvic.ca

DEAN, SUSAN DAY
PERSONAL Born 02/05/1937, Richmond, VA, d, 2 children **DISCIPLINE** ENGLISH LITERATURE, AMERICAN LITERATURE **EDUCATION** Sweet Briar Col, BA, 58; Bryn Mawr Col, MA, 68, PhD, 75. **CAREER** Librn, New York Pub Libr, 61-66; ASSOC PROF ENGLISH & AMERICAN LITERATURE, BRYN MAWR COL, 76-. **MEMBERSHIPS** MLA; Northeast Mod Lang Asn; Thomas Hardy Soc Am; Soc Values Higher Educ. **RESEARCH** Walt Whitman and the American long poem; American Romanticism; Thomas Hardy; Native American literature. **SELECTED PUBLICATIONS** Auth, Hardy's Poetic Vision in The Dynasts: The Diorama of A Dream, Princeton Univ, 77; ed, From Hardy to Max Gate: Ten Unpublished Hardy Letters, Bryn Mawr Col, 79. **CONTACT ADDRESS** Dept of English, Bryn Mawr Col, 101 N Merion Ave, Bryn Mawr, PA, 19010-2899. **EMAIL** sdean@brynmawr.edu

DEAN MOORE, KATHLEEN
PERSONAL m, 2 children **DISCIPLINE** LEGAL REASONING **EDUCATION** Univ Colo, PhD. **CAREER** Philos, Oregon St Univ. **HONORS AND AWARDS** Burlington Northern Found Fac Achievement Award; Meehan Excellence Tchg Award., Chair, dept Philos. **RESEARCH** Philos law. **SELECTED PUBLICATIONS** Auth, Pardons: Justice, Mercy, and the Public Interest, NY: Oxford UP, 89; Reasoning and Writing, Macmillan, 93; Inductive Arguments: The Critical Thinking Skills; Riverwalking, Lyons and Burford, 95. **CONTACT ADDRESS** Dept Philos, Oregon State Univ, Corvallis, OR, 97331-4501. **EMAIL** kmoore@orst.edu

DEANE, SEAMUS
DISCIPLINE IRISH STUDIES **EDUCATION** Cambridge Univ, PhD. **CAREER** Donald and Marilyn Keough Prof Irish Stud, Univ Notre Dame; dir, Field Day Theatre and Publ Co. **SELECTED PUBLICATIONS** Auth, Celtic Revivals: Essays in Modern Irish Literature 1880-1980; A Short History of Irish Literature; The French Revolution and Enlightenment in England 1789-1832; ed, The Field Day Anthology of Irish Writing. **CONTACT ADDRESS** Univ Notre Dame, Notre Dame, IN, 46556.

DEARIN, RAY DEAN
PERSONAL Born 12/17/1941, Paragould, AK, m, 1964, 2 children **DISCIPLINE** SPEECH **EDUCATION** Harding Col, BA, 63; Univ Ill, Champaign, MA, 65, PhD, 70. **CAREER** From instr to assoc prof, 65-77, PROF SPEECH, IA STATE UNIV, 77-; Consult ed, Cent States Speech J, 73-74. **MEMBERSHIPS** Cent States Commun Asn; Nat Commun Asn. **RESEARCH** Rhetoric; public address. **SELECTED PUBLICATIONS** Auth, Aristotle on Psychology and Rhetoric, Cent States Speech J, 11/66; The Philosophical Basis of Chaim Perelman's Theory of Rhetoric, Quart J Speech, 10/69; Justice in Ethics, Politics and Rhetoric, IA J Speech, fall 69; auth, The Fourth Stasis in Greek Rhetoric, In: Rhetoric and Communication, Univ IL, 76; Public address history as part of the speech communication discipline, Commun Educ, 9/80; The New Rhetoric of Chaim Perelman, 89. **CONTACT ADDRESS** Program in Speech Communication, Iowa State Univ, Ames, IA, 50011-2204. **EMAIL** rdearin@iastate.edu

DECATUR, LOUIS AUBREY
PERSONAL Born 04/27/1931, Washington, DC, m, 1965, 2 children **DISCIPLINE** RENAISSANCE LITERATURE **EDUCATION** Univ Md, College Park, BA, 54, MA, 63, PhD, 70. **CAREER** Lectr English, Univ Md, Europ Div, 63-65; instr, Univ Md, College Park, 65-68; asst prof, US Naval Acad, 68-70; asst prof, 70-80, assoc prof Eng, Ursinus Col, 80-. **HONORS AND AWARDS** Christian & Mary Lindback Award for Outstanding Teaching, 78. **MEMBERSHIPS** MLA; AAUP; Renaissance Soc Am. **RESEARCH** Renaissance prose fiction; folklore, prose; Renaissance drama. **SELECTED PUBLICATIONS** Art, West German Shakespeare as Seen by a Teacher Abroad, Shakespeare Quarterly, 82; art, The New Japanese Hamlet, Shakespeare Yearbook IX, 98. **CONTACT ADDRESS** Dept of English, Ursinus Col, PO Box 1000, Collegeville, PA, 19426-2562. **EMAIL** ldecatur@acad.ursinus.edu

DECKER, PHILIP H.
PERSONAL Born 04/19/1932, Lakewood, OH, m, 1955, 2 children **DISCIPLINE** SPEECH & DRAMA **EDUCATION** Knox Col, BA, 54; Northwestern Univ, MA, 55, PhD(theatre), 66. **CAREER** From asst prof to assoc prof, 57-71, chemn dept, 66-73, prof speech & theatre arts, MacMurray Col, 71-84-, chemn dept, 76-84; prof of English & Drama, 84-97, chair, dept English & Drama, 88-91, 94-97, prof emer, MacMurray Col, 97-, development officer, 97-. **HONORS AND AWARDS** Northwestern Univ fel, 54-55, 60-61; ISTA Pres Award for Outstanding Service, 85; MacMurray Col Wilkins Award for Excellence in Teaching, 86, 91; IL Col Citation in the Arts for distinguished contributions to the Fine Arts, 91; IL State Hist Soc Cert of Excellence for A Window on the Past, 91; Phi Beta Kappa, 94; Dept Honors, 94; listed in: Outstanding Educators of America, 90; Personalities in the Midwest. **MEMBERSHIPS** Speech Commun Asn; Am Educ Theatre Asn; Cent States Speech Asn. **RESEARCH** Dramatic literature, especially 20th century English, American and Elizabethan; theatre history; aesthetics of performance. **SELECTED PUBLICATIONS** Coauth, An Annotated Bibliography of Sources for Period Patterns, Educ Theatre J, 3/62; A Window on the Past: Residences of Jacksonville, IL, Their History and Design, 90. **CONTACT ADDRESS** Dept Theatre Arts, MacMurray Col, 477 E College Ave, Jacksonville, IL, 62650-2510. **EMAIL** pdecker@mac.edu

DECKER, WILLIAM
DISCIPLINE 19TH CENTURY AMERICAN LITERATURE **EDUCATION** Iowa, PhD, 84. **CAREER** Engl, Okla St Univ. **RESEARCH** Poetry of Whitman, Dickinson and their contemporaries. **SELECTED PUBLICATIONS** Auth, The Literary Vocation Of Henry Adams, Univ N Carolina Press, 90; Epistolary Practices: Letter Writing In America Before The Era Of Telecommunications, Univ N Carolina Press, 98. **CONTACT ADDRESS** Oklahoma State Univ, 101 Whitehurst Hall, Stillwater, OK, 74078.

DEE, JULIET L.
DISCIPLINE COMMUNICATION **EDUCATION** Princeton Univ, AB, 74; Northwestern Univ, MA, 75; Temple Univ, PhD, 81. **CAREER** Asst prof, Rugers Univ, 80-82; vis asst prof, Univ Calif, 82-84; asst prof, 84-92; assoc prof, 92-; dir, Legal Stud prog, 96-. **HONORS AND AWARDS** Award, Del Hum Forum, 86; grant, 86., Ch, fac senate comm on cult act and pub events, 94-95, 97-. **RESEARCH** Communications and law. **SELECTED PUBLICATIONS** Co-auth, Mass Communs Law in a Nutshell, West, 88; To Avoid Charges of Indecency, Please Hang Up Now: An Analysis of Legislation and Litigation Involving Dial-a-Porn, Commun and the Law, 94; Reconciling the Preferences of Environmental Activists and Corporate Policymakers, Jour of Pub Rel Res, 96; News Coverage of Abortion between Roe and Webster: Public Opinion and Real-World Events, Commun Res Rpt, 97; auth, Subliminal Lyrics in Heavy Metal Music: More Litigation, Anyone?, Commun and the Law, 94; Little Red Riding Hood, Justice Rehnquist and the NEA, Free Speech Yrbk, 95; Twins Separated at Birth: The Strange Cases of Michael Levin and Leonard Jeffries, The Howard Jour Commun, 95; Identifying a Victim when the Criminal is at Large: Is It Negligent or Newsworthy?, Commun and the Law, 96; When Classified Ads Lead to Murder: Hitmen, Soldier of Fortune, and the Question of Commercial Speech, Commun and the Law, 96. **CONTACT ADDRESS** Dept of Commun, Univ Delaware, 162 Ctr Mall, Newark, DE, 19716.

DEESE, HELEN R.
DISCIPLINE ENGLISH **EDUCATION** David Lipscomb Coll, BA, 65; Univ Tenn, MA, 67; George Peabody Coll, PhD, 73. **CAREER** PROF, ENG, TENN TECH UNIV **MEMBERSHIPS** Am Antiquarian Soc **SELECTED PUBLICATIONS** Ed & intro, Jones Very: The Complete Poems, 93. **CONTACT ADDRESS** Dept of Eng, Tenn Tech Univ, Cookeville, TN, 38505.

DEETZ, STANLEY A.
DISCIPLINE COMMUNCATION STUDIES **EDUCATION** Manchester Col, BS, 70; Univ Ohio, MA, 72, PhD, 73. **CAREER** Prof. **HONORS AND AWARDS** Outstanding Res Bk Awd, 94. **RESEARCH** Organizational communication. **SELECTED PUBLICATIONS** Auth, Describing differences in approaches to organizational science: Rethinking Burrell and Morgan and their legacy, 96; Transforming communication, transforming business: Building responsive and responsible workplaces, Hampton, 95; Democracy in an age of corporate colonization: Developments in communication and the politics of everyday life, Univ NY, 92. **CONTACT ADDRESS** Dept of Communication, Univ Colo Boulder, Boulder, CO, 80309. **EMAIL** Stanley.Deetz@Colorado.edu

DEKOVEN, MARIANNE
DISCIPLINE ENGLISH LANGUAGE AND LITERATURE **EDUCATION** Radcliffe Univ, BA; Stanford, PhD. **CAREER** Prof. **RESEARCH** Feminist theory and criticism; modernism and postmodernism; cultural history. **SELECTED PUBLICATIONS** Auth, A Different Language: Gertrude Stein's Experimental Writing; auth, Rich and Strange: Gender, History, Modernism. **CONTACT ADDRESS** Dept of English, Rutgers Univ, 510 George St, Murray Hall, New Brunswick, NJ, 08901-1167. **EMAIL** dekoven@rci.rutgers.edu

DELAHUNTY, GERALD
DISCIPLINE ENGLISH LITERATURE **EDUCATION** Univ Dublin, BA, MA; Univ Ca, PhD. **CAREER** Assoc prof. **SELECTED PUBLICATIONS** Auth, pubs on syntactic theory; sociolinguistics; functional grammar; Irish archaeology; co-auth, Communication Language and Grammar, McGraw Hill, 94. **CONTACT ADDRESS** Dept of English, Colorado State Univ, Fort Collins, CO, 80523. **EMAIL** delahunty@vines.colostate.edu

DELANEY, PAUL
DISCIPLINE ENGLISH **EDUCATION** Emory University, PhD, 72. **CAREER** Prof, 72-. **HONORS AND AWARDS** Danforth fel, Emory Univ, 69-72; fac res award, 92. **MEMBERSHIPS** Mem, Nat CCL Bd Dir, 93-96. **RESEARCH** Modern drama; modern poetry; Shakespeare; 19th & 20th cent Am lit; 20th cent Irish lit. **SELECTED PUBLICATIONS** Auth, Tom Stoppard in Conversation, Univ Mich Press, 94; Tom Stoppard: Craft and Craftiness, PMLA 107, 92; Structure and Anarchy in Tom Stoppard, PMLA 106, 91; Tom Stoppard: The Moral Vision of the Major Plays, London: Macmillan Press, New York: St. Martin's Press, 90. **CONTACT ADDRESS** Dept of Eng, Westmont Col, 955 La Paz Rd, Santa Barbara, CA, 93108-1099.

DELANY, PAUL
PERSONAL Born 07/18/1937, Purley, England **DISCIPLINE** ENGLISH **EDUCATION** McGill Univ, BComm, 57; Stanford Univ, AM, 58; Univ Calif Berkeley, MA, 61, PhD, 65. **CAREER** Econ, Int Labour Off Geneva, 58-59; instr, Columbia Univ, 64-66; asst to assoc prof, 66-77, PROF ENGLISH, SIMON FRASER UNIV, 77-; exch prof, Univ Waterloo, 85-86. **HONORS AND AWARDS** Guggenheim fel, 73; Killam res fel, 92-93; vis fel, Corpus Christi Col, Cambridge, 95-96; fel, Royal Soc Lit; fel, Royal Soc Can. **MEMBERSHIPS** MLA; ACUTE; DH Lawrence Soc Am (pres 90-92). **SELECTED PUBLICATIONS** Auth, British Autobiography in the Seventeenth Century, 69; auth, D.H. Lawrence's Nightmare, 78; auth, The Neo-Pagans, 87; ed, Vancouver: Representing the Postmodern City, 94; co-ed, Hypermedia and Literary Studies, 91; co-ed, The Digital Word, 93. **CONTACT ADDRESS** Dept of English, Simon Fraser Univ, Burnaby, BC, V5A 1S6.

DELANY, SHEILA
PERSONAL New Haven, CT **DISCIPLINE** ENGLISH **EDUCATION** Wellesley Col, BA, 61; Univ Calif Berkley, MA, 63; Columbia Univ, PhD, 67. **CAREER** Queen's Col, City Univ NY, 67-69; PROF, SIMON FRASER UNIV 70-. **HONORS AND AWARDS** Woodrow Wilson fel, 61-62; Fiction Award, Berkley, 63; Killam Res fel, 93-95. **MEMBERSHIPS** MLA; Medieval Academy Am; New Chaucer Soc; Can Col Univ Tchrs Eng. **SELECTED PUBLICATIONS** Auth, Counter-Tradition: The Literature of Dissent and Alternatives, 70; auth, Chaucer's House of Fame: The Poetics of Skeptical Fideism, 72; auth, Writing Women: Women Writers and Women in Literature, Medieval to Modern, 83; auth, The Naked Text: Chaucer's Legend of Good Women, 94. **CONTACT ADDRESS** Dept of English, Simon Fraser Univ, Burnaby, BC, V5A 1S6. **EMAIL** sdelany@sfu.ca

DELASANTA, RODNEY
PERSONAL Born 11/06/1932, Winchendon, MA, m, 1953, 4 children **DISCIPLINE** ENGLISH LITERATURE **EDUCATION** Providence Col, AB, 53; Brown Univ, AM, 55, PhD, 62. **CAREER** Teaching asst, Brown Univ, 55-57, instr English, 57-61; from asst prof to assoc prof, 61-70 PROF ENGLISH LITERATURE, PROVIDENCE COL, 70-; Vis prof English literature, Univ Fribourg, 68-70; Univ Neuchatel, 69-70; Vis prof, Brown Univ, 83. **HONORS AND AWARDS** Sears Roebuck Prize, Distinguished Teaching, 91. **MEMBERSHIPS** MLA; Medieval Acad Am; New Chaucer Soc. **RESEARCH** English medieval and Renaissance literature. **SELECTED PUBLICATIONS** Auth, The Epic Voice, Mouton, 67; Christian affirmation in the Book of the Duchess, PMLA, 1/69; The theme of judgment in the Canterbury Tales, Mod Lang Quart, 9/70; And of great reverence: Chaucer's Man of Law, Chaucer Rev, spring 71; Sacrament and sacrifice in the Pardoner's Tale, Ann Mediaevale, 73; Penance and poetry in the Canterbury Tales, PMLA, 3/78; Alisoun and the saved harlots: A Cozening of our expectations, Chaucer Rev, spring 78; Chaucer and the problem of universals, Medievalia, 82; Chaucer and Strode, Chaucer Rev, 91; Nominalism and typology in Chaucer, in Typology and English Medieval Literature, AMS Press, 92; co-auth, Chaucer's Orygnes Upon the Maudeleyne: A Translation, Chaucer Rev, 96; Nominalism and the Clerk's Tale Revisited, Chaucer Rev, 97. **CONTACT ADDRESS** Dept of English, Providence Col, 549 River Ave, Providence, RI, 02918-0002. **EMAIL** delasant@providence.edu

DELAURA, DAVID JOSEPH
PERSONAL Born 11/19/1930, Worcester, MA, m, 1961, 3 children **DISCIPLINE** ENGLISH LITERATURE **EDUCATION** Boston Col, AB, 55, AM, 58; Univ Wis, PhD, 60 **CAREER** From instr to prof English, Univ Tex, Austin, 60-74; AVALON FOUND PROF HUMANITIES & PROF ENGLISH, UNIV PA, 74-, Guggenheim Found fel, 67-68; Nat Endowment for Humanities fel, 78-79. **HONORS AND AWARDS** First William Riley Parker Prize of the Mod Lang Asn, Outstanding Article, PMLA, 64. **MEMBERSHIPS** MLA **RESEARCH** Nineteeth and 20th century English literature. **SELECTED PUBLICATIONS** Auth, Arnold and Carlyle, PMLA, 3/64; The place of the classics in T S Eliot's Christian humanism, In: Hereditas: Seven Essays on the Modern Experience of the Classical, Univ Tex, 64; The ache of modernism in Hardy's later novels, ELH, 9/67; Hebrew and Hellene in Victorian England: Newman, Arnold, and Pater, Univ Tex, 69; ed, Victorian prose: a guide to research, MLA, 73; The context of Browning's painter poems: Asthetics, polemics and historics, PMLA, 5/80; Arnold and Goethe: The one on the intellectual throne, In: Victorian Literature and Society, Ohio State Univ, 84; Ruskin, Arnold and Browning's Grammarian: Crowded with culture, In: Victorian Perspectives, Macmillan, 89. **CONTACT ADDRESS** Dept of English, Univ of Pa, 3340 Walnut St, Philadelphia, PA, 19104-6273.

DELBANCO, ANDREW
DISCIPLINE CLASSIC AMERICAN LITERATURE **EDUCATION** Harvard Univ, AB, 73, PhD, 80. **CAREER** Vis prof, Yale Univ; Julian Clarence Levi prof, 85-. **HONORS AND AWARDS** Grants, Guggenheim found; NEH; NH Ctr; Lionel Trilling award., Ed, The Portable Abraham Lincoln, 92; co-ed, The Puritans in America, 85; contrib, The New Republic. **SELECTED PUBLICATIONS** Auth, The Puritan Ordeal, 89;William Ellery Channing, 81; The Death of Satan: How Americans Have Lost the Sense of Evil, Farrar, Straus, and Giroux, 95; Required Reading: Why Our American Classics Matter Now, 97. **CONTACT ADDRESS** Dept of Eng, Columbia Col, New York, 2960 Broadway, New York, NY, 10027-6902.

DELL, CHAD E.
DISCIPLINE COMMUNICATION ARTS **EDUCATION** Univ of Wis at Madison, BA, 87, MA, 91, PhD, 97. **CAREER** Asst prof, Dept of Commun, Monmouth Univ, 96-. **HONORS AND AWARDS** Award for Outstanding Teaching by a Grad Student, 92-93. **MEMBERSHIPS** Am Studies Asn; Asn for Ed in Journalism and Mass Commun; Int Commun Asn; Nat Commun Asn; NJ Commun Asn; Soc for Cinema Studies; Union for Democratic Commun. **RESEARCH** Media audiences and fandom **SELECTED PUBLICATIONS** Auth, Lookit That Hunk of Man!: Subversive Pleasures, Female Fandom and Professional Wrestling, Theorizing Fandom: Fans, Subculture and Identity, Hampton, 98; coauth, Big Differences on the Small Screen: Race, Class, Gender, Feminine Beauty and the Characters at Frank's Place, Women Making Meaning: New Feminist Directions in Commun, Routledge, 92. **CONTACT ADDRESS** Communication Dept, Monmouth Univ, 400 Cedar Ave, West Long Branch, NJ, 07764-1898. **EMAIL** cdell@mondec.monmouth.edu

DEMARIA, ROBERT
PERSONAL Born 11/30/1948, New York, NY, m, 1977, 2 children **DISCIPLINE** ENGLISH **EDUCATION** Amherst College, BA, 70; Rutgers Univ, PhD, 75. **CAREER** Asst, Assoc, Prof, Henry Noble MacCracken Prof, 75-, Vassar College. **HONORS AND AWARDS** Guggenheim Fel; ASBS Fel. **MEMBERSHIPS** MLA; ALSC; ASELS; Samuel Johnson Soc. **RESEARCH** 18th Cent British Literature; History of English. **SELECTED PUBLICATIONS** Auth, British Literature: A Critical Reader, Oxford, Blackwell, 99; auth, Samuel Johnson and the Life of Reading, Baltimore, JHU Press, 97; British Literature 1640-1789: An Anthology, Oxford, Blackwell, 96; auth, The Life of Samuel Johnson, Oxford, Blackwell, 93; Johnson's Dictionary and Dictionary Johnson, Yearbook of Eng Studies, 98; Johnson's Dictionary and the Teutonic Roots of English, in: Language and Civilization, ed Claudia Bank, Berne, Peter Lang 92. **CONTACT ADDRESS** Vassar Col, Box 140, Poughkeepsie, NY, 12604. **EMAIL** demaria@vassar.edu

DEMARR, MARY JEAN
PERSONAL Born 09/20/1932, Champaign, IL **DISCIPLINE** ENGLISH **EDUCATION** Lawrence Col, BA, 54; Univ Ill, Urbana, AM, 57, PhD(English), 63. **CAREER** Asst prof English, Willamette Univ, 64-65; from asst prof to assoc prof, 65-75, PROF ENGLISH, IND STATE UNIV, TERRE HAUTE, 75-. **MEMBERSHIPS** MLA; Mod Humanities Res Asn; NCTE; AAUP; Popular Cult Asn. **RESEARCH** American literature; women's studies. **SELECTED PUBLICATIONS** Auth, Chopin,Kate Reconsidered--Beyond the Bayou, Jour Pop Cult, Vol 0027, 94. **CONTACT ADDRESS** Dept of English, Indiana State Univ, Terre Haute, IN, 47809.

DEMASTES, WILLIAM
DISCIPLINE MODERN DRAMA, AMERICAN LITERATURE, SHAKESPEARE **EDUCATION** Wis, PhD, 86. **CAREER** Prof, La State Univ; dir, MA in Hum prog, 96-, dir, grad stud, 92-94, dir, LSU in London, 95, ser ed, Mod Dramatists Res and Prod Sourcebooks. **RESEARCH** Modern dramatists. **SELECTED PUBLICATIONS** Auth, The Future of Avant-Garde Drama and Criticism: The Case of Sam Shepard, J of Dramatic Theory and Criticism, 90; Of Sciences and the Arts: From Influence to Interplay Between Natural Philosophy and Drama, Stud in the Lit Imagination, 91; Clifford Odets, 91; 'We Gotta Hang Together': Horovitz and the National Cycles of Violence, Israel Horovitz, 94; Re-Inspecting the Crack in the Chimney: Chaos Theory From Ibsen to Stoppard, New Theatre Quart, 94; Jessie and Thelma Revisited: Marsha Norman's Conceptual Challenge in 'night, Mother, Mod Drama, 94; Arthur Miller's Use and Modification of the American Realist/Naturalist Tradition, in Approaches to Teaching Arthur Miller's Death of a Salesman, 95; Theatre of Chaos, 97; ed, American Playwrights, 1880-1945, 94; British Playwrights, 1956-1995, 96; Realism and the American Dramatic Tradition, 96; coed, British Playwrights, 1880-1956, 96; Irish Playwrights, 1880-1995, 97. **CONTACT ADDRESS** Dept of Eng, Louisiana State Univ, 244 Hodges Hall, Baton Rouge, LA, 70803.

DEMERS, FRANCOIS
PERSONAL Born 07/14/1943, Sudbury, ON, Canada **DISCIPLINE** COMMUNICATIONS **EDUCATION** Univ Montreal, BA(Theol), 65; Laval Univ, BA(Phil), 77. **CAREER** Journalist, 65-80; PROF, LAVAL UNIV, 80-, dean arts, 87-96. **SELECTED PUBLICATIONS** Auth, Chroniques impertinentes du troisieme Front commun syndical, 82; auth, Communication et syndicalisme-des imprimeurs aux journalistes, 88; co-ed, America and the Americas, 92; co-ed, Challenges for International Broadcasting, 93. **CONTACT ADDRESS** Pavillon Casault, Laval Univ, Sainte-Foy, PQ, G1K 7P4. **EMAIL** Francois.Demers@com.ulaval.ca

DEMING, ROBERT HOWARD
PERSONAL Born 10/12/1937, Hartford, CT, m, 1962, 3 children **DISCIPLINE** ENGLISH **EDUCATION** Union Col, BA, 59; Univ KS, MA, 61, Univ WI, PhD, 65. **CAREER** Asst prof Eng, Miami Univ, 65-70; assoc prof, 70-72, prof eng, State Univ NY Col Fredonia, 72, ch person, 75-81, 97-00. **RESEARCH** Film study; non-fiction film; cult studies; feminism; TV studies. **SELECTED PUBLICATIONS** Auth, A Bibliography of James Joyce Studies, Univ Kans Libr, 64, 65, rev ed, 77; ed, Joyce: The Critical Heritage, Routledge & Kegan Paul, 70; auth, Ceremony and Art: Robert Herrick's Poetry, Mouton, Hague, 74; Love and knowledge in the Renaissance lyric, Tex Studies Lang & Lit, 74. **CONTACT ADDRESS** Dept of Eng, State Univ of NY Col, 1 Suny at Fredonia, Fredonia, NY, 14063-1143. **EMAIL** deming@ait.fredonia.edu

DENDINGER, LLOYD N.
PERSONAL Born 07/28/1929, New Orleans, LA, m, 1951, 3 children **DISCIPLINE** ENGLISH **EDUCATION** Tulane Univ, BA, 53; Vanderbilt Univ, MA, 61; La State Univ, PhD(English), 66. **CAREER** Instr English, Nicholls State Col, 61-64 & La State Univ, 64-66; from asst prof to assoc prof, 66-76, prof English & chmn dept, Univ S Ala, 76-85. **HONORS AND AWARDS** NEH Scholar, Princeton, Summer 76; Univ S Ala Alum Assn Prof of the Year. **MEMBERSHIPS** MLA; S Atlantic Mod Lang Asn. **SELECTED PUBLICATIONS** Auth, The Irrational Appeal of Frost's Dark Deep Woods, Southern Rev, Fall 66; Crane's Inverted Use of Images of The Rime of the Ancient Mariner, Studies Short Fiction, Winter 68; Robert Frost: The Popular and Central Poetic Images, Am Quart, Winter 69; Robert Frost in Birmingham, Ball State Forum X1V, Summer 73; The Ghoul-Haunted Woodland of Robert Frost, S Atlantic Bull, 11/73; Emerson's Influence on Frost Through William Dean Howells, In: Frost: Centennial Essays, Univ Press of Miss, 74; ed, E E Cummings: The Critical Reception, Burt Franklin, 81. **CONTACT ADDRESS** Dept of English, Univ of Southern Alabama, 307 University Bvd N, Mobile, AL, 36688-3053. **EMAIL** ldending@jaguarl.usouthal.edu

DENEEF, LEIGH A.
DISCIPLINE ENGLISH LITERATURE **EDUCATION** PA State Univ, PhD, 69. **CAREER** Assoc prof, Duke Univ. **RESEARCH** Psychoanalytical approaches to lit. **SELECTED PUBLICATIONS** Auth, This Poetick Liturgie: Robert Herrick's Ceremonial Mode, Duke, 74; Spenser and the Motives of Metaphor, Duke, 82; Traherne in Dialogue: Heidegger, Lacan, and Derrida, Duke, 88. **CONTACT ADDRESS** Eng Dept, Duke Univ, Durham, NC, 27706.

DENNISTON, DOROTHY L.
PERSONAL Born 08/10/1944, Springfield, MA, d **DISCIPLINE** ENGLISH **EDUCATION** Northeastern Univ, BA 1967; Simmons College, MA 1975; Brown Univ, PhD 1983. **CAREER** Secondary Schools, teacher of English, 1967-71; Simmons Coll, asst to dir of admiss, 1971-72, instr of English, 1972-74, assoc dean, 1974-76, 79-80; Univ of TN, asst prof of English, 1983-86; Brown Univ, vstg prof English, 1987-88, asst prof, 1988-94, assoc prof, 1994-. **HONORS AND AWARDS** Omega Psi Phi Fraternity Scholarship Boston Chptr 1962; J Rosen Scholarship Award Boston Chptr NE Univ 1965; Fellow Natl Fellowship Fund 1976-79; Brown University, Dorothy Danforth Compton Fellowship, 1981-82, Howard Post-doctoral Fellowship, 1986-87, Wriston Fellowship for Excellence in Teaching, 1990; University of TN, Faculty Rsch Awd, 1985, Faculty Rsch Awd Dept of English, 1984; Ford Foundation, Summer Seminar for Coll Professors, Fellow, 1993. **MEMBERSHIPS** Nat Assoc Foreign Student Affairs, 1972; Assoc for Study of Negro Life & History, 1972-; Modern Lang Assn, 1975-; Alpha Kappa Alpha Sorority, 1963-67; adv com for scholars-internship prog Martin L King Jr Cntr for Social Change, 1976-; Natl Assoc of Interdisciplinay Ethnic Studies 1977-; standing comm on black studies Coll Lang Assoc 1983-86; SE Lang Assoc, 1984-86; Langston Hughes Center for the Arts, 1988-; NE Lang Association 1991-; college bd, English Composition Test Committee 1984-87; Coll Language Assn, 1984-. **SELECTED PUBLICATIONS** Auth, The Fiction of Paule Marshall: History, Culture & Gender, Univ Tenn Press, 1995; "Paule Marshall," American Women Writers from Colonial Times to Present, 1980, updated 1992; assoc ed, Langston Hughes Review; assoc ed, Abafazi: The Simmons College Review of Women of African Descent; "Paule Marshall," Black Women in America: An Historical Encyclopedia, 1992; Early Short Fiction by Paule Marshall, Short Story Criticism, 1990; Faulkner's Image of Blacks in Go Down Moses, Phylon, March, 1983. **CONTACT ADDRESS** Brown Univ, Box 1852, Providence, RI, 02912.

DENNISTON, ELLIOTT AVERETT
PERSONAL Born 06/08/1940, Philadelphia, PA, m, 1966, 2 children **DISCIPLINE** ENGLISH **EDUCATION** Princeton Univ, BA, 62; Univ Mich, Ann Arbor, MA, 67, PhD, 70. **CAREER** Asst prof English Ky Wesleyan Col, 70-74; PROF ENGLISH, MO SOUTHERN STATE COL, 74-, Ed, Green River Rev, 73-75. **RESEARCH** Ben Jonson; English Renaissance drama; British drama. **CONTACT ADDRESS** Dept of English, Missouri Southern State Col, 3950 Newman Rd, Joplin, MO, 64801-1512.

DENT, GINA
DISCIPLINE AFRICAN DIASPORIC LITERATURE **EDUCATION** Univ Calif, BA, 89; Columbia, PhD, 97. **CAREER** English and Lit, Columbia Univ **SELECTED PUBLICATIONS** Ed, Black Popular Culture, 92. **CONTACT ADDRESS** Columbia Univ, 2960 Broadway, New York, NY, 10027-6902.

DEPORTE, MICHAEL VITAL
PERSONAL Born 04/24/1939, Albany, NY, m, 1992, 2 children **DISCIPLINE** ENGLISH LITERATURE **EDUCATION** Univ Minn, BA, 60; Stanford Univ, MA, 65, PhD, 66. **CAREER** From instr to asst prof English & humanities, Univ Chicago, 65-72; from asst prof to assoc prof, 72-81, prof English, Univ NH, 81-, Dir Grad Studies, 81-87, Chair, 87-97. **HONORS AND AWARDS** Woodrow Wilson Fel, 60; Lindberg Award for Outstanding Schol-Teacher, Univ NH, 86. **MEMBERSHIPS** MLA; Am Soc Eighteenth Century Studies; Friends of the Ehrenpreis Ctr for Swift Studies. **RESEARCH** English literature 1660-1800. **SELECTED PUBLICATIONS** Auth, Swift. God, and Power, In: Walking Naboth's Vineyard, Notre Dame Univ Press, 95; Vinum Daemonum: Swift and the Grape, Swift Studies, 97; Contemplating Collins: Freethinking in Swift, In: The Third Munster Symposium Papers, Wilhelm Fink Verlag, 98; author of numerous other articles. **CONTACT ADDRESS** Dept of English, Univ NH, 95 Main St, Durham, NH, 03824-3574. **EMAIL** mdeporte@christa.unh.edu

DEPROSPO, RICHARD CHRIS
PERSONAL Born 02/06/1949, Glen Cove, NY **DISCIPLINE** AMERICAN LITERATURE **EDUCATION** Yale Univ, BA, 71; Univ Va, PhD(Am lit), 77. **CAREER** ASST PROF ENGLISH, WASHINGTON COL, 75-. **MEMBERSHIPS** MLA. **RESEARCH** Eighteenth-and 19th-century American literature. **SELECTED PUBLICATIONS** Auth, American Women-Writers to 1800, Early Amer Lit, Vol 0031, 96. **CONTACT ADDRESS** Washington Col, 300 Washington Ave, Chestertown, MD, 21620-1197.

DERESIEWICZ, WILLIAM
PERSONAL Born 01/13/1964, Englewood, NJ, m **DISCIPLINE** JOURNALISM **EDUCATION** Columbia Univ, BA, 85, MS, 87, MA, 90, MPhil, 93, PhD, 98. **CAREER** Asst prof, 98-, Yale Univ. **RESEARCH** 19th & early 20th century Brit fict. **CONTACT ADDRESS** 54 Highland Ave, Guilford, CT, 06437. **EMAIL** william.deresiewicz@yale.edu

DERITTER, JONES
DISCIPLINE ENGLISH **EDUCATION** Oberlin Col, AB, 77; Univ VA, MA, 80, PhD, 88. **CAREER** Asst to assoc prof, Univ Scranton, 90-; vis asst prof, Skidmore Col, 89-90 & New Col, Univ S FL, 88-89; grad instr to instr, Univ VA, 81-88. **MEMBERSHIPS** MLA; Am Soc 18th-century Stud; Gp Early Mod Cult Stud. **RESEARCH** A collective biog of sev early mod women Pocahontas, Mary Jemison and Frances Slocum; who moved across the cult divide between Anglo-Am and native Am soc. **SELECTED PUBLICATIONS** Auth, Wonder not, princely Gloster, at the notice this paper brings you': Women, Writing, and Politics in Rowe's Jane Shore, Comp Drama 37, 97; Blaming the Audience, Blaming the Gods: Unwitting Incest in Three Eighteenth-century English Novels, Illicit Sex: Identity Politics in Early Modern Culture Athens, Univ GA Press, 96; The Embodiment of Characters: The Representation of Physical Experience on Stage and In Print, Univ Pa Press, 94; Not the Person she conceived me': The Public Identities of Charlotte Charke, Genders 19, 94; How Came This Muff Here: A Note on Tom Jones, Eng Lang Notes 26, 89 & A Cult of Dependence: The Social Context of The London Merchant, Comp Drama 21, 88. **CONTACT ADDRESS** Dept of Eng, Univ of Scranton, Scranton, PA, 18510.

DERRICK, CLARENCE
PERSONAL Born 04/08/1912, New Britain, CT, m, 1945, 2 children **DISCIPLINE** ENGLISH, HUMANITIES **EDUCATION** Trinity Col, Conn, AB, 35; Western Reserve Univ, MA, 38; Univ Chicago, PhD (educ), 53. **CAREER** Teacher, Avon Sch, Conn, 35-41 and Univ Sch, Shaker Heights, Ohio, 41-47; asst dir dept exam, Bd of Educ, Chicago, 48-49; supvr humanities sect, Test Develop, Educ Testing Serv, Princeton, NJ, 49-53; assoc prof, 53-59, chmn dept humanities, 62-75, PROF HUMANITIES, UNIV FLA, 59-. **RESEARCH** Evaluation; general education. **SELECTED PUBLICATIONS** Auth, Race and Touch of Evil, Sight Sound, Vol 6, 96. **CONTACT ADDRESS** Dept of Humanities, Univ of Fla, Gainesville, FL, 32601.

DERRY, JAMES
DISCIPLINE COMMUNICATION STUDIES **EDUCATION** Univ ND, BA; Univ Wis, MA; Purdue Univ, PhD. **CAREER** Assoc prof. **MEMBERSHIPS** Int Sociol Asn; Nat Asn Higher Edu. **SELECTED PUBLICATIONS** Auth, pubs on assessment of education and training. **CONTACT ADDRESS** Dept of Communication, Utah State Univ, 3580 S Highway 91, Logan, UT, 84321. **EMAIL** derry@cc.usu.edu

DERRYBERRY, BOB R.
PERSONAL Born 07/19/1937, Wardville, OK, m, 1958, 2 children **DISCIPLINE** SPEECH COMMUNICATION **EDUCATION** East Central State Univ Okla, BA, 60; East Central State Univ, MT, 62; Univ Ark, MA, 66; Univ Mo, PhD, 73 **CAREER** Instr, Southwest Baptist Col, 61-69; instr, Univ Mo, 69-70; assoc prof, Southwest Baptist Univ, 70-78; prof & chair, Ouachita Baptist Univ, 78-81; senior prof, dept chair, dir Forensics, Southwest Baptist Univ, 81- **HONORS AND AWARDS** Mo Gov Award Excellence in Teaching, 92, 97; Ed Board,

Southern Jrn Forensics, 97-98; Keynote Address Presenter, Pi Kappa Delta Ntl Convention Develop Conf, 93; Loren Reid Serv Award, 92; E.R. Nichols Award Outstanding Forensics Educator, Pi Kappa Delta, 90 **MEMBERSHIPS** Speech & Theatre Assoc Missouri President, 90; Pi Kappa Delta Ntl Forensic Fraternity; **SELECTED PUBLICATIONS** Auth, "Linking department and forensics directing in the small college," Speech Communication Assoc Annual Meeting, ERIC, 96; auth, "Future considerations for multidimensional forensic programs," Speech Theatre Assoc Mo Jrnl, 96; auth, "Understanding and utilizing academic freedom in the religious affiliated university," Speech Communication Assoc Annual Meeting, ERIC, 95 **CONTACT ADDRESS** 341 S Chicago Place, Bolivar, MO, 65613.

DERRYBERRY, BOX R.
DISCIPLINE SPEECH **EDUCATION** E Ctr State Univ Okla, BA, 60, MT, 62; Univ Ark, MA, 66; Univ Mo, PhD, 73. **CAREER** Instr, Southwest Baptist Col, 61-69; instr, Univ Mo, 69-70; asst to assoc prof, Southwest Baptist Univ, 70-78; prof, chair, speech, drama, Ouachita Baptist Univ, 78-81, PROF, DEPT CHAIR, DIR FORENSICS, DEPT COMMUN, 81-. **CONTACT ADDRESS** 341 S Chicago Pl, Bolivar, MO, 65613. **EMAIL** Bderrybe@sbuniv.edu

DESALVO, LOUISE ANITA
PERSONAL Born 09/27/1942, Jersey City, NJ, m, 1963, 2 children **DISCIPLINE** MODERN LITERATURE, WOMEN'S STUDIES **EDUCATION** Douglass Col, BA, 63; New York Univ, MA, 72, PhD(English educ), 77. **CAREER** Teacher English, Wood-Ridge High Sch, NJ, 63-67; coordr, English educ, Fairleigh Dickinson Univ, Teaneck, 77-82; ASSOC PROF ENGLISH, HUNTER COL, CITY UNIV NEW YORK, 82-, Contrib ed, Media & Methods Mag, 80-81. **HONORS AND AWARDS** Feature Article Award, Educ Press Asn Am, 80; Scholarly Ed Award, MLA, 80. **MEMBERSHIPS** Virginia Woolf Soc (treas, 79-82); MLA; NCTE; Bronte Soc. **RESEARCH** Virginia Woolf; Women's fiction; memoir. **SELECTED PUBLICATIONS** auth, Virginia Woolf's First Voyage: A Novel in the Making, Rowman & Littlefield & Macmillan, London, 80; auth, Nathaniel Hawthorne, Harvester, Humanities, 87; auth, Virginia Woolf: The Impact of Childhood Sexual Abuse on her Life and Work, Beacon, 89, Women's Press, 89; auth, Conceived with Malice, Literature as Revenge, Dutton, 94; auth, Vertigo: A Memoir, Dutton, 96; auth, Breathless, Beacon, 97; auth, Writing as a Way of Healing, Harper San Francisco, 99; ed, Virginia Woolf: Melymbrosia, NY Publ Libr, 82; ed, Between Women, Routledge, 93; ed, Territories of the Voice, Beacon, 89; ed, The Letters of Vita Sackville-West to Virginia Woolf, Morrow, 85. **CONTACT ADDRESS** Hunter Col, CUNY, 695 Park Ave, New York, NY, 10021.

DESBARATS, PETER
PERSONAL Born 07/02/1933, Montreal, PQ, Canada **DISCIPLINE** COMMUNICATIONS **EDUCATION** Loyola Col **CAREER** Journalist, var publs, 53-73; Ottawa bureau chief, Global Television, 74-80; Dean, Grad Sch Jour, Univ Western Ont, 81-96. **MEMBERSHIPS** Asn Dirs Jour Prog Can Univ (founding pres, 83-96). **SELECTED PUBLICATIONS** Auth, The State of Quebec, 65; auth, The Canadian Illustrated News, 70; auth, Rene: A Canadian in Search of a Country, 76; auth, The Hecklers, 79; auth, Canada Lost/Canada Found: The Search for a New Nation, 81; auth, Guide to Canadian News Media, 90, 2nd ed, 96; auth, Somalia Cover-Up: A Commissioner's Journal, 97.

DESJARDINS, MARY
DISCIPLINE FILM STUDIES **EDUCATION** Univ S CA, PhD. **CAREER** Fac, Univ CA Santa Barbara; fac, Univ Tex Austin; Asst prof, Dartmouth Col. **RESEARCH** Film and television stardom; feminist theory; gender and media; feminist filmmaking; melodrama. **SELECTED PUBLICATIONS** Auth, articles in Film Quart, The Velvet Light Trap, Quart Rev Film and Video, The Spectator, On Film, and Montage; book chapters in Questioning the Media, Fires Were Started: British Cinema and Thatcherism, and Television and Cultural History; entries in The Encyclopedia of TV. **CONTACT ADDRESS** Dartmouth Col, 3529 N Main St, #207, Hanover, NH, 03755. **EMAIL** Mary.Desjardins@Dartmouth.edu

DESMOND, JOHN F.
DISCIPLINE AMERICAN LITERATURE, SOUTHERN LITERATURE, MODERN IRISH LITERATURE, AND THE **EDUCATION** Univ Detroit, PhD, 60; Univ Okla, MA; PhD, 71. **CAREER** Instr, Ohio Univ; exec comm, Soc Stud S Lit; prof-. **HONORS AND AWARDS** Founder, pres, The Walker Percy Soc; ed bd, Bd of Adv for the Flannery O'Connor Soc; ed bd, Lit and Belief. **RESEARCH** Modern South, modern Irish poetry, and ethical and religious themes in 20th century writers. **SELECTED PUBLICATIONS** Ed, contribu, A Still Moment:Essays on the Art of Eudora Welty, auth, Risen Sons: Flannery's O'Connor's Vision of History, 87; At the Crossroads: Ethical and Religious Themes in the Writings of Walker Percy, 97. **CONTACT ADDRESS** Dept of Eng, Whitman Col, 345 Boyer Ave, Walla Walla, WA, 99362-2038. **EMAIL** desmond@whitman.edu

DESSEN, ALAN CHARLES
PERSONAL Born 11/16/1935, Baltimore, MD, m, 1963, 2 children **DISCIPLINE** ENGLISH **EDUCATION** Harvard Univ, BA, 57; Johns Hopkins Univ, MA, 61, PhD (English), 63. **CAREER** From instr to assoc prof English, Univ Wis-Madison, 63-69; assoc prof, Northwestern Univ, 69-73; PROF ENGLISH, UNIV NC, CHAPEL HILL, 73-, Nat Endowment for the Humanities Sr Res fel, Folger Shakespeare LIbr, 77-78. **MEMBERSHIPS** MLA; AAUP; S Atlantic Mod Lang Asn; Renaissance Soc Am; Shakespeare Asn Am. **RESEARCH** Shakespeare; Ben Jonson; Elizabethan-Jacobean drama and dramatic history. **SELECTED PUBLICATIONS** Auth, Resisting the Script, Shakespeare Onstage in 1991, Shakespeare Quart, Vol 43, 92; Reading Shakespeare in Performance--King Lear, Shakespeare Quart, Vol 44, 93. **CONTACT ADDRESS** Dept of English, Univ North Carolina, Chapel Hill, NC, 27514.

DESSNER, LAWRENCE JAY
PERSONAL Born 03/29/1934, New York, NY, m, 1961, 2 children **DISCIPLINE** ENGLISH LITERATURE **EDUCATION** Yale Univ, BA, 55; NY Univ, BA, 67, PhD (English), 69. **CAREER** From asst prof to assoc prof, 69-77, PROF ENGLISH, UNIV TOLEDO, 77-. **MEMBERSHIPS** MLA. **RESEARCH** British Victorian literature; popular culture. **SELECTED PUBLICATIONS** Auth, Arthur Havisham or Mr Arthur, Dickensian, Vol 91, 95; Gender and Structure in Cheever, John The Country Husband, Stud Short Fiction, Vol 31, 94. **CONTACT ADDRESS** Dept of English, Univ of Toledo, Toledo, OH, 43606.

DETENBER, BENJAMIN H.
DISCIPLINE COMMUNICATION **EDUCATION** Stanford Univ, AB, 83; PhD, 95. **CAREER** Consult, producer/dir, Stanford Instructional TV Network, 89-92; TV producer/dir, SITN, 83-89; tchg asst, Stanford Univ, 91-94; lectr, Stanford Univ, 94-95; asst prof, 95-. **MEMBERSHIPS** Mem, Broadcast Educators Assn; Intl Commun Assn. **RESEARCH** Social and individual level effects of media. **SELECTED PUBLICATIONS** Co-auth, A Bio-informational Theory of Emotion: Motion and Image Size Effects on Viewers, Jour Commun, 96; The Effects of Picture Motion on Affective Judgments and Psychophysiological Responses, Info Sys Div Intl Commun Assn, Montreal, Canada, 97. **CONTACT ADDRESS** Dept of Commun, Univ Delaware, 162 Ctr Mall, Newark, DE, 19716.

DETTMAR, KEVIN
DISCIPLINE ENGLISH LITERATURE **EDUCATION** Univ Calif, PhD, 90. **CAREER** Dept Eng, Clemson Univ **RESEARCH** 20th Century British and American Literature. **SELECTED PUBLICATIONS** Auth, The Rise and Fall of ono Vox and the Spiders from Dublin; Or, the Musical Logic of Late Capitalism, SAQ, 97); The Illicit Joyce of Postmodernism: Reading Against the Grain, Univ Wis, 96; Ulysses and the Preemptive Power of Plot, Pedagogy, Praxis, Ulysses: Using Joyce's Text to Transform the Classroom, Univ Mich, 95; Joyce/Irishbess Modernism, Bucknell Rev, 94; The Joyce That Beckett Built, James Joyce Quart; To Pirate The Pirate: Kathy Acker and the Politics of (post) Modernist Appropriation in Perspectives on Plagiarism and Intellectual Property in a Postmodern World, SUNY P; Alternative Rock Cello and the Importance of Being Earnest, Rocking Theory/Theorizing Rock: Literary Theory Meets Rock and Roll; H.G. Wells, British Short Fiction 1880-14: The Romantic Tradition, Dic Lit Biog, 96; James Joyce in British Short Fiction Writers 1914-1945, Dic Lit Biog. **CONTACT ADDRESS** Clemson Univ, 305 Strode, Clemson, SC, 29634. **EMAIL** dkevin@clemson.edu

DEVENYI, JUTKA
DISCIPLINE THEATER HISTORY **EDUCATION** Eotvos Lorand Univ Liberal Arts, MA; Univ CA Santa Barbara, PhD, 92. **CAREER** Asst prof, Cornell Univ; fac Actors Studio, Eugene Lang Col, present. **RESEARCH** Dramatic theory; contemp French and Eastern Europ drama. **SELECTED PUBLICATIONS** Auth, Metonymy and Drama: Essays on Language and Dramatic Strategy, Bucknell UP, 96; articles on contemp Hungarian and 19th century Ger drama. **CONTACT ADDRESS** Eugene Lang Col, New Sch for Social Research, 66 West 12th St, New York, NY, 10011.

DEVIN, LEE
PERSONAL Born 04/28/1938, Glendale, CA, m, 1958, 2 children **DISCIPLINE** DRAMA **EDUCATION** San Jose State Col, AB, 58; Ind Univ, MA, 61, PhD(speech & drama), 67. **CAREER** Lectr speech & drama, Ind Univ Exten, 60-62; instr & tech dir, Univ Va, 62-66; from instr to asst prof drama, Vassar Col, 66-71; assoc prof, 71-80, prof English, Swarthmore Col, 80-, Dir Theatre, 71-, Vis artist, Ball State Univ, 64; guest dir, High Tor Opera Co, fall 67; NEA fel grant, 74, Librettist's grants, 73, 74 & 76; artist in residence, People Light & Theatre Co, 77- **HONORS AND AWARDS** NEA Librettist's grants, 73, 74, 76; Mellon Fel 73, 77; Lang Fel, 90. **MEMBERSHIPS** Am Theatre Asn; Actors Equity Asn; Am Theatre Asn; Lit Mgrs and Dramaturgs of the Americas. **RESEARCH** Acting; dramaturgy. **SELECTED PUBLICATIONS** Composer: Ballad for Wanton Boy, 72 & Elegy for Irish Jack, 73, Earplay; Vox populous, St Paul Chamber Orchestra, 73; Where The Time Comes, 79, Frankenstein, 82, Earplay, St Carmen of the Main, Guelph Festival and G Shirmer, 87. **CONTACT ADDRESS** Dept of English Lit, Swarthmore Col, 500 College Ave, Swarthmore, PA, 19081-1306. **EMAIL** ldevin1@swarthmore.edu

DEVITT, AMY J.
PERSONAL Born 02/14/1955, Fort Collins, CO, m, 1991 **DISCIPLINE** ENGLISH **EDUCATION** Trinity Univ, BA, 77; Univ Kans, MA, 79; Univ Mich, PhD, 82. **CAREER** Asst prof, Univ Tulsa, 82-85; assoc dir, assoc prof, dir, 85-, Univ Kans. **HONORS AND AWARDS** Phi Beta Kappa; Rackham Fel; CLAS Grad Mentor Award; Kemper Tchg Fel. **MEMBERSHIPS** NCTE; MLA; DDS; CCCC. **RESEARCH** Genre theory; composition and rhetoric; English language; standardization. **SELECTED PUBLICATIONS** Auth, Standardizing Written English: Diffusion in the Case of Scotland, 1520-1659, 89; auth, art, Genre as Textual Variable: Some Historical Evidence from Scots and American English, 89; auth, art, Intertexuality in Tax Accounting: Generic, Referential, and Functional, 91; auth, art, Generalizing About Genre: New Conceptions of an Old Concept, 93; auth, art, Genre as Language Standard, 97. **CONTACT ADDRESS** Dept of English, Univ of Kansas, Lawrence, KS, 66045. **EMAIL** devitt@ukans.edu

DEVLIN, ALBERT J.
DISCIPLINE ENGLISH **EDUCATION** Univ Kans, PhD, 70. **CAREER** Prof; ed bd(s), Miss Quart & Tennessee Williams Lit J. **SELECTED PUBLICATIONS** Auth, Eudora Welty's Chronicle, Miss, 83 & Conversations with Tennessee Williams, UP Miss, 86; essays on, southern lit; co-ed, The Selected Letters of Tennessee Williams; acad adv, PBS documentary, Tennessee Williams: Orpheus of the American Stage, Amer Masters Ser, 94. **CONTACT ADDRESS** Dept of English, Univ of Missouri-Columbia, 309 University Hall, Columbia, MO, 65211.

DEVLIN, JAMES E.
DISCIPLINE ENGLISH **EDUCATION** Harvard; SUNY Binghamton. **CAREER** Fac, SUNY Col at Oneonta. **HONORS AND AWARDS** Ed, Satire Newsletter; chr, prog comm, SUNY Col Oneonta. **RESEARCH** Am lit; crime fiction. **SELECTED PUBLICATIONS** Auth, articles in Am lit from the Transcendentalist period to the present. **CONTACT ADDRESS** SUNY Col at Oneonta, 321 Netzer Admin Bldg, Oneonta, NY, 13820. **EMAIL** mayerae@oneonta.edu

DEVLIN, KIMBERLY J.
DISCIPLINE AMERICAN LITERATURE **EDUCATION** Bryn Mawr Univ, BA; Univ Mich, PhD. **CAREER** PROF, ART HIST, UNIVE CALIF, RIVERSIDE. **RESEARCH** James Joyce, feminist and psychoanalytic theory. **SELECTED PUBLICATIONS** Auth, Wandering and Return in "Finnegans Wake," Princeton Univ Press, 91; "'See Ourselves As Others See Us': Joyce's Look at the Eye of the Other," PMLA, 89; "Pretending in 'Penelope': Masquerade, Mimicry, and Molly Bloom," Novel, 91; "Castration and its Discontents: A Lacanian Approach to Ulysses," spec issue of James Joyce Quart on Joyce and Lacan, 91; "The Eye and the Gaze in Heart of Darkness: A Symptomological Reading," Mod Fiction Stud, 94; Bloom and the Police, Novel, 95. **CONTACT ADDRESS** Dept of Eng, Univ Calif, 1156 Hinderaker Hall, Riverside, CA, 92521-0209.

DI MAIO, IRENE STOCKSIEKER
DISCIPLINE GERMAN LANGUAGE, LITERATURE AND CULTURE/HISTORY, AND FILM **EDUCATION** La State Univ, PhD, 76. **CAREER** Assoc prof Ger, A&S fac senate, univ fac senate, A&S CAPPE comt, ch, Women's and Gender stud, Delta Phi Alpha, La State Univ. **RESEARCH** Eighteenth to twentieth century German literature with focus on the nineteenth century. **SELECTED PUBLICATIONS** Auth, The Multiple Perspective in Wilhelm Raabe's Third-Person Narratives of the Braunschweig Period, J. Benjamins, 81; Reclamations of the French Revolution: Fanny Lewald's Literary Response to the Nachmaumlrz in Der Seehof, Geist und Gesellschaft. zur Rezeption der Franzoumlsiszhen Revolution, ed Eitel Timm, Munich Fink, 90; Borders of Culture: The Native American in Friedrich Gerst&aumlcker's North American Narratives, in Yearbk of Ger Am Stud 28, 93. **CONTACT ADDRESS** Dept of For Lang and Lit, Louisiana State Univ, 124 C Prescott Hall, Baton Rouge, LA, 70803.

DIAMOND, ELIN
DISCIPLINE FEMINIST THEORY AND FEMINIST THEATER, AMERICAN DRAMA, EARLY MODERN DRAMA, M **EDUCATION** Brandeis, BA; Univ Calif, Davis, MA, PhD. **CAREER** Prof Eng, Rutgers, The State Univ NJ, Univ Col-Camden. **RESEARCH** Drama and performance; dramatic theory; critical theory. **SELECTED PUBLICATIONS** Auth, Unmaking Mimesis: Essays on Feminism and Theater; Performance and Cultural Politics; ed, Printer's Comic Play. **CONTACT ADDRESS** Dept of Lit in Eng, Rutgers, The State Univ New Jersey, Univ Col-Camde, Murray Hall 205B, New Brunswick, NJ, 08903. **EMAIL** ediamond@rci.rutgers.edu

DICENZO, MARIA
DISCIPLINE 20TH-CENTURY BRITISH LITERATURE; THEATRE **EDUCATION** McMaster, BA; Queen's, MA; McMaster, PhD. **CAREER** Asst Prof **SELECTED PUBLICATIONS** Auth,: The Politics of Alternative Theatre: The Case of 7:84 (Scotland), Cambridge Univ Press, 96; The Charabanc Theatre Company: Placing Women Centre-Stage in Northern Ireland; The Company of Sirens: Feminist Theatre for Social Change; Battle Fatigue: Notes from the Funding Front. **CONTACT ADDRESS** Dept of English, Wilfrid Laurier Univ, 75 University Ave W, Waterloo, ON, N2L 3C5. **EMAIL** mdicenzo@mach1.wlu.ca

DICK, DONALD
PERSONAL Born 06/21/1932, Lincoln, NE, m, 1955, 3 children **DISCIPLINE** SPEECH **EDUCATION** Union Col, NE, BA, 55; Univ NE, MA, 57; Mich State Univ, PhD, 65. **CAREER** From instr to assoc prof speech, La Sierra Col, 57-67; assoc prof, Loma Linda Univ, 67-68; prof speech & head, dept commun, 68-81; prof Commun, Southern Missionary Col, 81-82; Southern Col of Seventh-Day Adventists, 82-96; Southern Adventist Univ, 96-97, retired 9/30/97, ADJUNCT PROF EMERITUS, SOUTHERN ADVENTIST UNIV, 97, Pres, Adventist Radio Network, 65-74, mem bd dir, 74-81; secy-treas adv bd, Faith For Today, 71-74, producer, 75-76. **MEMBERSHIPS** Speech Commun Asn; Broadcast Educ Asn. **RESEARCH** Broadcasting audience research; religious radio broadcasting. **SELECTED PUBLICATIONS** Auth, Religious broadcasting: 1920-1965, A bibliography, J Broadcasting, fall 65, spring 66 & summer 66. **CONTACT ADDRESS** PO Box 370, Collegedale, TN, 37315-0370. **EMAIL** donandjoyce@mindspring.com

DICK, ERNST S.
DISCIPLINE GERMANIC PHILOLOGY, MEDIEVAL LITERATURE **EDUCATION** Univ Munster, PhD. **CAREER** Instr, Univ VA; affil, Johns Hopkins Univ, Univ MT, Univ WI; prof, 68. **RESEARCH** Germanic word studies and medieval Ger lit. **SELECTED PUBLICATIONS** Publ(s), etymological and semantic study on central terms of Germanic relig and cult; co-ed bk(s), and numerous articles on medieval Ger lit, Germanic philol, reception studies, and folklore; auth, articles on Annette von Droste-Hulshoff and Friedrich Durrenmatt. **CONTACT ADDRESS** Dept of Ger Lang and Lit, Univ Kansas, Admin Building, Lawrence, KS, 66045. **EMAIL** esdick@kuhub.cc.ukans.edu

DICK, ROBERT C.
DISCIPLINE COMMUNICATION STUDIES **EDUCATION** Emporia State Univ, BA, 60; Univ NMex, MA, 61; Stanford Univ, PhD, 69. **CAREER** Prof. **MEMBERSHIPS** World Commun Asn. **SELECTED PUBLICATIONS** Auth, pubs on the argumentation process; black intellectual and social history. **CONTACT ADDRESS** Dept of Communication, Indiana Univ-Purdue Univ, Indianapolis, 425 Univ Blvd, Indianapolis, IN, 46202. **EMAIL** rdick@iupui.edu

DICK, SUSAN M.
PERSONAL Born 11/06/1940, Battle Creek, MI **DISCIPLINE** ENGLISH **EDUCATION** Western Mich Univ, BA, 63; Northwestern Univ, MA, 64, PhD, 67. **CAREER** PROF ENGLISH, QUEEN'S UNIV, 67- **HONORS AND AWARDS** Fel, Royal Soc Can, 89 **RESEARCH** Virginia Woolf. **SELECTED PUBLICATIONS** Auth, Virginia Woolf, 89; ed, Confessions of a Young Man (George Moore), 72; ed, To the Lighthouse: The Original Holograph Draft (Virginia Woolf), 82; The Complete Shorter Fiction of Virginia Woolf, 85, 2nd enl ed, 89; co-ed, Omnium Gatherum: Essays for Richard Ellman, 89; To the Lighthouse (Virginia Woolf), 92. **CONTACT ADDRESS** English Dept, Queen's Univ, Kingston, ON, K7L 3N6.

DICKEN GARCIA, HAZEL F.
DISCIPLINE MASS COMMUNICATION STUDIES **EDUCATION** Univ Mich, MA; Univ Wis Madison, PhD. **CAREER** Prof **SELECTED PUBLICATIONS** Auth, To Western Woods, 91; Journalistic Standards in Nineteenth-Century America, 89; co-auth, Communication History, 80. **CONTACT ADDRESS** Mass Communication Dept, Univ of Minnesota, Twin Cities, 111 Murphy Hall, 206 Church St SE, Minneapolis, MN, 55455. **EMAIL** dicke003@maroon.tc.umn.edu

DICKEY, JAMES
PERSONAL Born 02/02/1923, Atlanta, GA, 3 children **DISCIPLINE** ENGLISH **EDUCATION** Vanderbilt Univ, BA, 49, MA, 50. **CAREER** Instr English and creative writing, Rice Univ, 50, 52-54 and Univ Fla 55-56; copywriter to creative dir var adv agencies, NY and Atlanta, 56-62; writer-in-residence, Reed Col, 63-64, San Fernando Valley State Col, 64-66 and Univ Wis-Madison, 66; consult poetry, Libr Cong, Washington, DC, 66-68; writer-in-residence, Wash Univ, 68; Franklin distinguished prof English, Ga Inst Technol, 68; POET-IN-RESIDENCE AND PROF ENGLISH, UNIV SC, 69-, Guggenheim fel, 62-63; Nat Inst Arts and Lett grant, 67. **HONORS AND AWARDS** Nat Bk Award for Poetry, 66; Levinson Prize, 81. **MEMBERSHIPS** Am Acad Arts and Sci; Nat Inst Arts and Lett. **SELECTED PUBLICATIONS** Auth, The Cancer Match, Lit Med, Vol 13, 94; Treadwell, Sophie Versus Barrymore, John, Playwrights, Plagiarism and Power in the Broadway Theater of the 1920s, Theatre Hist Stud, Vol 15, 95; Saar the Yellow Boat, Theatre J, Vol 46, 94; Contemporary Poets, Dramatists, Essayists, and Novelists of the South--A Biobibliographical Sourcebook, Essays Theatre Etudes Theatrales, Vol 14, 95; American Playwrights, 1880-1945A Research and Production Sourcebook, Essays Theatre Etudes Theatrales, Vol 14, 95; Diabetes, Lit Med, Vol 13, 94. **CONTACT ADDRESS** 4620 Lelia's Ct, Columbia, SC, 29206.

DICKEY, WILLIAM
PERSONAL Born 12/15/1928, Bellingham, WA **DISCIPLINE** ENGLISH **EDUCATION** Reed Col, BA, 51; Harvard Univ, MA, 55; State Univ Iowa, MFA, 56. **CAREER** Instr English, Cornell Univ, 56-59; from asst prof to assoc prof, 62-69, chmn creative writing dept, 74-77, PROF ENGLISH and CREATIVE WRITING, SAN FRANCISCO STATE UNIV, 69-, Mem deleg assembly, MLA, 74-77; creative writing fel, Nat Endowment for the Arts, 77-78. **HONORS AND AWARDS** Union League Found Prize, Poetry Mag, 62; Juniper Prize, Univ Mass Press, 78; Creative Writing award, Am Inst Arts and Lett, 80. **MEMBERSHIPS** MLA; Philol Asn of Pac Coast. **RESEARCH** English and American poetry; 18th century English literature; Willa Cather. **SELECTED PUBLICATIONS** Auth, Bungee Jumping, Antioch Rev, Vol 54, 96; Plum, Antioch Rev, Vol 54, 96; Theory and Substance of the Night, Ga Rev, Vol 49, 95; Building the Great Wall of China, North Am Rev, Vol 282, 97; Coming Back by Night, Poetry, Vol 170, 97; Calibans Second Song, Poetry, Vol 171, 97; Theft, Ga Rev, Vol 49, 95; The Death of Berryman, John, Poetry, Vol 167, 96; Semi Private, Poetry, Vol 166, 95; Hat, Poetry, Vol 166, 95; The Arrival of the Titanic, Poetry, Vol 167, 95; Coming of Television News and the National Guard, Poetry, Vol 166, 95. **CONTACT ADDRESS** Dept of English, San Francisco State Univ, San Francisco, CA, 94132.

DICKIE, M.
PERSONAL Born 09/13/1935, Bennington, VT, d, 2 children **DISCIPLINE** AMERICAN LITERATURE **EDUCATION** Middlebury College, BA, 56; Brown Univ, PhD, 65. **CAREER** Helen S Lanier Dist Prof, 87 to 98-, Univ Georgia; Asst Prof, Assoc Prof, Prof, hd Dept eng, 67-87, Univ IL. **HONORS AND AWARDS** Dist Fulbright Fel; Forester Prize; Phi Beta Kappa; Dist Alumni Awd. **MEMBERSHIPS** MLA; ASA; SAMLA; EBS. **RESEARCH** 20th Century American Poetry. **SELECTED PUBLICATIONS** Auth, Stein Bishop & Rich: Lyrics of Love War and Peace, Chapel Hill, Univ Of N Carolina Press, 97; Lyric Contingencies: Emily Dickinson and Wallace Stevens, Philadelphia, Univ of Penn Press, 91; On the Modernist Long Poem, Iowa City, Univ of Iowa Press, 86. **CONTACT ADDRESS** 125 Princeton Mill Rd, Athens, GA, 30602. **EMAIL** mmdickie@parcllel.uga.edu

DICKINSON, LOREN
PERSONAL Born 09/01/1932, Bemidji, MN, m, 1957, 2 children **DISCIPLINE** SPEECH **EDUCATION** Union Col, BA, 57; Univ Nebr, MA, 60; Univ Denver, PhD(speech), 68. **CAREER** Instr speech & dir pub rels, Columbia Union Col, 58-62; PROF SPEECH, WALLA WALLA COL, 62- **MEMBERSHIPS** Nat Speech Commun Asn. **CONTACT ADDRESS** Dept of Speech, Walla Walla Col, 204 S College Ave, College Place, WA, 99324-1198.

DICKS, VIVIAN I.
DISCIPLINE COMMUNICATION **EDUCATION** Wayne State Univ, BA; Ohio State Univ, MA, PhD; Detroit Col Law, JD. **CAREER** Prof, dept ch; Univ Detroit Mercy, 79-. **CONTACT ADDRESS** Dept of Communications, Univ of Detroit Mercy, 4001 W McNichols Rd, PO Box 19900, Detroit, MI, 48219-0900. **EMAIL** DICKSVI@udmercy.edu

DICKSON, DONALD R.
PERSONAL Born 08/19/1951, Biloxi, MS, m, 1990, 1 child **DISCIPLINE** ENGLISH LITERATURE **EDUCATION** Univ of Conn, BA, 73; Univ of Ill, AM, 76; PhD, 81. **CAREER** Prof, Tx A&M Univ, 81-; Ed, Seventeenth-Century News, 96-. **HONORS AND AWARDS** Res fel, Alexander von Humboldt-Stiftung, 92-93; teacher-scholar award, Univ honors prog, 98. **MEMBERSHIPS** MLA; SCMLA; Renaissance Soc of Am; South-Central Renaissance Conf; John Donne Soc; Usk Valley Vaughan Asn. **RESEARCH** Seventeenth-century studies. **SELECTED PUBLICATIONS** Auth, The Tessera of Antilia: Utopian Brotherhoods & Secret Societies in the Early Seventeenth Century, E.J. Brill, 98; The Hunt for Red Elixir: An Early Collaboration Between Fellows of the Royal Society, Endeavour, 98; The Alchemistical Wife: The Identity of Thomas Vaughan's Rebecca, The Seventeenth Century, 98; Thomas Henshaw, Sir Robert Paston and the Red Elixir: An Early Collaboration Between Fellows of the Royal Society, Notes and Records of the Royal Soc, 97; Johann Valentin Andreae's Utopian Brotherhoods, Renaissance Quart, 96; Johannes Saubert, Johan Valentin Andreae and the Unio Christiana, German Life & Letters, 96; coauth, The Variorum Edition of the Poetry of John Donne: The Anniversaries, Epicedes and Obsequies, Ind Univ Press, 95. **CONTACT ADDRESS** English Dept, Texas A&M Univ, College Station, TX, 77843-4227. **EMAIL** d-dickson@tamu.edu

DICKSTEIN, MORRIS
PERSONAL Born 02/23/1940, New York, NY, m, 1965, 2 children **DISCIPLINE** ENGLISH & COMPARATIVE LITERATURE **EDUCATION** Columbia Univ, AB, 61; Yale Univ, MA, 63, PhD, 67. **CAREER** From instr to asst prof Eng & comp lit, Columbia Univ, 66-71; from Assoc Prof to Prof, 71-94, Distinguished Prof Eng, Queens Col, NY, 94-; vis prof Am studies, Univ Paris, 80-81; dir, Ctr for the Hum, CUNY Grad Sch, 93-. **HONORS AND AWARDS** Soc Relig Higher Educ fel, 69-70; Chamberlain fel, Columbia Univ, 69-70; Guggenheim fel, 73-74; Am Coun Learned Socs fel, 77; Rockefeller Found Hum fel, 81-82; NEH Fel, 86-87; Mellon Fel, Nat Hum Ctr, 9-90. **MEMBERSHIPS** MLA; PEN Club; Nat Book Critics Circle (bd mem 83-89); Nat Soc Film Critics. **RESEARCH** Eng and Europ romanticism; mod lit and criticism; film and lit; Am cult hist. **SELECTED PUBLICATIONS** Auth, Allen Ginsberg and the 60's, Commentary, 1/70; Keats and His Poetry: A Study in Development, Univ Chicago, 71; The Black aesthetic in white America, Partisan Rev, winter 71/72; Coleridge, Wordsworth, and the conversation poems, Centennial Rev, fall 72; Fiction hot and kool: Dilemmas of the experimental writer, Tri Quart, 75; Seeds of the sixties: The growth of Freudian radicalism, Partisan Rev, 76; Gates of Eden: American Culture in the Sixties, Basic Bks, 77; co-ed, Great Film Directors: A Critical Anthology, Oxford Univ, 78; auth, Double Agent: The Critic and Society, Oxford Univ, 92; ed, The Revival of Pragmatism: New Essays on Social Thought, Law, and Culture, Duke Univ, 98; coauth, Cambridge History of American Literature, Vol 8, Cambridge Univ, 99. **CONTACT ADDRESS** Center for the Hum, Graduate Sch and Univ Ctr, CUNY, 33 W 42 St, New York, NY, 10036. **EMAIL** mdickste@email.gc.cuny.edu

DIEHL, HUSTON
PERSONAL Born 10/01/1948, Greenville, PA **DISCIPLINE** ENGLISH, ICONOGRAPHY **EDUCATION** Colo Col, BA, 70; Duke Univ, MA, 71, PhD (English), 75. **CAREER** ASsst prof English, State Univ NY Genesco, 75-79; asst prof, 79-82, ASSOC PROF ENGLISH, UNIV OKLA, 82-, Nat Endowment Humanities fel in residence, Univ Chicago, 78-79. **MEMBERSHIPS** Renaissance Soc Am; MLA. **RESEARCH** Tudor and Stuart drama; sixteenth and seventeenth century literature; Renaissance iconography. **SELECTED PUBLICATIONS** Auth, Bewhored Images and Imagined Whores--Iconophobia and Gynophobia in Stuart Love Tragedies, Eng Lit Renaissance, Vol 26, 96. **CONTACT ADDRESS** Dept of English, Univ of Okla, Norman, OK, 73069.

DIEHL JONES, CHARLENE
DISCIPLINE ENGLISH LITERATURE **EDUCATION** Univ Manitoba, BS, 82; PhD, 93. **CAREER** Prof **HONORS AND AWARDS** S. Warhaft Memorial Thesis Prize, 86. **SELECTED PUBLICATIONS** Auth, There's More Nothing to Say: Unspeaking Douglas Barbour's Story for a Saskatchewan Night; After Your Words; All in the Family: Modernism and its Progeny; Barbour's Story for a Saskatchewan Night: Silence & Bliss & the Untenable Text; Body/Language in Lola Lemire Tostevin's 'sophie; Cafe Companions (rev); Can(N)on: februaryish (rev); Charting the Labyrinth (rev); Critical contamination, or going boudoir: a diallage, **CONTACT ADDRESS** Dept of English, St. Jerome's Univ, Waterloo, ON, N2L 3G3. **EMAIL** cdiehljo@watarts.uwaterloo.ca

DIGAETANI, JOHN LOUIS
PERSONAL Born 06/23/1943, Chicago, IL, d **DISCIPLINE** ENGLISH **EDUCATION** Univ Ill, BA, 65; Northern Ill Univ, MA, 67; Univ Wisc, PhD, 73. **CAREER** Inst. Providence Col, 67-69; Inst. Univ New Orleans, 73-76; Guest Assoc, Harvard Univ, 81-82; PROF, ENGLISH, HOFSTRA UNIV, 1978-; DIR. HOFSTRA UNIV LONDON PROG, 1990-. **MEMBERSHIPS** MLA. **RESEARCH** 20th century theater; Opera; British lit. **SELECTED PUBLICATIONS** Ed, Penetrating Wagner's Ring: An Anthology, Fairleigh Dickinson Univ, 78; auth, Richard Wagner and the Modern British Novel, Fairleigh Dickinson Univ, 78; Writing Out Loud: A Self-Help Guide to Clear Business Writing, Dow Jones-Irwin, 83; Writing for Action: A Guide for the Health Care Professional, Dow-Jones-Irwin, 84; ed, Handbook of Executive Communication, Dow-Jones-Irwin, 86; auth, An Invitation to the Opera, Facts on File, 86; Puccini the Thinker, Peter Lang Press, 87; Carlo Gozzi: Translations of "The Love of Three Oranges," "Turandot," and "The Snake Lady" with a Bio-Critical Introduction, Greenwood, 88; ed, A Companion to Pirandello Studies, Greenwood, 91; auth, A Search for a Postmodern Theater: Interviews with Contemporary Playwrights, Greenwood, 92; ed, Opera and the Golden West, Fairleigh Dickinson Univ, 94; Money: Lure, Lore, and Literature, Greenwood, 94. **CONTACT ADDRESS** 523 W. 121 St., No. 24, New York, NY, 10027. **EMAIL** JDiGaetani@aol.com

DIGBY, JOAN
DISCIPLINE EIGHTEENTH CENTURY BRITISH LITERATURE, ART AND LITERATURE **EDUCATION** NY Univ, PhD. **CAREER** Prof, dir, honors prog, Long Island Univ, C.W. Post Campus. **SELECTED PUBLICATIONS** Auth, Philosophy in the Kitchen; or, Problems in Eighteenth-Century Culinary Aesthetics; Reading Goya's Dispartes; A Sound of Feathers; coauth, The Collage Handbook; coed, Permutations, Food for Thought; Inspired by Drink. **CONTACT ADDRESS** Long Island Univ, C.W. Post, Brookville, NY, 11548-1300.

DIJKSTRA, BRAM
PERSONAL Born 07/05/1938, Tandjung Pandan, Indonesia, m, 1964 **DISCIPLINE** AMERICAN & COMPARATIVE LITERATURE **EDUCATION** Ohio State Univ, BA, 61, MA, 62; Univ Calif, Berkeley, PhD, 67. **CAREER** From actg instr to asst prof, 66-73, assoc prof, 73-85, prof Am & comp lit, Univ Calif, San Diego, 85-. **RESEARCH** Visual arts and literature; sociology of literature; literature and ideology. **SELECTED PUBLICATIONS** Auth, Faces in Skin, Oyez, 65; The Hieroglyphics of a New Speech; Cubism, Stieglitz and the early Poetry of William Carlos Williams, Princeton, 69; contribr, Encounters: Essays in Literature and the Visual Arts, Studio Vista, London, 71; Un Reve Americain: Norman Mailer et l'esthetique de la domination, Temps Mod, Paris 4/72; The androgyne in nineteenth-century art and literature, Comp Lit, winter 74; Painting and ideology: Picasso and Guernica, Praxis, 76; ed, William Carlos Williams on Art and Artists, New Directions, 78; Nicht-repressive rhythmische Strukturen in einigen Formen afro-amerikanischer und westindischer Musik, Die Zeichen, Fischer Verlag, Frankfurt, 81; auth Idols of Perversity: Fantasies of Feminine Evil in Fin-de-siecle Culture. Oxford Univ, 86; Defoe and Economics: The Fortunes of ROXANA in the History of Interpretation, MacMillan, 87; The High Cost of Parasols: Images of Women in Impressionist Art, California Light, Chronicle Books, 90; America and Georgia O'Keefe, Georgia O'Keefe, The New York Years, A A Knopf, 91; Early Modernism in Southern California: Provincialism or Eccentricity Modernist Art 1900-1950, Univ Calif, 96; Evil Sisters: The Threat of Female Sexuality and the Cult of Manhood, A A Knopf, 96; Georgia O'Keefe and the Eros of Place, Princeton Univ, 98. **CONTACT ADDRESS** Dept Lit, Univ Calif San Diego, 9500 Gilman Dr., La Jolla, CA, 92093-5003.

DILLARD, JOEY L.
PERSONAL Born 06/26/1924, Grand Saline, TX, m **DISCIPLINE** ENGLISH **EDUCATION** So Methodist Univ, BA (Highest Hon) 1949, MA 1951; Univ of TX Austin, PhD 1956. **CAREER** Quito Ecuador, fulbright lecturer 1958-59; Bujumbura Burundi, fulbright lecture 1967-68; Yaounde Cameroun, linguist with AID 1964-65; Inst of Caribbean Studies of Univ of PR Rio Piedras, rsch assoc 1961-75; Northwestern State Univ, assoc prof 1975-83; Northwestern State Univ Natchitoches LA, prof of english 1983-89. **HONORS AND AWARDS** Alumnus Awd Phi Beta Kappa 1964; research grant Amer Philosophical Soc 1986-87; workshop grant Louisiana Endow for the Humanities 1987; Hendrix- Murphy Lecturer, Hendrix Coll, Conway AR, 1989. **MEMBERSHIPS** Dir Urban Language Study Ctr for Applied Linguistics 1967; visiting lecturer Ferkauf Graduate School Yeshiva Univ 1968-73. **CONTACT ADDRESS** Dept of Language & Arts, Northwestern State Univ, Natchitoches, LA, 71457.

DILLINGHAM, WILLIAM B.
PERSONAL Born 03/07/1930, Atlanta, GA, m, 1952, 3 children **DISCIPLINE** AMERICAN LITERATURE **EDUCATION** Emory Univ, AB, 55, AM, 56; Univ Pa, PhD, 61. **CAREER** From asst to assoc prof, 55-68, chmn, dept English, 79-82, PROF ENGLISH, EMORY UNIV, 68-, Fulbright lectr, Univ Oslo, 64-65, Nat Endowment for Humanities res fel, 78-79; Guggenheim fel, 82-83. **MEMBERSHIPS** MLA; SAtlantic Mod Lang Asn; Melville Soc. **RESEARCH** Nineteenth century American literature. **SELECTED PUBLICATIONS** Auth, Dreaming Revolution, Transgression in the Development of American Romance, Am Lit, Vol 66, 94; The Civil War World of Melville, Herman, Sewanee Rev, Vol 103, 95p; Melville, Herman Malcolm Letter--Mans Final Lore, Rsrcs Am Lit Stud, Vol 22, 96; The Pluralistic Philosophy of Crane, Stephen, Am Lit, Vol 66, 94. **CONTACT ADDRESS** Dept of English, Emory Univ, Atlanta, GA, 30322.

DILLON, BERT
PERSONAL Born 06/23/1937, Cherokee, OK, m, 1966 **DISCIPLINE** ENGLISH **EDUCATION** Univ Colo, BA, 60; Columbia Univ, MA, 63; Duke Univ, PhD (English), 72. **CAREER** From instr to asst prof, 65-74, ASSOC PROF ENGLISH, UNIV SC, 75-. **MEMBERSHIPS** MLA; Mediaeval Acad Am. **RESEARCH** Chaucer; Middle English literature; Malory. **SELECTED PUBLICATIONS** Auth, My Brothers Voice, Virg Quart Rev, Vol 73, 97; Never Having Had You, I Cannot Let You Go, Olds, Sharon Poems of a Father Daughter Relationship, Lit Rev, Vol 37, 93. **CONTACT ADDRESS** Dept of English, Univ of SC, Columbia, SC, 29205.

DILWORTH, THOMAS
PERSONAL Born 03/31/1945, Detroit, MI **DISCIPLINE** ENGLISH **EDUCATION** St Michael's Col, BA, 69; Univ Toronto, MA, 71, PhD, 77. **CAREER** Lectr, St John Fisher Col (NY), 70-72; asst to assoc prof, 77-86, ch comp lit prog, 79-96, PROF ENGLISH, UNIV WINDSOR, 86-. **HONORS AND AWARDS** Woodrow Wilson fel, 69; SSHRC res grants, 86-89, 89-94; Killam fel, 92-94. **SELECTED PUBLICATIONS** Auth, The Liturgical Parenthesis of David Jones, 79; auth, The Shape of Meaning in the Poetry of David Jones, 88; coauth, The Talented Intruder: Wyndham Lewis in Canada 1939-45, 92; ed, Inner Necessities: The Letters of David Jones to Desmond Chute, 84. **CONTACT ADDRESS** Dept of English, Univ of Windsor, Windsor, ON, N9B 3P4.

DIMMITT, JEAN POLLARD
PERSONAL Born 11/22/1941, Richmond, VA, m, 1991, 2 children **DISCIPLINE** ENGLISH **EDUCATION** Longwood Col, BA, 63; Univ of Va, MA, 66; Univ of Kans, PhD, 88. **CAREER** Asst prof of education, Kans Wesleyan Univ, 88-90; ASST PROF OF ENGLISH TO ASSOC PROF OF ENGLISH, WASHBURN UNIV, 90-. **MEMBERSHIPS** Nat Coun of Teachers of English; Kans Asn of Teachers of English; Confr on Col Composition and Commun. **RESEARCH** English pedagogy; composition; young adult Lit. **SELECTED PUBLICATIONS** Auth, Leaving Cold sassy: A Writer's Valediction, Kans English, 98; Cooperating Teachers: A guide and a Plea, Kans English, 96; More on Model Writers in Adolescent Lit, The ALAN Rev, 93; coauth, Energizing Social Studies Through Writing: A Handbook for Middle and High School Teachers, GSP Inc., 93; Integrating Writing and Social Studies: Alternatives to the Formal Research Paper, Soc Ed, 92. **CONTACT ADDRESS** Washburn Univ, 1700 College Ave, Topeka, KS, 66621. **EMAIL** zzdimm@washburn.edu

DIMOND, ROBERTA R.
PERSONAL Born 03/25/1940, Bakersfield, CA, s, 3 children **DISCIPLINE** LIBERAL ARTS **EDUCATION** Stanford Univ, AB, MA; Univ of Pa, MS, EdD. **CAREER** Teacher, Kumehancha schools, Honolulu, 63-65; prof, Temple Univ, 70-73; PROF OF LIBERAL ARTS, DELAWARE VALLEY COL, 86-. **HONORS AND AWARDS** Listed in Who's Who in Am Ed, Who's Who Am Women. **MEMBERSHIPS** Am Asn of Univ Profs; Am Psychol Asn; Nat Org of Women; Am Asn of Retired Persons; World Wild Life Fund, Philadelphia Area Tennis Asn. **RESEARCH** Dream interpretation; sports psychology; gestalt cognitive psychology. **SELECTED PUBLICATIONS** Auth, Mnemonic Devices, Nat Inst of Tchg of Psychol, 96; Sexual Responsibility in the 1990s, Rampages, 97; Dominance, Imagery & Focus-Sports Psychology, SWATH, 98. **CONTACT ADDRESS** Delaware Valley Col, Rt 202 E. Butler Ave, Doylestown, PA, 18901. **EMAIL** dimondr@devalcol.edu

DINNERSTEIN, MYRA
PERSONAL Born 04/19/1934, Philadelphia, PA, m, 1961, 2 children **DISCIPLINE** WOMEN'S STUDIES **EDUCATION** Univ Pa, AB, 56; Columbia Univ, MA, 63, PhD (hist), 71. **CAREER** Lectr hist, Univ Ariz, 71-74, CHAIRPERSON WOMEN'S STUDIES, UNIV ARIZ, 75-, CONSULT, NAT ENDOWMENT FOR HUMANITIES AND FUND FOR IMPROVEMENT OF POSTSECONDARY EDUC, 79-, NAT REV BD, PROJECT ON WOMEN IN THE CURRIC, MONT STATE UNIV, 81-, PRES, NAT ADV BD, NEW DIR YOUNG WOMEN, 81-. **MEMBERSHIPS** AHA; Nat Women's Studies Asn. **RESEARCH** American women's history. **SELECTED PUBLICATIONS** Auth, The Overworked American--The Unexpected Decline of Leisure, J Am Hist, Vol 79, 93. **CONTACT ADDRESS** Univ Ariz, 1 University of Az, Tucson, AZ, 85721-0001.

DIONISOPOULOS, GEORGE N.
DISCIPLINE COMMUNICATIONS **EDUCATION** San Diego State Univ, BA, 76, MA, 80; Purdue Univ, PhD, 84. **CAREER** Grad tchg asst, , 77-79; instr, San Diego Miramar Col, 80-81; grad tchg asst, Purdue Univ, 81-82; asst prof, Stae Univ NJ, 84-85; asst prof, 85-91; assoc prof, 91-. **HONORS AND AWARDS** Student choice award, San Diego Miramar Col, 80-81; David Ross fel, Purdue Univ, 82-83; scholar and creative activity award, CA State Univ Res, 89; aff action fac develop prog award, 89; Meritorious perf and prof promise awards, 87, 90; B Aubrey Fisher award, outstanding article yr, W Jour Commun, 92; cert of appreciation, San Diego AIDS Network for Edu, 93., Assoc ed, W Jour of Speech Commun, 89-94; ch, W Jour of Speech Commun, Rhetoric and Pub Address interest gp, 89-90; ch, Col Curriculum Comm, 93-; assoc ed, W Jour of Speech Commun, 94-. **MEMBERSHIPS** Mem, Speech Commun Assn; W States Commun Assn. **SELECTED PUBLICATIONS** Co-auth, Enthymematic Solutions to the Lockshin Defection Story: A Case Study in the Repair of a Problematic Narrative, Commun Stud 41, 90; The Meaning of Vietnam: Political Rhetoric as Revisionist Cultural History, Quart Jour of Speech 78, 92; Martin Luther King, The American Dream and Vietnam: A Collision of Rhetorical Trajectories, W Jour Commun 56, 92; Crisis at Little Rock: Eisenhower, History, and Mediated Political Realities, Eisenhower's War of Words: Rhetoric and Leadership Mich State UP, 94. **CONTACT ADDRESS** Dept of Commun, San Diego State Univ, 5500 Campanile Dr, San Diego, CA, 92182. **EMAIL** dionisop@mail.sdsu.edu

DIPASQUALE, THERESA M.
DISCIPLINE LYRIC POETRY, THE CULTURE AND RELIGION OF THE ENGLISH RENAISSANCE, 16TH- AN **EDUCATION** Univ Notre Dame, BA, 83; Univ Va, MA, 83; PhD, 89. **CAREER** Instr, Carleton Col; Fla Intl Univ; asst prof-. **RESEARCH** English Renaissance culture and religion; cross cultural reception of shakespeare. **SELECTED PUBLICATIONS** Auth, Heavens Last Best Gift, Eve and Wisdom in Paradise Lost, Mod Philol, 97. **CONTACT ADDRESS** Dept of Eng, Whitman Col, 345 Boyer Ave, Walla Walla, WA, 99362-2038. **EMAIL** cwis@whitman.edu

DIRCKS, PHYLLIS T.
DISCIPLINE RESTORATION AND EIGHTEENTH CENTURY LITERATURE, DRAMA **EDUCATION** NY Univ, PhD. **CAREER** Prof, Long Island Univ, C.W. Post Campus. **SELECTED PUBLICATIONS** Auth, David Garrick; Shakespeare's Use of Catch as Dramatic Metaphor; ed, Midas: An English Burletta; American Society for Theatre Research Newsletter. **CONTACT ADDRESS** Long Island Univ, C.W. Post, Brookville, NY, 11548-1300.

DIRCKS, RICHARD J.
PERSONAL Born 05/22/1926, New York, NY, m, 1963, 5 children **DISCIPLINE** ENGLISH **EDUCATION** Fordham Col, AB, 49, Fordham Univ, MA, 50, PhD, 61. **CAREER** From instr to asst prof English, Seton Hall Univ, 50-56; from asst prof to assoc prof, 56-65, dept rep, 62-64, chmn dept, 64-67, assoc dean grad sch arts & sci, 73-75, dir, Humanities Res Ctr, 75-77, PROF ENG, ST JOHN'S UNIV, 65-, Danforth assoc, 78-. **MEMBERSHIPS** MLA; Am Soc 18th Century Studies; Am Soc Theater Res. **RESEARCH** Criticism and aesthetics; 18th century literature. **SELECTED PUBLICATIONS** Coauth, Functional English, Republic, 59; auth, Gulliver's tragic rationalism, Criticism, 60; co-ed, Dodsley's An essay on fable, Augustan Reprint Soc, 65; auth, The perils of heartfree: A sociological review of Fielding's adaptation of dramatic convention, Tex Studies in Lit & Lang, 66; Richard Cumberland's political associations, Studies Burke & His Times, 70; Literary and theatrical perspectives, Philol Quart, 71; Richard Cumberland, Twayne, 76; The genesis and date of Goldsmith's Retaliation, Mod Philol, 77; Henry Fielding, Twayne, 78; ed, The Letters of Richard Cumberland, AMS Press, 88; ed, The Unpublished Plays of Richard Cumberland, 2 vol, AMS Press, 91-92; ed, The Memoirs of Richard Cumberland, AMS Press, 98. **CONTACT ADDRESS** Dept of English, St John's Univ, 8000 Utopia Pky, Jamaica, NY, 11439-0002. **EMAIL** dircksr@mail.stjohns.edu

DITSKY, JOHN M.
DISCIPLINE ENGLISH LANGUAGE; LITERATURE **EDUCATION** Detroit, PhB, MA; NY Univ, PhD, 67. **CAREER** Prof **SELECTED PUBLICATIONS** Auth, essays on East of Eden; John Steinbeck: Life, Work and Criticism; The Onstage Christ; The Grapes of Wrath; Friend & Lover; poetry ed, The Windsor Rev. **CONTACT ADDRESS** Dept of English Language and Literature, Univ of Windsor, 401 Sunset Ave, Windsor, ON, N9B 3P4.

DIXON, KATHLEEN
PERSONAL Born 01/23/1955, Richland, WA **DISCIPLINE** ENGLISH **EDUCATION** Univ Mich, PhD, 91 **CAREER** Asst prof, E Ore St Col, 84-85; asst prof, Ohio St Univ, 89-91; asst prof, Univ N Dak, 91-96; assoc prof, Univ N Dak, 96- **MEMBERSHIPS** Modern Lang Assoc; Ntl Council Teachers of English; **RESEARCH** Ntl Women's Studies Assoc; Rhetoric; Culture Studies **SELECTED PUBLICATIONS** Outbursts in Academe: Multicuturalism and Other Conflicts, Heinemann/Boynton/Cook, 98; Making Relationships: Gender in the Forming of Academic Community, Lang Publ, 97 **CONTACT ADDRESS** Univ N Dak, Box 7209, Grand Forks, ND, 58202. **EMAIL** dixon@badlands.nodak.edu

DIXON, LYNDA D.
PERSONAL Enid, OK, d, 2 children **DISCIPLINE** COMMUNICATION **EDUCATION** Southwest Mo State Univ, BS, 66, MA, 69; Univ of Ok, PhD, 90. **CAREER** Vis lectr/asst prof, Univ of Ok, 88-91; asst prof, Univ of New Mex, 91-92; asst prof/vis prof, Indiana Univ South Bend, 91-96; Assoc prof, Grad coord, Bowling Green State Univ, 96-. **HONORS AND AWARDS** Alumni Fel, Bowling Green State Univ, 97; doctoral minority fel, Ok State Regents for Higher Ed, 87-88. **MEMBERSHIPS** Nat Commun Asn; Central States Commun Asn; Ohio State Commun Asn; Int Commun Asn; Int Asn of Intercultural Studies. **RESEARCH** Health communication; intercultural communication; organizational communication; Native Americans in Society. **SELECTED PUBLICATIONS** Coauth, Icons of Bureaucratic Therapy: An application of Eco's Semiotic Methodology in an Intercultural Health Care Setting, Intercultural Commun Studies, 99; I Can Walk Both Ways: Identity Integration of American Indians in Oklahoma, Human Commun Res, 98; Signs in the Organization: Architectural Changes as Organizational Rhetoric in a Public Health Facility, Commun and Identity Across Cultures: Int and Intercultural Commun Annual NCA 23, Sage, 98; Patterns of Communication and Interethnic Integration: A Study of American Indians in Oklahoma, Canadian J of Native Ed, 98; The Cultural Deprivation of an Oklahoma Chrokee Family, Commun and Identity Across Cultures: Int and Intercultural Commun Annual NCA 22, Sage, 97; The Dilemma of Oklahoma Indian Women Elders: Women's Traditional Roles and Sociocultural Roles, Cross-cultural Aging in the U.S., Erlbaum, 97; The Language Culture of Rap Music, Language, Rhythm, and Sound, Univ of Pittsburgh Press, 97; Strategic Communication in Business and the Professions, Houghton Mifflin, 97. **CONTACT ADDRESS** Dept of Interpersonal Commun, Bowling Green State Univ, 313 West Hall, Bowling Green, OH, 43403. **EMAIL** lyndad@bgnet.bgsu.edu

DIXON, MIMI S.
PERSONAL m, 4 children **DISCIPLINE** ENGLISH **EDUCATION** Sarah Lawrence Col, AB, Chicago, MA, PhD. **CAREER** Prof, 80-; dept chair. **RESEARCH** Writing programs, composition theory and teaching. **SELECTED PUBLICATIONS** Auth, Tragicomic Recognitions: From Medieval Liturgy to Shakespearean Romance; Seeing and Saying in The Winter Tale; Thys Body of Mary: Femynyte and Inward Mythe, The Digby Mary Magdalene; Not Know me Yet?: Looking at Cleopatra, Three Renaissance Tragedies. **CONTACT ADDRESS** Wittenberg Univ, Springfield, OH, 45501-0720.

DIXON, WHEELER WINSTON
PERSONAL Born 03/12/1950, New Brunswick, NJ, m, 1986 **DISCIPLINE** ENGLISH **EDUCATION** Livingston Col, AB, 72; Rutgers Univ, MA, Mphil, 80, PhD, 82. **CAREER** Inst, Livingston Col, 69-72; inst, Rutgers Univ, 74-84; Lect, New Sch for Social Res, 83; asst prof, Univ Neb, 84-88, assoc prof, 88-92, CHMN, FILM STUDIES PROGRAM, 88- ; PROF, ENGLISH, UNIV NEB, 92-; guest lect, New Sch for Social Res, 97. **HONORS AND AWARDS** Col of Arts & Sci Award for Distinguished Teaching, 93; Recognition Award for Contributions to Students, 90-91, 91-92, 93-94, 94-95, 95-96, 96-97. **MEMBERSHIPS** Southwest Popular Culture Assn; Univ Film & Video Assn, Soc for Cinema Studies; Modern Lang Assn; Amer Assn of Univ Profs. **RESEARCH** Film studies. **SELECTED PUBLICATIONS** Auth, The Early Films of Andy Warhol, in Classic Images, 93; auth, It looks At You: Notes on the 'Look Back' in Cinema, in Post Script, 93; auth, The Early Film Criticism of Francois Truffaut, Ind Univ Pr, 93; auth, Re-Viewing British Cinema 1900-1992: Essays and Interviews, St of NY Univ Pr, 94; auth, The Marginalized Vision of Montgomery Tully Part One, in Classic Images, 94; auth, The Marginalized Vision of Montgomery Tully Part Two, in Classic Images, 94; auth, Act of Violence and the Early Films of Fred Zinnemann, in Film Criticism, 94; auth, Twilight of the Empire: The Films of Roy Ward Baker Part One, in Classic Images, 94; auth, It Looks at You: The Returned Gaze in Cinema, St Univ of NY Pr, 95; auth, Twilight of the Empire: The Films of Roy Ward Baker Parts Two and Three, in Classic Images, 95; auth, Femmes Vivantes and the Marginalized Feminine 'Other' in the Films of Reginald LeBorg, in Cinefocus, 95; auth, The Digital Domain: Image Mesh and Manipulation in Hyperreal Cinema/Video, in Film Criticism, 95-96; auth, Maurren Blackwood, Isaac Julien and the Sankofa Collective, in Film Criticism, 95-96; auth, Ida Lupino: In the Director's Chair, in Classic Images, 96; auth, Gender Approaches to Directing the Horror Film: Women Filmmakers and the Machanisms of the Gothic, in Popular Culture Review, 96; auth, Interview with Ralph Thomas: British Film Director, in Classic Images, 96; auth, Surviving the Studio System: The Films of Actor/Director Alex Nicol, in Classic Images, 96; auth, The Curious Case of John H.Collins, in Classic Images, 97; auth, The Films of Jean-Luc Godard, St Univ of NY Pr, 97; auth, Moving the Center: Notes Towards the Decentering of Eurocentric and American Cinema, in Popular Culture Review, 97; auth, An Interview with Bryan Forbes, in Classic Images, 97; auth, The Commercial Instinct: New Elstree Studios and The Danziger Brothers, 1956-1961, in Popular Culture Review, 98; auth, For Ever Godard: Notes on Godard's 'For Ever Mozart', in Literature/Film Q, 98; auth, The Transparency of Spectacle, in St Univ of Ny Pr, 98; auth, Disaster and Memory: Celebrity Culture and the Crisis of Hollywood Cinema, Columbia Univ Pr, forthcoming; auth, Film Genre in the 1990s, St Univ of Ny Pr, forthcoming; auth, The Colonial Bision of Edgar Wallace, in J of Popular Culture, forthcoming; aauth, The Invisible Man, Secret Agent, and the Prisoner: Three British Teleseries of the 1950s and 60s, in Classic Images, forthcoming; auth, The Man Who Created 'The Avengers': An Interview with Brian Clemens, in Classic Images, forthcoming; auth, The Auteur as Elegist: Richard Carlson's 'Riders to the Stars', in Pupular Culture Review, forthcoming; auth, Compromise and Triumph: The Films of Paul Robeson, in Classic Images, forthcoming; auth, When I'm 63: An Interview with Jonathan Miller, in Popular Culture Review, forthcoming. **CONTACT ADDRESS** Dept of English, Univ of Nebraska, 202 Andrews Hall, PO Box 880333, Lincoln, NE, 68588-0333. **EMAIL** wdixon@unlinfo.unl.edu

DJWA, SANDRA A.
PERSONAL St. John's, NF, Canada **DISCIPLINE** ENGLISH **EDUCATION** Memorial Univ, tchr A level, 56; Univ British Columbia, BEd, 64, PhD, 68. **CAREER** Elementary sch tchr, 57-60; PROF ENGLISH, SIMON FRASER UNIV, 68-, ch, Eng, 86-94, bd govs, 90-96. **HONORS AND AWARDS** Sr. Killam Res Fel, 81-83. **MEMBERSHIPS** Asn Can & Quebec Lits; Can Asn Chs Eng; Asn Can Tchrs Eng; Royal Soc Can. **SELECTED PUBLICATIONS** Auth, E.J. Pratt: The Evolutionary Years, 74; auth, Saul and the Selected Poetry of Charles Heavysege, 76; auth, The Politics of the Imagination: A Life of F.R. Scott, 87; co-ed, Complete Poems of E.J. Pratt: A Definitive Edition, 2 vols, 89. **CONTACT ADDRESS** Dept of English, Simon Fraser Univ, Burnaby, BC, V5A 1S6. **EMAIL** djwa@sfu.ca

DOAK, ROBERT
DISCIPLINE ENGLISH LITERATURE **EDUCATION** Ark State Univ, BA; Univ Ark, MA, PhD. **CAREER** Prof. **HONORS AND AWARDS** Pres, Newsletter Pop Cult in the S. **RESEARCH** Popular literature and film. **SELECTED PUBLICATIONS** Ed, Newsletter of the Pop Cult in the South. **CONTACT ADDRESS** Dept of Eng, Wingate Univ, Campus Box 3059, Wingate, NC, 28174. **EMAIL** robdoak@wingate.edu

DOANE, ALGER NICOLAUS
PERSONAL Born 08/16/1938, Fairfield, CA, m, 1979, 4 children **DISCIPLINE** ENGLISH & MEDIEVAL EUROPEAN LITERATURE **EDUCATION** Univ CA, Berkeley, BA, 61, MA, 63; Univ Toronto, PhD, 71. **CAREER** Lectr Eng, Victoria Univ Wellington, 65-71; asst prof, 71-77, assoc prof, 77-89, prof eng, Univ WI-Madison, 90, Am Coun Learned Soc fel, 73-74. **HONORS AND AWARDS** NEH summer stipend, 76; NEH proj grant, 94. **MEMBERSHIPS** Mediaeval Acad Am; ISAS. **RESEARCH** Old Eng poetry. **SELECTED PUBLICATIONS** Auth, Anglo Saxon Manuscripts, Orality and Texuality, 74; ed, Genesis A: A New Edition, Univ Wis, 78; The Saxon Genesis 991, 91; co-auth (with C P Posterneck) Vox Intexta: Orality and Texuality in the Middle Ages, 91; co-ed, Anglo-Saxon Manuscripts in Microfiche Facsimile. **CONTACT ADDRESS** Dept of Eng, Univ of Wisconsin, 600 North Park St, Madison, WI, 53706-1403. **EMAIL** andoane@facstaff.wisc.edu

DOBSON, JOANNE
DISCIPLINE 19TH-CENTURY AMERICAN LITERATURE **EDUCATION** Univ MA/Amherst, PhD. **CAREER** Assoc prof, Fordham Univ. **RESEARCH** Emily Dickinson, the canon. **SELECTED PUBLICATIONS** Auth, Sex, Wit and Sentiment: Frances Osgood and the Poetry of Love, Amer Lit 65, 93; The American Renaissance Reenvisioned, American Traditions: Nineteenth Century Women Writers, Rutgers UP, 93. **CONTACT ADDRESS** Dept of Eng Lang and Lit, Fordham Univ, 113 W 60th St, New York, NY, 10023.

DODD, WAYNE DONALD
PERSONAL Born 09/23/1930, Clarita, OK, m, 1958, 2 children **DISCIPLINE** ENGLISH **EDUCATION** Univ Okla, BA, 55, MA, 57, PhD(English), 63. **CAREER** Teaching asst English, Univ Okla, 55-59; from instr to prof English, 60-73, Univ Colo; Prof to Distinguished Prof English, Ohio Univ, 73-; Ed, Abstr English Studies, 62-65; Am Coun Learned Soc study fel, 64-65; ed, Ohio Rev, 71-; lit adv, Ohio Arts Coun, 75-. **HONORS AND AWARDS** NEA Fel in Poetry; Fel, Rockefeller Found, Italy; Individual Artist Fel, Ohio Arts Coun; Krauss Award for Lifetime Contributions to Poetry; CCLM Award for Distinguished Editing. **RESEARCH** Contemporary poetry. **SELECTED PUBLICATIONS** Auth, The Names You Gave It, LSU Press, 80; General Mule Poems, 81; Sometimes Music Rises, Univ Ga Press, 85; Echoes of the Unspoken, Univ Ga Press, 90; Of Desire & Disorder, Carnegie Mellon Univ Press, 94; Toward the End of the Century, Univ Iowa Press, 95; The Blue Salvages, Carnegie Mellon Univ Press, 98. **CONTACT ADDRESS** Dept of English, Ohio Univ, Athens, OH, 45701-2979.

DODGE, ROBERT KENDALL
PERSONAL Born 03/29/1941, Cortland, NY, m, 1963, 2 children **DISCIPLINE** ENGLISH **EDUCATION** Rice Univ, BA, 63; Univ Tex, Austin, MA, 64, PhD(English), 67. **CAREER** Asst prof English, Wis State Univ, Stevens Point, 67-70; asst prof, 70-76, assoc prof to prof English, Univ Nev, Las Vegas, 76-. **RESEARCH** Literature of the American Indian; Herman Melville; Early American Almanacs. **SELECTED PUBLICATIONS** Auth, Didactic Humor in the Almanacs of Early America, J Popular Cult, winter 71; co-ed, Voices from Wah' Kontah, An Anthology of Native American Poetry, Int Publ, 74; co-ed, New and Old Voices from Wah' Kon-tah, Int Publ, 84; ed, Early American Almanac Humor, The Popular Press, Bowling Green State Univ, 87; coauth, A Tale Type and Motif Index of Early U.S. Almanac Narrative, Greenwood Press, 92; auth, A Topical Index of Early U.S. Almanacs, 1776-1800, Greenwood Press, 97. **CONTACT ADDRESS** Dept of English, Univ of Nev Maryland Pkwy, PO Box 455011, Las Vegas, NV, 89154-5011. **EMAIL** dodge@nevada.edu

DOERFEL, MARYA L.
DISCIPLINE COMMUNICATION **EDUCATION** SUNY, Buffalo, PhD, 96. **CAREER** Asst prof, Univ NC, Charlotte. **RESEARCH** The impact of soc networks and competition on relationships, both inside and among organizations. **SELECTED PUBLICATIONS** Publ(s) have contrib to both organizational commun and methodological advances in network analysis. **CONTACT ADDRESS** Univ N. Carolina, Charlotte, Charlotte, NC, 28223-0001.

DOERKSEN, DANIEL WILLIAM
PERSONAL Born 11/27/1931, Winnipeg, MB, Canada, m, 1959, 3 children **DISCIPLINE** ENGLISH **EDUCATION** Univ Man, BA, 57, BEd, 62; Univ Wis, Madison, MA, 66, PhD (English), 73. **CAREER** Teacher English, Man schs, 57-76; asst prof, 68-75, assoc prof, 75-82, PROF ENGLISH, UNIV NB, 82-, Assoc ed, English Studies Can, 77-. **MEMBERSHIPS** MLA; Asn Can Univ Teachers English; Conf Christianity and Lit; Milton Soc Am; Spencer Soc Am. **RESEARCH** Seventeenth century poetry; literature of the English Renaissance; Christianity (especially the Bible) and literature. **SELECTED PUBLICATIONS** Auth, Authority, Church, and Society in Herbert, George--Return to the Middle Way, J Eng Germ Philol, Vol 96, 97; Donne and the Politics of Conscience in Early Modern England, 16th Century J, Vol 27, 96; Preaching Pastor Versus Custodian of Order, Donne, Andrewes, and the Jacobean Church, Philol Quart, Vol 73, 94; The Laudian Interpretation of Herbert, George, LitH ist 3rd Ser, Vol 3, 94; Preaching Pastor Versus Custodian of Order, Donne, Andrewes, and the Jacobean Church, Philol Quart, Vol 73, 94. **CONTACT ADDRESS** Dept of English, Univ of NB, PO Box 4400, Fredericton, NB, E3B 5A3.

DOLAN, FRANCES E.
PERSONAL Chicago, IL **DISCIPLINE** ENGLISH **EDUCATION** Univ Chicago, PhD, 88. **CAREER** Asst prof, eng, 89-95, assoc prof, eng, Affil Women's Studies and Hist, 95-, Miami Univ. **HONORS AND AWARDS** Monticello Found fel, Newberry Libr, 91; NEH/Folger Libr fel, 96; Soc for the Study of Early Mod Women, Best Article, 96. **MEMBERSHIPS** Mod Lang Asn; Shakespeare Asn of Amer. **RESEARCH** Early modern women; Law; Popular culture; Violence. **SELECTED PUBLICATIONS** Ed, The Taming of the Shrew: Texts and Contexts, Boston, Bedford Books, 96; article, Reading, Writing, and Other Crimes, Feminist Readings of Early Modern Culture: Emerging Subjects, Cambridge Univ Press, 96; article, Ridiculous Fictions: Making Distinctions in the Discourses of Witchcraft, Differences: A Journal of Feminist Cultural Studies, 7.2, 82-110, 95; auth, Dangerous Familiars: Representations of Domestic Crime in England, 1550-1700, Ithaca, Cornell Univ Press, 94; ed, Renaissance Drama, Renaissance Drama and the Law, 94; article, Gentlemen, I Have One Thing More to Say, Women on Scaffolds in England, 1563-1680, Mod Philol, 92.2, 157-78, 94; article, Taking the Pencil Out of God's Hand: Art, Nature, and the Face-Painting Debate in Early Modern England, Publ of the Mod Lang Asn, 108, 2, 224039, 93; article, The Subordinate's Plot: Petty Treason and the Forms of Domestic Rebellion, Shakespeare Quart, 43.3, 317-40, 92; article, Home-rebels and House-traitors: Murderous Wives in Early Modern England, Yale Jour of Law and the Humanities, 4.1, 1-31, Winter, 92. **CONTACT ADDRESS** Dept. of English, Miami Univ, Oxford, OH, 45056. **EMAIL** dolanfe@aol.com

DOMVILLE, ERIC W.
PERSONAL Born 04/27/1929, Liverpool, England **DISCIPLINE** ENGLISH **EDUCATION** Univ London, BA, 61, PhD, 65. **CAREER** Lectr to prof, 64-94, PROF EMER ENGLISH, TRINITY COL, UNIV TORONTO, 94-. **SELECTED PUBLICATIONS** Ed, A Concordance to the Plays of W.B. Yeats, 2 vols, 72; ed, Editing British and American Literature 1880-1920, 76; co-ed, The Collected letters of W.B. Yeats, vol 1, 86. **CONTACT ADDRESS** 342 Brunswick Ave, Toronto, ON, M5R 2Y9.

DONALDSON, JEFFERY
DISCIPLINE ENGLISH LITERATURE **EDUCATION** Univ Toronto, BA, MA, PhD. **RESEARCH** Mod and contemp Amer and Brit poetry; W.H. Auden, poetry and poetics; criticism of Northrop Frye. **SELECTED PUBLICATIONS** Auth, Mark Strand. American Writer's Supplement IV, Scribner, 96; auth, Waterglass, 99; auth, Once Out of Nature, 91. **CONTACT ADDRESS** English Dept, McMaster Univ, 1280 Main St W, Hamilton, ON, L8S 4L9.

DONALDSON, PETER SAMUEL
PERSONAL Born 11/21/1942, New York, NY, m, 1965, 3 children **DISCIPLINE** ENGLISH, HISTORY **EDUCATION** Columbia Univ, AB, 64, PhD (English), 74; Cambridge Univ, BA, 66, MA, 70. **CAREER** Preceptor English, Columbia Col, 67-68; from instr to asst prof, 69-78, assoc, 78-88, PROF LIT, MASS INST TECHNOL, 88-, Amm Fetter Friedlaender Prof Hum, 93-98, dept Hhead, 89-, dir, Shakespeare Elect Arch, 92-; Lectr comp lit, City Col New York, 67-69; Old Dom fel lit, Mass Inst Technol, 73; Nat Endowment for Humanities fel, 75; Am Counc Learned Soc fel, 82. **HONORS AND AWARDS** Fel, Royal Hist Soc, (UK), 79-. **MEMBERSHIPS** MLA; SAA. **RESEARCH** Rensaissance thought and letters: Machiavellian political tradition; Shakespeare in film and digital media. **SELECTED PUBLICATIONS** Auth, Staging the Gaze--Postmodernism, Psychoanalysis and Shakespearean Comedy, Renaissance Quart, Vol 47, 94; auth, Machiavelli and Mystery of State, Cambridge Univ Press, 88; auth, Shakespearean Films/Shakespearean Directors, Urwin Hyman, 90. **CONTACT ADDRESS** Massachusetts Inst Tech, 77 Massachusetts Ave, Cambridge, MA, 02139-4307. **EMAIL** psdlit@mit.edu

DONALDSON, SCOTT
PERSONAL Born 11/11/1928, Minneapolis, MN **DISCIPLINE** AMERICAN LITERATURE, AMERICAN STUDIES **EDUCATION** Yale Univ, Ba, 51; Univ Minn, MA, 52, PhD (Am studies), 66. **CAREER** Reporter, Minneapolis Star, 55-57; ed and publ, Bloomington Sun, 58-63; from asst prof to assoc prof English, 66-74, PROF ENGLISH, COL WILLIAM AND MARY, 74-, Fulbright lectr, Turku Univ, 70-71; vis prof, Univ Leeds, 72-73; Fulbright lectr, Univ Milan, 79. **MEMBER-**

SHIPS MLA; Am Studies Asn; Fulbright Alumni Asn; Int PEN; Auths Guild. **RESEARCH** Fitzgerald and Hemingway; American poetry; modern American fiction. **SELECTED PUBLICATIONS** Auth, The Road to West 43rd Street, Sewanee Rev, Vol 104, 96; Behind the Times--Inside the New York Times, Sewanee Rev, Vol 103, 95; Events Leading up to my Death--The Life of A 20th Century Reporter, Sewanee Rev, Vol 104, 96; One of the Family, Sewanee Rev, Vol 101, 93; Hemingway and Suicide, Sewanee Rev, Vol 103, 95; A Good Life--Newspapering and Other Adventures, Sewanee Rev, Vol 104, 96; The Murrow Boys--Pioneers on the Front Lines of Broadcast Journalism, Sewanee Rev, Vol 104, 96; My Times--Adventures in the News Trade, Sewanee Rev, Vol 103, 95; The Girls in the Balcony--Women, Men, and the New York Times, Sewanee Rev, Vol 103, 95; Parallel Time-Growing Up in Black and White, Sewanee Rev, Vol 103, 95; Brinkley, David--11 Presidents, 4 Wars, 22 Political Conventions, 1 Moon Landing, 3 Assassinations, 2,000 Weeks of News and Other Stuff on Television and 18 Years of Growing up in North Carolina, Sewanee Rev, Vol 104, 96; A Love Affair With Life and Smithsonian, Sewanee Rev, Vol 104, 96p; The Plagiarist, Sewanee Rev, Vol 101, 93. **CONTACT ADDRESS** Dept of English, Col of William and Mary, Williamsburg, VA, 23185.

DONATELLI, JOSEPH M.P.
DISCIPLINE ENGLISH LITERATURE **EDUCATION** State Univ NY Binghamton, BA; Univ NMex, MA; Univ Toronto, PhD. **CAREER** Assoc prof **RESEARCH** Fourteenth and fifteenth century narrative poetry; Anglo-Latin literature; reception of medieval texts in eighteenth century fiction. **SELECTED PUBLICATIONS** Auth, pubs on textual studies, media and communications theory, popular culture, and the effects of digital technology on literary forms. **CONTACT ADDRESS** Dept of English, Manitoba Univ, Winnipeg, MB, R3T 2N2.

DONAVIN, GEORGIANA
DISCIPLINE ENGLISH LITERATURE **EDUCATION** Ca State Univ, BA, 83, MA, 85; Univ Oregon, PhD, 92. **CAREER** Tchg asst, 84-85; instr, Ca State Univ, 86; grad tchg fel, Univ Oregon, 87-92; asst prof, 92-97; assoc prof, Westminster Col, 97-. **HONORS AND AWARDS** Manford A. Shaw Publ Prize. **SELECTED PUBLICATIONS** Auth, De sermone sermonem fecimus: Alexander of Ashby's De artificioso modo predicandi, 97; Locating a Public Forum for the Personal Letter in Malory's Morte Darthur, 96; The Medieval Rhetoric of Identification: A Burkean Reconception, 96. **CONTACT ADDRESS** Westminster Col Salt Lake City, 1840 S 1300 E, Salt Lake City, UT, 84105. **EMAIL** g-donavi@wcslc.edu

DONOVAN, JOSEPHINE
PERSONAL Born 03/10/1941, Manila, Philippines **DISCIPLINE** LITERATURE **EDUCATION** Bryn Mawr Col, BA, 62; Univ Wisc, Madison, MA, 67, PhD, 71. **CAREER** Prof, Univ Maine, Orono, 87- . **RESEARCH** Critical theory; women's literature (early modern, American). **SELECTED PUBLICATIONS** Auth, Sarah Orne Jewett, Ungar, 80; auth, New England Local Color Literature: A Women's Tradition, Ungar, 83; auth, After the Fall: The Demeter-Persephone Myth in Cather, Wharton and Glasgow, Penn State Univ, 89; auth, Gnosticism in Modern Literature: A Study of Selected Works of Camus, Sartre, Hesse, and Kafka, Garland, 90; auth, Uncle Tom's Cabin: Evil, Affliction, and Redemptive Love, Twayne, 91; auth, Feminist Theory: The Intellectual Traditions of American Feminism, expanded ed, Continuum, 92; auth, Women and the Rise of the Novel, 1405-1726, St. Martin's, 98. **CONTACT ADDRESS** Univ of Maine, 5752 Neville Hall, Orono, ME, 04469-5752.

DONOVAN, MAUREEN H.
PERSONAL Born 12/13/1948, Boston, MA, m, 1978, 1 child **DISCIPLINE** LIBRARY SCIENCE **EDUCATION** Manhattanville Col, BA, 70; Columbia Univ, MA, 73, MS, 74. **CAREER** Librn, Princeton Univ, 74-78; Librn, Ohio State Univ, 78-. **MEMBERSHIPS** Council East Asian Librys; Asn Asian Stud. **RESEARCH** Digital library; Japanese studies librarianship. **SELECTED PUBLICATIONS** Auth, art, East Asian Libraries Cooperative World Wide Web: An Experiment in Collaboration to Build Interdependence, 96. **CONTACT ADDRESS** Main Library, 1858 Neil Ave Mall, Columbus, OH, 43210. **EMAIL** donovan.1@osu.edu

DOOB, PENELOPE
PERSONAL Hanover, NH **DISCIPLINE** ENGLISH **EDUCATION** Harvard Univ, BA, 64; Stanford Univ, MA, 67, PhD, 69. **CAREER** Asst prof, 74-84, assoc prin, 81-85, PROF ENGLISH & MULTIDISCIPLINARY STUDS,YORK UNIV, 85-. **HONORS AND AWARDS** Guggenheim Fel, 74; Kent Fel, Danforth Found, 66-69; Woodrow Wilson Fel, 65-69; Medical Res Fel, Nat Sci Found, 64, 65. **MEMBERSHIPS** Actors' Fund of Can; Soc Tchg & Learning in Higher Educ; Sr Women Acad Admins Can; Am Asn Higher Educ; World Dance Alliance; Soc Dance Hist Scholars; MLA. **SELECTED PUBLICATIONS** Auth, Nebuchadnezzar's Children: Conventions of Madness in Middle English Literature, 74; auth, The Idea of the Labyrinth from Classical Antiquity through the Middle Ages, 90; coauth, Karen Kain: Movement Never Lies, 94. **CONTACT ADDRESS** Dept of English, York Univ, North York, ON, M3J 1P3. **EMAIL** prdoob@vm2.yorku.ca

DOODY, MARGARET A.
DISCIPLINE RESTORATION AND 18TH-CENTURY BRITISH LITERATURE, THE NOVEL **EDUCATION** Dalhousie Univ, BA, 60; Oxford Univ, BA, 62; MA, 67; DPhil, 68. **CAREER** Instr, 62-64; asst prof, Univ Victoria, Can, 68-69; lectr, Univ Col Swansea, UK, 69-70.; vis assoc prof, 76-77, assoc prof, UCLA, Berkeley, 77-80; prof, Princeton Univ, 80-89; vis prof, Columbia Univ, 81, 87; vis prof, Stanford Univ, 83; Andrew W Mellon Prof Hum and Eng, 89-; dir, comp lit prog, Vanderbilt Univ, 92-. **HONORS AND AWARDS** Atlantic Provinces scholar, 56-60; Commonwealth fel, 60-62; Can Coun grad fel, 64-65; Imperial Oil fel, 65-68; Can Coun postdoctoral res and travel grant, 69; John Simon Guggenheim Mem Found fel, 78; Ford Found Women's Stud grant, 85; Hon LLD, Dalhousie Univ, 85; Rose Mary Crawshay Prize, Brit Acad, 86; ACLS grant, 88; vis fel, Univ Otago, NZ, 93. **RESEARCH** Hymns; Venice; Apuleius. **SELECTED PUBLICATIONS** Auth, The True Story of the Novel, Rutgers Univ Press, 96; coauth, A Portrait of Jane Austen, Henry Rice, 95; ed, Frances Burney's Evelina or The History of a Young Lady's Entrance into the World, Penguin Bks, 94; co-ed, Hester Lynch Thrale Piozzi. The Two Fountains. A Fairy Tale in Three Acts, Johnsoniana, 94. **CONTACT ADDRESS** Comp Lit, Vanderbilt Univ, 130 Furman Hall, Nashville, TN, 37203-1727.

DOOLEY, PATRICIA
DISCIPLINE MASS COMMUNICATION, AND MEDIA ETHICS AND LAW **EDUCATION** Univ Minn, MA, PhD. **CAREER** Writer, Minn Hist Soc; asst prof, Univ Maine; dir, Kans Scholastic Press Assn District Four; asst prof. **RESEARCH** History of mass communication; media ethics and law. **SELECTED PUBLICATIONS** Auth, book on the history of journalism as an occupational group. **CONTACT ADDRESS** Dept of Commun, Wichita State Univ, 1845 Fairmont, Wichita, KS, 67260-0062. **EMAIL** dooley@elliott.es.twsu.edu

DOPP, JAMES A.
DISCIPLINE CANADIAN LITERATURE **EDUCATION** Univ Laurier, BA; Univ Victoria, MA; Univ York, PhD. **CAREER** Asst prof **RESEARCH** Contemporary Canadian poetry and fiction; critical theory; popular culture. **SELECTED PUBLICATIONS** Auth, On the Other Hand, 96; pub(s), articles in Mosaic, Double-Talking: Essays on Verbal and Visual Ironies, Encycl of Contemp Lit Theory, Eng Stud in Can, Open Lett, Stud Can Lit, Mattoid, Text Stud in Can, Can Lit. **CONTACT ADDRESS** Dept of English, Victoria Univ, PO Box 3070, Victoria, BC, V8W 3W1.

DORAN, MADELEINE
PERSONAL Born 08/12/1905, Salt Lake City, UT **DISCIPLINE** ENGLISH **EDUCATION** Stanford Univ, AB, 27, PhD, 30; Univ Iowa, AM, 28. **CAREER** Instr English lit, Wellesley Col, 30-33; from instr to prof English, 35-67, Ruth C Wallerstein prof English lit, 67-75, EMER PROF ENGLISH, UNIV WIS-MADISON, 75-, Am Coun Learned Soc fel, 33-34; Am Asn Univ Women fel, 46-47; Calkins vis prof, Wellesley Col, 57; vis prof, Stanford Univ, 60; Huntington Libr grant, 60 and 64; Folger Shakespeare Libr fel, 64; Guggenheim fel, 67-68; mem, Inst Res in Humanities, Univ Wis, 70-75. **HONORS AND AWARDS** LittD, Wheaton Col, Mass, 63, Carthage Col, 75 and Regis Col, 77. **MEMBERSHIPS** MLA; Renaissance Soc Am; Shakespeare Asn Am (pres, 74); Am Acad Arts and Sci. **RESEARCH** Shakespeare; Elizabethan drama; Renaissance literature. **SELECTED PUBLICATIONS** Auth, Orr Piano Trios Nos.1-3, Tempo, Vol 201, 97; Vw9 and the St. Matthew Passion, Tempo, Vol 201, 97. **CONTACT ADDRESS** 4238 Wanda Pl, Madison, WI, 53711.

DORGAN, HOWARD
PERSONAL Born 07/05/1932, Ruston, LA, m, 1961, 2 children **DISCIPLINE** RHETORIC AND PUBLIC ADDRESS, THEATRE **EDUCATION** Univ Tex, El Paso, BA, 53; Univ Tex, Austin, MFA, 57; La State Univ, PhD (speech), 71. **CAREER** Asst prof speech, lamar Univ, 66-69; teaching asst, La State Univ, 69-71; assoc prof speech, 71-77, PROF COMMUN ARTS, APPALACHIAN STATE UNIV, 77-, Ed, NC J Speech and Drama, 73-. **MEMBERSHIPS** Southern Speech Commun Asn; Speech Commun Asn. **RESEARCH** Southern rhetoric and public address: theatre history. **SELECTED PUBLICATIONS** Auth, Taking Up Serpents--Snake Handlers of Eastern Kentucky, J Am Hist, Vol 83, 96. **CONTACT ADDRESS** Dept of Commun Arts, Appalachian State Univ, Boone, NC, 28607.

DORLAND, MICHAEL
DISCIPLINE COMMUNICATIONS **EDUCATION** McGill Univ; Univ London; Concordia Univ, PhD. **CAREER** Vis scholar, Duke Univ; assoc prof. **HONORS AND AWARDS** Res, Univ du Quebec a Montreal. **RESEARCH** History of the Canadian public sphere **SELECTED PUBLICATIONS** Auth, many articles on Can film and cult policy; ed, Can Cult Ind: Policies, Problems and Prospects, 96; So Close To The State/s: The Emergence of Can Feature Film Policy, 98. **CONTACT ADDRESS** Dept of Commun, Carleton Univ, 1125 Colonel By Dr, Ottawa, ON, K1S 5B6.

DORNAN, CHRISTOPHER
DISCIPLINE COMMUNICATIONS **EDUCATION** Bachelor of Journalism from Carleton University, an M.A. in the History and Philosophy of Science from the University of Cambridge and a Ph.D. in Communication from McGill University **CAREER** Instr,Cornell Univ; dir; prof, 87. **HONORS AND AWARDS** Reporter, Edmonton Jour; sci writer, Globe and Mail; ed, edit writer, Ottawa Citizen; contributor, CBC Radio's Prime Time. **RESEARCH** News media as cultural form. **SELECTED PUBLICATIONS** Auth, Newspaper Publishing, The Cult Industries in Can, James Lorimer Publ, 96; Television Coverage: A History of the Election in 65 Seconds, The Can Gen Election of 1997, Dundurn Press, 97; **CONTACT ADDRESS** Dept of Commun, Carleton Univ, 1125 Colonel By Dr, Ottawa, ON, K1S 5B6.

DORNSIFE, ROB
DISCIPLINE ENGLISH **EDUCATION** Penn State Univ, MA; Lehigh, PhD. **CAREER** Dir, Grad Study & Writing Ctr. **HONORS AND AWARDS** Robert F Kennedy Stud Awd for Excellence Tchg, Creighton Univ, 96; Greek Awards banquet, 97 & 98; Outstanding Young Alumni Awd, Shippensburg Univ, 94; 1st Annual Creighton Univ Greek Commun Awd; Alpha Sigma Nu & Omicron Delta Kappa, 97. **SELECTED PUBLICATIONS** Publ in, J Adv Compos, Comput-Assisted Compos J, Writing Lab Newsl, NEJ, KE, MEJ, Nat Tchg and Lrng Forum, Tchg Prof. **CONTACT ADDRESS** Dept of Eng, Creighton Univ, 2500 CA Plaza, CA 306D, Omaha, NE, 68178. **EMAIL** robert@creighton.edu

DORSEY, LEROY
DISCIPLINE POLITICAL COMMUNICATION, PRESIDENTIAL RHETORIC **EDUCATION** Ind Univ, PhD. **CAREER** Asst prof, Texas A&M Univ. **HONORS AND AWARDS** Aubrey Fisher Awd, 95. **SELECTED PUBLICATIONS** Publ in, Quart J Speech; Presidential Stud Quart & Southern Commun J; contribur, African American Orators. **CONTACT ADDRESS** Dept of Speech Communication, Texas A&M Univ, College Station, TX, 77843-4234. **EMAIL** csnidow@tamu.edu

DORSEY, PETER
DISCIPLINE AMERICAN AUTOBIOGRAPHY, AFRICAN AMERICAN LITERATURE **EDUCATION** Univ Pa, PhD. **CAREER** Dept Eng, Mt Saint Mary's Col **SELECTED PUBLICATIONS** Auth, Sacred Estrangement: The Rhetoric of Conversion in Modern American Autobiography. **CONTACT ADDRESS** Dept of English, Mount Saint Mary's Col, 16300 Old Emmitsburg Rd, Emmitsburg, MD, 21727-7799. **EMAIL** dorsey@msmary.edu

DORSINVILLE, MAX
PERSONAL Born 01/30/1943, Port-au-Prince, Haiti, m, 1964, 1 child **DISCIPLINE** ENGLISH, COMPARATIVE LITERATURE **EDUCATION** Univ Sherbrooke, BA, 66, MA, 68; City Univ New York, PhD (comp lit), 72. **CAREER** Lectr, 70-72, asst prof, 72-75, dir, Ctr for French-Can Studies, 75-80, ASSOC PROF ENGLISH, MCGILL UNIV, 75-, Can Coun fel, 77-78. **MEMBERSHIPS** Can Comp Lit Asn (treas, 75-77); Asn Can Univ Teachers English. **RESEARCH** Twentieth century American novel; comparative Canadian literature; comparative African literature. **SELECTED PUBLICATIONS** Auth, Haiti--Its Literature and Way of Life, Can Rev Comparative Lit Rev Canadienne Litterature Comparee, Vol 21, 94. **CONTACT ADDRESS** Dept of English, McGill Univ, 853 Sherbrooke W, Montreal, PQ, H3A 2T6.

DOSKOW, MINNA
DISCIPLINE ENGLISH **EDUCATION** Univ Md, PhD. **CAREER** Dean, Lib Arts, Univ Baltimore; dean, Lib Arts, instr, Rowan Col of NJ. **RESEARCH** Japanese literature. **SELECTED PUBLICATIONS** Auth, William Blake's "Jerusalem:" Structure and Meaning in Poetry and Picture. **CONTACT ADDRESS** Rowan Col of NJ, Glassboro, NJ, 08028-1701.

DOTY, GRESDNA ANN
PERSONAL Born 02/22/1931, Oelwein, IA, m, 1980 **DISCIPLINE** THEATRE **EDUCATION** Iowa State Teachers Col, BA, 53; Univ Fla, MA, 57; Ind Univ, PhD (theatre), 67. **CAREER** From instr to asst prof speech & theatre, Southwest Tex State Col, 57-65; asst prof, 67-72, assoc prof, 72-79, prof Theatre, La State Univ, Baton Rouge, 79-, alumni prof Theatre, 84-96, Nat comt chmn, Am Col Theatre Festival, 76-79; Research grantee Nat Endowment Humanities, 81; Exxon Edn Found, 81. **MEMBERSHIPS** Am Soc Theatre Res, member exec comm, 88-91, vice-pres, 94-97; Speech Commun Asn; Am Theatre Asn; col of Fellows of Am Theatre. **RESEARCH** Theatre history. **SELECTED PUBLICATIONS** Auth, Anne Brunton in Bath and London, Theatre Surv, 5/67; Anne Merry and the Beginning of Stardom in the United States, Quart J Speech, 68; The Career of Anne Brunton Merry in the American Theatre, La State Univ, 71; coauth, Theatre Festivals: Practical Education for Actors, Directors and Designers, The Speech Teacher, 73; Contemporary Speech: A Comprehensive Approach to Communication, Nat Bk Co, 76; Southern Theatre History: A Bibliography of Theses and Dissertations, Southern Speech

Commun J, 77; An interview with Geral Freedman, Lit in Performance, 80; Anne Brunton Merry: First Star, In: Women in American Theatre, Crown, 81; co-auth, Inside the Royal Court Theatre, 1956-81: ArtistsTalk, LA State Univ, 90; . **CONTACT ADDRESS** Dept of Theatre, Louisiana State Univ, Baton Rouge, LA, 70803-0001.

DOUDNA, MARTIN KIRK
PERSONAL Born 06/04/1930, Louisville, KY, m, 1962, 3 children **DISCIPLINE** ENGLISH LITERATURE, AMERICAN CULTURE **EDUCATION** Oberlin Col, AB, 52; Univ Louisville, MA, 59; Univ Mich, PhD (Am cult), 71. **CAREER** Asst prof English, Mackinac Col, 66-69; assoc prof, 71-78, PROF ENGLISH, UNIV HAWAII, HILO, 78-. **MEMBERSHIPS** MLA; Thoreau Soc; Thoreau Lyceum. **RESEARCH** Nineteenth century American literature; American liberalism and radicalism; American magazine journalism. **SELECTED PUBLICATIONS** Auth, Nay Lady Sit, The Dramatic and Human Dimensions of Comus, Anq A Quart J Short Articles Notes Revs, Vol 8, 95. **CONTACT ADDRESS** Humanities Div, Univ of Hawaii, Hilo, HI, 96720.

DOUGHERTY, JAMES P.
DISCIPLINE 19TH-CENTURY AMERICAN LITERATURE **EDUCATION** Univ Pa, PhD. **CAREER** Instr, Univ Notre Dame; coed, Relig and Lit. **RESEARCH** Connections between religion and literature. **SELECTED PUBLICATIONS** Auth, The Fivesquare City; Walt Whitman and the Citizen's Eye. **CONTACT ADDRESS** Univ Notre Dame, Notre Dame, IN, 46556.

DOUGLAS, GEORGE HALSEY
PERSONAL Born 01/09/1934, East Orange, NJ, m, 1961, 1 child **DISCIPLINE** AMERICAN LITERATURE & STUDIES **EDUCATION** Lafayette Col, AB, 56; Columbia Univ, MA, 66; Univ Ill, PhD(philos), 68. **CAREER** From instr to prof, 66-88, prof English, Univ Ill, Urbana, 88-. **MEMBERSHIPS** MLA; Am Soc Aesthet; Am Studies Asn; Popular Cult Asn. **RESEARCH** American culture and social history. **SELECTED PUBLICATIONS** Auth, H L Mencken: Critic of American Life, Archon, 78; Rail city: Chicago and the Railroad, Howell-North Bks, 82; All Aboard: The Railroad in American Life, Paragon House, 92; Education Without Impact, Birch Lane Press, 92; Skyscraper Odyssey, McFarland, 96; Postwar America, Krieger Publishing, 98. **CONTACT ADDRESS** Dept of English, Univ of Illinois, 608 S Wright St, Urbana, IL, 61801-3613. **EMAIL** ghdougla@vivc.edu

DOWDEY, DIANE
DISCIPLINE NINETEENTH-CENTURY LITERATURE **EDUCATION** TX Christian Univ, BA, 76; Univ MS, MA, 77; Univ WI, PhD, 84. **CAREER** EngDept, Sam Houston State Univ **HONORS AND AWARDS** Delta Kappa Gamma Soc Int; Who's Who in Am Educ; Outstanding Young Women Am; Who's Who Am Women; Domestic Travel Fel Univ WI; Master's Fel Univ MS; Phi Beta Kappa, Sigma Tau Delta. **MEMBERSHIPS** S Central Mod Lang Asn, Nat Coun Tchrs Engl, Conf Col Compos & Comm, TX Coun Tchrs Engl, Conf Col Tchrs Eng, Nat Asn Develop Educs. **SELECTED PUBLICATIONS** Auth, The Researching Reader: Source-Based Writings Across the Disciplines, Holt, Rinehart, & Winston, 90; Instructor's Manual, Holt, Rinehart, & Winston, 91; I Do Not Want to Leave Alone, Pawn Rev, 76; Song for a Widow, Descant, 79-80; Bridging the Gap: Science for a Popular Audience, IA State Univ, 85; Rhetorical Techniques Audience Adaptation in Popular Science Writing, Jour Technical Writing in Popular Sci Writing, 87; Stephen Jay Gould: 'This View Science,' Markham Rev, 87; Society Mind by Marvin Minsky, Masterplots II: Nonfiction Series, Salem Press, 89; Citation and Documentation Across the Curriculum, Southern IL Univ Press, 92. **CONTACT ADDRESS** Sam Houston State Univ, Huntsville, TX, 77341.

DOWELL, PETER W.
DISCIPLINE ENGLISH LANGUAGE AND LITERATURE **EDUCATION** Univ Minn, PhD, 65. **CAREER** Assoc prof/ assoc dean Emory Col. **RESEARCH** 20th century American literature; American poetry and poetics; American studies. **SELECTED PUBLICATIONS** Ed, "Ich Kuss Die Hand:" The Letters of H L Mencken to Gretchen Hood. **CONTACT ADDRESS** English Dept, Emory Univ, 1380 Oxford Rd NE, Atlanta, GA, 30322-1950.

DOWELL, RICHARD WALKER
PERSONAL Born 11/26/1931, Bloomington, IN, m, 1957, 4 children **DISCIPLINE** ENGLISH, AMERICAN LITERATURE **EDUCATION** Ind State Univ, BS, 57; Univ Colo, MA, 60; Ind Univ, PhD (English), 68. **CAREER** Instr English, Univ Colo, 57-60; from instr to assoc prof, 63-74, PROF ENGLISH, IND STATE UNIV, TERRE HAUTE, 74-, Ed, Dreiser Newsletter, 69-. **RESEARCH** American literature 1875-1925; Theodore Dreiser. **SELECTED PUBLICATIONS** Auth, Mechanism and Mysticism, The Influence of Science on the Thought and Wok of Dreiser, Theodore, Am Lit, Vol 66, 94. **CONTACT ADDRESS** Dept of English, Indiana State Univ, Terre Haute, IN, 47809.

DOWLING, WILLIAM C.
DISCIPLINE ENGLISH LANGUAGE AND LITERATURE **EDUCATION** Dartmouth Univ, BA; Harvard Univ, PhD. **CAREER** Prof. **MEMBERSHIPS** SHEAR; Henry Sweet Soc; ALSC. **RESEARCH** 18th-Century English literature; American literature of the Revolution and early republic; semantic theory and philosophy of language. **SELECTED PUBLICATIONS** Auth, The Critic's Hornbook, The Boswellian Hero, Language and Logos in Boswell's Life of Johnson, Jameson/ Althusser/ Marx, Poetry and Ideology in Revolutionary Connecticut, The Epistolary Moment: the Poetics of the Eighteenth-Century Verse Epistle, Literary Federalism in the Age of Jefferson **CONTACT ADDRESS** Dept of English, Rutgers Univ, 510 George St, Murray Hall, New Brunswick, NJ, 08901-1167. **EMAIL** wcdowling@aol.com

DOWNES, DAVID ANTHONY
PERSONAL Born 08/17/1927, Victor, CO, m, 1949, 3 children **DISCIPLINE** ENGLISH **EDUCATION** Regis Col, BA, 49; Marquette Univ, MA, 50; Univ Wash, PhD (English), 55. **CAREER** Instr English, Gonzaga Univ, 50-53; from asst prof to assoc prof, Seattle Univ, 53-64, prof and chmn dept, 64-67; coordr humanities prog, 73-77, PROF ENGLISH, CALIF STATE UNIV, CHICO, 68-, Seattle Univ res grants, 61-63; dean humanities, Calif State Univ, Chico, 68-72, res grant, 70, dean educ develop, 72-73, ed, Univ J, 74-77, dir English dept grad progs 77-79, chair, Dept English, 79-; Lilly grant for Stanford Sem Lit and Art, 82. **MEMBERSHIPS** MLA. **RESEARCH** The genius of John Ruskin; criticism; western novel. **SELECTED PUBLICATIONS** Auth, Natures Covenant, Figures of Landscape in Ruskin, 19th Century Lit, Vol 48, 94. **CONTACT ADDRESS** Dept of English, California State Univ, Chico, Chico, CA, 95926.

DOWNEY, JAMES
PERSONAL Born 04/20/1939, Winterton, NF, Canada **DISCIPLINE** ENGLISH **EDUCATION** Memorial Univ Nfld, BA, 62, BEd 63, MA, 64, DLitt(hon), 91; Univ London, PhD, 1966; DHL(hon), Univ Maine, 87; LLD(hon), Univ NB, 91. **CAREER** Ch, dept Eng, 72-75, dean arts, 75-78, vice pres acad, Carleton Univ, 78-80; pres, Univ NB, 80-90; PRES, UNIV WATERLOO, 93-. **HONORS AND AWARDS** Fel, Univ Georgia, 85; off, Order Can, 97. **SELECTED PUBLICATIONS** Auth, The Eighteenth Century Pulpit, 69; co-ed, Fearful Joy, 74. **CONTACT ADDRESS** Univ of Waterloo, Waterloo, ON, N2L 3G1.

DOWNING, DAVID
PERSONAL Born 05/03/1947, Newton, MA, m, 1974, 2 children **DISCIPLINE** ENGLISH **EDUCATION** Beloit Coll, BA, 70; San Francisco State Univ, MA, 74; SUNY/Buffalo, PhD, 80. **CAREER** Asst, assoc, prof, 79-88, Eastern IL Univ; Prof, 88-, Indiana Univ of PA **HONORS AND AWARDS** Innovative Excellence in Teaching, Learning and technology Award, 98; Teaching Excellence Award for Outstanding Teaching: Innovative Practice, 93; Soc for Critical Exchange Grant for the Symposium, Problemss of Affirmation in Cultural Theory, 91; Soc for Critical exchange Grant for the conference, The Role of Theory in the Undergraduate Literature Classroom, 90. **MEMBERSHIPS** Soc for Critical Exchange, member, board of directors; The GRIP Project, member, Steering committee; Alternative Educational Environments, assoc dir; MLA, Midwest MLA; Soc for the Advancement of Amer Phil; Natl Council of Teachers of Eng. **SELECTED PUBLICATIONS** Auth, Image and Ideology in Modern/Postmodern Discourse, 91; Practicing Theory in Introductory College Literature Courses, 91; Founding ed Work and Days, 84; Changing Classroom Practices: Resources for Literary and Cultural Studies, 94; The TicToc Project: Teaching in Cyberspace Through On-Line Courses, Spring/Fall 97; co auth, Coming to Terms with Terms in Academic Cyberculture, The Emerging Cyberculture: Literacy, Paradigm, and Paradox, forthcoming.. **CONTACT ADDRESS** 1252 Malvern Ave., Pittsburgh, PA, 15217. **EMAIL** downing@grove.iup.edu

DOXEY, WILLIAM S.
PERSONAL Born 01/20/1935, Coral Gables, FL, d, 3 children **DISCIPLINE** ENGLISH **EDUCATION** Fla State Univ, BA, 61, MA, 65; Univ NC, Chapel Hill, PhD, 70. **CAREER** Prof English, State Univ of W Ga, 68-. **RESEARCH** Heurolinguistics; metaphor; early human art, sci-fi. **SELECTED PUBLICATIONS** Ed/pub, Notes on Contemporary Literature. **CONTACT ADDRESS** Dept English, State Univ of W Ga, Carrolton, GA, 30118. **EMAIL** bdoxey@westga.edu

DOYLE, CHARLES CLAY
PERSONAL Born 07/20/1943, Marlin, TX **DISCIPLINE** ENGLISH, FOLKLORE **EDUCATION** Univ Tex, Austin, BA, 64, PhD (English), 69.. **CAREER** Asst prof, Univ Southern Calif, 69-74; asst prof, 74-79, ASSOC PROF ENGLISH, UNIV GA, 79-. **MEMBERSHIPS** MLA; Am Folklore Soc; Am Dialect Soc; Amici Thomae More; Male-dicta: Int Res Ctr Verbal Aggression. **RESEARCH** Renaissance literature; European and American folklore; the English language. **SELECTED PUBLICATIONS** Auth, More Epigrams in the 16th Century and 17th Century 94p; Bourbon Nugae and More Epigrammata, Moreana, Vol 32, 95; The Long Story of the Short End of the Stick , Am Speech, Vol 69, 94; Another Elliptic with aand an Elliptic to, Am Speech, Vol 72, 97; Duck Butter Redux , Am Speech, Vol 72, 97; The Proverbial Hole in the Ground, Anq A Quart J Short Articles Notes Revs, Vol 8, 95; He That Will Swear Will Lie, Chaucer Rev, Vol 32, 97. **CONTACT ADDRESS** Dept of English, Univ Ga, 0 Georgia University, Athens, GA, 30602-0001.

DOYLE, ESTHER M.
PERSONAL Born 03/21/1910, Boston, MA **DISCIPLINE** ENGLISH, SPEECH **EDUCATION** Emerson Col, BLI, 35; Boston Univ, MA, 40; Northwestern Univ, PhD, 64. **CAREER** Tchr elem schs, Mass 29-37; oral English supvr & teacher, high schs, NY, 37-44; hosp recreation worker, Mil Welfare Serv, Am Red Cross, 44-45; from instr to prof English, 45-71, chmn dept, 67-75, Dana prof, 71-75, emer prof eng, 75-, Juniata Col; lectr, 60-61, Bethany Bible Sem; partic, Nat Humanities Series Progs, 69-73; vis prof, 71, Univ Ariz. **MEMBERSHIPS** Speech Commun Assn; AAUP. **RESEARCH** Verse drama. **SELECTED PUBLICATIONS** Co-ed, Studies in Interpretation, Vol I, 72 & Vol II, Amsterdam, 77. **CONTACT ADDRESS** Dept of English, Juniata Col, Huntingdon, PA, 16652.

DOYLE, JAMES
DISCIPLINE BIOGRAPHY AS A LITERARY GENRE **EDUCATION** Laurentian, BA; Toronto, MA; British Columbia, PhD. **CAREER** Prof **SELECTED PUBLICATIONS** Auth,: North of America: Images of Canada in the Literature of the United States, 1775-1900, ECW Press, 83; Stephen Leacock: The Sage of Orillia , ECW Press, 92; The Fin de Si?cle Spirit: Walter Blackburn Harte and the American/Canadian Literary Milieu of the 1890s, ECW Press, 95; Margaret Fairley and the Canadian Literary Tradition; Red Letters: Notes Toward a Literary History of Canadian Communism. **CONTACT ADDRESS** Dept of English, Wilfrid Laurier Univ, 75 University Ave W, Waterloo, ON, N2L 3C5. **EMAIL** jdoyle@mach1.wlu.ca

DOYLE, KENNETH
DISCIPLINE MASS COMMUNICATION STUDIES **EDUCATION** Univ Minn, PhD. **CAREER** Assoc prof **SELECTED PUBLICATIONS** Auth, Wealth Accumulation and Management, 95; co-auth, Communication in the Language of Flowers, Horticulture Tech, 94; ed, The Meanings of Money, 92. **CONTACT ADDRESS** Mass Communication Dept, Univ of Minnesota, Twin Cities, 111 Murphy Hall, 206 Church St SE, Minneapolis, MN, 55455. **EMAIL** kendoyle@maroon.tc.umn.edu

DRAGGA, SAM A.
DISCIPLINE TECHNICAL COMMUNICATION **EDUCATION** Univ OH, PhD, 82. **CAREER** Prof, TX Tech Univ; ser ed, Allyn & Bacon Ser in Tech Commun. **MEMBERSHIPS** Vice-pres, Asn of Tchr of Tech Writing. **SELECTED PUBLICATIONS** Coauth, Ed: The Design of Rhetoric, Baywood, 89; A Writer's Repertoire, HarperCollins, 95; A Reader's Repertoire, HarperCollins, 96; ed, Technical Writing: Student Samples and Teacher Responses, ATTW, 92. **CONTACT ADDRESS** Texas Tech Univ, Lubbock, TX, 79409-5015. **EMAIL** ditsd@ttacs.ttu.edu

DRAINE, BETSY
PERSONAL Born 08/21/1945, Boston, MA, m, 1981 **DISCIPLINE** BRITISH AND AMERICAN LITERATURE **EDUCATION** Mt Holyoke Col, AB, 67; Temple Univ, MA, 72, PhD (English), 77. **CAREER** Instr, 76-77, asst prof, 77-82, ASSOC PROF ENGLISH LIT, UNIV WIS-MADISON, 82-, Bk rev ed, Contemp Lit, 78-81, assoc ed, 79-; consult, Feminist Studies, 78-82. **HONORS AND AWARDS** Mark H Ingraham Prize, Univ Wis Press, 82. **MEMBERSHIPS** MLA; Doris Lessing Soc. **RESEARCH** British and American novel, 20th century; women novelists; literary theory. **SELECTED PUBLICATIONS** Auth, Lessing, Doris--The Poetics of Change, Mod Fiction Stud, Vol 42, 96; Lessing, Doris, Mod Fiction Stud, Vol 42, 96. **CONTACT ADDRESS** 1446 Rutledge St, Madison, WI, 53703.

DRAKE, ROBERT Y., JR.
PERSONAL Born 10/20/1930, Ripley, TN, s **DISCIPLINE** ENGLISH **EDUCATION** Vanderbilt Univ, BA, 52, MA, 53; Yale Univ, MA, 54, PhD, 55. **CAREER** Instr, Univ of Mich, 55-58; instr, Northwestern Univ, 58-69; asst prof, Univ of Tex, Austin, 61-65; assoc prof, 73-95, prof, 73-, Lindsay Young Prof, Univ Tenn, 98-. **HONORS AND AWARDS** Visiting Prof, Hendrix Col, Conway, Ark. **MEMBERSHIPS** Phi Beta Kappa; MLA; SAMLA; SSSL; CEA. **RESEARCH** Southern literature; shape and form of fiction. **SELECTED PUBLICATIONS** Auth, Amazing Grace, 65; The Single Heart, 71; The Burning Bush, 75; Survivors and Others, 87; My Sweetheart's House, 93; What Will You Do for an Encore?, 96; The Home Place: A Momory and a Celebration, 80 & 98. **CONTACT ADDRESS** English Dept, Univ of Tenn, Knoxville, TN, 37916.

DREHER, DIANE ELIZABETH
PERSONAL Born 05/06/1946, Louisville, KY, m, 1997 **DISCIPLINE** ENGLISH **EDUCATION** Univ Calif, Riverside, BA, 68; Univ Calif, Los Angeles, MA, 70, PhD, 73. **CAREER** Tchg asst, Univ Calif, Los Angeles, 69-71; from asst to assoc prof English, 74-92, prof English, 92- , chemn Dept of English, 92-97, Santa Clara Univ. **HONORS AND AWARDS** Phi Beta Kappa, 68; Danforth Assoc, 81; Outstanding Young Woman of Am, 78, 82; Graves Award in the Hum, 82; Sisterhood is Powerful Award, Santa Clara Univ, Women's Stud Prog, 96. **MEMBERSHIPS** MLA; Nat Writers' Union; AAUP. **RESEARCH** Early modern literature; feminist studies; autobiography; creative nonfiction. **SELECTED PUBLICATIONS** Auth, The Fourfold Pilgrimage: The Four Estates in Seventeenth-Century Literature, Univ Press of Am, 82; auth, Domination and Defiance: Fathers and Daughters in Shakespeare, Kentucky, 86; auth, The Tao of Inner Peace, HarperCollins, 91; auth, The Tao of Personal Leadership, HarperCollins, 96; auth, The Tao of Womanhood, Morrow, 98. **CONTACT ADDRESS** Dept of English, Santa Clara Univ, 500 El Camino Real, Santa Clara, CA, 95053. **EMAIL** ddreher@scu.edu

DREKONJA, OTMAR MAXIMILIAN
PERSONAL Born 11/30/1934, Austria, m, 1961, 3 children **DISCIPLINE** LITERATURE **EDUCATION** Univ Salzburg/ Austria, PhD, 71. **CAREER** TA, 62-63, Kent St Univ; SW at Memphis, Rhoades Col, 63-64; res asst, 64-67, Univ Innsbruck/ Austria; St John's Univ, 67-; CUNY Richmond Col, 72-. **RESEARCH** Austrian lit; Central Europe, GDR tradition, exile lit. **CONTACT ADDRESS** SJU, Collegeville, MN, 56321. **EMAIL** odrekonja@sbsju.edu

DREW, SHIRLEY K.
DISCIPLINE ORGANIZATIONAL COMMUNICATION **EDUCATION** Bowling Green State Univ, BA, MA, PhD. **CAREER** Assoc prof. **RESEARCH** Relationship disengagement. **SELECTED PUBLICATIONS** Publ, health commun, personal narratives. **CONTACT ADDRESS** Dept of Commun, Pittsburg State Univ, 1701 S Broadway St, Pittsburg, KS, 66762.

DREWRY, CECELIA HODGES
PERSONAL New York, NY, m **DISCIPLINE** ENGLISH **EDUCATION** Hunter Coll, AB 1945; Columbia U, AM 1948; Shakespeare Univ of Birmingham, England, Cert 1949; Northwestern U, PhD 1967; Univ of Ghana, Cert 1969. **CAREER** Princeton Univ, asst dean, asst prof; Haverford Coll, visiting prof of english 1977; Teachers Coll Columbia Univ, visiting instructor 1968; African & Afro-Amer Studies Prog, chairperson 1969-70; Rutgers Univ, assoc prof 1962-70; High School of Performing Arts NY, teacher 1952-59; Talladega Coll, instrutor 1945-47; Penthouse Dance & Drama Theatre NY, dir of speech 1948-52; Princeton High School, teacher 1959-61; various theatre appearances. **HONORS AND AWARDS** Award for excellence in oral interpretation of literature Northwestern Univ Sch of Speech; Alpha Psi Omega Hon Soc; Danforth Assn; Honoree Phi Delta Kappa. **MEMBERSHIPS** Mem AAVP; AAUW, MLA, SCA; trustee Cedar Crest Coll PA; mem Carnegie Found for Advmt of Tching; NAACP; Nat Council of Negro Women; Princeton Assn of Hum Rights. **CONTACT ADDRESS** Princeton Univ, 408 W College, Princeton, NJ, 08540.

DRIVER, MARTHA WESTCOTT
PERSONAL Born 10/24/1952, New York, NY, m, 1982 **DISCIPLINE** MEDIEVAL AND RENAISSANCE LITERATURE **EDUCATION** Vassar Col, AB, 74; Univ Pa, MA, 75, PhD (English), 80. **CAREER** Asst, Inst Medieval Studies Paleography, 76; lectr English, Univ Pa, 77-79 and Vassar Col, 80-81; ASST PROF ENGLISH, PACE UNIV, 81-, Reader, Pierpont Morgan Libr, 79-; mem, Inst Res Hist, 81-; intern, Nat Endowment Humanities, 82; writer, Publ Weekly, 82-. **MEMBERSHIPS** MLA; New Chaucer Soc; Midwest Mod Lang Asn. **RESEARCH** Manuscripts and early printed editions, particularly of Chaucer's works; medieval and Renaissance book illustration; paleography and early printing. **SELECTED PUBLICATIONS** Auth, A Directory of London Stationers and Book Artisans, 1300-1500, Speculum, J Medieval Stud, Vol 67, 92; The Pilgrimage of Prayer--The Texts and Iconography of the Exercitium Super Pater Noster, Speculum J Medieval Stud, Vcl 67, 92; The Pilgrimage of Prayer--The Texts and Iconography of the Exercitium Super Pater Noster, Speculum J Medieval Stud, Vol 67, 92; A Directory of London Stationers and Book Artisans, 1300-1500, Speculum J Medieval Stud, Vol 67, 92. **CONTACT ADDRESS** 100 W 57th St No 20-21E, New York, NY, 10019.

DRIVER, TOM FAW
PERSONAL Born 05/31/1925, Johnson City, TN, m, 1952, 3 children **DISCIPLINE** THEOLOGY, LITERATURE **EDUCATION** Duke Univ, AB, 50; Union Theol Sem, NY, MDiv, 53; Columbia Univ, PhD, 57. **CAREER** Instr drama, 56-58, from asst prof to assoc prof theol, 58- 67, prof theol & lit, 67-73, Paul J Tillich Prof Theol & Cult, 73-93, emeritus, 93- , Union Theol Sem; Kent fel, 53-56; Mars lectr, Northwestern Univ, 61; Guggenheim fel, 62; Earl lect, Pac Sch Relig, 62; vis assoc prof, Columbia Univ, 64-65; vis prof, Univ Otago, NZ, 76, Vassar Col, 78 & Montclair State Col, 81. **HONORS AND AWARDS** DLitt, Dennison Univ, 70. **MEMBERSHIPS** Soc Values Higher Educ; Am Acad Relig; New Haven Theol Discussion Gp; Witness for Peace. **RESEARCH** Classical and modern drama; contemporarv theology; ritual studies. **SELECTED PUBLICATIONS** Auth, The Sense of History in Greek and Shakespearean Drama, Columbia Univ, 60; co-ed, Poems of Belief and Doubt, Macmillan, 64; auth, The Shakespearian Clock, Shakespeare Quart, fall 64; Jean Genet, Columbia Univ, 66; History of the Modern Theatre, Delta, 71; The Twilight of Drama: From Ego to Myth, In: Humanities, Religion and the Arts, 72; Patterns of Grace: Human Experience as Word of God, Harper & Row, 77; Christ in a Changing World, Crossroad, 81; auth, The Magic of Ritual, Harper San Francisco, 91; auth, Liberating Rites: Understanding the Transformative Power of Ritual, Westview, 97. **CONTACT ADDRESS** 501 W 123rd St, #14G, New York, NY, 10027. **EMAIL** tfd2@columbia.edu

DROUT, MICHAEL D.C.
PERSONAL Born 05/03/1968, Neptune, NJ, m, 1994 **DISCIPLINE** ENGLISH **EDUCATION** Carnegie Mellon Univ, BA, 90; Stanford Univ, MA, 91; Univ of Mo-Columbia, MA, 93; Loyola Univ, PhD, 97. **CAREER** ASST PROF OF ENGLISH, WHEATON COL, 97-. **HONORS AND AWARDS** Alpha Sigma Nu nat Jesuit honor soc; Arthur G. Schmitt fel. **MEMBERSHIPS** Int Soc of Anglo-Saxonists; MLA; Medieval Acad. **RESEARCH** Anglo-Saxon and medieval Lit; linguistics; J.R.R. Tolkien; fantasy and science fiction. **SELECTED PUBLICATIONS** Auth, Hoisting the Arm of Defiance: Beowulfian Elements in ken Kesey's Sometimes a Great Notion, Western Am Lit, 93; The Influence of J.R.R. Tolkien's Masculinist Medievalism, Medieval Feminist Newsletter, 96; Reading the Signs of Light: Anglo-Saxonism, Education and obedience in Susan Cooper's The Dark is Rising, The Lion and the Unicorn, 97; The Fortunes of Men 4a: Reasons for Adopting a Very Old Emendation, Modern Philol, 98. **CONTACT ADDRESS** Wheaton Col, Norton, MA, 02766. **EMAIL** mdrout@wheatonma.edu

DRYDEN, EDGAR A.
PERSONAL Born 06/28/1937, Salisbury, MD, m, 1959, 3 children **DISCIPLINE** AMERICAN LITERATURE **EDUCATION** Wash Col, BA, 59; Univ RI, MA, 61; Johns Hopkins Univ, PhD(Am lit), 65. **CAREER** Asst prof English, Johns Hopkins Univ, 65-57; asst prof English, State Univ NY, Buffalo, 67-68, assoc prof, 68-78, assoc provost fac arts & lett, 72-78; prof English & Dept Head, Univ Az, 78-86, Guggenheim fel, 82-83. **MEMBERSHIPS** MLA. **RESEARCH** American literature; the novel. **SELECTED PUBLICATIONS** Auth, Melville's Thematics of Form, Johns Hopkins Univ, 68; Hawthorne's Castle in the Air: Form and Theme in The House of the Seven Gables, ELH, 6/71; History and Progress: Some Implications of Form in Cooper's Littlepage Novels, Nineteenth-Century Fiction, 6/71; Nathaniel Hawthorne: The Poetics of Enchantment, Cornell, 77; The entangled text: Melville's Pierre and the Problem of Reading, Boundary, spring 79; The Image of the Mirror: The Double Economy of James' Portrait, Genre, spring 80; The Form of American Romance, John Hopkins, 87; Editor, Arizona Quarterly, 88-. **CONTACT ADDRESS** Dept of English, Univ of Ariz, 1 University of Az, Tucson, AZ, 85721-0001. **EMAIL** edryden@u.arizona.edu

DRYDEN, M.
PERSONAL Born 01/11/1946, San Antonio, TX, d, 1 child **DISCIPLINE** FOREIGN LANGUAGE EDUCATION; ENGLISH EDUCATION; ENGLISH **EDUCATION** Univ Tex-Austin, BA, 80; MA, 92. **CAREER** Instr, Austin Commun Col; refugee ESL coordinator, 97- . **HONORS AND AWARDS** Phi Zeta Kappa teaching excellence, 93. **MEMBERSHIPS** TESOL **RESEARCH** Adult education ESL; refugee ESL. **SELECTED PUBLICATIONS** Auth, Teaching Language Teachers to be More Collaborative: The Second Language Learner Course at the University of Texas at Austin, MLA J, 97. **CONTACT ADDRESS** Dept of Adult Educ, Austin Comm Col, Austin, TX, 78741. **EMAIL** mdryden@mail.utexas.edu

DUBAN, JAMES
PERSONAL Born 03/14/1951, Paris, France **DISCIPLINE** AMERICAN LITERATURE **EDUCATION** Univ Mass, Amherst, BA, 72; Cornell Univ, MA, 75, PhD (Am lit), 76. **CAREER** Lectr English and Am lit, Cornell Univ, 76-77; ASST PROF AMERICAN LIT, UNIV TEX, AUSTIN, 77-, Am Coun Learned Soc grant, 78. **MEMBERSHIPS** MLA; Nathaniel Hawthorne Soc; Herman Melville Soc. **RESEARCH** Nineteenth-century American literature. **SELECTED PUBLICATIONS** Auth, Transatlantic Counterparts, The Diptych and Social Inquiry in Melville Poor Mans Pudding and Rich Mans Crumbs, New England Quart Hist Rev New England Life Letters, Vol 66, 93; The Father--A Life of James, Henry, New England Quart Hist Rev New England Life Letters, Vol 68, 95; Darwin, Charles, James, Henry, Sr, and Evolution, Harvard Lib Bull, Vol 7, 96. **CONTACT ADDRESS** Dept of English, Univ of Tex, Austin, TX, 78712.

DUBEY, MADHU
DISCIPLINE ENGLISH **EDUCATION** Ill Univ, PhD. **CAREER** Prof, Northwestern Univ. **RESEARCH** African American literature; women's fiction; feminist theory. **SELECTED PUBLICATIONS** Auth, Black Women Novelists and the National Aesthetic, 94; Carlene Polite, Black Women in the US, 93; essays on, African-Am culture. **CONTACT ADDRESS** Dept of English, Northwestern Univ, 1801 Hinman, Evanston, IL, 60208.

DUBINO, JEANNE
PERSONAL Born 05/07/1959, Bethesda, MD **DISCIPLINE** ENGLISH **EDUCATION** Boston Col, BA, English, 81; Univ Delaware, MA, 87; Univ Maryland, PhD, 92. **CAREER** Grad instr, 82-83, Univ of Delaware; grad instr, 84-92, Univ of Maryland; adj asst prof, 92-, Westfield St Col & Holyoke Comm Col; asst prof, 93-97, Plymouth St Col; vis asst prof, 97-99, Bilkent Univ Ankara Turkey. **HONORS AND AWARDS** Who's Who among Amer Tchrs, 98; Who's Who in Turkey, 98; Alternate Natl Endowment for the Humanities Sum Sem on Postcolonial Lit and Theory, 96; Fac Grant Award, 94; honor Society of Phi Kappa Phi, 92; PhD with Distinction, 89. **MEMBERSHIPS** Virginia Woolf Soc; Popular Culture Asn; Modern Language Asn; Natl Womens Studies Asn; Northeast Popular Culture Asn; Northeast Modern Language Asn; New Hampshire Humanities Council. **RESEARCH** 19th & 20th Century British lit; postcolonial lit; gender stud and feminist theory; victorian culture; cultural criticism. **SELECTED PUBLICATIONS** Rev, Virginia Woolf a Literary Life, Virginia Woolf Miscellany 40, 93; art, Wicked Workers Nasty Nannies and Lethal Lesbians The Backlash against Feminism in Fatal Attraction the Hand that Rocks the Cradle and Basic Instinct, Soc for Phil Stud of the Cont Visual Arts, 93; art, The Cinderella Complex Romance Fiction Patriarchy and Capitalism, Jour of Popular Culture, 93; art, On Illness as Carnival? The Body as Discovery in Virginia Woolfs On Being Ill and Mikhail Bakhtins Rabelais and His World, Virginia Woolf Emerging Persp: Selected Papers from the 3rd Ann Conf on Virginia Woolf, Pace Univ Press, 94; art, Waynes World Postmodern or Nostalgic, Pop Cult Rev, 95; art, Creating the Conditions of Life Virginia Woolf and the Common Reader, Selected Papers from the 4th Ann Conf on Virginia Woolf, 95; art, Travelogue Piece, Plymouth St Col Update, 96; art, From Reviewer to Literary Critic Virginia Woolfs Early Career as a Book Reviewer 19004-1918, Selected Papers from the 5th Ann Conf on Virginia Woolf, Pace Univ Press, 96; art, The Wheelbarrow, Writes of Passage, Plymouth Writers Group Pub, 96; art, Rambling through A Room of Ones Own vs Marching through I A Richards Practical Criticism on the Essay as an Anti Institutional Form, Selected Papers from the 6th Ann Conf on Viriginia Woolf, Pace Univ Press, 97; guest ed, Virginia Woolf Miscellany 50, 97; art, Virginia Woolf From Book Reviewer to Literary Critic 1904-1918, Virginia Woolf and the Essay; coed, Virginia Woolf and the Essay, St Martins 97; art, The Influence of Something upon Somebody Reflections on the 7th Ann Conf on Virginia Woolf, Pace Univ Press, 98. **CONTACT ADDRESS** Dept of English, Plymouth State Col, Univ System of New Hampshire, Plymouth, NH, 03264. **EMAIL** jdubino@bilkent.edu.tr

DUBROVSKY, GERTRUDE
PERSONAL Born 03/10/1926, New York, NY, d, 3 children **DISCIPLINE** ENGLISH LITERATURE **EDUCATION** Georgian Court Col, AB, 56; Rutgers Univ, MA, 59; Columbia Univ, EdD, 73. **CAREER** Yiddish instr, Princeton Univ Ctr for Jewish Life, 75-95; res, YIVO Inst for Jewish Res and Carnegie Found for Advan of Tchg; YIVO, 74-80, and CFAT, 84-86, independent scholar; social historian, 74- ; pres, DOCUMENTARY III, 84- . **HONORS AND AWARDS** Oxford Ctr for Jewish Stud fel, 94; NEH grant 76-78. **MEMBERSHIPS** Natl Coalition of Indep Scholars; Princeton Res Forum; Am Jewish Hist Soc; NJ Hist Soc. **RESEARCH** American Jewish experience; Kindertransport, Holocaust history. **SELECTED PUBLICATIONS** Auth, The Farmingdale Collection, YIVO Inst, 77; auth, The Land Was Theirs, Univ Alabama Pr, 92; auth numerous articles and book reviews. **CONTACT ADDRESS** 244 Hawthorne Ave., Princeton, NJ, 08540. **EMAIL** gdubrovsky@aol.com

DUCHARME, ROBERT
DISCIPLINE ENGLISH **EDUCATION** NY Univ; Univ Notre Dame, PhD. **CAREER** Dept ch. **HONORS AND AWARDS** Develop crs(es) in, Japanese Lit and Cult & Latin Amer fiction. **SELECTED PUBLICATIONS** Publ bk on, novels of Bernard Malamud & study of Joseph Conrad's Lord Jim. **CONTACT ADDRESS** Dept of English, Mount Saint Mary's Col, 16300 Old Emmitsburg Rd, Emmitsburg, MD, 21727-7799.

DUCKWORTH, ALISTAIR MCKAY
PERSONAL Born 08/04/1936, Balmullo, Scotland, m, 1964, 2 children **DISCIPLINE** ENGLISH **EDUCATION** Univ Edinburgh, MA, 58; Johns Hopkins Univ, MA, 64, PhD (English), 67. **CAREER** Instr English, Johns Hopkins Univ, 63-67; asst prof, Univ Va, 67-73; assoc prof, 73-80, PROF ENGLISH, UNIV FLA, 80-, Sesquicentennial assoc, Ctr Advan Studies, Univ Va, 71-72; vis prof prog in mod lit, State Univ NY, Buffalo, summer 74; Guggenheim Mem Found fel, 77-78; patron, Jane Austin Soc NAm, 79-. **HONORS AND AWARDS** Presidential Scholar, Univ Fla, Gainesville, 76-77. **MEMBERSHIPS** MLA; SAtlantic Mod Lang Asn; Am Soc 18th Century Studies; Asn Scottish Lit Studies. **RESEARCH** English novel; literature and landscape. **SELECTED PUBLICATIONS**

Auth, Domestic Realities and Imperial Fictions, Austen, Jane Novels in 18th Century Contexts, 19th Century Lit, Vol 50, 95; A Fry, Roger Reader, Eng Lit Transition 1880-1920, Vol 40, 97; Aspects of the Novelist, Forster, E. M. Pattern And Rhythm, Eng Lit Transition 1880-1920, Vol 39, 96; Space and the 18th Century English Novel, Scriblerian Kit Cats, Vol 25, 92; Women, Writing About Money--Womens Fiction in England, 1790-1820,19th Century Literature, Vol 52, 97; The Beautiful, Novel, and Strange--Aesthetics and Heterodoxy, Albion, Vol 29, 97. **CONTACT ADDRESS** Dept of English, Univ of Florida, Gainesville, FL, 32601.

DUCLOW, DONALD F.
PERSONAL Born 01/11/1946, Chicago, IL, m, 1970 **DISCIPLINE** ENGLISH, PHILSOSOPHY, MEDIEVAL STUDIES **EDUCATION** DePaul Univ, BA, English, philosophy, 68, MA, philosophy, 69; Bryn Mawr Coll, MA, medieval studies, 72, PhD, philosophy, 74. **CAREER** Visiting prof, philosophy, Fordham Univ, 78; asst prof of philosophy, 74-79, assoc prof of philosophy, 79-89, prof of philosophy, 89-, Gwynedd-Mercy Coll. **HONORS AND AWARDS** Mellon Fellow in the Humanities, Univ Pa, 80-81; NEH summer seminars, 87, 93. **MEMBERSHIPS** Amer Acad Religion; Medieval Acad Am; sec, Amer Cusanus Soc; Amer Assn Univ Profs; pres, Gwynedd-Mercy Coll Chap, 96-97. **RESEARCH** Medieval philosophy and religion. **SELECTED PUBLICATIONS** Auth, "Divine Nothingness and Self-Creation in John Scotus Eriugena," The Journ of Religion, vol 57, 77; "'My Suffering Is God': Meister Eckhart's Book of Divine Consolation," Theological Studies, vol 44, 83, reprinted in Classical and Medieval Literature Criticism, 93; "Into the Whirlwind of Suffering: Resistance and Transformation," Second Opinion, Nov 88; "Nicholas of Cusa," in Medieval Philosophers, vol 15, Dictionary of Literary Biography, 92; "Isaiah Meets the Seraph: Breaking Ranks in Dionysius and Eriugena?" in Eriugena: East and West, 94. **CONTACT ADDRESS** Gwynedd-Mercy Col, Gwynedd Valley, PA, 19437-0901.

DUDLEY, EDWARD J.
PERSONAL Born 07/18/1926, St. Paul, MN, m, 1959, 2 children **DISCIPLINE** SPANISH, ENGLISH **EDUCATION** Univ MN, Minneapolis, BA, 49, MA, 51, PhD, 63. **CAREER** Tchr, Am Sch, Managua, Nicaragua, 54-55; instr Span, St John's Univ, MN, 56-60; asst prof, UCLA, 63-70; chmn & prof Hisp lang & lit & dir comp lit prog, Univ Pittsburgh, 70-74; chmn dept Span, Ital & Port, 74-77, chmn dept French & Dept Ger & Slavic, 76-77, Prof Span & Comp Lit, State Univ NY Buffalo, 74-, Chmn Dept Mod Lang & Lit, 77-, Consult, Nat Bd Consult, Nat Endowment for Hum, 76. **MEMBERSHIPS** MLA; Mediaeval Acad Am; Asn Int Hispanistas; Cervantes Soc Am; Conrad Soc Am. **RESEARCH** Cervantes; early prose fiction; comp lit. **SELECTED PUBLICATIONS** Auth, Three patterns of imagery in Conrad's Heart of Darkness, Rev des Langues Vivantes, 65; coauth, El cuento, Holt, 66; auth, Court and country: The fusion of two images of love in Juan Rodriguez's El siervo libre de amor, PMLA, 67; Don Quixote as magus: The rhetoric of interpolation, Bull Hisp Studies, 72; co-ed, The Wild Man Within: An Image in Western Thought from the Renaissance to Romanticism, Univ Pittsburgh, 72; co-ed, 2nd ed, El cuento, Holt, 84; co-ed, American Attitudes toward Foreign Languages and Foreign Cultures, Bouvier, Bonn, 83; auth, The Endless Text: Don Quijote and The Hermeneutics of Romance, SUNY Press, 97; various other articles and essays on Cervantes. **CONTACT ADDRESS** Dept of Mod Lang & Lit, State Univ of NY, PO Box 604620, Buffalo, NY, 14260-4620. **EMAIL** edudley@acsu.buffalo.edu

DUDT, CHARMAZEL
PERSONAL Born 08/30/1940, Allahabad, India **DISCIPLINE** ENGLISH LITERATURE **EDUCATION** Allahabad Univ, India, BA, 59, MA, 61; Tex Tech Univ, PhD(English), 71. **CAREER** Lectr English, St John's Col, Agra, India, 62-63, Isabella Thoburn Col, Lucknow, India, 63-64; asst prof, 70-78, assoc prof, 78-84, PROF ENGLISH, WTEX STATE UNIV, 84-, CHAIR, SHAKESPEARE STUDIES, 95-. **MEMBERSHIPS** MLA; Conf Christianity & Lit; Asn Asian Studies; SCent Renaissance Soc **RESEARCH** Shakespeare; nineteenth century British literature; Asian studies. **SELECTED PUBLICATIONS** Auth, Of that time, of that place: Shakespeare's Illyria, Conf Col Teachers English, 5/75. **CONTACT ADDRESS** Dept of English, West Texas A&M Univ, 2501 4th Ave, Canyon, TX, 79016-0001. **EMAIL** cdudt@wtamu.edu

DUFFY, ANDREW ENDA
DISCIPLINE ENGLISH LITERATURE **EDUCATION** Harvard Univ, PhD, 90. **CAREER** ASSOC PROF, ENG, UNIV CALIF, SANTA BARBARA. **RESEARCH** Post-colonial lit and cult; Irish lit; Modernism and postmodernism; cult stud; Joyce. **SELECTED PUBLICATIONS** Auth, "Engendering Monsters," The South Asian Rev, 92; "The Japanese Car as Postcolonial Novel," Col Lit, 93; The Subaltern Ulysses, Univ Minn Press, 94. **CONTACT ADDRESS** Dept of Eng, Univ Calif, Santa Barbara, CA, 93106-7150. **EMAIL** duffy@humanitas.ucsb.edu

DUFFY, DENNIS
PERSONAL Born 10/08/1938, Louisville, KY **DISCIPLINE** ENGLISH **EDUCATION** Georgetown Univ Wash, 56-60; Univ Toronto, MA, 62, PhD, 64. **CAREER** Prin, Innis Col, 79-84, PROF ENGLISH, UNIV TORONTO; lectr, Shastri Indo-Can Inst, 82; lectr, Indian Asn Can Stud, 92-93; Fulbright fel, 93; Craig Dobbin Prof Can Stud, Univ Col, Dublin, 95-97. **RESEARCH** Canadian literature; John Richardson. **SELECTED PUBLICATIONS** Auth, Marshall McLuhan, 68; auth, Gardens, Covenants, Exiles: Loyalism in the Literature of Upper Canada, 82; auth, John Richardson and His Works, 83; auth, Sounding the Iceberg, 86; auth, Introducing John Richardson's 'Wacousta', 93; auth, A World Under Sentence: John Richardson and the Interior, 95. **CONTACT ADDRESS** Innis Col, Univ of Toronto, Toronto, ON, M5S 1J5.

DUGGAN, JOSEPH JOHN
PERSONAL Born 09/08/1938, Philadelphia, PA, m, 1981, 3 children **DISCIPLINE** MEDIEVAL LITERATURE, PHILOLOGY **EDUCATION** Fordham Univ, AB, 60; Ohio State Univ, PhD(Romance lang), 64. **CAREER** Instr French, 64-65, asst prof, 65-66, asst prof, French & comp lit, 66-71, assoc prof, 71-78, prof French, Comp Lit & Romance Philol, Univ Calif, Berkeley, 78-, assoc dean, Graduate Div, 89-; Nat Humanities Found younger scholar fel, 68-69; Guggenheim fel, 79-80; ed, Romance Philol, 82-87. **HONORS AND AWARDS** Mythopoesis: Literatura, totalidad, ideologia. Ofrecido a Joseph J. Duggan por su distinguida aportacion a los estudios literarios, Anthropos, 92. **MEMBERSHIPS** Mediaeval Acad Am; Soc Rencesvals. **RESEARCH** Medieval French and Spanish literatures; Romance philology. **SELECTED PUBLICATIONS** Auth, Formulas in the Couronnement de Louis, Romania, 66; Yvain's good name: The unity of Chretien de Troyes Chevalier au Lion, Orbis Litterarum, 69; A Concordance to the Chanson de Roland, Ohio State Univ Press, 70; The Song of Roland: Formulaic Style and Poetic Craft, Univ Calif Press, 73; ed & contribr, Oral Literature: Seven Essays, Scottish Acad Press, 75; auth, Ambiguity in Twelfth and Thirteenth-Century French and Provencal Literature: A Problem or a Value?, In: Studies in Honor of John Misrahi, Fr Lit Publ, 77; The Generation of the Episode of Baligant, Romance Philol, 77; A Guide to Studies on the Chanson de Roland, Grant & Cutler, 77; auth, A New Fragment of Les Enfances Vivien, Univ Calif Press, 85; auth, Medieval Epic as Popular Historiography: Appropriation of Historical Knowledge in the Vernacular Epic, In: Grundriss der romanischen Literatureu des Mittelalters, vol 2, Carl Winter, 86; auth, The Cantar de mio Cid: Poetic Creation in its Economic and Social Contexts, Cambridge Univ Press, 89; auth, L' episode d'Aupais dans Girart de Roussillou, In: Reading Around the Epic, King's Col, London. 98. **CONTACT ADDRESS** Dept of Comp Lit, Univ of Calif, 4118 Dwinelle Hall, Berkeley, CA, 94720-2510. **EMAIL** roland@socrates.berkeley.edu

DUNAWAY, DAVID KING
PERSONAL Born 10/03/1948, New York, NY **DISCIPLINE** MEDIA STUDIES, LITERATURE, ORAL HISTORY AND BROADCASTING **EDUCATION** Univ Wisc Madison, BA, 70; Univ Calif Berkeley, MAT, 72; PhD, Amer Studies, 81. **CAREER** Asst and assoc prof, Eng and Comm, Univ Nmex, 81; vis lectr, Fulbright, Univ Nairobi Kenya, 84; vis prof, Univ NC Chapel Hill, 96; visiting lectr, Fulbright, Univ Colombia, 97, vis lectr, Roskilde Univ, Denmark, 97. **HONORS AND AWARDS** Steager prize in folklore, Univ Calif Berkeley, 81; broadcasting awards, Golden Mike, Major Armstrong, Gabriel, Silver Rell. **MEMBERSHIPS** Amer Folklore Soc; Oral Hist Asn; Broadcast Educ Asn; Intl Assoc for Media and Comm. **RESEARCH** The entation of broadcasting and represing history and literature; Radio studies; Contemporary literature and folklore. **SELECTED PUBLICATIONS** Coauth, Writing the Southwest, with S. Spurgeon, Plume/Penguin, 95; auth, Aldous Huxley Recollected, Carroll & Graf, NY, 95, Sage, 98; Huxley in Hollywood, Harper, Bloomsbury, London, 89; Coauth, Oral History: An Interdisciplinary Anthology, with W. K. Baum, Amer Asn for State and Local Hist, Nashville, 84, Sage, 96; How Can I Keep From Singing: Peter Seeger, McGraw Hill, 81, 82, Harrap, London, 85, Shakai Shiso Sha, Tokyo, 85, Jucar, Barcelona, 88; World's Non-Physical Heritage: A Typology, UNESCO, Paris, 84; articles, Radio and Biography, Biog, Winter, 97; Communications Bill Tunes Out Public, Albuquerque Jour, 8 Feb, 96; Broadcasting History, Proceedings of IX International Oral History Conference Goreborg, Sweden, 96; Radio Management and University Neglect, Col Broadcasting, Dec. 92. **CONTACT ADDRESS** 33 S. Modoc Av., Medford, OR, 97504. **EMAIL** dunaway@unm.edu

DUNCAN, BONNIE I.
DISCIPLINE ENGLISH **EDUCATION** Columbus Col, BA, 81; Univ Iowa, MA, 85, PhD, 88. **CAREER** Assoc pro, 96-97 & asst prof, 91-96, Millersville Univ; asst prof & ch, Upper Iowa Univ, 89-91. **HONORS AND AWARDS** NEH Summer Inst, Northwestern Univ, 95 & Stanford Univ, 91; **MEMBERSHIPS** Mem, Engl Inst, Harvard Univ, 95; SSHE Fac Prof Develop Symp, 92; Fac Develop Coun of the State Syst Higher Educ Workshop, 92. **SELECTED PUBLICATIONS** Gen ed, The Political and Satirical Poems of Harley 2253: A Diplomatic Edition, Univ Pa Press, 96. **CONTACT ADDRESS** Dept of English, Millersville Univ, Pennsylvania, PO Box 1002, Millersville, PA, 17551-0302. **EMAIL** bduncan@marauder.millersv.edu

DUNCAN, CHARLES
DISCIPLINE ENGLISH LITERATURE **EDUCATION** Emory Univ, PhD. **CAREER** Sr prof Eng; coord, DAH prog. **HONORS AND AWARDS** Proj dir, NEH Focus grant, 97. **RESEARCH** Popular culture and global literature. **SELECTED PUBLICATIONS** Ed, Global Literature, One World, Many Voices. **CONTACT ADDRESS** Clark Atlanta Univ, 223 James P Brawley Dr, SW, Atlanta, GA, 30314.

DUNCAN, JEFFREY LIGHT
PERSONAL Born 01/26/1939, Tulsa, OK, m, 1969, 2 children **DISCIPLINE** AMERICAN LITERATURE **EDUCATION** Calif State Univ, Long Beach, AB, 61; Univ Va, MA, 62, PhD (Am lit), 65. **CAREER** Asst prof Am lit, Washington Univ, 65-69; temp lectr Am civilization, Univ Leeds, Eng, 70-71; assoc prof Am lit, 71-78, prof Am lit, 78-79, PROF ENGLISH LANG and LIT, EASTERN MICH UNIV, 79-, Bruern fel, Univ Leeds, Eng, 69-70; Nat Endowment for Arts fel, 78-79. **MEMBERSHIPS** Midwest Mod Lang Asn; MLA. **RESEARCH** American literature; language theory. **SELECTED PUBLICATIONS** Auth, Sutro Baths, Smithsonian, Vol 24, 93. **CONTACT ADDRESS** Dept of English, Eastern Michigan Univ, 612 Pray Harrold, Ypsilanti, MI, 48197-2201.

DUNCAN, KIRBY LUTHER
PERSONAL Born 12/02/1936, Deport, TX, m, 1966 **DISCIPLINE** ENGLISH **EDUCATION** Arlington State Col, BA, 63; Tex Technol Col, MA, 64; Univ SC, PhD (English),. **CAREER** Instr English, Univ SC, 66-67; asst prof, 67-72, assoc prof, 72-80, PROF ENGLISH, STEPHEN F AUSTIN STATE UNIV, 80-. **MEMBERSHIPS** MLA; NCTE; Am Studies Asn. **RESEARCH** Novels of Henry James; Pamela Hansford Johnson; teaching college composition. **SELECTED PUBLICATIONS** Auth, Lies, Damned Lies, and Statistics--Psychological Syndrome Evidence in the Courtroom After Daubert, Indiana Law Journal, Vol 71,96. **CONTACT ADDRESS** Dept of English and Philos, Stephen F Austin State Univ, Nacogdoches, TX, 75962.

DUNLAP, ISAAC H.
PERSONAL Chapel Hill, NC **DISCIPLINE** LIBRARY AND INFORMATION STUDIES **EDUCATION** Univ of NC, MLIS, 96 **CAREER** Asst Prof, 97-, Wstrn IL Univ **HONORS AND AWARDS** Beta Phi MU, 97 **MEMBERSHIPS** ALA, ACRL, ILA, IACRL **RESEARCH** Medieval Scholarship **SELECTED PUBLICATIONS** Auth, Gerard of Cremona: A manuscript Location Guide and Annotated Bibliography, Bulletin of Bibliography, 53:4, 96 **CONTACT ADDRESS** Macomb, IL, 61455-1239. **EMAIL** ih-dunlap@win.edu

DUNLAP, KAREN F. BROWN
PERSONAL Born 07/13/1951, Nashville, Tennessee **DISCIPLINE** JOURNALISM **EDUCATION** Michigan State University, East Lansing, MI, BA, 1971; Tennessee State University, Nashville, TN, MS, 1976; University of Tennessee, Knoxville, TN, PhD, 1982. **CAREER** Nashville Banner, Nashville, TN, staff writer, 1969, 1971, 1983-85 (summers); Macon News, Macon, GA, staff writer, 1972-73; Tennessee State University, Nashville, TN, assistant professor, 1976-85; University of South Florida, Tampa, FL, assistant professor, 1985-; The Poynter Institute, St Petersburg, FL, associate professor, 1989-. **HONORS AND AWARDS** McKnight Fellow, Florida Endowment Fund, 1986-87; Karl A. & Madira Bickel Fellow, Bickel Foundation, 1979-80. **MEMBERSHIPS** Society of Professional Journalists, 1980-; Delta Sigma Theta Sorority, 1982-; National Association of Black Journalists, 1985-; Association of Educators in Journalism and Mass Communications, 1981-. **CONTACT ADDRESS** Poynter Institute for Media Studies, 801 3rd St, S, St Petersburg, FL, 33701.

DUNN, ELLEN CATHERINE
PERSONAL Born 07/30/1916, Baltimore, MD **DISCIPLINE** ENGLISH **EDUCATION** Col Notre Dame, Md, AB, 38; Cath Univ Am, MA, 40, PhD, 47. **CAREER** Lectr English, Col Notre Dame, Md, 45-47; from instr to asst prof, 47-63, prof, 68-81, chmn dept, 69-78, EMER PROF ENGLISH, CATH UNIV AM, 81-, Vis lectr, Folger Shakespeare Libr, fall 81. **MEMBERSHIPS** MLA; Mediaeval Acad Am; AAUP; SAtlantic Asn Depts English (pres, 72-73). **RESEARCH** Medieval English and Latin drama; Renaissance English drama; saints' legends. **SELECTED PUBLICATIONS** Auth, The Farced Epistle as Dramatic Form in The 12th Century Renaissance, Comparative Drama, Vol 29, 95. **CONTACT ADDRESS** Dept of English, Catholic Univ of America, Washington, DC, 20064.

DUNN, RICHARD JOHN
PERSONAL Born 06/08/1938, Pittsburgh, PA, m, 1961, 3 children **DISCIPLINE** NINETEENTH CENTURY ENGLISH **EDUCATION** Allegheny Col, BA, 60; Western Reserve Univ, MA, 61, PhD (English), 64. **CAREER** Lectr English, Univ Colo, Colorado Springs, 66-67; instr, US Air Force Acad Prep Sch, 64-67; asst prof, US Air Force Acad, 65-67; asst prof, 67-71, assoc prof, 71-81, assoc chmn dept, 76-80, dean, summer, 80-82, PROF ENGLISH, UNIV WASH, 81-, CHMN DEPT, 82-, Assoc bibliogr, MLA Bibliog, 70-75. **MEMBERSHIPS** MLA; Philol Asn Pac Coast; Dickens Soc; Dickens Fel. **RE-**

SEARCH English novel; Victorian literature. **SELECTED PUBLICATIONS** Auth, The Night Side of Dickens, Cannibalism, Passion, Necessity, 19th Century Literature, Vol 50, 95; Dandies and Desert Saints--Styles of Victorian Manhood, Dickens Quarterly, Vol 14, 97; Trollope--A Biography, Stud Novel, Vol 25, 93; New Casebooks, David Copperfield and Hard Times, Dickens Quart, Vol 13, 96. **CONTACT ADDRESS** Dept of English, Univ of Washington, Seattle, WA, 98195.

DUNN, ROBERT P.
DISCIPLINE ENGLISH **EDUCATION** Pacific Union Col, BA, 63; MA, 65, PhD, 70, Univ Wisconsin-Madison **CAREER** Asst Prof, 68-73, Assoc Prof, 73-79, Prof, 79-90, Chr English, 77-81 and 87-90, Loma Linda Univ; Prof, 90-, Assoc Dean, Col Arts & Sciences, 90-94, Chr, Eng & Communication, 95-99, La Sierra Univ. **CONTACT ADDRESS** Dept of Eng, La Sierra Univ, 4700 Pierce St., Riverside, CA, 92515-8247. **EMAIL** rdunn@lasierra.edu

DUNN, ROBERT P.
PERSONAL Born 11/18/1941, Rockford, IL, m, 1963, 2 children **DISCIPLINE** ENGLISH **EDUCATION** Pacific Union Col, BA, 63; Univ Wis, Madison, MA, 66, PhD, 70; Sch Theol, Claremont, RelM, 77. **CAREER** Prof, 80-, Chemn, 77-81, 87-90, 95-99, assoc dean, 90-94, La Sierra Univ. **MEMBERSHIPS** Modern Lang Asn; Shakespeare Asn Am; Conference on Christianity and Lit. **RESEARCH** English renaissance; religion & literature. **CONTACT ADDRESS** Dept of English, La Sierra Univ, 4700 Pierce St, Riverside, CA, 92515-8247. **EMAIL** rdunn@lasierra.edu

DUNNE, JOSEPH FALLON
PERSONAL Born 12/12/1941, St. Louis, MO, m, 1964, 5 children **DISCIPLINE** ENGLISH, COMMUNICATIONS **EDUCATION** St Benedict's Col, AB, 63; Univ Kans, MA, 67; St Louis Univ, MA, 75. **CAREER** Prof English, St Louis Community Col, MERAMEC, 64-. **HONORS AND AWARDS** Fac Lect Award, 96; Gov Award for Excellence in Teaching, 96. **MEMBERSHIPS** Soc Tech Commun. **CONTACT ADDRESS** Dept of English, St Louis Community Col, 11333 Big Bend Rd, Saint Louis, MO, 63122-5799. **EMAIL** jdunne@mcmail.stlcc.cc.mo.us

DUPRIEST JR., TRAVIS TALMADGE
DISCIPLINE ENGLISH LITERATURE AND COMPOSITION **EDUCATION** Richmond Univ, BA; Harvard Divinity Sch, MTS; Univ Ky, PhD. **CAREER** English, Carthage Col. **HONORS AND AWARDS** Grants: Nat Endowment Hum; Univ Chicago Midwest Fac Seminar., Danforth fel, Pres Nat Huguenot Soc; Fel Huguenot, Fel Ctr Renaissance & Reformation Studies; Vis/Occas fel Univ Chicago, Cambridge Univ. **MEMBERSHIPS** MLA; Conference Christianity & Literature; former dir Honors Prog Carthage. **SELECTED PUBLICATIONS** Auth, Noon at Smyrna; Summer Storm; Soapstone Wall. **CONTACT ADDRESS** Carthage Col, 2001 Alford Dr., Kenosha, WI, 53140.

DURER, CHRISTOPHER
PERSONAL Born 09/15/1928, Warsaw, Poland, m, 1967, 1 child **DISCIPLINE** ENGLISH, COMPARATIVE LITERATURE **EDUCATION** Chicago Teachers Col, BEd, 61; Univ Calif, Berkeley, MA, 63, PhD (comp lit), 69. **CAREER** Instr humanities, Univ Mo, Rolla, 63-64; instr comp lit, San Francisco State Col, 65-67, Univ Calif, Berkeley, 68-69; asst prof English, 69-73, ASSOC PROF ENGLISH and MOD LANG, UNIV WYO, 73-. **MEMBERSHIPS** MLA; Am Comp Lit Asn; Int Comp Lit Asn; Am Soc 18th Century Studies. **RESEARCH** Comparative theory and history; English 18th century literature; 20th century drama. **SELECTED PUBLICATIONS** Auth, Musical Metamorphoses--Forms and History of Arrangement, Musik und Kirche, Vol 63, 93; The International Glen Gould Festival in Groningen , Musica, Vol 47, 93; Report on the 17th Edition of the Tage Alter Musik Held in Herne, December 1992, Musica, Vol 47, 93; Kagel Die Erschopfung Der Welt, Musica, Vol 48, 94; Freyer Distanzen, Musica, Vol 48, 94; 100 Years of Opera in Essen 1893-1993, Musica, Vol 47, 93; Fortner in Seinem Garten Liebt Don Perlimplin Belisa, Musica, Vol 48, 94; Geister Der ModerneReport on a Recent Concert Series in Recklinghausen March 7-14, 1993, Musica, Vol 47, 93; Hummel Gorbatschow, Musica, Vol 48, 94; Freyer Flugel Schlage, Musica, Vol 48, 94. **CONTACT ADDRESS** Dept of English, Univ of Wyo, Laramie, WY, 82070.

DUSSINGER, JOHN ANDREW
PERSONAL Born 11/18/1935, Reading, PA, m, 1959, 2 children **DISCIPLINE** ENGLISH **EDUCATION** Lehigh Univ, AB, 58; Oxford Univ, IIE, 59; Princeton Univ, MA, 61, PhD (English), 64. **CAREER** Instr English, Douglass Col, 62-65; asst prof, 65-68, ASSOC PROF ENGLISH, UNIV ILL, URBANA-CHAMPAIGN, 68-, Lectr English lit, Aarhus Univ, 70-72. **MEMBERSHIPS** MLA; Johnson Soc Midwest (pres, 68-69); Am Soc 18th Century Studies. **RESEARCH** Eighteenth century prose; the novel; history of ideas. **SELECTED PUBLICATIONS** Auth, Her Bread to Earn--Women, Money and Society from Defoe to Austen, Modern Lan Rev, Vol 90, 95;Clarissa, Jacobitism, and the Spirit of the University, Studies in the Literary Imagination, Vol 28, 95; Gulliver in Japan, Another Possible Source, Notes Queries, Vol 39, 92; The Working Class of People--An Early 18th Century Source, Notes Queries, Vol 43, 96; Austen, Jane Novels, The Art of Clarity, 19th Century Lit, Vol 48, 93. **CONTACT ADDRESS** 1612 Chevy Chase Dr, Champaign, IL, 61820.

DUST, PATRICK
DISCIPLINE TWENTIETH-CENTURY SPANISH LITERATURE **EDUCATION** Univ Chicago, PhD. **CAREER** Literature, Carleton Univ. **MEMBERSHIPS** Auth, Ortega y Gasset and the Question of Modernity. **CONTACT ADDRESS** Carleton Col, 100 S College St., Northfield, MN, 55057-4016.

DUST, PHILIP CLARENCE
PERSONAL Born 12/13/1936, Centralia, IL, m, 1967, 3 children **DISCIPLINE** ENGLISH RENAISSANCE LITERATURE **EDUCATION** St Mary of the Lake Sem, BA, 59; Eastern Ill Univ, BS, 61; Univ Ill, MA, 64, PhD (English), 68. **CAREER** Teacher Latin, Pekin Community High Sch, 61-63; teaching asst English, Univ Ill, 64-68; asst prof, 68-74, ASSOC PROF, NORTHERN ILL UNIV, 74-. **MEMBERSHIPS** MLA. **RESEARCH** Renaissance neo-Latin poetry and prose; Renaissance English poetry and prose; Renaissance pacifism. **SELECTED PUBLICATIONS** Auth, Burton, Richard Philosophaster, 16th Century J Vol 26, 95. **CONTACT ADDRESS** Dept of English, No Illinois Univ, 1425 W Lincoln Hwy, De Kalb, IL, 60115-2825.

DUTTON, WILLIAM H.
DISCIPLINE COMMUNICATION AND PUBLIC ADMINISTRATION **EDUCATION** Univ MO, BA; SUNY Buffalo, MA, PhD. **CAREER** Prof; USC, 80-; vis prof, Brunel Univ, 86-87; Nat dir, UK's Prog on Information & Commun Technol, 93-95; taught & conducted res, Univ S Fl, San Diego State Univ, & Univ CA at Irvine. **HONORS AND AWARDS** Fulbright Scholar, 86-87. **SELECTED PUBLICATIONS** Auth, Society on the Line: Information Politics in the Digital Age, Oxford UP; coauth, The Management of Information Systems, Columbia UP, 81; Computers and Politics, Columbia UP, 82; Modeling as Negotiating, Ablex, 85 & The Social Shaping of Information Superhighways, Campus Verlay/St Marten's Press, 97; ed, Information and Communication Technologies- Visions and Realities, Oxford UP; co ed, Wired Cities, GK Hall, 85. **CONTACT ADDRESS** Annenberg School for Commun, Univ of Southern California, University Park Campus, Los Angeles, CA, 90089. **EMAIL** wdutton@bcf.usc.edu

DUYFHUIZEN, BERNARD
DISCIPLINE ENGLISH LITERATURE **EDUCATION** Univ Tulsa, PhD, 83. **CAREER** Fac, 83-; to prof; chr, 92-. **HONORS AND AWARDS** Ed, Jour Pynchon Notes. **RESEARCH** Narrative literature; literary criticism; the reader and Thomas Pynchon's Gravity's Rainbow. **SELECTED PUBLICATIONS** Auth, Narratives of Transmission, Fairleigh Dickinson UP, 92; articles on critical theory, especially in the areas of feminism and narratology. **CONTACT ADDRESS** Dept of English, Univ of Wisconsin, Eau Claire, Hibbard Hall 433, PO Box 4004, Eau Claire, WI, 54702-4004. **EMAIL** pnotesbd@uwec.edu

DYE, GLORIA
PERSONAL Born 04/15/1950, Detroit, MI, s, 1 child **DISCIPLINE** LITERATURE **EDUCATION** Univ of MI, PhD, 89; Wayne St Univ, MA, 76, Bph, 73 **CAREER** Assoc Prof, 88-, Univ of NM; Inst, 82-88, Sinte Gleska Col **HONORS AND AWARDS** Phi Beta Kappa, 73; Hopwood awd, 82 **MEMBERSHIPS** Am Asn of Univ Prof **RESEARCH** Native Am Lit **SELECTED PUBLICATIONS** Auth, The War, At Home, Seven Hundred Kisses: A Yellow Silk Book of Erotic Writing, Harper, 97; Granola Whites, Polyester Indians, Southwestern Women: New Voices, Javelina Press, 96 **CONTACT ADDRESS** Dept of Humanities, Univ of New Mexico, Gallup, Gallup, NM, 87301-5697. **EMAIL** goyc@unm.edu

DYER, JOYCE
PERSONAL Born 07/20/1947, OH, m, 1969, 1 child **DISCIPLINE** ENGLISH **EDUCATION** Wittenberg Univ, BA, 69; Kent State Univ, PhD, eng, 77. **CAREER** Lake Forest Col, instr, 78-79; Western Res Acad, teacher, 79-90; Hiram Col, dir writing, assoc prof eng, 91-98. **HONORS AND AWARDS** NEH; fel, OH Arts Counc, 97; Appalachian Stud Awd, 97; Michael Starr Awd, 96; Md west writ Conf, first place, Cleveland Plain Dealer, essay, first place. **MEMBERSHIPS** MLA; AWP; NCTE; Appala Stud Asn. **RESEARCH** Nonfiction; medical humanities; Appala studies; contemp fiction; Am lit; southern letters; nonfiction films; Alzheimer's disease. **SELECTED PUBLICATIONS** The Awakening: A novel of Beginnings, Twayne/Macmillian, 93; In a Tangled Wood: An Alzheimer's Journey, SO Meth Press, 96; Bloodroot: Reflections on Place, By Appalachian Women Writers, Univ Press KY, 98. Hundreds of essays. **CONTACT ADDRESS** 30 Church St, Hudson, OH, 44236-3007. **EMAIL** dyerja@hiram.edu

DYER, KLAY
DISCIPLINE NINETEENTH-CENTURY CANADIAN AND AMERICAN LITERATURE AND CULTURE **EDUCATION** Univ Ottawa, PhD, 98. **CAREER** Asst prof. **RESEARCH** Influence of Cervantine thought and Don Quixote on the North American imagination. **SELECTED PUBLICATIONS** Ed, Joanna Ellen, The Untempered Wind, Early Can Women Writers Series, Tecumseh Press, 94; auth, "Passing Time and Present Absence: Looking to the Future in In the Village of Viger," Can Lit 141, 94; M.G. Vassanji, Contemp Novelists, St. James Press, 95; Joseph Howe, Peter McArthur, The Week, Encyc of the Essay, Fitzroy Dearborn, 96; Alice Munro, Encyc Pop Fiction, Beacham, 96; The Albanian Virgin; The Beggar Maid: Stories of Flo and Rose,; About the Author,; Lives of Girls and men; Jack McClelland, McClelland and Stewart, Oxford Companion to Can Lit, Oxford UP, 97; co-auth, Biographies and Memoirs in English, Oxford Companion to Can Lit, Oxford UP, 97; Canadian Women's History Bibliography, Can Inst for Hist Microreproductions, 97; rev(s), E.K. Brown: A Study in Conflict, by Laura Smyth Groening, Jour Can Poetry 10, 95; Touch Monkeys: Nonsense Strategies for Reading Twentieth-Century Poetry, by Marnie Parsons, Jour Can Poetry 11, 96; Rev of Voice, by Marie Elise St. George and Anne Szumigalski, Jour of Can Poetry 12, 97. **CONTACT ADDRESS** Dept of Eng Lang and Lit, Brock Univ, 500 Glenridge Ave, St Catharines, ON, L2S 3A1. **EMAIL** kdyer@spartan.ac.brocku.ca

DYKEMAN, THERESE B.
PERSONAL Born 04/11/1936, Anamosa, IA, d, 3 children **DISCIPLINE** RHETORIC **EDUCATION** Creighton Univ, BS; Loyola Univ, MA; Union Inst, PhD. **CAREER** Rhetoric and lit, Univ Bridgeport, 81-90; adj prof rhetoric and lit, Univ Conn, Stamford, 82; adj prof, Fairfield Univ, 85- ; adj prof, Sacred Heart Univ, 94- . **HONORS AND AWARDS** Distinguished Service Award, Marycrest Int Univ, Iowa, 93. **MEMBERSHIPS** Danforth Assoc of New England; Ctr for Independent Stud, New Haven; Nat Coalition of Independent Scholars; Soc for the Stud of Women Philosophers; Rhetoric Soc of Am. **RESEARCH** Philosophy by women or women philosophers; rhetorical theory. **SELECTED PUBLICATIONS** Auth, American Women Philosophers 1650-1930: Six Exemplary Thinkers, Mellen, 93; auth, The Neglected Canon: Nine Women Philosophers First to the Twentieth Century, Kluwer, 98; auth, The Infant Famished: Mary Moody Emerson, A Review, Transactions of the C.S. Peirce Society, 98; auth, The American Aesthetics of Ednah Dow Cheney, in Tougas, ed, Hearing Women Philosophers, forthcoming. **CONTACT ADDRESS** 47 Woods End Rd, Fairfield, CT, 06430. **EMAIL** TDykeman@fairl.Fairfield.edu

E

EADIE, WILLIAM F.
PERSONAL Born 09/22/1946, Evanston, IL, s **DISCIPLINE** COMMUNICATION **EDUCATION** Univ Calif Los Angeles, AB, 68, MA, 71; Purdue Univ, PhD, 74. **CAREER** Asst prof, Oh Univ, 74-79; prof & chemn, Calif State Univ, 79-93; assoc dir, Nat Comm Asn, 93-. **HONORS AND AWARDS** Ed, Jour of Applied Commun Res, 91-93; pres, Western States Commun Asn, 93-94; Phi Kappa Phi, Golden Key, Golden Anniversary award, Nat Commun Asn, 81. **MEMBERSHIPS** Nat Commun Asn; Intl Commun Asn; Western States Commun Asn. **RESEARCH** Applied Communication; Individual differences in communication. **SELECTED PUBLICATIONS** Rev, Conditions of Liberty: Civil Society and its Rivals, Jour of Applied Commun Res, 96; auth, Making a difference: The status and challenges of applied communication research, Applied communication in the 21st century: Report of the Tampa conference on applied communication, Lawrence Erlbaum Assoc, 95; auth, On having an agenda, Jour of Applied Commun Res, 22, 94; coauth, Communication research: Making a difference in the real world, Jour of Commun, 93; auth, Being applied: Communication research comes of age, Jour of Applied Commun Res, 90; auth, Hearing what we ought to hear, Vital Speeches, 89. **CONTACT ADDRESS** National Communication Association, 5105 Backlick Rd, Annandale, VA, 22003-6005. **EMAIL** weadie@natcom.org

EAKIN, PAUL JOHN
PERSONAL Born 03/08/1938, Cleveland, OH, m, 1964, 4 children **DISCIPLINE** ENGLISH **EDUCATION** Harvard Univ, AB, 59, AM, 61, PhD (English), 66. **CAREER** Asst prof, 66-72, assoc prof, 72-79, PROF ENGLISH, IND UNIV, BLOOMINGTON, 79- ,Sr Fulbright-Hays lectr, Univ Paris XII, Val de Marne, 72-73 and Univ Athens, Greece, 78-79. **MEMBERSHIPS** MLA; Am Asn Univ Profs; Am Fedn Teachers. **RESEARCH** Autobiography; 19th century American fiction; structural analysis of narrative. **SELECTED PUBLICATIONS** Auth, The Trial of Curiosity--James, Henry, James, William, and the Challenge Of Modernity, 19th Century Literature, Vol 47, 92. **CONTACT ADDRESS** Dept of English, Indiana Univ, Bloomington, Bloomington, IN, 47401.

EARLY, GERALD
PERSONAL Born 04/21/1952, Philadelphia, Pennsylvania, m, 1982 **DISCIPLINE** ENGLISH, AFRICAN-AMERICAN STUDIES **EDUCATION** University of Pennsylvania, Philadelphia, PA, BA, 1974; Cornell University, Ithaca, NY, MA, 1982, PhD, 1982. **CAREER** Washington University, St Louis, MO, professor of English & African & Afro-American studies, 1982; Randolph Macon College for Women, Lynchburg, VA, writer in residence, 1990. **HONORS AND AWARDS** Whiting Foundation Writer's Award, Whiting Foundation, 1988; CCLM/General Electric Foundation Award for Younger Writers, 1988; The Passing of Jazz's Old Guard, published in Best American Essays, 1986; University of Kansas Minority Postdoctoral Fellowship, 1985-87. **SELECTED PUBLICATIONS** Daughters: On Family and Fatherhood, Addison-Wesley, 1994. **CONTACT ADDRESS** Professor, African and Afro-American Studies, Washington Univ, One Brookings Dr, Box 1109, St Louis, MO, 63130-4899.

EARNEST, STEVE
DISCIPLINE ENGLISH LITERATURE **EDUCATION** Univ N Ala, BA, 82; Univ Miami, MFA, 86; Univ Colo, PhD, 95. **CAREER** Asst prof. **MEMBERSHIPS** Actors' Equity Asn; Asn Theatre Higher Edu; Ga Independent Theatre Asn. **SELECTED PUBLICATIONS** Auth, The Image of Caesar-Production Approaches to Julius Caesar, 92; An Enemy of the People and Current Environmental Issues, 91; Julius Caesar, 91. **CONTACT ADDRESS** Dept of Foreign Languages, State Univ W Ga, Carrollton, GA, 30118. **EMAIL** searnest@westga.edu

EATON, CHARLES EDWARD
PERSONAL Born 06/25/1916, Winston-Salem, NC, m, 1950 **DISCIPLINE** ENGLISH **EDUCATION** Univ NC, AB, 36; Harvard Univ, MA, 40. **CAREER** Instr English, Univ Mo, 40-42; vconsul, Am Embassy, Brazil, 42-46; ASST PROF ENGLISH, UNIV NC, 46-51; RES AND WRITING, 51-, Lectr, NC Poetry Circuit, 63. **HONORS AND AWARDS** Ridgely Torrence Award, 51; Golden Rose, New England Poetry Club, 72; Alice Fay Di Castagnoba Award, Poetry Soc Am, 74; Arvon Found Int Poetry Competition Award, London, 81. **MEMBERSHIPS** American literature. **SELECTED PUBLICATIONS** Auth, Petrified Forest, Centennial Rev, Vol 38, 94; La Vie En Rose, Ariel Rev Int Eng Lit, Vol 27, 96; The Truss, Centennial Rev, Vol 37, 93; The Winged Eye, Ariel Rev Int English Lit, Vol 24, 93; The Liaison, Sewanee Rev, Vol 104, 96; Metronome, Sewanee Rev, Vol 104, 96; Epitaphs, Ariel Rev Int Eng Lit, Vol 25, 94; The Gold Tooth, Centennial Rev, Vol 38, 94; Red Carpet Treatment, Col Eng, Vol 56, 94;Tapeworm, Centennial Rev, Vol 41, 97. **CONTACT ADDRESS** 808 Greenwood Rd, Chapel Hill, NC, 27514.

EAVES, MORRIS
DISCIPLINE ENGLISH **EDUCATION** Tulane Univ, PhD. **CAREER** Prof & dept ch; taught at, Univ NM & Tulane Univ. **HONORS AND AWARDS** William Riley Parker prize, Mod Lang Asn; Best Spec Issue awd, Conf Ed(s) Scholarly J; presidential prof of Eng, Univ NM; Nat Hum Ctr fel; NEH Summer sem co-dir; co-dir, Inst for High Sch Tchrs of Eng, Nat Hum Ctr & Assoc fel, Inst Advanced Technol in the Hum, Univ VA., Proj dir, The Blake Arch, an online, hypermedia ed of William Blake's illuminated bk(s), **RESEARCH** Lit and the visual arts; cult contexts of Brit Romanticism; hist of technol and commerce; institutionalization of the arts; organized work. **SELECTED PUBLICATIONS** Auth, William Blake's Theory of Art, The Counter-Arts Conspiracy: Art and Industry in the Age of Blake; ed, Romantic Texts, Romantic Times: Homage to David V. Erdman & S. Foster Damon's Blake Dictionary; co-ed, Romanticism and Contemporary Criticism & The Early Illuminated Books of William Blake; articles on, Romanticism, art and tec hnology, publishing history, the audience, & textual criticism; co-ed, Blake/An Illustrated Quart. **CONTACT ADDRESS** Dept of Eng, Univ of Rochester, 601 Elmwood Ave, Ste. 656, Rochester, NY, 14642. **EMAIL** meav@db1.cc.rochester.edu

EBBITT, WILMA ROBB
PERSONAL Born 06/29/1918, Can, m, 1942 **DISCIPLINE** ENGLISH **EDUCATION** Univ Sask, BA, 38, MA, 40; Brown Univ, PhD (English), 43. **CAREER** Instr English, Brown Univ, 43-45; from instr to prof, Univ Chicago, 45-68; lectr, Univ Colo, 68-69; vis prof, Univ Tex, Austin, 73-74; PROF ENGLISH, PA STATE UNIV, 74-. **MEMBERSHIPS** NCTE; MLA. **RESEARCH** American literature; rhetorical theory; editing. **SELECTED PUBLICATIONS** Auth, Vital Signs--Essays on American Literature and Criticism, Sewanee Rev, Vol 105, 97; Forms of Uncertainty--Essays in Historical Criticism, Sewanee Rev, Vol 101, 93; American Trajectories--Authors And Readings, 1790-1970, Sewanee Rev, Vol 104, 96; The Problem of American Realism--Studies in the Cultural History of a Literary Idea, Sewanee Rev, Vol 102, 94. **CONTACT ADDRESS** Dept of English, Pennsylvania State Univ, University Park, PA, 16802.

EBERHART, RICHARD
PERSONAL Born 04/05/1904, Austin, MN, m, 1941, 2 children **DISCIPLINE** ENGLISH **EDUCATION** Dartmouth Col, AB, 26; Cambridge Univ, BA, 29, MA, 33. **CAREER** Tutor to son of King of Siam, 31; master English, St Mark's Sch, 33-41; poet in residence, Univ Wash, 52-53; prof, Univ Conn, 53-54; vis prof and poet in residence, Wheaton Col, 54-55; Gauss lectr and resident fel, Princeton Univ, 55-56; prof, 56-68, class of 25 prof, 68-70, EMER PROF ENGLISH, DARTMOUTH COL, 70-, POET IN RESIDENCE, 56-, Asst mgr, Butcher Polish Co, 46-52, vpres, 52-58, dir, 58-; founder and pres, Poet's Theatre, Inc, Cambridge, Mass, 50; dir, YADDO, Saratoga Springs, NY, 55-; consult poetry, Libr Cong, 59-61, hon consult Am lett, 63-66, 66-69; mem adv comt, John F Kennedy Mem Ctr, Washington, DC, 59-; Elliston lectr, Univ Cincinnati, 61; lectr, Washington and Lee Univ, Trinity Col, Swarthmore Col and Col William and Mary, 63; Robert Frost mem lect, San Francisco Pub Libr, 64 and Wallace Stevens Prog, Univ Conn, 65; vis prof poetry, Univ Wash, 72 and Univ Fla, 74; adj prof, Columbia Univ, spring 75. **HONORS AND AWARDS** Shelley Award, Poetry Soc Am, 51; Harriet Monroe Mem Award, Univ Chicago, 55; Bollingen Prize, Yale Univ, 62; Pulitzer Prize, 66; Nat Bk Award, 77; president's Medallion, Univ Fla, 77., DLitt, Skidmore Col, 66, Col Wooster, 69 and Colgate Univ, 74; DHL, Franklin Pierce Col, 78. **MEMBERSHIPS** Fel Acad Am Poets; Poetry Soc Am; MLA; Am Inst Arts and Lett; Nat Acad Arts and Sci. **SELECTED PUBLICATIONS** Auth, A Dream, New England Rev Middlebury Series, Vol 15, 93. **CONTACT ADDRESS** Dept of English, Dartmouth Col, Hanover, NH, 03755.

EBERWEIN, JANE DONAHUE
PERSONAL Born 09/13/1943, Boston, MA, m, 1971 **DISCIPLINE** AMERICAN LITERATURE AND STUDIES **EDUCATION** Emmanuel Col, AB, 65; Brown Univ, PhD (Am civilization), 69. **CAREER** Asst prof, 69-75, ASSOC PROF ENGLISH, OAKLAND UNIV, 75-. **MEMBERSHIPS** MLA; Midwest Mod Lang Asn; Col English Asn; Am Studies Asn. **RESEARCH** Colonial American literature; American poetry; Emily Dickinson. **SELECTED PUBLICATIONS** Auth, Bradstreet, Anne C.1612-1672, Legacy, Vol 11, 94; The Poems of Dickinson, Emily--An Annotated Guide to Commentary Published in English, 1978-1989, Anq A Quart J Short Articles Notes Rev, Vol 8, 95; A New World of Words--Redefining Early American Literature, Am Lit, Vol 67, 95; Harvardine Quil , Early Am Lit, Vol 28, 93; Richard Beale Davis Prize for 1996 Awarded to Carroll, Lorrayne, Early Am Lit, Vol 32, 97; Sinful Self, Saintly Self--The Puritan Experience of Poetry, Am Lit, Vol 66, 94. **CONTACT ADDRESS** Dept of English, Oakland Univ, Rochester, MI, 48063.

EBY, CECIL DEGROTTE
PERSONAL Born 08/01/1927, Charles Town, WV, m, 1956, 2 children **DISCIPLINE** AMERICAN LITERATURE AND STUDIES **EDUCATION** Shepherd Col, BA, 50; Northwestern Univ, MA, 51; Univ Pa, PhD, 58. **CAREER** From instr to asst prof English, High Point Col, 55-57; from asst prof to assoc prof, Madison Col, Va, 57-60; from asst prof to assoc prof, Washington and Lee Univ, 60-65; assoc prof, 65-68, PROF ENGLISH, UNIV MICH, ANN ARBOR, 68-, Fulbright lectr Am lit, Lit Univ Salamanca, 62-63; Fulbright lectr Am studies, Univ Valencia, 67-68; Rackham res grants, 67, 71 and 77; chmn, Dept English, Univ Miss, 75-76. **RESEARCH** Literature of the First World War; Spanish Civil War in literature; midwestern literature. **SELECTED PUBLICATIONS** Auth, Popular Fiction in England, 1914-1918, Eng Lit Transition 1880-1920, Vol 36, 93; Hemingway the Short Happy Life of Francis Macomber, Explicator, Vol 51, 92; Fitzgerald Babylon Revisited, Explicator, Vol 53, 95. **CONTACT ADDRESS** Dept of English, Univ of Mich, Ann Arbor, MI, 48104.

ECCLES, MARK
PERSONAL Born 07/13/1905, Oxford, OH **DISCIPLINE** ENGLISH LITERATURE **EDUCATION** Oberlin Col, AB, 27; Harvard Univ, AM, 28, PhD, 32. **CAREER** Am Coun Learned Soc traveling fel, 33-34; lectr, 34-36, from asst prof to R E Neil Dodge prof, 37-76, R E NEIL DODGE EMER PROF ENGLISH, UNIV WIS, MADISON, 76-, Res fel, Huntington Libr, Calif, 40-41; Guggenheim fel, 55; Fulbright lectr, Stratford-on-Avon, 55-56. **MEMBERSHIPS** MLA, Int Asn Univ Prof English. **RESEARCH** Shakespeare; Elizabethan poetry and drama; medieval drama. **SELECTED PUBLICATIONS** Auth, Elizabethan Actors .4. S To End, Notes and Queries, Vol 40, 93. **CONTACT ADDRESS** 2 N Roby Rd, Madison, WI, 53706.

ECHERUO, MICHAEL
PERSONAL Born 03/14/1937, Umunumo, Nigeria, m, 1968, 5 children **DISCIPLINE** ENGLISH LITERATURE **EDUCATION** Univ London, BA, 60; Cornell Univ, MA, 63; Cornell Univ, PhD, 65 **CAREER** Prof English, Univ Nigeria, Univ Ibadan, Indiana Univ, Syracuse Univ, 73-; dean Grad School, Univ Ibadan, 78-80; President, IMO State Univ, 81-88; William Safire prof Modern Letters, Syracuse Univ, 90- **HONORS AND AWARDS** Phi Beta Kappa; Phi Kappa Phi, 65; Hon D. Litt, Lincoln Univ, 91; Hon LL. D, Abia State Univ, 97 **MEMBERSHIPS** Modern Lang Assoc Amer; African Studies Assoc; African Lit Assoc **RESEARCH** African Literature and Culture; 17th Century English Literature; African Linguistics **SELECTED PUBLICATIONS** Comprehensive Dictionary of the Igbo Language, 98; Mortality and Other Poems, 95; The Tempest, Longman, 80 **CONTACT ADDRESS** 401 HL, Syracuse, NY, 13244. **EMAIL** mecheuo@syr.edu

ECKHARDT, CAROLINE DAVIS
PERSONAL Born 02/27/1942, New York, NY, m, 1964, 4 children **DISCIPLINE** ENGLISH AND COMPARATIVE LITERATURE **EDUCATION** Drew Univ, BA, 63; Ind Univ, Bloomington, MA, 65; Univ Mich, Ann Arbor, PhD (comp lit), 71. **CAREER** Asst prof, 71-76, ASSOC PROF ENGLISH and COMP LIT, PA STATE UNIV, 76-, DIR COMP LIT PROG, 77-, Co-ed, JGE (jour), 74-; fel palaeography, Univ Pa Medieval Inst, 76. **MEMBERSHIPS** MLA; Mediaeval Acad Am; Int Arthurian Soc; Am Comp Lit Asn; Conf Ed Learned Jours. **RESEARCH** Medieval romance; medieval lyric; Chaucer. **SELECTED PUBLICATIONS** Auth, The Meaning of Ermonie in Sir Tristrem, Stud Philol, Vol 93, 96; The Historia Regum Britannie of Geoffrey of Monmouth, Vol 4--Dissemination and Reception in the Later Middle Ages, Speculum J Medieval Stud, Vol 69, 94; Comparative Poetics--An Intercultural Essay on Theories of Literature, World Lit Today, Vol 67, 93; The Meaning of Ermonie in Sir Tristrem, Stud in Philol, Vol 93, 96; The Historia Regum Britannie of Geoffrey of Monmouth, Vol 4--Dissemination and Reception in The Later Middle Ages, Speculum J Medieval Stud, Vol 69, 94. **CONTACT ADDRESS** Dept of English, Pennsylvania State Univ, 434n Burrowes Bldg, University Park, PA, 16802-6204.

EDDINGS, DENNIS WAYNE
PERSONAL Born 06/07/1938, Everett, WA, m, 1960, 2 children **DISCIPLINE** AMERICAN AND BRITISH LITERATURE **EDUCATION** Univ Wash, BA, 66, MA, 68; Univ Ore, PhD (English), 73. **CAREER** Instr, 68-71, asst prof, 71-75, ASSOC PROF HUMANITIES, WESTERN ORE STATE COL, 75-. **MEMBERSHIPS** MLA; New England Mod Lang Asn; Poe Studies Asn. **RESEARCH** Edgar Allan Poe; Mark Twain; James Boswell. **SELECTED PUBLICATIONS** Auth, The 19th Century American Short Story--Language, Form and Ideology, Am Lit, Vol 66, 94. **CONTACT ADDRESS** 4560 18th Place S, Salem, OR, 97302.

EDE, LISA
DISCIPLINE RHETORIC/COMPOSITION HISTORY **EDUCATION** Ohio State Univ, BS, 69; Univ Wisc, MA, 70; Ohio State Univ, PhD, 75 **CAREER** Engl, Oregon St Univ. **SELECTED PUBLICATIONS** Coauth, Perspectives on Collaborative Writing, Southern Ill Univ Press, 90; Coed, Classical Rhetoric and Modern Discourse. Southern Ill Univ Press,84. **CONTACT ADDRESS** Oregon State Univ, Corvallis, OR, 97331-4501. **EMAIL** lede@orst.edu

EDELMAN, DIANE PENNEYS
DISCIPLINE LEGAL WRITING **EDUCATION** Princeton Univ, AB, 79; Brooklyn Law Sch, JD, 83. **CAREER** Prof, Villanova Univ Sch Law, 93-. **HONORS AND AWARDS** Brooklyn J Int Law, 81-83; Ed-in-Ch, 82-83; Philip C. Jessup Int Law Moot Ct Team,82; Best Oralist, Eastern Region; First Runner-Up Team, Eastern Region; Alexander Mehr Mem prize; Oceana Publ prize; Moot Ct Honor Soc; Honorable Mention, Best Brief awd, 81. **MEMBERSHIPS** Amer Soc Int Law; co-founder and Vice Ch, Innovations in Tchg Int Law Interest Gp Ch, 96-98; bd ed, Legal Writing: The Journal of the Legal Writing Institute, 98-; Philadelphia and Amer Bar Asn; Princeton Univ, Alumni Schools Comt; bd dir, Trinity Nursery and Kindergarten, 94-; Wayne Art Ctr, 94-98; Philadelphia Volunteer Lawyers for the Arts & Philadelphia Area Repertory Theatre, 89-95. **RESEARCH** Teaching international law moot court as an alternative to traditional legal writing instruction. **SELECTED PUBLICATIONS** Auth, How They Write:Our Students' Reflections on Writing, 6:1 Perspectives 24, 97; Opening Our Doors to the World:Introducing International Law in Legal Writing and Legal Research Courses,5:1 Perspectives 1, 96; Coauth, Overcoming Language and Legal Differences in the Global Classroom:Teaching Legal Research and Legal Writing to International Law Graduates and International Law Students, 96 Proceedings Issue,3 Legal Writing: J Legal Writing Inst 127, 97; From Product to Process:Evolution of a Legal Writing Program, 58 Pittsburgh Law Rev 719, 97. **CONTACT ADDRESS** Law School, Villanova Univ, 800 Lancaster Ave, Villanova, PA, 19085-1692. **EMAIL** edelman@law.vill.edu

EDELSTEIN, ARTHUR
PERSONAL New York, NY **DISCIPLINE** AMERICAN LITERATURE, AMERICAN STUDIES **EDUCATION** Brooklyn Col, BA, 56; Stanford Univ, MA, 63, PhD (Englisb), 77. **CAREER** Lectr English, Hunter Col, City Univ NY, 63-66; asst prof English and Am studies, Brandeis Univ, 66-76; assoc prof English, Col William and Mary, 77-78; ADJ PROF ENGLISH, BRANDEIS UNIV, 79-, Dir writing prog, Brandeis Univ, 71-74; Nat Endowment for Humanities fel Am social hist, 73-74; mem adv comt to bd trustees humanities, Suffolk Univ, Boston, 78-79; vis prof English, Wellesley Col, fall, 81; CONSULT, MASS FOUND HUMANITIES AND PUBLIC POLICY, 80-. **MEMBERSHIPS** MLA. **RESEARCH** American realist fiction; American working class history; contemporary world literature. **SELECTED PUBLICATIONS** Auth, Weber, Max and the Jewish Question--A Study of the Social Outlook of His Sociology, Am Hist Rev, Vol 99, 94. **CONTACT ADDRESS** 2 Dale St, Wellesley, MA, 02181.

EDEN, MELISSA
DISCIPLINE 18TH AND 19TH CENTURY LITERATURE, WOMEN'S LITERATURE **EDUCATION** Middlebury Col, AB; Univ VA, MA, PhD. **CAREER** Asst prof, Hanover Col, 97. **SELECTED PUBLICATIONS** Auth, Studies in Afro-Am Lit: An Annual Annotated Bibliography, 1986, Callaloo 10, 86. **CONTACT ADDRESS** Hanover Col, Hanover, IN, 47243. **EMAIL** edenm@hanover.edu

EDER, DORIS LEONORA
PERSONAL Born 05/12/1936, Teplitz, Czechoslovakia, m, 1961 **DISCIPLINE** MODERN AND CONTEMPORARY LITERATURE **EDUCATION** Barnard Col, BA, 61; Hunter Col, MA, 65, PhD (English and comp lit), 68. **CAREER** From instr to asst prof English, Ohio State Univ, 66-70; from asst prof to assoc prof, Univ Rochester, 70-77; dean fac, Schenectady County Community Col, 77-78; dean prog develop and grad studies, Keene State Col, 78-82; DEAN, SCH ARTS AND SCI, UNIV NEW HAVEN, 82-. **MEMBERSHIPS** MLA; AAUP; Am Asn Higher Educ; Am Asn Univ Women. **SELECTED PUBLICATIONS** Auth, In Pursuit of the Phd, Virg Quart Rev, Vol 69, 93. **CONTACT ADDRESS** Sch of Arts and Sci, Univ of New Haven, New Haven, CT, 06516.

EDGERTON, GARY R.
PERSONAL Born 07/21/1952, Pittsfield, MA, m, 1983, 2 children **DISCIPLINE** COMMUNICATION ; THEATRE ARTS **EDUCATION** Univ of London, BA, 74; Univ of Mass, MA, 79, PhD, 81. **CAREER** From tchg asst to assoc, Univ of Mass, 76-80; from instr to asst prof, Bowling Green State Univ, 80-85; from assoc prof and ch to prof and ch, Goucher Col, 85-94; vis prof, Univ of Exeter, 90-91; prof and ch, Old Dominion Univ, 94- . **HONORS AND AWARDS** Outstanding Tchr in Commun, 82-83; Goucher Col Distinguished Tchg Award in the Hum, 89; Phi Kappa Phi Nat Hon Soc for Special Distinction in Scholar and Tchg, 96. **MEMBERSHIPS** Am Culture Asn; Asn for Commun Admin; Asn for Educ in Journalism and Mass Commun; Broadcast Educ Asn; Internat Commun Asn; Internat Asn for Media and Hist; Nat Commun Asn; Popular Culture Asn; Univ Film and Video Asn; Soc for Cinema Studies. **RESEARCH** Media History; Critical Analysis of Television; Film Theory and Criticism, and Theories and Issues in Cultural Studies; Qualitative Methods; The Documentary Tradition; Electronic Journalism; Mass Media and the Political Process; Mass Media and Social Impact; Making Sense of Popular Culture, and Art, Media, and Postmodernist Culture. **SELECTED PUBLICATIONS** Coauth, Redesigning Pocahontas: Disney, the White Man's Indian, and the Marketing of Dreams, Jour of Popular Film and Television 24.2, 96; In the Eye of the Beholder: Critical Perspectives in Popular Film and Television, 97; auth, Ken Burn's America: Style, Authorship, and Cultural Memory, Jour of Popular Film and Television 21.2, 93; Revisiting the Recordings of Wars Past: Remembering the Documentary Trilogy of John Huston, Reflections in a Male Eye: John Huston and the American Experience, ed G. Studlar and D. Desser, 93; A Breed Apart: Hollywood, Racial Stereotyping, and the Promise of Revisionism in The Last of the Mohicans, Jour of Am Culture 17.2, 94; Ken Burns -- A Conversation with Public Television's Resident Historian, Jour of Am Culture 18.1, 95; Quelling the Oxygen of Publicity: British Broadcasting and the Troubles During the Thatcher Years, Jour of Popular Culture 30.1, 96; Digital Color Imaging and the Colorization Controversy: Culture, Technology, and the Popular as Lightning Rod, Technohistory: Using the History of American Technology in Interdisciplinary Research, ed C. Hables Gray, 96; Ken Burn's The Civil War: Public Television, Popular History, and the Academy, An American Mosaic: Rethinking American Culture Studies, ed M. Fishwick, 97; guest ed, Spec Issue on Ethical Issues in Popular Film and Television, Jour of Popular Film and Television 21.3, 93; Spec Issue on Television as Historian, Film & Hist: An Interdisciplinary Jour of Film and Television Studies 29.1-4, forthcoming. **CONTACT ADDRESS** Dept of Communication and Theatre Arts, Old Dominion Univ, 4100 Powhatan Ave, Norfolk, VA, 23529-0087. **EMAIL** Gedgerto@ODU.EDU

EDWARDS, CLARK
DISCIPLINE COMMUNICATION STUDIES **EDUCATION** Southern IL Univ, BS, 66; Univ MO, MA, 71; Univ NM, PhD, 89. **CAREER** Assoc prof commun, Duquesne Univ. **SELECTED PUBLICATIONS** Auth, articles in Presidential Studies Quarterly; Polit Sci; Polit; Jour Mediated Commun; News Comput Jour; publ(s) on broadcast news writing and style. **CONTACT ADDRESS** Dept of Commun, Duquesne Univ, Forbes Ave, PO Box 600, Pittsburgh, PA, 15282.

EDWARDS, CLIFFORD DUANE
PERSONAL Born 01/20/1934, Atwood, KS, m, 1954, 3 children **DISCIPLINE** ENGLISH **EDUCATION** Ft Hays Kans State Col, AB, 58; Univ Mich, MA, 59, EdD, 63. **CAREER** Lectr English, Univ Mich, 63; from asst prof to assoc prof, Ft Hays Kans State Col, 63-69; prof & head, Dept English, Univ Wis-Platteville, 69-74; prof Eng & dir compos, Ft Hays State Univ, 74-83; Danforth assoc, 66-78; dir, NDEA Inst English, 68; English Inst Educ Prof Develop grant, US Off Educ, 69, chmn Eng, Ft. Hays State Univ, 83-. **MEMBERSHIPS** NCTE. **RESEARCH** American literature; literary criticism; composition. **SELECTED PUBLICATIONS** Auth, Arnold and Pater discuss Dylan Thomas: A conversation in limbo, LIT, 59; art, Existential absurdity on the campus, Christianity Today, 5/67; auth, Conrad Richter's Ohio Trilogy, Mouton, 70; art, Left brain and the teaching of writing, Improving Instr, 9/77. **CONTACT ADDRESS** Dept of English, Fort Hays State Univ, 600 Park St, Hays, KS, 67601-4009.

EDWARDS, EMILY D.
DISCIPLINE BROADCASTING/CINEMA **EDUCATION** Florence State Univ, BA, 74; Univ London, Postbaccalaureate stud, 74; Univ TN, Knoxville, MA, 77, PhD, 84. **CAREER** Grad tchg asst, 74-77, 81-82, PR mgr, dept Speech and Theatre, 79-81, instr, Univ TN, Knoxville, 80-81; dir Broadcast Sequence, dept Commun Stud, Univ AL, Birmingham, 83-87; asst prof, 87-, dir Graduate Stud, Univ NC, Greensboro, 92-95; nat adv bd, Birmingham Int Educ Film Festival, 87-; assoc ed, Southern Speech Commun J, 88-89. **HONORS AND AWARDS** Alpha Gamda Delta; Sigma Tau Delta; acad award, dept Art, 74; acad award, dept Speech and Drama, 74; Bickel Scholar, 83; Prog Dir Award, BIEFF, 86-87; Spec Achievement Award, Smokey Mt Film Festival, 92; New Works Proj Scriptwriting Award, Charolotte Theatre, 94; Bronze Apple Award, Nat Educ Media Network, 97. **MEMBERSHIPS** Univ Film and Video Asn; Asn for Edu in Jour and Mass Commun; Broadcast Edu Asn; Int Commun Asn; ITVA Int TV Asn Society of Prof Journalists; Sigma Delta Chi; Southern Sociol Asn; Speech Commun Asn; Southern Speech Commun Asn. **SELECTED PUBLICATIONS** Auth, No more slack jaws before the tube: a case for tech literacy, Speech Asn Minn J, 15, 1-13, 88; Ecstasy of Horrible Expectation: Correlations between Sensation-seeking and interest in horror movies, in, B. Austin, ed, Current Research In Film, Vol 5, Ablex Press, 91; Love Stinks: The Mean World of Love and Sex in Popular Music of the1980s, in, J. Epstein, ed, Teenagers and Their Music, Garland Press, 94; coauth, Mass Media Images in Popular Music, Popular Mus and Soc, 9, 4, 84; Children's construction of fantasy stories, Sex Roles, 18, 88; Life's Soundtracks: Correlations Between Music Subcultures and Listener Belief Systems, Southern Speech Commun J, 89; The Incubus in Experience, Folklore and Film, Southern Folklore, 52, 96. **CONTACT ADDRESS** Univ N. Carolina, Greensboro, Greensboro, NC, 27412-5001.

EDWARDS, GRACE TONEY
DISCIPLINE APPALACHIAN LITERATURE, APPALACHIAN FOLKLORE, AMERICAN LITERATURE, COMPOSIT **EDUCATION** Appalachian State Univ, BS, MA; Univ VA, PhD. **CAREER** Prof, dir, Appalachian Reg Stud Ctr, ch, Appalachian Stud prog, Radford Univ. **SELECTED PUBLICATIONS** Auth, Emma Belle Miles: Feminist Crusader in Appalachia, in the anthology Appalachia Inside Out; Our Mother's Voices: Narratives of Generational Transformation, in the J of Appalachian Stud. **CONTACT ADDRESS** Radford Univ, Radford, VA, 24142. **EMAIL** gedwards@runet.edu

EDWARDS, JANIS
DISCIPLINE MEDIA CRITICISM **EDUCATION** PhD. **CAREER** Univ Albany - SUNY **SELECTED PUBLICATIONS** Auth, Womanhouse: Making the Personal Story Political in Visual Form, Women & Lang, 96; Coauth, The Visual Ideograph: The Iwo Jima Image in Editorial Cartoons, Quart Jour Speech, 97; Political Cartoons in the 1988 Presidential Campaign: Image, Metaphor, and narrative, Garland Press, 97. **CONTACT ADDRESS** Univ Albany-SUNY, 1400 Washington Ave, Albany, NY, 12222. **EMAIL** jedwards@csc.albany.edu

EDWARDS, LEE R.
PERSONAL Born 04/30/1942, Brooklyn, NY, m, 1964, 1 child **DISCIPLINE** ENGLISH LITERATURE **EDUCATION** Swarthmore Col, BA, 62; Univ CA, Berkeley, MA, 65; Univ CA, San Diego, PhD, 69. **CAREER** Asst prof, 67-75, assoc prof, 75-80, prof eng & Am lit, Univ MA, Amherst, 80, Ed, Mass Rev, 74-80; Nat Endowment for Humanities independent study & res fel, 78; Dean, col umanities and Fine Arts, 91. **HONORS AND AWARDS** Phi Beta Kappa; Council of col of arts and sci. **MEMBERSHIPS** MLA; Women's Caucus Mod Lang Asn. **RESEARCH** Mod fiction; women's studies. **SELECTED PUBLICATIONS** Contribr, Twentieth Century Interpretations of Moll Flanders, Prentice-Hall, 70; ed, Charles Brockden Brown's Alcuin, Grossman, 71; co-ed, Woman: An Issue, Little, 72; auth, Women, Energy and Middlemarch, Mass Rev, winter-spring 72; American Voices, American Women, Avon, 73; co-ed, An Authority of Experience: Essays in Feminist Criticism, Univ Mass, 77;Psyche as Hero: Female Heroism and Fictional Form, Wesleyan Univ Press, 84. **CONTACT ADDRESS** Deans Office CHFA South Col, Univ of Massachusetts, Amherst, MA, 01003-0002. **EMAIL** lee.edwards@cas.umass.edu

EDWARDS, MARY-JANE
DISCIPLINE ENGLISH **EDUCATION** Univ Toronto, BA, 60, PhD, 69; Queen's Univ, MA, 63. **CAREER** Lectr, Acadia Univ, 61-63; instr, Univ BC, 66-69; asst prof, 70-73, assoc prof, 73-82, PROF, CARLETON UNIV, 82-. **MEMBERSHIPS** Bibliog Soc Can; Shastri Indo-Can Inst. **SELECTED PUBLICATIONS** Auth, The Evolution of Canadian Literature in English: Beginnings to 1867, 73; auth, The Evolution of Canadian Literature in English : 1867-1914, 73; auth, Canadian Literature in the 70's, 80. **CONTACT ADDRESS** Dept of English, Carleton Univ, 1125 Colonel By Dr, Ottawa, ON, K1S 5B6. **EMAIL** mary-jane-edwards@carleton.ca

EGAN, JAMES J.
PERSONAL Born 10/09/1945, Cleveland, OH, m, 1968, 1 child **DISCIPLINE** ENGLISH **EDUCATION** St. Joseph's Col, BA, 67; Univ Notre Dame, MA, 68; Univ Notre Dame, PhD, 71. **CAREER** Asst prof English, Univ of Akron, 71-77; assoc prof English, Univ of Akron, 77-83; prof English, Univ of Akron, 84-present; Coordr, Grad Studies in English, Univ of Akron, 87-93; dir, Arts & Sciences Careers Prog, Univ of Akron, 97-present. **HONORS AND AWARDS** Grants-in-Aid of Research, Newberry Libr; Grants-in-Aid of Research, Am Philosophical Soc., Assoc ed, Seventeenth-Century News. **MEMBERSHIPS** Milton Soc. **RESEARCH** Milton; Renaissance prose; contemporary popular culture; fantasy and science fiction. **SELECTED PUBLICATIONS** Auth, 'A Single Powerful Spectacle': Stephen King's Gothic Melodrama, in Extrapolation: A Journal of Science Fiction and Fantasy 27, 86; auth, The Dark Tower: Stephen King's Gothic Western, in The Gothic World of Stephen King, Bowling Green: Popular Press, 87; auth, Technohorror: The Dystopian Vision of Stephen King, in Extrapolation: A Journal of Science Fiction and Fantasy 29, 88; auth, Sacral Parody in the Fiction of Stephen King, in Journal of Popular Culture 23, 89; auth, 'Romance of a Darksome Type': Versions of the Fantastic in the Novels of Joyce Carol Oates, in Studies in Weird Fiction 7, 90; auth, Sanctuary: Shirley Jackson's Domestic and Fantastic Parables, in Studies in Weird Fiction 6, 93; auth, Proto-Fictive Structures in Joseph Hall's Contemplations, in WEVSARA: Selected Papers of the Shakespeare and Renaissance Association of West Virginia 16, 93; auth, Creator-Critic: Aesthetic Subtexts in Milton's Antiprelatical and Regicide Pamphlets, in Milton Studies 30, 93; auth, The Rhetoric of Animadversion in Andrew Marvell's Pamphlets, in WEVSARA: Selected Papers of the Shakespeare and Renaissance Association of West Virginia 17, 94; auth, Andrew Marvell Refashions the Marprelate Tradition: An Aesthetic Reading of the Rehearsal Transpros'd. in Prose Studies 18, 95; auth, Milton's Aesthetic of Plainness, 1659-1673, in The Seventeenth Century 12, 97; auth, Poetical Historiography: Milton's History of Britain as a Literary Text, in WEVSARA: Selected Papers of the Shakespeare and Renaissance Association of West Virginia 21, 98. **CONTACT ADDRESS** Dept of English, Univ of Akron, Olin Hall 301, Akron, OH, 44325-1906. **EMAIL** ejames@uakron.edu

EGAN, MARY JOAN
PERSONAL Born 06/23/1932, Tuscaloosa, AL, m, 1974 **DISCIPLINE** ENGLISH LITERATURE, IRISH STUDIES **EDUCATION** Univ Ala, BA, 52; Cath Univ Am, MA, 58, PhD (English and philos), 69. **CAREER** Instr English, Univ Md, 66-69; asst prof, Centenary Col La, 69-72; asst prof, 72-80, ASSOC PROF ENGLISH, SLIPPERY ROCK STATE COL, 80-, Instr English, Wiley Col, 69-70. **MEMBERSHIPS** Wallace Stevens Soc; Irish Am Cult Inst. **RESEARCH** Modern poetry; myth and archetype. **SELECTED PUBLICATIONS** Auth, Stevens, Wallace Homunculus et la Belle Etoile--An Echo of Goethe Faust, Eng Lang Notes, Vol 31, 93. **CONTACT ADDRESS** Dept of English, Slippery Rock State Col, Slippery Rock, PA, 16057.

EHRSTINE, JOHN
DISCIPLINE LITERATURE **EDUCATION** Wayne State Univ, PhD. **CAREER** Prof, Washington State Univ. **RESEARCH** Literary criticism, Old English, British romantic, and modern literature **SELECTED PUBLICATIONS** Auth, William Blake's Poetical Sketches, 67 & The Metaphysics of Byron: A Reading of the Plays, 75; co-ed, The HBJ Reader, 87. **CONTACT ADDRESS** Dept of English, Washington State Univ, 1 SE Stadium Way, PO Box 645020, Pullman, WA, 99164-5020. **EMAIL** ehrstine@mail.wsu.edu

EIGNER, EDWIN MOSS
PERSONAL Born 04/03/1931, Boston, MA, m, 1956, 2 children **DISCIPLINE** ENGLISH AND AMERICAN LITERATURE **EDUCATION** Cornell Univ, BA, 53; State Univ Iowa, MFA, 55, PhD (English), 63. **CAREER** Instr English, Univ Md Overseas Prog, 56-57; instr, Northwestern Univ, 60-63; from asst prof to assoc prof, Univ Kans, 63-70; chmn dept English, 72-75, dir, Study Ctr for UK and Ireland, 75-77, PROF ENGLISH, UNIV CALIF, RIVERSIDE, 70-, Fulbright-Hays grant and Fulbright lectr, Univ Erlangen, Ger, 67-68; Nat Endowment for Humanities younger scholar fel, 69. **MEMBERSHIPS** MLA. **RESEARCH** History of prose fiction. **SELECTED PUBLICATIONS** Auth, Vanishing Points--Dickens, Narrative, and the Subject of Omniscience, Victorian Stud, Vol 36, 92; On Becoming Pantaloon, Vol 89, 93; The Dickens Hero--Selfhood and Alienation in the Dickens World, Victorian Studies, Vol 36, 92; Creating Characters With Dickins, Charles, Victorian Stud, Vol 36, 92; Dickens and the Grown Up Child, Dickensian, Vol 90, 94. **CONTACT ADDRESS** Dept of English, Univ of Calif Riverside, Riverside, CA, 92502.

EISNER, SIGMUND
PERSONAL Born 12/09/1920, Red Bank, NJ, m, 1949, 6 children **DISCIPLINE** ENGLISH **EDUCATION** Univ Calif, Berkeley, BA, 47, MA, 49; Columbia Univ, PhD, 55. **CAREER** From instr to asst prof English, Ore State Col, 54-58; Fulbright award, Ireland, 58-59; from asst prof to assoc prof, Dominican Col San Rafael, 60-66; assoc prof, 66-67, PROF ENGLISH, UNIV ARIZ, 67-. **MEMBERSHIPS** MLA; Int Arthurian Soc; Mediaeval Acad Am; NCTE. **RESEARCH** Arthurian period and Chaucer. **SELECTED PUBLICATIONS** Auth, Colonial Ireland in Medieval English Literature, Speculum J Medieval Stud, Vol 71, 96, Pelerin De Prusse on The Astrolabe--Text and Translation of His Practique De Astralabe, Speculum J Medieval Stud, Vol 72, 97; The Ram Revisited, Chaucer Rev, Vol 28, 94. **CONTACT ADDRESS** Dept of English, Univ of Ariz, 1 University of Az, Tucson, AZ, 85721-0001.

EISS, HARRY EDWIN
PERSONAL Born 05/17/1950, Minneapolis, MN, m, 5 children **DISCIPLINE** ENGLISH **EDUCATION** Univ of Minn, BA, 75; Mankato State Univ, MS, 76; Univ of NDak, PhD, 82. **CAREER** NEH Inst, 89-90; NEH Tchr Scholar Prog, 90-91; Northern Mont Col, 82-87; prof, Eastern Mich Univ, 87- . **HONORS AND AWARDS** MCH Grant for Children's Lit Conf, 82-82; Merit Award to Outstanding Fac, NMC, 83-84; 86-87; Res Grant, NMC, 85; Fac Ctr for Instructional Effectiveness Grant for Tchg Innovations, EMU, 88; Spec Serv Award, Sigma Tau Delta, 93. **MEMBERSHIPS** Chdn. Area Popular Cult Asn; Mich Col Engl Asn; Soc of Children's Book Writers; Int Res Soc of Children's Lit; MLA; Nat Coun of Tchrs of Eng. **RESEARCH** Mythology; Children's and Young Adult Lit. **SELECTED PUBLICATIONS** Auth, Dictionary of Language Games, Puzzles and Amusements, 86; Dictionary of Mathematical Games, Puzzles and Amusements, 88; Literature for Youth On War and Peace, 89; Images of the Child: Past, Present, Future, 94. **CONTACT ADDRESS** Dept of English, Eastern Michigan Univ, Ypsilanti, MI, 48197.

ELDER, ARLENE ADAMS
PERSONAL Born 05/11/1940, Los Angeles, CA, 1 child **DISCIPLINE** AFRICAN, ETHNIC AMERICAN, & AUSTRALIAN-ABORIGINAL LITERATURE **EDUCATION** Immaculate Heart Col, AB, 61; Univ Denver, MA, 62; Univ Chicago, PhD(English), 70. **CAREER** Instr English, Emmanuel Col, 62-65; lectr, 70-71, asst prof, 71-76, assoc prof, 76-90, prof English & comp lit, Univ Cincinnati, 91-, affiliated with the Center for Women's Studies Certificate program; vis Fulbright lectr lit, Univ Nairobi, Kenya, 76-77. **MEMBERSHIPS** MLA, member exec coun, division of African lit, 95-2000; Soc Study Multi-Ethnic Lit US; AAUP; member, exec coun, African Lit Asn, 94-2000. **RESEARCH** African lit; ethnic Americans; Australian-Aboriginal lit. **SELECTED PUBLICATIONS** Auth, The Hindered Hand: Cultural Implications of Early African-American Fiction, Greenwood, 79; and many essays on African, African-Am, and women's literature. **CONTACT ADDRESS** Dept of English, Univ of Cincinnati, PO Box 210069, Cincinnati, OH, 45221-0069. **EMAIL** elder2@fuse.net

ELDER, JOHN
PERSONAL Born 03/22/1947, Louisville, KY, m, 1970, 3 children **DISCIPLINE** ENGLISH **EDUCATION** Pomona Coll, BA 69; Yale univ PhD 73. **CAREER** Middlebury Col, Stewart Prof eng environ studies 73. **HONORS AND AWARDS** Danforth Fellow; NEH Fellow. **MEMBERSHIPS** MLA; Assn Study Lit Environ. **RESEARCH** Environmental educ. **SELECTED PUBLICATIONS** Imagining the Earth: Poetry and the Vision of Nature, Urbana, Chicago, Univ of IL Press, 85, exp 2d ed, Univ GA Press 96; Following the Brush, Boston, Beacon Press, 93, Jap trans, Bunjinsha, 98; The Family of Earth and Sky:Indigenous Tales of Nature from Around the World, Boston, co ed Hertha Wong, Beacon Press, 94; American Nature Writers, NY Chas Scribner's Sons, 96; Reading the Mountains of Home, Cambridge, Harvard Univ Press, 98. **CONTACT ADDRESS** Dept of Eng, Middlebury Col, Middlebury, VT, 05753. **EMAIL** elder@middlebury.edu

ELIA, RICHARD LEONARD
PERSONAL Born 06/30/1941, Boston, MA, m, 1969 **DISCIPLINE** ENGLISH LITERATURE **EDUCATION** Providence Col, AB, 64; Northeastern Univ, AM, 65; Univ Mass, PhD(English), 73. **CAREER** Instr English, Northeastern Univ, 64-69; ASSOC PROF ENGLISH, SALEM STATE COL, 69-, Publ & ed, The Quart Rev of Wines, 81-. **MEMBERSHIPS** MLA; Col English Asn; Victorian Periodical Soc; Victorian Soc Am; Browning Soc, Boston **RESEARCH** Newspapers of victorian age; 19th century English; American painting. **SELECTED PUBLICATIONS** Auth, Platonic irony in Sidney's Apology, 72 & Three symbols in Snows of Kilimanjaro, 73, Rev del Lang Vivantes; T B Macaulay & W M Praed, 75 & W M Praed & B Disraeli, 76, Notes & Queries; Disraeli & Marylbone, Disraeli Newsletter, 77; Edward Clark Cabot: Watercolorist, Mag Antiques, 78; Some leaders of the Morning Post, Victorian Periodicals Newsletter, 78; Marshall Johnson, Jr, Marine Artist, Mag Antiques, 11/81. **CONTACT ADDRESS** Dept of English, Salem State Col, 352 Lafayette St, Salem, MA, 01970-5353.

ELKINS, MICHAEL R.
PERSONAL Born 02/03/1959, Knoxville, TN, s **DISCIPLINE** SPEECH COMMUNICATION **EDUCATION** Univ of Tenn-Knoxville, BS, 8/82, MA, 12/85; South Ill Univ-Carbondale, PhD, Speech Communication, 8/97. **CAREER** Teaching asst, Univ of Tenn-Knoxville, 83-85; lecturer, Tex A&M Univ, 86-89; course/coord/visiting instr/lecturer, Texas A&I Univ, 89-92; instructor, 97-, asst prof & ch, 97-, Tex A&M Univ, 95-97. **HONORS AND AWARDS** South Ill Univ Dept of Speech Commun Thomas J Pace, Jr, Outstanding Teacher Award, 95., Ch, Dept of Commun & Theatre Arts, Tex A&M Univ Kingsville, 97. **MEMBERSHIPS** Nat Commun Assoc; Cent Speech Commun Assoc; Southern States Commun Assoc; Tex Speech Commun Assoc; Int Soc for Gen Semantics; Pac & Asian Commun Assoc; Commun Educ Assoc; Am Assoc of Univ Women; Phi Kappa Phi; Golden Key; Kappa Delta Pi; Phi Delta Kappa; Pi Kappa Delta; Gamma Beta Pi; Alpha Zeta. **RESEARCH** Communication. **SELECTED PUBLICATIONS** Auth, Communication apprehension, teacher preparation, and at-risk students: Revealing South Texas secondary school teacher perceptions, Tex Speech Commun J, vol 20, 3-10, 95; auth, I will fear no audience: General semantics to the rescue, J of the Ill Speech & Theatre Assoc, vol 47, 41-43, 96; co-auth, Perceptions of cultural differences from international faculty in selected colleges and universities in South Texas, Tex Speech Commun J, vol 21, 3-12, 97; co-auth, The Texas Speech Commun J: A twenty year retrospective, Tex Speech Commun J, vol 23, 73-77, 98; Cultural issues in the workplace, J of the Ill Speech & Theatre Assoc. **CONTACT ADDRESS** Dept of Commun & Theatre Arts, Tex A&M, Kingsville, Campus Box 178, Kingsville, TX, 78363. **EMAIL** kfmre00@tamuk.edu

ELLEDGE, PAUL
DISCIPLINE BRITISH ROMANTICISM, AUTOBIOGRAPHY **EDUCATION** Tulane Univ, PhD. **CAREER** Instr, Vanderbilt Univ. **RESEARCH** Byron at Harrow School; child-actor William W. H. Betty. **SELECTED PUBLICATIONS** Essays published in ELH, Texas Stud in Lang and Lit; Essays on Criticism on Childe Harold's Pilgrimage. **CONTACT ADDRESS** Vanderbilt Univ, Nashville, TN, 37203-1727.

ELLER, JONATHAN R.
DISCIPLINE ENGLISH LITERATURE **EDUCATION** Univ Md, BA; Univ Ind, MA, PhD. **CAREER** Adj prof. **SELECTED PUBLICATIONS** Auth, pubs on contemporary American authors. **CONTACT ADDRESS** English Dept, Indiana Univ-Purdue Univ, Indianapolis, 425 Univ Blvd, Indianapolis, IN, 46202. **EMAIL** uplace@iupui.edu

ELLERBY, JANET MASON
DISCIPLINE AMERICAN LITERATURE **EDUCATION** Univ Ore, BS; Calif State Univ, Northridge, MA; Univ Wash, PhD. **CAREER** Assoc prof, Univ NC, Wilmington. **RESEARCH** Contemporary fiction by and about women. **SELECTED PUBLICATIONS** Her publishing has, for the most part, involved theoretical analysis of 20th century literature, theory, and pedagogy with gender as an overarching theme. **CONTACT ADDRESS** Univ N. Carolina, Wilmington, Morton Hall, Wilmington, NC, 28403-3297. **EMAIL** ellerbyj@uncwil.edu

ELLIOTT, CLARK ALBERT
PERSONAL Born 01/22/1941, Ware, MA, m, 1965, 2 children **DISCIPLINE** ARCHIVES, BIBLIOGRAPHY, HISTORY OF SCIENCE **EDUCATION** Marietta Col, AB, 63; Western Reserve Univ, MSLS, 65; Case Western Reserve Univ, MA, 68, PhD(libr & info sci), 70. **CAREER** Archivist, Case Inst Technol, 64-66; asst prof libr sci, Sch of Libr Sci, Simmons Col, 69-71; assoc cur, Harvard Univ archives, 71-97; LIBRN, BURNDY LIBR, DIBNER INST FOR THE HIST OF SCI AND TECHNOL, 97- . **HONORS AND AWARDS** Rep, Joint Comt on Archives of Sci & Technol, Hist of Sci Soc, 78-83; ed, Hist of Sci in Am: News and Views, 80-87. **MEMBERSHIPS** Soc Am Archivists; New England Archivists; Hist Sci Soc; Forum for the Hist of Sci in Am, chm, 97- . **RESEARCH** History of science in America, especially scientific careers, and institutions; documentation and historiography in history of science. **SELECTED PUBLICATIONS** Auth, The Royal Society Catalogue as an Index to Nineteenth Century American Science, J of Am Soc for Info Sci, 11-12/70; Sources for the History of Science in the Harvard University Archives, Havard Libr Bull, 1/74; Experimental Data as a Source for the History of Science, Am Archivist, 1/74; A Descriptive Guide to the Harvard University Archives, Harvard Univ Libr, 74; The American scientist in Antebellum Society: A Quantitative View, Social Studies of Sci, 1/75; Biographical Dict of American Science: The Seventeenth Through the Nineteenth Centuries, Greenwood Press, 79; Citation patterns and Documentation for the History of Science: Some Methodological Considerations, Am Archivist, Spring 81; Models of the American scientist: A look at Collective Biography, Isis, 3/82; auth, Biographical Index to American Science: The Seventeenth Century to 1920, Greenwood, 90; co-ed, Science at Harvard University: Historical Perspectives, Lehigh, 92; auth, History of Science in the United States: A Chronology and Research Guide, Garland, 96. **CONTACT ADDRESS** Burndy Library, Dibner Inst for the History of Science and Tech, MIT E56-100, Cambridge, MA, 02139.

ELLIOTT, EMORY B.
PERSONAL Born 10/30/1942, Baltimore, MD, m, 1966, 5 children **DISCIPLINE** AMERICAN LITERATURE & STUDIES **EDUCATION** Loyola Col, Md, AB, 64; Bowling Green State Univ, MA, 65; Univ Ill, Urbana, PhD(English), 72. **CAREER** Instr English, US Mil Acad, 67-69; asst prof, 72-77, assoc prof, 77-81, PROF ENGLISH, 81- , Chm Am Studies, 77-82, Princeton Univ; master, 82-86, chm, Eng, 86-98, Lee D Butler Col; DISTINGUISHED PROF ENG, UNIV CALIF, RIVERSIDE, 89- ; dir Center for Ideas and Society, 96- . **HONORS AND AWARDS** Guggenheim Found fel, 76; Richard Stockton Bicentennial Preceptorship, Princeton Univ, 76; Nat Humanities Ctr fel, 79-80; Nat Hum Sr Fel, 86-87; Univ Calif Hum Res Inst fel, 90-91; Nat Book Award, 88; Ford Found grant, 98-99. **MEMBERSHIPS** Am Studies Asn; MLA; Am Soc Eighteenth-Century Studies;Asn for Multi-Ethnic Lit of the US. **RESEARCH** American literature; American Colonial history and culture; 17th century English literature. **SELECTED PUBLICATIONS** Auth, Power and the Pulpit in Puritan New England, Princeton Univ, 75; Unity in Donne's Satyres, J English & Ger Philol, 76; contrib, Literary Uses of Typology, Princeton Univ, 77; auth, Puritan Influences in American Literature, 79; ed & contrib, Puritanism and American Literature, Univ Ill, 79; auth, Charles Brockden Brown, Am Writers, 79; The Clergy in the American Revolution, Am Quart, 79; Revolutionary Writers: Literature and Authority in the New Republic, 1725-1810, Oxford Univ, 82; ed, The Dictionary of Literary Biography, 1620-1810, 3 v, 84-85; ed, The American Novel Series, 85- ;ed, Penn Studies in Contemporary American Fiction Series, 87- ;ed, The Columbia Literary History of the United States, 88; ed and intro, Upton Sinclair's The Jungle, 90; ed, The Columbia History of the American Novel, 91; ed, American Literature: A Prentice-Hall Anthology, 3 v, 91; auth, The Literature of Puritan New England, In; The Cambridge History of American Literature, v 1, 94; co-ed, Readers' Guide to English and American Literature, 94; ed and intro, Charles Brockden Brown's Weiland and Carwin the Biloquist, 94; ed and intro, Mark Twain's The Adventures of Huckleberry Finn, 98. **CONTACT ADDRESS** Dept of English, Univ Calif Riverside, 1202 Humanities & Science Bldg, Riverside, CA, 92521.

ELLIOTT, GARY D.
PERSONAL Born 10/10/1940, Chickasha, OK, m, 1963, 2 children **DISCIPLINE** AMERICAN LITERATURE **EDUCATION** Harding Univ, BA, 62; Univ N Tex, MA, 68; Kans State Univ, PhD, 73. **CAREER** Sen Dev Off, Pepperdine Univ, 91-93; vp, 93-97, prof, 67-81, 97-, chemn, 73-81, Harding Univ; dean, 82-86, pres, Columbia Christian Col, 86-91. **HONORS AND AWARDS** Dist Tchg Award; Outstanding Alumnus Award; NEH Summer Grant. **MEMBERSHIPS** Conference on Christianity & Literature; Asn Literary Scholars & Critics. **RESEARCH** Ernest Hemingway; William Dean Howells. **CONTACT ADDRESS** Harding Univ, Box 10847, Searcy, AZ, 72149. **EMAIL** gelliott@harding.edu

ELLIOTT, MICHAEL
DISCIPLINE ENGLISH LANGUAGE AND LITERATURE **EDUCATION** Amherst Col, BA, 92; Columbia Univ, PhD, 98. **CAREER** Asst prof **RESEARCH** 19th and 20th century American literature, Native American literature, and cultural studies; ties between literature and social science in the history of ideas about "race" and "culture" in the United States. **SELECTED PUBLICATIONS** Auth, pubs about Native American literature in arts/revs for Am Quart, Early Am Lit, Studies Am Indian Lits, and Biography. **CONTACT ADDRESS** English Dept, Emory Univ, 1380 Oxford Rd NE, Atlanta, GA, 30322-1950.

ELLIS, DONALD
PERSONAL Born 09/10/1947, Burbank, CA, m, 1987, 2 children **DISCIPLINE** COMMUNICATION **EDUCATION** Univ Utah, PhD **CAREER** Asst prof, Purdue Univ, 76-80; assoc prof, Michigan State, 80-83; prof, Univ Hartford, 83-present **MEMBERSHIPS** Natl Communication Assoc; Assoc for Applied Linguistics; Intl Communication Assoc **RESEARCH** Language and social interaction; communication theory **SELECTED PUBLICATIONS** Auth, Fixing Communicative Meanning: A Coherentist Theory, Communication Research, 95; Coherence Patterns in Alzheimer's Discourse, Communication Research, 96; Research on Social Interaction and the Micro-Macro Issue, Research on Language and Social Interaction, in press; Language and Civility: The Semantics of Anger, Conflict and Communication, in press. **CONTACT ADDRESS** Dept of Communication, Univ of Hartford, West Hartford, CT, 06117. **EMAIL** dellis@mail.hartford.edu

ELLIS, FRANK HALE
PERSONAL Born 01/18/1916, Chicago, IL, m, 1940, 1 child **DISCIPLINE** ENGLISH **EDUCATION** Northwestern Univ, BS, 39; Yale Univ, PhD, 48. **CAREER** Instr English lit, Univ Buffalo, 41-42; from instr to asst prof, Yale Univ, 46-51; from asst prof to prof, 58-75, MARY AUGUSTA JORDAN PROF ENGLISH LIT, SMITH COL, 75-, Morse fel, 50-51; Huntington Libr fel, 75. **MEMBERSHIPS** MLA; Am Soc Eighteenth Century Studies. **SELECTED PUBLICATIONS** Auth, A J The Plague Year, Rev Eng Stud, Vol 45, 94; Defoe De Attributions--A Critique of Moore, J. R. Checklist Furbank, Pn, Owens, Wr, Rev Eng Stud, Vol 47, 96. **CONTACT ADDRESS** Dept of Eng, Smith Col, Northampton, MA, 01063.

ELLIS, KATHERINE
DISCIPLINE THE GOTHIC NOVEL, WOMEN WRITERS, ROMANCE AS A GENRE, CREATIVE WRITING **EDUCATION** Columbia Univ, BA, MA, PhD. **CAREER** Instr, Rutgers, State Univ NJ, Livingston. **RESEARCH** Genre theory as it applies to the Gothic, to "romance" and to first-person writing. **SELECTED PUBLICATIONS** Auth, The Contested Castle: Gothic Novels and the Subversion of Domestic Ideology. **CONTACT ADDRESS** Dept of Eng, Rutgers, State Univ NJ, Livingston Col, 36 Union St., Piscataway, NJ, 29232. **EMAIL** lcdean@rci.rutgers.edu

ELLISON, JEROME
PERSONAL Born 10/28/1907, Maywood, IL, m, 1934, 2 children **DISCIPLINE** ENGLISH **EDUCATION** Univ Mich, Ab, 30; Southern Conn State Col, MA, 64. **CAREER** Asst ed, Life Mag, 32-33; assoc ed, Reader's Digest, 35-42; ed-in-chief, Liberty Mag, 42-43; managing ed, Collier's Mag, 43-44; ed dir, bur overseas publ, Off War Info, 44-45; instr, night sch, NY Univ, 45; founder and publ, Mag of the Year, 45-47; writer, 47-55; assoc prof jour, Ind Univ, 55-60; writer, 60-64; from assoc prof to prof English and Humanities, Univ New Haven, 64-74; PRES and FOUNDER, PHENIX SOC, INC, 73-, Ed and publ, Best Articles and Stories Mag, 57-61; lectr, Div Continuing Educ, Univ Conn, 61-62. **RESEARCH** Literary criticism; contemporary fiction; literature of social protest. **SELECTED PUBLICATIONS** Auth, The Supplement of Reading, Wordsworth Cir, Vol 23, 92; Gorchakova, Galina, Tchaikovsky and Verdi Arias, Opera, Vol 47, 96; Feeling Strange, Anq A Quart J Short Articles Notes Rev, Vol 6, 93; A Short History of Liberal Guilt, Critical Inquiry, Vol 22, 96; From Reconstruction to Integration, Britain and Europe Since 1945, Albion, Vol 26, 94; Catos Tears, Elh Eng Lit Hist, Vol 63, 96; Race and Sensibility in the Early Republic, Am Lit, Vol 65, 93; Paleoenvironmental Evidence for Human Colonization of Remote Oceanic Islands, Antiq, Vol 68, 94. **CONTACT ADDRESS** 43 Wallingford Rd, Cheshire, CT, 06410.

ELLSWORTH, RALPH E.
DISCIPLINE LIBRARY SCIENCE **EDUCATION** Oberlin Univ, AB, 74; W Reserve Univ, BS, 31; Univ Chicago, PhD, 37. **MEMBERSHIPS** Amer Libr Assoc **RESEARCH** Student reading behavior **SELECTED PUBLICATIONS** 6 books; 21 jour articles **CONTACT ADDRESS** 801 Gillespie Dr, Apt 233, Boulder, CO, 80303.

ELSBREE, LANGDON
PERSONAL Born 06/23/1929, Trenton, NJ, m, 1952, 1 child **DISCIPLINE** ENGLISH **EDUCATION** Earlham Col, BA, 52; Cornell Univ, MA, 54; Claremont Grad Sch, PhD (English), 63. **CAREER** Instr English, Miami Univ, 54-57, Harvey Mudd Col, 58-59 and humanities, Scripps Col, 59-60; from instr to assoc prof, 60-71, PROF ENGLISH, CLAREMONT MEN'S COL, 71-, Hays-Fulbright lectr Am lit, Cairo, 66-67; lectr grad English prog, Calif State Univ, Los Angeles, 68-70. **MEMBERSHIPS** MLA; Thomas Hardy Soc. **RESEARCH** Science fiction; the sacred and profane in the fiction and poetry of Thomas Hardy and D H Lawrence; archetypal actions in narrative. **SELECTED PUBLICATIONS** Auth, A Long the River-run--Selected Essays, D H Lawrence Rev, Vol 24, 92; Lawrence, D. H. Literary Inheritors, D H Lawrence Rev, Vol 23, 91. **CONTACT ADDRESS** Dept of English, Claremont Men's Col, Claremont, CA, 91711.

ELTON, WILLIAM R.
PERSONAL Born 08/15/1921, New York, NY **DISCIPLINE** ENGLISH LITERATURE **EDUCATION** Brooklyn Col, AB, 41; Univ Cincinnati, AM, 42; Ohio State Univ, PhD, 57. **CAREER** Asst, Ohio State Univ, 42-45, instr, 45-46; instr, Brown Univ, 46-50; instr, NY Univ, 50-51; vis asst prof English, Univ Conn, 52-53; asst prof, Ohio State Univ, 53-55; from asst prof to prof, Univ Calif, Riverside, 55-69; vis prof, Columbia Univ, summer, 69; PROF ENGLISH LIT, GRAD SCH, CITY UNIV NEW YORK, 69-, Huntington Libr grants, 59-62 and 76, sem, 63; Folger Shakespeare Libr grants, 59, 70 and 71; Am Coun Learned Soc grants, 60-61; Am Philos Soc grant, 61; Fulbright lectr, India, 61-62; prof, City Col, New York, 63-64; ed, Shakespearean Res and Opportunities, Univ Calif, 65-69; adv ed, Shakespeare Studies, 65-; ed, New Veriorum Shakespeare Timon of Athens; Folger Shakespeare Libr sr fel, 75-76; Nat Endowment for Humanities fel, Huntington Libr, 76 and Folger Libr, 77; mem exec comt, Shakespeare Div, MLA, 78, NEH, 78; MEM, UNIV SEM IN RENAISSANCE, COLUMBIA UNIV, 70-, Acad Coun, New Shakespeare Globe Theater Ctr, South Bank, London, 81. **MEMBERSHIPS** PEN Club; Malone Soc; Renaissance Soc Am; Shakespeare Asn Am; MLA. **RESEARCH** Shakespeare and Renaissance drama; Renaissance intellectual history, especially philosophy and theology; modern poetry. **SELECTED PUBLICATIONS** Auth, Home From India, Partisan Rev, Vol 64, 97; Aristotle Nicomachean Ethics and Shakespeare Troilus And Cressida, J Hist Ideas, Vol 58, 97. **CONTACT ADDRESS** PhD Prog English, Graduate Sch and Univ Ctr, CUNY, 33 W 42nd St, New York, NY, 10036.

ELY, ROBERT EUGENE
PERSONAL Born 08/18/1949, Fort Wayne, IN, m, 1973, 1 child **DISCIPLINE** ENGLISH **EDUCATION** Manchester Col, BA, 71, MA, 75; Purdue Univ, PhD studies, 75-77; Ind Univ, JD, 85. **CAREER** Journalist & publications ed, Lincoln Nat Corp, 71-73; INSTR TO PROF OF ENGLISH & HUMANITIES, 77-81 & 84-, VP FOR ACADEMIC AFFAIRS, ALA STATE UNIV, 84-85; ATTORNEY IN PRIVATE PRACTICE, 85-. **HONORS AND AWARDS** Listed in Who's Who Among America's Teachers & Marquis' Who's Who in Am Law; Shaw-Montgomery Prize for Poetry, 85. **MEMBERSHIPS** Montgomery County Bar Asn; Ala State Bar; Ala Writers' Forum; Phi Eta Sigma; Lower Audubon Brook Soc. **RESEARCH** Aesthetics; modern poetry and drama; law, Lit, and society; phenomenology. **SELECTED PUBLICATIONS** Auth, The Wordy Shapes of Women in the Poetry of Dylan Thomas, English Studies Collections Series, Esco, 76; A Grammar of Narrative for Synge's Riders to the Sea, Standpoints: Essays in Honor of Charles Klingler, Manchester CP, 95; Mose T's Slapout Family Album, Black Belt, 96; coauth, The Humanities: A Cross-cultural Approach, 79. **CONTACT ADDRESS** Dept of Humanities, Alabama State Univ, TH 106, PO Box 271, Montgomery, AL, 36101-0271.

EMANUEL, JAMES ANDREW
PERSONAL Born 06/15/1921, Alliance, NE, d, 1950 **DISCIPLINE** ENGLISH **EDUCATION** Howard Univ, Washington DC, AB, 1950; Northwestern Univ, MA, 1953; Columbia Univ, PhD, 1962. **CAREER** US War Dept, Office of Inspector General, Washington DC, confidential secretary to asst inspector general of the Army, 1942-44; Army and Air Force Induction Station, Chicago IL, chief of pre-induction section (as civilian), 1950-53; YWCA Business School, New York City, teacher of English and commercial subjects, 1954-56; CITY COLL OF THE CITY UNIV OF NY, instructor, 1957-62, asst prof, 1962-70, assoc prof, 1970-73, PROF OF ENGLISH, 1973--. **HONORS AND AWARDS** John Hay Whitney Found Opportunity fellowship, 1952-54; Eugene F. Saxon Memorial Trust fellowship, 1964-65. **MEMBERSHIPS** Mem, Fulbright Alumni Assn. **SELECTED PUBLICATIONS** Author of Langston Hughes (essays), Twayne, 1967; author of The Treehouse and Other Poems, Broadside Press, 1968; author ofA Chisel in the Dark: Poems, Selected and New, Lotus Press, 1980; author of A Poet's Mind, Regents Publishing, 1983; author of The Broken Bowl: New and Uncollected Poems, Lotus Press, 1983; works have been published in many anthologies and periodicals. **CONTACT ADDRESS** Dept of English, City Col, CUNY, Convent Ave at 138th St, New York, NY, 10031.

EMBLETON, SHEILA
PERSONAL Ottawa, ON, Canada **DISCIPLINE** LANGUAGE/LITERATURE/LINGUISTICS **EDUCATION** Univ Toronto, BS, 75, MS, 76, PhD, 81. **CAREER** Lectr, 80-81, asst prof, Grad Prog Interdisciplinary Studs, 83-84, asst prof, 82-84, ASSOC PROF LANGS, LIT & LING, YORK UNIV 84-, assoc dean, Fac Arts, 94-97. **HONORS AND AWARDS** Queen Elizabeth II Scholar, 79-80; Gov Gen Gold Medal, 75; Dr. Harold C. Parsons Scholar, 72-73; Archibald Young Scholar, 73-74. **MEMBERSHIPS** Can Soc Stud Names; Finno-Ugic Stud Asn; Int Soc Hist Ling Asn; Ling Soc Am; Int Coun Onomastic Sci; Can Friends Finland. **SELECTED PUBLICATIONS** Auth, Statistics in Historical Linguistics, 86; auth, Lexicostatistics Applied to the Germanic, Romance, and Wakashan Families, in Word, 85; auth, Mathematical Methods of Genetic Classification, in Sprung From Some Common Source: Investigations into the Prehistory of Languages, 91. **CONTACT ADDRESS** Dept of Language, Literature & Linguistics, York Univ, North York, ON, M3J 1P3. **EMAIL** embleton@yorku.ca

EMERY, SARAH W.
PERSONAL Born 08/08/1911, Pleasant City, OH, w, 1948, 2 children **DISCIPLINE** PHILOSOPHY, ENGLISH **EDUCATION** Emory Univ, AB, 33; Ohio State Univ, MA, 38; PhD, 42. **CAREER** Tchg asst, Ohio State Univ, 38-42; tchg asst, Univ Ill, 42-43; instr, Packer Collegiate Inst, 43-46; instr, Syracuse Univ, 46-47; asst prof, Hollins Coll, 47-48; asst prof, Duke Univ, 51-52. **MEMBERSHIPS** Am Philos Asn; Phi Beta Kappa, The Poetry Soc of Tex. **SELECTED PUBLICATIONS** Auth, A Donkey's Life, A Story for Children, 79; They Walked into the Rose Garden and Other Poems, 92; Plato's Euthyphro, Apology and Crito, Arranged for Dramatic Presentation from the Jowett Translation with Chornses, 96. **CONTACT ADDRESS** Box 683, Denton, TX, 76202-0683.

EMMA, RONALD DAVID
PERSONAL Born 07/21/1920, London, England, m, 1948, 1 child **DISCIPLINE** ENGLISH, PHILOLOGY **EDUCATION** City Col New York, BBA, 41; Duke Univ, MA, 51, PhD, 60. **CAREER** Instr English, Col William & Mary, 54-60; asst prof, Cent Mich Univ, 60-61; from asst prof to assoc prof, Southern Conn State Col, 61-66; prof English, Windham Col, 66-78, chmn dept English, 66-70, chmn div humanitites, 66-74; ASST PROF ACCT, ALBERTUS MAGNUS COL, 81-, Asst, Duke Univ, 52-53; Col William & Mary res grants-in-aid, 58 & 59; vis lectr English, Univ Mass, 76-77; consult ed, English Literary Renaissance. **MEMBERSHIPS** MLA; Milton Soc Am; Yeats Soc; Int Asn Philos & Lit; Am Acct Asn. **RESEARCH** Grammar and style in Milton; Milton and 17th century poetry; contemporary Irish poetry. **SELECTED PUBLICATIONS** Auth, Milton's Grammar, Mouton The Hague, 63; co-ed, Language and Style in Milton, Ungar, 67 & Seventeenth-Century English Poetry, Lippincott, 69; The exordium and Paradise Lost, S Atlantic Quart, autumn 72; Milton's grammar, In: Milton Encyclopedia, Vol II; Poetry (a variety), in var Jours, US & Abroad. **CONTACT ADDRESS** 61 Elizabeth St, West Haven, CT, 06516.

EMMITT, HELEN
DISCIPLINE ENGLISH **EDUCATION** Univ Calif, Berkeley, PhD **RESEARCH** Women's Studies and Irish literature. **SELECTED PUBLICATIONS** Articles on, Pound, Eliot, Kate Chopin, & Woolf. **CONTACT ADDRESS** Dept of English and Fine Arts, Virginia Military Inst, Lexington, VA, 24450.

ENGBERG, NORMA J.
DISCIPLINE MEDIEVAL LITERATURE, OLD ENGLISH, LATIN **EDUCATION** George Washington Univ, BA, 61; Univ Fla, MA, 63; Univ Pa, Philadelphia, PhD, 69. **CAREER** Instr, George Washington Univ, 64-67; asst prof, Calif State Col, 68; asst prof, 69-75, assoc prof, 75-, dir, grad stud, 76-83, pres, past pres, Phi Kappa Phi, 79-81, ch, grad coun, Univ Nev, Las Vegas, 81-83. **MEMBERSHIPS** UNLV corp rep, Am Assn Univ Women, 82-84. **RESEARCH** Translations from Latin. **SELECTED PUBLICATIONS** Auth, Exposing Readers of Beowulf-in-Translation to the Original Poem's Phonology, Morphology, and Syntax, Old Eng Newsl; vol15, no 2, 82; Mod-Maegen Balance in Elene, The Battle of Maldon and The Wanderer, Neuphilologische Mitteilungen, vol 85, no 2, 84; PE100-408 Anglo Saxon Language, PE1075-1400 History, and PR1490-1799 Anglo-Saxon Literature, in 3rd ed of Books for College Libraries, Virginia Clark, ed, Am Libr Asn, 88. **CONTACT ADDRESS** Dept of Eng, Univ Nev, Las Vegas, 4505 Maryland Pky, PO Box 455011, Las Vegas, NV, 89154-5011. **EMAIL** adamsc@nevada.edu

ENGEL, ARTHUR JASON
PERSONAL Born 08/27/1944, Weehawken, NJ **DISCIPLINE** ENGLISH HISTORY **EDUCATION** Clark Univ, AB, 66; Princeton Univ, MA, 71, PhD, 75. **CAREER** Instr, 76-79, asst prof hist, 79-, Va Commonwealth Univ. **RESEARCH** English social history; history of education. **SELECTED PUBLICATIONS** Contribr, Emerging Concepts of the Academic Profession at Oxford 1800-54, The University in Society, Princeton Univ Press, Vol I, 305-52; auth, Oxford College finances 1871-1913: A Comment, Econ Hist Rev, 78; art, Immoral intentions: The University of Oxford and the Problem of Prostitution 1827-1914, Victorian Studies, 79; art, The University System in Modern England: Historography of the 1970's and Opportunities for the 1980's, Rev Higher Educ, Vol III, No 3, 80; art, Political Education in Oxford 1823-1914, Hist Educ Quart, 80; contribr, The English Universities and Professional Education, The Transformation of Higher Learning 1860-1930, Elsivir, 82; auth, From Clergyman to Don: The Rise of the Academic Profession in 19th century Oxford, Clarendon Press, 82. **CONTACT ADDRESS** Dept of History, Virginia Commonwealth Univ, Box 2001, Richmond, VA, 23284-9004. **EMAIL** aengel@atlas.vcu/edu

ENGEL, KIRSTEN H.
PERSONAL Born 11/28/1961, Chicago, IL, m, 1997 **DISCIPLINE** ENGLISH **EDUCATION** Brown Univ, BA, 83; Northwestern Sch of Law, JD, 86. **CAREER** Assoc Prof, 92-, Tulane Law Sch; staff att, 90-92, Sierra Club Legal Def Fund DC; staff att, 87-90, US EPA Gen Coun DC; clerk, 86-87, Judge MH Bright US CT Appeals. **RESEARCH** Environmental Law; Intl Envtl Law; Federalism; Environ Justice; Utility Restructuring; The Environment. **SELECTED PUBLICATIONS** Coauth, An Empirical Palliative for Theoretical hubris in the Race-to-the-Bottom Debate Over State Environmental Standard-Setting, Cornell J L, and Pub Policy, 98; auth, Brownfields Initiatives and the Requirements of Markets Based Rights Based and Pragmatic Conceptions of Environmental Justice, J Ntl Res, and Envtl L, 98; State Environmental Standard-Setting: Is There A Race and Is It to the Bottom?, Hastings L J 97; rev, Intl Mgmt of Hazardous Waste: The Basel Convention and Related Legal Rules, Intl Envtl L, 96; auth, Reconsidering the Ntl Market in Solid Waste: Trade-offs In Equity Efficiency Envtl Protection and State Autonomy, N C L Rev, 95; coauth, Intl Envtl Law Anthology, Anderson, 96. **CONTACT ADDRESS** Law School, Tulane Univ, 6329 Freret St, New Orleans, LA, 70118. **EMAIL** Kengel@law.tulane.edu

ENGELBERG, EDWARD
PERSONAL Born 01/21/1929, Germany, m, 1950, 3 children **DISCIPLINE** COMPARATIVE LITERATURE AND ENGLISH **EDUCATION** Brooklyn Col, BA, 51; Univ Ore, MA, 52; Univ Wis, PhD, 57. **CAREER** From instr to assoc prof English, Univ Mich, 57-65; assoc prof, 65-67, chmn, Comp Lit Prog, 65-72, chmn, Dept Romance and Comp Lit, 71-75, chmn, Joint Prog Lit Studies, 71-75, PROF COMP LIT, BRANDEIS UNIV, 67-, Nat Endowment for Humanities sr fel, 75; fac rep, Bd Trustees, Brandeis Univ, 76-78, mem, Acad Planning Comt, 75-78; mem, exec comt, Eastern Comp Lit Conf. **MEMBERSHIPS** MLA; Am Comp Lit Asn; AAUP. **RESEARCH** Ro-

manticism and literary history; modern poetry; English-German relations. **SELECTED PUBLICATIONS** Auth, Running to Paradise, Yeats Poetic Art, Eng Lit Transition 1880-1920, Vol 38, 95; Collected Letters, Vol 6, Beitrage Geschichte Arbeiterbewegung, Vol 36, 94. **CONTACT ADDRESS** Dept of Romance and Lit Comp, Brandeis Univ, Waltham, MA, 02154.

ENGESTROM, YRJO
DISCIPLINE COMMUNICATIONS **EDUCATION** Univ Helsinki, Finland, PhD, 87. **CAREER** PROF, COMMUN, UNIV CALIF, SAN DIEGO. **RESEARCH** Teams and networks in a variety of work settings and cultures. **SELECTED PUBLICATIONS** Auth, Learning, Working and Imagining: Twelve Studies in Activity Theory, Orienta-Konsultit, 90; Training for Change: New Approach to Learning and Teaching in Working Life, Intl Labour Office, 94. **CONTACT ADDRESS** Dept of Commun, Univ Calif, San Diego, 9500 Gilman Dr, La Jolla, CA, 92093. **EMAIL** yengestr@weber.ucsd.edu

ENGLAND, ANTHONY BERTRAM
PERSONAL Born 07/29/1939, m, 1964, 2 children **DISCIPLINE** ENGLISH LITERATURE **EDUCATION** Univ Manchester, BA, 61, MA, 63; Yale Univ, PhD (English), 69. **CAREER** Asst lectr English, Univ Manchester, 63-64; instr, Univ BC, 64-66; asst prof, 69-76, ASSOC PROF ENGLISH, UNIV VICTORIA, BC, 76-. **RESEARCH** Swift's poetry; Byron and the 18th century; early 18th century burlesque poetry. **SELECTED PUBLICATIONS** Auth, Byron and the Emergence of Japhet in Heaven and Earth, Eng Stud Can, Vol 21, 95. **CONTACT ADDRESS** Dept of English, Univ of Victoria, Victoria, BC, V8W 2Y2.

ENGLAND, MICHAEL TIMOTHY
DISCIPLINE MASS COMMUNICATION **EDUCATION** Western KY Univ, BA, 78; IN Univ, MA, 82; Univ TN, PhD, 94. **CAREER** Vis Lect/Assoc Instr, IN Univ, 79-82; Asst prof, Western KY Univ, 86-90, Instr/Grad Tchg Asst, Univ TN, 90-93; Asst prof, Southwest TX State Univ, 93-. **HONORS AND AWARDS** Nat Asn Television Prog Execs fel; Nat Alumni Asn Grad fel; Public Radio News Dirs Asn Award; Am Heart Asn award; KY Educ Asn award. **MEMBERSHIPS** Asn Educ Journalism & Mass Comm, Broadcast Educ Asn; Tex Asn Broadcast Educators, Radio Television News Dirs Asn; Nat Asn Col Broadcasters. **SELECTED PUBLICATIONS** Auth, Your Hit Parade and Gospel Music Formats, Greenwood Publ, 98; Rev, Pioneer of Television, Mass Comm Quart, 95; High-Definition Television: A Global Perspective, Int Comm Res. **CONTACT ADDRESS** Southwest Texas State Univ, 601 University Dr, San Marcos, TX, 78666-4604.

ENTERLINE, LYNN
DISCIPLINE GENDER STUDIES, CLASSICAL, MEDIEVAL, AND EARLY MODERN LITERATURE **EDUCATION** Cornell, PhD. **CAREER** Instr, Vanderbilt Univ. **RESEARCH** Theories of rhetoric, language, and poetics from the classical period through the 17th century; contemporary intersections between feminist, queer, materialist and psychoanalytic critiques of literature and culture. **SELECTED PUBLICATIONS** Auth, The Tears of Narcissus: Melancholia and Masculinity in Early Modern Writing; The Rhetoric of the Body in Renaissance Ovidian Poetry. **CONTACT ADDRESS** Vanderbilt Univ, Nashville, TN, 37203-1727.

ENTZMINGER, ROBERT L.
PERSONAL Born 02/25/1948, Charleston, WV, m, 1972, 2 children **DISCIPLINE** ENGLISH **EDUCATION** Wash & Lee Univ, BA, 70; Rice Univ, PhD, 75. **CAREER** Instr, 75-76, Rice Univ; asst prof, 76-82, assoc prof, 82-87, Virginia Tech; TK Young Prof Eng, chmn eng dept, 87-, Rhodes Col. **RESEARCH** 17th century British lit; Milton; Ben Jonson. **CONTACT ADDRESS** Dept of English, Rhodes Col, 2000 North Parkway, Memphis, TN, 38112. **EMAIL** entzminger@rhodes.edu

EPPERLY, ELIZABETH ROLLINS
PERSONAL Born 04/23/1951, Martinsville, VA **DISCIPLINE** HUMANITIES, ENGLISH LITERATURE **EDUCATION** Univ PEI, BA, 73; Dalhousie Univ, MA, 74; Univ London, PhD (English novel), 78. **CAREER** Lectr, 76-77; ASST PROF ENGLISH, UNIV PEI, 77-. **MEMBERSHIPS** Asn Can Univ Teachers English; Can Coun Teachers English. **RESEARCH** The importance of literary allusion in the novel, the works of Anthony Trollope, and the works of L M Montgomery. **SELECTED PUBLICATIONS** Auth, At the Altar--Matrimonial Tales, University Toronto Quart, Vol 65, 95. **CONTACT ADDRESS** Dept of English, Univ of PEI, Charlottetown, PE, C1A 4P3.

EPSTEIN, EDMUND LLOYD
PERSONAL Born 10/15/1931, New York, NY, m, 1965, 3 children **DISCIPLINE** ENGLISH, LINGUISTICS **EDUCATION** Queens Col, NY, BA, 51; Yale Univ, MA, 53; Columbia Univ, PhD(English), 67. **CAREER** Ed dict, various publ, 53-55; instr English, Univ Buffalo, 55-57; ed trade-and-text-bks, B P Putnam's Sons, 57-63 & Farrar, Straus & Giroux, 63-65; from assoc prof to prof English, Southern Ill Univ, Carbondale, 65-74; prof English, Queens Col City Univ New York 74-; Ed-in-chief, James Joyce Rev, 57-61; consult, James Joyce Quart, 63-; ed-in-chief, Lang & Style, 68-; vis scholar, Univ Col, Univ London, 71-72; prof English,Grad Ctr., City Univ New York, 81-; exchange prof , Univ Paris, 82, 95. **HONORS AND AWARDS** Excellence in Teaching Award, Standard Oil Found, Ind, 71, nominated Distinguished Prof of English, 97; nominated for Award for Excellence in Teaching, 97. **MEMBERSHIPS** MLA; Ling Soc Am; Mediaeval Acad Am. **RESEARCH** Modern British literature; linguistics, the analysis of style, structural semantics, the analysis of meaning. **SELECTED PUBLICATIONS** Coauth, Linguistics and English prosody, Studies Ling, 58; Interpretation of Finnegans Wake, James Joyce Quart, summer 66; auth, The Ordeal of Stephen Dedalus: Conflict of the Generations in James Joyce's A Portrait of the Art as a Young Man, Southern Ill Univ, 71; Language and Style, Methuen, London, 78; auth Women's Language and Style: Studies in Contemporary Language #1, Queens Col, 78; auth A Starchamber Quiry: a Joyce Centennial Publication, 1882-1982, Methuen, London, 82; auth Joyce Centenary Essays, Southern Ill Univ, 1983; auth Mythic Worlds, Modern Worlds: the Writings of Joseph Campbell on James Joyce, Harper-Collins, 93; auth The Language of African Literature, Africa World Press, 98. **CONTACT ADDRESS** Dept of English, Queens Col, CUNY, 6530 Kissena Blvd, Flushing, NY, 11367-1597. **EMAIL** epstein@qcvaxa.acc.qc.edu

EPSTEIN, WILLIAM HENRY
PERSONAL Born 10/31/1944, Easton, PA, m, 1968 **DISCIPLINE** ENGLISH LITERATURE, LITERARY THEORY **EDUCATION** Dartmouth Col, BA, 66; Columbia Univ, MA, 67, PhD (English, comp lit), 72. **CAREER** Asst prof, 70-76, ASSOC PROF ENGLISH LIT, PURDUE UNIV, WEST LAFAYETTE, 76-. **MEMBERSHIPS** MLA; Am Soc 18th Century Studies; Johnson Soc Cent Region. **RESEARCH** Eighteenth century British literature; biography; the novel. **SELECTED PUBLICATIONS** Auth, Embodied Knowing, Biography Interdisciplinary Quart, Vol 18, 95; Imitating Art--Essays in Biography, Biography Interdisciplinary Quart, Vol 19, 96; The Center for Tomorrow, Disciplining Victorian Biography, 19th Century Prose, Vol 22, 95. **CONTACT ADDRESS** Dept of English, Purdue Univ, Lafayette, IN, 47907.

ERDMAN, HARLEY M.
DISCIPLINE THEATRE STUDIES **EDUCATION** Univ Tex Austin, MA, PhD. **CAREER** Asst prof. **SELECTED PUBLICATIONS** Auth, Staging the Jew, Rutgers Univ, 97. **CONTACT ADDRESS** Theatre Dept, Univ of Massachusetts, Amherst, 720 Massachusetts Ave, Amherst, MA, 01003. **EMAIL** harley@theater.umass.edu

ERICKSON, DARLENE E. WILLIAMS
PERSONAL Born 11/05/1941, Bay City, MI, m, 1962, 2 children **DISCIPLINE** ENGLISH **EDUCATION** BA, Aquines Col, 63; MA, Western MI Univ, 70; PhD, Miami Univ, 89. **CAREER** Chair/Assoc Prof Ohio Dominican Col, 89-98. **HONORS AND AWARDS** Conley Award; Outstanding Tchg, 91; PhD awarded with Distinction in all areas, 89; Phi Kappa Phi. **MEMBERSHIPS** MLA; MMLA; AAHE; ISCLT. **RESEARCH** Marianne Moore; Women in Lit; Contemporary Novals; Usin Tech in the Univ Classrooms. **SELECTED PUBLICATIONS** Illusion is More Precise than Precision: Poetry of Marianne Moore, Univ Alabama Press, 92; With Skill, Endurance and Generosity of Heart: Frank McCourt's Angela's Ashes, 98; ed of The Dolphin ed by Kari-Heinz Westarp and Michael Boss, Aarhus Univ Press, title of Ireland: Towards New Identities, Low Countries of the Mind: Richard Powers's Galatea 2,2, 98; Co-presented with Dr Larry Cepek, Educom Conference in Milwaukee WI, Using Technology to Enhance Teaching and Learning, 98. **CONTACT ADDRESS** Ohio Dominican Col, 1216 Sunbury Rd, room 223 E, Columbus, OH, 43219. **EMAIL** ericksoa@ODC.EDU

ERICKSON, NANCY LOU
PERSONAL Born 07/14/1941, Berea, OH, m, 1964, 2 children **DISCIPLINE** HISTORY, ENGLISH **EDUCATION** Kent State Univ, BS, 61; Univ IL, Urbana, AM, 64; Univ NC, Chapel Hill, PhD(hist), 70. **CAREER** Teacher hist, Champaign Sr High Sch, IL, 63-64; teacher, Maine Twp High Sch West, Des Plaines, IL, 64-66; assoc prof to prof hist, Erskine Col, 74-, dir of institutional res, 88-; Lilly Scholar Hist, Duke Univ, 76-77. **HONORS AND AWARDS** Excellence in Teaching Award, 78; Renaissance Person of the Year, 92. **MEMBERSHIPS** Am Hist Asn; Orgn Am Historians; Coun Faith & Hist. **RESEARCH** Comparative cultures; United States-Soviet Union; national character; 17th century America. **CONTACT ADDRESS** Erskine Col, Hc 60, Due West, SC, 29639-9801. **EMAIL** nde@erskine.edu

ERICKSON, ROBERT A.
DISCIPLINE SEVENTEENTH- AND EIGTHTEENTH-CENTURY ENGLISH LITERATURE **EDUCATION** Yale Univ, PhD, 66. **CAREER** PROF, ENG, UNIV CALIF, SANTA BARBARA. **RESEARCH** Lit and relig; Lit and med. **SELECTED PUBLICATIONS** Auth, Mother Midnight: Birth, Sex, and Fate in Eighteenth-Century Fiction, AMS Press, 86; "Mrs. A. Behn and the Myth of Oroonoko-Imoinda," Eighteenth-Century Fiction, 93; "William Harvey's De motu cordis and the 'Republick of Literature'," Lit and Med During Eighteenth Century, Routledge, 93; "Lady Fulbank and the 'Poet's Dream'," Aphra Behn's The Lucky Chance, Broken Boundaries, Univ, Press of Ky, 96; The Language of the Heart, 1600-1750, Penn Press, 97; co-ed, John Arbuthnot's The History of John Bull, Clarendon Press, 76. **CONTACT ADDRESS** Dept of Eng, Univ Calif, Santa Barbara, CA, 93106-7150. **EMAIL** erickson@humanitas.ucsb.edu

ERISMAN, FRED RAYMOND
PERSONAL Born 08/30/1937, Longview, TX, m, 1961, 1 child **DISCIPLINE** AMERICAN STUDIES & LITERATURE **EDUCATION** Rice Inst, BA, 58; Duke Univ, MA, 60; Univ Minn, Minneapolis, PhD(Am studies), 66. **CAREER** From instr to assoc prof, 65-77, actg dean, Col Arts & Sci, 70-71 & 72-73, dir honors prog, 72-74, prof English, Tex Christian Univ, 77-, Co-ed, The French-American Rev J, 76-; book rev ed, Soc Sci J, 78-82; publ ed & mem exec bd, Int Res Soc Children's Lit, 81-83; Hess fel, Univ Minn, 81; Kinnucan Arms Chair fel, Buffalo Bill Hist Ctr, 82; chrmn, dept English. **HONORS AND AWARDS** Lorraine Sherley Prof of Literature, 86; Phi Beta Kappa, 88. **MEMBERSHIPS** Am Studies Asn; MLA; Orgn Am Historians; Western Lit Asn; Popular Cult Asn. **RESEARCH** American popular literature; American regional and environmental literature; detective and suspense fiction. **SELECTED PUBLICATIONS** Auth, The environmental crisis and presentday romanticism, Rocky Mountain Soc Sci J, 73; The romantic regionalism of Harper Lee, Ala Rev, 73; Frederic Remington, Western Writers Ser, Boise State Univ, 75; Prolegomena to a theory of American life, Southern Quart, 76; Romantic reality in the spy stories of Len Deighton, Armchair Detective, 77; Jack Schaefer: The writer as ecologist, Western Am Lit, 78; Western regional writers and the uses of place, J of the West, 80; co-ed (with Richard W Etulain), Fifty Western Writers, Greenwood Press, 82; Barnboken i USA, 86; contribur, A Literary History of the American West, 87; Laura Ingalls Wilder, Western Writers Ser, 94; Updating the Literary West; 97. **CONTACT ADDRESS** Dept of English, Texas Christian Univ, Box 297270, Fort Worth, TX, 76129-0002. **EMAIL** f.erisman@tcu.edu

ERLER, MARY C.
PERSONAL Born 11/15/1937, Tiffin, OH, m, 1963, 2 children **DISCIPLINE** ENGLISH LITERATURE **EDUCATION** St. Mary's Col, BA, 59; Univ Chicago, MA, 63; PhD, 81. **CAREER** Prof, Fordham Univ, 80- . **HONORS AND AWARDS** Grants from NEH, Amer Philos Soc, John Rylands Res Inst, and Folger Shakespeare Library; "Best Teacher" mention, Lisa Birnbach's New and Improved College Book, 90; English dept chair, 94-96. **MEMBERSHIPS** MLA; Medieval Acad of Am; Early Book Soc. **RESEARCH** Women's reading and book ownership 15th-16th century; medieval drama. **SELECTED PUBLICATIONS** ed, Robert Copland: Poems, 93; Exchange of Books between Nuns and Laywomen: Three Surviving Examples in New Science Out of Old Books: Studies...in Honour of A.I. Doyle, 95; 'Chaste Sports, Juste Prayses & All Softe Delight': Harefield 1602 and Ashby 1607, Two Female Entertainments in The Elizabethan Theatre XIV, 96; A London Achorite, Simon Appulby: His Fruyte of Redempcyon and Its Milieu, Viator, 98; Devotional Literature in Cambridge History of the Book in Britain, 99. **CONTACT ADDRESS** Dept of English, Fordham Univ, Bronx, NY, 10458.

ERLICH, RICHARD DEE
PERSONAL Born 02/07/1943, Terre Haute, IN **DISCIPLINE** ENGLISH LANGUAGE & LITERATURE **EDUCATION** Univ Ill, Urbana, AB, 65, PhD(English), 71; Cornell Univ, MA, 66. **CAREER** Instr English, Univ Ill, Urbana, 68-70; from Asst Prof to Assoc Prof, 71-86, PROF ENGLISH, MIAMI UNIV, 86-. **HONORS AND AWARDS** Woodrow Wilson Fel, 65; Danforth Fel, 65. **MEMBERSHIPS** Shakespeare Asn Am; Popular Cult Asn; Sci Fiction Res Asn; Soc Utopian Studies; AAUP; Int Asn Fantastic in the Arts. **RESEARCH** Shakespeare's plays; fantasy and science fiction; film criticism. **SELECTED PUBLICATIONS** Coauth, Words of binding: patterns of integration in Earthsea, In: Ursula K Le Guin, Taplinger, 79; co-ed, The Mechanical God: Machines in Science Fiction, Greenwood, 82; auth, Moon-Watcher, Man, and Star-Child: 2001 as Paradigm, In: Patterns in the Fantastic: Academic Programming at CHICON IV, Starmont, 83; coauth, Clockworks: A Multimedia Bibliography of Works Useful for the Study of the Human/Machine Interface in SF, Greenwood, 93; If Pornography is bad, exactly what is the matter with it?, The Cincinatti Post, 9/5/95; Coyote's Song: The Teaching Stories of Ursula K. Le Guin, The Borgo Press (in press); author of numerous articles and book chapters. **CONTACT ADDRESS** Dept of English, Miami Univ, Oxford, OH, 45056-1633. **EMAIL** ErlichRD@muohio.edu

ERVIN, HAZEL A.
DISCIPLINE HUMANITIES **EDUCATION** Guilford Col, AB, 80; N.C. A&T State Univ, MA, 85; Howard Univ, PhD, 93. **CAREER** Asst prof, 85-96, chemn, 93-96, Shaw Univ; assoc prof, Morehouse Col, 96-. **HONORS AND AWARDS** UNCF/Mellon fellow; John Lennon Grant for Summer Enrich-

ment; Who's Who Among African Am; World Who's Who of Women; Nat Consortium Educ Access Fellow. **MEMBERSHIPS** MLA; CLA; MELUS; The Langston Hughes Society. **RESEARCH** Ann Petry and literary criticism. **SELECTED PUBLICATIONS** Auth, Ann Petry: A Bio-Bibliography; auth, Tituba of Salem Village by Ann Petry; auth, Adieu, Harlem's Adopted Daughter Ann Petry, 97; auth, African American Literary Criticism, 97; auth, Race and Desire as New Paridigm in New Biography of Jean Toomer, 99. **CONTACT ADDRESS** Dept of English, Morehouse Col, 830 Westview Dr SW, Atlanta, GA, 30314. **EMAIL** hervin@morehouse.edu

ERWIN, D. TIMOTHY
DISCIPLINE 18TH CENTURY LITERATURE **EDUCATION** Marquette Univ, AB; Univ Chicago, MA, PhD, 84. **CAREER** Ch, adv, guest ed, Chicago Rev, 75-81; resident hd, univ housing, Univ Chicago, 76-81; instr, Univ San Diego, 81-84; asst prof, Rutgers Univ, 85-90; prof, ch, Multidisciplinary stud prog, Univ Nev, Las Vegas; ed, Stud in 18th-Century Cult, Johns Hopkins Univ Press. **HONORS AND AWARDS** Ellison Fund scholar, Univ Chicago, 75-76; Fels Award, Coord Coun of Lit Mag, 76; Chicago Rev, Best Ill Mag, Ill Arts Coun, 76; ed grantee, Nat Endowment for the Arts, 78; grant, Am Soc for 18th-Century Stud/Clark Libr, 85; NEH summer inst, Hobart and William Smith Col, 87; NEH summer sem UCSB, 93; short-term fel, Clark Libr, UCLA, 96; NEH fel, Aston Magna Acad, Yale Univ, 97; short-term fel, Yale Ctr for Brit Art, 98. **MEMBERSHIPS** MLA. **RESEARCH** Aspects of poetic diction 1660-1820. **SELECTED PUBLICATIONS** Auth, The Extraordinary Language of Robert Pinsky, Halcyon /94; J of the Hum 16, 94; Alexander Pope and the Disappearance of the Beautiful, in So Rich a Tapestry: The Sister Arts and Cultural Studies, eds, Kate Greenspan and Ann Hurley, 13ucknell UP, 95; A Memoir, Chicago Rev: Fifty Years: A Retrospective Issue 42, 96; six articles, in Hanoverian Britain: An Encyclopedia, Garland, 97; coauth, Restoration and Eighteenth-Century Literature, The Reader's Adviser, 14th ed, Bowker, 94. **CONTACT ADDRESS** Dept of Eng, Univ Nev, Las Vegas, 4505 Maryland Pky, PO Box 455011, Las Vegas, NV, 89154-5011. **EMAIL** timothy@nevada.edu

ESPOSITO, STEVEN
PERSONAL Born 07/15/1959, Cincinnati, OH, m, 1991, 3 children **DISCIPLINE** COMMUNICATION **EDUCATION** Miami Univ, BS, 81; Univ Cincinnati, MA, 93; Wayne State Univ, PhD, 96. **CAREER** Broadcast Journalist; Asst Prof and Dir of Univ TV, Capital Univ. **HONORS AND AWARDS** Production, Aesthetics and Criticism Competitive Paper, Broadcast Ed Asn, 97. **MEMBERSHIPS** Broadcast Educ Asn; Nat Commun Asn; Asn Educ in Jour and Mass Commun. **RESEARCH** Media criticism. **SELECTED PUBLICATIONS** Auth, Cohesion & Adaptability in the non-custodial father/child relationship: The effects of interaction quality, Jour Divorce & Remarriage, 23, 95; auth, Presumed innocent?: A comparative analysis of network news', prime time newsmagazines', and tabloid tv's pretrial coverage of the O.J. Simpson criminal case, Commun and the Law, 18, 96; auth, Source Utilization in Legal Jounalism: Network TV news coverage of the Timothy McVeigh Oklahoma City Bombing Trial, Commun and the Law, 20, 98. **CONTACT ADDRESS** Capital Univ, 2199 E Main St, Bexley, OH, 43209. **EMAIL** sesposit@capital.edu

ESSICK, ROBERT N.
DISCIPLINE BRITISH ROMANTIC LITERATURE AND ART **EDUCATION** UCLA, BA; Univ Calif-San Diego, PhD. **CAREER** Fac res lectr, 90-91; PROF, ART HIST, UNIV CALIF, RIVERSIDE. **HONORS AND AWARDS** Outstanding Acad bk, Choice, 80-81; outstanding bk, Chioce, 91-92; fel(s), NEH; Amer Coun of Learned Soc; Guggenheim., On-line fel, Inst Adv Tech in the Hum, Univ Va. **MEMBERSHIPS** Mem, Bd of Overseers Huntington Lib; ed bd, Stud Eng Lit. **RESEARCH** William Blake, Blake electronic archive. **SELECTED PUBLICATIONS** Auth, William Blake, Printmaker, Princeton Univ Press, 80; William Blake and the Language of Adam, Oxford Univ Press, 89; William Blake's Commercial Book Illustrations, Oxford Univ Press, 91; William Blake at the Huntington, 94; **CONTACT ADDRESS** Dept of Eng, Univ Calif, 1156 Hinderaker Hall, Riverside, CA, 92521-0209. **EMAIL** ressick@ucrac1.ucr.edu.

ESTERHAMMER, ANGELA
DISCIPLINE ENGLISH LITERATURE **EDUCATION** Univ Toronto, BA; Princeton Univ, PhD. **RESEARCH** Romantic literature and theory; philosophy of language; speech-act theory; performativity. **SELECTED PUBLICATIONS** Auth, Creating States: Studies in the Performative Language of John Milton and William Blake, Toronto, 94. **CONTACT ADDRESS** Dept of English, Western Ontario Univ, London, ON, N6A 5B8.

EUBA, FEMI
PERSONAL Born 01/02/1941, Lagos, Nigeria, m, 1992 **DISCIPLINE** THEATRE; ENGLISH **EDUCATION** Yale Sch of Drama, 73; Yale Grad Sch, 82; Univ of Ife, PhD, 86. **CAREER** Sr Lecturer, Univ Ife, Ile-Ife, Nigeria, 76-86; Vis Prof, William & Mary, 86-88; Asst Prof, 88-91, Assoc Prof, 91-96, Prof, 96-, La State Univ, 88-91. **HONORS AND AWARDS** LSU Alum Asn Fac Excellence Award, 97; Kennedy Ctr/Am Col Theatre

Festival Reg Award in Dir, 93; LSU Manship Fellow, 89. **MEMBERSHIPS** Asn of Theatre in Higher Educ; Black Theatre Asn; African Lit Asn; SW Theatre Convention; Crib Lit Asn; Phi Kappa Phi; British Actors' Equity. **RESEARCH** Comparative Black drama; myth & ritual; the creative process. **SELECTED PUBLICATIONS** Auth, Archetypes, Imprecators and Victims of Fate: Origins and Developments of Satire in Black Drama, Greenwood Press, 89; auth, The Gulf, full-length play, Longman, Ltd, 91; auth, The Theatre of Edouard Glissant: Resolving the Problems of Monsieur Toussaint at LSU Theatre, Horizons D'Edouard Glissant, J&D Editions, 473-482, 92; auth, Soyinka's Satiric Development and Maturity, Mapping Intersections: African Literature & Africa's Development, no 2, Africa World Press, 175-187, 98. **CONTACT ADDRESS** Louisiana State Univ, PO Box 16352, Baton Rouge, LA, 70893. **EMAIL** theuba@unix1.sncc.lsu.edu

EVANS, ARTHUR B.
DISCIPLINE HUMANITIES **EDUCATION** Tufts Univ, BA 70; Goddard Col, MA 72; Middlebury Col, MA 79; Columbia Univ, MPhil 82, PhD 85. **CAREER** Tufts Univ, tchg asst, 69-70; Montpelier HS, HS tchr 70-78; Community Col VT, adj inst, 74-75; Columbia Univ, preceptor 81-83; DePauw Univ, asst prof, assoc prof, ch romance lang, ch mod lang, 85 to 98-. **MEMBERSHIPS** MLA; SJV; AATF; CELJ; AI. **SELECTED PUBLICATIONS** Auth, On Philip K Dick, coed, SF-TH Inc, 92; Jules Verne, TCLC 52: Twentieth Century Literary Criticism, Gale 94; Verne's Vehicular Utopias, Metamorphoses Of Utopia, Lausanne, Switzerland, forthcoming; Scholarly SF Jours as Authorities, Science Fiction and Contests for Authority, U of Georgia Press, forthcoming; Jules Verne and the French Literary Canon, Jules Verne: Narratives of Modernity, Liverpool UP, forthcoming; Jules Verne Misunderstood Visionary, Sci Amer, 97; Modern Mystery Fantasy and Science Fiction Writers, ed, Bruce Cassidy, in: Sci Fic Studies, 94. **CONTACT ADDRESS** Dept of Modern Languages, DePauw Univ, Greencastle, IN, 46135. **EMAIL** aevens@depauw.edu

EVANS, DAVID ALLAN
PERSONAL Born 04/11/1940, Sioux City, IA, m, 1958, 3 children **DISCIPLINE** AMERICAN LITERATURE **EDUCATION** Morningside Col, BA, 62; Univ Iowa, MA, 64; Univ Ark, MFA, 76. **CAREER** Asst prof English, Adams State Col, 66-68; asst prof, 68-75, assoc prof, 75-78, PROF ENGLISH, SOUTH DAK STATE UNIV, 78-, Writer-in-residence, SDak Arts Coun, 73- and Iowa Arts Coun, 75; writer and scholar, Wayne State Col, 80. **MEMBERSHIPS** Assoc Writers Progs. **RESEARCH** Comtemporary American and English poetry. **SELECTED PUBLICATIONS** Auth The Kiss, South Dakota Rev, Vol 34, 96;, Semi Retirement, South Dakota Rev, Vol 34, 96. Ghost in the End Zone, South Dakota Rev, Vol 35, 97; On Milton, John, South Dakota Rev, Vol 33, 95; At The Ymca, South Dakota Rev, Vol 34, 96. **CONTACT ADDRESS** 1222 3rd St, Brookings, SD, 57006.

EVANS, GWYNNE BLAKEMORE
PERSONAL Born 03/31/1912, Columbus, OH, m, 1943, 2 children **DISCIPLINE** ENGLISH **EDUCATION** Ohio State Univ, AB, 34; Univ Cincinnati, AM, 36; Harvard Univ, PhD, 40. **CAREER** Asst & tutor, Brooklyn Col, 40-41; instr Univ Wis, 41-42, 45-56, asst prof, 46-47; from asst prof to prof English, Univ Ill, Urbana, 47-67; prof English, 67-75, CABOT PROF ENGLISH LIT, HARVARD UNIV, 75-, Dexter traveling fel, Harvard Univ, 40 & Guggenheim Mem Found, 48-49; ed, J English & Ger Philol, 55-63. **MEMBERSHIPS** Am Acad Arts Scis, 88-. **RESEARCH** Elizabethan drama; Shakespeare; 17th century prompt materials. **SELECTED PUBLICATIONS** Auth, Plays and Poems of William Cartwright, Univ Wis; Shakespearean Promptbooks of the 17th Century, Vols I-VIII, Univ Va; ed, Supp, In: Variorum I Henry IV, Shakespeare Asn Am; textual ed, Complete Works of Shakespeare, Houghton, 74, gen and text ed, second ed, 97; ed, Elizabethan-Jacobean Drma, A New Mermaid Background Book, 88; ed, New Cambridge Shakespeare's Sonnets, 96. **CONTACT ADDRESS** Barker Center, Harvard Univ, Cambridge, MA, 02138.

EVANS, JAMES EDWARD
PERSONAL Born 09/25/1946, Savannah, GA, m, 1969, 3 children **DISCIPLINE** ENGLISH LITERATURE **EDUCATION** Univ NC, Chapel Hill, BA, 67; Univ Pa, MA, 68, PhD, 71. **CAREER** Asst prof, 71-76, assoc prof Eng, 76-88, dir, grad studies Eng, 81-88, prof, 88, dept head, 90-99, Univ NC, Greensboro. **HONORS AND AWARDS** Phi Beta Kappa **MEMBERSHIPS** MLA; Am Soc 18th Century Studies; S Atlantic Mod Lang Assn. **RESEARCH** Early English periodicals; 18th century English novel; comedy. **SELECTED PUBLICATIONS** Art, Resisting a Private Tyranny in Two Humane Comedies, Broken Boundaries: Women & Feminism in Restoration Drama, University Press of Kentucky, 96; ed, John Gay and Oliver Goldsmith, Encyclopedia of British Humorists, S. Gale, Garland, 96. **CONTACT ADDRESS** Dept of English, Univ of North Carolina, 1000 Spring Garden, Greensboro, NC, 27412-0001. **EMAIL** evansj@fagan.uncg.edu

EVANS, JOHN MARTIN
PERSONAL Born 02/02/1935, Cardiff, England, m, 1963, 2 children **DISCIPLINE** ENGLISH LITERATURE **EDUCA-**

TION Oxford Univ, BA, 58, MA and DPhil(English), 63. **CAREER** From asst prof to assoc prof, 63-75, assoc dean humanities and sci, 77-81, PROF ENGLISH, STANFORD UNIV, 75-, Harmsworth scholar, Oxford Univ, 61-63. **MEMBERSHIPS** Renaissance Soc Am. **RESEARCH** Renaissance English, Old English and medieval English literature; Milton. **SELECTED PUBLICATIONS** Auth, Moral Fiction in Milton and Spencer, Review of Eng Stud, Vol 48, 97; A Poem of Absences, Milton Quart, Vol 27, 93; The Humanism of Milton Paradise Lost, Rev Eng Stud, Vol 46, 95; Heirs of Fame--Milton and Writers of the English Renaissance, Rev Eng Stud, Vol 48, 97. **CONTACT ADDRESS** Dept of English, Stanford Univ, Stanford, CA, 94305-1926.

EVANS, LAWRENCE
DISCIPLINE ENGLISH **EDUCATION** Harvard Univ, PhD. **CAREER** Prof, Northwestern Univ. **RESEARCH** Victorian and 20th century fiction. **SELECTED PUBLICATIONS** Ed, The Letters of Walter Pater, 70. **CONTACT ADDRESS** Dept of English, Northwestern Univ, 1801 Hinman, Evanston, IL, 60208.

EVANS, ROBLEY JO
PERSONAL Born 11/28/1933, Portland, OR, 1 child **DISCIPLINE** ENGLISH **EDUCATION** Reed Col, BA, 56; Univ Wash, MA, 61, PhD (English), 68. **CAREER** From instr to assoc prof, 64-78, PROF ENGLISH, CONN COL, 78-, Fulbright scholar, France, 56-57. **RESEARCH** Romantic poets; Victorian poets and critics; American Indian literature. **SELECTED PUBLICATIONS** Auth, Cholera in Medicine and Pharmacy in the Time of Vonpettenkofer, Isis, Vol 86, 95; Languages of Labor and Gender--Female Factory Work in Germany, 1850-1914, Labor Hist, Vol 38, 97; Cholera in Medicine and Pharmacy in the Time of Vonpettenkofer, Max, Isis, Vol 86, 95; The Police, Politics, and Society in Germany, 1700-1933, Geschichte Gesellschaft, Vol 22, 96; A German Womens Movement--Class and Gender in Hanover, 1880-1933, J Mod Hist, Vol 69, 97; Control, Connectionism and Cognition--Towards a New Regulatory Paradigm, Brit J Philos Sci, Vol 43, 92; An Autumn of German Romanticism , Hist Today, Vol 44, 94; Nipperdey 19th Century , Geschichte Gesellschaft, Vol 20, 94. **CONTACT ADDRESS** Dept of English, Connecticut Col, 270 Mohegan Ave, New London, CT, 06320-4125.

EVELEV, JOHN
DISCIPLINE ENGLISH **EDUCATION** Bowdoin Coll, BA, 87; Duke Univ, MA, 90, PhD, 95. **CAREER** VIS ASST PROF, ENG, UNIV TENN **MEMBERSHIPS** Am Antiquarian Soc **RESEARCH** Herman Melville **SELECTED PUBLICATIONS** Auth, "Made in the Marquesas: Typee, Tattooing and Melville's Critique of the Literary Marketplace," Ariz Quart 48:4, 92; auth, "The Contrast: The Problem of Theatricality and Political and Social Crisis in Postrevolutionary America," Early Am Lit 31:1, 96. **CONTACT ADDRESS** Dept of Eng, Univ of Tenn, 301 McClung Tower, Knoxville, TN, 37996.

EVENSON, BRIAN
DISCIPLINE ENGLISH AND CRITICAL THEORY **EDUCATION** Wash, PhD, 93. **CAREER** Engl, Okla St Univ. **HONORS AND AWARDS** NEA Creative Writer's Fel; Grant Lilly Library Helm Fel., Ass ed, Conjunctions Mag Fiction Ed The Cimarron Rev. **RESEARCH** Creative writing; critical theory; 18th cent Brit lit. **SELECTED PUBLICATIONS** Auth, Altmann's Tongue: Stories and Novella, Knopf, 94; The Space of Silence: Selected Poems of Rafael Cadenas, Pyx Press, 95; The Din of Celestial Birds: Early Stories,Wordcraft, 97; Prophets and Brothers, Chapbook , Rodent Press, 97; Father of Lies, New York, Four Walls Eight Windows, 98. **CONTACT ADDRESS** Oklahoma State Univ, 101 Whitehurst Hall, Stillwater, OK, 74078.

EVETT, DAVID HAL
PERSONAL Born 06/17/1936, Denver, CO, m, 1960, 3 children **DISCIPLINE** ENGLISH **EDUCATION** Univ South, BA, 58; Harvard Univ, AM, 62, PhD(English), 65. **CAREER** Asst prof English, Univ Wis, Madison, 65-70; ASSOC PROF ENGLISH, CLEVELAND STATE UNIV, 70-, Am Philos Soc grant-in-aid, 68-69. **HONORS AND AWARDS** British Cnl Prz in the Human **MEMBERSHIPS** MLA; Shakespeare Asn of Am; Renaissance Soc Am. **RESEARCH** Spenser and his contemporaries; visual imagery; Shakespeare. **SELECTED PUBLICATIONS** Auth, Paradise's Other map: Marvell's Upon Appleton House and the Topos of the Locus Amoenus, Pub Mod Lang Asn Am, 5/70; Travail of a Department, In: Academic Supermarkets, Jossey-Bass, 71; Types of King David in Shakespeare's Lancastrian Tetralogy, Shakespeare Studies, 10/81; Mammon's Grotto: Renaissance Grotesque Decor and Some Features of Spenser's Faerie Queene, English Lit Renaissance; auth, Literature and the Visual Arts in Tudor England, Univ of Ga, 91. **CONTACT ADDRESS** Dept of English, Cleveland State Univ, 1983 E 24th St, Cleveland, OH, 44115-2440. **EMAIL** d.evett@csuohio.edu

EWALD, HELEN ROTHSCHILD
PERSONAL Born 04/30/1947, Berwyn, IL, m, 1976 **DISCIPLINE** RHETORICAL THEORY, COMPOSITION **EDUCA-**

TION Valparaiso Univ, BA, 69; Univ Ariz, MA, 71; Ind Univ, PhD (drama and Renaissance lit), 77. **CAREER** Grad asst compos, Univ Ariz, 69-71; instr English and Am lit, Valparaiso Univ, 71-73; instr compos and Shakespeare, Ind Univ, 74-76; asst prof compos and lit, Washburn Univ, Topeka, 77-80; ASST PROF COMPOS, IOWA STATE UNIV, 80-. **MEMBERSHIPS** NCTE; Am Soc Theater Res. **RESEARCH** Rhetorical theory, specifically cognitive processes and composition; error-analysis: a conceptual approach to miscues in writing; role of convention in communication situations. **SELECTED PUBLICATIONS** Auth, Exploring Agency in Classroom Discourse or, Should David Have Told his Story, Coll Compos Comm, Vol 45, 94; Waiting for Answerability--Bakhtin and Composition Studies, Coll Compos Comm, Vol 44, 93; Interpreting Interpretations of Divergence, Coll Compos Comm, Vol 46, 95. **CONTACT ADDRESS** 1208 Park Way, Ames, IA, 50010.

EWELL, BARBARA CLAIRE
PERSONAL Born 03/10/1947, Baton Rouge, LA **DISCIPLINE** ENGLISH RENAISSANCE AND WOMEN'S LITERATURE **EDUCATION** Univ Dallas, BA, 69; Univ Notre Dame, PhD (English), 74. **CAREER** Asst prof English, Loyola Univ South, 74-75; instr, Newcomb Col, 75-76; asst prof, Univ Col, Tulane Univ, 76-79; ASST PROF ENGLISH, UNIV MISS, 79-, Lectr and instr, writing workshops, Mobil, Erns and Erns and Save the Children Conf, 77-79; consult, Allen Johnson and Assoc, 77-79; Monticello Col Found fel, Newberry libr, 82-83. **MEMBERSHIPS** MLA, Women's Caucus; SCent Mod Lang Asn; Nat Women's Studies Asn; NCTE; SCent Renaissance Asn. **RESEARCH** Michael Drayton and related poets; Kate Chopin in the context of 19th century popular fiction; women writers of the English Renaissance. **SELECTED PUBLICATIONS** Auth, The Family Saga in the South--Generations and Destinies, New Orleans Rev, Vol 21, 95; A Mixed Race--Ethnicity in Early America, Am Lit, Vol 66, 94; Becoming Southern--The Evolution of a Way of Life, Warner County and Vicksburg, Mississippi, 1770-1860, New Orleans Rev, Vol 21, 95. **CONTACT ADDRESS** Dept of English, Univ of Miss, University, MS, 38677.

F

FAAS, EKBERT
PERSONAL Born 05/07/1938, Berlin, Germany **DISCIPLINE** LITERATURE **EDUCATION** Univ Munich, Drphil; Univ Wurzburg, Drhabil. **CAREER** FAC MEM, YORK UNIVERSITY. **SELECTED PUBLICATIONS** Auth, Towards a New American Poetics, 78; auth, Ted Hughes, 80; auth, Young Robert Duncan, 83; auth, Tragedy and After: Euripides, Shakespeare, Goethe, 84; auth, Shakespeare's Poetics, 86; auth, Retreat into the Mind: Victorian Poetry and the Rise of Psychiatry, 88; auth, Woyzeck's Head, 91. **CONTACT ADDRESS** York Univ, 4700 Keele St, North York, ON, M3J 1P3.

FABER, J. ARTHUR
DISCIPLINE MEDIEVAL AND RENAISSANCE LITERATURE **EDUCATION** Calvin, AB, Bowling Green, MA; Univ Mass, PhD. **CAREER** Prof; **RESEARCH** Interplay of language and thought, comparative linguistics, English language and style. **SELECTED PUBLICATIONS** Areas: poetry, literary criticism. **CONTACT ADDRESS** Wittenberg Univ, Springfield, OH, 45501-0720.

FABER, RONALD
DISCIPLINE MASS COMMUNICATION STUDIES **EDUCATION** Univ Pa, MS; Univ Wis Madison, PhD. **CAREER** Prof **SELECTED PUBLICATIONS** Co-auth, For the Good of Others: Censorship and the Third-Person Effect, Int J Public Opinion Res, 96; The Future of Advertising After the Millennium, Marketing Rev, 96; Two Forms of Compulsive Compunction: Comorbidity Between Compulsive Buying and Binge Eating, J Consumer Res, 95. **CONTACT ADDRESS** Mass Communication Dept, Univ of Minnesota, Twin Cities, 111 Murphy Hall, 206 Church St SE, Minneapolis, MN, 55455. **EMAIL** faber001@maroon.tc.umn.edu

FABRICANT, CAROLE
DISCIPLINE IRISH LITERATURE **EDUCATION** Bard Coll, BA; Johns Hopkins Univ, PhD. **CAREER** PROF, ART HIST, UNIV CALIF, RIVERSIDE. **HONORS AND AWARDS** James L. Clifford prize winner. **RESEARCH** Postcolonial studies, 18th century studies. **SELECTED PUBLICATIONS** Auth, Swift's Landscape, Johns Hopkins Univ Press, 82; reissued, Univ Notre Dame Press, 95; Augustan landscape design, Stud 18th-Century Cult; Gulliver's Travels, St Martin's Press series; Case Studies, Contemp Criticism, 95; The Shared Worlds of ¤Delariviere| Manley and Swift, Pope, Swift, and Women Writers, 96; Defining Self and Others: Pope and 18th-Century Gender Ideology, Criticism, 98. **CONTACT ADDRESS** Dept of Eng, Univ Calif, 1156 Hinderaker Hall, Riverside, CA, 92521-0209. **EMAIL** finaid@pop.ucr.edu

FACKLER, HERBERT VERN
PERSONAL Born 01/23/1942, Monroe, LA, m, 1964, 2 children **DISCIPLINE** ANGLOIRISH & MODERN LITERATURE **EDUCATION** Centenary Col, LA, BA, 64; NM Highlands Univ, MA, 65; Univ NC, Chapel Hill, PhD(English), 72. **CAREER** Teaching asst English, NMex Highlands Univ, 65; instr, Centenary Col, La, 65-68; asst prof, Northwestern State Univ, LA, 69-70; asst prof, Univ Tulsa, 70-71; asst prof English & dir creative writing, 71-76, assoc prof, 76-96, PROF, UNIV SOUTHWESTERN LA, 97-; NDEA fel, Univ NC, Chapel Hill, 72; dir, Deep South Writers Conf, 80, 8, 94. **HONORS AND AWARDS** Phi Kappa Phi; Phi Eta Sigma; Sigma Tau Delta; NDEA Fellow Univ NC, Chapel Hill, 68-69; USL Found Distinguished Prof, 81; Highlands Distinguished Alumnus, 91; Assoc Samuel P. Peters Int Lit Res Center, 92. **MEMBERSHIPS** Col English Asn (treas, 72-74); SCent Mod Lang Asn; Am Comt Irish Studies; MLA; Deep South Writers Conf (dir 80 & 81); Popular Culture Asn. **RESEARCH** Nineteenth and twentieth century British and Am literature; AngloIrish lit; mystery and detective fiction. **SELECTED PUBLICATIONS** Auth, Series of studies of Deirdre works, Eire-Ireland, spring 72; Proust and Celine, Studies, by Mem SCent Mod Lang Asn, winter 73; The Dierdre legend in Anglo-Irish lit: A prolegomenon, Univ Southwestern La Res Ser, 74; That Tragic Queen: the Deirdre in Anglo-Irish Literature, Univ Salzburg, 79; ed, Modern Irish Novel, excluding Joyce, Univ Southwestern La Res Ser, 80; Reflections on a Slender Volume, in Lawrence Durrell: Comprehending the Whole, ed, Julian Raper, et al; Dialectic in the Corpus of Robert B. Parker's Spenser Novels, Clues, 94; Spenser's New England Conscience, Colby Quart, 98; novels: The Snow Pirates, The Last Long Pass, and Virginia Creeper, Dancing Jester Press, 99. **CONTACT ADDRESS** Dept of English, Univ of Southwestern, Box 44691 USL, Lafayette, LA, 70504-8401.

FADERMAN, LILLIAN
PERSONAL Born 07/18/1940, Bronx, NY **DISCIPLINE** ENGLISH **EDUCATION** Univ Calif, Berkeley, BA, 62; Univ Calif, Los Angeles, MA, 64, PhD, 67. **CAREER** Chmn dept English, 71-72, dean, Sch Humanities, 72-73, asst vpres acad affairs, 73-76, prof English, Calif State Univ, Fresno, 67-. **HONORS AND AWARDS** Lambda Literary Awards, 91, 94; ALA awards, 81, 91. **MEMBERSHIPS** MLA. **RESEARCH** Gay studies; American ethnic writing; women's studies. **SELECTED PUBLICATIONS** Auth, Odd Girls and Twilight Lovers: A History of Lesbian Life in Twentieth Century America, 91; ed, Chloe Plus Olivia: An Anthology of Lesbian Literature from the Seventeenth Century to the Present, 94; auth, I Begin My Life All Over: The Hmong and the American Immigrant Experience, 98. **CONTACT ADDRESS** Dept of English, California State Univ, Fresno, 5245 N Baker, Fresno, CA, 93740-8001. **EMAIL** lillian_faderman@csufresno.edu

FAGLES, ROBERT
PERSONAL Born 09/11/1933, Philadelphia, PA, m, 1956, 2 children **DISCIPLINE** COMPARATIVE LITERATURE, ENGLISH **EDUCATION** Amherst Col, AB, 55; Yale Univ, MA, 56, PhD (English), 59. **CAREER** Instr English, Yale Univ, 59-60; from instr to asst prof, 60-65, assoc prof English and comp lit, 65-70, dir prog comp lit, 65-76, PROF ENGLISH and COMPLIT, PRINCETON UNIV, 70-. **RESEARCH** The epic tradition; Greek tragedy; Greek, Latin and English lyric poetry. **SELECTED PUBLICATIONS** Auth, Rain, Steam, and Speed, Sewanee Rev, Vol 101, 93; The Pair Oared Shell, Sewanee Rev, Vol 101, 93. **CONTACT ADDRESS** Dept of English and Comp Lit, Princeton Univ, Princeton, NJ, 08540.

FAGUNDO, ANA MARIA
PERSONAL Born 03/13/1938, Santa Cruz de Tenerife, Spain **DISCIPLINE** COMPARATIVE LITERATURE, SPANISH AND ENGLISH LITERATURE **EDUCATION** Univ Redlands, BA, 62; Univ Wash, MA, 64, PhD (comp lit), 67. **CAREER** Asst prof Span lit, 67-76, ASSOC PROF CONTEMP SPAN LIT, UNIV CALIF, RIVERSIDE, 76-, Ed-in-Chief, Alaluz. **HONORS AND AWARDS** Carabela de Oro poetry prize. **MEMBERSHIPS** Am Asn Teachers Span and Port; Sociedad Colegial de Escritores. **RESEARCH** Contemporary Spanish poetry; contemporary American poetry. **SELECTED PUBLICATIONS** Auth, Cantico or a Tribute to Mother, Insula Revista De Letras Y Ciencias Humanas, Vol 48, 93. **CONTACT ADDRESS** Dept of Span, Univ Calif, Riverside, CA, 92502.

FAIGLEY, LESTER
PERSONAL Charleston, WV, m, 1969, 2 children **DISCIPLINE** ENGLISH; LINGUISTICS **EDUCATION** Univ Wash, PhD, 76. **CAREER** Prof English, Univ Tex at Austin, 79-; Dir, Div of Rhet & Composition. **HONORS AND AWARDS** MLA Mina P Shaughnessy Prize, 92; Conf of Col Composition & Commun Outstanding Book Award, 94. **MEMBERSHIPS** Conf of Col Composition & Commun; Modern Language Asn; Rhet Soc of Am. **RESEARCH** Rhetorical theory; impacts of technology on writing; visual rhetoric. **SELECTED PUBLICATIONS** Auth, Fragments of Rationality: Postmodernity and the Subject of Composition, Univ Pittsburgh Press, 92; auth, Yours for the Revolution (probably Pepsi, but never mind), J of Adv Composition, 14, 593-596, 94; co-auth, Going Electric: Creating Multiple Site for Innovation in a Writing Program, Resituating Writing: Constructing and Administering Writing Programs, Boynton/Cook, 46-58, 95; co-auth, Discursive Strategies for Social Change: An Alternative Rhetoric of Argument, Rhet Rev, 14, 142-72; 95; auth, Literacy After the Revolution, Col Composition & Commun, 48, 30-43, 97. **CONTACT ADDRESS** Div of Rhet & Composition, Univ Tex at Austin, Austin, TX, 78712-1122. **EMAIL** faigley@uts.cc.utexas.edu

FAIRBANKS, CAROL
PERSONAL 3 children **DISCIPLINE** ENGLISH LITERATURE **EDUCATION** Univ Mich, BA; Univ Wis Eau Claire, MA; Univ Minn, PhD. **CAREER** Fac. **RESEARCH** Japanese women fiction writers in translation. **SELECTED PUBLICATIONS** Auth, seven books: two on African-American writers, two on women in literature, and three on American and Canadian farm women in literature. **CONTACT ADDRESS** Dept of English, Univ of Wisconsin, Eau Claire, Hibbard Hall 359, PO Box 4004, Eau Claire, WI, 54702-4004. **EMAIL** fairbacf@uwec.edu

FAIRLEY, IRENE R.
PERSONAL Born 01/02/1940, Brooklyn, NY **DISCIPLINE** LINGUISTICS, ENGLISH **EDUCATION** Queens Col, NY, AB, 60; Harvard Univ, MA, 61, PhD (ling), 71. **CAREER** From instr to asst prof English, C W Post Col, Long Island Univ, 68-73; asst prof English and ling, 73-76, ASSOC PROF ENGLISH, NORTHEASTERN UNIV, 76-, Am Coun Learned Soc grant-in-aid, 77-78; Guggenheim fel, 79-80. **MEMBERSHIPS** Ling Soc Am; MLA; Semiotic Soc Am; Millay Colony for Arts. **RESEARCH** Linguistic approaches to literature, stylistics, poetics. **SELECTED PUBLICATIONS** Auth, Millay, Edna, Stvincent Gendered Language and Form, Sonnets from an Ungrafted Tree, Style, Vol 29, 95. **CONTACT ADDRESS** 34 Winn St, Belmont, MA, 02178.

FALK, THOMAS HEINRICH
PERSONAL Born 09/25/1935, Frankfurt, Germany, m, 1967, 2 children **DISCIPLINE** CONTEMPORARY LITERATURE **EDUCATION** Wagner Col, BA, 58; Univ S Calif, AM, 63, PhD, 70. **CAREER** Instr, 65-70, asst prof, 70-79, assoc prof, 79-92, ASSOC PROF EMER DEPT LINGUISTICS & LANGUAGES-GERMAN, MICH STATE UNIV. **MEMBERSHIPS** Am Asn Tchr Ger **RESEARCH** Contemporary Literature **SELECTED PUBLICATIONS** auth Elias Canetti: A Critical Study, 93. **CONTACT ADDRESS** Thomas Heinrich Falk, 2100 E Holt Rd, Williamston, MI, 48895. **EMAIL** falk@pilot.msu.edu

FALLER, GREG
DISCIPLINE FILM, MEDIA AND CULTURAL STUDIES **EDUCATION** Northwestern Univ, PhD, 87. **CAREER** Instr, Towson Univ; coordr, TU Stud Media Arts Festival, MCOM grad prog. **MEMBERSHIPS** Coordr, TU Film & Video Soc; SCS; UFVA; L/FA. **SELECTED PUBLICATIONS** Essayist and advisor of an internattional film dictionary (St James Press). **CONTACT ADDRESS** Towson Univ, Towson, MD, 21252-0001. **EMAIL** gfaller@towson.edu

FALLON, JEAN
DISCIPLINE 16TH CENTURY FRENCH LITERATURE, 19TH CENTURY POETRY **EDUCATION** Univ VA, PhD. **CAREER** Instr, Hollins Col, 90. **RESEARCH** French lyric poets of the 16th century. **SELECTED PUBLICATIONS** Auth, Voice and Vision in Ronsard's Les Sonnets pour Helene. **CONTACT ADDRESS** Hollins Col, Roanoke, VA, 24020.

FALLON, RICHARD GORDON
PERSONAL Born 09/17/1923, New York, NY, m, 1946, 2 children **DISCIPLINE** SPEECH & DRAMA **EDUCATION** Columbia Univ, BA, 48, MA, 51. **CAREER** Asst prof speech & theatre & dir theater, Hartwick Col, 48-51, Md State Teachers Col, 51-54; gen dir, Little Theater, Jacksonville, Fla, 54-56; asst prof speech & theater, 57-60, assoc prof theater, 60-65, dean sch theatre, 73-82, PROF SPEECH & THEATER & DIR THEATER, FLA STATE UNIV, 65-, EMER DEAN & DIR PROF PROGS, 82-, Gen dir, Asolo Theater Festival, 62; mem, Princeton Conf Theater Res, 66; chmn Theater Res Coun Am, 66-68; theater consult, New England Cols, 67; dir grant, Cult Enrichment Through Live Theatre, 67-69; dir, Burt Reynolds Inst Theatre Training. **HONORS AND AWARDS** Nat Conf Christians & Jews Gold Medal Award, 62; E Harris Harbison Award for Gifted Teaching, 71. **MEMBERSHIPS** Am Nat Theatre & Acad; Am Theatre Asn (pres-elect, 81-82, pres, 82-83); Speech Commun Asn; Nat Theatre Conf; Univ Resident Theatre Asn **RESEARCH** Development of cultural enrichment through live theatre in high schools of Florida; development of Eddie Dowling University Theatre Foundation for new playwrights; quantitative research in theater audiences in Miami, Florida. **SELECTED PUBLICATIONS** Assoc-ed, Works in progress, Theatre Documentation, 67. **CONTACT ADDRESS** Office of the Dean, Florida State Univ, 600 W College Ave, Tallahassee, FL, 32306-1096.

FALLON, ROBERT THOMAS
PERSONAL Born 06/06/1927, New York, NY, m, 1972, 2 children **DISCIPLINE** ENGLISH AND COMPARATIVE LITERATURE **EDUCATION** US Mil Acad, BS, 49; Canisius Col, MA, 60; Columbia Univ, PhD, 65. **CAREER** Asst prof English, US Mil Acad, 61-64; chmn dept mil sci, 69-70, asst to the pres, 70-71, assoc prof, 70-79, prof English, 79-95, PROF EMER, 95- , LASALLE COL, 79- ; neh FEL, 90-91. **HONORS AND AWARDS** James Holly Hanford Award, 94, Outstanding Acad Book, Choice, 96. **MEMBERSHIPS** Milton Soc Am (treas, 77-86, vpres, 87, & pres, 88); MLA; John Donne Soc; ALSC. **RESEARCH** John Milton--military and political imagery; English history -- The Interregnum; contrib ed, The Variorum Edition of the Poetry of John Donne. **SELECTED PUBLICATIONS** Auth, John Milton and the honorable artillery company, Milton Quart, 5/75; Filling the gaps: New perspectives on Mr Secretary Milton, Milton Studies XII, 78; Miltonic documents in the public records office, London, Studies Bibliog, 78; Milton's defenseless doors: The limits of irony, Milton Quart, 12/79; Milton in the anarchy, 1659-1660: A question of consistency, Studies English Lit, winter 81; Milton's Epics and the Spanish War: Toward a Poetics of Experience, In: Milton Studies XV, Univ Pittsburgh Press, 82; Captain or Colonel: The Soldier in Miltons Life and Art, Univ Missouri Press, 84; Milton in Government, Penn State Univ Press, 93; Divided Empire: Miltons Political Imagery, Penn State Univ Press, 95; Shakespeare: Appreciations for the Playgoer. **CONTACT ADDRESS** River Rd, Lumberville, PA, 18933. **EMAIL** fallon@lasalle.edu

FALLON, STEPHEN
DISCIPLINE LITERATURE **EDUCATION** Univ Va, PhD. **CAREER** Instr, Univ Notre Dame. **HONORS AND AWARDS** NEH fel. **RESEARCH** Philosophical and theological contexts of early modern poetry and prose. **SELECTED PUBLICATIONS** Auth, Milton among the Philosophers: Poetry and Materialism in Seventeenth-Century England. **CONTACT ADDRESS** Univ Notre Dame, Notre Dame, IN, 46556.

FANG, IRVING E.
PERSONAL Born 05/04/1929, New York, NY, d, 2 children **DISCIPLINE** SPEECH **EDUCATION** UCLA, PhD, 66. **CAREER** Eight years as a newspaper reporter & editor; one year with Reuters, London; eight years with ABC-TV News as news writer then as asst mgr of political unit; Porf, School of Journalism, Univ Minn, 69-. **HONORS AND AWARDS** Mitchell Charnley Award, 84; Distinguished Broadcast J Ed, Asn for Ed in Journalism and Mass Commun, 90; Fulbright Prof, Univ of the Philippines, 96-97. **RESEARCH** Broadcast journalism; history of media technology. **SELECTED PUBLICATIONS** Auth, A History of Mass Communication: Six Information Revolutions, Focal Press, 97; Television News, Radio News, Rada Press, 85; Those Radio Commentators, Iowa State Univ Press, 77. **CONTACT ADDRESS** School of Journalism and Mass Commun, Univ of Minn, Minneapolis, MN, 55455. **EMAIL** fangx001@tc.umn.edu

FANGER, DONALD LEE
PERSONAL Born 12/06/1929, Cleveland, OH, m, 1955, 3 children **DISCIPLINE** RUSSIAN & COMPARATIVE LITERATURE **EDUCATION** Univ CA, Berkeley, BA, 51, MA, 54; Harvard Univ, PhD, 62. **CAREER** Instr Russ lang & lit, Brown Univ, 60-62; from asst prof to assoc prof Russ lang & lit & dir Slavic Div, Stanford Univ, 66-68; chmn slavic dept, 73-82, Prof Slavic & Comp Lit, Harvard Univ, 68-98, Harry Levin Research Prof of Lit, 98-, Mem nat adv comt, Inter-Univ Comt Travel Grants, 67-68; Am Coun Learned Soc res grant, 68-69; mem prog comt, Int Res & Exchanges Bd, 69-73; Guggenheim fel, 75-76; fel, Am Acad Arts & Sci, 80-; res fel, Rockefeller Found Ctr Advan Study, Bellagio, summer 81. **HONORS AND AWARDS** Christian Gauss Award, Phi Beta Kappa, 80. **MEMBERSHIPS** MLA; Am Asn Tchr(s) Slavic & East Europ Lang; Am Comp Lit Asn, Am Acad of Arts & Sci. **RESEARCH** Develop of the Russ novel. **SELECTED PUBLICATIONS** Auth, Dostoevsky today, Survey, 4/61; Romanticism and comparative literature, Comp Lit, spring 62; ed, Brown Univ Slavic Reprint Series, 61-66; auth, Dostoevsky and Romantic Realism, Harvard Univ, 65 & Univ Chicago, 67; The Peasant in 19th Century Russia, Stanford Univ, 68; The Creation of Nikolai Gogol, Harvard Univ, 79. **CONTACT ADDRESS** Dept of Slavic Lang & Lit, Harvard Univ, Boylston Hall, Cambridge, MA, 02138-3800. **EMAIL** fanger@fas.harvard.edu

FANNING, CHARLES F.
DISCIPLINE ENGLISH **EDUCATION** Harvard Univ, BA, 64; MAT, 66; Univ Penn, MA, 68, PhD, 72. **CAREER** Assoc, prof, Eng, Bridgewater State Univ; current, PROF, ENG & HIST & DIR IRISH STUD, SO ILL UNIV CARBONDALE. **HONORS AND AWARDS** Am Book Award, 89; Am Conf for Irish Stud Book Prize for Lit Criticism, 91. **MEMBERSHIPS** Am Antiquarian Soc **SELECTED PUBLICATIONS** Auth, Finley Peter Dunne and Mr. Dooley: The Chicago Years, 78; auth, Mr. Dooley and the Chicago Irish: An Anthology, 76; ed, The Exiles of Erin: Nineteenth-Century Irish-American Fiction, Dofour Editions, 87 & 97; auth, The Irish Voice in America: Irish-American Fiction from the 1760s to the 1980s, 90. **CONTACT ADDRESS** Dept of Eng, So Ill Univ, Carbondale, IL, 62901. **EMAIL** celtic42@siu.edu

FARBER, CAROLE
DISCIPLINE COMMUNICATION STUDIES **EDUCATION** Univ British Columbia, BA; PhD. **RESEARCH** Feminist theory and pedagogy; social organization of anthropological knowledge; cultural studies; cultural performances. **SELECTED PUBLICATIONS** Auth, Subject Matters: Critical Essays in Feminist Teaching, Curriculum and Ethnography. **CONTACT ADDRESS** Dept of Communication, Western Ontario Univ, London, ON, N6A 5B8.

FARBER, GERALD HOWARD
PERSONAL Born 03/21/1935, El Paso, TX, m, 1967, 4 children **DISCIPLINE** COMPARATIVE LITERATURE, ENGLISH & AMERICAN LITERATURE **EDUCATION** Univ CA, Los Angeles, BA, 58; CA State Univ, Los Angeles, MA, 62; Occidental Col, PhD, 70. **CAREER** Lectr English, 62-65, asst prof, CA State Univ, Los Angeles, 66-68; from lectr to asst prof, 68-74, assoc prof, 74-81, PROF COMP LIT, SAN DIEGO STATE UNIV, 81-; Maitre assistant associe, 74 & maitre de conferences associe, 77, Univ Paris VII. **RESEARCH** Aesthetics; the teaching of literature; comedy; eighteenth-century European lit; Marcel Proust. **SELECTED PUBLICATIONS** Auth, The Student as Nigger, 70 & The University of Tomorrowland, 72, Simon & Schuster; A Field Guide to the Aesthetic Experience, Foreworks Press, 82; The Third Circle: On Education and Distance Learning, Sociological Perspectives, vol 41, no 4, 98; Aesthetic Resonance: Beyond the Sign in Literature, Reader: Essays in Reader-Oriented Theory, Criticism, and Pedagogy, no 32, fall, 94; Golden Grove Unweaving (and not a moment too soon), Fiction International, no 27, 94; Learning How To Teach: A Progress Report, College English, vol 52, no 2, Feb 90. **CONTACT ADDRESS** Dept of English and Comp Lit, San Diego State Univ, San Diego, CA, 92182-8140. **EMAIL** jfarber@mail.sdsu.edu

FARNHAM, ANTHONY EDWARD
PERSONAL Born 07/02/1930, Oakland, CA, m, 1957, 2 children **DISCIPLINE** ENGLISH, PHILOLOGY **EDUCATION** Univ Calif, Berkeley, AB, 51; Harvard Univ, MA, 57, PhD(English), 64. **CAREER** From instr to assoc prof, 61-72, PROF ENGLISH, MT HOLYOKE COL, 72-, Vis asst prof, Amherst Col, 64-65; lectr, Smith Col, 65-66; vis asst prof, Univ Calif, Berkeley, 66-67. **MEMBERSHIPS** Mediaeval Acad Am; MLA; Am Cath Hist Asn; Asn Literary Scholars & Critics; Dante Soc Am; New Chaucer Soc; Phi Beta Kappa **RESEARCH** Old and Middle English language and literature; history of the English language. **SELECTED PUBLICATIONS** Ed, A Sourcebook in the History of English, Holt, Rinehart & Winston, 69; auth, Statement and Search in the Confessio Amantis, Mediaevalia, 93. **CONTACT ADDRESS** Dept of English, Mount Holyoke Col, 50 College St, South Hadley, MA, 01075-1461.

FARR, JUDITH BANZER
PERSONAL Born 03/13/1937, New York, NY, m, 1962, 1 child **DISCIPLINE** ENGLISH & AMERICAN LITERATURE, AMERICAN PAINTING & LITERATURE **EDUCATION** Marymount Manhattan Col, BA, 57; Yale Univ, MA, 59, PhD(English & Am lit), 65. **CAREER** Instr English, Vassar Col, 61-63; asst prof, St Mary's Col, CA, 64-68; from asst prof to assoc prof, State Univ NY Col New Paltz, 68-76; vis assoc prof, assoc prof, 77-88, PROF ENGLISH, GEORGETOWN UNIV, 89-; State Univ NY res award fel, 72; grant-in-aid, Am coun Learned Soc, 74, 83, 86; Am Philos Soc Award, 86; Georgetown Univ Center for German Studies award, 93. **HONORS AND AWARDS** Alumnae Award for Achievement in Arts and Letts, Marymount-Manhattan Col, 76; Honorary LL D, Marymount Manhattan Col, 92. **MEMBERSHIPS** Cosmos Club. **RESEARCH** 19th century Am lit & painting; modern poetry & fiction; Brit fiction. **SELECTED PUBLICATIONS** Auth, The Passion of Emily Dickinson, Harvard Univ Press, 92; I Never Came to You in White: A Novel, Houghton Mifflin, 96; The Life and Art of Elinor Wylie, LA State Univ Press, 83; poems, fiction, & essays in professional & commercial publications; ed, Twentieth Century Interpretations of Sons and Lovers, Prentice-Hall, 69; Emily Dickinson: New Century Views, Simon & Schuster, 95. **CONTACT ADDRESS** English Dept, Georgetown Univ, Box 571131, Washington, DC, 20057-1131.

FARRAR, RONALD
PERSONAL AR, m, 2 children **DISCIPLINE** JOURNALISM AND MASS COMMUNICATIONS **EDUCATION** Univ AR, BS; Univ IA, MA; Univ MO, PhD. **CAREER** Reynolds-Faunt Memorial prof, Jour & assoc dean, Grad Stud & Res; worked as reporter, ed & mgr, newspapers in AR & IA; past dir, jour prog, Southern Methodist Univ, Univ MS & Univ KY. **RESEARCH** Media law; press hist; reporting; community journalism. **SELECTED PUBLICATIONS** Auth, 6 bk(s). **CONTACT ADDRESS** Col of Journalism & Mass Commun, Univy of S. Carolina, Carolina Coliseum rm 2044, Columbia, SC, 29208. **EMAIL** ron_farrar@jour.sc.edu

FARRED, GRANT
DISCIPLINE ENGLISH **EDUCATION** Univ Western Cape, South Africa, BA, 87 & 88; Columbia Univ, MA, 90; Princeton Univ, PhD, 96. **CAREER** Vis asst prof. **RESEARCH** South African literature and politics; contemporary African-American film, with a special focus on postcolonialism; cultural studies and the construction of intellectuals. **SELECTED PUBLICATIONS** Auth, What's My Name: Vernacular and Organic Intellectuals; First Stop Port-au-Prince: Mapping Postcolonial Africa Through Tousssaint L'Ouverture and his Black Jacobins; It's an X-Thing: The Culture of Black Nationalism in Contemporary South Africa; The Intellectual As Outsider; Take Back The Mike: Producing a Language for Date Rape. **CONTACT ADDRESS** Dept of English, Williams Col, B-10 Stetson, Williamstown, MA, 01267. **EMAIL** gfarred@williams.edu

FARRELL, JOHN PHILIP
PERSONAL Born 11/19/1939, New York, NY, m, 1964, 2 children **DISCIPLINE** ENGLISH **EDUCATION** Fordham Univ, BA, 61; Ind Univ, PhD(English), 67. **CAREER** From asst prof English to assoc prof, Univ Kans, 66-74; from assoc prof to prof English, Univ Tex, 74-83, **HONORS AND AWARDS** Outstanding Fac Mem, Col of Humanities, Univ Tex, 77; Nat Endowment for Humanities younger humanist fel, 72-73; Am Coun Learned Soc fel, 81. **RESEARCH** Victorian literature; modern American poetry. **SELECTED PUBLICATIONS** Auth, Hamlet's Final Role, Bucknell Rev, 5/66; Mathew Arnold's Tragic Vision, Publ of the Mod Lang Asn of Am, 70; The Beautiful Changes in Richard Wilbur's Poetry, Contemporary Lit, 71; Arnold, Byron and Taine, English Studies, 10/74; Revolution as Tragedy: The Dilemma of the Moderate from Scott to Arnold, Cronell Univ Press, 80; Reading the Text of Community in Wuthering Heights, ELH, 89; Dickens and Our Mutual Friend, ELH, 99. **CONTACT ADDRESS** Dept of English, Univ of Texas, Austin, TX, 78712-1026. **EMAIL** farrel@utexas.edu

FAULKNER, THOMAS CORWIN
PERSONAL Born 01/02/1941, Celina, OH, m, 1977 **DISCIPLINE** ENGLISH LITERATURE **EDUCATION** Hope Col, BA, 62; Miami Univ, MA, 64; Univ Wis, Madison, PhD(English), 72. **CAREER** Instr English, Wis State Univ, Whitewater, 64-67; lectr, Loyola Col, Montreal, 67-71; asst prof, 71-76, assoc prof, 76-81, prof English, Wash State Univ, 81-, dir, Humanities Res Ctr, Washington State Univ, 80-. **HONORS AND AWARDS** W K Kellogg Nat fel, 81-84. **MEMBERSHIPS** MLA; Am Soc Eighteenth-Century Studies; Bibliog Soc Am; Bibliog Soc, London; Renaissance Soc Am. **RESEARCH** Iconography and literature; eighteenth-century English literature; bibliography and textual editing. **SELECTED PUBLICATIONS** Auth, Halifax's The Character of a Trimmer and L'Estrange's Attack on Trimmers in the Observator, Huntington Libr Quart, 73; Letters of George Crabbe and Francis Fulford, Rev English Studies, 75; George Crabbe: Murray's 1834 edition of the life and poems, Studies Bibliog, 78; coauth, The Classical and Mythographic Sources of Pope's Dulness, Huntington Libr Quart, 80; auth, Computer Applications for an edition of Robert Burton's The Anatomy of Melancholy: A System for Scholarly Publishing, Comput & the Humanities, 81; ed, The Letters and Journals of George Crabbe, Oxford, Clarendon, 85; ed, Robert Burton, The Anatomy of Melancholy, 3 vols, Oxford, Clarendon, 89-94. **CONTACT ADDRESS** Dept of English, Wash State Univ, PO Box 645020, Pullman, WA, 99164-5020. **EMAIL** rlblair@wsu.edu

FAVOR, J. MARTIN
DISCIPLINE ENGLISH LITERATURE **EDUCATION** Univ MI Ann Arbor, PhD, 93. **CAREER** Asst prof, Dartmouth Col. **RESEARCH** Eng and African lit; African Am Studies. **SELECTED PUBLICATIONS** Auth, Ain't Nothin Like the Real Thing, Baby: Trey Ellis' Search for New Black Voices; Callaloo, 93; Inventions of Africa: A Selective Bibliography in Ann Arbor: Center for Afro-American and African Studies, Univ MI, 92. **CONTACT ADDRESS** Dartmouth Col, 3529 N Main St, #207, Hanover, NH, 03755.

FAWZIA, MUSTAFA
DISCIPLINE POST-COLONIAL LITERATURES **EDUCATION** IN Univ, PhD. **CAREER** Assoc prof, Fordham Univ. **RESEARCH** Cult studies, contemp critical theory. **SELECTED PUBLICATIONS** Auth, V.S. Naipaul, Cambridge UP, 95. **CONTACT ADDRESS** Dept of Eng Lang and Lit, Fordham Univ, 113 W 60th St, New York, NY, 10023.

FEARN-BANKS, KATHLEEN
PERSONAL Born 11/21/1941, Chattanooga, TN, d **DISCIPLINE** COMMUNICATIONS **EDUCATION** Wayne State Univ, BA, Journalism, 1964; UCLA, MS, Journalism, 1965; University of Southern California, Los Angeles, CA, ABD for PhD, 1978-81. **CAREER** NBC Publicity Dept, mgr, media relations, 1969-90; KNXT-TV News LA, newswriter, producer, 1968-69; Los Angeles Ctn Coll, instructor, Journalism, English, Creative Writing, 1965-; Los Angeles Times, Feature Writer, 1968; University of Washington, Seattle, WA, asst professor, 1990-; freelance motion picture publicist, currently. **HONORS AND AWARDS** CA Sun Magazine writers Award, UCLA 1965; Will Rogers Fellowship, UCLA, 1964-65. **MEMBERSHIPS** Member, Public Relations Society of America 1989-; mem, Writers Guild Amer; mem, Publicists Guild; member, Acad of TV & Sciences; bd of dir, vice pres, Neighbors of Watts; mem, Delta Sigma Theta Sorority, chapter vp; member, Association for Education in Journalism & Mass Comm, 1990-.

SELECTED PUBLICATIONS Numerous freelance magazine & journal articles; 3 Textbooks, The Story of Western Man, co-authored w/David Burleigh; Woman of the Year, Los Angeles Sentinel (newspaper) 1986; Author: Crisis Communications; A Case Book Approach; Teacher of the Year, School of Communications, University of Washington, 1993, 1995. **CONTACT ADDRESS** Univ of Washington, DS-40, Seattle, WA, 98101.

FEARNOW, MARK
PERSONAL Born 01/24/1958, Wabash, IN, s **DISCIPLINE** THEATRE AND DRAMA **EDUCATION** Indiana Univ, PhD, 90. **CAREER** Lehigh Univ, 90-91; Penn State Univ, 91-98. **MEMBERSHIPS** Amer Soc Theatre Res; Asn Theatre in Higher Educ; Lit Mgr and Drama of the Amer. **RESEARCH** Twentieth century Amer theatre; riots as theatre. **SELECTED PUBLICATIONS** The American Stage and the Great Depression, Cambridge, 97; Clare Booth Luce, Greenwood, 95. **CONTACT ADDRESS** 103 Arts Bldg., University Park, PA, 16802. **EMAIL** maf8@psu.edu

FEDDER, NORMAN JOSEPH
PERSONAL Born 01/26/1934, New York, NY, m, 1955, 2 children **DISCIPLINE** PLAYWRITING, DRAMA THERAPY **EDUCATION** Brooklyn Col, BA, 55; Columbia Univ, MA, 56; NY Univ, PhD, 62. **CAREER** Asst prof English, Trenton State Col, 60-61; assoc prof English & speech, Ind State Col, Pa, 61-64; assoc prof English, Fla Atlantic Univ, 64-67; assoc prof drama, Univ Ariz, 67-70; assoc prof, 70-80, prof speech & theatre, Kansas State Univ, 80-89, Distinguished prof, 89-, Registered Drama Therapist/Board Certified Trainer, 89-, chmn, Relig and Theatre Prog, Am Theatre Asn, 75-80; pres, Kans Asn Relig Communities and the Arts, 76-77; mem, Theatre Adv Bd, Kans Arts Comn, 76-81; dir, Israel Theatre Program, 95. **HONORS AND AWARDS** Kans Bicentennial Comn, 75-76; Nat Found Jewish Culture, 77-78 Res; Outstanding Teacher Award, 88; Kansas Theatre Hall of Fame, 90. **MEMBERSHIPS** Assoc for Theatre in Higher Education, National Assoc for Drama Therapy (Board of Directors), Jewish Theatre Asn. **RESEARCH** Jewish Theatre; playwriting; creative dramatics, drama therapy. **SELECTED PUBLICATIONS** Auth, We Can Make Our Lives Sublime, produced by CBS TV, 70; The Planter May Weep, produced by Univ Judaism, 70; Some Events Connected with the Early History of Arizona, produced by Ariz Pioneers Hist Soc, Kans State Univ & Sacramento State Col, 70; Earp!, produced by Kans State Hist Theatre, 71, Manhattan Civic Theatre, 78; Tennessee Williams' Dramatic Technique, In: Tennessee Williams: A tribute, Univ Miss, 77, reprinted, 80; The Betryal, Baker's Plays, Boston, 78; A Jew in Kansas, produced by National Jewish Theatre Festival, New York, 80; The Buck Stops Here!, produced by AMAS Repertory Theatre, New York, 83; Out of the Depths, produced by Univ of Tx--El Paso, 98. **CONTACT ADDRESS** Dept of Speech, Communication, Theatre and Dance, Kansas State Univ, 129 Nichols Hall, Manhattan, KS, 66506-2301. **EMAIL** fedder@ksu.edu

FEDERMAN, RAYMOND
PERSONAL Born 05/15/1928, Paris, France, m, 1960, 1 child **DISCIPLINE** ENGLISH, COMPARATIVE LITERATURE **EDUCATION** Columbia Univ, BS, 57; Univ Calif, MA, 59, PhD, 63. **CAREER** Tchg asst French, Univ CA, Los Angeles, 57-59; lectr, Univ CA, Santa Barbara, 59-62, asst prof, 62-64; from Assoc Prof to Prof French, 64-68, Prof English & Comp Lit, 73-90, Distinguished Prof Eng and Comp Lit, State Univ NY-Buffalo, 90-, Melodia E. Jones Ch of Lit, 94-; mem bd consult, Coord Coun Lit Mags, 73-76. **HONORS AND AWARDS** Guggenheim fel, 66-67; Frances Steloff Fiction Prize, 71; Panache Exp Fiction Prize, 72; Fulbright Fel, Israel, 82-83; NEH Fel/Fiction, 86; Am Bk Award, 86; DAAD Fel, Berlin, 89-90. **MEMBERSHIPS** PEN Am; MLA; Am Comp Lit Asn; Am Asn Tchr(s) Fr. **RESEARCH** Twentieth century French lit; contemp fiction; creative writing. **SELECTED PUBLICATIONS** Auth, Double or nothing (novel), 71 & ed, Surfiction (essays on modern fiction), 75, Swallow; auth, Amer Eldorado (novel), Ed Stock, 74; Take it or leave it (novel), Fiction Collective, 76; Me too (poems), Westcoast Rev, 76; co-ed, Cahier de L'herne: Samuel Beckett, Eds L'Herne Paris-France, 77; auth, Imagination as plagiarism, New Lit Hist, 77; The voice in the closet (fiction), Tri-Quart, 77; The Two Fold Vilration (novel), Ind Univ Press, 82; Smiles on Washington Square, 85; To Whom it May Concern, 90; CRITIFICTION, 94; La Fourrure de una Taute Rachel, 96. **CONTACT ADDRESS** Dept of Eng, State Univ NY, PO Box 604610, Buffalo, NY, 14260-4610. **EMAIL** moinous@aol.com

FEENEY, JOSEPH JOHN
PERSONAL Born 10/08/1934, Philadelphia, PA **DISCIPLINE** AMERICAN & MODERN BRITISH LITERATURE **EDUCATION** Fordham Univ, AB, 58, MA, 61; Woodstock Col, STB, 64, STL, 66; Univ Pa, PhD, 71. **CAREER** Teacher English & math, St Joseph's Prep Sch, 59-60; teacher English & Latin, Loyola High Sch, Md, 60-62; from lectr to assoc prof, 69-83, prof Eng, St Joseph's Univ, PA, 83-, Trustee, St Joseph's Prep Sch, 76-82, Fordham Univ, 94-, Loyola Sch (NYC), 97-; vis prof Georgetwon Univ, 86-87; vis prof, Santa Clara Univ, 98. **HONORS AND AWARDS** Lindback Award for Distinguished Teaching, 83; Apha Sigma Nu, 88. **MEMBERSHIPS** MLA; Northeast Mod Lang Assn; AAUP; Int Hopkins Assn; Am Cult Assn. **RESEARCH** American novel; G M Hopkins; Politics, war and the American imagination, 1900-1935. **SELECTED PUBLICATIONS** art, His Father's Son: Common Traits in the Writing of Manley Hopkins and Gerard Manley Hopkins, Gerard Manley Hopkins and Critical Discourse, AMS Press, 93; auth, Hopkins: A Religious and a Secular Poet, Studies, Dublin, 95; auth, My dearest Father: Some unpublished letters of Gerard Manley Hopkins, TLS: The Times Literary Supplement, 95; auth, The Bischoff Collection at Gonzaga University: A Preliminary Account, The Hopkins Quarterly, 96; auth, I Do Otherwise: Hopkins' Patterns of Creativity, Studies, Dublin, 97; auth, Martin McDonagh: Dramatist of the West, Studies, Dublin, 98; **CONTACT ADDRESS** Dept of English, St. Joseph's Univ, 5600 City Ave, Philadelphia, PA, 19131-1376. **EMAIL** jfeeney@sju.edu

FEIN, RICHARD J.
PERSONAL Born 12/05/1929, Brooklyn, NY, m, 1955, 2 children **DISCIPLINE** ENGLISH **EDUCATION** Brooklyn Col, BA, 53, MA, 55; NY Univ, PhD, 60. **CAREER** Teaching fel, NY Univ, 56-57; lectr English, Hunter Col, 58-60; instr, Fairleigh Dickinson Univ, 60-61; asst prof, Univ PR, 61-63; from asst prof to assoc prof, 63-77, PROF ENGLISH, STATE UNIV NY COL NEW PALTZ, 77-, Fulbright lectr Am lit, Univ Madras, India, 71-72. **HONORS AND AWARDS** Founders' Day Distinguished Scholar Award, NY Univ, 61. **MEMBERSHIPS** MLA. **RESEARCH** Am Lit; modern Jewish literature. **SELECTED PUBLICATIONS** Auth, Glatshteyn, Yankev Critical Motive , Yiddish, Vol 9,94. **CONTACT ADDRESS** Dept of English, State Univ of NY Col, New Paltz, NY, 12561.

FEINBERG, LEONARD
PERSONAL Born 08/26/1914, Vitebsk, Russia, m, 1938, 1 child **DISCIPLINE** ENGLISH **EDUCATION** Univ Ill, PhD (English), 46. **CAREER** Instr English, Univ Ill, 38-43; from asst prof to assoc prof, 46-57, PROF ENGLISH, IOWA STATE UNIV, 57-, DISTINGUISHED PROF, 73-, Lectr Am lit, Univ Ceylon, 57-58. **MEMBERSHIPS** Satire. **RESEARCH** Humor of the world. **SELECTED PUBLICATIONS** Auth, Vickery, Walter, Neef, 1921-1995, Slavic Rev, Vol 55, 96. **CONTACT ADDRESS** Dept of English, Iowa State Univ, Ames, IA, 50011.

FEINSTEIN, HERBERT CHARLES VERSCHLEISSER
PERSONAL Born 05/28/1927, New York, NY **DISCIPLINE** ENGLISH, MASS MEDIA OF COMMUNICATIONS **EDUCATION** Columbia Univ, AB, 48; Harvard Univ, JD, 51; Univ Calif, Berkeley, MA, 59, PhD, 68. **CAREER** Lawyer, Admiralty law off, Harry Kisloff, Boston, 51-53; mem res coun, Fund for Repub, Harvard Law Sch, 53-54; corp lawyer & adminr, Music Corp Am, Universal Studios, Calif, 55-56; lectr speech, Univ Calif, Berkeley, 57-59; asst prof English & jour, 59-66, assoc prof English, 66-72, PROF ENGLISH, SAN FRANCISCO STATE UNIV, 72-; Admitted to law practice, Bar of Mass, 51 & Calif, 55; mem, Fed Int Presse Cinematographique, 67-; Am Coun Learned Soc fel, 69-70, grant-in-aid, 72; Huntington Libr & Art Gallery fel, 73, film consult, 73-; lectr & tutor, Nat Film Sch, Eng, 74. **MEMBERSHIPS** MLA; Am Judicature Soc; Am Bar Asn; Am Studies Asn. **RESEARCH** Clemens scholarship; mass media communications, especially films; relationship between literature and the law. **SELECTED PUBLICATIONS** Auth, Two pair of gloves: Mark Twain and Henry James, Am Imago, winter 60; Mark Twain and the pirates, Harvard Law Sch Bull, 4/62; 3 in search of cinema, Columbia Univ Forum, summer 65. **CONTACT ADDRESS** Dept of English, San Francisco State Univ, 1600 Holloway Ave, San Francisco, CA, 94132-1740.

FELDMAN, IRVING
PERSONAL Born 09/22/1928, Brooklyn, NY, m, 1955, 1 child **DISCIPLINE** ENGLISH LITERATURE **EDUCATION** City Col NY, BS, 50; Columbia Univ, MA, 53. **CAREER** Instr English & Humanities, Univ PR, 54-56; asst prof English, Kenyon Col, 58-64; assoc prof, 64-68, prof English, State Univ NY, Buffalo, 68-, Fulbright scholar, 56; Ingram Merrill Found grant, 63; Guggenheim fel, 73-74; Creative Artists Pub Serv grant, 80. **HONORS AND AWARDS** Kovner Mem Award, Jewish Bk Counc Am, 62; Nat Inst Arts & Lett Award, 73; The Poetry of Irving Feldman: Nine Essays, Bucknell Univ Press, 92. **SELECTED PUBLICATIONS** Auth, Works and days, and other poems, Atlantic Monthly, 61; The Pripet Marshes, and other poems, Viking, 65; Magic Papers and other poems, Harper, 70; Lost Originals (poems), Holt, 72; Leaping Clear and other poems, Viking, 76; New and Selected Poems, Viking, 79; All of Us Here, Press of Appletree Alley, Lewisburg PA, 91 (reprint); The Life and Letters, Univ of Chicago, 94. **CONTACT ADDRESS** Dept of English, SUNY, Buffalo, PO Box 604610, Buffalo, NY, 14260-4610.

FELDMAN, PAULA R.
PERSONAL Born 07/04/1948, Washington, DC **DISCIPLINE** BRITISH LITERARY HISTORY, ENGLISH ROMANTICISM **EDUCATION** Bucknell Univ, BA, 70; Northwestern Univ, MA, 71, PhD (English), 74. **CAREER** Asst prof, 74-79, ASSOC PROF ENGLISH, UNIV SC, 79-. **MEMBERSHIPS** MLA; Byron Soc; Asn Documentary Editing; Keats Shelley Asn Am. **RESEARCH** English romanticism; biography. **SELECTED PUBLICATIONS** Auth, Hemans, Felicia and the Mythologizing of Blake Death, Blake Illustrated Quart, Vol 27, 94; The Poet and the Profits, Keats Shelley J, Vol 46, 97. **CONTACT ADDRESS** Dept of English, Univ of SC, Columbia, SC, 29208.

FELLUGA, DINO
DISCIPLINE ENGLISH LITERATURE **EDUCATION** Univ of Nice, France, 87; Univ Western Ont, BA, 89; Queen's Univ, MA, 90; UCLA, Santa Barbara, PhD, 95. **CAREER** Asst prof, Purdue Univ, 97-; asst ed, Romanticism on the Net. **HONORS AND AWARDS** Dissertation fel, Soc Sci and Hum Res Coun, 90-94; dissertation fel, postdoctoral fel, Univ Calgary, 94-95; postdoctoral fel; Stanford Univ, 95-97., Robert Poulet Prize, 87; Shakespeare Award, 87; Percivl Prize, 86, KIVO. **MEMBERSHIPS** Mem, MLA; Can Asn of Univ Tchr; Pacific Ancient and Mod Lang Asn; Brit Asn for Romantic Stud; North Am Soc for the Stud of Romanticism. **RESEARCH** The influence of popular narrative forms like the novel on British poetry from the beginning to the end of the nineteenth century. **SELECTED PUBLICATIONS** Auth, The Critic's New Clothes: Sartor Resartus as Cold Carnival, Criticism 37, 95; Tennyson's Idylls, Pure Poetry and the Market, SEL: Stud in Eng Lit 37, 97; Holocaust Iconoclasm and the Crisis of Representation, Theory and Psychol 7, 97. **CONTACT ADDRESS** Dept of Eng, Purdue Univ, 1080 Schleman Hall, West Lafayette, IN, 47907-1080. **EMAIL** felluga@omni.cc.purdue.edu

FELSTINER, JOHN
PERSONAL Born 07/05/1936, Mt. Vernon, NY, m, 1966 **DISCIPLINE** VERSE TRANSLATION, MODERN LITERATURE **EDUCATION** Harvard Univ, BA, 58, PhD (English), 65. **CAREER** Asst prof, 65-72, assoc prof, 72-79, PROF ENGLISH, STANFORD UNIV, 79-, Fulbright lectr Am Lit, Univ Chile, 67-68; Nat Endowment for Humanities jr fel, 71-72; vis prof English, Hebrew Univ, Jerusalem, 74-75; Rockefeller Found humanities fel, 80-81; Mem Found Jewish Cult scholar, 80-81. **HONORS AND AWARDS** Kenyon Rev Prize in Criticism, 67; Gold Medal Non-Fiction, Calif Commonwealth Club, 80. **MEMBERSHIPS** MLA; Latin Am Studies Asn; Asn Jewish Studies. **RESEARCH** Holocaust literature. **SELECTED PUBLICATIONS** Auth, Celan, Paul--Holograms of Darkness, Compar Lit, Vol 45, 93; Translation as Reversion--Celan, Paul Jerusalem Poems, Judaism, Vol 43, 94. **CONTACT ADDRESS** Dept of English, Stanford Univ, Stanford, CA, 94305-1926.

FELTES, NORMAN NICHOLAS
PERSONAL Born 03/20/1932, Chicago, IL, m, 1959, 3 children **DISCIPLINE** ENGLISH **EDUCATION** Univ Notre Dame, AB, 53; Univ Col, Dublin, MA, 57; Oxford Univ, BLitt, 59. **CAREER** Lectr English, Univ Col, Dublin, 60; asst prof, Loyola Col, Que, 60-63; asst prof, Kenyon Col, 63-65; asst prof, Emory Univ, 65-69; ASSOC PROF ENGLISH, YORK UNIV, 69-. **MEMBERSHIPS** MLA; Can Asn Univ Teachers; Asn Can Univ Teachers English. **RESEARCH** Victorian prose; Victorian fiction and social history; Marxist history criticism. **SELECTED PUBLICATIONS** Auth, Voyageuse, Gender and Gaze in the Canoe Paintings of Hopkins, Frances, Anne, Ariel Rev Int Eng Lit, Vol 24, 93; Visions of the People, Industrial England and the Question of Class, 1840-1914, Victorian Stud, Vol 35, 92. **CONTACT ADDRESS** Dept of English, York Univ, Downsview, ON, M3J 1P3.

FELTON, SHARON
DISCIPLINE ENGLISH, MODERN BRITISH AND AMERICAN LITERATURE, TECHNICAL WRITING **EDUCATION** Purdue Univ, PhD, 90. **CAREER** Asst prof. **RESEARCH** Modern and contemp American lit; Mod and Contemp Brit lit; Philos, especially existentialism, Women's Studies. **SELECTED PUBLICATIONS** Auth, 4 entries in The Robert Frost Encycl, Westport: Greenwood, 98; Portraits of the Artists as Young Defiers: James Joyce and Muriel Spark, Tenn Philol J 33, 96; Joan Didion: A Writer of Scope and Substance, Hollins Critic 26 4, 89; The Lie and the Liar: A Linguistic and Literary Analysis, Conn Rev 13, 91; ed, The Critical Response to Joan Didion, Westport, CT: Greenwood Press, 94; co-ed, The Critical Response to Gloria Naylor, Westport: Greenwood, 97; bk rev in, Stud in Short Fiction, Miss Quart & Mod Fiction Stud; essays in Criticism, Amer Lit, Thalia & Stud in the Humanities. **CONTACT ADDRESS** Dept of English, Middle Tennessee State Univ, 1301 E Main St, Murfreesboro, TN, 37132-0001. **EMAIL** sfelton@frank.mtsu.edu

FENNELL, FRANCIS L.
DISCIPLINE ENGLISH **EDUCATION** Univ Rochester, BA, 64; Northwestern Univ, MA, 65, PhD, 68. **CAREER** Prof. **RESEARCH** Victorian literature; rhetoric and composition; pedagogy. **SELECTED PUBLICATIONS** Auth, Rereading Hopkins: Selected New Essays, Univ Victoria Pres, Can, 96; Ladies Loaf Givers: Food, Women, and Society in the Novels of Charlotte Bronte and George Eliot, in Keeping the Victorian House, Garland, 95. **CONTACT ADDRESS** Dept of English, Loyola Univ, Chicago, 6525 N. Sheridan Rd., Chicago, IL, 60626. **EMAIL** ffennel@wpo.it.luc.edu

FERGENSON, LARAINE RITA
PERSONAL Born 10/25/1944, Newark, NJ, m, 1967, 3 children **DISCIPLINE** ENGLISH & AMERICAN LITERATURE **EDUCATION** Smith Col, BA, 66; Columbia Univ, MA, 67, PhD(English lit), 71. **CAREER** Lectr English, 70-71, asst prof, 71-77, assoc prof, 77-81, Prof English, 82-, & Coord of Writing, 95-, Bronx Cummunity Col. **HONORS AND AWARDS** Phi Beta Kappa, 65; Magna cum Laude at graduation, 66; Clara French Prize (co-awarded), Smith Col; NDEA fel, 66-70; NEH summer fel, 76; Mellon fel, 82, 87; Special Service Award from Student Gov Asn, Bronx Col, 92. **MEMBERSHIPS** MLA: Col English Asn; Thoreau Soc; Wordsworth-Coleridge Asn; Phi Beta Kappa. **RESEARCH** Nineteenth-century American literature; British Romantic literature; developmental composition. **SELECTED PUBLICATIONS** Auth, Was Thoreau rereading Wordsworth in 1851?, Thoreau J Quart, 7/73; To teach or not to teach the research paper, J Improvement Instr, spring 76; Wild nectar: The language of Thoreau's poetry, Concord Saunterer, spring 77; coauth, The state of the profession: a dialogue on the job market, Col English Asn Forum, 10/77; auth, Teaching Wordsworth in the open admissions Classroom, Wordsworth circle, fall 78; Wordsworth and Thoreau: The relationship between man and nature, Thoreau J Quart, 4/79; Margaret Fuller: Transcendental feminist, Concord Saunterer, winter 80; coauth, All in One: Basic Writing Text, Workbook, and Reader, Prentice-Hall, 80, 86, 92, 99; Writing With Style: Rhetoric, Reader, Handbook, Holt, Rinehart and Winston, 89; Headnote on Susanna Haswell Rowson and ed selection from Charlotte, A Tale of Truth in The Heath Anthology of American Literature, D. C. Heath, 90, 2nd ed, 93; A Danish Appreciation of Thoreau: Jacob Paludan's Foreword to Livet i Skovene (Life in the Woods: Walden), The Thoreau Soc Bull, no 205, autumn 93; The Politics of Fear on a CUNY Campus, Midstream, vol XXXX, no 4, May 94; Group Defamation: From Language to Thought to Action, Group Defamation and Freedom of Speech: The Relationship Between Language and Violence, eds Eric and Monroe Freedman, Greenwood Press, 95; Teaching Thoreau's Civil Disobedience (or is it Resistence to Civil Government?) to Composition Students, forthcoming in Approaches to teaching Thoreau, ed Richard Schneider, modern Lang Asn pub; and many other articles and reviews. **CONTACT ADDRESS** Dept of English, Bronx Comm Col, CUNY, 181st St and University Ave, Bronx, NY, 10453. **EMAIL** lfergens@bellatlantic.net

FERGUSON, MARGARET WILLIAMS
PERSONAL Born 12/28/1948, Columbus, OH **DISCIPLINE** ENGLISH LITERATURE, COMPARATIVE LITERATURE **EDUCATION** Cornell Univ, BA, 69; Yale Univ, MPhil, 72, PhD (comp lit), 74. **CAREER** ASST PROF ENGLISH, YALE UNIV, 74-, Morse fel, Yale Univ, 77-78. **MEMBERSHIPS** MLA; Shakespeare Asn Am. **RESEARCH** Renaissance literature; literary theory. **SELECTED PUBLICATIONS** Auth, Dangerous Familiars--Representations of Domestic Crime in England, 1550-1700, Mod Philol, Vol 94, 96. **CONTACT ADDRESS** Dept of English, Yale Univ, New Haven, CT, 06520.

FERGUSON, OLIVER WATKINS
PERSONAL Born 06/07/1924, Nashville, TN, m, 1949, 2 children **DISCIPLINE** ENGLISH **EDUCATION** Vanderbilt Univ, BA, 47, MA, 48; Univ Ill, PhD (English), 54. **CAREER** Instr English, Univ Ark, 48-50; asst prof Ohio State Univ, 54-57; from asst prof to assoc prof, 57-67, chmn dept, 67-73, PROF ENGLISH, DUKE UNIV, 67-, Guggenheim fel, 63-64; assoc ed, S Atlantic Quart, 61-72, ed, 72-. **MEMBERSHIPS** MLA; S Atlantic Mod Lang Asn; Southeastern Am Soc 18th Century Studies; Am Soc 18th Century Studies. **RESEARCH** Eighteenth century English literature. **SELECTED PUBLICATIONS** Auth, Jonathans Travels--Swift and Ireland, Scriblerian and the Kit Cats, Vol 28, 95. **CONTACT ADDRESS** 1212 Arnette Ave, Durham, NC, 27707.

FERGUSON, ROBERT A.
DISCIPLINE AMERICAN LITERATURE **EDUCATION** Harvard Col, AB, 64; Harvard Law Sch, JD, 68; Harvard Univ, PhD, 74. **CAREER** Instr, Stanford, Harvard Univ; Andrew W Mellon prof, Univ Chicago; George Edward Woodberry prof-. **HONORS AND AWARDS** NEH fel; Nati Hum Ctr; Guggenheim found; Willard Hurst award, Law and Soc Assn. **RESEARCH** Courtroom trial as a central ceremony in American life. **SELECTED PUBLICATIONS** Auth, Law and Letters, Amer Cult, 84; The American Enlightenment, 1750-1829, 94. **CONTACT ADDRESS** Dept of Eng, Columbia Col, New York, 2960 Broadway, New York, NY, 10027-6902.

FERGUSON, SHERILYN
DISCIPLINE COMMUNICATION **EDUCATION** BS, MA, PhD. **CAREER** Prof, Univ Northern CO. **MEMBERSHIPS** Speech Commun Asn; Western Speech Commun Asn; Am Asn of Marriage and Family therapists. **RESEARCH** Single parent families; organizational restructuring. **SELECTED PUBLICATIONS** Coauth, Children's Expectations of their single parents dating bahaviors: A premliminary investigation of emergent themes revelant to single parent dating, J of Appl Commun Res 23, 95. **CONTACT ADDRESS** Univ Northern Colorado, Greeley, CO, 80639.

FERGUSON, SUZANNE
DISCIPLINE MODERN AMERICAN AND ENGLISH LITERATURE **EDUCATION** Converse Col, BA; Vanderbilt Univ, MA; Stanford Univ, PhD. **CAREER** English, Case Western Reserve Univ. **HONORS AND AWARDS** Chair, Engl Dept. **SELECTED PUBLICATIONS** Auth or ed, The Poetry of Randall Jarrell; Literature and the Visual Arts in Contemporary Society; Critical Essays on Randall Jarrell. **CONTACT ADDRESS** Case Western Reserve Univ, 10900 Euclid Ave, Cleveland, OH, 44106.

FERNANDES, JAMES
PERSONAL Born 01/18/1947, Lihue, HI, m, 1988, 3 children **DISCIPLINE** SPEECH COMMUNICATION **EDUCATION** Univ Michigan, PhD, 80. **CAREER** Prof, commun, 75-, dir univ outreach, 95-96, Gallaudet Univ; adj prof, Univ Hawaii, 87-95; dir, Gallaudet Univ Pacific Reg Ctr, Univ Hawaii, 87-95. **HONORS AND AWARDS** Phi Beta Kappa, 69; pres award, Gallaudet Univ, 86; Nat Assoc of the Deaf, Golden Hand Award, 95. **MEMBERSHIPS** Nat Assoc of the Deaf; Nat Commun Assoc; ADARA. **RESEARCH** Deaf American public address; communication pedagogy with deaf students. **SELECTED PUBLICATIONS** Coauth, Guide to Better Hearing: A Resource Manual, City of Honolulu/GTE, 94; coauth, Signs of Eloquence: Selections from Deaf American Public Address, in, Readings in the Language, Culture, History, and Arts of Deaf People: Selected Papers from the Deaf Way Conference, Gallaudet, 94; auth, Communication Cops and Language Police, in Garretson, ed, Deafness: Life and Culture II, National Association of the Deaf, 95; auth, Partners in Education, Gallaudet Today, 96; auth, Creative Problem Solving--From Top to Bottom, Speech Commun Tchr, 98. **CONTACT ADDRESS** Dept of Communication Arts, Gallaudet Univ, 800 Florida Ave NE, Washington, DC, 20002. **EMAIL** JFernandes@gallua.gallaudet.edu

FERNS, JOHN
DISCIPLINE ENGLISH LITERATURE **EDUCATION** Oxford Univ, BA; Univ Western Ontario, MA, PhD. **RESEARCH** Victorian, Canadian and modern British poetry; literary criticism. **SELECTED PUBLICATIONS** Auth, The Poetry of L.M. Montgomery, 87. **CONTACT ADDRESS** English Dept, McMaster Univ, 1280 Main St W, Hamilton, ON, L8S 4L9.

FERRARI, RITA
DISCIPLINE ENGLISH **EDUCATION** PhD. **CAREER** Eng Dept, St. Edward's Univ **SELECTED PUBLICATIONS** Auth, Innocence, Power, and the Novels of John Hawkes, Univ Pa Press, 96; The Innocent Imagination in John Hawkes' Whistlejacket and Virginie: Her Two Lives, Ariz Quart, 90; Masking, Revelation, and Fiction in Katherine Anne Porter's 'Flowering Judas' and 'Pale Horse, Pale Rider', Jour Short Story Eng, 95. **CONTACT ADDRESS** St Edward's Univ, 3001 S Congress Ave, Austin, TX, 78704-6489.

FERRARI, ROBERTO
DISCIPLINE HUMANITIES **EDUCATION** Univ S Fla, BA, 92, MA (Humanities), MA (Library Sci), 97. **CAREER** Adj prof, Hillsborough Community Col, 94-97; assoc dean libr, Art Inst Fort Lauderdale, 97-99; HUM REF LIBR, FLA ATLANTIC UNIV, 99-. **CONTACT ADDRESS** 881 NW 95th Terr, #1608, Plantation, FL, 33324. **EMAIL** 6095237c@bc.seflin.org

FERRARO, THOMAS J.
DISCIPLINE ENGLISH LITERATURE **EDUCATION** Yale Univ, PhD, 88. **CAREER** Prof, Duke Univ. **SELECTED PUBLICATIONS** Auth, Ethnic Passages: Literary Immigrants in 20th-Century America, Chicago, 93; Ethnicity and the Literary Marketplace in the Columbia History of American Novel, Columbia, 91; ed, Catholic Lives Contemporary America, Duke, 97. **CONTACT ADDRESS** Eng Dept, Duke Univ, Durham, NC, 27706.

FERRE, JOHN P.
PERSONAL Born 10/29/1956, Charlottesville, VA, m, 1985, 2 children **DISCIPLINE** COMMUNICATIONS **EDUCATION** Mars Hill Coll, BA, Relig, 77; Purdue Univ, MA, Commun, 78; Univ Chicago, MA, Divinity, 82; Univ Ill-Urbana Champaign, PhD, Commun, 86. **CAREER** Vis instr, Eng, Philos, Purdue Univ Calumet, 79-80; asst prof, Commun, Univ Louisville, 85-90, assoc prof, Commun, Univ Louisville, 90-98; PROF, COMMUN, UNIV LOUISVILLE, 98-. **MEMBERSHIPS** Am Jour Hist Asn; Asn Educ Jour & Mass Commun; Soc Profess Jou **RESEARCH** Ethical, religious, & historical dimensions of mass media in US **SELECTED PUBLICATIONS** coauth, Good News: Social Ethics and the Press, Oxford Univ Press, 93; coauth, "Charles E. Coughlin," Historical Dictionary of American Radio, Greenwood, 98; auth, "Suicide," Censorship, Salem Press, 97; "Foremost in Service, Best in Entertainment," Television in America: Local Station History from Across the Nation, Iowa State Univ Press, 97; "Should Churches Boycott?" The Banner, 96; "Western Recorder," Popular Religious Magazines, Greenwood, 95. **CONTACT ADDRESS** Dept Commun, Univ Louisville, Louisville, KY, 40292. **EMAIL** ferre@louisville.edu

FETTERLEY, JUDITH
PERSONAL Born 11/28/1938, New York, NY **DISCIPLINE** AM LIT, WOMEN'S STUDIES **EDUCATION** Swarthmore Col, BA, 60; Ind Univ, MA, 66, PhD (English), 69. **CAREER** Asst prof English, Univ Pa, 67-73; asst prof, 73-78, ASSOC PROF ENGLISH, STATE UNIV NY, ALBANY, 78-. **MEMBERSHIPS** Nat Women's Studies Asn; MLA. **RESEARCH** Nineteenth century Am Lit; American women writers; Mark Twain. **SELECTED PUBLICATIONS** Auth, Cultures of Letters, Scenes of Reading and Writing in 19th Century America, Mod Philol, Vol 93, 96; 19th Century American Women Writers in the 21st Century, Legacy, Vol 14, 97; Entitled to More than Particular Praise--The Extravagance of Cary, Alice Clovernook, Legacy, Vol 10, 93; Not in the Least American--19th Century Literary Regionalism, Coll Eng, Vol 56, 94; Cultures of Letters, Scenes of Reading and Writing in 19th Century America, Mod Philol, Vol 93, 96; Commentary, 19th Century American Women Writers and the Politics of Recovery, Am Lit Hist, Vol 6, 94. **CONTACT ADDRESS** Dept of English, State Univ of NY, Albany, NY, 12222.

FIEDLER, LESLIE AARON
PERSONAL Born 03/08/1917, Neward, NJ, m, 1973, 8 children **DISCIPLINE** ENGLISH LITERATURE **EDUCATION** NY Univ, AB, 38; Univ Wis, AM, 39, PhD, 41. **CAREER** Asst English, Univ Wis, 40-41; instr, Univ Mont, 41-43; Rockefeller fel humanities, Harvard Univ, 46-67; from asst prof English to prof, Univ Mont, 47-65 & chmn dept, 54-56; prof English, State Univ NY, Buffalo, 64-, Fulbright fel & lectr, Univs Rome & Bologna, Italy, 52-54; jr fel, Sch Let, Ind Univ, 53-; resident fel creative writing & Gauss lectr, Princeton Univ, 56-67; Kenyon Rev fel criticism, 56-67; Am Coun Learned Soc grants-in-aid, 60-61; Fulbright fel, Univ Athens, Greece, 61-62; assoc ed, Ramparts; English adv, St Martin's Press; lit ed, The Running Man; vis prof Am Studies, Univ Sussex, Eng, 68; assoc fel, Calhoun Co, Yale Univ, 70-; vis prof, Univ Vincennes, Paris, 71-72; Samuel Clemens Prof of English, State Univ NY, Buffalo, 72- **HONORS AND AWARDS** Mod Lang Asn Hubbell Medal for Lifetime Contribution to the Study of American Literature; elected to Am Acad and Inst of Arts and Letters; Nat Book Critics Circle Award for Lifetime Contribution to American Arts and Letters. **RESEARCH** The novel; 19th and 20th century American and British literature; humanities. **SELECTED PUBLICATIONS** Auth, The Second Stone; Love and Death in the American Novel, 66, Nude Croquet and Other Stories, 69, The Stranger in Shakespeare, 72 & The Messengers Will Come No More, 74, Stein & Day; Freaks: Myths and Images of the Secret Self, Simon & Schuster, 78; Tyranny of the Normal, 96. **CONTACT ADDRESS** Dept of English, Univ of NY, PO Box 604610, Buffalo, NY, 14260-4610.

FIELDS, BEVERLY
PERSONAL Born 12/07/1917, Chicago, IL, m, 1940, 2 children **DISCIPLINE** ENGLISH **EDUCATION** Northwestern Univ, BA, 39, MA, 58, PhD (English romantic lit), 65. **CAREER** Instr English, Lake Forest Col, 61-62 and Northwestern Univ, 62-65; asst prof, 65-69, ASSOC PROF, UNIV ILL, CHICAGO, 69-. **MEMBERSHIPS** MLA. **RESEARCH** English romantic literature; English and American contemporary literature; literary criticism. **SELECTED PUBLICATIONS** Auth, Scientologists and Nazis, NY Rev Bks, Vol 44, 97. **CONTACT ADDRESS** Dept of English, Univ Ill, Chicago, IL, 60680.

FIELDS, DARIN E.
DISCIPLINE AMERICAN LITERATURE **EDUCATION** Univ Ariz, BA, 86; Univ Delaware, MA, 89; PhD, 92. **CAREER** Asst prof, Univ Delaware, 92-93; ch, grad stud comm, 97-98; asst prof, 93-. **HONORS AND AWARDS** Alsie Schulman and Edmund Schulman Mem scholar, Univ Ariz, 86; tchg asstship, Univ Del, 87-89; res asstship, Univ Del, 89-91; Mellon res fel, Va Hist Soc, 91; fel, Univ Del, 91-62; outstanding fac award, 94. **MEMBERSHIPS** Mem, Amer Lit Assn; Amer Soc Eighteenth Century Stud; Assn Doc Ed; Mod Lang Assn; Soc Eighteenth Century Amer Stud; Soc Stud S Lit; Va Hist Soc. **SELECTED PUBLICATIONS** Auth, Some Current Publications, Restoration: Studies in English Literary Culture, 93; George Alsop's Indentured Servant, A Character of the Province of Maryland, Md Hist Mag, 90; Two Spheres of Action and Suffering: Empire and Decadence in Little Dorrit, Dickens Quart, 90. **CONTACT ADDRESS** Dept of Eng, Wilkes Univ, 170 S Franklin St, Wilkes-Barre, PA, 18766.

FIFER, ELIZABETH
PERSONAL Born 08/05/1944, Pittsburgh, PA, m, 1970, 1 child **DISCIPLINE** COMPARATIVE LITERATURE, ENGLISH **EDUCATION** Univ MI, Ann Arbor, BA, 65, MA, 66, PhD, 69. **CAREER** Lectr hum, Res Col, Univ MI, 69-72; asst prof, 73-80, Assoc Prof Eng, Lehigh Univ, 80-, prof eng, Lehigh Univ. **MEMBERSHIPS** MLA; Asn Theater Res. **RESEARCH** Gertrude Stein; Contemp lit; Contemp drama; Contemp fiction (U S & World). **SELECTED PUBLICATIONS** Auth, The Confessions of Italo Sveno, Contemp Lit, 73: Sex-stereo Typing in Geography & Plays, Univ Mich Papers Women's Studies, 75; Tragedy into Melodrama, Lex et Scientia, 77; The Interior Theater of Gertrude Stein, Signs, 78; Rescued Readings: Reconstruction of Gertrude Stein's Difficult Texts, Wayne State Univ, 92. **CONTACT ADDRESS** Dept of Eng, Lehigh Univ, 35 Sayre Dr, Bethlehem, PA, 18015-3076. **EMAIL** EF00@lehigh.edu

FILEMYR, ANN
DISCIPLINE JOURNALISM/COMMUNICATIONS AND ENVIRONMENTAL STUDIES **EDUCATION** Thomas Jefferson Col, BA; Univ WI, Milwaukee, MA; Un Inst, PhD. **CAREER** Assoc prof, Antioch Col. **RESEARCH** Ecology. **SELECTED PUBLICATIONS** Auth, Loving Across the Boundary, in Skin Deep: Black Women and White Women Write About Race, Doubleday, 95; Media and Journalism, in Greening the College Curriculum: A Guide to Environmental Teaching in the Liberal Arts, Island Press, 95. **CONTACT ADDRESS** Antioch Col, Yellow Springs, OH, 45387.

FILIPOWICZ, HALINA
DISCIPLINE ENGLISH & AMERICAN LITERATURE **EDUCATION** Warsaw Univ, MA 69; Univ KS, PhD, 79. **CAREER** Prof Dept Slavic Lang & Lit, Univ Wisc, 97-; assoc prof Dept Slavic Lang & Lit, Univ Wisc, 89-97; asst prof Dept Slavic Lang & Lit, Univ Wisc, 82-89 **HONORS AND AWARDS** Univ Wisc Vilas Assoc Fel, 96-98; Ntl Endowment Humanities Fel, 92-93; Non-Tenured Fac Fel at Bunting Ist, Radcliffe Col, 85, 86; Univ Wisc Grad School Summer Res Grants, 87, 89, 90, 94; Univ Wisc Fac Recognition Award, 83; Intl Res & Exchanges Board Travel Grant, 83, 91, 93; Summer Stipend for Independent Res, Ntl Endowment Humanities, 82; Amer Council Learned Soc Fel, 81-82, 88-89; Oswald Prentiss Backus III Award, Univ KS, 81; Grad School Dissertation Fel, Univ KS, 78-79. **MEMBERSHIPS** Modern Lang Assoc; Amer Assoc of Tchrs of Slavic & East European Lang; Amer Assoc for Advancement of Slavic Studies. **RESEARCH** Polish Theatre & Drama; Polish Literature; Performance Studies; Gender Studies; Colonial/Postcolonial Cultural Studies; Critical Theory. **SELECTED PUBLICATIONS** A Laboratory of Impure Forms: The Plays of Tadeusz Rozewicz, Greenwood Pr, 91; Performing Bodies, Performing Mickiewicz: Theatre as a Drama Problem," Slavic and E European Jour, 99; Polska literatura emigracyjna' - proba teorii, Teksty Drugie, 98; Where is Gurutowski? Grotowski Sourcebook, Routledge, 97. **CONTACT ADDRESS** Dept of Slavic Languages & Literature, Univ of Wisconsin, Madison, Madison, WI, 53706. **EMAIL** hfilipow@falstaff.wisc.edu

FINDLAY, LEONARD MURRAY
PERSONAL Born 12/14/1944, Aberdeen, Scotland, m, 1968, 2 children **DISCIPLINE** ENGLISH **EDUCATION** Univ Aberdeen, MA, 67; Univ Oxford, DPhil, 72. **CAREER** Lectr English, City Birmingham Polytech, 70-72; ASST PROF ENGLISH, UNIV SASK, 72-. **MEMBERSHIPS** MLA; Asn Can Univ Teachers English; Victorian Studies Asn Western Can. **RESEARCH** Nineteenth century poetry and prose; literary theory and criticism; the interrelationship of the arts. **SELECTED PUBLICATIONS** Auth, Frye, Northrop, A Visionary Life, Eng Stud Can, Vol 21, 95; Runes of Marx and the University in Ruins, Univ Toronto Quart, Vol 66, 97; Retailing Petits Recits or Retooling for Revolution, Cultural Studies and the Knowledge Industries in Canada, Univ Toronto Quart, Vol 64, 95; Genre, Trope, Gender, Essays by Frye, Northrop, Hutcheon, Linda, Neuman, Shirley, Eng Stud Can, Vol 21, 95; Letter Bomb, Nuclear Holocaust and the Exploding Word, Dalhousie Rev, Vol 73, 93; The Divine Lagation of Frye, Northrop, English Studies in Canada, Vol 19, 93; Prairie Jacobin King, Carlyle and Saskatchewan English, Univ Toronto Quart, Vol 64, 95. **CONTACT ADDRESS** Dept of English, Univ of Sask, Saskatoon, SK, S7H 0W0.

FINDLAY, ROBERT
PERSONAL Born 08/16/1932, Joliet, IL **DISCIPLINE** THEATRE AND DRAMA **EDUCATION** Ill State Univ, BS, 57; Ohio Univ, MFA, 59; Univ Iowa, PhD (theatre), 64. **CAREER** Instr speech and drama, Allegheny Col, 59-60; from instr to asst prof, Bowling Green State Univ, 63-67; from asst prof to assoc prof, 67-73, PROF THEATRE and DRAMA, UNIV KANS, 73-, Nat Endowment for Humanities grants, 78 and 80; Kosciuszko Found grant, 80-81. **HONORS AND AWARDS** Amicus Poloniae badge, Poland mag, 76. **MEMBERSHIPS** Am Soc Theatre Res; Am Theatre Asn; Polish Inst Arts and Sci. **RESEARCH** Modern and contemporary theatre and drama. **SELECTED PUBLICATIONS** Auth, Christo Umbrellas--Visual Art Performance Ritual Real Life on a Grand Scale, Tdr Drama Rev A J Performance Stud, Vol 37, 93; The History of World Theater--From the English Restoration to the Present, Theatre J, Vol 44, 92. **CONTACT ADDRESS** Dept of Speech and Drama, Univ of Kans, Lawrence, KS, 66045-0001.

FINDON, JOANNE
PERSONAL Born 01/28/1957, Surrey, BC, Canada **DISCIPLINE** WRITING **EDUCATION** Univ BC, BA, 82; Univ Toronto, MA, 87, PhD, 94. **CAREER** Instr lit, dept Celtic stud, St Michael's Col, 86-89; instr, Univ Guelph, 94; instr, Univ Toronto & York Univ, 95-96. **HONORS AND AWARDS** IODE Award; York Univ res grant, 96-97. **MEMBERSHIPS** Ed Asn Can; Celtic Stud Asn N Am; Can Asn Irish Stud; Can Soc Medievalists. **SELECTED PUBLICATIONS** Auth, The Importance of Being Bracknell in The Blue Jean Collection, 92; auth, The Dream of Aengus, 94; auth, On the Road in Takes, 96; auth, Auld Lang Syne, 97; auth, A Woman's Words: Emer and Female Speech in the Ulster Cycle, 97. **CONTACT ADDRESS** 5886-128 St, Surrey, BC, V3X 1T3.

FINE, ELIZABETH C.
PERSONAL Born 12/20/1948, Cincinnati, OH, m, 1977 **DISCIPLINE** ORAL INTERPRETATION OF LITERATURE **EDUCATION** Univ Tex, Austin, BS, 71, PhD (commun), 78; Univ Calif, Berkeley, MA, 73. **CAREER** Teaching asst rhetoric, Univ Calif, Berkeley, 72-73; teaching asst speech, Univ Tex, Austin, 74-77; lectr and asst prof speech, Univ Ill, Urbana, 77-79; ASST PROF HUMANITIES and COMMUN, VA POLYTECH INST and STATE UNIV, 79-. **MEMBERSHIPS** Speech Commun Asn; Am Folklore Asn; Southern Speech Commun Asn. **RESEARCH** Ethnography of speaking; aesthetics of verbal act. **SELECTED PUBLICATIONS** Auth, The Politics of Public Memory--Tourism, History, and Ethnicity in Monterey, California, Semiotica, Vol 111, 96. **CONTACT ADDRESS** Dept of Commun, Studies Va Polytech Inst and State Univ, Blacksburg, VA, 24060.

FINE, LAURA
DISCIPLINE ENGLISH LITERATURE **EDUCATION** Univ Calif Davis, PhD. **CAREER** Dept Eng, Clark Atlanta Univ **RESEARCH** Autobiography; 20th century American and 20th century British literature. **SELECTED PUBLICATIONS** Auth, article on Richard Rodriguez. **CONTACT ADDRESS** Clark Atlanta Univ, 223 James P Brawley Dr, SW, Atlanta, GA, 30314.

FINE, MARLENE G.
PERSONAL Born 01/07/1949, NJ, s, 2 children **DISCIPLINE** COMMUNICATION **EDUCATION** Univ Mass, BA, 70; Univ Minn, MA, 72; Univ Mass, PhD, 80; MBA, 84. **CAREER** Dean Grad Studies, Emerson Col, 95-; Chair, Dept Marketing & Communication, Univ Mass, 93-95; assoc prof, Univ Mass, 91-95; asst prof, Univ Mass, 85-91; dir, Bus Admin Program, Univ Mass, 85-89; financial analyst, Small Bus Development Center, Univ Mass, 83. **HONORS AND AWARDS** Who's Who in Media & Communication, 96; Dictionary of Intl Biog, 95; Intl Who's Who Prof Bus Women, 94; World Who's Who of Women, 94; Who's Who of Amer Women, 94; Who Who in the East, 92; Univ Mass Prof of Year, 89; Beta Gamma Sigma, 84; Shaeffer Eaton Award for Academic Excellence, Univ Mass, 84; Pi Kappa Delta, 73; Delta Sigma Rho--Tau Kappa Alpha, 68. **RESEARCH** Organizational Communication; Cultural Diversity in Organizations **SELECTED PUBLICATIONS** Auth, Cultural diversity in the workplace: Organizational challenges and opportunities, Quorum, 95; Cultural diversity: The state of the field, Jour Bus Commun, 96; New voices in the workplace: Research directions in mulitcultural communication, Jour Bus Commun, 91; Epistemological and methodological commitments of a feminist perspective, Women and Lang, 91. **CONTACT ADDRESS** Dept of Graduate Studies, Emerson Col, 100 Beacon, Boston, MA, 02116. **EMAIL** mfine@emerson.edu

FINK, EDWARD L.
DISCIPLINE COMMUNICATIONS **EDUCATION** Univ WI-Madison, PhD, 75. **CAREER** Prof, Univ MD. **RESEARCH** Cognitive processes involved in persuasion. **SELECTED PUBLICATIONS** Co-auth, Cybernetics of Attitudes and Decisions, Dynamic Patterns, Commun Processes, Sage Publ, 96. **CONTACT ADDRESS** Dept of Commun, Univ MD, 4229 Art-Sociology Building, College Park, MD, 20742-1335. **EMAIL** elf@umdd.umd.edu

FINKE, L.A.
PERSONAL Born 03/07/1952, Dayton, OH, m, 1983, 2 children **DISCIPLINE** ENGLISH **EDUCATION** Univ Pa, PhD, 80 **CAREER** Inst, Univ Okla, 80-83; assoc prof, Lewis & Clark Coll, 84- 92; PROF WOMEN'S & GENDER STUD, Kenyon Coll, 92-. **MEMBERSHIPS** MLA; NWSA; Soc Medieval Fem Scholarship. **RESEARCH** Middle ages; literary theory; feminist theory. **SELECTED PUBLICATIONS** various **CONTACT ADDRESS** Women's & Gender Studies, Kenyon Col, Gambier, OH, 43022. **EMAIL** finkeL@kenyon.edu

FINKELPEARL, PHILIP J.
PERSONAL Born 06/09/1925, Pittsburgh, PA, m, 1948, 2 children **DISCIPLINE** ENGLISH **EDUCATION** Princeton Univ, AB, 48; Harvard Univ, AM, 49, PhD (English), 54. **CAREER** From instr to asst prof English, Brandeis Univ, 52-57; from asst prof to assoc prof, Vassar Col, 62-70; assoc prof, Lehman Col, 70-71; assoc prof, Univ Mass, Boston, 71-72, prof English, 72-82; PROF ENGLISH, WELLESLEY COL, 82-, Guggenheim fel, 71-72. **RESEARCH** Elizabethan drama and poetry. **SELECTED PUBLICATIONS** Auth, The Authorship of the Anonymous Coleorton Masque of 1618, Notes Queries, Vol 40, 93; The Fairies Farewell--The Masque at Coleorton 1618, Rev Eng Stud, Vol 46, 95. **CONTACT ADDRESS** Shaker Village, Harvard, MA, 01451.

FINKELSTEIN, NORMAN MARK
PERSONAL Born 05/30/1954, New York, NY **DISCIPLINE** CONTEMPORARY AMERICAN POETRY **EDUCATION** State Univ NY Binghamton, BA, 75; Emory Univ, PhD(English), 80. **CAREER** Prof English, dept chemn, Xavier Univ, 80-. **MEMBERSHIPS** MLA. **RESEARCH** 20th-Century Am Poetry; Jewish Lieterature; literary theory. **SELECTED PUBLICATIONS** Auth, Political commitment and poetic subjectification: George Oppen's test of truth, Contemp Lit, winter 81; Jack Spicer's ghosts and the Gnosis of history, Boundary 2, winter 81; George Oppen: Man and Poet, Nat Poetry Found, 81; William Bronk: The world as desire, Contemp Lit, fall 82; The Utopian Moment In Contemporary American Poetry, Bucknell, 88, 93; The Ritual of New Creation: Jewish Tradition and Contemporary Literature, SUNY, 92; Restlesss Messengers, Georgia, 92. **CONTACT ADDRESS** Dept of English, Xavier Univ, 3800 Victory Pky, Cincinnati, OH, 45207-4446. **EMAIL** finkelst@xavier.xu.edu

FINLAYSON, JOHN
DISCIPLINE ENGLISH LITERATURE **EDUCATION** Cambridge Univ, PhD. **CAREER** Dept Eng, Queen's Univ **RESEARCH** Medieval romance and allegory; Chaucer; editing medieval texts; historical contextualization. **SELECTED PUBLICATIONS** Auth, pubs on Arthurian romance, Chaucer, Pearl, Sir Gawain, Caxton, Petrarch, and Boccaccio; ed, Morte Arthure. **CONTACT ADDRESS** English Dept, Queen's Univ, Kingston, ON, K7L 3N6.

FINNEGAN, ROBERT EMMETT
DISCIPLINE ENGLISH LITERATURE **EDUCATION** St. Peter's Univ, MA; Univ Notre Dame, PhD. **CAREER** Prof **SELECTED PUBLICATIONS** Auth, pubs on old and middle English literature. **CONTACT ADDRESS** Dept of English, Manitoba Univ, Winnipeg, MB, R3T 2N2.

FINNERAN, RICHARD JOHN
PERSONAL Born 12/19/1943, New York, NY, m, 1976 **DISCIPLINE** ENGLISH AND AM LIT **EDUCATION** NY Univ, BA, 64; Univ NC, Chapel Hill, PhD, 68. **CAREER** Instr English, Univ Fla, 67-68; instr, NY Univ, 68-70; from asst prof to assoc prof, 70-77, PROF ENGLISH, NEWCOMB COL, TULANE UNIV, 77-, Lectr, Yeats Int Summer Sch, Sligo, Ireland, 72 and 76; Am Coun Learned Soc grants-in-aid, 73-74 and 77; Nat Endowment for Humanities summer grant, 75; Am Philos Soc res grants, 76 and 80; Huntington Libr fel, 78. **MEMBERSHIPS** MLA; Int Asn Studies Anglo-Irish Lit; Southern Atlantic Mod Lang Asn; Am Comt Irish Studies. **RESEARCH** Anglo-Irish literature, especially W B Yeats. **SELECTED PUBLICATIONS** Auth, That Word Known to All Men in Ulysses--A Reconsideration, James Joyce Quart, Vol 33, 96; The Yeats Sisters and the Cuala, Eng Lit Transition 1880-1920, Vol 39, 96; Family Secrets, Yeats, William, Butler and his Relatives, Eng Lit Transition 1880-1920, Vol 39, 96. **CONTACT ADDRESS** Dept of English, Tulane Univ, New Orleans, LA, 70118.

FIORDO, RICHARD A.
PERSONAL Born 11/02/1945, Chicago, IL, d, 1 child **DISCIPLINE** ENGLISH, SPEECH, COMMUNICATION **EDUCATION** Northern Ill, BA, 67; San Francisco State Univ, MA, 70; Univ Ill, PhD, 74 **CAREER** Instr, E Stroudsberg State Univ, 75; assoc prof, Univ Calgary, 75-95; assoc prof, Eureka Col, 95-97; prof, Univ N Dak, 97- **HONORS AND AWARDS** Distinguished Service **MEMBERSHIPS** Ntl Communication Assoc; Assoc Education in Jour & Mass Communication **RESEARCH** Human Relations; Public Relations; Cultural Commentary **SELECTED PUBLICATIONS** "Truth and Justice in Mass Media Reporting and Commentary: More Than One Master in American Adversarial Contests," Proceedings of the International Society for the Study of Argumentation, 98 **CONTACT ADDRESS** School of Communication, Univ North Dakota, PO Box 7169, Grand Forks, ND, 58203. **EMAIL** fiordo@prairie.nodak.edu

FIORE, PETER AMADEUS
PERSONAL Born 09/08/1927, Glens Falls, NY **DISCIPLINE** ENGLISH **EDUCATION** Siena Col, BA, 49; Cath Univ Am, MA, 55; London Univ, PhD, 61. **CAREER** From instr to prof, 56-75, chmn dept, 62-67, chmn div arts, 67-71, chmn Eng dept, 75-, Siena Col. **MEMBERSHIPS** MLA; Milton Soc Am; NCTE. **RESEARCH** Milton. **SELECTED PUBLICATIONS** Auth, Th'upright Heart and Pure, Duquesne Univ, 67; art, Freedom, Liability, and The State of Perfection in Paradise Lost, Milton Quart, 71; auth, Just So Much Honor, Pa State Univ, 72; auth, Milton and Kubrick: Eden's Apple Or Clockwork Orange, CEA Critic, 73; art, Account mee Man: The Incarnation in Paradise Lost, Huntington Lib Quart, 75; art, Eight Arts on Milton & the Church Fathers, Milton Encycl, 78; auth, Milton and Augustine, Pa St Univ, 81. **CONTACT ADDRESS** Dept of English, Siena Col, Loudonville, NY, 12211. **EMAIL** fiore@siena.edu

FIRCHOW, PETER EDGERLY
PERSONAL Born 12/16/1937, Needham, MA, 1 child **DISCIPLINE** ENGLISH & COMPARATIVE LITERATURE **EDUCATION** Harvard Univ, BA, 59, MA, 61; Univ Wis, PhD, 65. **CAREER** Asst prof English, Univ Mich, 65-67; from asst prof to assoc prof, 67-73, chmn comp lit prog, 72-78, PROF ENGLISH & COMP LIT, UNIV MINN, MINNEAPOLIS, 73-; Fel, Inst Advan Studies in Humanities, Univ Edinburgh, Scotland, 77; Distinguished vis prof, Chong King Univ, Taiwan, 82-83; vis prof, Jipin Univ, PRC, 87; vis prof, Univ Munidu, 88-89;

vis prof, Univ Graz, 90; Fulbright vis prof, Univ Bonn, 95-96. **MEMBERSHIPS** Midwest Mod Lang Asn (vpres, 76-77, pres, 77-78); Am Comp Lit Asn; Asn of Literary Scholars & Critics; Aldous Huxlery Literary Soc (mem, bd dir). **RESEARCH** Modern literature, English, European and American. **SELECTED PUBLICATIONS** Ed & transl, Friedrich Schlegel's Lucindo and the Fragments, Univ Minn Press, 71, partial reprint, 91; Aldous Huxley: Satirist and Novelist, Univ Minn Press, 72; auth, Wells, Lawrence and Brave New World, J Mod Lit, 4/76; Margaret Drabble's The Millstone: Rosamund's complaint, in Old Lines, New Forces, Fairleigh Dickinson Univ, 76; Conrad, Goethe and the German grotesque, Comp Lit Studies, 3/76; Private faces in public places: Auden's The Orators, PMLA, 3/77; ed & co-transl, East German Short Stories: An Introductory Anthology, Twayne, 79; Auth, Hilda Doolittle, in American Writers, Supplement I, Scribner's, 79; Germany and Germanic mythology in E M Forster's Howards End, Comp Lit, winter 81; Lewis Mumford, in American Writers, Supplement II, Scribner's, 81; The End of Utopia: A Study of Brave New World: Buckwell Univ Press, 84; The Death of the German Cousin, Buckwell Univ Press, 86; co-ed & transl, Alois Brandstetter, The Abbey, Ariadne Press, 98. **CONTACT ADDRESS** Dept of English, Univ of Minn, 207 Church St SE, Minneapolis, MN, 55455-0156. **EMAIL** firch002@maroon.tc.umn.edu

FISCHER, JOHN
DISCIPLINE RESTORATION & 18TH CENTURY ENGLISH LITERATURE, TEXTUAL SCHOLARSHIP **EDUCATION** Univ Fla, PhD, 68. **CAREER** Acad freedom comt, 79-80, actg ch, MLA, 81; mem, MLA Delegate Assembly, 83, 84-86; vpres, 84, pres, SCMLA, 85; adv bd, Friends of the Ehrenpreis Ctr for Swift Stud at Meunster, Ger, 85-; prof, ch, dept Eng, La State Univ, 92-95. **HONORS AND AWARDS** NEH sr fel, 83; Phi Beta Kappa; Woodrow Wilson fel; NDEA fel; Univ Fla fel. **MEMBERSHIPS** Mem, Phi Kappa Phi. **RESEARCH** Swift. **SELECTED PUBLICATIONS** Auth, On Swift's Poetry, 78; Dividing to Conquer: The Achievement of Irvin Ehrenpreis's Swift: The Man, His Works, and the Age, The 18th Century: Theory and Interp, 86; The Government's Response to an Epistle to a Lady, Philol Quart, 86; Swift's Early Odes, Dan Jackson's Nose, and 'The Character of Sir Robert Walpole,' Reading Swift, 93; coauth, The Full Text of Swift's On Poetry: A Rhapsody, Swift Stud, 94; coed, Contemporary Studies of Swift's Poetry, 81; Swift and His Contexts, 89. **CONTACT ADDRESS** Dept of Eng, Louisiana State Univ, 210O Allen Hall, Baton Rouge, LA, 70803. **EMAIL** enfisc@lsuvm.sncc.lsu.edu

FISCHER, JOHN IRWIN
PERSONAL Born 05/26/1940, Chicago, IL, m, 1976, 1 child **DISCIPLINE** ENGLISH **EDUCATION** Ohio St Univ, BA, 62; Univ Florida, PhD, 68. **CAREER** Asst prof, 68-76, assoc prof, 76-81, prof, 81-, chmn, 92-95, dir Grad Stud, 98-, Louisiana St Univ. **RESEARCH** Early 18th Century English Lit. **CONTACT ADDRESS** English Dept, Louisiana State Univ, Baton Rouge, LA, 70803. **EMAIL** enfisc@uhix1.sncc.lsu.edu

FISCHER, MICHAEL
DISCIPLINE LITERARY CRITICISM AND ENGLISH ROMANTICISM **EDUCATION** Northwestern Univ, PhD, 75. **CAREER** Instr, Univ NMex, 75-. **SELECTED PUBLICATIONS** Auth, Stanley Cavell and Literary Skepticism, 89. **CONTACT ADDRESS** Univ NMex, Albuquerque, NM, 87131.

FISH, STANLEY E.
DISCIPLINE ENGLISH LITERATURE **EDUCATION** Yale, PhD, 62. **CAREER** Arts and sci prof, law prof, Duke Univ. **SELECTED PUBLICATIONS** Auth, Doing What Comes Naturally, Duke, 89; There's No Such Thing as Free Speech and It's a Good Thing Too, Oxford, 94; Professional Correctness: Literary Studies and Political Change, 95. **CONTACT ADDRESS** Eng Dept, Duke Univ, Durham, NC, 27706.

FISHBURN, KATHERINE RICHARDS
DISCIPLINE BRITISH & AMERICAN LITERATURE **EDUCATION** Western MD Col, BA, 66; MI State Univ, MA, 71, PhD(English), 73. **CAREER** Team teacher English, Gov Thomas Johnson High Sch, 67-69; grad asst, 69-71, instr, 71-73, asst prof English, 73-85, prof English, MI State Univ, 86-; acad admin intern, MI State Univ, 78-79. **MEMBERSHIPS** MLA; Popular Cult Asn; Doris Lessing Soc. **RESEARCH** Contemporary literature; women's literature; Black literature; cultural criticism. **SELECTED PUBLICATIONS** Auth, Richard Wright's Hero: The Faces of a Rebel-Victim, Scarecrow, 77; Women in Popular Culture, In: A Handbook of American Popular Culture, Greenwood Press, 82; The Unexpected Universe of Doris Lessing: A Study in Narrative Technique, Greenwood Press, 85; Doris Lessing: Life, Work, and Criticism, York Press, 87; Reading Buchi Emecheta: Cross-Cultural Conversations, Greenwood Press, 95; The Problem of Embodiment in Early African American Narrative, Greenwood press, 97; The Dead Are So Disappointing, MI State Univ Press, forthcoming. **CONTACT ADDRESS** Dept English, Michigan State Univ, 201 Morrill Hall, East Lansing, MI, 48824-1036. **EMAIL** fishbur1@pilot.msu.edu

FISHER, EDITH MAUREEN
PERSONAL Born 07/29/1944, Houston, Texas, s **DISCIPLINE** LIBRARY SCIENCE **EDUCATION** University of Illinois, Urbana IL, MLS, 1972; Queens College CUNY, Certificate of Ethnicity and Librarianship, 1975; University of Pittsburgh, PhD 1991. **CAREER** University of California, San Diego, La Jolla CA, Central University Library, 1972-90, Contemporary Black Arts Program, adjunct lecturer, 1981-90; University of California, Los Angeles, School of Library and Information Science, lecturer, 1989; Evaluation and Training Institute, Los Angeles, CA, consultant/technical advisor, 1991; Tenge Enterprises, Encinitas, CA, president, currently. **HONORS AND AWARDS** Carnegie fellowship, 1971; PhD fellowship, 1987; Provost fellowship, Univ of CA, San Diego, 1987; Provost fellowship, Univ of Pittsburgh, 1988; Black Caucus of the American Library Association President's Award, 1990. **MEMBERSHIPS** Carleson Learning. **SELECTED PUBLICATIONS** Author of numerous publications. **CONTACT ADDRESS** President, Tenge Enterprises, 204 N El Camino Real, Encinitas, CA, 92024.

FISHER, JAMES
PERSONAL Born 11/08/1950, Long Branch, NJ, m, 1977, 2 children **DISCIPLINE** THEATER **EDUCATION** Monmouth Col, NJ, BA, 73; Univ NC Greensboro, MFA, 76. **CAREER** Prof, Wabash Col, Crawfordsville, IN, 78-. **HONORS AND AWARDS** Wabash Relig Center Summer grant, 98., Theater Person of the Year, IN, 97. **MEMBERSHIPS** Int Fedn of Theatre Res; S Theatre Conf; In Theatre Assoc; Theatre Libr Assoc; Soc for Theatre Res; Assoc for Theatre in Higher Educ; Assoc for Recorded Sound. **SELECTED PUBLICATIONS** Publ, The Theater of Yesterday and Tomorrow: Commedia Dell'arte on the Modern Stage, Mellen, 92, 98; auth, Al Jolson, Greenwood, 94; auth, Spencer Tracy, Greenwood, 94;auth, Eddie Cantor, Greenwood, 97; ed, The Puppetry Yearbook, three volumes. **CONTACT ADDRESS** Theatre Dept, Wabash Col, Crawfordsville, IN, 47933. **EMAIL** fisherj@scholar.wabash.edu

FISHER, JAMES RANDOLPH
PERSONAL Born 11/05/1906, Norfolk, VA **DISCIPLINE** ENGLISH LANGUAGE AND LITERATURE **EDUCATION** Howard Univ, AB, 31, AM, 33. **CAREER** Chmn dept lang and lit, Rust Col, 35-38; Allen Univ, 40-43; sophomore English, Tenn State Col, 45-47; prof, 47-72, chmn sophomore English, 48-74, chmn dept lang and lit, prof, 72-74, EMER PROF ENGLISH, SAVANNAH STATE COL, 74-. **MEMBERSHIPS** MLA; Mod Humanities Res Asn; Int Asn Univ Prof English; Col English Asn; Milton Soc Am. **SELECTED PUBLICATIONS** Auth, British Physicians, Medical Science, and the Cattle Plague, 1865-66, Bulletin of the History of Medicine, Vol 67, 93; Not Quite a Profession--The Aspirations of Veterinary Surgeons in England in the Mid 19th Century, Hist Rsch, Vol 66, 93. **CONTACT ADDRESS** Dept of English, Savannah State Col, Box 20434, Savannah, GA, 31404.

FISHER, JOHN HURT
PERSONAL Born 10/26/1919, Lexington, KY, m, 1942, 3 children **DISCIPLINE** ENGLISH **EDUCATION** Maryville Col, AB, 40; Univ Pa, AM, 42, PhD, 45. **CAREER** From asst to instr, Univ Pa, 42-45; instr, Washington Sq Col, NY Univ, 45-48, asst prof English, 48-55; from assoc prof to prof, Duke Univ, 55-60; prof, Ind Univ, 60-62 and NY Univ, 62-72; head dept, 76-78, JOHN C HODGES PROF ENGLISH, UNIV TENN, KNOXVILLE, 72-, Asst secy, MLA, 49-51, exec secy, 63-71; consult, US Off Educ, 62-65; ed, PMLA, 63-71; mem, US Comn, UNESCO, 63-69; chmn, Am Coun Learned Soc Conf Secys, 65-68; mem exec comt, Int Fed Mod Lang and Lit, 67-71, Am vpres, 72-78; trustee, Woodrow Wilson Nat Fel Found, 72-75; dir, Maryville Col, 72-75; Nat Endowment on Humanities sr fel, 75-76, consult, 76-; dir, New Chaucer Soc, 81-. **HONORS AND AWARDS** LittD, Middlebury Col, 70; LHD, Loyola Univ Chicago, 70. **MEMBERSHIPS** MLA (treas, 52-55, pres, 74); Mediaeval Acad Am; NCTE; New Chaucer Soc (pres, 82-). **RESEARCH** Medieval literature and the English language. **SELECTED PUBLICATIONS** Auth, England the Nation, Medium Aevum, Vol 66, 97; The New Humanism and Chaucer, Geoffrey, Soundings, Vol 80, 97; An Ars Legendi for Chaucer Canterbury Tales--A Reconstructive Reading, J Eng Ger Philol, Vol 92, 93; Textual Criticism and Middle English Texts, J Eng Ger Philol, Vol 95, 96; The Manuscripts of the Canterbury Tales, J Eng Ger Philol, Vol 92, 93; Early Chaucer Manuscripts, PMLA Publications of the Modern Language Association of America, Vol 108, 93; Textual Criticism and Middle English Texts, J Eng Ger Philol, Vol 95, 96. **CONTACT ADDRESS** Dept of English, Univ of Tenn, Knoxville, TN, 37916.

FISHER, JUDITH LAW
PERSONAL Born 08/31/1952, Montclair, NJ, m, 1982 **DISCIPLINE** VICTORIAN LITERATURE, THEORY OF WRITING **EDUCATION** Oberlin Col, AB, 74; Univ Tenn, MA, 75; Univ Ill, PhD (English), 80. **CAREER** Teaching asst English comp, Univ Tenn, 74-75, English, Univ Ill, 75-80; staff asst pub rel, Continuing Educ, Univ Ill, 76-79; fel English, Univ Kans, 80-82; LECTR ENGLISH, UNIV TEX AT SAN ANTONIO, 82-, Ed, Res Press, Champaign, Ill, 80. **MEMBERSHIPS** Mod Lang Asn. **RESEARCH** William Makepeace Thackeray; Victorian art history; history of the novel. **SELECTED PUBLICATIONS** Auth, The Making of Victorian Drama, Criticism Quart Lit Arts, Vol 35, 93; Theater in the Victorian Age, Criticism Quart Lit Arts, Vol 35, 93; Ethical Narrative in Dickens and Thackeray, Stud Novel, Vol 29, 97; Thackeray and Slavery, Stud Novel, Vol 27, 95; The Unwelcome Judicial Obligation to Respect Politics in Racial Gerrymandering Remedies, Mich Law Rev, Vol 95, 97; When Discretion Leads to Distortion--Recognizing Prearrest Sentence Manipulation Claims Under the Federal Sentencing Guidelines, Michigan Law Rev, Vol 94, 96. **CONTACT ADDRESS** Div English Classics and Philos, Univ of Texas, San Antonio, TX, 78285.

FISHER, LEONA
DISCIPLINE ENGLISH LITERATURE **EDUCATION** Stanford Univ, BA; Univ Ca, MA, PhD. **CAREER** Prof. **RESEARCH** Victorian literature; women writers; nonfiction prose; 19th century drama; children's literature; Latin American fiction; feminist theory. **SELECTED PUBLICATIONS** Auth, Mystical Fantasy for Children: Silence and Community, 90; Lemon, Dickens, and 'Mr. Nightingale's Diary': A Victorian Farce, 88; Mark Lemon's Three Farces on the 'Woman Question', 88; The Challenge of Women's Studies: Questions for a Transformed Future at Georgetown, 90; Women, Violence, and the Church, 90. **CONTACT ADDRESS** English Dept, Georgetown Univ, 37th and O St, Washington, DC, 20057.

FISHER, PHILIP
PERSONAL Born 10/11/1941, Pittsburgh, PA, d, 1 child **DISCIPLINE** ENGLISH & AMERICAN LITERATURE **EDUCATION** Univ Pittsburgh, AB, 63; Harvard Univ, AM, 66, PhD(English), 70. **CAREER** Asst prof English, Univ Va, 70-72; from Asst Prof to Assoc Prof, Brandeis Univ, 73-87; Prof English, 88-, Reid Prof English, Harvard Univ, 95-, Chair, Dept English, 90-93; Andrew Mellow asst prof, Harvard Univ, 76-77; vis scholar, Mass Inst Technol, 77-81; vis prof, Harvard Univ, summer 77; vis prof Frei Univ, Berlin, 81; mem, Cambridge Humanities Sem, 77-. **HONORS AND AWARDS** Fel, Inst Advanced Study, Berlin, 87-88; Guggenheim Fel, 96-97; Sr Fel, Getty Inst, 98-99. **MEMBERSHIPS** MLA. **RESEARCH** The novel; the city; theory of art objects. **SELECTED PUBLICATIONS** Contribr, Uses of Literature, 73 & The Worlds of Victorian Fiction, 75, Harvard Univ Press; auth, The future's past, New Lit Hist, 75; Hand-made space, Arts Mag, 77; Looking around to see who I am: Dreiser's territory of the self, J English Lit Hist, 78; Making Up Society, Univ Pittsburgh Press, 81; contribr, American Realism: New Essays, Johns Hopkins Univ Press, 82; Pins, a table, works of art, Representations, 82; Hard Facts, Oxford Univ, 87; Making and Effacing Art, Oxford Univ Press, 91; The New American Studies, Univ Calif Press, 91; Wonder, the Rainbow and the Aesthetics of Rare Experiences, Harvard Univ Press, 98; Still the New World: American Literature in a Culture of Creative Destruction, Harvard Univ Press, 99. **CONTACT ADDRESS** Dept English, Harvard Univ, Barker Center, Cambridge, MA, 02138-3800.

FISHER, WALTER R.
DISCIPLINE COMMUNICATION **EDUCATION** Univ IA, PhD. **CAREER** Prof & dir, Sch Commun; ed, Quart J Speech & Western J Commun. **HONORS AND AWARDS** Speech Commun Asn Distinguished Scholar Awd. **RESEARCH** Rhetorical theory and criticism; politic commun & argumentation; addressing in particular problems in reason and ethics. **SELECTED PUBLICATIONS** Co-ed, Rethinking Knowledqe: Reflections Across the Disciplines, SUNY Press, 95 & Human Communication as Narration: Toward a Philosophy of Reason, Value, and Action, Univ SCPress, 89. **CONTACT ADDRESS** Annenberg School for Commun, Univ of Southern California, University Park Campus, Los Angeles, CA, 90089. **EMAIL** wfisher@usc.edu

FISHERKELLER, JOELLEN
DISCIPLINE EDUCATION & COMMUNICATION **EDUCATION** Univ CA, Berkeley, PhD, 95. **CAREER** Asst prof, New York Univ, 95-. **RESEARCH** Young people; media cultures; media education. **SELECTED PUBLICATIONS** Auth, The Hidden Persistence of Immigrant Drop Outs: Distortions, Blank Spots and Blind Spots in Research on Schooling Careers, with Donald A Hansen and Vicky Johnson, Int J of Educational; Research, Pergamon Press, vol 23, no 1, 95; Representing Student's Thinking About Nutrient Cycles in Ecosystems, Bidimensional Coding of a Complex Topic, with Kathleen Hogan, J of Research in Science Teaching, vol 33, no 9, 96; Review of Children and the Movies: Media Influence and the Payne Fund Controversy, by Garth S Jowett, Ian C Jarvie, and Kathryn H Fuller, Cambridge Univ Press, 96, J of Commun, autumn 97; Review of Writing Superheroes: Contemporary Childhood, Popular Culture, and Classroom Literacy, by Anne Haas Dyson, Teachers Col Press, 97, Anthropology and Education Quart, 97; Learning from Young Adolescent TV Viewers, NJ J of Commun, fall 97; Everyday Learning About Identities Among Young Adolescents in TV Culture, Anthropology and Ed Quart, vol 28, no 4, winter 97; Learning About Power and Success: Young Adolescents Interpret TV Culture, The Commun Rev, March 98. **CONTACT ADDRESS** Dept of Culture and Commun, New York Univ, 239 Greene St, Rm 735, New York, NY, 10003-6674. **EMAIL** jf4@is2.nyu.edu

FISK, WILLIAM LYONS
PERSONAL Born 02/24/1921, Newark, OH, m, 1962, 2 children **DISCIPLINE** ENGLISH HISTORY **EDUCATION** Muskingum Col, AB, 41; Ohio State Univ, AM, 44, PhD (hist), 46. **CAREER** From asst prof to assoc prof hist, 46-55, dean and vpres, 68-76, PROF ENGLISH HIST, MUSKINGUM COL, 55-. **HONORS AND AWARDS** Distinguish Serv Award, Muskingum Col, 77. **MEMBERSHIPS** AHA; Conf Brit Studies. **RESEARCH** Twenty years of English labor legislation, 1795-1815; 17th and 18th century English history. **SELECTED PUBLICATIONS** Auth, Walker, John--Renaissance Man, Amn Presbyterians-J Presbyterian Hist, Vol 71, 93. **CONTACT ADDRESS** Dept of Hist, Muskingum Col, New Concord, OH, 43762.

FITCH, NOEL RILEY
PERSONAL Born 12/24/1937, New Haven, CT, m, 1958, 1 child **DISCIPLINE** AMERICAN LITERATURE **EDUCATION** Northwest Nazarene Col, BA, 59; Wash State Univ, MA, 65, PhD (Am studies), 69. **CAREER** Teacher lang arts and social studies, Moscow Jr High Sch, 59-62; teacher English, Moscow Sr High Sch, 62-63; assoc prof, Eastern Nazarene Col, 68-71; PROF LITERATURE, POINT LOMA COL, 71-, Assoc prof family literature, Family Studies Dept, San Diego State Univ, 76-78; Nat Endowment for Humanities fel, 80-81. **MEMBERSHIPS** AAUP; MLA; Am Studies Asn. **RESEARCH** Literary history in Paris in twenties and thirties. **SELECTED PUBLICATIONS** Auth, Silence and Power--A Reevaluation of Barnes, Djuna, Tulsa Stud Womens Lit, Vol 10, 91; Pound, Ezra in London and Paris, 1908-1925, Resources Am Lit Stud, Vol 21, 95. **CONTACT ADDRESS** 5383-105 Chelsea Ave, La Jolla, CA, 92037.

FITCH, RAYMOND E.
PERSONAL Born 01/23/1930, Boston, MA, m, 1952, 1 child **DISCIPLINE** NINETEENTH CENTURY LITERATURE, CRITISISM **EDUCATION** Harvard Univ, AB, 52; Univ MI, AM, 55; Univ PA, PhD, 65. **CAREER** Asst prof Eng, Pa Mil Col, 57-60; asst prof, SCT State Col, 61-66; assoc prof, 66-77, prof eng, OH Univ, 77, chmn grad prog, 78, emeritus prof 98. **MEMBERSHIPS** MLA; Int Phenomenol Soc. **RESEARCH** Lit and myth; works of Ruskin; critical theory. **SELECTED PUBLICATIONS** Ed, Dramatic romances and lyrics, : Complete Works of Robert Browning, OH Univ, 73; Literary Theory in the English Classroom, SCTE/NCTE, 81; The Poison Sky: Myth and Apocalypse in Ruskin, OH Univ, 82; Ed, Breaking With Burr: Harmon Blenner Hassett's Journal, 1801, Oh Univ, 1986. **CONTACT ADDRESS** Dept of Eng, Ohio Univ, Athens, OH, 45701-2979.

FITTER, CHRIS
DISCIPLINE SHAKESPEARE, 17TH CENTURY LITERATURE AND POLITICS, MARXIST AND NEW HISTORIC **EDUCATION** Oxford Univ, PhD. **CAREER** Instr, Rutgers, State Univ NJ, Camden Col of Arts and Sci. **RESEARCH** Shakespeare. **SELECTED PUBLICATIONS** Auth, Paradise Lost and the Tradition of Exile Consolation, Milton Stud, 84; The Landscape of Henry Vaughan, Essays in Criticism; Henry V, Ideology, and the Mekong Agincourt, Shakespeare Left and Right, Routledge, 91; Poetry, Space, Landscape, Cambridge, 95; W. J. Cash and the Southerner as Superman: Philosophic Influences on The Mind of the South, Southern Lit J, 95. **CONTACT ADDRESS** Rutgers, State Univ NJ, Camden Col of Arts and Sci, New Brunswick, NJ, 08903-2101. **EMAIL** fitter@camden.rutgers.edu

FITZSIMMONS, THOMAS
PERSONAL Born 10/21/1926, Lowell, MA, m, 1955, 2 children **DISCIPLINE** ENGLISH **EDUCATION** Stanford Univ, BA, 51; Sorbonne and Inst Sci Polit, cert Fr lit, philos and int affairs, 49 and 50; Columbia Univ, MA, 52. **CAREER** From staff writer to assoc ed, New Repub Mag, 52-55; dir res anthrop and publications, Human Relat Area Files, 55-59; from asst prof to assoc prof, 59-65, PROF ENGLISH, OAKLAND UNIV, 65-, Spec consult, Hist Div Dept of Defense, 52; res assoc, Yale Univ, 56-59; Fulbright prof, Tokyo Univ Educ and Tsuda-Juku Women's Col, Japan, 62-64; vis prof, Univ Bucharest, 67-68; prof, Tokyo Univ Educ and vis poet, Japan women's Univ and Keio Univ, Japan, 73-75. **HONORS AND AWARDS** Nat Found for Arts poetry grant, 67, world wide poetry reading tour, USIS, 75-76. **MEMBERSHIPS** PEN Club. **RESEARCH** Poetry; cultural anthropology; Asian poetry. **SELECTED PUBLICATIONS** Auth, Writing in the Margins--The Theatrical Voice of Women, Overland, Vol 136, 94. **CONTACT ADDRESS** Dept of English, Oakland Univ, Rochester, MI, 48063.

FIX, STEPHEN
DISCIPLINE ENGLISH **EDUCATION** Boston Col, BA, 74; Cornell Univ, PhD, 80. **CAREER** Prof. **RESEARCH** 18th-century British literature. **SELECTED PUBLICATIONS** Auth, Distant Genius: Johnson and the Art of Milton's Life; Johnson and the Duty of Reading Paradise Lost; The Contexts and Motives of Johnson's Life of Milton; Teaching Johnson's Critical Writing; Prayer, Poetry and Paradise Lost, Editing Johnson's Life of Milton, Yale Edition of the Works of Samuel Johnson. **CONTACT ADDRESS** Dept of English, Williams Col, Stetson C-12, Williamstown, MA, 01267. **EMAIL** sfix@williams.edu

FJELDE, ROLF GERHARD
PERSONAL Born 03/15/1926, Brooklyn, NY, m, 1964, 3 children **DISCIPLINE** MODERN DRAMA **EDUCATION** Yale Univ, BA, 46; Columbia Univ, MA, 47; Univ Copenhagen, 53; Univ Heidelberg, 53; Univ Oslo, 65. **CAREER** From instr to assoc prof, 54-69, PROF ENGLISH & DRAMA, PRATT INST, 69-, Am-Scand Found fel, Univ Copenhagen, 52-53; Yaddo Found fel, 52, 54; playwright-in-residence, Eugene O'Neill Mem Theatre Ctr; Nat Transl Ctr, Ford Found fel, 67-68; lectr drama, Juilliard Sch, 73-83; ed, Ibsen News & Comment, 79- **MEMBERSHIPS** Dramatists Guild; Auth League Am; Am Theatre Asn; Soc Advan Scand Studies; Ibsen Soc Am (pres, 79-). **RESEARCH** Henrik Ibsen; classic and modern drama; contemporary poetry and film. **SELECTED PUBLICATIONS** Auth, The image word, Ablib, 62; translr & ed, Peer Gynt, 64 & 80, Ibsen: Four major plays, Vol, 65 & Vol II, 70, New Am Libr; ed, Ibsen: A collection of critical essays, Prentice-Hall, 65; auth, Peer Gynt, naturalism and the dissolving self, Drama Rev, 69; The dimensions of Ibsen's dramatic world, Universitetsforlaget, 71; Ibsen: The complete major prose plays, New Am Libr/Farrar Straus & Giroux, 78. **CONTACT ADDRESS** Dept of English & Humanities, Pratt Inst, 200 Willoughby Ave, Brooklyn, NY, 11205-3899.

FLACHMANN, MICHAEL C.
PERSONAL Born 11/03/1942, St. Louis, MO, m, 1969, 2 children **DISCIPLINE** ENGLISH **EDUCATION** Univ of the South, BA, 64; Univ Va, MA, 65; Univ Chicago, PhD, 72. **CAREER** Instr, Southern Ill Univ, 65-68; Asst Prof to Assoc Prof, 72-81, Prof English, Calif State Univ, 81-, Dir Honors Prog, 81-. **HONORS AND AWARDS** Phi Beta Kappa; Philip Frances DuPont Schol, Univ Va, 65; William Raney Harper Doctoral Fel, Univ Chicago, 68; Outstanding Prof Award, Calif State Univ-Bakersfield, 92; Calif State Univ System-Wide Outstanding Prof Award, 93; U.S. Prof of the Year, Carnegie Found & Coun for the Advancement and Support of Educ, 95. **MEMBERSHIPS** Mod Lang Asn; Shakespeare Asn Am; Bibliographical Soc. **RESEARCH** Shakespeare, Renaissance literature; dramaturgy. **SELECTED PUBLICATIONS** Auth, Ben Jonson and the Alchemy of Satire, Studies English Lit, 77; coauth, Shakespeare's Lovers: A Text for Performance and Analysis, Southern Ill Press, 82; auth, Epicoene: A Comic Hell for a Comic Sinner, Medieval & Renaissance Drama in England I, 84; Teaching Shakespeare Through Parallel Scenes, Shakespeare Quart, 85; coauth, Shakespeare's Women: A Playscript for Performance and Analysis, Southern Ill Press, 86; auth, All Corners of the World: Spatial and Moral Geography in Cymbeline, On-Stage Studies XII, 89; The First English Epistolary Novel: The Image of Idleness (1555), Studies Philol, 90; Fitted for Death: Measure for Measure and the Contemplatio Mortis, English Lit Renaissance, 92; The Merchant of Ashland, On-Stage Studies, 92; Changing the W's in Shakespeare's Plays, Teaching Shakespeare Today, NCTE Press, 93; William Baldwin, Dictionary of Renaissance Biographies, 97; Suit the Action to the Word: Teaching Minds and Bodies in the English Classroom, Inspiring Teaching: Carnegie Professors of the Year Speak, Anker Press, 97; ed, Teaching Exellence: A Collection of Essays on College Education Written by Recipients of the California State University Trustees' Outstanding Professor Award, The Calif State Univ Inst Press, 98; coauth, The Prose Reader: Essays for Thinking, Reading, and Writing, Prentice Hall, 98; author of numerous other articles and publications. **CONTACT ADDRESS** English and Communications Dept, California State Univ, Bakersfield, 9001 Stockdale Hwy., Bakersfield, CA, 93311-1099. **EMAIL** mflachmann@csubak.edu

FLAHIVE, DOUG
DISCIPLINE ENGLISH LITERATURE **EDUCATION** Southern Ill Univ, BA, MA, PhD. **CAREER** Assoc prof. **SELECTED PUBLICATIONS** Auth, pubs on second language discourse processing; language testing; first and second language acquisition. **CONTACT ADDRESS** Dept of English, Colorado State Univ, Fort Collins, CO, 80523. **EMAIL** dflahive@vines.colostate.edu

FLANNAGAN, ROY C.
PERSONAL Born 12/02/1938, Richmond, VA, m, 5 children **DISCIPLINE** ENGLISH **EDUCATION** Washington & Lee Univ, BA, 60; Univ VA, MA, 61, PhD, 66. **CAREER** Asst prof English, Va Mil Inst, 65-66; assoc prof, 66-82, prof eng, OH Univ, 82; Ed, Milton Newslett, 67-69, Milton Quart, 70-; Pres, Coun Eds Learned Journals, 98. **HONORS AND AWARDS** OH Univ Baker Award, 67; Folger Shakespeare Libr fel, 67; Fulbright Travel grant, 70. **MEMBERSHIPS** MLA; Milton Soc Am (pres 90); Renaissance Soc Am. **RESEARCH** Milton; Renaissance Italian and Eng lit; ecology. **SELECTED PUBLICATIONS** Auth, Riverside Milton, Houghton Mifflin, 97. **CONTACT ADDRESS** Dept of Eng, Ohio Univ, Athens, OH, 45701-2979. **EMAIL** flannaga@oak.cats.ogiou.edu

FLANNERY, MICHAEL T.
DISCIPLINE LEGAL WRITING AND APPELLATE ADVOCACY **EDUCATION** Univ Del, BA, 87; Cath Univ Am Columbus Sch Law, JD, 91. **CAREER** Prof,Villanova Univ Sch Law, 96-; worked in, Wolf, Block, Schorr and Solis-Cohen; assoc, Gold-Bikin, Clifford and Young, 94; asst city solicitor, Philadelphia, 91-94. **CONTACT ADDRESS** Law School, Villanova Univ, 800 Lancaster Ave, Villanova, PA, 19085-1692. **EMAIL** flannery@law.vill.edu

FLECK, RICHARD F.
PERSONAL Born 08/24/1937, Philadelphia, PA, m, 1963, 3 children **DISCIPLINE** ENGLISH **EDUCATION** Rutgers Univ, BA, 59; Colo State Univ, MA, 62; Univ N Mex, PhD, 70. **CAREER** Instr, North Adams State Col, 63-65; prof, Univ Wyo, 65-90; dir, Teikyo Loretto Heights Univ, 90-93; dean, Commun Col, Denver, 93-. **HONORS AND AWARDS** Colo Arts Counc Award, 95; Who's Who West. **MEMBERSHIPS** Nat Asn Col Admin. **RESEARCH** Native American literature; natural history essay. **SELECTED PUBLICATIONS** Auth, Critical Perspectives on Native American Fiction, 93; auth, art, The World of N. Scott Momaday, 95; auth, John Muir's Mountaineering Essays, 97; auth, John Burroughs' Deep Woods, 98. **CONTACT ADDRESS** Dept of Arts and Humanities, Comm Col of Denver, Box 173363, Denver, CO, 80217. **EMAIL** cd_richard @cccs.cccoes.edu

FLEISHMAN, AVROM
PERSONAL Born 07/27/1933, New York, NY, m, 1960, 2 children **DISCIPLINE** ENGLISH **EDUCATION** Columbia Univ, BA, 54; Johns Hopkins Univ, MA, 56, PhD (English), 63. **CAREER** Instr English, Columbia Univ, 58-59; instr Hofstra Univ, 60-63; asst prof, Univ Minn, 63-66; asst prof, Mich State Univ, 66-67; assoc prof, 68-70, PROF ENGLISH, JOHNS HOPKINS UNIV, 70-, Belgian-Am Educ Found fel, 59-60; Guggenheim fel, 67-68; Explicator Lit Found Award, 75-76; sem dir, Nat Endowment for Humanities, 75 and 81. **MEMBERSHIPS** MLA. **RESEARCH** Modern and Victorian literature. **SELECTED PUBLICATIONS** Auth, Loose Canons--Notes on the Culture Wars, English Literature in Transition 1880-1920, Vol 36, 93; The Condition of English--Taking Stock in a Time of Culture Wars, Coll Eng, Vol 57, 95; Expanding Extending English Interdisciplinarity and Internationalism and Contact Zones and English Studies, Coll Eng, Vol 57, 95; Politics by Other Means--Higher Education and Group Thinking, English Literature in Transition 1880-1920, Vol 36, 93; Community of Learning--The American College and the Liberal Arts Tradition, Eng Lit Transition 1880-1920, Vol 36, 93; Conspiring with Forms--Life in Academic Texts, Eng Lit Transition 1880-1920, Vol 36, 93; The Blinding Torch--Modern British Fiction and the Discourse of Civilization, Clio J Lit Hist Philos Hist, Vol 24, 95; Openings--Narrative Beginnings from the Epic to the Novel, J Eng Ger Philol, Vol 93, 94; Narrativity--Theory and Practice, J Eng Ger Philol, Vol 93,94; Conrad, Joseph and the Anthropological Dilemma--Bewildered Traveler, Eng Lit Transition 1880-1920, Vol 39, 96; Narrativity--Theory and Practice, J Eng Ger Philol, Vol 93, 94; Expanding Extending English--Interdisciplinarity and Internationalism, Coll Eng, Vol 56, 94. **CONTACT ADDRESS** Dept of English, Johns Hopkins Univ, 3400 N Charles St, Baltimore, MD, 21218-2680.

FLEISSNER, ROBERT F.
PERSONAL Born 10/17/1932, Auburn, NY, d **DISCIPLINE** ENGLISH **EDUCATION** Cath Univ Am, BA, 57, MA, 58; Univ NC, 59-60; OH State Univ, 60-61; NY Univ, PhD, 64. **CAREER** Instr English, speech & drama, Spring Hill Col, 58-59; asst instr English, OH State Univ, 60-61; lectr English & World Lit, Bernard Baruch Sch, City Col NY, 62-64; asst prof English & chemn dept, Dominican Col, NY, 64-66; vis instr, Univ NM, 66-67; asst to assoc prof English, Cent State Univ, 67-; Dir, OH Shakespeare Conf, 77, co-dir, 96. **MEMBERSHIPS** MLA; Frost Soc; Shakespeare Asn Am; Col Lang Asn; T S Eliot Soc. **RESEARCH** Renaissance and Victorian periods; Robert Frost; T S Eliot. **SELECTED PUBLICATIONS** Auth, Dickens and Shakespeare, NY: Haskell House, 69; Frost on Frost ... at Midnight, Studies Humanities, 76; A Table of Greene Felds', Grasse-Greene/table, and Balladry, Shak Jahrbuch, East, 76; Herberts Aethiopesa and the Dark Lady, CLA J, 76; Stopping yet Again by Frost's Woods, Res Studies, 77; Nons sans Droict: Law and Heraldry, in Julius Caesar, Hartford Studies Lit, 77; The Malleable Knight and the Unfettered Friar: The Merry Wives of Windsor and Boccaccio, Shakespeare Studies XI, 78; Ruelle, In: Robert Frost: Studies of the Poetry, 80; Resolved to Love: The 1592 Edition of Henry Constable's Diana Critically Considered, Univ Salzburg Press, 80; The Prince and the Professor, Heidelberg: Carl Winter U P, 86; Ascending the Prufrockian Stair, NY: Peter Lang, 88; A Rose by Another Name, West Cornwall: Locust Hill Press, 89; Shakespeare and the Matter of the Crux, Lewiston: Mellon, 91; T S Eliot and the Heritage of Africa, NY: Peter Lang, 92; Frost's Road Taken, NY: Peter Lang, 96. **CONTACT ADDRESS** Dept of Humanities, Central State Univ, Ohio, Wilberforce, OH, 45384-9999.

FLEMING, DEBORAH DIANE
PERSONAL Born 05/29/1950, Steubenville, OH, m, 1991 **DISCIPLINE** ENGLISH **EDUCATION** Ohio State Univ, PhD, 85. **CAREER** Visiting asst prof, Denison Univ, 86-87; visiting asst prof, Ohio Wesleyan Univ, 88-89; academic counselor, Ohio State Univ, 90-93; asst prof, 93-98, assoc prof, 98-, Ashland Univ. **HONORS AND AWARDS** Vandewater Poetry Award, 83; Alumni Dissertation Research Award, 85; Amer Coun Learned Societies Conference Grant, 96; research grants, Ashland Univ, 95, 97. **MEMBERSHIPS** Amer Conf Irish Studies, 84-; Modern Lang Assn, 85-; Assn Study Literature Environment, 94-; Robinson Jeffers Assn 95-. **RESEARCH** W. B. Yeats; Irish studies; modern poetry in English; modern literature; environmentalist literature; ecofeminism; English Renais-

sance. **SELECTED PUBLICATIONS** Auth, "George Orwell and His Generation: Art and Political Purpose," Papers in Comparative Studies, vol 4, 85; ed & intro writer, Learning the Trade: Essays on W. B. Yeats and Contemporary Poetry, 92; auth, "The 'Common Ground' of Eamon Grennan," Eire-Ireland, winter 94; auth, A Man Who Does Not Exist: The Irish Peasant in the Work of W. B. Yeats and J. M. Synge, 95; auth, entries on Eamon Grennan and Seamus Deane, Dictionary of Irish Biography, 96. **CONTACT ADDRESS** Dept of English, Ashland Univ, Ashland, OH, 44805. **EMAIL** dfleming@ashland.edu

FLEMING, ROBERT
DISCIPLINE AMERICAN LITERATURE **EDUCATION** Univ Ill, PhD, 67. **CAREER** Instr, Univ NMex, 67-; ed, Am Lit Realism, 86-. **RESEARCH** African American literature. **SELECTED PUBLICATIONS** Auth, The Face in the Mirror: Hemingway's Writers, Univ Ala Press, 94. **CONTACT ADDRESS** Univ NMex, Albuquerque, NM, 87131.

FLETCHER, ALAN D.
DISCIPLINE ADVERTISING **EDUCATION** Univ Ill, PhD, 69. **CAREER** Prof, La State Univ; contributing ed, J of Advert, rev bd, J of Current Issues and Res in Advert; referee, Jour Quart, J Educr; steering comt, Freedom Forum Sem for New Prof of Advert; acad host, Very Important Prof sem, Promotional Products Asn Int. **MEMBERSHIPS** Pres, Am Acad of Advert; chemn, Acad Div of the Am Advert Fedn; chemn, Advert Div of the Asn for Educ in Journ and Mass Commun. **SELECTED PUBLICATIONS** Auth, Target Marketing Through the Yellow Pages, Yellow Pages Publ Asn, 91; Lessons in Promotional Products Marketing, Promotional Products Asn Int, 94; coauth, Fundamentals of Advertising Research, 4th ed Wadsworth, 91. **CONTACT ADDRESS** The Manship Sch of Mass Commun, Louisiana State Univ, Baton Rouge, LA, 70803. **EMAIL** adfletcher@aol.com

FLETCHER, ANGUS S.
PERSONAL Born 06/23/1930, New York, NY **DISCIPLINE** ENGLISH LITERATURE **EDUCATION** Yale Univ, BA, 50, MA, 52; Univ Grenoble, France, dipl, 51; Harvard Univ, PhD, 58. **CAREER** Instr English lit, Cornell Univ, 58-62; from asst prof to assoc prof, Columbia Col, Columbia Univ, 62-68; prof, State Univ NY Buffalo, 68-74; DISTINGUISHED PROF ENGLISH & COMP LIT, LEHMAN COL & GRAD CTR, CITY UNIV NEW YORK, 74-, Vis prof English & comp lit, Univ Calif, Los Angeles, 73-74; Dreyfuss vis prof humanities, Calif Inst Technol, 77-78. **MEMBERSHIPS** Renaissance Soc Am; English Inst. **RESEARCH** History of opera and mixed media; Renaissance studies; theory of literature. **SELECTED PUBLICATIONS** Auth, Allegory: Theory of a Symbolic Mode, 64 & The Transcendental Masque: An Essay on Milton's Comus, 71, Cornell Univ; The Prophetic Moment: An Essay on Spenser, Univ Chicago, 71; Positive negation: Threshold, sequence and personfication in Coleridge, English Inst, 72; I Richards and the Art of Critical Balance, Oxford Univ, 73; Allegory, Dictionary of the History of Ideas, Scribner, 73; On two words in the liberetto of the Magic Flute, Ga Rev, spring 75; ed, The Literature of Fact: English Institute Essays, Columbia Univ, 76; Colors of the Mind, Harvard Univ, 91. **CONTACT ADDRESS** 20 W 64th St, New York, NY, 10023.

FLETCHER, MARIE
PERSONAL Born 10/11/1913, New Verda, LA **DISCIPLINE** ENGLISH **EDUCATION** La State Normal Col, AB, 38; La State Univ, MA, 44, PhD, 63. **CAREER** Instr, High Schs, La, 32-48; from instr to assoc prof English, Nicholls State Col, 48-63; from assoc prof to prof, Northwestern State Col, La, 63-67; chmn dept, 73-77, PROF ENGLISH, NICHOLLS STATE UNIV, 77-. **HONORS AND AWARDS** Distinguished Service Award, La Coun Teachers Eng, 75. **MEMBERSHIPS** S Cent Mod Lang Asn. **RESEARCH** Am Lit. **SELECTED PUBLICATIONS** Auth At All Costs--Stories of Impossible Victories, Hist, Vol 57, 95; Segregated Skies, All Black Combat Squadrons of World War Ii, J Milit Hist, Vol 57, 93; A Rape of Justice--Macarthur and the New Guinea Hangings, Am Hist Rev, Vol 98, 93; The Spanish American War--An Annotated Bibliography, J Am Hist, Vol 79, 93; Double V--The Civil Rights Struggle of the Tuskegee Airmen, J Milit Hist, Vol 59, 95; The Late 19th Century United States Army, 1865-1898--A Research Guide, J Am Hist, Vol 79, 93; The Divided Skies, Establishing Segregated Flight Training at Tuskegee, Alabama, 1934-1942, J Mil Hist, Vol 57, 93; Pollard, Fritz--Pioneer in Racial Advancement, Hist, Vol 56, 94. **CONTACT ADDRESS** Dept of English, Nicholls State Univ, Thibodaux, LA, 70301.

FLETCHER, WINONA LEE
PERSONAL Born 11/25/1926, Hamlet, NC, m, 1952, 1 child **DISCIPLINE** SPEECH AND DRAMA **EDUCATION** J C Smith Univ, AB 47; State Univ, Iowa, MA, 51; Ind Univ, PhD (speech and theatre), 68. **CAREER** Instr English, Delwatt's Radio and Electronics Inst, 47-50; from instr to assoc prof English, Speech and Theatre, Ky State Univ, 51-68, dir theatre, 66-78, prof, 68-78; PROF DRAMA, THEATRE and AFRO-AM STUDIES, IND UNIV, 78-, ASSOC DEAN, COL ARTS and SCI, 81-, Consult, Ind Univ Bloomington, 70-71, vis assoc prof Afro-Am studies and theatre, 71-73; comnr, Ky Arts Comn, 76-80; mem task force, Comn on Blacks, Kennedy Ctr, 77-; coordr, Am Coun Teacher Fr and Black Col Proj, John F Kennedy Ctr, 81-. **MEMBERSHIPS** Fel Am Theatre Asn; Nat Asn Dramatic and Speech Arts (exec secy, 58-62); Speech Commun Asn; AAUP; Southeastern Theatre Conf. **RESEARCH** American theatre; Black drama and theatre; drama and theatre of the Federal Theatre Project. **SELECTED PUBLICATIONS** Auth, Sorrow is the Only Faithful one, The Life of Dodson, Owen, Theatre J, Vol 46, 94. **CONTACT ADDRESS** Dept of Fine Arts, Indiana Univ, Bloomington, Bloomington, IN, 47405.

FLIBBERT, JOSEPH THOMAS
PERSONAL Born 07/24/1938, Worcester, MA, m, 1963, 3 children **DISCIPLINE** AMERICAN LITERATURE **EDUCATION** Assumption Col, AB, 60; Boston Col, MA, 63; Univ IL, Urbana, PhD, 70. **CAREER** Instr Eng, Al-Hikma Univ, Bagdad, 61-62; instr French, Worcester Acad, MA, 62-63; asst prof Eng, Merrimack Col, 63-67; tchg asst, Univ IL, Urbana, 67-69; ch person dept, 74-77, dir advising & coun ctr, 77-78, assoc prof, 70-78, prof eng, Salem State Col, 70, Sr Fulbright-Hays scholar, 79. **MEMBERSHIPS** MLA; NEA; Melville Soc; Nathaniel Hawthorne Soc. **RESEARCH** Am lit, 1820-1860; Herman Melville; lit of the sea; Nathaniel Hawthorne. **SELECTED PUBLICATIONS** Auth, Hawthorne, Salem, and the Sea, Sextant, 94; Fragments From the Writings of a Solitary Man: Defeat and Death in Hawthorne's Shorter Works, Forum, 4/95; That Look Beneath: Hawthorne's Portrait of Benevolence in the House of the Seven Gables, In: Critical Essays on Hawthorne's House of the Seven Gables, G.K. Hall, 95; Poetry in the Mainstream, In: America and the Sea: A Literary History, Univ Ga, 95; The American Scholar: 1997, Values Realization J, 97. **CONTACT ADDRESS** Dept of Eng, Salem State Col, 352 Lafayette St, Salem, MA, 01970-5353. **EMAIL** jflibber@salem.mass.edu

FLICK, ROBERT GENE
PERSONAL Born 10/18/1930, Oblong, IL, m, 1951, 4 children **DISCIPLINE** ENGLISH, HUMANITIES **EDUCATION** Eastern IL State Col, BSEd, 52; Univ FL, MA, 54, PhD, 67. **CAREER** Tchr high sch, IL, 54-56; from instr to assoc prof Eng, Jacksonville Univ, 56-68; assoc prof & actg chmn hum, 68-69, chmn, Dept Hum, Philos & Relig, 69-79, prof hum, Univ Central L, 69-98; Tchr, State Univ System Study Center, Florence, Italy, 76, 81 & 85. **HONORS AND AWARDS** NEH Summer Seminar Grant, Univ MN, 80; Omicron Delta Kappa (hon mem 11/88); Phi Kappa Phi (hon mem 4/92); Excellence in Tchg Award, Col Arts and Sci, Founders Day, 4/26/90. **MEMBERSHIPS** AAUP, 57-77; SAtlantic Mod Lang Asn, 57-; Southern Hum Conf; FL Col Eng Asc, 64. **RESEARCH** Creative writing; Emily Dickinson and nineteenth century Am lit; Greek art and cult. **SELECTED PUBLICATIONS** Emily Dickinson: Mystic and Skeptic, Univ Microfilms, 67; Humanities Colloquium at SAMLA, In: Humanties in the South, Fall 72; Prospects for the Humanist in Public Policy Debate, Humanews, 77-78. **CONTACT ADDRESS** Dept of Hum, 1028 Golfside Dr, Winter Park, FL, 32792-5128. **EMAIL** rflick@pegasus.cc.ucf.edu

FLIEGELMAN, JAY
DISCIPLINE ENGLISH **EDUCATION** Ohio Wesleyan, BA, 71; Stanford Univ, PhD, 77. **CAREER** PROF, ENG, STANFORD UNIV **HONORS AND AWARDS** Mellon Distinguished Scholar-in-Res, 98-99. **MEMBERSHIPS** Am Antiquarian Soc **RESEARCH** Am Lib Bks, 1650-1860. **SELECTED PUBLICATIONS** Auth, Declaring Independence: Jefferson, Natural Language, and the Culture of Performance, Stanford Univ Press, 93; auth, Prodigals and Pilgrims: The American Revolution Against Patriarchical Authority, 1750-1800, Cambridge Univ Press, 82. **CONTACT ADDRESS** Dept of Eng, Stanford Univ, Stanford, CA, 94305.

FLIPPEN, CHARLES
DISCIPLINE COMMUNICATION **EDUCATION** Univ NC, PhD, 68. **CAREER** Instr, Towson Univ. **RESEARCH** Audience analysis of popular cult. **SELECTED PUBLICATIONS** Auth, Liberating the Media: The New Journalism. **CONTACT ADDRESS** Towson Univ, Towson, MD, 21252-0001. **EMAIL** cflippen@towson.edu

FLITTERMAN-LEWIS, SANDY
DISCIPLINE DEPARTMENT OF LITERATURES IN ENGLISH **EDUCATION** Berkeley, BA, MA, PhD. **CAREER** Assoc prof Eng, Rutgers, The State Univ NJ, Univ Col-Camden. **SELECTED PUBLICATIONS** Auth, To Desire Differently: Feminism and the French Cinema. **CONTACT ADDRESS** Dept of Lit in Eng, Rutgers, The State Univ New Jersey, Univ Col-Camde, Murray Hall 045, New Brunswick, NJ, 08903. **EMAIL** sweetsod@aol.com

FLORA, JOSEPH MARTIN
PERSONAL Born 02/09/1934, Toledo, OH, m, 1959, 4 children **DISCIPLINE** ENGLISH **EDUCATION** Univ Mich, BA, 56, MA, 57, PhD (English), 62. **CAREER** Instr English, Univ Mich, 61-62; from instr to assoc prof, 62-77, asst dean grad sch, 67-72, assoc dean, 77-78, actg chmn dept, 80-81, PROF ENGLISH, UNIV NC, CHAPEL HILL, 77-, CHMN DEPT, 81-, Mem adv bd, Studies in Short Fiction, 78-; mem adv bd, Southern Lit J. **MEMBERSHIPS** MLA; Soc Study Southern Lit; Western Lit Asn; Soc Study Midwestern Lit; James Branch Cabell Soc. **RESEARCH** Am Lit; 20th century drama; British literature 1880-1920. **SELECTED PUBLICATIONS** Auth, A Readers Guide to the Short Stories of Hemingway, Ernest, Rsrcs Am Lit Stud, Vol 21,96; The Modernist Short Story--A Study in Theory and Practice, Mod Fiction Stud, Vol 40, 94; Cabell, James, Branch and Richmond in Virginia, Mississippi Quart, Vol 47, 94; Wolfe, Thomas--An Annotated Critical Bibliog, Thomas Wolfe Rev, Vol 21, 97; Southern Writers and the Machine, Faulkner to Percy, Mississippi Quart, Vol 49, 96. **CONTACT ADDRESS** Dept of English, Univ of NC, Chapel Hill, NC, 27514.

FLORES, CAROL A.
PERSONAL Lockport, NY, m, 1968 **DISCIPLINE** ARCHITECTURE, HISTORY, THEORY & CRITICISM **EDUCATION** Univ NY Albany, BA, 66; Ga Inst of Tech, MS, 90; Ga Inst of Tech, PhD, archit, 96. **CAREER** Teacher, LaSalle Sch for Boys, 66-71; asst to pres, Environment/One Corp, 71; svc adv, N Eng Telephone, 72-76; chief svc adv, Southern Bell, 76-77; mgr, Southern Bell, 78-79; district mgr, Southern Bell, 80-82; operations mgr, Bell South Svc, 83-85; owner and commercial and residential designer, Design Options, 86-90; grad teaching asst, Col of Archit, Ga Inst of Tech, 89; doctoral fel, Col of Archit, Ga Inst of Tech, 90-94; asst prof, Col of Archit and Planning, Ball State Univ, 96-. **HONORS AND AWARDS** Outstanding rating, Mgt Assessment Prog, Southern Bell, 78; Outstanding Mgt Candidate, Southern Bell, 80; Individual Incentive award, BellSouth Svc, 84; Fel, Colonial Williamsburg Found, Antiques forum, 93; Ga Tech Alumni Asn Student Leadership travel award for Rome study, 93; Scholar, Nineteenth Century Studies Prog in London, Victorian Soc, 94; GTA teaching excellence award, col of archit, Ga Inst of Tech, 94; CETL/AMOCO Found GTA teaching excellence award, 94; pres fel, col of archit, Ga Inst of Tech, 90-94; doctoral fel, col of archit, Ga Inst of Tech, 91-94; Best Article Award, Southeast Chap, Soc of Archit Hist, 95; Outstanding Student in Archit, Ga Inst of Tech, dec, 96; Doctoral prog achievement award, Ga Inst of Tech, may, 97. **MEMBERSHIPS** Soc of Archit Hist; Southeast Chap, Soc of Archit Hist; Vernacular Archit Forum; Soc for Amer City and Regional Planning Hist; Asn of Coll Sch of Archit; Nineteenth-Century Studies Asn; Victorian Soc; Soc for Emblem Studies; Decorative Arts Soc; Intl Soc for Amer City and Regional Planning Hist; Wallpaper Hist Soc. **RESEARCH** 19th-Century British architecture, theory, and decorative arts; Architecture, theory and decorative arts of Owen Jones 1809-1874; Public housing; Symbolism in architecture. **SELECTED PUBLICATIONS** Auth, Owen Jones, Architect, Ga Inst of Tech, 96; contr, The Grammar of Ornament, Professional Artists' Edition, Pasadena, Direct Imagination Inc, 96; auth, US public housing in the 1930s: the first projects in Atlanta, Georgia, Planning Perspectives, 9, 405-430, 94. **CONTACT ADDRESS** College of Architecture and Planning, Ball State Univ, Muncie, IN, 47306-0305. **EMAIL** cflores@wp.bsu.edu

FLORY, WENDY STALLARD
PERSONAL Born 11/14/1943, Fulmer, England, m, 1966, 2 children **DISCIPLINE** ENGLISH/AMERICAN LITERATURE **EDUCATION** Univ of London, Bedford Col, BA Hons English, 65; Univ of Texas at Austin, PhD(English), 70. **CAREER** asst prof, English, Rutgers Univ, Doulgas Col 70-79; vis asst prof, English, Univ of Pa, 80-82; asst prof, English, Univ of Pa, 82-89; assoc prof, English, Purdue Univ, 89-93; PROF ENGLISH PURDUE UNIV, 90-. **HONORS AND AWARDS** Nat Endowment for the Humanities Fel, 82-83; Am Asn of Univ Women Fel, 79-80; Fulbright Grant, 65. **MEMBERSHIPS** MLA; Melville Soc. **RESEARCH** Poetry; American romance; literary symbolizing; Holocaust documents; psychology of persecutors. **SELECTED PUBLICATIONS** auth, The American Ezra Pound, Yale Univ Pr, 89; auth, Ezra Pound and The Cantos: A Record of Struggle, Yale Univ Pr, 80; auth, "A new Century-A New Symbol Criticism: Pierre and an A-Freudian Approach to Melville's Symbolizing," Melville Soc Extracts, 96; auth, "Maurice Sendak's Pierre Pictures," Melville Soc Extracts, 97; auth, "On Goldhagen's Refusal to Address the Psychological Dynamics of Holocaust Murder," Shofar: An Intedisciplinary Jour of Jewish Studies, 97. **CONTACT ADDRESS** Dept of English, Purdue Univ, 711 Hillcrest Rd, West Lafayette, IN, 47906. **EMAIL** wflory@sla.purdue.edu

FLOWER, DEAN SCOTT
PERSONAL Born 08/17/1938, Milwaukee, WI, 4 children **DISCIPLINE** ENGLISH **EDUCATION** Univ Mich, AB, 60; Stanford Univ, PhD(English), 66. **CAREER** Asst prof English, Univ Southern Calif, 64-69; assoc prof English, 69-85, PROF ENGLISH, 85-, chair English dept, 85-88, SMITH COL; Consult, Orff-Schulwerk Prof creativity & participation music educ, 65-67; advisory ed, The Hudson Review, 82-; chair, Advanced Placement Test Dev Com, 95-. **HONORS AND AWARDS** NEH award, 85, 87; NEH summer stipend, 89. **MEMBERSHIPS** MLA, SLE. **RESEARCH** American literature; contemporary prose fiction. **SELECTED PUBLICATIONS** Ed, The Great Short Works of Henry James, Harper, 66; Eight Short Novels, 67 & Counterparts: Classic and Contemporary American Stories, 71, Fawcett; auth, Henry James in Northampton: Visions and Revisions, Neilson Libr, 71; ed, Henry David Tho-

reau: Essays, Journals and Poems, Fawcett, 75; coauth, A Catalogue of American Paintings, Water Colors and Drawings, George Walter Vincent Smith Art Mus, 76. **CONTACT ADDRESS** Dept of English, Smith Col, Northampton, MA, 01060. **EMAIL** dflower@ernestine.smith.edu

FLOWER, LINDA S.
PERSONAL Born 03/03/1944 **DISCIPLINE** ENGLISH, WRITING **EDUCATION** Simpson Col, BA, 65; McGill Univ, BA, 64; Rutgers Univ, PhD, 72. **CAREER** Tchg asst Eng, Rutgers Univ, 70-71; lectr Eng, Univ Pittsburgh, 72-73; asst prof, 73-74, dir bus & prof commun, 74-80, prof eng, Carnegie-Mellon Univ, 80-, Dir, Center for Univ Outreach, 96-, Series ed, Res in Writing Series, Guilford Press; grants, Nat Inst Educ, 78-84. **MEMBERSHIPS** Conf Col Compos & Commun; Nat Coun Tchr(s) Eng; Am Educ Res Asn. **RESEARCH** Cognitive processes in writing--studying the thinking in writing--studying the thinking processes, the skills and strategies that distinguish experts and novices; tchg problem-solving strategies for writers. **SELECTED PUBLICATIONS** Coauth (with J R Hayes), Problem-solving strategies and the writing process, Col English, Vol 39, 449-461; auth, Writer-based prose: A cognitive basis for problems in writing, Col English, Vol 41, 19-37; coauth (with J R Hayes), The cognition of discovery: Defining a rhetorical problem, Col Compos & Commun, Vol 31, 21-32; auth, Problem-solving strategies for writing in college and community, Harcourt Brace Col Publ, 98; coauth (with J R Hayes), A cognitive process theory of writing, Col Compos & Commun, Vol 32, 365-387; coauth (with W C Peck, L Higgins), Community Literacy, Col Compos & Commun Vol 46, 199-222; auth Negotiating meaning of difference, Written Commun, Vol 13, 44-92; auth, The Construction of Negotiated Meaning: A Social Cognitive Theory of Writing, Univ Southern IL Press, 94. **CONTACT ADDRESS** Dept of Eng, Carnegie Mellon Univ, 5000 Forbes Ave, Pittsburgh, PA, 15213-3890. **EMAIL** lf54@andrew.cmu.edu

FLOWERS, BETTY SUE
PERSONAL Born 02/02/1947, Waco, TX, m, 1967 **DISCIPLINE** ENGLISH LITERATURE, CREATIVE WRITING **EDUCATION** Univ Tex, BA, 69, MA, 70; Univ London, PhD (English), 73. **CAREER** Teaching asst English, Univ Tex, 68-70; lectr drama and English, Beaver Col, London, 71-72; asst prof, 73-79, ASSOC PROF ENGLISH, UNIV TEX, 79-, ASSOC DEAN GRAD SCH, 79-, Mellon Found fel, 76. **MEMBERSHIPS** AAUP; MLA; Am Asn Advan Humanities. **RESEARCH** Nineteenth and 20th century poetry; psychological approaches to literature; women's studies. **SELECTED PUBLICATIONS** Auth, Victorian Women Poets, Writing Against the Heart, Mod Philol, Vol 92, 95; Victorian Women Poets, Writing Against the Heart, Mod Philol Vol 92, 95. **CONTACT ADDRESS** Dept of English, Univ of Tex, 0 Univ of Texas, Austin, TX, 78712-1026.

FOGEL, DANIEL
DISCIPLINE MODERN NOVEL, 19TH AND 20TH CENTURY ENGLISH AND AMERICAN LITERATURE, CREATI **EDUCATION** Cornell, PhD, 76. **CAREER** Prof, La State Univ; Ed Henry James Rev, 79-95; PMLA, adv comt, 86-90; exec Vice-Chancellor and Provost; exec comt, Div on Late 19th and Early 20th-Century Am Lit, MLA, 89-92. **HONORS AND AWARDS** LSU Alumni Asn Distinguished Fac Award, 88., Founder, Henry James Rev. **RESEARCH** Henry James; James Joyce; Virginia Woolf; Modern Poetry. **SELECTED PUBLICATIONS** Auth, Covert Relations: James Joyce, Virginia Woolf, and Henry James, 90; Daisy Miller: A Dark Comedy of Manners, 90; Schindler's List in Novel and Film: Exponential Conversion, the Hist J of Film, Radio, and TV 14, 94; The Editor as Teacher and Learner, the Henry James Rev 17, 96; ed, A Companion to Henry James Studies, 93. **CONTACT ADDRESS** Dept of Eng, Louisiana State Univ, 146 Thomas Boyd Hall, Baton Rouge, LA, 70803. **EMAIL** grdfoge@lsuvm.sncc.lsu.edu

FOGEL, STAN
DISCIPLINE ENGLISH LITERATURE **EDUCATION** Carleton Univ, BA, 68; Univ British Columbia, MA, 70; Purdue Univ, PhD, 73. **CAREER** Prof **RESEARCH** Contemporary literature; critical theory. **SELECTED PUBLICATIONS** Auth, Deconstruction and Theology (rev); I See England, I See France...: Robert Kroetsch's Alibi; And all the little typtopies': Notes on Language Theory in the Contemporary Experimental Novel; American Graffiti: Gass's in the Heart of the Heart of the Country; Biopsy: Biography (rev); Carpe Diem: Complain Daily; Don't Shoot the Dentist; Fidel Wakes Me Every Morning: A Cuban Update; Gobble, Gobble, Gobble: Critical Appetites (rev); Gringo Star. **CONTACT ADDRESS** Dept of English, St. Jerome's Univ, Waterloo, ON, N2L 3G3.

FOLEY, BARBARA
PERSONAL Born 03/29/1948, New York, NY, m, 1972, 2 children **DISCIPLINE** ENGLISH **EDUCATION** Radcliffe Col, BA, 69; Univ Chicago, MA, 71, PhD, 76. **CAREER** Asst prof, Eng, 76-79, Univ Wisc; asst prof, Eng & Amer stud, 80-87, Northwestern Univ; assoc prof, 87-95, tenured, 90, prof, 95-, Rutgers Univ. **HONORS AND AWARDS** Phi Beta Kappa; NH grants. **MEMBERSHIPS** MLA; AAUP. **RE-SEARCH** Amer Lit, African-Amer Lit; Marxist criticism, theory of the novel; politics & lit. **SELECTED PUBLICATIONS** Auth, Telling the Truth: The Theory and Practice of Documentary Fiction, Cornell UP, 86; auth, Radical Representations: Politics and form in US Proletarian Fiction 1929-1941, Duke UP, 93; art, Generic and Doctrinal Politics in the Proletarian Bildungsroman, Understanding Narrative, Ohio SUP, 94; art, Tillie Olsen, Companion to Amer Thought, Basil Blackwell, 95; art, Wayne Booth and the Politics of Ethics, Rhetoric & Pluralism: Legacies of Wayne Booth, Ohio SUP, 95; art, Jean Toomer's Sparta, Amer Lit 67, 95; art, Introduction to Myra Page, Moscow Yankee, Univ Ill Press, 96; art, Jean Toomer's Washington and the Politics of Class: From 'Blue Veins' to Seventh-Street Rebels, Modern Fiction Stud 42, 96; art, The Federal Writers Project, Encycl African-Amer Hist & Cult, Macmillan, 97; art, The Rhetoric of Anticommunism in Ralph Ellison's Invisible Man. Col Eng 59, 97; art, Interview with Barbara Foley, Conducted by Ron Strickland, Mediations 21, 98; art, Roads Taken and Not Taken: Anticommunism, Post-Marxism, an African American Literature, Cult Logic, 98; art, From Astor Place to Wall Street: Historicizing Melville's 'Bartleby', The Other Romance: Essays in Honor of James E. Miller, Jr, Univ Chicago Press 98; art, U.S. Proletarian Literature, SAMAR, 98; art, In The Land of Cotton; Economics and Violence in Jean Toomer's Cane, African Amer Rev 32, 98; art, Ralph Ellison as Proletarian Journalist, Sci & Soc, 99. **CONTACT ADDRESS** English Dept, Rutgers Univ, 360 Kings Blvd, Newark, NJ, 07102. **EMAIL** bfoley@andromeda.rutgers.edu

FOLEY, JOHN MILES
DISCIPLINE ENGLISH **EDUCATION** Univ Mass, PhD, 74. **CAREER** Prof **HONORS AND AWARDS** NEH, ACLS & Guggenheim fel., Founded, Ctr Stud in Oral Tradition. **MEMBERSHIPS** Russ Acad Sci. **SELECTED PUBLICATIONS** Auth, Traditional Oral Epic, Calif, 90; Immanent Art, Ind, 91 & The Singer of Tales in Performance, Ind, 95. **CONTACT ADDRESS** Dept of English, Univ of Missouri-Columbia, 309 University Hall, Columbia, MO, 65211. **EMAIL** foley@showme.missouri.edu

FOLKENFLIK, ROBERT
PERSONAL Born 05/23/1939, Newark, NJ, m, 1965, 2 children **DISCIPLINE** ENGLISH **EDUCATION** Rutgers Univ, BA, 61; Univ Minn, MA, 66; Cornell Univ, PhD (English), 68. **CAREER** From instr to asst prof English, Univ Rochester, 67-75, dir freshman English, 71-73; ASSOC PROF ENGLISH, UNIV CALIF, IRVINE, 75-, Asst ed, Studies in Burke and His Time, 72-74; Nat Endowment for Humanities younger humanist fel. **MEMBERSHIPS** MLA; Am Soc Eighteenth Century Studies; Western Soc Eighteenth Century Studies (vpres, 78-79). **RESEARCH** Eighteenth-century literature; the novel; biography. **SELECTED PUBLICATIONS** Auth, Rasselas and the Closed Field, Huntington Lib Quart, Vol 57, 94. **CONTACT ADDRESS** Dept of English and Comp Lit, Univ of Calif, Irvine, CA, 92664.

FOLKS, JEFFREY J
PERSONAL Born 10/16/1948, Tulsa, OK, 1 child **DISCIPLINE** AMERICAN AND SOUTHERN LITERATURE **EDUCATION** Reed Col, BA, 69; Ind Univ, MA, 72, PhD (English), 77. **CAREER** Assoc instr, Ind Univ, 70-72; instr, 76-79 asst prof, 79-82, ASSOC PROF ENGLISH, TENN WESLEYAN COL, 82-, Nat Endowment for Humanities summer sem, 79 and 82. **MEMBERSHIPS** MLA; Soc Study Southern Lit; Conf Christianity and Lit. **RESEARCH** American fiction. **SELECTED PUBLICATIONS** Auth, Agee, James Fashioning of Guilt--The Morning Watch, Southern Lit J, Vol 29, 96; Once Upon a Time, A Floating Opera, W Lit Today, Vol 69, 95; In the Jaws of Life, W Lit Today, Vol 66, 92; Mercy of a Rude Stream, W Lit Today, Vol 68, 94; A Diving Rock on the Hudson, W Lit Today, Vol 69, 95; The Damned Yard and Other Stories, W Lit Today, Vol 67, 93; Feather Crowns, W Lit Today, Vol 68, 94; Caldwell, Erskine--The Journey from Tobacco Road, W Lit Today, Vol 70, 96; The Collected Stories, W Lit Today, Vol 68, 94; The Archaeologist of Memory--Autobiographical Recollection in Tate Maimed Man Trilogy, Southern Lit J, Vol 27, 94; Crowd Types in Byrd, William Histories, South Lit J, Vol 26, 94. **CONTACT ADDRESS** English Dept, Tenn Wesleyan Col, Athens, TN, 37303.

FONTENOT, CHESTER J.
PERSONAL Los Angeles, CA, m, 3 children **DISCIPLINE** AMERICAN & AFRO-AMERICAN LITERATURE **EDUCATION** Whittier Col, BA, 72; Univ Calif, Irvine, PhD(comp cultures), 75. **CAREER** Asst prof, Univ Nebr-Lincoln, 75-77 & Cornell Univ, 77-79; assoc prof Lit, Univ Ill, Urbana-Champaign, 79-, vis scholar, Colgate Univ, Fall, 78, State Univ NY Binghamton, Spring, 78; vis artist, Purdue Univ, 80; reviewer & panelist, Nat Endowment for the Humanities, 81-, NSF, 82-. **HONORS AND AWARDS** Incomplete List of Teachers Rated Excellent By Their Students, The Univ Ill at Urbana-Champaign; Phi Beta Sigma Distinguished Faculty Award for Outstanding Teaching, The Univ Ill, Urbana-Champaign. **MEMBERSHIPS** MLA; Midwest Mod Lang Asn; Asn Study Afro-Am Life & Hist; Asn Study Multi-Ethnic Lit in the US; Col Lang Asn. **RESEARCH** Afro-American literature and cul-

ture; contemporary American literature; literary criticism and theory with emphasis on myth and symbolism. **SELECTED PUBLICATIONS** Ed, Writing About Black Literature, Nebr Curric Develop Ctr, 76; auth, Black fiction: From tragedy to romance, Cornell Rev, Spring 78; Ishmael Reed and the politics of Aesthetics, Black Am Lit Forum, Spring 78; Black fiction: Apollo or Dionysus, Twentieth Century Lit, Fall 78; Frantz Fanon and the Devourers, J of Black Studies, 9/78; Frantz Fanon: Language as the God Gone Astray in the flesh, Univ Nebr Studies, 79; Angelic dance or tug of war: The humanistic implications of cultural formalism, Black Am Lit and Humanism, 81; Mythic patterns in River Niger and Ceremonies in Dark Old Men, Melus, 81. **CONTACT ADDRESS** Dept of English, Univ of Illinois, 608 S Wright St, Urbana, IL, 61801-3613. **EMAIL** cfonten@uni.edu

FOOTE, BUD
PERSONAL Born 08/19/1930, Laconia, NH, m, 6 children **DISCIPLINE** MODERN LITERATURE, FOLKLORE & SCIENCE FICTION **EDUCATION** Princeton Univ, AB, 52; Univ Conn, MA, 58. **CAREER** Instr English, Univ Conn, 53-56; instr, Arnold Sch, Pembroke, Mass, 56-57; from instr to asst prof, 57-69, assoc prof, 69-85, PROF ENGLISH, GA INST TECHNOL, 85-, NEH proj staff, 71-72, 72-73; dir, 73, 74. **MEMBERSHIPS** S Atlantic Mod Lang Asn; MLA; Science Fiction Res Asn. **RESEARCH** American humor; science fiction. **SELECTED PUBLICATIONS** Auth, Richard Condon & David Karp, in Contemporary Novelists, St Martin, 72; The Connecticut Yankee in the Twentieth Century: Travel to the Past in Science Fiction, Greenwood Press, 91. **CONTACT ADDRESS** School of Lit, Commun & Culture, Georgia Inst of Tech, 225 North Ave NW, Atlanta, GA, 30332-0002.

FORBES, JOYCE
PERSONAL Trinidad, West Indies **DISCIPLINE** ENGLISH **EDUCATION** Howard Univ, BA, 61; Queen's Univ, MA, 64; Univ West Indies, PhD, 77. **CAREER** CHAIR, DEPT ENGLISH, LAKEHEAD UNIV 89-92. **HONORS AND AWARDS** Can Commonwealth Schol, 61-63; 3M Can Tchr Fel Outstanding Contrib Univ Tchr, 88. **MEMBERSHIPS** Can Asn Univ Tchrs; Ont Confed Univ Fac Adminr; Can Res Inst Advan Women; Caribbean African Asn. **SELECTED PUBLICATIONS** Auth, The Tears of Things in Arts & Lit Rev, 72; auth, Wilson Harris's Guyana Quartet: The Outsider as Character and Symbol, 86; auth, William Golding as Essayist in British Essays 1880-1960 in Dictionary of Lit Biog, 90. **CONTACT ADDRESS** Dept of English, Lakehead Univ, Thunder Bay, ON, P7B 5E1. **EMAIL** jforbes@flash.lakehead.ca

FORD, JAMES ERIC
PERSONAL Born 11/04/1943, Los Angeles, CA, m, 1973, 6 children **DISCIPLINE** ENGLISH LANGUAGE & LITERATURE **EDUCATION** Brigham Young Univ, BA, 68; San Francisco State Univ, MA, 71; Univ Chicago, PhD(English), 81. **CAREER** Asst prof to assoc prof, Brigham Young Univ, 76-81; asst prof English, Univ Nebr - Lincoln, 81-. **MEMBERSHIPS** MLA; Am Philol Asn. **RESEARCH** History and theory of criticism; literary criticism; research methods. **SELECTED PUBLICATIONS** Auth, On thinking about Aristotle's Thought, Critical Inquiry, spring 78; The Rebirth of Greek Tragedy and the Decline of the Humanities, Ga Rev, fall 80; A Generalized Model for Research Paper Instruction, Lit Res Newsletter, winter-spring 81; Barnardine's Nominal Nature in Measure for Measure, Papers on Lang & Lit, winter 82; ed, Teaching the Research Paper, Scarecrow Press; ed, The Foundations of Critical Plurlism, Critical Inquiry (spec ed) 96. **CONTACT ADDRESS** Dept English, Univ Nebr - Lincoln, Lincoln, NE, 68588-0333. **EMAIL** jford@unl.edu

FORD, THOMAS WELLBORN
PERSONAL Born 12/23/1924, Houston, TX, m, 1953, 2 children **DISCIPLINE** AM LIT **EDUCATION** Rice Univ, BA, 50; Univ Tex, MA, 51, PhD, 59. **CAREER** Instr, Kinkaid Prep Sch, Houston, Tex, 53-55; spec instr Eng, Univ Tex, 58-59; spec instr, Univ SC, 59-61; asst prof, 61-66; assoc prof, 66-71, PROF ENGLISH, UNIV HOUSTON, 71-. **MEMBERSHIPS** MLA; Am Studies Asn; Col English Asn; Western Lit Asn. **RESEARCH** Western Am Lit; nineteenth century and contemporary Am Lit. **SELECTED PUBLICATIONS** Auth, Guthrie, A. B. Additions of Shane, W Am Lit, Vol 29, 95; Leonor Park, W Am Lit, Vol 28, 94; Alligator Dance, W Am Lit, Vol 30, 95; Recollections of 1st Reading an Pound, Ezra Letter, Paideuma J Devoted Ezra Pound Scholarship, Vol 21, 92; Updike Ace in the Hole, Explicator, Vol 52, 94. **CONTACT ADDRESS** Dept of English, Univ of Houston, Houston, TX, 77004.

FOREMAN, KATHRYN S.
DISCIPLINE ENGLISH **EDUCATION** Yale Univ, BA, 80, MA, 85, PhD, 90. **CAREER** Asst prof, Univ the South, 90-92; asst prof, Univ Miami, 98- 98; ASSOC PROF, UNIV MIAMI, 98-. **CONTACT ADDRESS** Dept of English, Univ of Miami, PO Box 248145, Coral Gables, FL, 33124-4632. **EMAIL** kfreeman@miami.edu

FORKER, CHARLES RUSH
PERSONAL Born 03/11/1927, Pittsburgh, PA **DISCIPLINE** ENGLISH LITERATURE **EDUCATION** Bowdoin Col, AB, 51; Merton Col, Oxford, BA, 53, MA, 55; Harvard Univ, PhD, 57. **CAREER** Instr English, Univ Wis, 57-59; from asst prof to assoc prof, 59-68, PROF ENGLISH LIT, IND UNIV, BLOOMINGTON, 68-, Folger Shakespeare Libr fel, 68; Am Coun Learned Soc grant, 65-66; vis prof, Univ Mich, Ann Arbor, 68-69; Huntington Libr fel, 69; mem ed bd, Hamlet Studies and English Medieval and Renaissance Drama. **MEMBERSHIPS** MLA; Shakespeare Asn Am; Int Shakespeare Soc; Renaissance Soc Am; Malone Soc. **RESEARCH** Shakespeare studies; Elizabethan drama. **SELECTED PUBLICATIONS** Auth, The Tragedy of Coriolanus, Univ Toronto Quart, Vol 65, 95. **CONTACT ADDRESS** Dept of English, Indiana Univ, Bloomington, Bloomington, IN, 47401.

FORT, KEITH
DISCIPLINE ENGLISH LITERATURE **EDUCATION** Univ of South, BA; Univ Minn, MA, PhD. **CAREER** Prof. **SELECTED PUBLICATIONS** Auth, The Psychopathology of the Everyday Language of Literary Studies, 79; Form, Authority, and the Critical Essay, 71. **CONTACT ADDRESS** English Dept, Georgetown Univ, 37th and O St, Washington, DC, 20057.

FORTIER, JAN M.
PERSONAL Born 05/05/1946, Los Angeles, CA, m **DISCIPLINE** ENGLISH **EDUCATION** Univ Ore, MLS, 73; Temple Univ, PhD, 87. **CAREER** Instr, librn, Marylhurst Univ, 90-. **MEMBERSHIPS** ALA; ACRL; Asn Lit Scholar Critics. **RESEARCH** Literature of home. **CONTACT ADDRESS** 3112 SE Morrison St, Portland, OR, 97214-3045. **EMAIL** jfortier@marylhurst.edu

FOSHAY, TOBY
DISCIPLINE ENGLISH LITERATURE **EDUCATION** Acadia Univ, BA, MA; Dalhousie Univ, PhD. **CAREER** Assoc prof **HONORS AND AWARDS** Post-dr fel(s), Calgary Inst for the Hum, 87-88; SSHRCC, 89-90; Clare Hall, Cambridge Univ, 98. **RESEARCH** Literary theory; cultural theory. **SELECTED PUBLICATIONS** Auth, Lonergan Workshop VI, Scholars Press, 86; Isak Dinesen: A Reassessment of Her Work for the 1990's, Carleton UP, 93; Negation, Critical Theory, and Postmodern Textuality, Kluwer, 94; Shadow of Spirit: Postmodernism and Religion, Routledge, 92; Wyndham Lewis and the Avant-Garde: The Politics of the Intellect, McGill-Queen's, 92; co-ed, Derrida and Negative Theology, SUNY, 91; ed, Wyndham Lewis, Rude Assignment, Black Sparrow, 84. **CONTACT ADDRESS** Dept of English, Victoria Univ, PO Box 3070, Victoria, BC, V8W 3W1. **EMAIL** tfoshay@uvic.ca

FOSTER, DAVID
DISCIPLINE ENGLISH LITERATURE **EDUCATION** Univ WI, PhD. **CAREER** Assoc prof, Drake Univ. **RESEARCH** 19th and 20th century Brit lit. **SELECTED PUBLICATIONS** Auth, publ(s) on postmodernist rhet and aesthet; critiques of pedagog theory and practice. **CONTACT ADDRESS** Drake Univ, University Ave, PO Box 2507, Des Moines, IA, 50311-4505. **EMAIL** david.foster@drake.edu

FOSTER, DONALD W.
PERSONAL Born 06/22/1950, Chicago, IL, m, 1974, 2 children **DISCIPLINE** ENGLISH **EDUCATION** Wheaton Col, BA, 72; UC Santa Barbara, PhD, 85. **CAREER** Vis lectr, 85-86, UCSB; asst prof, 86-90, assoc prof, 90-, Vassar Col. **HONORS AND AWARDS** MLA, William Riley Parker Prize, 87; Delaware Shakespeare Prize, 87; Appointed to Jean Webster Chair, Vassar Col, 91. **MEMBERSHIPS** SAA; MLA; Malone Soc. **RESEARCH** Shakespeare; renaissance lit; forensic linguistics. **SELECTED PUBLICATIONS** Auth, Elegy by W S: A Study in Attribution, Assoc Univ Press, 89; auth, Resurrecting the Author: Elizabeth Tanfield Cary, Privileging Gender in Early Modern Britain, 16th Century Stud, 93; auth, Against the Perjured Falsehood Of Your Tongues: Frances Howard on the Course of Love, Eng Lit Renaissance 24.1, 94; auth, Shaxicon Update, SNL 45.2, 95; auth, Primary culprit, NY, 96; ed, A Funeral Elegy, PMLA 111.5, Shakespeare Stud, 97; auth, A Funeral Elegy: William Shakespeare's Best Speaking Witnesses, PMLA 11.5, Shakespeare Stud, 97; auth, Ward Elliot and Ron Valenza And Then There Were None: A Response, Computers and the Humanities 30, 96; ed & intro, William Shakespeare A Funeral Elegy, The Norton Shakespeare, Norton, 97; ed & intro, Elegie Funebre par William Shakespeare, Editions Stock, 96; auth, Shaxicon and Shakespeare's Acting Career, SNL 46.3, 96; auth, The Webbing of Romeo and Juliet, Critical Essays on Shakespeare's Romeo and Juliet, Hall, 97; auth, A Romance of Electronic Scholarship, part 1: The Words, EMLS, 98. **CONTACT ADDRESS** Vassar Col, PO Box 388, Poughkeepsie, NY, 12601. **EMAIL** foster@vassar.edu

FOSTER, EDWARD E.
PERSONAL Born 11/19/1939, West New York, NJ, m, 1966 **DISCIPLINE** ENGLISH **EDUCATION** St Peter's Col, NJ, AB, 61; Univ Rochester, PhD, 65. **CAREER** From instr to assoc prof English, Grinnell Col, 64-73; prof & dean, Col Arts & Sci, Univ San Diego, 73-76; chmn dept humanities, St Mary's Col, Md, 76-79; PROF & DEAN FAC, WHITMAN COL, WA, 79-. **MEMBERSHIPS** MLA; Medieval Acad Am. **RESEARCH** Middle English narrative; Restoration and 18th century political and religious poetry; literary taxonomy. **SELECTED PUBLICATIONS** Coauth, A Modern Lexicon of Literary Terms, Scott, 68; Humor in The Knight's Tale, Chaucer Rev, 68; Allegorical consolation in The Book of the Duchess, Ball State Univ Forum, 70; The text of William of Palerne, Neuphilol Mitt, 73. **CONTACT ADDRESS** Whitman Col, 345 Boyer Ave, Walla Walla, WA, 99362-2083. **EMAIL** fosteree@whitman.edu

FOSTER, FRANCES SMITH
PERSONAL Born 02/08/1944, Dayton, OH **DISCIPLINE** AM LIT, AFRO-AM LIT **EDUCATION** Miami Univ, BS, 64; Univ Southern Calif, MA, 71; Univ Calif, San Diego, PhD (Black and Am lit), 76. **CAREER** Instr lit, San Fernando State Col, 70-71; asst prof, 71-81, asst dean univ, 76-78, ASSOC PROF LIT, SAN DIEGO STATE UNIV, 81-. **MEMBERSHIPS** MLA; Col Lang Asn Res; NCTE. **RESEARCH** Slave narratives; women writers. **SELECTED PUBLICATIONS** Auth, Christian Recordings, Afro Protestantism, Its Press, and the Production of African Am Lit, Rel Lit, Vol 27, 95; The Schomburg Library of 19th Century Black Women Writers, Tulsa Stud in Womens Lit, Vol 11, 92. **CONTACT ADDRESS** Sch of Lit San Diego State Univ, San Diego, CA, 92182.

FOSTER, FRANCES SMITH
PERSONAL Born 02/08/1944, Dayton, OH, m **DISCIPLINE** AFRICAN-AMERICAN LITERATURE **EDUCATION** Miami Univ, BS, 1964; Univ of South CA, MA, 1971; Univ of CA, PhD, 1976. **CAREER** Cincinnati Public Schools, teacher, 1964-66; Detroit Public Schools, teacher, 1966-68; San Fernando Valley State Coll, instructor, 1970-71; San Diego State Univ, asst dean, 1976-79, prof, beginning 1971; Univ of California, San Diego, prof, currently. **HONORS AND AWARDS** Ford Found Fellowship; San Diego Fellowship; Gen Motors Scholar; SDSU Outstanding Faculty Awd; numerous articles and reviews on Afro-Amer literature. **MEMBERSHIPS** Humanities Adv Council; KPBS; San Diego State Univ, Career Plan & Placemt Ctr, Adv Comm; NAACP, Coll Lang Assn; Modern Lang Assn; Philological Assn of the Pac Coast; West Coast Women's Historical Assn; NEH Rsch Fellowship; CSU Faculty Rsch Fellowship; Phi Beta Kappa; Phi Kappa Pi; Althenoi Phi Kappa Delta; Alpha Kappa Alpha; Children's Literature Assoc; MELUS. **SELECTED PUBLICATIONS** "Changing Concepts of the Black Woman," "Charles Wright, Black Black Humorist," "The Black & White Masks of Franz Fanon & Ralph Ellison," "Witnessing Slavery, The Develop of the Ante-Bellum Slave Narrative," Greenwood Press, 1979; "Voices Unheard Stories Untold, Teaching Women's Literature from a Regional Perspective;" **CONTACT ADDRESS** Univ of California, San Diego, 9500 Gilman Dr, La Jolla, CA, 92093.

FOSTER, TEREE E.
PERSONAL Born 09/24/1947 **DISCIPLINE** ENGLISH LITERATURE AND HISTORY **EDUCATION** BA, Univ Ill Chicago Cir, 68; JD, Loyola Univ Chicago Sch of Law, 76. **CAREER** Admis off, Univ Ill Chicago Cir, nov 72-sep 73; co-dir, Dept of Defense, sep 69-sep 72; summer law intern, Off of the State Appelate Defender for the Fourth Jud Dist; jun 74-aug 74; law clerk, Philip H. Corboy and Assoc, sep 74-sep 76; instr, Loyola Univ Chic Sch of Law, sep 76-jan 77; jud law clerk, US Ct of Appeals for the Seventh Circuit, sep 76-aug 77; of coun, Hastie & Kirschner, feb 84-sep 90; vis prof, Oh State Univ Col of Law, 87-88, Univ Fla Col of Law, 88-89, Univ Denver Col of Law, 92-93; asst prof, aug 77-jul 80, assoc prof, jul 80-may 83, prof, may 83-, assoc dean, sep 90-aug 92, Univ Okla Col of Law; dean and prof of law, WV Univ Col of Law, 93-97; dean and prof of law, DePaul Univ Col of Law, jul 97-. **HONORS AND AWARDS** Phi Kappa Phi, 97; 1998 Distinguished Women in Law Award, WV Univ Col of Law Women's Law Caucus, Feb 27, 1998; Who's Who in Amer, 97-; Who's Who in Amer Law, 96-; Intl Who's Who in Prof, 96-. **MEMBERSHIPS** State of Ill Bar; State of Okla Bar; Northern Dist of Ill Bar; Western Dist of Okla Bar; US Ct of Appeals for the Seventh Circuit; US Ct of Appeals for the Tenth Circuit; Amer Law Inst; Soc of Amer Law Tchrs; Asn of Amer Law Sch; Scribes; Okla Bar Asn; WV Bar Asn; Ill Bar Asn; Amer Jud Soc. **SELECTED PUBLICATIONS** Contr, Law and Literature: An Annotated Bibliography of Law-related works, ed Elizabeth Villiers Gemmette, 98; auth, I Want to Live! Federal Judicial Values in Death Penalty Cases: Preservation of Rights or Punctuality of Execution?, A Symposium on Film and the Law, 21, Okla City, U.L. Rev, 63-87, 97; with Mayer-Schonberger, A Regulatory Web: Free Speech and the Global Information Infrastructure, ed Brian Kahin & Charles Nesson, MIT Press, 96; with Mayer-Schonberger, More Speech, Less Noise: Amplifying Contect-Based Speech Regulations Through Binding International Law, 43, BC Intl & Comp Law Rev, 59-135, 95; with Fallon, West Virginia's Pioneer Women Lawyers, 97, WV Law Rev, 702-23, 95; with M. D. Pfefferbaum, Child Witnesses in Okla, 88, Jour Okla State Med Asn, 479-86, 95; Beyond Victim Impact Evidence: A Modest Proposal Reprise, 45, Hastings Law Jour, 1305-27, 94. **CONTACT ADDRESS** 851 W. Roscoe, Chicago, IL, 60657. **EMAIL** tfoster@wppost.depaul.edu

FOSTER, VERNA A.
DISCIPLINE ENGLISH **EDUCATION** Univ London, BA, 67, MPhil, 70, PhD, 77. **CAREER** Assoc prof. **RESEARCH** Modern drama; Shakespeare; Renaissance drama; History and theory of drama; Comparative drama. **SELECTED PUBLICATIONS** Auth, Buckets o' Beckett in Chicago 1996, J Beckett Stud 5, 96; Sex, Power, and Pedagogy in Mamet's Oleanna and Ionesco's The Lesson, Am Drama 5, 95; Ibsen's Tragicomedy: The Wild Duck, Modern Drama 38, 95; A sad tale's best for winter: Storytelling and Tragicomedy in the Late Plays of Shakespeare and Beckett, in Past Crimson Past Woe: The Shakespeare-Beckett Connection, Garland Publ, Inc, 93; Sex Averted or Converted: Sexuality and Tragicomic Genre in the Plays of Fletcher, Stud in Engl Lit 32, 92. **CONTACT ADDRESS** Dept of English, Loyola Univ, Chicago, 6525 N. Sheridan Rd., Chicago, IL, 60626. **EMAIL** vfoster@wpo.it.luc.edu

FOULKE, ROBERT DANA
PERSONAL Born 04/25/1930, Minneapolis, MN, m, 1953, 3 children **DISCIPLINE** ENGLISH LITERATURE **EDUCATION** Princeton Univ, AB, 52; Univ Minn, MA, 57, PhD(English), 61. **CAREER** Teaching asst English, Univ Minn, 54-56, instr, 56-58, 60-61; from asst prof to assoc prof, Trinity Col, Conn, 61-70; prof English, 70-92 & chemn dept, 70-80, Skidmore Col; Vis prof lit criticism, NDEA Inst, Univ Minn, 65; vis prof stylistics, NDEA Inst, Macalester Col, 67; Nat Endowment Humanities Asian studies fel, 77-78. **HONORS AND AWARDS** Fulbright fel, 59-60; Asian Stud fel, cambridge Univ, 76-77; Skidmore Col Fac Res Grant, 82-83, 85-86, 86-87, 89-90; Odysssey project grant, 86; vis fel, Princeton Univ, 88. **MEMBERSHIPS** MLA; NCTE; New Eng Col English Asn; Col English Asn; Joseph Conrad Soc. **RESEARCH** Joseph Conrad; 19th and 20th century novel; theory of the novel; literary criticism; sea literature; maritime history. **SELECTED PUBLICATIONS** Auth, Conrad and the British Merchant Service: A Case History in Maritime History and Literary Interpretation, Bermuda J of Archaeol and maritime Hist, 93; coauth, Hong Kong Dragon Boas Festival and International Races, Sea History, 96; guest ed, special ed, James Fenimore Cooper: The Birth of American Maritime Experience, Am Neptune, 97; auth, The Sea Voyage Narrative, Twayne, 97; contribur, Gidmark, ed, An Encyclopedia of American Literature of the Sea and the Great Lakes, Greenwood, forthcoming. **CONTACT ADDRESS** 25 Dark Bay Ln, Lake George, NY, 12845.

FOURNIER, LUCIEN
DISCIPLINE VICTORIAN LITERATURE **EDUCATION** Univ Notre Dame, PhD. **CAREER** Eng Dept, St. Edward's Univ **SELECTED PUBLICATIONS** Auth, The Tragic Hero in a Naturalistic World, Notre Dame Juggler 64; "Introduction" to Charles Dickens and the Seven Deadly Sins, Interstate Press, 79. **CONTACT ADDRESS** St Edward's Univ, 3001 S Congress Ave, Austin, TX, 78704-6489.

FOWLER, DOREEN
PERSONAL Born 01/14/1948, Brooklyn, NY, m, 1972, 1 child **DISCIPLINE** ENGLISH **EDUCATION** Manhattanville Col, BA, 69; Brown Univ, PhD, 74. **CAREER** Asst, 70-72, Brown Univ; instr to asst prof, 74-76, Memphis St Univ; instr to assoc prof to prof, 79-97, Univ Miss; vis assoc prof, 85-86, Univ Calif Santa Barbara; vis prof to assoc prof, 94-, Univ Kan. **HONORS AND AWARDS** Grad fel, Brown Univ, 69-70, 73-74; teaching assistantship, Brown Univ, 70-71, 71-72; summer Stipend, Univ Ms, 84, 88, 90; faculty res grant, Univ Ms, 85, 87, 89. **MEMBERSHIPS** MLA; Amer Lit Assoc; Soc for Study of S Lit; Walker Percy Soc; Faulkner Soc; Eudora Welty Soc; Toni Morrison Soc; Richard Wright Soc; Carson McCullers Soc; Flannery O'Connor Soc. **RESEARCH** Lit of Amer South **SELECTED PUBLICATIONS** Auth, The Nameless Women of Go Down, Moses, Women's Stud, 93; art, I am dying: Faulkner's Hightower and the Oedipal Moment, Faulkner J 93, 94, 95; art, You Can't Beat a Woman: The Preoedipal Mother in Light in August, Faulkner J, 95, 96; art, Deconstructing Racial Difference: Flannery O'Connor's The Artificial Nigger, Flannery O'Connor Bull, 95-96; auth, Faulkner: The Return of the Repressed, Univ Press Va, 97. **CONTACT ADDRESS** Dept of English, Univ of Ks, Lawrence, KS, 66045. **EMAIL** dfowler@eagle.cc.ukans.edu

FOWLER, VIRGINIA C.
PERSONAL Born 03/29/1948, Lexington, KY, s **DISCIPLINE** ENGLISH **EDUCATION** Univ of Ky, BA, 69; Univ of Pittsburgh, MA, 71, PhD, 76. **CAREER** From asst prof to prof, Va Tech, 77- . **HONORS AND AWARDS** Phi Beta Kappa; Woodrow Wilson fel; NDEA fel; Sigma Tau Delta. **RESEARCH** African-Am lit, espec women's fiction. **SELECTED PUBLICATIONS** Auth, Henry James's American Girl: The Embroidery on the Canvas, 84; Nikki Giovanni, 92; Conversations With Nikki Giovanni, 92; Gloria Naylor: In Search of Sanctuary, 96. **CONTACT ADDRESS** Dept of English, Virginia Polytechnic Inst and State Univ, Blacksburg, VA, 24061-0112. **EMAIL** vfowler@vt.edu

FOX, ALICE
PERSONAL Born 07/29/1928, Trenton, NJ, 2 children **DISCIPLINE** SIXTEENTH AND SEVENTEENTH CENTURY ENGLISH **EDUCATION** Univ Mo, AB, 50; Univ Tenn, MA, 57;

Mich State Univ, PhD (English), 65. **CAREER** Instr English, Wash State Univ, 59-60; from instr to prof, Western Col, 61-74, chmn dept, 68-70; assoc prof, 74-80, PROF ENGLISH, MIAMI UNIV, 80-, Screening comt for Fulbrights to the UK, Inst Int Educ, 77-. **HONORS AND AWARDS** Outstanding Univ Woman, Miami Univ, 78. **MEMBERSHIPS** MLA; Shakespeare Asn Am; Spenser soc. **RESEARCH** Spenser; Shakespeare; seventeenth century English literature; Renaissance lyric, Virginia Woolf. **SELECTED PUBLICATIONS** Auth, Social Change in the Age of Enlightenment--Edinburgh, 1660-1760, Economic Hist Rev, Vol 48, 95; The Art of Rulership--A Study of Ancient Chinese Political Thought, J Chinese Philos, Vol 22, 95; Political Protest and Prophecy Under Henry VIII, Albion, Vol 24, 92; More, Thomas--The Search for the Inner Man, J Mod Hist, Vol 65, 93; Reflex and Reflectivity, Wuwei in the Zhuangzi, Asian Philos, Vol 6, 96; In the Mirror of Memory--Reflections on Mindfulness and Remembrance in Indian and Tibetan Buddhism, Philos East W, Vol 47, 97; Cranmer, Thomas--A Life, J Ecclesiastical Hist, Vol 48, 97; Rethinking Social History, English Society, 1570-1920, and its Interpretation, Economic Hist Rev, Vol 48, 95; The Local Origins of Modern Society--Gloucestershire, 1500-1800, Economic Hist Rev, Vol 49, 96; Popular Culture in England, C. 1500-1850, Hist, Vol 82, 97; Rumor, News and Popular Political Opinion in Elizabethan and Early Stuart England, Hist J, Vol 40, 97; Interpreting More, Thomas Utopia, J Mod Hist, Vol 65, 93; The Body, Self Cultivation, and Ki Energy, Asian Philos, Vol 6, 96. **CONTACT ADDRESS** Dept of English, Miami Univ, Oxford, OH, 45056.

FOX, CHRISTOPHER
DISCIPLINE LITERATURE **EDUCATION** SUNY, Binghamton, PhD. **CAREER** Instr, Univ Notre Dame. **HONORS AND AWARDS** ACLS fel. **RESEARCH** Interrelations of literature and the emerging human sciences, especially psychology and medicine, in the 18th century. **SELECTED PUBLICATIONS** Auth, Locke and the Scriblerians: Identity and Consciousness in Early Eighteenth-Century Britain; ed, Psychology and Literature in the Eighteenth Century; Teaching Eighteenth-Century Poetry; Gulliver's Travels: A Case Study in Contemporary Criticism; coed, Walking Nabob's Garden: New Studies of Swift. **CONTACT ADDRESS** Univ Notre Dame, Notre Dame, IN, 46556.

FOX, HUGH B.
PERSONAL Born 02/12/1932, Chicago, IL, m, 1988, 6 children **DISCIPLINE** ENGLISH AMERICAN LITERATURE **EDUCATION** Loyola Univ, Chica, BS, hum, 55, MA, 56; Univ IL, PhD, 58. **CAREER** Mich State Univ, prof, dept Am thought and lang, 68-99; Loyola Univ, Los Angeles, prof, eng, 58-68; Univ Sonora, Mexico, prof Am studies, 61. **HONORS AND AWARDS** John Carter Brown Lib fel, 58. **MEMBERSHIPS** COSMEP, founder, Bd mem, IAIP, 68-80. **RESEARCH** Contemp Am poetry; pre-Columbian trans oceanic contacts between new and old worlds in ancient times. **SELECTED PUBLICATIONS** The Gods of the Cataclysm, 76; First Fire: Central and South American Indian Poetry, 78; The Mythological Foundations of the Epic Genre: The Solar Voyage as the Hero's Journey, 96; Stairway to the sun, 96. **CONTACT ADDRESS** Michigan State univ, 1876 Melrose, E Lansing, MI, 48823.

FOX, PAMELA
DISCIPLINE ENGLISH LITERATURE **EDUCATION** Univ Ill, BA, MA; Univ Wash, PhD. **CAREER** Eng Dept, Georgetown Univ **RESEARCH** Cultural studies; feminist theory; working class writing and culture; British social novel; popular culture; 20th century writing by women. **SELECTED PUBLICATIONS** Auth, Recasting the 'Politics of Truth': Thoughts on Class, Gender, and the Role of Intellectuals, 93; Ethel Carnie Holdsworth's 'Revolt of the Gentle': Romance and the Politics of Resistance in Working-Class Women's Writing, 93; De/Refusing the Reproduction-Resistance Circuit of Cultural Studies: A Methodology for Reading Working-Class Narrative, 94; Class Fictions: Shame and Resistance in the British Working-Class Novel, 94. **CONTACT ADDRESS** English Dept, Georgetown Univ, 37th and O St, Washington, DC, 20057.

FOX, ROBERT CHARLES
PERSONAL Born 04/17/1920, Portland, OR **DISCIPLINE** ENGLISH **EDUCATION** Univ Portland, BA, 42; Columbia Univ, MA, 47, PhD (Eng), 56. **CAREER** Instr Eng, Wayne Univ, 47-49; lectr and instr, Rutgers Univ, 50-55; from instr to assoc prof, 55-68, PROF ENGLISH, ST FRANCIS COL, NY, 68-, CHMN DEPT, 73-. **MEMBERSHIPS** MLA; Milton Soc Am; NCTE; Renaissance Soc Am. **RESEARCH** English literature of the seventeenth century; Milton; Chaucer. **SELECTED PUBLICATIONS** Auth, Experiment Perilous--45 Years as a Participant Observer of Patient Oriented Clinical Research, Perspectives in Biology and Medicine, Vol 39, 96; Parsons, Talcott, My Teacher, Am Scholar, Vol 66, 97; Les Roses Mademoiselle, The Universe of Ghelderode, Michel, De, Am Scholar, Vol 63, 94. **CONTACT ADDRESS** 175 Adams St Apt 6F, Brooklyn, NY, 11201.

FOX GOOD, JACQUELYN
DISCIPLINE ENGLISH LITERATURE **EDUCATION** Northwestern Univ, BA; Univ Chicago, MA; Univ Va, PhD. **CAREER** Asst prof, 89-. **RESEARCH** Shakespeare and the English Renaissance; American autobiography and fiction. **SELECTED PUBLICATIONS** Auth, pubs on Shakespeare, and fiction. **CONTACT ADDRESS** Dept of Humanities, Illinois Inst of Tech, 3301 S Dearborn, Chicago, IL, 60616. **EMAIL** humfoxgood@minna.cns.iit.edu

FRADENBURG, LOUISE
DISCIPLINE MEDIEVAL ENGLISH AND SCOTTISH LITERATURE **EDUCATION** Univ Va, Phd, 82. **CAREER** PROF, ENG, UNIV CALIF, SANTA BARBARA. **RESEARCH** Crit theory; Gender and sexualities. **SELECTED PUBLICATIONS** Auth, City, Marriage, Tournament: Arts of Rule in Late Medieval Scotland, Univ Wis Press, 91; ed, Women of Sovereignty, Univ Edinburgh Press, 92; pub(s), articles on Chaucer, Dunbar, Henryson, and on psychoanalysis and medieval studies; co-ed, Premodern Sexualities, Routledge, 96. **CONTACT ADDRESS** Dept of Eng, Univ Calif, Santa Barbara, CA, 93106-7150. **EMAIL** lfraden@humanitas.ucsb.edu

FRAISTAT, NEIL RICHARD
PERSONAL Born 04/19/1952, Bronx, NY, m, 1979, 2 children **DISCIPLINE** ENGLISH LITERATURE **EDUCATION** Univ Conn, BA, 74; Univ Pa, MA, 76, PhD(English), 79. **CAREER** From asst prof to assoc prof, 79-91, prof English, 91- Univ MD, College Park. **HONORS AND AWARDS** Huntington Libr fel, 81; Am Coun Learned Soc fel, 82; fel for univ tchrs, NEH, 90; Fredson Bowers mem prize, Soc for Textual Scholar, 94. **MEMBERSHIPS** MLA; Keats-Shelley Soc; Milton Soc. **RESEARCH** British romantic poetry; 19th century British fiction; textual editing and bibliography. **SELECTED PUBLICATIONS** Auth, The Poem and the Book, 85; ed, Poems in Their Place, 86; ed, The Prometheus Unbound Notebooks, 91; ed, Romanticism, 93- ; ed, Stud in Romanticism, 95- ; ed, Keats-Shelley J, 96- . **CONTACT ADDRESS** Dept of English, Univ Md, College Park, MD, 20742. **EMAIL** nf5@umail.umd.edu

FRALEIGH, DOUGLAS
DISCIPLINE COMMUNICATION, ARGUMENTATION, FREEDOM OF SPEECH **EDUCATION** Univ CA, Berkeley, JD. **CAREER** Instr, dir, Forensics, CA State Univ. **MEMBERSHIPS** Pres, WSCA Freedom of Speech Interest Gp; exec coun, CEDA. **SELECTED PUBLICATIONS** Coauth, Freedom of Speech in the Marketplace of Ideas, St Martin's Press, 97. **CONTACT ADDRESS** California State Univ, Fresno, Fresno, CA, 93740.

FRANCO, JEAN
PERSONAL Born 03/31/1924, Dukinfield, England **DISCIPLINE** LITERATURE **EDUCATION** Univ Manchester, BA, 44, MA, 46; Univ London, BA, 60, PhD (Span), 64. **CAREER** Lectr Span, Queen Mary Col, Univ London, 60-64, reader, King's Col, 64-68; prof lit, Univ Essex, 68-72; PROF SPAN AND COMP LIT, STANDARD UNIV, 72-, Guggenheim fel, 76-77. **MEMBERSHIPS** MLA; Latin Am Studies Asn. **RESEARCH** Latin Am Lit and society; poetry; social theories of literature. **SELECTED PUBLICATIONS** Auth, Dr. No, Cineforum, Vol 35, 95; Masculine Feminine--Practices Concerning Differences and Democratic Culture, Hisp Revista Lit, Vol 23, 94; Outside in the Teaching Machine, Boundary 2 Int J Lit Cult, Vol 23, 96; Reading North by South--On Latin Am Lit, Culture and Politics, Revista Estudios Hisp, Vol 30, 96; Beyond Reservation Boundaries, Native American Laborers in World War II, J Southwest, Vol 36, 94; An Interview with Franco, Jess, Cineforum, Vol 35, 95; The Man who Killed Liberty Valance, Cineforum, Vol 35, 95. **CONTACT ADDRESS** Dept of Span and Port, Stanford Univ, Stanford, CA, 94305.

FRANK, DAVID A.
PERSONAL Born 03/23/1955, Topeka, KS, m, 1988, 2 children **DISCIPLINE** RHETORIC **EDUCATION** Western Washington Univ, BA, 78, MA, 79; Univ Oregon, PhD, 83. **CAREER** Grad asst, Western Washington Univ, 79-80; grad tchg fel,Univ Ore, 79-81, instr, 81, asst prof, 82, assoc prof, 88-. **HONORS AND AWARDS** Grad tchg fel awd for outstanding tchg, 91. **MEMBERSHIPS** Natl Commun Asn; Rhetoric Soc of Am. **RESEARCH** Israeli-Palestinian rhetoric; rhetorical theory and the new Rhetoric Project. **SELECTED PUBLICATIONS** Coauth, Lincoln-Douglas Debate, Natl Textbook, 93; auth, Debate as Rhetorical Scholarship, in CEDA 1991: 20th Anniversary Conference Proceedings, 93; auth, On the Study of Ancient Chinese Rhetoric, in Western J of Commun, 93; auth, Creative Speaking, Natl Textbook, 94; coauth, NonPolicy Debate, Gorsuch Scarisbrick, 94; auth, My Enemy's Enemy is My Friend: Palestinian Rhetoric and the Gulf Crisis, in Commun Stud, 95; auth, Diversity and the Public Space: A Response to Stepp, in Argumentation and Advocacy, 97; auth, The New Rhetoric, Judaism, and Post-Enlightenment Thought: The Cultural Origins of Perelmanian Philosophy, in Q J of Speech, 97; auth, A New Forensics for a New Millennium, in The Forensics, 97; auth, Dialectical Rapprochement in the New Rhetoric, in Argumentation and Advocacy, 98. **CONTACT ADDRESS** Robert D Clark Honors Col, Univ of Oregon, Eugene, OR, 97403. **EMAIL** dfrank@oregon.uoregon.edu

FRANK, JOSEPH
PERSONAL Born 12/20/1916, Chicago, IL, m, 1946, 3 children **DISCIPLINE** ENGLISH **EDUCATION** Harvard Univ, BA, 39, MA, 47, PhD (English), 53. **CAREER** From instr to prof English, Univ Rochester, 48-67; prof and chmn dept, Univ NMex, 67-69; head dept, 69-75, PROF ENGLISH, UNIV MASS, AMHERST, 69-, Huntington fel, 55-56; Guggenheim fels, 58-59, 61; Folger Shakespeare libr fel, 61-62; assoc ed, Seventeenth Century News, 61-69; consult, Univ Fla, City Col New York, Roger Williams, Ft Lewis and Mass Community Cols, 68-72; vis prof, Univ Kent, 76-77. **MEMBERSHIPS** MLA; Asn Depts English (pres, 69). **RESEARCH** Pedagogy; modern drama; seventeenth century literature. **SELECTED PUBLICATIONS** Auth, He Gambler, A Study in Ethnopsychology, Hudson Rev, Vol 46, 93; Dostoevsky, Anna Diary, NY Rev Bks, Vol 42, 95; The Comic Novel and the Poor--Fielding Preface to Joseph Andrews, 8th Century Stud, Vol 27, 94; Lampshade Time, Chicago Rev, Vol 38, 93; On Psychological Prose, NY Rev Bks, Vol 41, 94. **CONTACT ADDRESS** Dept of English, Univ Mass, Amherst, MA, 01002.

FRANK, MORTIMER HENRY
PERSONAL Born 01/14/1933, New York, NY, m, 1961, 1 child **DISCIPLINE** ENGLISH, MUSICOLOGY **EDUCATION** New York Univ, AB, 54, MA, 58, PhD (English), 68. **CAREER** Instr English, New York Univ, 62-65; from instr to assoc prof, 65-74, PROF ENGLISH, BRONX COMMUNITY COL, 74-, Fac res fel, State Univ NY, 73 and 74; producer, Rare Recordings, broadcast by WFUY, 75-; music ed, 17th Century News, 78- and Class Record, Chron Higher Educ, 78-80; cur, Toscanini Collection, Wave Hill, 81-. **MEMBERSHIPS** MLA; Northeast Mod Lang Asn. **RESEARCH** Am Lit; 17th century poetry; relationship between poetry and music. **SELECTED PUBLICATIONS** Auth, The Maestro Myth, Opera News, Vol 57, 93. **CONTACT ADDRESS** Dept of English, Bronx Comm Col, CUNY, 181st St and University Ave, Bronx, NY, 10453.

FRANK, ROBERT
DISCIPLINE ENGLISH ROMANTICS **EDUCATION** St. John's Univ, BA, 62; Univ Minn, MA, 68, PhD, 69. **CAREER** Engl, Oregon St Univ. **RESEARCH** Greek myth; poetry, nw lit. **SELECTED PUBLICATIONS** Auth, Don't Call Me Gentle Charles: A Reading of Lamb's Essays of Elia. Corvallis: Ore State Univ Press, 76; The Pacific Northewst: A Region in Myth and Reality. Ore State Univ Press, 83; The Grains or Passages in the Life of Ruth Rover, with Occasional Pictures of Oregon, Natural and Moral, Ore State Univ Press, 86; The Line in Postmodern Poetry, Univ Ill Press, 88. **CONTACT ADDRESS** Oregon State Univ, Corvallis, OR, 97331-4501. **EMAIL** rfrank@orst.edu

FRANK, ROBERTA
DISCIPLINE ENGLISH **EDUCATION** New York Univ, BA, 62, Harvard Univ MA, 64, PhD, 68. **CAREER** Asst prof, 68-73, assoc prof, 73-78, PROF ENGLISH & CTR MEDIEVAL STUDS, UNIV TORONTO, 78-. **HONORS AND AWARDS** Bowdoin Prize Hum, Harvard Univ, 68; Elliott Prize, Medieval Acad Am, 72. **MEMBERSHIPS** Fel, Royal Soc Can; Asn Advan Scand Studs Can; Medieval Acad Am; Int Saga Soc; MLA. **SELECTED PUBLICATIONS** Auth, Old Norse Court Poetry: The Drv. of Toronto, 78; auth, Old Norse Memorial Eulogies and the Ending of Beowulf, in ACTA, 79; auth, Did Anglo-Saxon Audiences Have a Skaldic Tooth?, in Scand Studs, 87; auth, On a Changing Field: Medieval Studies in the New World, in S African J Medieval and Renaissance Studs, 94. **CONTACT ADDRESS** Dept of English & Ctr Medieval Studies, Univ Toronto, Toronto, ON, M5S 1A1.

FRANKLIN, BENJAMIN
PERSONAL Born 09/10/1939, Gallipolis, OH, m, 1962, 2 children **DISCIPLINE** AM LIT **EDUCATION** Ohio State Univ, BA and BS, 65; Ohio Univ, MA, 66, PhD (English), 69. **CAREER** Asst prof English, Univ Mich, Ann Arbor, 69-76; assoc prof, 76-81, PROF ENGLISH, UNIV SC, 81-, Fulbright lectr, Univ Athens, Greece, 82-83; ed, Camden House, Inc. **HONORS AND AWARDS** Louis I Bredvold Award, Univ Mich, 75. **MEMBERSHIPS** MLA; Nathaniel Hawthorne Soc. **SELECTED PUBLICATIONS** Auth, Advertisements for Herself--The Anais Nin Press, Papers Bibliog Soc Am, Vol 91, 97; Learning Curve, Aba J, Vol 81, 95; A Tribunal Waiting for Work, Aba J, Vol 81, 95; Source Sought Notes Queries, Vol 40, 93; Brown, Goodman and the Puritan Catechism, Esq J Am Renaissance, Vol 40, 94. **CONTACT ADDRESS** Dept of English, Univ of SC, Columbia, SC, 29208.

FRANKLIN, H. BRUCE
PERSONAL Born 02/28/1934, Brooklyn, NY, m, 1956, 3 children **DISCIPLINE** ENGLISH & AMERICAN LITERATURE **EDUCATION** Amherst Col, BA, 55; Stanford Univ, PhD, 61. **CAREER** Asst prof English & Am lit, Stanford Univ, 61-64; asst prof English, Johns Hopkins Univ, 64-65; assoc prof, Stanford Univ, 65-72; vis fel, Ctr for Humanities, Wesleyan Univ, 74; prof English & Am stud, Rutgers Univ, Newark, 75-. **HONORS AND AWARDS** Alexander Cappon Prize, 78; Eaton Award, 81., Bd adv eds, Ser Wkg Papers Hist Sys, Nat, and Peoples, 98- ; adv bd, Viet Nam Gen, 94-; script consult, Sugarloaf Films, 93; pres, Melville Soc, 93. **MEMBERSHIPS** MLA;

ASA. **RESEARCH** Literature and society; American literature; science fiction; Vietnam War. **SELECTED PUBLICATIONS** Ed, The Essential Stalin, Doubleday, 72; Back Where You Came From: A Life in the Death of the Empire, Harper, 75; The Victim as Criminal and Artist: Literature from the American Prison, 78 & Robert A Heinlein: Amica as Science Fiction, Oxford Univ, 80; Prison Literature in Amica, Lawrence Hill, 82; ed, Countdown to Midnight, New Am Libr, 84; co-ed, Vietname and Amica, Grove/Atlantic, 85,95; auth, War Stars: The Superweapon and the American Imagination, Oxford Univ, 90; ed, The Vietnam War in American Stories, Songs, and Poems, Beford Books, 96; ed, Prison Writing in 20th Century Amica, Penquin, 98. **CONTACT ADDRESS** Dept of English, Rutgers Univ, 180 University Ave, Newark, NJ, 07102-1897. **EMAIL** jbfranklins@compuserve.com

FRANKLIN, RALPH WILLIAM
PERSONAL Born 08/20/1937, Ojus, FL **DISCIPLINE** ENGLISH, BIBLIOGRAPHY **EDUCATION** Univ Puget Sound, BA, 59; Northwestern Univ, MA, 60, PhD (Am lit), 65; Univ Chicago, MA, 68. **CAREER** Asst prof English, Univ Wis, 64-66; asst prof and cur Abernethy Libr, Middlebury Col, 68-70; asst chief tech serv and develop, Wash State Libr, 70-71; asst prof and dean students, Grad Libr Sch, Univ Chicago, 71-74; bibliog syst consult, Wash State Libr, 74-76; from assoc prof to prof and dir libr, Whitworth Col, 77-82; LIBRN, BEINECKE RARE BK and MANUSCRIPT LIBR, YALE UNIV, 82-, Consult, Wash State Libr, 71-74; Nat Endowment for Humanities grant, 78; Guggenheim fel, 80-81. **MEMBERSHIPS** Asn Col and Res Libr; Am Libr Asn; Bibliog Soc Am. **RESEARCH** Emily Dickinson; bibliography and textual criticism. **SELECTED PUBLICATIONS** Auth, High Churchmanship in the Church of England--From the 16th Century to the Late 20th Century, Theol Stud, Vol 57, 96. **CONTACT ADDRESS** Beinecke Rare Bk and Manuscript Libr, Yale Sta, PO Box 1603A, New Haven, CT, 06520.

FRANKLIN, ROSEMARY F.
PERSONAL Born 04/15/1941, Birmingham, AL, m, 1975 **DISCIPLINE** ENGLISH **EDUCATION** Birmingham Southern Col, AB, 63; Wake Forest Univ, MA, 64; Emory Univ, PhD, 68. **CAREER** Asst Prof, Ga State Univ, 67-69; ASST TO ASSOC PROF, UNIV OF GA, 69-. **HONORS AND AWARDS** Phi Beta Kappa; Sandy Beaver Assoc Prof of English; Humanities Center Fel. **MEMBERSHIPS** MLA; South Atlantic MLA; Hawthorne Soc; Melville Soc; Soc for the Study of Southern Lit. **RESEARCH** Am Lit; Lit by Am women writers. **SELECTED PUBLICATIONS** Auth, Edna as Psyche: The Self and the Unconscious, Approaches to Tchg Chopin's The Awakening, MLA, 88; An Index to Henry James's Prefaces to the New York Edition, Univ of Va Bibliographical Soc, 66; The Awakening and the Failure of Psyche, Am Lit, 84; The Minister's Black Veil: A Parable, Am Transcendental Quart, 85; Poe and Chopin's Awakening, Miss Quart, 94; Oates's Romantic Love Stories and Kristeva, South Atlantic Rev, 98. **CONTACT ADDRESS** Dept of English, Univ of Georgia, Park Hall, Athens, GA, 30602. **EMAIL** franklin@arches.uga.edu

FRANKLIN, WAYNE S.
DISCIPLINE AMERICAN LITERATURE **EDUCATION** Union Coll, BA, 67; Pittsburgh, MA, 68, PhD, 72. **CAREER** DAVIS DIST PROF, AM LIT, NORTHEASTERN UNIV **MEMBERSHIPS** Am Antiquarian Soc **RESEARCH** James Fenimore Cooper **SELECTED PUBLICATIONS** Auth, Discoverers, Explorers, Settlers, Univ Chicago Press, 79; auth, The New World of James Fenimore Cooper, Univ Chicago Press, 82; auth, A Rural Carpenter's World, Univ Iowa Press, 90; co-ed, Mapping American Culture, Univ Iowa Press, 92; auth, American Voices, American Lives: A Documentary Reader, WW Norton, 97. **CONTACT ADDRESS** Northeastern Univ, 406 Holmes Hall, Boston, MA, 02115. **EMAIL** wfrankli@lynx.neu.edu

FRANSON, JOHN KARL
PERSONAL Born 11/18/1941, Coalville, UT, m, 1965, 8 children **DISCIPLINE** ENGLISH LITERATURE **EDUCATION** Brigham Young Univ, BA, 66, MA, 69; Univ Ill, Urbana, PhD (English), 72. **CAREER** Grad asst English, Brigham Young Univ, 66-68; teaching asst, 68-72, res asst, Univ Ill, Urbana, 69-70; asst prof English, Ark State Univ, 72-75; asst prof, 75-77, assoc prof, 77-82, PROF ENGLISH, UNIV MAINE, FARMINGTON, 82-. **RESEARCH** Renaissance; Romantics. **SELECTED PUBLICATIONS** Auth, Too Soon Marrd, Juliets Age as Symbol in Romeo And Juliet, Papers on Language and Literature, Vol 32, 96; Coleridge Christabel, Lines 23-42, Explicator, Vol 52, 94. **CONTACT ADDRESS** Dept of English, Univ Maine, Farmington, ME, 04930.

FRANTZ, DAVID OSWIN
PERSONAL Born 08/16/1942, Lancaster, PA, m, 1970, 2 children **DISCIPLINE** RENAISSANCE LITERATURE **EDUCATION** Princeton Univ, BA, 64; Univ Mich, MA, 65; Univ Pa, PhD, 68. **CAREER** Asst prof, 68-75, assoc prof to prof Eng, Ohio State Univ, 75-. **HONORS AND AWARDS** Phi Beta Kappa **MEMBERSHIPS** Renaissance Soc Am; MLA; Mediaeval Acad Am; Dict Soc N Am. **RESEARCH** Renaissance. **SELECTED PUBLICATIONS** Auth, The Union of Houmell and Mariwell: The Triumph of Hearing, Spencer Studies, 86; auth, Festum Voluptatis: A Study of RennaissanceErotica, OSU Press, 89; art, Negotiating Florio's A Worlde of Words, Dictionaires 18, 97. **CONTACT ADDRESS** Dept of English, Ohio State Univ, 164 W 17th Ave, Columbus, OH, 43210-1326. **EMAIL** frantz.1@osu.edu

FRANTZEN, ALLEN J.
DISCIPLINE ENGLISH **EDUCATION** Loras Col, BA, 69; Univ Va, MA, 73, PhD, 76. **CAREER** Prof; dir, Loyola Literacy Center; co-ch, Medieval Stud Comt; exec secy, Ill Medieval Asn. **HONORS AND AWARDS** Guggenheim Fel, 94; Natl Endowment for Hum Fel, 90-91. **MEMBERSHIPS** MLA. **RESEARCH** Old and Middle English literature; literary history; history of sexuality; gay and lesbian Stud; literary theory and criticism; textual criticism. **SELECTED PUBLICATIONS** Auth, Desire for Origins: New Language, Old English, and Teaching the Tradition, Rutgers UP, 90; The Disclosure of Sodomy in the Middle English Cleanness, PMLA 111, 96; Co-ed, Anglo-Saxonism and the Construction of Soc Identity, UP Fla, 97. **CONTACT ADDRESS** Dept of English, Loyola Univ, Chicago, 6525 N. Sheridan Rd., Chicago, IL, 60626. **EMAIL** afrantz@luc.edu

FRAZER, JUNE
DISCIPLINE NINETEENTH AND TWENTIETH CENTURY BRITISH LITERATURE **EDUCATION** Stetson Univ , BA, 56; Univ N C Chapel Hill, MA, 58; PhD, 64. **CAREER** Prof, Western Ill Univ. **RESEARCH** Women's Literature, and Literary Criticism. **SELECTED PUBLICATIONS** . **CONTACT ADDRESS** Western Illinois Univ, 1 University Circle, Macomb, IL, 61455.

FRAZIER, LETA J.
PERSONAL IL, m, 1958, 2 children **DISCIPLINE** COMMUNICATION **EDUCATION** Tn Temple Col, BA, 59; Univ Tn, MAT, 61; Univ Mn, MA, 80, PhD, 88. **CAREER** Instr, 74-78, Crown Col; instr, 78-82, Normandale Commun Col; chair, prof, 83-, Bethel Col. **HONORS AND AWARDS** Phi Kappa Phi, Faculty Develop Coordinator, dir, grad program, Bethel Col; consultant in org commun. **MEMBERSHIPS** Nat Commun Assoc; Assoc for Supervision & Curric Devel. **RESEARCH** Family commun; cross cultural & gender; curric develop. **CONTACT ADDRESS** Bethel Dr, PO Box 13-3900, St. Paul, MN, 55112. **EMAIL** fralet@bethel.edu

FREDEMAN, WILLIAM E.
PERSONAL Born 07/19/1928, Pine Bluff, AR **DISCIPLINE** ENGLISH **EDUCATION** Hendrix Col (Ark), BA, 48; Univ Okla, MA, 50, PhD, 56. **CAREER** High sch tchr, Okla, 48-53; instr to prof, 56-90, PROF EMER ENGLISH, UNIV BRITISH COLUMBIA, 91-; SW Brooks vis lectr, Univ Queensland, 78. **HONORS AND AWARDS** SSHRCC res grants, 74-80, 83-88; Can Coun/SSHRCC leave fel, 59-60, 70-71, 78-79, 83-84; Guggenheim fel, 65-66, 71-72; Killam sr res fel, 70-71, 78-79, 83-84; UBC Isaak Walton Killam res prize, 88. **MEMBERSHIPS** MLA; Bibliog Soc (London); Int Asn Univ Profs Eng. **SELECTED PUBLICATIONS** Auth, A Pre-Raphaelite Gazette: A Bibliocritical Study, 65; auth, A Pre-Raphaelite Gazette: The Letters of Arthur Hughes, 67; auth, Prelude to the Last Decade: Dante Gabriel Rossetti in the Summer of 1872, 71; auth, The Letters of Pictor Ignotus: William Bell Scott's Correspondence with Alice Boyd 1859-1884, 76; ed, The P.R.B. Journal, 75; ed, Victorian Poetry, 75, 82, 87; ed, A Rossetti Cabinet, 91; co-ed, Dictionary of Literary Biography, 4 vols, 83-85. **CONTACT ADDRESS** 35269 McKee Place, Abbotsford, BC, V3G 1A7.

FREDERICKSON, RONALD Q.
DISCIPLINE THEATRE ARTS **EDUCATION** Univ Utah, MA, PhD. **CAREER** Prof, 72-. **MEMBERSHIPS** Asn Kans Theatre **SELECTED PUBLICATIONS** Auth, pubs on directing and acting. **CONTACT ADDRESS** Div of Communcation and Theatre Arts, Emporia State Univ, 1200 Commercial St, Emporia, KS, 66801-5087. **EMAIL** frederir@esumail.emporia.edu

FREDMAN, STEPHEN ALBERT
PERSONAL Born 05/20/1948, San Diego, CA, m, 1 child **DISCIPLINE** AMERICAN LITERATURE **EDUCATION** Calif Inst Arts, BFA, 71; Calif State Col, MA(English), 75; Stanford Univ, PhD(mod thought & lit), 80. **CAREER** Teaching asst English, Stanford Univ, 78-80; asst prof Am lit, Univ Notre Dame, 80-, Am Coun Learned Soc res fel, 82. **HONORS AND AWARDS** Nat Endowment for the Humanities Summer Stipend, 82 & 95; Lilly Fac Open Fel, 91-92; res fel, Recent Recipients of the PHD, ACLS, 82; Stanford fel, 77-80. **MEMBERSHIPS** MLA; Ed Board, Sagetrieb; Ed Board, William Carlos Williams Rev. **RESEARCH** Contemporary American poetry; Judaism & Modernism; the question of tradition in American poetry; poetry and performance; prose poetry; translation theory; the impact of Indic thought upon American literature. **SELECTED PUBLICATIONS** Auth, The Grounding of American Poetry: Charles Olson and the Emersonian Tradition, Cambridge Studies in American Literature and Culture; Cambridge Univ Press, 93; First Annotations to Edward Dorn's Gunslinger, Stephen Fredman and Grant Jenkins, Sagetrieb 15.3, 96; How to Get Out of the Room That Is the Book?: Paul Auster and the Consequences of Confinement, Postemodern Culture, 6.3, 5/96; Review of Lawrence Rainey and Robert von Hallberg, Sagetrieb 13.3, 96; Review of Barbara Einzig, Distance Without Distance, Talisman 14, fall 95; Review of Michael Davidson, The San Francisco Renaissance, Resources for Am Lit Study, 21.1, 95. **CONTACT ADDRESS** Dept of English, Univ of Notre Dame, 356 O'Shaugnessy Hall, Notre Dame, IN, 46556.

FREDRICKSON, ROBERT STEWART
PERSONAL Born 06/16/1940, Minneapolis, MN, m, 1964, 2 children **DISCIPLINE** ENGLISH AND AM LIT **EDUCATION** DePauw Univ, BA, 61; Univ Minn, MA, 64; Univ NC, Chapel Hill, PhD (English), 70. **CAREER** Instr English, Univ NC, Charlotte, 64-66; instr, Univ NC, Chapel Hill 66-69; asst prof, 69-78, ASSOC PROF ENGLISH, GETTYSBURG COL, 78-. **MEMBERSHIPS** MLA. **RESEARCH** Psychology and literature; 19th century realism. **SELECTED PUBLICATIONS** Auth, Stone, Robert Decadent Leftists, Papers on Lan Lit, Vol 32, 96. **CONTACT ADDRESS** Dept of English, Gettysburg Col, 300 N Washington St, Gettysburg, PA, 17325-1483.

FREE, KATHERINE B.
DISCIPLINE THEATRE HISTORY **EDUCATION** Marymount Col, BA; Univ Calif, Los Angeles, MA, PhD. **CAREER** Prof; consult & actress, theatre LA. **MEMBERSHIPS** Amer Soc Theatre Res, ASTR; Int Fedn for the Theatre Res, IFTR; Amer Edu Theatre Assoc, ATHE. **RESEARCH** Ancient Greek theatre & the folk theatre of India. **SELECTED PUBLICATIONS** Articles in, Theatre Res Int, Theatre J, & UCLA J of Dance Ethnol. **CONTACT ADDRESS** Dept of Theatre, Loyola Marymount Univ, 7900 Loyola Blvd, Los Angeles, CA, 90045.

FREE, WILLIAM JOSEPH
PERSONAL Born 03/18/1933, Chattanooga, TN, m, 1971 **DISCIPLINE** ENGLISH **EDUCATION** Univ Chatanooga, AB, 57; Univ NC, MA, 59, PhD, 62. **CAREER** From instr to asst prof, 62-68, ASSOC PROF ENGLISH, UNIV GA, 68-. **MEMBERSHIPS** SAtlantic Mod Lang Asn; Am Soc Aesthetics; Am Theatre Asn. **RESEARCH** Literary criticism; contemporary drama; literature and film. **SELECTED PUBLICATIONS** Auth, Confronting Williams, Tennessee a Streetcar Named Desire, Anq Quart J Short Articles Notes Rev, Vol 7, 94. **CONTACT ADDRESS** Dept of English, Univ of Ga, Athens, GA, 30601.

FREEBURG, ERNEST
DISCIPLINE HUMANITIES **EDUCATION** Middlebury Coll, BA, 80; Emory Univ, MA, 91, PhD, 95. **CAREER** ASST PROF, HUM, COLBY-SAWYER COLL **MEMBERSHIPS** Am Antiquarian Soc **RESEARCH** Blindness in Am **SELECTED PUBLICATIONS** Auth, "'An Object of Peculiar Interest:' The Education of Laura Bridgeman," Church Hist, Jun 92; "'More Important than a Rabble of Common Kings:' Dr Howe's Education of Laura Bridgeman," Hist of Ed Quart, Fall 94. **CONTACT ADDRESS** Hum Dept, Colby-Sawyer Col, 100 Main St, New London, NH, 03257. **EMAIL** efreeber@colby-sawyer.edu

FREEDMAN, CARL
DISCIPLINE CRITICAL THEORY **EDUCATION** Yale Univ, PhD, 83. **CAREER** Assoc prof, La State Univ. **HONORS AND AWARDS** Mem Prize, Margaret Church Mod Fiction Stud, 84. **RESEARCH** Modern culture; Marxist theory and science fiction. **SELECTED PUBLICATIONS** Auth, George Orwell: A Study in Ideology and Literary Form, 88; England as Ideology: from Upstairs Downstairs to A Room with a View, in Cultural Critique, 90-91; The Interventional Marxism of Louis Althusser, in Rethinking Marxism, 90; Power, Sexuality, and Race in All the King's Men, in Southern Lit and Lit Theory, 90; History, Fiction, Film, Television, Myth: the Ideology of M*A*S*H; Style, Fiction, Science Fiction: the Case of Philip K. Dick, in Styles of Creation, 92; Beyond the Dialect of the Tribe: James Joyce, Hugh MacDiarmid, and World Language, in Hugh MacDiarmid: Man and Poet, 92; Theory, the Canon, and the Politics of Curricular Reform: Teaching the Conflicts, 94; Science Fiction and the Question of the Canon, in Science Fiction and Market Realities, 95; How to Do Things with Milton: A Study in the Politics of Literary Criticism, in Critical Essays on John Milton, 95''. **CONTACT ADDRESS** Dept of Eng, Louisiana State Univ, 212D Allen Hall, Baton Rouge, LA, 70803. **EMAIL** cfreed2780@aol.com

FREEDMAN, MORRIS
PERSONAL Born 10/06/1920, New York, NY, d, 2 children **DISCIPLINE** ENGLISH & COMPARATIVE LITERATURE **EDUCATION** City Col New York, BA, 41; Columbia Univ, MA, 50, PhD, 53. **CAREER** Lectr & instr English, City Col New York, 46-54; assoc ed, Commentary, 54-55; from assoc prof to prof English, Univ NMex, 55-66; head dept, 67-72, prof English & Comp Lit, Univ Md, College Park, 66- **MEMBERSHIPS** MLA; NCTE; Milton Soc Am. **RESEARCH** Later sev-

enteenth century; Milton; creative writing and contemporary drama, American studies. **SELECTED PUBLICATIONS** Auth, Dryden's Miniature Epic, J English & Ger Philol, 58; Milton and Dryden on Rhyme, Huntington Libr Quart, 61; ed, Essays in the Modern Drama, Heath, 64; auth, The Compact English Handbook, McKay, 65; Success and the American Dramatist, Am Theatre, 67; The Moral Impulse, Southern Ill Univ, 67; co-ed, Controversy in Literature, Scribner's, 68; auth, American Drama in Social Context, Southern Ill Univ, 71. **CONTACT ADDRESS** Dept of English, Univ of Md, College Park, MD, 20742.

FREEMAN, BERNICE
PERSONAL Born 08/08/1909, La Grange, GA **DISCIPLINE** ENGLISH EDUCATION **EDUCATION** Tift Col, AB, 30; Univ NC, Chapel Hill, MA, 32; Columbia Univ, EdD(English educ), 52. **CAREER** Teacher high schs, Ga, 30-42; instr and critic, Demonstration High Sch, Ga Col, Milledgeville, 42-48, asst prof and prin, 48-51; co-dir, Ga Educ Ctr, 50-51; instructional supvr, Troup County Schs, Ga, 51-67; from assoc prof to prof educ, West Ga Col, 67-74, coordr, 69-73, chmn, Dept Sec Educ, 73-74; RETIRED., Mem high sch sect comt, NCTE, 52-54, mem bd dir elem sect, 66-69; mem, Publ and Constructive Studies Comt, Dept Rural Educ, NEA, 58-65, mem exec bd, 64-69, mem exec comt, 65-69. **MEMBERSHIPS** NCTE; NEA; MLA; SAtlantic Mod Lang Asn. **RESEARCH** The short story as a means of identifying a place; the Georgia short story. **SELECTED PUBLICATIONS** Auth, Precise Moments, Georg Rev, Vol 47, 93. **CONTACT ADDRESS** 305 Park Ave, La Grange, GA, 30240.

FREEMAN, JOANNA MAE
PERSONAL Born 03/22/1929, Kansas City, MO, m, 1951, 2 children **DISCIPLINE** ENGLISH LITERATURE, TECHNICAL WRITING **EDUCATION** Southwest Mo State Univ, BS in Educ, 49; Univ Colo, MA 52; Univ Kans, PhD (English), 73. **CAREER** PROF ENGLISH, PITTSBURG STATE UNIV, 58-. **MEMBERSHIPS** MLA; NEA; NCTE; Soc Tech Commun. **RESEARCH** Samuel Butler; Bible as literature; advanced technical writing. **SELECTED PUBLICATIONS** Auth, In Memoriam Smith, Malcolm 1941-94, Fr Stud, Vol 49, 95; Voices from Southeast Asia--The Refugee Experience in the United States, J Am Ethnic Hist, Vol 13, 94. **CONTACT ADDRESS** Dept of English, Pittsburg State Univ, 1701 S Broadway St, Pittsburg, KS, 66762.

FREEMAN, JOHN
DISCIPLINE RENAISSANCE LITERATURE **EDUCATION** Mich State Univ, BA; Wayne State Univ, MA, PhD. **CAREER** Prof, 87-. **RESEARCH** Holographic potential in the Arnolfini Portrait. **SELECTED PUBLICATIONS** Pub(s) on, Thomas More's Utopia, Shakespeare's Hamlet, and Stoppard's Rosencrantz and Guildenstern Are Dead; contribu, ELH, Moreana, and Modern Language Rev. **CONTACT ADDRESS** Dept of Eng, Univ Detrit Mercy, 4001 W McNichols Rd, PO BOX 19900, Detroit, MI, 48219-0900. **EMAIL** FREEMAJC@udmercy.edu

FREER, COBURN
PERSONAL Born 11/05/1939, New Orleans, LA, m, 1961, 2 children **DISCIPLINE** ENGLISH **EDUCATION** Lewis and Clark Col, BA, 60; Univ Wash, PhD (English), 68. **CAREER** Instr English, Univ Ariz, 65-67; from asst prof to assoc prof, Univ Mont, 67-76, prof, 76-80; PROF ENGLISH AND HEAD DEPT, UNIV GA, 80-, Fulbright lectr, Univ Oulu, 71-72; Nat Endowment for Humanities fel, 75. **MEMBERSHIPS** MLA; Milton Soc Am; SAtlantic Mod Lang Asn; Southeast Renaissance Conf. **RESEARCH** Renaissance and seventeenth century literature; modern poetry. **SELECTED PUBLICATIONS** Auth, Donne, John and Elizabethan Economic, Criticism Quart Lit Arts, Vol 38, 96. **CONTACT ADDRESS** Dept of English, Univ Ga, Athens, GA, 30602.

FREIBERT, LUCY MARIE
PERSONAL Born 10/19/1922, Louisville, KY **DISCIPLINE** AM LIT **EDUCATION** Spalding Col, AB, 57; St Louis Univ, MA, 62; Univ Wis-Madison, PhD (English), 70. **CAREER** Teacher, St Cecilia Sch, Louisville, Ky, 47-52; teacher, Holy Name Sch, 52-57; teacher, Presentation Acad, 57-60; asst prof English, Spalding Col, 60-65, 69-71; asst prof, 71-80, ASSOC PROF ENGLISH, UNIV LOUISVILLE, 81-. **MEMBERSHIPS** MLA; Melville Soc. **RESEARCH** Herman Melville; Am Lit; women's studies. **SELECTED PUBLICATIONS** Auth, Brutal Choreographies--Oppositional Strategies and Narrative Design in the Novels of Atwood, Margaret, Mod Fiction Stud, Vol 40, 94; A New Species--Gender and Science in Science Fiction, Tulsa Stud Womens Lit, Vol 13, 94; The Amber Gods and Other Stories, Resources Am Lit Stud, Vol 19, 93; Feminist Fabulation--Space, Postmodern Fiction, Tulsa Stud Womens Lit, Vol 13, 94. **CONTACT ADDRESS** Dept of English, Univ of Louisville, Louisville, KY, 40208.

FREIER, MARY P.
DISCIPLINE ENGLISH **EDUCATION** Univ of IL, MS, 98, PhD, 84, AM, 79; Millikin Univ, BA, 77 **CAREER** Coord, 98-, Jacksonville St Univ; Prof, 86-97, Dakota St Univ; Dir, 83-86, IN Univ E **HONORS AND AWARDS** Summer Study Grant, NEH, 95 **MEMBERSHIPS** Am Libr Asn; AL Lib Asn; Pop Cult Asn **RESEARCH** Infor anxiety **CONTACT ADDRESS** Houston Cole Libr, Jacksonville State Univ, Jacksonville, AL, 36265. **EMAIL** mfreier@jsucc.jsu.edu

FREIMARCK, VINCENT
PERSONAL Born 06/11/1918, New York, NY **DISCIPLINE** ENGLISH **EDUCATION** NY Univ, AB, 39; Columbia Univ, AM, 41; Cornell Univ, PhD, 50. **CAREER** Asst, NY Univ, 40, instr, 41-42; instr, Carnegie Inst Tech, 42-43; asst, Cornell Univ, 46-48; instr Eng, Wesleyan Univ, 48-52; from asst prof to assoc prof, 52-71, PROF ENGLISH, STATE UNIV NY BINGHAMTON, 71-. **MEMBERSHIPS** MLA. **RESEARCH** Am Lit of the eighteenth and nineteenth centuries; eighteenth century English criticism. **SELECTED PUBLICATIONS** Auth, The Letters of Bryant, William, Cullen, Vol 5, 1865-1871, Vol 6, 1872-1878, Am Lit, Vol 65, 93. **CONTACT ADDRESS** Dept of English, State Univ of NY, Binghamton, NY, 13901.

FREIMUTH, VICKI S.
DISCIPLINE HEALTH COMMUNICATION **EDUCATION** FL State Univ, PhD. **CAREER** Prof, Univ MD. **RESEARCH** Public's search for and use of health information. **SELECTED PUBLICATIONS** Co-auth, College Students' Awareness and Interpretation of the AIDS Risk, Sci, Tech, and Human Values 12, 87; Searching for Health Information: The Cancer Information Service Experience, Univ Pa Press, 89. **CONTACT ADDRESS** Dept of Commun, Univ MD, 4229 Art-Sociology Building, College Park, MD, 20742-1335.

FRENCH, ROBERTS WALKER
PERSONAL Born 07/16/1935, New York, NY, m, 1961, 2 children **DISCIPLINE** ENGLISH **EDUCATION** Dartmouth Col, BA, 56; Yale Univ, MA, 59; Brown Univ, PhD (English lit), 64. **CAREER** From asst prof to assoc prof, 64-77, PROF ENGLISH, UNIV MASS, AMHERST, 77-. **MEMBERSHIPS** MLA; Milton Soc Am. **RESEARCH** Modern poetry; Walt Whitman; Milton. **SELECTED PUBLICATIONS** Auth, The Western Canon, The Books and School of the Ages, Walt Whitman Quart Rev, Vol 12, 94; The Neglected Whitman, Walt--Vital Texts, Walt Whitman Quart Rev, Vol 11, 93; The Columbia History of American Poetry, Walt Whitman Quart Rev, Vol 11, 94. **CONTACT ADDRESS** Dept of English, Univ of Mass, Amherst, MA, 01003.

FRENCH, WILLIAM WIRT
PERSONAL Born 06/26/1932, Beckley, WV, m, 3 children **DISCIPLINE** ENGLISH LITERATURE **EDUCATION** WVa Univ, BA, 54; Univ Pittsburgh, MA, 60, PhD, 67. **CAREER** Asst to dean, Col Arts & Sci, Univ Pittsburgh, 62-64; from instr to asst prof, 64-71, asst chmn dept, 68-72, assoc prof English, 71-86, prof English, 86-, W Va Univ, 71-. **MEMBERSHIPS** MLA; Shakespeare Asn Am. **RESEARCH** Shakespeare; English Renaissance drama; American Drama. **SELECTED PUBLICATIONS** Auth, A Kind of Courage: King Lear at the Old Vic, London, 1940, Theatre Topics, 93; Murder Mystery Events: Playing, Myth-Making, and Smashing the Forth Wall, All At Once, Journal of Dramatic Theory & Criticism VIII:2, 94; EcoTheater: A Theater for the Twenty-First Century, Morgantown: W Va Univ, 98. **CONTACT ADDRESS** Dept English, West Virginia Univ, PO Box 6296, Morgantown, WV, 26506-6296.

FRENCH BAUMLIN, TITA
DISCIPLINE BRITISH DRAMA **EDUCATION** TX Christian Univ, BA, 76; Southern Methodist Univ, MA, 81; TX Christian Univ, PhD, 85. **CAREER** Southwest Tex State Univ **HONORS AND AWARDS** Ed, Explorations in Renaissance Cult. **SELECTED PUBLICATIONS** Coed, Ethos: New Essays in Rhetorical and Critical Theory, SMU Press, 94; Instructors' Manual for The HarperCollins World Reader sections on Medieval Europe, Early Modern Europe, and Modern Europe, HarperCollins, 94. **CONTACT ADDRESS** Southwest MS State Univ, 901 S. National, Ste. 50, Springfield, MO, 65804-0094.

FRENTZ, THOMAS S.
DISCIPLINE RHETORICAL STUDIES AND MASS MEDIA **EDUCATION** Univ Wisc, PhD. **CAREER** Comm Stu, Univ Ark **MEMBERSHIPS** Southern States Comm Asn. **SELECTED PUBLICATIONS** Articles, Quart Jour Speech; Critical Studies Mass Comm; Comm Monographs; Comm Quart; Western Jour Comm; Philosophy & Rhetoric; Southern Comm Jour. **CONTACT ADDRESS** Univ Ark, Fayetteville, AR, 72701.

FRESCH, CHERYL
DISCIPLINE 16TH- AND 17TH-CENTURY ENGLISH LITERATURE **EDUCATION** Cornell Univ, PhD; 76. **CAREER** Instr, Univ NMex, 76-. **RESEARCH** Blake's and Milton's visualizations of the scene of expulsion from the garden. **SELECTED PUBLICATIONS** Auth, 'Whither thou goest': Paradise Lost XXII 610-623 and The Book of Ruth, Milton Stud XXXII, 95. **CONTACT ADDRESS** Univ NMex, Albuquerque, NM, 87131.

FRESE, DOLORES
DISCIPLINE MEDIEVAL LITERATURE **EDUCATION** Univ Iowa, PhD. **CAREER** Instr, Univ Notre Dame. **RESEARCH** Figures of women in Old English and Middle English poetry. **SELECTED PUBLICATIONS** Auth, Re-Constructive Reading: An Ars Legendi for the Canterbury Tales; coed, Anglo-Saxon Poetry: Essays in Appreciation. **CONTACT ADDRESS** Univ Notre Dame, Notre Dame, IN, 46556.

FRIED, LEWIS FREDRICK
PERSONAL Born 01/29/1943, New York, NY **DISCIPLINE** AMERICAN LITERATURE **EDUCATION** Queens Col, NY, BA, 64, MA, 66; Univ MA, PhD, 69. **CAREER** Asst ed fiction, Tower Publ, 66; copy-ed, Mass Rev, 66; asst prof Am lit, 69-76, assoc prof, 76-89, prof Am lit, Kent State Univ, 89-, Vis prof, Int Grad Ctr Hebrew & Judaica, World Union Jewish Studies, Israel, 73-74. **HONORS AND AWARDS** Fulbright prof, 89-90, 93-94; Rapoport Fel, Hebrew Union Col, 97; Marcus Fel, Hebrew Union Col, 98. **RESEARCH** Am lit naturalism; Am proletarian fiction; Am-Jewish lit. **SELECTED PUBLICATIONS** Auth, James T Farrell: Shadow and Act, Jahrbuch Amerikastudien, 72; The disinherited: The worker as writer, New Lett, fall 72; The Golden Brotherhood of McTeague, Zeitschrift Fur Anglistik und Amerikanistik, 73; co-ed, American Literary Naturalism, Carl Winter Universitatsverlag, 75; auth, The Magician of Lublin: I B Singer's Ironic Man of Faith, Yiddish, 76; Bernard Carr and his trials of the mind, Twentieth Century Lit, 76; coauth, Jacob A Riis: A Reference Guide, G K Hall, 77; Jacob A Riis and the Jews, Am Studies, 79; ed-in-chief, Handbook of American Jewish Literature, Greenwood Press, 88; Makers of the City, Univ Mass Press, 90. **CONTACT ADDRESS** Dept of Eng, Kent State Univ, PO Box 5190, Kent, OH, 44242-0001. **EMAIL** dalamerica@aol.com

FRIEDENBERG, ROBERT VICTOR
PERSONAL Born 09/09/1943, Washington, DC **DISCIPLINE** POLITICAL COMMUNICATION, RHETORICAL THEORY **EDUCATION** Towson State Col, BS, 65; Temple Univ, MA, 67, PhD(speech), 70. **CAREER** Asst prof 70-74, assoc prof, 74-80, prof speech communication, Miami Univ, 80-, Speech consult, Republican Nat Cont, 76. **HONORS AND AWARDS** Outstanding Young Teacher Award, Cent States Speech Commun Asn, 74; pres, Relig Speech Assn, 90; variety of research grants from Shorenstein Cen of John F Kennedy School of Govern, Harvard Univ, Am Jewish Archives. **MEMBERSHIPS** Speech Commun Asn; Religious Speech Assn, Central States Speech Assn. **RESEARCH** Contemporary Political Communication; American Jewish Preaching; Political Debates. **SELECTED PUBLICATIONS** Auth, Communication Consultants in Political Campaigns: The Ballot Box Warriors, Hear O'Israel: The History of American Jewish Preaching 1642-1970; Rhetorical Studies of Political Debates: 1996; Rhetorical Studies of Political Debates: 1960-1992; Theodore Roosevelt and the Rhetoric of Militant Decency, with Judith S Trent, Political Campaign Communication: Principles and Practices. **CONTACT ADDRESS** Dept of Communication, Miami Univ, 1601 Peck Blvd, Hamilton, OH, 45011-3399. **EMAIL** friederv@muohio.edu

FRIEDMAN, ALAN
PERSONAL Born 06/08/1939, Brooklyn, NY, m, 1985, 4 children **DISCIPLINE** ENGLISH **CAREER** Creator, director, and teacher, Brasenose coll, Oxford, 84-87; exchange prof, 85, Universite, Paul Valery, Montpellier; chair, 87-89, UT faculty senate; exchange prof, 95, Univ Coll, Galway; Prof, Univ Tex, 76-. **HONORS AND AWARDS** Natl Endow for the Humanities Fell, 70-71; Fulbright research award, France, Dec-Jan 84-85; travel award, France, Spring 90; Parlin Fell, Plan II. **SELECTED PUBLICATIONS** Auth, Fictional Death and The Modernist Enterprise, Cambridge Univ Press, 95; auth, The Great War and Ritual, War and Literature, Stuttgart, 94; Standard English at the University of Texas, Situating College English, Greenwood, 96; Good Governance, Academe, July-Aug 96; Modernist Attitudes Toward Death, Death and the Quest for Meaning, 97. **CONTACT ADDRESS** Dept of English, Univ of Texas, Austin, TX, 78712. **EMAIL** friedman@uts.cc.utexas.edu

FRIEDMAN, BARTON ROBERT
PERSONAL Born 02/05/1935, Brooklyn, NY, m, 1958, 4 children **DISCIPLINE** MODERN LITERATURE **EDUCATION** Cornell Univ, BA, 56; Univ Conn, MA, 58; Cornell Univ, PhD(English), 64. **CAREER** Instr English, Bowdoin Col, 61-63; asst prof, Univ wis, 63-68, assoc prof, 68-77, prof, 77-78; prof & chemn dept English, Cleveland State Univ, 78-, Assoc ed, Literary Monographs, 69-76 & Irish Renaissance Annual, 80-. **MEMBERSHIPS** MLA; Am Comt for Irish Studies. **RESEARCH** History and literary narrative; post-war American literature; the Irish literary revival. **SELECTED PUBLICATIONS** Auth, to tell the sun from the druid fires imagery of good and evil, In: The Ring and the Book, Studies in English Lit, 66; Years, Johnson and Ireland's heroic dead, Eire-Ireland, 72; Fabricating history: Narrative strategy, In: The Lord of the rings, Clio, 73; On Baile's strand to At the hawk's well: Staging the deeps of the mind, J Mod Lit, 75; Adventures in the Deeps of the Mind, Princeton Univ Press, 77; You Can's Tell the Play-

ers, Cleveland State Univ Poetry Ctr, 79; Fabricating history or John Banim refights the Boyne, Eire-Ireland, 82; Tolkien and David Jones: The great war and the war of the ring, Clio, 82; Fabricating History, Princeton Univ Press, 88; Dissolving Surfaces, Yeats Annual, 89; Yeatsian, Metaphysics, Yeats Annual, 91; Esoteric Yeatsism, Yeats Annual, 93. **CONTACT ADDRESS** Dept of English, Cleveland State Univ, 1983 E 24th St, Cleveland, OH, 44115-2440. **EMAIL** b.friedman@csuohio.edu

FRIEDMAN, DONALD M.
PERSONAL Born 04/08/1929, New York, NY, m, 1959, 2 children **DISCIPLINE** ENGLISH **EDUCATION** Columbia Univ, BA, 49; Cambridge Univ, MA, 58; Harvard Univ, PhD, 60. **CAREER** Teaching fel, Harvard Univ, 56-60, instr English, 60-61; from asst prof to assoc prof, 61-73, PROF ENGLISH, UNIV CALIF, BERKELEY, 73-. **MEMBERSHIPS** MLA; Renaissance Soc Am; Milton Soc Am. **RESEARCH** Tudor poetry; seventeenth century poetry. **SELECTED PUBLICATIONS** Auth, Griswold, Erwin, Nathaniel--Inm Memoriam, Harvard Law Rev, Vol 108, 95; The World is a Garden--Garden Poetry of the English Renaissance, Renaissance Quart, Vol 49, 96. **CONTACT ADDRESS** Dept of English, Univ of Calif, Berkeley, CA, 94720.

FRIEDMAN, JOHN BLOCK
PERSONAL Born 12/08/1934, Troy, NY, m, 1962, 2 children **DISCIPLINE** MEDIEVAL ENGLISH LITERATURE **EDUCATION** Reed Col, BA, 60; Johns Hopkins Univ, MA, 61; Mich State Univ, PhD (English), 65. **CAREER** Asst prof English, Conn Col, 65-68; from asst prof to assoc prof, Sir George Williams Univ, 68-71; PROF ENGLISH, UNIV ILL, URBANA, 71-, Res, Ctr Study Medieval Civilization, Poiters, France, 73; Inst Southeastern Medieval and Renaissance Studies fel, 75; assoc, Ctr Advanced Studies, Univ Ill, 75-76; Guggenheim Mem Found fel, 79-80. **MEMBERSHIPS** MLA; Mediaeval Acad Am; Philol Asn Pac Coast. **RESEARCH** Medieval literature and iconography; survival of the classics. **SELECTED PUBLICATIONS** Auth, Courting Disaster--Astrology at the English Court and University in the Later Middle Ages, Speculumn J Medieval Stud, Vol 69, 94; The Middle English Weye of Paradys and the Middle French Voie De Paradis--A Parallel Text Edition, Speculum J Medieval Stud, Vol 69, 94; Dorigen Grisly Rokkes Blake Again , Chaucer Rev, Vol 31, 96; Virgil in Medieval England--Figuring the Aeneid from the 12th Century to Chaucer, Am Hist Rev, Vol 102, 97; Courting Disaster--Astrology at the English Court and University in the Later Middle Ages, Speculum J Medieval Stud, Vol 69, 94; The Middle English Weye of Paradys athe Middle French Voie De Paradis--A Parallel Text Edition , Speculum J Medieval Stud, Vol 69, 94. **CONTACT ADDRESS** Dept of English, Univ of Ill, Urbana, IL, 61801.

FRIEDMAN, MELVIN JACK
PERSONAL Born 03/07/1928, Brooklyn, NY, m, 1958, 2 children **DISCIPLINE** ENGLISH, COMPARATIVE LITERATURE **EDUCATION** Bard Col, AB, 49; Columbia Univ, AM, 52; Yale Univ, PhD (comp lit), 54. **CAREER** Assoc ed, French Studies, Yale Univ, 51-53; assoc prof comp lit, Univ Md, 62-66; PROF COMP LIT, UNIV WIS-MILWAUKEE, 66-, Vis sr fel, Univ EAnglia, 72; mem fel comt, Nat Endowment for Humanities, 73-74; Fulbright sr lectr, Univ Antwerp, 76. **MEMBERSHIPS** MLA; PEN. **RESEARCH** Twentieth century novel; 20th century literary criticism. **SELECTED PUBLICATIONS** Auth, 3 Views Of Modernism, Mississippi Quart, Vol 46, 93; Wandering and Home, Beckett Metaphysical Narrative, Contemporary Lit, Vol 36, 95; The Beckett Studies Reader, Contemporary Literature, Vol 36, 95; Beckett Dying Words, Contemporary Lit, Vol 36, 95; Nobodys Home, Speech, Self, and Place in American Fiction from Hawthorne to Delillo, Novel Forum Fiction, Vol 28, 95; Cabell, James, Branch and Richmond In Virginia, Am Lit, Vol 66, 94; Innovation in Beckett, Samuel Fiction, Contemporary Lit, Vol 36, 95; Accidents of Influence, Writing as a Woman and a Jew in America, Int Fiction Rev, Vol 20, 93. **CONTACT ADDRESS** Dept of Comp Lit, Univ of Wis, Milwaukee, WI, 53201.

FRIEDMAN, MICHAEL D.
DISCIPLINE ENGLISH **EDUCATION** Tulane Univ, BA, 82; Boston Univ, MA, 85, PhD, 90. **CAREER** Asst prof, Univ Scranton, 91-; vis asst prof, St John's Univ, 90-91; tchg fel, Boston Univ, 86-90. **HONORS AND AWARDS** Tchg improvt grant, Univ Scranton, 97; Stipend for Folger Shakespeare Libr Inst, Nat Endowment Hum, 96; internal res grant, Univ Scranton, 91 & 92; grad sch prize excellence tchg, Boston Univ, 89; Hum Found grant, 89; Presidential Univ tchg fel, 85-89 & grad fel, 84-85; Phi Beta Kappa & Engl Honor Soc, Tulane Univ. **MEMBERSHIPS** AAUP; MLA; Shakespeare Asn Am; Shakespeare and Renaissance Asn WV. **RESEARCH** Comprehensive oral examination in Renaissance lit; 17th-century lit; 19th-century Brit lit; literary theory. **SELECTED PUBLICATIONS** Auth, Prostitution and the Feminist Appropriation of Measure for Measure on the Stage, Shakespeare Bull 15 2, 97; Wishing a more strict restraint': Feminist Performance and the Silence of Isabella, Selected Papers from the W Va Shakespeare and Renaissance Asn 19, 96; O, let him marry her': Matrimony and Recompense in Measure for Measure, Shakespeare Quart 46, 95; Male Bonds and Marriage in All's Well and Much Ado, Stud in Eng Lit 35, 95; Service is no heritage': Bertram and the Ideology of Procreation, Stud in Philol 92, 95; To be slow in words is a woman's only virtue': Silence and Satire in The Two Gentlemen of Verona, Selected Papers from the W Va Shakespeare and Renaissance Asn 17, 94, repr in, Two Gentlemen of Verona: Critical Essays, NY, Garland, 95; rev, of Shakespearean Performance as Interpretation, by Herbert Coursen, Shakespeare Yearbk 4, 94. **CONTACT ADDRESS** Dept of Eng, Univ of Scranton, Scranton, PA, 18510. **EMAIL** FriedmanM1@Tiger.uofs.edu

FRIEDMAN, NORMAN
PERSONAL Born 04/10/1925, Boston, MA, m, 1945, 2 children **DISCIPLINE** ENGLISH **EDUCATION** Harvard Univ, AB, 48, AM, 49, PhD (English), 52; Adelphi Univ, MSW, 78. **CAREER** From instr to assoc prof English, Univ Conn, 52-63; assoc prof, 63-67, PROF ENGLISH, QUEENS COL GRAD CTR, NY, 68-; PROF ENGLISH, CITY UNIV NEW YORK, 68-, Am Coun Learned Soc grants, 59 and 60; Fulbright lectr, Univs Nantes and Nice, 66-67; consult, PMLA. **HONORS AND AWARDS** Bowdoin Prize, 48; Northwest Rev Annual Poetry Prize, 63; Borestone Mountain Poetry Awards, 64, 67. **MEMBERSHIPS** MLA; NCTE; AAUP. **RESEARCH** Literary criticism and critical theory; Victorian and modern literature; psychology and literature. **SELECTED PUBLICATIONS** Auth, Forum, PMLA Publications Mod Lan Assoc Am, Vol 111, 96. **CONTACT ADDRESS** Dept of English, Queens Col, CUNY, 6530 Kissena Blvd, Flushing, NY, 11367.

FRIEDMAN, PHILIP ALLAN
PERSONAL Born 07/19/1927, Brooklyn, NY **DISCIPLINE** ENGLISH LITERATURE, AMERICAN PHILOSOPHY **EDUCATION** NY Univ, BA, 48; Columbia Univ, MA, 49; Univ Heidelberg, cert ling and philol, 55. **CAREER** Reporter and bk reviewer, Jewish Examiner, 48-49; prof asst, Toby Press, New York, 50-51; asst ed, Random House, Inc, New York, 51-52; instr English compos and contemp lit, Wayne State Univ, 53-54, 55-58; from asst prof to assoc prof Am Lit and studies, Calif State Univ, Los Angeles, 59-77, prof, 77-80., Consult, State Dept Comt For Visitors, Mich, 53-54, 55-58; consult and mem bd, Jewish Community Libr, Jewish Fed Coun Greater Los Angeles, 72; consult drama, Henry Street Settlement Children's Theater, 77-; referee and consult history, Hist, 78-. **MEMBERSHIPS** AAUP. **RESEARCH** Am Lit and culture; philosophy of science. **SELECTED PUBLICATIONS** Auth, Slapping Back, Aba J, Vol 82, 96. **CONTACT ADDRESS** 100 N Detroit Los, Los Angeles, CA, 90036.

FRIEDMAN, SIDNEY JOSEPH
PERSONAL Born 06/08/1939, Des Moines, IA, m, 1962, 2 children **DISCIPLINE** ENGLISH, DRAMA **EDUCATION** Princeton Univ, AB, 61; Univ IA, MA, 63, PhD, 66. **CAREER** Assoc prof Eng & drama, WA Univ, 66-81; assoc prof, 81-98, Prof Theatre Arts, Boston Univ, 98. **MEMBERSHIPS** Asn Theatre in High Educ. **RESEARCH** Acting; directing; dramatic criticism. **CONTACT ADDRESS** Sch of Theatre Arts Boston Univ, 855 Commonwealth Ave, Boston, MA, 02215-1303.

FRIEDMAN, STANLEY
PERSONAL Born 05/03/1933, New York, NY, m, 1967, 2 children **DISCIPLINE** VICTORIAN & ENGLISH RENAISSANCE LITERATURE **EDUCATION** Columbia Univ, AB, 54, AM, 55, PhD, 63. **CAREER** Instr English, Univ NE, 55-56; lectr, 61-63, instr, 63-66, asst prof, 67-79, assoc prof, 80-98, ASSOC PROF EMERITUS ENGLISH, QUEENS COL, CITY UNIV NY, 98-; co-ed, Dickens Studies Annual, 96-. **HONORS AND AWARDS** Danforth Asn (with wife), 70-85. **MEMBERSHIPS** Dickens Soc. **RESEARCH** Dickens; Shakespeare. **SELECTED PUBLICATIONS** Auth, The motif of reading in Our Mutual Friend, Nineteenth Century Fiction, 6/73; Dickens' Mid-Victorian theodicy: David Copperfield, Dickens Studies Annual, Vol 7, 78; The Complex Origins of Pip and Magwitch, Dickens Studies Annual, Vol 15, 86; Estella's Parentage and Pip's Persistence: the Outcome of Great Expectations, Studies in the Novel, winter 87; A Considerate Ghost: George Rouncewell in Bleak House, Dickens Studies Annual, Vol 17, 88; Sad Stephen and Troubled Louisa: Paired Protagonists in Hard Times, Dickens Quart, 6/90; Heep and Powell: Dickensian Revenge?, Dickensian, spring 94; Recent Dickens studies: 1992, Dickens Studies Annual, Vol 23, 94. **CONTACT ADDRESS** Dept of English, Queens Col, CUNY, 6530 Kissena Blvd, Flushing, NY, 11367-1597.

FRIEDRICH, GUSTAV WILLIAM
PERSONAL Born 03/02/1941, Hastings, NB, Canada, m, 1962, 1 child **DISCIPLINE** COMMUNICATION **EDUCATION** Univ Minn, Minneapolis, BA, 64; Univ Kans, MA, 67, PhD(speech commun), 68. **CAREER** Teacher, St John's Lutheran Sch, Minn, 61-62; assoc prof commun, Purdue Univ, West Lafayette, 68-77; prof speech commun & chairperson dept, Univ Nebr-Lincoln, 77-81; prof Commun & Chemn dept, Univ Okla, 82-; asst prof hist, 75-79; from assoc prof to prof, 79-87; Cameron Univ. **MEMBERSHIPS** Am Educ Res Asn; Cent States Speech Asn; Int Commun Asn; National Commun Asn; Am Psychol AsnSoc for Historians of the Early American Republic, Phi Alpha Theta Int Honor Soc in History. **RESEARCH** Classroom communication; interpersonal communication; experimental research methodology. **SELECTED PUBLICATIONS** Coauth, Growing Together ... Classroom Communication, Charles E Merrill, 76; ed, Education in the 80's: Speech Communication, NEA, 81; coauth, Public Communication, Harper, 82; auth, Classroom interaction, In: Communication in the Classroom: Contemporary Theory and Practice, Prentice Hall, 82; Treachery or Hoax? The Rumored Southern Conspiracy to Confederate with Mexico, Civil War History, March, 89; Window on Washington in 1850: Tracking Newspaper Letter-Writers, American Journalism, Winter, 98. **CONTACT ADDRESS** Dept of Communication, Univ of Oklahoma, 610 Elm Ave Rm 101, Norman, OK, 73019-2081. **EMAIL** Fredrich@ou.edu

FRIEDRICH, PAUL
PERSONAL Born 10/22/1927, m, 1974, 6 children **DISCIPLINE** LINGUISTICS, ANTHROPOLOGY, POETRY **EDUCATION** Harvard Univ, BA, 50, MA, 51; Yale Univ, PhD, 57. **CAREER** Res assoc, Russ Res Ctr, 49-50; asst prof anthrop, Harvard Univ, 57-58; asst prof jr ling, Deccan Col, India, 58-59; asst prof anthrop, Univ Pa, 59-62; assoc prof, 62-67, prof anthrop & ling, Univ Chicago, 67-; prof anthrop, ling & soc thought, 92. **MEMBERSHIPS** Ling See Am; Amer Anthro Assoc; Amer Acad Arts & Sci . **RESEARCH** Homeric Greek; Russian; Mexican languages on cultures. **SELECTED PUBLICATIONS** Auth, Russia and Eurasia, Encyclopedic 1 World, Cultures, 94; auth, Music in Russian Poetry, Lang, 98. **CONTACT ADDRESS** Dept of Anthrop, Univ of Chicago, 1126 E 59th St, Chicago, IL, 60637-1539.

FRIEL, JAMES P.
PERSONAL Bronx, NY, m, 1976 **DISCIPLINE** PHILOSOPHY, LITERATURE **EDUCATION** Marist Col, BA, 56; Fordham Univ, MA, 65. **CAREER** Teacher English, Marist Bro Schs, 56-63 & Cent Sch Dist, Syosset, 63-68; prof philos, Marist Col & Col of Mt St Vincent, 68-69; Prof English & Philos, State Univ NY Farmingdale, 70-, Ed, Aitia Mag, 72-; State Univ NY grant, 73; Matchette Found grant & dir study group, 76-80; chmn two-yr teaching comt, Am Philos Asn, 77-82. **MEMBERSHIPS** Am Philos Asn; Nat Workshop Conf; Nat Info & Resource Ctr Teaching Philos. **RESEARCH** Metaphysics; humor; citizenship. **SELECTED PUBLICATIONS** Ed, Philosophy of Religion, State Univ NY, 73; auth, Citizen apprenticeship, Aitia Mag, 74-75; ed, Philosophy, Law, Modern Citizen, State Univ NY Farmingdale, 75; auth, Report on National Workship Conference, Aitia Mag, 76; Paying through the nose to lift those Sunday blues, Newday, 10/76; The mall the merrier, or is it?, NY Times, 11/76; ed, Nineteenth Century American Literature, State Univ NY, (in press). **CONTACT ADDRESS** SUNY, Farmingdale, 1250 Melville Rd, Farmingdale, NY, 11735-1389. **EMAIL** frieljp@suny.farmingdale.edu

FRIES, MAUREEN HOLMBERG
PERSONAL Born 07/14/1931, Buffalo, NY, d, 4 children **DISCIPLINE** ENGLISH LITERATURE **EDUCATION** D'Youville Col, AB, 52; Cornell Univ, MA, 53; State Univ NY Buffalo, PhD, 69. **CAREER** Instr English, State Univ NY Buffalo, 64-69; asst prof to assoc prof, 69-77, prof Eng, State Univ NY Col Fredonia, 77-90. **HONORS AND AWARDS** NEH fel, 75-76; res awards, State Univ NY, 72, 73, 79 & 80; co-dir, Conversation in the Disciplines, 80; distinguished teach prof, 90; distinguished prof emerita, 97-, Chancellor's Award for Excellence in Teaching, State Univ NY, 77. **MEMBERSHIPS** MLA; Int Arthurian Soc; Mediaeval Acad Am. **RESEARCH** Medieval English literature; Arthurian literature; women's studies. **SELECTED PUBLICATIONS** Co-ed, Approaches to Teaching the Arthurian Tradition, New York: Modern Language Association of America, 92; art, Sexuality and Women in the Old Irish Sagas, Celtic Connections, ACTA, Binghamton: SUNY Press, 93; Natural and art, Unnatural Childhoods in T.H. White's The Once and Future King, The Platte Valley Review, 93; art, How Many Roads to Camelot? The Married Knight in Malory's Morte Darthur,Culture and the King: The Social Implications of the Arthurian Legend, Essays in Honor of Professor Valerie M. LagorioAlbany: SUNY Press, 94; art, From the Lady to the Tramp: The Decline of Morgan le Fay in Medieval Romance, Arthuriana, 94; art, Geoffrey of Monmouth, The Dictionary of Literary Biography, Old and Middle English Literature, Detroit: Gale, 94; **CONTACT ADDRESS** Dept of English, SUNY, Fredonia, Fredonia, NY, 14063-1143.

FRITZ, DONALD WAYEN
PERSONAL Born 06/11/1933, Monroe, WI **DISCIPLINE** MEDIEVAL BRITISH LITERATURE **EDUCATION** Miami Univ, BA, 56, MA, 59; Stanford Univ, PhD(English), 68. **CAREER** Instr English, Southern Methodist Univ, 59-63, Stanford Univ, 67-68; prof english, Miami Univ, 68-; dir, Performing Arts Sci, 82-98. **MEMBERSHIPS** MLA; Midwest Mod Lang Asn; SAtlantic Mod Lang Asn; Chaucer Soc. **RESEARCH** Chaucer; Anglo-Saxon poetry; 14th century British poetry of Chaucer. **SELECTED PUBLICATIONS** Auth, Caedmon: A traditional poet, Mediaeval Studies, 69; Caedmon: A monastic exeget, Am Benedictine Rev, 74; The prioress's avowal of ineptitude, Chaucer Rev, 74; Chronological impossibilities in Widsith, Ger Notes, 75; The origin and meaning of pattern in Kells, J Anal Psychol, 77; Perspectives on Creativity and the Unconscious, Oxford Univ, 79; The Pearl and the sacredness of num-

ber, Am Benedictine Rev, 80; The animus-ridden wife of Bath, J Anal Psychol, 80; Reflection in a Golden Eye: Chaucer's Narcissistic Pardon, Chaucer Rev, 84. **CONTACT ADDRESS** Miami Univ, 4 Ives Woods Dr, Oxford, OH, 45052. **EMAIL** fritzdw@muohio.edu

FRITZELL, PETER ALGREN
PERSONAL Born 08/23/1940, Minneapolis, MN, m, 1962, 2 children **DISCIPLINE** AMERICAN LITERATURE **EDUCATION** Univ ND, BA, 62; Stanford Univ, MA, 66, PhD(English & humanities), 66. **CAREER** Chmn dept, 73-77, 87-90, asst prof, 66-73, assoc prof, 73-83, prof English, Lawrence Univ, 83-, Patricia Hamar Boldt Prof Liberal Studies, 89-; vis prof humanities, Stanford Univ, 68, 74 & 77; NEH fel, 72-73, 81-82 ; vis scholar environ studies, Dartmouth Col, 72-73; vis lectr, Univ WI-Green Bay, 74; dir, Lawrence Univ London Ctr, 77-78. **MEMBERSHIPS** MLA; Forest Hist Soc; ASLE; PBK. **RESEARCH** American literature of the seventeenth and eighteenth centuries, especially descriptive prose; nature writing. **SELECTED PUBLICATIONS** Auth, The Wilderness and the Garden, Forest Hist, 4/68; Introd to Henry Wansey's Journal of an Excursion, 1794, 69 & H B Mollhausen's Diary of a Journey (2 vols), 69, Johnson; Aldo Leopold's A Sand County Almanac and the Conflicts of Ecological Conscience, Trans Wis Acad Sci Arts & Lett, 76; American Wetlands as a Cultural Symbol, In: Wetland Functions and Values: The State of Our Understanding, 79; Walden and Paradox, New England Rev, 10/80; All Things are Natural, WI English J, 1/82; Changing Conceptions of the Great Lakes Forest, In: The Great Lakes Forest, 82; Nature Writing and America: Essays upon a Cultural Type, IA State, 90; Aldo Leopold, in American Nature Writers, 96. **CONTACT ADDRESS** Dept English, Lawrence Univ, 115 S Drew St, Appleton, WI, 54911-5798.

FROESE TIESSEN, HILDI
DISCIPLINE ENGLISH LITERATURE **EDUCATION** Univ Winnipeg, BA, 68; Univ Alberta, MA, 71, PhD, 81. **CAREER** Assoc prof **RESEARCH** Politics of art; literature of ethnic and religious minorities in Canada. **SELECTED PUBLICATIONS** Auth, pub(s) on new literatures in Canada, and individual authors such as Rudy Wiebe, Patrick Friesen and Di Brandt. **CONTACT ADDRESS** Dept of English, Conrad Grebel Col, 200 Westmount Rd, Waterloo, ON, N2L 3G6. **EMAIL** htiessen@uwaterloo.ca

FROMM, GLORIA GLIKIN
PERSONAL Born 11/14/1931, Newark, NY **DISCIPLINE** ENGLISH **EDUCATION** NY Univ, BA, 52, MA, 56, PhD (English), 61. **CAREER** Asst English, sch commerce, NY Univ, 57-59; instr, Brooklyn Col, 61-65, asst prof, 65-70; assoc prof, 70-78, PROF ENGLISH, UNIV ILL, CHICAGO CIRCLE, 78-, Am Coun Learned Soc grant, 67. **MEMBERSHIPS** MLA. **RESEARCH** Twentieth century novel, biography and autobiography. **SELECTED PUBLICATIONS** Auth, Richardson And Co , Library Chronicle Univ Texas Austin, Vol 23, 93; Women and Social Action in Victorian and Edwardian England, Eng Lit Transition 1880-1920, Vol 36, 93. **CONTACT ADDRESS** Dept of English, Univ Ill Chicago Circle, Box 4348, Chicago, IL, 60680.

FROSCH, THOMAS RICHARD
PERSONAL New York, NY **DISCIPLINE** ENGLISH LITERATURE **EDUCATION** Wesleyan Univ, BA, 64; Yale Univ, MA, 66, PhD (English), 68. **CAREER** Asst prof English, NY Univ, 68-71; PROF ENGLISH, QUEENS COL, 71-. **SELECTED PUBLICATIONS** Auth, Towards Reading Freud, Self Creation in Milton, Wordsworth, Emerson, and Freud, Stud Romanticism, Vol 33, 94. Writers Block - Leader,Z/, Studies In Romanticism, Vol 33, 94 **CONTACT ADDRESS** Dept of English, Queens Col, CUNY, 6530 Kissena Blvd, Flushing, NY, 11367-1597.

FROST, ELIZABETH
DISCIPLINE MODERN AND CONTEMPORARY AMERICAN POETRY **EDUCATION** UCLA, PhD. **CAREER** Asst prof, Fordham Univ. **RESEARCH** Feminist theory, experimental writing. **SELECTED PUBLICATIONS** Auth, Fetishism and Parody in Stein's Tender Buttons, Sexual Artifice, NY UP, 94; Mina Loy's Mongrel Poetics, Mina Loy: Woman and Poet, Nat Poetry Found, 97. **CONTACT ADDRESS** Dept of Eng Lang and Lit, Fordham Univ, 113 W 60th St, New York, NY, 10023.

FROST, LINDA ANNE
DISCIPLINE ENGLISH **EDUCATION** Bowling Green State Univ, BA, 85; SUNY at Stonybrook, PhD, 90. **CAREER** Asst prof, Eng, Penn State-Wilkes-Barre; current, ASST PROF, ENG, UNIV ALA B'HAM. **MEMBERSHIPS** Am Antiquarian Soc **SELECTED PUBLICATIONS** Auth, "'The Red Face of Man', The Penobscot Indian, and a Conflict of Interest in Thoreau's Maine Woods," ESQ 39, 93. **CONTACT ADDRESS** 3023 13th Ave S, No. 4, Birmingham, AL, 35205.

FROULA, CHRISTINE
DISCIPLINE ENGLISH **EDUCATION** Chicago Univ, PhD. **CAREER** Guggenheim fel; Herman and Beulah Pearce Miller res prof, Northwestern Univ. **RESEARCH** Interdisciplinary modernism, 19th and 20th century literature. **CONTACT ADDRESS** Dept of English, Northwestern Univ, 1801 Hinman, Evanston, IL, 60208.

FRUSHELL, RICHARD CLAYTON
PERSONAL Born 08/25/1935, Pittsburgh, PA, m, 1958, 5 children **DISCIPLINE** ENGLISH **EDUCATION** Duquesne Univ, PhD (English), 68. **CAREER** Teacher English, Oliver High Sch, Pittsburgh, Pa, 61-66; from asst prof to assoc prof, 68-71; PROF ENGLISH, IND STATE UNIV, TERRE HAUTE, 75-, Contribr, Annual Bibliog Eng Lang and Lit, Mod Humanities Res Asn, 71-75; fel, Lilly Libr, 77. **HONORS AND AWARDS** Caleb Mills Distinguished Teaching Award, Ind State Univ, 74. **MEMBERSHIPS** Am Soc 18th Century Studies; MLA; Mod Humanities Res Asn; Spenser Soc; Poe Studies Asn. **RESEARCH** Restoration and eighteenth century English literature; Renaissance English literature; bibliography. **SELECTED PUBLICATIONS** Auth, Swift 6 August 1735 Letter to Delany, Mary, Pendarves, All Other Days I Eat My Chicken Alone Like A King, Philol Quart, Vol 74, 95. **CONTACT ADDRESS** Dept of English, Indiana State Univ, Terre Haute, IN, 47809.

FRY, CARROL LEE
PERSONAL Born 07/31/1932, New Hampton, MO, m, 1957 **DISCIPLINE** ENGLISH **EDUCATION** Northwest Mo State Col, BS, 57; Univ Omaha, MA, 62; Univ Nebr, PhD (Eng), 70. **CAREER** Teacher hist and Eng, Maysville High Sch, Mo, 57-58; asst Eng, Univ Kans, 62-63; from instr to assoc prof, Mankato State Col, 63-72; ASSOC PROF and CHMN DEPT, NORTHWEST MO STATE UNIV, 72-, Ed consult, Houghton Mifflin Co, 71-; managing ed, Mo Eng Bull. **MEMBERSHIPS** AAUP; MLA; Midwest Mod Lng Asn. **RESEARCH** Eighteenth century English fiction; Jane Austen's novels; contemporary fiction. **SELECTED PUBLICATIONS** Auth, The Goddess Ascending--Feminist Neo Pagan Witchcraft in Bradley, Marion, Zimmer Novels, J Pop Cult, Vol 27, 93; Economic Issues in the Defense of Directors and Officers of Financial Institutions, Banking Law J, Vol 110, 93. **CONTACT ADDRESS** Dept of English, Northwest Missouri State Univ, Maryville, MO, 64469.

FRY, KATHERINE G.
PERSONAL Born 11/03/1961, Hamilton, MT, m, 1990, 1 child **DISCIPLINE** COMMUNICATIONS **EDUCATION** Univ Minn, BA, 85; Temple Univ, MA, 89, PhD, 94 **CAREER** Ed, Univ of Minn, 86-87; Ed asst, Temple Univ, 88; teaching & res asst, Temple Univ, 88-92; asst dir, Inst of Culture and Commun, Temple Univ, 88-91; ed asst, Critical Studies in Mass Commun, 89-91; tutor, Univ Writing Ctr, Temple Univ, 91-92; inst, Drexel Univ, 92; inst, Ursinus Col, 90-93; inst, Long Island Univ-Brooklyn, 93; inst, Brooklyn Col, 93-94; asst prof, Dept of Television & Radio, Brooklyn Col, CUNY, 94-. **MEMBERSHIPS** Nat Commun Assoc; Int Commun Assoc; Eastern Commun Assoc; NY State Commun Assoc. **RESEARCH** Cultural studies of mass media; cultural geography. **SELECTED PUBLICATIONS** Auth, Regional Magazines and the Ideal White Reader: Constructing and Retaining Geography as Text, Elec J of Commun, 4:2-3, 94; auth, Television and National Identity: The Case of Germany, ALMANAC, 96-97 ed; auth, essays in Encyclopedia of Television, Fitzroy Dearborn Publishers, 97; Myths of Nature and Place: Network Television News Coverage of the Great Flood of 1993, New Dimensions in Commun, vol 10, 54-68, 97. **CONTACT ADDRESS** 367 Bergen St. #3, Brooklyn, NY, 11217-2009. **EMAIL** kfrbc@cunyvm.cuny.edu

FRYE, JOANNE S.
DISCIPLINE ENGLISH LITERATURE **EDUCATION** Bluffton, BA, 66; Ind Univ, PhD, 74. **CAREER** Prof. **SELECTED PUBLICATIONS** Auth, Living Stories, Telling Lives; Tillie Olson; articles reflecting a feminist approach to literary texts. **CONTACT ADDRESS** Dept of Eng, Col of Wooster, Wooster, OH, 44691.

FRYE, ROLAND MUSHAT
PERSONAL Born 07/03/1921, Birmingham, AL, m, 1947, 1 child **DISCIPLINE** ENGLISH **EDUCATION** Princeton Univ, AB, 43, PhD (English), 52. **CAREER** Instr English, Howard Col, 47-48; from asst prof to prof, Emory Univ, 52-61; res prof, Folger Shakespeare Libr, 62-65; FELIX E SCHELLING PROF ENGLISH, UNIV PA, 65-, Guggenheim res fel, 56-57 and 73-74; Stone lectr and vis lectr, Princeton theol Sem; Am Coun Learned Soc grant, 66, 71 and 78; Am Philos Soc grant, 68, 71 and 78; Nat Endowment Humanities res grant, 73-74; mem, Inst Advan Study, Princeton Univ, 73-74 and 79; fels, Nat Endowment for Humanities, Huntington Libr, 81 and Ctr Theol Inquiry, Princeton, 82. **HONORS AND AWARDS** John Frederick Lewis Prize, Am Philos Soc, 79; James Holly Hanford Award, Milton Soc Am, 79. **MEMBERSHIPS** MLA; Renaissance Soc Am; Milton Soc Am (pres, 77-78); Shakespeare Soc Am; Am Philos Soc (secy, 78-81). **RESEARCH** Literature; art; theology. **SELECTED PUBLICATIONS** Auth, Bentley, Gerald, Eades September 15,1901 July 25, 94, Proceedings Am Philos Soc, Vol 140, 96; A Gust for Paradise, Milton Eden athe Visual Arts, Mod Philol, Vol 94, 96. **CONTACT ADDRESS** Dept of English, Univ of Pa, Philadelphia, PA, 19174.

FRYER, JUDITH
PERSONAL Born 08/05/1939, Minneapolis, MN, 2 children **DISCIPLINE** AM LIT AND HISTORY **EDUCATION** Univ Minn, PhD (Am studies), 73. **CAREER** Instr women's studies, Am studies and Am lit, Univ Minn, 68-73; asst prof, 74-78, ASSOC PROF AM STUDIES, MIAMI UNIV, OXFORD, OHIO, 78-, DIR AM STUDIES PROG, 74-, Instr Am lit, Macalester Col, St Paul, 72; guest prof Am studies, Univ T¤bingen, West Ger, 76-77; res grants, Miami Univ, summers, 75, 79 and 82, Nat Endowment for the Humanities, summers 76 and 78, 79-80; Fulbright grant, 76; fel, Bunting Inst, Harvard Univ, 79-80. **MEMBERSHIPS** Am Studies Asn; Nat Trust for Hist Preservation; Hist Keyboard Soc. **RESEARCH** Women's studies; early music. **SELECTED PUBLICATIONS** Auth, Review of Developments in State Securities Regulation, Business Lawyer, Vol 49, 93. **CONTACT ADDRESS** American Studies Prog, Miami Univ, Oxford, OH, 45056.

FUCHS, CYNTHIA
DISCIPLINE VISUAL ARTS **EDUCATION** Univ Pa, PhD. **CAREER** Assoc prof. **RESEARCH** African American studies; queer theory; postmodern theory; popular mass culture studies. **SELECTED PUBLICATIONS** Auth, Between the Sheets, In the Streets: Queer, Lesbian, Gay Documentary, 97; Death is Irrelevant: Cyborgs, Reproduction, and the Future of Male Hysteria, Genders, 93; The Buddy Politic, 93. **CONTACT ADDRESS** Dept of Film and Media Studies, George Mason Univ, 4400 University Dr, Fairfax, VA, 22030.

FUCHS, JACOB
PERSONAL Born 12/02/1939, New York, NY, m, 1963, 3 children **DISCIPLINE** ENGLISH LITERATURE **EDUCATION** Univ Calif, Berkeley, BA, 61, MA, 64; Univ Calif, Irvine, PhD (comp lit), 72. **CAREER** PROF ENGLISH, CALIF STATE UNIV, HAYWARD, 71-. **MEMBERSHIPS** Philol Asn of Pac Coast; Am Soc 18th Century Studies. **RESEARCH** Neoclassicism. **SELECTED PUBLICATIONS** Auth, The Greek Gang At Troy, Classical W, Vol 87, 93. **CONTACT ADDRESS** California State Univ, Hayward, 25800 Carlos Bee Bvd, Hayward, CA, 94542-3001.

FULK, JANET
DISCIPLINE COMMUNICATION **EDUCATION** OH State Univ, BA, 70, MBA, 77, PhD, 78. **CAREER** Assoc dir, Sch Commun, Univ Southern CA, 95-97 & asst, assoc & prof, 79-97; vis scholar, Stanford Univ, 97; res assoc, Univ Southern CA, 78-79; asst prof, Kent State Univ, 76-78 & vis lectr, Univ Aston Mgt Ctr, 78. **HONORS AND AWARDS** Best Res Article, OCIS Acad Mgt, 93; Int Commun Asn Top Paper Awd(s), 93, 91, 90 & 85; Speech Commun Asn Best Bk Awd, 90. **MEMBERSHIPS** Bd Gov, Acad Mgt, 90-93; Exec Comt, Orgn Behav Div, Acad Mgt, 88-90; div ch, Publ Sector Div, Acad Mgt, 81-82. **RESEARCH** Management and commun effectiveness in organizations and the interplay of organizational sys and commun technol. **SELECTED PUBLICATIONS** Auth, Social construct of commun tech, Acad Mgt Jl, 36, 93; coauth, Electronic Communication and Changing Organizational Forms, Orgn Sci, 95; A soc influence model of technol use, Orgn & commun technol, Newbury Park, Sage, 90; Cognitive elements in the soc construc of commun technol, Mgt Commun Quart, 94; Organizational colleagues, information richness, and electronic mail: A test of the soc influence model of technol use, Commun Res, 18, 91 & Emerging theories of commun in organizations, Yearly Rev J Mgt, 17, 91. **CONTACT ADDRESS** Annenberg School for Commun, Univ of Southern California, University Park Campus, Los Angeles, CA, 90089.

FULKERSON, RAYMOND GERALD
PERSONAL Born 02/19/1941, Owensboro, KY, m, 1960, 3 children **DISCIPLINE** RHETORICAL CRITICISM, AMERICAN PUBLIC ADDRESS **EDUCATION** David Lipscomb Col, BA, 63; Univ IL, Champaign-Urbana, MA, 66, PhD(speech), 71. **CAREER** CHMN DEPT, COMMUN & LIT, FREED-HARDEMAN COL, 65-. **MEMBERSHIPS** Speech Commun Asn; Asn Study Afro-Am Life & Hist; Southern Speech Commun Asn; Int Soc Gen Semantics; Int Commun Asn. **RESEARCH** Rhetoric of the Abolition Movement; Theories and Methods of Rhetorical Criticism. **SELECTED PUBLICATIONS** Auth, Frederick Douglass and the Kansas-Nebraska Act: A Case Study in Agitational Versatility, Cent State Speech J, winter 72; Exile as Emergence: Frederick Douglass in Great Britain, 1845-1847, Quart J Speech, 2/74; textual ed, Frederick Douglass Papers, Yale Univ Press. **CONTACT ADDRESS** Dept of Commun, Freed-Hardeman Univ, 158 E Main St, Henderson, TN, 38340-2306. **EMAIL** geraldf@aeneas,net

FULKERSON, RICHARD P.
PERSONAL Born 02/09/1942, Carterville, IL, m, 1963, 2 children **DISCIPLINE** ENGLISH **EDUCATION** SO Illinois Univ, BS 63; Ohio State Univ, PhD 70. **CAREER** Texas A&M Univ, prof 81-; East Texas State Univ, asst, assoc, prof 70-81.

HONORS AND AWARDS Dist Fac Awd; Outstanding tchr. **MEMBERSHIPS** NCTE; CCCC; RSA; ATAC; NCA. **RESEARCH** Written argumentation; Teaching College writing; English as a Profession. **SELECTED PUBLICATIONS** Auth, Teaching the Argument in Writing, Urbana, NCTE, 96; Call Me Horatio: Negotiating Between Cognition and Affect in Composition, Col Comp Comm, 98; The English Doctoral Metacurriculum: An Issue of Ethics, eds, Sheryl Fontaine and Susan Hunter, Foregrounding Ethical Awareness in Eng Studies, Portsmouth NH, Boynton/Cook, 98; Transcending Our Conception of Argument in light of Feminist Critiques, Argumentation and Advocacy, 96. **CONTACT ADDRESS** Dept of Lit And Languages, Texas A&M Univ, Commerce, TX, 75428. **EMAIL** dick_fulkerson@TAMU-commerce.edu

FULLER, LAWRENCE BENEDICT
PERSONAL Born 07/27/1936, Orange, NJ, m, 1971, 2 children **DISCIPLINE** ENGLISH, HISTORY **EDUCATION** Dartmouth Col, AB, 58; Columbia Univ, MA, 63; Pennsylvania State Univ, MA, 83; Johns Hopkins Univ, PhD(Educ), 74. **CAREER** Assoc prof English, Bloomsburg Univ, 71-. **HONORS AND AWARDS** Phi Betta Kappa; Phi Kappa Phi; Fulbright Scholar, Norway, 93-94. **MEMBERSHIPS** Hist Educ Soc; NCTE. **RESEARCH** History of education; literature for adolescents; methods of teaching secondary English. **SELECTED PUBLICATIONS** Auth, A sense of our own history, Independent Sch Bull, 12/71; Private secondary education: the search for a new model, 1880-1915, Foundational Studies, Spring 75; Research papers in English methods classes: introduction to varieties of opinion, English Educ, Summer 76; William M Sloane: A biographical study of turn of the century attitudes toward American education, Foundational Studies, Fall 78; Literature for adolescents: The early days, The ALAN Rev, Spring 79; Students' rights of expression: The decade since Tinker, English J, 12/79; Literature for adolescents: A historical perspective, English Educ, 2/80; Media Education: Where Have We Been? Where Are We Going?, English Education, February, 96. **CONTACT ADDRESS** Dept of English, Bloomsburg Univ of Pennsylvania, 400 E 2nd St, Bloomsburg, PA, 17815-1399. **EMAIL** lfuller@planetx.bloomu.edu

FULTON, GORDON D.
DISCIPLINE ENGLISH LITERATURE **EDUCATION** Univ Toronto, BA; Univ London, MA, PhD. **CAREER** Asst prof **RESEARCH** Restoration and 18th-century literature, literary stylistics. **SELECTED PUBLICATIONS** Ed, Benson and Greaves, Systemic Functional Approaches to Discourse, Ablex, 88; pub(s), articles in Lang and Lit, 93; Lumen, 94; Eighteenth-Century Life, 96. **CONTACT ADDRESS** Dept of English, Victoria Univ, PO Box 3070, Victoria, BC, V8W 3W1. **EMAIL** gdfulton@uvic.ca

FULTON, HENRY LEVAN
PERSONAL Born 04/16/1935, Pittsburgh, PA, m, 1974, 2 children **DISCIPLINE** ENGLISH LITERATURE **EDUCATION** Wesleyan Univ, BA, 57; Univ Mich, MA, 60, PhD (English), 67. **CAREER** Instr English, Univ Mich, 65-67; asst prof, 67-70, assoc prof, 70-78, PROF ENGLISH, CENT MICH UNIV, 78-. **MEMBERSHIPS** MLA; Johnson Soc Midwest; Scottish Church Hist Soc. **RESEARCH** Eighteenth century English culture; Scottish literature; Shakespeare. **SELECTED PUBLICATIONS** Auth, Education and the Scottish People, 1750-1918, Albion, Vol 29, 97; Scottish Universities--Distinctiveness and Diversity, Albion, Vol 25, 93. **CONTACT ADDRESS** Dept of English, Central Michigan Univ, Mt Pleasant, MI, 48858.

FULTON, RICHARD DELBERT
PERSONAL Born 12/05/1945, Missoula, MT, m, 1976, 2 children **DISCIPLINE** VICTORIAN LITERATURE AND STUDIES **EDUCATION** Eastern Mont Col, BA, 67; Univ SDak, AM, 69; Wash State Univ, PhD (English), 75. **CAREER** Lectr English, Univ Col, Univ Md, 70-71; instr, 76-78, ASST PROF ENGLISH, WASH STATE UNIV, 78-, ASST DEAN GRAD SCH, 75-, Dean in residence, Coun Grad Sch in the US, 82-83. **MEMBERSHIPS** MLA; Conf Brit Studies; Philol Asn Pac Coast; Res Soc Victorian Periodicals. **RESEARCH** Victorian periodicals research and bibliography; history of the Spectator. **SELECTED PUBLICATIONS** Auth, Press, Politics and Society, A History of Jourism In Wales, Albion, Vol 26, 94; A Wider Range--Travel Writing by Women in Victorian England, J Pre Raphaelite Stud New Series, Vol 5, 96. **CONTACT ADDRESS** NW 605 Charlotte St, Pullman, WA, 99163.

FULWEILER, HOWARD
DISCIPLINE ENGLISH **EDUCATION** Univ NC, PhD, 60. **CAREER** Prof; ed bd, Victorian Poetry & Explicator. **HONORS AND AWARDS** Purple Chalk awd, 92. **SELECTED PUBLICATIONS** Auth, a study of Arnold and Hopkins, Letters from the Darkling Plain, Univ Miss Press, 72 & Here a Captive Heart Busted: The Sentimental Journey of Modern Literature, Fordham UP, 93. **CONTACT ADDRESS** Dept of English, Univ of Missouri-Columbia, 309 University Hall, Columbia, MO, 65211.

FUMERTON, PATRICIA
DISCIPLINE SIXTEENTH- AND SEVENTEENTH-CENTURY CULTURE AND LITERATURE **EDUCATION** Stanford Univ, PhD, 81. **CAREER** ASSOC PROF, ENG, UNIV CALIF, SANTA BARBARA. **RESEARCH** Renaissance popular cult; Mobility; Space. **SELECTED PUBLICATIONS** Auth, Cultural Aesthetics: Renaissance Literature and Practice of Social Ornament, Univ Chicago Press, 92; "Subdiscourse; Jonson Speaking Low," Eng Lit Renaissance, 95. **CONTACT ADDRESS** Dept of Eng, Univ Calif, Santa Barbara, CA, 93106-7150. **EMAIL** pfumer@humanitas.ucsb.edu

FURIA, PHILIP
DISCIPLINE MODERN AMERICAN POETRY, THE JAZZ AGE **EDUCATION** Oberlin Col, BA, 65; Univ Chicago, MA 66; Iowa Writers Workshop, MFA, 70; Univ Iowa, PhD, 70. **CAREER** Instr, Univ NC, Wilmington. **RESEARCH** Use of songs in Hollywood films. **SELECTED PUBLICATIONS** Auth, Pound's Cantos Declassified, 84; The Poets of Tin Pan Alley: A History of America's Great Lyricists, 90; Ira Gershwin: The Art of the Lyricist, 96. **CONTACT ADDRESS** Univ N. Carolina, Wilmington, Morton Hall, Wilmington, NC, 28403-3297. **EMAIL** furiap@uncwil.edu

FURIA, PHILIP GEORGE
PERSONAL Born 11/15/1943, Pittsburgh, PA, m, 1966, 2 children **DISCIPLINE** AMERICAN LITERATURE **EDUCATION** Oberlin Col, BA, 65; Univ Chicago, MA, 66; Univ IA, MFA & PhD, 70. **CAREER** Asst prof, 70-76, assoc prof English, 76-83, prof of English, 84, Chair, Univ MN, 90-93, assoc Dean, Univ MN, 94-95; PROF AND CHAIR, UNIV NC AT WILMINGTON, 96-; Vis prof Am studies, Univ East Anglia, 76-77; Fulbright prof, Univ Graz, AUT, 82. **MEMBERSHIPS** MLA. **RESEARCH** Am popular song, modern Am poetry; literature and art. **SELECTED PUBLICATIONS** Auth, Is the Whited Monster Lowell's Quaker Graveyard Revisited, TX Studies in Lit & Lang, winter 76; coauth, Stevens' Fusky Alphabet, Publ Mod Lang Asn, 1/78; Paterson's progress, Boundary 2, winter 81; Pound's Cantos Declassified, PA State Press, 84; The Poets of Tin Pan Alley: A History of America's Great Lyricists, Oxford Univ Press, 90; Ira Gershwin: The Art of the Lyricist, Oxford Univ Press, 96; Something to Sing About: A Centenary Celebration of America's Great Lyricists, in Am Scholar, summer 97; Irving Berlin: A Life in Song, Schirmer/Simon & Schuster, 98. **CONTACT ADDRESS** Univ N. Carolina at Wilmington, 601 South College Rd, Wilmington, NC, 28403. **EMAIL** furiap@uncwil.edu

FURNESS, EDNA LUE
PERSONAL Born 01/26/1906, Knox Co, NE **DISCIPLINE** ENGLISH & SPANISH **EDUCATION** Univ CO, AB & BE, 28, MA, 39, EdD, 51. **CAREER** Teacher, High Schs, CO, 28-33 & WY, 33-39; instr Span, Pueblo Col, 42-45; instr English & mod lang, Casper Col, WY, 45-47; from asst prof to prof English & foreign lang educ, Univ WY, 47-61; prof English & Span, 61-72, EMER PROF LANG & LIT, WY STATE UNIV, 72-; Instr, Univ CO, 50-51; fac res grant, Univ WY, 57; Coe fel Am studies, Coe Found, 59; Delta Kappa Gamma res grant, 60-61; US Off Educ res grant, 66-67, humanities res grant, 71-72. **HONORS AND AWARDS** Haiku Award, Washington Poets Asn, 80. **MEMBERSHIPS** NEA; Int Platform Asn; Nat Coun Teachers English. **RESEARCH** Comparative literature; translation; children's literature. **SELECTED PUBLICATIONS** Coauth, New Dimensions in the Teaching of English, Pruett, 67; auth, Trends in Literature on Teaching the Language Arts, contribr, Teaching of Listening, Scarecrow, 71, Linguistics in the Elementary School Classroom, Macmillan, 71 & Language Arts in the Elementary School, Lippincott, 72; auth, Mediterranean magic, 74 & Spelling is Serious Stuff, 78, Delta Kappa Gamma Bull; contribr, Educational Assessment of Learning Problems, 78; Assessment and Correction of Language Arts Difficulties, 80; Spelling for the Millions, 66; Guide to Better English Spelling, 91. **CONTACT ADDRESS** 725 S Alton Way Windsor Gardens-6B, Denver, CO, 80231.

FURTWANGLER, ALBERT
PERSONAL Born 07/17/1942, Seattle, WA, m, 1968, 2 children **DISCIPLINE** ENGLISH LITERATURE **EDUCATION** Amherst Col, BA, 64; Cornell Univ, MA, 67, PhD (English), 68. **CAREER** Asst prof English and humanities, Univ Chicago, 68-71; asst prof English, 71-76, ASSOC PROF ENGLISH, MT ALLISON UNIV, 76-, Vis fel, Yale Univ, 77-78; vis prof, Linfield Col, 80-81. **RESEARCH** Rhetoric of American constitutional debates; 18th century periodicals. **SELECTED PUBLICATIONS** Auth, Undaunted Courage--Lewis, Meriwether, Jefferson, Thomas, and the Opening of the American West, J Am Hist, Vol 83, 96. **CONTACT ADDRESS** PO Box 1450, Sackville, NB, E0A 3C0.

FUSCO, RICHARD
DISCIPLINE NINETEENTH-CENTURY AMERICAN LITERATURE **EDUCATION** Univ PA, BA, 73, MA, 74;Univ MS, MA, 82; Duke Univ, Phd, 90. **CAREER** Engl, St. Joseph's Univ. **HONORS AND AWARDS** Fac adv, The Crimson and Gray. **MEMBERSHIPS** MLA, NEMLA, AAUP. **SELECTED PUBLICATIONS** Auth, Maupassant and the American Short Story: The Influence of Form at the Turn of the Century, Univ Park: Pa State Univ Press, 94; Fin de millenaire: Poe's Legacy for the Detective Story, Poe Soc, 93; Entrapment, Flight and Death: A Recurring Motif in Dickens with Plot and Interpretive Consequences for Edwin Drood, 91; On Primitivism in The Call of the Wild, Am Lit realism, 87. **CONTACT ADDRESS** St Joseph's Univ, 5600 City Ave, Philadelphia, PA, 19131. **EMAIL** fusco@sju.edu

FUSSELL, EDWIN
PERSONAL Born 07/04/1922, Pasadena, CA, m, 1971 **DISCIPLINE** ENGLISH AND AM LIT **EDUCATION** Pomona Col, AB, 43; Harvard Univ, AM, 47, PhD, 49. **CAREER** Instr English, Univ Calif, Berkeley, 49-51; asst prof, Pomona Col, 51-55; asst prof, Claremont Grad Sch, 55-56, from assoc prof to prof English and Am lit, 56-67; PROF AM LIT, UNIV CALIF, SAN DIEGO, 67-, Fulbright univ lectr, Univ Florence and Pisa, 67-68. **MEMBERSHIPS** MLA. **SELECTED PUBLICATIONS** Auth, The Beaten Track, European Tourism, Literature, and the Ways to Culture, 1800-1918, 19th Century Lit, Vol 49, 95. **CONTACT ADDRESS** Dept of Lit, Univ of Calif, San Diego La Jolla, CA, 92093.

G

GABBIN, JOANNE VEAL
PERSONAL Born 02/02/1946, Baltimore, Maryland, m, 1967 **DISCIPLINE** ENGLISH **EDUCATION** Morgan State Univ, Baltimore MD, BA, 1967; Univ of Chicago, Chicago IL, MA, 1970, PhD, 1980. **CAREER** Catalyst for Youth Inc, Chicago IL, prog dir, instructor, 1973-75; Lincoln Univ, University PA, asst prof of English, 1977-82, assoc prof of English, 1982-85; James Madison Univ, Harrisonburg VA, assoc prof of English, 1985-86, dir, Honors Program, 1986-, professor of English 1988-. **HONORS AND AWARDS** Outstanding Achievement Award, Black Conf on Higher Educ, 1982; Distinguished Teaching Award, The Christian R & Mary F Lindback Found, 1983; Creative Scholarship Award, Coll Language Assn, 1986; Women of Color Award, James Madison Uni, 1988; Honorary Mem, Golden Key Natl Honor Soc, 1988; Chairperson, Toni Morrison & The Supernatural, panel at the Middle Atlantic Writers Assn, 1988; Speaker, Creating a Masterpiece, Freshman Convocation James Madison Univ, 1988; Outstanding Faculty Award, VA State Council of Higher Educ, 1993; George Kent Award, Gwendolyn Brooks Ctr, Chicago State Univ, 1994. **MEMBERSHIPS** Langston Hughes Soc, Zora Neale Hurston Soc; Middle Atlantic Writer Assn Inc, the MAWA Journal; mem, Coll Language Assn; chair, Student Emergency Fund, First Baptist Church, 1989-; Board of the Virginia Foundation for the Humanities and Public Policy, chair. **SELECTED PUBLICATIONS** Sonia Sanchez: A Soft Reflection of Strength, Zora Neale Hurston Forum, 1987; A Laying on of Hands: Black Women Writers Exploring the Roots of their Folk & Cultural Tradition; Walk Together Children: Color and the Cultural Legacy of Sterling A Brown, 1988; Sterling A Brown: Building the Black Aesthetic Tradition, 1985 "A Laying on of Hands" Wild Women in the Whirlwind, Rutgers Univ Press, 1990, reprinted by Univ Press in VA, 1994. **CONTACT ADDRESS** Professor of English, Dir of the Honors Program, James Madison Univ, Hillcrest, Harrisonburg, VA, 22807.

GAFFNEY, FLOYD
PERSONAL Born 06/11/1930, Cleveland, OH, m **DISCIPLINE** DRAMA **EDUCATION** Adelphi Univ, BA 1959, MA 1962; Carnegie Inst of Tech, PhD 1966. **CAREER** Gilpin Players Karamu House, actor 1945-49; Pearl Primus African Dance Co, dancer 1950-51; Jerome School of Dancing, teaching asst 1960-62; Adelphi Univ, graduate teaching assistant of dance 1961; Waltann School of Creative Arts, teacher of dance & drama 1961; Clark Coll, asst prof, Speech 1961-63; William Balls Amer Conservatory Theatre, guest artist 1965; Univ of Pittsburgh, guest dance instructor 1966; OH Univ, asst prof in theatre 1966-69; FL A&M Univ, dir of fine arts project upward bound summer 1968; Univ of CA Santa Barbara, assc prof drama 1969-71, co-chmn of Black Studies dept. UC Santa Barbara. **HONORS AND AWARDS** Andrew Mellon Fellowship Drama 1964-65; OH Univ Bd Trustees Grant 1968; Fac Senate Grant Univ of CA Santa Barbara 1970; Ford Fnd Grant 1970; Faculty Sen Grant Univ of CA 1971-73; US Info Srv Cultural Exch Prof to Brazil 1972; Natl Humanities Fac 1974-75; grant Univ of CA Creative Arts Inst Grant 1974; Outstanding Educ of Amer Award; special proj grant Natl Endowment for the Arts 1977; Fulbright Scholar to Brazil 1979; Instr Improvement Grant 1979-81, 1984; participant Intl Congress of Black Communication Univ of Nairobi Kenya 1981; moderator Realism To Ritual, Form & Style in Black Theatre ATA Black Theatre Prog Panel 1982; Black Achievement Award forDrama Action Interprises Inc, 1984; Chancellor's Assocs, Merit Award; Outstanding Community Serv, Univ of California, San Diego, 1983; Natl Endowment for the Arts; US-Japan Alliance Best Director of Drama, 1986; NAACP Creative Arts Awards, 1986; UCSD Faculty Senate Research, Japan, Summer, 1987, 1988; Oxford Univ, Oxford, English, Summer; Institute for Shipboard Educ, Semester at Sea, Professor, Spring, 1992; mem, the National Faculty, 1990-93, reappointed 1994; Honorary mem, Golden Key National Honor Society, 1990; UCSD Faculty Sen-

ate Research Grants; England Summer 1990, 1993, 1994, Netherlands/Belgium, 1996, Paris, 1995, 1998; UCSD Humanities Center Grant, Teatro Mascara Magica, 1998-. **MEMBERSHIPS** UCSD Black Fac & Staff Assn 1979-94; Intercampus Cultural Exch Comm 1979-81; Third Clge Fac Comm UCSD 1980-94; Performing Arts Sub-Comm 1972-74; Fac Mentor Prog UCSD 1982; Pres Chair Search Comm UCSD 1982; San Diego Div of Acad Senate UCSD; bd dir Free Southern Theatre 1963-65; Amer Soc for Theatre Research 1966-69; Natl Humanities Fac 1974-75, 1994-; bd dir Combined Arts & Educ Council of San Diego Cty 1982-84; Amer Theatre Assn Black Theatre Prog 1966; artistic dir Southern CA Black Repertory Theatre Inc San Diego 1980-83; Confederation for the Arts 1983-; Steering Comm State & Local Partnership of San Diego Cty 1982-; bd dir, Educ Cultural Complex Theatre, 1981-83; bd mem, Horton Plaza Theatre Fnd, 198384, 1995-; panel mem, Natl Research Council for Minority Fellowship, 1984-87; Phi Lambda Rho Frat, 1958; Theatre Assn, 1966-85; Amer Assn of Univ Prof; mem Education Committee, Escondido Center of the Performing Arts 1995; Commissioner, Horton Plaza Theatre Foundation 1996-. **SELECTED PUBLICATIONS** Contributing Editor: Theatre Forum Journal, 1992-; Editorial Advisory Board-Lenox Avenue: A Journal of Interartistic Inquire, 1994-96; Associate Artistic Director, Teatro Mascara Magica; A Common Ground Theatre, 1994. **CONTACT ADDRESS** Univ of California, San Diego, PO Box 0344, La Jolla, CA, 92093.

GAINER, KIM
DISCIPLINE MEDIEVAL AND RENAISSANCE LITERATURE **EDUCATION** RI Col, BA; OH State Univ, MA, PhD. **CAREER** Prof, instr, Freshman Connections prog, Radford Univ. **RESEARCH** Censorship; adoption; archaeol. **SELECTED PUBLICATIONS** Auth, The Recalcitrance of Myth: The Conquest of the Americas in High School History Textbooks. **CONTACT ADDRESS** Radford Univ, Radford, VA, 24142. **EMAIL** kgainer@runet.edu

GAINES, BARRY
DISCIPLINE SHAKESPEARE AND TEXTUAL CRITICISM **EDUCATION** Univ Wis, PhD; 70. **CAREER** Instr, 79-, dir, bachelor of univ stud prog, Univ NMex. **SELECTED PUBLICATIONS** Coed, Revels Edition of A Yorkshire Tragedy. **CONTACT ADDRESS** Univ NMex, Albuquerque, NM, 87131.

GAINES, ELLIOT I.
PERSONAL Born 00/00/1950, d, 4 children **DISCIPLINE** MASS COMMUNICATION **EDUCATION** Ohio Univ, PhD 95, MA 94. **CAREER** Ashland Univ, prof, 3 years. **MEMBERSHIPS** NCA; SSA; PCA. **RESEARCH** Communication; culture and media. **SELECTED PUBLICATIONS** Auth, Communication for Osteopathic Manipulative Treatment: The Language of Lived Experience in OMT Pedagogy, Jour of Amer Osteopathic Assoc, 98. **CONTACT ADDRESS** Dept of Communications; Arts, Ashland Univ, Ashland, OH, 44805. **EMAIL** egaines@ashland.edu

GAINES, JANE M.
DISCIPLINE ENGLISH LITERATURE **EDUCATION** Northwestern Univ, PhD, 82. **CAREER** Prof, Duke Univ. **SELECTED PUBLICATIONS** Auth, Contested Culture: The Image, the Voice, and the Law, Univ NC, 91; ed, Classical Hollywood Narratives: The Paradigm Wars, Duke, 92; co-ed, Fabrications: Costume and the Female Body, Routledge, 90; pubs on feminist film theory. **CONTACT ADDRESS** Eng Dept, Duke Univ, Durham, NC, 27706.

GAINES, ROBERT N.
DISCIPLINE PHILOSOPHY OF COMMUNICATIONS **EDUCATION** Univ IA, PhD, 82. **CAREER** Assoc prof; grad dir, Univ MD. **RESEARCH** Rhetorical theory in ancient times. **SELECTED PUBLICATIONS** Auth, Cicero's Response to the Philosophers in De oratore, Book 1, Rhetoric and Pedagogy: Its History, Philosophy, and Practice. Essays in Honor of James J. Murphy, Lawrence Erlbaum Assoc, Inc, 95; Knowledge and Discourse in Gorgias' On the Non-Existent or On Nature, Philos & Rhet 30, 97. **CONTACT ADDRESS** Dept of Commun, Univ MD, 4229 Art-Sociology Building, College Park, MD, 20742-1335. **EMAIL** rg1@umail.umd.edu

GAINES, ROBERT N.
PERSONAL Born 01/15/1950, Sulphur, OK, m, 1993 **DISCIPLINE** COMMUNICATION **EDUCATION** Univ Iowa, PhD, 82. **CAREER** Acting asst prof, Univ Va, Charlottesville, 79-81; acting asst prof, Univ Wash, Seattle, 81-82; asst prof, 82-86; assoc prof, Univ Md, 86-. **MEMBERSHIPS** Am Soc for the Hist of Rhet; Am Soc of Papyrologists; Am Philol Assoc; Int Soc for the Hist of Rhet; Nat Commun Assoc; Rhet Soc of Am. **RESEARCH** History of rhetoric; textual criticism. **SELECTED PUBLICATIONS** Auth, Cicero's Response to the Philosophers in De oratore, Book 1, Rhetoric and Pedagogy: Its History, Philosophy, and Practice. Essays in Honor of James J. Murphy, Erlbaum, 43-56, 95; auth, Greek and Roman Rhetoric, The Encyclopedia of Classical Philosophy, Greenwood, 472-76, 97; auth, Knowledge and Discourse in Gorgia's On the Non-Existent or On Nature, Philos & Rhet, vol 30, 1-12, 97; auth, Aristotle's Rhetoric and the Contemporary Arts of Practical Discourse, Re-Reading Aristoltle's Rhetoric, Southern Ill Univ Press, (in press). **CONTACT ADDRESS** Dept of Speech Comm, Univ of Md, 2130 Skinner Bldg, College Pk, MD, 20742-7635. **EMAIL** rgl@umail.umd.edu

GAJOWSKI, EVELYN J.
DISCIPLINE SHAKESPEARE, RENAISSANCE **EDUCATION** Cleveland State Univ, BA, 71; Case Western Reserve Univ, MA, 74, PhD, 87. **CAREER** Asst prof, Wittenberg Univ, 79-81; Bd of Lit Lectr, Univ Calif, Santa Cruz, 88-91; asst prof, 91-94, asooc prof, Univ Nev, Las Vegas, 94-. **HONORS AND AWARDS** Grad Alumni Fund Award, 87, Dean's Commendation for Acad Excellence, Case Western Reserve Univ, 87; Best Feminist Essay Award, Rocky Mt MLA, 89; res grant, Univ Nev, Las Vegas, 92, 93, 94. **MEMBERSHIPS** Pres, Rocky Mt MLA. **RESEARCH** Women in Shakespeare. **SELECTED PUBLICATIONS** Auth, The Female Perspective in Othello, in Othello: New Perspectives, in eds, Virginia Mason Vaughan and Kent Cartwright, Fairleigh Dickinson Univ Press and Assoc UP, 91; The Art of Loving: Female Subjectivity and Male Discursive Traditions in Shakespeare's Tragedies, Univ Del Press and Assoc UP, 92. **CONTACT ADDRESS** Dept of Eng, Univ Nev, Las Vegas, 4505 Maryland Pky, PO Box 455011, Las Vegas, NV, 89154-5011. **EMAIL** shakespe@nevada.edu

GALCHINSKY, MICHAEL
DISCIPLINE ENGLISH **EDUCATION** Univ Calif at Berkeley, PhD. **CAREER** Dept Eng, Millsaps Col **RESEARCH** 19th-century Brit lit; novel; multiculturalism; Jewish cult stud & creative writing. **SELECTED PUBLICATIONS** Auth, The Origin of the Modern Jewish Woman Writer: Romance and Reform in Victorian England, Wayne State UP, 96. **CONTACT ADDRESS** Dept of English, Millsaps Col, 1701 N State St, Jackson, MS, 39210.

GALEF, DAVID
PERSONAL Born 03/27/1959, New York, NY, m, 1992, 1 child **DISCIPLINE** LITERATURE **EDUCATION** Columbia Univ, MA, PhD 83-89; Princeton Univ, BA 77-81 **CAREER** Univ MS, assoc prof 95, asst dir and asst prof 89-95; Master Sch Dobbs Ferry, hd creat writ 90; Columbia Univ, preceptor 88-89,tch 86-88; Japan Bus Seminars, tchr 85-86; Stanley H Kaplan Ed Cen, instr 83-85; Overseas Training Cen, Osaka JP, tchr 81-82. **HONORS AND AWARDS** MS Arts Coun Grnt; Guest Writ, The Writers Pl and Montclair ST Univ; Vis Sch Columbia Univ; Whatley Awd; Writers Exch Awd; 2 Columbia Pres Schl; Eng Dept Sch; HFG; Phi Beta Kappa. **MEMBERSHIPS** ED BD Twentieth Cen Lit; MLA; SO Cen MLA; NCTE; Assoc Writ Progs. **SELECTED PUBLICATIONS** Turning Japanese, The Perm Press, 98; Tracks, NY, William Morrow, 96; The Supporting Cast: A Study of Flat and Minor Characters, Univ Pk PA, PA St Press, 93; Observations on Rereading, Second Thoughts, ed, Detroit, Wayne ST Univ Press, 98; The Little Red Bicycle, NY Random House, 88; Abigaboo, The MacGuffin, 98; The Baby That Roared, Green's Mag, 96; Dishing it Out: Patterns of Women's Sadism in Literature, Psychoanalyses, Feminisms, ed Peter Rudnysky, forthcoming from SUNY Press 98; REVIEWS, All Saints, By Karen Palmer, NY Times Book Rev, 98; Audrey Hepburn's Neck, by Alan Brown, NY Times Book Rev, 96; If There is a Secret, Is There Love?, Bad Chemistry, by Gary Krist, Princ Alum Wkly, 98; numerous pub. **CONTACT ADDRESS** 1529 Jackson Av East, Oxford, MS, 38655. **EMAIL** dgalef@olemiss.edu

GALLANT, CHRISTINE
DISCIPLINE ENGLISH **EDUCATION** Univ Minn, BA, 62, MA, 66, PhD, 77. **CAREER** Asst prof, Va Commonwealth Univ, 77-84; PROF ENGLISH, GA STATE UNIV, 84-. **CONTACT ADDRESS** Dept of English, Georgia State Univ, Atlanta, GA, 30303. **EMAIL** engccg@panther.gsu.edu

GALLI, BARBARA E.
PERSONAL Born 12/01/1949, Montreal, PQ, Canada, d **DISCIPLINE** GERMANIC LANGUAGES; LITERATURE **EDUCATION** Carleton Univ Ottawa, BA 73; Univ Toronto, MA 76; McGill Univ, PhD 90. **CAREER** Univ Alabama, Aaron Aronov Ch 97-. **MEMBERSHIPS** AAR; AJS; ALA; MLA **RESEARCH** The thought of Franz Rosenzweig. **SELECTED PUBLICATIONS** Auth, Franz Rosenzweig and Jehuda Halevi: Translating Translation Translators, McGill-Queen's Univ Press, 95; God Man and the World: Lectures and Essays, trans and ed, Syracuse Univ Press, 98; Franz Rosenzweig and the New Thinking, trans and ed, Afterward by Alan Udoff, SUP, 98; Orientation in the Modern World: Franz Rosenzweig's Writings in a Cultural Vein, trans and ed, SUP, forthcoming, March 99. **CONTACT ADDRESS** Dept of Religious Studies, Univ of Alabama, 212 Manly Hall, Tuscaloosa, AL, 35487-0264. **EMAIL** bgalli@woodsquad.as.ua.edu

GALLO, LOUIS
PERSONAL New Orleans, LA **DISCIPLINE** CREATIVE WRITING AND MODERN AND CONTEMPORARY LITERATURE **EDUCATION** La State Univ, MA; Univ Mo, PhD. **CAREER** Prof, Radford Univ. **SELECTED PUBLICATIONS** His stories, poems, and essays have appeared in j(s) such as Glimmer Train, Greensboro Rev, Mo Rev, and New Orleans Rev. **CONTACT ADDRESS** Radford Univ, Radford, VA, 24142. **EMAIL** lgallo@runet.edu

GALPERIN, WILLIAM
DISCIPLINE ENGLISH LANGUAGE AND LITERATURE **EDUCATION** Univ Chicago, BA; Brown Univ, MA, PhD. **CAREER** Prof. **RESEARCH** Late 18th-century and early 19th-century British poetry and fiction; literary and cultural theory; film studies. **SELECTED PUBLICATIONS** Auth, Revision and Authority in Wordsworth; auth, The Return of the Visible in British Romanticism. **CONTACT ADDRESS** Dept of English, Rutgers Univ, 510 George St, Murray Hall, New Brunswick, NJ, 08901-1167. **EMAIL** whg1@ix.netcom.com

GANDAL, KEITH
DISCIPLINE AMERICAN LITERATURE AND CULTURE, FRESHMAN COMPOSITION, AND CREATIVE WRITING **EDUCATION** Univ Calif, Berkeley, MA, PhD. **CAREER** Dept Eng, Mt. Saint Mary's Col **RESEARCH** Lives and writings of modern literary rebels, Crane, Foucault; Bohemian writer Henry Miller; African-American folklorist Zora Neale Hurston. **SELECTED PUBLICATIONS** Publ on, Stephen Crane & Michel Foucault. **CONTACT ADDRESS** Dept of English, Mount Saint Mary's Col, 16300 Old Emmitsburg Rd, Emmitsburg, MD, 21727-7799. **EMAIL** gandal@msmary.edu

GANIM, JOHN MICHAEL
PERSONAL Born 02/18/1945, Weehawken, NJ **DISCIPLINE** ENGLISH, LINGUISTICS **EDUCATION** Rutgers Univ, BA, 67; IN Univ, MA, 69, PhD, 74. **CAREER** From asst prof to assoc prof, 74-88, prof eng, Univ CA, Riverside, 88, ch Eng Dept, 96. **HONORS AND AWARDS** Jr Fac Award, Ctr Medieval and Renaissance Studies, 77. **MEMBERSHIPS** MLA; Medieval Acad Am; Medieval Asn Pacific. **RESEARCH** Middle Eng lit; Chaucer; Old Eng lit. **SELECTED PUBLICATIONS** Auth, Disorientation, style and consciousness in Sir Gawain and the Green Knight, PMLA, 76; Tone and Time in Chaucer's Troilus, ELH, 76; Style and Consciousness in Middle English Narrative, Princeton Univ Press; Bakhtin, Chaucer, Carnival, Lent, Studies in the Age of Chaucer, 87; Chaucer, Boccaccio and the Problme of Popularity, In: Assays, Pittsburgh Univ Press, 87; Carnival Voices in the clerk's Envoy, Chaucer Rev, 87; Chaucer and the Noise of the People; Exemplaria, spring 90; Chaucerian Theatricality, Princeton Univ Press, 90; Forms of Talk in the Canterbury Tales, Poetica, 91; The Literary Uses of New History, In: The Idea of Medieval Literature: New Essays on Chaucer and Medieval Culture in Honor of Donald R Howard (James M Dean and Christian K Zacher, ed); Univ Del Press, 92; Chaucerian Ritual and Patriarchal Romance, Chaucer Yearbook, 92; Literary Anthropology at the Turn of the Centuries: E K Chambers' The Mediaeval Stage, Envoi, 93; The Devil's Writing Lesson, In: Oral Poetics in Middle English Poetry (Mark Amodio, ed), Garland, 94; Medieval Literature as Monster: The Grotesque Before and After Bakhtin, Exemplaria, 95; Recent Studies on Literature, Architecture, and Urbanism, MLQ, 9/95; The Myth of Medieval Romance, In: Medievalism and the Modernist Temper (R Howard Bloch and Stephen G Nichols, ed), Johns Hopkins Univ Press, 96; Double-Entry in the Shipman's Tale: Chaucer and Bookkeeping Before Pacioli, Chaucer Rev, 96. **CONTACT ADDRESS** Dept of Eng, Univ of California, 900 University Ave, Riverside, CA, 92521-0001. **EMAIL** john.ganim@ucr.edu

GANTAR, JURE
DISCIPLINE DRAMA **EDUCATION** Univ Ljubljana, BA, MA, Univ Toronto, PhD. **CAREER** Prof. **SELECTED PUBLICATIONS** Auth, Pred odprtimi vrati, (In Front of the Open Door), Pot v Rim, Aneks (The Passage to Rome. The Annexe), Zveza kulturnih organizacij Slovenije, 90; Atomska dramaturgija Vilija Ravnjaka, (Atomic Dramaturgy of Vili Ravnjak), Umetnost igre, Stirje eseji, (The Art of Playing. Four Essays), Ljubljana: Zveza kulturnih organizacij Slovenije, 91; Dramaturgija in smeh, (Dramaturgy and Laughter), Knjiznica Mestnega gledalisca ljubljanskega, 93; Creativity and Wit, Creativity and Discovery, Conf Proc, Cornerbrook: Memorial Univ Newfoundland, 94; Theatrical Laughter and the Concept of Cryptic Noise, Recherches semiotiques/Semiotic Inquiry, 94; Catching the Wind in a Net, The Shortcomings of Existing Methods for the Analysis of Performance, Mod Drama, 96; Postmodern Comedy: Tautology or Pleonasm?, Stud in the Hum, 97; Feydeau in razvoj motiva dvojckov, (Feydeau and the Development of the Motif of Twins), Gledaliski list Drame SNG Ljubljana, 97; rev(s), Review of Playtexts: Ludics in Contemporary Literature, by Warren Motte, Dalhousie Rev, 95; Review of Comedy: The Mastery of Discourse, by Susan Purdie, Dalhousie Rev, 94. **CONTACT ADDRESS** Dept of Theatre, Dalhousie Univ, Halifax, NS, B3H 3J5. **EMAIL** jgantar@is.dal.ca

GANZEL, DEWEY ALVIN
PERSONAL Born 07/05/1927, Albion, NE, m, 1955, 3 children **DISCIPLINE** ENGLISH LANGUAGE & LITERATURE **EDUCATION** Univ Nebr, Bsc, 49, MA, 53; Univ Chicago, PhD, 58. **CAREER** RETIRED PROF, ENG, OBERLIN COLL, 97. **RESEARCH** American fiction, Literary history. **SELECTED PUBLICATIONS** Mark Twain Abroad: The Cruise of the Quaker City, Univ Chicago Press, 68; Fortune and Men's Eyes: The Career of John Payne Collier, Oxford Univ Press, 82. **CONTACT ADDRESS** Dept Eng, Oberlin Col, Oberlin, OH, 44074. **EMAIL** dewey.ganzel@oberlin.edy

GARAY, MARY SUE
DISCIPLINE BUSINESS AND TECHNICAL COMMUNICATION, LITERACY **EDUCATION** Carnegie-Mellon Univ, PhD, 88. **CAREER** Asst prof, La State Univ; ch-Indust Outreach, Nat Coun of Tchr of Eng, 90-96; mem, Gov's Workforce Develop Comt, La, 93-95. **HONORS AND AWARDS** Excellence in Res Award, Cont Educ, LSU-BR, 94; summer fac grant, LSU-BR, 96; La's Workforce Develop Inst, 96. **RESEARCH** Workplace literacy; data interpretation. **SELECTED PUBLICATIONS** Auth, Workplace Literacy in the 90's: Definitions, Descriptions, Opportunities, and Cautions, in Stud in Tech Commun, 92; Meeting Workplace Needs in an Introductory Business Writing Course, Assoc of Bus Commun Quart, 95. **CONTACT ADDRESS** Dept of Eng, Louisiana State Univ, 212A Allen Hall, Baton Rouge, LA, 70803. **EMAIL** engara@unix1.sncc.lsu.edu

GARAY, RONALD
DISCIPLINE ELECTRONIC MEDIA HISTORY AND PUBLIC POLICY **EDUCATION** Ohio Univ, PhD, 80. **CAREER** Assoc dean, undergrad stud and admin, La State Univ. **RESEARCH** Electronic media history, law, and regulation. **SELECTED PUBLICATIONS** Auth, Congressional Television: A Legislative History, Greenwood Press, 84; Cable Television: A Reference Guide to Information, Greenwood Press, 88; Broadcasting of Congressional Proceedings, in Donald C. Bacon, et al, eds, The Encyclopedia of the United States Congress, Vol I, Simon & Schuster, 95; Guarding the Airwaves: Government Regulation of World War II Radio, in J of Radio Stud, 3, 95-96; Books, in William David Sloan, et al, eds, Mass Communication in the Information Age, Vision Press, 96; coauth, The Maverick of Radio, Greenwood Press, 92. **CONTACT ADDRESS** The Manship Sch of Mass Commun, Louisiana State Univ, Baton Rouge, LA, 70803. **EMAIL** rgaray@lsuvm.sncc.lsu.edu

GARCIA-GOMEZ, JORGE
PERSONAL Born 01/14/1937, Havana, Cuba, m, 1961, 3 children **DISCIPLINE** PHILOSOPHY, LITERATURE **EDUCATION** Univ Santo Tomas Villanueva, BA, 58; New Sch Social Res, MA, 65, PhD(Philos), 71. **CAREER** Asst prof Philos, Sacred Heart Univ, 66-69; assoc prof, 69-80, prof Philos, Southampton Col, Long Island Univ, 81-. **MEMBERSHIPS** Am Philos Asn; Am Cath Philos Asn; Am Asn Teachers Span & Port; AAUP. **RESEARCH** Metaphysics; phenomenology; aesthetics. **SELECTED PUBLICATIONS** Auth, A meditation of liberty, Abraxas, New York, fall 70; Ciudades, Ed Plenitud, Madrid, 74; ed & transl Aron Gurwitsch, El Campo de la Conciencia, Madrid, 78; Jose Ortega oy Gasset, Encyclopedia et Phenomenolozy, 97; A Bridge to Temporality, St Augustine's Confessions, Analecta Husser-liana, LII, 98 **CONTACT ADDRESS** Humanities Div Southampton Col, Long Island Univ, 239 Montauk Hwy, Southampton, NY, 11968-4198.

GARDAPHE, FRED L.
PERSONAL Born 09/07/1952, Chicago, IL, m, 1982 **DISCIPLINE** ENGLISH; CULTURAL STUDIES **EDUCATION** Univ of Wis at Madison, 76; Univ of Chicago, AM, 82; Univ of Ill Chicago, PhD, 93. **CAREER** Prof of English and Ed Studies, Columbia Col, 80-98; Prof of Italian/American Studies, SUNY Srony Brook, 98-. **HONORS AND AWARDS** Fac Development Grant, Columbia Col, 86; Dept of English Award, Univ of Chicago, 82; William F. Vilas Scholar, Univ of Wis, 75; Res fel, Immigration Hist Res Center, Minn, 86; Vis prof, Univ Sassari, Italy, 98; Road Scholar, Ill Humanities Counc, 96-98. **MEMBERSHIPS** Nat Book Critics Cr; MLA; Soc of Midland Authors; Midwast MLA; Soc for the Study of Multi-Ethnic Lit of the United States; Am Asn of Italian Studies; Nat Writers Union; Am Italian Hist Asn; Ill Ethnic Coalition. **RESEARCH** Italian/American culture; ethnic American cultures; immigration. **SELECTED PUBLICATIONS** Coauth, (Ex)tending or Escaping a Tradition: Don DeLillo and Italian/American Literature, Beyond the Margin, Farleigh Dickinson Univ Press, 98; (In)visibility: Cultural Representation in the Criticism of Frank Lentricchia, Differentia, 94; auth, Fascism and Italian/American Writers, Romance Languages Annual, Purdue Univ Press, 93; In Search of Italian/American Writers, Italian Am, 97; Here are the Italian/American Writers, Canadian J of Italian Studies, 96; Breaking and Entering: An Italian American's Literary Odyssey, Forkroads, 95, Beyond The Godfather, 97. **CONTACT ADDRESS** Dept of English/European Studies, State Univ of NY Stony Brook, Stony Brook, NY, 11794-3359. **EMAIL** fgar@aol.com

GARDINER, JUDITH KEGAN
PERSONAL Born 12/17/1941, Chicago, IL, m, 1963, 2 children **DISCIPLINE** ENGLISH LITERATURE, WOMEN'S STUDIES **EDUCATION** Radcliffe Col, AB, 62; Columbia Univ, MA, 64, PhD(English), 68. **CAREER** Asst prof English, Fisk Univ, 68-69; asst prof, 69-76, ASSOC PROF ENGLISH, UNIV ILL, CHICAGO, 76-, Vis res scholar Renaissance lit, Radcliffe Inst, 72-73; res assoc Renaissance lit, Newberry Libr, 78. **MEMBERSHIPS** Nat Asn Psychoanalytic Criticism; MLA; Nat Women's Studies Asn. **RESEARCH** 17th century English literature; psychology and literature; contemporary women's writing, especially mothers and daughters. **SELECTED PUBLICATIONS** Auth, Aging and Its Discontents--Freud and Other Fictions, Mod Fiction Stud, Vol 0038, 92; Caught-But-Not-Caught--Psychology and Politics in Stead, Christina the 'Puzzleheaded Girl,' Wlwe-World Lit Written in Eng, Vol 0032, 92; Dreams of Authority--Freud and the Fictions of the Unconscious, Mod Fiction Stud, Vol 0038, 92; Writing Womens Literary-History, Mod Philol, Vol 0093, 95. **CONTACT ADDRESS** Dept of English, Univ Ill Chicago Circle, Chicago, IL, 60680.

GARDNER, JOSEPH HOGUE
PERSONAL Born 09/15/1938, McDonough, GA, m, 1961, 2 children **DISCIPLINE** ENGLISH AND AMERICAN LITERATURE **EDUCATION** Harvard Univ, AB, 60; Univ Calif, Berkeley, MA, 63, PhD(English), 69. **CAREER** Actg instr English, Univ Calif, Berkeley, 65-66; from instr to asst prof, 66-71, ASSOC PROF ENGLISH, UNIV KY, 71-. **MEMBERSHIPS** MLA; AAUP; Dickens Fel; Dickens Soc; 1890's Soc Res; Victorian literature. **RESEARCH** Pre-Raphaelitism; aestheticism; decadence. **SELECTED PUBLICATIONS** Auth, American Notebook--Notes, G.R.G., 1877, Anq-A Quart J Short Articles Notes and Rev, Vol 0007, 94; From Student Club to National Society--the Founding of the London-Mathematical-Society in 1865, Hist Mathematica, Vol 0022, 95; Michelangelo Sweetness, Coleridge Flycatchers, Ligeia Eyes, and the Failure of Art in the 'House of Life,' J Pre-Raphaelite Stud-New Ser, Vol 0004, 95; A Selective Checklist of the Published Work of Beardsley, Aubrey, Anq-A Quart J Short Articles Notes and Rev, Vol 0009, 96. **CONTACT ADDRESS** Dept of English, Univ of Ky, 500 S Limestone St, Lexington, KY, 40506-0003.

GARNETT, MARY ANNE
DISCIPLINE 19TH CENTURY FRENCH LITERATURE **EDUCATION** Wisc State Univ, BA, 70; Univ Wisc, MA, 71, PhD, 80. **CAREER** English and Lit, Univ Ark **SELECTED PUBLICATIONS** Ed, Women in French Newsletter. **CONTACT ADDRESS** Univ Ark Little Rock, 2801 S University Ave., Little Rock, AR, 72204-1099. **EMAIL** magarnett@ualr.edu

GARRATT, ROBERT FRANCIS
PERSONAL Born 12/27/1941, San Francisco, CA, m, 1970, 1 child **DISCIPLINE** ENGLISH LITERATURE, MODERN IRISH LITERATURE **EDUCATION** San Jose State Univ, BA, 64, MA, 69; Univ Ore, PhD(lit), 72. **CAREER** Asst prof English, Univ Puget Sound, 72-77; vis assoc prof, Pitzer Col, 77-78; ASSOC PROF ENGLISH, UNIV PUGET SOUND, 78-, Nat Endowment for Humanities grant, Johns Hopkins Univ, 75 and Yale Univ, 79; Nat Endowment for Humanities fel, 81-82. **MEMBERSHIPS** Am Soc Eighteenth Century Studies; Brit Studies Conf Northwest (secy, 76-77); Am Comt Irish Studies; Philol Asn Pac Coast. **RESEARCH** Twentieth century Irish Poetry; modern poetry; modern literature (18th--20th century). **SELECTED PUBLICATIONS** Auth, Poetry as Archaeology--Heaney, Seamus Poetic Writings, Zeitschrift fur Anglistik und Amerikanistik, Vol 0042, 94. **CONTACT ADDRESS** Dept of English, Univ Puget Sound, 1500 N Warner St, Tacoma, WA, 98416-0005.

GARRETT, PETER K.
DISCIPLINE ENGLISH **EDUCATION** Haverford Col, BA, 62; MA, 63, PhD, 66, Yale Univ. **CAREER** Asst Prof, 68-75, Princeton Univ; Assoc Prof, 75-81, Prof, 81-, Univ Illinois **CONTACT ADDRESS** Dept of English, Univ of Illinois, 608 S Wright St, Urbana, IL, 61801. **EMAIL** pgarrett@uiuc.edu

GARRETT, PETER KORNHAUSER
PERSONAL Born 11/16/1940, Cleveland, OH, m, 1961, 2 children **DISCIPLINE** ENGLISH LITERATURE **EDUCATION** Haverford Col, BA, 62; Yale Univ, MA, 63, PhD(English), 66. **CAREER** From instr to asst prof English, Princeton Univ, 66-75; assoc prof, 75-81, PROF ENGLISH, UNIV ILL, URBANA, 81-, Fel, Am Coun Learned Soc, 74-75 and 82-83. **MEMBERSHIPS** MLA. **RESEARCH** Victorian and modern fiction; narrative theory. **SELECTED PUBLICATIONS** Auth, The Dialogics of Dissent in the English Novel, 19th-Century Lit, Vol 0050, 95. **CONTACT ADDRESS** Dept of English, Univ of Ill, 608 S Wright St, Urbana, IL, 61801-3613.

GARRISON, JAMES DALE
PERSONAL Born 01/10/1943, Bremerton, WA, m, 1969, 2 children **DISCIPLINE** ENGLISH **EDUCATION** Princeton Univ, AB, 65; Univ Calif, Berkeley, MA, 67, PhD(English), 72. **CAREER** Asst prof, 73-79, from assoc prof English, Univ Tex, Austin, 79-93; chmn English, 94. **MEMBERSHIPS** Am Soc Eighteenth-Century Studies. **RESEARCH** Restoration and eighteenth-century English literature; the Enlightenment. **SELECTED PUBLICATIONS** Auth, Dryden and the Tradition of Panegyric, Univ Calif, 75; Gibbon and the treacherous language of panegyrics, Eighteenth-Century Studies, 77; Lively and Laborious: Characterization in Gibbon's Metahistory, Modern Philol, 78; Dryden and the Birth of Hercules, Studies in Philol, 80; The Universe of Dryden's Fables, Studies in English Lit, 81; Pietas from Vergil to Dryden, Penn State Press, 92. **CONTACT ADDRESS** Dept of English, Univ of Texas, Austin, TX, 78712-1026. **EMAIL** jdgar@mail.utexas.edu

GARVEY, SHEILA HICKEY
PERSONAL Born 12/23/1949, Erie, PA, 2 children **DISCIPLINE** THEATER **EDUCATION** Emerson Col, BA, 71; Northwestern Univ, MA, 73; New York Univ, PhD, 75. **CAREER** Preceptor, English, NY Univ, 78-80; instr, theatre arts, Rutgers Univ, 80-81; asst prof, dramatic arts, Dickinson Col, 81-87; from assoc to full prof, 88- , app coord of theatre majors, 90, app coord of performance for Theatre Dept, 91, Southern Conn State Univ. **HONORS AND AWARDS** Dana Found grant, 87; AAUP/CSU res grants, 89, 90, 91, 95; John F. Kennedy Ctr for the Perf Arts, scholarship, 92; fac dev grants, 89, 90, 91, 92, 95, 97; summer curriculum grants, 91, 96, 98., Bd dir, New England Theatre Conf, 92-95; chemn Col Div of New England Theatre Conf, 92-95; mem Performance Rev Staff of New England Theatre Journal, 93- ; mem, Conn Critics Circle, 97- . **MEMBERSHIPS** New England Theatre Conf; Eugene O'Neill Soc; AAUP. **RESEARCH** Eugene O'Neill in performance; contemporary trends in actor training; women in theater. **SELECTED PUBLICATIONS** Auth, Documentation of Long Wharf Theatre 1993-4 Theatrical Season, New England Theatre J, 94; auth, Anna Christie and The Fallen Woman Genre: A Performance Perspective, Eugene O'Neill Rev, 95; auth, Documentation of Long Wharf Theatre 1994-1995 Theatrical Season, Hartford Stage 1994-1995 Theatrical Season, New England Theatre J, 95; auth, Documentation of Long Wharf Theatre 1995-1996 Theatrical Season, Hartford Stage 1995-1996 Theatrical Season and the Goodspeed Opera House 1995 Theatrical Season, New England Theatre J, 96; auth, Hughie Directed by (and starring) Al Pacino, Eugene O'Neill Rev, 96; auth, Documentation of Long Wharf Theatre 1995-1996 Theatrical Season and the Goodspeed Opera House 1995 Theatrical Season, New England Theatre J, 97; auth, Documentation of Long Wharf Theatre 1996-1997 Theatrical Season, and the Goodspeed Opera House 1996 Theatrical Season, New England Theatre J, 98; auth, A Long Century's Journey into Light: A Eugene O'Neill Performance Event at Long Wharf Theatre, Eugene O'Neill Rev, 98. **CONTACT ADDRESS** Dept of Theatre, Southern Connecticut State Univ, 501 Crescent St, New Haven, CT, 06515. **EMAIL** garvey@scsu.ctstateu.edu

GASTIL, JOHN WEBSTER
PERSONAL Born 02/07/1967, San Diego, CA **DISCIPLINE** COMMUNICATIONS **EDUCATION** Swarthmore Coll, BA, Polit Sci, 89; Univ Wis-Madison, PhD, Commun Arts, 94. **CAREER** Res mgr, Univ NMex, Inst Public Policy, 94-97; ASST PROF, UNIV WASH, SPEECH COMMUN, 98-. **RESEARCH** Public deliberation; participating democracy; public opinion **SELECTED PUBLICATIONS** Democracy in Small Groups: Participation, Decision Making, and Communication, New Soc Publ, 93; "Identifying Obstacles to Small Group Democracy," Small Group Research, 93; "A Meta-Analytic Review of the Productivity and Satisfaction of Democratic and Autocratic Leadership," Small Group Res, 94; " A Definition and Illustration of Democratic Leadership," Human Relations, 94; "Increasing Political Sophistication Through Public Deliberation," Political Communication, 98. **CONTACT ADDRESS** Dept Speech & Commun, Univ Wash, PO Box 353415, Seattle, WA, 98195. **EMAIL** jgastil@u.washington.edu

GATES, BARBARA TIMM
PERSONAL Born 08/04/1936, Sheboygan, WI, m, 1957, 2 children **DISCIPLINE** ENGLISH LITERATURE **EDUCATION** Northwestern Univ, BA, 58; Univ Del, MA, 61; Bryn Mawr Col, PhD(English), 71. **CAREER** Lectr English, Widener Col, 65-67; asst prof, 71-77, ASSOC PROF ENGLISH, UNIV DEL, 77-, Univ Del res grants, 72, 76, 79 and 81; Danforth assoc, 73-; consult Excellence in Teaching and Distinguished Acad Serv, Dept Educ, Commonwealth Pa, 75-76; Am Philos Soc grant, 76; DIMER res grant, 77; Am Coun Learned Soc grant, 79; Nat Endowment for Humanities grant, 81. **HONORS AND AWARDS** Lindback Award for Excellence in Teaching, Univ Del, 74. **MEMBERSHIPS** MLA; AAUP; Dickens Soc; Northeastern Mod Lang Asn; Bronte Soc. **RESEARCH** Victorian literature; early romanticism. **SELECTED PUBLICATIONS** Auth, The Facts of Life--The Creation of Sexual Knowledge in Britain, 1650-1950, J the Hist of Sexuality, Vol 0006, 96. **CONTACT ADDRESS** Dept of English, Univ of Del, Newark, DE, 19711.

GATES, HENRY LOUIS, JR.
PERSONAL Born 09/16/1950, Keyser, West Virginia, m, 1986 **DISCIPLINE** JOURNALISM **EDUCATION** Yale Univ, BA (summa cum laude), 1973; Clare Coll, Cambridge, England, MA, 1974, PhD, 1979. **CAREER** Time, London Bureau, London, England, staff correspondant, 1973-75; Amer Cyanamid Co, Wayne, NJ, public relations representative, 1975; Yale Univ, New Haven, CT, lecturer in English and Afro-American Studies, 1976-79, asst prof of English and Afro-American Studies, 1979-84, assoc prof of English and Afro-American Studies, 1984-85; Cornell Univ, Ithaca, NY, prof of English, Comparative Literature, and Aricana Studies, 1985-88, WEB Du Bois Prof of Literature, 1988-90; Duke University, Durham, NC, John Spencer Bassett Professor of English and Literature, beginning 1990; Harvard Univ, WEB Du Bois prof of the Humanities, chair, African-American Studies, dir, WEB Du Bois Institute for African-American Research, dir, 1991-. **HONORS AND AWARDS** Carnegie Found fellowship for Africa, 1970-71; Phelps fellowship, Yale Univ, 1970-71; Mellon

fellowship, Yale Univ, 1973-75, 1983-; A Whitney Griswold fellowship, Yale Univ, 1980; Natl Endowment for the Humanities grants, 1980-84, 1981-82; Rockefeller Found fellowship, 1980-81; MacArthur Prize fellowship, MacArthur Found, 1981-86; Whitney Humanities Center fellowship, 1982-84; Afro-Amer Cultural Center Faculty Prize, 1983; Ford Found grant, 1984-85; Zora Neale Hurston Soc Award for Creative Scholarship, 1986; Honorable Mention, John Hope Franklin Prize, Amer Studies Assn, 1988; Amer Book Award, 1989; Anisfield Book Award for Race Relations, 1989; Candle Award, Morehouse Coll, 1989; Natl Medal of Arts, presented by President Clinton, 1998. **MEMBERSHIPS** Council on Foreign Relations; board of directors, Lincoln Center Theater and Whitney Museum; European Institute for Literary & Cultural Studies, board of directors, 1990-; American Council for Learned Societies, board of directors, 1990-; American Antiquarian Society; Union of Writers of the African Peoples; Association for Documentary Editing; African Roundtable; African Literature Association; Afro-American Academy; American Studies Association; Association for the Study of Afro-American Life and History; Caribbean Studies Association; College Language Association; Modern Language Association; The Stone Trust; Zora Neale Hurston Society; mem, Pulitzer Prize Board. **SELECTED PUBLICATIONS** Author, Figures in Black: Words, Signs, and the Racial Self, 1987, The Signifying Monkey: Towards a Theory Afro-Amer Literary Criticism, 1988; Loose Canons: Notes on the Culture Wars, 1991; author, Colored People: A Memoir, 1994; The Future of the Race, 1996; editor, Our Nig, 1983, Black Literature and Literary Theory, 1984, "Race," Writing, and Difference, 1986, The Classic Slave Narratives, 1987; series editor, The Schomburg Library of Nineteenth-Century Black Women Writers, 1988; co-compiler, Wole Soyinka: A Bibliography of Primary and Secondary Sources, 1986; Colored People: A Memoir, Knopf, 1994; editor, The Norton Anthology of African-American Literature, 1996; co-editor, Transition: An International Review; author, editor, and contributor of articles and reviews to periodicals, books, and journals; George Polk Award, 1993; Lilliam Smith Award, Southern Literature, 1994; Chicago Tribune Heartland Award, 1994; 22 Honorary Degrees; Distinguished Editorial Achievement, Critical Inquiry, 1996; Tikkun National Ethics Award, 1996; The Richard Ellman Lectures, Emory University, 1996; Alternative Press Award for Transition, An Intl Review, 1995; Thirteen Ways of Looking At A Black Man, Random House, 1997. **CONTACT ADDRESS** Chair, Afro-American Studies Dept, Harvard Univ, 12 Quincy St, Cambridge, MA, 02138.

GATTA, JOHN, JR.
DISCIPLINE ENGLISH **EDUCATION** Univ Notre Dame, BA, 68; Cornell Univ, PhD, 73. **CAREER** Vis asst prof, Univ Mo, 73-74; asst prof, 74-79, assoc prof, 79-90, PROF ENG, 90-, dept head, 92-98, UNIV CONN; Fulbright lectr, Univ Dakar, Senegal, 87-88. **CONTACT ADDRESS** Dept of English, Univ of Connecticut, U-25, Storrs, CT, 06269. **EMAIL** Gatta@uconnvm.uconn.edu

GAULL, MARILYN
PERSONAL Born 02/06/1938, Boston, MA **DISCIPLINE** ENGLISH **EDUCATION** Univ Mass, BA, 58; Ind Univ, PhD(English), 64. **CAREER** Instr English, Col William and Mary, 63-64; lectr, Univ Mass, 64-66; asst prof, 67-72, ASSOC PROF ENGLISH, TEMPLE UNIV, 72-, Dir, Rydal Mt Summer Conf, 70-72; ed assoc, J Mod Lit, 70-; ed, The Wordsworth Circle, 70-; pres, Conf of Eds Learned J, 78-80. **MEMBERSHIPS** MLA; Keats-Shelley Asn Am; English Inst. **RESEARCH** Sociology of literature; romantic poetry; American studies. **SELECTED PUBLICATIONS** Auth, A Presence Which Is not To Be Put by, in Wordsworth, Richard, January 19, 1915 November 21, 1993, Wordsworth Circle, Vol 0025, 94; The State of Scholarly Publishing, PMLA-Publ of MLA of Am, Vol 0110, 95; The Profession of Romanticism, the Caverns Measureless and the Sunless Sea, Wordsworth Circle, Vol 0027, 96; The Wordsworth-Coleridge-Association 1995 Sessions, Wordsworth Circle, Vol 0027, 96. **CONTACT ADDRESS** Dept of English, Temple Univ, 1114 W Berks St, Philadelphia, PA, 19122-6029.

GAVIN, ROSEMARIE JULIE
PERSONAL Born 01/26/1917, Tropico, CA **DISCIPLINE** EDUCATION, ENGLISH **EDUCATION** Univ Calif, Los Angeles, BEd, cum laude, 39; Cath Univ Am, MA, 52; Stanford Univ, PhD(educ), 55. **CAREER** Teacher, Notre Dame High Schs, Calif, 42-51; prof educ & English, Col Notre Dame, Calif, 51-, dir grad studies, 63-, Acad Dean, 68-83, dir teacher educ, 52-70 & evening div, 55-65; deleg, Int Chap of Sisters of Notre Dame de Namur, Rome, 68 & 69; mem bd trustees, Col Notre Dame, Calif & Asn Independent Calif Cols & Univs, 68-. **HONORS AND AWARDS** BEd cum laude. **MEMBERSHIPS** AAUP; Am Asn Higher Educ; Nat Soc Study Educ; Nat Cath Educ Asn. **RESEARCH** Individualized instruction; single campus plan. **SELECTED PUBLICATIONS** Auth, Training Teachers of Secondary School English in Catholic Colleges for Women, Cath Educ Rev, 2/56; Chief Influences Shaping the Poetic Imagery of Thomas Merton, Renascence, 57; Hopkins' The Candle Indoors, Explicator, 2/62. **CONTACT ADDRESS** Col of Notre Dame, 1500 Ralston Ave, Belmont, CA, 94002-1997. **EMAIL** Sr.Gavin@cnd.edu

GAY, RICHARD R.
DISCIPLINE ENGLISH **EDUCATION** Univ Richmond, BA, 76, MA, 87; Univ NC, Greensboro, PhD, 91. **CAREER** From asst prof to asoc prof, Chowan Col, 91-97; tchr, Sussex County Public Sch(s), 90-91; tchg asst & campus-wide writing lab, Univ NC, Greensboro, 87-90; tchr, Prince George County Public Sch(s), Va, 87-88; tchr, Sussex County Public Sch(s), Va, 81-86; tchr, Cape Charles Public Sch(s), Va, 76-81; pres, Fac Forum, 95-97; secy, Steering Comt & ed, Strategic Self-Stud Rep for Reaffirmation of Accreditation, COC/SACS, 95-97; mem, Steering Committee for NCATE accreditation, 95-97; mem, Coop Instnl Res Prog Comt, CIRP, 93-94; actv mem, Lit Club, 91-95. **HONORS AND AWARDS** Tenure, Chowan Col, 95, Sussex County Public Sch(s), 83 & Cape Charles Public Sch(s), 79; Sigma Tau Delta tchg excellence, Chowan Col, 97. **MEMBERSHIPS** MLA; MCTE; S Atlantic Mod Lang Asn; Popular Cul Asn S. **RESEARCH** Curriculum develop and effective-sch(s) research. **SELECTED PUBLICATIONS** Auth, Arthurian Tragedy in Faulkner's Absalom, Absalom, Notes on Mississippi Writers, 90. **CONTACT ADDRESS** Dept of Eng, Chowan Col, 320 E Vance St, Murfreesboro, NC, 27855. **EMAIL** gayr@chowan.edu

GAYESKI, DIANE M.
DISCIPLINE COMMUNICATION STUDIES **EDUCATION** Univ Md, PhD. **CAREER** Assoc prof. **RESEARCH** Design and management of new technologies and practices. **SELECTED PUBLICATIONS** Auth, pubs on interactive media and the integration of internal and external communication, promotional strategies, and organizational learning. **CONTACT ADDRESS** Dept of Communication, Ithaca Col, 100 Job Hall, Ithaca, NY, 14850.

GAYLORD, ALAN T.
DISCIPLINE ENGLISH LITERATURE **EDUCATION** Princeton Univ, PhD, 59. **CAREER** Henry Winkley Prof of Anglo-Saxon and Eng Lang and Lit. **RESEARCH** Eng and Medievil lit. **SELECTED PUBLICATIONS** Auth, Portrait of a Poet, in The Ellesmere Chaucer: Essays in Interpretation, Huntington Lib, 95; From Dorigen to the Vavasour: Reading Backwards in The Olde Daunce, Love, Friendship, Sex & Marriage in the Medieval World, SUNY Press, 91; Imagining Voices: Chaucer on Cassette, Studies in the Age of Chaucer, 90. **CONTACT ADDRESS** Dartmouth Col, 3529 N Main St, #207, Hanover, NH, 03755.

GEHERIN, DAVID J.
PERSONAL Born 06/05/1943, Auburn, NY, m, 1964, 3 children **DISCIPLINE** 20TH CENT BRITISH AND AMERICAN NOVEL **EDUCATION** Univ Toronto, BA, 64; Purdue Univ, MA, 67, PhD, 70. **CAREER** Eastern Mich Univ, Prof eng, 69-. **RESEARCH** Contemp fiction; mystery; detective fiction. **SELECTED PUBLICATIONS** Sons of Sam Spade, 80; John D MacDonald, 82; The American Private Eye: The Image In Fiction, 85; Elmore Leonard, 89. **CONTACT ADDRESS** Eastern Michigan Univ, Dept English, Ypsilanti, MI, 48197. **EMAIL** eng_geherin@online.emich.edu

GEIST, JOSEPH E.
DISCIPLINE ENGLISH LANGUAGE AND LITERATURE **EDUCATION** Univ Kan, PhD. **CAREER** Prof and chr, Div English, For Langs, Comm-Theater Arts, and Art. **RESEARCH** American literature; contemporary theatre; and cinematic studies. **SELECTED PUBLICATIONS** Auth, articles on T.S. Eliot, the Liberal Arts, 20th Century Film and Drama. **CONTACT ADDRESS** Central Methodist Col, 411 Central Methodist Sq, Fayette, MO, 65248.

GEIST, PATRICIA
DISCIPLINE ORGANIZATIONAL COMMUNICATION, HEALTH COMMUNICATION **EDUCATION** Purdue Univ, PhD. **CAREER** Assoc prof, Fordham Univ. **RESEARCH** Negotiating ideology, control, and identity in organizations, predominantly in the health care professions. **SELECTED PUBLICATIONS** Co-auth, Negotiating the Crisis: DRGs and the Transformation of Hospitals, 92.; pub(s), Commun Monogr, Mgt Commun Quart, Health Commun, W Jour Commun, S States Speech Jour, Small Gp Behavior. **CONTACT ADDRESS** Dept of Commun, San Diego State Univ, 5500 Campanile Dr, San Diego, CA, 92182. **EMAIL** pgeist@ucsvax.sdsu.edu

GELERNT, JULES
PERSONAL Born 07/13/1928, Berlin, Germany, m, 1958, 2 children **DISCIPLINE** ENGLISH & COMPARATIVE LITERATURE **EDUCATION** City Col New York, BA, 49; Columbia Univ, MA, 50, PhD(comp lit), 63. **CAREER** Instr English, Hofstra Univ, 56-63; from asst prof to assoc prof, 63-71, PROF ENGLISH & CHMN DEPT, BROOKLYN COL, 75-78; Professor Emerites, 96; Mem, Comt Comp & World Lit, NCTE, 67-. **MEMBERSHIPS** Dante Soc Am; Renaissance Soc Am. **RESEARCH** Renaissance and comparative literature. **SELECTED PUBLICATIONS** Auth, Review Notes on Dante's Divine Comedy, Monarch, 63; World of Many Loves: The Heptameron of Marguerite de Navarre, Univ NC, 66. **CONTACT ADDRESS** Dept English, Brooklyn Col, CUNY, 2901 Bedford Ave, Brooklyn, NY, 11210-2813. **EMAIL** jrgelernt@worldnet.att.net

GELERNTER, JUDITH
PERSONAL Born 09/08/1967, Huntington, NY **DISCIPLINE** INFORMATION SCIENCE **EDUCATION** Yale, BA (Medieval Studies, magna cum laude), 89; Harvard, MA (Fine Arts), 92; Simmons, MS (Information Science), 94. **CAREER** Consultant, Metropolitan Museum of Art, Musical Instruments Dept, Performing Arts Index, 94-96; Librarian and Archivist, Dance Notation Bureau Research Library, 94-97; ed of newsletter, Channels, World Dance Alliance, Americas Center, 95-96; LIBRARY DIRECTOR AND ART CURATOR, UNION CLUB OF THE CITY OF NEW YORK, 97-. **HONORS AND AWARDS** Harvard Univ Scholarship, 89-92; Harvard Student travel grant, 90; Mellon grant, 92; Simmons College Scholarship, 93; Gadd/Merrill Endowment grant, 95. **MEMBERSHIPS** Soc of Dance Hist Scholars; Congress on res in Dance; Am Library Asn; Library Information Technology Asn; Art Librarians Soc, New York Chapter. **RESEARCH** Dance hist and criticism. **SELECTED PUBLICATIONS** Auth, Mannerist Aesthetics and the Court Dance of Fabritio Caroso, Proceedings of the Soc of Dance Hist Scholars, Feb 94; Database Management Software Rev: askSam, Special Libraries 85/4, fall 94; Metropolitan Museum of Art Performing Arts Index, Proceedings of the Soc of Dance Hist Scholars, published in joint authorship with Constance Olds in Dance and Technology III, ed A. William Smith, May 95; Images on Screen, Visual Resources Asn Bul, vol 22, no 1, spring 95, Storing Images, VRA Bul, vol 23, no 1, fall 96, Sharing Images Over a Network, VRA Bul, vol 24, no 1, spring 97; Channels, vol 1, no 2, fall 95, Channels, vol 2, no 1, spring 96, ed of World Dance Alliance Newsletter; co-auth with Constance Old, Performing Arts Index at the Metropolitan Museum of Arts, in The Art/MARC Sourcebook, Lynda S. White and Linda McRae, eds, 98; Partsche Bergsohn and Bergsohn: Early Dance, Dance Res J, 29/1, spring 97; White Oak Dance Project & The Shakers of Doris Humphrey, International Dictionary of Modern Dance, ed Taryn Benbow-Pfalzgraf, Gale, 98; Dance Notation, in A Core Collection in Dance, ed Mary Strow, an ARLIS pub, in press; Paul Taylor's Piazzolla Caldera, in progress for Ballet Rev. **CONTACT ADDRESS** 300 East 75th St., # 7F, New York, NY, 10021. **EMAIL** gelernter@att.net

GELLER, LILA BELLE
PERSONAL Born 10/06/1932, Chicago, IL, m, 1952, 3 children **DISCIPLINE** ENGLISH LITERATURE **EDUCATION** UCLA, BA, 52, PhD, 69; San Fernando Valley State Col, MA, 65. **CAREER** Asst prof, 69-73, assoc prof, 73-78, prof eng, CA State Univ, Dominguez Hills, 78. **MEMBERSHIPS** MLA. **RESEARCH** Eng Renaissance lit; Spenser; Shakespeare. **SELECTED PUBLICATIONS** Auth, The Acidalian Vision: Spenser's Graces in Book VI of The Faerie Queene, Rev English Studies, 8/72; Spenser's Theory of Nobility in Book VI of The Faerie Queene, English Lit Renaissance, winter 75; Venus and the Three Graces: a Neoplatonic Paradigm for Book III of The Faerie Queene, J English & Ger Philol, 1-4/76; Cymbeline and the imagery of covenant theology, Studies English Lit, 80; Reading Renaissance Drama; A Process Approach, with catherine Gannon, NY: Peter Lang publ, 91; Widows Vows and Middletons More Dissemblers Besides Women, Medieval and Renaissance Drama in England, p287-308, 91. **CONTACT ADDRESS** Dept of Eng, California State Univ, Dominguez Hills, 1000 E Victoria, Carson, CA, 90747-0005. **EMAIL** lgeller@csudh.edu

GELLRICH, JESSE M.
DISCIPLINE MEDIEVAL ENGLISH AND CONTINENTAL LITERATURE, HISTORY AND THEORY OF CRITICIS **EDUCATION** SUNY, Buffalo, PhD, 70. **CAREER** Prof, La State Univ; adv bd, Exemplaria, 87-. **HONORS AND AWARDS** Summer fac fel, Univ Calif, Irvine, 72, 73; pres grant, Univ Santa Clara, 80; ACLS fel, 86-87; John Nicholas Brown Prize, Medieval Acad of Am, 89; Manship fel, LSU, 90, 97; summer fac stipends, LSU, 94, 97; vis fel, Princeton Univ, 97. **RESEARCH** Medieval English and continental literature: orality and literacy in manuscript illumination, literature by women, and dream vision narrative in Latin, Old French, and Middle English. **SELECTED PUBLICATIONS** Auth, Deconstructing Allegory, Genre, 85; The Idea of the Book in the Middle Ages: Language Theory, Mythology, and Fiction, 85; Orality, Literacy and Crisis in the Later Middle Ages, Philol Quart, 88; Discourse and Dominion in the Fourteenth Century: Oral Contexts of Writing in Philosophy, Politics, and Poetry, 95; Figura, Allegory, and the Question of History, in Literary History and the Challenge of Philology: The Legacy of Erich Auerbach, 96. **CONTACT ADDRESS** Dept of Eng, Louisiana State Univ, 210A Allen Hall, Baton Rouge, LA, 70803. **EMAIL** jgellri@unix1.sncc.lsu.edu

GEMMETT, ROBERT J.
PERSONAL Born 03/11/1936, Schenectady, NY, m, 1964, 4 children **DISCIPLINE** ENGLISH **EDUCATION** Siena Col, BA, 59; Univ Mass, MA, 62; Syracuse Univ, PhD, 67. **CAREER** Instr English, Clarkson Univ, 64-65; assoc prof, 65-70, chemn dept, 75-79, prof English, SUNY, Brockport, 70-, dean humanities, 79-82, dean letters & scies, 82-92, SUNY, Buffalo, provst & VP, acad affairs, 92-97, prof 97-, SUNY, Brockport, Res grants, SUNY, 67 & 68; assoc ed, English Record, 67-69; res grant, SUNY, 77. **HONORS AND AWARDS** Chancellor's Award Excellence in Teaching, SUNY, 75. **RESEARCH** Brit-

ish 18th century studies and romantic period. **SELECTED PUBLICATIONS** Auth, The composition of William Beckford's Biographical Memoirs of Extraordinary Painters, Philol Quart, 1/68; ed, Biographical Memoirs of Extraordinary Painters, 69 & Dreams, Waking Thoughts and Incidents, 71, Fairleigh Dickinson Univ; Poets and Men of Letters, Mansell, London, 72; Vathek, The English Edition of 1786 and the French Editions of 1787, Scholars' Facsimiles, 72; auth, Beckford's Fonthill: The landscape as art, Gazette Beaux-Arts, 12/72; ed, The Episodes of Vathek, Fairleigh Dickinson Univ, 75; auth, William Beckford, Twayne, 77; The Consummate Collector, Michael Russell, 98. **CONTACT ADDRESS** Dept of English, SUNY, Brockport, 350 New Campus Dr, Brockport, NY, 14420-2914. **EMAIL** Rgemmet@po.brockport.edu

GENCARELLI, THOMAS F.
PERSONAL Born 07/02/1959, Mount Vernon, NY, m, 1994, 1 child **DISCIPLINE** MEDIA ECOLOGY **EDUCATION** New York Univ, PhD, 93. **CAREER** Inst, Iona Col, 89-93; ASST PROF, MONTCLAIR STATE UNIV, 93-. **MEMBERSHIPS** Int Communication Asn; Nat Communication Asn; Eastern Communication Asn, New Jersey Communication Asn; New York State Communication Asn; Nat Acad of Television Arts and Scis. **RESEARCH** Popular music; popular culture; media theory and criticism; media and culture. **SELECTED PUBLICATIONS** Coauth, Archetypal Criticism, Communication Ed, 90; auth, Taste Groups in the Real World: Media and Interpretive Communities, New Dimensions in Communication: Proceedings of the 47th Annual New York State Speech Communication Asn, 90; auth, Trying to Learn How to Walk Like the Heroes: Bruce Springsteen, Popular Music, and the Hero/Celebrity, American Heroes in the Media Age, Hampton Press, 94; auth, V-Chip, TV Ratings Just Simplistic Solutions, Herald Statesman, 96; auth, Kidding Ourselves With Solutions to TV Violence, Star Ledger, 96; auth, Television and Violence: Updating the Argument for the Future, Nat Communication Asn Conf, NY, 98; auth, Radio Continues to Eat Itself: An Analysis of the Music Radio Business and its Relationship to Culture in the United States, Int Communication Asn Conf, IL, 96; guest ed, Special Issue: Media Education, The New Jersey Journal of Communication, 98. **CONTACT ADDRESS** Dept of Broadcasting, Montclair State Univ, Upper Montclair, NJ, 07043. **EMAIL** gencarellit@saturn.montclair.edu

GENTRY, F.G.
PERSONAL Born 06/08/1942, Boston, MA, m, 1972 **DISCIPLINE** GERMAN AND ENGLISH **EDUCATION** Boston Col, BS, Ger and Eng, 63; Indiana Univ, MA, Ger, 66, PhD, Ger, 73. **CAREER** Instr, SUNY-Albany, 69-74; asst prof, SUNY-Albany, 74-75; asst prof, Univ Wis Madison, 75-80; assoc prof, Univ Wis Madison, 80-84; guest prof, Lehrstuhl Schupp, Univ Freiburg, 84; prof, Univ Wis Madison, 84-91; prof, Penn State Univ, 91-. **HONORS AND AWARDS** Alpha & Omega, Boston Col Sch of Educ Honor Soc, 62; Alpha Sigma Nu, Nat Jesuit Honor Soc, 62; Delta Phi Alpha, Nat Ger Honor Soc, 64, pres, Beta Chap, 68; Campion Distinguished Alumnus Award, Boston Col, 77; Seal of the Univ Freiburg, 85; fel, Vilas assoc, Univ Wis Madison, 86-88; Alexander von Humboldt-Stiftung fel, 78, 79, summer 82; Inst for Res in the Humanities, 77; Indiana Univ-Kiel Univ Exchange fel, 64. **MEMBERSHIPS** Alexander-von-Humboldt Assoc of Amer; Amer Assoc of Tchrs of Ger; Fulbright Assoc; Ger Studies Assoc; Gesellschaft fur interkulturelle Germnaistik; Intl Arthurian Soc; Intl Courtly Lit Soc; Intl Vereinigung fur Ger Sprachund Lit; Mediavisten-Verband; Medieval Acad of Amer; Mod Lang Asn; Oswald-von-Wolkenstein-Gesellschaft; Wolfram-von-Eschenbach-Gesellschaft. **RESEARCH** Medieval literature and culture. **SELECTED PUBLICATIONS** Co-ed, with James K. Walter, Heroic Epic, The Ger Libr, vol 1, NY, 95; Bibliographie zur fruhmittelhochdeutschen, Dichtung, Berlin, 92; ed, German Medievalism, Studies in Medievalism 3/4, Cambridge, 91; ed, Gottfried von Strasburg, The Ger Libr, vol 3, NY, 88; articles, Owe armiu phaffheite: Heinrich von Melk's Views on Clerical Life, Medieval Purity and Piety: Essays on Medieval Clerical Celibacy and Religious Reform, NY, Garland, 337-52, 98; Kaiserchronik, Dict of Lit Bio: Ger Writers and Works of the Early Middle Ages, 800-1170, vol 148, NY/London, Gale Res, 202-207,95; Notker von Zwiefalten, Dict of Lit Bio: Ger Writers and Works of the Early Middle Ages 800-1170, vol 148, NY/London, Gale Res, 106-109, 95; Der Arme Hartmann, Dict of Lit Bio: Ger Writers and Works of the Early Middle Ages, 800-1170, vol 148, NY/London, Gale Res, 10-13, 95; Silent that Others Might Speak: Notes on the Ackermann aus Bohmen, Ger Quart, 67, 484-492, 94. **CONTACT ADDRESS** Pennsylvania State Univ, 305 Burrowes Bldg., University Park, PA, 16802. **EMAIL** fggi@psu.edu

GENTRY, MARSHALL BRUCE
PERSONAL Born 07/28/1953, Little Rock, AR, m, 1989 **DISCIPLINE** ENGLISH, AMERICAN LITERATURE **EDUCATION** Univ AR, Fayetteville, BA, 75; Univ Chicago, MA, 76; Univ TX at Austin, PhD, 84. **CAREER** Graduate student teaching positions, Univ TX at Austin, 76-83; vis asst instr, 83-84, vis asst prof, TX A&M Univ, 84-85; asst prof, 85-91, assoc prof, 81-98, prof English, Univ of Indianapolis, 98-, English chair, 98-. **HONORS AND AWARDS** Lilly Summer Stipend for Development of New Courses, 87; Phi Beta Kappa, 74; Phi Kappa Phi, 82. **MEMBERSHIPS** MLA; SCMLA; MMLA; SAMLA; NEMLA; Am Lit Asn; Flannery O'Connor Soc; Writers' Center of Indianapolis, etc. **RESEARCH** 20th century Am fiction, especially E L Doctoron, Philip Roth, Flannery O'Connor. **SELECTED PUBLICATIONS** Auth, Flanery O'Connor's Religion of the Grotesque, Univ Press MS, 86; O'Connor's Legacy in Stories by Joyce Carol Oates and Paula Sharp, The Flannery O'Connor Bul 23, 94-95; Gender Dialogue and Ventriloquism in Julio Cortazar's Graffiti, The AR Rev 4, 95; Gender Dialogue in O'Connor, Flannery O'Connor: New Perspectives, ed Sura Rath and Mary Neff Shaw, Univ GA Press, 96; co-ed, the Practice and Theory of Ethics, Univ Indianapolis Press, 96; An Interview with Margaret Kingery, SD Rev 34.2, 96; review, The Good Doctor by Susan Onthank Mates, Studies in Short Fiction 33.3, 96; review, The Stories of Raymond Carver: A Critical Study by Kirk Nesset, Studies in Short Fiction 34.1, 97; auth, Ambition in the Poetry Boat: A Conversation with David Bottoms, conducted along with Alica Friman, The Southern Quart, forthcoming; author of numerous other articles, book reviews, and other publications. **CONTACT ADDRESS** Dept of English, Univ of Indianapolis, 1400 E Hanna Ave, Indianapolis, IN, 46227-3697. **EMAIL** bgentry@uindy.edu

GENTRY, THOMAS BLYTHE
PERSONAL Born 11/26/1922, Danville, KY, m, 1944, 2 children **DISCIPLINE** ENGLISH LITERATURE **EDUCATION** Centre Col, BA, 47; Univ KY, MA, 53, PhD, 62; VA Mil Inst, BA, 62. **CAREER** From instr to assoc prof, 48-66, PROF ENGLISH, VA MIL INST, 66-. **MEMBERSHIPS** Col English Asn. **CONTACT ADDRESS** Dept of English, Virginia Mil Inst, Lexington, VA, 24450.

GEOK-LIN LIM, SHIRLEY
PERSONAL Born 03/22/1952, Malacca, Malaysia, m, 1977, 2 children **DISCIPLINE** ENGLISH AND AMERICAN LITERATURE **EDUCATION** Univ of Malaya, Kuala Lumpur, BA, 67; Brandeis Univ, MA, 71; PhD, 73. **CAREER** Asst prof, Hostos Community Col, CUNY, 73-76; from asst prof to assoc prof, Westchester Col, NY, 76-90; prof, 90- ; ch, Women's Studies, Univ of Calif, 97-. **HONORS AND AWARDS** Fulbright scholar, 69-72; Wien Int Fel, 69-72; SUNY Chancellor's Award for Excellence in Teaching, 81; Commonwealth Poetry Prize, 80; Nat Univ of Singapore Fel, 82; Second Prize, Asiaweek Short Story Competition, 82; Mellon Fel, Univ of NY, 83; Inst of Southeast-Asian Studies Fel, 85-86; Mellon Fel, CUNY, 87; Asia Found Fel, Singapore, 89; Minorities Discourses Fel, Irvine, 93; U.S. Information Agency Acad Specialization Grant, 94; Curric Integration Grant, Univ of Calif, 95; Nat Endowment for the Hums Acad Consult for the Merchantile Library/New York Public Libraries, 95; Nominee, Distinguished Teacher Award, 97; UCSB Residential Life Outstanding Fac Member Award, 94-95, 96-97; Fulbright Distinguished Lecturership, 96; Finalist, Asn of Asian Am Studies Non-Fiction Book Prize, 97; Am Book Award, 97. **MEMBERSHIPS** MLA; ASA; NWSA. **RESEARCH** Asian-American cultural studies; women's studies; post-colonial literatures; autobiographies. **SELECTED PUBLICATIONS** Auth, Nationalism and Literature in English from the Philippines and Singapore, 93; Writing Southeast/Asia in English: Against the Grain, 94; Monsoon History: Selected Poems, 94; Life's Mysteries: The Best of Shirley Lim, 95; Among the White Moon Faces: An Asian-American Memoir of Homelands, 96; Two Dreams: Short Stories, 97; What the Fortune Teller Didn't Say, 97; Gender, Culture, and the Public Sphere, forthcom.; ed, The Forbidden Stitch: An Asian American Women's Anthology, 89; Approaches to Teaching Kingston's The Woman Warrior, 91; Reading the Literatures of Asian America, 92; One World of Literature, 93. **CONTACT ADDRESS** Dept of English, Univ of California, Santa Barbara, CA, 93106. **EMAIL** slim@humanitas.ucsb.edu

GEORGE, KEARNS
DISCIPLINE ENGLISH LANGUAGE AND LITERATURE **EDUCATION** Yale Univ, BA; Columbia Univ, MA; Boston Univ, PhD. **CAREER** Prof. **RESEARCH** Modernism; literature and philosophy; literary theory. **SELECTED PUBLICATIONS** Auth, Ezra Pound: The Cantos. **CONTACT ADDRESS** Dept of English, Rutgers Univ, 510 George St, Murray Hall, New Brunswick, NJ, 08901-1167. **EMAIL** gwkearns@aol.com

GEORGE, LAURA J.
DISCIPLINE LITERARY CRITICISM **EDUCATION** PhD. **CAREER** E Mich Univ **SELECTED PUBLICATIONS** Auth, Fashionable Figures: Rhetoric and Costume in British Romanticisms. **CONTACT ADDRESS** Eastern Michigan Univ, Ypsilanti, MI, 48197. **EMAIL** eng_George@online.emich.edu

GEORGE, SUSANNE K.
DISCIPLINE AMERICAN LITERATURE **EDUCATION** Univ Nebr, Lincoln, doctorate, 88. **CAREER** Assoc prof, Univ Nebr, Kearney. **MEMBERSHIPS** Nat pres, Western Lit Asn; fel, Ctr for Great Plains Stud; bd dir, Willa Cather Pioneer Mem and Educ Found; Nebr Hum Speaker's Bur. **RESEARCH** 19th century American Literature. **SELECTED PUBLICATIONS** Auth, The Adventures of The Woman Homesteader: The Life and Letters of Elinore Pruitt Stewart, Univ Nebr Press, 92; ed, Wellsprings: Poems by Six Nebraska Poets, Univ Nebr, Kearney, 95; coed, The Platte River: An Atlas of the Big Bend Region, Univ Nebr, Kearney, 93. **CONTACT ADDRESS** Univ Nebr, Kearney, Kearney, NE, 68849.

GERHART, MARY
PERSONAL Born 03/04/1935, Stacyville, IA **DISCIPLINE** THEOLOGY, LITERATURE **EDUCATION** Col St Teresa, Minn, BA, 62; Univ Mo, MA, 68; Univ Chicago, MA, 70, PhD(relig, lit), 73. **CAREER** Asst prof, 72-80, Assoc Prof Relig Studies, Hobart & William Smith Cols, 80-, Ed Chair, Relig Studies Rev, 78-, Nat Endowment for Humanities grant, 76 & Fulbright grant, 82-83. **HONORS AND AWARDS** D J Bowden lectr, Ind Univ, 72; Ida Mae Wilson lectr, Vanderbilt Univ, 80. **MEMBERSHIPS** AAUP; Am Acad Relig; Cath Theol Soc Am. **RESEARCH** Hermeneutical theory; the contemporary novel; metaphor and genre in science and religion. **SELECTED PUBLICATIONS** Auth, Paul Ricoeur's Hermeneutical theory as resource for theological reflection, Thomist, 7/75; Paul Ricoeur, la metaphore vive, Relig Studies Rev, 1/76; Paul Ricoeur's notion of diagnostics: Toward a philosophy of the human, J Relig, 4/76; Generic studies: Their renewed importance in religious and literary interpretation, J Am Acad Relig, 9/77; The ironic mode of religious imagination in Heinrich Boll, CTSA Proc, 77; The question of belief in literary criticism: An intorduction to the hermeneutical theory of Paul Ricoeur, Verlag Hans-Dieter Heniz, 79; The new literature and contemprorary religious conciousness, Angelican Theol Rev, 1/80; Resentfulness transformed: The religious vision of James Joyce, Cross Currents, 3/81. **CONTACT ADDRESS** Dept of Relig Studies, Hobart & William Smith Cols, Scandling Center, Box 4040, Geneva, NY, 14456-3382. **EMAIL** gerhart@hws.edu

GERLACH, JOHN CHARLES
PERSONAL Born 08/01/1941, Baltimore, MD, 2 children **DISCIPLINE** NINETEENTH CENTURY AMERICAN LITERATURE **EDUCATION** Kenyon Col, BA, 63; Columbia Univ, MFA, 65; Ariz State Univ, PhD, 69. **CAREER** Prof English, Cleveland State Univ, 68-, Asts Dean Col Arts & Sci, 79-85, Chmn, 90-94. **RESEARCH** Film; 19th century American fiction; fiction writing; Emily Dickinson; short story theory. **SELECTED PUBLICATIONS** Auth, Messianic nationalism in the early works of Herman Melville, Ariz Quart, 4/72; James Fenimore Cooper and the kingdom of God, Ill Quart, 4/73; The Critical Index, Teachers Col, Columbia Univ, 74; Simpson Among Angels, NAm Rev, 80; Toward the End: Closure & Structure in the American Short Story, Univ Ala Press, 85; Reading Dickinson: Fascicle 39, Emily Dickinson J, 94. **CONTACT ADDRESS** Dept of English, Cleveland State Univ, 1983 E 24th St, Cleveland, OH, 44115-2440. **EMAIL** j.gerlach@popmail.csuohio.edu

GERMAIN, EDWARD B.
PERSONAL Born 12/30/1937, Saginaw, MI, m, 1 child **DISCIPLINE** ENGLISH LANGUAGE; ENGLISH LITERATURE **EDUCATION** Univ Mich, PhD, 69. **CAREER** Instr, US Naval Reserve, 63-65; instr, Eastern Mich Univ, 64-66; teaching fel, Univ Mich Ann Arbor, 66-69; asst prof, eng, Pomona Col, 69-75; lectr, Wayne State Univ, 76; assoc prof, humanities, Nathaniel Hawthorne Col, 76-79; instr, eng, Rennes, France, 82-83; instr, eng, Phillips Acad, 79-. **HONORS AND AWARDS** Sabbatical grant, 97-98; Who's Who Among American Teachers, 96; appointment, sch yr abroad, France, 82-83; Keenan grant for writing, Phillips Acad, 82; sabbatical fel, Pomona Col, 75-76; fac res grant, Pomona Col, 70, 71, 75; Avery Hopwood award for creative writing, Univ Mich, 68; Phi Kappa Phi, 65. **MEMBERSHIPS** Intl James Joyce. **SELECTED PUBLICATIONS** Auth, The Annotated Sisters, teaching web site, http://www.andover.edu/english/joyce, 98; auth, Jane Kenyon, Ron Padgett, Lee Harwood, Robert Dana, Charles Henri Ford, Contemporary Poets of the English Language, St. James Press, London, revised, 96; ed, Surrealist Poetry in English, Penguin Books Ltd, London, 78; ed, Shadows of the Sun: the Diaries of Harry Crosby, Black Sparrow Press, Santa Barbara, Calif, 77; ed, Flag of Ecstasy: Selected Poems of Charles Henri Ford, Black Sparrow Press, 72. **CONTACT ADDRESS** PO Box 278, Dublin, NH, 03444. **EMAIL** egermain@andover.edu

GERNES, SONIA
DISCIPLINE ENGLISH AND LITERATURE **EDUCATION** Univ Wash, PhD. **CAREER** Instr, Univ Notre Dame. **HONORS AND AWARDS** Sheedy Award for Excellence in Tchg; Lilly fel; Fulbright sr lectr. **SELECTED PUBLICATIONS** Auth, The Mutes of Sleepy Eye; Brief Lives; Women at Forty; The Way to St. Ives. **CONTACT ADDRESS** Univ Notre Dame, Notre Dame, IN, 46556.

GERNES, TODD STEVEN
DISCIPLINE ENGLISH **EDUCATION** Univ Mass at Amherst, BA, 84; MA, 86; Brown Univ, AM, 87, PhD, 92. **CAREER** COORD, UPP LEVEL WRITING, UNIV MICH **MEMBERSHIPS** Am Antiquarian Soc **SELECTED PUBLICATIONS** Auth, "Recasting the Culture of Ephemera: Young Women's Literary Culture in 19th Century America, PhD diss, 92; **CONTACT ADDRESS** Eng Comp Board, Univ of Mich, 1111 Angell Hall, Ann Arbor, MI, 48109-1003. **EMAIL** tsgernes@umich.edu

GERRY, THOMAS M.F.
PERSONAL Born 01/31/1948, Toronto, ON, Canada **DISCIPLINE** ENGLISH **EDUCATION** Univ Toronto, BA, 71, BEd, 75; York Univ, MA, 73; Univ Western Ont, PhD, 83. **CAREER** Sch tchr, Hastings Co, 75-78; asst prof, Trent Univ, 85-87; asst prof, Acadia Univ, 87-88; ASSOC PROF ENGLISH, LAURENTIAN UNIV, 88-. **HONORS AND AWARDS** Laurentian Univ res awards, 90, 92, 94. **MEMBERSHIPS** Asn Can Stud; Proj Ploughshares. **SELECTED PUBLICATIONS** Auth, Contemporary Canadian and U.S. Women of Letters; ed, The York Pioneer, 85; ed bd, Stud Can Lit. **CONTACT ADDRESS** Dept of English, Laurentian Univ, 935 Ramsey Lake Rd, Sudbury, ON, P3E 2C6.

GERSHON, ROBERT
DISCIPLINE EMERGING COMMUNICATION TECHNOLOGIES **EDUCATION** Princeton Univ, BA; Boston Univ PhD. **CAREER** Comm Stu, Castleton St Univ. **SELECTED PUBLICATIONS** Auth, Documentary Style Narration, 80, Video Grammar, Educational and Industrial Television, October, 81; Gershon, Robert, State Humanities Councils as Patrons of Film and Video Production 85. **CONTACT ADDRESS** Castleton State Col, Seminary Street, Castleton, VT, 05735. **EMAIL** gershonr@sparrow.csc.vsc.edu

GERSTER, CAROLE
DISCIPLINE ENGLISH LITERATURE **EDUCATION** Univ MN, MA, PhD. **CAREER** Prof, Univ of WI. **RESEARCH** Am film; lit and films by and about women and ethnic minorities; Brit women's novels; literary theory. **SELECTED PUBLICATIONS** Auth, pubs about women and ethnic minorities in film and Brit lit. **CONTACT ADDRESS** Eng Dept, Univ Wisconsin, S 3rd St, PO Box 410, River Falls, WI, 54022-5001.

GERTZMAN, JAY ALBERT
PERSONAL Born 05/10/1939, Philadelphia, PA **DISCIPLINE** ENGLISH **EDUCATION** Univ Pa, BS, 61; Columbia Univ, MA, 63; Univ Pa, PhD(English), 72. **CAREER** Teacher English, Olney High Sch, Philadelphia, 62-68; from asst prof to assoc prof, 68-77, PROF ENGLISH, MANSFIELD UNIV, 77-. **HONORS AND AWARDS** Nat Endowment Humanities summer sem, 76 & 80; Summer Res Fel, Andrew Mellon Found Fel, Harry Ransom Humanities Res Ctr, Univ Tex Austin, June-July 94. **MEMBERSHIPS** D.H. Lawrence Soc of N Am. **RESEARCH** Cavalier poetry; literary censorship; publishing history; D.H. Lawrence. **SELECTED PUBLICATIONS** Auth, Commitment and sacrifice in Heart of Darkness: Marlowe's response to Kurtz, Studies in Short Fiction, 72; Robert Herrick's Recreative Pastoral, Genre, 74; Literature of courtesy and the cavalier persona, Proc Patristic, Medieval and Renaissance Conf, 78; Changes of dedication in Brathwait's English gentleman, analytical and enumerative bibliography, 79; Hemingway's writer-narrator in the denunciation, Res Studies, 79; Fantasy, Fashion, and Affection: Editions of Robert Herrick's Poetry For the Common Reader, 1810-1968, The Popular Press, 86; A Descriptive Bibliography of Lady Chatterley's Lover, With Essays Toward a Publishing History of the Novel, Greenwood Press, 89; Esoterica and The Good of the Race: Mail Order Distribution of Erotica in the Nineteen-Thirties, Papers of the Bibliog Soc of Am, 9/92; Erotic Novel, Liberal Lawyer, and Censor-Moron: Sex for Its Own Sake and Some Literary Censorship Adjudications of the Nineteen-Thirties, The D.H. Lawrence Rev, Fall 92; Postal Service Guardians of Public Morals and Erotica Mail Order Dealers of the Thirties: A Study in Administrative Authority in the United States, Publ Hist, 37, 95; A Trap for Young Book-leggers: The First American Printings of Frank Harris' My Life, Volumes Three and Four (1927), Papers of the Bibliog Soc of Am, 9/95. **CONTACT ADDRESS** Dept of English, Mansfield Univ, Belknap Hall, Mansfield, PA, 16933-1308. **EMAIL** jgertzma@epix.net

GEWANTER, DAVID
DISCIPLINE ENGLISH LITERATURE **EDUCATION** Univ Mich, BA; Univ Ca, MA, PhD. **CAREER** Assoc prof. **SELECTED PUBLICATIONS** Auth, In the Belly, Univ Chicago, 97. **CONTACT ADDRESS** English Dept, Georgetown Univ, 37th and O St, Washington, DC, 20057.

GHNASSIA, JILL DIX
DISCIPLINE ENGLISH LITERATURE **EDUCATION** Bucknell Univ, BA; Duke Univ, MA, PhD. **CAREER** Assoc prof, Hartford Univ. **RESEARCH** Humanities and literature; romanticism in the arts; interdisciplinary studies; discourse of the law. **SELECTED PUBLICATIONS** Auth, Metaphysical Rebellion in the Works of Emily Bronte (rev); pubs on Brontes, Percy Shelley, and Mary Wollstonecraft; co-auth, Epidemics and AIDS. **CONTACT ADDRESS** Univ of Hartford, 200 Bloomfield Ave, West Hartford, CT, 06117.

GHOSE, ZULFIKAR AHMED
PERSONAL Born 03/13/1935, Sialkot, Pakistan, m, 1964 **DISCIPLINE** ENGLISH LITERATURE **EDUCATION** Keele Univ, BA, 59. **CAREER** Lectr, 69-73, assoc prof English, 74-82, PROF ENGLISH, UNIV TX, AUSTIN, 83-. **RESEARCH** Writing novels and poetry. **SELECTED PUBLICATIONS** Auth, The Loss of India, Routledge & Kegan Paul, London, 64; The Murder of Aziz Khan, Macmillan, London, 67 & Day, 69; Jets from Orange, Macmillan, London, 67; The Incredible Brazilian, Macmillan, London, 72 & Holt, 72; The Beautiful Empire, Macmillan, London, 75; The Violent West, 72, Crump's Terms, 75 & A Different World, 78, Macmillan; Hamlet, Prufrock and Language, St Martin's, 78 & Macmillan, London, 78; Hulme's Investigations Into the Bogart Script, Curbstone Pub Co, Austin, 81; A New History of Torments, Hutchinson, London, 82 & Holt, 82; Don Bueno, Hutchinson, London, 83 & Holt, 83; A Memory of Asia, Curbstone Pub Co, Austin, 84; The Fiction of Reality, Macmillan, London, 83; Figures of Enchantment, Hutchinson, London, 86, and Harper & Row, 86; The Art of Creating Fiction, Macmillan, London, 91; Selected Poems, Oxford Univ Press, 91; The Triple Mirror of the Self, London, Bloomsburg, 92; Shakespeare's Mortal Knowledge, Macmillan, 93. **CONTACT ADDRESS** Dept of English, Univ Texas, 0 Univ TX, Austin, TX, 78712-1026.

GIANAKARIS, CONSTANTINE JOHN
PERSONAL Born 05/02/1934, Morenci, MI, m, 1957, 1 child **DISCIPLINE** ENGLISH **EDUCATION** Univ Mich, BA, 56, MA, 57; Univ Wis, PhD, 61. **CAREER** Asst to assoc dean Col Lett & Sci, Univ Wis, 58-60; from asst prof to assoc prof English, Ill State Univ, 61-66; assoc prof, 66-72, Western Mich Univ, prof English, 72-79, assoc dean, Col Arts & Sci, 79-82, prof English & Theatre, 89; Ill State Univ fac grant, 63-66; Westerm Mich fac res grant, 67-68; co-founder, co-ed, Comp Drama,66-91; jury panelist Nat Endowment for Humanities, 71-75. **HONORS AND AWARDS** Nat Endowment for Humanities Summer Award 82; Teaching Excellence Award, Western Mich Univ, 91. **MEMBERSHIPS** MLA; Renaissance Soc Am; NCent Renaissance Conf; Shakespeare Assn Am; Assn Higher Ed. **RESEARCH** Drama of Ben Jonson; modern British and American drama; Shakespeare. **SELECTED PUBLICATIONS** Auth, Rosencrantz and Guildenstern are dead: alterations in absurdism, Drama Surv, Fall 68; Identifying ethical values in Volpone, Huntington Libr Quart, 11/68; ed, Antony and Cleopatra, W C Brown, 69; auth, Plutarch, Twayne, 70; ed, Foundations of Drama, Houghton Mifflin, 75; auth, Mrozek's Tango and other savage comedies, In: Savage Comedy, Rodopi, 78; A playwright looks at Mozart: Peter Shaffer's Amadeus, Comp Drama, Spring 81; Peter Shaffer's treatment of Mozart in Amadeus, Opera News, 2/82; ed Peter Shaffer: A Casebook, Garland, 91; Peter Shaffer, Macmillan, UK & St Martin's SA, 92. **CONTACT ADDRESS** Dept of English, Western Michigan Univ, 1201 Oliver St, Kalamazoo, MI, 49008-3805. **EMAIL** gianakaris@wmich.edu

GIANNETTI, LOUIS DANIEL
PERSONAL Born 04/01/1937, Natick, MA, d, 2 children **DISCIPLINE** CINEMA, DRAMA **EDUCATION** Boston Univ, BA, 59; Univ Iowa, MA, 61, PhD(English), 67. **CAREER** Grad teaching asst rhetoric & lit, Univ Iowa, 62-66; asst prof English, Emory Univ, 66-69; asst prof humanities, 70-73, assoc prof film & English, 73-75, prof film & English, Case Western Reserve Univ, 77-. **MEMBERSHIPS** Soc Cinema Studies; Am Film Inst; Univ Film Asn. **RESEARCH** Film form; ideology; film acting. **SELECTED PUBLICATIONS** Auth, Cinematic Metaphors, J Aesthet Educ, 10/72; The Gatsby Flap, Lit & Film Quart, 1/75; Godard and Others: Essays in Film Form, Fairleigh Dickinson Univ Press & Tantivy Press, London, 75; Amarcord: The Impure Art of Federico Fellini, Western Humanities Rev, spring 76; The Member of the Wedding, Lit & Film Quart, winter 76; Fred Zinnemann's High Noon, Film Criticism, winter 76-77; Masters of the American Cinema, Prentice-Hall, 81; Understanding Movies, Prentice-Hall, 72, 2nd ed, 76, 3rd ed, 82, 4th ed, 87, 5th ed, 90, 6th ed, 93, 7th ed, 96. Co-auth, Flashback: A Brief History of Film, with Scott Eyman, Prentice Hall, 86, 2nd ed, 91, 3rd ed, 96. **CONTACT ADDRESS** 10900 Euclid Ave, Cleveland, OH, 44106-4901.

GIANNONE, RICHARD
PERSONAL Born 10/09/1934, Newark, NJ **DISCIPLINE** ENGLISH **EDUCATION** Cath Univ Am, AB, 56; Univ Mich, MA, 57; Univ Notre Dame, PhD(English), 64. **CAREER** Instr English, Univ Notre Dame, 58-60 & 61-62, asst prof, 64-67; assoc prof, 67-74, prof English, Fordham Univ, 74-, Vis scholar, Union Theol Sem, 75-76. **MEMBERSHIPS** MLA. **RESEARCH** American literature. **SELECTED PUBLICATIONS** Auth, One of ours: Willa Cather's suppressed Bitter Melody, SAtlantic Quart, winter 65; The quest motif in Thyrsis, Victorian Poetry, spring 65; Music in Willa Cather's Fiction, Univ Nebr, 68; The Shapes of Fiction, Holt, 71; John Keats: A Thematic Reader, Scott, 72; Vonnegut: A Preface to His Novels, Kennikat, 77; Flannery O'Connor and the Mystery of Love, Universtiy Press, 89. **CONTACT ADDRESS** Dept of English, Fordham Univ, 501 E Fordham Rd, Bronx, NY, 10458-5191.

GIARELLI, ANDREW
DISCIPLINE ENGLISH **EDUCATION** Yale Univ, BA, 75; State Univ NY, PhD, 84. **CAREER** Adj asst prof, 96-. **HONORS AND AWARDS** Contrib ed, World Press Rev. **SELECTED PUBLICATIONS** Ed, publ, Edging West; contrib ed,World Press Rev. **CONTACT ADDRESS** Dept of Eng, Portland State Univ, PO Box 751, Portland, OR, 97207-0751. **EMAIL** giarellia@pdx.edu

GIBALDI, JOSEPH
PERSONAL Born 08/20/1942, Brooklyn, NY, m, 1962, 2 children **DISCIPLINE** ENGLISH, COMPARATIVE LITERATURE **EDUCATION** City Col New York, BA, 65; City Univ New York, MA, 67; NY Univ, PhD(comp lit), 73. **CAREER** Instr English, Brooklyn Col, 71-73; asst prof comp lit, Univ Ga, 73-76; ASSOC DIR, BK PUBL AND RES PROG, MOD LANG ASN AM, 76-, Southeastern Inst Medieval and Renaissance Studies fel, 76; adj prof English, Fairleigh Dickinson Univ, 77- **MEMBERSHIPS** MLA; Am Comp Lit Asn; Renaissance Soc; New Chaucer Soc. **RESEARCH** Medieval and Renaissance literature; interdisciplinary studies; professional subjects. **SELECTED PUBLICATIONS** Auth, Don-Giovanni, Myths of Seduction and Betrayal, Philos and Lit, Vol 0017, 93. **CONTACT ADDRESS** Modern Language Association, 62 Fifth Av, New York, NY, 10011.

GIBBENS, E. BYRD
DISCIPLINE MODERN AMERICAN LITERATURE **EDUCATION** Univ NMex, PhD. **CAREER** English and Lit, Univ Ark. **SELECTED PUBLICATIONS** Auth, This Strange Country; "Strangers in the Arkansas Delta," The Arkansas Delta; "Beliefs and Customs," Folklore in Arkansas; Coauth, Far From Home. **CONTACT ADDRESS** Univ Ark Little Rock, 2801 S University Ave., Little Rock, AR, 72204-1099. **EMAIL** bxgibbens@ualr.edu

GIBBONS, REGINALD
DISCIPLINE ENGLISH **EDUCATION** Stanford Univ, PhD. **CAREER** Prof, Northwestern Univ; Guggenheim fel; Nat Endowment for the Arts fel. **HONORS AND AWARDS** Carl Sandburg Awd, 92; Anisfield-Wolf Book Awd, 95; Balcones Poetry Prize, 98. **SELECTED PUBLICATIONS** Auth, Criticism in the University, TriQuart Series on Criticism and Culture; Fiction of the Eighties: A Decade of Stories, TriQuart; Five Pears or Peaches; Guillen on Guillen: The Poetry and the Poet; Had I A Hundred Mouths: New & Selected Stories 47-83; Maybe It Was So; New Writing from Mexico; The Poet's Work: Twenty Nine Masters of Twentieth Century Poetry on the Origins and Practice of Their Art; The Ruined Motel: Poems; Saints; Sweetbitter: A Novel; TQ 20: Twenty Years of the Best Contemporary Writing and Graphics, TriQuart Magazine; TriQuarterly New Writers; William Goyen: A Study of the Short Fiction; The Writer in Our World: A TriQuarterly Symposium; Sparrow: New and Selected Poems; Kiss, The Atlantic Monthly, 97. **CONTACT ADDRESS** Dept of English, Northwestern Univ, 1801 Hinman, Evanston, IL, 60208.

GIBSON, CLAUDE LOUIS
PERSONAL Born 11/27/1940, Okmulgee, OK, m, 1986, 3 children **DISCIPLINE** ENGLISH **EDUCATION** Univ Ark, Fayetteville, BA, 64, MA, 65, PhD, 76. **CAREER** ASSOC PROF ENGLISH, TEX A&M UNIV, 76-, Dir Freshman English, 80-84, Dir Undergrad Studies, 94-; Managing ed, CEA Critic & CEA Forum, 77-80. **HONORS AND AWARDS** Distinguished Teaching Award, 93. **MEMBERSHIPS** Col English Asn; MLA; SCent Mod Lang Asn; Southern Comp Lit Asn; NCTE. **RESEARCH** Modern British literature; 19th century; rhetoric and composition. **SELECTED PUBLICATIONS** Contribr, The historical study of style: an annotated bibliography, summer 77 & Author style, winter 78, Style; auth, The undergraduate English curriculum three years later, CEA Critic, 5/78; The CEA 1978 National Survey of the Teaching of College English, CEA Forum, 10/78. **CONTACT ADDRESS** Dept of English, Tex A&M Univ, 1 Texas A and M Univ, College Station, TX, 77843-4227. **EMAIL** cgibson@tamu.edu

GIBSON, DONALD B.
PERSONAL Born 07/02/1933, Kansas City, MO, m, 1963 **DISCIPLINE** LITERATURE **EDUCATION** Univ of Kansas City, Kansas City MO, BA, 1955, MA, 1957; Brown Univ, Providence RI, PhD, 1962. **CAREER** Brown Univ, Providence RI, instructor, 1960-61; Wayne State Univ, Detroit MI, asst prof, 1961-67; Univ of Connecticut, Storrs CT, assoc prof, 1967-69, prof, 1969-74; RUTGERS UNIV, NEW BRUNSWICK NJ, DISTINGUISHED PROF, 1974-. **HONORS AND AWARDS** Postdoctoral Fulbright, Fulbright Hayes Comm, 1964-66; Study Grant, Natl Endowment for the Humanities, 1970; Research Grant, Amer Council of Learned Socities, 1970; National Endowment for the Humanities, fellowship, 1992-93. **MEMBERSHIPS** Coll Language Assn; Modern Language Assn 1964-; editorial bd, African American Review, 1972-; consultant, Educ Testing Serv, 1976-; Natl Council of Teachers of English, 1987-. **SELECTED PUBLICATIONS** Author, The Fiction of Stephen Crane, 1968; editor, Five Black Writers, 1970; editor, Twentieth-Century Interpretations of Modern Black Poets, 1973; author, The Politics of Literary Expression: A Study of Major Black Writers, 1981; author, The Red Bridge of Courage: Redefining The Hero, 1988; editor, W E B Du Bois, The Souls of Black Folk, 1989; Stephen Crane, The Red Badge of Courage, Editor, 1996. **CONTACT ADDRESS** English, Rutgers Univ, Murray Hall CN5054, New Brunswick, NJ, 08903.

GIBSON, DONALD BERNARD
PERSONAL Born 07/02/1933, Kansas City, MO, m, 1963, 2 children **DISCIPLINE** ENGLISH **EDUCATION** Univ Kan-

sas City, BA, 55, MA, 57; Brown Univ, PhD, 62. **CAREER** Instr English, Brown Univ, 60-61; from instr to asst prof English, Wayne State Univ, 61-66; from assoc prof to prof English, Univ Conn, 66-74; prof English, Rutgers Col, Rutgers Univ, 74-; Fulbright-Hayes Award, Krakow, Poland, 64-66; Nat Endowment for Humanities younger humanist fel, 70-71; vis prof English, Univ Iowa, 71. **MEMBERSHIPS** MLA; Col Lang Asn. **RESEARCH** Nineteenth century realism and naturalism; Black American writers. **SELECTED PUBLICATIONS** Ed, Five Black Writers: Essays on Wright, Ellison, Baldwin, Hughes and LeRoy Jones, New York Univ, 70; Twentieth Century Interpretations of Modern Black Poets, Prentice-Hall, 73; auth, The Politics of Literary Expression: A Study of Major Black Writers, Greenwood Press, 81; auth The Red Badge of Courage: Redefining the Hero. **CONTACT ADDRESS** Dept English, Rutgers Col Rutgers Univ, PO Box 5454, New Brunswick, NJ, 08903-0270. **EMAIL** dgibba@aol.com

GIBSON, MELISSA K.
PERSONAL Born 09/18/1969, Erie, PA, s **DISCIPLINE** ORGANIZATIONAL COMMUNICATION **EDUCATION** Edinboro Univ, BA, 92; Ohio Univ, MA, 95, PhD, 97. **CAREER** Asst Prof, Western Mich Univ, 97-. **HONORS AND AWARDS** Res Fel, 96-97; Central States Commun Asn Outstanding New Teacher Award, 98; Top Paper, Orgn Commun Div, Nat Commun Asn, 98. **MEMBERSHIPS** Nat Commun Asn; Central States Commun; Am Soc Training & Development; Int Commun Asn. **RESEARCH** Organizational communication; applied communication theory; training and development; nonprofit organizations. **CONTACT ADDRESS** Western Michigan Univ, 215 Sprau Tower, Kalamazoo, MI, 49008. **EMAIL** melissa.gibson@wmich.edu

GIBSON, STEPHANIE
DISCIPLINE COMMUNICATIONS **EDUCATION** NY Univ, PhD. **CAREER** Assoc prof, Univ Baltimore. **SELECTED PUBLICATIONS** Ed, Communication and Cyberspace. **CONTACT ADDRESS** Commun Dept, Univ Baltimore, 1420 N. Charles Street, Baltimore, MD, 21201.

GIFFORD, JAMES J.
PERSONAL Born 06/03/1946, Rome, NY **DISCIPLINE** HUMANITIES **EDUCATION** Fordham Univ, AB, 68; Columbia Univ, MA, 70; Syracuse Univ, PhD, 94. **CAREER** Prof, 72-, Mohawk Valley Commun Col. **HONORS AND AWARDS** Doctoral Prize, Syracuse Univ, 95 **RESEARCH** Amer lit; nineteenth-twentieth centuries; gay Amer writing; film. **SELECTED PUBLICATIONS** Auth, Dayneford's Library: American Homosexual Writing 1900-1913, Univ Ma Press, 95. **CONTACT ADDRESS** Humanities Dept, Mohawk Valley Commun Col, 1101 Sherman Dr, Utica, NY, 13501.

GIGLIOTTI, GILBERT L.
PERSONAL Born 11/07/1961, Allentown, PA, m, 1988, 1 child **DISCIPLINE** ENGLISH **EDUCATION** Xavier Univ, HAB, 81, MA, 85; Cath Univ Am, PhD, 92. **CAREER** From asst prof to assoc prof & asst chm, dept English, Central Conn State Univ, 92-. **MEMBERSHIPS** Int Asn Neo-Latin Studies; Am Asn Neo-Latin Studies; Soc Early Am; NE Mod Lang Asn. **RESEARCH** American Neo-Latin Verse; Frank Sinatra; The Connecticut Wits; Cotton Mather. **SELECTED PUBLICATIONS** Auth, Voyage to Maryland: Relation itineris in Marylandiam, Neo-Latin News, 97; auth, Nail-Gnawing in a New World Landscape: From Allusion to Disillusion in John Beveridge's Epistolae familiares, Conn Rev, 96; auth, Off a Strange, Uncoasted Strand: Navigating the Ship of State Through Freneau's Hurricane, Class & Mod Lit, 95; auth, The Alexandrian Fracastoro: Structure and Meaning in the Myth of Syphilus, Renaissance & Reformation, 90. **CONTACT ADDRESS** Dept of English, Central Connecticut State Univ, 1615 Stanley St., New Britain, CT, 06050. **EMAIL** Gigliotti@CCSU.edu

GILBERT, SANDRA MORTOLA
PERSONAL Born 12/27/1936, New York, NY, m, 1957, 3 children **DISCIPLINE** ENGLISH LITERATURE, WOMEN'S STUDIES **EDUCATION** Cornell Univ, BA, 57; NY Univ, MA, 61; Columbia Univ, PhD, 68. **CAREER** Lectr Eng, Queens Col, CUNY, NY, 63-64, 65-66; Lect Eng, CA State Univ, Sacramento, 67-68, Asst prof Eng, CA State Univ, Hayward, 68-71; Vis lectr Eng, St Mary's Col, Moraga, spring 72; assoc prof, IN Univ, Bloomington, 73-75; Assoc prof eng, Univ CA, Davis, 75-80; Vis prof, IN Univ, fall 80; Prof Eng, Univ Calif, Davis, 80-85; Margaret Bundy Scott vis prof, Williams Col, fall 84; Bonzall vis prof, Stanford Univ, winter 85; Vis prof, The Johns Hopkins Univ, fall 86; Prof Eng, Princeton Univ, 85-89, Charles Barnwell Strout Class of 1923 Professorship, 89; prof eng, Univ CA Davis, 89; Columbia Univ Pres Fel, 64; Am Assoc Univ Women's fel, 66-67; Nat Endowment for Hum fel, 80-81; Rockefeller Found Hum fel, 82; Guggenheim fel, 83; Hum Inst, Univ CA Davis, 87-88, Univ CA Pres Fel, 91-92. **HONORS AND AWARDS** Morrison Poetry Prize, Cornell Univ, 55; Guilford Essay Prize, Cornell Univ, 57; Van Rensselaer Poetry Prize, Columbia Univ, 64; Res Asst grant, CA State Hayward Found, 69-70; IN Univ Summer Fac Fel, 74; Univ CA Hum Inst, summer 76, 78; Finalist, Assoc Writing Prog Contest, 76-77; Univ CA Prog Develop Award, summer 79; Nominee, Nat Bk Critics' Circle Award, 80; Runner-up, Pulitzer Prize in Non-Fiction, 80; Eunice Tietjens Mem Prize, Poetry, 80; NEH Summer Seminar, Univ Calif Davis, summer 81; Univ CA Tchg Develop Award, summer 81; Gildersleeve Professorship, Barnard Col, Columbia Univ, fall 82; Joseph Warren Beach Lectr, Univ MN, May 84; Fac, School of Criticism & Theory, Northwestern Univ, Summer 84; USA Today, People Who Made a Difference, 85; Ms., Woman of the Year Award, 86; D. Litt., Wesleyan Univ, June 88; Paley Lectr, The Hebrew Univ, Jerusalem, 90; Charity Randall Award, Int Poetry Found, 1/90; Danz lectr, Univ WA Seattle, 92; Paterson Prize, 95; Union League Prize, 96; Fel, Am Acad Arts and Sci, 97. **MEMBERSHIPS** MLA. **RESEARCH** Nineteenth & 20th century Brit lit; mod poetry; feminist critical theory. **SELECTED PUBLICATIONS** Auth, All the Dead Voices: Krapp's Last Tape, Drama Survey, spring 68; Acts of Attention: The Poems of D H Lawrence, Cornell Univ, 73; My Name is Darkness: The Poetry of Self Definition, Contemporary Literature, autumn 77; Co-auth (with Susan Gubar), Novel, winter 77; Plain Jane's Progress: A Study of Jane Eyre, Signs: Jour Women in Culture and Socity, summer 77; Patriarchal Poetry and Women Readers: Reflections on Milton's Bogey, PMLA, 5/78; Horror's Twin: Mary Shelley's Monstrous Eve, Feminist Studies, summer 78; A Fine, White, Flying Myth: The Life/Work of Sylvia Plath, The Mass Rev, autumn 78; Co-auth (with Susan Gubar), The Madwoman in the Attic: The Woman Writer and the Nineteenth-Century Literary Imagination, Yale Univ Press, 79; In the Fourth World: Poems (intro by Richard Eberhart), Univ AL Press/AWP Poetry Series, 79; Co-ed (with Susan Gubar), Shakespear's Sisters: Feminist Essays on Women Poets, IN Univ Press, 79; Of Metaphors and Morals, Contemporary Lit, winter 79; Life Studies, or, Speech after Long Silence, Feminist Critics Today, Col Engl, 4/79; Mephistopheles in Maine: Rereading Lowell's Skunk Hour, In: A Book of Rereadings (Greg Kuzma, ed), Best Cellar Press, 79; Hunger/Pains: Women and Anorexia, Univ Publ, summer 79; Hell on Earth: Birds, Beasts, and Flowers as Subversive Narrative, The D H Lawrence Rev, fall 79; Costumes of the Mind: Transvestitism as Metaphor in Modern Literature, Critical Inquiry, winter 80; Glass Joints: A Meditation on the Line, Epoch, winter 80; What Do Feminist Critics Want? or A Postcard from the Volcano, ADE Bull, winter 80; D H Larence's Uncommon Prayers, In: New Essays on D H Lawrence, Southern Ill Univ Press, 81; Poetry, 1940-the Present: A Review of Scholarship, In: American Literary Scholarship: 1980, Duke Univ Press, 81; Wonder and Survival, Salmagundi, summer 82; Rider Haggard's Heart of Darkness, Partisan Rev, summer 82; The Second Coming of Aphrodite: Kate Chopin's Fantasy of Desire, Kenyon Rev, summer 83; The Summer Kitchen (drawings by Barbara Hazard), The Heyeck Press, 83; The Rediscovery of H D, The NY Times Book Rev, 8/7/83; D H Lawerence, In: The Dictionary of Literary Biography, 83; Soldier's Heart: Literary Men, Literary Women, and the Great War, Signs: Jour Women in Culture and Society, winter 83; The Wayward Nun Beneath the Hill: Emily Dickinson and the Mysteries of Womanhood, In: New Feminist Essays on Emily Dickinson (Suzanne Juhasz, ed), IN Univ Press, 83; H D, Who Was She?, Contemporary Lit, winter 83; Teaching Plath's Daddy to Speak to Undergraduates, ADE Bull, winter 83; The Melody of Quotidian, Parnassus, winter 83; Emily's Bread: Poems, W W Norton & Co, 84; Kate Chopin's The Awakening and Selected Stories, Penguin, 84; From Patria to Matria: Elizabeth Barrett Browning's Risorgimento, PMLA, 3/84; The Battle of the Books/The Battle of the Sexes: Virginia Woolf's Coeducational Vita Nuova, Mich Quart Rev, spring 84; In Yeat's House: The Death and Resurrections of Sylvia Plath, In: Critical Essays on Sylvia Plath (Linda Wagner, ed), G K Hall, 84; Co-auth (with Susan Gubar), Ceremonies of the Alphabet, NY Lit Forum, winter 84; Co-auth (with Susan Gubar), Tradition and the Female Talent, In: Proceedings of the Northeastern Center for Literary Studies, Northeastern Univ Press, 84; Co-ed (with Susan Gubar), The Norton Anthology of Literature by Women: The Tradition in English, W W Norton & Co, 85; Co-auth (with Susan Gubar), A Guide to the Norton Anthology of Literature by Women, W W Norton & Co, 85; Life's Empty Pack: Notes Toward a Literary Daughteronomy, Critical Inquiry, spring 85; Co-auth (with Susan Gubar) Sexual Linguistics: Women, Language, Sexuality, New Literary Hist, spring 85; Co-auth (with Susan Gubar), Forward into the Past: The Complex Female Affiliation Complex, In: New Essays on Literary History (Jerome J McGann, ed), Univ Wis Press, 85; Potent Griselda: D H Lawrence and the Great Mother, In: Centenary Essays on D H Lawrence (Peter Balbert and Philip Marcus, ed), Cornell Univ Press, 85; The Education of Henrietta Adams, Profession '84, MLA, 85; Co-auth (with Gerald Graff), Feminist Criticism in the University: An Interview with Sandra M Gilbert, In: Criticism in the University, Northwestern Univ Press, 85; Purloined Letters: William Carlos Williams and Cress, The William Carlos Williams Rev, fall 85; The American Sexual Poetics of Whitman and Dickinson, Reconstructing American Literary History (Sacvan Bercovitch, ed), Harvard Univ Press, 86; A Trantella of Theory, intro to Helene Cixous and Catherine Clement, In: The Newly Born Woman, Univ Minn Press, 86; Poetry and Politics: On Denise Levertov, Parnassus, spring 86; In Search of Our Mother's Libraries, NY Times Book Rev, 5/86; Co-ed (with Susan Gubar), Woman's Sentence, Man's Sentencing: Linguistic Fantasies in Woolf and Joyce, In: New Essays on Virginia Woolf (Jane Marcus, ed), Ind Univ Press, 86; Feminism and Modernism, Gordon and Breach, 87; Co-auth (with Susan Gubar), No Man's Land: The Place of the Woman Writer in the Twentieth Century, In: The War of the Words, vol 1, Yale Univ Press, 87; Co-auth (with Susan Gubar), The Man on the Dump versus the United Dames of America, or What Does Frank Lentricchia Want?, Critical Inquiry, winter 87; Blood Pressure: Poems, W W Norton & Co, 88; Co-auth (with Susan Gubar), The Mirror and the Vamp: Reflections on Feminist Criticism, In: The Future of Literary Theory (Ralph Cohen, ed), Methuen, 88; Glass Joints, A Meditation on the Line (rev), In: The Line in Postmodern Poetry (Robert Frank and Henry Sayre, ed), Univ IL Press, Urbana, 88; Co-auth (with Susan Gubar), Sexchanges, Col Engl, 11/88, and No Man's Land: The Place of the Woman Writer in the Twentieth Century, Yale Univ Press, 89; Look Ma! I'm Talking, In: The State of the Language (Leonard Michaels and Christopher Ricks, ed), Univ CA Press, 89; Co-auth (with Susan Gubar), Sweetness versus Light?, NY Rev of Books, 8/16/90; Marianne Moore as Female Female Impersonator, In: Marianne Moore: The Art of a Modernist (Joseph Parisi, ed), UMI Res Press, 90; Co-auth (with Susan Gubar), But oh! That Deep Romantic Chasm, Kenyon Rev, winter 91; Co-auth (with Susan Gubar), Masterpiece Theatre: An Academic Melodrama, Critical Inquiry, summer 91; Piacere Conoscerla: On Being an Italian American, In: From the Margin: Writings in Italian Americana (Anthony Julian Tamburri, Paolo A Girodano and Fred L Gardaphe, ed), Purdue Univ Press, 91; Co-auth (with Susan Gubar), A Simple Bedtime Story, Op-Ed, NY Times, 4/1/92; Virginia Woolf's Orlando, Penguin, 93; If a Lion Could Talk ...: Dickinson Translated, The Emily Dickinson Jour, 93; Co-auth (with Susan Gubar), Letters from the Front, In: No Man's Land: The Place of the Woman Writer in the Twentieth Century, vol 3, Yale Univ Press, 94; The Great Sanity, That Sun, The Feminine Power: May Sarton and the (New) Female Poetic Tradition, In: Essays in Honor of May Sarton's Eightieth Birthday (Constance Hunting, ed), Puckerbrush Press, 94; Now in a Moment I Know What I Am For: Rituals of Initiation in Whitman and Dickinson, In: Walt Whitman of Mickle Street (Geoffrey M Sill, ed), Univ Tex Press, 94; Wrongful Death: A Medical Tragedy, W W Norton & Co, 95; Ghost Volcano: Poems, W W Norton & Co, 95; Co-ed (with Susan Gubar and Diana O'Hehir), Mothersongs: Poems for, by and about Mothers, W W Norton & Co, 95; Co-auth (with Susan Gubar), Masterpiece Theatre: An Academic Melodrama, Rutgers Univ Press, 95; Co-ed (with Wendy Barker), The House is Made of Poetry: Essays on the Art of Ruth Stone, Southern Ill Univ Press, 95; Co-ed (with Susan Gubar), The Norton Anthology of Literature by Women: The Tradition in English, 2nd ed, W W Norton & Co, 95; Female Female Impersonator: Edna St Vincent Millay and the Theatre of Personality, In: New Essays on Edna St Vincent Millay (William Thesing, ed), G K Hall, 95; Directions for Using the Empress: Millay's Supreme Fiction(s), and Ad Feminam: Women and Literature (series intro), In: Millay at 100: A Critical Reappraisal (Diane P Freedman, ed), Southern Ill Univ Press, 95. **CONTACT ADDRESS** Dept of Eng, Univ of California, Davis, CA, 95616-5200. **EMAIL** sgilbert@ucdavis.edu

GILES, JAMES RICHARD
PERSONAL Born 10/26/1937, Bowie, TX, m, 1968, 1 child **DISCIPLINE** ENGLISH **EDUCATION** Tex Christian Univ, BA, 60, MA, 61; Univ Tex, PhD, 67. **CAREER** Instr English, 66, asst prof, 67-70, NTex State Univ; asst prof, 70-72, assoc prof, 72-80, prof Eng, Northern IL Univ, 80-. **MEMBERSHIPS** MLA. **RESEARCH** American literature; Black American literature; creative writing. **SELECTED PUBLICATIONS** Auth, Irwin Shaw: A Study of the Short Fiction, Twayne, 91; auth,The Naturalistic Inner-City novel in America, South Carolina, 95; auth, Understanding Hubert Selby, Jr., South Carolina, 98. **CONTACT ADDRESS** Dept of English, No Illinois Univ, 1425 W Lincoln Hwy, De Kalb, IL, 60115-2825.

GILL, ANN
DISCIPLINE COMMUNICATION STUDIES **EDUCATION** W State Univ, BA; Colo State Univ, MA; Univ Colo, JD; Univ Denver, PhD. **CAREER** Prof. **RESEARCH** Freedom of speech; law and policy of communication technologies; rhetorical theory. **SELECTED PUBLICATIONS** Auth, Rhetoric and Human Understanding; Public Policy and Public Concern: Freedom of Speech in the Workplace, Free Speech Yearbook, 90; In the Wake of 'Fraser' and 'Hazelwood', J Law Edu, 91; Renewed Concern for Free Speech on Campus, ACA Bul, 93; Revising Campus Speech Codes, Free Speech Yearbook, 93; The Oral Tradition of Gerry Spence in Pring v. Penthouse, SW Univ Law Rev, 98; co-auth, Help Wanted: An Inexperienced Job Seeker's Guide to Career Success. **CONTACT ADDRESS** Speech Communication Dept, Colorado State Univ, Fort Collins, CO, 80523. **EMAIL** agill@vines.colostate.edu

GILL, GLENDA ELOISE
PERSONAL Born 06/26/1939, Clarksville, TN, s **DISCIPLINE** ENGLISH **EDUCATION** Alabama A&M University, BS, 1960; University of Wisconsin-Madison, MA, 1964; University of Iowa, PhD, 1981. **CAREER** Alabama A&M University, assistant professor of English, 1963-69; University of Texas at El Paso, instructor of English, 1970-75; Simpson College, asst professor of English, 1981-82; Tuskegee University, associate professor and department head, 1982-83; Winston-Salem State University, associate professor of English, 1984-90; Michigan Technological University, associate professor of drama, 1990-. **HONORS AND AWARDS** National Endowment for the Hu-

manities, Summer Institute, Duke, 1991, Summer Institute, UNC-Chapel Hill, 1989, Summer Seminar, Yale, 1985, Summer Institute, Iowa, 1974; Rockefeller Foundation Grant, 1976, 1977. **MEMBERSHIPS** Modern Language Association, 1982-; American Society for Theatre Research, 1984-; The Association for Theatre in Higher Educ, 1987-; World Congress of Theatre, 1989-; Delta Sigma Theta, 1958-; National Council of Teachers of English, 1963-83; Conference of College Composition and Communication, 1963-83. **SELECTED PUBLICATIONS** "The African-American Student: At Risk," CCC, Vol 43, No 2, May 1992; "Canada Lee: Black Actor in Non-Traditional Roles," JPC, Winter, 1991; "View From My Window," Obsidian II, p 41-42, Winter 1990; "White Dresses, Sweet Chariots," Southern Literary Journal, Spring 1990; White Grease Paint on Black Performers, New York: Peter Lang, 1988; "Rosamond Gilder: Influential Talisman for African-American Performers," Theatre Survey, 1996; "The Alabama A & M Thespians, 1944-1963: Triumph of the Human Spirit," The Drama Review, 1994; "Her Voice Was Ever Soft, Gentle and Low, An Excellent Thing in Ruby Dee," Journal of Popular Culture, 1994; "Love In Black and White: Dramas of Miscegenation on the Stage," Journal of Amer Drama and Theater, fall, 1998; "Morgan Freeman's Resistance and Non-Traditional Roles," Popular Culture Review, vol 9, no 2, 45-58, August, 1998. **CONTACT ADDRESS** Associate Professor of Drama, Michigan Technological University, 1400 Townsend Dr, Department of Humanities, Walker 327, Houghton, MI, 49931.

GILLAN, JENIFFER
PERSONAL Born 09/01/1967, NJ, m, 1995 **DISCIPLINE** ENGLISH **CAREER** ASST PROF, ENG, BENTLEY COL, 95-. **HONORS AND AWARDS** Phi Beta Kappa, Bentley Col res, teach grants. **MEMBERSHIPS** MLA, MultiEthnic Lit Soc US; Am Lit Asn, Phi Beta Kappa, Alpha Sigma Nu. **RESEARCH** Am Lit; realism; Native Am Lit; Ethnic Am Lit. **SELECTED PUBLICATIONS** Co-ed, Growing Up Ethnic in America, Penguin, 99; co-ed, Identity Lessons, Penguin, 99; co-ed, Unsettling America, Penguin, 94; auth, Reservation Home Movies: Sherman Alexie's Poetry, Am Lit; auth, Hazards of Osage Fortunes: Gender and the Rhetoric of Compensation in Federal Policy and AMerican Indian Fiction, Az Q. **CONTACT ADDRESS** Dept of English, Bentley Col, Waltham, MA, 02452.

GILLESPIE, DIANE F.
DISCIPLINE MODERN BRITISH LITERATURE **EDUCATION** Alberta, PhD. **CAREER** Prof, Washington State Univ. **SELECTED PUBLICATIONS** Auth, Julia Duckworth Stephen: Stories for Children, Essays for Adults, 87; The Sisters' Arts: The Writing and Painting of Virginia Woolf and Vanessa Bell, 88; The Multiple Muses of Virginia Woolf, 93; edition of Woolf's Roger Fry, 96 & edition of selected papers from 6th annual Virginia Woolf conf, 97. **CONTACT ADDRESS** Dept of English, Washington State Univ, 1 SE Stadium Way, PO Box 645020, Pullman, WA, 99164-5020. **EMAIL** gillespi@wsu.edu

GILLESPIE, MICHAEL PATRICK
DISCIPLINE ENGLISH **EDUCATION** Univ Ill, BS, 68; Univ Wis, MA, 76, PhD, 80. **CAREER** From asst prof to assoc prof, 80-92, prof, English, 92-, Marquette Univ; vis res schol, Humanities Res Ctr, Univ Tex, 81, 82. **HONORS AND AWARDS** Summer Fac Fel, Marquette Univ, 83, 86, 90, 92, 97; NEH Fel for Individual Study and Res, 84-85; Fel, William Andrews Clark Memorial Libr, 87; Fel, Coun for Int Studies, 94; recipient of numerous grants. **MEMBERSHIPS** MLA; James Joyce Found; Am Conf Irish Studies. **SELECTED PUBLICATIONS** Auth, Oscar Wilde: Life, Work, and Criticism, York Press Ltd, 90; co-ed, Joycean Occassions: Essays from the Milwaukee James Joyce Conference, Univ Del Press, 91; auth, The Picture of Dorian Gray: "What the World Thinks Me", Twayne Publ, 95; coauth, James Joyce A to Z: The Essential Reference to His Life and Work, Facts on File, 95; auth, Oscar Wilde and the Poetics of Ambiguity, Univ Press Fla, 96; author of numerous articles and book reviews. **CONTACT ADDRESS** Dept English, Marquette Univ, PO Box 1881, Milwaukee, WI, 53201-1881. **EMAIL** Michael.Gillespie@marquette.edu

GILLESPIE, PATTI P.
PERSONAL Born 01/26/1938, Bowling Green, KY, d **DISCIPLINE** THEATRE **EDUCATION** Wellesley Coll, 55-56; Univ Ky, BS, 58; Western Ky Univ, MA, spec ed, 62-64; Indiana Univ, PhD, 70. **CAREER** Prof, head, Dept Theatre, Univ South Carolina, 79-82; prof, chair, Dept Commun Arts & Theatre, prof, Dept Theatre, Univ Maryland, 89-; Fulbright Scholar, Dept English, Univ Botswana, 92-93. **HONORS AND AWARDS** ACT-NUCEA Natl Award, 81; Omicron Delta Kappa, 83;; Mitchell Distinguished Visiting Prof, Trinity Univ, 87; Goodman Scholar, Peace Coll, 90; Lilly Fel, Univ Maryland, 92-93. **MEMBERSHIPS** Natl Commun Assn, pres, 86, 87; Amer Soc Theatre Research; AAUP. **RESEARCH** Women in theatre and drama; theatre historiograph; American theatre. **SELECTED PUBLICATIONS** Coauth, Western Theatre: Revolution and Revival, 84; auth, "Aristotle and Arimneste ('Nicanor's Mother'): Theatre Studies and Feminism," in Feminist Critiques in Speech Communication, 93; auth, "Feminist Theory of Theatre: Revolution or Revival," in Theatre and Feminist Aesthetics, 95; coauth, The Enjoyment of Theatre, 4th ed, 96, 5th ed, in progress; auth, "The Dilemma of Wedlock: African Marriage in Plays and Life," The McNeese Review, vol 35, 97. **CONTACT ADDRESS** Dept of Theatre, Univ of Maryland, College Park, MD, 20742.

GILLETT, MARGARET
PERSONAL Wingham, Australia **DISCIPLINE** EDUCATION **EDUCATION** Univ Sydney, BA, 50, Dip Educ, 51; New South Wales Tchr Cert, 52; Russell Sage, Troy, NY, MA, 58; Columbia Univ, EdD, 61. **CAREER** Tchr, Eng & Hist, 51-53, educ off, 54-57, Australia; asst prof, educ, Dalhousie Univ, 61-62; assoc prof, educ, 64-67, ch, dept hist & philos educ, 66-68, prof, 67-82, Macdonald Prof Educ, 82-94, PROF EMER, MCGILL UNIV, 95-. **HONORS AND AWARDS** 75th Anniversary Medal, contrib feminism & higher educ Women, Russell Sage NY, 91; Women Distinction, YWCA, 94; LLD, Univ Sask, 88. **MEMBERSHIPS** Comp Int Educ Soc Can; Am Educ Studs Asn; Can Hist Educ Asn; Can Res Inst Advan Women; Can Women's Studs Asn. **SELECTED PUBLICATIONS** Auth, A History of Education: Thought and Practice, 66; auth, We Walked Very Warily: A History of Women at McGill, 81; auth, Dear Grace: A Romance of History, 86; coauth, A Fair Shake Revisited, 96. **CONTACT ADDRESS** Dept of Educ Studies, McGill Univ, Montreal, PQ, H3A 1Y2. **EMAIL** ingi@musich.mcgill.ca

GILLMOR, DONALD M.
DISCIPLINE MASS COMMUNICATION STUDIES **EDUCATION** Univ Minn, MA, PhD. **CAREER** Prof **SELECTED PUBLICATIONS** Auth, Power, Publicity and the Abuse of Libel Law, 92; co-auth, Mass Communication Law: Cases and Comment, 90; co-ed, Media Freedom and Accountability, 89. **CONTACT ADDRESS** Mass Communication Dept, Univ of Minnesota, Twin Cities, 111 Murphy Hall, 206 Church St SE, Minneapolis, MN, 55455. **EMAIL** gillm001@maroon.tc.umn.edu

GILLON, ADAM
PERSONAL Born 07/17/1921, Kovel, Poland, m, 1946, 2 children **DISCIPLINE** ENGLISH AND COMPARATIVE LITERATURE **EDUCATION** Hebrew Univ, Jerusalem, MA, 48; Columbia Univ, PhD, 54. **CAREER** Lectr English, Sch Higher Studies, Jerusalem, 44-45; lectr English lang and lit, Hascalla Col, prin and teacher English, Montefiore Tech High Sch, Tel-Aviv, 49-50; instr English, Univ Kans, 56-57; assoc prof, Acadia Univ, 58-59, prof and head dept, 59-61; prof English and World Lit, 61-80, EMER PROF ENGLISH, STATE UNIV NY, NEW PALTZ, 80-; PROF ENGLISH LIT, UNIV HAIFA, ISRAEL, 81-, Can Res Coun grant-in-aid, 61; Polish ser ed, Twayne's World Auth Ser, 64-, Hebrew ser, 65-; State Univ NY Res Found res grants-in-aid, 65, 66, 68, 70 and 72-73; Alfred Jurzykowski Found award, 67; US Govt res grant, Israel, 68-69; Joseph Fels Found res grant, Israel, 68-69; ed, Joseph Conrad Today. **MEMBERSHIPS** Joseph Conrad Soc Am (pres, 75-82); MLA; Am Comp Lit Asn; NCTE; Int Comp Lit Asn. **RESEARCH** English, American, Polish, Russian and Hebrew literatures; creative writing of fiction, poetry and drama comparative and world literature. **SELECTED PUBLICATIONS** Auth, The 'Affair in Marseilles,' Another Polish Novel about Conrad, Conradiana, Vol 0025, 93. **CONTACT ADDRESS** Dept of English and World Lit, State Univ of NY Col, New Paltz, NY, 12561.

GILMAN, ERNEST B.
PERSONAL Born 04/20/1946, Denver, CO, m, 1968, 2 children **DISCIPLINE** ENGLISH LITERATURE **EDUCATION** Columbia Univ, BA, 68, MA, 71, PhD(English), 76. **CAREER** Asst prof English, Univ Va, 75-81; ASST PROF ENGLISH, NY UNIV, 81-. **MEMBERSHIPS** MLA. **RESEARCH** Renaissance literature and the visual arts. **SELECTED PUBLICATIONS** Auth, Junius, Franciscus, the Literature of Classical-Art, Vol 1, the Painting of the Ancients, 'De Pictura Veterum,' Vol 2, A Lexicon of Artists and Their Works, 'Catalogus Architectorum,' Renaissance Quart; Ekphrasis--the Illusion of the Natural Sign, Mod Lang Quart, Vol 0054, 93; The Rule of Art, Literature and Painting in the Renaissance, Mod Philol, Vol 0091, 93; Portraiture, Col Eng, Vol 0056, 94; Topics of Our Time--20th-Century Issues in Learning and in Art, Col Eng, Vol 0056, 94; The Arts, Education, and Aesthetic Knowing, Col Eng, Vol 0056, 94. **CONTACT ADDRESS** Dept English, New York Univ, 19 University Pl, New York, NY, 10003-4556.

GILMAN, OWEN W.
PERSONAL Born 04/02/1947, Farmington, ME, m, 1977, 2 children **DISCIPLINE** ENGLISH **EDUCATION** Univ NC, Chapel Hill, PhD eng 79, MA 73; Bowdoin Col, ME, AB eng 69. **CAREER** St Joseph's Univ, prof eng 79-, dept ch 97. **HONORS AND AWARDS** Linback Awd Excell in Tchg. **MEMBERSHIPS** MLA; SAMLA. **RESEARCH** Vietnam war lit; southern lit; native writing in Am. **SELECTED PUBLICATIONS** Vietnam and the Southern Imagination, Univ Press MS, 92; America Rediscovered; Critical essays on lit and films of the Vietnam War, with Lorrie Smith, Garland, 90; Barry Hannah, in: Contem Fic Writers of the South, Greenwood Press, 93. **CONTACT ADDRESS** Dept of Eng, St Joseph's Univ, 5600 City Av, Philadelphia, PA, 19131. **EMAIL** mthrice@sju.edu

GINSBERG, ELAINE KANER
PERSONAL Born 02/29/1936, New York, NY, d, 3 children **DISCIPLINE** AMERICAN LITERATURE, WOMEN WRITERS **EDUCATION** Trinity Univ, BA, 57; Univ Okla, MA, 66, PhD(English), 71. **CAREER** Instr, Univ Okla, 67-68; asst prof, 68-75, assoc prof English, 75-84, chmn dept, 78-84; asst vp, W VA Univ, 84-89; fel, Am Antiquarian Soc, 76, 90; chair, Grad Studies Forum, SAtlantic Mod Lang Asn, 81-82; evaluator, Humanities Found of WVa, 81-; consultant Evaluator, North Cen Assn of Cols and Schools, 89. **MEMBERSHIPS** MLA; Am Studies Asn; pres Women's Caucus of Mod Lang Assn, 98. **RESEARCH** American fiction; British and American women writers; Colonial American literature. **SELECTED PUBLICATIONS** Auth, The female initiation theme in American literature, Studies in Am Fiction, 75; Style and identification in Common Sense, WVa Philol Papers, 77; contribr, American Literature, 1764-1789, Univ Wis Press, 77; American Women Writers: A Critical Reference Guide, Vols I, II & IV, Frederick Ungar Publ Co, 79-82; Toward the Second Decade, Greenwood Press, 81; contrib Anti-Feminism in the Acedemy, Fuoutlege, 96; co-ed, Virginia Woolf: Centennial Essays, Whitston Publ Co, Inc, 83. **CONTACT ADDRESS** Dept of English, West Virginia Univ, PO Box 6296, Morgantown, WV, 26506-6296. **EMAIL** eginsber@wvu.edu

GINSBERG, LESLEY
DISCIPLINE ENGLISH **EDUCATION** Calif at Berkeley, BA, 87; Stanford Univ, PhD, 97. **MEMBERSHIPS** Am Antiquarian Soc **RESEARCH** Childhood & love in Am lit **CONTACT ADDRESS** 2035 Bowdoin St, Palo Alto, CA, 94306-1211.

GINTER, DONALD EUGENE
PERSONAL Born 12/04/1932, Fresno, CA, m, 1954, 7 children **DISCIPLINE** ENGLISH HISTORY **EDUCATION** Stanford Univ, AB, 54, AM, 58; Univ Calif, Berkeley, PhD(hist), 64. **CAREER** From instr to assoc prof hist, Duke Univ, 63-70; ASSOC PROF HIST, CONCORDIA UNIV, 70-, Soc Sci Res Coun fac res grant, 67-68. **MEMBERSHIPS** AHA; Conf Brit Studies; fel Royal Hist Soc. **RESEARCH** Modern English history; 18th century origins of political parties; comparative socio-economic analysis of Yorkshire, Georgia and Massachusetts. **SELECTED PUBLICATIONS** Auth, Fox, Charles, James, Am Hist Rev, Vol 0098, 93; Before the Luddites--Custom, Community, and Machinery in the English Woolen Industry, 1776-1809, J Interdisciplinary Hist, Vol 0024, 93. **CONTACT ADDRESS** Dept of Hist, Concordia Univ, Montreal, Montreal, PQ, H3G 1M8.

GIRAL, ANGELA
PERSONAL Madrid, Spain, 2 children **DISCIPLINE** LIBRARY SCIENCE **EDUCATION** Univ Mich, MSLS, 58. **CAREER** Ref libn, Biblioteca Central, Universidad Nacional Autonoma Mexico, 55-56; book scout, Princeton Univ in Brazil, 64-65; sr cataloger, 62-64, 65-67, libn, Urban And Environ Studies Library, Sch Archit Urban Planning, 67-75, Princeton Univ; upper school libn, Escola Americana, Rio de Janeiro, Brazil, 64-65; chief libn, Frances Loeb Library, Harvard Univ Grad Sch Design, 75-82; acting head, Sci and Eng Div, Columbia Univ Libraries, 90-91; acting asst vp human resources in info sci, 94-95, dir, 82-, Avery Archit Fine Arts Library, Columbia Univ. **HONORS AND AWARDS** Elected rep, Columbia Univ Senate, 98-01; principal invest, grant, Guastavino/Collins Archive Cataloguing and Preservation Project, Natl Endow Humanities, Getty Grant Prog, Gladys Kieble Delmas Found, 93-96; elected, Standing Comm Section Art Libraries Intl Fed. Library Assns Insts, 93. **MEMBERSHIPS** Intl Confed Archit Museums, 98-01, sec gen, 93-98; bd mem, Intl Coun Archit Museums, 91-; Athenaeum of Philadelphia on "Philadelphia Architects and Buildings Project," Steering Comm, 98; Columbia Univ Res Libraries Group Digital Image Access Project, 93-94; New York State Archit Records Needs Assessment Project, 92-93. **RESEARCH** Information science; technological advances in the study and research of art history and architecture. **SELECTED PUBLICATIONS** Auth, foreword to My Father Who Is on Earth, 94; coauth, "The Virtual Museum Comes to Campus: Two Perspectives on the Museum Educational Site Licensing Project," Art Libraries Journ, 96; auth, foreword, The Old World Builds the New: the Guastavino Company and the Technology of the Catalan Vault, 1885-1962, 96; auth, Avery's Choice: Five Centuries of Great Architectural Books, A Hundred Years of an Architectural Library, 97; ed, ICAM8 Proceedings, 98. **CONTACT ADDRESS** Avery Library, Columbia Univ, 1172 Amsterdam Ave, MC-0301, New York, NY, 10027. **EMAIL** giral@columbia.edu

GIRGUS, SAM B.
DISCIPLINE FILM STUDIES, PSYCHOANALYSIS, IDEOLOGY, AND FILM, AMERICAN LITERATURE AND C **EDUCATION** Univ NMex, PhD. **CAREER** Instr, Vanderbilt Univ. **SELECTED PUBLICATIONS** Auth, The Films of Woody Allen; Desire and the Political Unconscious; The New Covenant; The Law of the Heart; ed, The American Self. **CONTACT ADDRESS** Vanderbilt Univ, Nashville, TN, 37203-1727.

GISH, NANCY K.
PERSONAL Born 09/28/1942, Circleville, OH **DISCIPLINE** ENGLISH AND WOMAN'S STUDIES **EDUCATION** PhD, Eng, Univ Michigan, 73. **CAREER** Univ Southern Maine, Dir woman's Studies Prog, 95-, Prof, 85, Assoc Prof, 82-85, Asst Prof, 80-82; Dir Womans Studies, 87-89, Acting Dir Women's Studies Prog, Univ So ME, 85-86; Asst Prof, Univ Penn, 73-79; Coordin Rhetoric Inst, Univ Penn, 78-79; Lect, Univ Michigan, 72-73; Instr, Wayne State Univ, 66-72. **HONORS AND AWARDS** Russell Chair in Edu and Philos, 92-94; Schol to Sch of Criticism and Theory, 87; Univ southern ME Summer Faculty Fellowship, 84; Convocation Schol, 82-83; NEH Fellow, 79-80. **MEMBERSHIPS** MLA; ME Women's Studies Consortium. **RESEARCH** Mod and Contemp Poetry; Ident and Subjectivity; Scot Lit and Cult; Women's Poetry; Cross-cultural poetic Experimentation. **SELECTED PUBLICATIONS** Hugh MacDiarmid: Man and Poet, Nat Poet Found, Orono, Univ Edinburgh P, Edinburgh, 92; The Waste Land: A Poem of Memory and Desire, Twyane, Boston, 88; Hugh MacDiarmid: The Man and His Work, Macmillan, London, 84; Time in the Poetry of T S Elliot, Macmillan, London, 81. **CONTACT ADDRESS** 53 Lawn Ave, Portland, ME, 04103. **EMAIL** ngish@usm.maine.edu

GISH, ROBERT F.
PERSONAL Born 04/01/1940, Albuquerque, NM, m, 1968, 3 children **DISCIPLINE** ENGLISH LITERATURE **EDUCATION** Univ New Mexico, PhD 72. **CAREER** Cal Poly, dir, prof, 91-; Univ N Iowa, prof, 67-91. **HONORS AND AWARDS** Erna Fergusson Dist Alum Awd. **MEMBERSHIPS** PEN/WEST; Authors Guild; WALA; WWA. **RESEARCH** American Literature; ethnic literature; American West. **SELECTED PUBLICATIONS** Auth, Dreams of Quivira: Stories in Search of the Golden West, Clear Light Pub, 97; auth, Beautiful Swift Fox: Erna Fergusson and the Southwest, Texas A&M Univ Press, 96; auth, Bad Boys and Black Sheep: Fateful Tales from the West, Texas A&M Univ, 96; auth, Beyond Bounds: Cross Cultural Essays on Anglo American Indian and Chicano Literature, Univ New Mexico Press, 96; auth, Granada: Paul Horgan and the Southwest, Texas A&M Univ Press, 95; auth, When Coyote Howls: A Lavaland Fable, U of NM Press, 94; auth, First Horses: Stories of the New West, U of Nevada Press, 93; auth, William Carlos Williams: The Short Fiction, GK Hall 89. **CONTACT ADDRESS** Dept of English, California Polytech State Univ, PO Box 947, San Luis Obispo, CA, 93406. **EMAIL** rgish@calpoly.edu

GISSENDANNER, JOHN M.
PERSONAL Born 08/13/1939, d **DISCIPLINE** ENGLISH **EDUCATION** San Francisco State Univ, San Francisco, CA, BA, 1971, MA, 1972; Univ of California, San Diego, PhD, 1982. **CAREER** California State University, San Diego, CA, assistant professor, 1972-75; Towson State University, Towson, MD, assistant professor, beginning 1975, associate professor, 1991-98, prof, 1998. **HONORS AND AWARDS** University Merit Award, Towson State University, 1989; San Diego Fellowship Award, University of California, San Diego, 1971-74; Ford Foundation Fellowship Award, University of California, San Diego, 1973-74. **MEMBERSHIPS** American Association of University Professors, 1972-; National Association for the Advancement of Colored People, 1982-; Middle-Atlantic Writers' Association, 1978-; National Collegiate Honors Council, 1980-; Maryland Writers Council, 1980-. **CONTACT ADDRESS** English Dept, Towson Univ, Towson, MD, 21204.

GIULIANO, MICHAEL J.
DISCIPLINE COMMUNICATION **EDUCATION** Northwestern Univ, PhD, 93. **CAREER** Instr, Tenn Temple Univ, 81-84; asst prof, Trinity Col, 84-91; asst prof, Westmont Col, 91-. **RESEARCH** Film criticism; mass commun; commun ethics; televangelism. **SELECTED PUBLICATIONS** Auth, Reel History, Nixon, Audience Analysis in Debate; Prima Facie: A Guide to Value Debate; Smashing the Stone: When Christians Say Right Things in Wrong Ways. **CONTACT ADDRESS** Dept of Commun, Westmont Col, 955 La Paz Rd', Santa Barbara, CA, 93108-1099.

GIVNER, JOAN
PERSONAL Manchester, England **DISCIPLINE** ENGLISH **EDUCATION** London Univ, BA, 58, PhD, 72; Univ St. Louis, MA, 63. **CAREER** High sch tchr, 59-61; lectr, Port Huron Jr Col, 61-65; lectr to assoc prof, 65-81, PROF ENGLISH, UNIV REGINA, 81-95. **HONORS AND AWARDS** Mary Ingraham Bunting Fel, Radcliffe Col, 79; Herbert M. Umbach Award, 79; Award Excellence Res, Univ Regina Alumni Asn, 92. **SELECTED PUBLICATIONS** Auth, Katherine Anne Porter: A Life, 82; auth, Tentacles of Unreason, 85; auth, Unfortunate Incidents, 88; auth, Scenes From Provincial Life, 91; auth, In the Garden of Henry James, 96. **CONTACT ADDRESS** English Dept, Univ of Regina, Regina, SK.

GLADISH, ROBERT WILLIS
PERSONAL Born 02/19/1931, Colchester, England, m, 1962, 4 children **DISCIPLINE** ENGLISH **EDUCATION** Univ Chicago, MA, 56, PhD(English), 64. **CAREER** Instr English, Tex A&M Univ, 56-58; from instr to assoc prof, Univ Ill, Chicago Circle, 60-71; head, Dept English, 71-77, dean, Col of Acad of The New Church, 77-; dean, Bryn Athyn Coll New Church 77-89; prof Emeritus, 96. **MEMBERSHIPS** MLA; AAUP. **RESEARCH** Nineteenth century English language and literature. **SELECTED PUBLICATIONS** Auth, Mrs Browning's contributions to the New York Independent, Bull NY Pub Libr, 1/67; Mrs Browning's A Curse for a Nation, Victorian Poetry, Autumn 69; Elizabeth Barrett and the Centurion, Baylor Browning Interests, 1/73. **CONTACT ADDRESS** Bryn Athyn Col of the New Church, PO Box 717, Bryn Athyn, PA, 19009-0717.

GLANCY, DIANE
PERSONAL Born 03/18/1941, Kansas City, MO, d, 2 children **DISCIPLINE** ENGLISH **EDUCATION** Univ Missouri, Columbia, BA, English lit, 64; Univ Iowa, writer's workshop, MFA, 88. **CAREER** Artist-in-residence, State Arts Coun Oklahoma, 80-86; assoc prof, English, Macalester Coll, 88-; Native American Inroads Mentor, The Loft, 97; Edelstein-Keller Minnesota Visiting Writer of Distinction, Univ Minn, 98. **HONORS AND AWARDS** Lannan Found Fellowship, Provincetown Art Center, MA, 95; Career Initiative Grant, The Loft, 96; Minnesota Humanities Commission Grant, 97; Playwriting Award, prose, Wordcraft Circle of Native Writers, 97; Sundance Native Amer Screenwriting Fellowship, Univ Calif Los Angeles, 98. **MEMBERSHIPS** Poetry Soc Am; Associated Writing Programs; Modern Lang Assn. **RESEARCH** Writing; Native American critical thought. **SELECTED PUBLICATIONS** Auth, The Only Piece of Furniture in the House, 96; auth, The West Pole, 97; auth, Pushing the Bear, a Novel of the Trail of Tears, 98; auth, Flutie, 98; auth, The Cold-and-Hunger Dance, 98. **CONTACT ADDRESS** 261 Brimhall, St. Paul, MN, 55105. **EMAIL** glancy@macalester.edu

GLASER, HOLLIS F.
PERSONAL Born 12/08/1959, Champaign, IL, s **DISCIPLINE** COMMUNICATION **EDUCATION** Washington Univ, BA, 82; Univ Ill, PhD(Organizational Commun), 94. **CAREER** From asst prof to assoc prof, commun, Univ Nebr-Omaha, 94-. **MEMBERSHIPS** Nat Commun Asn. **RESEARCH** Sustainable food systems; democratic groups. **SELECTED PUBLICATIONS** Coauth, Bureaucatic Discourse and the Goddess: Toward an Ecofeminist Critique and Rearticulation, J Org Change & Management, 92; coauth, An Interdisciplinary Approach to Engendering Jewish Religious History, Shofar: An Interdisciplinary J Judaic Studies 5, 95; auth, Structure and Struggle in Egalitarian Groups: Dimensions of Power Relations, Small Group Res 27, 96; auth, Focusing the Students on Three Speech Topics, The Speech Communication Teacher: Ideas, Research, and Strategies for Learning 12, 98; auth, Organizing against Sexual Violence, in Sexual Aggression: Key Research and Activism, Charles C. Thomas (forthcoming); auth, A Multi-cultural Public Speaking Final Examination, The Speech Communication Teacher: Ideas, Research, and Strategies for Learning (forthcoming). **CONTACT ADDRESS** Dept Commun, Univ Nebr-Omaha, 6001 Dodge St., Omaha, NE, 68182-0112. **EMAIL** Hollis@unomaha.edu

GLASSER, THEODORE L.
DISCIPLINE COMMUNICATIONS **EDUCATION** Univ IA, PhD, 79. **CAREER** Fac, Univ MN, 81-89; assoc dir Silha Ctr Study Media Ethics Law, Univ MN; Assoc prof, Stanford Univ, 90. **HONORS AND AWARDS** Hillier Krieghbaum Awd, Assoc Educ Jour Mass Comm, 87; sr Fulbright scholar, Israel, 92-93., Vpres/ch mass commun div, Int Comm Ass. **MEMBERSHIPS** Int Comm Ass; Assoc Ed Jour Mass Comm. **RESEARCH** Press practices and performance, with emphasis on questions of media responsibility and accountability. **SELECTED PUBLICATIONS** Auth, academic and professional publications, including Journalism & Mass Communication Quarterly, Journal of Communication, Journal of Broadcasting & Electronic Media, Critical Studies in Mass Communication, Policy Sciences, Communication and the Law, The Quill, and The Nieman Reports; co-ed, Public Opinion and the Communication of Consent, Guilford, 95. **CONTACT ADDRESS** Dept Commun, Stanford Univ, McClatchy Hall, Stanford, CA, 94305.

GLAVAC, CYNTHIA
DISCIPLINE ENGLISH LITERATURE **EDUCATION** Bowling Green State Univ, PhD, 92. **CAREER** Assoc prof. **RESEARCH** Women's and world literature. **SELECTED PUBLICATIONS** Auth, In the Fullness of Life: A Biography of Dorothy Kazel, OSU. **CONTACT ADDRESS** Dept of English, Ursuline Col, 2550 Lander Road, Pepper Pike, OH, 44124. **EMAIL** cglavac@ursuline.edu

GLAVIN, JOHN
DISCIPLINE ENGLISH LITERATURE **EDUCATION** Georgetown Univ, BA; Bryn Mawr Col, MA, PhD. **CAREER** Assoc prof. **RESEARCH** 19th century British literature by women; literary theory. **SELECTED PUBLICATIONS** Auth, Intimacies of Instruction, Univ New England, 95; Fay Weldon: Leader of the Frivolous Band, Univ New England; Pickwick on the wrong side of the door, Dickens Studies Annual, 93; Caught in the Act: or The Prosing of Juliet, Harvester, 91. **CONTACT ADDRESS** English Dept, Georgetown Univ, 37th and O St, Washington, DC, 20057.

GLAZIER, LYLE EDWARD
PERSONAL Born 05/08/1911, Leverett, MA, m, 3 children **DISCIPLINE** ENGLISH **EDUCATION** Middlebury Col, AB, 33; Bread Loaf Sch English, AM, 37; Harvard Univ, PhD, 50. **CAREER** Prin graded sch, Northfield, Mass, 34-35; instr & housemaster, Mt Hermon Sch, 35-37; instr English, Bates Col, 37-42 & Tufts Col, 42-44; teaching fel, Harvard Univ, 45-47; from asst prof to assoc prof English & chm Am studies, 52-63, prof English, 65-72, EMER PROF ENGLISH, STATE UNIV NY BUFFALO, 72- . **HONORS AND AWARDS** Am Coun Learned Soc fac fel, 51-52; Fulbright prof & chm, Dept Am Lit, Univ Istanbul, 61-63; Fulbright lectr, Hacettepe Univ, Ankara, 68-69, vis prof 70, 71; Fulbright prof Univ Madras, India, 70, 71; USLS vol expert in Am Lit, India, 71; vis prof, Sana'a Univ, Yemen Arab Repub, fall 80. **MEMBERSHIPS** MLA; Am Studies Asn. **RESEARCH** American fiction; poetry; Black literature. **SELECTED PUBLICATIONS** Auth, Orchard Park and Istanbul (poems), Big Mountain Press, Swallow, 65; You Too (poems), 69, The Dervishes (poems), 71 & VD (poems), 71, Istanbul Matbaasi; Decadence and Rebirth, Hacettepe Univ, 71; Stills from a Moving Picture, Paunch, 74; Two Continents (poems), Vt Coun Arts, 76; auth, Great Day Coming, Raaj Prakashan, 87; auth, Summer for Joey, 88. **CONTACT ADDRESS** RD 3, Bennington, VT, 05201.

GLECKNER, ROBERT F.
DISCIPLINE ENGLISH LITERATURE **EDUCATION** Johns Hopkins Univ, PhD, 54. **CAREER** English, Duke Univ. **RESEARCH** Romantics. **SELECTED PUBLICATIONS** Auth, Poetical Sketches, Johns Hopkins, 82; Blake and Spenser, Johns Hopkins, 85; co-ed, Critical Essays on Byron, GK Hall, 91. **CONTACT ADDRESS** Eng Dept, Duke Univ, Durham, NC, 27706.

GLENN, GEORGE
DISCIPLINE THEATRE HISTORY **EDUCATION** Univ IL, PhD. **CAREER** Prof, ch, grad prog, dept Theater, dir, Iowa Regents London prog, Univ Northern IA, 91/92. **MEMBERSHIPS** Pres, Mid-Am Theatre Conf. **SELECTED PUBLICATIONS** Publ in a variety of areas from nautical drama to the use of firearms on stage. **CONTACT ADDRESS** Univ Northern IA, Cedar Falls, IA, 50614. **EMAIL** susan.chilcott@uni.edu

GLISERMAN, MARTIN
DISCIPLINE LITERATURE AND PSYCHOLOGY, THE BODY **EDUCATION** Colby, BA; Ind, MA, PhD. **CAREER** Instr, Rutgers, State Univ NJ, Livingston; ed in ch, Am Imago; fac Ctr for Mod Psychoanalytic Stud. **RESEARCH** Psychoanalysis; body studies. **SELECTED PUBLICATIONS** Auth, Psychoanalysis, Language, and the Body of the Text. **CONTACT ADDRESS** Dept of Eng, Rutgers, State Univ NJ, Livingston Col, Murray Hall CAC, Piscataway, NJ, 28094. **EMAIL** gliserma@rci.rutgers.edu

GLOVER, ALBERT GOULD
PERSONAL Born 11/19/1942, Boston, MA, d, 3 children **DISCIPLINE** AMERICAN POETRY **EDUCATION** McGill Univ, BA, 64; State Univ NY Buffalo, PhD(English), 68. **CAREER** Instr, State Univ NY Buffalo, 66-67; asst prof, 68-72, assoc prof, 72-78, prof English, ST Lawrence Univ, 78-. **HONORS AND AWARDS** Frank and Anne P. Piskor Professorship, 82. **MEMBERSHIPS** AAUP **RESEARCH** Contemporary American poetry; Our titan fathers: John Coltrane, Charles Olson, Jackson Pollock, and David Smith. **SELECTED PUBLICATIONS** Auth, A Trio in G, Frontier Press, 71; ed, Charles Olson: Letters for Origin, 71 & co-ed, Charles Olson: Archeologist of Morning, 72, Jonathan Cape; auth, Paradise Valley, Bellevue Pres, 75; Next, Burn Bks, 81; The Dinner Guest and Other Poems, Glover Publ, 91; Relax Yr Face, Glover Publ, 98; ed, River of Dreams. American Poems from the St. Lawrence Valley, Glover Publ, 91. **CONTACT ADDRESS** English Dept, St Lawrence Univ, Canton, NY, 13617-1499. **EMAIL** aglo@ccmaillink.stlawu.edu

GLOWKA, ARTHUR WAYNE
PERSONAL Born 03/18/1952, Weimar, TX, m, 1992, 2 children **DISCIPLINE** MEDIEVAL LITERATURE, ENGLISH LINGUISTICS **EDUCATION** Univ Tex, BA, 73, MA, 75; Univ Del, PhD(English), 80. **CAREER** Prof English, Ga Col and State Univ, 80-. **MEMBERSHIPS** S Atlantic Mod Lang Asn; New Chaucer Soc; Am Dialect Soc. **RESEARCH** Prosody; history of the English language; neology; medieval literature. **SELECTED PUBLICATIONS** Auth, Yachtjacking, Boatnapping, or Getting Seajacked by Ship-jackers, Am Speech 62, 87; A Simplified Model of Language Variation and Change: A History of the Bot People, Glowka and Lance; A Guide to Chaucer's Meter, Univ Press of Am, 91; co-ed, Language Variation in North American English: Research and Teaching, MLA, 93; auth, The Poetics of Layamon's Brut, In: Text and Tradition in Layamon's Brut, Arthurian Studies 33, 94; Lawman and the Sabellian Heresy, Int J for the Semiotics of Law 8.24, 95; Layamon's Heathens and the Medieval Grapevine, In: Literacy and Orality in Early Middle English Literature, ScriptOralia 83, 96; coauth, Among the New Words, Am Speech 72, Fall and Winter 97. **CONTACT ADDRESS** Dept of English & Speech, Georgia Col, PO Box 490, Milledgeville, GA, 31061-0490. **EMAIL** wglowka@mail.gac.peachnet.edu

GNAROWSKI, MICHAEL
PERSONAL Born 09/27/1934, Shanghai, China **DISCIPLINE** ENGLISH LITERATURE **EDUCATION** McGill Univ, BA, 56; Univ Montreal, MA, 60; Univ Ottawa, PhD, 67. **CAREER** Lectr English, Univ Sherbrooke, 61-62; asst prof, Lakehead Univ, 62-65; res assoc, Royal Comn Bilingualism & Biculturalism, 64-66; asst & assoc prof, Sir George Williams Univ, 66-72; vis prof, Univ Ottawa, 70-72; exch scholar & prof Can lit, Univ Leningrad, 77; exch scholar & prof Can lit, Univ Warsaw, 89; prof English, 72-96, ADJ RES PROF ENGLISH, CARLETON UNIV, 96-; founding co-ed, YES: A Magazine of Poetry and Prose, 65-70; co-founder & mng partner, Tecumseh Press, 73-81; publ, 72-, vice pres 95- The Golden Dog Press. **SELECTED PUBLICATIONS** Auth, Postscript of St. James Street, 65; The Gentlemen Are also Lexicographers, 69; ed, The Rising Village of Oliver Goldsmith, 66; Three Early Poems From Lower Canada, 69; Joseph Quesnel: Selected Poems and Songs, 70; Archibald Lampman, 70; Selected Stories of Raymond Knister, 72; New Provinces, 76; Leonard Cohen: The Artist and His Critics, 76; Selected Poetry of Archibald Lampman, 90; co-ed, The Making of Modern Poetry in Canada, 67; introd & annotations, Memoirs of Montparnasse, 95; introd & notes, John Glassco: Selected Poems with Three Notes on the Poetic Process, 97; co-transl Quebec Is Killing Me, 95. **CONTACT ADDRESS** Dept of English, Carleton Univ, 1125 Colonel By Dr, Ottawa, ON, K1S 5B6.

GOCHBERG, DONALD S.
PERSONAL Born 08/19/1933, Boston, MA, m, 1956, 4 children **DISCIPLINE** ENGLISH, HUMANITIES **EDUCATION** Bates Col, AB, 55; Univ Md, MA, 60, PhD, 66. **CAREER** Instr English, Univ Md, 60-65; from Asst Prof to Assoc Prof, 65-77, Prof Humanities, 77-90, Prof English, Mich State Univ, 90-. **HONORS AND AWARDS** Distinguished Educator Award, Mich State Univ, 73. **MEMBERSHIPS** AAUP. **RESEARCH** Seventeenth century English literature; Shakespeare; world literature and thought. **SELECTED PUBLICATIONS** Ed, The Twentieth Century, Harcourt Brace Javanovich, 80; The Ancient World, Harcourt Brace, 88; gen ed, World Literature and Thought, 4 vols, Harcourt Brace, 97-. **CONTACT ADDRESS** Dept of English, Michigan State Univ, 201 Morrill Hall, East Lansing, MI, 48824-1036. **EMAIL** gochberg@pilot.msu.edu

GODARD, BARBARA J.
PERSONAL Born 12/24/1941, Toronto, ON, Canada **DISCIPLINE** CANADIAN LITERATURE **EDUCATION** Univ Toronto, BA, 64; Univ Montreal, MA, 67; Univ Paris VIII Maitrise, 69; Univ Bordeaux, Doctorat 3e cycle, 71. **CAREER** Lectr, Univ Montreal, 64-67; lectr, Univ Paris, 68-70; asst prof, 71-81, ASSOC PROF ENGLISH, YORK UNIV 81-. **HONORS AND AWARDS** Gabrielle Roy Prize, Asn Can & Que Lits 88; Award of Merit, Asn Can Stud, 95. **MEMBERSHIPS** MLA; PEN Int; Asn Can & Que Lits; Asn Can Univ Profs Eng; Can Comp Lit Asn; Asn Lit Transl; Can Semiotic Asn; Can Women's Stud Asn; Can Res Inst Advan Women. **SELECTED PUBLICATIONS** Auth, Talking About Ourselves: The Literary Productions of Native Women of Canada, 85; Bibliography of Feminist 87; Audrey Thomas: Her Life and Work, 89; ed, Gynocritics/Gynocritiques: Feminist Approaches to the Writing of Canadian and Quebec Women, 87; Collaboration in the Feminine: Writing on Women and Culture from Tessera, 94; co-ed, Intersexions: Issues of Race and Gender in Canadian Women's Writings, 95. **CONTACT ADDRESS** Dept of English, York Univ, 4700 Keele St, North York, ON, M3J 1P3.

GODDU, TERESA
DISCIPLINE AMERICAN LITERATURE AND CULTURE **EDUCATION** Univ Pa, PhD. **CAREER** Instr, Vanderbilt Univ. **RESEARCH** American literature; American cultural study; African American literature. **SELECTED PUBLICATIONS** Auth, Gothic America, Columbia UP, 97. **CONTACT ADDRESS** Vanderbilt Univ, Nashville, TN, 37203-1727.

GODFREY, MARY F.
DISCIPLINE MEDIEVAL SERMON LITERATURE, MEDIEVAL DRAMA, PSYCHOANALYTIC CRITICISM **EDUCATION** Princeton, PhD. **CAREER** Asst prof, Fordham Univ. **RESEARCH** Post-conquest literary cult in Engl. **SELECTED PUBLICATIONS** Auth, Beowulf and Judith: Thematizing Decapitation in Old English Poetry, Tex Stud Lit and Lang 35, 93; Sir Gawain and the Green Knight: The Severed Head and the Body Politic, Assays: Critical Approaches to Medieval and Renaissance Texts 8, 95. **CONTACT ADDRESS** Dept of Eng Lang and Lit, Fordham Univ, 113 W 60th St, New York, NY, 10023.

GODSHALK, WILLIAM LEIGH
PERSONAL Born 07/12/1937, Pen Argyl, PA, m, 1967, 2 children **DISCIPLINE** ENGLISH LITERATURE **EDUCATION** Ursinus Col, BA, 59; Harvard Univ, MA, 60 PhD(English), 64. **CAREER** Instr English, Tufts Univ, 60-61; asst prof, Col William and Mary, 64-67; assoc prof, 67-73, PROF ENGLISH, UNIV CINCINNATI, 73-, Shakespeare consult, Widener Mem Collection, Harvard Col Libr, 63; fel coop prog in humanities, Duke Univ and Univ NC, Chapel Hill, 65-66; Taft Mem Fund grants, 68-71; assoc ed, Kalki, James Branch Cabell Soc, 72- **MEMBERSHIPS** MLA; Mod Humanities Res Asn; Renaissance Soc Am. **RESEARCH** English Renaissance literature; Shakespeare; modern fiction. **SELECTED PUBLICATIONS** Auth, Sidney, Philip--Courtier Poet, Renaissance Quart, Vol 0045, 92; Recent Studies in Daniel, Samuel (1975-1990), Eng Lit Renaissance, Vol 0024, 94; The 'Great Gatsby' and Thomas, Edward 'Rain': Fitzgerald, F. Scott, Eng Lang Notes, Vol 0032, 95; Bottoms Hold-or-Cut-Bow-Strings (A 'Midsummer Nights Dream' Act-1-Scene-2-Line-106): Shakespeare, William, Notes and Queries, Vol 0042, 95; Dating 'Edward III': Shakespeare, William, Notes and Queries, Vol 0042, 95. **CONTACT ADDRESS** Dept of English, Univ of Cincinnati, Cincinnati, OH, 45221.

GOELLNICHT, DONALD
DISCIPLINE ENGLISH LITERATURE **EDUCATION** Queen's Univ, BA; McMaster Univ, MA, PhD. **RESEARCH** Asian American and Asian Canadian writing; North American minority writing; Romantic poetry and critical theory; contemporary critical theory. **SELECTED PUBLICATIONS** Auth, The Poet-Physician: Keats and Medical Science, 84. **CONTACT ADDRESS** English Dept, McMaster Univ, 1280 Main St W, Hamilton, ON, L8S 4L9.

GOERING, ELIZABETH
DISCIPLINE COMMUNICATION STUDIES **EDUCATION** Bethel Col, BA, 79; Wichita State Univ, MA, 84; Purdue Univ, PhD, 91. **CAREER** Assoc prof. **SELECTED PUBLICATIONS** Auth, pubs on organizational communication, small group communication, the relationship between culture and communication, and communication and conflict. **CONTACT ADDRESS** Dept of Communication, Indiana Univ-Purdue Univ, Indianapolis, 425 Univ Blvd, Indianapolis, IN, 46202. **EMAIL** bgoering@iupui.edu

GOGWILT, CHRISTOPHER
DISCIPLINE 19TH TO 20TH CENTURY LITERATURE AND CULTURE **EDUCATION** Princeton, PhD. **CAREER** Assoc prof, Fordham Univ. **RESEARCH** Postcolonial studies, critical theory. **SELECTED PUBLICATIONS** Auth, Lord Jim and the Invention of the West, Conradiana 27, 95; The Invention of the West: Joseph Conrad and the Double-Mapping of Europe and Empire, Stanford: Stanford UP, 95. **CONTACT ADDRESS** Dept of Eng Lang and Lit, Fordham Univ, 113 W 60th St, New York, NY, 10023.

GOIST, PARK DIXON
PERSONAL Born 09/07/1936, Seattle, WA, m, 1987, 1 child **DISCIPLINE** AMERICAN STUDIES, THEATRE **EDUCATION** Univ WA, BA, 58; Univ Rochester, PhD, 67. **CAREER** Instr hist, Colgate Univ, 63 & Kent State Univ, 63-64; from instr to asst prof, 66-71, assoc prof Am studies, Case Western Reserve Univ, 71, Nat Am Studies Fac, 77. **MEMBERSHIPS** Am Studies Asn; Gt Lakes Am Studies Asn. **RESEARCH** Am intellectual hist; Am urban and community studies; Am drama. **SELECTED PUBLICATIONS** Co-ed, The Urban Vision: Selected Interpretations of the Modern American Dity, Dorsey, 70; auth, City and community: the urban theory of Robert Park, Am Quart, spring 71; Seeing things whole: a consideration of Lewis Mumford, 11/72 & Patrick Geddes and the city, 1/74, J Am Inst Planners: Town, City and Community, 1890-1920's, Am Studies, spring 73; Community and self in the Midwest town: Dell's Moon-Calf, Mid America II, 75; From Main Street to State Street: Town, City and Community in America, Kennikat, 77; Oregon Trail Diary, Reserve, 4/81. **CONTACT ADDRESS** Dep Theatre Arts, Case Western Reserve Univ, 10900 Euclid Ave, Cleveland, OH, 44106-4901.

GOLD, ELLEN REID
PERSONAL Kansas City, KS **DISCIPLINE** POLITICAL RHETORIC, TELEVISION CRITICISM **EDUCATION** Univ MO, BA, 60; Univ KS, MA, 65; Univ IL, PhD, 73. **CAREER** Asst dean, Col Lib Arts & Sci, KS Univ, 73-75; asst prof commun studies, 75-81, assoc prof commun studies, Univ KS, 81. **MEMBERSHIPS** Natl Commun Asn; Cent States Commun Asn. **RESEARCH** Presidential campaign rhetoric, Ronald Reagan, television criticism **SELECTED PUBLICATIONS** Auth, What debate reveals: An analysis of the Miller-Bennet Campaign, 1974, Kans Speech J, fall 76; coauth, Research and teaching about women and communication, SCA Women's Caucus Bibliog, 6/78; auth, Political apologia: The ritual of self-defense, Commun Monogr, 11/78; coauth (with Judith S Trent), Campaigning for President in New Hampshire: 1980, Exetasis, 4/1/80; auth, Recorded sound collections: New materials to explore the past, Centr States Speech J, summer 80; The Grimke Sisters and the emergence of the Woman's Rights Movement, Southern Speech Commun J, summer 81; Gladstone and the development of Stump oratory, Cent States Speech J, summer 82; Ronald Regan and the Oral Tradition, Commun Studies, 88. **CONTACT ADDRESS** Dept of Commun, Univ Kansas, Lawrence, KS, 66045-0001.

GOLD, JOEL JAY
PERSONAL Born 12/19/1931, Brooklyn, NY, m, 1956, 3 children **DISCIPLINE** ENGLISH **EDUCATION** Univ MO, AB, 55; IN Univ, PhD, 62. **CAREER** From instr to assoc prof, 62-74, prof eng, Univ KS, 72, Vis assoc prof Eng, Univ IL, Urbana-Champaign, 70-71; Am Coun Learned Soc grant, 70; Am Philos Soc grant, 70; Newberry Libr fel, 78; Bibliog soc of Am fel, 86. **HONORS AND AWARDS** Amoco Distinguished Tchg Award, 80; Distinguished Alum Award, Col Lib arts and Sci, univ MO, 98. **MEMBERSHIPS** MLA; AAUP; Am Soc Eighteenth-Century Studies. **RESEARCH** Humor **SELECTED PUBLICATIONS** Ed, A voyage to Abyssinia, In: Yale Edition of the Works of Samuel Johnson, Yale Univ, 85; auth, Johnson's translation of Lobo, PMLA, 3/65; In defense of single-speech Hamilton, Studies in Burke & Hist Time, winter 68-69; The return to Bath: Catherine Morland to Anne Elliot, Genre, fall 76; John Wilkes and the writings of Pensioner Johnson, Studies in Burke & His Time, spring 77; Mr Serjeant Glynn: Radical politics in the courtroom, Harvard Libr Bull, 5/81; auth, The Wayward Professor, univ Press Kansas, 89; The Battle of the Shorthand Books 1635-1800, publ hist, 84; Essays in The Chronicle of Higher Education, 82. **CONTACT ADDRESS** Dept of Eng, Univ Kansas, Lawrence, KS, 66045-0001. **EMAIL** jjg@kuhub.cc.ukans.edu

GOLD, JOSEPH
PERSONAL Born 06/30/1933, London, England **DISCIPLINE** ENGLISH **EDUCATION** Univ Birmingham (Eng), BA, 55; Univ Wisconsin, PhD, 59. **CAREER** Fac mem, Univ Man, 60-70; prof Eng, 70-94, ch, 70-73, PROF EMER, UNIV WATERLOO, 94-. **MEMBERSHIPS** Can Asn Am Stud (exec mem, 64-73); Asn Bibliotherapy Can. **SELECTED PUBLICATIONS** Auth, Faulkner: A Study in Humanism from Metaphor to Discourse, 66; auth, The Stature of Dickens: A Centenary Bibliography, 71; auth, Charles Dickens: Radical Moralist, 72; auth, Read For Your Life, 90; ed, King of Beasts and Other Stories, 67; ed, In the Name of Language, 75. **CONTACT ADDRESS** Box 1332, Haileybury, ON, P0J 1K0.

GOLDBECK, JANNE
DISCIPLINE ENGLISH LITERATURE **EDUCATION** Univ Okla, PhD, 72. **CAREER** Prof. **RESEARCH** Medieval literature; gender studies; 1930s in American film and autobiography. **SELECTED PUBLICATIONS** Auth, All the Ways. **CONTACT ADDRESS** Dept of English and Philosophy, Idaho State Univ, Pocatello, ID, 83209. **EMAIL** goldh@isu.edu

GOLDEN, ARTHUR
PERSONAL Born 08/22/1924, New York, NY, 1 child **DISCIPLINE** ENGLISH, AMERICAN LITERATURE **EDUCATION** NY Univ, BA, 47, PhD(English & Am lit), 62; Columbia Univ, MA, 48. **CAREER** Instr English, NY Univ, 59-63; from instr to assoc prof, 63-72, PROF ENGLISH, CITY COL NEW YORK, 73-, gen fac comt res and publ grant, 67., Nat Endowment Humanities grant, 70-71. **MEMBERSHIPS** MLA; Bibliog Soc Am; PEN; Int Asn Univ Prof English. **RESEARCH** American literature, especially 19th century and Walt Whitman. **SELECTED PUBLICATIONS** Auth, Allen, Gay, Wilson, 1903-1995, Walt Whitman Quart Rev, Vol 0013, 95; Whitman 'Repondez', a 'Ronded Catalogue Divine Complete', and Emerson, Etudes Anglaises, Vol 0048, 95. **CONTACT ADDRESS** Dept of English, City Col, CUNY, New York, NY, 10031.

GOLDEN, BRUCE
PERSONAL Born 06/18/1933, Rochester, NY, m, 1969 **DISCIPLINE** ENGLISH AND COMPARATIVE LITERATURE **EDUCATION** Northwestern Univ, BS, 55; Columbia Univ, AM, 58, PhD(English & comp lit), 66. **CAREER** Mem acad fac humanities, Juilliard Sch Music, 62-65; from instr to assoc prof English, 65-77, PROF ENGLISH, CALIF STATE COL, SAN BERNARDINO, 77-, Nat Endowment Humanities younger humanist fel, 71-72. **MEMBERSHIPS** MLA; Renaissance Soc Am; Malon Soc. **RESEARCH** Renaissance dramatic literature; literature and the other arts; popular culture. **SELECTED PUBLICATIONS** Auth, Mr-Mojo Risin--Morrison, Jim, the Last Holy Fool, Notes, Vol 0049, 93; Slowhand--The Life and Music of Clapton, Eric, Notes, Vol 0049, 93. **CONTACT ADDRESS** Dept of English, California State Univ, San Bernardino, 5500 University Pky, San Bernardino, CA, 92407-7500.

GOLDENBERG, ROBERT
PERSONAL Born 10/21/1942, Brooklyn, NY, m, 1986, 3 children **DISCIPLINE** ENGLISH LITERATURE **EDUCATION** Cornell Univ, BA, 63; Jewish Theol Seminary Am, MHL, 66; Brown Univ, PhD, 74. **CAREER** Eng Dept, SUNY Stony Brook **SELECTED PUBLICATIONS** Auth, Did the Amoraim See Christianity as Something New?, Sheffield Acad, 94; Patriarchat, Gruyter, 96; Eleazar ben Pedat; Shim'on ben Laqish; Talmud. **CONTACT ADDRESS** English Dept, SUNY Stony Brook, Stony Brook, NY, 11794.

GOLDFARB, JEFFREY C.
DISCIPLINE LIBERAL STUDIES **EDUCATION** Univ Chicago, PhD, 77. **CAREER** Prof, Eugene Lang Col. **RESEARCH** Soc of cult; comp polit; phenomenological soc; relationship between cult, polit, and democratic institutions. **SELECTED PUBLICATIONS** Auth, After the Fall: The Pursuit of Democracy in Central Europe, 92; The Cynical Society: The Culture of Politics and the Politics of Culture in American

Life, 91; Beyond Glasnost: The Post-Totalitarian Mind, 89; On Cultural Freedom: An Exploration of Public Life in Poland and America, 82; The Persistence of Freedom: The Sociological Implications of Polish Student Theater, 80. **CONTACT ADDRESS** Eugene Lang Col, New Sch for Social Research, 66 West 12th St, New York, NY, 10011.

GOLDGAR, BERTRAND ALVIN
PERSONAL Born 11/17/1927, Macon, GA, m, 1950, 2 children **DISCIPLINE** ENGLISH LITERATURE **EDUCATION** Vanderbilt Univ, BA, 48, MA, 49; Princeton Univ, MA, 57, PhD, 58. **CAREER** Instr English, Clemson Col, 48-50, asst prof, 51-52; from instr to assoc prof, 57-71, prof English, 71-80, JOHN N BERGSTROM PROF HUMANITIES, LAWRENCE UNIV, 80-, Nat Endowment for Humanities fel, 80-81. **MEMBERSHIPS** MLA; Am Soc 18th Century Studies. **RESEARCH** Eighteenth century English literature; Fielding's journalism. **SELECTED PUBLICATIONS** Auth, The Champion and the Chapter on Hats in 'Jonathan Wild,' Philol Quart, Vol 0072, 93; Reading Swift--Papers from the 2nd Munster Symposium on Swift, Jonathan, Scriblerian and the Kit-Cats, Vol 0027, 94; Telling People What to Think--Early 18th-Century Periodicals from the Review to the Rambler, Scriblerian and the Kit-Cats, Vol 0028, 95; The Patriot Opposition to Walpole--Politics, Poetry, and National Myth, 1725-1742, Mod Philol, Vol 0094, 97. **CONTACT ADDRESS** Dept of English, Lawrence Univ, Appleton, WI, 54912.

GOLDIN, FREDERICK
PERSONAL Born 11/03/1930, Brooklyn, NY, m, 3 children **DISCIPLINE** MEDIEVAL AND COMPARATIVE LITERATURE **EDUCATION** City Col New York, BA, 52; Columbia Univ, MA, 54, PhD(comp lit), 64. **CAREER** Instr English, Brooklyn Col, 60-61; from instr to asst prof, Rutgers Univ, 61-67; from asst prof to assoc prof English and comp lit, 67-76, Prof English and Comp Lit, City Col New York, 77-, PROF GER, FRENCH, ENGLISH AND COMP LIT, GRAD SCH, CITY UNIV NY, 77-, Fulbright sr res fel, Vienna, 68-69; Am Coun Learned Soc grant, 68-69; Fulbright sr res scholar, Vienna, 75-76; Am Coun Learned Soc travel grant, 78 and fel, 80-81; City Univ NY Res Found grant, 81. **MEMBERSHIPS** Soc Rencesvals; MLA; Mediaeval Acad Am; Int Arthurian Soc; Int Courtly Lit Soc. **RESEARCH** Medieval courtly literature; medieval and Renaissance epic; medieval and Renaissance drama **SELECTED PUBLICATIONS** Auth, The Age-de-Parage--Essay on Poetics in 13th-Century Occitania, Romance Philol, Vol 0047, 94. **CONTACT ADDRESS** Dept of Comp Lit Grad Sch, City Univ, NY 33 W 42nd St, New York, NY, 10036.

GOLDZWIG, STEVEN R.
PERSONAL Born 10/13/1950, San Antonio, TX, m, 1979, 2 children **DISCIPLINE** COMMUNICATION STUDIES **EDUCATION** Purdue Univ, PhD, 85. **CAREER** Asst prof, Univ of Southern Calif, 85-87; from asst prof to assoc prof, Marquette Univ, 87- . **HONORS AND AWARDS** Co-Recipient, M. Hochmut Nichols Award for Outstanding Scholarship in Public Address, 95; Outstanding article of the year, 96. **MEMBERSHIPS** Nat Commun Asn; Central States Commun Asn. **RESEARCH** Polit commun; Legal commun; Contemp residency & civil rights. **SELECTED PUBLICATIONS** Auth, Multiculturalism, Rhetoric, and the 21st Century, Southern Commun Jour, 64, 98; coauth, Constructing a Postmodernist Ethic: The Feminist Quest for a New Politics, Differences that Make a Difference: Examining the Assumptions in Gender Reseach, ed H. Sterk and L. Turner, 94; Crisis at Little Rock: Eisenhower, History, and Mediated Political Realities, Eisenhower's War of Words: Rhetoric and Leadership, ed M.J. Medhurst, 94. Idealism and Pragmatism in American Foreign Policy Rhetoric: The Case of John F. Kennedy and Vietnam, Presidential Studies Quart, 24, 94; In a Perilous Hour: The Public Address of John F. Kennedy, 95; Legitimating Liberal Credentials for the Presidency: John F. Kennedy and The Strategy of Peace, Southern Commun Jour, 60, 95; A Relational Approach to Moral Decision-Making: The Majority Opinion in Planned Parenthood v. Casey, Quart Jour of Speech, 81, 95; Post-Assassination Newspaper Editorial Eulogies: Analysis and Assessment, Western Jour of Commun, 59, 95; Undue Burdens and Abortion Decision-Making: Justice Sandra Day O'Connor and Judicial Decision-Making, Women and Politics, 16 (3), 96; Women's Reality and the Untold Story: Designing Women and the Revisioning of the Thomas/Hill Hearings, Outsiders Looking In: A Communication Perspective on the Hill/Thomas Hearings, ed P. Siegel, 96. **CONTACT ADDRESS** Dept of Communication Studies, Marquette Univ, PO Box 1881, Milwaukee, WI, 53201-1881. **EMAIL** goldzwigs@ums.csd.mu.edu

GOLIAN, LINDA MARIE
PERSONAL Born 03/27/1962, Woodbridge, NJ, m, 1988 **DISCIPLINE** LIBRARY **EDUCATION** Univ Miami, BA, 86; Florida St Univ, MA, 88; Florida Atlantic Univ, PhD, 98. **CAREER** Volunteer, 94-96, Family Literacy Specialist; serials consul, 96-97, SIRS, FL; prog specialist, 94-96, Marriott Stafford Court; adj instr, 94-, Univ S Florida; adj instr, 93-97, Florida Atlantic Univ. **RESEARCH** Mentoring, thinking style, learning styles, libr instruction, library admin. **CONTACT ADDRESS** 19245 Pine Run Lane, Ft Myers, FL, 33912. **EMAIL** lgolian@fgcu.edu

GOLLIN, RICHARD M.
DISCIPLINE ENGLISH **EDUCATION** Univ MN, PhD. **CAREER** Prof emer; taught at, Univ MN & Colgate Univ. **HONORS AND AWARDS** Fulbright scholar, Oxford Univ; Fore fel; Wilson fel; NYSCA, ACLS, Rockefeller & NEH grants. **RESEARCH** Structure and meaning of narrative films, and of other kinds as temporal sequences. **SELECTED PUBLICATIONS** Coauth, A Viewer's Guide to Film Arts, Artifices, and Issues: AH Clough: A Descriptive Catalogue; annotated re-ed of Clough's poetry; articles on, Arnold, Clough, Kipling, GB Shaw, Wallace Stevens, modern poetry & film criticism; contribur to New CBEL. **CONTACT ADDRESS** Dept of Eng, Univ of Rochester, 601 Elmwood Ave, Ste. 656, Rochester, NY, 14642. **EMAIL** ffff@db1.cc.rochester.edu

GOLLIN, RITA K.
PERSONAL Born 01/22/1928, New York, NY, m, 1950, 3 children **DISCIPLINE** ENGLISH LITERATURE **EDUCATION** Queens Col, NY, BA, 49; Univ Minn, MA, 50, PhD, 61. **CAREER** Asst, Univ Minn, 49-53; lectr English, univ sch, Univ Rochester, 55-62 & 63-64, part-time instr, 60-62, part-time asst prof, 63-64, asst prof, 64-67; from asst prof to assoc prof, 67-75, PROF ENGLISH, STATE UNIV NY COL, GENESEO, 75-95, DISTINGUISHED PROF ENGLISH, 95-, State Univ NY Res Found res grant, 68, 77, 80, 86, 87, 88, 91 & 98; fac exchange scholar, State Univ NY. **HONORS AND AWARDS** Phi Beta Kappa; AAUW fel; NEH fel, 84 & 88; Huntington Libr fel, 88; House of Seven Gables Hawthorne Award, 84; UUP travel grant, 98. **MEMBERSHIPS** MLA; Northeast Mod Lang Asn (vpres, 77-78, pres, 78-79); Nathaniel Hawthorne Soc (pres, 79-82); Am Women Writers. **RESEARCH** Nineteenth century American fiction, especially Hawthorne and Melville; 20th century American fiction; writers and shakers. **SELECTED PUBLICATIONS** Co-auth, Justice in an earlier treatment of the Billy Budd Theme, Am Lit, 57; co-auth, Exiles in India: An early Kipling variant, Notes and Queries, 65; Pierre's metamorphoses of Dante's Inferno, Am Lit, 68; Ed, A Little Journey in the World, 69 & Northwood: Or Life, North and South, 70, Johnson Reprint; The automobiles of The Great Gatsby, Studies in the Twentieth Century, 70; Modes of travel in Tender is the Night, Studies in the Twentieth Century, 71; contribr, Sarah Josepha Hale, Northwood, intro & bibliogr, Johnson, 72; auth, Dream-work in The Blithedale Romance, Emerson Soc Quart, 73; Little Souls Who Thirst for Fight in The Red Badge of Courage, Ariz Quart, 74; Understanding fathers in American Jewish fiction, Centennial Rev, 74; The forbidden fruit of Typee, Mod Lang Studies, 75; American Literature and An Introduction to Research and Bibliography in American Civilization, Everett Edwards, 75; auth, Painting and character in The Marble Faun, Emerson Soc Quart, 75; The Intelligence Offices of Hawthorne and Melville, Am Transcendental Quart, 75; The place of Walden in The Undiscovered Country, Thoreau Soc Bull, 76; The Quondam Sailor and Melville's Omoo, Am Lit, 76; Hawthorne on perception, lucubration , and reverie, Nathaniel Hawthorne J, 78; Hawthorne: The writer as dreamer, Studies in Am Renaissance, 78; Huckleberry Finn and The Time of the Evasion, Mod Lang Studies, 79; Nathaniel Hawthorne and the Truth of Dreams, La State Univ Press, 79; Nathaniel Hawthorne and the Truth of Dreams, La State Univ Press, 79; Arlin Turner, 1909-1980, Hawthorne Soc Newsletter, 80; Hester, Hetty, and the two Arthurs, Nathaniel Hawthorne J, 80; Getting a taste for pictures: Hawthorne at the Manchester Arts Exhibit, Nathaniel Hawthorne J, 80; Mathew Brady Photographs of Nathaniel Hawthorne, Studies in Am Renaissance, 82; Hawthorne's Golden Dora, Studies in Am Renaissance, 82; Louisa May Alcott's Hawthorne, Essex Inst Hist Collection, 82; co-ed, Hawthorne in Concord, Essex Inst Hist Collection Special Issue, 82; Malamud's Dubin and the Morality of Desire, PLL, 82; Standing on the Greensward: The Veiled Correspondence of Nathaniel Hawthorne and Henry Wadsworth Longfellow, in Papers Presented at the Longfellow Commemorative Conference, April 1-3, 1982, Longfellow Nat Hist Park, 82; Portraits of Nathaniel Hawthorne: An Iconography, Northern Ill Univ Press, 83; Twentieth-Century American Fiction: Men and Women Writers, in Reconstructing American Literature, Feminist Press, 83; Hawthorne contemplates the Shakers: 1831-1851, Nathaniel Hawthorne JOur, 84; A Hawthornean in Japan, Hawthorne Soc Newsletter, 84; On atropine poisoning in The Scarlet Letter, New England J Medicine, 84; Some reminiscences of Japan, Jimyukadori, 85; Hawthorne and the anxiety of aesthetic response, Centennial Rev, 85; co-ed, Thoreau Inter Alia: Essays in Honor of Walter Harding, SUNY Geneseo, 85; Teaching Women in American Literature, in Towards Equitable Education for Women and Men, 86; Nathaniel Hawthorne, in American Literary Scholarship 1982, 1983, 1984, 1985, Duke Univ Press, 84, 85, 86, 87; Hawthorne on the Isles of Shoals, Nathaniel Hawthorne Rev, 87; Teaching women, Geneseo Compass, Fac Forum, 4/87; Annie Field's Nathaniel Hawthorne: Grand as Ever, Postscript, 87; Legacy Profile: Annie Adams Fields (1834-1915), Legacy, 87; Again a Literary Man: Vocation and the Scarlet Letter, in Essays on the Scarlet Letter, G K Hall, 88; Subordinated Power: Mrs and Mr James T Fields, in Patrons and Protegees, Rutgers Univ Press, 88; Living in a world without Dickens, Huntington Libr Quart, 89; Pegasus in the Pound: The Editor, the author, their wives, and the Atlantic Monthly, Essex Inst Hist Collections, 89; First and last words on The Scarlet Letter, in From Cover to Cover: The Romances of Nathaniel Hawthorne, Essex Inst Hist Collection, 91; Nathaniel Hawthorne: The flesh and the spirit, or Gratifying Your Coarsest Animal Needs, Studies in the Novel, 91; co-auth, Prophetic Pictures: Hawthorne's Knowledge and Uses of the Visual Arts, Greenwood Press, 91; guest ed, Hawthorne in the Nineties, Studies in the Novel, special ed, 91; Ethan Brand's Homecomings, in New Essays on Hawthorne's Shorts Stories, Cambridge Univ Press, 93; Nathaniel Hawthorne, in Heath Anthology of American Literature, D C Heath, 90, 2nd ed, 93; Annie Adams Fields and Nathaniel Hawthorne, in American National Biography, Oxford Univ Press, forthcoming; Nathaniel Hawthorne and Annie Fields, in Scribbling Women: Engendering and Expanding the Hawthorne Tradition, Univ Mass Press, forthcoming. **CONTACT ADDRESS** Dept of English, State Univ of NY Col, 1 College Cir, Geneseo, NY, 14454-1401. **EMAIL** gollin@aol.com

GOLUMBIA, DAVID
PERSONAL Born 06/22/1963, Detroit, MI **DISCIPLINE** ENGLISH LANGUAGE AND LITERATURE **EDUCATION** Oberlin Col, BA, 95; Univ of Pennsylvania, PhD, 98. **CAREER** Independent scholar **MEMBERSHIPS** Modern Lang Assoc; Amer Phil Assoc; Linguistic Soc of Amer. **RESEARCH** Cultural studies; deconstruction; analytic philosophy (contemporary); linguistics (contemporary) as subjects for cultural studies; print and other media history **SELECTED PUBLICATIONS** Auth, Toward an Ethics of Cultural Acts: The Jamesian Dialectic in Broken Wings, the Henry James Review, 94; Black and White World: Race, Ideology, and Utopia in Triton and Star Trek, Cultural Critique 32, 95-96; Resisting the World: Philip K. Dick, Cultural Studies, and Metaphysical Realism, Science Fiction Studies 23:1, 96; Hypercapital, Postmodern Culture 7:1, 96; Rethinking Philosophy in the Third Wave of Feminism, Hypatia: A Journal of Feminist Philosophy, 97; Quines Ambivalence, Cultural Critique 38, 97-98; Feminism and Mental Representation: Analytic Philosophy, Cultural Studies, and Narrow Content, Is Feminist Philsophy Philosophy?, 99. **CONTACT ADDRESS** 502 Seminary Row, Apt 62, New York, NY, 10027. **EMAIL** dgolumbi@sas.uenn.edu

GOMEZ-MORIANA, ANTONIO
PERSONAL Born 09/13/1936, Malaga, Spain **DISCIPLINE** INTERDISCPLINARY STUDIES **EDUCATION** Univ Pontificia de Salamanca, Lic, 58, PhD, 62; Ludwig-Maximilians Univ (Munich, Ger), MA, 64, PhD, 65. **CAREER** Tchr, Sanlucar de Barrameda (Spain), 58-59; lectr, Spanisches Kulturinstitut (Munich, Ger), 62-65; Ruhr-Univ (Bochum, Ger), 65-71; prof, 71-74, ch Span, Univ Ottawa, 73-74, ; dir, dept d'etudes anciennes et mod, 74-78, prof, 74-96, prog de litt comp, 87-89, dir-fond, dep de litt comp, Univ Montreal, 89-90; ch Span & Latin Am stud, 92-94, PROF INTERDISCIPLINARY STUD, SIMON FRASER UNIV, 97-. **MEMBERSHIPS** Royal Soc Can; Acad Hum & Soc Sci; Inst Int Sociocritique; Asn Can Hispanistas; Can Semiotic Asn. **SELECTED PUBLICATIONS** Auth, uber den Sinn von 'Congoja' bei Unamuno, 65; auth, Derecha de resistencia y tiranicido, Estudio de una tematica en las 'comedias' de Lope de Vega, 68; auth, Die sprach- und literarhistorische Entwicklung des Spanischen, 73; auth, La subversion du discours rituel, 85; auth, Discourse Analysis as Sociocriticism, 93; coauth, Lecture ideologieue du Lazarillo de Tormes, 84. **CONTACT ADDRESS** Simon Fraser Univ, Burnaby, BC, V5A 1S6.

GONZALEZ, ALEXANDER G.
PERSONAL Born 05/29/1952, United Kingdom, m, 1998 **DISCIPLINE** ENGLISH **EDUCATION** Queens Col, CUNY, BA (magna cum laude), 76; Univ of Ore, MA, 78, PhD, 82. **CAREER** Half-time tutor of English Composition, 73-76, team-teacher, English Composition, Queens Col, 75-76; grad tchg fel, 77-80 & 81-82; dir, writing lab, 78-79, instr, Univ of Ore, 82-83; vis lectr, Univ of Calif at Santa Barbara, 80-81; asst prof of english, Ohio State Univ, 83-88; ASST PROF OF ENGLISH, 88-91, ASSOC PROF OF ENGLISH, 91-94; PROF OF ENGLISH, SUNY COL AT CORTLAND, 94-; distinguished scholar in residence, Pa State Univ, summer 91. **MEMBERSHIPS** MLA; South Atlantic MLA; Nat Coun of Teachers of English; Confr on Col Composition and Commun; James Joyce Found; Am Confr for Irish Studies; Irish-Am Cultural Inst; Int Asn for the Study of Anglo-Irish Lit. **RESEARCH** Irish Lit. **SELECTED PUBLICATIONS** Auth, Darrell Figgis: A Study of His Novels, Moder Irish Lit Monographs Series, 92; Short Stories from the Irish Renaissance: An Anthology, Whitston, 93; Assessing the Achievement of J.M. Synge, Greenwood, 96; Peadar O'Donnell: A Reader's Guide, Dufour, 97; Modern Irish Writers" A Bio-Critical Sourcebook, Greenwood, Aldwych Press, 97; Contemporary Irish Women Poets: Some Male Perspectives, forthcoming. **CONTACT ADDRESS** Dept of English, SUNY, Cortland Col, Box 2000, Cortland, NY, 13045. **EMAIL** gonzalez@snycorva.cortland.edu

GOOCH, BRYAN N.S.
PERSONAL Born 12/31/1937, Vancouver, BC, Canada **DISCIPLINE** ENGLISH/MUSIC **EDUCATION** Royal Conserv Music (Toronto), ARCT, 57; Trinity Col Music, (London), LTCL, 59, FTCL, 61; Univ BC, BA, 59, MA, 62; Univ London, PhD, 68. **CAREER** Instr to assoc prof, 64-86, asst dean, 72-75, PROF ENGLISH, UNIV VICTORIA, 86-; fac mem, Victoria Conserv Music, 67-70; res fel, Craigdarroch Col, 68-69; Master, Lansdowne Col, 69-72; vis prof, Univ BC, 94-96; fac mem,

Green Col, Univ BC, 95-99. **HONORS AND AWARDS** IODE Second World War mem post-grad schol, 62-64; Can Coun res grants, 73, 74, 75-78, leave fel, 76-77; SSHRCC grants, 78-80, 80-81, 82-88. **MEMBERSHIPS** Am Musicol Soc; Renaissance Soc Am; Shakespeare Asn Am; Can Asn Music Libr; life fel, Royal Commonwealth Soc. **SELECTED PUBLICATIONS** Co-ed, Poetry is for People; co-ed, Musical Settings of Late Victorian and Modern British Literature: A Catalogue; co-ed, Musical Settings of Early and Mid-Victorian Literature: A Catalogue; co-ed, Musical Settings of British Romantic Literature: A Catalogue; co-ed, A Shakespeare Music Catalogue; co-ed, The Emergence of the Muse: Major Canadian Poets from Crawford to Pratt; contribur, Encyclopedia of Music in Canada. **CONTACT ADDRESS** Univ of Victoria, PO Box 3070, Victoria, BC, V8W 3W1.

GOODALL, H. L. (BUD), JR.
PERSONAL Born 09/08/1952, Martinsburg, WV, m, 1984, 1 child **DISCIPLINE** COMMUNICATION **EDUCATION** Shepherd Col, BA, 73; Univ of NC at Chapel Hill, MA, 74; Pa State Univ, PhD, 80. **CAREER** Asst prof, Prog in Commun, 80-84, assoc prof and chair, Dept of Commun Arts, Univ of Ala, 84-89; assoc prof and dir of grad stud, Univ of Utah, 89-91; prof and coord, Prog in Speech and Commun Studies, Clemson Univ, 91-95; Prof and Head, Dept of Commun, Univ NC Greensboro, 95-. **HONORS AND AWARDS** Gerald M. Phillips Mentoring Award, Am Commun Asn, 95; Texty for Outstanding Textbook in Ed, Commun, Visual and Performing Arts, Textbook and Acad Authors Asn, 94; Article of the Year, Eastern Commun Asn, 84. **MEMBERSHIPS** Nat Commun Asn; Southern States Commun Asn. **RESEARCH** Communication ethnography; organizational studies; cultural studies. **SELECTED PUBLICATIONS** Coauth, Organizational Communication: Balancing Creativity and Constraint, Second Revised Edition, St Martin's Press, 97; The Death of Discourse in Our Own Chatroom: Sextext, Skillful Discussion, and Virtual Communities, The Death of Discourse in a Wired World, Sage, 98; Representation, Interpretation, and Performance: Opening the Text of Casing a Promised Land, Text and Performance Quart, 97; auth, Divine Signs: Connecting Spirit and Community, Southern Ill Univ Press, 96; Casing a Promised Land: Expanded Editions, Southern Ill Univ Press, 94; Transforming Communication Studies Through Ethnography, Commun: Views From the Helm For the Twenty-First Century, Allyn & Bacon, 97. **CONTACT ADDRESS** Communication Dept, Univ of N. Carolina, PO Box 26170, Greensboro, NC, 27402-6170. **EMAIL** HLGOODAL@UNCG.EDU

GOODHEART, EUGENE
PERSONAL Born 06/26/1931, New York, NY **DISCIPLINE** ENGLISH LITERATURE **EDUCATION** Columbia Univ, BA, 53, PhD, 61; Univ Va, MA, 54. **CAREER** From instr to asst prof, 58-62, Bard Col; asst prof, 62-66, Univ Chicago; assoc prof, 66-67, Mt Holyoke Col; from assoc to prof, 67-74, Mass Inst Technol; prof & chmn, 74-80, prof, 80-, Boston Univ; Edytha Macy Gross Prof of Hum, 83-, Brandeis Univ; Guggenheim Fel, 70-71; NEH panelist, 74, 81 & 82. **MEMBERSHIPS** MLA; AAUP. **RESEARCH** Ideology and literature. **SELECTED PUBLICATIONS** Auth, The Skeptic Disposition, Princeton Univ Press, 84; auth, Desire and Its Discontents, Columbia Univ Press, 87; auth, Pieces of Resistance, Cambridge Univ Press, 91; auth, The Reign of Ideology, Columbia Univ Press, 97. **CONTACT ADDRESS** 25 Barnard Ave, Watertown, MA, 02172.

GOODMAN, JENNIFER ROBIN
PERSONAL Born 01/19/1953, Urbana, IL **DISCIPLINE** LITERATURE **EDUCATION** Radcliffe Col, AB, 74; Univ Toronto, AM, 75; Harvard Univ, AM, 77, PhD(English), 81. **CAREER** Lectr English, Harvard Univ, 81-82; ASST PROF ENGLISH, TEX A&M UNIV, 82-. **MEMBERSHIPS** Medieval Acad Am; MLA; New Chaucer Soc. **RESEARCH** Medieval English literature; medieval studies; English and American literature. **SELECTED PUBLICATIONS** Auth, The New Arthurian Encyclopedia, Speculum-J Medieval Stud, Vol 0069, 94. **CONTACT ADDRESS** Dept of English, Tex A&M Univ, 1 Texas A and M Univ, College Station, TX, 77843.

GOODMAN, MICHAEL B.
DISCIPLINE ENGLISH LITERATURE **EDUCATION** SUNY Stony Brook, PhD. **CAREER** Fac, Fairleigh Dickinson Univ. **RESEARCH** Corporate commun(s), tech commun, contemp Am lit, and censorship. **SELECTED PUBLICATIONS** Auth, Write to the Point, Prentice Hall; Corporate Communications, SUNY P, 95; Working in a Global Environment, IEEE, 95. **CONTACT ADDRESS** Fairleigh Dickinson Univ, 1000 River Rd, Teaneck, NJ, 07666.

GOODMAN, RUSSELL B.
PERSONAL Born 05/20/1945, m, 1971, 2 children **DISCIPLINE** LITERATURE **EDUCATION** Univ Pa, AB, 66; Oxford Univ, MA, 70; Johns Hopkins, PhD, 71. **CAREER** Vis scholar, Cambridge Univ, 77-78; Fulbright Sr lectr, Central & Autonomous Univ of Barcelona, 93; asst prof to assoc prof to chair, to prof, Univ NM, 79- . **HONORS AND AWARDS** Edwin B. Williams School, Univ Pa, 62-66; Thouron British-Amer Exchange Fel, Oxford Univ, 66-68; William Montgomerie Prize in Philos, Jesus Col, Oxford, 67; Nat Defense Educ Act Fel, Johns Hopkins Univ, 68-71; Nat Endow for the Humanities travel to collections grant, 89-90; Fulbright Sr Lectr/Res award, Spain, 93. **MEMBERSHIPS** Amer Philos Assoc **RESEARCH** Amer philos; Wittgenstein; philos & lit. **SELECTED PUBLICATIONS** Auth, American Philosophy and the Romantic Tradition, Cambridge Univ Press, 90; Pragmatism: A Contemporary Reader, Routledge, 95; Wittgenstein and Pragmatism, Parallax, 98; Ralph Waldo Emerson, Routledge Encyclopedia of Philosophy, 98; Stanley Cavell: The Philosopher Responds to His Critics, Vanderbilt Univ Press, forthcoming; On the Tip of My tongue: Wittgenstein and William James, forthcoming. **CONTACT ADDRESS** Dept of Philosophy, Univ NM, Albuquerque, NM, 87131-1151. **EMAIL** rgoodman@unm.edu

GOODMAN, SUSAN
PERSONAL Born 03/20/1951, Boston, MA, m, 1995 **DISCIPLINE** AMERICAN LITERATURE **EDUCATION** Univ of NH, BA, 72, MEd, 74, MA, 85, PhD, 88. **CAREER** Acting asst prof, Univ of NH, 89; asst prof, 89-92, assoc prof, Calif State Univ, 92-94; asst prof, 94-96, assoc prof, 96-98, PROF OF ENGLISH, UNIV DELAWARE, 98-. **HONORS AND AWARDS** Resident fel, Va Center for the Humanities, 94. **MEMBERSHIPS** MLA; ALA; SSSL; Edith Wharton Soc; Ellen Glasgow Soc. **RESEARCH** Biography; American literature; Turn-of-the-century American writers. **SELECTED PUBLICATIONS** Auth, Ellen Glasgow: A Biography, The Johns Hopkins Univ Press, 98; Edith Wharton's Inner Circle, Univ of Tx Press, 94; Edith Wharton's Women: Friends and Rivals, Univ Press of New England, 90; co-ed, Edith Wharton: A Forward Glance, Univ of Delaware Press, forthcoming; Femmes de Conscience: Aspects du Feminisme Americain 1848-1875, Sorbonne Univ Press, 94. **CONTACT ADDRESS** Dept of English, Univ of Delaware, Newark, DE, 19711.

GOODNIGHT, G. THOMAS
PERSONAL Born 12/02/1948, Houston, TX, m, 1972, 3 children **DISCIPLINE** COMMUNICATION STUDIES; POLITICAL SCIENCE **EDUCATION** Univ of Houston, 71; Univ of Kansas, 77. **CAREER** Prof, Northwestern Univ, 75- ; dir of Forensics, 75-84; dir of grad studies, 83-86; 88-91. **HONORS AND AWARDS** Award for outstanding scholar, Am Forensic Asn, 74, 80, 82; Charles Wohlbert Res Award, SCA, 92; Outstanding Prof, Nat Speakers Asn, 94; Golden Monograph Award, SCA, 95. ORG Nat Commun Asn. **RESEARCH** Public Culture; Rhet; Argumentation; Policy Controversy; Commun Theory & Practice. **SELECTED PUBLICATIONS** Auth, Toward a Social Theory of Argumentation, Argumentation and Advocacy, 89; The Rhetorical Tradition, Modern Communication, and the Rhetoric of Assent, The Rhetoric of Assent, eds Williams and Hazen, 90; Controversy, Proceedings of the 6th Annual Conference on Argumentation, ed D. Parson, 91; Habermas, the Public Sphere, and Controversy, World Jour of Pub Opinion Res, 4, 92; Rhetoric, Legitimation, and the End of the Cold War: Ronald Reagan at the Moscow Summit, 1988, Reagan and Public Discourse in America, eds M. Weiler and B. Pearce, 92; Legitimation Inferences: An Additional Component for the Toulmin Model, Informal Logic, 15, 93; A New Rhetoric for a New Dialectic, Argumentation: An Int Jour on Reasoning, 7, 93; The Park, The Firm, and the University, Quart Jour of Speech, 81, 95; Reagan, Vietnam and Central America: On Public Memory and the Politics of Fragmentation, Rhet and the Presidency, ed M. Medhurst, 96; Hans J. Morgenthau In Defense of the National Interest and the Recovery of the Rhetorical Tradition, The Rhet of Realism, eds Hariman and Beer, 96; coauth, Entanglements of Consumption, Cruelty, Privacy and Fashion, The Social Controversy over Fur, Quart Jour of Speech, fall issue, 94; Studies in the Public Sphere, Quart Jour of Speech, fall isssue, 97. **CONTACT ADDRESS** Dept of Communication Studies, Northwestern Univ, 1809 Chicago Ave, Evanston, IL, 60201-4119. **EMAIL** GTQ@NWU.edu

GOODSON, ALFRED CLEMENT
PERSONAL Born 11/30/1946, Houston, TX **DISCIPLINE** COMPARATIVE LITERATURE, ENGLISH **EDUCATION** Rice Univ, BA, 68; State Univ NY Buffalo, PhD(comp lit), 73. **CAREER** Asst prof, 72-77, ASSOC PROF ENGLISH, MICH STATE UNIV, 77-, Alexander von Humboldt Stiftung res grant, Deutsches Seminar, Tubingen, 79. **RESEARCH** Romantic poetics; critical theory; myth. **SELECTED PUBLICATIONS** Auth, Frankenstein in the Age of Prozac: Artistic Creativity, Depression, Modern Medicine, Lit and Med, Vol 0015, 96. **CONTACT ADDRESS** 403 Kensington Rd, East Lansing, MI, 48823.

GOODSON, CAROL F.
PERSONAL Born 03/28/1947, Detroit, MI **DISCIPLINE** LIBRARY SCIENCE **EDUCATION** State Univ New York, BA, 70, MLS, 72; State Univ Ga, MA, 96. **CAREER** From libr intern to head librn, 70-72, SUNY; from readers serv librn to head libr to commun sch dir, 73-80, St Louis Public Libr and Board; ref librn, Ga Div Public Libr Serv, 81-84; head libr, Mercer Univ, 85; librn, St Henry Sch, 85-86; libr dir, Aguina Jr Col, 89-90; asst dir, Clayton Country Libr Syst, 90-91, coordr, head Librn, State Univ W Ga Libr, 91-. **HONORS AND AWARDS** Phi Kappa Phi; Beta Phi Mu; Sigma Taw Delta; Omicron Delta Kappa **MEMBERSHIPS** Am Libr Asn; LAMA; ACRL; Ga Libr Asn. **RESEARCH** Personal performance evaluation; work of film director Woody Allen. **SELECTED PUBLICATIONS** Auth, The Complete Guide to Performance Standards for Library Personnel, 97; auth, art, I Have Seen the Future, and It Is Us, 97; auth, art, Access Services at the State Univ of West Georgia, 97; auth, art, Putting the Service Back in Library Service, 97; auth, art, I'm Going to be in OCLC, 97 **CONTACT ADDRESS** 210 Oak Ave, Carrollton, GA, 30117. **EMAIL** cgoodson@westga.edu

GOPALAN, LALITHA
DISCIPLINE ENGLISH LITERATURE **EDUCATION** Madras Christian Col, BA; Univ Rochester, MA, PhD. **CAREER** Assoc prof. **RESEARCH** Film theory and practice; national cinemas; history of anthropology; postcolonial theory; feminist film theory and practice; cultural studies; Marxist theory. **SELECTED PUBLICATIONS** Auth, Putting Asunder: Marriage of Maria Braun, Deep Focus, 89; Indian Cinema, Afterimage, 92; Coitus Interruptus & the Love Story in Indian Cinema, 96. **CONTACT ADDRESS** English Dept, Georgetown Univ, 37th and O St, Washington, DC, 20057.

GOPEN, GEORGE D.
DISCIPLINE ENGLISH LITERATURE **EDUCATION** Harvard Univ, JD, 72, PhD, 75. **CAREER** Prof pract rhet, lectr fel. **RESEARCH** Rhetorical grammar. **SELECTED PUBLICATIONS** Auth, publ(s) on compos theory; rhet anal lit. **CONTACT ADDRESS** Eng Dept, Duke Univ, Durham, NC, 27706.

GORDON, ANDREW
PERSONAL Born 01/23/1945 **DISCIPLINE** LITERATURE AND PSYCHOLOGY **EDUCATION** Rutgers Univ, BA, 65; Univ Calif, MA, 67; PhD, 73. **CAREER** Tchg asst, Univ Calif, 68-70; Fulbright jr lectr, Univ Barcelona, Univ Valencia, Spain, 73-75; asst prof, 75-80; Fulbright jr lectr, Oporto, Portugal, 79; Fulbright sr lect, Univ Nis, Yugoslavia, 84-85; vis prof, Janus Pannonius Univ, Pecs, Hungary, 95; vis prof, Univ Alcala de Henares, Spain, 95; vis prof, Inst Superior de Psicologia Aplicada, Lisbon, Portugal, 95; vis prof, Ling Univ Nizhny Novgrorod, Russia, 97; assoc dir, IPSA, 85-93; dir, IPSA, 93-; ch, SAMLA, 84, 86; deleg assembly, MLA, 94-96; asst prof, 80-. **HONORS AND AWARDS** BA with high hon(s), Rutgers Univ, 65; Phi Beta Kappa, Rutgers, 65; NY State Regents tchg fel, 67-69; Fulbright jr lect, Spain, 73-75; Fulbright jr lect, Portugal, 79; Fulbright jr lect, Yugoslavia, 84-85; hum fac res award, 80; res award, 93. **SELECTED PUBLICATIONS** Auth, An American Dreamer: A Psychoanalytic Study of the Fiction of Norman Mailer, Fairleigh Dickinson Univ Press/ Assoc UP, 80; Smoking Dope with Thomas Pynchon: A Sixties Memoir, The Vineland Papers: Critical Takes on Pynchon's Novel, Dalkey Archv Press, 94; Cynthia Ozick's The Shawl and the Transitional Object, Lit and Psychol, 94; It's Not Such a Wonderful Life: The Neurotic George Bailey, The Amer Jour Psychoanalysis, 94; Shame in Saul Bellow's Something to Remember Me By, Saul Bellow Jour, 95; Close Encounters: Unidentified Flying Object Relations, The Psychoanalytic Rev, 95; Indiana Jones and the Temple of Doom: Bad Medicine, Foods of the Gods: Eating and the Eaten in Fantasy and Science Fiction, Ga Univ Press, 96; Herzog's Divorce Grief, Saul Bellow and the Struggle at the Center, AMS Press, 96; co-auth, Superior Intellect?: Sincere Fictions of the White Self, Jour Negro Edu, 95; The Beautiful American: Sincere Fictions of the White Messiah in the American Cinema, Lit and Psychoanalysis, Inst Superior de Psicologia Aplicada, 96; Les Mutines du Bounty: Malaise dans la civilisation, Gradiva: Revue Europeene d'Anthropolgie Litteraire 96; rev(s), Review of Science Fiction for Young Readers, Children's Lit, 96; Review of Family Plots: The De-Oedipalization of Popular Culture by Dana Heller, Yearbook of Comparative and General Literature, Ind Univ, 97. **CONTACT ADDRESS** Dept of Eng, Univ Fla, 226 Tigert Hall, Gainesville, FL, 32611. **EMAIL** agordon@nervm.nerdc.ufl.edu

GORDON, LOIS G.
PERSONAL Born 11/13/1938, Englewood, NJ, m, 1961, 1 child **DISCIPLINE** ENGLISH & COMPARATIVE LITERATURE **EDUCATION** Univ MI, AB, 60; Univ WI, MA, 62, PhD, 66. **CAREER** Lectr Eng, City Col NY, 64-66; asst prof, Univ MO, KS City, 66-68; from asst prof to assoc prof, 68-75, prof eng & comp lit, Fairleigh Dickinson Univ, 75-, vis prof, Rutgers Univ, 94, Asst ed, Lit & Psychol, 68-71. **MEMBERSHIPS** MLA; Nat Asn Psychoanal Criticism; Pinter Soc; Beckett Soc; PEN; Acad of Am Poets. **RESEARCH** Twentieth century Eng and comp lit; postmoderism. **SELECTED PUBLICATIONS** Auth, Death of a Salesman: An appreciation, In: The Forties, Everett Edwards, 69; Strateems to Uncover Nakedness: The Dramas of Harold Pinter, Univ MO Press, 69; Harold Pinter--Past and Present, Kans Quart, spring 71; Myth and meaning--The Sound and the Fury and the Wasteland, In: The Twenties, Everett Edwards, 74; Randall Jarrell, James Purdy & Richard Eberhart, In: Great Writers of England and America, St James, St Martins, 78; Elizabeth Bishop, Donald Davie, Gilbert Sorrentino, W S Merwin, Adrienne Rich, Muriel Rukeyser, In: Contemporary Writers: Poets, 80 & Donald Barthelme and William Gaddis, In: Contemporary Writers: Novelists, 81, St James, Macmillan; Donald Barthelme, G K Hall, 81; Robert Coover--The Universal Fictionmaking Process, South-

ern Ill Univ Press, 82; American Chronicle: Six Decades in American Life, 1920-1979, Atheneum/Random House, 87; American Chronicles: Seven Decades in American Life, 1920-1989, Random House, 80; Harold Pinter: A Handbook, Garland Publ, 90; The Columbia Chronicles of American Life, 1910-1992, Columbia Univ Press, 95; The World of Samuel Becket, 1906-1946, Yale Univ Press, 96; American Chronicle: The Twentieth Century, Yale Univ Press, 99. **CONTACT ADDRESS** Dept of Eng, Fairleigh Dickinson Univ, 1000 River Rd, Teaneck, NJ, 07666-1996.

GORDON, WALTER MARTIN
PERSONAL Born 03/05/1928, San Francisco, CA **DISCIPLINE** ENGLISH, THEOLOGY **EDUCATION** Gonzaga Univ, MA, 53; Col St Albert de Louvain, STL, 60; Univ London, PhD(English), 66. **CAREER** Instr English, Univ Santa Clara, 55-56; asst prof, Loyola Univ, Calif, 67-71; asst prof, 72-79, ASSOC PROF ENGLISH, UNIV GA, 79-. **MEMBERSHIPS** Amici Thomae More; Renaissance Soc Am; SAtlantic Mod Lang Asn; MLA. **RESEARCH** Dramatic form in Thomas More's writings; More's writings on the Eucharist; seriocomic art of More and Erasmus. **SELECTED PUBLICATIONS** Auth, The Complete Works of More, Thomas, Vol 7--The 'Letter to Bugenhagen', the 'Supplication of Souls', the 'Letter Against Frith,' Moreana, Vol 0029, 92; Maiestas in More, Thomas Political-Thought, Moreana, Vol 0034, 97. **CONTACT ADDRESS** Dept of English, Univ of Ga, 0 Georgia University, Athens, GA, 30602-0001.

GORFAIN, PHYLLIS
PERSONAL Born 10/09/1943, Houston, TX, M, 1965 **DISCIPLINE** ENGLISH, FOLKLORE **EDUCATION** Butler Univ, BA, 65; Univ Calif, Berkeley, MA, 67, PhD(English), 73. **CAREER** ASSOC PROF ENGLISH, OBERLINE COL, 71-, Am Coun Learned Soc study fel, 75-76. **MEMBERSHIPS** MLA. **RESEARCH** Shakespeare; folklore and literature; African folklore. **SELECTED PUBLICATIONS** Auth, Wedding Song, Henna Art among Pakistani Women in New York City, J Am Folklore, Vol 0109, 96. **CONTACT ADDRESS** Dept of English, Oberlin Col, 135 W Lorain St, Oberlin, OH, 44074-1076.

GORMELY SEMEIKS, JONNA
DISCIPLINE MODERN BRITISH LITERATURE **EDUCATION** Rutgers, PhD. **CAREER** Assoc prof, Long Island Univ, C.W. Post Campus. **SELECTED PUBLICATIONS** Auth, Visions of Solitude: D. H. Lawrence's Sun, St. Mawr, and The Man Who Loved Islands; Writing in Response to Reading in the Freshman Composition Course; coauth, The Goblin Child: Folktale Symbolism in Popular Art; Leather-Stocking in 'Nam: Rambo, Platoon, and the American Frontier Myth; coed, Discoveries: Fifty Stories of the Quest and Patterns in Popular Culture. **CONTACT ADDRESS** Long Island Univ, C.W. Post, Brookville, NY, 11548-1300.

GOSS, JAMES
PERSONAL Born 08/21/1939, San Pedro, CA, m, 1961, 3 children **DISCIPLINE** RELIGION & LITERATURE **EDUCATION** Univ Southern Calif, BA, 60; Southern Calif Sch Theol, MTh, 63; Claremont Grad Sch, PhD, 70. **CAREER** Assoc prof & campus minister, Cornell Col, 65-67; asst prof, 69-80, from prof to chemn, Relig Studies, Calif State Univ, Northridge, 80-98; exec assoc to the pres, 98. **MEMBERSHIPS** Soc Bibl Lit; Am Acad Relig. **RESEARCH** Religion in literature; New Testament. **SELECTED PUBLICATIONS** Auth, Camus, God and process thought, Process Studies, summer 74; art, O'Connor's redeemed man: Christus et/vel Porcus?, Drew Gateway, winter-spring 74; art, The double action of mercy in The Artificial Nigger, Christianity & Lit, spring 74; art, Eschatology, autonomy, and individuation: The evocative power of the kingdom, Jour Am Acad of Relig, 81. **CONTACT ADDRESS** President's Office, 18111 Nordhoff St, Northridge, CA, 91330-8200. **EMAIL** james.goss@exec.csun.edu

GOSSETT, SUZANNE
DISCIPLINE ENGLISH **EDUCATION** Smith Col, BA, 62; Princeton Univ, MA, 65, PhD, **CAREER** Prof. **RESEARCH** Renaissance drama; feminist and gender Stud; editorial theory. **SELECTED PUBLICATIONS** Auth, Recent Stud in the English Masque, ELR 26, 96; Thomas Middleton, A Fair Quarrel, in The Collected Works of Thomas Middleton, Oxford, 97; Why Should a Woman Edit a Man, Text, 96; coauth, Declarations of Independence: Women and Polit Power in Nineteenth-Century American Fiction, Rutgers UP, 90. **CONTACT ADDRESS** Dept of English, Loyola Univ, Chicago, 6525 N. Sheridan Rd., Chicago, IL, 60626. **EMAIL** sgosset@wpo.it.luc.edu

GOSSIN, PAMELA
DISCIPLINE ENGLISH LITERATURE **EDUCATION** Univ Wis, PhD, 89. **CAREER** Asst prof. **RESEARCH** History of science and literature and science; women and science; scientific biography and autobiography; popularization of science; rhetoric of science; astronomy and literature. **SELECTED PUBLICATIONS** Auth, Literature and Science: An Encyclopedic Companion, Garland; Literature and Astronomy; Literature & Science, Guide Hist Lit, 94. **CONTACT ADDRESS** Dept of Literature, Richardson, TX, 75083-0688. **EMAIL** psgossin@utdallas.edu

GOSSY, MARY S.
DISCIPLINE FEMINIST THEORY AND GOLDEN AGE LITERATURE, PROSE NARRATIVE, PSYCHOANALYTIC **EDUCATION** Bryn Mawr, BA, Harvard Univ, MA, PhD. **CAREER** Assoc prof, Rutgers, The State Univ NJ, Univ Col-Camden. **RESEARCH** Theory and practice of representation in feminist pornography; presence of Spain and Spanish in the unconscious of European modernism. **SELECTED PUBLICATIONS** Auth, The Untold Story: Women and Theory in Golden Age Texts, 89; Freudian Slips: Woman, Writing, the Foreign Tongue, 95. **CONTACT ADDRESS** Dept of Span and Port, Rutgers, The State Univ New Jersey, Univ Col-Camde, 205 Ruth Adams Bldg, New Brunswick, NJ, 08903. **EMAIL** mgossy@rci.rutgers.edu

GOTTESMAN, LES
DISCIPLINE ENGLISH COMPOSITION, AMERICAN LITERATURE, CULTURAL STUDIES, PHILOSOPHICAL A **EDUCATION** Columbia Univ, BA, MA; Univ San Francisco, EdD. **CAREER** Assoc prof Eng and Commun, dean, Sch of Arts & Sci, ch, dept Eng & Commun, Golden Gate Univ. **RESEARCH** Lit in Eritrea, Africa. **SELECTED PUBLICATIONS** Publ on lit in Eritrea, Africa and on hum pedag for students in professional degree programs. **CONTACT ADDRESS** Golden Gate Univ, San Francisco, CA, 94105-2968.

GOTTFRIED, ROY K.
DISCIPLINE MODERN LITERATURE, IRISH LITERATURE **EDUCATION** Yale Univ, PhD. **CAREER** Instr, Vanderbilt Univ. **SELECTED PUBLICATIONS** Auth, The Art of Joyce's Ulysses; Joyce's Iritis and the Irritated Text. **CONTACT ADDRESS** Vanderbilt Univ, Nashville, TN, 37203-1727.

GOUGEON, LEN GIRARD
PERSONAL Born 08/08/1947, Northampton, MA **DISCIPLINE** AMERICAN LITERATURE & STUDIES **EDUCATION** St Mary's Univ, Halifax, BA, 69; Univ Mass, Amherst, MA, 71, PhD(English), 74. **CAREER** Instr English, Univ Mass, Amherst, 70-74; asst prof, 74-77, assoc prof, 78-82, prof Am Lit, Univ Scranton, 82-. **MEMBERSHIPS** Thoreau Soc. **RESEARCH** Ralph Waldo Emerson and the American transcendentalists; reform movements of the nineteenth century; American romantic movement. **SELECTED PUBLICATIONS** Coauth, Emerson and the Anti-Slave, Negro Hist Bull, 3/79; auth, Emerson and Furness: Two Gentlemen of Abolition, Am Transcendental Quart, winter 79; Emerson and Thoreau: A Matter of Milk and Fish, Thoreau Soc Bull, summer 81; Emerson and the New Bedford Affair, Studies Am Renaissance, 81; Abolition, the Emersons and 1837, New England Quart, 9/81; Whitman's Leaves of Grass: Another Contemporary View, Walt Whitman Rev (in prep); Emerson, circle and the Ceisis of the Civil War in Emersonian Circles, ed, Wesley T Mott and Robert E Burkholder, Univ of Rochester Press, 97. **CONTACT ADDRESS** Dept of English, Univ of Scranton, 800 Linden St, Scranton, PA, 18510-4501. **EMAIL** gougeonli@uofs.edu

GOUGEON, LEONARD
DISCIPLINE ENGLISH **EDUCATION** St Mary's Univ, Halifax, BA; Univ MA, MA, PhD. **CAREER** Prof, Univ of Scranton. **MEMBERSHIPS** Am Lit Asn; Am Sec of the MLA; Thoreau Soc; Margaret Fuller Soc. **RESEARCH** 19th-century Am Transcendentalists and Romantics; relationships of major writers and their works to the var reform movements of the time. **SELECTED PUBLICATIONS** Auth, Virtue's Hero: Emerson, Antislavery, and Reform, Ga, 90; co-ed, Emerson's Antislavery Writings, Yale, 95; articles in jour(s), New Eng Quart, Amer Lit, Am Transcendental Quart, S Atlantic Rev, Walt Whitman Quart Rev, Mod Lang Stud, Emerson Soc Papers, Thoreau Soc Bull, Stud in the Am Renaissance, Col Lang Asn J; rev(s) in, J the Early Rep, New Eng Quart, J Am Hist, 19th-Century Contexts, Resources for Am Lit Study, African Am Rev. **CONTACT ADDRESS** Dept of Eng, Univ of Scranton, Scranton, PA, 18510. **EMAIL** GougeonL1@uofs.edu

GOULDING, DANIEL J.
DISCIPLINE FILM STUDIES AND THEATER ARTS **EDUCATION** Marshall Univ, BA, 57; Ohio Univ, MA, 59; PhD, 64. **CAREER** Prof, 66-. **HONORS AND AWARDS** Close-up award, Yugoslav Film Inst. **RESEARCH** Dancing and cultural theory. **SELECTED PUBLICATIONS** Auth, Liberated Cinema: The Yugoslav Experience, Ind Univ Press, 85; Five Filmmakers, Ind Univ Press, 94; ed, Post New Wave Cinema in the Soviet Union and Eastern Europe, Ind Univ Press 89. **CONTACT ADDRESS** Dept of Theatre and Dance, Oberlin Col, Oberlin, OH, 44074.

GOUNARIDOU, KIKI
PERSONAL Greece **DISCIPLINE** DRAMATIC ART **EDUCATION** Univ Calif, Davis, PhD, 92. **CAREER** Asst prof, Theatre and Performance Stud, Univ Pittsburgh, 92- . **HONORS AND AWARDS** Hewlett Int Res Awd; Chandler Awd for Acad Excellence; Best Dir Awd, Ithaca Int Theatre Festival. **MEMBERSHIPS** MLA; Int Fedn for Theatre Res; Am Soc for Theatre Res; Modern Greek Stud Asn. **RESEARCH** Theatre theory and performance studies; classical theatre; translation and translation theory. **SELECTED PUBLICATIONS** Auth, the Simulation of the Statue in Euripides' Alcestis, in Text and Presentation, 93; auth, Morris Coarnovsky, in Internatl Dictionary of Theatre, Gale, 95; auth, Hecuba, Spectrum, 95; co-auth, Euripides Hecuba: A Translation, Mellen, 95; auth, Lee Strasberg, in Internatl Dictionary of Theatre, Gale, 95; trans, the Crystal Spider, in Moderna Drama by Women: An Internatl Anthology, Routledge, 96; auth, Intertext and the Regendering of Nietzche's Superman in kostis Palamas' Trisevyeni, in J of Mod Greek Stud, 96; auth, (Dis)placing Classical Greek Theatre: An International Theatre Conference, in Ctre for W European Stud Newsl, 98; auth, the Sixth Festival of the Union of the Theatres of Wurope, in W European Stages, 98; auth, the Stranger of the house: Fin-de-Siecle Speculations on Euripides, in Millennium Responses: (Dis)placing Classical Greek Theatre, Aristotle Univ Pr, 98; auth, the Quest for Identity in Tennessee Williams' The Glass Menagerie, in Text and Presentation, 98; auth, Madame La Mort and Other Plays by Rachilde, Johns Hopkins, 98; auth, Euripides and Alcestis: Speculations, Simulations, and Stories of Love in the Athenian Culture, Univ Pr of Am, 98. **CONTACT ADDRESS** Cathedral of Learning 1617, Univ of Pittsburgh, Pittsburgh, PA, 15260. **EMAIL** kikigo@pitt.edu

GOURD, WILLIAM
PERSONAL Born 12/27/1934, Boston, MA, m, 1970, 3 children **DISCIPLINE** THEATRE AND COMMUNICATION **EDUCATION** Univ of Conn, BA, 60: The Ohio Univ, MFA, 64; Bowling Green State Univ, PhD, 73. **CAREER** Instr/asst prof, Univ of Tx at El Paso, 64-69; asst prof, Cleveland State Univ, 73-78; ASSOC PROF/PROF, 78-, DEPT CHAIR, 78-92, SAGINAW VALLEY STATE UNIV. **HONORS AND AWARDS** SVSU Fac Asn Service Award, 95; Professorial Continuing Achievement Award, 96. **MEMBERSHIPS** Nat Commun Asn; Mich Asn of Speech Commun; Central States Commun Asn. **RESEARCH** Actor/audience and director/cast communication; ethnographic performance & research. **SELECTED PUBLICATIONS** Auth, Information Processing in the Theatre: Subject Sex and Stimulus Complexity, Empirical Res in Theatre, 74; auth, Cognitive Complexity and Theatrical Information Processing: Audience Responses to Plays and Characters, Commun Monographs, 77; book review, Theatre Byways: Essays in Honor of Claude L. Shaver, Southern Speech Commun J, 81; auth, A Systems Theory Orientation to Director-Cast Commun, Empirical Res in Theatre, 84; narrator, Biological Procedures in Electron Microsopy, 71. **CONTACT ADDRESS** Dept of Commun & Theatre, Saginaw Valley State Univ, 7400 Bay Rd, University Center, MI, 48710.

GOURDINE, A.K.M.
DISCIPLINE AFRICAN-AMERICAN LITERATURE **EDUCATION** Mich State Univ, PhD, 94. **CAREER** Asst prof, La State Univ; ed bd, Calyx, 95. **RESEARCH** African literature; African diaspora studies; women's studies; post- colonial studies. **SELECTED PUBLICATIONS** Auth, Rhetoric of Resistance, The Writing Instr, 91; Postmodern Ethnography and the Womanist Mission: Post-colonial Sensibilities in Possessing the Secret of Joy, African Am Rev, 96; coauth, Strategies for Educating African American Males: The Detroit Model, 93. **CONTACT ADDRESS** Dept of Eng, Louisiana State Univ, 212J Allen Hall, Baton Rouge, LA, 70803. **EMAIL** insandy@unix1.sncc.lsu.edu

GOVAN, SANDRA YVONNE
PERSONAL Born 07/28/1948, Chicago, Illinois, s **DISCIPLINE** ENGLISH **EDUCATION** Valparaiso University, Valparaiso, IN, BA, 1970; Bowling Green University, Bowling Green, OH, MA, 1972; Emory University, Atlanta, GA, PhD, 1980. **CAREER** Luther College, Decorah, IA, instructor, 1972-75; University of Kentucky, Lexington, KY, assistant professor, 1980-83; University of North Carolina, Charlotte, NC, associate professor, 1983-. **HONORS AND AWARDS** Schomburg Scholar in Residence, NEH, Schomburg Center for Research in Black Culture, 1990-91; Outstanding Alumni Award, Valparaiso University, 1982; National Fellowship Fund Award, Ford Foundation, 1976-80; Emory University Fellowship, 1975. **MEMBERSHIPS** Member, Association for the Study of African American Life and History; member, Modern Language Association, 1980-; member, College Language Association, 1975-; member, Langston Hughes Society; coordinator, Ronald E McNair Postbaccalaureate Achievement Program. **CONTACT ADDRESS** Professor of English, Univ of North Carolina-Charlotte, Charlotte, NC, 28223.

GRACE, JOAN CARROLL
PERSONAL Born 03/06/1921, Brooklyn, NY **DISCIPLINE** ENGLISH **EDUCATION** Trinity Col, DC, AB, 43; Columbia Univ, MA, 51, PhD, 69. **CAREER** From asst to assoc to full prof, 68-91, prof emeritus, 91-, Eng, Fordham Univ. **MEMBERSHIPS** MLA. **RESEARCH** Shakespeare; Milton; modern British writers. **SELECTED PUBLICATIONS** Auth, Tragic Theory In The Critical Works Of Thomas Rymer, John Dennis and John Dryden, Fairleigh Dickinson Univ, 74. **CONTACT ADDRESS** 44 Morningside Dr, New York, NY, 10025.

GRACE, NANCY
DISCIPLINE ENGLISH LITERATURE **EDUCATION** Otterbein, BA, 73; Ohio State Univ, MA, 81, PhD, 87. **CAREER**

Assoc prof. **HONORS AND AWARDS** Dir, writing prog. **SELECTED PUBLICATIONS** Auth, The Feminized Male Character in Twentieth-Century Literature. **CONTACT ADDRESS** Dept of Eng, Col of Wooster, Wooster, OH, 44691.

GRACE, SHERRILL E.
DISCIPLINE ENGLISH **EDUCATION** Univ Western Ont, BA, 65; McGill Univ, MA, 70, PhD, 74. **CAREER** Asst prof, McGill Univ, 75-77; asst prof, 77-81, assoc prof, 81-87, PROF ENGLISH, UNIV BRITISH COLUMBIA 91-. **HONORS AND AWARDS** F.E.L. Priestley Award, 93; Killam Res Prize, 90; Killam Fac Res Fel, 90-91; Fel, Royal Soc Can. **MEMBERSHIPS** Asn Can Col Univ Tchrs Eng; Can Asn Am Studs; Asn Can Studs; Can Comp Lit Asn; Acad Women's Asn. **SELECTED PUBLICATIONS** Auth, Violent Duality: A Study of Margaret Atwood, 80; auth, The Voyage That Never Ends: Malcolm Lowry's Fiction, 82; auth, Regression and Apocalypse: Studies in North American Literary Expressionism, 89; auth, Sursum Corda: The Collected Letters of Malcolm Lowry, vol 1, 95, vol 2, 96. **CONTACT ADDRESS** Dept of English, Univ BC, Vancouver, BC, V6T 1Z1. **EMAIL** grace@arts.ubc.ca

GRADDY, WILLIAM E.
DISCIPLINE LITERATURE OF THE AMERICAN RENAISSANCE **EDUCATION** Southern IL Univ, BA, MA, PhD. **CAREER** Lit, Trinity Int Univ **SELECTED PUBLICATIONS** Articles, Reformed Jour, New Oxford Rev, Emerson Soc Quart, Eerdman's Handbook Christianity Am. **CONTACT ADDRESS** Trinity Int Univ, 2065 Half Day Road, Deerfield, IL, 60015.

GRADIN, SHERRIE L.
DISCIPLINE ENGLISH, COMPOSITION THEORY **EDUCATION** Casper Col, AA, 81; Portland State Univ, BA, 84; MA, 86; Univ NH, PhD, 90. **CAREER** Dir wrtg; assoc prof. **HONORS AND AWARDS** Nat wrtg prog admin grant, 95; fac devel grant, 95, 96, 97; Comm-based Dev. Grnt, 96. **RESEARCH** Gender studies, feminist theory **SELECTED PUBLICATIONS** Auth, Romancing Rhetorics: Social-expressivist Perspectives on the Teaching of Writing, Boynton/Cook, 95; A Writing Teacher Asks Some Questions Concerning Discourse Forms and the Culturally Diverse Classroom, CEA Critic, 94; What's Gender Got to Do With It?, National Forum: The Phi Kappa Phi, Jour, 94. **CONTACT ADDRESS** Dept of Eng, Portland State Univ, PO Box 751, Portland, OR, 97207-0751.

GRAHAM, JOYCE
PERSONAL Elliston, VA **DISCIPLINE** ENGLISH EDUCATION, ADOLESCENT LITERATURE **EDUCATION** Radford Univ, BS, MS; VA Tech, EdD. **CAREER** Prof, Radford Univ. **MEMBERSHIPS** Pres, VA Asn of Tchr of Eng. **SELECTED PUBLICATIONS** Contrib an essay to Writers for Young Adults, ed a column called "Global Issues" in the Eng J. **CONTACT ADDRESS** Radford Univ, Radford, VA, 24142. **EMAIL** jlgraham@runet.edu

GRAHAM, KENNETH WAYNE
PERSONAL Born 03/26/1938, Winnipeg, MB, Canada, m, 1963, 2 children **DISCIPLINE** ENGLISH LITERATURE AND BIBLIOGRAPHY **EDUCATION** Royal Mil Col Can, BA, 61; Univ London, MPh, 67, PhD(English), 71. **CAREER** Lectr English, 66-70, asst prof, 70-77, ASSOC PROF ENGLISH, UNIV GUELPH, 77-. **MEMBERSHIPS** Asn Can Univ Teachers English; Can Soc 18th Century Studies; Am Soc 18th Century Studies; Can Fedn of Humanities. **RESEARCH** Bibliography; 18th century literature; Gothic novel. **SELECTED PUBLICATIONS** Auth, The Godwins and the Shelleys--A Biography of a Family, Wordsworth Circle, Vol 0023, 92. **CONTACT ADDRESS** Dept of English, Univ of Guelph, Guelph, ON, N1G 2W1.

GRAHAM, MARYEMMA
DISCIPLINE ENGLISH **EDUCATION** Univ N Carolina at Chapel Hill, BA; Northwestern Univ, MA; Cornell Univ, MPS, PhD, 77. **CAREER** ASSOC PROF, ENG, NORTHEASTERN UNIV **MEMBERSHIPS** Am Antiquarian Soc **RESEARCH** Afro-Am authorship, 1746-1906. **CONTACT ADDRESS** PO Box 6248, Silver Spring, MD, 20916-6248.

GRAHAM, PETER W.
PERSONAL Born 02/11/1951, Manchester, CT, m, 1973, 2 children **DISCIPLINE** ENGLISH **EDUCATION** Davidson, AB, 73; Duke, MA, 74, PhD, 77. **CAREER** Asst Prof, Va Polytech Inst & State Univ, 78-84; Assoc Prof, 84-90; Prof, 90-. **HONORS AND AWARDS** James B Duke Fellow, Duke Univ, 73-76; Eli Lilly Post-doctoral Fellow, Univ Fla, 77-78; Andrew Mellon Post-doctoral Fellow, Duke Univ, 80-81; Elma Dangerfield Prize for Byron Stud, 92. **MEMBERSHIPS** Int Byron Soc. **RESEARCH** 19th cent Brit lit & culture; med hu; Byron; Darwin. **SELECTED PUBLICATIONS** Auth, Don Juan and Regency England, Va, 90; co-auth, Fictive Ills: Literary Perspectives on Wounds and Diseases, Lit & Med, vol 9, Johns Hopklins Univ Press, 90; co-auth, Articulating the Elephant Man: Joseph Merrick and His Interpreters, Johns Hopkins, 92; co-auth, Disorderly Eaters: Texts in Self-empowerment, Pa State, 92; co-auth, The Portable Darwin, Viking, 93; auth, Lord Byron, Twayne, 98. **CONTACT ADDRESS** Dept of English, Va Polytech Inst & State Univ, Blacksburg, VA, 24061. **EMAIL** pegraham@vt.edu

GRAHAM, THEODORA RAPP
PERSONAL Born 02/05/1938, Kearny, NJ, m, 1 child **DISCIPLINE** ENGLISH, HUMANITIES **EDUCATION** Rutgers Univ, NCAS, AB, 59; Columbia Univ, MA, 64; Univ Pa, PhD(English), 74. **CAREER** Teacher English & French, NJ schs, 60-63; instr English, Moravian Col, Bethelehem, Pa, 63-65 & Pa State Univ, University Park, 65-69; instr English & sec educ, 70-74, asst prof humanities & English, 74-77, Assoc Prof Humanities & English, PA State Univ, Capitol Campus, 77-, Coordr Grad Prog Humanities, 75-82; founding ed, William Carlos Williams Rev, 74-83; reviewer-panelist, Nat Endowment for Humanities, 77-. **HONORS AND AWARDS** Phi Beta Kappa; Provost's Award for Teaching Excellence, 87; Penn State's Achieving Women Award, 92; numerous Univ & campus research awards. **MEMBERSHIPS** MLA; Am Studies Asn; SAMLA; ALA; ALSC; Williams, Pound, Frost, Eliot, Stevens Societies; CELJ, 77-83; Pres WCW Soc, 88-89. **RESEARCH** Modern American poetry; 20th century American fiction; contemporary fiction and drama. **SELECTED PUBLICATIONS** Contribr, Composition and the disadvantaged, In: English and the Disadvantaged, International, 67; Louise Bogan, Grace King, Josephine Miles & Harriet Monroe, In: American Women Writers, Ungar, 79-80, rev 83; William Carlos Williams, Dict American Biography, 81; Louise Bogan (81 & 98) and Anita Brookner (93 & 98), Encycl of World Lit in the 20th Century; contribr, Teaching the Divine Comedy in an Interdisciplinary Context, MLA, 82; auth, Her Heigh Compleynt: The Cress Letters of Williams Paterson, In: Ezra Pound and William Carlos Williams, Univ of Pa Press, 83; Myra's Emergence in Williams' A Dream of Love, Sagetrieb, 84; Williams, Flossie, and the Others: The Aesthetics of Sexuality, Contemp Lit, 87; guest ed WCWR, devoted to Marianne Moore and WCW, Spring 98; auth, A Place for the Genuine: A Tribute to Mary Ellen Solt, In: WCWR, 93; editorials and reviews. **CONTACT ADDRESS** Sch of Humanities, Pa State Harrisburgh, 777 W Harrisburg Pike, Middletown, PA, 17057-4898. **EMAIL** trg1@psu.edu

GRANOFSKY, RONALD
DISCIPLINE ENGLISH LITERATURE **EDUCATION** Trent Univ, BA; Canterbury Univ, MA; Queen's Univ, PhD. **RESEARCH** Mod Brit lit; the novel; Canadian fiction. **CONTACT ADDRESS** English Dept, McMaster Univ, 1280 Main St W, Hamilton, ON, L8S 4L9.

GRANT, AUGUST E.
DISCIPLINE MASS COMMUNICATION TECHNOLOGY **EDUCATION** Univ FL, MA, JC; Univ Southern CA, PhD. **CAREER** Assoc prof & dir, Ctr Mass Commun Res; past fac, Univ TX at Austin; vis prof, USC, 96 & assoc prof, 97-; ed, Commun Technol Update. **RESEARCH** Convergence of commun forms through the application of new technol(s). **SELECTED PUBLICATIONS** Publ on, high-definition television, television audience behavior, television shopping serv, theories of new media & emerging commun technol(s). **CONTACT ADDRESS** Col of Journalism & Mass Commun, Univ of S. Carolina, Carolina Coliseum rm 3032A, Columbia, SC, 29208. **EMAIL** augie@.sc.edu

GRANT, BARRY KEITH
PERSONAL New York, NY, m, 1947 **DISCIPLINE** FILM, POPULAR CULTURE **EDUCATION** State Univ NY Buffalo, BA, 69, PhD(English, Am lit & film), 75. **CAREER** Lectr, 75-76, asst prof, 76-81, ASSOC PROF FILM AND POPULAR CULT, BROCK UNIV, 81-, CHMN, DEPT FINE ARTS, 82-, Asst dir, Media Study, Buffalo, 74-75; film critic, CJQR-FM, St Catharines, Ont, 80-; reader, Post-Script: Essays in Film and the Humanities, 82-. **MEMBERSHIPS** MLA; Popular Cult Asn; Film Studies Asn Can; Soc Educ Film and TV. **RESEARCH** American film; science fiction; popular music. **SELECTED PUBLICATIONS** Auth, Representing Reality--Issues and Concepts in Documentary, Film Quart, Vol 0046, 93; Theorizing Documentary, Film Quart, Vol 0048, 95; They Must Be Represented--The Politics of Documentary, Film Quart, Vol 0049, 96; Rich and Strange--The Yuppie Horror Film, J Film and Video, Vol 0048, 96; Replications--A Robotic History of the Science-Fiction Film, Film Quart, Vol 0051, 97. **CONTACT ADDRESS** Dept of Fine Arts, Brock Univ, St Catharines, ON, L2S 3A1.

GRANT, JOHN ERNEST
PERSONAL Born 08/28/1925, Newburyport, MA, m, 1974, 2 children **DISCIPLINE** ENGLISH **EDUCATION** Harvard Univ, AB, 51, AM, 54, PhD(English), 60. **CAREER** From instr to assoc prof English, Univ Conn, 56-65; PROF ENGLISH, UNIV IOWA, 65-, Am Coun Learned Soc fel, 68-69; Am Philos Soc fel 72; vis prof English, Univ Alta, 68 and 73 and Emory Univ, 76; Nat Endowment Humanities fel, 77; Yale Ctr British Arts fel, 81. **MEMBERSHIPS** MLA; AAUP; Midwest Mod Lang Asn. **RESEARCH** The poetry and painting of William Blake: the imagery of apocalypse; literary archetypes. **SELECTED PUBLICATIONS** Auth, The Poetry of Blake, William, Blake-Illustrated Quart, Vol 0028, 94. **CONTACT ADDRESS** Dept of English, Univ of Iowa, Iowa City, IA, 52242.

GRANT, JUDITH A.S.
PERSONAL Born 12/21/1941, Toronto, ON, Canada **DISCIPLINE** ENGLISH **EDUCATION** Univ Toronto, BA, 65, MA, 66, PhD, 74. **CAREER** Instr/lectr, Univ Toronto, 70-75; instr, Univ Toronto, Univ Guleph & Ryerson Polytech Inst, 75-80; asst prof, 80-82, adj prof Eng, Univ Guelph, 82-85; WRITER, 82-. **MEMBERSHIPS** Victorian Stud Asn Ont 69-. **SELECTED PUBLICATIONS** Auth, Robertson Davies, 78; auth, Robertson Davies: Man of Myth, 94; ed, The Enthusiasms of Robertson Davies, 79, rev ed 90; ed, The Well-Tempered Critic: One Man's View of Theatre and Letters in Canada, 81. **CONTACT ADDRESS** 17 Admiral Rd, Toronto, ON, M5R 2L4.

GRANT, PATRICK
DISCIPLINE ENGLISH LITERATURE **EDUCATION** Queen's Univ, Belfast, BA; Univ Sussex, PhD. **CAREER** Prof **HONORS AND AWARDS** Fel(s), Can Coun Leave; Killam Senior; Royal Soc Can. **RESEARCH** Renaissance and modern literature; literature and religion; literature and culture of modern Northern Ireland. **SELECTED PUBLICATIONS** Auth, The Transformation of Sin: Studies in Donne, Herbert, Vaughan and Traherne, Univ Mass Press, 74; Images and Ideas in Literature of the English Renaissance, Macmillan, 79); Six Modern Authors and Problems of Belief, Macmillan, 79; Literature of Mysticism in Western Tradition, Macmillan, 83; A Dazzling Darkness, An Anthology of Western Mysticism, Collins, 85; Literature and the Discovery of Method in the English Renaissance, Macmillan, 85; Reading the New Testament, Macmillan, 89; Literature and Personal Values, Macmillan, 92; Spiritual Discourse and the Meaning of Persons, Macmillan, 94; Personalism and the Politics of Culture, Macmillan, 96. **CONTACT ADDRESS** Dept of English, Victoria Univ, PO Box 3070, Victoria, BC, V8W 3W1.

GRANT, RAYMOND JAMES SHEPHERD
PERSONAL Born 05/26/1942, Aberdeen, Scotland, m, 1973 **DISCIPLINE** LANGUAGE AND LITERATURE **EDUCATION** Univ Aberdeen, MA, 64; Cambridge Univ, PhD(English), 71. **CAREER** Asst prof, 67-74, assoc prof, 74-80, PROF ENGLISH, UNIV ALTA, 80-. **RESEARCH** Anglo-Saxon verse; homilies; texts transcribed in the 16th and 17th centuries. **SELECTED PUBLICATIONS** Auth, A Copied Tremulous Worcester Gloss at Corpus: Cambridge Manuscript-41 from Corpus-Christi-College Library Containing Bede 'Historia Ecclesiastica,' Neuphilologische Mitteilungen, Vol 0097, 96; The Pedlar-Poet and the Prince of Editors--Mcfarlan, James and Dickens, Charles, Dickensian, Vol 0093, 97. **CONTACT ADDRESS** Dept of English, Univ of Alta, Edmonton, AB, T6G 2E5.

GRASSIAN, ESTHER
PERSONAL Born 02/15/1946, Columbus, GA, 2 children **DISCIPLINE** LIBRARY SCIENCE **EDUCATION** Univ California, Los Angeles, BA,67, MLS, 69. **CAREER** Reference and instruction librn, 69-95, electronic services coord, 95- , instruction services coord, 98- , Univ Calif Los Angeles Library. **HONORS AND AWARDS** Farland Award, Best graduating student in Hebrew, UCLA, 67; NEH reviewer, 94- ; Librarian of the Year Award, UCLA Librns Assoc, 95. **MEMBERSHIPS** ALA; ACRL; RLSA; LITA; Calif Clearinghouse on Libr Instruction. **RESEARCH** Information literacy; library instruction; critical thinking; Internet evaluation. **SELECTED PUBLICATIONS** Auth, Fear and Loathing on the Internet: Training the Trainers and Teaching the Users, Neal-Schuman, 96; auth, Appendix A: Thinking Critically About World Wide Web Resources, Greenwood, 97; auth, Teaching and the Virtual Library, in Laguardia, ed, Recreating the Academic Library, Neal-Schuman, 98. **CONTACT ADDRESS** College Library, Univ of California, Los Angeles, PO Box 951450, Los Angeles, CA, 90095-1450. **EMAIL** estherg@library.ucla.edu

GRAVEL, PIERRE
PERSONAL Born 03/13/1942, Montreal, PQ, Canada **DISCIPLINE** PHILOSOPHY, LITERATURE **EDUCATION** Univ Montreal, BPaed, 63; Univ Aix-Marseille, MA, 69, DPhil, 71. **CAREER** Asst lectr, Inst Am Univs and Univ Aix-Marseille, 68-71; prof, Col Maisonneuve, 71-73; asst prof, 73-78, ASSOC PROF PHILOS, UNIV MONTREAL, 78-, Consult philos, Rev Philos, 75-; mem, Comite de Lear, Rev Etudes Francaiscs, 78-; dir, Determinations, 82. **MEMBERSHIPS** Can Philos Asn. **RESEARCH** History of philosophy; aesthetics. **SELECTED PUBLICATIONS** Auth, 'Macbeth'--Shakespeare Depiction of the Workings of Power, Laval Theol et Philos, Vol 0051, 95. **CONTACT ADDRESS** 2910 Ed Montpetit, Montreal, PQ, H3C 3J7.

GRAVER, LAWRENCE
DISCIPLINE ENGLISH **EDUCATION** City Col NY, BA, 54; Univ Calif, Berkeley, PhD, 61. **CAREER** John Hawley Roberts prof & eme. **RESEARCH** Modern fiction and drama. **SELECTED PUBLICATIONS** Auth, Conrad's Short Fiction; Beckett: Waiting for Godot, An Obsession with Anne Frank. **CONTACT ADDRESS** Dept of English, Williams Col, Stetson d 21, Williamstown, MA, 01267. **EMAIL** lgraver@williams.edu

GRAVER, SUZANNE
DISCIPLINE ENGLISH **EDUCATION** Queen's Col CUNY, BA, 57; Univ Calif Berkeley, MA, 60; Univ Mass Amherst, PhD, 76. **CAREER** John Hawley Roberts prof. **RESEARCH** Victorian literature and culture & gender studies; women's studies; theory of fiction. **SELECTED PUBLICATIONS** Auth, Incarnate History: The Feminisms of Middlemarch; Writing in a Womanly' Way and the Double Vision of Bleak House, George Eliot and Community: A Study in Social Theory and Fictional Form. **CONTACT ADDRESS** Dept of English, Williams Col, Stetson d 11, Williamstown, MA, 01267. **EMAIL** sgraver@williams.edu

GRAVLEE, JACK
DISCIPLINE COMMUNICATION STUDIES **EDUCATION** Howard Col, BA; La State Univ, MA, PhD. **CAREER** Prof. **RESEARCH** Public speaking; television criticism. **SELECTED PUBLICATIONS** Auth, Pamphlets and the American Revolution: Rhetoric, Politics, Literature and the Popular Press; Myths in the Rhetorical Context of 1983 British Electioneering, 86; Watts' Dissenting Rhetoric of Prayer, Quarterly J Speech, 73; Bishop Jonathan Shipley's Charge to His Clergy 1774-1782, Anglican Episcopal Hist, 96. **CONTACT ADDRESS** Speech Communication Dept, Colorado State Univ, Fort Collins, CO, 80523. **EMAIL** jgravlee@vines.colostate.edu

GRAY, DONALD
PERSONAL Born 09/21/1927, Waukegan, IL, m, 1954, 2 children **DISCIPLINE** ENGLISH LITERATURE **EDUCATION** Loyola Univ, Ill, PhB, 50; Univ Minn, MA, 51; Ohio State Univ, PhD, 56. **CAREER** From instr to assoc prof English, 56-68, chmn dept, 68-73, PROF ENGLISH, IND UNIV, BLOOMINGTON, 68-, ED, COL ENGLISH, 78-. **MEMBERSHIPS** MLA; NCTE. **RESEARCH** Nineteenth century British literature; literary theory. **SELECTED PUBLICATIONS** Auth, The Pamphlets of Carroll, Lewis, Vol 1, the Oxford Pamphlets, Leaflets, and Circulars of Lutwidge, Charles, 19th Century Prose, Vol 0021, 94. **CONTACT ADDRESS** Dept of English, Univ of Ind, Bloomington, IN, 47401.

GRAY, JEFFREY
PERSONAL Seattle, WA **DISCIPLINE** ENGLISH **EDUCATION** Univ WA, MA; Univ CA, Riverside, PhD. **CAREER** Asst prof; dir, Poetry-in-the-Round; participant, NEH Summer Inst, San Juan, PR. **MEMBERSHIPS** Acad Am Poets; Nat Poetry Found; MELUS; MLA; Pac Ancient and Mod Lang Asn; Northeast MLA; Elizabeth Bishop Soc; Col Engl Asn. **RESEARCH** Poetry of Derek Walcott, Elizabeth Bishop, John Ashbery. **SELECTED PUBLICATIONS** Auth, Una Sesion Musical con Carli Munoz, El Nuevo Dia 19, San Juan, PR, 97; Steven Gould Axelrod, Greenwood Press, 97; It's Not Natural: Freud's Uncanny and O'Connor's Wise Blood, Southern Lit J 24 1, 96; Richard Hugo, Muriel Rukeyser, & Charles Reznikoff: three biographical essay for American National Biography, Oxford UP; Among the Amak, Ancient Love, & A Tunisian Story, Amer Poetry Rev 24 4, 95; John Ashbery's The Instruction Manual, Explicator 54, 96; Elizabeth Bishop's Brazil, January 1, 1502, Explicator 54, 95; Essence and the Mulatto Traveler: Europe as Embodiment in Nella Larsen's Quicksand, Novel: A Forum on Fiction 27 3, 94; Necessary Thought: Frank Bidart and the Post-Confessional, Contemp Lit 34 4, 93; ed, Memory and Imagination in Day by Day, The Critical Response to Robert Lowell. **CONTACT ADDRESS** Dept of Eng, Seton Hall Univ, Bayley Hall, 400 S. Ora, South Orange, NJ, 07079. **EMAIL** grayjeff@shu.edu

GRAYSON, JANET
PERSONAL Born 06/04/1934, Boston, MA, m, 1958, 4 children **DISCIPLINE** ENGLISH **EDUCATION** Brooklyn Col, BA, 58, MA, 62; Columbia Univ, PhD(English), 68. **CAREER** Lectr English, Brooklyn Col, 63-66; from asst prof to assoc prof, 66-75, PROF ENGLISH, KEENE STATE COL, 75-. **MEMBERSHIPS** Mediaeval Acad Am; Int Arthurian Soc. **RESEARCH** English and European medieval literature; Elizabethan literature; classical civilization. **SELECTED PUBLICATIONS** Auth, The Consecration of Stephen-Daedalus: Joyce, James A 'Portrait of the Artist as a Young Man,' Eng Lang Notes, Vol 0034, 96. **CONTACT ADDRESS** Keene State Col, Keene, NH, 03431.

GRAYSON, NANCY JANE
PERSONAL Born 02/10/1934, Abilene, TX **DISCIPLINE** ENGLISH **EDUCATION** Tex Christian Univ, BA, 56; Univ Tex, Austin, MA, 58, PhD(English), 68. **CAREER** Instr English, Tex Christian Univ, 60-61; teaching asst, Univ Tex, Austin, 61-66, teaching assoc, Univ Tex, Austin, 66-68; asst prof, 68-72, assoc prof English, Southwest Tex State Univ, 72-83, prof, Southwest Tex State Univ, 83-, dir freshman English, 73-79, dept chair, 87-93, Assoc Dean Of Liberal Arts, 98-. **MEMBERSHIPS** Col Conf Teachers English; SCent Mod Lang Asn; Col English Asn; MLA; Col Conf Compos & Commun. **RESEARCH** English Romantics; childrens' classics on film. **CONTACT ADDRESS** Dept of English, Southwest Texas State Univ, 601 University Dr, San Marcos, TX, 78666-4685. **EMAIL** NG01@swt.edu

GREAVES, GAIL-ANN
DISCIPLINE INTERCULTURAL COMMUNICATION AND RHETORIC **EDUCATION** Howard Univ, PhD. **CAREER** Asst prof and Dir of Forensics Prog, Long Island Univ, Brooklyn Campus. **HONORS AND AWARDS** Ten Years of Dedicated Service to Medgar Evers College and the Community; Outstanding Services to the Student Forensic, Academic Club Asoc at Brooklyn Col; Who's Who Int Students Certif of Merit; Award of Merit; Outstanding Young Woman of Am. **MEMBERSHIPS** Nat Forensic Asoc; Nat Commun Asoc; Trinidad and Tobago Working Women Asoc; Caribbean Studies Asoc. **RESEARCH** Calypso music; popular rhetoric. **SELECTED PUBLICATIONS** Auth, The Evolution of Calypso and Carnival, Trinidad and Tobago Working Women's Asoc Scholar Award Luncheon J, 93; auth, The Rhetoric of the Calypso of Political Commentary from the Republic of Trinidad and Tobago: An African-Centered Historical-Critical Analysis, Howard J Commun, 95; auth, Call-Response in Selected Calypsoes of Political Commentary from the Republic of Trinidad and Tobago, J Black Studies, 98. **CONTACT ADDRESS** 390 52nd St., Brooklyn, NY, 11203-4404.

GREBSTEIN, SHELDON NORMAN
PERSONAL Born 02/01/1928, Providence, RI, m, 1953, 2 children **DISCIPLINE** MODERN & AMERICAN LITERATURE **EDUCATION** Univ Southern Calif, BA, 49; Columbia Univ, MA, 50; Mich State Univ, PhD(English), 54. **CAREER** From instr to asst prof English, Univ Ky, 53-62; asst prof, Univ S Fla, 62-63; assoc prof, 63-68, dir grad English studies, 66-72, dean arts & sci, Harpur Col, 75-81; Prof English, State Univ NY, Binghamton, 68-81; Pres, 81-93, Prof Lit, SUNY Col Purchase, 93-95, DIR OF EDUC, WESTCHESTER HOLOCAUST CMN, 95- ; Fulbright-Hays lectr, Univ Rouen, France, 68-69. **RESEARCH** American and contemporary literature; Jewish-American literature; modern American fiction. **SELECTED PUBLICATIONS** Ed, Monkey Trial, Houghton, 60; auth, Sinclair Lewis, 62 & John O'Hara, 66, Twayne; ed, Perspectives in Contemporary Criticism, Harper, 68; Studies in For Whom the Bells Tolls, Merrill, 71; auth, Hemingway's Craft, Southern Ill Univ, 73. **CONTACT ADDRESS** Westchester Holocaust Cmn, 2900 Purchase St, Purchase, NY, 10577.

GREELEY, ANDREW MORAN
PERSONAL Born 02/05/1928, Chicago, IL **DISCIPLINE** SOCIOLOGY, ENGLISH LITERATURE, RELIGION **EDUCATION** St Mary Lake Sem, STL, 54; Univ Chicago, MA, Soc, 61, PhD, 62. **CAREER** Sr stud dir, Nat Opinion Res Center, Univ Chicago, 62-68; prog dir, High Educ, univ Chicago, 68-70; lectr, Soc dept, Univ Chicago, 63-72; PROF, SOC, UNIV ARIZ, 78-; PROF, SOC SCI, UNIV CHICAGO, 91-. **SELECTED PUBLICATIONS** Religion as Poetry, Trans Publ, 95; Sociology and Religion: A Collection of Readings, Harper Collins Coll Publ, 95; coauth, Common Ground, Pilgrim Press, 96; coauth, Forging a Common Future, Pilgrim Press, 1997; I Hope You're listening God, Crossroads Publ, 97. **CONTACT ADDRESS** Nat Opinion Res Center (NORC), Univ Chicago, 1155 E 60th St, Chicago, IL, 60637. **EMAIL** agreel@aol.com

GREEN, LAWRENCE DONALD
PERSONAL Born 07/14/1945, New York, NY **DISCIPLINE** RHETORIC, ENGLISH RENAISSANCE LITERATURE **EDUCATION** Univ Berkeley, BA, 69, MA, 71, PhD(rhet), 75. **CAREER** Lectr rhet, Univ Calif, Berkeley, 75-76; ASST PROF ENGLISH, UNIV SOUTHERN CALIF, 76-. **MEMBERSHIPS** MLA; Philol Asn Pac Coast; Shakespeare Soc; Rhet Soc Am; Nat Coun Teachers Educ. **RESEARCH** Elizabethan drama; Renaissance rhetoric and intellectual history; composition and language theory. **SELECTED PUBLICATIONS** Auth, The Elizabethan Courtier Poets--The Poems and Their Contexts, Huntington Libr Quart, Vol 0055, 92; Aristotle on Rhetoric--A Theory of Civic Discourse, Philos and Rhet, Vol 0026, 93; Renaissance Rhetoric, Philos and Rhet, Vol 0029, 96. **CONTACT ADDRESS** Dept of English, Univ of Southern Calif, Los Angeles, CA, 90007.

GREEN, LON C.
PERSONAL Born 07/27/1947, Salt Lake City, UT, m, 1993, 6 children **DISCIPLINE** RHETORIC; COMMUNICATION **EDUCATION** Univ of Nev, BA, 70; Utah State Univ, MS, 73; Kent State Univ, PhD, 83. **CAREER** Prof, ch, Dept of Speech & Theater, Lewis Univ, 77-85; prof, Ferris State Univ, 85- , head of dept of Hum, 85-93. **MEMBERSHIPS** AAHE; Nat Commun Asn; Am Soc for Sport Hist. **RESEARCH** Dispute resolution. **CONTACT ADDRESS** Dept of Humanities, Ferris State Univ, Big Rapids, MI, 49307. **EMAIL** lgreen@ferris.edu

GREEN, MARTIN
PERSONAL Born 11/13/1940, Brooklyn, NY, m, 1965 **DISCIPLINE** ENGLISH MEDIEVAL LITERATURE **EDUCATION** City Univ New York, BA, 61; Ind Univ, MA, 65, PhD(-English), 71. **CAREER** From instr to asst prof, 66-76, assoc prof English, Fairleigh Dickenson Univ, 76-83; prof English, 83; chmn English, 83-97; acting dean, Coll Arts & Sciences, 97; co-ed, Lit Rev, 76-. **MEMBERSHIPS** MLA; Medieval Acad Am; AAUP; Coord Coun Lit Mag. **RESEARCH** Old English poetry; myth and comparative literature; contemporary fiction; Literary & Popular magazines. **SELECTED PUBLICATIONS** Co-ed, The Other Sides of Reality, Boyd & Fraser, 72; auth, Man, time and apocalypse in the Wanderer, Seafarer, and Beowulf, J English Ger Philol, Fall 75; coauth, Vision and voice in the OE Christ III, Papers Lang & Lit, 76. **CONTACT ADDRESS** Dept of English, Fairleigh Dickinson Univ, 285 Madison Ave, Madison, NJ, 07940-1099. **EMAIL** green@alpha.fdu.edu

GREEN, WILLIAM
PERSONAL Born 07/10/1926, New York, NY, m, 1960, 2 children **DISCIPLINE** ENGLISH & DRAMA **EDUCATION** Queens Col, AB, 49; Columbia Univ, MA, 50, PhD(English), 59. **CAREER** Lectr English, Upsala Col, 53-56; tutor, 57-59, from instr to assoc prof, 59-72, prof English, Queens Col, NY, 72-, consult, col proficiency exam prog, NY State Educ Dept, 64-88; Andrew W Mellon Found fel, 82; Fulbright prof, Inst for Theatre Res, Univ of Vienna, Spring 83. **HONORS AND AWARDS** Phi Beta Kappa; PSC-CUNY Res Award, 86-90; Andrew W. Mellon Found joint fel with prof Leo Hershkowitz, 83-84. **MEMBERSHIPS** Col English Asn; MLA; Malone Soc; Shakespeare Asn of Am; Theatre Library Asn; Am Soc for Theatre Res; Int Fedn for Theatre Res; Am Theatre Critics Asn. **RESEARCH** Shakespeare; Elizabethan drama; modern European and American drama. **SELECTED PUBLICATIONS** Co-ed, Elizabethan Drama: Eight Plays, Applause Thetre Book Pub, 90; auth, The Use of Legal Records in Reproducing Theatrical Performances, Records and Images of the Art of the Performer, 92; Robert Edmond Jones, John Barrymore e l'Amleto del 1922, La Scena di Amleto, Biblioteca Teatrale, 90; Caliban by the Yellow Sands: Percy MacKay's Adaptation of The Tempest, Maske und Kothurn, 89; Venice Hosts International Hamlet Conference, Shakespeare Bulletin 7, May/June 89. **CONTACT ADDRESS** Dept of English, Queens Col, CUNY, 6530 Kissena Blvd, Flushing, NY, 11367-1597.

GREENBERG, ALVIN D.
PERSONAL Born 05/10/1932, Cincinnati, OH, m, 3 children **DISCIPLINE** ENGLISH **EDUCATION** Univ Cincinnati, BA, 54, MA, 60; Univ Wash, PhD(English), 64. **CAREER** Instr English, Univ Ky, 63-65; from asst prof to assoc prof, 65-72, chmn, English Dept, 88-93, PROF ENGLISH, MACALESTER COL, 72- . **HONORS AND AWARDS** Witter Bynner Found for Poetry, 79; Associated Writing Progs Short Fiction Award, 82; Stories in Best American Short Stories, 73 & 82; Nimrod/ Pablo Neruda Prize in Poetry, 88; Loft-McKnight Poetry Award, 91; Loft-McKnight Award of Distinction in Poetry, 94; Fulbright lectr Am lit, Univ Kerala, 66-67; ed, Minn Rev, 67-71; Northwest Area Found Grant for opera, 75; Nat Endowment Arts fel, 72 & 92, artists fel, Bush Found, 76 & 81; Fel in Non-Fiction, 97; Jerome Found Travel & Res Grant, 98. **MEMBERSHIPS** MLA; Asn Writing Prog. **RESEARCH** Literary criticism; 20th century literature; literature and psychology. **SELECTED PUBLICATIONS** Auth, Small Waves, El Corno Press, 65; Metaphysical Giraffe, New Rivers, 68; Going Nowhere, Simon & Schuster, 71; House of the Would-Be Gardener, New Rivers, 72; Dark Lands, Ithaca House, 73; Metaform, Univ Mass, 75; Invention of the West, Avon, 76; In/Direction, David R Godine, 78; Discovery of America & Other Tales, La State Univ, 80; And Yet, Juniper, 81; Delta q, Univ Mo, 83; Man in the Cardboard Mask, Coffee House, 85; Heavy Wings, Ohio Review, 88; Why We Live with Animals, Coffee House, 90; How the Dead Live, Graywolf, 98. **CONTACT ADDRESS** Dept of English, Macalester Col, 1600 Grand Ave, Saint Paul, MN, 55105-1899. **EMAIL** greenberg@macalester.edu

GREENBERG, BRADLEY
PERSONAL m, 3 children **DISCIPLINE** JOURNALISM **EDUCATION** Bowling Green Univ, BS, 56; MS, 57, PhD, 61, Univ WI **CAREER** Lectr, 60-61, research asst, 58-60, Univ WI; research assoc, 61-64, Stanford Univ; fel, 71-72, British Broadcasting Corp, senior fel, 78-79, 81, East-West Ctr, Communication Inst, research fel, 85-86, Independent Broadcasting Authority; Univ CA, fall 92; asst prof, 64-66, assoc prof, 66-71, chair of communication, 78-83, chair of telecommunication, 84-90, prof, 71, univ distinguished prof, 90, Michigan State Univ. **HONORS AND AWARDS** Univ of Wisc Chancellor's Award for Distinguished Service in Journalism, 78; Journalism Hall of Fame Inductee, Bowling Green Univ, 80; Mich State Univ Distinguished Prof Award, 90; MI State Univ Coll of Education Crystal Apple Award, 96; MI Assn of Governing Boards Distinguished Faculty member, 97; Natl Assn of Broadcasters Lifetime Achievement Award for Audience Research, 97; Intl Communication Assn, The B. Aubrey Fisher Mentorship Award, 98. **MEMBERSHIPS** Assn for Education in Journalism; Intl Communication Assn; Intl Assoc for Mass Communication Research. **SELECTED PUBLICATIONS** Auth, Desert Storm and the Mass Media, 93; Media, Sex and the Adolescent, 93; coauth, US Minorities and News, Cultural Diversity and the US Media, 98; The Valence of Close Relationships and the Focus on Individual Attributes in Six Months of Television Talk Show Topics, in press; A Quantitative Content Analysis of the Television Talk Show, Talking up a Storm: The Social Impact of Daytime Talk Programs, in press; Disclosures and Privacy Issues on Television Talk Shows, Balancing Disclosure, Privacy, and Secrecy, in press. **CONTACT ADDRESS** Dept of Telecommunication, Michigan State Univ, 477 Communication Arts Bldg, East Lansing, MI, 48824-1212. **EMAIL** bradg@pilot.msu

GREENBERG, MARC L.
PERSONAL Born 11/09/1961, Los Angeles, CA, m, 1988, 2 children **DISCIPLINE** LANGUAGE; LITERATURE **EDUCATION** Univ Calif Los Angeles, BA, 83, PhD, 90; Univ Chicago, MA, 84. **CAREER** Asst prof to assoc prof, Univ Ks, 90-. **HONORS AND AWARDS** Zahvala, Republic of Slovenia, 92, NEH Res Fel, 93; Fulbright-hays Fel, 88-89. **MEMBERSHIPS** Soc of Slovene Stud, Amer Assoc of Teachers of Slavic & E Eur Lang; SE Eur Stud Assoc; Amer Assoc for the Adv of Slavic Stud. **RESEARCH** Hist Slavic & Indo-Eur ling; dialectology. **SELECTED PUBLICATIONS** Auth, Archaisms and Innovations in the Dialect of Sredisce; In Slavic Stud, 95; The vowel system of the Sredisce dialect based on the descriptions of Karel Ozvald, Rodopi, 96; The Sociolinguistics of Sloven, intro, Mouton de Gruyter, 97; auth, Sound Repetition and Metaphorical Structure in the Igor' Tale, Slavic, 98; Is Slavic ceta an Indo-European Archaism? In J of Slavic Ling & Poetics, 99. **CONTACT ADDRESS** Dept Slavic Lang & Lit, Univ Ks, 2134 Wescoe Hall, Lawrence, KS, 66045-2174. **EMAIL** m-greenberg@ukans.edu

GREENE, DAVID LOUIS
PERSONAL Born 09/24/1944, Middletown, CT, m, 1974, 2 children **DISCIPLINE** ENGLISH LITERATURE **EDUCATION** Univ SFla, BA, 66; Univ Pa, MA, 67, PhD(English lit), 74. **CAREER** From asst prof to assoc prof English, 70-78, prof English, 78- , chemn dept, 72-92, chemn div humanities, 74-98, Piedmont Col. **MEMBERSHIPS** Am Antiquarian Soc. **RESEARCH** Restoration literature; children's literature; history of periodicals. **SELECTED PUBLICATIONS** Coauth, Introduction to L. Frank Baum's The Master Key, Hyperion Press, 74; auth, The concept of Oz, Children's Lit Ann, 74; auth, introd to William Godwin's Fables Ancient and Modern, 76 & Charles Lamb's The Adventures of Ulysses, Garland, 76; ed, L Frank Baum's The Purple Dragon & Other Fantasies, Fictioneer, 76; coauth, The Oz Scrapbook, Random, 77. **CONTACT ADDRESS** Dept of English, Piedmont Col, PO Box 10, Demorest, GA, 30535-0010. **EMAIL** dgreene@piedmont.edu

GREENE, DOUGLAS G.
DISCIPLINE HUMANITIES **EDUCATION** Univ Chicago, PhD. **CAREER** Engl, Old Dominion Univ. **SELECTED PUBLICATIONS** Auth, John Dickson Carr: The Man Who Explained Miracles, Otto Penzler Books/Simon and Schuster, 95. **CONTACT ADDRESS** Old Dominion Univ, 4100 Powhatan Ave, Norfolk, VA, 23058. **EMAIL** DGreene@odu.edu

GREENE, GAYLE JACOBA
PERSONAL Born 06/23/1943, San Francisco, CA **DISCIPLINE** ENGLISH LITERATURE **EDUCATION** Univ Calif, Berkeley, BA, 64, MA, 66; Columbia Univ, PhD(English lit), 74. **CAREER** Ed asst, Harper & Row Publ, 67-68; lectr English lit, Queens Col, 68-72 & Brooklyn Col, 72-74; from asst prof to assoc prof, 74-87, PROF ENGL ISH LIT, SCRIPPS COL, 87-; Beatrice M. Bain Vis Fel, Univ Calif, Berkeley, 92-93; Vis Prof, Univ Wash, Seattle, Spring 93. **HONORS AND AWARDS** Graves award, Pomona Col, 77. **RESEARCH** Shakespeare; women's studies; health and environment. **SELECTED PUBLICATIONS** Co-ed, The Woman's Part: Feminist Criticism of Shakespeare, Univ Ill, 80; auth, Feminist and Marxist Criticism: An Argument for Alliances, Women's Studies; Shakespeare's Sense of Language in Othello, Etudes Anglaises, 81; co-ed, Making a Difference: Feminist Literary Criticism, Methuen, 85; auth, Changing the Story: Feminist Fiction and the Tradition, Ind univ Pressm 91; co-ed, Changing Subjects: The Making of Feminist Literary Criticism, Routledge, 93; auth, Doris Lessing: The Poetics of Change, Univ Mich Press, 94; The Woman Who Knew Too Much: Alice Stewart and the Secrets of Radiation, Temple Univ Press (forthcoming); author of numerous journal articles and reviews. **CONTACT ADDRESS** Scripps Col, 1030 Columbia Ave, Claremont, CA, 91711-3948. **EMAIL** 74554,3526@compuserve.com

GREENE, JOHN
DISCIPLINE NINETEENTH-CENTURY FRENCH LITERATURE **EDUCATION** Univ Grenoble, PhD. **RESEARCH** Short fiction; novel and poetry; narrative technique. **SELECTED PUBLICATIONS** Auth, Structure et epistemologie dans Bouvard et Pecuchet, Flaubert et le Comble de l'art, SEDES, 1981; Le Sagittaire: symbolisme astrologique chez Barbey, Hommages a Jacques Petit, Les Belles Lettres, 85; co-ed, Barbey d'Aurevilly's Correspondance generale, 9 vols Les Belles Lettres, 81-89; Barbey d'Aurevilly, A Critical Bibliography of French Literature: The Nineteenth Century, Syracuse UP, 94. **CONTACT ADDRESS** Dept of French, Victoria Univ, PO Box 3045 STN CSC, Victoria, BC, V8W 3P4. **EMAIL** greenejc@uvvm.uvic.ca

GREENE, JOHN O.
PERSONAL Born 08/30/1954, Norfolk, VA, m, 1997 **DISCIPLINE** COMMUNICATION **EDUCATION** Purdue Univ, BA, 76; Pa State Univ, MA, 78; Univ of Wis, PhD, 83. **CAREER** Asst prof, Univ of Southern Calif, 83-85; asst prof, Purdue Univ, 85-88; assoc prof, Purdue Univ, 88-93; PROF, PURDUE UNIV, 93-. **HONORS AND AWARDS** Charles H. Woolbert Res Awd, Nat Commun Asn. **MEMBERSHIPS** Am Asn for the Advancement of Sci; Int Commun Asn; Nat Commun Asn; NY Acad of Sci. **RESEARCH** Communication theory; nonverbal communication; Interpersonal communication; Aging and communication; Cognitive processes and communication **SELECTED PUBLICATIONS** auth, "What sort of terms ought theories of human action incorporate?", Commun Studies, 94; auth, "Production of messages in pursuit of multiple social goals: Action assembly theory contributions to the study of cognitive encoding processes," Commun Yearbk, 95; auth, "Complexity effects on temporal characteristics of speech," Human Commun Res, 95; auth, "Adult acquisition of message-production skill," Commun Monogr, 97; ed, Message Production: Advances in Communication Theory, Lawrence Erlbaum, 97; auth, "The impact of individual differences on message-production skill acquisition," Commun Res, 98; auth, :The dawning of a new conception of the social actor," in Commun: Views from the helm for the Twenty-First Century, Allyn & Bacon, 98. **CONTACT ADDRESS** Dept of Commun, Purdue Univ, West Lafayette, IN, 47907. **EMAIL** greene@vm.cc.purdue.edu

GREENE, THOMAS R.
PERSONAL Born 10/17/1933, New York, NY, m, 1958, 2 children **DISCIPLINE** MEDIEVAL HISTORY, ENGLISH **EDUCATION** St Francis Col, NY, BA, 58; NY Univ, MA, 61, PhD(medieval hist), 67. **CAREER** Asst prof II Hist, Newark State Col, 63-64; instr, 64-66, ASST PROF II HIST, VILLANOVA UNIV, 66-. **MEMBERSHIPS** AHA. **RESEARCH** Twelfth century church history. **SELECTED PUBLICATIONS** Auth, Oriordan, Michael la 'Recente Insurrezione in Irlanda', 1916, Eire-Ireland, Vol 0028, 93; Starkey, Thomas and the Commonweal--Humanist Politics and Religion in the Reign of Henry-VIII, Church Hist, Vol 0063, 94; Starkey, Thomas and the Commonweal--Humanist Politics and Religion in the Reign of Henry-VIII, Church Hist, Vol 0063, 94; A Question of Character--A Life of Kennedy, John, F., Cath Hist Rev, Vol 0082, 96. **CONTACT ADDRESS** Dept of Hist, Villanova Univ, Villanova, PA, 19385.

GREENFIELD, BRUCE R.
DISCIPLINE ENGLISH **EDUCATION** York, BA, 73; McGill, MA, 77; Columbia Univ, PhD, 85. **CAREER** Asst prof, ASSOC PROF, ENG, DALHOUSIE UNIV **MEMBERSHIPS** Am Antiquarian Soc **SELECTED PUBLICATIONS** Auth, Narrating Discovery: The Romantic Explorer in American Literature, 1790-1855, Columbia Univ Press, 92; auth, "The Oral in the Written: The Irony of Representation in Louis Hennepin's Description de la Louisiane," Hist Reflections 21, 95. **CONTACT ADDRESS** Dept of Eng, Dalhousie Univ, Halifax, NS, B3H 3J5.

GREENFIELD, ROBERT MORSE
PERSONAL Born 08/11/1938, Chicago, IL, m, 1967, 2 children **DISCIPLINE** ENGLISH **EDUCATION** Occidental Col, BA, 60; Columbia Univ, MA, 61, PhD, 67. **CAREER** Lectr Eng, Queens Col, NY, 66-67; asst prof, 67-72, assoc prof Eng, Lake Forest Col, 72.- **RESEARCH** Sociology of literature; 20th century literature. **SELECTED PUBLICATIONS** Cooley's Genius, Fame and the Comparison of Races, In: Knowledge and Society, JAI Press, Vol 3, 81. **CONTACT ADDRESS** Dept of English, Lake Forest Col, 555 N Sheridan Rd, Lake Forest, IL, 60045-2399.

GREENFIELD, SUSAN
DISCIPLINE ENGLISH LITERATURE **EDUCATION** PA Univ, PhD. **CAREER** Prof, Fordham Univ. **RESEARCH** Women writers, familial relationships. **SELECTED PUBLICATIONS** Auth, Fanny's Misreading and the Misreading of Fanny: Women, Literature and Inferiority in Mansfield Park, Tex Stud Lit and Lang 36, 94; Aborting the 'Mother Plot': Politics and Generation in Absalom and Achitophel, Eng Lit Hist 62, 95. **CONTACT ADDRESS** Dept of Eng Lang and Lit, Fordham Univ, 113 W 60th St, New York, NY, 10023.

GREENSTEIN, MICHAEL
PERSONAL Born 06/27/1945, Toronto, ON, Canada **DISCIPLINE** ENGLISH **EDUCATION** SUNY Stony Brook, MA, 69; York Univ, PhD, 74. **CAREER** Asst-associe, Univ Bordeaux, 76-77; asst prof to assoc prof, 79-90, ADJ PROF ENGLISH, UNIV SHERBROOKE, 90-; vis lectr, Trent Univ, 85, 91; vis lectr, Univ Toronto Sch Cont Educ, 89-. **HONORS AND AWARDS** Toronto Jewish Cong Bk Award, 90. **MEMBERSHIPS** MLA; ACUTE; PEN. **SELECTED PUBLICATIONS** Auth, Adele Wiseman and Her Works, 85; auth, Third Solitudes: Tradition and Discontinuity in Jewish-Canadian Literature, 89. **CONTACT ADDRESS** Dept of English, Univ of Sherbrooke, Sherbrooke, PQ, J1K 251.

GREENWOOD, TINA EVANS
PERSONAL Born 01/06/1964, Tucson, AZ, m, 1989 **DISCIPLINE** LIBRARY SCIENCE **EDUCATION** Univ Arizona, BA, 87, MALib, 93; Tulane Univ, MA, 90. **CAREER** Instr, 91, Career Blazers Learning Ctr; instr, 91-92, Portable Practical Ed Preparation; grad res asst, 92, Univ Arizona Schl of Lib Sci; prog asst, libr skills, 93, grad tchng asst, 93, Univ Arizona, Main Libr; ref/tech svcs libr, 93-94, Rend Lake Col Learning Res Ctr; ref libr/asst prof, 94-96, Western Ill Univ Libr; adj fac mem, 96, Univ Arizona Schl Info Res; libr instr coord/ ref libr, asst prof, 96-, John F. Reed Libr, Fort Lewis Col. **RESEARCH** Using the Internet & other technologies in education. **CONTACT ADDRESS** John F Reed Library, Fort Lewis Col, 1000 Rim Dr., Durango, CO, 81301. **EMAIL** greenwood_t@fortlewis.edu

GREETHAM, DAVID CHARLES
PERSONAL Born 10/21/1941, Tilston, England, m, 1982, 2 children **DISCIPLINE** TEXTUAL CRITICISM AND BIBLIOGRAPHY **EDUCATION** Oxford Univ, BA, MA, 67; City Univ New York Grad Sch, PhD(English), 74. **CAREER** Head English Dept, Int Schule, Hamburg, Ger, 65-67; PROF ENGLISH, CITY UNIV NEW YORK, 67-, DOCTORAL FAC, 79-, Lectr, Brit Coun, WGer, 65-67; Andrew Mellon Found fel, City Univ New York Grad Ctr, 76-77; exec dir, Soc Textual Scholar, 81-; ed, text, AMS Press, 81-; dep exec off English, PhD Prog English, City Univ New York Grad Sch, 82-83. **MEMBERSHIPS** Medieval Acad Am; Asn Doc Ed; Renaissance English Text Soc; MLA. **RESEARCH** Interdisciplinary textual theory; paleography and codicology; editing of Middle English texts. **SELECTED PUBLICATIONS** Auth, If That Was Then, Is This Now: Editing Novels and Novelists, Now, Stud in Novel, Vol 0027, 95; Scribal Publication in 17th-Century England, Papers of Bibliogr Soc of Am, Vol 0089, 95; New Ways of Looking at Old Texts, Papers of Renaissance-Eng-Text-Soc, 1985-1991, Mod Philol, Vol 0093, 95; Coleridge and Textual Instability--The Multiple Versions of the Major Poems, J Eng and Ger Philol, Vol 0095, 96; Textual Forensics, PMLA-Publ of Mod Lang Asn of Am, Vol 0111, 96. **CONTACT ADDRESS** Graduate Sch and Univ Ctr, CUNY, New York, NY, 10036.

GREGORY, ELMER RICHARD
PERSONAL Born 09/25/1938, Baytown, TX, m, 1967, 1 child **DISCIPLINE** ENGLISH, COMPARATIVE LITERATURE **EDUCATION** Univ Tex, Austin, BA, 60; Rice Univ, MA, 61; Univ Ore, PhD(comp lit), 65. **CAREER** Asst prof English, Univ Ga, 65-67; from asst prof to assoc prof, 67-77, PROF ENGLISH, UNIV TOLEDO, 77-. **MEMBERSHIPS** Conf Christianity and Lit; Milton Soc Am; MLA. **RESEARCH** John Milton; 17th century British literature; detective stories. **SELECTED PUBLICATIONS** Auth, Milton and Tradition, Milton Stud, Vol 0029, 92; Moore, Marianne 'Poetry,' Explicator, Vol 0052, 93; Milton Protestant Sonnet Lady--Revisions in the Donna-Angelicata Tradition, Comp Lit Stud, Vol 0033, 96. **CONTACT ADDRESS** Dept of English, Univ of Toledo, Toledo, OH, 43606.

GREGORY, MICHAEL J.P.
PERSONAL Born 04/07/1935, Great Crosby, England **DISCIPLINE** ENGLISH **EDUCATION** Balliol Col, Oxford, BA, 58, MA, 63; Leeds Univ, PGCE, 59. **CAREER** Master, Oratory Sch, 59-61; lectr, Royal Col Sci Tech, Glasgow, 61-62; lectr, Leeds Univ, 61-66; assoc prof to prof 66-94, ch Eng, 66-71, 73-74, dir dramatic arts prog, 67-80, coordr ling & lang stud, 83-94, PROF EMER & SR SCHOLAR, YORK UNIV, 94-. **SELECTED PUBLICATIONS** Auth, What Is Good English?, 69; auth, English Patterns, 72; auth, Before and Towards Communication Linguistics, 96; coauth, Linguistics and Style, 64; Language and Situation, 78; co-ed, Discourse and Meaning in Society, 95. **CONTACT ADDRESS** RR1, Mount Uniacke, NS, B0N 1Z0.

GREGORY, MICHAEL STRIETMANN
PERSONAL Born 10/06/1929, Oakland, CA, m, 1962, 3 children **DISCIPLINE** ENGLISH LITERATURE & CRITICISM **EDUCATION** Univ Calif, Berkeley, BA, 52, PhD(cult anthrop), 69. **CAREER** Instr English, San Jose State Univ, 56-57; from instr to assoc prof, 59-71, prof English, San Francisco State Univ, 71-, Panel reviewer & site visitor humanities, Nat Endowment Humanities, 73-, proj dir planning grant, 73, consult humanities & mem, Nat Bd Consults, 74- & proj dir develop grant, 75-; panel reviewer ethical & value implications of sci & technol, NSF, 75- **MEMBERSHIPS** AAUP; MLA; AAAS; Am Anthrop Asn; Joseph Conrad Soc Am. **RESEARCH** Comparative values of China and the West; history of ideas, with emphasis on development of paradigms in science and humanities; comparative value structure, with emphasis on value-inversions in modern China. **SELECTED PUBLICATIONS** Auth, On style, Aperture, 4/60; Seachange (short story), San Francisco Rev, 6/60; Sisyphus in the classroom, Classroom J Conf Col Compos & Commun, 2/63; The Philosophy of light, Aperture, 2/64; Politics, Science and the Human Nature, J Calif Class Asn, 76; ed, Sociobiology and Human Nature, Jossey-Bass, 78; ed, Proceedings of the San Francisco State University Conference on Recombinant DNA, Blue Wind, 78; Science and Humanism, In: Beyond Two Cultures, Proc NEXA/CSUC Dissemination Conf, NEXA & San Francisco State Univ, 5/79; auth, The Science-Humanities Program at San Francisco State University, Leonardo, 80; auth, Science and Humanities: Toward a new World View, in Brock, ed, The Culture of Biomedicine, 84. **CONTACT ADDRESS** NEXA Prog Sch of Humanities, San Francisco State Un, 1600 Holloway Ave, San Francisco, CA, 94132-1740.

GREINER, DONALD JAMES
PERSONAL Born 06/10/1940, Baltimore, MD, m, 1974, 5 children **DISCIPLINE** AMERICAN LITERATURE **EDUCATION** Wofford Col, BA, 62; Univ VA, MA, 63, PhD(Am lit), 67. **CAREER** Tchg asst Eng, Univ VA, 65-66; from asst prof to assoc prof Am lit, 67-74, prof am lit, Univ Sc, 74-; chair am lit, 87-. **HONORS AND AWARDS** Award for Outstanding Tchg, 83; Award for Distinguished Research, 84, Univ SC. **MEMBERSHIPS** MLA; S Atlantic Mod Lang Asn. **RESEARCH** Am lit; John Updike, John Hawkes, Robert Frost; contemp Am fiction. **SELECTED PUBLICATIONS** Co-ed, The notebook of Stephen Crane, Univ VA, 69; auth, Comic terror: The novels of John Hawkes, Memphis State Univ, 73; Robert Frost: The poet and his critics, Am Libr Asn, 74; ed. American Poets Since 1945, two vols., Gale Research, 80; The Other John Updike, OH UP, 81; John Updike's Novels, OH UP, 83; Adultery in the American Novel: Updike, James, Hawthorne, Univ SCP, 84; Understanding John Hawkes, Univ SCP, 85; Domestic Particulars: The Novels of Frederick Busch, Univ SCP, 87; Women Enter the Wilderness: Males Bonding and the American Novel of the 1980s, Univ SCP, 91; Women without Men: Female bonding and the American Novel in the 1980s, Univ SCP, 93; coed, The Vineland Papers: Essays on Pynchon's novel, Dalkey Archive Press, 94. **CONTACT ADDRESS** Dept of English, Univ of SC, Columbia, SC, 29208. **EMAIL** greiner@sc.edu

GRELLA, GEORGE
DISCIPLINE AMERICAN LITERATURE, MODERN BRITISH LITERATURE, THE NOVEL, AND FILM **EDUCATION** Univ KS, PhD. **CAREER** Assoc prof; taught at, Bates Col & Univ KS. **HONORS AND AWARDS** NEH Younger Humanist awd & Nat Hum fac. **RESEARCH** 19th and 20th-century Am lit; 20th-century Eng lit; novel; film. **SELECTED PUBLICATIONS** Auth, hundreds rev(s), fiction, nonfiction & film, articles on, detective fiction, gangster novels, baseball, film & on authors as Edgar Allan Poe, Sir Arthur Conan Doyle, Ian Flem ing, Georges Simenon, Ross Macdonald, Dashiell Hammett, John le Carr, Len Deighton, John Irving; adv and contrib ed, 20th-century Crime and Mystery Writers. **CONTACT ADDRESS** Dept of Eng, Univ of Rochester, 601 Elmwood Ave, Ste. 656, Rochester, NY, 14642. **EMAIL** gjg5@db1.cc.rochester.edu

GRENBERG, BRUCE L
PERSONAL Born 04/14/1935, Rockford, IL, m, 1957, 1 child **DISCIPLINE** ENGLISH **EDUCATION** Beloit Col, BA, 57; Univ NC, Chapel Hill, MA, 58, PhD(English), 63. **CAREER** From instr to asst prof, 63-69, ASSOC PROF ENGLISH, UNIV BC, 69-, Can Coun res fel, 68-69. **MEMBERSHIPS** MLA. **RESEARCH** American and English literature. **SELECTED PUBLICATIONS** Auth, Melville Art of Democracy, Am Lit, Vol 0068, 96. **CONTACT ADDRESS** 6225 Yew, Vancouver, BC, V6M 3Z1.

GRENNEN, JOSEPH EDWARD
PERSONAL Born 09/03/1926, New York, NY, m, 1950, 6 children **DISCIPLINE** ENGLISH LITERATURE, MEDIEVAL SCIENCE **EDUCATION** Col Holy Cross, BS, 47; Fordham Univ, MA, 54, PhD, 60. **CAREER** Instr, High Sch, NY, 47-50; educ adv, Troop Info and Educ Div, US Army, Ger, 50-55; from asst prof to assoc prof, 56-76, chmn dept, 65-71, PROF ENGLISH, FORDHAM UNIV, 76-, Ed, Thought, 78-80. **MEMBERSHIPS** Mediaeval Acad Am; MLA; AAUP. **RESEARCH** Middle English literature; modern criticism; history of science. **SELECTED PUBLICATIONS** Auth, The Making of Works, Jones, David and the Medieval Drama, Renascence-Essays on Values in Lit, Vol 0045, 93. **CONTACT ADDRESS** Dept of English, Fordham Univ, New York, NY, 10458.

GRIFFEN, JOHN R.
DISCIPLINE BRITISH LITERATURE, INTRODUCTION TO LITERATURE, COMPOSITION **EDUCATION** Univ Ottawa, PhD, 63; Trinity, PhD, 72. **CAREER** Prof, Univ of Southern CO. **RESEARCH** Medieval and Victorian lit and hist; Engl 8th-19th centuries. **SELECTED PUBLICATIONS** Auth, A Commentary on the Cath Works of Cardinal Newman, 93; The Oxford Movement: A Revision, 2nd Ed, 84. **CONTACT ADDRESS** Dept of Eng, Univ of Southern Colorado, 2200 Bonforte Blvd, Pueblo, CO, 81001-4901.

GRIFFIN, CINDY
DISCIPLINE COMMUNICATION STUDIES **EDUCATION** Ca State Univ Northridge, BS; Univ Oregon, MA; Univ Ind, PhD. **CAREER** Prof. **RESEARCH** Women and communication; contemporary rhetorical theory; feminist theory and criticism. **SELECTED PUBLICATIONS** Auth, The Essentialist Roots of the Public Sphere: A Feminist Critique, W J Commun, 96; Beyond Persuasion: A Proposal for Invitational Rhetoric, Commun Monographs, 95; Rhetoricizing Alienation: Mary Wollstonecraft and the Rhetorical Construction of Women's Oppression, Quarterly J Speech, 94; Visual Communication Through a Feminist Lens: Anne Noggle's Photographs of Women and Aging, Women's Studies Commun, 94. **CONTACT ADDRESS** Speech Communication Dept, Colorado State Univ, Fort Collins, CO, 80523. **EMAIL** cgriffin@vines.colostate.edu

GRIFFIN, CLAUDIUS WILLIAMS
PERSONAL Born 03/24/1935, Brooklyn, NY, m, 1969, 4 children **DISCIPLINE** ENGLISH COMPOSITION AND RHETORIC **EDUCATION** Univ Richmond, BS, 58, MA, 60; Ind Univ, PhD (English), 72. **CAREER** Teaching assoc English, Ind Univ, Bloomington, 62-66; asst prof, 69-75, dir spec serv summer prog, 72-78, ASSOC PROF ENGLISH, VA COMMONWEALTH UNIV, 75-, DIR COMPOS AND RHET PROG, 70-, Va Commonwealth Univ grant, 78 and 80-82. **HONORS AND AWARDS** MLA excellence teaching award, 72. **MEMBERSHIPS** NCTE; SAtlantic Mod Lang Asn; Conf Col Compos & Commun. **RESEARCH** Composition and rhetoric, especially the teaching of composition in secondary schools and college; English literary criticism; Shakespeare. **SELECTED PUBLICATIONS** Auth, Henry-V Decision: Shakespeare, Branagh, Kenneth--Interrogative Texts, Lit-Film Quart, Vol 0025, 97. **CONTACT ADDRESS** Va Commonwealth Univ, Box 2005, Richmond, VA, 23284-9004.

GRIFFIN, EDWARD M.
PERSONAL Born 09/25/1937, Pittsburgh, PA, m, 1960, 3 children **DISCIPLINE** ENGLISH AND AMERICAN LITERATURE **EDUCATION** Univ San Francisco, BS, 59; Stanford Univ, MA & PhD(Am lit), 66. **CAREER** Asst prof English, 66-69, assoc prof, 69-80, dir grad studies, 72-75, prof English, 79-, chemn Prog Am Stud, 80-88, Univ Minn, Minneapolis; Vis assoc prof English, Standford Univ, 71-72; Fulbright prof, Univ Salzburg, 83-84; vis prof English & Am Stud, Univ Amsterdam, 97; asst ed Am lit, 18th Century: A Current Bibliog, 71-80; ed bd, Early Am lit, 77-80. **HONORS AND AWARDS** Danforth fel, 59-66; Univ Minn distinguished teacher, 88; Fulbright fel, 83-84; Univ San Francisco Edward J. Griffin Award, 98. **MEMBERSHIPS** MLA; Midwest Mod Lang Asn; Am Studies Asn; MidAm Am Stud Asn. **RESEARCH** American poetry; early American literature; American studies. **SELECTED PUBLICATIONS** Auth, Jonathan Edwards, Univ Minn, 71; auth, Old Brick: Charles Chauncy of Boston, 1705-1787, Univ Minn, 81; auth, Patricia Hearst and Her Foremothers: The Captivity Fable in America, Centennial Rev, 92; auth, Something Else in Place of All That, Am Stud, 94; auth, William Alfred's Hogan's Goat: Power and Poetry in Brooklyn, Prospects, 94; co-ed, and contribur, The Telling Image, AMS Press, 96. **CONTACT ADDRESS** Dept of English, Univ of Minn, 207 Church St SE, Minneapolis, MN, 55455-0156. **EMAIL** griffin@tc.umn.edu

GRIFFIN, JOHN R.
PERSONAL Born 03/31/1938 **DISCIPLINE** ENGLISH, HISTORY **EDUCATION** Xavier Univ, BS, 59, AM, 61; Univ Paris, cert, 60; Univ Ottawa, PhD(English), 63; Trinity Col, Dublin, PhD(hist), 72. **CAREER** Vis prof Am lit, Univ Torino, 59-60; from asst prof to assoc prof, 63-73, PROF ENGLISH LIT, SOUTHERN COLO STATE COL, 73-, Ital Govt fel, Circolo Italiano, Italy, 68; consult, Choice Mag, 73-74. **MEMBERSHIPS** MLA; Rocky Mountain Mod Lang Asn. **RESEARCH** Medieval, Renaissance and Victorian periods. **SELECTED PUBLICATIONS** Auth, Newman after 100-Years, Church Hist, Vol 0062, 93; Before Infallibility--Liberal Catholicism in Biedermeier Vienna, Church Hist, Vol 0062, 93; Thrown among Strangers--Newman,John,Henry in Ireland, Cath Hist Rev, Vol 0079, 93; Newman and Heresy--The Anglican Years, Church Hist, Vol 0064, 95; The Great-Dissent--Newman, John, Henry and the Liberal Heresy, Church Hist, Vol 0064, 95; Newman, John, Henry--Sermons 1824-1843, Church Hist, Vol 0065, 96; Newman, John, Henry--Selected Sermons, Church Hist, Vol 0065, 96; 2 Cardinals--Newman, J. H., Mercier, D. J., Church Hist, Vol 0066, 97, The Letters and Diaries of Newman, John, Henry, Vol 7--Editing the 'British Critic', January 1839 to December 1840, Church Hist, Vol 0066, 97. **CONTACT ADDRESS** Univ Southern Colo, Pueblo, CO, 81001.

GRIFFIN, LARRY D.
PERSONAL Born 10/12/1951, Vinita, OK, 1 child **DISCIPLINE** ENGLISH **EDUCATION** Univ of OK, PhD, 89, MA, 75; Northeast St Univ, BA, 73 **CAREER** Prof, Dyersburg St Commun Col **RESEARCH** Walt Whitman; prose poems, Richard Ford, PT Barnum **CONTACT ADDRESS** Dyersburg, TN, 38024. **EMAIL** lgriffin@dscclan.dscc.cc.tn.us

GRIFFIN, MICHAEL S.
DISCIPLINE MASS COMMUNICATION STUDIES **EDUCATION** Univ Pa, MA, PhD. **CAREER** Asst prof **SELECTED PUBLICATIONS** Auth, Picturing the Gulf War: Constructing an Image of the War in Time, Newsweek, and U.S. News and World Report, J Quarterly, 95; Gender Advertising in the U.S. and India: Exporting Cultural Stereotypes, 94; Looking at TV News: Strategies for Research, Commun, 92. **CONTACT ADDRESS** Mass Communication Dept, Univ of Minnesota, Twin Cities, 111 Murphy Hall, 206 Church St SE, Minneapolis, MN, 55455. **EMAIL** Michael.S.Griffin-1@tc.umn.edu

GRIFFITH, LARRY D.
PERSONAL Born 06/29/1946, Thayer, MO, m, 1966, 4 children **DISCIPLINE** PERFORMING ARTS **EDUCATION** Harding Univ, BA, 69; Univ Mo, MA, 71; Vanderbilt Univ, PhD, 84. **CAREER** Tchr, 69-71; assoc instr, Univ Mo 71-72; asst prof, York Col, 73-77; prof, chemn, 77-, Lipscomb Univ. **HONORS AND AWARDS** Outstanding Young Men of Am, Summer Grants, Lipscomb Univ. **MEMBERSHIPS** NATS; ACDA; MENC; IFCM. **RESEARCH** Choral music **CONTACT ADDRESS** Lipscomb Univ, 3901 Granny White, Nashville, TN, 37204. **EMAIL** larry.griffith@lipscomb.edu

GRIFFITH, MALCOLM A.
PERSONAL Born 08/27/1937, Lima, OH **DISCIPLINE** ENGLISH AND AMERICAN LITERATURE **EDUCATION** Oberlin Col, BA, 58; Ohio State Univ, MA, 62, PhD(English), 66. **CAREER** ASST PROF ENGLISH, UNIV WASH, 66-. **MEMBERSHIPS** MLA. **RESEARCH** American literature; fiction; aesthetics. **SELECTED PUBLICATIONS** Auth, A Deal for the Real-World, Humphreys, Josephine 'Dreams of Sleep' and the New Domestic Novel, Southern Lit J, Vol 0026, 93. **CONTACT ADDRESS** 4705 16th NE, Seattle, WA, 98105.

GRIMES, KYLE
DISCIPLINE BRITISH ROMANTIC LITERATURE **EDUCATION** Univ IL, PhD, 90. **CAREER** Dept Eng, Univ Ala **SELECTED PUBLICATIONS** Articles, Keats-Shelley Jour, JEGP, Nineteenth-Century Studies **CONTACT ADDRESS** Univ AL, 1400 University Blvd, Birmingham, AL, 35294-1150.

GRISWOLD, JEROME JOSEPH
PERSONAL Havre, MT **DISCIPLINE** CHILDREN'S & AMERICAN LITERATURE **EDUCATION** Seattle Univ, BA, 69; Univ Conn, MA, 73, PhD(English), 78. **CAREER** Asst prof & instr English, Northeastern Univ, 76-79; ed, Houghton Mifflin Publ Co, 79-80; prof English, San Diego State Univ, 80-. **MEMBERSHIPS** MLA; Children's Lit Asn; Wallace Stevens Soc. **RESEARCH** American children's literature; American popular culture; poetry of Wallace Stevens. **SELECTED PUBLICATIONS** The Children's Book of Randall Jarcel, Univ Ga Press, 88, Judicious Kids, Oxford Univ Press, 92; The Classic Am Children's Story, Penguin, 96. **CONTACT ADDRESS** Dept of English & Comp Lit, San Diego State Univ, 5500 Campanile Dr, San Diego, CA, 92182-0002.

GRISWOLD, WENDY
DISCIPLINE ENGLISH **EDUCATION** Harvard Univ, PhD. **CAREER** Prof, Northwestern Univ. **RESEARCH** Sociology of literature. **SELECTED PUBLICATIONS** Auth, Renaissance Revivals: City Comedy and Revenge Tragedy in the London Theatre, 1576-1980; Cultures and Societies in a Changing World. **CONTACT ADDRESS** Dept of English, Northwestern Univ, 1801 Hinman, Evanston, IL, 60208.

GROB, ALAN
PERSONAL Born 03/12/1932, New York, NY, m, 1958, 2 children **DISCIPLINE** ENGLISH LITERATURE **EDUCATION** Utica Col, BA, 62; Univ Wis, MA, 57, PhD, 61. **CAREER** From asst prof to assoc prof, 61-73, PROF ENGLISH, RICE UNIV, 73-, ASSOC OF HANSZEN COL, 76-. **MEMBERSHIPS** MLA. **RESEARCH** Romantic and Victorian poetry. **SELECTED PUBLICATIONS** Auth, Arnold the 'Scholar-Gipsy'--The Use and Abuse of History, Victorian Poetry, Vol 0034, 96. **CONTACT ADDRESS** Dept of English, Rice Univ, Houston, TX, 77001.

GROCH, JOHN R.
DISCIPLINE COMPUTER-MEDIATED COMMUNICATION **EDUCATION** PhD **CAREER** Coordr, Commun Stud in Continuing Educ. **RESEARCH** Film; mass cult; postmodernism. **SELECTED PUBLICATIONS** Written on, popularity of The Wizard of Oz & comic authorship in the films of the Marx Brothers. **CONTACT ADDRESS** Commun Dept, Chatham Col, Woodland Rd., Pittsburgh, PA, 15232.

GRODEN, MICHAEL
DISCIPLINE ENGLISH LITERATURE **EDUCATION** Univ Dartmouth, BA; Princeton Univ, MA; PhD. **RESEARCH** Narrative theory; film theory; hypertext and the physical presentation of texts. **SELECTED PUBLICATIONS** Auth, Ulysses, Princeton, 97; co-ed, Johns Hopkins Guide to Literary Theory and Criticism, Johns Hopkins, 94. **CONTACT ADDRESS** Dept of English, Western Ontario Univ, London, ON, N6A 5B8.

GROENING, LAURA S.
PERSONAL Born 08/29/1949, Winnipeg, MB, Canada **DISCIPLINE** ENGLISH **EDUCATION** Univ Man, BA, 72; Carleton Univ, MA, 79, PhD, 85. **CAREER** Asst prof, 90-94, ASSOC PROF ENGLISH, CONCORDIA UNIV, 94-. **HONORS AND AWARDS** Killam postdoctoral fel, 88-89; Can res fel, Dalhousie Univ, 89-90; QSPELL Award, 94. **SELECTED PUBLICATIONS** Auth, E.K. Brown: A Study in Conflict, 93; auth, The Annotated Bibliography of Duncan Campbell Scott, 94. **CONTACT ADDRESS** Dept of English, Concordia Univ, Montreal, 1455 de Maisonneuve Blvd W, Montreal, PQ, H3G 1M8.

GROGAN, CLAIRE
DISCIPLINE ENGLISH LITERATURE **EDUCATION** Trinity Col, BA; Univ Calgary, PhD. **CAREER** Engl, Bishop's Univ. **SELECTED PUBLICATIONS** Auth, pubs on construct of female appetite in the 1790s and works by Jane Austen and Elizabeth Hamilton. **CONTACT ADDRESS** English Dept, Bishop's Univ, Lennoxville, PQ, JIMIZ 7. **EMAIL** cgrogan@ubishops.ca

GROOME, MARGARET
DISCIPLINE ENGLISH LITERATURE **EDUCATION** McGill Univ, BA; MA; PhD. **CAREER** Asst prof **RESEARCH** Shakespeare; critical theory; dramatic theory; feminist theory; modern British drama; voice and text; Chekhov. **SELECTED PUBLICATIONS** Auth, Canada's Shakespeare Myth Unmasked: Mass Culture Shakespeare at the Stratford Festival. **CONTACT ADDRESS** Dept of English, Manitoba Univ, Winnipeg, MB, R3T 2N2.

GROPPE, JOHN DANIEL
PERSONAL Born 04/23/1933, New York, NY, m, 1962, 3 children **DISCIPLINE** ENGLISH **EDUCATION** City Col New York, BSEduc, 54; Columbia Univ, MA, 60. **CAREER** Instr English, Villanova Univ, 57-58; teaching asst, Notre Dame Univ, 58-60; from Asst Prof to Assoc Prof, 62-97, prof English, St Joseph's Col, Ind, 97-, chmn dept, 80-. **HONORS AND AWARDS** Fel, Instr Ecumenical & Cult Res, St John's Univ, Minn, 69-70; Nat Endowment Humanities fel-in-residence, Sem Am Autobiography, Dartmouth Col, 75-76. **MEMBERSHIPS** NCTE; Conf Col Compos & Commun; AAUP; Rhet Soc Am; Conf Christianity & Lit. **RESEARCH** Autobiographical theory; stylistics; rhetorical theory; religion and literature. **SELECTED PUBLICATIONS** Auth, A Shred of Decency, Western Humanities Rev, spring 68; Ritualistic Language, S Atlantic Quart, winter 70; You Can't Always Look It Up, Thought, 12/71. **CONTACT ADDRESS** Dept of English, St Joseph's Col, PO Box 929, Rensselaer, IN, 47978-0929. **EMAIL** johng@saintjoe.edu

GROSS, ALAN G.
PERSONAL Born 06/02/1936, New York, NY, m, 1978, 6 children **DISCIPLINE** ENGLISH **EDUCATION** Princeton Univ, PhD 62. **CAREER** Univ Minnesota, prof, 93-. **HONORS AND AWARDS** U of Pitts Cen Philo Fel; U of Minn Cen Philo Fel. **MEMBERSHIPS** MLA; NCA. **RESEARCH** Rhetorical theory and rhetoric of science. **SELECTED PUBLICATIONS** Auth, Rereading Aristotle's Rhetoric, coed, SO IL Press, 99; Rhetorical Hermeneutics: Invention and Interpretation in the Age of Science, coed, SUNY Press, 96; The Rhetoric of Science, 2nd ed, Cambridge, Harvard Univ Press, 96. **CONTACT ADDRESS** Dept of Rhetoric, Univ of Minnesota, 2482 N Sheldon, Roseville, MN, 55113. **EMAIL** grossalang@aol.com

GROSS, DANIEL D.
PERSONAL Born 02/02/1946, St. Paul, MN, m, 1991, 4 children **DISCIPLINE** COMMUNICATION; RHETORIC **EDUCATION** Bethel Col, BA, 68; Denver Theolog Sem, M.Div, 72; Univ Colo Denver, MA, 83; Univ Ore, PhD, 89. **CAREER** Ch and assoc prof Dept Communication & Theatre, Mont St Univ, 91-; asst prof Speech Communication, Tarleton St Univ, 90-91; Minister, Kimball & Dix Presbyterian Churches, Kimball & Dix, Nebraska, 87-90; teaching asst, Univ Ore, 86-87; intern, Clinical-Pastoral Education, Ft Logan Mental Health Center, 85-86; instr, Breckenridge Comm Col, 85-86; dir Educ, St James Presbyterian Church, Littleton, CO, 81-85; vis instr, Denver Sem, 75-80. **HONORS AND AWARDS** MSU-Billings tenured, 98; Fac Achievement Award, 97; Cetificate of Recognition, 96; Outstanding Fac Award, 95, 97; Cox Fel, 94; Merit Award Tchg Excellence, 93; Winston & Helen Cox Fel Nominee, MSU Billings, 92-93; Tchg Fel, Univ Ore, 86-87; Denver Sem Tuition Scholar Award, 68, 69. **MEMBERSHIPS** Ntl Communication Assoc, 90-; World Communication Assoc, 95-; Editorial Advisory Board Collgiate Pr, 95; Wadsworth Book Reviewers, 95; Conference of College Teachers of English, 94. **RESEARCH** Narrative Theory; Rhetorical Criticism; Communication and Law. **SELECTED PUBLICATIONS** Coauth, Oppression in Testing: An Examination of How Computer Adaptive Testing Alienates and Oppresses, Teaching in the Community Colleges Jour, 98; coauth, "Cybersex in the Wired Classroom: Facts, Issues, and Suggestions, Teaching in the Community Colleges Jour, 98; coauth, Language Boundaries and Discourse Stability: 'Tagging' as Form of Discourse Spanning International Borders, 97. **CONTACT ADDRESS** Dept of Communication and Theatre, Montana State Univ, MSU-B, 1500 N 30th St, Billings, MT, 54101. **EMAIL** ca_gross@vino.ememt.edu

GROSS, DAVID STUART
PERSONAL Born 02/22/1942, Mineola, NY, m, 1971, 1 child **DISCIPLINE** ENGLISH, COMPARATIVE LITERATURE **EDUCATION** Wesleyan Univ, BA, 65; Univ Iowa, MA, 69, PhD(comp lit), 73. **CAREER** Asst prof English, Winona State Col, 71-73; ASST PROF ENGLISH, UNIV OKLA, 73-. **MEMBERSHIPS** MLA; Soc Amis Flaubert. **RESEARCH** The novel; literature and society; Marxist theory. **SELECTED PUBLICATIONS** Auth, Minor Prophecies--The Literary Essay in the Culture Wars, World Lit Today, Vol 0067, 93; Rethinking Theory--A Critique of Contemporary Literary-Theory and an Alternative Account, World Lit Today, Vol 0067, 93; Cultural Criticism, Literary-Theory, Poststructuralism, World Lit Today, Vol 0068, 94; The Idea of the Postmodern--A History, World Lit Today, Vol 0069, 95; Public-Access--Literary-Theory and American Cultural Politics, World Lit Today, Vol 0069, 95; The Institution of Theory, World Lit Today, Vol 0069, 95. **CONTACT ADDRESS** Dept of English, Univ of Okla, Norman, OK, 73069.

GROSS, KENNETH
DISCIPLINE ENGLISH **EDUCATION** Yale Univ, PhD. **CAREER** Prof; taught at, Yale Univ. **HONORS AND AWARDS** Mellon fel; Am Coun Learned Soc fel; Folger Shakespeare Libr fel & Guggenheim fel. **RESEARCH** Intricate nature of literary fantasy. **SELECTED PUBLICATIONS** Auth, Spenserian Poetics: Idolatry, Iconoclasm, and Magic, The Dream of the Moving Statue; articles on, Dante, Shakespeare, Milton, Marvell & Romantic poetry. **CONTACT ADDRESS** Dept of Eng, Univ of Rochester, 601 Elmwood Ave, Ste. 656, Rochester, NY, 14642.

GROSSBERG, LAWRENCE
PERSONAL Born 12/03/1947, New York, NY, m, 1988, 1 child **DISCIPLINE** COMMUNICATION **EDUCATION** Univ Rochester, BA (philos, hist), 68; Univ IL, PhD (commun), 76. **CAREER** Asst prof, Purdue Univ, 75-76; asst, assoc, prof, Speech Commun, Communications Res, Criticism and Interpretive Theory, Univ IL, Champaign-Urbana, 76-94; Morris Davis distinguished prof of Commun Studies, Univ NC, Chapel Hill, 94-. **HONORS AND AWARDS** Fisher Mentorship Award, Int Commun Asn, 95; Distinguished Scholar Award, Nat Commun Asn, 97; ICA fel, Int Commun Asn, 98. **RESEARCH** Cultural studies; popular music; philos of culture & commun; neo-conservatism. **SELECTED PUBLICATIONS** Ed, with James Hay and Ellan Wartella, The Audience and Its Landscape, Westview Press, 96; auth, Toward a Geneology of the State of Cultural Studies: The Discipline of Communication and the Reception of Cultural Studies in the United States, in Cary Nelson and Dilip Gaonkar, Disciplinary and Dissent in Cultural Studies, Routledge, 96; Cultural Studies, Modern Logics, and Theories of Globalization, in Angela McRobbie, ed, Back to Reality: The Social Experience of Cultural Studies, Manchester Univ Press, 97; Re-placing Popular Culture, in The Clubcultures Reader: Readings in Popular Cultural Studies, ed, Steve Redhead with Derek Wynne and Justin O'Connor, Blackwells, 97; Doing Without Culture, or Cultural Studies in Helms' Country, in Judith S Trent, ed, Communication: Views from the Helm for the Twenty-First Century, Allyn & Bacon, 97; Configuring Space, in Unmapping The Earth: Catalog of the Kwang-ju Biennale 1997, Kwang-ju Biennale Press, 97; Dancing in Spite of Myself: Essays on Popular Culture, Duke Univ Press, 97; Bringing It All Back Home: Essays on Cultural Studies, Duke Univ Press, 97; with Ellen Wartella and Charles Whitney, MediaMaking, Sage, 98; The Cultural Studies' Crossroads Blues, European J of Cultural Studies 1, 98; numerous other books and articles, several publications forthcoming. **CONTACT ADDRESS** Dept of Commun Studies, Univ North Carolina, Chapel Hill, CB 3285 Bingham Hall, Chapel Hill, NC, 27599-3285. **EMAIL** docrock@email.unc.edu

GROSSKURTH, PHYLLIS M.
PERSONAL Toronto, ON, Canada **DISCIPLINE** ENGLISH **EDUCATION** Univ Toronto, BA, 46; Univ Ottawa, MA, 60; Univ London, PhD, 62. **CAREER** Lectr, Carleton Univ, 64-65; asst prof, 65-69, assoc prof, 69-72, PROF, UNIV TORONTO, 72-89. **HONORS AND AWARDS** Gov Gen Award nonfiction, 65; Univ BC Award Biog, 65; Hon Res Fel, Univ Kent, 91; Hon Fel, Univ Toronto, 92. **MEMBERSHIPS** Am Acad Psychoanalysis; PEN Int; Writer's Union Can. **SELECTED PUBLICATIONS** Auth, John Addington Symonds: A Biography, 64; auth, Gabrielle Roy, 69; auth, Melanie Klein: Her World and Her Work, 86; auth, Margaret Mead: A Life of Controversy, 89. **CONTACT ADDRESS** New College, Univ Toronto, Toronto, ON, M5A 2J6.

GROTH, JANET
DISCIPLINE ENGLISH **EDUCATION** Univ MN, BA; NY Univ, MA and PhD, 82. **CAREER** Fac, Plattsburgh State Univ of NY . **HONORS AND AWARDS** Former editorial assistant for New Yorker magazine. **RESEARCH** Magazine and article writing; Am lit; Shakespeare. **SELECTED PUBLICATIONS** Auth, two bks about Edmund Wilson. **CONTACT ADDRESS** SUNY, Plattsburgh, 101 Broad St, Plattsburgh, NY, 12901-2681.

GROVE, JAMES PAUL
PERSONAL Born 10/22/1949, Minneapolis, MN, m, 1972, 1 child **DISCIPLINE** AMERICAN LITERATURE, BRITISH FICTION **EDUCATION** Univ Minn, BA, 71; Col St Thomas, MAT, 74; Southern Ill Univ, Carbondale, MA, 76, PhD(English), 80. **CAREER** Instr English, Mt Mercy Col, 80-, full prof and chair, English Dept. **HONORS AND AWARDS** NEH grants, 86, 89, 93; Fulbright Lecturer, Czech Republic, 89-90. **MEMBERSHIPS** MLA; NCTE. **RESEARCH** Place in Literature, Evil in Contemporary American Literature, Southern Literature, Midwest Literature. **SELECTED PUBLICATIONS** Auth, Stepping Away From the Snug Sofa: Melvilles Vision of Death in Moby-Dick, New England Quart, 6/79; The Neglected Dinner in James' The Wings of the Dove, Am Notes & Queries, 9/79; Pastoralism and Anti-Pastoralism in Peter Matthiessen's Far Tortuga, Critique, Winter, 79; Articles on American, Czech, and Latin American Literature in journals (The New England Quart, American Lit, Critique, Am Notes and Queries, Prarie Schooner, Review of Contemporary Fiction, Iowa Woman, Crab Orchard Review, High Plains Literary Review); and in books, The Best of American Literature: Mark Twain, The Last Quarter: Contemporary Southern Fiction, Magill's Literary Annual. **CONTACT ADDRESS** English Dept, Mount Mercy Col, 1330 Elmhurst Dr N E, Cedar Rapids, IA, 52402-4797.

GROVE-WHITE, ELIZABETH M.
DISCIPLINE ENGLISH LITERATURE **EDUCATION** Trinity Col, Dublin, PhD. **CAREER** Assoc prof; dir, Wrtg Prog. **HONORS AND AWARDS** Peabody awd, 80; Hely-Hutchinson awd, 73; Found scholar, Trinity Col, Dublin, 70. **RESEARCH** Epistemic rhetoric; computer-mediated communication; transactional writing. **SELECTED PUBLICATIONS** Auth, Virginia Woolf's To the Lighthouse, Addison Longman, 80; articles and rev(s) in Globe and Mail, Amer Reporter, Hermathena, Hibernia, Brick. **CONTACT ADDRESS** Dept of English, Victoria Univ, PO Box 3070, Victoria, BC, V8W 3W1. **EMAIL** grovewhi@uvic.ca

GROVER, DORYS CROW
PERSONAL Born 09/23/1921, Pendleton, OR **DISCIPLINE** AMERICAN STUDIES, BRITISH LITERATURE **EDUCATION** Ore State Univ, BS, 51; Wash State Univ, PhD(Am studies), 69. **CAREER** Instr English, Wash State Univ, 64-69; prof, Drake Univ, 71-72; PROF ENGLISH, E TEX STATE UNIV, 72-, Fac res grants, 72-76 and 81-82. **HONORS AND AWARDS** Southwest Heritage Award, 77. **MEMBERSHIPS** MLA; Soc Study Midwest Lit; Rocky Mountain Mod Lang Asn; S Cent Mod Lang Asn; Am Studies Asn. **RESEARCH** American novel and novelists; Colonial American literature; Western literature. **SELECTED PUBLICATIONS** Auth, Brand, Max Best Poems--Verses from a Master of Popular Prose, Western Am Lit, Vol 0028, 93; The Texas Legacy of Porter, Katherine, Anne, J the W, Vol 0032, 93; Leadville, USA--An Intimate History of a Colorado Mining Town, Western Am Lit, Vol 0028, 94. **CONTACT ADDRESS** Dept of Lit and Lang, East Texas State Univ, Commerce, TX, 75428.

GROVES, JEFFREY D.
DISCIPLINE ENGLISH **EDUCATION** LaVerne, BA, 81; Claremont Grad Sch, MA, 83, PhD, 87. **CAREER** ASSOC PROF, ENG, HARVEY MUDD COLL **MEMBERSHIPS** Am Antiquarian Soc **SELECTED PUBLICATIONS** Auth, Ticknor-and-Fields-ism of all kinds: Thomas Starr King, Literary Promotion, and Canon Formation, New Eng Quart 68, 95; Judging Literary Books By Their Covers: House Styles, Ticknor and Fields, and Literary Promotion, in Reading Books: The Artifact as Text and Context, Univ Mass Press, 96. **CONTACT ADDRESS** Hum/Soc Sci, Harvey Mudd Col, Claremont, CA, 91711.

GROW, LYNN MERLE
PERSONAL Born 02/20/1945, Norfolk, VA **DISCIPLINE** ENGLISH LITERATURE **EDUCATION** Univ Southern Calif, BA, 67, MA, 68 & 72, PhD(English), 71. **CAREER** Teaching asst Englih, Univ Southern Calif, 70-71, instr, 71-72; asst prof English, Wichita State Univ, 72-77; lectr Univ Maryland, 77-81; LECTR, COL BAHAMAS, 81-. **MEMBERSHIPS** MLA; AAUP. **RESEARCH** Samuel Taylor Coleridge; scholarship in modern American philosophy; modern Philippine literature in English. **SELECTED PUBLICATIONS** Auth, The Automatic Glass Door and Other Poems, Dalhousie Rev, Vol 0073, 93. **CONTACT ADDRESS** Personnel Dept, Col of the Bahamas, PO Box N4912, Nassau, ., 67208.

GRUBER, WILLIAM E.
PERSONAL Born 09/26/1943, Hokendauqua, PA, m, 1968, 3 children **DISCIPLINE** ENGLISH **EDUCATION** Yale Univ BA, 65; Univ Idaho MA, 74; Washington State PhD, 79. **CAREER** Illinois State Univ asst prof eng, 79-80; Emory Univ asst prof, 80-86, assoc prof, 86-94, prof, 94-. **MEMBERSHIPS** MLA; SAMLA **RESEARCH** Drama; Hist of Drama. **SELECTED PUBLICATIONS** Comic theaters; Missing Persons: Character and Characterizations in Modern Drama. **CONTACT ADDRESS** Emory Univ, Dept Eng, Atlanta, GA, 30322. **EMAIL** wegrube@emory.edu

GRUBGELD, ELIZABETH
DISCIPLINE MODERN BRITISH LITERATURE, IRISH LITERATURE **EDUCATION** Univ Iowa, PhD, 83. **CAREER** Engl, Okla St Univ. **HONORS AND AWARDS** Prize Literary and Cultural Criticism, 95. **RESEARCH** Elizabeth Bowen and John Montague. **SELECTED PUBLICATIONS** Auth, George Moore and the Autogenous Self: The Autobiography and Fiction, Syracuse Univ Press. **CONTACT ADDRESS** Oklahoma State Univ, 101 Whitehurst Hall, Stillwater, OK, 74078.

GRUDIN, ROBERT
PERSONAL Born 03/04/1938, Newark, NJ, m, 1967, 2 children **DISCIPLINE** RENAISSANCE LITERATURE **EDUCATION** Harvard Univ, BA, 60; Univ Calif, Berkeley, Phd(comp lit), 69. **CAREER** Asst prof, 71-78, ASSOC PROF ENGLISH, UNIV ORE, 78-. **SELECTED PUBLICATIONS** Auth, The Elephants Teach--Creative-Writing since 1880, Philos and Lit, Vol 0020, 96. **CONTACT ADDRESS** English Dept, Univ Ore, Eugene, OR, 97403-1205.

GRUNDY, ISOBEL
PERSONAL Born 05/23/1938, Weybridge, England **DISCIPLINE** ENGLISH LITERATURE **EDUCATION** St Anne's Col, Oxford Univ, BA, 60, DPhil, 71. **CAREER** Tchr, Jamsankoski, Finland, 60-61; ed dept, JM Dent Publs, UK, 61-63; res asst, Columbia Univ, 63-66; asst lectr, St Anne's Col, Oxford Univ, 69-70; jr res fel, St Hugh's Col, Oxford Univ, 70-71; lectr to reader & head Eng, Queen Mary Col, London Univ, 71-90; HENRY MARSHALL TORY PROF, UNIV ALBERTA, 90-. **MEMBERSHIPS** Can Soc 18th Century Stud; Jane Austen Soc N Am. **SELECTED PUBLICATIONS** Auth, Lady Mary Wortley Montagu: Comet of the Englightenment; coauth, The Feminist Companion to Literature in English, 90; ed, Secrecy or the Ruin on the Rock (Eliza Fenwick), 94; ed, Romance Writings (Lady Mary Wortley Montagu), 96; ed, Selected Letters (Lady Mary Wortley Montagu), 97; co-ed, Women, Writing, History 1640-1740, 92. **CONTACT ADDRESS** Dept of English, Univ of Alberta, Edmonton, AB, T6G 2E5.

GRUNER, CHARLES R.
PERSONAL Born 11/06/1931, Pinckneyville, IL, m, 1958, 2 children **DISCIPLINE** SPEECH COMMUNICATION **EDUCATION** Southern Ill Univ, BS, 55, MA, 56; The Ohio State Univ, PhD, 63. **CAREER** Grad asst in Speech Dept, 55-56, res asst & res assoc, Southern Ill Univ, 63-64; teacher of speech, Webster Groves High School, 56-57; instr, 57-60, asst prof, St. Lawrence Univ, 60-64; asst prof, 64-66, assoc prof, Univ of Neb, 66-69; Ed, GA Speecj Commun J, 75-77, Assoc Prof, 69-74, Prof, Univ of GA, 74-. **HONORS AND AWARDS** Eagle Scout, 46-. **MEMBERSHIPS** Int Soc for General Semantics; Southern Speech Commun Asn; Ga Speech Asn; Am Inst of Parliamentarians; Workshop Libr on World Humor; Int Soc for Humor Studies. **SELECTED PUBLICATIONS** Auth, The Game of Humor: A Comprehensive Theory of Why We Laugh, Transaction Pub, 97; Parliamentary Procedure as the Major Part of a Course in Problem-Solving, Parliamentary J, 94; Appreciation and Understanding of Satire: Another Quasi-Experiment, Psychol Reports, 96; The Teachin/Research Symbiosis: A Two-Way Street, ERIC Clearinghouse on Reading, English, and Commun, 95; Satire as Persusion, ERIC Document ED, microfische; coauth, Evaluative Responses to Jokes in Informative Speech With and Without Laughter by an Audience: A Partial Replication, Psychol Reports, 94; Semantic Differential Measurements of Connotations of Verbal Terms and Their Doublespeak Facsimiles in Sentence Context, Psychol Reports, 95. **CONTACT ADDRESS** Dept of Speech Communication, Univ of Georgia, Athens, GA, 30602. **EMAIL** cgruner@uga

GRUPENHOFF, RICHARD
DISCIPLINE FILM PRODUCTION, FILM HISTORY, SCREENWRITING, AND AFRICAN AMERICAN FILM HIS **EDUCATION** Xavier Univ BA; Purdue Univ, MA; Ohio State Univ, PhD. **CAREER** Instr, 75-, ch, dept Radio-TV-Film, Rowan Col of NJ. **SELECTED PUBLICATIONS** Auth, The Black Valentino: The Stage and Screen Career of Lorenzo Tucker. **CONTACT ADDRESS** Rowan Col of NJ, Glassboro, NJ, 08028-1701. **EMAIL** grupenhoff@rowan.edu

GRUSHOW, IRA
PERSONAL Born 04/11/1933, New York, NY, m, 1965, 2 children **DISCIPLINE** ENGLISH **EDUCATION** City Col New York, BA, 54; Yale Univ, MA, 57, PhD, 63. **CAREER** Instr English, Carnegie-Inst Technol, 60-62; from instr to asst prof, 62-68, chmn dept, 74-80, assoc prof, 68-84, prof, 84-90, ALUMNI PROF ENGLISH BELLES LETTRES & LITERATURE, FRANKLIN & MARSHALL COL, 90-98, PROF EMER, 98-. **MEMBERSHIPS** MLA; Am Soc 18th Century Studies **RESEARCH** Satire; 18th century English literature; Sir Max Beerbohm **SELECTED PUBLICATIONS** Auth, The Imaginary Reminiscenses of Sir Max Beerbohm, Ohio Univ Press, 84. **CONTACT ADDRESS** Dept of English, Franklin and Marshall Col, PO Box 3003, Lancaster, PA, 17604-3003. **EMAIL** i_grushow@acad.fandm.edu

GRUSIN, R.
PERSONAL Born 09/29/1953, Chicago, IL, m, 2 children **DISCIPLINE** ENGLISH **EDUCATION** Univ Ill Urbana, BA, 76; Univ Calif Berkeley, PhD, 83. **CAREER** Asst prof, SAA, 86-91; assoc prof, SAA, 91-93; dir undergrad studies and assoc prof, SAA, 93-97; chair & assoc prof, sch of lit, comm & culture, Ga Inst of Tech, 97-. **HONORS AND AWARDS** Fel, NEH Inst on Image and Text in the Eighteenth Century, The John Hopkins Univ, summer, 88; fel, Sch of Criticism and Theory, summer, 85. **MEMBERSHIPS** Mod Lang Asn of Amer; South Atlantic Mod Lang Asn; Amer Studies Asn; Soc of Lit and Sci. **RESEARCH** New media studies; Ecocriticism; American cultural studies. **SELECTED PUBLICATIONS** Co-auth, Remediation: Understanding New Media, MIT Press, 98; auth, Transcendentalist Hermeneutics: Institutional Authority and the Higher Criticism of the Bible, Duke Univ Press, 91; co-auth, Remediation, Configurations, vol 4, no 3, 311-358, Fall, 96; article, Introduction, New Amer Studies in Sci and Tech: Essays in Cultural Historicism, Configurations, vol 3, no 3, 349-51, Fall, 95; article, Representing Yellowstone: Photography, Loss, and Fidelity to Nature, Configurations, vol 3, no 3, 415-36, Fall, 95; article, Theodore Parker, A Companion to American Thought, Blackwell, 516-17, 95; article, What Is an Electronic Author?, Configurations, vol 2, no 3, 469-83, Fall, 94. **CONTACT ADDRESS** School of Literature, Communication & Culture, Georgia Inst of Tech, 686 Cherry St, Atlanta, GA, 30332-0165. **EMAIL** richard.grusin@lcc.gatech.edu

GUDDING, GABRIEL
PERSONAL Born 06/16/1966, MN, 1 child **DISCIPLINE** AMERICAN STUDIES/CREATIVE WRITING (POETRY) **EDUCATION** Evergreen Coll, BA, 94; Purdue Univ, MA, 97. **CAREER** Grad stud, Purdue Univ, 95-97; Grad stud, Cornell Univ, 98-. **HONORS AND AWARDS** The Nation "Discovery" Award, 98. **MEMBERSHIPS** Poetry Society of America **RESEARCH** American poetry; history of science **SELECTED PUBLICATIONS** The Phenotype/Genotype Distinction and The Disappearance of the Body, Journal of the History of Ideas, John Hopkins Univ Press, July 96; The Wallace Stevens Jour, I See Your Hammer in the Horologe of Time and I Raise You a Westclock, Spring 97; The Iowa Review, One Petition Lofted into the Ginkgos, Fall 97; The Nation, The Parenthesis Inserts Itself into the Transcripts of The Committee on Un-American Activities, May 18, 1998; River Styx, The Bosun, August 1998; The Beloit Poetry Journal, The Footnote Reconnoiters the Piedmont. **CONTACT ADDRESS** Cornell Univ, 250 Goldwin Smith, Ithaca, NY, 14850. **EMAIL** gwg6@cornell.edu

GUENTHER, BARBARA J.
DISCIPLINE LIBERAL ARTS **EDUCATION** Nazareth Col, BS, 61; Univ MI, MA, 64; Univ WI, PhD, 74. **CAREER** Instr, Northwestern Univ; DePaul Univ; IN State Univ; Hillsdale Col; Univ N IA; Lake Forest Coll; assoc prof, 81. **HONORS AND AWARDS** Summer sem grant, NEH; travel res grants, Univ WI, Univ N IA; Fulbright award, 91. **SELECTED PUBLICATIONS** Pub(s), Ariz Eng Bulletin; Handbk of Exec Commun. **CONTACT ADDRESS** Dept of Lib Arts, Sch of the Art Inst of Chicago, 37 S Wabash Ave, Chicago, IL, 60603.

GUERIN, WILFRED LOUIS
PERSONAL Born 07/10/1929, New Orleans, LA, m, 1951, 6 children **DISCIPLINE** ENGLISH LITERATURE, CRITICISM **EDUCATION** Tulane Univ, BA, 51, MA, 53, PhD, 58. **CAREER** Instr, Holy Cross High Sch, New Orleans, 52-53; instr English, Centenary Col, 53-56, asst prof, 58-62; assoc prof, Univ Southwestern La, 62-63; prof, Centenary Col La, 63-74; prof English, La State Univ, Shreveport, 74-98, chair Dept English & For Langs, 78-85, vice-chancellor & provost, 85-91, dir Master's Prog, 93-98, coordr, Grad Studies, 94-98; fel, SEastern Inst Medieval and Renaissance Studies, Duke Univ, 66; fel, SEastern Inst Medieval and Renaissance Studies, NC Univ at Chapel Hill, 67; vis fac audit prog, Harvard Univ, 70. **HONORS AND AWARDS** Outstanding Teacher Award, Centenary Col, 68; H. M. Cotton Fac Excellence Award, La State Univ Found, 77; Phi Beta Kappa; Phi Sigma Iota; Kappa Delta Pi; Omicron Delta Kappa; Phi Kappa Phi; Sigma Tau Delta; Fac Achievement Award, LSUS, Spring 84; grant, La Comt for the Humanities, 84. **MEMBERSHIPS** MLA; SCent Mod Lang Asn; AAUP; SCent Renaissance Conf; Conf Christianity & Lit; SCentral Conf Christianity & Lit. **RESEARCH** Teilhard de Chardin; literary criticism; medieval and Renaissance literature. **SELECTED PUBLICATIONS** Auth, Christian Myth and Naturalistic Deity: The Great Gatsby, Renascence, 61; Irony and tension in Browning's Karshish, Victorian Poetry, 63; two chapters in Malory's Originality: A Critical Study of Le Morte Darthur, Johns Hopkins, 64; coauth, A Handbook of Critical Approaches to Literature, Harper & Row, 66 & 79, Oxford Univ Press, 92 & 99; auth, Death in the woods: Sherwood Anderson's Cold Pastoral, CEA Critic, 68; coauth, Mandala: Literature for Critical Analysis, Harper & Row, 70; auth, Browning's Cleon: A Teilhardian view, Victorian Poetry, 74; Dynamo, virgin and cyclotron: Henry Adams and Teilhard de Chardin on pilgrimage, Renascence, spring 76; coauth, L.I.T.: Literature and Interpretive Techniques, Harper & Row, 86; auth, Herbert's The Pulley, in Explicator 53.2, 95. **CONTACT ADDRESS** Dept of English, Louisiana State Univ, 1 University Pl, Shreveport, LA, 71115-2301. **EMAIL** wguerin@pilot.lsus.edu

GUERINOT, JOSEPH VINCENT
PERSONAL Born 02/18/1928, Rochester, NY **DISCIPLINE** ENGLISH LITERATURE **EDUCATION** St Bernard's Sem, Ba, 49; Fordham Univ, MA, 53; Yale Univ, PhD, 62. **CAREER** Asst, Fordham Univ, 51-52; asst English, Lycee Jules Ferry, France, 54-55; from instr to asst prof, Bucknell Univ, 55-65; asst prof, Hunter Col, 65-67; assoc prof, 67-71, PROF ENGLISH, UNIV WIS, MILWAUKEE, 71-. **RESEARCH** Pope; mediaeval Latin literature; Henry James. **SELECTED PUBLICATIONS** Auth, Wake, William Gallican Correspondence and Related Documents, 1716-1731, Scriblerian and the Kit-Cats, Vol 0028, 95. **CONTACT ADDRESS** Dept of English, Univ of Wis, Milwaukee, WI, 53201.

GUERRO, MARIA C.M. DE
PERSONAL Born 05/26/1950, Rosario, Argentina, m, 1974, 2 children **DISCIPLINE** ENGLISH AND LINGUISTICS **EDUCATION** Univ of Miss, MA, 73; Inter-Am Univ of Puerto Rico, EdD, 90. **CAREER** LECTR, 80-81, INSTR, 81-86, ASST PROF OF ENGLISH AND LINGUISTICS, 86-90, ASSOC PROF OF ENGLISH AND LINGUISTICS, 91-96, PROF OF ENGLISH AND LINGUISTICS, INTER AM UNIV METRO, 96-. **HONORS AND AWARDS** Scholars for the Dream Travel Awd, 95; Dr. Ilia Morales Awd for Acad Excellence, Inter Am Univ Doctoral prog, 91; fulbright scholar, Univ of Miss, 72-74. **MEMBERSHIPS** Am Asn of Applied Linguistics; Teachers of English to Speakers of Other Languages Int (TESOL); TESOL Puerto Rico; Int Reading Asn. **RESEARCH** Second language learning and tchg; socio-cultural theory. **SELECTED PUBLICATIONS** Coauth, Assessing the impact of peer revision on L2 writing, Applied Linguistics, 98; Peer revision in L2 classroom: Social-Cognitive activities, mediating strategies, and aspects of social behavior, J of Second Lang Writing, 96; Social-cognitive dimensions of interaction in L2 Peer Revision, Modern Lang J, 94; auth, Forma nd functions of inner speeech in adult second language learning, Vygotskian Approaches to Second Lang Rese, Ablex Press, 94; The din phenomenon: Mental rehearsal in the second language, Foreign Lang Annals, 87. **CONTACT ADDRESS** English Dept, Inter American Univ of Puerto Rico, PO Box 191293, San Juan, PR, 00919-1293. **EMAIL** mguerre@inter.edu

GUETTI, JAMES L.
DISCIPLINE ENGLISH LANGUAGE AND LITERATURE **EDUCATION** Amherst Univ, BA; MA; Cornell, PhD. **CAREER** Prof. **RESEARCH** Philosophy of language; critical theory; modern literature. **SELECTED PUBLICATIONS** Auth, Wittgenstein and the Grammar of Literary Experience; auth, The Limits of Metaphor; Word-Magic. **CONTACT ADDRESS** Dept of English, Rutgers Univ, 510 George St, Murray Hall, New Brunswick, NJ, 08901-1167.

GUIBBORY, ACHSAH
PERSONAL Born 06/30/1945, Norwalk, CT, m, 1972, 1 child **DISCIPLINE** ENGLISH **EDUCATION** Indiana Univ, BA, 66; Univ Calif, Los Angeles, MA, 67, PhD, 70. **CAREER** Asst prof, 70-76, PROF ENGLISH & RELIG STUDIES, UNIV ILL, URBANA-CHAMPAIGN, 76-. **HONORS AND AWARDS** Univ Ill Campus Award for Excellence Undergrad Teach, 79; William Prokasy College of LAS Award for Excellence Teaching, 95; Luckman Award, UIUC, Excellence in Undergrad Teach, 95. **MEMBERSHIPS** MLA; Milton Soc Am; John Donne Soc. **RESEARCH** Seventeenth-century English literature; views of history; religion. **SELECTED PUBLICATIONS** Auth, Dryden's views of history, Philol Quart, 73; Sir Thomas Browne's allusions to Janus, English Lang Notes, 75; Francis Bacon's view of history: The cycles of error and the progress of truth, J English & Ger Philol, 75; ed, The Ephesian Matron, Augustan Reprint Soc, 75; auth, The Poet as Myth-Maker: Ben Jonson's Poetry of Praise, Clio, 76; Sir Thomas Browne's Pseudodoxia Epidemica and the circle of Knowledge, Tex Studies Lang & Lit, 76; No lust theres like to poetry: Robert Herrick's passion for poetry, in Trust to Good Verses: Herrick Tercentenary Essays, 78; John Donne and memory as the art of salvation, HLQ, 80; A sense of the future: Projected audiences of Donne and Jonson, John Donne J, 83; The temple of Hesperides and Anglican Puritan controversy, in the Muses Commonweale: Poetry and Politics in the Earlier Seventeenth Century, 88; The Map of Time: Seventeenth Centruy English Literature and Ideas of Pattern in History, Univ Ill, 86; Imitation and originality: Cowley and Bacon's vision of progress, SEL, 89; Oh let me not serve so: The politics of love in Donne's Elegies, ELH, 90; A rationall of old rites: Sir Thomas Browne's Urn Burial and the conflict over ceremony, YES, 91; Donne, the idea of woman and the experience of love, John Donne J, 90; Sexual politics political sex: Seventeenth Century love poety, in Discoures of Desire: Sexuality in 17th Century Non-Dramatic Literature, 93; John Donne, in Cambridge Companion to English Poetry, Donne to Marvell, 94; Enlarging the units of the Religious Lyric: The case of Herrick's Hesperides, in New Perspectives on the Seventeenth-Century English Religious Lyric, 94; Charles's Prayer, idolatious imitation and true creation in Milton's Echonoulastes, in Of Poetry and Politics: New Essays on Milton and His World, 95; The Gospel according to Aemelia Lanyer: Women and the sacred in Aemelia Lanye's Salve Deis Rex Judaeouen, in Sacred and Profane: The Interplay of Secular and Devotional Literature 1500-1700, 95, rev ed in Aemelia Lanyer: Gender, Genre and the Canon, 98; Donne, Milton and holy sex, Milton Studies, 96; Fear of loving more: Death and the loss of sacremental love, in Donne's Desire of More: The Subject of Anne More Donne in His Poetry, 96; The Relique, The Song of Songs, and Donne's Songs and Sonets, John Donne J, 96; Ceremoney and Community from Herbert to Milton: Literature, Religion, and Cultural Conflict in 17th Century England, 98. **CONTACT ADDRESS** Dept of English, Univ of Ill, 608 S Wright St, Urbana, IL, 61801-3613. **EMAIL** aguibbor@uiuc.edu

GUILDS, JOHN C.
DISCIPLINE AMERICAN LITERATURE **EDUCATION** Duke Univ, PhD. **CAREER** English and Lit, Univ Ark. **SELECTED PUBLICATIONS** Ed, "Long Years of Neglect": The Work and Reputation of William Gilmore Simms, 88; Auth, Simms: A Literary Life, Ark, 92; Guy Rivers: A Tale of Georgia, Univ Ark, 93; The Yemassee: A Romance of Carolina (1994), and Richard Hurdis: A Tale of Alabama, 95. **CONTACT ADDRESS** Univ Ark, Fayetteville, AR, 72701.

GULLASON, THOMAS ARTHUR
PERSONAL Born 07/01/1924, Watertown, MA, m, 1955 **DISCIPLINE** ENGLISH **EDUCATION** Suffo'k Univ, BA, 48; Univ Wis, MA, 49, PhD, 53. **CAREER** Asst prof English, Heidelberg Col, 52-53; instr, Wis State Col, 53-54; from instr to assoc prof, 54-64, PROF ENGLISH, UNIV RI, 64-, Mem ed comt, Studies Short Fiction, 65-. **MEMBERSHIPS** MLA. **RESEARCH** Modern American literature; realism and naturalism; the short story. **SELECTED PUBLICATIONS** Auth, American Stories, Vol 2, Fiction from the Atlantic-Monthly, Stud in Short Fiction, Vol 0030, 93; Lardner, Ring and the Other, Am Lit, Vol 0065, 93; Prize Stories 1992--The O-Henry-Awards, Stud in Short Fiction, Vol 0030, 93; The Best American Short-Stories 1992, Stud in Short Fiction, Vol 0030, 93; Contemporary New-England Stories, Stud in Short Fiction, Vol 0031, 94; Currentgarcia, Eugene--In-Memoriam, Stud in Short Fiction, Vol 0032, 95; Crane, Stephen and the 'New York Tribune'--A Case Reopened, Rsrcs for Am Lit Stud, Vol 0022, 96. **CONTACT ADDRESS** Dept of English, Univ of RI, Kingston, RI, 02881.

GUMBRECHT, HANS ULRICH
PERSONAL Born 06/15/1948, Wurzburg, Germany, m, 1989, 4 children **DISCIPLINE** LITERARY THEORY; ROMANCE LITERATURES **EDUCATION** Univ Konstanz, Germany, Phd, 74. **CAREER** Prof, Univ Bochum, 75-82; prof, Univ Siegen, 83-89; prof, Stanford Univ, 89-. **HONORS AND AWARDS** Albert Gufkakh Prof of Lit; Amer Acad of Arts & Sci; Walker Ames Prof, Univ Washington. **MEMBERSHIPS** MLA **RESEARCH** Medieval Culture; Contemporary Culture; Philosophical Aesthetics. **SELECTED PUBLICATIONS** Romance Portraits, Johns Hopkins Univ Pr, forthcoming; The Non-Hermeneutic, Stanford Pr, 98; Corpo e forma. Per una epistemologia della presenza, Torino, 98; A Modernizacao dos Sentidos, Sa Paulo, 98. **CONTACT ADDRESS** Dept of Comparative Literature, Stanford Univ, Stanford, CA, 94305. **EMAIL** sepp@leland.stanford.edu

GUNN, GILES
DISCIPLINE AMERICAN LITERATURE **EDUCATION** Univ Chicago, PhD, 67. **CAREER** PROF, ENG, UNIV CALIF, SANTA BARBARA. **RESEARCH** Lit and relig; Am lit; Lit theory and critic; Am cult and relig stud. **SELECTED PUBLICATIONS** Auth, F.O. Matthiessen: The Critical Achievement, Univ Wash Press, 75; The Interpretation of Otherness: Literature, Religion, and the American Imagination, Oxford Univ Press, 79; The Culture of Criticism and the Criticism of Culture, Oxford Univ Press, 87; Thinking Across the American Grain: Ideology, Intellect, and the New Pragmatism, Univ Chicago Press, 92; co-ed, Redrawing the Boundaries: The Transformation of English and American Literary Studies, Mod Lang Assn, 92; ed, Early American Writing, Penguin, 94. **CONTACT ADDRESS** Dept of Eng, Univ Calif, Santa Barbara, CA, 93106-7150. **EMAIL** ggunn@humanitas.ucsb.edu

GURA, PHILIP F.
DISCIPLINE ENGLISH & AMERICAN STUDIES **EDUCATION** Harvard Univ, BA, 72, PhD, 77. **CAREER** PROF, ENG & AM STUD, UNIV NC AT CHAPEL HILL **MEMBERSHIPS** Am Antiquarian Soc **RESEARCH** Nathan Fiske; 19th century banjo. **SELECTED PUBLICATIONS** Auth, The Wisdom of Words: Language, Theology, and Literature in the New England Renaissance, Wesleyan, 81; auth, A Glimpse of Sim's Glory: Puritan Radicalism in New England, 1620-1660, Wesleyan, 84; auth, Early Nineteenth-Century Printing in Rural Massachusetts: John Howe of Greenfield and Enfield, ca. 1803-45, with a Transcription of his Printer's Book, ca. 1832, Procs of the AAS 101, 91; auth, The Crossroads of American History and Literature, Penn State Univ, 96. **CONTACT ADDRESS** Dept of Eng, Univ of North Carolina, CB#3520, Chapel Hill, NC, 27599-3520. **EMAIL** gura@email.unc.edu

GURAK, LAURA J.
DISCIPLINE RHETORIC STUDIES **EDUCATION** St Rose Col, BA, 89; Rensselaer Polytech Inst, MS, 90; PhD, 94. **CAREER** Assoc prof **HONORS AND AWARDS** Distinguished Tchg Awd, 97. **RESEARCH** Rhetoric of science and technology; rhetorical criticism; classical rhetorical theory; computer-mediated communication; social aspects of computing; intellectual property and electronic texts; technical and professional communication. **SELECTED PUBLICATIONS** Auth, Persuasion and Privacy in Cyberspace: The Online Protests over Lotus MarketPlace and the Clipper Chip, Yale, 97; Persuasion and Privacy (rev), Minn Daily's Arts. **CONTACT ADDRESS** Rhetoric Dept, Univ of Minnesota, Twin Cities, 64 Classroom Office Bldg, 1994 Buford Ave, St. Paul, MN, 55108. **EMAIL** gurakl@tc.umn.edu

GURALNICK, ELISSA SCHAGRIN
PERSONAL Born 03/04/1949, Philadelphia, PA, m, 1969, 2 children **DISCIPLINE** ENGLISH LITERATURE **EDUCATION** Univ Pa, AB & AM, 69; Yale Univ, MPhil, 71, PhD(English), 73. **CAREER** Asst prof, 73-80, assoc prof, 79-86, prof English, Univ Colo, Boulder, 86-. **HONORS AND AWARDS** Fellowship, Howard Foundation, 91-92. **MEMBERSHIPS** MLA. **RESEARCH** Modern and contemporary drama. **SELECTED PUBLICATIONS** Auth, Archimagical fireworks: The function of light imagery in Browning's Sordello, Victorian Poetry, 75; contribr, Improving student writing: A case history, Col English, 77; auth, Radical politics in Mary Wollstonecraft's A Vindication of The Rights of Woman, Studies in Burke and His Time, 77; The new segregation: A recent history of EOP at the University of Colorado, Boulder, Col English, 78; Rhetorical Strategy in Mary Wollstonecraft's A Vindication of the Rights of Woman, The Humanities Asn Review, 79; Radio Drama: The Stage of the Mind, Virginia Quart, 85; Artist Descending a Staircase: Stoppard Captures the Radio Station and Duchamp, PMLA 90; Sight Unseen: Beckett, Pinter, Stoppard, and Other Contemporary Dramatists on Radio, Athens: Ohio Univ Press, 96. **CONTACT ADDRESS** Univ Colo Hellems Bldg, Box 226, Boulder, CO, 80309-0226. **EMAIL** elissa.guralnick@colorado.edu

GURUSWAMY, ROSEMARY
DISCIPLINE EARLY AMERICAN LITERATURE AND AFRICAN-AMERICAN LITERATURE **EDUCATION** Univ MD, MA; Kent State Univ, PhD. **CAREER** Prof, Radford Univ. **MEMBERSHIPS** Pres, Soc of Early Americanists. **RESEARCH** Anne Bradstreet's poetry. **SELECTED PUBLICATIONS** Publ var articles in Early Am Lit, New Eng Quart, and Stud in Puritan Am Spirituality. **CONTACT ADDRESS** Radford Univ, Radford, VA, 24142. **EMAIL** rguruswa@runet.edu

GUSS, DONALD LEROY
PERSONAL Born 07/21/1929, New York, NY, m, 1960, 3 children **DISCIPLINE** ENGLISH LITERATURE **EDUCATION** City Col New York, BA, 50; Columbia Univ, MA, 52; Univ Wis, PhD, 61. **CAREER** Instr, Boston Col, 59-60; instr, Rutgers Univ, 60-63, res grant, 62-63; assoc prof, Wayne State Univ, 63-68; PROF ENGLISH AND CHMN DEPT, UNIV CALIF, SANTA BARBARA, 68-, Hungtington Libr grant, 63. **MEMBERSHIPS** MLA; Renaissance Soc Am; Am Asn Teachers Ital. **RESEARCH** Seventeenth century English; Renaissance Italian literature. **SELECTED PUBLICATIONS** Auth, The Power of Selfhood--Shakespeare 'Hamlet', Milton 'Samson,' Modern Lang Quart, Vol 0054, 93. **CONTACT ADDRESS** Dept of English, Univ of Calif, Santa Barbara, CA, 93106.

GUSTAFSON, SANDRA
DISCIPLINE AMERICAN LITERATURE **EDUCATION** Univ Calif, Berkeley, PhD. **CAREER** Instr, Univ Notre Dame. **HONORS AND AWARDS** Newcombe fel; Early Am Hist Asn fel. **SELECTED PUBLICATIONS** Published an essay on Margaret Fuller and Jonathan Edwards. **CONTACT ADDRESS** Univ Notre Dame, Notre Dame, IN, 46556.

GUTHRIE, JAMES ROBERT
PERSONAL Born 05/05/1951, Ann Arbor, MI, m, 1980 **DISCIPLINE** AMERICAN LITERATURE **EDUCATION** Univ Mich, BA, 73; State Univ NY Buffalo, MFA, 74, MA, 76, PhD(English), 79. **CAREER** ASST PROF ENGLISH, NORTH CENTRAL COL, 79-. **RESEARCH** Modern poetry; creative writing. **SELECTED PUBLICATIONS** Auth, Measuring the Sun, Dickinson, Emily Interpretation of her Optical Illness, Esq-J Am Renaissance, Vol 0041, 95; A Revolution in Locality, Astronomical Tropes in Dickinson, Emily Poetry, Midwest Quart-J Contemp Thought, Vol 0037, 96. **CONTACT ADDRESS** Dept of Eng, Wright State Univ, Dayton, OH, 45435.

GUTIEREZZ-JONES, CARL
DISCIPLINE ENGLISH LITERATURE **EDUCATION** Cornell Univ, PhD, 90. **CAREER** ASSOC PROF, ENG, UNIV CALIF, SANTA BARBARA. **RESEARCH** Chicano stud; contemp fiction; Pan-American stud; multiculturalism. **SELECTED PUBLICATIONS** Auth, "Provisional Historicity: Reading Through Terra Nostra," Rev of Contemp Fiction, 88; "Legal Rhetoric and Cultural Critique: Notes Toward Guerilla Writing," Diacritics, 90; Rethinking the Borderlands: Between Chicano Narrative and Legal Discourse, Univ Calif Press, 95. **CONTACT ADDRESS** Dept of Eng, Univ Calif, Santa Barbara, CA, 93106-7150. **EMAIL** carlgj@humanitas.ucsb.edu

GUTIERREZ, DONALD
PERSONAL Born 03/10/1932, Alameda, CA, m, 1953, 2 children **DISCIPLINE** MODERN BRITISH LITERATURE, NOVEL **EDUCATION** Univ Calif, Berkeley, BA, 56, MLS, 58; Univ Calif, Los Angeles, MA, 66, PhD(English), 68. **CAREER** Ref librn, Metrop Mus Art Libr, New York, 58-60; res and asst head librn, Tamiment Inst Libr, New York, 60-61; res librn, Grosset and Dunlap Bk Publ, 61-64; asst prof English, Univ Notre Dame, 68-75; asst prof, 75-79, ASSOC PROF ENGLISH, WESTERN NMEX UNIV, 80-. **MEMBERSHIPS** Rocky Mountain Mod Lang Asn; D H Lawrence Soc Am. **RESEARCH** D H Lawrence; Anthony Powell. **SELECTED PUBLICATIONS** Auth, World Outside the Window--The Selected Essays of Rexroth, Kenneth, Western Am Lit, Vol 0027, 92; An Autobiographical Novel, Western Am Lit, Vol 0027, 92; 'Flower Wreath Hill'--Later Poems, Western Am Lit, Vol 0027, 92; A Life of Rexroth, Kenneth, Lit Rev, Vol 0037, 93; Johnson, Spud and 'Laughing Horse,' D H Lawrence Rev, Vol 0025, 94; Rexroth 'Incartion,' Explicator, Vol 0053, 95. **CONTACT ADDRESS** Dept of English, Western New Mexico Univ, Silver City, NM, 88061.

GUTMAN, STANLEY T.
PERSONAL Born 12/24/1943, m, 2 children **DISCIPLINE** ENGLISH **EDUCATION** Hamilton Col, AB, 65; Duke Univ, PhD, 71. **CAREER** Prof English Chr Dept of English, Univ Vermont; Fulbright fel; Salzburg fel; vis speaker USIS. **MEMBERSHIPS** MLA. **RESEARCH** Modern poetry. **SELECTED PUBLICATIONS** Auth Mankind in Barbary: The Individual and Society in the Novels of Norman Mailer, Univ Press NE, 75; ed Technologies of the Self: A Seminar with Michel Foucault, Univ Mass Press, 88; As Others Read Us: International Perspectives on American Literature, Univ Mass Press, 91; coauth Outsider in the House, Verso, 97. **CONTACT ADDRESS** Dept of English, Univ Vt, PO Box 54030, Burlington, VT, 05405-4030.

GUTTENBERG, BARNETT
PERSONAL Born 12/10/1937, Boston, MA, m, 1967, 1 child **DISCIPLINE** MODERN AMERICAN AND SOUTHERN LITERATURE **EDUCATION** Columbia Univ, BA, 59; Cornell Univ, MA, 66, PhD(English), 71. **CAREER** Asst prof Am lit, Vanderbilt Univ, 67-74; asst pref, 74-77, ASSOC PROF AM LIT, UNIV MIAMI, 77-. **MEMBERSHIPS** MLA. **RESEARCH** William Faulkner; Southern literature. **SELECTED PUBLICATIONS** Auth, Waking Giants--The Presence of the Past in Modernism, D H Lawrence Review, Vol 0023, 91. **CONTACT ADDRESS** Univ Miami, Coral Gables, FL, 33124.

GUTTMAN, NAOMI E.
PERSONAL Born 07/10/1960, Montreal, PQ, Canada **DISCIPLINE** ENGLISH **EDUCATION** Concordia Univ, BFA, 85; Warren Wilson Col, MFA, 88; Univ S Calif LA, PhD stud, 93-. **CAREER** ASST PROF ENGLISH, HAMILTON COL, 96-. **HONORS AND AWARDS** Bliss Carman Award Lyric Poetry, 89; QSPELL (A.M. Klein) Award, 92. **SELECTED PUBLICATIONS** Auth, Reasons for Winter, 91. **CONTACT ADDRESS** Dept of English, Hamilton Col, 198 College Hill Rd, Clinton, NY, 13323.

GUY-SHEFTALL, BEVERLY
PERSONAL Memphis, Tennessee **DISCIPLINE** ENGLISH **EDUCATION** Spelman Coll, BA, 1966; Atlanta Univ, MA, 1968; Emory Univ, PhD. **CAREER** AL State Univ, faculty, 1968-71; Spelman coll, prof of English and women's studies, 1971-; Women's Research and Resource Center, Anna Julia Cooper prof of English, 1981; SAGE: A Scholarly Journal on Black women, founding co-editor; speaker. **HONORS AND AWARDS** Kellogg, fellow; Woodrow Wilson, fellow; Spelman College, Presidential Faculty Award for Outstanding Scholarship. **SELECTED PUBLICATIONS** Author: Daughters of Sorrow: Attitudes Toward Black Women, 1880-1920, Carlson, 1991; Words of Fire: An Anthology of African-American Feminist Thought; Spelman: A Centennial Celebration, 1981; co-edited Sturdy Black Bridges: Visions of Black Women In Literature, Anchor Books, 1979; Double Stitch: Black Women Write About Mothers & Daughters, Beacon Press, 1992. **CONTACT ADDRESS** Founding Director, Spelman Col, Atlanta, GA, 30314.

H

HAAHR, JOAN GLUCKAUF
PERSONAL Born 01/18/1940, New York, NY, m, 1963, 3 children **DISCIPLINE** MEDIEVAL LITERATURE **EDUCATION** Univ Copenhagen, 61-62; Harpur Col (SUNY), BA 61; MA, 63, PhD, 70, Harvard Univ. **CAREER** Prof, Chr Dept English, Yeshiva Univ, 69-. **HONORS AND AWARDS** NEH Summer Seminar, 89; Danforth Fdn Fel, 78-84; NEH Summer Stipend, 70; Woodrow Wilson Fel, 62-63; Fulbright Grant, 61-62. **MEMBERSHIPS** AAUP, Yeshiva Univ (Chapter Pres); MLA; Medieval Acad; Harvard Grad School Alumni Assoc; Soc for Medieval Feminist Scholarship **RESEARCH** Medieval literature **SELECTED PUBLICATIONS** Auth; Criseyde's Inner Debate: The Dialectic of Enamorment in the Filostrato and the Troilus, Studies in Philology, 92; auth, Justifying Love: The Classical Recusatio in Medieval Love Literature, Desiring Discourse: The Literature of Love, Ovid Through Chaucer, 98; auth, The Princess and the Pea, The Red Shoes, The Snow Queen, The Steadfast Tin Soldier, Oxford Companion to Fairy Tales, 99. **CONTACT ADDRESS** Dept of English, Yeshiva Univ, 500 W 185 St, New York, NY, 10033. **EMAIL** haahr@ymail.yu.edu

HAARBAUER, DON WARD
PERSONAL Born 09/17/1940, Charleroi, PA, m, 1964, 2 children **DISCIPLINE** THEATRE HISTORY **EDUCATION** Univ Ala, Tuscaloosa, BS, 62, MA, 65; Univ Wis, Madison PhD(theatre), 73. **CAREER** Asst prof speech & theatre, 68-73, asst dean sch humanities, 73-75, asst prof theatre, 73-77, chmn performing arts, 73-81, assoc prof, 77-80, prof theatre, Univ Ala, Birmingham, 80-, assoc dean sch arts & humanities, 81-, dir, Horn in the West, Boone, NC, 67-71. **MEMBERSHIPS** Southeastern Theatre Conf (admin vpres, 77-79, vpres, 79-80, pres, 80-81). **RESEARCH** Pre-twentieth century English theatre. **SELECTED PUBLICATIONS** Auth, The Birmingham theatres of Frank O'Brien, Southern Theatre, summer 77. **CONTACT ADDRESS** Univ of Alabama, 301 Humanities Bldg, Birmingham, AL, 35294-1260. **EMAIL** whaar@uab.edu

HAAS, JAMES M.
PERSONAL Born 09/16/1927, Milwaukee, WI, m, 1959 **DISCIPLINE** ENGLISH HISTORY **EDUCATION** Marquette Univ, PhB, 50; Univ Ill, AM, 55, PhD, 60. **CAREER** Instr hist, Univ Dayton, 59-61; from asst prof to assoc prof English hist, 61-75, PROF HIST, SOUTHERN ILL UNIV, EDWARDSVILLE, 75-, Am Philos Soc res grant, 70. **MEMBERSHIPS** Conf Brit Studies. **RESEARCH** Nineteenth-century English economic history. **SELECTED PUBLICATIONS** Auth, 18th-Century, Am Hist Rev, Vol 0100, 95; Traffic and Politics--The Role of Transportation in the Industrial-Revolution--A Comparison of England and France, Albion, Vol 0024, 92; The Origins of Railway Enterprise, the Stockton-and-Darlington Railway, 1821-1863, Albion, Vol 0026, 94; Bristol and the Atlantic Trade in the the Construction and Management of Rochester-Bridge, Ad-43-1993, Albion, Vol 0027, 95. **CONTACT ADDRESS** Dept of Hist, Southern Ill Univ, Edwardsville, IL, 62026.

HABA, JAMES
DISCIPLINE POETRY, FICTION, AND WORLD LITERATURE **EDUCATION** Reed Col, BA; Cornell Univ, PhD. **CAREER** Instr, Rowan Col NJ; poetry coordr, Geraldine R Dodge Found. **SELECTED PUBLICATIONS** Ed, The Language of Life, 95. **CONTACT ADDRESS** Rowan Col of NJ, Glassboro, NJ, 08028-1701.

HABIB, IMTIAZ
DISCIPLINE SHAKESPEARE **EDUCATION** Ohon Univ, MA, Indiana Univ, PhD. **CAREER** Engl, Old Dominion Univ. **HONORS AND AWARDS** Chair, Eng Undergrad Essay Constest. **MEMBERSHIPS** ODU Postcolonial Studies Gp. **RESEARCH** Shakespeare and Race; Race in the Early Modern Period; Postcolonial Theory and Literature; Modern American Drama. **SELECTED PUBLICATIONS** Auth, Shakespeare's Pluralistic Concepts of Character: A Study in Dramatic Anamorphism, 93; Tennessee Williams: A Descriptive Bibliography, 86. **CONTACT ADDRESS** Old Dominion Univ, 4100 Powhatan Ave, BAL 439, Norfolk, VA, 23058. **EMAIL** IHabib@odu.edu

HABIB, M.A. RAFEY
DISCIPLINE LITERARY THEORY, MODERN BRITISH LITERATURE, NON-WESTERN LITERATURE **EDUCATION** Oxford Univ, PhD. **CAREER** Instr, dir, Writing prog, Rutgers, State Univ NJ, Camden Col of Arts and Sci. **RESEARCH** T. S. Eliot; history of Western literary criticism, Urdu poetry. **SELECTED PUBLICATIONS** Auth, The Dissident Voice: Poems of N.M. Rashed: Translated from the Urdu, Oxford, 91; Classical Marxism, The Johns Hopkins Guide to Literary Theory, Johns Hopkins Univ Press, 93; Karl Marx, Friedrich Engels, Materialism, Antonio Gramsci, Gyorgy Lukas, Edward Said, Islamic Studies, The Blackwell Dictionary of Cultural and Critical Theory, Blackwell, 96; Aesthetics and Justice in Plato's Republic, Law and Literature: Perspectives, Peter Lang, 96; Bergson Resartus and T.S. Eliot's Manuscript, J of the Hist of Ideas; Horace's Ars Poetica and the Deconstructive Leech, Brit J of Aesthet; The Prayers of Childhood: T. S. Eliot's Manuscript on Kant, J of the Hist of Ideas. **CONTACT ADDRESS** Rutgers, State Univ NJ, Camden Col of Arts and Sci, New Brunswick, NJ, 08903-2101. **EMAIL** mhabib@camden.rutgers.edu

HACKMAN, MICHAEL
DISCIPLINE COMMUNICATIONS **EDUCATION** Univ Colo, BA; Univ Denver, MA, PhD. **CAREER** Vis sr lectr, Univ Waikato, New Zealand; prof; ch-. **HONORS AND AWARDS** CU-Colo Springs outstanding tchr award, 95. **RESEARCH** Impact of gender and culture on leadership behavior. **SELECTED PUBLICATIONS** Co-auth, Leadership: A Commun Perspective; Creative Commun; pub(s), Commun Edu, Commun Quart, Distance Edu, Perceptual and Motor Skills, S Speech Commun Jour. **CONTACT ADDRESS** Dept of Commun, Univ Colo, PO Box 7150, Colorado Springs, CO, 80933-7150.

HADAS, RACHEL
PERSONAL Born 11/08/1948, New York, NY, m, 1978, 1 child **DISCIPLINE** ENGLISH, LITERATURE **EDUCATION** Radcliffe Col, BA, 69; Johns Hopkins, MA, 77; Princeton, PhD, 82. **CAREER** ASSOC, ASST PROF, 82-87, PROF, 87-92, FULL PROF, 92-, RUTGERS UNIV. **HONORS AND AWARDS** Guggenheim fel, 88-89. **MEMBERSHIPS** MLA; PEN; Poetry Soc of Am; Acad of Am Poets. **RESEARCH** Poetry; literature; classics in translation. **SELECTED PUBLICATIONS** Auth, The Empty Bed, Wesleyan Univ Press, 95; auth, The Double Legacy, Faber & Faber, 95; auth, Halfway Down the Hall: New and Selected Poems, Wesleyan Univ Press, 98; auth, Starting from Troy, 75; auth, Slow Tansparency, 83; auth, Form, Cycle, Infinity: Lanscape Imagery in the Poetry of Robert Frost and George Seferis, 85; auth, A Son from Sleep, 87; auth, Pass It On, 89; auth, Living in Time, 90; auth, Unending Dialogue: Voices from an AIDS Poetry Workshop, 91; auth, Mirrors of Astonishment, 92; auth, Other Worlds Than This, 94; translator, Oedipus the King, Johns Hopkins Univ Press, 94; translator, Helen, Univ Press of Pa Press, 97. **CONTACT ADDRESS** Rutgers Univ, 520 Hill Hall, Newark, NJ, 07102. **EMAIL** rhadas@andromeda.rutgers.edu

HADDIN, THEODORE
PERSONAL m, 1961, 2 children **DISCIPLINE** AMERICAN LITERATURE **EDUCATION** Univ Mich, AB, 55, AM, 56, PhD(English), 68. **CAREER** Teacher English, Jackson High Sch, 58-61 and Ann Arbor High Sch, Mich, 61-63; instr, Univ Mich, 65-68; asst prof, St Louis Univ, 68-73; asst prof, 73-80, ASSOC PROF ENGLISH, UNIV ALA, BIRMINGHAM, 80-. **MEMBERSHIPS** MLA; S Atlantic Mod Lang Asn. **RESEARCH** American literature 19th century transcendentalism; early American literature, poetry and prose; 20th century American poetry. **SELECTED PUBLICATIONS** Auth, Cottonmouth, Southern Hum Rev, Vol 0027, 93. **CONTACT ADDRESS** Dept of English, Univ of Ala, Birmingham, AL, 35294.

HAEGERT, JOHN
DISCIPLINE TWENTIETH CENTURY ENGLISH LITERATURE **EDUCATION** Univ Chicago, PhD. **CAREER** Vis assoc prof, Univ Paris IV-Sorbonne; prof. **SELECTED PUBLICATIONS** Auth, scholarly articles on twentieth century British and American literary figures; pub(s), S Rev, Contemp Lit, Mod Philol, Criticism. **CONTACT ADDRESS** Dept of Eng, Univ Evansville, 1800 Lincoln Ave, Evansville, IN, 47714. **EMAIL** jh52@evansville.edu.

HAGEMAN, ELIZABETH H.
PERSONAL Born 05/20/1941, Vancouver, BC, Canada **DISCIPLINE** ENGLISH LITERATURE **EDUCATION** Simmons Col, BS, 63; Columbia Univ, MA, 64; Univ NC, PhD, 71. **CAREER** Instr English, Colby Jr Col, 64-65 & Col William & Mary, 65-68; asst prof English, 71-77, assoc prof English, 77-87, prof English, 87-, Univ NH, 78-. **HONORS AND AWARDS** Fel frp, Folger Shakespeare Libr, Newberry Libr, Am Philos Soc, ACLS, NEH. **MEMBERSHIPS** Soc Study of Early Mod Women, Renaissance Soc Am, Shakepeare Asn Am, Mod Lang Asn, Renaissance Eng Text Soc. **RESEARCH** Recent studies in Renaissance literature, English Lit Renaissance **SELECTED PUBLICATIONS** Auth, Robert Herrick: A Reference Guide, G K Hall, 82; art early mod women writers, Katherine Philips, Richard Crashaw. **CONTACT ADDRESS** Dept English, Univ NH, Durham, NH, 03824. **EMAIL** ehageman@cisunix.unh.edu

HAGGERTY, GEORGE E.
DISCIPLINE 18TH-CENTURY ENGLISH LITERATURE **EDUCATION** Holy Cross Coll, BA; Univ Calif-Berkeley, PhD. **CAREER** GRAD ADV, ART HIST, UNIV CALIF, RIVERSIDE. **HONORS AND AWARDS** Distinguished Tchg award, 87. **SELECTED PUBLICATIONS** Auth, Gothic Fiction/Gothic Form, Penn State, 89; Unnatural Affections: Women and Fiction in the Later 18th Century, Ind, 98; Men in Love; Masculinity and Sexuality in the 18th Century, Columbia, 98; co-ed, Professions of Desire: Lesbian and Gay Studies in Literature for the Modern Language Association, 95; edr, Encyclopedia of Gay Histories and Cultures, Garland Press. **CONTACT ADDRESS** Dept of Eng, Univ Calif, 1156 Hinderaker Hall, Riverside, CA, 92521-0209. **EMAIL** haggerty@ucrac1.ucr.edu

HAHN, H. GEORGE
PERSONAL Born 01/10/1942, Baltimore, MD, m, 1981, 1 child **DISCIPLINE** ENGLISH LITERATURE **EDUCATION** Mt. St. Mary's Col, BA, 63; Univ Md, MA, 66; Johns Hopkins Univ, MLA, 69; Univ Md, PhD, 79. **CAREER** Grad Asst, Univ Md, 63-66; Grad Fel, Johns Hopkins Univ, 69; from inst to prof, Towson Univ, 65-87; PROF, TOWSON UNIV, 87-; Dir Honors, 87-90, DIR ADVANCED WRITING COURSES, 1998-; EDITOR, ALL AHEAD FULL, NAVY LEAGUE OF THE UNITED STATES, 1993-. **HONORS AND AWARDS** Folger Shakespeare Library Fel, 74; Emmart Journalism Award for Writing About the Humanities, 94; Mackie Award for Navy League of U.S. Journalism 98. **MEMBERSHIPS** East-Central Soc for 18th-Century Studies. **RESEARCH** War and politics in 18th-century British literature; Classical rhetoric. **SELECTED PUBLICATIONS** Coauth, Towson: A Pictorial History, 78; auth, Henry Fielding: An Annotated Bibliography, 79; coauth, The Eighteenth-Century British Novel and Its Background, 85; auth, The Country Myth: Motifs in the English Novel From Defoe to Smollett, 91; "The Patriot's Flame": War Poetry and Nationalism in England, 1793-1815, forthcoming; auth, Character Development in Defoe's Narrative Prose, Philological Quart, 72; auth, Two Eighteenth-Century Modes in Scott's Waverly, Hartford Studies in Lit, 74; auth, The Political Mirror of the Tragic in Julius Caesar and Coriolanu & Auburn in Goldsmith's Deserted Village, Col Lang Assn J, 78 & 83; auth, Steele's Curs and Fielding's Hounds, Notes & Queries, 79; auth, Main Lines of Criticism in Fielding's Tom Jones, Brit Studies Monitor, 80; auth, Twilight Reflections: The Hold of Victorian Baltimore on Lizette Reese and H.L. Mencken, Southern Quart, 84; auth, Broadsides on the Thames: Pope's The Rape of the Lock, Anglia, 86; auth, A hagiographical Allusion in Joyce's Araby, Papers on Lang & Lit, 91; auth, Fielding, Parody, Satire, World Book Encycl, 96; auth, The Progress of Patriotism and Biography: The Battle of Trafalgar in Southey's Life of Nelson, War, Lit & the Arts, 97. **CONTACT ADDRESS** Dept of English, Towson Univ, Towson, MD, 21252. **EMAIL** Hahn@Towson.edu

HAHN, LAURA K.
PERSONAL Born 08/25/1968, CA **DISCIPLINE** COMMUNICATION **EDUCATION** San Francisco State Univ, CA, BA (magna cum laude), 91, MA (Speech Commun), 94; OH State Univ, Columbus, PhD (Commun), 99. **CAREER** Grad teaching assoc, Dept of Speech and Comminiction Studies, San Francisco State Univ, CA, 92-94; undergrad adv, Dept of Commun and Journalism, OH State Univ, Columbus, 95; Project coord, Center for the Advanced Study of Telecommun, OH State Univ, Columbus, 96-97; Dir of the Basic Course, Dept of Commun and Journalism, OH State Univ, Columbus, 96-98, grad teaching assoc, 94-98; vis prof, Int Col of Beijing, China, spring 98; LECT, DEPT OF COMMUN, HUMBOLDT STATE UNIV, ARCATA, CA, 98-. **HONORS AND AWARDS** Outstanding Scholastic Achievement, Golden Key Nat Honor Soc, 91; Outstanding Academic Achievement, San Francisco State Univ, 90-91; Prof Participation, OH State Univ, Columbus, 95, 96, 97. **SELECTED PUBLICATIONS** Auth, Status of the Animal Liberation Movement in the 1990's: The Rhetoric of Gandhi/Guerrilla, published through The 28th Annual CA State Univ Hayward Conf in Rhetorical Criticism, 93; Incorporating Theory and Practice: Student Involvement in a Social Movement, Speech Communication Teacher, 98. **CONTACT ADDRESS** Dept of Communication, Humboldt State Univ, Arcata, CA, 95521. **EMAIL** lkh9@axe.humboldt.edu

HAHN, THOMAS GEORGE O'HARA
PERSONAL Born 04/26/1946, New York, NY, 2 children **DISCIPLINE** ENGLISH LITERATURE & LANGUAGE **EDUCATION** Fordham Univ, AB, 68; Univ Calif Los Angeles, MA & PhD(English), 74. **CAREER** Asst prof, 73-80, assoc prof, 80-96, prof, Univ Rochester, 96, dir, Writing Prog, 76-81, dir, medieval sds ctr, 75-76, 83-84, 87-88, ch, cluster on premodern sds, 89-, dir grad sds Eng, 82-83, 96-97, , assoc, Susan B. Anthony Ctr for Women's Sds, 85-, gen ed, Chaucer Bibliographies, 84, gov brd, Robbins Lib, 87. **HONORS AND AWARDS** NEH Sum fel, ACLS fel, Vis mem, Wolfson Col, Cambridge; Ford Foun Tchg, PI, for NEH Prog Gra; E P Curtis Awd for Tchg Excel; Reach Teams Awd for Curricular Innov. **MEMBERSHIPS** Mediaeval Acad Am; MLA; New Chaucer Soc; Early English Text Soc; Index Mid English Prose. **RESEARCH** Old and Middle English language and literature; Medieval studies. **SELECTED PUBLICATIONS** Auth, Urian Oakes's Elegie and Puritan poetics, Am Lit, 73; General literary criticism--years work in Old English studies, Old English Newslett, 75 & 81; The audience in the medieval dramatic performance, Res Opportunities in Renaissance Drama, 77; I gentili e l'uom nasce a la riva de l'Indo, L'Alighierei, 77; The Indian tradition of the Middle Ages, Viator, 78; Primitivism and savagery in English discovery narratives of sixteenth century, J Medieval & Renaissance Studies, 78; ed, Me Letter of Alexander to Aristotle, Medieval Studies, 79; Upright Lives: Documents Concerning the Natural Virtue and Wisdom of the Indians, 81; coauth, Text and Context: Chaucer's Friar Tale; auth, Studies in the Age of Chaucer, 83; auth, Teaching the Resistant Woman: The Wife if Bath and the Academy, Exemplaria, 92; auth, The Performance of Gender in the Prioress, The Chaucer Yearbook, 92; auth, Traditional Religion, Social History, and Literary Study, Assays, 96; auth, Old Wives' Tales and Masculine Intuition, Retelling Stories, Lupack & Hahn, 97; auth, Early Middle English, Cambridge Hist of the Middle English Lit, Wallace, 98. **CONTACT ADDRESS** Dept of English, Univ of Rochester, 500 Joseph C Wilson, Rochester, NY, 14627-9000. **EMAIL** thhn@db3.cc.rochester.edu

HAIMES KORN, KIM
DISCIPLINE COMMUNICATION STUDIES **EDUCATION** FL State Univ, MA, PhD. **CAREER** Instr lit, Southern Polytech State Univ. **SELECTED PUBLICATIONS** Auth, publ(s) on response theory; collaborative lrng; literacy; multi cult pedag. **CONTACT ADDRESS** Hum and Tech Commun Dept, Southern Polytech State Univ, S Marietta Pkwy, PO Box 1100, Marietta, GA, 30060.

HAINES, ANNETTE L.
DISCIPLINE LIBRARY SCIENCE **EDUCATION** Wayne State Univ, MS, 77. **CAREER** Ref Libr, Central Mich Univ, 97-. **MEMBERSHIPS** ALA; Michigan Library Assoc. **RESEARCH** Library and information science **CONTACT ADDRESS** Park Library, Central Michigan Univ, Mt. Pleasant, MI, 48859. **EMAIL** annette.haines@cmich.edu

HAINES, VICTOR YELVERTON
PERSONAL Born 03/21/1941, Toronto, ON, Canada, 3 children **DISCIPLINE** MEDIEVAL ENGLISH AND CANADIAN LITERATURE **EDUCATION** Queen's Univ, Kingston, BA Hons, 65; Carleton Univ, MA, 66; McGill Univ, PhD(English), 75. **CAREER** Prof English, Acadia Univ, 66-67 and Royal Mil Col, St Jean, 67-73; PROF ENGLISH, DAWSON COL, 74-. **MEMBERSHIPS** Int Arthurian Soc; MLA; Asn of Can Univ Teachers English; Mediaeval Acad Am. **RESEARCH** Doctrine of the felix culpa; mediaeval romance; Can poetry **SELECTED PUBLICATIONS** Auth, Rhetoric and Existence, Philos and Rhet, Vol 0029, 96; The Dragon in The Fog--Play and Artworlds, Can Rev of Comp Lit-Rev Can de Lit Comparee, Vol 0023, 96. **CONTACT ADDRESS** Dawson Col, 1001 Sherbrooke, Montreal, PQ, H2L 1L3.

HAIR, DONALD SHERMAN
PERSONAL Born 11/24/1937, Strathroy, ON, Canada, m, 1966 **DISCIPLINE** ENGLISH **EDUCATION** Univ Western Ont, BA, 60; Univ Toronto, MA, 61, PhD(English), 64. **CAREER** Lectr 64-65, from asst prof to assoc prof, 65-73, assoc chmn dept, 67-73, PROF ENGLISH, UNIV WESTERN ONT, 73-, Can Coun leave fel, 73-74. **MEMBERSHIPS** Asn Can Univ Teachers English. **RESEARCH** Victorian literature; Canadian literature. **SELECTED PUBLICATIONS** Auth, The Languages of Paradise, Race, Religion, and Philology in the 19th-Century, Victorian Stud, Vol 0036, 93; Tennyson Fixations--Psychoanalysis and the Topics of the Early Poetry, 19th-Century Lit, Vol 0049, 94; Hardy Literary Language and Victorian Philology, Victorian Poetry, Vol 0032, 94; Soul and Spirit in 'In Memoriam,' Victorian Poetry, Vol 0034, 96. **CONTACT ADDRESS** Dept of English, Univ of Western Ont, London, ON, N6A 3K7.

HAKUTANI, YOSHINOBU
PERSONAL Born 03/27/1935, Osaka, Japan, m, 1967, 2 children **DISCIPLINE** AMERICAN LITERATURE, LINGUISTICS **EDUCATION** Hiroshima Univ, Japan, BA, 57; Univ Minn, Minneapolis, MA, 59; Pa State Univ, PhD(English), 65. **CAREER** Instr English, SDak State Univ, 59-61; asst prof, Calif State Univ, Northridge, 65-68; asst prof, 68-71, assoc prof, 71-80, PROF ENGLISH, KENT STATE UNIV, 80-, Res fel, Kent State Univ, 71-72. **MEMBERSHIPS** MLA; Ling Soc Am; Conf Col Compos & Commun; English Lit Asn Japan **RESEARCH** Japanese literature. **SELECTED PUBLICATIONS** Co-ed, The World of Japanese Fiction, Dutton, 73; co-ed, American Literary Naturalism: A Reassessment, Carl Winter, 75; auth, Young Dreiser: A Critical Study, Assoc Uiv Press, 80; ed, Critical Essays on Richard Wright, Hall, 82; ed, Selected Magazine Articles of Theodore Dreiser: Life and Art in the American 1890s, Assoc Univ Press, 85-87; ed, Selected English Writings of Youne Noguchi: An East-West Literary Assimilation, Assoc Univ Press, 90-92; co-ed, The City in African-American Literature, Assoc Univ Press, 95; auth, Richard Wright and Racial Discourse, Univ Mo Press, 96; co-ed, Haiku: This Other World by Richard Wright, Arcade/Little Brown, 98. **CONTACT ADDRESS** Dept of English, Kent State Univ, PO Box 5190, Kent, OH, 44242-0001. **EMAIL** yhakutan@kent.edu

HALABY, RAOUF J.
PERSONAL Born 11/22/1945, Jerusalem, Palestine, m, 1970, 2 children **DISCIPLINE** ENGLISH **EDUCATION** Ouachita Baptist Univ, Ar, BA, 68, MSE, 70; Texas A & M, EdD. **CAREER** Prof, chair, Ouachita Baptist Univ. **HONORS AND AWARDS** Who's Who, 71; Teacher of the Year, 79; Daughters of Amer Revolution Americanism Award; Notable Amer. **MEMBERSHIPS** Sixteenth Century Soc; NCTE; SCMLA; MLA. **RESEARCH** Arkansas dialects; near eastern immigration to US; sixteenth century educators; Richard Mulcaster; William Baziotes & abstract expressionism. **SELECTED PUBLICATIONS** Auth, Sneaking Books Under the Bedclothes, Christian Sci Monitor, 90; art, Language of the Heart Communicates Best, Ar Gazette, 90; auth, Myth, Ritual and Folklore in Pietro Didonato's Christ in Concrete, Les Presses de L'Universite Laval, Quebec, Canada, 90; art, America's Magical Shores, Ar Gazette, 90; auth, On Tents and Tapestries, Ar Catholic, 92. **CONTACT ADDRESS** 123 Evonshire, Arkadelphia, AR, 71923. **EMAIL** rrhalaby@iocc.com; halabyr@alpha.obu.edu

HALASZ, ALEXANDRA W.
DISCIPLINE ENGLISH LITERATURE **EDUCATION** Johns Hopkins Univ, PhD, 91. **CAREER** Assoc prof, Dartmouth Col. **RESEARCH** Shakespearean drama and Renaissance lit. **SELECTED PUBLICATIONS** Auth, The Marketplace of Print: Pamphlets and the Public Sphere in Early Modern England, Cambridge UP, 97;'So beloved that men use his picture for their signs': Richard Tarlton and the Uses of Sixteenth-Century Celebrity, Shakespeare Studies, 95; Wyatt's David, Tex Studies Lit and Lang, 88, rptd in Rethinking the Henrician Era, Univ II P, 93. **CONTACT ADDRESS** Dartmouth Col, 3529 N Main St, #207, Hanover, NH, 03755.

HALE, DAVID GEORGE
PERSONAL Born 03/25/1938, Worcester, MA, m, 1964, 2 children **DISCIPLINE** ENGLISH **EDUCATION** Wesleyan Univ, BA, 60; Duke Univ, MA, 61, PhD(English), 65. **CAREER** Tutor English, Duke Univ, 61-64; asst prof, Univ Cincinnati, 64-67; from asst prof to assoc prof, 67-75, PROF ENGLISH, STATE UNIV NY COL BROCKPORT, 75-, Folger Shakespeare Libr fel, 70; Southeastern Inst Medieval and Renaissance Studies fel, 75; Nat Endowment for Humanities fel, 77 and 81; vis prof English, Loughborough Univ, 79-80. **MEMBERSHIPS** MLA; Mod Humanities Res Asn; Resnaissance Soc Am. **RESEARCH** Renaissance. **SELECTED PUBLICATIONS** Auth, Hurston 'Spunk' and 'Hamlet,' Stud in Short Fiction, Vol 0030, 93; Malevolent Nurture--Witch-Hunting and Maternal Power in Early-Modern England, Renaissance Quart, Vol 0050, 97; Social Shakespeare--Aspects of Renaissance Dramaturgy and Contemporary Society, Renaissance Quart, Vol 0050, 97. **CONTACT ADDRESS** 350 New Campus Dr, Brockport, NY, 14420-2914.

HALE, JANE ALISON
PERSONAL Born 09/29/1948, Washington, DC, m, 2 children **DISCIPLINE** LITERATURE **EDUCATION** William & Mary, BA, 70, Univ Chicago, MST, 74; Stanford Univ, MA, 81, PhD, 84. **CAREER** Tchr, 70-72, Abeche, Chad, trainer, 72, St Thomas Virgin Isle, Peace Corps; tchr, 74-77, Pleasant Grove Union Elem Schl, NC; asst prof, 85-91, assoc prof, 91-, Brandeis Univ. **RESEARCH** Reading, writing, & tchng across cultures. **CONTACT ADDRESS** Dept of Romance & Comp Lit, Brandeis Univ, MS 024, Waltham, MA, 02254. **EMAIL** jhale@brandeis.edu

HALE, THOMAS ALBERT
PERSONAL Born 01/05/1942, Boston, MA, m, 1968, 1 child **DISCIPLINE** AFRICAN AND FRENCH LITERATURE **EDUCATION** Tufts Univ, BA, 64, MA, 68; Univ Rochester, PhD(French), 74. **CAREER** Agr co-op asst, Peace Corps, Union Nigerienne de Credit et de Cooperation, 64-66; admin asst, NDEA French Inst, Tufts Univ, 67; ASSOC PROF FRENCH AND COMP LIT, PA STATE UNIV, 73-, Co-ed, Cahiers Cesairiens, 74- and African Lit Asn Newsletter, 74-78; Fulbright sr lectr, Univ de Niamey, Niger, 80-81. **MEMBERSHIPS** MLA; African Lit Asn (secy-treas, 74-79, press, 81-82); Am Asn Teachers French; African Studies Asn; Am Comp Lit Asn. **RESEARCH** Caribbean literature; French literature outside France. **SELECTED PUBLICATIONS** Auth, The Negritude Poets--An Anthology of Translations from the French, Res in African Lit, Vol 0023, 92; A Comment Regarding Gadjigo,Samba Review of Scribe, Griots and Novelist, Res in African Lit, Vol 0023, 92; Griottes--Female Voices from West-Africa, Res in African Lit, Vol 0025, 94; African Novels and the Question of Orality, Res in African Lit, Vol 0025, 94; Oral Poetry--Its Nature, Significance and Social-Context, Res in African Lit, Vol 0026, 95; Status and Identity in West-Africa--Nyamakalaw of Mande, Res in African Lit, Vol 0027, 96; Misrepresenting and Misreading the 'Epic of Askia Mohammed,' Res in African Lit, Vol 0027, 96. **CONTACT ADDRESS** French Dept, Pennsylvania State Univ, 434 N Burrowes Bldg, University Park, PA, 16802-6204.

HALEWOOD, WILLIAM H.
PERSONAL Born 12/15/1929, Providence, RI, m, 1952, 3 children **DISCIPLINE** LITERATURE **EDUCATION** Univ Wichita, Ba, 53; Univ Minn, MA and PhD, 59. **CAREER** From asst prof to assoc prof lit, Reed Col, 59-67, chmn div lett and arts, 65-67; assoc prof, 67-72, PROF ENGLISH, UNIV COL, UNIV TORONTO, 72-, Am Coun Learned Socs fel, 63-64. **MEMBERSHIPS** MLA. **RESEARCH** Neoclassical aesthetics; early Protestant theology; 17th and 18th century English literature. **SELECTED PUBLICATIONS** Auth, Catching up with Bellamy, Edward, Univ Toronto Quart, Vol 0063, 94; The Predicament of the Westward Rider: Donne, John 'Good-Friday, 1613, Riding Westward,' Stud in Philol, Vol 0093, 96. **CONTACT ADDRESS** Dept of English, Univ Col Univ of Toronto, Toronto, ON, M5S 1A1.

HALIO, JAY LEON
PERSONAL Born 07/24/1928, New York, NY, 2 children **DISCIPLINE** ENGLISH **EDUCATION** Syracuse Univ, BA, 50; Yale Univ, MA, 51, PhD(English), 56. **CAREER** From instr to prof English, Univ Calif, Davis, 55-68; H Fletcher Brown Prof lib studies, 72, assoc provost instr, 75-81, PROF ENGLISH, UNIV DEL, 68-, Fulbright-Hays sr lectr, Univ Malaya, 66-67 & Buenos Aires, Arg, 74; mem, Del Humanities Coun, 75-78; cent exec comt, Folger Inst Renaissance & 18th Century Studies, 75-98; proj dir, Nat Endowment for Humanities develop grant, 78-82; Danforth assoc, 81- **HONORS AND AWARDS** Phi Beta Kappa. **MEMBERSHIPS** Int Shakespeare Asn; Shakespeare Asn Am; MLA; Am Lit Asn; Asn Lit Scholars and Critics. **RESEARCH** Elizabethan literature; contemporary English and American literature. **SELECTED PUBLICATIONS** Auth, Angus Wilson, 64; auth, Understanding Shakespeare's Plays in Performance, 88; auth, Philip Roth Revisited, 92; auth, Shakespeare in Performance: A Midsummer Night's Dream, 94; ed, The First Quarto of King Lear, 94; ed, Shakespeare's Romeo and Juliet: Texts, Contexts and Interpretation, 95; co-ed, Critical Essays on King Lear, 96; co-ed, Daughters of Valor: Contemporary Jewish American Women Writers, 97; ed, Shakespearean Illuminations, 98. **CONTACT ADDRESS** Dept of English, Univ of Del, Newark, DE, 19711. **EMAIL** jhalio@udel.edu

HALL, DENNIS R.
PERSONAL Born 10/24/1942, Columbus, OH, m, 1965, 3 children **DISCIPLINE** ENGLISH LITERATURE, RHETORIC **EDUCATION** Univ Notre Dame, BA, 64; Ohio State Univ, MA, 66, PhD, 70. **CAREER** Instr, 70-76, assoc prof, 76-85, PROF, 85-, dir of composition, 91-96, CHAIR, FAC SENATE & MEMBER B OF T, UNIV OF LOUISVILLE, 98-. **HONORS AND AWARDS** Univ Louisville Trustees Award, 96; Arts & Sciences Superior Performances Award, 97. **MEMBERSHIPS** Popular Culture Asn; Am Culture Asn; Popular Culture Asn/Am Culture Asn in the South. **RESEARCH** Popular culture. **SELECTED PUBLICATIONS** Ed, Studies in Popular Culture, 90-96; The Culture of the American South, 96; co-ed, Handbook of American Popular Culture, Greenwood, forthcoming; auth, The Triumph of Aesthetics, Eye on the Future: Popular Culture Scholar into the Twenty-First Century in Honor of Ray Browne, Popular Press, 94; No Laughing Matter: Values, Perception, and the Demise of AID jokes, J of Am Culture, 93; Lear's Vision of Modern Maturity: The Struggle for Modernity in the Context of Postmodernity, Pop Culture Rev, 93; ComPost: A Writing Program Newsletter and Its Rationale, WPA Writing Prog Admin, 93; Sm R. Watkins's Co. Aytch: A Literary Nonfiction, Ky Philol Rev, 93; Civil War Reenactors and the Postmodern Sense of History, J of Am Culture, 94; New Age Music: A Voice of Liminality in Postmodern Popular Culture, Popular Music and Soc, 94; Nicholson Baker's Vox: An Exercise in the Literature of Sensibility, Conn Rev, 95; Adertising as High Art, The Mid-Atlantic Almanack, 95; The Indeterminancy of the Question and Answer Format, Writing on the Edge, 95; 1996 Presidential ¤Kentucky Philological Associationl Address: Why Jane Austen? Why Now?, Ky Philol Rev, 96; Spanish Fly Redivivus: Dietary Supplements as Sexual Stimulants, J of Popular Culture, 96; A Garden of One's Own: The Ritual Consolations of the Backyard Garden, J of Am Culture, 96. **CONTACT ADDRESS** Dept of English, Univ Louisville, Louisville, KY, 40292.

HALL, JOAN H.
PERSONAL Born 07/21/1946, Akron, OH, m, 1971, 1 child **DISCIPLINE** ENGLISH **EDUCATION** College of Idaho, BA, 68; Emory Univ, MA, 71, PhD, 76. **CAREER** Gen editor 75-, Assoc editor 79-, Dictionary of Amer Regional Eng, Univ Wisc-Madison. **HONORS AND AWARDS** Dist Alum Awd; Verbatim DNSA Awd. **MEMBERSHIPS** DSNA; ADS. **RESEARCH** Lexicography; Amer English Dialects. **SELECTED PUBLICATIONS** Auth, Lags and Dare: A Case of Mutualism, in: Language Variety in the South Revisited, eds, Cynthia Bernstein, Thomas Nunnally, Robin Sabino, Tuscaloosa AL, U of AL Press, 97; Introduction to forum on Dialect Labeling in Dictionaries, Dictionaries, 97; coed, Dictionary of American Regional English, Cambridge MA, Belknap P of Harvard U Press, 85, 91, 96; rev, Heartland English, by Timothy C Frazer, J Eng Linguistics, 96; coed, Old English and New: Essays in Language and Literature in Honor of Frederick G Cassidy, NY, Garland, 92. **CONTACT ADDRESS** 600 N Park St, Madison, WI, 53706. **EMAIL** jdhall@facstaff.wisc.edu

HALL, KIM
DISCIPLINE ENGLISH LITERATURE **EDUCATION** Hood Col, BA; Univ Pa, PhD. **CAREER** Assoc prof. **RESEARCH** Sixteenth and seventeenth century British literature and culture; theories of race and ethnicity; feminism; literature and visual arts; material culture; cultural studies. **SELECTED PUBLICATIONS** Auth, Things of Darkness: Economies of Race and Gender in Early Modern England, 96; pubs on Shakespeare, theater history, visual culture, women writers, black feminist theory, food and material culture, pedagogy, and multiculturalism. **CONTACT ADDRESS** English Dept, Georgetown Univ, 37th and O St, Washington, DC, 20057.

HALL, KIM FELICIA
PERSONAL Born 12/25/1961, Baltimore, Maryland, s **DISCIPLINE** ENGLISH **EDUCATION** Hood College, Frederick, MD, BA (magna cum laude), 1983; Univ of Pennsylvania, Philadelphia, PA, PhD, 1990. **CAREER** Democratic Natl Convention, communications coord 1984; Univ of PA, graduate fellow 1985-86; Committee to re-elect Clarence Blount, campaign coord 1986; Swarthmore Coll, visiting instructor; Friends of Vera P Hall, public relations dir 1986-87; Georgetown Univ, Washington, DC, lecturer, 1989-90, assistant professor, 1990-. **HONORS AND AWARDS** Hood Scholar 1983; Mellon Fellowship in the Humanities, Woodrow Wilson Natl Fellowship Foundation; Folger Inst Fellowship, Washington DC 1986; Governor's Citation, Gov Harry Hughes MD 1986; Paul Robeson Award, University of Pennsylvania, 1989; Folger Institute Fellowship, Folger Shakespeare Library, 1991; Mellon Dissertation Fellowship, Woodrow Wilson National Fellowship Foundation, 1988-89. **MEMBERSHIPS** Vice pres Grad English Assoc Univ of PA 1985-86; mem Renaissance Soc of Amer; sec Grad English Assoc 1984-85; member, Modern Language Assn; member, Shakespeare Assn of America; member, American Society for Theatre Research. **CONTACT ADDRESS** English Dept, Georgetown Univ, 37 & O Streets, 328 New North, Washington, VT, 20057-0001.

HALL, LARRY JOE
PERSONAL Born 10/22/1937, Heavener, OK, m, 1959, 3 children **DISCIPLINE** AMERICAN LITERATURE & STUDIES **EDUCATION** Oklahoma City Univ, BA, 59; Garrett Theol Sem, MDiv, 62; NTex State Univ, MA, 70, PhD(Am Lit), 74. **CAREER** Asst prof, 74-81, from assoc prof to prof English, Okla Baptist Univ, 81-86. **HONORS AND AWARDS** Distinguished Teaching Award, 88. **MEMBERSHIPS** MLA; Am Studies Asn; Midcontinent Am Studies Assn; Conf on Christianity and Lit. **RESEARCH** Myth criticism and the contemporary novel. **CONTACT ADDRESS** Oklahoma Baptist Univ, 500 W University, Shawnee, OK, 74801-2558. **EMAIL** joehall@mail.okbu.edu

HALL, N. JOHN
PERSONAL Born 01/01/1933, Orange, NJ, m, 1968, 1 child **DISCIPLINE** ENGLISH LITERATURE **EDUCATION** Seton Hall Univ, AB, 55, MA, 67; Cath Univ Am, STB, 59; New York Univ, PhD, 70. **CAREER** Lectr, Sch Continuing Educ, New York Univ, 67-70; from asst prof to assoc prof, 70-78, prof English, 78-, Bronx Commun Col; prof English, 80-, Grad Sch & Univ Ctr; lectr, New Sch Social Res, 70-74; res award, City Univ New York, 71, 72; res award, City Univ New York Res Found, 71, 74, 76 & 77; Am Coun Learned Soc grant, 73, fel, 80; NEH fel, 74; Guggenheim fel, 77. **MEMBERSHIPS** MLA. **RESEARCH** Nineteenth century English literature; Anthony Trollope; the novel. **SELECTED PUBLICATIONS** Ed, Anthony Trollope's The New Zealander, Clarendon, 72; auth, Salmagundi, Byron, Allegra, and the Trollope Family, Beta Phi Mu, 75; auth, Trollope and His Illustrators, Macmillan, 80; ed, The Trollope Critics, 81, Macmillan; auth, The Letters of Anthony Trollope, Stanford Univ; auth, Trollepe: A Biography, Clarendon Press, 91; auth, Max Beerbohm Caricatures, Yale, 97. **CONTACT ADDRESS** Dept of English, Bronx Comm Col, CUNY, 2155 University Ave, Bronx, NY, 10453-2895. **EMAIL** nhall@email.gc.cuny.edu

HALL, WADE H.
PERSONAL Born 02/02/1934, Union Springs, AL **DISCIPLINE** ENGLISH **EDUCATION** Troy State Univ, BS, 53; Univ Ala, MA, 57; Univ Ill, PHD(English), 61. **CAREER** Instr English, Univ Ill, 57-61; asst prof, Univ Fla, 61-63; from assoc prof to prof, Ky Southern Col, 63-71; prof English, 71-96, prof emeritus, Bellarmine Col. **HONORS AND AWARDS** Ala Libr Asn Lit Award, 67. **MEMBERSHIPS** MLA; Conf Christianity & Lit; S Atlantic Mod Lang Asn. **RESEARCH** Literature of the South; American humor; theology and literature. **SELECTED PUBLICATIONS** Auth, Reflections of the Civil War in Southern humor, 62 & The Smiling Phoenix: Southern Humor, 1865-1914, 65, Univ Fla; The mirror of humor, Ala Librn, 1/68; The lonely world of Carson McCullers, Twigs, summer 68; The Truth is Funny: Jesse Stuart's Humor, Ind Coun Teachers English, 70; The High Limb, Ky Poetry Press, 73; coed, This Place Kentucky, Courier-J, 75; contribr, Jesse Stuart: Essays on His Work, Univ Ky, 77; The Kentucky Book, Courier J, 79; auth, The Rest of the Dream, Univ Kentucky, 88; auth, Hell-Bent for Music, Univ Kentucky, 96; auth, Conecuh People, Black Belt Press, 98. **CONTACT ADDRESS** Dept of English, Bellarmine Col, 2000 Norris Pl, Louisville, KY, 40205. **EMAIL** adeway@aol.com

HALLER, EVELYN
PERSONAL Born 03/07/1937, Chicago, IL, d, 2 children **DISCIPLINE** ENGLISH AND AMERICAN LITERATURE **EDUCATION** Barat Col of Sacred Heart, AB, 58; Emory Univ, MA, 59, PhD, 68. **CAREER** Lectr, Mission San Jose Campus, Col of the Holy Names, 63-67; asst prof, 68, lectr, 69, Creighton Univ; PROF, 83-, CHR ENGLISH, DOANE COL, 69-; AIFS London semester, 85, assoc fel Ctr for Great Plains Stud, 93, Univ v Nebraska; Newberry Libr fel, 84; NEH Summer, Princeton, 73, Brunnenburg, 94. **MEMBERSHIPS** Am Acad Relig; Mod Lang Asn; Nebraska Coun Hum, 76-80; Am Asn Univ Prof; AAUP Neb State Conf Pres; Assembly of State Conf treas. **RESEARCH** Modernism, especially Virginia Woolf, Willa Cather, and Exra Pound. **SELECTED PUBLICATIONS** Auth Isis Unveiled: Virginia Woolf USe of Egyptian Myth, Virginia Woolf: A Feminist Slant, Univ Nebraska Press, 83; Behind the Singer Tower: Willa Cather and Flaubert, Modern Fiction Studies, 90; Her Quill Drawn from the Firebird: Virginia Woolf and the Russian Dancers, The Multiple Muses of Virginia Woolf, Univ Missouri Press, 93; Octavia Wilberforce: A Portrain Unrealized, Women in the Milieu of Leonard and Virginia Woolf: Peace, Politics, and Education, Pace Univ Press, 98. **CONTACT ADDRESS** Doane Col, 1014 Boswell, Crete, NE, 68333. **EMAIL** ehaller@doane.edu

HALLET, CHARLES A.
DISCIPLINE RENAISSANCE DRAMATIC LITERATURE **EDUCATION** Yale, PhD. **CAREER** Prof, Fordham Univ. **RESEARCH** Mod utopianism. **SELECTED PUBLICATIONS** Auth, Analyzing Shakespeare's Action: Scene Versus Sequence, Cambridge UP, 91; Distinguishing Action from Narrative in Shakespeare's Multipartite Scenes, Shakespeare Quart 46, 95. **CONTACT ADDRESS** Dept of Eng Lang and Lit, Fordham Univ, 113 W 60th St, New York, NY, 10023.

HALLIN, DANIEL C.
DISCIPLINE POLITICAL COMMUNICATION **EDUCATION** Univ Calif-Berkeley, PhD, 80. **CAREER** PROF, DEPT CH, COMMUN, UNIV CALIF, SAN DIEGO. **RESEARCH** Comparative analysis of the news media's role in the public sphere. **SELECTED PUBLICATIONS** Auth, "The Uncensored War: The Media and Vietnam," Oxford, 86; We Keep America on Top of the World: Television Journalism and the Public Sphere, Routledge, 94. **CONTACT ADDRESS** Dept of Commun, Univ Calif, San Diego, 9500 Gilman Dr, La Jolla, CA, 92093. **EMAIL** dhallin@weber.ucsd.edu

HALLISSY, MARGARET
DISCIPLINE MEDIEVAL LITERATURE **EDUCATION** Fordham Univ, PhD. **CAREER** Prof, Long Island Univ, C.W. Post Campus. **SELECTED PUBLICATIONS** Auth, A Companion to Chaucer's Canterbury Tales; Clean Maids, True Wives, Steadfast Widows: Chaucer and Medieval Codes of Conduct; Venomous Woman: Fear of the Female in Literature; Poison Lore and Chaucer's Pardoner; Rappaccini's Venomous Beatrice; Marriage, Morality, and Maturity in Updike's Marry Me. **CONTACT ADDRESS** Long Island Univ, C.W. Post, Brookville, NY, 11548-1300.

HALLORAN, STEPHEN MICHAEL
PERSONAL Born 02/08/1939, Cohoes, NY, m, 1965, 2 children **DISCIPLINE** ENGLISH, SPEECH **EDUCATION** Holy Cross Col, BS, 60; Rensselaer Polytech Inst, PhD(commun & rhetoric), 73. **CAREER** English teacher, Hoosic Valley Cent Sch, 63-67; from instr to asst prof, 69-78, ASSOC PROF COMMUN, RENSSELAER POLYTECH INST, 78- **MEMBERSHIPS** NCTE; Coun Col Compos & Commun; Speech Commun Asn; Rhetoric Soc Am; Int Soc Hist of Rhetoric. **RESEARCH** Rhetorical criticism; theory of composition. **SELECTED PUBLICATIONS** Auth, History as Rhetoric--Style, Narrative, and Persuasion--Carpenter, Rhetorica-J Hist Rhet, vol 0015, 97. **CONTACT ADDRESS** Dept of Lang, Rensselaer Polytech Inst, Troy, NY, 12181.

HALLWAS, JOHN EDWARD
PERSONAL Born 05/24/1945, Waukegan, IL, m, 1966, 2 children **DISCIPLINE** AMERICAN AND BRITISH LITERATURE **EDUCATION** Western Ill Univ, BSEd, 67, MA, 68; Univ Fla, PhD(English), 72. **CAREER** Asst prof, 70-76, assoc prof, 76-81, prof english, Western Ill Univ, 81-, Dir regional collections, Western Ill Univ Libr; ed, Western Ill Regional Studies; columnist, Macomb J. **MEMBERSHIPS** Soc Study Midwestern Lit. **RESEARCH** Midwestern American Literature; Medieval British literature. **SELECTED PUBLICATIONS** Auth, The two versions of Hi sike, al wan hi singe, Neuphilol Mitteilungen, 76; Two autobiographical epitaphs in Spoon River Anthology, Great Lakes Rev, 76; co-ed, The Vision of This Land: Studies of Vachel Lindsay, Edgar Lee Masters and Carl Sandburg, Western Ill Univ, 76; auth, Poetry and prophecy: Vachel Lindsay's The Jazz Age, Ill Quart, 77; Childe Harold in the Mississippi Valley: Edmund Flagg's The Far West, Old Northwest, 77; The varieties of humor in John Hay's Pike County ballads, Mid-America, 78; The achievement of Virginia S Eifert, J Ill State Hist Soc, 78; The regional essays of Jerry Klein, Western Ill Regional Studies, 78; ed, The Poems of H: The Lost Poet of Lincoln's Springfield, Ellis Press, 82. **CONTACT ADDRESS** Dept of English, Western Illinois Univ, 1 University Cir, Macomb, IL, 61455-1390.

HALPERIN, JOHN
DISCIPLINE 19TH- AND 20TH-CENTURY BRITISH NOVEL, VICTORIAN LITERATURE **EDUCATION** Johns Hopkins Univ, PhD. **CAREER** Centennial Prof Eng, Vanderbilt Univ. **RESEARCH** Jane Austen, Thomas Hardy, Henry James, joseph Conrad. **SELECTED PUBLICATIONS** Auth, Jane Austen's Lovers, 88; Novelists in Their Youth, 90; Eminent Georgians, 95; ed, The Life of Jane Austen, 84. **CONTACT ADDRESS** Vanderbilt Univ, Nashville, TN, 37203-1727.

HALPERN, MARTIN
PERSONAL Born 10/03/1929, New York, NY, m, 1959, 2 children **DISCIPLINE** DRAMA **EDUCATION** Univ Rochester, BA, 50, MA 53; Harvard Univ, PhD, 59; Queens Col, MA, 97. **CAREER** From instr to asst prof English, Univ Calif, Berkeley, 59-64; asst prof, Univ Mass, 64-65; from asst prof to assoc prof, 65-77, chmn dept, 72-76, Schulman Prof Theater Arts, 77-94, prof emeritus, 94- , Brandeis Univ; Howard Found fel, 62-63; Fulbright travel grant, 62-63; theater panelist, Mass Coun Arts, 75-78; Mass Artists Found fel, 82. **HONORS AND AWARDS** Harold C Crain Award Playwriting, San Jose State Univ, 78. **RESEARCH** Dramatic literature, chiefly 19th and 20th century; playwriting; theory of poetry, chiefly metrics. **SELECTED PUBLICATIONS** Auth, Two Sides of an Island and Other Poems, Univ NC, 63; William Vaughn Moody, Twayne, 64; Keats and the Spirit That Laughest, Keat-Shelly J, winter 66; Verse in the theater, Mass Rev, winter 66; Aescylus, Atlantic Brief Lives; Selected Poems, Golden Quill, 76; Total Recall, In: Best Short Plays of 1978, Chilton, 78; What the babe said, Pioneer Drama Serv, 82. **CONTACT ADDRESS** 160 Henry St, Brooklyn, NY, 11201. **EMAIL** marhalp@aol.com

HALPERN, SHELDON
PERSONAL Born 07/16/1932, New York, NY, m, 1957, 2 children **DISCIPLINE** ENGLISH LITERATURE **EDUCATION** City Col NY, BA, 53; Columbia Univ, MA, 57, PhD(English), 63. **CAREER** Resident lectr English, Ind Univ, South Bend, 59-63; from asst prof to prof, Bowling Green State Univ, 63-78, vprovost, 74-78, vpres acad affairs, 78-80; VPRES COL PLANNING & RES, TRENTON STATE COL, 80-, Vis assoc prof, Tel-Aviv Univ, 68-69. **MEMBERSHIPS** MLA; Am Asn Higher Educ. **RESEARCH** English romantic literature. **SELECTED PUBLICATIONS** Auth, 'Eves Apple' (rev), NY Rev Bk, Vol 0044, 97; The 'Story of Junk' (rev), NY Rev Bk, Vol 0044, 97; The 'Kiss', NY Rev Bk, Vol 0044, 97. **CONTACT ADDRESS** Col Planning & Res, Trenton State Col, Trenton, NJ, 08625.

HALVERSON, JOHN
PERSONAL Born 01/16/1928, Cedar Rapids, IA **DISCIPLINE** ENGLISH **EDUCATION** Univ Denver, BA, 51; Columbia Univ, MA, 52; Univ Calif, Berkeley, PhD, 61. **CAREER** Supvr English compos, Univ Calif, Berkeley, 59-61; instr English, Princeton Univ, 61-65; from asst prof to assoc prof, 66-75, prof lit, 75-80, PROF ENGLISH & COMP LIT, UNIV CALIF, SANTA CRUZ, 80-, Fulbright lectr, Vidyalankara Univ, Ceylon, 65-66 & Univ Ceylon, 68-69. **RESEARCH** Medieval studies. **SELECTED PUBLICATIONS** Auth, Plato, The Athenian Stranger--Aspects of the So-Called Socratic Question, Arethusa, Vol 0030, 97; The Lamentable Comedy of 'Richard II, English Lit Renaissance, Vol 0024, 94; Literacy and Language Analysis, Lang Soc, Vol 0023, 94; Oral and Written Gospel--An Attempt at Superseding Oral Tradition by Creating a So-Called Literary Counterform Within an Oral Christology--A Critique Of Kelber, New Testament Studies, Vol 0040, 94. **CONTACT ADDRESS** Dept of Lit, Stevenson Col Univ of Calif, Santa Cruz, CA, 95064.

HAMALIAN, LEO
PERSONAL Born 01/13/1920, New York, NY, m, 1943, 3 children **DISCIPLINE** ENGLISH, COMPARATIVE LITERATURE **EDUCATION** Cornell Univ, BS, 42; Columbia Univ, MA, 47, PhD(English), 54. **CAREER** Instr English, New York Univ, 47-54; from instr to assoc prof, 54-67, PROF ENGLISH LIT, CITY COL NEW YORK, 67-, DIR, GRAD CREATIVE WRITING, 72-, Smith-Mundt grant, Syria, 62-64; Am Studies Sem fel, Columbia Univ, 68-; dean, Calif Inst of Arts, 70-72; mem, bd dir, Tuum Est Drug Rehabil Ctr, Venice, 71-; Fulbright lectr, Univ Tehran, 74-75 & Univ Hamburg, 80; ed, Ararat. **MEMBERSHIPS** MLA; NCTE; Am Studies Asn; English Union; PEN Club. **RESEARCH** T S Eliot; D H Lawrence; comparative continental literature. **SELECTED PUBLICATIONS** Auth, Wright, Richard and Racial Discourse, Am Lit, Vol 0069, 97. **CONTACT ADDRESS** Dept of English, City Col, CUNY, New York, NY, 10031.

HAMBLIN, ROBERT W.
DISCIPLINE ENGLISH LITERATURE **EDUCATION** NE Miss Community Col, AA, 58; Delta State Univ, BSE, 60; Univ MS, MA, 65, PhD, 76. **CAREER** Tchg asst, Univ MS, 64-65; mem, SE MO State Univ, 65-. **HONORS AND AWARDS** Governor's Awd, 77; SE Mo State Univ Alumni Asn Fac Merit Awd, 97; Halsell Prize, Miss Hist Soc,92. **RESEARCH** Am lit; merican Novel; Bible and lit; Faulkner studies; lit criticism; Poetry; southern lit; sport lit. **SELECTED PUBLICATIONS** Auth, publ(s) about Faulkner; sports; lit; poetry. **CONTACT ADDRESS** Eng Dept, SE MO State Univ, 1 University Plz, Cape Girardeau, MO, 63701. **EMAIL** rhamblin@semovm.semo.edu

HAMEL, MARY
DISCIPLINE ANCIENT AND MEDIEVAL EUROPEAN LITERATURE, CHAUCER, AND THE ENGLISH LANGUAGE **EDUCATION** Pa State Univ, PhD. **CAREER** Dept Eng, Mt. Saint Mary's Col **SELECTED PUBLICATIONS** Publ, a bk and articles on, Middle Engl lit; assoc ed, scholarly jour Chaucer Rev. **CONTACT ADDRESS** Dept of English, Mount Saint Mary's Col, 16300 Old Emmitsburg Rd, Emmitsburg, MD, 21727-7799. **EMAIL** hamel@msmary.edu

HAMILTON, ALBERT C.
PERSONAL Born 07/20/1921, Winnipeg, MB, Canada, m, 1950, 4 children **DISCIPLINE** ENGLISH **EDUCATION** Univ Man, BA, 45; Univ Toronto, MA, 48; Cambridge Univ, PhD, 53. **CAREER** Prof, Univ Wash, 52-68; fel, Huntington Libr, 59-60; PROF ENGLISH, QUEEN'S UNIV, 68-; fel, St John's Col, Cambridge, 74-75; fel, Hum Res Ctr, Canberra, 85; vis prof, Kumamoto Univ, 88. **MEMBERSHIPS** MLA; Renaissance Soc Am; Asn Can Univ Tchrs Eng; Spenser Soc Am. **RESEARCH** Renaissance literature; Shakespeare; Spenser. **SELECTED PUBLICATIONS** Auth, The Structure of Allegory in 'The Faerie Queene', 61; auth, The Early Shakespeare, 67; auth, Sir Philip Sidney: A Study of His Life and Works, 77; auth, Edmund Spenser's 'Faerie Queene', 77; auth, Northrop Frye: Anatomy of his Criticism, 90; gen ed, The Spenser Encyclopedia, 90; ed bd, English Literary Renaissance: Duquesne Studies in English. **CONTACT ADDRESS** Dept of English, Queen's Univ, Kingston, ON, K7L 3N6.

HAMILTON, JOHN MAXWELL
PERSONAL Born 03/28/1947, Evanston, IL, m, 1975, 1 child **DISCIPLINE** JOURNALISM **EDUCATION** Marquette Univ, BA, 69; Univ NH, 73; Boston Univ, MS, 74; Geo Washington Univ, PhD, 83. **CAREER** Reporter, Milwaukee J, 67-69; free-lance journalist, Washington DC, 73-75; for corresp, Lat Am, 76-78; spec asst/asst adm, Ag Int Dev, 78-81; staff assoc, House For Aff Subcomt Int Econ Policy, Trade, US Cong, 81-82; chief US For Policy Corresp Int Reporting Info Sys, Washing, 82-83; N Am Adv, Pub Aff, World Bank, 83-85; Dir Main St Am & Third World, Washington, 85-87; sen couns, World Bank, Washington, 83-85; DEAN, PROF, MANSHIP SCH MASS COMMUN, LA STATE UNIV, 92-. **HONORS AND AWARDS** Ford Fdn, Carnegie Inst, US AID grants; Hopkins P Brazeale Prof, 98; Los Angeles Time Critic's Choice Award; Frank Luther Mott-Kappa Tau Alpha Res Award, 88. **MEMBERSHIPS** MarketPlace Pub Rad Int; Int Ctr Journalists; US Info Svcs, Brazil; Asn Scholars Jornalism, Mass Commun; Soc Prof Journalists. **RESEARCH** Int aff **SELECTED PUBLICATIONS** Auth, Main Street America and the Third World, 86, 2d ed, 89; auth, Edgar Snow: A Biography, 88; auth, Entangling Alliances: How the Third World Shapes Our Lives, 90; co-auth, Hold the Press: The Inside Story on Newspapers, 96; various chapters in books, articles in prof journals inc Atlanta Constitution, Baltimore Sun, Bull Atomic Scientists, Boston Globe, Chicago Tribune, Christian Science Monitor, Columbia Journlism Rev, Jour Commerce, NY Times, The Nation. **CONTACT ADDRESS** Manship Sch Mass Commun, Louisiana State Univ, 221 Journalism Bldg, Baton Rouge, LA, 70803. **EMAIL** jhamilt@lsu.edu

HAMILTON, MARK A.
PERSONAL Born 04/13/1958, Stanford, CT, m, 1 child **DISCIPLINE** COMMUNICATION **EDUCATION** Michigan State Univ, PhD 87. **CAREER** Univ Connecticut, assoc prof, 10 years. **MEMBERSHIPS** ICA; NCA. **RESEARCH** Persuasion, attitude change, belief systems. **CONTACT ADDRESS** Dept of Communication Sciences, Univ of Connecticut, Storrs, CT, 06269-1085. **EMAIL** mhamil@uconnum.uconn.edu

HAMILTON, PETER K.
DISCIPLINE PUBLIC RELATIONS, ORGANIZATIONAL COMMUNICATION **EDUCATION** Wis-Whitewater, BA; University Nebr, MA; Univ Okla, PhD. **CAREER** Prof, ch, 72-. **RESEARCH** Communications theory, quantitative methods. **SELECTED PUBLICATIONS** Publ, Trade Jour articles and bk chap(s). **CONTACT ADDRESS** Dept of Commun, Pittsburg State Univ, 1701 S Broadway St, Pittsburg, KS, 66762.

HAMLIN, WILLIAM
DISCIPLINE ENGLISH LITERATURE **EDUCATION** Univ Wash, PhD, 89. **CAREER** Asst prof. **RESEARCH** Early Modern travel literature and ethnography; study of Renaissance skepticism; Jacobean tragedy. **SELECTED PUBLICATIONS** Auth, The Image of America in Montaigne; Spenser; Shakespeare: Renaissance Ethnography and Literary Reflection. **CONTACT ADDRESS** Dept of English and Philosophy, Idaho State Univ, Pocatello, ID, 83209. **EMAIL** hamlwill@isu.edu

HAMMER, MITCHELL R.
PERSONAL Born 08/07/1951, Appleton, WI, m, 1980, 2 children **DISCIPLINE** COMMUNICATION **EDUCATION** St Norbert Coll, BA, 73; Ohio Univ, MA, 74; Univ Minn, PhD, 82. **CAREER** Instr, Southern W Va Community Coll, 74-75; tchg assoc, Univ Minn, 75-76; res assoc, Univ Minn, 76-77; evaluation res, Univ Minn, 77-78; asst prof, Univ Vis Milwaukee, 82-87; vis prof, Indiana Univ Kuala Lumpur Malaysia, 87-88; assoc prof, Am Univ Washington DC, 88-. **HONORS AND AWARDS** Top Three honors, Int Commun Asn, 77, 87; Top Four honors, Speech Commun Asn, 84; Top Four honors Acad of Mgt, 89; Sr Interculturalist Award for Achievement, Soc of Intercultural Educ, Training and Res, 92; Top Three honors, Speech Commun Asn, 94; School of Int Service Award for Outstanding Scholar, Res, and Other Professional Contributors, 97-98; Outstanding Book Award, Int Asn of Conflict Mgt College Park Md, 98. **MEMBERSHIPS** Int Asn of Conflict Mgt; Int Commun Asn; Nat Commun Asn; Soc for Intercultural Educ, Training and Res; Int Acad of Intercultural Res. **RESEARCH** Negotiation dynamics involved in high density conflict situations; Discourse analysis of conflict escalation and de-escalation in hostage incidents; Patterns of cross-cultural adaptation; Effectiveness of international management training efforts. **SELECTED PUBLICATIONS** Auth, The Vietnam Experience, 91; numerous academic articles; coauth, Dynamic processes of crisis negotiation: Theory, research and practice, 97. **CONTACT ADDRESS** The School of International Service, American Univ, 4400 Massachusetts Ave NW, Washington, DC, 20016. **EMAIL** Docmitch@msn.com

HAMMERBACK, JOHN C.
PERSONAL Born 10/06/1938, San Francisco, CA, m, 1965, 2 children **DISCIPLINE** COMMUNICATION **EDUCATION** San Francisco State univ, BA, 62; Univ of Okla, MA, 65; Ind Univ, PhD, 70. **CAREER** Prof, ch, asst VP, assoc Dean, Calif State Univ, 68-97; prof & dept head, NC State Univ, 97-. **HONORS AND AWARDS** Outstanding Fac Lecturer, 71; 1st nn Exceptional Merit Service Award, 84; Who's Who in the W, Who's Who in Educ; Dist Schol Award, 95. **MEMBERSHIPS** Nat Commun Assoc; Western States Commun Assoc; Southern Commun Assoc; Rhet Soc of Am; Kenneth Burke Soc. **RESEARCH** Rhetorical criticism; discourse analysis; public communication. **SELECTED PUBLICATIONS** Auth, The Words of Cesar Chavez, Teacher of Truth, San Jose Studs, vol 20, 10-14, Spring 94; co-auth, Reies Tijerina, Leaders from the 1960s: A Biographical Sourcebook of American Activism, Praeger, 156-162, 94; co-auth, The Plan of Delano: Ethnic Heritage as Rhetorical Legacy, Quart J of Speech, vol 80, 53-70, 2/94; Jose Antonio's Rhetoric of Fascism, Southern Commun J, vol 59, 181-195, Spring 94; co-auth, Robert Parris Moses, African-American Orators, 261-269; co-auth, Leroy Eldridge Cleaver, African-American Orators: A Biocritical Sourcebook, Greenwood Press, 32-40, 96; co-auth, History and Culture as Rhetorical Constraint: Cesar Chavez' Letter from Delano, Alabama Press, (in press); co-auth, Your Tools Are Really the People: The Rhetoric of Robert Parris Moses, Commun Monographs, vol 65, 126-140, 6/97; auth, Future Research on Rhetoric and Intercultural Communication: Moving Forward from Starosta's Intersection, Int & Intercultural Commun Ann, 99. **CONTACT ADDRESS** 117 Raphael Dr, Cary, NC, 27511. **EMAIL** hammerback@social.chass.ncsu.edu

HAMMILL, GRAHAM L.
DISCIPLINE LITERARY THEORY **EDUCATION** Duke Univ, PhD. **CAREER** Instr, Univ Notre Dame. **SELECTED PUBLICATIONS** Auth, Consum'd to Nought: Naming, Bodies, and Subjectivity in The Faerie Queene; Faustus's Fortunes: Commodification, Exchange, and the Form of Literary Subjectivity; Being and Knowledge: Lacan and the Institution of Psychoanalysis; The Epistemology of Expurgation: Bacon and The Masculine Birth of Time; Stepping to the Temple. **CONTACT ADDRESS** Univ Notre Dame, Notre Dame, IN, 46556.

HAMMOND, ALEXANDER
DISCIPLINE NINETEENTH- AND TWENTIETH-CENTURY AMERICAN LITERATURE AND CULTURE **EDUCATION** Northwestern Univ, PhD **CAREER** Assoc prof & dir, Washington State Univ. **RESEARCH** Poe's fiction in relation to the patterns of representation, figuration, and production in the literary marketplace. **CONTACT ADDRESS** Dept of English, Washington State Univ, 1 SE Stadium Way, PO Box 645020, Pullman, WA, 99164-5020. **EMAIL** hammonda@wsu.edu

HAMNER, ROBERT DANIEL
PERSONAL Born 01/16/1941, Tuscaloosa, AL, m, 1963, 2 children **DISCIPLINE** ENGLISH & AMERICAN LITERATURE **EDUCATION** Wayland Baptist Col, BA, 64; Univ Tex, Austin, MA, 66, PhD(English), 71. **CAREER** Instr English, Wayland Baptist Col, 68-70; asst prof, 71-74, assoc prof English, 74-78, PROF ENGLISH & HUMANITIES, HARDIN-SIMMOND UNIV, 78-, Fulbright-Hays lectureship Am lit Univ Guyana, 75-76. **HONORS AND AWARDS** Piper Prof **MEMBERSHIPS** MLA; SCent Mod Lang Asn; African Lit Asn; Asn Caribbean Studies; Joseph Conrad Soc Am. **RESEARCH** Twentieth century American and English novel and poetry; British Commonwealth literature; British West Indian literature. **SELECTED PUBLICATIONS** Auth, Literary periodicals in world English: A selective checklist, World Lit Written in English, 68; contribr, Contemporary Novelists, St. Martin, 72; auth, V.S. Naipaul. Twayne, 73; auth, V.S. Naipaul, A selected bibliography, J Commonwealth Lit 751 ed, contribr, Critical Perspectives on V.S. Naipail, Three Contenints, 77; auth, Mythological aspects of Derek Walcott's drama, Ariel, 77; auth, Derek Walcott, Twayne, 81; autrh, Joseph Conrad and the colonial world: A selected bibliography, 82; Epic of the Dispossessed, Missouri Press, 97. **CONTACT ADDRESS** Dept of English, Hardin-Simmons Univ, Abilene, TX, 79698-0002. **EMAIL** rdh.engl@hsutx.edu

HANCHER, CHARLES MICHAEL
PERSONAL Born 05/20/1941, Newark, NJ **DISCIPLINE** ENGLISH **EDUCATION** Harvard Univ, AB, 63; Yale Univ, MA, 64, PhD(English), 67. **CAREER** Asst prof English, Johns Hopkins Univ, 67-72; asst prof, 72-73, assoc prof, 73-82, prof English, Univ Minn, Minneapolis, 82-, ed, Centrum, 73-77, coed, 79-83; Nat Endowment for Humanities fel, 77-78. **MEMBERSHIPS** MLA. **RESEARCH** Literary theory; pragmatics; Victorian literature. **SELECTED PUBLICATIONS** Auth, The Tenniel Illustrations to the Alice Books, Ohio State Univ Press, 85; Performative Utterance, the Word of God, and the Death of the Author, Semeia, 88; Judging Law and Literature, Univ Cincinnati Law Review, 90; Urgent Private Affairs': Millais's Peace Concluded, 1856, Burlington Mag, 91; Bailey and After: Illustrating Meaning, Word and Image, 92; The Law of Signatures, Law and Aesthetics, Lang, 92; Hunt's Awakening conscience, Journal of Pre-Raphaelite Studies, 95; The Century Dictionary: Illustrations, Dictionaries, 96; Tenniel's Allegorical Cartoons, The Telling Image: Explorations in the Emblem, AMS Press, 96; Gazing at The Imperial Dictionary, Book History, 98. **CONTACT ADDRESS** Dept of English, Univ of Minnesota, 207 Church St SE, Minneapolis, MN, 55455-0156. **EMAIL** mh@umn.edu

HAND, SALLY NIXON
PERSONAL Born 06/24/1933, Augusta, GA, m, 1953, 3 children **DISCIPLINE** 18TH CENTURY ENGLISH LITERATURE, COMPOSITION, WOMEN'S STUDIES **EDUCATION** Univ Ga, BA, 54; Fla State Univ, MA, 57; NY Univ, PhD, 73. **CAREER** Teaching asst English, Fla State Univ, 55-57; teacher, 64-76, chmn dept, 76-80, PROF ENGLISH, WILLIAM PATERSON UNIV, 80-. **HONORS AND AWARDS** Phi Beta Kappa; NEH. **MEMBERSHIPS** MLA. **RESEARCH** Samuel Johnson/Elizabeth Montague; Alex Pope's imitations of Horace; Shelley genealogy. **SELECTED PUBLICATIONS** Auth, When half gods to the god's arrive: feminine self sacrifice in the early fiction of Edith Wharton, Sociol & Arts Colloq Ser, William Paterson Col, 78; Timothy Shelley, merchant of Newark: the search for Shelley's American ancestor, Keats-Shelly J, spring 80. **CONTACT ADDRESS** William Paterson Col, 300 Pompton Rd, Wayne, NJ, 07470-2103. **EMAIL** SallyHand1@aol.com

HANDLING, PIERS G.P.
PERSONAL Born 07/21/1949, Calgary, AB, Canada **DISCIPLINE** FILM STUDIES **EDUCATION** Queen's Univ, BA, 71. **CAREER** Dir, res & info, 75-76, dir publs, 76-79, assoc dir, Can Film Inst, 80-81; lectr, Carleton Univ, 81-83; lectr, Queen's Univ, 84; dept dir & artistic dir, Festival of Festivals, Toronto, 87-94; DIR, TORONTO INT FILM FESTIVAL GP, 94-. **RESEARCH** Canadian film studies. **SELECTED PUBLICATIONS** Auth, The Films of Don Shebib, 78; auth, Canadian Feature Films 1913-1969, part 3 1964-69, 76; ed/auth, The Shape of Rage, The Films of David Cronenberg, 83; ed/auth, L'Horreur interieure: Les Films de David Cronenberg, 90; ed/auth, Self Portrait: Essays on the Canadian and Quebec Cinemas, 80. **CONTACT ADDRESS** Toronto Int Film Festival Gp, 2 Carlton St, 16th Fl, Toronto, ON, M5B 1J3.

HANENKRAT, FRANK THOMAS
PERSONAL Born 05/24/1939, Appomattox, VA, m, 1966 **DISCIPLINE** AMERICAN LITERATURE **EDUCATION** Univ Richmond, BA, 61, MA, 67; Emory Univ, PhD(English), 71. **CAREER** Inst English, Va Commonwealth Univ, 65-67; teaching asst, Emory Univ, 69-70; instr, Univ Ga, 70-71; assoc prof, 74-79, chmn, Dept English, 80-82, PROF ENGLISH & JOUR, LYNCHBURG COL, 79-, DIR, JOUR PROG, 81-84. **MEMBERSHIPS** MLA; Auth Guild & Auth League Am. **RESEARCH** Nineteenth and 20th century American literature. **CONTACT ADDRESS** Dept of English, Lynchburg Col, Lynchburg, VA, 24501. **EMAIL** hanenkrat@acavax.lynchburg.edu

HANKE, ROBERT
DISCIPLINE COMMUNICATION **EDUCATION** The Annenbey School for Commun, Univ of Pa. **CAREER** Res Assoc, McLuhan Prog for Culture & Tech; instr, Ryerson Polytechnic Univ. **MEMBERSHIPS** Int Commun Asn; Canadian Commun Asn. **SELECTED PUBLICATIONS** Auth, Theorizing Masculinity with/in the Media, Commun Theory, 98; auth, The Mock-macho Situation Comedy: Vengeance Masculinity and its Reiterations, Western J of Commun, 98; auth, Yo Quiero Mi MTV! Making Music Television for Latin America, Mapping the Beat: Popular Music and Contemporary Theory, 98; auth, Difference and Identity in Northern Exposure, Critical Approaches to Television, Houghton-Mifflin, 98. **CONTACT ADDRESS** 67 Chester Ave, Toronto, ON, M4K 2Z8. **EMAIL** bob@mcluhan.utoronto.ca

HANNAY, MARGARET PATTERSON
PERSONAL Born 12/20/1944, Rochester, NH, m, 1965, 2 children **DISCIPLINE** ENGLISH LITERATURE **EDUCATION** Wheaton Col, BA, 66; Col St Rose, MA, 70; State Univ NY, Albany, PhD(English), 76. **CAREER** Lectr, State Univ NY, Albany, 76-80; ASST PROF ENGLISH LIT, SIENA COL NY, 80- **MEMBERSHIPS** MLA; Conf Christianity & Lit (vpres 80-84); Milton Soc Am; C S Lewis Soc. **RESEARCH** Milton; women of the English renaissance; Sidney. **SELECTED PUBLICATIONS** Ed, As Her Wimsey Took Her: Critical Essays on Dorothy L. Sayers, Kent State Univ, 79; auth, C.S. Lewis, Frederick Unger Pub, 81; ed, Silent but for the Word: Tudor Women as Patrons, Translators, and Writers of Religious Works, Kent State Univ, 85; auth, Philip's Phoenix: Mary Sidney, Countess of Pembroke, Oxford Univ, 90; co-ed, The Collected Works of Mary Sidney Hervert, Countess of Pembroke, Clarendon, 98. **CONTACT ADDRESS** Dept of English, Siena Col, 515 Loudonville Rd, Loudonville, NY, 12211-1462. **EMAIL** hannay@siena.edu

HANNING, ROBERT W.
DISCIPLINE MEDIEVAL ENGLISH LITERATURE **EDUCATION** Columbia, BA, 58,; Oxford, BA, 68, MA, 64; Columbia, PhD, 64. **CAREER** English and Lit, Columbia Univ **HONORS AND AWARDS** Fel: ACLS, Guggenheim, NEH; Medieval Acad Am. **SELECTED PUBLICATIONS** Area: medieval historiography and romance. **CONTACT ADDRESS** Columbia Univ, 2960 Broadway, New York, NY, 10027-6902.

HANS, JAMES STUART
PERSONAL Born 05/06/1950, Elgin, IL, m, 1974, 1 child **DISCIPLINE** ENGLISH LITERATURE, PHILOSOPHY **EDUCATION** Southern IL Univ, Edwardsville, BA, 72, MA, 74; Washington Univ, St Louis, PhD(English), 78. **CAREER** Teaching asst English, Southern IL Univ, 72-74; asst prof, Kenyon Col, 78-82; asst to prof English, Wake Forest Univ, 82-; ed consult, Kenyon Rev, 79-82; dir, Kenyon & Exeter Prog, Exeter Univ, England, 80-81. **RESEARCH** Twentieth century literature; literary theory; contemporary philosophy. **SELECTED PUBLICATIONS** Auth, Gaston Bachelard and the Phenomenology of the Reading Consciousness, J Aesthetics & Art Criticism, spring 77; Hans-Georg Gadamer and Hermeneutic Phenomenology, Philos Today, spring 78; Derrida and Freeplay, Mod Lang Notes, 5/79; Presence and Absence in Modern Poetry, Criticism, fall 80; Hermeneutics, Play, Deconstruction, Philos Today, winter 80; The Play of the World, Univ MA Press, 81; Form and Measure in the Postmodern World, Kenyon Rev; Imitation and the Image of Man, John Benjaminis, 87; The Question of Value: Thinking Through Nietzsche, Heidegger and Freud, SIU Press, 89; The Value(s) of Literature, SUNY Press, 90; The Fate of Desire, SUNY Press, 90; The Origins of the Gods, SUNY Press, 91; Contextual Authority and Aesthetic Truth, SUNY Press, 92; The Mysteries of Attention, SUNY Press, 93; The Golden Mean, SUNY Press, 94; The Site of Our Lives: The Self and the Subject from Emerson to Foucault, SUNY Press, 95. **CONTACT ADDRESS** Dept English, Wake Forest Univ, PO Box 7387, Winston Salem, NC, 27109-7387. **EMAIL** hans@wfu.edu

HANSEN, BOB
DISCIPLINE THEATRE HISTORY, DRAMATIC LITERATURE **EDUCATION** Univ MN, BA; FL State Univ, MA; Univ MN, PhD. **CAREER** Instr, ch, dept Theatre, mng dir, Huron Playhouse, Bowling Green State Univ; instr, 86-, hd, dept, Broadcasting/Cinema and Theatre, Univ NC, Greensboro. **MEMBERSHIPS** NC Theatre Asn; USITT-Ohio; Am Theatre Asn; Southeastern Theatre Conf; Nat Asn Sch Theatre. **SELECTED PUBLICATIONS** Auth, Scenic and Costume Design for the Ballets Russes, UMI Res Press. **CONTACT ADDRESS** Univ N. Carolina, Greensboro, Greensboro, NC, 27412-5001. **EMAIL** rchansen@dewey.uncg.edu

HANSON, COLAN T.
DISCIPLINE COMMUNICATIONS **EDUCATION** Wayne State Univ, PhD, 78. **CAREER** Educator for 23 years; Prof & Dept Chair Mass Commun, Moorhead State Univ. **MEMBERSHIPS** NCA; PRSA; AAF. **RESEARCH** Public relations; advertising; persuasion. **CONTACT ADDRESS** Mass Communications Dept., Moorhead State Univ, 1104 7th Ave S, Moorhead, MN, 56563. **EMAIL** hansonc@mhd1.moorhead.msus.edu

HANSON, ELIZABETH
DISCIPLINE ENGLISH LITERATURE **EDUCATION** Johns Hopkins Univ, PhD. **CAREER** Dept Eng, Queen's Univ **HONORS AND AWARDS** Alumni Tchg Awd, 97. **RESEARCH** Social and economic contexts of Renaissance drama; early modern cultural studies. **SELECTED PUBLICATIONS** Auth, Discovering the Subject in Renaissance England, Cambridge, 98; pubs on economics and Jacobean drama, Renaissance women's writing, Shakespeare and early modern bureaucracy, the Elizabethan use of interrogatory torture, and Milton's poetry. **CONTACT ADDRESS** English Dept, Queen's Univ, Kingston, ON, K7L 3N6. **EMAIL** hansone@qsilver.queensu.ca

HAPKE, LAURA
PERSONAL Born 01/04/1946, New York, NY, m **DISCIPLINE** ENGLISH; AMERICAN STUDIES **EDUCATION** Brandeis Univ, BA, 67; Univ of Chicago, MA, 69; City Univ of NY, PhD, 74. **CAREER** Tchg fel, 72-74; adjunct instr, Queens Col, 78-81; instr, Nassau Comm Col, 78-81; from asst prof to prof Eng, Pace Univ, 81-91. **HONORS AND AWARDS** NEH awards, 80, 81; Choice Outstanding Acad Book Award, 92. **MEMBERSHIPS** PMLA; ASA; NYLNA. **RESEARCH** Labor lit; Women's studies; American & Victorian lit and cult. **SELECTED PUBLICATIONS** Auth, Girls Who Went Wrong: Prostitutes in American Fiction, 1885-1917, Bowling Green Univ, 89; Tales of the Working Girl: Wage - Earning Women in American Literature, 1890-1925, Twayne/Macmillan, 92; The Ideology of the Salvation Army, The Eighteen Nineties: An Encyclopedia of British Literature, Art and Culture, ed George Cevasco, Garland, 93; A Wealth of Possibilities: The Worker, the Text, and the Composition Classroom, Women's Studies Quarterly, 94; Homage to Daniel Horwitz, Liberating Memory: Working Class Intellectuals and Their Work, ed Janet Zandy, Rutgers Univ, 95; Daughters of the Great Depression: Women, Work, and Fiction in the American 1930s, Univ Georgia, 95. **CONTACT ADDRESS** Dept of English, Pace Univ, Pace Plaza, New York, NY, 10038-1502. **EMAIL** lhapke@tiac.net

HARBERT, EARL
PERSONAL Born 04/01/1934, Cleveland, OH **DISCIPLINE** ENGLISH, AMERICAN LITERATURE **EDUCATION** Hamilton Col, AB, 56; Johns Hopkins Univ, MA, 61; Univ Wis, PhD(English), 66. **CAREER** Instr English, George Washington Univ, 61-62; from asst prof to assoc prof, Tulane Univ, 65-77; PROF ENGLISH, NORTHEASTERN UNIV, 77- **MEMBERSHIPS** MLA; Northeast Mod Lang Asn. **RESEARCH** American literature; intellectual history. **SELECTED PUBLICATIONS** Auth, Better in Darkness--A Biography of Adams, Henry--His 2nd Life, 1862-1891, Hist Rev, Vol 0068, 95. **CONTACT ADDRESS** Dept of English, Northeastern Univ, Boston, MA, 02115.

HARBIN, BILL J.
DISCIPLINE DRAMATIC LITERATURE **EDUCATION** Ind Univ, PhD. **CAREER** Prof, dir, grad stud, La State Univ. **RESEARCH** American and British theatre and drama; notable gays and lesbians in US theatre history. **SELECTED PUBLICATIONS** Coed, Inside the Royal Court, 1956-1981. **CONTACT ADDRESS** Dept of Theatre, Louisiana State Univ, Baton Rouge, LA, 70803.

HARBIN, MICHAEL A.
PERSONAL Born 05/24/1947, Vincennes, France, m, 1971, 3 children **DISCIPLINE** BIBLICAL STUDIES, OLD TESTAMENT AND SEMITIC STUDIES, ENGLISH LITERATURE **EDUCATION** US Naval acad, BS, 69; Calif State Univ, MA, 93; Dallas Theol Sem, ThM, 80, ThD, 88. **CAREER** Adj prof of Bible, Le Tourneau Univ, 90-93; adj prof English, El Centro Col, 90-93; assoc prof Biblical Stud (s), Taylor Univ, 93- . **HONORS AND AWARDS** Who's Who in Amer, 98; Who's Who in Rel, 92-93; Who's Who in the Midwest, 95, 96; Phi Kappa Phi, 93. **MEMBERSHIPS** Soc Bibl Lit; Near East Archaeol soc; Inst Bibl res; Evangel Theol Soc. **RESEARCH** Old Testament History. **CONTACT ADDRESS** Dept of Biblical Studies, Taylor Univ, 269 W Reade Ave, Upland, IN, 46989. **EMAIL** mcharbin@tayloru.edu

HARDEN, EDGAR FREDERICK
PERSONAL Born 02/10/1932, Scranton, PA **DISCIPLINE** ENGLISH **EDUCATION** Princeton Univ, AB, 53; Harvard Univ, AM, 58, PhD, 60. **CAREER** From instr to asst prof English, Oberlin Col, 60-66; from asst prof to assoc prof, 66-77, actg head dept, 68-69, PROF ENGLISH, SIMON FRASER UNIV, 77-, Can Coun grant, 67-68, 69-70 & res grant, 74-75; Am Philos Soc res grant, 77; Soc Sci Humanities Res Coun Can res grant, 81-82. **MEMBERSHIPS** MLA; Tennyson Soc; Browning Soc; William Morris Soc. **RESEARCH** Victorian literature--novel, poetry & prose; visual art; William M Thackeray. **SELECTED PUBLICATIONS** Auth, Pegasus in Harness--Victorian Publishing And Thackeray, Bibliographical Soc Am, Vol 0088, 95. **CONTACT ADDRESS** Dept of English, Simon Fraser Univ, Burnaby, BC, V5A 1S6.

HARDER, BERNHARD D.
DISCIPLINE ENGLISH LANGUAGE; LITERATURE **EDUCATION** BC, BA, MA; NC Univ, PhD, 70. **CAREER** Assoc prof. **RESEARCH** International and Aboriginal literatures. **SELECTED PUBLICATIONS** Co-ed, Oxford UP ed of On the Properties of Things: John Trevisa's Translation of Bartholomaeus Anglicus De Proprietatibus Rerum: A Critical Text, 3 vols; pub (s), relationships between lang and soc and on Medieval and int lit. **CONTACT ADDRESS** Dept of English Language and Literature, Univ of Windsor, 401 Sunset Ave, Windsor, ON, N9B 3P4. **EMAIL** harder@uwindsor.ca

HARDER, HENRY LOUIS
PERSONAL Born 10/08/1936, Van Buren, AR, m, 1960, 5 children **DISCIPLINE** ENGLISH & AMERICAN LITERATURE **EDUCATION** Subiaco Col, BA, 58; Univ Ark, MA, 61; Univ Md, PhD, 70. **CAREER** Instr English, US Naval Acad, 65-69; asst prof, Anne Arundel Community Col, 69-70; asst prof, 70-73, assoc prof, 73-80, prof English, Mo Southern State Col, 80- **MEMBERSHIPS** MLA; AAUP; Mod Humanities Res Asn; Medieval Acad Am; Int Arthurian Soc. **RESEARCH** Middle English literature; Chaucer. **SELECTED PUBLICATIONS** Auth, Livy in Chaucer's and Gower's Lucrece Stories, Publ Mo Philol Asn, 77; Feasting in the Alliterative Morte Arthure, Chivalrie Literature, Medieval Inst Publ, 80. **CONTACT ADDRESS** 3950 Newman Rd, Joplin, MO, 64801-1512.

HARDER, SARAH
PERSONAL m **DISCIPLINE** ENGLISH LITERATURE **EDUCATION** Bowling Green State Univ, PhD. **CAREER** Fac, 68-. **HONORS AND AWARDS** Dir Women's Studies prog, Univ Wis Eau Claire, 84. **RESEARCH** Composition; drama; women in literature. **SELECTED PUBLICATIONS** Auth, published in journals such as Redbook and The American Woman. **CONTACT ADDRESS** Dept of English, Univ of Wisconsin, Eau Claire, Hibbard Hall 405, PO Box 4004, Eau Claire, WI, 54702-4004. **EMAIL** harderss@uwec.edu

HARDIN, JOHN ARTHUR
PERSONAL Born 09/18/1948, Louisville, Kentucky, m, 1973 **DISCIPLINE** HUMANITIES **EDUCATION** Bellarmine College, BA 1970; Fisk Univ, MA 1972; Univ of Michigan, PhD 1989. **CAREER** Univ of Louisville, lecturer 1972-84; KY State Univ, asst prof 1976-84, area coord 1978-80; Univ of KY, visiting asst prof 1980-81; Eastern WA Univ, asst prof 1984-90, assoc prof 1990-91; Western KY University, assoc professor, 1991-97, assistant dean, Potter College of Arts, Humanities and Social Sciences, 1997-. **HONORS AND AWARDS** Lenihan Awd for Comm Serv Bellarmine Coll 1969; Three Univ Fellowship Fisk Univ 1970-72; J Pierce Scholarshp Univ of MI Dept of History 1976; Distinguished Alumni Gallery Bellarmine Coll 1979-80; Pres Awd, Natl Council For Black Studies-Region X (1987); **MEMBERSHIPS** Mem exec comm KY Assoc of Teachers of History 1976-80, 1991-; state dir Phi Beta Sigma Frat Inc 1981-83; club pres Frankfort Kiwanis Club 1983-84; mem KY Historic Preservation Review Bd 1983-84, Publ Advisory Comm Kentucky Historical Soc 1983-84, Natl Council on Black Studies 1984-, KY Historical Soc 1984-; NAACP, 1984-; editorial advisory board member, Filson Club History Quarterly, 1989-92; life member, Phi Beta Sigma, 1980-; member, KY Oral History Commission, 1995-99; member, Phi Alpha Theta History Honor Society. **SELECTED PUBLICATIONS** author, Onward and Upward: A Centennial History of Kentucky State University 1886-1986, author, Fifty Years of Segregation: Black Higher Education in Kentucky, 1904-1954. **CONTACT ADDRESS** Potter College of Arts, Humanities & Social Sciences, Western Kentucky Univ, 1 Big Red Way, Bowling Green, KY, 42101-3576.

HARDIN, RICHARD F.
PERSONAL Born 11/09/1937, Los Angeles, CA, m, 1959, 6 children **DISCIPLINE** ENGLISH **EDUCATION** St Mary's Univ, BA, 59; Univ TX, MA, 64, PhD, 66. **CAREER** From asst prof to assoc prof to prof to chair, 66-00, Univ KS. **HONORS AND AWARDS** Diss Fel, Univ TX; Am Philos Soc Grant; Newberry Libr Grant; Marlowe Soc Award. **MEMBERSHIPS** AAUP; ALSC; Marlowe Soc; Sixteenth Century Studies; Southern Comp Lit Asn. **RESEARCH** English Renaissance lit; comparitive lit. **SELECTED PUBLICATIONS** Auth, Michael Drayton and the Passing of Elizabethan England; Civil Idolatry: Desacralizing and Monarchy in Spenser, Shakespeare, and Milton; ed, John Ross, Poems on Events of the Day 1582-1607; auth, Love in a Green Shade: Idyllic Romances Ancient to Modern; A Romance for Young Ladies: George Thornley's Translation of Daphnis and Chloe. **CONTACT ADDRESS** Dept of English, Univ of Kansas, Lawrence, KS, 66045. **EMAIL** rhardin@eagle.cc.ukans.edu

HARDY, DOROTHY C.
PERSONAL Town Creek, AL **DISCIPLINE** ENGLISH **EDUCATION** AL St U, BS; Xavier U, MEd; Univ of Cincinnati, EdD. **CAREER** Univ of Cincinnati, Grps & Univ Progams, asst dean stdnts 1973-77; KS St U, asst prof & emp/rcrtmnt Spec; Univ of Cincinnati, instr; Cincinnati Life Adj Inst, pres 1980-83; OH Dept Mental Hlth, comm div bus adm 1983-84; Southeast Missouri State Univ, 1984-89; Hardy Residential Rentals, 1986-96; Single Parent Program, Cape Gradeau Area Vocational Technical School, coord, 1991-95; UNIVERSITY OF N ALABAMA, ADJUNCT PROF OF ENGLISH, 1997. **HONORS AND AWARDS** Brodie Rsrch Award #1000 Plus 1975; Otstndg Comm Serv 1976; Otstndng Women NAACP 1981; Background Player "The Jesse Owens Story" Paramount Studio for ABC-TV 1984; Cert of Merit for the Fiction (Writer's Digest) Poetry (Creative Enterprise, World of Poetry) Pebble in the Pond 1985; Golden Poet Award 1986; Southwest Missouri State Univ Museum Exhibit, Black Women: Against the Odds, 1996; Alabama State Univ, Alumni of Distinction, 1997. **MEMBERSHIPS** Human Invlvmnt Prog 1979; bus act Madisonville Job Training 1982; consult Archdiocese of Grtr Cincinnati 1983; Prog Assoc for Economic Dev; mnrty coord Issues 2 & 3 Ctzns for Gov Richard F Celeste 1983-84; training dir Mondale/Ferraro Camp 1984. **SELECTED PUBLICATIONS** Fiction published in the Summerfield Journal Castalia Publishers & Ellipsis, Literary Journal; Poetry published in Essence Magazine, 1989, 1991-93.

HARDY, JOHN EDWARD
PERSONAL Born 04/03/1922, Baton Rouge, LA, m, 1942, 6 children **DISCIPLINE** ENGLISH & AMERICAN LITERATURE **EDUCATION** La State Univ, BA, 44; State Univ Iowa, MA, 46; Johns Hopkins Univ, PhD, 56. **CAREER** Instr English, Univ Detroit, 45-46, Yale Univ, 46-48 & Univ Okla, 48-52; instr writing, Johns Hopkins Univ, 52-54; from asst prof to prof English, 54-66, dir grad studies, Univ Notre Dame, 65-66; prof & head dept, Univ S Ala, 66-69; prof & chmn dept, Univ Mo-St Louis, 70-71; PROF ENGLISH, UNIV ILL, CHICAGO CIRCLE, 72-, Ford Found Fund Advan Educ fac studies fel, 52-53; Sewanee Rev fel poetry, 54; Fulbright prof Am lit, Am Inst, Univ Munich, 59-61; vis prof English, Univ Colo, 69-70. **MEMBERSHIPS** MLA. **RESEARCH** Poetry; literary criticism; modern fiction. **SELECTED PUBLICATIONS** Auth, Faunal Presences in the Poetry of Wilbur, Richard, Renascence Essays on Values in Literature, Vol 0045, 93. **CONTACT ADDRESS** Dept of English, Univ Ill Chicago Circle, Chicago, IL, 60680.

HARIMAN, ROBERT
PERSONAL Born 06/17/1951, Grand Forks, ND, m, 1982, 2 children **DISCIPLINE** RHETORIC **EDUCATION** Macalester Col, BA, 73; Univ MN, MA, 75, PhD, 79. **CAREER** Asst prof, 79-85, assoc prof, 85-93, full prof, Drake Univ, 93-.

HONORS AND AWARDS Case IA Professor of the Year; NCA Distinguished Scholarship Award. **MEMBERSHIPS** Nat Comm Asn; Rhetorical Soc Am. **RESEARCH** Classical and contemporary rhetorical theolry; stylistic analysis; twentieth-century political discourse. **SELECTED PUBLICATIONS** Auth, Popular Trials: Rhetoric, Mass Media, and the Law, ed vol, Univ AL Press, 90, paperback ed, 93; Post-Realism: The Rhetorical Turn in International Relations, co-ed with Francis A Beer, MI State Univ Press, 96; Political Style: The Artistry of Power, Univ Chicago Press, 95. **CONTACT ADDRESS** Dept of Rhetoric and Communication Studies, Drake Univ, Des Moines, IA, 50311-4505. **EMAIL** robert.hariman@drake.edu

HARK, INA RAE
PERSONAL Born 08/19/1949, Charleston, WV **DISCIPLINE** ENGLISH LITERATURE, FILM STUDIES **EDUCATION** Northwestern Univ, BA, 71; Univ Calif, Los Angeles, MA, 72, PhD(English), 75. **CAREER** Teaching asst, Univ Calif, Los Angeles, 72-74; asst prof, 75-80, ASSOC PROF ENGLISH, UNIV SC, 80-, Am Coun Learned Socs grant-in-aid, 77. **MEMBERSHIPS** MLA; Am Film Inst. **RESEARCH** Victorian literature; film; modern drama. **SELECTED PUBLICATIONS** Auth, Butler, Samuel--A Biography, 19th C Prose, Vol 0020, 93; The Annual of Bernard Shaw Studies, Vol 11, 93. **CONTACT ADDRESS** Dept of English, Univ of So Carolina, Welsh Bldg, Columbia, SC, 29208.

HARLAND, PAUL W.
PERSONAL Winnipeg, MB, Canada **DISCIPLINE** LITERATURE **EDUCATION** Univ Winnipeg, BA; Univ W Ontario, MA, PhD. **CAREER** Instr, Univ W Ontario; prof, Augustana Univ. **RESEARCH** Renaissance and twentieth century literature **SELECTED PUBLICATIONS** Co-ed,Dianoia. **CONTACT ADDRESS** Dept of English, Augustana Univ, 4901-46th Ave, Camrose, AB, T4V 2R3. **EMAIL** harlandp@augustana.ab.ca

HARMS, PAUL W.F.
DISCIPLINE HOMILETICS **EDUCATION** Concordia Sem, BA, 45, MDiv, 48, STM, 54; Northwestern Univ, MA, 57, PhD, 73; Valparaiso Univ, DA, 95. **CAREER** Assoc prof, Dir Drama and Forensics, Concordia Col, 52-56; prof, resident couns, Dir Drama, Concordia Sr Col, 56-76; prof, dean Community Life, Dir Drama, ELTS, 76-78; dean Community Life, 78-90; prof, 78-94; dir, Trinity Lutheran Sem Theater, 78-; prof emeri, Trinity Lutheran Sem, 94-. **SELECTED PUBLICATIONS** Auth, Seek Good Not Evil, CSS, 85; Presenting the Lessons, Augsburg, 80; ed, Praise of Preaching. CSS, 84. **CONTACT ADDRESS** Ministry Dept, Trinity Lutheran Sem, 2199 E Main St, Columbus, OH, 43209-2334. **EMAIL** pharms@trinity.capital.edu

HARNER, JAMES
PERSONAL Born 03/24/1946, Washington, IN, m, 1967, 1 child **DISCIPLINE** ENGLISH **EDUCATION** Ind State Univ, BS, 68; Univ Ill, MA, 70, PhD, 72. **CAREER** From asst prof to assoc prof to prof, 71-88, Bowling Green State Univ; prof, Tex A&M Univ, 88-. **HONORS AND AWARDS** Besterman Medal, outstanding bibliograpy published, 97, Libry Asn. **MEMBERSHIPS** Modern Lang Asn; Am Libry Asn; Bibliographical Soc London; Bibliographical Soc Am. **RESEARCH** Shakespeare; Bibliography. **SELECTED PUBLICATIONS** Auth, MLA Directory of Scholarly Presses in Language and Literature, 96; auth, World Shakespeare Bibliography on CD-ROM 1990-1993, 97; auth, World Shakespeare Bibliography on CD-ROM 1987-1994, 97; auth, World Shakespeare Bibliography on CD-ROM 1983-1995, 98; auth, Literary Research Guide: An Annotated Listing of Reference Sources in English Literary Studies, 98. **CONTACT ADDRESS** Dept of English, Texas A&M Univ, College Station, TX, 77843-4227. **EMAIL** j-harner@tamu.edu

HARPHAM, GEOFFREY GALT
DISCIPLINE ENGLISH LITERATURE **EDUCATION** Northwestern Univ, BA, 68; UCLA, PhD, 74. **CAREER** Prof, 86, Tulane Univ. **SELECTED PUBLICATIONS** Auth, On the Grotesque: A Critical Study, Princeton, 82; The Ascetic Imperative in Culture and Criticism, Chicago, 87; Getting It Right: Language, Literature and Ethics, Chicago, 92; So...What Is Enlightenment, Critical Inquiry, 94; Ethics, Critical Terms for Literary Study, Chicago, 95; Of Rats and Men; Or, Reason In Our Time, Raritan, 95; One of Us: The Mastery of Joseph Conrad, Chicago, 96; Ethics, Late Jameson, Salmagundi, 96. **CONTACT ADDRESS** Dept of Eng, Tulane Univ, 6823 St Charles Ave, New Orleans, LA, 70118. **EMAIL** harpham@mailhost.tcs.tulane.edu

HARPINE, WILLIAM
PERSONAL Born 09/15/1951, Washington, DC, m, 1977, 3 children **DISCIPLINE** SPEECH COMMUNICATION **EDUCATION** Coll of William and Mary, BA, 73; Northern IL Univ, MA, 74; Univ IL at Urbana-Champaign, PhD, 82. **CAREER** Temporary instr, 75-76, IA State Univ; asst prof, 79-82, Coll of William & Mary; prof, 82-present, Univ Akron. **MEMBERSHIPS** Natl Communication Assn; Amer Soc for the Hist of Rhetoric **RESEARCH** 19th century Amer public speaking; rhetoric theory. **SELECTED PUBLICATIONS** Auth, The Appeal to Tradition: Cultural Evolution and Logical Soundness, Informal Logic, 93; Stock Issues and Theories of Ethics, Southern Journal of Forensics, 96; Epideictic and Ethos in the Amarna Letters: The Withholding of Argument, Rhetoric Society Quarterly, 98. **CONTACT ADDRESS** Sch of Communication, Univ Akron, 108 Kolbe Hall, Akron, OH, 44325-1003.

HARPOLD, TERRY
DISCIPLINE LITERATURE, COMMUNICATION, AND CULTURE **EDUCATION** Univ Pa, PhD, 94. **CAREER** Asst prof, mem, Ctr for New Media Educ and Res, & Graphics, Visualization, & Usability Ctr, Ga Inst of Technol. **RESEARCH** Postmodern culture and literature. **SELECTED PUBLICATIONS** Publications include discussions of hypertextual narrative form and its graphical representations, the "inverted landscapes" of author J.G. Ballard, and the obscured political economies of cartographic depictions of the Internet. **CONTACT ADDRESS** Sch of Lit, Commun & Cult, Georgia Inst of Tech, Skiles Cla, Atlanta, GA, 30332. **EMAIL** terry.harpold@lcc.gatech.edu

HARRIENGER, MYRNA J.
DISCIPLINE COMPOSITION AND RHETORIC **EDUCATION** Purdue Univ, PhD, 91. **CAREER** Asst prof, TX Tech Univ. **RESEARCH** Writing in old age; writing in illness. **SELECTED PUBLICATIONS** Auth, Writing a Life: The Composing of Grace, in Feminist Principles and Women's Experience in Rhetoric and Composition, Univ Pittsburgh Press, 95. **CONTACT ADDRESS** Texas Tech Univ, Lubbock, TX, 79409-5015. **EMAIL** ditmh@ttacs.ttu.edu

HARRINGTON, E. MICHAEL
PERSONAL Born 02/02/1954, Cambridge, MA **DISCIPLINE** PERFORMING ARTS **EDUCATION** Univ Lowell, BM, 76; Univ Miami, MM, 78; Ohio State Univ, DMA, 85. **CAREER** Lectr, performed, taught master classes at Harvard Univ, Berkley Col Music, Eastman Sch Music, Emory Univ; assoc prof, Belmont Univ, currently. **HONORS AND AWARDS** Jemison Distinguished Prof Hum, 1995, Univ Ala; listed, Who's Who in the South, Who's Who Among Amer Teachers; Nashville Composer of the Year, 89. **MEMBERSHIPS** Board dir, Col Music Society Southern Chapter, Live Music in Am; ed board dir, Univ Ala Press. **RESEARCH** World music; copyright law; popular music. **SELECTED PUBLICATIONS** Articles publ, Col Music Symposium, Ex Tempore, Triad, Tenn Musician, Am Society Univ Composers Monograph Series, Ind Theory Review. **CONTACT ADDRESS** 2625 Link Dr, Franklin, TN, 37064-4942. **EMAIL** harringtone@mail.belmont.edu

HARRINGTON, HENRY R.
PERSONAL Born 12/23/1943, Evanston, IL, m, 1968, 1 child **DISCIPLINE** ENGLISH LITERATURE & THEOLOGY **EDUCATION** Williams Col, AB, 66; Stanford Univ, MA, 68, PhD, 71. **CAREER** Asst prof, 71-80, ASSOC PROF ENGLISH, UNIV MONT, 80- **MEMBERSHIPS** MLA; AAUP; Am Acad Relig. **RESEARCH** Victorian literature; comtemporary theology and literature; novel. **SELECTED PUBLICATIONS** Auth, English Travelers and the Oriental Crowd, Kinglake, Curzon, and the 'Miracle Of The Holy Fire', Harvard Library Bul, Vol 0005, 94; A Community of One, Masculine Autobiography and Autonomy in 19th-Century Britain, 19th C Prose, Vol 0022, 95. **CONTACT ADDRESS** Dept of English, Univ of Mont, Missoula, MT, 59801.

HARRIS, CHARLES BURT
PERSONAL Born 11/02/1940, LaGrange, TX, m, 1968, 2 children **DISCIPLINE** AMERICAN LITERATURE **EDUCATION** Tex Lutheran Col, AB, 63; Southern Ill Univ, MA, 65, PhD(English), 70. **CAREER** Instr English, Southern Ill Univ, 66-68; from asst prof to assoc prof, 68-78, PROF ENGLISH, ILL STATE UNIV, 78-, CHAIRPERSON ENGLISH, 79- **MEMBERSHIPS** MLA; Midwest Mod Lang Asn; Col English Asn; Asn Dept English; AAUP. **RESEARCH** Twentieth century American literature; the novel; recent American fiction. **SELECTED PUBLICATIONS** Auth, The Republic of Letters--Literary Organizations and Nea Support, Am Bk Rev, Vol 0017, 95. **CONTACT ADDRESS** Dept of English, Illinois State Univ, Normal, IL, 61761.

HARRIS, DANIEL A.
DISCIPLINE ENGLISH LANGUAGE AND LITERATURE **EDUCATION** Yale Univ, BA; MA; PhD. **CAREER** Prof. **RESEARCH** Jewish studies; Victorian poetry; modern and contemporary poetry; graduate student pedagogy. **SELECTED PUBLICATIONS** Auth, Yeats: Coole Park and Ballylee; auth, Inspirations Unbidden: the 'Terrible Sonnets' of Gerard Manley Hopkins. **CONTACT ADDRESS** Dept of English, Rutgers Univ, 510 George St, Murray Hall, New Brunswick, NJ, 08901-1167. **EMAIL** dharris@aol.com

HARRIS, DUNCAN SEELY
PERSONAL Born 02/22/1944, Worland, WY, m, 1966, 2 children **DISCIPLINE** ENGLISH & AMERICAN LITERATURE **EDUCATION** Stanford Univ, BA, 65; Boston Univ, MA, 66; Brandeis Univ, PhD, 73. **CAREER** Instr English, Tougaloo Col, 69; from instr to asst prof, 70-77, assoc prof Eng, 77-, Univ Wyo; Danforth Found Assoc, 80-; dir, honor's prog, 93. **MEMBERSHIPS** MLA; Melville Soc; Shakespeare Assn. **RESEARCH** Nineteenth century American literature; Shakespeare; allegory. **SELECTED PUBLICATIONS** Auth, The End of Lear and a Shape for Shakespearean Tragedy, Shakespeare Studies, 76; art, Again for Cydnus: The Dramaturgical Resolution of Antony and Cleopatra, Studies in English Lit, 77; co-ed, Teaching Shakespeare, Princeton Univ, 77; coauth, The Other Side Of The Garden: An Interpretive Comparison of the Book of the Duchess and the Daphnaida, J Medieval and Renaissance Studies, 78; auth, Tombs, Guidebooks and Shakespearean Drama: Death in the Renaissance, Mosaic, 82. **CONTACT ADDRESS** Dept of English, Univ of Wyoming, Box 3353, Laramie, WY, 82071. **EMAIL** dharris@wwyo.edu

HARRIS, ELIZABETH HALL
PERSONAL Born 11/27/1944, Ft. Worth, TX, m, 1995 **DISCIPLINE** CREATIVE WRITING (FICTION) & MODERN LITERATURE **EDUCATION** Carnegie-Mellon Univ, BS, 65; Stanford Univ, PhD(English), 76. **CAREER** Asst prof, 76-83, ASSOC PROF ENGLISH, UNIV TX, AUSTIN, 83-. **HONORS AND AWARDS** Honorable Mention, Best Short Stories of 1970 and Best Short Stories of 1985; New Stories from the South: The Year's Best, 86; The John Simmons Award, 91; The Best of Wind, 199?. **SELECTED PUBLICATIONS** Auth, The Ant Generator (stories), IA, 91. **CONTACT ADDRESS** Dept of English, Univ of Texas, 0 Univ of TX, Austin, TX, 78712-1026.

HARRIS, GIL W.
PERSONAL Born 12/09/1946, Lynchburg, Virginia, m **DISCIPLINE** COMMUNICATIONS **EDUCATION** Natl Acad of Broadcasting, dipl radio &TV 1964-65; Winston-Salem Coll, AS 1969-71; Shaw Univ, BA 1977-80; NC A&T St Univ, MS 1981-82; Pacific Western Univ, PhD 1986. **CAREER** WEAL/WQMG Radio Stations, oper dir 1972-79; Shaw Univ, dir of radio broadcasting 1979-81; Collegiate Telecommunications, system producer, sport dir 1981-84; SC St Coll, asst prof of broadcasting 1984-. **HONORS AND AWARDS** Citizen of the Week WGHP TV High Point NC 1977; Radio Announcer of the Year Dudley HS 1979; Outstanding Media Serv Triad Sickle Cell 1979; Outstanding Media Serv Mid-Eastern Athletic Conf 1983; Outstanding Media Serv Central Intercoll Athletic Assoc. **MEMBERSHIPS** Mem Omega Psi Phi, Prince Hall Mason, NAACP. **CONTACT ADDRESS** South Carolina St Col, PO Box 1915, Orangeburg, SC, 29117.

HARRIS, JANICE HUBBARD
PERSONAL Born 03/30/1943, Los Angeles, CA, m, 1966, 2 children **DISCIPLINE** BRITISH FICTION; WOMEN'S STUDIES; POST COLONIAL STUDIES **EDUCATION** Stanford Univ, AB, 65; Brown Univ, PhD, 73. **CAREER** Instr English, Tougaloo Col, 69-73; asst prof English, 75-81, Assoc prof English, 81-88, Assoc Dean Arts Sci. 83-84; Dir Univ Honors Prog, 82-86, prof English, 88-, dir Women's Studies, 95-,Univ Wyo, 80-, Danforth Teaching fel, 81. **MEMBERSHIPS** MLA; Nat Women's Studies Asn; Women's Caucus Mod Lang. **RESEARCH** Modern British fiction; women's studies; Post-Colonial Literatures. **SELECTED PUBLICATIONS** Auth, D H Lawrence and Kate Millett, Mass Rev, summer 74; Our mute, inglorious mothers, Midwest Quart, 4/75; Insight and experiment in D H Lawrence's early short fiction, Philol Quart, summer 76; Sexual antagonism in D H Lawrence's early leadership fiction, Mod Lang Studies, spring 77; The moulting of the plumed serpent, Mod Lang Quart, 3/79; Bushes, bears and the beast in the jungle, Studies in Short Fiction, spring 81; Gayl Jones' Corregidora, Frontiers, Vol 3; Feminist Representations of Wives and Work: An Almost Irreconcilable' Edwardian Debate, Women's Stud, 93; Challenging the Script of the Heterosexual Couple: Three Marriage Novels by May Sinclair, Papers on Lang & Lit, 93; Wifely Speech and Silence: Three Marriage Novels by H G Wells, Stud in Novel, 94; Edwardian Stories of Divorce, Rutgers Univ, 96. **CONTACT ADDRESS** Dept English, Univ Wyo, PO Box 3353, Laramie, WY, 82071-3353. **EMAIL** JHARRIS@vwyo.edu

HARRIS, JONATHAN GIL
DISCIPLINE ENGLISH LITERATURE **EDUCATION** Auckland Univ, BA, 83, MA, 86; Univ Sussex, PhD, 90. **CAREER** Assoc prof. **RESEARCH** Early modern English culture. **SELECTED PUBLICATIONS** Auth, Foreign Bodies and the Body Politic: Discourses of Social Pathology in Early Modern England, Cambridge, 98; Apples Beyond the Pale: The Irish Costermonger in the English Garden of Eden, Binghamton, 95; This is not a Pipe: Water Supply, Incontinent Sources, and the Leaky Body Politic, Cornell, 94; 'Narcissus in thy face': Roman Desire and the Difference it Fakes in Antony and Cleopatra, Cambridge, 94. **CONTACT ADDRESS** English Dept, Ithaca Col, 100 Job Hall, Ithaca, NY, 14850. **EMAIL** harrisj@ithaca.edu

HARRIS, JOSEPH
DISCIPLINE FOLKLORE AND ENGLISH **EDUCATION** Univ Ga, BA; Univ Frankfurt; Cambridge Univ, England; Har-

vard Univ, AM, PhD. **CAREER** Prof. **RESEARCH** Tradition and language. **SELECTED PUBLICATIONS** Co-ed, Prosimetrum: Cross-Cultural Perspectives on Narrative in Prose and Verse, 97. **CONTACT ADDRESS** Dept of English, Harvard Univ, 8 Garden St, Cambridge, MA, 02138. **EMAIL** harris@fas.harvard.edu

HARRIS, LAURILYN J.
DISCIPLINE THEATRE HISTORY AND DRAMATURGY **EDUCATION** Ind Univ, BA; Univ Iowa, MA, PhD. **CAREER** Prof & dir Grad Stud, Washington State Univ.. **SELECTED PUBLICATIONS** Publ in, Theatre Res Int; Theatre Hist Stud; J Creative Behavior; Theatre J; Notable Women in the Amer Theatre; Theatre Annual; Theatre Southwest; Amer Theatre Companies; Stud in Amer Drama; Nineteenth Century Theatre Res; Confronting Tenn Williams' Streetcar Named Desire. **CONTACT ADDRESS** Dept of Music and Theater, Washington State Univ, Pullman, WA, 99164-5300.

HARRIS, MARK
PERSONAL Born 11/19/1922, Mount Vernon, NY, m, 1946, 4 children **DISCIPLINE** ENGLISH **EDUCATION** Univ Minn, PhD, Am Studies, 56. **CAREER** Fac English, San Francisco State Col, 54-68; vis prof, Brandeis, 63; Purdue Univ, 67-79; Calif Inst Arts, 70-73; Immaculate Heart Col, 73-74; Univ Southern Calif, 73-75; prof, Univ Pittsburgh, 75-80; PROF ENGLISH, ARIZ STATE UNIV, 80-; **HONORS AND AWARDS** DHL, Ill Wesleyan Univ, 74., Fulbright prof, Univ Hiroshima, 57-58; Ford Found fel, 60; Nat Inst Arts & Letters fel, 61; Guggenheim Mem Found fel, 65, 74; Nat Endowment for Arts, 66. **SELECTED PUBLICATIONS** Auth, Trumpet to the World, 46; City of Discontent, 52; The Southpaw, 53; Bang the Drum Slowly, 56; Something About A Soldier, 57; A Ticket for a Seamstitch, 57; Wake Up, Stupid, 59; The Goy, 70; Killing Everybody, Dial Press, 73; It Looked Like Forever, McGraw-Hill Co, 79; Short Work of It: Selected Writing..., Univ Pittsburgh Press, 79; Saul Bellow: Drumlin Woodchuck, Univ Ga Press, 80; The Heart of Boswell, McGraw-Hill Co, 82; Lying in Bed, 84; Speed, 90; The Tale Maker, 94. **CONTACT ADDRESS** English Dept, Arizona State Univ, Tempe, Tempe, AZ, 85281.

HARRIS, RANDY ALLEN
DISCIPLINE ENGLISH LITERATURE **EDUCATION** Univ Alberta, MS, 85; Dalhousie Univ, MA, 82; Queen's Univ, BA, 80; Rensselaer Polytech Inst, MA, 86; DPhil, 90. **SELECTED PUBLICATIONS** Auth, The Chomskyan revolution 1: Science, syntax, and semantics, Perspectives Sci, 94; The Chomskyan revolution 2: Sturm und Drang, Perspectives Sci, 94; The linguistics wars, Oxford, 93; Acoustic dimensions of functor comprehension in Broca's aphasia, Univ Ind, 88; ed, Landmark essays in rhetoric of science: Case studies, Lawrence Erlbaum, 97; co-ed, Technical communication in Canada, Baywood, 94. **CONTACT ADDRESS** Dept of English, Waterloo Univ, 200 University Ave W, Waterloo, ON, N2L 3G1. **EMAIL** pwpmah@watarts.uwaterloo.ca

HARRIS, SUSAN KUMIN
PERSONAL Born 08/29/1945, Baltimore, MD, m, 1968 **DISCIPLINE** AMERICAN LITERATURE & STUDIES **EDUCATION** Antioch Col, BA, 68; Stanford Univ, MA, 72; Cornell Univ, PhD(English), 77. **CAREER** ASSOC PROF ENGLISH, QUEENS COL, 77- **MEMBERSHIPS** MLA. **RESEARCH** Mark Twain studies; women's studies (American, 19th century); rhetoric. **SELECTED PUBLICATIONS** Auth, The Modernist Madonna--Semiotics of the Material Metaphor, Tulsa Studies Womens Lit, Vol 0010, 91. **CONTACT ADDRESS** Dept of English, Queens Col, CUNY, Flushing, NY, 11367.

HARRIS, THOMAS E.
DISCIPLINE COMMUNICATION **EDUCATION** George Washington Univ, BA, 66; Univ of Maryland, MA, 67; Temple Univ, PhD, 80. **CAREER** Dir of Varsity Debate, George Washington univ, 67-71; lectr, dir of debate, Rutgers Univ, 71-77; prof, Univ of Evansville, 80-89; ASSO PROF, 89-96, PROF, 96-, UNIV OF ALA. **HONORS AND AWARDS** Outstanding Teach, Col of Continuing Studies, Univ of Ala, 96; last lecture honorary choice, Univ of Evansville, 87. **MEMBERSHIPS** Asn for Business Commun; Nat Commun Asn. **RESEARCH** Organizational change; communication; technology; leadership; teams. **SELECTED PUBLICATIONS** Coauth, Small Group and Team Communication, Allyn & Bacon, 99; auth, Diversity: Importance, Ironies, and Pathways, Conflict and Diversity, Hampton Press, 97; auth, Applied Organizational Communication: Perspectives, Principles, and Pragmatics, Lawrence Erlbaum Pubs, 93; auth, Analysis of the Clash over Issues Between Booker T. Washington and W.E.B Dubois, Garland, 93; auth, Toward Effective Employee Involvement: An Analysis of Parallel and Self-managing Teams, The J of Applied Business Res, Winter, 92-93. **CONTACT ADDRESS** PO Box 20305, Tuscaloosa, AL, 25402.

HARRIS, TRUDIER
PERSONAL Born 02/27/1948, Mantua, Alabama, s **DISCIPLINE** ENGLISH **EDUCATION** Stillman Coll, Tuscaloosa AL, BA, 1969; Ohio State Univ, Columbus OH, MA, 1972, PhD, 1973. **CAREER** The Coll of William and Mary, Williamsburg VA, asst prof, 1973-79; Univ of North Carolina, Chapel Hill NC, assoc prof, 1979-85, prof, 1985-88, J Carlyle Sitterson prof, 1988-; Univ of Arkansas, Little Rock AR, William Grant Cooper Visiting Distinguished, prof, 1987; Ohio State Univ, Columbus OH, visiting distinguished prof, 1988. **HONORS AND AWARDS** NEH Fellowship for Coll Teachers, 1977-78; Carnegie Faculty Fellow, The Bunting Inst, 1981-83; Fellow, Natl Research Council/Ford Found, 1982-83; Creative Scholarship Award, Coll Language Assn, 1987; Teaching Award, South Atlantic Modern Language Assn, 1987; Rockefeller Fellowship, Bellagio, Italy, 1994; National Humanities Center Fellowship, 1996-97. **MEMBERSHIPS** Mem, The Modern Language Assn of Amer, 1973-, Amer Folklore Soc, 1973-, Coll Language Assn, 1974-South Atlantic Modern Language Assn, 1980-, The Langston Hughes Soc, 1982-, Zeta Phi Beta Sorority Inc. **SELECTED PUBLICATIONS** Author of: From Mammies To Militants: Domestics in Black American Literature, 1982; Exorcising Blackness: Historical and Literary Lynching And Burning Rituals, 1984; Black Women In The Fiction of James Baldwin, 1985; Fiction and folklore: The Novels of Toni Morrison, 1991; The Power of the Porch : The Storyteller's Craft in Zora Neale Hurston, Gloria Naylor, and Randall Kenan, 1996; editor of: Afro-American Writers Before The Harlem Renaissance, 1986; Afro-American Writers From The Harlem Renaissance To 1940, 1987; Afro-American Writers From 1940 To 1955, 1988; editor, Selected Works of Ida B Wells-Barnett, 1991; Afro-American Fiction Writers After 1955 in the dictionary of Literary Biography Series, 1984; Afro-American Writers After 1955: Dramatist and Prose Writers, 1985; Afro-American Poets After 1955, 1985; The Oxford Companion to Women's Writing in the United States, 1994; The Oxford Companion to African American Literature 1997; Call and Response The Riverside Anthology of the African American Literary Tradition, 1997; The Literature of the American South: A Norton Anthology, 1997; New Essays on Baldwin's Go Tell It On the Mountian, 1996. **CONTACT ADDRESS** J Carlyle Sitterson Professor of English, Univ of North Carolina at Chapel Hill, CB# 3520 Greenlaw, Chapel Hill, NC, 27599-3520.

HARRIS, WILLIAM STYRON, JR.
PERSONAL Born 06/09/1936, Elizabeth City, NC, m, 1965, 1 child **DISCIPLINE** LIERATURE **EDUCATION** Wake Forest Univ, BA, 58; Duke Univ, AM, 63, PhD, 71 **CAREER** Inst, 68-69, Univ of VA; Asst Prof, 71-76, Assoc Prof, 76-82, Dir, 79-82, Prof, 82-, Chair, 82-, E TN St Univ **HONORS AND AWARDS** Fulbright Asoc, 85-86 **MEMBERSHIPS** MLA, SAMLA, AAUP **RESEARCH** Charles Kingsley **CONTACT ADDRESS** Dept of English, East Tennessee State Univ, PO Box 70683, Johnson CIty, TN, 37614-0683. **EMAIL** harris@etsu.edu

HARRISON, ANTONY HOWARD
PERSONAL Born 10/09/1948, London, England, m, 1974 **DISCIPLINE** ENGLISH LITERATURE, NINETEENTH CENTURY POETRY **EDUCATION** Stanford Univ, AB, 70; Univ Chicago, PhD(English), 74. **CAREER** Asst prof, 74-80, ASSOC PROF ENGLISH, NC STATE UNIV, 80-, Fel, Nat Humanities Ctr, 81-82. **MEMBERSHIPS** SAtlantic Mod Lang Asn; Victorians Inst; MLA. **RESEARCH** Victorian poetry; Victorian prose nonfiction; romantic poetry. **SELECTED PUBLICATIONS** Auth, Christina Rossetti in 1994-Introduction, Victorian Poetry, Vol 0032, 94; Epistolary Relations, The Correspondence of Christina Rossetti and Dante Gabriel Rossetti, J Pre-Raphaelite Studies-New Series, Vol 0004, 95; Annoying The Victorians, Criticism, Vol 0038, 96. **CONTACT ADDRESS** Dept of English, No Carolina State Univ, Raleigh, NC, 27650.

HARRISON, CAROL L.
PERSONAL Born 11/15/1946, Buffalo, NY **DISCIPLINE** ENGLISH **EDUCATION** English Psychology, BA 1968; PhD 1970. **CAREER** Medailla Coll English Dept, instructor, asst prof, chmn 1970-73; Media-Communications Medaille Coll, acting dir, assoc prof 1974-; SUNY AB English educ colloquim 1972-; Am Assn Univ Prof 1968-; Modern Language Assn 1969-; Intl Plaform Assn 1972-74; Univ Buffalo Alumni Assn 1968-; Academic Com Buffalo Philharmonic 1971-73. **HONORS AND AWARDS** Outstanding EDUCATIONs Am Award 1974. **MEMBERSHIPS** Vol work Buffalo Childrens Hosp 1972; Western NY Consortium English & Am Lit Prof 1974; Nomination Am Assn Univ Womens Educ Found. **CONTACT ADDRESS** 18 Agassiz Circle, Buffalo, NY, 14214.

HARRISON, CAROL LYNN
PERSONAL Born 11/15/1946, Buffalo, NY **DISCIPLINE** ENGLISH LITERATURE **EDUCATION** State Univ NY, Buffalo, BA(psychol) & BA(English), 68, PhD, 70. **CAREER** From instr to asst prof English, 70-74, chmn dept commun, 72-74, assoc prof & actg dir, media-commun, 74-76, prog dir lib studies, 76-78, assoc prof, 76-82, actg dean prof studies, 79-80 prof humanities, Medaille Col, 82-, Danforth Found assoc, 78. **MEMBERSHIPS** MLA; NCTE. **RESEARCH** Freshman composition development; 17th century British literature; advanced writing skills development. **SELECTED PUBLICATIONS** Auth, Eagle's Grass, in Heirloom Collection, 73 & Waiting, in Golden Book Verse, 74, Golden Eagle Press. **CONTACT ADDRESS** Medaille Col, 18 Agassiz Circle, Buffalo, NY, 14214-2695. **EMAIL** drcarole@buffnet.net

HARRISON, GARY
DISCIPLINE BRITISH ROMANTICISM, WORLD LITERATURE, AND LITERARY THEORY **EDUCATION** Stanford Univ, PhD, 87. **CAREER** Instr, Univ NMex, 87-. **RESEARCH** The culture of the early 1790s; Wordsworth and Godwin. **SELECTED PUBLICATIONS** Auth, Wordsworth's Vagrant Muse, 94; coed, Western Literature in a World Context, 95. **CONTACT ADDRESS** Univ NMex, Albuquerque, NM, 87131. **EMAIL** garyh@unm.edu

HARRISON, RANDALL PAUL
PERSONAL Born 02/03/1929, Eau Claire, WI, m, 1983 **DISCIPLINE** COMMUNICATION **EDUCATION** Univ Wisc, BS, 50; Mich State Univ, PhD, 64. **CAREER** Prof, Mich State Univ, 64-73; adjunct prof Communications, 73-78, CLIN FAC, UNIV CAL SAN FRAN, 78-, FAC CTR MEDIA & INDEPENDENT LEARNING, UNIV CAL BERKELEY, 78-; fel, Int Commun Asn; fel Am Asn Advan Sci; Helen Williams Award Excellence Col Independent Study, 95. **MEMBERSHIPS** Int Commun Asn **RESEARCH** Art; Non-verbal communication **SELECTED PUBLICATIONS** Beyond Words, Prentice Hall, 74; The Cartoon: Communication to the Quick, Saga, 80. **CONTACT ADDRESS** PO Box 22541, San Francisco, CA, 94122. **EMAIL** RandallHarrisonPhD@compuserve.com

HARRISON, VICTORIA
DISCIPLINE AMERICAN LITERATURE **EDUCATION** Rutgers Univ, PhD, 88. **CAREER** ASSOC PROF, ENG, UNIV CALIF, SANTA BARBARA. **RESEARCH** Ethnic Am identities and World War II; Mod women poets. **SELECTED PUBLICATIONS** Auth, Elizabeth Bishop's Poetics of Intimacy, Cambridge Univ Press, 93. **CONTACT ADDRESS** Dept of Eng, Univ Calif, Santa Barbara, CA, 93106-7150. **EMAIL** vgharr@humanitas.ucsb.edu

HARRISON, W. DALE
DISCIPLINE JOURNALISM **EDUCATION** Fullerton Col, 85; Tenn State Univ, BS 90; Univ Tenn, MA, 91; Univ Ga, PhD, . **CAREER** Inst, Univ Ga, 94-96; Adjunc inst, Truell-McConell Coll, 96; John B. Ashcroft instruc, Wingate Univ; Asst. Prof- **HONORS AND AWARDS** Georgia Press Asn; Alpha Chi Honor Prof; Fac Mem Month; Wingate Univ Student Govt Asn., Supvr, prof Writing & Editing Internships; adv, Jambar Writers Club; adv, Frontiers Newsl; adv, Lifelines Newsl; chair, acad senate charter & bylaws comt. **MEMBERSHIPS** Asn Educ Jour & Mass Comm; Col Media Advs; Tri-County Journalism Asn, Past: Ga Press Asn, Soc Collegiate Journalists, Tenn Press Asn. **SELECTED PUBLICATIONS** Articles, Rev Appeal; Knoxville Jour, Daily News Jour, Columbia Times. **CONTACT ADDRESS** Youngstown State Univ, One University Plaza, Youngstown, OH, 44555. **EMAIL** wdharris@cc.ysu.edu

HARRISON LELAND, BRUCE
DISCIPLINE LITERATURE AND COMPOSITION **EDUCATION** Hartwick Col , BA, 68; Rutgers Univ, PhD, 76. **CAREER** Tchg asst, Rutgers Col, 69-72; Asst prof, 72-86; Assoc prof, 86-91; prof, Western Ill Univ, 91-. **HONORS AND AWARDS** W IllUniv Fac Excellence Award, 91., Actg chair, Eng & Journalism, 92; Dir Writing, 83-97. **SELECTED PUBLICATIONS** Auth, Discovery: Writing to Learn; Kendall-Hunt, 93; Connections: Reading and Writing, Kendall-Hunt, 92; Discovery: Writing to Learn. Kendall-Hunt, 90; Partners in the Process: Professionalism for Writing Instructors, ERIC, 91. **CONTACT ADDRESS** Western Illinois Univ, 1 University Circle, Macomb, IL, 61455. **EMAIL** lelandb@ccmail.wiu.edu

HARSH, CONSTANCE D.
DISCIPLINE 20TH CENTURY ENGLISH LITERATURE, WOMEN AND LITERATURE **EDUCATION** Univ PA, BA, MA, 82, PhD, 87. **CAREER** Instr, Bryn Mawr Col; assoc prof, Univ PA, 88-. **RESEARCH** Victorian fiction, Eng indust novel. **SELECTED PUBLICATIONS** Auth, Subversive Heroines: Feminist Resolutions of Social Crisis in the Condition-of-England Novel, Univ Mich Press, 94; Gissing's In the Year of Jubilee and the Epistemology of Resistance, SEL, 94; Thyrza: Romantic Love and Ideological Co-Conspiracy, Gissing Jour, 94); Gissing's The Unclassed and the Perils of Naturalism, ELH, 92. **CONTACT ADDRESS** Dept of Eng, Colgate Univ, 13 Oak Drive, Hamilton, NY, 13346.

HART, EDWARD LEROY
PERSONAL Born 12/28/1916, Bloomington, ID, m, 1944, 4 children **DISCIPLINE** ENGLISH LITERATURE **EDUCATION** Univ Utah, BS, 39; Oxford Univ, DPhil, 50; Univ Mich, AM, 41. **CAREER** Asst prof English, Univ Wash, 49-52; from asst prof to assoc prof, 52-59, PROF ENGLISH, BRIGHAM YOUNG UNIV, 59-, Am Coun Learned Soc fel, 42; vis prof, Univ Calif, Berkeley, 59-60; Fulbright-Hays lectr, 73-74; mem, Utah State Fine Arts Bd & chmn Lit Arts Comt, 77- **HONORS AND AWARDS** Charles Redd Award in Humanities, Utah

Acad, 76; Distinguished Fac Award, Brigham Young Univ Col Humanities, 77. **MEMBERSHIPS** MLA; Rocky Mountain Mod Lang Asn; Am Soc 28th Century Studies. **RESEARCH** Some new sources of Johnson's Lives; contributions of John Nichols to Boswell's Life of Johnson; 18th century biographical works of John Nichols. **SELECTED PUBLICATIONS** Auth, James Hart, Contribution to our Knowledge of Oliver Crowdery and David Whitmer, Brigham Young Univ Studies, Vol 0036, 97. **CONTACT ADDRESS** Dept of English, Brigham Young Univ, A230 JKBA, Provo, UT, 84602.

HART, JOHN AUGUSTINE
PERSONAL Born 12/06/1917, New Haven, Conn, 1 child **DISCIPLINE** ENGLISH LITERATURE **EDUCATION** Yale Univ, AB, 40, AM, 42, PhD, 43. **CAREER** Instr English, Rensselaer Polytech Inst, 43-44; historian, Off Price Admin, Washington, DC, 44-46; from instr to asst prof English, 46-54, ASSOC PROF ENGLISH, CARNEGIE-MELLON UNIV, 54- **HONORS AND AWARDS** Golden Quill Awd **MEMBERSHIPS** MLA. **RESEARCH** Shakespeare; 18th century English literature; advanced placement program. **SELECTED PUBLICATIONS** Auth, Father-Daughter as Device in Shakespear's Romantic Comedies, Carnegie Series in English, 72; auth, Dramatic Structure in Shekespeare's Romantic Comedies, Carnegie Mellon Univ, 80; auth, As you like it, Shakespeare for Students, Gale Resm 92 **CONTACT ADDRESS** Dept of English, Carnegie Mellon Univ, 5000 Forbes Ave, Pittsburgh, PA, 15213-3890. **EMAIL** jh46@andrew.cmu.edu

HART, JOHN AUGUSTINE
PERSONAL New Haven, CT **DISCIPLINE** EUROPEAN FICTION IN TRANSLATION **EDUCATION** Yale Univ, PhD. **CAREER** Lit, Carnegie Mellon Univ. **MEMBERSHIPS** Area: Shakespeare. **CONTACT ADDRESS** Carnegie Mellon Univ, 5000 Forbes Ave, Pittsburgh, PA, 15213.

HART, JOY L.
PERSONAL Born 12/09/1959, Mt. Sterling, KY, s **DISCIPLINE** COMMUNICATION **EDUCATION** Univ Ky, PhD, 88. **CAREER** Asst prof, Univ Tulsa, 88-90; asst to ASSOC PROF, UNIV LOUISVILLE, 90-. **HONORS AND AWARDS** Gerald M. Phillips Mentoring Award, Am Comm Assoc, 98; Article of the Yr Award, Am Comm Asn, 98. **MEMBERSHIPS** South States Comm Asn, Nat Comm Asn, Am Comm Asn. **RESEARCH** Organizational and interpersonal communication. **SELECTED PUBLICATIONS** Co-auth, "When argument Fails: How Organizations deal with Incommensurabilities," in Proc of the Third Intl Conf on Argumentation, 95; co-auth, "The creation of, change in, and tension across narratives during organizational transformation: A longitudinal investigation," in Proc of the Third Ann Kentucky Conf on Narrative, 95; co-auth, "Detecting cultural knowledge in organization members' personal construct systems," in Jour of Constructivist Psych, 10, 97; co-auth, "Closings: Patient/provider communication about the end of life," in Patient Educ and Counseling, 98;co-auth, "Speaking for God: The functions of church leader storytelling in Southern Appalachia in the 1950s," in Am Comm Jour, 1, 98. **CONTACT ADDRESS** Dept of Communication, Univ of Louisville, Louisville, KY, 40292. **EMAIL** joy.hart@louisville.edu

HART, RODERICK P.
PERSONAL Born 02/17/1945, Fall River, MA, m, 1966, 2 children **DISCIPLINE** COMMUNICATION **EDUCATION** Univ MA, BA 66; PA State Univ, MA 68, PhD 70. **CAREER** 83, Liddell Prof Comm Gvt, 79-83, prof speech, Univ TX; 74-79, assoc prof, 70-74, asst prof, Purdue Univ. **HONORS AND AWARDS** Phi Kappa Phi Nat Schol of the Yr Awd; Diamond Ann Book Awd; Res Fell ICA; distg Schol Awd NCA; Winans-Wichelns Book Awd NCA; Adv Coun Res Awd; Chas H Woolbert Awd; Golden Ann Mono Awd; Phi Kappa Phi Nat Sch Hon; Woodrow Wilson Fell; NDEA Fell. **MEMBERSHIPS** NCA; ICA; APSA; Cen Stud Pres; RSA. **RESEARCH** Polit Commun; Rhetorical Studies. **SELECTED PUBLICATIONS** Software: Diction 4.0: The Text Analysis Program, Thousand Oaks, CA Sage, 97; Civic Hope: A Report on Citizenship, in preparation; Campaign Voices: The Language of Electoral Politics, Princeton Press, in preparation; Seducing America: How Television Charms the Modern Voter, NY Oxford Univ Press, 94,98; The Search for Intimacy in American Politics, in: M Salvador P Sias, eds, The Pub Voice in a Democrat at Risk, NY Praeger, 98; Community by Negation: An Agenda for Rhetorical Inquiry, in: M Hogan, ed, Rhetoric and Comm, Columbia, Univ SC Press, 98. **CONTACT ADDRESS** Dept of Speech, Univ Texas, Austin, TX, 78712. **EMAIL** rodhart@mail.utexas.edu

HARTLE, ANTHONY E.
PERSONAL Born 12/28/1942, Wichita, KS, m, 1964, 3 children **DISCIPLINE** PHILOSOPHY, LITERATURE **EDUCATION** US Mil Acad, BS, 64; Duke Univ, MA, 71; Univ of Texas, PhD, 82. **CAREER** PROF, DEP HEAD, ENGLISH, USMA. **MEMBERSHIPS** Am Philos Asn, Joint Serv Conf on Prof Ethics. **RESEARCH** Moral philosophy; applied ethics **SELECTED PUBLICATIONS** Auth, Moral Issues in Military Decision Making; Dimensions of Ethical Thought. **CONTACT ADDRESS** Dept of English, US Mil Acad, West Point, NY, 10996-1791. **EMAIL** ca5868@usma.edu

HARTMAN, CHARLES O.
PERSONAL Born 08/01/1949, Iowa City, IA **DISCIPLINE** ENGLISH LITERATURE **EDUCATION** Harvard Univ, AB, 71, MA, 72; WA Univ, PhD, 76. **CAREER** Tchg asst, 72-75; asst prof, 79-82; assoc prof, Univ WA, 82-84; assoc prof, 84-91, prof, Conn Col, 91-. **HONORS AND AWARDS** Andrews Narrative Poetry Prize, 88; Lloyd McKim Garrison Prize, 71. **SELECTED PUBLICATIONS** Auth, Russian Lessons, Yale, 98; Common Prayer, Ascent, 96; The Long View, Common Knowledge, 96; Virtual Muse: Experiments in Computer Poetry, Wesleyan Univ, 96; Glass Enclosure, Wesleyan Univ, 95; Honeydew, Orpheus, 95; Tuxedo, TriQuarterly, 94; Jazz Text: Voice and Improvisation in Poetry, Jazz, and Song, Princeton Univ, 91; co-auth, Sentences, Sun & Moon, 95. **CONTACT ADDRESS** Connecticut Col, Mohegan Ave, PO Box 270, New London, CT, 06320.

HARTOUNI, VALERIE
DISCIPLINE COMMUNICATIONS **EDUCATION** Univ Calif, Santa Cruz, PhD, 87. **CAREER** ASST PROF, COMMUN, UNIV CALIF, SAN DIEGO. **RESEARCH** Intersection of cultural and feminist studies. **SELECTED PUBLICATIONS** Auth, Reproductive Technologies and the Negotiation of Public Meanings, Univ Minn, 95; "Fetal Exposures: Abortion Politics and the Optics of Allusion," Camera Obscura, No 29, 94. **CONTACT ADDRESS** Dept of Commun, Univ Calif, San Diego, 9500 Gilman Dr, La Jolla, CA, 92093. **EMAIL** vhartoun@weber.ucsd.edu

HARTY, KEVIN JOHN
PERSONAL Born 07/20/1948, Brooklyn, NY **DISCIPLINE** ENGLISH LANGUAGE & LITERATURE **EDUCATION** Marquete Univ, AB, 70; Univ Pa, AM, 71, PhD(English), 74. **CAREER** Asst prof English, Centenary Col La, 74-76 & RI Col, 76-78; asst prof English, Temple Univ, 78-82; ASST PROF ENGLISH & COMMUN, LASALLE COL, 82-, Educ consult, Gino's Inc, 73-76; mem adv comt English, Dict Mid Ages, 76-; Folger fel, 76; Am Philos Soc grants-in-aid, 76-78; RI Col fac res grant, 77-78; educ consult, Fed Reserve Bank, First Pa Bank, RCA Corp, Blue Cross, 78-; Temple Univ res grant, 80. **MEMBERSHIPS** Medieval Acad Am; Mod Lang Soc; Col English Asn; Int Arthurian Soc; Early English Text Soc. **RESEARCH** Mediaeval literature, modern literature, writing skills. **SELECTED PUBLICATIONS** Auth, Chaucer, The Liturgy Again, and the Constance Ever-Increasing Pathos, the 'Man Of Laws Tale', Studies in Short Fiction, Vol 0031, 94; 'Till Eulenspiegel, His Adventures', Studies Short Fiction, Vol 0030, 93. **CONTACT ADDRESS** Dept of English, LaSalle Univ, 1900 W Olney Ave, Philadelphia, PA, 19103.

HARVEY, ELIZABETH D.
DISCIPLINE ENGLISH LITERATURE **EDUCATION** Smith Univ, BA; Johns Hopkins Univ, MA; PhD. **RESEARCH** Gender theory; psychoanalytic theory; history and theory of medicine; Renaissance literature and culture. **SELECTED PUBLICATIONS** Auth, Ventriloquized Voices: Feminist Theory and English Renaissance Texts, Routledge, 92; co-ed, Soliciting Interpretation: Literary Theory & 17th-Century English Poetry, Chicago, 90; Women & Reason, Michigan, 92. **CONTACT ADDRESS** Dept of English, Western Ontario Univ, London, ON, N6A 5B8.

HARWOOD, BRITTON JAMES
PERSONAL Born 07/12/1936, East Rutherford, NJ, m, 1985, 5 children **DISCIPLINE** MEDIEVAL LANGUAGE & LITERATURE **EDUCATION** Hamilton Col, BA, 59; Canisius Col, MS, 61; State Univ NY, Buffalo, PhD, 70. **CAREER** Instr English & French, Lyndonville, Cent High Sch, NY, 59-61; from instr to asst prof, 64-74, assoc prof, 74-79, prof English, 79-, chemn dept, 82, Miami Univ. **HONORS AND AWARDS** NEH and Ford Found grants. **MEMBERSHIPS** Mediaeval Acad Am; English Inst; Early English Text Soc; Mod Lang Asc; Soc Crit Exchange. **RESEARCH** Fourteenth century English literature; theories of interpretation; theory of genre. **SELECTED PUBLICATIONS** Auth, Piers Plowman and the Problem of Belief, Toronto, 92; art, Chaucer on Specke: House of Fame, The Friar's Tale, and the Summoner's Tale, Chaucer Rev, 92; co-ed and contribur, Class, Gender, and Early English Literature: Intersections, Indiana, 94; auth, The Alliterative Morte Arthure As A Witness to Epic, Orality in the Middle English Period, Garland, 94. **CONTACT ADDRESS** Dept of English, Miami Univ, 500 E High St, Oxford, OH, 45056-1602. **EMAIL** harwoobj@muohio.edu

HASHIMOTO, I.Y.
DISCIPLINE LANGUAGE AND WRITING **EDUCATION** Stanford Univ, BA, 67; Univ Wis, MA, 69; Univ Mich, PhD, 78. **CAREER** Instr, Univ Mich; Idaho State Univ; prof, 83-. **HONORS AND AWARDS** Dir, Whitman Col Wrtg Ctr; exec comm, Conf Col Compos and Commun. **RESEARCH** Academic writing, modern non-fiction prose. **SELECTED PUBLICATIONS** Auth, Thirteen Weeks: A Guide to Tchg Col Writing. **CONTACT ADDRESS** Dept of Eng, Whitman Col, 345 Boyer Ave, Walla Walla, WA, 99362-2038. **EMAIL** hashimiy@whitman.edu

HASKIN, DAYTON
PERSONAL Born 09/14/1946, Ann Arbor, MI **DISCIPLINE** ENGLISH LITERATURE, REFORMATION & PURITAN THEOLOGY **EDUCATION** Univ Detroit, BA, 68; Northwestern Univ, MA, 70; Univ London, BD, 75; Yale Univ, PhD(English), 78. **CAREER** Instr English, John Carroll Univ, 70-72; ASST PROF ENGLISH, BOSTON COL, 78- **MEMBERSHIPS** MLA; Milton Soc Am. **RESEARCH** Seventeenth century English literature; English puritanism; the English Bible. **SELECTED PUBLICATIONS** Auth, The Reinvention of Love--Poetry, Politics and Culture From Sidney to Milton, J English Germanic Philol, Vol 0095, 96; Politics, Poetics and Hermeneutics in Milton Prose - Lowenstein,D, Turner,Jg/, Heythrop Journal-A Quarterly Review Of Philosophy and Theology, Vol 0034, 93; Torah and Law in 'Paradise Lost', Theol Studies, Vol 0056, 95; Anxiety In Eden, A Kierkegaardian Reading of 'Paradise Lost', Comp Lit Studies, Vol 0032, 95; The Reinvention of Love--Poetry, Politics and Culture From Sidney to Milton, J English Germanic Philol, Vol 0095, 96; A History of Donne 'Canonization' From Izaak Walton to Cleanth Brooks, J English Germanic Philol, Vol 0092, 93. **CONTACT ADDRESS** Dept of English, Boston Col, Chestnut Hill, MA, 20167.

HASLAM, GERALD WILLIAM
PERSONAL Born 03/18/1937, Bakersfield, CA, m, 1961, 5 children **DISCIPLINE** AMERICAN LITERATURE, LINGUISTICS **EDUCATION** San Francisco State Col, AB, 63, MA, 65; Union Grad Sch, PhD, 80. **CAREER** Teaching asst English, Wash State Univ, 65-66; instr, San Francisco State Col, 66-67; from asst prof to assoc prof, 67-71, PROF ENGLISH, SONOMA STATE UNIV, 71-, Gen Semantics Found res grant, 66; invitational scholar, Polish Acad Sci, Warsaw, 66; mem nat acad adv bd, Multi-Cult Inst, 67-; dir, Okie Studies Proj & Arch, Sonoma State Col, 76-; ed, Lit Hist Am West, Nat Endowment for Humanities, 79- **HONORS AND AWARDS** Arizona Quart Award, 69. **MEMBERSHIPS** Col Lang Asn; Western Am Lit Asn; Multi-Ethnic Lit of US. **RESEARCH** The West in American literature; non-white American writers; American dialects. **SELECTED PUBLICATIONS** Auth, High Lonesome, the American Culture of Country-Music, Western Am Lit, Vol 0031, 96; Drink Cultura-Chicanismo, Western Am Lit, Vol 0028, 94. **CONTACT ADDRESS** Dept of English, Sonoma State Univ, Rohnert Park, CA, 94928.

HASLER, ANTONY
DISCIPLINE MEDIEVAL LITERATURE **EDUCATION** Cambridge Univ, PhD. **CAREER** Eng Dept, St. Edward's Univ **SELECTED PUBLICATIONS** Auth, William Dunbar: the Elusive Subject, Aberdeen Univ Press, 89; The Three Perils of Woman and John Wilson's Lights and Shadows of Scottish Life, Hogg and his World, 90; Hoccleve's Unregimented Body, Paragraph, 90; Reading the Land: James Hogg and the Highlands, Hogg and his World, 94; An introduction to James Hogg, The Three Perils of Woman, Edinburgh Univ Press, 95. **CONTACT ADDRESS** St Edward's Univ, 3001 S Congress Ave, Austin, TX, 78704-6489.

HASLETT, BETTY J.
DISCIPLINE SPEECH COMMUNICATION **EDUCATION** Univ Wis, MA, 68; Univ Minn, BA, 67; PhD, 71. **CAREER** Asst prof, 71-76; asoc prof, 76-86; prof, 87-; dept grad comm, 78-; ch, Univ Promotion & Tenure Comm, 92; dir, woman's stud prog, 96-. **HONORS AND AWARDS** Mortar Bd Award for tchg excellence, 84; UDRF grant, 87; dean's grant, 92., Reviewer, Jour Family Rel(s), 91; Commun Monogr(s), 90, 92 - 95; Jour Broadcasting and Electronic Media, 92, 93; Jour Lang and Soc Psychol, 87, 92, 96; Jour Commun, 86; Commun Yrbk, 95; Mayfield Press, 95; assoc ed, Commun Monogr(s), 86, 88; Human Commun Res, 82 86, 92-95; Commun Quart, 85, 87; Mgt Commun, 96-. **MEMBERSHIPS** Mem, Intl Commun Assn; Speech Commun Assn, E Commun Assn. **SELECTED PUBLICATIONS** Auth, Commentary, Commununication and Sex-Role Socialization, Garland Press, 93; Mary Anne Fitzpatrick, Women in Communication, Greenwood Press, 96; co-auth, Micro Inequities: Up Close and Personal, Subtle Discrimination: Principles and Practices, Sage, 97; **CONTACT ADDRESS** Dept of Commun, Univ Delaware, 162 Ctr Mall, Newark, DE, 19716.

HASSEL, JON
PERSONAL Born 01/28/1939, Fargo, ND, m, 1960, 1 child **DISCIPLINE** BALZAC AND THE ROMANTIC POETS **EDUCATION** Amherst Col, BA, 61, Brown Univ, MA, 64, PhD, 67. **CAREER** English and Lit, Univ Ark. **MEMBERSHIPS** The Romantic Movement bibliography team **SELECTED PUBLICATIONS** Area: middle-school language education. **CONTACT ADDRESS** Univ Ark, Fayetteville, AR, 72701.

HASSEL, R. CHRIS, JR.
DISCIPLINE SHAKESPEARE, RENAISSANCE LITERATURE **EDUCATION** Emory Univ, PhD. **CAREER** Instr, Vanderbilt Univ. **RESEARCH** Shakespeare's plays; Variorum Richard III. **SELECTED PUBLICATIONS** Auth, Renaissance Drama and the English Church Year; Faith and Folly in Shakespeare's Romantic Comedies, 80; Songs of Death, 87. **CONTACT ADDRESS** Vanderbilt Univ, Nashville, TN, 37203-1727.

HASSENCAHL, FRANCES J.
DISCIPLINE PUBLIC COMMUNICATION--RHETORIC **EDUCATION** Goshen Col, BA, Case-Western Reserve Univ, MA, Phd. **CAREER** Alfred Univ, Fac mem, 70-75; Old Dominion Univ, 76-. **RESEARCH** African-American Rhetoric, Public Speaking. **SELECTED PUBLICATIONS** Auth, Jane Addams, chapter Woman Public Speakers: 1830-1925, Greenwood Press, 93. **CONTACT ADDRESS** Old Dominion Univ, 4100 Powhatan Ave, Norfolk, VA, 23058. **EMAIL** FHassenc@odu.edu

HASSETT, CONSTANCE W.
DISCIPLINE ENGLISH LITERATURE **EDUCATION** Harvard Univ, PhD. **CAREER** Assoc prof, Fordham Univ. **RESEARCH** Victorian women's auto-biographies, pre-Raphaelite poetry and painting. **SELECTED PUBLICATIONS** Auth, The Style of Evasion: William Morris's The Defense of Guenevere, and Other Poems, Victorian Poetry 29, 91; Esthetic Autonomy in the Sister Arts: The Brotherly Project of Rossetti and Morris, Mosaic 25, 92. **CONTACT ADDRESS** Dept of Eng Lang and Lit, Fordham Univ, 113 W 60th St, New York, NY, 10023.

HATCH, JAMES V.
PERSONAL Born 10/25/1928, Oelwein, IA **DISCIPLINE** ENGLISH, THEATRE ARTS **EDUCATION** Northern Iowa State Univ, BA, 49; State Univ Iowa, MA, 55, PhD(theatre arts), 58. **CAREER** Asst prof theatre, Univ Calif, Los Angeles, 58-62; Fulbright lectr cinema, High Cinema Inst, Cairo, Egypt, 62-65; asst prof, 65-70, assoc prof, 71-76, PROF ENGLISH, CITY COL NEW YORK, 76-, US Dept State lectr theatre, India & Ceylon, 67-68; consult, Asian Theatre, JDR III Found, 69-70 & Drama Bk Specialist, New York, 70-73; res grant, City Col New York, 72-74; Nat Endowment Humanities grant, 73-74; exec secy, Hatch-Billops Collection, Inc 75-; guest prof English, Univ Hamburg, W Ger, 76; writing fel, MacDowell Colony, 76. **HONORS AND AWARDS** George Washington Honor Medal, Freedom Found, 58; Obie Award, Village Voice, 62. **MEMBERSHIPS** Am Theatre Asn. **RESEARCH** Black theatre history; East Indian theatre; Asian and Middle East cinema. **SELECTED PUBLICATIONS** Auth, Classic Plays from the Negro-Ensemble-Company, African Am Rev, Vol 0031, 97; Deep are the Roots, Memoirs of a Black Expatriot, Theatre Hist Studies, Vol 0014, 94; New Lost Plays by Bullins, African Am Rev, Vol 0029, 95; Digging the Africanist Presence in American Performance, Dance and Other Contexts, African Am Rev, Vol 0031, 97; The Jamaican Stage 1655-1900--A Profile of a Colonial Theater, Theatre Survey, Vol 0034, 93. **CONTACT ADDRESS** Dept of English, City Col, CUNY, 160 Convent Ave, New York, NY, 10031-9198.

HATHAWAY, RICHARD DEAN
PERSONAL Born 08/08/1927, Chillicothe, OH, 2 children **DISCIPLINE** AMERICAN LITERATURE **EDUCATION** Oberlin Col, AB, 49; Harvard Univ, AM, 52; Case Western Reserve Univ, PhD(Am studies), 64. **CAREER** Instr English, Maritime Col State Univ NY, 55 & Rensselaer Polytech Inst, 57-62; from asst prof to assoc prof, 62-70, PROF ENGLISH, STATE UNIV NY COL NEW PALTZ, 70-, Mem, Danforth assoc, 60-; assoc prof, Millsaps Col, 65-66. **MEMBERSHIPS** MLA; Am Studies Asn. **RESEARCH** New England literature and culture. **SELECTED PUBLICATIONS** Auth, Ghosts at the Windows--Ambiguity in the Fiction of Henry James--Shadow and Corona in the 'Ambassadors', Henry James Rev, Vol 0018, 97. **CONTACT ADDRESS** Dept of English, State Univ of NY, New Paltz, NY, 12562.

HATLEN, BURTON NORVAL
PERSONAL Born 04/09/1936, Santa Barbara, CA, m, 1961, 2 children **DISCIPLINE** ENGLISH **EDUCATION** Univ Calif, Berkeley, BA, 58; Columbia Univ, MA, 59; Harvard Univ, MA, 61; Univ Calif, Davis, PhD(English), 71. **CAREER** Acting asst prof English, King Col, 61-62; instr, Univ Cincinnati, 62-65; asst prof, 67-73, assoc prof, 73-81, PROF ENGLISH, UNIV MAINE, ORONO, 81-. **MEMBERSHIPS** MLA. **RESEARCH** Renaissance and modern American poetry. **SELECTED PUBLICATIONS** Ed & coauth, George Oppen: Man and poet, Nat Poetry Found, 81. **CONTACT ADDRESS** Dept of English, Univ of Maine, Orono, ME, 04473. **EMAIL** hatlen@maine.maine.edu

HAUSER, GERARD A.
PERSONAL Born 05/26/1943, Buffalo, NY, m, 1965, 2 children **DISCIPLINE** RHETORIC **EDUCATION** Canisius Col, BA, 65; Univ of Wis, Madison, MA, 66, PhD, 70. **CAREER** Asst prof, 69-73, assoc prof, 73-87, prof, 87-93, dir, Univ Scholars Prog, Pa State Univ, 87-93; PROF & CHEMN, COMMUN DEPT, UNIV OF COLO, BOULDER, 93-. **HONORS AND AWARDS** NY State Regents Scholar; NDEA Title IV Fel; CIC Traveling Fel; Phi Eta Sigma Scholastic Honorary; Liberal Arts Distinguished Teaching Award; Inst for Arts & Humanistic Studies Res Fel; Eastern Commun Asn Scholar, Temple Univ Visiting Excellence Scholar. **MEMBERSHIPS** Nat Commun Asn; Western States Commun Asn; Int Soc for the Hist of Rhetoric; Am Soc for the Hist of Rhetoric; Rhetoric Soc of Am; Nat Coun of Teachers of English; Conf on Col Composition & Commun. **RESEARCH** Rhetorical theory; rhetoric & the public sphere; critical theory. **SELECTED PUBLICATIONS** Auth, Vernacular Voices: The Rhetoric of Publics and Public Spheres, Univ of South Caroline Press, forthcoming; Introduction to Rhetorical Theory, Harper & Row, 86, Waveland Press, 91; auth, Civil Society and the Principle of the Public Sphere, Philosophy and Rhetoric, 98; auth, Vernacular Dialogue and the Rhetoricality of Public Opinion, Commun Monographs, 98; auth, On Publics and Public Spheres, Commun Monographs, 97; Between Philosophy and Rhetoric: Interpositions within the Tradition, Philosophy and Rhetoric, 95; Constituting Publics and Reconstituting the Public Sphere: The Meese Commission Report on Pornography, in Warranting Assent: Case Studies in Argument Evaluation, SUNY, 95; coauth, Communication of Values, Handbook of Rhetorical and Commun Theory, 84; auth, The New Rhetoric and New Social Movements, Emerging Theories of Human Communication, SUNY, 97; ed, The Body as Source and Site of Argument, Argument and Advocacy, forthcoming; ed, Theory and Praxis, Philosophy and Rhetoric, 91. **CONTACT ADDRESS** Commun Dept, Univ of Colorado, CB 270, Boulder, CO, 80309-2070. **EMAIL** hauserg@spot.colorado.edu

HAVEN, RICHARD P.
PERSONAL Born 05/03/1949, New Castle, IN, m, 1975, 3 children **DISCIPLINE** COMMUNICATION **EDUCATION** Ball State Univ, BS 71, MA 73; Univ Wis Madison, PhD 80. **CAREER** Univ Wis Whitewater, 72-, rank to prof, Comm Dept ch, 93-98, asst to chancellor, 91-93, assoc Dean 98-. **MEMBERSHIPS** NCA; ACE; NAPAHE; CAA. **RESEARCH** Speech writing; Public speaking; Persuasion. **SELECTED PUBLICATIONS** Auth, Working with a speech writer: Tips for Presidents and others in leadership roles, Ace Ntl Conf, 97, 98; Speech writing and Higher education: The role of the Presidential assistant, NAPAHE Ntl Conf with ACE, 95, 96, 98. **CONTACT ADDRESS** Dept of Communication, Univ of Wisconsin, Whitewater, CA 2029, Whitewater, WI, 53190. **EMAIL** havend@uwwvax.uww.edu

HAWES, WILLIAM K.
PERSONAL Born 03/06/1931, Grand Rapids, MI, d, 2 children **DISCIPLINE** SPEECH, RADIO TELEVISION, THEATER. **EDUCATION** Eastern Mich Univ, Ypsilanti, AB, 55; Univ Mich, Ann Arbor, MA, 56, PhD, 60. **CAREER** Univ Houston, Prof, 76-, assoc prof, 65-76, KUHF radio stn mgr 65-70, creator exec prod UH-TV, 67-; assoc prof, Univ NC, Chapel Hill, mgr WUNC, WTOP-TV, Washington, 64-65; Texas Christ Univ, Fort Worth, mgr found, KTCU, 60-64; asst prof, Eastern Mich Univ, 56-60; teach asst, Univ Mich, 56-57. **HONORS AND AWARDS** Eliz D Rockwell Fund, 96; UH NEH Granta, 80; Film Guest FRG, 81; UH London Prog, 84, 94; Avery Hopwood Awd, 57. **MEMBERSHIPS** Am Film Inst; Museum of Fine Arts, Houston; KUHT Pub TV. **RESEARCH** Hist amer tv, drama, cinema; pub tv; porn in film and TV. **SELECTED PUBLICATIONS** Public Television: America's First Station, Sunstone, 96; Television Performing, Ante La Camara, Focal, 91, 93; American Television Drama, Univ Alabama Press, 86. **CONTACT ADDRESS** Univ Houston, School of Communication, Houston, TX, 77204-4072.

HAWKINS, HUNT
PERSONAL Born 12/23/1943, Washington, DC, m, 1976, 2 children **DISCIPLINE** ENGLISH LITERATURE; AMERICAN LITERATURE **EDUCATION** Williams Col, BA, 65; Stanford Univ, MA, 69, PhD(English), 76. **CAREER** Teacher English, Kurasini Col, Tanzania, 66-67; instr, Tex Southern Univ, 68-70; teaching asst, Stanford Univ, 72-73; asst prof, Univ Minn, 77-78; from Asst Prof to Assoc Prof, 78-94, PROF ENGLISH, FLA STATE UNIV, 94-. **MEMBERSHIPS** MLA; SAtlantic Mod Lang Asn. **RESEARCH** Joseph Conrad; Mark Twain; colonial fiction. **SELECTED PUBLICATIONS** Auth, Mark Twain's involvement with the Congo reform movement, New England Quart, 78; Conrad's critique of imperialism in Heart of Darkness, Publ Mod Lang Asn, 79; Women in Heart of Darkness, Joseph Conrad Today, 81; Conrad and Congolese exploitation, Conradiana, 81; Joseph Conrad, Roger Casement and the Congo reform movement, J Mod Lit, 81; The issue of racism in Heart of Darkness, Conradiana, 82; E M Forster's critique of imperialism in A Passage to India, SAtlantic Rev, 83; Similarities between Mark Twain and Joseph Conrad, Polish Rev, 84; Conrad and the psychology of colonialism, Conrad Revisited, 85; Aime Cesaire's Lesson about Decolonization, CLA J, 86; Things Fall Apart and the Literature of Empire, Teaching Approaches to Things Fall Apart, 91; Joyce as a Colonial Writer, CLA J, 92; Teaching Heart of Darkness, Conradiana, 92; Mark Twain's Anti-Imperialism, ALR, 93. **CONTACT ADDRESS** English Dept, Florida State Univ, 600 W College Ave, Tallahassee, FL, 32306-1096. **EMAIL** hhawkins@english.fsu.edu

HAWKINS, KATE
DISCIPLINE SPEECH COMMUNICATION **EDUCATION** Univ Tex, PhD. **CAREER** Dir undergrad stud, Tex Tech Univ; assoc prof, asso dir, Elliot Sch Commun. **HONORS AND AWARDS** Awards tchg excellence, Wichita state Univ. **SELECTED PUBLICATIONS** Publ, areas of gender and power in language and leadership in small group communication. **CONTACT ADDRESS** Dept of Commun, Wichita State Univ, 1845 Fairmont, Wichita, KS, 67260-0062. **EMAIL** hawkins@elliott.es.twsu.edu

HAWKINSON, KENNETH S.
PERSONAL Born 06/14/1958, San Pedro, CA, s, 1 child **DISCIPLINE** COMMUNICATION **EDUCATION** Elgin Community Col, AA, 76; Western Ill Univ, BA, 78, MA, 79, PhD, 86. **CAREER** Grad asst, Western Ill Univ, 78-79; part-time instr, Univ of Md, 80; grad asst, Southern Ill Univ, 82-84; instr, Western Ill Univ, 84-85; lecturer, Southern Ill Univ, 85-86; Ecole Normale Superieur, Prof, 86-88. **HONORS AND AWARDS** Fulbright Scholar, 90-91; Faculty Excellence Awards, 92-93, 93-94, 94-95; Summer Stipend, 94; Phi Kappa Phi initiate, 95; Blue Key Fac Initiate, 95; Thompson professorship, 96-98. **MEMBERSHIPS** Nat Commun Assoc; Cent States Commun Assoc; Ill Speech & Theatre Assoc. **RESEARCH** Storytelling & oral tradition; African & Africam American folklore; Performance Studies; Rhetoric in fiction; literary criticism; creative writing. **SELECTED PUBLICATIONS** Auth, Two excercises on Diversity and gender, Speech Commun Teach, Fall 93; auth The Old Speech of the African Griot, Parabola, Spring, 94; auth, Performing Personal Narratives, Speech Commun Teach, Winter, 95; A New Individual Event: The Personal Narrative, J of the Ill Speech & Theatre Assoc, Spring 96; African Woman Grieves Dying Child, Eureka Lit Mag, Spring 98. **CONTACT ADDRESS** Dept of Commun, Western Illinois Univ, Western, IL, 61455. **EMAIL** kenneth_hawkinson@ccmail.wiu.edu

HAWTHORNE, LUCIA SHELIA
PERSONAL Baltimore, MD, d **DISCIPLINE** SPEECH **EDUCATION** Morgan State Univ, BS Lang Arts 1964; Washington State Univ, MAT Speech 1965; PA State Univ, PhD Speech Comm 1971. **CAREER** Washington State Univ, teaching asst 1964-65; Morgan State Univ, instructor 1965-67; PA State Univ, teaching asst 1967-69; Morgan State, asst prof 1969-72, assoc prof 1972-75, assoc dean of humanities 1974-75, prof 1975-, chmn dept of speech comm & theatre 1972-75, 1984-87. **HONORS AND AWARDS** Alpha Kappa Mu; Kappa Delta Pi; Lambda Iota Tau; Phi Alpha Theta; Promethean Kappa Tau; Alpha Psi Omega; Alpha Lambda Delta; Phi Eta Sigma; Danforth Assoc Danforth Found 1978-85; Academic Adminstrn Intern Amer Cncl on Educ 1974-75; Alumnus of the Year, Morgan State University, 1990-91; "Woman of The Year", Committee United to Save Sandtown, Inc, 1992. **MEMBERSHIPS** Chmn Commn on the Profession & Social Problems Speech Comm Assn 1972-75; mem Commn on Freedom of Speech Speech Comm Assn 1973-75; mem Bi-Lingual and Bi-Cultural Educ rep to TESOL for Speech Comm Assoc 1975-77; mem Speech Comm Assn, Eastern Comm Assn, MD Comm Assn, Assn of Comm Administrators; bd trustees Morgan Christian Ctr; life mem NAACP; Golden Heritage mem NAACP; Golden Life Member, Diamond Life Member, Delta Sigma Theta Sor Inc. **CONTACT ADDRESS** Dept of Speech Commun, Morgan State Univ, Baltimore, MD, 21251.

HAWTHORNE, MARK D.
PERSONAL Born 12/09/1938, Berea, OH, m, 1960, 1 child **DISCIPLINE** ENGLISH **EDUCATION** Wake Forest Univ, BA, 60; Univ Fla, MA, 62, PhD(English), 64. **CAREER** Asst prof English, NC State Univ, 64-67; from asst prof to assoc prof, Jacksonville Univ, 68-74, chmn div humanities, 73-74; head dept, 74-81, PROF ENGLISH, JAMES MADISON UNIV, 74- **MEMBERSHIPS** MLA; S Atlantic Mod Lang Asn. **RESEARCH** Anglo-Irish literature; British romantic and Victorian poetry and prose fiction. **SELECTED PUBLICATIONS** Auth, A Hermaphrodite Sort of Deity--Sexuality, Gender, and Gender Blending in Thomas Pynchon, Studies Novel, Vol 0029, 97. **CONTACT ADDRESS** Dept of English, James Madison Univ, Harrisonburg, VA, 22801.

HAYES, ANN LOUISE
PERSONAL Born 05/13/1924, Los Angeles, CA, w **DISCIPLINE** ENGLISH **EDUCATION** Stanford Univ, BA, 48, MA, 50. **CAREER** From instr to assoc prof, 58-74, prof eng, Carnegie-Mellon Univ, 74. **HONORS AND AWARDS** Irene Hardy poetry award, 43; Clarence Urmy Poetry, 43, 47, 50; Ina Coolbirth award, Univ CA, Stan, 43; 93 advan place award, mid states off, Philly. **RESEARCH** Advanced placement Eng programs: 17th and 20th century poetry. **SELECTED PUBLICATIONS** Auth, Essay on the sonnets in Starre of poets: discussions of Shakespeare, Carnegie Ser English, 66; coauth, Model for an Advanced Placement English course, ERIC, 68; auth, On reading Marianne Moore, Carnegie Ser English, 70; The dancer's step, Three Rivers Poetry J, 72; The Living and the Dead, Carnegie-Mellon Univ, 75; Witness: How All Occasions ..., Rook Press, 77; poems in Southern Rev, Am Scholar, Va Quart Rev & Three Rivers Poetry J; Progress Dancing, Robert L. Barth, 86; Circle of Earth, Robert L. Barth, 90. **CONTACT ADDRESS** Dept of Eng, Carnegie Mellon Univ, 5000 Forbes Ave, Pittsburgh, PA, 15213-3890. **EMAIL** Ah13@andrew.cmu.edu

HAYES-SCOTT, FAIRY CESENA
DISCIPLINE ENGLISH **EDUCATION** Univ Mich, BA, 72, MA, 73, PhD, 83; intern, Nat Tech Inst for the Deaf, 79. **CAREER** ED, INT J TEACHERS OF ENG WRITING SKILLS, 95-; consult, Direct Success (prog for hearing-impaired) Det Pub Schs, Mich Rehab, 94, 95, 96; OWN/PUB, ROBBIE DEAN PRESS, 91-; PROF, MOTT COMMUNITY COL, 75-. **CONTACT ADDRESS** 2910 E Eisenhower, Ann Arbor, MI, 48108. **EMAIL** FairyHa@aol.com

HAYMAN, DAVID
PERSONAL Born 01/07/1927, New York, NY, m, 1951, 2 children **DISCIPLINE** ENGLISH **EDUCATION** New York Univ, BA, 48; Univ Paris, DUniv, 55. **CAREER** From instr to assoc prof English, Univ Tex, 55-65; prof comp lit, Univ Iowa, 65-73, chmn dept, 66-68; prof Am lit, Univ Paris VIII, 72-73; PROF COMP LIT & CHMN DEPT, UNIV WIS-MADISON, 73-, Guggenheim fel, 58-59; Nat Endowment for Humanities fel, 79-80; fel, Wis Humanities Res Inst, 79. **MEMBERSHIPS** MLA; Mod Humanities Res Asn, Gt Brit; Am Comp Lit Asn. **RESEARCH** Comparative literature; British modern literature; critical theory. **SELECTED PUBLICATIONS** Auth, Jocoserious Joyce--The Fate of Folly in 'Ulysses', Modern Philol, Vol 0091, 94; Beckett 'Watt'--Genetic Criticism of the Doodles and Illuminations in Samuel Beckett 'Watt' Notebooks--The Graphic Accompaniment--Marginalia in the Manuscripts, Word & Image, Vol 0013, 97. **CONTACT ADDRESS** Dept of Comp Lit, Univ of Wis, 924 Van Hise Hall, Madison, WI, 53706.

HAYNES, CYNTHIA
DISCIPLINE LITERATURE STUDIES **EDUCATION** Univ Tex, PhD, 94. **CAREER** Asst prof. **RESEARCH** Rhetoric and composition; electronic pedagogy; critical theory; virtual rhetoric; Internet culture. **SELECTED PUBLICATIONS** Auth, The Ethico-Political Agony of Other Criticisms: Toward a Nietzschean Counter-Ethic, 90; Hanging Your Alias on Their Scene: Writing Centers, Graffiti, and Style, Writing Center Jour, 94; Inside the Teaching Machine: Actual Feminism and (Virtual) Pedagogy, 96; co-ed, High Wired: On the Design, Use, and Theory of Educational MOOS, Univ Mich, 97. **CONTACT ADDRESS** Dept of Literature, Richardson, TX, 75083-0688. **EMAIL** cynthiah@utdallas.edu

HAYNES, JONATHON
PERSONAL Born 12/04/1952, Bethleham, PA, m, 1998 **DISCIPLINE** LITERATURE **EDUCATION** McGill Univ, BA, 74; Yale Univ, MA, 74, PhD, 80. **CAREER** Vis asst prof, 80-82, Amer Univ, Cairo; vis asst prof, 82-83, Tufts Univ; asst prof, 83-85, Albion Col; fac mem, 85-94 Bennington Col; adj assoc prof, 95-96, Columbia Univ; assoc prof, 98-, Southampton Col. **RESEARCH** African film & lit; renaissance lit. **CONTACT ADDRESS** Humanities Div, Southampton Col, 239 Montauk Highway, Southampton, NY, 11968. **EMAIL** jhaynes@suffolk.lib.ny.us

HAYS, PETER L.
PERSONAL Born 04/18/1938, Bremerhaven, Germany, m, 1963, 3 children **DISCIPLINE** ENGLISH **EDUCATION** Univ Rochester, AB, 59; NY Univ, MA, 61; OH State Univ, PhD, 65. **CAREER** Instr Eng, OH State Univ, 65-66; asst prof, 66-72, assoc prof Eng, 72-76, chmn dept Eng, 74-77, prof eng, Univ CA, Davis, 77-, chmn dept Ger & Russ, 97-98, Fulbright lectr, Univ ME, Ger, 77-78. **HONORS AND AWARDS** Danforth Found Fel; Edith Wharton Soc board mem; Hemingway Found board mem. **MEMBERSHIPS** MLA; PAMLA; Wharton Soc; Davis Fac Asn; ASLC; Hemingway Soc. **RESEARCH** Am lit; drama. **SELECTED PUBLICATIONS** Auth, The complex pattern of redemption in The Assistant, Centennial Rev, spring 69; The Limping Hero, NY Univ, 71; Frost Centennial Essays, Univ Press Miss, 73; Hemingway and Fitzgerald, In: Hemingway in Our Time, Ore State Univ, 74; Arthur Miller and Tennessee Williams, Essays in Lit, fall 77; co-auth, Fugue as structure in Pynchon's Entropy, Pac Coast Philol, 10/77; co-auth, Fitzgerald's Vanity Fair, Fitzgerald/Hemingway Annual 1977; Gatsby, myth, fairy tale, and legend, Southern Folklore Quart, 77; Joseph Conrad and Stephen Crane, Etudes Anglaises, spring 78; co-auth, Pynchon's Spanish source for Entropy, Studies in Short Fiction, fall 79; co-auth, Something healing: Fathers and sons in Billy Budd, Nineteenth Century Fiction, 12/79; Yossarian and Gilgamesh, Notes on Modern Am Lit, fall 80; Self-reflexive laughter in A Day's Wait, Hemingway Notes, fall 80; Bearing the Lily: Wharton's names, Am Notes and Queries, 1/80; Frost and the critics: More revelation on All Revelation, English Lang Notes, 6/81; Hemingway, Faulkner, and a bicycle built for death, Notes on Modern American Lit, fall 81; Samson in Moby-Dick, Melville Soc Extracts, 9/81; Significant names in Delta Autumn, Notes on Modern Am Lit, winter 82; Exchange between rivals: Faulkner's influence on The Old Man and the Sea, In: Ernest Hemingway: The Writer in Context, Univ WI Press, 84; T S Eliot's Waste Land, Explicator, summer 84, Hemingway and London, Hemingway Rev, fall 84; Wharton's splintered realism, Edith Wharton Newsletter, spring 85; co-auth, No sanctuary: Hemingway's The Killers and Pinter's The Birthday Party, Papers on Lang and Lit, fall, 85; Santiago and Lear, Hemingway Newsletter, 1/86; Edith Wharton and F Scott Fitzgerald, Edith Wharton Newsletter, spring 86; Pynchon's Entropy: A Russian connection, Pynchon Notes, spring 85; Hemingway as Auteur, South Atlantic Quart, spring 87; Pynchon's cunning lingual novel: Communication in The Crying of Lot 49, Univ MS Studies in English, 84-87; The Manilius connection in Strange Interlude, O'Neill Newsletter, summer-fall 87; Shaffer's horses in Eqqus, the inverse of Swift's, Notes on Contemporary Lit, 9/87; Frost's Happiness Line if FWBT, Hemingway Newsletter, 6/88; Who is Faulkner's Emily?, Studies in Am Fiction, spring 88; Fuentes' use of False Dawn in The Old Gringo, Edith Wharton Newsletter, spring 88; Kesey's One Flew Over the Cuckoo's Nest and Dante's La Vita Nuova, Explicator, summer 88; Hemingway, Nick Adams, and David Bourne: Sons and writers, Ariz Quart, summer 88; Crippling and Lameness, In: Dictionary of Literary Themes and Motifs, Greenwood Press, 88; co-auth, Nostromo and The Great Gatsby, Etudes Anglaises, 10-12/88; Signs in Summer: Words and metaphors, Papers on Lang and Lit, winter 89; Hunting ritual in The Sun Also Rises, Hemingway Rev, spring 89; Garden of Eden allusion in Kipling, Hemingway Newsletter, 1/90; Ernest Hemingway, Unger, 6/90; A Concordance to Hemingway's In Our Time, G K Hall, 8/90; Ministrant Barkley, In: Hemingway in Italy and Other Essays, Praeger, 90; Error in Stoneback's FTA article, Hemingway Rev, spring 90; Child Murder and Incest in Modern American Drama, Twentieth Century Lit, winter 90; Who Removed Hemingway's ruptured spleen, Hemingway Rev, fall 91; Interview with Dr John H Jones, Hemingway Rev, fall 91; Catullus and The Sun Also Rises, Hemingway Rev, spring 93; The Grapes of Wrath and Ironweed, Steinbeck Newsletter, Summer 93; Undine is US, Etudes Anglaises, 1-3/94; Sherwood Anderson andOne Flew Over The Cuckoo's nest, Winesburg Eagle, summer 94; Huey Long's assassin and Hemingway, Hemingway Newsletter, 1/95; Hemingway in Cuba, video, Harmony Gold, 2/95; Hemingway's clinical depression: A speculation, Hemingway Rev, spring 95; Moral wavering in Babylon Revisited, F Scott Fitzgerald Soc Newsletter, 10/95; O'Neill and Hellman, Eugene O'Neill Rev, spirng & fall 94; Racial predestination: The elect and the damned in Light in August, English Lang Notes, 12/95; F Scott Fitzgerald, Feminist?, In: The Neglected Short Fiction of F Scott Fitzgerald, Univ Mo Press, 96; Malamud pays tribute to Hemingway, Hemingway Newsletter, 1/96; Tennessee Williams Outs Scott and Ernest, In: Author as Character, Assoc Univ Press, 98; Hemingway's exploitation of a natural resource: Indians, In: Hemingway and the Natural World, Univ ID Press, 99. **CONTACT ADDRESS** Dept of Eng, Univ of California, Davis, CA, 95616-5200. **EMAIL** plhays@ucdavis.edu

HAZEL, HARRY CHARLES
PERSONAL Born 05/28/1936, Seattle, WA, m, 1965, 6 children **DISCIPLINE** SPEECH COMMUNICATION **EDUCATION** Gonzaga Univ, AB, 60; Univ Wash, MA, 66; Wash State Univ, PhD(speech), 72. **CAREER** Instr speech, Yakima Valley Col, 66-70; asst prof speech, 71-76, dir summer sessions & continuing educ, 73-75, prof Commun Arts Dept, Gonzaga Univ, 76-, dean Sch Continuing Educ, 75-. **MEMBERSHIPS** Speech Commun Asn. **RESEARCH** Medieval communication theory and public address; American political campaigns; homiletics. **SELECTED PUBLICATIONS** Auth, The Bonaventuran Ars Concionandi, Western Speech, fall 72 & In: S Bonaventura 1274-1974, Vol II, Col St Bonaventure, Rome, 73; Harry Truman: Practical Persuader, Today's Speech, spring, 74; Images of War, Guilt, and Redemption in the First Crusade Speech of Urban II, Commun Quart, spring 78; Blending Speech, English and Logic, Commun, spring 81; The Art of Talking to Yourself and Others, Kansas City: Sheed and Ward, 87; Savonarola: The Disputatious Preacher, Journal of the Northwest Communication Asn, spring 87; The Power of Persuasion, Kansas City: Sheed and Ward, 89; Power and Constraint in the Rhetoric of Catherine of Siena, Journal of the NW Comm Asn, spring 91; Public Speaking Handbook: A Liberal Arts Perspective, co-auth by John Caputo, Dubuque, Iowa: Kendall/Hunt, 94; Interpersonal Communication: Competency Through Critical Thinking, co-auth by John Caputo and Colleen McMahon, Boston: Allyn & Bacon, 94. **CONTACT ADDRESS** Dept Commun Arts, Gonzaga Univ, 502 E Boone Ave, Spokane, WA, 99258-0001. **EMAIL** hazel@calvin.gonzaga.edu

HAZEN, JAMES F.
DISCIPLINE VICTORIAN AND MODERN BRITISH LITERATURE **EDUCATION** Princeton Univ AB, 57; Univ Wis, Madison, MS, 59, PhD, 63. **CAREER** Instr, Yale Univ, 63-66; asst prof, Univ Mo, St Louis, 66-71; assoc prof, 71-86, prof, 86-, actg dean, Grad Col, 72, chemn, dept Eng, 75-77, dir, grad stud Eng, 83-93, Univ Nev, Las Vegas; manuscript consult, Victorian Stud, Ind Univ, 70-80; assoc ed, 85-96, ed, Interim, 97-. **HONORS AND AWARDS** Fel, Silliman Col, Yale Univ, 64-69; Phi Kappa Phi, 80-;fac develop inst, Univ Nev, Las Vegas, NEH, 87, 88; William Morris Award for Excellence in Tchg, Univ Nev, Las Vegas, 90; Grad Fac Mem of the Yr, 93-94. **MEMBERSHIPS** MLA, 65-; Midwest MLA, 67-71; Rocky Mt MLA, 71-; Philol Asn Pacific Coast, 71-; Acad Am Poets, 92-; Jane Austen Soc of N Am, 93-; NCTE, 95-. **SELECTED PUBLICATIONS** Auth, A Colleague's Funeral, Piedmont Lit Rev, Vol XVII, No II, 94; Getting Used to It, Chattahoochee Rev, Vol 14, No 3, 94; The Pipe Burns Low, Cumberland Poetry Rev, Vol 13, No 2, 94; rev of Robert Cooperman, In the Household of Percy Blythe Shelley, Interim, Vol 13, No 1, 94; Portrait, Webster Rev, No 18, 94; The Snow, Hampden-Sydney Poetry Rev, 96; Bottle in the Shape of a Fish, The MacGuffin, 96; The Listeners, Yarrow, 96-97; Grandmother Thompson, Roanoke Rev, 97. **CONTACT ADDRESS** Dept of Eng, Univ Nev, Las Vegas, Las Vegas, NV, 89154. **EMAIL** adamsc@nevada.edu

HEARN, ROSEMARY
PERSONAL Born 05/01/1929, Indianapolis, IN, s **DISCIPLINE** ENGLISH **EDUCATION** Howard University, BA 1951; Indiana University, MA 1958, PhD 1973. **CAREER** LINCOLN UNIVERSITY, JEFFERSON CITY MO, ENGLISH PROF 1958-, dir of honors program 1968-72, executive dean/acad affairs 1983-85, spec asst to pres for acad affairs 1985-87, DEAN, COLLEGE OF ARTS AND SCIENCES 1989-, VP, ACADEMIC AFFAIRS, 1997-. **HONORS AND AWARDS** Outstanding teacher, Lincoln U, 1971; Development Proposals, Dept of HEW, district reader 1977-79; Phelps-Stokes (West Africa, 1975) NEH, grants received 1977-80; NEH, Division of Research Programs, proposal reviewer 1980-81; American Library Association, CHOICE, consultant-reviewer 1985-; Comm Serv Award, Jefferson City United Way, 1987. **MEMBERSHIPS** Natl Assn of Teachers of English; College Language Assn; Delta Sigma Theta; Jefferson City United Way, secretary, board of directors 1983-; Missouri Community Betterment Awards Competition, judge 1983; Mo State Planning Committee, American Council on Education, Natl Identification Program, member 1983-; Planning Committee, Natl Association of State Land Grant Colleges and Universities, member 1985-; Mid-Missouri Associated Colleges & Universities, vice-chairperson executive committee mid-Missouri; mem Missouri Assn for Social Welfare; reviewer/consultant, Amer Assn of Univ Women; advisory panel, MO Council on Arts, 1987-; reviewer, Amer Library Assn; reviewer/consultant, US Dept of HEW, 1977-79; Commission, Urban Agenda, NASVLGC, 1992-; pres-elect, bd of dir, Council of Colleges of Arts and Sciences, 1997-. **CONTACT ADDRESS** Academic Affairs, Lincoln Univ, 820 Chestnut St, Jefferson City, MO, 65102.

HEATH, WILLIAM
DISCIPLINE AMERICAN AND EUROPEAN LITERATURE AND CREATIVE WRITING **EDUCATION** Case Western Reserve, PhD. **CAREER** Adv, Lighted Corners, Col lit mag; Fulbright fel, Spain. **SELECTED PUBLICATIONS** Auth, The Children Bob Moses Led, 95 & The Walking Man. **CONTACT ADDRESS** Dept of English, Mount Saint Mary's Col, 16300 Old Emmitsburg Rd, Emmitsburg, MD, 21727-7799. **EMAIL** heath@msmary.edu

HEATH, WILLIAM WEBSTER
PERSONAL Born 07/01/1929, Buffalo, NY, m, 2 children **DISCIPLINE** ENGLISH **EDUCATION** Amherst Col, BA, 51; Columbia Univ, MA, 52; Univ Wis, PhD(English), 56. **CAREER** Teaching asst , Univ Wis, 52-56; from instr to assoc prof, 56-69, PROF ENGLISH, AMHERST COL, 69-, Grants, Am Philos Soc, 67-68, 72 & Am Coun Learned Socs, 72. **MEMBERSHIPS** MLA; AAUP. **RESEARCH** Nineteenth century poetry; contemporary British literature; autobiography. **SELECTED PUBLICATIONS** Auth, Elizabeth Bowen: An Introduction to Her Novels, Univ Wis, 61; ed, Discussions of Jane Austen, Heath, 61; auth, Wordsworth and Coleridge, Clarendon, 71; Major British Poets of the Romantic Period, Macmillan, 71; The Literary Criticism of John Middleton Murry, PMLA. **CONTACT ADDRESS** Dept of English, Amherst Col, Amherst, MA, 01002.

HEAVILIN, BARBARA A.
DISCIPLINE AMERICAN LITERATURE **EDUCATION** IN Wesleyan Univ, AB; VA Polytech Inst, MA; Ball State Univ, PhD. **CAREER** Engl, Taylor Univ. **RESEARCH** Women's studies; works by Toni Morrison, Isable Allende, and Amy Tan. **SELECTED PUBLICATIONS** Auth, Judge, Observer, Prophet: The American Cain and Steinbeck's Shifting Perspective, SDak Rev, 96. **CONTACT ADDRESS** Dept of Eng, Taylor Univ, 500 W Reade Ave., Reade Ctr , Upland, IN, 46989-1001. **EMAIL** BRHEAVILI@tayloru.edu

HECKENDORN COOK, ELIZABETH
DISCIPLINE EIGHTEENTH-CENTURY BRITISH AND FRENCH LITERATURE **EDUCATION** Stanford Univ, PhD, 90. **CAREER** ASSOC PROF, ENG, UNIV CALIF, SANTA BARBARA. **RESEARCH** Intersection of natural history; Landscape aesthetics; Property law in the period 1789-1832. **SELECTED PUBLICATIONS** Auth, "The Limping Woman and the Public Sphere," Body and Text in the Eighteenth Century, Stanford Univ Press, 94; Epistolary Bodies: Gender and Genre in the Eighteenth-Century Republic of Letters, Stanford Univ Press, 96. **CONTACT ADDRESS** Dept of Eng, Univ Calif, Santa Barbara, CA, 93106-7150. **EMAIL** ecook@humanitas.ucsb.edu

HEDGEPETH, CHESTER MELVIN, JR.
PERSONAL Born 10/28/1937, Richmond, VA, m, 1969 **DISCIPLINE** ENGLISH **EDUCATION** Blackburn Coll, BA 1960; Wesleyan Univ, MA 1966; Harvard Univ, EdD 1977. **CAREER** Maggie Walker HS, teacher 1960-65; Macalester Coll, instr in English 1968-71; VA Union Univ, instr English 1966-68, 1971-75; VA, Commonwealth Univ, coord of Afro-Amer studies 1978-; Univ of MD, dean arts & scis chmn English & languages 1983-95; African Language Project, principal investigator, 1992-98. **HONORS AND AWARDS** Danforth Assoc Danforth Found 1980-86; Certificate of Merit, Goddard Space Flight Center, 1990; Distinguished Alumnus, Harvard University, 1986; Distinguished Alumnus, Blackburn College, 1992. **MEMBERSHIPS** Mem Phi Delta Kappa Harvard Chap 1976-; mem Sigma Pi Phi (Gamma Theta); mem S Atlantic Modern Lang Assn 1978-; president, VA Humanities Conf 1982-83. **SELECTED PUBLICATIONS** Author: Afro-American Perspectives in the Humanities, Collegiate Pub Co,

1980, Theories of Social Action in Black Literature, Peter Lang Pub, 1986, 20th Century African American Writers & Artists, ALA, 1991; senior editor, Maryland Review, 1986-96. **CONTACT ADDRESS** Dept English & Languages, Univ of Maryland, Eastern Shore, Princess Anne, MD, 21853.

HEDGES, WILLIAM LEONARD
PERSONAL Born 02/16/1923, Arlington, MA, m, 1956 **DISCIPLINE** AMERICAN LITERATURE **EDUCATION** Haverford Col, BA, 46; Harvard Univ, PhD, 54. **CAREER** Teaching fel, Harvard Univ., 50-53; instr English, Univ Wis, 53-56; from asst prof to assoc prof, 56-67, chmn dept, 68-71, PROF ENGLISH, GOUCHER COL, 67-, CHMN AM STUDIES, 72-, Am Coun Learned Socs fel, 63-64. **MEMBERSHIPS** MLA. **RESEARCH** American Literature and intellectual history. **SELECTED PUBLICATIONS** Auth, Narrating Discovery--The Romantic Explorer in American Literature, 1790-1855, Am Lit, Vol 0066, 94. **CONTACT ADDRESS** Dept of Am, Studies Goucher Col, Towson, MD, 21204.

HEFFERNAN, JAMES ANTHONY WALSH
PERSONAL Born 04/22/1939, Boston, MA, m, 1964, 2 children **DISCIPLINE** ENGLISH **EDUCATION** Georgetown Univ, AB, 60; Princeton Univ, PhD(English), 64. **CAREER** Instr English, Univ Va, 63-65; from asst prof to assoc prof, 65-76, chmn dept, 78-81, prof English, Dartmouth Col, 76-; Frederick Session Beebe prof in the art of writing, 97-. **HONORS AND AWARDS** Woodrow Wilson Fel, 60-61; Franklin Murphy Fel, 61-62; R. K. Root Fel, 62-63; Dartmouth Fac fel, 67-69; NEH Grant for Res Conf on Lit and Visual Arts, 84; dir, NEH Summer Seminar on Eng Romantic Lit and the Visual Arts, 87, 89; NEH Grant for Res Conf on the Fr Revolution, 89; NEH Fel, 91. **MEMBERSHIPS** MLA; Coun of the Asn of Lit Schol and Critics. **RESEARCH** English romantic poetry and painting; theory of literature and the visual arts; European Romanticism. **SELECTED PUBLICATIONS** Auth, Wordsworth's Theory of Poetry: The Transforming Imagination, Cornell Univ, 68; Reflections on Reflections in English Romantic Poetry and Painting, 79 & The Geometry of the Infinite: Wordsworth, Coleridge and Taylor, 82, Bucknell Rev; Writing: A College Handbook, Norton, 4th ed, 94; auth, The Re-Creation of Landscape: A Study of Wordsworth, Coleridge, Constable, and Turner, Univ Press of New Eng, 85; ed, Space, Time, Image, Sign: Essays on Literature and the Visual Arts, Peter Lang, 87; ed, Representing the French Revolution: Literature, Historiography, and Art, Univ Press of New Eng, 92; auth, Museum of Words: The Poetics of Ekphrasis from Homer to Ashbery, Univ Chicago, 93; Writing: A Concise Handbook, W.W. Norton, 96. **CONTACT ADDRESS** Dept of English, Dartmouth Col, Hanover, NH, 03755-3533. **EMAIL** jamesheff@dartmouth.edu

HEFFERNAN, MICHAEL
DISCIPLINE POETRY WRITING, CONTEMPORARY POETRY **EDUCATION** Univ Mass, PhD. **CAREER** English and Lit, Univ Ark. **SELECTED PUBLICATIONS** Auth, The Cry of Oliver Hardy, Ga, 79; To The Wreakers of Havoc, Ga, 84; The Man at Home, Ark, 88; Love's Answer, Iowa, 94; The Back Road to Arcadia, Poobeg, 94. **CONTACT ADDRESS** Univ Ark, Fayetteville, AR, 72701.

HEFFERNAN, WILLIAM A.
DISCIPLINE ENGLISH **EDUCATION** BA, 59, MA, 61, St. John's Univ; Fordham Univ, PhD, 70. **CAREER** Assoc Prof, 70-71, Immaculate Heart Col; Assoc Prof, 73-, Saddleback Col. **CONTACT ADDRESS** Dept of Eng, Saddleback Col, 28000 Marguerite Pky, Mission Viejo, CA, 92692. **EMAIL** bheffernan@saddleback.cc.ca.us

HEIDENREICH, ROSMARIN
DISCIPLINE GERMAN/ENGLISH/LITERATURE **EDUCATION** Moorehead State Univ, BA, 64; Univ Man, MA, 66; Univ Toronto, PhD, 83. **CAREER** Prof, Schiller Univ, Ger, 68-69; prof, Univ Tubingen, Ger, 69; prof, Univ Freiburg, Ger, 69-74; PROF ENGLISH & TRANSLATION, ST. BONIFACE COL, UNIV MANITOBA, 83-. **HONORS AND AWARDS** Can Coun Doctoral Fel, 76-79. **MEMBERSHIPS** Can Asn Comp Lit; Can Asn Transl Studs. **SELECTED PUBLICATIONS** Auth, The Postwar Novel in Canada: Narrative Patterns and Reader Response, 89; auth, Recent Trends in Franco-Manitoban Fiction and Poetry, in Prairie Fire, 11, 90; auth, Causer l'amour dans le Far-West du Canada, in Poetiques de la Francophonie, 96. **CONTACT ADDRESS** Dept of English, St. Boniface Col, Winnipeg, MB.

HEILBRUN, CAROLYN G
PERSONAL East Orange, NJ, 3 children **DISCIPLINE** ENGLISH LITERATURE **EDUCATION** Wellesley Col, BA, 47; Columbia Univ, MA, 51, PhD(English), 59. **CAREER** Instr English, Brooklyn Col, 59-60; from instr to assoc prof, 60-72, PROF ENGLISH, COLUMBIA UNIV, 72-, Vis lectr, Union Theol Sem, 68-70; Swarthmore Col, 70-71; Guggenheim fel, 70-71; ed bd, Twentieth Century Lit, 72- & Signs, 74-; Radcliffe Inst fel, 76-; Rockefeller Found fel humanities, 76-77; mem exec coun, MLA, 76-79; vis prof, Princeton Univ, 82. **MEMBERSHIPS** MLA; Auth Guild; Auth League Am; PEN. **RESEARCH** Modern British literature, 1800-1950; English novel; biography; women. **SELECTED PUBLICATIONS** Auth, Is Biography Fiction, Soundings, Vol 0076, 93. **CONTACT ADDRESS** Dept of English, Columbia Univ, Philosophy Hall, New York, NY, 10027.

HEILMAN, ROBERT BECHTOLD
PERSONAL Born 07/18/1906, Philadelphia, PA, m, 1935, 1 child **DISCIPLINE** ENGLISH LITERATURE **EDUCATION** Lafayette Col, AB, 27; Ohio State Univ, AM, 30; Harvard Univ, AM, 31, PhD, 35. **CAREER** Teaching fel, Tufts Col, 27-28; instr English, Ohio Univ, 28-30, Univ Maine, 31-33, 34-35; from instr to prof, La State univ, 35-48; prof English, Univ Wash, 48-76, chmn dept, 48-71; Arnold Prof, Whitman Col, 77., Bk Reviewer, Key Reporter, 59-; Guggenheim fel, 64-65, 75-76; SAtlantic Grad Educ lectr, 71; Nat Endowment for Humanities sr fel, 71-72; vis scholar, Univ Ala, Birmingham, 78-. **HONORS AND AWARDS** Ariz Quart Best Essay Prize, 56; Explicator Bk Prize, 57; Longview Essay Award, 60; NCTE distinguished lectr, 68., DLitt, Lafayette Col, 67; LLD, Grinnell Col, 71; LHD, Kenyon Col, 73; DHum, Whitman Col, 77. **MEMBERSHIPS** MLA; NCTE; Philol Asn Pac Coast; Int Asn Univ Prof English; Shakespeare Asn Am. **RESEARCH** Criticism of drama; criticism of novel; history of English novel. **SELECTED PUBLICATIONS** Auth, We Scholars--Changing the Culture of the University, Am Scholar, Vol 0066, 97; The Fading Smile--Poets in Boston, From Robert Frost to Robert Lowell to Sylvia Plath, 1955-1960, Am Scholar, Vol 0065, 96. **CONTACT ADDRESS** Dept of English, Univ of Wash, Seattle, WA, 98195.

HEIN, ROLLAND NEAL
PERSONAL Born 09/12/1932, Cedar Rapids, IA, m, 1954, 2 children **DISCIPLINE** ENGLISH, THEOLOGY **EDUCATION** Wheaton Col, BA, 54; Grace Theol Sem, BD, 57; Purdue Univ, PhD, 71. **CAREER** Assoc prof English, Bethel Col, Minn, 62-70; from Assoc Prof to Prof English, 70-97, Fac Emeritus, Wheaton Col, Ill, 97-. **MEMBERSHIPS** MLA. **RESEARCH** Life and writings of George MacDonald, 1824-1905. **SELECTED PUBLICATIONS** Auth, A biblical view of the novel, Christianity Today, 1/73; Lilith: theology through mythopoeia, Christian Scholar's Rev, 74; ed, Life Essential: The Hope of the Gospel, 74, Creation in Christ: The Unspoken sermons of George MacDonald, 76 & George MacDonald's World: An Anthology from the Novels, 78, H Shaw; The Harmony Within 1982; Sunrise, 89; George MacDonald: Victorian Mythmaker, 93; G.K. Chesterton: Myth, Paradox, and the Commonplace, Seven: An Anglo-Am J, 96; Lilith: A Variorum Edition, Johannesen, 97; Christian Mythmakers, Cornerstone, 98. **CONTACT ADDRESS** Dept of English, Wheaton Col, 501 College Ave, Wheaton, IL, 60187. **EMAIL** Rolland N Hein@ Wheaton.edu

HEINEMAN, HELEN
PERSONAL Born 08/01/1936, Queens Village, NY, m, 1961, 4 children **DISCIPLINE** ENGLISH LITERATURE **EDUCATION** Queens Col, BA, 58; Columbia Univ, MA, 59; Cornell Univ, PhD, 67 **CAREER** Prof, Framingham St Col **HONORS AND AWARDS** Phi Bega Kappa; Woodrow Wilson Fel; Amer Assoc Univ Women Fel; Bunting Inst; Radcliffe Col Fel **RESEARCH** Victorian Literature **SELECTED PUBLICATIONS** Three Victorians in the New World: Dickens, Trollope and Mrs. Trollope In America, Lang, 90; Restless Angels: the Friendship of Six Victorian Women, Ohio Univ Pr, 84; Francees Trollope, GK Hall, 84 **CONTACT ADDRESS** Framingham State Col, 100 State, Framingham, MA, 01701. **EMAIL** hheineman@frc.mass.edu

HEISE, URSULA K.
DISCIPLINE POSTMODERN LITERATURE AND LITERARY THEORY **EDUCATION** Univ Cologne, BA, Univ Calif, MA, 85; Univ Cologne, MA, 87; Stanford Univ, PhD, 93. **CAREER** English and Lit, Columbia Univ **SELECTED PUBLICATIONS** Auth, Chronoschisms: Time, Narrative, Postmodernism; Cambridge Univ Press, 97. **CONTACT ADDRESS** Columbia Univ, 2960 Broadway, New York, NY, 10027-6902.

HELD, GEORGE
PERSONAL Born 01/28/1935, White Plains, NY **DISCIPLINE** ENGLISH & AMERICAN LITERATURE **EDUCATION** Brown Univ, AB, 58; Univ Hawaii, AM, 62; Rutgers Univ, PhD, 67. **CAREER** Instr English, Kamehameha Schs, 58-64; teaching asst, Rutgers Univ, 65-67; lectr, 67-68, asst prof English, 68-83, ASSOC PROF, QUEENS COL, NY, 83-; Fulbright lectr, Univ Bratislava, 73-74; Fulbright lectr, Charles Univ, Prague, Czech, 74-76; co-ed, The Ledge Poetry Magazine, 91-. **HONORS AND AWARDS** Second Prize, Tallahassee Writer's Asn Annual Int Poetry Competition, 96; A Directory of American Poets & Fiction Writers, 95-; Who's Who in the East, 98. **MEMBERSHIPS** MLA; ALBC; NCTE. **RESEARCH** Poetry. **SELECTED PUBLICATIONS** Auth, The Second Book of the Rhymer's Club, Rutgers Univ Libr J, 6/65; Jonson's Pindaric on friendship, Concerning Poetry, spring 70; Men on the moon: American novelists explore lunar space, Mich Quart Rev, spring 79; Heart to heart with nature: Ways of looking at A White Heron, Colby Libr Quart, 3/82; Conrad's Oxymoronic Imagination in The Secret Agent, Conradiana, 85; Brother Poets: The Relationship Between George and Edward Herbert, in Like Season'd Timber: Essays on George Herbert, Peter Lang, 87; In Defense of Homage to Catalonia, CN Rev, Dec/Jan 95-96; Poems in Commonmeal, Confrontation, Hellas, Modern Haiku, & dozens of other journals, 90-; Winged: Poems, Birnham Wood Graphics, 95; My Night with Dasha (short story), Ignite, Dec 97. **CONTACT ADDRESS** Dept of English, Queens Col, CUNY, 6530 Kissena Blvd, Flushing, NY, 11367-1597.

HELDMAN, JAMES M.
PERSONAL Born 07/15/1930, Durham, NC, m, 1952, 1 child **DISCIPLINE** ENGLISH **EDUCATION** Univ NC, BA, 56, MA, 58, PhD, 67. **CAREER** Instr English, Roanoke Col, 58-60, Univ Del, 64-66; asst prof, Univ Mo-Columbia, 66-72; chmn dept, 72-79, prof English, Western Ky Univ, 79- **MEMBERSHIPS** SAtlantic Mod Lang Asn. **RESEARCH** Victorian and British novel; Victorian prose and poetry; Edwardian novel. **SELECTED PUBLICATIONS** Auth, The last Victorian novel: technique and theme in Parade's End, Twentieth Century Lit, 72. **CONTACT ADDRESS** Dept of English, Western Kentucky Univ, 1 Big Red Way St, Bowling Green, KY, 42101-3576.

HELDRETH, LEONARD GUY
PERSONAL Born 04/08/1939, Shinnston, WV, m, 1964, 2 children **DISCIPLINE** ENGLISH & AMERICAN LITERATURE& FILM **EDUCATION** WVa Univ, BS, 62, MA, 64; Univ Ill, PhD, 73. **CAREER** Instr, 70-73, asst prof, 73-76, assoc prof, 76-81, prof English, 81-, asst Vpres Undergrad Affairs, 98-, assoc dean, Col Arts & Sci, 94-, interim dean, Sch Arts & Sci, 91-92, head, Dept English, 88-91, 92-98, N Mich Univ; abstract writer, NCTE/ERIC, 68-70. **HONORS AND AWARDS** English Dept fac merit award, 83, 87; Northern Mich Univ distinguished fac award, 87; bd mem, Mich Hum Coun, 89-93. **MEMBERSHIPS** Int Asn for Fantastic in the Arts; Am Cult Asn; Popular Cult Asn; Popular Cult Asn South. **RESEARCH** Film study; fantasy and science fiction. **SELECTED PUBLICATIONS** Auth, Films, Film Fantasies, and Fantasies: Spinning Reality from the Self in Kiss of the Spider Woman, J of the Fantastic in the Arts, 94; auth, Festering in Thebes: Elements of Tragedy and Myth in Cronenberg's Films, Post Script, 95; art, To Yokaichi and Beyond: part 1: The Yokaichi Experience; Getting to Know You, Marquette Monthly, 95; art, To Yokaichi and Beyond, part 2 Death, Life and Hiroshima Pizza, Marquette Monthly, 95; art, Architecture, Duality, and Personality: Mis-en-scene and Boundaries in Tim Burton's Films, Trajectories of the Fantastic, Greenwood, 97; auth, Anatomy of a Murder; From Fact to Fiction to Film, A Sense of Place, Northern Michigan, 97; auth, Memories! You're Talkin' About Memories! Retrofitting Blade Runner, Popular, 98. **CONTACT ADDRESS** Vice Pres for Undergraduate Affairs, No Michigan Univ, 1401 Presque Isle Ave, Marquette, MI, 49855-5301. **EMAIL** lheldret@nmu.edu

HELFAND, MICHAEL S.
PERSONAL Born 03/20/1942, New York, NY, m, 1965, 1 child **DISCIPLINE** VICTORIAN & MODERN ENGLISH LITERATURE **EDUCATION** Univ Va, BA, 64; Univ Iowa, PhD, 70. **CAREER** Asst prof English, 70-76, assoc prof English, Univ of Pittsburgh, 76-, Dir Grad Studies, 96-. **HONORS AND AWARDS** Fulbright Lectr Am Studies, China, 85-87, S Korea, 90-91. **MEMBERSHIPS** Northeast MLA. **RESEARCH** Modern fiction; victorian studies. **SELECTED PUBLICATIONS** Auth, Dickens at large, 1/72 & Architects of the self, 1/74, Novel: Forum on Fiction; Hemingway, a champ can't retire, Lost Generation J, 76; T H Huxley's Evolution and Ethics, Victorian Studies, 77; coauth, Anarchy and culture, Tex Studies Lit & Lang, 78; contribr, Victorian Poetry, yearly; coauth and co-ed, Oscar Wilde's Oxford Notebooks, Oxford Univ Press, 89. **CONTACT ADDRESS** Dept of English, Univ of Pittsburgh, 526 Cathedral/Learn, Pittsburgh, PA, 15260-2504. **EMAIL** msh@pitt.edu

HELGERSON, RICHARD
DISCIPLINE RENAISSANCE LITERATURE AND CULTURE **EDUCATION** Johns Hopkins Univ, PhD, 70. **CAREER** PROF, ENG, UNIV CALIF, SANTA BARBARA. **RESEARCH** Early mod Europ drama and paint; Renaissance lit and cult. **SELECTED PUBLICATIONS** Auth, The Elizabethan Prodigals, Univ Calif Press, 77; Self-Crowned Laureates: Spenser, Jonson, Milton, and the Literary System, Univ Calif Press, 83; Tasso on Spenser: The Politics of Chivalric Romance, Yrbk Eng Stud, 88; "Writing Against Writing: Humanism and the Form of Coke's Institutes," Mod Lang Quart, 92; "Camoes, Hakluyt, and the Voyages of Two Nations," Cult and Colonial, 92; Forms of Nationhood, Univ Chicago Press, 92; Doing Literary History on a Large Scale, Eng Stud and Hist, 94. **CONTACT ADDRESS** Dept of Eng, Univ Calif, Santa Barbara, CA, 93106-7150. **EMAIL** rhelgers@humanitas.ucsb.edu

HELLE, ANITA
DISCIPLINE ENGLISH EDUCATION **EDUCATION** Univ Puget Sound, BA, 70, MA, 72; Univ Ore, PhD, 86. **CAREER** Engl, Oregon St Univ. **SELECTED PUBLICATIONS** Auth, Reading Women's Autobiographies and Reconstructing Knowledge, Narrative and Dialogue in Education, Tchrs Col Press, 91; Reading the Rhetoric of Curriculum Transformation,

NWSA Jour, 94; William Stafford: On the Poet, His vocation, and Cultural Literacy, NCTE, 94. **CONTACT ADDRESS** Oregon State Univ, Corvallis, OR, 97331-4501. **EMAIL** ahelle@orst.edu

HELLEGERS, DESIREE
DISCIPLINE SIXTEENTH- AND SEVENTEENTH-CENTURY ENGLISH LITERATURE **EDUCATION** Univ Wash, PhD **CAREER** Asst prof, Washington State Univ. **RESEARCH** Literature and science, women writers, environmental issues in literature. **CONTACT ADDRESS** Dept of English, Washington State Univ, 1 SE Stadium Way, PO Box 645020, Pullman, WA, 99164-5020. **EMAIL** helleger@vancouver.wsu.edu

HELLENBRAND, HAROLD
DISCIPLINE EARLY AMERICAN LITERATURE, WORLD LITERATURES **EDUCATION** Stanford Univ, PhD. **CAREER** Prof, Dean, Col Liberal Arts, Univ Minn, Duluth. **SELECTED PUBLICATIONS** Auth, The Unfinished Revolution: Education and Politics in the Thought of Thomas Jefferson, Univ Del Press, 89. **CONTACT ADDRESS** Dept of Eng, Univ Minn, Duluth, Duluth, MN, 55812-2496.

HELLER, DANA
DISCIPLINE AMERICAN LITERATURE **EDUCATION** MFA, PhD. **CAREER** Engl, Old Dominion Univ. **RESEARCH** Gender Studies **SELECTED PUBLICATIONS** Areas: Cross Purposes: Lesbians, Feminists, and the Limits of Alliance; Family Plots: The De-oedipalization of Popular Culture; The Feminization of Quest-Romance: Radical Departures. **CONTACT ADDRESS** Old Dominion Univ, 4100 Powhatan Ave, BAL 425, Norfolk, VA, 23058. **EMAIL** DHeller@odu.edu

HELLER, LEE ELLEN
DISCIPLINE ENGLISH **EDUCATION** Scripps Coll, BA, 80; Brandeis Univ, MA, 82, PhD, 88. **CAREER** Asst prof, Eng, Mercer; current, EDUC CONSULT **MEMBERSHIPS** Am Antiquarian Soc **SELECTED PUBLICATIONS** Auth, "Cultural Criticism in the Classroom: Authority and Transcendent Truth after Poststructuralism," in College Literature, 90; auth, "Frankenstein and the Cultural Uses of Gothic," in Frankenstein: A Case Study in Contemporary Criticism, Bedford Books/St. Martin's Press, 91 & 92; auth, Instructor's Manual, Vol 1, Prentice-Hall Anthology of American Literature, 91; auth, "Recovering the Victorian Periodical," Nineteenth-Century Prose 20, 93; auth, "Conceiving the 'New' American Literature," Early Am Lit 29, 94. **CONTACT ADDRESS** 655 Circle Dr, Santa Barbara, CA, 93108. **EMAIL** leeheller@worldnet.att.net

HELLERSTEIN, NINA SALANT
PERSONAL Born 03/29/1946, New York, NY, m, 1970, 2 children **DISCIPLINE** MODERN FRENCH LITERATURE, FRENCH CIVILIZATION **EDUCATION** Brown Univ, BA, 68; Univ Chicago, MA, 69, PhD(Fr), 74. **CAREER** Adj asst prof Fr, Bernard Baruch Col, 74-75; vis asst prof, Vassar Col, 75-76; instr, Rosary Col & Roosevelt Univ, 76-78; asst prof to prof French, Univ Ga, 78-; dept head Romance Langs, Univ Ga, 92-93. **MEMBERSHIPS** S Atlantic Mod Lang Asn; MLA; Paul Claudel Soc; Soc Paul Claudel; Asn des Amis de la Fondation St John Perse; Am Asn of Teachers of French; NE Mod Lang Asn; Women in French; Pi Delta Phi (honorary); Simone de Beauvoir soc; Consiel International des Etudes Francophones. **RESEARCH** Paul Claudel; Modern French poetry; Simone de Beauvoir; Marguerite Duras; French and Francophone women's writing. **SELECTED PUBLICATIONS** Auth, Social, Sexual and Intellectual Revolt in the Works of Avante-Garde Dramatist Agnes Eschene, Women in Fr Studies, July 93; Le Poete et ses Interlocuteurs dans les Cing Grandes Odes, In: Paul Claudel: Les Odes, Les Editions Albion Press, 94; Narrative Innovation and the Construction of Self in Marguerite Audoux's Marie-Claire, Fr Rev, Dec 95; L'Ecriture des Conversations dans le Loir-et-Cher de Paul Claudel, In: Ecritures claudliennes: Actes du Colloque de Besancon, May 94; Food and the Female Existentialist Body, In: L'Invite, Fr Forum 22, 97; Phenomenology and Ekphrasis in Claudel's Connaissance de l'Est, Nottingham Fr Studies 36, 97. **CONTACT ADDRESS** Dept of Romance Lang, Univ Ga, Athens, GA, 30602-1815. **EMAIL** hellerst@arches.uga.edu

HELLINGER, BENJAMIN
PERSONAL Born 11/11/1933, Brooklyn, NY, m, 1969, 2 children **DISCIPLINE** ENGLISH LITERATURE **EDUCATION** Brooklyn Col, BA, 55, NY Univ, MA, 57, PhD, 69. **CAREER** Lectr Eng, Lehman Col, 65-68; asst prof, 69-73, assoc prof eng, John Jay Col Criminal Justice, 74. **RESEARCH** Eighteenth century Eng lit; hist of criticism. **SELECTED PUBLICATIONS** Auth, The Editing of Jeremy Collier's Short View of the Immorality and Profaneness of the English Stage, Papers Bibliog Soc Am, 73; Jeremy Collier's courage: A dissenting view, Yearbk English Studies, 75; Jeremy Collier's false and imperfect citations, Restoration & 17th Century Theatre Res, 11/75. **CONTACT ADDRESS** Dept of Eng, John Jay Col of Criminal Justice, CUNY, 445 W 59th St, New York, NY, 10019-1104.

HELLWIG, HAL
DISCIPLINE ENGLISH LITERATURE **EDUCATION** Univ Ca, PhD, 85. **CAREER** Assoc prof. **RESEARCH** American literature and computer applications in literature and in composition. **SELECTED PUBLICATIONS** Auth, pubs on composition studies, graduate programs in English, Seventeenth century English literature, computational linguistics, and business communications. **CONTACT ADDRESS** Dept of English and Philosophy, Idaho State Univ, Pocatello, ID, 83209. **EMAIL** hellharo@isu.edu

HELM, THOMAS EUGENE
PERSONAL Born 01/20/1943, Hammond, IN, m, 1966, 1 child **DISCIPLINE** RELIGION & LITERATURE **EDUCATION** Earlham Col, AB, 65; Havard Univ, STB, 68; Univ Chicago, AM, 72, PhD, 77. **CAREER** Asst prof, 74-80, assoc prof, 80-86, PROF RELIG STUDIES, WESTERN ILL UNIV, 86-, dir Univ Honors, 98-, Res Coun grant, Western Ill Univ, 78; jr fel, Inst Med & Renaissance Studies, 79. **MEMBERSHIPS** Am Acad Relig; Midwest Am Acad Relig; Renaissance Soc; Soc Values Higher Educ. **RESEARCH** Renaissance and reformation studies; rhetoric. **SELECTED PUBLICATIONS** Auth, The warp of piety, the woof of politics: American civil religion, Perkins J, spring 78; Enchantment and the banality of evil, Relig Life, spring 80; The Christian Religion, Prentice Hall, 91. **CONTACT ADDRESS** Dept of Philos & Relig Studies, Western Illinois Univ, 1 University Cir, Macomb, IL, 61455-1390. **EMAIL** te-helm@wiu.edu

HEMMER, JOSEPH
DISCIPLINE COMMUNICATION LAW **EDUCATION** Bradley Univ, MA; Univ Wisc, PhD, 78. **CAREER** Law, Caroll Col. **HONORS AND AWARDS** Marquette Univ DSR-TKA Outstanding Alumni Award, 68; Wisc Comm Asn Andrew T. Weaver Award, 82., Chair, Comm dept. **SELECTED PUBLICATIONS** Auth, Communication Law: Judicial Interpretation of the First Amendment. **CONTACT ADDRESS** Carroll Col, Wisconsin, 100 N East Ave, Waukesha, WI, 53186.

HEMMINGER, WILLIAM
DISCIPLINE ENGLISH LITERATURE **EDUCATION** Ohio Univ, PhD. **CAREER** Fulbright prof, Madagascar. **SELECTED PUBLICATIONS** Auth, A Friend of the Family; articles on African lit. **CONTACT ADDRESS** Dept of Eng, Univ Evansville, 1800 Lincoln Ave, Evansville, IN, 47714. **EMAIL** bh35@evansville.edu.

HENDERSON, JUDITH RICE
PERSONAL Born 09/24/1945, Bartlesville, OK, m, 1976, 3 children **DISCIPLINE** ENGLISH LITERATURE **EDUCATION** Univ Colo, BA, 67, BS, 67; Ind Univ, PhD(English lit), 74. **CAREER** Lectr, 71-74, asst prof, 74-81, ASSOC PROF ENGLISH, UNIV SASK, 81-, Can Coun res fel English, 75-76. **MEMBERSHIPS** MLA; Renaissance Soc Am; Int Soc Hist Rhet; Can Soc Renaissance Studies; Asn Can Univ Teachers English. **RESEARCH** Renaissance literature; stylistics; rhetoric. **SELECTED PUBLICATIONS** Auth, Medieval and Renaissance Letter Treatises and Form Letters--A Census of Manuscripts Found in Eastern-Europe and the Former Ussr, J Hist Rhet, Vol 0011, 93; Erasmian Ciceronians--The Intellectual Evolution of Renaissance Humanist Rhetoric--Reformation Teachers of Letter-Writing, J Hist Rhet, Vol 0010, 92; Vain Affectations, Bacon on Ciceronianism in the 'Advancement Of Learning', English Lit Renaissance, Vol 0025, 95. **CONTACT ADDRESS** Dept of English, Univ of Sask, Saskatoon, SK, S7N 0W0.

HENDRICK, GEORGE
PERSONAL Born 03/30/1929, Stephenville, TX, m, 1955, 1 child **DISCIPLINE** AMERICAN LITERATURE **EDUCATION** Tex Christian Univ, BA, 48, MA, 50; Univ Tex, PhD(-English), 54. **CAREER** Asst prof English, Southwest Tex State Col, 54-56, Univ Colo, 56-60; prof Am Studies, Frankfurt, 60-65; prof English, Univ Ill, Chicago, 65-67; head dept, 71-76, assoc dean grad col, 67-71, PROF ENGLISH, UNIV ILL, URBANA, 67-, Vis prof English, Univ Ill, Chicago, 64-65. **MEMBERSHIPS** MLA. **RESEARCH** American transcendentalism; twentieth century American literature and culture; medicine and literature. **SELECTED PUBLICATIONS** Auth, Hard Marching Every Day--The Civil-War Letters of Wilbur Fisk, 1861-1865, New England Quarterly, Vol 0065, 92; 'Adventures of Captain Simon Suggs, Late of the Tallapossa Volunteers'--Together with 'Taking The Census' and Other Alabama Sketches, Anq, Vol 0008, 95. **CONTACT ADDRESS** Dept of English, Univ of Ill, 608 S Wright St, Urbana, IL, 61801-3613.

HENDRIX, JERRY
DISCIPLINE SPEECH **EDUCATION** E Tex Univ, BA; Univ Okla, MA; La State Univ, PhD. **CAREER** Asst prof, Univ Southwest La; Instr, Westmar Col, Le Mars, Iowa; Prof, Am Univ. **SELECTED PUBLICATIONS** Areas: public relations case studies, public speaking. **CONTACT ADDRESS** American Univ, 4400 Massachusetts Ave, Washington, DC, 20016.

HENGEN, SHANNON
DISCIPLINE ENGLISH LITERATURE **EDUCATION** Univ Iowa, PhD. **RESEARCH** Canadian women's dramatic comedy; Margaret Atwood literature. **SELECTED PUBLICATIONS** Co-ed, Margaret Atwood's Power: Mirrors, Reflections and Images in Selected Fiction and Poetry, 93; auth, Approaches to Teaching Atwood's The Handmaid's Tale and Other Works, 94; auth, Theatre du Nouvel-Ontario and Francophone Culture in Sudbury, Ontario, Canada, Am Rev Can Studies, 91; art, 'your father the thunder / your mother the rain': Lacan and Atwood, Lit And Psychol, 86. **CONTACT ADDRESS** English Dept, Laurentian Univ, 935 Ramsey Lake Rd, Sudbury, ON, P3E 2C6.

HENIGHAN, THOMAS J.
PERSONAL Born 10/15/1934, New York, NY **DISCIPLINE** ENGLISH **EDUCATION** Columbia Univ, 56-57; Durham Univ, MLitt, 63; Univ Newcastle-upon-Tyne, PhD, 77. **CAREER** U.S. Foreign Ser, 59-61; instr, Central Mich Univ, 63-65; lectr to asst prof, 65-69, ASSOC PROF ENGLISH, CARLETON UNIV, 69-. **HONORS AND AWARDS** Can Coun fel, 69-70, grant, 83; Ont Arts Coun grants, 70, 72; Can Fedn Hum grant, 81. **SELECTED PUBLICATIONS** Auth, Natural Space in Literature, 82; auth, The Presumption of Culture, 96; auth, Ideas of North: A Guide to Canadian Arts and Culture, 97; contribur, Ottawa Rev, 76-79; ed/contribur, Brave New Universe, 80. **CONTACT ADDRESS** Dept of English, Carleton Univ, 1125 Colonel By Dr, Ottawa, ON, K1S 5B6.

HENNEDY, JOHN FRANCIS
PERSONAL Born 05/31/1936, Braintree, MA, m, 1963, 6 children **DISCIPLINE** ENGLISH **EDUCATION** Univ Notre Dame, BA, 58; Boston Univ, MA, 61; Univ Ill, Urbana, PhD(-English), 65. **CAREER** Asst prof English, 65-71, ASSOC PROF ENGLISH, PROVIDENCE COL, 71- **MEMBERSHIPS** MLA. **RESEARCH** Shakespeare; English Renaissance drama; 18th century. **SELECTED PUBLICATIONS** Auth, Virtues Own Feature--Shakespeare and the Virtue Ethics Tradition, Renaissance Quarterly, Vol 0050, 97. **CONTACT ADDRESS** Dept of English, Providence Col, 549 River Ave, Providence, RI, 02918-0002.

HENNESSY, MICHAEL
DISCIPLINE COMPOSTITION **EDUCATION** Marquette Univ, PhD. **CAREER** Southwest Tex State Univ **RESEARCH** James Joyce. **SELECTED PUBLICATIONS** Coauth, The Borzoi Handbook for Writers; The Borzoi Practice Book for Writers; The Random House Practice Book. **CONTACT ADDRESS** Southwest Texas State Univ, 601 University Dr, San Marcos, TX, 78666-4604. **EMAIL** mh17@swt.edu

HENNESSYVENDLER, HELEN
PERSONAL Born 04/30/1933, Boston, MA, d, 1 child **DISCIPLINE** LITERATURE **EDUCATION** Emmanuel Col, AB 54; Harvard Univ, PhD 60. **CAREER** Harvard Univ, vis prof 81-85, prof 85-90, univ prof 90-; Boston Univ, assoc prof 66-69, prof 69-85; Smith Col, asst prof 64-66; Swarthmore and Haverford Colleges, lectr 63-64; Cornell Univ, inst 60-63; The New Yorker, poetry critic, 78-. **HONORS AND AWARDS** Charles Stuart Parnell fel; Wilson Cen fel; several NEH; NIAL Awd; Guggenheim fel., Honorary Degrees from: Ntl Univ Ireland; Wabash Col; Univ Cambridge; Trinity Col Ireland; Univ Toronto; Dartmouth Col; Bates Col; Univ MA; Washington Univ; Fitchburg State Univ; Columbia Univ; Union Col; Univ Hartford; Kenyon Col; Univ Oslo; Smith Col **MEMBERSHIPS** MLA; AAAS; AAAL; APS. **RESEARCH** English and American **SELECTED PUBLICATIONS** Auth, Seamus Heaney, London Harper Collins, 98; The Art of Shakespeare's Sonnets, Cambridge MA, HUP, 97; Poems, Poets Poetry, Boston MA, Bedford Books, 96; The Breaking of Style: Hopkins, Heaney, Graham, Cambridge MA, HUP, 95; Soul Says: On Recent Poetry, Cambridge MA, HUP, 95. **CONTACT ADDRESS** Dept of English, Harvard Univ, Baker Center, Cambridge, MA, 02138.

HENSLEY, CARL WAYNE
PERSONAL Born 02/25/1936, Bristol, VA **DISCIPLINE** SPEECH COMMUNICATION **EDUCATION** Milligan Col, BA, 58; Christian Theol Sem, MDiv, 63; Butler Univ, MA, 66; Univ MN, PhD, 72. **CAREER** Minister, Christian Church, IN, 58-66; prof preaching, MN Bible Col, 66-73; aux prof, Bethel Theol Sem, 72-78; prof & chmn dept commun, Bethel Col, 73, Consult, 77, mediator, 86. **MEMBERSHIPS** Speech Commun Asn; Int Asn Bus Communicators; Relig Speech Commun Asn; Cent States Speech Asn; Disciples of Christ Hist Soc. **RESEARCH** Hist and criticism of public address; intellectual hist of Am relig movement; 19th century revivalism; conflict mgmt. **SELECTED PUBLICATIONS** Auth, Harry S Truman: Fundamental Americanism in foreign policy speechmaking, Southern Speech Commun J, 75; Rhetorical vision and the Persuasion of a historical movement, Quart J of Speech, 75; Alexander Campbell and the second coming of Christ: A footnote to history, Discipliana, 76; Illustration: The sermonic workhorse, New Pulpit Digest, 77; That board meeting at Corinth, Princeton Sem Bull, 79; Rhetoric and reality in the Restoration movement, Mission J, 82. **CONTACT ADDRESS** 3900 Bethel Dr, Saint Paul, MN, 55112-6999. **EMAIL** whensly@bethel.edu

HERBERT, CHRISTOPHER
DISCIPLINE ENGLISH **EDUCATION** Yale Univ, PhD. **CAREER** Prof, Northwestern Univ; NEH fel. **HONORS AND AWARDS** 2 CAS outstanding tchg awd(s). **SELECTED PUBLICATIONS** Auth, Trollope and Comic Pleasure, Chicago, 87, Culture and Anomie, Chicago, 91; articles on, Dickens; George Eliot; Trollope; 19th-century scientific thought. **CONTACT ADDRESS** Dept of English, Northwestern Univ, 1801 Hinman, Evanston, IL, 60208.

HERENDEEN, WYMAN H.
DISCIPLINE ENGLISH LANGUAGE; LITERATURE **EDUCATION** Brown, BA, MA; Toronto Univ, PhD, 84. **CAREER** Prof; dept head. **HONORS AND AWARDS** Choice best acad bk designation. **RESEARCH** Cultural studies; history of ideas; persistence of the classical tradition. **SELECTED PUBLICATIONS** Auth, From Landscape to Literature: The River and the Myth of Geography; co-ed, Ben Jonson's 1616 Folio. **CONTACT ADDRESS** Dept of English Language and Literature, Univ of Windsor, 401 Sunset Ave, Windsor, ON, N9B 3P4. **EMAIL** whh@uwindsor.ca

HERMANSSON, CASIE
DISCIPLINE 20TH CENTURY BRITISH LITERATURE **EDUCATION** Massey Univ, New Zealand, BA; Univ Toronto, MA, PhD. **CAREER** Full-time lectr. **RESEARCH** Women's literature, postcolonial literature, detective fiction **SELECTED PUBLICATIONS** Publ, article on The Great Gatsby, bk rev(s), Can fiction. **CONTACT ADDRESS** Dept of Eng, Pittsburg State Univ, 1701 S Broadway St, Pittsburg, KS, 66762. **EMAIL** chermans@pittstate.edu

HERNDON, SANDRA L.
DISCIPLINE COMMUNICATION STUDIES **EDUCATION** Southern Ill Univ, PhD. **CAREER** Prof. **MEMBERSHIPS** Eastern Commun Asn. **SELECTED PUBLICATIONS** Auth, pubs on organizational communication, impact of new technologies on organizations, and workplace diversity. **CONTACT ADDRESS** Dept of Communication, Ithaca Col, 100 Job Hall, Ithaca, NY, 14850.

HERNON, PETER
PERSONAL Born 08/31/1944, Kansas City, MO, m, 1972, 2 children **DISCIPLINE** LIBRARY AND INFORMATION SCIENCES **EDUCATION** Univ of Colo, BA, 66, MA, 68; Univ of Ill, advanced work in hist, 68-70; Univ of Denver, MA, 71; Ind Univ, PhD, 78. **CAREER** Ref libr, 71-75, instr, 71-74, asst prof, Univ of Nebr at Omaha, 74-75; assoc instr, Ind Univ, 75-78; vis lectr, Libr School, Univ of Wis at Madison, 78; ASSOC PROF, 81-83, ASST PROF, 78-81, PROF, GRAD SCHOOL OF LIBR AND INFOR SCI, SIMMONS COL, 86-; assoc prof, 83-85, prof, 85-86, vis prof, Grad Libr School, Univ of Az, 88; vis prof, Dept of Libr and Infor Studies, Victoria Univ of Wellington, 95-96. **HONORS AND AWARDS** Louise Maxwell Award, Indian Univ School of Libr and Infor Sci Alumni Asn, 93; winner of res paper competition, Libr Res Round Table, 86; res grant, Asn of Libr and Infor Sci Ed, 85; Asn of Am Libr Schools' Res Paper Competition Award, 82. **MEMBERSHIPS** Beta Phi Mu; Am Soc for Infor Sci; Am Libr Asn. **RESEARCH** Service quality; customer satisfaction; government information policy; research misconduct. **SELECTED PUBLICATIONS** Auth, Assessing Service Quality: Satisfying the Expectations of Library Customers, Am Libr Asn, 88; Research Misconduct: Issues, Implications, and Strategies, Ablex, 97; Federal Information Policies in the 1990s: Views and Perspectives, Ablex, 96; Service Quality in Academic Libraries, Ablex, 96; ed, Gov Infor Quart, J of Acad Librarianship, and Libr & Infor Sci Res. **CONTACT ADDRESS** Grad School of Libr & Infor Sci, Simmons Col, 300 The Fenway, Boston, MA, 02115-5898. **EMAIL** phernon@simmons.edu

HERRING, HENRY
DISCIPLINE AMERICAN LITERATURE **EDUCATION** Univ SC, BA, 61, MA, 64; Duke Univ, PhD, 68. **CAREER** Prof. **RESEARCH** Dept of Eng **SELECTED PUBLICATIONS** In the field of textual criticism. **CONTACT ADDRESS** Col of Wooster, Wooster, OH, 44691.

HERRING, PHILLIP F.
PERSONAL Born 06/30/1936, Fort Worth, TX, m, 1962, 2 children **DISCIPLINE** ENGLISH **EDUCATION** Univ of Tex, BA, 58, PhD, 66. **CAREER** Teaching asst and spec instr, Univ of Tex, 62-64; asst prof, Univ of Va, 65-70; from assoc prof to prof, Univ of Wis, 70-96; co-dir, Seventh Int James Joyce Symp , Zurich, 79; co-dir, NMex James Joyce Symp, 81; vis prof, Univ of NMex, 81-82; prog coord, Eight Int James Joyce Symp, Dublin, 82; adj prof, Univ of Tex, 96-. **HONORS AND AWARDS** A. Mellon Postdoctoral Fel, Univ of Pittsburgh, 68-69; Fel, Inst for Res in the Hums, 73; Romnes Fac Fel, 75-76; ACLS Travel Grant, 88; U.W.Fac Develop Grant, 89; NEH Summer Stipend, 91; Hilldale Undergrad Fac Award, 93; Djuna, Choice selection for one of the best acad books of the year, 95. **MEMBERSHIPS** James Joyce Found; MLA; Madison Lit Club. **SELECTED PUBLICATIONS** Auth, Joyce's ULYSSES notesheets in the British Museum, 72; Joyce's Notes and Early Drafts for ULYSSES: Selections from the Buffalo, in TLS, 78; Joyce's Uncertainty Principle, 87; Reply to Grace Eckley, in J. Joyce Lit Suppl 5, 91; Joyce's Sourcebooks for Ulysses in the Manuscripts, in 'Ulysse' a l'article: Joyce aux marges du roman, 91; Dubliners: The Trials of Adolescence, in J. Joyce: A Collection of Critical Essays, 92; Djuna Barnes Remembers James Joyce, In J. Joyce Quart 30, 92, Djuna Barnes and the Songs of Synge, in Eire-Ireland 28:2, 93; Djuna Barnes, Behind the Heart, in Library Chronicle 23:4, 93; Zadel Barnes, Journalist, in Rev of Contemp Fiction 13:3, 93; Djuna Barnes and Thelma Wood: The Vengeance of Nightwood, in J of Modern Lit 18:1, 94; 'I know of no writer as mean as I would be'!: Djuna Barnes' The Antiphon, in De Gits, 95; Djuna: The Life and Work of Djuna Barnes, 95; ed, The Collected Stories of Djuna Barnes, 96; coed, James Joyce: The Centennial Symposium, 86 **CONTACT ADDRESS** Harry Ransom Humanities Research Center, Univ of Texas, Austin, PO Drawer 7219, Austin, TX, 78713-7219. **EMAIL** PHerring@mail.utexas.edu

HERRNSTEIN SMITH, BARBARA
DISCIPLINE ENGLISH LITERATURE **EDUCATION** Brandeis Univ, PhD, 65. **CAREER** Braxton Craven prof comp lit. **SELECTED PUBLICATIONS** Auth, On the Margins of Discourse, Chicago, 78; Contingencies of Value, Harvard, 88; co-ed, South Atlantic Quarterly: Mathematics, Science, and Postclassical Theory, Duke, 95. **CONTACT ADDRESS** Eng Dept, Duke Univ, Durham, NC, 27706.

HERRON, CAROLIVIA
PERSONAL Born 0722, Washington, DC, s **DISCIPLINE** ENGLISH, AFRICAN-AMERICAN STUDIES **EDUCATION** Eastern Baptist College, BA, English lit, 1969; Villanova University, MA, English, 1973; University of Pennsylvania, MA, comparative lit & creative writing, 1983, PhD, comparative lit & lit theory, 1985. **CAREER** Harvard University, asst professor, African-American Studies and Comparative Literature, 1986-90; Mount Holyoke College, associate professor, English, 1990-92; Hebrew College, visiting scholar, 1994-95; Harvard University, visiting scholar, 1995. **HONORS AND AWARDS** US Information Service, Fulbright Post-Doctoral Research Award, 1985; NEH, Visit to Collections Award, 1987; Radcliffe College, Bunting Institute Fellowship, 1988; Yale University, Beineke Library Fellowship, 1988; Folger Shakespeare Library, Post-Doctoral Research Award, 1989. **MEMBERSHIPS** Classical Association of New England, 1986-93. **SELECTED PUBLICATIONS** Author: Thereafter Johnnie, novel, 1991; Selected Works of Angelina Weld Grimke, 1991. **CONTACT ADDRESS** Random House, 201 E 50th St, New York, NY, 10022.

HERZBERG, BRUCE
PERSONAL Born 07/19/1949, Vineland, NJ, m, 1977, 2 children **DISCIPLINE** ENGLISH LITERATURE, RHETORIC **EDUCATION** Amherst Col, BA, 72; Rutgers Univ, PhD, 78. **CAREER** Instr English, Clark Univ, 78-80; educ dir comput programming & tech writing, John M Nevison Assocs, 80-81; asst prof English, 81-90, prof eng, Bentley Col, 90. **HONORS AND AWARDS** Outstanding Bk Award, CCCC, for Rhetorical Tradition, 92. **MEMBERSHIPS** MLA; NCTE; SBL; WPA. **RESEARCH** Rhetoric and compos theory; Bibl lit. **SELECTED PUBLICATIONS** Auth, Selected articles on Thomas Pynchon: An annotated bibliography, Twentieth Century Lit, 5/75; contribr, Thomas Pynchon & Gravity's Rainbow, In: Academic American Encycl, Arete Publ Co, 79; coauth, Some problems in E D Hirsch's Philosophy of Composition, Mod Lang Notes, 12/80; contribr, Hal Clement & George O Smith, In: Dict of Literary Biography: 20th Century American Science Fiction, BC Res Co, 81; auth, Breakfast, death, feedback: Thomas Pynchon and the technology of interpretation, Bucknell Rev, fall 82; auth, michel Foucault's Theory of Rhetoric, In: Contending with Words, MLA, 91; auth, Composition and the Politics of the Curriculum, In: Politics of Writing Instruction, Heinemann, 91; Rhetoric Unbound, In: the Social Perspective in Professional Communication, Sage, 92; Community Service and Critical Teaching, Col Compos Commun, 10/94; Co-auth, The Rhetorical Tradition, Bedford, 90; Co-auth, Bedford Bibliography for Teachers of Writing, Bedford, 96; Co-auth, Negotiating Differences, 96. **CONTACT ADDRESS** Dept of Eng, Bentley Col, 175 Forest St, Waltham, MA, 02452-4705. **EMAIL** bherzberg@bentley.edu

HERZING, THOMAS WAYNE
PERSONAL Born 06/30/1939, St. Cloud, MN, m, 1961, 4 children **DISCIPLINE** BRITISH LITERATURE, ROMANTIC MOVEMENT **EDUCATION** St John's Univ, Minn, BA, 61; Marquette Univ, MA, 63; Univ Wis-Madison, PhD(English), 72. **CAREER** Instr English, St Joseph's Col, Ind, 62-67; from instr to asst prof, 67-74, assoc prof, 74-82, prof English, Univ Wis, Oshkosh, 82-, assoc dean, 96-, assoc, Ctr Activ Pub Sector, 74-. **MEMBERSHIPS** MLA; Am Soc 18th Century Studies; NCTE. **RESEARCH** Rhetorical analysis; the intellectual history behind Blake's poetry; the psychology of creativity. **SELECTED PUBLICATIONS** Coauth, Introduction to Basic Photography, Univ Wis, 75; Opportunities in a Recovering Economy, 3/76 & Riding the Future Curve: Forecasting Short-Term Markets, 5/76, Treas Dig; An Interdisciplinary Approach to Marketing and Business Communication, Midwest Bus Admin Asn, 77; ed, Investment Fundamentals, Irwin, 80; ed, Marketing Channels and Strategies, Grid Publ, 81; Conducting Fundamentals, Prentice-Hall, 82; auth, Test bank, In: Investments, Dryden, 82; ed, Strategies in Personal Finance, McGraw Hill, 83, 85, 88, 92; auth, The Leach Co.: The First 100 Years, 87; Don't Shoot the Decoys, 93; co-auth, The University of Oshkosh: The First 100 Years, 98. **CONTACT ADDRESS** Univ of Wis, 800 Algoma Blvd, Oshkosh, WI, 54901-8601. **EMAIL** herzing@uwosh.edu

HERZMAN, RONALD BERNARD
PERSONAL Born 11/17/1943, Brooklyn, NY, m, 1970, 2 children **DISCIPLINE** ENGLISH LITERATURE, MEDIEVAL STUDIES **EDUCATION** Manhattan Col, BA, 65; Univ Del, MA, 67, PhD(English), 69. **CAREER** Instr English, Univ Del, 68-69; asst prof, 69-79, ASSOC PROF ENGLISH, STATE UNIV NY, GENESEO, 79-, Fel in residence English, Univ Chicago, 78-79. **MEMBERSHIPS** Dante Soc Am. **RESEARCH** Dante; Chaucer; interdisciplinary medieval studies. **SELECTED PUBLICATIONS** Auth, Squaring the Circle--Exploring the Artistry of Dante in His 'Divine Commedia'--'Paradiso', and the Poetics of Geometry, Traditio-Studies Ancient Medieval Hist Thought Relig, Vol 0049, 94. **CONTACT ADDRESS** Dept of English, State Univ of NY, 1 College Cir, Geneseo, NY, 14454-1401.

HERZOG, KRISTIN
PERSONAL Born 03/01/1929, Germany, w, 1 child **DISCIPLINE** ENGLISH **EDUCATION** Duke Univ, MA, 73; Univ of NC, PhD, 80; State of Lower Saxony, Germany, Studien Assessorin, 56; Univ of Gottingen, Germany, Studien Referendarin, 54. **CAREER** Tchr of Secondary Sch, Germany; Independent Scholar and Writer. **MEMBERSHIPS** Modern Lang Assoc, AAR, GAAS, MELUS, NCIS. **RESEARCH** Ethnic-Amer Lit; Womens Stud; Feminist Theol. **SELECTED PUBLICATIONS** Auth, Women, Ethics, and Exotics: Images of Power in Mid-Nineteenth-Century American Fiction, Knoxville, Univ of Tennessee Press, 83; Finding Their Voice: Peruvian Women's Testimonies of War, Valley Forge, PA, Trinity Press International, 93; Contrib Ed to The Heath Anthology of American Literature, vol II and Instructor's Guide for this anthology, Lexington, MA, D.C. Heath, 90 & 94; Kraft des Uberlebens, Vielfaltige theologische Frauenforschung in den USA, Evangelische Kommentare, 97. **CONTACT ADDRESS** 2936 Chapel Hill Rd, Durham, NC, 27707. **EMAIL** kristinberzog@compuserve.com

HESLA, DAVID H.
PERSONAL Born 10/14/1929, Stevens Point, WI, m, 1956, 2 children **DISCIPLINE** LITERATURE; HISTORY OF IDEAS **EDUCATION** St Olaf Col, BA, 51; Univ Chicago, AM, 56, PhD, 64. **CAREER** Instr English, St Olaf Col, 55-56; from instr to asst prof, Cornell Col, 61-65; instr lit & theol, 65-70, assoc prof humanities, Emory Univ, 70-, consult, Miles Col, 71-72. **HONORS AND AWARDS** Fulbright lectr, US Educ Found, Finland, 72-73. **MEMBERSHIPS** Am Acad Relig. **RESEARCH** Religious dimensions of literature; modern British and American literature; literary criticism and theory. **SELECTED PUBLICATIONS** Auth, Theological ambiguity in the Catholic novels, In: Graham Greene, Univ KY, 63; The two roles of Norman Mailer, Adversity & Grace, 68; The Shape of Chaos: An Interpretation of the Art of Samuel Beckett, Univ Minn, 71. **CONTACT ADDRESS** Emory Univ, 1364 Clifton Rd NE, Atlanta, GA, 30322-0001. **EMAIL** iladhh@emory.edu

HESSELGRAVE, DAVID J.
PERSONAL Born 01/03/1924, N Freedom, WI, m, 1944, 3 children **DISCIPLINE** RHETORIC AND PUBLIC ADDRESS **EDUCATION** Evangelical Free Church Sem, Dipl, 44; Univ Minn, BA, 56, MA, 56, PhD, 65. **CAREER** Prof, of Mission, 65-91, chr, Dept Missions & Evangelism, 65-88, dir, School World Mission & Evangelism, 67-88, prof, emeritus, 92-, Trinity Evangelical Divinity School; Exrc Dir, Evangelical Missiological Soc, 89-94. **HONORS AND AWARDS** Acad prize, Univ Alumni Asn **MEMBERSHIPS** Ministerial Asn Evangelical Free Chruch Amer; Evangelical Theol Soc; Evangelical Missiological; Amer Soc Missiology. **RESEARCH** Cross-cultural studies; World Missions; World religions **SELECTED PUBLICATIONS** Auth, Communicating Christ Cross-Culturally: An Introduction to Missionary Communication; Planting Churches Cross-Culturally: A Guide for Home and Foreign Missions; coauth, Contextualization: Meanings, Methods, and Models; Todays Choices for Tomorrows Mission; auth, Scripture and Strategy: The Use of the Bible in Postmodern Church and Mission. **CONTACT ADDRESS** 5068 Valley Pines Dr., Rockford, IL, 61109. **EMAIL** DJHesselgrave@Juno.com

HESTER, MARVIN THOMAS
PERSONAL Born 07/22/1941, Owensboro, KY, m, 1968 **DISCIPLINE** RENAISSANCE LITERATURE **EDUCATION** Centre Col, Ky, BA, 63; Univ Fla, MA, 65, PhD(English lit), 72. **CAREER** Instr English, Univ Fla, 64-67; instr English, 71-72, asst prof English, 72-77, fac res fel, 73-74, ASSOC PROF ENGLISH, NC STATE UNIV, 77-, Nat Endowment for Humanities fel, 72-73 & 81-82; faculty res fel, 75-76 & 76-77; Southeast Medieval and Renaissance Inst fel, 78; co-ed, Renaissance Papers, 79-; ed, John Donne J, 82. **MEMBERSHIPS**

Southeastern Renaissance Soc; Renaissance Soc Am; SAtlantic MLA. **RESEARCH** English Renaissance satire; Donne; Thomas More. **SELECTED PUBLICATIONS** Auth, If-Thou-Regard-The-Same--Poem Between 'Amoretti' and 'Epithalamion'--Spenser Emblematic Centerfold, Anq, Vol 0006, 93; Miserrimum-Dictu, Donne Epitaph for His Wife, J English Germanic Philol, Vol 0094, 95; Donne and the Court-Of-Wards, Anq, Vol 0007, 94; Transfigured Rites in 17th-Century English Poetry, J English Germanic Philol, Vol 0092, 93; Let-Them-Sleep-- John Donne Personal Illusion in 'Holy Sonnet Iv', Papers Lang Lit, Vol 0029, 93. **CONTACT ADDRESS** No Carolina State Univ, Box 5308, Raleigh, NC, 27650.

HEUETT, BRIAN L.
PERSONAL Born 04/14/1960, Spokane, WA, m, 1984, 4 children **DISCIPLINE** COMMUNICATIONS **EDUCATION** Wash State Univ, BA, 93, MA, 95, PhD, 98. **CAREER** Acad adv, 95-98, grad asst, 96-98, asst coordr, 96-97, tchg asst, 93-98, Wash State Univ; asst prof, Southern Utah Univ, 98-. **HONORS AND AWARDS** Outstand Commun tchg asst, 95, 96, Edward R. Murrow Sch Commun; Katie Whitworth Scholar Award, 95, 96; tchg excellence award, 96, Wash State Univ; Outstanding Grad Stud Tchr, 96, Int Commun Asn. **MEMBERSHIPS** Nat Commun Asn; Western Speech Commun Asn. **RESEARCH** Communication apprehension and public speaking. **SELECTED PUBLICATIONS** Coauth, art, The relationship between visual imagery and public speaking apprehension, 97; coauth, art, Testing a refinement in an intervention for communication apprehension, 98. **CONTACT ADDRESS** Dept of Communications, Southern Utah Univ, Centrum 213f, Cedar City, UT, 84720. **EMAIL** heuett@suu.edu

HIBBARD, CAROLINE MARSH
PERSONAL Born 04/01/1942, Boston, MA **DISCIPLINE** ENGLISH HISTORY **EDUCATION** Wellesley Col, BA, 64; Oxford Univ, BA, 66; Yale Univ, PhD(hist), 75. **CAREER** Sessional lectr hist, Queen's Univ, 72-73; lectr, 73-75, asst prof, 75-81, assoc prof hist, Univ Ill, Urbana, 81-. **HONORS AND AWARDS** Article Prize, Berkshire Conf, 81; NEH Scholar Newberry, 88-89; Newberry Library/Brit. Acad. Fellowship summer 09; Fellow, Royal Historical Soc, 90. **MEMBERSHIPS** Am Cath Hist Asn; Conf Brit Studies; Cath Rec Soc, Gt Brit; AHA; Soc for Court Studies; Sixteenth Century Studies Society. **RESEARCH** Early Stuart English history; English Catholic history; early modern Europe. **SELECTED PUBLICATIONS** Auth, Early Stuart Catholicism: Revisions and Re-Revisions, J Mod Hist, 80; The Contribution of 1639, Recusant Hist, 82; Charles I and the Popish Plot, Chapel Hill, 83; Role of a Queen Consort: Household and Court of Henrietta Maria, 1625-42, in Court at the Beginning of the Modern Age, ed R. Asch, London, 91; Theatre of Dynasty, in Stuart Court and Europe, ed R.M. Smuts, Cambridge, 96. **CONTACT ADDRESS** Dept of Hist, Univ of Ill, 810 S Wright St, Urbana, IL, 61801-3611. **EMAIL** hibbardc@uiuc.edu

HICKSON, MARK
PERSONAL Born 08/10/1945, Macon, GA, m, 1986, 2 children **DISCIPLINE** COMMUNICATION **EDUCATION** Auburn Univ, BS, 66, MA, 68; S Ill, PhD, 71. **CAREER** Asst prof, Miss State Univ, 70-71; assoc prof, prof, chr, 74-87; prof, Univ of Ala at Birmingham, 87-. **HONORS AND AWARDS** S States Commun Assoc, Teaching Excellence Award, 98; Telly Award, 98. **MEMBERSHIPS** Nat Commun Assoc; Eastern Commun Assoc. **RESEARCH** Nonverbal communication; communication theory. **SELECTED PUBLICATIONS** co-auth, NVC: Nonverbal communication studies and applications, Brown/Benchmark, 93; co-auth, Compatible theory and applied research: Systems theory and triangulation, Qualitative Res: Applications in organizational commun, Hampton, 93; auth, The ethos of an academic department, J of the Assoc of Commun Admin, vol 83, 67-70, 93; co-auth, Active prolific scholars in communication studies: Analysis of research productivity, II, Commun Educ, vol 42, 224-233, 93; coauth, Modeling cultures: Toward grounded paradigms, An integrated approach to communication theory and research, Erlbaum, 96; co-auth, qualitative/descriptive (participation-observation) methodology, Essentials of commun res, Longman, 98; coauth, Organizational communication in the personal context: From interview to retirement, Allyn and Bacon, 98. **CONTACT ADDRESS** 2021 Shagbark Rd, Birmingham, AL, 35244. **EMAIL** hickson@uab.edu

HIEATT, ALLEN KENT
PERSONAL Born 01/21/1921, Indianapolis, IN, m, 1957, 2 children **DISCIPLINE** ENGLISH **EDUCATION** Univ Louisville, AB, 43; Columbia Univ, PhD(comp lit), 54. **CAREER** Instr English, Columbia Univ, 44-45; instr Col, 45-55, from asst prof to assoc prof, 55-69; vis prof, 68-69, PROF ENGLISH, UNIV WESTERN ONTARIO, 69-, Can Coun leave grant, 78. **MEMBERSHIPS** MLA; Renaissance Soc Am; Mod Humanities Res Asn; Asn Can Univ Teachers English. **RESEARCH** English, comparative literature and art history, 14th to 17th centuries. **SELECTED PUBLICATIONS** Auth, Cultural Aesthetics--Renaissance Literature and the Practice of Social Ornament, Renaissance Reformation, Vol 0017, 93; 'His Farewell to Military Profession', English Studies Can, Vol 0019, 93. **CONTACT ADDRESS** Dept of English, Univ of Western Ont, London, ON, N6A 3K7.

HIEATT, CONSTANCE B.
PERSONAL Born 02/11/1928, Boston, MA, m, 1958 **DISCIPLINE** LITERATURE **EDUCATION** Hunter Col (NY), AB, 53, AM, 57; Yale Univ, PhD, 59. **CAREER** Lectr, City Col NY, 59-60; asst to assoc prof, Queensborough Commun Col, 60-65; assoc prof to prof, St John's Univ (Jamaica), 65-69; prof, 69-93, PROF EMER ENGLISH, UNIV WESTERN ONTARIO, 93-. **HONORS AND AWARDS** Yale Univ fel, Lewis-Farmington fel, 57-59; Can Coun grants; SSHRCC grants. **MEMBERSHIPS** MLA; Medieval Acad Am; Asn Can Univ Tchrs Eng; Int Arthurian Asn; Soc Advan Scandinavian Stud; Anglo-Norman Text Soc; Int Saga Soc; Int Soc Anglo-Saxonists. **SELECTED PUBLICATIONS** Auth, The Realism of Dream Visions, 67; auth, Essentials of Old English, 68; auth, An Ordinance of Pottage, 88; coauth, The Canterbury Tales of Geoffrey Chaucer, 64, rev ed, 81; ed/transl, Pleyn Delit: Medieval Cookery for Modern Cooks, 76, rev ed, 79, rev 2nd ed, 96; ed/transl, Curye on Inglysch: English Culinary Manuscripts of the Fourteenth Century, 85; ed/transl, La novele cirurgerie, 90; ed/transl, Beginning Old English, 94; ed/transl, The Tale of the Alerion (Guillaume de Machaut), 94; transl, Beowulf and Other Old English Poems, 67, 2nd ed, 83; transl, Karlamagnus Saga, vols I-II, 75, vol III, 80. **CONTACT ADDRESS** 304 River Rd, Deep River, CT, 06417.

HIEBERT, RAY ELDON
DISCIPLINE JOURNALISM **EDUCATION** Stanford Univ, BA, 54; Columbia Univ Grad School of Journalism, MS, 57; Univ of Maryland, MA, 61, PhD, 62. **CAREER** Inst, Dept of English, Univ of Minn, Duluth, 57-58; asst prof, Dept of Commun, 58-62, chemn, assoc prof & prof, Dept of Commun, Amer Univ, 62-66; founding dir, Washington Journalism Center, 65-68; chemn & prof, Dept of Journalism, 68-72, founding dean, Col of Journalism, Univ of Md 73-79; ed, Public Relations Review, 75-; ed, The Communicator, Radio Television News Dir Asn, 70-77; series ed, Longman Series in Public Commun, Longman Co, NY, 75-90; series ed, Contemp Issues in Journalism, Acropolis Books, Washington DC, 70-74; series ed, Wiley Series on Gov and Commun, John Wiley & Sons, NY, 68-70; Acad Advisor, Voice of Am, 83-91; founding dir, Am Journalism Center, Budapest, Hungary, 91-95; member, selection comt, Freedom Support Act Fels for Journalists from Eastern Europe, Int Res and Exchange Board, 95-96; consult on journalism ed in Eastern Europe, The Freedom Forum, 95-97; PROF, 68-98, prof emeritus, 98-, COL OF JOURNALISM, UNIV OF MD. **MEMBERSHIPS** Cosmos Club, Washington D.C.; Int Commun Asn; Asn for Ed in Journalism and Mass Commun. **SELECTED PUBLICATIONS** Coauth, Eastern European Journalism: Before, During, and After Communism, Hampton Press, 98; auth, Exploring Mass Media, Lawrence Erlbaum Asn, 98; coauth, Stages of Post-Communist Media Transition in Hungary, Hungary: A New Nation, European Centre for Traditional Culture, 98; coauth, Remedial Education: The Remaking of Eastern European Journalists, in Journalism Educ in Europe and North Am: An Int Comparison, Inst fur Publizistick, forthcoming; ed, Impact of Mass Media, Longman Co. Inc., 87, 91, 94, & 98; auth, Transition: From the End of the Old Regime to 1996, in Journalism and the Educ of Journalists in the New East/Central Europe, Hampton Press, 98; auth, Blarus, Estonia, Hungary, Latvia, Lithuania, Ukraine, in Looking to the Future: A Survey of Journalism Educ in Central and Easter Europe and the Soviet Union, Freedom Forum, 94; auth, Growth of Advertising and Public Relations in Post-Communist Hungary, in Public Relations Rev, winter 94; auth, The Difficult Birth of a Free Press in Hungary, in Amer Journalism Rev, 94. **CONTACT ADDRESS** College of Journalism, Univ of Md, College Park, MD, 20742.

HIGDON, DAVID LEON
DISCIPLINE ENGLISH LITERATURE **EDUCATION** Univ KS, PhD, 68. **CAREER** Paul Whitfield Horn Prof Eng, TX Tech Univ; ed, Conradiana, 72-95. **HONORS AND AWARDS** Pres Excellence in Tchg Award; AMOCO Excellence in Tchg Award; YWES award. **RESEARCH** Postmodern narrative. **SELECTED PUBLICATIONS** Auth, Time and English Fiction, Shadows of the Past in Contemporary British Fiction. **CONTACT ADDRESS** Texas Tech Univ, Lubbock, TX, 79409-5015. **EMAIL** L.Higdon@ttu.edu

HIGGINS, ELIZABETH J.
DISCIPLINE ENGLISH LITERATURE **EDUCATION** Univ Calif Los Angeles, PhD, 68. **CAREER** Fac, Atlanta Univ, 68; fac, Clark Atlanta Univ, 88. **RESEARCH** British romantic literature; American literature; Victorian novel and poetry. **SELECTED PUBLICATIONS** Auth, The Living Novel, 82; bk revs, Jour Col Lang Asn. **CONTACT ADDRESS** Clark Atlanta Univ, 223 James P Brawley Dr, SW, Atlanta, GA, 30314.

HIGGINS, MARY ANNE
PERSONAL Born 01/22/1953, Barberton, OH, s **DISCIPLINE** COMMUNICATIONS **EDUCATION** Ohio State Univ, BS, 75; Univ Akron, MA, 85; Kent State Univ, PhD, 92. **CAREER** Vis inst, Kent State Univ, 91-92; Adj asst prof, 92-93; asst prof, Ind Purdue Ft Wayne, 93-97. **HONORS AND AWARDS** Finalist for Distinguished Teaching Award, KSU, 91; Recipient of Res Award, Kent State Univ, 92; Summer Grant Recipient, IPFW, 96. **MEMBERSHIPS** Nat Commun Assoc; Int Commun Assoc; Central States Commun Assoc. **RESEARCH** Rural/urban communication; health communication; communication with people with disabilities. **SELECTED PUBLICATIONS** Co-auth, Initiating and Reciprocating verbal aggression: Effects on credibility and credited valid arguments, Commun Studs, vol 43, 182-190, 93; auth, Common Ground, weekly newspaper column, The Independent, Massilon, OH, 92-94; New Trends, news values, and new models, NJ J of Commun, vol 4, (1)82-90, 96; auth, A critical rhetoric and the role of the critic, The Mich Academian, vol 29, 278-279, 97. **CONTACT ADDRESS** 14941 Marshallville Rd, Canal Fulton, OH, 44614. **EMAIL** farmmah@aol.com

HIGLEY, SARAH
DISCIPLINE ENGLISH **EDUCATION** Univ CA at Berkeley, PhD. **CAREER** Assoc prof & dir Undergrad Stud; taught at, Univ CA at Berkeley & Univ Geneva, Switzerland. **RESEARCH** Medieval northern lang and lit, Old Eng, Middle Eng, Welsh, Middle Welsh, Old Norse; contemp popular cult. **SELECTED PUBLICATIONS** Auth, Between Languages: The Uncooperative Text in Early Welsh and Old English Nature Poetry; The Legend of the Learned Man's Android, in Retelling Tales, Cambridge: DS Brewer, 97; Old Llwarch's Jawbone: Mediating Old and New Translation in Middle Welsh Studies, in The Formation of Culture in Medieval Britain, Lewiston, 96 & The Spoils of Annwn: Taliesin and Material Poetry, in A Celtic Florilegium, Lawrence, 96; articles on, Beowulf, Old Eng elegies, medieval Welsh poetry and prose including The Mabinogion and The Bk of Taliesin, transl theory, ling, Old Norse, medieval magic, film and television, and science fiction. **CONTACT ADDRESS** Dept of Eng, Univ of Rochester, 601 Elmwood Ave, Ste. 656, Rochester, NY, 14642. **EMAIL** slhi@troi.cc.rochester.edu

HIGONNET, MARGARET RANDOLPH
PERSONAL Born 10/02/1941, New Orleans, LA, m, 1974 **DISCIPLINE** COMPARATIVE LITERATURE, ENGLISH **EDUCATION** Bryn Mawr Col, BA, 63; Yale Univ, PhD(comp lit), 70. **CAREER** Instr English, George Washington Univ, 67-68; asst prof, 70-75, assoc prof, 75-81, PROF ENGLISH, UNIV CONN, 81-, CHMN, COMP LIT PROG, 78-, Fulbright prof, 81. **MEMBERSHIPS** MLA; English Inst (secy, 76-80); Am Comp Lit Asn. **RESEARCH** Jean Paul Richter; literary theory; Romanticism. **SELECTED PUBLICATIONS** Auth, Forum--Interdisciplinarity in Literary-Studies--Perspectives from Particular Fields, MLA Pubs, Vol 0111, 96; Academic Anorexia--Some Gendered Questions About Comparative Literature, Comp Lit, Vol 0049, 97. **CONTACT ADDRESS** Dept of English, Univ of Conn, Storrs, CT, 06268.

HILFER, ANTHONY CHANNELL
PERSONAL Born 10/19/1936, Los Angeles, CA, m, 1961, 1 child **DISCIPLINE** AMERICAN LITERATURE **EDUCATION** Middlebury Col, BA, 58; Columbia Univ, MA, 60; Univ NC, Chapel Hill, PhD(English), 63. **CAREER** Asst prof, 63-69, assoc prof English, Univ Tex, Austin, 69-, lectr Am Studies, Keele Univ, 70-71; ed, Texas Studies in Literature and Language, 92-. **MEMBERSHIPS** MLA. **RESEARCH** American literature, popular culture. **SELECTED PUBLICATIONS** Auth, George and Martha: Sad, sad, sad, In: Seven Contemporary Authors, Univ Tex, 66; coauth, Baby doll: A study in comedy and social awareness, Ohio Univ Rev, 69; auth, The Revolt from the Village, 1915-1930, Univ NC, 69; Absurdist language: The foregrounding of the symbol system, Sci/Technol & Humanities, 78; The Crime Novel, A Deviant Genre, U of Texas, 90; American Fiction Since 1940, Longman-Addison Wesley, 92. **CONTACT ADDRESS** Dept of English, Univ of Texas, Austin, TX, 78712-1026.

HILL, DAVID
DISCIPLINE ENGLISH LITERATURE **EDUCATION** IN Univ, PhD, 71. **CAREER** Prof Eng/dir lit studies, SUNY Oswego. **RESEARCH** 19th century Am lit; later 19th century Brit and Am fiction; lang and lit. **SELECTED PUBLICATIONS** Auth, essays on Emerson, James, Stevenson, and Eng compos; co-ed, The Journals and Miscellaneous Notebooks of Ralph Waldo Emerson (16 vol), Harvard UP, 60-82; The Poetry Notebooks of Ralph Walso Emerson, Univ MO P, 86. **CONTACT ADDRESS** SUNY Oswego, Oswego, NY, 13126. **EMAIL** dhill@Oswego.edu

HILL, EUGENE DAVID
PERSONAL Born 02/25/1949, New York, NY **DISCIPLINE** RENAISSANCE LITERATURE, INTELLECTUAL HISTORY. **EDUCATION** Columbia Univ, BA, 70; Princeton Univ, PhD(English), 80. **CAREER** Instr, 78-80, asst prof Eng, Mt Holyoke Col, 80-86; from asst prof to prof Eng, 86-94. **MEMBERSHIPS** Renaissance Soc Am. **RESEARCH** John Milton, John Donne, Thomas Kyd. **SELECTED PUBLICATIONS** Auth, The trinitarian allegory of the moral play of Wisdom, Mod Philol, 75; The place of the future, Sci Fiction Studies, 82; Parody and History in Arden of Feversham, Huntington Library Quarterly, 93. **CONTACT ADDRESS** Dept of English, Mount Holyoke Col, 50 College St, South Hadley, MA, 01075-6421.

HILL, HOLLY
PERSONAL Born 11/16/1938, Cleveland, OH, d **DISCIPLINE** THEATRE **EDUCATION** Stanford Univ, BA, 59; Columbia Univ, MFA, 71; Grad School of CUNY, PhD, 77. **CAREER** NY Theatre Correspondent, The Times of London, 83-95; actress, on, off, & off-off Broadway, dinner theater, tours, 59-74; DIR & CO-FOUND, ARABIC THEATER PROJECT, O'NEILL THEATER CENTER, 97-; PROF OF SPEECH & THEATRE, JOHN JAY COL OF CUNY, 81-; FREELANCE THEATRE CRITIC, 74-. **HONORS AND AWARDS** Jury of Cairo Int Festival for Experimental Theatre, 97; five awards from the Res Found of CUNY; Richard Rodgers Fel, Columbia Univ. **MEMBERSHIPS** Am Theater Critics Asn; Drama Desk; Isben Soc of Am. **RESEARCH** History of acting; the well made play; Arabic theater. **SELECTED PUBLICATIONS** Auth, Actors Lives, Theatre Communs Group, 94; auth, Playing Joan, Theatre Communs Group, 87; assoc ed & contribu, Encyclopedia of the New York Stage 1920-29, Garland, 82. **CONTACT ADDRESS** 250 E 87th St, 190, New York, NY, 10128-3115.

HILL, JAMES LEE
PERSONAL Born 12/10/1941, Meiga, GA, m, 1964, 2 children **DISCIPLINE** AMERICAN & AFRO-AMERICAN LITERATURE **EDUCATION** Ft Valley State Col, BS, 63; Atlanta Univ, MA, 68, Univ Iowa, PhD(Am civilization), 76. **CAREER** Instr English & French, Winder City Schs, 64-65; chair, Dept English, Hancock Cent High Sch; specialist compos, Paine Col, 68-71; dept chair English, Benedict Col, 74-77; CHAIR, DEPT ENGLISH, ALBANY STATE COL, 77-, DIV CHAIR ARTS & SCI, 81-, Ed, Paine Col J, 68-71 & Albany State Col J Arts & Sci, 79-; vchmn & exec comt, Ga Endowment for Humanities, 81- **MEMBERSHIPS** Conf Col Compos & Commun; NCTE; Col Lang Asn; Asn Dept English; SAtlantic Mod Lang Asn. **RESEARCH** Dialect interference in learning to write; style in the modern Afro-American novel; the history of Black literary criticism in America. **SELECTED PUBLICATIONS** Auth, An Interview With Garvin Frank Yerby, Resources Am Lit Study, Vol 0021, 95. **CONTACT ADDRESS** 504 College Dr, Albany, GA, 31705-2717.

HILL, JAMES LEE
PERSONAL Born 12/10/1941, Meigs, GA, m **DISCIPLINE** ENGLISH **EDUCATION** Fort Valley St Coll, BS English 1959-63; Atlanta Univ, MA English 1963-68; Univ of Iowa, PhD American CIV 1971-76, 1978; Purdue Univ, post doctoral study 1981; John Carroll Univ, post doctoral study 1984. **CAREER** Winder City Schs, instructor English 1964-65; Hancock Central High, chmn Eng dept 1965-68; Paine Coll, instructor English 1968-71; Benedict Coll, chmn Eng dept 1974-77; ALBANY STATE COLL, chmn Eng dept 1977-96, DEAN ARTS & SCIENCES 1981-. **HONORS AND AWARDS** NEH Fellow Atlanta Univ 1969; NEH Fellow Univ of IA 1971-74; Governor's Award in the Humanities, State of Georgia, 1987. **MEMBERSHIPS** Consultant, Natl Rsch Project on Black Women 1979-81; sec Albany Urban League Bd 1979-81; chair, assoc, asst chair, Conf on Coll Comp & Comm 1980-83; chair, vice chair GA Endowment for Humanities 1981-83; mem Exec Comm NCTE 1982-83; pres Beta Nu Sigma Phi Beta Sigma Frat 1983-; chair Academic Comm on English-GA 1983-84; vice pres S Atlantic Assn of Dept of English 1984-85; bd dir Natl Fed State Humanities Councils 1984-87; mem Coll Section Comm Natl Council of Teachers of English 1985-89, chair, 1993-95; Professional Service: dir NEA Writer-in-Resd Prog ASC 1982-91; dir NEH Summer Humanities Inst ASC, 1983, 1984, 1989; Regional dir Southern Region Phi Beta Sigma; visiting scholar Natl Humanities Faculty; Georgia Desoto Commission; Georgia Christopher Columbus Commission; NCTE Summer Inst for Teachers of Literature, dir. **SELECTED PUBLICATIONS** Publications: "Migration of Blacks to Iowa," "The Apprenticeship of Chester Himes," "The Antiheroic Hero in the Novels of Frank Yerby," A Sourcebook for Teachers of Georgia History; editor, Studies in African and African-American Culture; "Interview with Frank Garvin Yerby;" "Frank Yerby;" "The Foxes of Harrow;" "A Woman of Fancy." **CONTACT ADDRESS** Arts & Sciences, Albany State Univ, 504 College Dr, Albany, GA, 31705.

HILL, L. BROOKS
PERSONAL Born 10/21/1943, Grenada, MS, m, 1961, 2 children **DISCIPLINE** SPEECH COMMUNICATION **EDUCATION** Univ of Memphis, BA, 64; Univ of Ala, MA, 65; Univ of Ill, PhD, 68. **CAREER** Prof, Univ of Okla, 68-88; prof & ch, Trinity Univ, 88-. **HONORS AND AWARDS** Phi Kappa Phi; local teaching awards. **MEMBERSHIPS** Nat Commun Assoc; Int Assoc for Intercultural Commun Studs (pres); Int Commun Assoc. **RESEARCH** Intercultural commun. **SELECTED PUBLICATIONS** Co-auth, The Needs of the International Student, Teaching and Directing the Basic Communication Course, Kendall/Hunt, 263-270, 93; co-auth, various articles in Organization and Behavior in Cross-Cultural Settings, Sanshusha, 193-218, 219-242, 289-312, 94; co-auth, articles in Cross-Cultural Communication and Aging in America, Erlbuam, 5-23, 1143-161, 97. **CONTACT ADDRESS** Dept of Speech & Drama, Trinity Univ, 715 Stadium Dr, San Antonio, TX, 78212. **EMAIL** lhill@trinity.edu

HILL, LINDA MARIE
PERSONAL Born 07/13/1947, Vicksburg, MS **DISCIPLINE** 18TH CENTURY BRITISH LITERATURE **EDUCATION** Belhaven Col, BA, 69; Univ AR, MA, 71; Univ AL, PhD (18th Century British Lit), 89. **CAREER** English instr, L. B. Wallace Community Col, Andalusia, AL, 78-80; assoc prof English, Belhaven Col, Jackson, MS, 80-97; ENGLISH INSTR, HINDS COMMUNITY COL, RANKIN CAMPUS, PEARL, MS, 97-. **HONORS AND AWARDS** Dean's Scholar, Univ AL Grad School. **MEMBERSHIPS** SE Soc for Eighteenth-Century Studies; MS Women's Political Network. **RESEARCH** Women's studies, 18th century; Am lit, 19th century. **SELECTED PUBLICATIONS** Auth, dissertation, The Dramatic Daring of Susanna Centlivre: A Feminist Study of the Foremost Woman Playwright of the Eighteenth Century, Univ AL, 89. **CONTACT ADDRESS** Hinds Comm Col, 3805 Hwy 80 E., Pearl, MS, 39208-4295.

HILL, PATRICIA LIGGINS
PERSONAL Born 09/18/1942, Washington, DC, d **DISCIPLINE** ENGLISH **EDUCATION** Howard Univ Wash DC, BA cum laude 1965; Univ of San Francisco, MA English, 1970; Stanford Univ CA, PhD English/Amer Lit 1977. **CAREER** Univ of San Francisco, prof of English, 1985-, assoc prof English 1979-84, dir ethnic studies 1977-, asst prof English 1977-79, English instructor 1971-77; Upper Midwest Tri-Racial Center, University of MN, resource consultant 1977-78; Urban Inst for Human Service Inc, research consultant 1976-80; Stanford University, teaching asst English 1974-77. **HONORS AND AWARDS** Recipient of fellowship, Natl Endowment for Humanities 1978; **MEMBERSHIPS** Bd dir Westside Mental Health Center 1971-78; SF Community College Bd 1972-78; CA Council of Black Educ 1973-. **SELECTED PUBLICATIONS** Roots for a Third World Aesthetic Found in Black & Chicano Poetry, De Colores 1980; "The Violent Space, An Interpretation of the Function of the New Black Aesthetic in Etheridge Knight's Poetry," Black Amer Lit Forum 1980; General editor, "Call & Response: The Riverside Anthology of the African American Literary Tradition," Houghton Mifflin, 1997; "The Dark/Black-Bad Light/White-Good Illusion in Joseph Conrad's 'Heart of Darkness' & 'Nigger of the Narcissus," Western Journal of Black Studies 1979. **CONTACT ADDRESS** English Department, Univ of San Francisco, 2130 Fulton St, San Francisco, CA, 94117.

HILL, PHILIP GEORGE
PERSONAL Born 09/19/1934, Christiansburg, VA, m, 1957, 3 children **DISCIPLINE** DRAMA **EDUCATION** Univ Fla, BA, 56; Univ NC, Chapel Hill, MA, 60; Tulane Univ PhD(theatre), 64. **CAREER** Instr drama & speech, Allegheny Col, 60-62; PROF DRAMA & CHMN DEPT, FURMAN UNIV, 64- **HONORS AND AWARDS** Suzanne M Davis Mem Award, Southeastern Theatre Conf, 76. **MEMBERSHIPS** Am Theatre Asn (treas, 77-80); US Inst Theatre Technol; Southeastern Theatre Conf (vpres, 73-74, pres, 74-75). **SELECTED PUBLICATIONS** Auth, Doctoral Projects in Progress in Theater-Arts, Theatre J, Vol 0045, 93. **CONTACT ADDRESS** Dept of Drama, Furman Univ, 3300 Poinsett Hwy, Greenville, SC, 29613-0002.

HILL, THOMAS DANA
PERSONAL Born 05/06/1940, Boston, MA, m, 1960, 3 children **DISCIPLINE** ENGLISH **EDUCATION** Harvard Univ, BA, 61; Univ Ill, MA, 63; Cornell Univ, PhD(English), 67. **CAREER** From asst prof to assoc prof English, 67-78, PROF ENGLISH & MEDIEVAL STUDIES, CORNELL UNIV, 78-, Soc Humanities fac fel, Cornell Univ, 70-71; Am Coun Learned Soc fel, 73-74. **MEMBERSHIPS** Medieval Acad Am. **RESEARCH** Old and Middle English literature; Old French and Old Icelandic literature. **SELECTED PUBLICATIONS** Auth, The 'Liber Eliensis' Historical Selections and the Old-English 'Battle Of Maldon', J English Germanic Philol, Vol 0096, 97; Tormenting the Devil With Boiling Drops--An Apotropaic Motif in the Old-English 'Solomon And Saturn I' and Old Norse-Icelandic Literature, J English Germanic Philol, Vol 0092, 93; The Cult of the Virgin-Mary in Anglo-Saxon England, Rev English Studies, Vol 0046, 95. **CONTACT ADDRESS** Dept of English, Cornell Univ, 252 Goldwin Smith Hall, Ithaca, NY, 14853-0001.

HILL, W. SPEED
PERSONAL Born 01/19/1935, Louisville, KY, m, 1984, 3 children **DISCIPLINE** ENGLISH **EDUCATION** Princeton Univ, AB (with Honors), 57; Harvard Univ, AM, PhD, 64. **CAREER** Asst prof, English, Case Western Reserve Univ, 64-69; asst prof, English, Univ Col, New York Univ, 69-73; assoc prof, English, 73-78, PROF, ENGLISH, LEHMAN COL, CUNY 78-, PROF, ENGLISH, GRADUATE CENTER, CUNY, 80-; vis prof, English, Univ British Columbia, Vancouver, 96. **HONORS AND AWARDS** Phi Beta Kappa; Woodrow Wilson Fel (honorary), 57-58; Am Philos Soc Grant-in-aid, 69-70; Folger Library fel, summer 69; Newberry Library fel, summer 69; ACLS grant-in-aid, 70-71; ACLS Sr fel, 73-74; Folger Library-British Academy fel, spring 73; NEH fel, 81-82; Honorary Doctorate of Humane Letters, Seabury-Western Theol Sem, 93; listed in Who's Who in the East, 94-95, 95-96; Who's Who in American Education, 5th ed; Lehman Col, Award for Res and Scholarship, 94; Honorary Doctorate of Letters, Sewanee: The Univ of the South, 95; grants to the Hooker Edition: NEH; Fac Res Award Prog, CUNY. **SELECTED PUBLICATIONS** Auth, New Ways of Looking at Old Texts: Papers of the Renaissance English Text Soc, 1985-1991, ed, Medieval Renaissance Texts & Studies, 93; English Renaissance: Nondramatic Literature, in Scholarly Editing: A Guide to Research, ed D. C. Greetham, MLA, 95; Scripture as Text, Text as Scripture: The Example of Richard Hooker, TEXT 9, 96; Where We Are and How We Got Here: Editing After Poststructuralism, Shakespeare Studies, 24, 96; Commentary on Commentary on Commentary: Three Historicisms Annotating Richard Hooker, for Margins of the Text, ed D. C. Greetham, Univ MI Press, 97; Richard Hooker in the Folger Edition: An Editorial Perspective & Richard Hooker: A Selected Bibliography, 1971-1993, compiled with Egil Grislis, for a volume of Hooker Conference papers, Richard Hooker and the Construction of a Texts & Studies, 97; New Ways of Looking at Old Texts, II: Papers of the Renaissance English Text Soc, 1992-1996, ed, Medieval & Renaissance Texts & Studies, 98; numerous other articles, review articles, and reviews, also editor, co-ed, or supervisory editor of numerous volumes. **CONTACT ADDRESS** 33 C Tier St., Bronx, NY, 10464. **EMAIL** wshlc@cunyvm.cuny.edu

HILL DUIN, ANN
DISCIPLINE RHETORIC STUDIES **EDUCATION** Univ Minn, MA, PhD. **CAREER** Assoc prof **RESEARCH** Collaboration via emerging technologies; cognitive processes and computers; distance learning; virtual learning environments. **SELECTED PUBLICATIONS** Auth, Techniques for Evaluating the Usability of Documents; Computer-Supported Collaborative Work: The Workplace and the Writing Classroom. **CONTACT ADDRESS** Rhetoric Dept, Univ of Minnesota, Twin Cities, 64 Classroom Office Bldg, 1994 Buford Ave, St. Paul, MN, 55108. **EMAIL** ahduin@maroon.tc.umn.edu

HILL-LUBIN, MILDRED ANDERSON
PERSONAL Born 03/23/1933, Russell County, AL, m **DISCIPLINE** ENGLISH **EDUCATION** Paine Coll Augusta, GA, BA English Honors 1961; Western Reserve Cleveland, MA 1962; Indiana, 1964; Univ of Minnesota, 1965-66; Howard Univ & African-Amer Inst,1972; Univ of Illinois Urbana-Champaign, PhD English & African Studies 1974. **CAREER** Paine Coll, instructor/asst prof 1962-65 & 1966-70; Hamline Univ, exchange prof 1965-66; Paine Coll, asst prof English/dir EPDA program 1970-72; Univ of IL, tchng asst/instructor 1972-74; Univ of Florida, assoc prof of English/dir English program for special admit students 1974-77, asst dean of graduate sch 1977-80, assoc prof of English & African Studies 1982-. **HONORS AND AWARDS** Alpha Kappa Mu Honor Soc Paine Coll 1960; Travel-Study Grant to W Africa African-Amer Intl 19; Trainer of Teachers Fellowship Univ of Illinois 1973-74; Gainesville Area Women of Distinction Award, 1992; Univ of FL, Teacher of the Year, 1994; Gainesville Comm on the Status of Women, Susan B Anthony Award, 1994. **MEMBERSHIPS** Proj assoc Council of Chief State School Officers Washington, DC 1981-82; consultant Amer Council on Educ 1981-; panel mem Adv Cncl Mellon Humanities Grant UNCF College Fund 1980-90; discipline comm in African Lit Fulbright Awards 1983-86; exec comm Coll Comp & Comm (CCCC) 1977-80; exec comm African Lit Assn 1983-89; pres Gainesville Chap of the Links 1985-87; pres FOCUS 1978-79; bd dir Gainesville/Alachua Co Center of Excell 1985-; Alpha Kappa Alpha Sor; pres, African Literature Assn 1987-88; dir, Gainesville-Jacmel Haiti Sister Cities Program, 1987-92; pres, The Visionaires, 1988-91; FL Humanities Council, bd of dirs, 1991-95; Santa Fe Community Coll District, bd of trustees, 1993-. **SELECTED PUBLICATIONS** Co-ed, "Towards Defining the African Aesthetic" and articles in, "Southern Folklore Quarterly," "Coll Lang Assn Journal"; "Presence Africaine"; "Okike"; Leadership and Achievement Award, Nu Eta Lambda Chapter Alpha Phi Alpha Fraternity 1988; articles, "The Black Grandmother in Literature," in Ngambika, 1986. **CONTACT ADDRESS** Univ of Florida, 4008 TUR, Gainesville, FL, 32611.

HILL-MILLER, KATHERINE CECELIA
PERSONAL Born 01/24/1949, Granite City, IL, m, 1982, 1 child **DISCIPLINE** MODERN BRITISH & WOMEN'S LITERATURE **EDUCATION** Fordham Univ, BA, 71; Columbia Univ, MA, 72, MPhil, 74, PhD(English), 79. **CAREER** Teaching fel, Columbia Univ, 74; lect, Kingsborough Comm Col, 72-73; asst prof, Col William & Mary, 77-80; asst prof 80-84, assoc prof 84-89, PROF ENGLISH, CW POST CAMPUS LONG ISLAND UNIV, 89-; dir, poetry ctr, 82-85, DIR WRITING, CW POST CTR, 93-; guest lect, Rheinische Friedrich-Wilhelms-Universitat, Bonn, 86. **MEMBERSHIPS** MLA; Virginia Woolf Soc. **RESEARCH** Virginia Woolf; experimental fiction; women writers. **SELECTED PUBLICATIONS** Auth, My Hideous Progeny: Mary SHelley, William Godwin, and the Father-Daughter Relaationship, Univ Del Press, 95; auth, The Bantam Book of Spelling, Bantam Books, 86; co-auth, Writing Effective Paragraphs, Harper and Row, 74; auth, Virginia Woolf's Places: A Guide to Some English Literary Landscapes, fothcoming; auth, Virginia Woolf and Leslie Stephen: History and Literary Revolution, Pubs of the Mod Lang Asn, 96, no 3, 81. **CONTACT ADDRESS** Dept of English, Long Island Univ, C.W. Post, Greenvale, NY, 11548. **EMAIL** fkcmiller@aol.com

HILLARD, VAN E.
DISCIPLINE ENGLISH LITERATURE **EDUCATION** Univ Cincinnati, PhD, 87. **CAREER** Asst prof pract rhet; asst dir writing prog. **RESEARCH** Comp pedag; philos of rhetoric. **SELECTED PUBLICATIONS** Auth, publ(s) on rhet publ art; rhet photog; polit quilting. **CONTACT ADDRESS** Eng Dept, Duke Univ, Durham, NC, 27706.

HILLIARD, JERRY
DISCIPLINE COMMUNICATION STUDIES **EDUCATION** Kent State Univ, BA, MA; Univ Tennessee, PhD. **CAREER** Prof. **MEMBERSHIPS** Public Rel Soc Am. **SELECTED PUBLICATIONS** Auth, pubs in Journalism & Mass Communication Quarterly, Newspaper Research Journal; co-auth, Pressing Issues; ed, History of Tennessee Newspapers, Tennessee, 96. **CONTACT ADDRESS** Dept of Communication, East Tennesee State Univ, PO Box 70717, Johnson City, TN, 37614-0717. **EMAIL** saucemaf@etsu.edu

HILLIARD, RAYMOND FRANCIS
PERSONAL Born 11/13/1943, Washington, DC, m, 1969, 1 child **DISCIPLINE** ENGLISH **EDUCATION** Univ MD, BA, 66; Univ Rochester, PhD, 76. **CAREER** From asst prof to assoc prof 76-91, prof eng, Univ Richmond, 91. **MEMBERSHIPS** MLA; Am Soc 18th Century Studies. **RESEARCH** Eighteenth-century Brit lit. **SELECTED PUBLICATIONS** Auth, Emma: Dancing without space to turn in, In: Probability, Time, and Space in Eighteenth-Century Literature, AMS Press, 78; Desire and the structure of eighteenth-century fiction, Vol 9, Studies In Eighteenth Cent Cult, 79; The redemption of fatherhood in The Vicar of Wakefield, Studies in Engl Lit, 83; Pamela: Autonomy, subordination, and the State of Childhood, Studies in Philol, 86; Clarissa and ritual cannibalism, PMLA, 90; Laughter echoing from mouth to mouth: Symbalic cannibalism and gener in Evelina, Eighteenth Cent Life, 93. **CONTACT ADDRESS** Dept of Eng, Univ of Richmond, Richmond, VA, 23173-0002. **EMAIL** rhilliar@richmond.edu

HILLIARD, STEPHEN SHORTIS
PERSONAL Born 06/20/1939, Framingham, MA **DISCIPLINE** ENGLISH **EDUCATION** Harvard Univ, AB, 61; Princeton Univ, MA, 64, PhD(English), 67. **CAREER** Asst prof, 64-71, assoc prof English, Univ Nebr, Lincoln, 71-; from assoc prof to prof English, 71-84. **MEMBERSHIPS** MLA. **RESEARCH** Renaissance literature; critical theory. **CONTACT ADDRESS** Dept of English, Univ of Nebraska, 303 Andrews Hall, Lincoln, NE, 68588-0333. **EMAIL** hilliard@unlinfo.unl.edu

HILLIGOSS, SUSAN
DISCIPLINE ENGLISH LITERATURE **EDUCATION** Univ Pa, PhD, 77. **CAREER** Dept Eng, Clemson Univ **RESEARCH** Professional communication; visual communication. **SELECTED PUBLICATIONS** Auth, Robert Coles in US Authors Series, Twayne, 97; co-ed, Literacy and Computers: The Complications of Teaching and Learning with Technology, MLA, 94. **CONTACT ADDRESS** Clemson Univ, 708 Strode, Clemson, SC, 29634. **EMAIL** hillgos@clemson.edu

HILT, MICHAEL
DISCIPLINE COMMUNICATIONS **EDUCATION** Univ Kans, BS, 81, MS, 86; Univ Nebr, PhD, 94. **CAREER** Adj prof, Washburn Univ, 81-82; news producer/dir: KSNT-TV, Topeka, Kans, 82-86; adj prof, Rockhurst Col, 87; news producer: KCTV, Kansas City, Mo, 86-88; assoc prof, 88-, grad fel, Univ Nebr, Omaha, 93-; consult, Cox Commun, Omaha, Nebr, 97-. **SELECTED PUBLICATIONS** Auth, Television News and the Elderly: Broadcast Managers' Attitudes Toward Older Adults, Garland Publ Inc, 97. **CONTACT ADDRESS** Univ Nebr, Omaha, Omaha, NE, 68182. **EMAIL** MHilt@cwis.unomaha.edu

HILTY, DEBORAH PACINI
PERSONAL Born 07/23/1941, Boston, MA, m, 1965, 3 children **DISCIPLINE** ENGLISH LANGUAGE & LITERATURE **EDUCATION** Vassar Col, AB, 63; Columbia Univ, MA, 65; Case Western Reserve Univ, PhD(English lit), 69. **CAREER** Instr English, Col Wooster, 65-67; asst prof, Bradley Univ, 69-70; asst prof English, 70-74, assoc prof English & educ, 74-80, prof English & Educ, Col Wooster, 80-, exec asst to pres, 76-, Secy of col & bd trustees, Col Wooster, 76-. **MEMBERSHIPS** MLA; NCTE; Milton Soc Am. **RESEARCH** Seventeenth century poetry; history of genres; American women writers; Milton and genre. **CONTACT ADDRESS** Off of the Secy, Col of Wooster, 1189 Beall Ave, Wooster, OH, 44691-2363. **EMAIL** dhilty@acs.wooster.edu

HINCHCLIFFE, PETER
DISCIPLINE ENGLISH LITERATURE **EDUCATION** Univ British Columbia, BA, 58; Univ Toronto, MA, 60; PhD, 67. **CAREER** Assoc prof **SELECTED PUBLICATIONS** Auth, To Keep the Memory of So Worthy a Friend: Ethel Wilson As an Elegist; Coming to Terms with Kipling: Puck of Pook's Hill, Rewards and Fairies and the Shape of Kipling's Imagination; Elegy and Epithalamium in In Memoriam; Fathers and Children in the Novels of Evelyn Waugh; Fidelity and Complicity in Kipling and Conrad: Sea Constables' and 'The Tale. **CONTACT ADDRESS** Dept of English, St. Jerome's Univ, Waterloo, ON, N2L 3G3. **EMAIL** pmhinch@watarts.uwaterloo.ca

HINDEN, MICHAEL CHARLES
PERSONAL Born 06/05/1941, New York, NY **DISCIPLINE** ENGLISH & AMERICAN LITERATURE **EDUCATION** Ohio Univ, AB, 63; Sorbonne, Degre Superieur, 62; Brown Univ, PhD(English), 71. **CAREER** Instr English, Brown Univ, 68-69; asst prof, 70-75, assoc prof English, Univ Wis-Madison, 75-85, prof, 85-, chmn, Integrated Liberal Studies Prog, 80-84, assoc dean intl studies, 92-, dir, Bradley Learning Community, 95-, Fulbright prof Am lit, Univ Bucharest, Romania, 75-76. **HONORS AND AWARDS** Kiekhofer Distinguished Teaching Award, Wis, 72. **MEMBERSHIPS** MLA; The Eugene O'Neill Soc (chmn & bd dirs, 82-). **RESEARCH** Modern drama; nature of tragedy; contemporary literature. **SELECTED PUBLICATIONS** Auth, Byrd Thou Never Wert: The Collected Poems and Post Cards of Emmett Byrd, Ten Speed Press, 80; Long Day's Journey into Night: Native Eloquence, Twayne, 90. **CONTACT ADDRESS** Dept of English, Univ Wisconsin, Madison, 600 North Park St, Madison, WI, 53706-1403. **EMAIL** hinden@macc.wisc.edu

HINDMAN, KATHLEEN BEHRENBRUCH
PERSONAL Born 09/22/1942, South Bend, IN, m, 1967, 7 children **DISCIPLINE** LITERATURE **EDUCATION** Valparaiso Univ, BA, 65; La State Univ, MA, 67; Pa State Univ, PhD(English), 80. **CAREER** Asst, La State Univ, 65-67, instr, 67-73, asst prof, 73-81; Assoc Prof, 81-94, PROF ENGLISH, MANSFIELD UNIV, 94-. **HONORS AND AWARDS** Honors Program at Valparaiso Univ; Sabbatticals, Spring 78, Fall 90, Fall 94; SSHE grant to attend NAWE Conf, March 95. **MEMBERSHIPS** English Asn of the Penn State Universities; Asn of Penn State Colleges and Universities; Asn of Lit Schol and Critics; Traditional Cosmology Soc. **RESEARCH** Graham Greene; the modern novel; the short story; curriculum development; mythology. **SELECTED PUBLICATIONS** Auth, Erratic Glints (poem), Modern Haiku, winter 70; Jack London's The Sea-Wolf: Naturalism with a spiritual bent, The Jack London Newsletter, 9-12/73; Graham Green, In: British Dramatists Since World War II, Bruccoli-Clark, summer 82; Graham Greene and the Medieval Morality, Proceedings: The 1988 Conference of the English Association of the Pennsylvania State Universities, WestChester Univ, Oct 14-15, 88; Graham Greene, Read More About It, Vol 3, Pierian Press, 89; The Technique of Comparison in Crane's The Monster, Proceedings: The 1993 Conference of the Pennsylvania Universities, Mansfield Univ, Oct 1-2, 93. **CONTACT ADDRESS** English Dept, Mansfield Univ, Belknap Hall, Mansfield, PA, 16933-1308. **EMAIL** khindman@mnsfld.edu

HINES, RANDY
DISCIPLINE COMMUNICATION STUDIES **EDUCATION** Kent State Univ, BA, MA; Tex Univ, PhD. **CAREER** Assoc prof, 91-. **MEMBERSHIPS** Public Rel Student Soc Am. **SELECTED PUBLICATIONS** Auth, pubs in Mid Atlantic Bulletin of the Newspaper Advertising Marketing Executives; Southern Newspaper Publishers Association Bulletin; Business Journal; ed, A History of Tennessee Newspapers. **CONTACT ADDRESS** Dept of Communication, East Tennesee State Univ, PO Box 70717, Johnson City, TN, 37614-0717. **EMAIL** saucemaf@etsu.edu

HINKEL, HOWARD
DISCIPLINE BRITISH ROMANTICISM **EDUCATION** Tulane Univ, PhD, 68. **CAREER** Assoc prof & dept ch; past cha, campus Comt Undergrad Educ & Fac Develop Commt; past dir, Lower Div Stud & Campus Writing Program. **HONORS AND AWARDS** Purple Chalk awd, 86. **RESEARCH** Blake and the prophetic tradition and on the 19th century epistemologies of poets, clerics, and naturalists. **SELECTED PUBLICATIONS** Publ op, British Romanticism. **CONTACT ADDRESS** Dept of English, Univ of Missouri-Columbia, 309 University Hall, Columbia, MO, 65211.

HINNANT, CHARLES HASKELL
DISCIPLINE RESTORATION AND EIGHTEENTH-CENTURY ENGLISH LITERATURE, CRITICAL THEORY, HIS **EDUCATION** Columbia Univ, PhD, 66. **CAREER** Prof; dir, Grad Stud & Catherine Paine Middlebush ch; ed bd, Stud 18th-Century Cult & Restoration:Stud Engl Cult, 1660-1700. **HONORS AND AWARDS** Univ Mo res fel, 94-95. **SELECTED PUBLICATIONS** Auth, The Poetry of Anne Finch: An Essay in Interpretation, Newark: Univ Del Press, 94; Steel for the Mind: Samuel Johnson and Critical Discourse, Newark: Univ Del Press, 94; Samuel Johnson: An Analysis, London: Macmillan; NY St Martin's Press, 88; Purity and Defilement in Gulliver's Travels, London: Macmillan; NY: St Martin's Press, 87; Thomas Hobbes: A Reference Guide, Boston: GK Hall & Co, 80; Thomas Hobbes, Boston: GK Hall & Co, 77; Pleasure and the Political Economy of Consumption in Restoration Comedy, Restoration, 19, 95; Augustan Semiosis, in Cutting Edges: Postmodern Essays on Eighteenth-Century Satire, Knoxville: Univ Tenn Press, 95; Windsor Forest in Historical Context, in Approaches to Teaching Pope's Poetry, NY: MLA Amer, 93; Johnson and the Limits of Biography: Teaching the Life of Savage, in Approaches to Teaching the Works of Samuel Johnson, Kolb NY: MLA Amer, 93; Feminism and Femininity: A Reconsideration of Anne Finch's 'Ardelia's Answer to Ephelia', 18th Century: Theory and Interpretation, 33, 92; Swift and the 'Conjectural Histories' of the Eighteenth Century: the Case of the Fourth Voyage, Stud 18th-Century Cult, 21, 91 & Song and Speech in Anne Finch's 'To the Nightingale, Stud Engl Lit, 31, 91. **CONTACT ADDRESS** Dept of English, Univ of Missouri-Columbia, 309 University Hall, Columbia, MO, 65211. **EMAIL** enghh@showme.missouri.edu

HINZ, EVELYN J.
PERSONAL Born 12/07/1938, Humboldt, SK, Canada **DISCIPLINE** LITERATURE **EDUCATION** Univ Sask, BA, 61, MA, 67; Univ Mass, PhD, 73. **CAREER** Writer/producer, CFQC-TV(Saskatoon), 63-65; instr, Univ Sask, 66-68; PROF ENGLISH, UNIV MANITOBA, 72-; authorized biographer Anais Nin, second lit executor, Anais Nin estate, 77-. **HONORS AND AWARDS** Gov Gen Medal Acad Proficiency, 57; Killam post-doctroal res fel, 73-75; William Riley Parker Prize (PMLA), 77; RH Inst Award Interdisc Schol, 79; Coun Eds Learned Jours Best Special Issue Award, 96; Best Grad Tchr Award, 97. **MEMBERSHIPS** MLA; Asn Can Univ Tchrs Eng; Hum Asn Can; Conf Eds Learned Jours (pres, 88-90). **RESEARCH** Anais Nin **SELECTED PUBLICATIONS** Auth, The Mirror and the Garden: Realism and Reality in the Writings of Anais Nin, 71, repr, 73; ed, A Woman Speaks: The Lectures, Seminars and Interviews of Anais Nin, 75, 78, 79; ed, The World of Anais Nin: Critical and Cultural Perspectives, 78; ed, Beyond Nationalism: The Canadian Literary Scene in Global Perspective, 81; ed, Death and Dying, 82; ed, For Better or Worse, Attitudes Towards Marriage in Literature, 85; ed, Literature and Altered States of Consciousness, 86; ed, Data and Acta: Aspects of Life-Writing, 87; ed, Troops versus Tropes: War and Literature, 90; ed, Diet and Discourse: Eating, Drinking and Literature, 91; ed, Idols of Otherness: The Rhetoric and Reality of Multiculturalism, 96; co-ed, The Definitive Edition of Roger Williams, A Key into the Language of America, 73; co-ed, Henry Miller's The World of Lawrence: A Passionate Appreciation, 80, 85. **CONTACT ADDRESS** Dept of English, Univ of Manitoba, Winnipeg, MB, R3T 2N2.

HIRCH, JOHN C.
DISCIPLINE ENGLISH LITERATURE **EDUCATION** Boston Col, BA; Lehigh Univ, MA, PhD. **CAREER** Eng Dept, Georgetown Univ **RESEARCH** Chaucer and Middle English literature; medieval spirituality; American literature of the 19th and early 20th century; medieval culture and gender criticism. **SELECTED PUBLICATIONS** Auth, The Boundaries of Faith, The Development and Transmission of Medieval Spirituality, 96; Sursum Corda, Teaching Urban Youth to Read, 91; The Revelations of Margery Kempe, Paramystical Practices in Late Medieval England, 89; Hope Emily Allen, Medieval Scholarship and Feminism, 88; Barlam and Iosaphat, A Middle English Life of Buddha, 86. **CONTACT ADDRESS** English Dept, Georgetown Univ, 37th and O St, Washington, DC, 20057.

HIROKAWA, RANDY Y.
PERSONAL Born 09/23/1953, HI, m, 1978, 3 children **DISCIPLINE** COMMUNICATION STUDIES **EDUCATION** Univ WA, PhD, 80. **CAREER** Asst prof, PA State Univ, 80-84; prof, Univ IA, 84-. **HONORS AND AWARDS** Burlington Northern Fac Achievement Award, Univ IA, 89. **MEMBERSHIPS** Nat Commun Asn. **RESEARCH** Group decision-making. **SELECTED PUBLICATIONS** Ed, with M S Poole, Communication and Group Decision-making, Sage, 1st ed, 86, 2nd ed, 96; auth, Functional Approaches to the Study of Group Communication: Even Good Notions Have Their Problems, Small Group Res, 25, 94; Received Facilitators and Inhibitors of Effectiveness in Organizational Work Teams, Management Commun Quart, 8, 95; with L Erbert and A Hurst, Communication and Group Decision-Making Effectiveness, in Hirokawa and Poole, eds, Communication and Group Decision-making, 2nd ed, Sage, 96; with D S Gouran, Functional Theory and Communication in Decision-making and Problem-solving Groups, in Hirokawa and Poole, eds, Communication and Group Decision-making, 2nd ed, Sage, 96; with M S Poole, Communication and Group Decision-making, in Hirokawa and Poole, eds, Communication and Group Decision-making, Sage, 96; with A J Salazar, L Erbert, and R J Ice, Small Group Communication, in M B Salwen and D W Stacks, eds, An Integrated Approach to Communication Theory and Research, LEA, 96; with A J Salazar, An Integrated Approach to Communication and Group Decision-making, in L R Frey and J K Barge, eds, Managing Group Life: Communication in Decision-making Groups, Houghton-Mifflin, 97; auth, A Rose is a Rose By Any Other Name, But How Interdisciplinary Are Multi-professional Health Care Teams?, in E Swanson and R J Bulger, eds, Redefining Education in Primary Care, AAHC, in press; numerous other articles and book chapters, with several more publications forthcoming. **CONTACT ADDRESS** Dept of Commun Studies, Univ of Iowa, 117 BCSB, Iowa City, IA, 52242. **EMAIL** randy-hirokawa@uiowa.edu

HIRSCH, BERNARD ALAN
PERSONAL Born 10/03/1944, Chicago, IL, m, 1971, 1 child **DISCIPLINE** ENGLISH **EDUCATION** Univ Ill, Urbana, BS, 67, AM, 68, PhD, 75. **CAREER** Instr English, Northern Ill Univ, 68-70; lectr, Univ Ill, Urbana, 75-76; Asst Prof, 76-80, assoc prof English, Univ Kans, 80-. **HONORS AND AWARDS** Univ Kans res grant, 78; Edward F. Grier Teaching Award, 91; Vice-Chancellor's Fel, 97-98. **MEMBERSHIPS** MLA; Byron Soc; Keats-Shelley Asn; Western Lit Asn; NAm Soc Study Romanticism. **RESEARCH** English romantic movement; native American literature and culture. **SELECTED PUBLICATIONS** Co-ed, A Return to Vision, 71 & 74, The Shadow Within, 73 & The Essay: Structure and Purpose, 75, Houghton; auth, A want of that true theory: Julian and Maddalo as dramatic monologue, Studies Romanticism, winter 78; The Erosion of the Narrator's World View in Childe Harold's Pilgrimage, I-II, Mod Lang Quart, 12/81; Self-Hatred and Spritual Corruption in House Made of Dawn, Western Am Lit, 2/83; co-ed, The Essay: Readings for the Writing Process, Houghton Mifflin, 86; auth, The Telling Which Continues: Oral Tradition and the Written Word in Leslie Marmon Silko's Storyteller, Am Indian Quart, Winter 88, reprinted in Yellow Woman: Leslie Marmon Silko, Rutgers Univ Press, 93; Byron's Poetic Journal: Teaching Childe Harold's Pilgrimage, in Approaches to Teaching Byron's Poetry, MLA, 91. **CONTACT ADDRESS** Dept of English, Univ of Kans, Lawrence, KS, 66045-2115. **EMAIL** hirsch@falcon.cc.ukans.edu

HIRSCH, DAVID HARRY
PERSONAL Born 04/06/1930, Brooklyn, NY, m, 1954, 2 children **DISCIPLINE** ENGLISH & AMERICAN LITERATURE **EDUCATION** NY Univ, BA, 51, MA, 53. **CAREER** From instr to prof English, 61-78, NICHOLAS BROWN PROF ORATORY & BELLES LETTRES IN ENGLISH & CHMN DEPT ENGLISH, BROWN UNIV, 78-, Vis lectr, Bar-Ilan Univ, Israel, 66-67; Soc Relig Higher Educ fel, 71-72. **MEMBERSHIPS** MLA. **RESEARCH** Nineteenth century English and American literature; Poe; Melville; the Bible in English literature. **SELECTED PUBLICATIONS** Auth, Forgone Conclusions, Against Apocalyptic History, Criticism, Vol 0037, 95; Testimony--Crises of Witnessing in Literature, Psychoanalysis, and History, Holocaust Genocide Studies, Vol 0009, 95. **CONTACT ADDRESS** Dept of English, Brown Univ, 1 Prospect St, Providence, RI, 02912-9127.

HIRSCH, GORDON D.
PERSONAL Born 05/15/1943, Norwich, NY, m, 1972 **DISCIPLINE** ENGLISH **EDUCATION** Cornell Univ, AB, 65; Univ Calif, Berkeley, MA, 67, PhD(English), 71. **CAREER** From Asst Prof to Assoc Prof, 70-88, PROF ENGLISH, UNIV MINN, MINNEAPOLIS, 88-. **MEMBERSHIPS** MLA; Midwest Victorian Studies Asn. **RESEARCH** Victorian literature; the British novel; psychoanalytic literary criticism. **SELECTED PUBLICATIONS** Auth, Tennyson's Commedia, Victorian Poetry, 70; Charles Dickens' nurse's stories, Psychoanal Rev, 75; The mysteries in Bleak House: a psychoanalytic study, Dickens Studies Ann, 75; The monster was a lady: on the psychology of Mary Shelley's Frankenstein, Hartford Studies in Lit, 75; Organic imagery and the psychology of Mill's On Liberty, Mill News Lett, 75; The Laurentian double: images of D H Lawrence in the stories, D H Lawrence Rev, 77; Mr Pickwick's impotence, The Sphinx, 79; A psychoanalytic rereading of David Copperfield, Victorian Newslett, 80; Double Binds and Schizophrenogenic Conversations: Readings in Three Middle Chapters of Alice in Wonderland, Denver Quart, 84; History Writing in Carlyle's Past and Present, Prose Studies, 84; co-ed, Dr. Jekyll and Mr. Hyde After One Hundred Years, Univ Chicago Press, 88; auth, Shame, Pride, and Prejudice, Mosaic, 92; Robert Louis Stevenson, In: Dictionary of Literary Biography: British Travel Writers 1876-1909, 97. **CONTACT ADDRESS** Dept of English, Univ of Minn, 207 Church St SE, Minneapolis, MN, 55455-0156. **EMAIL** hirsc002@tc.umn.edu

HIRSCH, JAMES
PERSONAL Born 07/12/1946, Brooklyn, NY, m, 1969, 2 children **DISCIPLINE** ENGLISH **EDUCATION** Cornell Univ, BA (cum laude), 68; Univ Washington, PhD, 78. **CAREER** Asst prof English, 80-84, assoc prof English, 84-90, Univ Hawaii; scholar-in-residence, Oregon Shakespearean Festival, Ashland, 86; assoc prof English, Georgia State Univ, 90-. **HONORS AND AWARDS** Distinguished Honors Professor, Georgia State Univ, 98. **MEMBERSHIPS** Modern Language Assn; Shakespeare of America. **RESEARCH** Shakespeare; English Renaissance literature; theatrical history. **SELECTED PUBLICATIONS** Auth, "Morgann Greenblatt and Audience Response," Studies in the Literary Imagination, v 26, 93; auth, "Shakespeare and the History of Soliloquies," Modern Language Quarterly, v 58, 97; ed, "Cynicism and the Futility of Art in Volpone," New Perspectives o **CONTACT ADDRESS** Dept of English, Georgia State Univ, University Plaza, Atlanta, GA, 30303-3083. **EMAIL** jhirsh@gsu.edu

HIRSCH, JULIA
PERSONAL Born 01/01/1938, Antwerp, Belgium, 2 children **DISCIPLINE** ENGLISH **EDUCATION** Barnard Col, Columbia, Univ, BA, 59, MA, 60, PhD(English), 64. **CAREER** Lectr English & freshman adv, Barnard Col, Columbia Univ, 62-64; from instr to asst prof English, 64-73, ASSOC PROF ENGLISH, BROOKLYN COL, 73-, Am Coun Learned Soc study fel, 67-68; vis sr lectr English lit, Haifa Univ, 70-71; Nat Endowment Humanities fel, 77-78. **RESEARCH** History of nationalism; translation theory; medieval iconography. **SELECTED PUBLICATIONS** Auth, Grandmothers, Mothers, and Daughters--Oral Histories of 3 Generations of Ethnic Women, J Am Ethnic Hist, Vol 0013, 94. **CONTACT ADDRESS** Dept of English, Brooklyn Col, CUNY, 2901 Bedford Ave, Brooklyn, NY, 11210-2813.

HIRSH, JAMES
PERSONAL Born 07/12/1946, Brooklyn, NY, m, 1969, 2 children **DISCIPLINE** ENGLISH **EDUCATION** Cornell Univ, BA (cum laude), 68; Univ WA, PhD, 78. **CAREER** Asst prof, English, Univ HI, 80-84; Scholar-in-residence, OR Shakespearean Festival, Ashland, 86; assoc prof, English, Univ HI, 84-90; ASSOC PROF, ENGLISH, GA STATE UNIV, 90-. **HONORS AND AWARDS** GA State Univ Distinguished Honors Prof, 98. **MEMBERSHIPS** Modern Lang Asn; Shakespeare Asn of Am. **RESEARCH** Shakespeare; English Renaissance lit; theatrical hist. **SELECTED PUBLICATIONS** Auth, The Structure of Shakespearean Scenes, Yale Univ Press, 81; Othello and Perception, Othello, New Perspectives, ed Virginia Mason Vaughan and Kent Cartwright, Fairleigh Dickinson Univ Press, 91, paperback, 96, also in Shakespearean Criticism Yearbook 1991: A Selection of the Year's Most Noteworthy Studies, ed Ralph Berry, et al, Gale, 93; Morgann, Greenblatt, and Audience Response, Studies in the Literary Imagination 26, 93; ed, English Renaissance Drama and Audience Response, Studies in the Literary Imagination, Vol 26, no 1, spring 93; ed, New Perspectives on Ben Jonson, Fairleigh Dickinson Univ Press, 97; auth, Shakespeare and the History of Soliloquies, Modern Lang Quart 58, 97; Attributing a Funeral Elegy, a forum with Charles W. Hieatt, A. Kent Hieatt, Sidney Thomas, and Donald W. Foster, PMLA 112, 97. **CONTACT ADDRESS** Dept of English, Georgia State Univ, Atlanta, GA, 30303-3083. **EMAIL** jhirsh@gsu.edu

HIRSH, JOHN CAMPION
PERSONAL Born 06/26/1944, Hartford, CT **DISCIPLINE** MEDIEVAL & AMERICAN LITERATURE **EDUCATION** Boston Col, AB, 65; Lehigh Univ, MA, 66, PhD(English), 70. **CAREER** Instr, Lehigh Univ, 69-70; from asst prof to assoc prof, 70-84, PROF ENGLISH, GEORGETOWN UNIV, 84-. **HONORS AND AWARDS** Am Coun Learned Soc fel, 74-75. **MEMBERSHIPS** Medieval Acad Am; Am Studies Asn; Arthurian Soc; Int Reading Asn. **RESEARCH** Chaucer and Middle English literature; 19th and 20th century American literature; medieval Latin literature. **SELECTED PUBLICATIONS** Auth, Western Manuscripts 12-16 Centuries in Lehigh Univ, 70; Medieval Manuscripts in Lehigh University Libraries. Western Manuscripts of the Twelfth through the Sixteenth Centuries in Lehigh University Libraries, Lehigh Univ, 70; Barlam and Iosaphat. A Middle English Life of Buddha, Edited from MS. Peterhouse 257, Early English Text Soc, OS 290, Oxford Univ Press, 86; Hope Emily Allen. Medieval Scholarship and Feminism, Pilgrim Books, 88; The Revelations of Margery Kemp. Paramystical Practices in Late Medieval England, Medieval and Renaissance Authors Series, Vol 10, E.J. Brill, 89; Sursum Corda. Teaching Urban Youth to Read, Georgetown Univ Press, 91; The Boundaries of Faith. The Development and Transmission of Medieval Spirituality, Studies in the Hist of Christian Thought, Vol LXVII, E.J. Brill, 96; author of several journal articles and book contributions. **CONTACT ADDRESS** English Dept, Georgetown Univ, PO Box 571131, Washington, DC, 20057-1131. **EMAIL** hirsh@gusun.georgetown.edu

HOBSON, FRED COLBY, JR.
PERSONAL Born 04/23/1943, Winston-Salem, NC, d, 1 child **DISCIPLINE** ENGLISH **EDUCATION** Univ North Carolina, Chapel Hill, AB, English, 65, PhD, English, 72; Duke Univ, MA, history, 67. **CAREER** Prof of English, Univ of Ala, 72-86; prof of English, La State Univ, co-editor, Southern Review, 86-89; Lineberger Prof of English, Univ North Carolina, Chapel Hill, co-editor, Southern Literary Jour, 89-. **HONORS AND AWARDS** Jules F. Landry Award, for Tell About the South: A Southern Rage to Explain, 83; Lillian Smith Award, for South-Watching, 84; fellowship, Natl Endowment for the Humanities; fellowship, Natl Humanities Center. **MEMBERSHIPS** Modern Language Assn. **RESEARCH** American literature and intellectual history; biography; autobiography. **SELECTED PUBLICATIONS** Auth, Mencken: A Life, 94; co-editor, The Literature of the American South: A Norton Anthology, 97; auth, "Making Biography Out of Mencken," in Writing Lives: American Biography and Autobiography, 98; "The Early Wolfe: Realist and Satirist," Thomas Wolfe Review, fall 97; foreword to Southern Writers, 97; "Of Canons and Cultural Wars," in The Future of Southern Letters, 96; "Surveyors and Boundaries: Southern Literature and Literary Scholarship After Mid-Century," Southern Review, Autumn, 91. **CONTACT ADDRESS** Dept of English, Univ North Carolina, Chapel Hill, CB 3520, Chapel Hill, NC, 27599-3520. **EMAIL** fhobson@email.unc.edu

HOCHMAN, WILL
DISCIPLINE CREATIVE WRITING, COMPOSITION, ADVANCED COMPOSITION, SALINGER SEMINAR, INDE **EDUCATION** Hobart Col, BA, 74; Univ MT, MFA, 76; NY Univ, PhD, 94. **CAREER** Asst prof & dir, Writing, Univ of Southern CO. **HONORS AND AWARDS** Created, USC's 1st comput writing classroom. **RESEARCH** Writing; criticism; mod Am lit; computers and writing; writing centers; tchg teachers. **SELECTED PUBLICATIONS** Auth, Stranger Within, Boynton-Cook, 98; publ, Terminal Thinking; ed, War, Lit & the Arts. **CONTACT ADDRESS** Dept of Eng, Univ of Southern Colorado, 2200 Bonforte Blvd, Pueblo, CO, 81001-4901. **EMAIL** hochman@meteor.uscolo.edu

HOCKS, RICHARD
PERSONAL Born 06/30/1936, Cincinnati, OH, m, 1957, 4 children **DISCIPLINE** ENGLISH **EDUCATION** Univ NC, PhD, 67. **CAREER** Prof & Catherine Paine Middlebush prof Humanities at Mizzou. **HONORS AND AWARDS** Finalist, Nat Bk awd; Purple Chalk awd & fac alumni awd. **SELECTED PUBLICATIONS** Auth, Henry James & Pragmatistic Thought, NC, 74 & Henry James: A Study of the Short Fiction, Twayne '90; co-ed, Norton critical ed of The Wings of the Dove. **CONTACT ADDRESS** Dept of English, Univ of Missouri-Columbia, 309 University Hall, Columbia, MO, 65211.

HODGDON, BARBARA COVINGTON
PERSONAL Born 10/05/1932, Rochester, NY, 4 children **DISCIPLINE** ENGLISH LITERATURE, DRAMA **EDUCATION** Wellesley Col, BA, 53; Univ NH, MA, 70, PhD(English), 74. **CAREER** From asst prof to prof English, 74-81, Drake Univ, 80-, contrib ed, Shakespeare Newslett, 71-81, dir honor prog, 84-86, adv bd, Shakespeare on Film Newsl, 89-93; Shakespeare Interactive Hypermedia Archive Proj, 91-. **HONORS AND AWARDS** Madelyn Levitt Outstanding Teacher Award, 94; Trustee, Shakespeare Assoc. **MEMBERSHIPS** Shakespeare Asn Am; MLA; Midwest Mod Lang Asn. **RESEARCH** Shakespeare; drama in performance; film. **SELECTED PUBLICATIONS** Auth, The Mirror Up to Nature: Notes on Grigori Kozintsev's Hamlet, Comp Drama, Winter 75-76; Shakespeare's Directorial Eye, In: More Than Words Can Witness: Essays on Visual and Non-Verbal Enactment in Shakespeare, assoc Univ Presses, 78; In Search of the Performance Present, In: Shakespeare: The Theatrical Dimension, AMS Press, 78; Filming a Tragic Poem: Kozintsev's King Lear, Lit Film Quart, Spring 78; Landscape Viewed and Re-viewed: Antonioni's The Passenger, Fla State Univ, 78; Falstaff: History and his story, Iowa State J Res, 2/79; Of time and the arrow: A reading of Kurosawa's Throne of Blood, Univ Dayton Rev, Winter 79-80; Two King Lears: Un-Covering the film text, Lit/Film Quart, 82; Henry IV, Part One: Texts and Contexts, Bedford-St Martin's, 97; The Shakespeare Trade: Performances and Appropriations, Univ of Penn Press, 98; Making it New: Katie Mitchell Refashions Shakespeare-History, in Transforming Shakespeare: Twentieth-Century Women's Re-visions, ed, Marianne Novy, St Martin's, 99. **CONTACT ADDRESS** Dept of English, Drake Univ, 2507 University Ave, Des Moines, IA, 50311-4505. **EMAIL** barbara.hodgdon@drake.edu

HODGES, LOUIS WENDELL
PERSONAL Born 01/24/1933, Eupora, MS, m, 1954, 2 children **DISCIPLINE** RELIGION & JOURNALISM **EDUCATION** Millsaps Col, BA, 54; Duke Univ, BD, 57, PhD, 60. **CAREER** From asst prof to assoc prof, 60-68, prof relig, 68-97, dir ethics, 74-97, Knight Prof Journalism, 97-, Univ Prog Soc & Professions, Washington & Lee Univ. **MEMBERSHIPS** Am Soc Christian Ethics. **RESEARCH** Theology of race relations; theology and ethics, ethics and the press. **SELECTED PUBLICATIONS** Art, Christian Ethics and Non-Violence, Relig in Life, 62; art, The Roots of Prejudice, Christian Advocate, 62; coauth, The Christian and His Decisions, Abingdon, 69. **CONTACT ADDRESS** Dept of Journalism, Washington & Lee Univ, Lexington, VA, 24450. **EMAIL** hodgesl@wlu.edu

HODGINS, JACK S.
PERSONAL Born 10/03/1938, Comox, BC, Canada **DISCIPLINE** ENGLISH/WRITING **EDUCATION** Univ BC, BEd, 61, DLitt(hon), 95. **CAREER** High sch tchr, Nanaimo, BC, 61-80; writer-in-residence, Simon Fraser Univ, 77; writer-in-residence, 79, vis prof, Univ Ottawa, 81-83; vis prof, 83-85, PROF, UNIV VICTORIA, 85-. **HONORS AND AWARDS** Pres Medal, Univ Western Ont, 73; Eaton's BC Bk Award, 77; Gov Gen Award, 80; Can-Australia Award, 86. **MEMBERSHIPS** Writers' Union Can; Int PEN. **SELECTED PUBLICATIONS** Auth, The Barclay Family Theatre, 81; auth, Innocent Cities, 90; auth, A Passion for Narrative, 93; auth, The Macken Charm, 95; ed, The Frontier Experience, 75; ed, The West Coast Experience, 76. **CONTACT ADDRESS** Dept of Writing, Univ of Victoria, PO Box 1700, Victoria, BC, V8W 2Y2.

HOEFEL, ROSEANNE
DISCIPLINE AMERICAN LITERATURES, RHETORIC, POETRY AND WOMEN'S STUDIES **EDUCATION** Ohio State Univ, PhD. **CAREER** Assoc prof, Alma Col. **HONORS AND AWARDS** Barlow Award for Fac Excellence. **SELECTED PUBLICATIONS** Her articles have appeared in Stud in

Short Fiction, Emily Dickinson J, Transformations, Phoebe, Feminisms and The Women's Stud Rev. **CONTACT ADDRESS** Alma Col, Alma, MI, 48801.

HOENIGER, F. DAVID
PERSONAL Born 04/25/1921, Goerlitz, Germany, m, 1957, 2 children **DISCIPLINE** ENGLISH **EDUCATION** Univ Toronto, BA, 46, MA, 48; Univ London, PhD(English), 54. **CAREER** Lectr English, Univ Sask, 46-47; lectr, 48-51 & 53-55, from asst prof to assoc prof, 55-63, dir Ctr Reformation & Renaissance Studies, 64-69, PROF ENGLISH, VICTORIA COL, UNIV TORONTO, 63-, Humanities Res Coun Can fel, 56-57; Folger Shakespeare Libr fels, 59 & 63; Guggenheim fel, 64-65; Can Coun fel, 73-74. **MEMBERSHIPS** Renaissance Soc Am; Can Soc Renaissance Studies (pres, 76-78). **RESEARCH** Shakespeare; Renaissance biology and medicine; drama, 1500-1700. **SELECTED PUBLICATIONS** Auth, The Medical Mind of Shakespeare, Renaissance Reformation, Vol 0016, 92; Medieval and Early-Renaissance Medicine--An Introduction to Knowledge and Practice, Shakespeare Quarterly, Vol 0046, 95; Shakespeare, Harsnett, and the Devils of Denham, Shakespeare Quarterly, Vol 0046, 95; The Renaissance Print--1470-1550, ISIS, Vol 0086, 95. **CONTACT ADDRESS** Dept of English, Univ Toronto, Toronto, ON, M5S 1K7.

HOENIGER, FREDERICK J.D.
PERSONAL Born 04/25/1921, Goerlitz, Germany **DISCIPLINE** LITERATURE **EDUCATION** Univ Toronto, Victoria Col, BA, 46, MA, 48; Univ London, PhD, 54. **CAREER** Lectr, Univ Sask, 46-47; lectr to prof, 48-86, ch Eng, 69-72, dir, ctr Reformation & Renaissance stud, 64-69, 75-79, PROF EMER, VICTORIA COL, UNIV TORONTO. **HONORS AND AWARDS** Brit Coun scholar, 51-53; Guggenheim fel, 64-65. **MEMBERSHIPS** Can Soc Renaissance Stud; Int Shakespeare Asn. **SELECTED PUBLICATIONS** Auth, Medicine and Shakespeare in the English Renaissance, 92; coauth, A Gathering of Flowers from Shakespeare, 97; gen ed, The Revels Plays, 71-85. **CONTACT ADDRESS** Victoria Col, Univ of Toronto, Toronto, ON, M5S 1K7.

HOFFMAN, DANIEL
PERSONAL Born 04/03/1923, New York, NY, m, 1948, 2 children **DISCIPLINE** ENGLISH **EDUCATION** Columbia Col, AB, 47; Columbia Univ, AM, 49, PhD, 56. **CAREER** Lectr English, Columbia Univ, 47-48 & Rutgers Univ, 48-50; instr, Temple Univ, 50-52 & Columbia Univ, 52-56; vis prof Am lit & hist, Univ Dijon, 56-57; from asst prof to assoc prof English lit, Swarthmore Col, 57-66; PROF ENGLISH, UNIV PA, 66-, POET IN RESIDENCE, 78-, Fel sch lett, Ind Univ, 59; Am Coun Learned Soc res fels, 61-62 & 66-67; Elliston lectr poetry, Univ Cincinnati, 64; lectr, Sixth Int Sch Yeats Studies, Sligo, Ireland: 65; Ingram Merrill Found poetry grant, 71-72; chancellor, Acad Am Poets, 72-; Consult poetry, Libr of Congr, 73-74; Nat Endowment Humanities res fel, 75-76; coun, Auth Guild, 81- **HONORS AND AWARDS** Award, Yale Ser of Younger Poets, 53; Clarke F Ansley Award, 57; Medal excellence, Columbia Univ, 64; Award, Nat Inst Arts & Lett, 67; Poetry Mem Medal, Hungarian PEN, 80. **MEMBERSHIPS** MLA; PEN Club Am; English Inst; Auth Guild. **RESEARCH** Modern poetry, American literature. **SELECTED PUBLICATIONS** Auth, Bob, Hudson Rev, Vol 0047, 94; Blizzard, Hudson Rev, Vol 0047, 94; Scott Nearings Ninety-Eighth Year, Georgia Rev, Vol 0048, 94. **CONTACT ADDRESS** Dept of English, Univ of Pa, Philadelphia, PA, 19174.

HOFFMAN, MICHAEL JEROME
PERSONAL Born 03/31/1939, Philadelphia, PA, m, 1988, 4 children **DISCIPLINE** ENGLISH **EDUCATION** Univ Pa, AB, 59, MA, 60, PhD(English), 63. **CAREER** Instr English, Washington Col, 62-64; from instr to asst prof, Univ Pa, 64-67; from asst prof to assoc prof, 67-75, PROF ENGLISH, UNIV CALIF, DAVIS, 75-; ASST VCHANCELLOR, ACAD AFFAIRS, 76-83, Vis prof English, Sorbonne, 72-73; **HONORS AND AWARDS** USAR, 57-61; Nat Defense Ed Act fel, 59-62. **MEMBERSHIPS** MLA; Am Studies Asn; Am Lit Group; MLA. **RESEARCH** Nineteenth and 20th century American literature; modern fiction; modernism. **SELECTED PUBLICATIONS** Auth, The Development of Abstractionism in the Writings of Gertrude Stein, Univ Pa, 65; The Buddy System (novel), Holt, 71; The Subversive Vision: American Romanticism in Literature, Kennikat, 73; Themes, Topics, Criticism, Am Lit Scholar, 73-; Gertrude Stein, Twayne, 76; auth, Critical Essays on Gertrude Stein, 86; auth, Essentials of the Theory of Fiction, 88, rev, 96; auth, Critical Essays on American Modernism, 92. **CONTACT ADDRESS** Dept of English, Univ Calif Davis, Davis, CA, 95616-5200.

HOFFMAN, TYLER B.
DISCIPLINE 19TH- AND 20TH-CENTURY AMERICAN LITERATURE AND CULTURE, POETRY, AND POETICS **EDUCATION** Univ Va, PhD. **CAREER** Instr, Rutgers, State Univ NJ, Camden Col of Arts and Sci; poetry reviewer, South Atlantic Rev. **RESEARCH** The rhetoric of Robert Frost. **SELECTED PUBLICATIONS** Auth, Emily Dickinson and the Limit of War, in The Emily Dickinson J; contribu, Robert Frost Encyclopedia. **CONTACT ADDRESS** Rutgers, State Univ NJ, Camden Col of Arts and Sci, New Brunswick, NJ, 08903-2101. **EMAIL** tbhlhh@crab.rutgers.edu

HOFFMANN, JOYCE
DISCIPLINE JOURNALISM **EDUCATION** NY Univ, PhD. **CAREER** Engl, Old Dominion Univ. **HONORS AND AWARDS** Coordr, Journalism Emphasis. **RESEARCH** Reporting; media law and ethics; Vietnam & the press. **SELECTED PUBLICATIONS** Areas: Theodore H. White and Journalism as Illusion. **CONTACT ADDRESS** Old Dominion Univ, 4100 Powhatan Ave, BAL 313, Norfolk, VA, 23058. **EMAIL** JHoffman@odu.edu

HOFFPAUIR, RICHARD
PERSONAL Born 10/08/1942, Bell, CA, m, 1970 **DISCIPLINE** ENGLISH LITERATURE **EDUCATION** Univ Calif, Berkeley, BA, 65, MA, 67; Univ London, PhD(English), 69. **CAREER** Asst prof, 69-76, ASSOC PROF ENGLISH, UNIV ALTA, 76- **MEMBERSHIPS** Can Asn Univ Teachers; Asn Can Univ Teachers English. **RESEARCH** Poetic tradition, 18th to 20th centuries; Romantic idology; literary criticism. **SELECTED PUBLICATIONS** Auth, The Trivial Sublime--Theology and American Poetics, Univ Toronto Quarterly, Vol 0063, 93; Strategies of Knowing--The 'Proof' Sonnets of Yvor Winters, English Studies Can, Vol 0023, 97. **CONTACT ADDRESS** Dept of English, Univ of Alta, Edmonton, AB, T6G 2E1.

HOGAN, J. MICHAEL
PERSONAL Born 09/13/1953, Rapid City, SD **DISCIPLINE** COMMUNICATION **EDUCATION** Univ of Wis, Madison, PhD. **CAREER** Asst prof, Univ of Va, 81-86; Assoc prof, Ind Univ. **HONORS AND AWARDS** Winians-Wichelns Award for Distinguished Scholar in Rhet & Public Address. **MEMBERSHIPS** Nat Commun Assoc. **RESEARCH** Campaigns & social movements; public opinion & polling. **SELECTED PUBLICATIONS** Co-auth, Polling on the Issues: Public Opinion and the Nuclear Freeze, Public Opinion Quart, vol 55, 534-69, 91; auth, The Nuclear Freeze Campaign: Rhetoric and Foreign Policy in the Telepolitical Age, Mich State Univ Press, 94; auth, Eisenhower and Open Skies: A Case Study in Psychological Warfare, Eisenhower's War of Words: Rhetoric & Leadership, Mich State Univ Press, 94; co-auth, Woodrow Wilson, US Presidents as Orators: A Bio-Critical Sourcebook, Greenwood Press, 95; Demonization, Public Opinion, and the Gulf War, Argumentation and Values: Proceedings of the Ninth SCA/AFA Conf on Argumentation, Spch Commun Assoc, 96; co-auth, Defining the Enemy in Revolutionary America: From the Rhetoric of Protest to the Rhetoric of War, Southern Commun J, vol 61, 277-88, 96; Panama and the Panama Canal, The Encycl of US Foreign Rels, 97; auth, George Gallup and the Rhetoric of Scientific Democracy, Commun Monographs, vol 64, 161-79, 6/97; Ed, Rhetoric and Community: Studies in Unity and Fragmentation, Univ SC Press, 98. **CONTACT ADDRESS** Dept of Spch Commun, Pennsylvania State Univ, 234 Sparks Bldg, Univ Pk, PA, 16802-5201. **EMAIL** jmh32@psu.edu

HOGAN, ROBERT
PERSONAL Born 05/29/1930, Boonville, MO, m, 1950, 5 children **DISCIPLINE** ENGLISH **EDUCATION** Univ Mo, BA, 53, MA, 54, PhD(English), 56. **CAREER** Instr English, Univ Mo, 54-56 & Ohio Univ, 56-58; from instr to asst prof, Purdue Univ, 58-63; from asst prof to prof, Univ Calif, Davis, 63-70; PROF ENGLISH, UNIV DEL, 70-, Guggenheim fel, 61-62; vis prof Univ Rochester, 62-63; Fulbright vis prof, Univ Col, Dublin, 67-68; ed, J Irish Lit, 72- **RESEARCH** Anglo-Irish literature; modern drama. **SELECTED PUBLICATIONS** Auth, The Brave Timidity of Murray, Irish Univ Rev, Vol 0026, 96. **CONTACT ADDRESS** Dept of English, Univ of Del, Newark, DE, 19711.

HOGGARD, JAMES MARTIN
PERSONAL Born 06/21/1941, Wichita Falls, TX, m, 1976, 2 children **DISCIPLINE** ENGLISH; CREATIVE WRITING **EDUCATION** Southern Methodist Univ, BA, 63; Univ Kans, MA, 65. **CAREER** From instr to assoc prof, 66-77, PROF ENGLISH, MIDWESTERN STATE UNIV, 77-. **HONORS AND AWARDS** Hardin Prof of the Year, 77; NEA Creative Writing Fel, 81; TIL Short Story Award, 89; McMurty Dist Prof of English, 97. **MEMBERSHIPS** AAUP; SCent MLA; ALTA; TACWT; TIL. **RESEARCH** Modern literature; tragedy and comedy. **SELECTED PUBLICATIONS** Auth, Mesquite, Southwest Rev, spring 69; But the daddy doesn't get to cry, Redbook Mag, 6/72; contribr, The New Breed, Prickly Pear, 73; Tragedy as mediation, Southwest Rev, summer 75; auth, No accounting shall be asked, Southwest Rev, summer 76; Eyesigns: Poems, Trilobite Press, 77; Trotter Ross: Novel, Thorp Springs Press, 81; The Shaper Poems, Cedarshouse Press, 83; Two Gulls, One Hawk: Poems, 83; Elevator Man: Nonfiction, 83; Breaking an Indelicate Statue: Poems, 86; The Art of Dying: Translations, 88; Love Breaks: Translations, 91; Chronicle of My Worst Years: Translations, 94; Riding the Wind & Other Tales, 97; Alone Against the Sea: Translations, 98. **CONTACT ADDRESS** Dept of English, Midwestern State Univ, 3410 Taft Blvd, Wichita Falls, TX, 76308-2096. **EMAIL** fhoggardj@nexus.mwsu.edu

HOGLE, JERROLD EDWIN
PERSONAL Born 05/15/1948, Los Angeles, CA, m, 1970, 2 children **DISCIPLINE** ENGLISH LITERATURE **EDUCATION** Univ Calif, Irvine, AB, 70; Harvard Univ, MA, 71, PhD(English), 74. **CAREER** Asst prof, 74-80, assoc prof English, Univ Az, 80-89; prof English, Univ Az, 89-; assoc dean, coll of humanities, Univ Az, 90-93; Univ Distinguished Prof, Univ Az, 96-; Chair of the Faculty, Univ Az, 97-. **HONORS AND AWARDS** Burlington Northern Foundation Faculty Achievement Award, 88-89; Guggenheim Fellowship, 89-90; Mellon/Huntington Fellowship, 90; President, International Gothic Assoc, 95-97. **MEMBERSHIPS** MLA; NASSR; Keats-Shelley Assoc; International Gothic Assoc. **RESEARCH** Romantic literature; literary theory; 18th and 19th century novels; The Gothic. **SELECTED PUBLICATIONS** Shelley's Process, Oxford U P, 88; coed, Evaluating Shelley, Edinburgh, 96; articles in major essay collections and journals. **CONTACT ADDRESS** Dept of English, Univ of Ariz, PO Box 210067, Tucson, AZ, 85721-0067. **EMAIL** hogle@u.arizona.edu

HOLBEIN, WOODROW LEE
PERSONAL Born 01/01/1929, Gallipolis, OH, m, 1956, 2 children **DISCIPLINE** ENGLISH & AMERICAN LITERATURE **EDUCATION** Baldwin-Wallace Col, AB, 53; Western Reserve Univ, MA, 54. **CAREER** Instr English, Marshall Univ, 55-56 & Bethany Col, 56-57; asst prof, 57-68, assoc prof English, The Citadel, 68- **MEMBERSHIPS** S Atlantic MLA; Shakespeare Asn Am; Southeast Renaissance Conf. **RESEARCH** Shakespeare; American stage history; Renaissance. **CONTACT ADDRESS** Dept of English, The Citadel, 171 Moultrie St, Charleston, SC, 29409-0002.

HOLDEN, JONATHAN
PERSONAL Born 07/18/1941, Morristown, NJ, m, 1997, 2 children **DISCIPLINE** ENGLISH **EDUCATION** Oberlin Col, AB, 63; San Francisco State Col, MA, 70; Univ of Colorado, PhD, 74. **CAREER** Instr, Stephens Col, 74-77; PROF, 77-88, UNIV DISTINGUISHED PROF, KAN STATE UNIV,88-. **HONORS AND AWARDS** NEA Creative Writing Fel, 75 & 85; Devins Award, 72; Juniper Prize, 85; AWP Award, 83; Vassar Miller Prize, 95; Vassar Miller Prize in Poetry. **MEMBERSHIPS** Associated Writing Programs. **RESEARCH** Poetry; criticism; creative non-fiction. **SELECTED PUBLICATIONS** Auth, Landscapes of the Self: The Development of Richard Hugo's Poetry, Assoc Fac Press, 86; auth, Against Paradise, Univ of Utah Press, 90; auth, Jonathan Holden, Conversation, Initiation, Delight, 91; auth, The Fate of American Poetry, Univ of Ga Press, 91; auth, American Gothic, Univ of Ga Press, 92; auth, Brilliant Kids, Univ of Utah Press, 92; auth, The Sublime, univ of North Tx Press, 95; auth, Guns and Boyhood in America: A Memoir of Growing Up in the Fifities, Univ of Mich Press, 97; auth, Ur-Math, State St Press, 97. **CONTACT ADDRESS** Dept of English, Kansas State Univ, Manhattan, KS, 66506. **EMAIL** jonhold@ksu.edu

HOLDITCH, WILLIAM KENNETH
PERSONAL Born 09/18/1933, Ecru, MS **DISCIPLINE** AMERICAN LITERATURE **EDUCATION** Southwestern at Memphis, BA, 55; Univ Miss, MA, 57, PhD, 61. **CAREER** Asst, Univ Miss, 55-56, instr, 57-59; from instr to asst prof English, Christian Bros Col, Tenn, 61-65; asst prof, 65-72, ASSOC PROF ENGLISH, LA STATE UNIV, NEW ORLEANS, 72- **MEMBERSHIPS** SCent MLA; Am Fedn Teachers; MLA; Soc Study Southern Lit. **RESEARCH** Novels of Dos Passos; William Faulkner; literature of New Orleans. **SELECTED PUBLICATIONS** Auth, Tennessee Williams--A Descriptive Bibliography, Papers Bibliograph Soc Am, Vol 0090, 96. **CONTACT ADDRESS** 732 Frenchmen St, New Orleans, LA, 70116.

HOLLADAY, HILARY
PERSONAL Born 07/03/1961, Richmond, VA **DISCIPLINE** ENGLISH **EDUCATION** Univ Virginia, BA, 83; Col of William and Mary, MA, 87; Univ North Carolina, Chapel Hill, PhD, 93. **CAREER** Asst prof, Am Lit, 93-98, assoc prof, 98-, Univ Mass Lowell. **HONORS AND AWARDS** Humanities fel, Virginia Found for Hum and Public Policy, 98. **MEMBERSHIPS** MLA; Am Lit Assoc. **RESEARCH** African-American literature; modern vs. contemporary American poetry. **SELECTED PUBLICATIONS** Auth, Ann Petry, Twayne, 96; auth numerous articles. **CONTACT ADDRESS** English Dept, Univ of Mass, Lowell, Lowell, MA, 01854. **EMAIL** Hilary_Holladay@uml.edu

HOLLAHAN, EUGENE
PERSONAL Born 02/27/1933, Memphis, TN, m, 1963, 2 children **DISCIPLINE** ENGLISH & CONTINENTAL LITERATURE **EDUCATION** Memphis State Univ, AB, 59; Univ Tenn, MA, 61; Univ NC, PhD(English), 69. **CAREER** Instr English, NC State Univ, 62-69; asst prof, 69-77, ASSOC PROF ENGLISH, GA STATE UNIV, 77- **MEMBERSHIPS** MLA. **RESEARCH** Novel; poetry; structure and meaning in fiction. **SELECTED PUBLICATIONS** Auth, Proust and the Sense of Time, Studies Novel, Vol 0027, 95; Incident at a Border, S Dakota Rev, Vol 0033, 95. **CONTACT ADDRESS** Dept of English, Georgia State Univ, 33 Gilmer St SE, Atlanta, GA, 30303-3080.

HOLLAND, NORMAN N.
PERSONAL Born 09/19/1927, New York, NY, m, 1954, 2 children **DISCIPLINE** ENGLISH LITERATURE **EDUCATION** MIT, BS, 47; Harvard, LL.B, 50, PhD, 56; Boston Psychoanalytic Inst, Cert, 66. **CAREER** Inst, assoc prof, 55-66, MIT; prof, McNulty Prof, 66-83, SUNY Buf; Marston-Milbauer Eminent Scholar, Univ Florida, 83-. **HONORS AND AWARDS** Guggenheim Fel, 79-80; Amer Council of Learned Soc Sr Fel, 74-75. **MEMBERSHIPS** Shakespeare Asn of Amer; Intl Asn of Prof of Eng; Boston Psychoanlytic Soc and Inst; Amer Acad of Psychoanalysis; Asn Intl d'Esthetique Exp; Founder, Moderator, PSYART, online discus group; Founder, Ed in Chief, PSYART: Ahyperlink Jour for the Psychology of the Arts. **RESEARCH** Psychoanalytic criticism; reader-response criticism; movies, Shakespeare. **SELECTED PUBLICATIONS** Auth, 5 Readers Reading, Yale Univ Press, 75; auth, The I, Yale Univ Press, 85; auth The Dynamics of Literary Response, Columbia Univ Press, 89; auth, The Critical I, Columbia Univ Press, 92; auth, Death In a Delphi Seminar: A Postmodern Mystery, SUNY Press, 95. **CONTACT ADDRESS** Dept of English, Univ Florida, Gainesville, FL, 32611. **EMAIL** nholland@efl.eu

HOLLANDER, JOHN
PERSONAL Born 10/28/1929, New York, NY, m, 1982, 2 children **DISCIPLINE** ENGLISH **EDUCATION** Columbia Univ, AB, 50, MA, 52; Ind Univ, PhD, 59. **CAREER** Lectr English, Conn Col, 57-59; from instr to assoc prof, Yale Univ, 59-66; prof English, Hunter Col & Grad Ctr, City Univ New York, 66-67; prof English, 77-86, A Bartlett Giamatti Prof English, 86-95, Sterling Prof English, 95-, Yale Univ; mem Poetry Bd, Wesleyan Univ Press, 59-62; Bollingen Poetry Transl Prize Bd, 61-; Christian Gauss lectr, Princeton Univ, 63; Nat Inst Arts & Lett grant, 63; overseas fel, Churchill Col, Cambridge, 67-68; mem English Inst; sr fel, Nat Endowment for Humanities, 73-74; panelist, Nat Endowment for Arts, 76-. **HONORS AND AWARDS** Yale Series Younger Poets Award, 58; Poetry Chap-Book Award, 62; Levinson Award, Poetry Mag, 74; Nat Inst Arts & Letters Award in Literature, 63; Bollingen Prize, 83; Shenandoah Prize, 85; Melville Cane Award, 90; Governor's Arts Award for Poetry, Conn, 97; Morse Fel, Yale Univ, 62-63; MacArthur Fel, 90-95; Cleanth Brooks-Robert Penn Warren Award, 97., Marietta Col, LittD, 82. **MEMBERSHIPS** Am Acad Arts & Sci; Am Acad Inst Arts & Letters; chancellor, Acad Am Poets; Asn of Luterary Scholars and Critics. **RESEARCH** Poetry and the other arts; the Renaissance; romantic poetry. **SELECTED PUBLICATIONS** Auth, Selected Poetry, Knopf, 93; auth, Tesserae and Other Poems, Knopf, 93; auth, The Gazer's Spirit, Chicago, 95; ed, Animal Poems, Knopf, 96; ed, Garden Poems, Knopf, 96; ed, Nineteenth Century American Poetry, Library of America, 96; ed, Committed to Memory: 100 Best Poems to Memorize, Turtle Point, 96; ed, Marriage Poems, Knopf, 97; auth, the Work of Poetry, Columbia, 97; ed, Poems of Robert Frost, Knopf, 97. **CONTACT ADDRESS** PO Box 208302, New Haven, CT, 06520-8302. **EMAIL** john.hollander@yale.edu

HOLLANDER, ROBERT
PERSONAL Born 07/31/1933, Manhattan, NY, m, 1964, 2 children **DISCIPLINE** ENGLISH, COMPARATIVE LITERATURE **EDUCATION** Princeton AB, 55; Columbia PhD, 62. **CAREER** Col Sch, NYC, teacher, latin eng, 55-57; Colum Col, instr eng, 58-62; Princeton, lectur euro lit, dept RLL, 62; Princeton, prof euro lit, depots RLL and CL, 75-98; Butler Col, Master, 91-95, chmn comp lit, 94-98; Fellowships, Guggenheim, Fulbright, NEH 2, Rockefeller Found, Bellagio; Founding Memb of Intl Dante Seminar, pres, 92-2000; Mem, Bd trust, Collegiate Sch NYC, 90-96, 98-2001; Vs prof, Univ Florence, 88; Nat Humanities Cen, Mem, Bd trust, 81-, Chmn Comm on Schol Affairs, 87-88, Vice Chmn and VP of the center, 87-88, Chmn Bd, 88-91; Emer Stat, 91-. **HONORS AND AWARDS** The Howard T Behrman Award, Princ, 86; Gold Medal of the Cty Florence, behalf of Dante, 88; John Witherspoon Award in Humanities, NJ Comm, 88; Bronze Medal of the Cty of Tours, 93; Hon Cit of Certaldo, behalf of Boccaccio, 97. **MEMBERSHIPS** Dante Soc Am; Soc Dante Italiana; Am Boccaccio Asn. **RESEARCH** Dante; Boccaccio; late Medieval Europe **SELECTED PUBLICATIONS** Allegory in Dante's Commedia, Prin, 69; Boccaccio's Two Venuses, Colum, 77; Studies in Dante, Longo, 80; Il Virgilio dantesco, Oschki, 83; Boccaccio's Last Fiction, Il Corbaccio, Penn, 88; Dante's Letter to Cangrande, Mich, 93; Boccaccio's Dante and the Shaping Force of Satire, Mich, 97. **CONTACT ADDRESS** Princeton Univ, Dept Romance Languages, Princeton, NJ, 0854. **EMAIL** bobh@phoenix.princeton.edu

HOLLENBERG, DONNA KROLIK
PERSONAL Born 09/07/1942, Saskatoon, SK, Canada, m, 1989, 2 children **DISCIPLINE** ENGLISH **EDUCATION** Univ Manitoba, BA, 64; Boston Univ, MA, 68; Tufts Univ, PhD, 86. **CAREER** Instr, dept chmn, 70-, Mount Ida Jr Col; prof, 85-90, Simmons Col; prof, 91-, Univ Conn. **HONORS AND AWARDS** McGill Univ Scholar, 60-61; tuition scholar, Univ Stockholm, 61-62; HD Fel, Seinecke Lib, 91. **MEMBERSHIPS** AAUP; MLA; MELUE; ASCVS. **RESEARCH** Modern poetry; 20th century Amer lit; Canadian lit. **SELECTED PUBLICATIONS** Auth, Between History and Poetry: the Letters of H.D. and Norman Holmes Reneson, Univ Iowa Press, 97; auth, HD: The Poetics of Childbirth and Creativity, Northeastern Univ Press, 91. **CONTACT ADDRESS** Dept of English, Univ of Connecticut, Storrs, CT, 06269. **EMAIL** hollrub@world.std.com

HOLLEY, SANDRA CAVANAUGH
PERSONAL Born 03/30/1943, Washington, DC **DISCIPLINE** SPEECH **EDUCATION** George Washington University, AB 1965, AM 1966; Univ of CT, PhD 1979. **CAREER** Southern CT State Univ, speech/language pathologist, prof 1970-; Rehab Center of Eastern Fairfield Co, speech pathologist 1966-70. **HONORS AND AWARDS** Danforth fellow Southern CT State College 1973-80; Leadership in Communications Award Howard Univ 1987; Honorary Doctor of Public Service degree George Washington Univ 1989; Fellow, American Speech-Language-Hearing Association, 1980; SCSU, Multicultural Founders Award, 1994; National Coalition of 100 Black Women, Milestone Award, 1994; Distinguished Alumna Award, Dept. of Speech & Hearing, George Washington Univ, 1997. **MEMBERSHIPS** Chmn Humane Commission City of New Haven 1977-86; bd of dir American Natl Red Cross S Central Chap 1978-84; exec bd CT Speech & Hearing Assn 1971-83; bd dir New Haven Visiting Nurse Assn 1977-79; vice pres for adminstration, Amer Speech-Language-Hearing Assn 1983-85; mem bd of dir The Foote School Association 1985-89; pres American Speech-Language-Hearing Assn 1988. **CONTACT ADDRESS** Communication Disorders, Southern Connecticut State Univ, 501 Crescent St, New Haven, CT, 06515.

HOLLINGSWORTH, MARGARET
PERSONAL Sheffield, England **DISCIPLINE** WRITING **EDUCATION** Loughborough Univ, ALA; Lakehead Univ, BA, 71; Univ BC, MFA, 74. **CAREER** Freelance journalist & foreign corresp, 66-90; asst prof, 81-93, asst prof, 92-93, ASSOC PROF CREATIVE WRITING, UNIV VICTORIA, 94-. **HONORS AND AWARDS** Jessie Award, 95; Chalmers Award, drama, 85; Dora Mavor Moore Award, 86, 87; ACTRA Award, radio drama, 86, 88. **MEMBERSHIPS** Writers' Union Can; Playwrights' Union; ACTRA; Libr Asn; PEN; Betty Lambert Soc. **SELECTED PUBLICATIONS** Auth, Willful Acts, 85; auth, Smiling Under Water, 89; auth, Why We Don't Write: Where Are Our Women Playwrights?, in Can Theatre Rev, 91; auth, Numbrains, 94. **CONTACT ADDRESS** Dept of Writing, Univ Victoria, Victoria, BC, V8W 2Y2.

HOLLOWAY, KARLA F.C.
DISCIPLINE ENGLISH LITERATURE **EDUCATION** MI State Univ, PhD, 78. **CAREER** Prof, Duke Univ. **RESEARCH** Intersections between linguistics and lit. **SELECTED PUBLICATIONS** Auth, The Character of the Word, Greenwood, 87; New Dimensions of Spirituality, Greenwood, 87; Moorings and Metaphors: Figures of Culture and Gender in Black Women's Literature, Rutgers, 92. **CONTACT ADDRESS** Eng Dept, Duke Univ, Durham, NC, 27706.

HOLLSTEIN, MILTON C.
DISCIPLINE COMMUNICATION STUDIES **EDUCATION** Univ Iowa, PhD, 55. **CAREER** Prof. **HONORS AND AWARDS** Deseret News First Contributors Awd, 92. **MEMBERSHIPS** Soc Prof Jour; Asn Edu Jour and Mass Commun. **SELECTED PUBLICATIONS** Auth, Editing with Understanding, Macmillan, 81; Magazines in Search of an Audience: A Guide to Starting New Magazines, Magazine Publ Asn, 69. **CONTACT ADDRESS** Dept of Communication, Utah Univ, 100 S 1350 E, Salt Lake City, UT, 84112. **EMAIL** welch@admin.comm.utah.edu

HOLMER, JOAN OZARK
DISCIPLINE ENGLISH LITERATURE **EDUCATION** Univ Minn, BS; Princeton Univ, MA, PhD. **CAREER** Eng Dept, Georgetown Univ **RESEARCH** Renaissance literature; source study; fairy mythology; biblical allusion; moral philosophy; performance phenomenology; dramatic structure and genre; intellectual, cultural, religious and economic history. **SELECTED PUBLICATIONS** Auth, The Merchant of Venice: Choice, Hazard and Consequence, MacMillan & St Martin's, 95; pubs on Shakespeare, William Browne, Robert Herrick, and John Milton. **CONTACT ADDRESS** English Dept, Georgetown Univ, 37th and O St, Washington, DC, 20057.

HOLMES, CHARLOTTE A.
DISCIPLINE ENGLISH **EDUCATION** La State Univ, BA, 77; Columbia Univ, MFA, 80. **CAREER** Ed asst, Paris Rev, 79-80; assoc ed, Ecco Press, 80-82; Inst, Western Carolina Univ, 84-87; asst prof, 87-93, ASSOC PROF, 93-, PA STATE UNIV. **CONTACT ADDRESS** Dept of English, Pennsylvania State Univ, University Park, PA, 16802. **EMAIL** cxh18@psu.edu

HOLMES, DAVID
DISCIPLINE COMPOSITION **EDUCATION** B.A. OK Christian Col, BA, 86; CA State Univ Dominguez Hills, MA, 93; Univ S CA, PhD, 97. **CAREER** Dir, Am Studies Prog; asst prof. **SELECTED PUBLICATIONS** Auth, Nonfiction Prose, Encycl of Rhetoric, 95. **CONTACT ADDRESS** Dept of Eng, Pepperdine Univ, 24255 Pacific Coast Hwy, Malibu, CA, 90263. **EMAIL** dholmes@pepperdine.edu

HOLMES, MICHAEL E.
DISCIPLINE COMMUNICATION STUDIES **EDUCATION** Univ Minn, PhD, 91. **CAREER** Dept Comm, Utah Univ **MEMBERSHIPS** Int Commun Asn; Nat Commun Asn; NW Commun Asn; Western States Commun Asn. **RESEARCH** Organizational communication and nonroutine events; research methods and new communication technology; design theory. **SELECTED PUBLICATIONS** Auth, Optimal matching analysis of negotiation phase sequences in simulated and authentic hostage negotatiations, 97; Processes and patterns in hostage negotiations, Greenwood, 97; WinPhaser 1.0c: Interaction sequence description and analysis, 97; Naming virtual space in computer-mediated conversation, 95; Don't blink or you'll miss it: Issues in electronic mail research, 94; co-auth, Decision development in computer-assisted group decision making, Human Commun Res, 95; Negotiations in crisis, SUNY, 95. **CONTACT ADDRESS** Dept of Communication, Utah Univ, 100 S 1350 E, Salt Lake City, UT, 84112. **EMAIL** holmes@admin.comm.utah.edu

HOLTON, WILLIAM MILNE
PERSONAL Born 11/04/1931, Charlotte, NC, m, 1964 **DISCIPLINE** MODERN & AMERICAN LITERATURE **EDUCATION** Dartmouth Col, AB, 54, Harvard Univ, LLB, 57; Yale Univ, MA, 59, PhD, 65. **CAREER** From instr to assoc prof, 61-77, Prof English lit, Univ MD, College Park, 78-; Fulbright lectr, Univ Uppsala, 65-66; Fulbright prof, Univ Skopje, 70. **HONORS AND AWARDS** Golden Pen Award, Macedonian Cult Comn (for transl), 77. **MEMBERSHIPS** MLA; S Atlantic Mod Lang Asn; James Joyce Soc; PEN Club; Fr Asn Am St. **RESEARCH** Modern American literature; modern and contemporary poetry; modern poetry in translation. **SELECTED PUBLICATIONS** Auth, Sparrow's fall and sparrow's eye: Stephen Crane's Maggie, Studia Neophilologica, 69; coauth, Private Dealings: Eight Modern American Writers, Almqvist & Wiksell, Stockholm, 69; auth, Cylinder of Vision: The Fiction and Journalistic Writings of Stephen Crane, La State Univ, 72; Notes on Macedonia, Contempora, 72; coauth, New Perspectives, 74; ed, The Big House and Other Stories of Modern Macedonia, Univ Mo, 74; co-ed, Reading the Ashes: An Anthology of Modern Macedonian Poetry, 77 & The New Polish Poetry: A Bilingual Collection, 78, Univ Pittsburgh, 78; Co-ed, Austrian Poetry Today, Schocleen, NY, 85; Serbian Poetry from the Beginnings to the Present, Yale, NY, 89; The Songs of the Serbian People: From The Collections of Vuk Stefaneric Karadzic, Univ Pitts, 97. **CONTACT ADDRESS** Dept English, Univ Md, College Park, MD, 20742-0001. **EMAIL** wh25@umail.umd.edu

HOLTZ, WILLIAM
DISCIPLINE ENGLISH **EDUCATION** Univ Mich, PhD, 64. **CAREER** Prof; Catherine Paine Middlebush prof, 94; taught crs(es), sem in, Fielding, Sterne, Austen & Brontes. **HONORS AND AWARDS** 3 bk awds; ACLS & NEH fel. **SELECTED PUBLICATIONS** Auth, The Ghost in the Little House: A Life of Rose Wilder Lane, Univ Mo Press, 93; publ on, 18th-century lite, Engl novel & lit theory and criticism. **CONTACT ADDRESS** Dept of English, Univ of Missouri-Columbia, 309 University Hall, Columbia, MO, 65211.

HOLZBERGER, WILLIAM GEORGE
PERSONAL Born 01/06/1932, Chicago, IL, m, 1965, 2 children **DISCIPLINE** ENGLISH **EDUCATION** Northwestern Univ, Evanston, PhB, 60, MA(Philos), 65, MA(English), 66, PhD(English), 69. **CAREER** Asst prof, 69-74, assoc prof, 74-81, prof English, 81-97, PROF EMER, 97- , BUCKNELL UNIV. **HONORS AND AWARDS** Am Philos Soc grant-in-aid, 70; Am Coun Learned Soc grant-in-aid, 72 & 73; Nat Endowment for Humanities fel, 75-76. **MEMBERSHIPS** MLA; AAUP; Soc Advan Am Philos; Santayana Soc. **RESEARCH** English and American literature and intellectual history; 20th century literature. **SELECTED PUBLICATIONS** Auth, The Unpublished Poems of George Santayana: Some Critical and Textual Considerations, Southern Rev, 1/75; co-ed, Perspectives on Hamlet, 76 & ed, The Complete Poems of George Santayana: A Critical Edition, 79, Bucknell Univ; auth, Remembering the Bard of Boar's Hill, Mich Quart, winter 80; Accentuating the Positive, Southern Rev, 7/81; What is an Educated Person?, Eidos, 85; A E Housman & George Santayana, In: The Dict of Literary Biography; auth, The Significance of the Subtitle in Santayana's Novel The Last Puritan: A Memoir in the Form of a Novel, in Price, ed, Critical Essays on George Santayana, G.K. Hall, 91; auth, A.E. Housman, 1859-1936, in Gay and Lesbian Literature, Gale, 93; auth, George Santayana, 1863-1952, in Payne, ed, A Dictionary of Cultural and Critical Theory, Blackwell, 95; co-ed, The Works of George Santayana, 4 v, MIT. **CONTACT ADDRESS** Dept of English, Bucknell Univ, Lewisburg, PA, 17837.

HONEYCUTT, JAMES M.
DISCIPLINE DEPARTMENT OF SPEECH COMMUNICATION **EDUCATION** Univ Ill, PhD. **CAREER** Assoc prof, La State Univ. **RESEARCH** Relational conflict; marital interaction. **SELECTED PUBLICATIONS** Published over a dozen studies in intrapersonal communication processes in terms of covert dialogues or imagined interactions. **CONTACT ADDRESS** Dept of Speech Commun, Louisiana State Univ, Baton Rouge, LA, 70803.

HONIG, EDWIN
PERSONAL Born 09/03/1919, New York, NY, m, 1963, 2 children **DISCIPLINE** ENGLISH **EDUCATION** Univ Wis, BA, 41, MA, 47. **CAREER** Instr English, Purdue Univ, 42, Ill Inst Technol, 46 & Univ NMex, 47-48; instr Harvard Univ, 49-52, Briggs-Copeland asst prof, 52-57; assoc prof, 57-60, chmn dept, 67-68, prof, 60-82, EMER PROF ENGLISH & COMP LIT, BROWN UNIV, 82-, Guggenheim fel, 62; Bollingen Found grant, 63; vis prof, Univ Calif, Davis, 64-65; Nat Inst Arts & Lett grant, 66; Nat Transl Ctr Grant, 66; RI Comn on Arts, 67, sr poet, Poetry in Schs Prog, 67-72, mem spec comt, Arts-in-Educ, 70-72; Arts Award Comt, 72-73; Amy Lowell traveling scholar, 68-69; Nat Endowment for Humanities, co-transl fel, 77- & sr fel grant for independent studies, 75. **HONORS AND AWARDS** NEA Creative Writing Award, Nat Endowment of Arts, 77, Music Award, 80., MA, Brown Univ, 58. **MEMBERSHIPS** Dante Soc Am; PEN Club Am; Am Transl Asn; Poetry Soc Am. **RESEARCH** Renaissance; theory of translation; theory of persona in literature and other disciplines. **SELECTED PUBLICATIONS** Auth, Loafing, Mich Quarterly Rev, Vol 0036, 97. **CONTACT ADDRESS** Dept of English, Brown Univ, Providence, RI, 02912.

HOOPLE, ROBIN P.
DISCIPLINE ENGLISH LITERATURE **EDUCATION** Univ Syracuse, BA; MA; Univ Minn, PhD. **HONORS AND AWARDS** Co-ed, Mosaic; pres, Can Assn Am Studies. **RESEARCH** American Romanticism; American realism and naturalism. **SELECTED PUBLICATIONS** Auth, Distinguished Discord, 97; pub(s) on American literature. **CONTACT ADDRESS** Dept of English, Manitoba Univ, Winnipeg, MB, R3T 2N2.

HOPKINS, LEROY TAFT, JR.
PERSONAL Born 08/19/1942, Lancaster, PA **DISCIPLINE** ENGLISH, GERMAN **EDUCATION** Millersville St Coll, BA 1966; Harvard U, PhD 1974. **CAREER** Millersville State Coll, asst prof of German 1979-; Urban League of Lancaster Co Inc, acting exec dir 1979, asso dir 1976-79; Hedwig-Heyle-Schule (W Germany), instr English 1974-76; NE Univ, instructor German 1971-72. **HONORS AND AWARDS** Received Travelling Fellowship Harvard Univ 1969-70; Study/Visit Grant for Research, German Academic Exchange Service, 1989; Member of Honor Society, Phi Kappa Phi, 1991. **MEMBERSHIPS** Adv Com on Black History PA Hist & Mus Commn 1979-; com person City of Lancasters Overall Econ Devel Prog; Bd Mem Lancastger Co Library/Lancaster Neighborhood Hlth Ctr 1977-; chmn PA Delegation to White House Conf on Libraries 1978-79; 1st vice pres, Lancaster Historical Society, 1989-; mem, Pennsylvania Humanities Council, 1988-. **CONTACT ADDRESS** Dept of For Lang, Millersville Univ, Millersville, PA, 17551.

HOPPER, PAUL
DISCIPLINE ENGLISH AND LINGUISTICS **EDUCATION** Univ Tex, PhD. **CAREER** Lit, Carnegie Mellon Univ. **HONORS AND AWARDS** Ed, Jour Lang Scis; 's Language, Collitz Prof LSA's Linguistics Inst, Fulbright Fel; Guggenheim Fel. **MEMBERSHIPS** MLAl; Ling Soc Am. **SELECTED PUBLICATIONS** Coauth, Grammaticalization, Cambridge, 93. **CONTACT ADDRESS** Carnegie Mellon Univ, 5000 Forbes Ave, Pittsburgh, PA, 15213.

HORAN, ELIZABETH R.
PERSONAL Born 07/06/1956, Boston, MA, m, 1980, 1 child **DISCIPLINE** LITERATURE IN ENGLISH, SPANISH, LATIN, AND ITALIAN **EDUCATION** Barnard Col, BA 78; Univ Calif-Santa Cruz, MA, 84, PhD, 88. **CAREER** Lectr, Wheelock Col, 87-88; Vis Asst Prof, Tufts Univ, 88-89; Asst Prof, 89-95, Assoc Prof, Ariz State Univ, 95-. **HONORS AND AWARDS** Fulbright Schol, 85-87, 95-96; Gabriela Mistral Award, Org Am States, 90. **MEMBERSHIPS** MLA; ACLA; Letras Feministas; Emily Dickinson Int Soc. **RESEARCH** US & Latin American women writers; translations; biography. **SELECTED PUBLICATIONS** Co-transl, Happiness, White Pine Press, 93; auth, Gabriela Mistral, an Artist and Her People, Org Am States, 94; To Market: The Dickinson Copyright Wars, Emily Dickinson J, 96; Santa Maestra Muerta: Body and Nation in Portraits of Gabriela Mistral, Taller de Letras, 97; Reading the Book of Memory, Always from Somewhere Else: A Memoir of My Jewish Father, The Feminist Press at CUNY, 98; author of numerous other articles and publications. **CONTACT ADDRESS** English Dept, Arizona State Univ, Tempe, Tempe, AZ, 85287-0302. **EMAIL** elizabeth.horan@asu.edu

HORD, FREDERICK LEE
PERSONAL Born 11/07/1941, Kokomo, IN, d, 3 children **DISCIPLINE** BLACK STUDIES: LITERATURE/HISTORY **EDUCATION** Ind State Univ, BS, 63, MS, 65; Union Grad School, PhD, 87. **CAREER** Asst prof English, Wabash Col, 72-76; lectr, Howard Univ, 84-87; Dir Ctr Black Cult & Res, W Va Univ, 87-88; DIR BLACK STUDIES & FULL PROF, KNOX COL, 88- **HONORS AND AWARDS** ACM grant for Blacks-Jews Relationships; Ed bd, Jour of Black Stud; First Poets Series Award. **MEMBERSHIPS** Nat Asn Black Cult Ctrs; Nat Coun Black Studies; ILL Comm Black Concerns Higher Educ. **RESEARCH** African American literature; black philosophy; black psychology; history of black intellectuals; black culture centers. **SELECTED PUBLICATIONS** Auth, After Hours; Reconstructing Memory; coed, Life Sentences; I Am Because We Are: Readings in Black Philosophy. **CONTACT ADDRESS** Knox Col, 2 E South St, Galesburg, IL, 61401. **EMAIL** fhord@knox.knox.edu

HORNER, BRUCE
DISCIPLINE ENGLISH LITERATURE **EDUCATION** Univ Pittsburgh, PhD. **CAREER** Asst prof, 88-, Drake Univ. **RESEARCH** Criticism of popular and art music. **SELECTED PUBLICATIONS** Auth, publ(s) on polit writing instr. **CONTACT ADDRESS** Drake Univ, University Ave, PO Box 2507, Des Moines, IA, 50311-4505. **EMAIL** bruce.horner@drake.edu

HORTON, RONALD A.
PERSONAL Born 11/09/1936, Glendale, CA, m, 1968, 3 children **DISCIPLINE** ENGLISH **EDUCATION** Bob Jones Univ, BA, 58; UCLA, MA, 62; Univ NC Chapel Hill, PhD, 72. **CAREER** Instr, 60-66, prof, 69-, Bob Jones Univ. **HONORS AND AWARDS** Folger Shakespeare Libr Summer Fel, 70; S Atlantic Modern Lang Asn Book Award, 76., Pres, SC Asn Depts English, 76, 90; Head, English div, Bob Jones Univ, 69-. **MEMBERSHIPS** Modern Lang Asn; S Atlantic Modern Lang Asn; Renaissance Soc Am; Southeastern Renaissance Conference, Spenser Soc. **RESEARCH** English Renaissance Literature. **SELECTED PUBLICATIONS** Auth, The Unity of The Faerie Queene, Univ GA Press, 78; "Aristotle and His Commentators," The Spenser Encyclopedia, Univ Toronto Press, 90; "The Argument of Spenser's Garden of Adonis," Love and Death in the Renaissance, Dovehouse, 91; "Spenser's Farewell to Dido: The Public Turn," in Classical, Renaissance, and Postmodern Acts of the Imagination: Essays Commemorating O.B. Hardison, Jr., Univ DE Press, 96; "Herbert's Thy Cage, Thy Rope of Sands: An Hourglass," George Herbert Jour, 97-98. **CONTACT ADDRESS** 407 Library Dr, Greenville, SC, 29609. **EMAIL** rhorton@bju.edu

HORTON, SUSAN R.
PERSONAL Born 11/16/1941, Defiance, OH, d, 1 child **DISCIPLINE** ENGLISH; AMERICAN LITERATURE **EDUCATION** Brandeis Univ, PhD, 73. **CAREER** Prof English, Univ Mass at Boston, 72-. **HONORS AND AWARDS** Woodrow Wilson Dissertation Fel. **MEMBERSHIPS** MLA; Dickens Soc. **RESEARCH** 19th century cultural history; Dickens; African cross-cultural encounters. **SELECTED PUBLICATIONS** Auth, The Reader in the Dickens World, Macmillan Ltd/Univ Pittsburgh Press, 78; Interpreting Interpreting: Interpreting Dickens' Donkey, Johns Hopkins Univ Press, 79; Thinking Through Writing, Johns Hopkins Univ Press, 82, 85, 89; Literary Theory's Future, Literary Theory's Future, Univ Ill Press, 89; Difficult Women, Artful Lives: Olive Schreiner & Isak Dinesen, In and Out of Africa, Johns Hopkins Univ Press, 95; Victorian Optical Gadgetry, Modernist Selves, Victorian Literature & the Victorian Visual Imagination, Univ Calif Press, 97. **CONTACT ADDRESS** Harbor Campus, Univ Mass, Boston, MA, 02125. **EMAIL** horton@umbsky.cc.umb.edu

HORVATH, RICHARD P.
DISCIPLINE MIDDLE ENGLISH LITERATURE **EDUCATION** Stanford Univ, PhD. **CAREER** Asst prof, Fordham Univ . **RESEARCH** Chaucer, 15th century lit. **SELECTED PUBLICATIONS** Auth, Critical Interpretation of The Canterbury Tales B23981, Eng Lang Notes 24, 86; History, Narrative, and the Ideological mode of the Peterborough Chronicle, Mediaevalia 18, 93. **CONTACT ADDRESS** Dept of Eng Lang and Lit, Fordham Univ, 113 W 60th St, New York, NY, 10023.

HORWITZ, BARBARA
DISCIPLINE ENGLISH NOVEL **EDUCATION** SUNY, Stony Brook, PhD. **CAREER** Assoc prof, Long Island Univ, C.W. Post Campus. **SELECTED PUBLICATIONS** Auth, Jane Austen and the Question of Women's Education; The Unfit Mother in Lady Susan and The Juvenilia. **CONTACT ADDRESS** Long Island Univ, C.W. Post, Brookville, NY, 11548-1300.

HORWITZ, ROBERT
DISCIPLINE COMMUNICATIONS **EDUCATION** Brandeis Univ, PhD, 82 **CAREER** ASSOC PROF, COMMUN, UNIV CALIF, SAN DIEGO. **RESEARCH** Communication institutions. **SELECTED PUBLICATIONS** Auth, The Irony of Regulatory Reform: The Deregulation of American Telecommunications, Oxford, 89; "Begging the Question: Consistency and 'Common Sense' in the First Amendment Jurisprudence of Advertising and Begging," Stud in Law, Politics, and Society, Vol 13, 93. **CONTACT ADDRESS** Dept of Commun, Univ Calif, San Diego, 9500 Gilman Dr, La Jolla, CA, 92093. **EMAIL** rhorwitz@weber.ucsd.edu

HOSTETLER, MICHAEL J.
PERSONAL Born 08/19/1950, South Bend, IN, m, 1970, 3 children **DISCIPLINE** COMMUNICATION STUDIES **EDUCATION** Northwestern Univ, PhD, 93. **CAREER** Vis asst prof, Ind Univ Northwest, 93-94; S.U.N.Y. Oneonta; asst prof, St John's Univ, 95- . **MEMBERSHIPS** Nat Commun Asn; NY State Commun Asn; Relig Commun Asn. **RESEARCH** Am Pub Address; Relig and Rhet. **SELECTED PUBLICATIONS** Auth, John Calvin's Rhetorical Christianity and Sixteenth Century Religious Exiles: Constructing an Ethic of Refugees, Speech Commun Annual 10, 96; Liberty in Baptist Thought: Three Primary Texts, 1614-1856, The Am Baptist Quart 60, 96; Rethinking the War Metaphor in Religious Rhetoric: Burke, Black, and Berrigan's Glimmer of Light, The Jour of Commun and Relig 20, 97; The Enigmatic Ends of Rhetoric: Churchill's Fulton Address as Great Art and Failed Persuasion, Quart Jour of Speech 83, 97; Gov Al Smith Confronts the Catholic Question: The Rhetorical Legacy of the 1928 Campaign, Commun Quart 46, 98; William Jenning Bryan as Demosthenes: The Scopes Trial and the Undelivered Oration, On Evolution, Western Jour of Commun 62, 98. **CONTACT ADDRESS** Dept of Speech, St John's Univ, 8000 Utopia Pky, Jamaica, NY, 11439. **EMAIL** hostetlm@stjohns.edu

HOSTETTER, EDWIN C.
DISCIPLINE HUMANITIES **EDUCATION** John Hopkins Univ, PhD 92. **CAREER** Ecumenical Inst of Theol, prof, 89-; John Hopkins univ, adj prof 87-90. **HONORS AND AWARDS** Dunning Dist Fac lectr, St. Mary's Sem and Univ. **MEMBERSHIPS** IBR; SBL **RESEARCH** Habakkuk; Hebrew grammar; white collar crime. **SELECTED PUBLICATIONS** Auth, Amir, bikkura, bls, gabia, kad, kos, keli, s'p, abot, pag, perudot, prh, sws, so'ar and te'ena, in: New Intl Dictionary of Old Testament Theology Exegesis, ed Willem A. VanGemeren, Grand Rapids, Zondervan Pub House, 97; Mistranslation in Cant 1:5, Andrews Univ Sem Studies, 96; JUS230 Restorative Justice, coauth, Taylor Univ Fort Wayne, 96; Old Testament Introduction, IBR Bibliog, Grand Rapids, Baker Book House, 95; Nations Mightier and More Numerous: The Biblical View of Palestine's Pre-Israelite Peoples, Fort Worth, Bibla Press, 95; Geographic Distribution of the Pre-Israelite Peoples of Ancient Palestine, Biblische Zeitschrift, 94; Prophetic Attitudes toward Violence in Ancient Israel, Criswell Theol Rev, 94; Is American Justice Color-Blind?, ESA Advo, 93. **CONTACT ADDRESS** Dept of Biblical Studies, Ecumenical Inst of Theol, 28 Winehurst Rd, Catonsville, MD, 21228. **EMAIL** edwin@access.digex.net

HOUSE, KAY S.
DISCIPLINE ENGLISH **EDUCATION** Univ Ill, BA, 45; Univ Wash, MA, 45; Stanford Univ, PhD, 63. **CAREER** Prof, Eng, San Francisco State Univ; current, ED-IN-CH, THE WRITINGS OF JAMES FENIMORE COOPER. **MEMBERSHIPS** Am Antiquarian Soc **RESEARCH** James Fenimore Cooper **SELECTED PUBLICATIONS** Ed, James Fenimore Cooper's The Pilot, State Univ NY Press, 86, Lib Am, 91; auth, "Cooper's Indians After Yet Another "Century of Dishonor,'" in Letterature d'America, Univ Rome, 83; ed, James Fenimore Cooper's Satanstoe, State Univ NY Press, 90; auth, "The James Fenimore Cooper Collections at the American Antiquarian Society," in Serendipity and Synergy: Collection Development, Access and Research Opportunities at the American Antiquarian Society in the McCorison Era, Am Antiquarian Soc, 93. **CONTACT ADDRESS** PO Box 158, Payson, IL, 62360-0158.

HOVANEC, EVELYN ANN
PERSONAL Born 12/23/1937, Uniontown, PA **DISCIPLINE** ENGLISH, FOLKLORE, HISTORY AND LORE OF COAL MINERS **EDUCATION** Duquesne Univ, BEd, 62, MA, 66; Univ Pittsburgh, PhD, 73. **CAREER** Teacher social studies & English, Pittsburgh pub jr high schs, 62-66; ASSOC prof English, PA State Univ, Fayette, 66-88, dir Acad Aff, PA State, McKeesport 85-92. **HONORS AND AWARDS** PSF Awd for Pub Svc, 94; PSM Awd for Svc, 89; PSF Awd for Teach Excel, 97; PSF Min Stu Org Fac Awd, 98. **MEMBERSHIPS** Nat Coun Teachers English; Col English Asn; MLA. **RESEARCH** Mining literature and lore; mythology; Henry James. **SELECTED PUBLICATIONS** Auth, 3 poems, Earth & You, 72; coauth, Making the humanities human, WVa Rev Educ Res, fall 73; auth, Horses of the Sun (2 poems), In: Cathedral Poets II, Boxwood, 76; coauth, Patch/Work Voices: The Culture & Lore of a Mining People, Harry Hoffman, 77; auth, Coal culture & communities, Pa Oral Hist Newslett, 77; The Sea (poem), In: Strawberry Saxifrage, Nat Soc Publ Poets, 77; coauth, Making the Humanities Human, West VA Review of Educ Res 1, 46-47, 73; auth, A Mythological Approach to Tomorrow, Assoc of Teach Educ Review 3, 78; auth, Reader's Guide to Coal Mining Fiction and Selected Prose Narratives, Bul of Biblio, 41-57, Sept, 86; auth, Marie Belloc Lowndes, An Encyclopedia of British Women Writers, Garland, 297-298, 88. **CONTACT ADDRESS** Pennsylvania State Univ, PO Box 519, Uniontown, PA, 15401-0519. **EMAIL** eah2@psu.edu

HOWARD, ANNE BAIL
PERSONAL Born 11/19/1927, Albuquerque, NM, m, 1950, 2 children **DISCIPLINE** AMERICAN LITERATURE, COMPOSITION **EDUCATION** Univ NMex, MA, 53, PhD, 66. **CAREER** Teacher English, Espanola High Sch, 54-55 & Valley High Sch, Albuquerque, 55-57; instr & dir English A, Univ NMex, 59-63; from instr to asst prof, 63-71, dir Freshman English, 70-75, assoc prof, 71-85, PROF ENGLISH, UNIV NEV,

RENO, 85-, COORD WOMEN'S STUDIES, 79-85. **HONORS AND AWARDS** Distinguished teaching award, 92. **MEMBERSHIPS** MLA; NCTE; AAUP; Rocky Mountain Mod Lang Asn; Nat Women's Studies Asn. **RESEARCH** Women writers; biography. **SELECTED PUBLICATIONS** Coauth, A workbook for English A, Univ NMex, 62; The Long Campaign: A Biography of Anne Martin, Univ Nev Press, 85. **CONTACT ADDRESS** Dept of English, Univ of Nev, Reno, NV, 89557-0001. **EMAIL** abhoward@equinox.unv.edu

HOWARD, C. JERIEL
PERSONAL Born 03/14/1939, Wharton, TX **DISCIPLINE** ENGLISH **EDUCATION** Union Col, BA, 61; Tex Christian Univ, MA, 62, PhD(English), 67. **CAREER** Instr English, Southwestern Union Col, 62-64; instr, Union Col, 64-65, assoc prof, 65-66; instr, Tex Christian Univ, 66-67; guest instr, Tex Wesleyan Col, 67; chmn dept English, Tarrant County Jr Col, 67-68, chmn dept commun, 68-70; assoc prof, Bishop Col, 70-79; prof English, Northeastern Ill Univ, 79-. **MEMBERSHIPS** NCTE; Conf Col Compos & Commun; Conf Col Teachers English. **RESEARCH** Applied rhetoric; English methodology; American literature. **SELECTED PUBLICATIONS** Coauth, Contact: A Textbook in Applied Communications, 2nd ed, 74, 3rd ed, 78, Prentice-Hall; coauth (with Richard F Tracz), The Responsible Person, 2nd ed, Harper & Row, 75; Writing Effective Paragraph, Winthrop Press, 76; (with Elizabeth K Martin), Technique: Studies in Composition, 2nd ed, Harper & Row, 77; (with Dee Brock), Writing for a Reason, John Wiley & Sons, 77; Reprise: A Review of Basic Writing Skills, Goodyear Press, 80; (with Richard F Tracz), The Paragraph Book, Little-Brown, 82. **CONTACT ADDRESS** Dept of English, Northeastern Illinois Univ, 5500 N St Louis Ave, Chicago, IL, 60625-4625. **EMAIL** CJerielH@aol.com

HOWARD, ELIZABETH FITZGERALD
PERSONAL Born 12/28/1927, Baltimore, MD, m **DISCIPLINE** LITERATURE, LIBRARY SCIENCE **EDUCATION** Radcliffe Coll Harvard Univ, AB 1948; Univ of Pittsburgh, MLS 1971, PhD 1977. **CAREER** Boston Public Libr, childrens Librarian 1952-56; Episcopal Diocese of Pittsburgh, resource librn 1972-74; Pittsburgh Theol Sem, ref Librn 1974-77; Univ of Pittsburgh, visiting lecturer 1976-78; W VA Univ, asst prof 1978-85, on leave sr librarian Univ of Maiduguri Nigeria 1981-82, assoc prof 1985-89, professor, 1989-93, professor emerita, 1993-. **HONORS AND AWARDS** Library science honor soc Beta i Mu; candidate for bd of dirs Harvard Alumni Assoc 1987. **MEMBERSHIPS** Dir Radcliffe Alumnae Asso 1969-72; mem Brd of Trustees Ellis Sch Pittsburgh 1970-75; trustee Magee Womens Hosp 1980-94; Episcopal Diocese of Pittsburgh Cathedral Chapter 1984-86; Pittsburgh Chap of LINKS Inc; mem Amer Library Assoc, Children's Literature Assoc, Soc of Children's Book Writers; bd mem, QED Communications 1987-94; bd mem, Beginning With Books 1987-93. **SELECTED PUBLICATIONS** Author Articles in Professional Journals; author professional nonfiction, America as Story, 1988; author children's books, Train to Lulu's House, Chita's Christmas Tree, 1989, Aunt Flossie's Hats, 1991; Mac and Marie and the Train Toss Surprise, 1993; Papa Tells Chita a Story, 1995; What's in Aunt Mary's Room?, 1996; America as Story (2nd edition, with Rosemary Coffey), 1997.

HOWARD, HUBERT WENDELL
PERSONAL Born 09/22/1927, Anderson, IN, m, 1956, 3 children **DISCIPLINE** ENGLISH LITERATURE, MUSIC **EDUCATION** DePauw Univ, AB, 49; Stanford Univ, MA, 52; Juilliard Sch Music, dipl, 58; Univ Minn, Minneapolis, PhD(English, music), 70. **CAREER** Dir relig educ, First Methodist Church, Anderson, Ind, 49-50; plant mgr, Paglo Labs, NY, 58-60; instr English, Univ Minn, Minneapolis, 60-64; from asst prof to assoc prof English & music, 64-74, prof English & music, St John Fisher Col, 74-, vis prof, Eve Sch, Monroe Community Col, 68-71 & 73-74. **HONORS AND AWARDS** Winton Found Excellence Award, 62. **MEMBERSHIPS** MLA; Nat Asn Teachers Singing; NCTE; Northeast Am Soc 18th Century Studies. **RESEARCH** Renaissance British literature; 18th century British literature; Renaissance and Baroque music. **SELECTED PUBLICATIONS** Auth, He Loved Her (poem), Orphic Lute, spring 66; The Mystic (poem), Roanoke Rev, fall 72; The Parable, Col Compos & Commun, 12/73; Only Civil Disobedience, Alliance Witness, 4/74; Artistry or Snobbery, Sch Music News, 9/74; Aspasia & My Poem, Delta Epsilon Sigma Bull, 12/75; Becky and Bampfylde, Greyfriar, 77; Christina Rossetti: An Appreciation, Survivor, Arts and Lit Mag, July 77; Food and Drink as Subjects in the Literature, Painting , and Music of the Seventeenth and Eighteenth Centuries, Delta Epsilon Sigma Bull, Dec 78; Undermining the NFL, The Church Musician, Feb 79; Don't Just Get By, The Pioneer, St. John Fisher Col, Sept 80; Abraham Rothberg's The Song of David Freed, The Pioneer, Sept 80; An Answering Theology, Delta Epsilon Sigma Bull, Dec 80; Social Attitudes and Bad Writing, The Journal of English Teaching Techniques, winter 80; The Influence of the Music of Henry Purcell on the Poetry of Gerard Manley Hopkins, The Hopkins Quart, winter 82; Arthur Kober: 'No Regella Yenkee,' Polish American Studies, spring 83; A Good Dog Because It Has Hair, The College Board Review, summer 83; Songs For Learning, The College Board Review, summer 85; Progressive Education, Phi Delta Kappan, June 85; More Than a Name, Proteus, spring 85; Needed: A New Commitment to Public Service, Shared Purpose, The College Board News, summer 85; Bring Back Phil Silvers, The College Board Review, pp 6-9, fall 85; Hold the Phone, Young and Alive, March 86; Listen Up and Sound Off, American Way, April 86; Food and Drink as Subjects in the Paintings of the Eighteenth Century, Ball State Univ Forum, summer 86; Two Ways to Freedom, The College Board Rev, fall 86; Bach;s Detractors, Delta Epsilon Sigma Bull, March 87; The Filter of the Mind: The Edge Between the 'Written' and the 'Real," Midwest Quart, summer 87; Traditions, Col Brd Rev, summer 87; Jerome C. Hixson, Col Teaching, spring 88; The Enemy is Us, Col Brd Rev, fall 88; A Language With Spizzerinctum, Indiana English, spring 88; The Deeps Beneath the Depths, Ind English, winter 88; Guaranteed: The Right to Be A Student, Ind English, spring 89; A Context for Shock Art, City Newspaper (Rochester, NY), July 27, 89; A Re-reading of Ben Johnson's "Song to Celia," Col Lang Asn Journal, March 90; Lest We Forget: The Place of Roland Hayes in American Musical History, Delta Epsilon Sigma Journal, Oct 90; An English Professor's 'Spare' Time, Ind English, winter 90; Inside Communism and Zionism: Koestler's Darkness at Noon and Thieves in the Night, Delta Epsilon Sigma Journal, Jan 91; In Pursuit of the Real, San Jose Studies, spring 91; A Matter of Life and Death, Midwest Quart, autumn 91; Are Heroes Vanishing?, Forum for Honors, summer/fall 91; Hierarchic Systems as a Unifying Topic in the Writings of Arthur Koestler, Delta Epsilon Sigma J, Dec 91; The Fine Art of Baseball, DES Journal, March 92; Walcott MATCHED with Fisher, Nat Col Honors Council, NE Reg newsletter, summer 92; Making and Refining a Professor, Forum for Honors, summer/fall 92; Good Old American Politics, DES Journal, Oct 92; Quality Management, DES Journal, fall 93; Andrew Greeley's Literary Antecedents, DES Journal, winter 94; Technology: Artistic Medium and Muse, Research in Philosophy and Technology vol 14, 94; A Clockwork Shakespeare, Az English Bull, spring 94; Wings Instead of Clumsy Hooves, Ind English, spring 94; The Investigators, DES Journal, fall 94; The Mossad: The Enemy Within, DES Journal, fall 95; Remember the Sabbath, DES Journal, spring 95; The Creative Non-Fiction Essay, Ind English, fall 95; Paul Robeson Remembered, Midwest Quart, fall 96; Speaking of Editors..., DES Journal, fall 96; and author of many poems. **CONTACT ADDRESS** 3690 East Ave, Rochester, NY, 14618-3597.

HOWARD, JEAN E.
DISCIPLINE DRAMA; RENAISSANCE LITERATURE **EDUCATION** Brown Col, BA, 70; Univ London, MPhil, 72; Yale Univ, PhD, 75. **CAREER** Instr, Syracuse Univ, 75; prof **HONORS AND AWARDS** Marshall fel, 72; Danforth fel, 75; Wasserstrom prize, excellence tchr, Univ Syracusa, 75; NEH fel; Mellon fel; Folger fel; Newberry Library., Ed bd, Shakespeare Quart; Shakespeare Stud; Renaissance Drama. **RESEARCH** Feminist and Marxist literary theory. **SELECTED PUBLICATIONS** Auth, essays on Shakespeare, Pope, non-Shakespearean drama, contemporary criticism, new historicism, Marxism, postmodern political feminism; auth, Shakespeare's Art of Orchestration, 84; co-ed, Shakespeare Reproduced: The Text in History and Ideology, 87; NortonShakespeare, 97; co-auth, The Stage and Struggle in Early Modern England, 1994; Engendering a Nation: A Feminist Account of Shakespeare's English Histories, 97. **CONTACT ADDRESS** Dept of Eng, Columbia Col, New York, 2960 Broadway, New York, NY, 10027-6902.

HOWARD, LEIGH ANNE
PERSONAL Born 11/02/1964, Owensboro, KY, s **DISCIPLINE** ENGLISH, THEATRE **EDUCATION** Centre Col, BA, 86; Western Ky Univ, MA, 91; La State Univ, PhD, 95. **CAREER** Managing ed, Center Magazine, 86-90; ASST PROF OF COMMUN & COORD, PROG IN COMMUN STUDIES, SPALDING UNIV, 95-. **HONORS AND AWARDS** Outstanding Fac Member, Spalding Univ, 96-97. **MEMBERSHIPS** Nat Commun Asn; Southern States Commun Asn. **RESEARCH** Cultural/critical studies: film/media, women and body image, and ethnographic representation. **SELECTED PUBLICATIONS** Coauth, Krewe D'Elvis: LSU Folklore in the Making, La Folklore Miscellany, 93; coauth, The Political Correctness Controversy: Retreat from Argumentation and Reaffirmation of Critical Dialogue, The Am Behavioral Scientist, 95; auth, Playing Boal: Thetre, Therapy, Activism, Theatre Insight, 95; auth, Poetics and Petrochemicals: Organizational Performances of the Mississippi River, Corporate Advocacy: Rhetoric in the Communication Age, Greenwood Press, 97; auth, Ethics and Ethnography: Explicating Values in the Age of Postmodernity, The Am Behvioral Scientist, in press; auth, Stain Upon the Silence: Samuel Beckett's Deconstructive Inventions, Theatre Symposium, 97; auth, Learning to Recognize the Real Thing: Folklore as Persuasion in Magazine Advertising, Ky Journ of Commun, 98. **CONTACT ADDRESS** 501 Pine St, Apt. 1, Louisville, KY, 40204-1131.

HOWARD, LILLIE PEARL
PERSONAL Born 10/04/1949, Gadsden, Alabama, d **DISCIPLINE** ENGLISH **EDUCATION** Univ of South Alabama, Mobile, Al, BA, 1971; Univ of New Mexico, Albuquerque, NM, MA, 1972, PhD, 1975; Harvard University, Cambridge, MA, Grad of Institute for Educational Management, 1988 **CAREER** Wright State Univ, Dayton, OH, associate prof of English, 1980-85, assistant dean, coll liberal arts, 1982-83, associate dean coll liberal arts, 1983-87, professor of English, 1985-, assistant vice pres for academic affairs, 1987-88, associate vice pres for academic affairs, 1988-94; Undergraduate Educ & Academic Affairs, assoc provost, 1994-. **HONORS AND AWARDS** Woodrow Wilson Finalist, 1971; Ford Foundation Fellow, 1971-75; Grant Recipient, National Endowment for the Humanities, 1987-90; Grant Recipient, Ohio Board of Regents, 1990. **MEMBERSHIPS** Member, Modern Languages Association; member, American Association of Higher Education; member, Ohio Board of Regents Committee on the Enhancement of Undergrad education; member, Ohio Board of Regents Commission on Articulation and transfer; member, The National Association of Women Deans, Administrators, and Counselors; member, The National Association of Academic Affairs Administrators. **CONTACT ADDRESS** Undergraduate Education & Academic Affairs, 105E Allyn Hall, Dayton, OH, 45435.

HOWARD, THARON
DISCIPLINE ENGLISH LITERATURE **EDUCATION** Purdue Univ, PhD, 92. **CAREER** Dept Eng, Clemson Univ **RESEARCH** Professional communication; rhetoric. **SELECTED PUBLICATIONS** Auth, Designing Computer Classrooms for Technical Communication Programs in Computer and Technical Communication: A Sourcebook for Teachers and Program Directors, Ablex, 98; The Rhetoric of Electronic Communities, Ablex, 97; Mapping the Minefield of Electronic Ethics, The Nearness of You: Students and Teachers Writing On-Line, Teachers and Writers Collab, 96; Who Owns Electronic Texts?, Electronic Literacies in the Workplace: Technologies of Writing, NCTE Series Comput Comp, 96. **CONTACT ADDRESS** Clemson Univ, Clemson, SC, 29634. **EMAIL** tharon@clemson.edu

HOWARD, W. SCOTT
PERSONAL Born 11/06/1963, Englewood, NJ, m, 1988, 1 child **DISCIPLINE** ENGLISH **EDUCATION** Lewis & Clark Col, BA, 87; Portland St Univ, MA, 89; Univ Wa, PhD, 98. **CAREER** Instr, Sch Extended Stud, 94, Portland St Univ; asst prof, 98-, Univ Denver. **HONORS AND AWARDS** Res Grant, Lewis & Clark Col, 87; Phi Kappa Phi, 89; Travel Grant, Portland St Univ, 89; Fowler Travel Grant, Univ Wa, 95; Pew/PFF Teaching Fel, Univ Wa, 96; Travel Grant, Univ Wa, 97; Joan Webber Outstanding Teaching prize, honorable mention, Univ Wa; MLA Travel Grant, Modern Lang Assoc, 97; Humanities Dissertation Fel, Univ Wa, 98. **MEMBERSHIPS** Milton Soc of Amer; Modern Lang Assoc; Pacific NW Renaissance Conf; Phi Kappa Phi; Puget Sound Renaissance Colloquium; Textual Stud Group, Univ Wa. **SELECTED PUBLICATIONS** Auth, Writing Ghost Writing: A Discursive Poetics of History, Talisman, 95; auth The Paper Being: Animality & the Poetics of the Gift, Imprimatur, 96; auth, (T)rue priest(s) of the sense: Bacon, Donne, & the Anatomie of the Suprasensible, NW British Stud, 96; auth, A Fruit Most Rare: An Collins & the Politics of Elegiac Historiography, British Women's Writing 1640-1867, 97; auth, Whose Anatom(ie/y)?: Donne's Anniversaries & Bacon's Natural History, 1997 MLA Convention, John Donne Soc, 97. **CONTACT ADDRESS** Dept of English, Univ of Denver, Denver, CO, 80208. **EMAIL** showard@du.edu

HOWARD, WILLIAM J.
PERSONAL Born 05/21/1945, Prince George, BC, Canada **DISCIPLINE** ENGLISH **EDUCATION** Univ BC, BA, 67, MA, 69; Univ Leeds, PhD, 75. **CAREER** Asst prof to assoc prof, 75-85, dept head, 84-87, 90-91, PROF ENGLISH, UNIV REGINA, 85-. **MEMBERSHIPS** Wordsworth/Coleridge Asn; John Clare Soc; Byron Soc; ACCUTE. **RESEARCH** John Clare; William Wordsworth; writers of the Romantic Period. **SELECTED PUBLICATIONS** Auth, John Clare, 81; ed, Wascana Rev, 76-82; assoc ed, Prairie Forum, 77-81. **CONTACT ADDRESS** Dept of English, Univ of Regina, Regina, SK, S4S 0A2.

HOWELL, JOHN M.
PERSONAL Born 03/02/1933, Oshawa, ON, Canada, m, 1963, 1 child **DISCIPLINE** AMERICAN LITERATURE **EDUCATION** Millsaps Col, BA, 54; Univ Southern Calif, MA, 60; Tulane Univ, PhD(English), 63. **CAREER** Asst prof, 63-69, assoc prof, 69-80, Prof English, Southern Ill Univ, Carbondale, 81-, Chm Dept, 82-86, 95-98. **MEMBERSHIPS** MLA; NCTE. **RESEARCH** American literature. **SELECTED PUBLICATIONS** Auth, From Abercrombie & Fitch to The First Forty-Nine Stories: The text of Ernest Hemingway's Francis Macomber, Proof: Yearbk Am Bibliog & Textual Studies, 72; Hemingway's metaphysics in four stories of the thirties: A look at the manuscripts, Southern Ill Univ, fall-winter 73; Hemingway, Faulkner, and The Bear, Am Lit, 3/80; John Gardner: A Bibliographical Profile, Southern Ill Univ Press, 80; Faulkner, Prufrock, and Agamemnon: Horses, hell, and high water, In: Faulkner: The Unappeased Imagination, Whitston, 80; The Wound and the Albatross: John Gardner's Apprenticeship, In: Thor's Hammer: Essays on John Gardner, Univ Cent Ark Press, 85; McCaslin and Macomber: From Green Hills to Big Woods, Faulkner J, Fall 86; John Barth: An Interview, Papyrus, Southern Ill Univ, Spring 87; Hemingway and Chaplin: Monkey Business in The Undefeated, Studies in Short Fiction, Winter 90; Salinger in the Waste Land, In: Critical Essays on Salinger's

The Catcher in the Rye, G.K. Hall, 90; Understanding John Gardner, Univ of SC Press, 93. **CONTACT ADDRESS** Dept of English, Southern Ill Univ, Carbondale, IL, 62901-4300. **EMAIL** jmhowell@siu.edu

HOYT, CHARLES ALVA
PERSONAL Born 09/26/1931, Middletown, CT, m, 1974, 5 children **DISCIPLINE** ENGLISH LITERATURE **EDUCATION** Wesleyan Univ, AB, 53, MAT, 55; Columbia Univ, MA, 56, PhD(Eng), 61. **CAREER** Instr, Wayne State Univ, 57-60; from asst prof to assoc prof Eng, Bennett Col, 60-68, chmn dept, 68-77; assoc prof Eng, Marist Col, 77-79; Res & Writing, 79-, Consult hum, US govt, 72-; vis prof, State Univ NY Col New Paltz, 74. **RESEARCH** Ethnomusicology and jazz; Eng lit of the 19th century; contemp Eng and Am lit. **SELECTED PUBLICATIONS** Auth, Bernard Malamud and the new romanticism, In: Contemporary American Novelists, Southern Ill Univ, 64; Novelist or historian?, Columbia Univ Forum, 66; ed, Minor British Novelists, Southern Ill Univ, 67; auth, Contemporary British literature, In: Encycl Americana, Grolier, 68; ed, Minor American Novelists, Southern Ill Univ, 69; The Last Chance Jazz Band, Hudson Valley, 5/78; auth, Witchcraft, Southern Ill Univ Press, 81 & 82. **CONTACT ADDRESS** Southern IL Univ Press, PO Box 3697, Carbondale, IL, 62901.

HOZESKI, BRUCE WILLIAM
PERSONAL Born 02/28/1941, Grand Rapids, MI, m, 1967, 1 child **DISCIPLINE** ENGLISH LITERATURE, HISTORY OF LANGUAGE, MEDIEVAL BRITISH LITERATURE **EDUCATION** Aquinas Col, BA, 64; Mich State Univ, MA, 66, PhD(medieval English lit), 69. **CAREER** Grad asst English, Mich State Univ, 64-69; instr, Lansing Community Col, 68-69; PROF ENGLISH, BALL STATE UNIV, 69-, Chair, University Senate, 96-, Dir Grad Programs in English, 98-01; Exec Secy and Treas of Lambda Iota Tau, The Nat Honor Soc for Lit, 90-; founder and president, Int Soc of Hildegard von Bingen Studies, 84-89, lifetime mem of exec coun; mem Bd of Dir, Christian Ministries of Delaware County, 97-03. **MEMBERSHIPS** AAUP; MLA; Midwest Mod Lang Asn; NCTE; Medieval Acad Am. **RESEARCH** Medieval English literature; medieval drama; Hildegard of Bingen. **SELECTED PUBLICATIONS** Auth, Hildegard of Bingen's Ordo Virtutum: The earliest discovered liturgical morality play, Am Benedictine Rev, 75; A mathematical error in Jonathan Swift's A Modest Proposal, Am Notes & Queries, 76; The parallel patterns in Hrotsvitha of Gandersheim, a tenth century German playwright, and in Hildegard of Bingen, a twentieth century German playwright, Annuale Mediaevale, 78; The parallel patterns in Prudentia's Psychomachia and Hildegarde of Bingen's Ordo Virtutum, 14th Century, English Mystics Newslett, 82; Hildegard of Bingen's Scivias, 86; Hildegard von Bingen's Mystical Visions, 95; Hildegard of Bingen: The Book of the Rewards of Life: Liber Vitae Meritorum, 97; regular contribr to An Annotated Chaucer Bibliography - Studies in the Age of Chaucer, 91-present. **CONTACT ADDRESS** Dept of English, Ball State Univ, 2000 W University, Muncie, IN, 47306-0460. **EMAIL** 00bwhozeski@bsuuc.edu

HUANG, SHAORONG
PERSONAL Born 03/12/1951, China, m, 1978, 1 child **DISCIPLINE** COMMUNICATION, INTERPERSONAL COMMUNICATIONS **EDUCATION** Bowling Green State Univ, PhD, 94. **CAREER** Asst prof, Univ Cincinnati, 96-. **MEMBERSHIPS** Nat Commun Asn. **RESEARCH** Intercultural communication and rhetoric. **SELECTED PUBLICATIONS** Auth, Ritual, culture, and communication: Deification of Mao Zedong in China's cultural revolution movement, Politics, communication, and culture, Sage, Pub, 97; To rebel is justified: A rhetorical study of China's cultural revolution movement: 1966-1969, Univ Press of Am, 96; coauth, Expanding the knowledge base: Reconsidering the communication literature, J of the Asn for Commun Admin, 94; A brief survey of Chinese popular culture, J of Popular Culture, Bowling Green State Univ Popular Press, 93. **CONTACT ADDRESS** Univ of Cincinnati, 9555 Plainfield Rd, Cincinnati, OH, 45236. **EMAIL** Huangsn@ucrwcu.rwc.uc.edu

HUDGINS, CHRISTOPHER CHAPMAN
PERSONAL Born 03/22/1947, Richmond, VA, m, 1970, 1 child **DISCIPLINE** ENGLISH LITERATURE **EDUCATION** Davidson Col, AB, 68; Emory Univ, MA, 69, PhD, 76. **CAREER** Instr, Old Dominion Univ, 69-71; asst prof, 76-80, assoc prof English, 80-, chemn dept English, 83-94, chemn Nv Humanities Comm, 96, Univ Nv Las Vegas, 80-, Emory Univ Fel English, 68-69 & 71-75. **MEMBERSHIPS** MLA; Rocky Mt MLA; AAUP; Am Film Inst; vpres Harold Pinter Soc, 92; vpres David Monet Soc, 94. **RESEARCH** Harold Pinter; modern British and American drama; film studies. **SELECTED PUBLICATIONS** Auth, Dance to a cut-throat temper: Harold Pinter's poetry as index to intended audience response, Comp Drama, 12: 214-232; Inside out: Filmic technique and the theatrical depiction of a consciousness in Harold Pinter's Old Times, Genre, 13: 355-376; Intended audience response, The Homecoming, and the ironic mode of identification, Harold Pinter: A Collection of Critical Essays, Univ Mo, 90. **CONTACT ADDRESS** Dept English, Univ Nv, PO Box 455011, Las Vegas, NV, 89154-5011.

HUDSON, ROBERT J.
PERSONAL Born 06/11/1921, Selma, AL, m, 1944, 1 child **DISCIPLINE** ENGLISH EDUCATION **EDUCATION** Tenn State Col, BA, 46; NY Univ, MA, 47, PhD(English), 62. **CAREER** From instr to assoc prof English, 47-63, chmn dept, 71-77, asst dean, 68-74, PROF ENGLISH, TENN STATE UNIV, 63-, DEAN SCH ARTS & SCI, 74-, Prof English, Fisk Univ, 64-65, lectr Shakespeare & Elizabethan drama, 67- **HONORS AND AWARDS** NY Univ Founder's Day Award, 63. **MEMBERSHIPS** MLA; Col Lang Asn; NCTE; Shakespeare Asn Am; Conf Col Compos & Commun. **RESEARCH** Shakespeare, Elizabethan drama; sixteenth century non-dramatic literature. **SELECTED PUBLICATIONS** Auth, Publications by Cla Members, 1991-92, Cla J, Vol 0036, 92. **CONTACT ADDRESS** Dept of English, Tenn State Univ, Nashville, TN, 37203.

HUDSON-WEEMS, CLENORA
DISCIPLINE AFRICAN-AMERICAN LITERATURE **EDUCATION** Univ Iowa, PhD, 88. **CAREER** Assoc Prof; **MEMBERSHIPS** Ed bd, Western J for Black Stud. **SELECTED PUBLICATIONS** Auth, Africana Womanism: Reclaiming Ourselves, 93 & Emmett Till: The Sacrificial Lamb of the Civil Rights Movement, 94; essays on, Claude MacKay, Zora Neale Hurston, Richard Wright, Gwendolyn Brooks & Malcolm X; coauth, Toni Morrison, Twayne, 90. **CONTACT ADDRESS** Dept of English, Univ of Missouri-Columbia, 309 University Hall, Columbia, MO, 65211.

HUESCA, ROBERT
DISCIPLINE COMMUNICATIONS **EDUCATION** CA State Univ, BA, 82; Univ TX-Austin, MA, 88; OHio State Univ, PhD, 94. **CAREER** Tchg asst, OH State Univ, 90-91; tchg assoc, OH State Univ, 91-93; grad fel, OH State Univ, 93-94; asst prof, 94-. **HONORS AND AWARDS** Ed clinic award, The Columbus Dispatch, 89; multi-yr minority stud fel, OH State Univ, 90; travel grant, OH State Univ, 92; res travel grant, Intl Stud Fel prog, 92; travel grant, Tinker found, OH State Univ, 93 Walter B Emery scholar award, OH State Univ, 94; fac summer develop grant, 96., Res ch, Assn Edu in Jour and Mass Commun, 95-96; V hd, Assn Edu in Jour and Mass Commun, 96-97; hd, Assn Edu in Jour and Mass Commun, 97-98; manuscript feferee, Jour Intl Commun, 97; contribut ed, Commun Bknotes Quart, L Erlbaum Assoc, 97. **MEMBERSHIPS** Mem, Assn Edu in Jour and Mass Commun; Intl Assn for Mass Commun Res; Intl Commun Assn Nat Assn of Hisp Jour(s); Union for Democratic Commun. **SELECTED PUBLICATIONS** Co-auth, Theory and practice in Latin American alternative communication research, Jour Commun 44, 94; auth, A procedural view of participatory communication: Lessons from Bolivian tin miners' radio, Media, Cult and Soc 17, 95; Dying to make the paper, Rhetorical criticism: Exploration & practice, Waveland, 95; Honda: The ultimate trip, Rhetorical criticism: Exploration & practice, Waveland, 95; Subject-authored theories of media practice: The case of Bolivian tin miners' radio, Commun Stud 46, 95; Diversity in communication for social change, Peace Rev 8, 96; New directions for participatory communication for developmentm, Media Devel 43, 96; Participation for development in radio: An ethnography of the reporteros populares of Bolivia, Gazette: Intl Jour for Mass Commun Stud 57, 96; Low-powered television in rural Bolivia: New directions for democratic media practice, Stud Latin Am Pop Cult 16, 97. **CONTACT ADDRESS** Dept of Commun, Trinity Univ, 715 Stadium Dr, San Antonio, TX, 78212. **EMAIL** rhuesca @ trinity.edu

HUFFMAN, CLIFFORD CHALMERS
PERSONAL Born 06/05/1940, New York, NY, m, 1967 **DISCIPLINE** ENGLISH LITERATURE **EDUCATION** Columbia Univ, BA, 61, PhD(English), 69; Cambridge Univ, MA, 67. **CAREER** Instr English, Brandeis Univ, 68-70; asst prof, 70-73, ASSOC PROF ENGLISH, STATE UNIV NY, STONY BROOK, 73-, DIR SUMMER SESSION, 76-, Nat Endowment Humanities grant, 76. **MEMBERSHIPS** MLA. **RESEARCH** History of ideas; Renaissance history; English and comparative Renaissance literatures. **SELECTED PUBLICATIONS** Auth, Utter Antiquity--Perceptions of Prehistory in Renaissance England, Clio J, Vol 0024, 95. **CONTACT ADDRESS** Dept of English, State Univ of NY, 100 Nicolls Rd, Stony Brook, NY, 11794-0002.

HUFFMAN, JOHN L.
DISCIPLINE COMMUNICATION STUDIES **EDUCATION** Univ IA, PhD, 73. **CAREER** Instr, Bowling Green State Univ, Pepperdine Univ, Univ Tulsa; prof, Univ NC, Charlotte. **RESEARCH** Commun law and policy; First Amendment theory. **SELECTED PUBLICATIONS** His research efforts have appeared in numerous jour(s), including Jour Quart, J of Broadcasting and Electronic Media, Free Speech Yearbk, J of Commun Law and Policy, Jour Monogr, and Intellect. **CONTACT ADDRESS** Univ N. Carolina, Charlotte, Charlotte, NC, 28223-0001.

HUFMAN, MELODY J.
DISCIPLINE COMMUNICATION **EDUCATION** Wichita State Univ, BA, 77; Univ Denver, MA, 81, PhD, 83. **CAREER** Instr, Nat Col of Bus, Colorado, 82; instr, Metropolitan State Col, Colorado, 82; tchg fel, Univ Denver, 81-83; instr, Tarrant County Jr Col, Texas, 84; prof, Amber Univ, Texas, 84- . **MEMBERSHIPS** Natl Comm Asn; Western Comm Asn. **RESEARCH** Nonverbal communication; organizational communication; political communication. **SELECTED PUBLICATIONS** Auth, "Nonverbal Measures of self assessment," ERIC, 95; "Distance Learning Via a Modem," ERIC, 96; "Managerial Solutions," ERIC, 97; "Pet Adoption Experience a Dog-Gone Good Experience," Mansfield News Mirror, 97. **CONTACT ADDRESS** 1301 Wren Dr, Mansfield, TX, 76063. **EMAIL** drhufman@hotmail.com

HUGGINS, CYNTHIA
PERSONAL Born 06/23/1956, Greenville, SC, s **DISCIPLINE** ENGLISH **EDUCATION** Univ North Carolina at Greensboro, PhD, 97. **CAREER** Teaching asst, Univ North Carolina at Greensboro, 95-97; asst prof English, Univ Maine at Machias, 97-. **HONORS AND AWARDS** Lane Graduate Fel in English, Univ North Carolina at Greensboro; Mildred Kates Dissertation Award, Univ North Carolina at Greensboro; Bronte Soc Res Grant; Graduate Teaching Award, Dept of English, Univ North Carolina at Greensboro; Outstanding Graduate Teaching Asst Award, Col of Arts and Sciences, Univ North Carolina at Greensboro. **MEMBERSHIPS** Bronte Soc; Mod Lang Asn; Victorians Inst; North Atlantic, Mod Lang Asn; 18th and 19th Century British Women Writers Asn. **RESEARCH** Brontes; Victorian fiction and poetry; literary biography; Romantics; 18th century novel. **SELECTED PUBLICATIONS** Auth, "Behind the Mask of Branwell Bronte", in Bronte Newsletter 9, 90; auth, "Adam Bede: Author, Narrator and Narrative", in George Eliot Review 23, 92; auth, "Review of Rose Macaulay: A Writer's Life", in English Literature in Transition 1880-1820 37, 94; coauth, "Review of 'The Letters of Charlotte Bronte. With a Selection of Letters by Family and Friends. Volume One, 1829-1847' Recent work on the Brontes", in Victorians Institute Journal 24, 96; auth, "Witnessing by Example: Southern Baptists in Clyde Edgerton's 'Walking Across Egypt' and 'Killer Diller'", in The Southern Quart 35, 97; auth, "A. Mary F. Robinson (1857-1944)", in Dictionary of Literary Biography: Victorian Women Poets, Gale Research, 98. **CONTACT ADDRESS** Univ of Maine at Machias, 9 O'Brien Ave., Machias, ME, 046540. **EMAIL** CHUGGINS@ACAD.UMM.MAINE.EDU

HUGHES, DAVID YERKES
PERSONAL Born 11/12/1924, Berkeley, CA, m, 1955, 3 children **DISCIPLINE** ENGLISH **EDUCATION** Univ Calif, Berkeley, BA, 51; Columbia Univ, MA, 55; Univ Ill, Urbana, PhD(English), 62. **CAREER** Instr English, Univ NC, Chapel Hill, 61-64; asst prof, 64-69, assoc prof humanities, 69-78, PROF HUMANITIES, UNIV MICH, ANN ARBOR, 78- **MEMBERSHIPS** MLA. **RESEARCH** Science fiction; utopias; H G Wells. **SELECTED PUBLICATIONS** Auth, The Critical Response to Wells, SF Studies, Vol 0022, 95. **CONTACT ADDRESS** Dept of Humanities, Univ of Mich, Ann Arbor, MI, 48109.

HUGHES, DIANA L.
PERSONAL Born 02/09/1947, Hannibal, MO, m, 1983 **DISCIPLINE** SPEECH LANGUAGE **EDUCATION** E Illinois Univ, BS, 69; S Illinois Univ, MS, 71, MS, 72; Univ Wash, PhD, 82. **CAREER** Col level tchng, Univ Wisc, 72-82; tchr, 82-, Central Mich Univ. **HONORS AND AWARDS** Mich Assn of Gov Bds, Dist Fac Mem, 88. **MEMBERSHIPS** Amer Speech-Lang-Hearing Assn; Mich Speech-Lang-Hearing Assn. **RESEARCH** Child lang disorders; assessment of narrative discourse; lang intervention. **SELECTED PUBLICATIONS** Auth, Language Treatment and Generalization: A Clinician's Handbook, College-Hill, 85; coauth, Developmental Sentence Scoring: Still Useful After All These Years, Topics in Lang Disorders, 92; art, Interest Area 6: Intervention Programming and Efficacy, ASHA Spec Int Div #10, Ed/Learn Correlates of Comm Disorders 2:2, 92; coauth, A Case Study of Phonological Development in Language Delayed Twins Not Enrolled in Therapy, J of Childhood Comm Disorders 15:2, 93; coauth, Two Approaches to the Facilitation of Grammar in Children with Language Impairment: An Experimental Evaluation, J of Speech & Hearing Res 36, 93; art, Intervention Programming and Efficacy SIC #10, Newsl, 93; coauth, Computer Technology: Use in Training Programs, Asha 38-39, 93; coauth, Vowel Use of Phonologically Disordered Identical Twin Boys: A Case Study, Perceptual Motor Skills 79, 94; coauth, Computer Assisted Instruction for Learning Developmental Sentence Scoring: An Experimental Comparison, Amer J of Speech-Lang Path 3:3, 94; coauth, Guide to Narrative Language: Procedures for Assessment, Thinking Publ, 97. **CONTACT ADDRESS** Central Michigan Univ, Moore 416, Mt. Pleasant, MI, 48859. **EMAIL** diana.l.hughes@cmich.edu

HUGHES, LINDA K.
PERSONAL Born 07/09/1948, Dodge City, KS, m, 1966, 1 child **DISCIPLINE** ENGLISH **EDUCATION** Wichita State Univ, BA, 70; Univ Mo Columbia, MA, 71, PhD, 76. **CAREER** Instr, 76-80, asst prof, 80-84, eng, Univ Mo Rolla; asst prof, 84-85, assoc prof, 85-88, eng, Washburn Univ; assoc prof, 88-92, prof, 92-, dir grad studies, 92-, eng, Tex Christian Univ. **HONORS AND AWARDS** Phi Beta Kappa; Phi Kappa Phi; Phi Beta Delta; Dean's Teaching award, Tex Christian Univ,

92; pres, Res Soc of Victorian Periodicals, 97-99. **MEMBERSHIPS** Mod Lang Asn; South Central Mod Lang Asn; Res Soc of Victorian Periodicals; Interdisciplinary 19th-century studies; 1890s Soc. **RESEARCH** Victorian literature and culture; Victorian periodicals; Poetry; Women poets; Aestheticism and gender; Arthurian studies; Serial literature; Authorship; Tennyson; Rosamund Marriott Watson; Elizabeth Gaskell. **SELECTED PUBLICATIONS** Essay, Come Again, and Thrice as Fair, The Modern Return, Garland Publ, 51-64, 98; monogr, Strange Bedfellows: W. E. Henley and Feminist Fashion History, occasional series no 3, Eighteen Nineties Soc, 97; essay, Fair Hymen Holdeth Hid a World of Woes: Myth and Marriage in Poems by Graham R. Tomson, Victorian Women Poets: A Critical Reader, Basil Blackwell, 162-85, 96; essay, Textual/Sexual Pleasure and Serial Publication, Literature in the Marketplace: Nineteenth-Century British Publishing and Reading Practices, Cambridge Univ Press, 143-64, 95; article, A Fin-de-Siecle Beauty and the Beast: Configuring the Body in Works by Graham R. Tomson, Tulsa Studies in Women's Literature, 14.1, 95-121, Spring, 95; guest ed, Victorian Poetry: Victorian Women Poets, Spring, 95. **CONTACT ADDRESS** Dept. of English, Texas Christian Univ, TW, Box 297270, Ft. Worth, TX, 76129. **EMAIL** l.hughes@tcu.edu

HUGHES, ROBERT G.
DISCIPLINE HOMILETICS **EDUCATION** B.A. Lehigh Univ, 1959; MDiv, LTSP, 1962; ThM, Princeton Sem, 1974; PhD, 1981; Pastorates in Pa, 1962-71. **CAREER** Prof, 72; pres, 90; ch of the fac-. **HONORS AND AWARDS** Pastor, Christ's United Lutheran Church. **SELECTED PUBLICATIONS** Coauth, Preaching Doctrine: for the twenty-first Century, Fortress Press, 97. **CONTACT ADDRESS** Dept of Practical Theology, Lutheran Theol Sem, 7301 Germantown Ave, Philadelphia, PA, 19119 1794. **EMAIL** Mtairy@ltsp.edu

HULL, AKASHA
PERSONAL Shreveport, LA **DISCIPLINE** ENGLISH **EDUCATION** Southern University, BA (summa cum laude), 1966; Purdue University, MA, 1968, PhD, 1972 **CAREER** Univ of Delaware, prof of English 1972-88; University of California, Santa Cruz, professor, women studies 1988-. **HONORS AND AWARDS** Fellowship, Rockefeller Foundation 1979-80; Outstanding Woman of Color, Natl Institute of Women of Color 1982; Ford Foundation, Postdoctoral Fellowship 1987-88; AAUW Fellowship 1990. **MEMBERSHIPS** Co-project dir, Black Women's Studies project 1982-84; Mellon Scholar, Wellesley Ctr for Rsch on Women 1983; Fulbright Senior Lectureship, Univ of the West Indies-Jamaica 1984-86; commission co-chair, Modern Language Assn; Natl Women's Studies Assn; advisor/consultant, Black American Literature Forum, Feminist Studies. **SELECTED PUBLICATIONS** All the Women are White, All the Blacks are Men, but Some of Us are Brave, Black Women's Studies 1982; Give Us Each Day, the Diary of Alice Dunbar-Nelson 1984; Color, Sex, and Poetry: Three Women Writers of the Harlem Renaissance 1987; Healing Heart: Poems 1973-1988, 1989; Works of Alice Dunbar-Nelson, 3 vols, 1988. **CONTACT ADDRESS** Kresge Col, Univ of California, Santa Cruz, CA, 95064.

HULSE, CLARK
PERSONAL Born 06/01/1947, Pittsburgh, PA, m, 1969, 2 children **DISCIPLINE** ENGLISH **EDUCATION** Williams Col, BA, 69; Claremont Grad Sch, MA, 70, PhD(English), 74. **CAREER** Instr, 72-74, asst prof, 74-80, ASSOC PROF ENGLISH, UNIV ILL, CHICAGO CIRCLE, 80-, Univ Ill res grants, 76 & 78; Nat Endowment Humanities Newberry Libr fel, 79. **MEMBERSHIPS** MLA; Renaissance Soc Am. **RESEARCH** Elizabethan poetry; Shakespeare; interdisciplinary studies in Renaissance art and literature. **SELECTED PUBLICATIONS** Auth, The Portrait of Eccentricity--Archimboldo and the Mannerist Grotesque, Renaissance Quarterly, Vol 0046, 93; Habits of Thought in the English Renaissance, Religion, Politics, and the Dominant Culture, Modern Philol, Vol 0090, 93; The Elizabethan Courtier Poets--The Poems and Their Contexts, Anq, Vol 0006, 93. **CONTACT ADDRESS** Dept of English, Univ of Ill at Chicago Circle, Chicago, IL, 60680.

HUME, KATHRYN
PERSONAL Born 12/10/1945, Boston, MA, m, 1966 **DISCIPLINE** ENGLISH **EDUCATION** Harvard Univ, AB, 67; Univ Pa, MA, 68, PhD, 71. **CAREER** Lect, Cornell Univ, Univ Va, 69-73; asst prof, Cornell Univ, 73-77; assoc prof,77-86, prof, 86-93, DISTINGUISHED PROF, 93-, PA STATE UNIV. **CONTACT ADDRESS** Dept of English, Pennsylvania State Univ, Burrowes Bldg, University Park, PA, 16802.

HUME, ROBERT DAVID
PERSONAL Born 07/25/1944, Oak Ridge, TN, m, 1966 **DISCIPLINE** ENGLISH LITERATURE **EDUCATION** Haverford Col, BA, 66; Univ Pa, PhD(English), 69. **CAREER** From asst prof to assoc prof English, Cornell Univ, 69-77; PROF ENGLISH, PA STATE UNIV, 77-, ASSOC HEAD DEPT, 79-. **MEMBERSHIPS** MLA; Soc Theatre Res; Am Soc 18th Century Studies; Am Soc Theatre Res; Mod Humanities Res Asn. **RESEARCH** English drama, 1660-1800; 18th century novel and aesthetics; theory of literary criticism. **SELECTED PUBLICATIONS** Auth, Opera Salaries in 18th-Century London, J Am Musicol Soc, Vol 0046, 93; James Lewis Plans for an Opera-House in the Haymarket 1778, Theatre Res Int, Vol 0019, 94; Miscellanies (rev), Scriblerian Kit-Cats, Vol 0029, 96; Lovers, Clowns, and Fairies--An Essay on Comedies, Comp Lit, Vol 0048, 96; Thomas Doggett at Cambridge in 1701--Strolling Theater Companies in 18th-Century Britain, Theatre Notebk, Vol 0051, 97; A Profession of Friendship (rev), J English Germanic Philol, Vol 0096, 97; Before the Bard--Shakespeare in Early 18th-Century London, Elh-English Lit Hist, Vol 0064, 97. **CONTACT ADDRESS** Dept of English, Pennsylvania State Univ, University Park, PA, 16801.

HUMMA, JOHN BALLARD
PERSONAL Born 02/16/1940, Rosiclare, IL, m, 1968, 4 children **DISCIPLINE** NINETEENTH CENTURY AMERICAN LITERATURE **EDUCATION** George Washington Univ, BA, 63; Southern Ill Univ, Carbondale, MA, 65, PhD(English), 69. **CAREER** Assoc prof, 69-79, prof English, GA Southern Col, 80-. **HONORS AND AWARDS** Univ Excellence in Res Award, 89. **MEMBERSHIPS** MLA. **RESEARCH** British fiction; American literature. **SELECTED PUBLICATIONS** Auth, Poe's Ligeia: Glanvill's Will or Blake's Will, Miss Quart, winter 72-73; The Art and Meaning of Sarah Orne Jewett's The Courting of Sister Wisby, winter 73 & Gabriel and the Bedsheets: The Ending of the Dead, spring 73, Studies Short Fiction; D. H. Lawrence as Friedrich Nietzche, Philol Quart, 1/74; Melville's Billy Budd and Lawrence's The Prussian Officer: Old Adams and New, spring 74 & Pan and The Rocking-Horse Winner, 78, Essays Lit; The Narrative Framing Apparatus of Scott's Old Mortality, Studies in the Novel, winter 80; The Interpenetrating Metaphor: Nature and Myth in Lady Chatterley's Lover, PMLA, Jan 83; John Fowles' The Ebony Tower: In the Celtic Mood, Southern Humanities Rev, Winter 83; Of Bits, Beasts, and Bush: The Interior Wilderness in D. H. Lawrence's Kangaroo; S Atlantic Rev, Jan 86; James and Fowles: Tradition and Influence, Univ of Toronto Quart, Fall 88; Metaphor and Meaning in D. H. Lawrence's Later Novels, Univ of Mo Press, 90; Realism and Beyond: The Imagery of Sex and Sexual Oppression in Elizabeth Stoddard's Lemorne Versus Huell, S Atlantic Rev, Jan 93; Lawrence in Another Light: Women in Love and Existentialism, Studies in the Novel, Winter 92. **CONTACT ADDRESS** Dept of English, Georgia So Univ, PO Box 8023, Statesboro, GA, 30460-1000. **EMAIL** humma@gsaix2.cc.gasou.edu

HUMPHERYS, ANNE
PERSONAL Born 02/25/1937, Lehi, UT, m, 1967 **DISCIPLINE** ENGLISH LITERATURE **EDUCATION** Stanford Univ, BA, 59; Columbia Univ, MA, 62, PhD(English), 68. **CAREER** Assoc prof, 68-80, PROF ENGLISH, LEHMAN COL, 80- **MEMBERSHIPS** MLA; Res Soc Victorian Periodicals; Northeast Victorian Studies Asn. **RESEARCH** Victorian literature; history of the English novel. **SELECTED PUBLICATIONS** Auth, Locating the Popular Text--Popular-Culture, Victorian Lit Cult, Vol 0019, 91; 'Enoch Arden', the Fatal Return and the Silence Of Annie, Victorian Poetry, Vol 0030, 92; The Printed Image and the Transformation of Popular Culture, 1790-1860, Nineteenth-Century Lit, Vol 0047, 93. **CONTACT ADDRESS** Dept of English, Lehman Col, CUNY, 250 Bedford Park W, Bronx, NY, 10468-1527.

HUMPHRIES, JEFF
DISCIPLINE 19TH CENTURY LITERATURE, COMPARATIVE LITERATURE, LITERARY THEORY **EDUCATION** Yale Univ, PhD, 81. **CAREER** Prof, ch, La State Univ. **SELECTED PUBLICATIONS** Auth, Losing the Text, 86; Southern Literature and Literary Theory, 90; The Red and the Black: Mimetic Desire and Iconoclasm in Stendhal's Novel, 91; The Future of Southern Letters, 96. **CONTACT ADDRESS** Dept of Fr Grad Stud, Louisiana State Univ, Baton Rouge, LA, 70803.

HUNNING, ROBERT W.
DISCIPLINE ENGLISH LITERATURE **EDUCATION** Columbia Univ, BA, 58, PhD, 64; Oxford Univ, BA, 60, MA, 64. **CAREER** Instr, Middlebury Col; Yale Univ; Johns Hopkins Univ; NYU; Princeton Univ; dir, prof, Lincoln Col, Oxford, 80, 84, 86; prof, 63-. **HONORS AND AWARDS** ACLS fel; Guggenheim fel; NEH fel; elect fel, Medieval Acad Am, 86., Dir, NEH asummer sem, Col Tchr, 82, 85, 89; trustee, New Chaucer Soc, 97-01. **SELECTED PUBLICATIONS** Auth, books on medieval historiography and romance; co-ed, an anthology and two essay collections; co-transl, the Lais of Marie de France. **CONTACT ADDRESS** Dept of Eng, Columbia Col, New York, 2960 Broadway, New York, NY, 10027-6902.

HUNT, BARBARA ANN
PERSONAL Aberdeen, MS, d **DISCIPLINE** HUMANITIES **EDUCATION** Bennett Coll Greensboro NC, BA 1948-52; Syracuse U, MSLS 1952-54; MS Univ for Women, MA 1969-73; Univ of IL, CAS 1971-73; Northwestern University, PhD, 1988. **CAREER** MS Univ for Women, dir curr lab 1977-79; AL A&M Univ Huntsville, asst prof 1974-77; AL A&M University, acting dean, 1975-76; Bennett Coll Greensboro, head librn 1967-73; Dist 65 Evanston IL, librn cataloger 1961-66; Morgan State Coll, Baltimore MD, asst librn 1955-57; Rust Coll Holly Springs MS, head librn, assoc prof 1954-55; S Assn of Coll & Schools, consult 1968; Alabama State University, director of communications, 1983-85; University of Mississippi, African-American Novel Project, co-director, director, 1988-91; Knoxville College, Division of Arts & Humanities, head, 1993. **HONORS AND AWARDS** Cerf Lib Admin Dev Prog Univ of MD Coll Pk; University Fellowship, Northwestern University; Janet Green Flwshp, Nrthwstrn Univ 1980; Minority Flwshp St of MS 1979-81; Ford Found & Flwshp 1970-73; Minority Grant Univ of IL 1972; cadetship Syracuse Univ NY 1952-54. **MEMBERSHIPS** Mem bd of dir Wesley Found MS Univ for Women 1979-; mem bd of trustees Millsaps Coll Jackson MS 1979-; coord Wesley Found St James Meth 1979-; cert lay asso United Meth Ch; co-chrprsn Local United Negro Coll Fund 1978. **CONTACT ADDRESS** Div Arts and Humanities, Knoxville Coll, Knoxville, TN, 37921.

HUNT, JOHN DIXON
PERSONAL Born 01/18/1936, Gloucester, England, d, 2 children **DISCIPLINE** ENGLISH LITERATURE **EDUCATION** Bristol Univ UK, 57-59, PhD 64. **CAREER** Univ Michigan, tch fel, 59-60; Vassar Col, inst 60-62; Exeter univ, asst lectr, 62-64; Univ York, lectr 64-75; Univ London Bedford Col, reader, prof, 75-82; Leiden Univ Netherlands, prof, ch, 83-85; Univ E Anglia, prof, pub curator, 85-88; Dumbarton Oaks, dir, 88-91; Oak Spring Garden Library, acad adv, 91-94; Univ Penn, prof, ch, 94-. **HONORS AND AWARDS** Folger Shakespeare Lib Fel; John Hopkins Univ vis fel, vis prof; Leverhulme Trust Sr Fac Fel; Brit Acad Euro Ex Fund Gnt; Princeton Univ vis mem. **RESEARCH** Inter art Relationships; garden history and history. **SELECTED PUBLICATIONS** Editor since 81, Jour of Garden History, re-titled 98, Studies on the History of Gardens and Designed Landscapes; editor, Penn Studies in Landscape Architecture, Univ Penn Press, 96-; The Greater Perfection: A Theory of Gardens, Thames & Hudson conjunct with Univ Penn Press, forthcoming; The Oak Spring Hortis, Upperville VA, in press; Imagination: 1600-1750, J M Dent , 85, pbk, ed, Univ Penn Press, 96; The Italian Garden Art Design and Culture, essays by, Malcolm Campbell, Iris Lauterbach, Alessandro Tosi, Raymond Gastil, et al, Cambridge Univ Press, 93; Approaches New and Old to Garden History, in: Dumbarton Oaks Colloquim series, Garden Hist and Historiography, forthcoming; Garden Aesthetics, in: The Encycl of Aesthetics, ed Michael Kelly, OUP, forthcoming; Humphry Repton and Garden Historiography, Jour of Garden Hist, 96; Ruskin: The Design of Nature and the Transcription of its Manuscript, Assemblage, 97; The Garden as Virtual reality, Das Kunstliche Paradies, Gartenkunst im Spammungsfeld von Natur und Gesellschaft, ed, Marcus Kohler, spec issue, Die Gartenkunst, Hanover, 97. **CONTACT ADDRESS** Dept of Landscape Architecture, Univ Pennsylvania, Philadelphia, PA, 19104. **EMAIL** jdhunt@pobox.upenn.edu

HUNT, LINDA
PERSONAL m **DISCIPLINE** WRITING II, ESSAY WRITING, AND JOURNAL WRITING AND AUTOBIOGRAPHY **EDUCATION** Whitworth Col, MAT, Gonzaga Univ, PhD, 97. **CAREER** Asso prof. **HONORS AND AWARDS** Dir, Whitworth's Freshman Composition Prog. **SELECTED PUBLICATIONS** Auth, Rare Beasts, Unique Adventures: Reflections for College Students, Harper/Collins: Zondervan; contribu, Seattle Times, Reader's Digest, Psychology Today, Christian Science Monitor.. **CONTACT ADDRESS** Dept of Eng, Whitworth Col, 300 West Hawthorne Rd, Spokane, WA, 99251. **EMAIL** lhunt@whitworth.edu

HUNT, STEVEN B.
PERSONAL Dayton, OH **DISCIPLINE** COMMUNICATION **EDUCATION** Univ Kans, PhD, 73; Lewis & Clark NW Sch Law, JD, 85. **CAREER** Lewis & Clark Coll, 73- **HONORS AND AWARDS** Editor, Pi Kappa Delta Forensic, 92-97; pres, Cross Examination Debate Asn, 94-95; Pi Kappa Delta Scholarship, 96; L E Norton award, 96. **MEMBERSHIPS** National Commun Asn; Western States Commun Asn; Phi Beta Kappa; Cross Examination Debate Asn; Am Forensics Asn. **RESEARCH** Political campaign commun; argumentation and debate; legal commun. **SELECTED PUBLICATIONS** various **CONTACT ADDRESS** Commun Dept, Lewis & Clark Col, 0615 SW Palatine Hill Rd, Portland, OR, 97219. **EMAIL** hunt@lclark.edu

HUNT, TIMOTHY
DISCIPLINE AMERICAN LITERATURE AND CREATIVE WRITING **EDUCATION** Cornell Univ, PhD. **CAREER** Assoc prof, Washington State Univ. **RESEARCH** Robinson Jeffers and American modernism. **SELECTED PUBLICATIONS** Auth, Kerouac's Crooked Road: Development of a Fiction, 81; Lake County Diamond, 86; ed, 4 vol, The Collected Poetry of Robinson Jeffers, 88. **CONTACT ADDRESS** Dept of English, Washington State Univ, 1 SE Stadium Way, PO Box 645020, Pullman, WA, 99164-5020. **EMAIL** hunt@vancouver.wsu.edu

HUNTER, DIANNE MCKINLEY
PERSONAL Born 10/04/1943, Cleveland, OH **DISCIPLINE** ENGLISH **EDUCATION** Alfred Univ, BA, 66; Purdue Univ, MA, 68; State Univ NY, Buffalo, PhD(English), 72. **CAREER** Asst prof, 72-78, prof English, Trinity Col, Conn, 78-89, Nat

Endowment for Humanities fel, Univ Calif, 76; consult, Deakin Univ, Victoria, Australia. **MEMBERSHIPS** MLA; Int Shakespeare Assn. **RESEARCH** Metatheater; psychoanalytic criticism; women's literature; Psychoanalysis of drama; feminism; hysteria. PUB Auth, LeRoi Jones's Dutchman: Inter-racial ritual of sexual violence, American Imago, Fall 72 & In: The Practice of Psychoanalytic Criticism, Wayne State Univ, 76; co-ed, Gullibles Travels, Links Bks, 74; coauth (with Ian Reid), Myth in Literature and Society: Classical Antiquity, 79, auth, On Diving into the Wreck, In: The Makings of Modern Myth, 79, Is the Oedipus complex obsolescent?, In: Myth in Literature and Society: A Reader, 79 & Shakespearean mythmaking in Macbeth, In: Myth and Shakespeare: A Reader, 79, Deakin Univ Press; Hysteria, Psychoanalysis, and Feminism: The Case of Anna O, Writing on the Body, ed, Conboy etal, Columbia UP, 97; ed with intro and coauthor The Making of Dr Charcot's Hysteria Shows, Edwin Mellen, 98. **CONTACT ADDRESS** Dept of English, Trinity Col, 300 Summit St, Hartford, CT, 06106-3186. **EMAIL** dhunter@mail.trincoll.edu

HUNTER, LINDA
DISCIPLINE AFRICAN LITERATURE **EDUCATION** Univ Ind, BA, 70, MA, 72, PhD, 76. **CAREER** Dept African Lang, Wisc Univ **RESEARCH** Hausa language, linguistics, and literature; language in society; stylistics. **SELECTED PUBLICATIONS** Auth, Transformation in African Verbal Art: Voice, Speech, Language, Jour Am Folklore, 96; Uvulectomy-the making of a ritual, S African Jour al of Med, 95. **CONTACT ADDRESS** Dept of African Languages and Literature, Univ of Wisconsin, Madison, 500 Lincoln Drive, Madison, WI, 53706. **EMAIL** hunter@lss.wisc.edu

HURLEY, ANDREW
PERSONAL Born 11/27/1944, Dallas, TX, m **DISCIPLINE** ENGLISH **EDUCATION** Rice Univ, BA, 67, PhD, 73. **CAREER** Prof, English, Univ of Puerto Rico. **HONORS AND AWARDS** Magna cum laude, 67. **MEMBERSHIPS** MLA; ATA; ALTA; AATIA. **RESEARCH** Translation; translation studies. **SELECTED PUBLICATIONS** Transl, True and False Romances by Ana Lydia Vega, Serpent's Tail, 94; transl, The Assault by Reinaldo Arenas, Penguin, 94; transl, On Being Human: Interpretations of Humanism from the Renaissance to the Present, by Salvatore Puledda, Latitude Press, 97; transl, The Renunciation, by Edgardo Rodriguez Julia, 4 Walls, 8 Windows, 97; transl, Collected Fictions of Jorge Luis Borges, Viking, 98. **CONTACT ADDRESS** PO Box 21423 UPR Station, San Juan, PR, 00931-1423. **EMAIL** memail@coqui.net

HURST WILLIAMS, SUZANNE
DISCIPLINE COMMUNICATION ARTS **EDUCATION** Marquette Univ, BA, 79; Univ WI, MA, 82, PhD, 87. **CAREER** Tchg asst, Univ WI; 84-87; lectr, Univ WI, 83-84; prof, 87-. **HONORS AND AWARDS** Charlene Wackman summer scholar, Univ WI, 84; tchg award for grad stud, Univ WI, 84; outstanding female grad stud, Univ WI, 87; fac develop summer stipend, 90., Dir, Summer Media Inst, 91; co-coord, Trinity fac summer sem, 92; vice ch, 89-90, ch, 90-92, Broadcast Edu Assn; convention coord, Broadcast Edu Assn, 94; co-ch, Speech Commun Assn, 95; newsletter ed, Soc Animation Stud, 94-97; bd dir(s), Broadcast Edu Assn, 95-; co-founder, fac adv, TigerTV, 96-. **MEMBERSHIPS** Mem, Broadcast Edu Assn; Intl Commun Assn; Speech Commun Assn; Soc for Animation Stud; Tex Assn Broadcast Educators. **SELECTED PUBLICATIONS** Auth, Video Production Switchers, Special Effects Generators, and Digital Video Effects, Broadcast Tech Update, Focal Press, 97; Sustaining Program, Encycl of TV, Fitzroy Dearborn Publ, 97; The Howdy Doody Show, Encycl of TV, Fitzroy Dearborn Publ, 97;Captain Video and His Video Rangers, Encycl of TV, Fitzroy Dearborn Publ, 97; co-auth, The Encyclopedia of Television, Fitzroy Dearborn Publ, 97. **CONTACT ADDRESS** Dept of Commun, Trinity Univ, 715 Stadium Dr, San Antonio, TX, 78212.

HURT, JAMES RIGGINS
PERSONAL Born 05/22/1934, Ashland, KY, m, 1958, 3 children **DISCIPLINE** ENGLISH **EDUCATION** Univ Ky, AB, 56, MA, 57; Ind Univ, PhD(English), 65. **CAREER** Instr English, Univ Ky, 59-61; resident lectr, Ind Univ, 63-66; from asst prof to assoc prof, 66-73, prof English, Univ Ill, Urbana, 73-. **MEMBERSHIPS** MLA. **RESEARCH** Dramatic literature. **SELECTED PUBLICATIONS** Auth, Aelfric, Twayne, 72; Catiline's Dream: An essay on Ibsen's plays, Univ Ill, 72; Focus on Film and Theatre, Prentice, 74; Writing Illinois, Univ Ill, 92. **CONTACT ADDRESS** Univ of Illinois, 608 S Wright St, Urbana, IL, 61801-3613. **EMAIL** j-hurt@uiuc.edu

HUSE, NANCY LYMAN
PERSONAL Newark, NJ **DISCIPLINE** ENGLISH **EDUCATION** Caldwell Col, BA, 65; Duquesne Univ, MA, 71; Chicago Univ, PhD(English), 75. **CAREER** Teacher English, Newark Archdiocesan Schs, 58-68 & District 214, Arlington Heights, Ill, 68-69; asst prof English, Augustana Col, Ill, 72-, item writer English, Educ Testing Serv, 76-; consult lit, Centrum, Inc, 77-. **HONORS AND AWARDS** Sabbatical Award, Augustana Res Comt, 89-90; Harold T and Violet M Jaeke Award for Leadership, Augustana, 94; Invited Keynote Speaker, The Work of Tove Jansson Conference, 94; Lois Lenski Distinguished Lecture Series, Ill State Univ, 95; Kerlan Collection Children's Lit Forum, Univ Minnesota, Letters as Literary Criticism, 94. **MEMBERSHIPS** MLA; NCTE; Children's Lit Asn; Women's Caucus, Mod Lang Asn. **RESEARCH** Adolescent literature; feminist criticism; composition. **SELECTED PUBLICATIONS** Auth, Jesus saves and sells: Popular fiction and the Messianic Forties, Proceedings Popular Cult Asn, 75; John Hersey and James Agee: A Critical Bibliography, G K Hall 78. Noel Streatfeild, Twayne's English Authors Series, MacMillan, 94; co-ed, The Critical Response to Tillie Olsen, Greenwood Press, 94; auth, Of Nancy Hanks Born: Meridel LeSueur's Abraham Lincoln, ChLA Q, Spring 93; Re-fabricating Culture, Changing Images of Women, 94-95; The Heavier Book Sack, intro to The Phoenix Award, 1990-1995, Scarecrow Press/ ChLA, 95; Pioneer Myth Displaced: The Life of Rose Wilder Lane, The Lon and the Unicorn, 96. **CONTACT ADDRESS** Augustana Col, 639 38th St, Rock Island, IL, 61201-2210. **EMAIL** enhuse@augustana.edu

HUSSEY, JOHN
DISCIPLINE ENGLISH LITERATURE **EDUCATION** Univ Detroit, AB and MA; Univ FL, PhD. **CAREER** Prof, 71-, Fairleigh Dickinson Univ. **RESEARCH** Am cult in the two decades prior to the Civil War; transcendentalists. **SELECTED PUBLICATIONS** Auth, Neighbors in Eden (vid). **CONTACT ADDRESS** Fairleigh Dickinson Univ, 1000 River Rd, Teaneck, NJ, 07666. **EMAIL** jph@fscvax.fairmont.wvnet.edu

HUSSEY, MARK
PERSONAL Born 06/27/1956, London, England, m, 1992, 2 children **DISCIPLINE** ENGLISH LITERATURE **EDUCATION** Leeds Univ, BA, 78; Univ Nottingham, PhD, 82. **CAREER** Ed, English Tapes Prog, Sussex Publications, 76-82; asst to dir, Straus Thinking & Learning Ctr, 85-88; faculty, New School for Social Research, 87-90; oral Examiner, Gallatin Div., NY Univ, 88-90; faculty, Business Comm Prog, assoc prof to PROF ENGLISH, PACE UNIV, 84-; external examiner, honors thesis, Bates Col, 94; NY State Counc for the Humanities Speakers in the Humantities, 96-; **HONORS AND AWARDS** Faculty Recognition Award, Adult Education, 92;, Founding editor, Woolf Studies Annual, 94; organized first annual int Virginia Woolf conference at Pace Univ, 91 **MEMBERSHIPS** MLA, NCTE, Virginia Woolf Soc **RESEARCH** British modernism, feminist theory. **SELECTED PUBLICATIONS** Editor, Virginia Woolf Miscellany, 91-; Auth, Major Authors on CD-ROM: Virginia Woolf, Primary Source Media, 96; auth, Virginia Woolf A-Z: A Comprehensive Reference for Students, Teachers, and Common Readers to Her Life, Work and Critical Reception, Facts on File, 95; co-ed, Virginia Woolf: Emerging Perspectives. Selected Papers from the Third Annual Conference on Virginia Woolf, Pace UP, 94; auth, introduction to "Virginia Woolf: Themes and Variations. Selected Papers from the Second Annual Conference on Virginia Woolf, Pace UP, 93; auth, introduction to Virginia Woolf Miscellanies: Proceedings of the First Annual Conference on Virginia Woolf, Pace UP, 92; auth, "To the Lighthouse and Physics: The Corresponding Worlds of Virginia Woolf and David Bohm," in New Essays on Virginia Woolf, Contemporary Research Press, 95; auth, "A Violent Hunger for Lost Feelings," in Central Park, special issue, Spring 93; auth, "Refractions of Desire: The Early Fiction of Virginia and Leonard Woolf," in Modern Fiction Studies 38, Spring 92; auth, review of Defending Pornography: Free Speech, Sex, and the Fight for Women's Rights, in On the Issues, Summer 95; auth, review of Virginia Woolf: Critical Assessments, in Woolf Studies Annual, Routledge, 94; auth, review of No Man's Land and Letters from the Front in New York Times Book Review, Nov 6, 94. **CONTACT ADDRESS** Dept of English, Pace Univ, 1 Pace Plaza, New York, NY, 10038. **EMAIL** mhussey@pace.edu

HUSTON, JOHN DENNIS
PERSONAL Born 09/21/1939, New York, NY, m, 1964, 2 children **DISCIPLINE** ENGLISH LITERATURE **EDUCATION** Wesleyan Univ, BA, 61; Yale Univ, MA, 64, PhD(English), 66. **CAREER** From instr to asst prof English, Yale Univ, 66-69; assoc prof, 69-79, PROF ENGLISH, RICE UNIV, 79-. **MEMBERSHIPS** S Cent Mod Lang Asn; MLA. **RESEARCH** Elizabethan drama; Spenser; English Renaissance drama and poetry. **SELECTED PUBLICATIONS** Auth, Reading Football--How the Popular Press Created an American Spectacle, J Southern Hist, Vol 0061, 95. **CONTACT ADDRESS** Dept of English, Rice Univ, Houston, TX, 77001.

HUTCHEON, LINDA
PERSONAL Toronto, ON, Canada **DISCIPLINE** ENGLISH/ COMPARATIVE LITERATURE **EDUCATION** Cornell Univ , MA, 71; Univ Toronto, BA, 69, PhD, 75. **CAREER** Asst prof, 76-82, assoc prof, 82-85, prof, McMaster Univ, 85-88; PROF ENGLISH, UNIV TORONTO, 88-. **HONORS AND AWARDS** Woodrow Wilson Fel, 69-79; Killam Postdoc fel, 78-79; John P. Robarts Ch Can Studs, 88-89; Guggenheim Fel, 92-93. **MEMBERSHIPS** MLA; Int Comp Lit Asn; Can Comp Lit Asn; Toronto Semiotic Circle; Ctr Italian Can Studs; Asn Can Col Univs Tchrs Eng. **SELECTED PUBLICATIONS** Auth, Narcissistic Narrative: The Metafictional Paradox, 80; auth, The Canadian Postmodern: A Study of Contemporary English-Canadian Fiction, 88; auth, Irony's Edge: The Theory and Politics of Irony, 95; coauth, Opera: Desire, Disease, Death, 96. **CONTACT ADDRESS** Dept of English, Univ Toronto, Toronto, ON, M5S 1A1.

HUTCHINGS, WILLIAM
DISCIPLINE TWENTIETH CENTURY BRITISH FICTION **EDUCATION** Univ IL, PhD, 90. **CAREER** Dept Eng, Univ Ala **SELECTED PUBLICATIONS** Auth, The Plays of David Storey: A Thematic Study, Southern Ill, 88; David Storey: A Casebook, Garland, 92. **CONTACT ADDRESS** Univ AL, 1400 University Blvd, Birmingham, AL, 35294-1150.

HUTCHISSON, JAMES M.
PERSONAL Born 06/06/1961, Washington, DC, m, 1994, 1 child **DISCIPLINE** ENGLISH **EDUCATION** Redford Univ, BA, 82; Virginia Polytech Inst & St Univ, MA, 84; Univ Delaware, PhD, 87. **CAREER** Asst prof, 87-89, Wash & Jefferson Col; asst prof, 89-94, prof, 94-, Citadel. **CONTACT ADDRESS** Dept of English, The Citadel, Charleston, SC, 29409. **EMAIL** hutchissonj@citadel.edu

HUTTAR, CHARLES ADOLPH
PERSONAL Born 07/08/1932, Austin, TX, m, 1952, 7 children **DISCIPLINE** ENGLISH **EDUCATION** Wheaton Col, BA, 52; Northwestern Univ, MA, 53, PhD(English), 56. **CAREER** From asst prof to assoc prof English, Gordon Col, 55-66, from actg chmn to chmn dept, 55-66; chmn dept, 71-76, PROF ENGLISH, HOPE COL, 66-, Ed, Gordon Rev, 57 & 59, chmn, 65-66; Folger Shakespeare Libr grant-in-aid, 61; Am Philos Soc Penrose grant, 67, Johnson Fund grant, 78. **MEMBERSHIPS** MLA; Renaissance Soc Am; Conf Christianity & Lit (secy, 58-60; pres, 66-68); Milton Soc Am. **RESEARCH** Popular religious literature 1500-1700; Renaissance poetry. **SELECTED PUBLICATIONS** Auth, Planets in Peril, a Critical-Study of Lewis, Ransom Trilogy, Int Fiction Rev, Vol 0020, 93. **CONTACT ADDRESS** Dept of English, Hope Col, Holland, MI, 49423.

HUTTENSTINE, MARIAN L.
PERSONAL Born 01/26/1940, PA, s **DISCIPLINE** MASS COMMUNICATION; ENGLISH **EDUCATION** Bloomsburg State Univ, BS, 61, MEd, 67; Univ of NC at Chapel Hill, PhD, 85. **CAREER** Tchr, Lake-Lehman High School, 61-63; dept ch Engl, Lake-Lehman High School, 63-66; instr, Lock Haven State Univ, 66-70; from asst prof to assoc prof, Lock Haven State Univ, 70-74; tchg asst, Univ of NC, 74-75; lectr, Univ of NC, 75-77; asst prof, Univ of Ala, 77-93; adj instr, Shelton State Comm Col, 93; assoc prof, Jacksonville State Univ, 93-95; assoc prof, Radford Univ, 95-97; dept head and assoc prof, Miss State Univ, 97-. **HONORS AND AWARDS** Newspaper Fund fel, 62; Nat Defense Educ fel, 63; Int Who's Who of Women, 84, 89, 91, 93; Who's Who of World, 84, 89, 91; Who's Who of Am Women, 85, 87, 89, 91, 93; Student Press Freedom Serv Award, Ala Student Press Asn, 92; Sara Healey, Media Planning Bd Serv Award, UA, 92; First Amendment Award, Ala Media Professionals, 92; Cardinal Key Hon Soc, Hon Membership, 93; The Ken Knight Founder's Award, Minorities for Careers in Commun, 93; Who's Who in the South and Southwest, 80, 82, 84, cont.; Who's Who of Personalities in the South, 81, 83, 85, 87, 89, 92, 94, 96; Who's Who in Commun and Entertainment, 95, 97; Who's Who in Education, 96, 98; Who's Who in the Media and Commun, 98., Communicator of Achievement, Ala Media Professionals, 94. **MEMBERSHIPS** Nat Commun Asn; Asn for Educ in Journalism and Mass Commun; Investigative Reporters and Edits; Kappa Tau Alpha, Nat Fedn of Press Women; Ala Media Professionals; Miss Speech Commun Asn; Soc of Professional Journalists; Nat Asn of Exec Females; ACLU; PRAM. **RESEARCH** Commun Law, espec privacy, intellectual property, institutional liability; Journalism, espec writing styles; Media effectiveness, espec story structure effectiveness. **SELECTED PUBLICATIONS** Auth, Everywoman in the Journals of Joyce Maynard, 91; New roles, new problems, new concerns, NEW LAW, Southern Public Relations Jour 1/1, 93; coauth, How Public Relations Professionals View Men and Women Expert Source Credibility, 90; Nightmare in Copyright Law, 90; ADA: The Civil Rights Act for All, 92. **CONTACT ADDRESS** Dept of Communication, Mississippi State Univ, McComas Hall, PO Box PF, Mississippi State, MS, 39762. **EMAIL** mhuttenstine@comm.msstate.edu

HUXMAN, SUSAN S.
DISCIPLINE COMMUNICATION STUDIES **EDUCATION** Univ Kans, PhD. **CAREER** Asst prof, Wake Forest Univ; dir, basic course, Wichita State Univ; assoc prof-. **HONORS AND AWARDS** Awards tchg excellence, Univ Kans. **RESEARCH** Rhetorical criticism. **SELECTED PUBLICATIONS** Publ, in the field of rhetorical criticism and American Public. **CONTACT ADDRESS** Wichita State Univ, 1845 Fairmont, Wichita, KS, 67260-0062. **EMAIL** shuxman@elliott.es.twsu.edu

HYBELS, SAUNDRA
DISCIPLINE JOURNALISM **EDUCATION** Western Mich Univ, BA, 61; Univ Pa, MAC, 62; Univ Mich, PhD, 71. **CAREER** Asst prof, Jackson State Univ, 69-73; asst prof, Ithaca

Col, 73-76; prof, Lock Haven Univ Pa, 76-; bd mem, Ross Libr. **HONORS AND AWARDS** NEH fel, Claremont Univ, 81; NEH fel, Univ Md, 86, Fullbright lectr, Fed States of Micronesia, 88-89; Johnson Found grant, 90; grant, State Syst of Higher Educ, 93; Who's Who in the East, 95; Fullbright Lectureship, Albania, 95. **MEMBERSHIPS** Asn for Educ in Jour and Mass Commun; Popular Cult Asn. **SELECTED PUBLICATIONS** Coauth, Speech Communication, D. Van Nostrand, 74; Broadcasting: An Introduction, D. Van Nostrand, 78; auth, Polish Gardens, Christian Sci Monitor, 87; The Listener, in Sam G. Riley, ed, Consumer Magazines of the British Isles, Greenwood Press, 93; Communicating Effectively, 4th ed, McGraw-Hill, 95. **CONTACT ADDRESS** Journalism Dept, Lock Haven Univ, Pennsylvania, Lock Haven, PA, 17745. **EMAIL** shybels@eagle.lhup.edu

HYDE, VIRGINIA CROSSWHITE
PERSONAL Emporia, KS, m, 1987 **DISCIPLINE** ENGLISH **EDUCATION** Ariz State Univ, BA, 68; Univ Wis-Madison, PhD(English), 71. **CAREER** Asst prof, 70-75, assoc prof English, Wash State Univ, Pullman, 75-. **MEMBERSHIPS** MLA; AAUP; Int Arthurian Soc; Browning Inst; D H Lawrence Soc of North Am; Phi Kappa Phi. **RESEARCH** Victorian poetry and fiction; early 20th century poetry and fiction; especially D H Lawrence; Authurian literature and art; religion and myth in literature. **SELECTED PUBLICATIONS** Auth, Heroes and ideology in Middlemarch, Papers on Language and Literature, 88; auth, The Risen Adam, D H Lawrence's Revisionist Typology,Penn State Univ, 92; contribr, Introduction and Essay, In, Women and the Journey, The Female Travel Experience, Wash State Univ, 93; contribr, Essay, In; Images of Persephone; Feminist Readings in Western Literature, Univ Press of Florida, 94; contribr, Introduction, Lawrences's The Plumed Serpent, Penguin, 95; ed with L D Clark, Lawrence's The Plumed Serpent, Penguin, 95; auth, Variants Covers of The Secret Rose, Yeats Annual, 98; auth, The sense of an ending in The Plumed Serpent with L D Clark, D H Lawrence Rev, 93-94; auth, Kate and the goddess, Subtexts in The Plumed Serpent, D H Lawrence Rev, 95-96; ed, A Prairie Soul, Poems of Hazel Clawson Crosswhite, Professional Pres of Chapel Hill, 98; contrib, Essays, In, Approaches to Teaching D H Lawrence, MLA, 99; ed, Lawrence's Mornings in Mexico and Other Essays, Cambridge Univ, 2001 (contracted). **CONTACT ADDRESS** Dept of English, Washington State Univ, PO Box 645020, Pullman, WA, 99164-5020. **EMAIL** hydev@wsunix.wsu.edu

HYDE, VIRGINIA M.
DISCIPLINE VICTORIAN AND MODERN BRITISH LITERATURE **EDUCATION** Univ Wis, PhD. **CAREER** Prof, Washington State Univ. **SELECTED PUBLICATIONS** Auth, The Risen Adam: D. H. Lawrence's Revisionist Typology, 92. **CONTACT ADDRESS** Dept of English, Washington State Univ, 1 SE Stadium Way, PO Box 645020, Pullman, WA, 99164-5020. **EMAIL** hydev@wsunix.wsu.edu

HYDE, WILLIAM JAMES
PERSONAL Born 11/28/1924, Milwaukee, WI, m, 1950 **DISCIPLINE** ENGLISH **EDUCATION** Univ Wis, BS, 46, MA, 47, PhD, 53. **CAREER** Instr English, Univ Wis, Milwaukee, 46-47, Western Reserve Univ, 47-48 & State Univ Wash, 48-50; asst prof, Trinity Univ, 53-56; chmn dept, 60-64 & 67-72, PROF ENGLISH, UNIV WIS-LA CROSSE, 56- **MEMBERSHIPS** MLA; Midwest Mod Lang Asn; Tennyson Soc. **RESEARCH** English novel; Victorian literature and history. **SELECTED PUBLICATIONS** Auth, More on Scholarly Publishing, PMLA, Vol 0110, 95. **CONTACT ADDRESS** Dept of English, Univ of Wis, La Crosse, WI, 54601.

HYMAN, ROGER L.
DISCIPLINE ENGLISH LITERATURE **EDUCATION** York Univ, BA, MA; Univ Toronto, PhD. **RESEARCH** English-Canadian fiction; the novel. **SELECTED PUBLICATIONS** Art, Queen's Quarterly; art, Journal of Canadian Studies. **CONTACT ADDRESS** English Dept, McMaster Univ, 1280 Main St W, Hamilton, ON, L8S 4L9.

HYNES, JENNIFER
DISCIPLINE ENGLISH **EDUCATION** Texas A&M, BS, 88; MA, 92; Univ So Carol, PhD, 96. **CAREER** VIS INST, ENG, UNIV W VA **MEMBERSHIPS** Am Antiquarian Soc **CONTACT ADDRESS** 9305 Gardner St, Beaumont, TX, 77707.

HYNES, THOMAS J., JR.
PERSONAL Born 11/19/1949, Brighton, MA, d, 1 child **DISCIPLINE** COMMUNICATION STUDIES **EDUCATION** Univ Mass, BS, 71, PhD, 76; Univ NC- Chapel Hill, MA, 72. **CAREER** Full-time faculty member of Baylor Univ, Univ Louisville, and State Univ W Ga; Guest lecturer at over a dozen universities. **HONORS AND AWARDS** Outstanding Young Men of America: Debate Coach of the Year, 82, 83; Campus Impact Award, Univ Louisville, 84; Oustanding Administrative Performance Award, Univ Louisville, 90; Distinguished Service Award, Jefferson County Public Sch, 96. **MEMBERSHIPS** Am Forensic Asn; Int Commun Asn; Southern Speech Commun Asn; Speech Commun Asn; Int Soc Study Argumentation; Am Asn Higher Educ; Coun Undergraduate Res. **RESEARCH** Argument and public policy; higher education and communication. **SELECTED PUBLICATIONS** Coauth, American Educational Reform, Nat Textbook Co, 81; What Price Defense, Nat Textbook Co, 82; One Justice for All, Nat Textbook Co, 83; An End to Poverty, Nat Textbook Co, 84; Not a Drop to Drink, Nat Textbook Co, 85; American Agricultural Policy, Nat Textbook Co, 86; auth, Paths to Peace in Latin America, Nat Textbook Co, 87; Counterplan: Theory and Practice, Griffin Press, 87; Aging in America, Nat Textbook Co, 88; The Last Frontier, Nat Textbook Co, 90; author of numerous articles and book chapters. **CONTACT ADDRESS** Vice President for Acad Affairs, State Univ W Ga, Carrollton, GA, 30118. **EMAIL** thynes@westga.edu

I

IACOBUCCI, CHRISTINE
DISCIPLINE COMMUNICATION STUDIES **EDUCATION** Univ Albany, PhD. **CAREER** Asst prof. **SELECTED PUBLICATIONS** Auth, pubs on language use in social interactions, computer mediated communication, and human-computer interaction. **CONTACT ADDRESS** Dept of Communication, Ithaca Col, 100 Job Hall, Ithaca, NY, 14850.

IBELEMA, MINABERE
PERSONAL Born 12/09/1954, Bonny, Rivers State, Nigeria, m, 1994 **DISCIPLINE** JOURNALISM **EDUCATION** Wilberforce University, Wilberforce, OH, BA, 1979; Ohio State University, Columbus, OH, MA, 1980, PhD, 1984. **CAREER** Central State University, Wilberforce, OH, associate professor, 1984-91; Eastern Illinois University, Charleston, IL, associate professor, 1991-. **HONORS AND AWARDS** Honorable Mention, Munger Africana Library, African Thesis Competition, California Institute of Technology, 1982. **MEMBERSHIPS** NAACP member, association for Education in Journalism and Mass Communication, 1987-; member, Central States Communication Association, 1987-; member, Popular Culture Association, 1986-; corresponding secretary, American Association of University Professors, Central State University Chapter, 1990-. **SELECTED PUBLICATIONS** Author, Tribes and Prejudice: Coverage of the Nigerian Civil War, chapter in Africa's Media Image, 1991; author, Identity Crisis: The African Connection in African-American Sitcom Characters, chapter in Sexual Politics and Popular Culture, 1990. **CONTACT ADDRESS** Dept of Journalism, Eastern Illinois Univ, Buzzard Bldg, Charleston, IL, 61920.

IMBODEN, ROBERTA
PERSONAL Buffalo, NY **DISCIPLINE** ENGLISH **EDUCATION** Mercyhurst Col, BA, 56, MA, 61; Univ Toronto, MA, 77. **CAREER** Instr and PROF RYERSON POLYTECHNIC UNIV 65-. **MEMBERSHIPS** Can Hermeneutical Postmodern Soc. **SELECTED PUBLICATIONS** Auth, From the Cross to the Kingdom: Sartrean Dialectics and Liberation Theology, 87; auth, The Church, A Demon Lover: A Sartrean Critique of an Institution, 95. **CONTACT ADDRESS** Dept of English, Ryerson Polytechnic Univ, Toronto, ON, M5B 2K3. **EMAIL** rimboden@acs.ryerson.ca

IMBRIE, ANN ELIZABETH
PERSONAL Born 11/09/1950, Columbus, OH **DISCIPLINE** RENAISSANCE LITERATURE, LITERARY THEORY **EDUCATION** Smith Col, AB, 72; Univ NC, Chapel Hill, MA, 74, PhD(English), 79. **CAREER** Instr lit & writing, Univ NC, 78-79; ASST PROF ENGLISH, VASSAR COL, 79-, Nat Endowment for the Humanities fel, Brown Univ, 81-82. **MEMBERSHIPS** MLA. **RESEARCH** Nondramatic Renaissance literature, especially 17th century prose; Shakespeare; Renaissance literary theory and literary theory generally. **SELECTED PUBLICATIONS** Auth, What Shalimar Knew--Morrison, Toni 'Song of Solomon' as a Pastoral Novel, Col Engl, Vol 0055, 93. **CONTACT ADDRESS** Dept of English, Vassar Col, Poughkeepsie, NY, 12601.

INBODEN, ROBIN L.
PERSONAL Born 03/22/1957, Logan, OH, m, 1994 **DISCIPLINE** LITERATURE **EDUCATION** Cornell Univ, PhD, 85, MA, 82; Kenyon Col, AB, 79 **CAREER** Assoc Prof, 92-, Asst Prof, 89-92, Wittenberg Univ; Asst Prof, 85-89, Transylvania Univ **HONORS AND AWARDS** Sampson Excel in Tch Awd, Phi Beta Kappa; Nat merit Schol **RESEARCH** Victorian lit; Romantic lit; Classic Hollywood Cinema **CONTACT ADDRESS** Dept of English, Wittenberg Univ, PO Box 720, Springfield, OH, 45501. **EMAIL** rinboden@wittenberg.edu

INGE, M. THOMAS
PERSONAL Born 03/18/1936, Newport News, VA, m, 1998, 1 child **DISCIPLINE** ENGLISH **EDUCATION** Randolph-Macon Col, BA, 59; Vanderbilt Univ, MA, 60, PhD, 64. **CAREER** Instr, Vanderbilt Univ, 62-64; Asst Prof to Assoc Prof, Mich State Univ, 64-69; Assoc Prof to Prof English, Va Commonwealth Univ, 69-80, Dept Chair, 74-80; Prof English and Dept Head, Clemson Univ, 80-82; Resident Schol Am Studies, U.S. Infor Agency, 82-84; Robert Emory Blackwell Chair in Humanities, Randolph-Macon Col, 84-; Dir, USIA Summer Inst Am Studies Foreign Schol, 93-95. **HONORS AND AWARDS** Fulbright-Hays grants, 67-68, 71, 79, 88, 94; numerous research grants. **MEMBERSHIPS** Am Stud Asn; MLA; Am Humor Stud Asn; European Asn American Stud; Soc Stud Southern Lit; melville Soc; Mark Twain Circle, Southern Stud Forum; South Atlantic Mod Lang Asn. **SELECTED PUBLICATIONS** Auth, Donald Davidson: an Essay and a Bibliography, Vanderbilt Univ Press, 65; coauth, Donal Davidson, Twayne, 71; auth, The American Comic Book, Ohio State Libr, 85; Great American Comics, Smithsonian, 90; Comics as Culture, Univ Press Miss, 90; Faulkner, Sut, and Other Popular Southerners, Locust Hill Press, 92; Perspectives on American Culture: Essays on Humor, Literature, and the Popular Arts, Locust Hill Press, 94; Anything Can Happen in a Comic Strip: Centennial Reflections on an American Art Form, Univ Press Miss/Ohios State Univ, 95; author and editor of numerous other publications. **CONTACT ADDRESS** Humanities Dept, Randolph-Macon Col, Ashland, VA, 23005-5505. **EMAIL** tinge@rmc.edu

INGEBRETSEN, EDWARD J.
DISCIPLINE ENGLISH LITERATURE **EDUCATION** Loyola Univ, BA, MA; Duke Univ, PhD. **CAREER** Eng Dept, Georgetown Univ **RESEARCH** Edward American literature. **SELECTED PUBLICATIONS** Auth, Writing the Unholy: Lovecraft, Theology, and the 'Perfection of the Horrible', Fractal, 94; Psalms of the Still Country, 82; To Keep From Singing, 85; Love's Sentence: Domesticity as Religious Discourse in Robert Frost's Poetry, 89. **CONTACT ADDRESS** English Dept, Georgetown Univ, 37th and O St, Washington, DC, 20057.

INGERSOLL, EARL G.
PERSONAL Born 05/06/1938, Spencerport, NY, m, 1960, 2 children **DISCIPLINE** ENGLISH **EDUCATION** Univ Wisc Madison, PhD. **CAREER** Prof English, SUNY Col at Brockport, 64 to pres; dept adv, English Majors, 81-89; mem, Dept Constitution Rev Comt, 80-82; participant, Commun Skills Workshops, 80-84; mem, Dept APT Comt, 79-80, 82-83, 92-93, 95-98, chmn, APT Comt, 89-90, 95-96; Dept Scheduler, 75-86; mem, Student Appeals Rev Comt, 72-73, 80-81, 95-96, 98-; mem, Dept Curriculum Comt, 71-86, chmn, 72-73, 80-81, 98-. **MEMBERSHIPS** MLA; Col English Asn; NY Col English Asn; D.H. Lawrence Soc of N Am; Margaret Atwood Soc; Lawrence Durrell Soc; Doris Lessing Soc. **RESEARCH** 19th and 20th century British literature; Irish literature; Canadian literature. **SELECTED PUBLICATIONS** Auth, Lawrence Durrell: Conversations, 98; Engendered Trope in Joyce's Dubliners, 96; Putting the Question Differently, 96; Doris Lessing: Conversations, 94; Representations of Science and Technology in British Literature Since 1880, 92; Conversations with May Sarton, 91; Margaret Atwood: Conversations, 90, rev, 92; coauth, The Post-Confessionals: Conversations with American Poets of the Eighties, 89. **CONTACT ADDRESS** 173 Dewey St., Churchville, NY, 14428. **EMAIL** eingerso@po.brockport.edu

INGRAHAM, VERNON LELAND
PERSONAL Born 10/01/1924, Milfrod, NH, d, 3 children **DISCIPLINE** ENGLISH **EDUCATION** Univ NH, BA, 49; Amherst Col, MA, 51; Univ PA, PhD(English), 65. **CAREER** Instr English, Univ Del, 60-62, Haverford Col, 62-63 & Gettysburg Col, 63-65; from asst prof to assoc prof, 65-72, chemn dept, 68-72, prof emer, English, Univ MA, Dartmouth, 71-, assoc, Danforth Found, 73. **MEMBERSHIPS** MLA. **RESEARCH** Nineteenth and 20th century American literature; 20th century British literature. **SELECTED PUBLICATIONS** Auth, Survival: Readings on Environment, Holbrook, 71; ed, Literature from the Irish Literary Revival: An Anthology, Univ Press Am, 82. **CONTACT ADDRESS** Univ Massachusetts Dartmouth, 285 Old Westport Rd, North Dartmouth, MA, 02747-2300.

INGRAM, WILLIAM
PERSONAL Born 11/23/1930, Chicago, IL, m, 1 child **DISCIPLINE** RENAISSANCE LITERATURE & SOCIETY **EDUCATION** Grinnell Col, BA, 53; Columbia Univ, MA, 56; Univ Pa, PhD, 66. **CAREER** Instr Eng, Drexel Inst Technol, 57-65; from asst prof to assoc prof, 66-78, prof eng, Univ MI, Ann Arbor, 78. **HONORS AND AWARDS** Distinguished Tchg Award, 69; Am Coun Learned Socs, Folger Libr, Huntington Libr & Univ MI grants; Nat Endowment for Hum fel, 80-81; Excellence in Education Award, 97. **MEMBERSHIPS** Shakespeare Asn Am. **RESEARCH** Elizabethan drama; Renaissance cultl hist; computer-aided research. **SELECTED PUBLICATIONS** Co-ed, Concordance to John Milton's English Poetry, Clarendon, 73; auth, A London Life in the Brazen Age, Harvard Univ, 78; The Business of Playing, Cornell Univ Press, 92. **CONTACT ADDRESS** Dept of Eng, Univ of MI, Angel Hall, Ann Arbor, MI, 48109-1003. **EMAIL** ingram@umich.edu

INGWERSEN, NIELS
PERSONAL Born 05/18/1935, Horsens, Denmark, m, 1961 **DISCIPLINE** SCANDINAVIAN LITERATURE **EDUCATION** Copenhagen Univ, Cand Mag, 63. **CAREER** Adj Danish lit & lang, Hellerup Seminaruim, Denmark, 64-65; from asst

prof to assoc prof, 65-73, PROF SCAND LIT, UNIV WISMADISON, 73-, Res assoc, Odense Univ, Denmark, 71-72; assoc ed, Scand Studies, 71-; vis prof, Aarhus Univ, Denmark, 78-79. **MEMBERSHIPS** Soc Advan Scand Studies (pres, 69-71); Dansklaerer-foreningen; MLA. **RESEARCH** Danish novel; Danish prose of 1890's; theory of the novel. **SELECTED PUBLICATIONS** Auth, Sandemoses Ryg, World Lit Today, Vol 0067, 93; Ubekraeftede Forlydender, World Lit Today, Vol 0067, 93; Mellem ar og Dag, World Lit Today, Vol 0068, 94; Krigen, World Lit Today, Vol 0068, 94; The Rags--Studies on Common Danish-Norwegian Literature After 1814, Scand Stud, Vol 0067, 95; The Need for Narrative--The Folktale as Response to History, Scand Stud, Vol 0067, 95; Literary-Criticism, a Selection, Scanddinica, Vol 0034, 95; Peddling My Wares, J Engl and Germanic Philol, Vol 0096, 97. **CONTACT ADDRESS** Dept of Scand Studies, Univ of Wis, 1302 Van Hise Hall, Madison, WI, 53706.

INNESS, SHERRIE A.
PERSONAL Born 03/16/1965, Palo Alto, CA, s **DISCIPLINE** ENGLISH LITERATURE **EDUCATION** Wellesley Col, BA, 86; UC-San Diego, MA, 91; PhD, 93. **CAREER** Instr, 89-92, 93; Teach Asst, 90-92; UC San Diego;Miami Univ, Asst Prof English. 93-. **HONORS AND AWARDS** Regents' Fel, 88, Tuition Fel, 90, Teaching Escellence Award, 91, UCSD; Mellon Grants, 93, 94, NEH Fel, 95, Oregon Hum Cen Sum Res Fel, 96. **RESEARCH** Girls' culture; food studies; popular culture. **SELECTED PUBLICATIONS** Auth, Intimate Communities: Representation and Social Transformation in Women's College Fiction, 1895-1910, Bowling Green State Univ Popular Press, 95; Nancy Drew and Company: Culture, Gender, and Girls' Series, Bowling Green State Univ Popular Press, 97; The Lesbian Menace: Ideology, Identity, and the Representation of Lesbian Life, Univ Mass Press, 97; Breaking Boundaries: New Perspectives on Women's Regional Writing, Univ Iowa Press, 98; Tough Girls: Women Warriors and Wonder Women in Popular Culture, Univ Pa Press, 98; Delinquents and Debutantes: Twentieth-Century American Girls' Cultures, NY Univ Press, 98; Millenium Girls: Today' s Girls around the World, Rowman & Littlefield (forthcoming); author of numerous articles and other publications. **CONTACT ADDRESS** English Dept, Miami Univ, 1601 Peck Blvd, Hamilton, OH, 45011. **EMAIL** inness@muohio.edu

INSLEE, FORREST
PERSONAL Born 12/15/1961, Seattle, WA, s **DISCIPLINE** SPEECH **EDUCATION** Northwestern Univ, BA, 84, MA/PhD, 92; Regent Coll, MCS, 98 **CAREER** Asst Prof, Northwest Coll, 96-present. **MEMBERSHIPS** Natl Communication Assoc **RESEARCH** Cross-cultural Educ, leadership and management **CONTACT ADDRESS** Northwest Col, PO Box 579, Kirkland, WA, 98083. **EMAIL** forrest.inslee@ncag.edu

IORIO, SHARON
DISCIPLINE MASS COMMUNICATION **EDUCATION** Okla State Univ, MS, PhD. **CAREER** Grad coord, MA Commun Prog; assoc prof. **SELECTED PUBLICATIONS** Publ, sociology and the history of mass communication. **CONTACT ADDRESS** Wichita State Univ, 1845 Fairmont, Wichita, KS, 67260-0062.

IRONS, GLENWOOD H.
DISCIPLINE COMMUNICATIONS **EDUCATION** Brock Univ, BA; SUNY, MA, PhD. **CAREER** Prof, Brock Univ. **RESEARCH** Popular narrative genres (Detectives, sci-fi, horror, romance, western, thriller) and woman detectives. **SELECTED PUBLICATIONS** Auth, Gender, Language and Myth: Essays on Popular Narrative, Univ Toronto Press, 92; Feminism in Women's Detective Fiction, Univ Toronto Press, 95. **CONTACT ADDRESS** Dept of Applied Language Studies, Brock Univ, 500 Glenridge Ave, St. Catharines, ON, L2S 3A1. **EMAIL** girons@spartan.ac.BrockU.CA

IRSFELD, JOHN HENRY
PERSONAL Born 12/02/1937, Bemidji, MN, m, 1965, 1 child **DISCIPLINE** ENGLISH & AMERICAN LITERATURE & LANGUAGE **EDUCATION** Univ Tex, Austin, BA, 59, MA, 66, PhD(English), 69. **CAREER** From asst prof to assoc prof, 69-77, prof English & chemn dept, Univ Nevada, Las Vegas, 77- . **HONORS AND AWARDS** Barrick Scholar Award, Univ Nev, Las Vegas, 85-86; Nev Governor's Arts Award for Excellence in the Arts, 94. **MEMBERSHIPS** Nev Hum Comt, 81-87; NEH bd, 88, 89, 90, 92. **RESEARCH** Twentieth century English and American literature; poetry and poetics; fiction. **SELECTED PUBLICATIONS** Auth, Stop, rewind, and play (story), SDak Rev, 3/74; Ambivalence hardy fire (short story), Kans Quart, summer 74; The right thing: What it is, and how Theodore Roethke achieved it, Sparrow, 75; Coming Through (novel), 75 & Little Kingdoms (novel), 76, Putnam; The horse fountain (short story), Kans Quart, winter 76; Have you knocked on Cleopatra? (short story), 12/76 & The tourist (short story), 11/76, Las Vegas; auth, Rats Alley, 87. **CONTACT ADDRESS** Dept of English, Univ of Nev, PO Box 455011, Las Vegas, NV, 89154-5011. **EMAIL** irsfeld@nevada.edu

IRVINE, CAROLYN LENETTE
PERSONAL Born 03/07/1947, Quincy, Florida, m, 1977 **DISCIPLINE** SPEECH, ENGLISH EDUCATION Florida A&M University, Tallahassee, FL, BS, 1970; University of Florida, Gainesville, FL, MS, 1975; Florida State University, Tallahassee, FL, PhD, 1989. **CAREER** Shanks High School, Quincy, FL, speech & English teacher, 1976-77; Florida A&M University, Tallahassee, FL, speech teacher, 1975-76, 1983-, English teacher, 1978-83. **HONORS AND AWARDS** Certificate of Appreciation, Miracle Temple Daycare Center. **MEMBERSHIPS** Member, Jack and Jill of America, Inc, 1988-90; member, Associations of Teachers of America, 1989-90; member, Florida Speech Communication Association, 1984-91; member, Phi Delta Kappa, 1984-91; various others. **SELECTED PUBLICATIONS** "A Speech Recipe," The SGS Communicator, the School of General Studies, Florida A&M University, vol. 10, number 3, December 1990; "An Analysis of Speech," The SGS Communicator, the School of General Studies, Florida A&M University, vol. 8, number 4, December 1989; "Cooperative Education: Its Role and Scope in Vocational Education," ERIC Clearinghouse on Adult Career and Vocational Education, Research in Education, 1985; "Love," poem, in Anthology of Best Love Poetry, 1980. **CONTACT ADDRESS** Florida A&M Univ, Tallahassee, FL, 32304.

IRVINE, JAMES RICHARD
PERSONAL Born 03/04/1939, Port Arthur, TX, m, 1959 **DISCIPLINE** RHETORIC, SPEECH COMMUNICATION **EDUCATION** Stephen F Austin Univ, BS, 61, MA, 65; Univ Iowa, PhD(speech), 74. **CAREER** Teacher speech, Port Arthur pub schs, 61-63; teaching asst, Stephen F Austin Univ, 64-65; instr, Colo State Univ, 65-68; teaching asst rhetoric, Univ Iowa, 68-69; asst prof, 74-78, assoc prof, 78-82, PROF RHET & SPEECH, COLO STATE UNIV, 82-, Colo State Univ res grant, 76 & res sabbatical, 77. **HONORS AND AWARDS** Honors prof, Colo State Univ, 80. **MEMBERSHIPS** Speech Commun Asn Am; Rhet Soc Am; Western Speech Commun Asn; Conf Brit Studies. **RESEARCH** Rhetorical theory and criticism; 18th-century British rhetoric; enlightenment Scottish rhetorical theory. **SELECTED PUBLICATIONS** Auth, Campbell 'Philosophy of Rhetoric', bk-1, Associations With the Aberdeen-Philosophical-Society, Notes and Queries, Vol 0039, 92. **CONTACT ADDRESS** Dept of Speech Commun, Colorado State Univ, Fort Collins, CO, 80523-0001.

IRVINE, LORNA MARIE
PERSONAL Ottawa, ON, Canada, m, 1962, 2 children **DISCIPLINE** ENGLISH LITERATURE, PSYCHOLOGY **EDUCATION** McMaster Univ, BA, 59; Carleton Univ, MA, 65; Am Univ, PhD(lit studies), 77. **CAREER** Lectr English, Carleton Univ, 65-67 & 69-72; lectr, Am Univ, 75-77, prof lectr, 77-78; ASST PROF ENGLISH, GEORGE MASON UNIV, 78-. **MEMBERSHIPS** MLA; Asn Can Studies in US; Popular Cult Asn. **RESEARCH** English-Canadian fiction; women's studies; psychology of women. **SELECTED PUBLICATIONS** Auth, Other Solitudes--Canadian Multicultural Fictions, Mosaic-J Interdisciplinary Study Lit, Vol 0029, 96; Thresholds of Difference--Feminist Critique, Native Womens Writings, Postcolonial Theory, Mosaic-J Interdisciplinary Study Lit, Vol 0029, 96; Sounding Differences--Conversations With 17 Canadian Women-Writers, Mosaic-J Interdisciplinary Study Lit, Vol 0029, 96. **CONTACT ADDRESS** Dept of English, George Mason Univ, 4400 University Dr, Fairfax, VA, 22030-4444.

IRVINE, MARTIN
DISCIPLINE ENGLISH LITERATURE **EDUCATION** State Univ NY, BA; Brandeis Univ, MA; Harvard Univ, MA, PhD. **CAREER** Eng Dept, Georgetown Univ **RESEARCH** Media and cultural studies; Internet and information technology; educational technology; communications; literary theory; medieval literature; contemporary fiction. **SELECTED PUBLICATIONS** Auth, Grammatica and Literary Theory 350-1100, 93; Literate Subjectivity and Gender Conflicts in the Writings of Heloise and Abelard, 94; Medieval Textuality and the Archaeology of the Text, 90; Interpretation and the Semiotics of Allegory in the Works of Clement of Alexandria, Origen, and Augustine, 87; A Guide to the Sources of the Medieval Theories of Interpretation, Signs, and the Arts of Discourse: Aristotle to Ockham, 87. **CONTACT ADDRESS** English Dept, Georgetown Univ, 37th and O St, Washington, DC, 20057.

IRWIN, JOHN THOMAS
PERSONAL Born 04/24/1940, Houston, TX **DISCIPLINE** AMERICAN LITERATURE, HISTORY OF IDEAS **EDUCATION** Univ St Thomas, BA, 62; Rice Univ, MA & PhD, 70. **CAREER** Supvr pub affairs libr, Ling-Temco-Vought, NASA Manned Spacecraft Ctr, 66-67; asst prof Eng, Johns Hopkins Univ, 70-74; Ed, Ga Rev, Univ GA, 74-77; Prof Lit & English, 77-84, Decker Prof in the Humanities, The Writing Seminars, Johns Hopkins Univ, 84-, Chmn Dept, 77-96; ed, Johns Hopkins Fiction and Poetry Series, 79. **HONORS AND AWARDS** Danforth fel, Rice Univ, 70; Guggenheim fel, 91; Christian Gauss Prize, Phi Beta Kappa, 94; Scaglione Prize in Comparative Lit, MLA, 94. **MEMBERSHIPS** MLA. **RESEARCH** Mod Am poetry; 19th century Am novel; 20th century Am novel. **SELECTED PUBLICATIONS** Coauth, The structure of Cleanness: Parable as effective sign, Medieval Studies, 73; auth, Doubling and Incest/Repetition and Revenge, Johns Hopkins Univ, 75; The Heisenberg Variations, Univ Ga, 76; American Hieroglyphics, Yale Univ Press, 80; The Mystery to a Solution, Johns Hopkins Press, 94; Just Let Me Say This About That, Overlook Press, 98. **CONTACT ADDRESS** The Writing Seminars Johns Hopkins Univ, 3400 N Charles St, Baltimore, MD, 21218-2680.

ISAACS, NEIL D.
PERSONAL Born 08/21/1931, New York, NY, m, 1953, 4 children **DISCIPLINE** ENGLISH LITERATURE **EDUCATION** Dartmouth Col, AB, 53; Univ Calif, Berkeley, AM, 56; Brown Univ, PhD, 59. **CAREER** From inst to asst prof English, City Col New York, 59-63; from asst prof to assoc prof, Univ Tenn, 63-71; PROF ENGLISH, UNIV MD, 71-. **MEMBERSHIPS** SAtlantic MLA. **RESEARCH** Old English and Middle English poetry; fiction; film. **SELECTED PUBLICATIONS** Auth, Jim Dandy, Va Quart Rev, Vol 0071, 95; Bathgate in the Time of Coppola + Doctorow, American Gangster Films, Lit-Film Quart, Vol 0024, 96; Malle Eye for Rose 'Storyville' + The Books Influence on 'Pretty Baby', Lit-Film Quart, Vol 0024, 96; Passing off, Va Quart Rev, Vol 0073, 97. **CONTACT ADDRESS** Dept of English, Univ of Md, College Park, MD, 20742-0001.

ISANG, S. AKPAN
PERSONAL Itak, Nigeria, 3 children **DISCIPLINE** ORGANIZATIONAL COMMUNICATION **EDUCATION** Howard Univ, PhD 96. **CAREER** Nyack College, asst prof, 97-. **HONORS AND AWARDS** Aids Short Story Awd; Aids Video Awd **MEMBERSHIPS** ICA; IMA; IPA **RESEARCH** Audience influence on media; mentoring in organization **SELECTED PUBLICATIONS** Auth, Mentoring as Interpersonal Communication: An Application of a Mentoring Model to a Black Cultural Environment. **CONTACT ADDRESS** Dept of Communication, Nyack Col, 1 South Blvd, Nyack, NY, 10960-3698. **EMAIL** isang@nyack.edu

IVES, EDWARD DAWSON
PERSONAL Born 09/04/1925, White Plains, NY, m, 1951, 3 children **DISCIPLINE** FOLKLORE; ORAL HISTORY **EDUCATION** Hamilton Col, AB, 48; Columbia Univ, MA, 50; Ind Univ, PhD, 62. **CAREER** Instr English, Ill Col, 50-53; lectr English, City Col New York, 53-54; from instr to assoc prof English, 55-67, assoc prof, 67-70, PROF FOLKLORE, UNIV MAINE, ORONO, 70-, Coe res fund grant & Guggenheim fel, 65-66; lectr, NY State Hist Asn; Sem Am Cult, Cooperstown, NY, 67; assoc ed, J Am Folklore, 68-73; dir, Northeast Arch of Folklore & Oral Hist, 72-; folk arts panelist, Nat Endowment Arts, 77-80; ed, Northeast Folklore; LLD Univ Prince Edward Is, 86; Litt D, Mem Univ Nfld, 96. **HONORS AND AWARDS** Marius Barbeau Medal, Can Fol Stud Asn, 91. **MEMBERSHIPS** Am Folklore Soc; Can Folk Studies Asn; Can Folk Music Coun; Northeast Folklore Soc; Oral Hist Asn. **RESEARCH** All aspects of the folklore of the Northeast; the authorship of folksongs; oral history. **SELECTED PUBLICATIONS** Auth, Twenty-one folksongs from Prince Edward Island, Northeast Folklore, 63; Larry Gorman: The Man Who Made the Songs, Ind Univ, 64; coauth, Folksongs and Their Makers, Bowling Green Univ, 70; auth, Lawrence Doyle: Farmer poet of Prince Edward Island, Maine Studies, 71; Argyle boom, Northeast Folklore, 76; Joe Scott: The Woodsman Songmaker, Univ Ill, 78; The tape-recorded interview, 80; George Magoon and the Down East Game War, Univ Ill, 85; Folksongs of New Brunswick, Goose Lane, 89; The Bonn of Earl of Murray: The Man, The Murder, The Ballard, Univ Ill, 97. **CONTACT ADDRESS** Univ of Maine, South Stevens Hall, Orono, ME, 04473. **EMAIL** sandy_ives@vnut.maine.edu

IYER, NALINI
DISCIPLINE ENGLISH **EDUCATION** Univ Madras, BA, 86; Purdue Univ, MA, 88, PhD, 93. **CAREER** Eng, Seattle Univ. **MEMBERSHIPS** Midwest MLA; MLA. **SELECTED PUBLICATIONS** Auth, American Indian: Metaphors of the Self in Bharati Muckherjee's Holder of the World, Ariel, 96. **CONTACT ADDRESS** Dept of Eng, Seattle Univ, 900 Broadway, Seattle, WA, 98122-4460. **EMAIL** niyer@seattleu.edu

J

JACKA, ELIZABETH
DISCIPLINE MEDIA COMMUNICATIONS **EDUCATION** PhD. **CAREER** Prof, Univ Tech, Sydney; mem, Natl Adv Comt, Australian Key Ctr Cult and Media Policy. **MEMBERSHIPS** Rep, Natl Indigenous Media Asn Australia. **SELECTED PUBLICATIONS** Coauth, Australian Television and International Mediascapes, Cambridge Univ, 96; co-ed, New Patterns in Global Television: Peripheral Vision, Oxford Univ, 96.

JACKMAN, SYDNEY W
PERSONAL Born 03/25/1925, Fullerton, CA **DISCIPLINE** ENGLISH HISTORY **EDUCATION** Univ Wash, BS, 46, MA, 47; Harvard Univ, AM, 48; PhD(hist), 53. **CAREER** Tutor hist,

Harvard Univ, 49-52; instr, Phillips Exeter Acad, 52-56; from instr to assoc prof, Bates Col, 56-64; assoc prof, 64-65, PROF HIST, UNIV VICTORIA, BC, 65-, Rockefeller res grant, 61-62; Am Philos Soc Penrose fel, 64; mem fac bd hist & assoc Clare Hall, Cambridge Univ, 70-71; vis fel, Australian Nat Univ, 75; mem bd dirs, Humanities Res Coun Can, 77; vis scholar, Trinity Hall, Cambridge Univ, 77-78. **MEMBERSHIPS** Am Antiq Soc; fel Soc Antiq London; fel Royal Soc Antiq Ireland; fel Royal Hist Soc; Royal Soc Tasmania. **RESEARCH** British history, 17th century to end of 19th century; American colonial history; imperial history. **SELECTED PUBLICATIONS** Auth, Higgins, Andrew, Jackson and the Boats that Won the War, Amer Neptune, Vol 0056, 96. **CONTACT ADDRESS** 1065 Deal St, Victoria, BC, V8S 5G6.

JACKSON, ALLAN STUART
PERSONAL Born 04/24/1934, Pittsburgh, PA **DISCIPLINE** THEATER **EDUCATION** Univ Colo, BA, 56; Ohio State Univ, MA, 59, PhD(theater), 62. **CAREER** Instr theater, Ohio State Univ, 62; asst prof, 64-69, ASSOC PROF THEATER, STATE UNIV NY, BINGHAMTON, 69-. **MEMBERSHIPS** Am Educ Theater Asn; Am Soc Theater Res; Class Asn Am; Int Fed Theater Res. **RESEARCH** Theater **SELECTED PUBLICATIONS** Auth, Pizarro, Bridges and the Gothic Scene, Theatre Notebk, Vol 0051, 97. **CONTACT ADDRESS** 132 Annetta St, Vestal, NY, 13850.

JACKSON, ARLENE M.
DISCIPLINE VICTORIAN LITERATURE **EDUCATION** Marygrove Col, AB, 60, Villanova Univ, MA, 62; Univ MI, PhD, 79. **CAREER** Engl, St. Joseph's Univ. **SELECTED PUBLICATIONS** Auth, Photography as Style and Metaphor, Art of Thomas Hardy, Thomas Hardy Annual 2, 84; The Question of Credibility in Anne Bronte's The Tenant of Wildfell Hall, Eng Studies 63, 82; Agnes Wickfield and the Church Leitmotif in David Copperfield, Dickens Studies Annual 9, 81; The Evolutionary Aspect of Hardy's Modern Men, Revue Belge de Philologie et d'Historie 56; Illustration and the Novels of Thomas Hardy, Rowman & Littlefield, 80. **CONTACT ADDRESS** St Joseph's Univ, 5600 City Ave, Philadelphia, PA, 19131. **EMAIL** ajackson@sju.edu

JACKSON, BLYDEN
PERSONAL Born 10/12/1910, Paducah, KY, m, 1958 **DISCIPLINE** ENGLISH **EDUCATION** Wilberforce Univ, AB, 30; Univ Mich, AM, 38, PhD, 52. **CAREER** Teacher, pub schs, Ky, 34-45; from asst prof to assoc prof English, Fisk Univ, 45-54; prof English & chmn dept, Southern Univ, 54-62, dean grad sch, 62-69; assoc dean grad sch, 73-76, PROF ENGLISH, UNIV NC, CHAPEL HILL, 69-, SPEC ASST TO GRAD DEAN, 76-, Ed bull, Col Lang Asn, 59-; chmn col sect, NCTE, 71-73. **HONORS AND AWARDS** DH, Wilberforce Univ, 77; LIHD, Univ Louisville, 78. **MEMBERSHIPS** NCTE; MLA; Col Lang Asn (pres, 57-59); Col English Asn; Speech Commun Asn. **RESEARCH** Negro literature, Mich Alumni Rev; College Language Association, PMLA, 12/58. **SELECTED PUBLICATIONS** Coauth, Black Poetry in America, 74 & auth, The Waiting Years, 76, La State Univ. **CONTACT ADDRESS** Dept of English, Univ of NC, Chapel Hill, NC, 27514.

JACKSON, BRUCE
PERSONAL Born 05/21/1936, Brooklyn, NY, 3 children **DISCIPLINE** FILM, AMERICAN STUDIES **EDUCATION** Rutgers Univ, BA, 60; Ind Univ, MA, 62; Harvard Univ, JF, 63. **CAREER** Asst prof, 67-68, assoc prof, 69-71, prof English, Comp Lit & Folklore, 71-, SUNY distinguished prof, 90-, Samuel P. Capen Prof of Am Culture, 97-, SUNY Buffalo; dir, Ctr Stud Am Culture, 74-, sr consult, President's Crime Comn, Arthur D Little Co, 66; dir, Newport Folk Found, 65-72; Guggenheim Found fel, 71-72; adv bd, Nat Proj II, FIPSE, 75-77, New York Comn on Corrections, 76-77 & Inst Am West, 76-82; exec dir, Doc Res Inc, 78-; exec bd, Am Folklore Soc, 79-82. **HONORS AND AWARDS** Ed, J of Am Folklore, 86-90; pres, Am Folklore Soc, 84. **RESEARCH** Afro-American folklore; criminology; documentary. **SELECTED PUBLICATIONS** Auth, Law and Disorder; Criminal Justice in America, Illinois, 85; auth, Rainbow Freeware, New South Moulton Press, 86; ed, Feminism and Folklore, American Folklore Society, 87; auth, Fieldwork, Illinois, 87; auth, A User's Guide: Freeware, Shareware, and Public Domain Software, New South Moulton Press, 88; co-ed, The Centennial Index: 100 Years of Journal of American Folklore, American Folklore Society, 88; auth, Disorderly Conduct, Illinois, 92; co-ed, The World Observed: Reflections on the Fieldwork Process, Illinois, 96. **CONTACT ADDRESS** Ctr for Studies in Am Cult, SUNY, Buffalo, 610 Samuel Clemens Hall, Buffalo, NY, 14260-7015. **EMAIL** bjackson@acsu.buffalo.edu

JACKSON, GORDON
PERSONAL South Africa **DISCIPLINE** COMMUNICATION STUDIES **EDUCATION** Wheaton Col, MA; Ind Univ, PhD. **CAREER** Prof. **RESEARCH** Media ethics in South Africa. **SELECTED PUBLICATIONS** Auth, bk, South African Press, 93. **CONTACT ADDRESS** Dept of Commun, Whitworth Col, 300 West Hawthorne Rd, Spokane, WA, 99251. **EMAIL** gjackson@whitworth.edu

JACKSON, JACQUELINE DOUGAN
PERSONAL Born 05/03/1928, Beloit, WI, 4 children **DISCIPLINE** LITERATURE, CLASSICS **EDUCATION** Beloit Col, BA, 50, Univ Mich, Ann Arbor, MA, 51. **CAREER** Lectr lit, Kent State Univ, 66-68; ASSOC PROF LIT, SANGAMON STATE UNIV, 70-, Consult, Rockford Teacher Develop Ctr, Ill, 68-70; radio lectr, Univ Wis, WHA Sch of the Air, 69-. **HONORS AND AWARDS** Dorothy Canfield Fisher Award, 67., DLitt, MacMurray Col, 76; DHL, Beloit LCol, 77. **MEMBERSHIPS** MLA **RESEARCH** Creativity in children and adults; children's literature, current and historical; fantasy. **SELECTED PUBLICATIONS** Auth, the Taste of Spruce Gum, 66, Missing Melinda, 67, Chicken Ten Thousand, 68 & auth & illusr, the Ghost Boat, 69, Little; auth, Spring Song, Kent State Univ, 69; The Orchestra Mice, Reilly & Lee, 70; coauth, The Endless Pavement, Seabury, 73; auth, Turn Not Pale, Beloved Snail, Little, 74. **CONTACT ADDRESS** Dept of English, Sangamon State Univ, Springfield, IL, 62708.

JACKSON, JAMES HARVEY
PERSONAL Born 06/24/1920, Stroll, SD, m, 1944, 2 children **DISCIPLINE** PUBLIC ADDRESS **EDUCATION** Pasadena Col, AB, 41, MA, 43; Univ Southern Calif, MA, 55, PhD, 57. **CAREER** Assoc prof speech, 49-57, chmn lett, 57-63, dean students, 60-78, PROF SPEECH, POINT LOMA COL, 57-, Danforth Found, teacher study grant, 55; mem acad coun, Speech Commun Asn. **MEMBERSHIPS** Western Speech Commun Asn. **RESEARCH** Evaluation of Speech delivery and content; speaking of Clarence Darrow. **SELECTED PUBLICATIONS** Auth, I Believe, Nazarene Publ House, 49; coauth, Too Young for Love?, Beacon Hill, 68. **CONTACT ADDRESS** Dept of Speech, Point Loma Nazarene Col, 3900 Lomaland Dr, San Diego, CA, 92106-2810.

JACKSON, JAMES R.
PERSONAL Born 07/14/1935, St. Andrew's, Scotland **DISCIPLINE** ENGLISH **EDUCATION** Queen's Univ, BA, 57, MA, 58; Princeton Univ, AM, 60, PhD, 61; Univ London, PhD, 63. **CAREER** Vis res fel, Univ London, 62-63; asst prof, McMaster Univ, 63-64; asst prof to prof, Victoria Col, 64-94, UNIV PROF, UNIV TORONTO, 94-. **HONORS AND AWARDS** Guggenheim fel, 72-73; Killam sr scholar, 75-76, res fel, 82-84; Connaught sr fel, 85-86. **SELECTED PUBLICATIONS** Auth, Poetry of the Romantic Period, 80; auth, Annals of English Verse 1770-1835, 85; auth, Historical Criticism and the Meaning of Texts, 89; auth, Romantic Poetry by Women: A Bibliography 1770-1835, 93; ed, Coleridge: The Critical Heritage Volume 2: 1834-1900, 91; co-ed, S.T. Coleridge Shorter Works and Fragments, 2 vols, 95. **CONTACT ADDRESS** Victoria Col, Univ of Toronto, Toronto, ON, M5S 1K7.

JACKSON, KATHY MERLOCK
PERSONAL Born 08/27/1955, Pittsburgh, PA, m, 1983, 1 child **DISCIPLINE** COMMUNICATIONS **EDUCATION** West VA Univ, BA (magna cum laude), 71; OH State Univ, MA, 79; Bowling Green State Univ, PhD, 84. **CAREER** Prof and coordinator of Communications, Virginia Wesleyan Col, 84-. **HONORS AND AWARDS** Eleanor T Donley Award, West VA Univ, 75-76; Graduate Col Dissertation res grant, Bowling Green State Univ, 83-84; Am Culture PhD prog nonservice fel, Bowling Green State Univ, 83-84; VA Wesleyan Col fac development grant, 86, 88, 95; Mednick Found res grant, 86; One of fifty academmics nationwide invited to participate in the Int Radio and Television Soc Fac/Industry Seminar, New York City, 88, 89; Samuel Nelson Gray Distinguished Teaching award, V Wesleyan Col, 89; Walt Disney: A Bio-Bibliography awarded honorable mention for the Ray and Pat Browne Nat Book Award of the Popular Culture Asn in the Text, Reference, and Resource Book Category. **MEMBERSHIPS** Am culture asn; Popular Culture Asn; VA Asn of Broadcast Educators. **RESEARCH** Media; children's culture. **SELECTED PUBLICATIONS** Auth, Reading the River: Film as a Socio-Cultural Artifact, with Gary Edgerton, J of Regional Cultures, 3,1, spring/summer 83; Harvey Comics: A Neighborhood of Little Girls and Boys, Media Sight 3, 1, summer 84; Book review of Children's Literature and the Movies ed by Douglas Street, The J of Popular Film and Television, 85; Images of Children in American Film: A Socio-Cultural Analysis, Scarecrow Press, 86; Frankie and Annette at the Beach: The Beach as a Locale in American Popular Film, in Beyond the Stars IV: Locals in American Popular Film, Popular Press, 93; Walt Disney: A Bio-Bibliography, Greenwood Press, 93; Oscar Wilde, The Dictionary of Literary Biography: British Children's Writers, 1880-1914, Bruccoli Clark Layman, Inc, 94; Mattel's TV Chatter: Selling Talking Dolls to Babyboom Children, in Childhood and Popular Culture, Popular Press, 94; book review of Out of the Garden: Toys and Children's Culture in the Age of Television Marketing by Stephen Kline in the J of Popular Film and Television, 95; co-auth, with Gary Edgerton, Redesigning Pocahontas: Disney, the White Man's Indian, and the Marketing of Dreams, J of Popular Film and Television, summer 96; auth, Introduction, in J of Popular Film and Television, summer 96; numerous other articles and publications. **CONTACT ADDRESS** Communications, Virginia Wesleyan Col, 1584 Wesleyan Dr, Norfolk, VA, 23502-5512. **EMAIL** kmjackson@vwc.edu

JACKSON, MARY E.
PERSONAL Born 11/20/1949, Oshkosh, WI, m, 1971 **DISCIPLINE** LIBRARY SCIENCE **EDUCATION** Carroll Col, BA (German and Sociology), 71; Drexel Univ, MLS, 74. **CAREER** Univ PA Libraries, 73-93, head, Interlibrary Loan Dept, 78-93; ASN OF RES LIBRARIES, 93-, CURRENTLY SENIOR PROG OFFICER FOR ACCESS SERVICES. **HONORS AND AWARDS** Beta Phi Mu; ALA Whitney-Carneghie Fund Award; PA Library Asn Certificate of Merit. **MEMBERSHIPS** Am Library Asn; Asn for Asian Studies. **RESEARCH** Academic/research libraries; interlibrary loan and document delivery; performance measures; Japanese studies. **SELECTED PUBLICATIONS** Auth, The NAILDD project and Interlibrary Loan Standards, SISAC News 11, summer/fall 96; Managing Resource Sharing in the Electronic Age, ed with Amy Chang, AMS Press, 96; Becoming a Published Author: Eight Simple Steps for Librarians, Library Administration & Management 11, winter 97; Copyright and Users: The Perspective of Users & Copyright in the United States: Current Developments & Initiatives, Copyright Issues in Libraries: Global Concerns, Local Solutions, IFLA Office for Universal Availability of Pubs and Int Lending, 97; The North American Interlibrary Loan and Document Delivery Project: Improving ILL/DD Services, Interlending and Document Supply 25, 97; Making Connections: An Update on Vendor Implementations of the ILL Protocol, ARL 194, Oct 97; Measuring the Performance of Interlibrary Loan and Document Delivery Services, ARL 195, Dec 97; ILL/DD: An Annual Review, co-ed, AMS Press, 98-; Loan Stars: ILL Comes of Age, Library J 123, Feb 98; Measuring the Performance of Interlibrary Loan Operations in North American Research and Academic Libraries, Asn of Res Libraries, 98; A Spotlight on High-Performing ILL/DD Operations in Research Libraries, ARL 198, June 98; several other publications. **CONTACT ADDRESS** 21 Dupont Circle NW, Ste. 800, Washington, DC, 20036. **EMAIL** Mary@arl.org

JACKSON, MICHELE
DISCIPLINE COMMUNCATION STUDIES **EDUCATION** Macalester Col, BA, 87; Univ Minn, MA, 90, PhD, 94. **CAREER** Asst prof. **RESEARCH** Group communication; computer based communication technology; philosophy of technology. **SELECTED PUBLICATIONS** Auth, Assessing the structure of communication on the World Wide Web, Jour Comput Mediated Commun, 97; The meaning of communication technology: The Technology Context scheme, 96; co-auth, Imagery on the World Wide Web: Representations of the former Yugoslavia, 97; Group decision support systems as facilitators of quality team efforts, 94; Communication theory and group support systems, 92. **CONTACT ADDRESS** Dept of Communication, Univ Colo Boulder, Boulder, CO, 80309. **EMAIL** mhjackso@mailer.fsu.edu

JACKSON, MILES MERRILL
PERSONAL Born 04/28/1929, Richmond, VA, m, 1954, 4 children **DISCIPLINE** LIBRARY AND INFORMATION SCIENCE; COMMUNICATIONS **EDUCATION** Virginia Union Univ, BA, 55; Drexel Univ, MS, 56. **CAREER** Free Library of Philadelphia, 56-58; head librn, Hampton Univ, 58-62; librn, Territorial Amer Samoa, 62-64; chief libn, Atlanta Univ, 64-69; assoc prof, State Univ New York, 69-75; prof to dean, SLIS, Univ Hawaii, 75-95. **HONORS AND AWARDS** Fulbright Scholar to Iran, 68-69; U.S. gvt. specialist to India and Pakistan, 84, 85. **MEMBERSHIPS** Amer Lib Assn; Assn Lib and Info Sci Edu. **RESEARCH** International flow of information. **CONTACT ADDRESS** PO Box 1602, Kaneohe, HI, 96744. **EMAIL** jackson@hawaii.edu

JACKSON, WALLACE
DISCIPLINE ENGLISH LITERATURE **EDUCATION** PA Univ, PhD, 64. **CAREER** Prof, Duke Univ. **MEMBERSHIPS** MLA. **SELECTED PUBLICATIONS** Auth, The Probable and the Marvelous: Blake Wordsworth and the Eighteenth-Century Critical Tradition, Ga, 78; Vision and Re-vision in Alexander Pope, Wayne State, 83. **CONTACT ADDRESS** Eng Dept, Duke Univ, Durham, NC, 27706.

JACOBI, MARTIN
DISCIPLINE RHETORIC AND ENGLISH LITERATURE **EDUCATION** Univ Ore, PhD, 84. **CAREER** Dept Eng, Clemson Univ **RESEARCH** Classical and modern rhetoric; American drama. **SELECTED PUBLICATIONS** Auth, Review of Rhetoric and Pluralism: Legacies of Wayne Booth, Rhetoric Soc Quart, 98; Professional Communication, Cultural Studies, and Ethics, S Atlantic Rev, 96; The Dramatist as Salesman: A Rhetorical Analysis of Miller's Intentions and Effects in Approaches to Teaching Miller's Death of a Salesman, MLA, 95; Ed Lemon: Prophet of Profit in Essays on Israel Horowitz, Greenwood, 94; The Monster Within in Lanford Wilson's Burn This, Lanford Wilson: A Casebook, Garland, 94; coauth, A Comprehensive Bibliography of Works by and about Richard M. Weaver, Rhetoric Soc Quart, 95; Richard Weaver in Encyclopedia of Rhetoric, Garlan, 96. **CONTACT ADDRESS** Clemson Univ, 806 Strode, Clemson, SC, 29634. **EMAIL** mjacobi@clemson.edu

JACOBIK, GRAY
DISCIPLINE 19TH AND 20TH CENTURY AMERICAN POETRY **EDUCATION** Brandeis Univ, PhD. **CAREER** Eng Dept, Eastern Conn State Univ **SELECTED PUBLICATIONS** Poems in: Ploughshares; Prairie Schooner; Georgia Rev; Midwest Quart Rev; Southern Hum Rev; Am Lit Rev; N Am Rev; Alaska Quart Rev; Confrontation. **CONTACT ADDRESS** Eastern Connecticut State Univ, 83 Windham Street, Willimantic, CT, 06226.

JACOBS, DOROTHY HIERONYMUS
PERSONAL Born 03/13/1928, Hinsdale, IL, m, 1950, 2 children **DISCIPLINE** ENGLISH LANGUAGE & LITERATURE **EDUCATION** Univ Mich, Ann Arbor, AB, 50, AM, 60, PhD(English), 68. **CAREER** PROF ENGLISH, UNIV RI, 68- **HONORS AND AWARDS** Phi Kappa Phi **MEMBERSHIPS** MLA; AAUP **RESEARCH** Seventeenth century literature; modern drama; Renaissance drama. **CONTACT ADDRESS** Dept of English, Univ of RI, Kingston, RI, 02881.

JACOBS, EDWARD
DISCIPLINE RESTORATION AND 18TH CENTURY BRITISH LITERATURE **EDUCATION** Univ Ill, PhD. **CAREER** Engl, Old Dominion Univ. **RESEARCH** 17th and 18th Century British Literature. **SELECTED PUBLICATIONS** Areas: The History of the Book; Cultural Historiography. **CONTACT ADDRESS** Old Dominion Univ, 4100 Powhatan Ave, BAL 202, Norfolk, VA, 23058. **EMAIL** EJacobs@odu.edu

JACOBS, JOHN T.
DISCIPLINE ENGLISH **EDUCATION** Univ Notre Dame, PhD, 76. **CAREER** Prof & prog dir, Engl and Am Stud; Shenandoah's fac, 74-; site dir, 7th Willa Cather Int Sem, Shenandoah Univ, 97. **RESEARCH** Mod Southern fiction; nature writing; Willa Cather. **SELECTED PUBLICATIONS** Auth, The Western Journey: Exploration, Education, and Autobiography in Irving, Parkman, and Thoreau, 88; publ or presented papers on, Faulkner, Thoreau, Annie Dillard, Francis Parkman & Willa Cather. **CONTACT ADDRESS** Dept of Eng, Shenandoah Univ, 1460 University Dr., Winchester, VA, 22601. **EMAIL** jjacobs@su.edu

JACOBSON, THOMAS L.
DISCIPLINE COMMUNICATIONS **EDUCATION** Western WA Univ, BA, 77; Univ WA, MA, 81; PhD 86. **CAREER** Vis asst prof, Nothwestern Univ, 85-87; asst prof, SUNY Buffalo, 87-93; to assoc prof, 93-95; to ch, 95. **RESEARCH** Quality of international news coverage; mass and international commun. **SELECTED PUBLICATIONS** Auth, Old and New Approaches to Participatory Communication for Development in Participation: A Key Concept in Development Communication, Sage, 94; Electronic Mail Networks and Services in Third World Countries: Availability, Problems, Opportunities, Revue Tiers-Monde, 94; The Electronic Publishing Revolution is Not Global, JASIS: Jour Am Soc Info Sci, 94; coauth, Q-Analysis Techniques for Content Analysis, Quality & Quantity, 98; An Examination of the International Telecommunication Network, Jour Int Comm, 96; Non-commercial Computer Networks and National Development, Telematics Informatics, 93; A Pragmatist Account of Participatory Communication Research for National Development, Comm Theory, 93; co-ed, Participatory Communication Research for Social Change, Sage, 96. **CONTACT ADDRESS** Commun Dept, SUNY Buffalo, 338 Millard Fillmore, Buffalo, NY, 14261.

JACOBUS, LEE ANDRE
PERSONAL Born 08/20/1935, Orange, NJ, m, 1958, 2 children **DISCIPLINE** ENGLISH, PHILOSOPHY **EDUCATION** Brown Univ, AB, 57, AM, 59; Claremont Grad Sch, PhD(English), 68. **CAREER** Instr, Western Conn State Col, 60-68; PROF ENGLISH, UNIV CONN, 68-. **MEMBERSHIPS** MLA; James Joyce Soc; Milton Soc Am; Am Comt Irish Studies. **RESEARCH** Milton; 17th century English authors; modern Irish literature. **SELECTED PUBLICATIONS** Auth, Milton, John Burden of Interpretation, Theolog Stud, Vol 0056, 95. **CONTACT ADDRESS** Dept of English, U-25 Univ of Conn, Storrs, CT, 06268.

JAHNER, ELAINE A.
DISCIPLINE ENGLISH LITERATURE **EDUCATION** IN Univ, PhD, 75. **CAREER** Prof, Dartmouth Col. **RESEARCH** Native Am lit. **SELECTED PUBLICATIONS** Auth, Indian Literature and Critical Responsibility, Studies in Am Indian Lit, 93; Lakota Myth, Univ Neb P, 83; Knowing All the Way Down to Fire in Feminist Measures: Soundings in Poetry and Theory, Women Cult Series, Univ Mich P, 95; coauth, Literary Themes in Indigenous Religions in HarperCollins Dictionary of Religion, 96. **CONTACT ADDRESS** Dartmouth Col, 3529 N Main St, #207, Hanover, NH, 03755.

JAMES, WILLIAM
DISCIPLINE LEGAL RESEARCH **EDUCATION** Morehouse Col, BA, 67; Howard Univ Sch Law, JD, 72; Atlanta Univ Sch Libr Sci, MSLS, 73. **CAREER** Prof, Villanova Univ; dir, Law Libr, 88-; assoc dean, Inf serv, 95-. **MEMBERSHIPS** Asn Amer Law Schools Comt on Libr; bd adv, Legal Reference serv Quart; Amer Asn Law Libraries, served on comt for Placement, Educ, Minorities, Scholarship and grants; chem, Minorities Comt, 85-87; past chep, Scholarship and Nomination Comt, Southeastern Asn Law Librarians **RESEARCH** Legal research. **SELECTED PUBLICATIONS** Auth, Law Libraries Which Offer serv to Prisoners, Am Ass'n of Law Libraries Comt on Law Libr serv to Prisoners, 75; Recommended Collections for Prison Law Libraries, 75;"Legal Reference Materials and Law Library servs, Am Ass'n of Law Libraries Comt on Law Libraries serv to Prisoners, 76; Legal Reference Materials and Law Library servs, U Ken Continuing Legal Educ, 76; contrib, Fundaments of Legal Research, 77; co-contrib, Law and Psychiatry, 79 & Natural Resources and Development, 87. **CONTACT ADDRESS** Law School, Villanova Univ, 800 Lancaster Ave, Villanova, PA, 19085-1692. **EMAIL** wjames@law.vill.edu

JAMES, WILLIAM CLOSSON
PERSONAL Born 05/20/1943, Sudbury, ON, Canada, m, 1964, 3 children **DISCIPLINE** RELIGION, ENGLISH LITERATURE **EDUCATION** Queen's Univ, Ont, BA, 65, BD, 68; Univ Chicago, MA, 70, PhD(relig & lit), 74. **CAREER** Lectr, 73-75, asst prof, 75-80, chmn undergrad studies relig, 78-81, ASSOC PROF RELIG & LIT, QUEEN'S UNIV, ONT, 80-, Exec bd mem relig, Can Soc for Study Relig, 75-78; mem bd dirs relig, Can Corp for Studies Relig, 78-; book rev ed, Studies in Relig, 79-. **MEMBERSHIPS** Can Soc for Study Relig; Am Acad Relig. **RESEARCH** Religion and literature; modern Canadian fiction; heroism and the quest in literature. **SELECTED PUBLICATIONS** Auth, Nature and the Sacred in Canada + Role of Geography and Climate in Shaping a Canadian Identity, Stud in Religion Sciences Religieuses, Vol 0021, 92. **CONTACT ADDRESS** Dept of Relig, Queen's Univ, Kingston, ON, K7L 3N6.

JAMME, ALBERT W.F.
PERSONAL Born 06/27/1916, Senzeille, Belgium **DISCIPLINE** ENGLISH, FRENCH **EDUCATION** Cath Univ Louvain, DTheol, 47, DOr, 52; Pontif Bibl Comm, Rome, Lic, 48. **CAREER** Res Prof Semitics, Cath Univ Am, 55-, Epigraphical adv, Govt Saudi Arabia, 68-69. **MEMBERSHIPS** Cath Bibl Asn Am; Am Orient Soc. **RESEARCH** Pre-Islamic Arabian sci. **SELECTED PUBLICATIONS** Auth, Pieces Epigraphiques de Heid bin Aqil, la Necropole de Timna, (Hagr Kohlan), Biblio Mus, Louvain, 52; La Kynastie de Sarahbiil Yakuf et la documentation epigraphique sud-arabe, Ned Hist Archaeol Inst, Istanbul, 61; Sabaean inscriptions from Mahram Bilquis (Marib), Johns Hopkins Univ, 62; Miscellanees d'ancient arabe, I-XX, Washington, 71-98; Carnegie Museum 1974-1975 Yemen Expedition, Carnegie Natural Hist Spec Publ No 2, Pittsburgh, 76. **CONTACT ADDRESS** Dept of Semitics, Catholic Univ of America, 620 Michigan Ave N E, Washington, DC, 20064-0002.

JANANGELO, JOSEPH
DISCIPLINE ENGLISH **EDUCATION** Manhattanville Col, BA, 81; NY Univy, MA, 83, PhD, 88. **CAREER** Asst prof. **RESEARCH** Rhetoric and composition; composition theory; computer-mediated instruction; autobiography. **SELECTED PUBLICATIONS** Co-ed, Resituating Writing: Constructing and Administering Writing Programs, Boynton, Cook, 95; Theoretical and Critical Perspectives on Teacher Change, Ablex, 93. **CONTACT ADDRESS** Dept of English, Loyola Univ, Chicago, 6525 N. Sheridan Rd., Chicago, IL, 60626. **EMAIL** jjanang@wpo.it.luc.edu

JANDT, FRED E.
PERSONAL Seguin, TX **DISCIPLINE** COMMUNICATIONS **EDUCATION** Texas Lutheran Univ, BA,66; Stephen F Austin State Univ, MA, 67; Bowling Green State Univ, PhD, 70. **CAREER** Prof, Calif State Univ, San Bernadino, 83- . **MEMBERSHIPS** Nat Commun Asn Soc of Professionals in Dispute Resolution; So Calif Mediation Asn. **RESEARCH** Mediation; intercultural communication; computer-mediated communication. **SELECTED PUBLICATIONS** Auth, Win-Win Negotiating: Turning Conflict into Agreement, Wiley, 85; auth, Effective Interviewing for Paralegals, Anderson, 94; auth, Intercultural Communication: An Introduction, Sage, 95, 98; co-auth, Using the Internet and World Wide Web in Your Job Search, JIST, 97; coauth, Constructive Conflict Management: Asian-Pacific Cases, Sage, 96; auth, Alternative Dispute Resolution for Paralegals, Anderson, 97. **CONTACT ADDRESS** Communications Dept, California State Univ, San Bernardino, San Bernadino, CA, 92407. **EMAIL** fjandt@wiley.csusb.edu

JANIK, DEL IVAN
PERSONAL Born 02/11/1945, Berwyn, IL, m, 1992, 2 children **DISCIPLINE** ENGLISH & AMERICAN LITERATURE **EDUCATION** Northwestern Univ, BA, 66; Univ Mich, MA, 67; Northwestern Univ, PhD(English), 71. **CAREER** From Asst Prof to Assoc Prof, 71-81, PROF ENGLISH, STATE UNIV NY COL, CORTLAND, 81-. **HONORS AND AWARDS** State Univ NY Res Found fel, 77, 80. **MEMBERSHIPS** D.H. Lawrence Soc. **RESEARCH** D.H. Lawrence; modern American poetry; literature and the natural environment; modern english novel. **SELECTED PUBLICATIONS** Auth, Flann O'Brien: The artist as critic, Eire Ireland, 69; Toward Thingness: Cezanne's painting and Lawrence's poetry, Twentieth Century Lit, 73; The two infinites: D H Lawrence's Twilight in Italy, D H Lawrence Rev, 74; D H Lawrence's Future Religion: The unity of Last Poems, Tex Studies Lit & Lang, 75; D H Lawrence's Etruscan Places: The Mystery of Touch, Essays in Lit, 76; Poetry in the Ecosphere, Centennial Rev, 76; The Curve of Return: D H Lawrence's Travel Books, ELS, 81. **CONTACT ADDRESS** Dept of English, State Univ NY Col, PO Box 2000, Cortland, NY, 13045-0900. **EMAIL** janikd@cortland.edu

JANKOWSKI, THEODORA
DISCIPLINE EARLY MODERN LITERATURE , SPECIALTY IN DRAMA AND SHAKESPEARE **EDUCATION** Syracuse Univ, PhD. **CAREER** Asst prof, Washington State Univ. **RESEARCH** Cultural studies, feminist, Marxist, and queer theory; women writers of the early modern period. **SELECTED PUBLICATIONS** Auth, Women in Power in the Early Modern Drama, 92. **CONTACT ADDRESS** Dept of English, Washington State Univ, 1 SE Stadium Way, PO Box 645020, Pullman, WA, 99164-5020. **EMAIL** tajankow@mail.wsu.edu

JANN, ROSEMARY
DISCIPLINE ENGLISH **EDUCATION** Duke Univ, BA, 71; MA, 72, PhD, 75, Northwestern Univ. **CAREER** Asst Prof, 75-79, Ripon Col; Asst Prof, 79-85, Assoc Prof, 85-86 Rutgers Univ; Assoc Prof 86-94, Prof, 94-, George Mason Univ. **CONTACT ADDRESS** Dept of English, George Mason Univ, Fairfax, VA, 22030. **EMAIL** rjann@gmu.edu

JANZEN, HENRY DAVID
DISCIPLINE ENGLISH LANGUAGE; LITERATURE **EDUCATION** Assumption Univ, BA; Univ Windsor, MA; Wayne State Univ, PhD, 70. **CAREER** Prof **RESEARCH** Renaissance literature; editing and textual criticism. **SELECTED PUBLICATIONS** Pub (s), Heywood, Middleton, Milton & Shakespeare; prepared ed 2 manuscript plays, Thomas Heywood's The Escapes of Jupiter and Francis Jaques's The Queen of Corsica. **CONTACT ADDRESS** Dept of English Language and Literature, Univ of Windsor, 401 Sunset Ave, Windsor, ON, N9B 3P4. **EMAIL** janzen4@uwindsor.ca

JANZEN, LORRAINE
DISCIPLINE LITERATURE **EDUCATION** Brock, BA; McMaster, MA, PhD. **CAREER** Assoc prof, Nipissing Univ. **HONORS AND AWARDS** SSHRC 3 yr grant. **RESEARCH** Illustrated books. **SELECTED PUBLICATIONS** Auth, The Artist as Critic: Bitextuality in Fin-de-Sie cle Illustrated Books, Scolar, 95. **CONTACT ADDRESS** Dept of English, Nipissing Univ, 100 College Dr, Box 5002, North Bay, ON, P1B 8L7.

JASKOSKI, HELEN
PERSONAL Born 05/13/1941, Tucson, AZ **DISCIPLINE** ENGLISH **EDUCATION** Mt St Mary's Col, Calif, BA, 63; Stanford Univ, MA, 67, PhD(English & Am lit), 69. **CAREER** Writer, Syst Develop Corp, 63-64; asst prof English, Calif State Univ, Los Angeles, 68-70; assoc prof, 70-80, PROF ENGLISH, CALIF STATE UNIV, FULLERTON, 80-, Fulbright lectr Am lit, Marie Curie-Sklodowska Univ, Poland, 73-74; co-dir, Calif State Univ Inst Prog, Florence, Italy, 82-83; mem adv bd, Poetry Therapy Inst, Los Angeles. **MEMBERSHIPS** MLA; Soc Study Multi-Ethnic Lit US. **RESEARCH** American ethnic literature; women's literature; psychology and literature. **SELECTED PUBLICATIONS** Auth, Blackbird, Andrew Smallpox Story, Genre-Forms of Discourse and Culture, Vol 0025, 92; Words Like Bones + Native-American Literature and Contextualization in Silko, Leslie,Marmon 'Storyteller', Cea Critic, Vol 0055, 92; The Dawn of the World--Myths and Tales of the Miwok Indians of California, Col Engl, Vol 0056, 94; The 'Catacombs' and the Debate Between the Flesh and the Spirit, Critique-Studies in Contemporary Fiction, Vol 0035, 94; Looking-Glass, Col Engl, Vol 0056, 94; Annikadel--The History of the Universe as Told to the Achumawi Indians of California, Col Engl, Vol 0056, 94; The Destruction of California Indians, Col Engl, Vol 0056, 94; Cuero, Delfina--Her Autobiography, An Account of her Last Years and her Ethnobotanic Contributions, Col Engl, Vol 0056, 94; The Sharpest Sight, Col Engl, Vol 0056, 94; Keeping Slug-Woman Alive, Col Engl, Vol 0056, 94; The Maidu Indian Myths and Stories of Hancibyjim, Col Engl, Vol 0056, 94; Posey, Alex--Creek Poet, Journalist and Humorist, Resources for Amer Lit Study, Vol 0022, 96. **CONTACT ADDRESS** Dept of English, California State Univ, Fullerton, Fullerton, CA, 92634.

JASON, PHILIP KENNETH
PERSONAL Born 12/25/1941, New York, NY, m, 1962, 2 children **DISCIPLINE** ENGLISH LITERATURE **EDUCATION** New Sch Soc Res, BA, 63; Georgetown Univ, MA, 65; Univ Md, PhD(lit), 71. **CAREER** From instr to asst prof English, Georgetown Univ, 66-73; asst prof, 73-77, assoc prof English, 77-83, prof, US Naval Acad, 83- **MEMBERSHIPS** MLA; Assoc Writing Progs. **RESEARCH** Sociology and literature; 18th century British literature; 20th century expatriate literature. **SELECTED PUBLICATIONS** Auth, Thawing Out,

Dryad, 79; Near the Fire, Dryad, 83; Nineteenth Century American Poetry: An Annotated Bibliography, Salem, 89; coauth, Creative Writer's Handbook, Prentice Hall, 90, 99; ed, Fourteen Landing Zones: Approaches to Vietnam War Literature, Univ Iowa, 91; auth, The Vietnam War in Literature, An Annotated Bibliography of Criticism, Salem, 92; Anais Nin and Her Critics, Camden House, 93; The Separation: Poems, Viet Name Generation, 95; ed, The Critical Response to Anais Nin, Greenwood, 96; co-ed, Open Door: A Poet Lore Anthology 1980-1996, Writer's Center Editions, 97. **CONTACT ADDRESS** Dept of English, US Naval Acad, Annapolis, MD, 21402. **EMAIL** pjason@aol.com

JAUSS, DAVID
DISCIPLINE CREATIVE WRITING **EDUCATION** Univ Iowa, PhD. **CAREER** English and Lit, Univ Ark **SELECTED PUBLICATIONS** Auth, Black Maps; Improvising Rivers; Crimes of Passion; Glossolalia; Shards; Ed, Strong Measures: Contemporary American Poetry in Traditional Forms; The Best of Crazyhorse: 30 years of Poetry and Fiction. **CONTACT ADDRESS** Univ Ark Little Rock, 2801 S University Ave., Little Rock, AR, 72204-1099.

JAY, GREGORY S.
PERSONAL Born 08/01/1952, North Hollywood, CA, m, 1979, 1 child **DISCIPLINE** ENGLISH **EDUCATION** Univ of Calif at Santa Cruz, BA, 75; State Univ of NY, PhD, 80. **CAREER** Asst prof, Univ of Ala, 80-84; assoc prof, Univ of SC, 84-87; prof, Univ of Wis, 87- ; vis prof, Northwestern Univ, 91; schol in residence, Free Univ of Berlin, 91; contr ed, Am Lit Hist. **HONORS AND AWARDS** Summer Travel grant, Univ of Ala, 81; Summer Fac Res fel, Univ of Ala, 82; Res Conf grant, Nat Endowment for the Hums, 82; Summer Res grant, Univ of Ala, 83; Travel to Collections grant, Nat Endowment for the Hums, 83; NEH fel, 85; Ctr for 20th Centry Studies fel, 88-89; Res Incentive grant, UWM, 91; Ctr for 20th Century Studies, UWM, 94-95; Proj dir Rethinking American Studies: Connecting the Differnces, Nat Endowment for the Hums, 95-96; Res grant, Univ of Wis. **MEMBERSHIPS** Am Studies Asn; Midwest Modern Lang Asn; Mod Lang Asn; Multi-Ethnic Lit of the United States Soc. **SELECTED PUBLICATIONS** Auth, T.S. Eliot and the Poetics of Literary History, 83; America the Scrivener: Deconstruction and the Subject of Literary History, 90; American Literature and the New Historicism: The Example of Frederick Douglass, Boundary 2 17:1, 90; Hegel and the Dialectics of American Literary Historiography, Theorizing Am Lit: Hegel, the Sign, and History, ed B. Cowan and J. Kronick, 91; The End of American Literature: Toward a Multicultural Practice, Col Eng 53:3, 91; Response, Col Eng 54:2, 92; The First Round of the Culture Wars, Chronicle of Higher Educ, 26, 92; Catching Up With Whitman, South Atlantic Rev 57:1, 92; Postmodernism in The Waste Land: Woman, Mass Culture and Others, Rereading the New: A Backward Glance at Modernism, ed K. Dettmar, 92; Ideology and the New Historicism, Ariz Quart 49:1, 93; The Use of Literature in the Composition Classroom: A Response, Col Eng 55:6, 93; Knowledge, Power, and the Struggle for Representation, Col Eng 56:1, 94; Taking Multiculturalism Personally: Ethnos and Ethos in the Classroom, Am Lit Hist 6:4, 94; Response, Col Eng 57:1, 95; Not Born on the Fourth of July: Cultural Differences and American Literary Studies, After Political Correctness: The Hums and Soc in the 1990s, ed. C. Newfield and R. Strickland, 95; Recent Fictions in Theory, Studies in the Novel 27:2, 95; The Discipline of the Syllabus, Reconceptualizing Am Lit/Cult Studies, ed W. E. Cain, 96; Jewish Writers in the Multicultural Literature Class, Heath Anthology Newsletter 16, 97; American Literature and the Culture Wars, 97; Women Writers and Resisting Readers, Legacy 15:1, 98; coauth, Critical Pedagogy: A Reassessment, Higher Educ Under Fire: Politics, Economics, and the Crisis of the Humanities, ed M. Berube and C. Nelson, 94; Where Do We Go From Here?, Political Correctness: A Response from the Cultural Left, ed R. Bernstein, 97; ed, Modern American Critics: 1920-1955, vol 63, Dictionary of Lit Biog, 88; Modern American Critics Since 1955, vol 67, Dictionary of Lit Biog, 88; coed, After Strange Texts: The Role of Theory in the Study of Literature, 85. **CONTACT ADDRESS** Dept of English, Milwaukee, WI, 53201. **EMAIL** gjay@uwm.edu

JAY, PAUL
DISCIPLINE ENGLISH **EDUCATION** Univ Calif, Santa Cruz, BA, 75; Univ Calif, Berkeley, MA, 76; Univ Calif, Santa Cruz, PhD, 81. **CAREER** Prof. **RESEARCH** Literary criticism and theory; modernism and modernity; American literature; comparative literature of the Americas, border Stud. **SELECTED PUBLICATIONS** Auth, Contingency Blues: The Search for Foundations in American Criticism, Univ Wis Press, 97; Translation, Invention, Resistance: Rewriting the Conquest in Carlos Fuentes The Two Shores, Modern Fiction Stud 47, 97; Posing: Autobiography and the Subject of Philosophy in Postmodernism and Autobiography, Univ Mass Press, 94. **CONTACT ADDRESS** Dept of English, Loyola Univ, Chicago, 6525 N Sheridan Rd, Chicago, IL, 60626. **EMAIL** pjay@orion.it.luc.edu

JEFCHAK, ANDREW TIMOTHY
PERSONAL Born 01/25/1936, East Chicago, IN, m, 1959, 3 children **DISCIPLINE** AMERICAN LITERATURE, FILM STUDY **EDUCATION** IN Univ, Bloomington, AB, 59; DePaul Univ, MA, 65; MI State Univ, PhD, 70. **CAREER** Instr Eng, Am Inst Banking, Chicago, 64-65; grad asst & asst to dir inquiry & expression, Justin Morrill Col, MI State Univ, 65-68; Prof Eng & Film Study, Aquinas Col, 68-, Kellogg Found-Asn Independent Cols & Univs of MI fel, 71-72; Danforth assoc, 77-83. **MEMBERSHIPS** Am Film Inst; AAUP; Univ Film Asn. **RESEARCH** Family relationships in mod fiction; lit and motion pictures, comp art forms; struct and irony in motion pictures. **SELECTED PUBLICATIONS** Film Critic, Grand Rapids Press, 1977. **CONTACT ADDRESS** Dept of Eng, Aquinas Col, Michigan, 1607 Robinson Rd S E, Grand Rapids, MI, 49506-1799. **EMAIL** jefchand@aquinas.edu

JEFFRES, LEO
DISCIPLINE MASS COM THEORY, JOUNALISM, INTERNATIONAL COM, METHODS **EDUCATION** Univ ID, BA; Univ WA, MA; Univ MN, PhD. **CAREER** Commun res ctr dir. **SELECTED PUBLICATIONS** Auth, Mass Media Processes, Waveland Press, 94; co-auth, Separating People's Satisfaction With Life and Public Perceptions of the Quality of Life in the Environment, Soc Indicators Res, 95; The Impact of New and Traditional Media on College Student Leisure Preferences. World Commun, 95; Predicting use of Technologies for Communication and Consumer Needs, Jour Broadcasting and Electronic Media, 96. **CONTACT ADDRESS** Commun Dept, Cleveland State Univ, 83 E 24th St, Cleveland, OH, 44115. **EMAIL** l.jeffres@csuohio.edu

JEFFREY, DAVID LYLE
PERSONAL Born 06/28/1941, Ottawa, ON, Canada **DISCIPLINE** ENGLISH LITERATURE, ART HISTORY **EDUCATION** Wheaton Col, Ill, BA, 65; Princeton Univ, MA, 67, Ph-D(English), 68. **CAREER** Asst prof, Univ Victoria, BC, 68-69 & Univ Rochester, 69-72; assoc prof English & chmn dept, Univ Victoria, BC, 73-78; chmn dept, 78-81, PROF ENGLISH, UNIV OTTAWA, 78-, Gen ed, Dict Biblical Tradition in English Lit, 77-; Can Coun leave fel, 77-78; adj prof, Regent Col, 78-, **HONORS AND AWARDS** Bk of Year Award, Conf Christianity & Lit, 75; Solomon Katz Distinguished Lectr in Humanities, Univ Wash, 77. **MEMBERSHIPS** MLA; Conf Christianity & Lit; Mediaeval Acad Am; Asn Can Univ Teachers English; Am Acad Relig & Soc Biblical Lit. **RESEARCH** Medieval, modern and biblical literature. **SELECTED PUBLICATIONS** Auth, A History of the Bible as Literature, Vol 1, From Antiquity to1700, Vol 2, From 1700 tothe Present Day, J Rel, Vol 0075, 95. **CONTACT ADDRESS** Dept of English, Univ of Ottawa, Ottawa, ON, K1N 6N5.

JEFFREYS, MARK
DISCIPLINE MODERNIST POETRY AND POETICS **EDUCATION** Emory, PhD, 90. **CAREER** Dept Eng, Univ Ala **SELECTED PUBLICATIONS** Ed, New Definitions of Lyric, Garland, 97; Coauth, Teacher's Guide to the Norton Anthology of Poetry. **CONTACT ADDRESS** Univ AL, 1400 University Blvd, Birmingham, AL, 35294-1150.

JEHLIN, MYRA
DISCIPLINE ENGLISH LANGUAGE AND LITERATURE **EDUCATION** CUNY, BA; Univ Calif Berkeley, MA; PhD. **CAREER** Prof. **RESEARCH** Transatlantic cultural relations; literature and history. **SELECTED PUBLICATIONS** Auth, American Incarnation: The Individual, the Nation, and the Continent; auth, The English Literatures of America; ed, Papers of Empire. **CONTACT ADDRESS** Dept of English, Rutgers Univ, 510 George St, Murray Hall, New Brunswick, NJ, 08901-1167. **EMAIL** jehlen@rci.rutgers.edu

JEMIELITY, THOMAS J.
PERSONAL Born 12/17/1933, Cleveland, OH, m, 1965, 3 children **DISCIPLINE** ENGLISH **EDUCATION** John Carroll Univ, MA, 58; Cornell Univ, PhD, 65. **CAREER** Lectr English, Carleton Univ, Can, 62-63; from instr to asst prof, 63-70, chmn comt acad prog, Col Arts & Lett, 76-80, assoc prof to prof English, Univ Notre Dame, 70-. **HONORS AND AWARDS** Allen Seymour Olmsted fel, Cornell Univ, 60-61; Pres, Johnson Soc of the Cent Region, 85. **MEMBERSHIPS** Am Soc for Eighteenth-Century Studies; Jane Austen Soc of N Am; Eighteenth-Century Scottish Studies Soc; The Johnson Soc, Lichfield, England; The Johnson Soc of London; The Johnson Soc of the Cent Region; Midwest Am Soc for Eighteenth-Century Studies; NE Am Soc for Eighteenth-Century Studies. **RESEARCH** Alexander Pope and the Bible; satire; Samuel Johnson **SELECTED PUBLICATIONS** Auth, Savage Virtues and Barbarous Grandeur, Cornell Libr J, winter 66; I sing of a Maiden: God's courting of Mary, Concerning Poetry, 69; More in Notions Than Facts, Dalhousie Rev, fall 69; Dr Johnson and the Uses of Travel, Philol Quart, 4/72; Samuel Johnson, the Second Sight, and His Sources, Studies English Lit, summer 74; A Mock-Biblical Controversy: Sir Richard Blackmore in the Dunciad, PQ, 74; Post no bills (short story), Juggler, winter 78; Thomas Pennant's Scottish Tours and the Journey to the Western Islands of Scotland, In: Fresh Reflections on Samuel Johnson: Essays in Criticism, 87; More Disagreeable for Him to Teach or the Boys to Learn? The Vanity of Human Wishes in the Classroom, In: Teaching Eighteenth Century Poetry, AMS, 90; Satire and the Hebrew Prophets, 92; Teaching a Journey to the Western Islands of Scotland, In: Approaches to Teaching the Works of Samuel Johnson, MLA, 93; Gibbon Among the Aeolists: Islamic Credibility and Pagan Fanaticism in The Decline and Fall, In: Studies in Eighteenth-Century Culture; A Keener Eye on Vacancy: Boswell's Second Thoughts About Second Sight, Prose Studies. **CONTACT ADDRESS** Dept of English, Univ of Notre Dame, 356 Oshaugnessy Hall, Notre Dame, IN, 46556. **EMAIL** Thomas.J.Jemielity.1@nd.edu

JENKINS, ANTHONY W.
PERSONAL Born 07/08/1936, Sutton Coldfield, England, m, 1960, 2 children **DISCIPLINE** MEDIEVAL LITERATURE **EDUCATION** Cambridge Univ, MA; Univ Calif, Berkeley, PhD. **CAREER** Adj prof **RESEARCH** Renaissance; 19th and 20th-century drama; the British novel. **SELECTED PUBLICATIONS** Auth, Modern British Drama, 1890-1990, Modern Drama, Vol 0036, 93. **CONTACT ADDRESS** Dept of English, Victoria Univ, PO Box 3070, Victoria, BC, V8W 3W1.

JENKINS, CHARLES M.
PERSONAL Born 05/31/1948, Denver, CO, m, 1969, 2 children **DISCIPLINE** ENGLISH **EDUCATION** Univ Calif, Santa Barbara, BA, 70, MA, 74; Claremont Grad Univ, PhD, 94. **CAREER** Sec Eng Teacher, 71-72, 85-90; ASSOC PROF, LOCK HAVEN UNIV, 94-. **MEMBERSHIPS** Mod Lang Asn; Nat counc Teach Eng. **RESEARCH** Mysticism, medieval lit; cognition & literacy. **SELECTED PUBLICATIONS** Auth, Bizarre Mnemonics: Implications for the Classroom, J Mental Imagery, 99. **CONTACT ADDRESS** English Dept, Lock Haven Univ, Pennsylvania, Lock Haven, PA, 17745. **EMAIL** ejenkins@eagle.lhup.edu

JENKINS, JOYCE O.
DISCIPLINE AMERICAN LITERATURE **EDUCATION** Univ MI, BA, Ed, 71, MEd, 72; Bowling Green State Univ, PhD, 78. **CAREER** Assoc prof; co-ch, Black Hist Observance Comm, 93-94; hd lang(s). **HONORS AND AWARDS** Tchg fel, Bowling Green State Univ, 74-77; fel, NEH, Univ NC, 89; fel, Acad Leadership Acad, 93-95, Recognition for excellence in leadership, Off Acad Aff, 89; co-ch, Annual Black Hist Month Scholar Observance Comm, 93-96. **MEMBERSHIPS** Mem, AAUP; Nat Coun Tchr(s) Eng; Mod Lang Assn; Nat Col Hon(s) Coun; S Reg Hon(s) Coun; Phi Delta Kappa; Eng Hon Soc; For Lang Assn Ga; Ga-SC Col Eng Assn. **SELECTED PUBLICATIONS** Auth, Black History Month, Artsline: Macon Arts Alliance, Calendar/Newsletter, 90; Readers Will Ask for More of Taulbert's Once Upon a Time, Review of Once Upon a Time When We Were Colored, 90; Fort Valley State College Cooperative Developmental Energy Program: The Only One of Its Kind, Macon Mag, 92. **CONTACT ADDRESS** Dept of Eng, Fort Valley State Univ, 600 Park St, Fort Valley, GA, 310030.

JENKINS, KENNETH VINCENT
PERSONAL Elizabeth, NJ, d **DISCIPLINE** ENGLISH, AFRICAN-AMERICAN STUDIES **EDUCATION** Columbia Coll NY, AB; Columbia Univ NY, AM; Columbia Univ, PhD candidate. **CAREER** South Side High School, Rockville Centre NY, chmn English dept 1965-72; NASSAU COMMUNITY COLL, SUPVR ADJUNCT FACULTY, PROF ENGLISH AND AFR0-AMERICAN LITERATURE, CHMN AFRO-AMER STUDIES DEPT 1974-. **HONORS AND AWARDS** Baker Award, Columbia Univ; community awards; "Last Day in Church"; Martin Luther King Jr Award, Nassau County, 1989. **MEMBERSHIPS** Consultant in Eng, convener, chmn bd dir, Target Youth Centers Inc NY, 1973-75; Natl Bd Pacifica Found, mem 1973-80, chmn, pres 1976-80; chmn, Nassau County Youth Bd, 1979-; Phi Delta Kappa; Assn for the Study of Afro-Amer Life and History; Afro-Amer Inst NY; Mensa, 1968-70; Coun Black Amer Affairs; exec bd, NY African Studies Assn; African Heritage Studies Assn; mem, Governor's New York State Council on Youth, 1986-; advisory bd mem, Radio Station WBAI-FM NY, 1972-85; member, Schomburg Corp, 1989-; board member, Long Island Community Foundation, 1989-98; bd mem, New York State Youth Support Inc. **SELECTED PUBLICATIONS** author of essays, reviews **CONTACT ADDRESS** African-American Studies Dept, Nassau Comm Col, Garden City, NY, 11530.

JENKINS, RONALD BRADFORD
PERSONAL Born 11/14/1941, Rockingham, NC, m, 1973, 2 children **DISCIPLINE** RENAISSANCE LITERATURE **EDUCATION** Wake Forest Univ, BA, 64; NC State Univ, MA, 70; Univ NC, Chapel Hill, PhD(English), 76. **CAREER** Teacher English, E Southern Pines High Sch, NC, 64-66; instr, Vardell Hall Jr Col, 66-68, Winthrop Univ, SC, 70-72 & Univ NC, Chapel Hill, 75-76; asst prof, Campbell Col, 76-77, assoc prof, 77-78, Victor R Small prof & chmn dept, 78-79; PROF ENGLISH & CHMN DEPT ENGLISH & SPEECH, GA COL & STATE UNIV, 79- **MEMBERSHIPS** MLA; SAtlantic Mod Lang Asn; Milton Soc Am; Renaissance Soc Am; Southeastern Renaissance Conf. **RESEARCH** Milton studies; Medieval and Renaissance theology; Victorian and Romantic poetic theory. **SELECTED PUBLICATIONS** Auth, A new look at an old tombstone (The Scarlet Letter), New Eng Quart, 9/72; Milton and the Theme of Fame, Studies English Lit Ser, Mouton, The Hague, 73; Invulnerable virtue in Wieland and Comus, SAtlan-

tic Bull, 5/73; The Zerilla Dewey Subplot in The Rise of Silas Lapham, Explicator, spring 78; Robert Frost and the Agitated Heart, Notes on Contemp Lit, 3/80; The devil's advocate: A different approach to My Last Duchess, J English Teaching Tech, winter 80; Shakespeare's Measure for Measure: Cucullus non Facit Monachum, Explicator, summer 81; Four stages in the writing of expository prose, Freshman English Resource Notes, vol 7, no 1, 83; Henry Smith: England's Silver-Tongued Preacher, Mercer Univ Press, 83; Revelation in Paradise Regained, J of Evolutionary Psych, 85; The Case Against the King: The Family of Ophelia vs. His Majesty King Claudius of Denmark, J of Evolutionary Psych, 96. **CONTACT ADDRESS** P O Box 505, Milledgeville, GA, 31061-0505. **EMAIL** rjenkins@mail.gac.peachnet.edu

JENNINGS, LAWRENCE CHARLES
PERSONAL Born 11/10/1912, Exeter, MO, m, 1938, 3 children **DISCIPLINE** ENGLISH LITERATURE, ENGLISH LANGUAGE **EDUCATION** Southwest Mo State Col, BS, 34; Nazarene Theol Sem, BD, 48; Northwestern Mo State Col, MS, 60; Univ Okla, EdD(English), 71. **CAREER** Teacher English, Midway High Sch, Mo, 35-41; prin, Butterfield High Sch, 41-43; teacher bus, Maryville High Sch, 54-55; asst prof English, Can Nazarene Col, 55-63; from asst prof to assoc prof English, 64-69, chmn, div lang, lit & speech, 76-78, prof, 69-79, head dept, 72-79, EMER PROF ENGLISH, BETHANY NAZARENE COL, 79-. **MEMBERSHIPS** S cent Mod Lang Asn; S Cent Renaissance Conf; Southwest Lit Asn. **RESEARCH** Image of the professor in English literature from Carlyle to Snow; literary figures of the Mississippi River South. **CONTACT ADDRESS** Dept of English, Bethany Nazarene Col, Bethany, OK, 73008.

JENSEN, EJNER JACOB
PERSONAL Born 01/28/1937, Omaha, NE, 2 children **DISCIPLINE** ENGLISH **EDUCATION** Carleton Col, BA, 59; Tulane Univ, MA, 60, PhD(English), 65. **CAREER** From instr to asst prof, 64-70, assoc prof, 70-79, PROF ENGLISH, UNIV MICH, ANN ARBOR, 79- **MEMBERSHIPS** MLA; Malone Soc. **RESEARCH** English Renaissance drama; Shakespeare. **SELECTED PUBLICATIONS** Auth, Theme and imagery in The Malcontent, Studies English, Lit 70; The wit of Renaissance satire, Philol Quart, 72; The changing faces of love in English Renaissance drama, Comp Drama, 73; Lamb, Poel, and Our Post-War Theatre, Renaissance Drama, 79; John Marston, Dramatist, Salzburg, 79; Encounters with experience, New England Rev, 80; ed, The Future, UMI Press, 83; auth, Shakespeare and the Ends of Comedy, Indiana, 91; auth, Ben Jonson's Comedies on the Modern State, UMI. **CONTACT ADDRESS** Dept of English, Univ of Mich, 505 S State St, Ann Arbor, MI, 48109-1045. **EMAIL** ejjensen@umich.edu

JENSEN, J. VERNON
PERSONAL Born 09/29/1922, Scandia, MN, m, 1954, 2 children **DISCIPLINE** SPEECH COMMUNICATION **EDUCATION** Augsburg Col, BA, 47; Univ Minn, MA, 48, PhD(speech, hist), 59. **CAREER** Instr speech & hist, Augsburg Col, 48-51; teaching asst hist, 51-53, instr commun, 53-59, from asst prof to assoc prof speech & commun, 59-67, dir, Commun Prog, 70-73, PROF SPEECH & COMMUN, UNIV MINN, MINNEAPOLIS, 67-, Fulbright lectr, State Training Col Teachers, Rangoon, Burma, 61-62. **MEMBERSHIPS** Speech Commun Asn; Am Asn Advan Humanities; Am Forensic Asn; Hist Sci Soc. **RESEARCH** Rhetorical criticism; British and Commonwealth public speaking; Thomas Henry Huxley as a communicator. **SELECTED PUBLICATIONS** Auth, Huxley, Thomas, Henry Address at the Opening of the Johns-Hopkins-University in September 1876, Notes and Records of the Royal Soc of London, Vol 0047, 93; Sir Raleigh, Walter Speech From the Scaffold--A Translation of the 1619 Dutch Ed, and Comparison With English Texts, Rhetorica-J Hist Rhetoric, Vol 0015, 97. **CONTACT ADDRESS** Dept of Speech Commun, Univ of Minn, Minneapolis, MN, 55455.

JENSEN, KATHARINE
DISCIPLINE 17TH AND 18TH CENTURY LITERATURE, WOMEN'S WRITING, FEMINIST THEORY **EDUCATION** Columbia Univ, PhD, 88. **CAREER** Assoc prof, La State Univ. **SELECTED PUBLICATIONS** Auth, Male Models of Feminine Epistolarity, Writing the Female Voice, 88; The Inheritance of Masculinity and the Limits of Heterosexual Revision, 18th Century Life, 92; Writing Love: Letters, Women, and the Novel, 95. **CONTACT ADDRESS** Dept of Fr Grad Stud, Louisiana State Univ, Baton Rouge, LA, 70803.

JENSEN, ROBERT W.
PERSONAL Born 07/14/1958, Devils Lake, ND, d, 1 child **DISCIPLINE** JOURNALISM, MASS COMMUNICATION **EDUCATION** Univ MN, PhD, 92. **CAREER** Asst prof, 92-98, assoc prof, Univ TX, 98-. **MEMBERSHIPS** AEJMC; ICA; NCA. **RESEARCH** Freedom of speech; media law; feminism; sexuality; radical politics. **SELECTED PUBLICATIONS** Ed with David S Allen, Freeing the First Amendment: Critical Perspectives on Freedom of Expression, NY Univ Press, 95; coauth with Elvia R Arriola, Feminism and Free Expression: Silence and Voice, and auth, Embracing Uncertainty/Facing Fear, in Freeing the First Amendment, NY Univ Press, 95; auth, Pornography and the Limits of Experimental Research, in Gail Dines and Jean M Humez, eds, Gender, Race, and Class in Media: A Text Reader, Sage, 95; auth, The Politics and Ethics of Lesbian and Gay Wedding Announcements in Newspapers, Howard J of Commun, Jan-March 96; Knowing Poronography, Violence Against Women, March 96; What Are Journalists For?, Peace Rev, 96; Journalists and the Overtime Provisions of the Fair Labor Standards Act, Journalism and Mass Communications Quart, summer 96; Priviledge, Power, and Politics in Research, Int J of Qualitative Studies in Ed, 97; co-auth, with Gail Dines and Ann Russo, Pornography: The Production and Consumption of Inequality, Routledge, 97; numerous other publications and several forthcoming. **CONTACT ADDRESS** Dept of Journalism, Univ of Texas, Austin, TX, 78712. **EMAIL** rjensen@uts.cc.utexas.edu

JERRED, ADA D.
PERSONAL Born 04/14/1937, Ruston, LA, d, 1 child **DISCIPLINE** LIBRARY AND INFORMATION STUDIES **EDUCATION** La Col, BA, 55; Univ Denver, MA, 61; Tex Women's Univ, PhD, 85. **CAREER** Dir, La Col Libry, 59-62; cat, Emory Univ Libry, 62-63; cat, LSU, 63-70; from vis asst prof to asst librn to sen librn to head librn and prof, 72-87, LSU; grad asst, Tex Women's Univ, 81, dir, librys, Northwestern State Univ, 87-. **HONORS AND AWARDS** Enhancement of Watson Libry, 90, Expanded CD-ROM Network for Business Databases, 93, Expanded Res Capability Hum, 94, Electronic Imaging Melrose Documents, 95, Technological Enhancement Tchr Educ, 96; Telecommunications Capabilities for Access to and Sharing of Nursing Resources, LEQSF; Micrographics Enhancement of Social Sciences, 97, La Board Regents. **MEMBERSHIPS** Am Libry Asn; Asn Col Res Librys; Col Libry Standards Committee; La Libry Asn; Acad Section Chair; Constitution and By-Laws Committee; Libry Development Committee; Continuing Educ Committee; La Lit Award Committee; La Acad Libry Infor Consortium; La Libry Network Commission; Beta Phi Mu; Delta Kappa Gamma; Phi Kappa Phi; Phi Alpha Theta. **RESEARCH** Library management. **SELECTED PUBLICATIONS** Auth, art, The Past is Prologue: Designing Information Services for Historic Preservationists, 95; auth, art, Connecting Historic Preservationists: A Proposed Partnership Based on the ERIC Model, 95; auth, art, Fee vs. Free: Maintaining the Balance, 95, a **CONTACT ADDRESS** 324 Mr Ed Ln, Natchitoches, LA, 71457. **EMAIL** jarred@alpha.nsula.edu

JERZ, DENNIS G.
DISCIPLINE ENGLISH LITERATURE **EDUCATION** Univ Va, BA, 90; MA, 92; Univ Toronto, PhD, 98. **CAREER** Instr, Univ Toronto, 96-98; asst prof, 98-. **HONORS AND AWARDS** Open Fellow, Univ Toronto, 93-97; Simcoe Special Fellow, Univ Toronto, 92-93. **RESEARCH** Plays of Sam Shepard; religious studies. **SELECTED PUBLICATIONS** Auth, Towards a Pro-active Technical Writing Curriculum, Can Soc Mech Engineering Forum, 98; PSim 2.0: A Computer Simulation of Wagon Motion in the York Corpus Christi Pageant, (Re)Soundings: A World Wide Web Publication, 97. **CONTACT ADDRESS** Dept of English, Univ of Wisconsin, Eau Claire, Hibbard Hall 419, PO Box 4004, Eau Claire, WI, 54702-4004. **EMAIL** jerzdg@uwec.edu

JEWELL, JAMES EARL
PERSONAL Born 07/26/1929, Los Angeles, CA **DISCIPLINE** THEATER LIGHTING; ENGINEERING **EDUCATION** Univ of the Pacific, BA 51; Yale Univ, School of Drama. **CAREER** Holzmueller Corp SF, enginr div head, 57-67; Univ Cal Berke, sr lect, 63-67; Bolt Beranek Newmman SF & NY, sr consul, 67-69; Pacific Gas & Elec Co SF, Light Ser Admin, 69-87. **HONORS AND AWARDS** Lewis B Marks Awd; CIE; Coll Fell Amer Theater; CIE Dist Ser Awd. **MEMBERSHIPS** IES of NA; IES of China; SAH; AAAS; NTHP; NTS; ICI. **RESEARCH** History of lighting and lighting design; theater history. **SELECTED PUBLICATIONS** Auth, The Visual Arts in Bohemia: 125 Years of Artistic Creativity in the Bohemian Club, ed, Bohemian Club SF, CA, 97; Relighting Hearst Castle, SF Designers Light Forum, 96; Increasing fixture efficiency with connective venting in compact fluorescent downlights, Ninth Intl Conf, Varna Bulgaria, 93. Control system performance in a modern daylighted office building, with C. Benton, M. Fountain, S. Selkowitz, Proceedings of the 22nd CIE Sess, Melbourne Aus, Vic Aus, 91; Getting a Fix On Fixtures, APPA Lighting Wkshp, Omaha NE, Morgan Sys, Berkeley, 89; **CONTACT ADDRESS** 749 Rhode Island St, San Francisco, CA, 94107-2629. **EMAIL** j_jewell@arch-light.com

JEWINSKI, EDWIN
DISCIPLINE CANADIAN PROSE; POETRY **EDUCATION** Waterloo, BA, MA; Toronto, PhD. **CAREER** Prof **SELECTED PUBLICATIONS** Auth,: Milton Acorn: His Life and His Works; ECW Press, 91; The Politics of Art, Rudopi Press, 92; Co-ed, Joyce 'n Beckett, Fordham Press, 92; Auth, Joe Rosenblatt: His Life and His Works, ECW Press, 92; Michael Ondaatje: Express Yourself Beautifully, ECW Press, 94. **CONTACT ADDRESS** Dept of English, Wilfrid Laurier Univ, 75 University Ave W, Waterloo, ON, N2L 3C5.

JIAN-ZHONG, ZHOU
DISCIPLINE PHYSICS; LIBRARY & INFORMATION SCIENCE **EDUCATION** Beijing Normel Univ, BS, 85; Dominican Univ, MLIS, 90; Univ Del, MBA, 96. **CAREER** Info spec, Chinese Acad Science, 85-88; proj copy cataloger, Am Libr Asn, 88-89; intern librn, Northwestern Univ, 89-90; science librn, Univ Del, 90-. **MEMBERSHIPS** Am Libr Asn; Asn Col Res Libs; Libr & Info Technol Asn; Patent & Trademark Depository Libr Asn; Chinese-Am Librn Asn. **RESEARCH** Hitech and the libraries; organization and the retrieval of information in the web-based system; cost and the quality of electronic publications; copyright and the fair use of scholarly information; establishing of a good market for the intellectual properties. **SELECTED PUBLICATIONS** Ed and compiler, Research Report of the Institute of Physics, Chinese Academia Sinica, 85-88; auth, art, The Development of Library and Information Technologies in Southeast Asia, 97; auth, art, A New Subclass for Library of Congress Classification, QF: Computer Science, 98. **CONTACT ADDRESS** 10 Woodward Dr, Wilmington, DE, 19808. **EMAIL** joezhou@udel.edu

JIMOH, A. YEMISI
DISCIPLINE AMERICAN LITERATURE **EDUCATION** Univ Houston, PhD. **CAREER** English and Lit, Univ Ark. **SELECTED PUBLICATIONS** Auth, African American Literature: The African Continuum--Folklore, Myths, and Legends, Western Jour Black Studies, 89. **CONTACT ADDRESS** Univ Ark, Fayetteville, AR, 72701.

JIN, XUEFEI
DISCIPLINE ENGLISH LANGUAGE AND LITERATURE **EDUCATION** Brandeis Univ, PhD, 93. **CAREER** Asst prof **RESEARCH** Creative writing; poetry. **SELECTED PUBLICATIONS** Auth, Between Silences; Facing Shadows; Oceans of Words. **CONTACT ADDRESS** English Dept, Emory Univ, 1380 Oxford Rd NE, Atlanta, GA, 30322-1950.

JITENDRA, ASHA
DISCIPLINE 17TH AND 18TH CENTURY BRITISH AMERICA **EDUCATION** BA, Univ Madras,76; MS, Purdue Univ, 86; PhD, Univ Ore, 91. **CAREER** Asst prof, Texas Tech Univ, 91-93; Asst prof, Lehigh Univ, 93-. **MEMBERSHIPS** Ed bd, Remedial & Spec Ed, 1995-; ed bd, Ed & Treatment of Children, 96-. **SELECTED PUBLICATIONS** Co-au, Language Assesment of Linguistically Diverse Students, Scho Psy Rev, 25, 96; An Exploratory Evaluation of Dynamic Assesment and the Role of Basals on Comprehension of Mathematical Operations, 94. **CONTACT ADDRESS** Lehigh Univ, Bethlehem, PA, 18015. **EMAIL** AKJ2@leigh.edu

JOBE, STEVE
DISCIPLINE 19TH CENTURY AMERICAN LITERATURE, 18TH CENTURY BRITISH LITERATURE **EDUCATION** Univ S, BA, 78; Univ NC, Chapel Hill, MS, 81, PhD, 88. **CAREER** Assoc prof, Hanover Col, 90. **RESEARCH** 20th century Sourthern lit. **SELECTED PUBLICATIONS** Auth, The Discrimination of Stoicisms in The American, Stud in Am Fiction 16, 88; Henry James and the Philosophic Actor, Am Lit 62, 90; A Calendar of the Published Letters of Henry James, Henry James Rev 11, 90; Representation and Performance in The Tragic Muse, Am Lit Realism 1870-1910 26, 94; Henry James and the Innocence of Daisy Miller: A Corrected Text of the Letter to Eliza Lynn Linton, Am Lit Realism, 1870-1910 29, 97. **CONTACT ADDRESS** Hanover Col, Hanover, IN, 47243. **EMAIL** jobe@hanover.edu

JOCH ROBINSON, GERTRUDE
DISCIPLINE COMMUNICATION STUDIES **EDUCATION** Swarthmore Col, BA; Univ Chicago, MA; Univ Ill, PhD. **CAREER** Prof. **HONORS AND AWARDS** Ed, Can J Commun **RESEARCH** History/theory of communication; media industries and globalization; media and gender; comparative broadcast regulation; high/low culture; audiencing behavior. **SELECTED PUBLICATIONS** Auth, West Germany: The End of Public Service Broadcasting as we Know It, Longman, 93; auth, The Study of Women and Journalism: From Positivist to Feminist Approaches, Ablex, 94; co-auth, Women Politicians and their Media Coverage: A Generational Approach, Dundee, 92; co-ed, Women and Power: Canadian and German Experiences, 90. **CONTACT ADDRESS** Dept Communications, McGill Univ, 845 Sherbrooke St, Montreal, PQ, H3A 2T5.

JOHANNESEN, RICHARD LEE
PERSONAL Born 08/14/1937, Davenport, IA, 2 children **DISCIPLINE** COMMUNICATION **EDUCATION** Augustana Col, Ill, BA, 59; Univ Kans, MA, 60, PhD(speech), 64. **CAREER** Instr speech, Univ Kans, 61-62; from instr to asst prof, Ind Univ, Bloomington, 64-71; assoc prof, 72-77, prof Commun Studies, Northern Ill Univ, 77-, dept chair, 88-96. **MEMBERSHIPS** Speech Commun Asn; Cent States Speech Asn; Nat Soc Studies Commun; Rhet Soc Am. **RESEARCH** Contemporary theories of rhetoric; rhetorical criticism; ethical problems in communication. **SELECTED PUBLICATIONS** Ed, Ethics and Persuasion, Random, 67; co-ed, Language is Sermonic: Richard M Weaver on the Nature of Rhetoric, La State Univ, 70; ed, Contemporary Theories of Rhetoric, Harper, 71;

auth, The Emerging Concept of Communication as Dialogue, Quart J Speech, 12/71; Attitude of Speaker Toward Audience: A Significant Concept for Contemporary Rhetorical Theory & Criticism, Cent States Speech J, summer 74; Ethics in Human Communication, Waveland Press, 4th ed, 96; co-ed, Contemporary American Speeches, Kendall-Hunt, 8th ed, 97; **CONTACT ADDRESS** Dept of Communication, No Illinois Univ, De Kalb, IL, 60115-2825. **EMAIL** rjohannesen@niu.edu

JOHN, BRIAN
DISCIPLINE ENGLISH LITERATURE **EDUCATION** Univ Wales, BA, MA, PhD. **RESEARCH** Mod Irish lit; mod British lit. **SELECTED PUBLICATIONS** Auth, Supreme Fictions: Studies in the Work of William Blake, Thomas Carlyle, W.B. Yeats, and D.H. Lawrence, 74; auth, The World as Event: the Poetry of Charles Tomlinson, 89. **CONTACT ADDRESS** English Dept, McMaster Univ, 1280 Main St W, Hamilton, ON, L8S 4L9.

JOHNDAN, JOHNSON-EILOLA
DISCIPLINE PROFESSIONAL WRITING, COMPUTERS AND WRITING **EDUCATION** Mich Technol Univ, BS, 87; MS, 89; PhD, 93. **CAREER** Tchg asst, Mich Technol Univ, 87-90; asst prof Eng, dir, tech writing, NMex Inst of Mining and Technol, 93-94; asst prof Eng, 94-, dir, tech writing, Purdue Univ, 97-. **HONORS AND AWARDS** Outstanding Ph.D. Student, Mich Technol Univ, 93; Hugh Burns Award, Comput and Compos. 94; Nell Ann Picket Award, Asn of Tchr of Tech Writing, 96; Ellen Nold Award, Comput and Compos, 97; curric develop grant, Purdue Univ, 97; re-investment grant, Purdue Univ, 97, Curric develop; www site support, Purdue Univ. **MEMBERSHIPS** Nat Coun of Tchr of Eng; Conf on Col Compos and Commun; Asn of Tchr of Tech Writing; Am Asn of Univ Prof; Asn for Bus Commun; Coun for Prog in Tech and Sci Commun; Asn for Tchr of Advan Compos; Alliance for Comput and Writing; Soc for Tech Commun. **RESEARCH** Philosophies of instructional writing; intellectual property. **SELECTED PUBLICATIONS** Auth, An Overview of Reading and Writing in Hypertext: Vertigo and Euphoria,, Literacy and Computers, MLA, 94; Relocating the Value of Work: Technical Communication in a Post-Industrial Age, Tech Commun Quart 5.3, 96; Stories and Maps: Postmodernism and Professional Communication, Kairos 1.1, 96; Nostalgic Angels: Rearticulating Hypertext Writing, Ablex Press, 97; coauth, Our Colleagues Interact on a MOO, Computers and the Teaching of Writing in American Higher Education 1979-1994: A History, Ablex Press; Hypertext and Group Writing Processes in Corporate Settings, Multidisciplinary Research in Workplace Writing: Challenging the Boundaries, Lawrence Erlbaum, 95; Online Support Systems: Help, Documentation, and Tutorials.CRC Handbook of Computer Science and Computer Engineering, CRC Press, 96; Automating and Informating Hypertexts: Examining Interactions Between Corporate Structures and Computer Technologies, Electronic Literacies in the Workplace: Technologies of Writing, NCTE Press, 96; Policing Ourselves: Defining the Boundaries of Appropriate Discussion in Online Forums, Comput and Compos, 13.3, 96; Core Issues for Developing Online Support Systems, ACM Comput Surv 28.1, 96. **CONTACT ADDRESS** Dept of Eng, Purdue Univ, 1080 Schleman Hall, West Lafayette, IN, 47907-1080. **EMAIL** johndan@purdue.edu

JOHNSON, ALEX C.
PERSONAL Born 08/14/1943, Freetown, Sierra Leone, m, 2 children **DISCIPLINE** ENGLISH **EDUCATION** Univ Durham, BA, 68; Kent Univ, Canterbury, MA, 71; Univ Leeds, MPhil, 74; Univ Ibadan, PhD, 82. **CAREER** High Schls Tchr, 68-69, 71-72, Freetown, Sierra Leone; sr lectr, lectr, Eng dept, 74-88, FBC-USL; prof, Eng lang & Creole stud, 82-84, Univ Bayreuth, W Germany; sr lectr, actg head, class/phil dept, 87-88, assoc prof & head, Eng dept, 88-91, actg vice prin 89-90, dean, fac of arts, 89-91, Fourah Bay Col, Univ Sierra Leone; vis prof, 91-92, prof, Eng, 92-, SC St Univ. **HONORS AND AWARDS** Who's Who in Amer, 98; Who's Who in the South & Southwest, 97-98; Tchr of Year, 93, SCSU. **MEMBERSHIPS** CLA; ALA; NCTE; AAUP; WALS. **RESEARCH** Linguistic and sociolinguistic situation of Krio in Sierra Leone multilingualism; language of W African lit. **SELECTED PUBLICATIONS** Auth, Creative Tension in West African Drama in English: The Linguistic Dimension, World Lit Written in Eng, 84; auth, The Development of Sierra Leone Krio, Bayreuth African Stud Ser: Towards African Authenticity, 85; auth, Multilingualism and Language Policy in Sierra Leone, Bayreuth African Stud Ser: Lang and Ed in Africa, 86; auth, Varieties of Krio and Standard Krio, Reading & Writing Krio, Uppsala, 92; auth, Two Historical Plays From West Africa, Komparatistische Heft 8, 93; auth, The Krio Language, Oxford Com to African Lit, Oxford Univ Press, 97. **CONTACT ADDRESS** Dept of Communications & Languages, South Carolina State Univ, 300 College St NE, Orangeburg, SC, 29117. **EMAIL** Jonsonac@scsu.edu

JOHNSON, BOBBY HAROLD
PERSONAL Born 11/09/1935, Overton, TX, m, 1959, 2 children **DISCIPLINE** AMERICAN & JOURNALISM HISTORY **EDUCATION** Abilene Christian Col, BA, 58; Univ Okla, MA, 62, PhD(hist), 67. **CAREER** From asst prof to assoc prof, 66-77, PROF HIST, STEPHEN F AUSTIN STATE UNIV, 77-, Dir, Off Univ Info, Stephen F Austin State Univ, 79-82. **MEMBERSHIPS** Orgn Am Historans; Western Hist Asn **RESEARCH** American West, especially Oklahoma territory; history of American journalism; history of aviation. **SELECTED PUBLICATIONS** Auth, The Cartwrights of San-Augustine--3 Generations of Agricultural Entrepreneurs in 19th-Century Texas, Southwestern Hist Quart, Vol 0098, 95. **CONTACT ADDRESS** Dept of Hist, Stephen F Austin State Univ, Box 3013, Nacogdoches, TX, 75962.

JOHNSON, CHRISTOPHER G.
DISCIPLINE ENGLISH LITERATURE **EDUCATION** Univ British Columbia, BA; MA; Leeds Univ, PhD. **CAREER** Prof. **HONORS AND AWARDS** Merit Awd; Outreach Awd. **RESEARCH** Theatrical production; dramatic theory; Canadian and Commonwealth drama. **SELECTED PUBLICATIONS** Auth, George F. Walker: Playing With Anxiety; pub(s) on Canadian and Commonwealth plays, playwrights, and theatres. **CONTACT ADDRESS** Dept of English, Manitoba Univ, Winnipeg, MB, R3T 2N2.

JOHNSON, CLAUDIA DURST
PERSONAL Born 01/11/1938, Gastonia, NC, m, 1956, 2 children **DISCIPLINE** AMERICAN LITERATURE **EDUCATION** Western Ill Univ, BS, 59; George Peabody Col, MA, 62; Univ Ill, PhD(English), 73. **CAREER** Instr humanities, Shimer Col, 68-70; from asst to instr English, Univ Ill, Urbana, 71-73; asst prof, 73-77, ASSOC PROF ENGLISH, UNIV ALA, 77-, CHMN, DEPT ENG, 81-, Res stimulation, 80-81. **HONORS AND AWARDS** Grad Fac Res Award, Univ Ala, 77. **MEMBERSHIPS** MLA; S Atlantic Mod Lang Asn; Nathaniel Hawthorne Soc; Am Studies Asn. **RESEARCH** Nineteenth century and Puritan American literature. **SELECTED PUBLICATIONS** Auth, Resolution in the Marble Faun, Univ Ill Press, 78; Enter the Harlot, in: Women in the American Theatre, Crown, 80; The Productive Tension of Hawthorne's Art University, Univ Ala Press, 81; Nationalism & the Burlesque of Shakespeare, Theatre Survey, Am J Theatre Hist, 81; Oline Logan and Clara Morris, in: American Women Writers, Frederick Unger, 81; William Dunlap and John Bernard, Dict Lit Biog (in press); Nineteenth Century Theatrical Memoirs, Greenwood Press (in press); Nineteenth Century Actress in America, Nelson Hall, 83. **CONTACT ADDRESS** Dept of English, Univ of Ala, Morgan Hall, University, AL, 35486.

JOHNSON, DEWAYNE BURTON
PERSONAL Born 04/18/1920, Newman Grove, NE, m, 1942, 3 children **DISCIPLINE** JOURNALISM **EDUCATION** Univ Calif, Berkeley, BA, 48; Univ Calif, Los Angeles, MA, 50, EdD, 55. **CAREER** Corresp, United Press Asn, Tacoma, Wash, 48-49; res assoc, Univ Calif, Los Angeles, 51; instr English, El Camino Col, 52-53; asst prof English & dir pub rels, Southern Ore Col, 53-55; asst prof jour, San Diego State Col, 55-59; pub rels dir, La Mesa-Spring Valley Sch Dist, Calif, 59-60; instr English, San Diego City Col, 60; asst prof, 61-65, PROF JOUR, CALIF STATE UNIV, NORTHRIDGE, 61-, FAC PRES, 74-, Copy ed, San Diego Union, 55-59 & Los Angeles Times, 61-. **HONORS AND AWARDS** Outstanding Prof Jour, Calif Newspaper Publ Asn, 73 & 77. **MEMBERSHIPS** Soc Prof Journalists. **RESEARCH** Photojournalism; future of the mass media; problems in mass communication. **SELECTED PUBLICATIONS** Auth, Historical analysis of the criticisms concerning teaching about the United Nations Educational, Scienfific and Cultural Organizations in the Los Angeles city schools. **CONTACT ADDRESS** 10118 Aldea Ave, Northridge, CA, 91325.

JOHNSON, ERIC
DISCIPLINE ENGLISH LITERATURE **EDUCATION** PhD, Univ Notre Dame. **CAREER** Prof , Dakota State Univ, Dean, Col Lib Arts, Dakota State Univ. **SELECTED PUBLICATIONS** Areas: writing and teaching with computers, classic works of children's literature. **CONTACT ADDRESS** Dakota State Univ, 820 N. Washington Ave, Madison, SD, 57042. **EMAIL** johnsone@jupiter.dsu.edu. 2

JOHNSON, JAMES WILLIAM
PERSONAL Born 03/01/1927, Birmingham, AL, m, 1957, 2 children **DISCIPLINE** ENGLISH LITERATURE **EDUCATION** Birmingham-Southern Col, AB, 50; Harvard Univ, AM, 50; Vanderbilt Univ, PhD, 54. **CAREER** Instr English, Vanderbilt Univ, 52-54; from instr to assoc prof, 55-65, prof eng, Univ Rochester, 65-70, prof Emeritus, 71-, Fulbright scholar, UK, 54-55; fel, Folger Libr, 63, Am Coun Learned Socs, 49-50, 66-67 & Guggenheim, 70-71. **HONORS AND AWARDS** Whos Who in America; Matzdorf Award. **MEMBERSHIPS** English Inst; MLA; Northeastern Am Soc 18th Century Studies. **RESEARCH** Women's lit; mod drama; eighteenth century Engl & restoration lit and Southern Lit. **SELECTED PUBLICATIONS** Auth, Logic and Rhetoric, Macmillan, 62; The Formation of English Neo-Classical Thought, Princeton Univ, 67; Utopian Literature, Random, 68; Concepts of Literature, Prentice-Hall, 71; What was neo-classicism?, J Brit Studies, 71; Prose in Practice, Harcourt, 72; Gibbon's architectural metaphor, J Brit Studies, 73; Letters from the Countess of Rochester, Rochester Libr Bull, 74; ed, The Plays of John Dennis, 80. **CONTACT ADDRESS** Dept of Eng, Univ of Rochester, 500 Joseph C Wilson, Rochester, NY, 14627-9000. **EMAIL** jwjnhj@worldnet.att.net

JOHNSON, JEFFREY
DISCIPLINE 17TH AND 18TH CENTURY BRITISH LITERATURE **EDUCATION** Univ MS, PhD. **CAREER** Engl, Col Misericordia **SELECTED PUBLICATIONS** Contrib ed, The Variorum Edition of the Poetry of John Donne. **CONTACT ADDRESS** Col Misericordia, 301 Lake St., Dallas, PA, 18612-1098. **EMAIL** jjohnson@miseri.edu

JOHNSON, KENNETH E.
DISCIPLINE ENGLISH LITERATURE **EDUCATION** Univ Ca, BA, 75; Brown Univ, MA, 77, PhD, 81. **CAREER** Instr, Rhode Island Jr Col, 78-80; instr, Stonehill Col, 76-81; asst prof, 81-82; assoc prof, Fla Int Univ, 82-. **HONORS AND AWARDS** Tchg Incentive Prog Awd, 96. **SELECTED PUBLICATIONS** Auth, Teaching to the Postmodern, Jour Curriculum Theorizing, 94; Point of View of the Wandering Camera, Cinema Jour, 93; Tina Howe's Feminine Discourse, 92; There's No Basement in the Alamo, or , Pee-wee's Hermeneutics, 92. **CONTACT ADDRESS** Dept of English, Florida State Univ, 11200 SW 8th St, Miami, FL, 33174. **EMAIL** johnsonk@fiu.edu

JOHNSON, LEE MILFORD
PERSONAL Born 04/22/1944, Alexandria, MN, m, 1966, 4 children **DISCIPLINE** ENGLISH LITERATURE **EDUCATION** Hamline Univ, BA, 66; Princeton Univ, PhD(English), 70. **CAREER** Asst prof, 70-74, ASSOC PROF ENGLISH, UNIV BC, 74-. **RESEARCH** Prosody; Romantic poetry, 17th century poetry. **SELECTED PUBLICATIONS** Auth, The Passion of Meter, a Study of Wordsworth Metrical Art, 19th-Century Lit, Vol 0051, 96. **CONTACT ADDRESS** Dept of English, Univ of BC, Vancouver, BC, V6T 1W5.

JOHNSON, LEMUEL A.
PERSONAL Born 12/15/1941, Nigeria, m **DISCIPLINE** ENGLISH **EDUCATION** Oberlin Clg, BA 1965; PA St U, MA 1966; Univ of MI, PhD 1969. **CAREER** Dept of English Univ of MI, prof; English Univ of Sierra Leone Fourah Bay Clol, lecturer 1970-72; Radio Forum, host 1970-71. **HONORS AND AWARDS** Recipient hopwood awds for Short Story & Essay Cont 1967-68; Bredvold Prize for Scholar Publ; Dept of Eng Univ of MI awd 1972; pub num poems & translations. **MEMBERSHIPS** Sierra Leone Broad Serv Freetown; Pres African Lit Assc 1977-78. **SELECTED PUBLICATIONS** "The Devil, the Gargoyle & the Buffoon, The Negro as Metaphor in West Lit" 1971; Highlife for Caliban, 1973; "Hand on the Navel" 1978. **CONTACT ADDRESS** Univ of Michigan, Ann Arbor, MI, 48109.

JOHNSON, LINCK CHRISTOPHER
PERSONAL Born 02/02/1946, Evanston, IL **DISCIPLINE** AMERICAN LITERATURE **EDUCATION** Cornell Univ, AB, 69; Princeton Univ, MA, 71, PhD(English), 75. **CAREER** Instr, 74-76, asst prof, 76-83, assoc prof, 83-88, prof English, Colgate Univ, 88- . **HONORS AND AWARDS** Henry E Huntington Libr vis fel, 76; NEH fel Am Antiq Soc, 85. **MEMBERSHIPS** MLA; Am Lit Asn; Ralph Waldo Emerson Soc; Margaret Fuller Soc; Thoreau Soc of Am. **RESEARCH** Emerson; Thoreau; nineteenth century American literature and society. **SELECTED PUBLICATIONS** Auth, Thoreau's Complex Weave: The Writing of A Week on the Concord and Merrimack Rivers, with the Text of the First Draft, Virginia, 86; auth, Revolution and Renewal: The Genres of Walden, in Critical Essays on Henry David Thoreau's Walden, G.K. Hall, 88; auth, Reforming the Reformers: Emerson, Throeau, and the Sunday Lectures at Amory hall, Boston, in, ESQ: A J of the Am Renaissance, 91; contribur, The Cambridge Companion to Henry David Thoreau, Cambridge, 95; auth, Walden and the Construction of the American Renaissance, in, Approaches to Teaching Thoreau's Walden and Other Writings, MLA, 96; contribur, Biographical Dictionary of Transcendentalism, and, Encyclopedia of Transcendentalism, Greenwood, 96. **CONTACT ADDRESS** Dept of English, Colgate Univ, 13 Oak Dr, Hamilton, NY, 13346-1379. **EMAIL** LJohnson@mail.colgate.edu

JOHNSON, LUCILLE MARGUERITE
PERSONAL Born 04/03/1919, Hatton, ND, m, 1948 **DISCIPLINE** ENGLISH LITERATURE, RHETORIC **EDUCATION** Concordia Col, Moorhead, Minn, BA, 40; Wash State Univ, MA, 43; Univ Mont, EdD(rhet & hist & philos of educ), 67. **CAREER** Chmn dept English, Austin Col, Minn, 43-46; asst prof, Ohio Univ, 46-48 & Univ Wash, 48-50; chmn dept, Centralia Col, 50-53; assoc prof, 53-67, PROF ENGLISH & CHMN DEPT, PAC LUTHERAN UNIV, 67-, Consult, Teacher Educ Liaison Comt, Wash, 69-72; Can Embassy grant, 82. **MEMBERSHIPS** Am Asn Univ Women; MLA; NCTE Conf English Educ; Conf Col Compos & Commun. **RESEARCH** Chauceriana, Canadian literature. **SELECTED PUBLICATIONS** Auth, The Inner Life of Henry Vaughan as Revealed in His Religious Verse, Wash State Univ, 43; Teach them, 47 & The World's slow stain, 47, Lutheran Herald; A Neo-Aristotelian Study of Resources and Qualities of Descriptive Writing, Univ Mont, 67; Washington of the West, Wash State Hist Soc, 76. **CONTACT ADDRESS** Dept of English, Pac Lutheran Univ, Park Ave, Tacoma, WA, 98447.

JOHNSON, MICHAEL LILLARD
PERSONAL Born 06/29/1943, Springfield, MO, m, 1965 **DISCIPLINE** ENGLISH **EDUCATION** Rice Univ, BA, 65, PhD(English), 68; Stanford Univ, MA, 67. **CAREER** Lectr English, Rice Univ, 68-69; asst prof, 69-72, assoc prof, 72-78; PROF ENGLISH, UNIV KANS, 78-. **MEMBERSHIPS** Popular Cult Asn; NCTE. **RESEARCH** New journalism; lyric poetry; technology and literature. **SELECTED PUBLICATIONS** Auth, The New Journalism, Univ Kans, 71; Prometheus Reborn, 77 & Holistic Technology, 77, Libra; Dry season, 77 & The Unicorn Captured, 80, Cottonwood Rev. **CONTACT ADDRESS** Dept of English, Univ of Kans, Lawrence, KS, 66045-0001.

JOHNSON, RHODA E.
PERSONAL Born 11/14/1946, Bessemer, Alabama, m, 1968 **DISCIPLINE** FEMINIST STUDIES **EDUCATION** Tuskegee Institute, Tuskegee, AL, BS, 1968; University of Michigan, Ann Arbor, MI, AM, 1970; University of Alabama, Tuscaloosa, AL, PhD, 1980. **CAREER** University of Michigan, Ann Arbor, MI, student research asst, 1969-70; Tuskegee Institute, Tuskegee, AL, instructor, 1970-77, asst prof, 1977-81, assoc prof, dir of MARC, 1982-85; University of Alabama, Tuscaloosa, AL, visiting prof, acting dir, 1985-86, assoc prof, chair, 1986-92; assoc prof, 1992-. **HONORS AND AWARDS** Minority Access to Research Careers Grant, ADAMHA, 1982-85; Higher Education Component Grant, Southern Education Foundation, 1980-81; Poverty and Mental Health in the Rural South, CSRS/USDA, Carver Foundation, 1978-83; editor, Women's Studies in the South, Kendall/Hunt, 1991. **MEMBERSHIPS** Member, steering committee, 21st Century Leadership Project, 1989-; bd member, National Voting Rights Museum, 1994-; bd member, National Review Bd, Alabama Historical Commission. **CONTACT ADDRESS** Former Chair, Women's Studies, Univ of Alabama, Box 870272, 101 Manly, Tuscaloosa, AL, 35487-0272.

JOHNSON, SIMON
DISCIPLINE CREATIVE WRITING **EDUCATION** Colo State Univ, BA, 62; Columbia Sch Journalism, MS, 63; Univ Iowa, MFA, 69, PhD, 72. **CAREER** Engl, Oregon St Univ. **SELECTED PUBLICATIONS** Auth, Modern Technical Writing, Pentice-Hall, 90. **CONTACT ADDRESS** Oregon State Univ, Corvallis, OR, 97331-4501. **EMAIL** sjohnson@orst.edu

JOHNSON JR., J. THEODORE
DISCIPLINE NINETEENTH- AND TWENTIETH-CENTURY POETRY **EDUCATION** Univ WI, PhD. **CAREER** Prof, Univ KS. **HONORS AND AWARDS** Chancellor's award for excellence in tchg; Mortar Board's recognition as an oustanding educator, 92; sr class HOPE award to hon an outstanding progressive educator, Ed, Proust Res Assn Newsletter. **RESEARCH** Proust, and interrelations of lit and the visual arts. **SELECTED PUBLICATIONS** Publ(s), on Proust. **CONTACT ADDRESS** Dept of French and Italian, Univ Kansas, Admin Building, Lawrence, KS, 66045. **EMAIL** kufacts@ukans.edu

JOHNSON-SHEEHAN, RICHARD
DISCIPLINE RHETORIC AND PROFESSIONAL COMMUNICATION **EDUCATION** Iowa State Univ, PhD, 95. **CAREER** Instr, Univ NMex, 95-. **RESEARCH** The rhetoric of modern physics. **SELECTED PUBLICATIONS** Publishing articles exploring the rhetoric of modern physics. **CONTACT ADDRESS** Univ NMex, Albuquerque, NM, 87131.

JOHNSTON, ALEXANDRA F.
PERSONAL Born 07/19/1939, Indianapolis, IN **DISCIPLINE** ENGLISH/DRAMA **EDUCATION** Univ Toronto, BA, 61, MA, 62, PhD, 64; LLD(hon), Queen's Univ, 84. **CAREER** Asst prof, Queen's Univ, 64-67; asst prof to assoc prof, 67-77, PROF ENGLISH, VICTORIA COL, UNIV TORONTO, 78-. **HONORS AND AWARDS** Fel, Royal Soc Can, 97. **MEMBERSHIPS** Index Middle Eng Prose (adv comt); Int Soc Medieval Theatre (pres, 82-92); Medieval Renaissance Drama Soc, MLA (pres, 89-91); dir, Records Early Eng Drama, 76-. **SELECTED PUBLICATIONS** Auth, The York Records, Records of Early English Drama, 2 vols, 79; coauth, English Parish Drama, 96; coauth, Civic Ritual and Drama, 97. **CONTACT ADDRESS** Victoria Col, Univ of Toronto, 150 Charles St W, Toronto, ON, M5S 1K9.

JOHNSTON, ARNOLD
PERSONAL m **DISCIPLINE** PLAYWRITING **EDUCATION** Univ Del, PhD. **CAREER** Prof **HONORS AND AWARDS** Two WMU Fac Res Fel; Two Mich Counc Arts Grants; Two NEA/Arts Fund Kalamazoo Grants; Irving S. Gilmore Found Emerging Artist Grant, Kalamazoo's Community Arts Medal; NMU Alumni Assn Excellence in Teaching Award, 90. **MEMBERSHIPS** Dramatists' Guild. **RESEARCH** Fiction, and poetry. **SELECTED PUBLICATIONS** Auth, Of Earth and Darkness, Miss, 80; What the Earth Taught Us, March Street Press, 96; Writer/editor for NPR.. **CONTACT ADDRESS** Kalamazoo, MI, 49008. **EMAIL** arnie.johnston@wmich.edu

JOHNSTON, CAROL ANN
DISCIPLINE RENAISSANCE LITERATURE **EDUCATION** Harvard Univ, PhD. **CAREER** Asst prof-. **RESEARCH** Relationship between poetry and visual culture during the seventeenth century in England. **SELECTED PUBLICATIONS** Auth, Eudora Welty's short fiction, 97. **CONTACT ADDRESS** Dept of Eng, Dickinson Col, PO Box 1773, Carlisle, PA, 17013-2896.

JOHNSTON, GEORGIA
DISCIPLINE 20TH CENTURY BRITISH LITERATURE **EDUCATION** Rutgers Univ, PhD. **CAREER** Eng Dept, St. Edward's Univ **SELECTED PUBLICATIONS** Auth, After the Invention of the Gramophone; Hearing the Woman in Stein's Autobiography and Woolf's Three Guineas, Pace Univ Press, 92; Reading 'Anna' Backwards: Gertrude Stein Writing Modernism Out of the Nineteenth Century, Defining Modernism, 92; Women's Voice: Three Guineas as Autobiography, Pace Univ Press, 93; Narratologies of Pleasure: Gertrude Stein's Autobiography of Alice B. Toklas, Mod Fiction Studies, 96; Virginia Wolf's Autobiographers: Sidonie Smith, Shoshana Felman, and Shari Benstock, Pace Univ Press, 96; Virginia Woolf Revising Roger Fry into the Frames of 'A Sketch of the Past, Biography, 97; Class Performance in Between the Acts: Audiences for Miss La Trobe and Mrs. Manresa, Woolf Studies Annual, 97; Introduction: The Productions of Audience and Transgression, Edwin Mellen Press, 97. **CONTACT ADDRESS** St Edward's Univ, 3001 S Congress Ave, Austin, TX, 78704-6489.

JOHNSTON, JOHN
DISCIPLINE ENGLISH LANGUAGE AND LITERATURE **EDUCATION** Columbia Univ, PhD, 84. **CAREER** Prof **RESEARCH** Modern fiction; British and American Poetry; critical theory. **SELECTED PUBLICATIONS** Auth, Carnival of Repetition; trans, On the Line; co-trans, In the Shadow of the Silent Majorities. **CONTACT ADDRESS** English Dept, Emory Univ, 1380 Oxford Rd NE, Atlanta, GA, 30322-1950.

JOHNSTON, JOHN H.
PERSONAL Born 01/18/1921, Norfolk, VA, m, 1948, 7 children **DISCIPLINE** ENGLISH **EDUCATION** BA, 47; Univ Chicago, MA, 50; Univ WI, PhD, 60. **CAREER** Instr, 54-56 & 57-60, from asst prof to assoc prof, 60-69, Prof Eng, W VA Univ, 69-89; Prof emer Eng, 1989-. **MEMBERSHIPS** MLA; NCTE **RESEARCH** Eng poetry of World War I; Brit poetry, 1920-1939; urban poetics. **SELECTED PUBLICATIONS** Auth, Charles Sorley's bright promise, W VA Univ Philol Papers, 12/61; David Jones: The heroic vision, Rev Polit, 1/62; English Poetry of the First World War, Princeton Univ, 64; The Poet and the City, Univ GA Press, 84. **CONTACT ADDRESS** West Virginia Univ, Stansbury Hall, Morgantown, WV, 26506. **EMAIL** jhj21@aol.com

JOHNSTON, KENNETH R.
PERSONAL Born 04/20/1938, Marquette, MI, m, 1961, 3 children **DISCIPLINE** ENGLISH **EDUCATION** Augustana Col, Ill, BA, 59; Univ Chicago, MA, 61; Yale Univ, AM, 62, PhD(English), 66. **CAREER** Instr English, Augustana Col, Ill, 62-63; from asst prof to assoc prof English, 66-75, dir undergrad studies, 68-70, assoc dean col arts & sci, 73-74, PROF ENGLISH, IND UNIV, BLOOMINGTON, 75-, Fulbright prof Am lit, Univ Bucharest, Romania, 74-75; mem, English Romantic Exec Comn, MLA, 78- **HONORS AND AWARDS** Distinguished Teaching Award, Amoco Found, 73. **MEMBERSHIPS** MLA; Keats-Shelley Asn; Wordsworth-Coleridge Asn (pres, 74-76). **RESEARCH** English and American romantic poetry; Wordsworth; humanistic institutions. **SELECTED PUBLICATIONS** Auth, Romantic Voices--Identity and Ideology in British Poetry, 1789-1850, 19th-Century Lit, Vol 0047, 93; The Cambridge Companion toBritish Romanticism, Stud in Romanticism, Vol 0033, 94. **CONTACT ADDRESS** Dept of English, Indiana Univ, Bloomington, Bloomington, IN, 47401.

JOHNSTON, PAUL
DISCIPLINE ENGLISH **EDUCATION** Grand Valley State Col, BA; Univ MI Ann Arbor, MA; PhD,88. **CAREER** Chp, 97-99, Plattsburgh State Univ of NY. **RESEARCH** Am lit. **SELECTED PUBLICATIONS** Auth, publ(s) about representation of the environment in early Am lit and the relationship between cognitive sci and literary criticism. **CONTACT ADDRESS** SUNY, Plattsburgh, 101 Broad St, Plattsburgh, NY, 12901-2681.

JOHNSTON, STANLEY HOWARD
PERSONAL Born 04/28/1946, Cleveland, OH, m, 1976 **DISCIPLINE** ENGLISH LANGUAGE AND LITERATURE: ARCHIVES AND ACADEMIC LIBRARIES FOR THE LI **EDUCATION** BA, Columbia Univ, 68; MA, 70, PhD, 77, Univ Western Ontario; MSLS Case Western Reserve Univ, 79. **CAREER** Tchg Asst, Dept English, Univ Western Ontario, 71-72; Asst ed, Spenser Newsletter, Univ Western Ontario, 84-90; Bibliog The Cleveland Herbals Proj Hist Div Cleveland Hea Sci Library, 90-; Cur of Rare Books, the Holden Arboretum. **HONORS AND AWARDS** Phi Beta Mu. **MEMBERSHIPS** The Bibilo Soc, Bibilo Soc Of Am, Council on Bot and Horticulture Libraries, Am Library Assoc(Rare Gooks and Manuscript Div), Soc for the Hist of Natural Hist. **RESEARCH** Analytical and Descritptive Biblio; Book and Printing Hist, Bot and Horticultural Hist; Medical Hist; Hist of Bot Illus. **SELECTED PUBLICATIONS** A Study of the Career and Literary Publications of Richard Pynson, Dissertation, UWO 1977; The Cleveland Herbal, Botanical and Horticultural Collections, Kent State Univ Press, 92; Cleveland's Treasures of Botanical Literature, Orange Frazer Press, 98; Inter column in CBHL Newsletter, 95. **CONTACT ADDRESS** Holden Arboretum, 9500 Sperry Rd, Mentor, OH, 44060. **EMAIL** stanley177@aol.com

JOLLY, ROSEMARY J.
DISCIPLINE ENGLISH LITERATURE **EDUCATION** Univ Toronto, PhD. **CAREER** Dept Eng, Queen's Univ **HONORS AND AWARDS** Frank Knox Awd. **RESEARCH** Postcolonial literatures and theory; theories of violence, philosophical, psychoanalytical and clinical; intersections between gender and nationalism in minority literatures; interdisciplinarity in the postcolonial context; African, especially South African literatures; status of oral testimony. **SELECTED PUBLICATIONS** Auth, Colonization, Violence and Narration in White South African Writing: Breyten Breytenbach, Andre Brink and J.M. Coetzee, Ohio Univ, 96; Bessie Head and homophobia in Cross Addressing: Discourse on the Border, SUNY, 96; co-ed, Writing South Africa, Cambridge, 97. **CONTACT ADDRESS** English Dept, Queen's Univ, Kingston, ON, K7L 3N6.

JOLY, RALPH ROBERT
PERSONAL Born 02/03/1940, Salem, MA, m, 1959, 2 children **DISCIPLINE** ENGLISH **EDUCATION** William Tyndale Col, BRE, 64; Eastern Mich Univ, MA, 65; Univ NC, Chapel Hill, PhD(English), 73. **CAREER** Asst prof English, Harrisburg Area Community Col, 67-68; asst prof, Bethel Col, 70-74; assoc prof, Northwestern Col, 76-77; assoc prof, 77-79, prof English, Asbury Col, 79-. **MEMBERSHIPS** MLA; NCTE. **RESEARCH** Literary archetypalism; James Joyce; compositional strategies. **CONTACT ADDRESS** Asbury Col, 1 Macklem Dr, Wilmore, KY, 40390-1198. **EMAIL** rjoly@worldnet.att.edu

JONES, ANNE HUDSON
PERSONAL Born 11/14/1944, El Dorado, AR, m, 1971 **DISCIPLINE** LITERATURE & MEDICINE **EDUCATION** La State Univ, BA, 65; Univ NC, PhD(comp lit), 74. **CAREER** Asst prof English, Va Wesleyan Col, 70-71; lectr, New River Community Col, 71-72; instr, Va Polytech Inst & State Univ, 73-75, asst prof, 75-78, asst dir, Ctr Prog in Humanities, 78-79; ASST PROF LIT & MED, INST MED HUMANITIES, UNIV TEX MED BR, 79-, Assoc ed, Lit & Med, 80-; consult, Nat Bd Consult, Nat Endowment for the Humanities & Col Health Related Professions, Univ PR, 81- **MEMBERSHIPS** MLA; Am Comp Lit Asn; Southern Comp Lit Asn; Science Fiction Res Asn; Soc Health & Human Values. **RESEARCH** Medicine and the physician in American (popular) culture; feminist science fiction. **SELECTED PUBLICATIONS** Auth, A question of ethic: Materials and methods, Proc 27th Int Tech Community Conf, Inst Humanitic Studies, 80; Thomas Szasz' myth of mental illness and Peter Shaffer's Equus, Asclepius at Syracuse: Thomas Szasz, Libertarian Humanist, 81; Ethics and medical writing: A prolegomenon, Proc 28th Int Tech Community Conf, 81; Alexei Panshin's almost non-sexist Rite of Passage, in: Future Females: A Critical Anthology, Bowling Green Univ Press, 81; Salome: the decadent ideal, Comp Lit Studies, 81; Medicine and the physician in popular culture, in: The Handbook of American Popular Culture, Greenwood Press, 81; Women in science fiction: An annotated secondary bibliography, Extrapolation, spring 82; The cyborg (r)evolution in science fiction, in: The Mechanical God: Machines in Science Fiction, Greenwood Press, 82. **CONTACT ADDRESS** Inst Med Humanities, Univ Tex Med Br, 301 University Blvd, Galveston, TX, 77550-2708.

JONES, BUFORD
DISCIPLINE ENGLISH LITERATURE **EDUCATION** Harvard Univ, PhD, 62. **CAREER** Bibliogr. **SELECTED PUBLICATIONS** Auth, articles on Melville, Thoreau, Poe and Hawthorne. **CONTACT ADDRESS** Eng Dept, Duke Univ, Durham, NC, 27706.

JONES, CHRISTOPHER
DISCIPLINE ENGLISH LITERATURE **EDUCATION** Univ Toronto, PhD, 95. **CAREER** Asst prof. **RESEARCH** Old English literature; Anglo-Saxon England **SELECTED PUBLICATIONS** Auth, Aelfric's Letter to the Monks of Eynsham. **CONTACT ADDRESS** Dept of English and Philosophy, Idaho State Univ, Pocatello, ID, 83209. **EMAIL** jonechri@cwis.isu.edu

JONES, DAN CURTIS
PERSONAL Born 12/18/1942, Chattanooga, TN, m, 1964, 1 child **DISCIPLINE** ENGLISH **EDUCATION** Carson-Newman Col, BA, 64; Vanderbilt Univ, MA, 67; Ind Univ Pa, PhD, 79. **CAREER** Instr, Univ Tenn, Nashville, 66-69; instr, Univ Tenn, Chattanooga, 69-72; Eng fac, 75-89, div chmn, 89-, Wytheville Community Col. **HONORS AND AWARDS** Woodrow Wilson Fel, 65 **MEMBERSHIPS** NCTE; Conf Col Com-

pos & Commun; Two yr co-chmn Eng Assoc Southwest. **RESEARCH** Literary reading process of inexperienced readers; comm col leadership. **SELECTED PUBLICATIONS** Auth, Preparing Students To Write About Poems, Col Compos & Commun, 5/79; art, Affective Response: A Plea For A Balanced View, Winter 80; art, Helping Students Enter The World Of The Poem, Fall 81. **CONTACT ADDRESS** Wytheville Comm Col, 1000 E Main St, Box 1-A, Wytheville, VA, 24382-3308. **EMAIL** wcjoned@wc.cc.va.us

JONES, DARYL
PERSONAL Born 07/26/1946, Washington, DC, m, 1979, 2 children **DISCIPLINE** ENGLISH **EDUCATION** Mich State Univ, BA, 68, MA, 70, PhD, 74. **CAREER** Grad Tchng Asst, Asst to the Dean, Mich State Univ, 68-73, 70-73; Asst to Assoc to Prof & Ch, Tex Tech Univ, 73-79, 79-82, 82-83, 83-86; Prof & Dean, Col of Arts & Sci, Boise State Univ, 86-91; Prof & Provost & VP for Acad Affairs, Boise State Univ, 91-. **HONORS AND AWARDS** Phi Beta Kappa; Phi Kappa Phi; Creative Writing Fellow Grant, NEA, 85; Pres Acad Ach Award, Tex Tech Univ, 86; Natalie Ornish Poetry Award, 90; Writer in Residence, State of Idaho, 92, 93; Lifetime Hon Member, Golden Key Honorary, 97-, Elected member, Tex Inst of Letters. **MEMBERSHIPS** WICHE NW Acad Forum; Tex Inst of Letters; Pres, Tex Asn of Creative Writing Tchrs, 84-86; Ch, S-Cent Asn of Dept of Eng, 83-84; Pres, S Plains Area Counc, 83-84. **RESEARCH** American literature; creative writing; the popular western novel. **SELECTED PUBLICATIONS** Clenched Teeth and Curses: Revenge of the Dime Novel Outlaw Hero, J of Popular Culture, 652-65, 7, 73; auth, The Dime Novel Western, Bowling Green Univ Pop Press, 78; Two Years Behind the Lectern: On the Road as Idaho's Writer-in-Residence, Writer's NW Handbook, 6th ed, Media Weavers LLC, 75-77, 95. **CONTACT ADDRESS** Office of the Provost, Boise State Univ, 1910 Univ Dr, Boise, ID, 83725. **EMAIL** aprjones@bsu.idbsu.edu

JONES, DOUGLAS GORDON
PERSONAL Born 01/01/1929, Bancroft, ON, Canada, 4 children **DISCIPLINE** CANADIAN & MODERN LITERATURE **EDUCATION** McGill Univ, BA, 52; Queen's Univ, Ont, MA, 54. **CAREER** Lectr English, Royal Mil Col, 54-55; asst prof, Ont Agr Col, 55-61; lectr, Bishop's Univ, Que, 61-63; assoc prof, 63-73, PROF ENGL, UNIV SHERBROOKE, 73-. **HONORS AND AWARDS** Gov Gen Award Poetry, 77., PhD, Univ Guelph. **MEMBERSHIPS** Asn Can Univ Teachers English; League Can Poets; Asn Can & Que Literatures; fel Royal Soc Can. **RESEARCH** Canadian poetry in French and English. **SELECTED PUBLICATIONS** Auth, The sun is axeman (poetry), Univ Toronto, 61; Phrases from Orpheus (poetry), Oxford Univ, 67; Butterfly on Rock: A Study of Themes and Images in Canadian Literature, Univ Toronto, 70; in Search of America, Boundary, 74; transl, the Terror of the Snows (poetry), Univ Pittsburgh, 76; auth, Under the Thunder the Flowers Light up the Earth (poetry), Coach House, 77. **CONTACT ADDRESS** Dept of English Fac of Arts, Univ of Sherbrooke, Sherbrooke, PQ, J1K 2R1.

JONES, EDWARD T.
DISCIPLINE LITERATURE **EDUCATION** Juniata Col, BA; Univ Md, PhD. **SELECTED PUBLICATIONS** Areas: literature/film. **CONTACT ADDRESS** York Col, Pennsylvania, 441 Country Club Road, York, PA, 17403.

JONES, ELLEN
DISCIPLINE TWENTIETH-CENTURY BRITISH AND IRISH LITERATURE **EDUCATION** Cornell Univ, PhD. **CAREER** Eng Dept, St. Edward's Univ **HONORS AND AWARDS** Ed, Feminism & Mod Fiction; Feminist Readings Joyce, Virginia Woolf, Politics Modernism. **SELECTED PUBLICATIONS** Auth, Feminist Readings of Joyce: Preface, Mod Fiction Studies, 89; The Letter Selfpenned to One's Other: Joyce's Writing, Deconstruction, Feminism, Ohio State Univ Press, 89; Figuring Woolf, Mod Fiction Studies, 92; Writing the Modern: The Politics of Modernism, Mod Fiction Studies, 92; Textual Mater: Writing the Mother in Joyce, Cornell Univ Press, 93; Commodious Recirculation: Commodity and Dream in Joyce's Ulysses, James Joyce Quart, 93; The Flight of a Word: Narcissism and the Masquerade of Writing in Virginia Woolf's Orlando, Women's Studies: Interdisciplinary Jour, 94. **CONTACT ADDRESS** St Edward's Univ, 3001 S Congress Ave, Austin, TX, 78704-6489.

JONES, GRANVILLE HICKS
PERSONAL Born 04/08/1932, Jefferson, TX **DISCIPLINE** ENGLISH & AMERICAN LITERATURE **EDUCATION** Baylor Univ, BA, 54; Columbia Univ, MA, 61; Univ Pittsburgh, PhD(English), 69. **CAREER** Instr, 60-64, lectr, 66-68, asst prof, 68-72, ASSOC PROF ENGLISH, CARNEGIE-MELLON UNIV, 72-. **HONORS AND AWARDS** Teaching Award, MLA, 70; Ryan Teaching Award, Carnegie-Mellon Univ, 81. **MEMBERSHIPS** NCTE; Col Commun & Compos. **RESEARCH** Nineteenth and 20th century American literature; business and professional communication. **SELECTED PUBLICATIONS** Auth, Jack Kerouac and the American conscience, Carnegie Series in English, 63; Post mortem: Student-directed courses I and II, Col English, 71; Henry James's Georgina's reasons: the underside of Washington Square, Studies Short Fiction, 74; Henry James' Psychology of Experience, Mouton, 74. **CONTACT ADDRESS** Dept of English, Carnegie Mellon Univ, Pittsburgh, PA, 15213.

JONES, JAMES H.
PERSONAL Born 07/31/1929, Wheeling, WV, m, 1959, 5 children **DISCIPLINE** ENGLISH **EDUCATION** Kenyon Col, AB, 51; Univ Buffalo, MA, 57; Ind Univ, PhD(English), 65. **CAREER** From asst prof to assoc prof, 62-70, PROF ENGLISH, NORTHERN MICH UNIV, 70-, Nat Endowment for Humanities fel, 67-68. **MEMBERSHIPS** Shakespeare Asn Am; MLA. **RESEARCH** Shakespeare; ballads; Renaisssance Soc Am; Conf Christianity & Lit. **SELECTED PUBLICATIONS** Auth, Commonplace and memorization in the oral tradition of the English and Scottish popular ballad, J Am Folklore, 61; Lear and Leir: Matthew V: 30-37, the turning point and the rescue theme, Comp Drama, 70. **CONTACT ADDRESS** Dept of English, No Michigan Univ, 1401 Presque Isle Ave, Marquette, MI, 49855.

JONES, JOHN F.
PERSONAL Born 03/29/1929, Dublin, Ireland, m, 1974, 2 children **DISCIPLINE** HUMANITIES **EDUCATION** National Univ of Ireland, BA 53; Univ Michigan, MSW 66; Univ Minnesota, MAPA, PhD, 68. **CAREER** Univ of Minnesota-Duluth, dean/prof, 71-76; Chinese Univ of Hong Kong, dir/ch, 76-87; Univ of Denver, dean/prof, 87-96, prof, 96-. **HONORS AND AWARDS** Inter Univ Consortium for Intl Development Founders Award. **MEMBERSHIPS** IUCISD; CSWE **RESEARCH** Intl soc development; community development; training. **SELECTED PUBLICATIONS** Auth, New Training Design for Local Social Development, with T. Yogo, Nagoya, United Nat Cen for Reg Dev, 95; Call To Competence: Child Protective Services Training and Evaluation, et al, Englewood, CO, Amer Hum Assoc, 95; Glossary of Social Work Terms in Chinese and English, with Wang Shek, Hong Kong, Chinese Univ Press, 90. **CONTACT ADDRESS** Graduate Sch of Social Work, Univ of Denver, 2148 South High St, Denver, CO, 80208. **EMAIL** jojones@du.edu

JONES, LEANDER CORBIN
PERSONAL Born 07/16/1934, Vincent, Arkansas, m **DISCIPLINE** ENGLISH **EDUCATION** Univ of AR at Pine Bluff, AB 1956; Univ of IL, MS 1968; Union Graduate Institute, PhD 1973. **CAREER** Chicago Public Schools, English teacher 1956-68; Peace Corps Volunteer, English teacher 1964-66; City Colls of Chicago, TV producer 1968-73; Meharry Medical Coll, media specialist 1973-75; Western Michigan Univ, assoc prof Black Amer studies, 1975-89, prof 1989-. **HONORS AND AWARDS** "Roof Over My Head" TV Series WDCN Nashville 1975; acted in and directed several plays Kalamazoo 1979-86; exec producer & host for TV series "Fade to Black" 1986. **MEMBERSHIPS** Mem Kappa Alpha Psi 1953-; mem exec comm DuSable Mus African Amer History 1970-; designer of programs in theatre andTV for hard-to-educate; pres TABS Ctr 1972-; mem AAUP 1973-; mem Natl Council of Black Studies 1977-, MI Council of Black Studies 1977-, Popular Culture Assoc 1978-; chmn Comm Against Apartheid 1977-; mem South African Solidarity Org 1978-; mem MI Org African Studies 1980-; commander Vets for Peace Kalamazoo 1980-; pres Black Theatre Group of the Kalamazoo Civic Players 1980-83; bd of dirs Kalamazoo Civic Players 1981-83, MI Commn on Crime and Delinquency 1981-83; pres Corbin 22 Ltd 1986; Lester Lake Corp, secretary of the bd, 1992. **SELECTED PUBLICATIONS** Author "Africa Is for Reel," Kalamazoo 1983. **CONTACT ADDRESS** Prof, Black Amer Studies, Western Michigan Univ, Kalamazoo, MI, 49008.

JONES, LOUIS CLARK
PERSONAL Born 06/28/1908, Albany, NY, m, 1932, 3 children **DISCIPLINE** HISTORY, LITERATURE **EDUCATION** Hamilton Col, BA, 30; Columbia Univ, MA, 31, PhD(Eng lit), 42. **CAREER** From instr to assoc prof English & Am lit, NY State Col Teachers, Albany, 34-46; dir, 46-72, EMER DIR, NY STATE HIST ASN & FARMERS MUS, 72-; PROF AM FOLK ART, COOPERSTOWN GRAD PROG, STATE UNIV NY COL ONEONTA, 73-, Guggenheim fel, 46; mem, NY Coun on Hist Sites, 54-58, NY Coun on Arts, 60-72 & NY State Hist Trust, 66-72; dir, Coopertown Grad Prog, State Univ NY col Oneonta, 64-72; Nat Endowment for Humanities res grant, 72-73. **HONORS AND AWARDS** Award of Distinction, Am Asn State & Local Hist, 70; Katherine Coffee Prize, 81., LHD, Hamilton Col, 62. **MEMBERSHIPS** Am Asn Mus (vpres, 52-68); Am Asn State & Loal Hist (vpres, 50-57); fel Am Folklore Soc. **RESEARCH** Eighteenth century social history; New York state folklore; folklore of the supernatural; American folk art. **SELECTED PUBLICATIONS** Auth, Clubs of the Georgian Rakes, Columbia Univ, 42; Spooks of the Valley, Houghton, 48; Things that Bump in the Night, Hill & Wang, 59; ed, Growing up in the Cooper Country, Syracuse Univ, 65; Murder at Cl-earry Hill, 82; Three Eyes on the Past, Syracuse Univ Press, 82. **CONTACT ADDRESS** 11 Main St, Box 351, Cooperstown, NY, 13326.

JONES, MARK
DISCIPLINE ENGLISH LITERATURE **EDUCATION** Columbia Univ, PhD. **CAREER** Dept Eng, Queen's Univ **RESEARCH** Romantic poetry; literature and economics; pastoral; elegy; parody; history of literary criticism and theory. **SELECTED PUBLICATIONS** Auth, Lucy Poems, Univ Toronto, 95; Parody and its Containments, Representations, 96; Double Economics: Ambivalence in Wordsworth's Pastoral, PMLA, 93; Spiritual Capitalism: Wordsworth and Usury, JEGP, 93; Interpretation in Wordsworth, 91; co-auth, Wordsworth Scholarship: An Annotated Bibliography, Garland, 85. **CONTACT ADDRESS** English Dept, Queen's Univ, Kingston, ON, K7L 3N6. **EMAIL** jonesmc@qsilver.queensu.ca

JONES, MARY E.
DISCIPLINE BRITISH ROMANTIC AND VICTORIAN LITERATURE AND THE NOVEL **EDUCATION** Duke Univ, AB, MA; Union Grad Sch, PhD. **CAREER** Asso prof; dir, Am Stud prog. **HONORS AND AWARDS** Navy Commendation for work as liason, Sixth Fleet and people of Corfu, Fulbright scholar, Greece. **SELECTED PUBLICATIONS** Auth, Christopher Columbus and His Legacy, 92; Seeds of Change: Readings on Cultural Exchange after 1492, 93; The American Frontier, 94; John Jakes: A Critical Companion, 96; Daily Life on the Nineteenth Century American Frontier, 98. **CONTACT ADDRESS** Wittenberg Univ, Springfield, OH, 45501-0720.

JONES, NICHOLAS
DISCIPLINE ENGLISH LITERATURE **EDUCATION** Harvard Col, BA, 67; MA, 69; PhD, 73. **CAREER** Asso prof, Oberlin Coll, 76. **MEMBERSHIPS** Trustee, Northern Ohio Youth Orchestras. **RESEARCH** British Romantic period, Shakespeare and Renaissance drama, romantic women poets. **SELECTED PUBLICATIONS** Publ, anthology of 17th century New England sermons; articles on Milton and Herbert; biog essays on Felicia Hemans, Mary Russell Mitford, Mary Howitt, Hannah More in Dictionary of Lit Biog. **CONTACT ADDRESS** Dept of Eng, Oberlin Col, Oberlin, OH, 44074. **EMAIL** Nicholas_Jones@qmgate.cc.oberlin.edu

JONES, ROBIN A.
PERSONAL Born 08/16/1958, Anadarko, OK, m, 3 children **DISCIPLINE** COMMUNICATION; GENDER **EDUCATION** Okla State Univ, BS, 80; SW Baptist Theol Seminary, MA, 84; Okla Univ, PhD, 97. **CAREER** Adjunct Prof, Okla City Community Col, 97; Asst Prof, SWestern Okla State Univ, 97-. **HONORS AND AWARDS** Top Student Paper, Instructional Div, NCA, 96, CSCA, 96. **MEMBERSHIPS** Nat Commun Asn; AAUW; Central States Commun Asn; Delta Kappa Gamma. **RESEARCH** Gender issues; communication. **CONTACT ADDRESS** SWestern Okla State Univ, 100 Campus Dr., Weatherford, OK, 73096-3098. **EMAIL** jonesra@swosu.edu

JONES, SIDNEY C.
PERSONAL Born 09/03/1934, Atlantic, IA, 2 children **DISCIPLINE** ENGLISH LITERATURE **EDUCATION** State Univ, Iowa, BA, 56; Univ Wis, MS, 59. **CAREER** Asst, dept polit sci, State Univ, Iowa, 55-56; asst, dept integrated lib studies, Univ Wis, 57-61; from asst prof to assoc prof, 61-67, prof English, Carroll Col, Wis, 67-, retired, 98-. **MEMBERSHIPS** NCTE; MLA; AAUP; English Inst; Midwest Mod Lang Asn. **RESEARCH** Contemporary European literature; Renaissance literature; philosophy and literature. **CONTACT ADDRESS** 100 N East Ave, Waukesha, WI, 53186-5593. **EMAIL** sjones@cc1.edu

JONES, STANLEY E.
DISCIPLINE COMMUNCATION STUDIES **EDUCATION** State Univ Iowa, BA, 57, MA, 62; Northwestern Univ, PhD, 64. **CAREER** Prof. **RESEARCH** Nonverbal communication; applied communication; relationship of verbal and nonverbal codes. **SELECTED PUBLICATIONS** Auth, The Right Touch: Understanding and Using the Language of Physical Contact, Hampton, 94; Problems of validity in questionnaire studies of nonverbal behavior: Jourard's tactile body-accessibility scale, Southern Commun Jour, 92; co-auth, Touch attitudes and behaviors, recollections of early childhood touch, and social self confidence, Jour Nonverbal Behavior, 86. **CONTACT ADDRESS** Dept of Communication, Univ Colo Boulder, Boulder, CO, 80309. **EMAIL** Stanley.Jones@Colorado.edu

JONES, STEVEN
DISCIPLINE ENGLISH **EDUCATION** Univ Okla, BA, 80; Columbia Univ, PhD, 88. **CAREER** Assoc prof; ed, Keats-Shelley J; co-ed, Romantic Circles. **RESEARCH** Romantic-period literature and culture; textual criticism; editing; hypertext theory. **SELECTED PUBLICATIONS** Auth, Shelley's Satire: Violence, Exhortation, and Authority, Northern Ill UP, 94; The Black Dwarf as Satiric Performance, in Romanticism, Radicalism, and the Press, Wayne State UP, 97; The Book of Myst in the Late Age of Print, Postmodern Culture, 97; Satire and Countersatire in Crabbe and Wordsworth, The Wordsworth Circle, 98. **CONTACT ADDRESS** Dept of English, Loyola Univ, Chicago, 6525 N Sheridan Rd, Chicago, IL, 60626. **EMAIL** sjones1@orion.it.luc.edu

JONES, SUZANNE W.
PERSONAL Born 05/26/1950, Richmond, VA, m, 1986, 2 children **DISCIPLINE** ENGLISH **EDUCATION** Col of William and Mary, BA 72, MA 75; Univ Virginia, PhD 84. **CAREER** Univ Richmond, co-or women's stud 85-94, asst prof, assoc prof, 84 to 92-. **HONORS AND AWARDS** Phi Beta Kappa; Dist EDU Awd; Outstanding Fac Awd; Tchg Awd. **MEMBERSHIPS** MLA; SSSL **RESEARCH** Lit of the Amer South; Twentieth Cent Women Writers and Literature. **SELECTED PUBLICATIONS** Auth, Growing Up in the South: An Anthology of Modern Southern Literature, NY, Mentor/ Penguin USA, 91; Reading the Endings in Katherine Anne Porter's Old Mortality, Famous Last Words: Changes in Gender and Narrative Closure, ed Allison Booth, Charlottesville, VA UPV, 93, reprinted, in Critical Essays on American literature: Katherine Anne Porter, ed, Darlene Unrue, NY, G. K. Hall, 97; Edith Wharton's Secret Sensitiveness, The Decoration of Houses and Her Fiction, Jour of Modern Lit, 97; Reconstructing Manhood: Race, Masculinity, and Narrative Closure, in: Ernest Gaine's A Gathering of Old Men and A Lesson Before Dying, Masculinity's, 95. **CONTACT ADDRESS** Dept of English, Richmond Univ, Richmond, VA, 23173. **EMAIL** sjones@richmond.edu

JOOS, ERNEST
PERSONAL Born 01/06/1923, Uraiujfalu, Hungary, m, 1949, 6 children **DISCIPLINE** PHILOSOPHY, LITERATURE **EDUCATION** McGill Univ, MA, 59; Inst d'Etudes Medievales, Montreal, Lic en Phil, 66; Univ Montreal, PhD(medieval philos), 70. **CAREER** Asst prof philos, Loyola Col, Montreal, 67-75; PROF PHILOS, CONCORDIA UNIV, 75-, Vis prof philos, Univ Laval, Quebec, 77-78 & Univ de Montreal, 79-81. **MEMBERSHIPS** Can Philos Asn; Am Cath Philos Asn. **RESEARCH** Intentionality; metaphysics-ontology. **SELECTED PUBLICATIONS** Auth, The Words for Preaching--Homiletics Lectures Given in Findenwalde, Laval Theologique Et Philosophique, Vol 0049, 93; Might the End of History Be the Beginning of Wisdom--The Alienation of the Mind in Hegel 'Phenomenology of the Spirit', Laval Theologique Et Philosophique, Vol 0051, 95; Notes on Nietzsche, Laval Theologique et Philosophique, Vol 0051, 95. **CONTACT ADDRESS** Concordia Univ, Montreal, 130 Kenaston Ave, Montreal, PQ, H3R 1M2.

JORDAN, ROSAN
DISCIPLINE FOLKLORE, WOMEN'S AND GENDER STUDIES **EDUCATION** Ind Univ, PhD, 75. **CAREER** Assoc prof, La State Univ; bk rev ed, Southern Folklore, 86-92; ed bd, Revista de Investigaciones Folkloricas, 87-. **HONORS AND AWARDS** Centennial Award, Am Folklore Soc, 89; Lynwood Montell Prize, Southern Folklore, 92. **MEMBERSHIPS** Exec bd, La Folklore Soc, 81-; nominating comt, Am Folklore Soc, 93-96. **RESEARCH** Folklore; women's and gender studies. **SELECTED PUBLICATIONS** Auth, Folklore and Ethnicity: Some Theoretical Considerations, in, Louisiana Folklife: A Guide to the State, 85; Louisiana Folk Crafts: An Overview; Louisiana Folklife: A Guide to the State, 85; The Vaginal Serpent and Other Themes from Mexican-American Women's Lore, in Women's Folklore, Women's Culture, 85; Not into Cold Space: Zora Neale Hurston and J. Frank Dobie as Holistic Folklorists, Southern Folklore, 92; 'In This Folk-Lore Land': Race, Class, Identity, and Folklore Studies in Louisiana, J of Am Fo lklore, 96; coauth, Louisiana Traditional Crafts, 80; Comentarios Acerca del Folklore de una Elite Colonial, Cuadernos Inst Nac de Antropologia, 91; coed, Women's Folklore, Women's Culture, 85. **CONTACT ADDRESS** Dept of Eng, Louisiana State Univ, 237E Allen Hall, Baton Rouge, LA, 70803. **EMAIL** enrosan@unix1.sncc.lsu.edu

JORGENS, JACK J.
PERSONAL Born 01/04/1943, Minneapolis, MN, m, 1965, 2 children **DISCIPLINE** ENGLISH, FILM STUDIES **EDUCATION** Carleton Col, BA, 65; City Col NY, MA, 67; NY Univ, PhD, 70. **CAREER** Asst prof Eng, Univ CT, 70-71 & Univ MA, Amherst, 71-75; Assoc prof eng. AM Univ, 75-, Prof, Shakespeare Inst, Univ Bridgeport, 76-77. **HONORS AND AWARDS** Outstanding Prog Develop Cinema Studies, Am Univ, 76. **MEMBERSHIPS** Am Film Inst; MLA; Soc Cinema Studies; Shakespeare Asn Am. **RESEARCH** Shakespeare in performance; film and theatre; video production. **SELECTED PUBLICATIONS** Auth, Alice Our Contemporary, Great Excluded: Critical Essays Children's Lit, 72; Champlain Shakespeare Festival, autumn 73, New York Shakespeare Festival, autumn 73, New York Shakespeare Festival, autumn 74, Champlain Shakespeare Festival, winter 76 & Champlain Shakespeare Festival, spring 77, Shakespeare Quart; Shakespeare on Film, Ind Univ, 77. **CONTACT ADDRESS** Dept of Lit, American Univ, 4400 Massachusetts Ave NW, Washington, DC, 20016-8200. **EMAIL** accent2@accentmediainc.com

JOSLIN, KATHERINE
DISCIPLINE AMERICAN LITERATURE **EDUCATION** Northwestern Univ, PhD. **CAREER** Prof **HONORS AND AWARDS** Dir, Grad Studies; Grad Adv. **RESEARCH** Elizabeth Wharton, literary criticism. **SELECTED PUBLICATIONS** Auth, Wretched Exotic: Essays on Edith Wharton in Europe, Peter Lang, 93; Edith Wharton; Women Writers Series, Macmillan Publs Limited; St. Martin's Press, 91.. **CONTACT ADDRESS** Kalamazoo, MI, 49008. **EMAIL** joslin@wmich.edu

JOY, DONALD MARVIN
PERSONAL Born 08/20/1928, Gray County, KS, m, 1948, 2 children **DISCIPLINE** CIRRICULUM DEVELOPMENT; EDUCATIONAL PSYCHOLOGY; ENGLISH **EDUCATION** Cent Col, AA, 47; Greenville (IL) Col, BA, 49; Asbury Sem, BD, 54; Ind Univ, PhD, 69. **CAREER** Pastoral Min, 49-51 & 54-58; public school music, 49-51; Exec ed Free Methodist Church NA, 58-71; prof Human Develop Fam Studies, Asbury Sem, 71-98; DIR CTR FOR THE STUDY OF THE FAMILY, 98-; Phi Beta Kappa. **MEMBERSHIPS** Assoc Prof & Res in Relig Educ; Nat Assoc Prof Christians Educ. **RESEARCH** Moral development; consicience formation; spiritual direction. **SELECTED PUBLICATIONS** Becoming A Man!, Ventura: Regal, 90; Men Under Construction, Victor Chariot, 93; Women at Risk, with Dr. David Hager, Bristol House Ltd, 93; Celebrating the New Woman in the Family, Bristol House Ltd, 94; Rsik-Proffing Your Family, US Ctr for World Mission, 95; Re-Bonding: Preventing and Restoring Broken Relationships, Evangel Publ House, 96; Bonding: Relationships in the Image of God, Evangel Publ House, 96; Beyond Adolescence! Hope for Teens and Families, Asbury Theol Sem, 96; How to Use Camping Experiences in Religious Education: Transformation Through Christian Camping, Relig Educ Press, 98. **CONTACT ADDRESS** Ctr fo the Study of the Family, Donald Marvin Joy, 600 N Lexington Ave, Wilmore, KY, 40390. **EMAIL** rodojoy@juno.com

JOYCE, DONALD FRANKLIN
PERSONAL Born 11/04/1938, Chicago, IL, s **DISCIPLINE** LIBRARY SCIENCES **EDUCATION** Fisk Univ, BA 57; Univ Illinois, MS 60; Univ Chicago, PhD 78. **CAREER** Chicago Pub Lib, curator 60-81; Tenn State Univ Dwtnbr, coord 81-87; Austin Peay State Univ, dean lib and media 87-. **HONORS AND AWARDS** Distg Ser Awd; Black Caucus; Am Lib Asn. **MEMBERSHIPS** Am Lib Asn; Tenn Lib Asn. **RESEARCH** African Am Hist. **SELECTED PUBLICATIONS** Black Book Publishers in the United States: A Historical Dictionary of the Presses, 1817-1990, Westport Ct, Greenwood Press, 91; Gatekeepers of Black Culture: Black Owned Book Publishing in the United States, 1817-1981, Westport Ct, Greenwood Press, 83. **CONTACT ADDRESS** Felix G Woodward Library, Austin Peay State Univ, Sixth and College Sts, Clarksville, TN, 37044. **EMAIL** joyceD@apsu.edu

JUHL, M.E.
PERSONAL Born 03/18/1957, El Dorado, AR, m, 1989 **DISCIPLINE** LIBRARIANSHIP **EDUCATION** Univ Texas, BA, 79; Columbia Univ, MLS, 86. **CAREER** Ref librn, N Y Pub Libr, 86-87; ref librn, Columbia Univ, 87-93; ref dir, Univ Arkansas Libr, 93- . **HONORS AND AWARDS** Magna cum Laude, 79. **MEMBERSHIPS** Am Philol Asn; ALA. **RESEARCH** Classics and computing; humanities computing. **SELECTED PUBLICATIONS** "Ex Machina: Electronic Resources for the Classics," Choice, 95; "Red, White, and Boolean," Choice, 98. **CONTACT ADDRESS** Library, Univ of Arkansas, Fayetteville, AR, 72701. **EMAIL** bjuhle@comp.uark.edu

JUHNKE, JANET ANN
PERSONAL Born 11/26/1942, Halstead, KS, m, 1975, 2 children **DISCIPLINE** ENGLISH **EDUCATION** Bethel Col, BA, 64; Northwestern Univ, MAT, 65; Univ Kans, PhD(English), 74. **CAREER** Instr English, Bethel Col, 65-67; from Asst Prof to Assoc Prof, 73-87, Prof English, 87-95, Asst Dean Fac, 80-82, VPres, Dean of Fac, Kans Wesleyan, 95-, Chmn Humanities Div, 75-79, 83-86, 89-92. **HONORS AND AWARDS** The Sears-Roebuck Found Teaching Excellence and Campus Leadership Award, 91. **MEMBERSHIPS** AAHE; CIC; Children's Lit Asn. **RESEARCH** Satire; eighteenth century British literature; women's studies. **SELECTED PUBLICATIONS** Contribr, The Classic American Novel and the Movies, Ungar, 77; Inge's Women, Kans Quart, 86; contribr, Notable Women in the American Theater, Greenwood, 89. **CONTACT ADDRESS** Office of the Vice-President/Dean of Faculty, Kansas Wesleyan Univ, 100 E Claflin, Salina, KS, 67401-6196. **EMAIL** juhnke@diamond.kwu.edu

JUNG, DONALD J.
DISCIPLINE COMMUNICATION STUDIES **EDUCATION** Univ Mo St Louis, BA; Univ Portland, MA; Purdue Univ, PhD. **CAREER** Asst prof **SELECTED PUBLICATIONS** Auth, The Federal Communications Commission, the Broadcast Industry, and the Fairness Doctrine: 1981-1987, Univ Am; Centering the mass as a social condition: Technologies mediate humans communicate, 95; Is interactivity a function of human communication or computer mediation?, 95. **CONTACT ADDRESS** Communication Dept, Univ of Missouri, St. Louis, 590 Lucas Hall, St. Louis, MO, 63121. **EMAIL** sdjjung@umslvma.umsl.edu

JUNKER, KIRK W.
PERSONAL Born 05/02/1959, Pittsburgh, PA, s **DISCIPLINE** LAW; RHETORIC **EDUCATION** Penn State Univ, BA, 81; Duquesne Univ, JD, 84; Univ of Pittsburg, PhD, 96. **CAREER** Asst counsel, Pennsylvania Dept of Environmental Protection, 88-96; Adjunct Prof, Duquesne Univ, 95-present; lectr, The Open Univ, London, 96-98; lectr, Dublin City Univ, 98-present. **MEMBERSHIPS** British Assoc for the Advancement of Sci; Amer Assoc for the Advancement of Sci; Natl Communication Assoc; Internatl Soc for the Hist of Rhetoric; Society for the Social Study of Science; German-American Lawyers Assoc. **RESEARCH** Rhetoric; rhetoric and communication of sci; law; environmental policy. **SELECTED PUBLICATIONS** auth, Future Works '95: Fakten, Wege, Visionen, Citizen Participation in Environmental Protection, Amerika Haus, Munich, 96; auth, Juris, Environmental Regulation and Risk Mgt for Expansion and Direct Investment in Business in the U.S., 96; coauth, Science and the Public, More than Just Doing What's Right: Ethics in Science, The Science Wars, auth, Science, Regulation, and Standards, Informing Publics about Ozone Pollution, Open University Press, 98; Ed, Law and Science Special Issue of Social Epistemology, 99; auth, Science Communication, Scientists Communicating With Other Professionals, Open Univ Press, 99; auth, Rescuing All Our Futures: The Future of Future Studies, Cloning the Future, Adamantine Press, London, 98; coed, Science Communication: Professional Contexts, Routledge, London, 98. **CONTACT ADDRESS** 39 Palewell Pk, London, ., SW14 8JQ. **EMAIL** k.w.junker@open.ac.uk

JUNKINS, DONALD A.
PERSONAL Born 12/19/1931, Saugus, MA, m, 1958, 3 children **DISCIPLINE** AMERICAN LITERATURE, CREATIVE WRITING **EDUCATION** Univ Mass, BA, 53; Boston Univ, STB, 56, STM, 57, AM, 59, PhD(Am lit), 63. **CAREER** From instr to asst prof English, Emerson Col, 61-63; asst prof, Chico State Col, 63-66; from asst prof to assoc prof English, 66-74, dir MFA Grad Prog, 70-78, PROF ENGLISH, UNIV MASS, AMHERST, 74-, Assoc poetry ed, Mass Rev, 68-70; NEA creative writing fel grant, 74, 79; poetry ed, New Am Rev, 81- **HONORS AND AWARDS** Jennie Tane Award for poetry, 67; Nat Endowment for Arts award, 68; John Masefield Mem Award, Poetry Soc Am, 72. **MEMBERSHIPS** Poetry Soc Am; Hemingway Soc. **RESEARCH** Colonial and 19th century American literature; creative writing, poetry; contemporary world poetry. **SELECTED PUBLICATIONS** Auth, Hawthorne's House of Seven Gables: A prototype of the Human mind, Lit & Psychol, 67; Should stars woo and lobster claws?: Edward Taylor's poetic theory, Early Am Lit, 11/68; The Graves of Scotland Parish (poetry), Heron, 69; Walden, 100 Years After Thoreau (poetry), Yorick, 69; And Sandpipers She Said (poetry), Univ Mass, 70; ed, The Contemporary World Poets, Harcourt, 76; auth, The Uncle Harry Poems and Other Maine Reminiscences, Outland Press, 77; Crossing by Ferry, Poems New and Selected Univ Mass, 78; auth, Playing for Keeps, Lynx House Press, 91; auth, Journey to the Corrida, Lynx House Press, 98; trans, Euripides Andromache (Euripides I), Pa Univ Press, 98. **CONTACT ADDRESS** 63 Hawks Rd., Deerfield, MA, 01342.

JUSTUS, JAMES HUFF
PERSONAL Born 04/22/1929, Newport, TN **DISCIPLINE** ENGLISH **EDUCATION** Univ Tenn, AB, 50, AM, 52; Univ Wash, PhD, 61. **CAREER** From instr to assoc prof, 61-69, PROF ENGLISH, IND UNIV, BLOOMINGTON, 70-, Contribr, American literary scholarship, an annual 1968-, Duke Univ, 70-. **MEMBERSHIPS** MLA; Soc Study Southern Lit; AAUP; SAtlantic Mod Lang Asn. **RESEARCH** Twentieth century American novel; American literature, 1800-1900. **SELECTED PUBLICATIONS** Auth, The American Vision of Warren, Robert, Penn, Miss Quart, Vol 0046, 93; Percy, Walker--Books of Revelations, Amer Lit, Vol 0065, 93; Warren, Robert, Penn, A Study of the Short-Fiction, Modern Fiction Stud, Vol 0039, 93; The Way We Read Now--The American Legacy of the 1980s, Sewanee Rev, Vol 0102, 94; Southern Modernism and the Battle of Literary Succession, Southern Lit J, Vol 0027, 94; Warren 'Terra', Miss Quart, Vol 0048, 95. **CONTACT ADDRESS** Dept of English, Indiana Univ, Bloomington, Bloomington, IN, 47401.

K

KADLEC, DAVID
DISCIPLINE ENGLISH LITERATURE **EDUCATION** Univ Ind, BA; Univ Chicago, MA, PhD. **CAREER** Eng Dept, Georgetown Univ **RESEARCH** Modern British and American literature and culture; 20th century American poetry; literature and science; Victorian literature. **SELECTED PUBLICATIONS** Auth, pubs on Ezra Pound, James Joyce, Marianne Moore, Muriel Rukeyser and other 19th and 20th Century writers. **CONTACT ADDRESS** English Dept, Georgetown Univ, 37th and O St, Washington, DC, 20057.

KAGLE, STEVEN EARL
PERSONAL Born 09/15/1941, New York, NY, m, 1965, 2 children **DISCIPLINE** ENGLISH **EDUCATION** Cornell Univ, AB, 63; Univ Mich, MA & PhD(Am cult), 67. **CAREER** Asst prof English, Richmond Col, NY, 67-69; assoc prof, 69-80, PROF ENGLISH, ILL STATE UNIV, 80-, Chmn sem lit exploration, MLA, 72-. **MEMBERSHIPS** MLA; Am Studies Asn; Sci Fiction Res Asn. **RESEARCH** Autobiographical literature; American literary history; creative writing. **SELECTED PUBLICATIONS** Auth, An Examination of 8 Personal Narratives By Women in the Antebellum South, Miss Quart, Vol 0049, 96. **CONTACT ADDRESS** Dept of English, Illinois State Univ, Stevenson Hall, Normal, IL, 61761.

KAHANE, CLAIRE
PERSONAL New York, NY, 1 child **DISCIPLINE** ENGLISH **EDUCATION** City Col NY, BA, 56; Univ Calif, Berkeley, MA, 63, PhD, 75. **CAREER** Assoc prof English, SUNY, 74-. **MEMBERSHIPS** MLA **RESEARCH** Psychoanalytic criticism; feminist criticism; British and American fiction. **SELECTED PUBLICATIONS** Auth, Flannery O'Connor's rage of vision, Am Lit, 3/74; Review: Essays in Creativity, Psychoanal Quart, 75; The artificial niggers, Mass Rev, 4/78; Comic vibrations and self-construction in grotesque literature, XXIX: 114-120 & The nuptials of metaphor and To the Lighthouse, XXX: 72-82, Lit and Psychol; The maternal legacy, the grotesque tradition in Flannery O'Connor's female gothic, Female Gothic, Eden Press Women's Publ, fall 81; coauth (with Janice Doane), Psychoanalysis and American fiction: The subversion of Q E D, Studies Am Fiction, 8/81; ed, Psychoanalyse und das Unheimliche: Essays aus der amerikanischen Literaturkritik, An anthology of Psychoanalytic Criticism, Bouvier Press, WGermany, 81; co-ed In Dora's Case: Freud-Hysteria-Feminism, Columbia UP, 85; The Mother Tongue: Essays in Feminist-Psychoanalytic Interpretation, Cornell UP, 85; Auth, Passions of the Voice: Hysteria, Narrative and the Figure of the Speaking Woman, 1850-1915, Johns Hopkins, 95. **CONTACT ADDRESS** Dept English, SUNY, PO Box 604610, Buffalo, NY, 14260-4610. **EMAIL** ckahane@acsu.buffalo.edu

KAHN, COPPELIA
PERSONAL Born 08/17/1939, Seattle, WA, d, 1 child **DISCIPLINE** ENGLISH **EDUCATION** Barnard Col, BA (with honors), 61; Univ CA, Berkeley, MA, 64, PhD, 70. **CAREER** Teaching asst, acting instr, lect, English dept, Univ CA, Berkeley, 62-71; asst prof, English dept, Univ MA, 71-72; asst prof, assoc prof, prof, English dept, Wesleyan Univ, 73-86; vis assoc prof, Yale Univ, fall 83; vis prof, UCLA, 86-87; prof, English Dept, Brown Univ, 87-; vis prof, Universita' di Torino, April-May 96. **HONORS AND AWARDS** Fel, Oregon Center for the Humanities, 93; Fletcher Jones fel in the Humanities, Huntingdon Library, 88-89. **MEMBERSHIPS** Shakespeare Asn of Am; Renaissance Soc of Am; MLA. **RESEARCH** Gender studies; English Renaissance lit; Shakespeare; cultural studies. **SELECTED PUBLICATIONS** Auth, Representing Shakespeare: New Psychoanalytic Essays, co-ed with Murray Schwartz, Johns Hopkins Univ, 80; Man's Estate: Masculine Identity in Shakespeare, Univ CA Press, 81; Shakespeare's 'Rough Magic': Renaissance Essays in Honor of C L Barber, co-ed with Peter Erickson, Univ DE Press, 85; Making a Difference: Feminist Literary Criticism, co-ed with Gayle Greene, Methuen, 85, trans into Jpanese, 91, Chinese trans forthcoming; Changing Subjects: The Making of Feminist Literary Criticism, co-ed with Gayle Greene, Routledge, 93; Magic of Bounty: Timon of Athens, Jacobean Patronage, and Maternal Power, rpt in Shakespearean Tragedy and Gender, ed Madelon Sprengnether and Shirley Nelson Garner, IN Univ Press, 95; The Rape in Shakespeare's Lucrece, rpt in Shakespeare and Gender: A History, ed Ivo Kamps and Deborah Barker, Verso Press, 95; Roman Shakespeare: Warriors, Wounds, and Women, in the series Feminist Readings of Shakespeare, ed Ann Thompson, Routledge, 98; Thomas Middleton and Thomas Dekker, The Roaring Girl, ed with intro, in The Complete Works of Thomas Middleton, ed Gary Taylor, Oxford Univ Press, forthcoming 99; Coming of Age in Verona, in Shakespeare's Early Tragedies: A Collection of Critical Essays, ed Mark Rose, Prentice-Hall, forthcoming. **CONTACT ADDRESS** Dept of English, Brown Univ, Box 1852, Providence, RI, 02912. **EMAIL** coppelia_kahn@brown.edu

KAHN, MADELEINE
DISCIPLINE ENGLISH **EDUCATION** Swarthmore Col, BA, 77; Stanford Univ, PhD, 89. **CAREER** Assoc prof; Mills Col, 89-. **RESEARCH** 18th century English literature; the novel; feminist theory; gender studies; the Gothic and the sublime. **SELECTED PUBLICATIONS** Auth, Narrative Transvestism: Rhetoric and Gender in the Eighteenth-Century English Novel, Cornell UP, 91; A by-stander often sees more of the game than those that play: Ann Yearsley Reads The Castle of Otranto, in Questioning History: Postmodern Perspectives on 18th-Century Lit and Cult, Assoc UPresses, 97; Teaching Charlotte Charke: Pedagogy, Feminism, and the Construction of Self, in Now Introducing Charlotte Charke, Univ Ill Press, 97; The Milkmaid's Voice: Ann Yearsley and the Romantic Notion of the Poet, Approaches to Teaching Women Poets of the British Romantic Period, MLA Press, 97; Hannah More and Ann Yearsley: A Collaboration Across the Class Divide, Stud in 18th-Century Cult 25, 95; The Politics of Pornography, in American Women in the 90s: Today's Critical Issues, Northeastern UP, 93, sec ed, 94. **CONTACT ADDRESS** Dept of English, Mills Col, 5000 MacArthur Blvd, Oakland, CA, 94613-1301. **EMAIL** mkahn@mills.edu

KAHN, SY M.
DISCIPLINE THEATRE ARTS **EDUCATION** Univ PA, BA; Univ CT, MA; Univ WI, PhD. **CAREER** Prof emer, Univ Pacific. **HONORS AND AWARDS** UOP. **SELECTED PUBLICATIONS** Auth, publ(s) in lit jour(s). **CONTACT ADDRESS** Dept of Theatre Arts, Univ Pacific, Pacific Ave, PO Box 3601, Stockton, CA, 95211.

KAILING, JOEL
PERSONAL Atlanta, GA, m, 4 children **DISCIPLINE** SPEECH, INTERCULTURAL COMMUNICATION **EDUCATION** Univ Ky, PhD. **CAREER** Assoc prof, Lee Univ, 94-. **MEMBERSHIPS** Lee Comm Club; Lee Univ Vindagua, Missions Alive. **SELECTED PUBLICATIONS** Inside, Outside, Upside Down, Int Rev Missions, 88; A New Solution to the African Christian Problem; Missiology, 94. **CONTACT ADDRESS** Lee Univ, 1120 N. Ocoee St, Cleveland, TN, 37320-3450. **EMAIL** jkailing@leeuniversity.edu

KAIVOLA, KAREN
DISCIPLINE ENGLISH LITERATURE **EDUCATION** Univ Wash, PhD. **CAREER** Assoc prof, 97-. **RESEARCH** 20th century literature; British Modernism; postcolonial literature; women's writing. **SELECTED PUBLICATIONS** Auth, Virginia Woolf, Vita Sackville-West, and the Question of Sexual Identity, 97; Reconstructing Androgyny's 'Blind Spot': Technology, Gender B(l)ending, and Emerging Liminal Identities, MOSAIC, 97. **CONTACT ADDRESS** English Dept, Stetson Univ, Unit 8378, DeLand, FL, 32720-3771.

KALAIDJIAN, WALTER
DISCIPLINE ENGLISH LANGUAGE AND LITERATURE **EDUCATION** Univ Ill Urbana-Champaign, PhD, 92. **CAREER** Prof **RESEARCH** 20th-century American literature and culture. **SELECTED PUBLICATIONS** Auth, American Culture Between the Wars: Revisionary Modernism and Postmodern Critique; Languages of Liberation: The Social Text in Contemporary American Poetry; Understanding Theodore Roethke. **CONTACT ADDRESS** English Dept, Emory Univ, 1380 Oxford Rd NE, Atlanta, GA, 30322-1950.

KALBFLEISCH, PAMELA J.
PERSONAL Born 10/05/1956, Twin Falls, ID, m, 1987 **DISCIPLINE** COMMUNICATION **EDUCATION** Michigan State Univ, PhD 85; Univ New Mexico, MA 79; Boise State Univ, BA cum laude 78. **CAREER** Univ Wyoming, assoc prof 94-; Univ Kentucky, asst prof 89-94; Cal State Univ, asst prof 87-89; Univ Montana, vis asst prof 86-87. **HONORS AND AWARDS** Phi Kappa Phi; Sec Vice WSCA. **MEMBERSHIPS** WSCA; NCA; ICA. **RESEARCH** Mentoring, social support; deceptive communication, gender. **SELECTED PUBLICATIONS** Auth, Interpersonal Communication, Needham Hts MA, Allyn & Bacon, under contract; Mentoring as a Personal Relationship, NY, Guilford, under contract; Gender Power and Communication in Human Relationships, co-ed, Mahwah NJ, Lawrence Erlbaum Assoc, 95; auth, Perceived Equity Satisfaction and Related Maintenance Strategies in Parent Adolescent Dyads, coauth, Jour of Youth Adolescence, in press; auth, Appeasing the Mentor, Aggressive Behavior, 97; auth, The Language of Detecting Deceit, Jour of Lang and Social Psychol, 94; auth, Communication in Interracial Relationships, Tina M Harris, ed, When I Look at You I Don't See Color, Newbury Park, Sage, forthcoming; Sex Differences in Presenting and Detecting Deceptive Messages, coauth, D Canary, K Dindia, eds, Sex Differences and Similarities, Mahwah NJ, Lawrence Erlbaum Assoc, 98; auth, Mentoring Across Generations: Culture Family and Mentoring Relationships, coauth, in: H Nooral-Deen ed, Cross Cult Comm and Aging in Amer, Mahwah NJ, Lawrence Erlbaum Assoc, 97; auth, Beyond Boundaries: Sex and Gender Diversity in Communication, rev, Women's Stud Comm, 97; auth, Women as Leaders, documentary, with Karen H Bonnell, in preparation. **CONTACT ADDRESS** Dept of Communication, Univ of Wyoming, PO Box 430, Laramie, WY, 82070-0430. **EMAIL** pamelak@uwyo.edu

KALETA, KENNETH C.
PERSONAL Born 04/11/1948, Chicago, IL, w **DISCIPLINE** HUMANITIES **EDUCATION** New York Univ, PhD, 85. **CAREER** ASSOC PROF, ROWAN UNIV, RADIO/FILM/TV, 85-. **MEMBERSHIPS** UFVA; BEA **RESEARCH** Independent filmmaking. **SELECTED PUBLICATIONS** David Lynch, Twayne Publ, 93; Hanif Kureishi: Postcolonial Storyteller, Univ Tx Press, 98. **CONTACT ADDRESS** Rowan Univ, 201 Mullica Hill Rd, Glassboro, NJ, 08021. **EMAIL** kaleta@rowan.edu

KALLENDORF, CRAIG
PERSONAL Born 06/23/1954, Cincinnati, OH, m, 1993, 1 child **DISCIPLINE** ENGLISH **EDUCATION** Valparaiso Univ, BA, 75; Univ NC, Chapel Hill, MA, 77, PhD, 82. **CAREER** From asst prof to assoc prof to prof, 82-, TX A&M Univ. **HONORS AND AWARDS** Fel, Delmas Found, 87; Incentive Award, 89, Classical and Modern Lit; Fel, Nat Endowment Hum, 91, 92; Am Council Learned Soc, 92; **MEMBERSHIPS** Renaissance Soc Am; Am Philol Asn. **RESEARCH** Classical tradition in the Renaissance. **SELECTED PUBLICATIONS** Auth, Latin Influences on English Literature from the Middle Ages to the Eighteenth Century: An Annotated Bibliography of Scholarship, 1945-79, 82; Petrarch: Selected Letters, 86; A Bibliography of Venetian Editions of Virgil, 1470-1599, 91; "A Bibliography of Renaissance Italian Translations of Virgil, 94; Aldine Press Books at the Harry Ransom Humanities Research Center, 98. **CONTACT ADDRESS** Dept of English, Texas A&M Univ, College Station, TX, 77843-4227. **EMAIL** kalendrf@tamu.edu

KAMBOURELI, SMARO
DISCIPLINE 20TH-CENTURY CANADIAN LITERATURE **EDUCATION** Univ Thessaloniki, Greece, BA; Univ Manitoba, MA, PhD. **CAREER** Assoc prof; dir, Eng Grad Stud. **RESEARCH** Literary; feminist, and postcolonial theory; women's writing. **SELECTED PUBLICATIONS** Ed, Making a Difference: Canadian Multicultural Literature, 96; On the Edge of Genre: The Contemporary Canadian Long Poem, 91; co-ed, A Mazing Space: Writing Canadian Women Writing, 87. **CONTACT ADDRESS** Dept of English, Victoria Univ, PO Box 3070, Victoria, BC, V8W 3W1. **EMAIL** kamboure@uvic.ca

KAMENISH, PAULA K.
DISCIPLINE WORLD LITERATURE, EUROPEAN LITERATURE, DRAMA, NOVELLA, AND NOVEL **EDUCATION** Ctr Col Ky, BA; Univ NC, Chapel Hill, MA, PhD. **CAREER** Assoc prof, Univ NC, Wilmington. **RESEARCH** German and French theatre of the 20th century; Dada movement. **SELECTED PUBLICATIONS** Published articles on Shakespeare, French Canadian author Roch Carrier, and various modern dramatists. **CONTACT ADDRESS** Univ N. Carolina, Wilmington, Morton Hall, Wilmington, NC, 28403-3297. **EMAIL** kamenishp@uncwil.edu

KAMINSKI, THOMAS
PERSONAL Born 08/22/1950, Chicago, IL, m, 1980, 1 child **DISCIPLINE** EIGHTEENTH CENTURY ENGLISH LITERATURE **EDUCATION** Univ Ill, Urbana, BA, 72; Harvard Univ, AM, 73, PhD(English), 77. **CAREER** Asst prof English, Loyola Univ, Chicago, 77-86; assoc prof, 86-. **RESEARCH** Samuel Johnson; neo-classicism. **SELECTED PUBLICATIONS** Auth, Striving with Vergil: The Gennesis of Milton's Blind Mouths, Modern Philology 92, 95; Rehabilitating Augustanism: On the Roots of Polite Letters in England, Eighteenth-Century Life 20, 96; Opposition Augustanism and Pope's Epistle to Augustus, Studies in Eighteenth Century Culture, 26, 97. **CONTACT ADDRESS** Dept of English, Loyola Univ, 6525 N Sheridan Rd, Chicago, IL, 60626-5385. **EMAIL** tkamins@luc.edu

KAMINSKY, ALICE R.
PERSONAL New York, NY, m, 1947, 1 child **DISCIPLINE** LITERATURE **EDUCATION** NY Univ, BA, 46, MA, 47, PhD, 52. **CAREER** Instr English, Hunter Col, 52-53, Cornell Univ, 54-57, 59-63; asst prof, 63-64, assoc prof, 64-68, PROF ENGLISH, STATE UNIV NY COL, CORTLAND, 68-, Fac exchange scholar, State Univ NY, New York. **MEMBERSHIPS** MLA; New Chaucer Soc. **RESEARCH** Philosophy of literature; Chaucer; Shakespeare. **SELECTED PUBLICATIONS** Auth, Lewes, G.H.--A Life, 19th-Century Lit, Vol 0047, 92; James, Henry, Stein, Gertrude, and the Biographical Act, English Lit in Transition 1880-1920, Vol 0040, 97. **CONTACT ADDRESS** Dept of English, State Univ NY, Cortland, NY, 13045.

KANE, PETER
PERSONAL Born 02/27/1932, Beverly Hills, CA, m, 1982, 4 children **DISCIPLINE** LIBERAL ARTS; COMMUNICATION **EDUCATION** Univ CA Santa Barbara, BA, 54; Univ CA Los Angeles, MA, 60; Purdue Univ, PhD, 67. **CAREER** Asst prof, speech, 61-65, St Joseph's College (Indiana); asst prof, rhetoric, 65-68, SUNY Binghamton; prof, assoc prof, prof, SUNY Brockport, 68-96, prof of communications emeritus 96-. **HONORS AND AWARDS** Franklyn Haiman Award for Distinguished Scholarship Freedom of Expression, Natl Communication Assn, 93; Everett Lee Hunt Scholarship Award, 87. **MEMBERSHIPS** Nat Communication Assn; Eastern Communication Assn. **RESEARCH** Freedom of Expression, Media Law **SELECTED PUBLICATIONS** Auth, Errors, Lies, and Libel, Southern Ill Univ Press, 92; Murder, Courts, and the Press, Southern Ill Univ Press 92. **CONTACT ADDRESS** 5268 County Rd. #11, Rushville, NY, 14544. **EMAIL** kanepp@frontiernet.net

KANELLOS, NICOLAS
DISCIPLINE LANGUAGE, LITERATURE **EDUCATION** Univ Autonoma Mex, Mex Lit & Cult, 64-65; Farleigh Dickinson Univ, BA, Span, 66; Univ Tex, MA, Roman Lang, 68; Univ Lisboa Portugal, Portuguese Lit & Cult, 69070; Univ Tex, PhD, Span & Portuguese, 74. **CAREER** PROF, UNIV HOUSTON,

80-. **SELECTED PUBLICATIONS** America's Hispanic People: Their Images Through History, 97; edr, Biographical Dictionary of Hispanic Literature in the United States, Greenwood Press, 89; Mexican-American Theater Legacy and Reality, Lat Am Rev Press, 87; Hispanic-American Almanac: A Reference Work on Hispanics in the United States, Gale Res, 93, Hispanic Firsts, Gale Res, 97.. **CONTACT ADDRESS** Dept Hisp & Class Lang, Univ Houston, Houston, TX, 77204-3128.

KANWAR, ANJU
PERSONAL Born 09/18/1962, Delhi, India, s **DISCIPLINE** ENGLISH **EDUCATION** Jesus & Mary Col, Univ of Delhi, BA (honors), 83; Univ of Delhi, MA, 86; Northern Ill Univ, PhD, 95. **CAREER** Lectr, Univ of Delhi, 86-88; tchg asst, 88-93, vis asst prof, Northern Ill Univ, 88-93; instr, Triton Col, 93; instr, Coll of Du Page, 93-94; vis lectr, North Central Col, 98 & 99; INSTR, WAUBONSEE COMMUNITY COL, 93 & 96-. **HONORS AND AWARDS** Outstanding Service Awd, Children's World, 95-96; Arnold B. Fox Awd for Res Writing, Northern Ill Univ, 90. **MEMBERSHIPS** MLA. **RESEARCH** Modern British Lit; issues of gender; pedagogy; Indian writing in English. **SELECTED PUBLICATIONS** Auth, Speech and Silence: Representations of Unmarried Women in the Short Fiction of D.H. Lawrence, Peter Lang Inc., 99; Gender in the Classroom: Boundaries Real or Imagined?, Thresholds in Education, 95; Briscoe's Alternative: Durga or Sati? Woolf and Hinduism in to the Lighthouse, Virginai Woolf: Texts and Contexts: Selected Papers from the 5th Annual Virginia Woolf Confr, Pace UP, 96. **CONTACT ADDRESS** 30W49 Granada Ct. #104, Naperville, IL, 60563.

KAPLAN, CAREY
DISCIPLINE COLLABORATIVE COMPOSITION **EDUCATION** Univ MA, PhD. **CAREER** Eng, St. Michaels Col. **SELECTED PUBLICATIONS** Auth, The Canon and the Common Reader. **CONTACT ADDRESS** St. Michael's Col, Winooski Park, Colchester, VT, 05439. **EMAIL** ckaplan@smcvt.edu

KAPLAN, FRED
PERSONAL Born 11/04/1937, New York, NY, m, 1993, 3 children **DISCIPLINE** ENGLISH **EDUCATION** Brooklyn Col, BA, 59; Columbia Univ, MA, 61, PhD, 66. **CAREER** Instr English, Lawrence Univ, 62-64; asst prof, Calif State Univ, Los Angeles, 64-67; from asst to assoc prof, 67-75, PROF ENGLISH, QUEENS COL, CITY UNIV NY, 75-; PROF ENGLISH, GRAD CTR, CITY UNIV NY, 80-; City Univ New York fac res grant, 68-69, 74-77 & 79-82, 84-98; Fulbright lectr, Univ Copenhagen, 73-74; Guggenheim Found Fel, 76-77; ed, Dickens Studies Annual, 79-94; NEH fel, Huntington Libr, 81-82; fel, Nat Humanities Center, 85-86; ed, Proj edition works Thomas Carlyle, 81- **HONORS AND AWARDS** Dickens Soc, pres, 91, 97. **MEMBERSHIPS** MLA; Dickens Fellowship; Dickens Soc. **RESEARCH** 19th and 20th century British and American literature; biography. **SELECTED PUBLICATIONS** Auth, Miracles of Rare Device: The poet's Sense of Self in Nineteenth-Century Poetry, Wayne State Univ, 72; Dickens and Mesmerism: The Hidden Springs of Fiction, Princeton Univ, 75; Thomas Carlyle, A Biography, Cornell Univ Press, 82; Sacred Tears: Sentimentality in Victorian Literature, Princeton, 87; Charles Dickens, A Biography, William Morrow, 88; Henry James, The Imagination of Genius, A Biography, William Morrow, 93; Gore Vidal, A Biography, Doubleday, 99. **CONTACT ADDRESS** Graduate Center, Queens Col, CUNY, 33 W 42nd St, New York, NY, 10036.

KAPLAN, JUSTIN
PERSONAL Born 09/05/1925, New York, NY, m, 1954, 3 children **DISCIPLINE** AMERICAN LITERATURE **EDUCATION** Harvard Univ, BS, 44. **CAREER** Free-lance work with various NY publ, 46-54; ed, Simon & Schuster, 54-59; WRITER, 59-, Vis lectr, Harvard Univ, 69, 73 & 76; writer-in-residence, Emerson Col, Boston, 77-78; Guggenheim Mem fel, 75-76. **HONORS AND AWARDS** Pulitzer Prize in Biography, 67; Nat Bk Award in Arts & Lett, 67; Am Bk Award, 81. **MEMBERSHIPS** Am Acad Arts & Sci. **SELECTED PUBLICATIONS** Ed, With Toward Women, Dodd, 52; The Pocket Aristotle, Pocket Bks, 58; auth, Mr Clemens and Mark Twain, Simon & Schuster, 66; ed, Great Short Works of Mark Twain, Harper, 67; Mark Twain: Profile, Hill & Wang, 67; auth, Lincoln Steffens, a biography, 74 & Mark Twain and His World, 74, Simon & Schuster; Walt Whitman: A life, 80. **CONTACT ADDRESS** 16 Francis Ave, Cambridge, MA, 02138.

KAPLAN, LINDSAY
DISCIPLINE ENGLISH LITERATURE **EDUCATION** Johns Hopkins Univ, BA, 81; Univ Ca, PhD, 90. **CAREER** Eng Dept, Georgetown Univ **RESEARCH** Renaissance drama; Renaissance English law; race and gender in Renaissance culture; Jews in Early Modern England; Bible as literature. **SELECTED PUBLICATIONS** Auth, pubs on slander, women and slander; co-ed, Feminist Readings in Early Modern England, Cambridge, 96; The Culture of Slander in Early Modern England, Cambridge, 97. **CONTACT ADDRESS** English Dept, Georgetown Univ, 37th and O St, Washington, DC, 20057.

KAPLAN, NANCY
DISCIPLINE LITERATURE **EDUCATION** Cornell, PhD. **CAREER** Assoc prof, Univ Baltimore. **RESEARCH** Computing technology. **SELECTED PUBLICATIONS** Auth, E-Literacies. **CONTACT ADDRESS** Commun Dept, Univ Baltimore, 1420 N. Charles Street, Baltimore, MD, 21201.

KAPLAN, SYDNEY JANET
PERSONAL Born 12/28/1939, Los Angeles, CA, 1 child **DISCIPLINE** ENGLISH **EDUCATION** Univ Calif, Los Angeles, AB, 61, MA, 66, PhD(English), 71. **CAREER** Asst prof, 71-78, ASSOC PROF ENGLISH, UNIV WASH, 78-, DIR, WOMEN STUDIES PROG, 82-, Vis prof, Grad Inst Mod Letters, Univ Tulsa, summer, 80. **MEMBERSHIPS** MLA; Women's Caucus for Mod Lang; Nat Women Studies Asn. **RESEARCH** Twentieth century women writers; Virginia Woolf and Katherine Mansfield; women's studies. **SELECTED PUBLICATIONS** Auth, No Mans Land, the Place of the Woman Writer in the 20th-Century, Vol 3, Letters From the Front, Modern Lang Quart, Vol 0057, 96. **CONTACT ADDRESS** Dept of English, Univ of Wash, Seattle, WA, 98195.

KARCHER, CAROLYN LURY
PERSONAL Born 02/25/1945, Washington, DC, m, 1965 **DISCIPLINE** AMERICAN LITERATURE & STUDIES **EDUCATION** Johns Hopkins Univ, MA, 67; Univ Md, PhD(Am studies), 80. **CAREER** ASST PROF ENGLISH, TEMPLE UNIV, 81-. **MEMBERSHIPS** MLA; Am Studies Asn; Melville Soc. **RESEARCH** Nineteenth and early 20th century American literature; women's studies; slavery. **SELECTED PUBLICATIONS** Auth, Reconceiving 19th-Century American Literature--The Challenge of Women Writers, Amer Lit, Vol 0066, 94; Stowe, Harriet, Beecher--A Life, Legacy, Vol 0012, 95; Correspondent Colorings--Melville in the Marketplace, New England Quarterly a Historical Review of New England Life and Letters, Vol 0069, 96; Correspondent Colorings--Melville in the Marketplace, New Eng Quart-Hist Rev New Eng Life and Letters, Vol 0069, 96; Melville--A Biography, New Engl Quart-Hist Rev New Engl Life and Letters, Vol 0069, 96; Conceived By Liberty, Maternal Figures and 19th-Century American Literature, 19th-Century Lit, Vol 0051, 96. **CONTACT ADDRESS** Dept of English, Temple Univ, 1114 W Berks St, Philadelphia, PA, 19122-6029.

KARI, DAVEN M.
PERSONAL Born 09/24/1953, Hot Springs, SD, m, 1988, 3 children **DISCIPLINE** ENGLISH LITERATURE **EDUCATION** Fresno Pacific Univ, BA, 75; Baylor Univ, MA, 83; Purdue Univ, MA, 85, PhD, 86; So Baptist Theol Sem, MDiv, 88, PhD, 91. **CAREER** Tchg asst, Baylor Univ, 78-79; tchg asst, Purdue Univ, 79-85; lectr Univ Louisville, Spalding Univ, Jefferson Commun Col, 86-90; asst prof, Missouri Baptist Col, 91; prof, Eng, Christian Stud, Fine Arts, Calif Baptist Univ, 91-98; Acad Dean, Washington Bible Col, 98- . **HONORS AND AWARDS** Fac Mem of the Year, 93; Outstanding Young Men of Am, 85; listed, Who's Who in Am, 99; listed, Contemporary Authors, 97; listed Who's Who in the World, 97, 98, 99. **MEMBERSHIPS** Am Acad Relig; Conf on Christianity and Lit. **RESEARCH** Christianity and the arts; Trinity and the visual arts; stained glass windows; T.S. Eliot's drama; Christianity and literature; Bible and literature. **SELECTED PUBLICATIONS** Founder and contribur, The English Accent: Newsletter for Purdue Univ Dept of Eng, 85; asst ed, Business Writing Strategies and Samples, Macmillan, 88; auth, T.S. Eliot's Dramatic Pilgrimage: Progress in Craft as an Expression of Christian Perspective, Edwin Mellen, 90; auth, A Bibliography of Sources in Christianity and the Arts, Edwin Mellen, 95; contribur and co-ed, Baptist Reflections on Christianity and the Arts: Learning from Beauty: A Tribute to William L. Hendricks, Edwin Mellen, 97. **CONTACT ADDRESS** Washington Bible Col, 6511 Princess Garden Pky, Lanham, MD, 20706-3599. **EMAIL** dkari@bible.edu

KAROLIDES, NICHOLAS J.
PERSONAL Born 08/05/1928, Albany, NY, m, 1962, 2 children **DISCIPLINE** ENGLISH **EDUCATION** NY Univ, BS, 50, MA, 51, PhD(English), 63. **CAREER** Teacher & guid coun, Jr High Schs, NY, 54-64; from asst prof to assoc prof English, 64-69, asst dean Col Arts & Sci, 76-82, prof English, Univ Wis-River Falls, 69-, assoc dean, Col Arts & Sci, 82-, instr, NY Univ, 60-64; ed, Wis English J, 65-,& JM Newsletter, 72-75. **HONORS AND AWARDS** Univ Wis-River Falls Distinguished Teaching Award, 71; WCTE Award for Meritorius Serv, 72-88; Myers Center Award for the Study of Human Rights in North American for outstanding work on intolerance for Censored Books: Critical Viewpoints; 94; Outstanding Faculty Award, Humanities Div, Univ Wisconsin-River Falls, 97. **MEMBERSHIPS** NCTE; Conf English Educ. **RESEARCH** Literature; American pioneer related to American history and culture; teaching of minority literature in Wisconsin; censorship; application of literary theory. **SELECTED PUBLICATIONS** Auth, The Pioneer in the American Novel, 1900-50, Univ Okla, 67; Changing conceptions of the pioneer in the contemporary American novel, Wis Studies Lit, 67; Inside techniques-realizing purpose, English Educ, 75; The American frontier: A focus for interdisciplinary studies, Wis English J, 76; The trouble with parents, Wis English J, 78; Reading Process: Transactional Theory in Action in Reader Response in Elementary Classrooms, 96; Challenging Old Habits of Mind: Revisiting Reader's Stance, The New Advocate, Spring, 97. **CONTACT ADDRESS** Dept of English, Univ of Wisconsin, 410 S 3rd St, River Falls, WI, 54022-5013. **EMAIL** nicholas.karolides@uwrf.edu

KARRE, IDAHLYNN
DISCIPLINE INSTRUCTIONAL COMMUNICATION, COMMUNICATION IN EDUCATION, INTERPERSONAL COMM **EDUCATION** Univ CO, PhD, 70. **CAREER** Prof, 69-, ch, dept Speech Commun, Univ Northern CO. **SELECTED PUBLICATIONS** Wrote on tchg and learning in the col classroom. **CONTACT ADDRESS** Univ Northern Colorado, Greeley, CO, 80639.

KASKE, CAROL VONCKX
PERSONAL Born 02/05/1933, Elgin, IL, m, 1958, 1 child **DISCIPLINE** ENGLISH & COMPARATIVE LITERATURE **EDUCATION** Wash Univ, AB, 54; Smith Col, MA, 55; Johns Hopkins Univ, PhD(English), 64. **CAREER** Instr English, Duke Univ, 59-60, Women's Col, Univ NC, 61 & Univ Ill, Urbana, 61-64; from lectr to sr lectr, 64-73, asst prof English, Cornell Univ, 73-, Am Philos Soc grant-in-aid, 75; Am Coun Learned Soc travel grant, 79-86; from assoc prof to prof English, Cornell, 85-92. **MEMBERSHIPS** MLA; Renaissance Soc Am; Spenser Soc; Int Assn Neo-Latin Studies; AAUP. **RESEARCH** Renaissance literature; theology; Edmund Spenser. **SELECTED PUBLICATIONS** Auth, with John R Clark: Marsilio Ficino, Three Books on Life, a Critical Edition and Translation with Introduction and Notes, Binghamton, NY: Medieval and Renaissance Texts and Studies, 89; The dragon's spark and sting and the structure of Red Cross's dragon fight, Studies Philol, 69; Mount Sinai and Dante's Mount Purgatory, Dante Studies, 71; contribr, Spenser's Pluralistic Universe, In: Contemporary Thought on Spenser, Univ Southern Ill, 75; Getting around the Parson's Tale, In: Chaucer at Albany, Burt Franklin, 75; auth, The Bacchus who wouldn't wash, Renaissance Quart, 76; Spenser's Amoretti and Epithalamion of 1595, English Lit Renaissance, 78; Religious Reverence doth Buriall Teene, Rev English Studies, 79; **CONTACT ADDRESS** Dept of English, Cornell Univ, 252 Goldwin Smith Hall, Ithaca, NY, 14853-0001. **EMAIL** cvk2@cornell.edu

KASKE, ROBERT EARL
PERSONAL Born 06/01/1921, Cincinnati, OH, m, 1958, 1 child **DISCIPLINE** ENGLISH, COMPARATIVE LINGUISTICS **EDUCATION** Xavier Univ, Ohio, AB, 42; Univ NC, MA, 47, PhD(English & comp ling), 50. **CAREER** Instr English, Mediaeval lit & comp ling, Wash Univ, 50-52, asst prof, 52-57; asst prof Mediaeval lit, Pa State Univ, 57-58; assoc prof, Univ NC, 58-61; prof, Univ Ill, 61-64; prof, 64-75, AVALON FOUND PROF HUMANITIES, CORNELL UNIV, 75-, Guggenheim fel, 62-63 & 77-78; assoc mem, Ctr Advan Studies, Univ Ill, 62-63; Soc for Humanities fel, Cornell Univ, 72-73; chief ed, Traditio, 75-; Nat Endowment for Humanities res materials grant, 77; Southeastern Inst Medieval & Renaissance Studies sr fel, 79. **MEMBERSHIPS** Acad Lit Studies; MLA; fel Mediaeval Acad Am; Dante Soc Am; Int Asn Univ Prof English. **RESEARCH** Old and Middle English language and literature; Medieval Biblical exegesis and mythography; Dante. **SELECTED PUBLICATIONS** Auth, Amnon and Thamar on a Misericord in Hereford-Cathedral + The Decorative, Iconographic and Religious Significance of Medieval Centerpieces and Supporters, Remarks on Their Enigmatic Aspects, Traditio-Studies in Ancient and Medieval History Thought and Rel. **CONTACT ADDRESS** Dept of English, Cornell Univ, Ithaca, NY, 14853.

KASTAN, DAVID SCOTT
DISCIPLINE ENGLISH AND COMPARATIVE LITERATURE **EDUCATION** Princeton Univ, AB, 67; Univ Chicago, MA, 68 PhD, 74. **CAREER** Instr, Dartmouth Col, 73; prof, 87. **HONORS AND AWARDS** Gen ed, Arden Shakespeare. **SELECTED PUBLICATIONS** Auth, essays on Shakespeare and Renaissance lit, Daedalus, ELH, Renaissance Drama, Shakespeare Quarty, Shakespeare Stud, Stud in Philol; auth, Shakespeare and the Shapes of Time, 82; co-ed, Staging the Renaissance: Essays on Elizabethan and Jacobean Drama, 91; ed, Critical Essays on Shakespeare's Hamlet, 95; New History of Early English Drama, 97. **CONTACT ADDRESS** Dept of Eng, Columbia Col, New York, 2960 Broadway, New York, NY, 10027-6902.

KATZ, SANDRA
DISCIPLINE ENGLISH LITERATURE **EDUCATION** Smith Col, BA; Trinity Col, MA; Univ Mass, PhD. **CAREER** Prof, Hartford Univ. **RESEARCH** Biography ; American studies. **SELECTED PUBLICATIONS** Auth, biography of Elinor White Frost. **CONTACT ADDRESS** English Dept, Univ of Hartford, 200 Bloomfield Ave, West Hartford, CT, 06117.

KAUFER, DAVID S.
DISCIPLINE ARGUMENT THEORY **EDUCATION** Univ Wisc, PhD. **CAREER** Lit, Carnegie Mellon Univ. **SELECT-**

ED PUBLICATIONS Area: author-reader interactions across a variety of organizational contexts. **CONTACT ADDRESS** Carnegie Mellon Univ, 5000 Forbes Ave, Pittsburgh, PA, 15213.

KAUFFMAN, BETTE J.
PERSONAL Born 05/14/1945, Washington, IA, m, 1998 **DISCIPLINE** COMMUNICATIONS **EDUCATION** Univ Iowa, BA, 80; Univ Pa, MA, 82; PhD, 92. **CAREER** Assoc prof, head, 97-, NE La Univ. **HONORS AND AWARDS** Pi Sigma Alpha Nat Honor Soc; Kappa Tau Alpha Nat Honor Soc; Omicron Delta Kappa Nat Leadership Honor Soc; Univ Iowa Hancher-Finkbine Medallion; Phi Beta Kappa., Leon Barnes Commun J Honor Award, 79; Ruth Baty & Maurice Barnett Jones Scholar, 79, 80; cum laude grad, 80; tuition scholar, 80-86; grad teaching assistantships, 81-85; Fac Marshall for Broadcast/Cable, 91; faculty develop prog grant, 99. **MEMBERSHIPS** Assoc for Educ in Journ & Mass Commun; Publ Relations Soc of Amer; Int commun Assoc; founding member, Coalition for Multicultural Feminist Stud in Commun. **RESEARCH** Critical media stud; soc identity (race, class, gender) in culture & commun; visual commun. **SELECTED PUBLICATIONS** Auth, Feminist Facts: Interview Strategies and Political Subjects in Ethnography, Commun Theory, 92; art, Woman Artist: Between Myth and Stereotype, On the Margins of Art Worlds, Westview Press, 95; art, Missing Persons: Working Class Women and the Movies, 1940-1990, Feminism, Multiculturalism and the Media: Global Diversities, Sage Publ, 95; art, Media Realities: The Social Context of Visual Competence, J of Visual Literacy, 97; art, Angelica Kauffman, & Berenice Abbott, Women in World History, Yorkin Publ, 98. **CONTACT ADDRESS** Northeast Louisiana Univ, 120A Stubbs Hall, Monroe, LA, 71209. **EMAIL** jokauffman@alpha.nlu.edu

KAVANAGH, PETER
PERSONAL Born 03/19/1916, Inniskeen, Ireland, m, 1963, 2 children **DISCIPLINE** ENGLISH **EDUCATION** Univ Col, Dublin, A BA, 40, HDE and MA, 41; Trinity Col, Dublin, PhD(English), 44. **CAREER** Master, Dublin Nat Schs, 37-45; asst prof English, St Francis Col, NY, 46-47, Loyola Univ, Ill, 47-49 and Gannon Col, 49-50; ed and writer, Encycl Amna, 50-53; eng, Cementation Co, London, 53-57; prof English, Fairleigh Dickinson Univ, 57-58; RES and WRITING, 58-, Assoc prof English, Stout State Univ, 66-68. **MEMBERSHIPS** Assoc Brit Soc Engineers; MLA; Int Fedn Jists. **SELECTED PUBLICATIONS** Spaziergang Am Kanalufer, Akzente-Zeitschrift fur Literatur, Vol 44, 97; In Gedenken an Meine Mutter, Akzente-Zeitschrift fur Literatur, Vol 44, 97; Epos, Akzente-Zeitschrift fur Literatur, Vol 44, 97; Shancoduff, Akzente-Zeitschrift fur Literatur, Vol 44, 97; 'Spritzen Der Kartoffeln,' Akzente-Zeitschrift fur Literatur, Vol 44, 97; 'Innocence,' Poetry Rev, Vol 84, 94; Unschuld, Akzente-Zeitschrift fur Literatur, Vol 44, 97; 'Field Work,' Southerly, Vol 56, 96; Praludium, Akzente-Zeitschrift fur Literatur, Vol 44, 97. **CONTACT ADDRESS** Peter Kavanagh Hand Press 250 E 30th St, New York, NY, 10016.

KAWIN, BRUCE FREDERICK
PERSONAL Born 11/06/1945, Los Angeles, CA **DISCIPLINE** FILM HISTORY; MODERN LITERATURE **EDUCATION** Columbia Univ, AB, 67; Cornell Univ, MFA, 69, PhD, 70. **CAREER** Asst prof English, Wells Col, 70-73; lectr English & Film, Univ Calif, Riverside, 73-75; assoc prof, 75-80, prof English & Film, Univ Co, Boulder, 80-, Specialist, Ctr for Advan Film Studies, Am Film Inst, 74. **MEMBERSHIPS** MLA; SCS. **RESEARCH** Narrative theory; relations between literature and film. **SELECTED PUBLICATIONS** Auth, Slides (poem), Angelfish, 70; Telling It Again and Again: Repetition in Literature and Film, Cornell Univ, 72, repr Univ Press Co, 89; Faulkner and Film, Ungar, 77; Me Tarzan, you junk, Take One, 78; Mindscreen: Bergman, Godard and First-Person Film, Princeton Univ, 78; ed, To Have and Have Not--The Screenplay, Univ Wis, 80; The Mind of the Novel: Reflexive Fiction and the Ineffable, Princeton Univ, 82; Faulkner's MGM Screenplays, Univ Tenn, 82; How Movies Work, MacMillan, 87, repr Univ Ca Press, 92; co-auth, A short History of the Movies, 5th ed, MacMillan, 92; 6th ed, Allyn & Bacon, 96; 7th ed Allyn & Bacon, 99. **CONTACT ADDRESS** Dept of English, Univ Co, Box 226, Boulder, CO, 80309-0226. **EMAIL** bkawin@aol.com

KAY, JAMES F.
PERSONAL Born 05/18/1948, Kansas City, MO **DISCIPLINE** HOMILETICS; SYSTEMATIC THEOLOGY **EDUCATION** Pasadena Col, BA 69; Harvard Univ M Div 72; Union Theol Sem, M Phil 84, PhD 91. **CAREER** Northern Lakes Presby Parish MN, 74-78; Bemidji State Univ MN, campus pastor 77-79; Presby Hlth Edu Wel Assoc NY, consultant 80-82; Princeton Theological Sem, inst homiletics, asst prof, assoc prof, 88-97, Joe R Engle assoc prof, 97-. **HONORS AND AWARDS** Phi Delta Lambda; BA magna cum laude; Warrack Lectr. **MEMBERSHIPS** AH; AAR; DTS; Karl Barth Soc of N Amer. **RESEARCH** Apocalypticism; Greco-Roman rhetoric; Pauline theology. **SELECTED PUBLICATIONS** Auth, Women Gender and Christian Community, co-ed, Louisville, Westminster John Knox Press, 97; Seasons of Grace: reflections from the Christian Year, Grand Rapids, William B. Eerdmans Pub Co, 94; Christus Praesens: A Reconsideration of Rudolf Bultmann's Christology, Grand Rapids, William B. Eerdmans Pub Co, 94; Preaching at the Turn of the Ages, St Mary's Col Bull, 98; In Whose Name: Feminism and Trinitarian Baptismal Formula, Theology Today, 93. **CONTACT ADDRESS** Dept of Theology, Princeton Theol Sem, PO Box 821, Princeton, NJ, 08542. **EMAIL** james.kay@ptsem.edu

KAY, W. DAVID
PERSONAL Born 03/28/1939, Philadelphia, PA, m, 1959, 2 children **DISCIPLINE** ENGLISH LITERATURE **EDUCATION** Univ Pa, BA, 61; Princeton Univ, MA, 63, PhD, 68. **CAREER** Instr English, 65-68, asst prof, 68-78, assoc prof English, Univ Ill, Urbana, 78-; Danforth fel, Yale Div Sch, 69-70. **MEMBERSHIPS** Renaissance Soc Am; Shakespeare Asn Am. **RESEARCH** Renaissance humanism; Elizabethan and Jacobean drama; Ben Jonson. **SELECTED PUBLICATIONS** Auth, Bartholomew Fair: Ben Jonson in Praise of folly, English Lit Renaissance, spring 76; Erasmus learned joking: Ironic use of classical wisdom in Praise of Folly, Tex Studies in Lit & Lang, fall 77; Ben Jonson & Elizabethan dramatic convention, Mod Philol, 8/78; Ben Jonson: A Literary Life, Macmillan/St Martin's Press, 95; ed, John Marston, The Malcontent, New Mermaids, A&C Black/W.W. Norton, 98. **CONTACT ADDRESS** Dept of English, Univ of Ill, 608 S Wright St, Urbana, IL, 61801-3613. **EMAIL** w-kay@uiuc.edu

KAYE, FRANCES WELLER
PERSONAL Born 04/04/1949, Englewood, NJ, m, 1973 **DISCIPLINE** AMERICAN STUDIES AND AMERICAN LITERATURE **EDUCATION** Cornell Univ, BA, 70, MA, 72, PhD(Am studies), 73. **CAREER** Vis asst prof Am studies, Univ Iowa, 76-77; asst prof English, 77-80, ASSOC PROF ENGLISH, UNIV NEBR-LINCOLN, 81-, ASSOC ED, GREAT PLAINS QUART, 80- **RESEARCH** Great Plains studies; Aman studies; Canadian literature. **SELECTED PUBLICATIONS** Letters By Lamplight--A Womans View of Everyday Life in South Texas, 1873-1883, Legacy, Vol 10, 93; Bachelor Bess--The Homesteading Letters of Corey, Elizabeth, 1909-1919, Legacy, Vol 10, 93; The Left and Labor on the Plains--An Introduction, Great Plains Quart, Vol 16, 96; Plains Folk-II--The Romance of the Landscape, New Mexico Hist Rev, Vol 68, 93; Gone-Back-to-Alberta--Kroetsch, Robert Rewriting the Great-Plains, Great Plains Quart, Vol 14, 94; Int Influences on the Great-Plains--An Introduction, Great Plains Quart, Vol 14, 94. **CONTACT ADDRESS** Dept of English, Univ of Nebr, P O Box 880333, Lincoln, NE, 68588-0333.

KEATEN, JAMES A.
DISCIPLINE INTERCULTURAL COMMUNICATION **EDUCATION** PA State Univ, PhD, 70. **CAREER** Prof, Univ Northern CO. **MEMBERSHIPS** Speech Commun Asn; Western States Commun Asn; Japanese Psychol Asn. **RESEARCH** Commun apprehension; cross-cultural commun. **SELECTED PUBLICATIONS** Coauth, Teaching people to speak well: Training and remediation of communication reticence, Hampton Publ Co, 95; Komyunikeishon fuan to wa nanika? ¤A definition of communication apprehension and related constructsl, Hokuriku Daiguku Kiyo, 20, 96; Development of an instrument to measure reticence, Commun Quart, 45, 97; Communication apprehension in Japan: Grade school through secondary school, Int J of Intercultural Rel, 21, 97; Assessing the cross-cultural validity of the Personal Report of Communication Apprehension scale (PRCA-24), Japanese Psychol Res, 40, 98; Fundamentals of communication: An intercultural perspective, Kawashima Shotem, 98. **CONTACT ADDRESS** Univ Northern Colorado, Greeley, CO, 80639. **EMAIL** jkeaten@bentley.unco.edu

KEEFE, ROBERT
PERSONAL Born 03/11/1938, Framingham, MA, m, 1960 **DISCIPLINE** ENGLISH **EDUCATION** Brandeis Univ, AB, 64; Princeton Univ, PhD(English), 68. **CAREER** Asst prof, 67-77, ASSOC PROF ENGLISH, UNIV MASS, AMHERST, 78-, Guest prof, English lit, Univ Freiburg, Ger, 72-73 and 77-78. **MEMBERSHIPS** Soc Relig Higher Educ; MLA. **RESEARCH** Victorian literature; Matthew Arnold; 19th century concepts of time. **SELECTED PUBLICATIONS** Aestheticism and Deconstruction-Pater, Derrida, and Deman, Engl Lit Transition 1880-1920, Vol 36, 93. **CONTACT ADDRESS** UNIV MASSACHUSETTS, AMHERST, MA, 01003.

KEEHNER, MARY
DISCIPLINE RHETORICAL THEORY AND CRITICISM **EDUCATION** Purdue Univ, PhD. **CAREER** Asst prof, Purdue Univ. **RESEARCH** Feminist and other ideological approaches to the study of discourse. **SELECTED PUBLICATIONS** Auth, The lost passages of Kenneth Burke's Permanence and Change, Commun Stud, 91; Arguing about fetal versus women's rights: An ideological evaluation, Warranting Assent: Case Stud in Argument Evaluation, 95. **CONTACT ADDRESS** Dept of Commun, Purdue Univ, 1080 Schleman Hall, West Lafayette, IN, 47907-1080. **EMAIL** keen@vm.cc.purdue.edu

KEENAN, HUGH THOMAS
PERSONAL Born 01/16/1936, Humboldt, TN **DISCIPLINE** MEDIEVAL LITERATURE **EDUCATION** Memphis State Univ, BS, 57, MA, 60, BA, 63; Univ Tenn, PhD(English), 68. **CAREER** Instr English, Delta State Col, 60-62, Memphis State Univ, 62-63 & Univ Tenn, 63-67; assoc prof English, GA State Univ, 68-, Fel, Ctr Mediaeval & Renaissance Studies, Calif State Univ, 74; bk rev ed, SAtlantic Bull, 78-81. **MEMBERSHIPS** MLA; Mediaeval Acad Am; Mod Lang Soc Finland; SAtlantic Mod Lang Asn; Children's Lit Asn. **RESEARCH** Old English literature; Middle English Literature. **SELECTED PUBLICATIONS** Auth, The Ruin as Babylon, Tenn Studies Lit, 66; The of The Lord of the Rings, Tolkien & Critics, 68; Old English and Children's Literature, In: The Great Excluded, 71; ed, Typology and Medieval Literature, Studies in Lit Imagination, 75; auth, Christ and Satan: Some vagaries, Studies Medieval Cult, 75; The General Prologue, lines 345-346, Neuphilologische Mitteilungen, 78; ed, Dearest Chums and Partners, 93; Typology and English Medieval Literature, 92. **CONTACT ADDRESS** Dept of English, Georgia State Univ, 33 Gilmer St SE, Atlanta, GA, 30303-3080.

KEENAN, RICHARD CHARLES
PERSONAL Born 04/28/1939, Philadelphia, PA, m, 1967, 2 children **DISCIPLINE** ENGLISH LITERATURE, CINEMA **EDUCATION** Temple Univ, BS, 62; St Joseph's Col, Pa, MA, 66; Temple Univ, PhD(English), 74. **CAREER** Instr, Devon Prep Sch, Devon, Pa, 64-67, Temple Univ, 67-72, asst prof, 72-94, PROF ENGLISH, UNIV MD, EASTERN SHORE, 94-, Assoc ed, Lit/Film Quart, 77-. **MEMBERSHIPS** Literature/Film Asn; British Film Inst; MLA; Col English Asn **RESEARCH** American film studies; 19th century English & American literature. **SELECTED PUBLICATIONS** Auth, Browning and Shelley, 73 & coauth, Robert & Elizabeth Barrett Browning: An Annotated Bibliography for 1971, 73, Browning Inst Studies; auth, Cinema on Campus, Campus on Cinema, Lit/Film Quart, 4/73; Directors and Directions: Cukor, Ford and Kubrick, Lit/Film Quart, 74; Comments and Queries: No 5, (error in Browning biography by Irvine & Honan), Studies Browning & His Circle, spring 75; Negative Image: Black Actors and American Film, Lit/Film Quart, fall 75; coauth, Browning Without Words: D W Griffith's Filming of Pippa Passes, Browning Inst Studies, 76; The sense of an ending: Jan Kadar's distortion of Stephen Crane's The Blue Hotel, Lit/Film Quart, 88; Matthew Arnold, In: Survey of World Literature, Cavendish Press, 92; Colonial life and thought: Benjamin Rush, In: American Portraits: History through Biography Volume 1 to 1877, Kendall Hunt, 93; Salvador: Oliver Stone and the center of indifference, In: The Films of Oliver Stone, Scarecrow Press, 97. **CONTACT ADDRESS** Univ of Md, 11868 Academic Oval, Princess Anne, MD, 21853-1299. **EMAIL** rkeenan@umes-bird.umd.edu

KEENER, FREDERICK M.
PERSONAL Born 12/28/1937, New York, NY, m, 1961, 2 children **DISCIPLINE** ENGLISH, COMPARATIVE LITERATURE **EDUCATION** St John's Univ, NY, AB, 59; Columbia Univ, MA, 60, PhD(English), 65. **CAREER** From instr to asst prof English, St John's Univ, NY, 61-66; from asst prof to assoc prof, Columbia Univ, 66-72, dean summer session, 72-74; from assoc prof to prof, 74-78; PROF ENGLISH, HOFSTRA UNIV, 78-, Lectr, Hunter Col, 66; Nat Endowment for Humanities res fel, 76-77; vis prof, Columbia Univ, 81. **MEMBERSHIPS** MLA; Conf Brit Studies; Am Soc 18th Century Studies. **RESEARCH** Eighteenth century British literature; 18th century comparative literature. **SELECTED PUBLICATIONS** Critical Essays on Pope, Alexander, Scriblerian and the Kit-Cats, Vol 27, 95. **CONTACT ADDRESS** Dept of English, Hofstra Univ, 1000 Fulton Ave, Hempstead, NY, 11550-1091.

KEEP, CHRISTOPHER J.
DISCIPLINE 19TH; 20TH CENTURY BRITISH LITERATURE **EDUCATION** York Univ, BA, MA; Queen's Univ, PhD. **CAREER** Asst prof **HONORS AND AWARDS** Izaak Walton Killam Memorial post dr fel; post dr fel, SSHRC; AC Hamilton. **RESEARCH** Cultural studies; critical theory; film. **SELECTED PUBLICATIONS** Pub(s), Victorian Stud, Victorian Rev, Mosaic, Cinemas, Frontenac Rev; auth, Being on Line: Net Subjectivity, 97; Postmodern Apocalypse, 95; Litterature et informatique: La Litterature generee par ordinateur, 95; Dictionary of Literary Biography: Late-Victorian and Edwardian British Novelists, 95. **CONTACT ADDRESS** Dept of English, Victoria Univ, PO Box 3070, Victoria, BC, V8W 3W1. **EMAIL** ckeep@uvic.ca

KEGL, ROSEMARY
DISCIPLINE 16TH AND 17TH CENTURY ENGLISH LITERATURE **EDUCATION** Cornell Univ, PhD. **CAREER** Assoc prof; taught at, Cornell Univ & WA Univ in St Louis. **HONORS AND AWARDS** Newberry Libr/Nat Endowment Humanities fel & Newberry Libr short-term fel. **RESEARCH** 16th and 17th century Eng lit; contemp marxist and feminist theory. **SELECTED PUBLICATIONS** Auth, Rhetoric of Concealment: Figuring Gender and Class in Renaissance Literature; articles on, Marvell, Puttenham, Shakespeare & 16th and 17th century women's intellectual activ. **CONTACT ADDRESS** Dept of Eng, Univ of Rochester, 601 Elmwood Ave, Ste. 656, Rochester, NY, 14642. **EMAIL** kegl@troi.cc.rochester.edu

KEHL, DELMAR GEORGE
PERSONAL Born 09/12/1936, Mt Carroll, IL, m, 1963, 2 children **DISCIPLINE** AMERICAN LITERATURE **EDUCATION** Univ Wis-Madison, MS, 58; Univ Southern Calif, PhD(English), 67. **CAREER** Instr English, Roosevelt Sch, Conn, 58-59; teaching asst, Univ Southern Calif, 61-64, lectr, 64-65; from asst prof to assoc prof, 65-70, PROF ENGLISH, ARIZ STATE UNIV, 75-, Fac grants-in-aid, 69, 70, 72, 74, 76, 77 and 81; vis scholar, Harvard, 79; res fel, Yale, 79. **HONORS AND AWARDS** Elizabeth K Pleasants Award Excellence in Teaching, Univ Southern Calif, 62. **MEMBERSHIPS** NCTE; MLA; Rocky Mountain Mod Lang Asn. **RESEARCH** Literature and theology; rhetoric; popular culture. **SELECTED PUBLICATIONS** Oconnor, Flannery 4th-Dimension, the Role of Sexuality in Her Fiction, Mississippi Quart, Vol 48, 95; The Southwest Viewed from the Inside-Out--A Conversation With Noble, Marguerite, J Southwest, Vol 36, 94. **CONTACT ADDRESS** Dept of English, Arizona State Univ, Tempe, PO Box 870302, Tempe, AZ, 85287-0302.

KEISER, GEORGE ROBERT
PERSONAL Born 02/26/1941, Pottsville, PA **DISCIPLINE** ENGLISH AND AMERICAN LITERATURE **EDUCATION** Lehigh Univ, BA, 62, MA, 64, PhD(English), 71. **CAREER** From instr to asst prof, Canisius Col, 67-73; asst prof, 73-75, assoc prof, 75-81, PROF ENGLISH, KANS STATE UNIV, 81-, Am Coun Learned Soc fel, 79 and Huntington Libr fel, 82. **MEMBERSHIPS** MLA; Mediaeval Acad Am; Int Authurian Soc. **RESEARCH** Medieval English literature. **SELECTED PUBLICATIONS** An Unnoticed Middle-English Version of the 2nd Anglo-Norman Prose Lapidary, Manuscripta, Vol 38, 94; Reconstructing Thornton, Medium Aevum, Vol 65, 96; An Unnoticed Middle-English Version of the 2nd Anglo-Norman Prose Lapidary, Manuscripta, Vol 38, 94; Studies in the Vernon Manuscript, J Engl Ger Philol, Vol 92, 93; Printing the Written Word--The Social-Hist of Books, C.1450-1520, Speculum-A J Medieval Studies, Vol 69, 94; Illing a Lacuna in a Middle-English 'Secretum Secretorum,' Neuphilologische Mitteilungen, Vol 96, 95; Through a 14th-Century Gardener's Eyes, Chaucer Rev, Vol 31, 96; Printing the Written Word--The Social History of Books, C.1450-1520, Editor, Speculum-A J Medieval Studies, Vol 69, 94; Studies in the Vernon Manuscript, J Engl Ger Philol, Vol 92, 93; A New Text of, and New Light on, the 'Supplement to the Index of Middle English Verse,' 4106.5, Notes and Queries, Vol 43, 96. **CONTACT ADDRESS** Dept of English, Kansas State Univ, 106 Denison Hall, Manhattan, KS, 66506-0701.

KELLEGHAN, FIONA
PERSONAL Born 04/21/1965, West Palm Beach, FL, m, 1994, 1 child **DISCIPLINE** ENGLISH, LIBRARY & INFORMATION SCIENCE **EDUCATION** Univ Miami, BA, 87; **CAREER** Regional Reporter, ACRL Newsletter, 94-98; Consult Ed, Sci Fiction Studies; librn, assoc prof, Univ Miami, 89-. **MEMBERSHIPS** Am Libr Asn; Imagineering Interest Group; Sci Fiction Research Asn; Int Asn for the Fantastic in the Arts; S Fla Sci Fiction Soc. **RESEARCH** Lit criticism sci fiction, fantasy, horror fiction and film. **SELECTED PUBLICATIONS** Auth, "Lethem, Jonathan (Allen)" and "Williams, Walter Jon," in St. James Guide to Science Fiction Writers, St. James Press, 95; auth, "Good News from Outer Space (John Kessel)" and "The Deathworld Trilogy (Harry Harrison)," in Magill's Guide to Science Fiction and Fantasy Literature, Salem Press, 96; auth, "Kenrick, Tony" and "O'Connell, Carol," in St. James Guide to Crime & Mystery Writers, St. James Press, 96; coauth, "Fantasy Literature" and "Horror Literature," in Genre and Ethnic Collections: Collected Essays, JAI Press, 97; auth, "Roald Dahl," in Cyclopedia of World Authors, JAI Press, 97; auth, "Postcyberpunk Lost: The Pure Cold Light," in Nova Express, Winter/Spring 98; auth, "The Secret in the Chest: With Tests, Maps, Mysteries, & Intermittent Discussion Questions," in Realms of Fantasy, Oct 98; auth, "Coleridge Meets Carroll, in Mythprint: The Monthly Bulletin of the Mythopoeic Society, Jun 97; auth "Interview with John Kessel," in Science-Fiction Studies, Mar 93; auth, "Hell's My Destination: Imprisonment in the Works of Alfred Bester," in Science-Fiction Studies, Winter 94; auth, "Ambiguous News From the Heartland: John Kessel's Good News from Outer Space," in Extrapolation, Winter 94; auth, "Camouflage in Fantastic Fiction and Film," in Extrapolation, Summer 96; auth, "John Kessel's Screwball SF," in The New York Review of Science Fiction, Oct 97; auth, "Interview with Tim Powers," in Science-Fiction Studies, Spring 98; auth, "Getting a Life: Haunted Spaces in Two Novels of Tim Powers," in The New York Review of Science Fiction, Mar 98; auth, "Private Hells and Radical Doubts: An Interview with Jonathan Lethem," in Science-Fiction Studies, July 98; **CONTACT ADDRESS** Otto G. Richter Library, Univ of Miami, Coral Gables, FL, 33124. **EMAIL** fkelleghan@library.miami.edu

KELLER, ARNOLD
DISCIPLINE ENGLISH LITERATURE **EDUCATION** Sir George Williams Univ, BA; Claremont Grad Sch, MA; Univ Concordia, PhD. **CAREER** Assoc prof **HONORS AND AWARDS** Co-developer, Computer Software: DynaMark, Intellimation, 93. **RESEARCH** Writing instruction; computer applications to the teaching of English; Web publishing; intelligent tutoring systems. **SELECTED PUBLICATIONS** Pub(s),

articles in McGill Jour of Edu; Cmpt(s) and Edu, Jour of Edu Commun, Encycl of the Essay; auth, When Machines Teach: Designing Computer Courseware, Harper, 87; English Simplified, US and Canadian Editions, Harper, 87-96. **CONTACT ADDRESS** Dept of English, Victoria Univ, PO Box 3070, Victoria, BC, V8W 3W1. **EMAIL** akeller@uvic.ca

KELLER, DALE
DISCIPLINE COMMUNICATIONS **EDUCATION** AR State Univ, BA, 72; Fuller Theol Sem, Mdiv, 79; Wheaton Col, MA, 85; Univ KS, PhD, 97. **CAREER** Asst prof, 89, Truman State Univ. **HONORS AND AWARDS** Co-adv, Intl Assn Bus Commun. **MEMBERSHIPS** Mem, Assn Bus Commun. **RESEARCH** Evaluating how an e-mail user's choice of lang may impact a reader's perceptions of the sender. **SELECTED PUBLICATIONS** Auth, A rhetorician ponders technology, or why Kenneth Burke never owned a personal computer, Electronic Jour Commun. **CONTACT ADDRESS** Dept of Commun, Truman State Univ, 100 E Normal St, Kirksville, MO, 63501-4221. **EMAIL** Dkeller@Truman.edu

KELLER, EVE
DISCIPLINE ENGLISH LITERATURE **EDUCATION** Columbia Univ, PhD. **CAREER** Asst prof, Fordham Univ. **RESEARCH** Discourses of early mod sci, gender and sci. **SELECTED PUBLICATIONS** Auth, In the service of Truth and Victory: Geometry and Rhetoric in the Political Works of Thomas Hobbes, Prose Stud 15, 92; Mrs. Jane Sharp: Midwifery and the Critique of Medical Knowledge in Seventeenth-Century England, Women's Wrtg 2, 95. **CONTACT ADDRESS** Dept of Eng Lang and Lit, Fordham Univ, 113 W 60th St, New York, NY, 10023.

KELLER, KARL
PERSONAL Born 05/29/1933, Manti, UT, m, 1956, 5 children **DISCIPLINE** ENGLISH **EDUCATION** Univ Utah, BA, 58, MA, 59; Univ Minn, PhD(English), 64. **CAREER** Instr English, Univ Minn, 59-64; asst prof, State Univ NY Col, Cortland, 64-66; from asst to assoc prof, 66-69, PROF ENGLISH, SAN DIEGO STATE UNIV, 69-, San Diego State Found res grants, 70, 75, 79 and 81; Nat Endowment for Humanities fel, 79 and 82 and Am Coun Learned Soc fel, 80-81. **MEMBERSHIPS** MLA **RESEARCH** Early Am literature. **SELECTED PUBLICATIONS** Iaje Curious in Membership Inquiry, Down Beat, Vol 63, 96. **CONTACT ADDRESS** Dept of English, San Diego State Univ, San Diego, CA, 92182.

KELLETT, PETE
DISCIPLINE ORGANIZATIONAL COMMUNICATION **EDUCATION** Sheffield City Polytech, Eng, BA, 83; Southern IL Univ, Carbondale, MA, 85, PhD, 90. **CAREER** Asst prof, Univ NC, Greensboro; consult, Piedmont Triad area of NC. **MEMBERSHIPS** Speech Commun Asn; Int Commun Asn. **RESEARCH** Organizational commun; organizational change management. **SELECTED PUBLICATIONS** Author of approximately 20 book chapters, journal articles, and convention papers in organizational commun and related areas. **CONTACT ADDRESS** Univ N. Carolina, Greensboro, 102 Fergus, Greensboro, NC, 27412-5001. **EMAIL** Kellettp@iris.uncg.edu

KELLEY, DELORES G.
PERSONAL Born 05/01/1936, Norfolk, VA, m **DISCIPLINE** ENGLISH **EDUCATION** VA State Coll, BA Philos 1956; New York Univ, MA Educ 1958; Purdue Univ MA Comm (grad tchg fellow) 1972; Univ of MD, PhD, Am Studies 1977. **CAREER** New York City Protestant Council, dir Christian Educ 1958-60; Plainview JHS, tchr of English 1965-66; Morgan State Univ, instr of English 1966-70; Purdue Univ, grad teaching fellow in speech 1971-72; Coppin State Coll, dept chmn lang lit & philos 1976-79, dean of lower div, 1979-89, prof, communications, 1990-; MD State Delegate (elected from 42nd district), 1991-94; MD State Senator, 10th District, 1995-. **HONORS AND AWARDS** Gov's apptmt State Com on Values Educ 1980; fellow Amer Council on Educ 1982-83; mem Baltimore Jewish Council Fact-Finding Mission to Israel 1987; Coppin Critical Reading Grant, National Endowment for the Humanities, 1988-89. **MEMBERSHIPS** Mem Alpha Kappa Alpha 1955-; vol host family Baltimore Council Intl Visitors 1976-; Roots Forum project grant MD Com on Humanities & Pub Policy 1977; mem evaluation team Hood Coll MD State Dept of Educ 1978; reviewer & panelist Natl Endowment for the Humanities 1979-80; chairperson adv council Gifted & Talented Educ Baltimore City Sch 1979-; bd mem Harbor Bank of MD 1982-; exec bd Baltimore Urban League; sec MD Dem Party 1986-90; pres, Black/Jewish Forum of Baltimore, 1990-92; chair, Baltimore Chapter, Natl Political Congress of Black Women, 1993-95; MD Commissioner on Criminal Sentencing Policy, 1996-98; bd, Institute Christian Jewish Studies, 1989-; pres-elect, Women Legislators of MD, 1997-98; pres, Women Legislators of MD, 1998-99. **CONTACT ADDRESS** 3100 Timanus Lane, Ste 101, Baltimore, MD, 21244.

KELLEY, MICHAEL ROBERT
PERSONAL Born 08/20/1940, Washington, DC, 1 child **DISCIPLINE** ENGLISH LITERATURE, LINGUISTICS **EDUCATION** Cath Univ Am, BA, 62, MFA, 65, PhD(English), 70.

CAREER Asst prof, 70-75, assoc prof, 75-80, prof English, George Mason Univ, 80-, Contrib ed, Mod Humanities Res Asn Bibliog, 75-. **MEMBERSHIPS** MLA; Mediaeval Acad Am. **RESEARCH** Medieval English drama; Chaucer; literary aesthetics. **SELECTED PUBLICATIONS** Auth, Fifteenth Century Flamboyant Style and the Castle of Perseverance, Comp Drama, spring 72; English for Foreign Speakers--a Television Solution, AV instr, 11/72; Flamboyant Drama, Southern Ill Univ, 78. **CONTACT ADDRESS** Dept of English, George Mason Univ, 4400 University Dr, Fairfax, VA, 22030-4444. **EMAIL** mkelley@gmu.edu

KELLEY, SAMUEL L.
DISCIPLINE COMMUNICATOIN STUDIES **EDUCATION** Univ Ark, BA, MA; Univ Mich, PhD. **CAREER** Prof. **SELECTED PUBLICATIONS** Auth, pubs on African Americans; films of Spike Lee; human communication. **CONTACT ADDRESS** Dept of Communication, State Univ NY Cortland, PO Box 2000, Cortland, NY, 13045-0900. **EMAIL** Kelleys@cortland.edu

KELLOGG, DAVID
DISCIPLINE ENGLISH LITERATURE **EDUCATION** UNC Chapel Hill, PhD, 94. **CAREER** Assoc prof, Duke Univ. **SELECTED PUBLICATIONS** Auth, publ(s) on contemp poetry; poetics; theory of poetic; Perloff's Wittgenstein: W(h)ither Poetic Theory?, Diacritics, 97. **CONTACT ADDRESS** Eng Dept, Duke Univ, Durham, NC, 27706.

KELLY, ERNA
DISCIPLINE ENGLISH LITERATURE **EDUCATION** SUNY Albany, PhD. **CAREER** Fac, Univ Calif Los Angeles, 80-82; Univ Wis Eau Claire, 83-. **RESEARCH** Pre-19th Century women writers, poetry; non-fiction prose; drama. **SELECTED PUBLICATIONS** Auth, articles on writing and computers and 17th Century women poets. **CONTACT ADDRESS** Dept of English, Univ of Wisconsin, Eau Claire, Hibbard Hall 421, PO Box 4004, Eau Claire, WI, 54702-4004. **EMAIL** ekelly@uwec.edu

KELLY, ERNECE BEVERLY
PERSONAL Born 01/06/1937, Chicago, Illinois, s **DISCIPLINE** ENGLISH **EDUCATION** University of Chicago, AB, 1958, MA, 1959; Northwestern University, PhD, 1972. **CAREER** University of Wisconsin, assistant professor, 1978-81; Kingsborough Community College, associate professor, 1984-. **HONORS AND AWARDS** Humanities Council of New York; Speakers in the Humanities, 1992-99; City University of New York, research grant, 1989; Schomburg Center for Research in Black Culture, scholar in residence, 1988; National Endowment on the Humanities, awarded summer seminar, 1978. **MEMBERSHIPS** College Language Association, 1972-; National Council of Teachers of English, director, task force on racism & bias in teaching of English, 1970-80; Conference on College Composition and Communication, executive committee, 1971-74. **SELECTED PUBLICATIONS** Film reviews, Crisis Magazine and New York area newspapers, 1991-; 138 Commonly Used Idioms, student booklet, 1989; Searching for America, National Council of Teachers of English, 1972; Points of Departure, John Wiley & Sons, 1972. **CONTACT ADDRESS** Kingsborough Community Col, CUNY, 2001 Oriental Blvd, Brooklyn, NY, 11235.

KELLY, HENRY ANSGAR
PERSONAL Born 06/06/1934, Fonda, IA, m, 1968, 2 children **DISCIPLINE** ENGLISH **EDUCATION** St. Louis Univ, AB, 59, AM, PhL, 61; Harvard Univ, PhD, 65. **CAREER** Asst prof, 67-69, assoc prof, 69-72, PROF, ENGLISH DEPT, UCLA, 72-, DIR, CENTER FOR MEDIEVAL AND RENAISSANCE STUDIES, 98-. **HONORS AND AWARDS** Guggenheim fel, 72; NEH fel, 80-81, 96-97. **MEMBERSHIPS** Fel, Medieval Academy of Am. **RESEARCH** Medieval and Renaissance lit and hist. **SELECTED PUBLICATIONS** Auth, The Devil, Demonology, and Witchcraft: The Development of Christian Beliefs in Evil Spirits, Doubleday, 68; Divine Providence in the England of Shakespeare's Histories, Harvard Univ Press, 70; Love and Marriage in the Age of Chaucer, Cornell Univ Press, 75; The Matrimonial Trials of Henry VIII, Stanford Univ Press, 76; Canon Law and the Archpriest of Hita, SUNY, 84; The Devil at Baptism: Ritual, Theology, and Drama, Cornell Univ Press, 85; Chaucer and the Cult of St. Valentine, Davis Medieval Texts and Studies no 5, E. J. Brill, 86; Tragedy and Comedy from Dante to Pseudo-Dante, Univ CA Press, 89; Ideas and Forms of Tragedy from Aristotle to the Middle Ages, Cambridge Univ Studies in Medieval Lit, Cambridge Univ Press, 93; Chaucerian Tragedy, Chaucer Studies no 24, D. S. Brewer, 97. **CONTACT ADDRESS** Dept of English, Univ of California, Los Angeles, Los Angeles, CA, 90095. **EMAIL** kelly@humnet.ucla.edu

KELLY, JUSTIN J.
DISCIPLINE ENGLISH **EDUCATION** Yale Univ, PhD, 74 **CAREER** Univ Detroit-Mercy, 72-. **CONTACT ADDRESS** 10600 Fenkell, Detroit, MI, 48238. **EMAIL** kellyjj@udmercy.edu

KELLY, R. GORDON
DISCIPLINE AMERICAN LITERATURE **EDUCATION** DePauw Univ, BA, 61; Claremont Grad Sch, MA, 62; Univ IA, PhD, 70. **CAREER** Am Stud Dept, Univ Md **RESEARCH** Lit works as evidence in the serv of cultl analysis. **SELECTED PUBLICATIONS** Auth, Mother Was a Lady: Self and Society in Selected American Children's Periodicals, 1865-1890, Greenwood Press, 74; Literature and the Historian, Amer Quart, 74, reprinted, John Hopkins UP, 98; Edited Children's Periodicals of the United States, Greenwood Press, 84; Children's Literature and Historical Fiction, Handbook of Amer Pop Cult, Greenwood Press, 98; Mystery Fiction and Modern Life, Univ Press Miss, 98. **CONTACT ADDRESS** Am Stud Dept, Univ MD, Col Park, College Park, MD, 20742. **EMAIL** rk12@umail.umd.edu

KELLY, REBECCA
DISCIPLINE COMMUNICATION STUDIES **EDUCATION** GA State Univ, MA; PhD. **CAREER** Prof, 81-, Southern Polytech State Univ. **MEMBERSHIPS** Am Med Writers Asn. **SELECTED PUBLICATIONS** Auth, publ(s) on tchg tech; lit; about William Golding; about Anne Tyler. **CONTACT ADDRESS** Hum and Tech Commun Dept, Southern Polytech State Univ, S Marietta Pkwy, PO Box 1100, Marietta, GA, 30060.

KELLY, ROBERT LEROY
PERSONAL Born 02/06/1937, Shelton, NB, Canada, m, 1964, 2 children **DISCIPLINE** MEDIEVAL & RENAISSANCE LITERATURE **EDUCATION** St Benedict's Col, AB, 59; Univ Kans, MA, 62; Univ Ore, PhD, 69. **CAREER** Instr English, ID State Univ, 59-61 & Mt Angel Col, 66-68; asst prof, 68-74, assoc prof eng, Univ NC, Greensboro, 74. **MEMBERSHIPS** Mediaeval Acad Am; SAtlantic Mod Lang Asn; Southeastern Medieval Asn. **RESEARCH** Arthurian romance; Shakespeare; Spenser. **SELECTED PUBLICATIONS** Auth, Dactyls and curlews: Satire in A grammarian's funeral, Victorian Poetry, summer 67; Shakespeare's Scroops and the spirit of Cain, Shakespeare Quart, winter 69; Arthur, Galahad and the scriptural pattern in Malory, Am Benedictine Rev, 3/72; Hugh Latimer as Piers Plowman, Studies English Lit, 1500-1900, winter 77; Malory's Tale of Balin reconsidered, Speculum, 1/79; Malory and the Common Law: Hasty Judgement in the Tale of the Death of King Arthur, p111-139, 95; Patience as a Remedy for War in Malorys Tale of the Death of King Arthur, Studies in Philology, p111-135, 94; Wounds Healing and Knighthood in Malorys Tale Lancelot and Guinevere, Studoes in Malory, Medieval Publ, p 183-199, 85. **CONTACT ADDRESS** Dept of Eng, Univ of N. Carolina, 1000 Spring Garden, Greensboro, NC, 27412-0001. **EMAIL** kellyr@fagan.uncg.edu

KELVIN, NORMAN
PERSONAL Born 08/27/1924, New York, NY, m, 1956, 2 children **DISCIPLINE** ENGLISH LITERATURE **EDUCATION** Columbia Univ, AB, 48, MA, 50, PhD, 60. **CAREER** From Instr to Distinguished Prof English, City Col New York, 60-; from Prof to Distinguished Prof English, Grad Ctr, City Univ of New York, 84-. **HONORS AND AWARDS** Nat Endowment for Humanities sr fel, 67-68; Guggenheim fel, 74-75. **MEMBERSHIPS** MLA **RESEARCH** Nineteenth and 20th century British literature; letters of William Morris. **SELECTED PUBLICATIONS** Auth, A Troubled Eden: Nature and Society in the Works of George Meredith, Stanford Univ, 61; E M Forster, Southern Ill Univ, 67; The Collected Letters of William Morris, 4 vols, Princeton Univ Press, 84-86. **CONTACT ADDRESS** Dept of English, City Col, CUNY, 160 Convent Ave, New York, NY, 10031-9198.

KEMP, FRED O.
DISCIPLINE RHETORIC AND COMPOSITION **EDUCATION** Univ TX, Austin, PhD, 88. **CAREER** Dir, Comput Writing Res Lab, Univ TX, Austin; assoc prof, dir, Compos and Rhet, TX Tech Univ; pres, The Daedalus Gp, Inc. **HONORS AND AWARDS** EDUCOM/NCRIPTAL award, 90., Founder, The Daedalus Gp, Inc, Comput Writing Res Lab, Univ TX, Austin. **MEMBERSHIPS** Co-dir, Alliance for Comput and Writing; NCTE Instr Technol Comt; CCCC Comput in Compos Comt. **SELECTED PUBLICATIONS** Writen about computer-based writing pedag(s); coauth of Daedalus Integrated Writing Environment (software). **CONTACT ADDRESS** Texas Tech Univ, Lubbock, TX, 79409-5015. **EMAIL** F.Kemp@ttu.edu

KEMP, THERESA D.
DISCIPLINE LATE-MEDIEVAL AND EARLY MODERN BRITISH LITERATURE **EDUCATION** IN Univ, PhD, 94. **CAREER** Dept Eng, Univ Ala **HONORS AND AWARDS** Co-exec ed, Feminist Teacher; Prog Dir, UAB in Scotland. **SELECTED PUBLICATIONS** Articles: The Bloomsbury Guide Women's Lit, Shakespeare Quart, Sixteenth Century Studies, Renaissance Quart. **CONTACT ADDRESS** Univ AL, 1400 University Blvd, Birmingham, AL, 35294-1150.

KENDALL, CALVIN B.
PERSONAL Born 02/13/1935, Bronxville, NY, m, 1959, 2 children **DISCIPLINE** ENGLISH **EDUCATION** Bowdoin Col, BA, 56; Univ Calif, Berkeley, MA, 61, PhD(English), 66. **CAREER** Asst prof, 67-71, assoc prof, 71-82, prof English, Univ Minn, Minneapolis, 82-. **HONORS AND AWARDS** Horace T. Morse-Minnesota Alumni Assoc Award for Outstanding Contributions to Undergraduate Education. **MEMBERSHIPS** MLA; ISAS. **RESEARCH** Bede; Beowulf; medieval Latin poetics and rhetoric; Old English metrics; Romanesque verse inscriptions. **SELECTED PUBLICATIONS** Ed, Beda Venerabilis, De Arte Metrica et De Schmatibus et Tropis, in Corpus Christianorum 123A, Turnout, 75; auth, Bede's Historia Ecclesiastica: The Rhetoric of Faith, in Medieval Eloquence: Studies in the Theory and Practice of Medieval Rhetoric, Berkeley and Los Angelos, 78; Imitation and the Venerable Bede's Historia Ecclesiastica, in Saints, Scholars, and Heroes, Collegeville, Mn, vol 1, 79; The Prefix un-- and the Metrical Grammar of Beowulf: in Anglo-Saxon England 10 (39-52), 82; The Metrical Grammar of Beowulf: Displacement, in Speculum 58, 83; Let us Now Praise a Famous City: Wordplay in the OE Durham and the Cult of St. Cuthbert, in Journal of English and Germanic Philology 87, 88; Dry Bones in a Cathedral: The Story of the Theft of Bede's Relics and the Translation of Cuthbert into the Cathedral of Durham in 1104, in Medievalia 10, 88; The Voice in the Stone: The Verse Inscriptions of Ste.-Foy of Conques and the Date of the Tympanum, in Hermeneutics and Medieval Culture, Albany, 89; Bede's Art of Poetry and Rhetoric: The Latin Text with an English Translation, Introduction, and Notes, Saarbrucken, 91; The Metrical Grammar of Beowulf, Cambridge, 91; ed, with Peter Wells, Voyage to the Other World: The Legacy of Sutton Hoo, Minneapolis, 92. Auth, The Gate of Heaven and the Fountain of Life: Speech-Act Theory and portal Inscriptions, in Essays in Medieval Studies 10, 93; The Plan of St. Gall: An Argument for a 320-Foot Church Prototype, In Medieval Studies 56, 94; Literacy and Orality in Anglo-Saxon Poetry: Horizontal Displacement in Andreas, in Journal of English and Germanic Philology 95, 96; The Verse Inscriptions of the Tympanum of Jaca and the PAX Anagram, Mediaevalia 19, 96; The Allegory of the Church: Romanesque Portals and Their Verse Inscriptions, Toronto, 98. **CONTACT ADDRESS** Dept of English, Univ of Minn, 207 Church St S E, Minneapolis, MN, 55455-0156. **EMAIL** kenda001@maroon.tc.umn.edu

KENDALL, KATHLEEN E.
DISCIPLINE COMMUNICATION **EDUCATION** Oberlin Col, BA, 58; Univ So Miss, Hattiesburg, MA, 60; Indiana Univ, Bloomington, PhD, 66. **CAREER** Instr, speech and theatre, Allegheny Col, 60-62; tchg asst, speech and theatre, Indiana Univ, 62-64; assoc prof, dept commun, 64- , actg chemn, 69-70, 82-83, chemn, 83-86, SUNY Albany; vis scholar, dept speech commun, Univ Texas, Austin, 86; vis res scholar, Univ Maryland, College Park, 94. **HONORS AND AWARDS** Res fel, grants SUNY Albany, 67, 70, 79, 83-84, 87-88, 94-95; Goldsmith res award, Harvard Univ, 94; res fel, Harvard Univ, Joan Shorenstein Center on the Press, Politics and Public Policy, 97. **MEMBERSHIPS** Natl Commun Asn; Int Commun Asn; Am Polit Sci Asn. **RESEARCH** Political communication; presidential campaign discourse; communication in the presidential primary campaigns. **SELECTED PUBLICATIONS** Auth, Public Speaking in The Presidential Primaries Through Media Eyes, Am Behav Sci, 93; ed, Presidential Campaign Discourse: Strategic Communication Problems, SUNY, 95; coauth, Sex Differences in Political Communication During Presidential Campaigns, Commun Quart, 95; coauth, Political Images and Voting Decisions, in Hacker, ed, Candidate Images in Presidential Elections, Praeger, 95; auth, The Problem of Beginnings in New Hampshire: Control Over the Play, in Kendall, ed, Presidential Campaign Discourse: Strategic Communication Problems, SUNY, 95; coauth, Lyndon Johnson and the Problem of Politics: A Study in Conversation, in Medhurst, ed, The Future of the Rhetorical Presidency, Texas A & M, 96; auth, Presidential Debates Through Media Eyes, Am Behav Sci, 97; coauth, Influence of Communication During the Distant Phase of the 1996 Republican Primary Campaign, Jour of Commun, 97; auth, Communication Patterns in Presidential Primaries, 1912-2000: Knowing the Rules of the Game, Harvard, 98. **CONTACT ADDRESS** Dept of Communications, SUNY Univ, BA 119, Albany, NY, 12222. **EMAIL** kk724@cnsvax.albany.edu

KENDRICK, CHRISTOPHER
DISCIPLINE ENGLISH **EDUCATION** Univ Ill at Urbana, BA, 75; Yale Univ, PhD, 81. **CAREER** Assoc prof. **RESEARCH** Milton; 16th and 17th-century British literature; Marxism and theory. **SELECTED PUBLICATIONS** Auth, Preaching Common Grounds: Winstanley and the Diggers as Concrete Utopians, in Writing and the English Renaissance, Longman, 96; Agons of the Manor: Symbolic Responses to the Agrarian Crisis in mid-Seventeenth-Century England,in The Production of Renaissance Culture, Cornell UP, 94. **CONTACT ADDRESS** Dept of English, Loyola Univ, Chicago, 6525 N Sheridan Rd, Chicago, IL, 60626. **EMAIL** ckendri@wpo.it.luc.edu

KENDRICK, WALTER
DISCIPLINE VICTORIAN LITERATURE **EDUCATION** Yale Univ, PhD. **CAREER** Prof, Fordham Univ. **RESEARCH** Popular cult, pornography and censorship. **SELECTED PUBLICATIONS** Auth, The Thrill of Fear: 250 Years of Scary Entertainment, Grove Press, 91; Return to Sender: The Myth of the Death of the Letter, Village Voice Lit Supplement, 94. **CONTACT ADDRESS** Dept of Eng Lang and Lit, Fordham Univ, 113 W 60th St, New York, NY, 10023.

KENNAN, JR., WILLIAM R.
DISCIPLINE ENGLISH **EDUCATION** Dartmouth, BA, 67; Harvard Univ, PhD, 72. **CAREER** Prof. **RESEARCH** Humor; comedy; Joyce; Shakespeare; Milton; 18th century; Kingsley Amis. **SELECTED PUBLICATIONS** Auth, Jocoserious Joyce: The Fate of Folly in Ulysses; Bertrand Russell and the Eliots; Metamorphoses of Spritual Autobiography; Blushing Like the Morn: Milton's Human Comedy in Paradise Lost; James Boswell's Notes Toward a Supreme Fiction; David Hume's Fables of Identity; Dryden's Aeneid as English Augustan Epic; Sterne's Etristramolgy; Rousseau: Prophet of Sincerity. **CONTACT ADDRESS** Dept of English, Williams Col, Oakley Center, Williamstown, MA, 01267. **EMAIL** rbell@williams.edu

KENNEDY, CHRISTOPHER
DISCIPLINE ENGLISH LITERATURE **EDUCATION** Duke Univ, PhD, 79. **CAREER** Asst VP. **SELECTED PUBLICATIONS** Auth, articles on Old and Middle English lit; acad support spec admis students; intercollegiate athletics. **CONTACT ADDRESS** Eng Dept, Duke Univ, Durham, NC, 27706.

KENNEDY, GEORGE E.
DISCIPLINE LITERATURE **EDUCATION** NY Univ, PhD. **CAREER** Assoc prof & vice ch, Washington State Univ. **RESEARCH** Teaches technical writing, courses in the theory and methods of technical and professional communication. **SELECTED PUBLICATIONS** Coauth, Solving Problems Through Technical and Professional Writing, 93 & Correcting Common Errors in Writing, 96. **CONTACT ADDRESS** Dept of English, Washington State Univ, 1 SE Stadium Way, PO Box 645020, Pullman, WA, 99164-5020. **EMAIL** gkennedy@mail.wsu.edu

KENNEDY, J. GERALD
DISCIPLINE ENGLISH **EDUCATION** Grove City Col, BA, 69; Duke Univ, MA, 70, PhD, 73. **CAREER** From asst prof to assoc prof, 73-85, Prof of English, 85-97, dir, Master of Arts in Hum Prog, 84-87, William A. Read Professor of English, 97-, chemn dept, 95-98, Louisiana State Univ. **HONORS AND AWARDS** Phi Beta Kappa, 73; LSU summer res grants, 74, 76, 80, 90; NEH summer stipend, 77; Pushcart Prize Selection, 82; NEH travel grant, 88; LSU Found Distinguished Faculty Award, 93. **MEMBERSHIPS** Hemingway Found; Poe Studies Asn. **SELECTED PUBLICATIONS** Auth, The Narrative of Arthur Gordon Pym and Related Tales, Oxford, 94; auth, The Narrative of Arthur Gordon Pym and the Abyss of Interpretation, Twayne, 95; auth, Modern American Short Story Sequences: Composite Fictions and Fictions of Community, Cambridge, 95; co-ed, French Connections: Hemingway and Fitzgerald Abroad, St Martin's, 98; auth, Oxford Historical Guide to Edgar Allan Poe, Oxford, 99. **CONTACT ADDRESS** Dept of English, Louisiana State Univ, Baton Rouge, LA, 70803.

KENNEDY, WILLIAM JOHN
PERSONAL Born 04/26/1942, Brooklyn, NY, m, 1967, 2 children **DISCIPLINE** RENAISSANCE & COMPARATIVE LITERATURE **EDUCATION** Manhattan Col, BA, 63; Yale Univ, PhD(comp lit), 69. **CAREER** Instr Eng, Fairleigh Dickinson Univ, 67-70; asst prof comp lit, 70-76, assoc prof, 76-82, Prof comp lit, Cornell Univ, 82-, Vis assoc prof comp lit, NY Univ, 82. **HONORS AND AWARDS** Guggenheim fel 87-88; Villa Serbelloni, 98. **MEMBERSHIPS** MLA; Am Comp Lit Asn; Renaissance Soc Am. **RESEARCH** Lit theory; rhetorical criticism; lyric poetry. **SELECTED PUBLICATIONS** Auth, Rhetorical Norms in Renaissance Literature, Yale Univ Press, 78; Jacopo Sannazaro, VNIV New England Press, 83; Authorizing Petrarch, Cornell Univ Press, 94. **CONTACT ADDRESS** Comp Lit Dept, Cornell Univ, Ithaca, NY, 14850. **EMAIL** WJK3@cornell.edu

KENNELLY, LAURA B.
DISCIPLINE ENGLISH **EDUCATION** Univ N Texas, PhD, 75. **CAREER** Adj prof, Eng, Univ N Texas; current, IND SCH. **MEMBERSHIPS** Am Antiquarian Soc **CONTACT ADDRESS** PO Box 626, Berea, OH, 44017. **EMAIL** LKennelly@aol.com

KENT, CAROL FLEISHER
DISCIPLINE ENGLISH LITERATURE **EDUCATION** Univ NY, BA; Bread Loaf Sch English, MA; Brown Univ, PhD. **CAREER** Eng Dept, Georgetown Univ **RESEARCH** Modern literature and film. **SELECTED PUBLICATIONS** Auth, pubs on O'Connor and Hitchcock. **CONTACT ADDRESS** English Dept, Georgetown Univ, 37th and O St, Washington, DC, 20057.

KERBY-FULTON, KATHRYN
DISCIPLINE MIDDLE ENGLISH LITERATURE **EDUCATION** Univ York, BA, Bed; York, Eng, PhD. **CAREER** Prof

RESEARCH Medieval Latin religious writings; medieval women's literature. **SELECTED PUBLICATIONS** Auth, Reformist Apocalypticism and Piers Plowman, Cambridge UP, 90; Written Work: Langland, Labour and Authorship, U of Pennsylvania P; 97; Iconography and the Professional Reader: The Politics of Book Production in the Donce Piers Plowman, U of Minnesota P, 98. **CONTACT ADDRESS** Dept of English, Victoria Univ, PO Box 3070, Victoria, BC, V8W 3W1.

KERN-FOXWORTH, MARILYN L.
PERSONAL Born 03/04/1954, Kosciusko, Mississippi, m, 1982 **DISCIPLINE** SPEECH **EDUCATION** Jackson State Univ, BS Speech 1974; FL State Univ, MS Mass Communications 1976; Univ of WI-Madison, PhD Mass Communications 1982. **CAREER** FL State Univ, comm specialist 1974-76; General Telephone, personnel rep 1976-78; Univ of TN, asst prof 1980-87; Texas A&M Univ, assoc prof, 1987-. **HONORS AND AWARDS** Valedictorian of graduate class 1974; Readers Digest travel grant 1979; 1st prize Alan Bussel Rsch Competition 1980; Leadership Award Assn of Black Comm 1980; Kizzy Award Black Women Hall of Fame Found 1981; PR Fellow Aloca Professional 1981; Amon Carter Evans Awd Scholar 1983; Women of Achievement Univ of TN 1983; Unity Awards in Media 2nd Place Lincoln Univ 1984. **MEMBERSHIPS** Exec comm Assn for Educ in Journalism 1980-; mem Natl Council of Negro Women 1980-; mem Assn of Black Communicators 1980-; mem Natl Comm Assn 1982-; mem Intl Platform Assn 1982-; advisor Campus Practitioners 1982; mem Public Relations Soc of Amer 1982-; consultant/assoc editor Nashville Banner 1983; minister of educ Mt Calvary Baptist Church 1983; staff mem Graduate Teaching Seminary 1983-; adviser Public Relations Student Soc of Amer 1983-; mem Natl Fed of Press Women 1983-; mem Natl Assn of Media Women 1983-; mem Natl Fed of Exec Women 1983-; advisory comm Phillis Wheatley YWCA 1983-; mem Black Media Assn; Black Faculty & Staff Assn newsletter editor; regional corres Still Here. **SELECTED PUBLICATIONS** "Helping Minorities, Student Organizations Can Fill Gaps in Minority Programs" Journalism Editor 1982, "Advertising More Than a Black Face" Black Journalism Review 1981, "A Challenge to Your Future GTE Automatic Electric" 1977, "All Minority Grads-Opportunity Is Knocking" 1982; 1st & only black in the nation to receive a PhD in Mass communications with a concentration in advertising & public relations; Speciaward Recognition of Excellence PRSA Chap Knoxville TN 1985; author Alex Haley's bio for Dictionary of Literary Biography, Afro-American Writers After 1955 published 1985; PRSA, advisor of the year 1985; Poynter Institute Fellow, 1988; Amer Press Institute Fellow, 1988; Pathfinder Award, Public Relation Institute, 1988; Agnes Harris AAUW Postdoctoral Fellow, 1991-92. **CONTACT ADDRESS** Texas A&M Univ, 230 Reed McDonald Building, College Station, TX, 77843-4111.

KERSHNER, R. BRANDON
PERSONAL m, 3 children **DISCIPLINE** ENGLISH AND COMPARATIVE LITERATURE **EDUCATION** Johns Hopkins Univ, BA, 66; MA, 66; Stanford Univ, MA, 68; PhD, 72. **CAREER** Grad tchg asst, Stanford Univ, 68-69; asst prof, 71-76; vis prof, Univ Utrecht, 78; vis prof, Univ Col Dublin, 84; vis prof, Univ Utrecht, 94; ch, SAMLA, 90; assoc prof, 76-90; prof, 90-. **HONORS AND AWARDS** Danforth fel, 66-72; Woodrow Wilson fel, 66; Amer Conf on Irish Stud award, 90; res grant, 93. **MEMBERSHIPS** Mem, SSAMLA; MLA; Intl James Joyce Found; Amer Conf Irish Stud. **RESEARCH** James Joyce. **SELECTED PUBLICATIONS** Auth, Dylan Thomas: The Poet and His Critics Chicago: Amer Lib Assn, 77; Joyce, Bakhtin and Popular Literature: Chronicles of Disorder, Univ NC Press, 89; The Twentieth-Century Novel: An Introduction, St Martin's Press, 97; ed, James Joyce, A Portrait of the Artist as a Young Man, St. Martin's Press, 92. **CONTACT ADDRESS** Dept of Eng, Univ Fla, 226 Tigert Hall, Gainesville, FL, 32611. **EMAIL** rbkersh@nervm.nerdc.ufl.edu

KESHISHIAN, FLORA
PERSONAL Born 07/23/1954, Tehran, Iran **DISCIPLINE** COMMUNICATION **EDUCATION** NYU, PhD, 95. **CAREER** Adj Asst Prof, 91-, NYU & Queens Coll, Asst Prof, 97-, Montclair State Univ. **HONORS AND AWARDS** Reviewer, Critical Studies in Mass Communication. **MEMBERSHIPS** ICA, NCA, ECA, NYSCA. **RESEARCH** Culture & communication technology, language & culture, orality, politico-economic systems & culture. **SELECTED PUBLICATIONS** Auth, Political Bias and Nonpolitical News, A Content Analysis of an Armenian and Iranian Earthquake in the New York Times and the Washington Post, in: Critical Studies in Mass Communication, 97. **CONTACT ADDRESS** 167-09 65th Ave, Flushing, NY, 11365. **EMAIL** keshishianf@saturn.montclair.edu

KESSLER, ROD
PERSONAL Born 09/15/1949, Brooklyn, NY, m, 1990, 1 child **DISCIPLINE** ENGLISH **EDUCATION** Harvard, AB, 71; Univ Mass - Amherst, MS, 77; Univ Arizona, MFA, 81. **CAREER** Instr, 78, Greenfield Comm Col; writer in res, 82, Phillips Exeter Acad; prof, 83-87, Salem St Col. **CONTACT ADDRESS** English Dept, Salem St Col, 352 Lafayette St, Salem, MA, 01970-5353. **EMAIL** rkessler@salem.mass.edu

KESTERSON, DAVID BERT
PERSONAL Born 09/02/1934, Dundonald, Northern Ireland, m, 1961, 1 child **DISCIPLINE** ENGLISH **EDUCATION** Univ Liverpool, BA, 56; Univ Birmingham, PhD(English), 63. **CAREER** Instr English, Univ MI, 59-61; lectr, Univ Western Ont, 61-63; from asst prof to assoc prof, Univ MI, 63-69; assoc prof, 69-75, Prof English, Gwent Allen Smith Prof English, Mt Holyoke Col, 75-; vis assoc prof English, Dartmouth Col, 68-69. **MEMBERSHIPS** Int Byron Soc; Renaissance Soc of Am; Renaissance English Text Soc; Byron Soc; Chesterton Soc. **RESEARCH** Shakespeare; Skelton; Southwell; music and literature. **SELECTED PUBLICATIONS** Auth, Two Shakespearean Sequences, Macmillan & Univ Pittsburgh, 77; Shakespeare, Harsnett, and the Devils of Denham, DE Univ Press, 93; Robert Southwell, Twayne, 96; ed, Skelton, The Book of the Laurel, DE Univ Press, 91. **CONTACT ADDRESS** Mount Holyoke Col, 50 College St, South Hadley, MA, 01075-1461. **EMAIL** fbrownlo@mhc.mtholyoke.edu

KETNER, KENNETH LAINE
PERSONAL Born 03/24/1939, Mountain Home, OK, m, 1963, 1 child **DISCIPLINE** PHILOSOPHY, FOLKLORISTICS **EDUCATION** OK State Univ, BA, 61, MA, 67; Univ CA, Los Angeles, MA, 68; Univ CA, Santa Barbara, PhD(philos), 72. **CAREER** Instr philos, OK State Univ, 64-67; res asst folklore, Univ CA, Los Angeles, 67-68; teaching asst philos, Univ CA, Santa Barbara, 69-70; asst prof, 71-75, assoc prof, 75-77, Prof, 77-81, Peirce Prof Philos, TX Tech Univ, 81-, Dir Iinst Studies In Pragmaticism, 72-. **HONORS AND AWARDS** Research Merit Award, TX Tech Univ, 80. **MEMBERSHIPS** Am Philos Asn; Charles S Pierce Soc (pres, 78). **RESEARCH** Am philos, philosophical anthropology; folkloristic method and theory. **SELECTED PUBLICATIONS** Auth, The role of Hypotheses in Folkloristics, J Am Folklore, 86: 114-130; An Emendation of R G Collingwood's doctrine of asolute presuppositions, Grad Studies TX Tech Univ, 7/73; A Comprehensive Bibliography of the Published Works of Charles S Peirce, KTO Microform, 77; Charles S Peirce: Contributions to the Nation, TX Tech Univ, 78; Proceedings, Peirce Bicentennial Int Congress, TX Tech Univ, 81. **CONTACT ADDRESS** Institute for Studies in Pragmaticism, Texas Tech Univ, Room 304A Library, Lubbock, TX, 79409-0002. **EMAIL** B90Ky@ttacs.ttu.edu

KETROW, SANDRA M.
PERSONAL Born 05/20/1949, Indianapolis, IN **DISCIPLINE** SPEECH COMMUNICATION **EDUCATION** AB, 71, MS, 78, PhD, 82, Ind Univ. **CAREER** Teacher, eng, Lawrenceburg High Sch, 76-78; assoc instr/ed asst, dept of speech comm, Ind Univ & Central States Speech Jour, 78-81; asst prof & dir of pub speaking, dept of speech, Univ Fla, 81-84; visiting asst & adjunct prof, dept of speech, Butler Univ, 84-86; asst prof, 86-92, assoc prof, 92-98, prof & dir of grad prog, 98-, dept of speech comm, Univ RI. **HONORS AND AWARDS** Fel, Teaching & Tech, Univ RI, 97-98; World Who's Who of Women, 95-; Who's Who of Intl Women, 94-; Who's Who of Bus & Professional Women, 93-; Who's Who of Amer Women, 93-. **MEMBERSHIPS** Nat Comm Asn; Intl Comm Asn; Eastern Comm Asn. **RESEARCH** Nonverbal communication; Argumentation in groups. **SELECTED PUBLICATIONS** Co-auth, Processes and Outcomes Related to Non-Rational Argument in Societal Groups, Argument in a Time of Change: Proceedings of the Tenth AFA/SCA Argumentation Conference, 103-109, Nat Comm Asn, 98; co-auth, Social Anxiety and Performance in an Interpersonal Perception Task, Psychological Reports, 81, 991-996, 97; co-auth, Improving Decision Quality in the Small Group: The Role of the Reminder, Small Group Communication, 404-410, 97; auth, Is it Homophobia, Heterosexism, Sexism, or Can I Pass?, Lesbians in Academia: Degrees of Freedom, 106-112, NY, Routledge, 97; co-auth, Improving Decision Making in the Group: Arguing with Constructive Intent, Proceedings of the Ninth AFA/SCA Argumentation Conference, Speech Comm Asn, 95; co-auth, Improving Decision Quality in the Small Group: The Role of the Reminder, Small Group Research, 26, 4, 521-541, 95; co-auth, Using Argumentative Functions to Improve Decision Quality in the Small Group, Argument and the Postmodern Challenge: Proceedings of the Eighth AFA/SCA Argumentation Conference, 218-225, Speech Comm Asn, 93. **CONTACT ADDRESS** Dept. of Communication Studies, Univ of Rhode Island, 60 Upper College Rd., Suite 1, Kingston, RI, 02881-0812. **EMAIL** ketrow@uriacc.uri.edu

KEY, WILSON B.
PERSONAL Calif, s, 5 children **DISCIPLINE** COMMUNICATION **EDUCATION** Mex City Col, BA, 51; UCLA, MA, 53; Denver Univ, PhD, 71. **CAREER** Asst prof of Journalism, Boston Univ; res dir, Publicidad Badillo; pres, res & market development; assoc prof of mass commun, Univ of Western Ontario; Pres, Mediaprobe Inc. **MEMBERSHIPS** Mensa Int; Speech-Commun Asn; AAUP. **RESEARCH** Subliminal aspects of communication; general semantics. **SELECTED PUBLICATIONS** Auth, Age of Manipulation, Henry Holt; Clam-Plate Orgy, Prentice Hall; Media Sexploitation, Prentice Hall; Subliminal Seduction, Prentice Hall. **CONTACT ADDRESS** 150 E Laramie Dr., Reno, NV, 89511.

KEYES, CLAIRE J.
PERSONAL Born 11/02/1938, Boston, MA, m, 1987 **DISCIPLINE** ENGLISH **EDUCATION** Boston State College, BS 60, MA 63; Univ Mass, PhD 80. **CAREER** Salem State College, prof eng, 66-96, prof emer, 96-. **HONORS AND AWARDS** Helene Wurlitzer Gnt; Poetry Finalist MA Artist Foun; Awd for Excell Grad Sch. **MEMBERSHIPS** MELUS; ASA; NEMLA; ASAIL; Phi Beta Phi. **RESEARCH** Amer Women Poets; American Indian Lit. **SELECTED PUBLICATIONS** Auth, I'm a Montano: Leslie Marmon Silko's Transformation of the Yellow Women Muth in Ceremony, Jour of Lit Stud, Capetown SA, 98; Pattian Rogers and the New Science, Sycamore, 98; Between Ruin and Celebration, Joy Hardjo's, in: In Mad Love and War, Borderlines, Swansea Wales, 97; Geronimo Jerome, Sextant, Jour of Salem State Coll, 96. **CONTACT ADDRESS** Dept of English, Salem State Col, 12 Higgins Rd, Marblehead, MA, 01945. **EMAIL** CKEYES@salem.mass.edu

KEYISHIAN, HARRY
PERSONAL Born 04/09/1932, New York, NY, m, 1966, 4 children **DISCIPLINE** ENGLISH LITERATURE **EDUCATION** Queens Col (NY), BA, 54; NY Univ, MA, 57, PhD, 65. **CAREER** Asst instr English, Univ Md Overseas Proj, Newfoundland, 57-58; lectr, City Col New York, 59-60; instr, Bronx Community Col, 61 & Univ Buffalo, 61-64; from asst prof to assoc prof, 65-73, chmn dept, 72-74, Prof English, Fairleigh Dickinson Univ, Madison, 73-, dir, Fairleigh Dickinson Univ Press, 76-; ed, The Lit Rev, 76-. **HONORS AND AWARDS** Grants from NEH, NJ Coun on the Humanities, NJ Dept of Higher Educ, Mennen Found. **MEMBERSHIPS** MLA; Renaissance Soc Am; Northeast Mod Lang Asn; Shakespeare Asn Am. **RESEARCH** Elizabethan drama and Shakespeare; revenge themes in literature; 20th century fiction; film; performance criticism; advertising. **SELECTED PUBLICATIONS** Auth, Michael Arlen, Twayne, 75; Cross-Currents of Revenge in James's The American, in Mod Lang Studies, Spring 87; The NJ Shakespeare Festival's The Merchant of Venice: A Case Study, in On-Stage Studies, Spring 87; Vindictiveness and the Search for Glory in Frankenstein, in Am J Psychoanalysis, 9/89; The Shapes of Revenge: Victimization, Vengeance, and Vindictiveness in Shakespeare, Humanities Press, 95; ed, Critical Essays on William Saroyan, Twayne Publ, 95; Performing Violence in King Lear, in Shakespeare Bull, Summer 96; Michael Arlen, in Am Nat Biog, Oxford Univ Press, 98; author of several other journal articles. **CONTACT ADDRESS** Dept of English, Fairleigh Dickinson Univ, 285 Madison Ave, Madison, NJ, 07940-1099. **EMAIL** harry@alpha.fdu.edu

KEYSSAR, HELENE
DISCIPLINE COMMUNICATIONS **EDUCATION** Univ Iowa, PhD, Mod Letters, 74. **CAREER** PROF, COMMUN, UNIV CALIF, SAN DIEGO. **RESEARCH** Feminist theatre. **SELECTED PUBLICATIONS** Auth, Feminist Theatre: An Introduction to Plays of Contemporary British and American Women, Macmillan, 85; Robert Altman's America, Oxford, 91; co-auth, Remembering War: A US-Soviet Dialogue on World War II, Oxford, 90. **CONTACT ADDRESS** Dept of Commun, Univ Calif, San Diego, 9500 Gilman Dr, La Jolla, CA, 92093. **EMAIL** hkeyssar@weber.ucsd.edu

KEZAR, DENNIS
DISCIPLINE ENGLISH RENAISSANCE LITERATURE **EDUCATION** Univ Va, PhD. **CAREER** Instr, Vanderbilt Univ. **RESEARCH** Shakespeare's poetic responses to early modern theatricalism; Milton's representations of death and violence. **SELECTED PUBLICATIONS** Auth, The Properties of Shakespeare's Globe, Eng Lit Renaissance; Shakespeare's Rome in Milton's Gaza?, Eng Lang Notes; Milton's 'Careful Ploughman', Notes & Queries; John Skelton's Fictive Text and the Manufacture of Fame, Renaissance Papers; Radical Letters and Male Genealogies in Johnson's Dictionary, Stud in Eng Lit. **CONTACT ADDRESS** Vanderbilt Univ, Nashville, TN, 37203-1727.

KHARPERTIAN, THEODORE
PERSONAL Born 01/21/1949, Jersey City, NJ, m, 1982, 2 children **DISCIPLINE** LITERATURE **EDUCATION** Univ of PA, Ba, 70; Mcgill Univ, MA, 71, PhD, 85 **CAREER** Prof, 79-, Hudson Co Comnty col; Lect, 88-93, Rutgers Univ **MEMBERSHIPS** Mod Lang Asn **RESEARCH** Satire **SELECTED PUBLICATIONS** Auth, A Hand to Turn the Time: The Menippean Satires of Thomas Pynchon, Associated Univ Presses, 90; Hagop: A Memoir of my Father, National Association for Armenian Studies and Research, forthcom **CONTACT ADDRESS** Dept of Eng and Humanities, Hudson County Comm Col, Jersey City, NJ, 07306. **EMAIL** tkharpertian@hotmail.com

KHATIB, SYED MALIK
PERSONAL Born 05/07/1940, Trenton, NJ **DISCIPLINE** COMMUNICATIONS **EDUCATION** Trenton State Coll, BA 1962; UCLA, diploma African Studies 1962; MI State Univ, MA 1966, PhD 1968. **CAREER** Stanford Univ, asst prof 1969-75; SF State Univ, assoc prof 1978-82; Princeton Univ, visiting lecturer 1984; Trenton State Prison MCC, instructor 1985; Rahway State Prison MCC, instructor 1985; Mercer Coll, adjunct assoc prof; SUNY at New Paltz, Department of African-

American Studies, associate professor, chairman, 1985-88; MARIST COLLEGE, ASSOCIATE PROF OF COMMUNICATION, 1988-. **HONORS AND AWARDS** Dean's Honor List Trenton State Univ 1960; NDEA Fellow MI State Univ 1965-67; Postdoctoral Fellow Univ of PA 1968; Issue Editor Journal of Social Issues vol 29, 1973; mem editorial bd Journal of Black Psychology, 1974-76; recipient, Comm Serv Award Bay Area, 1975. **MEMBERSHIPS** Mem editorial bd Assn of Black Psychologists 1970; consultant SRI 1970; SSRC 1971; HEW 1972; 10 publications in the areas of methodology philosophy & psychology. **CONTACT ADDRESS** PO Box 878, New Paltz, NY, 12561.

KIBLER, JAMES EVERETT, JR.
DISCIPLINE ENGLISH **CAREER** PROF OF ENGLISH, UNIV GA. **SELECTED PUBLICATIONS** Ed, Selected Poems of William Gilmore Simms, Univ Ga Press, 90; Poetry and the Practical, Univ Ark Press, 96; The Simms Review 1993-1998; auth, Our Fathers' Fields, Univ SC Press, 98. **CONTACT ADDRESS** Dept of English, Univ Ga, Park Hall, Athens, GA, 30602.

KIEFER, KATE
DISCIPLINE ENGLISH LITERATURE **EDUCATION** Univ Dayton, BA; Ohio State Univ, MA, PhD. **CAREER** Prof. **SELECTED PUBLICATIONS** Auth, pubs on computers and composition. **CONTACT ADDRESS** Dept of English, Colorado State Univ, Fort Collins, CO, 80523. **EMAIL** kkiefer@vines.colostate.edu

KIEFER, LAUREN
DISCIPLINE ENGLISH **EDUCATION** Stanford Univ, BA; Cornell Univ, PhD, 93. **CAREER** Eng Dept, Plattsburgh State Univ **RESEARCH** Middle Eng, medieval Latin, and Old French lit(s), particularly from the 14th century. **SELECTED PUBLICATIONS** Auth, publ(s) on Medieval lit; articles on John Gower's Confession. **CONTACT ADDRESS** SUNY, Plattsburgh, 101 Broad St, Plattsburgh, NY, 12901-2681.

KIERNAN, MICHAEL TERENCE
PERSONAL Born 06/14/1940, New York, NY, m, 1964, 1 child **DISCIPLINE** ENGLISH LITERATURE **EDUCATION** Fairfield Univ, BA, 62; Marquette Univ, MA, 64; Harvard Univ, PhD(English), 71. **CAREER** Ed asst, Renascence, 62-64; teaching fel English, Harvard Univ, 67-71; Mather house resident tutor, 70-71, assoc mem grad fac, 73-79, asst prof, 71-77, assoc prof English, Pa State Univ, University Park, 77-, sr mem grad fac, 79-, Am Coun Learned Soc grant-in-aid, 72 & 78; Nat Endowment for Humanities-Folger Shakespeare Libr fel, 78; Am Philos Soc grant, 79, 87; Nat Endowment for Humanities-Huntington Libr res fel, 80; res fel, Huntington Libr, 86. **MEMBERSHIPS** Malone Soc; Renaissance Soc Am; Renaissance English Text Soc. **RESEARCH** Francis Bacon; Renaissance drama, especially Shakespeare; textual editing. **SELECTED PUBLICATIONS** Ed asst, The Plays of George Chapman: The Comedies: A Critical Edition, Univ Ill, Urbana, 70; auth, The order and dating of the 1613 editions of Bacon's Essays, Library, London, 12/74; ed, Henry the Fourth, Part One: A Bibliography to Supplement the New Variorum Edition of 1936 and the Supplement of 1956, Mod Lang Asn Am, 77; ed, Sir Francis Bacon: The Essayes or Counsels, Harvard Univ Press & Clarendon Press, 85; Sir Francis Bacon: The Advancement of Learning Vol 4, The Oxford Francis Bacon, Oxford, forthcoming; Sir Francis Bacon: The Essayes or Counsels Vol 15, The Oxford Francis Bacon, Oxford, forthcoming. **CONTACT ADDRESS** Dept of English, Pennsylvania State Univ, 117 Burrowes Bldg, University Park, PA, 16802-6200. **EMAIL** mtk@psu.edu

KIESSLING, NICOLAS
DISCIPLINE MEDIEVAL AND RENAISSANCE LITERATURE **EDUCATION** Univ Wis, PhD. **CAREER** Prof & actg dir Grad Stud, Washington State Univ. **SELECTED PUBLICATIONS** Auth, The Incubus in English Literature, 77; The Library of Robert Burton, 88 & The Legacy of Democritus Junior, Robert Burton, 90; co-ed, 3 vol critical ed, Burton's The Anatomy of Melancholy, Clarendon Press, 88-94. **CONTACT ADDRESS** Dept of English, Washington State Univ, 1 SE Stadium Way, PO Box 645020, Pullman, WA, 99164-5020. **EMAIL** kiesslin@wsu.edu

KIJINSKI, JOHN
DISCIPLINE ENGLISH LITERATURE **EDUCATION** Univ Wis, PhD, 85. **CAREER** Assoc prof. **RESEARCH** Victorian literature. **SELECTED PUBLICATIONS** Auth, pubs in Victorian Literature and Culture, Victorian Studies, and English Literature in Transition. **CONTACT ADDRESS** Dept of English and Philosophy, Idaho State Univ, Pocatello, ID, 83209. **EMAIL** kijijohn@isu.edu

KILLAM, G. DOUGLAS
PERSONAL Born 08/26/1930, New Westminster, BC, Canada **DISCIPLINE** ENGLISH **EDUCATION** Univ BC, BA, 54; Univ London, PhD, 64. **CAREER** Tchr, Sierra Leone, 63-65; tchr, Nigeria, 67-68; fac mem, York Univ, 68-73; tchr, Tanzania, 70-72; fac mem, 74-77, head Eng, 74-76, dean arts, Acadia Univ, 76-77; PROF ENGLISH, UNIV GUELPH, 77-. **MEMBERSHIPS** Asn Commonwealth Lit Lang Stud; Asn Can Univ Tchrs Eng; Can Asn African Stud; Int Asn Univ Profs Eng. **SELECTED PUBLICATIONS** Auth, Africa in English Fiction, 68; auth, Novels of Chinua Achebe, 68; auth, African Writers on African Writing, 72; auth, An Introduction to the Writings of Ngugi, 80; auth, Critical Perspectives on Ngugi, 85; ed, The Oxford Companion to African Literature: East and Central African Literatures in English, 79-89; co-ed, Can J African Stud, 79-81. **CONTACT ADDRESS** PO Box 112, Portland, ON, K0G 1V0.

KIM, SOON JIN
DISCIPLINE COMMUNICATION **EDUCATION** Univ MD, PhD, 82. **CAREER** Instr, Towson Univ. **HONORS AND AWARDS** 5 major grants from Tinker Found and US State Dept. **RESEARCH** China's world news agency, XINUA. **SELECTED PUBLICATIONS** Auth of a hardback on Spain's world news agency, EFE. **CONTACT ADDRESS** Towson Univ, Towson, MD, 21252-0001. **EMAIL** skim@towson.edu

KIME, WAYNE R.
DISCIPLINE ENGLISH LITERATURE **EDUCATION** Stanford Univ, BA; Univ DE, MA and PhD. **CAREER** Prof, 78-, Fairleigh Dickinson Univ. **RESEARCH** Literary and historical research in early Am studies; Richard Irving Dodge; Fitz-James O'Brien; and James Kirke Paulding. **SELECTED PUBLICATIONS** Auth, articles and books with subject matter addressing early Am studies. **CONTACT ADDRESS** Fairleigh Dickinson Univ, 1000 River Rd, Teaneck, NJ, 07666. **EMAIL** wrk@fscvax.fairmont.wvnet.edu

KIMNACH, WILSON H.
DISCIPLINE ENGLISH **EDUCATION** Brown Univ, BA, 60; Univ Penn, MA, 62, PhD, 71. **CAREER** Affil prof, Eng, Clark; current, PROF, ENG & PRESIDENTIAL PROF, HUM, BRIDGEPORT. **MEMBERSHIPS** Am Antiquarian Soc **SELECTED PUBLICATIONS** Ed, Sermons and Discourses, 1720-1723, vol 10 of the Works of Jonathan Edwards, Yale Univ Press, 92. **CONTACT ADDRESS** 59 Beecher Rd, Woodbridge, CT, 06525.

KING, JAMES
DISCIPLINE ENGLISH LITERATURE **EDUCATION** Univ Toronto, BA; Princeton Univ, MA, PhD. **RESEARCH** 20th century English lit and art; biography. **SELECTED PUBLICATIONS** Auth, William Cowper: a Biography, 86; auth, Interior Landscapes: a Life of Paul Nash, 87; auth, The Last Modern: a Life of Herbert Read, 90; auth, William Blake: His Life, 92; auth, Virginia Woolf, 94; auth, Margaret Laurence, 97. **CONTACT ADDRESS** English Dept, McMaster Univ, 1280 Main St W, Hamilton, ON, L8S 4L9.

KING, KATHLEEN
DISCIPLINE ENGLISH LITERATURE **EDUCATION** Univ Nebr, PhD, 84. **CAREER** Assoc prof. **RESEARCH** Computers and education; the writing of fiction and poetry; online teaching; and distance learning. **SELECTED PUBLICATIONS** Auth, Cricket Sings; Going Online: Computerized Courses for Distant Learners. **CONTACT ADDRESS** Dept of English and Philosophy, Idaho State Univ, Pocatello, ID, 83209. **EMAIL** kingkath@isu.edu

KING, PAUL E.
PERSONAL Born 10/07/1955, Fort Stockton, TX, m, 1977, 2 children **DISCIPLINE** SPEECH COMMUNICATION **EDUCATION** Univ North Tx, PhD, 85. **CAREER** ASSOC PROF, TX CHRISTIAN UNIV, 85-. **HONORS AND AWARDS** Fine Arts & Commun Col Teaching Award; Pi Kappa Delta; Pi Gamma Mu. **MEMBERSHIPS** ICA; SCA; SSCA. **RESEARCH** Information processing; interpersonal influence. **SELECTED PUBLICATIONS** Auth, Surviving an appointment as department chair, J of the Asn for Commun Admin, 97; coauth, Mindfulness, mindlessness, and communication instruction, Commun Ed, 98; A case study of the Weberian leadership of Joseph Smith, The J of Commun and Religion, 98; Compliance-gaining strategies, communication satisfaction, and willingness to comply, Commun Reports, 94; Contagion theory and the communication of public speaking anxiety, Commun Ed, 94. **CONTACT ADDRESS** Speech Commun Dept, Texas Christian Univ, Box 298000, Ft. Worth, TX, 76129.

KING, ROGER
PERSONAL Born 03/14/1947, London, England **DISCIPLINE** SOCIO-ECONOMICS; CREATIVE WRITER **EDUCATION** Univ Nottingham, UK, BSc, 69; Univ Mass, MS, 72; Univ Reading, UK, PhD, 77. **CAREER** Lectr, res fel, agric econ, Ahmadu/Bello Univ, Nigeria, 72-74; res off, rural develop, Univ Reading, UK, 74-79; consult, rural develop in Africa and Asia for UN, 79-90; vis prof, creative writing, Eastern Washington Univ, 90-91; assoc prof, creative writing, San Francisco State Univ, 94-97; self-employed writer, 97-. **HONORS AND AWARDS** Yaddo Fel; Breadloaf Fel. **MEMBERSHIPS** PEN. **RESEARCH** Relationship between international economic change, the lives of the poor, and the movement of people; relationship of social change, creative expression and freedoms. **SELECTED PUBLICATIONS** Auth, Horizontal Hotel, Andre Deutsch, 83; auth, The Development Game, Grantazo, 86; auth, Written on A Stranger Map, Grafton-Collins, 87; auth, Sea Level, Poseidon, 92. **CONTACT ADDRESS** 154 Shutesbury Rd, Leverett, MA, 01056. **EMAIL** rogerking1@aol.com

KING, SHELLEY
DISCIPLINE ENGLISH LITERATURE **EDUCATION** Univ Toronto, PhD. **CAREER** Dept Eng, Queen's Univ **RESEARCH** Romantic and Victorian fiction; children's literature. **SELECTED PUBLICATIONS** Co-ed, Adeline Mowrbray, 98. **CONTACT ADDRESS** English Dept, Queen's Univ, Kingston, ON, K7L 3N6. **EMAIL** kings@qsilver.queensu.ca

KINNAMON, KENETH
DISCIPLINE AFRICAN AMERICAN LITERATURE **EDUCATION** Harvard Univ, PhD. **CAREER** English and Lit, Univ Ark. **SELECTED PUBLICATIONS** Auth, Black Writers of America: A Comprehensive Anthology, Macmillan, 72; The Emergence of Richard Wright, Ill, 72; A Richard Wright Bibliography: Fifty Years of Criticism and Commentary, 1933-1982, Greenwood, 82; How Native Son Was Born, Writing Am Classics, 90; Ed, New Essays on Native Son, Cambridge, 90; Conversations With Richard Wright, Miss, 93; Critical Essays on Richard Wright's "Native Son", G K Hall, 97. **CONTACT ADDRESS** Univ Ark, Fayetteville, AR, 72701.

KINNAMON, NOEL JAMES
PERSONAL Born 09/06/1943, Winston-Salem, NC **DISCIPLINE** ENGLISH **EDUCATION** Duke Univ, AB, 65; Univ NC, Chapel Hill, MA, 66, PhD(English), 76. **CAREER** ASSOC PROF ENGLISH, MARS HILL COL, 66- **MEMBERSHIPS** MLA; SAtlantic Mod Lang Asn; Southeastern Renaissance Conf. **RESEARCH** Renaissance English literature; medieval English literature. **SELECTED PUBLICATIONS** Auth, Recent Studies in Renaissance English Manuscripts, Eng Lit Renaissance 2, 97; God's Scholer: The Countess of Pembroke's Psalms and Beza's Psalmorum Davidis... Libri Quinque, Notes and Queries, 1, 97; The Collected Works of Mary Sidney Herbert, Countess of Pembroke, Clarendon Press, 98. **CONTACT ADDRESS** Dept of English, Mars Hill Col, Mars Hill, NC, 28754. **EMAIL** nkinnamon@mhc.edu

KINNEY, ARTHUR F.
PERSONAL Born 09/05/1933, Cortland, NY **DISCIPLINE** ENGLISH **EDUCATION** Syracuse Univ, BA, 55; Columbia Univ, MS, 56; Univ Mich, Ann Arbor, PhD, 63. **CAREER** Act instr, Yale Univ, 63-66; from asst prof, 66-68, to assoc prof, 69-75, prof, 75- and Thomas W. Copeland Prof of Lit Hist, Univ Mass, Amherst; adj prof Engl, NY Univ; dir, Mass Ctr for Renaissance Stud, 97- . **HONORS AND AWARDS** Magna cum Laude, 55; Chancellor's Medal; Univ Res Fel; Distinguished Tchg Award; Morse Fel; NEH Sr Fel; Folger Sr Fel; Huntington Sr Fel; Bread Loaf Scholar. **MEMBERSHIPS** Renaissance Eng Text Soc; Shakespeare Asn of Am; Renaissance Soc of Am; ed, Eng Lit Renaissance; ed, Mass Stud in Early Modern Culture series; ed, Twayne Eng Authors in the Renaissance series. **RESEARCH** English literary history and cultural studies; Faulkner and the American South. **SELECTED PUBLICATIONS** Auth, John Skelton: The Priest as Poet; auth, Rogues, Vagabonds, and Sturdy Beggars; auth, Renaissance Historicism; auth, Classical, Renaissance and Postmodernist Acts of the Imagination: Essays Commemorating O.B. Hardison, Jr.; auth, Poetics and Praxis: Understanding and Imagination: The Collected Essays of O.B. Hardison, Jr.; auth, Critical Essays on William Faulkner: The Sutpen Family; auth, Go Down, Moses: The Miscegenation of Time: auth, Approaches to Teaching The Sound and the Fury; ed, The Witch of Edmonton; ed, Cambridge Companion to English Literature, 1500-1600; auth, Dorothy Parker, Revisited, 2d ed. **CONTACT ADDRESS** 25 Hunter Hill Dr, Amherst, MA, 01002. **EMAIL** afkinney@english.umass.edu

KINNEY, JAMES JOSEPH
PERSONAL Born 03/11/1942, Utica, NY **DISCIPLINE** ENGLISH **EDUCATION** St Bonaventure Univ, BA, 64; Univ TN, PhD(English), 72. **CAREER** Instr English, Univ TN, 69-71; div chm humanities, Columbia State Col, TN, 71-76; vis assoc prof English, Univ FL, 74-75; prof English, VA Commonwealth Univ, 77-; Nat Endowment for Humanities fel English, Univ MA, 76-77. **MEMBERSHIPS** Rhetoric Soc Am; MLA; Conf Col Compos & Commun; NCTE. **RESEARCH** Rhetoric; American literature; pedagogy. **SELECTED PUBLICATIONS** Auth, Training Teachers to Teach Composition, Freshman English News, fall 75; Tagmemic Rhetoric: A Reconsideration, Col Compos & Commun, 5/78; On Duty in an Age of Dilemma, Col English, 12/78; Classifying Heuristics, Col Compos & Commun, 12/79; Scientism and the Teaching of English, New Students in the Two-year Colleges, NCTE, 79; Composition Research and the Rhetorical Tradition, Rhet Soc Quart, summer 80; Why bother? The Importance of Critical Thinking, in: Fostering Critical Thinking, Jossey-Bass, 80; Understanding Writing, Random House, 82; Amalgamation!, Greenwood Press, 85. **CONTACT ADDRESS** Dept English, Virginia Commonwealth Univ, Box 842005, Richmond, VA, 23284-2005. **EMAIL** jkinney@vcu.edu

KINNEY, KATHERINE
DISCIPLINE AMERICAN AND AFRICAN AMERICAN LITERATURE **EDUCATION** Univ Wash, BA; Univ Pa, MA, PhD. **HONORS AND AWARDS** Fel, Post Nat Amer Stud Res Gp, Univ Calif Hum Res Inst, Irvine. **SELECTED PUBLICATIONS** Auth, "Foreign Affairs: Women, War, and the Post-National," Univ Calif Press; "Making Capital: War, Labor, and Whitman in Washington, D.C.," Breaking Bounds: A Whitman Centennial Volume; "Tim O'Brien's Going After Cacciato," Amer Lit Hist; Friendly Fire: American Identity and the Literature of the Vietnam War, 99. **CONTACT ADDRESS** Dept of Eng, Univ Calif, 1156 Hinderaker Hall, Riverside, CA, 92521-0209. **EMAIL** kkinney@ucrac1.ucr.edu.

KINZIE, MARY
DISCIPLINE ENGLISH **EDUCATION** Johns Hopkins Univ, PhD. **CAREER** Prof, Northwestern Univ; Guggenheim fel; Koldyke outstanding tchg prof. **SELECTED PUBLICATIONS** Auth, Threshold of the Year, 82; Masked Women, 90; Summers of Vietnam, 90; Autumn Eros and Other Poems, 91; Ghost Ship, 96; The Cure of Poetry in an Age of Prose, 93; The Judge Is Fury: Dislocation and Form in Poetry, 94. **CONTACT ADDRESS** Dept of English, Northwestern Univ, 1801 Hinman, Evanston, IL, 60208.

KIPPERMAN, MARK
PERSONAL Brooklyn, NY, m, 1996 **DISCIPLINE** ENGLISH LITERATURE **EDUCATION** Univ Penn, PhD 81; Univ NY Bingham, BA 73. **CAREER** Northern IL Univ, prof 86-; Princeton Univ, asst prof 80-86. **HONORS AND AWARDS** NEH Fel; NEH sun Fel; ACLS Fel. **MEMBERSHIPS** MLA; Keats-Shelley Assoc Amer. **RESEARCH** British romantic poetry. **SELECTED PUBLICATIONS** Auth, Beyond Enchantment: The Structure of Idealism and the Meaning of Romantic Quest, U of Penn Press, 86; auth, Coleridge Shelley Davey and Science's Millennium, Criticism, 98; auth, Shelley and the Ideology of the Nation: The Authority of the Poet, in: Shelley: Poet and Legislator of the World, ed Betty Bennet, Stuart Curran, Baltimore, John Hopkins Univ Press, 96; auth, Absorbing a Revolution: Shelley Becomes a Romantic, 1889-1903, Nineteenth Cent Lit, 92; auth, History and Ideality: The Politics of Shelleys's Hellas, Studies in Romanticism, 91; auth, Keats, Biography in Dictionary of Literary Biography, ed John Greenfield, Detroit, Gale Research, 90. **CONTACT ADDRESS** Dept of English, No Illinois Univ, DeKalb, IL, 60115. **EMAIL** makipper@niu.edu

KIRALYFALVI, BELA
DISCIPLINE THEATER AND DRAMA **EDUCATION** Univ Kans, PhD. **CAREER** Chp, speech commun; dir, Univ theatre; prof. **HONORS AND AWARDS** Adjudicator, ch, playwriting awards in the Amer Col Theatre Fest. **RESEARCH** Dramatic theory, criticism, and playscript analysis. **SELECTED PUBLICATIONS** Publ, aesthetics and theatre topics, nat and intl jour(s). **CONTACT ADDRESS** Dept of Commun, Wichita State Univ, 1845 Fairmont, Wichita, KS, 67260-0062.

KIRBY, DAVID
PERSONAL Born 11/29/1944, Baton Rouge, LA **DISCIPLINE** AMERICAN LITERATURE, CREATIVE WRITING **EDUCATION** La State Univ, BA, 66; Johns Hopkins Univ, PhD, 69. **CAREER** Asst prof, 69-74, assoc prof, 74-79, dir writing prog, 73-77, asst exec vpres, 75-77, PROF ENGLISH, FLA STATE UNIV, 79-. **RESEARCH** Writings of Henry James; late 19th century American literature; modern poetry. **SELECTED PUBLICATIONS** Co-ed, Individual and Community: Variations on a Theme in American Fiction, Duke Univ, 75; auth, American Fiction to 1900: A Guide to Information Sources, Gale Res, 75; The Opera Lover, Anhinga Press, 77; Grace King, Twayne Publ, 80; America's Hive of Honey: Foreign Sources of American Fiction through Henry James, 80 & The Sun Rises in the Evening: Monism and Quietism in Western Culture, 82, Scarecrow. **CONTACT ADDRESS** Dept of English, Florida State Univ, 600 W College Ave, Tallahassee, FL, 32306-1580. **EMAIL** dkirby@english.fsu.edu

KIRKWOOD, WILLIAM
DISCIPLINE COMMUNICATION STUDIES **EDUCATION** Northwestern Univ, BA, MA, PhD. **CAREER** Prof. **SELECTED PUBLICATIONS** Auth, pubs in Quarterly Journal of Speech, Communication Monographs, Communication Education, Journal of Communication, Rhetoric Society Quarterly, and Journal of Applied Communication Research. **CONTACT ADDRESS** Dept of Communication, East Tennesee State Univ, PO Box 70717, Johnson City, TN, 37614-0717. **EMAIL** saucemaf@etsu.edu

KIRSCHNER, TERESA
PERSONAL Barcelona, Spain **DISCIPLINE** HUMANITIES **EDUCATION** Lycee Francis de Barcelone, Baccalaureate Studs; Roosevelt Univ, Chicago, BA, 62; Univ Chicago, MA, 64, PhD, 73. **CAREER** Lectr, Spanish, Ind Univ, 66-67; instr, 67-74, asst prof, 74-81, assoc prof, 81-90, PROF, SIMON FRASER UNIV, 90-. **HONORS AND AWARDS** Univ Fel, Univ Chicago, 65-66; Prize, best book, Can Asn Hispanists, 81; Excellence in Tchg Award, Simon Fraser Univ, 87; Killam Res Fel, 95. **MEMBERSHIPS** Can Comn UNESCO; SSHRCC; Can FedN Hum; Can Asn Hispanists; MLA; Can Asn Univ Tchrs; N Am Catalan Soc; Can Asn Latin Am & Caribbean Studs. **SELECTED PUBLICATIONS** Auth, El protagonista colectivo en Fuenteovejuna de Lope de Vega, 79; auth, The Mob in Shakespeare and Lope de Vega, in Parallel Lives: Spanish and English National Drama, 1580-1680, 91; auth, The Staging of the Conquest in a Play by Lope de Vega, in Pacific Coast Philol, 92; auth, Typology of Staging in Lope de Vega's Theatre, in The Golden Age Comedia Text, Theory and Performance, 94. **CONTACT ADDRESS** Hum Prog, Simon Fraser Univ, Burnaby, BC, V5A 1S6. **EMAIL** tkirschn@sfu.ca

KISER, LISA J.
PERSONAL Born 07/21/1949, Chicago, IL, m, 1990 **DISCIPLINE** ENGLISH LIT **EDUCATION** Univ WI, BA 72; Univ VA, PhD 77 **CAREER** OH State Univ, asst prof 77-83, assoc prof 83-91, prof eng 91. **HONORS AND AWARDS** Alumni Distg Tch Awd; Honors Facul Ser Awd. **MEMBERSHIPS** Mod Lang Assn; Medieval Acad Am; Medieval Assn Midwest; New Chaucer Soc; Intl Court Lit Soc; AAUP. **RESEARCH** Medieval Lit and cult. **SELECTED PUBLICATIONS** Telling Classical Tales: Chaucer and the Legend of Good Women, Ithaca, Cornell Univ Press, 83; Truth and Textuality in Chaucer's Poetry, Hanover and London, Univ Press of New Eng, 91; several other books and articles. **CONTACT ADDRESS** Dept of Eng, Ohio State Univ, 164 West 17th ST, Columbus, OH, 43210. **EMAIL** kiser@osu.edu

KITELEY, BRIAN
PERSONAL Born 09/26/1956, Minneapolis, MN, m, 1991 **DISCIPLINE** ENGLISH **EDUCATION** Carleton Col, BA; City Col of NY, MA. **CAREER** Lectr, Am Univ in Cairo, 87-89; asst prof, Ohio Univ, 92-94; ASST PROF, 94-98, ASSOC PROF, UNIV OF DENVER, 98-. **HONORS AND AWARDS** Whiting Awd, 96; Guggenheim Fel, 92; NEA Fel, 91. **SELECTED PUBLICATIONS** Auth, I Know Many Songs, But I cannot Sing, Simon & Schuster, 96; Still Life With Insects, Graywolf Press, 93, The Bodley Head, 90, Ticknor & Fields, 89; short fiction in Ohio Rev, 99, The Denver Quart, 94, Iowa Rev, 93, Provincetown Arts, 93, Fiction, 89 & 87, and The Best Am Stories of 1988, Houghton Mifflin. **CONTACT ADDRESS** English Dept, Univ of Denver, Denver, CO, 80208. **EMAIL** bkiteley@du.edu

KITTREDGE, WILLIAM ALFRED
PERSONAL Born 08/14/1932, Portland, OR **DISCIPLINE** ENGLISH, CREATIVE WRITING **EDUCATION** Ore State Univ, BS, 53; Univ Iowa, MFA, 69. **CAREER** ASSOC PROF ENGLISH, UNIV MONT, 69-; Stegner fel, Stanford Univ, 73-74; Nat Endowment Arts award, 74. **SELECTED PUBLICATIONS** Auth, Hermitage, SDak Rev, Vol 0031, 93. **CONTACT ADDRESS** Dept of English, Univ of Mont, Missoula, MT, 59812.

KIZER, ELIZABETH J.
DISCIPLINE COMMUNICATION STUDIES **EDUCATION** Angelo State Univ, BA; Tex Tech Univ, MA; Purdue Univ, PhD. **CAREER** Assoc prof **SELECTED PUBLICATIONS** Auth, The Women's Room: A Readers Theatre Script with Production Notes (rev), Univ Mo, 82; Protest Song Lyrics as Rhetoric, Popular Music Soc, 83; co-auth, Multi-Image and Live Performance: Some Connections, Storyboard, 85; Audio-Visual Effects in Readers Theatre: A Case Study, Int J Instructional Media, 87. **CONTACT ADDRESS** Communication Dept, Univ of Missouri, St. Louis, 590 Lucas Hall, St. Louis, MO, 63121. **EMAIL** sejkize@umslvma.umsl.edu

KLAWITTER, GEORGE
DISCIPLINE RENAISSANCE LITERATURE **EDUCATION** Univ Notre Dame , AB, 63; Univ MI, AM, 69; Univ Chicago, PhD, 81. **CAREER** Eng Dept, St. Edward's Univ **HONORS AND AWARDS** 3 NEH fel; Burlington-Northern Fac Award Tchg Sch, 89, Tchr Year, 94., Contrib ed, John Donne Variorum, Brown Univ Women Writers Proj. **MEMBERSHIPS** MLA, Milton Soc, S Central Mod Lang Asn; John Donne Soc, Tex Medieval Soc; Medieval Acad Am; S Central Renaissance Asn, Renaissance Soc Am. **SELECTED PUBLICATIONS** Auth, The Poetry of Richard Barnfield. Selinsgrove: Susquehanna Univ Press, 90; Adapted to the Lake: Letters by the Brother Founders of Notre Dame, 1841-1849, Peter Lang, 93; The Enigmatic Narrator: The Voicing of Same-Sex Love in the Poetry of John Donne, Peter Lang, 94. **CONTACT ADDRESS** St Edward's Univ, 3001 S Congress Ave, Austin, TX, 78704-6489. **EMAIL** georgek@admin.stedwards.edu

KLEIN, JARED S.
PERSONAL Born 08/05/1946, Cleveland, OH, m, 1974, 2 children **DISCIPLINE** ENGLISH **EDUCATION** Case Western Reserve Univ, BA, 68; Yale Univ, MPhil, 71, MA, 72, PhD, 74. **CAREER** Asst prof, 74-79, assoc prof, 79-84, prof, class, 84-91, prof ,ling, class, Germanic & Slavic lang, 91-, Univ Georgia; Lady Davis Vis Prof, Hebrew Univ of Jerusalem, 85; dir, 93, d'Etudes Associe' Ecole Pratique des Hautes Etudes, Paris. **MEMBERSHIPS** Ling Soc Amer; Amer Oriental Soc; Amer Philol Assn; Philol Soc, Great Britain; Societe de Linguistique de Paris; Indogermanische Gesellschaft; Societas Linguistica Europea. **RESEARCH** Indo-European ling, esp Vedic Sanskrit, Greek, Latin, class Armenian, gothic & old Iranian. **SELECTED PUBLICATIONS** Auth, The Particle u in the Rigveda, A Synchronic and Diachronic Study, Vandenhoeck & Ruprecht, 78; auth, Toward a Discourse Grammar of the Rigveda, vol 1: Coordinate Conjunctions, parts 1 & 2, Heidelberg, Carl Winter, 85; auth, On Verbal Accentuation in the Rigveda, New Haven, Amer Oriental Soc, 92; auth, On Personal Deixis in Classical Armenian, A Study of the Syntax and Semantics of the n-, s-, and d- Demonstratives in Manuscripts E and M of the Old Armenian Gospels, Dettelbach, JH Roll, 96; art, Homeric Greek: A Synchronic and Diachronic Study, Historische Sprachforschung, 89; art, Some Indo-European Systems of Conjunction: Rigveda, Old Persian, Homer, Harvard Stud in Class Philol, 92; coauth, Gothic -(u)h: A Synchronic and Comparative Study, Trans of the Philol Soc, 93. **CONTACT ADDRESS** Dept of Classics, Univ of Georgia, Park Hall, Athens, GA, 30602-6203. **EMAIL** jklein@arches.uga.edu

KLEIN, JOAN LARSEN
PERSONAL Menominee, MI, 2 children **DISCIPLINE** ENGLISH LITERATURE **EDUCATION** Univ Mich, BA, 53; Harvard Univ, MA, 56, PhD(English), 58. **CAREER** Asst prof English, Univ Wis, 58-62; asst prof, Duquesne Univ, 63-64; lectr, Bryn Mawr Col, 64-70; asst prof, 70-79, ASSOC PROF, UNIV ILL, URBANA, 79-; Mellon fel English, Univ Pittsburgh, 61-62. **MEMBERSHIPS** MLA; Spenser Soc; Shakespeare Soc. **RESEARCH** Spenser; Shakespeare. **SELECTED PUBLICATIONS** Auth, The Invention of the Renaissance Woman, Renaissance Quart, Vol 0047, 94. **CONTACT ADDRESS** 2209 Vawter St, Urbana, IL, 60801.

KLEIN, WILLIAM FRANCIS
PERSONAL Born 11/21/1936, Dwight, IL, m, 1962, 3 children **DISCIPLINE** ENGLISH LITERATURE, LITERARY THEORY **EDUCATION** Butler Univ, BA, 59; Univ Chicago, MA, 62, PhD, 75. **CAREER** Instr English, DePaul Univ, 62-64; asst prof, St Xavier Col, 65-67; assoc prof English, Kenyon Col, 68-. **MEMBERSHIPS** Medieval Acad Am. **RESEARCH** Anglo-Saxon poetry; Henry James; the English modal system. **SELECTED PUBLICATIONS** Auth, Purpose and the poetics of The Wanderer and The Seafarer, Anglo-Saxon Poetry, Univ Notre Dame, 75; Fiction and the figures of life, 76 & The story of Audun and the great bear, 77, Perspective; A Critic Nearly Anomalous, Sewanee Rev, 94. **CONTACT ADDRESS** Dept English, Kenyon Col, Sunset Cottage, Gambier, OH, 43022-9623. **EMAIL** KLEIN@kenyon.edu

KLEINBERG, SEYMOUR
PERSONAL Born 01/05/1933, New York, NY **DISCIPLINE** ENGLISH LITERATURE **EDUCATION** City Col New York, BA, 53; Univ Conn, MA, 55; Univ Mich, PhD, 63. **CAREER** Instr, 59-62, Flint Jr Col; from asst prof to assoc prof, 62-72, prof Eng, 72-, Long Island Univ. **HONORS AND AWARDS** Nat Endowment for Humanities fel, 79. **MEMBERSHIPS** PEN **RESEARCH** Renaissance literature. **SELECTED PUBLICATIONS** Ed, The Other Persuasion, Vintage Books, 77; auth, Alienated Affections, St Martin's Press, 81. **CONTACT ADDRESS** Dept of English, Long Island Univ, Brooklyn, NY, 11201.

KLEINER, ELAINE LAURA
PERSONAL Born 05/02/1942, Portland, OR **DISCIPLINE** ENGLISH LANGUAGE & LITERATURE **EDUCATION** OR State Univ, BA, 64; Univ Chicago, MA, 66, PhD, 71. **CAREER** Tchg asst Eng, Univ WI-Madison, 67-68; from Asst Prof to Assoc Prof, 69-81, prof IN State Univ, 82, Dir, Interdisciplinary Univ Studies Gen Educ Prog, 76-85; Managing ed, Sch Rev, 68-70 & Sci-Fiction Studies, 72-74. **HONORS AND AWARDS** NDEA Fel, 65; Tchg Assistantship and Scholarship, Univ WI, 66; Ford Found Dissertation Year Schol, 68; Ellison Scholarship, Univ Chicago, 68; NEH Consult Grant, 77; Quality in Liberal Learning Grant, 78; NEH Summer Res Fel, Princeton Univ, 79; IN Arts Comn Grant, 83; IN Comt for the Hum Grant, 85; Fulbright Sr Scholarship Grant, Romania, 89-90; Univ Res Grant, IN State Univ, 95; Univ Arts Endowment Grant, IN State Univ, 96. **MEMBERSHIPS** IN Col Eng Asn; Asn Lit Scholarship & Critics; Soc Romanian Studies; IN Tchr-(s) Writing; Nat Coun Tchr(s) Eng; IN Writers Asn; Asn Tchr-(s) Tech Writing; **RESEARCH** Mod Eng lit; acad, creative, and professional writing; narrative theory; sci in lit. **SELECTED PUBLICATIONS** Auth, George Russell, In: Nationalism in Literature, New Brunswick, 96; Beside Great Waters: Poems from the Highlands and Islands, Avon Books, 97; This Sacred Earth and Other Poems, Mellen Poetry Press, 97; co-ed, Sacramental Acts: The Collected Love Poems of Kenneth Rexroth, Copper Canyon Press, 97; auth, Gadget Science Fiction: Technological Issues in Popular Culture, Simon and Schuster, 98; auth numerous other articles and publ. **CONTACT ADDRESS** Dept of Eng, Indiana State Univ, 210 N 7th St, Terre Haute, IN, 47809-0002. **EMAIL** ejelk@root.indstate.edu

KLEINER, JOHN
DISCIPLINE ENGLISH **EDUCATION** Amherst Col, BA, 83; Cornell Univ, MS, 85; Stanford Univ, PhD, 90. **CAREER** Assoc prof. **RESEARCH** Classical and medieval literature;

Latin, English, Italian traditions. **SELECTED PUBLICA-TIONS** Auth, Mismapping the Underworld: Error in Dante's Comedy. **CONTACT ADDRESS** Dept of English, Williams Col, Stetson d-25, Williamstown, MA, 01267. **EMAIL** jkleiner@williams.edu

KLEINMAN, NEIL
DISCIPLINE RENAISSANCE LITERATURE **EDUCA-TION** Univ Conn, PhD; Univ Pa, JD. **CAREER** Prof, Univ Baltimore. **HONORS AND AWARDS** Univ Maryland System Regents Awd for Distinguished Tchg, 98., Dir, Inst Lang, Technol, & Publs Design; Codir, Sch Comm Design; Dir, Doctorate Coms Design. **RESEARCH** Renaissance literature; propaganda; intellectual property; influence of new tecchnologies in modern society. **SELECTED PUBLICATIONS** Auth, The Dream that Was No More a Dream: A Search for Aesthetic Reality in Germany, 1890-1945. **CONTACT ADDRESS** Commun Dept, Univ Baltimore, 1420 N. Charles Street, Baltimore, MD, 21201.

KLENE, MARY JEAN
PERSONAL Born 09/08/1929, Hannibal, MO **DISCIPLINE** RENAISSANCE LITERATURE & ART **EDUCATION** St Mary's Col, Ind, BA, 59; Notre Dame Univ, MA, 66; Univ Toronto, PhD(English), 70. **CAREER** Elementary and secondary teacher, 52-65; Instr, 65-66, from asst prof to assoc prof, 70-81, Prof English, St Mary's Col, Ind, 81-, Chm Dept, 72-77, 81-85; adj assoc prof, Hofstra Univ, 78-79. **HONORS AND AWARDS** Nat Endowment for Humanities fel, 77-78; Lilly Fac Fel, London, 85-86; NEH summer fac fel in Stratford, England, 81, Princeton, 84; SMC "Spes Unica". **MEMBERSHIPS** MLA; Renaissance Soc Am; Chaucer Soc; Int Courtly Lit Soc; Shakespeare Asn of Am; Soc for Textual Schol; Soc for Values in Higher Educ. **RESEARCH** The tradition of the world upside-down; Shakespearean drama; editing Elizabethan entertainments. **SELECTED PUBLICATIONS** Auth, Othello: A fixed figure for the time of scorn, Shakespeare Quart, 75; Chaucer's contribution to a popular topos: The World up-so-doun, Viator, Vol XI, 80; RSC slides and sun images in Richard II, Shakespeare Film Newslett, Vol V, No 1; The fool, folly, and the world upside-down in Shakespeare's Measure for Measure, Upstart Crow, Vol III, 80; Instructor's guide for the Slide Set: Shakespeare: New Productions (1975-1980), Royal Shakespeare Co, Stratford-upon-Avon, England & KaiDib Films Int, 81; An Approach through Visual Stimuli and Student Writing, In: Approaches to Teaching Shakespeare's King Lear, Mod Lang Asn of Am, 86; Recreating the Letters of Lady Anne Southwell, repr from Renaissance English Text Soc 1990 MLA Panel: Voices of Silence: Editing the Letters of Renaissance Women, In: New Ways of Looking at Old Texts: Papers of the Renaissance English Text Society, 1985-1991, Binghampton, New York: Medieval & Renaissance Texts & Studies in conjunction with Renaissance English Text Soc, 93; The Southwell-Sibthorpe Commonplace Book: Folger MS, V.b. 198, Medieval & Renaissance Textual Studies #149, 97. **CONTACT ADDRESS** Dept of English, St Mary's Col, Notre Dame, IN, 46556. **EMAIL** jklene@saintmarys.edu

KLENOTIC, JEFFREY F.
PERSONAL Born 08/12/1963, New Castle, PA, s **DISCIPLINE** COMMUNICATION **EDUCATION** Pa State Univ, BA, 85; Univ of Mass, Amherst, MA, 88, PhD, 96. **CAREER** INSTR, COMMUN, 92-96, ASST PROF OF COMMUN, 96-98, ASSOC PROF OF COMMUN, 98-, UNIV OF NH MANCHESTER. **HONORS AND AWARDS** Excellence in Teaching Award, Univ of NH Manchester, 97; Phi Beta Kappa, 85-. **MEMBERSHIPS** Soc for Cinema Studies; Domitor; Nat commun Asn; Int Commun Asn; Northeast Historic Film Asn. **RESEARCH** Film history; media audiences; cultural studies. **SELECTED PUBLICATIONS** Auth, The Sensational Acme of Realism: Talker Pictures as Early Cinema Sound Practice, 99; auth, Class Markers in the Mass Movie Audience: A Case Study in the Cultural Geography of Moviegoing 1926-1932, The Commun Rev, 98; The Place of Rhetoric in New Film Historiography: The Discourse of Corrective Revisionism, Film Hist: An Int J, 94; auth, Milos Forman, The Encycl of Film, Perigee Books, 91; auth, Miklos Jancso, The Encycl of Film, Perigee Books, 91. **CONTACT ADDRESS** Dept of Commun, Univ of NH at Manchester, 400 Commercial St., Manchester, NH, 03101.

KLIGERMAN, JACK
PERSONAL Born 08/28/1938, Atlantic City, NJ, m, 1960, 2 children **DISCIPLINE** ENGLISH, PHOTOGRAPHY, LINGUISTICS **EDUCATION** Syracuse Univ, BA, 60, MA, 62; Univ Calif, Berkeley, PhD, 67. **CAREER** Asst prof, 67-75, assoc prof, 75-88, prof English, 89-, dept chemn, 97-, Lehman Col; Va Ctr for Creative Arts residency, summer 82. **MEMBERSHIPS** John Burroughs Memorial Asn. **RESEARCH** Photography; American and English literature; stylistics. **SELECTED PUBLICATIONS** Auth, Photography as a Celebration of Nature, The Structurist, 80; auth, Photography and Technology, The Structurist, 82; auth, Photographic Exhibitions: Paris in the Nineties, Godwin-Ternbach Museum, Queens Col. **CONTACT ADDRESS** Dept of English, Lehman Col, CUNY, Bronx, NY, 10468.

KLINE, DANIEL
DISCIPLINE MEDIEVAL LITERATURE **EDUCATION** Indiana Univ, PhD. **CAREER** Univ Alaska. **SELECTED PUBLICATIONS** Articles: Comparative Drama; Essays in Medieval Studies; MLA's Profession 95. **CONTACT ADDRESS** Univ Alaska Anchorage, 3211 Providence Dr., Anchorage, AK, 99508.

KLINE, JOHN A.
PERSONAL Born 07/24/1939, Marshalltown, IA, m, 1974, 5 children **DISCIPLINE** SPEECH COMMUNICATION **EDUCATION** Iowa St Univ, BS, 67; Univ of Iowa, MS, 68, PhD, 70; Federal Executive Inst, Sr Exec, 86. **CAREER** Tchr, 66-67, Iowa St Univ; Grad NDEA/Res Fel, 67-70 Univ of Iowa; Asst Prof, Dir, 70-71, Fundamentals of Speech Com, Univ of New Mexico; Asst Prof, Dir, 71-75, Grad Stud, Univ of Missouri-Columbia; Assoc Prof, Dean, Communication, 75-82, Prof, Dir, Academic Affairs, 82-92, Provost, 92-, United States Air Univ. **HONORS AND AWARDS** Undergrad Scholar Fel, Iowa St Univ, 65-67; NDEA Fel, Univ of Iowa, 67-70; Central States Speech Assoc Outstanding Tchr, 72; Phi Kappa Phi Honor Soc, 76; Fed Employee of the Year Montgomery AL, 79; Awd for Meritous Civilian Svc, 84; Whos Who in America 45th Ed, 88; Decoratin for Exceptional Civilian Svc, 88. **MEMBERSHIPS** Natl Comm Assoc; Phi Delta Kappa; Amer Coun on Ed **SELECTED PUBLICATIONS** Art, Indicators of Good Marriages, Home Life, 93; auth, Parlez Pour Quon Vous Ecoute (French Trans Speaking Effectively), 93; auth, Listening Effectively, Air Univ Press, 96. **CONTACT ADDRESS** USAF Air Univ, 55 LeMay Plaza South, Maxwell AFB, AL, 36112-6335. **EMAIL** jkline@hq.au.af.mil

KLINK, WILLIAM
PERSONAL Born 07/04/1945, Ft. Myers, FL, m, 1991, 1 child **DISCIPLINE** LITERATURE **EDUCATION** Montclair St Univ, BA, 67; Cathol Univ, MA, 71, PhD, 72 **CAREER** Prof, Charles Co Commun Col, 27 yrs **HONORS AND AWARDS** Authored approx 100 books, articles and scholarly presentations **MEMBERSHIPS** Popular Culture Asn **RESEARCH** Am lit **CONTACT ADDRESS** Charles County Comm Col, La Plata, MD, 20646. **EMAIL** billk@charles.cc.md.us

KLINKOWITZ, JEROME
PERSONAL Born 12//241943, Milwaukee, WI, m, 1966, 2 children **DISCIPLINE** AMERICAN LITERATURE, CONTEMPORARY STUDIES **EDUCATION** Marquette Univ, BA, 66, MA, 67; Univ Wis-Madison, PhD(Am lit), 70. **CAREER** Asst prof English, Northern Ill Univ, 69-72; from assoc prof to prof, 72-76, PROF ENGLISH, UNIV NORTHERN IOWA, 78-. **MEMBERSHIPS** MLA; PEN Club; Nathaniel Hawthorne Soc; Fiction Collective. **RESEARCH** Innovative American fiction; contemporary American culture, jazz and popular music. **SELECTED PUBLICATIONS** Auth, What Comes Next and Feminist Writings, Anq-A Quart J Short Articles Notes Rev, Vol 0005, 92; Am Fiction in The Cold War, Mod Fiction Studies, Vol 0038, 92; Rewriting America in Vietnam Authors and Their Generation, Mod Fiction Studies, Vol 0038, 92; Price,Reynolds in a Bibliography, 1949-1984, Rsrcs Am Lit Study, Vol 0019, 93; Firesticks, Am Indian Cult Res Jour, Vol 0017, 93; Doctorow, E.L. in An Annotated-Bibliography, Rsrcs Am Lit Study, Vol 0019, 93; As The Wolf Howls At My Door, Am Book Rev, Vol 0015, 93; The Harry and Sylvia Stories, N Am Rev, Vol 0278, 93; Pub Roth, Philip Anti-Baseball Novel, W Hum Rev, Vol 0047, 93; Taylor,Peter in A Descriptive Bibliography, 1934-87; Rcrs Am Lit Study, Vol 0019, 93; Gover, Robert in A Descriptive Bibliography, Rcrs Am Lit Study, Vol 0019, 93; Elvis Presley Calls His Mother After The Ed Sullivan Show, Am Book Rev, Vol 0015, 93; Absolutely Nothing To Get Alarmed About in The Complete Novels of Wright, Charles; Am Book Rev, Vol 0015, 94; Major, Clarence Innovative Fiction, African Am Rev, Vol 0028, 94; Fire and Power in The American Space Program as Postmodern Narrative; Am Lit, Vol 0067, 95; Sorrentino, Gilbert in A Descriptive Bibliography, Rcrs Am Lit Study, Vol 0021, 95; Containment Culture in American Narratives, Postmodernism, and the Atomic Age, Am Lit, Vol 0068, 96; The Scourging of W. H.D. Wretched Hutchinson, Am Book Rev, Vol 0017, 96; Literary Luxuries in American Writing at the End of the Millennium, Am Book Rev, Vol 0017, 96; Playtexts in Ludics in Contemporary Literature, Mod Fiction Studies, Vol 0042, 96; Life of Death, African Am Rev, Vol 0030, 96; Beyond Suspicion in New Am Fiction Since, Am Book Rev, Vol 0017, 96. **CONTACT ADDRESS** 1904 Clay St, Cedar Falls, IA, 50613.

KLOB, GWIN JACK
PERSONAL Born 10/09/1946, Chicago, IL, d **DISCIPLINE** ENGLISH LITERATURE **EDUCATION** BA, Hon, Univ of Chicago, 67; PhD Univ of VA, 71. **CAREER** Asst Prof, 71-79; Assoc Prof, 79-, UCLA. **MEMBERSHIPS** ALSC, The Tennyson Soc. **RESEARCH** Tennyson, Joyce, Victorian Poetry and Prose. **SELECTED PUBLICATIONS** Rev of Leonee Ormond, Alfred Tennyson: A Literary Life , ANQ 8, 95; Rev of Paul Fry, A Defense of Poetry: Relectins on the Occasion of Writing, Philosophy and Literature 20, 96; Tennyson, Carlyle, and the Morte d'Arthur, Carlyle Studies Annual 17, 97; An Unpublished Tennyson Letter, The Tennyson Research Bulletin 7, 97; Laureate Envy: TS Eliot on Tennyson, ANQ 11, 98; New

Light on Arthur Hallam and Ann Wintour, Tennyson Research Bulletin 6, 95; On First Look into Pope's Iliad: Hallam's Keatsian Sommet Victorian Poetry 29, 91. **CONTACT ADDRESS** Dept Eng, UCLouisiana, 405 Hilgard Ave, Los Angeles, CA, 90024. **EMAIL** kolb@ucla.edu

KLOTMAN, PHYLLIS RAUCH
PERSONAL Galveston, TX, m, 2 children **DISCIPLINE** AMERICAN LITERATURE **EDUCATION** Case Western Reserve Univ, BA, 61, MA, 63, PhD(English, Am and Afro-Am lit), 69. **CAREER** Instr English, Lawrence Inst Technol, 67-68; asst prof, Ind State Univ, Terre Haute, 69-70; asst prof Afro-Am studies, 70-73, assoc prof, 73-78, PROF AFRO-AM STUDIES, IND UNIV, BLOOMINGTON, 78-; Vis prof, Univ Hamburg, Ger, 78. **MEMBERSHIPS** MLA; Col Lang Asn; Col English Asn; Nat Coun Black Studies; Soc Cinema Studies. **RESEARCH** Afro-American literature, fiction, drama, biography and autobiography; Blacks in films. **SELECTED PUBLICATIONS** Auth, Black Cinema Treasures in Lost And Found, Film Quart, Vol 0046, 93; Making Movies Black in The Hollywood Message Movie from World War II to The Civil-Rights Era, Film Quart, Vol 0048, 94. **CONTACT ADDRESS** Dept of Afro-Am Studies, Indiana Univ, Bloomington, Bloomington, IN, 47401.

KLOTZ, MARVIN
PERSONAL Born 02/06/1930, New York, NY, m, 1953, 2 children **DISCIPLINE** AMERICAN LITERATURE **EDUCATION** Columbia Univ, BS, 51; Univ Minn, MA, 52; NY Univ, PhD, 59. **CAREER** Instr English, NY Univ, 56-59; from asst prof to assoc prof, 59-69, PROF ENGLISH, CALIF STATE UNIV, NORTHRIDGE, 69-; Fulbright lectr, Saigon, South Vietnam and Taipei, Taiwan, 67-68 and Univ Tehran, Iran, 75-76. **RESEARCH** Faulkner; fictional realism; American prose style. **SELECTED PUBLICATIONS** Auth, Longman Language Activator, Zeitschrift Anglistik Amerikanistik, Vol 0042, 94; Oxford Dictionary of Phrasal Verbs, Zeitschrift Anglistik Amerikanistik, Vol 0042, 94; Pons Pictorial English-German Spanish Dictionary, Zeitschrift Anglistik Amerikanistik, Vol 0043, 95; Duden-Oxford Picture Dictionary German And English, Zeitschrift Anglistik Amerikanistik, Vol 0044, 96; New German Documentary in The Impossible Struggle for a Fascism-Verite, Arachne, Vol 0003, 96. **CONTACT ADDRESS** Dept of English, California State Univ, Northridge, Northridge, CA, 91324.

KLUMPP, JAMES F.
DISCIPLINE RHETORICAL THEORY **EDUCATION** Univ MN, PhD, 73. **CAREER** Assoc prof, Univ MD. **RESEARCH** Kenneth Burke and the Europ continental critics. **SELECTED PUBLICATIONS** Co-auth, Rhetorical Criticism as Moral Action, Quart Jour Speech 75, 89. **CONTACT ADDRESS** Dept of Commun, Univ MD, 4229 Art-Sociology Building, College Park, MD, 20742-1335. **EMAIL** jk44@umail.umd.edu

KNAPP, GERHARD PETER
PERSONAL Bad Kreuznach, Germany, 4 children **DISCIPLINE** LITERARY CRITICISM, FILM **EDUCATION** Tech Univ, Berlin, MA, 68, Dr Phil, 70. **CAREER** Asst prof Ger, Tech Univ, Berlin, 68-70; asst prof, Lakehead Univ, 70-72; asst prof, 72-74, assoc prof, 74-79, Prof Ger & Comp Lit, Univ Utah, 79-; vis prof Ger, Univ Amsterdam, 77-78. **HONORS AND AWARDS** Phi Beta Kappa (hon mem, 95). **MEMBERSHIPS** MLA; Am Asn Tchr(s) Ger; Can Asn Univ Tchr(s) Ger; Int Brecht Soc. **RESEARCH** 19th and 20th century lit; theory of literary criticism; film studies. **SELECTED PUBLICATIONS** Auth & coauth of 21 books, auth of 65 articles & ed & co-ed of 42 bks on Ger & comp lit. **CONTACT ADDRESS** Dept of Lang & Lit, Univ of UT, 255 S Central Campus Dr, Rm 1400, Salt Lake City, UT, 84112-8916. **EMAIL** gerhard.knapp@m.cc.utah.edu

KNAPP, JAMES FRANKLIN
PERSONAL Born 10/10/1940, Chicago, IL, m, 1 child **DISCIPLINE** MODERN LITERATURE, MODERNISM, IRISH LITERATURE **EDUCATION** Drew Univ, BA, 62; Univ Conn, PhD(English), 66. **CAREER** Asst prof, 66-71, assoc prof English, Univ Pittsburgh, 71-89. **MEMBERSHIPS** MLA. **RESEARCH** Modern British and American poetry; contemporary poetry; myth theory. **SELECTED PUBLICATIONS** Auth, The meaning of Sir Orfeo, Mod Lang Quart, 68; Delmore Schwartz: Poet of the orphic journey, Sewanee Rev, 70; The poetry of R S Thomas, Twentieth Century Lit, 71; Proteus in the classroom: Myth and literature today, Col English, 3/73; Eliot's Prufrock and the form of modern poetry, Ariz Quart, Spring 74; Myth in the powerhouse of change, Centennial Rev, Winter 76; Ezra Pound, Twayne, 79; Literary Modernism and the Transformation of Work, Northwestern U Press, 96. **CONTACT ADDRESS** Dept of English, Univ of Pittsburgh, 526 Cathedral/Learn, Pittsburgh, PA, 15260-2504. **EMAIL** jkna+@pitt.edu

KNAPP, JOHN VICTOR
PERSONAL Born 05/03/1940, Syracuse, NY, m, 1977, 4 children **DISCIPLINE** MODERN LITERATURE **EDUCATION** State Univ NY, Cortland, BS, 63, MS, 66; Univ Ill, Urbana, PhD(English lit), 71. **CAREER** Teacher English, Chittenango

Cent High Sch, NY, 63-66; grad asst English and educ, Univ Ill, Urbana, 66-71; asst prof, 71-79, ASSOC PROF ENGLISH, NORTHERN ILL UNIV, DE KALB, 79-. **MEMBERSHIPS** MLA; Nat Coun Teachers English. **RESEARCH** Psychological approaches to literary criticism; modern British and American literature; English education and composition. **SELECTED PUBLICATIONS** Auth, Creative Reasoning in the Interactive Classroom in Experiential Exercises for Teaching Orwell, George Animal Farm, Col Lit, Vol 0023, 96. **CONTACT ADDRESS** 701 W Jefferson St, Stoughton, WI, 53589.

KNAPP, PEGGY ANN
PERSONAL Born 07/06/1937, Brainerd, MN, m, 1967, 3 children **DISCIPLINE** ENGLISH & AMERICAN LITERATURE **EDUCATION** Univ Wis-Madison, BS, 59, MA, 61; Univ Pittsburgh, PhD, 65. **CAREER** Lectr English, Mt Mercy Col, 65-66 & Univ Pittsburgh, 66-68; asst prof, Univ Conn, 68-69; from asst prof to assoc prof, 70-88, prof English, Carnegie-Mellon Univ, 88-. **MEMBERSHIPS** Mediaeval Acad Am; MLA. **RESEARCH** Middle English literature; Shakespeare; drama. **SELECTED PUBLICATIONS** Auth, Alisoun Weaves a Text, Phitol Quart, 86; Alisoun of Bath and the Reappropriation of Tradition, Chaucer Rev 24, 89; Deconstruction and the Canterbury Tales, Studies in the Age of Chaucer, 87; Chaucer and the Social Contest, Routledge, 90; Time Bound Words: Semantic and Social Economies from Chaucer's England to Shakespeare's, St. Martin's Press (forthcoming); author numerous other articles. **CONTACT ADDRESS** Dept of English, Carnegie Mellon Univ, 5000 Forbes Ave, Pittsburgh, PA, 15213-3890. **EMAIL** pk07@andrew.cmu.edu

KNAPP, ROBERT STANLEY
PERSONAL Born 03/29/1940, Alamosa, CO, m, 1965 **DISCIPLINE** ENGLISH **EDUCATION** Univ Colo, BA, 62; Univ Denver, MA, 63; Cornell Univ, PhD, 68. **CAREER** From instr to asst prof English, Princeton Univ, 66-74, Donald A Stauffer bicentennial preceptor, 70-73; asst prof, 74-77, assoc prof English, Reed Col, 77-, fel, Nat Endowment Humanities, Univ Chicago, 78-79. **MEMBERSHIPS** MLA, SAA, RSA. **RESEARCH** Shakespeare; critical theory. **SELECTED PUBLICATIONS** Auth, Samuel Beckett's allegory of the uncreating word, Mosaic, winter 73; Horestes: The uses of revenge, J English Lit Hist, summer 73; The monarchy of love in Lyly's Endymion, Miscellaneous Papers, 5/76; Love allegory in Grange's Golden Aphroditis, English Lit Renaissance, 78; Penance, irony & Chaucer's Retraction, Assays, 83; Shakespeare: The Theater and The Book, Princeton, 89; There's Letters from my Mother, Reading & Writing on Shakespeare, Delaware, 96; Is It Appropriate for a Man to Fear His Wife: Joan Case on Marriage, English Lit Renaissance, 98. **CONTACT ADDRESS** Dept English, Reed Col, 3203 SE Woodstock Blvd, Portland, OR, 97202-8199. **EMAIL** knapp@reed.edu

KNIES, EARL ALLEN
PERSONAL Born 07/11/1936, White Haven, PA, m, 1959, 3 children **DISCIPLINE** ENGLISH **EDUCATION** Muhlenberg Col, BA, 58; Lehigh Univ, MA, 60; Univ IL, PhD (English), 64. **CAREER** From asst prof to assoc prof, 64-74, chm dept, 74-78, prof English, OH Univ, 74-. **MEMBERSHIPS** MLA; Tennyson Soc. **RESEARCH** Victorian novel; Tennyson. **SELECTED PUBLICATIONS** Auth, Art, Death and the Composition of Shirley, Victorian Newsletter, fall 65; The Artistry of Charlotte Bront%, OH Univ Rev, 65; The I of Jane Eyre, Col English, 4/66; The Art of Charlotte Bront%, OH Univ, 69; The Diary of James Henry Mangles, Tennyson Res Bull, 11/81; Tennyson at Aldworth, OH Univ, 84. **CONTACT ADDRESS** Dept of English, Ohio Univ, Athens, OH, 45701-2979. **EMAIL** eknies1@ohiou.edu

KNIGHT, CHARLES ANTHONY
PERSONAL Born 09/03/1937, San Francisco, CA, m, 1958, 4 children **DISCIPLINE** ENGLISH **EDUCATION** Haverford Col, BA, 58; Univ Pa, MA, 60, PhD(English), 64. **CAREER** Instr English, Cath Univ Am, 61-62 and Univ Mass, Amherst, 62-65; asst prof, 65-69, assoc dean acad affairs, 72-75, actg dean, 75-76, assoc prof, 69-79, PROF ENGLISH, UNIV MASS, BOSTON, 79-. **MEMBERSHIPS** MLA; Am Soc Eighteenth-Century Studies. **RESEARCH** Eighteenth century English literature; British fiction. **SELECTED PUBLICATIONS** Auth, The Spectators Moral Economy, Mod Phil, Vol 0091, 93; Satire in A Critical Reintroduction, Scriblerian Kit-Cats, Vol 0027, 95; The Correspondence of Fielding,Henry and Fielding,Sarah J English Germanic Phil, Vol 0094, 95; Radical Satire And Print Culture 1790-1822, Eighteenth-Century Studies, Vol 0030, 96; Literature, Education, and Romanticism in Reading as Social Practice, 1780-1832, J English Germanic Philol, Vol 0095, 96. **CONTACT ADDRESS** Dept of English, Univ of Mass, Boston, MA, 12125.

KNIGHT, DENISE D.
DISCIPLINE ENGLISH **EDUCATION** SUNY, Albany, BA (summa cum laude), 83, MA, 85, DA, 86. **CAREER** Lect, Sienna Col, English dept, Loudonville, NY, 88-90; lect, SUNY, Albany, English Dept, 86-90; asst prof, 90-94, assoc prof, 94-97, PROF, SUNY, CORTLAND, ENGLISH DEPT, 97-. **HONORS AND AWARDS** Outstanding Reference Source Award, Am Library Asn, References and Adult Services div, 93; Phi Kappa Phi, 94; Radcliffe Col Res Support Grant Recepient, 94-95; Who's Who in the East, 95-96; speaker, NY Coun for the Humanities Speakers Prog, 96-98; Outstanding Book Award for Nineteenth-Century American Women Writers, Greenwood Press, 97, from CHOICE, 97., Founder, Central NY Conf on Lang and Lit, SUNY Col at Cortland, 91; ed, Gilman Soc Newsletter, 95-98; selection comm, Nat Women's Hall of Fame, 95, 96; dir, Center for Multicultural and Gender Studies, SUNY Col, Cortland, 96-98; BBC Radio Interview on Charlotte Perkins Gilman, Jan 98. **MEMBERSHIPS** Modern Lang Asn; Northeast Modern lang Asn; Charlotte Perkins Gilman Soc (pres, 98-2001); Am Lit Asn. **RESEARCH** Charlotte Perkins Gilman (1860-1935); 19th century Am women writers. **SELECTED PUBLICATIONS** Auth, The Yellow Wall-Paper and Selected Stories of Charlotte Perkins Gilman, Univ DE Press, 94; The Diaries of Charlotte Perkins Gilman, a two-volume critical ed, Univ Press VA, 94; The Later Poetry of Charlotte Perkins Gilman, Univ DE Press, 96; Unpunished: A Detective Novel by Charlotte Perkins Gilman, co-ed with Catherine J. Golden, Feminist Press, 97; Charlotte Perkins Gilman: A Study of the Short Fiction, Twayne Studies in Short Fiction, Twayne Pubs, 97; Nineteenth-Century American Women Writers: A Bio-Bibliographical Critical Sourcebook, Greenwood Press, 97; The Abridged Diaries of Charlotte Perkins Gilman, Univ Press VA, 98; The Dying of Charlotte Perkins Gilman, Am Transcendental Quart, June 99; Charlotte Perkins Gilman's First Book: A Biographical Gap, in ANQ, 99; Herland and Selected Stories of Charlotte Perkins Gilman, Penguin Classics, forthcoming 99; numerous other publications. **CONTACT ADDRESS** English Dept, SUNY, Cortland, Cortland, NY, 13045.

KNIGHT, WILLIAM NICHOLAS
PERSONAL Born 04/18/1939, Mt. Vernon, NY, m, 1961, 4 children **DISCIPLINE** MEDIEVAL & RENAISSANCE ENGLISH **EDUCATION** Amherst Col, BA, 61; Univ Calif, Berkeley, MA, 63; Ind Univ, PhD, 68. **CAREER** From instr to asst prof, 66-73, Wesleyan Univ; asst chmn dept, 70-71, fel, 71-72, Ctr Humanities; prof legal & common law hist, 73-75, Univ Bridgeport; assoc prof, 75-77, prof, 77-, chmn human, 75-, Univ Mo-Rolla; consult Renaissance lit, Choice; Ford Found fel, 70-71; scholar-in-residence English, Wesleyan Univ, 74-75; chmn, Policy Bd Joint Ctrs Aging, Univ Mo Syst, 77-. **MEMBERSHIPS** MLA; NCTE; Renaissance Soc Am. **RESEARCH** Shakespearean revenge tragedy; Shakespearean biography; equity in law and drama. **SELECTED PUBLICATIONS** Auth, The Death of J K (play), London Rev, 70; auth, Equity and Mercy in English Drama 1400-1641, Comp Drama, 72; auth, Spenserian Chivalric Influence in Paradise Regained, Costerus Essays, 72; art, Toward Archetype in the Joseph Colombo Shooting, Brit J Soc Psychiat & Community Health, 72; auth, Shakespeare at the Law: A Hidden Life, 1585-1595, Mason & Lipscomb, 73; art, Equity, The Merchant of Venice, and William Lambarde, Shakespeare Sur, 74; art, Lady That In Her Prime--Identified, Mo Philol Assn, 76; art, Legal Relationships Between Shakespeare's Life And His Works Since Schoenbaum's Life Records, Ark Philol Assn, 76. **CONTACT ADDRESS** Dept of English, Univ of Missouri, Rolla, Rolla, MO, 65401. **EMAIL** knight@umr.edu.com

KNIGHTON, ROBERT TOLMAN
PERSONAL Born 02/23/1935, Bountiful, UT, m, 1958, 3 children **DISCIPLINE** ENGLISH LITERATURE; AMERICAN LITERATURE **EDUCATION** Utah State Univ, BS, 61, MS, 62; Univ Colo, Boulder, PhD(English), 72. **CAREER** Instr English, Utah State Univ, 61-62; asst prof, 67-73, assoc prof, 73-80, PROF ENGLISH, UNIV OF THE PAC, 80-. **HONORS AND AWARDS** Faye and Alex G. Spanos Outstanding Teaching Award, 93. **MEMBERSHIPS** Am Soc Eighteenth Century Studies. **RESEARCH** Restoration and 18th century English literature; English romantic poetry; modern critical theory. **SELECTED PUBLICATIONS** Auth, Radical sublimation: The structure of community growth and alienation, Pac Hist, 76. **CONTACT ADDRESS** Dept of English, Univ of the Pacific, 3601 Pacific Ave, Stockton, CA, 95211-0197. **EMAIL** rknighto@uop.edu

KNIPP, THOMAS RICHARD
PERSONAL Born 02/27/1929, Chicago, IL, m, 1952, 6 children **DISCIPLINE** ENGLISH **EDUCATION** DePaul Univ, AB, 51, MA, 55; Mich State Univ, PhD (English), 66. **CAREER** Asst prof English, Univ Col, Ethiopia, 56-61; asst instr, Mich State Univ, 61-63; from asst prof to assoc prof, Kent State Univ, 63-73, asst dean arts and sci, 66-73; dean col arts and sci, 73-80, PROF ENGLISH, ST LOUIS UNIV, 73-; Regional Coun Int Educ Studies grant African lit, 66; Fulbright lectr English, Haile Sellassie I Univ, 68-69. **MEMBERSHIPS** African Studies Asn; African Lit Asn. **RESEARCH** American literature; African literature. **SELECTED PUBLICATIONS** Auth, Okigbo and Labyrinths in The Death of a Poet and the Life of a Poem, Res African Lit, Vol 0026, 95. **CONTACT ADDRESS** Col of Arts and Sci, St Louis Univ, 221 N Grand Blvd, Saint Louis, MO, 63103-2097.

KNOBLAUCH, CYRIL H.
PERSONAL Born 10/05/1945, Minneapolis, MN, m, 1984, 1 child **DISCIPLINE** ENGLISH **EDUCATION** Brown Univ, PhD, 73. **CAREER** Asst prof, Columbia Univ, 73-79; NYU, 79-82; assoc prof, 82-91, prof, 91-98, interim dean, Col of Arts and Sciences, State Univ of New York at Albany, 94-98; Dept of English, Univ NC at Charlotte, 98-. **RESEARCH** Rhetoric; literary studies; pedagogy. **SELECTED PUBLICATIONS** Auth, Rhetorical Traditions and the Teaching of Writing, Boynton/Cook, 84; Critical Teaching and the Idea of Literacy, Heinneman, 94; author of thirty articles. **CONTACT ADDRESS** Dept of English, Univ of North Carolina, Charlotte, Charlotte, NC, 28223. **EMAIL** knoblauch@email.uncc.edu

KNOELLER, CHRISTIAN
PERSONAL New York, NY **DISCIPLINE** ENGLISH LITERATURE **EDUCATION** Univ Calif Berkeley, PhD, 93. **CAREER** Fac, 93-. **HONORS AND AWARDS** Educ Yr, Alaska, 87; NCTE Tchr Res Found, 92; Russo Prize, Bucknell Univ, 76. **SELECTED PUBLICATIONS** Auth, Song in Brown Bear Country; publications include poetry, textbooks, school district curricula, and educational research. **CONTACT ADDRESS** Dept of English, Univ of Wisconsin, Eau Claire, Hibbard Hall 413, PO Box 4004, Eau Claire, WI, 54702-4004. **EMAIL** knoellcp@uwec.edu

KNOEPFLMACHER, U.C.
PERSONAL Born 06/26/1931, Munich, Germany, m, 4 children **DISCIPLINE** ENGLISH LITERATURE **EDUCATION** Univ CA, Berkeley, AB, 55, MA, 57; Princeton Univ, PhD, 61. **CAREER** From instr to assoc prof, Univ CA, Berkeley, 61-69, prof, 69-79; prof, 79-87, PATON FOUND PROF OF ANCIENT & MODERN LIT, PRINCETON UNIV, 88-; Am Coun Learned Soc fel, 65; Humanities Res Prof, 66-67 & 77; Guggenheim fel, 69-70, 87-88; sr fel, Nat Endowment Humanities, 72-73, 91-92; Nat Humanities Center NC, 95-96; adv bd, Pub Mod Lang Asn, 77-81, ed bd, 83-85; vis prof, Harvard Univ, summer, 71, Tulsa Univ, Grad Prof, 79 & Bread Loaf Sch English, 81, 83, 85, 87; dir, NEH Summer Seminars for Col Teachers, 75, 84, 86, 89; dir, NEH Summer Seminars for School Teachers, 90, 91, 95. **HONORS AND AWARDS** Distinguished Teaching Award, Acad Senate, Univ CA, Berkeley, 77; Children's Literature Asn Best Essay, 84. **MEMBERSHIPS** MLA; NCTE; NE Victorian Asn; CHLA. **RESEARCH** Nineteenth century English literature; English novel; children's literature. **SELECTED PUBLICATIONS** Auth, Religious Humanism and the Victorian Novel, Princeton Univ, 65; George Eliot's Early Novels: The Limits of Realism, Univ Calif, 68; ed, Francis Newman: Phases of Faith, Leicester Univ, 70; auth, Laughter and Despair: Readings in Ten Novels of the Victorian Era, 71, co-ed, Nature and the Victorian Imagination, 77; The Endurance of Frankenstein: Essays on Mary Shelley's Novel, Univ CA, 78; Forbidden Journeys: Fairy Tales and Fantasies by Victorian Women Writers, Chicago Univ, 93; Wuthering Heights: A Study, OH Univ, 94; Cross-writing the Child and the Adult, Yale Univ, 97; Ventures Into Childland: Victorians, Fairy Tales, and Femininity, Chicago Univ, 98. **CONTACT ADDRESS** Dept of English, Princeton Univ, Mccosh Hall 22, Princeton, NJ, 08544-1098. **EMAIL** uknopf@ariel.princeton.edu

KNOLES, LUCIA
DISCIPLINE ENGLISH **EDUCATION** St Mary's Coll, BA, 72; Rutgers, MA, 76, PhD, 79. **CAREER** ASSOC PROF, ENG, ASSUMPTION COLL **MEMBERSHIPS** Am Antiquarian Soc **CONTACT ADDRESS** Dept of English, Assumption Col, 500 Salisbury St, Worcester, MA, 01615-0005. **EMAIL** lknoles@eve.assumption.edu

KNOPP, SHERRON ELIZABETH
PERSONAL Born 04/11/1947, Fort Worth, TX **DISCIPLINE** MEDIEVAL & COMPARATIVE LITERATURE **EDUCATION** Loyola Univ, Chicago, AB, 71; Univ Calif, Los Angeles, MA, 72, PhD(English), 75. **CAREER** Asst prof, 75-80, assoc prof, 80-86, prof English, Williams Col, 86-. **MEMBERSHIPS** Mediaeval Acad Am; MLA; New Chaucer Soc. **RESEARCH** Chaucer; medieval romance; medieval dream poetry. **SELECTED PUBLICATIONS** Auth, Chaucer and Jean de Meun as Self-Conscious Narrators, Comitatus, 73; Catullus 64 and the Conflict Between Amores and Virtutes, Class Philol, 76; Artistic design in the stanzaic Morte Arthur, English Literary Hist, No 45; The Narrator and His Audience in Chaucer's Troilus and Criseyde, Studies in Philol, 78; A Zeer Zernes Ful Zerne: Teaching Sir Gawain and the Green Knight in the Survey for Majors, Approaches to Teaching Sir Gawain and the Green Knight, MLA, 86; Augustinian Poetic Theory and the Chaucerian Imagination, The Idea of Medieval Literature, Univ of Del Press, 91. **CONTACT ADDRESS** Dept of English, Williams Col, 880 Main St, Williamstown, MA, 01267-2600. **EMAIL** Sherron.E.Knopp@williams.edu

KNOWLES, RICHARD ALAN JOHN
PERSONAL Born 05/17/1935, Southbridge, MA, m, 1958, 2 children **DISCIPLINE** ENGLISH RENAISSANCE **EDUCATION** Tufts Univ, BA, 56; Univ Pa, MA, 58, PhD, 63. **CAREER** From instr to assoc prof, 62-90, prof eng, Dickson-Bascom prof of hum, 90; Univ WI-Madison, 75, Folger Shakespeare Libr fel, 68; Guggenheim Found fel, 76-77; NEH fel, 83-97, hum res inst, 90; mem, Variorum Shakespeare Comt, 72-; Gen ed, Variorum Shakespeare, 78. **MEMBERSHIPS** MLA; Shakespeare Asn Am; Intl Asoc Univ Profs of Eng; assoc Lit

Critics and scholars. **RESEARCH** Shakespeare; Renaissance mythography. **SELECTED PUBLICATIONS** Auth, Myth and type in As You Like It, English Lit Hist, 66; Unquiet and the double plot of 2 Henry IV, Shakespeare Studies, 66; Rough notes on editions collated for As You Like It, Shakespearean Res & Opportunities, 68-69; coauth, Shakespeare Variorum Handbook, MLA, 71; co-ed, English Renaissance Drama: Essays in Honor of Madeleine Doran & Mark Eccles, S Ill Univ, 76; ed, A New Variorum Edition of As You Like It, MLA, 77; auth, The Printing of the Second Quarto (Q2) of King Lear, Studies in Bibliography, 82; ed, A New Variorum Editions of Measure for Measure, 80, Anthony and Cleopatra, 90, The Winters Tale, 99; ed, New Variorum Supplimentary Bibliographies of 1 Henry IV, 2 Henry IV, Julius Caesar, Richard II, 77, Twelfth Night, 84. **CONTACT ADDRESS** Dept of Eng, Univ of Wisconsin, 600 North Park St, Madison, WI, 53706-1403. **EMAIL** rknowles@macc.wisc.edu

KNUTSON, ROSLYN L.
DISCIPLINE ENGLISH RENAISSANCE LITERATURE **EDUCATION** Univ Tex, PhD. **CAREER** English and Lit, Univ Ark **HONORS AND AWARDS** Dir, Cooper Honors Prog. **SELECTED PUBLICATIONS** Auth, The Repertory of Shakespeare's Company; "Falconer to the Little Eyases, Shakespeare Quart, 95; A Caliban in St. Mildred Poultry, Shakespeare & Cult Traditions; Telling the Story of Shakespeare's Playhouse World, Shakespeare Survey; The Commercial Significance of the Payments for Playtexts, Medieval & Renaissance Drama England; Elizabethan Documents, Captivity Narratives, and the Market for Foreign History Plays, English Literary Renaissance, 96. **CONTACT ADDRESS** Univ Ark Little Rock, 2801 S University Ave., Little Rock, AR, 72204-1099. **EMAIL** rlknutson@ualr.edu

KNUTSON, SUSAN
PERSONAL Vancouver, BC, Canada **DISCIPLINE** ENGLISH **EDUCATION** Simon Fraser Univ, BA, 75, MA, 83; Univ BC, PhD, 89. **CAREER** Proj Coordr & Ed, The Kootenay Community Printing Proj, Argenta, BC, 72; prod & script writer, WomenVision, CFRO FM, 80-81; asst prof, 88-93, ch, 93-, ASSOC PROF ENGLISH, UNIV SAINTE-ANNE, 93-. **HONORS AND AWARDS** Morris & Tim Wagner Fel, 84-85. **MEMBERSHIPS** Asn Can Studs; Can Women's Studs Asn; Can Res Inst Advan Women; Asn Can Univ Tchrs Eng; Asn Can & Quebec Lits. **SELECTED PUBLICATIONS** Auth, Challenging the Masculine Generic in Contempory Verse, 88; auth, For Feminist Narratology, 89; auth, Not for Lesbians Only: Reading Beyond Patriarchal Gender in Weaving Alliances: Selected Papers Presented for the Canadian Women's Studies Association at the 1991 and 1992 Learned Societies Conferences, 93. **CONTACT ADDRESS** Dept of English, Univ Sainte-Anne, Pointe-de-l'Eglise, NS, B0W 1M0.

KOBLER, JASPER FRED
PERSONAL Born 04/06/1928, Niagara Falls, NY, m, 1952, 2 children **DISCIPLINE** ENGLISH, AMERICAN LITERATURE **EDUCATION** La State Univ, BS, 49, BA, 51; Univ Houston, MA, 59; Univ Tex, PhD(English), 68. **CAREER** Reporter, Shreveport La Times, 51-52; res analyst, Defense Dept, Washington, DC, 52-54; reporter, United Press, New Orleans, 55-56; indust ed, Shell Oil Co, Houston, 56-59; instr English, Univ Houston, 59-61; from instr to asst prof, 64-70, ASSOC PROF ENGLISH, NTEX STATE UNIV, 70-. **MEMBERSHIPS** Col English Asn (treas, 78-81); NCTE; SCent Mod Lang Asn; Am Asn Advan Humanities. **RESEARCH** Nineteenth century American short story; American writers of 20s and 30s, especially Hemingway and Faulkner. **SELECTED PUBLICATIONS** Auth, Soldiers Home Revisited, A Hemingway, Mea-Culpa, Studies in Short Fiction, Vol 0030, 93. **CONTACT ADDRESS** Dept of English, No Texas State Univ, Denton, TX, 76203.

KOCH, CHRISTIAN HERBERT
PERSONAL Born 06/27/1938, St. Paul, MN, m, 1972 **DISCIPLINE** COMMUNICATION THEORY **EDUCATION** Northwestern Col, BA, 59; Univ Minn, Minneapolis, MA, 64; Southern Methodist Univ, MFA, 67; Univ Iowa, PhD (speech and drama), 70. **CAREER** Instr music, Dr Martin Luther Col, 59-60, 61-62 and Wis Lutheran Col, 62-66; asst prof, 70-74, ASSOC PROF COMMUN STUDIES, OBERLIN COL, 74-; Dir, Oberlin Int Conf Film Studies, 71-73. **MEMBERSHIPS** Speech Commun Asn; Int Asn Semiotic Studies; Soc Cinema Studies. **RESEARCH** Semiotics; general systems theory; nonmechanistic cybernetics. **SELECTED PUBLICATIONS** Auth, Administrative Presiding officials Today, Admin Law Rev, Vol 0046, 94; Landis,James in the Administrative Process, Admin Law Rev, Vol 0048, 96; **CONTACT ADDRESS** Dept of Commun Studies, Oberlin Col, 135 W Lorain St, Oberlin, OH, 44074-1076.

KOCH, KENNETH
PERSONAL Born 02/27/1925, Cincinnati, OH, m, 1957, 1 child **DISCIPLINE** ENGLISH, COMPARATIVE LITERATURE **EDUCATION** Harvard Univ, AB, 48; Columbia Univ, MA, 53, PhD, 59. **CAREER** Asst, Univ Calif, Berkeley, 51; from instr to assoc prof, 59-71, PROF ENGLISH and COMP LIT, COLUMBIA UNIV, 71-; Guggenheim fel, 61; Fulbright grant, 78, 82. **HONORS AND AWARDS** Harbison Award, Danforth Found, 70. **RESEARCH** Twentieth century American poetry; modern European literature. **SELECTED PUBLICATIONS** Auth, The Villino, Raritan-a Quart Rev, Vol 0012, 93; One Train May Hide Another, NY Rev Books, 93; One Train May Hide Another, Parabola-Myth Tradition and the Search for Meaning, Vol 0019, 94; Introduction to the Green Lake is Awake, Selected Poems, Am Poetry Rev, Vol 0023, 94; A Heroine of the Greek Resistance, Am Poetry Rev, Vol 0023, 94; A New Guide, Am Poetry Rev, Vol 0023, 94; Your Genius Made Me Shiver, Am Poetry Rev, Vol 0025, 96; An Interview With Koch, enneth, Am Poetry Rev, Vol 0025, 96; The True Life, Am Poetry Rev, Vol 0025, 96; How in Her Pirogue She Glides, Am Poetry Rev, Vol 0025, 96; What Makes This Statue Noble Seeming, Am Poetry Rev, Vol 0025, 96; Au Coconut School, Am Poetry Rev, Vol 0025, 96; Allegheny Menaces, Am Poetry Rev, Vol 0025, 96; Might I Be the First, Am Poetry Rev, Vol 0025, 96; In Ancient Times, Am Poetry Rev, Vol 0025, 96; Vous Etes Plus Beaux Que Vous Ne Pensiez, Poetry, Vol 0168, 96; Diving Along, Am Poetry Rev, Vol 0025, 96; Lets Pour, Am Poetry Rev, Vol 0025, 96; They Say Prince Hamlets Found a Southern Island, Am Poetry Rev, Vol 0025, 96; Mediterranean Suns, Am Poetry Rev, Vol 0025, 96; Africa Paese Notturno, Am Poetry Rev, Vol 0025, 96; Let Us Praise The Elephant, Am Poetry Rev, Vol 0025, 96. **CONTACT ADDRESS** Dept of English, Columbia Univ, New York, NY, 10027.

KOEHLER, G. STANLEY
PERSONAL Born 03/27/1915, West Orange, NJ, m, 1951, 5 children **DISCIPLINE** ENGLISH **EDUCATION** Princeton Univ, BA, 36, MA, 38, PhD, 42; Harvard Univ, MA, 37. **CAREER** Instr English, Okla State Univ, 38-40, Univ Kans, 46 & Yale Univ, 46-50; from asst prof to assoc prof, 50-62, PROF ENGLISH, UNIV MASS, AMHERST, 62-, Vis prof English, Univ Feiburg, Ger, 76-77. **MEMBERSHIPS** MLA; Milton Soc Am. **SELECTED PUBLICATIONS** Auth, A Curious Quire, Univ Mass, 63; The Art of Poetry: William Carlos Williams, Paris Rev, Fall 64; The Perfect Destroyers: A Signature of Poems, Mass Rev, summer 66; Milton's Milky Stream, J Am Folklore, 4-6/69; The Fact of Fall (poetry), Univ Mass, 69; Milton's Use of Color and Light, Milton Studies III, Pittsburgh Univ, spring 71; Milton and the Art of Landscape, Milton Studies VIII, 75; auth, Countries of the Mind: The Poetry of William Carlos Williams, Bucknell, 98. **CONTACT ADDRESS** Dept of English, Univ Mass, Amherst, MA, 01002.

KOGLER HILL, SUSAN E.
DISCIPLINE COMMUNICATIONS **EDUCATION** Bowling Green State Univ, BA, MA; Univ Denver, PhD. **CAREER** Dept ch, Cleveland State Univ. **SELECTED PUBLICATIONS** Co-auth, A Model of Mentoring and other Power Gaining Communication Strategies and Career Success, Organizational Communication: Emerging Perspectives, Vol IV, 94; The Impact of Mentoring and Collegial Support on Faculty Success: An Analysis of Support Behavior, Information Adequacy, and Communication Apprehension, Commun Edu, 38, 94. **CONTACT ADDRESS** Commun Dept, Cleveland State Univ, 83 E 24th St, Cleveland, OH, 44115. **EMAIL** s.hill@csuohio.edu

KOLB, GWIN JACKSON
PERSONAL Born 11/02/1919, Aberdeen, MS, m, 1943, 2 children **DISCIPLINE** ENGLISH **EDUCATION** Millsaps Col, AB, 41; Univ Chicago, AM, 46, PhD, 49. **CAREER** From instr to prof English, 49-77, chmn dept, 63-72, CHESTER D TRIPP PROF HUMANITIES, UNIV CHICAGO, 77-; Guggenheim fel, 56-57; vis assoc prof, Northwestern Univ, 58 and Stanford Univ, 60; Am Coun Learned Soc grant-in-aid, 61-62; chmn comt advan test in lit, Educ Testing Serv, 69-78; CO-ED, MOD PHILOL, 73-; vis prof, Univ Wash, 73. **MEMBERSHIPS** MLA; NCTE; Asn Depts English (pres, 67-68); Johnson Soc Midwest (pres, 65-66); Am Soc 18th Century Studies (pres, 76-77). **RESEARCH** English literature of the 18th century. **SELECTED PUBLICATIONS** Auth, Warton,Thomas Observations on the Faerie Queen of Spenser, Johnson, Samuel History of the English Language, and Warton History of English Poetry in Reciprocal Indebtedness, Philol Quart, Vol 0074, 95. **CONTACT ADDRESS** Dept of English, Univ of Chicago, Chicago, IL, 60637.

KOLB, JACK
PERSONAL Born 10/09/1946, Chicago, IL, m, 1999 **DISCIPLINE** ENGLISH **EDUCATION** Univ Chicago, BA, 67; Univ Va, PhD, 71. **CAREER** Asst prof, 71-76, ASSOC PROF, UNIV CALIF LOS ANGELES, 76-. **MEMBERSHIPS** ALSC; Tennyson Soc. **RESEARCH** Victorian poetry and prose; James Joyce. **SELECTED PUBLICATIONS** Ed, The Letter of Arthur Henry Hallam, Ohio State Univ Press, 81; auth, Laureate Envy: T.S. Eliot on Tennyson, ANQ 11, 98; auth, Tennyson, Carlyle, and the Morte d'Arthur, Carlyle Stud Ann 17, 97; auth, auth, New Light on Arthur Hallam and Anna Wintour, Tennyson Res Bull 6, 95; auth, On First Looking into Pope's Iliad: Hallam's Keatsian Sonnet, Victorian Poetry 29, 91; auth, The Love of Letters, underdone: Two Tennyson Studies, Victorians Inst J 15, 87; auth, Morte d'Arthur: The Death of Arthur Henry Hallam, Biog 9, 86; auth, Tennyson's Epithalamion: Another Account, Philol Q 64, 85; auth, Arthur Henry Hallam, Dictionary of Literary Biography 32: Victorian Poets Before 1850, 84; auth, Portraits of Tennyson, Modern Philol 81, 83; auth, Arthur Hallam and Emily Tennyson, Rev Eng Stud 28, 77; auth, The Hero and His Worshippers: The History of Arthur Henry Hallam's Letters, Bull John Rylands Libr 56, 73. **CONTACT ADDRESS** Dept of English, Univ of California, Los Angeles, Los Angeles, CA, 90095-1530. **EMAIL** kolb@ucla.edu

KOLIN, PHILIP CHARLES
PERSONAL Born 11/21/1945, Chicago, IL, d, 2 children **DISCIPLINE** AMERICAN DRAMA, SHAKESPEARE, TECHNICAL WRITING **EDUCATION** Chicago State Univ, BS, 66; Univ Chicago, MA, 67; Northwestern Univ, PhD, 73. **CAREER** Instr English, Western IL Univ, 67-68 & IL State Univ, 68-70; asst prof, Milton Col, 73-74; from Asst Prof to Prof Eng, Univ Southern MS, 74-, Charles W. Moorman Distinguished Prof in the Hum, 91-93; Co-ed, Miss Folklore Regist, 76. **HONORS AND AWARDS** Bk-of-the-Year Award, Am Jour Nursing, 81. **RESEARCH** Tech writing; Shakespeare; Tennessee Williams. **SELECTED PUBLICATIONS** Auth, sev entries in The Cambridge Guide to American Theatre, including Sticks and Bones, Streamers, Basic Training of Pavlo Hummel, A Streetcar Named Desire, Glass Menagerie, Rose Tattoo, and others, Cambridge Univ Press, 92; Roses for Sharron: Poems, Colonial Press, 93; Confronting Tennessee Williams's A Streetcar Named Desire: Essays in Critical Pluralism, Greenwood, 93; Titus Andronicus: Critical Essays, Garland, 95; co-ed, Speaking on Stage - Interviews With Contemporary American Playwrights, Univ Ala Press, 96; auth, Venus and Adonis: Critical Essays, Garland, 97; Tennessee Williams: A Guide to Research and Performance, Greenwood, 98; Tennessee Williams--Streetcar Named Desire (Plays in Performance Series), Cambridge Univ Press, 99; author of numerous articles and other publications. **CONTACT ADDRESS** Dept of Eng, Univ of S MS, S S Box 5037, Hattiesburg, MS, 39406-8395.

KOLKER, DELPHINE
PERSONAL Born 04/12/1918, Dayton, OH **DISCIPLINE** ENGLISH **EDUCATION** Univ Dayton, BS, 42; Cath Univ Am, MA, 44, PhD(English), 52. **CAREER** Instr English and chmn dept, Immaculata Col, Ohio, 44-59; asst prof English and humanities, St Joseph Col, Ind, 59-61; from asst prof to prof English and philos, St John Col Cleveland, 61-75; PROF ENGLISH, CLEVELAND STATE UNIV, 75-; CONSULT, CHOICE, 64-. **MEMBERSHIPS** MLA; Am Cath Philos Asn. **RESEARCH** Translations; philosophy; childrens literature. **SELECTED PUBLICATIONS** Auth, To Pay or Not to Pay in Local Governments Stake in Legislation to Reauthorize Superfund, Urban Lawyer, Vol 0025, 93. **CONTACT ADDRESS** Dept of English, Cleveland State Univ, Cleveland, OH, 44115.

KOLKO, BETH E.
DISCIPLINE RHETORIC AND COMPOSITION **EDUCATION** Oberlin Col, BA, 89; Univ TX at Austin, MA, 91, PhD, 94. **CAREER** Asst prof, Univ TX at Arlington, 96-; asst prof, Univ WY, Laramie, 94-96; adj asst instr, Univ TX, Austin, 91-94 & tchg asst, 89-91; tchg asst, Techn Commun, Mech Eng Dept, Univ TX, Austin, 90-92; asst dir, Lower Div Eng Off, Univ TX at Austin, 92-93; staff mem, Eng Dept Comp Writing and Res Lab, Univ TX at Austin, 92; lower div Eng Adv Bd, Univ TX at Austin, 90-92; manuscript rev, J Adv Composition, 96-; ed bd mem, Kairos: A J For Tchrs of Writing in Webbed Env, 97-; adv bd mem, CULTSTUD-L listserv, 96-; owner & moderator, Ada-l, Listserv for women in technol within Eng dept, 96-; mem, Rocky Mt ACW Exec Bd, 94-96; coordr, Front Range Composition Reading Gp, 95. **SELECTED PUBLICATIONS** Auth, Bodies in Place: Real Politics, Real Pedagogy, and Virtual Space, High Wired: On the Design, Use, and Theory of Educational MOOs, Univ Mich Press, Ann Arbor, 97; Building a World With Words: The Narrative Reality of Virtual Communities, Works and Days 25/26, 95; Intellectual Property in Collaborative Virtual Space, Computers and Composition, 98; Using Inter Change Transcripts Recursively in the Writing Classroom, Wings 1 1:4, 93; Written Argumentation, Hyperard application, Design team mem, Intellimation Libre Macintosh, Santa Barbara, 93. **CONTACT ADDRESS** Dept of Eng, Univ of Texas at Arlington, 203 Carlisle Hall, PO Box 19035, Arlington, TX, 76019-0595.

KOLODNY, ANNETTE
PERSONAL Born 08/21/1941, New York, NY **DISCIPLINE** AMERICAN LITERATURE, WOMENS STUDIES **EDUCATION** Brooklyn Col, BA, 62; Univ Calif, Berkeley, MA, 65, PhD(Am lit), 69. **CAREER** Asst prof English, Yale Univ, 69-70 and Univ BC, 70-74; admin coordr womens studies prog, Univ BC, 72-74; assoc prof English, Univ NH, 74-82; VIS ASSOC PROF ENGLISH, UNIV MD, 82-; UNIV BC SR RES GRANTS, 70-; Can Coun sr res grant, 73-74; MEM ADV BD, AM LIT, 74-; consult grants and fels, Can Coun, 74-77 and NAT ENDOWMENT HUMANITIES, 75-; fel study women soc, Ford Found, 75-76; Rockefeller found, 78-79; Guggenheim found, 79-80. **HONORS AND AWARDS** Florence Howe Essay Prize, 79. **MEMBERSHIPS** MLA; Am Studies Asn; Can Asn Am Studies; Nat Womens Studies Asn. **RESEARCH** Early and contemporary American literature; women writers. **SELECTED PUBLICATIONS** Auth, Inventing a Feminist Discourse, Rhetoric and Resistance in Fuller, Margaret Woman in the Nineteenth Century, New Literary Hist, Vol 0025, 94;

Response to Hartman, Rome, New Literary Hist, Vol 0027, 96; 60 Minutes at the University of Arizona in the Polemic Against Tenure, New Literary Hist, Vol 0027, 96. **CONTACT ADDRESS** Dept of English, Univ of Md, College Park, MD, 20742.

KOMAR, KATHLEEN LENORE
PERSONAL Born 10/11/1949, Joliet, IL **DISCIPLINE** MODERN GERMAN AND ENGLISH LITERATURE **EDUCATION** Univ Chicago, BA, 71; Princeton Univ, MA, 75, PhD(comp lit), 77. **CAREER** Asst Prof Ger Lang and Comp Lit, Univ Calif, Los Angeles, 77, Am Coun Learned Soc grant, 78. **MEMBERSHIPS** MLA; Am Comp Lit Asn; Philol Asn Pac Coast; Western Asn Ger Studies. **RESEARCH** Fragmented, multilinear narratives in the early 20th century: German and American; the poetry of Rainer Maria Rilkc and Wallace Stevens; the works of Hermann Broch. **SELECTED PUBLICATIONS** Auth, Through the Lens of the Reader in Explorations of European Narrative, J Ger Studies, Vol 0029, 93; Naturalism in the European Novel in New Critical Perspectives, Mod Fiction Studies, Vol 0039, 93; Countercurrents on the Primacy of Texts in Literary-Criticism, J Ger Studies, Vol 0030, 94; Lesarten in New Methodologies and Old Texts, J Ger Studies, Vol 0030, 94; Why There are so Few Men in My Comparative Literature Courses on Women-Writers, Womens Studies, Interdisciplinary J, Vol 0023, 94; Klytemnestra In Germany in Revisions of a Female Archetype by Reinig, Christa and Bruckner,Christine, Ger Rev, Vol 0069, 94; Es-War-Mord in Schroeter Film Malina in the Murder of Bachmann, Ingeborg at the Hands of an Alter-Ego, Mod Austrian Lit, Vol 0027, 94; The Kunstmarchen of Hofmannsthal, Musil, And Doblin in German, Mod Austrian Lit, Vol 0027, 94; The State of Comparative Literature in Theory and Practice 94, World Lit Today, Vol 0069, 95; The Beginning of Terror in a Psychological-Study of Rilke, Rainer, Maria Life and Work, J Engl Ger Philol, Vol 0094, 95 Comparative Literature in Introduction to Comparative Literature as an Academic Discipline in German, Germanisch-Romanische Monatsschrift, Vol 0045, 96; Experimental Setups in the Experimental Relationship Between Literature and Reality in Musil, Robert Drei Frauen, Mod Austrian Lit, Vol 0030, 97. **CONTACT ADDRESS** Dept of Ger Lang, Univ of Calif, Los Angeles, CA, 90024.

KOMECHAK, MICHAEL E.
PERSONAL Born 08/19/1932, Gary, IN **DISCIPLINE** ENGLISH & AMERICAN LITERATURE **EDUCATION** Univ Notre Dame, MA, 61; Cardinal Stritch Col, BFA, 78. **CAREER** Chmn dept English, St Procopius Acad, 59-65; chaplain, bldg coordr & teacher English, 65-75, assoc prof Fine Arts, Benedictine Univ, 80-98, chmn div, 78-96, retired May, 98, continues to be curator of the univ art collection and coordinator of campus art exhibitions. **RESEARCH** Nineteenth century American and English literature; contemporary journalism. **SELECTED PUBLICATIONS** Auth, Portfolio Format, Scholastic Ed, 12/62; Organize Student Press Bureau for Better Public Relations, Bull Columbia Scholastic Press Adv Asn, 1/66; Raise Funds Via Attractive Ad Book, Scholastic Ed, 12/66; Milwaukee's Pabst Theatre, 6/77 & Dart's Last Church, 10/77, Inland Architect. **CONTACT ADDRESS** Fine Arts Program, Benedictine Univ, 5700 College Rd, Lisle, IL, 60532-0900.

KONEK, CAROL WOLFE
PERSONAL Born 01/06/1934, Meade, KS, 4 children **DISCIPLINE** WOMENS STUDIES, ENGLISH **EDUCATION** Univ Kans, BS, 60; Wichita State Univ, MA, 68; Univ Okla, PhD(admin), 77. **CAREER** Instr compos, 68-76, ASST PROF WOMENS STUDIES, WICHITA STATE UNIV, 70-; Proj dir, proj DELTA, Womens Educ Equity Act, Wichita State Univ, 76-78. **MEMBERSHIPS** Am Educ Asn; Nat Asn of Women Deans, Adminrs and Counr; Nat Womens Studies Asn. **SELECTED PUBLICATIONS** Auth, The Creation of Feminist Consciousness From the Middle Ages, Historian, Vol 0056, 94; Contemporary Western-European Feminism, Historian, Vol 0056, 94. **CONTACT ADDRESS** Wichita State Univ, Wichita, KS, 67208.

KONICK, STEVE
DISCIPLINE COMMUNICATIONS **EDUCATION** Univ Md, Col Park, BA, 82, MA, 89, PhD, 93. **CAREER** Tchg asst, Univ Md, 86-91; lectr, Towson State Univ, 91-92; asst prof, SUNY, Geneseo, 92-96; asst prof, 96-, gen mgr, fac adv, Linfield Col, 96-; exec producer/news ed, Tuesday Weekly TV, 86-91; gen mgr/fac dir, WGSU-FM, 93-96, fac adv, NBS-AERho Honors Soc, SUNY, Geneseo, 94-96. **HONORS AND AWARDS** Prince Georgians on Camera First Place Video Award, Tuesday Weekly, 87; Geneseo Orgn Leadership Develop Award, 94. **MEMBERSHIPS** Asn for Educ in Jour and Mass Commun,89-. **SELECTED PUBLICATIONS** Auth, A Visual Thematic Analysis of Network News Coverage of AIDS, in Media-Mediated AIDS, ed Linda Fuller, 96. **CONTACT ADDRESS** Linfield Col, 900 SE Baker St, McMinnville, OR, 97128-6894. **EMAIL** skonick@linfield.edu

KONIGSBERG, IRA
PERSONAL Born 05/30/1935, New York, NY, m, 1957 **DISCIPLINE** ENGLISH **EDUCATION** City Col NY, BA, 56; Columbia Univ, MA, 57; Stanford Univ, PhD(English), 61. **CAREER** Instr English and Am lit, Brandeis Univ, 61-63; from asst prof to assoc prof, 63-74, PROF ENGLISH LANG and LIT, UNIV MICH, ANN ARBOR, 74-; Fulbright-Hays lectr Am lit, Univ Vienna, 66-67. **MEMBERSHIPS** MLA; Am Soc Eighteenth-Century Studies; Am Film Inst. **RESEARCH** Critical theory; film; restoration and 18th century English literature. **SELECTED PUBLICATIONS** Auth, The Movies, Introduction, Mich Quart Rev, Vol 0034, 95; Cinema, Psychoanalysis, and Hermeneutics, Secrets of The Soul, Mich Quart Rev, Vol 0034, 95; The Movies, a centennial issue, 2, Introduction, Mich Quart Rev, Vol 0035, 96; Cave Paintings and the Cinema, Wide Angle Quart J Film Hist Theory Criticism and Pract, Vol 0018, 96; The Only I in the World in Religion, Psychoanalysis, and the Dybbuk, Cinema J, Vol 0036, 97. **CONTACT ADDRESS** Dept of English, Univ of MIch, Ann Arbor, MI, 48104.

KOOISTRA, JOHN
DISCIPLINE ENGLISH **EDUCATION** Brock Univ, BA; McMaster, MA, PhD. **CAREER** Lectr, Nipissing Univ; McMaster; King Saud Univ, Riyadh, Saudi Arabia; Niagara Col; Brock Univ, 82-94. **SELECTED PUBLICATIONS** Auth, Shoo-fly Dyck, Summertime Stories from Front Porch Al, Penguin, 95. **CONTACT ADDRESS** Dept of English, Nipissing Univ, 100 College Dr, Box 5002, North Bay, ON, P1B 8L7.

KOON, G.W.
DISCIPLINE ENGLISH LITERATURE **EDUCATION** Univ Ga, PhD, 73. **CAREER** Dept Eng, Clemson Univ **RESEARCH** Modern American and Southern literature. **SELECTED PUBLICATIONS** Auth, Old Glory and The Stars and Bars, Univ SC Press, 95; Readings for a New Southern Renaissance, SCR, 93; 14 Types of Ambiguity, Southern Cult, 95. **CONTACT ADDRESS** Clemson Univ, 316 Strode, Clemson, SC, 29634. **EMAIL** badk@clemson.edu

KOONTZ, CHRISTIAN
DISCIPLINE ENGLISH LITERATURE, LINGUISTICS **EDUCATION** Mercyhurst Col, BA; Cath Univ Amer, MA, PhD. **CAREER** Prof, 80-. **RESEARCH** Writing to learn, heal, and create. **SELECTED PUBLICATIONS** Auth, Cultivating Multiple Intelligences through the Living Journal. **CONTACT ADDRESS** Dept of Eng, Univ Detroit Mercy, 4001 W McNichols Rd, PO BOX 19900, Detroit, MI, 48219-0900. **EMAIL** KOONTZC2@udmercy.edu

KOONTZ, THOMAS WAYNE
PERSONAL Born 07/09/1939, Ft. Wayne, IN, m, 1998, 5 children **DISCIPLINE** LITERATURE; FOLKLORE **EDUCATION** Miami Univ, BA, 61; Ind Univ, Bloomington, MA, 65, PhD(English), 70. **CAREER** Instr English, George Washington Univ, 65-67; PROF ENGLISH, BALL STATE UNIV, 67-; Nat Endowment Humanities educ grant & proj dir, Ball State Univ, 72-73. **HONORS AND AWARDS** Ely Lilly Fel. **RESEARCH** American studies and poetry; Black American literature. **SELECTED PUBLICATIONS** Auth, To Begin With; Charms; In Such a Light; ed, The View From The Top of The Mountain: Poems After Sixty, Barnwood Press, 81. **CONTACT ADDRESS** Dept of English, Ball State Univ, 2000 W University, Muncie, IN, 47306-0002. **EMAIL** tkoontz@wp.bsu.edu

KOPACZ, PAULA D.
DISCIPLINE ENGLISH **EDUCATION** Mt. Holyoke, AB, 69; Univ Conn, MA, 70; Columbia Univ, PhD, 75. **CAREER** Assoc prof, PROF & FOUND PROF, ENG, E KENTUCKY UNIV **MEMBERSHIPS** Am Antiquarian Soc **SELECTED PUBLICATIONS** Auth, "'To Finish What's Begun': Bradstreet's Last Words," Early Am Lit 23, 88; auth, "Men Can Do Best and Women Know It Well: Anne Bradstreet and Feminist Aesthetics," Kent Philological Rev 2, 87; auth, "Feminist at the Tribune: Margaret Fuller as Professional Writer," Studies in the American Renaissance, 91. **CONTACT ADDRESS** Eastern Kentucky Univ, 467 Case Annex, Richmond, KY, 40475. **EMAIL** engkopac@acs.eku.edu

KOPFMAN, JENIFER E.
DISCIPLINE COMMUNICATION **EDUCATION** Miami Univ, BA, 91; MI State Univ, MA, 94, PhD, 95. **CAREER** Adjunct asst prof, Univ AZ, 95-97; asst prof, Univ Toledo, 97-99. **HONORS AND AWARDS** Dissertation of the Year Award for Health Commun from the Speech Commun Asn and the Int Commun Asn, 95. **MEMBERSHIPS** Nat Commun Asn; Int Commun Asn; Western States Commun Asn. **RESEARCH** Health commun; persuasion & cognition; nonverbal commun. **SELECTED PUBLICATIONS** Auth, with S W Smith, K Morrison, and L A Ford, The Influence of Prior Thought and Intent on the Memorability and Persuasiveness of Organ Donation Message Strategies, Health Commun, 16, 94; with S W Smith, C L Medendorp, S Ranck, and K Morrison, The Prototypical Features of the Outstanding Professor from the Female and Male Undergraduate Perspective: The Roles of Verbal and Nonverbal Communication, J on Excellence in Col Teaching, 5, 94; with K Witte, H Bidol, M Casey, K Maduschke, A Marshall, G Meyer, K Morrison, K Ribisl, and S Robbins, Bringing Order to Chaos: Communication and Health, Commun Studies, 47, 96; S W Smith, and J K Ah Yun, Encouraging Feedback in the Large College Class: The Use of a Question/Comment Box, J of the Asn for Commun Administration, 3, 96; with S W Smith, Understanding the Audiences of a Health Communication Campaign: A Discriminant Analysis of Potential Organ Donors Based on Intent to Donate, J of Applied Commun Res, 24, 96; Persuading Potential Organ Donors to Sign Donor Cards: A Case History in Developing Effective Campaigns, in R J Knecht & E M Wiley, eds, Professional Business Communication: An Audience Centered Approach, Simon & Schuster Custom Pub, 97; with S W Smith, J K Ah Yun, and A Hodges, Affective and Cognitive Reactions to Narrative Versus Statistical Evidence Organ Donation Messages, J of Applied Commun Res, 26, 98. **CONTACT ADDRESS** Dept of Communication, Univ of Toledo, Libbey Hall, Toledo, OH, 43606. **EMAIL** jkopfma@pop3.utoledo.edu

KOPTAK, PAUL E.
PERSONAL Born 04/01/1955, Denville, NJ, m, 1983 **DISCIPLINE** COMMUNICATION **EDUCATION** Rutgers Univ, BA, Psychology, with honors, 77; N Park Theol Seminary, Master of Divinity, highest honors, 86; Garrett-Evangelical Theol Seminary/Northwestern Univ, PhD, Philosophy, 90. **CAREER** Part time instr in biblical and commun studs, N Park Col, 88-93; visiting lecturer, Carib Grad Sch of Theol, Kingston, Jam, 89-90; part-time instr in biblical studs, N Park Theol Seminary, 89-93; Interim Dean of studs, N Park Theol Seminary, 93-94; Asst prof of Commun & Biblical interpretation, Paul & Bernice Brandel Chr in Preaching, N Park Theol Seminary, 93-. **MEMBERSHIPS** Acad of Homeletics; Assoc for Commun in Theol Educ; Chicago Soc of Biblical Res; Evangelical Homelitic Soc; Inst for Biblical Res; Kenneth Burke Soc; Relig Speech and Commun Assoc; Soc of Biblical Lit; Nat Commun Assoc. **SELECTED PUBLICATIONS** auth, Rhetorical Identification in Paul's Autobiographical Narrative: Galatians 1:13-2:14, Journal for the Study of the New Testament, vol 40, 97-115, 90; auth, What's New in Interpreting Genesis? A Survey of Recent Commentaries and Books, Covenant Quarterly, vol 53 no 1, 3-16, 2/95; auth, Preaching Lawfully, Litany on Law and Liberty: A Response to Psalm 119, Ex Audita, vol 11, 145-152, 95; auth, The Temple, the Scribe, and the Widow, Preaching On-Line, 3/96; Rhetorical Criticism of the Bible: A Resource for Preaching, Covenant Quarterly, vol 54 no 3, 26-36, 7/96; On Namings and New Years, Preaching, 43-46, 11/96; co-ed, co-auth, To Hear and Obey: Essays in Honor of Frederick Carlson Holmgren, Covenant Pubs, 84-94, 97; Rhetorical Identification in Preaching, Preaching, 11/98. **CONTACT ADDRESS** No Park Theol Sem, 3225 W Foster Ave, #14, Chicago, IL, 60625-4895. **EMAIL** pkoptak@northpark.edu

KORCHECK, ROBERT
PERSONAL m, 1 child **DISCIPLINE** MEDIEVAL AND RENAISSANCE LITERATURE **EDUCATION** St Bonaventure Univ, BA; WVA Univ, Morgantown, MA, PhD. **CAREER** Instr, Duquesne Univ; instr, Fairmont State Col; instr, CA State Univ PA. **RESEARCH** Milton. **SELECTED PUBLICATIONS** Wrote a bk-length study of a coal mining community in southwestern PA (Nemacolin); also contrib an assortment of materials on coal mining to numerous organizations and publ. **CONTACT ADDRESS** California Univ of Pennsylvania, California, PA, 15419. **EMAIL** korcheck@cup.edu

KORENMAN, JOAN SMOLIN
PERSONAL Born 09/05/1941, Brooklyn, NY, m, 1968, 1 child **DISCIPLINE** AMERICAN LITERATURE **EDUCATION** Brandeis Univ, BA, 63; Harvard Univ, AM, 64, PhD(English), 70. **CAREER** Asst prof, 69-76, ASSOC PROF ENGLISH, UNIV MD BALTIMORE COUNTY, 76-; DIR WOMENS STUDIES MINOR, 81-. **MEMBERSHIPS** Soc Study Southern Lit; MLA; NCTE. **RESEARCH** American fiction; womens studies. **SELECTED PUBLICATIONS** Auth, African American Women Writers, Black Nationalism, and the Matrilineal Heritage, Cla J College Lang Asn, Vol 0038, 94. **CONTACT ADDRESS** Dept of English, Univ of Md Baltimore County, Baltimore, MD, 21228.

KORG, JACOB
PERSONAL Born 11/21/1922, New York, NY, m, 1953, 1 child **DISCIPLINE** ENGLISH **EDUCATION** City Col New York, BA, 43; Columbia Univ, MA, 47, PhD, 52. **CAREER** Instr English, Bard Col, 47-49 and City Col New York, 51-55; from asst prof to prof, Univ Wash, 55-68; prof, Univ Md, 68-70; PROF ENGLISH, UNIV WASH, 70-; Exchange prof, Nat Taiwan Univ, 60; travel grant, Am Coun Learned Soc, 81. **MEMBERSHIPS** Int Asn Univ Prof English; MLA. **RESEARCH** Victorian contemporary and comparative literature. **SELECTED PUBLICATIONS** Auth, The Writings of Thoreau, Henry,D. J, Vol 3, 1848-1865, Nineteenth Century Prose, Vol 0020, 93; The Thoreau Log in a Documentary Life of Thoreau, Henry,David 1817-1862, Nineteenth Century Prose, Vol 0020, 93; The Writings of Thoreau, Henry,D. J, Vol 4, 1851-1852, Nineteenth Century Prose, Vol 0020, 93; Jewish Life in Renaissance Italy, Clio-A J Lit Hist Phil Hist, Vol 0024, 95; The Myth of the Renaissance in 19th-Century Writing, Clio-A J Lit History Phil Hist, Vol 0025, 95; Shakespeare and the Jews in Shapiro,J, Clio-A J Lit Hist Philos Hist, Vol 0025, 96; The Collected Letters of Gissing, George, Vol 3, 1886-1888, Vol 4, 1889-1891, Vol 5, 1892-1895, Vol 6, 1895-1897, Nineteenth-Century Lit, Vol 0051, 96. **CONTACT ADDRESS** Dept of English, Univ of Wash, Seattle, WA, 98195.

KORITZ, AMY
DISCIPLINE MODERN LITERATURE, DRAMA **EDUCATION** Univ NC, PhD, 88. **CAREER** Instr, 89. **SELECTED PUBLICATIONS** Auth, Dancing the Orient for England: Maud Allan's 'The Vision of Salome, Theatre Jour 46.1, 94; Gendering Bodies/Performing Art: Dance and Literature in Early Twentieth-Century British Culture, AnnArbor: Univ Mich Press, 95; (Re)Moving Boundaries: From Dance History to Cultural Studies, Moving Words: Dance Criticism in Transition, Routledge, 96. **CONTACT ADDRESS** Dept of Eng, Tulane Univ, 6823 St Charles Ave, New Orleans, LA, 70118. **EMAIL** akoritz@mailhost.tcs.tulane.edu

KOROM, FRANK J.
PERSONAL Born 12/15/1957, Kikinda, Yugoslavia, s **DISCIPLINE** FOLKLORE AND FOLKLIFE **EDUCATION** Univ Col, BA, 84; Univ Penn, MA, 87, PhD, 92. **CAREER** Postdoc fel, Smithsonian Inst, 92-93; adj lec, Santa Fe Commun Col, 94-98; cur, Museum of Int Folk Art, 93-98; asst prof, Boston Univ, 98- **HONORS AND AWARDS** Phi Beta Kappa, Univ Col, 84. **MEMBERSHIPS** All India Folklore Cong; Am Acad of Relig; Am Folklore Soc; Asn of Asian Stud; Folklore Fels of Finland; Int Asn for Tibetan Stud; Int Soc for Folk Narrative Res; Int Union of Anthrop and Ethnol Sci; Phi Beta Kappa. **RESEARCH** Hinduism; Islam; Buddhism; ritual, muth, folklore and material culture. **SELECTED PUBLICATIONS** Auth, "A Festive Mourning: Moharram in Trinidad," India Mag, 93; Report on a Planned Exhibit of Tibetan Material Culture in Diaspora," Asian Folklore Stud, 94; "Community Process and the Performance of Muharram Observances in Trinidad," Drama Rev, 94; "Memory, Innovation and Emergent Ethnicities: The Creolization of an Indo-Trinidadian Performance," Diaspora, 94; "Transformation of Language to Rhythm: The Hosay Drums of Trinidad," World of Music, 94; "Recycling in India: Status and Economic Realities," Recycled, Reseen, Reseen: Folk Art from the Global Scrap Heap, Abrams, 96; "Oral Canon Formation in a Bengali Religious Community," Suomen Anthrop, 96; "Place, Space and Identity: The Cultural, Economic and Aesthetic Politics of Tibetan Diaspora," Tibetan Culture in the Diaspora, Austrian Acad of Sci, 97; "Old Age Tibet in New Age America," Constructing Tibetan Culture: Contemporary Perspectives, 97; "Tibetans," American Immigrant Cultures: Builders of a Nation, Macmillan, 97; "Language, Belief and Experience in Bengali Folk Deity," Western Folklore, 97; "Editing Dharmaraj: Academic Genealogies of a Bengali Folk Deity," Western Folklore, 97; Oral Exegesis, Western Folklore, 97; "Foreword," The Art of Exile, Mus of New Mexico Pr, 98 **CONTACT ADDRESS** Dept of Religion, Boston Univ, 745 Commonwealth Ave., Boston, MA, 02215. **EMAIL** korom@bu.edu

KORSHIN, PAUL J.
PERSONAL Born 07/24/1939, New York, NY, m, 1998 **DISCIPLINE** ENGLISH **EDUCATION** City Col New York, AB, 61; Harvard Univ, AM, 62, PhD(English), 66. **CAREER** Asst prof, 66-71, assoc prof, 71-80, prof English, Univ Penn, 80- ; Am Philos Soc grant-in-aid, 70; Am Coun Learned Soc grant-in-aid, 71 & 77; Guggenheim fel, 87-88; fel, Bellagio Ctr, Rockefeller Found, 88; co-chmn, Anglo-Am Organizing Comt, 18th Century Short Title Catalogue, 76-80. **MEMBERSHIPS** MLA; Mod Humanities Res Asn; Am Soc 18th Century Studies (exec secy, 73-78); Bibl Soc Am; Bibl Soc London. **RESEARCH** Eighteenth century English literature and intellectual history; 18th century literary patronage; Samuel Johnson, 1709-1784. **SELECTED PUBLICATIONS** Ed & contribr, Studies In Change and Revolution: Aspects of English Intellectual History, 1640-1800, 72 & auth, From Concord to Dissent: Major Themes in English Poetic Theory, 1640-1700, 73, Scolar Press, England; ed, The Widening Circle, Univ Penn, 76; Typologies in England, 1650-1820, Princeton Univ, 82; ed & gen ed, The Eighteenth Century: A Current Bibliography, AMS Press, 82; ed, contribur, Johnson After 200 Years, Univ Penn, 86; ed, The Age of Johnson: A Scholarly Annual, AMS, 87- . **CONTACT ADDRESS** Dept of English, Univ of Pa, 3340 Walnut St, Philadelphia, PA, 19104-6203. **EMAIL** pkorshin@english.upenn.edu

KOVARIK, BILL
DISCIPLINE PRINT AND WEB MEDIA **EDUCATION** VA Commonwealth Univ, BS; Univ SC, MA; Univ MD, PhD. **CAREER** Assoc prof, Radford Univ. **SELECTED PUBLICATIONS** Publ a bk on the hist of environmental conflict in the mass media. **CONTACT ADDRESS** Radford Univ, Radford, VA, 24142. **EMAIL** wkovarik@runet.edu

KOWALCZYK, RICHARD L.
DISCIPLINE VICTORIAN AND MODERN BRITISH LITERATURE **EDUCATION** Wayne State Univ, PhD. **CAREER** Prof, 61-. **RESEARCH** Technical writing based on professional consulting and publications. **SELECTED PUBLICATIONS** Pub(s), articles on writers' response to cultural issues; ed reader, Mod Lit. **CONTACT ADDRESS** Dept of Eng, Univ Detroit Mercy, 4001 W McNichols Rd, PO BOX 19900, Detroit, MI, 48219-0900. **EMAIL** KOWALR@udmercy.edu

KOWALEWSKI, MICHAEL
PERSONAL Born 11/02/1956, San Francisco, CA, m, 1983, 3 children **DISCIPLINE** ENGLISH **EDUCATION** Rutgers Univ, PhD 86, MA 82; Amherst Col, BA 78. **CAREER** Carleton Col, asst prof, assoc prof, 91 to 95-; Princeton Univ, asst prof 86-91. **HONORS AND AWARDS** Acls Fel. **MEMBERSHIPS** MLA; WLA; CSA; CHS. **RESEARCH** American regionalism; American film; the literature of place. **SELECTED PUBLICATIONS** Auth, Popular Classics of American Literature, Tokyo, Eihsha Ltd, 96; auth, Gold Rush: A Literary Exploration, ed, Berkeley CA, Heydey Books, conjunct with CA Council for the Humanities, 97; auth, Temperamental Journeys: The Modern Literature of Travel, ed, Athens GA, U of GA Press, 92; auth, Reading the West: New Essays on the Literature of the American West, ed, NY, Cambridge Univ Press, 96; auth, Deadly Musings: Violence and Verbal Form In American Fiction, Princeton NJ, P U Press, 93. **CONTACT ADDRESS** Dept of English, Carleton Col, Northfield, MN, 55057. **EMAIL** mkowalew@carleton.edu

KOZIKOWSKI, STANLEY JOHN
PERSONAL Born 04/16/1943, Fall River, MA, m, 1965, 2 children **DISCIPLINE** ENGLISH, COMMUNICATIONS THEORY **EDUCATION** Southeastern Mass Univ, BS, 65; Univ Mass, MA 68, PhD(English), 71. **CAREER** Instr English, Col of Our Lady of the Elms, 68-71, asst prof, 71-75; asst prof, 75-77, DEAN OF UNDERGRAD FAC, BRYANT COL, 78-. **MEMBERSHIPS** Am Bus Commun Asn; Am Inst Decision Sci; MLA; NCTE; New England Asn Instnl Res. **RESEARCH** English Renaissance drama and poetry; modern American literature; communications theory. **SELECTED PUBLICATIONS** Auth, Damned in a Fair Life, Cheever the Swimmer, Studies Short Fiction, Vol 0030, 93; Shakespeare Hamlet, Explicator, Vol 0055, 97. **CONTACT ADDRESS** 7 Cider Lane, Greenville, RI, 02828.

KRAFT, ELIZABETH
PERSONAL Born 10/05/1954, Atlanta, GA, m, 1989 **DISCIPLINE** ENGLISH **EDUCATION** Ga Southern Col, BA, 75; Ga State Univ, MA, 78; Emory Univ, PhD, 85. **CAREER** Asst prof, Univ of SC Spartanburg, 85-87; ASST PROF, 87-92, ASSOC PROF, 92-98, PROF, UNIV OF GA, 98-. **HONORS AND AWARDS** Outstanding honors prof, Univ of Ga, 98; Biblio Soc of Am Fel, 95; NEH Summer Stipend, 87; William Andrews Clark Memorial Libr Fel, 87. **MEMBERSHIPS** MLA; Am Soc for 18th Century Studies; SAMLA. **RESEARCH** Restoration and 18th Century British Lit. **SELECTED PUBLICATIONS** Co-ed, The Poems of Anna Letitia Barbauld, Univ of Ga, 94; ed, The Young Philosopher, Eighteenth-Century Novels by Women, Univ of Ky Press, 99; auth, Character and Consciousness in Eighteenth-Century Comic Fiction, Univ of Ga, 92; Laurence Sterne Revisited, Twayne, 96; Ooronoko in the Classroom: A Review of Texts, Restoration, 98; The Pentecostal Moment in A Sentimental Journy, Critical Essays on Laurence Sterne, G.K. Hall, 98; The Two Amelias: Henry Fielding and Elizabeth Justice, ELH, 95. **CONTACT ADDRESS** Dept of English, Univ of Georgia, Athens, GA, 30602. **EMAIL** ekraft@arches.uga.edu

KRAFT, RUTH NELSON
PERSONAL St. Louis, MO, m, 1966 **DISCIPLINE** ENGLISH, MUSIC **EDUCATION** Northwestern Univ, BM, 35, MM, 40; Columbia Univ, MA, 61. **CAREER** Teacher, Woodmere Acad, NY, 43-56; teacher English and creative writing, G W Hewlett High Sch, NY, 56-68, coordr Humanities, 68-74; INSTR MOD FICTION and HIST MUSIC, FIVE TOWNS COL, MERRICK, 75-. **HONORS AND AWARDS** Nat Award, Outstanding Sec Educr Am, 75. **SELECTED PUBLICATIONS** Auth, Humor in American Literature in A Selected Annotated-Bibliography, Metaphor Symbolic Activ, Vol 0008, 93; Illuminating Shadows in The Mythic Power of Film, Metaphor Symbolic Activ, Vol 0009, 94. **CONTACT ADDRESS** Beverly Rd, Douglaston, NY, 11363.

KRAHNKE, KARL
DISCIPLINE ENGLISH LITERATURE **EDUCATION** Univ Mich, BA, MA, PhD. **CAREER** Assoc prof. **RESEARCH** Discourse analysis of ESL writing; function of non standard Englishes in business and industry. **SELECTED PUBLICATIONS** Auth, puns on language and language teaching. **CONTACT ADDRESS** Dept of English, Colorado State Univ, Fort Collins, CO, 80523. **EMAIL** kkrahnke@vines.colostate.edu

KRAJEWSKI, BRUCE
DISCIPLINE ENGLISH LITERATURE **EDUCATION** Univ Iowa, PhD. **RESEARCH** Philos hermeneutics; hist of interpretation; film; rhetoric. **SELECTED PUBLICATIONS** Auth, Traveling with Hermes: Hermeneutics and Rhetoric, 92; auth, The Musical Horizon of Religion: Blumenberg's Matthieuspassion, Hist Human Sci, 93; auth, Postmodernism, Allegory, and Hermeneutics in Brazil, 89. **CONTACT ADDRESS** English Dept, Laurentian Univ, 935 Ramsey Lake Rd, Sudbury, ON, P3E 2C6.

KRAMER, AARON
PERSONAL Born 12/13/1921, Brooklyn, NY, m, 1942, 2 children **DISCIPLINE** ENGLISH **EDUCATION** Brooklyn Col, BA, 41, MA, 51; NY Univ, PhD(English), 66. **CAREER** From instr to assoc prof English, Adelphi Univ, 61-70; PROF ENGLISH, DOWLING COL, 70-; Chmn, Ficke Award Comt, Poetry Soc Am, 56 and Reynolds Award Comt, 57; lectr, Queens Col, NY, 66-69; co-dir, Poetry Therapy Progs, Cleary Sch Deaf, 69-78 and Cent Islip State Hosp, 70-78; lectr, Univ Guanajuato, 74; adj prof, Grad Union Col, 75-77; grad prof English, Adelphi Univ, 75-80; co-ed, West Hills Rev; fel, Mem Found Jewish Cult, 78. **HONORS AND AWARDS** Standard Panel Award, Am Soc Composers, Auths and Publs, 72, 73, 74, 77 and 81; All Nations Poetry Award, Triton Col, 75, 76, 77 and 78; Marshall Honorable Achievement Award, Professional Theatre Prog, Univ Mich, 78. **MEMBERSHIPS** PEN Club; Int Acad Poets; New England Mod Lang Asn; Asn Poetry Therapy; Am Soc Composers, Auths and Publs. **RESEARCH** World poetry, past and present; American history; aesthetic philosophy. **SELECTED PUBLICATIONS** Auth, Chekhov the Seagull, Theatre J, Vol 0045, 93; The Concept of Diskurswandel in the Works of Einstein, Carl in A Study of the History and Theory of the European Avant-Garde, J European Studies, Vol 0024, 94; German Atrocities and Franco-German Opinion, 1914 in The Evidence of German Soldiers Diaries, J Mod Hist, Vol 0066, 94; Pix, Mary Nebulous Relationship To Zelmane, Notes And Queries, Vol 0041, 94; Architectural Criticism in Time and Going Beyond Time in Texts 1913-1946, J European Studies, Vol 0025, 95; Hausmann, Raoul Correspondence with Jolas, Eugene, German Life and Letters, Vol 0048, 95; A Small Potatoes Avant Garde in Towards a New Assessment of German Dadaism - The Early Huelsenbeck,Richard, His Life And Works Through 1916 In Presentation and Interpretation, Mod Lang Rev, Vol 0091, 96; The Literary Motif of a Reflected Look in Leisegang, Dietrich Poetry, Archiv fur das Studium der Neueren Sprachen und Literaturen, Vol 0233, 96; Vasari, Giorgio in Art and History, Sixteenth Century J, Vol 0027, 96; Prismatic Thought, J European Studies, Vol 0026, 96; Freedom with Responsibility in The Social Market Economy in Germany, 1918-1963, Econ Hist Rev, Vol 0049, 96; A Living Shadow in Film in Literature to 1938, J European Studies, Vol 0026, 96; Carl Einstein Conference 94, J European Studies, Vol 0027, 97. **CONTACT ADDRESS** Dept of English, Dowling Col, 150 Idle Hour Blvd, Oakdale, NY, 11769-99.

KRAMER, DALE VERNON
PERSONAL Born 07/13/1936, Mitchell, SD, m, 1960, 2 children **DISCIPLINE** ENGLISH **EDUCATION** SDak State Univ, BS, 58; Western Reserve Univ, MA, 60, PhD(English), 63. **CAREER** From instr to asst prof English, Ohio Univ, 62-65; from asst prof to assoc prof, 65-71, prof English, Univ Ill, Urbana, 71-96; Vis prof English, Reading Univ, England, 66-67; Univ Ill fac study grant, 67; Am Philos Soc res grant, 69, 86; assoc fel, Ctr Advan Studies, Univ Ill, 71-72. **MEMBERSHIPS** MLA; AAUP; Midwest Mod Lang Asn. **RESEARCH** Textual scholarship; aesthetics of fiction; Thomas Hardy; Joseph Conrad. **SELECTED PUBLICATIONS** Auth, Marlow, myth and structure in Lord Jim, Criticism, 66; Revisions and vision: Thomas Hardy's The Woodlanders, Bull NY Pub Libr, 71; Charles Robert Maturin, Twayne, 73; Thomas Hardy: The Forms of Tragedy, Macmillan, 75; ed, Critical Approaches to the Fiction of Thomas Hardy, Macmillan, 79; The Woodlanders, Thomas Hardy, Oxford Univ Press, 81; ed, The Mayor of Casterbridge, Oxford, 87; ed, Critical Essays on Thomas Hardy, G.K. Hall, 90; ed, Hardy: Tess of the d'Urbervilles, Cambridge, 91; ed, Cambridge Companion to Hardy, Cambridge, 99. **CONTACT ADDRESS** Dept of English, Univ of Ill, 608 S Wright St, Urbana, IL, 61801-3613.

KRAMER, JENNIFER
PERSONAL Born 08/19/1964, Newark, NJ, m, 1992 **DISCIPLINE** CINEMA AND MASS MEDIA **EDUCATION** Univ Chicago, MA, 94 **CAREER** Assoc ed, video reviews counterpoise, amer libr asn, 97-. **MEMBERSHIPS** Nat Coalition Independent Scholars **RESEARCH** Cognitive science; Geometric modeling; Mass media conglomerates. **SELECTED PUBLICATIONS** Auth, The Spherical Burning Mirror, Premonitions, 93; Schroedingers Albatross, Puck, 94; The Method of Exhaustion, Trivia: A Jour of Ideas, 95; auth, Fairyland in the Kitchen, Jour Unconventional Hist, 96; Ongoing Support & The World Wide Web, Multimedia Producers Bible, 96; The Weeping Icon: Gender and Generic Conventions in the Film Bram Stokers Dracula, Dracular 97; Shadowboxing, Cyber-Psychos AOD, Lammas 97; Cold Comfort: Stephen W Hawking and The Bible, The Montrous and the Unspeakable: The Bible as Fantastic Literature, Sheffield Acad Press, 97; rev, Teh Nobel Legacy, Event Horizon, 98. **CONTACT ADDRESS** PO Box 281, Caldwell, NJ, 07006. **EMAIL** picpal@picpal.com

KRAMER, JOSEPH ELLIOT
PERSONAL Born 12/21/1934, New York, NY **DISCIPLINE** ENGLISH LITERATURE **EDUCATION** Princeton Univ, BA, 56, MA, 58, PhD, 65. **CAREER** Asst Prof English, Univ CA, Berkeley, 61-69; Assoc Prof, 69-88, prof eng, Bryn Mawr Col, 88. **HONORS AND AWARDS** Fulbright Fel, London Univ, 59-61. **MEMBERSHIPS** MLA. **RESEARCH** Shakespeare; Brit drama to 1642; mod drama; lit of sexual minorities. **SELECTED PUBLICATIONS** Auth, Damon and Pithias: An

apology for art, ELH, 12/68; Titus Andronicus: The flykilling incident, Shakespeare Studies, 69. **CONTACT ADDRESS** Dept of Eng, Bryn Mawr Col, 101 N Merion Ave, Bryn Mawr, PA, 19010-2899.

KRAMER, MARY DUHAMEL
PERSONAL Born 06/12/1944, Columbus, WI, m, 1968, 2 children **DISCIPLINE** ENGLISH LITERATURE **EDUCATION** Univ WI-Madison, BA, 66; Univ KS, MA, 67, PhD, 69. **CAREER** Prof eng, Univ MA Lowell, 69-, Fiction bk reviewer-freelance auth, lectr. **HONORS AND AWARDS** Phi Beta Kappa **MEMBERSHIPS** AAUP **RESEARCH** Medieval and Renaissance lit. **SELECTED PUBLICATIONS** Auth, The Roman Catholic Cleric on the Jacobean stage, 71 & The American Wild West Show and Buffalo Bill Cody, 72, Costerus; local & nat jour & newspapers; textbook, Human Values in Western Culture. **CONTACT ADDRESS** Dept of Eng, Univ Massachusetts Lowell, 1 University Ave, Lowell, MA, 01854-2893. **EMAIL** kramerm@woods.uml.edu

KRAMER, MAURICE
PERSONAL Born 04/04/1930, Philadelphia, PA, m, 1959 **DISCIPLINE** ENGLISH **EDUCATION** Univ Pa, AB, 51, AM, 53; Harvard Univ, PhD(English), 58. **CAREER** Instr English, Rutgers Univ, 57-61; from instr to assoc prof, 61-73, chmn dept, 70-75, exec off, Spec Baccalaureate Degree Prog Adults, 77-78, dean, Sch Humanities, 78-80, prof English, Brooklyn Col, 73-. **MEMBERSHIPS** MLA. **RESEARCH** American literature. **SELECTED PUBLICATIONS** Co-ed, Library of Literary Criticism: Modern American Literature, Ungar, 69 & 76; auth, Alone at Home with Elizabeth Stoddard, Am Transcendental Quart, 80. **CONTACT ADDRESS** Dept of English, Brooklyn Col, CUNY, 2900 Bedford Ave, Brooklyn, NY, 11210-2813. **EMAIL** mkramer@brooklyn.cuny.edu

KRAMER, MICHAEL W.
DISCIPLINE COMMUNICATION **EDUCATION** Concordia Jr Col, AA, 74; Concordia Col, BS, 76; NE Ill Univ, MA, 82; Univ Tex, PhD, 8/91. **CAREER** Teacher, Martin Luther HS, NY, 76-78; dept ch, Eng dept, Luther High School S, 78-84; asst prof, Concordia Lutheran Col, 84-91; assoc prof, Dept Commun, Univ Mo-Columbia, 91-. **HONORS AND AWARDS** Phi Kappa Phi, 87; Top competitive papers in Org Commun, SCA, 92, 94, 96; Top Competitive paper in the Basic Course, NCA, 97; Provost Outstanding Jr Fac Award, 95. **MEMBERSHIPS** Int Commun Assoc; Speech Commun Assoc; Acad of Management. **RESEARCH** Organizational communication; group communication; interpersonal commununication. **SELECTED PUBLICATIONS** Auth, Communication and uncertainty reduction during job transfers: Leaving and joining processes, Commun Monographs, vol 60, 178-198, 93; auth, Communication after job transfers: Social exchange processes in learning new roles, Human Commun Res, vol 20, 147-174, 93; auth, Uncertainty reduction during job transitions: An exploratory study of the communication experiences of newcomers and transferees, Management Commun Quart, vol 7, 384-412, 94; co-auth, Information-giving and information-receiving during job transitions, Western J of Commun, vol 59, 151-170, 95; co-auth, Communication during employee dismissals: Social exchange principals and group influences on employee exit, Management Commun Quart, vol 9, 156-190, 95; auth, A longitudinal study of peer communication during job transfers: The impact of frequency, quality, and network multiplexity on adjustment, Human Commun Res, vol 23, 59-86, 96; co-auth, The differential impact of a basic public speaking course on percieved communication competencies in class, work, and social contexts, Basic Commun Course Ann, Am Press, vol 8, 1-25, 96; co-auth, The impact of brainstorming on subsequent group decision-making: Beyond generating ideas, Small Grp Res, vol 28, 218-242, 97; co-auth, The impact of self-directed videotape feedback on students' self-reported levels of communication competence and apprehension, Commun Educ, vol47, 151-161, 98; co-auth, A framework for the study of emotions in organizational contexts, Management Commun Quart, vol 11, 336-372, 98. **CONTACT ADDRESS** Dept of Commun, Univ of Mo, Columbia, 115 Switzler Hall, Columbia, MO, 65211. **EMAIL** commmwk@showme.missouri.edu

KRAMER, VICTOR ANTHONY
PERSONAL Born 10/21/1939, Youngstown, OH, m, 1963, 1 child **DISCIPLINE** AMERICAN LITERATURE, LITERARY CRITICISM **EDUCATION** St Edwards Univ, AB, 61; Univ Tex, Austin, MA, 63, PhD(English), 66. **CAREER** Asst prof English, Marquette Univ, 66-69; asst prof, 69-76, assoc prof, 76-81, PROF ENGLISH, GA STATE UNIV, 81-; Am Philos Soc grant, 73; sr Fulbright lectr, Univ Regensburg, West Ger, 74-75. **MEMBERSHIPS** MLA; Am Studies Asn; SAtlantic Mod Lang Asn; AAUP; Conf Christianity and Lit. **RESEARCH** Modern American literature; American studies and literary criticism. **SELECTED PUBLICATIONS** Auth, Patterns of Adaptation in Place and Placelessness in Contemporary Southern Fiction, Studies Literary Imagination, Vol 0027, 94; The Literary Percys in Family, History, Gender, and the Southern Imagination, Southern Literary J, Vol 0028, 96; The House of Percy in Honor, Melancholy, and Imagination in a Southern Family, Southern Literary J, Vol 0028, 96. **CONTACT ADDRESS** Dept of English, Georgia State Univ, 33 Gilmer St SE, Atlanta, GA, 30303-3080.

KRANIDIS, RITA
DISCIPLINE VICTORIAN STUDIES, CULTURAL STUDIES, FEMINIST THEORY AND CRITICISM, AND POS **EDUCATION** Mount Holyoke Col, BA; Long Island Univ, MA; SUNY, Stony Brook, PhD. **CAREER** Prof, Radford Univ. **SELECTED PUBLICATIONS** Auth, Subversive Discourse: The Cultural Production of Late Victorian Feminist Novels, St Martin's, 95; ed, Imperial Objects: Essays on Victorian Women's Emigration and the Unauthorized Imperial Experience, Twayne Publ, 97. **CONTACT ADDRESS** Radford Univ, Radford, VA, 24142. **EMAIL** mkranidi@runet.edu

KRAPF, NORBERT A.
DISCIPLINE AMERICAN POETRY **EDUCATION** Notre Dame, PhD; St Joseph's Col, DHL honoris causa, 95. **CAREER** Prof, Long Island Univ, C.W. Post Campus. **SELECTED PUBLICATIONS** Auth, Arriving on Paumanok; The Playfair Book of Hours; Lines Drawn from Durer; Heartwood, A Dream of Plum Blossoms; Circus Songs; ed, Under Open Sky: Poets on William Cullen Bryant; Beneath the Cherry Sapling: Legends from Franconia; Finding the Grain: Pioneer Journals, Franconian Folktales, Ancestral Poems; transl, Shadows on the Sundial: Selected Early Poems of Rainer Maria Rilke. **CONTACT ADDRESS** Long Island Univ, C.W. Post, Brookville, NY, 11548-1300.

KRASNER, DAVID
PERSONAL Born 03/01/1952, Brooklyn, NY **DISCIPLINE** THEATER **EDUCATION** Carnegie-Mellon Univ, BFA, 74; Va Commonwealth Univ, 90; Tufts Univ, PhD, 96. **CAREER** Asst prof, Yale Univ **HONORS AND AWARDS** Amer Soc for Theater Res Errol Hill Award, 98, Dir, Undergraduate Theater Stud, Yale Univ **MEMBERSHIPS** ASTR; ATHE; MLA. **RESEARCH** African-American theater; performance. **SELECTED PUBLICATIONS** Auth, Whose Role Is It, Anyway?, African Amer Rev, 95; The Mirror Up To Nature: Modernist Aesthetics and Racial Authenticity in African American Theatre, 1895-1900, Theatre Hist Stud, 96; Re-writing the Body: Aida Overton Walker and the Social Formation of Cakewalking, Theatre Survey, 96; Walter Benjamin and the Lynching Play: Allegory and Mourning in Angelina Weld Grimke's Rachel, J of Comparative Drama, 97; Resistance, Parody, and Double Consciousness in African-American Theater, 1895-1910. **CONTACT ADDRESS** Theater Studies, Yale Univ, 254 York St, New Haven, CT, 06520-8296. **EMAIL** david.krasner@yale.edu

KRATZ, DENNIS
DISCIPLINE LITERATURE STUDIES **EDUCATION** Harvard Univ, PhD, 70. **CAREER** Prof. **RESEARCH** Medieval literature; classical tradition; fantasy/science fiction. **SELECTED PUBLICATIONS** Auth, The Romances of Alexander, Garland, 91; Waltharius and Ruodlieb, Garland, 84; Mocking Epic: Waltharius, Alexandreis and the Problem of Christian Heroism, Ediciones Jose Porrua Turanzas, 80; Development of the Fantastic Tradition through 1811, Garland, 90. **CONTACT ADDRESS** Dept of Literature, Richardson, TX, 75083-0688. **EMAIL** dkratz@utdallas.edu

KRAUS, SIDNEY
DISCIPLINE POLITICAL COMMUNICATION, MASS COMMUNICATION, PUBLIC RELATIONS **EDUCATION** Art Inst Chicago, BFA, MFA; Univ IA, PhD. **CAREER** Comm, Cleveland St Univ. **SELECTED PUBLICATIONS** Auth; Televised Presidential Debates and Public Policy, Lawrence Erlbaum & Assoc, 88; Mass Communication and Political Information, Lawrence Erlbaum & Assoc, 90. **CONTACT ADDRESS** Commun Dept, Cleveland State Univ, 83 E 24th St, Cleveland, OH, 44115. **EMAIL** s.kraus@csuohio.edu

KRAUSE, DAVID H.
DISCIPLINE AMERICAN LITERATURE **EDUCATION** Yale Univ, MA, MPhil, PhD. **CAREER** English, Carthage Col. **HONORS AND AWARDS** Nat Endowment Hum fel. **SELECTED PUBLICATIONS** Auth, Noon at Smyrna; Summer Storm; Soapstone Wall. **CONTACT ADDRESS** Carthage Col, 2001 Alford Dr., Kenosha, WI, 53140. **EMAIL** krause1@carthage.edu

KRAUSE, SYDNEY JOSEPH
PERSONAL Born 07/22/1925, Paterson, NJ, m, 1952 **DISCIPLINE** ENGLISH AND AMERICAN LITERATURE **EDUCATION** Univ Mo, BA, 49; Yale Univ, MA, 51; Columbia Univ, PhD(English), 56. **CAREER** Instr English, Univ Mo, 50-52; asst dir English prog foreign students, Col William and Mary, 53; instr, Ohio State Univ, 53-55, dir continuity, Wosu, 55; asst prof, Univ Akron, 55-62; assoc prof, 62-66, dir bibliog and textual ctr, 66-69, PROF ENGLISH, KENT STATE UNIV, 66-; Am Coun Learned Soc grant, 61; gen ed, C B Brown ed, Kent State Univ and MLA, 66-; Fulbright lectr, Copenhagen, 68-69 and T¤bingen, Gdr, 82; exchange prof, Leipzig, Gdr, 82. **MEMBERSHIPS** MLA. **RESEARCH** American literature; Mark Twain; Charles Brockden Brown. **SELECTED PUBLICATIONS** Auth, Penn Elm and Edgar Huntly in Dark Instruction to the Heart and The Staging of Pivotal Scenes at The Foot of Said Tree in The Brown, Charles, Brockden Novel Edgar Huntly and the Short Story Somnambulism A Fragment, Am Lit, Vol 0066, 94; Punishing the Press in Using Contempt of Court to Secure the Right to a Fair Trial, Boston Univ Law Rev, Vol 0076, 96. **CONTACT ADDRESS** Dept of English, Kent State Univ, Kent, OH, 44240.

KREISEL, HENRY
PERSONAL Born 06/05/1922, Vienna, Austria, m, 1947, 1 child **DISCIPLINE** ENGLISH **EDUCATION** Univ Toronto, BA, 46, MA, 47; Univ London, England, PhD, 54. **CAREER** Lectr English, 47-50, from asst prof to prof, 50-75, head dept, 61-67, sr assoc dean, Grad Studies, Fac Grad Studies and Res, 67-69, actg dean, 69-70, vpres, 70-75, Univ PROF ENGLISH, UNIV ALTA, 75-; CHMN, SCHOLAR COMT, CAN COUN, 63-; mem, Awards Jury, Gov-Gen Prizes in Lit, 66-68; mem, Bd Gov, Univ Alta, 66-69; consult, Acad Planning, Ont Coun Grad Studies, 73-74; vis fel, Wolfson Col, Cambridge Univ, 75-76. **HONORS AND AWARDS** Pres Medal, Univ Western Ont, 60. **MEMBERSHIPS** Asn Can Univ Teachers English(-pres, 62-63); MLA; fel Int Inst Arts and Lett; fel Royal Soc Arts. **RESEARCH** Early 20th century British literature; Canadian literature; history of modern European drama. **SELECTED PUBLICATIONS** Auth, Maimonidean Studies, Vol 1, Jewish Quart Rev, Vol 0083, 93; Maimonides Ethics in The Encounter of Philosophic and Religious Morality, J Medieval Studies, Vol 0069, 94; On the Term Kol All in Ibn-Ezra, Abraham and General Observations Concerning Neoplatonic Philosophy and the Problem of Divine Immanence as Analyzed from a Textual Standpoint, Rev Des Etudes Juives, Vol 0153, 94. **CONTACT ADDRESS** Dept of Comp Lit, Univ of Alberta, Edmonton, AB, T6G 2E6.

KREISWIRTH, MARTIN
DISCIPLINE ENGLISH LITERATURE **EDUCATION** Hamilton Col, BA; Univ Chicago; Univ Toronto, PhD. **RESEARCH** Narrative theory; literary theory; philosophy of history; Faulkner. **SELECTED PUBLICATIONS** Auth, William Faulkner: The Making of a Novelist, Ga, 83; co-ed, Theory Between the Disciplines: Authority/Vision/Politics, Mich, 90; Johns Hopkins Guide to Literary Theory and Criticism, Johns Hopkins, 94; Constructive Criticism: The Human Sciences in the Age of Theory, Toronto, 95. **CONTACT ADDRESS** Dept of English, Western Ontario Univ, London, ON, N6A 5B8.

KREMER, S. LILLIAN
PERSONAL Born 06/30/1939, New York, NY, m, 1960, 2 children **DISCIPLINE** AMERICAN AND JEWISH-AMERICAN LITERATURE **EDUCATION** State Univ NY Albany, BA, 59; City Univ NY, MA, 64; Kans State Univ, PhD(English), 79. **CAREER** Teaching asst compos, Kans State Univ, 75-78, grad instr lit and compos, 78-79; TEACHER BRIT and AM LIT and ADVAN COMPOS, MANHATTAN HIGH SCH, 79-. **RESEARCH** Holocaust in American literature; Jewish American writers; Jewish American writers. **SELECTED PUBLICATIONS** Auth, Post-Alienation, Recent Directions in Jewish-American Literature, Contemp Lit, Vol 0034, 93; Holocaust Survivors in Psychiatric and Literary Parallels, Proteus, Vol 0012, 95; Writing Mothers, Writing Daughters in Tracing the Maternal in Stories by American Jewish Women, Am Lit, Vol 0069, 97. **CONTACT ADDRESS** 1615 Osage, Manhattan, KS, 66502.

KREPS, GARY L.
DISCIPLINE COMMUNICATION **EDUCATION** City Col of San Francisco, 71-73; Univ of Colo, BA, 75, MA, 76; Univ of Southen Calif, 79. **CAREER** Instr, Chapman Univ, 76-78; teaching assoc, Unif of Southern Calif, 77-78; asst prof, Purdue Univ Calumet, 78-80; assir prof, 80-81, assoc prof, 80-83, dir of Organizational Commun, acting chemn, dept of Communicaton & Theatre, 81; dir of Health Studies Prog & adjunct prof of nursing, Ind Univ at Indianapolis, 82-83; asst prof, dir of the Health Commun Res Group, grad fac member, fel of the Inst for Health, Rutgers Univ, 83-87; dir of grad studies, 88-89, assoc prof, 87-88, prof, Northern Ill Univ, 87-95; exec dir & prof, Greenspun School of Commun, Univ of Nevada at Las Vegas, 95-97; ADJUNCT PROF, DOCTORAL PROG FACULTY, UNION INT, 96-; FOUNDING DEAN & PROF, SCHOOL OF COMMUN, HOFSTRA UNIV, 97-. **HONORS AND AWARDS** Gerald M. Phillips Award for Distinguished Applied Commun Scholar, nat Commun Asn; listed in Who's Who in Entertainment, 3rd edition, 98-99; honorary mem of Lambda Pi Eta, Nat Commun Honor Soc, 97; listed in Int Who's Who of Professionals, 96; Applied Commun Book of the Year Award, NCA Applied Commun Section, 95. **MEMBERSHIPS** Asn for Commun Admin; Asn for Ed in J and Mass Commun; Broadcast Ed Asn; Central States Commun Asn; Commun Inst for Online Scholar; Int Commun Asn; Nat Commun Asn; Eastern Commun Asn; Public Relations Professionals of Long Island; Western States Commun Asn; World Commun Asn. **RESEARCH** Organizational communication, intervention, & learning; health communication; health education and promotion; interpersonal/group interaction; multicultural relations; communication theory; leadership & empowerment; conflict management; communication and public policy, research methods. **SELECTED PUBLICATIONS** Auth, Disability and Culture: Effects on Multicultural Relations in Modern Organizatons, Handbook of Commun and People with Disablities:

Res and Application, Lawrence Erlbaum, 98; auth, Social Responsibility and the Modern Health Care System: Promoting a Consumer Orientation to Health Care, Organizational Commun and Change, Hampton Press, 98; auth, Information and Organizational Development: Enhancing Reflexivity at the Alexander Center, Case Studies in Organizational Commun, Guilford Press, 97; auth, Communicating to Promote Justice in the Modern Health Care System, J of Health Commun: Int Perspectives, 96; guest ed, The Interface Between Health Commun and Health Psychology, J of Health Psychology, 96; coauth, Preventing Sexual Harassment in Educational Organizations: A Communication Perspective, Organizational Commun for Human Resource Managers in Higher Ed: A Manual for Commun Behave, Col & Univ Personnel Asn, 98; coauth, The History and Development of the Field of Health Communication, Health Commun Res: A Guide to Developments and Direction, Greenwood Press, 98; coauth, Listening: A Crucial CommunicationCompetency for Effective Health Care Delivery, Listening in Everyday Life: A Personal and Professional Approach, Univ Press of Am, 97; coauth, Testing a Relational Model of Helth Communication Competence Among Caregivers for Individuals with Alzheimer's Disease, J of Health Psychology, 96. **CONTACT ADDRESS** School of Commun, Hofstra Univ, Dempster Hall, Hempstead, NY, 11549. **EMAIL** comglk@hofstra.edu

KRETSCHMAR, WILLIAM A., JR.
PERSONAL Born 09/13/1953, Ann Arbor, MI, m, 1976, 2 children **DISCIPLINE** ENGLISH; LINGUISTICS **EDUCATION** Univ Chicago, PhD 80; Yale Univ, MA 76; Univ Mich, BA high honors 71-75. **CAREER** Univ Georgia, asst prof, assoc prof, prof, 86 to 95-; Univ Wis, asst prof, 82-86. **MEMBERSHIPS** ADS; MLA; LSA. **RESEARCH** Language variation; dialectology; medieval lit. **SELECTED PUBLICATIONS** Auth, Concise Dictionary of Pronunciation, co-ed, Oxford, Oxford Univ Press, 98; auth, American English for the 21st Century, in: Englishes Around the World, ed, Edgar Schneider, Amsterdam, John Benjamins, 97; auth, Dimensions in Variation in American English Vocabulary, English World-Wide, 96; auth, Foundations in American English,, in: Focus on the USA, ed, Edgar Schneider, Phil, John Benjamins, 96; auth, Quantitative Areal Analysis of Dialect Features, Lang Variation and Change, 96; auth, Intro to Quantitative Analysis of Linguistic Survey Data, w/E Schneider, Thousand Oaks CA, Sage, 96; auth, Handbook of the Linguistic Atlas of the Middle and South Atlantic States, co-ed, Chicago, Univ Chicago Press, 93. **CONTACT ADDRESS** Dept of English, Univ of Georgia, Athens, GA, 30602. **EMAIL** billk@atlas.uga.edu

KREYLING, MICHAEL
DISCIPLINE AMERICAN AND SOUTHERN LITERATURE **EDUCATION** Cornell Univ, PhD. **CAREER** Prof Eng, Vanderbilt Univ. **RESEARCH** Southern intellectual and literary history. **SELECTED PUBLICATIONS** Auth, Eudora Welty's Achievement of Order, 80; Author and Agent: Eudora Welty and Diarmuid Russell, 91; The Figure of the Hero in Southern Narrative. **CONTACT ADDRESS** Vanderbilt Univ, Nashville, TN, 37203-1727. **EMAIL** hickmald@ctrvax.vanderbilt.edu

KRIEGEL, ABRAHAM DAVID
PERSONAL Born 02/15/1938, New York, NY, m, 1965, 2 children **DISCIPLINE** MODERN ENGLAND **EDUCATION** Hunter Col, BA, 58; Duke Univ, MA, 60, PhD, 65. **CAREER** From asst prof to assoc prof, 64-77, prof hist, Univ Memphis, 77-. **HONORS AND AWARDS** Am Philos Soc Grant, 66-67; John Simon Guggenheim fel, 79-80; Walter D Love Prize N Am Conf Brit Stud, 88. **MEMBERSHIPS** AHA; Conf Brit Studies; S Hist Asn; S Conf Brit Studies. **RESEARCH** Nineteenth century British politics; the English aristocracy. **SELECTED PUBLICATIONS** Auth, The Politics of the Whigs in Opposition 1834-1835, J Brit Studies, 5/68; The Irish Policy of Lord Grey's Government, Eng Hist Rev, 1/71; ed, The Holland House Diaries, 1831-1840, Routledge & Kegan Paul, 77; Liberty and Whiggery in Early Ninteenth Century England, J Modern Hist, 6/80; Edmund Burke and the Quality of Honor, Albion, 12/80; A Convergence of Ethnics: Saints and Whigs in British Antislavery, J Brit Studies, 87; Biography and the Politics of the Early Nineteenth Century, J Brit Studies, 90; Whiggery in the Age of Reform, J Brit Studies, 93; Up for Grabs, Va Quart Rev, 97. **CONTACT ADDRESS** Dept Hist, Univ Memphis, 3706 Alumni St, Memphis, TN, 38152-0001. **EMAIL** akriegel@memphis.edu

KRIEGEL, LEONARD
PERSONAL Born 05/25/1933, New York, NY, m, 1957, 2 children **DISCIPLINE** ENGLISH **EDUCATION** Hunter Col, BA, 55; Columbia Univ, MA, 56; NY Univ, PhD(Am civilization), 60. **CAREER** Asst prof English, Long Island Univ, 60-61; from instr to assoc prof, 61-72, PROF ENGLISH, CITY COL NEW YORK, 72-; Fulbright lectr, Neth, 64-65 and 68-69; Guggenheim fel, 71-72; Rockefeller fel, 76; Fulbright lectr, France, 81. **MEMBERSHIPS** Pen; MLA; Am Studies Asn. **RESEARCH** Politics and literature; creative writing; writing on education. **SELECTED PUBLICATIONS** Auth, From the Catbird Seat, Football, Baseball, and Language, Sewanee Rev, Vol 0101, 93; Supermarket Modern, Antioch Rev, Vol 0051, 93; Gender and Its Discontents and Sex and Gender Questions Increasingly Dominate Cultural Discourse, Partisan Rev, Vol 0060, 93; Imaginary Others, Blacks and Jews in New York, Partisan Rev, Vol 0060, 93; Graffiti, Tunnel Notes of a New Yorker, Am Scholar, Vol 0062, 93; The Face Beneath the Window, One Mans View of Abortion, Va Quart Rev, Vol 0069, 93; Geography Lessons and The Physical Landscape in Literary Fiction, Sewanee Rev, Vol 0102, 94; Walking Light in Essays and Memoirs, Sewanee Rev, Vol 0102, 94; Forgive Me, Mrs. Reilly, or How a New York Jew Learned to Love the South, Kenyon Rev, Vol 0016, 94; Beaches in Winter, Va Quart Rev, Vol 0070, 94; Boundaries of Memory in Liberals, Patriotism, and Melting Pots, Va Quart Rev, Vol 0071, 95; North On 99 and California and New York Remain the Raw Alternatives for Our American Future, Partisan Rev, Vol 0062, 95; Confessions of a Might-Have-Been Conservative, Or, How Newt and Rush Helped 1 New-York Liberal See the Light wnd Keep the Faith, Va Quart Rev, Vol 0072, 96; Immigrants, Partisan Rev, Vol 0063, 96; New York Losers and Winners, Va Quart Rev, Vol 0072, 96. **CONTACT ADDRESS** 355 Eighth Ave, New York, NY, 10001.

KRIEGER, MURRAY
PERSONAL Born 11/27/1923, Newark, NJ, m, 1947, 2 children **DISCIPLINE** ENGLISH LITERATURE/LITERARY THEORY **EDUCATION** Rutgers Univ, 40-42; Univ Chicago, MA, 48; Ohio State Univ, univ fel, PhD, 52. **CAREER** Instr, English, Kenyon Coll, 48-49; instr, Ohio State Univ, 51-52; asst to assoc prof, Univ Minn, 52-58; prof, English, 58-63, assoc mem, Center Advanced Study, 61-62, Univ Ill; M. F. Carpenter Prof Lit Criticism, Univ Iowa, 63-66; prof, English, dir. program in criticism, Univ Calif Irvine, 66-85; prof, English, UCLA, 73-82; prof, 74-94, co-dir, Sch Criticism and Theory, 75-77, dir, 77-81, hon sr fel, 81-, Univ. Calif; dir, Univ Calif Humanities Res Inst, 87-89. **HONORS AND AWARDS** Postdoctoral fel, Amer Coun Learned Socs, 66-67; humanities fel, Rockefeller Found, 78; fel, Amer Acad Arts and Scis, counc and exec comm, 87-88; resident scholar, Rockefeller Study Center, Bellagio, 90. **MEMBERSHIPS** Modern Lang Assn; Intl Assn Univ Profs English; Amer Acad Art and Scis. **RESEARCH** Literary theory **SELECTED PUBLICATIONS** Auth, Theory, Criticism and the Literary Test, 88; auth, A Reopening of Closure: Organicism against Itself, 89; auth, Ekphrasis: The Illusion of the Natural Sign, 92; auth, The Ideological Imperative: Repression and Resistance in Recent American Theory, 93; auth, The Institution of Theory, 94. **CONTACT ADDRESS** 407 Pinecrest Dr, Laguna Beach, CA, 92651. **EMAIL** mkrieger@uci.edu

KRING, HILDA ADAM
PERSONAL Born 01/03/1921, Munich, Germany, m, 1946 **DISCIPLINE** FOLKLORE & FOLKLIFE, ENGLISH **EDUCATION** Millersville State Col, BS, 42; Univ Pittsburgh, MLitt, 52; Univ PA, PhD(folklore, folklife), 69. **CAREER** Teacher English, social studies & Ger, Salisbury Twp High Sch, Gap, PA, 42-46; teacher English, Westmont-Upper Yoder High Sch, Johnstown, 46-47, Adams Twp High Sch, Sidman, 47-48 & Conemaugh Twp High Sch, Davidsville, 48-56; suprv, Slippery Rock State Col, 56-68; teacher, Slippery Rock Area Joint High Sch, 58-64 & 66-67; PROF ENGLISH & COMMUN ARTS, GROVE CITY COL, 67-. **HONORS AND AWARDS** PA Teacher of the Year, 67; Florence E. MacKenzie Campus-Community Award, 83; Mercer Co Medical Soc -Benjamin Rush Award for Outstanding Community Service, 87; A. G. Sikorsky Award-Leadership through Education -United Community Hospital, 92; Grove City Area Chamber of Commerce, 96; Daughters of the Am Revolution, Excellence in Community Service, 96. **SELECTED PUBLICATIONS** Auth, The Bird That Couldn't Sing (playette), Plays, 57; Another Approach to Poetry, English J, 1/61; The Mountain Wreath, Delta Kappa Gamma J, winter 65; Mary Goes Over the Mountain, PA Folklife, summer 70; The Harmonists: A Folk Cultural Approach, Scarecrow, 73; The Cult of St Walburga in Pennsylvania, PA Folklife, winter 74-75; The Many Faces of Teaching, Univ SC, 78; The Harmonist Kuche, 98. **CONTACT ADDRESS** Dept of English, 5 Kring Dr., Grove City, PA, 16127.

KROEBER, KARL
PERSONAL Born 11/24/1926, Oakland, CA, m, 1953, 3 children **DISCIPLINE** ENGLISH **EDUCATION** Univ CA, AB, 47; Columbia Univ, MA, 51, PhD, 56. **CAREER** Lectr & instr, Columbia Univ, 52-56; from instr to prof English, Univ Wis, 56-70, assoc dean grad sch, 63-65; chmn, dept English, 73-76, PROF ENGLISH & COMP LIT, COLUMBIA UNIV, 70-; Fulbright res fel, Italy, 60-61; US Off Educ grant, 65-66, Guggenheim fel, 66-67; vis prof English, Univ Wash, 68; NEH fel, 76; ed, Newslett, Asn Study Am Indian Lit, 77-, Kiekhofer Teaching Award, 59. **HONORS AND AWARDS** Fulbright fel, Guggenheim fel, US Office Educat grant, NEH grant. **MEMBERSHIPS** MLA; Mod Humanities Res Asn, Gt Brit; Am Comp Lit Asn; Int Asn Univ Prof English. **RESEARCH** Nineteenth century English literature; native American Indian literature; theory and history of fiction. **SELECTED PUBLICATIONS** Auth, Romantic Narrative Art, 61 & The Artifice of Reality, 64, Univ Wis; Styles in Fictional Structure, Princeton Univ, 71; Constable and Wordsworth: Romantic Landscape Vision, Univ Wis, 74; Images of Romanticism: Verbal and Visual Affinities, Yale Univ, 78; Traditional Literature of the American Indian, Univ Nebr Press, 81, 2nd ed, 97; Retelling/Rereading, Rutgers, 92; Ecological Literary Criticism, Columbia, 94; Artistry in Native American Myths, NE, 98. **CONTACT ADDRESS** Dept of English & Comp Lit, Columbia Univ, 2960 Broadway, New York, NY, 10027-6900. **EMAIL** kk17@columbia.edu

KROETSCH, ROBERT P.
DISCIPLINE ENGLISH LITERATURE **EDUCATION** Univ Alberta, BA; Middlebury Univ, MA; Univ Iowa, PhD. **CAREER** Prof emer. **HONORS AND AWARDS** Governor General's Awd, 69. **SELECTED PUBLICATIONS** Auth, pubs about Canadian writing, modern and contemporary literature, and creative writing. **CONTACT ADDRESS** Dept of English, Manitoba Univ, Winnipeg, MB, R3T 2N2.

KRONENFELD, JUDY
PERSONAL Born 07/17/1943, New York, NY, m, 1964, 2 children **DISCIPLINE** ENGLISH **EDUCATION** Smith Col, BA, 64; Stanford Univ, PhD, 71. **CAREER** Asst prof, English, Purdue Univ, 76-77; vis assoc prof, English and Comp Lit, Univ of Calif Irvine, 80-81, 87; vis asst prof, English, Univ of Calif Riverside, 88-89, and lect, Creative Writing Dept, 84- . **HONORS AND AWARDS** Summa cum Laude, Phi Beta Kappa, 64; Distinguished Res Awd, 96-97. **MEMBERSHIPS** MLA; RSA; ALSC. **RESEARCH** Literature of the English Renaissance, particularly poetry and Shakespeare; the new historicism; historicism in relation to challenges from postmodern critical/linguistic theory. **SELECTED PUBLICATIONS** Auth, Shadow of Wings, Bellflower, 91; auth, King Lear and the Naked Truth: Rethinking the Language of Religion and Resistance, Duke, 98; auth of numerous articles and poems. **CONTACT ADDRESS** Dept of Creative Writing, Univ of California, Riverside, Riverside, CA, 92521-0318. **EMAIL** jkronen@citrus.ucr.edu

KRONICK, JOSEPH
DISCIPLINE 19TH AND 20TH CENTURY AMERICAN LITERATURE **EDUCATION** UCLA, PhD, 81. **CAREER** Prof, La State Univ; coed, Horizons in Theory and Am Cult, LSU Press ser. **HONORS AND AWARDS** Summer grant, Ctr for Fr and Francophone Stud, 87; NEH summer stipend, 88. **RESEARCH** Critical theory; philosophy and literature. **SELECTED PUBLICATIONS** Auth, American Poetics of History: From Emerson to the Moderns, 84; Dr. Heidegger's Experiment, Boundary 2, 90; Resembling Pound: Mimesis, Translation, Ideology, Criticism, 93; Telling the Difference: Stanley Cavell's Resistance to Theory, Am Lit Hist, 93; Libra and the Assassination of JFK, Ariz Quart, 94; coed, Theorizing American Literature: Hegel, the Sign and History, 91; America's Modernisms: Revaluing the Canon, 96. **CONTACT ADDRESS** Dept of Eng, Louisiana State Univ, 212G Allen Hall, Baton Rouge, LA, 70803. **EMAIL** jkronic@unix1.sncc.lsu.edu

KROPF, CARL R.
PERSONAL Born 12/07/1939, Canton, OH **DISCIPLINE** EIGHTEENTH CENTURY LITERATURE **EDUCATION** Otterbein Col, BA, 61; Kent State Univ, MA, 63; Ohio State Univ, PhD(English), 68. **CAREER** Teaching asst English, Ohio State Univ, 63-68; asst prof, 68-72, assoc prof, 72-81, PROF ENGLISH, GA STATE UNIV, 81-. **MEMBERSHIPS** MLA; S Atlantic Mod Lang Asn; Am Soc 18th Century Studies. **RESEARCH** Restoration drama; 18th century novel and poetry. **SELECTED PUBLICATIONS** Auth, Editors Comment and After Genette, Current Directions in Narrative Analysis and Theory, Studies Literary Imagination, Vol 0025, 92. **CONTACT ADDRESS** Dept of English, Georgia State Univ, Atlanta, GA, 30303.

KRUCKEBERG, DEAN A.
PERSONAL Born 12/25/1946, Owatonna, MN, d, 2 children **DISCIPLINE** COMMUNICATIONS **EDUCATION** Wartburg Col BA, 69; Northern Ill Univ, MA, 74; Univ Iowa, PhD, 85. **CAREER** PR, Lutheran General Hosp, Il, 69-73; instr, and extension infor spec, Univ Minn, 73-76; instr, jour, Univ Iowa, 76-79; asst prof, jour and PR, Northwest Mo State Univ, 79-83; prof, coord, PR Degree Prog, Univ Northern Iowa, 83- . **HONORS AND AWARDS** Public Rel Soc of Am, Natl Outstanding Educator Award, 95; Pathfinder Award, Inst for Public Rel Res and Educ, 97; Iowa Regents Award for Fac Excellence, 97. **MEMBERSHIPS** Public Rel Soc Am; Int Commun Asn; Natl Commun Asn; Asn for Educ in Jour and Mass Commun; Central States Commun Asn. **RESEARCH** International public relations; international public relations ethics; public relations community building and other pr theories. **SELECTED PUBLICATIONS** Auth, Public Relations and Community, in Image Und PR: Kann Image Gegenstand Einer Public Relations-Wissenschaft Sein?, Westdeutscher Verlag, 93; auth, Professional Profile, in Journalism, Writing Conference, 94; co-auth, Principles of Public Relations, United Arab Emirates Univ Pr, 94; coauth, Case studies in Public Relations, United Arab Emirates Univ Pr, 94; auth, International Journalism Ethics, in Global Journalism: Survey of International Journalism, Longman, 95; coauth, This is PR: The Realities of Public Relations, Wadsworth, 95; coauth, European Public Relations: An Evolving Paradigm, in International Public Relations: A Comparative Analysis, Erlbaum, 96; auth, Transnational Corporate Ethical Responsibilities, in International Public Relations: A Compara-

tive Analysis, Erlbaum, 96; auth, Public Relations, in Media Education Assessment Handbook, Erlbaum, 97; auth, Using the Case Study Method in the Classroom, in Learning to Teach: What You Need to Know to Develop a Successful Career as a Public Relations Educator, Public Relations Soc of Am, 98; auth numerous articles. **CONTACT ADDRESS** Dept of Communication Studies, Univ of Northern Iowa, 260 CAC, Cedar Falls, IA, 50614-0357. **EMAIL** kruckeberg@uni.edu

KRUK, LAURIE
DISCIPLINE ENGLISH **EDUCATION** York Univ, BA; McMaster, MA; Western Univ, PhD. **CAREER** Asst prof, Nipissing Univ; Post-Doctoral Scholar, Simon Fraser & Univ in Burnaby, BC. **HONORS AND AWARDS** Northern Prospects Poetry prize., Organized a poetry celebration and fund-raiser for the League of Canadian Poets, The (W)rites of Spring. **RESEARCH** Canadian literature; women's writing; short story. **SELECTED PUBLICATIONS** Auth, Theories of the World, 92. **CONTACT ADDRESS** Dept of English, Nipissing Univ, 100 College Dr, Box 5002, North Bay, ON, P1B 8L7.

KRUPAT, ARNOLD
PERSONAL Born 10/22/1941, NY, d, 2 children **DISCIPLINE** ENGLISH **EDUCATION** NYU, BA, 62; Columbia Univ, PhD, 67. **CAREER** Prof, Sarah Lawrence Col **HONORS AND AWARDS** Flik, Sarah Law Col Field Gnt, 95; Mellon Found, 93, 81; NEH 90, 87, 70; Leopold Schepp Found fel, 78; Columbia Univ Woodbridge fel, 66; Columbia Pres fel, 65; Woodrow Wilson fel, 62; Fulbright fel; Phi Beta Kappa. **RESEARCH** Am Cult Stud; Native Am Lit. **SELECTED PUBLICATIONS** Everything Matters: Autobiographical Essays by Native American Writers, ed, with Brian Swann, NY, Random House, 98; The Turn to the Native: Studies in Criticism and Culture, Lincoln, Univ Nebraska press, 96; Woodsmen or Thoreau and the Indians, a novel, Norman, Univ Oklahoma Press, 94; Native American Autobiography: An Anthology, ed, Madison Univ Wisconsin Press, 94. **CONTACT ADDRESS** Sarah Lawrence Col, 1 Mead Way, Bronxville, NY, 10708. **EMAIL** akrupat@mail.slc.edu

KUCICH, JOHN RICHARD
PERSONAL Born 04/05/1952, San Francisco, CA **DISCIPLINE** VICTORIAN LITERATURE, LITERARY THEORY **EDUCATION** Univ CA, Santa Cruz, BA, 74; State Univ NY, Buffalo, MA, 76, PhD, 78. **CAREER** From Asst Prof to Assoc Prof, 79-90, Prof Eng, Univ MI, Ann Arbor, 90. **HONORS AND AWARDS** Nat Endowment for Hum fel, 83; Guggenheim Fel, 87-88. **MEMBERSHIPS** MLA; Narrative Soc; Dickens Soc. **RESEARCH** The novel. **SELECTED PUBLICATIONS** Auth, Action in the Dickens ending: Bleak House and Great Expectations, 19th Century Fiction, 6/78; Death worship among the Victorians: The Old Curiosity Shop, Publ Mod Lang Asn, 11/80; The purity of violence: A Tale of Two Cities, Dickens Studies Annual, 80; Excess and Restraint in the Novels of Charles Dickens, Univ Ga Press, 81; Repression in Victorian Fiction, Univ Calif Press, 87; The Power of Lies: Transgression in Victorian Fiction, Cornell Univ Press, 94. **CONTACT ADDRESS** Dept of Eng, Univ of MI, 505 S State St, Ann Arbor, MI, 48109-1003. **EMAIL** jkucich@umich.edu

KUCZYNSKI, PETER
DISCIPLINE ENGLISH **EDUCATION** Humboldt Univ, Berlin, Dipl, 64; Pedagogische Hochschule, Potsdam, Dr, 78; Humboldt Univ, Berlin, DrSC, 84. **CAREER** Author **RESEARCH** Nathaniel Hawthorne **SELECTED PUBLICATIONS** Papers and articles on Shakespeare, Pope, Godwin, Cocaigne, Luberland, Irving, Melville, Dreiser; ed, sel writings of G. Weerth. **CONTACT ADDRESS** Richard Wagner Strasse 23, Halle, ., 4020.

KUEHL, LINDA KANDEL
DISCIPLINE AMERICAN LITERATURE AND WORLD DRAMA **EDUCATION** City Col NY, BA and MA; Lehigh Univ, PhD. **CAREER** Prof, Delaware Valley Col. **RESEARCH** Southern writers; Peter Taylor; Robert Hazel; authoring fiction. **SELECTED PUBLICATIONS** Auth, criticism and fiction in sev j(s) and books including Studies in Short Fic, Contemp Lit, Reader's Encyclopedia of Am Lit, and The Cimarron Rev. **CONTACT ADDRESS** Delaware Valley Col, 700 E Butler Ave, Doylestown, PA, 18901-2697. **EMAIL** KuehlL@devalcol.edu

KUENZLI, RUDOLF ERNST
PERSONAL Born 07/28/1942, Switzerland, m, 1968, 2 children **DISCIPLINE** ENGLISH LITERATURE, COMPARATIVE LITERATURE **EDUCATION** Univ Wis-Madison, MA(English), 68, MA(Ger), 69, PhD(comp lit), 71. **CAREER** Asst prof 70-76, assoc prof, 76-82, Prof English and Comp Lit, Univ Iowa, 82-; Res fel English and comp lit, Univ Iowa, 76; fel, Sch Criticism and Theory, Univ Calif, 78; DIR, DADA ARCH RES CTR, 78-; Inst Res Humanities fel, 79-80; chmn program comp lit, Univ Paul Valery, 80-83; vis prof, Montpellier, France, 81-82. **MEMBERSHIPS** MLA; Midwestern Mod Lang Asn; Comp Lit Asn; Asn Study Lit and Philos; Asn Study Dada and Surrealism. **RESEARCH** Avant-garde; Nietzsche; philosophies of language. **SELECTED PUBLICATIONS** Auth, Identities and Introduction, J Midwest Mod Lang Asn, Vol 0028, 95. **CONTACT ADDRESS** Dept of Lit, Univ of Iowa, 308 English Phil Bld, Iowa City, IA, 52242-1492.

KUFTINEC, SONJA
DISCIPLINE THEATRE ARTS **EDUCATION** Stanford Univ, PhD. **CAREER** Asst prof **SELECTED PUBLICATIONS** Auth, pubs on performance art, 19/20th century American theatre, performance theory, women in theatre, and alternative forms of theatre. **CONTACT ADDRESS** Theatre Arts and Dance Dept, Univ of Minnesota, Twin Cities, 106 Norris Hall, 172 Pillsbury Dr SE, Minneapolis, MN, 55455. **EMAIL** skuftinec@aol.com

KUIST, JAMES MARQUIS
PERSONAL Born 04/21/1935, White Plains, NY, m, 1960, 1 child **DISCIPLINE** BRITISH LITERATURE **EDUCATION** Davidson Col, AB, 57; Duke Univ, MA, 59, PhD(English), 65. **CAREER** Instr English, Col of William & Mary, 59-61 & Univ NC, 64-65; asst prof, Univ Western Ont, 65-67; from asst prof to assoc prof, 67-78, Prof English, Univ Wis-Milwaukee, 78-, Nat Endowment for Humanities Younger Humanist fel, 72-73, Res Tools grant, 78-79. **MEMBERSHIPS** MLA; Am Soc for 18th Century Studies; Johnson Soc Cent Region. **RESEARCH** British Periodicals; Samuel Johnson; 18th century novel. **SELECTED PUBLICATIONS** Auth, New light on Sterne: An old man's recollections of the young vicar, Pmla, 65; ed, Cursory Observations on the Poems Attributed to Thomas Rowley, Augustan Reprint Soc, 66; auth, The Works of John Nichols: An Introduction, Kraus Reprint Corp, 68; co-ed, Essays in Eighteenth-Century Literature in Honor of Benjamin Boyce, 71 & auth, The conclusion of Gray's Elegy, 71, SAtlantic Quart; auth, The Gentleman's Magazine in the Folger Library: The history and significance of the Nichols family collection, Studies Bibliog, 76; The Nichols File of the Gentleman's Magazine, Wis Press, 82. **CONTACT ADDRESS** Dept of English, Univ of Wis, PO Box 413, Milwaukee, WI, 53201-0413. **EMAIL** jmkuist@csd.uwm.edu

KULLMAN, COLBY HAIGHT
PERSONAL Born 05/22/1945, New York, NY **DISCIPLINE** ENGLISH LITERATURE, COMPOSITION **EDUCATION** DePauw Univ, BA, 66; Univ Chicago, MA, 68; Univ Kans, MPhil, 73, PhD(English), 81. **CAREER** Asst instr English, Univ Kans, 69-79; CHIEF ED, THEATRE COMPANIES OF THE WORLD: SELECTED PROFILES, GREENWOOD PRESS, 79-; BK REVER, AM REF BK ANNUAL, 76-. **MEMBERSHIPS** MLA; NCTE; Col English Asn; Am Soc 18th Century Studies; Am Theatre Asn. **RESEARCH** Eighteenth century studies; dramatic literature; interdisciplinary studies. **SELECTED PUBLICATIONS** Auth, Rule By Power in Big Daddyism in The World of Williams, Tennesse Plays, Miss Quart, Vol 0048, 95; Boswell in Citizen of The World, Man of Letters, Albion, Vol 0028, 96. **CONTACT ADDRESS** 107 Barstow Pl, Lawrence, KS, 66044.

KULYK KEEFER, JANICE
PERSONAL Toronto, ON, Canada **DISCIPLINE** ENGLISH **EDUCATION** Univ Toronto, BA, 74; Univ Sussex, MA, 76, DPhil, 83. **CAREER** Tutor, Univ Sussex, 77-78; lectr, 81-82, tchr, 82-83, asst prof, 83-84, postdoc fel, Univ Sainte-Anne, 84-86; Writer-in-Residence, Douglas Col, Vancouver, 87; Writer-in-Residence, Univ PEI, 89; assoc prof, 90-92, PROF, UNIV GUELPH 92-. **HONORS AND AWARDS** James Harris Entrance Scholar, 70-74; Woodhouse Scholar, 72, 73, 74; First Prize, PRISM Int Fiction Comp, 84; First prize & Top Prize, NS Writers' FedN, 85; Found Advan Can Letters Author's Award, 86; Joseph B. Stauffer Prize, 88-89; Winning Entry, Malahat Long Poem Competition, 91. **MEMBERSHIPS** Eden Mills Writers' Festival Comt. **SELECTED PUBLICATIONS** Auth, The Paris Napoli Express, 86; auth, Under Eastern Eyes: A Critical Reading of Canadian Maritime Fiction, 87; auth, Traveling Ladies, 90; auth, The Green Library, 96. **CONTACT ADDRESS** Dept of English, Univ Guelph, Guelph, ON, N1G 2W1.

KUMMINGS, DONALD D.
PERSONAL Born 07/28/1940, Lafayette, IN, m, 1987, 2 children **DISCIPLINE** ENGLISH **EDUCATION** Purdue Univ, BA, 62, MA, 64; Ind Univ, Bloomington, PhD, 71. **CAREER** Teach assoc, Purdue Univ, 63-64; Instr English, Adrian Col, 64-66; assoc instr, Ind Univ, 66-70; asst to assoc to PROF, ENGLISH, UNIV WIS, PARKSIDE, 70-. **HONORS AND AWARDS** Stella C. Gray Dist Teach Award, Univ Wis, Parkside, 77, 90; Posner Poetry Prize Council Wis Writers, 90; Univ Wis Regents Teach Excel Award, 92; Carnegie Fnd for Adv of Teach, Wis Prof of the Year, 97., Frederick L. Hovde Award for Poetry, Purdue Univ, 63; Sch Letters Univ Fel, Ind Univ, 67; Acad Am Poets Prize, Ind Univ, 69. **MEMBERSHIPS** Acad Am Poets; Am Lit Asn; Mod Lang Asn Am; Walt Whitman Asn. **RESEARCH** Walt Whitman, Am poetry and poetics; 19th century Am lit. **SELECTED PUBLICATIONS** Co-ed, Walt Whitman: An Encyclopedia, 98; ed, Approaches to Teaching Whitman's "Leaves of Grass", 90. **CONTACT ADDRESS** Dept of English, Univ Wisconsin, Parkside, 900 Wood Rd, Box 2000, Kenosha, WI, 53141. **EMAIL** kummings@uwp.edu

KUNITZ, STANLEY
PERSONAL Born 07/29/1905, Worcester, MA, m, 1930, 1 child **DISCIPLINE** ENGLISH **EDUCATION** Harvard Univ, AB, 26, AM, 27. LitD, Clark Univ, 61 and Anna Maria Col, 77. **CAREER** Mem fac lit, Bennington Col, 46-49; prof English, State Teachers Col, Potsdam, 49-50; lectr, New Sch Soc Res, 50-57; vis prof, Brandeis Univ, 58-59, Danforth vis lectr, 61-63; lectr, 63-66, ADJ PROF WRITING, GRAD SCH ARTS, COLUMBIA UNIV, 67-; Guggenheim fel, 45; Lowell Poetry traveling fel, 54; vis prof, Univ Wash, 55-57, Queens Col, NY, 56-57, Yale Univ, 72, Rutgers Univ, 74 and Vassar Col, 81; Ford Found grant, 58-59; ed, Yale Ser of Younger Poets, 69-77; CHANCELLOR, ACAD AM POETS, 70-; consult poetry, Libr Congr, 74-76, hon consult Am letts, 76-79; vis prof and sr fel humanities, Princeton Univ, 78, Vassar Col, 81. **HONORS AND AWARDS** Garrison Medal, Harvard Univ, 26; Blumenthal Prize, 41; Levinson Prize, 56; Harriet Monroe Award, Univ Chicago, 58; Pulitzer Prize, poetry, 59; Brandeis Univ Creative Arts Medal for poetry, 65; Lenvre Marshall Award, 80. **MEMBERSHIPS** Nat Acad Inst Arts and Lett. **RESEARCH** Creative writing; modern British and American literature. **SELECTED PUBLICATIONS** Auth, Take Our Advice ad Veteran Teachers Give Solutions to Common Teaching Problems, Clavier, Vol 0032, 93; Hornworm, Autumn Lamentation, Am Poetry Rev, Vol 0024, 95; Hornworm, Summer Reverie, Am Poetry Rev, Vol 0024, 95; An Interview With Kunitz, Stanley, Mich Quart Rev, Vol 0036, 97. **CONTACT ADDRESS** 37 W 12th St, New York, NY, 10011.

KUNTH, DEBORAH J.
DISCIPLINE 18TH-CENTURY BRITISH LITERATURE, SHAKESPEARE, BRITISH FICTION **EDUCATION** Smith Col, AB, 74; Yale Univ; PhD, 80. **CAREER** Assoc prof, Colgate Univ. **HONORS AND AWARDS** Sears-Roebuck found tchg excellence and campus ldrship award, Colgate Univ, 90; younger scholars awards, NEH, 92. **MEMBERSHIPS** Mem, MLA Delagate Assembly, 85-87. **RESEARCH** Brit novelists. **SELECTED PUBLICATIONS** Publ, The Dictionary of British Literary Characters, Bruccoli-Clark-Layman, 93; rev(s), C. High Holman and Willian Harmon, A Handbook to Literature, Macmillian, 91; articles, Friendship in Jane Austin's Juvenilia and Lady Susan, Jane Austin's Beginnings, UMI Res Press, 89; The Duncaid and Smart Students: Learning the Importance of Dunces, Approaches to Teaching Alexander Pope, Modern Language Stidies. **CONTACT ADDRESS** Dept of Eng, Colgate Univ, 13 Oak Drive, Hamilton, NY, 13346.

KUNZ, DON
PERSONAL Born 11/23/1941, Kansas City, MO, m, 1965, 1 child **DISCIPLINE** ENGLISH LITERATURE **EDUCATION** Kans State Univ, BA, 64; Univ Tex, Austin, MA, 65; Univ Wash, PhD, 68. **CAREER** From asst prof to assoc prof, 68-82, prof English, Univ RI, 82-, dir Grad Studies English, 79-83, dir Univ Honors Prog, 84-87, Honors Fac Fel, 89-92, coordr, Film Studies Prog, 93-97. **MEMBERSHIPS** Am Asn Univ Prof; Acad Am Poets; Lit/Film Asn; Phi Kappa Phi. **RESEARCH** British drama 1660-1780; 20th century American novel; film. **SELECTED PUBLICATIONS** Auth, The Drama of Thomas Shadwell, Inst English Sprache & Lit, Univ Salzburg, 72; Oliver Stone's Film Adaptation of Born on the Fourth of July: Redefining Masculine Heroism, in War, Lit, and the Arts 2.2, 90; Singing the Blues in A Soldier's Story, in Lit/Film Quart 19.1, 91; Nutty Professors, in Forum for Honors, Summer/Fall 92; ed, The Films of Oliver Stone, Scarecrow Press, 97; Oliver Stone's Talk Radio, in Lit/Film Quart 25.1, 97; author of numerous other journal articles, poetry, and reviews. **CONTACT ADDRESS** English Dept, Univ of RI, Kingston, RI, 02881-0812. **EMAIL** dkunz@uriacc.uri.edu

KUPERSMITH, WILLIAM ROGER
PERSONAL Born 10/21/1941, Evanston, IL **DISCIPLINE** ENGLISH LITERATURE **EDUCATION** Georgetown Univ, AB, 63; Univ Tex, Austin, PhD, 69. **CAREER** Lectr English, Rice Univ, 69-70; asst prof, Gonzaga Univ, 70-72; asst prof, 72-76, assoc prof, 76-81, Prof English, Univ Iowa, 81-, Philol Quart managing ed, 73-75 & ed, 75- **MEMBERSHIPS** Am Soc Eighteenth-Century Studies; Mid-West Am Soc Eighteenth-Century Studies (pres, 76-77); MLA; Johnson Soc of the Central Region (pres, 87-88). **RESEARCH** Neoclassical literature; English satire. **SELECTED PUBLICATIONS** Co-ed, Henry Fielding Pasquin, Univ Iowa, 73; ed, From Chaucer to Gibbon: Essays in Memory of Curt A Zimansky, Philol Quart, 75; auth, Rhetorical structure in The Vanity of Human Wishes, Studies in Philol, 75; Vice and folly in neoclassical satire, Genre, 78; Augustan literature, Philological Quart, Vol 57, 473-491; What makes a paper publishable, Bull of Midwest Mod Lang Asn, Vol 12, 15-19; Juvenal amoung the whigs, Forum, Vol 17, 43-51; ed, George Chapman's Translation of the Fifth Satire of Juvenal, Windhover Press, 79; Roman Satirists in Seventeenth-Century England, Univ Nebr Press, 85. **CONTACT ADDRESS** Dept of English, Univ of Iowa, 308 English Phil Bld, Iowa City, IA, 52242-1492. **EMAIL** william-kupersmith@uiowa.edu

KURATA, MARILYN J.
DISCIPLINE NINETEENTH-CENTURY BRITISH LITERATURE **EDUCATION** Carnegie-Mellon, BS; Univ WI, PhD, 76. **CAREER** Grad dir, Univ AL. **SELECTED PUBLICATIONS** Auth, Models and Methods for Writing About Literature. **CONTACT ADDRESS** Univ AL, 1400 University Blvd, Birmingham, AL, 35294-1150.

KURITZ, PAUL
PERSONAL Born 10/01/1948, Hazleton, PA, m, 1971, 4 children **DISCIPLINE** THEATER **EDUCATION** Univ VA, AB, 70; Ind Univ, MA, PhD. **CAREER** Instr, Moorehead State Univ, 73-75; instr, Univ Pittsburgh, 75-78; from asst to assoc prof, Bates Col, 78-. **SELECTED PUBLICATIONS** Auth, Playing, An Introduction to Acting; auth, The Making of Theater History; auth, Fundamental Acting. **CONTACT ADDRESS** RR 1, Box 1940, Hebron, ME, 04238. **EMAIL** pkuritz@abacus.bates.edu

KURIYAMA, CONSTANCE B.
DISCIPLINE ENGLISH LITERATURE **EDUCATION** Univ CA, Berkeley, PhD, 73. **CAREER** Assoc prof, TX Tech Univ. **RESEARCH** Marlowe; comp study of the films of Charles Chaplin and Buster Keaton. **SELECTED PUBLICATIONS** Auth, Hammer or Anvil: Psychological Patterns in Christopher Marlowe's Plays. **CONTACT ADDRESS** Texas Tech Univ, Lubbock, TX, 79409-5015. **EMAIL** cbcbk@ttacs.ttu.edu

KURPIUS, DAVID
DISCIPLINE BROADCAST JOURNALISM PRACTICES AND PRODUCTION, RACE AND MEDIA, MASS COMMUNI **EDUCATION** Univ Wis, PhD, 97. **CAREER** Asst prof, La State Univ, 97-. **HONORS AND AWARDS** Top Paper Award, Asn for Educ in Jour and Mass Commun Nat Conv. **RESEARCH** Broadcast journalism practices and production; race and media; mass communication theory. **SELECTED PUBLICATIONS** Coauth, Diversity in the News: A Conceptual and Methodological Framework, in Jour and Mass Commun Quart, 95; The Synthetic Crisis: Media and Influences on Perception of Crime, Asn for Educ in Jour and Mass Commun Nat Conv, 95. **CONTACT ADDRESS** The Manship Sch of Mass Commun, Louisiana State Univ, B-6 Hodges Hall, Baton Rouge, LA, 70803. **EMAIL** dkurpiu@unix1.sncc.lsu.edu

KUTZER, M. DAPHNE
DISCIPLINE ENGLISH **EDUCATION** Mt Holyoke, BA; IN Univ, MA and PhD,79. **CAREER** Fac, Plattsburgh State Univ of NY. **HONORS AND AWARDS** NY State Univ Chancellor's Awd Excellence Tchg, 96; Phi Eta Sigma Disting Fac Awd, 97. **RESEARCH** Children's lit; writing by women; 19th century lit. **SELECTED PUBLICATIONS** Auth, children's lit; articles on women's writing and feminist literary theory. **CONTACT ADDRESS** SUNY, Plattsburgh, 101 Broad St, Plattsburgh, NY, 12901-2681.

KUYK JR., DIRK ADRIAAN
PERSONAL Born 04/27/1934, Roanoke, VA **DISCIPLINE** AMERICAN & ENGLISH LITERATURE **EDUCATION** Univ Va, AB, 55; Brandeis Univ, PhD(English), 70. **CAREER** Asst prof, 70-74, assoc prof, 74-78, PROF ENGLISH, TRINITY COL (CONN), 78-. **RESEARCH** Faulkner; Yeats; the symbolist movement. **CONTACT ADDRESS** Dept of English, Trinity Col, 300 Summit St, Hartford, CT, 06106-3186.

KUYPERS, JIM A.
DISCIPLINE COMMUNICATION **EDUCATION** LA State Univ, PhD, 95. **CAREER** Dir of Speech, Dartmouth Col, 95-. **MEMBERSHIPS** Am Commun Asn; Southern States Commun Asn; Nat Commun Asn. **RESEARCH** Political communication; communication criticism; media framing. **SELECTED PUBLICATIONS** Auth, "The Press and James Dobson: Contextual Reconstruction after the Ted Bundy Interview," FL Commun Jour, 90; coauth, "Of Mighty Mice and Meek Men: Contextual Reconstruction of the Iranian Airbus Shootdown," Southern Commun Jour, 94; auth, "Doxa and a Realistic Prudence for a Critical Rhetoric," Commun Quart, 96; auth, Presidential Crisis Rhetoric and the Press in the Post-Cold War World, Praeger, 97. **CONTACT ADDRESS** Dartmouth Col, HB 6046 Bartlett Hall, Hanover, NH, 03755. **EMAIL** jim.kuypers@dartmouth.edu

KWASNY, ANDREA
DISCIPLINE AMERICAN LITERATURE **EDUCATION** SUNY, PhD. **CAREER** English and Lit, Univ Ark **SELECTED PUBLICATIONS** Auth, On the Margins: Postmodernist positions in Faulkner's 'other' representation. **CONTACT ADDRESS** Univ Ark Little Rock, 2801 S University Ave., Little Rock, AR, 72204-1099. **EMAIL** adkwasny@ualr.edu

KYDD, ELSPETH
DISCIPLINE THEATRE ARTS **EDUCATION** Northwestern Univ, MA, PhD. **CAREER** Asst prof, Univ Toledo. **RESEARCH** Film theory; film hist; film and video production. **SELECTED PUBLICATIONS** Auth, publ(s) on racial representation in film and television. **CONTACT ADDRESS** Univ Toledo, Toledo, OH, 43606. **EMAIL** ekydd@uoft02.utoledo.edu

L

LA MOY, WILLIAM T.
PERSONAL Born 01/27/1953, Hartford, CT, s **DISCIPLINE** LIBRARY, INFORMATION SCIENCE **EDUCATION** Yale Univ, BA, 76; Simmons Col, MS, 88. **CAREER** James Duncan Phillips Libr, ed, dir of publ, Peabody Essex Mus Collections. **RESEARCH** Librarianship and info svc; colonial soc of Mass; colonial Amer hist & lit. **CONTACT ADDRESS** Phillips Library, Peabody Essex Musuem, East India Square, Salem, MA, 01970. **EMAIL** will_lamoy@pem.org

LABRIOLA, ALBERT C.
DISCIPLINE ENGLISH LITERATURE **EDUCATION** Duquesne Univ, BEd, 61; Columbia Univ, MA, 62; Univ VA, MA, 63, PhD, 66. **CAREER** Prof, Duquesne Univ. **MEMBERSHIPS** Milton Soc; John Donne Soc. **SELECTED PUBLICATIONS** Co-auth, Biblia Pauperum, 90; co-ed, Milton's Legacy in the Arts, 88. **CONTACT ADDRESS** Dept of Commun, Duquesne Univ, Forbes Ave, PO Box 600, Pittsburgh, PA, 15282.

LABUZ, RONALD
DISCIPLINE ADVERTISING DESIGN **EDUCATION** SUNY, Oswego, BA, 75; Ohio State Univ, MA, 77; Syracuse, MA, 95; PhD, 97. **CAREER** Prof, adv des, PROF, GRAPHIC COMM, MOHAWK VLY COMM COLL **MEMBERSHIPS** AM Antiquarian Soc **RESEARCH** Am Graphic Des, 1830-70. **SELECTED PUBLICATIONS** Auth, Contemporary Graphic Design, Van Nostrand Reinhold, 92; auth, The Computer in Graphic Design, Van Nostrand Reinhold 93; auth, Digital Typography, Digital Design. **CONTACT ADDRESS** Dept of Graphic Comm, Mohawk Valley Commun Col, 1101 Sherman Dr, Utica, NY, 13501. **EMAIL** rlabuz@mvcc.edu

LADD, BARBARA
DISCIPLINE ENGLISH LANGUAGE AND LITERATURE **EDUCATION** Univ NC Greensboro, MFA, 81; Univ Tex Austin, MA, 85; Univ NC Chapel Hill, PhD, 90. **CAREER** Prof **RESEARCH** Late nineteenth- and twentieth-century southern literature especially with history and literary texts; applications of New Historicism to the writing of literary histories, to the inscription of race, ethnicity, and gender in conceptions of the literary; classification and mis-classification of literature in terms of nation and region. **SELECTED PUBLICATIONS** Auth, Nationalism and the Color Line in the Work of George W. Cable, Mark Twain, and William Faulkner, LSU, 96; essays and reviews in Am Lit, Miss Quart, So Quart, and So Atlantic Rev. **CONTACT ADDRESS** English Dept, Emory Univ, 1380 Oxford Rd NE, Atlanta, GA, 30322-1950. **EMAIL** bladd@emory.edu

LADEFOGED, PETER
PERSONAL Born 09/17/1925, Sutton, England, m, 1953, 3 children **DISCIPLINE** LINGUISTICS, ENGLISH **EDUCATION** Univ Edinburgh, MA, 51, PhD, 59. **CAREER** Lectr phonetics, Univ Edinburgh, 53-61; W African Lang Surv fel, 61-62; from asst prof to assoc prof English, 62-65, PROF LING, UNIV CALIF, LOS ANGELES, 65-, Team leader, Uganda Lang Surv, 68. **MEMBERSHIPS** Acoust Soc Am; Int Phonetic Asn; Int Asn Voice Identification; Am Speech and Hearing Asn; Ling Soc Am (pres). **RESEARCH** Experimental phonetics; African languages; phonology. **SELECTED PUBLICATIONS** Auth, Another View of Endangered Languages, Lang, Vol 0068, 92; Clicks and Their Accompaniments, J Phonetics, Vol 0022, 94; The Status of Phonetic Rarities, Lang, Vol 0072, 96; Phonetic Structures of Banawa, an Endangered Language, Phonetica, Vol 0054, 97; Abercrombie, David and the Changing Field of Phonetics, J Phonetics, Vol 0025, 97. **CONTACT ADDRESS** Dept of Ling, Univ of Calif, Los Angeles, CA, 90024.

LAFFOON, ELIZABETH ANNE
DISCIPLINE COMMUNCATION STUDIES **EDUCATION** Rice Univ, BA, 86; Univ Houston, MA, 88; Northwestern Univ, PhD, 93. **CAREER** Asst prof. **RESEARCH** Rhetorical theory and criticism. **SELECTED PUBLICATIONS** Auth, Are those real? Reconsidering Habermas's conception of performance, Speech Commun, 95; Towards a rhetoric of indirection: Exploring the enthymematic character of Habermas's model of therapeutic critique, 95; The Rhetoric of Ecofeminism, 94. **CONTACT ADDRESS** Dept of Communication, Univ Colo Boulder, Boulder, CO, 80309. **EMAIL** Elizabeth.Laffoon@Colorado.edu

LAGO, MARY MCCLELLAND
PERSONAL Born 11/04/1919, Pittsburgh, PA, m, 1944, 2 children **DISCIPLINE** MODERN ENGLISH AND BENGALI LITERATURE **EDUCATION** Bucknell Univ, BA, 40; Univ Mo-Columbia, MA, 65, PhD(English), 69. **CAREER** Instr, 64-70, lectr, 70-75, res grants, 71-74, assoc prof, 75-78, PROF ENGLISH, UNIV MO-COLUMBIA, 78-, Am Philos Soc res grants, 67, 68 and 70; Am Coun Learned Soc/Ford Found Joint SAsia Prog grant, 72-73; Nat Endowment for Humanities grant, 80-83. **HONORS AND AWARDS** DLitt, Bucknell Univ, 81. **MEMBERSHIPS** MLA; Midwest Mod Lang Asn; Asn Asian Studies; Soc of Authors, London; Virginia Woolf Soc. **RESEARCH** Modern Indian literature; late 19th and early 20th century English literature and art history. **SELECTED PUBLICATIONS** Auth, A 'River Called Titash', World Lit Today, Vol 0069, 95. **CONTACT ADDRESS** Dept of English, Univ Missouri, Columbia, MO, 65201.

LAGOUDIS PINCHIN, JANE
DISCIPLINE WOMEN IN LITERATURE **EDUCATION** Harpur Col, SUNY, BA, 64; MA, Columbia Univ, MA, 65, PhD,73. **CAREER** Instr, Brooklyn Col, 66-67, prof(pt-time), 69; dir, div univ studies, 87-91; div hum, 91-94; dean, 94-. **RESEARCH** The cotton novels of mid-nineteenth century England. **SELECTED PUBLICATIONS** Auth, Alexandria Still: Forster, Durrell and Cavafy, Princeton UP, 77, Am Univ Cairo Press, 89; Lawrence and Gerald Durrell, Blood Brothers: Siblings as Writers, 83; publ, Twentieth Century Lit Criticism, Mod Fiction Studies, Critical Essays on Lawrence Durrell, 87. **CONTACT ADDRESS** Dept of Eng, Colgate Univ, 13 Oak Drive, Hamilton, NY, 13346.

LAHOOD, MARVIN JOHN
PERSONAL Born 03/21/1933, Auburn, NY, m, 1959, 3 children **DISCIPLINE** ENGLISH **EDUCATION** Boston Col, BS, 54; Univ Notre Dame, MA, 58, PhD(English), 62. **CAREER** From instr to assoc prof English, Niagara Univ, 60-64; from assoc prof to prof, State Univ NY Col Buffalo, 64-71, assoc acad develop, 68-71; prof English and acad dean, Col Misericordia, 71-72 and Salem State Col, 72-75; prof English and dean fac, D'Youville Col, 75-78; PROF ENGLISH, STATE UNIV NY COL, BUFFALO, 78-. **MEMBERSHIPS** MLA. **RESEARCH** American fiction; modern fiction. **SELECTED PUBLICATIONS** Auth, The Lives of Mailer, Norman, World Lit Today, Vol 0066, 92; Leviathan, World Lit Today, Vol 0067, 93; Very Old Bones, World Lit Today, Vol 0067, 93; Van Goghs Room at Arles, World Lit Today, Vol 0068, 94; A 'Frolic of his Own', World Lit Today, Vol 0068, 94; Riding the Yellow Trolley Car, World Lit Today, Vol 0068, 94; Brazil, World Lit Today, Vol 0069, 95; The Collected Stories of Auchincloss, Louis, World Lit Today, Vol 0069, 95; Mr Vertigo, World Lit Today, Vol 0069, 95; Palimpsest--a Memoir, World Lit Today, Vol 0070, 96; Vidal, Gore--Writer Against the Grain, World Lit Today, Vol 0070, 96; Talking Horse--Malamud, Bernard on Life and Work, World Lit Today, Vol 0071, 97; The 'Flaming Corsage', World Lit Today, Vol 0071, 97; Mrs Ted Bliss, World Lit Today, Vol 0071, 97. **CONTACT ADDRESS** State Univ NY Col, 93 Parkhaven Dr, Amherst, NY, 14222.

LAIN, LAURENCE B.
PERSONAL Crown Point, IN, m, 1969, 3 children **DISCIPLINE** COMMUNICATION **EDUCATION** Ind State Univ, BS, 69; Ball State Univ, MAE, 73; Ohio State Univ, PhD, 84. **CAREER** Dir, undergrad stud; fac adv; prof, 76-. **HONORS AND AWARDS** Laurence Campbell res award, Assn Edu in Journ Mass Commun, 92. **RESEARCH** Media history; journalism education; newspaper design and photography. **SELECTED PUBLICATIONS** Co- auth, Journalism Kids Do Better; Going to London?, London for Families, 97. **CONTACT ADDRESS** Dept of Commun, Univ Dayton, 300 Col Park, Dayton, OH, 75062. **EMAIL** Lain@udayton.edu

LAIRD, DAVID
PERSONAL Born 10/16/1927, Marshfield, WI, m, 1955, 1 child **DISCIPLINE** ENGLISH LITERATURE **EDUCATION** Univ Wis, BA, 50, MA, 51, PhD, 55. **CAREER** From instr to asst prof English, Oberlin Col, 55-58; FROM ASST PROF TO ASSOC PROF ENGLISH, CALIF STATE UNIV, 58-78, PROF, 68-73, CHMN DEPT, 69-72, COORDR AM STUDIES, 77-79. Fel, Nat Humanities Inst, Univ Chicago, 78-79; sr Fulbright lectr, Univ Tunis, Tunisia, 79-80; Inst Renaissance and 18th Century Studies fel, Folger Shakespeare Libr, 82. **MEMBERSHIPS** MLA; Philol Asn PACIFIC Coast; Am Studies Asn; Malone Soc **RESEARCH** Shakespeare; rhetoric and style; American literature and cultural history. **SELECTED PUBLICATIONS** Auth, Cather, Willa Women, Gender, Place, and Narrativity in 'O Pioneers' and 'My Antonia', Great Plains Quart, Vol 0012, 92; The Midwestern Ascendancy in American Writing, Amer Lit, Vol 0067, 95. **CONTACT ADDRESS** Dept of English, California State Univ, Los Angeles, Los Angeles, CA, 90032.

LAIRD, EDGAR
DISCIPLINE MEDIEVAL LITERATURE **EDUCATION** Southwest TX State Univ, BA, MA; Rutgers, PhD. **CAREER** Southwest Tex State Univ **RESEARCH** James Joyce. **SELECTED PUBLICATIONS** Auth, Astrology and Irony in Chaucer's Complaint of Mars, Chaucer Rev, 72; Chaucer's Complaint of Mars, 1.145: 'Venus valaunse,' Philol Quart, 72; Astronomical 'Proporcioneles' in the Franklin's Tale, Eng Lang Notes, 88; A Note on Planetary Tables and a Planetary Conjunction in Troilus and Criseyde, Chaucer Rev, 90; Boethius, Boece, and Bootes, Mod Philol, 90; "Robert Grosseteste, Albumasar, and Medieval Tidal Theory, Isis, 81; Mars in Taurus at the Nativity of the Wife of Bath, Eng Lang Notes, 90; "Astrology in the Court of Charles V of France , Manuscripta, 90; "Columbus and the Sky of January 17, 1493, Sky & Telescope, 91;

Love 'Elemented' in John Donne's 'Valediction: Forbidding Mourning,' , Am Notes & Queries, 91; Pelerin de Prusse on the Astrolabe, Medieval and Renaissance Texts and Studies, Binghamton, 95; Cosmic Law and Literary Character in Chaucer's Knight's Tale, Mellen, 95; Right Ascension, Am Jour, Physics, 96. **CONTACT ADDRESS** Southwest Texas State Univ, 601 University Dr, San Marcos, TX, 78666-4604.

LAKE PRESCOTT, ANNE
DISCIPLINE ENGLISH LITERATURE **EDUCATION** Barnard Col, BA, 59; Columbia Univ, MA, 61, PhD, 67. **CAREER** Prof, Bernard Col, 61; Columbia, 79-. **HONORS AND AWARDS** Trustee, Renaissance Soc of Am; past pres, Spenser Soc; ed bd, SEL; CLS; Spenser Stud; Amer Notes and Queries; Moreana; adv coun, PMLA. **RESEARCH** Anthology of Renaissance texts with focus on gender. **SELECTED PUBLICATIONS** Auth, French Poets, English Renaissance, and Imagining Rabelais in the English Renaissance, Yale UP, 98. **CONTACT ADDRESS** Dept of Eng, Columbia Col, New York, 2960 Broadway, New York, NY, 10027-6902.

LAKIN, BARBARA
DISCIPLINE ENGLISH LITERATURE **EDUCATION** Kansas State Univ, BS; Colo State Univ, MA, PhD. **CAREER** Assoc prof. **RESEARCH** New Historicism; occult in English Renaissance literature. **SELECTED PUBLICATIONS** Auth, pubs on Gender and Power in Macbeth, Othello, and The Merchant of Venice; influence of Giordaano Bruno's thought on several English Renaissance writers; Graham Greene. **CONTACT ADDRESS** Dept of English, Colorado State Univ, Fort Collins, CO, 80523. **EMAIL** blakin@vines.colostate.edu

LAMB, JONATHAN
DISCIPLINE ENGLISH LITERATURE **CAREER** Prof English, Princeton Univ; vis fel, Ctr Cross-Cult Res, Australian Natl Univ, 98. **RESEARCH** 18th century travel literature. **SELECTED PUBLICATIONS** Ed, Eighteenth Century Life, 94; auth, The Rhetoric of Suffering, Oxford Univ, 95; Eyewitnessing in the South Seas, In: The Eighteenth Century: Theory and Interpretation, pending. **CONTACT ADDRESS** Dept of Education, Australian National Univ. **EMAIL** Jonathan.Lamb@anu.edu.au

LAMB, MARGARET
DISCIPLINE DRAMATIC LITERATURE AND DRAMA THEORY **EDUCATION** NY Univ, PhD **CAREER** Assoc prof, Fordham Univ. **RESEARCH** Creative writing and the writer's process. **SELECTED PUBLICATIONS** Auth, Garrick's Anthony and Cleopatra, Shakespearean Criticism, 17, 92. **CONTACT ADDRESS** Dept of Eng Lang and Lit, Fordham Univ, 113 W 60th St, New York, NY, 10023.

LAMMERS, DONALD N.
PERSONAL Born 04/27/1930, Chicago, IL, m, 1952, 3 children **DISCIPLINE** ENGLISH HISTORY **EDUCATION** Cornell Univ, AB, 52; Stanford Univ, MA, 53, PhD, 60. **CAREER** Actg instr hist Western civilization, Stanford Univ, 59-60; asst prof hist, Univ Ariz, 60-67; assoc prof, Mich State Univ, 67-71 and Univ Waterloo, 71-73; assoc prof, 73-78, PROF HIST, MICH STATE UNIV, 78-, CHMN DEPT, 80-, Jr fel, Ctr Advan Studies Behav Sci, 64-65. **MEMBERSHIPS** Conf Brit Studies. **RESEARCH** British foreign and imperial relations since 1900. **SELECTED PUBLICATIONS** Auth, Winning the Peace--British Diplomatic Strategy, Peace Planning, and the Paris Peace Conference, 1916-1920, Amer Hist Rev, Vol 0098, 93; The Spoils of War--the Politics, Economics, and Diplomacy of Reparations, 1918-1932, J Mod Hist, Vol 0065, 93; British Policy and European Reconstruction After the 1st World War, J Mod Hist, Vol 0065, 93; Portrait of an Appeaser--Hadow, Robert, First Secretary in the British Foreign Office, 1931-1939, Int Hist Rev, Vol 0019, 97. **CONTACT ADDRESS** Dept of Hist, Michigan State Univ, East Lansing, MI, 48824.

LAMMERS GROSS, NANCY
PERSONAL m, 2 children **DISCIPLINE** HOMILETICS **EDUCATION** Willamette Univ, BS; Princeton Theol Sem, MDiv, PhD. **CAREER** Assoc prof, E Baptist Theol Sem. **HONORS AND AWARDS** Parish assoc, First Presbyterian Church of Plainsboro, New Jersey **MEMBERSHIPS** Mem, Acad of Homilectics; Governing Coun for the Acad of Preachers. **CONTACT ADDRESS** Eastern Baptist Theol Sem, 6 Lancaster Ave, Wynnewood, PA, 19096.

LAMPARSKA, RENA A.
DISCIPLINE LITERATURE **EDUCATION** Univ Wroctaw, Poland, LLM; Catholic Univ of America, MA; Harvard Univ, PhD. **CAREER** Assoc prof, Boston College. **RESEARCH** Italian literature. **CONTACT ADDRESS** Dept of Romance Languages and Literatures, Boston Col, Chestnut Hill, MA, 02167.

LANCASHIRE, ANNE
PERSONAL Montreal, PQ, Canada **DISCIPLINE** ENGLISH **EDUCATION** McGill Univ, BA, 62; Harvard Univ, MA, 63, PhD, 65. **CAREER** Lectr, 65-67, asst prof, 67-71, assoc prof, 71-76, PROF UNIV TORONTO 76-, acting ch, Eng dept, 83-84, vice princ & prog dir, University Col, 90-93. **HONORS AND AWARDS** Can Coun leave fel, 71-72; SSHRCC leave fel, 86-87. **MEMBERSHIPS** MLA; Shakespeare Asn Am; Malone Soc; Film Studs Asn Can: ACCUTE; Massey Col. **SELECTED PUBLICATIONS** Auth & ed, Galathea & Midas, 69; auth & ed, The Second Maiden's Tragedy, 78; ed, Editing Renaissance Dramatic Texts: English , Italian, Spanish, 76. **CONTACT ADDRESS** Dept of English, Univ Toronto, Toronto, ON, M5S 1A1. **EMAIL** anne@epas.utoronto.ca

LANCASHIRE, IAN
PERSONAL Born 11/29/1942, Winnipeg, MB, Canada, m, 1968, 2 children **DISCIPLINE** ENGLISH **EDUCATION** Univ Man, BA, 64; Univ Toronto, MA, 65, PhD(English), 69. **CAREER** Lectr, 68-69, asst prof, 69-74, ASSOC PROF ENGLISH, ERINDALE COL, UNIV TORONTO, 74-, Can Coun leave fel, 73, grant Reed, 76; proj bibliographer theatre hist, Rec Early English Drama, 75- **MEMBERSHIPS** Medaieval Acad Am; Early English Text Soc; MLA; Can Soc Renaissance Studies. **RESEARCH** Records of early English drama, minstrelsy and ceremony; Medieval and Tudor drama; bibliography. **SELECTED PUBLICATIONS** Auth, Patrons and Performance, Early Tudor Household Revels, Mod Philol, Vol 0091, 93. **CONTACT ADDRESS** Univ Toronto, Toronto, ON, M5S 1A1.

LANDAU, NORMA BEATRICE
PERSONAL Born 09/13/1942, Toronto, ON, Canada **DISCIPLINE** ENGLISH HISTORY **EDUCATION** Univ Toronto, BA, 64, MA, 65; Univ Calif, Berkeley, PhD(hist), 74. **CAREER** Lectr hist, Duke Univ, 72-74; vis lectr, Univ Calif, Los Angeles, 75-76; asst prof Hist, Univ Calif, Davis, 76-. **MEMBERSHIPS** Conf Brit Studies. **RESEARCH** English history, 1660-1832; legal and political history. **SELECTED PUBLICATIONS** Auth, The Justices of the Peace, 1679-1760, Univ Calif Press, 84; articles in Countercity and Change, Agricultural Hist Review, Historical Journal, Bull Lost Hist Res. **CONTACT ADDRESS** Dept of Hist, Univ Calif, Davis, CA, 95616-5200. **EMAIL** nblandau@ucdavis.edu

LANDES, W. DANIEL
PERSONAL Born 04/26/1950, Harrisonburg, VA **DISCIPLINE** PERFORMING ARTS **EDUCATION** Shenandoah Conservatory of Music, BM, 72; Univ Md, MM, 77; Southern Baptist Theolog Sem, DMA, 83. **CAREER** Assoc prof, Belmont Univ, 83-. **MEMBERSHIPS** Hymn Society; Society Electro-Acoustic Music. **RESEARCH** Hymnology; music technology. **SELECTED PUBLICATIONS** Coed, Electronic Encyclopedia of Hymnology. **CONTACT ADDRESS** School of Music, Belmont Univ, 1900 Belmont Blvd, Nashville, TN, 37212. **EMAIL** landesd@mail.belmont.edu

LANDOW, GEORGE PAUL
PERSONAL Born 08/25/1940, White Plains, NY, m, 1966, 2 children **DISCIPLINE** ENGLISH LITERATURE, DIGITAL CULTURE, ART HISTORY **EDUCATION** Brandeis Univ, MA, 62; Princeton Univ, AB, 61, MA, 63, PhD(English), 66; Brown Univ, MA, 72. **CAREER** Instr English, Columbia Univ, 65-68, asst prof, 69-70; vis assoc prof, Univ Chicago, 70-71; assoc prof, 71-78, Prof English & Artist Hist, Brown Univ, 78-; Fel, Soc for Humanities, Cornell Univ, 68-69; Guggenheim Found fels, 73 & 78; consult lit & art, Museum Art, RI Sch Design, 76-79; vis fel, Brasenose Col, Oxford Univ, 77; fac fel, Brown Univ Inst for Res in Information and Scholarship (IRIS), 85-92; NEA, 84-85; NEH Summer Inst, Yale, 88, 91; British Academy vis prof, Univ of Lancaster, vis res fel, Electronics and Computer Science, Univ of Southampton (UK), vis prof Univ of Zimbabwe, 97: IL SU, 98; Distinguished vis prof, Nat Univ of Singapore, 98. **HONORS AND AWARDS** Gustave O Arldt Award, Coun Grad Schs US, 72; .EDUCOM/NCRIPTAL award innovative courseware in the humanities, 90; many awards for websites. **MEMBERSHIPS** ACM; Tennyson Soc; Trollope Soc. **RESEARCH** Hypertext and digital culture; Victorian British poetry and nonfiction; Victorian painting and visual arts; theology and literature. **SELECTED PUBLICATIONS** Auth, Your Good Influence on Me: The Correspondence of John Ruskin and W H Hunt, John Rylands Libr, England, 76; William Holman Hunt and Typological Symbolism, Yale Univ, 79; ed, Approaches to Victorian Autobiography, Ohio Univ, 79; Victorian Types, Victorian Shadows: Biblical Typology and Victorian Literature, Art and Thought, Routledge & Kegan Paul, 80; Images of Crisis: Literary Iconology 1750 to the Present, Routledge & Kegan Paul, 82; Ruskin, Oxford Univ Press, 85; ed with others, Pre-Raphaelite Friendship, UMI, 85; ed, Ladies of Shalott: A Victorian Masterpiece and its Contexts, Brown, 86; Elegant Jeremiahs: The Sage from Carlyle to Mailer, Cornell, 86; ed with P. Delany, Hypermedia and Literary Studies, MIT, 91; Hypertext: The Convergence of Contemporary Critical Theory and Technology, Johns Hopkins, 92; ed with P. delany, Digital Word: Text-Based Computing in the Humanities, MIT, 93; Hyper/Text/Theory, Johns Hopkins, 94; Hypertext 2.0, Johns Hopkins, 97. **CONTACT ADDRESS** Dept of English, Brown Univ, Box 1852, Providence, RI, 02912-9127. **EMAIL** george@landow.com

LANDY, MARCIA
PERSONAL Born 06/24/1931, Cleveland, OH, m, 1953, 2 children **DISCIPLINE** ENGLISH **EDUCATION** Ohio Univ, AB, 53; Univ Rochester, MA, 61, PhD, 62. **CAREER** From instr to asst prof English, Univ Rochester, 63-67; asst prof, 67-70, assoc prof, 70-79, PROF ENGLISH, UNIV PITTSBURGH, 79-, Ed, Milton Studies, 67-; Danforth Found Assoc, 75. **MEMBERSHIPS** MLA. **RESEARCH** Milton; women studies; literary and film criticism. **SELECTED PUBLICATIONS** Auth, Fascism in Film: The Italian Commercial Cinema 1930-1943, Princeton, 86; British Genres: Cinema and Society 1930-1960, Princeton, 91; Imitations of Life: A Reader on Film and Television Melodrama, Wayne State, 91; Film, Politics and Gramsci, Minn, 94; Queen Christina, BFJ, 96; Cinematic Uses of the Past, Minn, 96; The Folklore of Consensus: Theatricality in the Italian Cinema 1930-1943, SUNY, 98. **CONTACT ADDRESS** Dept of English, Univ Pitt, 443 Cathedral/Lear, Pittsburgh, PA, 15260-0001. **EMAIL** mlandy@pitt.edu

LANE, CHRISTOPHER
DISCIPLINE ENGLISH LANGUAGE AND LITERATURE **EDUCATION** Univ London, PhD. **CAREER** Fac, Univ Wisc Milwaukee; Mellon Fel Hum, Univ Penn, 95-96; assoc prof, 88-. **RESEARCH** Victorian literature; British colonial fiction; critical theory. **SELECTED PUBLICATIONS** Auth, The Ruling Passion, Duke UP, 95; The Burdens of Intimacy, Univ Chicago, 98; ed, The Psychoanalysis of Race, Columbia UP, 98. **CONTACT ADDRESS** English Dept, Emory Univ, 1380 Oxford Rd NE, Atlanta, GA, 30322-1950.

LANE, EUGENE N.
DISCIPLINE EPIGRAPHY AND COMPARATIVE GRAMMAR **EDUCATION** Princeton Univ, AB; Yale Univ, PhD. **CAREER** Prof & dir Grad Stud; Univ Mo, 66-; taught at, Univ Va; **RESEARCH** Ancient religion; comparative grammar; Late Antiquity. **SELECTED PUBLICATIONS** Auth, Corpus Monumentorum Religionis Dei Menis, 4 vols, Leiden, Brill, 71-78 & Corpus Cultus Iovis Sabazii, vols 2 & 3, Leiden Brill, 85-89; coauth, Paganism and Christianity, 100-425 CE: a Sourcebook; ed, Cybele, Attis, and Related Cults: Essays in Memory of MJ Vermaseren. **CONTACT ADDRESS** Dept of Classical Studies, Univ of Missouri-Columbia, 309 University Hall, Columbia, MO, 65211.

LANE, PINKIE GORDON
PERSONAL Born 01/13/1923, Philadelphia, PA **DISCIPLINE** ENGLISH **EDUCATION** Spelman Col, BA, 49; Atlanta Univ, MA, 56; La State Univ, PhD(English), 67. **CAREER** PROF ENGLISH, SOUTHERN UNIV, BATON ROUGE, 67-80, CHMN DEPT, 74-80. Vpres, South and West, Inc, ed-in-chief, South and West: Int Lit Quart. **MEMBERSHIPS** Poetry Soc Am. **SELECTED PUBLICATIONS** Auth, Mississippi River Poems, African Amer Rev, Vol 0027, 93; Remembrances of Spring, African Amer Rev, Vol 0030, 96. **CONTACT ADDRESS** Southern Univ, 2738 77th Ave, Baton Rouge, LA, 70807.

LANG, CECIL Y.
PERSONAL Born 09/18/1920, NC, m, 1952, 1 child **DISCIPLINE** ENGLISH LITERATURE **EDUCATION** Duke Univ, AB, 41, MA, 42; Harvard Univ, PhD, 49. **CAREER** From instr to asst prof English, Yale Univ, 49-57; assoc prof, Claremont Grad Sch, 57-59; prof, Syracuse Univ, 59-65 and Univ Chicago, 65-67; prof, Ctr Advan Studies, 67-70, COMMONWEALTH PROF ENGLISH, UNIV VA, 70-, Guggenheim and Fulbright fels, 51-52; Morse fel, Yale Univ, 56-57; mem adv bd, Victorian Poetry, 63-; mem adv bd, Victorian Studies, 64-66; mem ed comt, Pmla, 68-73. **MEMBERSHIPS** MLA. **RESEARCH** Nineteenth century English literature. **SELECTED PUBLICATIONS** Ed, The Swinburne Letters (6 vols), Yale Univ, 59-62; New Writings by Swinburne, Syracuse Univ, 64; The Pre Raphaelites and their Circle, Houghton, 68, 2nd ed, Univ Chicago, 75; introd, Tennyson in Lincoln, Tennyson Res Ctr, Lincoln, Eng, 71; co-ed (with E F Shannon Jr), the Tennyson Letters, Harvard Univ, Vol 1, 81 and Clarendon Press, 82. **CONTACT ADDRESS** 1820 Edgewood Lane, Charlottesville, VA, 22903.

LANG, ROBERT
PERSONAL Born 10/25/1957, Zimbabwe, s **DISCIPLINE** FILM **EDUCATION** Columbia Univ, PhD, 86. **CAREER** ASSOC PROF OF CINEMA, UNIV OF HARTFORD. **HONORS AND AWARDS** Fulbright Sr Scholar Awd, Univ of Tunis, 93-94. **MEMBERSHIPS** Soc for Cinema Studies. **RESEARCH** Hollywood cinema; African cinema; queer studies; contemporary French studies. **SELECTED PUBLICATIONS** Auth, American Film Melodrama: Griffith Director, Princeton Univ Press, 89; ed, The Birth of a Nation: D.W. Griffith Director, Rutgers Univ Press, 94. **CONTACT ADDRESS** 25 Frederick St, 302, Hartford, CT, 06105. **EMAIL** lang@mail.hartford.edu

LANGBAUM, ROBERT
PERSONAL Born 02/23/1924, New York, NY, m, 1950, 1 child **DISCIPLINE** ENGLISH **EDUCATION** Cornell Univ, AB, 47; Columbia Univ, MA, 49, PhD(English), 54. **CAREER**

From instr English to asst prof, Cornell Univ, 50-60; from assoc prof to prof, 60-67, JAMES BRANCH CABELL PROF ENGLISH, UNIV VA, 67-, Ctr Advan Studies Behav Sci fel, 61-62; vis prof, Columbia Univ, 65-66; Guggenheim fel, 69-70; sr fel, Nat Endowment for Humanities, 72-73; mem Supv Comt, English Inst, 70-71, chmn, 72. **MEMBERSHIPS** MLA; Aaup; Acad Lit Studies. **RESEARCH** Nineteenth and 20th century English literature; literary criticism. **SELECTED PUBLICATIONS** Auth, Wordsworth, William--Intensity and Achievement, J Engl and Ger Philol, Vol 0093, 94; Coordinates of Anglo American Romanticism--Wesley, Edwards, Carlyle and Emerson, Wordsworth Circle, Vol 0025, 94; Wordsworth and the Prose Tradition in Poetry, Wordsworth Circle, Vol 0027, 96; Victorian Poetry, Poetry, Poetics, and Politics, 19th-Century Lit, Vol 0051, 96. **CONTACT ADDRESS** Dept of English, Univ of VA, Charlottesville, VA, 22903.

LANGELLIER, KRISTIN M.
DISCIPLINE COMMUNICATIONS **EDUCATION** Southern IL Univ, PhD, 80. **CAREER** Mark and Marcia Bailey Prof, grad coordr, Univ ME. **RESEARCH** Personal narrative. **SELECTED PUBLICATIONS** Auth, Personal narratives: Perspectives on theory and research, Text and Performance Quart, 9, 89; Appreciating phenomenology and feminism: Researching quiltmaking and communication, Human Stud, 17, 94; Responding to ethnicity: Franco-American studies in Maine, in H. Barthel ed, Logon didonai. Marz: Voraussichtlicher Erscheinungstermin, 96; coauth, Spinstorying: An analysis of women storytelling, in E. Fine and J. Speer eds, Performance, cult, and identity, Praeger, 92; Family storytelling as a strategy of soc control, in D. Mumby, ed, Narrative and soc control, Sage, 93. **CONTACT ADDRESS** Univ ME, Orono, ME, 04469-5752. **EMAIL** kristin@maine.edu

LANGENDOEN, DONALD TERENCE
PERSONAL Born 06/07/1939, Paterson, NJ, m, 1984, 1 child **DISCIPLINE** LINGUISTICS, ENGLISH **EDUCATION** Mass Inst Technol, BS, 61, PhD, 64. **CAREER** From asst prof to assoc prof ling, OH State Univ, 64-69; Prof Eng, Brooklyn Col, City Univ New York, 69-88, Prof Ling, Grad CTR, 71- Vis assoc prof, Rockefeller Univ, 68-69; sr Fulbright lectr, Rijksuniv Utrecht, The Neth, 77; vis scientist IBM TJ Watson Res Ctr, York Town Heights, 86-87; Univ of AZ, 88-, head linguistics dept 88-97, vis prof, Univ of Hong Kong, 98. **HONORS AND AWARDS** Fel NY Acad Sci, NYC 77, Named Ptnr in Edn, Bd of Edn, NYC 82. **MEMBERSHIPS** Ling Soc Am; Asn Comput Ling. AAAS, chair 99-; Asn for Linguistic and Lit Computing. **RESEARCH** Eng syntax; linguistic theory; psycholinguistics. **SELECTED PUBLICATIONS** Auth, The London School of Linguistics, 68; The Study of Syntax, 69, Essentials of English Grammar, 70 & coed, Studies in Linguistic Semantics, 71, Holt; coed, An Integrated Theory of Linguistic Ability, Crowell, 76, co-auth, The Vastness of Natural Languages, Blackwell, 84; ed, Linguistics Abstracts, 97-, co-ed, Optimality Theory: An Overview, Blackwell, 97. **CONTACT ADDRESS** Dept of Linguistics, Univ of AZ, PO Box 210028, Tucson, AZ, 85721. **EMAIL** langendt@arizona.edu

LANGER, LAWRENCE L.
PERSONAL Born 06/20/1929, New York, NY, m, 1951, 2 children **DISCIPLINE** LITERATURE **EDUCATION** City Col New York, BA, 51; Harvard Univ, AM, 52, PhD, 61. **CAREER** Instr English, Univ CT, 57-58; from instr to assoc prof, 58-72, prof English, Simmons Col, 72-, Alumnae Prof English, 76-92, PROF EMERITUS, 92-; Fulbright lectr Am lit, Univ Graz, Austria, 63-64; Nat Endowment for Humanities advan study & res fel, 78-79, 89-90. **HONORS AND AWARDS** Nat Book Critics Circle Award for Criticism, 91. **MEMBERSHIPS** MLA; Pen. **RESEARCH** Holocaust studies; literature of the holocaust. **SELECTED PUBLICATIONS** Auth, The Holocaust and the Literary Imagination, Yale Univ, 75; The Age of Atrocity: Death in Modern Literature, Beacon, 78; Versions of Survival: The Holocaust and the Human Spirit, State Univ NY, 82; Holocaust Testimonies: The Ruins of Memory, Yale, 91; Admitting the Holocaust: Collected Essays, Oxford, 95; Art from the Ashes: A Holocaust Anthology, Oxford, 95; Landscapes of Jewish Experience: The Painting of Samuel Bak, Univ Press of New England, 97; Preempting the Holocaust, Yale, 98. **CONTACT ADDRESS** 249 Adams Ave., West Newton, MA, 02115. **EMAIL** LLanger@world.std.com

LANGFORD, GERALD
PERSONAL Born 10/20/1911, Montgomery, AL, m, 1938, 2 children **DISCIPLINE** ENGLISH **EDUCATION** Univ Va, AB, 33, AM, 34, PhD, 40. **CAREER** Instr, Univ Ky, 36-38 & NC State Col, 38-40; assoc prof, Winthrop Col, 40-43; from asst prof to assoc prof, 46-50, prof English, Univ Tex, Austin, 62-. **RESEARCH** Creative writing; modern English and American literature. **SELECTED PUBLICATIONS** Auth, Alias O Henry a Biography of William Sidney Porter, Macmillan, 57; auth, The Richard Harding Davis Years, Holt, 61; auth, The Murder of Stanford White, Bobbs, 62; auth, Ingenue among the Lions: The Letters of Emily Clark to Joseph Hergesheimer, 65; auth, Faulkner's Revision of Absalom, Absalom!, Univ Tex, 71; auth, Faulkner's Revision of Sanctuary, 72, Univ Tex; auth, Destination, A Novel, Stonehenge, 81. **CONTACT ADDRESS** Dept of English, Univ of Texas, Austin, TX, 78712.

LANGFORD, THOMAS
PERSONAL Born 10/20/1930, Alice, TX, m, 1953, 2 children **DISCIPLINE** ENGLISH VICTORIAN LITERATURE **EDUCATION** Univ CA, BA, 56; TX Tech Univ, MA, 63; TX Christian Univ, PhD, 67. **CAREER** Minister, Churches Christ, 56-59; tchr Eng, Chas Page High Sch, OK, 58-61; fel, US Off Educ, 67-68; asst prof, 67-70, asst dean, 68-71, prof eng, TX Tech Univ, 70-, Assoc dean, grad sch, 71-95, Dean, grad sch, 95-86, Consult & reviewer, US Off Educ, 68-72; reviewer educ, Nat Coun Accreditation Tchr Educ, 68. **HONORS AND AWARDS** Outstanding Contrib to Graduate Educ in the South, 97; TTU Fac Leadership Award, 93; TTU Tchg Acad, 98. **MEMBERSHIPS** MLA; Col Eng Asn; Tennyson Res Soc; Browning Inst; Conf Christianity & Lit. **RESEARCH** Victorian lit; Milton studies; Christianity and lit. **SELECTED PUBLICATIONS** Auth, The temptations in Paradise Regained, Tex Studies Lang & Lit, spring 67; Johnson's Rasselas and The Vanity of Human Wishes, Christianity & Lit, fall 70; The phases of passion in Tennyson's Maud, SCent Mod Lang Asn Studies, winter 70; Prophetic imagination and the unity of Jane Eyre, Studies Novel, summer 74; John Ruskin and the doctrine of imperfection, Restoration Rev, 10/76; Assessing a new general studies master's program, Tex Tech J Educ, summer 78; Milton on ministry, Restoration Quart, Vol 22, 79; Literacy and belief, Lit & Belief, 1/81; Interdisciplinary study in the fine arts, Jour Aesthetic Educ, 82; Tennyson's The Hesperides and Milton, Victorian Inst Jour, 87; Trollope's satire, Stud in Novel, 87; A new letter from Matthew Arnold, Victorian Prose, 89; Cordelia and the rhetoric of righteousness, Lit and Belief, 91; Graduate Education in the South, 91. **CONTACT ADDRESS** Eng Dept, Texas Tech Univ, Lubbock, TX, 79409-1030. **EMAIL** kqtal@ttacs.ttu.edu

LANGIULLI, NINO FRANCIS
PERSONAL Born 10/09/1932, Brooklyn, NY, m, 1959, 3 children **DISCIPLINE** PHILOSOPHY, ENGLISH **EDUCATION** Maryknoll Col, AB, 55; Hunter Col, MA, 60; NY Univ, MA, 65, PhD(philos), 73. **CAREER** Instr English, St Augustine's High Sch, Brooklyn, 57-60; instr theol, 61-65, asst prof philos, 66-71, assoc prof, 72-76, Prof Philos, St Francis Col, NY, 76-, Danforth Assoc, 66-72. **HONORS AND AWARDS** Fulbright 60-61; Sears Roebuck Teaching Exc, 91; assoc ed, Measure, 89-96; book rev ed, Telos, 98. **MEMBERSHIPS** Am Philos Asn; AAUP. **RESEARCH** Contemporary philosophy; history of philosophy; metaphysics. **SELECTED PUBLICATIONS** Auth, Machiavelli, In: Shakespeare Encycl, Crowell, 66; ed & translr, Critical Existentialism, 69 & ed, The Existentialist Tradition, 71, Doubleday; translr, Existentialism, In: Encycl Britannica, Univ Chicago, 73; Possibility, Necessity, and Existence, Temple, 92; European Existentialism, Transaction, 97. **CONTACT ADDRESS** 32 Farnum St, Lynbrook, NY, 11563.

LANGLEY, STEPHEN G.
PERSONAL Born 12/25/1938, Gardner, MA **DISCIPLINE** THEATRE, SPEECH **EDUCATION** Emerson Col, BA, 60, MA, 61; Univ Ill, Urbana, PhD, 65. **CAREER** Lectr speech, 63-65, from instr to assoc prof, 65-76, bus mgr, Theatre Div, 66, gem mgr, Ctr Performing Arts, 68-75, prof theatre, Brooklyn Col, 76-, dir div Performing Arts Mgt, 75-, grad dept chp, Theatre Dept, 78-. **MEMBERSHIPS** Dramatists Guild; Am Theatre Asn. **RESEARCH** Puritanism and the American drama; performing arts administration. **SELECTED PUBLICATIONS** Auth, Theatre management in America: Principle and practice, and producers on producing, Drama Bk Specialists, 73, rev ed, 80. **CONTACT ADDRESS** Performing Arts Ctr, Brooklyn Col, CUNY, 2901 Bedford Ave, Brooklyn, NY, 11210-2813.

LANGSTRAAT, LISA
DISCIPLINE ENGLISH LITERATURE **EDUCATION** Purdue Univ, PhD, 96. **CAREER** Asst prof. **RESEARCH** Rhetoric and composition; cultural studies; feminist theory. **SELECTED PUBLICATIONS** Auth, pubs in Rhetoric and Composition, Composition Forum, and Works and Days. **CONTACT ADDRESS** Dept of English and Philosophy, Idaho State Univ, Pocatello, ID, 83209. **EMAIL** langlisa@isu.edu

LANHAM, RICHARD ALAN
PERSONAL Born 04/26/1936, Washington, DC, m, 1957 **DISCIPLINE** ENGLISH **EDUCATION** Yale Univ, AB, 56, MA, 60, PhD(English), 63. **CAREER** From instr to asst prof, Dartmouth Col, 62-65; from asst prof to assoc prof, 65-71, PROF ENGLISH, UNIV CALIF LOS ANGELES, 71-, DIR WRITING PROG, 79-, Sr fel, Nat Endowment for Humanities, 73-74. **MEMBERSHIPS** MLA. **RESEARCH** Medieval and Renaissance literature; Rhetoric; higher education in America. **SELECTED PUBLICATIONS** Auth, Introduction to Fish, Stanley, Milton Quart, Vol 0026, 92; The Economics of Attention, Mich Quart Rev, Vol 0036, 97. **CONTACT ADDRESS** Dept of English, Univ of Calif, Los Angeles, CA, 90024.

LANIER, PARKS
PERSONAL GA **DISCIPLINE** BRITISH ROMANTICISM, APPALACHIAN STUDIES, ADVANCED GRAMMAR, THE STUDY OF PO **EDUCATION** Pfeiffer Col, AB; Univ TN Knoxville, MA, PhD. **CAREER** Prof, Radford Univ. **SELECTED PUBLICATIONS** Ed, Poetics of Appalachian Space. **CONTACT ADDRESS** Radford Univ, Radford, VA, 24142. **EMAIL** planier@runet.edu

LANKEWISH, VINCENT A.
DISCIPLINE ENGLISH **EDUCATION** NY Univ, BA, 84; Merton Col, Oxford, MPhil, 86; Rutgers Univ, New Brunswick, PhD, 97. **CAREER** ASST PROF ENG, PA STATE UNIV, UNIV PARK, 98- **CONTACT ADDRESS** English Dept, Pennsylvania State Univ, Burrowes Bldg, University Park, PA, 16802-6200. **EMAIL** v214c@psu.edu

LANKFORD, GEORGE E.
PERSONAL Born 08/18/1938, Birmingham, AL **DISCIPLINE** JOURNALISM **EDUCATION** La St Univ, BA, 60; Princeton Theolog Sem, BD, 63; Ind Univ, PhD, 75. **CAREER** Instr to asst prof, Spring Hill Col, 66-67; chair, to Pauline M. & Brooks Bradley Prof, Lyon Col, 85- . **HONORS AND AWARDS** Prof of the Year, 91 **RESEARCH** Native American culture; Ozarks culture; iconography. **SELECTED PUBLICATIONS** Auth, A Documentary Study of Native American Life in the Lower Tombigbee Valley, Univ S Al, 83; Native American Legends, August House, 87; The Bates in Batesville, Ind Co Chronicle, 96; A brief History of Block 3, Old Town, Batesville, Ind Co Chronicle, 97; From Maryland to Batesville: The Hynson Brothers, Ind Co Chronicle, 98. **CONTACT ADDRESS** Lyon Col, 300 Highland Rd, Batesville, AR, 72501. **EMAIL** glankford@lyon.edu

LANOETTE, WILLIAM JOHN
PERSONAL Born 09/14/1940, New Haven, CT, m, 1969, 2 children **DISCIPLINE** ENGLISH LITERATURE **EDUCATION** Fordham Col, AB, 63; London Sch of Econ, MS, 66, PhD, 73. **CAREER** Res and reporter, Newsweek, 61-64; professional staff mem and legis asst, Res and Tech Prog Subcomt, US House of Representatives, 67-68; staff writer, The Nat Observ, Dow Jones & Co, 69-70, 72-77; staff correspondent and contrib ed, Nat Jour, 77-83; comm dir and sr assoc, World Resources Inst, 83-85; auth, Genius in the Shadows: A Biography of Leo Szilard, The man Behind the Bomb, 86-89; Wash correspondent, Bull of the Atomic Sci, 89-90; sr eval, Energy and Sci Issues, US General Acctg Office, 91-. **HONORS AND AWARDS** Guest scholar, Woodrow Wilson Intl Ctr for Scholars, Smithsonian Inst, 89; fel, John F. Kennedy Sch of Govt, Harvard Univ, 88-89; Forum award, 74. **RESEARCH** Interactions of science and politics, especially relating to the military and civilian applications of atomic energy; The rise and corruption of professional rowing in 19th Century America. **SELECTED PUBLICATIONS** Auth, Leo Szilard: A Comic and Cosmic Wit, Leo Szilard Centenary Volume, Eotvos Physical Soc, Budapest, 98; auth, Why We Dropped the Bomb, Civilization, Mag of the Libr of Congress, Jan/Feb, 95; auth, Reporting on Risk: Who Decides What's News?, Risk: Health, Safety & Environment, Quart, Franklin Pierce Law Ctr, vol 5, no 3, Summer, 94; auth, Genius in the Shadows: A Biography of Leo Szilard, The Man Behind the Bomb, Charles Scribner's Sons, 92, Univ Chicago Press, 94. **CONTACT ADDRESS** 326 Fifth St. SE, Washington, DC, 20003. **EMAIL** lanouette@erols.com

LARSON, CHARLES RAYMOND
PERSONAL Born 01/14/1938, Sioux City, IA, m, 1971, 2 children **DISCIPLINE** LITERATURE **EDUCATION** Univ Colo, BA, 59, MA, 61; Ind Univ, PhD, 70. **CAREER** Tchr, 62-64, US Peace Corps, Oraukwu, Nigeria; instr, 65-67, Am Univ; lectr, 67-70, Ind Univ; assoc prof, 70-74, prof, 74-, Am Univ; gen ed, Collier Bks African-Am Libr, 68-; prin juror, English-Speaking Union Lit Award for Third World Writers, 72-; Younger Humanist fel, NEH, 74-; Guggenheim fel, 76-77; individual res fel, NEH, 85-86; fiction & bk rev ed, 96-, Worldview. **HONORS AND AWARDS** Fulbright lectr, Africa, 72. **MEMBERSHIPS** MLA; African Lit Assn. **RESEARCH** African literature; Third World fiction; native American fiction. **SELECTED PUBLICATIONS** Auth, Arthur Dimmesdale, A & W Publ, 82; co-ed, Worlds of Fiction, Macmillan, 93; auth, Invisible Darkness: Jean Toomer and Nella Larsen, Univ Iowa Press, 93; auth, Under African Skies: Modern African Stories, FSG & Payback, 97. **CONTACT ADDRESS** 3600 Underwood St, Chevy Chase, MD, 20815. **EMAIL** crlarson@erols.com

LARSON, CLINTON F.
PERSONAL Born 09/22/1919, American Fork, UT, m, 1942, 2 children **DISCIPLINE** ENGLISH **EDUCATION** Univ Utah, BA, 43, MA, 47; Univ Denver, PhD(English), 56. **CAREER** From instr to assoc prof, 47-62, PROF ENGLISH, BRIGHAM YOUNG UNIV, 62-. **SELECTED PUBLICATIONS** Auth, Lower Campus, Brigham Young Univ Stud, Vol 0033, 93. **CONTACT ADDRESS** Dept of English, Brigham Young Univ, Provo, UT, 84601.

LARSON, DAVID MITCHELL
PERSONAL Born 10/21/1944, Marshall, MN, m, 1967, 1 child **DISCIPLINE** AMERICAN & BRITISH LITERATURE **EDUCATION** Univ Minn, Morris, BA, 66; Univ Minn, Minneapolis, MA, 69, PhD, 73. **CAREER** Asst prof English, Franklin & Marshall Col, 71-75; assoc prof Eng, Cleveland State Univ, 75-79. **MEMBERSHIPS** MLA; Col English Assn. **RESEARCH** Early American literature, especially writers of the later eighteenth century; contemporary science fiction. **SELECTED PUBLICATIONS** Art, Eighteenth Century Tales Of Sheep's Tails And One of Benjamin Franklin's American jokes, Philol Quart, spring 80; art, Thematic structure and conventions

in science fiction, The Sphinx, 81; art, Behevolent Persuaasion: the Art of Benjamin Franklin's Philanthropic Papaers, PMHB, CX, 86; art, Benjamin Franklin's touth, His Biographers, and the Autobiography, PMHB CXIX, 95 **CONTACT ADDRESS** Dept of English, Cleveland State Univ, 1983 E 24th St, Cleveland, OH, 44115-2440.

LARSON, ORVILLE K
PERSONAL Born 03/07/1914, Chicago, IL, m, 1946, 4 children **DISCIPLINE** DRAMA **EDUCATION** Univ Wis, BS, 41; Western Reserve Univ, MA, 42; Univ Ill, PhD(speech), 56. **CAREER** Instr speech and theatre, Univ Md, 46-49; instr speech and drama, Univ Conn, 51-56; asst prof speech, Mich State Univ, 56-59; assoc prof fine arts, Ohio Univ, 59-61; assoc prof speech and theatre and head div theatre, Univ Mass, 61-65; prof speech and theatre and chmn dept, Univ Bridgeport, 65-67; PROF SPEECH AND THEATRE, KENT STATE UNIV, 69-. **MEMBERSHIPS** Am Soc Theatre Res; Am Theatre Asn; Col Art Asn Am; Speech Commun Asn. **RESEARCH** Stage machinery and spectacle in the theatre of the Renaissance; history of theatrical art in 20th century American theatre; relationship between art and theatre of the Renaissance. **SELECTED PUBLICATIONS** Auth, The James Adams Floating Theater, Theatre Survey, Vol 0033, 92; The Simple Stage, its Origins in the Modern American Theater, Theatre Survey, Vol 0035, 94. **CONTACT ADDRESS** Theatre Div Dept of Speech, Kent State Univ, Kent, OH, 44242.

LARSON, RICHARD LESLIE
PERSONAL Born 01/19/1929, Stevens Point, WI, m, 1962 **DISCIPLINE** ENGLISH **EDUCATION** Harvard Univ, AB, 49, AM, 50, PhD(English), 63. **CAREER** Instr, Harvard Univ, Grad Sch Bus Admin, 56-59, lectr, 59-63; from asst prof to prof English, Univ Hawaii, 63-73; assoc dean educ, 73-75, actg dean, 75-78, dean, 78, PROF EDUC, LEHMAN COL, 73-, DEAN PROF STUDIES, 78-, Compiler ann bibliog on teaching of compos, Col Compos and Commun, 75-78. **MEMBERSHIPS** NCTE; Nat Conf Res English; MLA; Conf Col Compos and Commun; Speech Commun Asn. **RESEARCH** Rhetoric; teacher education in English; evaluation of teaching in English composition. **SELECTED PUBLICATIONS** Auth, Rhetorical Guide to the Borzoi College Reader, Knopf, 67; Discovery through questioning: a plan for teaching rhetorical invention, Col English, 11/68; Toward a linear rhetoric of the essay, Com Compos and Commun, 5/71; The evaluation of teaching: College English, MLA, 71; Process or product: the evaluation of teaching or the evaluation of learning, Bull Asn Depts English, 12/72; ed, Children and Writing in the Elementary School: Theories and Techniques, Oxford Univ, 75; auth, Structure and form in nonfiction prose, in: Teaching Composition: Ten Bibliographical Essays, Tex Christian Univ, 76. **CONTACT ADDRESS** 30 Greenridge Ave Apt 5-M White, Plains, NY, 10605.

LASARENKO, JANE
DISCIPLINE ENGLISH **EDUCATION** SUNY, Binghamton, BA, 72, MA, 74; OH State Univ, Columbus, PhD, 88. **CAREER** Asst prof, WTX A & M Univ, 91- & St Anselm Col, Manchester, 88-91; tchg asst, OH State Univ, Columbus, 84-88. **HONORS AND AWARDS** Dir, Writing-Across-the-Curric Prog, Webmistress, Slippery Rock Univ, 91-96; ed, TX Voices, TX Coun Tchr(s) Engl newsl, WTAMU, 95-97; Webmistress, dept Engl and Mod Lang, WTAMU; taught 1st univ completely online crse in, 96, WTAMU. **SELECTED PUBLICATIONS** Auth, Wired for Learning, Que Corp, 97; Teaching Literature in Cyberspace, Chapter for Integrating Information Technology Tools in Instruction, Microsoft Corp CD-ROM, 97; Collaborative Strategies in A Networked Classroom, Tchg in The Commun Col Elec J 1 3, 96; So, You Wanna MOO, Kairos 1 2, 96; Prowling Around, Kairos 1 1, 96; Computers and Writing: A Student's Perspective, Epiphany Guidebk, The Epiphany Gp, 96; Teaching Plagiarism, Paraphrase, and Summary: A Computer-Based Integrated Approach, The Exercise Exch 41 2, 96; The Red Scream: A Mystery Lover's Dream, Bk(s) in Tex, 96; Under The Beetle's Cellar, Bk(s) in Tex, 96; Horseshoe Sky, Women in Libr 25 1, 95; From Invitation to Experience: A Narrative of (Dis)Engagement, Midwest Quarterly 36 1, 94; coauth, Traveling the Virtual Terrain: Practical Strategies for Survival in the Electronic Classroom, The Online Classroom, Hampton Press, 98; Publishing on The World Wide Web: A Call for Standards and Guidelines, Kairos 1 3, 96. **CONTACT ADDRESS** Dept of Eng, Slippery Rock Univ, 102 Maltby Center, Slippery Rock, PA, 16057.

LASSLO, ANDREW
PERSONAL Born 08/24/1922, Mukacevo, Czechoslovakia, m, 1955, 1 child **DISCIPLINE** LIBRARY SCIENCE **EDUCATION** Univ Il, MS, 48, PhD, 52, MSLS, 61. **CAREER** Res chemist, Monsanto Chemical Co, St. Louis, Mo, 52-54; asst prof, Emory Univ, Atlanta, Ga, 54-60; prof to emeritus prof, chair, dir, 60-, Univ Tn. **HONORS AND AWARDS** Fel, Univ Il, Chicago, 51-52; Americanism Medal, Daughters of the Amer Revolution, 76; Sigma Xi Excellence in Res Award, Univ Tn, 89; Alumni Distinguished Svc Prof & Chairman, Univ Tn, 89-90; Beta Phi Mu; Rho Chi; Phi Lambda Sigma; Sigma Xi; awardee, res and training grants, Nat Inst of Health, 58-64, 66-72, 82-89, National Sci Found, 64-66, Geschickter Fund for Medical Res, 59-65, Gustavus and Louise Pfeiffer Res Found, 81-87. **MEMBERSHIPS** Acad Pharm Res & Sci; Amer Assoc Advan of Sci; Amer Assoc of Pharm Scientists; Amer Inst of Chemists; Amer Chem Soc, Amer Libr Assoc, Amer Pharm Assoc, Amer Soc for Pharm & Experimental Therapeutics. **RESEARCH** Science information & library resources. **SELECTED PUBLICATIONS** Ed, Blood Platelet Function and Medicinal Chemistry, 84; coauth, Inhibition of Thrombus Formation in Vivo by a Novel Antiplatelet Agent, Arterosclerosis, 90; art, Inhibition of Platelet Adhesion and Thrombus Formation on a Collagen-Coated Surface by Novel Carbamoylpiperidine Antiplatelet Agents, 92; auth, Research, Relevance and Reason, Res Commun in Psychol, Psych & Behavior, 94; auth, Travel at Your Own Risk - Reflections on Science, Research, and Education, PJD Publ, 98. **CONTACT ADDRESS** 5479 Timmons Ave, Memphis, TN, 38119. **EMAIL** alasslo.Memphis.24822@worldnet.att.net

LATIMER, DAN RAYMOND
PERSONAL Born 07/15/1944, San Angelo, TX, m, 1970, 1 child **DISCIPLINE** COMPARATIVE LITERATURE, ENGLISH STUDIES **EDUCATION** Univ Tex, Austin, BA, 66; Univ Mich, Ann Arbor, MA, 67, PhD(comp lit), 72. **CAREER** Asst prof, 72-78, ASSOC PROF ENGLISH, AUBURN UNIV, 78-; RES AND WRITING, 82-, Asst Ed, Southern Humanities Rev. **MEMBERSHIPS** MLA; Am Comp Lit Asn; Southern Comp Lit Asn. **RESEARCH** Symbolism; modern criticism; Goethe. **SELECTED PUBLICATIONS** Auth, Editors Comment + A Narrative Can Have a Powerful Rhetorical Appeal, Southern Humanities Rev, Vol 0028, 94; Editors Comment + National Epics, Southern Humanities Rev, Vol 0030, 96; Editors Comment + an Approach to the Work of Gauchet, Marcel, Southern Humanities Rev, Vol 0031, 97. **CONTACT ADDRESS** Dept of English, Auburn Univ, University, AL, 36849.

LATTA, KIMBERLY
DISCIPLINE SEVENTEENTH-CENTURY BRITISH LITERATURE **EDUCATION** Rutgers Univ, PhD. **CAREER** Eng Dept, St. Edward's Univ **SELECTED PUBLICATIONS** Auth, Such is My Bond: Maternal and Paternal Debt in Anne Bradstreet, Univ KY Press. **CONTACT ADDRESS** St Edward's Univ, 3001 S Congress Ave, Austin, TX, 78704-6489.

LATTA, SUSAN M.
DISCIPLINE ENGLISH LITERATURE AND LINGUISTICS **EDUCATION** Ind State Univ, BA, MA; Purdue Univ, PhD. **CAREER** Dir, wrtg prog; asst prof, 96-. **RESEARCH** Participatory action research and computer assisted instruction. **SELECTED PUBLICATIONS** Pub(s), essays on mass media in the classroom, student self-assessment, and critical research methodologies. **CONTACT ADDRESS** Dept of Eng, Univ Detroit Mercy, 4001 W McNichols Rd, PO BOX 19900, Detroit, MI, 48219-0900. **EMAIL** LATTAS7@udmercy.edu

LAUBENTHAL, PENNE J.
PERSONAL Born 08/02/1944, Athens, AL, m, 1961, 2 children **DISCIPLINE** ENGLISH, SPEECH **EDUCATION** Athens Col, Ala, BA, 65, MAT, 68; George Peabody Col, PhD(English), 72. **CAREER** Tutor & instr, 65-68, from asst prof to assoc prof, 68-72, PROF ENGLISH, ATHENS COL, ALA, 72-, CHAIRPERSON HUMANITIES DEPT, 80-. **HONORS AND AWARDS** Outstanding Committment to Teaching, 91; NEH Fel, 80, 88, 97. **MEMBERSHIPS** MLA; AAUP; SAtlantic Mod Lang Asn; Speech Commun Asn. **RESEARCH** Modern drama; comparative literature; modern French literature. **SELECTED PUBLICATIONS** Auth, A Humanist Looks at the Mind-Body Connection, J Med Asn Ga, 11/94; Biography of C. Eric Lincoln, In: A Bibliographical Guide to Alabama Literature; author of poetry published in Poet magazine and Elk River Review; reviews published in Myhtosphere and J Poetry Therapy. **CONTACT ADDRESS** Dept of English, Athens State Col, 300 N Beaty St, Athens, AL, 35611-1999. **EMAIL** laubepj@athens.edu

LAUTERBACH, CHARLES EVERETT
PERSONAL Born 03/08/1934, Denver, CO, m, 1962 **DISCIPLINE** DRAMA **EDUCATION** Univ Colo, BA, 56, MA, 61; Mich State Univ, PhD(Theatre), 66. **CAREER** Instr Drama, Univ Colo, 61; asst instr, Mich State Univ, 63-64; asst prof, Cent Wash State Col, 64-66 & Univ Calif, Riverside, 66-71; prof Theatre, Boise State Univ, 71-. **MEMBERSHIPS** Am Theatre Asn; Am Soc Theater Res. **RESEARCH** The drama of Thornton Wilder; trends in dramatic styles in American drama of the 1920's; 19th century American theatre history. **CONTACT ADDRESS** Dept of Theatre, Boise State Univ, 1910 University Dr, Boise, ID, 83725-0399. **EMAIL** clauter@micron.net

LAUZEN, MARTHA M.
DISCIPLINE MASS COMMUNICATION, PUBLIC COMMUNICATION **EDUCATION** Univ IA, BA, MA; Univ MD, PhD. **CAREER** Comm, San Diego St Univ. **MEMBERSHIPS** Mem, The Naisbitt Gp. **SELECTED PUBLICATIONS** Auth, numerous articles on issues mgt and pub rel(s), Jour Pub Rel(s) Res; Mgt Commun Quart; Jour Quart. **CONTACT ADDRESS** Dept of Commun, San Diego State Univ, 5500 Campanile Dr, San Diego, CA, 92182. **EMAIL** comments@sdsu.edu

LAVALLEY, AL
DISCIPLINE FILM STUDIES **EDUCATION** Yale Univ, PhD, 61. **CAREER** Fac, Yale Univ; fac, San Francisco State Univ; fac, Rutgers Univ; fac, Univ CA Santa Barbara; chr film studies, Darmouth Col, 84-95; prof. **HONORS AND AWARDS** Founder, Limelight film and theatre bookstore. **RESEARCH** Billy Wilder and Fritz Lang. **SELECTED PUBLICATIONS** Auth, publ(s) about Am film, gay film and gay theory, and German film; ed, books on Hitchcock and the screenplays of Mildred Pierce and Invasion of the Body Snatchers. **CONTACT ADDRESS** Dartmouth Col, 3529 N Main St, #207, Hanover, NH, 03755. **EMAIL** Al.LaValley@Dartmouth.edu

LAVASSEUR, DAVID G.
PERSONAL Born 02/23/1966, Baltimore, MD, s **DISCIPLINE** COMMUNICATION STUDIES **EDUCATION** Univ Md, BA, 88; Univ Md, MA, speech and comm, 90; Univ Kans, PhD, comm studies, 94. **CAREER** Asst prof, Villanova Univ, 94-97; asst prof, West Chester Univ, 97-. **HONORS AND AWARDS** Outstanding Communication Prof award, Nat Speakers Asn, 98. **MEMBERSHIPS** Nat Comm Asn. **RESEARCH** Public policy communication. **SELECTED PUBLICATIONS** Co-auth, Accounting for Dole's Humor in the 1976 Vice Presidential Debate: A Response to Gruner, Southern Jour of Comm, 64, 243-247, 97; auth, A Reconsideration of Edmund Burke's Rhetorical Art: A Rhetorical Struggle Between Prudence and Heroism, Quart Jour of Speech, 83, 332-350, 97; co-auth, The Dole Humor Myth and the Risks of Recontextualizing Rhetoric, Southern Jour of Comm, 62, 56-72, 96; coauth, The Use of Evidence in Presidential Debates: What Level and Type of Evidence Maximize a Candidate's Effectiveness?, Argumentation and Advocacy, 32, 129-142, 96; auth, Edifying Arguments and Perspective by Incongruity: The Perplexing Argumentation Method of Kenneth Burke, Argumentation and Advocacy, 29, 195-203, 93; co-auth, Addressing the Needs of Academically Talented Students: A Forensics Model for the Basic Public Speaking Course, Nat Forensic Jour, 7, 133-142, 89; co-auth, A Defense of Questions in Rhetorical Criticism, Nat Forensic Jour, 7, 151-158, 89; auth, Justice and the Balance, Principles and Types of Speech Communication, 11th ed, Glenview, Scott, Foresman/Little, Brown Higher Educ, 186-198, 90. **CONTACT ADDRESS** Dept. of Communication Studies, West Chester Univ, West Chester, PA, 19383. **EMAIL** dlevasseur@wcopa.edu

LAW, JULES
DISCIPLINE ENGLISH **EDUCATION** Johns Hopkins Univ, PhD. **CAREER** Prof, Northwestern Univ. **SELECTED PUBLICATIONS** Auth, The Rhetoric of Empiricism from Locke to I. A. Richards, 93; articles on, James Joyce; George Eliot; Derrida; Wittgenstein. **CONTACT ADDRESS** Dept of English, Northwestern Univ, 1801 Hinman, Evanston, IL, 60208.

LAW, RICHARD G.
DISCIPLINE MODERN AMERICAN LITERATURE **EDUCATION** Wash Univ, PhD. **CAREER** Prof & dir Gen Educ, Washington State Univ. **HONORS AND AWARDS** Developed, Virtual WSU learning module, What is Culture. **SELECTED PUBLICATIONS** Contrib ed, collection, Time's Glory: Original Essays on Robert Penn Warren, 86. **CONTACT ADDRESS** Dept of English, Washington State Univ, 1 SE Stadium Way, PO Box 645020, Pullman, WA, 99164-5020. **EMAIL** rlaw@wsu.edu

LAWLER, TRAUGOTT
PERSONAL Born 03/08/1937, Nyack, NY, m, 1958, 4 children **DISCIPLINE** ENGLISH **EDUCATION** Col Holy Cross, AB, 58; Univ Wis, MA, 62; Harvard Univ, PhD(English), 66. **CAREER** From instr to asst prof English, Yale Univ, 66-72; from assoc prof to prof, Northwestern Univ, Evanston, 72-81; PROF ENGLISH, YALE UNIV, 81-, Am Coun Learned Sic fel, 77-78. **MEMBERSHIPS** Medieval Acad Am; Soc Study Medieval Lang and Lit. **RESEARCH** Old and middle English; medieval Latin; Chaucer. **SELECTED PUBLICATIONS** Auth, The 'Canterbury Tales'--a Unified Work, Speculum-J Medieval Stud, Vol 0071, 96; A History of Anglo-Latin Literature, Ad1066-1422, Speculum-J Medieval Stud, Vol 0071, 96. **CONTACT ADDRESS** Dept of English, Yale Univ, P O Box 208302, New Haven, CT, 06520-8302.

LAWRENCE, ELIZABETH ATWOOD
PERSONAL Born 10/01/1929, Boston, MA, m, 1957, 2 children **DISCIPLINE** ENGLISH **EDUCATION** Mt Holyoke Col, BA, 51; Univ Pa, Sch of Vet Med, VMD, 56; Brown Univ, MA, 76, PhD, 79. **CAREER** Vet med practice, 56-80; full-time fac mem, Tufts Univ, Sch of Vet Med, 81-; prof, dept of environ & population health, Tufts Univ Sch of Vet Med. **HONORS AND AWARDS** James Mooney award, Southern Anthrop Soc; Woman Vet of the Yr award, Asn for Women Vet; Intl Distinguished Scholar award, Intl Asn of Human-Animal interactions Orgn. **MEMBERSHIPS** Amer Vet Med Asn; Amer Anthrop Asn; Amer Vet Hist Soc. **RESEARCH** Human relationships with animals and nature; Human-animal continuity; Animal symbolism. **SELECTED PUBLICATIONS** Auth, A Woman Veterinary Students in the 50s: The View from the Millennium, Anthrozoos, vol 10, no 4, 97; auth, Human and Horse Medicine

Among Some Native America Groups, Agr and Human Values, Jun, 98; auth, Cultural Perceptions of Differences Between People and Animals: A Key to Understanding Human-Animal Relationships, Jour of Amer Culture, vol 18, no 3, 95; auth, Love For Animals and the Veterinary Profession, Jour of the Amer Vet Med Asn, vol 205, no 7, 94; auth, Seeing in Nature What Is Ours: The Human-Animal Bond in Poetry, Jour of Amer Culture, vol 17, no 4, 94; auth, Conflicting Ideologies: Views of Animal Rights Advocates and Their Opponents, Soc and Animals, vol 2, no 2, 94; auth, Euthanasia and the Human-Equine Bond, Equine Practice, vol 15, no 10, 93; auth, A Seventh Cavalry Veterinarian, Custer, and Rain-in-the-Face: The Story Behind A Legend, Jour of the West, vol 32, no 2, 93. **CONTACT ADDRESS** PO Box 35, Adamsville, RI, 02801.

LAWRENCE, KATHLEEN
DISCIPLINE COMMUNICATOIN STUDIES **EDUCATION** Boston Col, BA, 80; Univ Ind, MA; 84, PhD. **CAREER** Assoc prof. **SELECTED PUBLICATIONS** Auth, pubs on intercultural, rhetorical, and health communication. **CONTACT ADDRESS** Dept of Communication, State Univ NY Cortland, PO Box 2000, Cortland, NY, 13045-0900. **EMAIL** lawrencek@cortland.edu

LAWRENCE, SAMUEL G.
DISCIPLINE INTERPERSONAL AND INTERCULTURAL COMMUNICATION **EDUCATION** PhD. **CAREER** Univ Albany - SUNY **SELECTED PUBLICATIONS** Auth, Normalizing stigmatized practices: Achieving co-membership by 'doing being ordinary, Res Lang & Soc Interaction, 96. **CONTACT ADDRESS** Univ Albany-SUNY, 1400 Washington Ave, Albany, NY, 12222. **EMAIL** jedwards@csc.albany.edu

LAWSON, DARREN P.
PERSONAL Born 08/18/1964, Asheboro, NC, m, 1988, 1 child **DISCIPLINE** ORGANIZATIONAL COMMUNICATION **EDUCATION** Bob Jones Univ, BA, 86, MA, 88; Univ Kans, PhD, 96. **CAREER** Fac, Bob Jones Univ, 88-93; Grad Teaching Asst, Univ Kans, 93-96; Assoc Dean, 96-97, Dean, Sch Fine Arts, Bob Jones Univ, 97-. **HONORS AND AWARDS** Am Legion Award, 86; Employee Merit Award, Bob Jones Univ, 93; Distinguished Technical Commun Award, SC Chapter Soc Tech Commun, 93; Departmental Award for Teaching Excellence, Univ Kans, 95; Outstanding Grad Teaching Asst Award, Univ Kans, 96; Employee Merit Award, Bob Jones Univ, 97; Pac Bell Knowledge Network Learning Application Award, 97; Education World Best of the Month Award, Virtual Presentation Asst website, 97. **MEMBERSHIPS** Nat Commun Asn; Int Commun Asn. **RESEARCH** Organizational assimilation; communication technology; training and development. **SELECTED PUBLICATIONS** Coauth, The Relationship Between Prisonization and Social Skills Among Prison Inmates, The Prison J, 96; auth, Netiquette: Understanding and Using Electronic Mail, Handbook of Business Communication, 97; Electronic Mail: Attributes, Guidelines, and Educational Applications, Balance 17, 98. **CONTACT ADDRESS** School of Fine Arts, Bob Jones Univ, Greenville, SC, 29614. **EMAIL** dplawson@bju.edu

LAWSON, LEWIS ALLEN
PERSONAL Born 11/13/1931, Bristol, TN, m, 1957, 2 children **DISCIPLINE** ENGLISH **EDUCATION** ETenn State Col, BS, 57, MA, 59; Univ Wis, PhD(English), 64. **CAREER** From instr to assoc prof, 63-71, PROF ENGLISH, UNIV MD, COLLEGE PARK, 72-, Fulbright prof English, Univ Copenhagen, 71-72. **MEMBERSHIPS** Soc Study Southern Lit; SAtlantic Mod Lang Asn. **RESEARCH** Southern and American literature. **SELECTED PUBLICATIONS** Auth, Pilgrim in the Ruins, a Life of Percy, Walker, Miss Quart, Vol 0046, 93; Essays on Humphreys, Josephine--Introduction, Miss Quart, Vol 0047, 94; Will Barrett and the Fat Rosy Temple of Juno + Percy,Walker the 'Last Gentleman', Southern Lit J, Vol 0026, 94; The Dream Screen in the 'Moviegoer', Papers on Lang and Lit, Vol 0030, 94; Signposts in a Strange Land, Resources for Amer Lit Study, Vol 0022, 96; Direct Liability as an Arranger Under Cercla 107--the Efficacy of Adhering to the Tenets of Traditional Corporate Law, Notre Dame Law Rev, Vol 0071, 96; Welty,Eudora Aesthetics of Place, Sewanee Rev, Vol 0105, 97. **CONTACT ADDRESS** Dept of English, Univ of Md, College Park, MD, 20742-0001.

LAY, MARY M.
DISCIPLINE RHETORIC STUDIES **EDUCATION** Univ NMex, MA, PhD. **CAREER** Prof **RESEARCH** Gender and communication; reproductive technologies; feminist theory and rhetoric of science and technology. **SELECTED PUBLICATIONS** Co-auth, The Rhetoric of Midwifery: Conflicts and Conversations in the Minnesota Home Birth Community in the 1990s, Quarterly J Speech, 96; The Emergence of the Feminine Voice, 1526-1640: The Earliest Published Books by English Renaissance Women, J Advanced Composition, 95. **CONTACT ADDRESS** Rhetoric Dept, Univ of Minnesota, Twin Cities, 64 Classroom Office Bldg, 1994 Buford Ave, St. Paul, MN, 55108. **EMAIL** mmlay@maroon.tc.umn.edu

LAYMAN, LEWIS M.
DISCIPLINE ENGLISH LITERATURE **EDUCATION** Middlebury Univ, BA; Univ Minn, MA; Univ British Columbia, PhD. **CAREER** Assoc prof **RESEARCH** William Faulkner. **SELECTED PUBLICATIONS** Auth, pub(s) on Whitman, Joyce and Faulkner. **CONTACT ADDRESS** Dept of English, Manitoba Univ, Winnipeg, MB, R3T 2N2.

LAYMAN, RICHARD
DISCIPLINE ENGLISH, AMERICAN LITERATURE **EDUCATION** Ind Univ, BA, 71; Univ Louisville, MA, 72; Univ SC, PhD, 75. **CAREER** Manly Inc, VPres, 83-; Bruccoli, Clark, Laymen, VPres, 76-. **CONTACT ADDRESS** Bruccoli Clark Layman, Inc, 2006 Sumter St, Columbia, SC, 29201. **EMAIL** rlayman@BCL-Manly.com

LAZAR, MOSHE
DISCIPLINE DRAMA AND COMPARATIVE LITERATURE **EDUCATION** Sorbonne, Paris, PhD. **CAREER** Prof, Univ Southern Calif; diplomado de Filologia Hispanica, Salamanca, Spain; res assoc, Ctr for Medieval and Renaissance Stud, UCLA. **RESEARCH** Spanish and Judeo-Spanish biblical and para-biblical texts. **SELECTED PUBLICATIONS** Auth, Provencal literature: Amour Courtois et Fin'Amors; Bernard de Ventadour; Lo Jutgamen General. **CONTACT ADDRESS** Col Letters, Arts & Sciences, Univ Southern Calif, University Park Campus, Los Angeles, CA, 90089. **EMAIL** lazar@.usc.edu

LEACH, JIM
DISCIPLINE COMMUNICATIONS **EDUCATION** Univ Exeter, BA; Univ Birmingham, MA, PhD. **CAREER** Prof, Brock Univ. **RESEARCH** Canadian cinema, European cinema, film theory, and cultural theory. **SELECTED PUBLICATIONS** Auth, A Possible Cinema: The Films of Alain Tanner, Scarecrow Press, 84; Everyone's an American now: Thatcherist Ideology in the Films of Nicolas Roeg, Fires Were Started: British Cinema and Thatcherism, Univ Minn Press, 93; North of Pittsburgh: Genre and National Cinema in the Canadian Context, Film Genre Reader, Univ Tex Press, 95. **CONTACT ADDRESS** Dept of Film Stud, Dramatic and Visual Arts, Brock Univ, 500 Glenridge Ave, St. Catharines, ON, L2S 3A1. **EMAIL** jimleach@spartan.ac.BrockU.CA

LEACH, JOSEPH
PERSONAL Born 05/02/1921, Weatherford, TX **DISCIPLINE** AMERICAN LITERATURE **EDUCATION** Southern Methodist Univ, AB, 42; Yale Univ, PhD, 48. **CAREER** Assoc prof, 47-55, PROF ENGLISH, UNIV TEX, EL PASO, 55-, HEAD DEPT, 60-. **MEMBERSHIPS** Am Folklore Soc; Rocky Mountain Mod Lang Asn; NCTE; Col Conf Compos and Commun; MLA. **RESEARCH** American cultural history. **SELECTED PUBLICATIONS** Auth, The typical Texan; Farewell to Horseback, Muleback, Footback and Prairie Schooner; Bright Particular Star, Yale Univ, 70. **CONTACT ADDRESS** Dept of English, Univ of Tex, El Paso, TX, 79968.

LEARS, T.J. JACKSON
PERSONAL Born 07/26/1947, Annapolis, MD, m, 1969, 1 child **DISCIPLINE** AMERICAN HISTORY AND LITERATURE **EDUCATION** Univ Va, BA, 69; Univ NC, Chapel Hill, MA, 73; Yale Univ, PhD(Am studies), 78. **CAREER** Instr Am studies, Yale Univ, 77-79; ASST PROF US HIST, UNIV MO, COLUMBIA, 79-. **MEMBERSHIPS** Am Studies Asn. **RESEARCH** American advertising; literary modernism; cultural impact of modernization. **SELECTED PUBLICATIONS** Auth, Making Fun of Popular Culture, Amer Hist Rev, Vol 0097, 92. **CONTACT ADDRESS** 212 N William St, Columbia, MO, 65201.

LEARY, JAMES PATRICK
PERSONAL Born 08/19/1950, Rice Lake, WI **DISCIPLINE** FOLKLORE, AMERICAN STUDIES **EDUCATION** Univ Notre Dame, AB, 72; Univ NC, MA, 73; Ind Univ, PhD(folklore), 77. **CAREER** ASST PROF FLOKLORE, UNIV KY, 77-. **MEMBERSHIPS** Am Folklore Soc; Maledilta Soc. **RESEARCH** Folk narrative; ethnic folklore; folklore of the upper midwest. **SELECTED PUBLICATIONS** Auth, Images of Loggers + Recent Videos on Historic Lumbering, J Amer Folklore, Vol 0106, 93. **CONTACT ADDRESS** Dept of English, Univ of KY, Lexington, KY, 40502.

LEBARON, CURTIS D.
DISCIPLINE COMMUNCATION STUDIES **EDUCATION** Young Univ, BA, 89; Univ Utah, MA, 93; Univ Tex, PhD, 97. **CAREER** Asst prof. **HONORS AND AWARDS** Top Three Paper Awd; Orea B. Tanner Memorial Awd, 88. **MEMBERSHIPS** Int Commun Asn; Speech Commun Asn; Western States Commun Asn; Int Pragmatics Asn. **RESEARCH** Language and social interaction within institutional settings; multimedia analysis of communication processes; micro ethnography of communication; deceptive communication. **SELECTED PUBLICATIONS** Co-auth, Looking for Verbal Deception in Clarence Thomas's Testimony, Univ Ill, 96. **CONTACT ADDRESS** Dept of Communication, Univ Colo Boulder, Boulder, CO, 80309. **EMAIL** Curtis.Lebaron@ Colorado.edu

LEBOFSKY, DENNIS STANLEY
PERSONAL Born 10/28/1940, Philadelphia, PA, m, 1965, 5 children **DISCIPLINE** LINGUISTICS; ENGLISH **EDUCATION** Temple Univ, BA, 61; Princeton Univ, MA, 65, PhD(ling), 70. **CAREER** From Instr to Asst Prof, 65-84, Assoc Prof English, Temple Univ, 84-. **RESEARCH** Philadelphia English. **CONTACT ADDRESS** Dept of English, Temple Univ, 1114 W Berks St, Philadelphia, PA, 19122-6029. **EMAIL** dlebofsk@nimbus.temple.edu

LECHE, EMMA JEAN
PERSONAL Mobile, AL **DISCIPLINE** COMMUNICATION **EDUCATION** Harvard Univ, PhD, 94. **CAREER** US Federal Government Wash DC, program and management, 78-94. **MEMBERSHIPS** AOM, ABC, NCA, SVHE. **RESEARCH** Industrial Chaplaincy. **SELECTED PUBLICATIONS** Auth, Industrial Chaplains as Change Agents and Ethics Officers, forthcoming. **CONTACT ADDRESS** Dept of Program and Management, 2401 H St NW, Apt 808, Washington, DC, 20037-2541. **EMAIL** ejlisadove@aol.com

LEDERER, KATHERINE
PERSONAL Born 03/19/1932, Trinity, TX, 2 children **DISCIPLINE** ENGLISH **EDUCATION** Sam Houston State Univ, BA, 52; Univ Ark, MA, 58, PhD(English), 67. **CAREER** Teacher pub schs, Tex, 54-56; asst English, Univ Ark, 56-59, instr, 59-60; from instr to assoc prof, 60-68, PROF ENGLISH, SOUTHWEST MO STATE UNIV, 68-. **MEMBERSHIPS** MLA; Aaup; NCTE; Sci Fiction Writers Asn; Sci Fiction Res Asn. **RESEARCH** American drama and novel; science fiction; Afro-American history and literature. **SELECTED PUBLICATIONS** Auth, Lillian Hellman, Twayne; the foxes were waiting for Horace, not Lefty: Irony in Hellman's the Little Foxes, Philol Papers, WVa Univ Bull, 8/80; and then they sang a Sabbath song: the Easter weekend lynchings of 1906, Springfield Mag, spring 81. **CONTACT ADDRESS** Dept of English, Southwest Mo State Univ, Springfield, MO, 65802.

LEE, ALVIN A
PERSONAL Born 09/30/1930, Woodville, ON, Canada, m, 1957, 5 children **DISCIPLINE** ENGLISH LANGUAGE AND LITERATURE **EDUCATION** Univ Toronto, BA, 53, MA, 58, PhD, 61; Victoria Univ, BD, 57. **CAREER** From asst prof to assoc prof, 60-70, dean grad studies, 71-73, PROF ENGLISH, MCMASTER UNIV, 70-, VPRES ACAD, 74-, Can Coun sr fel, 66-67. **MEMBERSHIPS** Mediaeval Acad Am; MLA; Asn Can Univ Teachers English. **RESEARCH** Old English poetry; contemporary Canadian poetry. **SELECTED PUBLICATIONS** Auth, Good Hall and Earth Dragon, 'Beowulf' and the 1st-Phase Language, Engl Stud in Can, Vol 0019, 93; Taking Life Seriously, a Study of the Argument of the 'Nichomachean Ethics', Engl Stud in Can, Vol 0022, 96. **CONTACT ADDRESS** Dept of English, McMaster Univ, 1280 Main St W, Hamilton, ON, L8S 4L8.

LEE, CHUAN
DISCIPLINE MASS COMMUNICATION STUDIES **EDUCATION** Univ Hawaii, MA; Univ Mich, PhD. **CAREER** Prof **SELECTED PUBLICATIONS** Auth, Sparking a Fire: The Press and the Ferment of Democratic Change in Taiwan, J Monographs, 93; Media Imperialism Reconsidered, 80; co-auth, Hong Kong Journalists in Transition, 95; Mass Media and Political Transition: The Hong Kong Press in China's Orbit, 91; ed, China's Media, Media's China, 94; Voices of China: The Interplay of Politics and Journalism, 90. **CONTACT ADDRESS** Mass Communication Dept, Univ of Minnesota, Twin Cities, 111 Murphy Hall, 206 Church St SE, Minneapolis, MN, 55455. **EMAIL** leexx010@tc.umn.edu

LEE, DAVID
PERSONAL Born 08/13/1944, Matador, TX, m, 1971, 2 children **DISCIPLINE** 17TH AND 18TH CENTURY BRITISH LITERATURE **EDUCATION** Colorado State Univ, BA, 67; Idaho State Univ, MA, 70; Univ of Utah, PhD, 73. **CAREER** Prof of English, Dept Head, Southern Utah Univ, 71-. **HONORS AND AWARDS** Outstanding Educator, 74, 81 & 94; Prof of the Year, 96; Governor's Award for Lifetime Achievement in the Arts; Poet Laureate, 97; Western States Book Award, 96; Critic's Choice Award, 96; Mountain and Plains States Bookseller's Award, 97. **MEMBERSHIPS** Utah Acad of Arts and Sci; Rocky Mountain Modern Language Asn; Assoc Writing Programs. **RESEARCH** Modern poetry; Pound and the development of modern poetics. **SELECTED PUBLICATIONS** Auth, The Porcine Legacy, Copper Canyon Press; Driving and Drinking, Copper Canyon Press; The Porcine Canticles, Copper Canyon Press; Shadow Weaver, Brooding Heron Press; Paragonah Canyon Autumn, Brooding Heron Press; Wayburne Pig, Brooding Heron Press, The Fish, Wood Works Press; Day's Work, Copper Canyon Press; My Town, Copper Canyon Press. **CONTACT ADDRESS** Dept of Language and Lit, Southern Utah Univ, Ceder City, UT, 84720.

LEE, DOROTHY A. H.
PERSONAL Born 01/22/1925, Columbia, Missouri, w, 1950 **DISCIPLINE** ENGLISH **EDUCATION** Wayne State Univ, BA, 1945, MA, 1947; Radciiffe College, MA, 1948; Radcliffe

College & Harvard Univ, PhD, 1955. **CAREER** Wayne State Univ, asst professor, 1952-62; Henry Ford Comm College, instructor, 1963-72; Univ of MI-Dearborn, professor, 1972-93. **HONORS AND AWARDS** Univ of MI-Dearborn, Susan B Anthony Award, 1985; Distinguished Teaching Award, 1985; MI Assn of Governing Boards of Colleges & Universities, Distinguished Facility Award, 1987; F Cousens Retired Person Award, U of M-Dearborn, 1993. **SELECTED PUBLICATIONS** Essays published in Michigan Quarterly Review, Black Women Writers; Callaloo Black American Literary Forum; College Language Assn Journal; Journal of Spanish Studies-Twentieth Century; Critique; Modern Drama. **CONTACT ADDRESS** Professor Emeritus, The Univ of Michigan - Dearborn, 4901 Evergreen Rd, Dearborn, MI, 48128. **EMAIL** dahl@umich.edu

LEE, HELEN ELAINE
PERSONAL Born 03/13/1959, Detroit, MI, s **DISCIPLINE** LITERATURE **EDUCATION** Harvard College, BA, 1981; Harvard Law School, JD, 1985. **CAREER** Various law-related and attorney jobs, 1985-94; Univ of Michigan, Dearborn, adjunct lecturer, 1995; MA INSTITUTE OF TECHNOLOGY, ASST PROF, WRITING & HUMANISTIC STUDIES, currently. **HONORS AND AWARDS** American Library Assn, Black Caucus, First Novel Award, 1994, 1995; DC Commission on the Arts and Humanities, $5,000 Grant-in-Aid Award, 1991; Phi Beta Kappa. **SELECTED PUBLICATIONS** Author, novel, The Serpent's Gift, Atheneum Publishers, 1994, London Headline Press, 1994; Marriage Bones, The African Diaspora in Short Fiction, ed; Charles Rowell Westview Press, 1995; Silences, The Best Short Stories by Black Writers vol II, ed, Gloria Naylor, Little, Brown and Co, 1995; novel Water Marked, Scirbner, forthcoming, 1998. **CONTACT ADDRESS** Program in Writing and Humanistic Studies, MIT, Rm 14E-303, Cambridge, MA, 02139-4307.

LEE, HSIAO-HUNG
PERSONAL Born 09/11/1953, Shanghai, China, m, 1979, 1 child **DISCIPLINE** ENGLISH LITERATURE; LIBRARY SCIENCE **EDUCATION** Shangai Tchrs Univ, BA, 76; Drew Univ, Mphil, 88 PhD, 90; Rutgers Univ, MLS, 91. **CAREER** Ref librn, Univ Central Ark, 91-95; asst prof, Troy State Univ, 96-. **HONORS AND AWARDS** Buckminster Fuller Scholar, 84-85; United Nations Scholar, 84-85; Drew Univ Full Scholar, 85-89. **MEMBERSHIPS** Ala Libr Asn; Am Libr Asn; Modern Language Asn. **RESEARCH** Victorian literature; uterary theory; information science. **SELECTED PUBLICATIONS** Auth, Chinese Herbal Medicine, Handbook of Popular Culture in China, Westport: Greenwood Press, 94; auth, The Possibilities of Hidden Things, Narrative Transgressions in Victorian Fictional Autobiographies, Peter Lang Publishing, 96. **CONTACT ADDRESS** 211 Glenwood Ave, Troy, AL, 36081. **EMAIL** hhlee@trojan.troyst.edu

LEE, JAE-WON
DISCIPLINE JOURNALISM, POLITICAL COM, INTERNATIONAL COMMUNICATION **EDUCATION** Seoul Nat Univ, BA, MA; Marquette Univ, MA; Univ IA, PhD. **CAREER** Comm, Cleveland St Univ. **SELECTED PUBLICATIONS** Co-auth, A Critical Look at Mass Communication in Korea, Nanam Publ, 94; Modernization vs Revolution, Sung Kyon Kwan UP, 93. **CONTACT ADDRESS** Commun Dept, Cleveland State Univ, 83 E 24th St, Cleveland, OH, 44115. **EMAIL** j.lee@csuohio.edu

LEE, JAMES WARD
PERSONAL Born 02/12/1931, Birmingham, AL, d, 2 children **DISCIPLINE** ENGLISH **EDUCATION** Mid TN State Univ, BS, 56; Auburn Univ, MA, 57, PhD, 64. **CAREER** Prof, Eng, Univ N TX, 70-, ch, Eng, 86-92, Dir, Center TX Studies, 86-94, Dir UNT Press, 88-90, Ed, Studies in Novel, 66; ed, New TX, 91-; Ed, Amer Lit Review, 88-90; Ed, TX Studies, 92-94; Ed, TX Traditions Series, 85-; Acquisitions consult, TCU Press, 97-; Member Natl Faculty, 73-; TX Inst Letters, 74-. **HONORS AND AWARDS** St Andrews Acad of Distinguished Scholars; President's Award UNT, 87; **MEMBERSHIPS** TX Folklore Soc; SCMLA; CCTE; Swestern Historical Assoc. **RESEARCH** Novel; folklore; TX Lit and cult. **SELECTED PUBLICATIONS** Coauth, J D Salinger and the Critics, Wadsworth, 62; auth, William Humphrey, Steck, 67; John Braine, Twayne, 68; Poetry: A Thematic Approach, Wadsworth, 68; co ed, Swestern American Literature: A Bibliography, OH univ Press, 80; Classics of Texas Fiction, E-Heart, 86; Texas: My Texas, UNT Press, 90; ed, 1941: Texas Goes to War, UNT Press, 91. **CONTACT ADDRESS** Dept of Eng, No Texas State Univ, PO Box 311307, Denton, TX, 76203-1307. **EMAIL** J.Lee@tcu.edu

LEE, PATRICIA-ANN
PERSONAL East Orange, NJ **DISCIPLINE** ENGLISH HISTORY **EDUCATION** Kean Col Union, BS; Columbia Univ, MA & PhD, 66. **CAREER** Asst prof hist, Newark State Col, 66-67; asst prof, 67-71, prof hist, Skidmore Col, 71, Ch Hist Dept. **MEMBERSHIPS** AHA; Conf Brit Studies. **RESEARCH** Tudor-Stuart English hist, espec the early Stuart Period. **SELECTED PUBLICATIONS** Auth, Play and the English Gentleman in the Early Seventeenth Century, Historian, 5/69; Some English Academies: An Experiment in Renaissance Education, Hist Educ Quart, fall 70; Reflections of Power, Margaret Fayou and the Dark Side of Queenship, Renaissance Quart, summer 89; A Bodye Politique to Governe: Aylmer, Knox and the Debate on Queenship, The Historian, winter 90; England: An Unfinished Revolution, In: Establising Democracies, Westview Press, 96; Mistress Stagg's Petitioners: February 1642, The Historian, winter 98. **CONTACT ADDRESS** 815 N Broadway, Saratoga Springs, NY, 12866-1698. **EMAIL** plee@skidmore.edu

LEE, RONALD E.
PERSONAL Born 02/07/1952, Wyandotte, MI, m, 1980, 1 child **DISCIPLINE** COMMUNICATION STUDIES **EDUCATION** Wayne Univ (Detroit), BA, 74, MA, 76; Univ Iowa, PhD, 81. **CAREER** Asst prof, Ind Univ-Bloomington, 83-91; Assoc prof, Univ Nebr-Lincoln, 91-. **HONORS AND AWARDS** Obermann Fellow, Iowa Ctr for Adv Studs, Univ Iowa, 91; Recipient of Medwest Forensic Assoc Award for Outstanding Schol, 89, 92; Outstanding Young teach, Cent States Commun Assoc, 87. **MEMBERSHIPS** Am Forensic Assoc; Cent States Commun Assoc; DSR-TKA; Nat Commun Assoc. **RESEARCH** Contemporary rhetorical theory; rhetorical criticism; contemporary American public discourse. **SELECTED PUBLICATIONS** Co-auth, Arguing about patriotism in a liberal community, Argument in Controversy, Speech Commun Assoc, 135-39, 91; co-auth, Visions of community, arguments for solidarity, and the structure of the new racist discourse, Argument and the postmodern challenge, Speech Commun Assoc, 443-49, 93; auth, Images of civic virtue in the new political Rhetoric, Presidential campaigning and American self-image, Westview, 40-59, 94; auth, Commencement addresses, I gotta tell you: The collected speeches of Lee Iacocca, Wayne State Univ Press, 259-284, 94; auth, Electoral politics and visions of community: Jimmy Carter, virtue, and the small town myth, West J of Commun, vol 59, 39-60, 95; auth, Humility and the political servant: Jimmy Carter's post-presidential rhetoric of virtue and power, Southern Commun J, vol 60, 120-130, 95; co-auth, Christian tradition, Jeffersonian democracy, and the myth of the sentimental family: An exploration of the premises of social-conservative argumentation, Argumentation and Values, Speech Commun Assoc, 36-42, 95; co-auth, Technical discourse in defense of public virtue: Ronald Reagan's explanation of the Iran/Contra affair, Pol Commun, vol 13, 115-129, 96; co-auth, The environmental rhetoric of balance: A case study of regulatory discourse and the colonization of the public, tech Commun Quart, vol 6, 25-40, 97; auth, Governing without passion: Willard's call for a rhetoric of competence, Argumentation and Advocacy, vol 33, 135-146, 97; co-auth, Myths of blood, property, and maternity: Exploring the public argumentation of anti-adoption advocates, Argument in a time of change: Definitions, frameworks, and critiques, Nat Commun Assoc, 256-261, 98; Getting down to the meat: Associational clusters and symbolic alignments in the discourse of meat consumption, Commun Studs, (in press); co-auth, Multicultural education in the little red schoolhouse: A rhetorical exploration of ideological justification and mythic repair, Commun Studs, (in press). **CONTACT ADDRESS** Univ Nebr, 437 Oldfather Hall, Lincoln, NE, 68588.

LEE, WILLIAM DAVID
PERSONAL Born 08/13/1944, Matador, TX, m, 1971, 2 children **DISCIPLINE** LITERATURE **EDUCATION** CO St Univ, BA, 67; ID St Univ, MA, 70; Univ of UT, PhD, 73 **CAREER** Head Prof, 71-, S UT Univ **HONORS AND AWARDS** Poet laureate of UT, 97, Nat Endow for Humanities Fels; Prof of the Year **MEMBERSHIPS** RMMLA, AWP **RESEARCH** Contemp poetry **SELECTED PUBLICATIONS** Auth, Covenants, Spoon River Press, 96; The Fish, Woodworks Press, 97; The Wayburne Pig, Brooding Heron Press, 98 **CONTACT ADDRESS** Dept of English, So Utah Univ, Cedar City, UT, 84790.

LEE-RIFFE, NANCY M.
PERSONAL Born 01/16/1933, Danville, KY, d, 5 children **DISCIPLINE** ENGLISH **EDUCATION** Agnes Scott Col, BA, 54; Radcliffe Col, AM, 55; Univ Ky, PhD, 63. **CAREER** Instr English, Temple Univ, 60-64; prof asst test develop, Educ Testing Serv, 64-65; asst prof English, Ursinus Col, 65-67; assoc prof, LaSalle Col, 67-68; assoc prof, 68-71, Prof English, 71-98, Eastern KY Univ; Mem col bd, Consult writing exam questions English Compos Test & reader advan placement English exams & English compos essay exams, 65-; Henry E Huntington Libr fel, 77. **HONORS AND AWARDS** Outstanding Young Women in Am Award, 67. **MEMBERSHIPS** ASECS; SEASECS. **RESEARCH** English literature especially Shakespeare, drama to 1642 and Milton; 18th century English periodicals and essayists. **SELECTED PUBLICATIONS** Auth, The Elizabethan stage: A bibliography, Shakespeare Newslett, 63; A finding list of some 18th century periodicals, Bull NY Pub Libr, 63; A fragment of Milton, from the Italian, Mod Philol, 66; Shall and will, Am Speech, spring-summer 76; Anecdotes about Scriblerians and Kit-Cats, Scriblerian, spring 77; The heavenly plantation: A seventeenth century mention of Florida, Fla Hist Quart, 10/77. **CONTACT ADDRESS** 406 Jackson St, Berea, KY, 40403-1726. **EMAIL** retleeri@acs.eku.edu

LEEDOM, TIM C.
PERSONAL Born 04/23/1945, Plainfield, NJ, d, 1 child **DISCIPLINE** POLITICAL SCIENCE, JOURNALISM **EDUCATION** Univ KS; Univ Hawaii, BS, 69. **CAREER** Aide, Gov John A. Burns, St of Hawaii; aide, Lt. Gov Thomas P. Gill, St of Hawaii; aide, Off of Sen John Leopold, St of Hawaii; ed, The Truthseeker, Freethought J. **HONORS AND AWARDS** Ford Found Legisl Internship; Exec Internship; PBS Internship, Univ Hawaii; Bk of Yr, 94. **RESEARCH** Religion; history. **SELECTED PUBLICATIONS** Auth, The Book Your Church Doesn't Want You To Read; auth, World's Apart; The Main Man. **CONTACT ADDRESS** PO Box 5009, Balboa Island, CA, 92662.

LEEDS, BARRY HOWARD
PERSONAL Born 12/06/1940, New York, NY, m, 1968, 2 children **DISCIPLINE** ENGLISH & AMERICAN LITERATURE **EDUCATION** Columbia Univ, BA, 62, MA, 63; Ohio Univ, PhD, 67. **CAREER** Lectr, 63-64, CUNY; instr, 64-65, Univ Tex, El Paso; tchng fel, 65-67, Ohio Univ; from asst prof to assoc prof, 68-71, prof, 76-, dist prof, 81-, Cent Conn St Col; Consult Am lit, Choice Mag, 68-; consult, Am Lit, Univ Tex Press, 79. **HONORS AND AWARDS** CCSU Dist Srvc Award, 82. **MEMBERSHIPS** AAUP; Ct Acad of Arts; Hemingway Soc. **RESEARCH** Contemporary American fiction; 20th century literature; American literature. **SELECTED PUBLICATIONS** Auth, The Test Of Manhood in Hemingway, Columbia Rev, 62; auth, The Structured Vision of Norman Mailer, NY Univ, 69; auth, Ken Kesey, Ungar, 81; rev, The Proselytizer, D Keith Mano, Saturday Rev, 7/72; American Book Review, Mod Fiction Studies, 73-74; contribr, Contemporary Literary Criticism (Vol I, Vol 2 & Vol 6), Gale, 76; auth, Will The Real Norman Mailer Please Stand Up, Kennikat, 74; auth, Theme and Technique in One Flew Over the Cuckoo's Nest, Conn Rev, 74. **CONTACT ADDRESS** 133 Jerome Ave, Burlington, CT, 06013. **EMAIL** Leeds@ccsu.ctstateu.edu

LEEDS-HURWITZ, WENDY
PERSONAL Born 06/17/1953, Indianapolis, IN, m, 1979, 1 child **DISCIPLINE** FOLKLORE, SOCIAL INTERACTION **EDUCATION** Univ of Pa, PhD, 83. **CAREER** ASST PROF, 82-88, ASSOC PROF, 88-95, PROF, 95-, UNIV OF WIS PARKSIDE. **HONORS AND AWARDS** Stella C. Gray Excellence in Teaching Award, 95. **MEMBERSHIPS** Nat Commun Asn; Int Commun Asn; Am Authors Asn; Am Folklore Soc. **RESEARCH** Language and social interaction; communication theory; intercultural communication; history of communication semiotics. **SELECTED PUBLICATIONS** Auth, Social Approaches to Communication, Guilford, 95; auth, Semiotics and Communication, Lawrence Erlbaum, 93; auth, Communication in Everyday Life, Ablex, 89; auth, Notes in the History of Intercultural Communication: The Foreign Service Institute and the Mandate for Intercultural Training, Readings in Cultural Contexts, Mayfield, 98; auth, Social Theories, Social Interpretations, Communication: Views from the Helm for the Twenty-First Century, Allyn-Bacon, 98; auth, The Concept of Context in Social Communication Theory, Context and Commun Behavior, Context Press, 97; auth, A Social Account of Symbols, Beyond the Symbol Model: Reflections on the Representational Nature of Language, State Univ of NY Press, 96; auth, Crossing Disciplinary Boundaries: The Macy Foundation Conferences on Cybernetics as a Case Study in Multidisciplinary Communication, Cybernetica, 94; coauth, Social Communication Theory: Communication Structures and performed Invocations, The Consequentiality of Commun, Lawrence Erlbaum Assocs, 95. **CONTACT ADDRESS** Commun Dept, Univ of Wisconsin Parkside, 900 Wood Rd., Kenosha, WI, 53141-2000. **EMAIL** wendy.leeds-hurwitz@uwp.edu

LEEMAN, RICHARD W.
PERSONAL Born 06/16/1955, Oak Park, IL, m, 1990, 2 children **DISCIPLINE** COMMUNICATION STUDIES **EDUCATION** Univ of Md, PhD, 90. **CAREER** ASST PROF, 89-95, ASSOC PROF, UNC AT CHARLOTTE, 95-. **HONORS AND AWARDS** Daniel M. Rohrer Award, Am Forensic Asn, 91. **MEMBERSHIPS** Nat Commun Asn; Southern Commun Asn; Carolinas Commun Asn. **RESEARCH** African-American oratory; American public address; rhetoric. **SELECTED PUBLICATIONS** Auth, African-American Orators: A Bio-Critical Sourcebook, Greenwood Press, 96; auth, Do Everything Reform: The Oratory of Frances E. Willard, Greenwood, 92; auth, The Rhetoric of Terrorism and Counterterrorism, Greenwood, 91; coauth, The Art and Practice of Argumentation and Debate, Mayfield, 97. **CONTACT ADDRESS** Dept of Commun Studies, Univ of N. Carolina, Charlotte, NC, 28223. **EMAIL** rwleeman@email.unccvm.uncc.edu

LEER, NORMAN ROBERT
PERSONAL Born 02/25/1937, Chicago, IL **DISCIPLINE** ENGLISH, COMPARATIVE LITERATURE **EDUCATION** Grinnell Col, AB, 58; Ind Univ, MA, 60, PhD(English), 64. **CAREER** Instr English, State Univ NY Stony Brook, 63-65; asst prof, Beloit Col, 65-67; assoc prof Roosevelt Univ, 67-72, assoc prof, 72-78, prof English, 78-, mem bd, Urban Life Ctr, 72-; coordr, Educ Network, Asn Humanistic Psychol, 72-74 & Midwest Regional Newslett, 78-; Fulbright lectr English, Odense Univ, Denmark, 74-75; lectr, Center for Older Adults, Fourth

Presbyterian Church of Chicago, 96-. **HONORS AND AWARDS** Phi Beta Kappa, Grinnell College, 58; Poetry Prize, All Nations Poetry Contest, Triton Col, 76, 77, 78, 79 & 81; Burlington Northern Award, Roosevelt Univ (for teaching and scholarship), 86; Illinois Significant Poet's Award, 90; Samuel Ortrowski Award, Roosevelt Univ (for best creative work), 98. **RESEARCH** Modern literature in the light of existential philosophy and humanistic psychology; writing poetry; application of some of the techniques of humanistic psychology to college teaching. **SELECTED PUBLICATIONS** Auth, Escape and Confrontation in the Stories of Philip Roth, Christian Scholar, summer 66; The Limited Hero in the Novels of Ford Madox Ford, Mich State Univ, 67; The Double Theme in Malamud's Assistant: Dostoevsky with Irony, Mosaic, spring 71; Innovation and power struggles: An Experiential Deadlock, J Humanistic Psychol, winter 73; To Doris Lessing: Inside the Apocalypse, Oyez Rev, spring 75; Riding Commas to the Moon: Teaching Maleness and Imagination, New Directions in Teaching, winter 78; Slightly Crumpled Survival Flower (poems), Spoon River Poetry Press, 85; I Dream My Father in a Stone (poems), Mellen Poetry Press, 91; Second Lining (poems), Mellen Poetry Press, 97; Over 100 individual poems in Spoon River Quart, Willow Review, Rhino, Oyez Review, The Wolf Head Quart, Poetry Digest, and American Poets and Poetry. **CONTACT ADDRESS** Dept of English, Roosevelt Univ, 430 S Michigan Ave, Chicago, IL, 60605-1394.

LEESON, TED

DISCIPLINE WRITING **EDUCATION** Marquette Univ, BA, 76; Univ Va, MA, 79, PhD, 84. **CAREER** Engl, Oregon St Univ. **SELECTED PUBLICATIONS** Auth, The Habit of Rivers. Lyons & Burford, 94. **CONTACT ADDRESS** Oregon State Univ, Corvallis, OR, 97331-4501. **EMAIL** tleeson@orst.edu

LEETS, LAURA

DISCIPLINE COMMUNICATIONS **EDUCATION** Univ CA Santa Barbara, BA; MA; PhD, 95. **CAREER** Asst prof/dir grad prog media studies, Stanford Univ. **RESEARCH** Effects of deprecating speech; consequences and coping mechanisms associated with this genre of lang. **SELECTED PUBLICATIONS** Auth, publ in mainstream commun jour(s) such as Human Communication Research and Communication Yearbook as well as interdisciplinary journals such as the Journal of Language and Social Psychology and the Journal of Multilingual and Multicultural Development; coauth, an introductory statistics bk. **CONTACT ADDRESS** Dept Commun, Stanford Univ, McClatchy Hall, Stanford, CA, 94305-2050. **EMAIL** leets@leland.stanford.edu

LEFF, LEONARD J.

PERSONAL Born 01/23/1942, Houston, TX, m, 1969, 1 child **DISCIPLINE** FILM STUDIES **EDUCATION** Univ Tex Austin, BA, 63; Univ Houston, MA, 65; Northern Ill Univ, PhD(English), 71. **CAREER** Instr English Lit, McNeese State Univ, 65-68 & Northern Ill Univ, 68-69; asst prof English Lit & Film, Bellevue Col, 73-79; asst prof English Lit & Film, Okla State Univ, 79-; prof English, 91-. **HONORS AND AWARDS** The Dame in the Kimono, New York Times Book Review Notable Books of the Year, 90. **MEMBERSHIPS** MLA; Soc Cinema Studies. **RESEARCH** American film history; American film censorship. **SELECTED PUBLICATIONS** Auth, Hollywood lives, Southern Quart, 4/78; Who's Afraid of Virginia Woolf?: A test of American film censorship, Cinema J, Spring 80; I hear America typing: A survey of scriptwriting manuals, Quart Rev Film Studies, Summer 81; Instant movies: The short, unhappy life of William Sargent's Electronovision, J Popular Film & TV, Spring 81; Play into film: Warner Brothers' Who's Afraid of Virginia Woolf?, Theatre J, 12/81; Hemingway and His Conspirators: Hollywood, Scribners, and the Making of American Celebrity Culture, Rowman & Littlefield, 97; Hitchcock and Selznick: The Rich and Strange Collaboration of Alfred Hitchcock and David O Selznick in Hollywood, Weidenfeld & Nicolson, 87, rpt University of California Press, 98. **CONTACT ADDRESS** Dept of English, Oklahoma State Univ, Stillwater, OK, 74078-0002. **EMAIL** leff_osu@osu.net

LEGGETT, B. J.

PERSONAL Born 02/25/1938, Alamo, TN, m, 1960, 2 children **DISCIPLINE** MODERN LITERATURE **EDUCATION** Lambuth Col, BA, 60; Univ Fla, MA, 62, PhD(English), 65. **CAREER** From asst prof to assoc prof, 65-77, PROF ENGLISH, UNIV TENN, KNOXVILLE, 77-, Nat Found Arts and Humanities fel 67; Hunington Libr fel, 81. Lindsay Young Prof English, 82-83. **MEMBERSHIPS** SAtlantic Mod Lang Asn; MLA. **RESEARCH** Modern poetry. **SELECTED PUBLICATIONS** Auth, Larkin Blues--Jazz and Modernism, 20th Century Lit, Vol 0042, 96. **CONTACT ADDRESS** Dept of English, Univ of Tenn, Knoxville, TN, 37916.

LEHMAN, PAUL ROBERT

PERSONAL Born 04/18/1941, Mansura, LA, m **DISCIPLINE** ENGLISH **EDUCATION** LA City Coll, AA 1966; Central State Coll, BA 1969; Central State U, ME 1971; Lehigh U, PhD 1976. **CAREER** Central State U, dean of grad coll 1985-88, prof dept of English 1984, 1988-, assoc prof dept of Eng 1976-; NCACC, adjunct prof 1974-76; CSU, instr 1971-73;CSU, lecturer 1969-71; KWTV, newsman reporter writer editor photographer producer & weekend anchorman 1968-70; KOFM radio, music newsman 1968-69; Standard Oil of CA, credit dept 1966-67; Western Electric Co, tester insptct 1963-66; Northampton Co Area Community Coll, dev co-ordinated coll orientation wkshp for minority stud 1975; Blk Am Lit, vol lecturer coll pub private sch (Jr & Sr) churches on Radio/TV News 1974-75; member, Edmond Arts & Humanities, 1991-; board member, Oklahoma Arthritis Foundation, 1991-; board member, Oklahoma Alliance for Art Education, 1989-. **HONORS AND AWARDS** Best actor in minor roll CSC 1968; dean's honor roll CSC 1968; 1st blk Am to rec PhD in Eng from Lehigh 1976; 1st blk Am to teach at CSU 1969; 1st blk in OK to anchor weekend TV news 1969; listed in Contemporary Authors for 1977-78; Lehigh Univ Fellowship 1973-76; 1st dissertation on John Oliver Killens 1976; 2nd place all-coll speech contest 1965; Awd for Serv to Urban League of Greater Okla City 1984; Awd for Serv to Boy Scouts of Amer 1985. **MEMBERSHIPS** Natl Jay-Cees; NAACP; Urban League; Heart Assn Natl Assn of Press Photographers; stud exec officer LACC 1966; mem NEA, OEA, CSEA, NCTE; vice chmn, Oklahoma Foundation for the Humanities 1988-89; treasurer, Oklahoma Alliance for Arts Education 1988-; Oklahoma Folklife Council; Edmond Community Housing Resource Board; Afro-American Southern Assn; Edmond Arts & Humanities, 1991-; Oklahoma Arthritis Foundation, 1991-. **CONTACT ADDRESS** Dept of English, Central State Univ, Oklahoma, 100 University Dr, Edmond, OK, 73034.

LEIDHOLDT, ALEX S.

DISCIPLINE JOURNALISM HISTORY, MESSAGE DESIGN/PRODUCTION **EDUCATION** Old Dominion Univ, PhD, 91. **CAREER** Asst prof, Purdue Univ. **SELECTED PUBLICATIONS** Auth, Standing Before the Shouting Mob: Lenoir Chambers and Virginia's Massive Resistance to Public School Integration, Univ Ala Press; USA/USSR Youth Summit Series, PBS; Doing Business with the Soviet Union, PBS ALSS; Prophets and Translators; Symbols, Stories and Visual Images, PBS ALSS. **CONTACT ADDRESS** Dept of Commun, Purdue Univ, 1080 Schleman Hall, West Lafayette, IN, 47907-1080. **EMAIL** aleidhol@vm.cc.purdue.edu

LEIGH, DAVID

DISCIPLINE ENGLISH **EDUCATION** Gonzaga Univ, BA, 61, MA, 62; Regis Col, Toronto, MA, 69; Yale Univ, PhD, 72. **CAREER** Ch, Eng dept, Seattle Univ. **MEMBERSHIPS** MLA; URAM; Christianity and Lit; NCTE. **SELECTED PUBLICATIONS** Auth, Literature, Imagination, and the Study of Ultimate Reality, URAM J, 95; Writing for a Live Audience, Ind Engl, 93; TS Eliot's Struggle Toward a Still Point, URAM J, 95; Malcolm X and the Black Muslim Search for Ultimate Reality, URAM J, 90; 2 articles for anthologies on Rel & Lit, 96. **CONTACT ADDRESS** Dept of Eng, Seattle Univ, 900 Broadway, Seattle, WA, 98122-4460. **EMAIL** dleigh@seattleu.edu

LEIGHTON, LAUREN GRAY

PERSONAL Born 06/21/1934, Virginia, MN, m, 1960, 2 children **DISCIPLINE** RUSSIAN LITERATURE, ROMANTICISM **EDUCATION** Univ Wis-Madison, BA, 60; Ind Univ, MA, 62; Univ Wis-Madison, PhD(Slavic lang), 68. **CAREER** Instr Russian, Mercer Univ, 62-63; instr, Grinnell Col, 63-64; asst prof Slavic, Univ Va, 67-72; assoc prof, Northern Ill Univ, 72-78; PROF SLAVIC, UNIV ILL, CHICAGO CIRCLE, 78-, US-USSR Acad Exchange, IREX-USSR Ministry Higher Educ, 70 and IREX-USSR Acad Sci, 77; ed, Slavic and East Europ J, 75-78. **MEMBERSHIPS** MLA; Asn Advan Slavic Studies; Am Asn Univ Prof, Am Asn Teachers Slavic and East Europ Lang. **RESEARCH** Russian romanticism; Pushkin; modern Russian fiction. **SELECTED PUBLICATIONS** Auth, Schiller and Zhukovskii--Aesthetic Theory in Poetic Translation, Slavic and E Europ J, Vol 0037, 93; Translation and Plagiarism, Pushkin and Thomas, D.M., Slavic and E Europ J, Vol 0038, 94; Speculative Freemasonry and the Enlightenment--a Study of the Craft in London, Paris, Prague and Vienna, Slavonic and East Europ Rev, Vol 0073, 95; A History of Russian Translation Fiction--Old Russia 18th-Century, Vol 1, Prose, Slavic Rev, Vol 0055, 96; The Lyric Poetry of Pushkin Time--the Elegiac School, Slavic and E Europ J, Vol 0040, 96. **CONTACT ADDRESS** Dept of Slavic Lang and Lit, Univ of Ill, Chicago Circle, Chicago, IL, 60680.

LEITER, SAMUEL LOUIS

PERSONAL Born 07/20/1940, Brooklyn, NY, m, 1963, 2 children **DISCIPLINE** THEATRE **EDUCATION** Brooklyn Col, BA, 62; Univ Hawaii, MFA, 64; NY Univ, PhD(dramatic art), 68. **CAREER** Lectr theatre, 65-68, from asst prof to assoc prof, 68-76, Prof Theatre, Brooklyn Col, 77-, **HONORS AND AWARDS** Fulbright Senior Res Sch, 74-75, Choice Awd Outstand Acad Book, Claire and Leonard Tow Prof 97-98 **MEMBERSHIPS** Am Soc Theatre Res; Asn for Theatre in Higher Educ; Cnl of Ed of Learned Jou; Int Fed of Theatre Res **RESEARCH** Japanese theatre; American theatre history; directing theory. **SELECTED PUBLICATIONS** auth, Four Interviews with Kabuki Actors, Educ Theater Jou, 66; auth, The Frozen Moment: A Kabuki Technique, Drama Survey, 67; auth, Brooklyn as an American Theater City 1861-1898, Jou of Long Island Hist, 68; auth, The Depiction of Violence on the Kabuki Stage, Educ Theater Jou,69; auth, Theater in the City of Churchesm Players, 69; auth, Keren: Spectacle and Trickery on the Kabuki Stage, Educ Theater Jou, 76; auth, Tha Kabuki Juhachiban, Lit East and West, 76; auth, Ichikawa Danjuro IX, A Life in Kabuki, Educ Theater Jou, 77; auth, Get Someone to Teach You How to Act! Sir John Gielgud Directs, Theater Hist Stu, 88; auth, Kumagai's Battle Camp: Form and Tradition in Kabuki Acting, Asian Theater Jou, 91; auth, The International Symposium of Traditional Theaters of Asia, Beijing, 91, Asian Theater Jou, 92; auth, Theater on the Homefront: World War II on New York's Stages, 1941-1945, Jou of Am Drama and Theater, 93; auth, Daniel S.P. Yang of the Hong Kong Repertory Theater, Asian Theater Jou, 93; The Kanamaru-za: Japan's Oldest Kabuki Theater, Asian Theater Jou 97; auth, What really Happens Backstage: A Nineteenth-Century Kabuki Document, Theater Survey, 97; auth, From the London Patents to the Edo Sanza: A Partial Comparison of British Theater and Kabuki, ca. 1650-1800, Theater Symposium VI, 98; auth, Trans and Commentary of the Birth of the Hanamichi, Theater Res Int, 99; auth, Japan: In the History of the Theater, 68; auth, Brooklyn Academy of Music: When Theater spelled SIN at BAM, In Brooklyn, 79; auth, Kabuki: An Introduction, In Kabuki, 82; auth, Brooklyn Theater Co, 1871-1875, Brooklyn Theater Co; auth, Brooklyn Theater Co, 1875-1876, Park Theater Co in American Theater Companies, 1749-1887, 86; auth, Kabuki: What's in it for us? Proceedings: East Asian Festival, Sta Univ of NY Brockport, 91; auth, Sol Hurok, Wiliam Inge, Diana Sands, Herman Shumlin, Samuel Spewack, and Margret Webster, Dictionary of American Biography, 94; auth, Kermit Bloomgarden, Alfred Lunt, Mary Pickford, Rosalind Russell, and Herman Shumlin, Dictionary of Americanb Biography, 95; auth, David Belasco and James A. Herne, American National Biography, 96; auth, Bando Mitsugoro, Bando Tamasaburo, Bunraku, Hanamichi, Ichikawa Danjuro, Ichikawa Ennosuke, Japanese Traditional Schools, Jidaimono, Kabuki Theater, Kurogo, Kataoka Tako, Matsumoto Joshiro, Nakamura Ganjiro, Nakamura Kankuro, Nakamura Kanzaburo, Nakamura Kichiemon, Nakamura Tomijuro, Nakamura Utaemon, Okuni Onnagata, Onoe Baiko, Onoe Kikugoro, One Shoroku, Sewamono, and Shishimai, Oxford Int Encyc of Dance, 98; auth, Directors and Directing: 1945- present, Cambridge History of the American Theater, 99; auth, Ethel Merman, Bette Davis, Lotte Lenya, Alan Schneider, Joshua Logan, Charles Ludlam, Lee Strasberg, Geraldine Page, and Danny Kaye, Scribner Encyclopedia of American Lives, 99; auth, The Art of Kabuki: Famous Plays, Performance, Univ of Calif Press, 79, reprint, Dover, 99; auth, Kabuki Encyclopedia: An English-Language Adaptation of Kabuki Jiten, Grenwood, 79; auth, The Encyclopedia of the New York Stage, 1920-1930, Greenwood, 86; ed, Shakespeare Around the Globe: A Guide to Notable Postwar Productions, Greenwood, 86; auth, Ten Seasons: New York Theater in the Seventies, Greenwood, 86; auth, From Belasco to Brook: Representative Directors of the English-Speaking Stage, Greenwood, 91; auth, From Stanislavsky to Barrault: Representative Directors of the European Stage, Greenwood, 91; auth, The Encyclopedia of the New York Stage, 1940-1950, Greenwood, 92; auth, The Great Stage Directors: 100 Distingused Careers of the Theater, Facts on File, 94; auth, New Kabuki Encyclopedia: A Revised Adaptation of Kabuki Jiten, Greenwood, 97; ed, Japanese Theater in the World, Japan Society, 97; ed, Zeami and the No Theater in the World, 98; ed, Asian Theater Jou, 91-. **CONTACT ADDRESS** Dept of Theatre, Brooklyn Col, CUNY, 2900 Bedford Ave, Brooklyn, NY, 11210-2813. **EMAIL** sleiter@brooklyn.cuny.edu

LEITH, LINDA J.

PERSONAL Born 12/13/1949, Belfast, Northern Ireland **DISCIPLINE** ENGLISH **EDUCATION** McGill Univ, BA, 70; Univ London(Eng), PhD, 76. **CAREER** TEACHER ENGLISH, JOHN ABBOTT COL, 75-; lectr, Concordia Univ, 82-83; lectr, McGill Univ, 88. **MEMBERSHIPS** Dir, Que Soc Promotion Eng Lang Lit, 88-94, 96-98; vice pres, Fedn Eng Lang Writers Que, 93-94, 97-98; mem, exec, Can Asn Irish Stud, 92-95; nat coun, Writers Union Can, 94-96; mem, Union des crivaines et ecrivains quebecois, 95-. **SELECTED PUBLICATIONS** Auth, Introducing Hugh MacLennan's Two Solitudes, 90; ed, Matrix, 88-94; ed, Telling Differences: New English Fiction from Quebec, 89; ed, Vehicule Fiction Ser, 89-94; founding assoc ed, Montreal Rev, 78-79, mem, bd consult, Science-Fiction Stud, 81-91. **CONTACT ADDRESS** Dept of English, John Abbott Col, PO Box 2000, Ste Anne de Bellevue, PQ, H9X 3L9.

LEITZ, ROBERT C.

PERSONAL Born 10/28/1944, New Orleans, LA, m, 1968 **DISCIPLINE** ENGLISH **EDUCATION** Univ New Orleans, BA, 67; Texas A&M Univ, MA, 69; Texas A&M, PhD, 73 **CAREER** Asst prof, Louisiana State Univ, 73-77; assoc prof, Louisiana State Univ, 77-82; prof, Louisiana State Univ, 82-; Curator, James Smith Noel Collection, Noel Memorial Libr **HONORS AND AWARDS** Henry E Huntington Libr Fel, 79; LSU Distinguished Fac Fel, 85 **MEMBERSHIPS** Frank Norris Soc; Jack London Soc; Assoc Documentary Editing **RESEARCH** Documentary Editing; American literature **SELECTED PUBLICATIONS** Coauth, The Letters of Charles W. Chestnutt, 1906-1932, Stanford Univ; coauth, The Essays and Speeches of Charles W. Chestnutt, Stanford Univ, 99;

coauth, To Be an Author! The Letters of Charles W. Chestnutt, 1889-1905, Princeton Univ, 97 **CONTACT ADDRESS** Dept Eng, Louisiana State Univ, Shreveport, 1 University Pl, Shreveport, LA, 71115. **EMAIL** rleitz@pilot.lsus.edu

LELAND, CHARLES WALLACE
PERSONAL Born 03/22/1928, Culver, IN **DISCIPLINE** ENGLISH LITERATURE, SCANDANAVIAN DRAMA **EDUCATION** Oberlin Col, AB, 50; Oxford Univ, BA, 53, MA, 56; Univ Toronto, STB, 58. **CAREER** Lectr English, 59-62, asst prof, 62-69, ASSOC PROF ENGLISH, UNIV TORONTO, 69-, Roman Cath priest, Congregation of St Basil, 59-. **MEMBERSHIPS** Asn Advan Scand Studies Can; Ibsen Soc Am; Soc Advan Scand Study. **RESEARCH** Ibsen; Strindberg; literature of the English Renaissance. **SELECTED PUBLICATIONS** Auth, Catiline and the Burial Mound, Mod Drama, Vol 0038, 95. **CONTACT ADDRESS** St Michael's Col Univ of Toronto, Toronto, ON, M5S 1J4.

LEMASTER, JIMMIE R.
PERSONAL Born 03/29/1934, Pike County, OH, m, 1966, 3 children **DISCIPLINE** ENGLISH LANGUAGE AND LITERATURE **EDUCATION** Defiance Col, BS, 59; Bowling Green State Univ, 62, PhD(English), 70. **CAREER** Teacher English, Stryker High Sch, 59-61; teacher, Bryan High Sch, 61-62; prof and chmn dept, Lang and Lit, Defiance Col, 62-77; Dir Am Studies Prog, Baylor Univ, 77-, Ed, Tex Writers Newsletter, 79-80; lectr Am lit, Second Foreign Lang Inst, Peking, 80-81; EXECUTIVE SECY, SOUTHWEST CONF HUMANITIES CONSORTIUM, 81-. **HONORS AND AWARDS** Publs Award, South and West, Inc, 70; Ohio Poet of Year, 76; Dean of Col Award Acad Excellence, 77. **MEMBERSHIPS** MLA; Aaup; Am Studies Asn; SCent Mod Lang Asn; Conf Col Teachers English. **RESEARCH** Twentieth century American literature; Jesse Stuart. **SELECTED PUBLICATIONS** Auth, A Chinese London Connection + A Conversation With Zhang, Bao, Anq-Quart J Short Articles Notes And Rev(s), Vol 0010, 97. **CONTACT ADDRESS** Am Studies Prog, Baylor Univ, Waco, TX, 76798.

LEMAY, JOSEPH ALBERIC LEO
PERSONAL Born 01/17/1935, Bristow, VA, m, 1965, 3 children **DISCIPLINE** AMERICAN LITERATURE **EDUCATION** Univ MD, AB, 57, AM, 62; Univ PA, PhD(English), 64. **CAREER** From instr to asst prof, George Washington Univ, 63-65; from asst prof to prof, Univ CA, 65-77; H F DU PONT WINTERTHUR PROF ENGLISH, UNIV DE, 77-; Coun, Inst Early Am Hist & Cult, 78-81; Inst Adv Study, Univ Del, 80-81, 98-99. **HONORS AND AWARDS** John Simon Guggenheim fellowship, 74-75; Sr fellow, Nat Endowment for the Humanities, 83-84, 94-95. **MEMBERSHIPS** MLA; Am Lit Asn; Bibliog Soc Am; Am Humor Studies Assn (pres, 81). **RESEARCH** American literature; Benjamin Franklin; Edgar Allan Poe. **SELECTED PUBLICATIONS** Auth, Men of Letters in Colonial Maryland, Univ TN, 72; The American Origins of Yankee Doodle, William & Mary Quart, 76; ed, The Oldest Revolutionary: Essays on Benjamin Franklin, Univ PA, 76; Essays in Early Virginia Literature Honoring Richard Beale Davis, Burt Franklin, 77; Benjamin Franklin, Universal Genius, In: The Renaissance Man in the Eighteenth Century, W A Clark Libr, 78; The Frontiersman from Lout to Hero: Notes on the Significance of the Comparative Method and Stage Theory in Early American Literature and Culture, Proc Am Antiq Soc, 78; ed, The Autobiography of Benjamin Franklin: A Genetic Text, Univ TN, 81; The Psychology of The Murders in the Rue Morgue, Am Lit, 82; New England's Annoyances: America's First Folk Song, Univ DE Press, 85; The Canon of Benjamin Franklin 1722-1776: New Attributions and Reconsiderations, Univ DE Press, 86; Deism, Masonry, and the Enlightenment: Essays Honoring Alfred Owen Aldridge, Univ DE Press, 87; Benjamin Franklin: Writings, NY: Library of Am, 87; An Early American Reader, Washington, DC: US Information Agency, 88; Robert Bolling Woos Anne Miller: Love and Courtship in Colonial Virginia, Univ Press VA, 90; The American Dream of Captain John Smith, Univ Press VA, 91; Did Pocahontas Save Captain John Smith?, Univ GA Press, 92; Reappraising Benjamin Franklin: A Bicentennial Perspective, Univ DE Press, 93; A Documentary History of Benjamin Franklin, vol 1, Printer: 1706-1730, vol 2, Rising Citizen: 1730-1747, 97. **CONTACT ADDRESS** Dept of English, Univ of Del, Newark, DE, 19711. **EMAIL** lemay@udel.edu

LEMIRE, ELISE V.
DISCIPLINE ENGLISH **EDUCATION** Yale Univ, BA, 86; Rutgers Univ, MA, 90, MPhil, 92, PhD, 96. **CAREER** ASST PROF, LIT, STATE UNIV NY-PURCHASE **HONORS AND AWARDS** Charlotte W. Newcombe Fellowship **MEMBERSHIPS** Am Antiquarian Soc **SELECTED PUBLICATIONS** Auth, "Making Miscegenation: Discourses of Interracial Sex and Marriage in the U.S., 1790-1865" **CONTACT ADDRESS** Hum Div, SUNY, Purchase, 735 Anderson Hill Rd, Purchase, NY, 10577-1400. **EMAIL** Lemire@Brick.Purchase.Edu

LEMIRE, EUGENE D.
PERSONAL Born 05/18/1929, Burton Twp, MI **DISCIPLINE** ENGLISH **EDUCATION** Univ Detroit, PhB, 51, MA, 54; Wayne State Univ, PhD, 62. **CAREER** Teaching fel, Univ Detroit, 51-54; from instr to asst prof English, 54-62; instr, Wayne State Univ, 58-61; from asst prof to prof, Univ Windsor, 61-80; sr lectr, 70-71, reader, 72-74, chmn sch humanities, 80-82, PROF ENGLISH AND CHMN DEPT, FLINDERS UNIV S AUSTRALIA, 74-, Can Coun fel, 68-69; fel-mem, Ctr Res in New Lit; mem, Mgt Comt in English, 77-, **MEMBERSHIPS** William Morris Soc and Kelmscott Fel; Australasian Univs Lang and Lit Asn; English Asn, Gt Brit; Australasian Victorian Studies Asn; Australia and NZ American Studies Asn. **RESEARCH** Victorian literature; William Morris; Jane Austen. **SELECTED PUBLICATIONS** Auth, Morris, William in America, a Publishing History From Archives, Bk Collector, Vol 0043, 94. **CONTACT ADDRESS** Sch of Humanities, Flinders Univ of So Australia, Bedford Pk, SA, 5042.

LEMIRE, MAURICE
PERSONAL Born 01/21/1927, Saint-Gabriel-de-Brandon, PQ, Canada **DISCIPLINE** LITERATURE **EDUCATION** Col Jean-de-Brebeuf, BA, 49; Univ Montreal, LTh, 53; Sorbonne, LL, 57; Univ Laval, DES, 62, DL, 66. **CAREER** Fac, Univ Montreal, 60-64; ch Fr dept, Univ Sherbrooke, 64-66; prof, 69-93, ch Can stud, 71-72, PROF EMER LITTERATURES, UNIV LAVAL, 94-. **HONORS AND AWARDS** Medaille Lorne Pierce, SRC, 89; Prix Raymond Klibansky, 92; Medaille de l'Academie des Lettres du Que, 94; Prix du Conseil Int des etudes canadiennes, 96. **MEMBERSHIPS** Soc d'histoire du theatre du Que; Asn des etudes canadiennes; Asn pour l'etude de l'imprime. **SELECTED PUBLICATIONS** Auth, Les grands themes nationalistes du roman historique canadien -francais, 70; auth, Charles Guerin de P.J.O. Chaveau, 75; auth, Les Contes de Louis Frechette, 2 vols, 76, 78; auth, Introduction a la litterature quebecoise 1900-1940, 80; auth, L'Institution litteraire, 86; auth, Le poids des politiques culturelles, 87; auth, Formation de l'imagination litteraire quebecoise, 93; auth, La litterature quebecoise en projet, 94; dir, Dictionnaire des oeuvres litteraires du Quebec, 5 vols, 71-85; dir, La Vie litteraire au Quebec, 3 vols, 91-95. **CONTACT ADDRESS** Dep litteratures, Univ Laval, Ste-Foy, PQ, G1K 7P4.

LENARD, MARY
DISCIPLINE RHETORIC, PROSE, AND BRITISH LITERATURE **EDUCATION** Univ Tex, Austin, PhD. **CAREER** Vis instr, Alma Col. **RESEARCH** Women's literature; feminist and cultural criticism. **SELECTED PUBLICATIONS** Published work in 19th-century British literature. **CONTACT ADDRESS** Alma Col, Alma, MI, 48801.

LENNOX, JOHN W.
PERSONAL Born 06/14/1945, Toronto, ON, Canada **DISCIPLINE** ENGLISH **EDUCATION** York Univ, BA, 67; Univ Sherbrooke, MA, 69; Univ NB, PhD, 76. **CAREER** Lectr, 70-77, assoc prof, 77-90, dir Robarts ctr Can stud, 85-88, dir grad prog Eng, 87-90, PROF ENGLISH, YORK UNIV, 91-. **MEMBERSHIPS** Asn Can Que Lit (pres 82-84); Asn Can Stud (pres 92-94); Int Coun Can Stud (pres 95-97). **SELECTED PUBLICATIONS** Coauth, William Arthur Deacon: A Canadian Literary Life, 82; ed, Margaret Laurence-Al Purdy: A Friendship in Letters, 93; co-ed, Dear Bill: The Correspondence of William Arthur Deacon, 88; co-ed, Selected Letters of Margaret Laurence and Adele Wiseman, 97. **CONTACT ADDRESS** Dept of English, York Univ, 4700 Keele St, North York, ON, M3K 1P3.

LENOSKI, DANIEL S.
DISCIPLINE ENGLISH LITERATURE **EDUCATION** Univ Manitoba, BA; MA; Queen's Univ, PhD. **CAREER** Assoc prof **RESEARCH** Aesthetic theories of W. B. Yeats. **SELECTED PUBLICATIONS** Auth, pub(s) on Anglo-Irish literature, late Victorian and early 20th century British literature, and Canadian novel. **CONTACT ADDRESS** Dept of English, Manitoba Univ, Winnipeg, MB, R3T 2N2.

LENT, JOHN ANTHONY
PERSONAL Born 09/08/1936, East Millsboro, PA, 5 children **DISCIPLINE** MASS COMMUNICATIONS, ASIAN STUDIES **EDUCATION** Ohio Univ, BSJ, 58, MS, 60; Univ Iowa, PhD, 72. **CAREER** Instr English & J, WVa Inst Technol, 60-62; lectr jour, De La Salle Col, Manila, Philippines, 64-65; asst prof English & jour, WVa Inst Technol, 65-66; asst prof jour, Wis State Univ-Eau Claire, 66-67 & Marshall Univ, 67-69; vis assoc prof jour, Univ Wyo, 69-70; assoc ed, Int Commun Bull, Univ Iowa, 70-72; cooodr mass commun prog, Univ Sains Malaysia, Penang, 72-74; assoc prof, 74-76, Prof Mass Commun, Temple Univ, 76-, Fulbright grant, Philippines, 64-65; ed, J, Malaysia/Singapore/Brunei Studies Group; Asn Asian Studies; Int Asn Mass Commun Res; chair, Asian Cinema Studies Soc; ed, Asian Cineme; managing ed, WittyWorld; assoc ed, Asian Thought and Soc; chair, IAMCR Comic Art Working Group. **HONORS AND AWARDS** Paul Eberman res award; 2 Broadcast Preceptor awards; Ray and Pat Browne Nat Book award. **RESEARCH** Mass media in Third World, especially in Caribbean and Asia; use of folk media; history of mass communications. **SELECTED PUBLICATIONS** Ed, The Asian Newspapers' Reluctant Revolution, Iowa State Univ/ Azumi Shoppan, 71, 72; auth, Philippine Mass Communications ..., Philippine Inst, 71, 72; Asian Mass Communications: A Comprehensive Bibliography, Temple Univ, 75, Suppl, 78; ed, Cultural Pluralism in Malaysia, Northern Ill Univ, 77; auth, Third World Mass Media and Their Search for Modernity, Bucknell Univ/Assoc Iniv Presses, 77; ed, Broadcasting in Asia and the Pacific, Temple Univ/Heinemann, 78; Asian Popular Culture, Different Road Taken, Global Productions (with G Sussman), Transnational Commun, and 40 others and over 500 journal articles. **CONTACT ADDRESS** Dept of Broadcast, Telecommun & Mass Media, Temple Univ, 2020 N 13th St, Philadelphia, PA, 19122-6029.

LENZ, WILLIAM ERNEST
PERSONAL Born 06/26/1950, New York, NY, m, 1975, 2 children **DISCIPLINE** ENGLISH AND AMERICAN LITERATURE **EDUCATION** BA magn cum laude Amherst College 73, MA Univ of Virginia 74, PhD Univ of Virginia 80. **CAREER** Prof and Chair Dept of English Chatham College. **HONORS AND AWARDS** Prof of English 97-98, NEH Project Director 96-97. **MEMBERSHIPS** MLA; ASA; NEMLA; SHARP; ALA. **RESEARCH** Explanations and Travel Literature. **SELECTED PUBLICATIONS** The Poetics of the Antarctic; A Study in Nineteenth-Century American Cultural Perceptions "Garland Studies in Nineteenth-American Literature", New York Garland, 95; Fast Talk and Flush Time: The Confidence Man As A Literary Convention, Columbia Univ of Missouri Press, 85; Identity in John Lloyd Stephen's Incidents of Travel in Central America,Chiapas and Yucatan in Travel Culture: Essays on What Makes Us Go; ed, Carol Traynor Williams Westport Connecticut and London Praeger, 79-87, 98; The Function of Wonem in Old Southwestern Humor:Re-reading Porter's Big Bear and Quarter Race Collections Mississippi Quarterly XLVI, 4, 598-600, 93; Poe's Arthur Gordon Pym and the Narrative Techniques of Antarctic Gothic, CEA Critic 53, 3, 41-63, 91; The Galapagos Islands: The Encantadas of Darwin and Melville Animal Talk, 9, 1, 26 91. **CONTACT ADDRESS** Dept of English, Chatham Col, Woodland Rd., Pittsburgh., PA, 15232. **EMAIL** lenz@CHATHAM.edu

LEON, PHILIP WHEELER
PERSONAL Born 12/28/1944, Memphis, TN, m, 1967, 1 child **DISCIPLINE** AMERICAN LITERATURE **EDUCATION** Wake Forest Univ, BA, 66, MA, 70; Peabody Col, PhD(English), 74. **CAREER** Instr English, Winston-Salem State Univ, 69-71, asst prof, 73-75; asst prof, 75-80, ASSOC PROF ENGLISH, THE CITADEL, 80-. **MEMBERSHIPS** Ncte; Col English Asn; Soc for Study Southern Lit. **RESEARCH** American fiction; bibliographic study. **SELECTED PUBLICATIONS** Auth, Mark Twain Weapons of Satire, Anti Imperialist Writings on the Philippine-American War, Miss Quart, Vol 0046, 93. **CONTACT ADDRESS** Dept of English, 171 Moultrie St, Charleston, SC, 29409-0002.

LEONARD, JAMES S.
PERSONAL Born 07/02/1947, Bristol, VA, m, 1979 **DISCIPLINE** ENGLISH LITERATURE **EDUCATION** Univ Tenn, BA, 69, MA, 79; Brown Univ, PhD, 83. **CAREER** Asst prof, 83-88, assoc prof, 88-93, prof, 93-, The Citadel. **HONORS AND AWARDS** SAMLA Stud Award, hon mention, 84; Huntington Lib fel, 84; fac achievement awards, 88, 90, 92, 94, 97. **MEMBERSHIPS** MLA; South Atlantic Mod Lang Assoc; Am Lit Assoc; Am Humor Stud Assoc; Wallace Stevens Soc; Mark Twain Circle. **RESEARCH** Wallace Stevens; Mark Twain; literary criticism. **SELECTED PUBLICATIONS** Coauth, The Fluent Mundo: Wallace Stevens and the Structure of Reality, Georgia, 88; co-ed, Satire or Evasion? Black Perspectives on Huckleberry Finn, Duke, 92; coed, Author-ity and Textuality: Current Views of Collaborative Writing, Locust Hill, 94; ed, Mark Twain Circular, 87- . **CONTACT ADDRESS** Dept of English, The Citadel, Charleston, SC, 29409. **EMAIL** leonardj@citadel.edu

LEONARDI, SUSAN J.
PERSONAL Born 04/27/1946, CA, 4 children **DISCIPLINE** ENGLISH LITERATURE **EDUCATION** Univ Cal, Davis, PhD, 86, MA, 82, eng lit; Immaculata Col, PA, BA, 68. **CAREER** Univ MD, Col Pk, asst prof, 87-89, assoc prof, 90-97, prof, 98-. **SELECTED PUBLICATIONS** The Diva's Mouth: Body, Voice, Prima Donna Politics, with Rebecca A Pope, Rutgers Univ Press, 97; Dangerous By Degrees: Women at Oxford and the Summerville College Novelists, Rutgers Univ Press, 89; The Long Distance Runner, Tulsa Studies in Women's Lit, 94; The Party's Over, Southwest Rev, 90; Recipes For Reading: Summer Pasta, Lobster a' la Riseholme and Key Lime Pie, PMLA, 89; Bernie Becomes a Nun, in: The Voices We Carry, Recent Italian/American Women's Fiction, ed Mary Jo Bono, Guernica Press, 92; Too Tall for Grace, in: Slow Hand, ed Michele Slung, NY, Harper Collins, 92; many other pub and articles. **CONTACT ADDRESS** Dept Eng, Univ Maryland, College Park, MD, 20742. **EMAIL** sl18@umail.umd.edu

LEPLEY, DOUG
DISCIPLINE ENGLISH LITERATURE **EDUCATION** Susquehanna Univ, BA; Bucknell Univ, MA; Lehigh Univ, PhD. **CAREER** Prof, 78, vice-pres, Acad Aff, Thomas Col. **SELECTED PUBLICATIONS** Publ articles on Geoffrey Chaucer and John Gower. Also edited for Shoestring Press and Mainely Local. **CONTACT ADDRESS** Thomas Col, Admin Bldg, Waterville, ME, 04901-5097. **EMAIL** lepley@thomas.edu

LESSER, WENDY
PERSONAL Born 03/20/1952, CA, m, 1985, 1 child **DISCIPLINE** ENGLISH **EDUCATION** Harvard, BA, 73; Univ Cal Berkeley, PhD, 82. **CAREER** Ed, THE THREEPENNY REVIEW, 80-; Guggenheim fel; ACLS fel; NEH fel; OSI fel; fel Am Acad Arts & Sci; Morton Darwen Zabel Award. **RESEARCH** Literature; Visual arts; Performing arts. **SELECTED PUBLICATIONS** His Other Half; Pictures at an Execution; The Amateur. **CONTACT ADDRESS** Threepenny Review, PO Box 9131, Berkeley, CA, 94709.

LESTER, MARK
DISCIPLINE ENGLISH **EDUCATION** Univ CA, PhD. **CAREER** Found ch, dept Eng Sec Lang, Eastern WA Univ . **SELECTED PUBLICATIONS** Auth, Grammar in the Classroom. **CONTACT ADDRESS** Eastern Washington Univ, Cheney, WA, 99004-2431.

LESTOURGEON, DIANA E.
PERSONAL Born 04/06/1927, Covington, KY **DISCIPLINE** ENGLISH **EDUCATION** Univ Pa, AB, 49, AM, 50, PhD(English), 60. **CAREER** Instr, Ala Polytech Inst, 53-54 & Univ Mo, 54-55; asst instr, Pa State Univ, 55-56; from asst instr to instr, Univ Pa, 56-63; from asst prof to assoc prof, 65-77, Prof English, Widener Univ, 77- . **MEMBERSHIPS** MLA **RESEARCH** Twentieth century British fiction; psychological fiction; 18th century prose and poetry. **SELECTED PUBLICATIONS** Auth, Rosamond Lehmann, Twayne, 65; coauth, The Figure in The Carpet, Albion, 76. **CONTACT ADDRESS** Dept of English, Widener Univ, 1 University Pl, Chester, PA, 19013-5792.

LETTIS, RICHARD
PERSONAL Born 06/30/1928, Springfield, MA, m, 1951, 5 children **DISCIPLINE** ENGLISH **EDUCATION** Univ Mass, BA, 52; Yale Univ, MA, 53, PhD(English), 57. **CAREER** Instr English, Ohio Univ, 56-60; from asst prof to assoc prof, 60-67, exec dean, 71-73, PROF ENGLISH, C W POST COL, LONG ISLAND UNIV, 67-, Humanities ed, Pennant Studies Guides, Educ Res Assoc and Bantam, 66-67. **RESEARCH** English novel of 18th and 19th centuries. **SELECTED PUBLICATIONS** Auth, How I Work, Dickens in the Writers Chair, Dickensian, Vol 0089, 93. **CONTACT ADDRESS** Long Island Univ, C.W. Post, Greenvale, NY, 11548.

LETZRING, MONICA
PERSONAL Born 02/01/1935, Grafton, ND **DISCIPLINE** ENGLISH AND COMPARATIVE LITERATURE **EDUCATION** Col St Scholastica, BA, 57; Univ Md, MA, 60, PhD, 63. **CAREER** Instr English lit, Col Notre Dame, Md, 63; instr English, Ctr Ling, Bergamo, Italy, 63-65; asst prof, 65-75, ASSOC PROF ENGLISH, TEMPLE UNIV, 75-. **MEMBERSHIPS** MLA; Am Soc 18th Century Studies. **RESEARCH** Eighteenth century English literature. **SELECTED PUBLICATIONS** Auth, Behn, Aphra--Selected Poems, Scriblerian and the Kit-Cats, Vol 0028, 95; 'Indamora' to' Lindamira', Scriblerian and the Kit-Cats, Vol 0028, 95; Behn, a the 'Rover', Scriblerian and the Kit-Cats, Vol 0028, 95; Behn,Aphra 'Oroonoko', the 'Rover' and Other Works, Scriblerian and the Kit-Cats, Vol 0028, 95; The Dramatic Works of Lillo, George, Scriblerian and the Kit-Cats, Vol 0028, 95; Restoration and 18th-Century Plays by Women, Scriblerian and the Kit-Cats, Vol 0028, 95. **CONTACT ADDRESS** Dept of English, Temple Univ, 1114 W Berks St, Philadelphia, PA, 19122-6029.

LEUPIN, ALEXANDRE
DISCIPLINE MEDIEVAL LITERATURE, LITERARY CRITICISM AND THEORY, PSYCHOANALYSIS, EPISTEM **EDUCATION** Univ Gen(ve, Doctorat, 71. **CAREER** Prof, La State Univ. **SELECTED PUBLICATIONS** Auth, Le Graal et la litt?rature, 83; Barbarolexis: Medieval Literature and Sexuality, 89; Lacan and the Human Sciences, 91; Fiction et incarnation, th?ologie et litt?rature au Moyen Age, 93. **CONTACT ADDRESS** Dept of Fr Grad Stud, Louisiana State Univ, Baton Rouge, LA, 70803.

LEUTHOLD, STEVEN M.
PERSONAL Born 05/24/1957, Houston, TX, m, 1981, 2 children **DISCIPLINE** COMMUNICATIONS **EDUCATION** Univ Montana, BA, 80; Wash State Univ, MA, 89; Univ Penn, PhD, 92. **CAREER** Instr, Intensive Am Lang Ctr, 88, instr, Murrow Sch for Commun, 87-89, Wash State Univ; instr, Annenberg Sch for Commun, Univ Penn, 89-92; asst prof, Syracuse Univ Sch of Art and Design, 92-. **MEMBERSHIPS** Col Art Asn. **RESEARCH** Art theory; aesthetics; indigenous issues; color; media studies. **SELECTED PUBLICATIONS** Auth, An Indigenous Aesthetic? Two Noted Native Videographers: George Burdeau and Victor Masayesva, Wicazo Sa: A Rev of Native Am Stud, 94; auth, Social Accountability and the Production of Native American Film and Video, Wide Angle, 94; auth, Native American Responses to the Western, Am Indian Cult and Res Jour, 95; auth, Native American Art and Artists in Visual Arts Documentaries from 1973-1991, On the Margins of Artworlds, Westview, 95; auth, The Book and the Peasant: Visual Representation and Social Change in German Woodcuts, 1521-1525, Printing Hist, 95; auth, Is There Art in Indigenous Aesthetics? Jour of Arts Mgt, Law and Soc, 96; auth, Representing Truth and History in Native American Documentary, Film and Hist, 97; auth, Native American Documentary: An Emerging Genre, Film Criticism, 97; auth, Native Media's Communities, Am Indian Cult and Res Jour, 97; auth, Indigenous Aesthetics: Representation and Conditions of Reception, Dialogue and Universalism, 97; auth, Crossing the Lines: Toward a Curriculum of Comparative Deisign, Multicultural Educ, 97; auth, Historical Representation in Native American Documentary: A Review Essay, Ethnohistory, 97; auth, Genre-lizing about Realism, Art Criticism, 98; auth, Indigenous Aesthetics: Native Art, Media and Identity, Texas, 98. **CONTACT ADDRESS** School of Art and Design, Syracuse Univ, Syracuse, NY, 13244. **EMAIL** smleutho@mailbox.syr.edu

LEV, PETER
PERSONAL Born 06/15/1948, Cleveland, OH, m, 1976, 2 children **DISCIPLINE** MASS COMMUNICATION **EDUCATION** Wesleyan Univ, BA, 70; Univ Calif, Los Angeles, MA, 74, PhD, 80. **CAREER** Vis Asst Prof, Univ Tex at Dallas, 80-82; Asst Prof, 83-88, Assoc Prof, 88-93, Prof Mass Commun, Towson Univ. **HONORS AND AWARDS** Fac Excellence Award, Towson, 96-97., Past Pres, Lit/Film Asn; Ed Bd, Lit Film Quart; Crse file ed, J of Film & Video. **MEMBERSHIPS** Lit/Film Asn; Int Asn for Media & Hist; Univ Film & Video Asn; Soc for Cinema Stud. **RESEARCH** History of American & European film; international film & television; film & ecology. **SELECTED PUBLICATIONS** Auth, The Euro-American Cinema, Univ Tex Press, 93; auth, Whose Future?, Lit/Film Quart, 26.1, 98; 7 essays in The Encyclopedia of Novels into Film, 98; auth, Conflicting Visions: American Films of the 1970s, Univ Tex Press, in process. **CONTACT ADDRESS** Dept of Mass Commun, Towson Univ, Towson, MD, 21252. **EMAIL** plev@towson.edu

LEVACK, BRIAN PAUL
PERSONAL Born 04/06/1943, New York, NY, m, 1966, 2 children **DISCIPLINE** ENGLISH HISTORY **EDUCATION** Fordham Col, BA, 65; Yale Univ, MA, 67, PhD(hist), 70. **CAREER** From instr to asst prof, 69-74, assoc prof, 74-94, John Green Regents Prof Hist, Univ Tx, Austin, 94-; . **HONORS AND AWARDS** Guggenheim fel, 75-76; Scholorin Residence, Washington and Lee Univ School of Law, 94. **MEMBERSHIPS** AHA; Conf Brit Studies; Am Soc Legal Hist; Stair Soc; Sixteenth Century Studies Conference. **RESEARCH** Early modern British history; English legal history; Scottish history. **SELECTED PUBLICATIONS** Auth, The Civil Lawyers in English, 1603- 1641: A Political Study, Oxford, 73; The Formation of the British State: England, Scotland, and the Union, 1603-1707, Oxford, 87; Law, Sovereignty and the Union, in Scots and Britons, Cambridge, 94; The Great Witch Hunt, in Handbook of European History in the Later Middle Ages, Renaissance and Reformation, 1400-1600, vol 2, Brill, 95; The Witch in Baroque Personae, Chicago, 95; The Witch Hunt in Early Modern Europe, London: Longman, 2nd ed, 95; Possession, Witchcraft and the Law in Jacobean England, Washington and Lee Law Rev 52, 96; Possession and Exorcism, Oxford Encyclopedia of the Reformation, 96; State-Building and Witch Hunting in Early Modern Europe, in Witchcraft in Early Modern Europe: Studies in Culture and Belief, Cambridge, 96; Law in The History of the University of Oxford, Vol IV: The Seventeenth Century, Oxford, 97. **CONTACT ADDRESS** Dept Hist, Univ Texas, Austin, TX, 78712-1026. **EMAIL** levack@mail.utexas.edu

LEVENDUSKI, CRISTINE
DISCIPLINE ENGLISH LANGUAGE AND LITERATURE **EDUCATION** Univ Minn, PhD, 89. **CAREER** Assoc prof/dir grad studies. **RESEARCH** American studies; early American literature. **SELECTED PUBLICATIONS** Auth, Peculiar Power: A Quaker Woman Preacher in 18th Century America, Smithsonian, 96. **CONTACT ADDRESS** English Dept, Emory Univ, 1380 Oxford Rd NE, Atlanta, GA, 30322-1950. **EMAIL** cmleven@emory.edu

LEVENSON, CARL
DISCIPLINE ENGLISH LITERATURE **EDUCATION** Univ Chicago, PhD, 86. **CAREER** Assoc prof. **RESEARCH** Plato; Old Testament; continental philosophy. **SELECTED PUBLICATIONS** Auth, Socrates and the Corybantes; Dionysian Spirituality in the Philosophy of Plato; co-ed, Reality of Time and of Life and Death. **CONTACT ADDRESS** Dept of English and Philosophy, Idaho State Univ, Pocatello, ID, 83209.

LEVENSON, JACOB CLAVNER
PERSONAL Born 10/01/1922, Boston, MA, m, 1946, 3 children **DISCIPLINE** ENGLISH **EDUCATION** Harvard Univ, AB, 43, PhD, 51. **CAREER** Tutor, 46-50, Harvard Univ; instr, 50-54, Univ Conn; from asst prof to prof, 54-67, chmn prog Am studies, 63, Univ Minn; chmn dept, 71-74, Edgar Allan Poe Prof English, 67-, Univ Va; mem fac Am Studies Sem, Salzburg, Austria, 47 & 49; vis lectr English & gen educ, 51-52, Harvard Univ; Am Philos Soc Penrose grant, 56; fac res grant, Univ Minn, 56; Guggenheim fel, 58-59; Am Coun Learned Soc fel, 61-62; mem English Inst; mem comt consult, Notable American Women, 1607-1950, Radcliffe Col, 63-72. **HONORS AND AWARDS** E Harris Harbison Distinguished Tchng Award, Danforth Found, 66; Univ Va Soc of Fels, 78-. **MEMBERSHIPS** MLA; Am Studies Assn. **RESEARCH** American literature; American cultural history. **SELECTED PUBLICATIONS** Auth, The Sadness of Sister Carrie, Morphologies of Faith, Scholars Press, 90; art, American Literature 1865-1914, Reader's Encycl of Amer Hist, Houghton, 91; auth, Passage to Modernity: Cranes Red Badge and Norris's McTeague, Cambridge Companion to American Realism and naturalism, Cambridge, 95. **CONTACT ADDRESS** Univ of Virginia, 219 Bryan Hall, Charlottesville, VA, 22903. **EMAIL** jcl3g@virginia.edu

LEVENSON, JILL
DISCIPLINE ENGLISH **EDUCATION** Queen's Col City, Univ New York, BA, 63; Harvard Univ, MA, 64, PhD, 67. **CAREER** Lectr, Queen's Col City, Univ New York, 64; tutor, Harvard Univ, 65-66; asst prof, Trinity Col, 67-74, assoc prof, 74-82, PROF ENGLISH, UNIV TORONTO 82-. **HONORS AND AWARDS** Cert Merit, Conf Ed Learned J, 86; Outstanding Tchr Award, Fac Arts Sci, Univ Toronto, 94. **MEMBERSHIPS** MLA; Shakespeare Asn Am; Int Shakespeare Asn; Am Soc Theatre Res. **SELECTED PUBLICATIONS** Auth, Shakespeare's Troilus and Cressida and the Monumental Tradition in Tapestries and Literature in Renaissance Drama No. 7, 76; auth, The Narrative Format of Benoit's Roman de Troie in Romania No. 1, 79; auth, Shakespeare in Performance: Romeo and Juliet, 87. **CONTACT ADDRESS** Trinity Col, Univ Toronto, Toronto, ON, M5S 1H8. **EMAIL** jilleven@uhura.trinity.toronto.edu

LEVERNIER, JAMES
DISCIPLINE AMERICAN LITERATURE AND AMERICAN STUDIES **EDUCATION** SUNY, PhD. **CAREER** English and Lit, Univ Ark **SELECTED PUBLICATIONS** Coauth, The Indian Captivity Narrative; Structuring Paragraphs; Coed, The Indians and Their Captives; American Writers Before 1800: A bibliographical and critical dictionary. **CONTACT ADDRESS** Univ Ark Little Rock, 2801 S University Ave., Little Rock, AR, 72204-1099.

LEVIN, CHARLES
DISCIPLINE COMMUNICATION STUDIES **EDUCATION** McGill Univ, BA, MA; Concordia Univ, PhD. **CAREER** Fac lectr. **MEMBERSHIPS** Can Psychoanalytic Soc. **RESEARCH** European social thought and aesthetics since the enlightenment. **SELECTED PUBLICATIONS** Auth, Jean Baudrillard: A Study in Cultural Metaphysics, Prentice Hall, 96; auth, Entre la Chaire et l'Esprit: le Corps Social du Nouveau-ne, 92; auth, Thinking through the Hungry Baby: Towards a New Pleasure Principle, 92. **CONTACT ADDRESS** Dept Communications, McGill Univ, 845 Sherbrooke St, Montreal, PQ, H3A 2T5.

LEVIN, JONATHAN
DISCIPLINE 19TH-AND 20TH-CENTURY AMERICAN LITERATURE **EDUCATION** Mich, BA, 83; UCLA, MA, 85; Rutgers, PhD, 95. **CAREER** English and Lit, Columbia Univ **HONORS AND AWARDS** Fel, Nat Hum Ctr; Assoc ed, Raritan Rev. **SELECTED PUBLICATIONS** Auth, Walt Whitman, an illustrated selection of Whitman's poetry, 97. **CONTACT ADDRESS** Columbia Univ, 2960 Broadway, New York, NY, 10027-6902.

LEVIN, RICHARD A.
PERSONAL Born 04/04/1944, Brooklyn, NY, m, 1975, 2 children **DISCIPLINE** ENGLISH LITERATURE **EDUCATION** Univ NC, Chapel Hill, BA, 65; Oxford Univ, BA, 67; Stanford Univ, PhD, 72. **CAREER** From instr to asst prof Eng, Univ New Orleans, 71-74; asst prof, 74-81, Assoc Prof Eng, Univ CA, Davis, 81. **MEMBERSHIPS** MLA; Shakespeare Asn Am. **RESEARCH** Early mod Eng Lit. **SELECTED PUBLICATIONS** Love and Society in Shakespeare Comedy, Univ of DE Press, 85; articles on Sponsor Sidney Shakespears dramatic contemporaries. **CONTACT ADDRESS** Dept of Eng, Univ of California, Davis, CA, 95616-5200. **EMAIL** ralevin@ucdavis.edu

LEVINE, BERNARD
PERSONAL Born 07/15/1934, Boston, MA, m, 1963 **DISCIPLINE** ENGLISH LITERATURE **EDUCATION** Harvard Univ, AB, 56; Brown Univ, PhD, 65. **CAREER** Asst English, Brown Univ, 61-63; from instr to asst prof, 63-71, assoc prof English, Wayne State Univ, 71-. **MEMBERSHIPS** MLA **RESEARCH** Nineteenth and twentieth century romantic poetry; W B Yeats. **SELECTED PUBLICATIONS** Auth, High talk: Concentrative analysis of a poem by Yeats, James Joyce Quart, winter 66; Yeats' Aesthetics and His Concept of Self, 66 & The Dissolving Image: Yeats' Spiritual-Aesthetic Development, 69, Wayne State Univ; Yeats' Leda and the Swan: A psychopoetic analysis, Bucknell Rev, 69. **CONTACT ADDRESS** Dept of English, Wayne State Univ, 431 State Hall, Detroit, MI, 48202-1308.

LEVINE, GEORGE L.
DISCIPLINE ENGLISH LANGUAGE AND LITERATURE **EDUCATION** NY Univ, BA; Univ Minn, MA; PhD. **CAREER** Kenneth Burke Prof Engl. **RESEARCH** Victorian literature and culture; novel and narrative; science and culture; Darwin. **SELECTED PUBLICATIONS** Auth, Darwin and the Novelists; auth, The Realistic Imagination; Lifebirds. **CONTACT ADDRESS** Dept of English, Rutgers Univ, 510 George St, Murray Hall, New Brunswick, NJ, 08901-1167. **EMAIL** gelevine@compuserve.com

LEVINE, GEORGE RICHARD
PERSONAL Born 08/05/1929, Boston, MA, m, 1958, 2 children **DISCIPLINE** ENGLISH **EDUCATION** Tufts Col, BA, 51; Columbia Univ, MA, 52, PhD(English), 61. **CAREER** Instr, Northwestern Univ, 59-63; from asst prof to assoc prof, 63-70, assoc provost fac Arts & Lett, 71-72, provost & dean fac Arts & Lett, 75-81, prof English, State Univ NY Buffalo, 70-, Fulbright lectr, Univ Cologne, 69-70, Chancellor's Award for Excellence in Teaching, State Univ NY, 74. **MEMBERSHIPS** MLA; Am Soc 18th Century Studies. **RESEARCH** Eighteenth century English literature; English novel; dynamics of the teaching-learning process. **SELECTED PUBLICATIONS** Coauth, Riverside Readings, Columbia Univ, 58; Readings in American English, Prentice-Hall Int, 60; auth, Henry Fielding and the Dry Mock: A Study of the Techniques of Irony in his Early Works, Mouton, 67; coauth, Poetic and pictorial design in Two Songs of Innocence, Pmla, 5/67; auth, Dryden's Inarticulate Poesy: music and the Davidic King in Absalom and Achitophel, 18th Century Studies, Summer 68; Satiric intent and Baroque design in Donne's Go and Catch a Falling Star, Neuren Sprachen, 71; coauth, Poetry and the group process: an experiment in classroom dynamics, New Directions in Teaching, Winter 74; Introduction to Jonathan Swift, A Modest Proposal and Other Satires, Prometheus Press, 95. **CONTACT ADDRESS** Dept of English, SUNY, Buffalo, PO Box 604610, Buffalo, NY, 14260-4610.

LEVINE, PHILIP
PERSONAL Born 01/10/1928, Detroit, MI, m, 1945, 3 children **DISCIPLINE** CREATIVE WRITING **EDUCATION** Wayne State Univ, BA, 50, MA, 55; Univ Iowa, Mfa, 57. **CAREER** Instr English, Univ Iowa, 55-57; Stegnar fel, Stanford Univ, 57-58; PROF ENGLISH, CALIF STATE UNIV, FRESNO, 58-, Guggenheim fel, 73; Nat Endowment for the Arts grant, 76. **HONORS AND AWARDS** Joseph Henry Jackson Award, 63; Chaplebrook Award, 68; Frank O'Hara Mem Award, 72; Nat Inst Arts and Lett Award, 73; Lenore Marshall Award, Saturday Rev and New Hope Found, 76. **RESEARCH** Poetry; contemporary Spanish and Spanish American poetry; translation. **SELECTED PUBLICATIONS** Auth, 1933, Atheneum, 74; on the Edge and Over, Cloud Marauder, 76; The Names of the Lost, 76, Seven Years from Somewhere, 79 and Ashes: Poems New and Old, 79, Atheneum; Pili's Wall, Unicorn Press, rev ed, 80; Don't Ask, Univ Mich Press, 81; One for the Rose, Atheneum, 81. **CONTACT ADDRESS** Dept of English, California State Univ, Fresno, Fresno, CA, 93710.

LEVINE, RICHARD ALLAN
PERSONAL Born 05/13/1932, Malden, MA, m, 1954, 2 children **DISCIPLINE** ENGLISH **EDUCATION** Univ Mass, BA, 53; Univ Conn, MA, 55; Ind Univ, PhD, 61. **CAREER** Assoc, Ind Univ, 55-57, resident lectr English, 57-59; from instr to asst prof, Miami Univ, 59-64; asst prof, Univ Calif, Riverside, 64-69; assoc prof, 69-72, dir grad studies, 70-73, PROF ENGLISH, STATE UNIV NY STONY BROOK, 72-, CHMN DEPT, 75-. **MEMBERSHIPS** MLA; NCTE; Int Asn Univ Prof English. **RESEARCH** Victorian literature; the English novel; literature and society. **SELECTED PUBLICATIONS** Auth, A World of Possibilities, Romantic Irony in Victorian Literature, 19th Century Prose, Vol 0019, 92. **CONTACT ADDRESS** Dept of English, State Univ of NY, Stony Brook, NY, 11794.

LEVINE, ROBERT
PERSONAL Born 05/09/1933, New York, NY, m, 1958, 3 children **DISCIPLINE** ENGLISH **EDUCATION** City Col NY, BA, 54; Columbia Univ, MA, 58; Univ CA, Berkeley, PhD, 63. **CAREER** Instr Eng, Rensselaer Polytech Inst, 58-59 & Cornell Univ, 62-64; from Asst Prof to Assoc Prof, 64-88, Prof English, Boston Univ, 88-, Actg Chmn, Classics Dept, 71-73, Chmn, Medieval Studies Comt, 74-76, Asst Dean, Advising Office, Col Liberal Arts, 78-79, Spring 87, 89-95; Vis Asst Prof English, Brown Univ, Spring 66; Vis Assoc Prof, Universite Paul Valery, France, Fall 84. **MEMBERSHIPS** MLA. **RESEARCH** Old Eng; Middle Eng; Medieval Latin. **SELECTED PUBLICATIONS** Transl, France Before Charlemagne, Mellen Press, 90; A Thirteenth-Century Minstrel's Chronicle, Mellen Press, 90; A Thirteenth-century Life of Charlemagne, Garland Press, 91; The Deeds of God through the Franks, Boydell & Brewer, 97; auth, Gower as Gerontion: Oneiric Autobiography in the Confessio Amantis, Medieaevistik 5, 92; Who composed Havelok for whom?, Yearbook for English Studies XXII, 92; The Pious Traitor: the Man who Betrayed Antioch, Mittellateinisches Jahrbuch XXXIII, 98; author or numerous other articles. **CONTACT ADDRESS** Dept of Eng, Boston Univ, 236 Bay State Rd, Boston, MA, 02215-1403. **EMAIL** bobl@bu.edu

LEVITIN, ALEXIS
DISCIPLINE ENGLISH **EDUCATION** Columbia Univ, BA; MA; Phd, 71. **CAREER** Fac, Plattsburgh State Univ of NY. **RESEARCH** Creative writing; Shakespeare; world lit. **SELECTED PUBLICATIONS** Auth, transl(s) of poetry from the Portuguese. **CONTACT ADDRESS** SUNY, Plattsburgh, 101 Broad St, Plattsburgh, NY, 12901-2681.

LEVITT, MORTON PAUL
PERSONAL Born 12/22/1936, Brooklyn, NY, m, 1963 **DISCIPLINE** ENGLISH **EDUCATION** Dickinson Col, BA, 58; Columbia Univ, MA, 60; Pa State Univ, PhD(English), 65. **CAREER** Instr English, Pa State Univ, 60-62; from instr to asst prof, 62-71, assoc prof, 71-79, PROF ENGLISH, TEMPLE UNIV, 80-, Assoc, Ctr Neo-Hellenci Studies, 72-; Fulbright lectr Am lit, Zagreb Univ, Yugoslavia, 74-75. **RESEARCH** The novels and verse of Nikos Kazantzakis; fiction of James Joyce; literary modernism. **SELECTED PUBLICATIONS** Auth, Joyce and Vuillard--the Music of Painting, James Joyce Quart, Vol 0030, 93. **CONTACT ADDRESS** Dept of English, Temple Univ, 1114 W Berks St, Philadelphia, PA, 19122-6029.

LEVITTI, STEVEN R.
DISCIPLINE COMMUNICATION **EDUCATION** MT State Univ, BA, 82; WV Univ, MA, 83; OH State Univ, PhD, 88. **CAREER** Assoc prof, Univ TX at San Antonio, 97-& asst prof, 91-97; asst prof, Univ KY, 86-91; grad tchg asst, OH State Univ, 83-86 & W V Univ, 82-83; undergrad tchg asst, MT State Univ, 82; proj asst, Commun Enterprises, OH news Network, 84; fac adv, Univ TX at San Antonio, Public Relations Stud Soc of Am, 95-; UTSA mentor, 92-94; mem, Bd Dir, Publ Relations Soc Am, 95-; co-ch, Ushers Comt, Annual Conv of the Speech Commun Asn, San Antonio, 95; plan comt, Publ Rel Soc Am sem, 95; guest lectr, Univ WI-Oshkosh, 92 & 95; VIP, Usher for featured speaker George Gilder, EDUCOM '94 Conf, San Antonio, 94; reviewer, Int Commun Asn, 40th Annual Conf Int Commun Asn, Dublin, Ireland, 90; ch & organizer, Interdisciplinary Prog, Presented at the 39th Annual Conf Int Commun Asn, San Francisco, 89; adv bd, Paisano stud newspaper, 96-; selection comt, Becas Eckerd Scholar Prog, 93; commun workshop, Alamo Heights Manor, 92. **HONORS AND AWARDS** Phi Kappa Phi Nat Hon Soc, WV Univ, 83; Nat Commun Forum Univ Fac Grant, 89., Formed, 1st Publ Relations Stud Soc Chap in San Antonio. **SELECTED PUBLICATIONS** Auth, Technology transfer and media imperialism: The US-Canadian case, Media criticism: Journeys in interpretation, Dubuque, Kendall/Hunt Publ Comp, 92; Satellite technology, N M Satellite telecommunications and their potential for vocational education, OH State Univ: Nat Ctr Vocational Educ, 84; coauth, International teleconferencing: Its role in university-level education, Teleconferencing and electronic communications V: Applications, technologies, and human factors, Madison, Ctr Interactive Prog, Univ WI-Extension, 86; Improving intelligibility and user satisfaction in audioconferencing: Wireless microphone vs speakerphone input signals, Teleconferencing and electronic communications IV: Applications, technologies, and human factors, Madison, Ctr Interactive Prog, Univ WI-Extension, 85; Designing videoconferencing facilities for improved eye contact: A case study in technological development, J Broadcasting and Electronic Media, 31 2, 87; Risky shift and gender of the advocate: Information theory versus normative theory, Gp and Organizational Stud, 9 2, 84; rev, Issues in new information technology, 89; Measuring the information society, J Broadcasting & Electronic Media, 33 2, 89. **CONTACT ADDRESS** Col of Fine Arts and Hum, Univ Texas at San Antonio, 6900 N Loop 1604 W, San Antonio, TX, 78249. **EMAIL** slevitt@lonestar.utsa.edu

LEVY, ALFRED J.
PERSONAL Born 11/15/1926, Boston, MA, m, 2 children **DISCIPLINE** ENGLISH & AMERICAN LITERATURE **EDUCATION** Clark Univ, AB, 49; Univ WI, AM, 50, PhD(English), 57. **CAREER** Assoc English, IN Univ, 55-57, from instr to asst prof, 57-61; from asst prof to assoc prof, 61-71, assoc dean arts & sci, 68-76, prof English, Univ Hawaii, Manoa, 71-. **MEMBERSHIPS** AAUP. **RESEARCH** American prose fiction; world literature. **SELECTED PUBLICATIONS** Coauth, Manuscripts of Hawthorne's short stories, Studies Bibliog, 61; auth, Ethan Brand and the unpardonable sin, Boston Univ Studies English, autumn 61; The House of the Seven Gables: the religion of love, 19th-Century Fiction, 12/61. **CONTACT ADDRESS** Dept English, Univ Hawaii at Manoa, 1733 Donaghho Rd, Honolulu, HI, 96822-2368.

LEVY, ANITA
DISCIPLINE 19TH CENTURY NOVEL, GOTHIC FICTION, EARLY MODERN AND VICTORIAN CULTURE **EDUCATION** Univ CA at San Diego, PhD. **CAREER** Asst prof; taught at, Williams Col & Univ CA at San Diego. **RESEARCH** Late-18th and 19th century Brit lit, espec the novel, gender studies, and cult studies. **SELECTED PUBLICATIONS** Auth, Other Women: The Writing of Class, Race, and Gender, 1832-1898; articles on, early mod print cult, Brontes, Victorian anthrop, Dorothy Richardson & gendered labor. **CONTACT ADDRESS** Dept of Eng, Univ of Rochester, 601 Elmwood Ave, Ste. 656, Rochester, NY, 14642. **EMAIL** levy@db1.cc.rochester.edu

LEVY, JACQUES
DISCIPLINE THEATER **EDUCATION** BA CCNY, BA, 56; MI State Univ, MA, 58, PhD, 61. **CAREER** Dir, writer, prof theater, 30 yr(s); instr, Yale, Columbia Univ, Hunter Col; prof; dir, the Theater, 92. **HONORS AND AWARDS** Obie award; Drama Desk and Outer Critics Circle award; 4 BMI awards for bk and lyrics of a produced musical., Grammy nominations. **SELECTED PUBLICATIONS** Auth, Fame...The Musical, Lyricist, 95. **CONTACT ADDRESS** Dept of Eng, Colgate Univ, 13 Oak Drive, Hamilton, NY, 13346.

LEVY, MICHAEL MARC
PERSONAL Born 04/15/1950, Chicago, IL, m, 1983, 2 children **DISCIPLINE** SCIENCE FICTION, RENAISSANCE, AND CHILDREN'S LITERATURE **EDUCATION** Univ IL, Champaign, BA, 72; OH State Univ, MA, 74; Univ MN, Minneapolis, PhD(English), 82. **CAREER** Lectr English, 80-84, assist prof, 85-86, assoc prof, 87-89, PROF, UNIV WI-STOUT, 90-. **MEMBERSHIPS** MLA; Sci Fiction Res Asn; Children's Lit Asn; MMLA. **RESEARCH** Science fiction, particularly when related to gender; children's lit, particularly when related to science fiction, gender, and Southeast Asian children's lit; seventeenth century poetry. **SELECTED PUBLICATIONS** Auth, Philip Francis Nowlan & Gary K Wolf, 20th Century Sci Fiction Writers, 81; coauth, Modern Science Fiction and Fantasy: A Study Guide, Univ Minn Exten, 81; auth, Sir William Davenant, Francis Beaumont, Thomas Middleton & Thomas Randolph, Critical Survey of Poetry, 82; Who, What, and Why? Character Motivation in Doctor Who, Children's Lit Asn Quart, 85; Paradise Lost in Northern Wisconsin, Approaches to Paradise Lost, 86; Modern Science Fiction and Fantasy: A Study Guide, 3rd ed, with Patricia C. Hodgell, 94; From Darkness to Light: Judy Chicago's Holocaust Project, with Sandra Lindow, Kaleidoscope, 94, Natalie Babbitt, 91; The New Wave, Cyberpunk and Beyond, Anatomy of Wonder, 95; George R. R. Martin: I Want to Provide a Journey We Haven't Taken Before, Pubs Weekly, 96; Lois McMaster Bujold: Science Fiction and Disability, Kaleidoscope, 97; Who Killed Science Fiction? A Spectrum of Responses, NY Review of SF, 97; Lois Lowry's The Giver: Interrupted Bildungsroman or Ambiguous Dystopia?, Foundation, 97; Science Fiction in 1997, What Do I Read Next?, 98; Ophelia Triumphant: the Survival of Adolescent Girls in Recent SF by Butler and Womack, Foundation, 98; Refugees and Immigrants: The Southeast Asian Experience as Depicted in Recent Children's Books, Mellon, forthcoming; Annotated Bibliography of Young Adult Science Fiction: History and Criticism, Young Adult Science Fiction, forthcoming; Young Adult Science Fiction as Bildungsroman, Young Adult Science Fiction, forthcoming. **CONTACT ADDRESS** Dept English, Univ Wisconsin-Stout, Po Box 790, Menomonie, WI, 54751-0790. **EMAIL** levym@uwstout.edu

LEVY, WILLIAM TURNER
PERSONAL Born 11/03/1922, Far Rockaway, NY **DISCIPLINE** ENGLISH **EDUCATION** City Col New York, BA, 42; Columbia Univ, MAj 47, PhD, 52. **CAREER** From instr to assoc prof English, Baruch Col, 46-77; priest, Protestant Episcopal Church, 52-; sr ed, The Churchman, 59-76. **SELECTED PUBLICATIONS** Auth, The Idea of the Church in T S Eliot, Christian Scholar, 58; auth, William Barnes: The Man and the Poems, Longmans Ltd, Dorchester, 60;art, Jeffers as prophet, Robinson Jeffers, Grabhorn, 62; coauth, Affectionately, T S Eliot, Lippincott, 68; auth, The Films of Frank Capra, Citadel, 77. **CONTACT ADDRESS** 22121 Lanark St, Canoga Park, CA, 91304.

LEWALSKI, BARBARA KIEFER
PERSONAL Born 02/22/1931, Chicago, IL, m, 1956, 1 child **DISCIPLINE** ENGLISH LITERATURE, RENAISSANCE **EDUCATION** Kans State Teachers Col, Emporia, Bsed, 50; Univ Chicago, AM, 51, PhD, 56. **CAREER** PROF, 82-, WILLIAM R KENAN PROF ENG, 82-, DIR GRAD STUD, 97- , HARVARD UNIV. **HONORS AND AWARDS** MLA James Russell Lowell Prize, 79; Milton Society, James Holly Hanford Award, 83, 85; Am Acad Arts & Scis; Am Philos Soc; Intl Asn Univ Prof Eng. **MEMBERSHIPS** MLA; Milton Soc Am; Renaissance Soc Am; Soc Study Early Mod Women. **RESEARCH** Milton; 17th cent lit; early modern women's writing. **SELECTED PUBLICATIONS** Auth, Milton's Brief Epic; The Genre, Meaning, and Art of Paradise Regained, Methuen and Brown Univ Press, 66; auth, Donne's Anniversaries and the Poetry of Praise: The Creation of a Symbolic Mode, Princeton Univ Press, 73; auth, Protestant Poetics and the Seventeenth-Century Religious Lyric, Princeton Univ Press, 79, paperback 84, reprint 86; auth, Paradise Lost and the Rhetoric of Literary Forms, Princeton Univ Press, 85, paperback, 86; auth, Writing Women in Jacobean England, 1603-1625, Harvard Univ Press, 93, paperback, 95; auth, Rensaissance Genres: Essays on Theory, History, and Interpretation, Harvard English Studies 14, Harvard Univ Press, 86; auth, Norton Anthology of English Literature, Sixteenth Century Seciton, Norton, 86, 93, 00; auth, The Polemics and Poems of Rachel Speght, Oxford Univ Press, 96. **CONTACT ADDRESS** Dept of Eng, Harvard Univ, Barker Ctr, Cambridge, MA, 02138. **EMAIL** lewalski@fas.harvard.edu

LEWES, ULLE ERIKA
PERSONAL Born 03/22/1942, Tallinn, Estonia **DISCIPLINE** MEDIEVAL & COMPARATIVE LITERATURE **EDUCATION** Cornell Univ, AB, 64; Harvard Univ, MA, 65, PhD, 72. **CAREER** Instr, Temple Univ, 71-72, asst prof, 72-78; Assoc Prof, 78-82, Prof English, Ohio Wesleyan Univ, 82-, Dir Writing Ctr, Ohio Wesleyan Univ; writing consult, Muskingum Col, Denison Col, Col DuPage & Rice Univ; Dir, Project Writing across the Curriculum, Mellon Found Grant, 79-82; Lead Prof, NEH Summer Inst on Renaissance Drama, Secondary School Teachers-Ohio Wesleyan, 86; dir, various Ohio Wesleyan grants, 84, 85, 86, 94. **HONORS AND AWARDS** Phi Beta Kappa, 63; S.A. Potter Award, Harvard Univ, 72; Younger Schol grant, Int 12th Century Renaissance Conf, Medieval Acad, 77; Benjamin T. Spencer Lectureship, 94-96. **MEMBERSHIPS** MLA; Medieval Acad Am; Asn Teachers Advanc Compos; Conf Col Comp and Commun; Coun Writing Prog Admin; Estonian Learned Soc; Nat Coun Teachers English; Tristan Soc. **RESEARCH** The Tristan legend; mutual influences between medieval romances and Saints' lives; the theory and practice of teaching composition. **SELECTED PUBLICATIONS** Auth, Is America Losing Her Folklore Heritage?, Town and Country, 78; The Life in the Forest: Influence of the Saint Giles Legend on the Courtly Tristan Story, Univ Tenn, Chattanooga, 79; A Rejoinder to C.S. Jaeger on the Tristan Story, Tristania, 81; The Uses of Peer Editing in Advanced Writing Courses, J Advanced Comp, 85; The Originality of the Farewell Scene in Gottfield's Tristan, Tristania, 89; Writing as Learning: A Workbook for Teachers of Jefferson County Schools, 90. **CONTACT ADDRESS** Dept of English, Ohio Wesleyan Univ, 61 S Sandusky St, Delaware, OH, 43015-2398.

LEWIS, CYNTHIA
PERSONAL Born 10/11/1951, Middleton, OH, m, 4 children **DISCIPLINE** ENGLISH **EDUCATION** Ohio State Univ, BA, 74; Harvard Univ, MA, 75, PhD, 80. **CAREER** From asst prof to assoc prof to prof to chemn, 80-, Davidson Col. **HONORS AND AWARDS** Omicron Delta Kappa; Best Tchr Award; CASE; Love of Tchg Award. **MEMBERSHIPS** Shakespeare Asn Am **RESEARCH** Shakespeare in Renaissance drama **SELECTED PUBLICATIONS** Auth, art, Dark Deeds Darkly Answered, 83; auth, art, With Simular Proof Enough, 91; auth, art, Heywood's Gunaikeion and Women-Kind in A Women Killed With Kindness, 94; auth, Particular Saints: Shakespeare's Four Antonios, Their Context and Their Plays, 97. **CONTACT ADDRESS** Dept of Cent English, Davidson Col, PO Box 1719, Davidson, NC, 28036. **EMAIL** cylewis@davidson.edu

LEWIS, GLADYS SHERMAN
PERSONAL Wynnewood, OK, m, 1955, 4 children **DISCIPLINE** LITERATURE **EDUCATION** St Anthony's Sch Nursing, RN, 53; Texas Christian Univ, BA, 56; Cent St Univ, OK, MA, 85; Okla St Univ, PhD, 92; Southwest Baptist Theol Sem, TX, MDiv. **CAREER** Instr, 61-70, Baptist Hosp Sch; tchng asst, 84-85, adj fac, 91, Cent St Univ, OK; adj fac, 86, Okla Christian Univ of Sci & Arts; instr, 91, asst prof, 92-96, assoc prof, 96-, eng dept, Uiv Cent Okla. **HONORS AND AWARDS** Two Thousand Notable Am Women; Who's Who in Am; Who's Who in Am Women; Who's Who in Relig; Who's Who in Am Nursing; Who's Who Med & Healthcare; World's Who's Who of Women; Intl Who's Who of Intellectuals; Intl Authors and Writers; Gladys Lewis Day in Midwest City, 3/18/79; Outstanding Woman of the Yr; Midwest City Pilot Club, 79; Outstanding Grad Stud, Cent St Univ, 85; Pres Excel Tchng Award, Univ Cent Okla, 96-97. **MEMBERSHIPS** AAR; Am Lit Asn; Am Stud Asn; Christianity & Lit; John Bunyan Soc; Harriet Beecher Stowe Soc; Hemingway Soc; Mid Am Am Stud Asn; Modern Lang Asn; Natl Council Tchrs of Eng; Soc of Bibl Lit; S Cent Modern Lang Asn. **RESEARCH** Middle English & 16th century British; 17th - 19th Century American; 19th Century British fiction. **SELECTED PUBLICATIONS** Auth, Message, Messenger, and Response: Puritan Forms and Cultural Reformation in Harriet Beecher Stowe's Uncle Tom's Cabin, UPA, 94; auth, See the Multitudes Reap the Harvest, Okla St Missions Week of Prayer, 92; auth, Declare Hope, Natl Missions Week of Prayer, 92. **CONTACT ADDRESS** 2220 NE 131st St, Edmond, OK, 73013-5728. **EMAIL** GSLPHD@aol.com

LEWIS, JANE ELIZABETH
PERSONAL Born 08/24/1961, Kansas City, MO, m, 1998 **DISCIPLINE** ENGLISH **EDUCATION** Univ Colo, BA, 83; Col Wm & Mary, MA, 84; Princeton Univ, PhD, 88. **CAREER** Asst prof, 88-94, ASSOC PROF, ENG, 94-, UNIV CALIF, LOS ANGELES. **HONORS AND AWARDS** NEH summer stipend, 90; NEH fel, 97-98; ACLS fel, 90; Univ Calif Pres fel, 90., Ed bd, journalx **MEMBERSHIPS** Mod Lang Asn; Am Soc 18th cent Stud. **RESEARCH** 18th cent Br lit; lit & hist. **SELECTED PUBLICATIONS** Auth, The English Fable: Aesop and Literary Culture, 1651- 1740, Cambridge Univ Press, 96; auth, The Trial of Mary Queen of Scots, Bedford, 98; auth, Mary Queen of Scots: Romance and Nation, Routledge, 98. **CONTACT ADDRESS** Dept of English, Univ of California, Los Angeles, Los Angeles, CA, 90095. **EMAIL** jlewis@humnet.ucla.edu

LEWIS, JON
DISCIPLINE FILM STUDIES **EDUCATION** Hobard Col, BA, 77; SUNY, MFA, 79, UCLA, PhD, 83. **CAREER** Engl, Oregon St Univ. **SELECTED PUBLICATIONS** Auth, Punks in L.A.: It's Kiss or Kill, Jour Popular Cult, 88; Voices From a Steeltown: Tony Buba's Lightning Over Braddock Aferimage, 89; The Road to Romance and Ruin: Teen Films and Youth Culture, Routledge, 92; The Crisis of Authority in Francis Coppola's Rumble Fish, in Crisis Cinema, Maisonneuve Press, 92; Disney After Disney: From Family Business to the Business of Family, in Disney Discourses, Routledge ,94; Whom God Wishes to Destroy... Francis Coppola and The New Hollywood Duke Univ Press, 95; The New American Cinema, Duke Univ Press, 98. **CONTACT ADDRESS** Oregon State Univ, Corvallis, OR, 97331-4501. **EMAIL** jlewis@orst.edu

LEWIS, LISA
DISCIPLINE CREATIVE WRITING & POETRY **EDUCATION** Univ Houstin, PhD, 93. **CAREER** Engl, Okla St Univ. **HONORS AND AWARDS** Univ Wis Press' Brittingham Prize Poetry; Jessica Nobel Maxwell prize; Lynda Hull Memorial prize; Best Am Poetry, The Pushcart Prize anthology. **SELECTED PUBLICATIONS** Auth, The Unbeliever; Silent Treatment, Viking/Pelikan, 98. **CONTACT ADDRESS** Oklahoma State Univ, 101 Whitehurst Hall, Stillwater, OK, 74078.

LEWIS, NATHANIEL
DISCIPLINE AMERICAN LITERATURE AND IMAGES OF THE WEST **EDUCATION** Harvard Univ, PhD. **CAREER** Eng, St. Michaels Col. **SELECTED PUBLICATIONS** Area: cult of the Am West. **CONTACT ADDRESS** St. Michael's Col, Winooski Park, Colchester, VT, 05439. **EMAIL** nlewis@smcvt.edu

LEWIS, ROBERT WILLIAM
PERSONAL Born 12/15/1930, Elrama, PA, m, 1955, 2 children **DISCIPLINE** ENGLISH **EDUCATION** Univ Pittsburgh, BA, 52; Columbia Univ, MA, 58; Univ Ill, PhD, 63. **CAREER** Asst, Columbia Univ, 55; instr English, Univ Nebr, 55-58; asst, Univ Ill, 58-63; from instr to asst prof, Univ Tex, Austin, 63-69; chmn dept, 69-78, 96-99, assoc prof, 69-71, Prof English, 71-, Univ North Dak; asst ed, Abstr English Studies, 65-66; coordr Peace Corps, Univ Tex, 65-67; Fulbright-Hays lectr, Italy, 67-68; consult, Nat Endowment for Humanities, 71-77; res prof, Univ NDak, 71; vis prof Am studies & Fulbright-Hays lectr, Ain Shams Univ, Cairo, 75-76; vis prof English, Am Univ in Cairo, 75-76. **MEMBERSHIPS** MLA; NCTE; Aaup; Hemingway Soc. **RESEARCH** American literature; literary criticism; American Indian literature. **SELECTED PUBLICATIONS** Art, Hemingway in Italy: Making It Up, J Mod Lit, 4/82; ed, Hemingway in Italy and Other Essays, Praeger, 90; auth, A Farewell to Arms: The War of the Words, Twayne, 92. **CONTACT ADDRESS** Dept of English, Univ of NDak, PO Box 7209, Grand Forks, ND, 58202-7209. **EMAIL** rolewis@badlands.nodak.edu

LEWIS, THOMAS SPOTTSWOOD WELLFORD
PERSONAL Born 05/29/1942, Philadelphia, PA, m, 1964, 1 child **DISCIPLINE** ENGLISH & AMERICAN LITERATURE **EDUCATION** Univ New Brunswick, CAN, BA, 64; Columbia Univ, MA(honors), 65, PhD, 70. **CAREER** Instr English, Iona Col, 67; res asst English, Columbia Univ, 67-68; from instr to asst prof, 68-75, assoc prof English, 75-82, PROF, SKIDMORE COL, 83-; Am Philos Soc res grant, 71 & 75; NY Coun for Humanities grant, 77, 87; dir, Brooklyn Bridge and Am Cult Symposium, 77; CONSULT, FLORENTINE FILMS, 78-; NEH grants, 85, 86, 89, 93, 95-96, 97; Corp for Public Broadcasting grant, 89; various grants for The Empire of the Air radio prog, private donor, WETA, Wash, 88, General Motors, 90, 91, Am Public Radio, 90; support, WETA, 92; OR Coun for the Humanities grant, 93; TX Coun for the Humanities grant, 93; Arthur Vining Davis Found grant, 95-96. **HONORS AND AWARDS** Fac fel, Columbia Univ, 64-68; Paul Klingenstein fel, Columbia Univ, 65-66; Woodrow Wilson Dissertation fel, 68; Skidmore Col Fac Res Lect, 85; W. C. D. Pacey Lect, Univ New Brunswick, 90; Harry Houck Award, Antique Radio Club of Am, 92; fel, Radio Club of Am, 92; Marconi Award, Veteran Wireless Operators Asn, 92; Divided Highways film, 98: George Foster Peabody Award; Best Documentary, New England Film Festival; Bronze Apple, Nat Ed Asn; honorable mention, San Francisco Film Festival & Chicago Film Festival. **MEMBERSHIPS** MLA. **RESEARCH** Biography; modern British and American literature; literature and technology. **SELECTED PUBLICATIONS** Auth, Hart Crane and His Mother: A Correspondence, Salmagundi, no 9, spring 69; Some new letters of John Butler Yeats, in Modern Irish Literature, Twayne, 72; The Letters of Hart Crane and His Family, Columbia Univ Press, 74; ed, Virginia Woolf: A Collection of Criticism, McGraw-Hill, 75; auth, The Brooklyn Bridge: Lewis Mumford and Hart Crane, Hart Crane Newlett, 4/78; Lewis Mumford and the Academy, Salmagundi, 80; Homeric Epic and the Greek Vase, in The Greek Vase, Hudson-Mohawk Asn Cols & Univs, 81; The Brothers of Ganymede, Salmagundi, 82; Virginia Woolf and the Sense of the Past, Salmagundi, no 68-69, 85-86; Radio Revolutionary: Edwin Howard Armstrong's Invention of FM Radio, Am Heritage of Invention and Technology, fall 85, reprinted, Skidmore Voices, fall 86; To Do, To Be, To Suffer: The Memoirs of Ulysses S. Grant, Saratoga Springs, Skidmore Col Fac Res Lect, 87; Rudolph Arnheim's Snippets and Seeds, Salmagundi, no 78-79, spring/summer 88; Rev of Ruth Hoberman, Modernizing Lives: Experiments in English Biography, vol 11, no 3, summer 88; Empire of the Air: The Men Who Made Radio, NY, Harper/Burlingame Books, 91; A Godlike Presence: The Impact of Radio on the Nineteen Twenties and Thirties, Magazine of History, vol 6, no 4, spring 92; Triumph of the Idol - Rush Limbaugh and a Hot Medium, Media Studies J, vol 7, no 3, summer 93; Divided Highways: The Interstate Highway System and the Transformation of American Life, NY, Viking Books, 97; various positions on several films and radio broadcasts. **CONTACT ADDRESS** Dept of English, Skidmore Col, 815 N Broadway, Saratoga Springs, NY, 12866-1698.

LEWIS, TODD VERNON
PERSONAL Born 01/12/1949, Lynwood, CA, m **DISCIPLINE** SPEECH COMMUNICATION **EDUCATION** Biola Univ, BA, 72; Ohio State Univ, MA, 74; Louisiana State Univ, PhD, 80. **CAREER** Teaching asst speech, Ohio State Univ, Columbus, 73-74; teaching asst, Louisiana State Univ, Baton Rouge, 77-78; prof & chm, commun, Biola Univ, La Mirada, Calif, 74-. **HONORS AND AWARDS** AFA-NIET Distinguished Serv Award, 90 **MEMBERSHIPS** Speech Commun Assn; Am Forensics Assn; Relig Speech Commun Assn; Nat Forensics Assn. **RESEARCH** Religious communication (rhetoric); readers theatre; forensics; film history. **SELECTED PUBLICATIONS** Auth, Communicating Literature, 3rd ed, Kendall/Hunt Pub co, 99. **CONTACT ADDRESS** Dept of Communication, Biola Univ, 13800 Biola Ave, La Mirada, CA, 90639-0001. **EMAIL** todd_lewis@peter.biola.edu

LEYASMEYER, ARCHIBALD I
PERSONAL Born 12/15/1935, Riga, Latvia, m, 1964 **DISCIPLINE** ENGLISH **EDUCATION** Harvard Univ, BA, 57; Eastern Baptist Theol Sem, Mre, 60; Princeton Univ, MA, 64, PhD(-English), 67. **CAREER** From instr to asst prof, 64-68, Morse-Alumni Dist Tchg Prof, 96-, Faculty Dir, 79, Assoc Prof English, Univ Minn, Minneapolis, 68-, Fac Dir, Univ Without Walls, 79-, Morse-Amoco Award, 82. **HONORS AND AWARDS** Danforth Assoc, Gordon L. Starr Awd, Univ Col Disting Tchg Awd, Ruth Christie Tchg Awd. **MEMBERSHIPS** Asn Eighteenth Century Studies; Asn Advan Baltic Studies; Johnsonian Soc; MLA. **RESEARCH** Modern drama; eighteenth century; satire. **CONTACT ADDRESS** Dept of English, Univ of Minn, 207 Church St S E, Minneapolis, MN, 55455-0156. **EMAIL** leyas002Wtc.umn.edu

LHAMON, W.T.
DISCIPLINE ENGLISH **EDUCATION** Johns Hopkins Univ, BA, 66; Univ Ind, PhD, 73. **CAREER** PROF, ENG, FLA STATE UNIV **MEMBERSHIPS** Am Antiquarian Soc **CONTACT ADDRESS** Dept of Eng, Florida State Univ, Tallahassee, FL, 32306-1036.

LIBERMAN, TERRI
PERSONAL Brooklyn, NY **DISCIPLINE** AMERICAN AND MODERN LITERATURE **EDUCATION** William Smith Col, BA, 64; Purdue Univ, MA, 66; Case Western Reserve Univ, PhD(English), 76. **CAREER** Instr English, Col Wooster, 66-68; Asst Prof English, Norwich Univ, 76- **MEMBERSHIPS** MLA; Pop Culture Asn; Phi Beta Kappa. **RESEARCH** Contemporary literature; women's studies; popular culture. **CONTACT ADDRESS** Dept of English, Norwich Univ, 65 S Main St, Northfield, VT, 05663-1035.

LICKONA, THOMAS E.
PERSONAL Born 04/04/1943, Poughkeepsie, NY, m, 1966, 2 children **DISCIPLINE** ENGLISH, PSYCHOLOGY **EDUCATION** Siena Col, BA, 64; Ohio Univ, MA, 65' State Univ NY, Albany, PhD, 71. **CAREER** PROF, EDUC, STATE UNIV NY, CORTLAND, 70-; vis prof, Harvard Univ, Boston Univ, 78-79; DIR, CTR 4TH, 5TH R'S, STATE UNIV NY, CORTLAND, 94-. **MEMBERSHIPS** Character Education Partnership; Nat Asn Scholars; Soc of Cath Soc Scientists. **RESEARCH** Moral development, character education. **SELECTED PUBLICATIONS** Moral Development and Behavior, 76; Raising Good Children, 83; Educating for Character: How Our Schools Can Teach Respect and Responsibility, 91; Character Development in Schools and Beyond, 92; Sex, Love, and You: Making the Right Decision, 94. **CONTACT ADDRESS** Educ Dept, SUNY, Cortland, Cortland, NY, 13045. **EMAIL** C4n5RS@Cortland.edu

LIDDELL, JANICE LEE
DISCIPLINE ENGLISH LITERATURE **EDUCATION** Univ Mich, MA and PhD. **CAREER** Chp Dept Eng. **RESEARCH** African women's literature, particularly African American and Caribbean. **SELECTED PUBLICATIONS** Auth, Imani: and the Flying Africans; various children's books. **CONTACT ADDRESS** Clark Atlanta Univ, 223 James P Brawley Dr, SW, Atlanta, GA, 30314.

LIEBERMAN, LAURENCE
PERSONAL Born 02/16/1935, Detroit, MI, m, 1956, 3 children **DISCIPLINE** ENGLISH, MODERN POETRY **EDUCATION** Univ Mich, BA, 56, MA, 58. **CAREER** Instr English, Orange Coast Col, 60-64; from asst prof to assoc prof, Col Virgin Islands, 64-68; assoc prof, 68-70, Prof English, Univ Ill, Urbana, 70-; consult & poetry ed, Univ Ill Press, 70-; poetry reviewer, Yale Rev, 71-75. **HONORS AND AWARDS** Major Hopwood Award poetry writing, 58; Fel, Yaddo, NY, 63 & 67; Huntington-Hartford Found fel, 64; Nat Endowment for Arts Award for poem, 67; assoc fel, Univ Ill Ctr Advan Study, Japan & Hawaii, 71-72; Ill Arts Coun Proj Completion grant, 80, writing fel, 82-83; NEH Fel, 86; Jerome Shestack Award, Am Poetry Rev, 86. **MEMBERSHIPS** MLA. **RESEARCH** Contemporary American poetry; poetry criticism. **SELECTED PUBLICATIONS** Auth, The Osprey Suicides (a volume of poems), Macmillan & Collier, 73; The Osprey Suicides (poem), New Yorker, 11/72; Whispers out of time: A reading of John Ashbery's Self-Portrait in a Convex Mirror, Am Poetry Rev, 5/77; Unassigned Frequencies: American Poetry in Review (1964-77), Univ Ill, 12/77; Joren: The Volcanic Falls, a long poem, Hudson Rev, winter 77-78; Sea Caves of Dogashima, a long poem, Am Poetry, fall 78; God's Measurements (a volume of poems), 80 & Eros at the World Kite Pageant: Poems (1979-82), 82, MacMillan; The Mural of Wakeful Sleep, poems, Macmillan, 85; The Creole Mephistopheles, Macmillan, 89; New and Selected Poems, Univ Ill Press, 93; The St. Kitts Monkey Feuds, book-length poem, The Cummington Press, 95; Beyond the Muse of Memory: Essays on Contemporary American Poets, Univ Mo Press, 95; Dark Songs: Slave House and Synagogue, Univ Ark Press, 96; Compass of the Dying, Univ Ark Press, 98; The Regatta in the Skies: Selected Poems, Univ Ga Press, 98. **CONTACT ADDRESS** Dept of English, Univ Ill, 608 S Wright St, Urbana, IL, 61801-3613.

LIEPE-LEVINSON, KATHERINE
DISCIPLINE THEATER-ACADEMIC AND PRACTICAL **EDUCATION** Empire State Col, BA, 84; Hunter Col, MA, 86; CUNY, PhD, 93. **CAREER** Art dir, Terra Firma Studiotheatre; dir, Synergy Performance Group; instr, Hunter Col, Empire State Col; vis asst prof, 93. **HONORS AND AWARDS** Arts grants, NY State Coun; grant, NYSCA; John Golden playwriting award, Hunter Col. **SELECTED PUBLICATIONS** Auth, Aphrodite's Last Visit: A Period Piece, Twenty-three Plays from the New Play Development Workshop, Miss State UP, 94; Multiple Perspectives in Motion, Peer Helping: The Vision, The Mission, MIT Press, 93; rev(s), Biomechanics: Meyerhold's System of Movement Training, Taking the Myster out of Sensory Technique, Theatre Service, 94. **CONTACT ADDRESS** Dept of Eng, Colgate Univ, 13 Oak Drive, Hamilton, NY, 13346.

LIGGETT, SARAH
DISCIPLINE WRITING AND THE TEACHING OF WRITING INCLUDING THEORY, PEDAGOGY, AND ASSESSM **EDUCATION** Purdue Univ, PhD, 82. **CAREER** Prof, La State Univ. **HONORS AND AWARDS** Phi Beta Kappa; NCTE Award, Comput & Composing, 86. **RESEARCH** Technical writing; research methodology in composition and writing pedagogy. **SELECTED PUBLICATIONS** Auth, Preventing Meltdown: Licensee Event Reports in the Nuclear Energy Industry, Stud in Tech Commun, 90; Creativity and Non-Literary Writing: The Importance of Problem Finding, J of Tchg Writing, 91; coauth, Computers & Composing: How the New Technologies Are Changing Writing, 84; Power Relations, Technical Writing Theory, and Workplace Writing, J of Bus and Tech Commun, 93; Changing Institutions, Changing Teachers, ADE Bull, 96. **CONTACT ADDRESS** Dept of Eng, Louisiana State Univ, 219A Allen Hall, Baton Rouge, LA, 70803. **EMAIL** enligg@unix1.sncc.lsu.edu

LIGHTFOOT, JEAN HARVEY
PERSONAL Born 11/29/1935, Chicago, IL, d **DISCIPLINE** ENGLISH **EDUCATION** Fisk Univ, BA 1957; Univ of Chgo, MA 1969; Northwestern Univ Evanston IL, PhD 1974. **CAREER** Chicago Public Schools, English teacher 1957-69; Kennedy King Campus Chicago City Coll, prof English 1969-; Citizens Comm on Public Educ, exec dir 1975-76; Comm on Urban Affair Spec Projects AME Church, exec dir 1978-80; The Neighborhood Inst, educ coordinator 1979-. **HONORS AND AWARDS** Outstanding Young Women of Amer 1968; Ford Fellowship Univ of Chicago 1968-69; TTT Fellowship Northwestern Univ 1972-73. **MEMBERSHIPS** Counselor Hillcrest Ctr for Children NY 1958-61; asst prof ed Northeastern Univ Chicago 1974-76; consult Prescription Learning Inc 1977-; featured soloist Park Manor Cong Church 1958-, John W Work Chorale 1959-; staff dir, convener The S Shore Schools Alliance 1979-80. **CONTACT ADDRESS** Education Coordinator, The Neighborhood Inst, 1950 E 71st St, Chicago, IL, 60649.

LIGHTFOOT, MARJORIE JEAN
PERSONAL Born 04/24/1933, Oak Park, IL **DISCIPLINE** CONTEMPORARY ENGLISH, AMERICAN LITERATURE **EDUCATION** Brown Univ, AB, 55; Northwestern Univ, MA, 56, PhD(English), 64. **CAREER** Instr freshman English, Univ Ariz, 60-63, asst prof Am lit & humanities, 64-69, assoc prof English, 69-74, Prof English, Ariz State Univ, 74- **MEMBERSHIPS** MLA; Rocky Mountain Mod Lang Asn; Western Humor & Irony; WestCent Mod Lang Asn. **RESEARCH** Twentieth century British and American literature; Chaucer and the Bronte's; 20th century women authors. **SELECTED PUBLICATIONS** Auth, Prosody and Performance, Quart J Speech, 2/67; The Uncommon Cocktail Party, Mod Drama, 2/69; Numerical Sequential and Temporal Patterns in English Verse, Quart J Speech, 4/71; Description and Transcription of Temporal Patterns of Rhythm in English Verse, summer 74 & Temporal Prosody, fall 74, Lang & Style; Breakthrough in Doris Lessing's The Golden Notebook, Studies in the Novel, summer 75; Fiction vs Reality: Clues and Conclusions in The Golden Notebook, Mod Brit Lit, fall 77; Geoffrey Chaucer's Troilus and Criseyde: A Dramatic Adaptation and Translation of the Poem, 2nd ed, 1/78; Glimpses of the Brontes: A Biography on Stage, privately publ, 79, 2nd ed, 80. **CONTACT ADDRESS** Dept of English, Arizona State Univ, Tempe, PO Box 870302, Tempe, AZ, 85287-0302.

LIKES, TERRY
PERSONAL m **DISCIPLINE** BROADCAST JOURNALISM **EDUCATION** Maryville Univ, St. Louis BA 88; W Ky Univ, MA, 88; Univ Ky, PhD, 96. **CAREER** Asst prof, Western Ky Univ, 88-; TV sports announcer, broadcast consult, 88-. **HONORS AND AWARDS** Ky Press award for news coverage, 86, 87. **RESEARCH** News reporting, Radio/TV performance, writing; producing/directing Western News for WKYU-TV. **SELECTED PUBLICATIONS** Areas: Radio and Television **CONTACT ADDRESS** Western Kentucky Univ, 1526 Big Red Way Street, Bowling Green, KY, 42101. **EMAIL** terry.likes@wku.edu

LILLY JR., PAUL R.
DISCIPLINE ENGLISH **EDUCATION** Holy Cross Col, BA; Boston Col, MA; Fordham Univ, PhD. **CAREER** Dept Eng, SUNY Col at Oneonta **HONORS AND AWARDS** Fulbright Lectureship, Spain 73-75, Belgium 85-86, India 95; fellow, NEH; 78-79; NEH Summer Inst, 95; SUNY res grant. **RESEARCH** Contemp and mod Am fiction, the Am Renaissance, and Am humor. **SELECTED PUBLICATIONS** Auth, Words in Search of Victims: The Achievement of Jerzy Kosinski, Kent State UP, 88; articles on William Faulkner, Richard Bausch, Elizabeth Tallent, Mary Gordon, John Updike, Jerzy Kosinski, 19th century humorists Augustus Baldwin Longstreet, William Tappan Thompson, Petroleum V. Nasby, and others. **CONTACT ADDRESS** SUNY Col at Oneonta, 304 Fine Arts Bldg, Oneonta, NY, 13820. **EMAIL** maniscsj@oneonta.edu

LIMBACHER, JAMES L.
PERSONAL Born 11/30/1926, St. Marys, OH **DISCIPLINE** DRAMA, FILM **EDUCATION** Bowling Green State Univ, BA, 49, MA, 54; Ind Univ, MS, 55; Wayne State Univ, MS in LS, 72. **CAREER** Mem Audio-Visual Div, Dearborn Dept Libr, 55-; INSTR FILM HIST, WAYNE STATE UNIV, 73-. **MEMBERSHIPS** Am Fed Film Soc (pres, 62-65); Educ Film Libr Asn (pres, 66-69); Soc Cinema Studies. **RESEARCH** History and appreciation of the motion picture; audio-visual media. **SELECTED PUBLICATIONS** Auth, Lulu in Berlin, J Popular Film and Television, Vol 0020, 92; Almonds and Raisins, J Popular Film and Television, Vol 0020, 92; Pioneers of the French Cinema, Vol 1, J Popular Film and Television, Vol 0020, 92; Dead of Night, J Popular Film and Television, Vol 0020, 92; The 'Whales of August', J Popular Film and Television, Vol 0022, 94; 'Orphans of the Storm', J Popular Film and Television, Vol 0022, 94; 'Indianapolis--Ship of Doom', J Popular Film and Television, Vol 0022, 94; Grey Gardens, J Popular Film and Television, Vol 0022, 94; 'Dizzy Gillespie--a Night in Tunisia', J Popular Film and Television, Vol 0022, 94; The 'Patti Page Songbook', J Popular Film and Television, Vol 0022, 94; Color Adjustment, J Popular Film and Television, Vol 0022, 94; Night of the Hunter, J Popular Film and Television, Vol 0022, 94; The 'Man You Loved to Hate', J Popular Film and Television, Vol 0022, 94; The 'Origins of American Films', J Popular Film and Television, Vol 0023, 95. **CONTACT ADDRESS** 21800 Morley Ave, Dearborn, MI, 48124.

LIMON, JOHN
DISCIPLINE ENGLISH **EDUCATION** Harvard Univ, BA, 73; Univ Calif Berkeley, PhD, 81. **CAREER** Prof & ch, Amer Stud. **RESEARCH** American Literature and the history and philosophy of science and of war; stand-up comedy. **SELECTED PUBLICATIONS** Auth, The Place of Fiction in the Time of Science, Writing After War, Journey to the End of Night: David Letterman and Celine, Kristeva, Scorsese. **CONTACT ADDRESS** Dept of English, Williams Col, Stetson d-16, Williamstown, MA, 01267. **EMAIL** jlimon@williams.edu

LIN, CAROLYN
DISCIPLINE ADVERTISING, MASS COM THEORY, TELECOMMUNICATIONS **EDUCATION** Nat Cent Univ, BA; IA State Univ, MS; MI State Univ, PhD. **CAREER** Grad prog dir, Cleveland State Univ. **SELECTED PUBLICATIONS** Auth, Network Prime-Time Programming Strategies in the 80's, Jour Broadcasting & Electronic Media, 95; Audience Fragmentation in a Competitive Video Marketplace, Jour Advt Res, 94. **CONTACT ADDRESS** Commun Dept, Cleveland State Univ, 83 E 24th St, Cleveland, OH, 44115. **EMAIL** c.a.lin@csuohio.edu

LINCOLN, KENNETH
PERSONAL Born 07/22/1943, Lubbock, TX, 1 child **DISCIPLINE** ENGLISH LITERATURE **EDUCATION** Stanford Univ, BA, 65; Indiana Univ, MA, 67, PhD, 69. **CAREER** Prof English and American Indian Studies, UCLA, 69- . **HONORS AND AWARDS** Fulbright res and lectr, Italy, 84; delegate, Sino-American Writers' Conf, China, 88; Professore Contratto, Univ Piza, 90, Univ Florence, 93, Univ Rome, 97; Distinguished tchg award, 91; Rockefeller res, Bellagio, Italy, 92; USIS German lect tour, 93. **RESEARCH** Native American studies; modern poetry. **SELECTED PUBLICATIONS** Auth, Indi'n Humor: Bicultural Play in Native America, Oxford, 93; auth, Men Down West, Capra, 97; auth, A Writer's China: Bridges East & West, Capra, 99; auth, Sing with the Heart of a Bear: Fusions of Native and American Poetry 1890-1999, California, 99. **CONTACT ADDRESS** Dept of English, Univ of California, Los Angeles, 405 Hilgard Ave, Los Angeles, CA, 90095-1530. **EMAIL** lincoln@humnet.ucla.edu

LINDAHL, CARL
PERSONAL Born 12/02/1947, Boston, MA **DISCIPLINE** FOLKLORE, ENGLISH, MEDIEVAL STUDIES **EDUCATION** Harvard Univ, BA, 71; Indiana Univ, Bloomington, MA, 76, PhD, 80. **CAREER** Asst prof, 80-86, assoc prof, 86-97, prof, 97- , English Dept, Univ Houston. **HONORS AND AWARDS** Magna Cum Laude, 71; fel, Am Coun Learned Soc, 83; tchg excellence awd, 93; Alcee Fortier Awd, Am Folklore Soc, 96; fel, Virginia Found for Hum, 97; Lib of Cong Parsons Grant, 98., Founder and ed, World Folktale Library, Garland and Univ Pr Miss; editorial bd, Folklore; dist ed bd, Medieval Folklore. **MEMBERSHIPS** Am Folklore Soc; Folklore Soc, London; Int Soc for Contemp Legend Res; Int Soc for Folk Narrative Res; New Chaucer Soc; Nordic Inst of Folklore, **RESEARCH** Folk narrative; medieval literature; medieval folklore; American folklore. **SELECTED PUBLICATIONS** Auth, Earnest Games: Folkloric Patterns in the Cantebury Tales, Indiana, 87; auth, Jacks: the Name, the Tales, the American Traditions, in Jack in Two Worlds, Univ NC Pr, 94; auth, the Oral Undertones of Late Medieval Romance, in Oral Tradition in the Middle Ages, Medival and Renaissance Texts Series, 95; auth, Bakhtin's Carnival Laughter and The Cajun Country Mardi Gras, in Folklore, 96; auth, the Presence of the Past in the Cajun Country Mardi Gras, in J of Folklore Res, 96; auth, Some Uses of Numbers, in J of Folklore Res, 97; auth, the Oral Aesthetic and the Bicameral Mind, in Gilgamesh: A Reader, Bolchazy-Carducci, 97; auth, the Power of Being Outnumbered, in La Folklore Miscellany, 97; auth, Chaucer and the Shape of Performance, in Critical Essays on Geoffrey Chaucer, GK Hall, 98; auth, Sir Gawain and the Green Knight, Robert Burns's 'Halloween,' and Myth in its Time, in telling Tales, Medieval Narratives and the Folk Tradition, St Martins, 98; ed, Outlaws and Other Medieval Heroes, Southern Folklore, 96; co-ed, Swapping Stories: Folktales from Louisiana, Mississippi, 97; co-auth, Cajun Mardi Gras Masks, Mississippi, 97. **CONTACT ADDRESS** Dept of English, Univ of Houston, Houston, TX, 77204-3012. **EMAIL** clindahl@uh.edu

LINDEN, STANTON J.
DISCIPLINE MILTON AND SEVENTEENTH-CENTURY NONDRAMATIC LITERATURE **EDUCATION** Univ Minn, PhD. **CAREER** Prof, Washington State Univ. **RESEARCH** 15th-century alchemist George Ripley and the Ripley Scrolls. **SELECTED PUBLICATIONS** Auth, Darke Hierogliphicks: Alchemy in English Literature from Chaucer to the Restoration, 96; ed, William Cooper's A Catalogue of Chymicall Books, 1673-88, 87 & The Mirror of Alchemy, attributed to Roger Bacon, 92; gen ed, rep series English Renaissance Hermeticism & ed, Cauda Pavonis: Studies in Hermeticism. **CONTACT ADDRESS** Dept of English, Washington State Univ, 1 SE Stadium Way, PO Box 645020, Pullman, WA, 99164-5020. **EMAIL** linden@wsu.edu

LINDER, LAURA R.
PERSONAL Born 07/13/1954, Albuquerque, NM, m, 1991, 1 child **DISCIPLINE** MASS COMMUNICATION **EDUCATION** Univ of NC, PhD, 97. **CAREER** Asst prof, Univ of NC. **MEMBERSHIPS** NCA; ICA; UFVA; BEA; IRTS; ACM; ACJMC; AAUP; AAUW; RTWOA. **RESEARCH** Public access television; Situation comedies. **SELECTED PUBLICATIONS** Auth, Now on the Net, Tune-In, fall, 95; Video User's Guide for Mass Communication, 96; Thomas Edison, The Hist of Mass Media in the United States: An Encycl, ed M.A. Blanchard, 98; Radio Corporation of America, The Hist of Mass Media in the U.S.: An Encycl, ed M.A. Blanchard, 98; Community Access Television, The Hist of Mass Media in the U.S.: An Encycl, ed M.A. Blanchard, 98. **CONTACT ADDRESS** Dept of Communication, Univ of No Carolina, 100 Carmichael Dorm, PO Box 26170, Greensbboro, NC, 27402-6170. **EMAIL** lrlinder@uncg.edu

LINDNER, CARL MARTIN
DISCIPLINE AMERICAN LITERATURE AND CULTURE **EDUCATION** Univ WI-Madison, PhD. **CAREER** Prof, Univ of WI, Parkside. **HONORS AND AWARDS** UW-Parkside Awd, Exellence in Res and Creative Act 96; Univ WI Regents Tchg Exellence Awd, 92; Stella C Gray Distinguished Tchg Awd, 90-91; Ragdale Found fel, 90; WI Arts Bd Creative Writ-

ing fel for Poetry, 80; Standard Oil Distinguished Tchr Awd, 69-70. **SELECTED PUBLICATIONS** Essays on, lit; publ approx 200 poems in var lit jour, 2 chapbks of poetry, Vampire & The Only Game; bk of poetry, Shooting Baskets in a Dark Gymnasium. **CONTACT ADDRESS** Dept of Eng, Univ of Wisconsin, Parkside, 900 Wood Rd, 218 Commun, PO Box 2000, Kenosha, WI, 53141-2000. **EMAIL** lindner@uwp.edu

LINDSAY, STAN A.
PERSONAL Born 12/09/1949, Canton, IL, m, 1970, 4 children **DISCIPLINE** RHETORIC **CAREER** Lectr and vis instr, Purdue Univ, 87-98; vis lectr, Indiana Univ, 97-98; instr, Loyola Univ-Chicago, 98-. **MEMBERSHIPS** Nat Commun Asn; Rhetoric Soc Am; Kenneth Burke Soc; Cent States Commun Asn; Am Acad Relig; Soc Bibl Lit. **RESEARCH** Exploring the implications of Kenneth Burkes concept of entelechy. **SELECTED PUBLICATIONS** Auth Prayer as Proto-Rhetoric, The Jour of Commun and Relig, 97; Implicit Rhetoric: Kenneth Burkes Extension of Aristotles Concept of Entelchy, Univ Press Am, 98; The Twenty-One Sales in a Sale, Oasis Books, 98. **CONTACT ADDRESS** PO Box 2421, West Lafayette, IN, 47906. **EMAIL** slindsa@luc.edu

LINDSKOLD, JANE M.
PERSONAL Born 09/15/1962, Washington, DC, m, 1997 **DISCIPLINE** ENGLISH **EDUCATION** Fordham Univ, BA, 84, MA, 86, PhD, 89. **CAREER** Teaching Fel, 86-88, Adj Prof, Fordham Univ, 88, 89; Vis Asst Prof, 89-91, Asst Prof, Lynchburg Col, 91-94; Full-time author, 94-. **HONORS AND AWARDS** Dean's List, 82-83, 83-84; Henry Luce Fel, 84-85, 85-86; Presidential Fel, 86-87, 87-88. **RESEARCH** Modern British, Medieval, and Renaissance literature; science fiction; mythology; drama; composition and computers. **SELECTED PUBLICATIONS** Auth, Brother to Dragons, Companion to Owls, AvoNova, 94; Marks of Our Brothers, AvoNova, 95; Pipes of Orpheus, AvoNova, 95; Chronomaster (authored the novel, computer game, and strategy guide), Prima, 96; Smoke and Mirrors, AvoNova, 96; When the Gods Are Silent, AvoNova, 96; coauth, Donnerjack, AvoNova, 97; auth, Changer, Avon Eos, 98; coauth, Lord Demon, Avon Eos (forthcoming 99); auth, Changer's Daughter, Avon Eos (forthcoming); author of numerous other publications. **CONTACT ADDRESS** 3900 75th St. NW, Albuquerque, NM, 87120.

LING, CHEN
DISCIPLINE COMMUNICATION **EDUCATION** Oh State Univ, PhD, 91. **CAREER** Asst prof, Univ Okla, 91-97; assoc prof, Hong Kong Bapt Univ, 97-. **MEMBERSHIPS** Intl Comm Asn; Nat Comm Asn; Asn for Chinese Comm Studies. **RESEARCH** International communication; Language and social interaction; Interpersonal communication; Organizational communication. **SELECTED PUBLICATIONS** Auth, Verbal Adaptive Strategies in US American Dyadic Conversations with US American or East-Asian Partners, Comm Monogr, 64, 302-323, 97; co-auth, Managerial Emotionality in Chinese Factories, Mgmt Comm Quart, 11, 6-50, 97; co-auth, Approaches to Managerial Influences in the People's Republic of China, Jour of Bus Comm, 34, 289-315, 97; auth, Cognitive Complexity and Situational Influences on Topic Selection in Intracultural and Intercultural Interactions, Comm Reports, 9, 1-12, 96; auth, Interaction Involvement and Patterns of Topical Talk: A Comparison of Intercultural and Intracultural Dyads, Intl Jour of Intercultural Relations, 19, 463-482, 95; co-auth, Topic Management, Shared Knowledge and Accommodation: A Study of Communication Adaptability, Res on Lang and Social Interaction, 27, 389-417, 94; co-auth, Intercultural Organizational Communication Research in Multinational Corporations: A Preliminary Agenda, Comm in Multinational Orgn, 12-29, 94; co-auth, Managerial Communication Practices in Chinese Factories: A Preliminary Study, Jour of Bus Comm, 29, 229-252, 92; auth, The Door Opens to a Thousand Blossoms: A Preliminary Study on Communication and Development in Rural China 1979-1988, Asian Jour of Comm, 1, 103-121, 91. **CONTACT ADDRESS** Dept. of Communication Studies, Hong Kong Baptist Univ, 224 Waterloo Rd., Kowloon, .. **EMAIL** chling@hkbu.edu.hk

LINK, FREDERICK M.
PERSONAL Born 09/02/1930, Reno, NV **DISCIPLINE** ENGLISH LITERATURE **EDUCATION** Southwestern at Memphis, AB, 52; Boston Univ, MA, 54, PhD(English), 57. **CAREER** Asst prof English, Boston Univ, 60-63; asst prof, 63-65, assoc prof, 65-68, PROF ENGLISH, UNIV NEBR-LINCOLN, 68-, CHMN DEPT ENGLISH, UNIV NEBR-LINCOLN, 81-. **MEMBERSHIPS** MLA; Midwest Mod Lang Asn; Aaup. **RESEARCH** English drama, 1660-1837; English poetry, 1660-1798. **SELECTED PUBLICATIONS** Auth, Editing Cather, Stud in the Novel, Vol 0027, 95. **CONTACT ADDRESS** Dept of English, Univ of Nebr, Lincoln, NE, 68588.

LINN, WILLIAM JOSEPH
PERSONAL Born 10/10/1943, Pittsburgh, PA, m, 2 children **DISCIPLINE** ENGLISH LITERATURE **EDUCATION** Long Island Univ, BA, 65; Hunter Col, MA, 67; NY Univ, PhD, 70. **CAREER** Lectr Eng, Hunter Col, 70-74; asst prof, Brooklyn Col, City Univ NY, 74-77; coordr, Learning Ctr, Passaic County Community Col, 77-78; Asst Prof Eng & Dir Core Writing Prog, Univ MI, Dearborn, 79-81; assoc prof eng, Univ of MI-Dearborn, 81. **HONORS AND AWARDS** Fulbright lectr, Am lit, Univ of Yaounde (Cameroon), 85; Fulbright lectr, Am lit, Univ of eliko-Turnovo (Bulgaria), 88-90; Fulbright lectr, Am lit, Univ of Ouagadougou (Burkina Fusa), 95-96; Creative Artists Public Service, Grant in Fiction, 79; Michigan Council for the Arts, Grant in Fiction, 84. **RESEARCH** Anglo-Irish lit; Psych of learning. **SELECTED PUBLICATIONS** Auth, The pendulum of power: dynamics within the classroom & Remediation and the remedial process, In: Yearbook (1975) of Improving College and University Teaching; Contrastive approaches: An experiment in pedagogical technique, Col Engl, 10/76; The war veteran's reaction to Conrad's The Tale, Teaching Engl in the 2-year college, fall 77; Creativity and remediation: The nexus of change, Col Engl, 12/77; Psychological variants of success, Col Engl, 4/78; The use of personality and taste in teaching writing, Teaching English in the 2-year college, winter 78; Numbers and Angela II, Col Engl, 1/81; Zen and the art of composing, Teaching Engl in the 2-year college, fall 81; Shamrocks and semicolons, AZ Engl Bull, winter 85; various entries in Dictionary of Irish Literature (orig and rev ed), Greenwood Press, 79 & 96; Missing in Action (novel), Avon Books (USA) and Sphere Books (Gr Brit), 81 & 83; Kambe Hai (novel), Sphere Books (Gr Brit), 87. **CONTACT ADDRESS** Eng Dept, Univ of MI-Dearborn, 4901 Evergreen Rd, Dearborn, MI, 48128-1491. **EMAIL** wjlinn@ca-fl.umd.umich.edu

LINTON, CALVIN DARLINGTON
PERSONAL Born 06/11/1914, Kensington, MD, m **DISCIPLINE** ENGLISH LITERATURE **EDUCATION** George Washington Univ, AB, 35; Johns Hopkins Univ, AM, 39, PhD, 40. **CAREER** From jr instr to instr English, Johns Hopkins Univ, 39-40; prof & head dept, Queens Col, NC, 40-41; from asst dean to assoc dean, 45-57, Prof English, George Washington Univ, 47-, Dean, Columbian Col Arts & Sci, 57-, Consult report writing, Nat Security Agency, US Air Force, US Civil Serv Comn & US Army Chem Corps; comnr, Comn Insts of Higher Educ, Mid States Asn Cols & Sec Schs, 62-71, vchm, 67-71; lectr, Folger Inst Renaissance & 18th Century Studies. **HONORS AND AWARDS** DHumLett, Erskine Col, 95. **MEMBERSHIPS** MLA; Mod Humanities Res Asn, Gt Brit (Am secy, 63-); Eastern Asn Deans; Am Conf Acad Deans. **RESEARCH** Milton; government writing; T S Eliot. **SELECTED PUBLICATIONS** Auth, How to Write Reports: Effective Revenue Writing, US Govt Printing Off, 61; The Bible As Literature, In: The Expositor's Commentary, Zondervan, 74; The Bicentennial Almanac, 75 & The American Almanac, 77, Thomas Nelson; Humor in the Bible, In: The International Standard Bible Encycl, Eerdmans, 82. **CONTACT ADDRESS** 5216 Farrington Rd Westmoreland Hills, Bethesda, MD, 20816.

LINTON, PATRICIA
DISCIPLINE CONTEMPORARY LITERATURE **EDUCATION** Indiana Univ Pa, PhD. **CAREER** Univ Alaska. **SELECTED PUBLICATIONS** Articles: MELUS; Am Indian Lit. **CONTACT ADDRESS** Univ Alaska Anchorage, 3211 Providence Dr., Anchorage, AK, 99508.

LIPKING, LAWRENCE
DISCIPLINE ENGLISH **EDUCATION** Cornell Univ, PhD. **CAREER** Chester D. Tripp prof Humanities, Northwestern Univ. **HONORS AND AWARDS** Christian Gauss Awd, Abandoned Women and Poetic Tradition, 88; William Riley Parker prize, MLA. **SELECTED PUBLICATIONS** Auth, The Ordering of the Arts in Eighteenth-Century England 70; The Life of the Poet: Beginning and Ending Poetic Careers, 81; Samuel Johnson: The Life of an Author, 98; ed; Norton Anthology of English Literature; The Genius of the Shore: Lycidas, Adamastor, and the Poetics of Nationalism. **CONTACT ADDRESS** Dept of English, Northwestern Univ, 1801 Hinman, Evanston, IL, 60208.

LIPS, ROGER C.
DISCIPLINE AMERICAN LITERATURE, WORLD LITERATURE **EDUCATION** Univ Wis, Madison, PhD. **CAREER** Assoc prof, Univ Minn, Duluth. **SELECTED PUBLICATIONS** Auth, Orestes A. Brownson, in American Literary Critics and Scholars,1800-1850, Gale, 87; Francis Fisher Browne, in American Magazine Journalists, 1850-1900. Gale. 89. **CONTACT ADDRESS** Dept of Eng, Univ Minn, Duluth, Duluth, MN, 55812-2496.

LIPSCHULTZ, JEREMY HARRIS
DISCIPLINE COMMUNICATIONS **EDUCATION** Southern Ill Univ, PhD, 90. **CAREER** Assoc prof, 89-, grad prog ch, dept Commun, Univ Nebr, Omaha. **RESEARCH** Broadcast regulation. **SELECTED PUBLICATIONS** Broadcast Indecency: FCC Regulation and the First Amendment, Focal Press, 97. **CONTACT ADDRESS** Univ Nebr, Omaha, Omaha, NE, 68182. **EMAIL** jeremy@cwis.unomaha.edu

LIPSCOMB, DREMA RICHELLE
DISCIPLINE ENGLISH **EDUCATION** Rensselaer Polytech Inst, PhD. **CAREER** Asst prof; taught at, Northern MI Univ, SUNY at Albany & Rensselaer Polytech Inst. **HONORS AND AWARDS** Rockefeller fel. **RESEARCH** Literary studies; rhetorical and cult criticism; African Am feminist theory. **SELECTED PUBLICATIONS** Publ on, rhetorical criticism; discourse and soc; race and writing & African Am feminist theory. **CONTACT ADDRESS** Dept of Eng, Univ of Rochester, 601 Elmwood Ave, Ste. 656, Rochester, NY, 14642. **EMAIL** dbbe@db1.cc.rochester.edu

LISBY, GREGORY C.
DISCIPLINE MASS COMMUNICATION, JOURNALISM **EDUCATION** Auburn Univ, BA; Univ Miss, MA; Univ Tenn, doctorate, 88. **CAREER** Assoc prof, dir, Grad Stud, Ga State Univ; ed bd, Am Jour. **HONORS AND AWARDS** Outstanding Jr Fac Award, Ga State Univ; Henry W Grady Prize for Res in Jour Hist, 90. **MEMBERSHIPS** Past hd, Law Div, Asn for Educ in Jour & Mass Commun. **RESEARCH** Communication law and legal history. **SELECTED PUBLICATIONS** Auth, Mass Communication Law in Georgia, New Forums Press, 95. **CONTACT ADDRESS** Georgia State Univ, Atlanta, GA, 30303. **EMAIL** glisby@gsu.edu

LISTON, WILLIAM THOMAS
PERSONAL Born 10/07/1930, Mt Kisco, NY, m, 1958, 5 children **DISCIPLINE** ENGLISH **EDUCATION** State Univ NY Albany, BA, 57; Univ Ill, MA, 60, PhD, 65. **CAREER** Instr, Univ Ill, 64-65; asst prof, 65-70, assoc prof, 70-80, prof English, Ball State Univ, 80-, dir, Ball State Univ London Ctr, 79-80; exch prof English, Yeungman Univ, Spring 84, Bucknell Univ, 87-88. **MEMBERSHIPS** Shakespeare Asn Am; AAUP; Int Shakespeare Asn; Am Theatre Critics Asn; MLA. **RESEARCH** Shakespeare; drama. **SELECTED PUBLICATIONS** Auth, Her Brother's Keeper, in Southern Humanities Rev, spring 77; Success at Stratford, in Commonweal, 9/77; John Proctor's Playing in The Crucible, in Midwest Quart, summer 79; On Laertes' Advice to Ophelia: Hamlet, I.iii.12-14, in Col Lit 12, 85; Male and Female Created He Them: Sex and Gender in Macbeth, in Col Lit 16, 89; Paradoxical Chastity in a Midsummer Night's Dream, in Univ Dayton Rev 21, 91; Francis Quarles' Divine Fancies: A Critical Edition, Garland, 92; Not Just Personal: Platonism in The Great Gatsby, in The Midwest Quart 35, 94; Paraphrasing Shakespeare, in Teaching Shakespeare Into the Twenty-First Century, Ohio Univ Press, 97; Shakespeare's Plays in Performance from 1970, Appendix B, in The Riverside Shakespeare, Houghton Mifflin, 2nd ed, 97. **CONTACT ADDRESS** Dept of English, Ball State Univ, Muncie, IN, 47306-0460. **EMAIL** 00wtliston@bsu.edu

LITTLE, ANNE COLCLOUGH
PERSONAL Born 08/04/1944, Florence, SC, m, 1965, 2 children **DISCIPLINE** ENGLISH **EDUCATION** Univ So Carolina, BA, 65; Auburn Univ, MA, 80; Univ So Carolina, PhD, 89. **CAREER** Asst prof, 89-95, assoc prof, 95- , Auburn Univ, Montgomery. **MEMBERSHIPS** So Atlantic MLA; F. Scott Fitzgerald Soc; Asn of Col English Tchrs of Ala. **RESEARCH** Twentieth-century American poetry; twentieth-century American fiction. **SELECTED PUBLICATIONS** Auth, The Crystal Lens of Time: Andrew Hudgins' The Glass Hammer, Chattahoochee Rev, 95; auth, The Manuscripts of James Gould Cozzens' By Love Possessed, Resources for Am Lit Stud, 95; co-ed, The Muses Female Are; Martha Moulsworth and Other Women Writers of the English Renaissance, Locust Hill, 95; auth, Alice Perrin, in Naufftus, ed, British Short Fiction Writers, 1880-1914: The Romantic Tradition, Dict of Lit Biog, v. 156, Gale, 96; coauth, Short Fiction: A Critical Companion, Locust Hill, 97; auth, Old Impulses, New Expressions: Duality and Unity in the Poetry of Denise Levertov, Renascence, 97; co-ed, A Collection of Essays on the Poetry of Denise Levertov, Locust Hill, 99. **CONTACT ADDRESS** Dept of English and Philosophy, Auburn Univ, Montgomery, Montgomery, AL, 36117-3596. **EMAIL** alittle@mickey.aum.edu

LITTLEFIELD, DAN F.
DISCIPLINE NATIVE AMERICAN LITERATURE & HISTORY **EDUCATION** SUNY, PhD. **CAREER** English and Lit, Univ Ark **SELECTED PUBLICATIONS** Auth, Alex Posey: Creek poet, journalist and humorist; The Life of Okah Tubbee; Coauth, A Biobibliography of Native American Writers; Coed: The Heath Anthology of American Literature; Kamaha Omaha Stories by Francis LaFlesche; The Fus Fixico Letters by Alex Posey. **CONTACT ADDRESS** Univ Ark Little Rock, 2801 S University Ave., Little Rock, AR, 72204-1099. **EMAIL** dflittlefiel@ualr.edu

LITTLEFIELD, DAVID J.
PERSONAL Born 08/22/1928, Tupper Lake, NY, m, 1953, 4 children **DISCIPLINE** ENGLISH **EDUCATION** Spring Hill Col, AB, 51; Yale Univ, MA, 53, PhD, 61. **CAREER** Instr Eng, 53-56 & 59-61, from asst prof to prof, 61-71, dir freshman Eng, 64-65 & 66-68, chmn, Div Hum, 67-70, chmn, Dept Eng & Drama, 71-74, Stewart Prof Eng, Middlebury Col, 71-95, Vis fel classics, Princeton Univ, 65-66; educ consult, Kinney Nat Serv, Inc, 68-; chmn, Vt Coun on Hum & Pub Issues, 72-76; consult-panelist, Media Prog, Div Pub Progs, Nat Endowment for Hum, 75-; summer fel, Stanford Univ, 75; vis prof, Antioch Sch Law, summer, 76 & fall, 78. **MEMBERSHIPS** MLA; Am Philol Asn. **RESEARCH** Aristophanes; Ovid; Eng neoclassical lit; law and lit. **SELECTED PUBLICATIONS** Auth, Pomona and Vertumnus: A fruition of hist in Ovid's Metamorphoses,

Arion, 65; ed, Twentieth Century Interpretations of the Frogs, Prentice-Hall, 68; auth, Metaphor and myth: The unity of Aristophanes' Knights, Studies Philol, 68. **CONTACT ADDRESS** 346 Sperry Rd, Cornwall, VT, 05753-9447. **EMAIL** djl@shoreham.net

LITTLEJOHN, DAVID
PERSONAL Born 05/08/1937, San Francisco, CA, m, 1963, 2 children **DISCIPLINE** JOURNALISM **EDUCATION** Univ Calif, Berkeley, BA, 59; Harvard Univ, MA, 60, PhD(English), 63. **CAREER** Asst prof English, 63-68 and English and jour, 68-69, from asst prof to assoc prof jour, 69-76, assoc dean, 74-78, PROF JOUR, UNIV CALIF, BERKELEY, 76-, Weekly critic, Kqed-TV, 65-75; Fulbright lectr, Univ Montpellier, 66-67; critic-at-large, PBS Network, 71-72; Am Coun Learned Soc fel, London and Paris, 72-73; consult Aspen Prog Commun and Soc, 74-76. **RESEARCH** Eighteenth and 20th century literature; English, American and French literature; criticism and aesthetics. **SELECTED PUBLICATIONS** Auth, The Queens Throat--Opera, Homosexuality, and the Mystery of Desire, Notes, Vol 0050, 93; The Angels Cry--Beyond the Pleasure Principle in Opera, Notes, Vol 0050, 93; The Barnes Collection, Smithsonian, Vol 0024, 93; International Dictionary of Opera, Notes, Vol 0051, 95; The Viking Opera Guide, Notes, Vol 0051, 95; The New Grove Dictionary of Opera, Notes, Vol 0051, 95; The Oxford Dictionary of Opera, Notes, Vol 0051, 95; Whats So Great about Vermeer--Reflections on the Washington Exhibition, Hudson Rev, Vol 0049, 96; **CONTACT ADDRESS** Sch of Jour, Univ of Calif, 121 Northgate Hall, Berkeley, CA, 94720-5861.

LITZ, ARTHUR WALTON
PERSONAL Born 10/31/1929, Nashville, TN **DISCIPLINE** ENGLISH **EDUCATION** Princeton Univ, BA, 51; Oxford Univ, DPhil, 54. **CAREER** Assoc prof, 56-67, chmn dept 75-81, PROF ENGLISH, PRINCETON UNIV, 67-, Am Coun Learned Soc fel, 60-61; Nat Endowment for Humanities sr fel, 74-75; ed, the James Joyce Archive, 78-80. **HONORS AND AWARDS** Danforth Gifted Teaching Award, 72. **MEMBERSHIPS** MLA; English Inst. **RESEARCH** James Joyce; 19th century novel; modern poetry and fiction. **SELECTED PUBLICATIONS** Auth, an Unpublished Poem of 1909 by Pound, Ezra, Paideuma-J Devoted to Ezra Pound Scholarship, Vol 0022, 93; Pater, Walter--Lover of Strange Souls, Sewanee Rev, Vol 0103, 95; Brooks, Cleanth October-16,1906 May-10, 1994, Proc Amer Philos Soc, Vol 0140, 96. **CONTACT ADDRESS** Dept of English, Princeton Univ, Princeton, NJ, 08544.

LIU, ALAN
DISCIPLINE ENGLISH LITERATURE **EDUCATION** Stanford Univ, PhD, 80. **CAREER** PROF, ENG, UNIV CALIF, SANTA BARBARA. **RESEARCH** Cultural criticism and postmodernism. **SELECTED PUBLICATIONS** Auth, "The Voice of the Shuttle: Web Page for Humanities Research," Wordsworth: The Sense of History, Stanford Univ Press, 89; "The Power of Formalism: The New Historicism," ELH, 89; "Wordsworth and Subversion, 1793-1804: Trying Cultural Criticism," The Yale Jour of Criticism, 89; "Local Trancendence: Cultural Criticism, Postmodernism, and the Romanticism of Detail," Representations; 89. **CONTACT ADDRESS** Dept of Eng, Univ Calif, Santa Barbara, CA, 93106-7150. **EMAIL** ayliu@humanitas.ucsb.edu

LIU, YAMENG
DISCIPLINE CONTEMPORARY RHETORICAL STUDIES **EDUCATION** Univ Southern Calif, PhD. **CAREER** Lit, Carnegie Mellon Univ. **SELECTED PUBLICATIONS** Areas: Aristotle and John Donne. **CONTACT ADDRESS** Carnegie Mellon Univ, 5000 Forbes Ave, Pittsburgh, PA, 15213.

LIUZZA, ROY
DISCIPLINE ANGLO-SAXON LITERATURE, MEDIEVAL LITERATURE **EDUCATION** Northeast La Univ, BA, 78; Yale University, MA, 79, PhD, 88. **CAREER** Instr, 90, Tulane Univ. **SELECTED PUBLICATIONS** Auth, The Old English Version of the Gospels Early English Text Society, EETS O.S. 304, Oxford, 94; Representation and Readership in the Middle English Havelok, JEGP 93, 94; The Return of the Repressed: New and Old Theories in Old English Literary Criticism, Old English Shorter Poems: Basic Readings on Anglo-Saxon Lit 3, Garland Press, 94; On the Dating of Beowulf, Beowulf: Basic Readings on Anglo-Saxon Lit 1, Garland Press, 95; Orthography and Historical Linguistics, Jour Eng Ling 24, 96; co-ed, Anglo-Saxon Manuscripts in Microfiche, Facsimile vol 6: Gospels, MRTS, 95. **CONTACT ADDRESS** Dept of Eng, Tulane Univ, 6823 St Charles Ave, New Orleans, LA, 70118. **EMAIL** rliuzza@mailhost.tcs.tulane.edu

LIVATINO, MELVIN W.
PERSONAL Born 06/27/1940, Chicago, IL, 3 children **DISCIPLINE** ENGLISH **EDUCATION** Univ Ill, BA, 66; Loyola Univ Chicago, MA, 68. **CAREER** Inst, 68-71, asst prof, 71-76, Wright Col, City Col Chicago; asst prof, 76-86, assoc prof, 86-91, PROF ENG, 91-, TRUMAN COL, CITY COL CHICAGO. **HONORS AND AWARDS** Phi Theta Kappa, 62; Truman Col Dist Prof Award, semifinalist, 96, 97, 98., Ed, Discourse, City Cols Chicago fac magazine, 90-94. **MEMBERSHIPS** ALSC; C.G. Jung Inst Chicago, Jos Campbell Soc. **RESEARCH** Teaching creative writing; creative nonfiction; John Cheever, Raymond Carver; 20th cent Am lit; film studies. **SELECTED PUBLICATIONS** Ed, pub, classroom anthology student writing, 88-; ed, pub, chapbook series students' work, 98-; ed, pub These Foreign Shores, Eng Sec Lang mag, 97, columnist, Keenager, 71-75. **CONTACT ADDRESS** English Dept, Truman Col, 1145 Wilson Ave, Chicago, IL, 60640.

LIVINGSTON, JAMES L.
PERSONAL Born 10/21/1940, Detroit, MI, m, 1962, 4 children **DISCIPLINE** RENAISSANCE LITERATURE **EDUCATION** Univ Detroit, AB, 62; Univ NC, Chapel Hill, MA, 65; Univ Buffalo, PhD, 70. **CAREER** Instr, Detroit Country Day Sch, 65-66; instr, Clemson Univ, 66-67; inst, Fredonia State Col, 67-68; asst prof, 69-73, assoc prof, 73-82, prof English, 82-, Northern Mich Univ. **HONORS AND AWARDS** Woodrow Wilson Fel, 62; NEH grants, 85, 88, 91, 94. **MEMBERSHIPS** Renaissance Soc Am; Milton Soc. **RESEARCH** Mythology; Shakespeare; Ben Jonson; poetry and music. **SELECTED PUBLICATIONS** Auth, Walt Whitman's Epistle to the Americans, Am Lit, 1/69; art, With Whitman Around the Campfire, Walt Whitman Rev, 6/70; Auth, Names in Twain's Mysterious Stranger, Notes & Queries, 6/71. **CONTACT ADDRESS** Dept of English, No Michigan Univ, 1401 Presque Isle Ave, Marquette, MI, 49855-5301. **EMAIL** jlivings@nmu.edu

LJUNGQUIST, KENT PAUL
PERSONAL Born 06/22/1948, Worcester, MA **DISCIPLINE** AMERICAN LITERATURE **EDUCATION** Clark Univ, BA, 70; Univ Conn, MA, 72; Duke Univ, PhD(English), 75. **CAREER** Asst prof English, Bluefield Col, 75-77; asst prof, 77-81, assoc prof to prof English, Worcester Polytech Inst, 81-, co-ed, Passing of fairyland, Poe Studies Asn Newslett, 78-84, 91-97. **MEMBERSHIPS** Poe Studies Asn; Hawthorne Soc; Soc Study Southern Lit. **RESEARCH** Poe; Melville; literary attitudes toward landscape; New England writers. **SELECTED PUBLICATIONS** Auth, Poe's Raven and Bryant's Mythology, Am Transcendental Quart, winter 76; coauth, Monsieur Dupin: Further Details on the Reality Beyond the Legend, Southern Lit J, fall 76; auth, The Influence of Adonais on Eleonora, Poe Studies, 6/77; Poe's The Island of the Fay: The Passing of Fairyland, Studies Short Fiction, summer 77; Burke's Enquiry and The Pit and the Pendulum, Poe Studies, 6/78; How to write a Poe thriller, Southern Literary J, spring 80; Jack Burden's Kingdom by the Sea, Notes on Comtemp Lit, 1/80; Uses of the Daeman in Selected Works by Poe, Interpretations, 80; The Grand and the Fair: Poe's Landscape Aesthetics and Pictorial Techniques, 84; co-ed, J. F. Cooper's The Deerslayer, 87; auth, The Identity of Outis: A Further Chapter in the Poe-Longfellow War, Am Lit, 88; ed, Facts on File Bibliography of America Fiction to 1865, 94; auth, Surveys of Poe Criticism, American Literary Scholarship 1983-86, 95; The Little War and Longfellow's Dilemna: New Documents in the Plagiarism Controversy of 1845, Resources for Am Lit Study, 97. **CONTACT ADDRESS** Dept of Humanities, Worcester Polytech Inst, 100 Institute Rd, Worcester, MA, 01609-2247. **EMAIL** kpl@wpi.edu

LOBB, EDWARD
DISCIPLINE ENGLISH LITERATURE **EDUCATION** Princeton Univ, PhD. **CAREER** Dept Eng, Queen's Univ **HONORS AND AWARDS** ASUS Tchg Awd. **RESEARCH** Modern literature; T.S. Eliot; modern art and photography. **SELECTED PUBLICATIONS** Auth, T.S. Eliot and the Romantic Critical Tradition; pubs on modern fiction and poetry; ed, Words in Time: New Essays on Eliot's Four Quartets. **CONTACT ADDRESS** English Dept, Queen's Univ, Kingston, ON, K7L 3N6.

LOCHHEAD, DOUGLAS GRANT
PERSONAL Born 03/25/1922, Guelph, ON, Canada, m, 1949, 2 children **DISCIPLINE** ENGLISH **EDUCATION** McGill Univ, BA, 43, Bls, 51; Univ Toronto, MA, 47. **CAREER** Librn and lectr sociol, Univ Victoria, BC, 51-52; librn cataloguer, Cornell Univ, 52-53; chief librn and prof, Dalhousie Univ, 53-60; chief librn and prof English, York Univ, Ont, 60-63; Librn, Massey Col, Univ Toronto, 63-75, prof English, bibliog and palaeography, Univ Col, 65-75; DAVIDSON PROF CAN STUDIES, MT ALLISON UNIV, 75-, DIR CTR FOR CAN STUDIES, 77-, Sr fel, Massey Col, Univ Toronto, 64-75, emer fel, 75-, spec lectr fac libr sci, 65-75; Can Coun Res grants, 67, 68, 78 and 79; mem bd, Inst of Can Hist Reproductions, Ottawa, 78-. **MEMBERSHIPS** Asn Can Univ Teachers English; fel Royal Soc Can; Bibliog Soc Can; Bibliog Soc Am; League Can Poets. **RESEARCH** Canadian printing history; 19th century Canadian literature. **SELECTED PUBLICATIONS** Auth, The History of the Book in Canada--a Bibliography, Papers of the Bibliographical Soc Amer, Vol 0088, 94; Studies in Maritime Literary History, 1760-1930, Engl Stud in Can, Vol 0021, 95. **CONTACT ADDRESS** Ctr Can Studies, Mount Allison Univ, Sackville, NB, E0A 3C0.

LOCHMAN, DAN
DISCIPLINE NON-CHAUCERIAN MEDIEVAL LITERATURE **EDUCATION** Loyola Univ Chicago, BA, MA; Univ WI, PhD. **CAREER** Southwest Tex State Univ **RESEARCH** Tudor humanists, espec John Colet and Thomas More. **SELECTED PUBLICATIONS** Areas: Milton; John Colet; Thomas More; Desiderius Erasmus. **CONTACT ADDRESS** Southwest Texas State Univ, 601 University Dr, San Marcos, TX, 78666-4604.

LOCHRIE, KARMA
DISCIPLINE ENGLISH **EDUCATION** DePauw Univ, BA, 77; Princeton Univ, MA, 78, PhD, 81. **CAREER** Assoc prof. **RESEARCH** Chaucer; Old English language and literature; Middle English literature; Women's Stud; Cultural Stud; Queer Stud. **SELECTED PUBLICATIONS** Co-ed, Constructing Medieval Sexuality, Univ Minn Press, 97; Margery Kempe and Translations of the Flesh, Univ Pa Press, 91; essays, Mystical Acts, Queer Tendencies, in Constructing Medieval Sexuality, Univ Minn Press, 97; Desiring Foucault, J Medieval and Early Modern Stud 27.1, 97; Don't Ask, Don't Tell: Murderous Plots and Medieval Secrets, in Premodern Sexualities, Routledge, 96; Women's 'Pryvetees' and Fabliau Politics in the Miller's Tale, Exemplaria, 95; Sexual Violence and the Politics of War in the Old English Judith, Ind UP, 95. **CONTACT ADDRESS** Dept of English, Loyola Univ, Chicago, 6525 N Sheridan Rd, Chicago, IL, 60626. **EMAIL** klochri@wpo.it.luc.edu

LOCK, F.P.
DISCIPLINE ENGLISH LITERATURE **EDUCATION** McMaster Univ, PhD. **CAREER** Dept Eng, Queen's Univ **RESEARCH** Restoration and eighteenth century literature; politics; intellectual history; Jonathan Swift; Edmund Burke. **SELECTED PUBLICATIONS** Auth, Susanna Centlivre, The Politics of 'Gulliver's Travels', Reflections on the Revolution in France, (rev); pubs on Swift, Burke, and Austen; co-ed, Collected Poems of Thomas Parnell. **CONTACT ADDRESS** English Dept, Queen's Univ, Kingston, ON, K7L 3N6. **EMAIL** lockfp@qsilver.queensu.ca

LOCKETTE, AGNES LOUISE
PERSONAL Born 04/21/1927, Albany, GA, m **DISCIPLINE** ENGLISH **EDUCATION** Albany State Coll, Albany, GA, BS, 1948; Univ of Nevada, Las Vegas, MEd, 1967; Univ of Arizona, Tucson, EdD, 1972. **CAREER** Carver HS Dawson, GA, teacher, 1948-49; Clark County School Dist, Las Vegas, NV, teacher, 1952-70; Univ of Nevada, Las Vegas, prof of educ, 1972-84, prof, 1971-. **HONORS AND AWARDS** Honors Hazard Training School, Albany State Coll, GA; diploma, Albany State Coll HS Albany State Coll, GA; class valedictorian; first woman appointed to Clark County Air Pollution Hearing Bd, 1972-; Keynote speaker Annual Honor Convocation Univ of NV Las Vegas 1984; Disting Teaching Awd Coll of Educ Univ of NV Las Vegas 1984; Outstanding Service Award, Westside School Alumni Assn, 1988; Recipient of one of UNLV's First Master's Degrees, Elem Educ, MEd, 1967. **MEMBERSHIPS** Kappa Delta Pi; Delta Kappa Gamma Soc; Natl Concil of Teachers of English; Amer Assn Univ Women; mem, Phi Kappa Phi; Assn of Childhood Educ Intl; Natl Soc of Profs; Natl Educ Assn; Grace Community Church, Boulder City, NV, church council, mem, financial section, 1989-; chairperson, Clark Co Air Pollution Hearing Bd, Las Vegas, NV. **CONTACT ADDRESS** Education, Univ of Nevada, Las Vegas, 4505 Maryland Parkway, Las Vegas, NV, 89154.

LOCKLIN, GERALD IVAN
PERSONAL Born 02/17/1941, Rochester, NY, 7 children **DISCIPLINE** ENGLISH **EDUCATION** St John Fisher Col, BA, 61; Univ Ariz, MA, 63, PhD, 64. **CAREER** Prof English, Calif State Univ, Long Beach, 65-. **HONORS AND AWARDS** Borestone Mt Best Poem Award, 67. **RESEARCH** Twentieth century literature; poetry. **SELECTED PUBLICATIONS** Auth, Locklin Biblio: A Bibliography on the Work of Gerald Locklin, 1963-1990, Zerx Press, 91; co-ed, A New Geography of Poets, Univ Ark Press, 92; auth, Woman Trouble, a longstory chapbook, Event Horizon Press, 94; Charles Bukowski: A Sure Bet (essays, memoirs, and poems), Water Row Books, 3/96; Locklin Biblio 2: A Bibliography on the Work of Gerald Locklin, Vol 2, 1990-1997, Zerx Press, 97; The First Time He Saw Paris, In: Two Novellas, Event Horizon Press, 97; author of over 200 articles, essays, reviews, books of poetry, poetry in anthologies, and other works including audio, video, and alternative media. **CONTACT ADDRESS** Dept of English, California State Univ, Long Beach, 1250 N Bellflower, Long Beach, CA, 90840-0001. **EMAIL** glocklin@csu16.edu

LOCKRIDGE, LAURENCE SHOCKLEY
PERSONAL Born 07/01/1942, Bloomington, IN **DISCIPLINE** ENGLISH LITERATURE; AMERICAN LITERATURE **EDUCATION** Ind Univ, AB, 64; Harvard Univ, MA, 68, PhD(English), 69. **CAREER** Asst prof, Rutgers Univ, New Brunswick, 69-76; vis lectr English, Northwestern Univ, 77-78; Assoc Prof to Prof English, NY Univ, 78-. **HONORS AND AWARDS** Phi Beta Kappa, 63; Woodrow Wilson Fel, 64-65; Danforth Fel, 64-69; NEH Summer Stipend, 78; Guggenheim Fel, 84-85; The MidAmerica Award, 98. **MEMBERSHIPS** NY Inst for the Humanities; The Biog Seminar; PEN Am Ctr; Authors' Guild; The Manuscript Soc; Soc for the Study of Midwestern Lit; Am Asn of Suicidologists; Am Suicide Found. **RESEARCH** Literature and philosophy; biography and autobiography; ethics and literature; British and American Romanticism;

history of critical theory. **SELECTED PUBLICATIONS** Auth, Coleridge the Moralist, Cornell Univ, 77; The Ethics of Romanticism, Cambridge Univ Press, 89; Shade of the Raintree: The Life and Death of Ross Lockridge, Jr., Viking Penguin, 94, Penguin Books, 95; ed, Raintree County, Penguin Books, 94; co-ed, Nineteenth-Century Lives, Cambridge Univ Press, 89. **CONTACT ADDRESS** Dept of English, New York Univ, 19 University Pl, Rm 200, New York, NY, 10003-4556.

LOE, THOMAS
DISCIPLINE ENGLISH LITERATURE **EDUCATION** Univ IA, PhD, 74. **CAREER** Prof Eng/Dir grad progs, SUNY Oswego. **RESEARCH** Tchg and research interests; 19th and early 20th-century narratives; film; short fiction. **SELECTED PUBLICATIONS** Auth, articles on narrative, narrative theory, film. **CONTACT ADDRESS** SUNY Oswego, Oswego, NY, 13126. **EMAIL** loe@Oswego.edu

LOE, THOMAS BENJAMIN
PERSONAL Born 06/14/1943, Perham, Minn, m, 1964, 3 children **DISCIPLINE** ENGLISH LITERATURE **EDUCATION** St Olaf Col, BA, 65; Univ Iowa, MA, 71, PhD(English), 74. **CAREER** From instr to asst prof, 71-77, actg chmn dept, 78-80, 96, assoc prof, 77-89, prof, 89-, English, State Univ NY Col Oswego; vis res schol, Cambridge Univ 87-88. **HONORS AND AWARDS** SUNY Chancellor's Awd for Excel in Tchg. **MEMBERSHIPS** MLA. **RESEARCH** 19th and 20th century English novel; narrative theory. **CONTACT ADDRESS** Dept of English, State Univ of NY, 7060 State Route 104, Oswego, NY, 13126-3599. **EMAIL** loe@oswego.edu

LOEFFLER, DONALD LEE
DISCIPLINE COMMUNICATIONS **EDUCATION** Univ of Dayton, BS, 52; Teachers Col, Columbia Univ, MA, 53; State Univ of Iowa, 60; Bowling Green State Univ, PhD, 69. **CAREER** Teacher, public schools of Durand, Mich, 55-57; U.S. Army, Personnel Sergeant Major (E-5), 53-55; teacher, Gunston Jr High School, 57-58; chief speech therapist, Barney Children's Medical Center, 60-64; asst prof of speech, Mass State Col at Worcester, 64-67; part-time speech therapist, Public Schools of New Reigel, 67-68; teaching fel, supervisor of Speech Instructional Center, visiting instr, Bowling Green State Univ, 68-69; dir of theatre, 69-92, tenured, 74; assoc prof, 69-75, prof, 75-92, head, Dept of Speech and Theatre Arts, Western NC Univ, 70-88. **HONORS AND AWARDS** Alpha Psi Omega; Boss of the Year, NCAEOP, 80-81; Secretary Suzanne M. Davis Memorial Award for Outstanding Service to Theatres in the Southeast, 88; Exceptional Service Trophy, 88, Herman Middleton Distinguished Career Award, 92. **MEMBERSHIPS** Am Asn of Univ Prof; Am Speech and Hearing Asn; Nat Asn Schools of Theatre; Asn of Commun Admin; Am Theatre Asn; Am Theatr in Higher Education; Carolina Speech Commun Asn; NC Theatre Conf; Southeastern Theatre Conf; Speech Commun Asn; Univ and Col Theatre Asn. **SELECTED PUBLICATIONS** Auth, Homosexual Character in Drama, Arno Press, 75; auth, Coming Out-1950-1970, Southern Theatre, 74; auth, Theatre Perspectives on the Field of Communication, ACA Bull, 84; auth, Figuring Workload Equivalencies of Performance/Production Assignments for Theatre Faculty, ACA Bull, 84; auth, Strategies for Tenure/Promotion of Technical Theatre Faculty, ACA Bull, 85; auth, Censorship in College and University Theatres: the Administrative Point of View, ACA Bull, 86; auth, The Tenuring of Technical Theatre Faculty: A Call for Assistance, ACA Bull, 86; auth, Departmental Administrations: Chairing, Managing, and Running the Academic Enterprise, ACA Bull, 87; auth, Closing the Gap: How Colleges and Universities Can Help Improve Secondary Theatre Education, ACA Bull, 87. **CONTACT ADDRESS** Dept of Commun and Theatre Arts, Western Carolina Univ, Cullowhee, NC, 28723. **EMAIL** dllcfm@gte.net

LOESBERG, JONATHAN
DISCIPLINE BRITISH LITERATURE **EDUCATION** Cornell Univ, PhD, 77; Cornell Univ, MA, 75; Brown Univ, AB, 72. **CAREER** Ch, Amer Univ Dept Lit, 96- dir, Univ Honors Program, Amer Univ, 92-95; prof, Amer Univ, 91-; deputy chair, Amer Univ Dept Lit, 90-92; dir, MA Program Lit, Amer Univ, 84-86, 91; assoc prof, Amer Univ, 86-91; asst prof, Amer Univ, 82-86; asst prof, Col of Holy Cross, 80-82; vis asst prof, Brandeis Univ, 79-80; asst prof, Cornell Univ, 77-79. **HONORS AND AWARDS** ACLS Fel, 95-96; Amer Univ Award for Achievement in Scholarship, 91; NEH Summer Inst Co-Dir, 90; AU NEH Colloquium Participant, 88; Amer Univ Summer Grant, 87; Mellon Grant, 85; NEH Summer Stipend, 84; NEH Summer Sem Fel, 82; School of Criticism & Theory Fel, 81; Cornell Summer Fel, 73, 74, 75, 76; Phi Kappa Phi, 76; Cornell Grad Fel, 72-73. **MEMBERSHIPS** Northeast Victorian Studies Ass Ch, 96-97; Duke Univ Pr Reader; Univ Virginia Pr Reader; Univ Ga Pr Reader; Columbia Univ Pr Reader. **RESEARCH** Literary theory, connections between literature and philosophy. **SELECTED PUBLICATIONS** Cultural Studies, Victorian Studies and Formalism, Victorian Studies & Cultural Studies, 99; Materialism and Aesthetics: Paul de Man's Aesthetic Ideology, Diacritics, 98; Dickensian Deformed Children and the Hegelian Sublime, Victorian Studies, 97; Aestheticism and Deconstruction: Pater, Derrida and de Man, Princeton Univ Pr, 91. **CONTACT ADDRESS** Dept of Literature, American Univ, 3717 Windon Pl, NW, Washington, DC, 20016. **EMAIL** jloesbe@american.edu

LOGAN, DEBORAH
DISCIPLINE NINETEENTH-CENTURY BRITISH LITERATURE **EDUCATION** Hamilton Col, BA; Univ NC Chapel Hill, MA, PhD. **CAREER** Prof **RESEARCH** Romantic and Victorian Literature; Harriet Martineau, Thomas Hardy. **SELECTED PUBLICATIONS** Auth, Fallenness in Victorian Women's Writing, Univ Miss Press, 98. **CONTACT ADDRESS** Western Kentucky Univ, 1526 Big Red Way Street, Bowling Green, KY, 42101. **EMAIL** Deborah.Logan@wku.edu

LOGAN, GEORGE
DISCIPLINE ENGLISH LITERATURE **EDUCATION** Harvard Univ, PhD. **CAREER** Dept Eng, Queen's Univ **RESEARCH** Renaissance humanism; English literary Renaissance. **SELECTED PUBLICATIONS** Auth, The Meaning of More's 'Utopia'; pubs on Renaissance literature, Renaissance humanism, and computer applications to literary studies; co-ed,The Norton Anthology of English Literature; Utopia; Unfolded Tales: Essays on Renaissance Romance. **CONTACT ADDRESS** English Dept, Queen's Univ, Kingston, ON, K7L 3N6.

LOGSDON, LOREN
DISCIPLINE ENGLISH LITERATURE **EDUCATION** Eureka Col, BA; Univ IL, MA; OH Univ, PhD. **CAREER** Prof, Eureka Col . **HONORS AND AWARDS** Ed, Eureka Lit Mag. **RESEARCH** Am lit. **SELECTED PUBLICATIONS** Auth, articles on sci fiction, espec on the work of Ray Bradbury. **CONTACT ADDRESS** Eureka Col, 300 E College Ave, PO Box 280, Eureka, IL, 61530.

LOHAFER, SUSAN
PERSONAL Born 06/23/1942, Goshen, NY **DISCIPLINE** SHORT FICTION THEORY, LITERARY NONFICTION **EDUCATION** Radcliffe Col, AB, 64; Stanford Univ, MA, 66; NY Univ, PhD, 70. **CAREER** Vis asst prof English, Ohio State Univ, 72-73; asst prof, 73-77, Assoc Prof 77- 82, prof, English, Univ Iowa, 82-. **MEMBERSHIPS** MLA; M/MLA; Soc for the Stu of the Short Story. **RESEARCH** Short fiction theory. **SELECTED PUBLICATIONS** Auth, Knave, Fool, and Genius, Univ NC, 73; auth, Coming to terms with the Short Story, LSUP, 83; co-ed, Short Story Theory at a Crossroads, LSUP, 89; co-ed, The Tales We Tell, Greenwood, 98. **CONTACT ADDRESS** Dept of English, Univ of Iowa, 308 English Phil Blvd, Iowa City, IA, 52242-1492. **EMAIL** slohafer@compuserve.com

LOHRLI, ANNE
PERSONAL Born 02/09/1906, Bake Oven, OR **DISCIPLINE** ENGLISH LANGUAGE AND LITERATURE **EDUCATION** Occidental Col, AB, 27, AM, 28; Columbia Univ, AM, 32; Univ Southern Calif, PhD, 37. **CAREER** Res and collaboration, 27-37; teacher, Los Angeles City Schs, 38-45; prof, 45-65, EMER PROF ENGLISH, N MEX HIGHLANDS UNIV, 65-, Vis prof, Univ Trieste, 54. **MEMBERSHIPS** MLA. **RESEARCH** Victorian periodicals. **SELECTED PUBLICATIONS** Auth, Fresh Fields and Pastures New + Misquoting Milton Line From 'Lycidas', Notes and Queries, Vol 0041, 94; The Divine Williams--Query, Notes and Queries, Vol 0044, 97. **CONTACT ADDRESS** New Mexico Highlands Univ, 790 Baylor Ave, Claremont, CA, 91711.

LOISELLE, ANDRE
DISCIPLINE FILM **EDUCATION** Univ Brit Columbia, PhD. **CAREER** Asst prof. **RESEARCH** Canadian and Quebecois cinema. **SELECTED PUBLICATIONS** Co-ed, Auteur/Provocateur: The Films of Denys Arcand, Flicks Bk(s)/Praeger, 95; pub(s), articles on film and theatre in jour(s), The Can Jour of Film Stud; Quebec Stud; Post Script; Theatre Res in Can; Essays in Theatre and L'Annuaire theatral; auth, articles on Michel Brault's Les Ordres; auth, bk on Anne Claire Poirier's film Mourir a tue-tete, Flicks Bk(s). **CONTACT ADDRESS** Dept of Art and Cult, Carleton Univ, 1125 Colonel By Dr, Ottawa, ON, K1S 5B6.

LOIZEAUX, ELIZABETH BERGMANN
PERSONAL Born 12/16/1950, New York, NY, m, 1982 **DISCIPLINE** ENGLISH LITERATURE **EDUCATION** Mt Holyoke Col, BA, 72; Univ Mich, Ann Arbor, MA, 74, PhD(English), 80. **CAREER** ASST PROF ENGLISH, UNIV MD, COLLEGE PARK, 80-. **MEMBERSHIPS** MLA; SAtlantic Modern Lang Asn; Victorians Inst. **RESEARCH** William Butler Yeats; relations of poetry and the visual arts; modern poetry. **SELECTED PUBLICATIONS** Auth, The Book of Yeats Vision--Romantic Modernism and Antithetical Tradition, English Lit in Transition 1880-1920, Vol 0040, 97. **CONTACT ADDRESS** 51 Walnut Ave, Takoma Park, MD, 20912.

LOMAS, RONALD LEROY
PERSONAL Born 05/21/1942, Rock Island, IL **DISCIPLINE** SPEECH **EDUCATION** Western IL Univ, BA 1965, MA 1967; Bowling Green State Univ, PhD 1976. **CAREER** Western IL Univ, grad asst dept of speech 1965-66; Bowling Green State Univ, grad asst dept of speech 1969-70; Lorain Cty Comm Coll instr speech & dir forensics, reg adv 1969; Bowling Green State Univ, instr speech & ethnic studies 1970-, asst to dir of ethenic studies 1970-75; Univ of Cincinnati Med School, coord of supportive serv 1975-76; TX So Univ Houston, assoc prof speech comm. **HONORS AND AWARDS** Foreign Serv Scholar 1964; Omicron Delta Kappa 1973; Disting Faculty Awd 1974; Outstanding Instr TSU 1980. **MEMBERSHIPS** Chmn faculty eval comm Lorain Cty Comm Coll 1968-69; chmn Minority Affairs Comm 1968-69; adv Black Progressives 1968-69; consult & lectr Black Culture St Pauls Episcopal Church Maumee OH 1972-73; leadership consult B'nai B'rith Youth Org S Euclid OH 1972-73, Lorain Council 1970-71, MI Council 1973; communication consult Title I Grant Toledo Minority Businessmen 1974-75; mem Intl Commun Assoc, Speech Commun Assoc; producer Black Perspectives WBGU Channel 70 1971;producer, host & writer of prog WBGU Channel 57 1973. **CONTACT ADDRESS** Texas So Univ, 3100 Cleborne St, Houston, TX, 77004.

LONDON, BETTE
DISCIPLINE ENGLISH **EDUCATION** Univ CA at Berkeley, PhD. **CAREER** Assoc prof & dept ch; taught at, Univ CA at Berkeley. **RESEARCH** 19th and 20th century Brit lit; feminist and postcolonial theory; gender studies; hist of authorship. **SELECTED PUBLICATIONS** Auth, The Appropriated Voice: Narrative Authority in Conrad, Forster, and Woolf; Mary Shelley, Frankenstein, and the Spectacle of Masculinity, PMLA 108, 93 & Of Mimicry and English Men: EM Forster and the Performance of Masculinity, in A Passage to India, Theory in Practice Series, Open UP, 94; articles on, Bronts, Mary Shelley, colonialist and postcolonialist discourse, Virginia Woolf & feminist criticism. **CONTACT ADDRESS** Dept of Eng, Univ of Rochester, 601 Elmwood Ave, Ste. 656, Rochester, NY, 14642. **EMAIL** bldn@db1.cc.rochester.edu

LONDRE, FELICIA HARDISON
PERSONAL Born 04/01/1941, Fort Lewis, WA, m, 1967, 2 children **DISCIPLINE** THEATER HISTORY, DRAMATIC LITERATURE **EDUCATION** Univ Mont, Missoula, BA, 62; Univ Wash, Seattle, MA, 64; Univ Wis-Madison, PhD(theater), 69. **CAREER** Asst prof speech & theater, Univ Wis-Rock County, 69-75; asst prof theater & film, Univ Tex, Dallas, 75-78; assoc prof to prof, 78-87, Curator's Prof Theater, Univ Mo-Kansas City, 87-; partic, Avant Garde Theatre, 79; partic, Soviet & Polish drama, 82; dramaturg, Mo Repertory Theatre, 75-; app, Comn Theatre Res, Am Theatre Asn, 81-84; traveling respondant, Am Col Theatre Festival, Region 5-S, 80-; Wis Arts Bd, theatre & film adv bd, 74-75. **HONORS AND AWARDS** Carnegie Corp Scholarship, McGill Univ French Summer Sch, Montreal, 60; Consul General's Award in French, 61, 62; Daniel E. Bandmann Achievement Award for Outstanding Success in All Phases of Theatre, Univ Mont, 62; Daughter of Mark Twain Soc, elected 81; Recipient of numerous grants and fellowships from UMKC, NEH, Mo Humanities Coun, and others. **MEMBERSHIPS** Am Soc Theatre Res; Mark Twain Soc; Asn for Theatre in Higher Educ. **RESEARCH** Nineteenth & 20th century French, Spanish and Russian theatre history and dramatic literature; American entertainment of the silent film era, 1895-29; playwriting and dramaturgy. **SELECTED PUBLICATIONS** Auth, Tennessee Williams, Frederick Ungar Publ Co, 79; Tom Stoppard, Frederick Ungar Publ Co, 81; transl, The Show-Man, Ubu Repertory Theater Publications, 84; auth, Federico Garc?a Lorca, Frederick Ungar Publ Co, 84; assoc ed, Shakespeare Around the Globe: A Guide to Notable Postwar Revivals, Greenwood Press, 86; auth, Tennessee Williams: Life, Work, and Criticism, York Press, 89; The History of World Theater: From the English Restoration to the Present, Continuum, 91; coauth, Shakespeare Companies and Festivals: An International Guide, Greenwood Publ Group, 95; ed, Love's Labour Lost: Critical Essays, Garland Publ, 97; coauth, The History of North american Theater: From Pre-Columbian Times to the Present, Continuum (forthcoming 98); author of numerous scholarly articles, book and theater reviews. **CONTACT ADDRESS** Dept of Theatre, Univ of Mo, 5100 Rockhill Rd, Kansas City, MO, 64110-2499. **EMAIL** fhlondre@cctr.umkc.edu

LONEY, GLENN MEREDITH
PERSONAL Born 12/24/1928, Sacramento, CA **DISCIPLINE** THEATRE & SPEECH **EDUCATION** Univ Calif, Berkeley, AB, 50; Univ Wis-Madison, MA, 51; Stanford Univ, PhD, 54. **CAREER** Instr, 55-56, San Francisco State Col; instr, 56, Univ Nev, Las Vegas; lectr, Europe, 56-59, Univ Md; instr, 59-61, Hofstra Univ; from asst prof to assoc prof, 61-70, prof, 70-, Brooklyn Col; prof, 70-, emeritus prof, 91, Grad Ctr, CUNY; hon fel, 60, Am Scand Found. **MEMBERSHIPS** Am Theatre Assn; Am Soc Theatre Res; Theatre Libr Assocs; Int Fed Theatre Res; Theatre Hist Soc; AAUP; Am Music Critics Assn, Am Theatre Critics Assn; Drama Desk; Outer Critics Circle; Muni Art Soc NY; Phi Beta Kappa; Alpha Mu Gamma, Phi Eta Sigma, Phi Delta Phi. **RESEARCH** Opera as theatre; preservation of historic theatres; dance theatre. **SELECTED PUBLICATIONS** Auth, Your Future in the Performing Arts, Rosen, 80; The House of Mirth-the Play of the Novel, Assoc Univ Presses, 81; auth, 20th Century Theatre, Facts on File, 82; auth, California Gold Rush Drama, Musical Theatre in America, 84; auth, Creating Careers in Music Theatre, 88; auth, Staging Shakespeare, 90; auth, Peter Brrok: Oxford To Orghast, 98;

ed, Art Deco News & The Modernist, 81-94; chief corresp, New York Theatre - Wire, NY Museum Wire, online, 96. **CONTACT ADDRESS** 3 E 71st St, New York, NY, 10021.

LONG, ADA
DISCIPLINE EIGHTEENTH-CENTURY LITERATURE AND WOMEN'S LITERATURE **EDUCATION** Stanford, BA, 67; SUNY, PhD, 76. **CAREER** Dir, Univ honors prog, Univ AL. **SELECTED PUBLICATIONS** Auth, Off the Map: Selected Poems of Gloria Fuertes; Stepping Out: An Introduction to the Arts; A Handbook for Honors Directors. **CONTACT ADDRESS** Univ AL, 1400 University Blvd, Birmingham, AL, 35294-1150.

LONG, RICHARD ALEXANDER
PERSONAL Born 02/09/1927, Philadelphia, PA **DISCIPLINE** ENGLISH, HUMANITIES **EDUCATION** Temple Univ, AB, 47, MA, 48; Univ Poitiers, DesL, 65. **CAREER** Instr, WVa State Col, 49-50; asst prof English, Morgan State Col, 51-64; lectr, Univ Poitiers, 64-65; prof English and French, Hampton Inst, 66-68; Prof English, Atlanta Univ, 68-, Fulbright scholar, Univ Paris, 57-58; vis lectr, Harvard Univ, 70-71; ADJ PROF, EMORY UNIV, 72-. **MEMBERSHIPS** MLA; Mod Humanities Res Asn; Mediaeval Acad Am; Col Lang Asn (pres, 69-71); Ling Soc Am. **RESEARCH** Theory of art; Afro-American culture; medieval literature. **SELECTED PUBLICATIONS** Auth, Race Contacts and Interracial Relations, African Amer Rev, Vol 0029, 95. **CONTACT ADDRESS** Emory Univ, ATLANTA, GA, 30322.

LONGENBACH, JAMES
DISCIPLINE ENGLISH **EDUCATION** Princeton Univ, PhD. **CAREER** Joseph Henry Gilmore prof; taught at, Princeton Univ & Oxford Univ. **HONORS AND AWARDS** Guggenheim & Mellon fel; NEH st fel. **RESEARCH** Mod lit. **SELECTED PUBLICATIONS** Auth, Modern Poetry After Modernism, Wallace Stevens: The Plain Sense of Things; Stone Cottage: Pound, Yeats, and Modernism, Modernist Poetics of History; articles on, Elizabeth Bishop, Amy Clampitt, Jorie Graham, Hart Crane, Richard Howard, Randall Jarrell, TS Eliot, Ford Madox Ford, James Joyce, Walter Pater, Robert Pinsky, Ezra Pound, Wallace Stevens, Richard Wilbur & WB Yeats; poems in, Nation, New Rep, Paris Rev & Yale Rev. **CONTACT ADDRESS** Dept of Eng, Univ of Rochester, 601 Elmwood Ave, Ste. 656, Rochester, NY, 14642. **EMAIL** jlgb@db1.cc.rochester.edu

LONGEST, GEORGE CALVIN
PERSONAL Born 02/17/1938, Richmond, VA, 4 children **DISCIPLINE** AMERICAN LITERATURE **EDUCATION** Univ Richmond, Ba, 60, MA, 61; Univ GA, PhD(Am lit), 69. **CAREER** Instr Eng, VA Polytech Inst & State Univ, 62-63; from instr to asst prof, 63-77, asst chmn dept, 73-80, actg chmn dept, 80-82, Assoc Prof Eng, VA Commonwealth Univ, 77-, Assoc Chmn Dept, 82-, Managing ed, Resource for Am Literary Study, 78-81; Ed, Annual Bibliog in Southern Lit, Miss Quart. **HONORS AND AWARDS** Tchg Excellence Award, Asn Dept Eng & MLA, 73. **MEMBERSHIPS** S Atlantic Mod Lang Asn; Soc Study Southern Lit. **RESEARCH** Southern and mod Am lit; nineteenth century Am lit. **SELECTED PUBLICATIONS** Contribr, Soc Study, 76-82; Annual bibliography Southern literature, Miss Quart, winter 77; auth, Three Virginia Writers: Mary Johnston, Thomas Nelson Page, Amelie Rives Trochetzkoy, G K Hall, 78; Genius in the Garden: Chartes F. Gillette and Landscape Architecture in Virginia, 92. **CONTACT ADDRESS** 1136 West Ave, Richmond, VA, 23220. **EMAIL** glongest@vcu.edu

LONGMIRE, SAMUEL
DISCIPLINE ENGLISH LITERATURE **EDUCATION** Ind Univ, PhD. **CAREER** Fulbright lectr, Romania; dept ch; dean, Col Arts and Sci; prof, Univ Evansville. **HONORS AND AWARDS** Founder, UE Chapter, Samuel Johnson Soc. **SELECTED PUBLICATIONS** Auth, scholarly articles on eighteenth century literary figures; pub(s), short fiction, in Cottonwood, The Flying Island, And Down The River; **CONTACT ADDRESS** Dept of Eng, Univ Evansville, 1800 Lincoln Ave, Evansville, IN, 47714. **EMAIL** sl27@evansville.edu.

LONGO, BERNADETTE
DISCIPLINE ENGLISH LITERATURE **EDUCATION** Rensselaer Polytech Inst, PhD, 96. **CAREER** Dept Eng, Clemson Univ **RESEARCH** Professional communication and technical writing. **SELECTED PUBLICATIONS** Auth, Design Collaboration Network User Manual, Rensselaer Polytech Inst, 94; Advanced System Operation Courseware Trainer's Manual, Power Tech, 93; Technical Communication Constituted as an Object of Cultural Study, Tech Comms Quart, 98; From Secrets to Science: Technical Writing, Utility, and the Hermetic Tradition in Agricola's De Re Metallica, Jour Tech Writing Comm, 97; Who Makes Engineering Knowledge?, IEEE Int Prof Comm Conf Proceedings, 97; coauth, Extending the Boundaries of Rhetoric in Legal Pedagogy, Jour Bus Tech Comm, 96. **CONTACT ADDRESS** Clemson Univ, Clemson, SC, 29634. **EMAIL** blongo@clemson.edu

LOPEZ, TIFFANY ANA
DISCIPLINE 20TH CENTURY AMERICAN LITERATURE AND DRAMA **EDUCATION** Calif State Univ, BA; Univ Calif-Santa Barbara, PhD. **CAREER** PROF, UNIV CALIF, RIVERSIDE. **RESEARCH** Chicana/o and Latina/o popular culture, and feminist and minority discourses. **SELECTED PUBLICATIONS** Ed, anthol, Growing Up Chicana/o, William & Morrow, 93; auth, "Imaging Community: Video in the Installation Work of Pepo Osorio," Art Jour, 95; "A Tolerance for Contradictions: The Short Stories of Mare Cristina Mena," 19th Century Amer Writers: A Critical Reader, Oxford Univ Press, 98; "Performing Aztla: The Female Body as Cultural Critique in the Teatro of Cherre Moraga," Performing America: Cultural Nationalism in American Theatre, Univ Mich Press, 98. **CONTACT ADDRESS** Dept of Eng, Univ Calif, 1156 Hinderaker Hall, Riverside, CA, 92521-0209. **EMAIL** talopez@ucrac1.ucr.edu.

LOTT, RAYMOND
PERSONAL Born 07/07/1936, Orlando, FL, m, 1958, 2 children **DISCIPLINE** ENGLISH LITERATURE **EDUCATION** Univ Miami, BA, 58, MA, 59; Duke Univ, PhD, 62. **CAREER** Res asst, Duke Univ, 61; from instr to assoc prof, 61-73, PROF ENGLISH, FLA SOUTHERN COL, 73-. **MEMBERSHIPS** NCTE; Col English Asn; MLA. **RESEARCH** Shakespeare; English, American and French novel; modern drama. **SELECTED PUBLICATIONS** Auth, The 'Crucifix Fish', Lit Rev, Vol 0037, 93. **CONTACT ADDRESS** Dept of English, Florida So Col, Lakeland, FL, 33802.

LOUCKS, JAMES F.
PERSONAL Born 02/07/1936, Lakewood, OH, m, 1989, 2 children **DISCIPLINE** ENGLISH **EDUCATION** Yale Univ, BA 57; Ohio State Univ, PhD 67. **CAREER** Ohio State Univ, assoc prof, asst vpres reg ser, assoc dean, 77 to 83-; Val Univ IN, ch, assoc prof, 71-77; Drexel Univ PA, assoc prof 70-71; Univ VA, asst prof, dir soph eng prog, 67-70; Ohio State Univ Colum, tchg asst, instr, 60-67. **HONORS AND AWARDS** Univ Prof Val Univ. **MEMBERSHIPS** TS Eliot Soc. **RESEARCH** Victorian and 20th Cent Poetry. **SELECTED PUBLICATIONS** Auth, Robert Brownings Poetry: A Norton Critical Edition, NY, Norton, 79 reprint, 83; auth, The Exile's Return: Fragment of a TS Eliot Chronology, ANQ, 96; auth, Eliot's Burbank with a Baedeker: Bleistein with a Cigar, ANQ, 95; Eliot's Ash Wednesday, ANQ, 95; auth, The Ring and the Book and the Land and the Book, ANQ, 94; rev, The Varieties of Metaphysical Poetry, by TS Eliot, Ronald Schchard, ed, London, Faber, 93, ANQ, 96. **CONTACT ADDRESS** Dept of English, Ohio State Univ, 1179 University Dr, Newark, OH, 43055-1797. **EMAIL** loucks.1@osu.edu

LOUGY, ROBERT E.
PERSONAL Born 09/11/1940, San Francisco, CA, m, 1962, 2 children **DISCIPLINE** ENGLISH **EDUCATION** Univ Calif, Davis, AB, 62, MA, 64, PhD(English), 66. **CAREER** Asst, Univ Calif, Davis, 62-65, fel, 65-66; asst prof, 66-72, ASSOC PROF ENGLISH, PA STATE UNIV, UNIVERSITY PARK, 72-, Asst ed, Seventeenth-Century News, 66-67, abstr ed, 67-68; jr fel, Inst Arts and Humanistic Studies, Pa State Univ, 70-73; Nat Endowment for Humanities fel, 73-74. **MEMBERSHIPS** MLA. **RESEARCH** Nineteenth century British novel and theory of the novel; aesthetics and poetic theory of the 19th and 20th centuries; British Romantic Poetry. **SELECTED PUBLICATIONS** Auth, Vanishing Points--Dickens, Narrative, and the Subject of Omniscience, Dickens Quart, Vol 0011, 94; Desire and Ideology of Violence, America in Dickens, Charles 'Martin Chuzzlewit', Criticism-Quart for Lit and the Arts, Vol 0036, 94. **CONTACT ADDRESS** Dept of English, Pennsylvania State Univ, 117 Burrowes Bldg, Univ Park, PA, 16802-6200.

LOUIS, MARGOT K.
DISCIPLINE ENGLISH LITERATURE **EDUCATION** Univ Toronto, PhD. **CAREER** Assoc prof **RESEARCH** 19th-century poetry; 19th-century women poets. **SELECTED PUBLICATIONS** Pub(s), articles in Victorian Poetry, Victorian Newsletter, Nineteenth-Century Lit, Explicator, Mythlore, Victorian Lit and Cult; auth, Swinburne and his Gods: The Roots and Growth of an Agnostic Poetry, McGill-Queen's UP; co-ed, Influence and Resistance in Nineteenth-Century English Poetry, Macmillan. **CONTACT ADDRESS** Dept of English, Victoria Univ, PO Box 3070, Victoria, BC, V8W 3W1.

LOVE, GLEN A.
PERSONAL Born 07/04/1932, Seattle, WA, m, 1956, 2 children **DISCIPLINE** ENGLISH **EDUCATION** Univ Wash, BA, 54, MA, 59, PhD(Am lit), 64. **CAREER** Teacher pub schs, Seattle, Wash, 55-59; asst English, Univ Wash, 59-60, asst dean students, 60-63; asst prof English, San Diego State Col, 63-65; from asst prof to assoc prof, 65-74, dir compos, 65-70 and 73-74, assoc dean grad sch, 70-71, actg head dept, 78, PROF ENGLISH, UNIV ORE, 74-, Fulbright lectr, Univ Regensburg, WGer, 78-79. **MEMBERSHIPS** NCTE; Am Studies Asn; PACIFIC Northwest Am Studies Asn (pres, 76-78); Western Lit Asn. **RESEARCH** American literature; Western American literature; rhetoric. **SELECTED PUBLICATIONS** Auth, Et in Rcadia Ego--Pastoral Theory Meets Ecocriticism, Western Amer Lit, Vol 0027, 92; Slouching Towards Altruria, Evolution, Ecology, and Howells, William, Dean, Harvard Libr Bull, Vol 0005, 94; Muir, John 'Stickeen' and the Lessons of Nature, Western Hist Quart, Vol 0028, 97. **CONTACT ADDRESS** Dept of English, Univ of Ore, Eugene, OR, 97403.

LOVELADY, EDGAR JOHN
PERSONAL Born 11/12/1937, Grand Rapids, MI, m, 1958, 2 children **DISCIPLINE** ENGLISH, GREEK **EDUCATION** Toronto Bible Col, dipl bible, 58; Grace Col, BA, 60; Grace Theol Sem, MDiv, 63; St Francis Col, MA, 66; Purdue Univ, PhD(English), 74; Grace Theol Sem, ThM, 76. **CAREER** Teacher English, W Noble Sch Corp, 63-66; Prof English & Greek, Grace Col, 66-. **HONORS AND AWARDS** Alva J McClain Award, Grace Col, 75; Distinguished Alumnus, 75; Delta Epsilon Chi; Phi Kappa Phi; Int Who's Who in Educ. **MEMBERSHIPS** MLA; Ind Coun of Teachers of English. **RESEARCH** Old English grammar; Greek grammar. **SELECTED PUBLICATIONS** Auth, The Logos concept in John 1:1, Grace J, spring 63; The rise of Silas Lapham as problem novel, Ind English J, 73-74. **CONTACT ADDRESS** Grace Col, 200 Seminary Dr., Box 397, Winona Lake, IN, 46590-1294. **EMAIL** lovelaej@grace.edu

LOVERIDGE-SANBONMATSU, JOAN
PERSONAL Born 07/05/1938, Hartford, CT, m, 1964, 2 children **DISCIPLINE** RHETORIC AND COMMUNICATION; BRITISH AND IRISH HISTORY. **EDUCATION** Univ Vermont, BA, 60; Ohio Univ, MA, 63; Penn State Univ, PhD, 71. **CAREER** Tchg asst, Commun Stud, Ohio Univ, 62-63; instr Commun Stud & ESL, Penn State Univ, 66-67; vis asst prof Commun Stud, RIT, 71; adj prof Commun Stud, Monroe Commun Col, 72-76; asst prof Commun Stud & Womens Stud, SUNY Brockport, 63-77; Prof Commun Stud & Women,s Stud, SUNY Oswego, 77-. **HONORS AND AWARDS** Postdoctoral fel Multicult Womens Summer Sem, Univ Chicago, 83; Trailblazer Higher Educ Award, Nat Orgn Women, Cent NY State, 87; Womens Ctr Award Extraordinary Commitment Womens Issues, 96, Womens Ctr Award Outstanding Dedication to Womens Ctr, 98, SUNY Oswego ; SUNY Oswego Intensive Eng Prog, 95, 96; SEED Award, 98; Am Red Cross Overseas Asn Pres Citation Award Soc Change, 98. **MEMBERSHIPS** Nat Commun Asn; Nat Womens Stud Asn; E Commun Asn; NY State Speech Asn; Soc Int Educ, Trng & Res; Am Red Cross Overseas Asn; Speech Commun Asn Puerto Rico. **RESEARCH** Japanese American women interned at Poston in World War II; Womens studies, English as a second language; Rhetoric and social change. **SELECTED PUBLICATIONS** Auth, Multicultural Dilemnas of Language Usage, Why Don't You Talk Right, Multicultural Commun Perspectives, Kendall Hunt, 92; Benazir Bhutto: Feminist Voice for Democracy in Pakistan, Howard Jour Commun, 94; Helen Broinowski, Caldicott: pediatrician, peace activist, catalyst for the nuclear disarmament movement, Women Public Speakers in the United States, Greenwood Press, 94; coauth Feminism and Womans Life, Minerva Publ Co, 95. **CONTACT ADDRESS** 23 McCracken Dr., Oswego, NY, 13126. **EMAIL** sanbonma@oswego.edu

LOVERING, JOSEPH PAUL
PERSONAL Born 02/16/1921, Calais, ME, m **DISCIPLINE** ENGLISH **EDUCATION** Col Holy Cross, AB, 43; Boston Univ, MA, 48; Ottawa Univ, PhD, 56. **CAREER** Instr English, St Anselm's Col, 46-48; asst prof, St Michael's Col, 48-56, assoc prof, 56-60, prof english & chm dept, Canisius Col, 60-, chm fac senate, 73-, Dir Grad English, 76- **MEMBERSHIPS** Col English Asn. **RESEARCH** American novel and poetry. **SELECTED PUBLICATIONS** Auth, S Weir Mitchell, Twayne, 71; Dorothy Canfield Fisher, Vt Hist; Gerald Warner Brace, S K Hall, 81. **CONTACT ADDRESS** Dept of English, Canisius Col 2001 Main St, Buffalo, NY, 14208.

LOVING, JEROME MACNEILL
PERSONAL Born 12/25/1941, Philadelphia, PA, 2 children **DISCIPLINE** AMERICAN LITERATURE **EDUCATION** Pa State Univ, BA, 64; Duquesne Univ, MA, 70; Duke Univ, PhD, 73. **CAREER** Teaching asst English, Duke Univ, 71-73; asst prof, 73-76, assoc prof, 76-81, Prof English, Tex A&M Univ, 81-; Fulbright to USSR, 78, France, 89-90; vis prof, Sorbonne, 84, Univ Tex, Austin, 86. **MEMBERSHIPS** MLA; AAUP. **RESEARCH** Transcendentalism; American poetry. **SELECTED PUBLICATIONS** Auth, Civil War Letters of George Washington Whitman, Duke Univ, 75; Walt Whitman's Champion: William Douglas O'Connor, Tex A&M Univ, 78; Emerson, Whitman and the American Muse, Univ NC, 82; Whitman and Dickinson, Am Lit Scholar, 80-85; Emily Dickinson: The Poet on the Second Story, Cambridge Univ Press, 86; Lost in the Customhouse: Authorship in the American Renaissance, Univ Iowa Press, 93; Walt Whitman: The Song of Himself, Univ Calif Press, 99 (in press); ed, Walt Whitman: Leaves of Grass, Oxford Univ Press, 90; Frank Norris' McTeague, Oxford Univ Press, 95; author of numerous journal articles. **CONTACT ADDRESS** Dept of English, Tex A & M Univ Col, College Station, TX, 77843. **EMAIL** j-loving@tamu.edu

LOVITT, CARL
DISCIPLINE ENGLISH LITERATURE **EDUCATION** Univ Wis, PhD, 81. **CAREER** Dept Eng, Clemson Univ **RESEARCH** International professional communication. **SELECTED PUBLICATIONS** Auth, The Rhetoric of Murderers' Confessional Narratives: The Model of Pieere Rivdere's Memoir, Jour Narr Techs, 92; Using Journals to Redefine Public and Private Domains in the Literature Classroom, When Writing Teachers Teach Literature, Boynton/Cook, 95; Defoe's Almost Invisible Hand: Narrative Logic as a Structuring Principle in Moll Flanders, 18th Century Fic, 93; coauth, Helping Student Writers Get Things Done: Teaching Genre in the First-Year Composition Course, MLA, 97; Portfolios in the Disciplines: Sharing Knowledge in the Contact Zone, New Directions in Portfolio Assessment, Boynton/Cook, 94. **CONTACT ADDRESS** Clemson Univ, Clemson, SC, 29634. **EMAIL** lcarl@clemson.edu

LOW, ANTHONY
PERSONAL Born 05/31/1935, San Francisco, CA, m, 1961, 13 children **DISCIPLINE** ENGLISH LITERATURE **EDUCATION** Harvard Univ, AB, 57, MA, 59, PhD(English), 65. **CAREER** Asst prof, Seattle Univ, 65-68; from asst prof to assoc prof, 68-78, prof English, NY Univ, 78-, asst ed, Seventeenth-Century News, 68-73; vis scholar, Jesus Col, Cambridge, 74-75. **HONORS AND AWARDS** Pew Evangelical Fel 95; Honored M Hon Scholar, 95. **MEMBERSHIPS** MLA; Milton Soc Am; Spenser Soc Am; Mod Humanities Res Asn; Renaissance Soc Am. **RESEARCH** Milton; Renaissance and 17th century literature; modern literature. **SELECTED PUBLICATIONS** Auth, Action and suffering: Samon Agonistes and the irony of alternatives, Pmla, 5/69; The image of the tower in Paradise Lost, Studies English Lit, Winter 70; Augustine Baker, Twayne, 70; Milton's God: Authority in Paradise Lost, Milton Studies, 72; The Blaze of Noon: A Reading of Samson Agonistes, Columbia Univ, 74; Milton's Samson and the Stage, with implications for dating the play, Huntington Libr Quart, 8/77; Love's Architecture: Devotional Modes in Seventeenth-Century English Poetry, NY Univ, 78; The unity of Milton's Elegia Sexta, English Lit Renaissance, Spring 81; The Reinvention of Love: Poetry, Politics and Culture from Sidney to Milton, Cambridge Univ, 93. **CONTACT ADDRESS** Dept of English, New York Univ, 19 University Pl, New York, NY, 10003-4556. **EMAIL** low@compuserve.com

LOW, LISA
PERSONAL Born 05/20/1952, Boston, MA, m, 1991, 2 children **DISCIPLINE** ENGLISH **EDUCATION** Univ Wisc, BA, 74; Univ Mass, MA, PhD, 86. **CAREER** Asst prof, 86-87, Cornell Col; asst prof, 87-89, Colby Col; asst prof, 89-94, assoc prof, 94-98, prof, 98-, Pace Univ. **HONORS AND AWARDS** Kenan Award, Scholarly and Sum Res Grants, Pace Univ, 89-97; Univ Fel, Univ Mass, 84-85; Charles Peters Shakespeare Award, Univ Mass, 83; Dist Qualifying Exam, Univ Mass, 82; Lucy Stebbins Ward Mem Scholarship, Univ CA Berkley, 72. **MEMBERSHIPS** MLA; Milton Soc of Amer; Intl Virginia Woolf Soc; Soc Study of Women in the Renaissance (SSWR). **RESEARCH** John Milton & Virginia Woolf. **SELECTED PUBLICATIONS** Auth, Milton, the Metaphysicals, and Romanticism, Cambridge Univ Press, 94; coed, Andrew Marvell and the Early Modern Meditation Poem, Milton the Metaphysicals and Romanticism, Cambridge UP, 94; coed, Reading the past, Reflecting the Present, Milton, the Metaphysicals and Romanticism, Cambridge UP, 94; art, Milton and Woolf in the Women's Studies and English Literature Classroom, (Re)Reading, (Re)Writing, (Re)Thinking Virginia Woolf, Pace UP, 95; art, Two Figures in Dense Violet Night: Virginia Woolf, John Milton, and the Epic Vision of Marriage, Woolf Stud Ann, 95; art, Refusing to Hit Back: Virginia Woolf and the Impersonality Question, Virginia Woolf and the Essay, St. Martin's Press, 97; art, Woolf's Allusion to Hedda Gabler in the Voyage Out, Virginia Woolf Miscellany 50, 97; art, Woolf's Allusion to Comus in the Voyage Out, Virginia Wool: Renaissance Woman, OH Univ Press. **CONTACT ADDRESS** Pace Univ, One Pace Plaza, New York, NY, 10038-1502. **EMAIL** lisalow@aol.com

LOWANCE, MASON IRA
PERSONAL Born 06/02/1938, Atlanta, GA, m, 1963, 2 children **DISCIPLINE** ENGLISH AND AMERICAN LITERATURE **EDUCATION** Westminster School, 56-60; Princeton Univ, AB (cum laude), 60); Oxford Univ, BA, 64, MA, 67; Emory Univ, PhD, 67. **CAREER** Consult to Office of Ed, 65-78; instr in religion and English, Punahou School, 60-61; instr in English, Morehouse Col, 64-67; ASST TO PROF OF ENGLISH, UNIV OF MASS. **HONORS AND AWARDS** Guggenheim Fel, 82-83; Am Antiquarian Soc NEH Fel, 77; Nat Humanities Inst, Yale, 77-78; Distinguished Alumnus Award, Westminster School, 92. **MEMBERSHIPS** MLA; Am Antiquarian Soc; Am Studies Asn; Soc of Early Americanists. **RESEARCH** American religion and literature; American religious history; nineteenth century American slavery and abolitionism; metaphor and symbolism in American literature. **SELECTED PUBLICATIONS** Auth, The Typological Writings of Jonathan Edwards, Yale Univ Press, 93; auth, The Stowe Debate: Rhetorical Strategies in Uncle Tom's Cabin, Univ of Mass Press, 94; auth, A House Divided: the Antebellum Slavery Debates in America 1776-1865, Princeton Univ Press, 99; auth, Spirituals, Encyclo of Am Poetry, Chicago, 98. **CONTACT ADDRESS** Dept of English, Univ of Massachusetts, Bartlett Hall, Amherst, MA, 01003.

LOWE, JOHN
DISCIPLINE AFRICAN AMERICAN, SOUTHERN, AND ETHNIC LITERATURE **EDUCATION** Columbia, PhD, 81. **CAREER** Prof, La State Univ. **HONORS AND AWARDS** Fulbright scholar, India, 83; NEH summer sem, Berkeley, 84; Andrew W. Mellon Fac Fel in the Hum, Harvard Univ, 85-86; fac fel, Ford Found, 86-87; LSU Fac Res Awards, Summer, 89, 91; NEH travel to collections grant, 90; La Endowment for the Hum grant, 92; fel, Am Coun of Learned Soc, 92-93; Sr Fulbright Professorship, Univ Munich, Germany, 95-96. **MEMBERSHIPS** Pres, La Folklore Soc, 91-92; pres, MELUS, 97-. **RESEARCH** Humor; Hurston; Wright; Faulkner; Gaines; Louisiana literature; native American literature. **SELECTED PUBLICATIONS** Auth, Jump at the Sun: Zora Neale Hurston's Cosmic Comedy, 94; Coyote's Jokebook: Humor in Native American Literature and Culture, The Dictionary of Native Am Lit, 94; Wright Writing Reading: Narrative Strategies in Uncle Tom's Children, in The Modern American Short Story: Sequence as a Genre, 94; An Interview with Brenda Marie Osbey, The Southern Rev, 94; From Mule Bones to Funny Bones: the Plays of Zora Neale Hurston, Southern Quart, 95; I am Joaquin! Space and Freedom in Yellow Bird's Joaquin Murieta, Early Native Am Lit, 96; Humor and Ethnicity in Ethnic Autobiography: Zora Neale Hurston and Jerre Mangione, in Cul Difference and the Lit Text, 96; 'Change the Joke and Shift the Yoke': The Tradition of African American Humor, Presses Universitaires, 96; ed, Conversations with Ernest Gaines; coed, The Future of Southern Letters, 96. **CONTACT ADDRESS** Dept of Eng, Louisiana State Univ, 240C Allen Hall, Baton Rouge, LA, 70803. **EMAIL** jlowe@unix1.sncc.lsu.edu

LOWRY, DAVID
PERSONAL m, 2 children **DISCIPLINE** MASS COMMUNICATION **EDUCATION** Abilene Christian Univ, BA, 76, MA, 78; Univ N TX, PhD, 82. **CAREER** Ex-instr, OK Christian Univ; dir, Edu Tech, Pepperdin; prof, 85-. **MEMBERSHIPS** Mem, Univ Acad Coun; Seaver Acad Coun; tchg, Pepperdine Overseas Intl Coun. **RESEARCH** Family commun, impact of new tech upon a variety of commun variables. **SELECTED PUBLICATIONS** Publ, area of interpersonal commun. **CONTACT ADDRESS** Pepperdine Univ, 24255 Pacific Coast Hwy, Malibu, CA, 90263. **EMAIL** dlowry@pepperdine.edu

LU, MIN-ZHAN
DISCIPLINE CULTURAL AND CRITICAL STUDIES **EDUCATION** Univ Pittsburgh, PhD. **CAREER** Assoc prof, 89, Drake Univ. **HONORS AND AWARDS** Mina P Shaughnessy Awd. **SELECTED PUBLICATIONS** Auth, feminist and post colonial theory in rel pedag; educ non-mainstream col students; fiction. **CONTACT ADDRESS** Drake Univ, University Ave, PO Box 2507, Des Moines, IA, 50311-4505. **EMAIL** min.lu@drake.edu

LU, XING L.
PERSONAL Born 05/26/1956, Beijing, China, m, 1981, 1 child **DISCIPLINE** RHETORIC; COMMUNICATION **EDUCATION** Beijing Second Foreign Language Inst, China, BA, 82; Canberra Col, Australia, MA, 84; Univ of Ore, PhD, 91. **CAREER** Vis prof, Univ of Puget Sound, 91-91; from asst prof to assoc prof, DePaul Univ, 92- . **MEMBERSHIPS** Nat Commun Asn; Am Soc of the Hist of Rhet. **RESEARCH** Class Chinese Rhet; Chinese commun studies; Intercult commun; Lang and cult; Polit discourse. **SELECTED PUBLICATIONS** Auth, On the Study of Chinese Rhetoric, The Western Jour of Commun, vol 57, 93; Theory of Persuasion in Han Fei Tzu and Its Impact on Chinese Communication Behaviors, The Howard Jour of Communs, vol 5, 93; Identity Negotiation in the Classroom, I Have a Story to Tell, eds S. Jackson and J. Solis, 98; Rhetoric and Philosophy in Ancient China: A Comparison with Ancient Greek Rhetoric from 5th-3rd Centuries BCE, 98; In Interface Between Individualistic and Collectivistic Orientations in Chinese Cultural Values and Social Relations, The Howard Jour of Communs, vol 9(2), 98; An Ideological/Cultural Analysis of Political Slogans in Communist China, Discourse & Soc, forthcoming. **CONTACT ADDRESS** Dept of Communication, DePaul Univ, 8506 Avers Ave, Skokie, IL, 60076-2226. **EMAIL** xlu@condor.depaul.edu

LUCAS, ALEC
PERSONAL Born 06/20/1913, Toronto, ON, Canada, m, 1939, 2 children **DISCIPLINE** ENGLISH **EDUCATION** Queen's Univ, Ont, BA, 43, MA, 45; Harvard Univ, AM, 47, PhD, 51. **CAREER** From asst prof to assoc prof English, Univ NB, 50-57; from asst prof to assoc prof, 57-64, prof English, 64-81, EMER PROF ENGLISH, MCGILL UNIV, 81-, Can Coun fel, 73-74; vis lectr Am lit, Laval Univ, 65; univ exchange lectr, Univ Toronto, 67; mem ed adv bd, English Studies in Canada, 77-. **MEMBERSHIPS** Asn Can Univ Teachers English; Asn Quebec and Can Lit. **RESEARCH** Nineteenth century English fiction; Canadian literature. **SELECTED PUBLICATIONS** Coauth, Literary History of Canada, Univ Toronto, 65; ed, The Best of Peter McArthur, Clarke, Irwin, 67; auth, Hugh MacLennan, McClelland and Stewart, 70; ed, Great Canadian Short Stories, Dell, 71; auth, Peter McArthur, Twayne, 75; Farley Mowat, McClelland and Stewart, 76; The Otonabee School, Mansfield Bk Mart, 77; K M Wells, P McArthur and Canadian Nature Writing, the Oxford Companion to Can Lit, 82. **CONTACT ADDRESS** Univ of Nantes, Nantes, ., F-44035.

LUCAS, HENRY CAMERON
PERSONAL Born 04/04/1944, Omaha, NE, m, 1968, 2 children **DISCIPLINE** INFORMATION SYSTEMS **EDUCATION** Yale Univ, BS (magna cum laude), 66; MIT, MS, 68; PhD, 70. **CAREER** Consult to Arthur D. Little Inc, 66-70; ASST PROF, STANFORD UNIV, 70-74; ASSOC PROF, 74-78, PROF & CHEMN, 84-88, RES PROF OF INFOR SYSTEMS, 88-98, PROF, 98-, INFOR SYSTEMS, NY UNIV; on leave, IBM European Systems Res Inst, 81; visiting res, Bell Commun res, 91; Shaw Found Prof, Nanyang Tech Univ, 97-98. **HONORS AND AWARDS** Phi Beta Kappa; Tau Beta Pi; Schools of Business Award for Excellence in Teaching, 82; Arthur Anderson Chair, Univ of Antwerp Lect Series, 86; Westside Alumni Hall of Fame Award, 91. **MEMBERSHIPS** Asn for Computing Machinery; Inst of Managemnt Scis; IEEE; Asn for Infor Systems. **SELECTED PUBLICATIONS** Auth, Information Technology: The Search for Value, Oxford Univ Press, 99; auth, The T-Form Organization: Using Technology to Design Organizations for the 21st Century, Jossey-Bass, 96; auth, Information Technology for Management, McGraw-Hill Inc, 97; coauth, A Reengineering Framwork for Evaluating a Financial Imaging System, Commun of the ACM, 96; coauth, How Open Data Networks Influence Business Performance and Market Structure, Commun of the ACM, 96; coauth, Differential and Cross-Competitive Performance Effects of Airline Computer Reservation Systems, ICIS Proceedings, 96; coauth, What is a Virtual Organization, Stern Business, 98. **CONTACT ADDRESS** New York Univ, New York, NY, 10003. **EMAIL** hlucas@stern.nyu.edu

LUCAS, JAMES L.
PERSONAL Born 10/20/1923, Canton, OH, d **DISCIPLINE** ENGLISH **EDUCATION** Boston Univ, AB 1947; Cornell Univ Law School, LLB 1950; Univ of Chgo, MA English 1965; Univ of Chicago Divinity School, MA 1970; No IL Univ, PhD 1980. **CAREER** OH Indust Commiss, atty examiner 1953-57; Wittenberg Univ Springfield OH, instr english & humanites 1957-60; Harper Coll Palatine IL, instr english 1967-; TV Coll Chicago City Coll,TV instr 1970-74,84-; Chicago City Coll Wilbur Wright Coll, prof english 1965-. **HONORS AND AWARDS** Martin Luther Fellow United Lutheran Church of Amer 1950; author 2 manuals in Amer Literature for televised college courses publ by Chicago Ed TV Assoc 1970-,71; author The Religious Dimension of Twentieth-Century & Amer Lit publ by Univ Press of Amer 1982-; listed in Men of Acheivement 1977; author Executive Seizure Power Constitutional Power of the President to Seize Private Industry publ JAG Bulletin USAF 1959. **MEMBERSHIPS** Mem Bar of US Supreme Court 1955-, US Court of Military Appeals 1955-, Supreme Court of OH 1952-; lecturer fine arts, lit, humanites Chgo-Area Orgs 1965-; mem United Lutheran Church of Amer 1960, Sigma Tau Delta Natl English Honors Soc; Modern Lang Assoc 1975-, Natl Council of Teachers of English 1980-. **CONTACT ADDRESS** Wilbur Wright Col, Chicago City Col, 3400 N Austin Ave, Chicago, IL, 60634.

LUCAS, MARK T.
DISCIPLINE ENGLISH LITERATURE **EDUCATION** Centre Col, BA, 75; Univ NC Chapel Hill, PhD. **CAREER** Fac 81, prof, current. **HONORS AND AWARDS** Hughes and Kirk Awds, Centre Col; Sears Found Tchg Prize; NEH Fellow; Hartsell Award, Univ NC. **RESEARCH** Southern literature; William Faulkner. **SELECTED PUBLICATIONS** Auth, The Southern Vision of Andrew Lytle, La State Univ Press, 87; contrib, Fifty Southern Writers after 1900, Greenwood, 87; Companion to Southern Literature, La State Univ Press, 88; ed, Home Voices: A Sampler of Southern Writing, Univ Press, 91. **CONTACT ADDRESS** Centre Col, 600 W Walnut St, Danville, KY, 40422. **EMAIL** lucasmrk@centre.edu

LUCAS, STEPHEN E.
PERSONAL Born 10/05/1946, White Plains, NY, m, 1969, 2 children **DISCIPLINE** COMMUNICATION **EDUCATION** Univ CA, Santa Barbara, BA, 68; PA State Univ, MA, 71, PhD, 73. **CAREER** Asst prof, 72-76, assoc prof, 76-82, prof, Dept Commun Arts, Univ WI, 82-; vis assoc prof, Univ VA, 79. **MEMBERSHIPS** Pulitzer Prize nomination for Portents of Rebellion, 76; Speech Commun Asn Golden Anniversary Award for Portents of Rebellion: Rhetoric and Revolution in Philadelphia, 1765-1776, 77; Chancellor's Award for Excellence in Teaching, Univ WI, 88; IW Student Asn Excellence in Teaching Award, 92; elected to WI Teaching Academy, 97. **RESEARCH** Am political rhetoric; rhetorical criticism. **SELECTED PUBLICATIONS** Auth, Portents of Rebellion: Rhetoric and Revolution in Philadelphia, 1765-1776, Temple Univ Press, 76; The Schism in Rhetorical Scholarship, Quart J of Speech, Feb 81; Genre Criticism and Historical Context: The Case of George Washington's First Inaugural Address, Southern Commun J, summer 86; The Renaissance of American Public Address: Text and Context in Rhetorical Criticism, Quart J of Speech, May 88; Justifying America: The Declaration of In-

dependence as a Rhetorical Document, in Thomas W Benson, ed, American Rhetoric: Context and Criticism, Southern IL Univ Press, 89; The Stylistic Artistry of the Declaration of Independence, Prologue, spring 90; The Art of Public Speaking, 6th ed, McGraw-Hill, 98; The Rhetorical Ancestry of the Declaration of Independence, Rhetoric and Public Affairs, summer 98; George Washington: The Wisdom of an Anmerican Patriot, Madison Housem 98. **CONTACT ADDRESS** Dept of Commun Arts, Univ of Wisconsin, Madison, Madison, WI, 53706. **EMAIL** selucas@facstaff.wisc.edu

LUCID, ROBERT FRANCIS
PERSONAL Born 06/25/1930, Seattle, WA, m, 1954, 1 child **DISCIPLINE** ENGLISH **EDUCATION** Univ Wash, BA, 54; Univ Chicago, MA, 55, PhD, 58. **CAREER** Instr English, Univ Chicago, 57-59; asst prof, Wesleyan Univ, 59-64; from asst prof to assoc prof, 64-75, PROF ENGLISH, UNIV PA, 75-, CHMN DEPT, 80-. **MEMBERSHIPS** Am Studies Asn (exec secy, 64-69); MLA; Aaup. **RESEARCH** American literature; modern literature. **SELECTED PUBLICATIONS** Auth, In Memoriam--Cohen, Hennig--1919-1996, Amer Quart, Vol 0049, 97. **CONTACT ADDRESS** Dept of English, Univ of Pa, Philadelphia, PA, 19104.

LUDWIG, RICHARD MILTON
PERSONAL Born 11/24/1920, Reading, PA **DISCIPLINE** ENGLISH **EDUCATION** Univ Mich, AB, 42; Harvard Univ, Am, 43, PhD(English), 50. **CAREER** From instr to assoc prof, 50-68, Prof English, Princeton Univ, 68-, Asst Librn Rare Bks & Spec Collections, 74-, Princeton preceptor, 54-57, Eng, 55-56, McCosh fac fel, 67-68. **MEMBERSHIPS** Am Studies Asn; MLA; Grolier Club. **RESEARCH** American and English novel; American poetry; American drama. **SELECTED PUBLICATIONS** Co-ed, Major American Writers, Harcourt, 52; ed, Aspects of American Poetry, Ohio State Univ, 63; Letters of Ford Madox Ford, Princeton Univ, 65; auth, Guide to American Literature and Its Backgrounds since 1890, Harvard Univ, 72; co-ed, Literary History of the United States, Macmillan, 74; ed, Dr Panofsky & Mr Tarkington, Princeton Univ Libr, 74; co-ed, Advanced Composition, Harcourt, 77. **CONTACT ADDRESS** Princeton Univ, 22 McCosh Hall, Princeton, NJ, 08540.

LUEBKE, STEVE
DISCIPLINE ENGLISH LITERATURE **EDUCATION** Univ WI, MA, PhD. **CAREER** Prof, Univ of WI. **RESEARCH** Contemp Am lit; fiction and poetry writing; lit and music; travel lit. **SELECTED PUBLICATIONS** Auth, pubs on Paul Theroux, Stephen Minot, Jack London; critical thinking. **CONTACT ADDRESS** Eng Dept, Univ Wisconsin, S 3rd St, PO Box 410, River Falls, WI, 54022-5001.

LUEY, BETH EDELMANN
PERSONAL Born 02/23/1946, Columbus, OH, m, 1967, 1 child **DISCIPLINE** SCHOLARLY PUBLISHING **EDUCATION** Radcliffe Col, BA, 67; Harvard Univ, AM, 68; Nat Hist Publ & Records Comn, cert, 81. **CAREER** Managing ed, World Law Fund; asst & assoc ed, Univ Pittsburgh Press, 73-77; DIR SCHOL PUBL PROG, ARIZ STATE UNIV, 80-. **MEMBERSHIPS** Asn Doc Ed; Women in Scholarly Publ; Soc Hist Authorship, Reading, and Publ; Soc Schol Publ. **SELECTED PUBLICATIONS** Auth, Handbook for Academic Authors, Cambridge Univ Press, 87, 90, 95; Editing Documents and Texts, Madison House, 90; coauth, The Structure of International Publishing in the 1990's, Transaction, 92. **CONTACT ADDRESS** Dept of Hist, Arizona State Univ, Tempe, PO Box 872501, Tempe, AZ, 85287-2501. **EMAIL** aabel@asuvm.inre.asu.edu

LUHR, WILLIAM GEORGE
PERSONAL Born 03/31/1946, Brooklyn, NY, m, 1981, 1 child **DISCIPLINE** ENGLISH LITERATURE, FILM STUDY **EDUCATION** Fordham Univ, BA, 67; NY Univ, MA, 69, PhD(Eng), 78. **CAREER** Tchr & chmn, Film Dept, Parsons Jr High Sch, 68-76; Assoc Prof Eng & Film, ST Peter's Col, 78-82, Adj lectr, Queens Col, New York, 70-73; consult, Films Inc, 73-76; panelist & interviewer, Athens Int Film Festival, 76-; lectr, Hudson County Community Col, 77; juror, Am Film Festival, 77-; videotape consult, Fac Med, Columbia Univ, 81; lectr, the Hum Inst, SUNY, Prof Eng, St. Peter's Col, 88-; vis prof of comm, Hunter Col, 91. **MEMBERSHIPS** MLA; Soc Cinema Studies; Univ Film & Video Asn; Col Eng Asn; Am Film Inst. **RESEARCH** Victorian lit; aesthetics and ideological study. **SELECTED PUBLICATIONS** Coauth, Authorship and Narrative in the Cinema: Issues in Contemporary Aesthetics and Criticism, GP Putnam's Sons, 77; auth, Howard Hawks, Hawkshief: Patterns of continuity in Rio Bravo, El Dorado and Rio Lobo, 77 & In the shadow of the Apocalypse, 79, Wide Angle; The function of narrative in literature and film: Some issues, In: Ideas of Order in Literature and Film, Univ Press Fla, 80; coauth, Blake Edwards, Ohio Univ Press, 81; auth, David Copperfield: Novel and film, In: The English Novel in Film, 81 & Raymond Chandler and Film, 82, Frederick Ungar Publ Co; Nosferatu and post-war German film, Mich Academician, World Cinema Since 1945, Frederick Ungar Publishing Co, 87;co-auth, Returning to the Scene: Blake Edwards, Vol II, Ohio Univ Press, 89; ed, The Maltese Falcon: John Houston, Director, Rutgers Univ Press, 95; co-auth, Thinking About Movies: Watching, Questioning, Enjoying, Harcourt, Brace and Co, 99. **CONTACT ADDRESS** 180 W Poplar St, Floral Park, NY, 11001. **EMAIL** LUHR_W@spcvxa.spc.edu

LUKACHER, NED
PERSONAL Born 09/03/1950, York, PA, m, 1978 **DISCIPLINE** ENGLISH LITERATURE, COMPARATIVE LITERATURE **EDUCATION** Dickinson Col, BA, 72; Univ Ariz, MA, 74; Duke Univ, PhD(English), 78. **CAREER** ASST PROF ENGLISH, UNIV ILL, CHICAGO, 80-. **SELECTED PUBLICATIONS** Auth, The 3rd Wound, Bowie, Malcolm, Brooks, Peter, and the Myth of Actaeon, Comp Lit, Vol 0048, 96. **CONTACT ADDRESS** Univ Illinois, Chicago, IL, 60680.

LUKENBILL, WILLIS B.
PERSONAL Born 03/27/1939, Smith Cty, TX, m, 1968, 1 child **DISCIPLINE** LIBRARY AND INFORMATION SCIENCE **EDUCATION** Univ N Tex, BS, 61; Univ Okla, MLS, 64; Ind Univ, PhD, 73. **CAREER** Lbn, Seguin HS, 61-63; Asst Lbn, Austin Col, 64; Inst, La Tech Univ, 64-68; Asst Prof, Univ Md, 72-74; Asst Prof, 75-80, Assoc Prof, 80-96, Prof, 96-, Grad Sch Lib & Inf Sci, Univ Tex at Austin. **HONORS AND AWARDS** Temple Tchng Fellow, Univ Tex, 87-88; Hall of Fame, Grad Sch Lib & Inf Sci, Univ N Tex. **MEMBERSHIPS** Am Lib Asn; Tex Lib Asn. **RESEARCH** Popular culture; youth media & literature; sociology of information delivery; AIDS-HIV information delivery. **SELECTED PUBLICATIONS** Auth, AIDS-HIV Information Services and Programs in Libraries, Lib Ultd, 94; auth, Providing HIV-AIDS Information for Rural Communities: A Role for the Rural Public Library, Pub Libraries, 34, 284-290, 10/95; auth, AIDS-HIV Services and Programs in Libraries, Encycl of Lib & Info Sci, vol 60, Marcel Dekker, Inc, 97; auth, Erotized AIDS-HIV Information on Cable Television: A Study of Obscenity, State Censorship and Cultural Resistance, AIDS Educ & Prevention, 10, 229-244, 6/98. **CONTACT ADDRESS** Grad Sch of Lib & Info Sci, Univ Tex at Austin, SZB 564, D7000, Austin, TX, 78712. **EMAIL** luke@uts.cc.utexas.edu

LUMSDEN, LINDA
PERSONAL Born 12/22/1953, Hartford, CT, 2 children **DISCIPLINE** MASS COMMUNICATION **EDUCATION** Central Ct St Univ, BA, 78; Syracuse Univ, MA, 89; Univ NC Chapel Hill, PhD, 95. **CAREER** Asst prof, W Ks Univ, 96- **HONORS AND AWARDS** Minnie Rubinstein Grad Res Fel, 94 **MEMBERSHIPS** AEJMC; AJHA. **RESEARCH** Women's hist; jour hist; first amendment hist. **SELECTED PUBLICATIONS** Auth, Adirondack Craftspeople, Adirondack Publ Co, 83; Playing with Fire: A legal Analysis of Cross Burning in RAV w. St. Paul, Free Speech Yearbook, 93; Rampant Women: Suffragists and the Right of Assembly, Univ Tn Press, 97; Suffragist, Equal Rights, in Women's Periodicals of the US, Greenwood Press, 97; Feminist Press, New York Times, New York Herald Tribune, Suffrage Press, in History of the Mass Media in the US, Fitzroy Dearborn, 98. **CONTACT ADDRESS** Dept of J, W KY Univ, Bowling Green, KY, 42101. **EMAIL** linda.lumsden@wku.edu

LUNDE, ERIK SHELDON
PERSONAL Born 10/16/1940, Hanover, NH, m, 1963, 2 children **DISCIPLINE** AMERICAN HISTORY, FILM HISTORY, FILM STUDIES **EDUCATION** Harvard Univ, AB, 63; Univ Md, MA, 66, PhD(Am Hist), 70. **CAREER** Asst prof Am Hist, Marquette Univ, 69-70; asst prof, 70-74, assoc prof, 74-79, prof Am Thought & Lang, Mich State Univ, 79-. **HONORS AND AWARDS** Outstanding Teacher Award, Mich State Univ Chapter, Golden Key National Honor Society, 94. **MEMBERSHIPS** Orgn Am Historians. **RESEARCH** Auth, Horace Greeley, G K Hall, 81; Civil War and Reconstruction; American intellectual history; American studies. **SELECTED PUBLICATIONS** Co-ed with Douglas Noverr, Film Studies and Film History, Markus Wiener, 89; **CONTACT ADDRESS** Dept of American Thought & Lang, Michigan State Univ, 289 Bessey Hall, East Lansing, MI, 48824-1033.

LUNSFORD, ANDREA ABERNETHY
PERSONAL Born 09/17/1942, Ardmore, OK, m, 1972 **DISCIPLINE** ENGLISH, RHETORIC **EDUCATION** Univ Fla, BA, 62, MA, 64; Ohio State Univ, PhD(English and rhet), 77. **CAREER** Instr English and debate, Colonial High Sch, Fla, 65-68; assoc prof English, Hillsborough Community Col, Fla, 68-72; grad res assoc, Ohio State Univ, Columbus, 72-77; asst prof, 77-80, ASSOC PROF ENGLISH AND COORDR COMPOS, UNIV BC, 80-. **MEMBERSHIPS** MLA; Nat Coun Teachers English; Rhet Soc Am; Int Soc Hist Rhet; Can Coun Teachers English. **RESEARCH** Nineteenth and 20th century rhetoric; theory of composition. **SELECTED PUBLICATIONS** Auth, Teachers Rhetorical Comments on Student Papers, Coll Composition and Commun, Vol 0044, 93; Hypertext--the Convergence of Contemporary Critical Theory and Technology, Mod Philol, Vol 0092, 94; Representing Audience, Successful Discourse and Disciplinary Critique, Coll Composition and Commun, Vol 0047, 96; Intellectual Property and Composition Studies, Coll Composition and Commun, Vol 0047, 96; Rhetoric and Pluralism, Philos and Lit, Vol 0020, 96. **CONTACT ADDRESS** Ohio State Univ, Columbus, OH, 43210.

LUPACK, ALAN
DISCIPLINE ENGLISH **EDUCATION** Univ PA, PhD. **CAREER** Cur, Rossell Hope Robbins Libr & Koller-Collins grad ctr; taught at, St John's Univ, Wayne State Col NE & Univ Wroclaw Poland. **HONORS AND AWARDS** Developer, Camelot Proj WWW. **MEMBERSHIPS** Ed bd, Arthuriana and TEAMS Middle Eng Texts. **RESEARCH** Mod versions of the Arthurian legends, particularly the Arthurian legend in Am; medievalism in lit and the arts. **SELECTED PUBLICATIONS** Auth, The Dream of Camelot, poems; ed, Three Middle English Charlemagne Romances, Arthur the Greatest King: An Anthology of Modern Arthurian Poetry; Arthurian Drama: An Anthology, Lancelot of the Laik and Sir Tristrem, A Round Table of Contemporary Arthurian Poetry & special issue of Arthuriana on King Arthur in America; articles on, Sir Tristrem, Amer Arthurian lit & Arthurian youth groups. **CONTACT ADDRESS** Dept of Eng, Univ of Rochester, 601 Elmwood Ave, Ste. 656, Rochester, NY, 14642. **EMAIL** alpk@db1.cc.rochester.edu

LURIE, ALISON
PERSONAL Born 09/03/1926, Chicago, IL, m, 1996, 3 children **DISCIPLINE** CHILDREN'S LITERATURE, FOLKLORE **EDUCATION** Radcliffe Col, AB, 47. **CAREER** Lectr Eng, 69-73, adj assoc prof, 73-76, assoc prof, 76-79, Prof Eng, Cornell Univ, 79-, Frederic J Whiton Prof Am Lit, Cornell Univ, Yaddo Found fel, 63, 64 & 66; Guggenheim fel, 65; Rockefeller Found fel, 67. **HONORS AND AWARDS** New York State Cultural Coun Found Grant (CAPS), 72-73; Am Ac Arts & Lett Award, Fiction, 84; Pulitzer Prize, Fiction, 85; Radcliffe Col Alumnae Recognition Award, 87; Prix Femina Etranger, 89 **MEMBERSHIPS** MLA; Aaup; Children's Lit Asn; Pen Club; Author's Guild. **SELECTED PUBLICATIONS** Auth, Love and Friendship, Macmillan, 62; The Nowhere City, Coward McCann, 65; Imaginary Friends, 67, Coward McCann; Real People, 69 & The War Between the Tates, 74, Random House; V R Lang: Poems and Plays, with Memoir by Alison Lurie, Random House, 75; co-ed, The Garland Library of Children's Classics (73 vols), Garland Publ, 76; auth, Only Children, Random House, 79; Clever Gretchen and Other Forgotten Folk Tales, Crowell, 80; The Heavenly Zoo, Farrar Strauss, 81; The Language of Clothes, Random House, 81; Foreign Affairs, Random House, 84; The Truth abut Lorin Jones, Little Brown, 88; Don't Tell the Grownups: Subversive Children's Literature, Little Brown, 90; Women and Ghosts, Doubleday, 94; The Last Resort, Holt, 98; ed, The Oxford Book of Modern Fairy Tales. **CONTACT ADDRESS** Eng Dept, Cornell Univ, 252 Goldwin Smith Hall, Ithaca, NY, 14853-0001. **EMAIL** al28@cornell.edu

LUSARDI, JAMES P.
PERSONAL Born 09/03/1931, Morristown, NJ, m, 1953, 2 children **DISCIPLINE** ENGLISH **EDUCATION** Lafayette Col, AB, 55; Yale Univ, MA, 57, PhD(English), 63. **CAREER** Instr English, Williams Col, 58-61; asst prof, Wesleyan Univ, 62-66; ASSOC PROF ENGLISH, LAFAYETTE COL, 66-, Am Coun Learned Soc grant, 65. **MEMBERSHIPS** Renaissance Soc Am; MLA. **RESEARCH** English Renaissance; dramatic and non-dramatic literature, especially Thomas More, Shakespeare and Milton. **SELECTED PUBLICATIONS** Auth, The Pictured Playhouse, Reading the Utrecht Engraving of Shakespeare London, Shakespeare Quart, Vol 0044, 93. **CONTACT ADDRESS** Dept of English, Lafayette Col, Easton, PA, 18042.

LUSCHER, ROBERT M.
PERSONAL San Diego, CA **DISCIPLINE** AMERICAN LITERATURE **EDUCATION** Univ Calif, San Diego, BA; Duke Univ, MA, PhD. **CAREER** Instr, La State Univ; instr, dir, Honors, ch, dept Eng, Catawba Col; instr, ch, dept Eng, Univ Nebr, Kearney. **RESEARCH** The short story sequence. **SELECTED PUBLICATIONS** Published a book on John Updike's short fiction, as well as articles on Ernest Gaines, J.D. Salinger, Mary Wilkins Freeman, and Emily Dickinson. **CONTACT ADDRESS** Dept of Eng, Univ Nebr, Kearney, Kearney, NE, 68849-1320. **EMAIL** luscherr@platte.unk.edu

LUSTIG, MYRON W.
DISCIPLINE INTERPERSONAL COMMUNICATION **EDUCATION** Univ WI, PhD. **CAREER** Comm, San Diego St Univ. **HONORS AND AWARDS** Assoc ed, Commun Monogr; assoc ed, W Jour Commun. **SELECTED PUBLICATIONS** Auth, Intercultural Competence: Interpersonal Communication Across Cultures, 96. **CONTACT ADDRESS** Dept of Commun, San Diego State Univ, 5500 Campanile Dr, San Diego, CA, 92182. **EMAIL** rlustig@mail.sdsu.eduy

LUTKUS, ALAN
PERSONAL Born 09/28/1940, East Chicago, IN, m, 1966 **DISCIPLINE** ENGLISH, LINGUISTICS **EDUCATION** Harvard Univ, BA, 62; Ind Univ, MA, 66, PhD, 75. **CAREER** Ndea Lectr Ling, Trinity Col, Conn, 68; Instr Eng & ling, Northern IL Univ, 69-71; Assoc Prof Eng & Ling, State Univ NY Col Geneseo, 73-; Chief Ling Consul, Amer Inst Tech, vocab series Wordscape, 90; media consilt, NEH Amer radio Project, 96-97. **RESEARCH** Stylistics; compos. **SELECTED PUBLICATIONS** Coauth, Arts and Skills of English: Daybook, Grades 3-6, Holt, 72-73; auth, Troublespeaking the ap-

proach to public doublespeaking: Purism and our concept of language, Col English, 76; coauth, Spelling Matters, 77 & The World of Spelling, Grades 1-8, 78, Heath; coauth, Spelling Worlds, Grades 2-6, Ditto Master Series, Heath, 79; Buster Keaton, p265-272, Sir John Falstaff, p176-184, Touchstone, p466-470, in Fools and jesters in Literature, Art, and History: A Bio-Biographical Sourcebook, Greenwood Press, 98; Composition Theory Meet sPractice and They Pretty Well Get Along Twice, Journal of Teaching Writing, 3, 84; Literacy Reconsidered For Better and Worse, Review essay, Journal of Teaching Writing, 2, 83. **CONTACT ADDRESS** Dept of Eng, SUNY, Geneseo, 1 College Cir, Geneseo, NY, 14454-1401. **EMAIL** lutkus@uno.cc.genesco.edu

LUTZ, MARY ANNE
DISCIPLINE ENGLISH **EDUCATION** LaSalle, BA, 75; Rutgers, MA, 82, PhD, 86. **CAREER** ASSOC PROF, ENG, FROSTBURG STATE UNIV **MEMBERSHIPS** Am Antiquarian Soc **CONTACT ADDRESS** Dept of Eng, Frostburg State Univ, Frostburgh, MD, 21532-1099.

LUTZ, REINHART
DISCIPLINE ENGLISH LITERATURE **EDUCATION** Univ Berlin, BA, 83; Univ CA, MA, 85; PhD, 91. **CAREER** Assoc prof, Univ Pacific. **MEMBERSHIPS** MLA; UOP; Soc Cinema Studies. **SELECTED PUBLICATIONS** Auth, publ(s) on Barry Malzberg; J.G. Ballard; Ohm Krueger. **CONTACT ADDRESS** Eng Dept, Univ Pacific, Pacific Ave, PO Box 3601, Stockton, CA, 95211.

LUTZ, WILLIAM
DISCIPLINE RHETORIC AND COMPOSITION, 19TH-CENTURY BRITISH LITERATURE **EDUCATION** Rutgers Sch Law, JD; Nev, Reno, PhD. **CAREER** Instr, Rutgers, State Univ NJ, Camden Col of Arts and Sci; ed, Quart Rev of Doublespeak 80-94. **HONORS AND AWARDS** Warren I. Sussman Award for Excellence in Tchg, 91; George Orwell Award for Distinguished Contribution to Honesty and Clarity in Pub Lang, 96. **SELECTED PUBLICATIONS** Auth, Beyond Nineteen Eighty-Four, NCTE, 89; Doublespeak , HarperCollins, 89; The New Doublespeak, HarperCollins, 96; The Assessment of Writing: Politics, Policies, and Practices, Mod Lang Asn, 96; ed, Webster's New World Thesaurus, Simon and Schuster, 86; The Cambridge Thesaurus of American English, Cambridge, 94. **CONTACT ADDRESS** Rutgers, State Univ NJ, Camden Col of Arts and Sci, New Brunswick, NJ, 08903-2101. **EMAIL** wlutz@camden.rutgers.edu

LUXON, THOMAS H.
PERSONAL Born 04/26/1954, Darby, PA, m, 1988, 2 children **DISCIPLINE** ENGLISH, LITERATURE **EDUCATION** Brown Univ, AB, 77; Univ Chicago, AM, 78, PhD, 84. **CAREER** William Rainey Harper Instr, 84-85, Univ Chicago; vis asst prof, 85-86, St. Lawrence Univ, NY; asst prof, 87-88, Franklin and Marshall Col; asst prof, 88-94, assoc prof, 94-, Dartmouth Col. **HONORS AND AWARDS** The Robinson Potter Dunn Premium in Eng, Brown Univ, 76; The Ratcliffe Hicks Premium in Eng, Brown Univ, 77; Univ Chicago Scholar for Grad Stud, 78-79, 81-82, 83-84; The Charlotte W. Newcombe Diss fel, The Woodrow Wilson Fel Found, 83-84; Nat Endowment for the Hum Fel for Independent Stud & Res, 86-87; Jr Fac fel, Dartmouth Col, 92; Venture Fund for Acad Computing, Dartmouth Col, 97. **MEMBERSHIPS** Modern Lang Asn; John Bunyan Soc of North Am; John Milton Soc; Renaissance Soc of Am. **RESEARCH** Early modern culture, especially relig and lit; critical theory; teaching writing; electronic editions of literary works. **SELECTED PUBLICATIONS** Auth, Other Men's Words and Bunyan's New-Birth, Texas Stud in Lang & Lit, 36, 94; auth, Literal Figures: Puritan Allegory and the Reformation Crisis in Representation, Univ Chicago Press, 95; auth, Rough Trade: Milton as Ajax in the Place of Punishment, Prose Stud: Lit, Hist, Theory 19, 96; auth, Single Imperfection: Manliness in the Age of Milton, Univ Chicago Press; A Second Daniel: The Jew and the True Jew in The Merchant of Venice, Early Modern Lit Studies 4.3, 99; Not Words Alone: Milton and Carnal Conversation. **CONTACT ADDRESS** Dartmouth Col, 6032 Sanborn House, Hanover, NH, 03755. **EMAIL** thomas.h.luxon@dartmouth.edu

LVOVICH, NATASHA
PERSONAL Born 06/11/1956, Moscow, Russia, m, 1980, 2 children **DISCIPLINE** ENGLISH **EDUCATION** Moscow Ling Univ, BA, 76, MA, 78; Union Grad School, PhD, 95. **CAREER** Instr, Moscow Lang Training Ctr, 80-88; transl, Hebrew Immigrant Aid Soc, 88-89; instr, Sutton Bus School, 89-90; instr, Michel Thomas Lang Ctr, 89-94; instr, Touro Col, 90-94; consult, Jews for Racial & Econ Justice, 94-96; adj asst prof Dept Tchg & Learning, NY Univ, 95-97; adj lectr, 91-94, substitute instr, 94-95, adj asst prof, 95-97, substitute asst prof English, 97, ASST PROF ENGLISH, 97- , KINGSBOROUGH COMM COL, CUNY. **MEMBERSHIPS** MLA; TESOL Int; NYS TESOL; CUNY ESL Coun; Ctr Appl Ling. **RESEARCH** Second language acquisition: Psycho-and sociolinguistic perspectives; Inter-cultural and affective dimensions of bilingualism; Acculturation and language learning; Socio-cultural identity and language. **SELECTED PUBLICATIONS** Auth, The Effect of the Affect: Psychosocial Factors in Adult ESL Student Language Performance, College ESL, CUNY, 95; The Multilingual Self: An Inquiry into Language Learning, Lawrence Erlbaum Assoc Publi, 97; Acculturation and Learning: A Multilingual View, CenterPieces, Kingsborough Comm Col, CUNY, 98. **CONTACT ADDRESS** Dept of English, Kingsborough Comm Col, CUNY, 2001 Oriental Blvd, Brooklyn, NY, 11235. **EMAIL** NLvovich@kbcc.cuny.edu

LYNCH, KATHRYN
PERSONAL Born 03/30/1951, Los Angeles, CA, m, 1974, 3 children **DISCIPLINE** ENGLISH **EDUCATION** Stanford Univ, BA, 73; Univ Virginia, MA, 78, PhD, 82. **CAREER** Asst Prof, Assoc Prof, Prof, 83 to 98-, Wellesley College; Lectr, 82-83, UCLA. **HONORS AND AWARDS** NEH 87, 97. **MEMBERSHIPS** MLA; MAA; Chaucer Soc. **RESEARCH** Chaucer; Medieval Lit; Dreams in Lit. **SELECTED PUBLICATIONS** Auth, The Logic of the Dream Vision in Chaucer's, House of Flame, Literary Nominalism and the Theory of Rereading Medieval Texts, Lewiston NY, 95; auth, East Meets West in Chaucer's Squire's and Franklin's Tales, Speculum, 95; Partitioned Fictions: The Meaning and Importance of Walls in Chaucer's Poetry, Art and the Context in Late Medieval English Narrative, ed, R R Edwards, Cambridge, 94; auth, The High Medieval dream Vision: Poetry Philosophy and Literary Form, Stanford, 88. **CONTACT ADDRESS** Dept of English, Wellesley Col, Wellesley, MA, 02481. **EMAIL** klynch@wellesley.edu

LYNCH, ROSE MARIE
PERSONAL Born 09/09/1942, Linton, IN, m, 1977, 2 children **DISCIPLINE** ENGLISH **EDUCATION** Ind State Univ, BS, 64, MS, 64; Ball State Univ, PhD(English), 75. **CAREER** Instr English, Olney Central Col, 64-68; teaching fel, Ball State Univ, 68-70; Instr English & Jour, Ill Valley Community Col, 70-, newspaper advisor, Tech Prep team leader. **HONORS AND AWARDS** Connections 2000, Ill State Board of Educ, 93; Outstanding Fac Mem Award, Ill Comm Col Trustees Asn, 94. **MEMBERSHIPS** Nat Sch Board Asn; Am Fedn of Teachers; Lassalle-Perm High Sch Board of Educ. **RESEARCH** Freshman composition programs, particularly in junior colleges. **SELECTED PUBLICATIONS** Auth, We Can't wish it away, ADE Bull, 5/76; Junior college instructors do need special training, Conf Col Compos & Commun, 5/76; The Advisor's Nightmare, Community Col Journalist, 88; Reliving the past, Col English, 9/77; Did I Miss Anything, Eng J, 4/91. **CONTACT ADDRESS** Illinois Valley Comm Col, 2578 E 350th Rd, Oglesby, IL, 61348-1074. **EMAIL** rmlynch@ivcc.edu

LYNCH, THOMAS PATRICK
PERSONAL Born 08/19/1930, Brooklyn, NY **DISCIPLINE** ENGLISH LITERATURE **EDUCATION** Fordham Univ, MA, 58; Columbia Univ, MA, 64, PhD, 69. **CAREER** Prof Eng, Greek & Latin, San Jose Sem, Quezon City, Philippines, 55-58; ch Eng, Ateneo Davao, Davao City, Philippines, 64-66; asst prof, Ateneo Manila, Philippines, 70-74; Prof Eng, St Peter's Col, Jersey City, NJ, 74-, Chmn Dept, 78. **MEMBERSHIPS** MLA; Col Eng Asn. **RESEARCH** Nineteenth and 20th century Am; Brit 20th century; Chaucer. **SELECTED PUBLICATIONS** Auth, Still needed: A Tuckerman text, Papers Bibliog Soc Am, 75. **CONTACT ADDRESS** St Peter's Col, 2641 Kennedy Blvd, Jersey City, NJ, 07306-5997. **EMAIL** lynch_pspcvxa@spc.edu

LYNGSTAD, SVERRE
PERSONAL Born 04/30/1922, Norway, 1 child **DISCIPLINE** ENGLISH **EDUCATION** Univ Oslo, Norway, BA(English), 43, BA(hist), 46; Univ Wash, MA, 49; NY Univ, PhD(English), 60. **CAREER** Asst English compos, NY Univ, 49-53; lectr English compos and lit, City Col New York, 54-55; instr English, Hofstra Col, 55-60 and Queens Col, NY, 60-62; from asst prof to assoc prof, 62-68, PROF ENGLISH, NJ INST TECHNOL, 68-, Ed consult Scand lit, Grove Press, NY, 63-68. **MEMBERSHIPS** MLA; Am Comp Lit Asn; Soc Advan Scand Studies; Int Soc Study Time. **RESEARCH** The novel, especially British, Scandinavian and Russian; time in literature; technology and human values. **SELECTED PUBLICATIONS** Auth, Helvetesfabel, World Lit Today, Vol 0066, 92; Min Steilende Love, Noveller Om Kjaerlighet, World Lit Today, Vol 0067, 93; 'Brekasjer'--Collected Poems 1970-1985, World Lit Today, Vol 0067, 93; A History of Norwegian Literature, World Lit Today, Vol 0068, 94; Dikt Og Spelmannsmusikk 1968-1993, World Lit Today, Vol 0068, 94; 'Dimension'--Special Issue, Scand Stud, Vol 0067, 95; Frokost I Det Skjonne, World Lit Today, Vol 0069, 95; Omrade Aldri Fastlagt, World Lit Today, Vol 0069, 95; Fimbul, World Lit Today, Vol 0069, 95; Kalenderdikt, World Lit Today, Vol 0070, 96; En 'Annen Vei', World Lit Today, Vol 0071, 97. **CONTACT ADDRESS** Dept of Humanities, New Jersey Inst of Tech, 323 High St, Newark, NJ, 07102.

LYNN, PENROD
PERSONAL Piqua, OH **DISCIPLINE** SOCIAL SCIENCES/HUMANITIES **EDUCATION** Ohio State Univ, BA, 67, PhD, 75; Yale Univ, MAT, 68; Univ Alberta, LLB, 80, LLM, 86; BAR: Alta, 84. **CAREER** Tchr, Paul Dunbar High Sch, 68-69; tchr, Oakwood St. High, 70-72; adj asst prof, Fr, Wright State Univ, 70-72; grad tchg asst, Ohio State Univ, 72-75; asst prof, Univ South Carolina, 75-77; lectr, Romance langs, 77-79, asst prof, 79-83, assoc prof, 83-89, LECTR, FAC LAW, UNIV ALBERTA, 86-, PROF ROMANCE LANGS 89-. **HONORS AND AWARDS** Fullbright Fel; Outstanding Grad, Tchr Assoc Award; Novice G. Fawcett President's Gold Medal; Col Arts & Scis Coun Gold Medal; Women's Panhellenic Scholar Gold Medal, Ohio State Univ. **MEMBERSHIPS** Law Soc Alta; MLA; Am Asn Tchrs Fr; Can Comp Lit Asn; The Friends of George Sand; Nat Asn Women Educ; Can Asn Law Soc; Can Asn Law Tchrs; Nat Asn Women & Inst Law Res & Reform Law. **SELECTED PUBLICATIONS** Auth, Divorce Mediation: Helping to Ease the Pain, in Network of Sask Women, 86; auth, Canadian Children's Literature in French: an Annotated Bibliography; auth, Experiences Litteraires, 89; auth, Helene Cixous: The Future Feminine, 94. **CONTACT ADDRESS** SSHRCC, 350 Albert St, Box 1610, Ottawa, ON, K1P 6G4. **EMAIL** lpenrod@vm.ucs.ualberta.ca

LYON CLARK, BEVERLY
DISCIPLINE ENGLISH **EDUCATION** Swarthmore Col, BA; Brown Univ, PhD. **CAREER** Engl, Wheaton Col. **RESEARCH** Rel between feminist theory and criticism of children's lit. **SELECTED PUBLICATIONS** coed, Little Women And The Feminist Imagination And Nobody's Baby: Feminist Theory And Children's Culture; co-auth, Feminist Criticism; Reading Romance, Reading Ourselves. **CONTACT ADDRESS** Dept of Eng, Wheaton Col, 26 East Main St, Norton, MA, 02766. **EMAIL** Beverly_Clark@wheatonma.edu

LYONS, BRIDGET G.
PERSONAL Born 08/28/1932, Prague, Czechoslovakia, m, 1971 **DISCIPLINE** ENGLISH LANGUAGE AND LITERATURE **EDUCATION** Radcliffe Univ, BA; Oxford Univ, MA; Columbia, PhD. **CAREER** Prof. **RESEARCH** 16th-17th century English literature; European Renaissance. **SELECTED PUBLICATIONS** Auth, Orson Welles: Chimes at Midnight, Reading in an Age of Theory; ed, Voices of Melancholy. **CONTACT ADDRESS** Dept of English, Rutgers Univ, 510 George St, Murray Hall, New Brunswick, NJ, 08901-1167. **EMAIL** lyons@fas-english.rutgers.edu

LYONS, TIMOTHY JAMES
PERSONAL Born 07/06/1944, Framingham, MA, m, 1967, 2 children **DISCIPLINE** FILM HISTORY AND HISTORIOGRAPHY **EDUCATION** Univ Calif, Santa Barbara, BA, 66, MA, 68; Univ Iowa, PhD(speech and dramatic art), 72. **CAREER** From instr to asst prof radio, TV and film, Temple Univ, 72-76, chmn dept, 76-78, assoc prof, 76-80. ED, J UNIV FILM ASN 76-. **MEMBERSHIPS** Soc Cinema Studies (secy, 75-77, pres, 77-79); Univ Film Asn. **RESEARCH** American silent film; Charles Chaplin. **SELECTED PUBLICATIONS** Auth, The Complete Guide to American Film Schools and Cinema and Television Programs, J Film and Video, Vol 0047, 95. **CONTACT ADDRESS** 2534 Poplar, Philadelphia, PA, 19130.

LYRA, FRANCISZEK
DISCIPLINE ENGLISH **EDUCATION** Warsaw Univ, MA, 58; Univ Ind, PhD, 62. **CAREER** Sr lect, Eng, M. Curie-Sklodowska Univ, Poland; ADJ PROF, AM STUD CTR & ENG, WARSAW UNIV. **MEMBERSHIPS** Am Antiquarian Soc **SELECTED PUBLICATIONS** Trans: Maria Dzielska, Hypatia, Harvard Univ Press, 95; Trans, Ralph Waldo Emerson, "Manners," "Politics," "Nominalist and Realist," "New England Reformers," Wydawnictwo Test, Lublin. **CONTACT ADDRESS** Amer Stud Ctr, Warsaw Univ.

LYTAL, BILLY D.
PERSONAL Born 10/01/1939, Prentiss County, MS, m, 1961, 2 children **DISCIPLINE** COMMUNICATIONS **EDUCATION** Miss Col, BA, 61; Univ Miss, MA, 64; Univ Southern Miss, PhD, 80. **CAREER** Instr, chemn, Miss Col, 65-. **HONORS AND AWARDS** Chemn, Advertising comm, Public Relations comm; chemn, Miss Col. **MEMBERSHIPS** Miss Speech; Comm Asn. **RESEARCH** Audience profile **CONTACT ADDRESS** 115 E Lakeview, Clinton, MS, 39056. **EMAIL** lytal@mc.edu

M

MA, MING-QIAN
DISCIPLINE AMERICAN POETRY, LITERATURE **EDUCATION** Brigham Young Univ, MA, 87; Stanford Univ, PhD; 93. **CAREER** Exchange fac, 84-86, instr, Brigham Young Univ, 86-88; tchg asst/instr, 89-90, tutor, 90-91, tchg fel, 92-93, tchg asst/tutor, 94-95, tchg asst, Stanford Univ, 95-96; instr, Univ Nev, Las Vegas, 96-. **HONORS AND AWARDS** The Ed M and Minnie Berry Rowe Award for Excellence in Tchg, Brigham Young Univ, 87; Phi Kappa Phi, 87; grad fel, Stanford Univ, 89-90; John Sias dissertation fel, 93-94. **MEMBERSHIPS** MLA; Am Lit Asn; Am Comp Lit Asn; Am Asn of Chinese Comp Lit. **RESEARCH** The study of Postmodern experimental poetry and poetics in relation to art, science, and philosophy. **SELECTED PUBLICATIONS** Auth, Poetry as

History Revised: Susan Howe's Revisionist Approach to History in 'Scattering As Behavior Toward Risk', Am Lit Hist 6:4, 94; An Epistolary Road Map for a Modern-Day Moses: The Kierkegardian Strait Gates in Saul Bellow's Herzog, Saul Bellow J 13: 1, 95; Articulating the Inarticulate: Singularities and the Counter-Method in Susan Howe, Contemp Lit 36;3, 95; A 'no man's land!': Postmodern Citationality in Zukofsky's 'Poem beginning "The"', in Upper Limit Music: The Writing of Louis Zukofsky, Mark Scroggins ed, Univ Ala Press, 97. **CONTACT ADDRESS** Dept of Eng, Univ Nev, Las Vegas, 4505 Maryland Pky, PO Box 455011, Las Vegas, NV, 89154. **EMAIL** ma1@nevada.edu

MA, QIAN
DISCIPLINE ENGLISH LITERATURE **EDUCATION** Emory Univ, PhD. **CAREER** Dept Eng, Clark Atlanta Univ **RESEARCH** Comparative literature (Chinese and English); feminist literary criticism, especially feminist utopian studies; Chinese literature; 18th century British literature. **SELECTED PUBLICATIONS** Auth, published a book in China on the history of English literature. **CONTACT ADDRESS** Clark Atlanta Univ, 223 James P Brawley Dr, SW, Atlanta, GA, 30314.

MACDONALD, MARGARET R.
PERSONAL Born 01/21/1940, Seymour, IN, m, 1965, 2 children **DISCIPLINE** FOLKLORE; CHILDREN'S LITERATURE **EDUCATION** Ind Univ, AB, 62, PhD, 79; Univ Wash, Seattle, MLS, 64; Univ Hawaii, MEdEc, 68. **CAREER** Children's Specialist, 64-65, Childrens Lbn, 77-, King Co Lib System, Seattle, Wash; Vis Lecturer, Univ Wash, Seattle, 75-79. **HONORS AND AWARDS** Fulbright Schol, 95-96; Nat Storytelling Asn Leadership Award, 98. **MEMBERSHIPS** Am Folklore Soc; Am Library Asn; Nat Storytelling Asn; Int Bd on Books for Youth; Soc of Children's Book Writers & Illustrators. **RESEARCH** Personal narrative; performance theory; the folktale. **SELECTED PUBLICATIONS** Auth, The Storyteller's Sourcebook: A Subject, Title, and Motif Index to Folklore Collections for Children, Gale, 82; auth, Scipio, Indiana: Threads from the Past, Ye Galleon, 88; auth, The Folklore of World Holidays, Gale, 91; auth, The Storyteller's Start-up Book: Finding, Learning, Performing, and Using Folktales, Aug Hse, 93; auth, Scipio Storytelling: Talk in a Southern Indiana Community, Univ Press of Am, 96; ed, Thai Tales: Folktales of Thailand by Supaporn Vathanaprida, Libraries Unltd, 94; auth, Traditional Storytelling Today: An International Sourcebook, Fitzroy Dearborn, 98. **CONTACT ADDRESS** 11507 NE 104th, Kirkland, WA, 98083. **EMAIL** margmacd@kcls.org

MACDONALD, ROBERT HUGH
PERSONAL Born 06/15/1934, Manchester, England, m, 1959, 2 children **DISCIPLINE** ENGLISH LITERATURE **EDUCATION** NY Univ, AB, 59; Univ Edinburgh, dipl English studies, 63, PhD(English), 69. **CAREER** Asst prof, 68-71, assoc prof, 71-79, PROF ENGLISH, CARLETON UNIV, 79-. **RESEARCH** The novel; myth and symbol. **SELECTED PUBLICATIONS** Auth, Representing War--Form and Ideology in First World War Narratives, Engl Stud in Can, Vol 0022, 96. **CONTACT ADDRESS** Dept of English, Carleton Univ, 1125 Colonel By Dr, Ottawa, ON, KIS 5B6.

MACHANN, CLINTON JOHN
PERSONAL Born 07/18/1947, Bryan, Tex, m **DISCIPLINE** BRITISH & AMERICAN LITERATURE **EDUCATION** Tex A&M Univ, BA, 69; Univ Tex, Austin, PhD(English), 76. **CAREER** Asst Prof English, Tex A&M Univ, 76-, Proj dir, Tex Czechs Symp, Tex Comt for Humanities, 78-79. **MEMBERSHIPS** MLA; Soc for Study of Multi-Ethnic Lit US; Col English Asn; Conf Col Teachers English. **RESEARCH** British Victorian prose; American ethnic literature; structuralism in literary theory. **SELECTED PUBLICATIONS** Auth, John Stuart Mill's mental crisis: Adlerian interpretation, J of Adlerian Psychol, 73; T J Wise and Browning's Helen's Tower, Papers Bibliog Soc Am, 74; contribr, The present state of the Czech language in Texas, In: Southwest Areal Linguistics Then and Now, Trinity Univ, 77; ed, The Czechs in Texas: A Symposium, Tex A&M Univ, 77; auth, Multiethnic literature, CEA Forum, 78; Ruskin's Praeterita and nineteenth-century autobiographical genre, English Lang Notes, 78; Hugo Chotek and Czech-American fiction, Melus, 79; The foliate pattern: Evidence of natural process in Thoreau, Thoreau Quart, 81; coauth, Krasna Amerika: A Study of the Texas Czechs, 1851-1939, Eakin Press, 83; auth, Czech Music in Texas: A Sesquicentennial Symposium, Komensky Press, 87; coauth, Matthew Arnold in His Time and Ours: Centenary Essays, Univ of VA, 88; auth, Katherine Anne Porter and Texas: An Uneasy Relationship, Texas A&M Univ, 90; auth, Czech Voices: Stories from Texas in the Amerikan narodni kalendar, Texas A&M, 91; auth, Selected Letters of Matthew Arnold, Univ of Mich, 93; auth, The Genre of Autobiography in Victorian Literature, Univ of Mich, 95; auth, Matthew Arnold: A Literary Life, St. Martin's, 97. **CONTACT ADDRESS** Dept of English, Tex A&M Univ, Dept. of Eng, College Station, TX, 77843-4227. **EMAIL** c-machann@tamu.edu

MACHOR, JAMES LAWRENCE
PERSONAL Born 10/13/1950, Cleveland, OH, m, 1972, 1 child **DISCIPLINE** ENGLISH LITERATURE **EDUCATION** OH Univ, BA, 72; Univ ID, MA, 74; Univ IL, PhD, 80. **CAREER** Asst prof, 80-86, assoc prof, OH State Univ, Lima, 86-90; assoc prof, 90-95, prof, KS State Univ, 95-. **HONORS AND AWARDS** Nat Endowment for the Humanities, summer, 86; Sr Fulbright fel, Univ Brussels, Belgium, 91. **MEMBERSHIPS** Modern Lang Asn; Am Studies Asn; Am Lit Asn. **RESEARCH** Nineteenth-century Am lit and culture; reader-oriented criticism and theory; fiction and narratology. **SELECTED PUBLICATIONS** Auth, Patoral Cities: Urban Ideals and the Symbolic Landscape of America, Univ WI press, 87; Historical Hermeneutics and Antebellum Fiction: Gender, Response Theory, and Interpretive Contexts, Readers in History, ed James L Machor, Johns Hopkins Univ Press, 93; ed, Readers in History: Nineteenth-Century American Literature and the Contexts of Response, Johns Hopkins Univ Press, 93; auth, Searching for Targets with a Loaded Canon, ESQ: A J of the Am Renaissance, 39, 93; Canon Exchanges and the Changing Profession, J of the Midwest Modern Language Asn, 31 2, 98; many other articles and chapters. **CONTACT ADDRESS** Dept of English, Kansas State Univ, Denison Hall, Manhattan, KS, 66506. **EMAIL** machor@ksu.edu

MACK, ROBERT
DISCIPLINE 18TH-CENTURY BRITISH LITERATURE **EDUCATION** Princeton Univ, PhD. **CAREER** Instr, Vanderbilt Univ. **RESEARCH** Biography of Thomas Gray. **SELECTED PUBLICATIONS** Ed, Oriental Tales; Arabian Nights' Entertainments; Horace Walpole's The Castle of Otranto; co-ed, Frances Burney's The Wanderer. **CONTACT ADDRESS** Vanderbilt Univ, Nashville, TN, 37203-1727.

MACK, S. THOMAS
DISCIPLINE AMERICAN LITERATURE **EDUCATION** W Chester Univ, BA, 69; John Carroll Univ, MAT, 70; Villanova Univ, 73; Lehigh Univ, PhD. **CAREER** Prof, Univ SC Aiken, 76- ; lectr, Shanxi Univ, Taiyuan, People's Repub of China **HONORS AND AWARDS** Outstanding Teacher of the Year, 79-80; Amoco Found Outstanding Teaching Award, 80; Univ Svc Award, 88-89; Comm Svc Award, 92-93. **SELECTED PUBLICATIONS** Auth, Percival Everett, in Contemporary Southern Writers, St. James Press, 98; Fine Tuning the Senior Thesis, SC Higher Educ Assess Conf, 98; William Least Heat-Moon, in Encyclopedia of Multiculturalism, Supplement, Marshall Cavendish, 98; Alnilam, in Cyclopedia of Literary Characters, Salem Press, 98; Tripmaster Monkey: His Fake Book, in Cyclopedia of Literary Characters, Salem Press, 98. **CONTACT ADDRESS** 53 Deerwood Ct, Aiken, SC, 29803.

MACKAY, CAROL HANBERY
PERSONAL Born 07/01/1944, San Francisco, CA **DISCIPLINE** ENGLISH LITERATURE, RHETORIC AND COMPOSITION **EDUCATION** Stanford Univ, BA, 66, MA, 67; Univ Calif, Los Angeles, PhD(English), 79. **CAREER** ASST PROF ENGLISH, UNIV TEX, AUSTIN, 79-, Teach assoc and fel, Univ Calif, Los Angeles, 74-78; consult, Nat Inst Educ Writing Proficiency Assessment, 80-. **HONORS AND AWARDS** Outstanding New Teacher, Amoco Found, 81. **MEMBERSHIPS** MLA; NCTE; Conf Col Compos and Commun. **RESEARCH** The novel; 19th century English literature. **SELECTED PUBLICATIONS** Auth, Soaring Between Home and Heaven + Victorian Photography--Cameron, Julia, Margeret Visual Meditations on the Self, Libr Chronicle of the Univ Tex at Austin, Vol 0026, 96. **CONTACT ADDRESS** Dept English, Univ Tex, 0 Univ of Texas, Austin, TX, 78712-1026.

MACKENDRICK, LOUIS KING
DISCIPLINE ENGLISH LANGUAGE; LITERATURE **EDUCATION** Western Ontario, BA, MA; Toronto, PhilM, PhD, 71. **CAREER** Prof **RESEARCH** Canadian short story. **SELECTED PUBLICATIONS** Auth, Robert Harlow and His Works; Al Purdy and His Works & Some Other Reality: Alice Munro's Something I've Been Meaning to Tell You; ed, Probable Fictions: Alice Munro's Narrative Acts & issue of Essays on Canadian Writing on Al Purdy. **CONTACT ADDRESS** Dept of English Language and Literature, Univ of Windsor, 401 Sunset Ave, Windsor, ON, N9B 3P4.

MACKETHAN, LUCINDA HARDWICK
PERSONAL Born 09/12/1945, Akron, OH, m, 1969, 2 children **DISCIPLINE** AMERICAN LITERATURE, BRITISH LITERATURE **EDUCATION** Hollins Col, BA, 67; Univ NC, Chapel Hill, MA, 69, PhD(English), 74. **CAREER** Instr, 71-74, asst prof, 74-79, ASSOC PROF ENGLISH, NC STATE UNIV, 80-, Nat Endowment for Humanities fel, 81. **MEMBERSHIPS** MLA; Soc Study Southern Lit; S Atlantic MLA. **SELECTED PUBLICATIONS** Auth, Redeeming Blackness--Urban Allegories of Oconnor, Percy, and Toole, Stud in the Lit Imagination, Vol 0027, 94. **CONTACT ADDRESS** Dept of English, No Carolina State Univ, Raleigh, NC, 27695.

MACKEY, BARBARA S.
PERSONAL Born 01/27/1941, Los Angeles, CA, m, 1971, 1 child **DISCIPLINE** THEATRE **EDUCATION** Bowling Green State Univ, PhD, 96. **CAREER** Head of English and Speech div, John Woolman School, Nevada city, CA, 63; instr, Southern Univ LA, 65-67; Dir of Hancock County Speech Improvement Prog (GA), 67-68; asst prof, Shippensburg State Col, 68-69; teaching asst, PA State Univ, 69-71; instr, PA State Dept of Continuing Ed, 71-73; instr, Shippensburg State Col, 76-77; Int vis prof, Kolej Damansara Utama, Malaysia, spring 89; instr, Millersnvilee Univ, spring 93; Bowling Green State Univ, 93-96; currently part-time at Univ of Toledo, Owens Community Col, and Univ of Findlay. **HONORS AND AWARDS** First managing dir of Old Bedford Village Opera House, 82-84; creator and dir, Oral Interpretors Project, Old Bedford Village, 82-84. **MEMBERSHIPS** Asn for Theatre in Higher Ed; Speech Commun Asn; Central States Commun Asn; Theatre Asn of PA; Am Soc for Eighteenth-Century Studies. **RESEARCH** Theatre hist; 18th century; dramalurgy; dramatic lit. **SELECTED PUBLICATIONS** Auth, Classroom Across the World, Univ MI School of Ed Innovator, vol 23, no 1, spring-summer 92; Personality Assessments as a Guide to Acting Pedagogy, Communication and Theatre Asn of MN J, vol 22, summer 95; book review of The First English Actresses: Women and Drama 1660-1700, by Elizabeth Howe, Restoration and Eighteenth Century Theatre Research, series 2, vol 10, no 2, winter 95; The Antigone TV Interviews: An Activity for the Introductory Theatre Class, Commun and Theatre Asn of MN J, vol 24, 97; book review of Getting Into the Act: Women Playwrights in London 1776-1829, by Ellen Donkin, Restoration and Eighteenth Century Theater Research, series 2, vol 12, no 1, summer 97; book review of John Barrymore, Shakespearean Actor, by Michael A Morrison, in Text and Performance Quart, July 98; book review, Broken Boundaries: Women and Feminism in Restoration Drama, ed by Katherine M Quinsey, Restoration and Eighteenth Century Theatre Research, summer 98; The Lost Acting Treatise of Charles Manklin, Speech and Theatre Asn of MN, Aug 98; book review, Playwrights and Plagiarists in Early Modern England, by Laura J Rosenthal, Theatre J, Oct 98; numerous other publications. **CONTACT ADDRESS** 1058 Orchard Rd, Adrian, MI, 49221.

MACKILLOP, JAMES JOHN
PERSONAL Born 05/31/1939, Pontiac, MI, m, 1964, 2 children **DISCIPLINE** IRISH MYTHOLOGY & LITERATURE **EDUCATION** Wayne State Univ, AB, 62, MA, 68; Syracuse Univ, PhD(Eng), 75. **CAREER** Instr English, MI Technol Univ, 63-66; from asst prof to assoc prof, 69-78, Prof Eng, Onondaga Community Col, 78-, Vis fel, Harvard Univ, 75; drama & film critic theater, Wono, 76-80; lectr cinema, State Univ NY at Cortland, 79-. **HONORS AND AWARDS** Trustees' Award for Distinguished Fac Serv, Onondaga Community Col, 6/81; SUNY Award for Excellence in Tchg, State Univ of NY, 83. **MEMBERSHIPS** MLA; Am Conf for Irish Studies, Pres, 95-97; Can Asn Irish Studies. **RESEARCH** A dictionary of Celtic mythology; glossary of Celtic words in Eng usage; mythological theory. **SELECTED PUBLICATIONS** Contribr, Ulster violence in fiction, In: Conflict in Ireland, Univ Fla, 76; Finn MacCool: The hero & the anti-hero, In: Views of the Irish Peasantry, Archon, 77; contribr & ed, Speaking of Words, Holt, Rinehart & Winston, 78, 2nd ed, 82; Yeats, Joyce and the Irish Language, Eire-Ireland, spring 80; coauth (with T Friedmann), The Copy Book, Holt, Rinehart & Winston, 80; contribr, World Book Encyclopedia, 80; Richard Power's Pastoral Elegy, Eire-Ireland, summer 82; ed, Celtic Scholarship, Fionn mac Cumhaill: Celtic Myth in English Literature, Syracuse Univ, 86; co-ed, Irish Literature: A Reader, Syracuse Univ, 87; A Dictionary of Celtic Mythology, Oxford Univ, 98; Envisioning Ireland: Essays on Contemporary Irish Cinema, Syracuse Univ, 99. **CONTACT ADDRESS** 108 Limestone Ln, Syracuse, NY, 13219. **EMAIL** mackillj@aurora.sunyocc.edu

MACKINNON, PATRICIA L.
DISCIPLINE LIBERAL ARTS, GENERAL EDUCATION, INTERDISCIPLINARY STUDIES **EDUCATION** Univ CA, Irvine, BA; Univ CA, Santa Cruz, PhD. **CAREER** Instr, UCLA, Stanford Univ, Clarkson Univ, St Lawrence Univ, Univ CA, Davis; asst prof Hum, Golden Gate Univ. **SELECTED PUBLICATIONS** Auth of articles in medieval and renaissance studies. **CONTACT ADDRESS** Golden Gate Univ, San Francisco, CA, 94105-2968.

MACKSEY, RICHARD ALAN
PERSONAL Born 07/25/1931, Glen Ridge, NJ, m, 1956, 1 child **DISCIPLINE** COMPARATIVE LITERATURE, ENGLISH **EDUCATION** Johns Hopkins Univ, MA, 53, PhD, 57. **CAREER** Jr instr English, Johns Hopkins Univ, 53-55; from instr to asst prof, Loyola Col, 56-58; asst prof writing sem, 58-63, assoc prof humanistic studies, 64-73, Carnegie lectr sem hist ideas, 62-64, chmn sect lang, lit and cult, 66-72, actg dir humanities ctr, 68-69, PROF HUMANISTIC STUDIES AND CHMN HUMANITIES CTR, JOHNS HOPKINS UNIV, 73-, Chmn comt internal evidence, Bibliog Conf, 62; lectr, Baltimore Mus Art, 64-65; dir, Bollingen Poetry Festival, Turnbull lect, Theatre Hopkins, Center Stage, Tantamount Films, Carroll House and Levering Hall; moderator, Dialogue of the Arts, CBS; ed comp lit, Mod Lang Notes and Structure. **MEMBERSHIPS** MLA; Am Soc Aesthet; Renaissance Soc Am; Mediaeval Acad Am; Col English Asn. **RESEARCH** European and English novel; poetics, rhetoric, and theory of literature; interrelation of arts, comparative methodology and intellectual history. **SELECTED PUBLICATIONS** Auth, Mcclain, William ,H. 1917-1994--in Memoriam, Mln-Mod Lang Notes, Vol 0110, 95. **CONTACT ADDRESS** Ctr for Humanities, Johns Hopkins Univ, 3400 N Charles St, Baltimore, MD, 21218-2680.

MACKY, NANCY
DISCIPLINE DRAMA AND IRISH LITERATURE **EDUCATION** Kent State Univ, PhD. **CAREER** Asst prof. **HONORS AND AWARDS** Lady Gregory, scholar. **RESEARCH** Approaches to teaching. **SELECTED PUBLICATIONS** Publ in, nat textbook on teaching techniques; other journals. **CONTACT ADDRESS** Dept of Eng, Westminister Col, New Wilmington, PA, 16172-0001.

MACLAINE, ALLAN HUGH
PERSONAL Born 10/24/1924, Montreal, PQ, Canada, m, 1949 **DISCIPLINE** ENGLISH **EDUCATION** McGill Univ, BA, 45; Brown Univ, PhD(English), 51. **CAREER** Instr English, McGill, 46-47, Brown Univ, 47-50 & Univ MA, 51-54; from asst prof to prof, TX Christian Univ, 54-62; PROF ENGLISH, UNIV RI, 62-, DIR GRAD STUDIES ENGLISH, 71-, Chmn dept English, 66-67, actg dean div univ exten, 67-68, dean, 68-71. **MEMBERSHIPS** MLA; Col English Asn (dir, 61-, pres, 65-66); Int Asn Univ Prof English; fel Nat Univ Exten Asn; Asn for Scottish Literary Studies. **RESEARCH** Scottish poetry, especially Burns; middle English literature, especially Chaucer; 18th century English literature. **SELECTED PUBLICATIONS** Auth, Burn's use of Parody in Tam O'Shanter, Criticism, 59; The Student's Comprehensive Guide to the Canterbury Tales, Barron's, 64; Robert Fergusson, Twayne, 65; The Christis Kirk tradition: Its evolution in Scots poetry to Burns, Studies in Scottish Lit, 65-66; Allan Ramsay, Twayne, 85; ed, The Christis Kirk Tradition: Scots Poems of Folk Festivity, Asn for Scottish Literary Studies, 96. **CONTACT ADDRESS** Dept of English, Univ of RI, Kingston, RI, 02881.

MACLEAN, HUGH NORMAN
PERSONAL Born 03/24/1919, Aguilas, Spain, m, 1949, 2 children **DISCIPLINE** ENGLISH **EDUCATION** Princeton Univ, BA, 40; Univ Toronto, MA, 47, PhD(English), 50. **CAREER** Lectr English, Univ Toronto, 49-50; asst prof, Royal Mil Col, 50-56, Univ Cincinnati, 56-60 and York Univ, 60-63; prof, 63-74, DISTINGUISHED TEACHING PROF ENGLISH, STATE UNIV NY ALBANY, 74-, Huntington Libr res fel, 54-55; ED, SPENSER NEWSLETTER, 82-. **MEMBERSHIPS** MLA; Renaissance Soc Am; Int Asn Univ Profs English; Shakespeare Asn Am; Spenser Soc; Milton Soc. **RESEARCH** Literature of the English Renaissance. **SELECTED PUBLICATIONS** Ed, Edmund Spenser's Poetry, 69, 82 and Ben Jonson and the Cavalier Poets, 74, Norton. **CONTACT ADDRESS** Dept of English, State Univ of NY, Albany, NY, 12222.

MACLEOD, ALISTAIR
DISCIPLINE ENGLISH LANGUAGE; LITERATURE **EDUCATION** St F X, BA, BEd; New Brunswick, MA; Univ Notre Dame, PhD; St F X, LLD, 69. **CAREER** Prof; fiction ed, The Windsor Review; tchr, advanced writing in the summer prog at, Banff; Can participant in the Can Scotland Writers-in-Residence Exchange Prog, 84-85. **RESEARCH** 19th-century literature; Creative Writing. **SELECTED PUBLICATIONS** Auth, The Lost Salt Gift of Blood, 76; As Birds Bring Forth the Sun, 86. **CONTACT ADDRESS** Dept of English Language and Literature, Univ of Windsor, 401 Sunset Ave, Windsor, ON, N9B 3P4.

MACMILLAN, CARRIE H.
PERSONAL Born 11/03/1945, Fredericton, NB, Canada **DISCIPLINE** ENGLISH **EDUCATION** Univ NB, BA, 67; Dalhousie Univ, MA, 70; McMaster Univ, PhD, 77. **CAREER** Asst prof, 77-83, assoc prof, 84-93, head dept, 94-, PROF ENGLISH, MT ALLISON UNIV 94-. **HONORS AND AWARDS** Tucker Tchr Award, Mt Allison Univ, 90. **MEMBERSHIPS** Asn Can Col Univ Tchrs Eng; Asn Can Que Lits; Hum Asn Can. **SELECTED PUBLICATIONS** Coauth, Silenced Sextet: Six Nineteenth-Century Canadian Women Novelists, 93. **CONTACT ADDRESS** Dept of English, Univ Mount Allison, Sackville, NB, E4L 1B8. **EMAIL** cmacmillan@mta.ca

MACNAUGHTON, WILLIAM ROBERT
PERSONAL Born 11/14/1939, Moncton, NB, Canada, m, 1962, 3 children **DISCIPLINE** ENGLISH, AMERICAN LITERATURE **EDUCATION** Univ Toronto, BA, 62; Univ Wis, MA, 63, PhD(English), 69. **CAREER** Asst prof, 70-75, ASSOC PROF ENGLISH, UNIV WATERLOO, ONT, 75-, CHMN, 79-, Can Coun res fel, 71 and 76. **MEMBERSHIPS** Asn Can Univ Teachers English; Can Asn Am Studies. **RESEARCH** Nineteenth and 20th century American literature, particularly writers of realistic and naturalistic fiction. **SELECTED PUBLICATIONS** Auth, Meaning in James, Henry, Amer Lit, Vol 0064, 92; Wharton, Edith Bad Heroine, Sophy Viner in the 'Reef', Stud in the Novel, Vol 0025, 93; Wharton the 'Reef', Explicator, Vol 0051, 93; Wharton, Edith, the 'Reef' and James, Henry, Amer Lit Realism 1870-1910, Vol 0026, 94; The Disruption of the Feminine in James, Henry, Univ Toronto Quart, Vol 0064, 94. **CONTACT ADDRESS** Dept of English, Univ of Waterloo, Waterloo, ON, N2L 3G1.

MACOVSKI, MICHAEL
DISCIPLINE LITERATURE OF THE ROMANTIC PERIOD **EDUCATION** Univ CA, Berkeley, PhD. **CAREER** Assoc prof, Fordham Univ. **RESEARCH** Byron, M. Bakhtin. **SELECTED PUBLICATIONS** Auth, Byron, Bakhtin, and the Translation of History, Re-reading Byron, Garland Press, 93; Dialogue and Literature: Apostrophes, Auditors, and the Collapse of Romantic Discourse, Oxford UP, 94. **CONTACT ADDRESS** Dept of Eng Lang and Lit, Fordham Univ, 113 W 60th St, New York, NY, 10023.

MACPHEE, LAURENCE EDWARD
PERSONAL Born 12/02/1934, Jersey City, NJ, m, 1960, 3 children **DISCIPLINE** ENGLISH **EDUCATION** St Peter's Col, NJ, BS, 56; NY Univ, MA, 59; Rutgers Univ, PhD(English), 67. **CAREER** From instr to asst prof, 59-68, Assoc Prof English, Seton Hall Univ, 68- **HONORS AND AWARDS** Swiss Government Fel, 56-57; Woodrow Wilson Fel, 58-59; Danforth Fel, 58-61. **MEMBERSHIPS** MLA; AAUP. **RESEARCH** J F Cooper; 19th century American novel. **SELECTED PUBLICATIONS** Auth, The Great Gatsby's romance of motoring: Nick Carraway and Jordan Baker, Mod Fiction Studies, summer 72. **CONTACT ADDRESS** Dept of English, Seton Hall Univ, South Orange, 400 S Orange Ave, South Orange, NJ, 07079-2697.

MACPHERSON, JAY
PERSONAL Born 06/13/1931, London, England **DISCIPLINE** ENGLISH **EDUCATION** Carleton Col, Ont, BA, 51; McGill Univ, BLS, 53; Univ Toronto, MA, 55, PhD(English), 64. **CAREER** Lectr, 57, from asst prof to assoc prof, 58-73, PROF ENGLISH, VICTORIA COL, UNIV TORONTO, 73-. **MEMBERSHIPS** Asn Can Univ Teachers English; League Can Poets. **RESEARCH** Eighteenth century to present romance fictions. **SELECTED PUBLICATIONS** Auth, A Dictionary of Biblical Tradition in English Literature, Univ Toronto Quart, Vol 0065, 95; Sparshott, Francis, Poet, J Aesthet Educ, Vol 0031, 97. **CONTACT ADDRESS** Victoria Col, Univ of Toronto, Toronto, ON, M5S 1A1.

MACRAE, SUZANNE H.
DISCIPLINE MEDIEVAL LITERATURE **EDUCATION** Univ N Carolina, PhD. **CAREER** English and Lit, Univ Ark. **SELECTED PUBLICATIONS** Auth, Thomas Berger's Mythical Arthur Rex, Popular Arthurian Traditions, 92; Yeelen: A Political Fable of the Komo Blacksmiths/Sorceres, Res African Lit, 95; Mature and Older Women in African Film, Res African Lit, 96. **CONTACT ADDRESS** Univ Ark, Fayetteville, AR, 72701.

MADDEN, DAVID
PERSONAL Born 07/25/1933, Knoxville, TN, m, 1956, 1 child **DISCIPLINE** ENGLISH **EDUCATION** Univ Tenn, BA, 57; San Francisco State Col, MA, 58. **CAREER** Instr English and drama, Appalachian State Teachers Col, 58-59; instr English, Centre Col, 60-62; lectr creative writing, Univ Louisville, 62-64, Kenyon Col, 64-66 and Ohio Univ, 66-68; WRITER IN RESIDENCE, LA STATE UNIV, 68-, Asst ed, Kenyon Rev, 64-66; assoc ed, Film Heritage, 65, Film J, 71 and Fiction Int, 73; Rockefeller grant fiction, 69; mem bd, Assoc Writing Progs, 76-79. **HONORS AND AWARDS** Nat Coun on Arts Selection in Fiction, 70. **MEMBERSHIPS** Auth Guild; Soc Studies Southern Lit; Popular Cult Asn (pres, 76-78); Pen Club. **RESEARCH** English, especially contemporary literature; drama; creative writing. **SELECTED PUBLICATIONS** Auth, Nonfiction Rediscoveries--Introduction, Georgia Rev, Vol 0047, 93; Lost Men + Wolfe,Thomas Civil-War Short-Stories, 'Four Lost Men' and 'Chickamauga'--From Gettysburg to Chickamauga, Thomas Wolfe Rev, Vol 0021, 97. **CONTACT ADDRESS** Louisiana State Univ, Baton Rouge, LA, 70803.

MADDEN, DEIDRE
PERSONAL Born 01/08/1936, Washington, DC, m, 3 children **DISCIPLINE** SPEECH & LANGUAGE **EDUCATION** Ohio Univ, BA, 58; Western Reserve, MA, 67; Kent St, PhD, 82 **CAREER** Speech Pathol, 60-68, Parochial; Lect, 67-68, Com Col; Asst, Full Prof, 67-98, Baldwin-Wallace Col **HONORS AND AWARDS** Chair-Dept-BW; Co-Chair, Faculty-BW; Chair-Sexual Harrassment Com-BW **MEMBERSHIPS** ASHA; OSHA; ASTD **CONTACT ADDRESS** Medina, OH, 44256.

MADDEN, KATE
DISCIPLINE COMMUNICATION STUDIES **EDUCATION** Colby Col, BA; Univ Pa, MA; Pa State Univ, PhD. **CAREER** Asst prof. **RESEARCH** International mass communication; media and cultural diversity; communication technology and cultural change. **SELECTED PUBLICATIONS** Auth, Video and Cultural Identity: the Inuit Broadcasting Corporation Experience. **CONTACT ADDRESS** Dept of Communication, State Univ NY Col Brockport, Brockport, NY, 14420. **EMAIL** kmadden@po.brockport.edu

MADDOX, LUCY
DISCIPLINE ENGLISH LITERATURE **EDUCATION** Furman Univ, BA; Duke Univ, MA; Univ Va, PhD. **CAREER** Eng Dept, Georgetown Univ **RESEARCH** 19th and 20th century American literature; Native American literature. **SELECTED PUBLICATIONS** Auth, Susan Fenimore Cooper and the Plain Daughters of America, 88; Gilbert White and the Politics of Natural History, 86; Nabokov's Novels in English, 83; Removals: Nineteenth-Century American Literature and the Politics of Indian Affairs, 91. **CONTACT ADDRESS** English Dept, Georgetown Univ, 37th and O St, Washington, DC, 20057.

MADDUX, STEPHEN
DISCIPLINE MODERN LANGUAGE AND LITERATURE **EDUCATION** Univ Dallas, BA, 71; Univ Chicago, MA, 73; PhD, 79; addn stud, Univ Paris, 71-72; Univ Toronto, 75-76; Wilhelms Univ, 77-78. **CAREER** Assoc prof; hd, Fr prog. **RESEARCH** Montaigne, Pascal. **SELECTED PUBLICATIONS** Auth, The Fiction of the Livre in Robert de Boron's Merlin, Jour Rocky Mountain Medieval and Renaissance Assn, 85; Satan With and Without a Human Face in the Novels of Georges Bernanos, Claudel Studies, 86; Cocteau's Tristan and Iseut: A Case of Overmuch Respect, Tristan and Isolde: A Casebook New York: Garland, 95. **CONTACT ADDRESS** Dept of Mod Lang and Lit, Univ Dallas, 1845 E Northgate Dr, Irving, TX, 75062. **EMAIL** maddux@acad.udallas.edu

MADGETT, NAOMI LONG
PERSONAL Born 07/05/1923, Norfolk, VI, w, 1972 **DISCIPLINE** ENGLISH **EDUCATION** VA State Coll, BA 1945; Wayne State Univ, MEd 1955; Intl Inst for Advanced Studies (Greenwich Univ), PhD 1980. **CAREER** Poet and author, 1941-; MI Chronicle, staff writer 1946-47; MI Bell Tel Co, serv rep 1948-54; Detroit Pub Sch, teacher 1955-65, 1966-68; public speaker, poetry readings only 1956-; Oakland Univ, res assoc 1965-66; EAST MI UNIV, assoc prof English 1968-73; Univ of MI, lectr 1970; East MI Univ, prof 1973-84, PROF EMERITUS 1984-; Lotus Press, publ & editor 1974-; editor, Lotus Poetry Series, MI State Univ Press, 1993-98. **HONORS AND AWARDS** Distinguished English Teacher of the Year, Met Detroit; 1st recipient Mott Fellowship in English 1965; Disting Soror Award, Alpha Rho Omega Chap, Alpha Kappa Alpha Sor, 1969; papers being collected in Special Collections Libr Fisk Univ; Resolutions from Detroit Cty Cncl 1982 and MI State Legisl 1982 & 1984; Key to the City of Detroit 1980; Recognition by Black Caucus of Natl Cncl of Teachers of English 1984; Natl Coalition of 100 Black Women 1984; Induction into Stylus Society Howard Univ 1984; Disting Artist Award, Wayne State Univ, 1985; Robert Hayden Runagate Awd, 1985; Creative Artist Award, MI Council for the arts, 1987; Creative Achievement Award, College Language Assn, 1988; "In Her Lifetime" Award, Afrikan Poets Theatre Inc, 1989; Literature Award, Arts Foundation of Michigan, 1990; Honorary Degree, Loyola University, Chicago, 1993; Recognition by Black Caucus of American Library Assn, 1992; honorary degree, MI State Univ, 1994; MI Artist Award, 1993; Amer Book Award, 1993. **MEMBERSHIPS** Coll Language Assn; Alpha Kappa Alpha Sor; NAACP; Detroit Women Writers; Southern Poverty Law Center; Langston Hughes Society; Zora Neale Hurston Society. **SELECTED PUBLICATIONS** Editor of two anthologies including: Adam of Ife: Black Women in Praise of Black Men, 1992; eight books published including: Remembrances of Spring: Collected Early Poems, 1993; Octavia and Other Poems, 1988; Star by Star; Pink Ladies in the Afternoon; Exits & Entrances; poems widely anthologized & translated. **CONTACT ADDRESS** Lotus Press Inc, PO Box 21607, Detroit, MI, 48221.

MADIGAN, MARK J.
PERSONAL Born 01/16/1961, Hartford, CT **DISCIPLINE** ENGLISH **EDUCATION** St. Michael's Col, BA, 83; Univ Vt, MA, 87; Univ Mass, PhD, 91. **CAREER** Lectr, Univ Vt, 91-96; Asst Prof English, Nazareth Col of Rochester, 96-. **HONORS AND AWARDS** Frederick Tupper Award, Univ Vt, 87; Drad Sch Fel, Univ Mass, 90-91; Phi Kappa Phi, 91; Seminar Fel, Sixth Int Seminar on Willa Cather, 95; Colloquium Fel, 1998 Int Willa Cather Colloquium. **MEMBERSHIPS** Dorothy Canfield Fisher Soc (Pres 93-98); Herman Melville Soc; NEast Pop Cult Asn (Exec Coun 92-98); Richard Wright Circle; Willa Cather Soc. **RESEARCH** African American literature; modern and contemporary American literature; popular culture. **SELECTED PUBLICATIONS** Auth, Then everything was dark?: The Two Endings of Nella Larsen's Passing, Papers of the Bibliog Soc Am, 89; Miscegenation and the dicta of race and class: The Rhinelander Case and Nella Larsen's Passing, Mod Fiction Studies, 90; Willa Cather and Dorothy Canfield Fisher: Rift, Reconciliation, and One of Ours, Cather Studies I, Univ Nebr Press, 90; Profile: Dorothy Canfield Fisher, Legacy: A J Am Women Writers, 92; ed, Keeping Fires Night and Day: Selected Letters of Dorothy Canfield Fisher, Univ Mo Press, 93; auth, As true and direct as a birth or death certificate: Richard Wright on Jim Thompson's Now and On Earth, Studies Am Fiction, 94; A Newly-Discovered Robert Frost Letter to Dorothy Canfield Fisher, The Robert Frost Rev, 94; ed, Seasoned Timber, Univ Press New England, 96; The Bedquilt and Other Stories by Dorothy Canfield Fisher, Univ Mo Press, 96; auth, From the Prarie to the Pulps: The Cather-Thompson Connection, Willa Cather Newsletter, 97. **CONTACT ADDRESS** English Dept, Nazareth Col, Rochester, 11 Rowley St, Rochester, NY, 14618.

MADSEN, DEBORAH
DISCIPLINE AMERICAN STUDIES & ENGLISH **EDUCATION** Univ Adelaide, BA, 81, MA, 84; Univ Sussex, DPhil, 88. **CAREER** Dir, Am stud prog, Univ Leicester; DEPT ENG, SO BANK UNIV, LONDON. **MEMBERSHIPS** Am Antiquarian Soc **RESEARCH** Hist of Pynchon & Hawthorne families **CONTACT ADDRESS** 2 Croft Close, Histon, ., CB4 4HU.

MAERTZ, GREGORY
DISCIPLINE ENGLISH **EDUCATION** Northwestern Univ, BA, 81; Harvard Univ, MA, 83, PhD, 88. **CAREER** ASSOC PROF, ENG, ST JOHN'S UNIV **MEMBERSHIPS** Am Antiquarian Soc **SELECTED PUBLICATIONS** Ed, Cultural Interactions in the Romantic Age: Critical Essays in Comparative Literature, SUNY Press; Goethe, British Romanticism, and Cultural Identity, Univ Press Ky. **CONTACT ADDRESS** Eng Dept, St John's Univ, 8000 Utopia Pkwy, Jamaica, NY, 11439. **EMAIL** gregmaertz@aol.com

MAGID, LAURIE
DISCIPLINE LEGAL WRITING AND APPELLATE ADVOCACY **EDUCATION** Wharton Sch Bus, Univ Pa, BS, 82; Columbia Law Sch, JD, 85. **CAREER** Instr, Villanova Univ, 97-; clerked, Honorable James Hunter III Ct Appeals Third Circuit; asst dist atty, Philadelphia Dist Attorney's Off, 86-95; past prosecutor, tried cases, wrote briefs; argued in the Pa Supreme and Superior Courts; past adj prof, Temple Law Sch; assoc prof and co-dir Legal Writing Dept, Widener Law Sch, 95. **SELECTED PUBLICATIONS** Publi in, Columbia Law Rev, Ohio State Law J, Wayne Law Rev & San Diego Law Rev, on Miranda Rights, Discriminatory Selection of Juries, Legal Writing Pedagogy and First Amendment Protections. **CONTACT ADDRESS** Law School, Villanova Univ, 800 Lancaster Ave, Villanova, PA, 19085-1692. **EMAIL** magid@law.vill.edu

MAGNUSON, PAUL ANDREW
PERSONAL Born 04/10/1939, Newton, MA, m, 1965, 2 children **DISCIPLINE** ENGLISH LITERATURE **EDUCATION** Brown Univ, AB, 61; Univ Minn, PhD, 69. **CAREER** Asst prof English, Univ Pa, 69-74, asst prof, 74-76; assoc prof English, 76-88, prof, 88-, NY Univ, 76-. **MEMBERSHIPS** MLA; Wordsworth-Coleridge Asn; Keats-Shelley Asn. **RESEARCH** English Romantic lit. **SELECTED PUBLICATIONS** Auth, Coleridge's Nightmare Poetry, Univ Va, 74; Coleridge and Wordsworth: A Lyrical Dialogue, Princeton, 88; Reading Public Romanticism, Princeton, 98. **CONTACT ADDRESS** Dept of English, New York Univ, 19 University Pl, New York, NY, 10003-4556. **EMAIL** pm1@is3.nyu.edu

MAGUIRE, JAMES HENRY
PERSONAL Born 04/02/1944, Denver, CO, m, 1967, 2 children **DISCIPLINE** AMERICAN LITERATURE AND STUDIES **EDUCATION** Univ Colo, Boulder, BA, 66; Ind Univ, Bloomington, MA, 69, PhD(English and Am studies), 70. **CAREER** Asst prof, 70-75, ASSOC PROF ENGLISH AND AM LIT, BOISE STATE UNIV, 75-, CO-ED, BOISE STATE UNIV WESTERN WRITERS SER, 72-; CO-ED, LIT HIST AM WEST, 80-. **MEMBERSHIPS** MLA; Am Studies Asn; Western Lit Asn. **RESEARCH** American realism; Western American literature; the novel. **SELECTED PUBLICATIONS** Auth, Prose and Poetry of the American West, New Mex Hist Rev, Vol 0068, 93; In Mountain Shadows--a History of Idaho, J West, Vol 0032, 93; The Dancing Ground of Sky--the Selected Poetry of Church, Peggy, Pond, Western Amer Lit, Vol 0028, 94; Traven, B.--the Life Behind the Legends, J West, Vol 0033, 94; Harte, Bret California--Letters to the Springfield-Republican and Christian-Register, 1866-67, Resources for Amer Lit Study, Vol 0021, 95; Stegner, Wallace--Man and Writer, New Mex Hist Rev, Vol 0072, 97; Where the Morning Lights Still Blue--Personal Essays about Idaho, J West, Vol 0036, 97; The 'Yellowstone Meditations', Western Amer Lit, Vol 0032, 97. **CONTACT ADDRESS** Dept of English, Boise State Univ, Boise, ID, 83725.

MAHONEY, IRENE
PERSONAL Born 05/05/1921, Brooklyn, NY **DISCIPLINE** ENGLISH **EDUCATION** Col New Rochelle, BA, 41; Fordham Univ, MA, 48; Cath Univ Am, PhD, 58. **CAREER** Assoc prof, 62-69, prof English, 69-, Writer-In-Residence, 70-, Col New Rochelle. **RESEARCH** French Renaissance; contemporary fiction. **SELECTED PUBLICATIONS** Auth, Marie of the Incarnation: Mystic and Missionary, Doubleday, 64; auth, Royal Cousin: Life of Henry IV of France, Doubleday; auth, Life of Catherine de Medici, Coward, 74. **CONTACT ADDRESS** Dept of English, Col of New Rochelle, New Rochelle, NY, 10801.

MAHONEY, JOHN FRANCIS
PERSONAL Born 05/19/1929, Detroit, MI, m, 1980 **DISCIPLINE** ENGLISH, CLASSICS **EDUCATION** Univ Detroit, BA, 50, MA, 52; Univ NC, PhD, 56. **CAREER** Instr English, Univ NC, 53-56; instr Latin, Duke Univ, 54-56; asst prof Mid English, Duquesne Univ, 56-59, assoc prof English & chm grad studies, 59-61; assoc prof English & comp lit, Univ Detroit, 61-63, chm grad comt, 61-64, dean col arts & sci, 69-73, prof English & comp lit & chm dept, 64-73; dean, Walden Univ, 73-74;

vpres acad affairs, William Paterson Col NJ, 74-78; Dean, Walden Univ, 79-, Southern Fels Fund fel, 56; mem bd, Am Grad & Prof Comn, 66-; pres, Vri, Inc, 79-; admin dir, Beli-Laddi farm, 80- ; ed & publ Imperial Beach & South County Times, 85-98; columnist, Imperial Beach Eagle & Times, 98- ; PROJECT DEVELOP OFFICER, B.E.L.I., Inc., 96- . **MEMBERSHIPS** MLA; Mediaeval Acad Am; Dante Soc Am; Soc Exceptional Children. **RESEARCH** Mixed media; mediaeval languages; Dante. **SELECTED PUBLICATIONS** Ed, The Structure of Purgatorio, Dante Soc Bull, 62; Chaucerian Tragedy and the Christian Tradition, Ann Mediaevale, 62; American Authors and Critics (12 vols), Holt, 62-; coauth, Studies in Honor of V T Holmes, Jr, Univ NC, Chapel Hill, 66; The Insistent Present, Houghton, 70; co-ed, New Poets, New Music, Winthrop, 71; coauth, Early Help (film), Medianovations, 73; The House of Tenure (play), Medianovations, 80. **CONTACT ADDRESS** PO Box 5429, Playa del Rey, CA, 92293. **EMAIL** mahwis@gte.net

MAHONEY, JOHN L.
PERSONAL Born 02/04/1928, Somerville, MA, m, 1956, 3 children **DISCIPLINE** ENGLISH **EDUCATION** Boston Col, AB, 50, AM, 52; Harvard Univ, PhD, 57. **CAREER** From instr to assoc prof English, 55-65, chmn dept, 62-67 & 69-70, dir PhD studies, 70-72, prof English, 65-, Thomas F. Rattigan prof English, 94- , Boston Col; vis prof English, Harvard Univ sum sess, 63, 65, 67, 71, 80, 83, 86. **HONORS AND AWARDS** Phi Beta Kappa; hon mem, Golden Key Soc; Mass Prof of the Year award, 89; Am Philos Soc grant, 87; Boston Col fac fel, 86, 94; hon mem, Alpha Sigma Nu, 82; NEH lectr, 83, 86; Mellon Found grant, 81-82. **MEMBERSHIPS** MLA; Wordsworth-Coleridge Asn; Am Soc 18th Cent Studies; Northeast Soc for Eighteenth-Century Stud; Interdisciplinary Nineteenth-Century Stud; Keats-Shelley Asn of Am; NCTE; AAUP; The Johnsonians. **RESEARCH** British Enlightenment and Romantic Literature; tragedy and drama; religion and literature. **SELECTED PUBLICATIONS** Ed and contribur, The Enlightenment and English Literature, Heath, 80; auth, The Persistence of Tragedy: Episodes in the History of Drama, Boston Public Library/NEH, 85; auth, The Whole Internal Universe: Imitation and the New Defense of Poetry in British Criticism and Aesthetics, 1660-1830, Fordham, 85; co-ed, Coleridge, Keats, and the Imagination: Romanticism and Adam's Dream, Missouri, 89; auth, William Wordsworth: A Poetic Life, Fordham, 97; ed and contribur, Seeing Into the Life of Things, Fordham, 97. **CONTACT ADDRESS** 8 Sutherland Rd, Lexington, MA, 02173. **EMAIL** mahoney@bc.edu

MAHONY, ROBERT E.P.
PERSONAL Born 09/08/1946, Bronxville, NY, m, 1973, 1 child **DISCIPLINE** ENGLISH LITERATURE & IRISH STUDIES **EDUCATION** Georgetown Univ, AB, 68; Trinity Col, Dublin, PhD, 74. **CAREER** Asst prof, Univ IL, Chicago Circle, 74-80; asst prof, 80-82, Assoc Prof Eng, Cath Univ Am, 82. **MEMBERSHIPS** Am Center for Irish Studies; Int Soc for Study of Irist Lit; Am Soc 18th Century Studies. **RESEARCH** Eighteenth century poetry and poetics; Anglo-Irish lit; bibl; Swift. **SELECTED PUBLICATIONS** Auth, Ed, Different Styles of Poetry, Cadenus, Dublin, 78; coauth (with Betty Rizzo), Christopher Smart: An Annotated Bibliograhy, Garland, 84; The Annotated Letters of Christopher Smart, Southern Ill Univ Press, 91; Jonathan Swift: The Irish Identity, Yale, 95. **CONTACT ADDRESS** Dept of Eng, Catholic Univ of America, 620 Michigan Ave N E, Washington, DC, 20064-0002. **EMAIL** mahony@cua.edu

MAIER, JOHN
PERSONAL Born 06/14/1943, Charleston, WV, m, 1966, 1 child **DISCIPLINE** ENGLISH **EDUCATION** Duquesne Univ, BA, 65, PhD, 70; Univ PA, AM, 66. **CAREER** Instr Eng, Duquesne Univ, 66-69; asst prof, Clarion State Col, 69-71; from Asst Prof to Assoc Prof, 71-85, Prof Eng, State Univ Ny Col Brockport, 85-; Co-ed, Lit Onomastics Studies, 74-78; Fulbright-Hays lectr, Syria & Jordan, 79-80, Morocco, 89-; Dir, NEH Summer Seminar, 86, 93. **HONORS AND AWARDS** State Univ NY Res Found grants, 76, 79, 81 & 82; Nat Endowment of Humanities fel, 77; SUNY Chancellor's Award for Excellence in Tchg, 96. **MEMBERSHIPS** Soc Bibl Lit; Am Orient Soc; MLA; Int Asn Philos & Lit; Mediaeval Acad Am. **RESEARCH** Eng Renaissance lit; lit of the ancient Near East; lit theory and criticism. **SELECTED PUBLICATIONS** Auth, Mesopotamian names in The Sunlight Dialogues, or, Mama makes it to Batavia, New York, Lit Onomastics Studies, 77; Image and Paradox in Venus and Adonis and The Rape of Lucrece, English Studies Collections, 77; The file on Leonidas Le Cenci Hamilton, Am Lit Realism, 1870-1910, 78; co-ed, The Bible in Its Literary Milieu: Contemporary Essays, Eerdmans, 80; Is Tiamat really Mother Huber?, Lit Onomastics Studies, 82; The Truth of a most ancient work: Interpreting a poem addressed to a holy place, Centrum, 82; coauth, Gilgamesh, Translated from the Version of Sinleqi unninni, 84; Myths of Enki, The Crafty God, 89; co-ed, Mappings of the Biblical Terrain: The Bible as Text, 90; auth, Desert Songs: Western Images of Morocco and Moroccan Images of the West, 96; ed, Gilgamesh: A Reader, 97; author of numerous other articles. **CONTACT ADDRESS** Dept of Eng, State Univ, 350 New Campus Dr, Brockport, NY, 14420-2914. **EMAIL** jmaier@ACSPR1.ACS.Brockport.edu

MAITZEN, ROHAN AMANDA
DISCIPLINE 19TH-CENTURY BRITISH NOVEL, VICTORIAN LITERATURE **EDUCATION** Univ Brit Columbia, BA, 90; Cornell Univ, MA, 93, PhD, 95. **CAREER** Tchg asst, Cornell Univ; asst prof, 95-. **HONORS AND AWARDS** Mellon Dissertation Yr fel, 94-95; Sage grad fel, 93-94; Mellon fel, 90-92; Commonwealth scholar, Cambridge Univ, 90; Eng hon(s) medal and prize, Univ Brit Columbia, 90., Ch, Nominating Comm, 97-98; Undergrad Comm, 96-97; undergrad adv, Dept Eng, 96-97; **MEMBERSHIPS** Mem, Inter Unit Rev Comm, 98; Acad Develop Comm, 98-01; Adv Comm, 98-01; Undergrad Comm, 98-99; Acad Fin and Plan Comm, 97-98; Lib and Arch Comm, Univ King's Col, 96-98; Int Unit Rev Comm, 96-97. **SELECTED PUBLICATIONS** Auth, "This Feminine Preserve: Historical Biographies by Victorian Women," Victorian Stud, 95; "By No Means An Improbable Fiction: Redgauntlet's Novel Historicism," Stud in the Novel, 93; rpt, Critical Essays on Sir Walter Scott: The Waverley Novels, G.K. Hall, 96; Gender, Genre, and Victorian Historical Writing, Garland, 98; rev, Review of Rosemarie Bodenheimer, The Real Life of Mary Ann Evans: George Eliot, Her Letters and Fiction, Cornell UP, 94; Victorian Rev, 95. **CONTACT ADDRESS** Dept of Eng, Dalhousie Univ, Halifax, NS, B3H 3J5. **EMAIL** rmaitzen@is.dal.ca

MAJOR, CLARENCE
PERSONAL Born 12/31/1936, Atlanta, GA, m, 1980 **DISCIPLINE** ENGLISH **EDUCATION** State Univ of New York at Albany, BS; Union Institute, PhD. **CAREER** Writer; Sarah Lawrence College, Bronxville, NY, lecturer, 1972-75; Howard University, Washington, DC, lecturer, 1975-76; University of Washington, Seattle, WA, assistant professor, 1976-77; University of Colorado, Boulder, CO, associate professor, 1977-81, professor, 1981-89; UNIVERSITY OF CALIFORNIA AT DAVIS, PROF, 1989-; has held numerous other positions as visiting professor, consultant, and lecturer. **HONORS AND AWARDS** Nat'l Council on the Arts Award, Assn of Univ Presses, 1970; Pushcart prize for poem "Funeral," 1976; Fulbright-Hays Inter-Univ Exchange Award, Franco-Amer Comm for Educational Exchange, 1981-83; Western State Book Award for Fiction (My Amputations), 1986. **SELECTED PUBLICATIONS** All-Night Visitors (novel), 1969; Dictionary of Afro-American Slang, 1970; Swallow the Lake (poetry), 1970; Symptoms and Madness (poetry), 1971; Private Line (poetry), 1971; The Cotton Club: New Poems, 1972; No (novel), 1973; The Dark and Feeling: Black American Writers and Their Work (essays), 1974; The Syncopated Cakewalk (poetry), 1974; Reflex and Bone Structure (novel), 1979; Emergency Exit (novel), 1979; Inside Diameter: The France Poems, 1985; My Amputations: A Novel, 1986; Such Was the Season: A Novel, 1987; Surfaces and Masks (poetry), 1987; Some Observations of a Stranger at Zuni in the Latter Part of the Century (poetry), 1988; Painted Turtle: Woman with Guitar (novel), 1988; Juba to Jive: A Dictionary of African-American Slang, Penguin, 1994; Calling the Wind, Anthology, 1993; The Garden Thrives, Anthology, 1996; Dirty Bird Blues, Novel, 1996; Configurations: New and Selected Poems: 1958-1998; author of numerous articles, reviews and anthologies; editor. **CONTACT ADDRESS** Dept of English, Univ of California, Davis, Davis, CA, 95616.

MAKAU, JOSINA M.
PERSONAL Born 04/11/1950, Oostzahn, Netherlands **DISCIPLINE** RHETORIC, PHILOSOPHY **EDUCATION** Calif State Univ, Northridge, BA, 73; Univ Calif, Los Angeles, MA, 73; Univ Calif, Berkeley, MA, 76, PhD(rhetoric), 80. **CAREER** ASST PROF COMMUN, OHIO STATE UNIV, 79-. **MEMBERSHIPS** Speech Commun Asn; Rhetoric Soc Am; Int Soc Hist Rhetoric; Cent States Speech Asn. **RESEARCH** Rhetoric and philosophy of law; modern theories of argumentation; rhetorical criticism. **SELECTED PUBLICATIONS** Auth, Argumentation, Communication, and Fallacies--a Pragma-Dialectical Perspective, Philos and Rhetoric, Vol 0028, 95. **CONTACT ADDRESS** Dept of Commun, Ohio State Univ, Columbus, OH, 43210.

MALACHUK, DANIEL S.
DISCIPLINE ENGLISH LITERATURE AND COMPOSITION **EDUCATION** Bowdoin Col, BA, 89; Rutgers Univ, MA, 94; PhD, 96. **CAREER** Asst prof and wtg dir, Daniel Webster Col, 97-; adj prof comp and Am hist, Hesser Col, 96-97; ed and mktg wtr, Houghton Mifflin and DC Heath, 89-97. **HONORS AND AWARDS** Univ Dissertation Fel, Rutgers Univ, 95-96; Barry V. Qualls Dissertation Fel, 94-95; grad fel, 91-92; Mitchell & Webb Scholar Grad Study, Bowdoin Col, 91. **RESEARCH** Ser learning, experiential learning, and internet-based learning. **SELECTED PUBLICATIONS** Auth, The Republican Philosophy of Emerson's Early Lectures, New England Quart, 98. **CONTACT ADDRESS** Daniel Webster Col, 20 University Dr., Nashua, NH, 03063. **EMAIL** malachuk@dwc.edu

MALEK, ABBAS
DISCIPLINE COMMUNICATIONS **EDUCATION** • Amer Univ, PhD. **CAREER** Assoc profr. **MEMBERSHIPS** Pres, Int Commun sect, IAMCR. **RESEARCH** International communication; cross cultural communication; communication policy.

SELECTED PUBLICATIONS Auth, News Media & Foreign Relations, Ablex, 97; ed, bk series, Contemp Stud in Int Political Commun. **CONTACT ADDRESS** School of Communications, Howard Univ, 2400 Sixth St NW, Washington, DC, 20059.

MALOF, JOSEPH FETLER
PERSONAL Born 05/26/1934, Riga, Latvia, m, 1957, 3 children **DISCIPLINE** ENGLISH **EDUCATION** Kenyon Col, BA, 56; Univ Calif, Los Angeles, MA, 57, PhD(English), 62. **CAREER** Asst English, Univ Calif, Los Angeles, 60-61; from instr to assoc prof, 61-73, Prof English, Univ Tex, Austin, 73-, E Harris Harbison Prize, Danforth Found, 70. **RESEARCH** Twentieth century poetry in English; American literature; English versification. **SELECTED PUBLICATIONS** Auth, The native rhythm of English meters, Tex Studies Lit & Lang, Winter 64; Meter as organic form, Mod Lang Quart, 3/66; A Manual of English Meters, Ind Univ, 70; Haiku in heroics, Lit East & West 3/71. **CONTACT ADDRESS** Dept of English, Univ of Texas, Austin, TX, 78712-1026.

MALONE, DUMAS
PERSONAL Born 01/10/1902, Coldwater, MS, m, 1925, 2 children **DISCIPLINE** HISTORY, BIOGRAPHY **EDUCATION** Emory Univ, BA, 10; Yale Univ, BA, 16, MA, 21, PhD, 23. **CAREER** Instr hist, Yale Univ, 19-23, asst prof, 23; from assoc prof to prof, Univ Va, 23-29; ed, Dict Am Biog, 29-31, ed-in-chief, 31-36; dir and chmn bd Syndics, Harvard Univ Press, 36-43; prof hist, Columbia Univ, 45-59; Jefferson Found prof hist, 59-62, BIOGRAPHER IN RESIDENCE, UNIV VA, 62-, Vis prof, Yale Univ, 27, Sterling sr fel, 27-28; ed, Hist Bk Club, 48-; Guggenheim fels, 51-52 and 58-59; managing ed, Polit Sci Quart, 53-58; hon consult, Am hist, Libr Congr, 68. **HONORS AND AWARDS** Porter Prize, Yale Univ, 23, Wilbur L Cross Medal, 72; Thomas Jefferson Award, Univ Va, 64; John F Kennedy Medal, Mass Hist Soc, 72; Pulitzer Prize in Hist, 75., DLitt, Emory Univ and Rochester Univ, 36, Dartmouth Col, 37 and Col William and Mary, 77; LLD, Northwestern Univ, 35 and Univ Chattanooga, 62. **MEMBERSHIPS** AHA; Southern Hist Asn(pres, 67-68); Am Antiq Soc; Am Acad Arts and Sci; Soc Am Hist. **RESEARCH** Early American history. **SELECTED PUBLICATIONS** Auth, A Linguistic Approach to the Bakhtinian Hero in Martin, Steve 'Roxanne', Lit-Film Quart, Vol 0024, 96. **CONTACT ADDRESS** Alderman Libr, Univ of Va, Charlottesville, VA, 22901.

MALONE, M.J.
PERSONAL Born 05/26/1950, New Brunswick, NJ, m, 1972, 2 children **DISCIPLINE** HUMANITIES **EDUCATION** NYU, BA 72; SIU, MA 76; IU, PhD 85. **CAREER** Mount St. Mary's Col, asst prof, assoc prof, ch, 85 to 98-. **HONORS AND AWARDS** ACLS Trav Gnt; ASA Trav Gnt; Choice Outstanding Book of the Year Awd. **MEMBERSHIPS** ASA; SSSI; Alpha Kappa Delta; Intl Sociol Hon Soc. **RESEARCH** Sociology of language; discourse and conversation analysis; Sociol of emotions and the body; symbolic interaction; modern theory. **SELECTED PUBLICATIONS** Auth, Worlds of Talk: The Presentation of Self in Everyday Conversation, London, Polity Press, 97; Semiotics, in: D. Levinson and M. Ember, eds, The Encycl of Cultural Anthro, Henry Holt, 96; How to do things with friends: Altercasting and recipient design, Res On Language and Soc Interaction, 95; Conflicting Demands in Writing Response Groups, with Margaret Tipper, The Writing Instructor, 95; Small disagreements: Character contests and working consensus in informal talk, Symbolic Interaction, 94. **CONTACT ADDRESS** Dept of Sociology, Mount St. Mary's Col, Emmitsburg, MD, 21727. **EMAIL** malone@msmary.edu

MALOUF, MELISSA
DISCIPLINE ENGLISH LITERATURE **EDUCATION** Univ CA Irvine, PhD, 79. **CAREER** Prof, Duke Univ. **HONORS AND AWARDS** Pushcart Prize, 89. **SELECTED PUBLICATIONS** Auth, It Had to Be You, Press, 97; No Guarantees, William Morrow, 90. **CONTACT ADDRESS** Eng Dept, Duke Univ, Durham, NC, 27706.

MAMA, RAOUF
DISCIPLINE AFRICAN LITERATURE **EDUCATION** Univ MI, PhD. **CAREER** Eng Dept, Eastern Conn State Univ **SELECTED PUBLICATIONS** Tales in: Storytelling Mag; Parabola; CT Rev; Facts & Fiction. **CONTACT ADDRESS** Eastern Connecticut State Univ, 83 Windham Street, Willimantic, CT, 06226. **EMAIL** MAMA@ECSU.CTSTATEU.EDU

MAMAN, MARIE
PERSONAL Born 12/27/1931, Norway, m, 1957, 4 children **DISCIPLINE** INFORMATION SCIENCE **EDUCATION** Degree, Stockholms Tekniska Inst, 54; Rutgers Univ, BA, 74, MLS, 76. **CAREER** Chem Techn, Norwegian Col Agriculture, 55-56; chem techn, Inst Nat de la Recherche Agronomique, 57; ref librn, 82-, circ libr, 84- Rutgers Univ. **MEMBERSHIPS** ALA; USAIN **RESEARCH** Women-bibliography **SELECTED PUBLICATIONS** Coauth, Women in Agriculture: A Guide to Research, 96; auth, art, Survey of the Literature on Women in Agriculture at the Rutgers University Libraries, 93; auth, art, Elise Boulding: A Bibliography, 92; coauth, art, Aims of User Education: Special Library Results, 92; auth, art, Cora Sandel (1890-1947), 91. **CONTACT ADDRESS** Mabel Smith Douglass Library, Rutgers Univ, 8 Chapel Dr, New Brunswick, NJ, 08901-8521.

MANCHEL, FRANK
PERSONAL Born 07/22/1935, Detroit, MI, m, 1958, 2 children **DISCIPLINE** ENGLISH, COMMUNICATION **EDUCATION** Oh State Univ, BA, 57; Hunter Col, MA, 60; Columbia Univ, EdD, 66. **CAREER** Instr high sch, NY, 58-64; asst prof English, Southern Conn State Col, 64-67; assoc prof, 67-72, Prof Commun, Univ Vt, 72-, Assoc Dean, Col Arts & Sci, 77-, Prog Coord, Commun Dept, 81-, Dir grad English inter prof, Univ Vt, & La Mancha proj, 68; mem nat comt innovative practices in English educ, 68; critic-at-large, WEZF-TV, 81-83. **MEMBERSHIPS** Am Fed Film Soc; Soc Cinema Studies (treas, 72-75); Am Film Inst; Brit Film Inst. **RESEARCH** Motion picture; Black studies; comedy. **SELECTED PUBLICATIONS** Auth, Terrors of the Screen, 70 & Cameras West, 71, Prentice-Hall; Film Study: A Resource Guide, Fairleigh Dickinson Univ, 73; Yesterday's Clowns, 73, The Talking Clowns, 76, An Album of Great Science Fiction Films, 76, Women on the Hollywood Screen, 77 & Gangsters on the Screen, 78, Watts; Box-Office Clowns, 79 & An Album of Great Sports Movies, 80, Watts; Film Study: An Analytical Bibliography, 4 vol, 90. **CONTACT ADDRESS** English Dept, Univ Vt, Old Mill, Burlington, VT, 05405-0001. **EMAIL** fmanchel@200.uvm.edu

MANCINI, ALBERT NICHOLAS
PERSONAL Born 09/15/1929, Trenton, NJ, m, 1968, 2 children **DISCIPLINE** LITERARY HISTORY **EDUCATION** Univ Naples, DLett, 57; Univ Calif, Berkeley, PhD(Romance lit), 64. **CAREER** Teaching asst Ital lang, Univ Calif, Berkeley, 57-61; instr Ital lang and lit and comp lit, Princeton Univ, 62-64; from asst prof to assoc prof, 64-72, consult, Sch Educ, 65-66, PROF ITAL LANG AND LIT, OHIO STATE UNIV, 72-, Assoc ed, Forum Italicum, 78-; consult, Univ Toronto Press, Univ Calif Press, Princeton Univ Press and Ohio State Univ Press; evaluator, Nat Endowment for Humanities; vis prof, Ital Sch Middlebury Col, 78 and 82. **MEMBERSHIPS** MLA; Am Asn Teachers Ital; Dante Soc Am; Renaissance Soc Am; Am Boccaccio Asn. **RESEARCH** Italian literature of the 15th, 16th and 17th centuries; cross-influences in Romance literatures in the same periods; bibliography. **SELECTED PUBLICATIONS** Auth, Translation Theory and Practice in 17th Century Italy--the Case of the French Novel, Symposium-Quart J in Mod Lit(S), Vol 0047, 93. **CONTACT ADDRESS** Dept of Romance Lang, Ohio State Univ, 1841 Millikin Rd, Columbus, OH, 43210-1229.

MANGANIELLO, DOMINIC
PERSONAL Born 11/04/1951, Cimitile, Italy, m, 1979, 1 child **DISCIPLINE** MODERN ENGLISH LITERATURE **EDUCATION** McGill Univ, BA, 74; Univ Oxford, DPhil, 78. **CAREER** Lectr, Univ Laval, 78-79; ASST PROF ENGLISH LIT, UNIV OTTAWA, 79-. **RESEARCH** T S Eliot and Dante. **SELECTED PUBLICATIONS** Auth, The Birth of Modernism, Pound, Ezra, Eliot, T.S., Yeats, W.B. and the Occult, Engl Stud in Can, Vol 0020, 94. **CONTACT ADDRESS** Dept of English, Univ of Ottawa, Ottawa, ON, K1N 6N5.

MANHEIM, MICHAEL
PERSONAL Born 03/04/1928, New York, NY, m, 1955, 2 children **DISCIPLINE** ENGLISH **EDUCATION** Columbia Col, AB, 49; Columbia Univ, MA, 51, PhD, 61. **CAREER** Instr English, Univ Del, 53-61; from asst prof to assoc prof, 61-67, assoc dean humanities, 63-66, chmn dept English, 66-72 and 79-82, PROF ENGLISH, UNIV TOLEDO, 67-, Danforth grant, 59-60; proj dir, Nat Endowment for Humanities Planning Proj, WGTE-TV-FM, Toledo, 76-78; mem, Chancellor's adv comt tele-commun higher educ, 81. **HONORS AND AWARDS** Outstanding Teachers Award, Univ Toledo, 74. **MEMBERSHIPS** Shakespeare Asn Am; Aaup; MLA; Midwest Mod Lang Asn. **RESEARCH** Shakespeare; Elizabethan drama; modern drama. **SELECTED PUBLICATIONS** Auth, Oneill, Eugene Creative Struggle, the Decisive Decade, 1924-1933, Mod Drama, Vol 0037, 94; The Function of Battle Imagery in Kurosawa Histories and the 'Henry V' Films, Lit-Film Quart, Vol 0022, 94. **CONTACT ADDRESS** Dept of English, Univ of Toledo, Toledo, OH, 43606.

MANIQUIS, ROBERT MANUEL
PERSONAL Born 09/04/1940, Newark, NY, m, 1961, 2 children **DISCIPLINE** ENGLISH LITERATURE, COMPARATIVE LITERATURE **EDUCATION** Rutgers Univ, BA, 62; Columbia Univ, MA, 63, PhD(English), 67. **CAREER** Asst prof English, 66-77, dir freshman English, 75-76, ASSOC PROF ENGLISH, UNIV CALIF, LOS ANGELES, 77-, Am Coun Learned Soc fel, 72-73. **MEMBERSHIPS** MLA; Philol Asn PACIFIC Coast. **RESEARCH** Nineteenth century Romanticism, English, French, and German; 19th century novel, English, French, and German. **SELECTED PUBLICATIONS** Auth, In the Theater of Romanticism--Coleridge, Nationalism, Women, Mod Lang Quart, Vol 0057, 96; Sacramental Commodities--Gift, Text and the Sublime in De-Quincey, Stud in Romanticism, Vol 0036, 97. **CONTACT ADDRESS** Dept of English, Univ of Calif, Los Angeles, CA, 90024.

MANLEY, FRANK
DISCIPLINE ENGLISH LANGUAGE AND LITERATURE **EDUCATION** Johns Hopkins Univ, PhD, 59. **CAREER** Charles Howard Candler Prof Ren Lit. **RESEARCH** Shakespeare; Donne; Renaissance drama and poetry. **SELECTED PUBLICATIONS** Ed/Trans, Epistola Ad Pomeranum; ed, All Fools; The Anniversaries; co-ed/trans, De Fructu qui ex Doctrina Percipitur. **CONTACT ADDRESS** English Dept, Emory Univ, 1380 Oxford Rd NE, Atlanta, GA, 30322-1950.

MANN, DAVID DOUGLAS
PERSONAL Born 09/13/1934, Oklahoma City, OK, m, 1983 **DISCIPLINE** ENGLISH **EDUCATION** Okla State Univ, BS, 56, MA, 63; Ind Univ, PhD(English), 69. **CAREER** Teacher Leelanau Schs, Mich, 62-63; instr English, Wabash Col, 65-67; asst prof, 68-73, assoc prof, 73-78, Prof English, Miami Univ, 78-; fac Am Asn Higher Educ Humanities Conf, 77; asst ed, Old Northwest, 75-78; scholar in residence, Univ Luxembourg, 78-80, 85-87. **HONORS AND AWARDS** Folger Shakespeare Libr fel, 70-71; NEH grant restoration stage, 76-77; Fel, Bibliog Soc Am, 88; Beinecke Libr Fel, 89; Lilly Libr Fel, 91. **MEMBERSHIPS** MLA; Midwestern Mod Lang Asn; Midwestern Soc for 18th century Studies; Samuel Johnson Soc Midwest; Charles Lamb Soc. **RESEARCH** Restoration and 18th-century drama and literature; modern American poetry; Robert Louis Stevenson. **SELECTED PUBLICATIONS** Auth, The Pugh Gift of the George Hewitt Myers Collection of Robert Louis Stevenson Materials, Yale Univ Libr Gazette, Spring 90; Checklist of Female Dramatists, 1660-1823, Restoration and Eighteenth-Century Theatre Research, Summer 90; coauth, The Publisher William Turner, Female Playwrights, and Mary Pix's The Adventures in Madrid, Rev English Studies 46, 95; A Possible Allusion in The Beaux Stratagem to Mary Pix's The Adventures in Madrid, The Scriblerian, Fall 96; auth, Odds on Treasure Island, Studies in Scottish Lit 29, 97; author of numerous other articles and reviews. **CONTACT ADDRESS** Dept of English, Miami Univ, 500 E High St, Oxford, OH, 45056-1602. **EMAIL** manndd@muohio.edu

MANN, JOHN STUART
PERSONAL Born 09/12/1945, Washington, DC, m, 1969, 2 children **DISCIPLINE** ENGLISH & AMERICAN LITERATURE **EDUCATION** Col Wooster, BA, 67; Univ PA, MA, 68, PhD, 72. **CAREER** Asst prof, 71-77, dir grad studies, dept Eng, 78-82, Assoc Prof Eng, Western IL Univ, 77-, Poetry & Ed ed, Miss Valley Rev Creative Writing, 73-95. **MEMBERSHIPS** MLA; Col Eng Asn; Am Asn Univ Prof. **RESEARCH** Nineteenth century Am fiction and poetry; contemp Ampoetry. **SELECTED PUBLICATIONS** Auth, Dream in Emily Dickinson's poetry, Emily Dickinson Bull, 78; Dickinson's Letters to Higginson: Motives for Metaphor, Higginson J Poetry, 78; The theme of the double in The Call of the Wild, Markham Rev, 78; Emily Dickinson, Emerson, and the poet as namer, New Eng Quart, 78; Carolyn Forche: Poetry & Survival in America, Poetry, 86; numerous poems in lit mags. **CONTACT ADDRESS** Dept of Eng, Western Illinois Univ, 1 University Circle, Macomb, IL, 61455-1390. **EMAIL** mfjsmx@uxa.ecn.bgu.edu

MANN, KAREN BERG
PERSONAL Born 04/20/1945, Waukegan, IL, m, 1969 **DISCIPLINE** ENGLISH **EDUCATION** Northwestern Univ, BA, 67; Univ Pa, MA, 68, PhD(English), 71. **CAREER** Asst prof, 71-76, ASSOC PROF ENGLISH, WESTERN ILL UNIV, 77-. **MEMBERSHIPS** MLA; Aaup. **RESEARCH** Nineteenth century British literature; prose fiction; women's studies. **SELECTED PUBLICATIONS** Auth, The Matter With Mind--Violence and the 'Silence of the Lambs', Criticism-Quart for Lit and the Arts, Vol 0038, 96. **CONTACT ADDRESS** Dept of English, Western Illinois Univ, 1 University Cir, Macomb, IL, 61455-1390.

MANN, THOMAS J.
PERSONAL Born 02/21/1948, Chicago, IL, s **DISCIPLINE** LIBRARY SCIENCE **EDUCATION** Saint Louis Univ, BA, 70; Loyola Univ Chicago, PhD, 75; LA State Univ, MLS, 79. **CAREER** Private investigator, 76-77; reference librarian, 80, LSU; Catholic Univ of Amer, 80-81; Library of Congress, 81-. **MEMBERSHIPS** Amer Library Assn **SELECTED PUBLICATIONS** Auth, A Guide to Library Research Methods, 87; auth, Library Research Models, 93; auth, The Oxford Guide to Library Research, 98. **CONTACT ADDRESS** 2030 F St. NW, #102, Washington, DC, 20006. **EMAIL** tman@loc.gov

MANNING, PETER J.
PERSONAL Born 09/27/1942, New York, NY, m, 1967 **DISCIPLINE** ENGLISH **EDUCATION** Harvard Univ, BA, 63; Yale Univ, MA, 65, PhD(English), 68. **CAREER** Asst prof English, Univ Calif, Berkeley, 67-75; ASSOC PROF ENGLISH, UNIV SOUTHERN CALIF, 77-, Guggenheim fel, 81-82. **MEMBERSHIPS** MLA; Byron Soc; Wordsworth-Coleridge Asn; Keats-Shelley Asn. **RESEARCH** English romantic poetry. **SELECTED PUBLICATIONS** Auth, Childe Harold in the Marketplace + 'Childe Harolds Pilgrimage' by Byron, George, Gordon--From Romaunt to Handbook, Mod Lang Quart, Vol 0052, 91; Byron, the Bible, and Religion--Essays From the 12th-Int Byron Sem, Wordsworth Circle, Vol 0023, 92; Poor Polidori, Keats-Shelley J, Vol 0041, 92; Wordsworth, William

'Lyrical Ballads' and Other Poems, 1797-1800, Wordsworth Circle, Vol 0025, 94; Byron Historical Dramas, J Engl and Ger Philol, Vol 0094, 95. **CONTACT ADDRESS** Dept of English, Univ of Southern Calif, Los Angeles, CA, 90089.

MANNING, SUSAN
DISCIPLINE ENGLISH **EDUCATION** Columbia Univ, PhD. **CAREER** Prof, Northwestern Univ. **RESEARCH** 19th- and 20th-century dance, theatre and drama in Europe and the United States. **SELECTED PUBLICATIONS** Auth, Ecstasy and the Demon: Feminism and Nationalism in the Dances of Mary Wigman, 93. **CONTACT ADDRESS** Dept of English, Northwestern Univ, 1801 Hinman, Evanston, IL, 60208.

MANOGUE, RALPH ANTHONY
PERSONAL Born 08/05/1935, New York, NY **DISCIPLINE** ENGLISH LITERATURE **EDUCATION** Georgetown Univ, BS, 58; Univ Va, MA, 60; NY Univ, PhD(English), 71. **CAREER** Teacher and dept head, Congressional High Sch, Falls Church, Va, 59-64; adj lectr, Queens Col, NY, 64-72; PROF ENGLISH, MIDDLESEX COUNTY COL, NJ, 71-. **MEMBERSHIPS** Wordsworth-Coleridge Asn; Keats-Shelley Asn; Conf Brit Studies. **RESEARCH** British Romantics; freedom of the press: England 1780-1832; radical English publishers 1780-1832. **SELECTED PUBLICATIONS** Auth, The Treason Trials, 1794, Albion, Vol 0026, 94; Ridgway, James and America, Early Amer Lit, Vol 0031, 96; The Plight of Ridgway, James, London Bookseller and Publisher, and the Newgate Radicals 1792-1797, Wordsworth Circle, Vol 0027, 96. **CONTACT ADDRESS** Middlesex County Col, Edison, NJ, 08818.

MANSELL, DARREL
DISCIPLINE ENGLISH LITERATURE **EDUCATION** Yale Univ, PhD, 63. **CAREER** Prof, Dartmouth Col. **RESEARCH** Victorian and Brit lit. **SELECTED PUBLICATIONS** Auth, Telling It Like It Was in English 83, AWP Chron, 93; Metaphor as Matter, Lang and Lit, 92; Trying to Bring Literature Back Alive: The Ivory in Joseph Conrad's Heart of Darkness, Criticism, 91. **CONTACT ADDRESS** Dartmouth Col, 3529 N Main St, #207, Hanover, NH, 03755.

MANSO, LEIRA ANNETTE
DISCIPLINE LITERATURE **EDUCATION** Univ Puerto Rico, BA, 87; New York Univ, MA, 89; SUNY (Binghamton), PhD, 96. **CAREER** Adjunct Prof, 96-, Broome Community Col. **CONTACT ADDRESS** 100 Roberts St 22-11, Binghamton, NY, 13901. **EMAIL** manso_l@sunybroome.edu

MANY, PAUL
DISCIPLINE COMMUNICATION STUDIES **EDUCATION** St John's Univ, BA; OH State Univ, MA, PhD. **CAREER** Prof, Univ Toledo. **SELECTED PUBLICATIONS** Auth, These Are the Rules, 97; The Fine Art of Saying No, Academe, 96; Literary Journalism: Newspapers' Last, Best Hope, Conn Rev, 96; Rabbits, Live and Dressed. **CONTACT ADDRESS** Dept of Commun, Univ Toledo, Toledo, OH, 43606. **EMAIL** pmany@uoft02.utoledo.edu

MAPP, EDWARD C.
PERSONAL Born 08/17/1929, New York, NY **DISCIPLINE** THEATER **EDUCATION** City Coll of NY, BA 1953; Columbia Univ, MS 1956; NY Univ, PhD 1970. **CAREER** NY City Bd of Educ, tchr 1957-64; NY City Tech Coll, dir of Library Learning Resources Center 1964-77; Borough of Manhattan Community Coll, dean of faculty 1977-82; City Colleges of Chicago, vice chancellor 1982-83; BOROUGH OF MANHATTAN COMMUNITY COLL, prof 1983-92, PROF EMERITUS, 1994-. **HONORS AND AWARDS** Founders Day Award for Outstanding Scholarship NY Univ 1970; Distinguished Serv Award Borough of Manhattan Community Coll The City Univ of NY 1982; elected to NY Acad of Pub Educ 1978; Black Collectors Hall of Fame, 1992. **MEMBERSHIPS** Dir Natl Serv Corp 1984-87; bd of dir United Nations Assoc of NY 1975-78; bd of trustees NY Metro Ref & Rsch Agency 1980-81; feature columnist Movie/TV Mktg 1979-91; 100 Black Men Inc 1975-85; bd mem (Brooklyn Region) Natl Conf of Christians & Jews 1975-81; treas City Univ of NY Fac Senate 1972-77; Brooklyn Borough Pres Ed Adv Panel 1981; commissioner, New York City Human Rights Commission, 1988-94, vice chair, 1992-94. **SELECTED PUBLICATIONS** Author: Blacks in American Films, 1972; Puerto Rican Perspectives, 1974; Blacks in Performing Arts, 1978, 2nd edition, 1990; co-author: A Separate Cinema, 1992; curator: Edward Mapp African-American Film Poster Collection, presented to Center for Motion Picture Study of the Academy of Motion Picture Arts and Sciences, 1996. **CONTACT ADDRESS** Manhattan Comm Col, CUNY, 199 Chambers St, New York, NY, 10007.

MAQBOOL, AZIZ
DISCIPLINE ENGLISH LITERATURE **EDUCATION** Punjab Univ, BA, MA; Oxford Univ, PhD. **RESEARCH** Nineteenth and twentieth century literature; Henry James; modern fiction; critical theory; textual criticism. **SELECTED PUBLICATIONS** Auth, The Tales of Henry James, 84. **CONTACT ADDRESS** English Dept, McMaster Univ, 1280 Main St W, Hamilton, ON, L8S 4L9.

MARCHANT, PETER L.
PERSONAL Born 05/14/1928, London, England, m, 1961, 2 children **DISCIPLINE** ENGLISH **EDUCATION** Cambridge, BA, 53, MA, 56; Univ Iowa, PhD(English), 66. **CAREER** Lectr English, Univ BC, 54-55; instr Coe Col, 57-58; from instr to asst prof, Pa State Univ, 63-68; from asst prof to assoc prof, 68-74, prof English, State Univ NY Col Brockport, 74-; prof Emeritus, ret, 93. **HONORS AND AWARDS** Chancellor's Award for Excellence in Teaching, 78. **RESEARCH** Fiction; the English novel; teaching English to the disadvantaged. **SELECTED PUBLICATIONS** Auth, Give Me Your Answer, Do, Michael Joseph, 60. **CONTACT ADDRESS** SUNY, Brockport, 350 New Campus Dr, Brockport, NY, 14420-2914. **EMAIL** pmarchant@alsbrockport@edu

MARCHIONE, MARGHERITA FRANCES
PERSONAL Born 02/19/1922, Little Ferry, NJ **DISCIPLINE** ROMANCE LANGUAGES; AMERICAN HISTORY **EDUCATION** Georgian Court Col, AB, 43; Columbia Univ, AM, 49, PhD(Ital), 60. **CAREER** Teacher parochial & private high schs, 43-54; instr lang, Villa Walsh Col, 54-67; assoc prof, 67-77, chmn dept lang, 67-68, Prof Ital, Fairleigh Dickinson Univ, Florham-Madison Campus, 77-, Res grants, Fairleigh Dickinson Univ, 68-69, 71-82; NDEA grant Ital inst undergrad, US Off Educ, 68; consult & rep, Gallery Mod Art, 68, 69; dir Ital Inst, Univ Salerno, 72, Tivoli, 73, Rome, 74; mem exec coun, Am Ital Hist Asn, 77-79; mem adv bd, NJ Cath Hist Rec Comn, 77-; NJ Hist Comn, 78-; Nat Hist Publ & Records Comn, 78, 79, 80 & 81; Nat Endowment for Humanities grant, 80-83. **HONORS AND AWARDS** Am-Ital Achievement Award in Educ, 71; UNICO Nat Rizzuto Award, 77; Star of Solidarity of Ital Repub, Pres Italy, 77. **MEMBERSHIPS** Am Asn Teachers Ital; MLA; Am Coun Teaching Foreign Lang; Am Inst Ital Studies (pres, 77-80); Am Ital Hist Asn. **RESEARCH** Contemporary Italian Culture and literature; Dante; the papers of Philip Mazzei. **SELECTED PUBLICATIONS** Transl & ed, Philip Mazzei: Jefferson's Zelous Whig, Am Inst Ital Studies, 75; ed, Lettere di Clemente Rebora, Ed di Storia e Letteratura, Rome, vol I, 76, vol II, 82; auth, Clemente Rebora, G K Hall, 78; ed, Philip Mazzei: My life and wanderings, Am Inst Ital Studies, 80; Philip Mazzei: The comprehensive microfilm edition of his papers, Kraus-Thomson Orgn Ltd, 82; Guiseppe Prezzolini: Un secodo, di attivita, Ruscovi Books, Milan, 82; Philip Mazzei: Selected Writings and Correspondence, 1730-1816, Ed di Storia a Letteratura, Rome, vol I, 82. **CONTACT ADDRESS** Col of Arts & Sci Fairleigh, Fairleigh Dickinson Univ, Madison, NJ, 07940.

MARCUS, LEAH
DISCIPLINE RENAISSANCE/EARLY MODERN LITERATURE, SHAKESPEARE, TEXTUAL STUDIES, THE RECO **EDUCATION** Columbia Univ, PhD. **CAREER** Edwin Mims Prof Eng, Vanderbilt Univ. **RESEARCH** The writings of Queen Elizabeth I. **SELECTED PUBLICATIONS** Auth, Childhood and Cultural Despair, 78; The Politics of Mirth, 86; Puzzling Shakespeare, 88; Unediting the Renaissance, 96. **CONTACT ADDRESS** Vanderbilt Univ, Nashville, TN, 37203-1727.

MARCUS, MORDECAI
PERSONAL Born 01/18/1925, Elizabeth, NJ, m, 1955, 2 children **DISCIPLINE** ENGLISH **EDUCATION** Brooklyn Col, BA, 49; NY Univ, MA, 50; Univ Kans, PhD, 58. **CAREER** Asst, Rutgers Univ, 51-52; from asst instr to instr, Univ Kans, 52-58; from instr to asst prof, Purdue Univ, 58-65; from asst prof to assoc prof, 65-72, PROF ENGLISH, UNIV NEBR, LINCOLN, 72-. **MEMBERSHIPS** MLA. **RESEARCH** Modern poetry; literature and psychology; writing of poetry. **SELECTED PUBLICATIONS** Auth, What is an initiation story?, J Aesthet Art Criticism, winter 60; Walt Whitman and Emily Dickinson, Personalist, autumn 62; Five Minutes to Noon (poems), Best Cellar, 71; The whole pattern of Robert Frost's Two Witches, Lit and Psychol, No 2, 76; Return from the Desert (poems), Newedi, 77; Conversational Basketball (poems), Nebr Rev, 80; Talisman (poems), Sparrow, 81; A Midsummer Night's Dream: the Dialectic of Eros-Thanatos, Am Imago, fall 81. **CONTACT ADDRESS** Dept of English, Univ of Nebr, Lincoln, NE, 68588.

MARCUS, SHARON
DISCIPLINE ENGLISH AND COMPARATIVE LITERATURE **EDUCATION** Brown Univ, BA, 86; Johns Hopkins Univ, PhD, 95. **CAREER** Assoc prof, eng dept, Univ Calif Berkeley. **RESEARCH** 19th century British and French novel; Feminist theory; Lesbian and gay studies; Urban and architectural history. **SELECTED PUBLICATIONS** Auth, Apartment Stories: City and Home in Nineteeth Century, Paris and London. **CONTACT ADDRESS** Dept. of English, Univ of California, Berkeley, Berkeley, CA, 94720-1030. **EMAIL** smarcus@socrates.berkeley. Edu

MARCUS, STEVEN
DISCIPLINE 19TH-CENTURY LITERATURE AND CULTURE **EDUCATION** Columbia Univ, AB, 48, AM, 49, PhD, 61; Clark Col, DHL, 86. **CAREER** Sci assoc, Amer Acad psychoanalysts.George Delacorte prof. **HONORS AND AWARDS** Fel, Amer Acad Arts and Sci; Acad Lit Stud; Fulbright fel; Amer Coun Learned Soc; Guggenheim award; Ctr Advan Stud Behavioral Sci; Rockefeller grant; Mellon grants., Ch, exec comm Bd Trustees, NEH; hon mem, Amer Psychoanalytic Assn, 79; Inst psychoanalytic trng and res, 91; assoc ed, Partisan Rev; ed bd, Prose; Stud,Psychoanalysis and Contemporary Thought; Psychoanalytic Bk, Psyche. **SELECTED PUBLICATIONS** Auth, 200 publ; Freud and the Culture of Psychoanalysis, 84; Medicine and Western Civilization, 95; Dickens From Pickwick to Dombey; The Other Victorians; Engels; Manchester and the Working Class; Doing Good; Representations: Essays on Literature and Society; co-ed, Ernest Jones's The Life; Work of Sigmund Freud. **CONTACT ADDRESS** Dept of Eng, Columbia Col, New York, 2960 Broadway, New York, NY, 10027-6902.

MARDER, HERBERT
DISCIPLINE ENGLISH **EDUCATION** Columbia Univ, PhD(English), 64. **CAREER** ASSOC PROF ENGLISH, UNIV ILL, URBANA, 65-. **RESEARCH** Modern fiction; feminist literature; improvisation in contemporary poetry. **SELECTED PUBLICATIONS** Auth, The Biographer and the Angel + Finding the Guiding Force Behind Writing about Real Life, Amer Scholar, Vol 0062, 93; Woolf,Leonard and Woolf, Virginia as Publishers--the Hogarth-Press, 1917-41, J Engl and Ger Philol, Vol 0093, 94. **CONTACT ADDRESS** Univ of Ill, Champaign, IL, 61820.

MARES, CHERYL
DISCIPLINE ENGLISH **EDUCATION** Univ CO, BA; Princeton Univ, MA; PhD. **CAREER** Assoc prof, Sweet Briar Col. **HONORS AND AWARDS** Stu Govt Assn Excellence Tchg Awd, Sweet Briar Col, 88. **RESEARCH** Literary theory; 20th century women writers; Virginia Woolf. **SELECTED PUBLICATIONS** Auth, articles on Virginia Woolf. **CONTACT ADDRESS** Sweet Briar Col, Sweet Briar, VA, 24595.

MARES, E.A.
DISCIPLINE CREATIVE WRITING/POETRY **EDUCATION** Univ NMex, PhD, 74. **CAREER** Instr, Univ NMex. **SELECTED PUBLICATIONS** Auth, The Unicorn Poem and Flowers and Songs of Sorrow, 92; There Are Four Wounds, Miguel, 94. **CONTACT ADDRESS** Univ NMex, Albuquerque, NM, 87131. **EMAIL** tmares@unm.edu

MARGOLIES, ALAN
PERSONAL Born 10/12/1933, New York, NY **DISCIPLINE** ENGLISH AND AMERICAN LITERATURE **EDUCATION** City Col New York, BA, 54; NY Univ, MA, 60, PhD(English), 69. **CAREER** Lectr English, Brooklyn Col, 61-68; lectr, City Col New York, 69-70; asst prof, 70-75, assoc prof, 76-80, PROF ENGLISH, JOHN JAY COL CRIMINAL JUSTICE, 81-, City Univ New York fac res award, 71-74 and 81-82; Am Coun Learned Soc grant-in-aid, 72; Nat Endowment for Humanities grant, 79-81. **MEMBERSHIPS** MLA; Bibliog Soc Am; Am Lit Sect, MLA; Am Studies Asn; Northeast Mod Lang Asn. **RESEARCH** American literature; bibliography; film. **SELECTED PUBLICATIONS** Auth, The Maturing of Fitzgerald, F.Scott, 20th Century Lit, Vol 0043, 97. **CONTACT ADDRESS** Dept of English, John Jay Col of Criminal Justice, CUNY, 445 W 59th St, New York, NY, 10019.

MARGULIES, IVONE
DISCIPLINE FILM STUDIES **EDUCATION** Univ do Estado do Rio de Janeiro, BA; Univ Federal do Rio de Janeiro, MA; NY Univ, 92. **CAREER** Taught at, NY Univ, Barnard Col & Sch Visual Arts; past ed, Motion Picture J; **HONORS AND AWARDS** Soc Cinema Stud awd, 92-93. **RESEARCH** Feminist film practice; Independent film; performance in film and video and cinema verite strategies. **SELECTED PUBLICATIONS** Auth, Instead Nothing Happens: Chantal Akerman's Hyperrealist Everyday, Duke UP, 96. **CONTACT ADDRESS** Dept of Film and Media Studies, Hunter Col, CUNY, 695 Park Ave, New York, NY, 10021.

MARIANI, PAUL L.
PERSONAL Born 02/29/1940, New York, NY, m, 1963, 3 children **DISCIPLINE** MODERN POETRY, BIOGRAPHY **EDUCATION** Manhattan Col, BA, 62; Colgate Univ, MA, 64; City Univ New York, PhD(English), 68. **CAREER** Lectr English, Colgate Univ, 63; from instr to asst prof, John Jay Col, 66-68; from asst prof to assoc prof, 68-71, dir grad studies, 72-74, prof English, Univ Mass, 75-; assoc ed, William Carlos Williams Rev; Sagetribe, Bread Loaf Sch of English, 82-84; Bread Loaf Writer's Conf, Poetry Staff, 85-96; dir, The Glen, 95, 96, & 98. **HONORS AND AWARDS** Dist Univ Prof, Univ Mass/Amherst; NEH Fel for Independent Res, 82, 72, 73, 81 & 82; New Jersey Writers' Award for Williams Bio, 82; NEA Fel, 84; Guggenheim Fel, 85 & 86; Healy Res Grant, 84; Univ Mass Res Fel, 86 & 87; Choice Award from Prairie Schooner, 89 & 95. **MEMBERSHIPS** MLA; Hopkins Soc; Poetry Soc Am. **RESEARCH** Twentieth century American poetry and poetics; Gerard Manley Hopkins; William Carlos Williams; John Berryman; Robert Lowell; Hart Crane. **SELECTED PUBLICATIONS** Auth, William Carlos Williams: A New World Naked, McGraw-Hill, 81; Dream Song: The Life of John Berryman, William Morrow, 90; Timing Devices: Godline, 79;

Crossing Cocytus, Grove Press, 82; Prime Mover: Grove Press, 85; Salvage Operations: New and Selected Poems, WW Norton & Co, 90; The Great Wheel, WW Norton, 96; The Broken Tower: A Life of Hart Crane: WW Norton, 99. **CONTACT ADDRESS** Dept of English, Univ of Massashusetts, Amherst, Amherst, MA, 01003. **EMAIL** pmarianai@english.umass.edu

MARINELLI, PETER V.
PERSONAL Born 07/30/1933, New York, NY **DISCIPLINE** ENGLISH **EDUCATION** Fordham Univ, BA, 55, MA, 60; Princeton Univ, PhD(English), 64. **CAREER** PROF ENGLISH, UNIV COL, UNIV TORONTO, 63-. **RESEARCH** Medieval period; English and Italian Renaissance. **SELECTED PUBLICATIONS** Auth, Selections From Boiardo 'Orlando Innamorato', Italica, Vol 0069, 92. **CONTACT ADDRESS** Univ of Toronto, English Sect Univ Col, Toronto, ON, M5S 1A1.

MARK, REBECCA
DISCIPLINE PERFORMANCE STUDIES, SOUTHERN LITERATURE **EDUCATION** B.A.: SUNY Col at Purchase, 1978 Ph.D, Stanford Univ, 1986. **CAREER** Instr, 89, Tulane Univ. **SELECTED PUBLICATIONS** Auth, The Dragon's Blood: Feminist Intertextuality, Eudora Welty's The Golden Apples. **CONTACT ADDRESS** Dept of Eng, Tulane Univ, 6823 St Charles Ave, New Orleans, LA, 70118. **EMAIL** rmark@mailhost.tcs.tulane.edu

MARKELS, JULIAN
PERSONAL Born 06/24/1925, Chicago, IL, m, 1963, 3 children **DISCIPLINE** ENGLISH **EDUCATION** Univ Chicago, BS, 48; Univ Minn, MA, 52, PhD(English), 57. **CAREER** Instr English, Univ Minn, 52-56; from instr to assoc prof, 56-67, PROF ENGLISH, OHIO STATE UNIV, 67-, CHMN DEPT, 76-, Elizabeth Clay Howald fel, 65-66. **MEMBERSHIPS** MLA. **RESEARCH** Shakespeare; American literature; American cultural history. **SELECTED PUBLICATIONS** Auth, 'Moby Dick' White Elephant + Melville, Herman, Amer Lit, Vol 0066, 94; Toward a Marxian Reentry to the Novel, Narrative, Vol 0004, 96. **CONTACT ADDRESS** Dept of English, Ohio State Univ, 164 W 17th Ave, Columbus, OH, 43210.

MARKEN, JACK WALTER
PERSONAL Born 02/11/1922, Akron, OH, m, 1946, 3 children **DISCIPLINE** ENGLISH **EDUCATION** Univ Akron, BA, 47; Ind Univ, MA, 50, PhD(English), 53. **CAREER** Instr, Univ Ky, 52-54; asst prof English and humanities, Ohio Wesleyan Univ, 54-55; asst prof, Cent Mich Univ, 55-60; prof English, Slippery Rock State Col, 60-67; PROF ENGLISH, S DAK STATE UNIV, 67-, Am Philos Soc grant, 59, res grants, 65, 67; Fulbright lectr, Univ Jordan, 65-66; US Info Serv-Finnish-Am Soc lectr Am Indian lit, Finland, 70; lectr, Univ Jordan, 82; GEN ED, NATIVE AM BIBLIOG SERIES, SCARECROW PRESS, 80-, Distinguished Award in Humanities, SDak Comt on Humanities, 77. **MEMBERSHIPS** MLA; Aaup. **RESEARCH** The late 18th century; literature of the American Indian. **SELECTED PUBLICATIONS** Auth, Walking the Rez Road, Amer Indian Culture and Res J, Vol 0017, 93. **CONTACT ADDRESS** S Dakota State Univ, Brookings, SD, 57007.

MARKI, IVAN
PERSONAL Born 06/14/1934, Budapest, Hungary, m, 1965, 2 children **DISCIPLINE** LITERARY CRITICISM, AMERICAN LITERATURE **EDUCATION** Univ Alta, BA, 61; Columbia Univ, MA, 63, PhD(English), 74. **CAREER** From instr to asst prof, 65-75, assoc prof, 75-77, Margaret Bundy Scott Assoc Prof, 77-83, English, Hamilton Col, 83-; Fulbright Visit Prof, KLTE, Debreccen, hungary, 91-92. **MEMBERSHIPS** MLA; Am-Hungarian Educr Asn; ALSC **RESEARCH** Nineteenth-century American literature; twentieth-century American literature; critical theory. **SELECTED PUBLICATIONS** Auth, The Trial of the Poet: An Interpretation of the First Edition of Leaves of Grass, Columbia Univ, 76. **CONTACT ADDRESS** Dept of English, Hamilton Col, 198 College Hill Rd, Clinton, NY, 13323-1292. **EMAIL** imarki@ruby.hamilton.edu

MARKOS, LOUIS
DISCIPLINE ENGLISH **CAREER** Assoc prof; fac, Houston Baptist Univ, 7 yrs. **HONORS AND AWARDS** Who's Who Among Amer Tchr(s), 96; NEH Summer Inst Virgil's Aeneid, Emory Univ, 94; Opal Goolsby Outstanding tchg awd, 92. **MEMBERSHIPS** Phi Beta Kappa. **RESEARCH** Marriage of his evangelical Christian faith and his love for humanistic pursuits. **SELECTED PUBLICATIONS** Auth, My Icon Case: Literary Sketches of a Greek American Family, 95 & Life to the Full: The Search for Joy in a Fallen World, 91; coauth, Witness to the Truth: A Literary Critical Approach to the Gospel of John, 97. **CONTACT ADDRESS** Language Dept, Houston Baptist Univ, 7502 Fondren Rd, Houston, TX, 77074.

MARKS, LAURA U.
DISCIPLINE FILM STUDIES **EDUCATION** Univ Rochester, MA, PhD. **CAREER** Asst prof. **SELECTED PUBLICATIONS** Pub(s), Screen; Camera Obscura; Cinemas; Wide Angle; Jump Cut. **CONTACT ADDRESS** Dept of Art and Cult, Carleton Univ, 1125 Colonel By Dr, Ottawa, ON, K1S 5B6.

MARKS, PATRICIA
DISCIPLINE BRITISH NOVEL, VICTORIAN POETRY AND PROSE, RESEARCH AND CRITICISM, MODERN D **EDUCATION** Douglass Univ, BA, 65; Mich State Univ, PhD, 70. **CAREER** Prof Eng, fac senate, acad comt, grad exec comt, grievance comt, core curric subcomt, Women's Stud comt, Valdosta State Univ; Regents Distinguished Prof for Tchg and Lrng, Asheville Inst, 96; fac develop adv comt, fac develop comt, Univ Syst of Ga. **HONORS AND AWARDS** NDEA Title IV fel, Mich State Univ, 67-70; NEH fel in Residence, Univ Pa, 77-78; fac develop grants and res grants, Valdosta State Univ fac, 85-; IISP travel sem, 89; NEH summer sem, Univ Calif, Berkeley, 93; Am Asn of Higher educ Faculty Citizenship Award, 94; NEH summer stud grant, 95. **MEMBERSHIPS** Trustee, Dickens Soc, 94; secy, Hawthorne Soc, 97. **SELECTED PUBLICATIONS** Auth, American Literary and Drama Reviews: An Index to Late Nineteenth Century Periodicals, G K Hall, 84; Bicycles, Bangs, and Bloomers: The New Woman in the Popular Press, UP Kentucky, 90; coauth, The Smiling Muse: Victoriana in the Comic Press, Assoc UP/Art Alliance, 85; Paul Dombey and the Milk of Human Kindness, in Dickens Quart 9.1, 94; Rev of Victorian American Women 1840-1880: An Annotated Bibliography, by Karen Rae Mehaffey, in Victorian Per Rev 27, 94; Rev of George Cruikshank's Life, Times, and A rt, Vol I: 1792-1835, by Robert Patten, in Victorian Per Rev 27, 94; The Boy on the Wooden Horse: Robert Audley and the Failure of Reason, in Clues, 94; Rev of Parentage and Inheritance in the Novels of Charles Dickens, by Anny Sadrin, in Dickens Quart 12, 95; Rev of Dickens and the Grown-up Child, by Malcolm Andrews, in S Atlantic Rev 60, 95; Rev of The Afterlife of Property: Domestic Security and the Victorian Novel, by Jeff Nunokawa, in ANQ, 95; Americanus Sum: Life Attacks Anglomania, in Victorian Per Rev 28, 95; 'Mon Pauvre Prisonnier': Becky Sharp and the Triumph of Napoleon, in Stud in the Novel 28.1, 96; Painting a Classroom, Reaching Through Tchg 10.1, 97. **CONTACT ADDRESS** Dept of Eng, Valdosta State Univ, 1500 N. Patterson St, Valdosta, GA, 31698. **EMAIL** pmarks@valdosta.edu

MARLANE, JUDITH
DISCIPLINE COMMUNICATION **EDUCATION** Columbia Univ, BFA, 58; MA, 62, PhD, 74. **CAREER** WNET Television, 62-66; founder, pres, JSG Prod, 66-82; producer, MCA/WWOR-TV, NY, 82-87; pres, Juroco, 89- ; chair, prof, Calif St Univ Northridge, 87- . **HONORS AND AWARDS** Who's Who; Broadcast Preceptor Award, 77; Front Page Award Judge, 80; Int Film & Television Festival Silver Medallion, 83; Silver Angel Awards, 82, 83, 84, 85, 86 **MEMBERSHIPS** Nat Acad of Television Arts & Sci; Int Radio & Television Soc; Broadcast Educ Assoc; Hollywood Radio & Television Soc; Hollywood women's Press club; Amer Women in Radio & Television; Amer Assoc of Univ Prof; Nat Assoc of Broadcasters; Nat Educ Assoc; Pi Lambda Theta; Kappa Delta Pi. **SELECTED PUBLICATIONS** Auth, Lawyer Advertising on Television, Trial Diplomacy J, 89; The world of Chinese Television, Television Quart, 92; Women in Television News, Columbia Univ Press, 76; Women in Television News Revisited, Univ Tx Press, 99. **CONTACT ADDRESS** Dept of Radio-Television-Film, California State Univ, Northridge, 18111 Nordhoff St, Northridge, CA, 91330-8317.

MARLIN, JOHN
DISCIPLINE ENGLISH **EDUCATION** US Mil Acad, BS; Univ Chicago, AM, PhD. **CAREER** Asst prof, Col St. Elizabeth. **RESEARCH** Medieval drama. **SELECTED PUBLICATIONS** Auth, Virtual Ritual: History, Drama, and the Spirit of the Liturgy in the Flenny Playbook, Amer Benedictine Rev, Dec 97; Monastic Spirituality and 12th century Drama, Int Medieval Cong, 97. **CONTACT ADDRESS** Dept of Eng, Col of Saint Elizabeth, 2 Convent Rd., Morristown, NJ, 07960. **EMAIL** jmarlin@liza.st-elizabeth.edu

MARLING, WILLIAM H.
DISCIPLINE AMERICAN LITERATURE, MODERNISM **EDUCATION** Univ Utah, BA, MA, Univ Calif, PhD. **CAREER** English, Case Western Reserve Univ. **HONORS AND AWARDS** Dir, Grad Studies. **SELECTED PUBLICATIONS** Auth or ed, The American Roman Noir; Raymond Chandler; Dashiell Hammett; William Carlos Williams and the Painters. **CONTACT ADDRESS** Case Western Reserve Univ, 10900 Euclid Ave, Cleveland, OH, 44106.

MARLOW, JAMES ELLIOTT
PERSONAL Born 02/14/1938, Belle Rive, IL, m, 1965, 2 children **DISCIPLINE** ENGLISH LITERATURE **EDUCATION** Dartmouth Col, BA, 60; Univ Calif, Davis, MA, 68, PhD, 72. **CAREER** Asst prof English, Col William & Mary, 69-73; asst prof, 73-76, assoc prof, 76-80, prof English, Univ Mass, Dartmouth, 80-. **HONORS AND AWARDS** Dartmouth Class of 1960 Poet; NEH Seminar, 73, 80. **MEMBERSHIPS** MLA; Dickens Soc; Victorian Inst. **RESEARCH** Novels of Charles Dickens; theory of the novel; contemporary literature. **SELECTED PUBLICATIONS** Auth, Franklin, Dickens, and solitary monster, Dickens Studies Newslett, 81; The response of Victorian periodicals to the fate of Franklin, Victorian Periodicals Rev, 82; Pickwick, Pugilism, and Popular Culture, J Popular Culture, 82; The Second Disk, Am Heritage, 12/82; English Cannibalism: Dickens After 1859, Studies in English Lit 23, 83; Pickwick's Writing: Propriety and Language, English Lit Hist 53, 86; Social Harmony and Dickens' Revolutionary Coding, Dickens Studies Annual 17, 89; Charles Dickens: The Uses of Time, Asn Univ Presses, 94. **CONTACT ADDRESS** Dept of English, Univ Mass, Dartmouth, 285 Old Westport Rd, North Dartmouth, MA, 02747-2300. **EMAIL** jmarlow@umassd.edu

MAROTTI, ARTHUR FRANCIS
PERSONAL Born 04/03/1940, New York, NY, m, 1964, 2 children **DISCIPLINE** ENGLISH **EDUCATION** Fordham Univ, AB, 61; Johns Hopkins Univ, PhD, 65. **CAREER** Asst prof English, Wash Univ, 65-70; assoc prof English, full prof English, 85-, Wayne State Univ, 70-85, Fel, Humanities Ctr, Johns Hopkins Univ, 70-71; Guggenheim fel, 75-76; fac res award, Wayne State Univ, 78-88. **HONORS AND AWARDS** ACLS Fel, 88-89; Wayne State Univ Charles Gershenson Distinguished Fac Fel, 95-97. **MEMBERSHIPS** Mla; Midwest Mod Lang Asn; Renissance Soc Am; Meton Soc Am; Renaissance Eng Text Soc; Soc Textual Scholar. **RESEARCH** Sixteenth and 17th century poetry and drama; John Donne's poetry; Transmission of texts in manuscript & print; Religious discourses in early modern England. **SELECTED PUBLICATIONS** Auth, All about Jonson's poetry, ELH, 72; contribr, Donne and the extasie, The Rhetoric of Renaissance Poetry, Univ Calif, 74; auth, Countertransference, the communication process, and the dimensions of psychoanalytic criticism, Critical Inquiry, 78; John Donne and the Rewards of Patronage, Patronage in the Renaissance, Princeton Univ, 81; Love is not love: Elizabethan Sonnet Sequences and the Social Order, Elh, 82; co-ed,Reading With a Difference: Gender, Race, and Cultural Identity, Wayne State Univ, 93; ed, Critical Essays on John Donne, GK Hall, 94; Manuscript, Print, and the English Renaissance Lyric, Cornell Univ, 95; coed, Texts and Cultural Change in Early Modern England, MacMillan, 97. **CONTACT ADDRESS** Dept of English, Wayne State Univ, 51 W Warren, Detroit, MI, 48202-1308. **EMAIL** a_marotti@wayne.edu

MAROVITZ, SANFORD E.
PERSONAL Born 05/10/1933, Chicago, IL, m, 1964 **DISCIPLINE** ENGLISH **EDUCATION** Lake Forest Col, BA, 60; Duke Univ, MA, 61, PhD(English), 68. **CAREER** Instr English, Temple Univ, 63-65; Fulbright lectr, Univ Athens, Greece, 65-67; asst prof, 67-70, assoc prof, 70-75, chmn grad studies, 72-74 and 80-82, PROF ENGLISH, KENT STATE UNIV, 75-, Vis prof English, Shimane Univ, Matsue, Japan, 76-77. **MEMBERSHIPS** Mla; Am Studies Asn; Melville Soc Am; Western Lit Asn; Northeast Mod Lang Asn. **RESEARCH** Nineteenth century American literature; American frontier and Western fiction; Jewish-American literature. **SELECTED PUBLICATIONS** Auth, Playing Cowboys--Low Culture and High Art in the Western, Amer Lit, Vol 0065, 93; The Essential Fuller, Margaret, Legacy, Vol 0011, 94; Ambivalent Authors, Ambiguous America in Selected American Jewish Writings to 1930, Yiddish, Vol 0009, 94; The Civil War World of Melville, Herman, Civil War Hist, Vol 0041, 95; The Columbia Book of Civil War Poetry, Civil War Hist, Vol 0041, 95; A Melville Encyclopedia--the Novels, Resources for Amer Lit Study, Vol 0021, 95; Western American Novelists, Vol 1, Clark, Walter, Van, Tilburg, Cushman, Dan, Davis, H.L., Fisher, Vardis, Guthrie, A.B., Jr, Humphrey, William, and Johnson, Dorothy, M., Western Amer Lit, Vol 0031, 97. **CONTACT ADDRESS** Dept of English, Kent State Univ, Kent, OH, 44242.

MARQUEZ, ANTONIO
DISCIPLINE AMERICAN AND COMPARATIVE LITERATURE **EDUCATION** Univ Nmex, PhD, 77. **CAREER** Instr, Univ NMex, 77-. **HONORS AND AWARDS** Fulbright scholar/lectr. **SELECTED PUBLICATIONS** Auth, Richard Rodriguez's Hunger of Memory and New Perspectives on Ethnic Autobiography, Tchg Am Ethnic Lit, UNM, 95. **CONTACT ADDRESS** Univ NMex, Albuquerque, NM, 87131.

MARREN, SUSAN M.
DISCIPLINE MODERN AMERICAN FICTION **EDUCATION** Univ Mich, PhD. **CAREER** English and Lit, Univ Ark. **SELECTED PUBLICATIONS** Auth, Subversive Mothering in Harriet Jacob's Incidents in the Life of a Slave Girl and Toni Morrison's Beloved, Mich Feminist Studies, 91; Between Slavery and Freedom: The Transgressive Self in Olaudah Equiano's Autobiography, PMLA, 93. **CONTACT ADDRESS** Univ Ark, Fayetteville, AR, 72701.

MARRON, MARIA B.
DISCIPLINE COMMUNICATIONS **EDUCATION** Univ Col Dublin, BA; OH Univ, MA, PhD. **CAREER** Comm Dept, Southwest Tex State Univ **SELECTED PUBLICATIONS** Auth, The Founding of Investigative Reporters and Editors, Inc., and the Fledgling Organization's Conduct of the Arizona Project: A Time of Trial and Triumph, Asn Educ Journalism & Mass Comm Annual Conf, 93; Investigative Journalism, Journalism Professionalism, and Professional Efficacy in Ireland, Int Comm Asn, 94. **CONTACT ADDRESS** Southwest Texas State Univ, 601 University Dr, San Marcos, TX, 78666-4604.

MARRS, SUZANNE
DISCIPLINE COMPOSITION, 19TH AND 20TH CENTURY AMERICAN LITERATURE, AND 20TH CENTURY SO **EDUCATION** Univ Okla, PhD. **CAREER** Welty Scholar-in-Residence, Miss Dept Archives and Hist, 85-86; lectr, in Russia & Fr; consul, BBC documentary on Eudora Welty, 87. **RESEARCH** South. **SELECTED PUBLICATIONS** Auth, bk The Welty Collection & articles on Eudora Welty's fiction. **CONTACT ADDRESS** Dept of English, Millsaps Col, 1701 N State St, Jackson, MS, 39210.

MARRUS, FRANCINE E.
DISCIPLINE COMMUNICATION THEORY **EDUCATION** Ohio Univ PhD 89. **CAREER** Living Legacy, researcher; writer, 98-; Clemson Univ, asst prof 90-98; FU, vis asst prof 90; UT, instr 85-88. **HONORS AND AWARDS** Appreciation Awd; Community Serv Awd. **MEMBERSHIPS** NCA; SCW. **RESEARCH** Spiritual Communications; half contexts and representations; ethnomorphic methods. **SELECTED PUBLICATIONS** Auth, Living in the Light: Myths in Alcoholics Anonymous that communicate a member's view of wellness in recovery, Communication in Recovery: Studies in Personal Transformation, eds, L Eastland, S. Herndon, J. Barr, Hampton Press, in progress; auth, In the Spirit: Communication Performance in a twelve step program, Communication in Recovery: Studies in Personal Transformation, eds, L. Eastland, S. Herndon, J. Barr, Hampton Press, in progress; auth, Leading classroom discussion in the basic course, Teaching and directing the basic comm course, eds, L.W. Hugenberg, P.L. Gray, D.N. Trank, Dubuque IA, Kendall and Hunt Pub, 93. **CONTACT ADDRESS** 167 Cedar Creek Circle, Central, SC, 296330 9467. **EMAIL** learnangel@aol.com

MARSH, JAMES H.
PERSONAL Born 09/10/1943, Toronto, ON, Canada **DISCIPLINE** EDITOR/CANADIAN STUD **EDUCATION** Carleton Univ, BA, 74. **CAREER** Ed, Holt, Rhinehart & Winston, 65-67; ed, Collier Macmillan, 67-70; exec ed, Carleton Libr Ser, 70-80; Ed-in-chief, Junior Encyclopedia of Canada, 87-91. **HONORS AND AWARDS** Secy State Can Prize Excellence, 86; Medal Royal Soc Can, 86; mem, Order Can, 89; Canada 125 Medal. **SELECTED PUBLICATIONS** Auth, Fishermen of Lunenburg, 68; auth, The Fur Trade, 69; auth, The Discoveries, 70; coauth, New Beginnings, 2 vols, 81, 82; contribur, The Canadian Encyclopedia; ed-in-chief, The Canadian Encyclopedia: Multimedia Edition, 95. **CONTACT ADDRESS** 9708 - 92 St, Edmonton, AB, T6C 3S4.

MARSHALL, ALICIA A.
DISCIPLINE HEALTH COMMUNICATION **EDUCATION** Purdue Univ, PhD. **CAREER** Asst prof, Texas A&M Univ. **HONORS AND AWARDS** National Inst Health grant; US Army Dept grant. **SELECTED PUBLICATIONS** Publ in, Health Commun; Commun Monographs; Acad Med; J Gen Internal Med; contribur, Health Communication and the Disenfranchised; Integrated Approaches to Communication Theory and Research; Case Studies in Health Communication. **CONTACT ADDRESS** Dept of Speech Communication, Texas A&M Univ, College Station, TX, 77843-4234. **EMAIL** csnidow@tamu.edu

MARSHALL, DAVID
DISCIPLINE ENGLISH **EDUCATION** Johns Hopkins Univ, PhD. **CAREER** Prof, Northwestern Univ. **RESEARCH** 18th century fiction and aesthetics, narrative theory; Shakespeare; lyric poetry; autobiography; Philosophy and literature. **SELECTED PUBLICATIONS** Auth, The Figure of Theater: Shaftesbury, Defoe, Adam Smith and George Eliot, Columbia Univ Press, 86; The Surprising Effects of Sympathy: Marivaux, Diderot, Rousseau and Mary Shelley, Univ Chicago Press, 88. **CONTACT ADDRESS** Dept of English, Northwestern Univ, 1801 Hinman, Evanston, IL, 60208.

MARSHALL, DONALD G.
PERSONAL Born 09/09/1943, Long Beach, CA, m, 1975, 2 children **DISCIPLINE** ENGLISH **EDUCATION** Harvard Univ, AB, 65; Yale Univ, PhD, 71. **CAREER** Asst prof, UCLA, 69-75; from assoc prof to prof, 75-90, Univ Iowa; prof, head, UIC, 90-. **HONORS AND AWARDS** NEH Fel, 73-74 **MEMBERSHIPS** Modern Lang Asn; Conference on Christianity and Literature. **RESEARCH** Literary theory and its history; words worth; literature and religion. **SELECTED PUBLICATIONS** Ed, Literature as Philosophy, Philosophy as Literature, 87; ed, Hans-Georg Gadamer. Truth and Method, 89; auth, Contemporary Critical Theory: A Selective Bibliography, 93. **CONTACT ADDRESS** Dept of English, Univ of Illinois, Chicago, 601 S Morgon, Rm 2027, Chicago, IL, 60607-7120. **EMAIL** marshall@uic.edu

MARSHALL, GROVER EDWIN
PERSONAL Born 03/28/1930, Portland, ME, m, 1966, 1 child **DISCIPLINE** FRENCH; ITALIAN **EDUCATION** Bowdoin Col, BA, 51; Princeton Univ, MA, 54, PhD(French), 71. **CAREER** Instr French & Ital, Princeton Univ, 54-58; instr, Williams Col, 58-60, asst prof Romanic lang, 60-64, lectr, 64-65; Asst Prof, 65-90, Assoc Prof French & Ital, Univ NH, 95-, Chmn Dept, 73-80, 81-83, 88-91. **HONORS AND AWARDS** Phi Beta Kappa, 50. **MEMBERSHIPS** Am Asn Teachers Fr; NE Mod Lang Asn. **RESEARCH** Francophone Caribbean **CONTACT ADDRESS** Dept of French, Univ of New Hampshire, 15 Library Way, Durham, NH, 03824-3596. **EMAIL** groverm@christa.unh.edu

MARSHALL, LINDA EDITH
PERSONAL Born 04/25/1941, London, ON, Canada, m, 1965, 1 child **DISCIPLINE** ENGLISH **EDUCATION** Univ Western Ont, BA, 63, MA, 65; Univ Toronto, PhD(Medieval studies), 74. **CAREER** Lectr, 65-72, asst prof, 72-79, ASSOC PROF ENGLISH, UNIV GUELPH, 79-, Can Coun leave fel Medieval poetic theory, 77. **MEMBERSHIPS** Medieval Acad Am; Asn Can Univ Teachers English; Keats-Shelley Asn Am. **RESEARCH** Poetic theory, Medieval and Romantic. **SELECTED PUBLICATIONS** Auth, Transfigured to his Likeness, Sensible Transcendentalism in Rossetti, Christina 'Goblin Market', Univ Toronto Quart, Vol 0063, 94; Abstruse the Problems, Unity and Divisions in Rossetti, Christina 'Later Life, a Double Sonnet of Sonnets', Victorian Poetry, Vol 0032, 94. **CONTACT ADDRESS** Dept of English, Univ of Guelph, Guelph, ON, N1G 2W1.

MARSHALL, W. GERALD
PERSONAL Statesville, NC **DISCIPLINE** ENGLISH **EDUCATION** Lenoir-Rhyme Coll, BA; Appalachian State Univ, MA; State Univ NY at Binghamton, PhD. **CAREER** Assoc prof, Univ of Hawaii **MEMBERSHIPS** MLA **RESEARCH** Restoration and Eighteenth Century Lit and Culture **SELECTED PUBLICATIONS** Auth, A Great Stage of Fools: Theatricality and Madness in the Plays of William Wycherley, AMS Press, 94; The Restoration Mind, Univ of Delaware Press, 97. **CONTACT ADDRESS** Dept of English, Univ of Hawaii at Manoa, Honolulu, HI, 96822-2453.

MARTIN, BRUCE KIRK
PERSONAL Born 05/28/1941, Jersey City, NJ, m, 1965, 2 children **DISCIPLINE** ENGLISH AND AMERICAN LITERATURE **EDUCATION** Univ Cincinnati, AB, 63, MA, 66, PhD(English), 67. **CAREER** From asst prof to assoc prof, 67-78, PROF ENGLISH, DRAKE UNIV, 78-, Summer sem, Nat Endowment for Humanities, 78. **MEMBERSHIPS** MLA **RESEARCH** Nineteenth and 20th-century British literature; literary theory. **SELECTED PUBLICATIONS** Auth, Vincy, Fred and the Unraveling of 'Middlemarch', Papers on Lang and Lit, Vol 0030, 94. **CONTACT ADDRESS** Dept of English, Drake Univ, 2507 University Ave, Des Moines, IA, 50311-4505.

MARTIN, DONALD R.
DISCIPLINE COMMUNICATIONS **EDUCATION** OH State Univ, PhD. **CAREER** Instr, CA Polytechnic State Univ; OH Wesleyan Univ; assoc prof, 93-. **HONORS AND AWARDS** Telecommun mgr, KPBS. **SELECTED PUBLICATIONS** Auth, bk chapters and jour articles in area of new telecommun technol. **CONTACT ADDRESS** Dept of commun, San Diego State Univ, 5500 Campanile Dr, San Diego, CA, 92182. **EMAIL** dmartin@mail.sdsu.edu

MARTIN, HERBERT WOODWARD
PERSONAL Born 10/04/1933, Birmingham, AL, m, 1979, 2 children **DISCIPLINE** MODERN POETRY, CREATIVE WRITING **EDUCATION** Univ Toledo, BA, 64; Middlebury Col, MLitt, 72; Carnegie-Mellon Univ, DA, 79. **CAREER** Tchg fel freshman compos, State Univ NY, Buffalo, 64-67; from instr to asst prof freshman compos, sophmore English & creative writing, Aquinas Col, 67-70; from asst to assoc prof, 70-80, prof poet in residence, creative writing, Drama, mod poetry & mod drama, Univ Dayton, 70; distinguished visiting prof, central MI univ, 73-; Fulbright fell, Janus Pannonius univ, Pecs, ungary, 90-91. **HONORS AND AWARDS** Paul Laurence Dunbar humanitarian award, 96; Opus award, Poetry and performance, 96; Elmer Lackner award, Univ sevice, 96; OH Hum couns Bjornson Hum award, 96; First writer in residence at Paul Laurence Dunbar Memorial House, 96; Paul Laurence Dunbar Laureate Peot for Dayton, OH, 96; Hon PhD of Humane letters from Urbana univ, 98; Ohioana Award for Theatrical Performance, 98. **RESEARCH** In His Own Voiuce: The Dramatic and Other Uncollected Works of Paul Laurence Dunbar. **SELECTED PUBLICATIONS** Auth, New York, The Nine Million and other Poems, Abracadabra Press, 68; The Shit-Storm Poems, Pilot Press, 72; The Persistence of the Flesh, 76 & The Forms of Silence, 80, Lotus Press; Paul Laurence Dunbar: A Singer of Songs, State of Ohio Libr, 79; Paul Laurence Dunbar: Common Ground, opera, 95; It Pays to Advertise, opera, 96. **CONTACT ADDRESS** Univ of Dayton, 300 College Park, Dayton, OH, 45469-0002. **EMAIL** Martinh@checkov.hm.udayton.edu

MARTIN, JOHN SAYRE
PERSONAL Born 11/25/1921, England, m, 1956, 3 children **DISCIPLINE** ENGLISH **EDUCATION** Univ Calif, Berkeley, AB, 43, MA, 48, PhD(English), 58. **CAREER** Lectr English, Univ Calif, Berkeley, 55-56; instr, Univ Ill, Urbana, 57-62; asst prof, Hiram Col, 62-65; assoc prof, 65-79, PROF ENGLISH, UNIV CALGARY, 80-. **MEMBERSHIPS** MLA; Philol Asn Pac Coast; Asn Can Univ Teachers English. **RESEARCH** Nineteenth and twentieth century literature. **SELECTED PUBLICATIONS** Auth, Mrs Moore and the Marabar Caves, Mod Fiction Studies, winter 65-66; Peter Bayley and the lyrical ballads, English Studies, 12/67; Wordsworth's echoes, English Lang Notes, 3/68; E M Forster, the Endless Journey, Cambridge Univ, 76. **CONTACT ADDRESS** Dept of English, Univ of Calgary, Calgary, AB, T2N 1N4.

MARTIN, RONALD EDWARD
PERSONAL Born 06/30/1933, Chicago, IL, m, 1956, 3 children **DISCIPLINE** ENGLISH; AMERICAN STUDIES **EDUCATION** Carroll Col, Wis, BA, 55; Boston Univ, AM, 57, PhD(Am lit), 63. **CAREER** Instr English, Boston Univ, 61-62; from instr to asst prof, 62-68, assoc prof, 68-81, PROF ENGLISH, UNIV DEL, 81-99; Am Coun Learned Soc grant-in-aid, 67-68; dir, Ctr Sci & Cult, 81-85; Fulbright Distinguished Chr, Am Stud, Odense Univ, Denmark, 93-94. **MEMBERSHIPS** AAUP; AAAS. **RESEARCH** American literature since 1880; relationships of science, philosophy, and literature. **SELECTED PUBLICATIONS** Auth, The Fiction of Joseph Hergesheimer, Univ Pa, 65; American Literature and the Universe of Force, Duke Univ, 81; American Literature and the Destruction of Knowledge, Duke Univ, 91. **CONTACT ADDRESS** 234 W Main, Newark, DE, 19711. **EMAIL** rmartin@udel.edu

MARTIN, RUSSELL L.
DISCIPLINE ENGLISH **EDUCATION** S Methodist Univ, BA, 78, MA, 86. **CAREER** NAIP CATALOGUER, RES ASST, A HISTORY OF THE BOOK IN AMERICA, AAS **MEMBERSHIPS** Am Antiquarian Soc **SELECTED PUBLICATIONS** Auth, Mr, Jefferson's Business: The Farming Letters of Thomas Jefferson and Edmund Bacon, 1806-1826; auth, Two American Farmers: Thomas Jefferson and Edmund Bacon, Mag of Albemarle Co Hist 50, 92. **CONTACT ADDRESS** Am Antiquarian Soc, 185 Salisbury St, Worcester, MA, 01609. **EMAIL** rlm@mwa.org

MARTIN, SEAN CHARLES
PERSONAL Born 02/24/1954, San Francisco, CA, s **DISCIPLINE** ENGLISH **EDUCATION** Univ of Dallas, BA, 76; Univ of Notre Dame, MA, 77 **CAREER** Asst Prof, 93-98, Univ of St. Thomas Sch of Theol; Vis Asst Prof, 98-pres, Univ of Dallas **MEMBERSHIPS** Am Acad of Relig; Soc of Bibl Lit; Cath Bibl Assoc **RESEARCH** Deutero-Pauline Literature **SELECTED PUBLICATIONS** Auth, Pauli Testamentum 2 Timothy and the Last Words of Moses, Editrice Pontifica Universita Gregoriana, 97 **CONTACT ADDRESS** Dept Theology, Univ Dallas, 1845 E Northgate Dr, Irving, TX, 75062. **EMAIL** martin@acad.udallas.edu

MARTIN, TERRY J.
PERSONAL Born 10/26/1958, Berkeley, CA, m, 1982, 2 children **DISCIPLINE** ENGLISH **EDUCATION** SUNY, Buffalo, PhD, 88. **CAREER** Instr, Universidad Industrial de Santander, Colombia, 81-82; asst prof, Idaho State Univ Pocatello, 88-89; assoc prof, Baldwin-Wallace Coll, 89-. **HONORS AND AWARDS** Phi Beta Kappa, 79; Chancellor's Award for Excellence in Teaching, SUNY/Buffalo, 86; Omicron Delta Kappa, 95. **MEMBERSHIPS** Soc Study of the Short Story; Midwest MLA. **RESEARCH** 19th-century American literature; African-American literature; literature theory. **SELECTED PUBLICATIONS** Auth, "A Slave in Form. . .¤But Not| in Fact': Frederick Douglass and the Paradox of Transcendence," Proteus, A Journal of Ideas: The Legacy of Frederick Douglass, spring 95; auth, "John Barth's 'Petition' as Microcosm," Short Story, spring 96; auth, "Harriet Jacobs," Nineteenth-Century American Women Writers, 97; auth, "John Barth," An International Companion to the Contemporary Short Story in English, 98; auth, Rhetorical Deception in Three Stories by Hawthorne, Poe, and Melville, forthcoming. **CONTACT ADDRESS** Dept of English, Baldwin-Wallace Col, Berea, OH, 44017. **EMAIL** tmartin@bw.edu

MARTIN, TIMOTHY
DISCIPLINE MODERN BRITISH LITERATURE, IRISH LITERATURE, JAMES JOYCE **EDUCATION** Univ Pa, PhD. **CAREER** Instr, Rutgers, State Univ NJ, Camden Col of Arts and Sci; dir, James Joyce Conf, Philadelphia, 89; invited lectr, James Joyce Summer Sch, Dublin, 93, 95, 96; invited lectr, Trieste Joyce Sch, 97. **RESEARCH** James Joyce **SELECTED PUBLICATIONS** Auth, Joyce and Wagner: A Study of Influence, Cambridge, 91; coed, Joyce in Context, Cambridge, 92. **CONTACT ADDRESS** Rutgers, State Univ NJ, Camden Col of Arts and Sci, New Brunswick, NJ, 08903-2101. **EMAIL** timartin@camden.rutgers.edu

MARTIN, W.R.
PERSONAL Born 04/06/1920, Durban, South Africa, m, 1970, 3 children **DISCIPLINE** ENGLISH **EDUCATION** Univ SAfrica, BA, 41, MA, 47, DLitt et Phil(English), 65. **CAREER** Sr lectr English, Univ Stellenbosch, 59-61; asst prof, Ont Agr Col, 61-62; from asst prof to assoc prof, 62-69, dep chmn dept, 67-69, assoc chmn dept, 77-80, PROF ENGLISH, UNIV WATERLOO, 69-. **MEMBERSHIPS** Asn Can Univ Teachers English **RESEARCH** Twentieth century British, especially W B Yeats,

D H Lawrence, Conrad and Henry James. **SELECTED PUBLICATIONS** Auth, Bugles, Trumpets and Drums: English Poetry and the Wars, Mosaic, vol XIII, 79; The Narrator's Retreat, In: James's Four Meetings, Studies in Short Fiction, fall 80; Conrad's Management of Narration, Conradiana, vol XIV, No 1. **CONTACT ADDRESS** Dept of English, Univ of Waterloo, Waterloo, ON, N2L 3G1.

MARTIN, WANDA
DISCIPLINE COMPOSITION AND RHETORIC **EDUCATION** Univ Louisville, PhD, 87. **CAREER** Instr, dir, freshman Eng prog, Univ NMex. **SELECTED PUBLICATIONS** Recent articles on teaching an ethical approach to argumentation have appeared in Tech Commun Quart and Issues in Writing. **CONTACT ADDRESS** Univ NMex, Albuquerque, NM, 87131.

MARTIN, WILLIAM BIZZELL
PERSONAL Born 05/12/1926, Waxahachie, TX, m, 1950, 2 children **DISCIPLINE** ENGLISH LITERATURE **EDUCATION** Southern Methodist Univ, BA, 48; Univ Edinburgh, Scotland, dipl, 50, PhD, 53. **CAREER** Instr English, Tarleton State Col, 50-51; from instr to asst prof, Agr & Mech Col Tex, 52-55; assoc prof, Northeast Mo State Teachers Col, 55-56; prof English & dept head, Tarleton State Univ, 56-86, prof emeritus, 87-, Smith-Mundt lectr English & Am lit, Lebanese Nat Univ, 60-61. **MEMBERSHIPS** MLA; S.C. M.L.A. **RESEARCH** Eighteenth century English drama, Modern British and American drama. **SELECTED PUBLICATIONS** Ed, Texas Plays, SMU Press, 90; Chapters in Grider and Rodenberger, Texas Women Writers: A Tradition of Their Own, Tx A&M Univ Press, 97 and in Updating the American West (a supp to A Literary History of the American West), Tx Christian Univ Press, 97. **CONTACT ADDRESS** Dept of English & Lang, Tarleton State Univ, Stephenville, TX, 76402-0002. **EMAIL** martin@tarleton.edu

MARTIN MURREY, LORETTA
DISCIPLINE ENGLISH **EDUCATION** Western Ky Univ, BA, MA; Univ Ky, PhD, 91. **CAREER** Prof, Western Ky Univ, 84-. **HONORS AND AWARDS** Dir W Ky Univ-Glasgow Writing Center; ed, Broomsedge Chronicles. **MEMBERSHIPS** Rawsticks, Bale Boone Poetry Group. **RESEARCH** Quilting in Southern Literature, writing, poetry, and Japanese language and culture. **SELECTED PUBLICATIONS** Areas: Eudora Welty, Mary Lee Settle, and Joy Bale Boone. **CONTACT ADDRESS** Western Kentucky Univ, 1526 Big Red Way Street, Bowling Green, KY, 42101.

MARTINE, JAMES JOHN
PERSONAL Born 07/23/1937, Philadelphia, PA, m, 1961, 3 children **DISCIPLINE** AMERICAN LITERATURE, ENGLISH **EDUCATION** Temple Univ, BA, 67; Pa State Univ, MA, 68, PhD(English), 71. **CAREER** Asst prof, 71-74, assoc prof, 74-79, prof am lit, St Bonaventure, 80-, Reviewer, Philadelphia Sunday Bull Bk Sect, 71-82 & Libr J, 73-; adv ed, Studies Am Fiction, 72-; Nat Endowment for Humanities grant, summer, 76. **MEMBERSHIPS** MLA; Aaup; Northeast Mod Lang Asn. **RESEARCH** Twentieth century American fiction; 19th century American literature; history of American literature. **SELECTED PUBLICATIONS** Auth, The Courage to Defy, In: Critical Essays on Catch-22, Dickenson, 73; Fred Lewis Pattee and American Literature, Pa State Univ, 73; American Literature: Student Guide 1 & 2, Intext, 77; All in a boiling soup: An interview with Arthur Miller, In: Critical Essays on Arthur Miller, 79 & ed, Critical Essays on Arthur Miller, 79, G K Hall; Dict of Literary Biography: American Novelists 1910-1945, Vol 9, Part 1-3, Gale, 81; Rich boys and Rich Men: The Bridal Party, In: The Short Stories of F Scott Fitzgerald: New Approaches in Criticism, Univ Wis Press, 82; The Window, Delta Epsilon J, 82; auth, The Crucible: Politics, Poverty, and Prestense, Twayne, 93; Drama, In: Am Lit Scholar, 93-96. **CONTACT ADDRESS** Dept of English, St Bonaventure Univ St, St Bonas, NY, 14778-9999. **EMAIL** jmartine@sbu.edu

MARTINES, LAURO
PERSONAL Born 11/22/1927, Chicago, IL, m, 1957, 1 child **DISCIPLINE** RENAISSANCE HISTORY, ENGLISH LITERATURE **EDUCATION** Drake Univ, AB, 50; Harvard Univ, PhD(hist), 60. **CAREER** From instr to asst prof hist, Reed Col, 58-62; PROF HIST, UNIV CALIF, LOS ANGELES, 66-, Am Philos Soc grants, 60, 61, 66; Am Counc Learned Soc fel, 62-63; Harvard Ctr Ital Renaissance Studies fel, Villa I Tatti, Florence, Italy, 62-65; John Simon Guggenheim Mem Found fel, 64-65; Ford Found grant, 68-69; Nat Endowment for Humanities sr fel, 71, fel, 78-79. **MEMBERSHIPS** AHA; Renaissance Soc Am; fel Mediaeval Acad Am. **RESEARCH** Seventeenth century Europe; the Italian Renaissance; the social analysis of English Renaissance verse. **SELECTED PUBLICATIONS** Auth, Law, Family, and Women, J Mod Hist, vol 0066, 94; On the Practice or Art of Dancing, J Mod Hist, vol 0067, 95; The Revolt of the Ciompi, Amer Hist Rev, vol 0100, 95; Love and History--The Renaissance Italian Connection, Annales-Hist Sci Sociales, vol 0051, 96; Family Memoirs--The Castellani Family of 14th Century Florence, Speculum-J Medieval Stud, vol 0071, 96; The District of Green Dragon, J Interdisciplinary Hist, vol 0027, 97; The Fortunes of the Courtier--The European Reception of Castiglione Cortegiano, Amer Hist Rev, vol 0102, 97. **CONTACT ADDRESS** Dept of Hist, Univ of Calif, Los Angeles, CA, 90024.

MARTINEZ, NANCY CONRAD
PERSONAL Born 03/25/1944, Corvallis, OR, m, 1971 **DISCIPLINE** BRITISH LITERATURE **EDUCATION** Southern Ore State, BA, 71; Univ NMex, MA, 72, PhD(English), 76. **CAREER** Adj asst prof English, 77-79, dir, Develop Acad Prog & asst prof English, 80-81, ASSOC DEAN, COL GEN STUDIES, UNIV ALBUQUERQUE, 82-. **MEMBERSHIPS** Conf Col Compos & Commun; NCTE; SCent Soc Eighteenth Century Studies; Western Col Reading Asn. **RESEARCH** Satire; composition. **SELECTED PUBLICATIONS** Auth, Shakespeare Sonnet-99, a Blighted Flower Garden in a Winters Tale, Explicator, vol 0051, 93. **CONTACT ADDRESS** Univ Albuquerque, Albuquerque, NM, 87131.

MARTZ, LOUIS LOHR
PERSONAL Born 09/27/1913, Berwick, PA, m, 1941, 3 children **DISCIPLINE** ENGLISH **EDUCATION** Lafayette Col, AB, 35; Yale Univ, PhD, 39. **CAREER** From instr to prof English, 38-57, Douglas Tracy Smith prof English & Am lit, 57-71, dir Beinecke Rare Bk & Manuscript Libr, 72-77, STERLING PROF ENGLISH, YALE UNIV, 71-, Guggenheim fel, 48-49; William Lyon Phelps lectr, Yale Univ, 67; Ward-Phillips lectr, Notre Dame Univ, 68; Nat Endowment for Humanities fel, 77-78. **HONORS AND AWARDS** LittD, Lafayette Col, 60. **MEMBERSHIPS** Am Acad Arts & Sci; MLA; Renaissance Soc Am; Antiqn Soc; Amici Thomae Mori. **RESEARCH** Renaissance; 17th and 20th centuries. **SELECTED PUBLICATIONS** Auth, Holy Living and Holy Dying, vol 1, Holy Living, vol 2, Holy Dying, Mod Philol, vol 0090, 92. **CONTACT ADDRESS** Yale Univ, 994 Yale Station New, Haven, CT, 06520.

MARTZ, WILLIAM J.
DISCIPLINE SHAKESPEARE, TWENTIETH-CENTURY LITERATURE, DRAMA, CREATIVE WRITING, COMPOSI **EDUCATION** Univ, Rochester, BA; Northwestern Univ, MA; Yale Univ, PhD. **CAREER** Prof, Ralph Hale Ruppert Distinguished Prof Am Hist, Ripon Col. **SELECTED PUBLICATIONS** Auth, The Distinctive Voice. **CONTACT ADDRESS** Ripon Col, Ripon, WI. **EMAIL** MartžW@mac.ripon.edu

MARVIN, ELIZABETH W.
PERSONAL Born 11/10/1955, Denton, TX, m, 2 children **DISCIPLINE** PERFORMING ARTS **EDUCATION** Col Wooster, BA, 77; Eastman Sch Music, MA, 81, PhD, 89. **CAREER** Instr, Marymount Palos Verdes Col, 80-82; from tchg asst to instr to asst prof to assoc prof to chemn, Eastman Sch Music, 82-. **HONORS AND AWARDS** NEH; Nat Grad Fel Prog Fel, US Dept Edu, 86-87; Young Scholar Award, 93; Bridging Fel, 93; Res leave, 94, 98. **MEMBERSHIPS** Col Music Society; Music Theory Society of NY State; Society Music Perception & Cognition; Phi Beta Kappa; Pi Kappa Lambda; Society Music Theory. **SELECTED PUBLICATIONS** Auth, art, Research on Tonal Perception and Memory: What Implications for Music Theory Pedagogy, 95; coauth, art, Sex Differences in Memory for Timbre. An Event-Related Potential Study, 96; coauth, art, CD-ROMS, HyperCard, and the Theory Curriculum: A Retrospective Review, 96; coauth, art, Absolute Pitch and Sex Affect Event-Related Potential Activity for a Melodic Interval Discrimination Task, 97; auth, Tonal/Atonal: Cognitive Strategies for Recognition of Transposed Melodies, 97. **CONTACT ADDRESS** Eastman Sch of Music, 26 Gibbs St, Rochester, NY, 14604. **EMAIL** betsy@theory.esm.rochester.edu

MARX, PAUL
PERSONAL Born 12/24/1930, New York, NY, m, 1955, 2 children **DISCIPLINE** ENGLISH **EDUCATION** Univ MI, BA, 53; Univ IA, MFA, 57; New York Univ, PhD, 66. **CAREER** Lectr Eng, Southern IL Univ, 57-60; asst prof, Lehigh Univ, 63-67; assoc prof, 67-73, Prof Eng & Chmn Dept, Univ New Haven, 73. **MEMBERSHIPS** MLA; NCTE. **RESEARCH** Romantic, Victorian and mod Brit lit. **SELECTED PUBLICATIONS** Ed, Twelve Short Story Writers, Holt, 70; auth, Eduora Welty & Harvey Swados, In: Contemporary Novelists, St James Press, 72; Modern and Classical Essayists, Mayfield, 96. **CONTACT ADDRESS** Dept of Eng, Univ of New Haven, 300 Orange Ave, West Haven, CT, 06516-1999. **EMAIL** pmarx@snet.net

MASLAN, MARK
DISCIPLINE AMERICAN LITERATURE **EDUCATION** Univ Calif-Berkeley, PhD, 90. **CAREER** ASST PROF, ENG, UNIV CALIF, SANTA BARBARA. **RESEARCH** Lit and cult theory. **SELECTED PUBLICATIONS** Auth, "Foucault and Pragmatism," Raritan, 88; "Whitman's 'Strange Hand': Body as Text in Drum-Taps," ELH, 91; "Whitman and his Doubles," Amer Lit Hist, 94. **CONTACT ADDRESS** Dept of Eng, Univ Calif, Santa Barbara, CA, 93106-7150. **EMAIL** mmaslan@humanitas.ucsb.edu

MASON, BOBBIE ANN
PERSONAL Born 05/01/1940, Mayfield, KY, m, 1969 **DISCIPLINE** ENGLISH **EDUCATION** Univ Conn, PhD, 72. **CAREER** Writer, fiction. **HONORS AND AWARDS** PEN Hemingway Award; Southern Book Award. **MEMBERSHIPS** PEN; Author's Guild. **RESEARCH** American and Irish Literature 20th Century. **SELECTED PUBLICATIONS** Auth, In Country; Feather Crowns; Shiloh and Other Stories; Clear Springs, 99. **CONTACT ADDRESS** Intl Creative Mgt, 40 W 57th St, New York, NY, 10019.

MASSA, RICHARD WAYNE
PERSONAL Born 05/02/1932, Carona, KS, m, 1971, 3 children **DISCIPLINE** ENGLISH **EDUCATION** Univ Mo-Columbia, BJ, MA, 54. **CAREER** Instr jour, Univ Mo, 55; instr, Miss State Col Women, 57-58; assoc prof Eng, Okla Col Lib Arts, 58-69; consult & vpres, Interpersonal Commun Consults, 69-72; prof jour, Mo Southern State Col, 72-, head, dept commun, 80-, spec instr jour, Northeast Mo State Univ, 72; dir, intl studies, 96. **HONORS AND AWARDS** Govenor's Award for Excellence in Education, 96 **RESEARCH** Communications; crime reporting; international journalism. **SELECTED PUBLICATIONS** Coauth & co-ed, Contemporary Man in World Society, 69; co-ed, Aesthetic Man, 69; auth, Philosophical Man, McCutcheon, 69; auth, Inquisitive Man, McCutcheon, 70. **CONTACT ADDRESS** Inst of Int Studies, Missouri Southern State Col, 3950 Newman Rd, Joplin, MO, 64801-1512. **EMAIL** massar@mail.mssc.edu

MASSE, MICHELLE
DISCIPLINE NARRATIVE, FEMINIST AND PSYCHOANALYTIC THEORY, FICTION **EDUCATION** Brown Univ, PhD, 81. **CAREER** Assoc prof, La State Univ; assoc ed, NOVEL: A Forum on Fiction, 77-81; ser ed, Feminist Theory and Criticism (SUNY Press). **HONORS AND AWARDS** NEH Fel, 83-84; fel, Newberry Libr, Monticello Col Found, 89; La Enhancement grant, 91, 94. **RESEARCH** Narcissism and the bildungsroman. **SELECTED PUBLICATIONS** Auth, In the Name of Love: Women, Masochism, and the Gothic, 92. **CONTACT ADDRESS** Dept of Eng, Louisiana State Univ, 212P Allen Hall, Baton Rouge, LA, 70803. **EMAIL** mmasse@unix1.sncc.lsu.edu

MASSELINK, NORALYN
DISCIPLINE 17TH CENTURY ENGLISH LITERATURE **EDUCATION** Calvin Coll, BA, 81; Univ Ill, Urbana, MA, 83, PhD, 87. **CAREER** Lectr, Interboro Inst, 87; asst prof, Hofstra Univ, 87-88; ASSOC PROF ENGLISH, SUNY, CORTLAND, 88-. **MEMBERSHIPS** John Donne Soc. **RESEARCH** John Donne **SELECTED PUBLICATIONS** Auth, Donne's Epistemology and the Art of Memory, The John Donne J, 8.1, 89; auth, Apparition Head vs. Body Bush: The Prosodical Theory and Practice of John Crowe Ransom, The Southern Q, winter 91; auth, Wormseed Revisited: Glossing Line Forty of Donne's Farewell to Love, Eng Lang Notes, 30.2, Dec 92; auth, A Matter of Interpretation: Example and John Donne's Role as Preacher and as Poet, The John Donne J, 11.1&2, 92; co-ed, The Cortland Composition Handbook, McGraw-Hill, 96; auth, Teaching Donne's Devotions Through the Literature of AIDS, Studies in Medieval and Renaissance Teaching, 6.1, spring 98; auth, Memory in John Donne's Sermons: Readie or Not? S Atlantic Rev, 63.2, spring 98. **CONTACT ADDRESS** Dept of English, SUNY, Cortland, PO Box 2000, Cortland, NY, 13045. **EMAIL** masselinkn@snycorva.cortland.edu

MATABANE, PAULA W.
DISCIPLINE COMMUNICATIONS **EDUCATION** Howard Univ, PhD. **CAREER** Assoc prof. **RESEARCH** TV audience characteristics; social learning from tv; African Americans in tv and film. **SELECTED PUBLICATIONS** Documentary producer-writer, Africa in the Holy Land: Significant Connections, producer of informational video/film programs. **CONTACT ADDRESS** School of Communications, Howard Univ, 2400 Sixth St NW, Washington, DC, 20059.

MATANLE, STEPHEN
DISCIPLINE LANGUAGE AND LITERATURE **EDUCATION** Johns Hopkins Univ, MA; Am Univ, PhD. **CAREER** Assoc prof, Univ Baltimore; ch, Div Lang, Lit & Comm Design, 95-. **CONTACT ADDRESS** Commun Dept, Univ Baltimore, 1420 N. Charles Street, Baltimore, MD, 21201.

MATAR, NABIL
PERSONAL Born 11/04/1949, Beirut, Lebanon, m, 1986, 2 children **DISCIPLINE** ENGLISH **EDUCATION** Cambridge Univ, PhD, 76. **CAREER** Prof, Florida Inst Technol, 88- ; dept head, 97- . **RESEARCH** Anglo-Islamic relations; the Renaissance. **SELECTED PUBLICATIONS** Auth, Muslims in Seventeenth-Century England, J Islamic Studies, 97; auth, Wives, Captive Husbands and Turks: The First Women Petitioners in Caroline England, Explor in Renaissance Cult, 97; auth, Alexander Ross and the First English Translation of the Qur'an, The Muslim World, 98; auth, Islam in Britain: 1558-1685; auth, The Renaissance Triangle: Muslims, Britons and American Indians, 98. **CONTACT ADDRESS** Humanties Dept, Florida Inst of Tech, Melbourne, FL, 32901. **EMAIL** nmatar@fit.edu

MATES, JULIAN
PERSONAL Born 06/24/1927, New York, NY, m, 3 children **DISCIPLINE** DRAMATIC LITERATURE **EDUCATION** Brooklyn Col, BA, 49; Columbia Univ, MA, 50, PhD, 59. **CAREER** Lectr Eng, City Col NY, 51-52; lectr, Hofstra Col, 52-53, instr, 53-58; asst prof, 59-61, assoc prof, 62-66, Prof Eng, C W Post Col, Long Island Univ, 67-, Dean Sch Of Arts, 68-, Dir, Am Theatre Festival, C W Post Col, 68-. **MEMBERSHIPS** Am Soc Theatre Res; Theatre Libr Asn. **RESEARCH** Am lit; musical theatre. **SELECTED PUBLICATIONS** Auth, The American Musical Stage before 1800, Rutgers Univ, 62; coauth, Renaissance Culture: A New Sense of Order, Braziller, 66; auth, Dramatic anchor: Research opportunities in the American drama before 1800, Early American Lit, 71; American musical theatre: Beginnings to 1900, In: American Theatre: The Sum of Its Parts, Samuel French, 72; Sam Harris, In: Dictionary of AmBiography, Scribner, 73; contribr, Renaissance literature, In: Europe Reborn, Mentor, 75; ed, William Dunlap: 4 Plays, Scholars' Facsimiles & Reprints, 76; contribr, Theatre vs drama: popular entertainment in early America, In: Discoveries & Considerations, State Univ NY, 76; ed, Musical works of William Dunlap, Scholars Facsimiles & Reprints, 80. **CONTACT ADDRESS** Eng Dept, Long Island Univ, 720 Northern Blvd, Greenvale, NY, 11548-1300. **EMAIL** jmates@earthlink.net

MATHENY, DAVID LEON
PERSONAL Born 10/15/1931, El Reno, OK, m, 1954, 2 children **DISCIPLINE** SPEECH **EDUCATION** Kans State Teachers Col, Ba, 53, MS, 57; Univ Okla, PhD(speech), 65. **CAREER** From instr to asst prof speech, Tex Christian Univ, 57-67; PROF SPEECH, EMPORIA STATE UNIV, 67-, ED, THE PRESUMPTION, 77-. **MEMBERSHIPS** Speech Commun Asn; Am Forensic Asn; Cent States Speech Asn. **RESEARCH** American public address; argumentation and debate. **SELECTED PUBLICATIONS** Auth, Douglass, Frederick, Abolition Orator, Proteus, vol 0012, 95. **CONTACT ADDRESS** Dept of Speech, Emporia State Univ, Emporia, KS, 66801.

MATHEWSON, DAVE L.
DISCIPLINE ENGLISH **EDUCATION** Colo Crhsitian Col, BA, 86; Denver Sem, MA, 89; Univ Aberdeen, Scotland, PhD, 98. **CAREER** Lect, Univ Aberdeen, Scotland, 97; INST, NEW TESTAMENT, OAK HILLS CHRISTIAN COL, 98. **CONTACT ADDRESS** Oak Hills Christian Col, 1600 Oak Hills Rd SW, Bemidji, MN, 56601. **EMAIL** Ohfaclty@northernnet.com

MATOTT, GLENN
DISCIPLINE ENGLISH LITERATURE **EDUCATION** Tufts Univ, BA; Univ Mont, MA; Univ Nothern Colo, PhD. **CAREER** Prof emer. **SELECTED PUBLICATIONS** Auth, pubs on philosophy, practice of teaching writing. **CONTACT ADDRESS** Dept of English, Colorado State Univ, Fort Collins, CO, 80523. **EMAIL** gmattot@vines.colostate.edu

MATRO, THOMAS G.
PERSONAL Hammonton, NJ, m, 4 children **DISCIPLINE** ENGLISH **EDUCATION** Rutgers Univ, BS, 62: MA, 66, PhD(English), 75. **CAREER** Instr English, Rutgers Col, Rutgers Univ, 70-71, lectr, 71-73; lectr, 73-74, asst prof, 74-80, Assoc Prof English, Cook Col, Rutgers Univ, 80-. **MEMBERSHIPS** MLA; Virginia Woolf Soc; Humanities & Techol Asn (pres, 97-99). **RESEARCH** Modern British literature; literature and technology; Am lit of 19th and 20th centuries. **SELECTED PUBLICATIONS** Auth, Only Relations: Vision & Achievement, In: To the Lighthouse, PMLA, 3/84; Constituting Tension & Uncertainty in Walker Percy's The Thanates Syndrome, Humanities and Technol Rev, Fall 94. **CONTACT ADDRESS** Dept of Humanities & Commun, Rutgers Univ, 70 Lipman Dr., New Brunswick, NJ, 08901-8525. **EMAIL** matro@aesop.rutgers.edu

MATTESON, ROBERT STEERE
PERSONAL Born 11/19/1931, New Paltz, NY, m, 1958, 3 children **DISCIPLINE** ENGLISH **EDUCATION** Haverford Col, BA, 53; Univ Pa, MS, 59, MA, 61; Univ Okla, PhD(English), 68. **CAREER** Spec instr English, Univ Okla, 63-64; from instr to assoc prof, 65-75, PROF ENGLISH, ST LAWRENCE UNIV, 75-. **MEMBERSHIPS** Am Soc Eighteenth Century Studies; Am Comt Irish Studies. **RESEARCH** Restoration and 18th century literature; Irish literature. **SELECTED PUBLICATIONS** Auth, King, William, Basiraeana and Lanaeana, Libr, vol 0017, 95. **CONTACT ADDRESS** Dept of English, St Lawrence Univ, Canton, NY, 13617.

MATTHEWS, JACK
PERSONAL Born 06/17/1917, Winnipeg, MB, Canada, m, 1942, 2 children **DISCIPLINE** COMMUNICATION AND PSYCHOLOGY **EDUCATION** Heidelberg, AB, 38; Ohio Univ, MA, 40, PhD, 46 **CAREER** Asst Dir, 46-48, Purdue Univ; Asst Prof, Prof, 48-88, Univ of Pittsburgh **HONORS AND AWARDS** Dr Sci, Heidelberg **MEMBERSHIPS** Am Phychol Assoc; Speech Assoc of Am **RESEARCH** Speech Pathology; Social Psychology **SELECTED PUBLICATIONS** Auth, The Speech Communications Process, Scott, Foresmans; The Emeritus Professor: Old Rank-New Meaning, George Washington U Press & ASHE; The Professions of Speech-Language Pathology in Human Communications Disorders, McMillan; Communication Disorders in the Mentally retarded, Appleton Century Crofts **CONTACT ADDRESS** Verona, PA, 15147-3851. **EMAIL** jmatthws@pitt.edu

MATTHIAS, JOHN EDWARD
PERSONAL Born 09/05/1941, Columbus, OH, m, 1967, 2 children **DISCIPLINE** ENGLISH LITERATURE **EDUCATION** OH State Univ, BA, 63; Stanford Univ, MA, 66. **CAREER** Assoc prof, 67-79, Prof Eng, Univ Notre Dame, 80-; Mem, London Poetry Secretariat, London Arts Asn, poets & writers prog, NY State Coun Arts & prog poetry readings, Ill Arts Coun, 70-; vis fel, Clare Hall, Cambridge Univ, England, 76-77, assoc, 77-; vis prof, Skidmore Col 78 & Univ Chicago, 80. **HONORS AND AWARDS** O-Brien Award, Ctr for Study Man, Notre Dame, 75; Columbia Univ Transl Ctr Award, 78; Swedish Inst Award, 81; Poetry Award, Soc Midland Authors, 84; Ingram Merrill Found Award, 84, 90; Slobodan Janovic Literary Prize in Translation, 89; George Bogin Award, Poetry Soc Am, 90; Lily Endowment Fel, 93; Ohio Libr Asn Poetry Award: Best volume of poetry publ, 95, 96. **RESEARCH** Mod Brit poetry; mod Am poetry; creative writing. **SELECTED PUBLICATIONS** Auth, Bucyrus, 70 & ed, Twenty-Three Modern British Poets, 71, Swallow; Contemporary British Poetry, Northwestern Univ, 71; auth, Turns, 74 & Crossing, 79, Swallow; ed, Introducing David Jones, Faber & Faber, 80; Five American Poets, Carcanet, 80; co-ed, Contemporary Swedish Poetry, Anvil, 80; Bathory & Lermontov, Kalejdoskop forlag, 80; auth, Nothern Summer, Swallow Press, 84; co-ed & transl, The Battle of Kosovo, Swallow Press, 87; ed, David Jones: Man and Poet, Nat Poetry Found, 89; auth, Tva Dikter, Ellerstrom Publ, 89; ed, Selected Works of David Jones, Nat Poetry Found, 93; auth, Swimming at Midnite: Selected Shorter Poems, Swallow Press, 95; Beltane at Aphelion: Collected Longer Poems, Swallow Press, 95. **CONTACT ADDRESS** Dept of Eng, Univ of Notre Dame, 356 Oshaugnessy Hall, Notre Dame, IN, 46556. **EMAIL** John.E.Matthias.1@nd.edu

MATYNIA, ELZBIETA
DISCIPLINE LIBERAL STUDIES **EDUCATION** Univ Warsaw, PhD, 79. **CAREER** Sr Lctr Liberal Studies and dir New Schl Transregional Ctr for Democratic Studies. **RESEARCH** The hist of soc thought and the soc of art; origins of nationalism and the emergence of gender issues in the new Europ democracies. **SELECTED PUBLICATIONS** Auth, Poetics of the Revolution, Perf Arts Jour; Hitler and the Artists, Am Jour Soc. **CONTACT ADDRESS** Eugene Lang Col, New Sch for Social Research, 66 West 12th St, New York, NY, 10011.

MAURER, A.E. WALLACE
PERSONAL Born 09/11/1921, Grenfell, SK, Canada, m, 1963, 2 children **DISCIPLINE** ENGLISH **EDUCATION** Univ Man, BA, 42, MA, 48; Univ Wis, PhD, 54. **CAREER** Teaching asst English, Univ Wis, 48-53; from asst instr to assoc prof, 53-69, PROF ENGLISH, OHIO STATE UNIV, 69-. **MEMBERSHIPS** MLA. **RESEARCH** John Dryden and the Restoration. **SELECTED PUBLICATIONS** Auth, Shaw, the Annual of Shaw Studies, vol 11, Shaw and Politics, Mod Drama, vol 0037, 94. **CONTACT ADDRESS** Dept of English, Ohio State Univ, Columbus, OH, 43210.

MAURER, MARGARET
DISCIPLINE SHAKESPEARE, 16TH AND 17TH CENTURY ENGLISH LITERATURE **EDUCATION** Seton Hall Col, BA, 69; Cornell Univ, PhD, 73. **CAREER** Dir, Div Univ Studies, 84-87; prof, 74-.; ch. **HONORS AND AWARDS** Summer Inst fel, NEH, 78. **RESEARCH** 16th and early 17th century Eng lit. **SELECTED PUBLICATIONS** Publ, Mod Lang Quart, Studies in Phliogy, Studies in Eng Lit, ELH, Genre. **CONTACT ADDRESS** Dept of Eng, Colgate Univ, 13 Oak Drive, Hamilton, NY, 13346.

MAXFIELD, JAMES F.
PERSONAL Born 12/25/1936, Omaha, NE, m, 1958, 3 children **DISCIPLINE** ENGLISH **EDUCATION** Knox Col, BA, 59; Univ Iowa, MA, 61, Phd(English), 67. **CAREER** Instr English, Knox Col, 64-66; from instr to asst prof, 66-71, assoc prof, 71-82, PROF ENGLISH, WHITMAN COL, 82-. **HONORS AND AWARDS** Graves Award, 70-71. **MEMBERSHIPS** MLA; Am Film Inst. **RESEARCH** Victorian novel, Dickens, Hardy; 20th century literature; cinema. **SELECTED PUBLICATIONS** Auth, Out of the Past--The Private Eye as Tragic Hero, New Orleans Rev, vol 0019, 92; The Worst Part + Scorsese, Martin 'Mean Streets', Lit-Film Quart, vol 0023, 95. **CONTACT ADDRESS** Dept of English, Whitman Col, Walla, WA, 99362.

MAY, CHARLES EDWARD
PERSONAL Born 02/18/1941, Paintsville, KY, m, 1980, 3 children **DISCIPLINE** ENGLISH & AMERICAN LITERATURE **EDUCATION** Morehead State Univ, BA, 63; Ohio Univ, MA, 64, PhD(English), 66. **CAREER** Asst prof English, Ohio Univ, 66-67; from asst prof to assoc prof, 67-77, PROF ENGLISH, CALIF STATE UNIV, LONG BEACH, 77-. **HONORS AND AWARDS** Outstanding Prof Award, 84; Fulbright fel, Dublin, Ireland, 96-97. **RESEARCH** The short story. **SELECTED PUBLICATIONS** Auth, Short Story Theories, Ohio Univ, 76; The Modern European Short Story, 89; Edgar Allan Poe: A Study of the Short Fiction, 91; Fiction's Many Worlds, 93; The New Short Story Theories, 94; The Short Story: The Reality of Artifice, 94; Interacting with Essays, 96. **CONTACT ADDRESS** Dept of English, California State Univ, Long Beach, 1250 N Bellflower, Long Beach, CA, 90840-0001. **EMAIL** cmay@csulb.edu

MAY, JILL P.
PERSONAL Born 08/23/1943, Rocky Ford, CO, m, 1967, 2 children **DISCIPLINE** CHILDREN'S LITERATURE, LIBRARY **EDUCATION** **EDUCATION** Wis State Univ-Eau Claire, BA, 65, Univ Wis-Madison, Msls, 66. **CAREER** Vis asst prof, 70-75, asst prof, 75-82, ASSOC PROF CHILDREN'S LIT, PURDUE UNIV, 82-, Nat Endowment for the Humanities, Ind Libr Asn, 79; ed, Ind Libraries: A Quart J, 80-82; assoc ed, Children's Lit Asn Quart, 82-. **MEMBERSHIPS** Children's Lit Asn; MLA; NCTE; Int Reading Asn. **RESEARCH** Historical children's literature; film in children's literature; minority children's literature. **SELECTED PUBLICATIONS** Auth, Feminism and Childrens Literature, Fitting 'Little Women' Into the American Literary Canon, Cea Critic, vol 0056, 94; Theory and Textual Interpretation--Childrens Literature and Literary Criticism, J Midwest Mod Lang Asn, vol 0030, 97. **CONTACT ADDRESS** Dept of Children's Lit, Purdue Univ, West Lafayette, IN, 47907-1968.

MAY, JOHN R.
DISCIPLINE RELIGIOUS STUDIES, ENGLISH IN RELIGION AND LITERATURE **EDUCATION** Emory Univ, PhD, 71. **CAREER** Alumni prof Eng and Relig Stud, La State Univ; ed, Paulist. **HONORS AND AWARDS** Alpha Sigma Nu; Phi Kappa Phi. **RESEARCH** Southern literature; religion and film. **SELECTED PUBLICATIONS** Auth, The Pruning Word: The Parables of Flannery O'Connor, Notre Dame, 76; Ed, Image and Likeness: Religious Visions in American Film Classics, Paulist, 92. **CONTACT ADDRESS** Dept of Philos and Relig S tud, Louisiana State Univ, 106 Coates Hall, Baton Rouge, LA, 70803.

MAY, JOHN RICHARD
PERSONAL Born 09/16/1931, New Orleans, LA, m, 1977, 4 children **DISCIPLINE** LITERATURE & RELIGION, FILM CRITICISM **EDUCATION** Loyola Univ, La, BBA, 51; Spring Hill Col, MA, 57; St Louis Univ, STL, 65; Emory Univ, PhD(Lit & Theol), 71. **CAREER** Lectr Humanities, Spring Hill Col, 65-68; from asst prof to assoc prof Relig Studies, Loyola Univ, La, 71-76, dir Mat Social Studies, 74-76; assoc prof & chmn Freshman English, 76-81, prof English, La State Univ, Baton Rouge, 81-; dept chmn, 83-92; alumni prof, 88; assoc ed, Horizons, 74-80; prog dir, La Comt on Humanities, 75-77. **MEMBERSHIPS** Col Theol Soc; Conf Christianity & Lit; Southeastern Am Acad Relig; Walker Percy Soc; Flannery O'Connor Soc. **RESEARCH** Theological literary criticism; American literature; religion and film. **SELECTED PUBLICATIONS** Auth, Toward a New Earth; Apocalypse in the American Novel, Univ Notre Dame, 72; contribr, Mark Twain, 74; Disguises of the Demonic, Association, 75; auth, The Pruning Word: The Parables of Flannery O'Connor, Univ Notre Dame, 76; coauth, Film Odyssey: The Art of Film as Search for Meaning, 76 & The Parables of Lina Wertmuller, 77, Paulist; ed, The Bent World: Essays on Religion and Culture, Scholars Press, 81; co-ed, Religion in Film, Univ Tenn Press, 82; ed, Image and Likeness: Religious Visions in Am Film Classics, Paulist, 92; ed, New Image of Religious Film, Sheed & Ward, 97. **CONTACT ADDRESS** Dept of English, Louisiana State Univ, Baton Rouge, LA, 70803-0001. **EMAIL** jmay2@lsuvm.1su.edu

MAYER, ROBERT
DISCIPLINE EIGHTEENTH-CENTURY BRITISH LITERATURE **EDUCATION** Northwestern Univ, PhD, 87. **CAREER** Engl, Okla St Univ. **RESEARCH** Historiography and fiction and the links between them. **SELECTED PUBLICATIONS** Auth, History and the Early English Novel: Matters of Fact from Bacon to Defoe, Cambridge Univ Press, 97. **CONTACT ADDRESS** Oklahoma State Univ, 101 Whitehurst Hall, Stillwater, OK, 74078.

MAYNARD, JOHN ROGERS
PERSONAL Born 10/06/1941, Williamsville, NY, 1 child **DISCIPLINE** ENGLISH LITERATURE, BIOGRAPHY **EDUCATION** Harvard Col, BA, 63; Harvard Univ, PhD(English), 70. **CAREER** Tutor English, Harvard Univ, 65-69, asst prof English, hist & lit, 69-74; asst prof English, 74-76, ASSOC PROF ENGLISH, NY UNIV, 76-, Nat Endowment Humanities sr res grant, Robert Browning Biog, 72-73; Guggenheim fel, 80-81. **HONORS AND AWARDS** Thomas J Wilson Prize, Bd Syndics, Harvard Univ Press, 76. **MEMBERSHIPS** MLA; Browning Inst. **RESEARCH** Nineteenth and twentieth-century English literature; biography; sexuality in literature. **SELECTED PUBLICATIONS** Auth, Child Loving--The Erotic Child and Victorian Culture, Albion, vol 0025, 93. **CONTACT ADDRESS** Dept of English, New York Univ, 19 University Pl, New York, NY, 10003-4556.

MAYO, CHARLES M.
DISCIPLINE PUBLIC RELATIONS AND ADVERTISING **EDUCATION** Univ Ala, PhD, 93. **CAREER** Asst prof, La State Univ, hosp dir, Commun, dir, col PR. **RESEARCH** Public relations; advertising; organizational communication. **SELECTED PUBLICATIONS** Coauth, Changes in Global Focus of U.S. Business Magazines, in Jour Quart, 91; Measuring Advertising's Effectiveness, Franchising Update, 92; Game Time, Soap Time, and Prime Time TV Ads: Treatment of Women in Sunday Football and Rest-of-Week Commercials, in Jour Quart, 93. **CONTACT ADDRESS** The Manship Sch of Mass Commun, Louisiana State Univ, Baton Rouge, LA, 70803.

MAZZARO, JEROME
PERSONAL Born 11/25/1934, Detroit, MI **DISCIPLINE** RENAISSANCE AND CONTEMPORARY LITERATURE **EDUCATION** Wayne State Univ, AB, 54, PhD(English), 63; Univ Iowa, MA, 56. **CAREER** Instr English, Univ Detroit, 58-61; asst prof, State Univ NY Col Cortland, 62-64; FROM ASST PROF TO ASSOC PROF, STATE UNIV NY BUFFALO, 64-72, PROF ENGLISH, 72-80., Guggenheim fel, 64-65. **MEMBERSHIPS** Dante Soc Am. **RESEARCH** Contemporary poetry; Renaissance poetry. **SELECTED PUBLICATIONS** Auth, The Arts of Memory and Hogarth, William Line of Beauty, Essays in Lit, vol 0020, 93; Mnema and Forgetting in Euripides the 'Bacchae', Comp Drama, vol 0027, 93; Morality in Pirandello 'Come Tu Mi Vuoi', Mod Drama, vol 0036, 93; Whitman, Walt and the Citizens Eye, Sewanee Rev, vol 0102, 94; Play and Pirandello Il 'Giuoco Delle Parti', Comp Drama, vol 0027, 94; The Growth of 'Leaves of Grass', Sewanee Rev, vol 0102, 94; Whitman and the American Idiom, Sewanee Rev, vol 0102, 94; Tapping God Other Book, Wordsworth at Sonnets, Stud in Romanticism, vol 0033, 94; Disseminating Whitman, Sewanee Rev, vol 0102, 94; Mathematical Certainty and Pirandello 'Cosi E Se Vi Pare, Comp Drama, vol 0028, 95; Euripides and the Poetics of Sorrow, Comp Drama, vol 0029, 95; Pirandello I 'Giganti Della Montagna' and the Myth of Art, Essays in Lit, vol 0022, 95; Pirandello and Film, Comp Drama, vol 0030, 96; Whitman, Walt America--A Cultural Biography, Sewanee Rev, vol 0104, 96; Road Thoughts, Hudson Rev, vol 0049, 96; Pirandellos 'Sei Personaggi' and Expressive Form, Comp Drama, vol 0030, 96; Duets, Hudson Rev, vol 0050, 97. **CONTACT ADDRESS** SUNY, 147 Capen Blvd, Buffalo, NY, 14260.

MCALEAVEY, DAVID WILLARD
PERSONAL Born 05/27/1946, Wichita, KS, m, 1977, 2 children **DISCIPLINE** ENGLISH & AMERICAN LITERATURE **EDUCATION** Cornell Univ, BA, 68, MFA, 72, PhD(English), 75. **CAREER** Instr, 74-75, asst prof , 75-88, PROF ENGLISH & AM LIT, GEORGE WASHINGTON UNIV, 89-. **MEMBERSHIPS** MLA. **RESEARCH** Creative writing, twentieth century English and American poetry and poetics. **CONTACT ADDRESS** Dept of English, George Washington Univ, 801 22nd St NW, Washington, DC, 20052-0001. **EMAIL** dmca@gwu.edu

MCALEXANDER, HUBERT HORTON
PERSONAL Born 10/27/1939, Holly Springs, MS, m, 1970, 1 child **DISCIPLINE** LITERATURE **EDUCATION** Univ of Miss, BA, 61, MA, 66; Univ of Wis, PhD, 73. **CAREER** Instr, Univ of Miss, 66-69; asst prof, Tex A & M, 73-74; ASST PROF, 74-80, ASSOC PROF, 80-93, PROF, UNIV OF GA, 93-. **HONORS AND AWARDS** Josiah Meigs Awd for Excellence in Tchg, Univ of Ga, 97. **MEMBERSHIPS** MLA; ALA; SAMLA; Soc for Study of Southern Lit. **RESEARCH** Literary biography; Southern culture and Lit. **SELECTED PUBLICATIONS** Auth, The Prodigal Daughter: A Biography of Sherwood Bonner, La Univ Press, 81, Univ of Tenn Press, 99; History, Gender, and the Family in A Stand in the Mountains, The Craft of Peter Taylor, Univ of Ala Press, 95; Peter Taylor: The Undergraduate Years at Kenyon, The Kenyon Rev, 99; ed, Conversations with Peter Taylor, Univ Press of Miss, 87; Critical Essays on Peter Taylor, G.K. Hall, 93. **CONTACT ADDRESS** 125 Bearing st, Athens, GA, 30605-1006. **EMAIL** hmealexa@arches.vga.edu

MCALEXANDER, PATRICIA JEWELL
PERSONAL Born 01/26/1942, Johnstown, NY, m, 1970, 1 child **DISCIPLINE** ENGLISH **EDUCATION** State Univ NY, Albany, BA, 64; Columbia Univ, MA, 66; Univ Wis-Madison, PhD(English) 73. **CAREER** Instr English, Univ Colo, 66-68; LECTR ENGLISH, UNIV GA, 77-. **MEMBERSHIPS** MLA; S Atlantic Mod Lang Asn. **RESEARCH** American literature; literature of the early republic; Charles Brockden Brown. **SELECTED PUBLICATIONS** Auth, Faking It--A Look Into the Mind of a Creative Learner, Coll Compos and Commun, vol 0044, 93; Written Language Disorders, Coll Compos and Commun, vol 0044, 93. **CONTACT ADDRESS** Dept of English, Univ of Ga, Athens, GA, 30602.

MCALLISTER, MATTHEW P.
DISCIPLINE ADVERTISING **EDUCATION** Purdue Univ, BA, 83, MA, 86; Univ IL, Phd, 90. **CAREER** Grad Tchg Asst, Purdue Univ, 83-85; Grad Tchg Asst, Univ IL, 85-90; Adj Fac Mem, 89, 90; Vis Asst Prof, Denison Univ, 90-91; Asst Prof, VA Tech, 91-97; Assoc Prof with tenure; VI Tech, 97-. **HONORS AND AWARDS** Outstanding Academic Bk 96; Certificate Tchg Excellence Award; Adv Year, VA Tech Univ Student Leadership Awards, Cited tchg excellence Comm 220 Cited tchg excellence Speech Comm 112; Nat Sci Found fel, Purdue Univ., Ed Board, Crit Studies Mass Comm, 96-; Vice-Chair, Int Comm Asn, 96-; Secy, Int Comm Asn, 94-96; Panel Respondent,Int Comm Asn; 93, 95, 96; panel chair, Int Comm Asn. **MEMBERSHIPS** Kappa Tau Alpha, National Commun(s) Honorary. **SELECTED PUBLICATIONS** Auth, The Commercialization Am cult: New advertising, control and democracy. Thousand Oaks, CA: Sage Publs, Inc. Hardback and paperback ed, 96. **CONTACT ADDRESS** Virginia Polytech Inst & State Univ, Blacksburg, VA, 24061. **EMAIL** mattm@vt.edu

MCALPIN, SARA
DISCIPLINE ENGLISH **EDUCATION** Clarke Col, BA, 56; Marquette Univ, MA, 64; Univ Pa, PhD, 71. **CAREER** St Joseph Acad, 59-61; teach fel, Univ Pa, 67-71; CLARK COL, 61-67, 71-. **CONTACT ADDRESS** 1550 Clark Dr, Dubuque, IA, 52001. **EMAIL** smcalpin@keller.clarke.edu

MCALPINE, MONICA ELLEN
PERSONAL Born 08/14/1940, Rochester, NY, m, 1974, 1 child **DISCIPLINE** ENGLISH LITERATURE **EDUCATION** Nazareth Col, Rochester, BA, 62; Univ Rochester, MA, 67, PhD, 72. **CAREER** Instr Eng, Univ Rochester, 67-68; from instr to asst prof, 68-77, assoc prof, 77-91, Prof Eng, Univ MA, Boston, 91. **MEMBERSHIPS** MLA; Mediaeval Acad Am; New Chaucer Soc. **RESEARCH** Chaucer; Middle Eng lit. **SELECTED PUBLICATIONS** Auth, The Genre of Troilus and Criseyde, Cornell Univ, 78; The pardoner's homosexuality and how it matters, Pmla, 95:8-22; Chaucer's Knight't Tale: An Annotated Bibliography, 1900-1985, Toronto Univ, 91. **CONTACT ADDRESS** Univ Massachusetts Harbor Campus, 100 Morrissey Blvd, Boston, MA, 02125-3300. **EMAIL** mcalpine@umbsky.cc.umb.edu

MCBRIDE, WILLIAM
DISCIPLINE ENGLISH LITERATURE **EDUCATION** Colo State Univ, BA; Univ Nothern Colo, MA; Univ Nebr, PhD. **CAREER** Prof. **SELECTED PUBLICATIONS** Auth, pubs on Charles Dickens; co-auth, Young Adult Literature: Background, Selection & Use. **CONTACT ADDRESS** Dept of English, Colorado State Univ, Fort Collins, CO, 80523. **EMAIL** bmcbride@vines.colostate.edu

MCCABE, BERNARD
PERSONAL Born 08/09/1923, Middlesbrough, England, m, 1952, 8 children **DISCIPLINE** ENGLISH **EDUCATION** Univ Manchester, Llb, 45; Stanford Univ, MA, 59, PhD(English), 61. **CAREER** Asst prof, 61-66, chmn, 72-76, assoc prof, 66-79, PROF ENGLISH, TUFTS UNIV, 79-. **MEMBERSHIPS** MLA. **RESEARCH** Novel of social protest; modern fiction; the eighteen-thirties and forties. **SELECTED PUBLICATIONS** Auth, End-End Heat + An Interview With Bird, Antonia on 'Face', Sight and Sound, vol 0007, 97. **CONTACT ADDRESS** Dept of English, Tufts Univ, Medford, MA, 02155.

MCCAFFREY, JERRINE A.
PERSONAL Sioux City, IA **DISCIPLINE** LITERATURE **EDUCATION** Univ ofNE, PhD, 96 **CAREER** Tchr, 90-, Des Moines Area Cmty Col **HONORS AND AWARDS** Ron Howard Master Tchr Awd **MEMBERSHIPS** WLA **CONTACT ADDRESS** DMACC, Des Moines, IA, 51401. **EMAIL** jamccaffrey@dmacc.cc.ia

MCCALEB, JOSEPH L.
DISCIPLINE COMMUNICATIONS **EDUCATION** Univ TX, PhD, 76. **CAREER** Assoc prof, Univ MD. **RESEARCH** Tchr effectiveness in the develop of their personal authority. **SELECTED PUBLICATIONS** Auth, How Do Teachers Communicate, Amer Assn Col Tche Edu, 87; Evaluating Teachers' Communications, Future of Speech Commun, SCA, 89. **CONTACT ADDRESS** Dept of Commun, Univ MD, 4229 Art-Sociology Building, College Park, MD, 20742-1335. **EMAIL** jm33@umail.umd.edu

MCCANN, RICHARD
DISCIPLINE CREATIVE WRITING **EDUCATION** Univ Iowa, PhD. **CAREER** Asso prof, Am Univ; co-dir, MFA program, creative writing. **HONORS AND AWARDS** Beatrice Hawley Award, 94, Capricorn Poetry Award, 93; NEA, Creative Writ Fel. **MEMBERSHIPS** Board of Trustees Jenny McKean Moore Fund Writers. **SELECTED PUBLICATIONS** Auth, Ghost Letters; Nights of 1990; Dream of the Traveler; Worlds of Fiction; Co-ed, Landscape and Distance: Contemporary Poets from Virginia. **CONTACT ADDRESS** American Univ, 4400 Massachusetts Ave, Washington, DC, 20016. **EMAIL** mccann@american.edu

MCCARREN, VINCENT PAUL
PERSONAL Born 03/22/1939, New York, NY, m, 1968 **DISCIPLINE** CLASSICAL STUDIES, MEDIEVAL LITERATURE **EDUCATION** Fordham Univ, AB, 60; Columbia Univ, AM, 67; Univ Mich, PhD(class studies), 75. **CAREER** Lectr Greek & Latin, Brooklyn Col, 63-68; instr, Hunter Col, 68-69, class lang & lit, Herbert H Lehman Col, 69-70; lcctr Greek & Latin, 75-76, acad coun gen acad areas, 77-78, RESEARCHER, MIDDLE ENGLISH DICT, UNIV MICH, 79-. **MEMBERSHIPS** Am Soc Papyrologists; Am Philol Soc. **RESEARCH** Documentary papyrology; Greek and Latin etymological studies. **SELECTED PUBLICATIONS** Aith, The Tanner Bede--The Old English Version of Bede 'Historia Ecclesiastica', Oxford Bodleian Library Tanner 10, Together With the Mediaeval Binding Leaves, Oxford Bodleian Library 10, and the Domitian Extracts, London British Libra, Speculum; Bristol University Ms Dm 1, a Fragment of the 'Medulla Grammaticae'--an dd, Traditio Stud in Ancient and Medieval Hist Thought and Relig, vol 0048, 93. **CONTACT ADDRESS** Middle English Dict, Univ Michigan, 555 S Forest, Ann Arbor, MI, 48109.

MCCARTHY, B. EUGENE
PERSONAL Born 05/03/1934, Grand Haven, MI, m, 1962, 3 children **DISCIPLINE** ENGLISH **EDUCATION** Univ Detroit, AB, 58, MA, 61; Univ Kans, PhD(English), 66. **CAREER** Instr English, Univ Detroit, 60-61; from instr to asst prof, 65-72, ASSOC PROF ENGLISH, COL OF THE HOLY CROSS, 72-. **RESEARCH** Milton; literary criticism of Restoration drama. **SELECTED PUBLICATIONS** Auth, Gray Music for the 'Bard' + Autograph Manuscript by Gray, Thomas, Revf Engl Stud, vol 0048, 97. **CONTACT ADDRESS** 422 Lovell, Worcester, MA, 01602.

MCCARTHY, JOHN F.
PERSONAL Born 02/25/1930, Newton, MA **DISCIPLINE** ENGLISH **EDUCATION** Harvard Univ, BA, 51; Yale Univ, MA, 53, PhD(English), 63. **CAREER** Instr English, Univ NH, 56-59; from instr to asst prof, 59-69, ASSOC PROF ENGLISH, BOSTON COL, 69-. **MEMBERSHIPS** MLA. **RESEARCH** Nineteenth century English poetry. **SELECTED PUBLICATIONS** Auth, The Canonical Meaning of the Recent Authentic Interpretation of Canon-230.2 Regarding Female Altar Servers, Sacred Mus, vol 0122, 95. **CONTACT ADDRESS** Dept of English, Boston Col, 140 Commonwealth Ave, Chestnut Hill, MA, 02167-3800.

MCCARTHY, JOHN P.
DISCIPLINE ENGLISH HISTORY **EDUCATION** Columbia Univ, PhD. **CAREER** Prof, Fordham Univ. **HONORS AND AWARDS** Organizer, ch, G K Chesterton Conf; exec coun, Am Irish Hist Soc. **SELECTED PUBLICATIONS** Auth, Hilaire Belloc: Edwardian Radical, 78; Dissent from Irish America 93; ed, volume of the Collected Works of G. K. Chesterton; pub(s), articles and reviews in Am, Cath Hist Rev, the Irish Times, Nat Rev, The Recorder. **CONTACT ADDRESS** Dept of Hist, Fordham Univ, 113 W 60th St, New York, NY, 10023.

MCCARTHY, PATRIC J.
DISCIPLINE ENGLISH LITERATURE **EDUCATION** Columbia Univ, PhD, 60. **CAREER** PROF EMER, UNIV CALIF, SANTA BARBARA. **HONORS AND AWARDS** Adv bd, Nineteenth-Century Prose; ed, Dickens-L, the e-group for Dickensians. **RESEARCH** Stud of the lang of value in Dickens. **SELECTED PUBLICATIONS** Auth, Matthew Arnold and the Three Classes, Columbia Univ Press, 64. **CONTACT ADDRESS** Dept of Eng, Univ Calif, Santa Barbara, CA, 93106-7150. **EMAIL** mccarthy@humanitas.ucsb.edu

MCCARTHY, PATRICK A.
PERSONAL Born 07/12/1945, Charlottesville, VA, m, 1997, 3 children **DISCIPLINE** ENGLISH **EDUCATION** Univ Virginia, BA, 67, MA, 68; Univ Wisc - Milwaukee, PhD, 73. **CAREER** Asst prof, 76-81, assoc prof, 81-84, prof, 84-, dir, grad stud, 86-95, dir, undergrad stud, Engl, 98-99, Univ Miami. **RESEARCH** Modern British & Irish lit, Irish stud, sci fiction. **CONTACT ADDRESS** Dept of English, Univ of Miami, Coral Gables, FL, 33124. **EMAIL** pmccarthy@umiami.ir.miami.edu

MCCARTHY, WILLIAM PAUL
PERSONAL Born 08/25/1942, Bronxville, NY **DISCIPLINE** EIGHTEENTH CENTURY BRITISH LITERATURE **EDUCATION** Hobart Col, BA, 64; Rutgers Univ, PhD, 74. **CAREER** From instr to assoc prof, 72-87, Prof English, Ia State Univ, 87-. **HONORS AND AWARDS** NEH Fel, 88. **MEMBERSHIPS** MLA; Am Soc Eighteenth-Century Studies. **CONTACT ADDRESS** Iowa State Univ, Ames, IA, 50011-0002. **EMAIL** Wpmccarthy@aol.com

MCCARTNEY, JESSE FRANKLIN
PERSONAL Born 11/29/1939, Duncan, OK, m, 1959, 2 children **DISCIPLINE** ENGLISH **EDUCATION** OK State Univ, BS, 63; Univ AR, MA, 65, PhD, 71. **CAREER** From asst prof to assoc prof Eng, Univ Southern MA, 68-77; dir, Off Instr Develop, Ball State Univ, 77-82; Prof Eng & Vpres Instnl Serv, Catawba Col, 82-85, Vpres Acad Affairs & Dean, 85-92; Chmn, Eng Dept & dir Inst Res, 92. **MEMBERSHIPS** MLA; South Cent Mod Lang Asn; Prof & Organizational Develop Network; Am Asn Higher Educ. **RESEARCH** Mod Brit and Am lit; tchg in the hum. **SELECTED PUBLICATIONS**

Guest-ed & contribr, Special Issue on Teaching the Humanities, Southern Quart, 1/74; auth, The Frank Arthur Swinnerton collection: A special literary collection, English Lit Transition, 75; The pedagogical style of T H Huxley in On the Physical Basis of Life, Southern Quart, 1/76; Barry Hannah, Miss Libr Comn, 77; The contributions of faculty development to humanistic teaching, Lib Educ, 12/77; Politics in Graham Green's The Destructors, Southern Humanities Rev, winter 78; Faculty Development: Planning for Individual and Institutional Renewal, Planning for Higher Educ, winter 80. **CONTACT ADDRESS** Eng Dept, Catawba Col, 2300 W Innes St, Salisbury, NC, 28144-2488. **EMAIL** jmccartn@catawba.edu

MCCLARTY, WILMA KING- DOERING

PERSONAL Born 07/21/1939, m, 1962, 1 child **DISCIPLINE** ENGLISH, ENGLISH EDUCATION **EDUCATION** Andrews Univ BA, 61, MA, 62; Univ MT, DEduc, 68. **CAREER** Asst prof Eng & educ, Southwestern Union Col, 68-72; assoc prof, 72-80, Prof Eng & Chmn Dept, Southern Adventist University, 80-; Coord, Seventh-day Adventist Sec Sch Eng Tchrs Conv, Southern Missionary Col, 73. **MEMBERSHIPS** NCTE. **SELECTED PUBLICATIONS** Auth, Why are you so peculiar?, Rev & Herald, 8/71; Open-minded or just empty headed, J Adventist Educ, 2-3/72; Urgency (poem), Ministry, 2/72. **CONTACT ADDRESS** Dept of Eng, Southern Adventist Univ, PO Box 370, Collegedale, TN, 37315-0370. **EMAIL** wmclarty@southern.edu

MCCLARY, BEN HARRIS

DISCIPLINE ENGLISH **EDUCATION** Univ Tenn, BA, 55; MA, 57; Sussex, PhD, 66. **CAREER** Prof, PROF EMER ENG, MIDDLE GEORGIA COLL **MEMBERSHIPS** Am Antiquarian Soc **SELECTED PUBLICATIONS** Auth, "William Cullen Bryant's Sketch of His Father in American Biography, " Am Lit 55, 83; "George Washington Harris's New York Atlas Series: Three New Items," Stud in Am Humor 2, 84; "Samuel Lorenzo Knapp and Early American Biography," Procs of the AAS 95, 85. **CONTACT ADDRESS** PO Box 80082, Chattanooga, TN, 37414.

MCCLUNG, WILLIAM A.

PERSONAL Born 01/22/1944, Norfolk, VA, s **DISCIPLINE** ENGLISH **EDUCATION** Willaims Col, BA, 66; Harvard Univ, AM, 67, PhD, 72. **CAREER** Asst prof to assoc prof to PROF ENG, MISS STATE UNIV, 71-. **HONORS AND AWARDS** Dexter Fel, Harvard Univ, 70; Am Phil Soc Grantee, 85; vis fel, The Huntington Libr, 85; ACLS Fel, 88; Andrew W. Mellon Fel, The Huntington Libr, 91. **MEMBERSHIPS** Phi Beta Kappa, Phi Kappa Phi, Am Asn Univ Prof; Mod Lang Asn, Soc of Arch Hist; Renaissance Soc of Am; Milton Soc of Am, John Donne Soc of Am, Nat Trust for Hist Pres. **RESEARCH** Literary/architectural relations **SELECTED PUBLICATIONS** Auth, "Designing Utopia," Moreana: Bulletin Thomas More (France), 94ed, commentary, The Variorum Edition of the Poetry of John Donne, Vol VIII: The Epigrams, Epithalamions, Epitaphs and Inscriptions, Indiana UP, 95; auth "The Decor of Power in Naples, 1747," Jour of Arch Educ 52.1, 98. **CONTACT ADDRESS** Mississippi State Univ, PO Drawer E, Mississippi State, MS, 39762-5505. **EMAIL** wam3@ra.msstate.edu

MCCLURE, CHARLES R.

PERSONAL Born 05/24/1949, Syracuse, NY, m, 1970, 1 child **DISCIPLINE** INFORMATION STUDIES **EDUCATION** OK State Univ, BA (Spanish), 71, MA (Hist), 73; Univ OK, MLS (Library Science), 74; Rutgers Univ, PhD (Information Studies), 77. **CAREER** Prof, Univ OK, School of Library Science, 78-86; DISTINGUISHED PROF, SYRACUSE UNIV, SCHOOL OF INFORMATION STUDIES, 86-. **HONORS AND AWARDS** Best Book of the Year, Am Soc for Information Science, 87; Distinguished Researcher, Nat Commission on Libraries and Information Science, 94. **MEMBERSHIPS** Am Library Asn; Information Industry Asn; Asn of Library and Information Science. **RESEARCH** Information policy; planning/evaluation of information services. **SELECTED PUBLICATIONS** Auth, with others, Libraries in the Internet/National Research and Education Network (NREN): Perspectives, Issues and Strategies, Meckler Pub, 94; with others, Internet Costs and Cost Models for Public Libraries, Nat Commission on Libraries and Information Science, 95; with Cynthia Lopata, Assessing the Academic Networked Environment: A Manual of Strategies and Options, Coalition for Networked Information, 96; with others, The 1996 National Survey of Public Libraries and the Internet: Issues Progress and Issues, Nat Commission on Libraries and Information Science, 96; co-ed and contrib with Peter Hernon and Harold Relyea, Federal Information Policies in the 1990's: Issues and Conflicts, Ablex Pub Corp, 96; with Bill Moen, An Evaluation of the Federal Government's Implementation of the Government Information Locator service (GILS), Government Printing Office, 97; with John Bertot, The 1997 Survey of Public Libraries and the Internet: Costs and Capabilities for the Electronic Networked Environment, Am Library Asn, 98; with John Bertot, Policy Issues and Stategies Affecting Public Libraries in the National Networked Environment, Nat Commission on Libraries and Information Science, 98; with John Bertot, The 1998 National Survey of Public Library Outlet Internet Connectivity, Nat Commission on Libraries and Information Science, 99. **CONTACT ADDRESS** School of Information Studies, Center for Science and Technology, Syracuse Univ, Syracuse, NY, 13244. **EMAIL** cmcclure@mailbox.syr.edu

MCCLURE, CHARLOTTE SWAIN

PERSONAL Born 07/30/1921, Newark, OH, m, 1945, 3 children **DISCIPLINE** AMERICAN AND COMPARATIVE LITERATURE **EDUCATION** Denison Univ, Ohio, BA, 44; Univ NMex, MA, 66, PhD(English), 73. **CAREER** Staff & feature writer state govt, Int News Serv, Columbus, 44-45; staff & feature writer local govt & gen news, J-Herald, Dayton, 46-47; instr English & chmn dept, Sandia Sch, Albuquerque, 66-68; from instr to asst prof, 69-75, dir honors prog admin, 75-79, asst prof for lang & comp lit, 78-82, ASSOC PROF COMP LIT, GA STATE UNIV, ATLANTA, 82-, Fac, Gerontology Ctr, Ga State Univ, 79-; Women's Educ Equity Act Prog grant, 79-82. **MEMBERSHIPS** MLA; SAtlantic Mod Lang Asn; Southern Comp Lit Asn; Western Lit Asn. **RESEARCH** Rediscovery of American writers, especially women of late 19th and early 20th centuries; comparison of types of literary characters portrayed in the literatures of the western world; comparative study of themes in western hemispheric literatures. **SELECTED PUBLICATIONS** Auth, The Adventures of the Woman Homesteader--The Life and Letters of Stewart, Elinore, Pruitt, Amer Lit, vol 0065, 93; Helen of the West Indies + Walcott, Derek and 'Omeros'--History or Poetry of a Caribbean Realm, Stud in the Lit Imagination, vol 0026, 93; California Daughter, Atherton, Gertrude and Her Times, Resources for Amer Lit Study, vol 0022, 96. **CONTACT ADDRESS** Georgia State Univ, 2674 Leslie Dr NE, Atlanta, GA, 30345.

MCCLURE, JOHN

DISCIPLINE ENGLISH LANGUAGE AND LITERATURE **EDUCATION** Tufts Univ, BA; Stanford, MA; PhD. **CAREER** Prof. **RESEARCH** Colonial cultural studies; religious cultural studies; contemporary fiction. **SELECTED PUBLICATIONS** Auth, Kipling and Conrad: The Colonial Fiction, Late Imperial Romance. **CONTACT ADDRESS** Dept of English, Rutgers Univ, 510 George St, Murray Hall, New Brunswick, NJ, 08901-1167. **EMAIL** jmcclure@rci.rutgers.edu

MCCOLLEY, DIANE K.

DISCIPLINE 17TH-CENTURY POETRY, RENAISSANCE AND REFORMATION CULTURAL CONTEXTS **EDUCATION** Univ Ill, PhD. **CAREER** Instr, Rutgers, State Univ NJ, Camden Col of Arts and Sci; ed bd, Milton Stud. **HONORS AND AWARDS** James Holly Hanford Award, 93. **MEMBERSHIPS** Pres, Milton Soc. **RESEARCH** Environmental poetics in early modern and modern poetry. **SELECTED PUBLICATIONS** Auth, Milton's Eve, Ill, 83; Milton and the Sexes, The Cambridge Companion to Milton, Cambridge, 92; A Gust for Paradise: Milton's Eden and the Visual Arts, Ill, 93; The Copious Matter of My Song, Literary Milton: Text, Pretext, Context, Duquesne Univ Press, 94; Beneficent Hierarchies: Reading Milton Greenly, Spokesperson Milton: Voices in Contemporary Criticism, Susquehanna, 94; Poetry and Music in Seventeenth-Century England, Cambridge Univ Press, 97. **CONTACT ADDRESS** Rutgers, State Univ NJ, Camden Col of Arts and Sci, New Brunswick, NJ, 08903-2101. **EMAIL** mccolley@camden.rutgers.edu

MCCONNELL, FRANK

DISCIPLINE AMERICAN LITERATURE **EDUCATION** Yale Univ, PhD, 68. **CAREER** PROF, ENG, UNIV CALIF, SANTA BARBARA. **RESEARCH** Film; Popular culture; Am lit; Brit roman; Lit theory. **SELECTED PUBLICATIONS** Auth, The Confessional Imagination: A Reading of Wordsworth's Prelude, Johns Hopkins, 74; The Spoken Seen: Film and the Romantic Imagination, Johns Hopkins, 75; Four Post-War Novelists, Univ Chicago Press, 77; Wells's Time Machine and War of the Worlds: A Critical Edition, Oxford Univ Press, 77; Storytelling and Mythmaking: Images from Film and Literature, Oxford Univ Press, 79; Lord Byron's Poetry, Norton, 79; The Science Fiction of H G Wells, Oxford Univ Press, 81. **CONTACT ADDRESS** Dept of Eng, Univ Calif, Santa Barbara, CA, 93106-7150. **EMAIL** mcconnel@humanitas.ucsb.edu

MCCORD, HOWARD

PERSONAL Born 11/03/1932, El Paso, TX, m, 1975, 4 children **DISCIPLINE** ENGLISH **EDUCATION** Univ Tex, El Paso, BA, 57; Univ Utah, MA, 58. **CAREER** Assoc prof English & humanities, Washington State univ, 60-71; dir creative writing prog, 71-80, 90-98; prof English, Bowling Green State Univ, 71-98; prof Emeritus, 98-, D H Lawrence fel, Univ NMex, 71; secy exec comn bd dir, Coord Coun Lit Mag, 72-77; adj prof, Union Grad Sch, 73-; res associateship for study in Iceland, Bowling Green Univ, 73; Nat Endowment arts fel, 76, 83; mem lit adv panel, 77-79; vis prof, Calif State Univ, 76; distinguished lectr, Univ Alaska, 78-81; chmn lit panel, Ohio Arts Coun, 79-81. spec achievement award, Bowling Green Univ, 75. **MEMBERSHIPS** MLA; Pen Club; Poetry Soc Am; Arctic Inst. **RESEARCH** Poetry; fiction; criticism. **SELECTED PUBLICATIONS** Auth, Fables and Transfigurations, 67, Longjaunes his Periplus, 68 & Maps, 71, Kayak; Selected Poems, 1955-1971, 75 & The Great Toad Hunt and Other Expeditions, 78, Crossing; The Arctic Desert, Stonemarrow, 78; The Arcs of Lowitz, Saltworks, 80; Walking Edges, Raincrow, 82; Dake of Chemical Birds, Bloody Twin, 89; The Man Who Walked to the Moon, McPherson, 97; Bone/Hueso, Logan Elim, 99. **CONTACT ADDRESS** Creative Writing Prog, Bowling Green State Univ, 1001 E Wooster St, Bowling Green, OH, 43403-0001. **EMAIL** mccord@bgnet.bgsu.edu

MCCORMACK, ERIC

DISCIPLINE ENGLISH LITERATURE **EDUCATION** Univ of Glasgow, MA; Univ Manitoba, PhD. **CAREER** Assoc prof **HONORS AND AWARDS** Commonwealth Writers Prize, 88; Arts Council Bk Prize; Governor General's Awd Fiction, 97. **SELECTED PUBLICATIONS** Auth, Black Water 2; First Blast of the Trumpet Against the Monstrous Regiment of Women; Gates of Paradise; I Shudder at Your Touch-Tales of Sex and Horror; Inspecting the Vaults; Likely Stories: A Post-modern Sample; Oxford Book of Canadian Detective Fiction; Oxford Book of Canadian Ghost Stories; Oxford Book of Scottish Short Stories; Paper Guitar; Short Fiction; The Mysterium; The Paradise Motel; The Story Begins The Story Ends. **CONTACT ADDRESS** Dept of English, St. Jerome's Univ, Waterloo, ON, N2L 3G3. **EMAIL** epmccorm@watarts.uwaterloo.ca

MCCOY, KEN

DISCIPLINE THEATRE ARTS **EDUCATION** Univ Ala, BA, 78; Univ Ill, MFA, 84; Bowling Green State Univ, PhD, 94. **CAREER** Dept Theater Arts, Stetson Univ **MEMBERSHIPS** Latin American Studies Comt. **SELECTED PUBLICATIONS** Auth, Liberating the Latin American Audience: The Conscientizacao of Enrique Buenaventura and Augusto Boal, 95; Diana Taylor's Theatre of Crisis (rev), 95; The Theatre of Mario Vargas Llosa: A Bibliography and Production History 1981-1994, Am Theatre Rev, 95; A Brief Guide to Internet Resources in Theatre and Performance Studies, 95; A Brief Bibliography of Internet Theatre Resources Beyond Email, 95. **CONTACT ADDRESS** Dept of Theatre Arts, Stetson Univ, Unit 8378, DeLand, FL, 32720-3771. **EMAIL** kmccoy@stetson.edu

MCCOY, KEN W.

PERSONAL AL, m, 1993 **DISCIPLINE** THEATRE **EDUCATION** Univ AL, Birmingham, BA, 82; IL Univ Carbondale, MFA, 84; Bowling Green St Univ, PhD, 94. **CAREER** Asst prof, Dept of Communication Stud and Theatre Arts, 94-, Stetson Univ, FL. **HONORS AND AWARDS** BGSU; Outstanding Grad Stud; Shanlelin Res Award Finalist Fel; Omicom Delta Kappa; Theta Alpha Phi; Alpha Psi Omega. **MEMBERSHIPS** NCA; Assoc for Theatre in Higher Education. **RESEARCH** Latin American theatre, internet and performance **SELECTED PUBLICATIONS** Contribur, Who's Who in the Contemporary World Theatre, Rutledge Publ, 2000; art, Strategies for Liberation in the Latin American Popular Theatre, Theatre InSight, 95; art Book Rev, Diana Taylors Theatre of Crisis, Theatre InSight, 95; art, A Guide to Internet Resources in Theatre and Performance Studies, The Internet Comp Subject Guides to Humanities Res, 95; art, The Theatre of Mario Vargas Llosa A Bibliography and Production History 1981-1994, Latin Amer Theatre Rev, 95; art, A Brief Bibliography of Internet Theatre Resources Beyond Email, Theatre Topics, 95. **CONTACT ADDRESS** Stetson Univ, 421 N Woodland Blvd, Unit 8374, Deland, FL, 32720. **EMAIL** Kmccoy@stetson.edu

MCCRACKEN, DAVID

PERSONAL Born 05/07/1939, Cincinnati, OH **DISCIPLINE** ENGLISH **EDUCATION** Oberlin Col, BA, 61; Univ Chicago, MA, 62, PhD(English), 66. **CAREER** Asst prof, 66-71, assoc prof, 71-80, PROF ENGLISH, UNIV WASH, 80-. **MEMBERSHIPS** MLA; Am Soc 18th century Studies; Wordsworth-Coleridge Asn. **RESEARCH** Late eighteenth century literature; Wordsworth. **SELECTED PUBLICATIONS** Auth, The Grasmere JS, 19th Century Prose, vol 0020, 93; Narration and Comedy in the Book of Tobit, J Bibl Lit, vol 0114, 95. **CONTACT ADDRESS** Dept of English, Univ of Wash, Seattle, WA, 98195.

MCCRACKEN FLETCHER, LUANN

DISCIPLINE EIGHTEENTH CENTURY BRITISH LITERATURE **EDUCATION** Lehigh Univ, BA, MA; UCLA, PhD. **CAREER** English Lit, Cedar Crest Col. **SELECTED PUBLICATIONS** Areas: Charlotte Bronte, Charles Dickens, and Virginia Woolf. **CONTACT ADDRESS** Cedar Crest Col, 100 College Drive, Allentown, PA, 18104.

MCCULLEN, MAURICE

DISCIPLINE ENGLISH LITERATURE **CAREER** Prof, Univ Pacific. **SELECTED PUBLICATIONS** Auth, E. M. Delafield, 85; co-auth, George Meredith: Characters and Characteristics, Garland, 79. **CONTACT ADDRESS** Eng Dept, Univ Pacific, Pacific Ave, PO Box 3601, Stockton, CA, 95211.

MCCULLOUGH, JOSEPH B.

PERSONAL Born 09/08/1943, Spokane, WA, m, 1980 **DISCIPLINE** AMERICAN LITERATURE & HUMOR **EDUCATION** Gonzaga Univ, BEd, 66; Ohio Univ, MA, 67, PhD(English), 69. **CAREER** Asst prof, 69-72, assoc prof, 72-79, actg dean, Grad Col, 77-80, prof English, Univ Nev, Las Vegas, 79-98, Fulbright lectr Am Lit, Helsinki Univ, 80-81; U of Athens, 85-86. **RESEARCH** Hamlin Garland; American literary realism and Mark Twain. **SELECTED PUBLICATIONS** Auth, Mark Twain and the Hy Slocum-Carl Byng controversy, Am Lit, 3/71; A listing of Mark Twain's contributions to the Buffalo Express, 1869-1871, Am Lit Realism, Winter 72; co-ed (with Robert K Dodge), Voices From Wah 'Kon-Tah: Contemporary Poetry of Native Americans, Int Publ, 74; auth, Madam Merle: Henry James' White Blackbird, Papers Lang & Lit, Summer 75; coauth (with Robert K Dodge), The Puritan myth and the Indian in the early American novel, Pembroke Mag, Summer 76; Pudd'nhead Wilson: A search for identity, Mark Twain J, Summer 77; Hamlin Garland, Twayne, 78; Hamlin Garland's romantic fiction, In: Critical Essays on Hamlin Garland, G K Hall, 82; Selected Letters of Hamlin Govland, co-ed with Keith Newlin, U of Neb Press, 98. **CONTACT ADDRESS** Dept of English, Univ of Nevada, PO Box 455011, Las Vegas, NV, 89154-5011. **EMAIL** JoeMcc@nevada.edu

MCCUTCHEON, ELIZABETH NORTH
PERSONAL Born 11/13/1932, New York, NY, m, 1959, 2 children **DISCIPLINE** ENGLISH LITERATURE **EDUCATION** William Smith Col, BA, 54; Univ Wis, MA, 56, PhD(English), 61. **CAREER** From asst prof to assoc prof, 66-74, Prof English, Univ Hawall, 74-95; prof Emeritus; Guggenheim fel, 79-80. **HONORS AND AWARDS** DHL, Hobart & William Smith Col, 80. **MEMBERSHIPS** MLA; Bibliog Soc Eng; Renaissance Soc Am; Amici Thomae Mori; Int Asn Neo-Latin Studies. **RESEARCH** English literature of the 16th and 17th centuries; Neo-Latin literature; rhetoric. **SELECTED PUBLICATIONS** Auth, Lancelot Andrewes' Preces Privatae: A journey through time, Studies Philol, 68; Thomas More, Raphael Hythlodaeus, and the Angel Raphael, Studies English Lit, 69; Denying the contrary: More's use of litotes in the Utopia, Moreana, 71; Bacon and the Cherubim: An iconographical reading of the New Atlantis, English Lit Renaissance, 72; Sir Nicholas Bacon's Great House Sententiae (Latin text with first English transl & introd, notes and bibliog), English Lit Renaissance Suppl No 3, 77; Recent studies in Andrewes, Eng Lit Renaissance, 81; The Apple of My Eye: Thomas More to Antonio Bonvisi: A Reading and a Translation, Moreana, 81; My Dear Peter: More's Ars Poetica and Hermeneutics for Utopia, Angers, France, 82. **CONTACT ADDRESS** Dept of English, Univ of Hawaii, Manoa, 1733 Donaghho Rd, Honolulu, HI, 96822-2368. **EMAIL** mccutch@aloha.net

MCDANIEL, JUDITH M.
DISCIPLINE HOMILETICS **EDUCATION** Univ Tex, BA, 58-61; Univ Wash, grad stud, 70-71; Diocese of Olympia, Sch Theol, Cert of Grad, 74-77; Col Preachers, 82; Gen Theol Sem, MDiv, 83-85; Univ Wash, PhD, 86-94. **CAREER** Assoc rector, St John's Parish, 85-86; tchg asst, Univ Wash, 85-86; rector, St John's Parish, 87-90; asst prof, 90-93; assoc prof, Va Theol Sem, 93-. **HONORS AND AWARDS** Parish administrator, St Barnabas Parish, 77-78; deacon, St Barnabas Parish, 78-79; deacon & priest assoc, St Mark's Cathedral, 79-83; **SELECTED PUBLICATIONS** Auth, Sermon: What you See is what you Get, Sermons that Work V, Forward Movement Publ, 95; The Rhythm of Rhetoric: Cache of the Middle Ages, Univ Microfilms, Ann Arbor, 94; Speaking on Controversial Issues, A Wholesome Example: Sexual Morality & the Episcopal Church, Bristol Bk(s), 93; rev(s), Review of: A Captive Voice: The Liberation of Preaching by David Buttrick, Sewanee Theol Rev, 94; Review of Intersections: Post-Critical Studies in Preaching, Sewanee Theol Rev, 96; Review of Marcus J. Borg, Meeting Jesus Again for the First Time, Va Sem Jour, 95. **CONTACT ADDRESS** Va Theol Sem, 3737 Seminary Rd, Alexandria, VA, 22304. **EMAIL** JMcDaniel@vts.edu

MCDERMOTT, DOUGLAS
PERSONAL Born 09/25/1936, Los Angeles, CA, m, 1958, 6 children **DISCIPLINE** DRAMATIC ART **EDUCATION** Pomona Col, AB, 58; Univ NC, MA, 60; Univ Iowa, PhD(drama), 63. **CAREER** From asst to assoc prof dramatic art, Univ Calif, Davis, 63-70; PROF DRAMA, CALIF STATE COL, STANISLAUS, 70-. **MEMBERSHIPS** Am Soc Theatre Res; Am Theatre Asn. **RESEARCH** Eighteenth and 19th century American and British theatre history; dramatic theory and criticism. **SELECTED PUBLICATIONS** Auth, The Impact of Working Conditions Upon Acting Style, Theatre Res Int, vol 0020, 95. **CONTACT ADDRESS** Dept of Drama, California State Univ, Stanislaus, Turlock, CA, 95380.

MCDONALD, KELLY M.
PERSONAL Born 10/28/1970, Auburn, WA, s **DISCIPLINE** COMMUNICATION STUDIES **EDUCATION** Kansas Univ PhD 98. **CAREER** Kansas Univ, grad tchg asst, 94-97; Western Washington Univ, asst prof, 97-. **MEMBERSHIPS** AFA; ASR; CSSA; ICA; NCA. **RESEARCH** Criticism; political communication; argumentation and persuasion. **SELECTED PUBLICATIONS** Auth, Getting the Story Right: The Role of Narrative in Academic Debate, coauth, Rostrom, 98; auth, Extending the Conversation: Continuity and Change with Debate and Forensics Organizations Entering the 21st Century, Argumentation and Advocacy, 96; auth, Arguing Across Spheres: The Impact of Electronic LISTSERV'S on the Public Sphere Argument, coauth, Proceedings of the Ninth SCA/AFA Conf on Argumentation, 95. **CONTACT ADDRESS** Dept of Communication, Western Washington Univ, Bellingham, WA, 98225-9102. **EMAIL** kmmcdon@cc.wwu.edu

MCDONALD, SHEILA
DISCIPLINE ROMANTIC POETRY, BLACK AMERICAN LITERATURE **EDUCATION** SUNY, Stony Brook, PhD. **CAREER** Assoc prof, Long Island Univ, C.W. Post Campus. **SELECTED PUBLICATIONS** Auth, The Impact of Libertinism on Byron's Don Juan. **CONTACT ADDRESS** Long Island Univ, C.W. Post, Brookville, NY, 11548-1300.

MCDONALD, VERLAINE
DISCIPLINE COMMUNICATION **EDUCATION** Seattle Pac Univ, BA, 87; USC, MA, 93; Univ Southern Calif, PhD, 94. **CAREER** Asst Prof, Seattle Pac Univ, 94-95; Asst Prof, Berea Col, 95-. **MEMBERSHIPS** Nat Commun Asn; Southern States Commun Asn. **RESEARCH** Rhetorical theory & criticism; the history of American Communism. **CONTACT ADDRESS** Berea Col, CPO 1333, Berea, KY, 40404-0001. **EMAIL** verlaine_mcdonald@berea.edu

MCDONALD, WALT
DISCIPLINE CREATIVE WRITING **EDUCATION** Univ IA, PhD, 66. **CAREER** Paul Whitfield Horn Prof Eng, dir, Creative Writing, TX Tech Univ. **HONORS AND AWARDS** Three Western Heritage Awards, the Nat Cowboy Hall of Fame; Tex Prof of the Yr, CASE, 92; two NEA fel. **SELECTED PUBLICATIONS** Auth, Counting Survivors, Univ of Pittsburgh Press, 95; Night Landings, Harper & Row; After the Noise of Saigon, The Juniper Prize, Univ of Mass Press; The Flying Dutchman, Ohio State UP; A Band of Brothers: Stories from Vietnam. **CONTACT ADDRESS** Texas Tech Univ, Lubbock, TX, 79409-5015. **EMAIL** walt@ttu.edu

MCDONALD, WALTER ROBERT
PERSONAL Born 07/18/1934, Lubbock, TX, m, 1959, 3 children **DISCIPLINE** ENGLISH **EDUCATION** Tex Technol Col, BA, 56, MA, 57; Univ Iowa, PhD(English) 66. **CAREER** Instr English, US Air Force Acad, 60-62 & 65-66, from asst prof to assoc prof, 66-71; assoc prof, 71-75, Prof English, Tex Tech Univ, 75-, lectr, Univ Colo, 67-69. **HONORS AND AWARDS** Three National Cowboy Hall of Fame's Western Heritage Award for All That Matters; Ohio State Univ Press/ The Journal Award for Blessings the Body Cave, 98. **MEMBERSHIPS** MLA; The Texas Instit of Letters; Western Writers of America; PEN; Assoc Writing Progs; Texas Assoc of Creative Writing Teachers. **RESEARCH** Creative Writing; twentieth century Am fiction and poetry. **SELECTED PUBLICATIONS** Co-ed, A Catch-22 casebook, Crowell, 73; auth, Coincidence in the novel, Col English, 2/68; The functional comedy of Catch-22, CEA Critic, 1/72; Caliban in Blue, Tex Tech, 76; The redemption novel: Suffering and hope in The Assistant and House Made of Dawn, CCTE Proceedings, 76; Snow job, Quartet, 76; The track, Sam Houston Lit Rev, 76; Anything, Anything, L'Eperiren, 80; Burning the Fence, Tex Tech, 81. **CONTACT ADDRESS** Dept of English, Texas Tech Univ, Lubbock, TX, 79409-0001. **EMAIL** walt@ttu.edu

MCDONOUGH, ANN
DISCIPLINE THEATRE **EDUCATION** Univ Minn, PhD. **CAREER** Hd, sr adult theatre prog, Univ Nev, Las Vegas. **SELECTED PUBLICATIONS** Auth, The Golden Stage: Dramatic Activities For Older Adults, Kendall-Hunt Publ, 95. **CONTACT ADDRESS** Univ Nev, Las Vegas, Las Vegas, NV, 89154.

MCDOUGALL, WARREN
DISCIPLINE ENGLISH **EDUCATION** Western Ontario, BA; Edinburgh, PhD. **CAREER** HON FELL, ENG LIT, EDINBURGH **MEMBERSHIPS** Am Antiquarian Soc **CONTACT ADDRESS** 53 Ladysmith Rd, Edinburgh, EH9 3EY.

MCDOWELL, EARL E.
DISCIPLINE RHETORIC STUDIES **EDUCATION** W Va Univ, MA; Univ Nebr, PhD. **CAREER** Prof **RESEARCH** Technical communication apprehension; technical communication programs; employment cycle interviewing; conflict; gender and psychological sex. **SELECTED PUBLICATIONS** Auth, Interviewing Practices for Technical Writers, Baywood, 91; Research in Scientific and Technical Communication, Burgess Int, 93; Scientific and Technical Communicators' Perceptions of the Performance Appraisal Interview, J Tech Writing Commun, 95; co-auth, An Exploratory Study of the Communication Behaviors of Japanese and US College Students, 97. **CONTACT ADDRESS** Rhetoric Dept, Univ of Minnesota, Twin Cities, 64 Classroom Office Bldg, 1994 Buford Ave, St. Paul, MN, 55108. **EMAIL** mcdow001@maroon.tc.umn.edu

MCDOWELL, FREDERICK PETER WOLL
PERSONAL Born 05/29/1915, Philadelphia, PA, m, 1953, 5 children **DISCIPLINE** ENGLISH **EDUCATION** Univ Pa, BS, 37, MA, 38; Harvard Univ, PhD(English), 49. **CAREER** Instr English, Washington & Jefferson Col, 38-39 & Univ Del, 39-41; from instr to assoc prof, 49-63, PROF ENGLISH, UNIV IOWA, 63-, Nat Endowment for Humanities sr fel, 73-74; exchange prof, Universite Paul Valery, Montpellier, France, 80-81. **MEMBERSHIPS** MLA; Ellen Glasgow Soc (pres, 77); Virginia Woolf Soc; Joseph Conrad Soc; Am Shaw Soc. **RESEARCH** British and American literature since 1850; George Bernard Shaw; Bloomsbury group. **SELECTED PUBLICATIONS** Auth, Heartbreak House--Preludes and Apocalypse, Engl Lit in Transition 1880-1920, vol 0038, 95; 'Pygmalion'--Shaw Spin on Myth ond Cinderella, Engl Lit in Transition 1880-1920, vol 0039, 96. **CONTACT ADDRESS** Dept of English, Univ of Iowa, Iowa City, IA, 52242.

MCELRATH, JOSEPH R.
PERSONAL Born 06/10/1945, Jesup, GA, m, 1966, 2 children **DISCIPLINE** ENGLISH **EDUCATION** LeMoyne Col, BA, 67; Duquesne Univ, MA, 69; Univ of South Carolina, PhD, 73. **CAREER** Asst Prof, 73-74, SUNY; Asst Prof, 74-77, Assoc Prof, 77-81, Prof, 81-, Florida St Univ. **HONORS AND AWARDS** John Frederick Lewis Awd of the Amer Philos Soc, 96. **MEMBERSHIPS** Stephen Crane Soc; Frank Norris Soc; Assoc for Documentary Editing; Soc for Textual Scholarship; Charles Waddel Chesnutt Assoc **RESEARCH** Amer lit 1870-1910. **SELECTED PUBLICATIONS** Auth, Frank Norris Revisited, Twayne, 92; auth, Frank Norris A Descriptive Bibliography, Univ of Pit Press, 92; auth, John Steinbeck The Contemporary Reviews, Cambridge Univ Press, 96; auth, The Apprenticieship Writings of Frank Norris, Amer Philosophical Soc, 96; auth, To Be An Author: Letters of Charles W Chesnutt, Princeton Univ Press, 97. **CONTACT ADDRESS** Florida State Univ, Dept of English, Tallahassee, FL, 32306-1580. **EMAIL** jmcelrath@english.fsu.edu

MCELREATH, MARK
DISCIPLINE COMMUNICATION, PUBLIC RELATIONS **EDUCATION** Univ WI, Madison, PhD, 75. **CAREER** Instr, fac adv, PR Gp, Towson Univ; ed bd, J of PR Res. **MEMBERSHIPS** Hd, Ethics Comt, Int Asn of Bus Communicators. **SELECTED PUBLICATIONS** Auth, The Management of Systematic Ethical Public Relations Campaigns. **CONTACT ADDRESS** Towson Univ, Towson, MD, 21252-0001. **EMAIL** mmcelreath@towson.edus

MCELROY, COLLEEN J.
PERSONAL Born 10/30/1935, St Louis, Missouri, d **DISCIPLINE** ENGLISH **EDUCATION** Kansas State Univ, Manhattan KS, BS, 1958, MS, 1963; Univ of Washington, Seattle WA, PhD, 1973. **CAREER** Rehabilitation Inst, Kansas City MO, chief, Speech & Hearing Serv, 1963-66; Western Washington Univ, Bellingham WA, asst prof, Speech, 1966-74; Univ of Washington, Seattle WA, supvr, EOP Composition, 1972-83, dir, Creative Writing, 1984-87, prof of English, 1983-. **HONORS AND AWARDS** NEA Creative Writing Fellowship for Poetry, 1978; Fiction 1st place, Callalvo Magazine, 1981; Poetry 1st place, Cincinnati Poetry R, 1983; Creative Writing Residency, MacDowell Colony, New Hampshire, 1984, 1986; Before Columbus Amer Book Award, 1985; Women of Achievement, Theta Sigma Phi, 1985; Creative Writing Residency Yugoslavia, Fulbright Fellowship, 1988; Washington State Governor's Award for Fiction and Poetry, 1988; NEA Creative Writing Fellowship for Fiction, 1991; Rockefeller Fellowship to Bellagio Institute, Lake Como, Italy, 1991; DuPont Distinguished Scholar in Residence, Hollins College, Virginia, 1992; Fulbright Research Fellowship, Madagascar, 1993; Arts America, Jordan & Morocco, 1996. **MEMBERSHIPS** Mem, Writers Guild of Amer East, 1978-, Dramatists Guild, 1986-, PEN Writers, 1989-; member, Author's Guild, 1989-; member, Writer's Union, 1989-. **SELECTED PUBLICATIONS** The Wild Gardens of the Loup Garou, 1983; Queen of the Ebony Isles, 1984; Jesus and Fat Tuesday, 1987; Follow the Drinking Gourd, 1987; Driving Under the Cardboard Pines, 1990; What Madness Brought Me Here, 1990; A Long Way from St Louie, 1996. **CONTACT ADDRESS** Professor of English, Univ of Washington, Seattle, WA, 98109.

MCELROY, JOHN HARMON
PERSONAL Born 03/28/1934, Parker's Landing, PA, m, 1957, 4 children **DISCIPLINE** AMERICAN LITERATURE **EDUCATION** Princeton Univ, AB, 56; Duke Univ, MA, 62, PhD(Am lit), 66. **CAREER** Instr English, Punahou Sch, 58-60; asst prof Am lit, Univ Wis-Madison, 66-70; from asst prof to assoc prof, 70-76, PROF AM LIT, UNIV ARIZ, 76-, Fulbright lectr Am lit, Univ Salamanca, 68-69. **MEMBERSHIPS** MLA; Melville Soc; Poe Soc. **RESEARCH** Textual criticism; literary criticism; American literature, 1760-1860. **SELECTED PUBLICATIONS** Auth, Sea Changes, British Emigration and American Literature, 19th Century Prose, vol 0022, 95. **CONTACT ADDRESS** Dept of English, Univ of Ariz, 1 University of Az, Tucson, AZ, 85721-0001.

MCFAGUE, SALLIE
PERSONAL Born 05/25/1933, Quincy, MA **DISCIPLINE** THEOLOGY, RELIGION AND LITERATURE **EDUCATION** Smith Col, BA, 55; Yale Divinity Sch, BD, 59; Yale Grad Sch, PhD(theol), 64. **CAREER** Asst prof, 72-75, dean, 75-79, assoc prof, 75-79, PROF THEOL, VANDERBILT DIVINITY SCH, 80-. Ed, Soundings, 67-75; Nat Endowment for

Humanities fel, Oxford, 80-81. **MEMBERSHIPS** Am Acad Relig; Soc Values Higher Educ; Soc Arts, Relig & Contemp Cult; Am Theol Soc. **RESEARCH** Religious language; contemporary theology, religion and literature. **SELECTED PUBLICATIONS** Auth, Barbour, Ian--Theologians Friend, Scientists Interpreter, Zygon, vol 0031, 96; The Loving Eye Versus the Arrogant Eye--Christian Critique of the Western Gaze on Nature and the Third World, Ecumenical Rev, vol 0049, 97. **CONTACT ADDRESS** Vanderbilt Univ, 221 Kirkland Hall, Nashville, TN, 37232.

MCFARLAND, RONALD E.
DISCIPLINE ENGLISH LITERATURE **EDUCATION** Fla State Univ, BA, 63; MA, 65; PhD, 70. **CAREER** Prof, Harford Univ. **SELECTED PUBLICATIONS** Auth, Certain Women, Confluence, 77; Composting At Forty, Confluence, 84; The Haunting Familiarity of Things, Singular Speech, 93; ed, Eight Idaho Poets, Univ Idaho, 79; co-ed, Idaho's Poetry: A Centennial Anthology, Univ Idaho, 88; Deep Down Things: Poems of the Inland Pacific Northwest, Wash State Univ, 90. **CONTACT ADDRESS** English Dept, Univ Idaho, 415 W 6th St, Moscow, ID, 83844. **EMAIL** ronmcf@uidaho.edu

MCGEE, CHRISTOPHER EDWARD
DISCIPLINE ENGLISH LITERATURE **EDUCATION** Univ Toronto, BA; MA; PhD. **CAREER** Assoc prof **SELECTED PUBLICATIONS** Auth, Strangest consequence from remotest cause: The Second Performance of The Triumph of Peace; The Visit of the Nine Goddesses: A masque at Sir John Crofts' House; A Canadian Reports on the Stratford Festival (rev); A Matter of Time (rev); ABCs of ABCs: Two Canadian Exemplars; Against the Stream (rev); An Entertainment for Elizabeth I at Greenwich. **CONTACT ADDRESS** Dept of English, St. Jerome's Univ, Waterloo, ON, N2L 3G3. **EMAIL** cemcgee@watarts.uwaterloo.ca

MCGINTY, CAROLYN
PERSONAL Born 01/07/1921, Chicago, IL **DISCIPLINE** LITERARY CRITICISM, AMERICAN LITERATURE **EDUCATION** Loyola Univ Chicago, PhB, 43, MA, 49; Cath Univ Am, PhD(English), 63. **CAREER** From instr to assist prof, 63-75, assoc prof English & chemn dept, Rosary Col, 76-; res dir semester in London, 73, 73-75; consult, Scholastic Testing Serv, Bensenville, IL, 67-. **MEMBERSHIPS** Aaup; Col English Asn; MLA; NCTE. **RESEARCH** Linguistics and stylistics; Henry James' prose style. **CONTACT ADDRESS** Dept of English, Rosary Col, River Forest, IL, 60305.

MCGJEE, JAMES
DISCIPLINE LITERATURE **EDUCATION** Montclair State Col, AB; Bowling Green State Univ, PhD. **CAREER** Prof; dir, theater. **SELECTED PUBLICATIONS** Area: critical study of Sam Shepard. **CONTACT ADDRESS** York Col, Pennsylvania, 441 Country Club Road, York, PA, 17403.

MCGLONE, EDWARD L.
DISCIPLINE COMMUNICATION STUDIES **EDUCATION** Univ Ohio, BA, PhD. **CAREER** Prof, 87-. **HONORS AND AWARDS** Outstanding Young Tchr Awd; Paideia Awd; **MEMBERSHIPS** Central States Commun Asn; Speech Commun Asn. **SELECTED PUBLICATIONS** Auth, pubs on communication theory and interpersonal communication. **CONTACT ADDRESS** Div of Communcation and Theatre Arts, Emporia State Univ, 1200 Commercial St, Emporia, KS, 66801-5087. **EMAIL** mcglonee@esumail.emporia.edu

MCGLYNN, PAUL DUMON
PERSONAL Born 07/11/1937, Detroit, MI, m, 1963, 2 children **DISCIPLINE** ENGLISH **EDUCATION** Univ Detroit, PhB, 59, MA, 61; Rice Univ, PhD, 67. **CAREER** Instr Eng, Univ Detroit, 61-62; from instr to assoc prof, 64-77, Prof Eng, Eastern MI Univ, 77. **MEMBERSHIPS** MLA; Midwestern Mod Lang Asn. **RESEARCH** Eighteenth century Brit lit; the novel; cinema; Irish lit. **SELECTED PUBLICATIONS** Auth, Orthodoxy versus anarchy in Sterne's Sentimental Journey, Papers on Lang & Lit, summer 71; Point of view and the craft of cinema: Notes on some devices, J Aesthet & Art Criticism, winter 73; Rhetoric as metaphor in The Vanity of Huamn Wishes, Studies English Lit, summer 75; since 1987, a published poet. Over 200 poems in over 92 journals in the U.S., Canada, and Great Britain, including Chiron Rev, Bouillabaisse, Windsor Rev, Sepia, Poetry Motel, and Santa Barbara Rev. **CONTACT ADDRESS** Dept of Eng, Eastern Michigan Univ, 612 Pray Harrold, Ypsilanti, MI, 48197-2201. **EMAIL** eng_mcglynn@online.emich.edu

MCGOWAN, JOHN
PERSONAL Born 07/12/1953, New York, NY, m, 1983, 2 children **DISCIPLINE** ENGLISH **EDUCATION** Georgetown Univ, BA, Eng, 74; SUNY at Buffalo, PhD, Eng, 78. **CAREER** Asst prof, Humanities Dept, Univ Mich, Ann Arbor, 79-83; assoc prof Eng, Eastman Sch of Music, Univ Rochester, 84-92; prof Eng and Comparative Lit, Univ NC, Chapel Hill, 92-. **HONORS AND AWARDS** Sr fel, NEH, 88-89; dir, NEH Summer Sem, 97. **MEMBERSHIPS** MLA; SAMLA; Intl Asn for Philos and Lit. **RESEARCH** Literary theory; political philosophy; American pragmatism; Victorian literature. **SELECTED PUBLICATIONS** Auth, Hannah Arendt: An Introduction, 98; Co-ed, Hannah Arendt and the Meaning of Politics, 97; auth, Post modernism and its Critics, 91; Representation and Revelation: Victorian Realism from Carlyle to Yeats, 86. **CONTACT ADDRESS** Univ of North Carolina, CB #3520, Chapel Hill, NC, 27599-3520. **EMAIL** JPM@email.unc.edu

MCGOWAN, JOSEPH P.
DISCIPLINE ENGLISH **EDUCATION** Villanova Univ, BA, 88; Univ PA, PhD, 91. **CAREER** Asst prof, Univ San Diego, 93-; instr, Villanova Univ, 92-93; tchg fel, Univ Pa, 89-92; tchg apprentice, Univ PA, 88-89. **SELECTED PUBLICATIONS** Auth, Anglo-Saxon Manuscripts in Microfiche Facsimile: Legal and Grammatical Manuscripts at London & Oxford, Binghamton, NY:SUNY/Medieval & Renaissance Texts & Stud, 98; More Glosses from Early Medieval English Manuscripts, Notes & Queries, 98; Anglo-Saxon Manuscripts in Microfiche Facsimile, vol 8: Manuscripts in Switzerland, Binghamton, SUNY/ Medieval & Renaissance Texts & Stud, 98; Augustine of Ancona, Sermones dominicales, Sermones de sanctis adclerum, Collationes pro defunctis 2 vols, Rome/Villanova:Augustinian Press, 98 & Readings from the Beowulf Manuscript, fols. 94r-98r, the St Christopher folios, Manuscripta, 97; coauth, Four Unedited Prayers from British Library,MS Cotton Tiberius A. iii, Mediaeval Stud 56, 94; rev, Apollonius of Tyre: Medieval and Renaissance Themes and Variations, in J of Medieval Latin 7, 97. **CONTACT ADDRESS** Dept of Eng, Univ of San Diego, 5998 Alcal Park, San Diego, CA, 92110-2492. **EMAIL** mcgowan@teetot.acusd.edu

MCGRAIN, JOHN W.
PERSONAL Born 07/25/1931, Baltimore, MD, s **DISCIPLINE** ENGLISH **EDUCATION** Loyola Col, 49. **CAREER** Technical Publ, Bendix Corp, Technical Service Corp DMS-Int, 55-70; County Historian & Hist Preservation Planner, Office of Planning, Baltimore County, Md, 76-98. **MEMBERSHIPS** Soc Archit Hist; Soc Industrial Archeol; Md Hist Soc. **RESEARCH** State and local history; gristmills; industries; agriculture; architecture. **SELECTED PUBLICATIONS** Auth, Lewis Mill Goes to Pottery, Old Mill News, 4/84; Pig Iron/ Cotton Duck: The Company Towns of Baltimore County, Baltimore County Public Libr, 85; The Man Who "Invented" Automation, Evening Sun, 5/23/87; The English Consul Mansion and Its Owners, Md Hist Mag, Spring 89; History of Agriculture in Baltimore County, limited edition, Towson Libr & Md Hist Soc, 90; Pig Iron/Cotton Duck, vol 2 (in prep); author of numerous other articles and publications. **CONTACT ADDRESS** 34 Willow Ave., Towson, MD, 21286-5226.

MCGUIRE, PETER
DISCIPLINE AUDIENCE ANALYSIS, DOCUMENTATION DESIGN, AND MULTIMEDIA DESIGN **EDUCATION** Brown Univ, PhD, 75. **CAREER** Prof, Ga Inst of Technol; consult, Europ-Asian Multimedia Commun of Interest. **RESEARCH** The impact of design theory on multimedia. **SELECTED PUBLICATIONS** Coauth, Functional Writing, Readings in Technical Writing; A Guide to Technical Writing. **CONTACT ADDRESS** Sch of Lit, Commun & Cult, Georgia Inst of Tech, Skiles Cla, Atlanta, GA, 30332. **EMAIL** peter.mcguire@lcc.gatech.edu

MCGUIRE, PHILIP CARROLL
PERSONAL Born 08/23/1940, Pittsburgh, PA, m, 1971, 1 child **DISCIPLINE** ENGLISH **EDUCATION** LaSalle Col, BA, 62; Stanford Univ, MA, 65, PhD(English), 68. **CAREER** Asst prof, 66-71, ASSOC PROF ENGLISH, MICH STATE UNIV, 71-. **MEMBERSHIPS** MLA; Aaup; Renaissance Soc Am; Shakespeare Asn Am. **RESEARCH** English poetry of the Renaissance; Shakespeare. **SELECTED PUBLICATIONS** Auth, Recent Studies in Tudor and Stuart Drama, Studies in Engl Lit 1500-1900, vol 0034, 94. **CONTACT ADDRESS** Dept of Englishe, Michigan State Univ, East Lansing, MI, 48824.

MCHANEY, THOMAS LAFAYETTE
PERSONAL Born 10/17/1936, Paragould, AR, m, 1962, 3 children **DISCIPLINE** AMERICAN LITERATURE **EDUCATION** Miss State Univ, BA, 59; Univ NC, Chapel Hill, MA, 62; Univ SC, PhD(English), 68. **CAREER** Instr English, Univ Miss, 63-65; asst prof, 68-73, assoc prof, 73-78, PROF ENGLISH, GA STATE UNIV, 78-. **HONORS AND AWARDS** Spec Award for Fiction, Henry Bellaman Found, 70. **MEMBERSHIPS** MLA; S Atlantic Mod Lang Asn. **RESEARCH** William Faulkner; economics of authorship. **SELECTED PUBLICATIONS** Auth, 'Yoknapatawpha'--The Function of Geographical and Historical Facts in Faulkner, William Fictional Picture of the Deep South, Miss Quart, vol 0046, 93; Selected Poems of Simms, William, Gilmore, Resources for Amer Lit Study, vol 0020, 94. **CONTACT ADDRESS** Dept of English, Georgia State Univ, 33 Gilmer St SE, Atlanta, GA, 30303.

MCILVAINE, ROBERT MORTON
PERSONAL Born 12/28/1943, Vernon, TX, m, 1966, 2 children **DISCIPLINE** ENGLISH & AMERICAN LITERATURE **EDUCATION** Davis & Elkins Col, BA, 66; Univ Pa, MA, 67; Temple Univ, PhD, 72. **CAREER** Tchg asst Eng, Temple Univ, 68-72; from Asst Prof to Prof Eng, Slippery Rock Univ, 72-, Chmn Dept, 77-79. **RESEARCH** Am realism and naturalism; Am novel; Victorian lit. **SELECTED PUBLICATIONS** Auth, Robert Herrick and Thorstein Veblen, WA State Univ Res Studies, 6/72; Dos Passo's reading of Thorstein Veblen, Am Lit, 11/72; Edith Wharton's American beauty rose, J Am Studies, 12/73. **CONTACT ADDRESS** Dept of Eng, Slippery Rock Univ, SWC Bldg, Slippery Rock, PA, 16057-1326. **EMAIL** robert.mcilvaine@sru.edu

MCINTOSH, ANNE
DISCIPLINE SPEECH COMMUNICATION **EDUCATION** UNC Chapel Hill, BA, 88; Univ of Mont Missoula, MA, 91; Univ of Tex Austin, PhD, 95. **CAREER** Res consult; instr. **HONORS AND AWARDS** Lucia Morgan Scholar, 88. **MEMBERSHIPS** Nat Commun Asn; Western States Commun Asn. **RESEARCH** Male-female communication; interpersonal communication; deafness; health communication. **SELECTED PUBLICATIONS** Auth, Getting Back into a Career Again, Hearing Health, 97; Putting ALDs on the Menu, Hearing Health, 97; And Now a Word on Auto Safety..., Hearing Health, 96; Semantic Mapping Across the Curriculum: Helping Students Discover Connections, Perspectives in Ed and Deafness, 95; In Memory of Steve Hodges: An Interview, Hearing Health, 95; Making Science Accessible to Deaf Students, Am Annals of the Deaf, 95. **CONTACT ADDRESS** PO Box 1961, Davidson, NC, 28036. **EMAIL** mcintosh@vnet.net

MCINTOSH, JAMES HENRY
PERSONAL Born 02/04/1934, New York, NY, 1 child **DISCIPLINE** ENGLISH **EDUCATION** Harvard Univ, AB, 55; Yale Univ, PhD, 66. **CAREER** Instr Eng & Ger, 60-61, Scattergood Sch; from instr to asst prof Eng, 62-67, Tufts Univ; from asst prof to assoc prof, 67-75, Yale Univ; dir undergrad stud Am stud, 72-75, assoc prof Eng, 75-, Univ Mich; prof, 88-, actg dir Am stud, 82-, dir, 84-92, Morse Human fel, 71-72, Yale Univ; mem fac, Bread Loaf Sch, 73, 74 & 78; NEH sr fel, 76. **MEMBERSHIPS** Soc Values Higher Educ. **RESEARCH** 19th century American literature; international Romanticism; North & South American literary relations. **SELECTED PUBLICATIONS** Auth, Thoreau as Romantic Naturalist, Cornell Univ, 74; auth, Emerson's Unmoored Self, Yale Rev, 76; auth, Hawthorne's Search for a Wider Public and a Select Society, Forum, Houston, 76; auth, Melville's Use and Abuse of Goethe: The Weaver-Gods in Faust and Moby-Dick, Amerikastudien/ American Studies, 80; ed, Nathaniel Hawthorne's Tales, 87; auth, The Mariner's Multiple Guest, New Essays on Moby Dick, 86; auth, Billy Budd, Sailor, Melville's Last Romance, Critical Essays on Billy Budd, Sailor, 89. **CONTACT ADDRESS** Univ of Michigan, Ann Arbor, 505 S State St, Ann Arbor, MI, 48109-1003. **EMAIL** jhmci@umich.edu

MCINTOSH, MARJORIE KENISTON
PERSONAL Born 11/15/1940, Ann Arbor, MI, m, 1961, 3 children **DISCIPLINE** ENGLISH HISTORY **EDUCATION** Radcliffe Col, AB, 62; Harvard Univ, MA, 63, PhD, 67. **CAREER** Res assoc, Radcliffe Inst, 67-68; lectr Europ hist, Simmons Col, 68-70; lectr, Univ Colo, Denver, 71-72; vis lectr English hist, 77-79; asst to assoc prof, English hist, 79-92, prof, 92-, exec dir, Ctr for British Stud, 88-90, Univ Colorado, Boulder. **HONORS AND AWARDS** Magna cum laude, 62; Phi Beta Kappa; President's Award for Outstanding Service, 90; Essex Book Award, 91; Excellence in Tchg Award, 95; elected fel, British Royal Hist Soc, 96. **MEMBERSHIPS** AHA; Conf Brit Studies; Medieval Acad Am; Soc Sci Hist Asn; Am Soc Legal Hist. **RESEARCH** Local and social history of late medieval and early modern England; poverty in England, 1480-1660. **SELECTED PUBLICATIONS** Auth, Autonomy and Community: The Royal Manor of Havering, 1200-1500, Cambridge, 86; auth, A Community Transformed: The Manor and Liberty of Havering, 1500-1620, Cambridge, 91; auth, Controlling Misbehavior in England, 1370-1600, Cambridge, 98. **CONTACT ADDRESS** Dept of History, Univ of Colo, Box 234, Boulder, CO, 80309-0234.

MCJANNET, LINDA
PERSONAL Born 02/16/1943, Washington, DC, d, 2 children **DISCIPLINE** ENGLISH LITERATURE **EDUCATION** Wellesley Col, BA, 64; Harvard Univ, MA, 66; Harvard Univ, PhD, 71 **CAREER** Asst prof, Cath Univ Amer, 72-75; Expository Writing Prog, Harvard Col, 75-78; assoc Communication, Harvard Grad Sch Bus Admin, 85-91; asst prof, Bentley Col, 81-88; assoc prof, Bentley Col, 88-96; prof English, Bentley Col, 96- **HONORS AND AWARDS** Woodrow Wilson Fel, 64-65; Bentley Col Inst Fel, 90-91; Bentley Col Scholar of Year, 88; Phi Beta Kappa, 63 **MEMBERSHIPS** Mod Lang Assoc; Shakespeare Assoc Amer; **RESEARCH** English Renaissance; Early Modern Drama **SELECTED PUBLICATIONS** Auth, "Genre and Geography: The Eastern Mediterranean in Pericles and The Comedy of Errors." Playing Across the Globe: Genre and Geography in English Renaissance Drama, Fairleigh Dickinson, 98; auth, The Voice of Elizabethan Stage Directions: The Evolution of a Theatrical Code, Univ Delaware, 98; auth, Management Communication, McGraw-Hill, 96 **CONTACT ADDRESS** 338 Walden St., Cambridge, MA, 02138. **EMAIL** lmcjannet@bentley.edu

MCKEE, PATRICIA
DISCIPLINE ENGLISH LITERATURE **EDUCATION** Brandeis Univ, PhD, 78. **CAREER** Prof, Dartmouth Col. **RESEARCH** Am and Brit lit; the novel; Toni Morrison. **SELECTED PUBLICATIONS** Auth, Public and Private: Gender, Class, and the British Novel (1764-1878), Univ Minn P, 97; Spacing and Placing Experience in Toni Morrison's Sula, Mod Fic Studies, 96; William Faulkner's As I Lay Dying: Experience in Passing, S Atlantic Quart, 91; Heroic Commitment in Richardson, Eliot, and James, Princeton UP, 86. **CONTACT ADDRESS** Dartmouth Col, 3529 N Main St, #207, Hanover, NH, 03755.

MCKENDRICK, NORMAN G.
DISCIPLINE ENGLISH COMPOSITION AND LITERATURE **EDUCATION** Loyola Univ, BA, MA; Fordham Univ, PhD; W Baden Pontifical Univ, licentiates. **CAREER** Assoc prof, 62-. **SELECTED PUBLICATIONS** Pub(s), modern poetry, folk singers, and the texts of Greek Fathers. **CONTACT ADDRESS** Dept of Eng, Univ Detroit Mercy, 4001 W McNichols Rd, PO BOX 19900, Detroit, MI, 48219-0900.

MCKENZIE, ALAN TABER
PERSONAL Born 07/07/1940, Arlington, MA, m, 1962, 2 children **DISCIPLINE** ENGLISH LITERATURE **EDUCATION** Harvard Univ, BA, 62; Univ Pa, MA, 66, PhD(English), 68. **CAREER** Asst prof, 68-73, actg asst head dept, 73-74, asst head dept, 76-79, ASSOC PROF ENGLISH, PURDUE UNIV, WEST LAFAYETTE, 73-, Leverhulme fel, Univ Dundee, 81-82. **MEMBERSHIPS** Am Soc 18th Century Studies; MLA; Johnson Soc; Mid-West Am Soc 18th Century Studies. **RESEARCH** Eighteenth century English literature; Samuel Johnson; word processing. **SELECTED PUBLICATIONS** Auth, The English Poetic Epitaph--Commemoration and Conflict from Jonson to Wordsworth, Scriblerian and the Kit-Cats, vol 0025, 92; The Embodiment of Characters--The Representation of Physical Experience on Stage and in Print, 1728-1749, Scriblerian and the Kit-Cats, vol 0028, 95; The Crisis of Courtesy--Studies in the Conduct-Book in Britain, 1600-1900, Scriblerian and the Kit-Cats, vol 0028, 95. **CONTACT ADDRESS** Dept of English, Purdue Univ, West Lafayette, IN, 47907.

MCKEON, MICHAEL
DISCIPLINE ENLIGHTENMENT, EARLY NOVEL, THEORY OF THE NOVEL, PASTORAL POETRY, POLITICAL **EDUCATION** Univ Chicago, BA; Columbia Univ, MA; PhD. **CAREER** Prof Eng, Rutgers, The State Univ NJ, Univ Col-Camden. **RESEARCH** Marvell, Defoe, Swift, pre-history of domestic fiction, and early modern "division of knowledge." **SELECTED PUBLICATIONS** Auth, The Origins of the English Novel. **CONTACT ADDRESS** Dept of English, Rutgers, The State Univ New Jersey, Univ Col-Camde, Murray Hall 202, New Brunswick, NJ, 08903. **EMAIL** complit@rci.rutgers.edu

MCKERNAN, JOHN JOSEPH
PERSONAL Born 05/11/1942, Omaha, NE, m, 1967, 1 child **DISCIPLINE** POETRY **EDUCATION** Univ Omaha, BA, 65; Univ Ark, MA, 67; Columbia Univ, MFA, 71; Boston Univ, PhD, 80. **CAREER** Prof Eng, 67-, Marshall Univ; NEH fel, 80; Yale Univ sum res sem, 82. **MEMBERSHIPS** MLA; Southern Mod Lang Assn. **RESEARCH** Epistolary verse in the English renaissance; the poetry of Weldon Kees; contemporary American poetry. **SELECTED PUBLICATIONS** Auth, Walking Along the Missouri, Lost Roads Press, 77; auth, Erasing the Blackboard: Annex 21, Univ Nebr, Omaha, 78; auth, Postcard from Dublin, Dead Metaphor Press, 98; ed, Essays on R S Thomas, Little Rev Press, 79; auth, Notes on George Turberville as a Translator of Ovid, Shakespeare and Renaissance Assn WVa, 82. **CONTACT ADDRESS** Dept of English, Marshall Univ, Huntington, WV, 25701. **EMAIL** mckernan@marshall.edu

MCKINLEY, JAMES COURTRIGHT
PERSONAL Born 12/08/1935, Omaha, NE, m, 1959, 4 children **DISCIPLINE** BRITISH & AMERICAN LITERATURE **EDUCATION** Univ Mo-Columbia, BA & BJ, 59, MA, 68, PhD(English), 70. **CAREER** Copy supvr, Procter & Gamble, Inc, 60-64; acct exec, Young & Rubicam Advert, Inc, 64-66; asst prof, 70-77, assoc prof, 77-83, prof and dir, prof writing prog, 89- English, Univ Mo-Kansas City. **HONORS AND AWARDS** Nat Endowment for Humanities fel, 72-73; Fulbright fel, 83, 89, 92; McDowell Colony fel, 84, 89. **MEMBERSHIPS** MLA; PEN; Nat Book Critics Circle; Assoc Writing Progs. **RESEARCH** Twentieth century British poetry. **SELECTED PUBLICATIONS** Auth, Interview with Robert Graves, Playboy, 70; Each New Springtime, Each New Summer, New Lett, 75; Playboy's History of Assassination, Playboy, 76; Child's Play, Choteau Rev, 76; Assassination in America, Harper, 77; Inside Sirhan, Playboy, 78; Foreign Farming, Atlantic Monthly, 78; auth, Act of Love, Baertenbush, 89; auth, The Ficklean Suite and Other Stories, Arkansas, 93. **CONTACT ADDRESS** Univ Mo, Kansas City, 510 Rockhill Rd, Kansas City, MO, 64110-2499.

MCLEAN, ANDREW MILLER
PERSONAL Born 05/25/1941, Brooklyn, NY, 1 child **DISCIPLINE** ENGLISH RENAISSANCE LITERATURE & HISTORY **EDUCATION** St Olaf Col, BA, 63; Brooklyn Col, MA, 67; Univ NC, Chapel Hill, PhD(English), 71. **CAREER** Asst prof, 71-76, Assoc Prof English, 77-82, prof, 82- ,Univ Wis-Parkside; Rev ed, Clio: An Interdisciplinary Jour of Lit, Hist, and Philos of Hist, 71-93; res prof, Catholic Univ Louvain, 75-76. **MEMBERSHIPS** MLA; Soc Studies Midwestern Lit; Renaissance Soc Am; Shakespeare Asn Am. **RESEARCH** Sixteenth century English literature; interdisciplinary studies, film-Shakespeare. **SELECTED PUBLICATIONS** Auth, Emerson's Brahma, New England Quart, 3/69; James Joyce & A Doblin, Comp Lit, spring 73; English translation of Erasmus, Moreana, 11/74; Castiglione, Cicero & English dialogues, Romance Notes, 75; Barlow, More & the Anglican episcopacy, Moreana, 2/76; contribr, Bibliography on teaching Shakespeare, In: Teaching Shakespeare, Princeton Univ, 77; Barlow & the Lutheran Factions, Renaissance Quart, summer 78; auth, Shakespeare: Annotated Bibliographies and Media Guide for Teachers, MCTE, 80; ed, Work of William Barlowe, Sutton Courtenay press, 81; co-ed, Redefining Shakespeare: Literary Theory and Theater Practice in the German Democratic Republic. Univ Delaware, 98. **CONTACT ADDRESS** Dept of English, Univ of Wiscosin, Parkside, Box 2000, Kenosha, WI, 53141-2000. **EMAIL** andrew.mclean@uwp.edu

MCLEAN, KEN
DISCIPLINE ENGLISH LITERATURE **EDUCATION** Waterloo Lutheran Univ, BA; McMaster Univ, MA; York Univ, PhD. **CAREER** Engl, Bishop's Univ. **SELECTED PUBLICATIONS** Auth, pubs on John Richardson, William Kirby, Joyce Marshall, Patrick Lane and Margaret Laurence. **CONTACT ADDRESS** English Dept, Bishop's Univ, Lennoxville, PQ, JIMIZ 7. **EMAIL** kmclean@ubishops.ca

MCLEOD, ALAN L.
PERSONAL Born 03/13/1928, Sydney, Australia, m, 1954, 2 children **DISCIPLINE** ENGLISH, SPEECH **EDUCATION** Univ Sydney, Australia, BA, 50, MA, 52, Dipl Ed, 51; Univ Melbourne, Australia, BEd, 56; Pa State Univ, PhD, 57. **CAREER** Lectr English & speech, Wagga State Teachers Col, Australia, 52; asst speech, Pa State Univ, 52-53 & 54-56; lectr English & speech, Balmain State Teachers Col, 56-57; from asst prof to assoc prof, State Univ Col Fredonia, 57-62; prof, Lock Haven State Col, 62-66; PROF ENGLISH & SPEECH, RIDER COL, 66-, State Univ NY res fel, 62. **MEMBERSHIPS** Speech Commun Asn; MLA; Book Collectors Soc, Australia. **RESEARCH** Seventeenth and eighteenth century poetry and drama; commonwealth literature; rhetorical criticism. **SELECTED PUBLICATIONS** Auth, It So Happen, World Lit Today, vol 0066, 92; South of the West--Postcolonialism and the Narrative Construction of Australia, World Lit Today, vol 0067, 93; One of Bens, a Tribe Transported, World Lit Today, vol 0068, 94; Divina Trace, World Lit Today, vol 0068, 94; Spirits in the Dark, World Lit Today, vol 0069, 95; The 'Longest Memory', World Lit Today, vol 0069, 95; The 'Assistant Professor', World Lit Today, vol 0071, 97; 'How Loud Can the Village Cock Crow' and Other Stories, World Lit Today, vol 0071, 97. **CONTACT ADDRESS** Dept of English, Rider Coll, Lawrenceville, NJ, 08648.

MCLEOD, ARCHIBALD
PERSONAL Born 11/05/1906, Edinburg, Scotland, m, 1943, 1 child **DISCIPLINE** DRAMA **EDUCATION** Oberlin Col BA, 33; State Univ Iowa, MA, 34; Cornell Univ, PhD(speech & drama), 42. **CAREER** Instr speech & drama, Kans State Teachers Col, 34-35; assoc prof, Tex State Col Women, 35-39 & 41-43; asst prof, La State Univ, 43-47; chmn dept theatre, 59-75, PROF SPEECH & DRAMA, SOUTHERN ILL UNIV, CARBONDALE, 47-; Exec Secy, Ill State Theatre CO, 75-, Fulbright lectr dramatic art, Natya Sangh, Madras, India, 62-63. **MEMBERSHIPS** Am Theatre Asn. **RESEARCH** Dramatic literature; theatre audience; aesthetics of the theatre. **SELECTED PUBLICATIONS** Auth, The New Zealand Novels of Langley, Eve, Southerly, vol 0055, 95. **CONTACT ADDRESS** Southern Ill Univ, 907 W Schwartz St, Carbondale, IL, 62901.

MCLEOD, DOUGLAS M.
DISCIPLINE COMMUNICATIONS **EDUCATION** Univ Wis, BA, 83; Univ Minn, MA, 86; PhD, 89. **CAREER** Res supervr, Univ Minn, 86-89; secy, Intl Commun Assn, 94-96; div hd, Assn Edu in Jour and Mass Commun, 95-96; chair, Assn Edu in Jour and Mass Commun, 95; assoc prof, 89-. **HONORS AND AWARDS** Elliston scholar, Univ Minn, 84-85; Bell and Howell sudent res award, Spec Lib(s) Assn, 87; Casey dissertation award, Univ minn, 88-89; arts and sciences dean's grant, 91, 92., Res consult, St Paul Cable Access, 89; co-ed, Minn Jour, 84. **RESEARCH** Journalism and mass communication. **SELECTED PUBLICATIONS** Co-auth, The Expanding Boundaries of Political Communication Effects, Media Effects: Advances in Theory and Research, Lawrence Erlbaum Assoc(s), 94; Reporters vs Undecided Voters: An Analysis of the Questions Asked During the 92 Presidential Debates, Commun Quart, 94; Direct and Indirect Effects of Socioeconomic Status on Public Affairs Knowledge, Jour Quart, 94; Cultivation in the Newer Media Environment, Commun Res, 94; Gender Stereotypes in MTV Commercials: The Beat Goes On, Jour Broadcasting and Electronic Media, 94; Conflict and Public Opinion: Rallying Effects of the Persian Gulf War, Jour Quart, 94; rev(s), Review of P. Thaler's The Watchful Eye: American Justice in the Age of the Television Trial, Jour Broadcasting and Electronic Media, 39, 95; Review of J. Mueller's, Policy and Opinion in the Gulf War, Amer Jour, 94; A Comparative Analysis of the Use of Corporate Advertising in the United States and Japan, Intl Jour Advt, 94; Actual and Perceived U.S. Public Opinion: The Spiral of Silence During the Persian Gulf War, Intl Jour of Pub Opinion Res, 95; Anarchists Wreak Havoc in Downtown Minneapolis: A Multi-level Study of Media Coverage of Radical Protest, Jour Monogr(s), 95; The Effects of Spokesperson Gender, PSA Appeal, and Involvement on Eevaluations of Safe-sex Public Service Announcements, Health Commun, 96; auth, Communicating Deviance: The Effects of Relevision News Coverage of Social Protest, Jour Broadcasting and Electronic Media, 95. **CONTACT ADDRESS** Dept of Commun, Univ Delaware, 162 Ctr Mall, Newark, DE, 19716. **EMAIL** dmcleod@udel.edu

MCLEOD, SUSAN
DISCIPLINE RHETORIC AND COMPOSITION THEORY **EDUCATION** Wis Univ, PhD. **CAREER** Prof & dept ch, Washington State Univ. **SELECTED PUBLICATIONS** Auth, Dramatic Imagery in the Plays of John Webster, 77 & Notes on the Heart: Affect and the Writing Classroom, 96; ed, Strengthening Programs for Writing Across the Curriculum, 88; sr ed, Writing About the World, text for freshman comp, 91, 2nd ed, 94, & Writing Across the Curriculum: A Guide to Developing Programs, 92. **CONTACT ADDRESS** Dept of English, Washington State Univ, 1 SE Stadium Way, PO Box 645020, Pullman, WA, 99164-5020. **EMAIL** mcleod@wsunix.wsu.edu

MCMAHON, ROBERT
DISCIPLINE EPIC, PLATONIST LITERATURE, PHILOSOPHY AND LITERATURE **EDUCATION** Univ Calif, Santa Cruz, PhD, 86. **CAREER** Prof, La State Univ. **HONORS AND AWARDS** Robert L (Doc) Amborski Award, 87; Phi Kappa Phi Award, 90; Award for Excellence in Tchg Freshmen, 94; Alpha Lambda Delta, Nat Freshman Honor Soc; Amoco Award, 95; Tiger Athletic Found Award, Honors Col, 96. **RESEARCH** Voegelinian essays; Milton; Dante. **SELECTED PUBLICATIONS** Auth, Homer/Pound's Odysseus and Virgil/Ovid/Dante's Ulysses: Pound's First Canto and the Commedia, Paideuma, 87; Kenneth Burke's Divine Comedy: The Literary Form of The Rhetoric of Religion, PMLA, 89; Augustine's Prayerful Ascent: An Essay on the Literary Form of the Confession, 89; Satan as Infernal Narcissus: Interpretative Translation in the Commedia, in Dante and Ovid: Essays in Intertextuality, 91; 'Coloss. 3.3' as Microcosm, George Herbert J, 93; The Structural Articulation of Boethius' Consolation of Philosophy, Medievalia et Humanistica, 94; The Two Poets of Paradise Lost, 98. **CONTACT ADDRESS** Dept of Eng, Louisiana State Univ, 212K Allen Hall, Baton Rouge, LA, 70803.

MCMASTER, JULIET
PERSONAL Kenya **DISCIPLINE** ENGLISH **EDUCATION** Oxford Univ, BA, 59, MA, 62; Univ Alta, MA, 62, PhD, 70. **CAREER** Asst prof, 65-70, assoc prof, 70-76, PROF ENGLISH, UNIV ALBERTA 76-. **HONORS AND AWARDS** Molson Prize Hum Soc Sci, 94. **SELECTED PUBLICATIONS** Auth, Thackery: The Major Novels, 71; auth, Trollope's Pallister Novels: Theme and Form, 78; auth, Dickens the Designer, 87; auth, Jane Austen the Novelist: Essays Past and Present, 95; ed adv bd, Nineteenth Century Literature; ed adv bd, Eighteenth Century Fiction. **CONTACT ADDRESS** Dept of English, Univ of Alberta, Edmonton, AB, T6G 2E5. **EMAIL** juliet.mcmaster@ualberta.ca

MCMASTER, ROWLAND DOUGLAS
PERSONAL Born 12/05/1928, Sydney, Australia **DISCIPLINE** ENGLISH **EDUCATION** Univ Toronto, BA, 53, MA, 54, PhD(English), 59. **CAREER** Instr, Univ Toronto, 54-56; assoc prof English, Acadia Univ, 57-58; from asst prof to assoc prof, 58-67, PROF ENGLISH, UNIV ALTA, 67-. **MEMBERSHIPS** Asn Can Univ Teachers English (pres, 72-74); Int Asn Univ Professors English; MLA; Dickens Soc. **RESEARCH** Victorian novel Dickens; Victorian thought. **SELECTED PUBLICATIONS** Auth, Little Dorrit: experience and design, Queen's Quart, 61; ed, Great Expectations by Charles Dickens, Macmillan, 65; auth, Criticism of civilization in the structure of Sartor Resartus, Univ Toronto Quart, 68; ed, Little Dorrit, Macmillan, 69; Women in the Way We Live Now, English Studies Can, 81; Trollope and the terrible meshes of the law: Mr Scarborough's Family, Nineteenth-Century Fiction, 81; coauth (with Juliet McMaster), The novel from Sterne to James, Macmillan, 81. **CONTACT ADDRESS** Dept of English, Univ of Alta, Edmonton, AB, T6G 2E5.

MCMULLEN, LORRAINE
PERSONAL Born 07/27/1926, Ottawa, ON, Canada **DISCIPLINE** ENGLISH **EDUCATION** Univ Ottawa, BS, 48, BA, 63, MA, 67, PhD, 70. **CAREER** Asst prof, assoc prof, prof, dept English, Univ Ottawa, 69-92; adj prof, Univ Victoria, 92-; PROF EMER ENGLISH, UNIV OTTAWA, 92-. **MEMBERSHIPS** SSHRCC Comt Res Tools, 85-87 **SELECTED PUB-**

LICATIONS Auth, An Introduction to the Aesthetic Movement in English Literature 1971, 75; auth, Sinclair Ross 1979, 90; auth, An Old Attempt in a Woman, 83; auth, Francis Brooke and Her Works, 83; auth, Ernest Thompson Seton and His Works, 89; coauth, Silenced Sext **CONTACT ADDRESS** Dept of English, Univ Victoria, PO Box 3070, Victoria, BC, V8W 3W1.

MCMULLEN, MARGARET

PERSONAL Born 02/19/1960, Newton, MS, m, 1993, 1 child **DISCIPLINE** ENGLISH **EDUCATION** Grinnell Col, BA, 82; Radcliffe Col, 82; Univ Arkansas, MFA, 89. **CAREER** Assoc Entertainment Ed, Glamour, 82-85; Asst prof English, Univ Arkansas, 89-90; Asst prof English, 90-96, ASSOC PROF ENGLISH, UNIV EVANSVILLE, 96- ; vis fac, Harlaxton Col, Grantham, Eng, 95; Individual Artist fel, 94 & 96; Dean's Tchr Yr, Univ Evansville, 96. **HONORS AND AWARDS** First Prize Non-Fiction, My Right Breast, New Press Lit Quart & Lit Soc, 93. **MEMBERSHIPS** Auth Guild; Assoc Writing Prog; MLA. **RESEARCH** Creative fiction; Creative nonfiction. **SELECTED PUBLICATIONS** Auth, My Sister's Problem with Food and Me, Eating Our Hearts Out: Women and Food, The Crossing Press, 93; auth, When Warhol Was Still Alive, The Crossing Press, 94; auth, Lifeguarding, Bless Me, Father, Plume/Penguin, 94; Saying Goodbye to Joey, Breaking Up is Hard to Do, The Crossing Press, 94; coauth, Sacred Hearts, Am Mongrel Filmmakers, 95; auth, When My Friend Died of AIDS, A Loving Testimony: Remembering Loved Ones Lost to AIDS, The Crossing Press, 95; ed World Cultures Faculty Handbook, Univ Evansville, 96; auth, To Be Sad Like Ilma, Boulevard, St. Louis Univ, 97; auth, The Past is Present in the Pass, Southern Accents, 97; Our Mission, Evansville Rev, 97. **CONTACT ADDRESS** English Dept, Univ of Evansville, 1800 Lincoln Ave, Evansville, IN, 47722. **EMAIL** mm44@evansville.edu

MCMULLEN, WAYNE J.

PERSONAL Born 12/10/1954, Trenton, NJ **DISCIPLINE** SPEECH COMMUNICATION **EDUCATION** Penn State, PhD 89; Auburn Univ, MA 82; Temple Univ, BA 80. **CAREER** Penn State, asst prof, assoc prof, 91 to 98-; West Chester Univ, asst prof, inst, 88-91; Penn State, inst/res asst, 82-87. **HONORS AND AWARDS** Outstanding Tchr, 97 **MEMBERSHIPS** NCA; ORWC **RESEARCH** Rhetoric of Film **SELECTED PUBLICATIONS** Auth, Portrayals of Women's Friendships in Thelma and Louise, coauth, forthcoming; Sleep No More: Issues of Paranoia and Conformity in Invasion of the Body Snatchers, coauth, forthcoming; Reconstruction of the Frontier Myth in Witness, The SO Comm Jour, 96; Gender and the American Dream in Kramer vs Kramer, Women's Stud In comm, 96; Mythic Perspectives in Film Criticism, Jour of the NW Comm Assoc, 96; The China Syndrome: Corruption to the Core, Lit/Film Quart, 95; The Politics of Adaptation: Steven Speilberg's Appropriation of The Color Purple, coauth, Text and Perf Quart, 94. **CONTACT ADDRESS** Dept of Communication, Pennsylvania State Univ, Media, PA, 19063. **EMAIL** wjm11@psu.edu

MCMURTRY, JOSEPHINE

PERSONAL Born 12/07/1937, Bristol, VA, d, 1 child **DISCIPLINE** ENGLISH LITERATURE **EDUCATION** Tex Woman's Univ, BA, 59; Rice Univ, PhD(English), 69. **CAREER** Asst prof, 69-74, assoc prof, 74-86, PROF ENGLISH, UNIV RICHMOND, 86-. **MEMBERSHIPS** Shakespeare Asn Am **RESEARCH** Shakespeare; 16th century narrative poetry, 19th century British fiction. **SELECTED PUBLICATIONS** Auth, Victorian Life and Victorian Fiction, Archon Bks, 79; English Language, English Literature, Archon Books, 85; Understanding Shakespeare's England, Archon Books, 89; Shakespeare Films in the Classroom, Archon Books, 94. **CONTACT ADDRESS** Dept of English, Univ of Richmond, 28 Westhampton Way, Richmond, VA, 23173-0002.

MCNAMEE, MAURICE BASIL

PERSONAL Born 06/05/1909, Montello, WI **DISCIPLINE** ENGLISH **EDUCATION** St Louis Univ, AB, 33, AM, 34, STL, 41, PhD, 45. **CAREER** Instr, 36-37, Creighton Prep Sch; from asst prof to assoc prof Eng, 44-60, prof, 60-77, chmn dept, 56-77, Emer Prof Eng, Art & Art History & Dir, 77-, Cupples House, ST Louis Univ; Fulbright res fel, Belgium, 65-66; Am Philos Soc res grants, 65-66 & 78; Ford Found Jesuit Fac Fund res grant, St Louis Univ, 66-68; dir, Cupples House Mus, 74-77. **HONORS AND AWARDS** Nancy McNeir Ring Outstanding Fac Award, St Louis Univ, 73. **MEMBERSHIPS** MLA; Col Art Assn Am; Mediaeval Acad Am. **RESEARCH** Symbolism in Flemish painting; mannerism and surrealism in art and literature. **SELECTED PUBLICATIONS** Auth, Literary Decorum in Francis Bacon, St Louis Univ, 50; Reading for Understanding, 68; auth, Honor and the Epic Hero, 59; auth, Literary Types and Themes, Holt, 60; art, Bacon's Inductive Method and Humanistic Grammar, Studies Lit Imag, 71; art, The Origin of the Vested Angel as a Eucharistic Symbol in Flemish Painting, Art Bull, 73; auth, Medieval Latin Liturgical Drama and the Annunciation by the Aix-en-Provence Master, Gaz des Beaux-Arts, 74; art, Good Friday Liturgy and the Hans Memling Antwerp Triptych, J Warburg & Courtauld Insts, 74; auth, Vested Angels, Deeters Loresen, 97. **CONTACT ADDRESS** Dept of Art History, St. Louis Univ, 221 Grand Ave St, Louis, MO, 63103.

MCNARON, TONI ANN HURLEY

PERSONAL Born 04/03/1937, Birmingham, AL **DISCIPLINE** ENGLISH **EDUCATION** Univ Ala, BA, 58; Vanderbilt Univ, MA, 60; Univ Wis, PhD(English), 64. **CAREER** Instr English & geog, All Saint's Episcopal Col, 59-61; asst prof, 64-67, Assoc Prof English, Univ Minn, Minneapolis, 67-**HONORS AND AWARDS** Distinguished Teacher Award, Univ Minn, 67. **MEMBERSHIPS** MLA; Nat Women's Studies Asn; NCTE; Aaup; Am Asn Higher Educ. **RESEARCH** Emily Dickinson; Shakespeare's women; lesbian poetry. **SELECTED PUBLICATIONS** Auth, Finding and studying lesbian culture, Radical Teacher, winter 78; co-ed, Voices in the Night: Women's Writings on Incest, Cleis Press, 82; auth, I Dwell in Possibility, Feminist Press, 84; co-ed, New Lesbian Studies: Into the 21st Century, Feminist Press, 97; Poisoned Ivy: Lesbian and Gay Academics Confronting Homophobia, 97. **CONTACT ADDRESS** Dept of English, Univ of Minnesota, 207 Church St SE, Minneapolis, MN, 55455-0156. **EMAIL** mcnar001@maroon.tc.umn.edu

MCPHAIL, MARK L.

DISCIPLINE COMMUNICATION STUDIES **EDUCATION** Univ Mass, PhD, 87. **CAREER** Prof. **RESEARCH** Rhetorical theory and epistemology; language of race relations. **SELECTED PUBLICATIONS** Auth, Zen and the Art of Rhetoric; The Rhetoric of Racism. **CONTACT ADDRESS** Dept of Communication, Utah Univ, 100 S 1350 E, Salt Lake City, UT, 84112. **EMAIL** welch@admin.comm.utah.edu

MCPHAIL, THOMAS LAWRENCE

DISCIPLINE COMMUNICATION STUDIES **EDUCATION** McMaster Univ, BA; State Univ NY Buffalo, MA; Purdue Univ, PhD. **SELECTED PUBLICATIONS** Auth, Population Shift Plus Pay-Per-View: The New Dynamics of American TV, Intermedia, 92; Issues and Opportunities for Telecoms in Rural Areas, Telecommunication Rev, 93; co-auth, Communication: The Canadian Experience, Copp Clark Pitman, 90; Teleconferencing in Rural America: Major Obstacles, 91; The Future of Broadcasting: The Effect of Pay-Per-View, Feedback, 92. **CONTACT ADDRESS** Communication Dept, Univ of Missouri, St. Louis, 590 Lucas Hall, St. Louis, MO, 63121. **EMAIL** stlmcph@umslvma.umsl.edu

MCPHERSON, DAVID

DISCIPLINE RENAISSANCE LITERATURE **EDUCATION** Univ Tex, PhD, 66. **CAREER** Instr, Univ NMex, 72-. **SELECTED PUBLICATIONS** Auth, Shakespeare, Jonson, and the Myth of Venice, 90. **CONTACT ADDRESS** Univ NMex, Albuquerque, NM, 87131.

MCPHERSON, JAMES ALAN

PERSONAL Born 09/16/1943, Savannah, GA, d, 1 child **DISCIPLINE** LITERATURE, HISTORY, LAW **EDUCATION** Morris Brown Col, BA, 65; Harvard Law School, LLB, 68; Writers Workshop, Univ IA, MFA, 71. **CAREER** Lect, Univ CA at Santa Cruz, 69-71; asst prof, Morgan State Univ, 75-76; assoc prof, Univ VA, 76-81; prof, Univ IA, 81-. **HONORS AND AWARDS** Pulitzer Prize, 78; MacArthur Prize Fellows Award, 81. **MEMBERSHIPS** ACLU; NAACP; Authors Guild; Am Academy of Arts and Sciences; fel, Center for Advanced Studies, Stanford Univ, 97-98. **RESEARCH** Law. **SELECTED PUBLICATIONS** Auth, Crabcakes, 98; Fatherly Daughter, 98. **CONTACT ADDRESS** Dept of English, Univ of Iowa, Iowa City, IA, 52242.

MCTAGGART, WILLIAM

DISCIPLINE WRITING **EDUCATION** Ohio Univ, PhD. **CAREER** Dept ch, 90-95; prof. **HONORS AND AWARDS** Fulbright scholar, Oxford, 68-69., Fac adv, rugby, Alpha Sigma Phi. **RESEARCH** Autobiographical writing. **SELECTED PUBLICATIONS** Auth, History of 100 years of Titan football. **CONTACT ADDRESS** Dept of Eng, Westminister Col, New Wilmington, PA, 16172-0001.

MCVEIGH, PAUL J.

PERSONAL Born 10/10/1947, Philadelphia, PA, s, 1 child **DISCIPLINE** HUMANITIES **EDUCATION** Am Univ, BA, 71; Univ Va, MA, 72; Trinity Col, Dublin, PhD, 84 **CAREER** Chemn, Northern Va Commun Col, 89-. **HONORS AND AWARDS** Chancellor's Common Wealth Prof, 89-91; Excellence Tchg Award, Northern Va Commun Col Educ Found, 89., Dir, Inst Tchr as Learner, State Council Funds for Excellence Grant, 94-96. **CONTACT ADDRESS** Humanities Div, No Virginia Comm Col, 3001 N Beauregard St, Alexandria, VA, 22311. **EMAIL** nvmcvep@nu.cc.va.us

MCWILLIAMS, JOHN P.

PERSONAL Born 07/22/1940, Cleveland, OH, m, 1985, 6 children **DISCIPLINE** ENGLISH **EDUCATION** Princeton Univ, AB 62; Harvard Univ, PhD 68. **CAREER** Univ CA Berkeley, asst prof 68-74; Univ IL, assoc prof 74-77; Middlebury Col, prof 77. **HONORS AND AWARDS** Phi Beta Kappa; 3 NEH fellowships. **MEMBERSHIPS** ALA; MLA; ASA. **RESEARCH** Early Am Lit, Cult to 1860. **SELECTED PUBLICATIONS** The Last of the Mohicans: Civil Savagery and Savage Civility, Twayne-Macmillan, 94; ed, James Fenmore Cooper, The Last of the Mohicans, Oxford Univ Press, 90, 2d ed, rev expanded 94, 3d ed 98; The American Epic: Transforming a Genre, Cambridge Univ Press, 89; Indian John and the Northern Tawnies, New Eng Quarterly, 96; Poetry, Columbia Univ Press, 93; The Epic in the Nineteenth Century, Columbia History of America. **CONTACT ADDRESS** Dept of Am Lit, Middlebury Col, Middlebury, VT, 05753. **EMAIL** john.mcwilliams@middlebury.edu

MEADOWS, MICHAEL

DISCIPLINE JOURNALISM, MEDIA ENTERTAINMENT **CAREER** Sr lectr Journalism, Griffith Univ. **MEMBERSHIPS** Jour Educ Asn; Media Entertainment and Arts Alliance. **RESEARCH** Indigenous media; journalistic practices and ethics. **SELECTED PUBLICATIONS** auth, A Watering Can in the Desert-Issues in Indigenous Broadcasting Policy in Australia, 92; Northern Voices, Northern Choices: Television Northern Canada-A Background Report, 95; auth, Representation and Resistance: Aborigines, the Media and Cultural Resource Management (Univ Qld, 97; coauth, The Way People Want to Talk: Indigenous Media in Australia, the Pacific, and Canada, Pluto Press, 96.

MEATS, STEPHEN EARL

PERSONAL Born 03/16/1944, LeRoy, KS, m, 1964, 3 children **DISCIPLINE** AMERICAN LITERATURE **EDUCATION** Univ SC, BA, 66, MA, 68, PhD(Am lit), 72. **CAREER** Asst prof English, US Air Force Acad, 68-72; assoc prof, Univ Tampa, 72-74, chp, Humanities Div, 74-79; prof & chp, English Dept, Pittsburg State Univ, 79-, vis res prof, Southern Studies Prog, Univ SC, 75 & 76. **HONORS AND AWARDS** Cert of Commendation, Am Asn State & Local Hist, 77. **MEMBERSHIPS** MLA; Asn Depts English. **RESEARCH** Nineteenth century American literature; William Faulkner. **SELECTED PUBLICATIONS** Auth, Who Killed Joanna Burden?, Miss Quart, summer 71; Addenda to Van Winkle: Henry William Herbert (Frank Forester), Publ Bibliog Soc Am, spring 73; Introduction and explanatory notes for Simms' Joscelyn, A Tale of the Revolution, Univ SC Press, 75; co-ed, Revolutionary War Novels of William Gilmore Simms, 8 vols, Reprint Co, 76; auth, Artist vs historian: Simms and the Revolutionary South, In: 18th Century Florida and the Revolutionary South, Univ Presses of Fla, 78; auth & ed, South Carolina Writers in the Spirit of the Times, Gyascutas, Humanities Press, 78; auth, Henry William Herbert (Frank Forester), In: Dict of Literary Biography, Gale Res, 79; ed, Selected Writings of Benjamin F Perry, 3 vols, Reprint Co, 80. **CONTACT ADDRESS** English Dept, Pittsburg State Univ, 1701 S Broadway St, Pittsburg, KS, 66762-7500. **EMAIL** smeats@pittstate.edu

MEDHURST, MARTIN J.

PERSONAL Born 10/15/1952, Alton, IL, m, 1989, 2 children **DISCIPLINE** SPEECH COMMUNICATION **EDUCATION** Wheaton Col, BA, 74; Northern Ill Univ, MA, 75; Penn State Univ, PhD, 80. **CAREER** Asst prof, 79-85, assoc prof, 85-88, Univ of Calif at Davis; ASSOC PROF, 88-91, PROF, 91-, TEXAS A&M UNIV; coordr, Prog in Presidential Rhetoric, Bush School of Gov and Public Service, 93-. **HONORS AND AWARDS** Nat Commun Asn Golden Anniversary Prize Fund Award, 82; Religious Speech Commun Asn Pub Award, 83; Marie Hochmuth Nichols Award for Outstanding Scholar in Public Address, 95 & 97; Naomi Lews Fac Fel in Liberal Arts, Tex A&M Univ, 93-94 & 94-95; Speech Commun Asn Anniversary Prize Fund Award, 82; Paul K. Crawford Award for Outstanding Graduate Student, Northern Ill Univ, 75. **MEMBERSHIPS** Nat Commun Asn; Southern Commun Asn; Western Commun Asn; Int Soc for the Hist of Rhetoric; Rhetoric Soc of Am; Soc for Historians of Am Foreign Relations. **RESEARCH** Cold War rhetoric; Presidential rhetoric; rhetoric of film. **SELECTED PUBLICATIONS** Ed, Beyond the Rhetorical Presidency, Tex A&M Univ Press, 96; ed, Eisenhower's War of Words: Rhetoric and Leadership, Mich State Univ Press, 94; auth, Martial Decision Making: MacArthur, Inchon, and the Dimensions of Rhetoric, in Rhetoric and Community: Studies in Unity and Fragmentation, Univ of South Carolina Press, 98; auth, A Tale of Two Constructs: The Rhetorical Presidency versus Presidential Rhetoric, Beyond the Rhetorical Presidency, Tex A&M Univ Press, 96; auth, Dwight D. Eisenhower, U.S. Presidents as Orators: A Bio-Critical Sourcebook, Greenwood Press, 95; auth, Eisenhower's Rhetorical Leadership: An Interpretation, Eisenhower's War of Words: Rhetoric and Leadership, Mich State Univ Press, 94; coauth, Rhetorical Reduplication in MTV's Rock the Vote Campaign, Commun Studies 49, 98; auth, The Rhetorical Renaissance: A Battlefield Report, Southern Commun Journal 64, 98; auth, Rhetorical Education in the 21st Century, Southern Commun Journal, 98. **CONTACT ADDRESS** Dept of Speech Commun, Texas A&M Univ, College Station, TX, 77843. **EMAIL** m-medhurst@tamu.edu

MEDINE, PETER ERNEST

PERSONAL Born 03/30/1941, DeKalb, IL, 1 child **DISCIPLINE** LITERATURE OF THE ENGLISH RENAISSANCE **EDUCATION** Northwestern Univ, Evanston, BA, 63; Univ Wis-Madison, MA, 65, PhD, 70. **CAREER** From instr to asst prof, 69-75, assoc prof 75-94, PROF ENGLISH, UNIV ARIZ,

94-; Folger Shakespeare Libr fel; Huntington Libr fel. **MEMBERSHIPS** MLA; Renaissance Soc Am; Philol Asn Pac Coast. **RESEARCH** Renaissance poetry, prose and drama. **SELECTED PUBLICATIONS** Ed, Horace His Arte of Poetrie, Scholars' Facsimiles & Reprints, 72; auth, Praise and blame in Renaissance satire, Pac Coast Philol, 72; ed, De Satyrica Graecorum Poesi et Romanorum Satira, Scholars' Facsimiles & Reprints, 73; auth, Object and intention in Jonson's Famous Voyage, Studies English Lit, 75; Casaubon's Prolegomena to the Satires of Persius: An introduction, text & translation, English Lit Renaissance, 76; Martial's Epigrammata and the Poematium: An hypothesis, Pac Coast Philol, 77; auth, Thomas Wilson, Twayne, 86; ed, Thomas Wilson's Art of Rhetoric, Penn State, 94; ed, Soundings of Things Done, Del, 97. **CONTACT ADDRESS** Dept of English, Univ of Ariz, Tucson, AZ, 85721-0001. **EMAIL** medine@u.arizona.edu

MEEKER, JOSEPH W.
DISCIPLINE ENGLISH LITERATURE **EDUCATION** Univ Calif Berkeley, BA; Occidental Col, MA, PhD. **CAREER** Prof. **RESEARCH** Twentieth century literature and philosophy; environmental ethics; human ecology; comedy and tragedy; mythology; systems theory. **SELECTED PUBLICATIONS** Auth, The Comedy of Survival: Studies in Literary Ecology, Guild, 80; Spheres of Life: An Introduction to World Ecology, Charles Scribner's, 75; Ancient Roots of the Modern World, Athabasca Univ, 75. **CONTACT ADDRESS** English Dept, Union Inst, 440 E McMillan St, Cincinnati, OH, 45206-1925.

MEEKER, MICHAEL W.
DISCIPLINE MODERN BRITISH AND AMERICAN LITERATURE **EDUCATION** Northern Ill Univ, BA, MA; Univ Wisc, PhD. **CAREER** Tchng Asst, Northern Ill Univ,65-67; Instr, Elgin Community Col, 67-69; Tchng Asst, Univ Wisc, 69-73; Asst prof, Moorhead State Univ, 73-77; Prof, Winona State Univ, 77-. **HONORS AND AWARDS** Acceleration Grant; Grant develop computerized student portfolio system; IDEALS Multimedia Workshop; MSUS Challenge Grant, Hypertext Portfolios; Fac Improvement Grant; Summer Res Grant, Hypercard, WSU; Merit Award, WSU; Fac Improvement Grant Summer; Release time grant res; Bush Grant release time work Minn Writing Proj; Award best essay pub Minn Engl Jour; Fac Improvement Grant, NEH Summer Fel; Fac Res Grant; Bush Grant release time work Minn Writing Proj; Bush Grant release time work Great River Writing Proj; Merit Performance Award, Moorhead State Univ; Awarded Tenure, Moorhead State Univ; Promoted Asst Prof, Moorhead State Univ; Fac Improvement Grant, Moorhead State Univ; Fac Improvement Grant, Moorhead State Univ; D.Yale Beach Fel; Excellence Scholarship & Tchng, Univ Wisc. **MEMBERSHIPS** Nat Coun Tchrs Engl; Minn Coun Tchrs Eng; Col Comp & Comm ; Network Cooperative Learning Higher Educ; Asn Writing Ctrs. **RESEARCH** Modern British and American literature, literary theory, composition. **SELECTED PUBLICATIONS** Auth, Readers as Authors in a Hypertext Literature Classroom, Proceedings Conference Comp & Writing, 94; Comp-Mediated Class Jour, An Apple Writer Database Manager,Collegiate. **CONTACT ADDRESS** Winona State Univ, 600 W Franklin Street, Richmond, VA, 23220. **EMAIL** meeker@vax2.winona.msus.edu

MEHAFFEY, KAREN RAE
PERSONAL Born 03/16/1959, Ann Arbor, MI, m, 1989 **DISCIPLINE** LIBRARY SCIENCE **EDUCATION** Univ Mich, AB, AMLS. **CAREER** Res coord, Gale Research, 82-84; librn, Univ Mich, 85; librn, St Hedwig High Sch, 86-88; asst librn to libr dir, Sacred Heart Major Sem, 88-. **HONORS AND AWARDS** Appointed to US Civil War Center Panel of Experts, 98. **MEMBERSHIPS** Amer Libr Assoc; Amer Theol Libr Assoc; Mich Libr Assoc; Libr Admin & Mgmt Assoc; Assoc of Col & Res Libr. **RESEARCH** Victorian Amer women 1840-1870; Civil War soc hist; Victorian mourning rituals; nineteenth century temperance movement. **SELECTED PUBLICATIONS** Auth, The Genteel State: Victorian Manners and the Civil War, Part II, Citizens' Companion, 95; auth, Collecting the Carte-de-Visite, Citizens' Companion, 96; auth, Civility in War Time Washington, Camp Chase Gazette, 97; auth, The Genteel State: Victorians Manners and the Civil War, Citizens' Companion, 98; auth, Knowing Ourselves: Understanding the People and History We Portray, Citizens' Companion, 98. **CONTACT ADDRESS** Sacred Heart Major Sem, Szoka Libr, 2701 Chicago Blvd, Detroit, MI, 48206-1704. **EMAIL** krmehaffey@yahoo.com

MEINERS, ROGER K.
PERSONAL Born 12/05/1932, Forreston, IL, m, 1958, 2 children **DISCIPLINE** ENGLISH **EDUCATION** Wheaton Col, Ill, BA, 54; Univ Denver, MA, 57, PhD, 61. **CAREER** From instr to asst prof English, Ariz State Univ, 59-64; asst prof, Univ Mo-Columbia, 64-65, assoc prof, 66-70, dir grad study, 67-70; assoc prof, 70-71, PROF ENGLISH, MICH STATE UNIV, 71- **MEMBERSHIPS** MLA. **RESEARCH** Twentieth century American and English literature; literary criticism; 19th and 20th century philosophy, psychology and literature. **SELECTED PUBLICATIONS** Auth Bird Shadows, Centennial Rev, Vol 39, 95; Eikampfs Dialectic, Centennial Rev, Vol 39, 95; Material History, Centennial Rev, Vol 39, 95; Eikampf Singing at the End, Centennial Rev, Vol 39, 95; Dialectics at a Standstill--Orwell, Benjamin and the Difficulties of Poetry, Boundary 2, Int Jour Lit Cult, Vol 20, 93. **CONTACT ADDRESS** Dept of English, Michigan State Univ, 201 Morrill Hall, East Lansing, MI, 48824-1036.

MEINKE, PETER
PERSONAL Born 12/29/1932, Brooklyn, NY, m, 1957, 4 children **DISCIPLINE** AMERICAN LITERATURE **EDUCATION** Hamilton Col, AB, 55; Univ of Mich, MA, 61; Univ of Minn, PhD, 65. **CAREER** Asst prof of English, Hamline Univ, 61-66; prof of lit & dir of The Writing Workshop, Eckerd Col, 66-93; WRITER, 93-. **HONORS AND AWARDS** NEA Fel in poetry, 76 & 89; Flannery O'Conner Award for Short Fiction, 86; Emily Dickinson Award, Poetry Soc of Am, 92; Sow's Ear Prize, 95. **MEMBERSHIPS** Poetry Soc of Am; Acad of Am Poets. **RESEARCH** Literature. **SELECTED PUBLICATIONS** Auth, The Legend of Larry the Lizard, John Knox Press, 68; auth, Howard Nemerov, Univ of Minn Press, 69; auth, Very Seldom Animals, Possum Press, 70 & 72; auth, Lines from Neuchatel, Konglomerati Press, 74; auth, The Night Train and the Golden Bird, Univ of Pittsburgh Press, 77; auth, The Rat Poems, Bits press, 78; auth, Trying to Surprise God, Univ of Pittsburgh Press, 81; auth, Underneath the Lantern, Heatherstone Press, 86; auth, The Piano Tuner, Univ of Ga Press, 86; auth, Night Watch on the Chesapeake, Univ of Pittsburgh Press, 87; auth, Far From Home, Heatherstone Press, 88; auth, Liquid Paper: New & Selected Poems, Univ of Pittsburgh Press, 91; auth, Camporcorto, Sow's Ear Press, 96; auth, Scars, Univ of Pittsburgh Press, 96. **CONTACT ADDRESS** 147 Wildwood Ln, SE, St. Petersburg, FL, 33705-3222. **EMAIL** meinkep@acasun.eckerd.edu

MEISEL, MARTIN
PERSONAL Born 03/22/1931, New York, NY, m, 1957, 3 children **DISCIPLINE** ENGLISH, COMPARATIVE LITERATURE **EDUCATION** Queens Col, NY, BA, 52; Princeton Univ, MA, 57, PhD(English), 60. **CAREER** Army, 54-56; instr English, Rutgers Univ, 57-58; from instr to assoc prof, Dartmouth Col, 59-65; prof, Univ WI, 65-68; vchm dept, 73-76, prof English, 68-86, chm dept English & comp lit, 80-83, vice pres arts and sciences, 86-87, 89-93, Brander Matthews prof of dramatic lit, Columbia Univ, 87-; Guggenheim fel, 63-64, 87-88; Am Coun Learned our Carribean Poets, Duluth: Poetry Harbor, 96; Lawrence Ferlinghetti, Gregory Corso and Gwendolyn Brooks, in Frank N Magill, ed, Cyclopedia of World Authors, Revised Edition, Pasadena, CA: Salem Press, 97; If Beale Street Could Talk, in Frank N Magill, ed, Masterplots II: Juvenile and Young Adult Literature Series, Supplement, 3 vols, Pasadena, CA: Salem Press, 97; The Wapshot Scandal, The Country Husband, and John Cheever, in David Peck, ed, Identities and Issues in Literature, 3 vols, Pasadena, CA: Salem Press, 97; The Beat Generation: A Bibliographical Teaching Guide, Lanham, MD: Scarecrow Press, 98. **CONTACT ADDRESS** Dept of English, Univ of Wisconsin, 2100 Main St, Stevens Point, WI, 54481-3897. **EMAIL** wlawlor@uwsp.edu

MEISEL, PERRY H.
PERSONAL Shreveport, LA **DISCIPLINE** ENGLISH **EDUCATION** Yale Univ, BA, 70, MPhil, 73, PhD(English), 75. **CAREER** Carnegie teaching fel English, Yale Univ, 70-71, acting instr, 73, teaching fel, 73-74; vis instr, Wesleyan Univ, 74; asst prof, 75-80, assoc prof, 80-87, prof English, NY Univ, 87-, Fel, NY Inst Humanities, 78-81. **MEMBERSHIPS** MLA; PEN; Phi Beta Kappa. **RESEARCH** Modern literature; contemporary literature; theory of fiction and criticism. **SELECTED PUBLICATIONS** Auth, Thomas Hardy: The Return of the Repressed, 72 & The Absent Father, 80, Yale Univ; Freud, Prentice-Hall, 81; Bloomsbury/Freud, Basic, 85; The Myth of the Modern, 87; The Cowby and the Dandy, 98. **CONTACT ADDRESS** Dept of English, New York Univ, 19 University Pl, New York, NY, 10003-4556.

MEISER, MARY
PERSONAL WI **DISCIPLINE** ENGLISH LITERATURE **EDUCATION** Harvard Univ, PhD. **CAREER** Comp dir, Acad Skills Ctr, 76-; dir comp, Eng dept, 86-. **RESEARCH** Applied linguistics; composition; English as a second language; English education. **SELECTED PUBLICATIONS** Auth, textbooks dealing with applied linguistics and English education. **CONTACT ADDRESS** Dept of English, Univ of Wisconsin, Eau Claire, Hibbard Hall 358, PO Box 4004, Eau Claire, WI, 54702-4004. **EMAIL** meiserm@uwec.edu

MELADA, IVAN
DISCIPLINE VICTORIAN LITERATURE **EDUCATION** Univ Calif, Berkeley, PhD, 67. **CAREER** Instr, Univ NMex, 67-. **SELECTED PUBLICATIONS** Auth, Sheridan Le Fanu, 87. **CONTACT ADDRESS** Univ NMex, Albuquerque, NM, 87131.

MELDRUM, BARBARA H.
DISCIPLINE ENGLISH **EDUCATION** Westmont Coll, BA, 56; Claremont Grad Sch, MA, 57, PhD, 64; Univ Idaho, BA, 89. **CAREER** Prof, PROF EMER, ENG, UNIV IDAHO **MEMBERSHIPS** Am Antiquarian Soc **SELECTED PUBLICATIONS** Auth, "Structure in Moby-Dick: The Whale Killings and Ishmael's Quest, " ESQ 21, 75; auth, Sophus K. Winther, 83; auth, Under the Sun, Myth and Realism in Western American Literature, 85; Old West - New West: Centennial Essays, 93. **CONTACT ADDRESS** 420 N Polk St, Moscow, ID. **EMAIL** bmeldrum@uidaho.edu

MELIA, DANIEL FREDERICK
PERSONAL Born 03/02/1944, Fall River, MA **DISCIPLINE** CELTIC LANGUAGES AND LITERATURE **EDUCATION** Harvard Col, BA, 66, Harvard Univ, MA, 70, PhD(Celtic lang and lit), 72. **CAREER** Asst prof, 72-78, ASSOC PROF RHETORIC, UNIV CALIF, BERKELEY, 78-, ASSOC DEAN, COL LETT AND SCI, 81-, Vis asst prof English, Univ Calif, Los Angeles, 73-74; Nat Endowment for Humanities jr res fel Celtic and Regents fac fel humanities, Univ Calif, 75. **MEMBERSHIPS** Celtic Studies Asn (secy treas, 77-79); fel Medieval Acad Ireland; MLA; Medieval Acad Am; Am Folklore Soc. **RESEARCH** Medieval Celtic literature; folklore and mythology; rhetoric and poetics. **SELECTED PUBLICATIONS** Auth, Celtic Languages and Literature See Vol III, The Irish Literary Tradition, Speculum J Medieval Stud, Vol 72, 97; The Irish Tradition in Old English Literature, Speculum J Medieval Stud, Vol 72, 97; From Scythia to Camelot--A Radical Reassessment of the Legends of King Arthur, The Knights of the Round Table, and The Holy Grail, W Folklore, Vol 55, 96. **CONTACT ADDRESS** Dept of Rhetoric, Univ of Calif, 2125 Dwinelle Hall, Berkeley, CA, 94720-2671.

MELL, DONALD CHARLES
PERSONAL Born 05/20/1931, Akron, OH, m, 1957, 2 children **DISCIPLINE** ENGLISH LITERATURE **EDUCATION** Yale Univ, BA, 53, MA, 59; Univ Pa, PhD(English), 61. **CAREER** Instr English, Rutgers Univ, 61-65; asst prof, Middlebury Col, 65-68; asst prof, 68-73, ASSOC PROF ENGLISH, UNIV DEL, 73- **MEMBERSHIPS** MLA; Am Soc 18th Century Studies. **RESEARCH** Augustan satire; Swift; 18th century literature. **SELECTED PUBLICATIONS** Auth, Reader Entrapment in 18th Century Literature, Scriblerian Kit Cats, Vol 25, 93. **CONTACT ADDRESS** Dept of English, Univ of Del, Newark, DE, 19711.

MELLARD, JAMES MILTON
PERSONAL Born 01/30/1938, West Monroe, LA, m, 1958, 3 children **DISCIPLINE** ENGLISH, AMERICAN LITERATURE **EDUCATION** Lamar Univ, BA, 60; Univ Okla, MA, 61; Univ Tex, PhD(English), 64. **CAREER** Spec instr English, Univ Tex, 63-64; asst prof, Univ Southern Calif, 64-67; from asst prof to assoc prof, 67-73, dir, Freshman English, 68-72, dir, Grad Studies, 76-78, Prof English, Northern Ill Univ, 73-, Chmn Dept English, 78-84, Acting Dean, Liberal Arts & Sci, 84-85, Athletic Dir (interim), 87. **HONORS AND AWARDS** The John Gray Award, for graduating athlete with highest scholastic average, 60; The Bingman Award for Outstanding Achievement, 60; Grad Fund Award, Univ Southern Calif, 65-66, 66-67; NEH Summer Stipend Award, 68; Dean's Fund Grant, Northern Ill Univ, 72-73; Grad Sch Summer Stipend Award, 86, 87, 89, 90. **MEMBERSHIPS** MLA; Midwest MLA; Assoc Dept English; Soc Study Southern Lit. **RESEARCH** 20th century American literature; prose fiction/ rhetoric of fiction; critical theory; psychoanalytic (particularly Lacanian) theory; William Faulkner. **SELECTED PUBLICATIONS** Auth, Four Modes: A Rhetoric of Modern Fiction, Macmillan, 73; coauth, The Authentic Writer: English Rhetoric and Composition, D.C. Heath, 77; auth, Quaternion: Stories, Poems, Plays, Essays, Scott, Foresman, 78; The Exploded Form: The Modernist Novel in America, Univ Ill Press, 80; Doing Tropology: Analysis of Narrative Discourse, Univ Ill Press, 87; Using Lacan, Reading Fiction, Univ Ill Press, 91; author of over 60 journal articles and reviews. **CONTACT ADDRESS** Dept of English, No Illinois Univ, 1425 W Lincoln Hwy, De Kalb, IL, 60115-2825. **EMAIL** jmellard@niu.edu

MELLEN, JOAN
PERSONAL Born 09/07/1941, New York, NY **DISCIPLINE** FILM, LITERATURE **EDUCATION** Hunter Col, BA, 62; City Univ New York, MA, 64, PhD, 68. **CAREER** Assoc prof, 67-77, prof English, Temple Univ, 77-. **MEMBERSHIPS** Soc Cinema Studies; MLA. **RESEARCH** Film criticism; contemporary fiction. **SELECTED PUBLICATIONS** Auth, Natural Tendencies: A Novel, Dial, 81; auth, Privilege: The Enigma of Sasha Bruce, Dial, 82; auth, Bob Knight: His Own Man, 88; auth, Kay Boyle: Author of Herself, 94; auth, Hellman and Hammett, 96. **CONTACT ADDRESS** Dept of English, Temple Univ, 1114 W Berks St, Philadelphia, PA, 19122-6029. **EMAIL** joanmellen@aol.com

MELLOR, ANNE KOSTELANETZ
PERSONAL Born 07/15/1941, m, 1969, 1 child **DISCIPLINE** ENGLISH AND COMPARATIVE LITERATURE **EDUCATION** Brown Univ, BA (summa cum laude, English & Philos), 63; Columbia Univ, MA (English & Comparative Lit), 64, PhD (English & Comparative Lit), 68; Courtauld Inst of Art, London, Fulbright-Hays Scholar, 64-65. **CAREER** Asst prof of English, Stanford Univ, 66-73, assoc prof, 73-80, founding dir of Feminist Studies Prog, 82-84, Howard H. and Jessie T. Watkins Univ Prof of English and Feminist Studies, 83-85; vis assoc prof of Humanities, 77, PROF OF ENGLISH, UNIV CA, LOS

ANGELES, 84-, DISTINGUISHED PROF OF ENGLISH, 96-, dir of Women's Studies Prog, 86-87. **HONORS AND AWARDS** Phi Beta Kappa, 63; Guggenheim fel, 72-73, 83-84; NEH fel for Younger Humanists (declined), 72-73; NEH Summer Stipend, 76; NEH/Huntington Library Fel, 77-78; dir, NEH Summer Seminar for College Teachers, 82, 89, 94; Stanford Univ Deans' Award for Excellence in Teaching, 82; exec comm, 82-87, Romantics Div, MLA, chair of comm, 86; Howard H. and Jessie T. Watkins Univ Prof of English and Feminist Studies, 83-85; English Lit and Lang Selection Comm, Coun for Int Exchange of Scholars, 87-90, chair of comm, 89-90; Humanities Res Centre fel, Nat Univ of Austalia, Canberra, 90; Rockefeller Found Fel, Bellagio Study Centre (declined), 91; Clark Prof, Clark Library, UCLA, 92. **MEMBERSHIPS** Modern Lang Asn; North Am Soc for the Study of Romanticism; Int Asn of Univ Profs of English; Am Conference on Romanticism; Interdisciplinary Nineteenth Century Studies Asn. **RESEARCH** British Romantic Writing; Women's Studies; 19th Century Art and Lit. **SELECTED PUBLICATIONS** Ed, with Audrey Fisch and Esther Schor, The Other Mary Shelley: Beyond Frankenstein, Oxford Univ Press, 93; auth, Romanticism and Gender, Routledge, Chapman & Hall, 93, paperback, 93, chapter 2 reprinted in Romanticism: A Critical Reader, ed Duncan Wu, Blackwell Pubs, 95; ed, with Richard Matlak, British Literature, 1780-1830, Harcourt Brace Pubs, 96; ed, with Maximillian Novak, The Age of Sensibility in a Time of Terror, Univ DE Press, in press; auth, Mothers of the Nation--Women's Political Writing in England, 1780-1830, IN Univ Press, in press. **CONTACT ADDRESS** 2620 Mandeville Canyon Rd., Los Angeles, CA, 90049. **EMAIL** mellor@ucla.edu

MELLOWN, ELGIN WENDELL
PERSONAL Born 12/29/1931, Selma, AL, m, 1957, 2 children **DISCIPLINE** ENGLISH LITERATURE **EDUCATION** Emory Univ, AB, 54; Univ London, MA, 58, PhD(English), 62. **CAREER** Instr English, Univ Ala, 58-60, asst prof, 62-65; asst prof, 65-68, ASSOC PROF ENGLISH, DUKE UNIV, 68- **MEMBERSHIPS** MLA. **RESEARCH** Twentieth century British literature. **SELECTED PUBLICATIONS** Auth Disease and Distinctiveness in the American South, Am Speech, Vol 70, 95. **CONTACT ADDRESS** Dept of English, Duke Univ, Durham, NC, 27706.

MELTON, FRANK TOMPKINS
PERSONAL Born 05/09/1939, Columbia, SC **DISCIPLINE** ENGLISH HISTORY **EDUCATION** Univ of South, BA, 61; Vanderbilt Univ, MA, 63; Univ Wis, PhD(hist), 69. **CAREER** Lectr, 67-69, asst prof, 69-78, ASSOC PROF HIST, UNIV NC, GREENSBORO, 78- **MEMBERSHIPS** AHA; Southern Conf Brit Studies; Conf Brit Studies. **RESEARCH** History of banking; Stuart England; Sir Robert Clayton. **SELECTED PUBLICATIONS** Auth, Chancery Equity Records and Proceedings, 1600-1800--A Guide to Documents in the Public- Record Office, Albion, Vol 28, 96; The Bank of England and Public Policy, 1941-1958, Am Hist Rev, Vol 99, 94; A Domestic History of the Bank of England, 1930-1960, Am Hist Rev, Vol 99, 94; The History of the Haberdashers Company, Albion, Vol 24, 92.

MENDELSON, EDWARD
DISCIPLINE 19TH-AND 20TH-CENTURY LITERATURE **EDUCATION** Univ Rochester, BA, 66; Johns Hopkins Univ, PhD, 69. **CAREER** Instr, Yale Univ; Harvard Univ; prof 81-. **HONORS AND AWARDS** Grants & fels: Guggenheim, NEH, Am Coun Learned Socs. **SELECTED PUBLICATIONS** Ed, volume of essays on Pynchon; novels by Hardy, Bennett, Meredith; co-ed, Homer to Brecht: The European Epic and Dramatic Traditions; Romanic Rev; Yale Fr Stud; TLS, Raritan; Gravity's Rainbow. **CONTACT ADDRESS** Dept of Eng, Columbia Col, New York, 2960 Broadway, New York, NY, 10027-6902.

MENGXIONG, LIU
PERSONAL Born 12/17/1946, Shanghai, China, m, 1973, 1 child **DISCIPLINE** LIBRARY/INFORMATION SCIENCE **EDUCATION** Univ Mich, PhD, 90 **CAREER** Librn, San Jose St Univ, 89-. **HONORS AND AWARDS** Beta Phi Mu Int Honors Soc **MEMBERSHIPS** Amer Libr Assoc **RESEARCH** Digital libr; infor technol; infor seeking behav; svc & technol rsrc. **CONTACT ADDRESS** Clark Libr, San Jose St Univ, One Washington Sq, San Jose, CA, 95192. **EMAIL** mliu@email.sjsu.edu

MENIKOFF, BARRY
PERSONAL Born 01/02/1939, Brooklyn, NY, 3 children **DISCIPLINE** ENGLISH **EDUCATION** Brooklyn Col, BA, 60; Univ Wis, MS, 62, PhD(English), 66. **CAREER** Asst prof, 65-70, ASSOC PROF ENGLISH, UNIV HAWAII, 70-, Fulbright-Hays grant lectr, Univ Santiago, 68-69; vis assoc prof English, Univ Southern Calif, 76-78; Huntington fel, 80; Newberry fel, 81. **MEMBERSHIPS** MLA; Aaup; Am Philos Soc. **RESEARCH** Nineteenth and twentieth century American literature; late Victorian and modern British literature; Henry James and Robert Louis Stevenson. **SELECTED PUBLICATIONS** Auth, Toward the Production of a Text, Time, Space, and David Balfour, Studies in the Novel, Vol 27, 95; Grub Street in a Velvet Coat, The Letters of Robert Louis Stevenson, Vols 1-6, 19th Century Lit, Vol 50, 96. **CONTACT ADDRESS** Dept of English, Univ of Hawaii, 1733 Donaghho Rd, Honolulu, HI, 96822-2368.

MENTO, JOAN
DISCIPLINE THEATRE, SHAKESPEARE, IRISH DRAMA **EDUCATION** MA, PhD. Dipl, Anglo-Irish Studies, Trinity Coll, Dublin. **RESEARCH** Children's theatre, Irish drama. **SELECTED PUBLICATIONS** Rev, plays, Shakespeare Bulletin and NEng Theatre Jour. **CONTACT ADDRESS** Dept of Engl, Westfield State Col, 577 Western Ave., Westfield, MA, 01085.

MERIVALE, PATRICIA
PERSONAL Born 07/19/1934, Derby, England **DISCIPLINE** ENGLISH, COMPARATIVE LITERATURE **EDUCATION** Univ Calif, Berkeley, BA, 55; Oxford Univ, BA, 58, MA, 62; Harvard Univ, PhD(comp lit), 63. **CAREER** From instr to assoc prof, 62-70, PROF ENGLISH, UNIV BC, 70-, Can Coun fels, 69-70. **MEMBERSHIPS** Can Comp Lit Asn (secy-treas, 77-79); MLA; Asn Can Univ Teachers English; Am Comp Lit Asn. **RESEARCH** Artifice and the artist parable; thematics; narrative structure in contemporary fiction. **SELECTED PUBLICATIONS** Auth The Works of Auster, Paul--Approaches and Multiple Readings, Contemporary Lit, Vol 38, 97; The Telling of Lies and the Sea of Stories Haroun, Pinocchio and the Postcolonial Artist Parable, Ariel Rev Int Eng Lit, Vol 28, 97; Literature and the Body, Can Rev Comp Lit Revue Can Litterature Comparee, Vol 22, 95; Atwood, Margaret Fairy Tale Sexual Politics, Eng Stud Can, Vol 22, 96; Beyond the Red Notebook--Essays on Auster, Paul, Contemporary Lit, Vol 38, 97. **CONTACT ADDRESS** Dept of English, Univ of BC, Vancouver, BC, V6T 1W5.

MERKUR, DAN
PERSONAL Born 05/26/1951, Toronto, ON, Canada, m, 1997, 3 children **DISCIPLINE** HUMANITIES **EDUCATION** Stockholm Univ, PhD, 85. **CAREER** Syracuse Univ, asst prof, 86-90; adj prof, Univ of Toronto, York Univ, McMaster Univ, Queens Univ, 92-. **MEMBERSHIPS** CSSR, CSBS, AAR, SBL. **RESEARCH** Religious uses of altered states of consciousness. **SELECTED PUBLICATIONS** Auth, Powers Which We Do Not Know, 91; auth, Becoming Half Hidden, 92; auth, Gnosis, 93; auth, The Ecstatic Imagination, 98; auth, Mystical Moments and Unitive Thinking, 99. **CONTACT ADDRESS** Dept of History of Religion, Toronto Univ, 630 Vesta Dr Apt 103, Toronto, ON, M5N 1J1. **EMAIL** dan.merkur@utoronto.ca

MERRIAM, ALLEN H.
PERSONAL Born 07/28/1942, Orange, NJ, m, 1992, 2 children **DISCIPLINE** SPEECH COMMUNICATION **EDUCATION** Drew Univ, BA, 64; Ohio Univ, MA, 70, PhD, 72. **CAREER** Asst prof, The Col of NJ, 72-77; vis asst prof, Univ of Va, 77-78; asst pro, Va Tech, 78-82; assoc prof, Va Tech, 82-88; prof, Mo S State Col, 88-. **MEMBERSHIPS** Nat Commun Assoc; Assoc for Asian Studs. **RESEARCH** Intercultural rhetoric; history of oratory; third world studies. **SELECTED PUBLICATIONS** Ghandi v0s. Jinnah, The Debate over the Partition of India, 80; numerous articles. **CONTACT ADDRESS** 1419 Marzelle Ct, Joplin, MO, 64801. **EMAIL** merriam-a@mail.mssc.edu

MERRILL, THOMAS F.
PERSONAL Born 01/05/1932, Maplewood, NJ, m, 1957, 4 children **DISCIPLINE** ENGLISH **EDUCATION** Princeton Univ, AB, 54; Univ Nebr, MA, 60; Univ Wis, PhD(English), 64. **CAREER** Asst prof English, Univ Calif, Los Angeles, 64-66; Fulbright-Hays lectr Am lit, Univ Bordeaux, 66-67; asst prof English, DePauw Univ, 67-69; PROF ENGLISH, UNIV DEL, 69-, Fulbright-Hays lectr Am lit, Argentina, 82-83. **MEMBERSHIPS** MLA. **RESEARCH** Modern poetry; Renaissance literature; stylistics. **SELECTED PUBLICATIONS** Auth, Yeats Vision Papers, J Irish Lit, Vol 22, 93; Kavanagh, Patrick--A Critical, J Irish Lit, Vol 22, 93. **CONTACT ADDRESS** Dept of English, Univ of Del, Newark, DE, 19711.

MESEROLE, HARRISON TALBOT
PERSONAL Born 07/25/1921, Brooklyn, NY, m, 1943 **DISCIPLINE** ENGLISH **EDUCATION** Wilson Col, DC, BS, 42; Univ Md, MA, 54, PhD, 60. **CAREER** Instr English, Univ Md, 56-57; from instr to assoc prof, 57-63, assoc head dept, 72-75, PROF ENGLISH, PA STATE UNIV, UNIVERSITY PARK, 63-, HEAD, AM STUDIES PROG, 75-, Assoc bibliogr, MLA, 63-66, bibliogr-in-chief and ed ann MLA Int Biblog, 66-75; COED, SEVENTEENTH-CENTURY NEWS, 69-; ED, WORLD SHAKESPEARE BIBLIOG, 75- **MEMBERSHIPS** MLA; Am Studies Asn; Bibliog Soc Am; Malone Soc; Mod Humanities Res Asn. **RESEARCH** American literature of the 17th, 18th and 19th centuries; bibliography. **SELECTED PUBLICATIONS** Auth, World Shakespeare Bibliography 95, Shakespeare Quart, Vol 47, 96. **CONTACT ADDRESS** Dept of English, Pennsylvania State Univ, University Park, PA, 16802.

MESSBARGER, PAUL ROBERT
PERSONAL Born 10/08/1934, Parnell, MO, m, 1959, 6 children **DISCIPLINE** AMERICAN LITERATURE **EDUCATION** St Benedict's Col Kans, BA, 56; Univ Notre Dame, MA, 58; Univ Minn, Minneapolis, PhD, 69. **CAREER** Instr English, St Ambrose Col, 60-61; asst prof, 65-69, dir honors prog, 66-69, Marquette Univ; assoc prof English & chmn dept, St Mary's Col Ind, 69-73; assoc prof English, Loyola Univ Chicago, 73-. **MEMBERSHIPS** Am Studies Assn; Midwest Mod Lang Assn; AAUP. **RESEARCH** American literary history; American religious history. **SELECTED PUBLICATIONS** Auth, Fiction With a Parochial Purpose, Boston Univ, 71. **CONTACT ADDRESS** Dept of English, Loyola Univ, Chicago, 6525 N Sheridan Rd, Chicago, IL, 60626-5385. **EMAIL** pmessba@orion.it.luc.edu

MESSENGER, CHRISTIAN KARL
PERSONAL Born 01/16/1943, East Orange, NJ, m, 1968, 2 children **DISCIPLINE** AMERICAN AND MODERN FICTION **EDUCATION** Trinity Col, Conn, BA, 65; Northwestern Univ, PhD(English), 74. **CAREER** Asst prof English, Wittenberg Univ, 74-76; asst prof, 76-82, ASSOC PROF ENGLISH, UNIV ILL, CHICAGO, 82- **MEMBERSHIPS** MLA; Popular Cult Asn. **RESEARCH** American fiction; contemporary fiction; popular culture. **SELECTED PUBLICATIONS** Auth, Football as Narrative--Review Article, A Lit Hist, Vol 7, 95; Sporting with the Gods--The Rhetoric of Play and Game in American Culture, Am Hist Rev, Vol 98, 93. **CONTACT ADDRESS** Dept of English, Univ of Ill, Box 4348, Chicago, IL, 60680.

MESTELLER, JEAN C.
DISCIPLINE AMERICAN LITERATURE, AMERICAN STUDIES, WOMEN WRITERS **EDUCATION** Lynchburg Col, BA; Univ Va, MA; Univ Minn, PhD 78. **CAREER** Instr, Univ Minn; Ill State Univ; prof, 78-. **HONORS AND AWARDS** Sally Ann Abshire Awards (3). **RESEARCH** Nineteenth-century popular fiction and the working girl. **SELECTED PUBLICATIONS** Auth, Romancing the Reader: From Laura Jean Libbey to Harlequin Romance and Beyond. **CONTACT ADDRESS** Dept of Eng, Whitman Col, 345 Boyer Ave, Walla Walla, WA, 99362-2038. **EMAIL** mastellerj@whitman.edu

METCALF, ALLAN ALBERT
PERSONAL Born 04/18/1940, Clayton, MO, d, 4 children **DISCIPLINE** ENGLISH, LINGUISTICS **EDUCATION** Cornell Univ, BA, 61; Univ Calif, Berkeley, MA, 64, PhD(English), 66. **CAREER** Asst prof English, Univ Calif, Riverside, 66-73; assoc prof, 73-81, prof English & chmn dept, MacMurray Col, IL, 81-, exec sec, Am Dialect Soc, 81-. **HONORS AND AWARDS** Phi Beta Kappa, Cornell, 61. **MEMBERSHIPS** MLA; Ling Soc Am; Mediaeval Acad Am; Am Dialect Soc; NCTE. **RESEARCH** American English dialects and Lexicography; California dialects; medieval English literature. **SELECTED PUBLICATIONS** Auth, Sir Gawain andyou, Chaucer Rev, Winter 71; The Sopken Language of a Southern California Community, Univ Calif, Riverside, 71; Directions of change in Southern California English, J English Ling, 3/72; Poetic Diction in the Old English Meters of Boethius, Mouton, The Hague, 73; Silent Knight: Sum for Cortaysye? Archiv For das Studium der neueren Sprchen und Literaturen, 76; Chicano English, Ctr Appl Ling, 79; A guide to the California-Nevada field records of the linguistic atlas of the Pacific Coast, Univ Calif, Berkeley, 79; Gawain's number, In: Essays in the Numerical Analysis of Medieval Literature, Bucknell Univ Press, 80; Typography of the Century Dictionary, Dictionaries, v 17, 96; The South in the Dictionary of American Regional English, in: Language Variety in the South Revisited, Univ of Alabama Press, 97; America in So Many Words: Words that Have Shaped America, with David K Barnhart, Houghton Mifflin, 97. **CONTACT ADDRESS** Dept of English, MacMurray Col, 477 E College Ave, Jacksonville, IL, 62650-2510. **EMAIL** aallan@aol.com

METLITZKI, DOROTHEE
PERSONAL Koenigsberg, Germany, 1 child **DISCIPLINE** MIDDLE ENGLISH AND AMERICAN LITERATURE **EDUCATION** Univ London, BA, 36, MA, 38; Yale Univ, PhD(Am studies), 56. **CAREER** Instr English, Hebrew Univ, Jerusalem, 39-44; lectr, British Coun, Cairo, 45-47; press officer, Ministry Foreign Affairs, Israel, 48-51; secy for affairs of Arab women, Israel Fedn Labor, 51-53; William Coe and Sterling fel Am studies, Yale Univ, 53-57; lectr English, Univ Calif, Berkeley, 57-65, assoc prof, 65-67; sr lectr, 65-76, PROF ENGLISH, YALE UNIV, 76-, Am Coun Learned Soc fel, 63. **MEMBERSHIPS** MLA; Mediaeval Acad Am; Am Orient Soc. **RESEARCH** Arabic material in medieval literature; the study of the Bible in the Middle Ages; American orientalism. **SELECTED PUBLICATIONS** Auth On the Meaning of Hatem in Goethe the West Ostlicher Divan, J Am Orient Soc, Vol 0117, 97. **CONTACT ADDRESS** English Dept, Yale Univ, New Haven, CT, 06520.

METZGER, DAVID
DISCIPLINE RHETORIC AND COMPOSITION **EDUCATION** Emporia State Univ, BA; Univ Miss, PhD. **CAREER** Engl, Old Dominion Univ. **HONORS AND AWARDS** Ed, Bien Dire: Jour Lacanian Orientation; Coordr Tchg; Found dir Writing Tutorial Services; English Dept Coun. **RESEARCH** Biblical rhetoric; History of poetics; Psychoanalytical theory; Chaucer. **SELECTED PUBLICATIONS** Ed., Medievalism as an Integrated Study; Lacan and the Question of Writing; Auth,

The Lost Cause of Rhetoric, SIUP 1195 ; Teaching as a Test of Knowledge, Yale UP, 97; Kushner's Angels in America and Queer Mysticism, 97; Freud's Jewish Science and Lacan's Sinthome, Am imago, 97; The Drives and Sexuation, Umbra, 97. **CONTACT ADDRESS** Old Dominion Univ, 4100 Powhatan Ave, Norfolk, VA, 23058. **EMAIL** MMourao@odu.edu

METZGER, LORE
PERSONAL Born 05/08/1925, Frankfurt, Germany **DISCIPLINE** ENGLISH AND COMPARATIVE LITERATURE **EDUCATION** Hunter Col, BA, 46; Columbia Univ, MA, 47, PhD, 56. **CAREER** Instr English, Mt Holyoke Col, 56-59; Am Asn Univ Women fel, 59-60; from instr to asst prof English, Univ Wash, 60-64; assoc prof English and comp lit, Mich State Univ, 64-68; PROF ENGLISH, EMORY UNIV, 68-, Huntington Libr res grant, 63; fel consult, Nat Endowment for Humanities, 71-74. **MEMBERSHIPS** MLA; Am Comp Lit Asn; Southern Comp Lit Asn; Northeast Mod Lang Asn. **RESEARCH** Romanticism; literary theory; modern drama. **SELECTED PUBLICATIONS** Auth, Korinth, Studies in Eighteenth Century Culture, Vol 22, 92. **CONTACT ADDRESS** Dept of English, Emory Univ, Atlanta, GA, 30322.

MEYER, JOHN C.
PERSONAL Born 10/11/1964, Tulsa, OK, m, 1991, 1 child **DISCIPLINE** COMMUNICATION STUDIES **EDUCATION** Phillips Univ, BS, 86; Univ Kans, MA, 88, PhD, 91. **CAREER** Asst prof Speech Commun, Univ S Miss, 91-96; assoc prof of Speech Commun, 96-. **MEMBERSHIPS** Southern States Commun Assoc; Cent States Commun Assoc; Nat Commun Assoc. **RESEARCH** Organizational communication; humor & communication; communication & conflict. **SELECTED PUBLICATIONS** Co-auth, The impact of formats on voter reaction, The 1992 presidential debates in focus, Praeger, 69-83, 94; auth, Tell me a story: Eliciting organizational values fom narratives, Commun Quart, vol 43, 210-224, 95; auth, Seeking organizational unity: Building bridges in response to mystery, South Commun J, vol 61, 210-219, 95; coauth, Children and relationship development: Communication strategies in a day care center, Commun Reports, vol 10, 75-85, 97; Humor in member narratives: Uniting and Dividing at work, West J of Commun, vol 61, 188-208, 97. **CONTACT ADDRESS** Speech Commun Dept, Univ of Southern Miss, Box 5131, Hattiesburg, MS, 39406-5131. **EMAIL** jmeyer@ocean.otr.usm.edu

MEYER, RUSSELL J.
DISCIPLINE ENGLISH LITERATURE **EDUCATION** Ohio State Univ, BA, MA; Univ Minn, PhD. **CAREER** Prof. **RESEARCH** Renaissance Literature; rhetoric; computing. **SELECTED PUBLICATIONS** Auth, Edmund Spenser's Faerie Queene: Educating the Reader, 91; pubs on Spenser, Shakespeare; co-auth, Voices and Visions: An Integrated Approach to Reaching and Writing, 95. **CONTACT ADDRESS** Div of Communcation and Theatre Arts, Emporia State Univ, 1200 Commercial St, Emporia, KS, 66801-5087. **EMAIL** MeyerRus@esumail.emporia.edu

MEYERING, SHERYL L.
DISCIPLINE ENGLISH **EDUCATION** Michigan State Univ, PhD, 86. **CAREER** Asst Prof, 86-88, Michigan State Univ; Asst Prof, 88-93, Assoc Prof, 93-, Southern Illinois Univ Edwardsville **CONTACT ADDRESS** Dept of Eng, Southern Illinois Univ Edwardsville, Box 1431, Edwardsville, IL, 62026. **EMAIL** meyering@aol.com

MEYERS, MARIAN J.
DISCIPLINE MASS COMMUNICATION **EDUCATION** Univ Wis, Madison, MA; Univ Iowa, PhD, 89. **CAREER** Asst prof, Ga State Univ. **RESEARCH** The representation of women and minorities within the news. **SELECTED PUBLICATIONS** Auth, News Coverage of Violence Against Women: Engendering Blame, Sage, 96. **CONTACT ADDRESS** Georgia State Univ, Atlanta, GA, 30303. **EMAIL** joumjm@panther.gsu.edu

MEYERS, RONALD J.
PERSONAL Born 03/01/1936, m, 1959, 2 children **DISCIPLINE** ENGLISH **EDUCATION** Brooklyn Col, BA, 57; Columbia Univ, MA, 59; NY Univ, PhD, 63. **CAREER** Lectr English, Pratt Inst, 59-60; instr, Brooklyn Col, 60-63; asst prof, Temple Univ, 63-66; assoc prof, 66-70, Prof English, East Stroudsburg State Col, 70-, Lectr, Hunter Col, 62-63; NJIT, 68; Rutgers, 69. **MEMBERSHIPS** MLA; PA Assoc of Eng Tchr(s); Dramatists Guild. **RESEARCH** Shakespeare; Eng lit; cult studies. **SELECTED PUBLICATIONS** Auth, O'Neill's use of the Phedre legand in Desire under the elms, Revue de Lit Comp, 1-3/67; The conflict of generations, Apscuf J, 5-6/70; Is symbiosis between technology and letters possible?, Dialogist, spring 71; Catherine de Medici and the Massacre of Paris (hist play), 78; Isabellas Duplicity: Discord of Love Marriage and Family in Shakespears Problem Plays, selected papers from West Virginia Shakespear ans Renaissance assoc, 87; Spout as Ritual and Fantasy, Mosaic, 98. **CONTACT ADDRESS** Dept of Eng, East Stroudsburg Univ of Pennsylvania, 200 Prospect St, East Stroudsburg, PA, 18301-2999. **EMAIL** meyers@esu.edu

MEYERS, TERRY L.
DISCIPLINE ENGLISH **EDUCATION** Lawrence Univ, AB, 67; Univ Chicago, MA, 68, PhD, 73. **CAREER** Instr, 70-73; asst prof, 73-79; assoc prof, 79-94 & prof, 94-, Col William and Mary; assoc dean fac Arts and Sci, 81-84 & ch, Engl Dep, 95-, Col William and Mary. **HONORS AND AWARDS** Ford Found fel; NDEA Title IV fel & Danforth Tutor, Univ Chicago; Alumni fel, 73-74 & Thomas Jefferson Tchg Awd, 80, Col William and Mary; Fac Speaker, Commencement Candlelight Ceremony, 79, 81; Fac Recognition Awd, Swem Libr, 93; VP, 76-78 & pres, 78-80, Victorians Inst; bus ed, Victorians Inst J, 77-79; Reader, article on Swinburne for Victorian Stud, 76; article on Swinburne for Philol Quart, 78; bk on Swinburne for Univ NC Press, 79; PBK Competition entry Letters of Tennyson, Univ Va, 82; lit text for St Martin's Press, 83; AP Engl Exams, ETS, 72-84; preliminary AP Engl Exams, 87 & article on Swinburne for Victorian Poetry, 97, Victorians Inst; rev, NEH, a proposal for a conf at Yale, 89; NEH, a proposal for a conf at the New York Publ Libr, 91 & NEH, grant proposal to support an edition of the collected letters of Christina Rossetti, 94, Victorians Inst; ACLS grant-in-Aid, est $1100, 75; NEH Summer Stipend, est $3700, 87; NEH Travel To Collections grant, $750, 90 & semester res grant, Col William and Mary, 74 & 90. **SELECTED PUBLICATIONS** Auth, Swinburne, Shelley, and Songs before Sunrise, The Whole Music of Passion, Aldershot, England: Scolar Press, 93; Swinburne Shapes His Grand Passion: A Version by 'Ashford Owen, Victorian Poetry 31 1, 93; Two Poems by Swinburne: 'Milton' and On Wagner's Music, Victorian Poetry 31 2, 93; Swinburne's Copyright: Gone Missing, Victorian Poetry 31 2, 93; Found: Swinburne's Copyright, Victorian Poetry, 33 1, 95; Second Thoughts On Rossetti: Tennyson's Revised Letter of October 12, 1882, Tennyson Res Bull, 93; Swinburne and Whitman: Further Evidence, Walt Whitman Quarterly Review, 14 1, 96 & Comments on Amy Clampitt's 'Matoaka, William and Mary Mag, 61 5, 94; ed, The Sexual Tensions of William Sharp: A Study of the Birth of Fiona Macleod, Incorporating Two Lost Works, 'Ariadne in Naxos' and 'Beatrice, NY: Peter Lang Publ, 96; rev, Swinburne's Medievalism: A Study in Victorian Love Poetry, The Daily Press and Times-Herald, 88 & Vanishing Lives: Style and Self in Tennyson, DG Rossetti, Swinburne and Yeats, Engl Lit in Transition, 32 3, 89. **CONTACT ADDRESS** Dept of English, Col of William and Mary, PO Box 8795, Williamsburg, VA, 23187. **EMAIL** tlmeye@facstaff.wm.edu

MEYERS, WALTER EARL
PERSONAL Born 07/01/1939, Pittsburgh, PA, m, 1961, 3 children **DISCIPLINE** SCIENCE FICTION, ENGLISH LINGUISTICS **EDUCATION** Duquesne Univ, BA, 64; Univ Fla, PhD(English), 67. **CAREER** From asst prof to assoc prof, 67-78, PROF ENGLISH, NC STATE UNIV, 78- **HONORS AND AWARDS** SAtlantic Mod Lang Asn Studies Award, 78. **MEMBERSHIPS** Am Dialect Soc; MLA; Sci Fiction Res Asn. **RESEARCH** Medieval drama; modern English usage. **SELECTED PUBLICATIONS** Auth, Linguistics in TextbooksA 40-Year Comparison, Am Speech, Vol 70, 95;The Work of Aldiss, Brian, W.--An Annotated Bibliography and Guide, Sci Fiction Stu, Vol 20, 93; The Grammarians Desk--Krankor, Sci Fiction Stud, Vol 24, 97. **CONTACT ADDRESS** Dept of English, No Carolina State Univ, Raleigh, NC, 27650.

MEZEY, ROBERT
PERSONAL Born 02/28/1935, Philadelphia, PA, m, 1963, 3 children **DISCIPLINE** AMERICAN & EUROPEAN POETRY **EDUCATION** Univ Iowa, BA, 59. **CAREER** Instr English, Western Reserve Univ, 63-64; asst prof, Franklin & Marshall Col, 65-66; asst prof, Fresno State Univ, 67-68; assoc prof, Univ Utah, 73-76; prof Eng & poet in res, Pomona Col, 76-; vis poet, Beaver Col, 64. **HONORS AND AWARDS** Ingram-Merrill Found grantee, 73-74; Guggenheim fel, 77-78; Lamont Poetry Award, 60, Poetry Prize, Am Acad of Arts & Letters, 82. **RESEARCH** Spanish poetry; Thomas Hardy. **SELECTED PUBLICATIONS** Auth, Evening Wind, Wesleyan, 87; ed, Selected Poems of Thomas Hardy, Penguin, 98; ed, Selected Poems of E.A. Robinson, Modern Library, 99. **CONTACT ADDRESS** Dept of English, Pomona Col, 140 W Sixth St, Claremont, CA, 91711-6319. **EMAIL** rmezey@pomona.edu

MICHAEL, JOHN
DISCIPLINE ENGLISH **EDUCATION** Johns Hopkins Univ, PhD. **CAREER** Assoc prof & dir grad stud; taught at, Univ Warsaw Poland, Johns Hopkins Univ & SUNY at Geneseo. **RESEARCH** Contemp rel between academic intellectuals and popular polit; problematics of national identity in Am literary romances and films; complex interrelations between the interpretation of lit and the reading of hist. **SELECTED PUBLICATIONS** Auth, Emerson and Skepticism: The Cipher of the World; articles on, Emerson, Hawthorne, Poe, neo-pragmatism, the Frankfur t School, Eastern Europe, Stephen Hawking, intellectuals & contemporary cultural politics. **CONTACT ADDRESS** Dept of Eng, Univ of Rochester, 601 Elmwood Ave, Ste. 656, Rochester, NY, 14642. **EMAIL** jnml@troi.cc.rochester.edu

MICHAEL, MARION C.
PERSONAL Born 05/17/1930, Monroe, GA, m, 1957, 2 children **DISCIPLINE** ENGLISH **EDUCATION** Univ Ga, AB, 50, PhD (English), 63; Univ Va, MA, 55. **CAREER** Instr English, Univ Ga, 55-57, 59-61; from asst prof to assoc prof, Southeastern La Col, 61-65; from asst prof to assoc prof, Auburn Univ, 65-71, chmn freshman English, 66-71; prof English and chmn dept, Tex Tech Univ, 71-82; DEAN SCH LIBERAL ARTS AND PROF ENGLISH, AUBURN UNIV, MONTGOMERY, 82-, ASSOC ED, CONRADIANA, UNIV MD, 68- **MEMBERSHIPS** MLA; SAtlantic Mod Lang Asn; Joseph Conrad Soc. **RESEARCH** Conrad. **SELECTED PUBLICATIONS** Auth, The Political Paradox Within Deillo, Don Libra, Critique Stud Contemporary Fiction, Vol 35, 94; Carter, Angela Nights at the Circus, An Engaged Feminism Via Subversive Postmodern Strategies, Contemporary Lit, Vol 35, 94. **CONTACT ADDRESS** Dept of English, Auburn Univ, Montgomery, AL, 36117.

MICHAELS, LEONARD
PERSONAL Born 01/02/1933, New York, NY, m, 1965, 2 children **DISCIPLINE** ENGLISH **EDUCATION** NY Univ, BA, 53; Univ Mich, MA, 56, PhD(English), 67. **CAREER** Asst prof English, Paterson State Col, 62-63 and Univ Calif, Davis, 67-69; from asst prof to assoc prof, 69-76, PROF ENGLISH, UNIV CALIF, BERKELEY, 76-, Mem, Univ Calif Inst Creative Art, 68 and Nat Found on Art, 68; Guggenheim fel, 70-71. **MEMBERSHIPS** Am Acad Arts and Sci. **RESEARCH** Romantic poetry and prose; modern literature. **SELECTED PUBLICATIONS** Auth, Editors Note , Film Criticism, Vol 17, 93 The Confidence Man in Modern Film, University of Toronto Quarterly, Vol 62, 93; A Girl With a Monkey, Partisan Rev, Vol 63, 96; Shooting a Melon, The Target Practice Sequence in the Day of the Jackal, Film Criticism, Vol 18, 94; Goldsworthy,James--InMemoriam, Film Criticism, Vol 20, 96; An Interview with Michaels, Leonard, New England Rev Middlebury Series, Vol 15, 93 **CONTACT ADDRESS** Dept of English, Univ of Calif, Berkeley, CA, 94720.

MICHAELSON, PAT
DISCIPLINE LITERATURE STUDIES **EDUCATION** Univ Chicago, PhD, 85. **CAREER** Asst prof. **RESEARCH** Comparative studies in literature; 18th century literature and women's studies. **SELECTED PUBLICATIONS** Auth, Women in the Reading Circle, Eighteenth Century Life, 89; Reading Pride and Prejudice, Eighteenth Century Fiction, 90. **CONTACT ADDRESS** Dept of Literature, Richardson, TX, 75083-0688. **EMAIL** pmichael@utdallas.edu

MICHALCZYK, JOHN JOSEPH
PERSONAL Born 06/26/1941, Scranton, PA, m, 3 children **DISCIPLINE** FRENCH LITERATURE, CINEMA **EDUCATION** Boston Col, BA, 66, MA, 67; Harvard Univ, PhD (French lit & cinema), 72; Weston Col, MDiv, 74. **CAREER** Instr & chmn French & cinema, Loyola High Sch, Towson, Md, 67-69; instr, int French through film, Harvard Univ, 71-71; instr, graduate summer program in French, Rivier Col (Nashua, NH), 72-76; asst prof French & cinema, 74-80, assoc prof Fine Arts Dept, Boston Col, 80-, dir of film studies, Boston Col, 84-, prof & chmn Fine Arts Dept, 96-. **HONORS AND AWARDS** 2 New England Emmy Nominations for films: "Of Stars and Shamrocks: Boston's Jews & Irish" and "In the Shadow of the Reich: Nazi Medicine"; Distinguished documentary award from TASH (The Asn for the Severely Handicapped) for "Nazi Medicine"; "Palmes Academiques" from French Government for 25 years of contributions to French culture; Directory of American Scholars; Contemporary Authors; Fulbright (Italy); Mellon (Costa-Gavras). **MEMBERSHIPS** Malraux Soc. **RESEARCH** Issues of Social Justice in art, literature, and film; documentary film production. **SELECTED PUBLICATIONS** Auth, Malraux, le cinema, et La Condition humaine, 1/74 & Le cinema polonais en '73, 4/74, Cinema '74; Camus/Malraux: A staged version of Le Temps du mepris, 10/76 & Robbe-Grillet, Michelet and Barthes: From La Sorciere to Glissements progressifs du plaisir, 12/77, Fr Rev; Andre Malraux's Film Espoir: The Propaganda/Art Film and the Spanish Civil War, Romance Monogr, 77; Ingmar Bergman: La, Passion d'etre homme aujourd'hue, Beauchesne, Paris, 77; Recurrent Imagery of the Labyrinth in Robbe-Grillet's Films, Stanford Fr Rev, spring 78; The French Literary Filmmakers, Asn Univ Press, 80; Costa-Gavras: The Political Fiction Film, Arts Alliance Press, 84; Italian Political Filmmakers, Fairleigh Dickinson Univ Press, 86; Medicine, Ethics, and the Third Reich: Historical and Contemporary Issues, Sheed and Ward, 94; The Resisters, the Rescuers, and the Refugees, Sheed and Ward, 97; and articles on film and its relation to literature and the arts in: American Soc Legion of Honor; Annali d'Iliansistica; Cineaste; Cinema (Paris); Cinema and Soc (Paris); Contemporary French Civ; Current Research in Film; French Review; Lit/Film Quart; Magill's Cinema Annual; Melanges Malraux Miscellany; Stanford French Review; Twentieth Century Lit. **CONTACT ADDRESS** Fine Arts Dept, Boston Col, 140 Commonwealth Ave, Chestnut Hill, MA, 02167-3800. **EMAIL** john.michalczyk@bc.edu

MICHELSON, BRUCE FREDERIC
PERSONAL Born 10/19/1948, Baltimore, MD, m, 1973, 2 children **DISCIPLINE** AMERICAN & MODERN LITERATURE, MARK TWAIN **EDUCATION** Williams Col, AB, 70; Univ WA, MA, 73, PhD, 76. **CAREER** Asst prof English & dir Undergrad Advising, Univ IL, Urbana, 76-82; assoc prof

English, Univ IL, 83-93; Fulbright Lecturer, BEL, 83-84; PROF ENGLISH, UNIV IL, URBANA, 93-; DIR CAMPUS HONORS PROG, 96-. **MEMBERSHIPS** MLA; Am Lit Asn; Mid America Am Studies Asn; Fulbright Asn; Richard Wilbur Soc; Mark Twain Circle. **RESEARCH** Mark Twain; contemporary poetry. **SELECTED PUBLICATIONS** Auth, Mark Twain the Tourist: The Form of The Innocents Abroad, Am Lit, 11/77; Richard Wilbur: The Quarrel with Poe, Southern Rev, 4/78; Richard Wilbur's, The Mind-Reader, Southern Rev, 7/79; Huck and the Games of the World, Am Libr Rev, 3/80; Deus Ludens: The Shaping of Mark Twain's Mysterious Stranger, Novel, 10/80; The Myth of Gatsby, Modern Fiction Studies, 1/81; Wilbur's Words, MA Rev, 4/82; auth, Wilbur's Poetry: Music in a Scattering Time, 91; Mark Twain on the Loose: A Comic Writer and the American Self, 95; articles on Twain, Hawthorne, Bellow, Wharton, Jarrell, Frederic, Keillor, and others. **CONTACT ADDRESS** Honors House, Univ Illinois, 1205 W Oregon, Urbana, IL, 61801-3613. **EMAIL** brucem@staff.uiuc.edu

MICHIE, ELSIE B.
DISCIPLINE VICTORIAN NOVEL **EDUCATION** Yale Univ, PhD, 84. **CAREER** Assoc prof, assoc ch, dept Eng, mem, women's and gender stud fac, adj mem, comp lit fac, La State Univ. **RESEARCH** Women, property, and narrative in novels and film; race, class and gender. **SELECTED PUBLICATIONS** Auth, Production Replaces Creation: Market Forces and Frankenstein as a Critique of Romanticism, in 19th-Century Contexts, 89; Frankenstein and Marx's Theories of Alienated Labor, in Approaches to Teaching Frankenstein, 90; From Simianized Irish to Orient Despots: Heathcliff, Rochester, and Racial Difference, Novel, 92; Outside the Pale: Cultural Exclusion, Gender Difference, and the Victorian Woman Writer, 93; White Chimpanzees and Oriental Despots: Racial Stereotyping and Edward Rochester, in Jane Eyre, 96. **CONTACT ADDRESS** Dept of Eng, Louisiana State Univ, 210G Allen Hall, Baton Rouge, LA, 70803. **EMAIL** enmich@unix1.sncc.lsu.edu

MICKELSON, SIG
DISCIPLINE MASS COMMUNICATIONS **EDUCATION** Univ Minn, MA, 40; Augustana Col, hon LLD, 87. **CAREER** Distinguished prof, ch, The Manship Sch of Mass Commun, La State Univ; pres, CBS News; hd, Radio Free Europe/Radio Liberty; vpres, CBS, Inc, Time-Life Broadcast Inc, The Encycl Britannica Educ Corp. **SELECTED PUBLICATIONS** Auth, America's Other Voice, the Story of Radio Free Europe and Radio Liberty, Praeger, 83; The First Amendment and the Challenge of New Technology, Praeger, 89; From Whistlestop to Sound Bite: Four Decades of Politics and Television, Praeger, 89; The Northern Pacific Railroad and the Selling of the West: A Case Study of a Nineteenth Century Public Relations Venture, Ctr for Western Stud, 93. **CONTACT ADDRESS** The Manship Sch of Mass Commun, Louisiana State Univ, Baton Rouge, LA, 70803.

MIDDENDORF, JOHN HARLAN
PERSONAL Born 03/31/1922, New York, NY, m, 1943, 2 children **DISCIPLINE** ENGLISH **EDUCATION** Dartmouth Col, AB, 43; Columbia Univ, AM, 47, PhD, 53. **CAREER** From instr to assoc prof English, Columbia Univ, 50-65, prof, 65-80, dir grad studies English and comp lit, 71-74, vchmn dept, 75-80. Co-ed, Johnsonian Newslett, 50-78, ed, 78-; Coun Res in Humanities res grant, 58-59; Am Philos Soc grant, 62; Am Coun Learned Soc grant-in-aid, 62; mem English compos test comt, Col Entrance Exam Bd, 61-67, chmn, 67-69; assoc ed, Yale Ed Works of Samuel Johnson, 62-66, gen ed, 66-; chmn, The Johnsonians, 69 and 79; chmn, Sem Eighteenth Century Cult, Columbia Univ, 73-75; NAT ENDOWMENT FOR HUMANITIES RES GRANT, 76- **MEMBERSHIPS** The Johnsonians (secy-treas, 58-68); Grolier Club; MLA; Oxford Bibliog Soc; Am Soc 18th Century Studies. **RESEARCH** Samuel Johnson and his circle; economic theory and attitudes in 18th century English literature; bibliography and editing. **SELECTED PUBLICATIONS** Auth, Johnson, Samuel in the Medical World--The Doctor and the Patient, 18th Century Studies, Vol 26, 93. **CONTACT ADDRESS** 404 Riverside Dr, New York, NY, 10025.

MIDDLEBROOK, JONATHAN
PERSONAL Born 10/06/1940, New York, NY, m, 1973, 2 children **DISCIPLINE** ENGLISH LITERATURE **EDUCATION** Harvard Univ, BA, 61; Yale Univ, MA, 63, PhD, 65. **CAREER** Asst prof English, Univ Calif, Berkeley, 65-69; lectr, 69-71, assoc prof, 71-76, prof English San Francisco State Univ, 76-, res fel, Univ Reading, UK, 71. **HONORS AND AWARDS** Magna Cum Laude, PBK, Woodrow Wilson Fellow. **MEMBERSHIPS** MLA, American Name Society. **RESEARCH** African-American lit; Shakespeare; 19th century British and American literature. **SELECTED PUBLICATIONS** Ed, Matthew Arnold Dover Beach, C E Merrill, 70; auth, Mailer and the Times of his time, Bay Bks, 76. **CONTACT ADDRESS** Dept of English, San Francisco State Univ, 1600 Holloway Ave, San Francisco, CA, 94132-1740. **EMAIL** nonce@sfsu.edu

MIDDLETON, ANNE LOUISE
PERSONAL Born 07/14/1940, Detroit, MI **DISCIPLINE** ENGLISH **EDUCATION** Univ Mich, BA, 62; Harvard Univ, MA, 63, PhD, 66. **CAREER** From Asst Prof to Assoc Prof, 66-80, Prof English, Univ Calif, Berkeley, 81-. **MEMBERSHIPS** MLA; Mediaeval Acad Am; Medieval Asn Pac; New Chaucer Soc. **RESEARCH** Old and Middle English literature. **CONTACT ADDRESS** Dept of English, Univ of Calif, 322 Wheeler Hall, Berkeley, CA, 94720-1030. **EMAIL** medieval@socrates.berkeley.edu

MIDDLETON, JOYCE IRENE
DISCIPLINE ENGLISH **EDUCATION** Univ MD, PhD. **CAREER** Asst prof; taught at, Univ MD at Col Park & Penn State Univ; postdoctoral fel, Univ MD. **RESEARCH** Lit of African Am women writers; Toni Morrison; hist and contemp theories of rhetoric; tchg, orality; literacy; memory. **SELECTED PUBLICATIONS** Articles and rev(s) on, Toni Morrison, Zora Neale Hurston, rhetoric & compos. **CONTACT ADDRESS** Dept of Eng, Univ of Rochester, 601 Elmwood Ave, Ste. 656, Rochester, NY, 14642. **EMAIL** jmdt@db1.cc.rochester.edu

MIESZKOWSKI, GRETCHEN
PERSONAL Born 06/13/1938, Plainfield, NJ, m, 1963, 2 children **DISCIPLINE** ENGLISH LITERATURE **EDUCATION** Vassar Col, BA, 60; Yale Univ, MA, 62, PhD, 65. **CAREER** Instr Eng, Univ Chicago, 64-65; from instr to asst prof, Yale Univ, 65-71; asst prof, Queen's Univ, 72-73; assoc prof, 74-79, Prof Lit, Univ Houston Clear Lake, 79-, Am Coun Learned Soc fel, 78-79; Inst Independent Study fel, Radcliffe Col, 78-79. **HONORS AND AWARDS** Piper Award for Excellence in Tchg, Piper Found, 78. **MEMBERSHIPS** MLA; S Cent Mod Lang Asn; New Chaucer Soc; S Cent Womens Studies Asn **RESEARCH** Medieval lit; Shakespeare; women in lit. **SELECTED PUBLICATIONS** Auth, The Reputation of Criseyde: 1155-1500, Conn Acad Arts & Sci, 71; Pandras in Deschamp's Ballade for Chaucer, Chaucer Rev, 75; R K Gordon and the Troilus and Criseyde Story, Chaucer Rev, 80; Chaucer's Pandarus and Jean Brasdefer's Houdee, Chaucer Rev, 85; No Longer By a Miracle, a Twin: Helen Vendler's Reviews of Adrienne Rich's Recent Poetry, South Central Rev, 88; Chaucer's Much Loved Criseyde, Chaucer Rev, 91; The Prose Lancelot's Galehot, Malory's Lavain, and the Queering of Late Medieval Literature, Arthurian, 95. **CONTACT ADDRESS** Univ of Houston Clear Lake, 2700 Bay Area Blvd, Houston, TX, 77058-1025. **EMAIL** mieszkowski@uhcl.cl.uh.edu

MIGNON, CHARLES WILLIAM
PERSONAL Born 12/11/1933, New York, NY, m, 1959, 2 children **DISCIPLINE** ENGLISH **EDUCATION** Kenyon Col, BA, 56; Univ Conn, MA, 59, PhD(English), 63. **CAREER** Asst prof English, Univ Ill, 63-67; from asst prof to assoc prof, 67-73; actg chmn dept, 77-78, PROF ENGLISH, UNIV NEBR, LINCOLN, 73-, Fulbright lectr, Inst English, Warsaw Univ, 72-73. **RESEARCH** Edward Taylor; American transcendentalists; Ralph W Emersn. **SELECTED PUBLICATIONS** Auth, Design in Puritan American Literature, New England Quart Histl Rev New England Life Letters, Vol 66, 93. **CONTACT ADDRESS** Dept of English, Univ of Nebr, Lincoln, NE, 68508.

MIKA, JOSEPH JOHN
PERSONAL Born 03/01/1948, McKees Rocks, PA, s, 3 children **DISCIPLINE** LIBRARY EDUCATION **EDUCATION** Univ Pitts, BA, 69, MLS, 71, PhD, 80. **CAREER** Asst librn & instr, Ohio State Univ, 71-73; asst librn & asst prof, Johnson State Col, 73-75; grad asst, tchg fel School Libr & Info Sci, Univ Pitts, 75-55; asst dean, assoc prof libr sci, Univ S Miss, 77-86, dir libr & info sci prog, PROF, 94- , WAYNE STATE UNIV; CO-ED JOUR EDUC LIBR & INFO SCI, 95- . **MEMBERSHIPS** Phi Delta Kappa. **SELECTED PUBLICATIONS** Articles to prof jour. **CONTACT ADDRESS** Libr & Info Sci Prog, Wayne State Univ, 106 Kresge Library, Detroit, MI, 48202.

MIKELONIS-PARASKOV, VICTORIA M.
DISCIPLINE RHETORIC STUDIES **EDUCATION** Ind Univ Pa, MA, PhD. **CAREER** Prof **RESEARCH** Intercultural communication; design of training materials; schema theory. **SELECTED PUBLICATIONS** Auth, The Role of Models in Technical Writing; co-auth, Procedure for Designing and Writing Training Materials. **CONTACT ADDRESS** Rhetoric Dept, Univ of Minnesota, Twin Cities, 64 Classroom Office Bldg, 1994 Buford Ave, St. Paul, MN, 55108. **EMAIL** vmikel@hhh.tc.umn.edu

MIKO, STEPHEN
DISCIPLINE ENGLISH LITERATURE **EDUCATION** Yale Univ, PhD, 67. **CAREER** ASSOC PROF, ENG, UNIV CALIF, SANTA BARBARA. **RESEARCH** Modern novel. **SELECTED PUBLICATIONS** Auth, Toward Women in Love, Yale Univ Press, 71; ed, Twentieth-Century Interpretations of Women in Love, Prentice-Hall, 69. **CONTACT ADDRESS** Dept of Eng, Univ Calif, Santa Barbara, CA, 93106-7150.

MILDER, ROBERT
PERSONAL Born 06/03/1945, New York, NY, m, 1970, 2 children **DISCIPLINE** AMERICAN LITERATURE **EDUCATION** Union Col, BA, 67; Harvard Univ, MA, 68, PhD, 72. **CAREER** From asst prof to assoc prof, 72-90, prof, 90- , Washington Univ. **HONORS AND AWARDS** Summa Cum Laude, 67; Phi Beta Kappa; Harvard Graduate Prize fel; NEH fel, 80. **MEMBERSHIPS** MLA; ALA; Melville Soc; Emerson Soc; Thoreau Soc; Hawthorne Soc. **RESEARCH** Nineteenth century American literature. **SELECTED PUBLICATIONS** Ed, Critical Essays on Melville's Billy Budd, Sailor, G.K. Hall, 89; auth, Reimagining Thoreau, Cambridge, 95; auth, The Scarlet Letter and Its Discontents, Nathaniel Hawthorne Rev, 96; ed and intro, Billy Budd, Sailor and Selected Tales, Oxford, 97; co-ed, Melville's Evermoving Dawn: Centennial Essays, Kent State, 97; auth, Melville and the Avenging Dream, in Levine, ed, The Cambridge Companion to Melville, Cambridge, 98; auth, The Radical Emerson? in Porte, ed, The Cambridge Companion to Emerson, Cambridge, 99; auth, An Arch Between Two Lives: Melville in the Mediterranean, 1856-57, Arizona Q, 99; auth, Hawthorne's Winter Dreams, Nineteenth-Century Lit, 99. **CONTACT ADDRESS** Washington Univ, PO Box 1122, St. Louis, MO, 63130. **EMAIL** rmilder@artsci.wustl.edu

MILES, JOSEPHINE
PERSONAL Born 06/11/1911, Chicago, IL **DISCIPLINE** ENGLISH PHILOLOGY AND CRITICISM **EDUCATION** Univ Calif, Los Angeles, AB, 32; Univ Calif, AM, 34, PhD, 38. **CAREER** From instr to prof, 40-52, UNIV PROF ENGLISH, UNIV CALIF, BERKELEY, 52-, Am Asn Univ Women res fel, 39-40; Guggenheim fel, 48-49; Am Coun Learned Soc fel, 64-65; Nat Found Arts fel, 67-68 and 79-80. Shelley Award, 35; Nat Inst Arts and Lett Award, 56; Lowell Award, MLA, 75. **HONORS AND AWARDS** DLitt, Mills Col, 66. **MEMBERSHIPS** MLA; Am Soc Aesthet; Philol Asn Pac Coast; Am Acad Arts and Sci; fel Acad Am Poets. **RESEARCH** Literary history; linguistics; modern poetry. **SELECTED PUBLICATIONS** Auth, The Sound of Silence, Lingua Fr, Vol 7,94; What Makes God God Like, Parnassus Poetry Rev, Vol 19, 94. **CONTACT ADDRESS** Dept of English, Univ of Calif, Berkeley, CA, 94720.

MILEUR, JEAN-PIERRE
DISCIPLINE ENGLISH LITERATURE **EDUCATION** Univ Calif-Berkeley, BA; Yale Univ, PhD. **CAREER** DEAN, GRAD DIV, UNIV CALIF, RIVERSIDE. **RESEARCH** Connections between romanticism and critical theory. **SELECTED PUBLICATIONS** Auth, Vision and Revision: Coleridge's Art of Immanence, Univ Calif Press, 82; Literary Revisionism and the Burden of Modernity, Univ Calif Press, 85; The Critical Romance, Univ Wis Press, 90; co-auth, Nietzsche's Case: Philosophy as/and Literature, Routledge, 92. **CONTACT ADDRESS** Dept of Eng, Univ Calif, 1156 Hinderaker Hall, Riverside, CA, 92521-0209.

MILIC, LOUIS TONKO
PERSONAL Born 09/05/1922, Split, Yugoslavia, m, 3 children **DISCIPLINE** ENGLISH, STYLISTICS **EDUCATION** Columbia Univ, AB, 48, MA, 50, PhD, 63. **CAREER** Instr English, Mont State Col, 52-54; lectr, Columbia Univ, 55-58, from instr to asst prof, 58-67, assoc prof, Teachers Col, 67-69; chmn dept, 69-78, PROF ENGLISH, CLEVELAND STATE UNIV, 69-, Rev ed, Comput and Humanities, 66-71; Am Coun Learned Soc/Int Bus Mach fel, 67-68; GEN ED, NEW HUMANISTIC RES SER, TEACHERS COL; CO-ED, THE GAMUT, 79-; Nat Endowment for Humanities fel, summer, 80. **MEMBERSHIPS** Int Asn Univ Professors English; Am Soc 18th Century Studies; Asn Comput in Humanities; Asn Appl Ling. **RESEARCH** Rhetoric; 18th century English literature; computer-assisted literary research. **SELECTED PUBLICATIONS** Auth, Quantitative Aspects of Genre in the Century of Prose Corpus, Style, Vol 28, 94; Words of Ones Own, Some Evidence Against Mens Use of Language as a Tool of Domination, Style, Vol 29, 95 A Comment on Finch, Alison Article, Style, Vol 29, 95; A Comment on Finch, Alison Article, Style, Vol 29, 95. **CONTACT ADDRESS** 3111 Chelsea Dr, Cleveland Heights, OH, 44118.

MILLEDGE, LUETTA UPSHUR
PERSONAL Savannah, GA **DISCIPLINE** ENGLISH **EDUCATION** Ft Valley State Coll, BA English 1948; Atlanta Univ, MA English 1949; Univ Georgia, PhD English 1971. **CAREER** SAVANNAH STATE COLL, asst instructor 1949-, assoc prof, prof, chr div humn 1973-80, hd dept English 1972-80, hd dept humnl/fine arts 1980-84, head department of humanities 1984-91, PROF EMERITA 1991-. **HONORS AND AWARDS** Regent's Scholarship 1944-48; Ford Found Fellowship 1969-71; George Washington Honor Medal; Freedoms Found Valley Forge Speech Vital Spchs 1973; Phi Kappa Phi, Phi Beta Kappa, Univ of GA; Co-Teacher of the Year School of Humanities 1989. **MEMBERSHIPS** Brd mem GA Endowment for Humanities 1980-83; Elder Butler Presbytery Church; mem Presid Comm Futr Savannah State Coll. **CONTACT ADDRESS** Savannah State Col, Savannah, GA, 31404.

MILLER, CAROLYN R.
PERSONAL Born 04/29/1945, Boston, MA, m, 1967 **DISCIPLINE** COMMUNICATION AND RHETORIC **EDUCA-**

TION Rensselaer Polytechnic Inst, PhD, 80. **CAREER** Visiting assoc prof, Dept of Humanities, Mich Tech Univ, spring quarter, 88; visiting assoc prof, Dept of English, Penn State Univ, summer 88; visiting prof, Dept of Lit, Commun, and Culture, Ga Inst of Tech, winter & spring quarters, 91; INST, DEPT OF ENGLISH, 77-79, ASST PROF, 80-83, ASSOC PROF, 83-90, PROF, NC STATE UNIV, 90-. **HONORS AND AWARDS** Best Article in the Philos or Theory of Tech and Sci Commun, Nat Coun of Teachers of English, 1975-1980, 81 and Best Collection of Essays in Sci and Tech Commun, 84; Outstanding Teacher Award, NC State Univ, 84; Fel for Col Teachers, Nat Endowment for the Humanities, 92-93; Fel, Asn of Teachers of Tech Writing, 95. **MEMBERSHIPS** Asn of Teachers of Tech Writing; Conf on Col Composition and Commun; Coun for Progs in Tech and Sci Commun; Int Soc for the Hist of Rhetoric; MLA; Nat Coun of Teachers of English; Rhetoric Soc of Am; Soc for Social Studies of Sci; Nat Commun Asn. **RESEARCH** Rhetorical theory; rhetoric of science and technology; rhetoric of professions and disciplines. **SELECTED PUBLICATIONS** Auth, Opportunity, Opportunism, and Progress: Kairos in the Rhetoic of Technology, Argumentation, 94; auth, "Learning from History: World War II and the Culture of High Technology," Journal of Business and Tech Commun, 98; auth, Rhetorical Community: The Cultural Basis of Genre, Genre and the New Rhetoric, Taylor and Francis, 94; auth, Classical Rhetoric without Nostalgia: A Response to Gaonkar, Rhetorical Hermeneutics, SUNY Press, 96; coauth, Reading Darwin, Reading Nature or On the Ethos of Historical Science, Understanding Scientific Prose, Univ of Wis Press, 93; auth, The Low-Level Radioactive Waste Siting Controversy in North Carolina: Toward a Rhetorical Model of Risk Communication, in Green Culture: Environmental Rhetroric in Contemporary America, Univ of Wis, 96; co-ed, Making and Unmaking the Prospects for Rhetoric: Selected papers from the 1996 Rhetoric Society of America Conference, Lawrence Erlbaum, 97. **CONTACT ADDRESS** English Dept, No Carolina State Univ, Box 8105, Raleigh, NC, 27695-8105. **EMAIL** crmiller@ncsu.edu

MILLER, CLARENCE HARVEY
PERSONAL Born 08/04/1930, Kansas City, MO, m, 1959, 4 children **DISCIPLINE** ENGLISH LITERATURE, HUMANISM **EDUCATION** St Louis Univ, AB, 51; Harvard Univ, MA, 52, PhD(English), 55. **CAREER** From instr to assoc prof, 57-66, PROF ENGLISH, ST LOUIS UNIV, 66-, Fulbright prof English, Univ Wuerzburg, WGer, 60-61; Guggenheim fel, 66-67; guest prof English, Ruhr-Univ, WGer, 76-77. **MEMBERSHIPS** MLA; Amici Thomae Mori; Mod Humanities Res Asn; Renaissance Soc Am. **RESEARCH** Renaissance nondramatic English literature; Thomas More; Erasmus. **SELECTED PUBLICATIONS** Auth, An Unpublished Note from Robinson, Edwin, Arlington to Beach, Stewart, Editor of The Independent, Anq Quart J Short Articles Notes Revs, Vol 6, 93; More, Thomas Letters to Vancranevelt, Frans, Including 7 Recently Discovered Autographs--Latin Text, English Translation, and Facsimiles of the Originals, Moreana, Vol 31, 94; The Devils Bow and Arrows--Another Clue to the Identity of the Yeoman in Chaucer Friars Tale, Chaucer Rev, Vol 30, 95; Humanist Play and Belief--The Seriocomic Art of Erasmus, Desiderius, Renaissance Quart, Vol 46, 93. **CONTACT ADDRESS** Dept of English, St Louis Univ, St Louis, MO, 63108.

MILLER, EDMUND
PERSONAL Born 07/18/1943, Queens, NY, s **DISCIPLINE** ENGLISH **EDUCATION** C.W. Post Campus Long Island Univ, BA (summa cum laude), 65; Ohio State Univ, MA, 69; State Univ of NY at Stony Brook, PhD, 75. **CAREER** ASST PROF, 81-86, ASSOC PROF, 86-90, PROF, 90-, CHEMN, C.W. POST CAMPUS, LONG ISLAND UNIV, 93-. **SELECTED PUBLICATIONS** Auth, Drudgerie Divine: The Rhetoric of God and Man in George Herbert, Universitat Salzburg, 79; George Herbert's Kinships: An Ahnentafel with Annotations, Heritage Press, 93; Exercises in Style, Ill State Univ, 80, privately printed, 90; The School for Coeds, Key, 72; co-ed, Like Season'd Timber: New Essays on George Herbert, Peter Lang, 87; ed, Mount-Orgueil or, Divine and Profitable Meditations, Scholars' Facsimiles & Reprints, 84. **CONTACT ADDRESS** English Dept, Long Island Univ, C.W. Post, Brookville, NY, 11548-1300. **EMAIL** Edmiller@phoenix.liunet.edu

MILLER, EDWIN HAVILAND
PERSONAL Born 09/02/1918, Johnstown, PA, m, 1946, 1 child **DISCIPLINE** ENGLISH LITERATURE **EDUCATION** Lehigh Univ, AB, 40; Pa State Col, AM, 42; Harvard Univ, PhD, 51. **CAREER** Instr English, Pa State Col, 40-42 and 45-46; from instr to prof, Simmons Col, 47-61; assoc prof, 61-62, chmn dept, 68-73, PROF ENGLISH, NY UNIV, 62-, Res fel, Folger Shakespeare Libr, 53; Am Coun Learned Soc fel, 59-60; Guggenheim fels, 67-68 and 78-79. **MEMBERSHIPS** MLA; Col English Asn. **RESEARCH** American literature; literature and psychology. **SELECTED PUBLICATIONS** Auth, Symphony New Brunswick--Quartets, Quintets and Full Orchestra, Performing Arts and Entertainment in Canada, Vol 30, 96; Allen, Gay, Wilson, 1903-95, Walt Whitman Quart Rev, Vol 13, 95; Federal Sentencing Guidelines for Organizational Defendants, Vanderbilt Law Rev, Vol 46, 93. **CONTACT ADDRESS** Dept of English, New York Univ, New York, NY, 10003.

MILLER, ELIZABETH A.
PERSONAL Born 02/26/1939, St. John's, NF, Canada **DISCIPLINE** LITERATURE **EDUCATION** Memorial Univ Nfld, MA, 75, PhD 88. **CAREER** High sch tchr & prin, 58-68; dir comm, Nfld Tchrs Asn, 68-70; PROF ENGLISH, MEMORIAL UNIV NFLD, 70-. **MEMBERSHIPS** Asn Can Col & Univ Tchrs Eng; Int Asn Fantastic Arts; Int Bram Stoker Soc; British Gothic Soc. **SELECTED PUBLICATIONS** Auth, The Life and Times of Ted Russell, 81; auth, The Frayed Edge: Norman Duncan's Newfoundland, 92; auth, Reflections on Dracula, 97; ed, The Chronicles of Uncle Mose, 75; ed, Tales from Pigeon Inlet, 77; ed, The Best of Ted Russell, 82; ed, Stories from Uncle Mose, 83; ed, A Fresh Breeze from Pigeon Inlet, 88; ed, The Holdin' Ground and Ground Swell, 90; ed, Arms and the Newfoundlander, 94; co-ed, Banked Fires, 89; co-ed, Tempered Days, 96. **CONTACT ADDRESS** Dept of English, Memorial Univ of Newfoundland, St. John's, NF, A1C 5S7. **EMAIL** emiller@morgan.ucs.mun.ca

MILLER, EUGENE ERNEST
PERSONAL Born 04/18/1930, Akron, OH, m, 1962, 2 children **DISCIPLINE** ENGLISH **EDUCATION** Univ Notre Dame, BA, 55; Ohio Univ, MA, 62; Univ Ill, Urbana, PhD(English), 67. **CAREER** ASSOC PROF ENGLISH, ALBION COL, 67-, Nat Endowment for Humanities fel, Howard Univ, 71-72. **MEMBERSHIPS** MLA; Col English Asn. **RESEARCH** English; Afro-American literature; aesthetics. **SELECTED PUBLICATIONS** Auth, Wright, Richard, Community, and the French Connection,20th Century Lit, Vol 41, 95; Native Son, African Am Rev, Vol 27, 93; Minor Casualities, African Am Rev, Vol 30, 96. **CONTACT ADDRESS** Dept of English, Albion Col, Albion, MI, 49224.

MILLER, GABRIEL
PERSONAL Born 08/03/1948, Bronx, NY, m, 1974, 2 children **DISCIPLINE** MODERN AMERICAN FICTION, AMERICAN DRAMA & FILM **EDUCATION** Queens Col, BA, 70; Brown Univ, PhD, 75. **CAREER** Asst prof Eng & film, AZ State Univ, 75-76; asst prof Eng, IL State Univ, 77-80; from Asst Prof to Assoc Prof, 80-96, prof eng, Rutgers Univ, Newark, 96, Dept Ch, 92. **MEMBERSHIPS** MLA; ADE. **RESEARCH** Polit and the novel; film hist and theory. **SELECTED PUBLICATIONS** Auth, Hitchcock's wasteland vision: An examination of Frenzy, Film Heritage, spring 76; A laugh gains the upper hand: Woody Allen's Love and Death, Bright Lights, No 7, 78; Daniel Fuchs, Twayne, 79; Screening the Novel, Frederick Ungar, 80; John Irving, Frederick Ungar, 81; auth, introd to Alvah Bessie's Solo Flight & The Serpent Was More Subtil, Chandler & Sharp, 82; Clifford Odets, Continuum, 89; ed, Critical Essays on Clifford Odets, G.K. Hall, 91; auth, Fanfare for the Common Man: The Films of Martin Ritt, Univ Press KY. **CONTACT ADDRESS** Dept of Eng, Rutgers Univ, 180 University Ave, Newark, NJ, 07102-1897. **EMAIL** gamiller@andromeda.rutgers.edu

MILLER, GREG
DISCIPLINE ENGLISH **EDUCATION** Vanderbilt Univ, BA; Stanford Univ, MA; Univ Calif at Berkeley, PhD. **CAREER** Dept ch. **SELECTED PUBLICATIONS** Auth, Iron Wheel, Univ Chicago Press, 98. **CONTACT ADDRESS** Dept of English, Millsaps Col, 1701 N State St, Jackson, MS, 39210.

MILLER, JEANNE-MARIE A.
PERSONAL Born 02/18/1937, Washington, DC, m **DISCIPLINE** ENGLISH **EDUCATION** Howard Univ, BA 1959, MA 1963, PhD 1976. **CAREER** Howard Univ, instr English 1963-76, grad asst prof English 1977-79; Inst for the Arts & the Humanities Howard Univ, asst dir 1973-75, grad assoc prof of English 1979-92; asst for academic planning office of the vice pres for academic affairs 1976-90, grad professor of English, 1992-. **HONORS AND AWARDS** Advanced Study Fellowship Ford Found 1970-72; Fellow So Fellowship Fund 1972-74; Grantee Amer Council of Learned Societies; 1978-79; Grantee Natl Endowment for the Humanities 1981-84; Grantee, Howard University Faculty Research Fund, 1994-95, 1996-97; edited book From Realism to Ritual: Form & Style in Black Theatre 1983; Pi Lambda Theta Natl Honor and Professional Assn in Education 1987. **MEMBERSHIPS** Ed Black Theatre Bulletin Amer Theatre Assoc 1977-86; mem exec council Black Theatre Prog Amer Theatre Assoc 1977-86; proposal reviewer Natl Endowment for the Humanities 1979-; adv bd WETA-TV Ed prog on Black Folklore 1976-77; mem Friends of JF Kennedy Ctr for Performing Arts, Amer Assoc of Univ Women, Amer Civil Liberites Union, Amer Film Inst; assoc mem Arena Stage, Washington Performing Arts Soc, Eugene O'Neill Memorial Theatre Ctr, Amer Soc of Business and Exec Women; assoc Art Inst of Chicago, Boston Museum of Fine Arts, Metropolitan Museum of Art, Corcoran Gallery of Art, Smithsonian Inst, Washington Performings Arts Soc, The Washington Opera Guild, World Affairs Council of Washington DC, Drama League of New York, Modern Language Assoc, Amer Studies Assoc, Coll Lang Assoc, Natl Council of Teachers of Engli Amer Assoc for Higher Educ, Natl Assoc for Women Deans Administrators and Counselors, Natl Women's Studies Assoc. **SELECTED PUBLICATIONS** 60 articles in various jrnls & mags **CONTACT ADDRESS** Dept of English, Howard Univ, 2400 6th St NW, Washington, DC, 20059.

MILLER, KATHERINE I.
DISCIPLINE COMMUNICATION **EDUCATION** Univ Southern Calif, PhD. **CAREER** Prof, Texas A&M Univ. **SELECTED PUBLICATIONS** Auth, Organizational Communication: Approaches and Processes; contribur, Organizational Communication and Change: Challenges in the NextCentury; Case Studies in Organizational Communication: Perspectives on Contemporary Work Life; Communication and Disenfranchisement: Social Health Issues and Implications; past ed, Mgt Commun Quart. **CONTACT ADDRESS** Dept of Speech Communication, Texas A&M Univ, College Station, TX, 77843-4234.

MILLER, MARY JANE
PERSONAL Born 10/09/1941, Beamsville, ON, Canada **DISCIPLINE** FILM STUDIES **EDUCATION** Univ Toronto, BA, 63, MA, 64; Univ Birmingham (UK), PhD, 73. **CAREER** Fac mem, Univ Western Ont, 64-66; fac mem, 68-86, ch 75-78, PROF FILM STUD, DRAMATIC & VISUAL ARTS, BROCK UNIV, 86-; consult, Nat Arch Can, 79. **HONORS AND AWARDS** Woodrow Wilson fel, 63. **MEMBERSHIPS** Asn Can Theatre Res; Film Stud Asn Can; Asn Can Stud; Asn Commun Stud. **SELECTED PUBLICATIONS** Auth, Turn Up the Contrast: CBC Television Drama Since 1952, 87; auth, Rewind and Search: Conversations with Makers and Decision-Makers of CBC TV Drama, 96. **CONTACT ADDRESS** Dept of Film Studies, Dramatic & Visual Arts, Brock Univ, St. Catharines, ON, L2S 3A1.

MILLER, RONALD BAXTER
PERSONAL Born 10/11/1948, Rocky Mount, NC, m **DISCIPLINE** ENGLISH **EDUCATION** NC Central Univ, BA (Magna Cum Laude) 1970; Brown Univ, AM 1972, PhD 1974. **CAREER** Haverford Coll, asst prof English 1974-76; State Univ Coll of NY, lecturer 1974; Univ of TN, assoc prof, 1977-81, prof of English, 1982-92, dir of Black Literature Program, prof; Univ of GA, prof of English & African American studies, 1992-, dir of Institute for African American Studies, currently. **HONORS AND AWARDS** Black Scholar Lectures Le Moyne Coll 1985, Univ of UT 1985; ACLS Conf Grant Black Amer Literature and Humanism Research 1978; NEH Summer Research 1975; Haverford Coll Rsch 1975; Natl Fellowships Fund Dissertation Grant 1973-74; Univ of TN Committee Awards for Excellence in Teaching of English 1978-79; United Negro Coll Fund, Distinguished Scholar, Xavier Univ, 1988; Honored teacher, Alpha Delta Pi, 1988; Natl Rsch Council, Ford Found, Sr Fellowship, 1986-87; Irvine Foundation Visiting Scholar, University of San Francisco, 1991; author: Reference Guide to Langston Hughes and Gwendolyn Brooks, 1978; Ed & Contra Black American Literature and Humanism, 1981; Black American Poets Between Worlds, 1986; Author, Art and Imagination of Langston Hughes, 1989; Southern Trace of Black Critical Theory, 1991; co-author: Call and Response: Riverside Anthology in African American Literary Tradition, 1997; University of Tennessee, Golden Key Award for Excellence, 1990; American Book Award, 1991; ACOG Cultural Olympiad, 1994; University of Georgia, Golden Key Award for Excellence, 1995; Sr Lilly Teaching Fellowship, 1995-96. **MEMBERSHIPS** Consultant, NEH sponsor, TV Series "The South" 1977-78; evaluator Div of Publ Programs Harlem Exec Comm Afro-Am Lit Discuss Group MLA 1980-83; chr/founder/1st chr Div on Black Amer Lit and Culture 1982-84; mem MLA delegate Assembly 1984-86, 1997-99; participant/consultant Black Writers South (GA Cncl for the Arts and Humanities) 1980-; vice pres Black History Month Lecture Series 1980; reader Univ of TN Press 1980-; chr Black Studies CLA 1982-; pres The Langston Hughes Soc 1984-88; Zora Neale Hurston Review 1986-; Committee on Languages and Literatures of America, 1994-97. **SELECTED PUBLICATIONS** Advisor, contrib ed "WATU: A Cornell Journ of Black Writing" 1978-79, "Obsidian: Black Literature in Review" 1979-, "Callaloo" 1981-, "Black American Literature Forum," African American Review, 1982-, "Middle Atlantic Writers Assn Review" 1982-, "Langston Hughes Review" 1982-. **CONTACT ADDRESS** English & African American Studies, Univ of Georgia, Athens, GA, 30602-3012.

MILLER, TICE LEWIS
PERSONAL Born 08/11/1938, Lexington, NE, m, 1963, 1 child **DISCIPLINE** THEATRE HISTORY **EDUCATION** Kearney State Col, BA, 60; Univ Nebr, Lincoln, MA, 61; Univ Ill, Urbana, PhD(Theatre), 68. **CAREER** Instr speech & theatre, Kansas City Jr Col, 61-62; asst prof theatre, Univ WFla, 68-72; assoc prof, 72-79, prof Theatre & Drama, Univ Nebr, Lincoln, 79-, fel, Ctr Great Plains Studies, 78. **HONORS AND AWARDS** Fellow, College of Fellows of American Theatre, JFK Center, Washington, D.C., 92; Sam Davidson Theatre Award, Lincoln Arts Council, 98. **MEMBERSHIPS** Am Soc Theatre Res; Am Theatre Asn; Univ & Col Theatre Asn; Mid-Am Theatre Conf. **RESEARCH** American theatre; 19th century American theatre; American theatre critics. **SELECTED PUBLICATIONS** Auth, John Ranken Towse: Last of the Victorian critics, Educ Theatre J, 5/70; Towse on Reform in the American Theatre, Cent States Speech Commun J, winter 72; Early Cultural History of Nebraska: The Role of the Opera House, Nebr Speech Commun J, 74; Alan Dale: The Hearst critic, Educ Theatre J, 3/74; From Winter to Nathan: The Critics Influence on the American Theatre, Southern Speech Commun J, winter 76; Identifying the Dramatic Writers for Wilkes's

Spirit of the Times, 1859-1902, Theatre Survey, 5/79; Bohemians and Critics: Nineteenth Century Theatre Criticism, Scarecrow Press Inc, 81; Fitz-James O'Brien: Irish Playwright & Critic in New York, 1851-1862, Nineteenth Century Theatre Res, fall 82; co-ed, Cambridge Guide to American Theatre, 93; co-ed, The American Stage, Cambridge, 93; editorial advisory board & major contributor, Cambridge Guide to Theatre, 88, 92, 95. **CONTACT ADDRESS** Dept of Theatre Arts, Univ of Nebr, PO Box 880201, Lincoln, NE, 68588-0201. **EMAIL** tmiller@unlinfo.unl.edu

MILLER, VERNON D.
PERSONAL Born 02/26/1955, Houston, TX, d, 2 children **DISCIPLINE** ORGANIZATIONAL COMMUNICATION **EDUCATION** Baylor Univ, BA, 77, MA, 79; Univ Tx at Austin, PhD, 88. **CAREER** Univ Wis at Milwaukee, 86-90; Mich State Univ, 90-98. **MEMBERSHIPS** Int Commun Asn; Acad of Management; Nat Commun Asn. **RESEARCH** Organizational assimilation; employment interviewing; role leavening; role negotiation. **SELECTED PUBLICATIONS** Coauth, Antecedents to willingness to participate in a planned organizational change, J of Applied Commun, 94; The maternity leave as a role negotiation process: A conceptual framework, J of Managerial Issues, 96; The role of communication in managing reducations in work force, J of Applied Commun Res, 96; Toward a research agenda for the second employment interview, J of Applied Commun Res, 96; The role of a conference in integrating a contractual network of health services organizations, J of Business Commun, 96; An experimental study of newcomers' information seeking behaviors during organizational entry, Commun Studies, 96; Communicating and Connecting: The functions of human communication, Harcourt Brace Col Pub, 96; Testing two contrasting models of innovativeness in a contractual network, Human Commun Res, 97; Survivors' information seeking following a reduction in workforce, Commun Res, 97; Downsizing and structural holes: Their impact on layoff survivors' perceptions of organizational chaos and openess to change, Commun Res, 98; The case of the aggrieved expatriate case analysis: Miller analysis, Management Commun Quart, 98. **CONTACT ADDRESS** Dept of Commun, Michigan State Univ, East Lansing, MI, 48824-1212.

MILLGATE, MICHAEL
PERSONAL Born 07/19/1929, Southampton, England, m, 1960 **DISCIPLINE** ENGLISH & AMERICAN LITERATURE **EDUCATION** Cambridge Univ, BA, 52, MA, 56; Univ Leeds, PhD, 60. **CAREER** Tutor English & polit, Workers' Educ Asn, Eng, 53-56; lectr English, Univ Leeds, 58-64; prof English & chmn dept, York Univ, 64-67; prof English, Univ Toronto, 67-94; Can Coun leave grant, 68-69; S W Brooks fel, Univ Queensland, 71; Can Coun Killam Prog senior res scholar, 74-75; Guggenheim fel, 77-78; Connaught Sr Fel Hum, 79-80; SSHRCC Leave Fel, 81-82; aid to Publications Comt, Can Federation for Hum, 84-90; vis scholar, Meiji Univ, 85; Killam res fel, 86-88; prof, 87-94, prof Emeritus, 94-, Univ Toronto; Bd of Dir, Mark Twain Project, 91-; Educ Adv Bd, Guggenheim Found, 94-; Exec Comt, Toronto centre for the Book, 94-. **HONORS AND AWARDS** Fel, Royal Soc Can, 81; Fel, Royal Soc of Lit, 83. **MEMBERSHIPS** MLA; Victorian Stud Asn of Ontario; Thomas Hardy Soc; Tennyson Soc; Bibliog Soc Am; Soc Textual Scholarship. **RESEARCH** Thomas Hardy; William Faulkner; Alfred Tennyson; Book history. **SELECTED PUBLICATIONS** Ed, Selected Letters of Thomas Hardy, Clarendon, 90; auth, Testamentary Acts; auth, Browning, Tennyson, James, Hardy, Clarendon, 92; co-ed, Thomas Hardy's Studies, Specimens &c Notebook, Clarendon, 94; ed, Letters of Emma and Florence Hardy, Clarendon, 96; auth, Faulkner's Place, Georgia, 97. **CONTACT ADDRESS** 1 Balmoral Ave, Apt 809, Toronto, ON, M4V 389.

MILLICAN, ARTHENIA J. BATES
PERSONAL Born 06/01/1920, Sumter, SC, w **DISCIPLINE** ENGLISH **EDUCATION** Morris Coll Sumter, SC, BA (Magna Cum Laude) 1941; Atlanta Univ, MA 1948; LA State Univ Baton Rouge, PhD 1972. **CAREER** Westside HS Kershaw, SC, English teacher 1942-45; Butler HS Hartsville, SC, civics/ English teacher 1945-46; Morris Coll, head English dept 1947-49; Mary Bethune HS Halifax, VA, English teacher 1949-55; MS Valley State Univ, English instructor 1955-56; Southern Univ, English instructor 1956-59, asst prof 1959-63, assoc prof 1963-72, prof English 1972-74; Norfolk State Univ, prof English 1974-77; Southern Univ Baton Rouge, LA, prof English & creative writing 1977-80; researcher, writer, freelancer. **HONORS AND AWARDS** National Endowment for the Arts Award, 1 out of 165 in the nation, 1976; Delta Sigma Theta Sorority Inc, Silver Anniversary Award, 1991, Baton Rouge Sigma Alumnae Chapter, first, Delta Pearl Award in Literature, 1989. **MEMBERSHIPS** Mem Baton Rouge Alumnae Chap of Delta Sigma Theta; mem comm Arts and Letters Baton Rouge Sigma Alumnae Chapt; serve as poet prose reader and exhibitor of creative works for programs; mem Les Gayettes Civic and Social Club; executive committee member, Societas Docta, Inc, 1988-90; life member, College Language Assn, 1948-; member, Society for the Study of Southern Literature, 1986-; committee member, Louisiana Folklore Society, 1973-; Modern Language Assn of America; Natl Council of Teachers of English; Assn for the Study of Afro-American Life & History; Phillis Wheatley Club. **SELECTED PUBLICATIONS** Author, works include: prize short story "Where You Belong" publ in "Such Things From the Valley" 1977; cover story Black World July 1971; cover picture and interview "Nuance" with Adimu Owusu March 1982; contributing author, James Baldwin, A Critical Evaluation; Sturdy Black Bridges, Visions of Black Women in Literature; author, The Deity Nodded 1973, Seeds Beneath the Snow, Vignettes of the South 1975, Journey to Somewhere 1986, Trek to Polaris 1989; contributing ed, Heath Anthology of American Literature; Prepared Black Culture Registry, Louisiana, a first, 1985; author, Hand on the Throttle, 1993; works have been included in several anthologies including Revolutionary Tales (1995); editor, Bill Mullen.

MILLICHAP, JOE
DISCIPLINE AMERICAN LITERATURE **EDUCATION** St Petrs Col, BA, 61; Univ Notre Dame, MA, 62, PhD, 70. **CAREER** Univ NC, 65-68; Univ Mont, 68-71; vis prof, Univ Tulsa, 79-82; Prof, Western Ky Univ, 84-. **HONORS AND AWARDS** Fullbright Prof, Univ Finland, 78-79. **RESEARCH** American literature, film, and culture. **SELECTED PUBLICATIONS** Areas: Southern Renaissance, Railroads,and American Literature. **CONTACT ADDRESS** Western Kentucky Univ, 1526 Big Red Way Street, Bowling Green, KY, 42101. **EMAIL** joseph.millichap@wku.edu

MILLS, JOHN ARVIN
PERSONAL Born 12/03/1931, Indianapolis, IN, m, 1961 **DISCIPLINE** ENGLISH **EDUCATION** Butler Univ, BA, 53; IN Univ, MA, 59, PhD, 61. **CAREER** Lectr speech & drama, IN Univ, 59-61; assoc prof drama, Univ AZ, 61-66; from asst prof to assoc prof theater, State Univ NY Binghamton, 66-74; Assoc Prof Eng, Univ AZ, 74-98 (ret), Found grant-in-aid, 68-69; Guggenheim res fel, London, 72-73. **MEMBERSHIPS** Am Soc Theatre Res. **RESEARCH** Dramatic criticism; mod drama; theatre hist. **SELECTED PUBLICATIONS** Auth, Shaw's Linguistic Satire, Shaw Rev, 1/65; The Comic in Words: Shaw's Cockneys, Drama Surv, summer 66; Language and Laughter: Shaw's Comic Diction, Univ Ariz, 68; Acting is Being: Bernard Shaw on the Art of the Actor, Shaw Rev, 5/70; The Modesty of Nature: Charles Fechter's Hamlet, Theatre Surv, 5/74; What. What-Not!: Absurdity in Saroyan's The Time of Your Life, Midwest Quart, winter 85; Hamlet on Stage: The Great Tradition, Greenwood Press, 85; Old Mr. Picklepin: Simon Gray's Butley, Amer Imago, winter 89. **CONTACT ADDRESS** Dept of Eng, Univ of AZ, 1 University of Az, Tucson, AZ, 85721-0001. **EMAIL** jamills@azstarnet.com

MILNER, JOSEPH O'BEIRNE
PERSONAL Born 06/18/1937, m, 1963, 3 children **DISCIPLINE** ENGLISH, EDUCATION **EDUCATION** Davidson Col, AB, 59; Univ NC, Chapel Hill, MA, 65, PhD, 71. **CAREER** Instr Eng, NC State Univ, 65-66; instr, Univ NC, Chapel Hill, 68-69; asst prof, 69-80, Assoc Prof Eng & Educ, Wake Forest Univ, 80, Ed, NC Eng Tchr, 72-; consult, Winston-Salem-Forsyth County Schs, 73. **MEMBERSHIPS** MLA; Aaup; Southeastern Mod Lang Asn. **RESEARCH** Am lit, 1960-1973. **CONTACT ADDRESS** Dept of Eng, Wake Forest Univ, PO Box 7266, Winston Salem, NC, 27109-7266. **EMAIL** milner@wfu.edu

MILOWICKI, EDWARD JOHN
PERSONAL Born 03/02/1932, Plains, PA **DISCIPLINE** ENGLISH **EDUCATION** Wilkes Col, BA, 58; Duquesne Univ, MA, 63; Univ Ore, PhD(English), 68. **CAREER** Asst English, Duquesne Univ, 59-61; instr, St Vincent Col, 61-63; instr, Univ Ore, 63-68; dir grad studies, 72-79, assoc prof English, Mills Col, 68-. **MEMBERSHIPS** MLA; Medieval Asn Pac; Int Courtly Lit Soc; Chaucer Soc. **RESEARCH** Medieval literature, especially Chaucer; classical literature, especially Ovid; character in Western literature. **SELECTED PUBLICATIONS** Auth, Some Medieval Light on Marshall McLukan, Studies in the Literary Imagination, Vol IV, pages 51-59; coauth (with Rawdon Wilson), Character in Paradise Lost: Milton's Literary Formalism, Milton Studies, Vol Xiv, pages 75-94; Characterization in Troilus and Coiseyde: Some Relationships Centered on Hope, Canadian Review of Comparative Lit 11, , 12-24, March 84; Reflections on a Symbolic Heritage: Ovid's Narcissus, Syllecta Classica, 7:155-66, 96; (with Rawdon Wilson) Troilus and Cressida: Voices in the Darkness of Troy, in Reading the Renaissance: Culture, Poetics and Drama, ed Johnathan Hart, New York: Garland, 96; (with Rawdon Wilson), Ovid's Shadow: Character and Characterization in Early Modern Literature, Neohelicon XXII/1, 9-47; (with Rawdon Wilson), Ovid through Shakespeare: The Divided Self, Poetics Today, Vol 12, num 2, 217-252, summer 95. **CONTACT ADDRESS** English Dept., Mills Col, 5000 MacArthur Blvd, Oakland, CA, 94613-1000. **EMAIL** milo@ella.mills.edu

MINER, MADONNE
DISCIPLINE AMERICAN LITERATURE AND WOMEN'S STUDIES **EDUCATION** SUNY, Buffalo, PhD, 82. **CAREER** Prof, ch, dept Eng, TX Tech Univ, 97-. **SELECTED PUBLICATIONS** Auth, Insatiable Appetites: Twentieth-Century American Women's Bestsellers, 84. **CONTACT ADDRESS** Texas Tech Univ, Lubbock, TX, 79409-5015. **EMAIL** M. Miner@ttu.edu

MINICH BREWER, MARIA
DISCIPLINE 20TH-CENTURY NARRATIVE, THEATER, AND CULTURAL THEORY **EDUCATION** Yale Univ, PhD. **CAREER** Instr, Univ Minn, Twin Cities. **RESEARCH** Issues of survival and writing in the aftermath of World War II. **SELECTED PUBLICATIONS** Auth, Claude Simon: Narrativities Without Narrative, Univ Nebr Press, 95. **CONTACT ADDRESS** Univ Minn, Twin Cities, Minneapolis, MN, 55455.

MINKOFF, HARVEY
PERSONAL New York, NY **DISCIPLINE** LINGUISTICS, ENGLISH **EDUCATION** City Col New York, BA, 65, MA, 66, Grad Ctr, PhD, 70. **CAREER** Asst prof English, Iona Col, 67-71; assoc prof English & Ling, 71-90, prof Eng and Ling, Hunter Col, 90-. **MEMBERSHIPS** Ling Soc Am; MLA. **RESEARCH** Applications of linguistics to language teaching and learning; theory and practice of literary translation. **SELECTED PUBLICATIONS** Ed, Teaching English Linguistically: Five Experimental Curricula, 71 & auth, The English Verb System, 72; (N)ever write like(?) you talk: Teaching the syntax of reading & composition, English Record, 74; coauth, Mastering Prestige English, Villa Press, 75; auth, Teaching the Transition From Print to Script Analytically, Elementary English, 75; Some Stylistic Consequences of Aelfric's Theory of Translation, Studies in Philol, 76; coauth, Transitions: A key to mature reading and writing, In: Classroom Practices in Teaching English, NCTE, 77; coauth, Complete Course in College Writing, Kendall-Hunt, 84; coauth, Visions and Revisions, Prentice-Hall, 90; ed, Approaches to the Bible, 2 Vols, Bibl Arch Soc, 95; coauth, Exploring America, Harcourt, 95; auth, Mysteries of the Dead Sea Scrolls, Ottenhenmer, 98. **CONTACT ADDRESS** Dept of English, Hunter Col, CUNY, 695 Park Ave, New York, NY, 10021-5085.

MINOT, WALTER S.
PERSONAL Woonsocket, RI, m, 1963, 1 child **DISCIPLINE** HUMANITIES **EDUCATION** Providence Col, AB, 62; Univ of Nebr, PhD, 70. **CAREER** Dir, 89-95, chemn, 93-98, prof, English, Gannon Univ, 79-. **HONORS AND AWARDS** NEH Sem, Rhetoric and Public Discourse., Referee, Col Composition and Commun, 89-94; referee, Focuses, 89-95; referee, Pa English, 88-97; bibliogr, Composition and Rhetoric: Annual Annotated Bibliogr, 84-87. **MEMBERSHIPS** NCTE; Rhetoric Society of Am; Wordsworth-Coleridge Asn. **RESEARCH** British romanticism; Rhetoric and Composition; Millay. **SELECTED PUBLICATIONS** Auth, Rhetoric: Theory and Practice for Composition, 81; auth, Personality and Persona: Developing the Self, 89; auth, The Marriage Hearse in Blake's London, 91; auth, Blake's Infant Joy: An Explanation of Age, 91; auth, Keat's Ode to a Nightingale, 92; auth, Puns, The Encyclopedia of Romanticism, 92. **CONTACT ADDRESS** Dept of English, Gannon Univ, Erie, PA, 16541. **EMAIL** minotool@mail1.gannon.edu

MINTER, DAVID LEE
DISCIPLINE ENGLISH **EDUCATION** N Texas State, BA, 57, MA, 59; Yale Univ, BD, 61, PhD, 65. **CAREER** Prof, Libbie Shearn Moody prof, Eng, Rice Univ **MEMBERSHIPS** Am Antiquarian Soc **RESEARCH** King Philip's War **SELECTED PUBLICATIONS** Auth, The Interpreted Design as a Structural Principle in American Prose, 69; auth, William Faulkner: His Life and Works, 82; auth, A Cultural History of the American Novel: Henry James to William Faulkner, Cambridge Univ Press; auth, biographical essays on Samuel Danforth, James Hammond, Jonathan Mitchell, Thomas Prince, William Stoughton, Patrick Tailfer, and St. George Tucker, in American Writers Before 1800: A Biographical and Critical Dictionary, vols 1-3, Greenwood Press, 83. **CONTACT ADDRESS** Dept of Eng, Rice Univ, Box 1892, Houston, TX, 77251. **EMAIL** dcmint@rice.edu

MINTZ, KENNETH A.
PERSONAL Born 03/15/1951, Plattsburgh, NY, d **DISCIPLINE** LIBRARY SCIENCE; ENGLISH **EDUCATION** Univ Redlands, BA, 73; S Ct St Univ, MLS, 78. **CAREER** Asst newsletter ed, First Unitarian Soc New Haven Ct, 79-80; newsletter ed, Unitarian Soc of Rutherford NJ, 84-85; head, Commun Church New York, 93- ; book rev, Libr J 88-93; librn, Bayonne Publ Libr, NJ, 80-88; cataloger, Hoboken Public Libr, 91- . **HONORS AND AWARDS** Guill Poetry Award, 91; Editor's Choice Award, 89, 96; Legion of Honor Award, 98; Decree of Merit, Int Biog Centre, Cambridge England, 97; Outstanding Achievement Diploma Cambridge England, 97; NJ Essay Writer of the Year, 97; Christmas Story Prize, 97; Essay Prize, 94; Bayonne Writers Legion of Honor Award, 89; Bayonne Writers Special Legion Award, 96. **MEMBERSHIPS** Acad of Amer Poets; Hoboken Creative Alliance, Bayonne Writers' Group; NY Acad of Sci; Poets' Guild. **RESEARCH** Lit; hist; philos. **CONTACT ADDRESS** 24 Belviders Ave, Apt 5, Jersey City, NJ, 07304-1325. **EMAIL** kmintz351@aol.com

MINTZ, LAWRENCE E.
DISCIPLINE AMERICAN STUDIES/ENGLISH **EDUCATION** Univ SC, BA, 66; MI State Univ, MA, 67, PhD, 69. **CAREER** Am Stud Dept, Univ Md **RESEARCH** Am popular cult and Am humor. **SELECTED PUBLICATIONS** Auth, The Standup Comedian as Social and Cultural Mediator, Amer

Quart, 85; Devil and Angel: Philip Roth's Humor, Stud in Amer Jewish Lit, 89; Ethos and Pathos in Chaplin's City Lights, Charles Chaplin: Approaches to Semiotics, Mouton deGryter, 91; Humor and Ethnic Stereotypes in Vaudeville and Burlesque, MELUS, 96; ed, Humor in America: A Research Guide to Genres and Topics, Greenwood Press, 88. **CONTACT ADDRESS** Am Stud Dept, Univ MD, Col Park, College Park, MD, 20742. **EMAIL** lm36@umail.umd.edu

MISSEY, JAMES L.
PERSONAL Born 07/09/1935, San Bernardino, CA, 1 child **DISCIPLINE** ENGLISH **EDUCATION** Pomona Col, BA, 57; Univ Pa, MA, 59, PhD(English), 63. **CAREER** Instr English, Beloit Col, 62-64; asst prof, Denison Univ, 64-66; asst prof, 66-68, assoc prof English, Univ Wis-Stevens Point, 68-96, prof English, 96-. **RESEARCH** The fiction of E M Forster. **SELECTED PUBLICATIONS** Auth, Forster's Redemptive Siren, Mod Fiction Studies, winter 64-65; Pacifist's and Revolutionary Violence, Win Peace and Freedom through Nonviolent Action 27: 10, Jan 67; The Connected and the Unconnected in Howards End, Wis Studies Lit, 69; A McCullers Influence on Albee's The Zoo Story, Am Notes & Queries, 4/75; The Rhodesian Woman, Wisc Acad Review 28.3: 4-5, 82; Theme and Speakers in Shumway's Song of the Archer, Transactions of the Wisc Acad of Sciences, Arts, and Letters 71, Pt 2: 131-135, 83; Thoreau's Turtledove and Mine, The Christian Science Monitor, 21, Dec 83: 30; Acting in Salinger's Franny and Zooey, Wisc English Journal 25.3: 16-18, 15, 83, cont 26.3: 6, 84; The Eve of Revolution: An Antiwar Memoir, Stevens Point WI: Portage County Hist Soc, 85; The London Theatre: Fall 1985, Wisc Acad Rev 32.3: 9-13, 86; Revisiting the Intensity of the 60's, The Christian Science Monitor, 4 May 90: 16; Hennacy, Ammon, The Book of Ammon, ed Jim Massey and Joan Thomas, 2nd ed, Baltimore: Forkamp, 94; Ammon Hennacy, Christian Anarchism, and the One-Person Revolution, The Small City and Regional Community 11: 305-310, 95. **CONTACT ADDRESS** Dept of English, Univ of Wis, 2100 Main St, Stevens Point, WI, 54481-3897. **EMAIL** jmissey@uwsp.edu

MITCHELL, ANGELYN
DISCIPLINE ENGLISH LITERATURE **EDUCATION** NC State Univ, BA; NC Central Univ, MA; Howard Univ, PhD. **CAREER** Eng Dept, Georgetown Univ **RESEARCH** American, African American and Caribbean literature; critical theory; cultural studies; women's studies; African American studies. **SELECTED PUBLICATIONS** Auth, pubs on William Wells Brown, Harriet Wilson, Kate Chopin, and Toni Morrison; ed, Within the Circle: An Anthology of African American Literary Criticism from the Harlem Renaissance to the Present, 94. **CONTACT ADDRESS** English Dept, Georgetown Univ, 37th and O St, Washington, DC, 20057.

MITCHELL, JUDITH I.
DISCIPLINE ENGLISH LITERATURE **EDUCATION** Univ Saskatchewan, BA, MA; Univ Alberta, PhD. **CAREER** Assoc prof; dir, Hon(s) Prog. **RESEARCH** 19th-century novel; women's poetry; gender studies; feminist theory. **SELECTED PUBLICATIONS** Auth, Hardy's Female Reader, A Sense of Sex: Feminist Perspectives on Hardy, U of Illinois P, 91; Naturalism in George Moore's A Mummer's Wife (1885), The New Nineteenth Century: Feminist Readings of Underread Victorian Fiction, Garland,96; The Stone and the Scorpion: The Female Subject of Desire in the Novels of Charlotte Bronte, George Eliot and Thomas Hardy, Greenwood Press, 94. **CONTACT ADDRESS** Dept of English, Victoria Univ, PO Box 3070, Victoria, BC, V8W 3W1. **EMAIL** mitchell@uvic.ca

MITCHELL, KENNETH R.
PERSONAL Born 12/13/1940, Moose Jaw, SK, Canada **DISCIPLINE** ENGLISH **EDUCATION** Univ Sask, BA, 65, MA, 67 **CAREER** English instr, Univ Regina, 67-70; Scott-Can Exchange Fel, 79-80; vis prof, Univ Nanjing, China, 80-81; PROF ENGLISH, UNIV REGINA, 84-. **HONORS AND AWARDS** Can Authors Asn Award Best Can Play, 85; Ottawa Little Theatre Prize Best One Act Play Can Heroes, 71. **MEMBERSHIPS** Playwrights Union Can; Can Asn Univ Tchrs **SELECTED PUBLICATIONS** Auth, Wandering Rafferty, 72; auth, The Meadowlark Connection, 75; auth, The Con Man, 79; auth, Stones of the Dalai Lama, 93; auth, Everybody Gets Something Here, 77; auth, The Shipbuilder, 90; auth, Davin, 79; auth, Gone the Burning Sun, 85; coauth, Cruel Tears, 77; coauth, The Plainsman, 92; coauth, Ken Mitchell Country, 84; coauth, Witches and Idiots, 90; ed, Horizon, Writings of the Canadian Prairie, 77. **CONTACT ADDRESS** Dept of English, Univ Regina, Regina, SK, S4S OA2. **EMAIL** Ken.Mitchell@uregina.ca

MITCHELL, W.J. THOMAS
PERSONAL Born 03/24/1942, Anaheim, CA, m, 1968, 2 children **DISCIPLINE** LITERATURE **EDUCATION** Mich State Univ, BA, 64; Johns Hopkins Univ, MA, 66, PhD(English), 68. **CAREER** From asst prof to assoc prof English, Ohio State Univ, 68-77; assoc prof, 77-79, prof English, Univ Chicago, 79-89, Gaylord Donnelley Distinguished Service prof, 90-, Humanities res fel, Ohio State Univ, 70-71; Am Philos Soc grant, 70-71, ed consult, Studies Romanticism, 73-; Nat Endowment for Humanities res fel, 78-79; Guggenheim fel, 81-82; ed, Critical Inquiry, 79-. **HONORS AND AWARDS** Outstanding Special Issue of a Scholarly Journal, from CELJ (Conference of Editors of Learned Journals), 80-81; Canterbury Visiting Fellow, Univ of Canterbury, New Zealand, 87; Fairchild Distinguished Scholar, Calicornie Institute of Technology, 94; Charles Rufus Morey Prize in Art History of the College Art Asn, for Picture Theory, 96; Gordon E. Laing Prize for a Chicago Press book by a University of Chicago Author, 97. **MEMBERSHIPS** MLA; Aaup; Am Soc 18th Century Studies. **RESEARCH** Poetry and painting in romantic period; theory of imagery; works of William Blake. **SELECTED PUBLICATIONS** Auth, Poetry and Pictoral Imagination in Blake, Eighteenth Century Studies, fall 69; Blake's Composite Art, In: Blake's Visionary Forms Dramatic, Princeton Univ, 70; Blake's Radical Comedy, In: Blake's Sublime Allegory, Univ Wis, 73; Style as Epistemology, Studies in Romanticism, spring 77; Blake's Composite Art, Princeton Univ, 78; Spatial Form in Literature, Critical Inquiry, winter 79; ed, The Language of Images, 80; On Narrative, 81; The Politics of Interpretation, 82; What is an Image?, New Lit Hist; Iconology, Univ of Chicago Press, 86; Picture Theory, Chicago, 94; The Last Dinosaur Book, Chicago, 98. **CONTACT ADDRESS** Dept of English, Univ of Chicago, 5540 Greenwood Ave, Chicago, IL, 60637-1506. **EMAIL** wjtm@midway.uchicago.edu

MOEHLMANN, JOHN FREDERICK
PERSONAL Born 12/23/1942, Conover, NC, m, 1965, 2 children **DISCIPLINE** ENGLISH **EDUCATION** Lenoir-Rhyne Col, BA, 65; Appalachian State Univ, MA, 67; Univ Tenn, PhD(English), 74. **CAREER** Instr English, Camp Lejeune Br, E Carolina Univ, 67-69 & Univ SC, Florence, 69-70; Asst Prof English, High Point Univ, 75-, Lilly scholar English, Duke Univ, 77-78. **HONORS AND AWARDS** Distinguished Teaching-Service Awayd, 81. **MEMBERSHIPS** MLA; S Atlantic Mod Lang Asn; Southeastern Asn 18th Century Studies; AAUP. **RESEARCH** Shakespeare; Restoration and eighteenth century literature. **SELECTED PUBLICATIONS** Auth, A Concordance to the Complete Poems of John Wilmot, Earl of Rochester, Whitston, 79. **CONTACT ADDRESS** High Point Univ, 933 Montlieu Ave, High Point, NC, 27262-3598. **EMAIL** jmoehlma@acme.highpoint.edu

MOFFATT, JOHN
DISCIPLINE ENGLISH LITERATURE **EDUCATION** Queen's Univ, PhD. **CAREER** Dept Eng, Queen's Univ **RESEARCH** Theories of oral-traditional narrative in early mediaeval Insular literature; Scottish Gaelic literature; contemporary minority language culture. **SELECTED PUBLICATIONS** Auth, A Commodified Antimodernism: Evangelism, The Gaelic Text, and the Construction of Ethnotourism in Nova Scotia, 97;co-ed, Inside Language: A Canadian Language Reader, Prentice Hall, 98. **CONTACT ADDRESS** English Dept, Queen's Univ, Kingston, ON, K7L 3N6. **EMAIL** moffatt-j@rmc.ca

MOGEN, DAVID LEE
PERSONAL Born 09/07/1945, Bremerton, WA **DISCIPLINE** AMERICAN LITERATURE, SCIENCE FICTION, NATIVE AMERICAN LITERATURE, FRONTIER **EDUCATION** Columbia Univ, BA, 67; Univ Colo, PhD, 77. **CAREER** Tchr Eng, Intermediate Sch, NY, 68-71; instr, Univ CO, 71-77; instr, GA State Univ, 77-79; Asst Prof English, 79-85, assoc prof, 85-90, prof eng, 90-; Asst ed, English Lang Notes, 71-73. **HONORS AND AWARDS** NDEA Fel, City Univ NY, 67-68; Eng Lang Notes fel, 71-76; Univ Fel, Univ CO, 74-75; Fac res grant, CO State Univ, 79-80; NEH Symposium, Univ CA, Berkeley, summer 87; Oliver P Pennock Award, Distinguished Service, CO State Univ, 94; NEH fac seminar, CSU Am Studies program, 8/97. **MEMBERSHIPS** MLA. **RESEARCH** Am lit; Am frontier mythology; sci fiction. **SELECTED PUBLICATIONS** Auth, Agonies of innocence: The Governess and Maggie Verver, Am Literary Realism, 1870-1910, summer, 76; Owen Wister's cowboy heroes, Southwestern Am Lit; Owen Wister's cowboy heroes, In: The Western: A Collection of Critical Essays, Prentice-Hall, 79; Re-evaluating the John W Campbell tradition: Elitism, parochialsim, and Calvinsim, Studies in Popular Culture, spring 80; Frontier Myth and American Gothic, Genre, fall 81; Wilderness Visions, Past and Future: Science Fiction Westerns, Borgo Press, 81, 2nd ed, 93; Owen Wister, In: Twentieth-Century Western Writers, Gale Research Co, 83; Ray Bradbury, Twayne United States Authors Series, G K Hall and Co, 86; Sex and true West in McMurtry's fiction, Southwestern Am Lit, spring 89; co-ed, The Frontier Experience and the American Dream, Tex A&M Univ Press, 89; Essay review of Other Destinies and The Heirs of Columbus, Colo Rev, fall 93; co-ed, Frontier Gothic, Assoc Univ Presses, 93; Essay review of Love Medicine, 2nd ed, and The Bingo Palace, Colo Rev, fall 94; Essay review of Sygo and Justice, Colo Rev, fall 96. **CONTACT ADDRESS** Dept of Eng, Colorado State Univ, Fort Collins, CO, 80523-0001. **EMAIL** dmogen@vines.colostate.edu

MOGLEN, HELENE
PERSONAL Born 03/22/1936, New York, NY, m, 1957, 3 children **DISCIPLINE** ENGLISH LITERATURE **EDUCATION** Bryn Mawr Col, BA, 57; Yale Univ, MA, 58, PhD(English lit), 64. **CAREER** From instr to asst prof English lit, NY Univ, 64-71; from assoc prof to prof, State Univ NY Col Purchase, 71-78, actg dean humanities, 76-77; prof English lit, 78-, dean humanities & arts, Univ CA, Santa Cruz, 78-82; fels, Am Coun Learned Soc, 73-74, Am Asn Univ Women, 93-94, & State Univ NY Found, 77. **MEMBERSHIPS** MLA; Pen. **RESEARCH** Victorian literature; English novel; feminist criticism. **SELECTED PUBLICATIONS** Auth, Laurence Sterne and the Contemporary Vision, In: The Winged Skull, Kent State Univ, 71; The Double Vision of Wuthering Heights: A Clarifying View of Female Development, Centennial Rev, 71; Disguise and Development: The Self and Society in Twelfth Night, Lit & Psychol, 73; The Philosophical Irony of Laurence Sterne, Univ FL, 73; Charlotte Bronte: The Self Conceived, Norton, 76; co-ed, with Jim Sleuth and Andrea Lunsford, The Future of Doctoral Studies in English, MLA, 89; co-ed, with Andrea Lunsford and Jim Sleuth, The Rights of Lirtacy, MLA: co-ed, with Elizabeth Abel and Barbara Chrunian, Female Subjects in Blade and ...., Race, Psychoanalysis, Feminism, Univ CA Press, 97. **CONTACT ADDRESS** Kresge Col, Univ California, Santa Cruz, CA, 95064-0001. **EMAIL** moglen@cab.ucsc.edu

MOHSEN, RAED
PERSONAL Born 12/15/1959, Lebanon, s **DISCIPLINE** INTERPERSONAL COMMUNICATION **EDUCATION** Bowling Green State Univ, BA 83, pub admin 84, PhD ; Gallaudet Univ, MSW 96. **CAREER** Gallaudet Univ, asst prof, assoc prof, 89-97; Lebanese American Univ, assoc prof, 97-. **HONORS AND AWARDS** Who's Who Among Amer Tchrs. **MEMBERSHIPS** NCA; NASW. **RESEARCH** Intimate Relationships; Communication Practices; Behavior of Deaf People. **SELECTED PUBLICATIONS** Auth, Out on Campus: A Challenging Public Speaking Experience, The Speech Comm Teacher, 93; auth, Communicating Like and Dislikes During the Intimate Encounters of Married Couples, FL Comm Jour, 93; Petitioning Governments for Redress of Grievances: A Communication Approach to Terrorism, Speech and Theater Assoc of MO Jour, 93; auth, Communication Issues in deaf/Hearing Intimate Relationships: Toward A Better Future, A Deaf Amer Mono, 93. **CONTACT ADDRESS** Dept of Communication, Lebanese American Univ, 475 Riverside Dr #1846, New York, NY, 10115-0065. **EMAIL** rmohsen@lau.edu.lb

MOISAN, THOMAS
DISCIPLINE RENAISSANCE LITERATURE **EDUCATION** Harvard Univ, PhD. **CAREER** Eng Dept, St. Edward's Univ **SELECTED PUBLICATIONS** Auth, 'Knock Me Here Soundly': Comic Misprision and Class Consciousness in Shakespeare, Shakespeare Quart, 91; Repetition and Interrogation in Othello: 'What needs this Iterance?' or, 'Can anything be made of this?', Fairleigh Dickinson Press, 91; O anything of nothing first create': Gender, Patriarchy, and the Tragedy of Romeo and Juliet, Scarecrow Press, 91; Monsters of the Deep: Social Dissolution in Shakespeare's Tragedies, Shakespeare Quart, 94; Interlinear Trysting and 'Household Stuff': The Latin Lesson and the Domestication of Learning in The Taming of the Shrew , Shakespeare Studies, 95; 'What's that to you?' or, Facing Facts: Anti-Paternalist Chords and Social Discords in The Taming of the Shrew, Renaissance Drama, 97, Antique Fables, Fairy Toys: Elisions, Allusion,and Translation in A Midsummer Night's Dream , Garland, 98. **CONTACT ADDRESS** St Edward's Univ, 3001 S Congress Ave, Austin, TX, 78704-6489.

MOLDENHAUER, JOSEPH JOHN
PERSONAL Born 02/09/1934, Rastatt, Germany, m, 1957, 2 children **DISCIPLINE** ENGLISH **EDUCATION** Amherst Col, BA, 56; Columbia Univ, MA, 57, PhD(English), 64. **CAREER** From spec instr to assoc prof, 57-72, prof English, 72-85, M C Boatright Regents Prof, Univ Tx, Austin, 86-, chemn, 79-83; Amherst Col fel, Columbia Univ, 56-57, Southern fel Fund fac fel, 59-60; Guggenheim fel, 68-69; textual ed, The writings of Henry D Thoreau, 72-. **MEMBERSHIPS** MLA; Bibliographical Soc Am; Thoreau Soc; ALA. **RESEARCH** Nineteenth century American literature; textual editing. **SELECTED PUBLICATIONS** Auth, Unity of Theme and Structure in The Wild Palms, In: William Faulkner: Three Decades of Criticism, MI State Univ, 60; Murder as a Fine Art, Basic Connections Between Poe's Aesthetics, Psychology, and Moral Vision, Pmla, 5/68; Paradox in Walden, In: The Recognition of H D Thoreau, Univ MI, 69; ed, H D Thoreau's The Maine Woods, Princeton Univ, 72; auth, A Descriptive Catalog of ... Poe Manuscripts, Univ TX, Austin, 73; co-ed, H D Thoreau, Early Essays and Miscellanies, Princeton Univ, 75; ed, Poe's The Spectacles: A New Text from Manuscript, In: Studies in the American Renaissance-1977, G K Hall, NY, 78; auth, Bartleby and the Custom-House, Delta No 7, 11/78; ed, H D Thoreau, Cape Cod, Princeton Univ, 88-; auth, Walden and Wordsworth's Guide to the Lake District, in Studies in the American Renaissance--1900, Univ Press VA, 90; Textual Instability in the Riverside Edition of Thoreau, Papers of the Bibliographical Soc of Am, 12/91; Pym, the Dighton Rock, and the Matter of Vinland, in Poe's Pym: Critical explorations, Duke Univ, 92; The Maine Woods, in Cambridge Companion to Henry David Thoreau, Cambridge Univ, 95. **CONTACT ADDRESS** Dept English, Univ Tex, Austin, TX, 78712-1164. **EMAIL** eiey567@uts.cc.utexas.edu

MOLETTE, BARBARA J.
PERSONAL Born 01/31/1940, Los Angeles, California, m, 1960 **DISCIPLINE** ENGLISH **EDUCATION** Florida A&M, Tallahasse FL, BA, 1966; Florida State Univ, Tallahassee FL, MFA, 1969; Univ of Missouri, Columbia MO, PhD 1989-. **CAREER** Spelman Coll, Atlanta GA, instructor, 1969-75; Texas Southern Univ, Houston TX, asst professor, 1975-85; Mayor's Advisory Committee on Arts & Culture, Baltimore MD, dir arts in educ programs, 1988-90; Baltimore City Community College, professor, 1990-93; Eastern Connecticut State Univ, 1993-. **HONORS AND AWARDS** Graduated with Highest Honors from Florida A&M, 1966; Graduate Fellowship, Florida State Univ, 1967-69; Graduate Fellowship, Univ of Missouri, 1986-87; Rosalee Pritchett, performed at Negro Ensemble Company, 1971, published in Black Writers of America. **MEMBERSHIPS** Mem, Dramatist Guild of Amer, 1971-; president, Natl Assn For African-American Theatre, 1989-91; consultant for workshops in theatre and mass communications. **SELECTED PUBLICATIONS** Author of Black Theatre, Wyndham Hall Publishers, 1986; Noahs Ark, published in Center Stage, 1981; Upstage/Downstage, column in Houston Informer, 1977-78; **CONTACT ADDRESS** English Dept, Eastern Connecticut State Univ, Willimantic, CT, 06226.

MOLETTE, CARLTON WOODARD, II
PERSONAL Born 08/23/1939, Pine Bluff, AR, m, 1960 **DISCIPLINE** DRAMA **EDUCATION** Morehouse Coll, BA 1959; Univ of KC, graduate study 1959-60; Univ of IA, MA 1962; FL State Univ, PhD 1968. **CAREER** Little Theatre Div of Humanities Tuskegee Inst, asst dir 1960-61; Des Moines Comm Playhouse, designer tech dir 1962-63; Howard Univ Dept of Drama, asst prof of tech production & design 1963-64; FL A&M Univ, asst prof & tech dir 1964-67, assoc prof 1967-69; Spelman Coll, assoc prof of drama, 1969-75; Div of Fine Arts, chmn 1974-75; School of Communications TX So Univ, dean 1975-84; Lincoln Univ, dean College of Arts & Sciences, 1985-87; Coppin State College, vice pres Academic Affairs, 1987-91; University of CT, Department of Dramatic Arts, prof, Institute for African-American Studies, senior fellow, 1992-; guest dir Univ of MI Feb-Mar 1974. **HONORS AND AWARDS** Graduate fellowship in theatre Univ of KC; Atlanta Univ Center Faculty Rsch Grant 1970-71; Rosalee Pritchett (play) produced by Negro Ensemble Company, 1970; other plays: Dr B S Black (musical), Booji, Noah's Ark; Fortunes of the Moor produced by The Frank Silvera Writers' Workshop, 1995. **MEMBERSHIPS** Mem The Dramatists Guild; National Conference on African American Theatre, past president; Natl Assn of Dramatic & Speech Arts; past editor of "Encore"; mem bd dir Atlanta Arts Festival; vice pres Greater Atlanta Arts Council; chmn bd trustees Neighborhood Arts Center, Miller Theatre Advisory Council; mem, bd dir, Young Audiences of Maryland, 1990-93. **SELECTED PUBLICATIONS** Co-auth, Black Theatre, Premise & Presentation, Wyndham Hall Press, 2nd ed, 1986. **CONTACT ADDRESS** Department of Dramatic Arts, 802 Bolton Rd, Storrs, CT, 06268.

MONKMAN, LESLIE G.
DISCIPLINE ENGLISH LITERATURE **EDUCATION** York Univ, PhD. **CAREER** Dept Eng, Queen's Univ **RESEARCH** Canadian and other post-colonial literatures. **SELECTED PUBLICATIONS** Auth, A Native Heritage: Images of the Indian in English-Canadian Literature; pubs on Canadian and other post-colonial literatures in English. **CONTACT ADDRESS** English Dept, Queen's Univ, Kingston, ON, K7L 3N6. **EMAIL** monkmanl@post.queensu.ca

MONROE, DEBRA
DISCIPLINE ENGLISH **EDUCATION** Univ WI, BA; KS State Univ, MA; Univ UT, PhD. **CAREER** Southwest Tex State Univ **HONORS AND AWARDS** Flannery O'Connor Award for Short Fiction. **RESEARCH** Tudor humanists, espec John Colet and Thomas More. **SELECTED PUBLICATIONS** Auth, The Source of Trouble, Univ Ga Press; A Wild, Cold State, Simon & Schuster. **CONTACT ADDRESS** Southwest Texas State Univ, 601 University Dr, San Marcos, TX, 78666-4604.

MONTAGNES, IAN
PERSONAL Born 03/11/1932, Toronto, ON, Canada **DISCIPLINE** COMMUNICATIONS **EDUCATION** Univ Toronto, BA, 53, MA, 56. **CAREER** Tchr, Ryerson Inst Tech, 57-59; Info off, Univ Toronto, 59-63; info off, ROM, 63-66; head ed dept, Univ Toronto Press, 72-82; lectr, Fac Lib Sci, Univ Toronto, 89-93. **MEMBERSHIPS** Secy, Asn Can Univ Presses; Asn Am Univ Presses, 75-91; adv bd, Int Fedn Sci Eds, 91-; assoc fel, Massey Col 89-; Arts & Letters, Toronto. **SELECTED PUBLICATIONS** Auth, An Uncommon Fellowship: The Story of Hart House, 69; auth, The University of Toronto: A Souvenir, 84; co-ed, Cold Iron and Lady Godiva: Engineering Education at Toronto, 1920-1972, 72. **CONTACT ADDRESS** 31 Baldwin St, Port Hope, ON, L1A 1S3.

MONTGOMERY, LYNA LEE
DISCIPLINE VICTORIAN LITERATURE **EDUCATION** Univ Ark, PhD. **CAREER** English and Lit, Univ Ark. **HONORS AND AWARDS** Assoc chair. **SELECTED PUBLICATIONS** Coed, The Phoenix: Its Use as a Literary Device in English from the 17th Century to the 20th Century, D H Lawrence Rev, 72; A Mystery Reader, Scribner's, 75. **CONTACT ADDRESS** Univ Ark, Fayetteville, AR, 72701.

MOONEY, JACK
DISCIPLINE COMMUNICATION STUDIES **EDUCATION** Univ Ga, MA, 70; Univ Tennessee, PhD, 84. **CAREER** Prof. **SELECTED PUBLICATIONS** Auth, International Printing Pressmen and Assistants' Union of North America, 84; ed, Tennessee's newspapers for the state's bicentennial celebration, 96. **CONTACT ADDRESS** Dept of Communication, East Tennesee State Univ, PO Box 70717, Johnson City, TN, 37614-0717. **EMAIL** saucemaf@etsu.edu

MOORE, DON
DISCIPLINE SHAKESPEARE, JACOBEAN DRAMA, MODERN DRAMA **EDUCATION** Tulane, PhD, 64. **CAREER** Prof, La State Univ. **HONORS AND AWARDS** Outstanding Tchg award. **MEMBERSHIPS** Exec comt, S Cent Renaissance Soc, 85-89. **RESEARCH** The stagings of Shakespeare. **SELECTED PUBLICATIONS** Auth, John Webster and His Critics; Webster: The Critical Heritage. **CONTACT ADDRESS** Dept of Eng, Louisiana State Univ, 212M Allen Hall, Baton Rouge, LA, 70803.

MOORE, JOHN DAVID
PERSONAL Born 08/20/1949, s **DISCIPLINE** NINETEENTH-CENTURY BRITISH LITERATURE **EDUCATION** Univ MT, BA, 73, MA, 77; Univ WA, PhD, 85. **CAREER** Tchg asst, Univ WA, 80-84; Instr, Univ WA, 85; asst prof, Univ WA , 85-90; Assoc prof, Univ WA, 91-. **HONORS AND AWARDS** Grad Sch Dissertation Fel Univ WA, 83; Ill Hum Coun Mini Grant, 90, 92, 94; EIU Booth Library Fel, 90; Coun Fac Res Grant, EIU, 90. **MEMBERSHIPS** MLA; Midwest Mod Lang Asn; Midwest Victorian Studies Asn; Children's Lit Asn; Col Lang Asn. **SELECTED PUBLICATIONS** Auth, The Vision of the Feminine in William Morris' The Waters of the Wondrous Isles, Pre-Raphaelite Rev, 80; Coleridge and the 'Modern Jacobinical Drama': Osorio, Remorse, and the Development of Coleridge's Critique of the Stage, 1797-1816, Bul Res Hum, 82; Pottering About in the Garden: Kenneth Grahame's Vision of Pastoral in The Wind in the Willows, Jour MMLA, 90; John Masefield's The Box of Delights, Masterplots II: Juvenile and Young Adult Fiction, 91; Angela Brazil's A Fourth Form Friendship, , Masterplots II: Juvenile and Young Adult Fiction, 91; Emphasis and Suppression in Stevenson's Treasure Island: Fabrication of the Self in Jim Hawkins' Narrative, CLA Jour, 91; Richard Peck's Close Enough to Touch, Beacham's Guide Lit For Young Adults, 94; Richard Peck's The Dreadful Future of Blossom Culp, Beacham's Guide Lit For Young Adults, 94; Laurence Yep's Kind Hearts and Gentle Monsters, Beacham's Guide Lit For Young Adults, 94; Donald Barthelme's Paradise, Beacham's Guide Lit For Young Adults, 94; The Indians in Our Cupboards: Images of Native Americans in Books for Children, Ill Eng Bull, 95. **CONTACT ADDRESS** Eastern Illinois Univ, 600 Lincoln Ave, Charleston, IL, 61920-3099.

MOORE, JUDITH
DISCIPLINE 18TH-CENTURY LITERATURE **EDUCATION** Cornell Univ, PhD. **CAREER** Univ Alaska. **SELECTED PUBLICATIONS** Auth, A Zeal for Responsibility: The Struggle for Professional Nursing in Victorian England, 1868-1883, Univ Ga Press, 88; The Appearance of Truth: The Story of Elizabeth Canning and Eighteenth-Century Narrative, Univ Delaware Press, 94. **CONTACT ADDRESS** Univ Alaska Anchorage, 3211 Providence Dr., Anchorage, AK, 99508.

MOORE, MICHAEL
DISCIPLINE GERARD MANLEY HOPKINS **EDUCATION** Carleton, BA, MA; Queen's, PhD. **CAREER** Prof **HONORS AND AWARDS** WLU Outstanding Tchr Awd, 91; Canada Natl Tchg Awd, 93. **SELECTED PUBLICATIONS** Coauth, A Writer's Handbook of Current English, 83, 88; Coed, Sir Philip Sidney and the Croom Helm, 84; Interpretation of Renaissance Culture; Vital Candle: Victorian and Modern Bearings in Gerard Manley Hopkins, Univ Waterloo Press, 94; Dangerous Beauty: Hopkins and Newman; George Whalley: Remembrances, Quarry Press, 89; Why Hopkins Matters, Hopkins Quart, 98. **CONTACT ADDRESS** Dept of English, Wilfrid Laurier Univ, 75 University Ave W, Waterloo, ON, N2L 3C5. **EMAIL** mmoore@mach1.wlu.cas

MOORE, NATHAN
PERSONAL Born 06/26/1931, Mayaro, Trinidad and Tobago, m, 1967 **DISCIPLINE** ENGLISH **EDUCATION** Caribbean Union Coll Trinidad, A 1958; Rockford Coll IL, BA 1963; Carleton Univ Ottawa, MA 1965; Univ of British Columbia, PhD 1972. **CAREER** Barbados Secondary Sch, hs tchr 1958-61; Carleton U, sessional lecturer 1964-65, teaching fellow 1963-65; Barrier Sch Dist British Col, hs tchr, 1966-67; Walla Walla Coll WA, coll tchr 1967-79; AL State U, professor of English, 1979-, chmn dept of Engl 1980-. **HONORS AND AWARDS** Schlrshp Rockford Coll 1961; schlrshp Readers Digest 1962; Carleton Fellow Carleton Univ 1963-65. **MEMBERSHIPS** Mem Modern Lang Assn 1965-; mem Am Soc for 18th Century Studies 1971-; mem South Atlantic MLA 1980-. **CONTACT ADDRESS** Dept of Lang and Lit, Alabama State Univ, S Jackson St, Montgomery, AL, 36101.

MOORE, PATRICK
DISCIPLINE INSTRUMENTAL DISCOURSE **EDUCATION** Univ Miss, PhD. **CAREER** English and Lit, Univ Ark **SELECTED PUBLICATIONS** Auth, Rhetorical versus Instrumental Approaches to Teaching Technical Communication, Technical Comm; Intimidation and Communication, JBTC; When Politeness is Fatal, JBTC; Coauth, Using Gestalt Theory to Teach Document Design and Graphics, TCQ. **CONTACT ADDRESS** Univ Ark Little Rock, 2801 S University Ave., Little Rock, AR, 72204-1099. **EMAIL** epmoore@aol.com

MOORE, RAYBURN SABATZKY
PERSONAL Born 05/26/1920, Helena, AK, m, 1947, 2 children **DISCIPLINE** AMERICAN & SOUTHERN LITERATURE **EDUCATION** Vanderbilt Univ, BA, 42, MA, 47; Duke Univ, PhD(Am Lit), 56. **CAREER** Res asst, Duke Univ, 52, asst, 52-54; from asst prof to prof English, Hendrix Col, 54-59; assoc prof, 59-65, dir grad studies English, 64-69, Prof English, Univ Ga, 65-, Chmn Am Studies Prog, 68-, Chmn Div Lang & Lit, 75-, Vis scholar, Duke Univ, 58 & 64; chmn, executive comt, S Atlantic Grad English Group, 71-72. **MEMBERSHIPS** Soc Study Southern Lit (vp, 81-); MLA; Am Studies Asn; Southern Hist Asn; S Atlantic Mod Lang Asn. **RESEARCH** Southern literature since 1820; American literary magazines, 1865-1890; 19th century American realism, especially Henry James. **SELECTED PUBLICATIONS** Auth, Don Joaquin, a forgotten story by George W Cable, Am Lit, 1154; Constance Fenimore Woolson, Twayne, 63; The full light of a higher criticism, S Atlantic Quart, winter 64; Paul Hamilton Hayne, Twayne, 72; The epistolary James, Sewanee Rev, fall 75; The strange irregular rhythm of life: James's late tales and Constance Woolson, Satlantic Rev, 1976; The literary world gone mad: Hayne on Whitman, Southern Lit J, 1977; ed, A Man of Letters in the 19th Century South: Selected Letters of Paul Hamilton Hayne, La State Univ Press, 82; Classics Of Civil-War Fiction - Madden,D, Bach,P, Editors, Mississippi Quarterly, Vol 0046, 1993; Meaning In James,Henry - Bell,M, Studies In The Novel, Vol 0027, 1995; Preston,Margaret,Junkin - A Biography - Coulling,Mp, Mississippi Quarterly, Vol 0049, 1996. **CONTACT ADDRESS** Dept of English, Univ of Georgia, Park Hall, Athens, GA, 30602.

MOORE, ROBERT HAMILTON
PERSONAL Born 01/03/1913, St. Matthews, KY, m, 1939 **DISCIPLINE** ENGLISH **EDUCATION** Ind Univ, AB, 34, AM, 38; Univ Ill, PhD, 48. **CAREER** Asst English, Ind Univ, 35-38; from asst to instr, Univ Ill, 38-49; from assoc prof to prof, 49-78, chmn compos, 49-77, Emer Prof English, George Wash Univ, 78-. **MEMBERSHIPS** NCTE; Conf Col Compos & Commun. **RESEARCH** Freshman English; linguistics; rhetoric. **SELECTED PUBLICATIONS** Auth, Plan before you write, 50, Effective writing, 55, 59, 65 & 71, Elements of composition, 60, Handbook of effective writing, 66, 71 & The research paper, 67, Holt. **CONTACT ADDRESS** 314 Van Buren St, Falls Church, VA, 22046.

MOORE, ROBERT HENRY
PERSONAL Born 09/16/1940, Madisonville, KY, m, 1964, 2 children **DISCIPLINE** AMERICAN LITERATURE & HISTORY **EDUCATION** Davidson Col, AB, 62; Univ NC, Chapel Hill, MA, 64; Univ Wis-Madison, PhD(English), 70. **CAREER** Instr English, US Mil Acad, 68-70; asst prof, Univ Md, College Park, 70-76, assoc prof, 76-80. Contrib-reader, Dict Am Regional English, 68-; exec secy, Faulkner Concordance Proj, 70-, ed, Faulkner Concordance Newslett, 72-; reviewer, Nat Endowment for Humanities, 72; fel, Inter-Univ Sem Armed Forces & Soc, 73-. **MEMBERSHIPS** MLA; Am Studies Asn; Am Civil Liberties Union. **RESEARCH** twentieth century American language and literature, American studies; armed forces and society. **SELECTED PUBLICATIONS** Coauth, Black puritan, William & Mary Quart, 467; ed, Ellison at West Point, Contempt Lit, spring 74; coauth, School for Soldiers, Oxford Univ, 74; Cameras in state courts, An historical-perspective, judicature, vol 0078, 1994. **CONTACT ADDRESS** 9202 Saybrook Ave Branwell Park, Silver Spring, MD, 20901.

MOORE, WILLIAM HAMILTON
PERSONAL Born 06/29/1937, Kansas City, MO, m, 1964, 1 child **DISCIPLINE** ENGLISH **EDUCATION** Southwestern Univ, Tex, BA, 59; Harvard Univ, MA, 60, PhD(English), 63. **CAREER** From instr to asst prof English, Duke Univ, 63-67; from asst prof to assoc prof, 67-76, Prof Humanities, Austin Col, 76- **MEMBERSHIPS** MLA. **RESEARCH** The poetry of Michael Drayton; Elizabethan drama. **SELECTED PUBLICATIONS** Auth, An allusion in 1593 to The Taming of the Shrew, Shakespeare Quart, winter 64; Sources of Drayton's conception of Poly-Olbion, Studies Philol, 10/68. **CONTACT ADDRESS** Dept of English, Austin Col, Sherman, TX, 75090. **EMAIL** wmoore@austinc.edu

MOORTI, SUJATA
DISCIPLINE WOMEN'S STUDIES **EDUCATION** Univ Md, PhD, 95. **CAREER** Old Dominion Univ. **SELECTED PUBLICATIONS** Auth, Cathartic Confessions or Emancipatory Texts: Talk Shows and TV Representations of Rape; Desire in a Lost Empire: Constructions of Gendered Identities in

The Jewel in the Crown; Newspaper Coverage of Global Climate Change, 1986-1991; Environ Jour, January, 93. **CONTACT ADDRESS** Old Dominion Univ, 4100 Powhatan Ave, 4100 Powha, Norfolk, VA, 23058. **EMAIL** smoorti@odu.edu

MORACE, ROBERT ANTHONY
PERSONAL Born 09/22/1947, Rockville Centre, NY, m, 1987, 3 children **DISCIPLINE** ENGLISH **EDUCATION** SUNY Cortland, BA, 69, MS, 72; Univ SC, PhD, 76. **CAREER** Tchr, 69-71, Homer High Schl; grad tchng asst, 72-74, 75-76, tchng assoc, 76-77, Univ of S Carolina; Sr Fulbright Lect, 85-87, Warsaw Univ, Poland; asst prof, English, 77-81, assoc prof, English, 81-, Chmn, English Dept, 82-85, 98-, Daemen Col. **HONORS AND AWARDS** Dist Fac Achievement Award, Daemen Col, 79; Sr Fulbright Lect, Warsaw Univ, 85-87; Burger Prize, Univ of Wyoming, best theatre essay, 96. **MEMBERSHIPS** Modern Language Asn; Northeast Modern Language Asn; Amer Lit Section; Soc for the Study of Narrative Lit; John Gardner Soc. **RESEARCH** Contemporary fiction; Amer lit; narrative theory; bibliography; critical reception; cultural criticism. **SELECTED PUBLICATIONS** Art, Play It Again Sam, Papers on Lang & Lit, 93; art, Dialogues and Dialogics, Modern Lang Stud, 93; art, Tales from the Crypt(o-autobiography) A Users Guide to John Cheevers Journals, The Critical Response to John Cheever, Greenwood, 94; Auth, Newor(1)der, ANQ 5, 92; art, The Facts in Black and White Cheevers Falconer and Widemans Philadelphia Fire, Powerless Fictions: Ethics Cultural Critique and American Fiction in the Age of Postmodernism, Rodopi, 96; art From Sacred Hoops to Bingo Palaces Louise Erdrichs Carnivalesque Fiction, The Chippewa Landscape of Louise Erdrich, Univ of Alabama Press, 99; rev, Gardner Studies, Papers on Lang & Lit, 99; art, Whither Gardner Studies, Essays on John Gardner, 99. **CONTACT ADDRESS** English Dept, Daemen Col, Amherst, NY, 14226. **EMAIL** rmorace@daemen.edu

MORALES DEGARIN, MARIA A.
PERSONAL Born 08/08/1946, San Juan, PR, m, 1970, 2 children **DISCIPLINE** LIBRARY SCIENCE **EDUCATION** Univ del Sagrado Corazon, BA; Univ Puerto Rico, MLS. **CAREER** Dir, Univ del Sagrado Corazon, 71, 72-; dir, Puerto Rico Junior Col, 71. **MEMBERSHIPS** Am Asn Univ Prof; Am Library Asn; Phi Delta Kappa; Asn of Carribean Univ and Res Libr. **CONTACT ADDRESS** Universidad del Sagrado Corazon, Box 12383, San Juan, PR, 00914-2383. **EMAIL** a_garin@uscac1.usc.clu.edu

MORAN, BARBARA B.
PERSONAL Born 07/08/1944, Columbus, MS, m, 1965, 2 children **DISCIPLINE** LIBRARY SCIENCE **EDUCATION** Mount Holyoke Col, AB, 66; Emory Univ, M Ln, 73; SUNY, Buffalo, PhD, 82. **CAREER** Grad asst, 72-73, Woodruff Grad Libr, Emory Univ; libr head & dir, audiovisual svc, 74-78, Park Schl Buffalo; intern, 80, office of head Lockwood Mem Libr SUNY, Buffalo; tchng asst, 80-81, Schl of Info & Libr Stud, SUNY; asst prof, 81-87, assoc prof & asst dean, 87-90, dean & prof, 90-98, prof, 99-, Schl of Info & Libr Sci, Univ N C, Chapel Hill. **RESEARCH** Organizational leadership, organizational restructuring, career progression patterns **CONTACT ADDRESS** Sch of Information & Library Sci, Univ of No Carolina, Chapel Hill, CB# 3360, 100 Manning Hall, Chapel Hill, NC, 27599-3360. **EMAIL** moran@ils.unc.edu

MORAN, CHARLES
PERSONAL Born 11/06/1936, New York, NY, m, 1964, 2 children **DISCIPLINE** ENGLISH LITERATURE, WRITING **EDUCATION** Princeton Univ, AB, 58; Brown Univ, PhD(English), 67. **CAREER** Actg chmn, 78-81, assoc prof English, Univ Mass, Amherst, 67-, dir Writing Prog, 82-, dir, Nat Endowment for the Humanities Inst Teaching Writing, Univ Mass, Amherst, 78-82; vis prof, State Univ NY Albany, 81-82. **HONORS AND AWARDS** Distinguished Teacher Award, 90; Computers & Composition; Pres, Award for Public Service, 98. **MEMBERSHIPS** MLA; Col English Asn; Nat Coun Teacher English; New England Asn Teachers English. **RESEARCH** The teaching of writing; reader-response theory and its implications for the teaching of writing. **SELECTED PUBLICATIONS** Co-ed (with Kathleen Kroll), The letters of Herman White, Mass Rev, Summer 77; auth, Orwell, Jaws and McKuen: A case for good writing, Col English Asn Forum, 2/80; Teaching writing/teaching literature, Col Compos & Commun, 2/80; Hanging out the shingle: The writing tutor, J English Teaching Techniques, Winter 80; Turnpike poem: For Mina, Col Compos & Commun, 10/80; coauth (with Joseph T Skerrett, Jr), English Departments and the in-service training of teachers, Col Eng, 4/81; The secondary-level writing laboratory: A report from the field, In: Tutoring Writing, Scott Foresman, 82; New compos texts: The anatomy of process, Rev & Proc Community Col Humanities Asn, 2/82; Computers and the Teaching of Writing in American Higher Education, 79-94; co-auth, Norwood, NJ: Ablex, 96. **CONTACT ADDRESS** Dept of English, Univ of Massachusetts, Amherst, MA, 01003-0515. **EMAIL** cmoran@english.umass.edu

MORAN, MARY H.
PERSONAL Born 05/01/1947, Boston, MA, m, 1977, 1 child **DISCIPLINE** ENGLISH **EDUCATION** Brown Univ, BA, 69; Univ NMex, MA, 75, PhD, 80. **CAREER** Asst prof, English, Clemson Univ, 82-86; teach to Assoc prof, Univ Ga, 88-. **HONORS AND AWARDS** Best Essay, Carolinas Symp on Brit Stud, 89; NEH Panelist, 98. **MEMBERSHIPS** S Atlantic MLA; Ga/SC Col English Assoc; Nat Asn of Devel Educ. **RESEARCH** Contemporary British Novel; composition & rhetoric; developmental writing. **SELECTED PUBLICATIONS** Auth, Penelope Lively, Twayne, 93; auth, James Burgh, Eighteenth-Century British and American Rhetorics and Rhetoricians, Greenwood Press, 36-41, 94; auth, The Role of Reading Aloud in the Composing Process, Selected Conf Papers from the 20th Ann NADE Conf, 29-30; auth, The Novels of Penelope Lively: A Case for the Continuity of the Experimental Impulse in Postwar British Fiction, S Atl Rev, 1.62, 101-20; auth, Connections Between Reading and Successful Revision, J of Basic Writing, 16.2, 76-89, 97; auth, Mina Shaughnessy, Twentieth-Century Rhetorics and Rhetoricians, Greenwood Press, (in press). **CONTACT ADDRESS** Div Acad Asst, Univ Ga, Athens, GA, 30602. **EMAIL** mhmoran@arches.uga.edu

MORAN, MICHAEL G.
PERSONAL Born 03/21/1947, Ft. Benning, GA, m, 1977, 1 child **DISCIPLINE** ENGLISH LITERATURE **EDUCATION** City Col NY, BA, 71; Univ New Mexico, MA, 73, PhD, 78. **CAREER** Asst prof English, Clemson Univ, 80-86; assoc prof English, Univ Rhode Island, 86-88; assoc prof English, Univ Georgia, 88- . **HONORS AND AWARDS** Natl Coun Tchrs of English res award, 86; NEH Summer Inst, 89; Newberry Lib/Columbian Quincentennial Fel, 89; GA-SC Col English Asn res award, 91; GA-SC Col English Asn Teacher/Scholar of the Year, 95. **MEMBERSHIPS** Conf on Col Composition and Commun. **RESEARCH** History of rhetoric and composition; history of technical communication. **SELECTED PUBLICATIONS** Co-ed, Research in Composition and Rhetoric, Greenwood, 84; co-ed, Research in Technical Communication, Greenwood, 85; co-ed, Research in Basic Writing, Greenwood, 90; ed, British and American Rhetorics and Rhetoricians, Greenwood, 94; co-ed, Four Keys to the Past, Ablex, 99. **CONTACT ADDRESS** Dept of English, Univ of Georgia, Athens, GA, 30602. **EMAIL** mgmoran@arches.uga.edu

MORANT, MACK BERNARD
PERSONAL Born 10/15/1946, Holly Hill, South Carolina, s **DISCIPLINE** ENGLISH **EDUCATION** Voorhees College, Denmark, SC, BS, business administration, 1968; University of Massachusetts, Amherst, MA, MEd Urban Education, 1972, CAGS, education administration, 1973, EdD, 1976. **CAREER** Belcher Town State School, mental health assistant I, 1974-76; University Masachusetts, graduate student, research assistant, 1971-74; South Carolina Public School System, history, English, business teacher, 1968-71; Dillion-Marion Human Resources Comm, deputy director, 1977-81; South Carolina State College, Orangeburg, SC, director small business development ct, 1982-85; Virginia State University, Petersburg, VA, placement director, 1985-92; Augusta College, assistant professor, teacher, Georgia, 1992-96; Voorhees College, student support services program, dir, 1997-. **MEMBERSHIPS** Vice-chairman, Virginia State University Assessment Committee, 1986-87; member, Prince Hall Mason, 1986-; member, American Philatelic Society, 1988-; member, Alpha Kappa Psi Fraternity, 1985-. **SELECTED PUBLICATIONS** SPA Articles Include: "Identifying and Evaluation of Black History in Textbooks," The Journal of Secondary School Principals News; "The Gigantic Asylumn," The Carolina Messenger, 1977; "Blues, Jazz, and American Blacks," The Chronicle of Higher Education, 1978; The Insane Nigger, R&M Publishing Co, 1979; Publications include "Demystification of Blackness," Exploration in Education, South Carolina State College, 1983; "Bookselling: Direct Mail Marketing," Interlit, Dec, 1991; Upcoming Book African-American on Stamps, McFarland Publishers, 2000. **CONTACT ADDRESS** Publisher, R&M Publishing Co, PO Box 1276, Holly Hill, SC, 29059.

MORELAND, RICHARD
DISCIPLINE AMERICAN LITERATURE **EDUCATION** Univ Calif, Berkeley, PhD, 87. **CAREER** Assoc prof, dir, grad stud Eng, La State Univ. **HONORS AND AWARDS** Leverhulme Commonwealth/USA vis fel, Univ Wales, Swansea, 91-92. **RESEARCH** Cross-cultural encounters; critical theory; W. Faulkner. **SELECTED PUBLICATIONS** Auth, Humor, Rage, and Anti-Semitism in Faulkner's Hamlet, Faulkner J, 87; Compulsory and Revisionary Repetition: Faulkner's 'Barn Burning' and the Craft of Writing Difference, in Faulkner and the Craft of Fiction, 89; Faulkner and Modernism: Rereading and Rewriting, 90; 'He Wants to Put His Story Next to Hers': Putting Twain's Story Next to Hers in Toni Morrison's Beloved, Mod Fiction Stud, 93; Teaching Cross-Cultural Encounters and Student Writing with Question- Hypothesis-Questions (QHQs), in Teaching a "New Canon?", 95; Faulkner and Modernism, in Cambridge Companion to Faulkner Studies, 95; coauth, A Continuity in the Southern White Dilemma: Would Huck Finn Vote for David Duke?," in Borderlines: Studies in American Culture, 94. **CONTACT ADDRESS** Dept of Eng, Louisiana State Univ, 213A Allen Hall, Baton Rouge, LA, 70803. **EMAIL** enmore@lsuvm.sncc.lsu.edu

MOREY, JAMES
DISCIPLINE ENGLISH LANGUAGE AND LITERATURE **EDUCATION** Hamilton Univ, AB, 83; Cornell Univ, MA, 87; PhD, 90. **CAREER** Fac, Tex Tech Univ; assoc prof/dir undergrad studies, Emory Univ, 94-. **HONORS AND AWARDS** Fulbright scholar, 87-88. **RESEARCH** Old and Middle English, including Chaucer; Old French and Old Norse literature; Renaissance literature with a concentration on religious literature and the vernacular Bible. **SELECTED PUBLICATIONS** Auth, articles in Speculum, JEGP, Studies in Philol, Chaucer Rev, Spenser Studies, and Shakespeare Quart. **CONTACT ADDRESS** English Dept, Emory Univ, 1380 Oxford Rd NE, Atlanta, GA, 30322-1950. **EMAIL** jmorey@emory.edu

MORGAN, BETSY
DISCIPLINE US LITERATURE **EDUCATION** PhD. **CAREER** Eastern Col **SELECTED PUBLICATIONS** Areas: El Salvador; Justice issues. **CONTACT ADDRESS** Eastern Col, 1300 Eagle Rd, St. Davids, PA, 19087-3696.

MORGAN, GERALD
PERSONAL Born 05/08/1925, London, England, m, 1957, 2 children **DISCIPLINE** ENGLISH, PHILOSOPHY **EDUCATION** Loyola Col, Que, BA, 51; Univ Montreal, MA, 55, MA, 59, PhD(English), 62. **CAREER** Lectr lit & lang, Royal Mil Col, Que, 55-57, lectr lang & philos, 57-60, asst prof, 60-63, prof & head dept, 63-65; Prof Lit & Philos & Head Dept, Royal Roads Mil Col, Victoria, 65-, Mem exec comt, Humanities Res Coun Can, 70-72; Can Coun leave fel, 71-72; fel, Can Int Acad Humanities & Soc Sci, 74-. **MEMBERSHIPS** Humanities Asn Can (pres, 69-71); Can Asn Slavists; Mod Humanities Res Asn; Int Asn Univ Prof English. **RESEARCH** Conrad and maritime history; analogy versus metaphor in literature and science; Aristotle and general systems theory. **SELECTED PUBLICATIONS** Auth Conrad, Madach et Calderon, Etudes Slaves et Est- Europeennes, spring 61; Narcissus afloat: Myth and symbol in Conrad, autumn 64 & Harlequin Faustus: Marlowe's comedy of hell, spring 67, Humanities Asn Bull; coauth, Of Several Branches, Part III, Univ Toronto, 68; auth, Soundings: An Introduction to Philosophy, Queen's Printer, 76; co-ed, Critical Edition of The Nigger of the Narcissus, Norton, 79; ed, The Franklins Tale from Canterbury Tales, Homes & Meier, 81; Dowries For Daughters In West Wales, 1500-1700, Welsh History Review, Vol 0017, 95. **CONTACT ADDRESS** Dept of English, Royal Roads Mil Col, Victoria, BC, V0S 1B0.

MORGAN, LESLIE ZURKER
PERSONAL Born 02/03/1954, Norfolk, VA, m, 1978 **DISCIPLINE** MODERN LANGUAGE & LITERATURE **EDUCATION** Mt Holyoke Col, AB, 74; Middlebury Col, MA, 75; Yale Univ, MA, 77, MPhil, 79, PhD, 83. **CAREER** Lectr to asst prof, 82-89, St Univ NY Stony Brook; asst prof to assoc prof, 89-, Loyola Col Md. **MEMBERSHIPS** AAIS; AATF; AATI; ACH; CALICO; Dante Soc of Amer; IAHS; ICLS; MLA; Societe Rencevals. **RESEARCH** Romance epic; computational philol; computer assisted lang learning. **SELECTED PUBLICATIONS** Coed, The Foreign Language Classroom: Bridging Theory and Practice; Garland Educ Series, 95; ed, Dante: Summa Medioevalis, Filalibrary, 95; auth, Berta ai piedi grandi: Historical Figure and Literary Symbol, Olifant, 94-95; auth, Bovo d'Antona in the Geste Francor: Unity of Composition and Clan Destiny, Italian Culture, 99. **CONTACT ADDRESS** Dept of Modern Lang & Lit, Loyola Col, 4501 N Charles St, Baltimore, MD, 21210-2699. **EMAIL** morgan@vax.loyola.edu

MORGAN, LYLE W., II
DISCIPLINE ENGLISH **EDUCATION** **EDUCATION** Doane Col, AB; M.Ed., Fla State Christian Col, MEd; Wayne State Col, MAE, MSE; University Nebr, PhD. **CAREER** Assoc prof. **RESEARCH** 19th and 20th Century British fiction, Walt Whitman. **SELECTED PUBLICATIONS** Auth, The Homeopathic Treatment of Sports Injuries, 86; Homeopathic Medicine and Emergency Care, 90; Treating Sports Injuries the Natural Way, 84; Homeopathy and Your Child, 92; articles on bk censorship; bk rev(s). **CONTACT ADDRESS** Dept of Eng, Pittsburg State Univ, 1701 S Broadway St, Pittsburg, KS, 66762. **EMAIL** lmorgan@pittstate.edu

MORGAN, PETER FREDERICK
PERSONAL Born 09/01/1930, Stafford, England, m, 1961, 4 children **DISCIPLINE** ENGLISH **EDUCATION** Univ Birmingham, BA, 51; Univ London, MA, 55, PhD(English), 58. **CAREER** Lectr English, Victoria Col, 58-59; from lectr to assoc prof, 59-74, Prof English, Univ Col, Univ Toronto, 74-. **RESEARCH** Nineteenth-century literature; film and poetry. **SELECTED PUBLICATIONS** Ed, Taylor and Hessey, Keats-Shelley J, winter 58; Wordsworth and Jeffrey, Humanities Asn Bull, fall 68; Scott as critic, Studies in Scottish Lit, 769; Letters of Thomas Hood, Univ Toronto, 73; The poetic in the early life of JS Mill, Wordsworth Circle, winter 78; Lewes,G.H. - A Life - Ashton,R, Albion, Vol 0024, 1992. **CONTACT ADDRESS** Univ Col Univ of Toronto, Toronto, ON, M5S 1A1.

MORLEY, PATRICIA
PERSONAL Born 05/25/1929, Toronto, ON, Canada **DISCIPLINE** ENGLISH **EDUCATION** Univ Toronto, BA, 51;

Carleton Univ, MA, 67; Univ Ottawa, PhD, 70; Univ Sudbury, DSLitt, 92. **CAREER** Asst prof, Sir George Williams Univ, 72-75; assoc prof, 75-80, prof Eng & Can Stud, 80-89, PROF EMER, CONCORDIA UNIV, 92-; fel, Lonergan Univ Col, 79-84; fel, 79-88, assoc fel, 88-89, lifetime hon fel, Simone de Beauvoir Inst, 89-. **HONORS AND AWARDS** Ottawa Citizen Award Non-fiction, 87; Ottawa-Carleton Lit Award, 88, 91; Can Council Non-fiction Award, 91. **MEMBERSHIPS** Manotick Art Asn; Writers Union Can; Can Asn Commonwealth Lang & Lit Stud. **RESEARCH** Canadian literature **SELECTED PUBLICATIONS** Auth, The Mystery of Unity: Theme and Technique in the Novels of Patrick White, 72; auth, The Immoral Moralists: Hugh MacLennan and Leonard Cohen, 72; auth, Roberston Davies, 76; auth, The Commedians: Hugh Hood and Rudy Wiebe, 77; auth, Morley Callaghen, 78; auth, Margaret Laurence: The Long Journey Home, 91; auth, As Though Life Mattered: Leo Kennedy's Story, 94; ed, Ernest Thompson Seton: Selected Stories, 78. **CONTACT ADDRESS** PO Box 137, Manotick, ON, K4M 1A2.

MORRAL, FRANK R.
PERSONAL Born 04/07/1937, Vanersborg, Sweden, m, 1961, 3 children **DISCIPLINE** ENGLISH **EDUCATION** Whitman Col, AB, 59; Columbia Univ, AM, 60, PhD(English), 65; Col of St Thomas, MA, 80. **CAREER** Instr English, Whitman Col, 62-64; from instr to assoc prof, 64-75, Prof English, Carleton Col, 76-. **RESEARCH** Shakespeare; 16th century literature; James Joyce. **CONTACT ADDRESS** 1 N College St, Northfield, MN, 55057-4044.

MORRIS, DAVID BROWN
PERSONAL Born 08/11/1942, New York, NY, m, 1966, 1 child **DISCIPLINE** EIGHTEENTH CENTURY ENGLISH LITERATURE **EDUCATION** Hamilton Col, BA, 64; Univ Minn, Minneapolis, PhD(English), 68. **CAREER** Asst prof English, Univ VA, 68-72; assoc prof lit, Am Univ, 72-74; Prof English, Univ Iowa, 74-, Nat Endowment for Humanities younger humanist fel, 72-73; Guggenheim fel, 76-77. **MEMBERSHIPS** Am Soc 18th Century Studies; MLA. **RESEARCH** Alexander Pope; history of criticism; eighteenth century literature. **SELECTED PUBLICATIONS** Auth, The Religious Sublime: Christian Poetry and Critical Tradition in Eighteenth Century England, Univ KY, 72; The Kinship of Madness in Pope's Dunciad, Philol Quart, 72; The Visionary Maid: Tragic Passion and Redemptive Sympathy in Pope's Eloisa to Abelard, Mod Lang Quart, 73; Virgilian Attitudes in Pope's Windsor-Forest, Tex Studies Lit & Lang, 73; The Neurobiology Of The Obscene - Miller,Henry And Tourette Syndrome, Literature And Medicine, Vol 0012, 1993; About Suffering - Voice, Genre, And Moral Community, Daedalus, Vol 0125, 1996; Environment - The White-Noise Of Health - Editors Introduction, Literature And Medicine, Vol 0015, 1996. **CONTACT ADDRESS** Dept of English, Univ of Iowa, Iowa City, IA, 52242.

MORRIS, FRANCIS J.
DISCIPLINE MEDIEVAL BRITISH; MODERN BRITISH; LITERARY **EDUCATION** Saint Joseph's Col, AB, 58, Columbia Univ, MA, 60; Univ PA, PhD, 77. **CAREER** Engl, St. Joseph's Univ. **SELECTED PUBLICATIONS** Auth, Platonic Elements in Chaucer's Parliament of Fowles, PCTE Journal 4, 77; In Critical Survey of Literary Theory, Salem, 88. **CONTACT ADDRESS** St Joseph's Univ, 5600 City Ave, Philadelphia, PA, 19131. **EMAIL** fmorris@sju.edu

MORRIS, HARRY
PERSONAL Born 08/09/1924, New York, NY, m, 1949, 2 children **DISCIPLINE** ENGLISH **EDUCATION** Univ Miami, AB, 49, AM, 50; Univ Minn, PhD, 57. **CAREER** Teaching fel English, Ind Univ, 52-55; instr, Ohio Univ, 55-56; from instr to asst prof, Tulane Univ, 56-61; from asst prof to assoc prof, 61-67, Prof English, Fla State Univ, 67-, Folger Libr fel, 58. **MEMBERSHIPS** MLA; S Atlantic Mod Lang Asn Res; Renaissance and modern poetry. **RESEARCH** Medieval and renaissance eschatology. **SELECTED PUBLICATIONS** Co-auth, Poetry: A critical and historical introduction, Scott, 62; auth, Richard Barnfield: Colin' child, Fla State Univ; The Snake Hunter, Univ GA, 69; 'Duesenberg, 1929', Poetry, Vol 0165, 1994; 'On The Plight Of Us In The Caravaggio', Kenyon Review, Vol 0016, 1994; 'Sometimes, Late', Antioch Review, Vol 0052, 1994. **CONTACT ADDRESS** Dept of English, Florida State Univ, Tallahassee, FL, 32306.

MORRIS, JOHN NELSON
PERSONAL Born 06/18/1931, Oxford, England, m, 1966, 3 children **DISCIPLINE** ENGLISH **EDUCATION** Hamilton Col, AB, 53; Columbia Univ, MA, 56, PhD(English), 64. **CAREER** Instr English, Univ Del, 56-58; from lectr to instr, Columbia Univ, 58-61; lectr, San Francisco State Col, 61-62; from instr to asst prof, Columbia Univ, 62-67; assoc prof, 67-71, Prof English, Washington Univ, 71-, Guggenheim fel, 79., Literature Award, Am Acad & Inst Arts & Letters, 79. **MEMBERSHIPS** MLA. **RESEARCH** Eighteenth century English literature; Milton. **SELECTED PUBLICATIONS** Co-ed, Modern short stories: The fiction of experience, McGraw, 62; auth, Paradise Lost now, Am Scholar, winter 63-64; Versions of the self: Studies in English autobiography from John Bunyan to John Stuart Mill, Basic Bks, 66; Green business: Poems, Atheneum, 70; Wishes as horses: A word for the Houhynhynms, Yale Rev, 73; Samuel Johnson and the artists work, Hudson Rev, 73; The life beside this one, 75 & The Glass Houses (poems) 80, Atheneum; Religious-Experience In The Philosophical Theology Of Farrer,Austin, J Of Theological Studies, Vol 0045, 1994. **CONTACT ADDRESS** Dept of English, Washington Univ, St Louis, MO, 63130.

MORRIS, PAUL
DISCIPLINE COMPUTER-ASSISTED WRITING INSTRUCTION **EDUCATION** Univ Calif Davis, BA; Univ Nev, MA, PhD. **CAREER** Asst prof **RESEARCH** Creative writing, popular culture, American literature. **SELECTED PUBLICATIONS** Auth, The New Literacy: Moving Beyond the 3Rs, 96; two articles about Vietnam; rev, Unforgiven. **CONTACT ADDRESS** Dept of Eng, Pittsburg State Univ, 1701 S Broadway St, Pittsburg, KS, 66762. **EMAIL** smorris@pittstate.edu

MORRIS, VIRGINIA BAUMGARTNER
PERSONAL Born 03/28/1942, Ballston Spa, NY, m, 1970, 2 children **DISCIPLINE** ENGLISH & IRISH LITERATURE **EDUCATION** Beaver Col, BA, 64; Columbia Univ, MA, 66, PhD(English), 73. **CAREER** Asst prof, 67-76, Assoc Prof English, John Jay Col Criminal Justice, 76- **MEMBERSHIPS** MLA; Renaissance Soc Am; Acja. **RESEARCH** Sixteenth century English literature; Irish literary Renaissance; Crime and Punishment in literature. **SELECTED PUBLICATIONS** International Perspectives On Social And Policy Issues - Introduction, J Of Arts Management Law And Society, Vol 0026, 1997. **CONTACT ADDRESS** John Jay Col of Criminal Justice, CUNY, 445 W 59th St, New York, NY, 10019.

MORRISON, TONI
PERSONAL Born 02/18/1931, Lorain, OH, d, 2 children **DISCIPLINE** WRITER **EDUCATION** Howard Univ, BA, 53; Cornell Univ, MA, 55. **CAREER** Tchr, Engl, Texas Southern Univ, 55-57; tchr, Howard Univ, 57-63; assoc ed, Syracuse, 64-66; sr ed, Random House, 67-83; assoc prof English, SUNY Purchase, 71-72; vis lectr, Yale Univ, 76-77; Albert Schweitzer Prof Hum, SUNY Albany, 84- ; Robert F. Goheen Prof, Coun of Hum, Princeton Univ, 87- . **HONORS AND AWARDS** Nobel Prize, Literature; Natl Book Critic's Circle Award; Am Acad and Inst of Arts and Lett Award; Natl Coun of the Arts; Pulitzer Prize, 88., Auth, The Bluest Eye, 70; Sula, 73; Song of Solomon, 77; Tar Baby, 81; Dreaming Emmett, 86; Beloved, 87; Jazz, 92; The Dancing Mind, 97; Paradise, 98. **CONTACT ADDRESS** Random House, 201 East 50th St, New York, NY, 10022.

MORRISSEY, LEE
PERSONAL Born 08/21/1964, Boston, MA **DISCIPLINE** ENGLISH **EDUCATION** Boston Col, BA, 86; Columbia Univ, MA, 88, 90, Mphil, 92, PhD, 95. **CAREER** Asst Prof, Clemson Univ, 95-. **HONORS AND AWARDS** Pres Fel, Columbia Univ, 90-93; Robert John Bennet Mem Award, 93; Mellon Found Sum Fe., 93; Grad Stu Essay Prize, Am Soc Eighteenth Cen Stu, 94. **MEMBERSHIPS** MLA; ASELA; ACSA. **RESEARCH** 18th century British literature; Milton; literary theory; literature & architecture. **SELECTED PUBLICATIONS** Ed & contribr, The Kitchen Turns Twenty: A Retrospective Anthology, The Kitchen, 92; auth, Robinson Crusoe and the South Sea Trade: 1710-1720, Money: Lure, Lore, and Literature, Greenwood Press, 94; Affectedly Unaffected: Eighteenth-Century Architectural Follies and Walpole's Castle of Otranto, Postmodern Perspectives on Eighteenth-Century Literature and Culture, Assoc Univ Presses, 98; From the Temple to the Castle: An Architectural History of English Literature, 1660-1760, Univ Press Va, 99; Approach and read the stone: Toward an Archaeology of Gray's Elegy, The Age of Johnson (forthcoming). **CONTACT ADDRESS** English Dept, Clemson Univ, 801 Strode Tower, Box 341503, Clemson, SC, 29634-1503. **EMAIL** lmorris@clemson.edu

MORRISSEY, THOMAS J.
DISCIPLINE ENGLISH **EDUCATION** SUNY Binghamton, BA; MA; Rutgers Univ, PhD, 77. **CAREER** Col wrtg dir, Plattsburgh State Univ of NY . **HONORS AND AWARDS** Disting Tchg Prof, Plattsburgh State Univ of NY, 96; NY State Univ Chancellor's Awd Excellence Tchg, 91. **RESEARCH** Sci Fiction; Irish Lit. **SELECTED PUBLICATIONS** Auth, publ(s) on writing pedag, Irish Lit, and Sci Fiction. **CONTACT ADDRESS** SUNY, Plattsburgh, 101 Broad St, Plattsburgh, NY, 12901-2681.

MORRISSON, MARK S.
DISCIPLINE ENGLISH **EDUCATION** Univ Tex, Austin, BA, 88; Univ Chicago, MA, 89, PhD, 96. **CAREER** ASST PROF ENG, PA STATE UNIV, UNIV PK, 96-. **CONTACT ADDRESS** Dept of English, Pennsylvania State Univ, 119 Burrows Bldg, University Park, PA, 16802-6200.

MORSBERGER, ROBERT E.
PERSONAL Born 09/10/1929, Baltimore, MD, m, 1955, 1 child **DISCIPLINE** ENGLISH **EDUCATION** Johns Hopkins Univ, BA, 50; Univ Iowa, MA, 54, PhD(English), 56. **CAREER** From instr to asst prof English, Miami Univ, 56-59; asst prof, Utah State Univ, 59-61; from asst prof to assoc prof Am Thought & Lang, Mich State Univ, 61-68; prof English, Eastern Ky Univ, 68-69; chmn dept, 74-78, prof English, Calif State Polytech Univ, Pomona, 69-, vis prof & adv, English, Mich State Univ-US Agency for Int Develop team, Univ Nigeria, 64-66; vis assoc prof, NMex State Univ, 67-68; adv Gloveville Proj, Nat Am Studies Fac, 73. **HONORS AND AWARDS** Winner of the Burkhardt Award for Outstanding Steinbeck Scholarship. **MEMBERSHIPS** Am Studies Asn; Rocky Mountain Mod Lang Asn; Western Literature Asn; John Steinbeck Soc Am; Pen. **RESEARCH** American and African literature; motion pictures; popular culture; Eighteenth Century Studies. **SELECTED PUBLICATIONS** Auth, The language of composition, 65 & coauth, Commonsense grammar and style, 65, rev ed, 72, Crowell; ed, Essays in exposition: an international reader, Univ Nigeria & US Agency for Int Develop, 66; The Wilkes expedition: 1838-1842, Am Hist Illus, 6/72; The Minister's Black Veil: Shrouded in a blackness, ten times black, New Eng Quart, 9/73; ed, John Steinbeck, Viva Zapata!, Viking, 75; coauth, Lew Wallace: Militant Romantic, McGraw-Hill, 80; co-ed, 2 volumes on American Screenwriters in the Dictionary of Literary Biography, et al. **CONTACT ADDRESS** Dept of English and Mod Lang, California State Polytech Univ, 3801 W Temple Ave, Pomona, CA, 91768-4001. **EMAIL** remorsberger@csupomona.edu

MORSE, CHARLOTTE COOK
PERSONAL Born 10/26/1942, Washington, DC **DISCIPLINE** ENGLISH LITERATURE, MEDIEVAL STUDIES **EDUCATION** Brown Univ, AB, 64; Stanford Univ, MA, 68, PhD(English), 70. **CAREER** From instr to asst prof English, Yale Univ, 68-76, Assoc Prof English, VA Commonwealth Univ, 76-, Morse fel English, Yale Univ, 72-73; prog officer div res grants, Nat Endowment for Humanities, 75-76. **MEMBERSHIPS** Mediaeval Acad Am; MLA; Southeastern Medieval Asn. **RESEARCH** Middle English literature; Old French literature; medieval intellectual history. **SELECTED PUBLICATIONS** Auth, The image of the vessel in Cleanness, Univ Toronto Quart, 71; The Pattern of Judgment in the Queste and Cleanness, Univ Mo, 78; The Manuscripts Of The 'Canterbury Tales', Notes And Queries, Vol 0040, 1993; Women Defamed And Women Defended - An Anthology Of Medieval Texts - Blamires,A, Pratt,K, Marx,Cw, Editors, Medium Aevum, Vol 0063, 1994; The Shorter Poems - Minnis,Aj, Notes And Queries, Vol 0043, 1996; Gender And Romance In Chaucer,Geoffrey 'Canterbury Tales' - Crane,S, Speculum-A J Of Medieval Studies, Vol 0071, 1996; Gender And Romance In Chaucer,Geoffrey 'Canterbury Tales' - Crane,S, Speculum-A J Of Medieval Studies, Vol 0071, 1996; Chaucer 'Clerks Tale' - The Griselda Story Received, Rewritten, Illustrated - Bronfman,J, Notes And Queries, Vol 0043, 1996; From 'Pearl' To 'Gawain' - Form And Fynisment - Blanch,Rj, Wasserman,Jn, Speculum-A J Of Medieval Studies, Vol 0072, 1997; From 'Pearl' To 'Gawain' - Form And Fynisment - Blanch,Rj, Wasserman,Jn, Speculum-A J Of Medieval Studies, Vol 0072, 1997. **CONTACT ADDRESS** Dept of English, VA Commonwealth Univ, Box 2005, Richmond, VA, 23284-9004.

MORSE, JONATHAN
PERSONAL Born 08/29/1940, New York, NY, 1 child **DISCIPLINE** AMERICAN LITERATURE **EDUCATION** Penn State Univ, BS, 62, MS, 65; Ind Univ, PhD, 75. **CAREER** Bacteriologist, Eli Lilly & Co, 64-69; from instr to asst prof English, Wayne State Univ, 73-77; from Asst Prof to Prof English, Univ Hawaii, Manoa, 77-. **MEMBERSHIPS** AAAS; AAUP; MLA; IAPL; Soc Critical Exchange; Emily Dickinson Int Soc. **RESEARCH** Literary history; literary criticism. **SELECTED PUBLICATIONS** Auth, Word by Word: The Language of Memory, Cornell Univ Press, 90; Typical Ashbery, In: The Tribe of John: John Ashbery and Contemporary Poetry, Univ Ala Press, 95; Some of the Things We Mean When We Say "New England", Emily Dickinson J 5.2, 96; Antisemitism as Discourse, H-Net list H-Antisemitism, 1/24/97; Six articles in: An Emily Dickinson Encyclopedia, Greenwood Press, 98; T.S. Eliot Says Jew, Am Lit Hist (in press); author of numerous other articles. **CONTACT ADDRESS** Dept of English, Univ of Hawaii, 1733 Donaghho Rd, Honolulu, HI, 96822-2368. **EMAIL** jmorse@hawaii.edu

MORSE, JOSIAH MITCHELL
PERSONAL Born 01/14/1912, Columbia, SC, m, 1936, 2 children **DISCIPLINE** ENGLISH **EDUCATION** Univ SC, AB, 32, MA, 33; Pa State Univ, PhD(English), 52. **CAREER** Reporter, Columbia Record, SC, 34; news ed, Am Banker, 35- 42; asst ed, The Nation, 43-45; UN correspondent, Free Press India, 46-47; from instr to prof, Pa State Univ, 48-67; prof, 67-79, Emer Prof English, Temple Univ, 79-, Am Coun Learned Soc fel, 51; Mem, Int Fed Mod Lang & Lit; bk rev ed, J Gen Educ, 60- 67; mem ed comt, Pmla, 70-74. **MEMBERSHIPS** MLA; Int Comp Lit Asn; Am Comp Lit Asn. **RESEARCH** James Joyce; comparative literature; problems of teaching English. **SELECTED PUBLICATIONS** Auth, The Sympathetic Alien, NY Univ, 59; Matters of style, Bobbs, 68; The irrelevant English teacher, 72 & Prejudice and Literature, 76, Temple Univ; Popular Science + Response To Johnson,Steven Article On The Vogue Of Chaos Theory Among Teachers Of Liberal-Arts, Lingua Franca, Vol 0006, 1996. **CONTACT ADDRESS** 115 Morris Rd, Ambler, PA, 19002.

MORTON, CARLOS
PERSONAL Born 10/15/1947, Chicago, IL, m, 1981, 2 children **DISCIPLINE** ENGLISH DRAMA **EDUCATION** Univ Tex El Paso, BA, eng, 75; Univ Calif San Diego, MFA, drama, 79; Univ Tex Austin, PhD, drama, 87. **CAREER** Instr, speech and drama dept, Laredo Jr Col, 86-88; asst prof, drama, Univ Tex El Paso, 88-89; assoc prof, 90-95, full prof, 96-, theatre, Univ Calif Riverside. **HONORS AND AWARDS** Fulbright lectr, Univ Nat Autonoma de Mex, 89-90; winner, second prize, James Baldwin Playwriting Contest, UMAS, 89; winner, first prize, Nat Latino Playwriting Contest, NY Shakespeare Festival Theatre, NY, 86; Mina Shaughnessy Scholar, FIPSE, Wash, DC, 81. **RESEARCH** U.S. Latino theatre; Chicano theatre; Mexican and Central American theatre. **SELECTED PUBLICATIONS** Play, Cuentos, Una Linda Raza, Fulcrum Publ, 163-172, 98; play, Rancho Hollywood, Great Scenes From Minority Playwrights, Meriwether Publ Ltd, 97-137, 97; play, The Many Deaths of Danny Rosales, Types of Drama, RR Donnelley & Sons, 809-832, 97; auth, At Risk, Players Press, 14, 97; auth, The Drop Out, Players Press, 15, 97; auth, Drug-O, Players Press, 18, 97; auth, Los Fatherless, Players Press, 23, 97; auth, The Fickle Finger of Lady Death and Other Plays, Peter Lang Press, NY, 133, 96. **CONTACT ADDRESS** Theatre Arts Dept., Univ of California, Riverside, CA, 92525.

MOSCO, VINCENT
DISCIPLINE COMMUNICATIONS **EDUCATION** Harvard Univ, PhD. **CAREER** Prof; supervisor of grad stud. **HONORS AND AWARDS** Ed bd(s), US, Can, Eng, Spain; contrib, ed adv bd of the Intl Encycl of Commun; res positions, US government with the White House Off of Telecommun Policy; Nat Res Coun and the US Congress Off of Tech Assessment; Can with the Fed Dept(s) of Commun, Labour, and Finance; consult, US Gen Accounting Off; the Commun Workers of Amer; Commun Workers of Can; Can Overseas Telecommun Union; pres, Polit Econ Section. **MEMBERSHIPS** Mem, governing coun of the Intl Assn for Mass Commun Res. **RESEARCH** Communication and critique, communication and social science. **SELECTED PUBLICATIONS** Auth, The Political Economy of Communication: Rethinking and Renewal, London: Sage, 96; pub(s), over fifty refereed articles and book chapters, Soc; Telecommun Policy; Jour Commun; Ind Rel(s); Columbia Jour Rev; Le Monde Diplomatique; Critical Stud in Mass Commun; Media Stud Jour. **CONTACT ADDRESS** Dept of Commun, Carleton Univ, 1125 Colonel By Dr, Ottawa, ON, K1S 5B6.

MOSELEY, JAMES G.
PERSONAL Born 03/24/1946, Atlanta, GA, m, 1968, 2 children **DISCIPLINE** RELIGION; LITERATURE **EDUCATION** Stanford Univ, BA, 68; Univ Chicago Div Sch, MA, 71, PhD, 73. **CAREER** Cord Amer stud (s) prog, 73-79, Ch Hum div, 79-86, asst, assoc, full prof, 73-86, New Col, Univ S Fla; prof Relig, 86-91, dir honors prog, 89-91, VP acad affairs, Dean fac, 86-89, Chapman Col, Calif; VP, Dean, prof Relig, Transylvania Univ, Ky, 91- . **HONORS AND AWARDS** Fel in res Col tchrs, Natl Endowment Hum, Princeton, 76-77; Ed proj grant, NEH, for curric devel, New Col, 77; summer sem Col tchrs, NEH, 79, Univ Calif, Irvine; summer sem Col tchrs, NEH, 82, Harvard Univ; res and creative scholar awd, Univ S Fla, Summer, 83; Co-dir, summer sem sch tchrs, NEH, 84, New Col; Core Fac, Revisioning Am: Relig and the Life of the Nation, series, Ind Univ, Lilly Endowment, 84-90; Proj Dir, Power and Morality conf for commun leaders and sec sch tchrs, Fla endowment Hum, New Col, 85; dir, summer sem sch tchrs, NEH, New Col, 86; dir, summer sem sch tchrs, NEH, Univ Calif Irvine, 90; dir, summer sem sch tchrs, Transylvania Univ, 92; Core fac, Cultural Diversity and Civic Responsibility, Wye High Sch fac sem, Transylvania Univ, 93; Core Fac, Pub Expressions of Rel in Amer, series, Ind Univ, Lilly Endowment, 92-94. **MEMBERSHIPS** Amer acad Relig; Amer Stud Asn; Org Amer Hist; Amer soc Church Hist; Natl Col honors coun; Amer conf acad Deans; Asn Amer Col Univ; Amer Asn higher educ. **RESEARCH** History of Religion. **SELECTED PUBLICATIONS** Auth, A Complex Inheritance: The Idea of Self-Transcendence in the Theology of Henry James, Sr, and the Novels of Henry James, Amer Acad Relig Diss Series, vol 4, Missoula, MT, AAR and Scholar Press, 75; Conversion through Vision: Puritanism and Transcendentalism in The Ambassadors, Jour Amer Acad Relig, XLIII/3, Sept 75; Religious Ethics and the Social Aspects of Imaginative Literature, Jour Amer Acad Relig, XL vol 3, Sept 77; Religion and Modernity: A Case Granted, Bull of the Couns on the Stud Relig, IX/1, Feb 78; Literature and Ethics: Some Possibilities for Religious Thought, Perspect Relig Stud (s), VI/1, Spring 79; The Social Organization of Religion in America: Then and Now, SEASA '79 Proceedings, Tampa, Fla, Amer Stud (s) Press, 79; Culture, Religion, and Theology, Theol Today, XXXVII/3, Oct 80; auth, A Cultural History of Religion in America, Westport, Conn, Greenwood Press, 81; From Conversion to Self-Transcendence: Religious Experience in American Literature, SEASA '83 Proceedings, Tampa, Fla, Amer Stud (s) Press, 83; Inerrantism as Narcissism: Biblical Authority as a Cultural Problem, Perspectives in Relig Stud (s), Fall 83; An Occasion for Changing One's Mind: A Response to Charles Long, Relig Studs and Theol, vol 3, Sept 85; Winthrop's Journal: Religion, Politics, and Narrative in Early America, in Religion and the Life of the Nation: American Recoveries, Sherrill, Illinois UP, 90, reprinted in Literature Criticism from 1400-1800, LC, vol 31, Bostrom, Detroit, Gale, 95; auth, John Winthrop's World: History as a Story as History, Madison, U of Wisconsin P, 92; Civil Religion Revisited, Relig and Amer Cult: A Jour of Interpretation, 4/1, Winter, 94; rev essay: Jenny Franchot's Roads to Rome: The Antebellum Protestant Encounter with Catholicism, Relig Stud (s) Rev, 23/3, July 97. **CONTACT ADDRESS** Dept of Dean, Transylvania Univ, Lexington, KY, 40508.

MOSELEY, MERRITT
PERSONAL m, 4 children **DISCIPLINE** ENGLISH LITERATURE AND LANGUAGE **EDUCATION** Huntingdon Col, BA; Univ NC, Chapel Hill, MA, PhD. **CAREER** Prof, dean, fac develop, Univ NC, Asheville. **SELECTED PUBLICATIONS** Auth, Understanding Julian Barnes, Univ SC Press, 97. **CONTACT ADDRESS** Univ N. Carolina, Asheville, Karpen Hall, Asheville, NC, 28804-8510. **EMAIL** MOSELEY@unca.edu

MOSER, HAROLD DEAN
PERSONAL Born 10/31/1938, Kannapolis, NC, m, 1964, 2 children **DISCIPLINE** AMERICAN HISTORY, AMERICAN LITERATURE **EDUCATION** Wake Forest Univ, BA, 61, MA, 63; Univ Wis-Madison, PhD(hist), 77. **CAREER** Instr hist, Chowan Col, 63-65; teaching asst, Univ Wis- Madison, 67-69; res asst, State Hist Soc Wis, 68-71; from asst ed to co-ed, Papers of Daniel Webster, Dartmouth Col, 71-78, ed corresp ser, Papers of Daniel Webster, 78-79; Ed & Dir, Papers of Andrew Jackson, Univ Tenn, 79-, Nat Hist Pub Comn fel, Dartmouth Col, 71-72. **HONORS AND AWARDS** Philip M Hamer Award, Soc Am Archivists, 75. **MEMBERSHIPS** Orgn Am Historians; Southern Hist Asn; AHA. **RESEARCH** Jacksonian America; the Old South; Daniel Webster. **SELECTED PUBLICATIONS** Auth, Reaction in North Carolina to the Emancipation Proclamation, NC Hist Rev, 67; New Hampshire and the ratification of the Twelfth Amendment, Dartmouth Libr Bull; co- ed, The Papers of Daniel Webster: Correspondence Series (Vols 1, 2 & 4), 75-78, ed, Vol 5, 82, Univ Press New Eng; The Papers of Andrew Jackson, Univ Tenn Press, Vol 2 (in prep); Liberty And Power - The Politics Of Jacksonian America - Watson,Hl, Virginia Magazine Of History And Biography, Vol 0101, 1993. **CONTACT ADDRESS** Papers of Andrew Jackson, Univ of Tenn, Hermitage, TN, 37066.

MOSES, MICHAEL VALDEZ
DISCIPLINE ENGLISH LITERATURE **EDUCATION** VA Univ, PhD, 87. **CAREER** English, Duke Univ. **RESEARCH** Mod comp and contemp lit, with emphasis on twentieth century Brit, Irish, postcolonial and Third World fiction and theory. **SELECTED PUBLICATIONS** Auth, The Novel and the Globalization of Culture, Oxford, 95; ed, The Writings of J.M. Coetzee, Duke, 94; publ(s) on Hardy; Stoker; Joyce; Beckett; DeLillo; Carpentier; Vargas Llosa; Ngugi; latin Am Lit rev; S Atlantic quart; mod fiction studies. **CONTACT ADDRESS** Eng Dept, Duke Univ, Durham, NC, 27706.

MOSIER, JOHN
PERSONAL Born 07/09/1944, Bentonville, Ark, m, 1986, 3 children **DISCIPLINE** ENGLISH **EDUCATION** Tulane Univ, BA, 64, MA, 66, PhD(English), 68. **CAREER** Instr, Tulane Univ, 66-68; instr 67-68, asst dean, 69-71, exec secy acad aff, 71-74, asst prof, 67-80; assoc dir, Film Inst, 75-85, dir, 85-93; editor, New Orleans, 86-93; chmn, 89-92, prof, Loyola Univ, 86-; contrib editor, Americas Mag, 80-90, contrib editor, New Orleans Art Rev, 92-. **RESEARCH** Flim and history **SELECTED PUBLICATIONS** Auth, Machine intelligence and the arts, New Orleans Rev, 69; coauth, Institute research: A review, Univ Southwestern La, 72; auth, Voando a Brasilia, 1ste e Espectaculo, 76; Depoe, Correio Brasiliense, 76; coauth, Women & men together, Houghton, 77; auth, Latin American film today, Americas, 78; Cineman 77, 1ste e Cinema, 78; The new Brasilian film, New Orleans Rev, 78; contrib auth, Handbook of Popular Culture in Latin America, Greenwood, 85; auth, World Cinema Since 1945, Ungar, 87; auth, Before the Wall Came Down Univ Press Amer, 90; coauth, Cinema polinais Editions du cerf, 89; ed, Artist Under Socialism, nor, 85; ayth Kafkas Ankommen, Kino, 92; auth, On the Edge of the Abyss, Cream City Rev, 89; auth Yankee Hustle, Variety, 80; auth, Sanitizing Stalin, Times Picayune, 97; auth, Surviving Art Films, New Orleans Art Rev, 96; auth, Un Secreto Bien Guardado, Americas, 89. **CONTACT ADDRESS** Loyola Univ, 6363 St Charles Ave, Box 50, New Orleans, LA, 70118-6195. **EMAIL** jmosier@loyno.edu

MOSS, JOHN E.
PERSONAL Born 02/07/1940, Waterloo County, ON, Canada **DISCIPLINE** ENGLISH **EDUCATION** Univ West Ont, BA, 61, MA, 69; Univ Waterloo, Mphil, 70; Univ NB, PhD, 73. **CAREER** Concordia Univ, 73-76; Univ BC, 77-78; Queen's Univ, 78-80; PROF ENGLISH (CAN LIT) UNIV OTTAWA 80-; Dobbin ch Can stud, Univ Dublin, 97-98. **MEMBERSHIPS** Asn Can Univ Tchrs Eng; Writers Union Can. **SELECTED PUBLICATIONS** Auth, Arctic Landscape and the Metaphysics of Geography; auth, Sex and Violence in the Canadian Novel; auth, Bellrock; auth, Enduring Dreams: An Exploration of Arctic Landscape; founding ed, J Can Fiction. **CONTACT ADDRESS** 1290 Hilliard St, Peterborough, ON, K9H 5S4.

MOSS, LAURA
DISCIPLINE ENGLISH LITERATURE **EDUCATION** Univ Toronto, BA; Univ Guelph, MA; Queen's Univ, PhD. **CAREER** Asst prof **RESEARCH** Postcolonial theories and literatures; resistance writing; nationalism; multiculturalism; realisms; intersection of postmodernism and postcolonialism; Southern African and Canadian fiction. **SELECTED PUBLICATIONS** Auth, pub(s) on Chinua Achebe, Ngg, Ian Wedde, Salman Rushdie, and postcolonial theory. **CONTACT ADDRESS** Dept of English, Manitoba Univ, Winnipeg, MB, R3T 2N2.

MOSS, S.
PERSONAL Born 02/29/1944, St. Paul, MN, d, 1 child **DISCIPLINE** THEATER, ENGLISH RENAISSANCE DRAMA **EDUCATION** Univ Calif, Los Angeles, BA, 65; Univ S Fla, MA, 93, PhD, 97. **CAREER** Actress, Los Angeles, New York regional theater, 65-90; prof, Univ S Fla, 97-. **MEMBERSHIPS** Shakespeare Asn; Actor's Asn; Marlow Soc. **RESEARCH** Renaissance medicine; literature; the occult. **SELECTED PUBLICATIONS** Auth, A Continuing Checklist of Multidisciplinary Scholarship on Aging, J Aging and Identity, 96, 97 ; auth, Biographical entry on Bram Stoker in Dictionary of Literary v 178: British Fantasy and Science-Fiction Writers before World War I, Bruccoli Clark Layman, 97; auth, The Psychiatrist's Couch: Hypnosis, Hysteria, and Proto-Freudian Performance in Dracula, in Sucking Through the Century, 1897-1997, Dundurn, 97; auth, Psychical Research and Psychoanalysis: Bram Stoker and the Early Freudian Investigation into Hysteria, in The Shade and the Shadow: A Critical Anthology, Desert Island Books, 98. **CONTACT ADDRESS** Dept Eng, CPR107, Univ S. Florida, 4202 E Fowler Ave, Tampa, FL, 33620. **EMAIL** moss@chuma.cas.usf.edu

MOSS, SIDNEY PHIL
PERSONAL Born 03/27/1917, Liverpool, England, m, 1946, 3 children **DISCIPLINE** ENGLISH **EDUCATION** Univ Ill, BS, 50, MA, 51, PhD, 54. **CAREER** From res asst to asst ed Am Lit, Univ Ill, 50-56; from head res dept to ed, Champaign, Ill, off, Spencer Press, 52-54; from asst prof to prof English, Murray State Univ, 56-64; vis prof, 64, Prof English, Southern Ill Univ, Carbondale, 65-, Am Philos Soc grants, 66 & 78; Fulbright lectr Am lit, Univ Col, Dublin, 69-70. **RESEARCH** American and English literature, especially of the nineteenth century. **SELECTED PUBLICATIONS** Coauth, Thy Men Shall Fall, Ziff-Davis, 48; auth, Poe's Literary Battles, Duke Univ, 63; Composition by Logic, 66 & Readings for Composition by Logic, 68, Wadsworth; Poe's Major Crisis, Duke Univ, 70; coauth, The New Composition by Logic, Southern Ill Univ, 78; Charles Dickens' Quarrel with America, Whitston, 82; Dickens,Frederick, From Courtship To Courtroom, Dickensian, Vol 0090, 1994. **CONTACT ADDRESS** Dept of English, Southern Ill Univ, Carbondale, IL, 62901.

MOULTHROP, STUART
DISCIPLINE COMMUNICATIONS **EDUCATION** Yale Univ, PhD. **CAREER** Yale; Univ Tx; Ga Inst Tech; assoc prof, Univ Baltimore. **SELECTED PUBLICATIONS** Auth, Victory Garden; Co-ed, Postmodern Culture On-Line Journal. **CONTACT ADDRESS** Commun Dept, Univ Baltimore, 1420 N. Charles Street, Baltimore, MD, 21201.

MOULTON, JANICE
DISCIPLINE ENGLISH, PHILOSOPHY **EDUCATION** Cornell Univ, BA, 63; Univ Chicago, MA, 68; PhD, 71. **CAREER** Asst prof, Univ Ky, 79-81; prof, Central China Tchrs Univ, 86-87; res fac, Smith Coll, 81-. **HONORS AND AWARDS** Executive Comm, Am Philos Asn, 78; Bd of Dir, Sino-Am Network for Educ Exchange. **MEMBERSHIPS** Am Philos Asn; Sino-Am Network for Educ Exchange; Soc for Women in Philos. **RESEARCH** Philosophy; Methodology; Ethics; Feminism; Philosophy Language; Research Methodology; Fraud. **SELECTED PUBLICATIONS** Auth, Plagiarism; Academic Freedom, Encycl of Ethics, 98; coauth, Scaling the Dragon, 94. **CONTACT ADDRESS** Dept of Philosophy, Smith Col, Northampton, MA, 01063. **EMAIL** jmoulton@sophia.smith.edu

MOUNT, ERIC, JR.
PERSONAL Born 12/07/1935, Versailles, KY, m, 1958, 4 children **DISCIPLINE** ENGLISH, CHRISTIAN ETHICS AND RELIGION **EDUCATION** Rhodes Col, BA, 57; Union Theol Sem in Va, BD, 60; Yale Divinity Sch, STM, 61; Duke Univ, PhD, 66. **CAREER** Asst prof, 66-70, assoc prof, 70-75, prof, 75-96, Rodes prof, 96-, relig, Centre Col; dir, Centre-in-Europe, 92-93; vpres and dean of students, Centre Col, 83-88; social studies div chair, 80-83, relig prog chair, 84-88, Centre Col. **HONORS AND AWARDS** BA with distinction; Phi Beta Kappa; Omicron Delta Kappa; NEH summer seminars, 76, 81; BD, second in class; Alsop fel; PhD two univ fel; one Kearns fel; Theologian-in-residence, Amer Church in Paris, 74-75; pres, southeast region, Amer Acad of Relig, 87-88; David Hughes distinguished svc award, Centre Col, 77. **MEMBERSHIPS** Soc of Christ Ethics; Amer Acad of Relig; Soc for Values in Higher Educ; Soc of Bus Ethics; Asn for Practical and Professional Ethics. **RESEARCH** Theological ethics; Social ethics; Contemporary theology; Medical ethics; Business ethics; Professional ethics. **SELECTED PUBLICATIONS** Arti-

cles, Homing in on Family Values, The Family, Religion and Culture Series, Theol Today, 98; article, European Community and Global Community: A View from Alsace and Beyond, Soundings, 96; article, The Currency of Covenant, Annual of the Soc of Christ Ethics, 96; article, Metaphors, Morals and AIDS, Jour of Ethical Studies, 93; article, Can We Talk? Contexts of Meaning for Interpreting Illness, Jour of Med Humanities, vol 14, no 2, 93; auth, Professional Ethics in Context: Institutions, Images and Empathy, John Knox Press, 90; auth, The Feminine Factor, John Knox Press, 73; auth, Conscience and Responsibility, John Knox Press, 69. **CONTACT ADDRESS** Centre Col, 600 W. Walnut St., Danville, KY, 40422. **EMAIL** mounte@centre.edu

MOURAO, MANUELA
DISCIPLINE 19TH CENTURY BRITISH LITERATURE **EDUCATION** Univ Porto, BA; Eastern Ill Univ, MA; Univ Ill, PhD. **CAREER** Engl, Old Dominion Univ. **SELECTED PUBLICATIONS** Areas: Representations of gender in fiction; 19th century women writers; Early-modern pornographic texts; Nuns and convents-historical and fictional. **CONTACT ADDRESS** Old Dominion Univ, 4100 Powhatan Ave, Norfolk, VA, 23058. **EMAIL** MMourao@odu.edu

MOWLANA, HAMID
DISCIPLINE INTERNATIONAL COMMUNICATION **EDUCATION** Northwestern Univ & Univ Teheran, BA; Northwestern Univ, MS, PhD. **CAREER** Prof, Am Univ, dir, Div of Int Commun. **HONORS AND AWARDS** Pres Int Asn Media Comm Res. **RESEARCH** Cultural and psychological aspects of international relations, and worldwide socio-economic development. **SELECTED PUBLICATIONS** Auth, The Passing of Modernity: Communication and the Transformation of Society, Longman, 90; The Global Media Debate: Its Rise, Fall, and Renewal, Ablex Publications, 93; Global Information and World Communication: New Frontiers in International Relations, Longman, 86; Communication Technology and Development; International Flow of News, UNESCO, 88; Triumph of the Image: The Media's War in the Persian Gulf, Westview, 92 and International Communication in Transition: The End of Diversity? and Invisible Crises: What Conglomerate Control of Media Means for America and the World, Westview, 96 **CONTACT ADDRESS** American Univ, 4400 Massachusetts Ave, Washington, DC, 20016.

MOYER, KERMIT W.
DISCIPLINE CREATIVE WRITING **EDUCATION** Northwestern Univ, PhD. **CAREER** Prof, Am Univ, 70-. **HONORS AND AWARDS** Outstanding Tchr Year. **MEMBERSHIPS** Board of Trustees Jenny McKean Moore Fund Writers. **SELECTED PUBLICATIONS** Auth, Tumbling, Univ Ill Press, 88; articles, F. Scott Fitzgerald, poetry, fiction. **CONTACT ADDRESS** American Univ, 4400 Massachusetts Ave, Washington, DC, 20016. **EMAIL** kmoyer@american.edu

MOYER, RONALD L.
DISCIPLINE THEATRE HISTORY, LITERATURE AND ACTINIG **EDUCATION** Univ IL, BA, 66, MA, 67; Univ Denver, PhD, 74. **CAREER** Prof & dir, Grad Stud; prof, Univ SD, 74-, dept ch, 78-83, 89-91, tenure, 80; dir, Black Hills Playhouse, 76- & assoc mng dir, 79 & 80; tchg fel, Univ Denver, 72-73; instr, Purdue Univ-Calumet, 67-71; grad asst, Univ IL, 66-67; local arrangements ch, SDHSAA One-Act Play Festival, 90 & 85; local arrangements supvr, Irene Ryan Competition, ACTF, Region V North, 89; hon mem, Bd Dir, The Black Hills Playhouse, 92-; second VP & mem, Bd Dir, The Black Hills Playhouse, 83-91; critic, Am Col Theatre Festival Region V N, 84; local arrangements ch, ACTF Region V North Festivention, 83; Univ/Col Theatre Asn Repr, Mid- Am Theatre Conf Coun, 81-83; treasurer, S Dakota Theatre Asn, 78-82, finance comt, 78-82 & nominating comt, 78; co-drafter, Const Rev, 78; local arrangements ch, SDHSAA One-Act Play Festival, 82; mem, Plan Comt, MATC Conv, 80-81; ch, Reg Theatre Auditions, MATC Conv, 81; critic & mem, Reg Screening Team, ACTF Region V North, 80-81; mem, Plan Comt, MATC Conv, 79-80; ch, Reg Theatre Auditions, MATC Conv, 80; local arrangements ch, SDHSAA One-Act Play Festival, 80; univ comt(s), Univ Graphics Rev Comt, 94-95; Grad Coun, 78-83,84-87, 89-; subcomt(s), Univ Senate, 77-78 & Rules and Nominating Comt, 87-89; Presidential-Alumni Scholar Selection Comt, 80, 81; Educ Media Comt, 76-77; Statewide Educ Serv Adv Comt, 75-77. **HONORS AND AWARDS** Sioux Falls Argus Leader, 95; USD Stud Theatre League Fac Appreciation Awd, 92; Courseware develop awd, IBM-Rochester, 91; The Divorce Colony, play won second prize, David Libr of the Am Revolution, 87; USD Stud Theatre League Fac Appreciation Awd, 86; first prize, 2 plays, David Libr Am Revolution nat contest, 76; NDEA Title IV fel, Univ Denver, 71-74; Bush Mini-Grant Prog, 95; USD fac develop prog, 93; vis prof, IBM-Rochester, 92 & 91; USD fac develop prog, 92; Bush Found grant, 89, 88 & 85; SD Arts Coun grant, 82-83. **RESEARCH** Use of the Internet for the study of theatre and drama; Shakespearean performance; methods of playscript analysis. **SELECTED PUBLICATIONS** Auth, American Actors, 1861-1910: An Annotated Bibliography of Books, Troy, NY, Whitston Publ Co, 79; coauth & ed advert brochure, IBM Ultimedia Video Delivery System/400, Rochester, MN, Int Bus Mach Corp, co 92. **CONTACT ADDRESS** Dept of Theatre, Univ SD, 414 E Clark St, Vermillion, SD, 57069. **EMAIL** rmoyer@charlie.usd.edu

MUELLER, ROGER
DISCIPLINE ENGLISH LITERATURE **EDUCATION** Macalester Col, BA, 57; Univ MN, MA, 65, PhD, 68. **CAREER** Prof, Univ Pacific. **HONORS AND AWARDS** UOP, 65-97. **SELECTED PUBLICATIONS** Auth, publ(s) on American Transcendentalism; college writing. **CONTACT ADDRESS** Eng Dept, Univ Pacific, Pacific Ave, PO Box 3601, Stockton, CA, 95211.

MUKERJI, CHANDRA
DISCIPLINE COMMUNICATIONS **EDUCATION** Northwestern Univ, PhD, Sociol, 68. **CAREER** PROF, COMMUN, UNIV CALIF, SAN DIEGO. **RESEARCH** Material aspects of human cult and commun processes. **SELECTED PUBLICATIONS** Auth, From Graven Images: Patterns of Modern Materialism, Columbia, 83; A Fragile Power: Scientists and the State, Princeton, 90; co-auth, Rethinking Popular Culture, Univ Calif, 91. **CONTACT ADDRESS** Dept of Commun, Univ Calif, San Diego, 9500 Gilman Dr, La Jolla, CA, 92093. **EMAIL** cmukerji@weber.ucsd.edu

MULCAIRE, TERRY
DISCIPLINE ENGLISH **EDUCATION** UC, Berkeley, PhD. **CAREER** Prof, Northwestern Univ. **RESEARCH** 19th century American literature, cultural studies, popular culture. **SELECTED PUBLICATIONS** Articles on, Stephen Crane & Walt Whitman. **CONTACT ADDRESS** Dept of English, Northwestern Univ, 1801 Hinman, Evanston, IL, 60208.

MULFORD, CARLA
DISCIPLINE ENGLISH **EDUCATION** Univ Del, BS, 77, MA, 79, PhD, 84. **CAREER** Adm, res asst, Univ Del, 77-80; vis instr, Temple Univ, 82- 84; asst prof, Villanova Univ, 84-86; asst prof, 86-92, ASSOC PROF, 92-, PA STATE UNIV. **CONTACT ADDRESS** Dept of English, Pennsylvania State Univ, University Park, PA, 16802. **EMAIL** cjm5@psu.edu

MULHALLEN, KAREN
PERSONAL Woodstock, ON, Canada **DISCIPLINE** ENGLISH **EDUCATION** Waterloo Lutheran Univ, BA, 63; Univ Toronto, MA, 67, PhD, 75. **CAREER** Lectr, 66-70, PROF ENGLISH, RYERSON POLYTECH UNIV 70-. **HONORS AND AWARDS** Maclean Hunter Arts Journ Fel, 94. **MEMBERSHIPS** Descant Arts & Letters Found; ASECS; CMPA; CSECS; PEN; Writers Union Can. **SELECTED PUBLICATIONS** Auth, Sheba and Solomon, 84; auth, Modern Love Poems 1970-1989, 90; auth, In the Era of Acid Rain, 93; ed, Descant, 73-. **CONTACT ADDRESS** Dept of English, Ryerson Polytechnic Univ, 350 Victoria St, Toronto, ON, M5B 2K3. **EMAIL** kmulhall@acs.ryerson.ca

MULL, DONALD L.
DISCIPLINE 19TH- AND 20TH-CENTURY AMERICAN LITERATURE **EDUCATION** Yale Univ, PhD. **CAREER** Instr, Rutgers, State Univ NJ, Camden Col of Arts and Sci. **SELECTED PUBLICATIONS** Auth, The Girl in the Black Raincoat, Doell, Sloan, and Pearce, 66; Henry James's Sublime Economy: Money as Symbolic Center in the Fiction, Wesleyan, 73. **CONTACT ADDRESS** Rutgers, State Univ NJ, Camden Col of Arts and Sci, New Brunswick, NJ, 08903-2101. **EMAIL** schiavo@crab.rutgers.edu

MULLEN, EDWARD
PERSONAL Born 07/12/1942, Hackensack, NJ, m, 1971, 2 children **DISCIPLINE** LITERATURE **EDUCATION** West Va Wesleyan, BA, 64; Northwestern, MA, 65, PhD, 68. **CAREER** Asst prof, Purdue Univ, 67-71; from assoc prof to prof, 71-, Univ Mo. **HONORS AND AWARDS** Woodrow Wilson Fel, 64-65; ACLS Grant in Aid, 79., Co-ed, The Afro-Hispanic Rev, 87-. **MEMBERSHIPS** MLA; Langston Hughes Soc; Col Lang Asn. **RESEARCH** Afro-Hispanic literature; African-American literature. **SELECTED PUBLICATIONS** Auth, art, Afro-Hispanic and Afro-American Literary Historiography: Comments on Generational Shifts, 95; auth, art, The Teaching Anthology and the Hermaneneutics of Race: The Case of Placido, 95; auth, art, Nicolas Guillen and the Notion of Race in Latin American Literature, 97; auth, Afro-Cuban Literature: Critical Junctures, 98; coauth, El Cuento Hispanico: A Graded Literary Anthology, 99. **CONTACT ADDRESS** Univ of Mo, 143 Arts & Science Bldg, Columbus, MO, 65211. **EMAIL** mullene@missouri.edu

MULLEN, KAREN A.
PERSONAL Born 07/05/1941 **DISCIPLINE** ENGLISH, LINGUISTICS **EDUCATION** Grinnell Col, BA, 63; Univ Iowa, MA, 66, PhD(English), 73. **CAREER** Asst rhet, 66-70, asst ling, 70-73, from instr to asst prof ling, 74-75, coord English as foreign lang prog, 75-77, assoc dir, Intensive English Prog, Univ Iowa, 76-78; Assoc Prof & Dir Intensive English, Univ Louisville, 78-, Ed, News lett for spec interest group lang anal & studies humanities, Asn Comput Mach, 71-75; consult ed, Comput & Humanities, 72-75. **MEMBERSHIPS** Asn Teachers English to Speakers Other Lang; Ling Soc Am; MLA; Nat Asn Foreign Student Affairs; Asn Comput Mach. **RESEARCH** Cloze-passage test; relationship between second-language proficiency and intelligence. **SELECTED PUBLICATIONS** Auth, In-core PLI sort and search procedures for lexical data, Siglash Newslett, 73; The Wanderer: Considered again, Neophilologus, 74; Rater reliability and oral proficiency evaluations, Occas Papers Ling, 77; Using rater judgments in the evaluation of writing proficiency for non-native speakers of English, Teaching & Learning English as 2nd Lang: Trends Res & Pract, 77; Direct evaluation of second language proficiency, Lang Learning, 79; More on Cloze tests, Concepts Lang Testing 79; An alternative to the Cloze test, TESOL, 79; Evaluating writing in ESL, chap 15 & Rater reliability and oral proficiency evaluations, chap 8, In: Research in Language Testing, Newbury House, 80; Making Progress In English - Furey,Pr, Menasche,L, Modern Language J, Vol 0077, 1993. **CONTACT ADDRESS** Dept of English, Univ of Louisville, Louisville, KY, 40208.

MULLEN, LAWRENCE J.
PERSONAL Born 02/02/1960, Schenectady, NY, m, 1990 **DISCIPLINE** COMMUNICATION STUDIES **EDUCATION** Univ IA, PhD, 92. **CAREER** Asst prof, Augustana Col, Sioux Falls, SD, 92-94; asst prof, UNLV, Las Vegas, NV, 94-. **HONORS AND AWARDS** Outstanding Fac Res Award, 96; NV Regents Outstanding Fac, 97. **MEMBERSHIPS** Nat Commun Asn; Int Commun Asn; Broadcast Ed Asn; Am Asn of Public Opinion Res. **RESEARCH** Visual literacy; Presidential political commun; mass commun processes and effects. **SELECTED PUBLICATIONS** Auth, An Overview of Political Content Analyses of Magazines, Electronic J of Commun/La Revue Electronique de Communication, 4, 94; with M Pfau, T Diedrich, & K Garrow, Television Viewing and Public Perceptions of Attorneys, Human Commun Res, 21 (3), 95 & the Influence of Television Viewing on Public Perceptions of Physicians, J of Broadcasting and Electronic Media, 39 (4), 95; with E W Rothenbuhler, R DeLaurell, & C R Ryu, Coimmunication, Community Attachment and Involvement, Journalism and Mass Communication Quart, 39 (4), 96; with R DeLaurell, The Audience in Television Production: A Review of 20 Current College Textbooks, Feedback, 37 (3), 96; The President's Visual Image from 1945 to 1974: An Analysis of Spatial Configuration in News Magazine Photographs, Presidential Studies Quart, 27 (4), 97; with R DeLaurell, The Concept of Audience in Radio & Audio Production Textbooks, Feedback, 38 (1), 97; Close-ups of the President: Photojournalistic Distance from 1945 to 1974, Visual Commun Quart, 5 (2), 98; African American Portrayals in Comic Books, Popular Culture Rev, forthcoming, 98; several other articles. **CONTACT ADDRESS** Hank Greenspun School of Connmunication, Univ of Nevada, Las Vegas, 4505 Maryland Pkwy, Las Vegas, NV, 89154-5007. **EMAIL** mullen@nevada.edu

MULLEN, RICHARD D.
PERSONAL Born 09/30/1915, Mountain View, MO, m, 1938 **DISCIPLINE** ENGLISH **EDUCATION** Univ Ala, AB, 49; Univ Miss, MA, 50; Univ Chicago, PhD, 55. **CAREER** Instr English, Univ Mass, 50-51, 53-56; from asst prof to assoc prof, 56-68, Prof English, Ind State Univ, Terre Haute, 68-. **MEMBERSHIPS** Sci Fiction Res Asn; MLA. **RESEARCH** English drama to 1642; English literature 1500-1660; science fiction. **SELECTED PUBLICATIONS** Auth, Blish, van Vogt and the uses of Spengler, Riverside Quart, 68; The undisciplined imagination: E R Burroughs and Lowellian Mars, In: Science Fiction: The Other Side of Realism, Bowling Green Popular Press, 71; The prudish prurience of Haggard and Burroughs, Riverside Quart, 73; ed, Science Fiction Studies, Ind State Univ, 73-; The Passage Of The Light, The Recursive Science-Fiction Of Malzberg,Barry,N. - Resnick,M, Lewis,Ar, Science-Fiction Studies, Vol 0021, 1994; A Modern Utopia - Italian - Wells,Hg, Science-Fiction Studies, Vol 0021, 1994; First-Fandom + Organization For Those Active In Science- Fiction Since Before 1938, Science-Fiction Studies, Vol 0023, 1996; Ufos - An Insiders View Of The Official Quest For Evidence - Craig,R, Science-Fiction Studies, Vol 0023, 1996; Outside The Human Aquarium - Masters Of Science-Fiction - Stableford,B, Science-Fiction Studies, Vol 0024, 1997; R.D.-Mullen Reply To Haycock,Christine,E. Criticism Of His Obituary Of Moskowitz,Sam, Science-Fiction Studies, Vol 0024, 1997; Moreau And Plaxy Redivius + Novels, Science-Fiction, Science-Fiction Studies, Vol 0024, 1997; Wells,H.G. And The Culminating Ape - Kemp,P, Science-Fiction Studies, Vol 0024, 1997; Recent Books From Borgo-Press + Science-Fiction Studies, Science-Fiction Studies, Vol 0024, 1997; Moskowitz,Sam, 1920-1997 + In-Memoriam, Science- Fiction Studies, Vol 0024, 1997; Islands In The Sky - The Space Station Theme In Science-Fiction Literature - Westfahl,G, Science-Fiction Studies, Vol 0024, 1997; Longer Views - Extended Essays - Delany,Sr, James,K, Science-Fiction Studies, Vol 0024, 1997; A Subtler Magick - The Writings And Philosophy Of Lovecraft,H.P. - Joshi,St, Science-Fiction Studies, Vol 0024, 1997. **CONTACT ADDRESS** Dept of English, Indiana State Univ, Terre Haute, IN, 47809.

MULLER, ADAM
DISCIPLINE ENGLISH LITERATURE **EDUCATION** Univ Calgary, BA; Univ Alberta, MA; McGill Univ, PhD. **CAREER** Asst prof **RESEARCH** Critical theory; American modernism; South African literature; narrative film and film theory; literary exile. **SELECTED PUBLICATIONS** Auth, pub(s) on literary theory, cultural studies, and aesthetics. **CONTACT ADDRESS** Dept of English, Manitoba Univ, Winnipeg, MB, R3T 2N2.

MULLER, GILBERT HENRY
PERSONAL Born 11/08/1941, Brooklyn, NY, m, 1964, 2 children **DISCIPLINE** AMERICAN LITERATURE **EDUCATION** Stanford Univ, PhD(Eng & Am lit), 67. **CAREER** Tchg asst Eng & Renaissance lit, Stanford Univ, 64-66; asst prof Am & comp lit, Pahlavi Univ, Iran, 67-71; asst prof, 71-73, Assoc Prof AM & Comp Lit, LaGuardia Community Col, City Univ, NY, 73-80, Prof, 80- Nat Endowment for Hum fel, 74-79; Fulbright-Hays exchange scholar, 78-79; fac res award, City Univ NY, 75-77. **MEMBERSHIPS** NEA; Am Studies Asn; MLA; Am Fed Tchrs. **RESEARCH** Interdisciplinary studies; Am studies; rhetoric and compos. **SELECTED PUBLICATIONS** Auth, Flannery O'Conner's Dantean Vision, Ga Rev, 6/69; Revolutionary romanticism, New Republic, 9/72; Nightmares and Visions: Flannery O'Connor and the Catholic Grotesque, Univ Ga, 72; Comparison and Contrast, Harper, 74; Faulkner's Red Leaves and the Garden of the South, Studies Short Fiction, 74; The Basic English Handbook, Harper, 78; The McGraw-Hill Short Prose Reader, McGraw, 79; Chester Himes, 89, John A. Williams, 84; New Strangers in Paradise: The Immigrant Experience in Contemporary AmLiterature, 94; Bridges: Literature Across Cultures, 94; Ways in Reading and Writing About Literature, 94; Major Modern Essayists, 94; The McGraw Hill Introduction to Literature, 95. **CONTACT ADDRESS** 21 Monfort Rd, Port Washington, NY, 11050. **EMAIL** gilmr@lagcc.cuny.edu

MULLIN, ANNE
DISCIPLINE ENGLISH LITERATURE **EDUCATION** Univ Mass, PhD, 90. **CAREER** Asst prof. **RESEARCH** Composition process; unconscious influences on language use; composition strategies for non-native speakers and for students with disabilities. **SELECTED PUBLICATIONS** Auth, pubs in Writing on the Edge, Presence of Mind, Nothing Begins with N, and Journal of the Assembly for Expanded Perceptions in Learning. **CONTACT ADDRESS** Dept of English and Philosophy, Idaho State Univ, Pocatello, ID, 83209. **EMAIL** mullanne@isu.edu

MULLIN, MICHAEL
PERSONAL Born 11/30/1944, Chicago, IL, m, 1966, 4 children **DISCIPLINE** ENGLISH LITERATURE, DRAMA **EDUCATION** Col Holy Cross, AB, 66; Yale Univ, MPhil, 70, PhD(English), 72. **CAREER** From instr to asst prof, 70-76, Assoc Prof English, Univ Ill, Urbana, 76-, Dir, Shakespeare Film Coop, 73-; observership, Royal Shakespeare Co, Stratford-upon-Avon, 75; graduate col res grants, Univ Ill, 75-82; consult var orgn, 76-; proj dir, Nehihc Symp Shakespeare in Performance, 77-78; res fel Theater, Prog Fac Study in Sec Discipline, 77-78. **HONORS AND AWARDS** Undergraduate Instruct Award, 78 & Excellent Teacher Award, 73-82, Univ Ill. **MEMBERSHIPS** Int Shakespeare Asn; Soc Theater Res England; Am Soc Theater Res; Shakespeare Asn Am; MLA. **RESEARCH** Shakespeare, Theater history, film. **SELECTED PUBLICATIONS** MacBeth on film, Lit Film Quart, winter 73; Auguries and understood relations: Theodore Komisarjevksy's Macbeth, Theater J, 74; Macbeth at Stratford-upon-Avon, 1955, Shakespeare Studies, 76; Tony Richardson's Hamlet: script and screen, Lit Film Quart, 76; Macbeth Onstage, Univ MO, 76; Strange images of death: Sir Herbert's Tree's Macbeth, 1911, Theater Survey, 1176; Macbeth in modern dress: Royal court Theater, 1928, Theater J, 78; Theatrical Stratford-Upon-Avon: A Catalogue Index to Productions, 1879-1978 (2 vols), Greenwood Press, 80; 'Everyday Life After The Revolution' .2., Theater J, Vol 0045, 1993; Genty 'Derives', Theater J, Vol 0045, 1993; Looking At Shakespeare - A Visual History Of 20th-Century Performance - Kennedy,D, Shakespeare Quarterly, Vol 0047, 1996. **CONTACT ADDRESS** Dept of English, Univ Ill, Urbana, IL, 61801.

MUMBY, DENNIS K.
DISCIPLINE ORGANIZATIONAL COMMUNICATION, PHILOSOPHY OF COMMUNICATION **EDUCATION** Southern Ill Univ, PhD, 84. **CAREER** Assoc prof, Purdue Univ. **SELECTED PUBLICATIONS** Auth, The Political Function of Narrative in Organizations, Commun Monogr, 87; Communication & Power in Organizations, Ablex, 88; ed, Narrative & Social Control, Sage, 93. **CONTACT ADDRESS** Dept of Commun, Purdue Univ, 1080 Schleman Hall, West Lafayette, IN, 47907-1080. **EMAIL** dmumby@purdue.edu

MUNKER, DONA FELDMAN
PERSONAL Born 03/08/1945, Los Angeles, CA **DISCIPLINE** ENGLISH **EDUCATION** Univ Southern CA, BA (drama), 66; IN Univ, Bloomington, MA (English), 67; New York Univ, PhD (English), 76. **CAREER** Lect or adjunct lect, Hunter Col and Univ of Giessen, Ger, 73-76; asst ed, Little, Brown & Co, 80-85; sr ed, Arbor House Pub Co, consult ed, Time-Life Books, 83-85; self employed, writer, consulting book ed, independent scholar, 85-. **HONORS AND AWARDS** Huntington Library Andrew Mellon Fel, 98-99. **MEMBERSHIPS** CA and Southern CA Hist Socs; The Biography Seminar of NY Univ; The Women Writing Women's Lives Seminar, City Univ Grad Center, NY. **RESEARCH** Biography as a genre; theories of creativity and the psychology of creative development; early 20th century social and cultural hist. **SELECTED PUBLICATIONS** Auth, Swift and the Traditions of Seventeenth Century Poetry, Seventeenth Century News, vol 32, nos 1-2, spring/summer, 75; Men are Only Men: Mary Renault's Theseus, Der historische Roman in England und Amerika, eds R Borgmeier and B Reitz, vol I, Carl Winter Verlag, 86; The Country of the Mind: Notes From a Persian-American Collaboration, Chanteh: A Transcultural J, vol 1, no 1, fall 92; Daughter of Persia: A Woman's Journey from Her Father's Harem through the Islamic Revolution, co-auth with Sattareh Farman-Farmaian, Crown Pubs, 92, Doubleday/Anchor, 93; Enchantment and the Biographical Passion, American Imago: Psycho-Analysis and Culture, vol 54, no 4, winter, 97-98; reviews in The New York Times Book Review, Publisher's Weekly, Chanteh. **CONTACT ADDRESS** 166 E 61st St, New York, NY, 10021-8510.

MUNN, PAUL
PERSONAL Born 11/21/1950, Seattle, WA **DISCIPLINE** ENGLISH **EDUCATION** Univ Minn, PhD, 88. **CAREER** Chemn, 92-94; vis prof, Shikoku Univ, 95; prof, Saginaw Valley State Univ, 96-. **MEMBERSHIPS** ALSC; MLA; NCTL; NAS. **RESEARCH** Poetry; pedogogy; Milton. **SELECTED PUBLICATIONS** Auth, art, Vestigial Forms in John Ashbery's A Wave, 92-; auth, art, Comment, 95; auth, art, The Feminist Classroom: A Critique, 95; coauth, art, Are Japanese Proverbs Intelligible to Americans, 96; auth, art, Giroux and Radical Pedagogy: A Humanist's Response, 97. **CONTACT ADDRESS** Saginaw Valley State Univ, University Center, MI, 48710. **EMAIL** ptmunn@svsu.edu

MURA, KAREN E.
DISCIPLINE ENGLISH LITERATURE **EDUCATION** Wellesley Col, BA, 79; Oxford Univ, MA, 81; Univ Toronto, MA, 82; Univ Wis, PhD, 90. **CAREER** Instr, Delta Col, 87-88; res ed, Univ Mich, 89-91; asst prof, 91-. **MEMBERSHIPS** Am Asn Univ Women; Early Bk Soc; Medieval Acad Am; MLA; Soc Medieval Feminist Scholar. **RESEARCH** Medieval literature; interdisciplinary studies. **SELECTED PUBLICATIONS** Auth, Thomas Wardon: A Mid-Fifteenth Century Reader, 1448-1462, Fifteenth-Century Studies, 95. **CONTACT ADDRESS** Susquehanna Univ, 514 University Ave, Selinsgrove, PA. **EMAIL** mura@susqu.edu

MURDICK, WILLIAM
DISCIPLINE RHETORIC AND LINGUISTICS **EDUCATION** SUNY, Albany, BA; Univ IA, MFA; IN Univ PA, PhD. **CAREER** Instr, CA State Univ PA. **SELECTED PUBLICATIONS** Auth, What English Teachers Need to Know about Grammar, Eng J, Nov 96; coauth, Evolution of a Writing Center, Writing Ctr J, 91; Placing Whole Language in a Workshop Setting, Eng Leadership Quart, Dec 91; Art, Writing, and Politics, Art Educ, Sept 92; Journal Writing and Active Learning, Eng Leadership Quart, Oct 93. **CONTACT ADDRESS** California Univ of Pennsylvania, California, PA, 15419s. **EMAIL** murdick@cup.edu

MURPHY, BRIAN
PERSONAL Born 05/25/1939, Detroit, MI, m, 1979, 3 children **DISCIPLINE** ENGLISH **EDUCATION** Univ Detroit, BA, 61, MA, 63; Harvard Univ, AM, 65; Univ London, PhD, 74. **CAREER** Instr, eng, 69-73, asst prof, eng, 73-76, assoc prof, eng, 76-96, prof, eng, 96-, dir of honors col and coord of cinema, 85-, Oakland Univ. **HONORS AND AWARDS** Teaching excellence award, 95. **RESEARCH** 19th Century British literature; Shakespeare; Film, Oscar Wilde, G. B. Shaw, C. S. Lewis. **SELECTED PUBLICATIONS** Auth, Critical study of C. S. Lewis, Starmont, 83; auth, The Enigma Variations, Scribner's 81, Blond & Briggs, 82, Het Spectrum, 85-86. **CONTACT ADDRESS** Oakland Univ, 112 Vandenberg Hall, Rochester, MI, 48309. **EMAIL** hc@oakland.edu

MURPHY, PATRICK D.
PERSONAL Born 01/16/1964, Cincinnati, OH, s, 1 child **DISCIPLINE** TELECOMMUNICATION **EDUCATION** Ohio Univ, PhD, 96. **HONORS AND AWARDS** Fulbright-Garcia Robles Fel. **MEMBERSHIPS** ICA; NCA; AEJMC; UDC. **RESEARCH** Transnational media; mass communication theory; cultural studies. **SELECTED PUBLICATIONS** Auth, Contrasting Perspectives: Cultural studies in Latin American and the U.S., a Conversation with Nestor Garcia Canclini, Cultural Studies, 97; Television and Cultural Politics in Mexico: Some notes on Televisa, the state, and transnational culture, Howard J of Commun, 95; coauth, Cultural Identity and Cyberimperialism: Computer Mediated Explorations of Ethnicity, Nation, and Citizenship, Cyberimperialism: Global Relations in the New Electronic Frontier, in press; The Study of Communication and Culture in Latin America: From laggards and the oppressed to resistance and hybrid cultures, The J of Int Commun, 97. **CONTACT ADDRESS** Dept of Mass Communications, Southern Ill Univ, Edwardsville, IL, 62026-1775. **EMAIL** pmurphy@slue.edu

MURPHY, PETER
DISCIPLINE ENGLISH **EDUCATION** Yale Univ, BA, 81; Johns Hopkins, PhD, 86. **CAREER** Lectr & dean of the Col. **RESEARCH** 18th and 19th century British literature; popular culture; literary culture broadly defined. **SELECTED PUBLICATIONS** Auth, Poetry as an Occupation and an Art in Britain, 1760-1830; Climbing Parnassus, and Falling Off; Scott's Disappointments: Reading The Heart of MidLothian. **CONTACT ADDRESS** Dept of English, Williams Col, Hopkins Hall and Stetson 410, Williamstown, MA, 01267. **EMAIL** pmurphy@williams.edu

MURPHY, RICHARD
DISCIPLINE TEACHING OF WRITING, THE STUDY OF FICTION, GRAMMAR, ENGLISH EDUCATION, AND **EDUCATION** Univ Santa Clara, BA, 67; Univ CA, Berkeley, PhD, 77. **CAREER** Prof, Radford Univ, 79-. **HONORS AND AWARDS** Donald N. Dedmon Award for Prof Excellence, 82. **SELECTED PUBLICATIONS** Auth, The Calculus of Intimacy: A Teaching Life, The Ohio State U P, 94; coauth, Symbiosis: Writing in an Academic Culture, Heinemann, 93. **CONTACT ADDRESS** Radford Univ, Radford, VA, 24142. **EMAIL** rmurphy@runet.edu

MURPHY, RUSSELL E.
DISCIPLINE AMERICAN AND BRITISH LITERATURE **EDUCATION** Univ Miss, PhD. **CAREER** English and Lit, Univ Ark **SELECTED PUBLICATIONS** Auth, Structure and Meaning: An introduction to literature; 'It is impossible to say just what I mean': The Wasteland as Transcendent Meaning; The 'Rough Beast' and Historical Necessity: A new consideration of Yeats's 'The Second Coming, Studies Literary Imagination. **CONTACT ADDRESS** Univ Ark Little Rock, 2801 S University Ave., Little Rock, AR, 72204-1099. **EMAIL** remurphy@ualr.edu

MURRAY, CATHERINE A.
PERSONAL Kitchener, ON, Canada **DISCIPLINE** COMMUNICATIONS **EDUCATION** Queen's Univ, PhD, 85. **CAREER** Sr proj dir, Decima Res, 85-89, VP, 89-91; ASSOC PROF, SIMON FRASER UNIV, 92-. **MEMBERSHIPS** WTN Found; OWL Children's Trust; BC Film. **SELECTED PUBLICATIONS** Auth, Information Security at Risk?, 93; auth, Privacy Potholes on the Information Highway, 96; coauth, Making Our Voices Heard: The Future of the CBC, NFB and Telefilm. **CONTACT ADDRESS** Simon Fraser Univ, Vancouver, BC, V5A 1S6. **EMAIL** catherine-murray@sfu.ca

MURRAY, HEATHER
PERSONAL Weston, ON, Canada **DISCIPLINE** ENGLISH **EDUCATION** Vic Col, Univ Toronto, BA, 73; York Univ, MA, 77, PhD, 84. **CAREER** Asst prof & postdoc fel, Queen's Univ, 85-87; ASSOC PROF TRINTY COL, UNIV TORONTO 87-, dir, Women's Stud Prog, 93-96. **SELECTED PUBLICATIONS** Auth, Working in English: History, Institution, Resources, 96. **CONTACT ADDRESS** Dept of English, Univ Toronto, Toronto, ON, M5S 1H8.

MURRAY, LAURA
DISCIPLINE ENGLISH LITERATURE **EDUCATION** Cornell Univ, PhD. **CAREER** Dept Eng, Queen's Univ **RESEARCH** American literature between the Revolution and the Civil War; contemporary American fiction and autobiography; Native North American literature; cultural theory; theoretical issues arising from scholarly editing; oral cultures in comparison to and in relation with writing-oriented cultures; diaries and correspondences as genres. **SELECTED PUBLICATIONS** Auth, pubs on early Native American writing, Washington Irving's Sketch Book, and phrasebooks for immigrants to America; ed, To Do Good to My Indian Brethren: The Writings of Joseph Johnson 1751-1776, Univ Mass, 98; co-ed, Talking on the Page: Editing Aboriginal Oral Texts, Univ Toronto. **CONTACT ADDRESS** English Dept, Queen's Univ, Kingston, ON, K7L 3N6. **EMAIL** lm19@post.queensu.ca

MURRAY, MICHAEL D.
DISCIPLINE COMMUNICATION STUDIES **EDUCATION** St Louis Univ, BA, MA; Columbia Univ, PhD. **SELECTED PUBLICATIONS** Auth, The Political Performers: CBS Broadcasts in the Public Interest, Praeger, 94; America's Unconventional Press Critic: Alistair Cooke, Jour Mass Commun Quarterly, 95; Creating a Tradition in Broadcast News: A Conversation with David Brinkley, Jour Hist, 95; Television News Encyclopedia, Oryx, 98; co-ed, Teaching Mass Communication, Praeger, 92; Television in America, Iowa State Univ, 97. **CONTACT ADDRESS** Communication Dept, Univ of Missouri, St. Louis, 590 Lucas Hall, St. Louis, MO, 63121. **EMAIL** smdmurr@umslvma.umsl.edu

MUSGROVE, LAURENCE E.
DISCIPLINE ENGLISH **EDUCATION** Univ OR, PhD. **CAREER** Asst prof & dir, Compos. **MEMBERSHIPS** Ex Bd mem, Ind Tchr(s) Writing, 96-98; Nat Coun Tchr(s) Engl; Sigma Tau Delta, Int Eng Honor Soc. **SELECTED PUBLICATIONS** Auth, Attitudes Toward Writing, J Assembly Expanded Perspectives Lrng, 98; Attitude, Eng J, Vol 87, 98; Portfolios, Self-Evaluation, and Student Lrng, Teaching Matters, Univ Southern IN, 97; Given All Things, a poem, The Flying Island, Vol 5, 97; You Ask Me, a poem, Southern IN Rev, Vol 4, 97; Should I Go or Should I Stay A Interview with Liam Rector,

Interview, Southern IN Rev, Vol 4, 97; Old Lonesome's Way of Drinking Needles, a poem, Southern IN Rev, Vol 3, 96; Blessed, a poem, Southern IN Rev, Vol 2, 95; For Immediate Release, a poem, Southern IN Rev, Vol 1, 94; Classical Topoi and the Academic Commonplace, ERIC Clearinghouse on Reading and Commun Skills, ED 357 366, 93; Composing Character in Composition, Rhet in the Vortex of Cultural Studies: Proc 5th Biennial Conf, Minneapolis, Rhet Soc Am, 93; The Rhet and Composition Handbook, Univ Southern IN, 97; Univ Southern IN, Dept Eng Web Site, 97; Univ Southern IN Rhet & Compos Prog Handbk On-Line, 97; Univ Southern IN Rhet & Compos Prog Web Site, 97 & 96; Fac Handbk for the Rhet & Compos Prog, Univ Southern IN, 96; Rhet & Compos Placement Exam Handbk with Guidelines Assessing the RCPE, 95; coauth, Proficiencies 2-3, IN High Sch Eng/Lang Arts Competencies, Ind Dept Educ, 97; Literature, Writing, Teaching, Creative Writing, Eng Dept Recruitment Brochure, 96; ed, Writing to Learn about Tchg Writing Secondary Sch, coll 17 stud essays from Eng 310, 95; rev, A Proposal for a Series of Short Thematic Readers for College Composition, Marjorie & John Ford, 96; Writing Essentials: The Norton Pocket Guide to Online Writing, 95. **CONTACT ADDRESS** Dept of Eng, Univ of Southern IN, 8600 University Blvd, Evansville, IN, 47712-3596. **EMAIL** lemusgro.ucs@smtp.usi.edu

MUSMANN, KLAUS
PERSONAL Born 06/27/1935, Magdeburg, Germany, m, 1986 **DISCIPLINE** LIBRARIANSHIP **EDUCATION** Wayne St Univ, BA, 62; Univ of MI, AMLS, 63, MA, 67; Univ of South CA, PhD, 81 **CAREER** Asst Librn, 65-67, MI St Univ; Asst Librn, 67-68, CA St Poly; Assoc Librn, 84-86, Librn, 86-94, Act Dir, 94-96, Dir, 96-, Univ of Redlands **HONORS AND AWARDS** Res grants **MEMBERSHIPS** ALA; ACRL **RESEARCH** Diffusion of technol innov **SELECTED PUBLICATIONS** Auth, The Ugly Side of Librarianship: Discrimination in Libraries from 1900-1950, Univ of IL, 98; Technological Innovations in Libraries, 1860-1960, Greenwood Press, 93 **CONTACT ADDRESS** Armacost Libr, Univ of Redlands, Redlands, CA, 92374. **EMAIL** kmusmann@uor.edu

MYERS, LINDA
DISCIPLINE COMPOSITION **EDUCATION** Lehigh Univ, PhD, 94. **CAREER** Asst prof, dir, Compos, TX Tech Univ. **RESEARCH** Writing programs; writing centers; writing across the curriculum programs. **SELECTED PUBLICATIONS** Ed, Approaches to Computer Classrooms: Learning from Practical Experience, SUNY Press, 93. **CONTACT ADDRESS** Texas Tech Univ, Lubbock, TX, 79409-5015. **EMAIL** L.Myers@ttu.edu

MYERS, MITZI
PERSONAL Sulphur Springs, TX, m, 1967 **DISCIPLINE** ENGLISH **EDUCATION** E Tex State Univ, BA, 61, MA, 62; Rice Univ, PhD(English), 69. **CAREER** Asst prof English, Univ Calif, Santa Barbara, 66-73; lectr, Calif State Col, San Bernardino, 74-77; lectr English, Calif State Univ, Fullerton, 76-78, Calif Polytech Inst, 78-80 & Univ Calif, Los Angeles, 80-82; Lectr English, Calif State Univ, Long Beach, 80-, Univ Calif res grant, 69-70. **MEMBERSHIPS** MLA; Philol Asn Pac Coast; Am Soc 18th Century Studies; Western Soc 18th Century Studies; Women's Caucus Mod Lang Asn; Conf British Studies. **SELECTED PUBLICATIONS** Auth, Godwin's changing conception of Caleb Williams, Studies English Lit, 72; contribr, Politics From the Outside: Mary Wollstonecraft's First Vindication, Studies 18th Century Culture, 77; auth, Mary McCarthy's evasive comedy, Regionalism Female Imagination, 77-78; contribr, Wollstonecraft's Letters Written ... in Sweden: Toward Romantic Autobiography, Studies 18th Century Culture, 79; contribr, The Lost Tradition & Women's Autobiography, 80; auth, Wollstonecraft's Maria, Wordsworth Circle, 80; Godwin on Wollstonecraft, Studies in Romanticism, 81; Reform or ruin: A revolution in female manners, Studies in 18th Century Culture, 82; The Shelley,mary Reader - Bennett,bt, Robinson,ce, Keats-shelley J, Vol 0041, 1992; Heaven Upon Earth - The Form of Moral And Religious Childrens-literature to 1850 - Demers,p, Lion And The Unicorn, Vol 0019, 1995. **CONTACT ADDRESS** 2206 Bedford Dr, Fullerton, CA, 92631.

MYERS, NORMAN J.
PERSONAL Canton, OH **DISCIPLINE** THEATRE **EDUCATION** Hiram Col, BA, 57; Univ Il, MA, 59, PhD, 62. **CAREER** Asst prof, Lycoming Col, 59-61; asst prof, Ky Wesleyan Col, 69-61; asst prof, SUNY, 62-63; asst prof, Univ New Orleans, 66-70; asst prof to assoc prof to prof Emeritus, Bowling Green St Univ, 70-98. **MEMBERSHIPS** Amer Soc for Theatre Res; Mid-Amer Theatre Assoc, Nat Commun Assoc; Col English Assoc. **RESEARCH** Theatre history; cultural stud; performance stud; dramatic theory & criticism. **SELECTED PUBLICATIONS** Auth, Two Kinds of Alaska: Pinter and Kopit Journey Through Another Realm, Pinter Rev, 93; Shoestring Shakespeare Meets the Apocrypha: Arden of Faversham at Bowling Green State University, 95; Proslavery Ideology and the Antebellum/Civil War Theatre, McNeese Rev, 95-96; Finding a Heap of Jewels in Lesser Shakespeare: The Wars of the Roses and Richard Duke of York, New England Theatre J, 96. **CONTACT ADDRESS** Theatre Dept, Bowling Green State Univ, Bowling Green, OH, 43403. **EMAIL** nmyers@bgnet.bgsu.edu

MYERS, NORMAN JERALD
PERSONAL Born 06/24/1935, Canton, OH, m, 1959, 2 children **DISCIPLINE** THEATRE **EDUCATION** Hiram Col, AB, 57; Univ Ill, Urbana, MA, 59, PhD, 62. **CAREER** Asst prof speech & drama, Lycoming Col, 59-61; asst prof theatre, Ky Wesleyan Col, 62-63; asst prof, State Univ NY Col Oswego, 63-66; asst prof drama, La State Univ, New Orleans, 66-70; Assoc Prof Theatre, Bowling Green State Univ, 70-91; prof Theatre, Bowling Green State Univ, 91-98; Prof Emeritus, 98; Managing dir, Huron Playhouse, 71-79. **MEMBERSHIPS** Am Theatre Asn. **RESEARCH** American theatre history; British theatre history; dramatic theory and criticism. **SELECTED PUBLICATIONS** Auth, A season at the John Street: From The Theatrical Register, Southern Speech J, winter 68; Early recognition of Gordon Craig in American periodicals, Educ Theatre J, 3/70; Shoestring Shakespeare,Meets the Apocrypha: Arden of Faversham at Bowling Green State University, Proceedings of Wretched Plays and Miserable Fragments, Exploring the Dark Corners of the Shakespeare Canon, Slippery Rock, PA, 95; Proslavery Ideology and the Antebellum/Civil War Theatre, McNeese Review 95-96; Finding a Heap of Jewels in Lesser Shakespeare: The Wars of the Roses and Richard Duke of York, New England Theatre J, 96. **CONTACT ADDRESS** Dept of Theatre, Bowling Green State Univ, 1001 E Wooster St, Bowling Green, OH, 43403-0001. **EMAIL** nmyers@bgnet.bqsu.edu

MYERSON, JOEL ARTHUR
PERSONAL Born 09/09/1945, Boston, MA **DISCIPLINE** AMERICAN LITERATURE **EDUCATION** Tulane Univ, AB, 67; Northwestern Univ, Evanston, MA, 68, PhD, 71. **CAREER** Asst prof, 71-76, assoc prof, 76-80, prof English, 80-90, Carolina Prof of Am Lit, 90-96, Carolina Distinguished prof of Am Lit, 96-, Univ SC; assoc ed, Northwestern-Newberry Ed of the Writings of Herman Melville, 70-77; consult, Ctr for Ed Am Authors, 74-76; Am Philos Soc res grantee, 72-73, 84-85; NEH grants, 76, 78-81, 88-92, 94-97, 97-99; ed, Studies in the Am Renaissance, GK Hall, 78-82, Univ Virginia, 83-96; Guggenheim fel, 81-82; ed bd, Pittsburgh Series in Bibl, 78-; consult, Comm on Scholarly Ed, MLA, 78-; consult, Concord Museum, 86-89, 91-97; assoc ed, Am Natl Biog, 89-98; consult Fruitlands Museums, 90-93. **HONORS AND AWARDS** Contemporary Authors, Who's Who in America; Distinguished Service Award of Asn for Documentary Ed, 86; Children's Lit Asn Book Award, 90; elected Mass Hist Soc, 94; elected, Am Antiq Soc, 95; Lyman H. Butterfield award, Asn for Documentary Ed, 95; teacher of the year award, 97. **MEMBERSHIPS** Melville Soc; MLA; Bibliog Soc Am; SAtlantic Mod Lang Asn; Asn for Documentary Ed; Northeast MLA; Philol Asn of Carolinas; Soc for Textual Scholarship; Poe Stud Asn; Ralph Waldo Emerson Soc; Margaret fuller Soc. **RESEARCH** New England Transcendentalism; textual and bibliographical studies; R W Emerson. **SELECTED PUBLICATIONS** Coauth, Ralph Waldo Emerson: An Annotated Bibliography of Criticism, 1980-1991, Greenwood, 94; co-ed, Emerson's Antislavery Writings, Yale, 95; ed, The Cambridge Companion to Henry David Thoreau, Cambridge, 95; co-ed, The Professions of Authorship: Essays in Honor of Matthew J. Bruccoli, South Carolina, 96; co-ed, Louisa May Alcott's The Inheritance, Dutton, 97; ed, The Selected Letters of Ralph Waldo Emerson, Columbia, 97; auth, Margaret Fuller: An Annotated Bibliography of Criticism, 1983-1995, Greenwood, 98. **CONTACT ADDRESS** Dept of English, Univ of South Carolina, Columbia, SC, 29208. **EMAIL** myerson-joel@sc.edu

N

NABHOLTZ, JOHN R.
PERSONAL Born 01/06/1931, Cleveland, OH **DISCIPLINE** ENGLISH **EDUCATION** Loyola Univ, Ill, AB, 51; Univ Chicago, MA, 52, PhD(Wordsworth), 61. **CAREER** Instr English, Cornell Univ, 59-63; asst prof, Univ Rochester, 63-69; assoc prof, 69-78, Prof English, Loyola Univ, Chicago, 78- **MEMBERSHIPS** MLA; Byron Soc; Charles Lamb Soc; Wordsworth-Coleridge Asn. **RESEARCH** English romanticism. **SELECTED PUBLICATIONS** Auth, Wordsworth's Guide to the lakes, Mod Philol, 64; ed, Selected Essays of Charles Lamb, 67 & Selected Essays of William Hazlitt, 70, AHM Pub; auth, The journeys homeward: Book IV of The Prelude, Studies Romanticism, 71; Drama and rhetoric in Lamb's essays, Studies English Lit, 72; ed, Prose of the British Romantic Movement, Macmillan, 74; auth, The integrity of Wordsworth's Tintern Abbey, J English & Ger Philol, 74; Romantic Prose and Classical Rhetoric, Wordsworth Circle, 80; Prose in The Age of Poets - Romanticism And Biographical Narrative From Johnson to Dequincey - Cafarelli,aw, Keats-shelley J, Vol 0041, 1992. **CONTACT ADDRESS** Dept of English, Loyola Univ, Chicago, IL, 60626.

NADEL, IRA BRUCE
PERSONAL Born 07/22/1943, Rahway, NJ, m, 1976 **DISCIPLINE** ENGLISH & AMERICAN LITERATURE **EDUCATION** Rutgers Univ, New Brunswick, BA, 65, MA, 67; Cornell Univ, PhD(English), 70. **CAREER** Asst prof English, 70-77, Assoc Prof English, Univ BC, 77-, Leave fels, Can Coun, 75-76 & Soc Sci & Humanities Res Coun Can, 82. **MEMBERSHIPS** MLA Victorian Studies Asn Western Can (pres, 80-82); Asn Can Univ Teachers English. **RESEARCH** Victorian literature and thought; biography. **SELECTED PUBLICATIONS** Auth, London in the Quick: Blanchard Jerrold and the text of London: A Pilgrimage, London J, 576; Wonderful Deception: Art and the artist in Little Dorrit, Criticism, winter 77; Renunciation and the perfect freedom of the Victorians, In: Interspace and the Inward Sphere: Essays on the Romantic and Victorian Self, Western Ill Univ, 78; Gustave Dore: English art and London life, In: Victorian Artists and The City, Pergamon, 80; Jewish Writers of North America, Gale, 81; Moments in The Greenwood: Maurice in Context, E M Forster Centenary Revaluations, 82 & Versions of the Life: George Eliot and Her Biographers, George Eliot: Centenary Essays, 82, Macmillan; Apologize or confess! The dilemma of Victorian autobiography, Biography, fall 82; Pound,ezra Poetry And Prose - Contributions to Periodicals - Baechler,l, Litz,aw, Longenbach,j, Paideuma-a J Devoted to Ezra Pound Scholarship, Vol 0022, 1993; Forget-me- not, Joycean Bibliography, James Joyce Quarterly, Vol 0032, 1995. **CONTACT ADDRESS** Dept of English, Univ of BC, Vancouver, BC, V6T 1W5.

NAESS, HARALD S.
PERSONAL Born 12/27/1925, Oddernes, Norway, m, 1950, 3 children **DISCIPLINE** SCANDINAVIAN STUDIES **EDUCATION** Univ Oslo, Cand Phil, 52. **CAREER** Lector Norweg, King's Col, Univ Durham, 53-58, lectr, 58- 59; vis lectr, 59-61, assoc prof, 61-67, Torger Thompson Prof Scand Studies, Univ Wis-Madison, 67-, Fulbright scholar, 59-61; mem ed comt, Nordic Trans Serv, Univ Wis, 64-; ed, Scand Studies, 73-77. **MEMBERSHIPS** Soc Advan Scand Studies; Norweg-Am Hist Soc. **RESEARCH** Scandinavian, particularly Norwegian, eighteenth and nineteenth century literature; American-Norwegian Immigration history. **SELECTED PUBLICATIONS** Auth, Knut Hamsuns brevveksling med postmaster Frydenlund (1862-1947), 59 & Forsok over Vesaas' prosastil, 62, Edda; Knut Hamsun og Amerika, Gyldendal, 69; ed, Norway number, Lit Rev, 69; co-ed, Americana-Norvegica III, 71 & auth, Norsk litteraturhistorisk bibliografi, 75, Universitetsforlaget; Norwegian Influence on the Upper Midwest, Univ Minn, 76; Denmark - Miller,ke, Scandinavian Studies, Vol 0065, 1993; Sweden - Sather,lb, Swanson,a, Scandinavian Studies, Vol 0065, 1993; a Bright Flash of Light - Abel,niels,henrik And His Times - Norwegian - Stubhaug,a, Scandinavica, Vol 0036, 1997. **CONTACT ADDRESS** Dept of Scand Studies, Univ Wis, Madison, WI, 53706.

NAFICY, HAMID
PERSONAL Born 02/02/1944, Isfahan, Iran, m, 1995, 2 children **DISCIPLINE** FILM AND TELEVISION **EDUCATION** Univ Southern Calif, BA, 68; Univ Calif Los Angeles, MFA, 71; PhD, 90. **CAREER** Assoc prof, Free Univ Iran, 73-79; vis assoc prof, Television and Cinema Coll Tehranm 74-78; vis asst prof, Univ Southern Calif, 80-81; vis asst prof, Univ Calif Santa Barbara, 90-91; vis asst prof, Univ Southern Calif, 91; asst prof, Rice Univ, 93-95; assoc prof, Rice Univ, 95-. **HONORS AND AWARDS** Numerous Awards from Rice Univ, Univ Calif, Am Film Inst; Rockefeller Fel, 92-93; Doctoral Res Grant, 88; Nat Endowment for Humanities, 85; UNESCO Fel, 76; Chris Award 33rd Annual Columbus Film festival, 85; Silver Prize Houston Int Film Festival, 85; Second Prize Int Film and TV Fetsival NY, 86. **MEMBERSHIPS** Middle Eastern Studies Asn of N Am; Soc for Cinema Studies; Soc for Iranian Studies; univ Film and Video Asn. **RESEARCH** Cultural studies of film and media, exilic and diasporic culture and cinema, television and media; Iranian cinema and culture, ethnographic and documentary films, ethnicity and media. **SELECTED PUBLICATIONS** Auth, The Making of Exile Cultures: Iranian Television in Los Angeles, 93; ed, Home, Exile, Homeland: Film, Media, and the Politics of Place, 98; co-ed, Otherness and the Media: The Ethnography of the Imagined and the Imaged, 93. **CONTACT ADDRESS** Dept of Art and Art History, Rice Univ, Box 1892, Houston, TX, 77251. **EMAIL** naficy@rice.edu

NAGEL, ALAN FREDERICK
PERSONAL Born 03/09/1941, Beverly, MA, m, 1973 **DISCIPLINE** COMPARATIVE LITERATURE, ENGLISH **EDUCATION** Harvard Col, BA, 63; Cornell Univ, MA, 65, PhD(comp lit), 69. **CAREER** Asst prof, 69-72, chmn, Grad Prog, 71-75, assoc prof, 72- 80, Prof English & Comp Lit, Univ Iowa, 80-, Chmn, BA Lett, Univ Iowa, 71-81, chmn, Interdiscipline Prog Lit, Sci & Arts; vis prof, Univ Paul Valery, Montpelier, France, fall, 82. **MEMBERSHIPS** MLA; Am Comp Lit Asn; Midwest Mod Lang Asn. **RESEARCH** Poetics; Renaissance literature, literary theory. **SELECTED PUBLICATIONS** Co-ed, The Three Crowns of Florence: Humanist Assessments of Dante, Petrarca, Boccaccio, Harper, 72; auth, Lies and the limitable inane Contradiction in More's Utopia, Renaissance Quart, 73; Literary and historical context in Ronsard's Sonnets pour Helene, Pub Mod Lang Asn, 79; Rhetoric, value and action in Alberti, Mod Lang Notes, 80; 'Mastro Don Gesualdo', Gender, Dialect, And The Body, Stanford Italian Review, Vol 0011, 1992; Countercurrents - on The Primacy of Texts in Literary-criticism - Prier,ra, Comparative Literature Studies, Vol 0031, 1994. **CONTACT ADDRESS** Dept of Comp Lit, Univ of Iowa, 308 English Phil Bld, Iowa City, IA, 52242-1492.

NAKADATE, NEIL EDWARD
PERSONAL Born 09/01/1943, East Chicago, Ind, 3 children **DISCIPLINE** AMERICAN LITERATURE, RHETORIC & COMPOSITION **EDUCATION** Stanford Univ, AB, 65; Ind Univ, Bloomington, MA, 68 PhD(English), 72. **CAREER** Asst instr English, Ind Univ, 67-70; asst prof, Univ Tex, Austin, 70-77; asst prof, 77-80, Assoc Prof English, Iowa State Univ, 80- **HONORS AND AWARDS** IA State Univ Fnd Awd for Career Achievement in Tchg; Golden Key, NHS; **MEMBERSHIPS** Conf Col Compos & Commun; Soc Study Southern Lit; MLA. **RESEARCH** Modern American literature; prose fiction; rhetorical theory. **SELECTED PUBLICATIONS** Auth, Robert Penn Warren and the confessional novel, Genre, 12/69; The function of colloquy in Robert Penn Warren's Brother to Dragons, Tenn Studies Lit, 76; ed, Robert Penn Warren: A Reference Guide, G K Hall, 77; auth, The decomposition of the liberal arts, the liberalization of composition, and an alternative course, ERIC, 3/77; ed, Robert Penn Warren: Critical Perspectives, Univ Press Ky, 81; auth, Identity, dream, and exploration: Warren's later fiction, in Robert Penn Warren: Critical Perspectives, 81; coauth, Writing in the Liberal Arts Tradition: A Rhetoric with Readings, Harper & Row, 85, 2nd ed, 90; coed, A Rhetoric of Doing: Essays on Written Discourse in Honor of James L. Kinneavy, S Illinois Univ, 92; auth, Understanding Hane Smiley, Univ SC, (in press). **CONTACT ADDRESS** Dept of English, Iowa State Univ, Ames, IA, 50011-0002. **EMAIL** neiln@iastate.edu

NALBANTIAN, SUZANNE
DISCIPLINE COMPARATIVE LITERATURE, CRITICAL THEORY **EDUCATION** Columbia Univ, PhD. **CAREER** Prof, Long Island Univ, C.W. Post Campus. **SELECTED PUBLICATIONS** Auth, Aesthetic Autobiography; The Symbol of the Soul from Holderlin to Yeats: A Study in Metonymy; Seeds of Decadence in the Late Nineteenth-Century Novel. **CONTACT ADDRESS** Long Island Univ, C.W. Post, Brookville, NY, 11548-1300.

NAPIERALSKI, EDMUND ANTHONY
PERSONAL Born 11/06/1937, Buffalo, NY, m, 1964, 3 children **DISCIPLINE** LITERATURE **EDUCATION** Canisius Col, BA, 61; Loyola Univ, Chicago, PhD(English), 67. **CAREER** From instr to asst prof English, Georgetown Univ, 64-71; asst prof, 71-80, Prof English, King's Col, Pa, 80-, Dir honors prog, Ctr Independent Learning; Coordr of the Core Curriculum Assessment. **MEMBERSHIPS** Asn Lit Schol and Critics; Multi-Ethnic Lit of the U.S.; Asn for the Study of Am Indian Lit. **RESEARCH** Tragedy; dramatic form; comparative literature. **SELECTED PUBLICATIONS** Auth, Restoration and 18th Century Theatre Research Bibliography, Restoration & 18th Century Theatre Res, 61-73; contribr, Restoration and Eighteenth Century Theatre Research: A Bibliographical Guide, 1900-1968, Southern Ill Univ, 71; auth, The tragic knot: Paradox in the experience of tragedy, J Aesthet & Art Criticism, 73; Tennessee Williams' The Glass Menagerie: The dramatic metaphor, Southern Quart, 10/77; Miss Julie: Strindberg's Tragic Fairy Tale, Mod Drama, 9/83, reprinted in Twentieth Century Lit Criticism, 47, 93; Thomas's A Refusal to Mourn the Death, by Fire, of a Child in London, The Explicator, Spring 92; Morrison's The Bluest Eye, The Explicator, Winter 94; coauth, Assessing Learning in Programs, In: Handbook of the Undergraduate Curriculum, Jossey-Bass Publ, 97. **CONTACT ADDRESS** Dept of English, King's Col, 133 N River St, Wilkes Barre, PA, 18711-0801. **EMAIL** eanapier@gw02.kings.edu

NARDO, ANNA
DISCIPLINE RENAISSANCE AND 17TH CENTURY, BRITISH LITERATURE **EDUCATION** Emory Univ, PhD, 74. **CAREER** Prof, dir, undergrad stud, La State Univ. **HONORS AND AWARDS** Fel, Nat Hum Ctr, 81; HM "Hub" Cotton Fac Excellence Award, 88; James Holly Hanford Award, 91; Nicholson Award, 93. **RESEARCH** John Milton; Shakespeare and film; George Eliot. **SELECTED PUBLICATIONS** Auth, Milton's Sonnets and the Ideal Community, 79; John Donne at Play in Between, The Eagle and the Dove, 86; Their Faith is Strong, but Their Prose is Weak: Teaching Paradise Lost at LSU, in Approaches to Teaching Paradise Lost, 86; George Herbert: Pulling For Prime, S Cent Rev, 86; Samson, 'Sung and Proverb'd for a Fool,' Mosaic, 88; Academic Interludes in Paradise Lost, Milton Stud, 91; The Ludic Self in Seventeenth-Century English Literature, 91; Milton and the Academic Sonnet, in Milton in Italy, 91; The Education of Milton's Good Angels,' Arenas of Conflict, 97. **CONTACT ADDRESS** Dept of Eng, Louisiana State Univ, 213C Allen Hall, Baton Rouge, LA, 70803. **EMAIL** anardo@unix1.sncc.lsu.edu

NASH, ELIZABETH
DISCIPLINE THEATRE ARTS **EDUCATION** Univ Ind, PhD. **CAREER** Assoc prof **SELECTED PUBLICATIONS** Auth, Always First Class: The Career of Geraldine Farrar. **CONTACT ADDRESS** Theatre Arts and Dance Dept, Univ of Minnesota, Twin Cities, 106 Norris Hall, 172 Pillsbury Dr SE, Minneapolis, MN, 55455. **EMAIL** nashx001@maroon.tc.umn.edu

NASS, CLIFFORD I.
DISCIPLINE COMMUNICATIONS **EDUCATION** Princeton Univ, BA, 81; PhD 86. **CAREER** Assoc prof/dir PhD progs dept commun, Stanford Univ. **HONORS AND AWARDS** Co-dir Soc Respon Commun Tech proj, research applied to Microsoft Office 97, meas instr, and Serengeti voice-based exec asst; prof magician. **RESEARCH** Human-computer interaction; soc responses to commun tech; statistical methods; organization theory. **SELECTED PUBLICATIONS** Auth, 35 publ on tech and statistical methodology; coauth, The Media Equation: How People Treat Computers, Television, Cambridge UP; New Media Like Real People and Places, Cambridge UP. **CONTACT ADDRESS** Dept Commun, Stanford Univ, McClatchy Hall Rm. 300D, Stanford, CA, 94305. **EMAIL** nass@leland.stanford.edu

NASSAR, EUGENE PAUL
PERSONAL Born 07/20/1935, Utica, NY, 3 children **DISCIPLINE** ENGLISH, CRITICISM **EDUCATION** Kenyon Col, BA, 57; Oxford Univ, MA, 60; Cornell Univ, PhD(English), 62. **CAREER** Instr English, Hamilton Col, 62-64; from asst prof to assoc prof, 64-71, Prof English, Utica Col, 71-, Nat Found Arts & Humanities fel, 73-74; Rhodes scholar; Woodrow Wilson fel. **RESEARCH** Literary criticism. **SELECTED PUBLICATIONS** Auth, Wallace Stevens: An Anatomy of Figuration, Univ Pa, 65; The Rape of Cinderella: Essays in Literary Continuity, Ind Univ, 70; The Cantos of Ezra Pound: The Lyric Mode, Johns Hopkins Univ, 75; Essays: Critical and Metacritical, Fairleigh Dickinson Univ Press, 82; Illustrations to Dante's Inferno, Fairleigh Dickinson Univ Press, 94. **CONTACT ADDRESS** Dept of English, Utica Col, 1600 Burrstone Rd, Utica, NY, 13502-4892. **EMAIL** enassar@utica.ucsu.edu

NATALLE, ELIZABETH
DISCIPLINE INTERPERSONAL COMMUNICATION, COMMUNICATION THEORY **EDUCATION** FL State Univ, MA, PhD. **CAREER** Assoc prof, dir, intercultural commun exchange prog, Univ NC, Greensboro. **HONORS AND AWARDS** Woman of Distinction Award, Univ NC, Greensboro, 96. **RESEARCH** Gender and interpersonal process; feminist criticism; women's commun networks. **SELECTED PUBLICATIONS** Auth, Gender and communication theory, Commun Educ, 40, 91; Gendered issues in the workplace, in J.T. Wood, ed, Gendered relationships, Mayfield Press, 96; coauth, Deconstructing gender differences in persuasibility: A bricolage, Women's Stud in Commun, 16, 93; Feminist philosophy and the transformation of organizational communication, in B. Kovacic, ed, New approaches to organizational communication, SUNY Press, 94; Sex differences, organizational level, and superiors' evaluation of managerial leadership, Mgt Commun Quart, 10, 97. **CONTACT ADDRESS** Univ N. Carolina, Greensboro, Greensboro, NC, 27412-5001. **EMAIL** ej_natalle@uncg.edu

NATHANSON, LEONARD
PERSONAL Born 09/22/1933, New York, NY **DISCIPLINE** ENGLISH LITERATURE **EDUCATION** Brooklyn Col, BA, 54; Duke Univ, MA, 55; Univ WI, PhD, 59. **CAREER** Instr Eng, Northwestern Univ, 59-60; asst prof, Univ Cincinnati, 60-66; Assoc Prof Eng, Vanderbilt Univ, 66-98, Prof Emer Eng, Vanderbilt Univ, 98-; Taft Mem Fund res grant, 62; mem exec comt, Milton Soc Am, 72-75. **MEMBERSHIPS** MLA; Mod Hum Res Asn; Renaissance Soc Am; S Atlantic MLA; Milton Soc Am. **RESEARCH** Seventeenth century lit; Milton. **SELECTED PUBLICATIONS** Auth, The Strategy of Truth: A Study of Sir Thomas Browne, Univ Chicago, 67; ed, Shakespeare, The Tempest, W C Brown, 69; ed & contribr, A Milton Encyclopedia (9 vols), Bucknell Univ, Vol Viii, 78-81. **CONTACT ADDRESS** Dept of English, Vanderbilt Univ, Nashville, TN, 37235.

NATOV, RONI
DISCIPLINE ENGLISH LITERATURE **EDUCATION** City Univ NY, BA, MA, PhD. **CAREER** Prof. **RESEARCH** Literature and psychology; women's studies; children's studies and fantasy; fairy tales and myths. **SELECTED PUBLICATIONS** Auth, Leon Garfield, Twayne/Macmillan, 94; Mothers and Daughters: Jamaica Kincaid's Pre-Oedipal Narrative, Children's Lit, 90; The Child Hero: Internal and External Journeys, Children's Lit Edu, 89; Living in Two Cultures: Bette Bao Lord's Stories of Chinese-American Experience, Lion Unicorn, 87; The Truth of Ordinary Lives: Autobiographical Fiction for Children, Children's Lit Edu, 86; Stories We Need to Hear, Or the Reader and the Tale, Lion Unicorn, 86; The Power of the Tale, Children's Lit, 85. **CONTACT ADDRESS** English Dept, Union Inst, 440 E McMillan St, Cincinnati, OH, 45206-1925.

NAUGHTON, JOHN
DISCIPLINE 19TH AND 20TH CENTURY FRENCH POETRY, THE CONTEMPORARY FRENCH NOVEL **EDUCATION** Stanford Univ, BA, MA; Univ CA, Santa Cruz, MA, PhD. **CAREER** Former instr, Univ Tours, France; Univ CA; consult, Univ Chicago Press, 87; dir, Dijon Study Group, 95; prof. **HONORS AND AWARDS** Picker sr fac grant, Colgate Univ, 87; medal, Col de France, Paris, 91; hon(s), Phi Eta Sigma., Nominee, Colgate prof yr, 91, 97. **SELECTED PUBLICATIONS** Transl, In the Shadows Light, Univ Chicago Press, 91; auth, Louis-Rene des Forets, Rodopi, 93; Yves Bonnefoy: New and Selected Poems, Univ Chicago Press and Carcanet Press, London, 95; articles, L'Esprit Createur; Sud; Temenos; Studies in 20th Century Literature; Dalhousie Fr Studies; transl(s), New Lit Hist; Critical Inquiry; Yale Fr Studies; Fr-Brit Studies; Poetry Rev; Tel-Aviv Rev; Graham House Rev; Mod Poetry in Translation; rev(s), World Lit Today; S Hum Rev; L'Esprit Createur; Fr Forum. **CONTACT ADDRESS** Dept of Romance Lang, Colgate Univ, 13 Oak Drive, Hamilton, NY, 13346. **EMAIL** jnaughton@center.colgate.edu

NEELD, ELIZABETH HARPER
PERSONAL Born 12/25/1940, Brooks, GA, m, 1983 **DISCIPLINE** ENGLISH **EDUCATION** Univ Chattanooga, MS, MS; Univ Tenn, Knoxville, PhD. **CAREER** Head, Hum Div, Cleveland State Commun Col, 67-73; dir, Eng Prog, MLA, 73-76; prof, Eng, Texas A&M Univ, 76-83; independent scholar, res and auth, 83-89; exec prof, Univ Houston, 90- . **HONORS AND AWARDS** Listed, Contemporary Authors, Who's Who in America, Who's Who in the World. **MEMBERSHIPS** MLA; NCTE. **RESEARCH** Eighteenth century; rhetoric. **SELECTED PUBLICATIONS** Auth, Writing, 3 eds; auth, Writing Brief, 3 eds; auth, Readings for Writing; auth, The Way a Writer Reads; auth, Options for the Teaching of English: The Undergraduate Curriculum; auth, Either Way Will Hurt & Other Essays on English; auth, Harper & Row Studies in Language and Literature; auth, Fairy Tales of the Sea; auth, From the Plow to the Pulpit; auth, Seven Choices, 3d ed; auth, Sacred Primer. **CONTACT ADDRESS** 6706 Beauford Dr, Austin, TX, 78750. **EMAIL** ENWriter@aol.com

NEELY, CAROL THOMAS
PERSONAL Born 05/16/1939, Philadelphia, PA, m, 1965, 3 children **DISCIPLINE** ENGLISH LITERATURE **EDUCATION** Smith Col, BA, 61; Yale Univ, MA, 63, PhD(English), 69. **CAREER** From instr to asst prof English, Univ Ill, Urbana Champaign, 65-73; instr, 75-76, Assoc Prof English, Ill State Univ, 80-. **MEMBERSHIPS** MLA; Shakespeare Asn Am. **RESEARCH** Shakespeare; poetry of the English Renaissance; feminist criticism. **SELECTED PUBLICATIONS** Auth, The Winter's Tale: The Triumph of Speech, Studies English Lit, 75; Detachment and Engagement in Shakespeare's Sonnets: 94, 116, 129, Pmla, 77; Women and Men in Othello, Shakespeare Studies, 77; The Structure of English Renaissance Sonnet Sequences, JEnglish Lit Hist, 78; Women and issue in The Winter's Tale, Philol Quart, 78; co-ed (with Carolyn Lenz & Gayle Greene), The Woman's Part: Feminist Criticism of Shakespeare, Univ Ill Press, 80; auth, Feminist Modes of Shakespearean Criticism: Compensatory, Justificatory, Transformational, Women's Studies, 81; Melancholy, Genius, And Utopia in The Renaissance - Schleiner,w, Shakespeare Quarterly, Vol 0044, 1993. **CONTACT ADDRESS** 708 Arlington Ct, Champaign, IL, 61820.

NEFF, JOYCE
DISCIPLINE MANAGEMENT WRITING **EDUCATION** Western Md Col, BA; Univ Md, MA; Univ Pa, PhD. **CAREER** Engl, Old Dominion Univ. **MEMBERSHIPS** Univ Interdisciplinary Studies Comt; Arts & Letters Practicum (CAP) Comt; Dept Curr & Instruction Comt. **SELECTED PUBLICATIONS** Coauth, Professional Writing in Context: Lessons from Teaching and Consulting in Worlds of Work, Lawrence Erlbaum; Literacy among Undergraduates: How We Represent Students as Writers and What It Means When We Don't, in Rhetoric, Cultural Studies, and Literacy. Earlbaum, 95; "Rhetoric in a Bureaucracy: Government Evaluators as Report Writers" in Studies in Technical Communication. Univ N Tex, 96. **CONTACT ADDRESS** Old Dominion Univ, 4100 Powhatan Ave, Norfolk, VA, 23058. **EMAIL** JNeff@odu.edu

NEIVA, EDUARDO
PERSONAL Born 08/31/1950, Brazil, m, 1993, 2 children **DISCIPLINE** COMMUNICATION **EDUCATION** Pontificia Universidade Catolica do Rio de Janeiro, BA, 79; Universidade Federal do Rio de Janeiro, MA, 83, PhD, 89. **CAREER** Assoc prof, Universidade Federal Fluminense, 75-93; assoc prof, St Univ of Rio de Janeiro, 89-93; chair, Catholic Univ of Rio de Janeiro, 87-89; vis prof, Universidade Fernando Pessoa, Oporto, Portugal, 95; vis prof, Ind Univ Bloomington, 90; asst prof to assoc prof to dir, Univ Al Birmingham, 93- . **HONORS AND AWARDS** Travel grant, Int Conf on Word & Image Stud, 96; Fulbright Scholar, Ind Univ, 90; Conselho Nacional de Pesquisa grant, 91-93. **MEMBERSHIPS** Assoc for Semiotic Res; Int Commun Assoc. **RESEARCH** Image & visual culture; semiotics; commun theory. **SELECTED PUBLICATIONS** Auth O que aprender com antigas catastrofes, Sao Paulo, Atica, 96; Comunicacao na era pos-moderna, Rio de Janeiro, Vozes, 97; O racionalismo critico de Karl Popper, Sao Paulo, Francisco Alves, 98; Mythologies of vision, Peter Lang, 99; Ideology, in Encyclopaedic Dictionary of Semiotics, Berlin, Mouton de Gruyter, 94. **CONTACT ADDRESS** Dept of Commun, Univ Al Birmingham, UAB Station, Birmingham, AL, 35294. **EMAIL** neiya@uab.edu

NELSEN, ROBERT
DISCIPLINE LITERATURE STUDIES **EDUCATION** Univ Chicago, PhD, 85. **CAREER** Assoc prof. **HONORS AND AWARDS** Ed, Common Knowledge. **SELECTED PUBLICATIONS** Auth, Miles Away From Home, TriQuart, 95; They Fly Up and Drop, Quart W, 94; We Bums Are Not Homeless, Chariton Rev, 93; Everybody Needs a Fine Dancer, SW Rev, 92; Something Big, Northwestern Univ, 90; The Story of a Mighty and Ferocious Warrior, Other Voices, 89. **CONTACT ADDRESS** Dept of Literature, Richardson, TX, 75083-0688. **EMAIL** nelsen@utdallas.edu

NELSON, CARY ROBERT
PERSONAL Born 05/15/1946, Philadelphia, PA **DISCIPLINE** ENGLISH & AMERICAN LITERATURE **EDUCATION** Antioch Col, BA, 67; Univ Rochester, PhD(English), 70. **CAREER** From asst to assoc prof, English, 70-82, Prof English & Criticism & Interpretive Theory, 82- ; Jubilee Prof of Liberal Arts and Sci, 91- ,Univ Ill, Urbana; Vis prof, State Univ NY Col Buffalo, 77; coordr, Fac Criticism Sem, Univ Ill, Urbana, 77-, assoc fel, Ctr Advan Studies, 78, dir, Unit for Criticism & Interpretive Theory, 81- **MEMBERSHIPS** MLA; AAUP; Midwest MLA; Tchrs for a Democratic Culture; Kenneth Burke Soc; Ernest Hemingway Soc; Natl Counc Tchrs English. **RESEARCH** Modern English and American literature; critical theory. **SELECTED PUBLICATIONS** Auth, The Incarnate Word: Literature as Verbal Space, Illinois, 73; auth, Our Last First Poets: Vision and History in Contemporary American Poetry, Illinois, 81; auth, Repression and Recovery: Modern American Poetry and the Politics of Cultural Memory, 1910-1945, Wisconsin, 89; auth, Shouts from the Wall: Posters and Photographs Brought Back from the Spanish Civil War by American Volunteers, Illinois, 96; auth, Manifesto of a Tenured Radical, New York Univ, 97; coauth, Academic Keywords: A Devil's Dictionary for Higher Education, Routledge, 99. **CONTACT ADDRESS** Dept of English, Univ of Ill, 608 S Wright St, Urbana, IL, 61801.

NELSON, CLAUDIA B.
PERSONAL Born 11/02/1960, Fort Belvoir, VA, 1 child **DISCIPLINE** ENGLISH **EDUCATION** Bryn Mawr Col, AB, 80; Indiana Univ, PhD, 89. **CAREER** Fac to assoc prof, English, Southwest Texas State Univ, 93- . **HONORS AND AWARDS** Pres Awd for Excellence in Scholarly/Creative Activity; SWT;, Memb, bd of dir, Children's Lit Asn. **MEMBERSHIPS** Children's Lit Asn; MLA. **RESEARCH** Victorian literature and culture; children's studies. **SELECTED PUBLICATIONS** Auth, Boys Will Be Girls: The Feminine Ethic and British Children's Fiction, 1857-1917, Rutgers, 91; co-ed, with Vallone, The Girl's Own: Cultural Histories of the Anglo-American Girl, 1830-1915, Univ Georgia, 94; auth, Invisible Men: Fatherhood in Victorian Periodicals, 1850-1910, Univ Georgia, 95; co-ed, with Holmes, Maternal Instincts: Visions of Motherhood and Sexuality in Britain, 1875-1925, Macmillan, 97. **CONTACT ADDRESS** 501 E Annie St, Austin, TX, 78704. **EMAIL** cho2@swt.edu

NELSON, DANA D.
DISCIPLINE ENGLISH LITERATURE **EDUCATION** MI State Univ, PhD. **CAREER** Vis prof, 98-99. **RESEARCH** Colonial to nineteenth century Am lit; promotional, travel and frontier lit; early national and early US Novel; multi ethnic US lit; women's lit and gender studies; femnist and gender theory; cult and race theory. **SELECTED PUBLICATIONS** Auth, The Word in Black and White: Reading Race in American Literature. **CONTACT ADDRESS** Eng Dept, Duke Univ, Durham, NC, 27706.

NELSON, DAVID C.
DISCIPLINE COMMUNICATIONS **EDUCATION** Purdue Univ, BA, MA, PhD. **CAREER** Ed, Col Media Rev, 88-93; Assoc ed, College Media Rev, 93-; Assoc ed, Newspaper Res Jour, 92-. **SELECTED PUBLICATIONS** Rev ed, Writing the News, Wadsworth Publ, 93; Understanding Grammar, Brown & Benchmark, 93, State of the Art: Issues in Contemporary Communication, St Martins Press, 92; A Handbook for Reporters, Allyn & Bacon, 92; Coauth, Viability and the Mass Communication Curriculum , 93; Designing client services for academic organizations , 92. **CONTACT ADDRESS** Southwest Texas State Univ, 601 University Dr, San Marcos, TX, 78666-4604.

NELSON, HARLAND S.
PERSONAL Born 08/11/1925, Hawley, MN, m, 1954, 3 children **DISCIPLINE** ENGLISH **EDUCATION** Concordia Col, Minn, BA, 49; Wash State Univ, MA, 51; Univ Minn, PhD, 59. **CAREER** Instr English, Univ Mo, 51-53 & Univ Conn, 59-62; from asst prof to assoc prof 62-67, Prof English, Luther Col, Iowa, 67-, Fulbright lectr, Univ Bergen, Norway, 67-68 & Univ Innsbruck, Austria, 72-73; dir, Consortium Agr & World Hunger, 81- **MEMBERSHIPS** MLA; NCTE; Aaup; Soc Values Higher Educ; Col English Asn. **RESEARCH** Victorian literature; Dickens; modern and contemporary fiction. **SELECTED PUBLICATIONS** Auth, Dickens' plots: The Ways of Providence or the influence of Collins?, Victorian Newslett, spring 61; Stephen Crane's achievement as a poet, Tex Studies Lit & Lang, winter 63; Dickens' Our Mutual Friend and Henry Mayhew's London Labour and the London Poor, 19th-Century Fiction, 1265; Steinbeck's politics then and now, Antioch Rev, spring 67; contribr, Shonfield and Forster's India: A controversial exchange, Encounter, 668; auth, Theology and the films of Ingmar Bergman, Dialog, summer 71; Staggs's Gardens: The railway through Dickens' World, Dickens' Studies Annual, 74; Dickens Studies Annual - Essays on Victorian Fiction, Vol 23 - Timko,m, Kaplan,f, Guiliano,e, Dickens Quarterly, Vol 0013, 1996; Charles Dickens, Twayne, 81; Dickens, Religion, And Nubile Girls, Dickens Quarterly, Vol 0014, 1997. **CONTACT ADDRESS** Dept of English, Luther Col, Decorah, IA, 52101.

NELSON, JAMES GRAHAM
PERSONAL Born 12/20/1929, Covington, KY **DISCIPLINE** ENGLISH LITERATURE **EDUCATION** Univ Ky, BA, 52; Columbia Univ, MA, 55, PhD, 61. **CAREER** Lectr English, Columbia Univ, 58-61; from instr to assoc prof, 61-69, Prof English, Univ Wis-Madison, 69-, Guggenheim fel, 65-66. **MEMBERSHIPS** MLA; Milton Soc Am. **RESEARCH** Romantic and Victorian literature; Pubishing history; John Milton. **SELECTED PUBLICATIONS** Auth, The Sublime Puritan: Milton and the Victorians, Univ Wis, 63; Sir William Watson, Twayne, 67; The Early Nineties: A View From the Bodley Head, Harvard Univ, 71; The Poetry of Newbolt,henry, Patriotism Is Not Enough - Jackson,vf, English Literature in Transition 1880-1920, Vol 0037, 1994. **CONTACT ADDRESS** Dept of English, Univ of Wis, Madison, WI, 53706.

NELSON, MALCOLM A.
PERSONAL Born 05/29/1934, Carbondale, IL, m, 1993, 5 children **DISCIPLINE** ENGLISH **EDUCATION** Williams Col, BA, 55; Northwestern Univ, MA, 57, PhD, 61 **CAREER** Asst, Northwestern Univ, 56-59; from instr to asst prof English, Miami Univ, 59-65; asst prof, Grinnell Col, 65-68; assoc prof, 68-73, prof, 73-83, DISTINGUISHED TEACHING PROF, STATE UNIV NY COL FREDONIA, 83-; State Univ NY Res Found grant, 69 & 71; Am Philos Soc grant, 71. **HONORS AND AWARDS** Chancellor's Award for Excellence in Teaching, State Univ NY, 75; distinguished teaching prof of Eng, 83. **MEMBERSHIPS** Renaissance Soc Am; MLA; Catch Soc Am (exec secy, 68-); Asn Gravestone Studies; Am Fedn Teachers **RESEARCH** Shakespeare; 16th-18th century poetry and music--catches, canons and glees; American gravestone poetry and art; Mari Sandoz and the American West. **SELECTED PUBLICATIONS** Auth, The Poet and the Goddess, Nous, 3/67; co-ed, A Collection of Catches, Canons and Glees, 1762-1793 (4 vols), Mellifont, 70; auth, Catches, glees and chaces: Cantici bibendi et alii, Lyric & Song, 6/71; The Robin Hood Tradition in the English Renaissance, Univ Salzburg, 73; coauth, Resurrecting the epitaph, Markers, Vol I, 80; auth, See an account by Sir G Esterling, 1598, Shakespeare Quart, Vol 31, No 1; coauth, Grinning skulls, smiling cherubs, bitter words, J Popular Cult, Vol 15, No 4; Epitaph and Icon: A Field Guide to the Old Burying Grounds of Cape Cod, Martha's Vineyard, and Nantucket, Parnassus, 83; Hamlet the Fool, In: Fools and Jesters in Literature, Art and History, Greenwood Press, 98. **CONTACT ADDRESS** Dept of English, State Univ of NY, SUNY at Fredonia, Fredonia, NY, 14063-1143. **EMAIL** nelson@cs.fredonia.edu

NELSON, NICOLAS HARDING
PERSONAL Born 07/07/1940, Nebraska City, NE, m, 1965, 2 children **DISCIPLINE** ENGLISH LITERATURE **EDUCATION** Stanford Univ, BA, 62; Univ Wis, Madison, MA, 65, PhD(English), 71. **CAREER** Lectr English, 69-71, asst prof, 71-76, Assoc Prof English, Ind Univ, Kokomo, 76-, Chmn Div Humanities, 71-. **MEMBERSHIPS** MLA; Am Soc 18th Century Studies; Johnson Soc Cent Region; Augustan Reprint Soc. **RESEARCH** Samuel Butler; Hudibras; 18th century English satire. **SELECTED PUBLICATIONS** Auth, Astrology, Hudibras, and the Puritans, J Hist Ideas, 7-976; Narrative Transformations, Prior Art of The Tale, Studies in Philology, Vol 0090, 1993; Narrative Transformations, Prior Art of The Tale, Studies in Philology, Vol 0090, 1993. **CONTACT ADDRESS** Div of Humanities, Indiana Univ, Kokomo, 2300 S Washington St, Kokomo, IN, 46902.

NELSON, RANDY FRANKLIN
PERSONAL Born 05/20/1948, Charlotte, NC, m, 1968, 1 child **DISCIPLINE** AMERICAN LITERATURE **EDUCATION** NC State Univ, BA, 70, MA, 72; Princeton Univ, MA, 75, PhD(English), 76. **CAREER** Asst prof English, Univ Louisville, 76-77; Asst Prof English, Davidson Col, 77-, Ed, Textual Res, Writings of Henry David Thoreau, 76-. **MEMBERSHIPS** MLA; Thoreau Soc; Mark Twain Soc; Southern Writers Conf; Poe Soc. **RESEARCH** H D Thoreau; Mark Twain; Southern literature. **SELECTED PUBLICATIONS** Slave Ship', African American Review, Vol 0030, 1996. **CONTACT ADDRESS** Dept of English, Davidson Col, Davidson, NC, 28036.

NELSON, RICHARD ALAN
DISCIPLINE MASS COMMUNICATIONS **EDUCATION** Fla State Univ, PhD, 80. **CAREER** Assoc dean, grad stud and res, La State Univ; Instr, assoc dir, Int Telecommun Res Inst, Univ Houston; hd, PR, Kans State Univ; Accredited PR Prof, PR Soc of Am. **MEMBERSHIPS** Pres, Int Acad of Bus Disciplines, 97-99. **SELECTED PUBLICATIONS** Auth, Lights! Camera! Florida! Ninety Years of Moviemaking and Television Production in the Sunshine State, Fla Endowment for the Hum, 87; Bias Versus Fairness: The Social Utility of Issues Management, in PR Rev 16,1, 90; Activist Groups and New Technologies: Influencing the Public Affairs Agenda, in Lloyd B. Dennis, ed, Practical Public Affairs in an Era of Change: A Communications Guide for Business, Government, and College, PR Soc of Am/UP of Am, 95; A Chronology and Glossary of Propaganda in the United States, Greenwood Press, 96; coauth, Issues Management: Corporate Public Policymaking in an Information Society, Sage Publ, 89. **CONTACT ADDRESS** The Manship Sch of Mass Commun, Louisiana State Univ, Baton Rouge, LA, 70803. **EMAIL** rnelson@unix1.sncc.lsu.edu

NEMETH, NEIL
DISCIPLINE COMMUNICATION **EDUCATION** Ohio Univ, BS; Ohio State Univ, MA; Ind Univ, PhD. **CAREER** Asst prof, 94-. **RESEARCH** Reporting, editing, mass communication law, mass communication ethics. **SELECTED PUBLICATIONS** Publ, Newspaper Res Jour, Southwestern Mass Commun Jour **CONTACT ADDRESS** Dept of Commun, Pittsburg State Univ, 1701 S Broadway St, Pittsburg, KS, 66762.

NERONE, JOHN
DISCIPLINE COMMUNICATIONS **EDUCATION** Xavier, HAB, 78; Univ Notre Dame, BA, 80, PhD, 82. **CAREER** Assoc prof, Inst Comm Res, PROF, UNIV ILL **MEMBERSHIPS** Am Antiquarian Soc **RESEARCH** US Newspapers **SELECTED PUBLICATIONS** Auth, Lessons from American History, in Journalists in Peril, Media Studies Rev, Fall 96; coauth, News Photography and the New Long Journalism," in Visual Representation and History; auth, The Culture of the Press in the Early Republic: Cincinnati, 1793-1848; auth, Violence Against the Press: Policing the Public Sphere in U.S. History; ed, Last Right: Revisiting Four Theories of the Press. **CONTACT ADDRESS** 505 E Armory Ave, Champaign, IL, 61820. **EMAIL** j-nerone@uiuc.edu

NESSET, KIRK
DISCIPLINE ENGLISH **CAREER** ASST PROF ENGLISH, ALLEGHENY COL **HONORS AND AWARDS** Pushcart Prize, 97. **MEMBERSHIPS** MLA; AWP **RESEARCH** Fiction writing; Poetry; Native American Literature. **SELECTED PUBLICATIONS** auth, "Reading Raymond Carver," Am Lit, 93; "The Final Stitch: Raymond Carver and Metaphor," Profils Am, 93; "Paradise for Sheep," Widener Rev, 93; "Cells of the Empire," Hawaii Rev, 93; "Record Shop Girl," Tampa Rev, 93; "Legally Dead," Oregon Rev, 93; "M. Casual," Oregon Rev, 93; "Mr. Excitement," Fiction, 94; Mr. Erotic, Witness, 94; Scream, Witness, 94; "I Want You to Kill Me," Chattahoochee Rev, 94; "Garlic," Potomac Rev, 94; The Highway, ZYZZYVA, 94; "Insularity and Self-Enlargement in Raymond Carver's Cathedral," Essay Lit, 94; "Gates to Buddhist Practive," Mountain Rec, 95; The Stories of Raymond Carver: A Critical Study, Ohio Univ Press, 95; School Bus, What's Become of Eden: Poems of Family at Century' End, Slapering Hol Press, 95; "Painting the Rain," The Ohio Poetry Rev, 95; "The End of the World is Los Angeles," The Ohio Poetry Rev, 95; "Invective," Black River Rev, 95; "The Stinging and Saving," New Orleans Rev, 95; Love Song, Descant, 95; "Regarding My Grandfather's Funeral, Which I Did Not Attend," Worcester Rev, 95; "Remember the Dead and the Dying," Karamu, 95; Paging Barry Badly, Witness, 96; The Noise That Wants to be Joy, Witness, 96; "Paradise Road," Tampa Rev, 96; "Snakes Having Babies," Indiana Rev, 96; Days Before Scanners, Anthology of New England Writers, 96; "The House With No Glass and No Curtains," Cimarron Rev, 96; "Mr. Ironic," Cimarron Rev, 96; "The Free Europeans," Green Mtn Rev, 96; "The No-Theory Theory," Phoebe, 96; "Jeremiad," Poet Lore, 95-96; "Thorn," Poet Lore, 95-96; "France in Tahiti," Poet Lore, 95-95; "The Collapse of the Heart is a Myth," Writer's Forum, 96; "Integrity," The Plum Rev, 96; "Burn," Free Lunch, 96; "Propinquity," Slant, 96; "Some of the Most Striking Women I Have Known Have Been Men," Antioch Rev, 96; "Timing," Nebraska Rev, 97; "Mr. Agreeable," Fiction, 97; "Crossroad," High Plains Lit Rev, 97; "Believing in People," W. Hum Rev, 97; "Behind the Wheel," S Carolina Rev, 97; "Style," Tempus, 97; "Archile Gorky at Forty," William and Mary Rev, 97; "Ultimate Sign," Laurel Rev, 97; "Wrong Number," Mudfish, 97; "Vultures," Seattle Rev, 97; "I Will, I Will Not," Boston Rev, 98; "Saint X," Pairie Schooner, 98; "To The Generous Anonymous Person Who Returned My Valise, Snatched From A Bench Near the Library," Nimrod, 98; "Mr Ecstatic," Nimrod, 98; "No Love at the Beach," Spoon River Poetry Rev, 98; "Backsliding," Spoon River Poetry Rev, 98; "Goat's Stomach," Spoon River Poetry Rev, 98; "Dance With Dave," Folio, 98; "Be With Somebody," Gettysburg Rev, 98. **CONTACT ADDRESS** Dept of English, Allegheny Col, Meadville, PA, 16335. **EMAIL** knesset@alleg.edu

NETTELS, ELSA
PERSONAL Born 05/25/1931, Madison, WI **DISCIPLINE** ENGLISH, AMERICAN LITERATURE **EDUCATION** Cornell Univ, AB, 53; Univ WI, MA, 55, PhD(Eng), 60. **CAREER** Instr Eng, Mt Holyoke Col, 59-62, asst prof, 63-67; from asst prof to assoc prof, 67-75, Prof Eng, Col William & Mary, 75-, S Atlantic MLA stud award, 75. **HONORS AND AWARDS**

S Atlantic MLA Studies Award, 75; NEH fel for col Tchrs, 83-84. **MEMBERSHIPS** MLA; NE MLA, S Atlantic MLA; Henry James Soc; Edith Wharton Soc, Am Stud Asn. **RESEARCH** Am lit; mod fiction. **SELECTED PUBLICATIONS** Auth, The ambassadors and the sense of the past, Mod Lang Quart, 6/70; Action and point of view in Roderick Hudson, English Studies, summer 72; James and Conrad on the art of fiction, Tex Studies Lit & Lang, fall 72; Heart of darkness and the creative process, Conradiana, summer 73; The scapegoats and martyrs of Henry James, Colby Libr Quart, 9/74; The grotesque in Conrad's fiction: Nineteenth-Century Fiction, 11/74; James and Conrad, Univ Ga, 77; William Dean Howells and the American language, New Eng Quart, fall 80; Language, Race, and Social Class in Howells's America, Univ Press of Ky, 88; Language and Gender in American Fiction: Howells, James, Wharton, and Cather, 97. **CONTACT ADDRESS** Dept of English, Col of William and Mary, Williamsburg, VA, 23185.

NEUENDORF, KIMBERLY A.
DISCIPLINE MASS COM THEORY, FILM **EDUCATION** MI State Univ, BA, MA, PhD. **CAREER** Comm, Cleveland St Univ. **SELECTED PUBLICATIONS** Arms Co-auth, TV Entertainment, News, and Racial Perceptions of College Students, Jour Commun, 92; Exposure Effects and Affective Responses to Music, Commun Monogr, 94. **CONTACT ADDRESS** Commun Dept, Cleveland State Univ, 83 E 24th St, Cleveland, OH, 44115. **EMAIL** k.neuendorf@csuohio.edu

NEUFELD, JAMES EDWARD
PERSONAL Born 12/09/1944, Niagara, ON, Canada, m, 1974, 2 children **DISCIPLINE** ENGLISH DRAMA, CANADIAN LITERATURE **EDUCATION** Univ Toronto, BA, 67; Univ Chicago, AM, 69, PhD(comp lit), 74. **CAREER** Assoc Prof English, Trent Univ, 72-, Vis assoc prof, Univ Victoria, summer, 82; prin, Catharine Parr Trail Col, Trent Univ, 82- **MEMBERSHIPS** Asn Can Univ Teacher English. **RESEARCH** Seventeenth century English comedy: Ben Jonson and the restoration; connections between English literature and other art forms; Canadian literature. **SELECTED PUBLICATIONS** Auth, Some pivot for significance in the poetry of Margaret Avison, 576 & Structural unity in the Dept for Trilogy: Robertson Davies as egoist, fall 76, J Can Studies; Some notes on Browning's Musical Poems, Studies in Browning and His Circle, spring 78; Scorecard + Anderson,reid Tenure at The National- ballet-of-canada - The Ballet in 1991-92, J of Canadian Studies- revue D Etudes Canadiennes, Vol 0027, 1992. **CONTACT ADDRESS** Dept of English, Trent Univ, Peterborough, ON, K9J7B8.

NEUFELDT, LEONARD N.
PERSONAL Born 11/03/1937, Yarrow, BC, Canada, m, 1961, 3 children **DISCIPLINE** ENGLISH **EDUCATION** Waterloo Univ Col, BA, 61; Univ Ill, AM, 62, PhD, 66. **CAREER** Asst prof English, Univ Wash, 66-72; assoc prof Am lit, Univ Tex of the Permian Basin, 73-78; prof Am lit, Purdue Univ, 78-, Fulbright prof Am studies, Univ Erlangen, 72-73; Am Coun Learned Soc grants, 75 & 77; Am Philos Soc grant, 77. **MEMBERSHIPS** MLA. **RESEARCH** American transcendentalism; unitarianism; poetry. **SELECTED PUBLICATIONS** Auth, The Vital Mind: Emerson's Epistemology, in Philol Quart, 4/71; Time and Man's Possibilities in Light in August, in Ga Rev, spring 71; Emerson and the Civil War, in J English & Ger Philol, 10/72; A Way of Walking, Univ NB, 72; ed, Ralph Waldo Emerson: New Appraisals, Transcendental Bks, 73; The Science of Power, in J Hist Ideas, 4/77; The House of Emerson, Univ Nebr, 82; Journal Vol II of H D Thoreau, Princeton, 87; The Economist: Henry Thoreau and Enterprise, Oxford, 89; Raspberrying, Black Moss, 91; Journal Vol IV of H.D. Thoreau, Princeton, 92; Yarrow, Black Moss, 93; Car Failure North of Nimes, 94; Trees Partly of Wood, Black Moss (in press). **CONTACT ADDRESS** Am Studies, Purdue Univ, West Lafayette, IN, 47907-1968. **EMAIL** neufeldt@purdue.edu

NEUFELDT, VICTOR A.
DISCIPLINE 19TH-CENTURY BRITISH LITERATURE **EDUCATION** Univ Brit Col, BA; Univ Ill, PhD. **CAREER** Adj prof. **HONORS AND AWARDS** Canada Council Leave fel, 74-75; Canada Council res grant, 72-73; SSHRCC grants, 80-81, 81-82, 88-90, 90-91, 91-92, 92-95, 97-99; vis fel, Clare Hall, Univ Cambridge, 95-96., Pres, Victorian Stud Assn of W Can. **MEMBERSHIPS** Ed bd, Eng Lit Stud Monogr and The Victorian Rev. **SELECTED PUBLICATIONS** Auth, George Eliot's Middlemarch Notebooks, U of California P, 79; The Poems of Charlotte Bronte, Garland, 85; The Poems of Patrick Branwell Bronte, Garland, 90; A Bibliography of the Manuscripts of Patrick Branwell Bronte, Garland, 93; The Works of Patrick Branwell Bronte, vol 1, Garland, 97. **CONTACT ADDRESS** Dept of English, Victoria Univ, PO Box 3070, Victoria, BC, V8W 3W1.

NEUMAN, SHIRLEY C.
PERSONAL Born 10/10/1946, Edmonton, AB, Canada **DISCIPLINE** CANADIAN/WOMEN'S LITERATURE **EDUCATION** Univ Alta, BA, 68, MA, 69, PhD, 76. **CAREER** Lectr, 76-77, asst prof, 77-81, assoc prof, 81-86, Prof Eng, Univ Alta, 86-, chair, Women's Stud, 87-89, McCalla Res Prof, 89-90, dept chair, 92-95; DEAN OF ARTS, UNIV BRITISH COLUMBIA, 96-. **HONORS AND AWARDS** Gabriel Roy Crit Essay Award, Asn Can & Que Lit, 84 **MEMBERSHIPS** Acad Hum & Soc Sci, Royal Soc Can (pres 94-96); Can Assoc Chairs Eng (pres, 93-94); Asn Can Univ Tchrs Eng (pres, 90-92). **SELECTED PUBLICATIONS** Auth, Gertrude Stein: Autobiography and the Problem of Narration, 79; auth, Some One Myth: Yeats' Autobiographical Prose, 82; coauth, Labyrinths of Voice: Conversations with Robert Kroetsch, 82; co-ed, A Mazing Space: Writing Canadian Women Writing, 86; co-ed, ReImagining Women, 94. **CONTACT ADDRESS** Faculty of Arts, Univ BC, 1866 Main Mall, B130, Vancouver, BC, V6T 1Z1. **EMAIL** shirley.neuman@ubc.ca

NEUMEYER, PETER F.
PERSONAL Born 08/04/1929, Munich, Germany, m, 1952, 3 children **DISCIPLINE** ENGLISH **EDUCATION** Univ Calif, Berkeley, BA, 51, MA, 54, PhD, 63. **CAREER** Teacher pub schs, Calif, 57-58, 60-61; assoc supvr dept educ, Univ Calif, Berkeley, 61-62, actg instr English, 62-63; asst prof educ & tutor English, Grad Sch, Harvard Univ, 63-69; assoc prof English, State Univ NY Stony Brook, 69-75, dir freshman English, 73-75; chmn dept, W VA Univ, 75-78, prof English, 75-78; Prof English & Comp Lit & Dir Freshman English, San Diego State Univ, 78-. **MEMBERSHIPS** Children's Lit Asn; MLA. **RESEARCH** German-English literary relations; freshman English; children's literature. **SELECTED PUBLICATIONS** Auth, Franz Kafka and England, Ger Quart, 67; A structural approach to the teaching of literature to children, Elem English, 67; Donald and the ..., Addison-Wesley, 69; The Faithful Fish, Young-Scott, 71; co-ed, Elements of Fiction, Wm C Brown, 74; auth, Thomas Mann, Max Brod and New York Pubic Library, Mod Lang Notes, 75; The art of the world, English J, 577; What makes a good children's book? The structure of Charlotte's Web, S Atlantic Bull, 79; Charlotte, Arachnida + 'Annotated Charlottes Web' - The Scientific Sources, Lion And The Unicorn, Vol 0019, 1995; 'We Are All in The Dumps With Jack And Guy' - 2 Nursery Rhymes With Pictures by Sendak,maurice, Childrens Literature in Education, Vol 0025, 1994. **CONTACT ADDRESS** Dept of English & Comp Lit, San Diego State Univ, San Diego, CA, 92182.

NEUSSENDORFER, MARGARET R.
DISCIPLINE LITERATURE & AMERICAN STUDIES **EDUCATION** Coll St Scholastica, BA, 55; St. Louis, MA, 63; Yale Univ, MPhil, 71, PhD, 75. **CAREER** Assoc prof, lit & Am stud, Texas Permian Basin; IND SCHOLAR. **MEMBERSHIPS** Am Antiquarian Soc **RESEARCH** Elizabeth Palmer Peabody **SELECTED PUBLICATIONS** Auth, Elizabeth Peabody Writes to Wordswoth, Stud in Am Renaissance, 84. **CONTACT ADDRESS** 23 Minthorne St, Worcester, MA, 01603.

NEVILLE, MARY EILEEN
PERSONAL Born 07/11/1930, York, NE **DISCIPLINE** ENGLISH **EDUCATION** Mt Marty Col, SDak, AB, 53; St Louis Univ, MA, 56, PhD, 58. **CAREER** Instr English, 57-68, chmn dept, 65-69, Prof English, Mt Marty Col, SDak, 68-, Dir Intercult Educ, 73-80; Vis prof English & educ, Univ Nebr, 69-70, fel, 69-70. **MEMBERSHIPS** NCTE; Conf Col Compos & Commun; Conf English Educ. **RESEARCH** Native American literature and culture; Afro-American literature; priorities in American values. **CONTACT ADDRESS** Mount Marty Col, 1100 W Eighth St, Yankton, SD, 57078. **EMAIL** eneville@rs6.mtmc.edu

NEW, MELVYN
PERSONAL Born 10/08/1938, New York, NY, m, 1959, 2 children **DISCIPLINE** ENGLISH **EDUCATION** Columbia Univ, BA, 59; Vanderbilt Univ, MA, 62, PhD, 66. **CAREER** Instr English, Univ Tenn, Martin, 62-63 & Vanderbilt Univ, 65-66; from asst prof to assoc prof, 66-76, prof English, Univ Fla, 76-, chmn, 79-88, Nat Endowment Humanities younger scholar fel, 73-74; Am Philos Soc grants, 68, 71 & 76; Nat Endowment for Humanities fel, 80-81, 94-95. **MEMBERSHIPS** Am Soc 18th Century Studies. **RESEARCH** Restoration and 18th century English literature; satire. **SELECTED PUBLICATIONS** Auth, Laurence Sterne as Satirist: A Reading of Tristram Shandy, Univ Fla, 69; co-ed, The Works of Laurence Sterne: Tristram Shandy: The Text (2 vols), Univ Fla, 78; The Commentary, 1 Vol, Univ Fla, 84; ed, ed, Sterne-Smollett, The Scriblerian, 86; advisory ed, The Shandeam, 89-; ed, Approaches to Teaching Sterne's Tristram Shandy, MLA, 89; ed, New Casebook on Tristram Shandy, Macmillan and St. Martin's, 92; Telling New Lies: Essays in Fiction, Past and Present, Univ Fl, 92; The Complete Novels and Selected Writings of Amy Levy, Univ Fl, 93; Tristram Shandy: A Book for Free Spirits, Twayne-Macmillan, 94; The Sermons: The Text (1 vol.), Univ Fl, 96; The Commentary (1 vol.), Univ Fl, 96; ed, Life and Opinions of Tristram Shandy, Penguin, 97; Critical Essays on Lawrence Sterne, G.K. Hall, 98.. **CONTACT ADDRESS** Dept of English, Univ of Florida, P O Box 117310, Gainesville, FL, 32611-7310. **EMAIL** melnew@nervm.nerdc.ufl.edu

NEW, WILLIAM H.
PERSONAL Born 03/28/1938, Vancouver, BC, Canada **DISCIPLINE** CANADIAN LITERATURE **EDUCATION** Univ BC, BEd, 61, MA, 63; Univ Leeds, PhD, 66. **CAREER** PROF ENGLISH, UNIV BRITISH COLUMBIA, 65-, asst dean, grad stud, 75-77, Brenda & David McLean Chair Can Stud, 95-97. **HONORS AND AWARDS** Killam Res Prize, 88; Gabrielle Roy Award, 88; Jacob Biely Prize, 95; Killam Tchg Prize, 96. **MEMBERSHIPS** Royal Soc Can **SELECTED PUBLICATIONS** Auth, Malcolm Lowry, 71; auth, Articulating West, 72; auth, Among Worlds, 75; auth, Critical Writings on Commonwealth Literature, 75; auth, Malcolm Lowry: A Reference Guide, 78; auth, Dreams of Speech and Violence, 87; auth, A History of Canadian Literature, 89; auth, Science Lessons, 96; auth, Land Sliding, 97; ed, Four Hemispheres, 71; ed, Dramatists in Canada, 72; ed, Modern Canadian Essays, 76; ed, Margaret Laurence, 77; ed, A Political Art, 78; ed, Canadian Writers in 1984, 84; ed, Canadian Short Fiction, 86, 2nd ed, 97; ed, Canadian Writers since 1960, 2 vols, 86, 87; ed, Canadian Writers, 1920-1959, 1st series 88, 2nd series 89; ed, Canadian Writers, 1890-1920, 90; ed, Canadian Writers Before 1890, 90; ed, Literary History of Canada, vol IV, 90; ed, Native Writers and Canadian Writing, 90; ed, Inside the Poem, 92; co-ed, Voice and Vision, 72; co-ed, Modern Stories in English, 75, 2nd ed, 86, 3rd ed, 91; co-ed, Active Voice, 80, 2nd ed 86, 3rd ed 91; co-ed, A 20th Century Anthology, 84; co-ed, Literature in English, 93. **CONTACT ADDRESS** Dept of English, Univ BC, 1873 East Mall, Vancouver, BC, V6T 1Z1.

NEWFIELD, CRISTOPHER
DISCIPLINE NINETEENTH- AND TWENTIETH-CENTURY AMERICAN LITERATURE **EDUCATION** Cornell Univ, PhD, 88. **CAREER** ASSOC PROF, ENG, UNIV CALIF, SANTA BARBARA. **RESEARCH** Lit and soc theory; Gender, sexuality, and race. **SELECTED PUBLICATIONS** Auth, "Corporate Pleasures for a Corporate Planet," Social Text, 95; "White Philosophy," Critical Inquiry, 94; Te Emerson Effect: Individualism and Submission in America, Univ Chicago Press, 95; co-ed, After Political Correctness: The Humanities and Society in the 1990s, Westview, 95; Mapping Multiculturalism, Univ Minn Press, 95. **CONTACT ADDRESS** Dept of Eng, Univ Calif, Santa Barbara, CA, 93106-7150. **EMAIL** cnewf@humanitas.ucsb.edu

NEWKIRK, GLEN A.
PERSONAL Born 08/23/1931, Strawn, KS, m, 1957, 3 children **DISCIPLINE** ENGLISH LITERATURE **EDUCATION** Kans State Col, AB, 53, MA, 56; Univ Denver, PhD(English), 66. **CAREER** Asst ed, Emporia Times, Kans, 53-54; instr English, Kans State Col, 55-57, Colo State Univ, 57-58 & Southwest Mo State Col, 58-60; dir Pubicity, Southwestern Col, Kans, 60-61; instr commun, Univ Denver, 61-63; from asst prof to assoc prof, 63-67, acting chmn dept, 68, grad coordr, 69-72, Prof English, Univ Nebr, Omha, 67- **MEMBERSHIPS** Renaissance Soc Am; MLA. **RESEARCH** Renaissance courtesy books, Shakespeare; Elizabethan drama. **SELECTED PUBLICATIONS** Ed, Contemporary Issues & auth, Instructors Manual, Scott, 71; Anaya Archetypal Women in 'Bless Me, Ultima', South Dakota Review, Vol 0031, 1993. **CONTACT ADDRESS** Dept of English, Univ of Nebr, Omaha, NE, 68101.

NEWMAN, BARBARA
DISCIPLINE RELIGION AND ENGLISH **EDUCATION** Yale Univ, PhD. **CAREER** Prof, Northwestern Univ. **RESEARCH** Repression of Heloise; child sacrifice and maternal matyrdom in saints' lives and romances; mystical womens' attitudes toward Hell and Purgatory. **SELECTED PUBLICATIONS** Auth, Sister of Wisdom: St Hildegard's Theology of the Feminine, Univ Calif Press, 87; ed, and transl, Symphonia Armonie Celestium Revelationum, Cornell UP, 88; From Virile Woman to WomanChrist: Studies in Medieval Religion and Literature, Univ Pa Press, 95; Sister of Wisdom: St Hildegard's Theology of the Feminine, 89. **CONTACT ADDRESS** Dept of Religion, Northwestern Univ, 1801 Hinman, Evanston, IL, 60208. **EMAIL** bjnewman@nwu.edu 9

NEWMAN, GEOFFREY W.
PERSONAL Born 08/29/1946, Oberlin, Ohio, s **DISCIPLINE** DRAMA **EDUCATION** Howard Univ, Washington DC, BFA, 1968; Wayne State Univ, Detroit MI, MA, 1970; Howard Univ, Washington DC, PhD, 1978. **CAREER** Actor, educator, consultant, theorist and director in theatre; Howard Univ, Wabash College, Drama Dept, chmn; Montclair State Coll, dean of School of the Arts, 1988-. **HONORS AND AWARDS** Directed world premiere of Owen Dodson's Sound of Soul and European premiere of Robert Nemiroff's Raisin; received Amoco Award for Theatrical Excellence, by John F Kennedy Center for the Permorming Arts in conjunction with Amer Theatre Assn; received special commendations from Mayor Marion Barry Jr, Washington DC, Mayor Pat Screen, Baton Rouge LA, and Gov Harry Hughes, State of Maryland; published articles in professional journals; served as nominator for Washington DC Awards Society's Helen Hayes Awards. **MEMBERSHIPS** Mem, grant screening panels, District of Columbia Commn on the Arts and Humanities, Pennsylvania State Council for the Arts, and Illinois State Arts Council; artistic dir and cofounder, Takoma Players, Takoma Theatre, Washington DC; artistic dir, Ira Aldridge Theatre, Howard Univ, Washington DC; artistic dir, Park Place Productions, Washington DC; artistic dir, Young Audiences of District of Columbia. **CONTACT ADDRESS** Dean, School of the Arts, Montclair State Col, 1 Normal Ave, Montclair, NJ, 07043-1624.

NEWMAN, LEA BERTANI VOZAR
PERSONAL Born 08/03/1926, Chicago, IL, m, 1976, 5 children **DISCIPLINE** AMERICAN LITERATURE **EDUCATION** Chicago Teachers Col, BA, 47; Wayne State Univ, Detroit, MA, 66; Univ Mass, Amherst, PhD(English), 79. **CAREER** Instr compos, Macomb Community Col, 65-66; instr compos & lit, Pa State Univ, Schuylkill, 66-68; instr, 68-73, asst prof, 73-79, assoc prof, 79-81, Prof Compos & Lit, 81-92, PROF EMER, 92- , Mass Col Lib Arts (N Adams State Col). **HONORS AND AWARDS** Fulbright Univ Bologna, 73-74; Dir NEH pilot grant, 81-82; pres, Hawthorne Soc, 89-90; Mass State Col Asn Sen Fac award, 93; pres, Melville Soc 96. **MEMBERSHIPS** Nathaniel Hawthorne Soc; MLA; Melville Soc. **RESEARCH** Nathaniel Hawthorne's fiction; Herman Melville's life and works; interdisciplinary approaches to teaching literature; Dante's influence on Hawthorne and Melville; Robert Frost's poetry of New England. **SELECTED PUBLICATIONS** Auth, Yeats, Swift, Irish Patriotism and rationalistic anti-intellectualism, Mass Studies English, III: 108-16; A Reader's Guide to the Short Stories of Nathaniel Hawthorne, G K Hall, 79; auth, A Readers Guide to the Short Stories of Herman Melville, G K Hall, 86; auth, Melville's Copy of Dante, Studies in the American Renaissance, Va Univ Press, 93; auth, Hawthorne's Summer in Florence, Florence in the Literary Imagination, Olschki, forthcoming; auth, A Sense of Place: Robert Frost's Poems of Vermont and New Hampshire, Images from the Past, forthcoming. **CONTACT ADDRESS** 120 Imperial Ave, Bennington, VT, 05201. **EMAIL** chick@sover.net

NEWMAN, ROBERT P.
PERSONAL Born 01/26/1922, Hannibal, MO, d, 3 children **DISCIPLINE** COMMUNICATION STUDIES **EDUCATION** Univ Redlands, BA 43; Oxford Univ BA 49; Univ Conn, PhD 56. **CAREER** Smith Col, inst 49-50; Univ Conn, inst 50-52; Univ Pitts, asst, assoc, prof, 52-95; Univ Iowa, Adj prof, 95-. **HONORS AND AWARDS** Pulitzer Nomination; Nat Book Awd nom; LA Times Bk Prize runner up; Import Bk on Civil Liberties; Diamond Ann Bk Awd; Dist Res Awd. **MEMBERSHIPS** AHA; SHAR; SMH; NCA; HESS; OAH **RESEARCH** US China Policy; Cold War; Amer Inquisition; Holocaust; Japanese Surrender **SELECTED PUBLICATIONS** Auth, Framing the Enola Gay Debate: Identity Ethnicity Obscurantism, in: Rhetoric and Public Memory, eds, Stephen Browne David Henry, Sage, in press; NSC National Insecurity 68: Nitze's Second Hallucination, in: Public Disclosure in Cold War America, eds, H. W. Brands Martin Medhurst, TX A&M, in press; Sinners in the Hands of an Angry Goldhagen: A Narrative of Guilt and Redemption, Rhetoric and Pub Affs, 98; Hiroshima and the Trashing of Henry Stimson, NEQ, 98; On the Enola Gay Symposium, letter to the editor, Jour of Amer Hist, 96; Roosevelt and Unconditional Surrender: An Analogy That Held, in: Argumentation and Values, ed Sally Jackson, SCA, 95; Truman and the Hiroshima Cult, MSUP, 95, ten known revs, Diamond Jub Book Awd, NCA 97; Ending the War with Japan: Paul Nitze's , Early Surrender Counterfactual, PHR, 95. **CONTACT ADDRESS** Dept of Communications, Univ of Iowa, 105 Becker Communication Bldg, Iowa City, IA, 52242. **EMAIL** robert-newman@uiowa.edu

NEWPORT, WILLIAM H.A.
PERSONAL Born 10/11/1965, Hartford, CT **DISCIPLINE** LIBERAL ARTS **EDUCATION** Univ New York, AS, 90, BS, 91; Southern Conn, MLS, 98, MA, 98. **CAREER** Ref librn, 97, Avon Free Public Libr; grad asst, 96-98, Southern Conn State Univ; Librn, 98-, Mashantucket Pequot Museum and Res Ctr. **HONORS AND AWARDS** Grad Asst, 96-98, SCSU; CVC/SLA, 97, Conference Travel Stipend; Elma Jean and John Wiacek Jr Scholar, 97, SCSU. **MEMBERSHIPS** Asn Col Res Libr; Am Libr Asn; Am Aviation Hist Society; Conn Aeronautical Hist Asn; Army Air forces Roundtable Conn. **RESEARCH** Military history; aviation history. **SELECTED PUBLICATIONS** Auth, Evolution of American Fighter Aircraft Armament, 98. **CONTACT ADDRESS** Mashantucket Pequot Mus and Research Ctr, 110 Pequot Trl, PO Box 3180, Mashantucket, CT, 06339-3180. **EMAIL** wnewport@mptn.org

NEWSOM, DOUGLAS ANN
PERSONAL Born 01/16/1934, Dallas, TX, m, 1993, 4 children **DISCIPLINE** PUBLIC RELATIONS **EDUCATION** Univ Texas, BJ, 54; Univ Texas, BFA, 55; Univ Texas, MJ, 56; Univ Texas, PhD, 78 **CAREER** Instr, Univ Texas, 61-62; visiting prof, Univ Okla, 79; Fulbright lectr, Osmania Univ, 88; **HONORS AND AWARDS** Kappa Tau Alpha; Phi Kappa Phi; Phi Beta Delta; Fine Arts Commun nominee for Chancellor's Award for Res & Creativity, 95; Named Scholarship, Public Relations Students, created by TCU PRSSA chapt, 93; First 25 Named to Public Relations Women Pioneers, 93; Public Relations Soc Amer Col of Fellows, 90; Fulbright Scholar to India, 88 **MEMBERSHIPS** Pub Rel Soc Amer; Comn Pub Rel Educ; Col of Fel; Center Pub Rel Task Force, 91-91; Friends of PRSSA; Assoc for Educ Jour and Mass Commun; Vanguard Found Board; Intl Commun Assoc; Intl Pub Rel Assoc; Fulbright Assoc; Amer Assoc Univ Women; Soc Prof Journalist; World Commun Assoc **RESEARCH** Public Relations; Women's Studies; Consumerism **SELECTED PUBLICATIONS** Co-ed, Silent Voices, Univ Press Amer, 95; coauth, This is PR: The Realities of Public Relations, Wadsworth, 96; coauth, Public Relations Writing: Form & Style, Wadsworth, 98; **CONTACT ADDRESS** Texas Christian Univ, TCU 298060, Fort Worth, TX, 76129. **EMAIL** d.newsom@TCU.edu

NEWTON, ADAM Z.
PERSONAL Born 03/23/1957, New York, NY, s **DISCIPLINE** ENGLISH **EDUCATION** Harvard Univ, 92; San Francisco State Univ, 89; Hartford Col, 80. **CAREER** Univ Texas, prof. **HONORS AND AWARDS** Thomas Wilson Prize; NS Perkins Prize. **MEMBERSHIPS** MLA; AJS; SSNL. **RESEARCH** 19th Century British Lit; 20th Century Amer lit; Modern Jewish Thought, lit, ethnicity; Eastern and Central European lit. **SELECTED PUBLICATIONS** Auth, The Fence and A Neighbor: Levinas Leibowitz and Israel Among the Nations, forthcoming; Facing Black and Jew: Literature as Public Space, 20th C Amer, Cambridge U Press, 99; auth, Narrative Ethics, Harvard U Press, 95. **CONTACT ADDRESS** Dept of English, Texas Univ, Austin, TX, 78712. **EMAIL** adam.zach@mail.utexas.edu

NEY, JAMES WALTER
PERSONAL Born 07/28/1932, Nakuru, Kenya, m, 1954, 3 children **DISCIPLINE** ENGLISH, LINGUISTICS **EDUCATION** Wheaton Col, Ill, AB, 55, AM, 58; Univ Mich, EdD(English), 63. **CAREER** English specialist, Dade County Pub Schs, Fla, 61-62 & Univ Ryukyus, 62-64; asst prof, Mich State Univ, 65-69; assoc prof, 69-75, Prof English, Ariz State Univ, 75-, Res grant, NCTE, 76, chmn comt to evaluate ling, 77-80. **MEMBERSHIPS** Can Ling Soc; Nat Asn Foreign Student Affairs; Teaching English to Speakers Other Lang; Ling Soc Am; MLA. **RESEARCH** Teaching English as a second language; teaching of written composition to native speakers of English. Coauth, Readings on American Society, 69, Readings from Samuel Clemens, 69, Blaisdell; Adventures in English, Laidlaw Bros, 72; Marckwardt, 72; Two apparent fallacies in current grammatical thought, Gen Ling, 74; Linguistics, Language Teaching and Composition in the Grades, Mouton, The Hague, 75; The modals in English: A floating Semantic feature analysis, JEnglish Ling, 76; Sexism in the English language: A biased view in a biased society, ETC, 76; Semantic Structures, Mouton, The Hague, 81; Generativity, The History of a Notion That Never Was, Historiographia Linguistica, Vol 0020, 1993; Letters - Resource Books For Teachers - Burbidge,n, Gray,p, Levy,s, Rinvolucri,m, Modern Language J, Vol 0081, 1997. **CONTACT ADDRESS** Dept of English, Arizona State Univ, Tempe, Tempe, AZ, 85281.

NICE, J.A.
DISCIPLINE COMMUNICATIONS **EDUCATION** Northwestern Univ, BS 82, JD 86. **CAREER** Univ Denver, asst prof, assoc prof, 91-97-; Northwestern Univ, clinical teaching fell, 89-91; Legal Asst Foun Chicago, staff att, 86-89. **HONORS AND AWARDS** 4 Years Prof of the year for teaching excellence. **MEMBERSHIPS** LSA; SALT **RESEARCH** Poverty and welfare reform; constitutional law. **SELECTED PUBLICATIONS** Auth, Poverty Law: Theory and Practice, West Pub, 97; Making Conditions Constitutional by Attaching Them to Welfare, Den Univ Law, 72, rev 95; Welfare Servitude, Georgetown Jour on Fighting Poverty, 94. **CONTACT ADDRESS** Dept of Law, Univ of Denver, 1900 Olive St, Denver, CO, 80220. **EMAIL** jnice@mail.law.du.edu

NICHOLL, JAMES ROBERT
PERSONAL Born 12/11/1938, Plainview, TX, m, 1967, 2 children **DISCIPLINE** ENGLISH LITERATURE **EDUCATION** Univ Tex, Austin, BA, 61, PhD(English), 70; post-doctoral studies: Columbia Univ, 90, Univ Va, 94, 96, The Shakespeare Centre, Stratford upon Avon, 96. **CAREER** Asst prof English, 70-77, dir freshman composition, 76-80, assoc prof, 77-82, Prof English, Western Carolina Univ, 82-, Dept Head, 83-90; exec secy, NC English Teachers Asn, 81-84; co-dir, Mountain ATCA Writing Project, 84-90. **HONORS AND AWARDS** Nat Endowment for Humanities summer sem, Huntington Lib, 78; Col Arts and Sci Superior Teaching Award, 94. **MEMBERSHIPS** Shakespeare Asn Am; NCTE; Conf Col Compos & Commun; Western Lit Asn; Nat Coun Teachers of English. **RESEARCH** Shakespearean drama, rhetoric and composition; history and literature of the American West. **SELECTED PUBLICATIONS** Auth, Community resources and the teaching of literature, NC English Teacher, spring 75; More Captivates America: The popular success of A Man for All Seasons, Moreana, 9/76; Shakespeare course for non-English majors, CEA Forum, 12/76; The case for local lore and literary magazines, or, Teaching without seeming to, In: Action Learning: English Language Arts, K-12, State Dept Pub Instr, 77; coauth, Rhetorical Models for Effective Writing, Winthrop, 78, 3rd ed, Little, Brown, 78, 81, & 85; auth, The in-class journal, College Composition and Communication, 10/79; Another time, another place: Imagination and Shakespearean drama, Exercise Exchange, spring 80; Walt Whitman's visit to Missouri, Kansas, and Colorado, Heritage of the Great Plains, winter 81; Computers in English Instruction: The Dream and the Reality, In: Micro to Main Frame: Computers in English Education, NCTE, 83; A Dedication to the Memory of Philip Ashton Rollins, 1869-1950, Ariz and the West, 84; The First Mexican American Fictional Hero, Res in Educ, 12/92; coauth, Effective Argument: A Writer's Guide with Readings, Allyn & Bacon, 2nd ed, 91, 98; Models for Effective Writing, Allyn & Bacon, 94. **CONTACT ADDRESS** Dept of English, Western Carolina Univ, Cullowhee, NC, 28723. **EMAIL** jnicholl@wcu.edu

NICHOLS, ASHTON
PERSONAL Born 06/07/1953, Washington, DC, m, 1975, 4 children **DISCIPLINE** ENGLISH **EDUCATION** Univ Va, BA, 75, MA, 79, PhD, 84. **CAREER** Asst prof, 84-85, Auburn Univ; asst prof to assoc prof to prof, 88-, assoc dean, 98-99, Dickinson Col. **HONORS AND AWARDS** Lindback Award for Distinguished Teaching; Ganoe Award for Inspirational Teaching; Who's Who, 99-00., Phi Beta Kappa, 75; DuPont Scholar, 71-75; vis scholar, Cambridge Univ, 83, Vis Res, William Morris Centre, London, 78. **MEMBERSHIPS** MLA; NASSR; ASLE; NCSA. **RESEARCH** Romanticism; Wordsworth; natural hist; nature writing. **SELECTED PUBLICATIONS** Auth, The Poetics of Epiphany: Nineteenth-Century Origins of the Modern Literary Moment, Univ of Al Press, 87; auth, Electronic Resources for Nineteenth-Century Studies: A Provisional Appraisal, Nineteenth-Century Stud, 97; auth, The Anxiety of Species: Toward a Romantic Natural History, The Wordsworth Circle, 97; auth, The Revolutionary "I": Wordsworth and the Politics of Self-Presentation, London: Macmillan, New York, St Martins, 98; auth, Cognitive and Pragmatic Linguistic Moments: Literary Epiphany in Thomas Pynchon and Seamus Heaney, Moments of Moment: Aspects of the Literary Epiphany, Amsterdam & Atlanta: Rodopi, 99. **CONTACT ADDRESS** Dept of English, Dickinson Col, Box 1773, Carlisle, PA, 17013. **EMAIL** nicholsa@dickinson.edu

NICHOLS, JAMES
DISCIPLINE LITERATURE **EDUCATION** Univ Miss, BA; Univ Birmingham, MA; Univ Wash, PhD, 64. **CAREER** Prof, 68-; **HONORS AND AWARDS** Chairperson dept English, 68-93. **SELECTED PUBLICATIONS** Area: satire and a novel **CONTACT ADDRESS** Winona State Univ, PO Box 5838, Winona, MN, 55987-5838.

NICHOLS, KATHLEEN L.
DISCIPLINE AMERICAN LITERATURE AND DRAMA **EDUCATION** Augustana Col, BA; Univ Nebr, MA, PhD. **CAREER** Prof. **RESEARCH** Minority women writers, women's studies. **SELECTED PUBLICATIONS** Publ, articles on Hemingway, Cather, Sexton, Susanna Rowson, Agnes Smedley, women dramatists; bk rev(s). **CONTACT ADDRESS** Dept of Eng, Pittsburg State Univ, 1701 S Broadway St, Pittsburg, KS, 66762. **EMAIL** knichols@pittstate.edu

NICHOLS, PATRICIA CAUSEY
PERSONAL Born 12/29/1938, Conway, SC, m, 1959, 2 children **DISCIPLINE** ENGLISH, LINGUISTICS **EDUCATION** Winthrop Col, BA, 58; Univ Minn, MA, 66; San Jose State Univ, MA, 72; Stanford Univ, PhD(ling), 76. **CAREER** Teacher, Hampton Pub Schs, Va, 58-60; Lectr English, Ling & Educ, San Jose State Univ, 76-, Co-ed, Women & Lang News, 76; vis asst prof English, Univ SC, 80-81; vis instr, Univ Calif, Santa Barbara, 82. **MEMBERSHIPS** MLA; Ling Soc Am; Am Dialect Soc. **RESEARCH** Gullah; gender and sex differences in speech; American dialects. **SELECTED PUBLICATIONS** Auth, A sociolinguistic perspective on reading and black children, Lang Arts, 54: 150-157; Ethnic consciousness in the British Isles, Lang Problems & Lang Planning, 1: 10-31; Black women in the rural south: Conservative and innovative, Int J Social Lang, Vol 17, 78; Planning for language change, San Jose Studies, 6: 18-25; Variation among Gullah speakers in rural South Carolina, In: Language Use and the Uses of Language, Georgetown Univ Press, 80; Women in their speech communities, In: Women and Language In Literature and Society, Praeger Pub, 80; Creoles in the USA, In: Language in the USA, Cambridge Univ Press, 81; Linguistic options and choices for black women in the rural South, In: Language, Gender and Society, Newbury House Pub (in press); a Syntactic Analysis of Sea-island Creole - Cunningham,iae, J of Pidgin And Creole Languages, Vol 0009, 1994. **CONTACT ADDRESS** 1430 Westmont Ave, Campbell, CA, 95008.

NICKELS, CAMERON C.
PERSONAL Born 08/20/1941, Sabetha, KS, 2 children **DISCIPLINE** AMERICAN SUTDIES, LITERATURE **EDUCATION** Ft Hays State Univ, Ba, 62; Southern IL Univ, MA, 64; Univ MN, PhD, 71. **CAREER** Instr Eng, Cent MO State Univ, 64-67; assoc prof, 71-82, Prof Eng, James Madison Univ, 82, Nat Endowment for Hum, summer sem, 79. **MEMBERSHIPS** MLA; Am Studies Asn; SAtlantic Mod Lang Asn; Am Humor Studies Asn. **RESEARCH** Am humor; early Am lit; nineteenth-century Am cult. **SELECTED PUBLICATIONS** Auth, Seba Smith embattled, Maine Hist Soc Quart, 73; contribr, The Oldest Revolutionary: Essays on Benjamin Franklin, Univ Pa, 76; ed, An early version of The Tar Baby story, J Am Folklore, 81; The idology of early New England Humor, Early Am Lit, 82; auth, New England Humor, From the Revolutionalry war to the civil war, 93; ed, To Wit, newsltr, 91. **CONTACT ADDRESS** Dept of Eng, James Madison Univ, 800 S Main St, Harrisonburg, VA, 22807-0002. **EMAIL** nickelcc@jmu.edu

NICKERSON, CATHERINE ROSS
DISCIPLINE ENGLISH LANGUAGE AND LITERATURE **EDUCATION** Yale Univ, PhD, 91. **CAREER** Dir undergrad studies/assoc prof Grad Inst Lib Arts/dept Engl. **RESEARCH** Detective fiction; Lizzie Borden; narrative and the representation of mystery, crime, and violence; Asian American literature.

SELECTED PUBLICATIONS Auth, 'The Cunning of Her Sex:' The Rhetoric of Guilt, Innocence, and Gender in the Trial of Lizzie Borden in Violence and American History, NY UP; Murder as Social Criticism, Am Lit Hist, 97; Serial Detection and Serial Killers in Twin Peaks, Lit/Film Quart, 93. **CONTACT ADDRESS** Grad Inst Lib Arts, Emory Univ, 1380 Oxford Rd NE, Atlanta, GA, 30322-1950. **EMAIL** cnicker@emory.edu

NICKS, JOAN P.

PERSONAL Cudworth, SK, Canada **DISCIPLINE** FILM STUDIES **EDUCATION** Brock Univ, BA, 79; Carlton Univ, MA, 84. **CAREER** Lectr, 78-84, asst prof, fine arts, 81-84, ASSOC PROF FILM STUDS, DRAMATIC & VISUAL ARTS, BROCK UNIV, 93-. **HONORS AND AWARDS** Kinnear Estate Scholar, 77-78, Harding Book Prize, 77-78, Gov Gen Medal, 78-79; Alumni Asn Excellence Tchg Award, 94, Brock Univ. **MEMBERSHIPS** Film Studs Asn Can. **SELECTED PUBLICATIONS** Auth, Aesthetic Memory in Mourir a tue-tete: Fragments from Screens of Silence in Responses, 92; auth, Sex, Lies and Landscape: Meditations on vertical tableaux in Joyce Wieland's The Far Shore and Jean Beaudin's J. A. Martin, Photographe in Can J Film Studs 1,2-3, 93. **CONTACT ADDRESS** Dept of Film Studies, Dramatic and Visual Arts, Brock Univ, St. Catherines, ON, L2S 3A1. **EMAIL** jpnicks@spartan.ac.brocku.ca

NICOL, CHARLES DAVID

PERSONAL Born 12/21/1940, St. Louis, MO, 2 children **DISCIPLINE** AMERICAN & CONTEMPORARY LITERATURE **EDUCATION** Univ KS, BA, 62, MA, 66; Bowling Green State Univ, PhD, 70. **CAREER** From instr to asst prof, 66-73, assoc prof, 73-79, PROF ENGLISH & HUMANITIES, IN STATE UNIV, 79-; Vladimir Nabokov Soc, Pres 79-81, board 79-; Assoc ed, Sci-Fiction Studies, 74-78, board 88-; Nabokovian , Annot ed, 80-95; Para-doxa, ed board 95-. **HONORS AND AWARDS** Fulbright Sr Lecturer, Tbilisi, 84. **MEMBERSHIPS** MLA; Sci Fiction Res Asn; Melville Soc; Nabokov Soc. **RESEARCH** Vladimir Nabokov; contemporary fiction; Am Renaissance. **SELECTED PUBLICATIONS** Auth, Don Juan Out of Hell, Atlantic Monthly, 6/69; Pnin's History, Novel, summer 71; A Study in Counterfeit, NY Times Book Rev, 7/77; Poets Grilled and Served, Chronicle Higher Educ, 1/78; ed Nabokov's Fifth Arc, Univ TX, 83; reprt Critical Essays on Vladimir Nabokov, ed Roth, G K Hall, 84; One Hundred Years on a Raft, Harper's, 7/86; ed, A Small Alpine Form, Garland, 93. **CONTACT ADDRESS** Dept of English, Indiana State Univ, 210 N 7th St, Terre Haute, IN, 47809-0002. **EMAIL** ejnicol@root.indstate.edu

NIEDZWIECKI, CHARISSA K.

DISCIPLINE COMMUNICATION STUDIES **EDUCATION** Univ Nebr-Lincoln, PhD, 96. **CAREER** Asst prof, Univ Wis-La Crosse, 94-. **HONORS AND AWARDS** Most Accessible Instructor Award, by Students Advocating Potential Ability, 97; recipient of numerous grants. **MEMBERSHIPS** Nat Commun Asn; Int Listening Asn; Central States Commun Asn. **RESEARCH** Family communication; gender; intercultural. **SELECTED PUBLICATIONS** Auth, Listen and You Will be Heard, Criss Cross Currents, 80; auth, Listening Comprehension Exercises, in International Listening Association's Teaching Ideas in Listening, 96, 97, 98; auth, Intercultural Review, The Nat Commun Asn J Ideas, Res and Strategies for Learning, Summer 98; auth, A Multicultural Shakespeare, In: Culture Shock in the Classroom: Stories from America's Schools (forthcoming). **CONTACT ADDRESS** 1725 State St, La Crosse, WI, 54601. **EMAIL** niedzwie@mail.uwlax.edu

NIELSEN, MICHAEL

DISCIPLINE COMMUNICATIONS **EDUCATION** Univ IL, BS, 72, PhD, 85. **CAREER** Tchg asst, Univ IL, 80-82, 84; asst prof, FL Atlantic Univ, 84-89; assoc prof, dept hd, 89-. **HONORS AND AWARDS** Tenure, 95; Kappa Tau Alpha; Phi Kappa Phi. **RESEARCH** A cult studies critique of derivative copyright works. **SELECTED PUBLICATIONS** Auth, Labor's Stake in the Electronic Cinema Revolution, Jump Cut, Rev Contemp Media, 90; The struggles of progressive union members in reforming the motion picture workers' union (IATSE) in the period 1937-1950, Hollywood's Other Blacklist, Brit Film Inst, London, 96; co-auth, Bright Lights, Low Wages, S Exposure, 92. **CONTACT ADDRESS** Dept of Commun, Wesley Col, 120 N State St, Dover, DE, 19901-3875. **EMAIL** mike.nielsen@dol.net

NIEMI, BOB

DISCIPLINE AMERICAN POPULAR CULTURE AND FILM **EDUCATION** Univ MA, PhD. **CAREER** Eng, St. Michaels Col. **SELECTED PUBLICATIONS** Auth, Bibliography of Weldon Kees. **CONTACT ADDRESS** St. Michael's Col, Winooski Park, Colchester, VT, 05439. **EMAIL** rniemi@smcvt.edu

NIGRO, AUGUST JOHN

PERSONAL Born 12/11/1934, Jersey City, NJ, m, 1967, 3 children **DISCIPLINE** ENGLISH **EDUCATION** Fairleigh Dickinson Univ, BA, 58; Univ Miami, MA, 60; Univ Md, PhD, 63. **CAREER** Asst English, Univ Miami, 58-60 & Univ Md, 60-63; lectr, Univ Md, Europe, 63-65; asst prof, Niagara Univ, 65-67; Prof English, Kutztown Univ Pa, 67-. **HONORS AND AWARDS** NEH Summer Seminar, 74, 81; NEH Fel-in-Residence, 76-77; NEH secondary school summer seminar directorship (88-91); USIA Summer Inst For Educ Directorship, 93. **RESEARCH** Modern poetry and American fiction; myth and psychological criticism. **SELECTED PUBLICATIONS** Auth, The long march: Expansive hero in closed world, Critique, winter 67-68; coauth, William Styron: A configuration, Minard, Rev Lett Mod, Paris, 68; The Diagonal Line: Separation and Reparation in American Literaturte, Susquehanna Univ Press, 84. **CONTACT ADDRESS** Dept of English, Kutztown Univ, Pennsylvania, Kutztown, PA, 19530. **EMAIL** nigro@kutztown.edu

NILES, LYNDREY ARNAUD

PERSONAL Born 05/09/1936, m **DISCIPLINE** SPEECH **EDUCATION** Columbia Union Coll, BA 1963; Univ of MD, mA 1965; Temple U, phD 1973. **CAREER** School of Communications Howard Univ, chmn Comm Arts & Sci Dept 1979-; Howard Univ, prof & asso dean 1975-79; Univ of MD, lectr 1971-75; Univ of DC, asst prof 1968-74, instr 1965-68; Columbia Union Coll, lectr 1964-65; Leadership Resources Inc, mgmt consult 1974-75. **MEMBERSHIPS** Mem Speech Commn Assn/InternatrA Commn Assn/Am Soc for Training & Devel/NAACP; pres Met Wash Commn Assn 1974-75; . **SELECTED PUBLICATIONS** "Listening & Note Taking Methods" 1965; "Black Rhetoric five yrs of growth, Encoder 1974; "Communication in Dental Office", article in Encoder 1979 **CONTACT ADDRESS** Sch of Commun, Howard Univ, 24 6th Street, NW, Washington, DC, 20059.

NIMS, JOHN FREDERICK

PERSONAL Born 11/20/1913, Muskegon, MI, m, 1947, 3 children **DISCIPLINE** ENGLISH LITERATURE **EDUCATION** Univ Notre Dame, AB, 37, AM, 39; Univ Chicago, PhD, 45. **CAREER** Asst prof, Univ Toronto, 45-46; assoc prof English, Univ Notre Dame, 39-45, 46-55, prof, 55-61; vis writer in residence, Univ Ill, Urbana, 61-62, prof English, 62-65; prof, Univ Ill, Chicago Circle, 65-73 & Univ Fla, 73-76; Prof English, Univ Ill, Chicago Circle, 76-, Fulbright lectr, Univ Milan, 52-53 & Univ Florence, 53-54; vis prof, Univ Madrid, 58-60; vis ed, Poetry, Chicago, 60-61, ed, 78-; vis prof, Harvard Univ, 64 & 68-69; Nat Found on Arts & Humanities sabbatical grant, 67-68; Nat Inst Arts & Lett grant, 68; Creative Arts Citation in Poetry, Brandeis Univ, 74; Phi Beta Kappa poet, Harvard Univ, 78. **RESEARCH** Creative writing; Elizabethan and Jacobean drama; comparative literature. **SELECTED PUBLICATIONS** Auth, Knowledge of the Evening, Rutgers Univ, 60; ed, Arthur Golding's transl of Ovid's Metamorphoses, Macmillan, 65; auth, Of Flesh and Bone, 67 & Sappho to Valery: Poems in Translation, 71, Rutgers Univ & Princeton Univ Press, 80; Western Wind: An Introduction to Poetry, Random, 74; The Harper Anthology of Poetry, Harper & Row, 81; The Kiss: A J Ambalaya, Houghton Mifflin, 82; Selected Poems, Univ Chicago, 82; Cultural Heritage', Georgia Review, Vol 0047, 1993; Mens Room, the Ritz', Georgia Review, Vol 0047, 1993; 'Strange', Hudson Review, Vol 0047, 1994; 'Two Madrigals by Michelangelo for Vittoria Colonna', Poetry, Vol 0171, 1997. **CONTACT ADDRESS** Dept English, Univ Ill Chicago Circle, Chicago, IL, 60680.

NIXON, CORNELIA

DISCIPLINE CREATIVE WRITING **EDUCATION** Univ Calif at Irvine, BA, 69; San Francisco State, MA, 73; Univ Calif at Berkeley, PhD, 81. **CAREER** NOVELIST **MEMBERSHIPS** Am Antiquarian Soc **SELECTED PUBLICATIONS** Res for a novel, "Martha's Version," set in Maryland, 1869. **EMAIL** nixon@indiana.edu

NIXON, ROB

DISCIPLINE AFRICAN AND BRITISH LITERATURES **EDUCATION** Rhodes Univ, S Africa, BA, 77; Univ Iowa, MA, 82; Columbia Univ, PhD, 89. **CAREER** Assoc prof. **SELECTED PUBLICATIONS** Auth, London Calling: VS Naipaul, Post-Colonial Mandarin, Oxford UP, 92; Homelands, Harlem, Hollywood: South African Culture and the World Beyond, Routledge, 94; auth, ninety essays and rev, New Yorker; Critical Inquiry; NY Times; TLS; London Rev of Bks; The Village Voice; S Atlantic Quart; Grand St; Nat; Black Renaissance/Renaissance Noire; Transition; The Independent. **CONTACT ADDRESS** Dept of Eng, Columbia Col, New York, 2960 Broadway, New York, NY, 10027-6902.

NNOLIM, CHARLES E.

PERSONAL Born 05/10/1939, Umuchu, Nigeria, m, 1966 **DISCIPLINE** ENGLISH **EDUCATION** Benedictine College, Atchison, KS, BA (honors), 1966; Bemidji State Univ, Bemidji, MN, MA, English, 1968; Catholic Univ of America, Washington, DC, PhD, 1975. **CAREER** Ferris State College, Big Rapids, MI, asst prof of English, 1969-70; Babson College, Wellesley, MA, asst prof of English, 1970-76; Univ of Port Harcourt, Port Harcourt, Nigeria, professor of English, 1980-. **HONORS AND AWARDS** Recipient, Doctoral Fellowship, Catholic Univ of Amer, 1968-72; author, Melville's Benito Cereno: A Study in Mng of Name-Symbolism, 1974; author, Pessimism in Conrad's Heart of Darkness, 1980; author, critical essays on African literature published in US and British journals. **MEMBERSHIPS** Mem, African Studies Assn; mem, Modern Lang Assn of Amer; mem, Natl Soc of Literature & the Arts; pres, Literary Society of Nigeria, 1986-; member, African Literature Assn, 1974-; member, West African Assn of Commonwealth Literature & Language Studies, 1988-. **CONTACT ADDRESS** Dept Eng, Univ of Port Harcourt, Port Harcourt, ..

NOBLE, DOUGLAS

DISCIPLINE COMPUTERS IN ARCHITECTURE, DESIGN, DESIGN THEORIES AND METHODS **EDUCATION** CA State Polytech Univ, Pomona, BS, 81, BA, 82; Univ CA, Berkeley, MA, 83, PhD, 91. **CAREER** Asst prof, USC, 91-; lectr, Univ CA, Berkeley, 84-91; Kenneth S Wing & Assoc, Arch, 85-86; CHCG Arch, 78-84. **HONORS AND AWARDS** William Van Alen Memorial Prize, 94; ACSA AIAS New Fac Tchg Awd, 94; PhD Comt Prize, UC Berkeley, 89; Distinguished Tchg Asst Awd, 87; Pasadena/Foothill AIA Design Awd, 83; 1st Prize-AISC Stud Design Competition, 80. **MEMBERSHIPS** Asn for Comput Aided Design in Arch; Am Inst Arch; Asn Collegiate Schools Arch. **RESEARCH** Design theories and methods; site analysis through digital photography. **SELECTED PUBLICATIONS** Auth, Issues Regarding Architectural Records of the Future: Planning for Change in Libraries, 94; Mission, Method, Madness; Computer Supported Design in Architecture, ACADIA, 92; Software for Architects: A Guide to Software for the Architectural Profession, 92; Issues in the Design of Tall Buildings, 91; User's Guide to Berkeley Architecture, Daily Calif, 90; coauth, Computer Aided Architectural Design, Univ Calif, Berkeley, 90; Shading Mask: A Teaching Tool for Sun Shading Devices, 95-96; Student Initiated Explorations in the Design Studio, ACADIA, 94; Issues Regarding Architectural Records of the Future: Planning for Change in Libraries, Architronic: Elec J Arch, 94; The Sorcerers Apprentice, Computer Graphics World, 90. **CONTACT ADDRESS** School of Archit, Univ of Southern California, University Park Campus, Los Angeles, CA, 90089. **EMAIL** dnoble@mizar.usc.edu

NOBLE, MARIANNE K.

DISCIPLINE AMERICAN LITERATURE **EDUCATION** Columbia Univ, PhD. **CAREER** Asst prof, Am Univ. **RESEARCH** American literature, culture and studies; construction of sexuality in 19th century American Women's literature.. **SELECTED PUBLICATIONS** Articles, Gothic and sentimental literature. **CONTACT ADDRESS** American Univ, 4400 Massachusetts Ave, Washington, DC, 20016. **EMAIL** mnoble@american.edu

NOHRNBERG, JAMES CARSON

PERSONAL Born 03/19/1941, Berkeley, CA, m, 1964, 2 children **DISCIPLINE** RENAISSANCE & MEDIEVAL LITERATURE, BIBLE STUDIES **EDUCATION** Harvard Col, BA, 62; Univ Toronto, PhD, 70. **CAREER** Tch fel Eng, Univ Toronto, 63-64; Jr fel, Soc of Fel, Harvard Univ, 65-68; adj Eng, Harvard Univ, 67-68; Actg instr Eng, Yale Univ, 68-69, lectr, 69-70, asst prof, 70-75; Prof Eng, Univ VA, 75-; Woodrow Wilson fel, Toronto, 62-63, Morse fel Eng, Yale Univ, 74-75; Ctr for Advan Studies fel, Univ VA, 75-78; Guggenheim fel, 81-82; Gauss Seminars in Criticism lctr, Princeton Univ, 87; Inst Adv Study fel, IN Univ, 91; lectr, 74-97, Yale, Princeton, MLA, Columbia, Hopkins, Kenyon, NEH Seminars, Cornell, Univ VA, Georgetown, Emory, Univ Calif Irvine, Ind Univ, Newberry Libr, Loyola Balitmore, Univ South. **HONORS AND AWARDS** Robert Frost Poetry Prize, Kenyon Col 60; Acad of Am Poets, harvard Col, 62. **MEMBERSHIPS** MLA; Spenser Soc. **RESEARCH** Bible; Dante; Shakespeare; Milton. **SELECTED PUBLICATIONS** Auth, On literature and the Bible, Centrum, fall 74; The Analogy of The Faerie Queene, Princeton Univ, 76, 1st cor ed, 81; The Tale Told by Twice-Told Tales, Yearbook of Comp and Gen Lit, Ind Univ, 90; Allegories of scripture, Shofar, winter 93; Like unto Moses: The Constituting of an Interruption, Ind Univ, 95; The Descent of Geryon: the Moral System of Inferno XVI-XXXI, Dante Studies, 98; Allegory D-Veiled: A New Theory for Construing Allegory's Two Bodies, Modern Philol, 11/98; contribr, Homer to Brecht: The European epic and dramatic traditions, In: The Iliad & In: The Inferno, Yale Univ, 77; contribr, Pynchon: A collection of critical essays, In: Pynchon's Paraclete, Prentice-Hall, 77; Moses, In: Images of Man and God: Old Testament Short Stories in LIterary Focus, Almond Press, 81; Centre and labyrinth: Essays in honour of Northrop Frye, In: Paradise Regained by One Greater Man: Milton's Wisdom Epic as a Fable of Identity, Univ Toronto, 83; Spenser Encyclopedia, In: Acidale, & In: The Faerie Queene Book IV, Univ Toronto, 90; The Book and the text: the Bible and literary theory, In: The Keeping of Nahor: The Etiology of Biblical Election in Genesis, Blackwell, 90; Annotation and its texts, In: Justifying Narrative: Commentary in Biblical Storytelling, Oxford Univ, 91; Not in heaven: Coherence and complexity in Biblical narrative, In: Princely Characters, Ind Univ, 91; Fortune and romance: Boiardo in America, In: Orlando's Opportunity: Chance, Luck, Fortune, Occasion, Boats, and Blows in Boiardo's Orlando Innamorato, Ariz State Univ, 98; Lectura Dantis, Inferno, In: Inferno XVIII: Introduction to Malebolge, Univ CA, 98. **CONTACT ADDRESS** Dept of Eng, Univ of Virginia, 219 Bryan Hall, Charlottesville, VA, 22903. **EMAIL** jnc@j1.mail.virginia.edu

NOLAN, BARBARA
PERSONAL Born 01/26/1941, Indianapolis, IN **DISCIPLINE** ENGLISH **EDUCATION** Trinity Col, DC, BA, 62; Univ Wis, Madison, MA, 63, PhD(English), 67. **CAREER** Teaching asst, Univ Wis, Madison, 62-65; from instr to asst prof English, 66-72, fac fel, 67-68, assoc prof English, Wash Univ, 72-78; Prof English, Univ Va, 78-, Nat Endowment for Humanities fel, summer, 68; Am Coun Learned Soc grant-in-aid, 72; Guggenheim fel, 78-79. **MEMBERSHIPS** MLA; Mediaeval Acad Am; Dante Soc. **RESEARCH** Thirteenth and fourteenth century religious poetry and art; Beowulf and Old English poetry; medieval romance. **SELECTED PUBLICATIONS** Auth, The Vita Nuova: Dante's Book of Revelation, Dante Studies, 70; The authorship of Pearl: two notes, Rev English Studies, 71; The Vita Nuova and Richard of St Victor's Phenomenology of Vision, Dante Studies, 74; The Gothic Visionary Perspective, Princeton Univ, 77; The judgment of Paris in the Roman d'Eneas: A new look at sources and significance, Class Bull, 80; coauth (with Morton W Bloomfield), Beotword, Gilpavide and the Gilplaeden Scop of Beowulf, J English & Ger Philol, 80. **CONTACT ADDRESS** Dept of English, Wash Univ, St Louis, MO, 63130.

NOLAN, EDWARD FRANCIS
PERSONAL Born 03/30/1915, Fernandina, FL **DISCIPLINE** ENGLISH **EDUCATION** Univ Fla, Bae, 37, AM, 38; Princeton Univ, PhD, 41. **CAREER** Head dept English, Presby Jr Col, 41-42; instr, Presby Col, 42-44, assoc prof, 46-47; adJprof, 47-48, assoc prof, 48-63, Prof English, Univ Sc, 63- **MEMBERSHIPS** Southeast Renaissance Conf; Southern Atlantic Mod Lang Asn. **RESEARCH** Old English; Renaissance. **SELECTED PUBLICATIONS** Auth, Shakespeare's Sonnet Lxxiii; Verdi's Macbeth; The death of Bryan Lyndon; Barron's Simplified Approach to Shakespeare: Romeo and Juliet, 67, Barron's Simplified Approach to Shakespeare: Othello, 67, coauth, Barron's Simplified Approach to Shakespeare: King Lear, 68 & auth, A Simplified Approach to Shakespeare: The Merchant of Venice, 71, Barron's; Browning 'Rabbi Ben Ezra', Lines 124-5, Explicator, Vol 0051, 1993. **CONTACT ADDRESS** Dept of English, Univ of SC, Columbia, SC, 29208.

NOLLER, DAVID K.
DISCIPLINE DEVELOPMENT OF CRITICAL AND CREATIVE THINKING **EDUCATION** PhD. **CAREER** Univ Albany - SUNY **SELECTED PUBLICATIONS** Articles, Inklings. **CONTACT ADDRESS** Univ Albany-SUNY, 1400 Washington Ave, Albany, NY, 12222. **EMAIL** noller@cnsunix.albany.edu

NOLLETTI, ARTHUR E., JR.
PERSONAL Born 05/17/1941, Wooster, OH, m, 1 child **DISCIPLINE** ENGLISH LITERATURE **EDUCATION** OH Univ, Athens, AB, 63; Univ WI, Madison, MA, 65, PhD, 73. **CAREER** Instr, Univ WI, Platteville, 65; teaching asst, Univ WI, Madison, 65-70; instr, English, Cleveland State Univ, OH, 70-71; prof, English, Framingham State Col, MA, 71-. **HONORS AND AWARDS** Nat Endowment for the Humanities fel, 79-80, in film; NEH Summer Seminar grant, 77, in film; Asian Cultural Coun for res in film, June-July 92; Northeast Asia Coun Awards Travel grants, July 85, June-July 92. **MEMBERSHIPS** MLA; Soc for Cinema Studies. **RESEARCH** Film (Japanese film, Am film, Int film). **SELECTED PUBLICATIONS** Ed with David Dresser, Reframing Japanese Cinema, IN Univ Press, 92; ed, Special Fred Zinnemann Issue of Film Criticism, spring/fall 94; auth, Spirituality and Style in the Nun's Story, Film Criticism, spring/fall 94; Ozu's Tokyo Story and the Recasting of McCarey's Make Way for Tomorrow, in Ozu's Tokyo Story, ed David Dresser, Cambridge Univ Press, 97; Book review of James Goodwin, ed, Perspectives on Akira Kurosawa, Film Quart 49, 4, summer 96; Once More and Gosho's Romanticism in the Early Occupation Period, in Wording the Image, ed Carole Cavanaugh and David Washburn, Cambridge Univ Press, forthcoming; ed, The Films of Fred Zinnemann: Critical Perspectives, SUNY Press, forthcoming. **CONTACT ADDRESS** Dept of English, Framingham State Col, 100 State St, Framingham, MA, 01701. **EMAIL** anollet@frc.mass.edu

NOONAN, JAMES S.
PERSONAL Born 08/26/1933, Ottawa, ON, Canada **DISCIPLINE** LITERATURE **EDUCATION** St. Patrick's (Ottawa), BA, 54; Univ Ottawa, BTh, 59, STL, 60; Cambridge Univ, MA, 71; Jules & Gabrielle Leger Fel, 86. **CAREER** PROF ENGLISH, CARLETON UNIV, 67- **MEMBERSHIPS** Oblates of Mary Immaculate, 54-84. **SELECTED PUBLICATIONS** Contribur, Supplement to the Oxford Companion to Canadian History and Literature, 73; contribur, The Oxford Companion to Canadian Literature, 83, 2nd ed, (updated) 97; contribur, The Oxford Companion to Canadian Theatre, 89; ed, Biography and Autobiography: Essays on Irish and Canadian History and Literature, 93; bk rev ed, Theatre History in Canada, 83-94; bk rev ed, English Studies in Canada, 89-95. **CONTACT ADDRESS** Dept of English, Carleton Univ, 1125 Colonel By Dr, Ottawa, ON, K1S 5B6.

NOONE, PAT
DISCIPLINE MODERN LITERATURE **EDUCATION** New Rochelle, BA, 60, Hunter Col, MA, 64; Univ NY, PhD, 71. **CAREER** Engl, Col Mt. St. Vincent **HONORS AND AWARDS** Adv, Fonthill Dial; Hum rep Undergrad Comt. **SELECTED PUBLICATIONS** Auth, 'Six Ways of Looking at a City': Literature and New York of the Late Nineteenth Century, Turn of the Century, 96. **CONTACT ADDRESS** Col of Mount Saint Vincent, 6301 Riverdale Ave, Riverdale, NY, 10471. **EMAIL** pnoone@cmsv.edu

NORBERG, PETER
DISCIPLINE AMERICAN ROMANTICISM **EDUCATION** Boston Col, BA, 90, Rice Univ, MA, 94, PhD, 97. **CAREER** Engl, St. Joseph's Univ. **SELECTED PUBLICATIONS** Auth, Post-Colonial Theory and the Problem of American Pluralism, Boston Univ, 97. **CONTACT ADDRESS** St Joseph's Univ, 5600 City Ave, Philadelphia, PA, 19131. **EMAIL** norberg@sju.edu

NORD, DAVID P.
DISCIPLINE JOURNALISM **EDUCATION** Valparaiso, BA, 69; Univ of Minn, MA, 72; Univ Wis, PhD, 79. **CAREER** Assoc prof, jour, PROF, JOUR & AM STUD, IND UNIV BLOOMINGTON Am stud. **HONORS AND AWARDS** Catherine Covert Award, 90 **MEMBERSHIPS** Am Antiquarian Soc **SELECTED PUBLICATIONS** Auth, "The Evangelical Origins of Mass Media in America, 1815-1835," Journ Monographs 88, 84; auth, "Working Class Readers: Family, Community and Reading in Late 19th- Century America," Comm Res 11, 86; auth, "A Republican Literature: A Study of Magazine Reading and Readers in Late Eighteenth-Century New York," Am Quart 40, 88; auth, "Theology and News: The Religious Roots of American Journalism, 1630-1730, Jour of Am Hist 77, 90; auth, "Systematic Benevolence: Religious Publishing and the Marketplace in Early Nineteenth-Century America," in Communications and Change in American Religious History, Eerdmans, 93; auth, "Reading the Newspaper: Strategies and Politics of Reader Response, Chicago, 1912-1917," Jour of Comm 45, Summer 95; auth, "Religious Reading and Readers in Antebellum America," Jour of the Early Rep 15, Summer 95; auth, "Readership as Citizenship in Late 18th-Century Philadelphia," in A Melancholy Scene of Devastation: The Public Response to the 1793 Yellow Fever Epidemic, Coll of Physicians of Phil; auth, "Free Books, Free Grace, Free Riders: The Economics of Religious Publishing in Early Nineteenth-Century America, " Procs of the AAS. **CONTACT ADDRESS** Sch of Jour, Indiana Univ, Bloomington, Bloomington, IN, 47405. **EMAIL** nord@indiana.edu

NORDLOH, DAVID JOSEPH
PERSONAL Born 05/03/1942, Cincinnati, OH, m, 1968, 2 children **DISCIPLINE** AMERICAN LITERATURE, BIBLIOGRAPHY **EDUCATION** Holy Cross Col, AB, 64; Ind Univ, PhD(English), 69. **CAREER** From instr to asst prof English, 68-75, assoc prof, 75-81, Prof English, Ind Univ, Bloomington, 81-, Textual ed, A selected edition of W D Howells, Ind Univ, 68-73, gen ed, 74-; textual expert, Ctr Eds Am Auth, MLA, 68-76; vis prof English, Univ Va, 78; ed, Twayne's United States Authors Series, 78-; chmn comt Scholarly Ed, MLA, 79- **MEMBERSHIPS** MLA; Soc Textual Scholar; Asn Doc Ed. **RESEARCH** Nineteenth century American literature; bibliography and textual editing; W D Howells. **SELECTED PUBLICATIONS** Co-ed, The Rise of Silas Lapham, 71, April Hopes, 75, ed, Years of My Youth, 75, co-ed, A Hazard of New Fortunes, 76, ed, A Modern Instance, 77 & The Minister's Charge, 78, Ind Univ; auth, On Crane Now Edited, Studies in the Novel, 78; W D Howells at Kittery Point, Harvard Lib Bull, 80; Setting Pages and Fixing Words - Bal and Critical Editing of American Literature, Papers of the Bibliographical Society of America, Vol 0086, 1992. **CONTACT ADDRESS** Dept of English, Indiana Univ, Bloomington, Bloomington, IN, 47401.

NORDQUIST, RICHARD
PERSONAL New York, NY **DISCIPLINE** ENGLISH & RHETORIC **EDUCATION** SUNY at Geneseo, BA; Univ of Leicester, MA; Univ of Ga, PhD, 91. **CAREER** Instr of English for European Div of the Univ of Md, 76-80; vis prof, Tallinn Pedagogical Univ, 98; PROF OF ENGLISH & RHETORIC, 80-, DIR OF COMPOSITION, 88-93, DIR OF WRITING CENTER, 82-88, DIR OF GENERAL STUDIES, 97-, DIR OF BRITISH STUDIES PROG, 96-, ASST DEAN OF ACADEMIC SERVICES & DIR OF NONTRADITIONAL LEARNING, ARMSTRONG ATLANTIC STATE UNIV, 93-98. **HONORS AND AWARDS** Armstrong Alumni Asn Outstanding Fac Awd, 94; Armstrong Student Govt Svc Awd, 96. **MEMBERSHIPS** MLA. **RESEARCH** Twentieth-century lit and lit nonfiction. **SELECTED PUBLICATIONS** Auth, Passages: A Writer's Guide, 4th edition, St. Martin's Press, 00; articles on the American essay, Encyclopedia of Am Lit, 99; Forms of Imposture in the Essays of E.B. White, Critical Essays on E.B. White, G.K. Hall, 95. **CONTACT ADDRESS** Dept of Lang & Lit, Armstrong Atlantic State Univ, Savannah, GA, 31419. **EMAIL** richard_nordquist@mailgate.armstrong.edu

NORLAND, HOWARD BERNETT
PERSONAL Born 03/01/1932, Palo Alto Co, IA **DISCIPLINE** ENGLISH **EDUCATION** St Olaf Col, BA, 54; Univ Wis, MS, 58, PhD(English), 62. **CAREER** Instr English, Univ Kans, 61-63; from asst prof to assoc prof, 63-71, Prof English, Univ Nebr, Lincoln, 71-, Folger Shakespeare Libr fel, 67; ed bd, Genre, 67-; Frank H Woods fel humanities, 74. **MEMBERSHIPS** MLA; Renaissance Soc Am; Int Asn Neo-Latin Studies. **RESEARCH** Renaissance drama and critical theory; modern drama. **SELECTED PUBLICATIONS** Auth, The text of The Maid's Tragedy, Papers Bibliog Soc Am, 67; ed, Critical Edition of Beaumont and Fletcher's The Maid's Tragedy, 68 & Study of Ben Jonson, 69, Univ Nebr; auth, The design of Ben Jonson's Catiline, Sixteenth Century J, 78; Vives critical view of drama, Humanistica Lovaniensia, J Neo- Latin Studies, 81; The role of drama in More's literary career, 16th Century J, 82; The role of drama in Erasmus' literary thought, Bologna Acta: Selected Papers Int Cong Neo-Latin Studies (in press); Lamentable-tragedy-mixed-ful-of-pleasant- mirth, the Enigma of 'Cambises', Comparative Drama, Vol 0026, 1993; Apocalypse and Armada in Kyd 'Spanish Tragedy' - Ardolino,f, Moreana, Vol 0033, 1996. **CONTACT ADDRESS** Dept of English, Univ of Nebr, Lincoln, NE, 68508.

NORMAN, JOANNE S.
DISCIPLINE ENGLISH LITERATURE **EDUCATION** Univ Calgary, BA; Univ Toronto, MA; Univ Ottawa, PhD. **CAREER** Engl, Bishop's Univ. **SELECTED PUBLICATIONS** Auth, pubs on medieval Scottish poetry, medieval manuscripts, and word and image studies. **CONTACT ADDRESS** English Dept, Bishop's Univ, Lennoxville, PQ, JIMIZ 7. **EMAIL** jnorman@ubishops.ca

NORTHROP, DOUGLAS A.
DISCIPLINE ELIZABETHAN LITERATURE, LITERARY CRITICISM, NATIVE AMERICAN LITERATURE **EDUCATION** Wesleyan Univ, BA; Univ Chicago, MA, PhD. **CAREER** Prof, Helen Swift Neilson Prof Cult Stud, ch, dept Eng, fac dean, Ripon Col. **HONORS AND AWARDS** NEH fac fel. **SELECTED PUBLICATIONS** Publ works on Shakespeare, Spenser, and Milton. **CONTACT ADDRESS** Ripon Col, Ripon, WI. **EMAIL** NorthropD@mac.ripon.edu

NORTON, CAMILLE
DISCIPLINE ENGLISH LITERATURE **EDUCATION** Univ MA, BA, 83; Harvard Univ, MA, 87, PhD, 92. **CAREER** Asst prof, Univ Pacific. **HONORS AND AWARDS** Grolier Prize, 81; Derek Bk Awd, 92. **SELECTED PUBLICATIONS** Co-ed, Resurgent: New Writing by Women, Univ IL, 92. **CONTACT ADDRESS** Eng Dept, Univ Pacific, Pacific Ave, PO Box 3601, Stockton, CA, 95211.

NORWOOD, JAMES
DISCIPLINE THEATRE ARTS **EDUCATION** Univ Calif Berkeley, PhD. **CAREER** Assoc prof **SELECTED PUBLICATIONS** Auth, pubs on Shakespeare, modern French theatre, and film criticism. **CONTACT ADDRESS** Theatre Arts and Dance Dept, Univ of Minnesota, Twin Cities, 106 Norris Hall, 172 Pillsbury Dr SE, Minneapolis, MN, 55455. **EMAIL** nowo001@maroon.tc.umn.edu

NOURIE, ALAN RAYMOND
PERSONAL Born 12/30/1942, Kankakee, IL, m, 1969, 1 child **DISCIPLINE** ENGLISH, LIBRARY SCIENCE **EDUCATION** Southern Ill Univ, Carbondale, BA, MA, PhD; Univ of Ill, Champaign-Urbana, MS. **CAREER** Instr & asst prof, Southeast Mo State Univ, 78-81; librarian III, head of Humanities dept, Auburn Univ, 81-85; ASSOC PROF TO PROF, SOCIAL SCI LIBRARIAN, ILL STATE UNIV, 85-. **MEMBERSHIPS** ACRL; T.S. Eliot Soc. **SELECTED PUBLICATIONS** Compiler, A Concordance to the Collected Poems of T.S. Eliot, 84; T.S. Eliot's Criterion Miscellany: A Lost Series, Serials Librarian, spring 87; co-ed, American Mass Market Magazines, 91; auth, Twentieth Century Literature in English, Guide to Infor Access: A Complete Res Handbook and Directory, Am Libr Asn/Random House, 94. **CONTACT ADDRESS** Milner Library, Illinois State Univ, Normal, IL, 61761. **EMAIL** alan@mhsgate.mlb.ilstu.edu

NOVAK, MAXIMILLIAN E.
PERSONAL Born 03/26/1930, New York, NY, m, 1966, 3 children **DISCIPLINE** ENGLISH LITERATURE **EDUCATION** Univ Calif, Los Angeles, BA, 52, MA, 54, PhD, 58; St John's Col, Oxford, DPhil, 61. **CAREER** Asst prof, Univ Mich, 58-62; from asst prof to prof, Univ Calif, Los Angeles, 62- . **HONORS AND AWARDS** Fulbright fel, 55-57; Guggenheim fel, 65-66, 85-86; NEH fel, 80-81; Clark Lib prof, 77-78; pres fel, UCLA, 91-92., Pres, Johnson Soc of Southern Calif; pres, Western Soc for Eighteenth Cent Stud. **MEMBERSHIPS** MLA; ASECS. **RESEARCH** Eighteenth century and Restoration English literature; Jewish American literature. **SELECTED PUBLICATIONS** Auth, Realism, Myth, and History in Defoe's Fiction, Nebraska, 83; auth, Eighteenth-Century English Literature, Schocken, 84; ed, The California Edition of the Works of John Dryden, v. 10, 13, California, 70, 84; co-ed, The Stoke Newington Edition of Daniel Defoe, v.1, AMS Press, 98. **CONTACT ADDRESS** English Dept, Univ of California, Los Angeles, PO Box 90095-1530, Los Angeles, CA, 90095-1530. **EMAIL** novak@humnet.ucla.edu

NOVERR, DOUGLAS ARTHUR
PERSONAL Born 05/13/1942, Battle Creek, MI, m, 1968 **DISCIPLINE** AMERICAN LITERATURE & STUDIES **EDUCATION** Cent Mich Univ, BA, 65, MA, 66; Miami Univ, PhD(English), 72. **CAREER** Instr English, Cent Mich Univ, 66-67 & Miami Univ Ohio, 67- 69; from instr to asst prof, 70-78, Assoc Prof English, Mich State Univ, 78-, Nat Endowment Humanities fel English, Miami Univ Ohio, 68-69; sr Fulbright lectr Am lit, Marie Curie Sklodowska Univ, Poland, 76-77. **MEMBERSHIPS** MLA; Am Studies Asn; Popular Cult Asn; Thoreau Soc; Soc Am Baseball Res. **RESEARCH** Nineteenth century American literature; American painting and literature; American sports history. **SELECTED PUBLICATIONS** Auth, Emily Dickinson and the art of despair, Emily Dickinson Bull, 73; Bryant and Cole in the Catskills, Bull NY Pub Libr, 75; Midwestern travel literature in the nineteenth century: Romance and reality, Mid America, 77; coauth, The athletic revolution reconsidered, Sport Social Bull, fall 77; The Relationship of Painting and Literature: A Guide to Information Sources, Gale Res, 78; Midwestern Regionalist Painting and the Origins of Midwestern Popular Culture, Mid Am, 80; coauth, Violence in American sports, In: Sports in Modern America, River City Pub Ltd, 81; Sports in the twenties, In: The Evolution of Mass Culture in America, Forum Press, 82; My Life in The Negro Leagues - an Autobiography - Fields,w, J of Popular Culture, Vol 0027, 1993; The Ultimate Fantasy Football League - 1992 Guide And Handbook - Chon,b, Colao,g, Morrison,r, Schilling,a, J of Popular Culture, Vol 0027, 1993; Sports in North-america - a Documentary History, Vol 3, The Rise of Modern Sports, 1840-60 - Kirsch,gb, J of Popular Culture, Vol 0027, 1993; Baseball - a History of America Game - Rader,bg, J of American History, Vol 0081, 1994; Football And Its Fans, Supporters And Their Relations With The Game, 1885-1985 - Taylor,r, J of Popular Culture, Vol 0029, 1996; The Annotated Baseball Stories of Lardner,ring, 1914-1919 - Hilton,ga, J of Popular Culture, Vol 0030, 1996; Sports in North-america, a Documentary History, Vol 4, Sports in War, Revival And Expansion, 1860-1880 - Kirsch,gb, J of American Culture, Vol 0019, 1996; Babe - The Life And Legend of Zaharias,babe,didrikson - Cayleff,se, J of American Culture, Vol 0019, 1996; White,sol History of Colored Baseball, With Other Documents on The Early Black Game, 1886-1936 - Malloy,j, J of American Culture, Vol 0019, 1996; Early Innings - a Documentary History of Baseball, 1825-1908 - Sullivan,da, J of American Culture, Vol 0019, 1996; A Kind of Grace - a Treasury of Sportswriting by Women - Rapoport,r, J of American Culture, Vol 0019, 1996. **CONTACT ADDRESS** Dept of Lang, Michigan State Univ, 229 Bessey Hall, East Lansing, MI, 48824-1033.

NUERNBERG, SUSAN M.
DISCIPLINE ENGLISH **EDUCATION** Miami Univ, BA, 68; Univ Mass, MA, 78, PhD, 90; Univ Dijon, France, 85. **CAREER** Asst prof, 90-96, ASSOC PROF ENG,96-, UNIV WIS, OSHKOSH. **CONTACT ADDRESS** English Dept, Univ of Wisconsin, Oshkosh, Oshkosh, WI, 54901. **EMAIL** nuernber@uwosh.edu

NULL, ELISABETH M.
PERSONAL Born 12/01/1942, Wercester, MA, 2 children **DISCIPLINE** FOLKLORE, HISTORY, LIBRARY SCIENCE **EDUCATION** Sarah lawrence Col, BA, MA, 85, Mphil, 89 **CAREER** Appoint, Lib of Congress, 95, Librn, 91-98, Georgetown Univ **MEMBERSHIPS** Am Folklore Soc **RESEARCH** Am Musical life **CONTACT ADDRESS** Silver Spring, MD, 20910-5534. **EMAIL** elisabeth.null@tcs.wap.org

NUNES, ZITA
DISCIPLINE AFRICAN-AMERICAN LITERATURE **EDUCATION** B.A., Brown, 83; M.A., Berkeley, 86; PhD, Berkeley, 93. **CAREER** Asst prof. **HONORS AND AWARDS** Fel, Soc Sci Res Coun; fel, Fulbright. **RESEARCH** Brazil on the modernist period. **SELECTED PUBLICATIONS** Auth, pubs on Brazilian modernism, racial theory, and the relationship between lit and anthrop. **CONTACT ADDRESS** Dept of Eng, Columbia Col, New York, 2960 Broadway, New York, NY, 10027-6902.

NUSSBAUM, FELICITY
PERSONAL Born 08/12/1944, Dayton, OH, d, 2 children **DISCIPLINE** ENGLISH **EDUCATION** Austia Col, BA, 65; IN Univ, MA, 67, PhD, 70. **CAREER** PROF OF ENGLISH, UCLA; advisory bd, Auto/biography Studies, 90-; ed bds, Studies in English Lit 1500-1900, 94-, 18th Century Studies, 90-93; advisory committee, PMLA, 97-2000; advisor ed, 18th Century Studies, 95-98. **HONORS AND AWARDS** NEH summer grant, 81; Rockefeller Humanist-in-Residence fel, 87; Co-recipient, Louis Gottschalk Prize, Am Soc for 18th Century Studies, for Autobiographical Subject, 89; Marta Sutton Weds fel, Stanford Humanities Center, 91-92; John Simon Guggenheim Memorial Found fel, 93; Andrew Mellon Short-term fel, Huntington Library, 97-98; NEH fel, 98; William Andrew Clara Library Prof, 99-2000. **MEMBERSHIPS** PMLA; ASECS. **RESEARCH** 18th century British lit; women's studies; critical theory; autobiography. **SELECTED PUBLICATIONS** Auth, The Plays of David Mallet (1705?-1765), facsimile ed with critical intro, Garland Press, 80; The Brink of All We Hate: English Satires on Women, 1660-1750, Univ Press KY, 84; The New Eighteenth Century: Theory/Politics/English Literature, co-ed with Laura Brown, Methuen, 87; The Politics of Difference, special issue of Eighteenth-Century Studies, ed and intro, 23.4, summer 90; The Autobiographical Subject: Gender and Ideology in Eighteenth-Century England, Johns Hopkins Univ Press, 89, paperback, 95; Torrid Zones: Maternity, Sexuality and Empire in Eighteenth-Century English Narrative, Johns Hopkins Univ Press, 95; Defects: Engendering the Modern Body, co-ed with Helen Deutsch, lead vol in Corporealities series, Univ MI Press, forthcoming 99; author of numerous essays. **CONTACT ADDRESS** Dept of English, Univ of California, Los Angeles, Box 951530, Los Angeles, CA, 90095.

NYCE, BENJAMIN M.
PERSONAL Born 04/25/1932, Buffalo, NY, m, 1967 **DISCIPLINE** ENGLISH **EDUCATION** Princeton Univ, AB, 54; Claremont Grad Sch, PhD(English), 67. **CAREER** Lectr English, Scripps Col, 61-63; instr, Univ Calif, Riverside, 63-64; asst prof, Calif State Polytech Col, 64-67; asst prof, 67-77, assoc prof, 77-80, prof English, Univ San Diego, 80-, Fulbright-Hays prof Am studies, Univ Mohammed V, Morocco, 69-70 & Univ Nairobi, 72-73. **MEMBERSHIPS** MLA. **RESEARCH** English and American novel, late 19th and 20th century; political fiction; African Literature and Film. **SELECTED PUBLICATIONS** Auth, Ignazio Silone's Political Trilogy, New Orleans Rev, 68; Joyce Cary's Political Trilogy: The Atmosphere of Power, Mod Lang Quart, 3/71; Joseph Conrad's Nostromo, Recovering Lit, spring 72; Satyajit Ray: A Study of his Films, Praeger, 89. **CONTACT ADDRESS** Dept of English, Univ of San Diego Alcala Park, 5998 Alcala Park, San Diego, CA, 92110-2492. **EMAIL** agardner@cts.com

O

O'BARR, WILLIAM M.
DISCIPLINE ENGLISH LITERATURE **EDUCATION** Northwestern Univ, PhD, 69. **CAREER** Prof, Duke Univ. **SELECTED PUBLICATIONS** Auth, Culture and the Ad: Representations of Otherness in the World of Advertising, Westview, 94; Language and Politics, 76; Language and Power, 84; Rules Versus Relationships: The Ethnography of Legal Discourse, 90; pubs on lang and commun domains law and polit. **CONTACT ADDRESS** Dept of Cult Anthrop, Duke Univ, Durham, NC, 27706.

O'BRIEN, CHARLES
DISCIPLINE FILM STUDIES **EDUCATION** Univ Iowa, PhD, 92 **CAREER** Dept Art & Cult, Carleton Univ **HONORS AND AWARDS** Chateaubriand FEL,a Soc Sci and Hum Res Coun; res fel, Camargo Found in Cassis, Fr. **RESEARCH** Analysis of the French reception of Japanese films. **SELECTED PUBLICATIONS** Auth, articles and bk chapters on silent films of the 1920s, film noir in Paris, French films of the German occupation, Jean Renoir's American films, and French colonial films; transl, Francesco Casetti's Within the Gaze, Univ Ind Press. **CONTACT ADDRESS** Dept of Art and Cult, Carleton Univ, 1125 Colonel By Dr, Ottawa, ON, K1S 5B6.

O'BRIEN, GEORGE
PERSONAL m, 2 children **DISCIPLINE** ENGLISH **EDUCATION** St Augustine's Coll, Ireland; Ruskin Coll, Eng; Univ Warwick, Eng, BA, PhD. **CAREER** Lect, Eng, Univ warwick, 76-80; vis asst prof, Vassar Coll, 80-84; asst prof, Georgetown Univ, 84-90; assoc prof, Georgetown Univ, 90-97; PROF, GEORGETOWN UNIV, 97-. **SELECTED PUBLICATIONS** The Village of Longing/Dancehall Days, Viking, 90; Dancehall Days, Blackstaff, 94; Out of Our Minds, Blackstaff, 94; co-edr, The Ireland Anthology, St. Martin's Press, 98. **CONTACT ADDRESS** Dept Eng, Georgetown Univ, Washington, DC, 20057. **EMAIL** obrien1@gusun.georgetown.edu

O'BRIEN, KEVIN
DISCIPLINE LITERATURE STUDIES **EDUCATION** Univ New Brunswick, BA, 61; Univ Notre Dame, MA, 66; PhD, 72. **CAREER** Dept Eng, Xavier Univ **RESEARCH** Biography of literary figures. **SELECTED PUBLICATIONS** Auth, Oscar Wilde 1854-1900; Robert Harborough Sherard 1861-1943; Irene Osgood 1869-1922. **CONTACT ADDRESS** St Francis Xavier Univ, Antigonish, NS, B2G 2W5. **EMAIL** kobrien@stfx.ca

O'BRIEN, SUSIE
DISCIPLINE ENGLISH LITERATURE **EDUCATION** Queen's Univ, BA, PhD; Queensland Univ, MA. **RESEARCH** Post colonial theory; Eco-criticism; Canadian literature; theory of popular culture. **CONTACT ADDRESS** English Dept, McMaster Univ, 1280 Main St W, Hamilton, ON, L8S 4L9.

O'BRIEN-O'KEEFFE, KATHERINE
DISCIPLINE OLD ENGLISH LITERATURE **EDUCATION** Univ Pa, PhD. **CAREER** Instr, Univ Notre Dame. **HONORS AND AWARDS** Nat Hum Ctr fel; Distinguished Achievement Award in Tchg, Tex A&M Univ. **RESEARCH** The intellectual milieu which produced the Old English Solomon and Saturn poems. **SELECTED PUBLICATIONS** Auth, Visible Song. **CONTACT ADDRESS** Univ Notre Dame, Notre Dame, IN, 46556.

O'CONNELL, BARRY
DISCIPLINE ENGLISH **EDUCATION** Harvard Univ, BA, 66; MA, 72; PhD, 76. **CAREER** PROF, ENG, AMHERST COLL **MEMBERSHIPS** AM Antiquarian Soc **SELECTED PUBLICATIONS** Auth, On Our Own Ground: The Complete Works of William Apess, A Pequot, Univ Mass Press, 92. **CONTACT ADDRESS** Amherst Col, Box 2234, Amherst, MA, 01002-5000. **EMAIL** boconnell@amherst.edu

O'CONNOR, JOHN E.
PERSONAL Born 08/13/1943, New York, NY, m, 1965, 2 children **DISCIPLINE** AMERICAN HISTORY, CINEMA **EDUCATION** St Johns Univ, NY, BA, 65; Queens Col, NY, MA, 67; City Univ New York, PhD(early Am hist), 74. **CAREER** Lectr hist, Queens Col, NY, 66-69; asst prof, 69-79, assoc prof hist, NJ Inst Technol, 79-89; coordr Man & Technol Prog, 77-89, assoc chmn, 70-76, chemn, 76- , Historians Film Comt, 70-76; co-ed, Film & Hist J, 71- . **HONORS AND AWARDS** AHA created John E. O'Connor Award for Best Film or TV Production about History, 91. **MEMBERSHIPS** AHA; Orgn Am Historians; Am Studies Asn; Soc Cinema Studies. **RESEARCH** Early American history; history and technology; motion pictures and television. **SELECTED PUBLICATIONS** Coauth, Teaching History With Film, AHA, 74; ed, Film & the Humanities, Rockefeller Found, 77; auth, Legal reform in the Early Republic: The New Jersey Experience, Am J Legal Hist, 78; William Paterson: Lawyer and Statesman 1745-1806, Rutgers Univ Press, 79; ed, American History/ American Film: Interpreting the Hollywood Image, Frederick Ungar Publ, 79; ed, I am a Fugitive From a Chain Gang, Univ Wis Press, 81; auth, Image as Artifact: The Historical Analysis of Film and Television, Kreiger, 91. **CONTACT ADDRESS** Dept of Humanities, New Jersey Inst of Tech, 323 M L King Jr Blvd, Newark, NJ, 07102-1824.

O'CONNOR, MARY E.
DISCIPLINE ENGLISH LITERATURE **EDUCATION** McGill Univ, BA; Univ Toronto, MA; PhD. **RESEARCH** Feminist theory; African-American women writers; Victorian and mod Brit lit. **SELECTED PUBLICATIONS** Auth, John Davidson, 87. **CONTACT ADDRESS** English Dept, McMaster Univ, 1280 Main St W, Hamilton, ON, L8S 4L9.

O'CONNOR, PATRICIA E.
DISCIPLINE ENGLISH LITERATURE **EDUCATION** Marshall Univ, BA; Georgetown Univ, MA, PhD. **CAREER** Eng Dept, Georgetown Univ **RESEARCH** Functions of story; Appalachian narratives; teaching writing; prison teaching; literacy struggles. **SELECTED PUBLICATIONS** Auth, pubs on narrative strategies, discourses of violence, and service learning; co-auth, Literacy Behind Prison Walls, 94. **CONTACT ADDRESS** English Dept, Georgetown Univ, 37th and O St, Washington, DC, 20057.

O'DEA, SHANE
PERSONAL Born 07/06/1945, St. John's, NF, Canada **DISCIPLINE** ENGLISH **EDUCATION** Memorial Univ, BA, 66, MA, 74. **CAREER** Lectr, 70-75, asst prof, 75-80, assoc prof, 80-89, PROF ENGLISH, MEMORIAL UNIV NFLD, 89-; CHAIR BD GOVS, HERITAGE CAN. **HONORS AND AWARDS** Southcott Award, 88; Heritage Can Comm Serv Award, 78; Lt-Gov Award, 90; Memorial Univ Distinguished Tchr Award, 88; Can 125 Medal, 92. **MEMBERSHIPS** Life mem, Nfld Hist Trust, 73; vice-ch, St John's Heritage Adv Comt, 77-91; pres, Nfld Hist Soc, 81-83; ch, Heritage Found Nfld & Lab, 89-92; Gov Heritage Can, 95-. **SELECTED PUBLICATIONS** Auth, The Domestic Architecture of Old St. John's, 74; coauth, A Gift of Heritage, 75; co-ed, Ten Historic Towns, 78; co-ed, Dimensions in Canadian Architecture, 83. **CONTACT ADDRESS** Dept of English, Memorial Univ of Newfoundland, St. John's, NF, A1C 5S7. **EMAIL** sodea@morgan.ucs.mun.ca

O'DONNELL, MABRY MILLER
PERSONAL Born 07/18/1945, Huntsville, AL, m, 1972, 3 children **DISCIPLINE** SPEECH COMMUNICATION, GENDER STUDIES **EDUCATION** La State Univ, BA, 67; Univ Ala, MA, 69; Bowling Green State Univ, PhD(interpersonal and public commun), 77. **CAREER** Instr to assoc prof, 69-88, PROF SPEECH, MARIETTA COL, 88-, Forensics Coach, 69-. **HONORS AND AWARDS** Outstanding Fac Award, 88, 97; Alpha Lambda Delta Fac Award, 89, 90; Outstanding Fac Mem in Continuing Educ, 91; Harness Fel, 92-95; McCoy Prof, 94-98; Speech Commun Asn of Ohio's 1994 Col Teacher of the Year; William R. and Marie Adamson Flescher Prof of Humanities, 95-99; Pi Kappa Delta Coaches Hon Roll, 95, 97; E.R. Nichols Award, Outstanding Forensics Instr in the Nation, presented by Pi Kappa Delta, 96. **MEMBERSHIPS** Nat Commun Asn; Ohio Acad of Hist; Ohio Forensic Asn; Alpha Epsilon Rho; Alpha Lambda Delta; Delta Gamma; Omicron Delta

Kappa; Order of Omega; Phi Alpha Theta; Pi Kappa Delta. **RESEARCH** Frances Wright; forensics; public address. **SELECTED PUBLICATIONS** Auth, Effective Interviewing or How to Get Your Client to Tell You What You Need to Know, Proc of Small Bus Inst Dir Asn, 2/94; Interpersonal Communication, In: Ready for the Real World. **CONTACT ADDRESS** 215 5th St., Marietta, OH, 45750-4025. **EMAIL** odonnelm@marietta.edu

O'DONNELL, THOMAS G.
DISCIPLINE ENGLISH **EDUCATION** Col Charleston, BA, 86; Fla State Univ, MA, PhD, 96. **CAREER** Asst prof. **RESEARCH** Contemporary theories of composition; classical rhetoric; history of rhetoric; philosophy and rhetoric. **SELECTED PUBLICATIONS** Auth, Politics and Ordinary Language: A Defense of Expressivist Rhetorics, Col Engl, 96; Putting Correctness in its Place: Justifications for Teaching and Learning Alternate Grammars in Elements of Alternate Style: Essays on Writing and Revision; Speech-Acts, Conventions, and Voice: Challenges to a Davidsonian Conception of Writing, J Advan(d) Composition, 94. **CONTACT ADDRESS** Dept of English, Loyola Univ, Chicago, 6525 N Sheridan Rd, Chicago, IL, 60626. **EMAIL** todonne@wpo.it.luc.edu

O'DONNELL, VICTORIA
PERSONAL Born 02/12/1939, Greensburg, PA, m, 1993, 2 children **DISCIPLINE** SPEECH COMMUNICATION **EDUCATION** Pa St Univ, BA 59, MA, 62, PhD, 68. **CAREER** Asst prof to prof, Dept of Commun/Pub Address, Univ of N Tex, 67-89; Dept Ch, 81-89, Dept of Commun/Pub Address, Univ of N Tex; Dept Ch, Dept of Speech Commun, Ore State Univ, 89-91; Prof, Dept of Speech Commun, Mo State Univ-Bozeman, 91-93; Dir, Univ Honors Prog, Mo State Univ-Bozeman, 93-. **HONORS AND AWARDS** Honors prof, Univ of N Tex, 76; Mortar Board Top Prof, 79, 86; Mo State Univ Alum Assoc & Bozeman Chamber of Com Excellence Award, 97. **MEMBERSHIPS** Nat Commun Assoc; Int Commun Assoc; Western States Commun Assoc; Nat Col Honors Coun. **RESEARCH** Television criticism; propaganda & persuasion; env commun; documentary filmmaker. **SELECTED PUBLICATIONS** Coauth, Persuasion and Propaganda, Sage, 86, 92, 93, 98; auth, Introduction to Public Communication, Kendall-Hunt, 92, 93; auth, Collective Memory and the End of the Cold War, The National Honors Report, 95. **CONTACT ADDRESS** Univ Honors Prog, Montana State Univ, PO Box 172140, Bozeman, MT, 59717-2140. **EMAIL** vodonnel@montana.edu

O'GRADY, JEAN
DISCIPLINE ENGLISH **EDUCATION** Yale Univ, MA, 65; Univ Toronto, BA, 64, PhD, 78. **CAREER** Lectr, York Univ, 65-66; lectr, Univ Toronto, 67-69; lectr, Ryerson Polytechnic, 80; postdoc fel, Collected Works of John Stuart Mill, 81-90; res assoc, Collected Works of Northrop Frye, 94-. **HONORS AND AWARDS** Gov General's Gold Medal in Eng, 64; Yale Univ Fel; Woodrow Wilson Fel; Can Coun Doctoral Award, 78. **MEMBERSHIPS** Victorian Studs Asn Ont. **SELECTED PUBLICATIONS** Auth, Special Writer: an Annotated Bibliography of the Writings of R.E. Knowles in the Toronto Daily Star and Star Weekly, 93; auth, A Pocket Guide to the Peerage in Newsl of the Victorian Studs Asn, 88; contribur, Oxford Companion to Canadian Literature; contribur, Canadian Encyclopedia; contribur, Victorian Britain: an Encyclopedia. **CONTACT ADDRESS** Victoria Col, Univ Toronto, 73 Queen's Park Cres, Toronto, ON, M5S 1K7.

O'HARA, MICHAEL M.
PERSONAL Born 10/10/1959, Princeton, NJ, d **DISCIPLINE** PERFORMING ARTS **EDUCATION** Fordham Univ, BA, 82; Univ Md, MA, 90, PhD, 97. **CAREER** Adj lectr, Mary Washington Col, 94; lectr, Univ Md, 95;, artist dir, Old Dominion Opry, 96; adj lectr, Univ Md, 97; consult, Theatre Resoure Productions, 94-; asst prof, Ball State Univ, 97-. **HONORS AND AWARDS** Pi Kappa Delta, 83, Honorary Forensics Fraternity; Omicron Delta Kappa, 90, Nat Honorary Leadership Fraternity; Nat 1st Place Winner, 92, NCI/ACTF; Who's Who Among Students, Am Univ Col, 92; Cert Recognition Outstanding Contrib to Students, 92, UMCP; nominee, Outstanding Teacher Year, 92, UMCP; Cert Teaching Excellence, 95, 96, UMCP. **MEMBERSHIPS** Nat Commun Asn; Am Theatre in Higher Educ; Am Society Theatre Res. **RESEARCH** Shaw and American Theatre; theatrical pedagogy and technology. **SELECTED PUBLICATIONS** Auth, On the Rocks and the Federal Theatre Project, 92; auth, Class of 29 and the American Dream, 93; auth, Arms and the Man and Federal Theatre: Love and War in Troubled Times, 94; auth, Federal Theatre's Androcles & The Lion, 99. **CONTACT ADDRESS** Dept of Theatre and Dance, Ball State Univ, Muncie, IN, 47306. **EMAIL** mohara@gw.bsu.edu

O'HEARN, CAROLYN
DISCIPLINE ENGLISH LINGUISTICS AND LITERATURE **EDUCATION** Univ Mo, BS; Ariz State Univ, MA, PhD; **CAREER** Assoc prof. **RESEARCH** Medieval literature, technical writing. **SELECTED PUBLICATIONS** Auth, Writing, Grammar and Usage, 89; articles on ling and lit. **CONTACT ADDRESS** Dept of Eng, Pittsburg State Univ, 1701 S Broadway St, Pittsburg, KS, 66762. **EMAIL** cohearn@pittstate.edu

O'KELL, ROBERT P.
DISCIPLINE ENGLISH LITERATURE **EDUCATION** Carleton Univ, BA; Univ Ind, MA; PhD. **CAREER** Prof **SELECTED PUBLICATIONS** Auth, pub(s) on cultural studies, relation between literature and social history, and rhetoric of politics in Victorian England. **CONTACT ADDRESS** Dept of English, Manitoba Univ, Winnipeg, MB, R3T 2N2.

O'MALLEY, SUSAN GUSHEE
PERSONAL Born 11/19/1942, Boston, MA, d, 2 children **DISCIPLINE** WOMEN'S STUDIES **EDUCATION** Smith Col, AB, 64; Tulane Univ, MA, 65, PhD, 73. **CAREER** ASST PROF TO PROF, KINGSBOROUGH COMMUNITY COL, 74-. **HONORS AND AWARDS** Fulbright Scholar; Mellon Fel; CUNY Collaborative Grant; Huntington Library Fel; Folger Seminar Fel; NEH Travel Grants; NEH Summer Seminar. **MEMBERSHIPS** MLA; NCTE; Soc for the Study of Women in the Renaissance; Shakespeare Asn of Am. **RESEARCH** English early modern pamphlets on women. **SELECTED PUBLICATIONS** Auth, Defences of Women: Jane Anger, Constantia munda, Ester Sowernam, Rachel Speght, The Printed Writings of Renaissance Englishwomen 1500-1640, Scolar Press, 96; A Critical Old-Spelling Edition of Thomas Goffe's The Courageous Turk 1618, Garland Pub, 79; Single Parent Maneuvers in Academia, The Family Track, Univ of Ill Press, 98; The Pamphlet Controversy about Women: Class and Gender, Attending to Women in Early Modern England, Univ of Delaware Press, 94; coauth, Politics of Education, SUNY Press, 90. **CONTACT ADDRESS** English Dept, Kingsborough Comm Col, CUNY, 2001 Oriental Blvd, Brooklyn, NY, 11235. **EMAIL** suokb@cunyvm.cuny.edu

O'MEALLY, ROBERT
DISCIPLINE AFRICAN AMERICAN LITERATURE **EDUCATION** Stanford Univ, BA, 70; Harvard Univ, PhD, 75. **CAREER** Zora Neale Hurston prof. **HONORS AND AWARDS** Co-ed, Norton Anthology of African Amer Lit. **SELECTED PUBLICATIONS** Auth, The Craft of Ralph Ellison, Harvard, 80; Seeing Jazz, Smithsonian, 97; ed, New Essays on Invisible Man Cambridge, 89; Tales of the Congaree, Univ NC, 90; The Jazz Cadence of American Culture, Columbia, 98; co-ed, History and Memory in African American Culture, Oxford, 94. **CONTACT ADDRESS** Dept of Eng, Columbia Col, New York, 2960 Broadway, New York, NY, 10027-6902.

O'NEILL, MEGAN
DISCIPLINE RHETORIC AND COMPOSITION **EDUCATION** Eastern WA Univ, BA, 90, MA, 92; Univ NM, PhD, 96. **CAREER** Adj asst prof; dir, Compos Rhet & Compos. **SELECTED PUBLICATIONS** Auth, The Listserv in the Networked Writing Classroom: Building Community, ACE J, 1:1, 97; Bibliog essay on Helen MacInnes, Dictionary Lit Biog 96, 98; regular rev(s), Star Trek novels, TV Zone, publ in UK; rev, essays of Romanticism scholar on New Bk(s)in 19th Century Stud Rev essay of Michael Macovski's Dialogue & Lit 94, Readerly/Writerly Texts 1:2, 94; textbk rev(s) & eval for, Addison-Wesley-Longman, Mayfield, Prentice-Hall, Houghton-Mifflin & McGraw-Hill. **CONTACT ADDRESS** Dept of Eng, Creighton Univ, 2500 CA Plaza, CA 306A, Omaha, NE, 68178. **EMAIL** moneill@creighton.edu

O'SHEA, EDWARD
DISCIPLINE ENGLISH LITERATURE **EDUCATION** Northwestern Univ, PhD, 75. **CAREER** Prof, SUNY Oswego. **HONORS AND AWARDS** Ch, fac assbly, SUNY Oswego. **RESEARCH** Mod Brit and Irish lit; lit criticism and theory. **SELECTED PUBLICATIONS** Auth, Descriptive Catalogue of W.B. Yeats's Library; Yeats as Editor; essays on Yeats, Shakespeare, pedagogical issues in Eng educ. **CONTACT ADDRESS** SUNY Oswego, 207C Swetman, Oswego, NY, 13126. **EMAIL** edoshea@Oswego.edu

O'SULLIVAN, MICHAEL K.
PERSONAL Born 05/31/1950, St. Louis, MO, m, 1977, 1 child **DISCIPLINE** LIBRARY AND INFORMATION SCIENCE **EDUCATION** Univ MO, Columbia, BJ, 72; Univ Northern IA, Cedar Falls, MA (Communications Media), MA, 76; Univ IA, Iowa City, MA (Library and Information Science), 96. **CAREER** INSTRUCTIONAL MEDIA COORDINATOR, ROSEMOUNT HIGH SCHOOL, ROSEMOUNT, MN, 96-; REFERENCE LIBRARIAN, HAMLINE UNIV, ST. PAUL, MN, 97-. **HONORS AND AWARDS** Outstanding Young Man of America, 75, 85; Iowa Volunteer of the Year Award, 94. **MEMBERSHIPS** ALA; ACRL. **RESEARCH** Information literacy; internet evaluation. **CONTACT ADDRESS** 4533 149th Ct., Apple Valley, MN, 55124. **EMAIL** mosullivan@gw.hamline.edu

OAKES, ELISABETH
PERSONAL m, 3 children **DISCIPLINE** SHAKESPEARE AND AMERICAN WOMEN POETS **EDUCATION** Vanderbilt Univ, PhD, 91. **CAREER** Assoc prof, Western Ky Univ. **RESEARCH** Shakespeare and early modern widows; Shakespere pedagogy, women's literature.. **SELECTED PUBLICATIONS** Auth, Polonius, the Man behind the Arras: A Jungian Study, New Essays on Hamlet, AMS Press, 94; Enacting Shakespeare's Language, Teaching Shakespeare Today: Practical Approaches and Productive Strategies, NCTE, 93. **CONTACT ADDRESS** Western Kentucky Univ, 1526 Big Red Way Street, Bowling Green, KY, 42101.

OAKS, HAROLD RASMUS
PERSONAL Born 06/20/1936, Provo, UT, m, 1960, 5 children **DISCIPLINE** THEATRE **EDUCATION** Brigham Young Univ, BA, 60, MA, 62; Univ Minn, PhD(Speech, Theatre Arts), 64. **CAREER** Instr Speech & Theatre Arts, Univ Minn, 62-64, admin asst Off Adv Drama res, 63-64; asst prof Speech & Drama, Frostburg State Univ, 64-66; assoc prof & dir Theatre, Univ Nebraska-Kearney, 66-68; assoc prof Dramatic Arts, Colo State Univ, 68-70; prof Theatre & Media Arts, 70-; chmn, 80-93; assoc prof Dramatic Arts & coord Child Drama, Bringham Young Univ, 70-, US Off Econ Humanities & Soc Sci Develop Prog grant-in-aid, 66-68; consult Integrated Arts Prog, Provo City Schs, 76-77. **HONORS AND AWARDS** Gold Medallion of Excellence, Am Col Theatre Festival, Amoco Oil Co, 78; Presidential Citation, Am Alliance for Theatre & Ed, 93. **MEMBERSHIPS** Am Theatre Asn (treas, 72-73); Rocky Mountain Theatre Asn (pres, 70-71); US Inst Theatre Technol; Children's Theatre Asn; Int Asn Theater for Children and Youth. **RESEARCH** Theatre administration: improvisation and child drama; puppetry as a teaching tool; US & int theatre for young audiences. **SELECTED PUBLICATIONS** Auth, Theatre management and administration training in American colleges and universities, US Inst Theatre Technol, 9/67; Introduction to the Theatre, Brigham Young Univ, 71; coauth, An evening of historical vignettes, Ensign, 10/72; auth, Puppets, Patterns, and Plays, Brigham Young Univ, 76, rev, 81; Puppets as a Teaching Tool, Welfare Serv, Latter-day Saints Church, 77; Using puppets in health teaching, Health & Elem Teaching, Appendix B, 77; Mormon Montage (play), produced at Brigham Young Univ, 3 & 8/78; Outstanding Plays for Young Audiences International Bibliography, vol IV, ed, ASSITEJ/USA, Provo, Utah, Brigham Young University Press, 93; What's Happening in Theatre for Young Audiences?, TYA Today, vol 9, no 2, March, 95; Vigilance Against Violence, the Ensign, vol 27, no 8, August, 97. **CONTACT ADDRESS** Dept of Theatre & Cinematic Arts, Brigham Young Univ, 581 Hfac, Provo, UT, 84602-0002. **EMAIL** harold_oaks@byu.edu

ODEN, GLORIA
PERSONAL Born 10/30/1923, Yonkers, NY, m **DISCIPLINE** ENGLISH **EDUCATION** Howard Univ, BA 1944, JD 1948; NY Univ, grad study. **CAREER** Amer Inst of Physics, editor 1961-66; Inst of Electric & Electronic Engrs, sr editor 1966-67; Appleton-Century-Crofts, supr 1967-68; Holt Rinehart & Winston, proj dir for science and language arts books 1968-71; Univ of MD Baltimore County, assistant prof, assoc prof, prof of English. **HONORS AND AWARDS** Creative Writing Fellowships John Hay Whitney Found 1955-57; Fellowship to Yaddo Saratoga Springs NY 1956; Breadloaf Writers Scholarship Middlebury College 1960; interviewed for Black Oral History Prog Fisk Univ Library 1973; Living Black American Authors 1973; Black Writers Past & Present 1975; Distinguished Black Women's Award, Towson University, 1984; William H Hastie Symposium Award, 1981; numerous others. **MEMBERSHIPS** PEN; The Poetry Soc of Amer; The Society for the Study of the Multi-Ethnic Literature of the United States. **CONTACT ADDRESS** English Dept, Univ of Maryland, Baltimore County, Baltimore, MD, 21228.

OGDEN, DUNBAR HUNT
PERSONAL Born 03/01/1935, Portsmouth, OH, m, 1957, 2 children **DISCIPLINE** DRAMATIC ART **EDUCATION** Davidson Col, AB, 55; Duke Univ, MA, 56; Yale Univ, PhD, 62. **CAREER** Instr English, Univ Md Overseas Prog, 58; instr Ger, Southern Conn State Col, 60-62; asst prof, 62-70, chmn Grad Studies, 69-79, dramatic art, 70-89, prof dramatic art, 89-, Univ Cal, Berkeley; Humanities Res Prog fel, Univ Calif, 67-68; Am Coun Learned Soc fel, 68-69; vis prof, Inst Dramatic Art, Univ Amsterdam, 74-75, 88; dramaturg, Berkeley Shakespeare Festival, 78-80; Humanities Res Prog fel, Univ Calif, 82. **MEMBERSHIPS** Int Fed Theatre Res; Am Theatre Asn; Am Soc Theatre Res; Theatre Lib Asoc. **RESEARCH** Classical, Medieval, and Renaissance theater and drama; German and Dutch theater and drama of the 20th century; Italian Baroque scene design. **SELECTED PUBLICATIONS** Auth, The Staging of Drama in the Medieval Church, Yale Univ; auth, The Italian Baroque Stage, 78; auth, Actor Training and Audience Response, 84; auth, Performance Dynamics and the Amsterdam Werkteater, 87; auth, Das Werkteater von Amsterdam, 93; ed The Theatre and Drama of Greece and Rome, James Butler, 72; auth, Theatre West: Image and Impact, 90; auth, The International Theatre Exhibition: Amsterdam, 1922, 92; auth, The Play of Daniel: Critical Essays, 97. **CONTACT ADDRESS** Dept of Dramatic Art, Univ of California, Berkeley, 101 Dwinelle Anx, Berkeley, CA, 94720-2560.

OGDEN, JOHN T.
DISCIPLINE ENGLISH LITERATURE **EDUCATION** Princeton Univ, BA; Johns Hopkins Univ, MA; Univ Ill, PhD. **CAREER** Assoc prof **RESEARCH** Poetry. **SELECTED PUBLICATIONS** Auth, pub(s) on Wordsworth, Coleridge, and 18th century aesthetic theory. **CONTACT ADDRESS** Dept of English, Manitoba Univ, Winnipeg, MB, R3T 2N2.

OGLES, ROBERT M.
DISCIPLINE SOCIAL PSYCHOLOGICAL EFFECTS OF MASS COMMUNICATION CONTENT, HISTORY OF

MASS **EDUCATION** Univ Wis, PhD, 87. **CAREER** Assoc prof, Purdue Univ. **RESEARCH** History of mass communications. **SELECTED PUBLICATIONS** Auth, Getting Research Out of the Classroom and Into the Newspaper, Col Media Rev, 91; MTV: Music Television in R.G. Picard (ed), The Cable Network Handbk, 93; coauth, Question Specificity in Studies of Television's Contributions to Viewers' Fear and Perceived Probability of Criminal Victimization", Mass Commun Rev, 93. **CONTACT ADDRESS** Dept of Commun, Purdue Univ, 1080 Schleman Hall, West Lafayette, IN, 47907-1080. **EMAIL** rogles@sla.purdue.edu

OHLGREN, THOMAS HAROLD
PERSONAL Born 11/08/1941, Minneapolis, MN, m, 1962, 2 children **DISCIPLINE** MEDIEVAL ENGLISH LITERATURE **EDUCATION** Univ Mich, BA, 63, MA, 65, PhD(English), 69. **CAREER** Asst prof, 69-75, asst dean interdisciplinary prog, chmn humanities, soc sci & educ, 78-82, Assoc Prof English, Purdue Univ, West Lafayette, 75-, Younger humanist fel art hist, Nat Endowment for Humanities, 73-74. **MEMBERSHIPS** Mediaeval Acad Am; Int Ctr for Medieval Art; MLA. **RESEARCH** Old English literature and art; computer applications in medieval art history. **SELECTED PUBLICATIONS** Coauth, Computers and the medievalist, Speculum, 474; Some new light on the Old English Caedmonian genesis, Studies Iconography, I: 38-73; co-ed, The New Languages: A Rhetorical Approach to the Mass Media and Popular Culture, Prentice-Hall, 77; ed, Illuminated Manuscripts: An Index to Selected Bodleian Library Color Reproductions, 77 & Illuminated Manuscripts and Books in the Bodleian Library: A Supplemental Index, 78, Garland; Computer Indexing of Illuminated Manuscripts for Use in Medieval Studies, Computers & Humanities, 12: 189-199; Subject Access to Iconographic Data Bases: Theory and Practice, In: Data Bases in the Humanities and Social Sciences, North-Holland Pub, 80; Index to iconographic Subjects in Anglo-Saxon Illuminated Manuscripts, Old English Newslett, fall 81; The Iconography of The Mouth of Hell - 8th-century Britain to The 15th-century - Schmidt,gd, J of English And Germanic Philology, Vol 0096, 1997; The Iconography of The Mouth of Hell - 8th-century Britain to The 15th-century - Schmidt,gd, J of English And Germanic Philology, Vol 0096, 1997. **CONTACT ADDRESS** Dept of English, Purdue Univ, West Lafayette, IN, 47907-1968.

OHLHAUSER, JON B.
PERSONAL Born 02/06/1966, Calgary, AB, Canada, m, 1991, 4 children **DISCIPLINE** COMMUNICATION **EDUCATION** Regent Univ, PhD, 97. **CAREER** Gov mem res, 90-93, Legisl Assembly of Alberta; asst prof, 96-, Atlantic Baptist Univ. **MEMBERSHIPS** Nat Commun Asn. **RESEARCH** Parlimentary debate; spirituality & commun. **SELECTED PUBLICATIONS** Auth, Human Rhetoric: Accounting for Spiritual Intervention, Howard J of Commun, 7, 96. **CONTACT ADDRESS** 159 Briggs Cross Rd, Box 6004, Lutes Mountain, NB, E1B 1E3. **EMAIL** johlhauser@abu.nb.ca

OKHAMAFE, IMAFEDIA
PERSONAL s **DISCIPLINE** PHILOSOPHY,. ENGLISH **EDUCATION** Purdue Univ, PhD, Philosophy and English, 1984. **CAREER** Univ of NE at Omaha, prof of philosophy & English 1993-. **MEMBERSHIPS** Modern Language Association of America; American Philosophical Association. **SELECTED PUBLICATIONS** Articles have appeared in periodicals such as Black Scholar, Journal of the British Soc for Phenomenology, UMOJA, Intl Journal of Social Educ, Auslegung, Rsch in African Literatures, Soundings, Philosophy Today, and Africa Today. **CONTACT ADDRESS** Prof of Philosophy & English, Univ of Nebraska-Omaha, Annex 39, Omaha, NE, 68182-0208.

OLBRICHT, THOMAS H.
PERSONAL Born 11/03/1929, Thayer, MO, m, 1951, 5 children **DISCIPLINE** RHETORIC, BIBLICAL THEOLOGY **EDUCATION** Northern IL, BS, 51; Univ IA, MA 53, PhD, 59; Harvard Divinity School, STB, 62. **CAREER** Chair speech, Univ Dubuque, 55-59; PA State Asn Prof speech and humanities, 62-67; Prof Biblical Theol, Abilene Christian Univ, 67-86, Dean, Col of Liberal and Fine Arts, 81-85; Distinguished Prof Relig, 94-97, chair, Relig div, 86-96, Pepperdine Univ, Distinguished Prod Relig, Emeritus, 97-. **MEMBERSHIPS** Soc of Biblical lit; Nat Commun Asn; Am Academy Relig. **RESEARCH** Rhetorical analysis of scripture; history of Biblical interpretation. **SELECTED PUBLICATIONS** Co-auth, with Stanley E Porter, Rhetoric and the New Testament 1991 Heidelberg Conference, Sheffield Academic Press, 93; auth, Hearing God's Voice: My Life with Scriptures in Churches of Christ, ACU Press, 96; co-auth, with Stanley E Porter, Rhetoric, Theology and the Scriptures, Pretoria Conf, Sheffield Academic Press, 96; with Stanley E Porter, The Rhetorical Analysis of Scripture: Essays from the 1995 London Conference, Univ of Sheffield, 97. **CONTACT ADDRESS** 14 Beaver Dam Rd, South Berwick, ME, 03908-1818. **EMAIL** Tolbrich@gw1.net

OLDANI, LOUIS JOSEPH
PERSONAL Born 03/01/1933, St. Louis, MO **DISCIPLINE** AMERICAN & ENGLISH LITERATURE **EDUCATION** St Louis Univ, AB, 57, PhL, 59, MA, 62, Stb, 66; Pa, PhD(English), 72. **CAREER** From instr to asst prof, 71-77, from assoc prof to prof English, Rockhurst Col, 77-85, Lilly grant fac develop, Eli Lilly Found, 75 & 77; Mellon sr fel, Univ Kans, 79; ed, Jesuit Drama Series, Inst Jesuit Sources. **HONORS AND AWARDS** Alpha Sigma Nu Distinguished Teaching Award, 95; AAUP, pres Rockhurst Chap; MLA; NCTE. **MEMBERSHIPS** MLA. **RESEARCH** Dreiser, descriptive and textual bibliography; the novel; Jesuit drama. **SELECTED PUBLICATIONS** Auth, Muriel Spark's delightful and savage heroes, Current Rev Catholicism, summer 64; Bibliographical description of Dreiser's The Genius, Libr Chronicle, winter 73; Dreiser and paperbacks: An unpublished letter, Dreiser Newsletter, fall 75; The lively state of Dreiser bibliography, Res Studies, 12/76; Two unpublished Pound letters: Pound's aid to Dreiser, Libr Chronicle, spring 77; Literary language and postmodern theories of semiotics, In: Semiotic Themes, Univ Kans Humanistic Studies, Vol 53, 81; ed, An introduction to the Jesuit theater & Jesuit Theater Englished, 89; Inst Jesuit Sources; Dreiser's Genius in the Making, Studies in Bibliography, 94; Jesuit Theater in Italy: A Bibliography, AHSI, 97. **CONTACT ADDRESS** Dept of English, Rockhurst Col, 1100 Rockhurst Rd, Kansas City, MO, 64110-2561. **EMAIL** oldani@vaxl.rockhurst.edu

OLIKER, MICHAEL A.
PERSONAL Born 01/09/1946, Philadelphia, PA, m, 1982 **DISCIPLINE** PHILOSOPHY OF EDUCATION, LIBRARY AND INFROMATION SCIENCE, ENGLISH **EDUCATION** Kutztown Univ of Penn, BA, 67; Temple Univ, EdM, 69; Univ Ill-Urbana, PhD, 76; Drexel Univ, MS, 80. **CAREER** Tchg asst, Syracuse Univ, 69-70; adj fac, Phila Commun Col, 70; vis fac, 70-71, adj fac, 83-84, Glassboro State Col; adj fac, Bloomsburg State Col, 74; tchg asst, 71-72, 73-75, adj fac, 76, Univ Ill-Urbana; vis fac, 76-77, adj fac, 80, 89-91, Loyola Univ Chicago; adj fac, 80 & 83, Temple Univ; adj fac, Ill State Univ, 84; asst prof, E Ill Univ, 95-97; adj fac, NE Ill Univ, 97-. **MEMBERSHIPS** Midwest Philos Educ Soc; Am Educ Stud Asn; Am Libr Asn; Am Philos Asn; Mod Lang Asn; Philos Educ Soc; Popular Cult Asn. **RESEARCH** Applied of critical thinking to: (1) Popular culture, (2) Educational administration and policy; Douglas McGregors 'Theory Y' approach to administration; Philosophy of Plato and John Dewey; History of American educational thought. **SELECTED PUBLICATIONS** Auth On the Images of Education in Popular Film, Educ Horizons, 93; Analytical Philosophy and the Discourse of Institutional Democracy, Proceedings of the Midwest Philosophy of Education Society 1991-92, The Society, 93; Popula Film as Educational Ideology: A Framework for Critical Analysis, Proceedings of the Midwest Philosophy of Education Society 1993-94, The Society, 95; Educational Policy and Administration, 96; Censorship, Philosophy of Education, Garland, 96; Superman, Adolescents, and the Metaphysics of Popular Culture, 97; The Language of Educational Policy and Administration, Proceedings of the Midwest Philosophy of Education Society, The Society, 97; Toward an Intellectual Understanding of Anti-Intellectual Popular Culture, Jour of Thought, 98. **CONTACT ADDRESS** 5006 W Grace St, Chicago, IL, 60641. **EMAIL** moliker@sprynet.com

OLIVER, EILEEN
DISCIPLINE ENGLISH LITERATURE **EDUCATION** Univ Tex at Austin, PhD. **CAREER** Assoc prof, Washington State Univ. **RESEARCH** Influence of assignment on the writing quality of nonmainstream students. **SELECTED PUBLICATIONS** Auth, Crossing the Mainstream: Multicultural Perspectives in Teaching Literature, 94. **CONTACT ADDRESS** Dept of English, Washington State Univ, 1 SE Stadium Way, PO Box 645020, Pullman, WA, 99164-5020. **EMAIL** olivere@wsu.edu

OLMSTED, JANE
DISCIPLINE AMERICAN LITERATURE, MULTICULTURALISM **EDUCATION** Bowling Green State Univ, BFA; Univ Louisville, MA; Univ Minn, PhD. **CAREER** Prof **RESEARCH** Women Writers. **SELECTED PUBLICATIONS** Auth, The Pull to Memory and the Language of Place in Paule Marshall's The Chosen Place, The Timeless People, and Praisesong for the Widow, African Am Rev, 97. **CONTACT ADDRESS** Western Kentucky Univ, 1526 Big Red Way Street, Bowling Green, KY, 42101. **EMAIL** jane.olmsted@wku.edu

OLNEY, JAMES
DISCIPLINE NARRATIVE THEORY, AUTOBIOGRAPHY, MODERN POETRY, AFRICAN LITERATURE **EDUCATION** Columbia Univ, PhD, 63. **CAREER** LSU Found Henry J. Voorhies Prof Eng, La State Univ. **SELECTED PUBLICATIONS** Auth, Metaphors of Self: the Meaning of Autobiography, 72; Tell Me Africa, 73; The Rhizome and the Flower, 80; Studies in Autobiography, 88; The Language(s) of Poetry, 93. **CONTACT ADDRESS** Dept of Fr Grad Stud, Louisiana State Univ, Baton Rouge, LA, 70803.

OLSEN, ALEXANDRA H.
PERSONAL Born 05/01/1948, Polson, MT, m, 1967 **DISCIPLINE** ENGLISH **EDUCATION** Univ Calif Berkeley, PhD, 77 **CAREER** Asst prof to assoc prof to prof, Univ Co Denver, 78-90. **HONORS AND AWARDS** Exemplary teaching award, 93; Methodist scholar/teacher award, 89., Phi Beta Kappa **MEMBERSHIPS** MLA; Medieval Acad; PAMLA; ISAS, RMMRA; RMMLA; WCBS. **RESEARCH** Old English lit; middle English, hagiography; sci fiction. **SELECTED PUBLICATIONS** Auth, Gender Roles, A Beowulf Handbook, Univ Nb, 97; Re-Vision: A Comparison of A Canticle for Leibowitz and the Novellas, Extrapolation, 97; The Homiletic Tradition in Old English, in Geardagum, 97; Texts with Roots in Oral Tradition in Teaching Oral Tradition, Modern Lang Assoc, 98; coauth, Poems and Prose from the Old English, Yale Univ Press, 98. **CONTACT ADDRESS** Dept of English, Univ Denver, Denver, CO, 80208. **EMAIL** aolsen@du.edu

OLSON, STEVEN
PERSONAL Born 09/07/1950, Morris, MN, m, 1972, 2 children **DISCIPLINE** ENGLISH **EDUCATION** Moorhead State Col, BA, 72; Univ of Tex El Paso, MA, 78; Univ of Ill Urbana-Champaign, PhD, 86. **CAREER** Asst prof of English, Northern Montana Col, 86-89; prof of English, Central Wash Univ, 89-. **RESEARCH** 19th Century American literature; William Faulkner. **SELECTED PUBLICATIONS** Auth, The Prairie in Nineteenth-Century American Poetry, Univ of Ok Press, 94; Now the wild prairie to the view Appears': Nineteenth-century Ill Poets of the Prairies, Western Ill Regional Studies, 88; A Perverted Poetics: Bryant's and Emerson's Concern for a Developing American Literature, Am Transcendental Quart, 86; William Cullen Bryant's View of Prairie America's Conflicting Values, NDak Quart, 85; Coming Home, SDak Rev, 82; several entries in The Walt Whitman Encyclopedia, forthcoming. **CONTACT ADDRESS** English Dept, Central Washington Univ, 400 E 8th Ave, Ellensburg, WA, 98926-7558. **EMAIL** olsons@cwu.edu

ONWUEME, TESS
PERSONAL Nigeria **DISCIPLINE** ENGLISH LITERATURE **EDUCATION** Univ Ife, MA; Univ Benin, PhD. **CAREER** Prof multicult lit studies, Montclair State Univ; prof African Studies/Eng, Vassar Col; Disting Prof Cult Diversity, Univ Wis Eau Claire, present. **HONORS AND AWARDS** Literary Prize in Drama, Assoc Nigerian Authors, 85; Distinguished Martin Luther King/Ceasar Chavez/Rosa Parks Writer and Scholar, Wayne State Univ, 88 and 90. **RESEARCH** African cultural traditions; contemporary socio-political issues as they relate to rural and urban women. **SELECTED PUBLICATIONS** Auth, The Desert Encroaches; A Hen Too Soon; Ban Empty Barn; Mirror for Campus; The Reign of Wazobia; The Artist's Homecoming; Some Day Soon; Legacies; Go Tell It to Women; Riot in Heaven; scholarly articles on African drama, culture, and literature. **CONTACT ADDRESS** Dept of English, Univ of Wisconsin, Eau Claire, Hibbard Hall 416, PO Box 4004, Eau Claire, WI, 54702-4004. **EMAIL** onwuemto@uwec.edu

ORAVEC, CHRISTINE
DISCIPLINE COMMUNICATIONS **EDUCATION** Lawrence, BA, 71; Univ Wis at Madison, MA, 72, PhD, 79. **CAREER** Asst prof, to PROF, DEPT COMM, UNIV UTAH **MEMBERSHIPS** Am Antiquarian Soc **SELECTED PUBLICATIONS** Auth, "Conservatism vs. Preservationism in the Controversy over the Hetch Hetchy Dam," Quart Jour of Speech 70, 84; auth, "The Democratic Critics: An Alternative American Rhetorical Tradition of the Nineteenth Century," Rhetorica 4, 86; auth, "William Leggett: A Benthamite Rhetorical Critic," in Visions of Rhetoric: History, Theory, and Criticism, Rhetoric Soc Am, 87; coauth, "A Prairie Home Companion and the Fabrication of Community," CSMC 4, 87, repr in Rhetorical Dimensions in Media: A Critical Casebook, Kendall Hunt, 91; auth, "The Sublimation of Mass Consciousness in the Rhetorical Criticism of Jacksonian America," Comm 11, 90; auth, "To Stand Outside of Oneself: The Sublime in the Discourse of Natural Scenery," in The Symbolic Earth: Discourse and Our Creation of the Environment, Univ Press Ky, 96. **CONTACT ADDRESS** Dept of Comm, Univ of Utah, Salt Lake City, UT, 84112. **EMAIL** c.oravec@m.cc.utah.edu

ORCHARD, LEE F.
DISCIPLINE THEATRE ARTS **EDUCATION** Concordia Univ, BA, BE; Northwestern Univ, MA; Univ OR, PhD. **CAREER** Act pedag;assoc prof, 91-, Truman State Univ. **HONORS AND AWARDS** Adjudicator, Am Col Theatre Fest, 88. **RESEARCH** Performance pedag, directing, theatre and cult, musical theatre. **SELECTED PUBLICATIONS** Auth, Acting: Onstage and Off **CONTACT ADDRESS** Theatre Dept, Truman State Univ, 100 E Normal St, Kirksville, MO, 63501-4221.

OREL, HAROLD
PERSONAL Born 03/31/1926, Boston, MA, m, 1951, 2 children **DISCIPLINE** ENGLISH LANGUAGE AND LIT **EDUCATION** UNH, BA, 48; Univ Mich, MA, 49, PhD, 52. **CAREER** Instr, Univ MD, Col Pk, 52-56; Info Spec, GE, Evendale OH, 56-57; Assoc prof, Univ Kansas, 57-62, prof, 63-97, dist prof, 74-. **HONORS AND AWARDS** Orator Poets Corner West Minster Abbey, 78, 86; Am Comm on Irish stud, Pres, 70-72; Thomas Hardy Soc, Eng, VP, 68-; Royal Soc Lit, Eng, fel, 86-; Higuchi Res Achmt Awd, 90. **RESEARCH** 19th and 20th C, Brit and Am Lit. **SELECTED PUBLICATIONS** The Brontes: Interviews and Recollections, ed, London, Macmillan, Iowa, Univ Iowa press, 97; The Historical Novel from Scott to Sabatini, London, Macmillan, 95; Critical Essays on Thomas

Hardy's Poetry, ed, NY, G K Hall, 95; Critical Essays on Sir Arthur Conan Doyle, NY, G K Hall, 92; numerous other books and articles. **CONTACT ADDRESS** Dept English, Univ Kansas, Lawrence, KS, 66045-2115.

ORENSTEIN, GLORIA FEMAN
DISCIPLINE WOMEN AND MEN IN SOCIETY AND COMPARATIVE LITERATURE **EDUCATION** NY Univ, PhD. **CAREER** Assoc prof, Univ Southern Calif. **RESEARCH** Feminist Scholar on a Spiritual Quest. **SELECTED PUBLICATIONS** Auth, The Theater of the Marvelous: Surrealism and The Contemporary Stage; The Reflowering of the Goddess; Multi-Cultural Celebrations: Betty La Duke Paintings 1972-1992; co-ed, Reweaving The World: The Emergence of Ecofeminism. **CONTACT ADDRESS** Col Letters, Arts & Sciences, Univ Southern Calif, University Park Campus, Los Angeles, CA, 90089. **EMAIL** orenstei@usc.edu

ORIARD, MICHAEL
DISCIPLINE AMERICAN LITERATURE **EDUCATION** Univ Notre Dame, BA, 70; Stanford Univ, PhD, 76. **CAREER** Engl, Oregon St Univ. **SELECTED PUBLICATIONS** Auth, Dreaming of Heroes: American Sports Fiction, 1868-1980, Nelson-Hall, 82; The End of Autumn: Reflections on My Life in Football, Doubleday, 82; Sporting With the Gods: The Rhetoric of Play and Game in American Culture, Cambridge Univ Press, 91; Reading Football: How the Popular Press Created an American Spectacle, Univ N Carolina Press, 93. **CONTACT ADDRESS** Oregon State Univ, Corvallis, OR, 97331-4501. **EMAIL** moriard@orst.edu

ORLIK, PETER B.
PERSONAL Born 09/30/1944, Hancock, MI, m, 1967, 2 children **DISCIPLINE** MASS COMMUNICATION **EDUCATION** Wayne St Univ, BA, 65, MA, 66, PhD, 68. **CAREER** Coordr, Wayne St Univ, 66-69; founder, prog head to prior learning coordr & resident consultant to chair, Cent Mich Univ, 70- . **HONORS AND AWARDS** Bd of gov Scholar, Wayne St Univ, 62-65; Wayne St Univ Symphony Orchestra Scholar, 65; Acad Excellence Award, Wayne St Univ, 65; Univ Achievement Award, Cent Mich Univ, 74; Outstanding Young Men of Amer, 79; Who's Who, 80-99; Outstanding People of the twentieth Century, 99. **MEMBERSHIPS** Alpha Epsilon Rho/Nat Broadcasting Soc; Assoc for Educ in J & Mass Commun; Broadcast Educ Assoc; Nat Assoc of Television Prog Exec; Phi Kappa Phi Honor Soc. **RESEARCH** Media writing; criticism; hist & prog. **SELECTED PUBLICATIONS** Auth, The Electronic Media: An Introduction to the Profession, Allyn & Bacon, 92, Iowa St Univ Press, 97; Broadcast/Cable Copywriting, Allyn & Bacon, 78, 82, 86, 90, 94, 98; Electronic Media Criticism: Applied Perspectives, Focal Press, 94; Evolving a Cost-Effective Assessment Course, Feedback, 95; Two Hockey Inaugurals: A Ritual comparison of Senators and Ducks, Mid-Atlantic Almanack, 96. **CONTACT ADDRESS** 613 Kane St, Mt. Pleasant, MI, 48858. **EMAIL** Peter.B.Orlik@cmich.edu

ORR, BRIDGET
DISCIPLINE ENGLISH LITERATURE **EDUCATION** PhD. **CAREER** Instr, English, Fordham Univ; vis fel, Ctr for Cross-Cult Res, Australian Natl Univ, 98. **RESEARCH** 18th century Literature. **CONTACT ADDRESS** Dept of Education, Australian National Univ.

ORR, LEONARD
DISCIPLINE MODERN BRITISH AND AMERICAN LITERATURE **EDUCATION** Ohio State Univ, PhD. **CAREER** Assoc prof, Washington State Univ. **RESEARCH** Narrative theory; cultural semiotics, psychoanalytic criticism. **SELECTED PUBLICATIONS** Auth, Problems and Poetics of the Non-aristotelian Novel; Yeats and Postmodernism; The Dictionary of Critical Theory, 91 & Critical Essays on Samuel Taylor Coleridge, 92. **CONTACT ADDRESS** Dept of English, Washington State Univ, 1 SE Stadium Way, PO Box 645020, Pullman, WA, 99164-5020. **EMAIL** orr@beta.tricity.wsu.edu

ORR, MARILYN
DISCIPLINE ENGLISH LITERATURE **EDUCATION** Univ Ottawa, PhD. **RESEARCH** Early nineteenth century British novel; women's writing. **SELECTED PUBLICATIONS** Auth, Almost Under the Immediate Eye: Framing Displacement, 93; auth, The Return of the Different: Rereading in Scott and Calvino, Dalhousie Rev, 92; auth, Real and Narrative Time: Waverley and the Education of Memory, 91; auth, Repetition, Reversal, and the Gothic: The Pirate and St. Ronan's Well, 90. **CONTACT ADDRESS** English Dept, Laurentian Univ, 935 Ramsey Lake Rd, Sudbury, ON, P3E 2C6.

ORTIZ, RICARDO L.
DISCIPLINE ENGLISH LITERATURE **EDUCATION** UCLA, PhD, 92. **CAREER** Asst prof, Dartmouth Col. **RESEARCH** Lit theory and criticism. **SELECTED PUBLICATIONS** Auth, John Rechy and the Grammar of Ostentation in Cruising the Performative: Interventions into the Representation of Ethnicity, Nationality, and Sexuality, Ind UP, 95; Rechy,

Isherwood and the Numbers Game in El Poder Hispano: Actas del V Congreso de Culturas Hispanas de los Estados Unidos, Servisio de Publicaciones y Centro de Estudios Norteamericanos de la Universidad de Alcala, 94; Fielding's 'Orientalist' Moment: Historical Fiction and Historical Knowledge in Tom Jones, Studies Eng Lit 1500-00, 93. **CONTACT ADDRESS** Dartmouth Col, 3529 N Main St, #207, Hanover, NH, 03755.

OSBERG, RICHARD H.
PERSONAL Born 01/25/1947, Boston, MA, m, 1969, 1 child **DISCIPLINE** LITERATURE **EDUCATION** Dartmouth Col, BA, 69; MA, 70, PhD, 74, Claremont Graduate School **CAREER** Asst Prof, 78-82, Hamilton Col; Asst Prof, 82-88, Assoc Prof, 88-96, Prof and Chr, Dept of English, 96-, Santa Clara Univ. **MEMBERSHIPS** MLA; PAPC; MAA **RESEARCH** Chaucer; 14th century English literature; 19th and 20th century Medievalism **SELECTED PUBLICATIONS** Auth, A Voice for the Prioress: The Context of English Devotional Prose, Studies in the Age of Chaucer, 96; auth, The Poems of Laurence Minot, TEAMS Middle English Texts Series, 96; auth, The Prosody of Middle English Pearl and the Alliterative Lyric Tradition, English Historical Metrics, 96; auth, The Maimed King, the Wasteland, and the Vanished Grail in Iris Murdoch's The Green Knight, The Year's Work in Medievalism X, 98; auth, Humanist Allusions and Medieval Themes: the Receyving of Queen Anne, Medievalism in the Modern World: Essays in Honour of Leslie Workman, 98. **CONTACT ADDRESS** Dept of English, Santa Clara Univ, Santa Clara, CA, 95053. **EMAIL** rosberg@scu.edu

OSEGUERA, ANTHONY
PERSONAL Born 09/09/1939, Bingham Canyon, UT, m, 1994 **DISCIPLINE** COMMUNICATION **EDUCATION** Univ Missouri, BS, 70; St Louis Univ, MA, 73; Univ Missouri, Columbia, PhD, 76. **CAREER** Asst prof, 76-80, Valdosta St Univ, GA; prof, mass comm, 80-, E Illinios Univ. **HONORS AND AWARDS** Paul Harris Fel; NCA, La Raza Caucus & Div, Cert of Recognition; A Better Place, Outstanding Unite Way Film, Lowndes County GA, 79. **MEMBERSHIPS** NCA; SCAPR. **RESEARCH** Intl broadcasting; political communication; and media criticism. **SELECTED PUBLICATIONS** Art, The Theory, Research, and Practice of Communication in Spain, ERIC's RIE, 87; art, Nicaragua: Political-Economy as Communication and Media Influence, ERIC's RIE, 88; art, Internationalizing the College and University Campus: Four Paradigms, Intlng Curricula, IL St Univ Publ, 88; art, Internationalizing the US College and University Curricula through the International Mass Communication Minor, ERIC's RIE, 90; art, Historicity, The Television Critic, and the third World Scholar, ERIC's RIE, 91; art, Classical Theatre and the TV Critic, formerly: A Critical View of Television Through the Eyes of Classical Drama, ERIC's RIE, 91. **CONTACT ADDRESS** Eastern Illinois Univ, 114 E Coleman Hall, Charleston, IL, 61920. **EMAIL** cfaao@eiu.edu

OSINUBI, OLUMIDE
DISCIPLINE ENGLISH LITERATURE **EDUCATION** Univ Lancaster, PhD. **CAREER** Asst prof. **RESEARCH** Language and literature, dialectology, psycholinguistics, critical linguistics, and statistical linguistics. **SELECTED PUBLICATIONS** Auth, African American Writers and the Use of Dialect in Literature: The Foregrounding of Ethnicity, Jour Commonwealth and Postcolonial Studies, 96. **CONTACT ADDRESS** Clark Atlanta Univ, 223 James P Brawley Dr, SW, Atlanta, GA, 30314.

OSTER, JUDITH
DISCIPLINE COMPOSITION AND ENGLISH AS A SECOND LANGUAGE TEACHING **EDUCATION** Case Western Reserve Univ, BA, MA, PhD. **CAREER** English, Case Western Reserve Univ. **HONORS AND AWARDS** Dir, Writing Ctr. **SELECTED PUBLICATIONS** Auth or ed, Toward Robert Frost: The Reader and the Poet; From Reading to Writing: A Rhetoric and Reader. **CONTACT ADDRESS** Case Western Reserve Univ, 10900 Euclid Ave, Cleveland, OH, 44106.

OSTERMEIER, TERRY H.
PERSONAL Born 04/15/1937, New London, WI, m, 1964, 2 children **DISCIPLINE** COMMUNICATION **EDUCATION** Wis State Univ, BS, 59; Marquette Univ, MA, 61; Mich State Univ, PhD, 66. **CAREER** Instr, State Univ of NY, 63-66; Commun Dept ch, Univ of Wis Whitewater, 68-88; from asst prof to assoc prof, Univ of Wis Whitewater, 68- . **HONORS AND AWARDS** Kappa Delta Phi, 59; Disting. Alumnus Award Pi Kappa Delta, 73; Phi Kappa Phi, 83; Wis Col Tchr of the Year, 95; Dean's Col Award, 97; Outstanding Col Res Award, 98. **MEMBERSHIPS** Int Listening Asn; World Commun Asn; Int Asn for Intercult Commun Studies; Nat Commun Asn; Wis Commun Asn; Central States Commun Asn. **RESEARCH** Intercult listening; Nonverbal commun; Intercult commun. **SELECTED PUBLICATIONS** Auth, Sprechnormen - Internationale Vergleiche, Sprechkultur im Medienzeitalter, ed Freyr Varwig, 86; Auditory Illusions and Confusions, Experimental Listening: Tools for Teachers and Trainers, ed C. Coakley and A. Wolvin, 89; Perceptions of Cultural Values and Communicating Interculturally: A Simulation Experience, World Commun, vol 18, 89; Auditory Illusions and Confusions: Impact on

Listening, Int Listening Jour, vol 3, 89; To Communicate in a Culturally Diverse World: A Curricular Approach to Gain Competency for the 1990s, Jour of the Wis Commun Asn, vol XXII, 91; Fast Talkers and Speeding Listeners: Television/ Radio Commercials, Int Listening Jour, vol 5, 91; Listening as a Theme of a Corporation Annual report, Jour of the Wis Commun Asn, vol XXIV, 93; Perception of Nonverbal Cues in Dialogic Listening in an Intercult Interview, Int Listening Jour, spec issue, 93; Meaning Differences for Nonverbal Cues: Easier or More Difficult for the Intercult Listener, Intercult Commun Studies, vol V:1, 95; A Short History of Speech at a Wisconsin Public University: The First 65 Years, Jour of the Wis Commun Asn, vol XXIX, 98. **CONTACT ADDRESS** 11258 E. State Rd 59, Whitewater, WI, 53190-3320. **EMAIL** Ostermet@uwwvax.uww.edu

OSTOVICH, HELEN
DISCIPLINE ENGLISH LITERATURE **EDUCATION** Univ Toronto, BA, MA, PhD. **RESEARCH** Renaissance drama; eighteenth century novel; detective fiction. **SELECTED PUBLICATIONS** Auth, Ben Jonson: Four Comedies. **CONTACT ADDRESS** English Dept, McMaster Univ, 1280 Main St W, Hamilton, ON, L8S 4L9.

OSTRIKER, ALICIA
DISCIPLINE ENGLISH LANGUAGE AND LITERATURE **EDUCATION** Brandeis, BA; Univ Wis, PhD. **CAREER** Prof Eng, Ctr for the Stud of Jewish Life, Rutgers, The State Univ NJ, Univ Col-Camden. **RESEARCH** Poetry; feminism; religion. **SELECTED PUBLICATIONS** Auth, Stealing the Language: the Emergence of Women's Poetry in America; The Nakedness of the Fathers: Biblical Visions and Revisions; The Mother/Child Papers; The Imaginary Lover; Green Age, The Crack in Everything. **CONTACT ADDRESS** Dept of Lit in Eng, Rutgers, The State Univ New Jersey, Univ Col-Camde, Murray Hall 203B, New Brunswick, NJ, 08903. **EMAIL** ostriker@rci.rutgers.edu

OSTROM, HANS
DISCIPLINE ENGLISH AND AMERICAN LITERATURE **EDUCATION** Univ Calif, Davis, BA, 75; Univ Calif, Davis, MA, 79; Univ Calif, Davis, PhD, 82. **CAREER** Instr, Univ Calif, Davis, 77-80 & 81-83; vis lectr, Johannes Gutenberg Univ, Ger, 80-81; instr, Univ Puget Sound, 83-; Fulbright sr lectr, Uppsala Univ, Sweden, 94. **HONORS AND AWARDS** Martin Nelson sabbatical fel, 78; Burlington Northern Fac Achievement Award, Univ Puget Sound, 86 & 89; Alumni Asn's Citation for Excellence, Univ Calif, Davis, 89; John Lantz fel, Univ Puget Sound, 96-97. **MEMBERSHIPS** Am Asn of Univ Prof; Conf on Col Compos and Commun; MLA; Nat Book Critics Circle; Nat Coun Tchr Eng; Alumni Asn, Univ of Calif, Davis. **SELECTED PUBLICATIONS** Auth, William Everson's Earth Poetry and the Progress Toward Feminism, in Essays in Honor of William Everson, Castle Peak Ed, 93; Langston Hughes: A Study of the Short Fiction, Twayne/Macmillan, 93; coauth, Water's Night: Poetry Chapbook, Mariposite Press, 94; coed, Colors of a Different Horse, Nat Counc Tchr Eng, 94. **CONTACT ADDRESS** Dept of Eng, Univ Puget Sound, 1500 North Warner, Tacoma, WA, 98416. **EMAIL** ostrom@ups.edu

OSTROWSKI, CARL
DISCIPLINE ENGLISH **EDUCATION** Wayne State Univ, BA, 90; Univ Tenn, MA, 92; Univ SC, PhD, 97. **CAREER** Teach assoc, 91, teach asst, 91-92, Univ Tenn; adj instr, Midlands Tech Col, 96-97; teach asst, Univ SC, 93-97; ASST PROF, CAMERON UNIV, 97-. **CONTACT ADDRESS** Dept of English, Cameron Univ, Lawton, OK, 73505. **EMAIL** carlo@cameron.edu

OTT, BRIAN L.
PERSONAL Born 03/22/1969, Erie, PA **DISCIPLINE** SPEECH COMMUNICATION **EDUCATION** PA State Univ, PhD, 97. **CAREER** Asst prof of Media Studies, CO State Univ, 98-. **HONORS AND AWARDS** Col of Liberal Arts Outstanding Teaching Award, PA State, 96. **MEMBERSHIPS** Nat Commun Asn; Int Commun Asn. **RESEARCH** Critical media studies; television criticism; cultural studies. **SELECTED PUBLICATIONS** Auth, Memorializing the Holocaust: Schindler's List and Public Memory, The Rev of Ed/Pedagogy/ Cultural Studies, 18, 96. **CONTACT ADDRESS** Dept of Speech Commun, Colorado State Univ, 202 Eddy Hall, Fort Collins, CO, 80523. **EMAIL** Bott@vines.colostate.edu

OTTEN, TERRY RALPH
PERSONAL Born 04/15/1938, Dayton, KY, m, 1960, 2 children **DISCIPLINE** ENGLISH **EDUCATION** Geoergetown Coll, BA, 59; Univ KY, MA, 61; Ohio Univ, PhD, 66; Georgetown Coll, DLTT, 97. **CAREER** Instr, Western KY State Univ, 61-63; instr, Ohio Univ, 65-66; PROF, WITTENBERG UNIV, 66-. **MEMBERSHIPS** Mod Lang Asn; Midwest MLA; Toni Morrison Soc; Arthur Miller Soc; Wordsworth and His Circle; North Am Soc Study Romanticism. **SELECTED PUBLICATIONS** "Arthur Miller and the Temptation of Innocence," The Achievement of Arthur Miller, Contemp Res Press, 95; "Morrison on Morrison," Modern Lang Asn, 97; Transfiguring the Narrative-Beloved from Slave Narrative to Tragedy," Critical

Essays on Toni Morrison's Beloved, GK Hall, 98; "Tar Baby and the Fall Myth," in Toni Morrison: Contemporary Critical Essays, MacMillan, 98; "Historical Drama and the Dimensions of Tragedy: A Man for All Seasons and The Crucible," Am Drama, 96. **CONTACT ADDRESS** Eng Dept, Wittenberg Univ, Springfield, OH, 45501. **EMAIL** totten@wittenberg.edu

OTTENHOFF, JOHN
DISCIPLINE RHETORIC, LINGUISTICS AND BRITISH LITERATURE **EDUCATION** Univ Chicago, PhD. **CAREER** Prof, adv, Sigma Tau Delta, Alma Col. **HONORS AND AWARDS** Outstanding Fac Mem in Hum Award. **RESEARCH** Shakespeare; Shakespeare on film. **SELECTED PUBLICATIONS** Publications in his specialty, Renaissance devotional poetry. **CONTACT ADDRESS** Alma Col, Alma, MI, 48801.

OTTER, MONIKA
DISCIPLINE ENGLISH LITERATURE **EDUCATION** Columbia Univ, PhD, 91. **CAREER** Assoc prof, Dartmouth Col. **RESEARCH** Brit and Medieval lit. **SELECTED PUBLICATIONS** Auth, Inventiones: Fiction and Referentiality in Twelfth-Century English Historical Writing, NC UP, 96; New Werke: St. Erkenwald, St. Albans, and the Medieval Sense of the Past, Jour Med and Ren Studies, 94. **CONTACT ADDRESS** Dartmouth Col, 3529 N Main St, #207, Hanover, NH, 03755.

OWER, JOHN
PERSONAL Born 01/17/1942, Palmerston North, New Zealand, m, 1986, 2 children **DISCIPLINE** ENGLISH **EDUCATION** Univ Alberta, BA, 63, MA, 66, PhD, 72. **CAREER** Asst Prof, Univ Tenn, 70-72; Lecturer, Univ Waikato, 72-73; Asst Prof, Univ SC, 73-78; Assoc Prof, Univ SC, 78-96; ret, 96. **HONORS AND AWARDS** Woodrow Wilson Fellow; Canada Counc Post-Doctoral Res Fellow; SC Arts Commision Individual Artist Fellow; Winthrop Col Award for Excellence in Writing in Poetry; Univ of SC Eng Dept Tchng Award. **RESEARCH** Romantic poetry; modernist literature; science fiction; Canadian literature. **SELECTED PUBLICATIONS** Auth, Edith Sitwell: Metaphysical Medium and Metaphysical Message, 20th Cent Lit, 16:4, 253-267, 10/70; auth, Sociology, Psychology, and Satire in The Apprenticeship of Duddy Kravitz, Mod Fiction Stud, 22:3, 413-428, 76; auth, The Aesthetic Hero: His Innocence, Fall, and Redemption, Bucknell Rev, 23:2, 96-115, 77; auth, Legendary Acts, Univ Ga Press, 77; auth, The Death-Fires, the Fire-Flags, and the Corposant in The Rime of the Ancient Mariner, Philol Quart, 70:2, 199-218, 91. **CONTACT ADDRESS** 142 Stafford Dr, Athens, GA, 30605-3718.

OWOMOYELA, OYEKAN
PERSONAL Born 04/22/1938, Ifon, Nigeria, m, 1975 **DISCIPLINE** AFRICAN LITERATURE **EDUCATION** Univ London, BA, 63; Univ Calif, Los Angeles, MFA, 66, PhD(theater hist), 70. **CAREER** Lectr audio visuals, Univ Ibadan, Nigeria, 68-71; asst prof, 72-75, assoc prof, 75-81, Prof Lit & Drama, Univ Nebr- Lincoln, 81-, Sr consult, Ctr Mgt Develop, Nigerian, 75. **MEMBERSHIPS** African Studies Asn; African Lit Asn; Am Folklore Soc. **RESEARCH** Sociology of African literature; Yoruba folklore and society. **SELECTED PUBLICATIONS** Auth, Folklore and Yoruba theater, Res in African Lit, fall 71; The Sociology of sex and crudity in Yorbua Proverbs, Proverbium: Bull d'information sur les recherches paremiologiques, 20: 751-758; coauth (with Bernth Lindfors), Yoruba Proverbs: Translations and Annotations, Ohio Univ Ctr Int Studies, 73; auth, Western humanism and African usage: A critical survey of non-African responses to African literature, Issue: A Quart J Opinion IV, winter 74; African Literatures: An Introduction, Crossroads Press, 79; Obotunde Ijimere, the phantom of Nigerian theater, 79 & Dissidence and the African writer: Commitment or dependency, 381, Studies Rev; The pragmatic humanism of Yoruba culture, J African Studies, fall 81; an Enchanting Darkness - The American Vision of Africa in The 20th-century - Hickey,d, Wylie,kc, African American Review, Vol 0029, 1995; African Philosophy in Search of Identity - Masolo,da, Research in African Literatures, Vol 0027, 1996; The Hermeneutics of African Philosophy - Horizon And Discourse - Serequeberhan,t, Research in African Literatures, Vol 0027, 1996; The Idea of Africa - Mudimbe,vy, Research in African Literatures, Vol 0027, 1996; The Wisdom of Many - Essays of The Proverb - Mieder,w, Dundes,a, Research in African Literatures, Vol 0027, 1996. **CONTACT ADDRESS** Dept of English, Univ Nebr, P O Box 880333, Lincoln, NE, 68588-0333.

OZSVATH, ZSUZSANNA
DISCIPLINE LITERATURE STUDIES **EDUCATION** Univ Tex, PhD, 68. **CAREER** Assoc prof. **RESEARCH** 19th and 20th century European literature and history; Holocaust studies. **SELECTED PUBLICATIONS** Coauth, Foamy Sky: The Major Poems of Miklos Radnoti, Princeton, 92; pubs in Partisan Review, Poetry, The Webster Rev, Judaism, The Canadian-American Rev of Hungarian Studies, Lit Rev, Ger Studies Rev, Res Studies. **CONTACT ADDRESS** Dept of Literature, Richardson, TX, 75083-0688. **EMAIL** zozsvath@utdallas.edu

P

PADDEN, CAROL
DISCIPLINE COMMUNICATIONS **EDUCATION** Univ Calif, San Diego, PhD, Ling, 83. **CAREER** ASSOC PROF, COMMUN, UNIV CALIF, SAN DIEGO. **RESEARCH** Symbolic develop in young children; Interplay of child develop and cult inst. **SELECTED PUBLICATIONS** Co-auth, Deaf in America: Voices from a Culture, Harvard, 88; auth, "Lessons To Be Learned from Young Deaf Orthographers," Ling and Edu, Vol 5, 93; "Folk Explanation in Language Survival," Collective Remembering, Sage, 90. **CONTACT ADDRESS** Dept of Commun, Univ Calif, San Diego, 9500 Gilman Dr, La Jolla, CA, 92093. **EMAIL** cpadden@weber.ucsd.edu

PADDON, ANNA R.
DISCIPLINE COMMUNICATIONS **EDUCATION** Wheaton Col, BA, 91; Columbia Univ, MS, 63; Univ Tenn, PhD, 85. **CAREER** Instr, Univ Tenn, 73-88; head journ dept, Benedict Col, 85- 88; PROF, SOUTHERN ILL UNIV, 88-. **CONTACT ADDRESS** Sch Journalism, So Illinois Univ, 102-C North Violet Ln, Carbondale, IL, 62901-1943. **EMAIL** paddona@siu.edu

PADOVANO, ANTHONY T.
PERSONAL Born 09/18/1934, Harrison, NJ **DISCIPLINE** THEOLOGY, LITERATURE **EDUCATION** Seton Hall Univ, AB, 56; Gregorian Univ, STD(theol), 62; Pontiff Univ St Thomas Aquinas, PhL, 62; NY Univ, MA, 71; Fordham Univ, PhD, 80. **CAREER** Prof syst theol, Darlington Sem, 62-74; Prof AM Lit & Relig Studies, Ramapo Col, 71-, Consultor, Nat Cath Off Radio & TV, 67; vis prof, Villanova Univ, 68, St Mary's Col, Ind, 69, Univ St Thomas, 69, Univ Wyo, 70, Barry Col, Fla, 71, Seattle Univ, 72, Fordham Univ, 73, Univ San Francisco, 73, Boston Col, 73, Assumption Col, Worcester, Mass 73 & Georgetown Univ, Washington, DC, 73; prof, Ramapo Col, NJ, 71-; rep US dialogue group, Lutheran-Roman Cath Theol Conversations, 70-72. **HONORS AND AWARDS** Nat Cath Press Asn Bk Award, 70. **MEMBERSHIPS** Cath Theol Soc Am. **RESEARCH** Systematic theology; American literature; contemporary philosophy. **SELECTED PUBLICATIONS** Auth, Dawn Without Darkness, 71, Free to be Faithful, 72 & Eden & Easter, 74, Paulist Press; A Case for Worship, Silver Burdett, 75; America, Its People, Its Promise, St Anthony Messenger Press, 75; Presence and Structure, Paulist Press, 75; The Human Journey, 82 & Trilogy, 82, Doubleday; Ace of Freedoms - Merton,thomas Christ - Kilcourse,g, Horizons, Vol 0021, 1994. **CONTACT ADDRESS** 9 Millstone Dr, Morris Plains, NJ, 07950.

PAGE, JUDITH W.
PERSONAL New Orleans, LA **DISCIPLINE** ENGLISH **EDUCATION** Newcomb Col; Univ Chicago, PhD. **CAREER** Teaches in Engl dept & assoc dean, div arts and letters. **HONORS AND AWARDS** 2 NEH grants. **SELECTED PUBLICATIONS** Auth, Wordsworth and the Cultivation of Women, Univ Calif Press, 94. **CONTACT ADDRESS** Dept of English, Millsaps Col, 1701 N State St, Jackson, MS, 39210.

PAGEN, MICHELE A.
PERSONAL Born 05/02/1968, Uniontown, PA, s **DISCIPLINE** THEATRE **EDUCATION** Calif Univ of Pa, BA, Theatre, 5/90, MA, 8/91; Bowling Green State Univ, Dr of Philos in Theatre, 9/94. **CAREER** Asst prof of theatre, Univ of Findlay, 94-95; asst prof of theatre, Calif Univ of Pa, 95-; admin dir, Cal Rep Pa, 96-. **HONORS AND AWARDS** Grad res grant, 94; Outstanding Young Alumni, Calif Univ of Pa, 95; Irene O'Brien Res Grant, 98., Alpha Psi Omega, Nat Theatre Honorary, 90. **MEMBERSHIPS** Nat Commun Assoc (secy, theatre div); Assoc for Theatre in Higher Educ; Am Col Theatre Fest; East Coast Theatre Conf; Theatre Commun Grp. **RESEARCH** Pedagogy in higher education. **SELECTED PUBLICATIONS** Auth, Life as a Performer: Ethnographic Qualities in the Performance of Self, ERIC Higher Educ Doc ED 368 030, 10/94. **CONTACT ADDRESS** Theatre Dept, California Univ of Pennsylvania, 250 Univ Dr, California, PA, 15419. **EMAIL** pagen@cup.edu

PAGLIA, CAMILLE
PERSONAL Born 04/02/1947, Endicott, NY **DISCIPLINE** ENGLISH **EDUCATION** SUNY, Binghamton, BA, 68; Yale Univ, MA, 71, PhD, 74. **CAREER** Dept Lib Arts, Univ of the Arts **HONORS AND AWARDS** Fac, Bennington Col, 72-80; Vis Lecturer, Wesleyan Univ, 80; Yale Univ, 80-84; Univ of the AArts, Asst Prof, Hum, 84-87, Assoc Prof, 87-91, Prof, 91. **SELECTED PUBLICATIONS** Auth, Sexual Personae: Art and Decadence from Nefertiti to Emily Dickinson, Yale Univ Press, 90; auth, Sex Art, and America Culture, Vintage Books, 92; auth, Vamps and Tramps: New Essays, Vintage Books, 94; auth, Alfred Hitchcock's The Birds, Brit Film Inst, 98. **CONTACT ADDRESS** Dept of Liberal Arts, Univ of the Arts, 320 S Broad St, Philadelphia, PA, 19102.

PAHL, DENNIS A.
DISCIPLINE NINETEENTH- AND TWENTIETH-CENTURY AMERICAN LITERATURE, CRITICAL THEORY **EDUCATION** SUNY, Buffalo, PhD. **CAREER** Assoc prof, Long Island Univ, C.W. Post Campus. **SELECTED PUBLICATIONS** Auth, Architects of the Abyss: The Indeterminate Fictions of Poe, Hawthorne, and Melville; Poe/Script: The Death of the Author in The Narrative of Arthur Gordon Pym; Rediscovering Byron: Poe's The Assignation; Flaming Poe: Fictions of Self and Self-Containment; Godard's Alphaville: A Journey through Film Space. **CONTACT ADDRESS** Long Island Univ, C.W. Post, Brookville, NY, 11548-1300.

PALMER, BARTON
DISCIPLINE ENGLISH LITERATURE **EDUCATION** NY Univ, PhD, 89. **CAREER** Dept Eng, Clemson Univ **RESEARCH** Medieval literature; film studies. **SELECTED PUBLICATIONS** Auth, Hollywood's Dark Cinema: The American Film Noir, Twayne, 94; Perspectives on Film Noir, G.K. Hall, 95; trans, Guiollaume de Machaut: Comfort d'ami, Garland, 92; co-trans and ed, Guiollaume de Machaut: Le Livre dou Voir Dit, Garlan, 92. **CONTACT ADDRESS** Clemson Univ, 802 Strode, Clemson, SC, 29634. **EMAIL** ppalmer@clemson.edu

PALMER, WILLIAM
DISCIPLINE RHETORIC, CREATIVE WRITING **EDUCATION** Mich State Univ, PhD. **CAREER** Prof, Alma Col. **HONORS AND AWARDS** Charles A Dana Prof Eng, 93. **SELECTED PUBLICATIONS** Published essays and poetry in Eng J, Col Compos and Commun and Detroit Free Press Mag. **CONTACT ADDRESS** Alma Col, Alma, MI, 48801.

PALMERI, FRANK
PERSONAL Born 08/06/1952, Denver, CO, m, 1990 **DISCIPLINE** ENGLISH **EDUCATION** Columbia Univ, BA, 74, MA, 75, PhD, 81. **CAREER** Vis asst prof, 82-83, Univ of Anhim, People's Rep of China; instr, adj asst prof, 83-84, Univ Denver, CO; asst prof, 84-90, assoc prof, 90-, Univ Miami. **RESEARCH** 18th & 19th century narrative; comparative lit. **CONTACT ADDRESS** Dept of English, Univ of Miami, Coral Gables, FL, 33124. **EMAIL** fpalmeri@miami.edu

PALMQUIST, MIKE
DISCIPLINE ENGLISH LITERATURE **EDUCATION** St Olaf Col, BA; Carnegie Mellon Univ, PhD. **CAREER** Assoc prof. **RESEARCH** Writing across the curriculum; the effects of computer and network technologies on writing instruction; the use of hypertext, hypermedia in instructional settings. **SELECTED PUBLICATIONS** Auth, pubs in Computers and Compositions; Written Communication; IEEE Transaction on Professional Communication; Engineering Education. **CONTACT ADDRESS** Dept of English, Colorado State Univ, Fort Collins, CO, 80523. **EMAIL** mpalmquist@vines.colostate.edu

PAPPANO, MARGARET
DISCIPLINE LATE MEDIEVAL ENGLISH LITERATURE **EDUCATION** Dartmouth Col, AB, 87; Sussex Univ, MA, 89; Columbia Univ, MA, 90; Columbia Univ, PhD, 98. **CAREER** English and Lit, Columbia Univ **SELECTED PUBLICATIONS** Auth, The Priest's Body: Literature and Popular Piety in Late Medieval England. **CONTACT ADDRESS** Columbia Univ, 2960 Broadway, New York, NY, 10027-6902.

PARINS, JAMES
DISCIPLINE NINETEENTH-CENTURY BRITISH STUDIES **EDUCATION** Univ Wisc, PhD. **CAREER** English and Lit, Univ Ark **SELECTED PUBLICATIONS** Auth, John Rolling Ridge; William Barnes; The British Colonial Press of the Eighteenth and Nineteenth Centuries, Victorian Periodicals Rev; Coauth, American Native and Alaska Native Newspapers and Periodicals, 1826-1985. **CONTACT ADDRESS** Univ Ark Little Rock, 2801 S University Ave., Little Rock, AR, 72204-1099. **EMAIL** remurphy@ualr.edu

PARINS, MARYLYN
DISCIPLINE ARTHURIAN LITERATURE **EDUCATION** Univ Mich, PhD. **CAREER** English and Lit, Univ Ark **SELECTED PUBLICATIONS** Auth, Malory: The critical heritage; Looking for Arthur: Theories of origin and historicity; King Arthur; Scholarship, Modern Arthurian, The New Arthurian Encyclopedia; Malory's Expurgations, Arthurian Tradition: Essays in Convergence. **CONTACT ADDRESS** Univ Ark Little Rock, 2801 S University Ave., Little Rock, AR, 72204-1099. **EMAIL** mjparins@ualr.edu

PARIS, BERNARD J.
PERSONAL Born 08/19/1931, Baltimore, MD, m, 1949, 2 children **DISCIPLINE** ENGLISH **EDUCATION** Johns Jopkins Univ, BA, 52; PhD, 59. **CAREER** Instr, Lehigh Univ, 56-60; asst, assoc and prof, Michigan State Univ, 60-81; prof, Univ Fl, 81-96; dir, Inst for Psychol Study of the Arts, 85-92; prof emer, 96- . **HONORS AND AWARDS** Phi Beta Kappa, 52; fel, NEH, 69-70; fel, Guggenheim Found, 74-75. **MEMBERSHIPS** MLA; Asn for Advanc of Psychoanalysis; Am Acad of Psychoanalysis; Int Karen Horney Soc. **RESEARCH** Litera-

ture and psychology; fiction; Shakespeare; Karen Horney; history of psychoanalysis. **SELECTED PUBLICATIONS** Auth, Experiments in Life: George Eliot's Quest for Values, Wayne State Univ, 65; auth, A Psychological Approach to Fiction: Studies in Thackeray, Stendhal, George Eliot, Dostoevsky, and Conrad, Indiana, 74; auth, Character and Conflict in Jane Austen's Novels: A Psychological Approach, Wayne State, 78; auth, Bargains with Fate: Psychological Crises and Conflicts in Shakespeare and His Plays, Plenum, 91; auth, Character as a Subversive Force in Shakespeare: The History and the Roman Plays, Fairleigh Dickinson, 91; auth, Karen Horney: A Psychoanalyst's Search for Self-Understanding, Yale, 94; auth, Imagined Human Beings: A Psychological Approach to Character and Conflict in Literature, NY Univ, 97; ed, Karen Horney: The Therapeutic Process, Yale, 99. **CONTACT ADDRESS** 1430 NW 94th St, Gainsville, FL, 32606. **EMAIL** bjparis@ufl.edu

PARISI, BARBARA
PERSONAL Born 03/31/1954, Brooklyn, NY, m, 1995 **DISCIPLINE** THEATER PERFORMANCE STUDIES **EDUCATION** New York Univ, PhD 91. **CAREER** Long Island Univ Bklyn, ch, speech and theater. **HONORS AND AWARDS** Shubert Archive Fel. **MEMBERSHIPS** NYSSCA; NCA; ATHE; Art NY. **RESEARCH** Women's History; Feminist Theater. **SELECTED PUBLICATIONS** Auth, Empowerment Through Communication, Kendall Hunt, Culture Inst of Brooklyn, BAM BCBD St Ann's as Performing Arts Culture Inst, Scarecrow Press. **CONTACT ADDRESS** Long Island Univ, 35 Brighton 8th Pl, Brooklyn, NY, 11235-6366.

PARISI, PETER
DISCIPLINE JOURNALISTIC WRITING AND PRESS CRITICISM, THEORY AND HISTORY **EDUCATION** Ind Univ, PhD, 74. **CAREER** Fac, Penn State Harrisburg, CW Post Campus of Long Island Univ & Hunter univ; taught Engl comp & lit at, Bucknell Univ and Rutgers Univ; 6 yrs, reporter, reviewer & ed; past ed, division's newsl, 2 yrs. **RESEARCH** Language and ideology in the press and the problem of expanding the scope of journalistic discourse. **SELECTED PUBLICATIONS** Publ on, journalism & popular culture; in, J Popular Cult, Jour Educator, Chronicle Higher Educ, Col Engl & Urban Geog; ed, Artist of the Actual: Essays on Paul Goodman, Scarecrow Press, 86. **CONTACT ADDRESS** Dept of Film and Media Studies, Hunter Col, CUNY, 695 Park Ave, New York, NY, 10021.

PARK-FULLER, LINDA M.
PERSONAL Born 08/18/1948, Minot, ND, m, 1975 **DISCIPLINE** SPEECH; THEATRE **EDUCATION** Univ of Ndak, BA, 70; Univ of Mo, MA, 71; Univ of Tex, PhD, 80. **CAREER** Instr, St Cloud State Univ, 71-81; prof, Mo State Univ, 81- . **HONORS AND AWARDS** Phi Beta Kappa; Phi Kappa Phi. **MEMBERSHIPS** Nat Commun Asn; Asn for Theatre in Higher Educ; Speech and Theatre Asn of Mo; Nat Wellness Asn. **RESEARCH** Performance Studies; Interactive Theatre; Theatre and Social and Health Issues; Playback Theatre, Narrative lit in performance. **SELECTED PUBLICATIONS** Auth, Understanding What We Know: A Production Record of Tillie Olsen's Yonnondio: From the Thirties, Lit in Performance, 4, 83; Between the Reflection and the Act: A Response to Mary S. Strine's essay, Between Meaning and Representation: Dialogical Aspects of Interpretation Scholarship, Renewal and Revision: The Future of Interpretation, ed Ted Colson, 86; Voices: Bakhtin's Heteroglossia and Polyphony, and the Performance of Narrative Literature, Lit in Performance, 7, 86; Performance as Praxis: The Intercollegiate Performance Festival, Text and Performance Quart, 14, 94; Narration and Narratization in a Cancer Story: Composing and Performing A Clean Breast of It, Text and Performance Quart, 15, 95; Towards and Interdisciplinary Performance Course: Process and Politics, forthcom. in Performance Studies in the Next Millenium, ed Sheron Dailey; Improvising Disciplines: Performance Studies and Theatre, forthcom. in Teaching Performance Studies, eds N. Stucky and C. Wimmer; Re-Valuing the Oral Tradition in Higher Education: Playback Theatre in the Academy, forthcom. in the Proceedings of the First Int Symposium on Playback Theatre, eds H. Dauber and J. Fox; ed, A Bibliography of Studies in Interpretation: 1979-1985, Lit in Performance, 7, 87; coauth, Minding the Stops: Performance and Affective Stylistics, Text and Performance Quart, 10, 90; Charting Alternative Performance and Evaluative Practices, Commun Educ, 44, 95. **CONTACT ADDRESS** Dept of Theatre and Dance, SW Missouri State Univ, Springfield, MO, 65804. **EMAIL** 1pf236f@mail.smsu.edu

PARKER, DOUGLAS
DISCIPLINE ENGLISH LITERATURE **EDUCATION** Univ Birmingham, PhD. **RESEARCH** Renaissance drama; Reformation lit; children's lit. **SELECTED PUBLICATIONS** Auth, From Reading to Writing: A Reader, Rhetoric and Handbook, 89;auth, The Third Suitor in King Lear, English Studies, 91; art, Bilingual Students: A Challenge for Canadian Universities, Can Modern Lang Rev, 87; art, Common Concerns in Marian Engel's Children's Stories and her Adult Fiction, Can Children's Lit, 86; co-auth, Rede me and be nott wrothe 1528, 92. **CONTACT ADDRESS** English Dept, Laurentian Univ, 935 Ramsey Lake Rd, Sudbury, ON, P3E 2C6.

PARKER, JO ALYSON
DISCIPLINE EIGHTEENTH-CENTURY NOVEL **EDUCATION** Univ CA, BA, 81; MA, 84; PhD, 89. **CAREER** Engl, St. Joseph's Univ. **SELECTED PUBLICATIONS** Auth, Complicating a Simple Story: Inchbald's Two Versions of Female Power, Eighteenth-Century Studies 30, 97; Spiraling Down 'the Gutter of Time': Tristram Shandy and the Strange Attractor of Death, Weber Studies 14, 97; Strange Attractors in Absalom, Absalom!" in Reading Matters: Narrative in the New Media Ecology, Cornell Univ Press, 97; Gendering the Robot: Stanislaw Lem's 'The Mask,' Science-Fiction Studies 19, 92. **CONTACT ADDRESS** St Joseph's Univ, 5600 City Ave, Philadelphia, PA, 19131. **EMAIL** jparker@sju.edu

PARKER, PATRICIA L.
DISCIPLINE ENGLISH **EDUCATION** Western Maryland Col, BA, 63; Univ Chicago, MA, 64; New York Univ, PhD, 81. **CAREER** Visiting Lectr, Osaka Jogakuin, Japan, 86-87; Visiting Lectr, Hiroshima Shudo Univ, Japan, 91-92 and 93-94; Asst Prof, 73-82, Assoc Prof, 82-88, Prof, 88-, Salem State Col. **SELECTED PUBLICATIONS** Auth, Inescapable Romance, a Study of Romance from Ariosto to Wallace Stevens; Literary Fat Ladies: Rhetoric, Gender, Property; Shakespeare from the Margins; co-ed, Shakespeare and the Question of Theory and Women; Race and Writing in the Early Modern Period. **CONTACT ADDRESS** English Dept, Salem State Col, Salem, MA, 01970. **EMAIL** pparker@salem.mass.edu

PARKER, STEPHEN JAN
PERSONAL Born 08/05/1939, Brooklyn, NY, m, 1965, 2 children **DISCIPLINE** RUSSIAN & COMPARATIVE LITERATURE **EDUCATION** Cornell Univ, BA, 60, MA, 62, PhD (Russ & comp lit), 69. **CAREER** Asst prof Russ, Univ Okla, 66-67; asst prof, 67-73, Assoc Prof Russ, Univ Kans, 73-, Assoc Chmn & Dir Grad Studies, 78-; mem nat selection comt, Coun Int Educ Exchange, Russ Lang Prof, 77; ed, The Nabokovian, 78-. **HONORS AND AWARDS** Nat Endowment for Humanities younger humanist fel, 70-71. **MEMBERSHIPS** MLA; Am Asn Advan Slavic Lang; Am Asn Teachers Slavic & East Europ Lang; Vladimir Nabokov Soc. **RESEARCH** Russian prose fiction of the 19th and 20th centuries; Europan and American modern novel; writings of Vladimir Nabokov. **SELECTED PUBLICATIONS** Coauth, Russia on Canvas: Ily a Repin, Pa State Univ Press, 81; co-ed, The Achievements of Vladimir Nabokov, Cornell Univ, 85; auth, Understanding Vladimir Nabokov, 89; author of numerous articles and reviews. **CONTACT ADDRESS** Dept of Slavic Lang & Lit, Univ of Kans, Lawrence, KS, 66045-0001. **EMAIL** sjparker@kuhub.cc.ukans.edu

PARKS, SHERI L.
DISCIPLINE COMMUNICATION **EDUCATION** Univ NC-Chapel Hill, BA, 78; Univ MA-Amherst, MA, 83, PhD, 85. **CAREER** Assoc dean in undergrad stud. **RESEARCH** Am aesthetics. **SELECTED PUBLICATIONS** Auth, Feminism in the Lives of Ordinary Women, Barnard Col Papers, 90; In My Mother's House: Traditional Black Feminism in the PBS Production Underlying 'A Raisin in the Sun, Feminism and Theater, Fairleigh Dickinson UP, 94. **CONTACT ADDRESS** Am Stud Dept, Univ MD, Col Park, College Park, MD, 20742. **EMAIL** sp10@umail.umd.edu

PARKS, STEPHEN ROBERT
PERSONAL Born 07/18/1940, Columbus, OH **DISCIPLINE** ENGLISH LITERATURE, BIBLIOGRAPHY **EDUCATION** Yale, BA, 61; Cambridge, England (King's Col), PhD, 65. **CAREER** Assoc curator, then curator, James M and Marie Louise Osborn Collection, Beinecke Rare Book and Manuscript Library, Yale Univ, 67-; librarian, Elizabethan Club of Yale Univ, 72-. **SELECTED PUBLICATIONS** Ed with intro, Sale catalogues of Libraries and Eminent Persons, gen ed, A N L Munby, vol 5: Poets and Men of Letters, London, 72; ed with bibliographical notes, The English Book Trade 1660-1853; Titles Relating to the Early History of English Publishing, Bookselling, the Struggle for Copyright and the Freedom of the Press, 38 vols, New York, 75-76; auth, John Dunton and the English Book Trade; A Study of His Career with a Checklist of His Publications, New York, 75; The Bibliographical Society of America 1904-1979; A Retrospective Collection, compiled by Stephen Parks for the Bibliographical Soc of Am, Charlottesville, 80; Literary Autographs, papers read ata a Clark Library Seminar by Parks and P J Croft, Stephen Parks, Charles Cotton and the Derby Manuscript, Los Angeles, 83; auth, The Elizabethan Club of Yale University and Its Library, Yale Univ Press, 86; auth, The Luttrell File: Narcissus Luttrell's Inscriptions of Dates of Publication on Contemporary Pamphlets, 1679-1720, supp to the Yale Univ Lib Gazette, winter 96-97; author of numerous articles. **CONTACT ADDRESS** Beinecke Library, Yale Univ, 1630A Yale Station, New Haven, CT, 06520. **EMAIL** stephen.parks@yale.edu

PARRY-GILES, TREVOR
DISCIPLINE COMMUNICATION **EDUCATION** Ripon Col, BA, 85; Univ Nmex, 87; Indiana Univ, PhD, 92. **CAREER** Asst prof, St Ambrose Univ, 91-97; asst prof, West Ill Univ, 97-98; SR WRITER,CAMPAIGN PERFORMANCE GROUP, 98-. **MEMBERSHIPS** Nat Commun Asn. **RESEARCH** Political communication; Rhetorical theory; Legal communication **SELECTED PUBLICATIONS** Auth, "Parliament, Puritans, and Protesters: The Ideological Development of the British Commitment to 'Free Speech'", Free Speech Yrbk, 93; auth, "Ideological Anxiety and the Censored Test: Real Lives-At the Edge of the Union," Critical Stud in Mass Commun, 94; auth, "Property Rights, Human Rights, and American Jurisprudence: The Rejection of John J. Parker's Nomination to the Supreme Court," South Commun Jour, 94; auth, "Idealogy and Poetics in Public Issue Construction: Thatcherism, Civil Liberties, and Terrorism' in Northern Ireland," Commun Q, 95; auth, "Character, the Constitution, and the Ideological Embodiment of Civil Rights' in the 1967 Nomination of Thurgood Marshall to the Supreme Court," Q Jour Speech, 96; coauth, "Gendered Politics and the Presidential Image Construction: A Reassessment of the 'Feminine Style,'", Commun Monogr, 96; coauth, "Political Scopophilia, Presidential Campaigning, and the Intimacy of American Politics," Commun Stud, 96; coauth, "'A Stranger to Its Laws': Freedom, Civil Rights, and the Legal Ambiguity of Romer vs. Evans," Argumentation & Advocacy, 97. **CONTACT ADDRESS** Campaign Performance Grp, Trevor Parry-Giles, 2600 Virginia Ave NW, Ste 303, Washington, DC, 20037-1905. **EMAIL** parrygiles@earthlink.net

PASCO, ALLAN H.
DISCIPLINE 19TH-CENTURY LITERATURE **EDUCATION** Univ MI, PhD. **CAREER** Prof, Univ KS. **RESEARCH** Prose fiction, cult studies, and comp lit. **SELECTED PUBLICATIONS** Auth, Proust and the Color-Keys to 'A la recherche du temps perdu,' Novel Configurations: A Study of French Fiction, Balzacian Montage, Allusion: A Literary Graft; Sick Heroes: French Society and Literature in the Romantic Age, 1750-1850; pub(s), jour(s) PMLA, New Lit Hist, MLN, Contemp Lit, Comp Lit, Jour Europ Stud, Va Quart Rev. **CONTACT ADDRESS** Dept of French and Italian, Univ Kansas, Admin Building, Lawrence, KS, 66045. **EMAIL** kufacts@ukans.edu

PATERSON, DOUGLAS L.
PERSONAL Born 10/26/1945, Omaha, NE **DISCIPLINE** THEATRE **EDUCATION** Yankton Col, Yankton, SD, BA, 68; Cornell Univ, MA, 70, PhD, 72. **CAREER** Asst prof, 72-75, Yankton Col; asst prof, 75-79, Willamette Univ; co-member, 79-81, The Dakota Theatre Caravan; assoc prof, prof, chair, 81-, Univ Neb Omaha; bd, 82-88, Alliance for Cultural Democracy; vice-pres, 90-92, Assoc for Theatre in Higher Educ; vice-pres, 94-96, ATHE; chair, 94-97, Pedagogy of the Oppressed Conf. **HONORS AND AWARDS** Ford Found Fel, 68-70; Teacher of the Year, 74; Isaacson Endowed Chair, 98., US leading practitioner/theorist of theatre techniques develop by Brazilian Dir Augusto Boal. **MEMBERSHIPS** Assoc Theatre in Higher Educ; Pedagogy & Theatre of the Oppressed. **RESEARCH** Theatre of the oppressed; techniques of Augusto Boal; theatre & soc change; post-moderism; cultural materialism; new historicism. **SELECTED PUBLICATIONS** Auth, A Role to Play for the Theatre of the Oppressed, Drama Rev, 94; coauth, We Are All Theatre: An Interview with Augusto Boal, High Performance, 96; auth, foreward, Hope is Vital, Heineman, 98; auth, The Embodiment of Embodied Pedagogy, Embodied Pedagogy, 99. **CONTACT ADDRESS** Dept of Theatre, Univ Nb Omaha, Fine Arts Bldg, Omaha, NE, 68182. **EMAIL** paterson@unomaha.edu

PATEY, DOUGLAS L.
PERSONAL Born 05/20/1951, New York, NY, s **DISCIPLINE** 18TH CENTURY BRITISH LITERATURE **EDUCATION** Hamilton Col, AB, 72; Univ Va, PhD, 79. **CAREER** Prof English, Smith Col, 79-. **HONORS AND AWARDS** NEH Fel; Guggenheim Fel. **MEMBERSHIPS** Am Soc 18th-Century Studies; Hist Sci Soc; SHARP; Asn Lit Schol & Critics. **RESEARCH** 18th-century British literature and culture. **SELECTED PUBLICATIONS** Auth, Probability and Literary Form: Philosophic Theory and Literary Practice in the Augustan Age, Cambridge Univ Press, 84; The Eighteenth-Century Invents the Canon, Mod Lang Studies, 88; Swift's Satire on "Science" and the Structure of Gulliver's Travels, ELH, 91; "Aesthetics" and the Rise of Lyric in the Eighteenth Century, SEL, 93; The Institution of Criticism, Cambridge History of Literary Criticism, vol 4: The Eighteenth Century, Cambridge Univ Press, 97; Ancients and Moderns, Cambridge History of Literary Criticism, vol 4: The Eighteenth Century, Cambridge Univ Press, 97; The Life of Evelyn Waugh: A Critical Biography, Blackwell, 98. **CONTACT ADDRESS** English Dept, Smith Col, Northampton, MA, 01063. **EMAIL** dpatey@hotmail.com

PATRAKA, VIVIAN
DISCIPLINE THEATER **EDUCATION** Brooklyn Col, BA; Univ Michigan, MA, PhD. **CAREER** Prof English & dir, Inst for the Study of Culture and Soc, Bowling Green State Univ. **HONORS AND AWARDS** Cum laude, BA; pres, Women and Theatre Program; vice-pres, Res and Publs, and mem, Bd of Governors, Asn for Theatre in Higher Educ; Am Soc for Theatre Res program comm, 96. **SELECTED PUBLICATIONS** Contribur, Making a Spectacle: Feminist Essays on Contemporary Women's Theatre, Michigan; contribur, Performing Feminism: The Critical Act, Johns Hopkins; contirbur, Critical Theory and Performance, Michigan; contribur, Acting Out: Feminist Performances, Michigan; contribur, Performance and Cultural

Politics, Routledge; contribur, Jews and Other Differences, Minnesota; auth, Spectacles of Suffering: Theatre, Fascism and the Holocaust, Indiana Univ, forthcoming. **CONTACT ADDRESS** Institute for the Study of Culture and Society, Bowling Green State Univ, Collete Park Office Bldg, Bowling Green, OH, 43403-0023. **EMAIL** vpatrak@bgnet.bgsu.edu

PATRICK, BARBARA
DISCIPLINE AMERICAN LITERATURE AND AMERICAN ENGLISH GRAMMAR **EDUCATION** Univ NC, Chapel Hill, PhD, 91. **CAREER** Instr, Rowan Col of NJ. **SELECTED PUBLICATIONS** Works on the dramatic poetry of W.H. Auden; on collaborative writing in the classroom. **CONTACT ADDRESS** Rowan Col of NJ, Glassboro, NJ, 08028-1701.

PATTEN, ROBERT LOWRY
PERSONAL Born 04/26/1939, Oklahoma City, OK, d, 2 children **DISCIPLINE** ENGLISH **EDUCATION** Swarthmore Col, BA, 60; Princeton Univ, MA, 62, PhD, 65. **CAREER** Lect, asst prof, 64-69, Bryn Mawr Col; asst prof, prof, 69-, Rice Univ; Lynette S Autrey Prof in Humanities, 96-. **HONORS AND AWARDS** Woodrow Wilson Fel, 60-61; Fulbright Scholarship, Univ of London, 63-64; NEH Fel 68-69, 77-78, 87-88; Guggenheim Fel, 80-81; Nat Humanities Center Fel, 87-88; Assoc Center for Advanced Study in the Visual Arts, Nat Gal of Art, 88-89; NEH Proj Grant Dir and PI, 87-90; George R Brown Award for Sup Tchng, Rice Univ, 88, 89, 91; Grad Stud Assoc Outstanding Serv Award, 94; Robert Lowry Patten Grad Stud Serv Awards est in honor, 96. **MEMBERSHIPS** Modern Language Assoc; Beta of TX Chapt, Phi Beta Kappa, Pres; Phi Beta Kappa Alumni of Gr Houston, Dir; The Dickens Proj, Univ of CA Santa Cruz, Dir; AAUP; Soc for History of Authorship Reading and Pub. Dir. **RESEARCH** Charles Dickens; George Cruikshank; British and European fiction to 1900; the illustrated book; the history of the book 19th cent British lit and art. **SELECTED PUBLICATIONS** Auth, George Cruikshanks Life Time and Art, New Brunswick Rutgers Univ Press, London, Lutterworth Press, 96; coauth, Literature in the Marketplace Nineteenth Century British Publishing and Reading Practices, Cambridge Univ Press, 95; coauth, Introduction Publishing History as Hypertext, Lit in the Marketplace; auth, Serialized Retrospection in the Pickwick Papers, ch 6, Lit in the Marketplace; art, When Is a Book Not a Book, Biblion the Bulletin of the NY Pub Lib 4, 96. **CONTACT ADDRESS** Dept of English, Rice Univ, 6100 Main St, PO Box 1892, Houston, TX, 77251-1892. **EMAIL** patten@rice.edu

PATTERSON, BECKY
DISCIPLINE CRITICAL CREATIVE THINKING **EDUCATION** Fielding Inst, PhD. **CAREER** Univ Alaska. **SELECTED PUBLICATIONS** Auth, Concentration, 93; Coauth, Developing Reading Versatility, 97. **CONTACT ADDRESS** Univ Alaska Anchorage, 3211 Providence Dr., Anchorage, AK, 99508.

PATTERSON, BOB E.
PERSONAL Born 08/29/1931, Kings Mountain, NC, m, 1953, 2 children **DISCIPLINE** LITERATURE AND THEOLOGY **EDUCATION** Gardner-Webb Univ, AA, 50; Baylor Univ, BA, 52, MA, 57; Southern Baptist Theol Seminary, Mdiv, 56, PhD, 60. **CAREER** Distinguished Prof of Rel, Dept of Rel, 61-, Baylor Univ. **HONORS AND AWARDS** Alpha Chi Scholastic Fraternity; Outstanding Educ Of Amer; Outstanding Faculty Member; Permanent Distinguished Prof of Rel; Regional Pres of AAR; Natl Pres of N.A.B.P.R. **MEMBERSHIPS** AAR, A.A.U.D., NABPR. **RESEARCH** Theology, Faith and Science, Biblical Studies, Philosophy of Religion. **SELECTED PUBLICATIONS** Auth, Science, Faith and Revelation; Perspectives on Theology; Discovering Ezekiel and Daniel; Discovering Matthew; Discovering Revelation; Theologians, Carl F. H. Henry, Reinhold Niebuhr; Who is Jesus Christ?, ed, 18 vol series, Makers of Modern Theological Mind. **CONTACT ADDRESS** Dept of Religion, Baylor Univ, Waco, TX, 76798. **EMAIL** Bob_Patterson@baylor.edu

PATTERSON, CELIA
DISCIPLINE TECHNICAL WRITING **EDUCATION** E Tex State Univ-Texarkana, BS, MS; Univ Tulsa, PhD. **CAREER** Asst prof. **RESEARCH** Modern American fiction, Anglo American WW1 literature. **SELECTED PUBLICATIONS** Publ, articles on tech wrtg, Chopin and Faulkner; bk rev(s). **CONTACT ADDRESS** Dept of Eng, Pittsburg State Univ, 1701 S Broadway St, Pittsburg, KS, 66762. **EMAIL** cpatters@pittstate.edu

PATTERSON, WARD L.
PERSONAL Born 12/26/1933, Killbuck, OH **DISCIPLINE** COMMUNICATION **EDUCATION** PhD, Ind Univ. **CAREER** Campus Minister, Ind Univ, 72-90; Prof, Cincinnati Bible Col & Seminary, 91-. **HONORS AND AWARDS** Rotary Student Exchange Fellow for Study in Australia. **RESEARCH** Church & culture; public speaking; humor; intercultural communication. **CONTACT ADDRESS** 2852 McKinley Ave, Cincinnati, OH, 45211.

PATTERSON-ISKANDER, SYLVIA W.
PERSONAL Born 06/27/1940, Boston, MA, m, 1982, 2 children **DISCIPLINE** ENGLISH **EDUCATION** La State Univ, BS, 61; Univ SW La, MA, 65; Fla State Univ, PhD, 69. **CAREER** Asst Prof Eng, 69-73, Assoc Prof, 73-81, Prof, 81-, Univ SW La. **HONORS AND AWARDS** Distinguished Prof, 91., Pres, Children's Lit Asn. **MEMBERSHIPS** Int Soc for Res in Children's Lit; MLA; SCMLA; NCTE; AAUP. **RESEARCH** Children's & young adult literature. **SELECTED PUBLICATIONS** Auth, Robert Cormier, 152-155, Cynthia Voigt, 669-671, Twentieth Century Young Adult Writers, St James, 94; auth, Mystery and Detective Fiction, Five Owls, 8.4, 73-80, 94; auth, Thomas Bewick, Hanoverian Britian: An Encyclopedia, Garland, 54, 97. **CONTACT ADDRESS** Dept of English, Univ Southwestern La, Lafayette, LA, 70504-4691. **EMAIL** sylvia.iskander@juno.com

PATTISON, EUGENE H.
PERSONAL Born 01/08/1935, Pontiac, MI **DISCIPLINE** ENGLISH **EDUCATION** Alma Col, BA, 56; Univ Mich, MA, 57, PhD, 63; Harvard Univ, STB, 64. **CAREER** From asst prof to assoc prof to prof to chemn 64-, Alma Col; ordained min, Presbyterian Church, 64-. **HONORS AND AWARDS** State Col Scholar; Presbyterian Grad Fel, 62-63; Dist Prof Year, 73, 81, Alma Col; NEH, 81; Grand Prytaniskey Ldr Award; Tau Kappa Epsilon, 75; Order of Omega; Phi Beta Kappa; Coolidge Res Fel, 95. **MEMBERSHIPS** Am Asn Univ Prof; Asn Relig Intellectual Life; Conf Col Compos Commun; Modern Lang Asn; Society Stud Midwestern Lit Culture. **RESEARCH** American literature, 1865-1920, Annie Dillard; Robinson Jeffers; Gene Stratton Porter; Booth Tarkington; Midwestern literature. **SELECTED PUBLICATIONS** Auth, art, A Century of Alma College Leadership, 86; auth, art, The Great Lakes Childhood: The Experience of William Dean Howells and Annie Dillard, 88-89; auth, art, Who is Blennerhassett: Three Twenthieth Century Novels Give Answer, 89; auth, art, The Landscape and the Sense of the Past in William Dean Howells, 93; auth, art, The Limberlost, Tinker Creek Science and Society: Gene Stratton-Porter and Annie Dillard, 94-95. **CONTACT ADDRESS** Alma Col, Alma, MI, 48801-1599. **EMAIL** pattison@alma.edu

PAULY, THOMAS HARRY
PERSONAL Born 03/06/1940, Missoula, MT, m, 1988, 1 child **DISCIPLINE** LITERATURE **EDUCATION** Harvard Col, BA, 62; Univ Calif Berkeley, MA, 65, PhD, 70. **CAREER** Asst prof, 70, assoc prof, 77, prof, 84, Univ Del. **RESEARCH** American literature. **SELECTED PUBLICATIONS** Auth, Maurine Watkins, Chicago and her Chicago Tribune articles, 98; article, The Criminal as Culture, Amer Lit Hist, 9, 776-85, Winter, 97; article, Murder Will Out, and It Did in Chicago, NY Times, sec 7, 5, 22 Dec, 96; article, Gatsby as Gangster, Studies in Amer Fiction, 21, 225-36, Autumn, 93; article, Man for Two Seasons: Bill Reid Jr., Harvard Mag, 67-72, Nov-Dec, 91; article, Black Images and White Culture During the Decade Before the Civil Rights Movement, Amer Studies, 31, 101-119, Fall, 90; book rev, Picture Book, Amer Quart, 41, 558-62, Sept, 89; article, American Art and Labor: The Case of Anshutz's The Ironworkers Noontime, Amer Quart, 40, 333-50, Sept, 88; auth, Maxwell Anderson Truckline Cafe, 85; auth, An American Odyssey: Elia Kazan and American Culture, Temple Univ Press, 83. **CONTACT ADDRESS** Univ of Delaware, Memorial Hall, Newark, DE, 19716. **EMAIL** thomas.pauly@mvs.udel.edu

PAVEL, THOMAS
PERSONAL Born 04/04/1941, Bucharest, Romania, m, 3 children **DISCIPLINE** ENGLISH **EDUCATION** Ecole Haute Etudes Scis Soc, Paris, doctorate, 71 **CAREER** Prof, Univ Ottawa, 70-80; prof, Univ Quebec, Montreal, 80- 86; prof, Univ Calif, Santa Cruz, 86-90; prof, Princeton Univ, 90-98; PROF, UNIV CHICAGO, 98-. **HONORS AND AWARDS** Rene Weller prize for best book in literary theory, 92; Am Comparative Lit Asn fel. **MEMBERSHIPS** MLA, ALCS **RESEARCH** Literary theory; Fr lit **SELECTED PUBLICATIONS** Co-auth, De Barthes a Balzac, Albin Michel, 98; auth, L'Art de l'eloignement. Essai sur l'imagination classique, Gallimard, 96; auth, The Feud of Language, Blackwell, 89, paperback 90, Fr ed, 88, Port trans, 90, Romanian trans, 94; auth, Fictional Worlds, Harvard Univ Press, 86, paperback ed, spring 89, Fr ed, 88, It trans, 92, Romanian trans, 94; Span trans, 96. **CONTACT ADDRESS** 851 W Gunnison #J, Chicago, IL, 60640. **EMAIL** ct-pavel@uchicago.edu

PAVITT, CHARLES
DISCIPLINE COMMUNICATION THEORY **EDUCATION** Queens Col-CUNY, BA, 76; Univ Wis, MA, 79; PhD, 83. **CAREER** Tchg asst, Univ Wis, 76-82; instr, George Mason Univ, 84; lectr, Howard Univ, 86; lectr, George Wash Univ, 86-87; asst prof, 87-94; assoc prof, 94-. **HONORS AND AWARDS** Univ Del Grant, 87, 89, 90., Paper reviewer, Commun Res, 87; Human Commun Res, 87, 88, 89; Commun Theory, 89, 91; Jour Soc and Personal Relships, 90. **MEMBERSHIPS** Mem, Intl Commun Assn; E Commun Assn. **RESEARCH** The Role of Belief Structures and Decision Processes in Face-to-face Interaction. **SELECTED PUBLICATIONS** Auth, A Controlled Rest of Some Complicating Factors Relevant to the Inferential Model for Evaluations of Communicative Competence, W Jour Speech Commun, 90; An Analysis of Artificial Intelligence Based Models for Describing Communicative Choice, Commun Theory, 91; co-auth, Implicit Theories of Marriage and Evaluations of Marriages on Television, Human Commun Res, 90; Implicit Theories of Leadership and Judgments of Leadership Among Group Members, Small Gp Res, 91. **CONTACT ADDRESS** Dept of Commun, Univ Delaware, 162 Ctr Mall, Newark, DE, 19716.

PAXMAN, DAVID B.
PERSONAL Born 12/31/1946, Salt Lake City, UT, m, 1996, 10 children **DISCIPLINE** ENGLISH LANGUAGE; LITERATURE **EDUCATION** Univ Chicago, PhD 82, MA 72; Brigham Young Univ, BA 71. **CAREER** Brigham Young Univ, assoc prof, 88-; Brigham Young Univ HI, asst prof, assoc prof, 76-83. **MEMBERSHIPS** ASECS; WSECS. **RESEARCH** Eighteenth-century British Literature; Intellectual History. **SELECTED PUBLICATIONS** Auth, Samuel Johnson Life's Incompleteness and the Limits of Representation, Lit and Belief, 98; auth, Failure as Authority: Poetic Voices and the Muse of Grace in William Cowper's The Task, 1650-1850, Ideas Aesthetics and Inquiries in the Early Modern Era, 98; auth, Writing about the Arts and Humanities, coauth, Needham Hts MA, Simon and Schuster Custom, 96; auth, Adam in a Strange Country: Locke's Language Theory and Travel Literature, Modern Philos, 95; auth, Oral and Literate Discourse in Aphra Behn's Oroonoko, Restoration: Studies in English Literary Culture, 1600-1700, 94; auth, A New Comer's Guide to Honolulu, Mutual Pub, 93. **CONTACT ADDRESS** Dept of Literature, Brigham Young Univ, 3136 JKHB, Provo, UT, 84602. **EMAIL** david_paxman@byu.edu

PAXTON, MARK
DISCIPLINE NEWSWRITING AND REPORTING **EDUCATION** Univ TN, PhD, 95. **CAREER** Southwest Tex State Univ **SELECTED PUBLICATIONS** Articles: Charleston Daily Mail; Nashville Banner; The Associated Press. **CONTACT ADDRESS** Southwest MS State Univ, 901 S. National, Ste. 50, Springfield, MO, 65804-0094.

PAYNE, F. ANNE
PERSONAL Born 08/28/1932, Harrisonburg, VA **DISCIPLINE** ENGLISH EUROPEAN MEDIEVAL LIT **EDUCATION** Shortor col, BA, BMUS, piano, 53; Yale Univ, MA, 54, PhD, 60. **CAREER** Instr, Coun Col, 56; Instr, Univ Buff, 67-75, Lect, 60; Asst Prof, SUNY, Buff, 60-67; Assoc Prof, SUNY, Buff, 67-75, Prof, 75-; Adj Fel St Anne's Col, 66-. **HONORS AND AWARDS** AAUW Fellowshp to Oxford, 66-67; SUNY, C S Fellowshp, 67, 68, 71, 72; Julian Park Pub Award, SUNY, 81; Who's Who Am Women. **MEMBERSHIPS** Medieval Acad; ISAS; New Chaucer Soc; Pi Kappa Lambda. **RESEARCH** Medieval late classical lit and satire. **SELECTED PUBLICATIONS** King Alfred and Boethius, WI Univ Press, 67; Chaucer and Menippean Satire, WI Univ Press, 81; 3 Aspects of Wyrd in Beowulf, Pope Festschrift. **CONTACT ADDRESS** State Univ NY at Buffalo, Dept Eng, Clemens hall, Buffalo, NY, 14260. **EMAIL** paynefa@acsu.Buffalo.edu

PAYNE, J. GREGORY
PERSONAL Born 09/18/1949, s **DISCIPLINE** COMMUNICATION **EDUCATION** Univ Ill-Urbana-Champaign, BA, 71, MA, 72, PhD, 77; Harvard Univ, MPA, 84. **CAREER** Grad asst, Dept Speech Commun, Univ Ill, Urbana-Champaign, 72-75; instr, USC, Calif State Univ, Los Angeles, Commun Col Dist, 76-83; asst prof & Dir Forensics, Commun Studies Dept, Calif Luth Col, 76-77; internship coordr, Mayor Tom Bradleys off, 76-77; instr Upward Bound Prog, 76-77; asst prof & Dir Forensics, Dept Theatre Arts & Rhet, Occidental Col, 77-83; Assoc Prof, Dept of Commun, Emerson Col, 83-. **HONORS AND AWARDS** Phi Beta Kappa; Phi Kappi Phi; Nat Defense Educ Act fel 72-76; Univ Ill Grad fel, 72-76; Big Ten Traveling Scholar; US Treas Patriotic Serv Award, 80; City Los Angeles Commendation Forensics Excellence, 82; Univ Ill Distinguished Alumni Award, 97; Loftsgordon Award Outstanding Tchg, Occidental Col, 82; R F Kennedy Award Commun, Polit, & Law Orgn, Emerson Col, 90; Emerson Col Award Leadership Friends of Emerson Majestic, 93. **MEMBERSHIPS** ACium; AAUP; E Commun Asn; Speech Commun Asn; Delta Sigma Rho-Tau Kappa Alpha; E States Commun Asn; Univ Ill Alumni Asn; Univ Ill LAS Alumni Comm; Harvard Univ Kennedy School Alumni. **SELECTED PUBLICATIONS** Coauth, Private Lives, Public Officials: The Challenge to Mainstream Media, Am Behav Sci, 93; auth, Introduction, Am Behav Sci, 93; coauth, Crisis in Communication: Coverage of Magic Johnson AIDS Disclosure, AIDS: Effective Health Communication for the 90s, Taylor & Francis Ltd, 93; AIDS: A Plan for the 21st Century-Thinking Globally, Acting Locally: AIDS Auth, Action 2000 Plan, AIDS: Effective Health Commun for the 90s, Taylor & Francis Ltd, 93; Education for the Health Communication Professional: A Collaborative Curricular Partnership, Am Behav Sci, 94; Effective Health Message Design: The America Responds to AIDS Campaign, Am Behav Sci, 94; Status and Scope of Health Communication, Jour Health Commun, 96; auth, Introduction: Media Coverage of Mad Cow Issue, The Mad Cow Crisis: Health and the Public Good, Univ Col London Press, 98. **CONTACT ADDRESS** Communication Dept, Emerson Col, 21 Commonwealth Ave., Boston, MA, 02116. **EMAIL** gpayne@emerson.edu

PAYNE, MICHAEL
PERSONAL Born 01/17/1941, Dallas, TX, 4 children **DISCIPLINE** ENGLISH LITERATURE **EDUCATION** South Ore Univ, BA, 62; Univ Ore, PhD, 69. **CAREER** Asst prof, Bucknell Univ, 69-86; JOHN P. CROZER PROF, ENG LIT, BUCKNELL UNIC, 86-. **MEMBERSHIPS** Inst Romance Stud, Coll Eng Asn, MLA **RESEARCH** Shakespeare; Renaissance Literature; Literature & Cultural Theory. **SELECTED PUBLICATIONS** Reading Theory: An Introduction to Lacan, Derrida, and Kristeva, Blackwell Publ, 93; co-edr, The Bucknell Lectures in Literary Theory, Blackwell Publ, 90-94; The Dictionary of Cultural and Critical Theory, Blackwell Publ, 96; Reading Knowledge: An Introduction to Barthes, Foucault, and Althusser, Blackwell Publ, 97. **CONTACT ADDRESS** Dept Eng, Bucknell Univ, Lewisburg, PA, 17837. **EMAIL** payne@bucknell.edu

PEARCE, RICHARD
DISCIPLINE MODERN FICTION, MODERN DRAMA **EDUCATION** Hobart Col, BA; Columbia Univ, MA, PhD. **CAREER** Engl, Wheaton Col. **SELECTED PUBLICATIONS** Publ, The Politics of Narration: James Joyce, William Faulkner, and Virginia Woolf; The Novel in Motion: An Approach to Modern Fiction; Stages of the Clown: Perspectives on Modern Fiction from Dostoyevsky to Beckett; William Styron; ed, James Joyce and Thomas Pynchon; A Forum on Fiction. **CONTACT ADDRESS** Dept of Eng, Wheaton Col, 26 East Main St, Norton, MA, 02766. **EMAIL** Richard_Pearce@wheatonma.edu

PEARSALL, DEREK A.
PERSONAL Born 08/28/1931, Birmingham, England, m, 1952, 5 children **DISCIPLINE** ENGLISH **EDUCATION** Univ of Birmingham, UK, BA, 51, MA, 52. **CAREER** King's Col, London, 59-65; Univ of York, 65-85; Harvard Univ, 85-2000. **HONORS AND AWARDS** Fel, AAAS; fel, Medieval Acad. **MEMBERSHIPS** New Chaucer Soc; Medieval Acad; IAUPE; Early Eng Text Soc. **RESEARCH** Medieval English literature. **SELECTED PUBLICATIONS** Auth, The Canterbury Tales, Allen & Unwin, 85; auth, The Life of Geoffrey Chaucer, Blackwell, 92; auth, Chaucer to Spenser: Writings in English, 1375-1575, Blackwell, 98. **CONTACT ADDRESS** Dept of English, Harvard Univ, 12 Quincy St, Cambridge, MA, 02138. **EMAIL** dpearsal@fas.harvard.edu

PEARSON, JOHN H.
DISCIPLINE AMERICAN LITERATURE **EDUCATION** Eckerd Col, BA; Boston Univ, PhD. **CAREER** Eng Dept, Stetson Univ **RESEARCH** Nineteenth and early twentieth century fiction; autobiography; literary theory and criticism. **SELECTED PUBLICATIONS** Auth, Framing the Modern Reader: The Prefaces of Henry James, Penn State; pubs on frame theory in literature and the other arts, American colonial literature, and Henry James. **CONTACT ADDRESS** English Dept, Stetson Univ, Unit 8378, DeLand, FL, 32720-3771.

PEARSON, JUDY C.
PERSONAL Born 09/02/1946, Pipestone, MN, m, 1977, 6 children **DISCIPLINE** COMMUNICATION **EDUCATION** St. Cloud State Univ, BA, 68; Ind Univ, MA, 73, PhD, 75. **CAREER** Dir, N Va Ctr & assoc dean grad sch & prof, Va Tech, 95-; from assoc prof to prof & dir grad studies, Ohio Univ, 81-95; vis prof, Mich State Univ, 81; asst prof & basic course dir, Ind Univ, 76-81. **HONORS AND AWARDS** Outstanding Women of Achievement, 76; Cent States Speech Asn Outstanding Young Tchr Award, 77; Distinguished Alumni Award, St. Cloud State Univ, 87; Honorary alumnus, Ohio Univ, 91; Scholar of the Year, Cent States Commun Asn, 95. **MEMBERSHIPS** Speech Commun Asn; Int Commun Asn; Am Educ Res Asn; Cent States Speech Asn; Ind Speech Asn; Ill Speech & Theater Asn; Am Asn Univ Prof; Iowa Commun Asn; Am Inst Parliamentarians; E Commun Asn; Speech Commun Asn Ohio; World Commun Asn; Commun Asn Japan; Counc Grad Sch; Nat Commun Asn; Nat Asn State Univ & Land Grant Col. **RESEARCH** Relational maintenance; higher education; the changing PhD; women in education. **SELECTED PUBLICATIONS** Coauth, Let's Go Krogering: Children's Compliance Gaining and Adults' Compliance Resistance in a Naturalistic Setting, Speech Commun Annual, 93; coauth, Sweet Pea and Pussy Cat: An Examination of Idiom Use and Marital Satisfaction Over the Life Cycle, Jour Soc & Personal Relationships, 93; coauth, Antecedent and Consequent Conditions of Student Questioning: An Analysis of Classroom Discourse Across the University, Comm Educ, 94; coauth, Children's Perspectives of the Family: A Phenomenological Inquiry, Human Studies, 94; coauth, Interpersonal Rituals in Marriage and Adult Friendship, Commun Monogr, 97; coauth, Confidence in Public Speaking, 93; auth, Communication and the Family: Seeking Satisfaction in Changing Times, 93; coauth, Understanding and Sharing: An Introduction to Speech Communication, 94; coauth, Understanding and Sharing: Audio Companion, 94; coauth, Gender and Communication, 95; auth, Marriage After Mourning: The Secrets of Surviving Couples, 95; coauth, Confidence in Public Speaking, 95; coauth, Understanding and Sharing, 97. **CONTACT ADDRESS** Va Tech/Va Univ, 7054 Haycock Rd., Falls Church, VA, 22043. **EMAIL** jcp@vt.edu

PEARSON, MICHAEL
DISCIPLINE CREATIVE WRITING (NON-FICTION) **EDUCATION** Fordham Univ, BA;Univ SF, MA; Pa State Univ. **CAREER** Engl, Old Dominion Univ. **RESEARCH** Literary non-fiction ; memoirs. **CONTACT ADDRESS** Old Dominion Univ, 4100 Powhatan Ave, Norfolk, VA, 23058. **EMAIL** MPearson@odu.edu

PEASE, DONALD E.
DISCIPLINE ENGLISH LITERATURE **EDUCATION** Univ Chicago, PhD, 73. **CAREER** Avalon Prof Hum and Prof Eng. **RESEARCH** Am drama, fiction, and criticism. **SELECTED PUBLICATIONS** Auth, Regulating Multi-adhoccerists, Fish('s) Rules, Crit Inquiry, 97; Negative interpellations: From Oklahoma City to the Trilling-Matthiessen Transmission, Boundary, 96; Visionary Compacts: American Renaissance Writings in Cultural Context, Univ Wis, 87; ed, National Identities and Post-Americanist Narratives, Duke UP, 94; New Americanists: Revisionist Interventions into the Canon, boundary 2, 89; co-ed, Cultures of United States Imperialism, Duke UP, 93; The American Renaissance Reconsidered: Selected Papers of the English Institute, Johns Hopkins UP, 85. **CONTACT ADDRESS** Dartmouth Col, 3529 N Main St, #207, Hanover, NH, 03755.

PEASE, TED
PERSONAL m **DISCIPLINE** COMMUNICATION STUDIES **EDUCATION** Univ New Hampshire, BA, 78; Univ Minn, MA, 81; Univ Ohio, PhD, 91. **CAREER** Prof, 94-. **SELECTED PUBLICATIONS** Auth, The Newsroom Barometer: Job Satisfaction and the Impact of Racial Diversity on U.S. Daily Newspapers, 91; No Train, No Gain: Continuing Education in Newspaper Newsrooms, 93; co-auth, The Forgotten Medium, Transaction, 95. **CONTACT ADDRESS** Dept of Communication, Utah State Univ, 3580 S Highway 91, Logan, UT, 84321. **EMAIL** tpease@wpo.hass.usu.edu

PECK, RUSSELL A.
DISCIPLINE ENGLISH **EDUCATION** IN Univ, PhD. **CAREER** John Hall Deane prof; taught at, IN Univ, Univ Hull Yorkshire, Col St Thomas & Colgate Univ; bibliogr, Stud in the Age of Chaucer & MLA; Mercer Brugler prof of Humanities, 82-85. **HONORS AND AWARDS** Edward Peck Curtis prize, 72; E. Harris Harbison awd, 72; Students' Asn awd, 82; prof of the Yr, Coun for the Advancement and Support Educ, 85; Guggenheim fel; Danforth Assoc fel & NEH sem dir, Bd of the Conf on Christianity and Lit MLA., Founder & gen ed, Middle Eng Text Ser; founding dir, Medieval House. **MEMBERSHIPS** Assoc ed Mediaevalia ed bd, Grad Record Examination; ch ed bd, TEAMS; dir, Drama House. **RESEARCH** Eng and Scottish lit of the 13th through the 15th centuries and var facets of medieval cult studies. **SELECTED PUBLICATIONS** Auth, Kingship and Common Profit in Gower's Confessio Amantis; Chaucer's Lyrics and Anelida and Arcite: An Annotated Bibli ography; Chaucer's Boece, Romaunt, Astrolabe, Equatorie, Lost Works and the Chaucer Apocrypha: An Annotated Bibliography; articles on, Chaucer, Gower, The Alliterative Morte Arthure, Parlement of the Three Ages, St Erkenwald, numerology, poetics, imagination, medieval intellectual hist, social unrest, medieval soc hist, Ecclesiastes, Shakespeare & Mike Nichols's Working Girl; ed, Gower's Confessio Amantis, Heroic Women from The Old Testament in Middle English Verse & Religious Typology in Recent Cinema. **CONTACT ADDRESS** Dept of Eng, Univ of Rochester, 601 Elmwood Ave, Ste. 656, Rochester, NY, 14642. **EMAIL** rpec@db1.cc.rochester.edu

PECORA, VINCENT P.
PERSONAL Born 09/07/1953, Baltimore, MD, m, 1992, 2 children **DISCIPLINE** ENGLISH **EDUCATION** Brown Univ, BA, 75; Columbia Univ, MA, 78, PhD, 83. **CAREER** Asst prof, Univ AR, 84-85; asst prof, 85-90, asoc prof, 90-95, PROF, UNIV CA, LOS ANGELES, 95-. **HONORS AND AWARDS** NEH Summer Stipend, 85; fel, Univ CA Humanities Res Inst, Univ CA, Irvine, 89; Nominated for Distinguished Teaching Award, Mortar Board Soc, UCLA, 92., Dir, Center for Modern and Contemporary Studies, UCLA, 96-; dir, Humanities Consortium and Mellon Postdoctoral Fellowship Prog, UCLA, 97-. **MEMBERSHIPS** Western Humanities Alliance (Bd of Dirs); Modern Lang Asn. **RESEARCH** Modern British and comparative lit; intellectual hist; literary theory. **SELECTED PUBLICATIONS** Auth, Self and Form in Modern Narrative, Johns Hopkins Univ Press, 89; Households of the Soul, Johns Hopkins Univ Press, 97. **CONTACT ADDRESS** Dept of English, Univ of California, Los Angeles, Los Angeles, CA, 90095-1530. **EMAIL** pecora@humnet.ucla.edu

PEDERSON, LEE
DISCIPLINE ENGLISH LANGUAGE AND LITERATURE **EDUCATION** Univ Chicago, PhD, 64. **CAREER** Charles Howard Candler Prof. **RESEARCH** Linguistics. **SELECTED PUBLICATIONS** Auth, East Tennessee Folk Speech; An Annotated Bibliography of Southern Speech; Pronunciation of English in Metropolitan Chicago; co-auth, A Manual for Dialect Research in the Southern States; ed, The Linguistic Atlas of the Gulf States, (v 1-4). **CONTACT ADDRESS** English Dept, Emory Univ, 1380 Oxford Rd NE, Atlanta, GA, 30322-1950.

PEEMOELLER, HELEN C.
PERSONAL Born 01/24/1939, Wilmington, DE, m, 1973 **DISCIPLINE** ENGLISH **EDUCATION** Bryn Mawr Coll, AB, 60; Univ Wis, MA, 61; Univ Pa, 61-67. **CAREER** Inst Moore Col Art, 65-66; inst Northampton County Area Community Col, 67-70; PROF, CHAIR HUM, READING AREA COMMUNITY COL, 71-. **HONORS AND AWARDS** NEH scholar **MEMBERSHIPS** MLA **RESEARCH** Film, writing, medieval & Renaissance **SELECTED PUBLICATIONS** various **CONTACT ADDRESS** Reading Area Comm Col, PO Box 1706, Reading, PA, 19606. **EMAIL** HPeemoeller@email.racc.cc.pa.us

PEIRCE, KATE L.
DISCIPLINE COMMUNICATIONS **EDUCATION** FL State Univ, BA, MS, Univ TX, PhD. **CAREER** Comm Dept, Southwest Tex State Univ **HONORS AND AWARDS** Ed, The Forim. **SELECTED PUBLICATIONS** Auth, A Feminist Theoretical Perspective on the Socialization Messages in Seventeen magazine, Sex Roles, 90; Forces That Inhibit Transformation to a Feminist Future, gender & Comm, 92; The Changing Portrayal of Suicide in the Media, Mid-South Sociol Asn, 92; Socialization of Teenage Girls Through Teen-magazine Fiction: The Making of a New Woman or an Old Lady?, Sex Roles, 93; Socialization Messages in Teen and Seventeen Magazines in Women and Media, Wadsworth Publ, 94; YM in Women's Periodicals in the United States, Greenwood Press, 94; Seventeen in Women's Periodicals in the United States, Greenwood Press, 94. **CONTACT ADDRESS** Southwest Texas State Univ, 601 University Dr, San Marcos, TX, 78666-4604.

PENCEAL, BERNADETTE WHITLEY
PERSONAL Born 12/16/1944, Lenoir, North Carolina, m, 1967 **DISCIPLINE** ENGLISH **EDUCATION** Syracuse Univ, Syracuse NY, BS, 1966; The City Coll, New York NY, MA, 1973, Letter of Completion, 1974; Fordham Univ, New York NY, PhD, 1989. **CAREER** Fashion Inst of Technology, New York NY, instructor of English, 1973-74; Green Haven Maximum Security Prison, Stormville NY, instructor of English, 1974-76; Malcolm-King Coll, New York NY, instructor of English, 1974-78; Hunter Coll, New York NY, instructor of reading, 1974-79; Coll of New Rochelle, New Rochelle NY, instructor of English, 1977-89; New York Univ, New York NY, mentor of English, 1980-. **HONORS AND AWARDS** "Bernadette Penceal Day," Office of the President of the Borough of Manhattan, City of New York, 1987. **MEMBERSHIPS** Mem, Assn of Black Faculty & Admin, New York Univ, 1981-, Phi Delta Kappa, 1981-; pres, Assn of Black Women in Higher Educ Inc, 1985-87, J & B Whitley's Inc, 1985-; bd mem, Urban Women's Shelter, 1985-87; mem, New York Urban League, 1987-, Amer Assn of Univ Women, 1989-. **SELECTED PUBLICATIONS** "Non-Intellective Factors as Predictions of Academic Performance of Non-Traditional Adult College Freshmen," 1989. **CONTACT ADDRESS** English Mentor, New York Univ, 239 Green St, 8th Floor, New York, NY, 10039.

PENDELL, SUE
DISCIPLINE COMMUNICATION STUDIES **EDUCATION** Fla State Univ, BS; Auburn Univ, MA; Univ Utah, PhD. **CAREER** Prof. **RESEARCH** Interpersonal communication; intercultural communication; nonverbal communication; group communication; communication theory. **SELECTED PUBLICATIONS** Auth, Deviance and Conflict in Small Group Decision Making, Small Group Res, 90; co-auth, The Myth of Viewer-Listener Disagreement in the First Kennedy-Nixon Debate, Central States Speech J, 87; An Introduction to Speech Communication; Winning Presidential Debates: An Analysis of Criteria Influencing Audience Response, W J Speech Commun, 87. **CONTACT ADDRESS** Speech Communication Dept, Colorado State Univ, Fort Collins, CO, 80523. **EMAIL** spendell@vines.colostate.edu

PEREZ-TORRES, RAFAEL
DISCIPLINE ENGLISH **EDUCATION** Loyola-Marymount Univ, BA, 82, MA, 84; Stanford Univ, 89. **CAREER** Asst prof, Univ Wis, Madison, 89-92; asst prof, Univ Pa, 92- 94; asst prof, 94-96, assoc prof, 96-97, dept Chicano stud, Univ Calif, Santa Barbara; ASSOC PROF, DEPT ENG, UNIV CALIF, LOS ANGELES, 98-. **HONORS AND AWARDS** Univ Calif, Santa Barbara, Regent's Hum Fac fel, 96; Univ Wis System Inst Race and Ethnicity res grant, 91, 92. **MEMBERSHIPS** Mod Lang Asn; Am Stud Asn; Lat Am Stud Asn. **RESEARCH** Postmodern theory and cult; Chicano cult stid; Chicano poetry; postcolonial stud; race and Chicano cult; multicult lit; contemp Am lit. **SELECTED PUBLICATIONS** Auth, Movements in Chicano Poetry-Against Myths, Against Margins, Cambridge Univ Press, 95; auth, Chicano Ethnicity, Cultural Hybridity, the Mestizo Voice, Am Lit 70.1, Spring 98; auth, Knitting and Knotting the Narrative Thread - Beloved as Postmodern Novel, reprint Reading Toni Morrison: Theoretical and Critical Approaches, Johns Hopkins Press, 98; Refiguring Aztlan, Aztlan: A J Chicano Stud 22.2, Fall 97; auth, Nomads and Migrants - Negotiating a Multicultural Postmodernism, Latinos and Education: A Critical Reader, Routledge, 97; auth, Tracing and Erasing: Race and Pedagogy in The Bluest Eye. Approaches to Teaching the Novels of Toni Morrison, Mod Lang Asn Pubs, 97; auth, Chicano/a Cultural Discourse: Coyotes at the Border, Am Lit 67,

Dec 95; auth, Feathering the Serpent: Chicano Mythic Memory, in Memory and Cultural Politics: New Approaches to American Ethnic Literatures, Northeastern Univ Press, 96; Nomads and Migrants - Negotiating a Multicultural Postmodernism, Cultural Critique 26, Winter93/94; auth, The Ambiguous Outlaw: John Rechy and Complicitous Homotextuality, in The Fiction of Masculinity: Crossing Cultures, Crossing Sexualities, NY Univ Press, 94; auth, Chicano Literature entry in Encyclopedia of English Studies and Language Arts, Scholastic, 94. **CONTACT ADDRESS** Dept of English, Univ of California, Los Angeles, 2319 Rolfe Hall, Los Angeles, CA, 90095. **EMAIL** perezt@humnet.ucla.edu

PERKINS, DAVID
PERSONAL Born 10/25/1928, Philadelphia, PA, s **DISCIPLINE** ENGLISH **EDUCATION** Harvard Univ, AB, 51, AM, 52, PhD, 55. **CAREER** Instr to Assoc Prof, 57-64, Prof English, Harvard Univ, 64-95, Chair, Dept English, 76-81, Chair, Dept Lit, 87-89; Vis Prof English, Gttingen Univ, 68-69; Vis Prof, Univ Calif-Irvine, 96-97. **HONORS AND AWARDS** Guggenheim Fel, 62, 73; ACLS Fel, 77; Fulbright Fel to Ger, 68-69; Walter Channing Cabot Award for Distinguished Achievement in the Humanities, 87; Distinguished Schol Award, Keats-Shelley Asn, 90. **MEMBERSHIPS** Keats-Shelley Asn; Byron Soc; Ed Bd, The Wordsworth Circle; Ed Bd, Mod Lang Quart. **RESEARCH** English Romanticism; Modern and Contemporary English; American Poetry. **SELECTED PUBLICATIONS** Auth, The Quest for Permanence: The Symbolism of Wordsworth, Shelley, and Keats, 59; Wordsworth and the Poetry of Sincerity, 64; English Romantic Writers, 67, 2nd ed, 94; A History of Modern Poetry, Vol I: From the 1890s to the High Modernist Mode, 76; Vol II, Modernism and After, 87; Is Literary History Possible?, 92; author of numerous other publications and articles. **CONTACT ADDRESS** English Dept, Harvard Univ, 12 Quincy St., Cambridge, MA, 02138.

PERKINS, GEORGE
DISCIPLINE REALISM AND NATURALISM IN THE AMERICAN NOVEL **EDUCATION** PhD. **CAREER** E Mich Univ **HONORS AND AWARDS** Fel, Inst Adv Studies Hum,Univ Edinburgh; Found Mem, Soc Study Narrative Lit; Assoc ed, Narrative; Fulbright Scholar. **SELECTED PUBLICATIONS** Auth, The American Tradition as Literature. **CONTACT ADDRESS** Eastern Michigan Univ, Ypsilanti, MI, 48197. **EMAIL** ENG_Perkins@online.emich.edu

PERKINS, JAMES ASHBROOK
PERSONAL Born 02/07/1941, Covington, KY, m, 1963, 2 children **DISCIPLINE** ENGLISH AMERICAN LIT **EDUCATION** Centre Col, BA 63; Miami Univ, MA 65; Univ Tenn, PhD 72. **CAREER** Memphis Univ, instr, 65-67; Univ Tenn, instr 67-72; Westminster Col, prof 73-. **HONORS AND AWARDS** Fulbright; NEH sem Prin, Yale, NYU; NEH Inst, NYU, Princ. **MEMBERSHIPS** MLA; SAMLA; Robert Penn Warren Circle. **RESEARCH** Robert Drake; Robert Penn Warren; Southern Lit. **SELECTED PUBLICATIONS** Robert Penn Warren's All the Kings Men: Three stage Vers, with James A Grimshaw Jr, Athens, Univ GA Press, 99; Southern Writers at Century's End, with Jeffery Folks, Lexington, Univ Press KY, 97. **CONTACT ADDRESS** Dept Eng, Westminster Col, Box 62, New Wilmington, PA, 16142. **EMAIL** jperkins@westminster.edu

PERLMUTTER, DAVID
DISCIPLINE MASS COMMUNICATIONS **EDUCATION** Univ Pa, MA; Univ Minn, PhD, 95. **CAREER** Asst prof, La State Univ, 95-. **RESEARCH** Political communication, public opinion, film, photography, history of visual representation of war. **SELECTED PUBLICATIONS** Published articles in Visual Communication Quarterly, Historical Methods, Communication, and Visual Anthropology. **CONTACT ADDRESS** The Manship Sch of Mass Commun, Louisiana State Univ, Baton Rouge, LA, 70803. **EMAIL** deprlmu@unix1.sncc.lsu.edu

PERLOFF, MARJORIE GABRIELLE
PERSONAL Born 09/28/1931, Vienna, Austria, m, 1953, 2 children **DISCIPLINE** ENGLISH LITERATURE **EDUCATION** Oberlin Coll, 48-52; Barnard Coll, AB, 53; Cath Univ Am, MA, 56, PhD, 65. **CAREER** Florence Scott prof, Eng, Univ South Calif, 76-85; prof, Eng & Compar Lit, Stanford Univ, 86-90; PROF, HUM, STANFORD UNIV, 90-. **MEMBERSHIPS** Mod Lang Asn; Am Compar Lit Asn; Stanford Hum Inst **RESEARCH** Modernism; Postmodernism; 20th century poetry. **SELECTED PUBLICATIONS** Radical Artifacе: Writing Poetry in the Age of Media, Univ Chicago Press, 94; The Dance of the Intellect: Studies in the Poetry of the Pound Tradition, Cambridge Univ Press, 96; Wittgenstein's Ladder: Poetic Language and the Strangeness of the Ordinary, Univ Chicago Press, 96; In Preparation: Poetry On & Off the Page: Essays for Emergent Occasions, Northwestern Univ Press, 98. **CONTACT ADDRESS** Dept Eng, Stanford Univ, Stanford, CA, 94305. **EMAIL** mperloff@earthlink.net

PERLOFF, RICHARD M.
DISCIPLINE POLITICAL COM, JOURNALISM, PERSUASUION **EDUCATION** PhD, Univ of WI, MA, Univ of Pittsburgh, BA, Univ of MI. **CAREER** Comm, Cleveland St Univ. **SELECTED PUBLICATIONS** Auth, Political Communication: Politics, Press, and Public in America, Lawrence Erlbaum Assoc, 97; Perceptions and Conceptions of Political Media Impact: The Third-person Effect and Beyond, The Psychology of Political Communication, Univ MI Press, 96; The Dynamics of Persuasion, Lawrence Erlbaum Assoc, 93. **CONTACT ADDRESS** Commun Dept, Cleveland State Univ, 83 E 24th St, Cleveland, OH, 44115. **EMAIL** r.perloff@csuohio.edu

PERRY, PATSY BREWINGTON
PERSONAL Born 07/17/1933, Greensboro, North Carolina, m, 1955 **DISCIPLINE** ENGLISH **EDUCATION** North Carolina Coll, Durham, NC, BA (magna cum laude), 1950-54; North Carolina Coll, Durham, NC, MA, 1954-55; Univ of North Carolina, Chapel Hill, NC, PhD, 1968-72. **CAREER** Georgetown High School, Jacksonville, NC, teacher, 1955-56; Duke University, visiting professor, 1975; North Carolina Central Univ, Durham, NC, reserve book librarian, 1956-58, instructor, 1959-63, asst prof, 1964-71, assoc prof, 1972-74, prof, 1974-, English dept chmn, 1979-90, special asst to the chancellor, currently. **HONORS AND AWARDS** Alpha Kappa Mu Honorary Soc, 1953; Danforth Scholarship Grant, Summer, 1967; Career Teaching Fellowship, Univ of North Carolina, 1968-69; Faculty Fellow, North Carolina Central Univ, 1968-71; nominee, ACE Fellow Program in Academic Admin, Amer Council on Educ, 1977; Ford Foundation Writing Fellow, Recognition for Excellence in Teaching Writing, 1989; Silver Medallion Award for Excellence in Education, YWCA of Durham, 1991; Research Award, North Carolina Central University, 1991. **MEMBERSHIPS** Mem, YWCA, 1976-; mem The Links Inc, l976-; life mem, Coll Language Assn; mem, senator 1986-, Philological Assn of the Carolinas; mem, South Atlantic Modern Language Assn; mem, Assn of Departments of English; mem, The Langston Hughes Soc; reader, College Board English Composition Test (ETS), 1985-; board member, Women in Action for the Prevention of Violence, 1990-. **SELECTED PUBLICATIONS** Author of "The Literary Content of Frederick Douglass' Paper Through 1860," CLA Journal 1973, "One Day When I Was Lost: Baldwin's Unfulfilled Obligation," chapter in James Baldwin: A Critical Evaluation, edited by Therman B O'Daniel, Howard Univ Press 1977, and biographical essays in Southern Writers-Biographical Dictionary, Louisiana State Univ Press 1979, The Dictionary of Literary Biography, 1986; Notable BlackAmerican Women, edited by Jessi Smith, 1991, Southern Writers of the Second Renascence--Poets, Dramatists, Essayists, and others, edited by Joseph Flora and Robert Bain, 1992. **CONTACT ADDRESS** Dept of English, North Carolina Central Univ, Communications Bldg, Rm 327, Durham, NC, 27707.

PERSE, ELIZABETH M.
DISCIPLINE TELECOMMUNICATIONS, MASS COMMUNICATION **EDUCATION** Northwestern Univ, BA, 71; Kent State Univ, MA, 85, PhD, 87. **CAREER** Rev, criticism asst, Jour of Broadcasting, 83-84; ed asst, Jour Broadcasting & Electronic Media, 84-86; secy, Speech Commun Assn, 87-88; act ch, 93; ch, Speech Commun Assn, 93-94; pres, Arts and Sci Col Senate, 93-94; ch, dept search comm. 91-92, 93-94; ch, Speech Commun Assn, 93-94; assoc prof, 87-. **HONORS AND AWARDS** David B Smith fel, Kent State Univ, 86; grad stud senate res award, Kent State Univ, 86; Univ fel, Kent State Univ, 86-87; doc hon(s) fel, Speech Commun Assn, 87; grad stud senate dissertation award, Kent State Univ, 87; grant, 88, 91, 94; top paper award, Assn Edu in Jour and Mass Commun, 92., Rev and Criticism ed, Jour Broadcasting & Electronic Media, 94-97. **MEMBERSHIPS** Mem, Assn Edu in Jour and Mass Commun; Broadcast Edu Assn; E Commun Assn; Intl Commun Assn; Speech Commun Assn; Amer Acad Advt. **SELECTED PUBLICATIONS** Auth, Uses of Erotica and Acceptance of Rape Myths, Commun Res, 94; Sensation Seeking the Use of Television for Arousal, Commun Rpt, 96; co-auth, Gratifications From Newer Television Technologies, Jour Quart, 94, repr, Ablex, 97; Direct and Indirect Effects of Socioeconomic Status on Public Affairs Knowledge, Jour Quart, 94;Cultivation in the Newer Media Environment, Commun Res, 94; Measures of Mass Communications, Commun Research Measures: A sourcebook, Guilford, 94; Sports and Media Events Orientations to the 92 Winter Olympics, Jour Intl Commun, 95; The stability of College Students' Implicit Theories of Marriage as Measured by the Relational Dimensions Instrument, Commun Quart, 95; Women in Communications, Greenwood, 96; The Effects of Spokesperson Gender, PSA Appeal, and Involvement on Evaluations of Safe-sex Public Service Announcements, Health Commun, 96; News Coverage of Abortion Between Roe and Webster: Public Opinion and Real-world Events, Commun Res Rpt 14, 97; Uses of Interpersonal Communication Motives and Humor by Elders, Commun Res Rpt 14, 97; Gender Differences in Television Use: An Exploration of the Instrumental-expressive Dichotomy, Commun Res Rpt 14, 97; Communicate Oonline, Mountain View, Mayfield, 98; The Mayfield Quick Guide to the Internet for Communnications Students, Mountain View, Mayfield, 98; rev(s), Review and Criticism Editor's Note, Jour Broadcasting & Electronic Media, 95, 96. **CONTACT ADDRESS** Dept of Commun, Univ Delaware, 162 Ctr Mall, Newark, DE, 19716. **EMAIL** eperse@udel.edu

PERSON, LELAND S.
DISCIPLINE 19TH-CENTURY AMERICAN LITERATURE **EDUCATION** IN, PhD, 77. **CAREER** Univ Ala **HONORS AND AWARDS** Pres, Henry James Soc. **SELECTED PUBLICATIONS** Auth, Aesthetic Headaches: Women and a Masculine Poetics in Poe, Melville, and Hawthorne, 88. **CONTACT ADDRESS** Univ AL, 1400 University Blvd, Birmingham, AL, 35294-1150.

PETERFREUND, STUART S.
PERSONAL Born 06/30/1945, Brooklyn, NY, d, 1 child **DISCIPLINE** CREATIVE WRITING, ENGLISH LITERATURE **EDUCATION** Cornell Univ, BA, 66; Unif of Calif at Irvine, MFA, 68; Univ of Wash, PhD, 74. **CAREER** Asst prof, Univ of Ark at Little Rock, 75-78; asst prof, 78-82, assoc prof, 82-91, prof and chr, Northeastern Univ, 91-. **HONORS AND AWARDS** School of Criticism and Theory Fel, 77; Southern Arts Agencies Fel, 77; 4 NEH summer seminars, 79, 83, 88, & 90-91; Dibner Fel, 95. **MEMBERSHIPS** MLA; ASECS; AWP; SLS; Wordsworth-Coleridge Asn; Keats-Shelley Soc; Byron Soc; HSS. **RESEARCH** Eighteenth and Nineteenth-century English literature; literature and science; social history of science. **SELECTED PUBLICATIONS** Auth, Literature and Science: Theory and Practice, 90; William Blake in a Newtonian World, 98; numerous essays published in JHI, Configurations, Criticism, ELH, TWC, Eighteenth-Century Life, and others. **CONTACT ADDRESS** English Dept, Northeastern Univ, 360 Huntington Ave, Boston, MA, 02115-5096. **EMAIL** speterfr@lynx.dac.neu.edu

PETERS, ERSKINE ALVIN
PERSONAL Born 03/16/1948, Augusta, Georgia, s **DISCIPLINE** ENGLISH **EDUCATION** Yale Univ, summer study 1968; Paine Coll, BA English 1969; Oberlin Coll, Postbaccalaureate study 1969-70; Princeton Univ, PhD English 1976; Sorbonne Paris, summer study 1984. **CAREER** Morristown Coll, tutor 1970-72; Univ of CA Berkeley, assoc prof of Afro-Amer Literature; Univ of Notre Dame, prof of English, currently. **HONORS AND AWARDS** First Recipient of Frank J Henry Award, Univ of GA 1968; Rockefeller Fellowship in Afro-Amer Studies 1972-76. **MEMBERSHIPS** Advisor Oakland Scholar Achiever Program 1980-82; discussion leader SATE Program at San Quentin Prison 1980-83. **SELECTED PUBLICATIONS** Auth, William Faulkner, The Yoknapatawpha World and Black Being 1983, African Openings to the Tree of Life 1983, Fundamentals of Essay Writing 1983. **CONTACT ADDRESS** Professor of English, Univ of Notre Dame, Notre Dame, IN, 46556.

PETERS, JULIE
DISCIPLINE DRAMA AND THEATRE HISTORY **EDUCATION** Yale Univ, AB, 81; Princeton Univ, PhD, 87. **CAREER** Asoc prof. **HONORS AND AWARDS** Fel, Fulbright found; fel, Folger Library; fel, Amer Coun Learned Soc; fel, Humboldt found. **RESEARCH** Law and literature. **SELECTED PUBLICATIONS** Auth, Congreve, the Drama, and the Printed Word, Stanford, 90; co-ed, Women's Rights, Human Rights: International Feminist Perspectives, Routledge, 95. **CONTACT ADDRESS** Dept of Eng, Columbia Col, New York, 2960 Broadway, New York, NY, 10027-6902.

PETERSON, BRENT O.
DISCIPLINE 19TH AND 20TH-CENTURY GERMAN LITERATURE **EDUCATION** Johns Hopkins Univ, BA; Univ IA, MA; Univ MN, PhD. **CAREER** Assoc prof, Ripon Col; instr, Humboldt Univ, Berlin. **HONORS AND AWARDS** NEH grants. **SELECTED PUBLICATIONS** Wrote a book on 19th-century Ger-Am(s). **CONTACT ADDRESS** Ripon Col, Ripon, WI. **EMAIL** PetersonB@mac.ripon.edu

PETERSON, ERIC E.
DISCIPLINE COMMUNICATIONS **EDUCATION** Southern IL Univ, PhD, 80. **CAREER** Assoc prof, ch, dept Commun and Jour, Univ ME. **RESEARCH** The integration of media consumption; interpersonal play. **SELECTED PUBLICATIONS** Auth, Media consumption and girls who want to have fun, Critical Stud in Mass Commun, 4, 87; The technology of media consumption, Am Behavioral Sci, 32, 88; Moving toward a gender balanced curriculum in basic speech communication courses, Commun Educ, 40, 91; Diversity and Franco-American identity politics, Maine Hist Soc Quart, 34, 94; Nonsexist language reform and "political correctness," Women and Lang, 17, No.2, 94. **CONTACT ADDRESS** Univ ME, Orono, ME, 04469-5752. **EMAIL** peterson@maine.edu

PETERSON, LINDA H.
PERSONAL Born 10/11/1948, Saginaw, MI **DISCIPLINE** ENGLISH **EDUCATION** Wheaton Col, BA, 69; Univ Rhode Island, MA, 73; Brown Univ, PhD, 78. **CAREER** Lectr, 77-78, asst prof, 78-85, assoc prof, 85-92, dir undergrad study in English, 90-94, Prof, 92- , chr Dept of English, 94- , Yale Univ, 77- ; Dir Bass Writing prog, Yale Col, 79-89 & 90-. **HONORS**

AND AWARDS Morse fel, 81-82; Mellon fel, 84-85 & 97-98; NEH fel, 89-90; vis fel, Clare Hall, Cambridge, 98. **MEMBERSHIPS** MLA; NCTE; WPA; RSVP. **RESEARCH** 19th Century British literature. **SELECTED PUBLICATIONS** Auth, Victorian Autobiography: The Tradition of Self-Interpretation, Yale Univ Press, 86; coauth, Writing Prose, Yale Col, 89; ed, Wuthering Heights: A Case Study in Contemporary Criticism, St Martin's Press, 92; ed The Norton Reader, & Instructors Guide to the Norton Reader, W W Norton, 92; coauth, A Struggle for Fame: Victorian Woman Artists and Authors, Yale Ctr Brit Art, 94; auth, Traditions of Autobiography: Womens Autobiography and Autobiographical Fiction in Nineteenth-Century England, Univ Press Va, 99. **CONTACT ADDRESS** English Dept, Yale Univ, PO Box 208302, New Haven, CT, 06520-8302.

PETERSON, LORNA INGRID
PERSONAL Born 07/22/1956, Buffalo, NY **DISCIPLINE** LIBRARY SCIENCE **EDUCATION** Dickinson College, Carlisle, PA, BA, 1977; Case Western Reserve Univ, Cleveland, OH, MS library science, 1980; Iowa State University, PhD, 1992. **CAREER** Wright State University, Dayton, OH, humanities reference librarian/special college cataloger, 1980-81; Ohio University, Athens, OH, special college cataloger, 1982-82; Iowa State University, Ames, IA, cataloger, 1983-85, bibliographic instructor, 1985-91; SUNY-BUFFALO, NY, assistant professor, ASSOC PROF, currently. **MEMBERSHIPS** Board member, Ames, ISU YWCA, 1984-89; chair communications committee, Iowa Library Assn/ACRL, 1984-86; chair membership committee, Iowa Library Assn/ACRL, 1987-88; representative to ALA/RTSD Org & Bylaws, American Library Assn, 1984-86; member, Black Caucus of ALA, 1980, 1988-; African American Librarian Assn of Western New York, 1990-; ALA-Lirt Research Committee, 1994-96; ALA-ACRL/BIS, Education for Bibliographic Instruction, 1994-96; ALA-RASD/MOPSS, Catalog Use Committee, 1992-96; Committee on Accreditation, 1997-2001. **CONTACT ADDRESS** Sch of Info & Library Studies, SUNY, Buffalo, 534 Baldy Hall, Buffalo, NY, 14260.

PETERSON, R.G.
PERSONAL Born 01/09/1936, Chicago, IL **DISCIPLINE** ENGLISH LITERATURE **EDUCATION** Univ Minn, BA, 56, PhD, 63; Northwestern Univ, MA, 58. **CAREER** Instr Eng, Univ Minn, 60-62; from asst prof to assoc prof, 63-76, Prof Eng & Classics, St Olaf Col, 76-96, prof emer, 96- ; book rev ed, Eighteenth-Century Studies, 79-83; exec secy, Am Soc for Eighteenth-Century Stud, 83-89; exec comt, Int Soc for Eighteenth-Century Stud, 83-94. **HONORS AND AWARDS** William Riley Parker Prize, MLA, 75-76. **MEMBERSHIPS** MLA; Am Soc 18th Century Stud; Johnson Soc Cent Region; Class Asn Midwest & South. **RESEARCH** The classics in the Restoration and eighteenth century; Latin literature, especially poetry and history; literary structure. **SELECTED PUBLICATIONS** Auth, Larger Manners and Events: Sallust and Virgil in Absolom and Achitophel, PMLA, 67; auth, The Unity of Horace Epistle 17, Class J, 68; auth, The Unavailing Gift: Dryden's Roman Farewell to Mr. Oldham, Mod Philol, 69; auth, The Unknown Self in the Fourth Satire of Persius, Class J, 73; auth, Renaissance Classicism in Pope's Duncaid, Studies Eng Lit, 75; auth, Samuel Johnson at War with the Classics, 18th Century Stud, 75; auth, Critical Calculations: Measure and Symmetry in Literature, PMLA, 76. **CONTACT ADDRESS** 1158 Fifth Ave, 12-A, New York, NY, 10029-6917. **EMAIL** Petersor@idt.net

PETERSON, RICHARD S.
PERSONAL Born 07/14/1938, Ayr, Scotland, m, 1965, 1 child **DISCIPLINE** ENGLISH **EDUCATION** Princeton Univ, BA 60; Univ Cal Berkeley, PhD 68. **CAREER** Princeton Univ, inst, asst prof, 66-72; Univ VA, lect, 72-75; Yale Univ, asst prof, 76-80; Univ Conn Storrs, assoc prof, prof, 80 to 84-. **HONORS AND AWARDS** Fulbright Fel; APS Fel; 2 NEH Fel; ACLS Fel; ABS Fel. **MEMBERSHIPS** MLA; RSA; Spenser Soc. **RESEARCH** Ben Johnson; Edmund Spenser; Renaissance English and French Lit; Latin Poetry; Hist; Archives. **SELECTED PUBLICATIONS** Auth, Rereading Colin's Broken Pipe, Spenser Studies, coauth, 99; Laurel crown and Apes tail-New Light on Spenser, Spenser Studies, 98; Spurting Froth Upon Coutiers, TLS, 97; In From the Cold: An Englishman at Rome, 1595, ANQ, 92. **CONTACT ADDRESS** Dept of English, Univ of Connecticut, Storrs, CT, 06268.

PETHICA, JAMES
DISCIPLINE ENGLISH **EDUCATION** Oxford Univ, BA, 80; DPhil, 87. **CAREER** Vis asst prof. **RESEARCH** Modern British literature; Irish studies; modern drama; contemporary Irish poetry; modernist and experimental fiction. **SELECTED PUBLICATIONS** Auth, WB Yeats: Last Poems, Manuscript Materials, Editor Lady Gregory's Diaries 1892-1902. **CONTACT ADDRESS** Dept of English, Williams Col, Statson d-18, Williamstown, MA, 01267. **EMAIL** jpethica@williams.edu

PETRAGLIA-BAHRI, DEEPIKA
DISCIPLINE ENGLISH LANGUAGE AND LITERATURE **EDUCATION** Bowling Green Univ, PhD, 92. **CAREER** Fac, Ga Inst Tech, 94; fac, Bowling Green Univ, 92-94; asst prof, Emory Univ, 95. **RESEARCH** Postcolonial literature and theory; technology, culture, and postcolonialism. **SELECTED PUBLICATIONS** Auth, Terms of Engagement: Postcolonialism, Transnationalism, and Composition Studies, Exploring Borderlands: Postcolonial and Composition Studies, Jour Comp Theory,, 98; Marginally Off-Center: Postcolonialism in the Teaching Machine, Col Engl, 97; Once more with Feeling: What is Postcolonialism?" ARIEL: Rev Int Engl Lit, 95; Disembodying the Corpus: Postcolonial Pathology in Tsitsi Dangarembga's Nervous Conditions, Postmod Cult: An Elec Jour Interdisc Crit, 94; Boethius and Sir Thomas Browne: The Common Ground, Mythes, Croyances et Religion dans le monde Anglo-Saxon, 92; The Reader's Guide to P.G. Wodehouse's America, Studies Am Humor, 89; coauth, "Swallowing for Twenty Years/the American Mind and Body:" An Interview with G. S. Sharat Chandra, Jour Commonwealth Postcolonial Studies, 97; co-ed, Between the Lines: South Asians and Postcoloniality, Temple UP, 96. **CONTACT ADDRESS** English Dept, Emory Univ, 1380 Oxford Rd NE, Atlanta, GA, 30322-1950. **EMAIL** dpetrag@emory.edu

PETRAGLIA-BAHRI, JOSEPH
DISCIPLINE RHETORIC AND COGNITIVE SCIENCE **EDUCATION** Carnegie Mellon Univ, PhD, 91. **CAREER** Asst prof, Ga Inst of Technol. **RESEARCH** The rhetoric of inquiry. **SELECTED PUBLICATIONS** Ed, Reconceiving Writing, Rethinking Writing Instruction, Lawrence Erlbaum, 95. **CONTACT ADDRESS** Sch of Lit, Commun, & Cult, Georgia Inst of Tech, Skiles Cla, Atlanta, GA, 30332. **EMAIL** joseph.petraglia@lcc.gatech.edu

PETRESS, KENNETH C.
PERSONAL Born 11/01/1939, Chicago, IL **DISCIPLINE** SPEECH COMMUNICATION **EDUCATION** Northern IL Univ, BS Ed, 77, MA, 79, CAS, 80; LA State Univ, PhD, 88. **CAREER** Instr, Northern IL Univ, 80-83; vis prof, Xi Dian Univ, Xian, China, 83-84; lect, Empora State Univ, 84-86; prof, Univ ME at Presque Isle, 88-. **MEMBERSHIPS** Nat Commun Asn; Southern States Commun Asn; Yale-China Asn. **RESEARCH** Rhetoriaty of political symbols. **SELECTED PUBLICATIONS** Auth, Coping with a New Educational Environment: Chinese Students' Imagined Interactions Before Beginning Studies in the US, J of Instr Psychol, 22 (1), 95; A Partial Solution to the University Journal Subscription Problem, J of Instr Psychol, 22 (3), 95; with Keith L Madore, College Faculty Absences Need to Be Treated More Seriously, College Student J, 29 (3), 95; Olympic Participation By Children: Is There A Dark Side?, ME Scholar, 8, 95; Questions of Obligation, Cost Effectiveness, and Efficiency: University Remedial Programs, Education, 116 (1), 95; The Multiple Roles of An Undergraduate's Academic Advisor, Education, 117 (1), 96; The Dilema of University Undergraduate Student Attendance Policies: To Require Class Attendance or Not, Col Student J 30 (3), 96; Broasdcasting in China, in Alan Wells, ed, World Broadcasting: A Comparative View, Ablex, 96; with Kurt O Hofmann, The Community Review Board Offers Students Fairness in Administrative Decision Appeals, Education, 118 (1), 97. **CONTACT ADDRESS** 181 Main St, Presque, ME, 04769-2888. **EMAIL** petress@polaris.umpi.maine.edu

PETRIE, NEIL
DISCIPLINE ENGLISH LITERATURE **EDUCATION** Univ Nothern Colo, BA; Kent State Univ, PhD. **CAREER** Assoc prof. **SELECTED PUBLICATIONS** Auth, pubs on drama and fiction writers. **CONTACT ADDRESS** Dept of English, Colorado State Univ, Fort Collins, CO, 80523. **EMAIL** npetrie@vines.colostate.edu

PETRONELLA, VINCENT F.
PERSONAL Born 01/10/1935, New York, NY, m, 1965 **DISCIPLINE** ENGLISH **EDUCATION** City Col of NY, BA, 62; Univ of Oregon, MA, 64; Univ of Mass at Amherst, PhD, 69. **CAREER** Tchg asst, Univ of Ore, 62-64; instr, Univ of Mass, 64-66; asst prof, 66-67, assoc prof, Boston State Col, 67-70; PROF OF ENGLISH, UNIV OF MASS, 70-. **HONORS AND AWARDS** Tchg Svc Awd, Boston State Col, Univ of Mass, 80; Healey Pub Svc Awd, Univ of Mass, 96. **MEMBERSHIPS** Boston Browning Soc, 93-98; Int Shakespear Asn; MLA. **RESEARCH** Shakespeare; The English Renaissance; the impact of the age of Shakespeare on the Nineteenth Century; Robert Browning; George Bernard Shaw. **SELECTED PUBLICATIONS** Auth, Shakespeare's Dramatic Chambers, Festschrift for G. Blakemore Evans, Fairleigh Dickinson Univ Press, 99; Shakespeare's The Comedy of Errors, Shakespearean Criticism 34, Gale Research, 97; William Archer and Bernard Shaw, British Playwrights 1880-1956: A Research and Production Sourcebooks, Greenwood Press, 96; Robert Browning and Julia Wedgwood: The Intellectual and Emotional Relationship, Ars Ceramica 14, 98. **CONTACT ADDRESS** Dept of English, Univ of Masschusetts, Boston, 100 Morrissey Blvd, Boston, MA, 02125-3393.

PETRUZZI, ANTHONY
DISCIPLINE RHETORIC AND COMPOSITION **EDUCATION** Franconia Col, BA, Middlebury Col, MA; Univ Conn, PhD. **CAREER** Instr, dir, Compos, Univ Nebr, Kearney. **HONORS AND AWARDS** Grad Stud Tchg Award, Univ Conn. **SELECTED PUBLICATIONS** Published articles on Plato, Emerson, and Dante. **CONTACT ADDRESS** Univ Nebr, Kearney, Kearney, NE, 68849. **EMAIL** petruzzia@platte.unk.edu

PETTEY, GARY R.
DISCIPLINE MASS COM THEORY, METHODS, JOURNALISM **EDUCATION** Univ WI, BA, MA, PhD. **CAREER** Comm, Cleveland St Univ. **SELECTED PUBLICATIONS** Co-auth, The Relationship of Perceived Physician Communicator Style to Patient Satisfaction, Commun Rep(s); Designing a commun campaign to teach intravenous drug users and sex partners about AIDS, Publ Health Rep(s), 91. **CONTACT ADDRESS** Commun Dept, Cleveland State Univ, 83 E 24th St, Cleveland, OH, 44115. **EMAIL** g.pettey@csuohio.edu

PETTIS, JOYCE
PERSONAL NC, m **DISCIPLINE** AFRICAN AMERICAN LITERATURE **EDUCATION** Winston Salem State Univ, BS, 68; East Carolina Univ, MA, 74; Univ N Carolina, Chapel Hill, PhD, 83. **CAREER** Pitt Commun Col, 72-74; East Carolina Univ, 74-85; assoc prof, Eng, North Carolina State Univ, 85-; vis assoc prof, Univ Ala, 94-96. **HONORS AND AWARDS** College Lang Asn For Scholarship Award, 95; 1997 nominee for Provost's African-American Prof Dev Award. **MEMBERSHIPS** Col Lang Asn; Charles Chesnutt Soc; MLA; George Moses Horton Soc. **RESEARCH** Festivity and celebration in fiction. **SELECTED PUBLICATIONS** Auth, Legacies of Community and History in Paule Marshall's Daughters, Stud in the Lit Imagination, 93; auth, The Marrow of Tradition: Charles Chesnutt's Novel of the South, No Carolina Lit Rev, 94; auth, Toward Wholeness in Paule Marshall's Fiction, Univ Virginia, 95; auth, An Interview with Gerald Barrax, Callaloo, 97; auth, Read Ann Petry's The Narrows into Black Literary Tradition, in Hubbard, ed, Recovered Writers/Recovered Texts, Univ Tenn, 97. **CONTACT ADDRESS** English Dept, No Carolina State Univ, PO Box 8105, Raleigh, NC, 27695. **EMAIL** pettis@social.chass.ncsu.edu

PFAFF, DANIEL W.
PERSONAL Born 05/19/1940, Nampa, ID, m, 1966, 2 children **DISCIPLINE** JOURNALISM, MASS COMMUNICATION **EDUCATION** Univ OR, BS, 62; Penn State Univ, MA, 68; Univ MN, PhD, 72. **CAREER** Penn State Univ, Asst to Prof Journalism, 71-98; Col Communications, Assoc Dean, 90-94. **HONORS AND AWARDS** Frank Luther Mott-Kappa Tau Alpha Research Award **MEMBERSHIPS** Am Journalism Hist Asn **RESEARCH** Am Hist and Biogr, 19 and 20th cent. **SELECTED PUBLICATIONS** Joseph Pulitzer II and the Post Dispatch: A Newspaperman's Life, Um¤inv Pk, PA, Penn State Press, 91; Essays for Oxford Univ Press on Joseph Pulitzer, Joseph Pulitzer II, George Jones and John Wien Forney for American National Biography; Essays for Onyx Press on Spiro Agnew's Anti Press Campaign, Edward P Morgan and Howard K Smith for the Encyclopedia of Television News, ed by Michael D Murray. **CONTACT ADDRESS** Pennsylvania State Univ, 260 Homan Av, State College, PA, 16801-6332. **EMAIL** dwp1@psu.edu

PFAU, MICHAEL
PERSONAL Born 03/14/1945, Washington, DC, m, 1968, 2 children **DISCIPLINE** COMMUNICATION/JOURNALISM **EDUCATION** Univ of NH, BA, 1970, MA, 1971; Uniz of Ariz, PhD, 87. **CAREER** Alexander Ramsey High Sch, Dept of Social Studs, Instructor, 71-75; Augustana Col, Dept of Commun & Theatre, asst prof, 75-81, dir of forensics, 75-84, assoc prof & dept head, 81-88, prof/dept head, 88-93; Univ of Ariz, Teaching Assoc, 84-86; Univ of Wisc-Madison, prof, 93-, Dir of Grad Studs, 95-. **HONORS AND AWARDS** Finalists, Nat Debate Tournament, 76, 80, 83; Top 3 Paper, Hlth Commun Div, Speech Commun Assoc, Int Commun Assoc, 87; finalist, dissertation award, Speech Commun Assoc, 88; Burlington North Found Fac Achievement Award, 90; Augustana Res and Artists's Fund grant, 84, 87-93; Golden Anniversary Award, Speech Commun Assoc, 91; Vilas Assoc App, 96-97; Top Four Paper, Info Sys Div, Int Commun Assoc, 98., Summa cum laude grad, Univ of NH. **MEMBERSHIPS** Assoc for Educ in J & Mass Commun; Broadcast Educ Assoc; Cent States Commun Assoc; Int Commun Assoc (sec, 95-97, membership ch, 97-99); Pub Relations Soc of Am; Nat Comun Assoc; Am Forensic Assoc; Speech Commun Assoc. **RESEARCH** Media influence. **SELECTED PUBLICATIONS** Co-auth, Persuasive Communication Campaigns, Allyn & Bacon, 93; co-auth, With Malice toward All? The Media and Public Confidence in Democratic Institutions, Praeger Pubs, (in press); co-auth, Communication and Public Opinion, Sage, (in progress); co-auth, Relational and Competence Perceptions of Presidential Candidates during Primary Election Campaigns, J of Broadcasting & Elec Media, vol 37, 275-292. 93; co-auth, The persistence of Inoculation in Conferring Resistance to Smoking Initiation among Adolescents: The Second Year, Hum Commun Res, vol 20, 413-430, 94; co-auth, Effectiveness of Adwatch Formats in Deflecting Targeted Political Attack Ads, Commun Res, vol 21, 325-341, 94; auth, Impact of Product Involvement, Message Format, and Receiver Sex of the Efficacy of Comparative Advertising Messages, Commun Quart, vol 42, 244-258, 94; co-

auth, Television Viewing and Public Perceptions of Attorneys, Hum Commun Res, vol 21, 307-330, 95; co-auth, Influence of Communication Modalities on Voters' Perceptions of Candidates during Presidential Primary Campaigns, J of Commun, vol 45, 122-133, 95; co-auth, An Innoculation Theory Explanation for the Effects of Corporate Issue/Advocacy Advertising Campaigns, Commun Res, vol 22, 485-505, 95; co-auth, The Influence of Television Viewing on Public Perceptions of Physicians, J of Broadcasting & Elec Media, vol 39, 441-458, 95; co-auth, Television Viewing and Perception of Social Reality among Native American Adolescents, Intercultural Commun Studs, vol 1, 1-7, 96; co-auth, Influence of Traditional and Non-Traditional News Media in the 1992 Election Campaign, West J of Commun, vol 60, 214-232, 96; co-auth, Enriching the Inoculation Construct: The Role of Critical Components in the Process of Resistance, Hum Commun Res, vol 24, 187-215, 97; co-auth, Influence of Communication During the Distant Phase of the 1996 Republican Presidential Primary Campaign, J of Commun, vol 47, 6-26, 97; co-auth, Nuances in Inoculation: The Role of Inoculation Approach, Ego-Involvement, and Message Processing Disposition in Resistance, Commun Quart, vol 45, 461-481, 97; co-auth, The Influence of Individual Communication Media on Public Confidence in Democratic Institutions, The South Commun J, vol 63, 91-112, 98; co-auth, Use of Political Talk Radio versus Other Media and Public Confidence in Democratic Institutions, J & Mass Commun Quart, (in press); co-auth, Media Use Public Confidence in Democratic Institutions, J of Broadcasting & Elec Media, (in press). **CONTACT ADDRESS** Sch of J & Mass Commun, Univ of Wisc-Madison, 17 Rye Cir, Madison, WI, 53717. **EMAIL** mwpfau@facstaff.wic.edu

PFAU, THOMAS
DISCIPLINE ENGLISH LITERATURE **EDUCATION** SUNY Buffalo, PhD, 89. **CAREER** Assoc prof, Duke Univ. **RESEARCH** 18th and 19th century intellectual and lit hist, with an emphasis on Eng Romanticism and on continental aesthetic and epistemological theory. **SELECTED PUBLICATIONS** Auth, Wordsworth's Profession: Form, Class, and The Logic of Early Romantic Cultural Production, Stanford UP, 97; ed, Friedrich Holderlin: Essays and Letters on Theory, SUNY, 87; Idealism and the Endgame of Theory: Three Essays (rev), SUNY, 94; co-ed, Rhetorical and Cultural Dissolution in Romanticism, a special issue of South Atlantic Quarterly, 96. **CONTACT ADDRESS** Eng Dept, Duke Univ, Durham, NC, 27706.

PFEIFFER, SANDY W.
DISCIPLINE COMMUNICATION STUDIES **EDUCATION** Amherst Col, BA; Kent State Univ, PhD. **CAREER** Prof, 80-, Southern Polytech State Univ. **RESEARCH** Am lit; international tech commun; proposal writing; Japan cult. **SELECTED PUBLICATIONS** Auth, Proposal Writing: The Art of Friendly Persuasion, Merrill, 89; Technical Writing: A Practical Approach, Prentice Hall, 97. **CONTACT ADDRESS** Hum and Tech Commun Dept, Southern Polytech State Univ, S Marietta Pkwy, PO Box 1100, Marietta, GA, 30060.

PFORDRESHER, JOHN P.
DISCIPLINE ENGLISH LITERATURE **EDUCATION** Georgetown Col, BA; Univ Minn, PhD. **CAREER** Eng Dept, Georgetown Univ **RESEARCH** Victorian literature; relationship of painting to literature in 19th century; Catholic studies. **SELECTED PUBLICATIONS** Auth, England in Literature, 89; Classics in World Literature, 89; Variorum Edition: Tennyson's Idylls of the King, 73. **CONTACT ADDRESS** English Dept, Georgetown Univ, 37th and O St, Washington, DC, 20057.

PHELAN, JAMES PIUS X.
PERSONAL Born 01/25/1951, New York, NY, m, 1972, 2 children **DISCIPLINE** ENGLISH LITERATURE **EDUCATION** Boston Coll, BA, Eng Lit, 72; Univ Chicago, MA, Eng Lang & Lit, 73, PhD, 77. **CAREER** Instr, Sch Art Inst Chicago, Lib Arts, 75-77; asst prof, Ohio State Univ, 77-83; assoc prof, Ohio State Univ, 83-89; PROF, OHIO STATE UNIV, ENG, 89-; Ch, Eng Dept, Ohio State Univ, 94-. **MEMBERSHIPS** Soc Study Narr Lit; MLA, NCTE, Midwest MLA **RESEARCH** Narrative theory; Critical theory; English & American novel. **SELECTED PUBLICATIONS** Narrative as Rhetoric: Technique, Audiences, Ethics, Ideology, Ohio State Univ Press, 96; co-edr, Understanding Narrative, Ohio State Univ Press, 94; co-edr, Adventures of Huckleberry Finn: A Case Study in Critical Controversy, Bedford Books, 95; "Now I Lay Me: Nick's Strange Monologue, Hemingway's Powerful Lyric, and the Reader's Disconcerting Experience," New Essays on the Short Stories of Ernest Hemingway, Cambridge Univ Press, 98; "Before Reading in its Own Terms," Before Reading: Narrative Conventions and the Politics of Interpretation, Ohio State Univ Press, 98; "Narrative as Rhetoric: Reading the Spells of Porter's Magic'," The Critical Tradition, Bedford Books, 98. **CONTACT ADDRESS** Dept Eng, Ohio State Univ, 164 W. 17th Ave, Columbus, OH, 43210-1370. **EMAIL** phelan.1@osu.edu

PHELPS, TERESA GODWIN
PERSONAL Born 05/29/1944, Bournemouth, England, m, 1964, 3 children **DISCIPLINE** LEGAL WRITING **EDUCATION** Univ Notre Dame, BA, 73, MA, 75, PhD(English), 80. **CAREER** Asst Prof Legal Writing, Law Sch, Univ Notre Dame, 80-, Ed, Notre Dame English J, 78-80. **MEMBERSHIPS** MLA; Law & Humanities Inst; Asn Am Law Sch. **RESEARCH** Legal language; law and humanities. **SELECTED PUBLICATIONS** Auth, Problems and Cases for Legal Writing, Nat Inst Trial Advocacy, 82; the Power of Persuasion, University of Cincinnati Law Review, Vol 0063, 1994. **CONTACT ADDRESS** Law Sch, Univ Notre Dame, Notre Dame, IN, 46556.

PHILLIPS, DENNY
DISCIPLINE COMMUNICATION STUDIES **EDUCATION** Hiram Col, BA; Univ Ohio, MA, PhD. **CAREER** Prof. **RESEARCH** Communication and popular culture; organizational communication; media programming and management. **SELECTED PUBLICATIONS** Auth, Meddling in Metal Music, Studies Social Sci, 92; The Organization Communication Perspective, Speech Tchr, 91; Communication Investments, Broadcast Cable Financial J, 91; co-auth, Strip Mining for Gold and Platinum: Record Sales and Chart Performance Pre- and Post-MTV, Popular Music Soc, 92; Influence in the Workplace: Maximizing Personal Empowerment; MTV and the New Artist: Bullet, Breaker or Bust?, Popular Music Soc, 92. **CONTACT ADDRESS** Speech Communication Dept, Colorado State Univ, Fort Collins, CO, 80523. **EMAIL** dphillips@vines.colostate.edu

PHILLIPS, GENE D.
DISCIPLINE ENGLISH **EDUCATION** Loyola Univ Chicago, MA, 57; Fordham Univ NY, PhD, 70. **CAREER** Prof. **RESEARCH** Modern novel, British & American; adaptation of fiction to film; film history, British & American. **SELECTED PUBLICATIONS** Auth, Hemingway and Film, Ungar, 80; Fiction, Film, and F. Scott Fitzgerald, Loyola UP, 86; Fiction, Film, and Faulkner: The Art of Adaptation, Univ Tenn Press, 88; Conrad and Cinema: The Art of Adaptation, Peter Lang, 95. **CONTACT ADDRESS** Dept of English, Loyola Univ, Chicago, 6525 N Sheridan Rd, Chicago, IL, 60626. **EMAIL** gphilli@wpo.it.luc.edu

PHILLIPS, KENDALL R.
PERSONAL Born 05/12/1969, San Antonio, TX, m, 1994 **DISCIPLINE** SPEECH COMMUNICATION **EDUCATION** Southwest Baptist Univ, BS, 90; Cent Mo State Univ, MA, 92; Pa State Univ, PhD, 95. **CAREER** Asst prof, Cent Mo State Univ, 95-. **HONORS AND AWARDS** Kathryn DeBoer Distinguished Teaching award; Top Paper, Rhetoric & Pub addres, E Commun Assoc. **MEMBERSHIPS** Nat Commun Assoc; Rhet Soc of Am; Am Forensics Assoc. **RESEARCH** Rhetorical theory/criticism; continental philosophy. **SELECTED PUBLICATIONS** Co-auth, Self-monitoring and argumentativeness: Using argument as impression management, Argument in Controversy, Speech Commun Assoc, 193-196, 91; co-auth, Impact and implications of parliamentary debate format on American debate, Advanced debate: Readings in theory, practice, and teaching, Net Textbook Co, 94-104, 92; co-auth, Cyberphobia and Education, Commun Law & Policy Newsletter, vol 7, no 1, 3, 96; auth, The spaces of public dissension: Reconsidering the public sphere, Commun monographs, vol 63, 231-248, 96; auth, Interpretive controversy and The Silence of the Lambs, Rhet Soc Quart, vol, 28, 33-47, 98; auth, Rhetoric, resistance and criticism: A response to Sloop and Ono, Philos & Rhet, (in press); auth, Tactical apologies: The American Nursing Association and assisted suicide, South Commun J, (in press). **CONTACT ADDRESS** Dept of Commun, Central Missouri State Univ, 136 Martin Hall, Warrensburg, MO, 64093. **EMAIL** phillips@cmsuvmb.cmsu.edu

PHILLIPS, ROBERT
PERSONAL Born 02/02/1938, Milford, DE, m, 1963, 1 child **DISCIPLINE** ENGLISH, COMMUNICATIONS **EDUCATION** Syracuse Univ, BA (English), 60, BA (Communications), 60, MA (English), 62. **CAREER** Prof of English and Dir of Creative Writing Program, 91-96; Moores Univ Scholar, Univ Houston, 98-; poetry rev ed, Modern Poetry Studies, 69-73; poetry reviewer, The Houston Post, 92-95; poetry rev, The Houston Chronicle, 95-. **HONORS AND AWARDS** Award in Lit, Am Academy of Arts and Letters; CAPS Award in Poetry. **MEMBERSHIPS** PEN; Poetry Soc of Am; Poets' House; ASCAP. **RESEARCH** 20th century Am poetry and fiction. **SELECTED PUBLICATIONS** Auth, Triumph of the Night, Carroll & Graf, 89, reissued as The Omnibus of 20th-Century Ghost Stories, Robison, 90, Italian, German, and Russian eds, 91, Carroll & Graf paperback, 92; Shenandoah and Other Verse Plays, BOA Eds, 92; Public Landing Revisited, Story Line Press, 92; Delmore Schwatz & James Laughlin: Selected Letters, W W Norton, 93 (Chosen as a Notable Book of the Year by the New York Times Book Review); Face to Face (poetry), Wings Press, 93; Breakdown Lane, Johns Hopkins Univ Press, 94 (Chosen as a Notable Book of the Year by the New York Times Book Review); William Goyen: Selected Letters from a Writer's Life, Univ TX Press, 95, with an afterword by Sir Stephen Spender; New & Selected Poems by Marya Zaturenska, Syracuse Univ Press, 99; News About People You Know, forthcoming; The Madness of Art: Literary Interviews, forthcoming; Fiction's Forms (textbook), forthcoming; numerous other publications. **CONTACT ADDRESS** Dept of English, Univ of Houston, Creative Writing Prog, Houston, TX, 77204-3012.

PHILLIPS MCGOWAN, MARCIA
DISCIPLINE FEMINIST CRITICISM **EDUCATION** CT Col, BA; Rutgers Univ, MA, PhD. **CAREER** Eng Dept, Eastern Conn State Univ **SELECTED PUBLICATIONS** Coed, Claribel Alegria and Central American Literature, OH Univ Press, 94. **CONTACT ADDRESS** Eastern Connecticut State Univ, 83 Windham Street, Willimantic, CT, 06226. **EMAIL** MCGOWAN@ECSU.CTSTATEU.EDU

PHILPOTT, JEFFREY S.
DISCIPLINE COMMUNICATIONS **EDUCATION** Lewis and Clark Col, BA, 80; Univ NE Lincoln, MA, 83; Univ WA, PhD, 95. **CAREER** Comm, Seattle Univ. **SELECTED PUBLICATIONS** Auth, Recurrent Form, Time, and Situation: Common Rhetorical Responses to Public Crisis as Synchronic Genre, Paper presented at the 2nd Int Symp on Genre, Simon Fraser Univ, Vancouver, BC, 98; Turning Tragedy into Triumph: Rhetorical Transformation and the Explosion of the Space Shuttle Challenger, Paper presented at the Western Speech Commun Asn Conv, Monterey, Calif, 97; Eternal Questions, Evolving Answers: Fifty Years of Seattle University Mission Statements, Gaffney Lect, Seattle Univ, 96; From 'Major Malfunction' to 'Bold Pioneers': Public Rhetoric in the Aftermath of the Challenger Disaster, Sharon James Mem Lect, Seattle Univ, 96; Edmund Burke, Thomas Paine, and the Motive for Political Action, Paper presented at the Northwest Conf on Brit Stud, Vancouver, Wash, 93; Defense Spending and the New World Order: Scenic Placement in Post-Cold War Military Rhetoric, Paper presented at Western Speech Commun Asn annual conv, Boise, 92; King George: Metaphoric Constructions of President Bush in Patrick Buchanan's 1992 Presidential Campaign, Presentation at the Western Speech Commun Asn annual conv, Boise, 92. **CONTACT ADDRESS** Dept of Commun, Seattle Univ, 900 Broadway, Seattle, WA, 98122-4460. **EMAIL** jphilpot@seattleu.edu

PICKENS, ERNESTINE W. MCCOY
PERSONAL Born 12/21/1936, Braden, TN, m, 1977 **DISCIPLINE** ENGLISH **EDUCATION** Tennessee State University, BS, 1958; Atlanta University, MA, 1975; Emory University, PhD, 1986. **CAREER** Shelby County Board of Education, Barret's Chapel High School, teacher, 1958-60; Cassopolis High School, teacher, 1961-62; Weaver High School, teacher, 1964-71; John Overton High School, teacher, 1971-73; Atlanta University, communications skills instructor, 1973; Clark College, assistant professor of English, 1975-86; CLARK-ATLANTA UNIV, PROF OF ENGLISH, 1987-. **HONORS AND AWARDS** United Negro College Fund, Lilly Grant, 1982, Dana Award, 1981; US Labor Department, Appreciation Award, 1992; National Council of Teacher's of English, Appreciation Award, 1990; Clark College, Outstanding Teacher Award, 1978. **MEMBERSHIPS** College Language Association Standing Committee: English Curriculum; American Studies Association; National Council of Teachers of English; Toni Morrison Society; Langston Hughes Society. **SELECTED PUBLICATIONS** Author: Charles W Chesnutt and the Progressive Movement, 1994; Charles W Chesnutt's "The Conjure Woman," Masterpieces African-American Literature, Harper and Collins Publishing, 1992; Charles W Chesnutt's "The House Behind the Cedars in Master Plots," Salem Press, 1993; Scholar in Residence, New York Univ, 1996; founding pres, Charles Waddell Chessnutt Assn. **CONTACT ADDRESS** English, Clark Atlanta Univ, James P Brawley Dr & Fair St, Atlanta, GA, 30314.

PICKENS, WILLIAM GARFIELD
PERSONAL Born 12/27/1927, Atlanta, Georgia, m, 1950 **DISCIPLINE** ENGLISH **EDUCATION** Morehouse College, BA (magna cum laude), 1948; Atlanta University, MA, 1950; University of Hartford, 1953-54, 1964-65; Trinity College, Summers, 1954-59; University of Connecticut, PhD, 1969. **CAREER** Hillside High School, Durham NC, teacher, 1950; Chandler Evans, W Hartford CT, clerk, 1952-54; Hartford Board of Education, Hartford CT, teacher & dept head, 1954-70; US Post Office, Hartford CT, clerk, 1954-56; Pickens Realty, Hartford CT, pres, 1956-71; Morehouse College, Atlanta GA, professor/dept chmn, 1970-84; prof, 1970-; Emory Univ, Atlanta, visiting prof of humanities, 1992-93. **HONORS AND AWARDS** Service plaque, Realty Bd of Greater Hartford, 1964; Author, Trends in Southern Sociolinguistics, 1975; Benj E Mays & Margaret Mitchell, A Unique Legacy in Medicine, 1996; Phi Beta Kappa, Delta of Georgia, 1984; Distinguished Faculty Scholar, UNCF, 1984-85; Dana Faculty Fellowship, Dana Foundation, 1992-93. **MEMBERSHIPS** College Language Assn, 1970-; Natl Council of Teachers of English, 1971-; Conference of College Composition & Communication, 1972-; American Dialect Society, 1975-; Friendship Baptist Church, 1977-; Peyton Woods Chalet Community Organization, 1978-; Langston Hughes Society, 1983-; Toni Morrison Society, 1992-; Phi Beta Kappa. **SELECTED PUBLICATIONS** Social Dialectology in Chesnutt's House behind Cedars, 1987; **CONTACT ADDRESS** Dept of English, Morehouse Col, 830 Westview Dr SW, Brawley Hall 224, Atlanta, GA, 30314.

PICKER, JOHN
PERSONAL Born 05/12/1970, New Brunswick, NJ, s **DISCIPLINE** ENGLISH **EDUCATION** Swarthmore Coll, BA, 92;

Univ Va, MA, 95, PhD (expected) **CAREER** Instr, Univ Va, 95-present. **HONORS AND AWARDS** DuPont Fel, 95-97; Arts and Sci Dissertation Year Fel, 98-99 **MEMBERSHIPS** MLA **RESEARCH** 19th and 20th century lit **SELECTED PUBLICATIONS** Auth, Judaism, Shylock and the Struggle for Closure, 94; Walt Whitman Quarterly Review, The Union of Music and Text in Whitman's Drum-Taps and Higginson's Army Life in a black Regiment, 95; Journal of Theatre and Drama, Shakespeare Divided: Revision and Transformation in Marowitz's Variations on The Merchant of Venice and Wesker's Shylock, 96; English Literary History, Disturbing Surfaces: Representations of the Fragment in The School for Scandal, 98. **CONTACT ADDRESS** English Dept, Univ Va, 219 Bryan Hall, Charlottesville, VA, 22903. **EMAIL** jmp7u@virginia.edu

PICKLESIMER, DORMAN
DISCIPLINE COMMUNICATION/HISTORY **EDUCATION** Morehead State Univ, AB, 60; Bowling Green State Univ, MA, 65; Ind Univ, PhD, 69. **CAREER** Prof, Boston Col, 69-. **HONORS AND AWARDS** Phi Kappa Delta; Gold Key Honor Soc. **MEMBERSHIPS** Nat Communication Asn; Eastern Communication Asn; World Communication Asn. **RESEARCH** History of American public address; classical rhetoric. **CONTACT ADDRESS** Dept of Communcations, Boston Col, Lyons Hall 215, Chestnut Hill, MA, 02167. **EMAIL** picklesi@bC.edu

PICOT, JOCELYNE
DISCIPLINE COMMUNICATION STUDIES **EDUCATION** Univ Montreal, BA; Univ Concordia, MA; Simon Fraser Univ, PhD. **CAREER** Adj prof. **RESEARCH** Communications technologies; evaluation and needs analysis; telehealth, telemedicine, tele-learning and telework; policy studies relevant to the information highway. **SELECTED PUBLICATIONS** Auth, Is There a Telehealth Industry in Canada?, Univ Vic, 96; auth, The Politics of Inter-institutional Cooperation: A Case study and some New Perspectives, 91; auth, Report of the Focus Group on Office Technology in Federal Government Establishments, 90. **CONTACT ADDRESS** Dept Communications, McGill Univ, 845 Sherbrooke St, Montreal, PQ, H3A 2T5.

PIEPHO, LEE
DISCIPLINE ENGLISH **EDUCATION** Kenyon Col, BA; Columbia Univ, MA; Univ VA, PhD. **CAREER** Sara Shallenberger Prof Eng. **HONORS AND AWARDS** Stu Govt Assn Excellence Tchg Awd, Sweet Briar Col, 91. **RESEARCH** Italian humanism in 16th-century Eng cult. **SELECTED PUBLICATIONS** Auth, transl and commentary of Mantuan's Epilogues; articles on Renaissance poetry. **CONTACT ADDRESS** Sweet Briar Col, Sweet Briar, VA, 24595.

PIERCE, JOHN
DISCIPLINE ENGLISH LITERATURE **EDUCATION** Univ Toronto, PhD **CAREER** Dept Eng, Queen's Univ **HONORS AND AWARDS** ASUS Tchg Awd. **RESEARCH** Romantic poetry; late 18th and early 19th century fiction. **SELECTED PUBLICATIONS** Auth, Flexible Design: Blake's Writing of Vala or The Four Zoas, McGill-Queen's Univ, 98. **CONTACT ADDRESS** English Dept, Queen's Univ, Kingston, ON, K7L 3N6. **EMAIL** piercej@qsilver.queensu.ca

PIERSON PRIOR, SANDRA
DISCIPLINE MEDIEVAL LITERATURE **EDUCATION** Wellesley Col, BA, 62; Columbia Univ, MA, 77, PhD, 83. **CAREER** Dir, compos; instr, NYU; Queens Col; prof, 77-. **HONORS AND AWARDS** Ed, Envoi. **RESEARCH** Guide for teaching logic and rhetoric. **SELECTED PUBLICATIONS** Auth, articles, Jour of Medieval and Renaissance Stud; Mod Philol; Jour Eng and Ger Philol; monogr, Twayne Authors Series; The Fayre Formez of the Pearl Poet, Mich State UP. **CONTACT ADDRESS** Dept of Eng, Columbia Col, New York, 2960 Broadway, New York, NY, 10027-6902.

PIFER, ELLEN
PERSONAL Born 06/26/1942, New York, NY, m, 1962, 1 child **DISCIPLINE** ENGLISH AND COMPARATIVE LITERATURE **EDUCATION** Mills Col, Oakland, CA; Univ CA, Berkeley, BA (English, with Distinction), MA, PhD (Comparative Lit, English, Russian, French), 76. **CAREER** Asst prof, dept of English, Univ DE, 77-81; asoc prof, English and Comparative Lit, dept of English, Univ DE, 81-89; vis prof, Comparative Lit, Univ CA, Berkeley, spring 90; Distinguished Vis Prof of Am Lit, Universite Jean Moulin, Lyon III, France, spring 92; prof of English and Comparative Lit, Dept of English, Univ DE, 89-. **HONORS AND AWARDS** Nominated for Excellence in Teaching Award, Univ DE, 77, 88, 86; General Univ Res grant, Univ DE, 78, 81, 86, 90; DE Humanities Forum Res fel, 87-88; DE Arts Coun Individual Artists fel (Non-Fiction Prose), 89-90; Nat Endowment for the Humanities summer stipend for res, 91; Outstanding Academic Book Award (for Saul Bellow Against the Grain), Choice Magazine, 90-91; Distinguished Vis Prof of Am Lit, Univ Lyon III, France, 92; Fulbright Scholar, France, 92; Rector's Distinguished Vis Prof in Am Lit, Univ Helsinki, Finland, March 28-April 8, 93; Center for Advanced Studies fel, Univ DE, 93-94; listed in Who's Who in the World, Who's Who in Ed, The International Authors and Writers Who's Who, Dictionary of Am Scholars, etc. **MEMBERSHIPS** Modern Language Asn; Am Lit Asn; Int Vladimir Nabakov Soc (pres, 98-2000, vice-pres, 96-98, member, bd of dirs). **RESEARCH** Modern and contemporary lit; the novel; the image of childhood in contemporary writing and culture. **SELECTED PUBLICATIONS** Auth, Nabokov and the Novel, Harvard Univ Press, 80, 81; ed and intro, Critical Essays on John Fowles, G K Hall, 86; auth, Saul Bellow Against the Grain, Univ PA Press, 90; Lolita, The Garland Companion to Vladimir Nabokov, ed Vladimir E Alexandrov, Garland, 95; Birds of a Different Feather: Nabakov's Lolita and Kosinski's Boy, Cycnos 12, 2, 95; Nabakov's Discovery of America: From Russia to Lolita, in The American Columbiad: Discovering America, Inventing the United States, eds Mario Materassi and Maria I Ramalho de Sousa Santos, VU Univ Press, 96; Winners and Losers: Bellow's Dim View of Success, in Saul Bellow and the Struggle at the Center, ed Eugene Hollahan, AMS Press, 96; The River and Its Current: Literary and Collective Memory in Toni Morrison's Beloved, Sounding the Depths: Water as Metaphor in North American Literatures, eds Gayle Wurst and Christine Raguet-Bouvart, Univ of Liege Press, 98; The Children: Wharton's Creative Ambivalence to Self, Society and the New World, in Edith Wharton: A Forward Glance, eds Clare Colquitt, Susan Goodman and Candace Waid, Univ DE Press, forthcoming, 98; Her Monster, His Nymphet: Nabakov, Mary Shelley, and the Specter of Sexism, Nabakov and His Fiction: New Perspectives, ed Julian W Connolly, Cambridge Univ Press, forthcoming, 99; many other essays, reviews, and articles. **CONTACT ADDRESS** English Dept, Univ of Delaware, Memorial Hall, Newark, DE, 19716. **EMAIL** epifer@udel.edu

PIKE, DAVID
DISCIPLINE MODERNISM, DANTE, AND FILM **EDUCATION** Columbia Univ, PhD. **CAREER** Asst prof, Am Univ. **HONORS AND AWARDS** Gustave O. Arlt Award, 97., Mellon Doc Fel, Columbia Univ, 93-95. **RESEARCH** Changing images of underground London and Paris. **SELECTED PUBLICATIONS** Auth, Passage through Hell: Modernist Descents, Medieval Underworlds Cornell Univ Press. **CONTACT ADDRESS** American Univ, 4400 Massachusetts Ave, Washington, DC, 20016. **EMAIL** dpike@american.edu

PINEDO, ISABEL
DISCIPLINE MEDIA **EDUCATION** Univ Chicago, MA; CUNY Grad Ctr, PhD. **CAREER** Dept Ed, Hunter Col City Univ NY **RESEARCH** Relation between Media and Society. **SELECTED PUBLICATIONS** Auth, Recreational Terror: Women and The Pleasures of Horror Film Viewing, Albany: SUNY Press, 97; Recreational Terror: Postmodern Elements of the Contemporary Horror Film, J Film Video, vol 48, 96 & And Then She Killed Him: Women and Violence in the Slasher Film, in Mediated Women: Representations in Popular Culture, Cresskill, NJ: Hampton Press, 97. **CONTACT ADDRESS** Dept of Education, Hunter Col, CUNY, 695 Park Ave, New York, NY, 10021.

PINKA, PATRICIA G.
PERSONAL Born 02/27/1935, Pittsburgh, PA, w, 1966, 1 child **DISCIPLINE** ENGLISH **EDUCATION** Univ Pittsburgh, BA 56; San Francisco State Univ, MA 64; Univ Pittsburgh, PhD 69. **CAREER** Agnes Scott College, asst prof, assoc prof, prof, 69 to 82-; Point Park College, inst, 66-67. **HONORS AND AWARDS** Mellon Fel; 2 NEH Fel; Outstanding Tchr; Who's Who Among Amer Tchrs. **MEMBERSHIPS** MLA; AAUP; MS; JDS. **RESEARCH** 17th century poetry; feminist lit and theory. **SELECTED PUBLICATIONS** Auth, John Donne, Micropedia, Encycl Britannica, 14th ed, 94, revised 98; Donne Idios and the Somerset Epithalamion, Studies in Philosophy, 93; Timely Timelessness in Two Nativity Odes, in: Bright Shoots of Everlastingness, eds TL Pebworth Claude Summers, CO, UMP, 87; This Dialogue of One: The Songs and Sonnets of John Donne, Tuscaloosa, UAP, 82; The Autobiographical Narrator in the songs and Sonnets, That Subtle Wreath, ed MW Pepperdene, Decatur GA, 74; **CONTACT ADDRESS** Dept of English, Agnes Scott Col, 141 E. College Ave, Decatur, GA, 30030. **EMAIL** ppinka@agnesscott.edu

PINNEY, CHRIS
DISCIPLINE VISUAL ARTS **CAREER** Sr lectr in Material Culture, Univ Col London; vis fel, Ctr Cross-Cult Res, Australian Natl Univ. **RESEARCH** Indian/Hindu culture; anthrop art. **SELECTED PUBLICATIONS** Camera Indica: The Social Life of Indian Photographs (Reaktion/Univ Chicago, 97; The Nation (Un)Pictured, In: Critical Inquiry, Summer 97. **CONTACT ADDRESS** Dept of Education, Australian National Univ. **EMAIL** Chris.Pinney@anu.edu.au

PINSKER, SANFORD
PERSONAL Born 09/98/1941, Washington, PA, m, 1968, 2 children **DISCIPLINE** LITERATURE **EDUCATION** Washington & Jefferson Col, BA, 1963; Univ Washington, PhD, 67 **CAREER** Teach asst, Univ Wash, 63-67; asst prof, Franklin & Marshall Col, 67-74; visiting prof, UC, Riverside, 73 & 75; assoc prof, Franklin & Marshall Col, 74-84; prof, Franklin & Marshall Col, 84-88; prof, Franklin & Marshall Col, 88- **HONORS AND AWARDS** Grad Inst Mod Lett, 68; NEH Younger Humanist, 70-71; NEH Sem Amer Humor 78-79; Fulbright Senior Lectr, 85-85; Pennsylvania Humanist, 85-87; Fulbright Senior Lectr, 90-91; Pennsylvania Humanist, 90-91, 96-97 **SELECTED PUBLICATIONS** Worrying About Race, 1985-1995: Reflections During a Troubled Time, Whitston, 96; Oedipus Meets the Press and Other Tragi-Comedies of Our Time, Mellon, 96; The Catcher in the Rye: Innocence Under Pressure, Twayne, 93; Sketches of Spain, Plowman, 92 **CONTACT ADDRESS** English Dept, Franklin and Marshall Col, 700 N Pine St., Lancaster, PA, 17603. **EMAIL** spinkster@aol.com

PINSKY, ROBERT
PERSONAL Born 10/20/1940, Long Branch, NJ, m, 3 children **DISCIPLINE** ENGLISH **EDUCATION** Rutgers Univ, BA 62; Stanford Univ, MA 65, PhD 66. **CAREER** Univ Chicago, asst prof 66-67; Wellesley Col, prof 67-80; Harvard Univ, vis lect 80; Univ Cal Berk, prof 80-89; Boston Univ, prof 88-; The New Republic, poetry ed 78-87; Slate, poetry ed 96-. **HONORS AND AWARDS** Woodrow Wilson fel; Fulbright fel; Guggenheim fel; Stegner fel; NEH; NEA; Shelly Mem Awd; Poet Laureate of the US; Lenore Marshall Prize; Oscar Blumenthal Prize; Nominated for 1995 Pulitzer Prize in Poetry; Ambassador Book Awd; Wm Carlos Williams Awd; Saxifrage Prize; Landon Translation Prize. **SELECTED PUBLICATIONS** Auth, The Handbook of Heartbreak, Wm Morrow and Co, 98; The Sounds of Poetry, Farrar Straus Giroux, 98; The Figured Wheel: New and Collected poems 1966-1996, FS&G, 95; The Inferno of Dante, Farrar Straus Giroux, 95; The Want Bone, The Ecco Press, 90; Mindwheel, interactive fiction for computer, with Stephen Hales and William Mataga programmers, pub by Broderbund Software. **CONTACT ADDRESS** Dept of English, Boston Univ, 236 Bat State Rd, Boston, MA, 02215.

PINSON, HERMINE DOLOREZ
PERSONAL Born 07/20/1953, Beaumont, TX, m, 1976 **DISCIPLINE** ENGLISH **EDUCATION** Fisk University,, BA, 1975; Southern Methodist University, MA, 1979; Rice University, PhD, 1991. **CAREER** Houston, Community Coll, 1977-79; Texas Southern Universitys, asst prof, 1979-92; COLLEGE OF WILLIAM & MARY, ASSOC PROF OF ENGLISH, 1992-. **HONORS AND AWARDS** Vermont Studio Ctr, fellowship, 1997; Macdowell Colony, fellow, 1996; Yaddo Colony, fellow, 1996; Ford Postdoctoral, fellow, 1991; National Endowment for the Humanities fellow, 1988. **MEMBERSHIPS** Modern Language Assn; Southern Conference on African-American Studies, Inc; American Literature Assn; Southern Modern Language Assn. **SELECTED PUBLICATIONS** Author: "Ashe," collection of poems, 1992; Mama Yetta and Other Poems, 1988; work published in anthologies: Common Bonds, 1986; Loss of Ground Note, Callaloo and African-American Review, 1989. **CONTACT ADDRESS** Dept of English, Col of William and Mary, PO Box 8795, Williamsburg, VA, 23187-8795. **EMAIL** hdpins@facstaff.wm.edu

PITCHFORD, NICOLA
DISCIPLINE ENGLISH LITERATURE **EDUCATION** Univ WI, PhD. **CAREER** Asst prof, Fordham Univ. **SELECTED PUBLICATIONS** Auth, Reading Feminism's Pornography Conflict: Implications for Postmodernist Reading Strategies, Genders, 96. **CONTACT ADDRESS** Dept of Eng Lang and Lit, Fordham Univ, 113 W 60th St, New York, NY, 10023.

PITT, DAVID G.
PERSONAL Born 12/12/1921, Musgravetown, NF, Canada **DISCIPLINE** LITERATURE **EDUCATION** Mt Allison Univ, BA, 46, LLD, 89; Univ Toronto, MA 48, PhD, 60. **CAREER** Assoc prof, 49-61, prof, 61-82, dept head 70-82, PROF EMERITUS ENGLISH, MEMORIAL UNIV NFLD, 82-. **HONORS AND AWARDS** Hum Res Coun Fel, 56; Can Coun Sr Fel, 69; Univ BC Medal Can Biog, 85; City Toronto Bk Award Finalist, 85; Nfld & Labrador Arts Coun Artist of the Yr Award, 89; Memorial Univ Eaton Honor Soc, 95. **MEMBERSHIPS** Hum Asn Can; Nfld Geneal Soc. **SELECTED PUBLICATIONS** Auth, Elements of Literacy, 65; auth, Windows of Agates, 66, 2nd ed, rev & enlarged, 90; auth, E.J. Pratt: The Truant Years 1882-1927, 84; auth, E.J. Pratt: The Master Years 1927-1964, 87; auth, Towards the First Spike: The Evolution of a Poet, 87; auth, Tales from the Outer Fringe: Five Stories and a Novella, 90; coauth, Goodly Heritage, 84; ed, Here the Tides Flow (E.J. Pratt), 62; ed, Critical Views on Canadian Writers: E.J. Pratt, 69; contribur, The Encyclopedia of Newfoundland and Labrador; contribur, The Canadian Encyclopedia; contribur, The Dictionary of Newfoundland and Labrador Biography; contribur, Encyclopedia of Post-Colonial Literatures in English. **CONTACT ADDRESS** Dept of English, Memorial Univ of Newfoundland, St. John's, NF, A1C 5S7.

PIZER, DONALD
PERSONAL Born 04/05/1929, New York, NY, m, 1966, 3 children **DISCIPLINE** ENGLISH **EDUCATION** Univ Calif, Los Angeles, BA, 51, MA, 52, PhD, 55. **CAREER** Asst Prof, 57, Assoc Prof, 61, Prof 64, Pierce Butler Prof of English, 72-, Tulane Univ. **HONORS AND AWARDS** Guggenheim Fellow, 62-65; Am Coun of Learned Soc Fellow, 71-72; NEH Fellow, 78-79; Fulbright Lectureships, 67-68, 85, 98. **MEMBERSHIPS** Modern Lang Asn; Am Lit Asn. **RESEARCH**

American literature, 1865-1940. **SELECTED PUBLICATIONS** Auth, Hamlin Garland's Early Work and Career, Univ Calif Press, 60; Realism and Naturalism in Nineteenth Century American Literature, S Ill Univ, 66; auth, The Novels of Frank Norris, Ind Univ Press, 74; auth, The Novels of Theodore Dreiser: A Critical Study, Univ Minn Press, 76; auth, Dos Passos' USA: A Critical Study, Univ Press of Va, 88; auth, American Expatriate Writing and the Paris Moment: Modernism and Place, La State Univ Press, 96. **CONTACT ADDRESS** Dept English, Tulane Univ, New Orleans, LA, 70118.

PIZZATO, MARK
DISCIPLINE THEATRE, PLAYWRIGHTING **EDUCATION** Univ Notre Dame, BA, 82; Cath Univ Am, MFA, 84; Univ WI, Milwaukee, PhD, 92. **CAREER** Prof, Univ NC, Charlotte. **SELECTED PUBLICATIONS** Publ articles on ritual in mod drama, on the edges of perception in stage and screen structures, and on violence in the mass media; his plays are available through Aran Press. **CONTACT ADDRESS** Univ N. Carolina, Charlotte, Charlotte, NC, 28223-0001.

PIZZO, JOSEPH S.
DISCIPLINE ENGLISH **EDUCATION** Trenton State Col, BA, 73, MA, 75. **CAREER** Eng teacher, Middlesex Pub Schs, 74-75; teac SAT prep, Bound Brook Comm Jointure Adult Sch, 77-81; ed, Morris County Counc Ed Asns, 82-83; TEACH, CHESTER TWP PUB SCHS, 75-; ADJ PROF, BUS, COMMUN, ENG, CENTENARY COL, 92-; adj teach trainer, Middlesex County Col, 95; FOUNDER, PRES, WORK SMART INC, 95-; ADJ PROF ENG, UNION COUNTY COL, 97-. **CONTACT ADDRESS** Black River Middle Sch, Rte 513, Chester, NJ, 07930. **EMAIL** pizzo@chester-nj.org

PLATH, JAMES
PERSONAL Born 10/29/1950, Chicago, IL, m, 1995, 5 children **DISCIPLINE** ENGLISH **EDUCATION** Cal State Univ, Chico, BA, 80; Univ Wis, Milwaukee, MA, 82, PhD, 88. **CAREER** Asst prof Ill Wesleyan Univ, 88-93, ASSOC PROF ENGLISH, 93-. **HONORS AND AWARDS** Fulbright Scholar, Caribbean Regional Lect Prog, Univ W Indies, 95-96; Graduate of Last Decade Award, UWN Alumni Asn, 92; Editor's Award Council of Lit Mag & Presses, 90. **MEMBERSHIPS** Acad Am Poets; Coun Lit Mag & Presses; Fitzgerald Soc; Fulbright Asn; Hemingway Soc; Soc of Midland Auths. **RESEARCH** John Updike, Ernest Hemingway, Raymond Carver, modernism and minimalism. **SELECTED PUBLICATIONS** Auth, "Shadow Rider: The Hemingway Hero as Western Archetype," in Hemingway and the Natural World, 99, Univ Idaho Press; auth, "Verbal Vermeer: Updike's Middle-Class Protraiture," in Rabbit Tales: Poetry and Politics in John Updike's 'Rabbit Novels, 98, Univ Ala Press; auth, "The Sun Also Rises as 'A Greater Gatsby': 'Isn't it Pretty to Think So?'" in French Connections: Hemingway and Fitzgerald Abroad, 98, St. Martin's; auth, "Le Torero and 'The Undefeated': Hemingway's Foray into Analytical Cubism," in Hemingway Repossessed, 94, Praeger, and Studies in Short Fiction, Summer 93; coauth, Remembering Ernest Hemingway, 99, Ketch & Yawl Press; auth, Conversations with John Updike, 94, Univ Press of Miss; auth, "Santiago at the Plate: Baseball in The Old Man and the Sea," The Hemingway Rev, Fall 96; auth, Fishing for Tension: The Dynamics of Hemingway's 'Big Two- Hearted River'," North Dakota Quarterly, Spring 94-95; auth, "After the Storm and After the Denim: Raymond Carver Comes to Terms with the Hemngway Influence," The Hemingway Rev, Spring 94. **CONTACT ADDRESS** Dept of English, Illinois Wesleyan Univ, Bloomington, IL, 61702-2900. **EMAIL** jplath@titan.iwu.edu

PLUMMER, JOHN F.
DISCIPLINE MEDIEVAL LITERATURE, TEXTUAL CRITICISM **EDUCATION** Univ Wash, PhD. **CAREER** Instr, Vanderbilt Univ. **RESEARCH** Signs and identity in the medieval romance. **SELECTED PUBLICATIONS** Auth, articles on Middle English Drama, ChrQtien de Troyes, Malory and Sir Gawain and the Green Knight; ed, Variorum Chaucer edition of The Summoner's Tale. **CONTACT ADDRESS** Vanderbilt Univ, Nashville, TN, 37203-1727.

PLUMSTEAD, WILLIAM
PERSONAL m, 3 children **DISCIPLINE** ENGLISH **EDUCATION** Western Univ, BA; Univ Rochester, MA, PhD. **CAREER** Asst prof, Nipissing Univ. **MEMBERSHIPS** Past ch steering comt, Nipissing's third annual Visions/Voices conf. **RESEARCH** American Renaissance literature. **SELECTED PUBLICATIONS** Auth, Loon, 92; Freddy Dimwhistle's, Northcountry Sketchbook, 97. **CONTACT ADDRESS** Dept of English, Nipissing Univ, 100 College Dr, Box 5002, North Bay, ON, P1B 8L7.

PODIS, JOANNE
DISCIPLINE ENGLISH LITERATURE **EDUCATION** Case Western Reserve Univ, PhD, 94. **CAREER** Prof. **RESEARCH** 19th century British literature. **SELECTED PUBLICATIONS** Auth, pubs on aspects of the student writing process; coauth, Writing: Invention, Style, and Form, 84; Rethinking Writing, 96. **CONTACT ADDRESS** Dept of English, Ursuline Col, 2550 Lander Road, Pepper Pike, OH, 44124. **EMAIL** jpodis@ursuline.edu

POE, ELIZABETH
PERSONAL CA **DISCIPLINE** CHILDREN'S AND YOUNG ADULT LITERATURE AND READER RESPONSE THEORY **EDUCATION** Pitzer Col, BA; CO State Univ, MA; Univ CO, PhD. **CAREER** Instr, Univ WI prof, Radford Univ; ed, SIGNAL (J of Int Reading Asn). **SELECTED PUBLICATIONS** Auth, Focus on Sexuality, 90; Focus on Relationships, 93. **CONTACT ADDRESS** Radford Univ, Radford, VA, 24142. **EMAIL** eapoe@runet.edu

POIRIER, RICHARD
PERSONAL Born 09/09/1925, Gloucester, MA **DISCIPLINE** ENGLISH LITERATURE **EDUCATION** Amherst Coll, BA, 49; Yale Univ, MA, 51; Cambridge Univ, Fulbright Scholar, 52-53; Harvard Univ, PhD, 60. **CAREER** Instr, 50-52, Williams Coll; teach Fel, 53-60, Instr, 60-61, Asst Prof, 61-63, Harvard; Prof & Chmn Rutgers Coll Eng Dept, 63-66, Disting Prof & Chmn Eng dept, 66-68, Disting Prof & chmn, New Brunswick Eng dept, 68-73, Disting Prof & Dir Eng Grad Studies, 73-77, Dir Eng Grad Studies, 77-81, Rutgers Univ; Beckman Prof, 76, Univ Cal Berkeley; Marius Bewley Prof of Amer & Eng Lit, 77-98, Prof Emeritus 98-; editor, 62-71, Partisan Review; editor, 81-, Raritan Qtly Review; co-founder, 83, Chmn of board, 84-, VP, 89-, Library of America. **HONORS AND AWARDS** Fulbright Scholar, Guggenheim Found Grant, NEH Fel, LLD Amherst Coll, Lindback Awd Rutgers Univ, AAAS Fel, AAIA&L, Achievement Awd, Pushcart Prize, NYIH Fel, J B Hubbell Awd. **MEMBERSHIPS** AAA&S, AAUP, MLA, PEN, Lit Class of US, NBCC, PMLA. **SELECTED PUBLICATIONS** Auth, A World Elsewhere, The Place of Style in American Literature, NY Oxford UP 66, reissued Madison Wis UP, 85; Norman Mailer, Modern Masters Series, NY, Viking, 72; Robert Frost, The Work of Knowing, NY, Oxford UP, 77; The Renewal of Literature, Emersonian Reflections, NY Random House, 87; Poetry and Pragmatism, Cambridge Harvard UP, 92; Trying It Out in America, Literary and Other Performances, Farrar Straus & Giroux, forthcoming 99. **CONTACT ADDRESS** Raritan Quarterly, 31 Mine St, New Brunswick, NJ, 08903.

POLAND, TIM
PERSONAL Findlay, OH **DISCIPLINE** AMERICAN LITERATURE **EDUCATION** OH Univ, BA; GA state Univ, MA, PhD. **CAREER** Prof, Radford Univ. **RESEARCH** Western Am lit; Native Am lit; fiction writing. **SELECTED PUBLICATIONS** Publ an assortment of critical essays and bk rev in var j(s) such as Western Am Lit, Am Lit, Southwestern Am Lit, The Explicator, and The Mark Twain Encycl. **CONTACT ADDRESS** Radford Univ, Radford, VA, 24142. **EMAIL** tpoland@runet.edu

POLHEMUS, ROBERT M.
PERSONAL Born 12/12/1935, San Francisco, CA, 4 children **DISCIPLINE** ENGLISH **EDUCATION** Univ of Calif at Berkeley, BA, 57, MA, 59, PhD, 63. **CAREER** Prof of English, 63-98, Howard and Jesse Watkins Univ Prof, Stanford Univ, 92-. **HONORS AND AWARDS** Guggenheim Fel; Dean's Teaching Award, Stanford Univ. **MEMBERSHIPS** MLA. **RESEARCH** Victorian and 19th century literature; film; psychology & art; cultural studies. **SELECTED PUBLICATIONS** Auth, Erotic Faith, 90; Comic Faith, 80; The Changing World of Anthony Trollope; Critical Reconstructions, 95; The Lot Complex, Rereading Texts, Rethinking Critical Presuppositions, 97. **CONTACT ADDRESS** English Dept, Stanford Univ, Stanford, CA, 94305. **EMAIL** polhemus@leland.stanford.edu

POLK, NOEL E.
PERSONAL Born 02/23/1943, Picayune, MS, d, 2 children **DISCIPLINE** ENGLISH **EDUCATION** Mississippi College, BA, 65, MA, 66; Univ SC, PhD, 70. **CAREER** Univ Texas at Arlington, 70-74; Univ S Carolina, S Studies Prog, 74-76; Assoc Prof, 80-81, Univ Strasbourg; vis Prof, 96, Univ Rennes; Prof, Univ Southern Miss. **MEMBERSHIPS** MLA **RESEARCH** Bibliography, Am Novel, Faulkner, Welty. **SELECTED PUBLICATIONS** Auth, Outside the Southern Myth, UP Miss, 96; Children of the Dark House, UP Miss, 95; Eudora Welty: A Bibliography of her work, UP Miss, 93. **CONTACT ADDRESS** English Dept, Univ S Miss, Hattiesburg, MS, 39406. **EMAIL** noel.polk@usm.edu

POOLE, JOHN R.
DISCIPLINE THEATRE ARTS **EDUCATION** Univ Ga, PhD, 95. **CAREER** Asst prof. **RESEARCH** Early twentieth century protest drama of the Depression era; southern regional minority drama. **SELECTED PUBLICATIONS** Auth, pubs in Theatre Studies Jour, Theatre Jour. **CONTACT ADDRESS** Dept of Theatre, Illinois State Univ, Normal, IL, 61761.

POOLE, MARSHALL SCOTT
DISCIPLINE COMMUNICATION **EDUCATION** Univ Wis, PhD. **CAREER** Prof, Texas A&M Univ. **HONORS AND AWARDS** Golden Anniversary Monograph Awd, Speech Commun Asn. **RESEARCH** Organizational communication, small group communication, communication technology. **SELECTED PUBLICATIONS** Coauth and co-ed, Research on the Management of Innovation; Communication and Group Decision-Making & Working Through Conflict; contribur, to Organizations and Communication Technology; Communication Perspectives on Negotiation; Communication and Organizations. **CONTACT ADDRESS** Dept of Speech Communication, Texas A&M Univ, College Station, TX, 77843-4234.

POPE, DEBORAH
DISCIPLINE ENGLISH LITERATURE **EDUCATION** WI Univ, PhD, 79. **CAREER** Prof, Duke Univ. **SELECTED PUBLICATIONS** Auth, A Separate Vision: Isolation in Contemporary Women s Poetry, LSU, 84; Ties That Bind: Essays on Mothering and Patriarchy, Univ Chicago, 90; Fanatic Heart, LSU, 92; Mortal World, LSU, 95. **CONTACT ADDRESS** Eng Dept, Duke Univ, Durham, NC, 27706.

POPE, REBECCA A.
DISCIPLINE ENGLISH LITERATURE **EDUCATION** Barat Col, BA; Oxford Univ, MA; Univ Chicago, PhD. **CAREER** Eng Dept, Georgetown Univ **RESEARCH** 19th century British literature; history and theory of gender and sexuality; the relations between illness, medicine, and culture. **SELECTED PUBLICATIONS** Auth, pubs on 19th century British writers, gothic fiction, detective fiction, opera and performance art, AIDS; co-auth, The Diva's Mouth: Body, Voice, Prima Donna Politics, 96. **CONTACT ADDRESS** English Dept, Georgetown Univ, 37th and O St, Washington, DC, 20057.

PORTER, JOSEPH A.
DISCIPLINE ENGLISH LITERATURE **EDUCATION** Univ CA Berkeley, PhD, 72. **CAREER** Prof, Duke Univ. **SELECTED PUBLICATIONS** Auth, Critical Essays on Shakespeare's Romeo and Juliet, GK Hall, 97; pubs on criticism; fiction. **CONTACT ADDRESS** Eng Dept, Duke Univ, Durham, NC, 27706.

PORTER, MICHAEL LEROY
PERSONAL Born 11/23/1947, Newport News, VI, s **DISCIPLINE** LITERATURE, HISTORY **EDUCATION** VA State Univ, BA, (hon) sociology 1969; Atlanta Univ, MA, hist 1972; Leonardo DaVinci Acad, Rome, Italy, MCP Contem 1983-84; Emory Univ, PhD hist/Amer studies 1974; Sorbonne Univ, postpoet, hist, Paris France, 1979; Thomas Nelson Community Coll, cert crim justice 1981; US Armed Forces Staff Coll, Norfolk VA, US Pres Appt, 1987. **CAREER** WA State Univ, asst prof of history, black studies prog 1974-75; Mohegan Comm Coll, Dept History lectr 1975-76; Newport News VA, asst education coord, education comp, target proj prog 1977; Hampton Univ, asst prof history 1977-80; NC Mutual Ins Co, life ins underwriter 1980-81; Mullins Prot Serv VA Bch, private investigator, 1981-83; Amer Biographical Inst Raleigh, media freelancer 1984-85, publications dir/deputy governor 1985-; Old Dominion Univ, Norfolk VA, consultant 1985; Michael Porter Enterprises International, president, founder, 1985-88; INTL BIOGRAPHICAL CTR, CAMBRIDGE ENGLAND, DEPUTY DIR GEN 1986-. **HONORS AND AWARDS** 1st Black Concert Pianist to play Carnegie Hall, 1963; Lyon Dissertation Prize, 1974; Ebony Magazine, Eligible Bachelor, 1975; Outstanding Black, 1992; Hero, 1992; International Honors Cup, 1992; Abira Genius Grant, 1992; World Greetings, 1992; Pioneer Award, 1992; Great American, 1991; World Intellectual, 1993; Golden Academy Award, 1991; One of 500 Leaders of Influence in the 20th Century; Intl Hall of Leaders, Amer Biographical Inst, 1988; participant (exhibit), DuSable Museum of Black History, 1988; honoree, Intl Exhibit, Singapore, Malaysia, 1988; Outstanding Man of the World, Ormiston Palace, Tasmania, Australia, 1989; Exhibit, Intl Music Museum, London, ENG, 1989; Poetry Reading, Royal Palace, Lisbon, Portugal, 1998; Michael Porter Poetry Exhibit, Internet Intl Poetry Hall of Fame, 1997-2002; Lecture, Oxford Univ, Oxford, ENG, 1997; Famous Quote, Leningrad, Russia, 1998; 20th Century Award for Achievement, 1990; Black History Maker, 1992; International Man of the Year, 1992; Most Admired Person of the Decade, 1990-99; Recipient, Grant For Exceptionally Gifted Poets, 1998; US Congress, Certificate of Appreciation, 1991; Honorary US Congressman, 1993; Hampton History Center, Historical Marker, 1992; Appearances before US President's Council of Economic Advisors & Senate Finance Committee, 1992; Honorary Knighthood, 1997; US Presidential Medal of Freedom, 1993. **MEMBERSHIPS** Life patron World Inst of Achievement 1985; curator "Michael L Porter Historical & Literary Collection"; World Literary Acad 1984-85; World Biographical Hall of Fame 1985; Federal Braintrust, 1990; Intl Advisory Council, 1989-; African American Hall of Fame, 1994; Elite International, 1992; bd of governors, Amer Biog Inst, 1986; Phi Beta Kappa; Intl Academy of Intellectuals, 1993; Famous Poet's Society, 1996; chairman, US Selective Service Bd #32, 1986-92; chief delegate, Intl Congress on Arts & Communications, Nairobi, Kenya, 1990. **SELECTED PUBLICATIONS** "African Leadership Ideology" (w/Ukandi Damachi) Praeger 1976; "Sacrificing Qual Lang Learn for Pol Exped" 1977;Television Programs: Cited On World News Tonight; Hard Copy; 60 Minutes; Current Affairs; Entertainment Tonight; CBS Evening News; The Remarkable Journey; Journey of African American Athelete, 1995; Eve's Bayou, 1997; 4 Little Girls; NBC Nightly News; Film: The Making of Black Atlanta, 1974; 1st Black Elected to Intl Academy of Intellectuals,

Paris, France, 1993; Radio: Empire State Bldg Broadcasting Ctr, WRIN, 1997; Publications: Ebony, Jet, Intl, Digest, Talent; Contemporary Authors. **CONTACT ADDRESS** Archives Administrator, 3 Adrian Circle, Hampton, VA, 23669-3814.

POSFAY, EVA
DISCIPLINE LITERATURE OF THE SEVENTEENTH CENTURY **EDUCATION** Princeton, PhD. **CAREER** Literature, Carleton Col. **SELECTED PUBLICATIONS** Auth, L'architecture du pouvoir feminin dans La Princesse de Cleves, Papers French Seventeenth Century Lit. **CONTACT ADDRESS** Carleton Col, 100 S College St., Northfield, MN, 55057-4016.

POST, JONATHAN F.S.
PERSONAL Born 05/11/1947, Rochester, NY, m, 1975, 2 children **DISCIPLINE** ENGLISH LITERATURE **EDUCATION** Amherst Col, AB, 70; Univ Rochester, PhD. **CAREER** Asst prof, Yale Univ, 75-79; assoc to full prof, 79- , Dept Chr, 90-93, UCLA, 79-. **HONORS AND AWARDS** NEH fel, 79-80; Guggenheim fel, 84-85. **MEMBERSHIPS** Renaissance Soc Am; Milton Soc Am. **RESEARCH** Renaissance-17th century English literature; modern poetry. **SELECTED PUBLICATIONS** Auth, Henry Vaughn: The Unfolding Vision, Princeton, 82; Sir Thomas Browne, G K Hall, 87; ed George Herbert in the Nineties: Reflections and Reassessments, George Herbert Monogr, 95. **CONTACT ADDRESS** English Dept, UCLouisiana, Los Angeles, CA, 90095-1530. **EMAIL** Post@humwet.UCLA.edu

POST, ROBERT M.
PERSONAL Buckhannon, WV **DISCIPLINE** DRAMATIC ARTS AND SPEECH **EDUCATION** West Virginia Wesleyan Col, BA, 56; Ohio Univ, MA, 58, PhD, 61. **CAREER** From Instr to assistant and assoc prof, Univ of Washington, 60- . **HONORS AND AWARDS** Phi Kappa Phi; Rose Lefcowitz Prize, 92-93. **MEMBERSHIPS** Northwest Commun Asn; Western States Commun Asn. **RESEARCH** Performance; literature. **SELECTED PUBLICATIONS** Auth, Politics, Prison, and Poetry: South Africa's Breyten Breytenbach, Poet Lore, 92-93; auth, Salvation or Damnation? Death in the Plays of Edward Albee, Am Drama, 93; auth, Victims in the Writing of Athol Fugard, in Draper, ed, Contemporary Literary Criticism, v.80, Gale, 94; auth, An Audience is an Audience: Gertrude Stein Addresses the Five Hundred, Kentucky Rev, 96. **CONTACT ADDRESS** Dept of Speech Communications, Univ of Washington, PO Box 353415, Seattle, WA, 98195. **EMAIL** bobpost@u.washington.edu

POSTER, CAROL
PERSONAL Born 08/05/1956, New York, NY **DISCIPLINE** ENGLISH **EDUCATION** Univ Missouri, PhD 94; E Wash Univ, MFA 92; Hollins College, BA cum laude, 77. **CAREER** Vis fel, 99, Univ Iowa; Assoc Prof, 97-, Montana State Univ; Asst Prof, Assoc Prof, 94 to 98-, Univ N Iowa; Instr, 92-94, Univ Missouri; teach Asst, 90-92, E Wash Univ; Pres, 84-89, Amaryllis Software. **HONORS AND AWARDS** Gildersleeve Prize; MCB Outstanding Contr Auth Recog Awd; George Blocker Pace Awd; G Ellsworth Huggins Doct Schshp; Phi Kappa Phi Hon Soc; Dan Walden Awd. **MEMBERSHIPS** MLA; Rocky Mtn MLA; RSA; ISHR; ASHR; NCA; APA; CAMW&S; CAPNW; ISSN. **SELECTED PUBLICATIONS** Coed, Letter Writing Manuals from Antiquity to the Present, U S Carolina Press, forthcoming; auth, Phila Epideictic Rhetoric and Epistolary Theory in Late Antiquity, in: coed, Letter Writing Manuals form Antiquity to the Present, Columbia SC, U of S Carolina Press, forthcoming; Re-Positioning Pedagogy: A Feminist Historiography of Aristotle's Rhetorica, Feminist Interpretations of Aristotle, ed, Cynthia Freeland, Univ Pk PA, Penn State U Press, simultaneous hrdcv and pbk editions, 98; auth, Being Time and Definition: Towards a Semiotics of Figural Rhetoric, Philo and Rhetoric, forthcoming; Silence as a Rhetorical Strategy for Neoplatonic Mysticism, Mystics Qtly, 98; Canonicity and the Campus Bookstore: Teaching Victorian Women Writers, Feminist Teach, 97; Aristotle's rhetoric against Rhetoric: Unitarian Reading and Esoteric Hermeneutics, Amer J of Philology, 97; Being and Becoming: Rhetorical Ontology in Early Greek Thought, Philo and Rhetoric, 96; rev, Christopher Lyle Johnston, ed, Theory Text Context, Rhetoric Soc Qtly, 98; Skiing: Faceplants Eggbeaters and Snowsnakes: A Guide to the Ski Bum Lifestyle, Merrillville IN, ICS Books, 95; The Basic Essentials of Alpine Skiing, Merrillville IN, ICS books, 93; Auth poetry, Surrounded by Dangerous Things, CT, Singular Speech Press, 95. **CONTACT ADDRESS** English Dept, Montana State Univ, Bozeman, MT, 59717-0230. **EMAIL** poster@english.montana.edu

POTTER, ELIZABETH
DISCIPLINE WOMEN'S STUDIES **EDUCATION** Agnes Scott Col, Atlanta, BA, 69; Rice Univ, Houston, MA, 73, PhD, 74. **CAREER** Alice Andrews Quigley prof; Mills Col, 92-. **HONORS AND AWARDS** AESA's Critic's Choice awd, 93. **RESEARCH** Gender and science; intersections of feminism and epistemology; philosophy. **SELECTED PUBLICATIONS** Auth, Underdetermination Undeterred, in Feminism, Science and the Philosophy of Science, Kluwer Acad Publ, 96; Good Science and Good Philosophy of Science, in Synthese,

Vol 104, 95; ethodological Norms in Traditional and Feminist Philosophy of Science, in PSA 94, Vol 2, 95; Locke's Epistemology and Women's Struggles, in Modern Engendering: Critical Feminist Essays in the History of Western Philosophy, SUNY Press, 94; coauth, Gender and Epistemic Negtiation, Elizabeth Potter, When Feminisms Intersect Epistemology; coed, Feminist Epistemologies, Routledge, 93. **CONTACT ADDRESS** Dept of Women's Studies, Mills Col, 5000 MacArthur Blvd, Oakland, CA, 94613-1301. **EMAIL** epotter@mills.edu

POTTER, ROBERT ALONZO
PERSONAL Born 12/28/1934, New York, NY, d, 5 children **DISCIPLINE** DRAMATIC ART **EDUCATION** Pomona College, BA, 56; Clavermont Grad Sch, MA, 63, PhD, 65. **CAREER** Asst Prof, Lectr, Assoc Prof, 66-81; Prof dramatic art, 81-, Univ California Santa Barbara; Instr, 65, Harvey Mudd College. **HONORS AND AWARDS** Fulbright Fel; Harold J Pious Awd; Vis Prof, Univ Kent at Canterbury. **MEMBERSHIPS** Dramatists Guild; SIET; MRDS; MLA; ATHE. **RESEARCH** Medieval and Renaissance drama; Playwriting. **SELECTED PUBLICATIONS** Auth, The Holy Spectacles of Hildegard of Bingen, Euro Medieval Drama, 98; Auth, The Auto da Fe as Medieval Drama, in: Festive Drama, ed Meg Twycross, Cambridge, DS Brewer, 96; EEn Esbattement van s'Menshen Sin en Verganckelijcke Schoonheit, Man's Desire and Fleeting Beauty, ed, Elsa Strietman, co translated, Leeds Medieval Studies, Leeds, Cen for Med Stud, 95; 24 original plays and stage adaptations including, Saint Barbara in the Flesh 95; La Celestina 90; The Lady in the Labyrinth 89; Just Across the Border 82; The Vision of Children 80. **CONTACT ADDRESS** Dept of Dramatic Art, Univ Calif Santa Barbara, Santa Barbara, CA, 93106. **EMAIL** potter@humanitas.ucsb.edu

POWELL, RONALD R.
PERSONAL Born 05/24/1944, Columbia, MO, m, 1967, 2 children **DISCIPLINE** LIBRARY SCIENCE **EDUCATION** Univ Mo, Columbia, AB, 62-67; Western Mich Univ, Kalamazoo, MS, 67-68; Univ Ill, PhD, 71-76. **CAREER** Libr dir, Univ Charleston, 76-79; asst prof, Univ Mich, 79-86; assoc prof, Univ Mo-Columbia, 86-92; from dir to chemn to prof, 87-, interim dir, Wayne State Univ. **HONORS AND AWARDS** Beta Phi Mu; Who's Who Libry & infor Sciences, 82; Sen Fel, UCLA, 82; Contemporary Authors, 85; Who's Who Midwest, 95-96, 96-97. **MEMBERSHIPS** Am Libry Asn; Asn Col Res Librys; Asn Libry Infor Science Educ Mich Libry Asn. **RESEARCH** Measurement and evaluation of library and information resources and services; education for library and information science; research methods; academic libraries. **SELECTED PUBLICATIONS** Coauth, Basic Reference Sources, a Self-Study Manual, 85; coauth, Success in Answering Reference Questions: Two Studies, 87; auth, art, Report on Russia Project-Moscow, 1996, 97; auth, art, Development of Research Abilities for PhD Students in Library and Information Science, 97; auth, Basic Research Methods for Librarians, 97. **CONTACT ADDRESS** Library and Information Science Program, Wayne State Univ, 106 Kresge Library, Detroit, MI, 48202. **EMAIL** ad5328@wayne.edu

POWER, MARY
DISCIPLINE IRISH AND WOMEN'S LITERATURE **EDUCATION** Univ Wis, PhD, 67. **CAREER** Instr, Univ NMex, 67-. **RESEARCH** James Joyce. **SELECTED PUBLICATIONS** Auth, Molly Bloom and Mary Anderson: The Inside Story, Europ Joyce Stud, 90. **CONTACT ADDRESS** Univ NMex, Albuquerque, NM, 87131.

POWERS, JOHN H.
PERSONAL Born 10/07/1947, Valparaiso, IN, m, 1987, 1 child **DISCIPLINE** SPEECH COMMUNICATION THEORY **EDUCATION** Milligan Col, BA, 69; Univ Denver, MA, 74, PhD, 77. **CAREER** Asst prof, TX A&M Univ, 77-83, assoc prof, 83-93; assoc prof, Hong Kong Baptist Univ, 93-. **MEMBERSHIPS** Nat Commun Asn; Int Commun Asn; World Commun Asn. **RESEARCH** Communication theory; language and commun; public/political commun. **SELECTED PUBLICATIONS** Auth, Public Speaking: The Lively Art, Harper Collins, 94; On the Intellectual Structure of the Human Communication Discipline, Communication Education, 44, 95; Conflict Genres and Management Strategies During China's Ten Years of Turmoil, Intercultural Commun Studies, 7, 97; ed with Randy Kluver, Civic Discourse, Civil Society and the Chinese World, Ablex, in press. **CONTACT ADDRESS** Comm Studies Dept, Hong Kong Baptist Univ, Kowloon, .. **EMAIL** JPowers@hkbu.edu.hk

PRAHLAD, SW. ANAND
DISCIPLINE POETRY AND FOLKLORE **EDUCATION** UCLA, PhD, 91. **CAREER** Asst prof **HONORS AND AWARDS** Grants to work on the production of multimedia packages for classroom instr. **SELECTED PUBLICATIONS** Auth, Hear My Story and Other Poems, Berkeley Poets Workshop, 82 & Under His Own Vine and Fig Tree: A Theory of Contextual Meaning in African-American Proverb Speech Acts, Univ Miss Ptes, 96; articles on, proverbs and African-Amer folklore. **CONTACT ADDRESS** Dept of English, Univ of Missouri-Columbia, 309 University Hall, Columbia, MO, 65211.

PRATLEY, GERALD
PERSONAL Born 09/03/1921, London, England **DISCIPLINE** FILM STUDIES **CAREER** Film critic & commentator, CBC, CTV, CFRB, 1948-75; dir, Ont Film Inst, 68-90; adv comt, film stud prog, 80-90, PROF FILM, RYERSON UNIV, 90-. **HONORS AND AWARDS** Mem, Order Can, 84; CFTA Award, 90; LLD(hon), York Univ, 91; LLD(hon), Univ Waterloo, 93; LLD(hon), Bowling Green State Univ, 94. **MEMBERSHIPS** Ont Film Asn; Film Stud Asn Can; Royal Commonwealth Soc; Acad Can Cinema; PEN; ACTRA; Writers Guild Can. **SELECTED PUBLICATIONS** Auth, John Frankenheimer, 70; auth, Cinema of Otto Preminger, 72; auth, Cinema of David Lean, 73; auth, Cinema of John Huston, 75; auth, Torn Sprockets: The Uncertain Projection of the Canadian Film, 84. **CONTACT ADDRESS** Performing Arts Lodge, 110 The Esplanade, Ste 213, Toronto, ON, M5E 1X9.

PRATT, JOHN
DISCIPLINE ENGLISH LITERATURE **EDUCATION** Univ Ca, BA; Columbia Univ, MA; Princeton Univ, PhD. **CAREER** Prof. **SELECTED PUBLICATIONS** Auth, The Laotian Fragments, 85; Vietnam Voices; pubs on modern poetry. **CONTACT ADDRESS** Dept of English, Colorado State Univ, Fort Collins, CO, 80523. **EMAIL** jcpratt@vines.colostate.edu

PRATT, LINDA RAY
DISCIPLINE ENGLISH **EDUCATION** Florida Southern Col, BA, 65; MA, 66, PhD, 71, Emory Univ. **CAREER** Asst Prof to Prof, 68-, Univ Nebraska-Lincoln **CONTACT ADDRESS** Dept of English, Univ of Nebraska, Lincoln, NE, 68588. **EMAIL** lpratt@unlinfo.unl.edu

PRATT, LOUIS HILL
PERSONAL Born 08/11/1937, Savannah, GA, m **DISCIPLINE** ENGLISH **EDUCATION** Savannah State College, BS (cum Laude), 1958; Columbia Univ Teacher Coll, MA, 1967; Florida State University, Tallahassee, PhD, 1974. **CAREER** Public School State of Georgia, teacher, 1958-62, 1964-69; US Army Air Def Command, operations assistant, 1962-64; Florida A&M University, Language Dept, instr, 1969-74; Florida A&M University, Freshman Comp Dept of Language & Lit, asst professor & director, 1974-75; FLORIDA A&M UNIVERSITY, DEPARTMENT OF ENGLISH, PROF OF ENGLISH, 1975-. **HONORS AND AWARDS** Recipient NDEA Fellowship, Florida State University, 1972-74; J Russell Reaver Award, Florida State University, best creative scholarship in American Literature in dissertation, 1974-75; National Endowment for the Humanities Stipend to attend Afro-Amer Culture Inst, Univ of Iowa, 1977; Man of the Year Award, Alpha Phi Alpha, 1979; Presidential Medallion, Excellence from the Savannah State Univ Natl Alumni Assn, 1990; Teacher of the Year, 1994; Advanced Teacher of the Year, Florida A&M University, 1995. **MEMBERSHIPS** Life member, College Language Association; Alpha Phi Alpha; pres, Middle Atlantic Writers Assn, 1994-96; charter member, Seven Hills Toastmasters Club. **CONTACT ADDRESS** English Dept, Florida A&M Univ, Rm 414, Tucker Hall, Tallahassee, FL, 32307-4800.

PRATT, MINNIE BRUCE
DISCIPLINE ENGLISH LITERATURE **EDUCATION** Univ Ala, BA; Univ NC Chapel Hill, PhD. **CAREER** Prof. **HONORS AND AWARDS** Lillian Hellman-Dashiell Hammett Awd, 91; Gay Lesbian Bk Awd, 91; Harriete Simpson Arnow Prize Poetry, 90. **SELECTED PUBLICATIONS** Auth, Rebellion: Essays 1980-1991, 91; Crime Against Nature, 90; The Child Taken from the Mother, 88; My Mother's Question, Frontiers, 88; Declared Unfit, Polit Heart, 87; We Say We Love Each Other, 85. **CONTACT ADDRESS** English Dept, Union Inst, 440 E McMillan St, Cincinnati, OH, 45206-1925.

PRENSHAW, PEGGY
DISCIPLINE SOUTHERN LITERATURE, AMERICAN LITERATURE **EDUCATION** Univ of Tex, Austin, PhD, 70. **CAREER** Fred C. Frey Prof, La State Univ; Ed, 73-91, adv ed, Southern Quart, 92-; gen ed, Lit Conversations series, 84-; secytreas, Conf of Eds of Learned J, 84-87; ch, Miss Hum Coun, 86-87; adv ed, J of Fla Lit, 89-; Pres, Soc for the Stud of Southern Lit, 90-92; bd of LEH, 92-95; exec comt, SCMLA, 93-95. **HONORS AND AWARDS** NEH grant, 86; outstanding spec issue prize (Southern Quart), CELJ, 86; guest lectr, Gorky Inst, Moscow, 90; Charles Frankel prize, NEH, 94. **MEMBERSHIPS** Pres, Soc for the Stud of Southern Lit, 90-92; pres, Eudora Welty Soc, 93-95. **RESEARCH** Autobiographical writings of Southern women; Eudora Welty. **SELECTED PUBLICATIONS** Auth, Sex and Wreckage in the Parlor: Welty's 'Bye-Bye Brevoort,' Southern Quart, 95; The True Happenings of My Life: Reading Southern Women Autobiographers, in Haunted Bodies: Rethinking the South through Gender, 97; The Construction of Confluence: The Female South and Eudora Welty's Art, in The Late Novels of Eudora Welty, 97; ed, More Conversations with Eudora Welty, 96. **CONTACT ADDRESS** Dept of Eng, Louisiana State Univ, 237C Allen Hall, Baton Rouge, LA, 70803. **EMAIL** enpren@unix1.sncc.lsu.edu

PRESTON, JOAN M.
DISCIPLINE COMMUNICATIONS **EDUCATION** Univ W Ontario, PhD. **CAREER** Prof, Brock Univ. **RESEARCH** Virtual reality, multimedia, media reality and fantasy, television. **SELECTED PUBLICATIONS** Auth, TV reality: The truth and nothing but?, Intl Commun Assn Conf, 95; co-auth, Selective viewing: Cognition, personality and TV genres, Brit Jour Soc Psychol, 94; Integration in personal constructions of television, Intl Jour Personal Construct Psychol, 90. **CONTACT ADDRESS** Dept of Communications Studies, Brock Univ, 500 Glenridge Ave, St. Catharines, ON, L2S 3A1. **EMAIL** jpreston@spartan.ac.brocku.ca

PRICE, ALAN
PERSONAL Born 05/11/1943, Rushville, IN, m, 1998 **DISCIPLINE** ENGLISH, AMERICAN LITERATURE **EDUCATION** Earlham Col, BA, 65; Penn State Univ, MA, 66; Univ of Rochester, PhD, 76. **CAREER** INSTR, 66-76, ASST PROF OF ENGLISH, 76-88, ASSOC PROF OF ENGLISH, 88-97, PROF OF ENGLISH, 97-, PENN STATE UNIV. **HONORS AND AWARDS** NEH Summer Seminar fels, 80 & 87; NEH Travel to Collections grants, 85 & 91; twice elected Hazleton Campus Teacher of the Year, Penn State; George W. Atherton Award for Excellence in Teaching, Penn State, 91; profiled in Who's Who in the World and Who's Who in the East; listed in Who's Who in America. **MEMBERSHIPS** MLA; Am Studies Asn; Nat Coun of Teachers of English; Col English Asn; Edith Whaton Soc; Am Lit Soc. **RESEARCH** American Literature; Edith Wharton; World War I. **SELECTED PUBLICATIONS** Auth, The End of the Age of Innocence: Edith Wharton and the First World War, St Martin's Press, 96; auth, Far More Than They Know: Current Wharton Studies, Review, Univ of Va Press, 97; auth, Frank Tuohy, British Short-Fiction Writers 1945-1980, The Dictionary of Literary Biography Vol 139, Gale Research Inc, Bruccoli Clark Layman, 94; auth, Dorothy Canfield Fisher, The Oxford Companion to Women's Writing in the United States, Oxford Univ Press, 94; auth, Literature, The Artworld and Its Audience: Art as Kaleidoscope, Haven Press, 93; co-ed & contribur, Wretched Exotic: Essays on Edith Wharton in Europe. **CONTACT ADDRESS** Hazelton Campus, Pennsylvania State Univ, Hazelton, PA, 18201. **EMAIL** pym@psu.edu

PRICE, BERNADETTE B.
PERSONAL Born 03/07/1959, White Plains, NY **DISCIPLINE** AMERICAN LITERATURE **EDUCATION** Manhatlunville Coll, M Liberal Arts. **CAREER** Sr Mngr, Orbis Books, NY. **HONORS AND AWARDS** Cath Press Asn Award of Merit; Special Promotion. **MEMBERSHIPS** Cath Book Publishers Asn; Asn Theol Bookssllers. **RESEARCH** 19th Century American Short Stories. **CONTACT ADDRESS** Orbis Books, Box 308, Maryknoll, NY, 10545-0308. **EMAIL** bpnce@maryknoll.org

PRICE, DAVID C.
DISCIPLINE COMMUNICATION STUDIES **EDUCATION** ID State Univ, BA, 87, MA, 88;Univ UT, PhD, 97. **CAREER** Asst prof commun studies, Doane Col, 93-. **HONORS AND AWARDS** Robert F. Kennedy Minority News Award. **MEMBERSHIPS** Nat Commun Asn; Western States Commun Asn; Soc Prof Jour; Nebr Col Media Asn. **RESEARCH** Commun in Crises; Rhetorical Commun in the News Media; Organizational Commun in Newsrooms; Commun Silence. **SELECTED PUBLICATIONS** Auth, The Death of Partisanship in Idaho? A Rhetorical Analysis of the 1986 Gubernatorial Election, Idaho State Univ, 88. **CONTACT ADDRESS** Commun Studies Dept, Doane Col, Boswell Ave, PO Box 1014, Crete, NE, 68333. **EMAIL** dprice@doane.edu

PRINCE, JOHN R.
DISCIPLINE LEGAL WRITING AND APPELLATE ADVOCACY **EDUCATION** Okla Baptist Univ, BA, 79; Duke Univ Sch Law, JD, 83. **CAREER** Prof, Villanova Univ; clerked, Honorable Thomas N. O'Neill, Jr. US Dist Ct Eastern Dist Pa; past assoc, firms in Philadelphia; private pract in his own firm; taught at, Rutgers-Camden Sch Law & St Thomas Univ Sch Law. **MEMBERSHIPS** Amer, Philadelphia & Dela Co Bar Asn. **CONTACT ADDRESS** Law School, Villanova Univ, 800 Lancaster Ave, Villanova, PA, 19085-1692. **EMAIL** prince@law.vill.edu

PRINEAS, MATTHEW
DISCIPLINE ENGLISH LITERATURE **EDUCATION** Univ Rochester, PhD, 95. **CAREER** Asst prof. **RESEARCH** Textual criticism; history and theory of rhetoric; Bible; Renaissance prosody. **SELECTED PUBLICATIONS** Auth, pubs on Henry Vaughan, Anna Trapnel, Andrew Marvell. **CONTACT ADDRESS** Dept of English and Philosophy, Idaho State Univ, Pocatello, ID, 83209. **EMAIL** prinmatt@isu.edu

PRITCHARD, SUSAN V.
PERSONAL Born 09/12/1943, Appleton, WI, m, 1994, 4 children **DISCIPLINE** LIBRARY SCIENCE **EDUCATION** Univ Ariz, MLS, 89; Ariz State Univ, BA, 95. **CAREER** Dir, Devry Inst of Technol, 89-. **HONORS AND AWARDS** ASU Acad Scholar; 1st recipient of $5000 scholar to obtain MLS. **MEMBERSHIPS** ALA; SLA; Ariz State Library Asn; Central Ariz Library Cooperative. **CONTACT ADDRESS** Devry Inst of Tech, 2149 W Dunlap Ave, Phoenix, AZ, 85021. **EMAIL** spritchard@devry-phx.edu

PRITCHARD, WILLIAM H.
PERSONAL Born 11/12/1932, Binghamton, NY, m, 1957, 3 children **DISCIPLINE** ENGLISH **EDUCATION** Amherst Col, BA, 53; Columbia Univ, 54; Harvard Univ, MA, 56; PhD, 60. **CAREER** Henry Clay Folger prof, Amherst Col, 1958- . **HONORS AND AWARDS** Phi Beta Kappa; Guggenheim fel, 73-74; ACLS fel, 63-64, 77-78; NEH fel, 77-78, 86; script writer for "Robert Frost: A Question of Place" (NPR), 78; Under Criticism: Essays for William H. Pritchard, 98. **MEMBERSHIPS** Asoc of Lit Scholars and Critics. **RESEARCH** English and American poetry, fiction, criticism--especially 20th century. **SELECTED PUBLICATIONS** Auth, Randall Jarell: A Literary Life, 90; auth, Playing It by Ear: Literary Essays and Reviews, 94; auth, English Papers: A Teaching Life, 95; auth, Talking Back to Emily Dickinson, and Other Essays, 98; ed, Mountain Interval and New Hampshire, 99. **CONTACT ADDRESS** English Dept, Amherst Col, Amherst, MA, 01002.

PROEHL, GEOFFREY
DISCIPLINE DEPARTMENT OF COMMUNICATION AND THEATRE ARTS **EDUCATION** George Fox Col, BS, 73; Wayne State Univ, MFA, 77; Stanford Univ, PhD, 88. **CAREER** Instr, 88-94, chemn, grad stud prog, Villanova Univ; instr, Univ Puget Sound, 94-. **RESEARCH** Dramaturgy and theatricality. **SELECTED PUBLICATIONS** Auth, Coming Home Again: American Family Drama and the Figure of the Prodigal, Fairleigh Dickinson Univ Press, 97; co-ed, Dramaturgy in American Theater: A Source Book, Harcourt Brace Jovanovich, 97. **CONTACT ADDRESS** Dept of Commun and Theatre Arts, Univ Puget Sound, 1500 North Warner, Tacoma, WA, 98416. **EMAIL** gproehl@ups.edu

PRUITT, VIRGINIA D.
PERSONAL Born 05/08/1943, Rochester, MN, d **DISCIPLINE** ENGLISH **EDUCATION** St. Olaf Col, BA, 65; Univ NC at Chapel Hill, 66; Univ Va, PhD, 74. **CAREER** Instr, Memphis State Univ, 68-71; prof, Washburn Univ, 74-. **HONORS AND AWARDS** Phi Beta Kappa, 65; Mayo Found Scholar Award, 71-74. **MEMBERSHIPS** MLA; popular Culture Asn. **RESEARCH** Doris Lissing; Alice Munro **SELECTED PUBLICATIONS** Auth, The Selected Correspondence of Karl A. Menninger: 1919-1945, 95; auth, The Selected Correspondence of Karl A. Menninger: 1946-1965, 95; auth, Dear Dr. Menninger: Women's Voices From the Thirties, 97. **CONTACT ADDRESS** Washburn Univ, Topeka, KS, 66621.

PURINTON, MARJEAN D.
DISCIPLINE ENGLISH LITERATURE **EDUCATION** TX A & M Univ, PhD, 91. **CAREER** Asst prof, TX Tech Univ. **MEMBERSHIPS** Pres, S Cent Women's Stud Asn. **RESEARCH** Brit romantic period. **SELECTED PUBLICATIONS** Auth, Romantic Ideology Unmasked: The Mentally Constructed Tyrannies in Dramas of William Wordsworth, Lord Byron, Percy Shelley, and Joanna Baillie, Delaware UP, 94. **CONTACT ADDRESS** Texas Tech Univ, Lubbock, TX, 79409-5015. **EMAIL** cbmdp@ttacs.ttu.edu

PUTNAM, LINDA L.
DISCIPLINE COMMUNICATION **EDUCATION** Univ Minn, PhD. **CAREER** Prof, Texas A&M Univ. **HONORS AND AWARDS** Amoco Found Awd for Distinguished Tchg; Speech Commun Association's Charles H. Woolbert Res Awd; ICA Fel, Int Commun Asn; gov bd, Acad Mgt & pres elect, Int Commun Asn., Mem ed bd 8 scholarly jour, Quart J Speech; Mgt Commun Quart & Commun Theory. **RESEARCH** Organizational communication, gender & communication, negotiation & conflict management. **SELECTED PUBLICATIONS** Co-ed, Communication and Negotiation; Handbook of Organizational Communication & Communication and Organization: An Interpretive Approach. **CONTACT ADDRESS** Dept of Speech Communication, Texas A&M Univ, College Station, TX, 77843-4234.

PYCHINKA, C.A. PRETTIMAN
PERSONAL Born 08/09/1968, Greensburg, PA, m, 1998 **DISCIPLINE** LITERATURE **EDUCATION** Pa State Univ, BA, 89, MA, 90; Princeton Univ, PhD, 95 **CAREER** Teaching asst, 89-90, Pa St Univ; asst, 90-94, Princeton Univ; asst prof, 94-96, Cedar Crest Col; vis asst prof, 95, 96, Muhlenberg Col & Allentown Col of St Francis de Sales; asst prof, chair, asst dir, 96-, Cedar Crest Col. **HONORS AND AWARDS** Univ Scholar Prog, 87-90; Samuel P Bayard Award for Excellence in Camparative Lit; Phi Beta Kappa, 89; Mary Cross Fel, 90; Andrew W Mellon Found Grant, 95-97; Culpeper Found Grant, 98. **MEMBERSHIPS** Modern Lang Assoc; Amer Comparative Lit Assoc; Renaissance Soc Amer; Assoc Literary Scholars & Critics. **RESEARCH** European Baroque era; Celtic lang & lit; modernism. **SELECTED PUBLICATIONS** Auth, John Dryden's Dramatic Theory and Its Debts to the Spanish Comedia; Renaissance Soc Amer, 96; art, The English Segismundo: Aphra Behn's The Young King, Amer Comparative Lit Assoc; 97; art, The Laws of Hywel Dda and the Portrayal of Women in Medieval Welsh Literature, Modern Lang Assoc, 97; art, The Influence of the Commedia dell'arte on the Early plays of Lope de Vega, Renaissance Soc Amer, 98; art, Micheal O Coileain, Sewanee Review, 98. **CONTACT ADDRESS** 100 College Dr, Allentown, PA, 18104. **EMAIL** CPrettiman@aol.com

Q

QUALLS, BARRY V.
DISCIPLINE ENGLISH LANGUAGE AND LITERATURE **EDUCATION** Fla State Univ, BA; Northwestern Univ, MA; PhD. **CAREER** Assoc Dean Hum. **RESEARCH** Victorian literature; Biblical literature; poetry. **SELECTED PUBLICATIONS** Auth, The Secular Pilgrims of Victorian Fiction: the Novel as Book of Life. **CONTACT ADDRESS** Dept of English, Rutgers Univ, 510 George St, Murray Hall, New Brunswick, NJ, 08901-1167.

QUIGLEY, AUSTIN E.
DISCIPLINE ENGLISH LITERATURE **EDUCATION** Univ Nottingham; BA, 67, MA, 69; Univ Calif, Santa Cruz, PhD, 71. **CAREER** Instr, Univ Nottingham; Univ Geneva; Univ Konstanz; Univ Mass; dept ch, Univ Va; H. Gordon Garbedian prof, 90; dean, Columbia Col, 95-. **HONORS AND AWARDS** Fel, Danforth; fel, NEH; assocship, Univ Va., Former ch, MLA Drama Div Exec Comm; ch, Columbia's Docl Subcomm on Theatre and Film; Interdept Comm on Drama and Theatre Arts; ed bd, New Lit Hist; Mod Drama; The Pinter Rev. **SELECTED PUBLICATIONS** Auth, The Pinter Problem and The Modern Stage and Other Worlds; auth, pub, articles on mod drama and lit theory **CONTACT ADDRESS** Dept of Eng, Columbia Col, New York, 2960 Broadway, New York, NY, 10027-6902.

QUIGLEY, AUSTIN F.
DISCIPLINE DRAMA, MODERN LITERATURE **EDUCATION** Univ Nottingham, BA, 67; Univ Birmingham, MA, 69; Univ Calif, PhD, 67. **CAREER** English and Lit, Columbia Univ **HONORS AND AWARDS** Dean, Columbia Col, 95-; Danforth fel, NEH fel. **SELECTED PUBLICATIONS** Auth, The Pinter Problem; The Modern Stage and Other Worlds. **CONTACT ADDRESS** Columbia Univ, 2960 Broadway, New York, NY, 10027-6902.

QUINLAN, KIERAN
DISCIPLINE MODERN AMERICAN AND IRISH LITERATURE **EDUCATION** Vanderbilt Univ, PhD, 84. **CAREER** Univ Ala **HONORS AND AWARDS** Pres, Henry James Soc. **SELECTED PUBLICATIONS** Auth, John Crowe Ransom's Secular Faith, LSU Press, 89; Walker Percy, The Last Catholic Novelist, LSU Press, 96. **CONTACT ADDRESS** Univ AL, 1400 University Blvd, Birmingham, AL, 35294-1150.

QUINN, WILLIAM A.
DISCIPLINE MEDIEVAL LITERATURE **EDUCATION** Ohio State Univ, PhD. **CAREER** English and Lit, Univ Ark. **HONORS AND AWARDS** Dir, Grad studies. **SELECTED PUBLICATIONS** Auth, Jongleur: A Modified Theory of Oral Improvisation and its Effects on the Performability and Transmission of Middle English Romance, Univ Press Am, 82; Chaucer's Rehersynges: The Performability of the "Legend of Good Women", Catholic Univ Press, 94. **CONTACT ADDRESS** Univ Ark, Fayetteville, AR, 72701.

QUINSEY, KATHERINE M.
DISCIPLINE ENGLISH LANGUAGE; LITERATURE **EDUCATION** Trent, BA; London, PhD, 89. **CAREER** Assoc prof **HONORS AND AWARDS** SSHRCC grant, 93-96. **RESEARCH** Pope, Dryden, print culture; seventeenth-century and Restoration rhetoric and linguistic philosophy; feminism 1600-1800. **SELECTED PUBLICATIONS** Ed, Broken Boundaries: Women and Feminism in Restoration Drama, 96. **CONTACT ADDRESS** Dept of English Language and Literature, Univ of Windsor, 401 Sunset Ave, Windsor, ON, N9B 3P4. **EMAIL** kateq4@uwindsor.ca

QUINTERO, RUBEN
PERSONAL Born 05/05/1949, Montebello, CA, m, 1973, 4 children **DISCIPLINE** ENGLISH; AMERICAN LITERATURE; LANGUAGE **EDUCATION** CSULA, BA, 78, 80; Harvard Univ, AM, 83, PhD, 88. **CAREER** ASSOC PROF, CSULA; Phi Kappa Phi. **HONORS AND AWARDS** Univ DE Press Manuscript Award 18th Century Studies, 90. **MEMBERSHIPS** ASECS; ASLSC; Int Soc Hist Rhet **RESEARCH** Restoration and eighteenth-century British literature. **SELECTED PUBLICATIONS** Literate Culture: Pope's Rhetorical Art, 82. **CONTACT ADDRESS** Dept of English, California State Univ, Los Angeles, 5151 State Univ Dr, Los Angeles, CA, 90032-8110. **EMAIL** rquint@calstatela.edu

QUIRK, RUTHMARIE
PERSONAL Born 06/12/1955, MA, s, 1 child **DISCIPLINE** LIBRARY SCIENCE **CAREER** Head librarian, Univ Hawaii,95-. **RESEARCH** Directory of Sacred Dance in Hawaii. **CONTACT ADDRESS** 7253 Nohili St, Honolulu, HI, 96825-2249.

QUIRK, THOMAS VAUGHAN
PERSONAL Born 12/28/1946, Houston, TX, m, 1986, 3 children **DISCIPLINE** ENGLISH **EDUCATION** AZ State Univ, BA, 70; Univ NM, MA, 72, PhD, 77. **CAREER** Asst prof, 78-79, New Mexio-Gallup; asst prof, prof, 79-88, Univ MO-Columbia. **MEMBERSHIPS** Melville Soc; Mark Twain Cir; Amer Lit Assn. **RESEARCH** 19th and early 20th Amer literature and culture **SELECTED PUBLICATIONS** Auth, American Realism and the Canon, 94; Selected Tales, Essays, Speeches and Sketches of Mark Twain, 94; Mark Twain, American Literary Scholarship, 94,95,96; Coed, Viking Portable American Realism 1865-1918, 97; Biographies of Books, 96; auth, Mark Twain: A Study of the Short Fiction, 97. **CONTACT ADDRESS** Dept of Eng, Univ MO, 107 Tate Hall, Columbia, MO, 65211. **EMAIL** engtq@showme.missouri.edu

QUIRK, WILLIAM J.
DISCIPLINE LEGAL RESEARCH **EDUCATION** Princeton Univ, AB, 56; Univ VA, LLB, 59. **CAREER** Prof, Univ of SC. **SELECTED PUBLICATIONS** Publ on, tax and financial policy. **CONTACT ADDRESS** School of Law, Univ of S. Carolina, Law Center, Columbia, SC, 29208. **EMAIL** law0159@univscvm.csd.scarolina.edu

R

RABILLARD, SHEILA M.
DISCIPLINE MODERN LITERATURE; DRAMA **EDUCATION** Queen's Univ, BA, MA; Univ W Ontario, Bed; Princeton Univ, PhD. **CAREER** Assoc prof. **RESEARCH** Theories of drama and performance; gender studies. **SELECTED PUBLICATIONS** Auth, Shepard's Challenge to the Modernist Myths of Origin and Originality: Angel City and True West, Rereading Shepard, Macmillan, 93; essays reprinted in Theatre Criticism Vol V, Gale, 95, Theatre Criticism Vol VI, Gale, 95. **CONTACT ADDRESS** Dept of English, Victoria Univ, PO Box 3070, Victoria, BC, V8W 3W1. **EMAIL** rabillar@uvic.ca

RADFORD, GARY P.
DISCIPLINE COMMUNICATION **EDUCATION** Sheffield Hallam Univ, Engl, BA, 83; Southern Ill Univ, Carbondale, MS, 84; State Univ NJ, PhD, 91. **CAREER** Assoc prof, 97-; asst prof, William Paterson Univ NJ, 90-97; instr, William Paterson Univ NJ, 89-90; grad tchg asst, State Univ NJ, 86-89; instr, State Univ NJ, 84-86; grad tchg asst, Sheffield Hallam Univ, Engl, 83-84; Southern Ill Univ Carbondale. **SELECTED PUBLICATIONS** Auth, Foucault inserted: Philosophy, struggle, and transgression, Transgressing discourses: Communication and the voice of other, Albany, NY: SUNY Press, 97; Science, the voice of other, and Kant's foggy island of truth, Transgressing discourses: Communication and the voice of other, Albany, NY: SUNY Press, 97; Characterizing the Mod library experience: Rationality or fantasia, Continuity and Transformation: The Promise of Confluence, Proceedings of the 7th Nat Conf of the Asn of Col and Res Libr(s), Chicago, IL: Amer Libr Asn, 95; A Foucauldian perspective of the relationship between communication and information, Between Communication and Information, Information and Behavior, 93; coauth, Transgressing discourses: Communication and the voice of other,Albany, NY: SUNY Press, 97; Instructor's manual: Communication and human behavior, 2nd ed, NY: Macmillan, 88; We do need a philosophy of Library and Information Science, we're not confused enough: A response to Zwadlo, Libr Quart, 97; Power, knowledge, and fear: Feminism, Foucault, and the stereotype of the female librarian, Libr Quart, 97; The impact of four conferencing formats on the efficiency and quality of small group decision making in a laboratory experiment setting, Telematics and Informatics, 94. **CONTACT ADDRESS** Dept of Communication, William Paterson Col, Hobart Hall, Room 211, Wayne, NJ, 07470. **EMAIL** radfordg@nebula.wilpaterson.edu

RADWAY, JANICE
DISCIPLINE ENGLISH LITERATURE **EDUCATION** MI State Univ, PhD, 77. **CAREER** Prof, Duke Univ. **RESEARCH** Cult studies; feminist theory. **SELECTED PUBLICATIONS** Auth, Reading the Romance and A Feeling for Books: The Book-of-the-Month Club; Literary Taste; Middle Class Desire. **CONTACT ADDRESS** Eng Dept, Duke Univ, Durham, NC, 27706.

RAE, PATRICIA
DISCIPLINE ENGLISH LITERATURE **EDUCATION** Oxford Univ, DPhil. **CAREER** Dept Eng, Queen's Univ **RESEARCH** Modern British and American poetry and fiction; early twentieth century philosophy and psychology; classical pragmatism and neopragmatism; modern literature and the visual arts; Imagism and Vorticism; literature and politics in the 1930s. **SELECTED PUBLICATIONS** Auth, The Practical Muse: Pragmatist Poetics in Hulme, Pound, and Stevens, 97; Mr. Charrington's Junk Shop: T.S. Eliot and Modernist Poetics in Nineteen Eighty-Four, 97; Cannon Aspirin: Wallace Stevens' Defense of Pleasure, 97; From Mystical Gaze to Pragmatic Game: Representations of Truth in Vorticist Art, 89; T.E. Hulme's French Sources: A Reconsideration, 89. **CONTACT ADDRESS** English Dept, Queen's Univ, Kingston, ON, K7L 3N6.

RAFAEL, VICENTE
DISCIPLINE COMMUNICATIONS **EDUCATION** Cornell Univ, PhD, Hist, 84. **CAREER** ASSOC PROF, COMMUN, UNIV CALIF, SAN DIEGO. **RESEARCH** Compar colonial discourses; Polit and cult of nationalisms. **SELECTED PUBLICATIONS** Auth, Contracting Colonialism: Translation and Christian Conversion in Tagalog Society Under Early Spanish Rule, Duke, 93; "White Love: Surveillance and Nationalist Resistance in the U.S. Colonization of the Philippines," Cultures of U S Imperialism, Duke, 93. **CONTACT ADDRESS** Dept of Commun, Univ Calif, San Diego, 9500 Gilman Dr, La Jolla, CA, 92093. **EMAIL** vrafael@weber.ucsd.edu

RAFFEL, BURTON
PERSONAL Born 04/27/1928, New York, NY, m, 1974, 5 children **DISCIPLINE** ENGLISH **EDUCATION** BA, Brooklyn Coll, 48; MA, OH State Univ, 49; JD, Yale Univ, 58. **CAREER** Distinguished Prof of Hum, Prof of Enf, Univ of SW LA, 89-; Dir, The Adirondack Mtn Found, 87-89; Prof of Eng, Univ of Denver, 86-87; Vis Prof, Eng, Emory Univ, 74; Vis Prof of Hum, York Univ(Toronto), 72-75; Sr Tutor, (Dean)Ontario Coll of Art(Toronto),71-72; Assoc Prof of Eng, State Univ of NY, Buffalo, 66-68; Inst of Eng, State Univ of NY, Stony Brood, 64-65; Attorney Milbank, Tweed, Hadley and McCloy, NY, 58-60. **SELECTED PUBLICATIONS** The Development of Modern Indonesian Poetry, State Univ of NY Press, 67; The Art of Translating Prose, Penn State Univ Press, 94; American Victorians: Explotations in Emotional History, Archon Books, 84; Politicians, Poets and Con Men, Archon Books, 86; The Annotated Milton: The Complete English Poems with annotations lexical, syhntactical, prosodic, and referential, Bantam Books, 99; Lyrics From the Old English, with Robert P.Creed, Folkways LP No FL, 9858; Metrical Dramaturgy in Shakespeares Early Plays, The CEA Critic, 95; A Lost Poem by Chairil Anwar, Indonesia Circle, 95; Translation and Creativity, Western Humanities Review, 96; Who Heard the Rhymes and How: Shakespeares Dramatrugical Signals, Oral Tradition, 98; Mark Twain's View of Huck Finn, Ball State U Forum, 83(XXIV:3). **CONTACT ADDRESS** Dept Eng, Univ of SW Louisiana, Lafayette, LA, 70504-4691. **EMAIL** bnraffel@net-connect.net

RAGSDALE, J. DONALD
DISCIPLINE COMMUNICATION THEORY, INTERPERSONAL COMMUNICATION, FILM **EDUCATION** Samford Univ, BA, 61; Univ Ill, MA, PhD. **CAREER** Prof, La State Univ. **MEMBERSHIPS** Pres, Southern States Commun Asn. **RESEARCH** Marital communication. **SELECTED PUBLICATIONS** Author of numerous scholarly articles and book chapters in communication theory, interpersonal communication, film, and marital communication. **CONTACT ADDRESS** Dept of Speech Commun, Louisiana State Univ, Baton Rouge, LA, 70803.

RAGUSSIS, MICHAEL
DISCIPLINE ENGLISH LITERATURE **EDUCATION** City Col NY, BA; Columbia Univ, MA; Johns Hopkins Univ, PhD. **CAREER** Eng Dept, Georgetown Univ **RESEARCH** Eighteenth and nineteenth centuries, with focus on fiction and drama; literary theory; Anglo Jewish studies; cultural studies. **SELECTED PUBLICATIONS** Auth, The Subterfuge of Art: Language and the Romantic Tradition, Johns Hopkins Univ, 78; Acts of Naming: The Family Plot in Fiction, Oxford, 86; Figures of Conversion: "The Jewish Question" and English National Identity, Duke, 95. **CONTACT ADDRESS** English Dept, Georgetown Univ, 37th and O St, Washington, DC, 20057.

RAHMAN, SHAFIQUR
PERSONAL Born 12/14/1946, Bangladesh, m **DISCIPLINE** COMMUNICATION **EDUCATION** Dhaka Univ, Bangladesh, MA, 68, 73; Simon Fraser Univ, Vancouver, BC, Canada; PhD, 87. **CAREER** Asst Prof, Chittagong Univ, 81-83; instr, La St Univ Baton Rouge, 87; asst prof to assoc prof & chair, Alcorn St Univ, Ms, 88- . **HONORS AND AWARDS** Freedom Forum J Educ Admin Workshop, San Francisco, Calif, 97; Amer Press Inst Critical Mgmt Skills Sem, Reston, Va, 98. **MEMBERSHIPS** Assoc Educ in J & Mass Commun; Assoc of Schools of J & Mass Commun; Black Col Commun Assoc; Assoc for Commun Admin; Int Commun Assoc; Asian Stud Assoc; Canadian Econ Assoc. **RESEARCH** Mass media analysis; audience stud; media & the minorities; political-economy of org & bureaucracy; inst, int, intercultural commun; third world commun; educ & develop; Asian media syst. **SELECTED PUBLICATIONS** Auth, Bureaucratic Organizational Communication: Implication of Definition-Building Roles of Bureaucracies in Development Programs, Dhaka Univ, Bangladesh, 90; The role of Selective Perception in Creating and Communicating Definitions of Development in Organizations, Univ Wi Oshkosh, 91; Comparative Content Analysis of Selected Mississippi Newspapers: Coverage of News About Afro-American People and Issues, Alcorn St. Univ, Ms, 92-95; State, Culture and Media: A Case of Bangladesh Television, Bangladesh-Amer J Soc Third Annual Conf, NY,98; Perceptions/Feedbacks of Bangladesh Television Viewers Towards Foreign News and Dubbed Foreign English Satellite Programs, Dhaka, Bangledesh, ongoing. **CONTACT ADDRESS** Dept of Commun, Alcorn State Univ, 1000 ASU Dr, #269, Lorman, MS, 39096-9402. **EMAIL** srahman@lorman.alcorn.edu

RAINEY, KENNETH T.
DISCIPLINE COMMUNICATION STUDIES **EDUCATION** OH State Univ, PhD. **CAREER** Prof tech commun, Southern Polytech State Univ. **HONORS AND AWARDS** Outstanding Faculty Awd, 92. **MEMBERSHIPS** STC; Asn Tchr Tech Writing; Soc Tech Commun; Nat Council Tchr Eng. **SELECTED PUBLICATIONS** Auth, articles on compos and rhet; Am cult; tech commun. **CONTACT ADDRESS** Hum and Tech Commun Dept, Southern Polytech State Univ, S Marietta Pkwy, PO Box 1100, Marietta, GA, 30060.

RAINWATER, MARY CATHERINE
PERSONAL Born 05/31/1953, Corpus Christi, TX **DISCIPLINE** LITERATURE **EDUCATION** Univ TX, Austin, BA 74, PhD 82; Univ CA, Irvine, MA 76. **CAREER** St Edward's Univ, adj prof 85-87, instr 87-88, asst prof 88-93, assoc prof 93; Univ TX, Austin, asst inst lectr 76-85; univ CA, Irvine, tch asst assoc 74-76. **HONORS AND AWARDS** Forester Prize; Dart Sch Criti Theor Fell; Distg Diss Awd; Phi Kappa Phi Hon Soc; Grad Honors 74; OutStnd Stu 72 **MEMBERSHIPS** MLA; ALA; ASAIL; EGS; SCMLA. **RESEARCH** Native am lit, hist and cult; contemp lit and cult; 19th 20th century Brit Am lit and cult; contem ethnic lis; contem nonfic writing. **SELECTED PUBLICATIONS** Dreams of Fiery Stars: The Transformations of Native American Fiction, Phil PA, Univ PA Press, 99; The Way to Rainy Mountain: The Sixties in America, ed Rowena Wildin, Pasadena, Salem Press, forthcoming 99; Ethnic Signs in Erdrich's Tracks and the Bingo Palace, forth coming 98, ed Allan Chavkin, Univ Alabama Press; Planes, lines, Shapes and Shadow's: N Scott Momaday's Iconological Imagination, TX Stud in Lit Lang, 95; Through a Gate and Into Another Life: Ellen Glasgow After 1945, eds, Welford Taylor George Longest, Richmond, Virginia State Lib, forthcoming, 99. **CONTACT ADDRESS** Sch of Hum, St Edward's univ, 3001 South Congress Av, Austin, TX, 78704.

RAISOR, PHILIP
DISCIPLINE 20TH CENTURY AMERICAN, BRITISH, AND WORLD POETRY, FICTION, DRAMA **EDUCATION** La State Univ, BA, MA; Kent State Univ, PhD. **CAREER** Engl, Old Dominion Univ. **HONORS AND AWARDS** Fac Rep, ODU Board Visitors; Chair Fac Form; Chair & Dir Grad Studies Eng; Pres New Virginia Rev; Mem Assoc Writing ProgBoard Dir; President ODU chapter Phi Kappa Phi. **RESEARCH** Poetry. **SELECTED PUBLICATIONS** Tuned and Under Tension: The Recent Poetry of W. D. Snodgrass. **CONTACT ADDRESS** Old Dominion Univ, 4100 Powhatan Ave, Norfolk, VA, 23058. **EMAIL** PRaisor@odu.edu

RAJAN, TILOTTAMA
PERSONAL NY **DISCIPLINE** ENGLISH/CRITICISM **EDUCATION** Univ Toronto, BA, 72, MA, 73, PhD, 77. **CAREER** Asst prof, Univ Western Ont, 77-80; asst prof, 80-83, assoc prof, Queen's Univ, 83-85; prof, Univ Wisconsin, Madison, 85-90; PROF ENGLISH/CTR THEORY & CRITICISM, UNIV WESTERN ONT, 90-. **HONORS AND AWARDS** John Simon Guggenheim Fel, 87-88; Res Fel, SSHRCC, 90-94. **MEMBERSHIPS** MLA; North Am Soc Stud Romanticism; Fel, Royal Society Can. **SELECTED PUBLICATIONS** Auth, Dark Interpreter: The Discourse of Romanticism, 80, 86; auth, The Supplement of Reading: Figures of Understanding in Romantic Theory and Practice, 90; co-ed, Intersections: Nineteenth Century Philosophy and Contempory Theory, 94. **CONTACT ADDRESS** CTR Stud Theory & Criticism, Univ Western Ont, London, ON, N6A 3K7. **EMAIL** trajan@bosshog.arts.uwo.ca

RALSTON, STEVEN
DISCIPLINE COMMUNICATION STUDIES **EDUCATION** Old Domnion Univ, BA; Univ Tennessee, MA; Ind Univ, PhD. **CAREER** Assoc prof. **MEMBERSHIPS** Am Soc Training Develop; , Med Off Managers Asn, Int Auditors Asn; Asn Bus Commun; Int Commun Asn; Speech Commun Asn. **SELECTED PUBLICATIONS** Auth, pubs on business and professional communication, applied organizational communication, interviewing, and communication education. **CONTACT ADDRESS** Dept of Communication, East Tennesee State Univ, PO Box 70717, Johnson City, TN, 37614-0717. **EMAIL** saucemaf@etsu.edu

RAMAZANI, JAHAN
PERSONAL Born 02/17/1960, Charlottesville, VA, m, 1995, 1 child **DISCIPLINE** ENGLISH **EDUCATION** Univ Virginia, BA, 81; Oxford, MA, 83; Yale, MA 85, PhD, 88. **CAREER** Asst prof, 88-94, Univ VA, prof, 94-present,. **HONORS AND AWARDS** Nominated, Natl Book Critics Circle; William Riley Parker Award, MLA, 97. **MEMBERSHIPS** MLA **RESEARCH** Modern poetry, post colonial literature **SELECTED PUBLICATIONS** Poetry of Mourning, Chicago, 94; Yeats: The Poetry of Death, Yale, 90. **CONTACT ADDRESS** Dept of English, Univ of Virginia, Bryan Hall, Charlottesville, VA, 22903. **EMAIL** ramazani@virginia.edu

RAMBUSS, RICHARD
DISCIPLINE ENGLISH LANGUAGE AND LITERATURE **EDUCATION** Johns Hopkins Univ, PhD. **CAREER** Assoc

prof, 96. **RESEARCH** Renaissance literaure and culture; cultural criticism; film; history of sexuality. **SELECTED PUBLICATIONS** Auth, Closet Devotions, Duke UP, 98; Spenser's Secret Career, Cambridge UP, 93; Spenser's Lives, Spenser's Careers in Spenser and the Subject of Biography, U Mass P, 97; Devotion and Defilement: The Haigiographics of Chaucer's 'Prioress' Tale' in Textual Bodies, SUNY P, 97; Homodevotion in Cruising the Performative, Indiana UP, 95; and Christ's Ganymede, Yale Jour Law Hum, 95. **CONTACT ADDRESS** English Dept, Emory Univ, 1380 Oxford Rd NE, Atlanta, GA, 30322-1950. **EMAIL** rrambus@emory.edu

RAMESH, CLOSPETH N.
DISCIPLINE INTERPERSONAL, INTERCULTURAL, AND MASS COMMUNICATION **EDUCATION** Bangalore Univ, India, BA, 77; Univ S MS, MS, 87; MI State Univ, PhD, 92. **CAREER** Assoc prof, 91-, Truman State Univ. **HONORS AND AWARDS** Kulapati award, Bharatiya Vidya Bhavan, India, 85; grad stud award for tchg excellence, Intl Commun Assn, 91. **MEMBERSHIPS** Mem, Nat Commun Assn; Consult Comm on Indic Traditions and Conflict Mgt, Columbia Univ. **RESEARCH** Asian Indians in the US, and hostage negotiations. **SELECTED PUBLICATIONS** Pub(s), Commun Res; Intl Jourf Gp Tensions; Media Devel; Jour Intl Commun. **CONTACT ADDRESS** Dept of Commun, Truman State Univ, 100 E Normal St, Kirksville, MO, 63501-4221. **EMAIL** LL88@Truman.edu

RAMP, STEVEN W.
DISCIPLINE HOMILETICS **EDUCATION** Col William and Mary, BA, 71; Vanderbilt Univ Sch, JD, 75; Princeton Theol Sem, MDiv, 90, PhD, 97. **CAREER** Assoc prof, 98-. **HONORS AND AWARDS** Sr pastor, J.J. White Memorial Presbyterian Church, 93-97; interm pastor, Hope Presbyterian Church, 90-93. **MEMBERSHIPS** Mem, Presbytery Comm; bd mem, Habitat for Humanity. **SELECTED PUBLICATIONS** Auth, The Uniform Commercial Code in Tennesse, 87. **CONTACT ADDRESS** Dept of Homiletics, Luther Sem, 2481 Como Ave, St. Paul, MN, 55108. **EMAIL** sramp@luthersem.edu

RAMPERSAD, ARNOLD
PERSONAL Born 11/13/1941, Port of Spain, Trinidad and Tobago, m **DISCIPLINE** ENGLISH **EDUCATION** Bowling Green State Univ, Bowling Green, OH, BA, 1967, MA, 1968; Harvard Univ, Cambridge, MA, 1969, PhD, 1973. **CAREER** Univ of VA, Charlotteville, VA, asst prof, 1973-74; Stanford Univ, Stanford, CA, prof, 1974-83; Rutgers Univ, New Brunswick, NJ, prof, 1983-88; Columbia Univ, New York, NY, prof, 1988-90; Princeton Univ, Princeton, NJ, Woodrow Wilson prof of literature, 1990-, dir, Program in Afro-American Studies, 1994-. **MEMBERSHIPS** Dir, Program in American Studies, Princeton Univ, 1990-95. **SELECTED PUBLICATIONS** The Collected Poems of Langston Hughes, editor, 1994; Jackie Robinson: A Biography, author, Knopf, 1998; Art & Imagination of W E B DuBois, Harvard Univ Press, 1976; Life of Langston Hughes (2 Vols), Oxford Univ Press, 1986, 1988. **CONTACT ADDRESS** Professor, Princeton Univ, McCosh 22, Princeton, NJ, 08544.

RAMSEY, C. EARL
DISCIPLINE EIGHTEENTH CENTURY LITERATURE **EDUCATION** Univ Fla, PhD. **CAREER** English and Lit, Univ Ark **HONORS AND AWARDS** Dir, Donaghey Scholars Prog. **SELECTED PUBLICATIONS** Auth, A Midsummer Night's Dream, Homer to Brecht; Ed, No More Elegies. **CONTACT ADDRESS** Univ Ark Little Rock, 2801 S University Ave., Little Rock, AR, 72204-1099. **EMAIL** ceramsey@ualr.edu

RAMSEY, JAROLD
PERSONAL Born 09/01/1937, Bend, OR, m, 1959, 3 children **DISCIPLINE** ENGLISH **EDUCATION** Univ OR, BA honors 59; Univ WA, PhD 66. **CAREER** Univ Rochester, asst, assoc, prof eng, 66-98, prof emeritus 98-; Univ Victoria, BC, vis prof 74-76; Univ WA, instr 63-65. **HONORS AND AWARDS** Lillian Fairchild Awd; Don Walker Awd; NEH Fell; Ingram Merrill writ Grant; QRL Intl Poetry Prize. **MEMBERSHIPS** MLA; AFS; Assn Studies of Amer Indian Lits. **RESEARCH** Shakespeare; Amer Indian Lit; Environmental Lit; Mod Poetry. **SELECTED PUBLICATIONS** The Stories We Tell: An Anthology Of Oregon Folk Literature, Ore St Press, 94; Nehalem Tillamook Tales, Ore St Press, 90; Reading the Fire: Essays in the Traditional Indian Literatures of the Far West, Univ Neb Press, revised and expanded edition forthcoming form Univ Wash Press, 99; Hand Shadows, Qtly Rev Press, 89; Coyote Goes Up River: A cycle for Story Theater and Mime, Georgia Rev, 81. **CONTACT ADDRESS** Eng Dept, Univ of Rochester, Rochester, NY, 14627. **EMAIL** ramsey@macmail.

RAMSEY, MARY K.
PERSONAL Born 05/23/1962, Okla City, OK, s **DISCIPLINE** ENGLISH **EDUCATION** Okla Baptist Univ, BA, 84; Univ St. Andrews, MPhil, 89; Univ Okla, MA, 93; Yale Univ, PhD, 98. **CAREER** ASST PROF ENG, GA STATE UNIV, 98- **MEMBERSHIPS** Int Soc Anglo-Saxonists; Medieval Acad Am; Southeastern Medieval Asn; S Atlantic Mod Lang Asn.

RESEARCH Old Eng lang, lit, cult; Dante stud; rel, lit. **SELECTED PUBLICATIONS** various **CONTACT ADDRESS** Dept English, Georgia State Univ, Atlanta, GA, 30303-2083. **EMAIL** mkramsey@gsu.edu

RANDALL, DALE B.J.
DISCIPLINE ENGLISH **EDUCATION** Western Reserve Univ, BA, 51; Rutgers Univ, MA, 53; Univ of Pa, PhD, 58. **CAREER** Instr, 57-60; asst prof, 60-65; assoc prof, 65-70; full prof, 70-. **HONORS AND AWARDS** Harrison Fel, 55-56; Duke Fac Res Fel, 64-65; Duke Endow Fel, 70-71; Guggenheim Memorial Found Fel, 70-71; NEH Senior fel, 78; senior fel, Folger Shakespeare Libr, 86. **MEMBERSHIPS** Asn of Lit Sch and Critics; Gypsy Lore Soc; Int Shakespeare Asn; Malone Soc; Marlowe Soc; Medieval and Renaissance Drama Soc; MLA; Shakespeare Asn of Am. **RESEARCH** Medieval and Renaissance literature; Shakespeare studies **SELECTED PUBLICATIONS** Auth, Soliloquy of a Farmer's Wife: The Diary of Annie Luella Perrin, 99; Winter Fruit: English Drama 1642-1660, 95; Renaissance Papers, 84-90; "Image-making and Image-breaking: Seeing 'The Minister's Black Veil' Through a Miltonic Glass Darkly" in Resources for Am Lit Study, 97; "American 'Mairzy' Dottiness, Sir John Falstolf's Secretary, and the 'Law French' of a Caroline Cavalier" in Am Speech, 95. **CONTACT ADDRESS** Duke Univ, Durham, NC, 27708.

RANES, BARBARA
DISCIPLINE VICTORIAN LITERATURE **EDUCATION** Univ IA, BA, 61, MA, 65, PhD, 70; TESL Cert, UW-WI, 84. **CAREER** Instr, Univ IA; UW-Oshkosh; UW-Milwaukee; UW-Waukesha; MATC-Madison; Loyola; DePaul; Vis lectr, 95-. **SELECTED PUBLICATIONS** Auth, Psyche: Contemporary Women Poets, 73; From Baba to Tovarishch: The Bolshevik Revolution and Women's Struggle for Liberation, 94. **CONTACT ADDRESS** Dept of Lib Arts, Sch of the Art Inst of Chicago, 37 S Wabash Ave, Chicago, IL, 60603.

RANK, HUGH DUKE
PERSONAL Born 11/03/1932, Chicago, IL, d, 4 children **DISCIPLINE** ENGLISH **EDUCATION** Notre Dame, BA, 54, MA, 56, PhD, 69. **CAREER** Univ Notre Dame, 59-60; Arizona State Univ, 61-63; St Josephs Col, 63-68; Fulbright prof, Denmark, 67-68; Sacred Heart Univ, 68-72; Governors State Univ, 68-. **HONORS AND AWARDS** Orwell Award, 76 NCTE; Prof Yr Award, 68, 72, 90. **MEMBERSHIPS** NCTE. **RESEARCH** Persuasion Analysis. **SELECTED PUBLICATIONS** Auth The Pitch; The Pep Talk; Persuasion Analysis; Language and Public Policy; Edwin O'Connor. **CONTACT ADDRESS** English Dept, Governors State Univ, University Park, IL, 60466. **EMAIL** HD-Rank@govst.edu

RANTA, RICHARD R.
PERSONAL MN **DISCIPLINE** FILM, COMMUNICATIONS **EDUCATION** Univ Minn, Duluth, BA, 65; Cornell Univ, MA; Univ Iowa, PhD, 74. **CAREER** Instr, Univ Va, 69-72; DIR OF COMMUN STUDIES, INTERIM DEAN, UNIV COL, ASST VP OF ACAD AFFAIRS, UNIV OF MEMPHIS, 72-; GENERAL MANAGER, HIGH WATER RECORDS; VICE CHEMN, GILLIAM COMMUN, INC. **HONORS AND AWARDS** Who's Who in Am. **MEMBERSHIPS** Memphis Shelby County Film and Tape Comn; Crossroads Music Expo; Tenn Film; Entertainment and Music Comn Advisory Board; Concerts Int; Libertyland/Mid-South Fair; Inst of Egyptian Art and Archaeol; Asn for Commun Admin Bulletin Ed Board; Citizens Law Enforcement Rev Comt; Crime Stoppers; Southern Arts Fed Folk Arts Advisory Board; Delta Sailing Asn; Southern States Commun Asn; Nat Acad of Recording Arts & Sci. **CONTACT ADDRESS** Col of Commun & Fine Arts, Univ Memphis, Campus Box 526546, Memphis, TN, 38152-6546.

RAO, NAGESH
DISCIPLINE INTERCULTURAL COMMUNICATION **EDUCATION** MI State Univ, PhD, 94. **CAREER** Asst prof, Univ MD . **RESEARCH** Role of cult appropriateness in designing effective health campaigns. **SELECTED PUBLICATIONS** Co-auth, Communication and Community in a City Under Seige: The AIDS Epidemic in San Francisco, Commun Res 22, 95. **CONTACT ADDRESS** Dept of Commun, Univ MD, 4229 Art-Sociology Building, College Park, MD, 20742-1335. **EMAIL** nr35@umail.umd.edu

RAO, SANDHYA
DISCIPLINE COMMUNICATIONS **EDUCATION** Banglore Univ, BS, BA, MS; Bowling Green State Univ, PhD. **CAREER** Comm Dept, Southwest Tex State Univ **SELECTED PUBLICATIONS** Auth, International Communication: History, Conflict and Control of the G Metropoliy, Wadsworth Publ, 93; Towards the Development of Computer Attitude Scales for Developing Countries, Int Comm Asn Conf, 94; Role of attitudes and perceptions of users in the implementation of NIC-NET, in Karnataka State, India, an example, Gazette, 94. **CONTACT ADDRESS** Southwest Texas State Univ, 601 University Dr, San Marcos, TX, 78666-4604.

RASKIN, JONAH
PERSONAL Born 01/03/1942, Brooklyn, NY **DISCIPLINE** COMMUNICATIONS **EDUCATION** Columbia Col, BA, 63; Columbia Univ, MA, 64; Univ Manchester, PhD, 67. **CAREER** Prof, chemn, Commun Stud Dept. **HONORS AND AWARDS** Fulbright prof, Belgium, 86-87. **SELECTED PUBLICATIONS** Auth, For the Hell of It: The Life and Times of Abbie Hoffman, 96. **CONTACT ADDRESS** 1801 E Cotati Ave, Rohmert Park, CA, 94928.

RASULA, JED
DISCIPLINE ENGLISH LITERATURE **EDUCATION** Univ Calif Santa Cruz, PhD. **CAREER** Dept Eng, Queen's Univ **HONORS AND AWARDS** Frank Knox Awd. **RESEARCH** Modernism; modern poetry and poetics; literary sociology; critical theory; cultural studies and history of ideas; jazz; film; architecture; literature and science. **SELECTED PUBLICATIONS** Auth, The American Poetry Wax Museum: Reality Effects 1940-1990, NCTE, 95; ed, Imagining Language, MIT, 96. **CONTACT ADDRESS** English Dept, Queen's Univ, Kingston, ON, K7L 3N6.

RATCLIFFE, STEPHEN
DISCIPLINE ENGLISH **EDUCATION** Univ Calif at Berkeley, BA, MA, PhD. **CAREER** Asst prof; Mills Col, 84-. **RESEARCH** Creative writing; Shakespeare; Renaissance Poetry; English Romantic poetry; contemporary poetry and poetics. **SELECTED PUBLICATIONS** Auth, Words and Music: Campion and the Madrigal Ayre Tradition, Approaches to Teaching Shorter Elizabethan Poetry, MLA Approaches to Teaching World Lit Ser, 97; What Doesn't Happen in Hamlet: The Queen's Speech, Exemplaria: A J Theory in Medieval and Renaissance Stud, 97; Eigner's Scores, Witz, 97; 'Shakespeare' and 'I., Exemplaria: A J Theory in Medieval and Renaissance Stud, Vol 8, 96; Conceal me what I am: Reading Act 1, Scene 2 of Twelfth Night, Univ Miss Stud in Engl, New Ser 11-12, 95; Grenier's Scrawl, Witz: A J Contemp Poetics, 96; Correspondences, Santa Barbara Rev, Vol 3, 95; Michael Gregory, Catalogue for Gail Severn Gallery, 95; Preface to Mallarme: poem in prose, Poetic Briefs, 94; Untitled, range/landscape, 94; Dahlen's Reading, Raddle Moon 13, Vol 6, 94; Writing ¤Echoesl Writing, Santa Barbara Rev, Vol 2, 94. **CONTACT ADDRESS** Dept of English, Mills Col, 5000 MacArthur Blvd, Oakland, CA, 94613-1301. **EMAIL** sratclif@mills.edu

RATHBURN, PAUL A.
DISCIPLINE LITERATURE **EDUCATION** Univ Wis, PhD. **CAREER** Instr, Univ Notre Dame. **RESEARCH** Performance theory. **SELECTED PUBLICATIONS** Publishes essays in Shakespeare-on-Film, and lectures on Shakespearean tragedy in the Notre Dame Great Teachers Series, Golden Dome Productions, 92. **CONTACT ADDRESS** Univ Notre Dame, Notre Dame, IN, 46556.

RATLIFF, GERALD LEE
PERSONAL Born 10/23/1944, Middletown, OH **DISCIPLINE** ENGLISH; COMMUNICATION **EDUCATION** Georgetown Col, BA, 67; Univ Cincinnati, MA, 70; Bowling Green St Univ, PhD, 75. **HONORS AND AWARDS** Medallion of Honor, Theta Alpha Phi, 89; Silver Medal of Honor, Int Biog Centere, 98; Teaching Fel, East Commun Assoc, 98; Man of Year, Amer Biog Inst, 998; Deputy Gen Dir Int Biog Centre, 99., Theta Alpha Phi Nat Theatre Honorary, 90; Fulbright Scholar, 90; Fel, Int Schools of Theatre Assoc, 91; US Delegate John F. Kennedy Center for Perf Arts, Int Scholar Exchange Prog, 91; Outstanding Graduate Alumni Award, Bowling Green St Univ, 94; Fel, Nat Fulbright Assoc, 97. **MEMBERSHIPS** E Commun Assoc; Nat Commun Assoc, NY Col English Assoc; Fulbright Assoc. **RESEARCH** Dramatic imagery in Mamet & O'Neill; Reader's Theatre approaches to visualization; literary themes in contemporary drama & poetry **SELECTED PUBLICATIONS** Coauth, An Introduction to Theatre, Rosen Press, 88; auth, The Politics of Machiavelli's The Prince, Barron's Publ Ltd, 86; A Sourcebook for Playing Scenes, Meriwether Publ Ltd, 93; Contemporary Scene Study, Meriwether Publ Ltd, 96; The Theatre Handbook, Meriwether Publ Ltd, 98. **CONTACT ADDRESS** English/Commun Dept, SUNY Potsdam, Potsdam, NY, 13676. **EMAIL** ratlifgl@potsdam.edu

RAUSCHENBERG, ROY A.
PERSONAL Born 10/07/1929, Chicago, IL, m, 1958, 4 children **DISCIPLINE** ENGLISH HISTORY **EDUCATION** Univ IL, BA, 51, MA, 56, PhD, 60. **CAREER** From instr to asst prof hist, E TX State Col, 59-61; asst prof, Chicago Teachers Col, 61-63; asst prof, Baldwin-Wallace Col, 63-64; asst prof, 64-68, assoc prof English Hist, OH Univ, 68-, retired. **MEMBERSHIPS** AHA; Hakluyt Soc; Conf Brit Studies; Asn Can Studies United States. **RESEARCH** Eighteenth century English science; 18th century English culture; John Ellis. **SELECTED PUBLICATIONS** Auth, Daniel Carl Solander, naturalist on the Endeavour voyage, Am Philos Soc Trans, Vol 58, No 8; A letter of Sir Joseph Banks describing the life of Daniel Solander, Vol 55, No 179 & Daniel Carl Solander, the naturalist on the Endeavour voyage, Vol 58, No 193, ISIS; ed, The journals of Joseph Bank's voyage up Great Britain's west coast to Iceland and to the Orkney Isles July to October 1772, Proc Am Philos

Soc, Vol 117, No 3; John Ellis, FRS: Eighteenth century naturalist and royal agent to west Florida, Notes & Rec Royal Soc, London, 3/78. **CONTACT ADDRESS** Dept Hist, Ohio Univ, Athens, OH, 45701-2979.

RAVITZ, ABE C.
PERSONAL Born 05/20/1927, New York, NY, m, 1989, 4 children **DISCIPLINE** AMERICAN LITERATURE **EDUCATION** CCNY, BA, 49; NY Univ, MA, 50, PhD, 55. **CAREER** Asst Prof, Pa State Univ, 53-58; Assoc Prof to Prof English, Hiram Col, 58-66; Prof English, 66-86, Dept Chair, 66-86, Calif State Univ - Dominguez Hills, Emeritus Prof English, 86-. **MEMBERSHIPS** MLA; ASA **RESEARCH** American literature; American popular culture. **SELECTED PUBLICATIONS** Auth, Alfred Henry Lewis, Boise State Univ Press, 86; Rex Beach, Boise State Univ Press, 95; Thunder on the Left: Leane Zugsmith's Prose, Int Publ, 95; Imitations of Life: Fannie Hurst's Gaslight Sonatas, Southern Ill Univ Press, 97. **CONTACT ADDRESS** English Dept, California State Univ, Dominguez Hills, Dominguez Hills, CA, 90747.

RAWLINS, WILLIAM K.
DISCIPLINE INTERPERSONAL COMMUNICATION AND COMMUNICATION THEORY **EDUCATION** Temple Univ, PhD, 81. **CAREER** Prof, dir, grad stud, Purdue Univ. **RESEARCH** The communicative achievement; management of friendship across the life course. **SELECTED PUBLICATIONS** Auth, A Dialectic Analysis of the Tensions, Functions, and Strategic Challenges of Communication in Young Adult Friendships, Commun Yearbk, 12, 89; Friendship Matters: Communication, Dialectics, and the Life Course, Aldine de Gruyter, 92. **CONTACT ADDRESS** Dept of Commun, Purdue Univ, 1080 Schleman Hall, West Lafayette, IN, 47907-1080. **EMAIL** rawlinsw@vm.cc.purdue.edu

RAY, EILEEN BERLIN
DISCIPLINE ORGANIZATIONAL COMMUNICATION, HEALTH COMMUNICATION **EDUCATION** Univ SC, BA, MEd; MI State Univ, MA; Iniv Wash, PhD. **CAREER** Undergrad prog dir, Cleveland State Univ. **SELECTED PUBLICATIONS** Auth, Communication and Disenfranchisement: Social Health Issues and Implications, Lawrence Erlbaum & Assoc, 96; Case studies in communication and disenfranchisement: Applications to social health issues, Lawrence Erlbaum & Assoc, 96; Case Studies in Health Communication, Lawrence Erlbaum & Assoc, 93. **CONTACT ADDRESS** Commun Dept, Cleveland State Univ, 83 E 24th St, Cleveland, OH, 44115. **EMAIL** e.berlinray@csuohio.edu

RAY, GEORGR B.
DISCIPLINE COMMUNICATION AND CULTURE, LANGUAGE AND COMMUNICATION, INTERPERSONAL COMMUN **EDUCATION** Bowling Green State Univ, BA; Cornell Univ, MPS; Univ WA, PhD. **CAREER** Comm, Cleveland St Univ. **SELECTED PUBLICATIONS** Co-auth, Shyness, Self-confidence and Social Interaction, Soc Psychol Quart, 93; auth, Identities in Crisis: Individualism, Disenfranchisement and the Self-help Culture, Communication and Disenfranchisement: Social Health Issues and Implications, Lawrence Erlbaum, 96. **CONTACT ADDRESS** Commun Dept, Cleveland State Univ, 83 E 24th St, Cleveland, OH, 44115. **EMAIL** g.ray@csuohio.edu

RAY, ROBERT H.
PERSONAL Born 04/29/1940, San Saba, TX, m, 2 children **DISCIPLINE** ENGLISH **EDUCATION** Univ of Tex at Austin, BA, 63, PhD, 67. **CAREER** From asst prof to prof, Baylor Univ, 67- . **HONORS AND AWARDS** Phi Beta Kappa. **MEMBERSHIPS** MLA; Asn of Lit Scholars and Critics; John Donne Soc. **RESEARCH** Donne; Herbert; Marvell; Shakespeare; Hooker. **SELECTED PUBLICATIONS** Auth, The Herbert Allusion Book: Allusions to George Herbert in the Seventeenth Century, Studies in Philol 83:4, 86; Approaches to Teaching Shakespeare's King Lear, 86; A John Donne Companion, 90; A George Herbert Companion, 95; An Andrew Marvell Companion, 98. **CONTACT ADDRESS** Dept of English, Baylor Univ, PO Box 97406, Waco, TX, 76798. **EMAIL** robert_ray@baylor.edu

RAYOR, DIANE J.
PERSONAL Born 04/18/1958, Cheyenne, WY, m, 1986, 1 child **DISCIPLINE** LITERATURE **EDUCATION** Univ CA, Santa Cruz, PhD, 87. **CAREER** Vis asst prof, , 88-91, Northwestern Univ; assoc prof, 91-98, Grand Valley St Univ. **MEMBERSHIPS** APA; Women's Classical Caucus. **RESEARCH** Translation; Greek poetry (Archaic & Hellenistic); women in antiquity. **SELECTED PUBLICATIONS** Transl, Latin Lyric and Elegiaic Poetry, Garland, 95; auth, Sappho's Lyre, 91; coauth, Callinachus, Johns Hopkins, 98. **CONTACT ADDRESS** English Dept, Grand Valley State Univ, 1 Campus Dr, Allendale, MI, 49401. **EMAIL** RayorD@GVSU.edu

REAL, MICHAEL
PERSONAL m, 1 child **DISCIPLINE** TELECOMMUNICATIONS **EDUCATION** St Paul Sem, BA; St Thomas Col, MA; Univ IL, PhD. **CAREER** Instr, Univ IL; prof, Univ CA; dept ch, 86-91; prof-, Fordham Univ. **RESEARCH** Media, cult, and soc responsibility. **SELECTED PUBLICATIONS** Auth, Mass Mediated Culture, Prentice Hall, 77; Global Ritual: Olympic Media Coverage and International Understanding, UNESCO, 86; Super Media: A Cultural Studies Approach, Sage, 89. **CONTACT ADDRESS** Dept of Commun, San Diego State Univ, 5500 Campanile Dr, San Diego, CA, 92182. **EMAIL** mreal@ sciences.sdsu.edu

REDDICK, ROBERT
DISCIPLINE ENGLISH **EDUCATION** Univ MN, BS, 66, MA, 69, PhD, 75. **CAREER** Assoc prof; assoc ed, Harold Frederic Edition, 78-85; ed, Market-Place, 81, Damnation of Theron Ware or Illumination, 85 & Gloria Mundi, 86; asst ed, Allegorica, 78-87; UTA Adv Bd, Pre/Text, 83-. **HONORS AND AWARDS** 1,642 Summer stipend, Univ TX, Arlington, 78. **MEMBERSHIPS** Int Soc Anglo-Saxonists; Ling Soc Am, 70-95; MLA; Tex Medieval Asn. **SELECTED PUBLICATIONS** Auth, On the Underlying Order of Early West Saxon, J Ling 18, 82; Old English unlae: A Note on Andreas, Engl Lang Notes 22, 85 The Grammar of Logic, Pre/Text 6, 85; Textlinguistics, Text Theory, and Language Users, Word 37, 86; rev, Techniques of Translation: Chaucer's Boece, Allegorica 9, 87-88; Clause-Bound Grammar and Old English Syntax, Stud Philol 87, 90; English Expository Discourse, Language in Context: Essays for Robert E. Longacre, Dallas, Summer Inst Ling, 92; Heavy Noun Phrases in Pre-900 Prose, Engl Stud 74, 93. **CONTACT ADDRESS** Dept of Eng, Univ of Texas at Arlington, 203 Carlisle Hall, PO Box 19035, Arlington, TX, 76019-0595.

REDDY, MAUREEN T.
PERSONAL Born 03/20/1955, Boston, MA, m, 1979, 2 children **DISCIPLINE** ENGLISH **EDUCATION** BA, 76, MA, 78, Boston Col; PhD, 85 Univ Minnesota. **CAREER** Asst Prof, 85-87, Haverford Col; Prof, 87-, Rhode Island Col. **HONORS AND AWARDS** Pioneer and Trailblazer Award, Rhode Island Commission on Women, 95; Koppelman Award for Excellence in Feminist Studies of Popular Culture and American Culture, 95; Minnesota Book Award for Mother Journeys, 95. **MEMBERSHIPS** Southern New England Consortium on Race and Ethnicity; Natl Women's Studies Assoc; Northeast Victorian Studies Assoc; Modern Lang Assoc. **RESEARCH** Race and interracial relationships in genre fiction **SELECTED PUBLICATIONS** Auth, Crossing the Color Line: Race, Parenting, and Culture, 94; Coauth, Mother Journey's: Feminists Write About Mothering, 94; ed, Everyday Acts Against Racism, 96; Auth, Elizabeth Cleghorn Gaskell, Dictionary of Literary Biography, 95; Racism, The Reader's Companion to US Women's History, 97; Invisibility/Hypervisibility: The Paradox of Normative Whiteness, Tranformations, 98. **CONTACT ADDRESS** Dept of English, Rhode Island Col, 600 Mt. Pleasant Ave., Providence, RI, 02908. **EMAIL** mreddy@grog.ric.edu

REDFIELD, MARC
PERSONAL NY **DISCIPLINE** LITERATURE **EDUCATION** Yale Univ, BA, 80; Cornell, PhD, 90. **CAREER** Asst prof, Univ Geneve, 86-90; asst prof, Claremong Grad Univ, 90-96; ASSOC PROF, 96- . **HONORS AND AWARDS** MLA Prize for a First Book, 97. **MEMBERSHIPS** MLA, N Am Soc for the Study of Romanticism. **RESEARCH** Comparative lit; lit theory. **SELECTED PUBLICATIONS** Auth, The Dissection of the State: Wilhelm Meisters Wanderjahre and the Politics of Aesthetics, The Ger Quart, 96; auth, Phantom Formations: Aesthetic Ideology and the Bildungsroman, 96; Addictions, Diacritics, 97; Spectral Romanticisms, Europ Romantic Rev, 98; Madame Bovary et le fetiche du langage, Romantic Rev, 98. **CONTACT ADDRESS** Dept of English, Claremont Graduate Sch, Claremont, CA, 91711. **EMAIL** marc.redfield@cgu.edu

REDMAN, TIM
DISCIPLINE LITERATURE STUDIES **EDUCATION** Univ Chicago, PhD, 87. **CAREER** Assoc prof. **RESEARCH** American and British modernism; American studies; medieval and renaissance Italian literature. **SELECTED PUBLICATIONS** Auth, Ezra Pound and Italian Fascism, Cambridge, 91; Louis Zukofsky, Charles Scribner's Sons, 91; ed, Offical Rules of Chess, 87. **CONTACT ADDRESS** Dept of Literature, Richardson, TX, 75083-0688. **EMAIL** redman@utdallas.edu

REECE, DEBRA J.
PERSONAL Born 04/10/1958, Denver, CO, m, 1994 **DISCIPLINE** COMMUNICATION **EDUCATION** Regent Univ, Va Bch, Va, MA, 90; Univ Ky, Lexington, PhD, 96. **CAREER** Asst prof, Bethel Col, St Paul, Minn, 96-. **MEMBERSHIPS** Nat Commun Assoc **RESEARCH** Media uses & gratifications within cross-cultural contexts; reception analysis of news programming. **SELECTED PUBLICATIONS** Auth, review of Mind Media Industry in Europe, J Quart, vol 72, 475-476, 95; auth, Covering and communication: The symbolism of dress among Muslim women, Howard J of Commun, vol 7, 35-52, 96; auth, The Gendering of Prayer: An Ethnographic Study of Muslim Women in the United States, J of Commun & Relig, vol 20, 37-47, 97. **CONTACT ADDRESS** Bethel Col, 3900 Bethel Dr, St. Paul, MN, 55112. **EMAIL** debra-reece@bethel.edu

REED, BILL
DISCIPLINE COMMUNICATION STUDIES **EDUCATION** Univ Memphis, BA; Univ Mich, MA, PhD. **CAREER** Asst prof. **RESEARCH** Argumentation and debate; business communication; early American political and religious rhetorical discourse. **SELECTED PUBLICATIONS** Co-auth, Speech Communication in a Democratic Society. **CONTACT ADDRESS** Dept of Communication, State Univ NY Col Brockport, Brockport, NY, 14420. **EMAIL** breed@po.brockport.edu

REED, JOHN R.
PERSONAL Born 01/24/1938, Duluth, MN, m, 1971 **DISCIPLINE** ENGLISH LITERATURE **EDUCATION** Univ of Minn at Duluth, double BA, 59; Univ of Rochester, PhD, 63. **CAREER** Instr, Univ of Cincinnati, 62-64; asst prof, Univ of Conn, 64-65; vis fel & lectr, Univ of Warwick, 66-67; asst prof, 65-68, assoc prof, 68-71, prof, Wayne State Univ, 71-. **HONORS AND AWARDS** Guggenheim Fel, 70-71 & 83-84; distinguished prof, Wayne State Univ, 90. **MEMBERSHIPS** MLA; AAUP; Dickens Soc; H.G. Wells Soc; Midwest Victorian Studies Asn; Victorians Inst. **RESEARCH** Nineteenth- and Twentieth-century British literature and culture. **SELECTED PUBLICATIONS** Auth, Old School Ties: The Public Schools in British Literature, Syracuse Univ Press, 64; Perception and Design in Tennyson's Idylls of the King, Ohio Univ Press, 70; Victorian Conventions, Ohio Univ Press, 75; The Natural History of H.G. Wells, Ohio Univ Press, 82; Decadent Style, Ohio Univ Press, 85; Victorian Will, Ohio Univ Press, 89; Dickens and Thackeray: Punishment and Forgiveness, Ohio Univ Press, 95; Hercules, Fiddlehead Poetry Books, 73; A Gallery of Spiders, Ontario Rev Press, 80; Stations of the Cross, Ridgeway Press, 92; Great Lake, Ridgeway Press, 95; Life Sentences, Wayne State Univ Press, 96. **CONTACT ADDRESS** English Dept, Wayne State Univ, 51 W. Warren, Detroit, MI, 48202. **EMAIL** j.reed@wayne.edu

REED, PETER J.
PERSONAL Born 05/14/1935, London, England, m, 1961 **DISCIPLINE** ENGLISH **EDUCATION** Univ Idaho, BA, 60; Univ Wash, MA, 62, PhD, 65; Harvard Univ, 62-63. **CAREER** Tchg asst, Univ Wash, 60-63; asst prof, San Diego State Col, 67-68; asst prof, 65-67 & 68-72, assoc prof, 72-79, PROF, 79-, Assoc Dean Col Language Arts, 91-96, UNIV MINN; Phi Beta Kappa; Phi Delta Kappa; Sigma Delta Chi; Phi Kappa Phi; Alpha Delta. **HONORS AND AWARDS** CLA Distinguished Tchr, 86. **MEMBERSHIPS** Soc Fantastic Arts; Int Air Hist Soc. **RESEARCH** 20th Century British fiction; Kurt Vonnegut **SELECTED PUBLICATIONS** coauth Kurt Vonnegut: A Checklist, 1985-92, Bulletin of Bibliog, 93; Kurt Vonnegut, Dictionary of Lit Biog 152, American Novelists Since World War II, Bruccoli Clark Layman, 95; auth The Responsive Shaman: Kurt Vonnegut and His World, The Vonnegut Chronicles, Greenwood Publ, 96, Lonersome Once More: The Family Theme in Kurt Vonnegut's Slapstick, The Vonnegut Chronicles, Greenwood Publ, 96; The Graphics of Kurt Vonnegut, The Vonnegut Chronicles, Greenwood Publ, 96; Kurt Vonnegut: A Selected Bibliography 1985-1994, The Vonnegut Chronicles, Greenwood Publ, 96; A Portrait of the Writer as a Busy Man, Star Tribune of the Twin Cities, 96; The Vonnegut Chronicles: Interviews and Essays, Greenwood Publ, 96; The Short Fiction of Kurt Vonnegut, Greenwood Press, 97; Collecting Kurt Vonnegut, Firsts: The Book Collectors Magazine, 98. **CONTACT ADDRESS** Dept of English, Univ Minn, Minneapolis, MN, 55455. **EMAIL** REEDX001@kc.umn.edu

REED, WALTER
DISCIPLINE ENGLISH LANGUAGE AND LITERATURE **EDUCATION** Yale Univ, BA, PhD. **CAREER** Fac, Yale Univ; fac, Univ Tex Austin; prof/chemn dept, Emory Univ, 87-. **HONORS AND AWARDS** Guggenheim fel, 77-78., Co-dir, NEH summer sem col tchrs, 95. **RESEARCH** British Romanticism; comparative literature. **SELECTED PUBLICATIONS** Auth, pubs on the Romantic hero in 19th century fiction, on the Quixotic and picaresque traditions in the history of the novel, and on the Bible as literature from a Bakhtinian perspective. **CONTACT ADDRESS** English Dept, Emory Univ, 1380 Oxford Rd NE, Atlanta, GA, 30322-1950. **EMAIL** wlreed@emory.edu

REEDER, HEIDI M.
DISCIPLINE INTERPERSONAL COMMUNICATION, RELATIONAL COMMUNICATION **EDUCATION** Univ OR, BS, summa cum laude, 91; Stanford Univ, MA, 93; AZ State Univ, PhD, 96. **CAREER** Dept Comm, Univ NC **RESEARCH** Interpersonal commun; male-female relationships. **SELECTED PUBLICATIONS** Auth, The subjective experience of love through adult life, Int J of Aging and Human Develop, 43, 96; coauth, Unwanted escalation of sexual intimacy: Male and female perceptions of connotations and relational consequences of resistance messages, Commun Monogr, 62, 95; Disclosure of sexual abuse by children and adolescents, J of Appl Commun, 24, 96. **CONTACT ADDRESS** Dept of Commun Stud, Univ N. Carolina, Greensboro, 102 Fergus, Greensboro, NC, 27412-5001. **EMAIL** hmreeder@hamlet.uncg.edu

REESMAN, J.C.
PERSONAL Born 09/19/1955, Shreveport, LA, m, 1982, 1 child **DISCIPLINE** ENGLISH **EDUCATION** Centenary College, BA 77; Baylor Univ, MA 79; Univ Penn, PhD 84. **CAREER** Univ Texas SA, asst prof, assoc prof, prof, dir div eng, interim dean, 86 to 98-; Univ Penn, tchg asst 79-84, vis asst prof, 85-96; Univ Hawaii, asst prof, 84-85; Baylor Univ, teach asst, 77-79. **HONORS AND AWARDS** Fac Dev Awd; Golden Key Hon Soc Mem; Jack London Woman of the Year Awd; Presidents Dist Ser Awd; Robt A Miller Awd; Who's Who In Amer; Omicron Delta Kappa; Sigma Tau Delta Awd; Mabel Campbell awd. **MEMBERSHIPS** MLA; SCMLA; ALS/MLA; ALA; Henry James Soc; Faulkner Soc; Jack London Soc. **RESEARCH** Jack London; Henry James; William Faulkner; Amer Women Writers; Amer Lit; 19th and 20th Century Amer Novel; Narrative Theory. **SELECTED PUBLICATIONS** Auth, Jack London: A Study of the Short Fiction, NY, Twayne, 99; Speaking the Other Self: American Women Writers, Athens, U of GA Press, 97; Rereading Jack London, co-ed, Stanford, Stanford Univ Press, 96; Jack London Revised Edition, coauth, NY, Twayne, 94; A Handbook of Critical Approaches to Literature, 3rd, 4th ed, coauth, Oxford, Oxford Univ Press, 92,98; Fiction 1900-1930, Amer Lit Schshp, Duke Univ Press, 97; Never Travel Alone: Naturalism Jack London and the White Silence, Amer Lit Realism, 97; Women Language and the Grotesque in Flannery O'Connor and Eudora Welty in: Flannery O'Connor: New Approaches, eds Sura Rath, Mary Neff Shaw, Athens, Univ GA Press, 96. **CONTACT ADDRESS** Dept of English, Univ Texas, San Antonio, TX, 78285. **EMAIL** reesman@lonestar.utsa.edu

REEVES, BYRON
DISCIPLINE COMMUNICATIONS **EDUCATION** Southern Methodist Univ, BA; MI State Univ, PhD. **CAREER** Dir grad studies/assoc chr Mass Comm Res Ctr, Univ Wis; fac, Stanford Univ, 85-; to Paul C. Edwards Prof, present. **RESEARCH** Psychological processing of television with emphasis on processes of attention, memory and emotion. **SELECTED PUBLICATIONS** Auth, publ in bks of collected studies and jour(s) such as Human Communication Research, Journal of Social Issues, Journal of Broadcasting, and Journalism Quarterly. **CONTACT ADDRESS** Dept Commun, Stanford Univ, McClatchy Hall Rm 300A, Stanford, CA, 94305. **EMAIL** reeves@leland.stanford.edu

REGE, JOSNA E.
DISCIPLINE ENGLISH LITERATURE **EDUCATION** Univ Ma Amherst, PhD, 95. **CAREER** Asst prof, Dartmouth Col. **RESEARCH** Am and Brit lit. **SELECTED PUBLICATIONS** Auth, Indian Literature in English in The Encyclopedia of English Studies and Language Arts, Scholas and NCTE, 94. **CONTACT ADDRESS** Dartmouth Col, 3529 N Main St, #207, Hanover, NH, 03755.

REICH, ROBERT D.
PERSONAL Born 04/25/1951, Miami, FL **DISCIPLINE** MASS MEDIA & COMMUNICATION; MEDIA STUDIES **EDUCATION** New School for Social Res, MA, 82; Temple Univ, PhD, 95. **CAREER** Advertising copywriter, Tech Graphics, 89; Rusiald & Assocs, 90-92; Wyeth-Ayerst Pharmaceuticals, 92-94; ASST PROF, MARY BALDWIN COL. **MEMBERSHIPS** Int Commun Asn; Am Advertising Asn; Nat Commun Asn. **RESEARCH** Psychology of advertising; advertising to children. **CONTACT ADDRESS** Dept of Communication, Mary Baldwin Col, Staunton, VA, 24401. **EMAIL** rreich@cit.mbc.edu

REID, LOREN
PERSONAL Born 08/26/1905, Gilman City, MO, m, 1930, 4 children **DISCIPLINE** COMMUNICATION **EDUCATION** BA, Grinnell Col, 27; PhD, Univ of Iowa, 32. **CAREER** Univ of Mo, 35-39; Syracuse Univ, 39-44; Univ of Mo, 44-75; Vis prof, Univ S Calif, 47, 54; Vis prof, Univ Utah, 52; Vis prof, Univ of Md, overseas, 52-53, 60-61; Vis prof, Univ Mich, 57; Vis prof, Univ of Ha, 57; Vis prof, Univ of Iowa, 58; Ret, 75-. **HONORS AND AWARDS** Distinguished Res or Serv, Grinnell Col, Univ of Mo, Ohio Univ, Speech & Theatre Asn of Mo, NY State Comm Asn, Cent States Comm Asn (pres, 42-40); Sesquicentennial prof, Univ of Mo; Fellowship, Roy Hist Soc. **MEMBERSHIPS** Cent States Comm Asn; Natl Comm Asn (exec sec 45-52, pres 57); Amer Comm Asn Univ Profs; Royal Hist Soc. **RESEARCH** British political speaking; Missouri social history. **SELECTED PUBLICATIONS** Auth, Charles James Fox, Longmans, 79; auth, Hurry Home Wednesday, Univ Mo Pres, 79; auth, Finally It's Friday, Univ Mo Press, 81, Jap ed (sels), 86; auth, Professor on the Loose, Mortgage Ln Press, 92; Reflections, Mortgage Ln Press, 98. **CONTACT ADDRESS** 200 E Brandon Rd, Columbia, MO, 65203. **EMAIL** commreid@showme.missouri.edu

REID, LOUANN
DISCIPLINE ENGLISH LITERATURE **EDUCATION** Linfield Col, BA; Wash State Univ, MA; NY Univ, PhD. **CAREER** Asst prof. **SELECTED PUBLICATIONS** Auth, pubs on interactive classroom; teachers as researchers; teaching of critical thinking in response to literature. **CONTACT ADDRESS** Dept of English, Colorado State Univ, Fort Collins, CO, 80523. **EMAIL** lreid@vines.colostate.edu

REID, PANTHEA
DISCIPLINE THE MODERN NOVEL **EDUCATION** Univ NC, PhD, 71. **CAREER** Prof, La State Univ. **HONORS AND AWARDS** Phi Beta Kappa; sr Fulbright lectr, Univ Porto, Port, 76; CIES res grant-in-aid to the UK, 83; NEH summer res grant, 83; NEH travel to collections grant, 85. **MEMBERSHIPS** Vice-pres, 92, pres, S Cent Mod Lang Asn, 93. **RESEARCH** The arts of biography; inter-artistic relations. **SELECTED PUBLICATIONS** Auth, The Blasphemy of Art: Fry's Aesthetics and Woolf's Post-Impressionist Short Stories, in Virginia Woolf's Multiple Muses, 93; The Shape of Language and the Scene of Writing for Faulkner when 'Matisse and Picasso Yet Painted,' in Faulkner and the Artist, 95; Art and Affection: A Life of Virginia Woolf, 97. **CONTACT ADDRESS** Dept of Eng, Louisiana State Univ, 210Q Allen Hall, Baton Rouge, LA, 70803. **EMAIL** preid@unix1.sncc.lsu.edu

REID, ROBERT L.
PERSONAL Born 10/11/1943, Charlotte, NC, m, 1968, 2 children **DISCIPLINE** ENGLISH **EDUCATION** Yale Univ, BA, 66; Univ VA, PhD, 71. **CAREER** English dept, VA Intermont Col, 71-81; English Dept, Emory & Henry Col, 81-, chair, 86-, Henry Carter prof English, 91-. **HONORS AND AWARDS** Yale English Honors prog, grad with high honors; Yale Honors Thesis ("H D & Imagism"), won Richard Schoenberg Award, 66; Teaching Excellence Award, 81; VA Shakespeare Lect (appointed by VA Found for Humanities), 89. **MEMBERSHIPS** MLA; SAMLA; Southeastern Renaissance Conf; Spenser Soc; Carolina Symposium of British Studies. **RESEARCH** Spenser's Fairie Queene; Shakespeare; Renaissance physiology & psychol; Renaissance dramaturgical structure & epic narrative structure. **SELECTED PUBLICATIONS** Auth, Man, Woman, Child or Servant: Family Hierarchy as a Figure of Tripartite Psychology in The Faerie Queene, Studies in Philol 79, 81; Alma's Castle and the Symbolization of Reason in The Faerie Queen, J of English and Germanic Philol 80, 81; Spenserian Psychology & the Structure of Allegory in Books I and II of The Faerie Queene, Modern Philol 79, 82; Eratic Interruptions: First Year in the Chair, ADE Bul, fall 88; Platonic Psychology, Soul, House of Holiness, in The Spenser Encyclopedia, Univ Toronto, 90; MacBeth's Three Murders: Shakespearean Psychology and Tragic Form, Renaissance Papers, 91; The Faerie Queene: Gloriana or Titania?, The Upstart Crow 13, 93; Lear's Three Shamings: Shakespearean Psychology and Tragic Form, Renaissance Papers, 96; Humoral Psychology in Shakespeare's Henriad, Comparative Drama, 96-97; Epiphanal Encounters in Shakespearean Dramaturgy, Comparative Drama, forthcoming. **CONTACT ADDRESS** English Dept, Emory & Henry Col, Emory, VA, 24327. **EMAIL** rlreid@ehc.edu

REID, RONALD F.
PERSONAL Born 07/24/1928, Herington, KS, w, 1953, 2 children **DISCIPLINE** SPEECH; RHETORIC **EDUCATION** George Pepperdine Univ, BA, 50; Univ of NMex, MA, 51; Purdue Univ, PhD, 54. **CAREER** From instr to asst prof, Washington Univ, 54-59; from asst prof to assoc prof, Purdue Univ, 59-66; prof, Univ of Mass, 66-91, dept head, 66-70. **HONORS AND AWARDS** Winans/Wichelms Award for Disting. Scholarship, 76; SCA Monograph Award, 83; Relig Speech Commun Award for Outstanding Publ, 96. **MEMBERSHIPS** Am Soc for the Hist of Rhet: Int Soc for the Hist of Rhet; Int Soc for the Class Tradition; Nat Commun Asn. **RESEARCH** Hist of Am Polit Rhet; Hist of Am Rhet Theory. **SELECTED PUBLICATIONS** The Boylston Professorship of Rhetoric and Oratory, 1806-1904, Quart Jour of Speech, 45, 59; Newspaper Response to the Gettysburg Addresses, Quart Jour of Speech, 53, 67; New England Rhetoric and the French War, 1754-1760: A Case Study in the Rhetoric of War, Commun Monographs, 43, 76; The American Revolution and the Rhetoric of History, 78; Prophecy in New England Victory Sermons, ca. 1760: A Study in American Concepts of Historic Mission, 80; Apocalypticism and Typology: Rhetorical Dimensions of a Symbolic Reality, Quart Jour of Speech, 69, 83; Three Centuries of American Rhetorical Discourse: An Anthology and a Review, 88; Edward Everett: Unionist Orator, 90; Edward Everett and Neoclassical Oratory in Genteel America, Oratorical Culture in Nineteenth-Century America: Transformations in the Theory and Practice of Rhetoric, eds G. Clark and S. M. Halloran, 93; Disputes Over Preaching Method, The Second Awakening, and Ebenezer Porter's Teaching of Sacred Rhetoric, Jour of Commun and Relig, 18, 95; Walter Edward Williams (1936-), Professor, Editorialist, African-American Orators: A Bio-Critical Sourcebook, ed R. W. Leeman, 96. **CONTACT ADDRESS** PO Box 209, Northfield, MA, 01360-0209.

REID, STEPHEN
DISCIPLINE ENGLISH LITERATURE **EDUCATION** Grinnell Col, BA; Univ Mo, MA; Univ Kans, PhD. **CAREER** Prof. **SELECTED PUBLICATIONS** Auth, The Prentice Hall Guide for College Writers, 95; Purpose and Process: A Reader for Writers, 94. **CONTACT ADDRESS** Dept of English, Colorado State Univ, Fort Collins, CO, 80523. **EMAIL** sreid@vines.colostate.edu

REIGELMAN, MILTON M.
PERSONAL m **DISCIPLINE** ENGLISH LITERATURE **EDUCATION** Col William and Mary, BA; Univ Pa, MA; Univ Iowa, MA, PhD. **CAREER** Fac, 71; vice pres planning and resources, 91-96; J. Rice Cowan Prof Eng, present; acting pres, 97-98. **HONORS AND AWARDS** Rookie of Yr Awd, Centre Col; David Hughes Outstanding Prof Awd, Centre, Col; Fulbright lectr., Pub and co-found, Danville Quart, 74-77; dean, Governor's Scholars Prog, Centre Col. **SELECTED PUBLICATIONS** Auth, The Midland: A Venture in Literary Regionalism, Univ Iowa P. **CONTACT ADDRESS** Centre Col, 600 W Walnut St, Danville, KY, 40422. **EMAIL** reigelma@centre.edu

REILLY, EDWARD J.
PERSONAL Born 12/22/1943, Darlington, WI, m, 1969, 2 children **DISCIPLINE** ENGLISH **EDUCATION** Loras Col, BA, 66; Univ Notre Dame, MA, 68, PhD, 74. **CAREER** Prof, 78-, St Joseph's Col. **HONORS AND AWARDS** St Joseph's Col Fac Develop Grants, 87, 89, 90, 91; St. Joseph's Col Distinguished Fac Award, 88; Hemingway Found Grant, 89; Award for Excellence in Teaching, 90; Fac of the Year, 92; NEH Grant, 94; **MEMBERSHIPS** Univ Continuing Educ Assoc; Coun for Adult & Experiential Learning; Assoc for Continuing Higher Educ; Amer Assoc for Higher Educ; Assoc for Integrative Stud; Modern Lang Assoc of Amer; Amer Soc for Eighteen Century Stud; Midwest, Northeast, & Canadian Soc for Eighteenth Stud, Delta Epsilon Sigma; Hemingway Soc; F Scott Fitzgerald Soc; Maine Writers & Publ Alliance, Haiku Soc of Amer; confer on Basic Writing; Consortium for Teaching of the Middle Ages; Maine Medievalists Assoc; Danforth Assoc of New England; Popular Cult Assoc. **RESEARCH** Medieval lit; 18th cent lit; Hemingway; Fitzgerald; Vietnam War; sports lit. **SELECTED PUBLICATIONS** Auth, The Breaking of Glass Horses and Other Poems, Great Elm, 88; art, Approaches to Teaching Swift's Gulliver's Travels, MLA, 88; auth, My Struggling Soil, Plowman Press, 94; auth, Anniversary Haiku, Brooks Books, 97; auth, How Sky Holds the Sun, AHA, 98. **CONTACT ADDRESS** Dept of English, St Joseph's Col, 278 Whites Bridge Rd, Standish, ME, 04084-5263. **EMAIL** erielly@sjcme.edu

REILLY, JOHN MARSDEN
PERSONAL Born 02/18/1933, Pittsburgh, PA, M, 1995, 3 children **DISCIPLINE** ENGLISH **EDUCATION** West Virginia Univ, BA 54, Wash Univ MA 63, PhD 67. **CAREER** Wash Univ, instr, 60; Univ Puerto Rico, asst prof, 61-63; SUNY Albany, asst prof, assoc prof, prof, 63-93, Howard Univ, Prof, 94-. **HONORS AND AWARDS** Edgar Allen Poe Awd; Dist Ethnic Stud Awd; Dist Pop Culture Awd. **MEMBERSHIPS** ASA; CLA; MLA; MELUS. **RESEARCH** African American Literature; Detective Fiction; Post Modern Fiction. **SELECTED PUBLICATIONS** Auth, Founding a Literature, Resources for Amer Lit Study, 96; auth, Stepping Out on the Stage of the World: Richard Wright and the Art of Non-Fiction, Callaloo, 86; auth, Tony Hillerman: A Critical Companion, 96; auth, Twentieth Century Crime and Mystery Writers, ed, 81, 2nd ed, 85; Richard Wright: The Critical Reception, 78. **CONTACT ADDRESS** Dept of English, Howard Univ, Washington, DC, 20059. **EMAIL** jreilly@gac.howard.edu

REINHARDT, JOHN EDWARD
PERSONAL Born 03/08/1920, Glade Spring, VA, m **DISCIPLINE** ENGLISH **EDUCATION** Knoxville Coll, AB 1939; Univ of WI, MS 1947, PhD 1950. **CAREER** VA State Coll, prof eng 1950-56; USIS Manila Philippines, cultural affairs officer 1956-58; Amer Cultural Ctr Kyoto Japan, dir 1958-63; USIS Tehran Iran, cultural attache 1963-66; Office E Asia & Pacific USIA, dep asst 1966-68; Nigeria, ambassador 1971-75; Washington DC, asst sec state 1975; Intl Comm Agency, dir 1976-81; Smithsonian Inst, asst sec for history & art 1981-84; Smithsonian Inst, dir, directorate of intl activities 1984-87; professor, Political Science, University of Vermont, 1987-91, professor, emeritus, 1991-. **MEMBERSHIPS** Mem, Amer Foreign Serv Assn, 1969-, Modern Language Assn, Intl Club, Cosmos Club.

REINHEIMER, DAVID
DISCIPLINE ENGLISH LITERATURE **EDUCATION** Univ Dallas, BA, 89, MA, 89; Univ CA, MA, 91, PhD, 95. **CAREER** Instr, 90-91; Assoc prof, 91-92; tchg asst, 93-94; adj prof, 94-95; adj lectr, Univ CA, 95-96; instr, Sacramento City Col, 95-96; asst prof, SE MO State Univ, 97-. **SELECTED PUBLICATIONS** Auth, The Roman Actor, Censorship, and Dramatic Autonomy,98; The N-Town Play: Cotton MS Vespasian D.8. (rev), 96; The Renaissance Bible: Scholarship, Subjectivity, and Sacrifice (rev); The English Faust Bookb (rev), 96; Ethical and Ontological Allusion: Shakespeare in The Next Generation, 95; Drama and the Market in the Age of Shakespeare (rev), 94; Last Things and Last Plays: Shakespearean Eschatology (rev), 93. **CONTACT ADDRESS** Eng Dept, SE MO State Univ, 1 University Plz, Cape Girardeau, MO, 63701.

REISS, JOHN
DISCIPLINE AMERICAN LITERATURE **EDUCATION** Univ WI, PhD. **CAREER** Eng, St. Michaels Col. **SELECTED PUBLICATIONS** Auth, Robert Frost. **CONTACT ADDRESS** St. Michael's Col, Winooski Park, Colchester, VT, 05439.

REITZ MULLENIX, ELIZABETH
DISCIPLINE THEATRE ARTS **EDUCATION** Univ Ill, PhD, 95. **CAREER** Asst prof. **RESEARCH** Nineteenth century American theatre history; gender studies and feminist theatre. **SELECTED PUBLICATIONS** Auth, pubs on cross dressing and gender feminist theory. **CONTACT ADDRESS** Dept of Theatre, Illinois State Univ, Normal, IL, 61761.

REMPEL, GERHARD
PERSONAL Soviet Union, m, 2 children **DISCIPLINE** ENGLISH LITERATURE **EDUCATION** Wheaton Col, BA, 59; Northwestern Univ, MA, 61; Univ Wis, PhD, 71. **CAREER** Admin tchg asst, Univ Wis, 67-69; asst prof, WNEC, 69-75; ch, fac personnel comm, 72-73; vis asst prof, Univ Md, 72-73; ch, fac devel comm, 74-76; ch, faculty senate, 75-76; assoc prof, WNEC, 75-81; ch, dept hist, govt, econ, 79-82; dir, cult prog, 78-90; prof, WNEC, 81-. **HONORS AND AWARDS** Non-Resident scholarship, Univ Wis, 66-68; spec summer fel, Univ Wis, 67-69; Ford res fel, 68-69; travel grant, Univ Wis, 68; summer res grant, WNEC, 91, 92; res grant, DAAD, 92. **SELECTED PUBLICATIONS** Auth, Hitler's Children: The Hitler Youth and the SS, Univ NC Press, 89; Gottlob Berger and Waffen-SS Recruitment, 33-45, Militaergeschichtliche Mitteilungen, 80; Training Teenage Spies and Policeboys: The Hitler-Jugend Streifendienst, The Citadel Devel Found, 82. **CONTACT ADDRESS** Dept of Eng, Western New England Col, 1215 Wilbraham Rd., Springfield, MA, 01119-2654. **EMAIL** grempel@wnec.edu

REMPEL, JOHN W.
DISCIPLINE ENGLISH LITERATURE **EDUCATION** Univ British Columbia, BA; Univ Tex Austin, MA; PhD. **CAREER** Assoc prof **RESEARCH** 18th century women writers; musical literary relations; bibliography; restoration comedy; book collecting. **SELECTED PUBLICATIONS** Auth, pub(s) on Shakespeare and Nahum Tate, Dryden, Swift, 18th and 20th century wine, 17th and 18th century poetry, Georgian silver, American, Victorian and continental 19th century music. **CONTACT ADDRESS** Dept of English, Manitoba Univ, Winnipeg, MB, R3T 2N2.

RENFRO, PAULA C.
DISCIPLINE COMMUNICATIONS **EDUCATION** Baylor Univ, BA, MA, Univ TX, PhD. **CAREER** Comm Dept, Southwest Tex State Univ **HONORS AND AWARDS** Ast Chair, Dept Mass Comm; Ed, Leadtime. **SELECTED PUBLICATIONS** Auth, Expectations of Change in the High School Press after Hazelwood, Southwestern Mass Comm Jour, 88; Coauth, Rupert Murdoch's Style: The New York Post, Newspaper Res, 88; Jour Post-Hazelwood: Survey Results Indicate Little Change, Hooray for High School Journalism, 89; Southwestern Art in Regional Magazines of the United States, Greenwood Press, 91; TV Guide Under Murdoch: Less Serious Analysis, More Entertainment, Southwestern Mass Comm Jour, 92; Chronicle of Higher Education, Greenwood Press, 94; Folio, Greenwood Press, 94; Southwestern Art in Regional Magazines of the United States, Southern Mag; **CONTACT ADDRESS** Southwest Texas State Univ, 601 University Dr, San Marcos, TX, 78666-4604.

RENFRO, R. BRUCE
DISCIPLINE COMMUNICATIONS **EDUCATION** Univ TX, BA, MA, PhD. **CAREER** Comm Dept, Southwest Tex State Univ **SELECTED PUBLICATIONS** Coauth, A Bibliometric Analysis of Public Relations Research, Jour Public Relations Res, 92; Auth, Public Relations Writing and Media Techniques, Harper/Collins Publ, 93; How to Get the Most Out of Press Releases, Tex Intercollegiate Press Asn/Southwest Journalism Congress Convention, 94. **CONTACT ADDRESS** Southwest Texas State Univ, 601 University Dr, San Marcos, TX, 78666-4604.

RENO, J. DAVID
PERSONAL Born 02/03/1949, Bethlehem, PA, m, 1995, 1 child **DISCIPLINE** COMMUNICATION STUDIES **EDUCATION** Emerson Col, BS, SP, 73, MA, 95. **CAREER** Alliance Independent Sch, Bd Dir, 93-95; Nat Alliance HUD Tenants, BD Dir, 95-97; Assoc Former Intelligence Officers, Bd Dir, 95-. **HONORS AND AWARDS** Awd Appreciation, AFIO. **MEMBERSHIPS** AIS; IRE; NCIS; CAJ; NWU; PEN; AFIO; IRE. **RESEARCH** Amer History; Investigative Reporting as Schshp; Literary Landmarks of Amer. **SELECTED PUBLICATIONS** Auth, The Magic of Accounting, IRE Jour, 85; auth, Yellowstone and the Presidency, Christian Sci Monitor, 89; auth, White Collar Crime, The Journalist's Guide to its Literature, IRE Jour, 86; auth, Secret New England, AFIO, 91; auth, To Protect Serve National Security, Investigative Reporters and Editors Jour, 90; auth, Erle Stanley Gardner and the Court of Last Resort, Mystery Writers of Amer, NY, The Players Club 95. **CONTACT ADDRESS** The Piano Factory, 791 Tremont St W-113, Boston, MA, 02118-1062. **EMAIL** renojo.bpd@cl.Boston.ma.us

RENZA, LOUIS A.
DISCIPLINE ENGLISH LITERATURE **EDUCATION** Univ CA Irvine, PhD, 72. **CAREER** Prof, Dartmouth Col. **RESEARCH** Am lit; Edgar Allen Poe; lit criticism. **SELECTED PUBLICATIONS** Auth, 'Ut Pictura Poe': Poetic Politics in 'The Island of the Fay' and 'Morning on the Wissahicon' in The American Face of Edgar Allan Poe, Johns Hopkins UP, 95; Poe's Masque of Mass Culture: Or, Other-Wise: A Review Essay, Poe Studies: Dark Romanticism: Hist, Theory, Interp, 95; Influence in Critical Terms for Literary Study, Univ Chicago P, 90; A White Heron and the Question of Minor Literature, Univ Wis P, 84; coauth, The Irish Stories of Sarah Orne Jewett; S Ill UP, 96. **CONTACT ADDRESS** Dartmouth Col, 3529 N Main St, #207, Hanover, NH, 03755.

REVELL, DONALD
PERSONAL Born 06/12/1954, Bronx, NY, m, 1992, 1 child **DISCIPLINE** ENGLISH **EDUCATION** SUNY, Buffalo, PhD (English), 80. **CAREER** Asst prof, English, Ripon Col, 82-85; asst prof to assoc prof, English, Univ Denver, 85-94; prof English, Univ UT, 94-. **HONORS AND AWARDS** NEA fel in Poetry, 88, 95; Guggenheim fel in Poetry, 92. **MEMBERSHIPS** Nat Book Critics Circle. **RESEARCH** Poetics. **SELECTED PUBLICATIONS** Auth, Erasures, Wesleyan/UPNE, 92; Beautiful Shirt, Wesleyan/UPNE, 94; Alcools, Wesleyan/UPNE, 95. **CONTACT ADDRESS** English Dept, Univ of Utah, Salt Lake City, UT, 84112.

REVERAND, CEDRIC D.
PERSONAL Born 12/03/1941, Brooklyn, NY, m, 1965 **DISCIPLINE** ENGLISH LITERATURE **EDUCATION** Yale Univ, BA, 63; Columbia Univ, MA, 64; Cornell Univ, PhD, 72. **CAREER** Lect, St. John's Univ, 66-67; inst, 71-72, asst prof, 72-77, assoc prof, 77-82, PROF, 82-, DIR CULTURAL PROGS, UNIV WYO, 78-. **HONORS AND AWARDS** Phi Beta Kappa; Ford fel, Cornell; hon fel, Cambridge; Univ Wyo for outstanding teaching, Andrew Mellow fel, Univ Calif Los Angeles, Yale. **MEMBERSHIPS** Mod Lang Asn; Am Soc for 18th cent Stud. **RESEARCH** Dryden; Pope; Restoration & 18th cent poetry; fine arts. **SELECTED PUBLICATIONS** various **CONTACT ADDRESS** Univ of Wyoming, Box 3353 Univ Sta, Laramie, WY, 82071. **EMAIL** reverand@uwyo.edu

REYNOLDS, DAVID S.
PERSONAL Born 08/30/1948, Providence, RI, m, 1983, 1 child **DISCIPLINE** ENGLISH; AMERICAN LITERATURE **EDUCATION** Amherst Col, BA, 70; Univ Calif Berkeley, PhD, 79 **CAREER** Asst prof, Northwestern Univ, 80-83; assoc prof, Rutgers Univ, 86-89; prof, Baruch Col, 89-95; distinguished prof, Baruch Col, 96- **HONORS AND AWARDS** Bancroft Prize; Ambassador Book Award; Finalist, Ntl Book Critics Circle Award; Christian Gauss Award **MEMBERSHIPS** Modern Lang Assoc; Amer Antiquarian Soc; Amer Studies Assoc **RESEARCH** American Literature and Culture; American Renaissance; American History **SELECTED PUBLICATIONS** Co-ed, The Serpent in the Cup: Temperance and American Literature, Univ Mass, 97; auth, Walt Whitman's America: A Cultural Biography, Vintage, 96; auth, Beneath the American Renaissance: The Subversive Imagination in the Age of Emerson and Melville, Knopf, 88 **CONTACT ADDRESS** 16 Linden Ln, Old Westbury, NY, 11568. **EMAIL** reyno45@ibm.net

REYNOLDS, RICHARD CLAY
PERSONAL Born 09/28/1949, Quana, TX, m, 1972, 2 children **DISCIPLINE** AMERICAN LITERATURE **EDUCATION** Univ TX Austin, BA, 71; Trinity Univ, MA, 74; Univ Tulsa, PhD, 79. **CAREER** Grad Tchng Fel, 74-77, Univ of Tulsa; instr, English, 77-78, Tulsa Junior Col; instr, English, 77-78 Claremore Col; assoc prof, 78-88 Lamar Univ Beaumont TX; Prof, novelist in res, 88-92, Univ of N TX; vis prof, writer in res, Spring 94, Villanova Univ; vis prof, writer, Summer Ses, 95, West TX A&M Univ; vis writer, consult, Fall 95, Univ of South Dakota; vis lect, Sept 96, Univ of TX at Austin; adj prof, Fall 96, TX Womans Univ; vis lect, Fall 97, Summer 98, Univ of TX Dallas; freelance writer, 92-; assoc prof, 98- Univ of TX Dallas. **HONORS AND AWARDS** Deans List, Univ of TX, 70; Grad Tchng Fel, 74-77, Comm intern, 76, Grad Res Intern, 77, Faculty Res Grant, 78, Univ of Tulsa; Beaumont Art Museum Scholarship for US Landscape Sem, 82; Top Prof Volunteer KVLU Lamar Univ, 81-82; Amer Biographical Inst Adv Board, 82-88; Dir of Amer School, 82-87; Col of Arts & Sciences Deans Merit Award, 82-87; Univ Mini Grant, Lamar Univ, 83; Sum Dev Leave, Lamar Univ, 83; Regents Merit Award, 86; Oppie Award for the Vigil, 87; Dev Leave Lamar Univ, 87; Col of Arts & Sciences Excellence in res Award, Lamar Univ, 88; TX Inst of Letters, 88; Western Writers of Amer, 89; The National Faculty, 90; WWA Spur Award, Finalist Best Western Short Fiction, 92; Key to the City of Fort Worth Friends of the Library Award, 92; Violet Crown Fiction Award, 92; ALE Award for Short Fiction, 93; Pulitzer Prize Entrant for Fiction, 92; WWA Spur Award Finalist Best Novel of the West, 93; Fel National Endowment for the Arts, 94; PEN Texas Awards for Essay and Fiction, 97; Texas Coun for the Arts/Austin Writers League Literature Grant, 97; Council on National Literatures Fiction Award, 98. **MEMBERSHIPS** The National Faculty; PEN West; Western Writers of Amer; TX Inst of Letters; Modern Lang Asn; The Authors Guild; South Central Modern Lang Asn; Western Amer Lit Asn; TX Asn of Creative Writing Tchrs; Asn Writing Programs. **RESEARCH** Amer West, Amer lit, Amer history. **SELECTED PUBLICATIONS** Auth, The Vigil, NY St Martins Press/Richard Marek, 86; auth, The Texas Blacklands Where the West Begins or Where the South Ends, Texas Blackland Prairie Land History Culture, Baylor Univ Press, 93; auth, Mexico, That's What I Like About the South and Other Stories for the Nineties, Univ of South Carolina Press, 93; auth, Summer Seeds, Careless Weeds, SMU Press, 93; auth, Fist Fight, Texas Short Fiction A World in Itself, ALE Pub 93; auth, Ettas Pond, Higher Elevations Stories from the West, Ohio Univ Press, 93; auth, Shechem, Cimarron Review, 93; auth, Andrew Hudgins 1951-, Oxford Companion to Twentieth Century Poetry in English, Oxford Univ Press, 94; auth, Early Innings, ie Magazine, 94; auth, Dogstar, Sulphur River Review, 94; auth, Forward, Coffee, How the Cimarron River Got Its Name and Other Stories about Coffee, Rep of TX Press, 95; auth, One Hundred Years of Heroes The Southwestern Exposition and Livestock Show, Fort Worth, TCU Press, 95; auth, Right Field Blues, Rev Texas Short Fiction a World in Itself II, ALE Pub, 95; auth, Nickleby, South Dakota Review, 96; auth, The First Tour, Texas Rev, 96; auth, Goodnight Sweetheart, Texas Short Stories, Browder Springs Press, 97; auth, The Last Wolf, Potpourri, 97; auth, The State of Publishing, Dict of Lit Biography Yearbook 1997, TX Review, Layman Press, 98; auth, Twenty Questions Answers for the Aspiring Writer, Browder Springs Press, 98; auth, Of Snakes and Sex and Playing in the Rain, Best Texas Writing, Rancho Loco Press, 98; auth, A Trilogy Blue Coach & The Player, Suddenly Prose Poetry and Sudden Fiction, Martin House, 98; auth, Agatite, NY St Martins Press, 86; auth, Franklins Crossing, NY Signet, 93; auth, Players, NY Carroll and Graf, 97; ed, Taking Stock A Larry McMurtry Casebook, SMU Press 89; ed, Sound Warehouse A Memoir The Early Years of an American Retailer, Privately Pub, 95; auth, Screenplay, Players, Daydream Entertain, 97; **CONTACT ADDRESS** 909 Hilton Pl, Denton, TX, 76201. **EMAIL** RclayR@aol.com.

RIBEIRO, ALVARO
DISCIPLINE ENGLISH LITERATURE **EDUCATION** Univ Hong Kong, BA; Weston Sch Theol, STL; Oxford Univ, PhD. **CAREER** Eng Dept, Georgetown Univ **RESEARCH** 17th and 18th century British literature and culture; analytical bibliography and textual criticism; music history; theology and literature. **SELECTED PUBLICATIONS** Ed, Tradition in Transition: Women Writers, Marginal Texts, and the Eighteenth-Century Canon, Oxford, 96; The Letters of Dr Charles Burney, Volume I: 1751-1784, Oxford, 91; co-ed, Evidence in Literary Scholarship, Oxford, 79. **CONTACT ADDRESS** English Dept, Georgetown Univ, 37th and O St, Washington, DC, 20057.

RICE, GRANTLAND S.
DISCIPLINE ENGLISH **EDUCATION** Colby, BA, 86; Univ Penn, MA, 87; Brandeis, MA, 91, PhD, 94. **CAREER** ASST PROF, ENG, OHIO STATE UNIV **MEMBERSHIPS** Am Antiquarian Soc **SELECTED PUBLICATIONS** Auth, H.S. Crevecoeur and the Politics of Authorship in Republican America," Early Am Lit 28; 93; auth, H. H. Brackenbridge and the Resistance to Textual Authority," Am Lit, 95; auth, The Transformation of Authorship in America, Univ Chicago Press, 97. **CONTACT ADDRESS** Dept of Eng, Ohio State Univ, 164 W 17th Ave, Columbus, OH, 43210. **EMAIL** rice.177@osu.edu

RICE, LOUISE ALLEN
PERSONAL Born 11/21/1940, Augusta, Georgia, m, 1965 **DISCIPLINE** ENGLISH **EDUCATION** Tuskegee Univ, BS 1963; Columbia Univ Teachers Coll, MA 1969; Univ of GA, PhD 1979. **CAREER** Washington High Sch, English teacher 1963-66; Lucy Laney High School, English Teacher 1966-68; Paine Coll, instructor/reading specialist 1968-71; Lansing School Dist, instructor/reading specialist 1971-72; Paine Coll, assoc prof/asst academic dean 1972-77, 1979-81; Lamar Elem Sch, instructional lead teacher 1981-84; Augusta Coll, assoc dir of admissions 1984-88, asst prof of educ and reading l988-, asst prof of developmental reading 1989-. **HONORS AND AWARDS** Black Womanhood Speaker's Awd Paine Coll 1983; Distinguished Serv Awd Augusta Pan-Hellenic Council 1984; Urban Builders Awd Augusta Black History Comm 1985; Outstanding Comm Svcs, Leadership and Achievement Certificate Amer Assoc of Univ Women 1986, Educ of the Year, Lincoln League, Augusta, 1988; Distinguished Leadership Award United Negro College Fund 1990; Woman of the Year Augusta Alumnae Ch Delta Sigma Theta Sorority 1991; National Secretary, Delta Sigma Theta Sorority, Inc., 1992-. **MEMBERSHIPS** Adv bd Richmond Co Bd of Educ 1982-; bd dirs CSRA Economic Opportunity Authority Inc 1984-; dir Southern Region Delta Sigma Theta Sor Inc 1986-91; Educ Comm Augusta Human Relations Comm, l989-90. **CONTACT ADDRESS** Department of Developmental Studies, Augusta State Univ, 2500 Walton Way, Augusta, GA, 30904-2200.

RICE WINDERL, RONDA
DISCIPLINE MEDIA ECOLOGY **EDUCATION** Olivet Nazarene Univ, BA; Emerson Col, MA; NY Univ, PhD. **CAREER** Eng Dept, Eastern Nazarene Col **HONORS AND AWARDS** Chair, Div Arts & Letters; Chair, Dept Comm Arts; Prod/Dir, Theatre Prog. **SELECTED PUBLICATIONS** Area: the influence of Western theatre on contemporary Japanese theatre. **CONTACT ADDRESS** Eastern Nazarene Col, 23 East Elm Ave, Quincy, MA, 02170-2999.

RICHARD, RON
DISCIPLINE DEVELOPMENTAL DRAMA EDUCATION Concordia Univ, MA, 92; McGill Univ, PhD, 94. CAREER Prof; actor; dir; playwright. RESEARCH Theatre for young audiences and drama for special populations. SELECTED PUBLICATIONS Pub(s), in Creating a Theatre in Your Classroom. CONTACT ADDRESS Dept Art Hist, Concordia Univ, Montreal, 1455 de Maisonneuve W, Montreal, PQ, H3G 1M8. EMAIL ronrich@alcor.concordia.ca

RICHARDS, JEFFREY H.
PERSONAL Born 12/04/1948, Libertyville, IL, m, 1978, 2 children DISCIPLINE ENGLISH EDUCATION Yale Univ, BA, 71; Univ North Carolina, PhD, 82. CAREER Asst dir, Dowling Col, 71-72; tchg asst to instr, 74-79, vis assoc prof, 86-87, Univ North Carolina; instr to asst prof to assoc prof, 79-87, dir, 80-83, chair, 83-87, Lakeland Col; vis foreign prof, Beijing Normal Univ, 84-85; vis lect, 87-92, asst dir, 88-92, North Carolina Univ; vis asst prof, Duke Univ, 92; asst prof, 92-95, assoc prof, 95-, chair, 95-, Old Diminion Univ. HONORS AND AWARDS Aurelian Honor Society, 70-71, Yale Univ; Outstanding Tchr, 82-83, Lakeland Col; Old Dominion Univ Fac Summer Grant, 93; Nature Conservancy Task Force Seed Grant, 93-94; Most Inspiring Fac Award, 96, Old Dominion Univ; Col Arts Letters Res Grant, 96-97, ODU; Phi Kappa Phi Honor Society, 97, Old Dominion Chapter. MEMBERSHIPS Mod Lang Asn; Am Stud Asn; South Atlantic Am Stud Asn; Society Early Am; Am Lit Asn. RESEARCH Early American literature; American drama; 19th century American literature. SELECTED PUBLICATIONS Auth, Theatre Enough: American Culture and the Metaphor of the World Stage, 1607-1789, 91; auth, Mercy Otis Warren, 95; auth, Early American Drama, 97; auth, art, How to Write An American Drama, 97; auth, art, How to Write An American Play: Murray's the Traveller Returned and its Source, 98; auth, art, Mercy Otis Warren, 99. CONTACT ADDRESS Dept of English, Old Dominion Univ, Norfolk, VA, 23529. EMAIL jhrichar@odu.edu

RICHARDS, PHILLIP M.
DISCIPLINE AFRO-AMERICAN LITERATURE EDUCATION Yale Univ, BA, 72; Univ Chicago MA, 74, PhD, 87. CAREER Instr, Howard Univ; Ar State Univ; assoc prof, 87-. RESEARCH Early Am lit. SELECTED PUBLICATIONS Auth, Nationalist Themes in the Preaching of Jupiter Hammon, Early Am Lit; ed, Julian Mayfield's The Hit and The Long Night. CONTACT ADDRESS Dept of Eng, Colgate Univ, 13 Oak Drive, Hamilton, NY, 13346.

RICHARDSON, ANNE
PERSONAL Born 12/22/1942, Berkeley, CA, d DISCIPLINE ENGLISH; LIBRARY SCIENCE EDUCATION Univ Calif Berkeley, BA, 65; Yale Univ, PhD, 76; Univ Calif Berkeley, Sch of Libr and Info Studies, MLS, 78. CAREER Instr, eng, Yale Univ,. 69; instr, eng, Albertus Magnus Col, 69-70; instr, eng, George Washington Univ, 71-74; instr, eng, Anna Head-Josiah Royce Sch, 76; asst reference libr, Univ Kans Libr, 78-79. HONORS AND AWARDS Phi Beta Kappa; Woodrow Wilson fel; Univ Calif Berkeley regents' fel. MEMBERSHIPS William Tyndale Proj; Renaissance Eng Text Soc; Hagiography Soc; Mod Lang Asn; Inst for Hist Study. RESEARCH William Tyndale; Early modern period. SELECTED PUBLICATIONS Auth, On Representing Tyndale's English, New Ways of Looking at Old Texts II: Papers of the Renaissance English Text Society, 1992-1996, Medieval & Renaissance Texts & Studies, 98; book rev, William Tyndale: A Biography, Moreana, 122, 99-109, Jun 95; co-ed, William Tyndale and the Law, William Tyndale and the Bill of Rights, Sixteenth Century Jour Publ, 94; auth, Tyndale's Quarrel with Erasmus: A Chapter in the History of the English Reformation, Fides et Hist, XXXV, 3, 46-65, Fall, 93; film rev, Hamlet, The Sixteenth Century Jour, 22, 862-64, Winter, 91; auth, Scripture as Evidence, The Obedience of a Christian Man, Moreana, 28, 106-107, 83-104, Jul, 91; auth, The Assault on Access: a Public Scholar attends the AHA, The Independent Scholar, 5, 2, 5-6, Spring, 91; film rev, Henry V, The Sixteenth Century Jour, 21, 500, Fall, 90; film rev, God's Outlaw: The Story of William Tyndale, The Sixteenth Century Jour, 733-34, Winter, 89; auth, The Evidence Against an English First Edition of Tyndale's Obedience, Moreana, 52, 47-52, 76. CONTACT ADDRESS 543 Vincente Ave., Berkeley, CA, 94702.

RICHARDSON, BETTY
PERSONAL Born 02/14/1935, Louisville, KY, d, 1 child DISCIPLINE ENGLISH EDUCATION Univ of Louisville, BA, 57; Univ of Nebr, MA, 63, PhD, 68. CAREER Tchg asst and instr, Univ of Nebr, 63-68; from asst prof to prof, Southern Ill Univ, 68-. HONORS AND AWARDS SIUE Tchg Excellence Award, 91; various local recognitions. MEMBERSHIPS Int Soc for Humor Studies; Nat Writers Club; Auths Guild; Popular Cult Asn. RESEARCH Popular fiction and cult hist; Detective fiction; Women's fiction; 19th and 20th century social and intellectual hist. SELECTED PUBLICATIONS Auth, Victoria, Queen of England, The 1890s: An Encycl of Brit Lit, ed G.A. Cevasco, 93; Leslie Ford, Great Women Mystery Writers, ed K. Gregory Klein, 94; Gladys Mitchell, Great Women Mystery Writers, ed K. Gregory Klein, 94; W. Somerset Maugham, Encycl of Brit Humorists, ed S. Gale, 96; Samuel Butler, Encycl

of Brit Humorists, ed S. Gale, 96; George Bernard Shaw, Encycl of Brit Humorists, ed S. Gale, 96; G.K. Chesterton, Encycl of Brit Humorists, ed S. Gale, 96; Moll Cutpurse: Mirror of Majesty, Popular Cult Asn Conv, 97; Ladies Unleashed, or The Daughter Also Rises, Popular Cult Asn Conv, 97; Highlights of Film Censorship, 5000-word filmography, Censorship, 97; Highlights of Film Propaganda, 5000-word filmography, Encycl of Propaganda, 97. CONTACT ADDRESS Dept of English, Southern Illinois Univ, Edwardsville, IL, 62025. EMAIL brichar@siue.edu

RICHARDSON, DON
PERSONAL Born 08/07/1938, Malta, OH, m, 3 children DISCIPLINE COMMUNICATION EDUCATION Auburn Univ, BA, 61; OH Univ, MA, 63, PhD, 64. CAREER Asst Prof, Univ GA, 64-66; Prof, Assoc Dean of grad school, Chair, div of Arts and Sciences, Chair, Dept of Communications, Auburn Univ, 66-91; CHAIR, DEPT OF PUBLIC COMMUNICATION, SAM HOUSTON STATE UNIV, 91-. MEMBERSHIPS Speech Communication Asn; Southern States Communication Asn. SELECTED PUBLICATIONS Auth, with others, The Multidimensionality of Presbycusis: Hearing Losses on the Content and Relational Dimensions of Speech, Jour of Int Listening Asn, VII, 93; Presbycusis and Conversation: Elderly Interactants Adjusting to Muliple Hearing Losses, with others, Res on Lang and Social Interaction, 39, 97; book chapter, The Production of Listening, Working Memory, and Hemispheric Lateralization, in TR5: An Introduction to Research Writing, Simon & Schuster Custom Pub, 98; ed, Conversations with Carter, Lynne Rienner Pubs, 98. CONTACT ADDRESS Dept of Public Communication, Sam Houston State Univ, Huntsville, TX, 77341. EMAIL scm_drr@shsu.edu

RICHARDSON, GRANETTA L.
DISCIPLINE LITERATURE EDUCATION Univ Akron, BA; Ohio State Univ, MA; Univ Tenn, Knoxville, PhD. CAREER Asst prof, Univ NC, Wilmington. RESEARCH Film theory and film criticism; Vietnam War literature. SELECTED PUBLICATIONS Wrote on topics as diverse as Puritan influences on Vietnam poetry to the Barbie doll. CONTACT ADDRESS Univ N. Carolina, Wilmington, Morton Hall, Wilmington, NC, 28403-3297. EMAIL richardsongr@uncwil.edu

RICHARDSON, MALCOLM
DISCIPLINE TECHNICAL WRITING EDUCATION Univ Tenn, PhD, 78. CAREER Dr. J.F. Taylor Prof Eng, dir, LSU Writing Ctr, La State Univ. HONORS AND AWARDS ACLS res grant, 82; LSU summer grant, 94. RESEARCH Chaucer; Shakespeare; history of writing and rhetoric. SELECTED PUBLICATIONS Auth, Medieval English Vernacular Correspondence, Allegorica, 89; The Earliest Known Owners of Canterbury Tales MSS and Chaucer's Secondary Audience, Chaucer Rev, 89; Early Equity Judges: Keepers of the Rolls in Chancery,1415-1437, Am J of Legal Hist, 92; Women Commercial Writers of Late Medieval England, Disputatio: A Transdisciplinary J of Medieval Stud, 96; Women, Commerce, and Rhetoric in Late Medieval England, in Essays in the Rhetorical Activities of Historical Women, ed Molly Meijer Wertheimer, 97; coauth, An Anthology of Chancery English, 84; Power Relations, Technical Writing Theory, and Workplace Writing, J of Bus and Tech Writing, 93. CONTACT ADDRESS Dept of Eng, Louisiana State Univ, 31G Coates Hall, Baton Rouge, LA, 70803. EMAIL enmric@lsuvm.sncc.lsu.edu

RICHARDSON, STEPHANIE A.
DISCIPLINE BRITISH LITERATURE EDUCATION Univ Akron, BA; Ohio State Univ, MA; PhD. CAREER Tchg asst, Ohio State Univ; asst prof, Univ NC, Wilmington. HONORS AND AWARDS Univ-wide tchg award, Ohio State Univ. RESEARCH Classical rhetoric; modern British literature. SELECTED PUBLICATIONS Write in the following areas: classical rhetoric; modern British literature; literary criticism; film studies; popular culture; Biblical studies. CONTACT ADDRESS Univ N. Carolina, Wilmington, Morton Hall, Wilmington, NC, 28403-3297. EMAIL richardsons@uncwil.edu

RICHMOND, HUGH M.
PERSONAL Born 03/20/1932, Burton-upon-Trent, England, m, 1958, 2 children DISCIPLINE LITERATURE EDUCATION Cambridge Univ, BA, 54; Oxford Univ, DPhil, 57. CAREER Lieutenant, Royal Artillery, 51-52; Youth Camp Warden, 54; Asst d'anglais, Lcee J. Perrin, Lyon, France, 54-55; Instr to Prof, 57-94, Prof Emeritus English, Univ Calif - Berkeley, 94- (recalled, 94-96), Dir, Shakespeare Prog, 73-, Dir Shakespeare Forum, 80-95, Chancellor's Adviser, Educ Development, 83-86; Dir, Educ Div, Shakespeare Globe Ctr, 95-. HONORS AND AWARDS UK State Schol, 48; Open Schol, Emmanuel Col, Cambridge, 49; Tripos Prize, 54; ACLS Fel, 64-65; UC Res Prof, 68, 75; UC Humanities Inst Awards, 73, 76, 87; UC Regents Teaching Grants, 73, 74, 76-78; UCB Teaching Grants, 75, 79, 83, 85, 95; NEH Educ Grants, 76-78, 84-86; NEH Res Fel, 77, 88; UCB Campus Award for Distinguished Teaching, 79; UCB Humanities Ctr Grant, 93; British Airways Travel Fel, 95, 96. MEMBERSHIPS NCalif Renaissance Conf; MLA. SELECTED PUBLICATIONS Auth, The School of Love, Princeton, 64; Shakespeare's Political Plays, Random House, 67, Peter Smith, 77; Shakespeare's Sexual

Comedy, Bobbs-Merrill, 71; Renaissance Landscapes, Mouton, 73; The Christian Revolutionary: John Milton, UC Press, 74; Puritans & Libertines, UC Press, 81; Shakespeare in Performance: King Richard III, Manchester Univ Press, 90; Shakespeare in Performance: King Henry VIII, Manchester Univ Press, 94; author of numerous journal articles. CONTACT ADDRESS Univ Calif - Berkeley, Berkeley, CA, 94720.

RICHMOND, MAUREEN
PERSONAL Born 12/08/1951, Texarkana, AR, m, 1997 DISCIPLINE ENGLISH AND WRITING EDUCATION Univ Ar., Little Rock, BA, Eng, 84. CAREER Consulting astrologer, 81-; founder and dir, Sch of Esoteric Astrology, 97-. HONORS AND AWARDS Phi Kappa Phi, Univ Ar., Little Rock. MEMBERSHIPS Amer Fed Astrols; Amer Acad Relig. RESEARCH The roots of esoteric philosophy in ancient sacred traditions. SELECTED PUBLICATIONS Auth, Sinius, Source Publ, 97. CONTACT ADDRESS 808 Dothan Ct., Raleigh, NC, 27614. EMAIL blueray@msn.com

RICHMOND, VELMA B.
PERSONAL Born 03/12/1931, New Orleans, LA, m, 1958, 2 children DISCIPLINE ENGLISH LITERATURE; MEDIEVAL STUDIES EDUCATION La State Univ, BA, 51, MA, 52; Oxford Univ, BLitt, 57; Univ NC, PhD, 59. CAREER Instr, La State Univ, 57-58; Instr to Prof, 58-96, Prof Emeritus English, Holy Names Col, 96-, Chmn English, 70-76, Dean Acad Affairs, 80-85. HONORS AND AWARDS Fulbright Schol, Oxford Univ, 55-57; ACLS Fel, 76; Project Dir, NEH Implementation Grant for Core Prog in Humanities Studies, 81-84. MEMBERSHIPS Medieval Acad; New Chaucer Soc; Medieval Asn Pac; Mod Lang Asn; Mod Humanities Res Asn; Christianity and Lit; Int Arthurian Soc. RESEARCH Chaucer; medieval romance; Shakespeare; children's literature; contemporary Catholic fiction. SELECTED PUBLICATIONS Auth, Laments for the Dead in Medieval Narrative, Duquesne Univ Press, 66; The Popularity of Middle English Romance, Bowling Green State Univ Press, 75; Muriel Spark, Frederick Ungar Publ Co, 84; Geoffrey Chaucer, Continuum, 92; The Legend of Guy of Warwick, Garland, 96; author of numerous articles and reviews. CONTACT ADDRESS 1280 Grizzly Peak Blvd., Berkeley, CA, 94708.

RICHTER, DAVID H.
PERSONAL Born 10/01/1945, Chicago, IL, m, 1983, 2 children DISCIPLINE ENGLISH EDUCATION BA, 65, MA, 66, PhD, English, 71, Univ of Chicago. CAREER Inst, Roosevelt Univ, 67-70; INST, 70-71, ASST PROF, 71-75, ASSOC PROF, 75-84, PROF, 84-, QUEENS COL; PROF, GRAD CENTER OF THE CITY UNIV OF NY, 95-. MEMBERSHIPS MLA; Am Soc for Eighteenth-Century Studies; Soc for the Study of Narrative Lit. RESEARCH Literary theory; prose fiction; eighteenth-century studies; biblical narrative. SELECTED PUBLICATIONS Auth, Ideology and Form in Eighteenth-Century Literature, Tex Tech Univ Press, 99; auth, The Critical Tradition: Classical Texts and Contemporary Trends, Bedford Books, 89 & 98; auth, The Progress of Romance: Literary Historiography and the Gothic Novel, Ohio State Univ Press, 96; auth, Narrative/Theory, Longman, 96; auth, Falling into Theory: Conflicting Views on Reading Literature, Bedford Books, 94; auth, Multiculturalism, Academic Radicalism, and the University Presses, Scholarly Publishing, 93; auth, Croce, The Johns Hopkins Guide to Literary Criticism and Theory, Johns Hopkins Univ Press, 93; auth, Background Action and Ideology: Grey Men and Dope Doctors in Raymond Chandler, Narrative 2, 94; auth, Wayne C. Booth and the Pragmatics of Literary Reviewing, in Rhetoric and Pluralism: Legacies of Wayne Booth, Ohio State Univ Press, 95; auth, Midrash and Mashal: Difficulty in the Blessing of Esau, Narrative 5, 96; auth, A Name by Any Other Rose: Umberto Eco and the Semiotics of Detection, in Reading Eco, Ind Univ Press, 96; auth, Farewell My Concubine: The Difficult, the Stubborn and the Outrage of Gibeah, in Agendas for Midrash in the Twenty-First Century, 98. CONTACT ADDRESS 201 W. 89th St., New York, NY, 10024. EMAIL david_richter@qc.edu

RICKE, JOSEPH M.
DISCIPLINE ENGLISH EDUCATION Rice Univ, PhD. CAREER Dept Eng, Hunter Col, City Univ NY MEMBERSHIPS MLA: Medieval and Renaissance Drama Soc & Conf Christianity and Lit. SELECTED PUBLICATIONS Publ on, from Shakespeare's Taming of the Shrew to the value of lit study in Christian higher educ. CONTACT ADDRESS Dept of English, Hunter Col, CUNY, 695 Park Ave, New York, NY, 10021. EMAIL jricke@huntington.edu

RICKLY, REBECCA
DISCIPLINE RHETORIC AND COMPOSITION EDUCATION Ball State Univ, PhD, 95. CAREER Instr, Univ MI; vis asst prof, TX Tech Univ. MEMBERSHIPS Ch, NCTE's Instruct Technol Comt. RESEARCH The influence of tech on pedag; research methodology. SELECTED PUBLICATIONS Auth, Reflection and Responsibility in (Cyber)Tutor Training: Seeing Ourselves Clearly On and Off the Screen, in Wiring the Writing Center, ed Eric H. Hobson; Promotion, Tenure, and Technology: Do We Get What We Deserve?, in Electronic Networks: Crossing Boundaries/Creating Communities, eds,

Tharon Howard, Dixie Goswami, Rocky Gooch; The Gender Gap in Computers and Composition Research: Must Boys Be Boys?, Comput and Compos. **CONTACT ADDRESS** Texas Tech Univ, Lubbock, TX, 79409-5015. **EMAIL** R.Rickly@ttu.edu

RIDDELL, RICHARD
DISCIPLINE ENGLISH LITERATURE **EDUCATION** Stanford Univ, PhD, 78. **CAREER** Mary D. B. T. and James H. Semans prof pract drama; dir drama prog. **HONORS AND AWARDS** Tony Awd; Drama Desk Awd; Maharam Awd. **SELECTED PUBLICATIONS** Auth, publ(s) on educ; Europ theater. **CONTACT ADDRESS** Eng Dept, Duke Univ, Durham, NC, 27706.

RIDLAND, JOHN
DISCIPLINE ENGLISH LITERATURE **EDUCATION** Claremont Grad Sch, PhD, 64. **CAREER** PROF, ENG, UNIV CALIF, SANTA BARBARA. **RESEARCH** Poetry; Creative writing; Robert Frost; Lit of Australia and New Zealand. **SELECTED PUBLICATIONS** Auth, Ode on Violence, 69; And Say What He Is, 75; In the Sadowless Light, 78; Elegy for my Aunt, 81; Palms, 93. **CONTACT ADDRESS** Dept of Eng, Univ Calif, Santa Barbara, CA, 93106-7150. **EMAIL** jridland@humanitas.ucsb.edu

RIEBLING, BARBARA
PERSONAL Born 11/13/1949, Columbus, OH, s **DISCIPLINE** ENGLISH LITERATURE **EDUCATION** Univ Pennsylvania, PhD, 93 **CAREER** Pierce Col, 75-87; visiting asst prof, Swarthmore Col, 91-92; assoc prof, Univ Toledo, 93-98 **MEMBERSHIPS** MLA; SAA; RSA **RESEARCH** Early Modern English Literature; History of Political Thought; Literary Theory **SELECTED PUBLICATIONS** Auth, "Milton on Machiavelli: Representations of the State in Paradise Lost," Renaissance Quart, 96; auth, "England Deflowered and Unmanned: The Sexual Image of Politics in Marvell's Last Instructions," SEL: Studies in English Lit, 1500-1900, 95; coauth, After Poststructuralism: Interdisciplinarity and Literary Theory, Northwestern, 93 **CONTACT ADDRESS** Dept of English Lang and Lit, Univ Toledo, Toledo, OH, 43606.

RIECKMAN, JENS
DISCIPLINE TWENTIETH-CENTURY LITERATURE **EDUCATION** Harvard Univ, PhD, 75. **CAREER** Asst prof, Univ Va, 75-81; instr, Univ Wash, 81-93; prof, 93-. **HONORS AND AWARDS** Mellon fac fel, Harvard Univ, 80-81; res grant, ACLS, 83-84; Guggenberg fel, 88-89. **RESEARCH** Critical biography of the young Hofmannsthal. **SELECTED PUBLICATIONS** Auth, Der Zauberberg: Eine geistige Autobiographie Thomas Manns, Stuttgart: Akademischer Verlag Heinz, 77, 79; Aufbruch in die Moderne: Die Anfange des Jungen Wien, osterreichische Literatur und Kritik im Fin de Siecle, Konigstein, Ts: Athenaum, 85, 86; Leopold von Andrian, osterreichische Tagebuchschriftsteller, Wien: Edition Atelier, 94. **CONTACT ADDRESS** Ger dept, Univ Calif, Irvine, CA, 92697. **EMAIL** jrieckma@uci.edu

RIELY, JOHN C.
PERSONAL Born 08/27/1945, Philadelphia, PA, m, 1969, 2 children **DISCIPLINE** ENGLISH LITERATURE; ART HISTORY **EDUCATION** Harvard Col, AB, 67; Univ Pa, MA, 68, PhD, 71. **CAREER** Assoc res ed, Yale Addition Horace Walpoles Correspondence, 71-79; lectr, Yale Univ, 73-79; asst prof, Columbia Univ, 79-80; vis prof, Univ Minn, 80-81; from asst to assoc prof, Boston Univ, 81-. **HONORS AND AWARDS** Huntington Lib Fel, 73; ACLS Grant; Vis Fel, 82-83, Yale Ctr for Brittish Art; NEH Senior Fel, 88-89, Boston Public Libr Fel, 95-96; Fel Soc Antiquanes London and Royal Soc Arts. **MEMBERSHIPS** ASECS; NEASECS; Asn Lit Scholar Critics; Col Art Asn; Walpole Soc; Johnsonines US and UK. **RESEARCH** Late 17th thru early 19th early literature and art history; Johnson and his circle; Sir Joshua Reynolds; Horace Walpole; Alex Pope; Biography and Portraiture; caricature and comic art; English country house and landscape garden. **SELECTED PUBLICATIONS** Auth, Rowlandson Drawings From the Paul Mellon Collection, 77; auth, The Age of Horace Walpole and Caricature 73, 90. **CONTACT ADDRESS** Dept of English, Boston Univ, 236 Bay State Rd, Boston, MA, 02215. **EMAIL** jriely@bu.edu

RIGOLOT, FRANCOIS
PERSONAL Born 05/21/1939, France, m, 1970, 2 children **DISCIPLINE** LITERATURE **EDUCATION** Ecole Des Hautes Etudes Commerciales, BA, 61; Northwestern Univ, MA, 63; Univ Wis, PhD, 69. **CAREER** Asst prof, Univ Mich, 69-74; from asst prof to assoc prof to prof, 74-, Princeton Univ. **HONORS AND AWARDS** NEH Fel, 80; Guggenheim Fel, 83; Gilbert Chinard Literary Prize, 84; Chevalier Des Palmes Academiques, 87; James Russell Lowell Prize, 90; Behrman Award for Distinguished Achievment, Hum, 93., Chemn, 84-91, 96-, Meridith Howland Pyne Prof, 81-, Princeton Univ. **MEMBERSHIPS** AATF; AIEF; RHR; MLA; RSA; SPFA; SAM; SARD; RHLF; SFS **RESEARCH** Renaissance studies; French literature; poetics; stylistics; history of rhetoric. **SELECTED PUBLICATIONS** Auth, Les Langages de Rabelais, 72; auth, Poetique et la poesie, 79; auth, Le Texte de la Renaissance, 82; auth, Les Metamorphoses de Montaigne, 88; auth, Louise Labe Lyonnaise, ou la Renaissance au feminin, 98. **CONTACT ADDRESS** Romance Languages Dept, Princeton Univ, 201 E Pyne, Princeton, NJ, 08544. **EMAIL** rigolot@princeton.edu

RIGSBY, ENRIQUE D.
DISCIPLINE RHETORICAL THEORY **EDUCATION** Univ Ore, PhD. **CAREER** Prof, Texas A&M Univ. **HONORS AND AWARDS** Outstanding New Teacher Awd, Southern States Commun Asn; Col of Liberal Arts Distinguished Teaching Awd, Asn Former Students at Texas A&M Univ & Univ-Wide Distinguished Achievement Awd in Tchg, Asn of Former Students and Texas A&M Univ. **RESEARCH** Rhetorical theory & criticism, civil rights rhetoric, media studies. **SELECTED PUBLICATIONS** Contribur, African American Orators & Television Criticism. **CONTACT ADDRESS** Dept of Speech Communication, Texas A&M Univ, College Station, TX, 77843-4234.

RILEY, SAM G.
PERSONAL Born 10/08/1939, Raleigh, NC, d, 2 children **DISCIPLINE** COMMUNICATIONS, JOURNALISM **EDUCATION** Davidson Coll, BA, 61; Univ NC-Chapel Hill, MBA, 62, PhD, 70. **CAREER** Asst prof, Jour, Temple Univ, 70-74; assoc prof, Jour, Georgia South Univ, 74-81; dept head, Va Tech, Jour, 81-85; PROF, VA TECH, COMMUN STUD, 81-. **MEMBERSHIPS** Asn educ Jour & Mass Commun; Am Jour Hist Asn; Res Soc Am Periodicals; Kappa Tau Alpha; Nat Soc Newspaper Column **RESEARCH** Mass media history; Journal writing. **SELECTED PUBLICATIONS** Consumer Magazines of the British Isles, Greenwood Press, 93; The Best of the Rest: Non-Syndicated Newspaper Columnists Select Their Best Work, Greenwood Press, 93; Dictionary of Literary Biography: American Magazine Journalists, 1900-1960, Gale Res, 94; Biographical Dictionary of American Newspaper Columnists, Greenwood Press, 95; The American Newspaper Columnist, Praeger, 98. **CONTACT ADDRESS** Virginia Polytechnic Inst & State Univ, Blacksburg, VA, 24061. **EMAIL** sriley@vt.edu

RIMAL, RAJIV N.
DISCIPLINE COMMUNICATION THEORY **EDUCATION** Stanford Univ, PhD. **CAREER** Asst prof, Texas A&M Univ. **HONORS AND AWARDS** Nathan Maccobby Awd for Excellence in Commun Res & Int Commun Association's Health Commun Div top 3 paper Awd. **RESEARCH** Health communication & public health campaigns, use of interactive technologies in health promotion, family communication & health, social psychology & persuasion, communication theory. **SELECTED PUBLICATIONS** Contribur, Using Interactive Computing in Health Promotion and Political Persuasionand Attitude Change. **CONTACT ADDRESS** Dept of Speech Communication, Texas A&M Univ, College Station, TX, 77843-4234.

RINEHART, LUCY
DISCIPLINE ENGLISH **EDUCATION** Barnard Coll, BA, 84; Columbia MA, 85, MPhil, 88, PhD, 94. **CAREER** ASST PROF, ENG, DEPAUL UNIV **MEMBERSHIPS** Am Antiquarian Soc **SELECTED PUBLICATIONS** Assoc ed & contr auth, The Cambridge Handbook of American Literature, Cambridge Univ Press, 86; auth, "A Nation's Noble Spectacle: Royall Tyler's The Contrast as Metatheatrical Commentary," American Drama, Spring 94; auth, "George Henry Boker," "James Kirke Paulding," in The Garland Companion to American Nineteenth-Century Verse, 95. **CONTACT ADDRESS** Dept of Eng, DePaul Univ, 802 W Belden, Chicago, IL, 60614. **EMAIL** lrinehar@wppost.depaul.edu

RISSER, JAMES V.
DISCIPLINE COMMUNICATIONS **EDUCATION** Univ NE, BA; Univ San Francisco Sch Law, JD. **CAREER** WA Bureau Chief, Des Moines Register, 76-85; prof and dir grad prog, Stanford Univ, 85; vis lctr, Wells Col, Mills Col, Drew Univ, and Bowdoin; res ed, Univ NE Sch Jour. **HONORS AND AWARDS** Pulitzer Prize,76 and 79; Raymond Clapper Mem Awd, 76 and 78; Thomas L. Stokes Awd, 71 and 78., Dir John S. Knight Fel Prog, Standford Univ. **MEMBERSHIPS** Pulitzer Prize bd, Soc Prof Jour; Investigative Rptrs Eds; Gridiron Club Washington; Ed Adv Bd Reuter Found London. **SELECTED PUBLICATIONS** Auth, articles and editorials for Des Moines Register. **CONTACT ADDRESS** Dept Commun, Stanford Univ, McClatchy Hall, Stanford, CA, 94305.

RITTER, KURT
DISCIPLINE POLITICAL RHETORIC, AMERICAN PUBLIC ADDRESS **EDUCATION** Ind Univ, PhD. **CAREER** Prof, Texas A&M Univ. **HONORS AND AWARDS** Amoco Found Awd ,Distinguished Tchg; Winans-Wichelns Awd , Distinguished Scholarship in Rhetoric and Public Address; Speech Commun Association's Karl R.Wallace Mem Res Awd & annual Aubrey Fisher Awd for the outstanding article in the Western J Commun. **SELECTED PUBLICATIONS** Coauth, Ronald Reagan: The Great Communicator & The American Idealogy: Reflections of the Revolution in American Rhetoric; Contribur, The Clinton Presidency: Images; Issues,and Communication Strategies, African American Orators; The Modern Presidency and Crisis Rhetoric; US Presidents as Orators; Inaugural Addresses of 20th Century American Presidents; Contemporary American Public Discourse; Rhetorical Studies of National Political Debates. **CONTACT ADDRESS** Dept of Speech Communication, Texas A&M Univ, College Station, TX, 77843-4234.

RITVO, HARRIET
DISCIPLINE HISTORY; ENGLISH **EDUCATION** Harvard Univ, AB, 68, PhD, 75. **CAREER** Arthur J. Conner Prof of Hist, MIT. **HONORS AND AWARDS** Guggenheim Fel; Nat Endowment for the Humanities Fel; Writing Writers Prize. **MEMBERSHIPS** AHA; SHNH; PEN; HSS. **RESEARCH** British cultural history; history of biology/natural history; human-animal relations. **SELECTED PUBLICATIONS** Auth, The Platypus and the Mermaid and Other Figments of Classifying Imagination, Harvard Univ Press, 97; The Animal Estate: The English and Other Creatures in the Victorian Age, Harvard Univ Press, 87, Penguin Books, 90; The Sincerest Form of Flattery, Dead or Alive: Animal Captives of Human Cultures, Princeton Univ Press, 99; The Roast Beef of Old England, Mad Cows and Modernity: Cross-disciplinary Reflections on the Crisis of Creutzfeldt-Jacob Disease, Humanities Res Centre, 98; Introduction, The Variation of Animals and Plants under Domestication, Johns Hopkins Univ Press, 98; Zoological Nomenclature and the Empire of Victorian Science, Contexts of Victorian Science, Univ of Chicago Press, 97; coed, The Macropolitics of Nineteenth-Century Literature: Nationalism, Imperialism, Exoticism, Univ of Pa Press, 91, Duke Univ Press, 95. **CONTACT ADDRESS** Massachusetts Inst of Tech, 77 Massachusettes Ave., E51-288, Cambridge, MA, 02139. **EMAIL** hnritvo@mit.edu

RIVERS, LOUIS
PERSONAL Born 09/18/1922, Savannah, Georgia, m **DISCIPLINE** SPEECH **EDUCATION** Savannah State Coll, BS 1946; New York Univ, MA 1951; Fordham Univ, PhD 1975. **CAREER** WV State Coll, instructor 1951-52; Southern Univ, instructor 1952-53; Tougaloo Coll, asst prof 1953-58; New York City Tech Coll, professor 1970-. **HONORS AND AWARDS** John Hay Whitney Theater 1957; Outstanding Teacher Plaque from Kappa Delta Pi 1983; Andrew Mellon Creative Writing Fellowship 1984. **MEMBERSHIPS** Mem Natl Writers Club, Dramatist Guild, Speech Communication Assn, College Language Assn, Phi Delta Kappa, Kappa Delta Pi. **CONTACT ADDRESS** Professor of Writing/Speech, New York City Tech Col, 300 Jay St, Brooklyn, NY, 11201.

ROBARDS, BROOKS
PERSONAL Born 08/21/1942, Mount Kisco, NY, m, 1988, 3 children **DISCIPLINE** COMMUNICATION **EDUCATION** Bryn Mawr, AB, 64; Hartford Univ, MA, 70; Univ Mass/Amherst, PhD, 82. **CAREER** Prof, Westfield St Col, 79-. **HONORS AND AWARDS** Fulbright, Beijing, 93-94. **MEMBERSHIPS** Natl Comm Assn; Intl Comm Assn; Popular Cult Assn; Soc for Prof Journalists. **RESEARCH** Film; TV journalism; women's studies. **SELECTED PUBLICATIONS** Auth, Arnold Schwarzenegger, Brompton, 92; auth, Sweet & Sour: One Women's Chinese Adventure; One Man's Chinese Torture, Summerset, 94; auth, The Medieval Knight at War, Barnes & Noble, 97; auth, A Magical Place: Poems, Paintings & Photographs of Martha's Vineyard, Summerset, 98. **CONTACT ADDRESS** Dept of Communication, Westfield State Col, Westfield, MA, 01086.

ROBB, STEPHEN
DISCIPLINE CONTEMPORARY PUBLIC ADDRESS, MASS COMMUNICATION **EDUCATION** Ind Univ, PhD, 67. **CAREER** Assoc prof, Purdue Univ. **RESEARCH** Advertising as goal-directed persuasion involving identification of demographic and psychographic groups; persuasion as a focus for understanding recent history as related to politics and art. **SELECTED PUBLICATIONS** Auth, The Voice of Black Rhetoric: Selections, 71; Fundamentals of Evidence and Argument, 76; Psychographics and the Liquor Industry, 83; coauth, Crisis Management and the Paradigm Case, in E. Toth and R. Heath (eds), Rhetorical and Critical Approaches to Public Relations, Erlbaum, 92. **CONTACT ADDRESS** Dept of Commun, Purdue Univ, 1080 Schleman Hall, West Lafayette, IN, 47907-1080. **EMAIL** srobb@purdue.edu

ROBBINS, HELEN W.
DISCIPLINE ENGLISH **EDUCATION** Smith Col, AB; Duke Univ, MA, PhD. **CAREER** Assoc prof, Lyon Col. **RESEARCH** Victorian lit; feminist theory; film. **SELECTED PUBLICATIONS** Auth, More Human Than I Am Alone: Womb Envy in The Fly and Dead Ringers in Screening the Male. **CONTACT ADDRESS** Dept of Eng, Lyon Col, 300 Highland Rd, PO Box 2317, Batesville, AR, 72503.

ROBBINS, KENNETH
PERSONAL Born 01/07/1944, Douglasville, GA, m, 1989, 2 children **DISCIPLINE** THEATRE; PLAYWRITING **EDUCATION** Univ Ga, MFA, 69; S Ill Univ-Carbondale, PhD, 82.

CAREER Prof, Dept Theatre, Univ S. Dakota, 85-98; dir, sch of perf arts, LA Tech Univ, 98-. **HONORS AND AWARDS** Japan Found Artists fel; S Dakota Sr Artist fel, Asoc Writing Prog Novel Award; Toni Morrison Award Fiction; SETC New Play Award. **MEMBERSHIPS** Dramatists Guild; PLaywrights Ctr; Asn Theatre in Higher Educ. **RESEARCH** Theatre of the Middle East. **SELECTED PUBLICATIONS** Auth, Calling the Cows, N Dakota Quart, 92; Leaving Prosperity, Briar Cliff Rev, 93; A Conversation with William Kloefkorn, S Dakota Rev, 94; The Hunger Feast, Palmetto Play Serv, 95; A Selection from The Baptism of Howie Cobb, Heritage of the Great Plains, 96; Atomic Field, S Theatre, 96; Mollys Rock, Palmetto Play Serv, 96; Vestiges of Power: Censorship in Contemporary Egyptian Theatre and Society, New Theatre Vistas, Garland Press, 96; The Closed Door Policy, S Quart, 96; Planespotting, S Quart, 97. **CONTACT ADDRESS** School of Perf Arts, Louisiana Tech Univ, Ruston, LA, 71272. **EMAIL** if45128@latech.edu

ROBERT, LUCIE
PERSONAL Born 05/22/1954, Jonquiere, PQ, Canada **DISCIPLINE** LITERATURE **EDUCATION** Laval Univ, BA, 76, MA, 80, PhD, 87. **CAREER** Res assoc, Dictionnaire des oeuvres litteraires du Quebec, Univ Laval, 78-86; PROF LITERARY STUDIES, UNIV QUEBEC AT MONTREAL, 86-. **HONORS AND AWARDS** Prix Edmond-de-Nevers, 80-91; Can Fedn Hum Best Bk Fre, 90-91. **MEMBERSHIPS** Ctr de Recherche en Litterature Quebecoise, Univ Laval **RESEARCH** Quebec literature **SELECTED PUBLICATIONS** Auth, Le Manuel de Mgr. Camille Roy, 82; auth, L'Institution du litteraire au Quebec, 89; coauth, Dictionnaire des oeuvres litteraires du Quebec, 78-87; coauth, La Vie litteraire au Quebec 1764-1914, 6 vols, 91-99; coauth, Litterature et societe Anthologie, 94; coauth, Litterature du Quebec, 94; contribur, Jeu; contribur, Poetics Today; contribur, Recherches Sociographiques; contribur, Etudes francaises; contribur, Etudes litteraires; contribur, Spirale; contribur, Lettres quebecoises; contribur, Voix & Images/Litterature quebecoise. **CONTACT ADDRESS** Dept Literary Stud, Univ Quebec at Montreal, Box 8888, Station Centre-Ville, Montreal, PQ, H3C 3P8. **EMAIL** robert.lucie@uqam.ca

ROBERTO, ANTHONY J.
DISCIPLINE COMMUNICATION **EDUCATION** Mich State Univ, PhD, 95. **CAREER** Violence prevention scientist, Mich Public Health Inst, 95-; ADJ ASST PROF, DEPT of COMMUN, Mich State Univ, 96-. **HONORS AND AWARDS** Outstanding Article Awd, 98; Bronze Telly Awd, 98; Awd of Merit, 98; Top-four Paper, 96; Garrison Mem Awd for Outstanding Scholar, 92. **MEMBERSHIPS** Am Pub Health Asn; Eastern Commun Asn; Int Asn of Conflict Mgt; Int Commun Asn; Nat Commun Asn. **RESEARCH** Health Communication; Conflict Management; Violence prevention; Persuasion/social influence. **SELECTED PUBLICATIONS** Coauth, "Relational Development as Negotiated Order in Hostage Negotiation," Human Commun Res, 93; coauth, "Revisiting mediator issue intervention strategies," Mediation Q, 94; coauth, "An Empirical Examination of Three Models of Integrative and Distributive Bargaining," Internatl J of Conflict Management, 96; coauth, "The Assessment of Argumentativeness and Verbal Aggressiveness in Adolescent Populations," Commun Q, 97; coauth, "The Firearm Injury Reduction Education (FIRE)Program: Formative Evaluation Insights and Implications," Social Marketing Q, 98. **CONTACT ADDRESS** Michigan Public Health Inst, 2438 Woodlake Cir, Ste. 240, Okemos, MI, 48864.

ROBERTS, BRIAN
DISCIPLINE ENGLISH **EDUCATION** Calif State Univ at Sacramento, BA, 86; MA, 89; Rutgers Univ, PhD, 95. **CAREER** ASST PROF, ENG, RUTGERS UNIV **MEMBERSHIPS** Am Antiquarian Soc **SELECTED PUBLICATIONS** Mus from the Colonial era through the Civil War **CONTACT ADDRESS** Dept of Hist, Rutgers Univ, New Brunswick, NJ, 08903-5059.

ROBERTS, CHARLES
DISCIPLINE COMMUNICATION STUDIES **EDUCATION** Davidson Col, BA; Temple Univ, MA, PhD. **CAREER** Prof, 90-. **MEMBERSHIPS** Int Listening Asn; Eastern Commun Asn; Southern Speech Commun Asn. **SELECTED PUBLICATIONS** Auth, A First Look At Communication Theory; co-auth, Intrapersonal Communication Processes; Intrapersonal Communication Processes: Original Essays. **CONTACT ADDRESS** Dept of Communication, East Tennesee State Univ, PO Box 70717, Johnson City, TN, 37614-0717. **EMAIL** robertsc@etsuarts.etsu-tn.edu

ROBERTS, DONALD F.
DISCIPLINE COMMUNICATIONS **EDUCATION** Columbia Univ, AB, 61; Univ CA Berkeley, MA, 63; Stanford Univ, PhD, 68. **CAREER** Fac, 68-; to dir Inst Comm Res, 85-90; to chr dept comm, 90-96; to Thomas More Storke Prof, 96-. **HONORS AND AWARDS** Consult, Filmation, Disney, MGM Animation, JP Kids; planner/panelist, Conf Families and Media. **RESEARCH** Children and adolescent use of and response to media. **SELECTED PUBLICATIONS** Auth, chaps in The Handbook of Communication, Learning from Television: Psychological and Education Research, International Encyclopedia of Communications; revs on effects of mass communication for the Annual Review of Psychology and Handbook of Social Psychology;coauth, chapter on public opinion processes in the Handbook of Communication Science; Television and Human Behavior; Its Not Only Rock and Roll: Popular Music in the Lives of Adolescents; co-ed, The Process and Effects of Mass Communication. **CONTACT ADDRESS** Dept Commun, Stanford Univ, McClatchy Hall, Stanford, CA, 94305.

ROBERTS, JOHN R.
PERSONAL Born 03/07/1934, IN, m, 1955, 6 children **DISCIPLINE** ENGLISH **EDUCATION** IN State Univ, 55; Univ IL, MA 57, PhD 62. **CAREER** Univ WI, instr 62-63, asst prof 63-66; Univ Detroit, assoc prof 66-68; Univ MO, assoc prof 68-72, prof 72. **HONORS AND AWARDS** Byler Distinguished Prof Awd; Cambridge Fel, Catherine Paine Middlebush Ch; 6 NEH Awards. **MEMBERSHIPS** MLA; IAUP; Milton Soc Amer; John Donne Soc; CRC. **RESEARCH** 17th century Brit Poetry; Eng Recusant Lit; bibli. **SELECTED PUBLICATIONS** The Variorum Edition of the Poetry Of John Donne, IND Univ Press, 99; New Perspectives on the Seventeenth-Century English Religious Lyric, ed, Univ MO Press, 94; New Perspectives on the Life and Art of Richard Crashaw, ed, Univ MO Press, 90. **CONTACT ADDRESS** Dept of Eng, Univ of MO, Tate Hall, Columbia, MO, 65211. **EMAIL** engjohn@showme.missouri.edu

ROBERTS, NANCY L.
DISCIPLINE MASS COMMUNICATION STUDIES **EDUCATION** Brown Univ, MA; Univ Minn, MA, PhD. **CAREER** Assoc prof **SELECTED PUBLICATIONS** Auth, American Peace Writers, Editors, and Periodicals: A Dictionary, 90; Dorothy Day and the 'Catholic Worker', 84; co-auth, As Ever, Gene: The Letters of Eugene O'Neill to George Jean Nathan, 87. **CONTACT ADDRESS** Mass Communication Dept, Univ of Minnesota, Twin Cities, 111 Murphy Hall, 206 Church St SE, Minneapolis, MN, 55455. **EMAIL** rober003@maroon.tc.umn.edu

ROBERTS, ROBIN
DISCIPLINE WOMEN'S STUDIES, AMERICAN STUDIES **EDUCATION** Univ Pa, PhD, 85. **CAREER** Prof, La State Univ. **HONORS AND AWARDS** Russell B. Nye Award, Popular Cult Asn, 87; Kathleen Gregory Klein Award, Popular Cult Asn, 90. **RESEARCH** Popular culture; music videos; Star Trek. **SELECTED PUBLICATIONS** Auth, A New Species: Gender and Science in Science Fiction, 93; Sisters in the Name of Rap: Rapping for Women's Lives, Black Women in Am, 94; Ladies First: Queen Latifah's Afrocentric Feminist Music Video, African Am Rev, 94; It's Still Science Fiction: Strategies of Feminist Science Fiction Criticism, Extrapolation, 95; Ladies First Women in Music Videos, 96; Anne McCaffrey: A Critical Study, 96. **CONTACT ADDRESS** Dept of Eng, Louisiana State Univ, 212H Allen Hall, Baton Rouge, LA, 70803. **EMAIL** rrobert@unix1.sncc.lsu.edu

ROBERTS, THOMAS J.
PERSONAL Born 06/10/1925, Omaha, NE, d, 3 children **DISCIPLINE** ENGLISH; AMERICAN LITERATURE **EDUCATION** Univ of Minn, BA, 48, MA, 52, PhD, 58. **CAREER** Instr, Univ of Kansas, 52-55; Univ of Minn, 55-58; from asst prof to assoc prof, Am Univ of Cairo, 58-63; assoc prof, Univ of Alaska, 60-61; from asst prof to prof, Univ of Conn, 63- . **HONORS AND AWARDS** Consult, Nat Survey of Undergrad Progs in Eng; Nat Endowment for the Hum fel for Independent Study and Res, 81-82. **RESEARCH** Lit Theory; Vernacular Lit. **SELECTED PUBLICATIONS** Auth, When Is Something Fiction, 72; The Network of Literary Identifications, New Lit Hist, 5(1), 73; An Aesthetics of Junk Fiction, 90; Gold Bullet Sport: A Dime Novel by Buffalo Bill; or, A Record of an Expedition into the Great Americn Literary Desert, Tex Studies in Lit and Language, 33, 91; Popular Fiction Under the Old Dispensation and The New, LIT 4, 93. **CONTACT ADDRESS** Dept of English, Storrs, CT, 06268. **EMAIL** roberts@uconnvm.uconn.edu

ROBERTSON, FIONA
DISCIPLINE ENGLISH **EDUCATION** Oxford Univ, BAL, 81; MPhil, 83, DPhil, 88. **CAREER** Lectr, Eng lit, Univ Durham; READER. **MEMBERSHIPS** Am Antiquarian Soc **SELECTED PUBLICATIONS** Ed and introd, Sir Walter Scott, The Bride of Lammermoor, Oxford Univ Press, 91; auth, Legitimate Histories: Scott, Gothic, and the Authorities of Fiction, Clarendon Press, 94; auth, "Keats' New World: An Emigrant Poetry," in Bicentenary Readings, Edinburgh Univ Press, 97; auth, "Of Speculation and Return: Scott's Jacobitzer, John Law, and the Company of the West," Scottish Lit Jour 24, 97; auth, Walter Scott, Lives of the Great Romantics by their Contemporaries, Pickering and Chatto, 97. **CONTACT ADDRESS** Dept of Eng Stud, Univ of Durham, Elvet Riverside, New Elvet, ., DH1 3JT. **EMAIL** Fiona.Robertson@durham.ac.uk

ROBEY, DAVID H.
DISCIPLINE SPEECH COMMUNICATION **EDUCATION** Pillsbury Col, BA, 70; Bob Jones Univ, MA, 72; Union Inst, PhD. **CAREER** Prof, Tennessee Temple Univ, 72-81; Prof, Cedarville Col, 81-. **SELECTED PUBLICATIONS** Auth, Two for Missions, Lillenas Publ Co, Kansas City, Miss, 88. **CONTACT ADDRESS** Cedarville Col, PO Box 601, Cedarville, OH, 45314.

ROBINSON, AMY
DISCIPLINE ENGLISH LITERATURE **EDUCATION** Oberlin Col, Univ Pa, MA, PhD. **CAREER** Eng Dept, Georgetown Univ **RESEARCH** Cultural studies; performance studies; African American literature and culture; gay and lesbian studies; feminist and literary theories; 19th and 20th century American literature. **SELECTED PUBLICATIONS** Auth, Authority and the Public Display of Identity: Wonderful Adventures of Mrs. Seacole in Many Lands, Feminist Studies, 94; It Takes One to Know One: Passing and Communities of Common Interest, Critical Inquiry, 94; Is She or Isn't She: Madonna and the Erotics of Appropriation, 93; The Trouble of Passing, 93. **CONTACT ADDRESS** English Dept, Georgetown Univ, 37th and O St, Washington, DC, 20057.

ROBINSON, DAVID
DISCIPLINE AMERICAN LITERATURE **EDUCATION** Univ Tex, BA, 70; Harvard Divinity School, MTS, 72; Univ Wisc, MA, 73; PhD, 76. **CAREER** Engl, Oregon St Univ. **HONORS AND AWARDS** Dir, Am Studies. **SELECTED PUBLICATIONS** Auth, Apostle of Culture: Emerson as Preacher and Lecturer, Univ Pa Press,82; Margaret Fuller and the Transcendental Ethos: Women in the Nineteenth Century, PMLA 97, 82; Unchronicled Nations: Agrarian Purpose and Thoreau's Ecological Knowing," Nineteenth Century Literature 48, 93; Emerson and the Conduct of Life: Pragmatism and Ethical Purpose in the Later Work. Cambridge Univ Press,93; World of Relations: The Achievement of Peter Taylor. Univ Press Ky, 98. **CONTACT ADDRESS** Oregon State Univ, Corvallis, OR, 97331-4501. **EMAIL** drobinson@orst.edu

ROBINSON, EDWARD A.
PERSONAL Born 06/13/1935, Gary, IN, m **DISCIPLINE** ENGLISH **EDUCATION** Howard University, BA, 1959; University of Chicago, MAT, 1970; Northwestern University, PhD, 1974. **CAREER** Northeastern Illinois University, assistant professor; Lake Forest College, IL, English instructor, 1970-72; Chicago Board of Education, HS English consultant, 1970-72; Wendell Phillips & Summer HS, Chicago, instructor, 1961-64; English Department, Harlan HS, Chicago, instructor & chairman, 1960-69; Carver HS, Chicago, instructor, 1959-60; Emmy Award Winning TV Prog, "The Giants", "The Common Men", narrator, 1967; "Like It Was the black man in America", teacher/host, 1969; Midwest Modern Language Association convention, presented paper, 1973; NDEA Institute, University of Chicago, summer participant, 1965. **HONORS AND AWARDS** Recipient, Experienced Teacher Fellowship, University of Chicago, 1969-70; Ford Foundation Fellowship for Black Americans, 1973-74. **MEMBERSHIPS** South Shore Valley Community Organization, 1969-74; Faulkner School Association, 1974-75; Faulkner School Father's Club, 1974-75; National Urban League, 1968-74; Operation PUSH, 1972. **SELECTED PUBLICATIONS** numerous publications **CONTACT ADDRESS** Ciriculum & Instruction, Northeastern Illinois Univ, 550 N St Louis Avenue, Chicago, IL, 60625-4625.

ROBINSON, ELLA S.
PERSONAL Born 04/16/1943, Wedowee, Alabama, w, 1980 **DISCIPLINE** ENGLISH **EDUCATION** AL State Univ, BS 1965; Univ of NE, MA 1970, PhD 1976. **CAREER** Univ of IL, assistant prof 1975-77; Atlanta Univ, assistant prof 1977-79; Univ of Nebraska-Lincoln, professor of English, beginning 1979; Tuskegee University, assoc prof, currently. **HONORS AND AWARDS** Travelled throughout Nigeria in order to do research for poetry, paintings and articles. **MEMBERSHIPS** Mem MLA 1974-87; chair afro-lite session MMLA 1985-86; life time mem NAACP 1986-; ALA; African Amer Poet for the Heritage Room, Bennet Martin Library, 1989. **SELECTED PUBLICATIONS** Painted 85 oils & acrylics; author, "Selected Poems," 1995; "To Know Heaven," 1996; "Love the Season and Death," 1996; "Heritage: Tuskegee Poems a Celebration," 1997; numerous articles. **CONTACT ADDRESS** Prof of English, Tuskegee Institute, Tuskegee Institute, AL, 36087.

ROBINSON, JAMES D.
DISCIPLINE COMMUNICATION **EDUCATION** W Valley Col, AA, 76; Univ Pacific, BA, 78; W Va Univ, MA, 79; Purdue Univ, PhD, 82. **CAREER** Prof, 82-. **SELECTED PUBLICATIONS** Co-auth, The Portrayal of Religion & Spirituality on Fictional Network Programming, Rev Rel Res, 94; The Image of Christian Leaders in Fictional Network Programming, Sociol of Rel, 94; Four Decades of Families on Television: A demographic Profile, Jour Broadcasting & Electronic Media, 94; Health Information Campaigns and the Elderly, Ohio Speech Jour, 94; Usage Patterns and Portrayals of the Elderly in the Mass Media, Handbook of Commun and Aging Research, Lawrence Erlbaum Assoc, 95; The Invisible Generation: Portrayals of the Elderly on Prime-time Television, Commun Rpt, 95.

CONTACT ADDRESS Dept of Commun, Univ Dayton, 300 Col Park, Dayton, OH, 75062. **EMAIL** Robinson@udayton.edu

ROBINSON, JAMES E.
DISCIPLINE LITERATURE **EDUCATION** Univ Ill, PhD. **CAREER** Instr, Univ Notre Dame. **RESEARCH** Cosmological, rhetorical and theatrical aspects of space and time in Shakespeare. **SELECTED PUBLICATIONS** Auth, Bruno and Beckett: Coincidence of Contraries; Samuel Beckett's Doomsday Play: The Space of Infinity. **CONTACT ADDRESS** Univ Notre Dame, Notre Dame, IN, 46556.

ROBINSON, LAURA
DISCIPLINE ENGLISH LITERATURE **EDUCATION** Queen's Univ, PhD. **CAREER** Dept Eng, Queen's Univ **RESEARCH** Women writers; feminist theory. **SELECTED PUBLICATIONS** Auth, pubs on L.M. Montgomery. **CONTACT ADDRESS** English Dept, Queen's Univ, Kingston, ON, K7L 3N6. **EMAIL** 3lmr5@qlink.queensu.ca

ROBINSON, WILLIAM HENRY
PERSONAL Born 10/24/1922, Newport, Rhode Island, m, 1948 **DISCIPLINE** ENGLISH **EDUCATION** New York Univ, BA, 1951; Boston Univ, MA, 1957; Harvard Univ, PhD, 1964. **CAREER** Prairie View Agr & Mech Coll, Prairie View TX, English instructor, 1951-53; NC Agr & Tech State Univ, Greensboro, mem of English faculty, 1956-61, 1964-66; Boston Univ, MA, assoc prof of English & humanities, 1966-68; Howard Univ, Washington DC, prof of English, 1968-70; Rhode Is Coll, Providence, prof of English and dir black studies, 1970-85; vis prof of Amer & English lit, Brown Univ, 1987--. **MEMBERSHIPS** Bd mem, RI Commn on the Humanities; Bd mem, RI Black Heritage Soc; Intl Lecture Platform Assn; mem, NSLCAH; Nat Com on Black Studies; NAACP; Urban League; Coll Language Arts Assn; Assn for Study of Negro Life & Culture. **SELECTED PUBLICATIONS** Editor of Early Black American Poets, W.C. Brown, 1969, Early Black American Prose, W.C. Brown, 1970, Nommo: An Anthol of Modern Black African & Black American Lit, Macmillan, 1972, Critical Essays on Phillis Wheatley, G.K. Hall, 1982; author of Phillis Wheatly in the Black American Beginnings, Broadside, 1975, Phillis Wheatley: A Bio-ibliography, G.K. Hall, 1981, Phillis Wheatley and Her Writings, Garland, 1984; also autho of num TV, stage, radio scripts; contr to journals. **CONTACT ADDRESS** English Dept, Rhode Island Col, 600 Mt Pleasant Ave, Providence, RI, 02908.

ROCKS, JAMES E.
DISCIPLINE ENGLISH **EDUCATION** Duke Univ, PhD. **CAREER** Assoc prof; sr assoc dean, Grad Sch. **RESEARCH** American literature and Southern literature. **SELECTED PUBLICATIONS** Auth, Whittier's Snow-Bound: The circle of our hearth and the Discourse on Domesticity, in Stud in the Am Renaissance 17, UP Va, 93. **CONTACT ADDRESS** Dept of English, Loyola Univ, Chicago, 6525 N Sheridan Rd, Chicago, IL, 60626. **EMAIL** jrocks@wpo.it.luc.edu

RODERICK, JOHN M.
DISCIPLINE ENGLISH LITERATURE **EDUCATION** Providence Col, BA; Rhode Island Col, MA; Brown Univ, PhD. **CAREER** Prof, Hartford Univ. **HONORS AND AWARDS** Larsen Awd, 96. **SELECTED PUBLICATIONS** Auth, The Welder; Clotheslines and Baseball, Alembic Magazine, 97. **CONTACT ADDRESS** English Dept, Univ of Hartford, 200 Bloomfield Ave, West Hartford, CT, 06117.

RODOWICK, DAVID N.
DISCIPLINE ENGLISH **EDUCATION** Univ IA, PhD. **CAREER** Prof & dir Film Stud Prog; taught at, Univ IA & Yale Univ. **HONORS AND AWARDS** Created & administered, Yale Film Stud Prog, Yale Univ. **RESEARCH** Film theory of Gilles Deleuze; philos implications of new commun technol. **SELECTED PUBLICATIONS** Auth, The Difficulty of Difference: Psychoanalysis, Sexual Difference, and Film Theory & The Crisis of Political Modernism: Criticism and Ideology in Contemporary Film Theory; articles on, film theory & cult criticism. **CONTACT ADDRESS** Dept of Eng, Univ of Rochester, 601 Elmwood Ave, Ste. 656, Rochester, NY, 14642. **EMAIL** rdwk@troi.cc.rochester.edu

ROGERS, JACK E.
PERSONAL Born 12/13/1957, Stillwater, OK, m, 1991, 4 children **DISCIPLINE** SPEECH COMMUNICATION, SOCIOLOGY **EDUCATION** La State Univ, PhD, 94. **CAREER** Assoc prof, Southern Univ, 86-95; ASST PROF, UNIV OF TX AT TYLER, 96-. **HONORS AND AWARDS** Pres, Int Debat Asn. **MEMBERSHIPS** NCA, SSCA, CEDA, IPDA. **RESEARCH** Debate; forensics. **SELECTED PUBLICATIONS** Auth, A Community of Unequals: An Analysis of Dominant and Subdominant Culturally Linked Perceptions of Participation and Success within Intercollegiate Competitive Debate, Contemporary Argumentations & Debate: The J of the Cross-Examination Debate Asn, 97; A Critique of the Lexis/Nexis Debate: What's Missing Here?, The Southern J of Forensics, 96; Interrogating the Myth of Multiculturalism: Toward Significant Membership and Participation of Afrian Americans in Forensics, The Forensic of Pi Kappa Delta, 95; The Minority Perspective: Toward the Future Forensics Participation of Historically Black College and Universities, Proceedings from the Pi Kappa Delta Development Conf, 95; Constructing the Deconstruction: Toward the Empowerment of Women and Minorities in Forensics, Pi Kappa Delta Nat Development Conf, 95; What do they have that I haven't got? Comparison Survey Data of the Resources and Support Systems of Top CEDA Programs and Directors, CEDA Yearbook, 91. **CONTACT ADDRESS** Univ Texas at Tyler, 3900 University Blvd, Tyler, TX, 75799.

ROGERS, JIMMIE N.
DISCIPLINE POLITICAL AND CULTURAL COMMUNICATION **EDUCATION** Fla State Univ, PhD. **CAREER** Comm Stu, Univ Ark. **SELECTED PUBLICATIONS** Auth, The Country Music Message Revisited, Univ Ark Press, 89. **CONTACT ADDRESS** Univ Ark, Fayetteville, AR, 72701.

ROGERS, KATHARINE MUNZER
PERSONAL Born 06/06/1932, New York, NY, m, 1956, 3 children **DISCIPLINE** ENGLISH LITERATURE **EDUCATION** Barnard Coll, BA, 52; Columbia Univ, PhD, 57. **CAREER** Prof, Brooklyn Coll CUNY, 58-88; PROF EMER, BROOKLYN COLL CUYN, 88-. **RESEARCH** Animals in literature; L Frank Baum's life 7 works; women writers; Women in literature **SELECTED PUBLICATIONS** edr, Meridian Anthology of Restoration and Eighteenth-Century Plays by Women, Penguin USA, 94; auth, The Cat and the Human Imagination: Feline Images from Bast to Garfield, Univ Mich Press, 98. **CONTACT ADDRESS** Dept Eng, Brooklyn Col, CUNY, Brooklyn, NY, 11210.

ROGERS, PHIL
DISCIPLINE ENGLISH LITERATURE **EDUCATION** Harvard Univ, PhD. **CAREER** Dept Eng, Queen's Univ **RESEARCH** Medieval literature; comparative literature. **SELECTED PUBLICATIONS** Auth, pubs on medieval and modern literature and language. **CONTACT ADDRESS** English Dept, Queen's Univ, Kingston, ON, K7L 3N6.

ROGNESS, MICHAEL
DISCIPLINE HOMILETICS **EDUCATION** Augustana Col, BA; Luther Sem, SD, 56, BD, 60; Erlangen/Nurnberg Univ, ThD, 63. **CAREER** Instr, Inst for Ecumenical Res, Lutheran World Federation, Strasbourg, France, 67-70; assoc prof, 85; prof, 93-. **HONORS AND AWARDS** Fulbright scholar, Erlangen/Nurnberg Univ, 63., Pastor, St John's Lutheran Church, 64-67; First Lutheran Church, 70-85. **SELECTED PUBLICATIONS** Auth, Philip Melanchthon, Reformer, 69; The Church Nobody Knows - The Shape of the Future Church, 71; Follow Me, 77; Lutheran Doctrine, 84; The Hand that Holds Me - How God's Grace Touches Our Lives, 84; Hope in a Threatening World, 91; Preaching to a TV Generation - The Sermon in the Electronic Age, 95. **CONTACT ADDRESS** Dept of Homiletics, Luther Sem, 2481 Como Ave, St. Paul, MN, 55108. **EMAIL** mrogness@luthersem.edu

ROLLIN, LUCY
DISCIPLINE ENGLISH LITERATURE **EDUCATION** Emory Univ, PhD, 89. **CAREER** Dept Eng, Clemson Univ **RESEARCH** Children's literature. **SELECTED PUBLICATIONS** Auth, The Antic Art: Enhancing Children's Literary Experiences with Film and Video, Highsmith Press, 94; Arthur Rackham, Dictionary of Literary Biography,94; Dreaming in Public: The Psychology of Nursery Rhyme Illustration, Children's Lit Asn Quart, 94; ed, Mark Twain's The Prince and the Pauper, Oxford Univ Press, 96. **CONTACT ADDRESS** Clemson Univ, 314 Strode, Clemson, SC, 29634. **EMAIL** rlucy@clemson.edu

ROLLINS, PETER
DISCIPLINE AMERICAN/FILM STUDIES **EDUCATION** Harvard, PhD, 72. **CAREER** Comm Stu, Okla St Univ. **RESEARCH** Ethnic experience--dissertations on the Boston Irish; Mexican-American literature. **SELECTED PUBLICATIONS** Auth, Hollywood's World War I, Popular Press; Hollywood's Indian, UP Ky; Hollywood as Historian, UP Ky. **CONTACT ADDRESS** Oklahoma State Univ, 101 Whitehurst Hall, Stillwater, OK, 74078.

ROLLYSON, CARL E., JR.
PERSONAL Born 03/02/1948, Miami, FL, m, 1981, 1 child **DISCIPLINE** ENGLISH **EDUCATION** Mich State Univ, BA, 69; Univ Toronto, MA, 70, PhD, 75. **CAREER** Prof eng, Prof art, 87 to 95-, CUNY Baruch; Asst Prof, Assoc Prof, Prof, 76-87, Wayne State Univ. **HONORS AND AWARDS** Phi Beta Kappa; NEH Fel; ACLS Gnt; APS Gnt. **MEMBERSHIPS** Authors Guild. **RESEARCH** Biography **SELECTED PUBLICATIONS** Auth, Rebecca West: A Life, 96; the Many Lives of Norman Mailer, 91; Nothing Ever Happens to the Brave: The Story of Martha Geilhorn, 90; Lillian Hellman: Her Legend and Her Legacy, 88; Marilyn Monroe: A Life of the Actress, 86. **CONTACT ADDRESS** Baruch Col, CUNY, 17 Lexington Ave, Box 6-0732, New York, NY, 10010. **EMAIL** crlp@bellatlantic.net

ROMAN, CAMILLE
DISCIPLINE TWENTIETH-CENTURY AMERICAN AND BRITISH LITERATURE **EDUCATION** Brown, PhD. **CAREER** Asst prof, Washington State Univ. **HONORS AND AWARDS** Founding co-ed, Twayne's Music Series. **RESEARCH** 1950s maternal ideologies and poetry. **SELECTED PUBLICATIONS** Co-ed, The Women and Language Debate: A Sourcebook for Rutgers UP. **CONTACT ADDRESS** Dept of English, Washington State Univ, 1 SE Stadium Way, PO Box 645020, Pullman, WA, 99164-5020. **EMAIL** roman@wsu.edu

ROMANOW, WALTER I.
PERSONAL Born 04/29/1924, Saskatoon, SK, Canada **DISCIPLINE** COMMUNICATION STUDIES **EDUCATION** Univ Sask, BA, 51; Univ Windsor, MA, 64; Wayne State Univ, PhD, 74. **CAREER** Sta mgr, CFQC-TV, Saskatoon, 53-63; aide-de-camp, lt gov Sask, 60-63; lectr Eng, dir media ctr, 64-67, prof, 68-81, dean soc sci, 81-86, dean stud affairs, 86-87, PROF EMER COMMUNICATION STUD, UNIV WINDSOR. **MEMBERSHIPS** Int Press Asn; Asn Educ Jour; Can Commun Asn. **SELECTED PUBLICATIONS** Coauth, Mass Media and Political Processes in Canada, 83; coauth, Media Canada: An Introductory Analysis, 92, 2nd ed, 96; dir, Can J Commun, 82-87. **CONTACT ADDRESS** 11135 - 83 Ave, Ste 2101 College Plaza, Edmonton, AB, T6G 2C6.

ROMBES, NICHOLAS
DISCIPLINE EARLY AMERICAN LITERATURE **EDUCATION** Bowling Green State Univ, BS; Pa State Univ, MA, PhD. **CAREER** Asst prof, 95-. **HONORS AND AWARDS** Contrib, Heath Anthology of Amer Lit. **RESEARCH** Terrors of the enlightenment in early American fiction. **SELECTED PUBLICATIONS** Pub(s), articles on The Federalist Papers, Thomas Jefferson, Robert Frost, Salman Rushdie, and numerous early American authors; co-ed, intl peer-reviewed jour, Post Identity. **CONTACT ADDRESS** Dept of Eng, Univ Detroit Mercy, 4001 W McNichols Rd, PO BOX 19900, Detroit, MI, 48219-0900. **EMAIL** nick@libarts.udmercy.edu

RONALD, ANN
DISCIPLINE ENGLISH **EDUCATION** Northwestern Univ, PhD 70; Univ Colorado, MA 66; Whitman Col, BA 61. **CAREER** Western Lit Assoc, exec sec, pres exec coun, 78-81, 83-84; Western Amer Lit, Studies in Short Fiction, ISLE: ed board. **CONTACT ADDRESS** Dept of English, Univ of Nevada, Reno, NV, 89557. **EMAIL** ronald@unr.edu

RONAN, JOHN J.
PERSONAL Born 06/18/1944, San Diego, CA, m, 1987, 2 children **DISCIPLINE** MEDIA AND COMMUNICATIONS **EDUCATION** Loyola Univ, Chicago, BA, 67; Univ IL, Chicago, MA, 69. **CAREER** PROF, CHAIR, MEDIA AND COMMUNICATIONS, NORTH SHORE COMMUNITY COLLEGE, DANVERS, MA. **HONORS AND AWARDS** UCROSS Fellow, 94; NEA Fellow in Poetry, 99. **MEMBERSHIPS** Poetry Soc of Am; Academy of Am Poetry. **RESEARCH** Contemporary French poetry. **CONTACT ADDRESS** Box 5524, Gloucester, MA, 01930. **EMAIL** jronan@nscc.mass.edu

RONDA, BRUCE
DISCIPLINE ENGLISH LITERATURE **EDUCATION** Hope Col, BA; Yale Univ, PhD. **CAREER** Assoc prof. **SELECTED PUBLICATIONS** Auth, Intellect and Spirit: The Life and Work of Robert Coles,89; ed, The Letters of Elizabeth Palmer Peabody, American Renaissance Woman, 84. **CONTACT ADDRESS** Dept of English, Colorado State Univ, Fort Collins, CO, 80523. **EMAIL** bronda@vines.colostate.edu

ROOKE, CONSTANCE M.
PERSONAL Born 11/14/1942, New York, NY **DISCIPLINE** ENGLISH **EDUCATION** Smith Col, BA, 64; Tulane Univ , MA, 66; Univ NC, PhD, 73. **CAREER** Lectr, 69, asst prof, 73, assoc prof, 81, ch Women's Stud Prog, 79, dir, Learning & Teaching Centre, 81-83, Univ Victoria; prof English, 88-, dept ch, 88-93, ASSOCIATE VICE-PRES ACADEMIC, UNIV GUELPH 94-. **MEMBERSHIPS** Mem, Can Per Publs Asn; dir, Asn Can Univ Tchrs Eng; Can Res Inst Advan Women; exec, Can Fed Hum; bd dir, PEN Int, Can Ctr. **SELECTED PUBLICATIONS** Auth, Reynolds Price, 83; auth, Fear of the Open Heart, 89; ed, Night Light: Stories of Aging, 86; ed, Writing Away: The PEN-Canada Travel Anthology, 97. **CONTACT ADDRESS** Dept of English, Univ Guelph, Guelph, ON, N1G 2W1. **EMAIL** connier@exec.admin.uoguelph.ca

ROPER, ALAN
PERSONAL Born 07/17/1933, Bridgend, Wales, m, 1957, 1 child **DISCIPLINE** ENGLISH **EDUCATION** Cambridge Univ, BA, 57, MA, 61; Dalhousie Univ, MA, 59; Johns Hopkins Univ, PhD (English), 61. **CAREER** Instr, English, Harvard Univ, 61-62; supervisor, English, Queens' Col, Cambridge, 62-65; asst prof, 65-58, assoc prof, 68-71, prof, 71-94, PROF EMERITUS, UNIV CA, LOS ANGELES, 94-. **HONORS AND AWARDS** Res fel, Queens' Col, Cambridge, 62-65; Guggenheim fel, 69-70; assoc gen ed, works of John Dry-

den, 75-78, gen ed, 78-89; assoc investigator, NEH, 76-78, principal investigator, 78-85, 87-89; Clark Library Prof, 79-80. **MEMBERSHIPS** MLA. **RESEARCH** Dryden and seventeenth-century political poetry. **SELECTED PUBLICATIONS** Auth, Dryden's Poetic Kingdoms, Routledge & KP, 65; Arnold's Poetic Landscapes, Johns Hopkins Univ Press, 69; Drawing Parallels and Making Applications in Restoration Literature, in Politics as Reflected in Literature, Clark Library, 89; Dryden, Sunderland, and the Metamorphoses of a Trimmer, Huntington Library Quart, 91; How Much Did Farquhar's Beaux Spend in London? Studies in Bibliography, 92; co-ed, The Works of John Dryden, Vol XVIII, Univ CA Press, 74, Vol XI, 78, Vol XIX, 79, Vol XIII, 84, Vols V & VI, 87, Vol XX, 89, Vol XIV, 92. **CONTACT ADDRESS** Dept of English, Univ of California, Los Angeles, Los Angeles, CA, 90095-1530. **EMAIL** roper@humnet.ucla.edu

ROSA, ALFRED
DISCIPLINE ENGLISH **EDUCATION** Univ Conn, BA, 64; Univ Mass, MA, 66, PhD, 71. **CAREER** Prof Eng, Univ Vt; Fulbright lectr, Univ Sassari, Sardinia, 73-74; found & pres, New England Press, 78- . **HONORS AND AWARDS** Found, Mass Stud in Eng, Univ Mass, 67; trustee, Dick Raymond Found; trustee, Vt Commons Sch; pres, Vt chap, Fulbright Asn. **SELECTED PUBLICATIONS** Co-ed, Language Awareness, St Martin's; co-ed, Language: Introductory Readings, St Martin's; co-ed, Subject and Strategy, St Martin's; co-ed, Models for Writers, St Martin's; co-ed, Outlooks and Insights, St Martin's; co-ed, Themes for Writers, St Martin's; co-ed, Controversies: Contemporary Arguments for College Writers, Allyn & Bacon; co-ed, The Writer's Brief Handbook, Allyn & Bacon; ed, The Old Century and The New: Essays in Honor of Charles Angoff; auth, Salem, Transcendentalism, and Hawthorne. **CONTACT ADDRESS** Dept of English, Univ of Vermont, 304 Old Mill, Burlington, VT, 05405-4030. **EMAIL** arosa@zoo.uvm.edu

ROSE, PHYLLIS DAVIDOFF
PERSONAL Born 10/26/1942, New York, NY, 1 child **DISCIPLINE** ENGLISH LITERATURE **EDUCATION** Radcliffe Col, BA, 64; Yale Univ, MA, 65; Harvard Univ, PhD(English), 70. **CAREER** Asst prof, 69-76, assoc prof, 76-81, PROF ENGLISH, WESLEYAN UNIV, 81- ; vis prof, Univ Calif, Berkeley, 81-82. **HONORS AND AWARDS** Nat Endowment for Humanities grant, 73-74 **RESEARCH** Nineteenth and 20th century English literature; biography. **SELECTED PUBLICATIONS** Auth, Woman of Letters: A Life of Virginia Woolf, Oxford Univ, 78; auth, Parallel Lives, Knopf, 83; auth, Writing of Women, Wesleyan, 85; auth, Jazz Cleopatra: Josephine Baker in He Time, 89; ed, The Norton Book of Women's Lives, Norton, 93; auth, The Year of Reading Proust, Scribner, 97. **CONTACT ADDRESS** Dept of English, Wesleyan Univ, Middletown, CT, 06457.

ROSEN, KENNETH MARK
PERSONAL Born 03/07/1938, New York, NY, 2 children **DISCIPLINE** AMERICAN LITERATURE **EDUCATION** Cornell Univ, BA, 59; San Francisco State Univ, MA, 64; Univ NM, PhD, 69. **CAREER** Asst prof, 69-73, Assoc Prof Eng, 73-80, prof eng, Dickinson Col, 80-, Ford Found hum grants, 70-71 & 72; ed, Hemingway Notes, 71-74; sr Fulbright lectr Am lit, Univ Thessaloniki, Greece, 75-76, Beijing Univ, China, 80-81, Mada Univ, Gadjah Yogyakarta, Indonesia, 90-91. **MEMBERSHIPS** Assn Studies Am Indian Lit; MLA; Am Studies Asn; AAUP. **RESEARCH** The Am novel; Am Indian lit; Hemingway. **SELECTED PUBLICATIONS** Auth, O'Neill's Brown and Wilde's Gray, Mod Drama, 2/71; Kate Chopin's The Awakening: Ambiguity as art, J Am Studies, 8/71; Ten eulogies: Hemingway's Spanish death, Bull NY Pub Libr, 74; The Man to Send Rain Clouds, 74 & Voices of the Rainbow, 75, Viking; Heminway Repossessed, Praeger, 94. **CONTACT ADDRESS** Dept of Eng, Dickinson Col, 1 Dickinson Col, Carlisle, PA, 17013-2897.

ROSEN, ROBERT CHARLES
PERSONAL Born 12/29/1947, Brooklyn, NY, m, 1992, 1 child **DISCIPLINE** ENGLISH **EDUCATION** MIT, BS, Math, 70; Rutgers Univ, MA, PhD, Eng, 78. **CAREER** PROF, ENG, WILLIAM PATERSON UNIV, 78-. **RESEARCH** American literature; politics and literature **SELECTED PUBLICATIONS** auth, John Dos passos: Politics and the Writer, Univ of Nebr, 81; co-ed, Politics of Education: Essays from "Radical Teacher", SUNY Press, 90; coauth, Literature and Society: An Introduction to Fiction, Poetry, Drama, Nonfiction, Prentice-Hall, 90; coauth, Against the Current: Readings for Writers, Prentice Hall, 98. **CONTACT ADDRESS** Dept of English, William Paterson Col, 300 Pompton Rd, Wayne, NY, 07470. **EMAIL** rcrosen@pilot.njin.net

ROSENBERG, BETH C.
DISCIPLINE 20TH CENTURY BRITISH LITERATURE **EDUCATION** PhD, 92. **CAREER** Instr, Univ Nev, Las Vegas. **RESEARCH** Virginia Woolf. **SELECTED PUBLICATIONS** Auth, How Should One Write a Memoir?: Virginia Woolfs 'A Sketch of the Past', in Re:Reading, Re:Writing. Re: Teaching Virginia Woolf, eds, Eileen Barrett and Patricia Cramer, Pace UP, 95; Virginia Woolf and Samuel Johnson: Common Readers, St Martin's Press and Macmillan Publ, 95; Virginia Woolf, in The St James Guide to Feminist Writers,St James Press, 96; Sandra Gilbert and Susan Gubar, in The St. James Guide to Feminist Writers, St James Press, 96; '...in the wake of the matrons': Virginia Woolf's Rewriting of Fanny Burney, in Virginia Woolf: Texts and Contexts, eds, Beth Rigel Daugherty and Eileen Barrett, Pace UP, 96; coed, Virginia Woolf and the Essay, St Martin's Press and Macmillan Publ, 97. **CONTACT ADDRESS** Dept of Eng, Univ Nev, Las Vegas, 4505 Maryland Pkwy, PO Box 455011, Las Vegas, NV, 89154. **EMAIL** drbeth@nevada.edu

ROSENBERG, BRUCE
PERSONAL Born 07/27/1934, New York, NY, m, 1981, 4 children **DISCIPLINE** ENGLISH; FOLKLORE **EDUCATION** Hofstra Univ, BA, 55; Pa State Univ, MA, 62; Ohio State Univ, PhD, 65. **CAREER** Instr English, Univ Wis-Milwaukee, 62; asst prof, Univ Calif, Santa Barbara, 65-67 & Univ Va, 67-69; prof English & comp lit, Pa State Univ, 69-77; prof English lit & American Civilization, Brown Univ, 77-. **HONORS AND AWARDS** Am Coun Learned Soc fel, 67-68; James Russell Lowell Prize, 70; Nat Endowment for Humanities fel, 72-73; Guggenheim fel, 82-83; **MEMBERSHIPS** MLA; Folklore Fel Int; Am Folklore Soc. **RESEARCH** Middle English literature; folklore; comparative literature. **SELECTED PUBLICATIONS** Auth, Annus Mirabilis distilled, PMLA, 6/64; Wandering Angus & Celtic renaissance, Philol Quart, fall 67; Lord of the fire Flies, Centennial Rev, winter 67; ed, The Folksongs of Virginia, Univ Va, 69; auth, The Art of the American Folk Preacher, Oxford Univ, 70; co-ed, Medieval Literature and Folklore Studies, Rutgers Univ, 71; auth, Custer and the Epic of Defeat, Penn State, 75; The Code of the West, Ind Univ, 82; Teh Neutral Ground, 94. **CONTACT ADDRESS** Dept English, Brown Univ, 82 Waterman St, Providence, RI, 02912-0001. **EMAIL** AC401000@brown.edu

ROSENBERG, JOHN D.
DISCIPLINE ENGLISH LITERATURE **EDUCATION** Columbia Univ, BA, 50, MA, 51; Clare Col, BA, 53; Cambridge Univ, MA, 58; Columbia Univ, PhD, 60. **CAREER** Instr, Harvard Univ; Princeton Univ; Univ Brit Columbia; William Peterfield Trent prof, 62. **HONORS AND AWARDS** Kellett award; award for distinguished serv, Columbia Col Core Curriculum; Amer Coun of Learned Soc; fel, Guggenheim; fel, NEH., Ch, Hum prog; ed bd, Victorian Stud; Nineteenth-Century Lit; exec comm, MLA Victorian div; adv bd, Victorians Inst Jour; The Carlyle Annual. **RESEARCH** John Ruskin. **SELECTED PUBLICATIONS** Ed, works by Ruskin, Mayhew, Swinburne, and Tennyson; auth, The Darkening Glass, 61; The Fall of Camelot, 73; Carlyle and the Burden of History, 85. **CONTACT ADDRESS** Dept of Eng, Columbia Col, New York, 2960 Broadway, New York, NY, 10027-6902.

ROSENBERG, MARVIN
PERSONAL Fresno, CA, 1 child **DISCIPLINE** DRAMATIC ART **EDUCATION** Univ CA, AB, MA, PhD(English). **CAREER** Ed, Off War Inform, 43-45; chief Thailand sect, int broadcasting div, US Dept State, 45-47; prof emer, dramatic art, Univ Ca, Berkeley, 48-. **HONORS AND AWARDS** Guggenheim fel, Falger Library-British Academy fel; NEH fel. **MEMBERSHIPS** Shakespeare Asn Am; MLA; Int Fed Theatres Res; Int Shakespeare Asn. **RESEARCH** Literature and criticism of drama; Shakespeare; theatre history. **SELECTED PUBLICATIONS** Auth, The Masks of Othello, 61, The Masks of King Lear, 72 & The Masks of Macbeth, 78, Univ CA; The Masks of Hamlet, 92; The Adventures of a Shakespeare Scholar, 97. **CONTACT ADDRESS** Dept Dramatic Art, Univ California, 3210 Tolman Hall, Berkeley, CA, 94720-1651.

ROSENBLATT, JASON PHILIP
PERSONAL Born 07/03/1941, Baltimore, MD, m, 1964, 2 children **DISCIPLINE** ENGLISH LITERATURE **EDUCATION** Yeshiva Univ, BA, 63; Brown Univ, MA, 66, PhD, 68. **CAREER** Asst prof English, Univ PA, 68-74; asst prof, 74-76, assoc prof eng, Georgetown Univ, 76-83, prof of English, 83-; Vis lectr, Swarthmore Col, 72-73, Univ MD, spring, 80; Guggenheim Mem Found fel, 77. **HONORS AND AWARDS** Natl Endowment for Hum Fel, 84, 90-91; Milton Soc Amer Hanford Award, 88; Milton Soc Amer, vice pres, 98, pres elect, 99; Editorial board, Milton Soc, 92. **MEMBERSHIPS** Milton Soc Am. **RESEARCH** The works of John Milton; 17th century Eng relig poetry. **SELECTED PUBLICATIONS** Auth, Celestial entertainment in Eden: Book V of Paradise Lost, Harvard Theol Rev, 10/69; Structural unity and temporal concordance: The war in heaven in Paradise Lost, PMLA, 1/72; Adam's pisgah vision, J English Lit Hist, 3/72; The mosaic voice in Paradise Lost, In: Eyes Fast Fixt, Univ Pittsburgh, 75; Audacious Neighborhood: Idolatry in Paradise Lost, Book I, Philol Quart, summer 75; Aspects of incest in Hamlet, Shakespeare Quart, 78; Sir Edward Dering's Milton, Mod Philol, 5/82; Angelic tact: Raphael on creation, In: Milton and the Middle Ages, Bucknell Univ Press, 82; co ed, Not in Heaven: Coherence and Complexity in Biblical Narrative, IN Univ Press, 91; auth, Torah and Law in Paradise Lost, Princeton Univ Press, 94. **CONTACT ADDRESS** Dept of Eng, Georgetown Univ, PO Box 571131, Washington, DC, 20057-1131. **EMAIL** rosenblj@gunet.georgetown.edu

ROSENHEIM, JAMES MORTON
PERSONAL Born 07/12/1951, Chicago, IL **DISCIPLINE** ENGLISH HISTORY **EDUCATION** Harvard Univ, BA, 72; Princeton Univ, MA, 78, PhD, 81. **CAREER** Instr, Westminster Choir Col, 78-81, asst prof, 81-82; Asst Prof, 82-89, assoc prof hist, TX A&M Univ, 89, Assoc Head Dept Hist, 96-, Dir, Interdisciplinary Group for Hum Studies, 98. **MEMBERSHIPS** AHA; NAm Conf Brit Studies; ASECS. **RESEARCH** Early mod Eng soc hist; early mod Brit cult studies. **SELECTED PUBLICATIONS** Auth, The Townshends of Raynham: Nobility in Transition in Restoration and Early Hanoverian england, Wesleyan Univ Press, 89; co-ed, The First Modern Society: Essays in English History in Honour of Lawrence Stone, Cambridge Univ Press, 89; auth, The Notebook of Robert Doughty 1662-1665, Norfolk Record Soc, vol LIV, 91; Landownership, the Aristocracy, and the Country Gentry, In: The Reigns of Charles II and James VII and II, Macmillan Press Ltd, 97; The Emergence of a Ruling Order: English Landed Society 1650-1750, Addison Wesley Longman, 98; auth of other articles and publi. **CONTACT ADDRESS** Dept of Hist, Texas A&M Univ, College Station, TX, 77843-4236. **EMAIL** j-rosenheim1@tamu.edu

ROSENHEIM, SHAWN
DISCIPLINE ENGLISH **EDUCATION** Oberlin, BA, 84; Yale Univ, PhD, 92. **CAREER** Assoc prof. **RESEARCH** Nonfiction film; technology and culture, Hollywood film. **SELECTED PUBLICATIONS** Auth, The Cryptographic Imagination: Secret Writing from Edgar Poe to the Internet; co-ed, The American Face of Edgar Allan Poe; essays on literature and film in, Persistence of Hist, Film Quart, NY Times **CONTACT ADDRESS** Dept of English, Williams Col, Statson d-24, Williamstown, MA, 01267. **EMAIL** srosenheim@williams.edu

ROSENTHAL, JUDITH ANN
PERSONAL Born 08/22/1945, Syracuse, NY **DISCIPLINE** ENGLISH & AMERICAN LITERATURE **EDUCATION** State Univ NY Binghamton, BA, 66; Univ Pittsburgh, MA, 67, PhD(English), 70. **CAREER** Asst instr English, Univ Pittsburgh, 70-71; asst prof, 71-77, assoc prof, 77-79, PROF, CALIF STATE UNIV, FRESNO, 79-, Ed, Anonymous: A Journal for the Woman Writer, 73-75. **MEMBERSHIPS** MLA **RESEARCH** Women in literature; modern drama; Renaissance literature. **SELECTED PUBLICATIONS** Coauth, Norman Mailer: Prisoner of Sexism, Lilith, 4/71; auth, Anaisnin: Beyond race, culture, Calif Advocate, 5/74. **CONTACT ADDRESS** Dept of English, California State Univ, Fresno, 5245 N Baker, Fresno, CA, 93740-8001. **EMAIL** judithr@csufresno.edu

ROSENTHAL, MARGARET F.
DISCIPLINE ITALIAN RENAISSANCE ITALIAN LITERATURE **EDUCATION** Yale Univ, PhD. **CAREER** Asso prof, Univ Southern Calif. **RESEARCH** Women writers in early-modern Venice; social, cultural, political forces in Venice in the 16th century. **SELECTED PUBLICATIONS** Auth, The Honest Courtesan, Veronica Franco, Citizen and Writer in Sixteenth-Century Venice, 92. **CONTACT ADDRESS** Col Letters, Arts & Sciences, Univ Southern Calif, University Park Campus, Los Angeles, CA, 90089.

ROSENTHAL, MICHAEL
DISCIPLINE BRITISH LITERATURE AND CULTURE **EDUCATION** Harvard Univ, BA, 58; Univ Wis, MA, 59; Columbia Univ, PhD, 67. **CAREER** Prof. **SELECTED PUBLICATIONS** Auth, Virginia Woolf and The Character Factory: Baden-Powell's Boy Scouts and the Imperatives of Empire. **CONTACT ADDRESS** Dept of Eng, Columbia Col, New York, 2960 Broadway, New York, NY, 10027-6902.

ROSENWALD, LAWRENCE A.
DISCIPLINE ENGLISH **EDUCATION** Columbia Coll, BA, 70; Columbia, MA, 71, PhD, 79. **CAREER** PROF, ENG, WELLESLEY COLL **MEMBERSHIPS** Am Antiquarian Soc **SELECTED PUBLICATIONS** Auth, "Cotton Mather as Diarist," Prospects 8; auth, "Sewall's Diary and the Margins of Puritan Literature," Am Lit, 86; auth, Emerson and the Art of the Diary, Oxford, 88; auth, Theory, Texted Music, Performance," Jour of Musicol, Winter 93; ed & trans, Martin Buber and Franz Rosenzweig, Scripture and Translation, Ind Univ Press, 94. **CONTACT ADDRESS** Dept of Eng, Wellesley Col, Wellesley, MA, 02181. **EMAIL** lrosenwald@wellesley.edu

ROSOWSKI, SUSAN JEAN
PERSONAL Born 01/02/1942, Topeka, KS, m, 1963, 2 children **DISCIPLINE** AMERICAN LITERATURE, BRITISH ROMANTICS **EDUCATION** Whittier Col, BA, 64; Univ Ariz, MA, 67, PhD, 74. **CAREER** Instr, 71-76, Univ NE, Lincoln, Asst prof Brit romantics and women's studies, Univ NE, Omaha, 76-78, assoc prof, Univ NE, Omaha, 78-82, Univ NE, Lincoln, 82-86, Prof, Univ NE, Lincoln, 86-91, Adele Hall Prof, 91-97, Adele Hall distinguished prof, Univ NE, Lincoln, 97; Danforth Found Assoc, 80; Berdahl-Rolvaag lectr, Augustana Col, 86; vis scholar, Willamette Univ, 89; Lectr Eng Scholar series, Univ CA Davis, 89; vis scholar, St Lawrence Univ, 90; script consult, Singing Cather's Song: A Portrait of Mildred R Bennett, 89-90, and O Pioneers, 89-91. **HONORS AND**

AWARDS Great Tchr Award, Univ NE Omaha, 81; Annis Chaikin Sorensen Award, Distinguished Tchg, Hum, Univ NE Lincoln, 86; Fletcher Pratt fel, nonfiction, Bread Loaf Writer's Conf, 89; Univ NE Lincoln Recognition Award, Contr to Students, 89, 90, 94; Mildred R Bennett NE Lit Award, Outstanding Leadership & Serv, NE Center for the Bk, 94; Nebr Literary Heritage Asn, Honorary NE Author, 95-96. **MEMBERSHIPS** Counc Edof Learned Jour; MLA; Am Lit Asn; Western Lit Asn; Willa Cather Pioneer Mem and Educ Found; AAUP; Margaret Fuller Soc; Ellen Glasgow Soc; Soc for Textual Editing; Nebra Center for the Bk. **RESEARCH** Willa Cather; Am lit; Western and Plains lit; Women's studies. **SELECTED PUBLICATIONS** Auth, Thematic development in the comedies of William Congreve, Studies English Lit, summer 76; Joyce's Araby and Imaginative Freedom, Res Studies, 76; Willa Cather's A Lost Lady: The paradoxes of change, Novel, fall 77; Narrative technique in Willa Cather's My Mortal Enemy, J Narrative Tech, spring 78; The novel of awakening, Genre, fall 79; Willa Cather's women, Studies Am Fiction, 81; The pattern of Willa Cather's novels, Western Am Lit, 2/81; Willa Cather--a pioneer in art, Prairie Schooner, spring-summer 81; Margaret Atwood's Lady Oracle: Social mythology and the gothic novel, Res Studies, 81; Willa Cather's women, Studies in American Fiction, 81; Willa Cather's A Lost Lady: Art versus the closing frontier, Great Plains Quart, 82; Discovering symbolic meaning: Teaching with Willa Cather, English Jour, 12/82; co-ed, Women and Western American Literature, Whitston, 82; The Novel of Awakening, In: The Voyage In: Fictions of Female Development, Univ Press New Engl, 83; Willa Cather's Plains legacy: The early Nebraska stories, Nebr Humanist, 83; Willa Cather's American Gothic: Sapphira and the Slave Girl, Great Plains Quart, 84; co-auth, Willa Cather's 1916 Mesa Verde essay: The genesis of The Professor's House, Prairie Schooner, 84; Willa Cather's female landscapes: The Song of the Lark and Lucy Gayheart, Women's Studies, 84; Willa Cather: Living history, In: Perspectives: Women in Nebraska History, NE Dept Educ and NE State Coun Soc Sci, 6/84; Prototypes for Willa Cather's Flavia and Her Artists: The Canfield connection, Am Notes and Queries, May/June 85; The Voyage Perilous: Willa Cather's Romanticism, Univ NE Press, 86; co-auth, The Writings of Willa Cather: A Statement of Editorial Principles and Procedures, Univ NE Lincoln, 86; rev 87 & 88; The scholarshop of L Brent Bohlke, Willa Cather Pioneer Mem Newsletter, fall 87; Willa Cather and the fatality of place: O Pioneers!, My Antonia, and A Lost Lady, Geography and Literature, Syracuse Univ Press, 87; Foreward, Cather's Kitchen, Univ Nebr Press, 87; The Awakening as a Prototype of the Novel Awakening, Approaches to Teaching Chopin's the Awakening, MLA Am, 88; Margaret Atwood's Lady Oracle: Fantasy and the modern gothic novel, In: Critical Essays on Margaret Atwood, G K Hall, 89; Every reader's story: Teaching the romanticism of My Antonia, In: Approaches to Teaching My Antonia, MLA Am, 89; Willa Cather's Magnificat: Matriarchal Christianity in Shadows on the Rock, Lit and Belief, 89; Willa Cather's Pioneer Children and Immigrant Experience, Augustana Col, 89; Writing against silences: Female adolescent development in the novels of Willa Cather, Studies in the Novel, 89; ed-in-chief, Cather Studies, vol 1, 90, vol 2, 93, vol 3, 96, Univ Nebr Press; The Guilty Enjoyments of a library: Willa Cather's idea of a book, Nebr Lib Asn Quart, summer 90; Willa Cather's New World fiction: Gendered times and subverted feelings, In: Cather Studies, 90; Willa Cather's Chosen Family: Fictional Formations and Transformations, In: The Family and Community in Willa Cather's Fictions, BYU, 90; Willa Cather: A review essay, Mod Fiction Studies, spring 90; Margaret Fuller, and Engendered West, and Summer on the Lakes, Western Am Lit, summer 90; Cather in the Classroom, Nebr English Jour, fall 91; James Leslie Woodress Jr, In: Dictionary of Literary Biography: Twentieth-Century American Literature Biographers, Bruccoli Clark Layman, 91; Willa Cather, In: Twentieth-Century Western Writers, 2nd ed, St James Press, 91; Adaptations of O Pioneers! in the clasroom: Novel, play, and film, Nebr English Jour, fall 91; gen ed, The Cather Edition: O Pioneers!, by Willa Cather, Univ Nebr Press, 92; Willa Cather's visions and re-visions of female selves, In: Women's Artistry: Reenvisioning the Female Self, Edwin Mellen Press, 92; Willa Cather and the intimacy of art, or: In defense of privacy, Willa Cather Pioneer Mem Newsletter, winter 92-93; La femme, la Frontiere, et l'ecriture, In: Le Mythe de L'Quest, Autrement, 10/93; gen ed, The Cather Edition, My Antonia, by Willa Cather, Univ Nebr Press, 94; Willa Cather as a city novelist, In: Writing the City: Literaure and the Urban Experience, Routledge, 94; Cather's Manifesto for art -- Coming, Aphrodite!, Willa Cather Pioneer Mem Newsletter, 94; Variations on as single theme: Faces in a Single Tree, Clayfeld Rejoices, Clayfeld Laments, and Before It Vanishes, In: At An Elevation: On the Poetry of Robert Pack, Middlebury Col Press, 94; Afterword, Cather's University Days, Center for Great Plains Studies, 95; Writing the love plot our way: Women and work, In: Private Voices, Public Lives: Women Speak on the Literary Life, Univ North TX, 95; sr ed, Editing Cather, Studies in the Novel, 95; Willa Cather's ecology of place, Wester Am Lit, 5/95; Molly's Truthtelling, or Jean Stafford rewrites the Western, In: Reading the West: New Essays on the Literature of the American West, Cambridge Univ Press, 96; Willa Cather editing Willa Cather: From Houghton Mifflin to the House of Knopf, Studies in the Literary Imagination, 96; Prospects for the study of Willa Cather, In: Resources for American Literature Study, 96, and In: Prospects for the Study of American Literature: a Guide for Scholars and Students, NY Univ Press, 97; The Western Hero as logos, or, Unmaking meaning, Western Am Lit, 11/97; New Wests, In: Updating the Literary West, Tex Christian Univ Press, 97; gen ed, The Cather Edition, A Lost Lady, by Willa Cather, Univ NE Press, 97; The Place of Literature and the Cultural Phenomenon of Willa Cather, monogr, Univ NE Ed Services, 98; gen ed, The Cather Edition, Obsucre Destinies, Univ NE Press, in press; The Cather Edition, Death Comes for the Archbishop, Univ Nebr press, in press; Birthing a Nation: Gender, Creativity, and the Significance of the West in American Literature, Univ NE Press, in press. **CONTACT ADDRESS** Eng Dept, Univ of NE, PO Box 880333, Lincoln, NE, 68588-0333. **EMAIL** srosowsk@unlinfo.unl.edu

ROSS, BILLY I.
DISCIPLINE COMPUTER-ASSISTED REPORTING, EMERGING MEDIA TECHNOLOGIES **EDUCATION** Southern Ill Univ, PhD, 64. **CAREER** Distinguished vis prof, La State Univ; Dir, Jour sch, Tex Tech Univ. **MEMBERSHIPS** Mem, Accrediting Coun in Jour and Mass Commun; pres, Am Soc of Jour Sch Adminr, Am Acad of Advert. **SELECTED PUBLICATIONS** Auth, The Case Approach to Problem Situations, Advert Educ Works, 89; The Status of Advertising Education, Advert Educ Works, 91; coauth, Where Shall I Go To Study Advertising and Public Relations?, Advert Educ Works, 65; ed, Seventy-Five Years of Journalism and Mass Communication Leadership, Asn of Sch of Jour and Mass Commun, 93. **CONTACT ADDRESS** The Manship Sch of Mass Commun, Louisiana State Univ, Baton Rouge, LA, 70803.

ROSS, CATHERINE S.
PERSONAL Born 11/04/1945, London, ON, Canada **DISCIPLINE** COMMUNICATIONS **EDUCATION** Univ Toronto, MA, 68; Univ W Ont, BA, 67, PhD, 76. **CAREER** Fac mem, 73-, assoc dean, grad stud, 95-96, acting dean, Communications Open Learning, 96-97, PROF UNIV WESTERN ONTARIO. **HONORS AND AWARDS** Sci Writers Can Award, 97. **MEMBERSHIPS** Ont Lib Asn **SELECTED PUBLICATIONS** Auth, Circles: Shapes in Math, Science and Nature, 92; auth, A Double Life: A Biography of Alice Munroe, 92; auth, Triangles: Shapes in Math, Science and Nature, 94; coauth, Communicating Professionally, 89; ed, Recovering Canada's First Novelist: Proceedings from the John Richardson Conference, 84. **CONTACT ADDRESS** Elborn College, Univ of Western Ontario, London, ON, N6A 5B8. **EMAIL** ross@julian.uwo.ca

ROSS, DANIEL W.
PERSONAL Born 05/29/1952, Atlanta, GA, m, 1976, 2 children **DISCIPLINE** ENGLISH **EDUCATION** Univ Ga, ABJ, 74, MA, 77; Purdue Univ, PhD, 84. **CAREER** Asst prof, eng, Allentown Col of St. Francis de Sales, 85-89; asst prof, eng, Columbus State Univ, 90-95; chair, dept of lang and lit, Columbus State Univ, 95-. **MEMBERSHIPS** Mod Lang Asn. **RESEARCH** Southern literature; Victorian literature. **SELECTED PUBLICATIONS** Auth, The Critical Response to William Styron, Greenwood Press, 95; auth, Seeking a Way Home: The Uncanny in Wordsworth's Immortality Ode, 625-43, 92. **CONTACT ADDRESS** 6860 Ranch Forest Dr., Columbus, GA, 31904. **EMAIL** ross_daniel@colstate.edu

ROSSMAN, CHARLES R.
PERSONAL Born 02/13/1938, Brookings, SD, m, 1963, 2 children **DISCIPLINE** ENGLISH **EDUCATION** Calif State Col Los Angeles, BA, 62; Univ Southern Calif, MA, 65, PhD(-English), 68. **CAREER** Teacher English, Colegio Abelardo Moncayo, Ecuador, 62-63; assoc, Univ Calif, Los Angeles, 67-68; asst prof, 68-75, ASSOC PROF ENGLISH, UNIV TEX, AUSTIN, 75-90, DIR PLAN II HONORS PROG, 77-, Fulbright prof, Nat Univ, Mex, 72-73, Fulbright Prof, Paul Valery Univ, Montpelier France, 82; Prof English, 90-; Distinguished Teaching Prof, 96-. **MEMBERSHIPS** MLA **RESEARCH** Modern Latin American fiction; 20th century British literature. **SELECTED PUBLICATIONS** Auth, The Gospel According to D H Lawrence, spring 70, Lawrence on the Critic's Couch, summer 70 & Four Versions of Lawrence, spring 73, D H Lawrence Rev; auth, Stephen Dedalus's Villanelle, James Joyce Quart, spring 75; Art and Life in Joyce's Portrait, In: Forms of Modern British Fiction, Univ Tex, 75; Myth and Misunderstanding D H Lawrence, Bucknell Rev, 77; ed, Mario Vargas Llosa: A Collection of Critical Essays, Univ Tex, 78; ed, D H Lawrence Rev, 96. **CONTACT ADDRESS** Dept English, Univ Tex, Austin, TX, 78712-1026. **EMAIL** rossman@mail.utexas.edu

ROSTECK, H. THOMAS
DISCIPLINE COMMUNICATION AND CULTURE AND RHETORICAL STUDIES **EDUCATION** Univ Wisc, PhD. **CAREER** Comm Stu, Univ Ark **HONORS AND AWARDS** Dir, Depts Undergrad Honors Prog. **SELECTED PUBLICATIONS** Auth, See It Now Confront McCarthyism: Television Documentary and the Politics of Representation, Univ Alab Press. **CONTACT ADDRESS** Univ Ark, Fayetteville, AR, 72701.

ROTH, LANE
PERSONAL Born 00/00/1943, New York, NY **DISCIPLINE** CINEMA, COMMUNICATIONS **EDUCATION** NY Univ, BA, 64; Fla State Univ, MA, 74, PhD, 76. **CAREER** Asst prof, Univ Evansville, 76-78; assoc prof, 78-82; ASSOC PROF, COMMUN, LAMAR UNIV, 82-. **HONORS AND AWARDS** National German Honors, 64; Regents' Merit Award for Teaching Excellence, Lamar Univ, 80. **MEMBERSHIPS** Intl Asn for the Fantastic in Arts, Bd, Mental Health Asn Jefferson Cty; pres of the bd, 1997- **RESEARCH** Jungian psychol, literary criticism, philos. **SELECTED PUBLICATIONS** Auth, Humanity, Technology and Comedy in Microbi, a Hungarian Animated Science Fiction Television Series, World Communication, 93; Co-auth, G. M. Broncho Billy" Anderson: The First Movie Cowboy Hero, in Back in the Saddle: Essays on Western Film and Television Actors, McFarland Publ, 98. **CONTACT ADDRESS** Communications Dept, Lamar Univ, PO Box 10050, Beaumont, TX, 77710-0050.

ROTH, LORNA
PERSONAL Montreal, PQ, Canada **DISCIPLINE** COMMUNICATION STUDIES **EDUCATION** McGill Univ, Cert Educ, 67, MA, 83; Concordia Univ, BA, 72, PhD, 94. **CAREER** Tchr, 68-73; cross-cultural Commun & Educ Consult, private sector, 77-93; lectr, 92-94, ASST PROF COMMUN STUDS, CONCORDIA UNIV, 94-. **MEMBERSHIPS** Ctr Res/Action Race Relations; Can Commun Asn; Asn Can Univs Northern Studs; Fel, Commun Studs & Public Affairs; Can Asn Journalists. **SELECTED PUBLICATIONS** Auth, Election Broadcasting in Canada, Vol 21, 91; auth, Mohawk Airwaves and Cultural Challenges: Some Reflections on the Politics of Recognition and Cultural Appropriation After the Summer of 1990, in Can J Commun, Vol 18, 93; auth, Seeing Ourselves: Media Power and Policy in Canada, 96. **CONTACT ADDRESS** Dept of Commun Studies, Concordia Univ, Montreal, Montreal, PQ, H4B 1R6. **EMAIL** roth@odyssee.net

ROTH, PHYLLIS ANN
PERSONAL Born 01/06/1945, New York, NY, d **DISCIPLINE** ENGLISH LITERATURE **EDUCATION** Clark Univ, AB, 66; Univ Conn, MA, 67, PhD(English), 72. **CAREER** Instr, Univ Conn, 67; from instr to asst prof, Northeastern Univ, 69-76; asst prof, 76-78, from assoc prof English, Skidmore Col, 78-85; dept chmn, 85-89; dean fac, 90-; act pres, 92; interim pres, 99. **MEMBERSHIPS** AAUP; MLA; NCTE. **RESEARCH** Literary theory; fiction. **SELECTED PUBLICATIONS** Auth, In search of aesthetic bliss: A rereading of Lolita, Col Lit, winter 75; The psychology of the double in Nabakov's Pale Fire, Essays in Lit, Fall 75; Suddenly sexual women in Bram Stoker's Dracula, Lit & Psychol, Fall 77; Nabokov: The man behind the mystification, In: Nabokov's Fifth Arc, 82; Bram Stoker, 82; G K Hall, Critical Essays on Vladimir Nahokov, ed, G K Hall, 84. **CONTACT ADDRESS** Dept of English, Skidmore Col, 815 N Broadway, Saratoga Springs, NY, 12866-1698. **EMAIL** paroth@skidmore.edu

ROTHFORK, JOHN G.
PERSONAL Born 12/18/1946, Holstein, IA, m, 1966, 1 child **DISCIPLINE** AMERICAN STUDIES, LITERATURE **EDUCATION** Morningside Col, BA, 68; Univ Iowa, MA, 70; Truman Univ, MA, 73; Univ NMex, PhD(Am studies), 73. **CAREER** Assoc prof philos & English, NMex Inst Mining & Technol, 70-98, asst prof English, Cent Ark Univ, 74-75; ed, NMex Humanities Rev, 78-82; lectr, Univ NMex, 79-80; Fulbright lectr, Indian Inst Technol, 81-82; Fulbright lectr, Tokyo Univ, Keio Univ, 85; prof Am Lit, Mukogawa Women's Univ, Japan, 98-. **MEMBERSHIPS** MLA; Am Philos Asn; Rocky Mountain Mod Lang Asn. **RESEARCH** Technology and values; comparative religion. **SELECTED PUBLICATIONS** Auth, Grokking god: Phenomenology in NASA & Science Fiction, Res Studies, 76; Transcendentalism and Henry Barnard's School Architecture, J Gen Educ, 77; The Buddha Center in Conrad's Youth, Lit East & West, 77; Indians (poems), Northwoods Press, 80; Having Everything is Having Nothing, Southwest Rev, 81; Uber Stanislaw Lem, Suhrkamp, 81; auth, V S Naipaul and the Third World, Res Studies, 81; Hindu Mysticism in the Twentieth Century: R K Narayan's The Guide, Philol Quart (in prep). **CONTACT ADDRESS** English Dept, Muskogawa Women's Univ, 6-46 Ikebiraki-cho, Nishinomiya, ., 663. **EMAIL** rothfork@zdnetmail.com

ROTHMAN, IRVING N.
PERSONAL Born 04/10/1935, Pittsburgh, PA, m, 1962, 2 children **DISCIPLINE** ENGLISH LITERATURE **EDUCATION** Univ Pittsburgh, BA, 57; Univ Pittsburgh, MA, 59; Univ Pittsburgh, PhD, 67. **CAREER** Asst prof, Univ Houston, 67-73; mem grad fac, Univ Houston, 71; assoc prof, Univ Houston, 73-80; prof, Univ Houston, 80-. **CONTACT ADDRESS** Department of English, Univ of Houston, Houston, TX, 77204-3012. **EMAIL** irothman@uh.edu

ROTHWELL, KENNETH SPRAGUE
PERSONAL Born 05/26/1921, Bay Shore, NY, m, 1954, 4 children **DISCIPLINE** ENGLISH **EDUCATION** Univ NC, BA, 48; Columbia Univ, Ma, 49, PhD(English), 56. **CAREER** Instr English, Univ Kans, 49-50, Univ Rochester, 52-55 & Univ Cincinnati, 55-57; asst prof, Univ Kans, 57-62, from assoc prof

to prof 62-70; chmn dept, 70-76, PROF ENGLISH, UNIV VT, 76-, Am Philos Soc grant-in-aid, 63 & 68; co-ed, Shakespeare on Film Newsletter, 76- **MEMBERSHIPS** Malone Soc; Renaissance Soc Am; MLA; Cent Renaissance Conf (pres, 69); Shakespeare Asn Am. **RESEARCH** Shakespeare and the Elizabethans; Shakespeare and film. **SELECTED PUBLICATIONS** Auth, Questions of Rhetoric and Usage, Little, 70; A Mirror for Shakespeare, IDC, 80; auth, Shakespeare on Screen: An International Filmography and Videography, 90. **CONTACT ADDRESS** Dept of English, Univ of Vt, Burlington, VT, 05405. **EMAIL** krothwell@zoo.uvm.edu

ROUSSELOW, JESSICA
DISCIPLINE COMMUNICATION ARTS **EDUCATION** Univ MN, PhD. **CAREER** Prof, 67-, assoc dean, Div Fine and Appl Arts, Taylor Univ. **SELECTED PUBLICATIONS** Coauth, God's Ordinary People, No Ordinary Heritage. **CONTACT ADDRESS** Taylor Univ, Upland, IN, 46989.

ROWAN, KATHERINE E.
PERSONAL Born 02/17/1954, Alexandra, VA **DISCIPLINE** ENGLISH, RHETORIC AND COMPOSITION, SPEECH COMMUNICATION **EDUCATION** George Mason Univ, Fairfax, VA, BA (English Lit), 75; Univ IL, Urbana-Champaign, MA (Speech Commun), 78; Purdue Univ, PhD (English), 85. **CAREER** Teaching asst, Dept of Speech Commun, Univ IL, Urbana, 76-79; lect, English div, Parkland Col, Champaign, Il, 78-79; lect, Dept of Rhetoric & Commun, SUNY, Albany, 79-81; lect, Master's in Managrment Prog, Col of St Rose, Albany, NY, 80; lect, Dept of English (evening div), Russell Sage Col, Troy, NY, 80-81; teaching asst, Dept of English, Purdue Univ, 82-84; graduate instr, 84-85, asst prof, 85-91, assoc prof, 91-95, prof, Dept of Commun, Purdue Univ, West Lafayette, IN, 96-. **HONORS AND AWARDS** Graduated magna cum laude, George Mason Univ, 75; listed, Who's Who Among American Colleges and Universities; Phi Kappa Phi, Purdue Univ, 83; David Ross Summer res fel, Dept of English, Purdue Univ, 84; Gannett Foun Teaching fel, IN Univ, Bloomington, 87; Poynter Inst Teaching fel, Poynter Inst for Media Studies, St Petersburg, FL, 88; X-L Summer res grant, Purdue Univ, 86, 90; Outstanding Young Teacher Award, Central States Commun Asn, 90; Purdue Univ School of Liberal Arts Educational Excellence Award, 91; Top 3 Paper, Public Relations Interest Group, Int Commun Asn, 92; directed two master's theses which won the Outstanding Master's Thesis Award, Health Commun Div of the Nat Commun Asn and Int Commun Asn (Rose G Campbell, 94, and Susan L Smith, 96). **MEMBERSHIPS** Asn for Ed in Journalism and Mass Commun; Int Commun Asn; Nat Commun Asn; Nat Coun of Teachers of English; Phi Kappa Phi; Soc of Professional Journalists. **SELECTED PUBLICATIONS** Auth, review of Psycholinguistics of Readable Writing, by Alice S Horning, Commun Theory, 4, 94; Why Rules for Risk Communication Fail: A Problem-Solving Approach to Risk Communication, Risk Analysis, 14, 94; The Technical and Democratic Approaches to Risk Situations: Their Appeal, Limitations, and Rhetorical Alternative, Argumentation, 8, 94; Expository Writing, in A C Purves, ed, Encyclopedia of English Studies and Language Arts, vol 1, Scholastic, Inc, 94; with M R Dennis, R A Feinberg, R Widdows, and R E Crable, Corporate Civil Disobedience in the Consumer Interest: The Case of Kellogg's Catalytic Defiance of FDA Health Claim Laws, Advancing the Consumer Interest, 6, 94; with D M Hoover, Communicating Risk to Patients: Detecting, Diagnosing, and Overcoming Lay Theories, Communicating Risk to Patients, US Pharmacopeial Convention, 94; What Risk Communicators Need to Know: An Agenda for Research, in B R Burleson, ed, Communication Yearbook, 18, Sage, 95; A New Pedagogy for Explanatory Speaking: Why Arrangement Should Not Substitute for Invention, Conmmunication Education, 44, 95; Exposition, in T Enos, ed, Encyclopedia of Rhetoric and Composition: Communication from Ancient Times to the Information Age, Garland Pub, 96; numerous other publications. **CONTACT ADDRESS** Dept of Commun, Purdue Univ, West Lafayette, IN, 47907. **EMAIL** rowan@purdue.edu

ROWAN, STEPHEN C.
DISCIPLINE ENGLISH LITERATURE **EDUCATION** Fairfield Univ, BA, 66; St Mary's Sem and Univ, STB, 68; Univ Brit Columbia, MA, 75, Doctorate, 85. **CAREER** Instr, Seattle Univ. **MEMBERSHIPS** Shakespeare Asn of Am; Pacific Northwest Renaissance Soc; Conf on Christianity and Lit; MLA. **SELECTED PUBLICATIONS** Auth, 'Religiously the Ask A Sacrifice': The Strategy and the Theme of the Scapegoat in Titus Androicus, Symp, Seattle Univ, 87; Words From the Cross, Twenty Third Publ, 88; The Nicene Creed: Poetic Words for a Prosaic World, Stu in Formative Spirituality, Duquesne Univ, 89; The Nicene Creed: Poetic words for a Prosaic World, Twenty third Publ, 90; Much Have I Travelled in the Realms of Gold, Spiritual Life, 94; The Parables of Calvary: Reflections on the Last Words of Jesus, Twenty Third Publ, 94. **CONTACT ADDRESS** Seattle Univ, Seattle, WA, 98122-4460. **EMAIL** srowan@seattleu.edu

ROWE, ANNE ERVIN
PERSONAL Born 09/05/1945, Gainesville, FL, m, 1963, 3 children **DISCIPLINE** AMERICAN LITERATURE **EDUCATION** Fla State Univ, BA, 67; Univ NC, Chapel Hill, MA, 69, PhD, 73. **CAREER** Vis Asst Prof, 72-73, from Asst Prof to Assoc Prof, 73-84, prof English, Fla State Univ, 84-. **MEMBERSHIPS** MLA; South Atlantic Mod Lang Asn; Col English Asn. **SELECTED PUBLICATIONS** Auth, The Enchanted Country: Northern Writers in the South, 1865-1910, 78 & Lefcadio Hearn, In: A Bibliographical Guide to Southern Literature, 79, La State Univ Press; The Idea of Florida in the American Literary Imagination, La State Univ Press, 86. **CONTACT ADDRESS** Dept of English, Florida State Univ, 600 W College Ave, Tallahassee, FL, 32306-1096.

ROWE, JOYCE A.
DISCIPLINE 19TH CENTURY AMERICAN LITERATURE AND CULTURE **EDUCATION** Columbia, PhD. **CAREER** Assoc prof; dept ch, Fordham Univ. **SELECTED PUBLICATIONS** Auth, Equivocal Endings in Classic American Novels Cambridge UP, 88; Social History and the Politics of Manhood in Melville's Redburn, Mosaic 26, 93. **CONTACT ADDRESS** Dept of Eng Lang and Lit, Fordham Univ, 113 W 60th St, New York, NY, 10023.

ROWE, KAREN E.
PERSONAL Born 07/26/1945, Philadelphia, PA **DISCIPLINE** ENGLISH **EDUCATION** Mount Holyoke Col, AB (with Great Distinction, Magna Cum Laude), 67; IN Univ, MA, 67, PhD, 71. **CAREER** Assoc instr, IN Univ, 69-70; asst prof, English, 71-79, assoc prof, 79-97, PROF OF ENGLISH, UCLA, 97-, Dir, UCLA Center for the Study of Women, 84-88. **HONORS AND AWARDS** Woodrow Wilson Dissertation Year fel, 70-71; NEH fel for Independent Study and Res, 77-78; fel, Radcliffe Inst for Independent study, 77-78; fel, Univ CA Management Inst, 81; Bryn Mawr/HERS Mid-America Inst for Women in Higher Ed Admin, 86., Sarah Williston Scholar, Phi Beta Kappa, 65. **RESEARCH** Early Am lit to 1800; women's lit (17th-20th Am and British); English Renaissance and seventeenth-century lit; English poetry; French and British fairy tales and folklore; curriculum and institutional multiculturalism. **SELECTED PUBLICATIONS** Auth, Sacred or Profane?: Edward Taylor's Meditations on Canticles, Modern Philol 72, 74; Feminism and Fairy Tales, Women's Studies: An Interdisciplinary J, 6, 79, numerous reprints; Fairy-born and Human-bred: Jane Eyre's Education in Romance, in The Voyage In: Fictions of Female Development, ed Elizabeth Abel, Marianne Hirsch, and Elizabeth Langland, Univ Press, New England, 83; Prophetic Visions: Typology and Colonial American Poetry, in Puritan Poets and Poetics: Seventeenth-Century American Poetry in Theory and Practice, ed Peter White, PA State Univ Press, 85; Saint and Singer: Edward Taylor's Typology and the Poetics of Meditation, Cambridge Univ Press, 86, numerous reprints; To Spin a Yarn: The Female Voice in Folklore and Fairy Tale, in Fairy Tales and Society: Illusion, Allusion, and Paradigm, ed Ruth B. Bottigheimer, Univ PA Press, 86; Shifting Models, Creating Visions: Process and Pedagogy for Curriculum Transformation, in Women of Color and the Multicultural Curriculum: Transforming the College Classroom, ed Liza Fiol-Matta and Mariam K. Chamberlain, The Feminist Press, 94; Multiculturalism and the Humanities Core: From Policy to Pedagogy, in Selected Papers from the Texas Seminar on the Core Curriculum, 1993, 1994, 1995, ed Shirley D. Ezell and Cay Smith Osmon, Univ Houston and NEH, 95; The Rise of Women's Education in the United States and Korea: A Struggle for Educational and Occupational Equality, co-auth with Byong-Suh Kim, Asian J of Women's Studies 3, 97; In The Heath Anthology of American Literature, ed Paul Lauter, Richard Yarborough, et al, 3rd ed, 2 vols, Houghton Mifflin, 98; numerous other publications. **CONTACT ADDRESS** Dept of English, Univ of California, Los Angeles, Box 90095-1530, Los Angeles, CA, 90095-1530.

ROWLAND, BERYL
PERSONAL Scotland **DISCIPLINE** ENGLISH **EDUCATION** Univ London, BA, 80; Univ Alta, MA, 58; Univ BC, PhD, 62. **CAREER** Asst prof, 62-68, assoc prof, 68-71, prof, 71-83, DISTINGUISHED PROF EMER ENGLISH, YORK UNIV, 83-; DLitt (hon), Mt St Vincent Univ, 82. **HONORS AND AWARDS** Alta Golden Jubilee Drama Award, 55; Am Univ Presses Bk Award, 74; Huntington Fel, Int Asn Univ Profs Eng, 76; Canada 125 Medal, 93. **MEMBERSHIPS** Asn Can Univ Tchrs Eng; Hum Asn; Eng Asn; MLA; New Chaucer Soc. **SELECTED PUBLICATIONS** Auth, Blind Beasts: Chaucer's Animal World, 71; auth, Animals with Human Faces, 73; auth, Birds with Human Souls, 78; auth, Earl Birney: Chaucerian Irony, 85; auth, Chaucer's Working Wyf: The Unraveling of a Yarn Spinner, in Chaucer in the Eighties, 96. **CONTACT ADDRESS** Dept of English, York Univ, North York, ON, V8W 2Y2.

ROWLAND, GORDON
DISCIPLINE COMMUNICATION STUDIES **EDUCATION** Univ Ind, PhD. **CAREER** Assoc prof. **SELECTED PUBLICATIONS** Auth, pubs on include design, learning systems, and design education. **CONTACT ADDRESS** Dept of Communication, Ithaca Col, 100 Job Hall, Ithaca, NY, 14850.

ROWLINSON, MATTHEW C.
DISCIPLINE ENGLISH LITERATURE **EDUCATION** Cornell Univ, PhD, 86. **CAREER** Assoc prof, Dartmouth Col. **RESEARCH** Romantic and Victorian Brit lit; Tennyson. **SELECTED PUBLICATIONS** Auth, Tennyson's Fixations: Psychoanalysis and the Topics of the Early Poetry, UP Va, 94; The Skipping Muse: Repetition and Difference in Two Early Poems of Tennyson, Victorian Poetry, 84, rptd in Critical Essays on Alfred Lord Tennyson, G.K. Hall, 93. **CONTACT ADDRESS** Dartmouth Col, 3529 N Main St, #207, Hanover, NH, 03755.

ROY, ABHIK
PERSONAL Born 01/26/1954, Calcutta, India, m, 1991 **DISCIPLINE** COMMUNICATIONS **EDUCATION** St Xavier's Col, BS, 72; Univ of Calcutta, LLB, 75; Univ of Kansas, MS, 85, PhD, 96. **CAREER** Acct exec, Phoenix Advert Ltd, 75-79; sen acct exec, Kenyon & Eckhardt, 79-81; Phoenix Advert Ltd, 81-82; asst prof, Mankato State Univ, 88-91; commun consult, 91-93; asst prof, Metrop State Univ, 93- . **HONORS AND AWARDS** Kappa Tau Alpha. **MEMBERSHIPS** Nat Commun Asn, Int Commun Asn. **RESEARCH** Media globalization and local resistance; Media representation of race, gender, ethnicity and age. **SELECTED PUBLICATIONS** Coauth, Underrepresented, positively portrayed: Older adults in television commercials, Jour of Applied Commun Res, 25, 97; auth, Marion Barry's road to redemption: A textual analysis of ABC's news story aired on 14 September 1994, The Howard Jour of Commun, 7, 96; Images of domesticity and motherhood in Indian television commercials: A critical study, Jour of Popular Cult, forthcom.; Images of women in Indian television commercials: A critical study, forthcom.; Indian press response to international satellite television: A textual analysis, Television in Asia, eds M. Richards & D. French, forthcom. **CONTACT ADDRESS** Dept of Communications, Metropolitan State Univ, 4920 Penn Ave S, Minneapolis, MN, 55409-2261. **EMAIL** royab001@metvax.metro.msus.edu

ROY, EMIL L.
PERSONAL Born 06/18/1933, Fremont, NE **DISCIPLINE** ENGLISH **EDUCATION** Univ Redlands, BA, 55; Univ Calif, Berkeley, MA, 56; Univ Southern Calif, PhD(English), 61. **CAREER** Instr English, Fullerton Jr Col, 57-59 & Cerritos Col, 60-61; from instr to asst prof, Univ Southern Calif, 61-66; assoc prof, Northern Ill Univ, 66-68; Purdue Univ, West Lafayette, 68-73 & Univ PR, Mayaguez, 73-74; prof English & chm dept, Univ Tenn, Martin, 74-75; prof English & Acad Dean, Univ Sc, Aiken, 75-, Fulbright prof, Univ Kiel, Ger, 64-65. **MEMBERSHIPS** MLA **SELECTED PUBLICATIONS** Coauth, Studies in Fiction, Harper, 65; auth, King Lear and Desire Under the Elms, Die Neueren Sprachen, 1/66; Studies in Drama, Harper, 68; Christopher Fry, 68 & British Drama Since Shaw, 72, Southern Ill Univ, War and Manliness in TrC, Comp Drama, 72; coauth, Literary Spectrum, Allyn & Bacon, 74; Literature I, Macmillan, 76. **CONTACT ADDRESS** Univ of S. Carolina, 171 University Pky., Aiken, SC, 29801-6309. **EMAIL** Emilroy@hotmail.com

ROY, GEORGE ROSS
PERSONAL Born 08/20/1924, Montreal, PQ, Canada, m, 1954, 1 child **DISCIPLINE** ENGLISH, COMPARATIVE LITERATURE **EDUCATION** Concordia Univ, BA, 50; Univ Montreal, MA, 51, PhD(English), 59; Univ Strasbourg, dipl, 54; Univ Paris, DUniv(comp lit), 58. **CAREER** Lectr English, Royal Mil Col, St Jean, 54-56; asst prof, Univ Ala, 58-61; from asst prof to assoc prof, Univ Montreal, 61-63; prof, Tex Technol Univ, 63-65; prof English & Comp Lit, Univ SC, 65-90; Huntington Libr grant, 62; Can Coun & Am Philos Soc grant, 63; founding mem bd gov & chmn libr comt, Am-Scottish Found, NY, 66-; founding ed, Studies in Scottish Lit, 63- ; gen ed, Scottish Poetry Reprints, Quarto Press, London & Dept English Bibliog Ser, Univ SC. **HONORS AND AWARDS** Founding vice-pres, Asn for Scottish Lit Stud; fel, Soc of Antiq of Scotland; hon life pres, Robert Burns Federation; Robert Burce Award, Old Dominion Univ; distinguished prof Univ S Carolina, 89. **MEMBERSHIPS** Int Comp Lit Asn; Am Comp Lit Asn; MLA; S Atlantic MLA; Edinburgh Bibl Soc; Thomas Carlyle Soc; James Boswell Soc. **RESEARCH** Comparative literature; Scottish literature; Robert Burns. **SELECTED PUBLICATIONS** Auth, Editing the Makars in the Eighteenth and Early Nineteenth Centuries, in Strauss, ed, Scottish Language and Literature, Medieval and Renaissance, Frankfurt am Main, 86; auth, The Bible in Burns and Scott, in Wright, ed, The Bible in Scottish Literature, Edinburgh, 88; auth, Scottish Poets and the French Revolution, Etudes Ecossaises, 92, auth, Editing Burns' Letters in the Twentieth Century, in Carnie, ed, Robert Burns: Some Twentieth-Century Perspectives, Calgary, 93; auth, Editing Robert Burns in the Nineteenth Century, in Simpson, ed, Burns Now, Edinburgh, 94. **CONTACT ADDRESS** Dept of English, Univ of SC, Columbia, SC, 29208.

ROY, PARAMA
DISCIPLINE ENGLISH LITERATURE **EDUCATION** Univ Delhi, BA; Univ Rochester, MA, PhD. **CAREER** PROF, UNIV CALIF, RIVERSIDE. **RESEARCH** Analysis of colonial discourse and postcolonial theory and literatures. **SELECTED PUBLICATIONS** Auth, The Victorians Inst Jour, 89; Studies

in English Literature 1500-1900, 89; Indian Traffic: Identities in Question in Colonial and Postcolonial India, Univ Calif Press, 99. **CONTACT ADDRESS** Dept of Eng, Univ Calif, 1156 Hinderaker Hall, Riverside, CA, 92521-0209. **EMAIL** proy@ucracl.ucr.edu.

ROZBICKI, MICHAEL J.
PERSONAL Born 06/24/1946, Gdynia, m, 1991, 1 child **DISCIPLINE** ENGLISH LITERATURE/HISTORY **EDUCATION** Warsaw Univ, Poland, MA, 70, PhD, 84; Maria Curie-Sklodowska Univ, Poland, 75. **CAREER** Asst prof to assoc prof, 76-92, Warsaw Univ; asst prof to assoc prof, 92-, St Louis Univ. **HONORS AND AWARDS** Free Univ Berlin Fel, 82, 89; Oxford Univ Fel, 84; Rockefeller Found Fel, 90; John Carter Brown Libr Fel, 86; Huntington Libr Fel, 91; Amer Coun of Learned Soc Fel, 79-80. **MEMBERSHIPS** AAUP; Org Amer Hist. **RESEARCH** Cultural hist of colonial British Amer **SELECTED PUBLICATIONS** Auth, Transformation of English Cultural Ethos in Colonial America: Maryland 1634-1720, Univ Press Amer, 88; auth, The Birth of a Nation: History of the United States of American to 1860, Interim Publ House, Warsaw, 91; art, Between East-Central Europe and Britain: Reformation, Science, and the Emergence of Intellectual Networks in Mid-Seventeenth Century, E Europe Quart, 96; art, The Curse of Provincialism: Negative Perceptions of Colonial American Plantation Gentry, J S Hist, 97; auth, A Bridge to a Barrier to American Identity? The Uses of European Taste among Eighteenth-Century Plantation Gentry in British American, Amerikastudien, Heidelberg, 98; auth, The Complete Colonial Gentleman: Cultural Legitimacy in Plantation America, Univ Press Va, 98. **CONTACT ADDRESS** Dept of History, St. Louis Univ, 3800 Lindell Blvd, PO Box 56907, St. Louis, MO, 63156-0907. **EMAIL** rozbicmj@slu.edu

ROZEMA, HAZEL J.
PERSONAL Born 10/16/1953, Grand Rapids, MI, m **DISCIPLINE** COMMUNICATION **EDUCATION** Calvin Col, BA, 75; Mich State Univ, MA, 76; Univ Kans, PhD, 81. **CAREER** Asst prof, Univ Ark, at Little Rock, 83-88; assoc prof & ch, commun dept, Millikin Univ, 88-95; prof & ch, Mankato State Univ, 95-97; asst prof, commun dept, Univ Ill, 97-. **HONORS AND AWARDS** Outstanding Teacher Award, Univ Kans, Millikin Univ; Faculty Scholar Award, Univ Ark. **MEMBERSHIPS** Nat Commun Assoc; CSSA; PCA. **RESEARCH** Interpersonal & organizational communications; diversity & gender communications; sex education. **SELECTED PUBLICATIONS** Var articles in Family Relations, The Speech Communication Teacher. **CONTACT ADDRESS** 11 Baker Lane, Decatur, IL, 62526. **EMAIL** rozema.hazel@uis.edu

RUBEN, BRENT DAVID
PERSONAL Born 10/17/1944, Cedar Rapids, IA, m, 1967, 2 children **DISCIPLINE** COMMUNICATION **EDUCATION** Univ Iowa, BA, 66, MA 68, PhD, 70. **CAREER** Inst of Mass Commun, 68-70, asst prof of Mass Commun, Univ of Iowa, 70-71; asst prof of Commun, 71-74, assoc prof of Commun, 74-80, asst chairperson, Dept of Commun, 76-80, prof of Commun, 80-87, fel, Douglass Col, 87-, chemn, Dept of Commun, 80-84, dir, PhD prog, school of Commun, Infor, and Libr Studies, 84-93, EXEC DIR, UNIV PROG FOR ORGANIZATIONAL QUALITY AND COMMUN IMPROVEMENT, 93-, DISTINGUISHED PROF OF COMMUN, 87-, JOINT FAC MEMBER, GRAD SCHOOL OF APPLIED AND PROFESSIONAL PSYCHOLOGY, RUTGERS UNIV, 97-. **HONORS AND AWARDS** Distinguished Service Award, School of Commun, Infor, and Libr Studies, 93-94; Distinguished Service Award, Rutgers Univ, 93-94; Distinguished Teaching Award, School of Commun, Infor, and Libr Studies, Rutgers Univ, 92-93; Excellence in Teaching Award, Dept of Commun, Rutgers Univ, 92-93; Distinguished Service Award, Coalition of Digestive Disease Orgns, 84. **MEMBERSHIPS** Inst for Health, Rutgers Univ; Quality New Jersey; Nat Inst of Sci and Tech; Nat Higher Ed Quality Coun; Speech Commun Asn; Am Asn for Higher Ed; Int Commun Asn; Am Asn for Higher Ed; Eastern Commun Asn; Nat/Speech Commun Asn; Acad for Intercultural Studies; Am Soc for Infor Sci; Kappa Tau Alpha; Alpha Kappa Psi. **SELECTED PUBLICATIONS** Coauth, Communication and Human Behavior, Fourth Edition, Allyn-Bacon, 98; auth, Organizational Communication and Systems Theory, Commun Theory: A Reader, 98; Quality in Higher Education, Transaction Books, 95; coauth, Excellence in Higher Education: A Guidebook for Self-Assessment, Strategic Planning and Improvement in Higher Education, Kendall-Hunt, 97; coauth, Excellence in Higher Education: A Workbook for Self-Assessment, Strategic Planning and Improvement in Higher Education, Kendall-Hunt, 97; coauth, Process Improvement in Higher Education, Kendall-Hunt, 97; auth, The Face of Higher Education: An Introduction to Service Excellence and Quality on the Front Line, Kendall-Hunt, 96; auth, Tradition of Excellence: Higher Education Quality Self-Assessment Guide, Kendall-Hunt, 94; coauth, The New Jersey Shore Cleanup Initiative: A Case of Quality Practice, Proceedings, Ocean Community Conference, Marine Tech Soc, Inc, 98; auth, The Quality Approach in Higher Education: Concepts and Context for Change, in Quality in Higher Ed, Transaction Books, 95; auth, Defining and Assessing Quality in Higher Education: Beyond TQM, in Quality in Higher Ed, Transaction Books, 95; auth, What Students Remember: Teaching, Learning and Human Communication, Quality in Higher Ed, Transaction Books, 95. **CONTACT ADDRESS** Office for Organizational Quality and Commun Impro, Rutgers Univ, 4 Huntington St/SCILS 222, New Brunswick, NJ, 08903. **EMAIL** ruben@qci.rutgers.edu

RUBENSTEIN, JILL
PERSONAL Born 05/14/1943, Pittsburgh, PA **DISCIPLINE** ENGLISH LITERATURE **EDUCATION** Univ Rochester, AB, 65; Harvard Univ, MAT, 66; Johns Hopkins Univ, MA, 68, PhD(English), 69. **CAREER** Asst prof English, Ill State Univ, 69-72; asst prof, 72-76, ASSOC PROF ENGLISH, UNIV CINCINNATI, 76-, ASSOC DEAN, ARTS & SCI, 81-. **MEMBERSHIPS** MLA; Wordsworth-Coleridge Asn; Asn Scottish Lit Studies. **RESEARCH** Works of Sir Walter Scott; Lady Louisa Stuart. **SELECTED PUBLICATIONS** Auth, Sound and Silence in Coleridge's Conversation Poems, English, 72; The Dilemma of History: A Reading of Scott's Bridal of Triermain, 72 & Wordsworth and Localised Romance, 76, Studies English Lit; Sir Walter Scott: A Reference Guide, G K Hall, 78; Scott's Journal and Its Critics, Wordsworth Circle, 78; Lady Louisa Stuart as Critic of Sir Walter Scott, Scottish Lit J, 80; Lady Louisa Stuart and Henry Lord Brougham, Wordsworth Circle, 81. **CONTACT ADDRESS** Dept of English, Univ of Cincinnati, PO Box 210069, Cincinnati, OH, 45221-0069.

RUBENSTEIN, ROBERTA
PERSONAL Born 11/05/1944, Milford, DE, m, 1971, 2 children **DISCIPLINE** ENGLISH LITERATURE **EDUCATION** Univ CO, BA (magna cum laude), 66; Univ London, PhD, 69. **CAREER** Instr, 69-70, asst prof, 70-74, assoc prof, 74-80, full prof, Dept of Lit, American Univ, Washington, DC, 80-, acting chair, 76-77, dir of women's studies prog, 82-88. **HONORS AND AWARDS** American Univ: Outstanding Teacher Award, Col of Arts and Sciences, 74, 79; Sr Scholar Award, CAS, 87; Univ Fac Award for Outstanding Contrib to Academic Development, 89; Am Univ Scholar/Teacher of the Year Award, 94. **MEMBERSHIPS** Modern Lang Asn; Phi Beta Kappa (Zeta chapter). **RESEARCH** Modern and contemporary fiction; women's lit and feminist theory; psychological approaches to lit. **SELECTED PUBLICATIONS** Auth, The Novelistic Vision of Doris Lessing: Breaking the Form of Consciousness, Univ IL Press, 79; Boundaries of the Self: Gender, Culture, Fiction, Univ IL Press, 87; Worlds of Fiction, co-ed, with Charles R Larson, Macmillan, 93; Fragmented Bodies/Selves/ Narratives: Margaret Drabble's Postmodern Turn, Contemporary Lit 35-1, 94; Fixing the Past: Yearning and Nostalgia in Woolf and Lessing, in Woolf and Lessing: Breaking the Mold, ed Ruth Saxton and Jean Tobin, St Martin's Press, Homeric Resonances: Longing and Belonging in Barabara Kingsolver's Animal Dreams, in Homemaking: Women Writers and the Politics and Poetics of Home, ed Catheine Wiley and Fiona R Barnes, Garland, 96; House Mothers and Haunted Daughters: Shirley Jackson and Female Gothic, Tulsa Studies in Women's Literature, 15-2, 96; History and Story, Sign and Design: Faulknerian and Postmodern Voice in Toni Morrison's Jazz, in Unflinching Gaze: Re-Invisioning Morrison and Faulkner, ed Carol A Kolmerton, Stephen M Ross, and Judith Bryant Wittenburg, Univ Press MS, 97; Singing the Blues/Reclaiming Jazz: Toni Morrison and Cultural Mourning, Mosaic: The Interarts Project, Part II: Cultural Agendas 31-2, 98; over ninety book reviews and review-essays published between 1970-1998 in the following scholarly journals and newspapers: J of Modern Lit, Modern Fiction Studies, Woolf Studies Annual, Doris Lessing Newsletter, Belles Lettres, The Women's Rev of Books, Books Abroad, The New Republic, The Progressive, Res in African Lits, World Lit Written in English, The Nat Observer, Chicago Tribune Book World, Washington Post Book World, The Detroit News, The World and I, Worldview. **CONTACT ADDRESS** Dept of Lit, American Univ, Gray Hall 214, Washington, DC, 20016. **EMAIL** rubenst@american.edu

RUBIN, REBECCA B.
PERSONAL Born 12/11/1948, York, PA, m **DISCIPLINE** SPEECH COMMUNICATION **EDUCATION** Penn St Univ, BA, 70, MA, 71; Univ IL UC, PhD, 75 **CAREER** Instr, 71-72, Messiah Col PA; tchng/res asst, Dept of Speech and Drama, 72-75, Univ of IL; asst prof, 75-76, Georgia Southern Col; instr, Dept of Drama & Speech, 76-77, Univ of NC; asst prof, Communication Discipline, 77-81, Univ of WI; asst prof, Dept of Communication, 81-82, Cleveland St Univ; assoc prof, School of Speech Comm, prof, School for Communication Stud, 88-, Kent St Univ. **HONORS AND AWARDS** Who's Who in the Media and Communications; Women in Communication a Biographical Sourcebook; Outstanding Merit Award Speech Comm Asn, 95; Kent St Univ Pres Honor Roll, 92; Phi Beta Delta Honor Soc for Intl Scholars, 92. **MEMBERSHIPS** Natl Comm Asn; Intl Comm Asn. **RESEARCH** Interpersonal communication; communication competence. **SELECTED PUBLICATIONS** Coauth, Communication Research Strategies and Sources, Wadsworth, 93; auth, Communication Competency Assessment Instrument High School Edition, Spectra Inc, 94; auth, Communication Competency Assessment Instrument, Spectra, 94; auth, SCA Summer Conference Proceedings and Prepared Remarks, Speech Comm Asn, 94; coauth, Communication Research Measures: A Sourcebook, Guilford, 94; coauth, Communication Research Strategies and Sources, Wadsworth, 96; coauth, Media Education Assessment Handbook, Erlbaum, 97; coauth, Preparing Competent College Graduates Setting New and Higher Expectations for Student Learning, 97; coauth, Communication and Personality Trait perspectives, Hampton Press, 98; coauth, Test of a Self-Efficacy Model of Interpersonal Communication Competence, Comm Quart 41, 93; coauth, The Role of Self-Disclosure and Self-Awareness in Affinity-Seeking Competence, Comm Res Reports 10, 93; coauth, Development of a Communication Flexibility Measure, South Comm Jour 59, 94; coauth, Development of a Measure of Interpersonal Communication Competence, Comm Res Reports 11, 94; coauth, Organizational Entry: An Investigation of Newcomer Communication Behavior and Uncertainty, Comm Res 22, 95; coauth, A New Measure of Cognitive Flexibility, Psychol Reports 76, 95; coauth, Performance Based Assessment of High School Speech Instruction, Comm Ed 44, 95; coauth, Effects of Instruction on Communication Apprehension and Communication Competence, Comm Ed 46, 97; coauth, Affinity-Seeking in Initial Interactions, South Jour of Comm, 98. **CONTACT ADDRESS** Kent State Univ, PO Box 5190, Kent, OH, 44242-0001. **EMAIL** rrubin@kent.edu

RUBIO, MARY H.
PERSONAL Born 10/02/1939, Mattoon, IL **DISCIPLINE** LITERATURE **EDUCATION** DePauw Univ, BA, 61; Univ Illinois, MA, 65; McMaster Univ, PhD, 82. **CAREER** PROF ENGLISH, UNIV GUELPH, 67-; co-founder & current co-ed, CCL: Canadian Children's Literature/Litterature canadienne pour la jeunesse, 75. **MEMBERSHIPS** ISRCL; ACUTE; ChLA. **SELECTED PUBLICATIONS** Co-auth, Writing a Life: L.M. Montgomery, 95; ed, The Genesis of Grove's 'Adventure of Leonard Broadus': a Text and Commentary, 83; ed, Harvesting Thistles: The Textual Garden of L.M. Montgomery, Essays on Her Journals & Novels, 94; co-ed, KANATA: An Anthology of Canadian Children's Literature, 76; co-ed, The Selected Journals of L.M. Montgomery, vol 1 85, vol 2 87, vol 3 92. **CONTACT ADDRESS** Dept of English, Univ Guelph, Guelph, ON, N1G 2W1. **EMAIL** mrubio@uoguelph.ca

RUDD, JILL
DISCIPLINE INTERPERSONAL COMMUNICATION, GROUP COMMUNICATION **EDUCATION** Kent State Univ, BA, MA, PhD. **CAREER** Comm, Cleveland St Univ. **SELECTED PUBLICATIONS** Auth, Divorce Mediation: One Step Forward Two Steps Back?, Communication and the Disenfranchised,L. Erlbaum Assoc, 96. **CONTACT ADDRESS** Commun Dept, Cleveland State Univ, 83 E 24th St, Cleveland, OH, 44115. **EMAIL** j.rudd@csuohio.edu

RUDE, CAROLYN D.
DISCIPLINE TECHNICAL COMMUNICATION **EDUCATION** Univ IL, PhD, 75. **CAREER** Prof Eng, 81-, dir, Tech Commun, TX Tech Univ. **MEMBERSHIPS** Assoc fel, Soc for Tech Commun; fel, Asn of Tchr of Tech Writing. **RESEARCH** Decision making. **SELECTED PUBLICATIONS** Auth, Technical Editing, 91; coauth, Technical Communication, 95. **CONTACT ADDRESS** Texas Tech Univ, Lubbock, TX, 79409-5015. **EMAIL** rude@ttu.edu

RUDE, DONALD W.
DISCIPLINE ENGLISH LITERATURE **EDUCATION** Univ IL, PhD, 71. **CAREER** Prof, dir, grad stud, TX Tech Univ. **SELECTED PUBLICATIONS** Auth, A Critical Edition of Sir Thomas Elyot's The Boke Named The Governour; articles on Joseph Conrad, Sir Thomas Elyot, T.S. Eliot, and William Shakespeare, as well as poetry. **CONTACT ADDRESS** Texas Tech Univ, Lubbock, TX, 79409-5015. **EMAIL** ditdr@ttacs.ttu.edu

RUDERMAN, JUDITH
DISCIPLINE ENGLISH LITERATURE **EDUCATION** Duke Univ, PhD, 77. **CAREER** Prof, Duke Univ. **MEMBERSHIPS** DH Lawrence Soc N Am. **SELECTED PUBLICATIONS** Auth, D. H. Lawrence and the Devouring Mother, Duke, 84; William Styron, Ungar, 87; Joseph Heller, Ungar, 91. **CONTACT ADDRESS** Eng Dept, Duke Univ, Durham, NC, 27706.

RUDOLPH, ROBERT SAMUEL
PERSONAL Born 10/05/1937, Philadelphia, PA, m, 1960, 1 child **DISCIPLINE** ENGLISH **EDUCATION** Temple Univ, BA, 59; Univ Wis, MA, 61, PhD(English), 66. **CAREER** Asst prof English, 65-69, from assoc prof to prof English Lang & Lit, Univ Toledo, 69-81. **MEMBERSHIPS** NCTE. **RESEARCH** Diachronic linguistics; Medieval English literature. **CONTACT ADDRESS** 2801 W Bancroft St, Toledo, OH, 43606-3390.

RUFFIN, PAUL
DISCIPLINE NINETEENTH-CENTURY LITERATURE **EDUCATION** MS State Univ, BS, 64, MA, 68; Univ Southern MS, PhD, 74. **CAREER** EngDept, Sam Houston State Univ **HONORS AND AWARDS** Dir, Eng Writing Option; Found & Dir, TX Rev Press; Fac adv, Sam Houston State Rev. **MEMBERSHIPS** TX Inst Letters; MS Inst Arts & Letters; S-Central Mod Lang Asn; Conf Col Tchrs Eng; Conf Eds Learned Jours; TX Asn Creative Writing Tchrs; Gulf Coast Asn Creative Writing Tchrs. **SELECTED PUBLICATIONS** Auth, Mississippi

Poets, 76; The Texas Anthology, 79; Lighting the Furnace Pilot, 82; Our Women, 85; Contemporary New England Poetry: A Sampler, 86-87; The Storm Cellar, 87; To Come Up Grinning: A Tribute to George Garrett, 89; Contemporary Southern Short Fiction: A Sampler, 91; Images of Texas in the Nation, 91; That's What I Like (About the South): Southern Fiction fbr the 1990's, Univ S Carolina Press, 93; The Man Who Would Be God, Southern Methodist Univ Press, 93; After The Grapes of Wrath: Essays on John Steinbeck, Ohio Univ Press, 95; Circling, Browder Springs Press, 96; A Goyen Companion: Appreciations of a Writers Writer, Univ Tex Press, 97. **CONTACT ADDRESS** Sam Houston State Univ, Huntsville, TX, 77341.

RUGGLES, MYLES A.
DISCIPLINE INSTITUTIONAL CONTEXT OF SOCIAL COMMUNICATION PROCESSES **EDUCATION** Simon Fraser, MA, PhD. **CAREER** Fac, Univ Windsor, 94-. **RESEARCH** Institutional context of social communication processes. **SELECTED PUBLICATIONS** Auth, Automating Interactions: Economic Reason and Social Capital in Addressable Networks, Hampton Press: Cresskill, NJ, Hampton Commun Series, 98; The Audience Reflected in the Medium of Law, Ablex Publ: Norwood, NJ: Ablex Commun and Inf Sci Series, 94; What kind of global culture? Mass Communication in a Changing Context, Can Jour Commun, 98; Mixed Signals: Personal Data Control in the Intelligent Network, paper in Media Inf Australia, 93; Personal Information Flows and Boundaries in the Intelligent Network, CIRCIT Policy Res Paper Series, Melbourne: Ctr for Int Res on Commun and Inf Technol, 92; coauth, Balance and Freedom of Speech: The Challenge for Canadian Broadcasting, paper in Can Jour Commun, 92. **CONTACT ADDRESS** Dept of Communication Studies, Univ of Windsor, 401 Sunset Ave, Windsor, ON, N9B 3P4. **EMAIL** ruggles@server.uwindsor.ca

RUGOFF, MILTON
PERSONAL Born 03/06/1913, New York, NY, m, 1937, 1 child **DISCIPLINE** HISTORY, ENGLISH **EDUCATION** Columbia Col, BA, 33; Columbia Univ, MA, 34, PhD, 40. **CAREER** Ed, Alfred E Knopf, Inc, 42-47; assoc ed, 47-48, Mag of the Year; ed, 53, Readers Subscription Bk Club; ed, vice pres, 48-93, Chanticleer Press, Inc, NY. **HONORS AND AWARDS** Literary Lion medal, NY Pub Lib, 90; Ohioana Bk Award, 82. **MEMBERSHIPS** Soc Amer Hist; Authors' Guild. **RESEARCH** American Biography; Elizabethan literature; history of traveland exploration. **SELECTED PUBLICATIONS** Auth, The Penguin Book of World Folk Tales, Viking, 49; ed & intro, The Great Travelers, S and S, 61; auth, Donne's Imagery: A Study in Creative Sources, Atheneum, 62; auth, Marco Polo's Adventures in China, Caravel Bks, 64; auth, Prudery and Passion: Sexuality in Victorian America, Putnam, 71; ed, Britannica Encycl of American Art, Simon, 73; auth, The Beechers: An American Family in the Nineteenth Century, Harper & Row, 81; auth, America's Gilded Age: Intimate Portraits from an Era of Extravagance and Change, Holt & Co, 89. **CONTACT ADDRESS** 18 Ox Ridge Rd, Elmsford, NY, 10523.

RULAND, RICHARD
PERSONAL Born 05/01/1932, Detroit, MI, m, 1989, 4 children **DISCIPLINE** ENGLISH **EDUCATION** Assumption Col, Univ W Ont, BA, 53; Univ Detroit, MA, 55; Univ Mich, PhD, 60. **CAREER** From instr to asst prof, English and Am Stud, Yale Univ, 60-68; prof English and Am Lit, 67- , chemn dept, 69-74, Washington Univ; pres, Asn of Depts of English, 74; vis Fulbright prof, Univ Groningen, 75; vis Fulbright prof Univ East Anglia, 78-79; Guggenheim fel, 82-83; actg chemn Comp Lit Prog, Washington Univ, 93-94. **HONORS AND AWARDS** Bruern Fel, 64; Morse Fel, 66; Fulbright Fel, 75, 78; ACLS travel grant, 81; Guggenheim res fel, 82. **RESEARCH** Literary history, tradition and canon formation; cultural nationalism; British-American cultural relations; the history, theory and method of literary study in the United States. **SELECTED PUBLICATIONS** Auth, Art and A Better America, Am Lit Hist, 91; auth, From Puritanism to Postmodernism: A history of American Literature, Routledge, 91; auth, Literary History and the Legacy of Pragmatism, Am Lit Hist, 94. **CONTACT ADDRESS** Dept of English, Washington Univ, One Brookings Dr, St. Louis, MO, 63130-4899.

RUMOLD, RAIUER
PERSONAL Born 10/29/1941, Elbihg, Germany, m, 2 children **DISCIPLINE** LITERATURE **EDUCATION** Stanford, PhD, 71 **CAREER** Vis asst prof, Stanford Univ, 73-76, assoc prof, Northwestern Univ. **MEMBERSHIPS** MLA **RESEARCH** 20th century lit & thought; modernism & avant-garde stud. **SELECTED PUBLICATIONS** Auth, Sprachliches Experiment und literarische Tradition, Stanford German Stud, 75; Gottfried Benn und der Expressionismus, Skriptor/Athenaem, 82; ed, The Ideological Crisis of Expressionism, Camden House 90; Man from Babel, Yale Univ Press, 98, gen ed, Series in the Study of the Avant-Garde and Modernism, Northwestern Univ Press, 93- . **CONTACT ADDRESS** Dept of German Lit & Critical Thought, Northwestern Univ, 1427 Noyes St, Evanston, IL, 60201. **EMAIL** r-rumold@nwu.edu

RUNGE, LAURA
PERSONAL Born 05/04/1966, Yonkers, NY **DISCIPLINE** ENGLISH **EDUCATION** Univer of Rochester, BA, 88; Emory Univ, MA, 91, PhD 93. **CAREER** Assoc prof, 93-, Univ of South Florida. **HONORS AND AWARDS** Phi Beta Kappa, 87; Undergraduate teach award, 95-96; USF Research & Creative Scholarship grant 98. **MEMBERSHIPS** MLA; ASECS; Aphra Behn Soc (exec secretary); AAVW **RESEARCH** Women's Literature; 18th century British literature, aesthetics **SELECTED PUBLICATIONS** Auth, Gender and Language in British Literary Critcism, 1660-1780, Cambridge Univ Press, 87. **CONTACT ADDRESS** Dept of English, Univ S Florida, 4202 E. Fowler Ave., Tampa, FL, 33620. **EMAIL** runge@chuma.cas.usf.edu

RUNYAN, WILLIAM RONALD
PERSONAL Born 07/18/1940, Steubenville, OH, 1 child **DISCIPLINE** EIGHTEENTH CENTURY ENGLISH LITERATURE, RHETORIC **EDUCATION** Wayne State Univ, BA, 63, MA, 65; Princeton Univ, PhD(English), 75. **CAREER** Grad asst English, Wayne State Univ, 63-65; instr, Wright State Univ, 65-69; instr humanities, Morgan State Col, 69-71; grad asst English, Princeton Univ, 74-75; vis lectr, Univ Wis, Parkside, 69-71; asst prof, 76-80, assoc prof English, Salem Col, 80-82, full prof, Salem-Teikyo Univ, 83-. **MEMBERSHIPS** MLA; AAUP **RESEARCH** The satirical element in English romantic poetry; rhetorical theory and classical translations; contemporary continental rhetorical theory. **SELECTED PUBLICATIONS** Auth, Bob Southey's diabolical doggerel: source and authorship, Wordsworth Circle, winter 76. **CONTACT ADDRESS** Dept of Liberal Studies, Salem-Teikyo Univ, Salem, WV, 26426.

RUPP, RICHARD HENRY
PERSONAL Born 11/16/1934, Indianapolis, IN, m, 1963, 5 children **DISCIPLINE** AMERICAN LITERATURE **EDUCATION** Univ Notre Dame, BA, 56, MA, 57; Ind Univ, Bloomington, PhD(English), 64. **CAREER** From instr to asst prof English, Georgetown Univ, 61-68; asst prof, Univ Miami, 68-72; assoc prof, Brooklyn Col, 72-75; grad dean, 75-80, prof English, Appalachian State Univ, 75-. **MEMBERSHIPS** MLA **RESEARCH** Anglo-Irish Literature. **SELECTED PUBLICATIONS** Auth, Celebration in Post-War American Fiction, Univ Miami, 70; ed, Nathaniel Hawthorne's The Marble Faun, Bobbs, 71; Critics on Whitman, 72 & Critics on Emily Dickinson, 72, Univ Miami; Getting Through College, 84; Deke (a novel), 99. **CONTACT ADDRESS** Dept of English, Appalachian State Univ, Boone, NC, 28608-0001. **EMAIL** rupprh@appstate.edu

RUPPERSBURG, HUGH
PERSONAL Born 03/01/1950, Atlanta, GA, m, 1978, 3 children **DISCIPLINE** AMERICAN LITERATURE **EDUCATION** Univ SC, AB, 72, MA, 74, PhD, 78. **CAREER** Asst prof, 79-84, assoc prof, 84-90, head, Eng Dept, 92-95; ASSOC DEAN, ARTS, SICS, UNIV GA, 96-; PROF, ENG, 90-, UNIV GA. **HONORS AND AWARDS** Outstanding honors prof, 83, 87; Franklin Col Arts, Scis Sandy Peaver teaching award; Asn Col Bookstores, Ga Author of Year, 92., Chair, exec comt, univ counc **MEMBERSHIPS** S Atlantic Mod Lang Asn; Soc Stud S Lit; Mod LangAsn; Counc Cols Arts, Scis, **RESEARCH** Am lit; Am novel; contemp fiction; Southern lit. **SELECTED PUBLICATIONS** Auth, A Reader's Companion to Faulkner's Light in August, Univ Press Miss, 94; ed, Georgia Voices II: Non-Fiction, Univ Ga Press, 94; ed, Georgia Voices I: Fiction, Univ Ga Press, 92; ed, Georgia Voices III: Poetry, Univ Ga Press, 99; auth, Visual Arts, Point of View, Stream of Consciousness, Burden, Robert Penn Warren and Sartoris, in A William Faulkner Encyclopedia, Greenwood Press, 99; auth, James P. Kilgo and James Wilcox, in Contemporary Southern Writers, St. James Press, 98; auth, Atlanta, Savannah, University of Georgia, Atlanta Constitution, in A Companion to Southern Literature, La State Univ Pres, 99; auth, The Normality of MAdness in James Wilcox's Modern Baptists in The Fourth Quarter Contemporary Southern Writers, Univ Ky Press, 97; preface to The Hawk and the Sun, Univ Ga Press, 94; preface to Better a Dinner of Herbs, Univ Ga Press, 92. **CONTACT ADDRESS** Dean's office, Col Arts & Scis, Univ of Georgia, 310 New College, Athens, GA, 30622. **EMAIL** hruppers@franklin.uga.edu

RUSHING, JANICE H.
DISCIPLINE RHETORICAL AND MASS MEDIA CRITICISM **EDUCATION** Univ S Calif, PhD. **CAREER** Comm Stu, Univ Ark **SELECTED PUBLICATIONS** Articles, Critical Studies in Mass Comm, Western Jour Comm, Quart Jour Speech, Southern Comm Journal, Comm Education, Comm Monographs, Comm Studies. **CONTACT ADDRESS** Univ Ark, Fayetteville, AR, 72701.

RUSSELL, ANNE
DISCIPLINE EARLY MODERN DRAMA; POETRY **EDUCATION** Trent, BA; York, MA, PhD. **CAREER** Assoc Prof **SELECTED PUBLICATIONS** Ed, The Rover by Aphra Behn , 94; Tragedy, Gender, Performance: Women as Tragic Heroes on the Nineteenth-Century Stage; Gender and Passion in Nineteenth-Century Romeos. **CONTACT ADDRESS** Dept of English, Wilfrid Laurier Univ, 75 University Ave W, Waterloo, ON, N2L 3C5. **EMAIL** arussell@mach1.wlu.ca

RUSSELL, CHARLES G.
DISCIPLINE COMMUNICATION STUDIES **EDUCATION** Southern IL Univ, BS, 59, MS, 65, PhD, 71. **CAREER** Asst prof, Eastern IL Univ, 65-71; asst prof, WV Univ, 71-75; assoc prof, 75-76; prof, Univ Toledo, 85-. **SELECTED PUBLICATIONS** Auth, The Interpersonal Process, Burgess Int Group, 96; Instructor's Guide for The Interpersonal Process, Burgess Int Group, 96; Language and Behavior, Burgess Int Group, 93; Interpersonal is Between, Burgess Int Group, 93. **CONTACT ADDRESS** Dept of Commun, Univ Toledo, Toledo, OH, 43606. **EMAIL** crussel@utnet.utoledo.edu

RUSSO, ADELAIDE
DISCIPLINE 19TH AND 20TH CENTURY POETRY, SEMIOTICS, INTERDISCIPLINARY STUDIES **EDUCATION** Columbia Univ, PhD, 80. **CAREER** Assoc prof, La State Univ. **SELECTED PUBLICATIONS** Auth, Instructor's Guide, French in Action: The Capretz Method, 94; Muthos et proph?tie, Mythe et pens?e surrealiste, 95; L'art et oscillation et l'oeil d'un certain philosophe, in Actes des Journ?e Artaud, 95. **CONTACT ADDRESS** Dept of Fr Grad Stud, Louisiana State Univ, Baton Rouge, LA, 70803.

RUSSO, JOHN PAUL
PERSONAL Born 05/31/1944, Boston, MA, s **DISCIPLINE** ENGLISH **EDUCATION** Harvard Univ, AB, 65, MA, 66, PhD, 69. **CAREER** Asst prof, 69-73, Harvard Univ; asst prof, 73-77, Univ Chicago; assoc prof, 77-78, prof, 80-82, Rutgers Univ Camden; prof, 82-, Univ Miami. **RESEARCH** history of criticism, representations of Italy. **SELECTED PUBLICATIONS** Auth, Am-Cath arts and fictions - culture, ideology, aesthetics - giles,p/, J of Am Hist, 1994; Imitating the Italians, Wyatt, Spenser, Synge, Pound, Joyce - Dasenbrock,rw/, Modern Philol, 1994. **CONTACT ADDRESS** Dept of English, Univ of Miami, Coral Gables, FL, 33124. **EMAIL** jprusso@miami.edu

RUSSO, MARY
DISCIPLINE LITERATURE AND CRITICAL THEORY **EDUCATION** Cornell Univ, PhD. **CAREER** Prof Lit and Critical Theory, dean, Sch of Hum, Arts and Cult Stud, Hampshire Col. **SELECTED PUBLICATIONS** Auth, Female Grotesque: Risk, Excess and Modernity, Routledge; coed, Nationalism and Sexualities, Routledge; Design in Italy: Italy in Europe, Africa, Asia and the Americas, Univ MN Press. **CONTACT ADDRESS** Hampshire Col, Amherst, MA, 01002.

RUST, RICHARD DILWORTH
PERSONAL Born 09/04/1937, Provo, UT, m, 1960, 3 children **DISCIPLINE** ENGLISH **EDUCATION** Brigham Young Univ, BS, 61; Univ Wis, MS, 62, PhD(English), 66. **CAREER** From asst prof to assoc prof, 66-77, PROF ENGLISH, UNIV NC, CHAPEL HILL, 77-, Sr Fulbright lectr, Univ Heidelberg, 71-72 & 77-78; gen ed, Complete Works of Washington Irving, 77- **MEMBERSHIPS** MLA; SAtlantic Mod Lang Asn; Nathaniel Hawthorne Soc; Melville Soc. **RESEARCH** Nineteenth century American literature, especially writers of the American Renaissance period; literature and art of the American Frontier. **SELECTED PUBLICATIONS** Auth, The Papers Of Smith,Joseph, J, 1832-1842 - Jessee,Dc, Ed/, Brigham Young Univ Studies, 1993; Taste And Feast - Images Of Eating And Drinking In The Book-Of-Mormon/, Brigham Young Univ Studies, 1993; The Papers Of Smith,Joseph, Vol 1 - Autobiographical And Historical Writings - Jessee,Dc, Ed/, Brigham Young Univ Studies, 1993. **CONTACT ADDRESS** Dept of English, Univ of NC, Chapel Hill, NC, 27514.

RUSZKIEWICZ, JOHN JOSEPH
PERSONAL Born 05/28/1950, Cleveland, OH **DISCIPLINE** RHETORIC AND COMPOSITION **EDUCATION** St Vincent Col, BA, 72; Ohio State Univ, MA, 73, PhD, 77. **CAREER** From Asst Prof to Assoc Prof, 77-95, prof English, Univ Tex, Austin, 95-. **MEMBERSHIPS** Rhet Soc Am; NCTE; Conf Col Teachers English. **RESEARCH** Renaissance drama; rhetoric and composition. **SELECTED PUBLICATIONS** Auth, Liberality, Friendship and Timon of Athens, Thoth, 75-76; Parody and pedagogy: Explorations in imitative literature, Col English, 40: 693-701; Well-Bound Words: A Rhetoric, Scott, Foresman, 81; The Scott, Foresman Handbook for Writers, Scott, Foresman, 91; The Presence of Others, St Martin's, 94; Everything's an Argument, Bedford/St Martin's, 99. **CONTACT ADDRESS** Div Rhetoric and Comp, Univ of Tex, Austin, TX, 78712-1026. **EMAIL** ruszkiewicz@mail.utexas.edu

RUTHERFORD, CHARLES SHEPARD
PERSONAL Born 09/10/1940, Chicago, IL, m, 1962, 2 children **DISCIPLINE** MEDIEVAL LITERATURE **EDUCATION** Carleton Col, BA, 62; Ind Univ, Bloomington, MA, 66, PhD(English), 70. **CAREER** Lectr, 68-70, Asst Prof English, Univ Md, College Park, 70-, Assoc Dean, Arts and Humanities, 80-. **HONORS AND AWARDS** Am Coun on Educ fel, 77-78. **MEMBERSHIPS** MLA; SAtlantic Mod Lang Asn; Medieval Acad Am. **RESEARCH** Chaucer; Middle English poetry; Old English poetry. **SELECTED PUBLICATIONS** Auth, Pandarus as a lover: A joly wo or loves shotes keene, Annuale Medaevale, 72; A new dog with an old trick: Archetypal patterns in

Sounder, J Popular Film, spring 73; The Boke of Cupide reopened, Neuphilologische Mitteilungen, 77. **CONTACT ADDRESS** Col of Arts and Humanities, Univ of Maryland, Col Park, College Park, MD, 20742-0001. **EMAIL** cruther@deans.umd.edu

RYALS, CLYDE DE L.
PERSONAL Born 12/19/1928, Atlanta, GA, m, 1971 **DISCIPLINE** ENGLISH **EDUCATION** Emory Univ, AB, 47, MA, 49; Univ Pa, PhD, 57. **CAREER** Instr English, Univ Md, 56-67; from instr to prof, Univ Pa, 57-73, grad chmn, 69-72; chmn dept, 79-82, PROF ENGLISH, DUKE UNIV, 73-, Guggenheim fel, 72-73. **MEMBERSHIPS** MLA; Am Soc Aesthet; NCTE. **RESEARCH** Nineteenth century literature. **SELECTED PUBLICATIONS** Auth, Development And Browning Philosophy Of Inadequacy/, Browning Inst Studies, 1990; Browning Hatreds - Karlin,D/, Nineteenth-Century Lit, 1994; The Brownings Correspondence, July 1845 January 1846, Letters 1982-2177 - Kelley,P, Lewis,S/, Nineteenth Century Prose, Vol 0022, 1995; Recent Studies In The 19th-Century + Recent Books On Romantic/Victorian Poets, Fiction, Drama, Art And Irish Lit/, Studies In English Lit 1500-1900, Vol 0036, 1996. **CONTACT ADDRESS** 1620 University Dr, Durham, NC, 27707.

RYAN, LAWRENCE VINCENT
PERSONAL Born 06/22/1923, St. Paul, MN, m, 1945, 4 children **DISCIPLINE** ENGLISH **EDUCATION** Col St Thomas, BA, 44; Northwestern Univ, MA, 46, PhD(English), 52. **CAREER** Instr English, Col St Thomas, 46-52; from instr to prof 52-77, dir grad prog humanities, 58-67, assoc dean sch humanities & sci, 67-70, actg dean, 74, chmn adv bd, 74-75, JOSEPH S ATHA PROF HUMANITIES, STANFORD UNIV, 77-, CHMN HUMANITIES SPEC PROG, 73-, Huntington Libr grants-in-aid, 53, 56 & 72; Am Philos Soc grant-in-aid, 57; co-ed, Neo Latin News, 57-; Guggenheim fel, 58; assoc Harvard Renaissance Ctr, Florence, 64; Am Coun Learned Soc grant-in-aid, 71. **MEMBERSHIPS** Dante Soc Am; Int Asn Neo-Latin Studies; MLA; Renaissance Soc Am; Conf Brit Studies. **RESEARCH** Literature of the English Renaissance; modern Latin literature; literature of the Italian Renaissance. **SELECTED PUBLICATIONS** Auth, The Renaissance Dialog - Literary Dialog In Its Soc And Political Contexts, Castiglione To Galileo - Cox,V/, Moreana, Vol 0030, 1993; Medievalia-Et-Humanistica - Studies In Medieval And Renaissance Cult - Clogan,Pm/, Moreana, Vol 0033, 1996; More,Thomas - Complete Epigrams - Italian - Firpo,L, Paglialunga,L, Translators/, Moreana, Vol 0033, 1996; Virgil In Medieval Eng, Figuring The 'Aeneid' From The 12th-Century To Chaucer - Baswell,C/, Albion, Vol 0028, 1996. **CONTACT ADDRESS** Dept of English, Stanford Univ, Stanford, CA, 94305.

RYAN, ROBERT ALBERT
PERSONAL Born 07/25/1930, Cleveland, OH **DISCIPLINE** ENGLISH HISTORY **EDUCATION** Western Reserve Univ, AB, 52, MA, 53, PhD, 56. **CAREER** Instr, Alfred Univ, 56; from asst prof to assoc prof hist, 56-69, PROF HIST, ITHACA COL, 69-98; PROF EMER, 98-; Grant-in-aid, Col Ctr Finger Lakes, 63. **MEMBERSHIPS** AHA; Conf Brit Studies. **RESEARCH** Tudor and Stuart England; Ancient Greece; Nazi Germany and the Holocaust. **CONTACT ADDRESS** 113 Crescent Place, Ithaca, NY, 14850.

RYAN, ROBERT M.
DISCIPLINE BRITISH ROMANTICISM, RELIGION IN LITERATURE **EDUCATION** Columbia Univ, PhD. **CAREER** Instr, Rutgers, State Univ NJ, Camden Col of Arts and Sci. **MEMBERSHIPS** Bd dir, Keats-Shelley Asn of Am, 19th-Century Stud Asn. **SELECTED PUBLICATIONS** Auth, Keats: The Religious Sense, Princeton Univ Press, 76; contribu, Mod Philol, keats-Shelley Jour, Wordsworth Circle, Jour of Rel. **CONTACT ADDRESS** Rutgers, State Univ NJ, Camden Col of Arts and Sci, New Brunswick, NJ, 08903-2101. **EMAIL** rmryan@camden.rutgers.edu

RYE, MARILYN
DISCIPLINE ENGLISH LITERATURE **EDUCATION** Rutgers Univ, PhD. **CAREER** Dir Freshman Wrtg, Fairleigh Dickinson Univ. **RESEARCH** Writing; native Am writers; detective fiction. **SELECTED PUBLICATIONS** Auth, Making Cultural Connections, Bedford Bks; essays and reviews in Murder is Academic, Oxford Dict Mystery and Crime Wrtg, Crit Survey Mystery and Detective Fic. **CONTACT ADDRESS** Fairleigh Dickinson Univ, 1000 River Rd, Teaneck, NJ, 07666.

RYKEN, LELAND
PERSONAL Born 05/17/1942, Pella, IA, m, 1964, 3 children **DISCIPLINE** ENGLISH **EDUCATION** Central Col, BA; Univ OR, PhD. **CAREER** Wheaton Col, IL, prof eng, 68-. **MEMBERSHIPS** Modern Lang Asn; Milton Soc Am; Conf on Christianity and Lit; Evangelical Theological Soc. **RESEARCH** Milton; Shakespeare; Christianity and Lit; The Bible as Lit; Puritanism. **SELECTED PUBLICATIONS** A Dictionary of Biblical Imagery, co ed, Inter Varsity, 98; Redeeming the Time: A Christian Approach to Work and Leisure, Baker 95; The Discerning Reader: Christian Perspectives on Literature and Theory, co ed, Inter-Varsity/Baker, 95; A Complete Literary Guide to the Bible, co ed, Zondervan, 93; numerous more books. **CONTACT ADDRESS** Dept Eng, Wheaton Col, Wheaton, IL, 60187. **EMAIL** leland.ryken@wheaton.edu

RYSKAMP, CHARLES ANDREW
PERSONAL Born 10/21/1928, East Grand Rapids, MI **DISCIPLINE** ENGLISH **EDUCATION** Calvin Col, AB, 50; Yale Univ, MA, 51, PhD(Eng), 56; Trinity Col, LittD, 75. **CAREER** From instr to assoc prof Eng, 55-59, John E Annan Bicentennial preceptor, 61-64, cur Eng & Am lit, Univ Libr, 67-79, Dir Pierpoint Morgan Libr, NY, 69-, Procter & Gamble fel, 58-59; Coun Hum jr fel, 60-61; publs chmn, Princeton Libr Chronicle, 62-70; Bollingen Found fel, 65-67; Guggenheim Found fel, 66-67; prof, Princeton, Univ, 69-. **MEMBERSHIPS** Keats-Shelley Asn Am; Am Soc 18th Century Studies; Asn Int Bibliophile; Asn Art Mus Dirs; MLA. **RESEARCH** Eighteenth century Eng lit; William Cowper. **SELECTED PUBLICATIONS** Coauth, Boswell: The Ominous Years, McGraw, 63; ed, The Cast-Away, 63 & Wilde and the Nineties, 66, Princeton Univ; William Blake, Engraver, 69; William Blake: The Pickering Manuscript, 72; The Pierpont Morgan Library: Gifts in Honor of the Fiftieth Anniversary, 74, coauth (with Van Hallelt), Rembrandt & His Century: Dutch Drawings of the Seventeenth Century, 78 & auth, Flowers in Books & Drawings, Nine Forty to Eighteen Forty, 80, Pierpont Morgan; A W William & Mary & Their House, Oxford Univ, 80. **CONTACT ADDRESS** 29 E 36th St, New York, NY, 10016.

S

SACCIO, PETER
DISCIPLINE ENGLISH LITERATURE **EDUCATION** Princeton Univ, PhD, 68. **CAREER** Leon D. Black Prof Shakespearean Studies and Prof Eng. **RESEARCH** Shakespearean drama; mod Brit drama; gay male lit. **SELECTED PUBLICATIONS** Auth, Shakespeare: The Word and the Action (vid lecs) in Superstar Tchrs Series, Teaching Co, 95; Modern British Drama (vid lecs) in Superstar Tchrs Series, Teaching Co, 94; Shakespeare's English Kings: History, Chronicle and Drama, Oxford UP, 77. **CONTACT ADDRESS** Dartmouth Col, 3529 N Main St, #207, Hanover, NH, 03755.

SACHDEVA MANN, HARVEEN
DISCIPLINE ENGLISH **EDUCATION** Government Col, India, BA, 77; Panjab Univ, India, MA, 79; Purdue Univ, West Lafayette,PhD, 86. **CAREER** Assoc prof. **RESEARCH** Postcolonial Stud; south Asian Stud; third world feminism; literary criticism and theory; Asian and Asian American Stud. **SELECTED PUBLICATIONS** Auth, Being Borne across: Translation and Salman Rushdie's The Satanic Verses, Criticism 37.2, 95; Women's Rights versus Feminism Postcolonial Perspectives, in Postcolonial Discourse and Changing Cultural Contexts: Theory and Criticism, Greenwood, 95; Bharat mein Mahila Lekhana, or Women's Writing in India: Regional Literatures, Translation, and Global Feminism, Socist Rev 24.4, 94; Cracking India: Minority Women Writers and the Contentious Margins of Indian Nationalist Discourse, The J Commonwealth Lit 29.2 , 94; articles on, gender and Sikh nationalism; ethics and Third World lit Stud; Saadat Hasan Manto and Mahasweta Devi. **CONTACT ADDRESS** Dept of English, Loyola Univ, Chicago, 6525 N. Sheridan Rd., Chicago, IL, 60626. **EMAIL** hmann@wpo.it.luc.edu

SACHSMAN, DAVID B.
PERSONAL Born 08/16/1945, New York, NY, m, 1967, 2 children **DISCIPLINE** COMMUNICATION **EDUCATION** Univ of Pa, BA, English, 67; Stanford Univ, AM, Commun, 68; Stanford Univ, PhD, Pub Aff Commun, 73. **CAREER** Teaching asst, Dept of Commun, Stanford Univ, 70; asst prof, Calif State Univ, Hayward, 69-71; asst prof, Rutgers Univ, 71-76; Sr Fulbright-Hays Schol, Univ of Nigeria, Nsukka, 78-79; assoc prof, Rutgers Univ, 76-88; assoc mem, grad faculty, Rutgers Grad Sch, 86-88; Adjunct assoc prof, Univ of Med & Dent of NJ-Robert Wood Johnson Med Ctr, 87-89; prof of commun, Calif State Univ, Fullerton, 88-91; prof of commun, UTC, 91-; adjunct prof, Univ Tenn, Knoxville, 96-. **HONORS AND AWARDS** Special award for Res about J and Journalistic Media, 84, 86, 88, 89., Ch of Excellence in Commun & Public Aff. **MEMBERSHIPS** Assoc for Educ in J and Mass Commun; Int Commun Assoc; Nat Commun Assoc; Soc of Env J; Invest Reporters and Eds; Radio-Television News Dirs Assoc; Chattanooga Press Assoc. **RESEARCH** Env jour; risk commun; mass commun & soc. **SELECTED PUBLICATIONS** Mass Communication Education: Moving Toward Diversity, Mass Comm Rev, vol 20, no 3 & 4, 180-91, 93; Communication Between Scientists and the Media: Introducing the Concepts of Risk, Risk Analysis, and Risk Communication to Journalists, Hazardous Waste and Pub Hlth: int Congress on the Health Effects of Hazardous Waste, Princeton Scientific Publishing Co., Inc, 945-52, 94; The Mass Media Discover the Environment: Influences on Environmental Reporting in the First Twenty Years, The Symbolic Earth: Discourse, and Our Creation of the Environment, Univ Press of Ky, 241-56, 96; Reporting Risks and Setting the Environmental Agenda, Environmental Education for the 21st Century: International and Interdisciplinary Perspectives, Peter Lang Publ, 129-141, 97; Co-auth, Proceedings of the Conference on Communication and Our Environment, Univ of Tenn at Chattanooga Graphic Svcs, 97. **CONTACT ADDRESS** West Ch of Commun, Univ of Tenn, 615 McCallie Ave, Chattanooga, TN, 37403-2504. **EMAIL** david-sachsman@utc.edu

SADDLEMYER, ANN
PERSONAL Born 11/28/1932, Prince Albert, SK, Canada **DISCIPLINE** DRAMA/COMPARATIVE LITERATURE **EDUCATION** Univ Sask, BA, 53(Eng & Psychol), 55(Eng Hons); Queen's Univ, MA, 56; Bedford Col, Univ London, PhD, 61. **CAREER** Lectr, 56-57, instr, Victoria (BC) Col, 60; asst prof, 62, assoc prof, 65, prof, Univ Victoria, 68-71; prof, 71-95, dir, grad drama ctr, 72-77, acting dir, 85-86, PROF EMER ENGLISH, GRAD CTR FOR STUD DRAMA, COMPARATIVE LITERATURE, 95-; vis prof Berg Ch, NY Univ, 75; sr fel, 75-88, master 88-95, MASTER EMER, MASSEY COL, 95-; **HONORS AND AWARDS** Guggenheim fel, 65, 77; Connaught sr res fel, 86; Distinguished Serv Award, Prov Ont, 85; Univ Toronto Alumni Award, 90; off, Order Can, 95; LLD(hon), Queen's Univ, 77; DLitt(hon), Univ Victoria, 89; DLitt(hon), McGill Univ, 89; DLitt(hon), Univ Windsor, 90. **MEMBERSHIPS** Int Asn Stud Anglo-Irish Lit (past chmn); Asn Can Theatre Res (founding pres); Can Asn Irish Stud. **RESEARCH** Anglo-Irish literature; theatre history **SELECTED PUBLICATIONS** Auth, In Defence of Lady Gregory, Playwright, 66; auth, The Plays of J.M. Synge, Books One and Two, 68; auth, Synge and Modern Comedy, 68; auth, The Plays of Lady Gregory, 70; auth, A Selection of Letters from J.M. Synge to W.B. Yeats and Lady Gregory, 71; auth, Letters to Molly: J.M. Synge to Maire O'Neill, 71; auth, Theatre Business, The Correspondence of the First Abbey Theatre Directors, 82; auth, The Collected Letters of J.M. Synge, vol I 83, vol II 84; coauth, The World of W.B. Yeats, 65; Lady Gregory Fifty Years After, 87; ed, Early Stages: Essays on Theatre in Ontario 1800-1914, 90; Later Stages: Essays on Theatre in Ontario World War I to the 1970s, 97; co-ed, The World's Classics J.M. Synge, 95; co-ed, Theatre Hist Can, 79-86; ed bd, Irish Univ Rev; ed bd, Can J Irish Stud; ed bd, The Shaw Rev. **CONTACT ADDRESS** Massey Col, Univ of Toronto, 4 Devonshire Pl, Toronto, ON, M5S 2E1. **EMAIL** saddlemy@chass.utoronto.ca

SAFER, ELAINE BERKMAN
PERSONAL Born 09/18/1937, Brooklyn, NY, d, 3 children **DISCIPLINE** ENGLISH **EDUCATION** Brooklyn Col, BA, 58; Univ Wis, MS, 59; Case Western Reserve Univ, MA, 61, PhD, 67. **CAREER** Teaching fel English, Case Western Reserve Univ, 61-63; instr, Northwestern Univ, 63-66; asst prof, 67-73, assoc prof English, 73-88; PROF ENGLISH, 88- , UNIV DEL, 73- ; Summer fac fel, Univ Del, 71, 78, 81, 92; NEH summer stipend, 83; Fulbright scholar, 90; Distinguished prof Univ Jean-Moulin Lyon III, 90, 92, 93, 94, 95, 96; fel Ctr Advan Stud, Univ Del, 97-98. **HONORS AND AWARDS** Univ Del Excellence Tchg Award, 93. **MEMBERSHIPS** MLA; Milton Soc; Renaissance Soc Am; AAUP; Int Soc Humor Studies; Am Lit Sect MLA; Am Lit Asn; Am Humor Stud Asn, pres 97-98; Pres Saul Bellow Soc Am Lit Asn, 92-95. **RESEARCH** Twentieth Century American literature; The Novel; John Milton. **SELECTED PUBLICATIONS** Coed John Milton: L'Allegro and Il Penseroso, Charles Merrill, 70; auth, Sufficient to have stood: Eve's responsibility in Book IX, Milton Quart, 10/72; The Socratic dialogue & knowledge in the making in Paradise Regained, Milton Studies, 74; Nativity Ode and the Ode as Genre, In: Milton Encycl, Bucknell Univ, 78; It's the truth even if it didn't happen: Ken Kesey's One Flew over the Cuckoo's Nest, Lit/Film Quart, 77; The Allusive Mode and Black Humor in Barth's Giles Goat-Boy and Pynchon's Gravity's Rainbow, Renascence, 80 & In: Critical Essays on Thomas Pynchon, G K Hall, 81; The Use of Contraries: Milton's Adaptation of Dialectic, In: Paradise Lost, Ariel, 81; The Allusive Mode and Black Humor in Barth's Sot-Weed Factor, Studies in Novel, 81; The Contemporary American Comic Epic: The Novels of Barth, Pynchon, Gaddis, and Kesey, Wayne State Univ Press, 88. **CONTACT ADDRESS** Dept of English, Univ of Del, Newark, DE, 19711. **EMAIL** safer@udel.edu

SAHA, PROSANTA KUMAR
PERSONAL Born 12/04/1932, Calcutta, India, m, 1958, 2 children **DISCIPLINE** ENGLISH, LINGUISTICS **EDUCATION** Univ Calcutta, BA, 56; Oberlin Col, MA 57; Western Reserve Univ, PhD(English), 66. **CAREER** Teacher, Hawken Sch, 57-62; instr English, 62-64, asst prof English & ling, 66-72, Assoc Prof English & Ling & Chmn Ling & Undergrad Humanities Prog, Case Western Reserve Univ, 72- **HONORS AND AWARDS** Carl F Wittke Award, Case Western Reserve Univ, 71. **MEMBERSHIPS** Ling Soc Am. **RESEARCH** English literature and linguistics; computer analysis of literature, especially stylistics; Bengali literature and linguistics. **SELECTED PUBLICATIONS** Auth, Reflexive Revisited + English Pronouns/, Am Speech, Vol 0068, 1993. **CONTACT ADDRESS** Dept of English, Case Western Reserve Univ, Clark Hall Rm 103 Case, Cleveland, OH, 44106.

SAHNI, CHAMAN LALL
PERSONAL Born 06/10/1933, Thatta, India, m, 1960, 2 children **DISCIPLINE** ENGLISH, FAR EASTERN LINGUISTICS **EDUCATION** Agra Univ, India, BA, 54; Lucknow Univ, India, MA, 56; Univ RI, MA, 68; Wayne State Univ, PhD, 74. **CAREER** Lectr Eng, Bareilly Col, India, 56-59; head dept, Seth Motilal Col, 59-60; lectr, S D Col, India, 60-62 & Kurukshetra Univ, 62-67; from instr to asst prof, Wayne State Univ, 71-75; asst prof, 75-78, assoc prof, 78-81, prof eng, Boise State Univ, 81. **MEMBERSHIPS** MLA; SAsian Lit Asn **RESEARCH** Mod Brit fiction. **SELECTED PUBLICATIONS**

Ed with introd & notes, Chaucer: The Prologue, 66 & Milton's Samson Agonistes, 67, Kitab Ghar, India; auth, The Marabar Caves in the light of Indian thought, In: Focus on Forster's A Passage to India, Humanities, 76; ed with introd & notes, Shelley's Adonais, 7th ed, 93, coauth, Advanced Literary Essays, 16th ed, 94 & auth, Principles and History of Literary Criticism, 3rd ed, 77, Bareilly U P, India; Forster's A Passage to India: The Religious Dimension, Arnold-Heinemann, India, 81, and Humanities Press 81; Gandhi and Tagore, SAsian Rev, 7/81; E M Forster's A Passage to India: The Islamic Dimension, South Asian Rev, 83, and Cahiers Victoriens & Edouardiens, 83; Indian Writers of English Fiction, Advanced Lit Essays, Prakash Book Depot, India, 85; Indian Poetry in English, Advanced Lit Essays, Prakash Book Depot, India, 85; The Images of Mahatma Gandhi in Indo-English Fiction, Advanced Lit Essays, Prakash Book Depot, India, 85; Rabindranath Tagor: Sidelights, Contemporary Authors, Gale Res Co, 87; Steppenwolf and Indian Thought, South Asian Rev, 88; Raja Rao: The Serpent and the Rope, Kamala Markandaya: Nectar in a Sieve, and Anita Desai: Fire on the Mountain, In: Cyclopedia of Literary Characters II, Salem Press, 90; R K Narayan, E M Forester, and Bharati Mukherjee, In: Critical Survey of Short Fiction, rev ed, Salem Press, 93; Sasthi Brata, In: Writers of the Indian Diaspora: A Bio-Bibliographical Source Book, Greenwood Press, 93; Donald Duk by Frank Chin, and Jasmine by Bharati Mukherjee, In: Masterplots II: American Fiction, supplement, Salem Press, 94; Krishna Janamashtami, Lala Hardayal, Gayatri Chakravorti Spivak, and Bharati Mukherjee, In: Asian American Encyclopedia, Marshall Cavendish, 95; Wife by Bharati Mukherjee, In: Masterplots II: Women's Literature, Marshall Cavendish, 95; Anita Desai, In: Magill's Survey of World Literature, Supplement, Salem Press, 95; Siddhartha by Hermann Hesse, In: Masterplots: Revised Second Edition, Salem Press; 96; Jasmine by Bharati Mukherjee, In: Masterplots II: Short Story, Supplement, Salem Press, 96; Kamala Markandaya and Anita Desai, In: Cyclopedia of World Authors, rev ed, Salem Press, 97. **CONTACT ADDRESS** Dept of Eng, Boise State Univ, 1910 University Dr, Boise, ID, 83725-0399. **EMAIL** csahni@bsu.idbsu.edu

SAID, EDWARD
DISCIPLINE ENGLISH **EDUCATION** Princeton Univ, AB, 57; Harvard Univ, AM, 60, PhD, 64. **CAREER** Instr, Harvard Univ; Johns Hopkins Univ; Yale Univ; Univ Chicago; ch, comp lit; prof 63-. **HONORS AND AWARDS** Fel, Stanford Ctr Advan Stud in Behavioral Sci; Columbia's Trilling award; Wellek prize, Amer Comp Lit Assn., Dir, NEH sem on lit criticism, 78; lect, Gauss sem, Princeton, 77; Eliot Memorial Lectures, Kent Univ, 85; Messenger Lectures, Cornell Univ, 86; Frye Lectures, Univ Toronto, 86; Davie Academic Freedom Lecture, Univ Cape Town, 91; Camp Lectures, Stanford Univ, 93; Northcliffe Lectures, Univ London, 93; Woolfson Lecture, Oxford, 93; BBC's Reith Lectures, BBC, 93. **MEMBERSHIPS** Mem, For Rel Coun; sr fel, Sch of Criticism and Theory. **SELECTED PUBLICATIONS** Auth, Beginnings; Orientalism; The Question of Palestine; Covering Islam; The World, the Text and the Critic; After the Last Sky; Blaming the Victims; Culture and Imperialism; The Politics of Dispossession; Wellek and Reith Lectures, Musical Elaborations and Representations of the Intellectual.Peace and Its Discontents, 96. **CONTACT ADDRESS** Dept of Eng, Columbia Col, New York, 2960 Broadway, New York, NY, 10027-6902.

SAILLANT, JOHN D.
PERSONAL Born 07/25/1957, Providence, RI, m, 3 children **DISCIPLINE** EARLY AMERICAN LITERATURE **EDUCATION** Brown Univ,BA, 79; MA, 81; DPhil, 89. **CAREER** Prof **HONORS AND AWARDS** NEHGrant, 97; Ames Fel, Univ Mass, 97; Am Acad Relig Grant, 96; The Huntington & British Acad Grant; RI Comt Hum Grant, 96; Va Hist Soc Mellon Res Grant, 94, 96; Am Counc Learned Socs Fel, 92-93; **MEMBERSHIPS** Am Acad Relig; Am Hist Asn; Am Soc Eighteenth-Century Studies; Am Studies Asn; Forum Eu Expansion & Global Interaction; Great Lakes Am Studies Asn; New England Hist Asn; Soc of Early Amists; Soc Historians Early Republic. **SELECTED PUBLICATIONS** Auth, The Black Body Erotic and the Republican Body Politic, 1790-1820, Jour Hist Sexuality, 95; Slavery and Divine Providence in New England Calvinism: The New Divinity and a Black Protest, New England Quart, 95; Explaining Syncretism in African American Views of Death: An Eighteenth-Century Example, Cult & Tradition, 95; Hymnody in Sierra Leone and the Persistence of an African American Faith, The Hymn, 97; The American Enlightenment in Africa: Jefferson's Colonizationism and Black Virginians' Migration to Liberia, 1776-1840, Eighteenth-Century Studies, 98. **CONTACT ADDRESS** Kalamazoo, MI, 49008. **EMAIL** john.saillant@wmich.edu

SAJDAK, BRUCE T.
PERSONAL Born 11/22/1945, Chicago, IL, m, 1979, 1 child **DISCIPLINE** ENGLISH, LIBRARY SCIENCE **EDUCATION** Loras Col, AB, 66; Univ of Mich, MA, 67, PhD, 74, AMLS, 75. **CAREER** Humanities libr, Univ of Houston, Victoria Campus, 75-77; reference libr, Univ of Md, Col Park, 77-80; REFERENCE LIBR, SMITH COL, 80-. **MEMBERSHIPS** Modern Humanities Res Asn; Asn of Col & Res Librs, New England. **RESEARCH** Bibliography; Shakespeare. **SELECTED PUBLICATIONS** Assoc Am ed, Annual Bibliography of English Language & Literature, 96-; contribur, World Shakespeare Bibliography, Shakespeare Quarterly, 92-; auth, Shakespeare Index, Kravs, 92; PhD dissertation: Silence on the Shakespearean Stage, Univ of Mich, 74. **CONTACT ADDRESS** Smith Col, 79 South St., Northampton, MA, 01060. **EMAIL** bsajdak@library.smith.edu

SALAZAR, ABRAN J.
DISCIPLINE COMMUNICATION **EDUCATION** Univ Iowa, PhD. **CAREER** Assoc prof, Texas A&M Univ. **HONORS AND AWARDS** Southern States Commun Association's annual awd for the best article in the Southern Commun J; Col Liberal Arts Distinguished Tchg Awd from the Former Students Asn Texas A&M Univ. **RESEARCH** Group organizational communication, interpersonal communication & health. **SELECTED PUBLICATIONS** Publ in, Health Commun; Human Commun Res, Southern Commun J; Small Gp Res. **CONTACT ADDRESS** Dept of Speech Communication, Texas A&M Univ, College Station, TX, 77843-4234.

SALEM, JAMES MORRIS
PERSONAL Born 11/15/1937, Portage, WI, m, 1958, 4 children **DISCIPLINE** ENGLISH, MODERN DRAMA **EDUCATION** Wis State Univ, La Crosse, BS, 61; La State Univ, PhD(English), 65. **CAREER** Asst prof English, Kent State Univ, 65-67; from asst prof to assoc prof English, 67-76, dir Am Studies, 68-76, PROF AM STUDIES, UNIV ALA, 76-, Consult Am lit, Scarecrow Press, NJ, 67- **MEMBERSHIPS** Am Studies Asn. **RESEARCH** American popular culture; American literature; American drama. **SELECTED PUBLICATIONS** Auth, Death And The Rhythm-And-Bluesman - The Life And Recordings Of Ace,Johnny/, Am Music, Vol 0011, 1993. **CONTACT ADDRESS** Dept of Am Studies, Univ Ala, University, AL, 35486.

SALEM, PHILIP
PERSONAL Born 08/07/1945, Sioux City, IA, d, 1 child **DISCIPLINE** COMMUNICATION STUDIES; SPEECH COMMUNICATION **EDUCATION** Northern State Col, BS, 68; Univ S Dakota, 80; Univ Denver, MA, 72; Univ Denver, PhD, 74 **CAREER** Radio Announcer, KABR Aberdeen, S Dak, 66-69; TV Newsman, KXAB Aberdeen S Dak, 68; Teacher, Webster Independent School District, S Dak, 69-71; Radio Announcer, KADX, 71-74; Graduate Teaching Asst, Univ Denver, 73-74; prof, Southwest Tex St Univ, 74- **HONORS AND AWARDS** Dir, "Organizational Communication and Change: Challenges in the Next Century," 96; President's Award Res, nominee to the SWTSU President, 84, 85, 88, 92, 95, 97; President's Award Teaching, nominee to the SWTSU President, 84, 95; Southwest Bus Syposium Award, 94; Fund for Improvement of Postsecondary Education Grant, 94 **MEMBERSHIPS** Tex Speech Comm Assoc; Western States Comm Assoc; Conflict Resolution Education Network; Acad Management; Ntl Comm Assoc; ;Int Comm Assoc **RESEARCH** Communication Theory; Organizational Communication; Interpersonal Communication; Information Systems; Communication and Technology; Communication and Conflict Management **SELECTED PUBLICATIONS** Ed, Organizational communication and change, Hampton Pr, forthcoming; Institutional factors influencing the success of Drug Abuse Education and Prevention Programs, US Dept Education, 91; Organizational communication and higher education, Amer Assoc Education, 81 **CONTACT ADDRESS** Dept Speech Comm, Southwest Tex St Univ, San Marcos, TX, 78666. **EMAIL** ps05@swt.edu

SALEM MANGANARO, ELISE
DISCIPLINE ENGLISH LITERATURE **EDUCATION** Univ NC, PhD. **CAREER** Fac, Fairleigh Dickinson Univ . **RESEARCH** 16th-18th century Brit lit, world lit, contemp Arab writers, ethnic Am lit, cult studies, and mass media. **SELECTED PUBLICATIONS** Auth, essays in Engl Studies, MELUS, Biog East and West. **CONTACT ADDRESS** Fairleigh Dickinson Univ, 1000 River Rd, Teaneck, NJ, 07666.

SALOMON, HERMAN PRINS
PERSONAL Born 03/01/1930, Amsterdam, Netherlands **DISCIPLINE** LITERATURE **EDUCATION** NY Univ, Am, 52, PhD(French), 61. **CAREER** From instr to asst prof French, Rutgers Univ, 61-65; asst prof French, Queens Col, NY, 65-68; asst prof French, 68-76, Assoc Prof Romance Lang, State Univ NY, Albany, 76- **MEMBERSHIPS** Am Asn Teachers Fr; MLA; Ned Ver Leraren in Levende Talen; Int Asn Fr Studies. **RESEARCH** Seventeenth century French literature; literature of the Netherlands; history of Spanish and Portuguese Judaism. **SELECTED PUBLICATIONS** Auth, Hist Of The Jews In The Netherlands - Dutch - Blom,Jch, Fuksmansfeld,Rg, Schoffer,I/, Studia Rosenthaliana, Vol 0030, 1996; Congregation-Shearith-Israel First Language + Uniting The Sephardim And Ashkenazim Congregation As A Linguistic Subculture Within New-York Dutch Society - Port/, Tradition-A J Of Orthodox Jewish Thought, Vol 0030, 1995; Another Lost Book Found - The Melo Haggadah, Amsterdam, 1622/, Studia Rosenthaliana, Vol 0029, 1995. **CONTACT ADDRESS** Dept of Romance Lang, State Univ of New York, Albany, NY, 12203.

SALOMON, ROGER B.
DISCIPLINE AMERICAN AND MODERN ENGLISH LITERATURE **EDUCATION** Harvard Univ, BA, Univ Calif, MA, PhD. **CAREER** English, Case Western Reserve Univ. **HONORS AND AWARDS** Dir, Writing Ctr. **SELECTED PUBLICATIONS** Auth or ed, Twain and the Image of History; Desperate Storytelling: Post-Romantic Elaborations of the Mock-Heroic Mode. **CONTACT ADDRESS** Case Western Reserve Univ, 10900 Euclid Ave, Cleveland, OH, 44106.

SALTZMAN, ARTHUR MICHAEL
PERSONAL Born 08/10/1953, Chicago, IL, d, 1 child **DISCIPLINE** ENGLISH & AMERICAN LITERATURE **EDUCATION** Univ Ill, AB, 75, AM, 76, PhD, 79. **CAREER** Prof English, Mo Southern State Col, 92-; from asst prof to assoc prof, 81-92. **HONORS AND AWARDS** Outstanding Teacher, MSSC Found, 92; 1st Annual Roy T. Ames Memorial Essay Award, 98. **MEMBERSHIPS** MLA. **RESEARCH** Contemporary fiction; 20th century literature. **SELECTED PUBLICATIONS** Auth, The Fiction of William Gass: The Consolation of Language, Southern Ill, 86; Understanding Raymond Carver, SC, 88; Designs of Darkness in Contemporary American Fiction, Penn, 90; The Novel in the Balance, SC, 93; Objects and Empathy, in Ohio Rev, 97; From the Letters to Gamma Man, in Evansville Rev, 98; Once More Upon a Time Again, in Contemp Educ, 98; The Girl in the Moon, in Literal Latte, 98; The Nightmare of Relation in William Gass' The Tunnel, in Into the Tunnel, Del, 98; Incipience and Other Alibis, in Gettysburg Rev, 99; Understanding Nicholson Baker, SC, 99; Avid Monsters: The Look of Agony in Contemporary Fiction, in Twentieth Century Lit, 99; author of numerous other journal articles and book reviews. **CONTACT ADDRESS** Dept of English, Missouri Southern State Col, 3950 Newman Rd, Joplin, MO, 64801-1595. **EMAIL** saltzman-a@mail.mssc.edu

SALWAK, DALE F.
PERSONAL Born 02/07/1947, Greenfield, MA, m, 1985, 1 child **DISCIPLINE** ENGLISH **EDUCATION** Purdue Univ, BA, 69; Univ Southern Calif, MA, 70, PhD, 74. **CAREER** Asst Ed, Dept Agricultural Info, 66-69; Instr, Univ Southern Calif, 72-73; Prof English, Citrus Col, 73-. **HONORS AND AWARDS** Paul A. Sidwell Award for Novel-in-Progress, Purdue, 69; NDEA Title IV Fel, Univ Southern Calif, 69-72; Teacher of the Year, Citrus Col, 76-77, 78-79, 82-83; NEH grant, 85; Res Fel, Citrus Col Found, 86; Distinguished Alumni Award, Purdue Univ, 87; Best Essay 96-97, Inside English. **RESEARCH** Bible; modern British literature; detective novel; biography; philosophy. **SELECTED PUBLICATIONS** Auth, The Wonders of Solitude, New World Libr, 95; ed, The Literary Biography: Problems and Solutions, Univ Iowa Press, 96; auth, The Words of Christ, New World Libr, 96; The Wisdom of Judaism, New World Libr, 97; ed, A Passion for Books, Macmillan/St. Martin's Press, 98; The Power of Prayer, New World Libr, 98; auth, In Defense of the Bible (forthcoming); author of numerous other publications. **CONTACT ADDRESS** Citrus Col, 1000 W Foothill Blvd., Glendora, CA, 91741. **EMAIL** dsalwak@citrus.cc.ca.us

SALZBERG, JOEL
PERSONAL Born 05/31/1934, Brooklyn, NY **DISCIPLINE** AMERICAN LITERATURE **EDUCATION** City Col New York, BA, 56; Ind Univ, MA, 60; Univ Okla, PhD(English), 67. **CAREER** Asst prof English, Univ Northern Iowa, 65-68; asst prof, 68-72, ASSOC PROF ENGLISH, UNIV COLO, DENVER CTR, 72- **MEMBERSHIPS** MLA **RESEARCH** American Romanticism; psychology and literary criticism; 19th century realism. **SELECTED PUBLICATIONS** Auth, Of Autobiographical Essence And Self-Parody, Malamud On Exhibition In 'Pictures Of Fidelman'/, Genre, Vol 0024, 1991; The Loathly-Landlady, Chagallian, Unions, And Malamudian Parody + Malamud,Bernard - The 'Girl Of My Dreams' Revisited/, Studies In Short Fiction, Vol 0030, 1993; Forging A New Self - A Adamic Protagonist And The Emergence Of A Jewish-Am Author As Revealed Through The Novels Of Malamud,Bernard - Ahokas,P/, Studies In Am Fiction, Vol 0022, 1994; Malamud,Bernard Revisited - Abramson,Ea/, Studies In Am Fiction, Vol 0023, 1995; American Iconology - New Approaches To 19th-Century Art And Lit - Miller,Dc/, English Language Notes, Vol 0032, 1995. **CONTACT ADDRESS** Dept of English, Univ of Colo, Denver, CO, 80210.

SAMMONS, MARTHA CRAGOE
PERSONAL Born 11/27/1949, Philadelphia, PA, m, 1973, 3 children **DISCIPLINE** ENGLISH **EDUCATION** Wheaton Col, BA, 71; Univ NC, Chapel Hill, PhD(English), 74. **CAREER** Teaching asst chem & grad asst English, Univ NC, 73-74; lectr, Duke Univ, 74; instr, Univ NC, 75; from asst prof to assoc prof, 75-87, PROF ENGLISH, WRIGHT STATE UNIV, 87-. **MEMBERSHIPS** C S Lewis Soc. **RESEARCH** Technical writing; online documentation; hypertext. **SELECTED PUBLICATIONS** Auth, A Guide Through Narnia, Shaw Publ, 79, Brendow, 98; A Guide Through C S Lewis' Space Trilogy, Cornerstone Bks, 80; A Better Country: The Worlds of Religious Fantasy and Science Fiction, Greenwood Press, 88; Multimedia Presentations on the Go: An Introduction and Buyer's Guide, Libr Unlimited, 96; The Internet Writer's Handbook, Allyn & Bacon, 99. **CONTACT ADDRESS** Dept of English, Wright State Univ, Dayton, OH, 45435-0002. **EMAIL** msammons@wright.edu

SAMPSON, EDWARD C.
PERSONAL Born 12/20/1920, Ithaca, NY, m, 1968, 2 children **DISCIPLINE** ENGLISH **EDUCATION** Cornell Univ, BA, 42, PhD, 57; Columbia Univ, MA, 48. **CAREER** Instr Eng, Hofstra Univ, 46-49; fel, Cornell Univ, 49-52; from instr to prof lib studies, Clarkson Col Technol, 52-66, prof hum, 66-69; Prof English, State Univ NY Col Oneonta, 69-, Fulbright lectr, Univ Panjab, Pakistan, 59-60. **MEMBERSHIPS** MLA; Nathaniel Hawthorne Soc. **RESEARCH** Hawthorne; E B White; Thomas Hardy. **SELECTED PUBLICATIONS** Auth, Motivation in The Scarlet Letter, Am Lit, 1/57; Afterword, The House of the Seven Gables, Signet, 61; Three unpublished letters by Hawthorne to Epes Sargeant, Am Lit, 3/62; Critical study of E B White, Vol 232, In: Twayne United States Authors Series, Twayne; Thomas Hardy: Justice of the peace, Colby Libr Quart, 12/77, E.B.White, Dictionary of Literary Biography, vol ii, American Humorists, part 2, Gale Research, 82. **CONTACT ADDRESS** 89 Hemlock Dr, Killingworth, CT, 06419. **EMAIL** crsampson@snet.net

SAMRA, RISE J.
PERSONAL Born 03/19/1952, Green Bay, WI, s **DISCIPLINE** COMMUNICATION STUDIES **EDUCATION** Univ Arizona, PhD, 85. **CAREER** Author **CONTACT ADDRESS** 4001 S Ocean Dr # 5L, Hollywood, FL, 33019. **EMAIL** rsamra@mail.barry.edu

SAMSON, DONALD
PERSONAL NY **DISCIPLINE** TECHNICAL WRITING AND EDITING, BRITISH AND AMERICAN LITERATURE **EDUCATION** Cornell Univ, BA; Univ NC, MA, PhD. **CAREER** Prof, Radford Univ; tech writer/ed, Lockheed Martin Corp. **SELECTED PUBLICATIONS** Auth, Editing Technical Writing, Oxford, 93; coauth, Professional Writing in Context: Lessons from Teaching and Consulting in Worlds of Work, Erlbaum, 95. **CONTACT ADDRESS** Radford Univ, Radford, VA, 24142. **EMAIL** dsamson@runet.edu

SAMSON, JOHN W.
DISCIPLINE AMERICAN LITERATURE **EDUCATION** Cornell Univ, PhD, 80. **CAREER** Assoc prof, TX Tech Univ; ed, The 18th Century: Theory and Interpretation. **HONORS AND AWARDS** Co-founder, Soc for 18th-Century Am Stud. **MEMBERSHIPS** Pres, Soc for 18th-Century Am Stud. **RESEARCH** The hist and theoretical study of Am novels and narratives. **SELECTED PUBLICATIONS** Auth, White Lies: Melville's Narratives of Facts, 89. **CONTACT ADDRESS** Texas Tech Univ, Lubbock, TX, 79409-5015. **EMAIL** ditjs@ttacs.ttu.edu

SAMTER, WENDY
DISCIPLINE INTERPERSONAL COMMUNICATION **EDUCATION** LaSalle Univ, BA, 81; Purdue Univ, MA, 83; PhD, 89. **CAREER** Tchg asst, Purdue Univ, 81-88; res asst, Purdue Univ; asst dir, Purdue Univ, 83-86; asst prof, 89-. **HONORS AND AWARDS** Univ fel, Purdue Univ, 81-82; David Ross Found summer dissertation res grant, Purdue Univ, 84; Intl Commun Assn award for outstanding grad stud tchr, 85; Bruce Kendall Award for excellence in tchg, Purdue Univ, 85; David Ross res fel, Purdue Univ, 84-85; Alan H Monroe scholar, Purdue Univ, 88-89; intl travel grant, 90; supplemental funds grant, 90, 91; award for distinguished achievement field of commun, Commun Dept, Lasalle Univ, 93., Pres, Tri-State Commun Assn, 1993 **MEMBERSHIPS** Mem, Intl Commun Assn; Speech Commun Assn; Tri-State Commun Assn. **RESEARCH** Individual differences in social cognition. **SELECTED PUBLICATIONS** Co-auth, Cognitive and Motivational Influences on Spontaneous Comforting Behavior, Brown & Benchmark, 93; A Social Skills Analysis of Relationship Maintenance: How Individual Differences in Communication Skills Affect the Achievement of Relationship Ffunctions, Communication and Relational Maintenance, Acad Press, 94; auth, Unsupportive Relationships: Deficiencies in the Support-giving Skills of the Lonely Pperson's Friends, Communication of Social Support: Messages, Interactions, Relationships, and Community, Sage, 94. **CONTACT ADDRESS** Dept of Commun, Univ Delaware, 162 Ctr Mall, Newark, DE, 19716.

SAMUELS, MARILYN S.
DISCIPLINE TECHNICAL COMMUNICATIONS **EDUCATION** Hunter Col, BA, MA; Univ NY, PhD. **CAREER** English, Case Western Reserve Univ. **HONORS AND AWARDS** Dir, Technical Writing. **SELECTED PUBLICATIONS** Auth or ed, The Technical Writing Process; Writing the Research Paper. **CONTACT ADDRESS** Case Western Reserve Univ, 10900 Euclid Ave, Cleveland, OH, 44106.

SAMUELS, SHIRLEY
DISCIPLINE ENGLISH **EDUCATION** Univ Calif at Berkeley, BA, 77, MA, 81, PhD, 86. **CAREER** Asst prof, Eng, to ASSOC PROF & DIR, WOMEN'S STUD, CORNELL UNIV **MEMBERSHIPS** Am Antiquarian Soc **SELECTED PUBLICATIONS** Auth, "Plague and Politics in 1793: Arthur Mervyn," Criticism, 85; auth, "The Family, the State, and the Novel in the Early Republic," Am Quart, 86; auth, "Infidelity and Contagion: The Rhetoric of Revolution," Early Am Lit, 87; auth, "Wieland: Alien and Infidel," Early Am Lit, 90; auth, "Generation through Violence," in New Essays on Last of the Mohicans, 92; auth, "The Identity of Slavery," in The Culture of Sentiment: Race, Gender and Sentimentality in 19th-Century America, Oxford Univ Press, 92, repr in Romances of the Republic: Women, the Family and Violence in the Literature of the Early American Nation, Oxford Univ Press, 96; auth, "Miscegenated America," Am Lit Hist, Fall 97. **CONTACT ADDRESS** Eng Dept, Cornell Univ, 335 Rockefeller, Ithaca, NY, 14853. **EMAIL** srs8@cornell.edu

SAMUELS, WILFRED D.
PERSONAL Born 02/07/1947, Puerto Limon, Costa Rica, m, 1980 **DISCIPLINE** ENGLISH **EDUCATION** Univ of California, Riverside, CA, BA, 1971; University of Iowa, Iowa City, IA, MA, PhD, 1971-77. **CAREER** Univ of Colorado, Boulder, CO, asst prof, 1978-85; Benjamin Banneker Honors Coll, Prairie View AM, TX, assoc prof, 1985-87; Univ of Utah, Salt Lake City, UT, assoc prof, 1987-. **HONORS AND AWARDS** Ford Foundation Post Doctoral Fellow, Ford, 1984, 1985; CAAS UCLA, Postdoctoral Fellow, 1982, 1983; NEH Symposium Grants, 1980, 1984, 1989; Outstanding Teacher Award, several, 1978-84; Ramona Cannon Award for teaching Excellence in the Humanities, 1992; Student's Choice Award, 1993; The University of Utah, Distinguished Teaching Award, 1994. **MEMBERSHIPS** Popular Culture; MLA; Am Literature Assn. **CONTACT ADDRESS** Professor, Department of English, Univ of Utah, 3407 LNCO, Salt Lake City, UT, 84112.

SANCHEZ-EPPLER, KAREN
DISCIPLINE AMERICAN LITERATURE **EDUCATION** Williams Col, BA; Cambridge Univ, BA; Johns Hopkins Univ, PhD. **CAREER** Instr, Amherst Col. **RESEARCH** Imagining rel(s) between lit, soc structures, and soc change. **SELECTED PUBLICATIONS** Auth, Touching Liberty: Abolition, Feminism and the Politics of the Body, 93. **CONTACT ADDRESS** Amherst Col, Amherst, MA, 01002-5000.

SAND, R.H.
PERSONAL Born 12/30/1936, New York, NY, m, 1964, 2 children **DISCIPLINE** ENGLISH **EDUCATION** Harvard Col, BA 58; Harvard Law Sch, JD 61. **CAREER** Kirye Schuler Fierman Hays Handler, 65-70; Allied signal Inc, 70-. **MEMBERSHIPS** Assoc of the Bar NYC **RESEARCH** Legal developments in occupational safety and health. **SELECTED PUBLICATIONS** Employee Relations Law Journal, columnist on Safety and Health. **CONTACT ADDRESS** Allied Signal Inc, 101 Columbia Rd, Morristown, NJ, 07962.

SANDERS, MARK
DISCIPLINE ENGLISH LANGUAGE AND LITERATURE **EDUCATION** Brown Univ, PhD, 92. **CAREER** Assoc prof **RESEARCH** African-American literature; 20th-century American literature. **SELECTED PUBLICATIONS** Ed, A Son's Return: Selected Essays of Sterling A. Brown. **CONTACT ADDRESS** English Dept, Emory Univ, 1380 Oxford Rd NE, Atlanta, GA, 30322-1950.

SANDERS, ROBERT E.
DISCIPLINE INTERPERSONAL COMMUNICATION **EDUCATION** PhD. **CAREER** Univ Albany - SUNY **SELECTED PUBLICATIONS** Auth, Cognitive Foundations of Calculated Speech, 87; The role of mass communication processes in the social upheavals in the Soviet Union, Eastern Europe, and China, SUNY Press, 92; Cognition, computation, and conversation, Human Comm Res, 92; Culture, communication, and preferences for directness in the expression of directives, Comm Theory, 94; A retrospective essay on the consequentiality of communication, Lawrence Erlbaum, 95; A neo-rhetorical perspective: The enactment of role-identities as interactive and strategic, Lawrence Erlbaum, 95; The sequential-inferential theories of Sanders and Gottman, SUNY Press, 95; An impersonal basis for shared interpretations of messages in context, Context Press , 97; The production of symbolic objects as components of larger wholes , Lawrence Erlbaum, 97; Children's neo-rhetorical participation in peer interactions, Falmer , 97; Find your partner and do-si-do: The formation of personal relationships between social beings, Jour Soc & Personal Relationships, 97. **CONTACT ADDRESS** Univ Albany-SUNY, 1400 Washington Ave, Albany, NY, 12222. **EMAIL** RES72@cnsvax.albany.edu

SANDERS, SCOTT P.
DISCIPLINE PROFESSIONAL WRITING AND EDITING **EDUCATION** Univ Colo, PhD, 80. **CAREER** Instr, Univ NMex, 84-; past ed, IEEE Transactions on Prof Commun. **HONORS AND AWARDS** NCTE Award for Best Article, 89. **RESEARCH** Technical communication. **SELECTED PUBLICATIONS** Coauth, The Physics of Skiing, Am Inst of Physics Press, 96; coed, Frontier Gothic, 93; Weber Studies, spec issue on Nat Am Lit; IEEETransPC issue on ethics and prof commun. **CONTACT ADDRESS** Univ NMex, Albuquerque, NM, 87131.

SANDIFORD, KEITH
DISCIPLINE EIGHTEENTH-CENTURY LITERATURE, THE NOVEL, AFRICAN -AMERICAN LITERATURE **EDUCATION** Univ Ill, Urbana-Champaign, PhD, 79. **CAREER** Prof, La State Univ. **HONORS AND AWARDS** Res fel, NEH, 87. **RESEARCH** Sugar and colonizing discourses; colonial (West Indian) literature; slavery and anti-slavery. **SELECTED PUBLICATIONS** Auth, Images of the African in his Literature from Renaissance to Enlightenment, Images de L'Africain de L'Antiquite au XXe Siecle, 87; The Sugared Muse or The Case of James Grainger, M.D. (1721-66), Nieuwe West-Indische Gids, 87; Measuring the Moment: Strategies of Protest in Eighteenth-Century Afro-English Writing, 88; Inkle and Yarico: The Construction of Alterity from History to Literature, Nieuwe West-Indische Gids, 90; Gothic and Intertextual Constructions in Gloria Naylor's Linden Hills, Ariz Quart, 91; Rochefort's History: The Poetics of Collusion in a Colonizing Narrative, Papers in Lang and Lit, 93; 'Our Caribs' are not Savages: The Use of Colloquy in Rochefort's Natural and Moral History of the Caribby-Islands, Stud in Western Civilization, 93. **CONTACT ADDRESS** Dept of Eng, Louisiana State Univ, 212V Allen Hall, Baton Rouge, LA, 70803. **EMAIL** ksandif@lsuvm.sncc.lsu.edu

SANDS, HELEN R.
DISCIPLINE COMMUNICATION **EDUCATION** Univ VT, BA; Southern IL Univ, MA, PhD. **CAREER** Prof & Coordr, Interpersonal-Orgn Commun; fac, Univ Southern IN, 69-; fac sponsor, Commun Arts Club & USI's chap Alpha Chi. **HONORS AND AWARDS** Alumni Teach of the Yr, 81; Order of Omega Teach of the Yr, 97. **MEMBERSHIPS** Speech Commun Assoc. **RESEARCH** Interpersonal communication; public address. **SELECTED PUBLICATIONS** Coauth, textbk, Public Conversations. **CONTACT ADDRESS** Dept of Commun, Univ South Ind, 8600 University Blvd, Evansville, IN, 47712. **EMAIL** hsands.ucs@smtp.usi.edu

SANDSTROEM, YVONNE LUTTROPP
PERSONAL Born 08/10/1933, Vasteras, Sweden, m, 1954, 2 children **DISCIPLINE** ENGLISH & SCANDINAVIAN LITERATURE **EDUCATION** Brown Univ, AM, 66, PhD(English), 70. **CAREER** Asst prof, 69-75, ASSOC PROF ENGLISH, SOUTHEASTERN MASS UNIV, 75- **MEMBERSHIPS** MLA; Soc Advan Scand Studies; Renaissance Soc Am; Am Literary Translr Asn. **RESEARCH** Seventeenth century English literature; modern Scandinavian literature; translations of Swedish literature. **SELECTED PUBLICATIONS** Auth Ett 'Andetag Djupt Ar Livet' - Swedish - Andersson,P/, World Literature Today, Vol 0066, 1992. **CONTACT ADDRESS** Dept of English, Southeastern Mass Univ, North Dartmouth, MA, 02747.

SANTOS, SHEROD
PERSONAL Born 09/09/1948, Greenville, SC, m, 1975, 2 children **DISCIPLINE** ENGLISH, PHILOSOPHY **EDUCATION** San Diego State Univ, BA, 71; MA, 74;, MFA, 78; Univ Utah, PhD, 82. **CAREER** Asst prof, Calif State Univ San Bernardino, 82-83; asst prof, Univ Mo Columbia, 83-86; vis prof, Univ Calif Irvine, 89-90; assoc prof, Univ Mo Columbia, 86-92; prof, Univ MO Columbia, 93-. **HONORS AND AWARDS** Utah Arts Council Award in Lit, 80; Discovery The Nation award, 78; Pushcart Prize in Poetry, 80; Oscar Blumenthal Prize, 81; Nat Poetry Series Selection, 82; Meralmikjen Fel in Poetry, Bread Loaf Writers' Conference, 82; Ingram Merrill Found Grant, 82; The Robert Frost Poet, 84; Mo Arts Council Award in Lit, 87; Fel to the Yaddo Center fort he Arts, 87; NBC Today Show Appearance, 87; Nat Endowment for the Arts Grant, 87; Weldon Springs Res Grant, Univ Mo, 91-92; Chancellor's Award for Outstanding Fac Res, Univ Mo, 93; Pushcart Prize in the Essay, 94; British Arts Council Int Travel Grant, 95; Appointed Mem, Nat Endowment for the Arts Lit Panel, 95; BF Conners Award in Poetry, 98. **MEMBERSHIPS** Acad Am Poets; Poetry Soc of Am; PEN Am Center; Robinson Jeffers Soc; Poets and Writers; Associated Writing Programs. **RESEARCH** Poetry and Poetics. **SELECTED PUBLICATIONS** Auth, The City of Women, 93; The Pilot Star Elegies, 98; numerous chapbooks, screenplay, poetry in journals and magazines. **CONTACT ADDRESS** Dept of English, Univ of Mo, 107 Tate Hall, Columbia, MO, 65211. **EMAIL** engss@showme.missouri.edu

SAPERSTEIN, JEFF
DISCIPLINE COMPOSITION, AMERICAN LITERATURE, SHAKESPEARE, AND FILM **EDUCATION** SUNY, Albany, BA; Northeastern Univ, MA; Univ NH, PhD. **CAREER** Prof, Radford Univ. **RESEARCH** Compos theory/pedag; gender studies; film theory; ethnic studies; Shakespeare. **SELECTED PUBLICATIONS** Publ articles in film studies, on films of Woody Allen, on Roth, Thoreau, Morrison, and Atwood. **CONTACT ADDRESS** Radford Univ, Radford, VA, 24142. **EMAIL** jsaperst@runet.edu

SARKODIE-MENSAH, KWASI
PERSONAL Born 06/13/1955, Ejisu, Ashanti, Ghana, m, 1980 **DISCIPLINE** LIBRARY SCIENCE **EDUCATION** Universidad Complutense, diploma, 1978; University of Ghana, BA (w/ honors), 1979; Clarion University, MSLS, 1983; University of

Illinois, PhD, 1988. **CAREER** Ahmadiyya Secondary School, teacher, 1979-80; Origbo Community High School, teacher, 1980-82; Clarion University, graduate asst, 1982-83; University of Illinois, graduate asst, 1984-86; Xavier University of Louisiana, head of public services, 1986-89; Northeastern University, library instruction coordinator, 1989-92; Boston College, chief reference librarian, 1992-95; Commonwealth of Massachusetts, court interpreter, 1992-; US Attorney General's Office, Boston, consultant, African languages; College of Advancing Studies, Boston College, faculty, 1996-; Boston College Libraries, manager of instructional services, 1995-. **HONORS AND AWARDS** University of Illinois, Fellow, 1986-87; Research Strategies, Top 20 Articles in Library Instruction, 1986; Origbo Community High School, Best Teacher, 1981, 1982; Spanish Government, Scholarship to study abroad, 1978; University of Ghana, Scholarship, 1975-79. **MEMBERSHIPS** American Library Assn, 1984-; Massachusetts Faculty Development Consortium, advsry bd mbr, 1992-; ACRL/IS Diverse Committee, chair, 1993-95; Northeastern University Committee to Improve College Teaching, 1989-92; Multicultural Network, 1992-; Boston College, Martin Luther King Committee, 1993-; ACRL/IS Committee on Education for Library Instructors, ACRL/IS Award Committee; African Pastoral Center, Archdiocese of Boston, bd mem. **SELECTED PUBLICATIONS** Author, works include: Making Term Paper Counseling More Meaningful, 1989; Writing in a Language You Don't Know, 1990; The Intl Ta: A Beat from a Foreign Drummer, 1991; Dealing with Intl Students in a Multicultural Era, 1992; Paraprofessionals in Reference Services: An Untapped Mine, 1993; editor: Library Instruction Roundtable Newsletter, 1991-92; consultant: Northeastern Univ Project on the History of Black Writing, 1990-; The International Student in the US Academic Library: Bldg Bridges to Better Bibliographic Instruction; Nigerian Americans, 1995; Human Aspect of Reference in the Era of Technology, 1997; Using Humor for Effective Library Instruction, 1998; International Students US Trends, Cultural Adjustments, 1998; Reference Services for the Adult Learner, 1999. **CONTACT ADDRESS** Manager, Instructional Services, Boston College, 307 O'Neill Library, Chestnut Hill, MA, 02167. **EMAIL** sarkodik@bc.edu

SARLOS, ROBERT KAROLY
PERSONAL Born 06/06/1931, Budapest, Hungary, m, 1962, 2 children **DISCIPLINE** THEATRE HISTORY **EDUCATION** Occidental Col, BA, 59; Yale Univ, PhD(hist of theatre), 65. **CAREER** Instr English, Mitchell Col, 62-63; from lectr to acting asst prof, 63-65, asst prof, 66-70, assoc prof, 70-79, PROF DRAMATIC ART, UNIV CALIF, DAVIS, 79-, Vpres, Woodland Opera House Inc, 80- **MEMBERSHIPS** Int Fed Theatre Res; Am Soc Theatre Res. **RESEARCH** Elizabethan, Baroque and American theatre. **SELECTED PUBLICATIONS** Auth The Impact Of Working-Conditions Upon Acting Style/, Theatre Res Int, Vol 0020, 1995. **CONTACT ADDRESS** Dept of Dramatic Art, Univ of Calif, Davis, CA, 95616.

SASSON, JACK MURAD
PERSONAL Born 10/01/1941, Aleppo, Syria **DISCIPLINE** FOREIGN LANGUAGES, HISTORY **EDUCATION** Brooklyn Col, BA, 62; Brandeis Univ, MA, 63, PhD, 66. **CAREER** From asst prof to assoc prof, 66-77, Prof Relig, Univ NC, Chapel Hill, 77-, Soc Relig Higher Educ fel, 69-70; assoc ed, J Am Orient Soc, 77. **MEMBERSHIPS** Soc Bibl Lit; Am Orient Soc; Israel Explor Soc; Dutch Orient Soc. **RESEARCH** Ancient Near Eastern societies. **SELECTED PUBLICATIONS** Auth, Albright As An Orientalist + Albright,William,Foxwell And Palestinian Archaeol/, Bibl Archaeol, Vol 0056, 1993; Jonah - A Commentary - Limburg,J/, Interpretation-A J Of Bible And Theol, Vol 0049, 1995. **CONTACT ADDRESS** Dept of Relig, Univ of NC, Chapel Hill, NC, 27514.

SASSON, SARAH DIANE HYDE
PERSONAL Born 08/27/1946, Asheville, NC, m, 1969, 3 children **DISCIPLINE** AMERICAN LITERATURE & HISTORY **EDUCATION** Univ NC, BA, 68, PhD(Eng), 80; Univ IL, Urbana, MA, 71. **CAREER** Instr Eng, 80-81, lectr Am studies, 81-82, Dir, Master of Arts in Lib Studies Prog, Duke Univ, 87-; Dir, Univ MAT Prog, Duke Univ, 91-95; Assoc of Graduate Lib Studies, Pres, 94-96. **HONORS AND AWARDS** Am Coun Learned Soc Fel. **MEMBERSHIPS** Am Folklore Soc; Am Studies Asn; MLA. **RESEARCH** Shaker Lit; Am autobiography; Am relig lit. **SELECTED PUBLICATIONS** Auth, The Shaker Personal Narrative, Univ TN Press (in prep). **CONTACT ADDRESS** Duke Univ, Box 90095, Durham, NC, 27708.

SASSON, VICTOR
PERSONAL Born 12/20/1937, Baghdad, Iraq, d, 1 child **DISCIPLINE** RELIGION; ENGLISH LITERATURE **EDUCATION** Univ London, BA honors, 73; New York Univ, PhD, 79. **CAREER** Univ S Africa, sr lectr, 81-85; Long Island Univ, asst prof, 90-91; Touro Col NY, asst prof, 90-96. **HONORS AND AWARDS** Thayer fel; AAR. **MEMBERSHIPS** Colum Univ Sem Hebrew Bible and Shakespeare; SOTS. **RESEARCH** Text and language of Hebrew bible; N W Semitic Epigraphy; tense and aspect in Biblical Hebrew and old Aramaic; ancient near east. **SELECTED PUBLICATIONS** Auth, The Literary and

Theological Function of Job's Wife in the Book of Job, Biblica, 98; Some Observations on the Use and Original Purpose of the Waw Consecutive in Old Aramaic and Biblical Hebrew, VT, 97; The Inscription of Achish Governor of Eqron and Philistine Dialect, Cult and Culture, UF, 97; The Old Aramaic Inscription for Tell Dan: Philological Literary and Historical Aspects, JSS, 95; The Book of Oraccular Visions of Balaam from Deir Alla, UF, 86. **CONTACT ADDRESS** Brighton 3F, Brooklyn, NY, 11235.

SAUCERMAN, JAMES RAY
PERSONAL Born 11/14/1931, Colorado Springs, CO, m, 1951, 1 child **DISCIPLINE** ENGLISH **EDUCATION** Univ Northern Colo, Greeley, BA, 57, MA, 58; Univ Mo-Columbia, PhD(English), 77. **CAREER** Teacher English & French, Scottsbluff High Sch, Nebr, 58-62; from instr to asst prof English, 62-75, assoc prof, 77-80, PROF ENGLISH, NORTHWEST MO STATE UNIV, 80- **MEMBERSHIPS** MLA; Midwest Mod Lang Asn; Thoreau Soc; Poe Studies Asn; Western Lit Asn. **RESEARCH** Nineteenth century American literature; twentieth century American literature; Western American literature. **SELECTED PUBLICATIONS** Auth, Critical Essays On Bly,Robert - Davis,Wv/, Western Am Lit, Vol 0029, 1995; 'Bone Dance' - New And Selected Poems, 1965-1993 - Rose,W/, Western Am Lit, Vol 0030, 1995; 'Facing The Music' - Berger,B/, Western Am Lit, Vol 0031, 1996. **CONTACT ADDRESS** Dept of English, Northwest Missouri State Univ, 800 University Dr, Maryville, MO, 64468-6015.

SAUER, ELIZABETH
PERSONAL Kitchener, ON, Canada **DISCIPLINE** ENGLISH **EDUCATION** Wilfred Laurier Univ, HBA, 86; Univ Western Ont, MA, 87, PhD, 91. **CAREER** Res asst, transl, Wilfred Lauier Univ, 82-86; tchg asst, 86-90, res asst, 90-91, Univ Western Ont; asst prof, 92-95, ASSOC PROF, BROCK UNIV 95-. **HONORS AND AWARDS** Can Fedn Hum Grant, 94-97; SSHRC Doc Fel, Univ Western Ont, 88-91; Gold Medal Eng, Wilfred Laurier Univ, 86. **MEMBERSHIPS** Milton Soc Am; Can Soc Renaissance Studs; Asn Can Col Univ Tchrs Eng; Renaissance Soc Am; Ctr Reformation Renaissance Studs. **SELECTED PUBLICATIONS** Auth, Barbarous Dissonance and Images of Voice in Milton's Epics, 96; auth, The Prodigious Births of Scylla, Mrs. Rump, and Milton's Sin, in The Ben Jonson J: Literary Contexts in the age of Elizabeth, James and Charles, 2, 96; co-ed, Agnostics: Arenas of Creative Contest, 97. **CONTACT ADDRESS** Dept of English, Brock Univ, St. Catherines, ON, L2S 3A1. **EMAIL** emsauer@spartan.ac. brocku.ca

SAUNDERS, DAVID
DISCIPLINE MASS COMMUNICATIONS **EDUCATION** PhD. **CAREER** Prof/hd Sch Media and Journalism, Fac Arts, Queensland Univ Tech, 96-; comnr, Australian Film Commission, 92-; dep dir, Australian Key Ctr Cult and Media Policy, 95-. **HONORS AND AWARDS** Recip, num natl res grants. **SELECTED PUBLICATIONS** Auth, Featuring Australia: The Cinema of Charles Chauvel, Allen and Unwin, 91; Framing Culture: Criticism and Policy in Australia, Allen and Unwin, 92; co-ed, The Media in Australia: Industries, Texts, Audiences, Allen and Unwin, 93; coauth, Contemporary Australian Television, Univ New South Wales, 94; coauth, Australian Television and International Mediascapes, Cambridge Univ, 96; co-ed, New Patterns in Global Television: Peripheral Vision, Oxford Univ, 96; coauth, The Missing Link: Australian Television Programmers and Schedulers, Australian FTR Sch, 97; co-ed, The Media in Australia: Industries, Texts, Audiences, 2nd ed, Allen and Unwin, 97; coauth, Cultural Policy, Sage Publ, 98.

SAUNDERS, WILLIAM
PERSONAL Born 11/05/1946, Port Chester, NY, m, 1977, 2 children **DISCIPLINE** ENGLISH **EDUCATION** Denison Univ, BA summa cum laude 68; Univ Iowa, MA 73, PhD 75; Harvard Univ, postdoc 79-80. **CAREER** Harvard Univ Grad Sch Design, editor, 94-, various responsibilities 82-93; program adv 80-82; Tchr at Harvard, Tufts, Boston and Whittenburg Univs 72-82. **HONORS AND AWARDS** Phi Beta Kappa; Environmentalist of the Year. **MEMBERSHIPS** AIA **RESEARCH** Architecture and the arts; criticism; cultural studies. **SELECTED PUBLICATIONS** Auth, Orthodoxies of the Anti-Orthodox: A Review of the Critical Landscape, Design Bk Rev, 98; auth, From Photograph to Place: Disappointment of Delight, Harv Design Mag, 98; The Early Work of Daniel Urban Kiley, ed, Princeton Archi Press, 99; auth, Richard Haag: Bloedel Reserve and Gas Works Park, ed, NY, Princeton Archi Press, 97; auth, Poetic Perception and Gnomic Fantasy in the Writing of Rem Koolhaas, Jour of Archi Edu, 97; auth, A Skeptic's Approach to Prayer, The World, 97; auth, Durability and Emphemerality: From the Editor, Harvard Design Mag, 97; auth, Recognizing Neglected Design: From the Editor, Harvard Design Mag, 97; auth, Changing Cities and New Urbanism: From the Editor, Harvard Design Mag, 97; auth, Reflections on Architectural Practices in the Nineties, ed, NY, Princeton Archi Press, 96; auth, Historic Auburndale, ed, 2nd rev exp edition, Auburndale Assoc Press, 96; auth, State of Design Publishing: From the Editor, GSD News, 96; auth, Architecture Teaching and Research: From the Editor, GSD News, 96. **CONTACT ADDRESS** Dept of External Relations, Harvard Univ, 228 Islington Rd, Newton, MA, 02466. **EMAIL** saunders@gsd. harvard.edu

SAUR, PAMELA S.
PERSONAL New York, NY, m, 1969, 2 children **DISCIPLINE** FOREIGN LANGUAGE; LITERATURE **EDUCATION** Univ Iowa, BA, 70, MA 72, PhD 82; Univ Mass, MEd 84. **CAREER** Auburn Univ, asst prof 84-88; Lamar Univ, asst prof, assoc prof, 89 to 95-. **HONORS AND AWARDS** Schtzkammer Ch Ed; TFLAB Ed. **RESEARCH** Modern Austrian Literature; Lang and Lit; Pedagogy; Comparative Lit. **SELECTED PUBLICATIONS** Auth, The Place of Asian Literature in Translation, in Amer Univ's, CLA Jour, 98; Barbara Frischmuth's Use of Mythology in Her Demeter Triology, Out from the shadows: Essays on Contemporary Aust Women Writers and Filmmakers, Margarette Lamb-Faffelbeger, ed, Riverside CA, Ariadne Press, 97; Real and Imaginary Journeys In Barbara Frischmuth's Writings, Ger Notes and Rev, 97; Amer Lit and Aust Lit, Two Histories, Geschichte der osterreichischen Lit, Teil I, Donald G. Daviau, Herbert Arlt, eds, St Ingbert, Rohrig Univ, 96; Regional dramas of Karl Schonherr and the Nazi Stigma, Ger Notes and Rev, 96; Property Wealth and the Amer Dream, in: Barn Burning, Teaching Faulkner, Cen for Faulkner Stud, MO State U, 95; Captain Anthony Forthcoming; Lucas: An Austrian Pioneer, Austrian Info, 95. **CONTACT ADDRESS** Dept of Literature, Lamar Univ, PO Box 10023, Beaumont, TX, 77710. **EMAIL** saurps@hal.lamar.edu

SAUTER, KEVIN O.
PERSONAL Born 03/29/1952, Minneapolis, MN, m, 1981, 3 children **DISCIPLINE** COMMUNICATION **EDUCATION** Moorehead State Univ, BA, 74; Miami Univ, MA, 76; Penn State Univ, PhD, 84. **CAREER** Instr, James Madison Univ, 79-82; Assoc Prof, Univ St. Thomas, 82-; reviewer, Houton Mifflin Publ, 92-93; reviewer, McGraw Hill Publ, 92. **HONORS AND AWARDS** Mem, Media Schol Roundtable, Central States Commun Asn Convention, 4/97; First place award in Original Arts Production category, for:: Stained Glass, Minn Community Television Awards, 9x. **MEMBERSHIPS** Nat Commun Asn; Broadcast Educr Asn; Central States Commun Asn; Minn Commun & Theater Asn; Screenwriters Workshop. **RESEARCH** Television criticism; politics and TV; Presidential public address. **SELECTED PUBLICATIONS** Auth, The 1976 Mondale-Dole Debate, Thetorical Studies of National Political Debates, Praeger Press, 89, 93; Local Television, Lighting in a Tube: The Television Industry in America, Allyn and Bacon, 96; Martha's Magic, 91; Stained Glass, 9x; A Couple of Blaguards, 93; Producer, Date of Birth, 98; producer of numerous other video/audio productions. **CONTACT ADDRESS** 2205 Dellwood St. N., Roseville, MN, 55113-4308. **EMAIL** kosauter@stthomas.edu

SAVAGE, ANNE
DISCIPLINE ENGLISH LITERATURE **EDUCATION** Calgary Univ, BA; Univ London, PhD. **RESEARCH** Old and Middle English lit and language; medieval allegory; semiotic theory. **SELECTED PUBLICATIONS** Trans, The Anglo-Saxon Chronicles, 82; trans, Anchoritic Spirituality, 91. **CONTACT ADDRESS** English Dept, McMaster Univ, 1280 Main St W, Hamilton, ON, L8S 4L9.

SAVAGE, ELIZABETH
PERSONAL Born 10/23/1939, Buffalo, NY **DISCIPLINE** ENGLISH **EDUCATION** Medaille Col, BA, 61; St Louis Univ, PhD(English), 71. **CAREER** From instr to asst prof, 71-75, chmn, Div Humanities, 74-81, assoc prof English, Medaille Col, 75-; coord general Education, 97-. **MEMBERSHIPS** MLA **RESEARCH** Renaissance literature. **SELECTED PUBLICATIONS** Ed, John Donne's Devotions upon Emergent Occasions: A Critical Edition with Introduction and Commentary, Inst English Speech & Lit, Salzburg, 75; compiler (with Walter Lehrman & Dolores Sarafinski), The Plays of Ben Jonson: A Reference Guide, G K Hall, 80. **CONTACT ADDRESS** Dept of English, Medaille Col, 18 Agassiz Circle, Buffalo, NY, 14214-2695.

SAVVAS, MINAS
PERSONAL Born 04/02/1939, Athens, Greece **DISCIPLINE** COMPARATIVE LITERATURE, CREATIVE WRITING **EDUCATION** Univ Ill, BA, 64, MA, 65; Univ Calif, Santa Barbara, PhD(English), 71. **CAREER** Asst prof English, Univ Calif, Santa Barbara, 65-68; assoc prof, 68-74, Prof English, San Diego State Univ, 74- **MEMBERSHIPS** MLA; Mod Greek Studies Asn; Hellenic Cult Soc. **RESEARCH** Modern Greek literature; continental novel; translation. **SELECTED PUBLICATIONS** Auth, Remembering Ritsos,Yannis + Poet/, Literary Review, Vol 0036, 1993; The 'Fourth Dimension' - Ritsos,Y, Green,P, Translator, Bardsley,B, Translator/, World Lit Today, Vol 0068, 1994; The Oldest Dead White Europ Males And Other Reflections On The Classics - Knox,B/, J Of Modern Greek Studies, Vol 0012, 1994; 'Vreghmeno Rouho' - Bramos,G/, World Lit Today, Vol 0068, 1994; 'Mavra Litharia' - Ganas,M/, World Lit Today, Vol 0068, 1994; I 'Mihani Ton Mistikon' - Siotis,D/, World Lit Today, Vol 0068, 1994; The Poetry And Poetics Of Cavafy,Constantine,P - Aesthetic Visions Of Sensual Reality - Anton,Jp/, World Lit Today, Vol 0070, 1996; 'Oudheteri Zoni' - Greek - Kariotis,M/, World Lit Today, Vol 0070, 1996; To 'Taxidi 1963-1992' - Greek - Tsaloumas,D/, World Lit Today, Vol 0070, 1996. **CONTACT ADDRESS** Sch of Lit, San Diego State Univ, San Diego, CA, 92115.

SAWAYA, FRANCESCA
DISCIPLINE AMERICAN LITERATURE **EDUCATION** Univ Calif, BA, 84; Univ York, Eng, MA, 86; Cornell Univ, MA, 88, PhD, 92. **CAREER** Asst prof, 95-. **SELECTED PUBLICATIONS** Auth, The Problem of the South: Economic Determination, Gender Determination, and the Politics of Genre in Glasgow's Virginia, Ellen Glasgow: New Perspectives, Tennessee Univ Press; Domesticity, Cultivation, and Vocation in Jane Addams and Sarah Orne Jewett, Nineteenth-Century Lit 48, 94; Between Revolution and Racism: Colonialism and the American Indian, The Prairie, James Finimore Cooper: His Country and His Art, The Bicentennial Papers, SUNY Oneonta, 91. **CONTACT ADDRESS** Dept of Eng, Portland State Univ, PO Box 751, Portland, OR, 97207-0751. **EMAIL** sawaya@nh1.nh.pdx.edu

SAWYER-LAUCANNO, CHRISTOPHER
PERSONAL Born 01/04/1951, San Mateo, CA, m, 1987, 2 children **DISCIPLINE** LITERATURE **EDUCATION** Univ Calif, Santa Barbara, BA, 71; Brandeis Univ, MA, 75, PhD, 82. **CAREER** Lecturer, Mass Inst of Tech, 82-90; Writer-in-residence, Mass Inst of Tech, Prog in Writing & Humanistic Stud, 90-. **HONORS AND AWARDS** NEA Translation Fellow, 91. **RESEARCH** Contemporary comparative literature; translation theory & practice; biography; ethnography. **SELECTED PUBLICATIONS** Auth, The World's Words: A Semiotic Reading of Joyce and Rabelais, Alyscamps, 93; trans, Rafael Alberti, Concerning the Angels, Alyscamps, 95; trans, Demons & Spirits: Contemporary Chol Mayan Chants & Incantations, Alyscamps. **CONTACT ADDRESS** Prog in Writing & Humanistic Stud, Massachusetts Inst of Tech, Cambridge, MA, 02139. **EMAIL** csl@mit.edu

SAYRE, ROBERT FREEMAN
PERSONAL Born 11/06/1933, Columbus, OH **DISCIPLINE** ENGLISH **EDUCATION** Wesleyan Univ, BA, 55; Yale Univ, MA, 58, PhD(English), 62. **CAREER** Vis instr English, Wesleyan Univ, 60; from instr to asst prof, Univ Ill, 61-65; from asst prof to assoc prof, 65-72, PROF ENGLISH, UNIV IOWA, 72-, Univ Ill res grant, Grad Col, 62; lectr Am lit, Lund Univ, Sweden, 63-64, res fel, 64-65; res prof, Univ Iowa, 69-70, 73-74; Guggenheim fel, 73-74; chmn Am lit sect, Midwest Mod Lang Asn, 73. **MEMBERSHIPS** MLA; Midwest Mod Lang Asn; NCTE; Am Studies Asn. **RESEARCH** American autobiography; self and social vision; American Indian literature. **SELECTED PUBLICATIONS** Auth, Writing In The New Nation - Prose, Print, And Politics In The Early United-States - Ziff,L/, Am Hist Rev, Vol 0098, 1993; The Cult Of Sentiment - Race, Gender And Sentimentality In 19th-Century Am - Samuels,S/, William And Mary Quart, Vol 0052, 1995; Franklin,Benjamin And His Enemies - Middlekauff,R/, Biog-An Interdisciplinary Quart, Vol 0020, 1997. **CONTACT ADDRESS** Dept of English, Univ of Iowa, 308 English Phil Bld, Iowa City, IA, 52242-1492.

SCANLAN, J.T.
DISCIPLINE EIGHTEENTH-CENTURY ENGLISH LITERATURE, LEGAL HISTORY **EDUCATION** Univ Mich, PhD. **CAREER** Vis asst prof, Vassar Col; asst prof Eng, Providence Col. **RESEARCH** The spirit of contradiction in 18th-century London; legal history, contemporary non-fiction. **SELECTED PUBLICATIONS** Writes on eighteenth-century English literature, legal history, and contemporary non-fiction. **CONTACT ADDRESS** Dept of Eng, Providence Col, EH 215, Providence, RI, 02918-0001. **EMAIL** hambone@providence.edu

SCANLAN, THOMAS
DISCIPLINE RHETORIC STUDIES **EDUCATION** Cornell Univ, MA, Univ Minn, PhD. **RESEARCH** Landscape as index to cultural values; agriculture and ideology; family and literature in America; technology and control of nature. **SELECTED PUBLICATIONS** Auth, Family, Drama, and American Dreams; The Prairie Eye. **CONTACT ADDRESS** Rhetoric Dept, Univ of Minnesota, Twin Cities, 64 Classroom Office Bldg, 1994 Buford Ave, St. Paul, MN, 55108.

SCHAAFSMA, DAVID
PERSONAL Born 01/06/1953, Grand Rapids, MI, m, 1994, 1 child **DISCIPLINE** ENGLISH **EDUCATION** Calvin Col, BA, 75; Univ of Mich, MA, 82, PhD, 90; Western Mich Univ, MFA, 84. **CAREER** English teacher, Holland Christian High School, 76-77; English teacher, Hudsonville Unity Christian High School, 77-81; English instr, Grand Valley State Univ, 81-85; English ed, Univ of Mich, 85-90; English ed, Univ of Wis-Madison, 90-95; English Ed, Teachers Col, Columbia Univ, 95-. **HONORS AND AWARDS** NCTE Richard A. Meade Award, 94. **MEMBERSHIPS** NCTE; MLA; AERA. **RESEARCH** Narrative inquiry; English education; community-based writing projects; teaching of writing. **SELECTED PUBLICATIONS** Auth, Eating on the Street: Teaching Literacy in a Multicultural Society, Pittsburgh Press, 93; coauth, Language and Reflection, MacMillan, 92; co-ed, Literacy and Democracy, NCTE, 98. **CONTACT ADDRESS** Teachers Col, Columbia Univ, 525 W 120th St., New York, NY, 10027. **EMAIL** ds339@columbia.edu

SCHABER, BENNET
DISCIPLINE ENGLISH LITERATURE **EDUCATION** Brown Univ, PhD, 87. **CAREER** Asst prof, SUNY Oswego. **RESEARCH** Theory; lit and the visual arts; earlier Eng lit. **SELECTED PUBLICATIONS** Auth, Postmodernism Across the Ages, Syracuse UP, 94; Vision Procured: Psychoananalysis and the Social History of Art in Vision and Textuality, Duke UP, 96; essays on Film, Freud, Chaucer, Boccaccio, Lacan. **CONTACT ADDRESS** SUNY Oswego, 213C Swetman, Oswego, NY, 13126. **EMAIL** schaber@Osw ego.edu

SCHACHTERLE, LANCE E.
DISCIPLINE ENGLISH **EDUCATION** Haverford, BA, 66; Univ Penn, PhD, 70. **CAREER** Asst prof, to prof, Eng, and provost, Worcester Polytech Inst **MEMBERSHIPS** Am Antiquarian Soc **RESEARCH** James Fenimore Cooper **SELECTED PUBLICATIONS** Auth, "The Three 1823 Editions of Cooper's The Pioneers," Procs of the AAS 84, 74; ed, Cooper's The Deerslayer, 84; ed, Cooper's 'The Spy', 85; co-ed, James Fenimore Cooper, The Pioneers, SUNY Press, 80, Lib Am, 85, Viking-Penguin, 87; coauth, "Fenimore Cooper's Literary Defenses: Twain and the Text of The Deerslayer," Stud in the Am Renaissance, 88; auth, "Bandwith as Metaphor for Consciousness in Pynchon's Gravity's Rainbow," Stud in the Lit Imagination 22, Spring 89; co-ed, The Meritorious Price of Our Redemption by William Pynchon; auth, "Cooper's Spy and the Possibility of American Fiction," Stud in the Hum, 91; auth, "Cooper and Wordsworth," Univ of Miss Stud in Eng, 92. **CONTACT ADDRESS** 32 Massachusetts Ave, Worcester, MA, 01602-2123.

SCHAEFER, JOSEPHINE O'BRIEN
PERSONAL Born 11/28/1929, New York, NY, d, 2 children **DISCIPLINE** ENGLISH LITERATURE **EDUCATION** Hunter Col, BA, 52; Smith Col, MA, 53; Stanford Univ, PhD, 62. **CAREER** Instr English, Univ Nebr, 53-55; lectr, Ind Univ, 60-61; asst prof, Western Col, Ohio, 61-65; assoc prof, Trinity Col, 67-70 & Western Col, 70-74; prof English, Univ Pittsburgh, 74-92. **HONORS AND AWARDS** Phi Beta Kappa, 52; Fulbright, 60, 65, 87; NEH, 69; Distinguished Teaching Award, 91. **MEMBERSHIPS** MLA; Northeast Mod Lang Asn. **RESEARCH** Modern British fiction; Virginia Woolf; James Joyce. **SELECTED PUBLICATIONS** Art, Vision in Virginia Woolf's biographies, Virginia Woolf Quart, 76; art, Sterne's A Sentimental Journey and Woolf's Jacob's Room, Mod Fiction Studies, summer 77; auth, The Great War and This Late Age of World's Experience in Cather and Woolf, Virginia Woolf: The Fiction, The Reality, and The Myth of War, Syracuse, 91. **CONTACT ADDRESS** 1790 West Crestline Dr, Littleton, CO, 80120.

SCHAFER, WILLIAM JOHN
PERSONAL Born 09/18/1937, Richmond, IN, m, 1958, 2 children **DISCIPLINE** ENGLISH **EDUCATION** Earlham Col, AB, 59; Univ Minn, MA, 64, PhD(English & art hist), 67. **CAREER** Instr, 64-73, assoc prof, 73-74, PROF ENGLISH & HUMANITIES, BEREA COL, 74-, Nat Endowment for Humanities younger humanist fel, 71-72; traveling humanist, Ky Coun for Humanities, 78-79. **MEMBERSHIPS** AAUP **RESEARCH** Black music and its influence on American popular culture; contemporary American and British fiction; history of ideas in American culture. **SELECTED PUBLICATIONS** Auth, 'Kentucky Straight' - Offutt,C/, Appalachian J, Vol 0021, 1993; The 'Same River Twice' - Offutt,C/, Appalachian J, Vol 0021, 1993; 'Gains And Losses'/, South Dakota Rev, Vol 0031, 1993; Appalachia Inside-Out, Vol 1, Conflict And Change, Vol 2, Cult And Custom - Higgs,Rj, Manning,An, Miller,Jw/, Appalachian J, Vol 0022, 1995; The Bridges Of Johnson,Fenton/, Appalachian J, Vol 0022, 1995; 'Sharpshooter' - A Novel Of The Civil-War - Madden,D/, Appalachian J, Vol 0024, 1997. **CONTACT ADDRESS** 101 Chestnut St, Berea, KY, 40404-0003.

SCHAGRIN, MORTON L.
PERSONAL Born 11/22/1930, Wilmington, DE, m, 1956, 3 children **DISCIPLINE** HUMANITIES **EDUCATION** Univ Chicago, BA, 51, BS, 52, MA, 53, Univ Calif Berk, PhD, 65. **CAREER** Univ Calif Berk, tchg asst, lectr, 58-61; Univ Fla, asst prof, 61-63; Denison Univ, asst prof, assoc prof, pres DSA, chemn H&FAC, 63-70; Harvard Univ, res assoc., 65-66; SUNY Fredonia, assoc prof, chemn, prof, assoc dean, dean, 70-. **MEMBERSHIPS** GLCA, NSF, T-SPA, APA, Fulbright Assoc. **RESEARCH** 18th and 19th century experimental science; modern logic. **SELECTED PUBLICATIONS** Auth, The Resistance to Ohm's Law, Am Jour of Physics, 63; auth, The Language of Logic, Random House, 79; auth, Early Observations and Calculations on Light Pressure, Am Jour of Physics, 74; auth, More Heat than Light, Syntheses, 94; auth, Logic: A Computer Approach, coauth, McGraw-Hill, NY, 85; Rumford's Experiments on the Materiality of Light, Realism and Antirealism in the Philosophy of Science, eds. R. S. Cohen, R. Hilpinen, Q. Renzong, Kluwer Academic Pub, Dordrecht, 95. **CONTACT ADDRESS** Dept of Philosophy, State Univ Col, 2140 Fenton Hall, Fredonia, NY, 14063. **EMAIL** schagrin@fredonia.edu

SCHALLER, KRISTI
DISCIPLINE COMMUNICATION **EDUCATION** Ill State Univ, BA, MA; Ohio Univ, PhD, 93. **CAREER** Asst prof, Ga State Univ. **HONORS AND AWARDS** Tchg award, Ohio Univ; tchg award, Int Commun Asn. **RESEARCH** Teacher-student communication. **SELECTED PUBLICATIONS** Published articles in Commun Rpt, Early Child Develop & Care, and J of Grad Tchg Asst Develop. **CONTACT ADDRESS** Georgia State Univ, Atlanta, GA, 30303. **EMAIL** kschaller@gsu.edu

SCHAMBERGER, ED
DISCIPLINE ENGLISH LITERATURE **EDUCATION** Colo State Univ, BS, MA; Univ Pa, PhD. **CAREER** Assoc prof. **SELECTED PUBLICATIONS** Auth, pubs on American literature; American authors. **CONTACT ADDRESS** Dept of English, Colorado State Univ, Fort Collins, CO, 80523. **EMAIL** jschamberger@vines.colostate.edu

SCHAPIRO, BARBARA
PERSONAL Born 03/04/1952, St. Louis, MO, m, 1979, 2 children **DISCIPLINE** ENGLISH **EDUCATION** MA, PhD, Tafts Univ; BA, Univ Mich. **CAREER** Prof English, Rhode Island Col, 87-. **HONORS AND AWARDS** Phi Beta Kappa. **MEMBERSHIPS** MLA; Mass Assoc for Psychoanalytic Psychol. **RESEARCH** Psychoanalysis and Lit; Modern & Contemporary Ficton. **SELECTED PUBLICATIONS** D H Lawrence and the Paradoxes of Psychic Life, SUNY Press, Forthcoming, 99; Literature and The Relational Self, NYU Press, 94; Narcissism and the Text: Studies in Literature and the Psychology of Self, co-ed, NYU Press, 86; The Romantic Mother: Narcissistic Patterns in Romantic Poetry, John Hopkins Univ Press, 83. **CONTACT ADDRESS** Dept English, Rhode Island Col, 60 Mount Pleasant Ave, Providence, RI, 02908. **EMAIL** busric@aol.com

SCHARFFENBERGER, ELIZABETH WATSON
PERSONAL Born 09/14/1957, Wheeling, WV, s **DISCIPLINE** THEATRE **EDUCATION** Univ Chicago, AB, 77; Columbia Univ, MA, 80, MPhil, 83, PhD, 88. **CAREER** Instr, 85-86, Clarkson Univ; instr, 86-88, NY Univ; asst prof, 88-94, Wash Univ; lectr, 95, 96, 98, 99, Columbia Univ; adj asst prof, 96, Barnard Col; vis asst prof, adj assoc prof, 96-98, Columbia Univ; lectr, 97-, NY Univ, Gallatin Schl; vis asst prof, 99, Yale Univ. **RESEARCH** Athenian Drama & Theatre; Comic Lit; Influence of Classics in renaissance & modern times. **CONTACT ADDRESS** 380 Riverside Dr, New York, NY, 10025.

SCHECHNER, RICHARD
PERSONAL Born 08/23/1934, Newark, NJ, m, 1987, 2 children **DISCIPLINE** THEATRE **EDUCATION** Cornell Univ, BA, 56; State Univ Iowa, MA, 58; Tulane Univ, PhD, 62. **CAREER** Asst to assoc prof Theatre, Tulane Univ, 62-67; prof drama, NY Univ, 67-79; prof perf stud, NY Univ, 80-; ed, Tulane Drama Rev, 62-67; ed. The Drama Rev, 67-69, 85-; co-dir, Free South Theatre, 64-66; co-fndr, dir, New Orleans Grp, 65-67; fndr, dir, The Performance Grp, NY, 67-80; fnde, dir, E Coast Artists, 92-. **HONORS AND AWARDS** Guggenheim fel, Fulbright Comn, Indo-Am fel, Hoffman Eminent Schol, NEH Sr fel, Asian Cult Coun, Whitney Halstead Schol, Emmens Prof, Hum fel, Old Dominion fel, Am Inst, Indian Stu Sr fel, Montgomery fel; Mondello Prize, Honorary Prof, Shanghai Theatre Acad, Special Awards. **MEMBERSHIPS** AAAS; Am Theatre Asn. **RESEARCH** Performance studies, relationship od ritual, play, performance in everyday life. **SELECTED PUBLICATIONS** Auth, Public Domain, Bobbs, 68; co-ed, The Free Southern Theatre, Bobbs, 69; ed, Dionysus in 69; Farrar, Straus, and Giroux, 70; auth, Environmental Theatre, Hawthorn, 73, Reprint Applause, 94; co-ed, Ritual, Play, and Performance, Seabury, 76; coauth, Theatres, Spaces, and Environments, 77; auth, Essays on Performance Theory, 77; Drama Bk Specialists, expanded as Performance Theory, Routledge, 88; auth, The End of Humanism, Perf Arts J, 82; auth, Performative Circumstances, Seagull, 83; auth, Between Theater and Anthropology, Univ of Pa, 85; co-ed, By Means of Performance, Cambridge Univ, 90; ed, Worlds of Performance, Routledge, 94; auth, The Future of Ritual, Routlaedge, 93; coed, The Grotowski Sourcebook, Routledge, 97. **CONTACT ADDRESS** Dept of Performance Studies, New York Univ, 721 Broadway, New York, NY, 10003. **EMAIL** richard.schechner@nyu.edu

SCHECHTER, JOEL
PERSONAL Born 06/21/1947, Washington, DC, m **DISCIPLINE** THEATRE ARTS **EDUCATION** Antioch Col, BA, 69; Yale Sch Drama, MFA, DFA, 72,73. **CAREER** Lit Adv, Am Place Theatre, 73-77; lectr, New Sch Social Res, 74; asst prof, SUNY, 74-77; ed chief, Theatre Magazine, 77-92; dramaturg, Yale Repertory Theatre, 77-92; prof, Yale Sch Drama, 77-92; prof, chemn, San Francisco State Univ, 92-. **HONORS AND AWARDS** Danforth Fel; John Gassner Prize Criticism; Fox Fellow Moscow Univ; **MEMBERSHIPS** Brecht Soc **RESEARCH** Political satire; circus history, popular theatre. **SELECTED PUBLICATIONS** Auth, Durov's Pig: Clowns, Politics and Theatre, 85; auth, Satiric Impersonations: From Aristophanes to the Guerilla Girls, 94; auth, The Congress of Clowns and Other Russian Circus Acts, 98. **CONTACT ADDRESS** Dept of Theatre Arts, San Francisco State Univ, 1600 Holloway Ave, San Francisco, CA, 94116.

SCHECKTER, JOHN
DISCIPLINE AUSTRALIAN LITERATURE, AMERICAN LITERATURE **EDUCATION** Iowa, PhD. **CAREER** Assoc prof, Long Island Univ, C.W. Post Campus. **SELECTED PUBLICATIONS** Auth, The Australian Novel 1830-1980: A Thematic Introduction; The Lost Child in Australian Fiction; Australia Lost and Founded: Versions of the First Settlement in Two Modern Novels; Now That the (Water) Buffalo's Gone: James Welch and the Transcultural Novel; History, Possibility, and Romance in The Pioneers. **CONTACT ADDRESS** Long Island Univ, C.W. Post, Brookville, NY, 11548-1300.

SCHEDLER, GILBERT W.
PERSONAL Born 03/11/1935, Vancouver, BC, Canada, m, 1975, 3 children **DISCIPLINE** LITERATURE **EDUCATION** Concordia Col, BA, 57; Concordia Sem, BD, 60; Washington Univ, MA, 63; Univ Chicago, PhD(lit & relig), 70. **CAREER** Instr Humanities, Wittenberg Univ, 63-64; asst prof, 67-71, assoc prof, 71-79, assoc prof relig, 79-81, PROF RELIG & ENGLISH, UNIV PAC, 81-, Guest lectr, Univ Bangalore, India, 69-70; dep dir, Callison Col, Overseas Ctr, India, 69-70. **RESEARCH** Contemporary religious thought; recent American poetry; Taoism and Eastern religions. **SELECTED PUBLICATIONS** Auth, College Study Guide in American Literature, Am Sch, 66; Southern California Has Never Been Christian (poem), Epos, spring-summer 74; Urban Man (poem), Contemp Quart, spring 77; Waking Before Dawn, Wampeter Press, 78; Extended Family (poem), In: Celebration: Best Poems of the 70's, Calif State Poetry Quart, spring 80; A Spring Day on Campus (poem), In: Anthology of Magazine Verse and Yearbook of American Poetry, 80; Sermons (poem), Christian Century, 9/81; Till Death Do Us Part (poem), Calif State Poetry Quart, winter 82. **CONTACT ADDRESS** English Dept, Univ of the Pacific, 3601 Pacific Ave, Stockton, CA, 95211-0197. **EMAIL** gschedle@uop.edu

SCHEELE, HENRY ZAEGEL
PERSONAL Born 08/27/1933, Sheboygan, WI, m, 1956, 2 children **DISCIPLINE** SPEECH, COMMUNICATION **EDUCATION** Lake Forest Col, BA, 56; Purdue Univ, MS, 58, PhD-(speech), 62. **CAREER** Asst prof, 62-72, assoc prof speech, Purdue Univ, West Lafayette, 72-, res grant, Purdue Univ, 64. **HONORS AND AWARDS** Excellence in Teaching Award, 79, 94. **MEMBERSHIPS** National Commun Asn; Cent States Speech Commun Asn; Center for the Study of the Presidency. **RESEARCH** Political communication. **SELECTED PUBLICATIONS** Auth, Ronald Reagan's 1980 Acceptance Address: A Focus on American Values, The Western Journal of Speech Communication, 84; The 1956 Nomination of Dwight D. Eisenhower: Maintaining the Hero Image, Presidential Studies Quart, 86; Response to the Kennedy Administration: The Joint Senate-House Republican Leadership Press conferences, Presidential Studies Quart, 89; President Dwight D. Eisenhower and U.S. House Leader Charles A. Halleck: An Examination of an Executive-Legislative Relationship, Presidential Studies Quart, 93; and Prelude to the Presidency: An Examination of the Gerald R. Ford-Charles A. Halleck House Minority Leadership Contest, Presidential Studies Quart, 95. **CONTACT ADDRESS** Dept of Commun, Purdue Univ, West Lafayette, IN, 47907-1998.

SCHEICK, WILLIAM JOSEPH
PERSONAL Born 07/15/1941, Newark, NJ, 2 children **DISCIPLINE** AMERICAN LITERATURE **EDUCATION** Montclair State Col, BA, 63; Univ Ill, Urbana, MA, 65, PhD(Am lit), 69. **CAREER** Asst prof, 69-74, assoc prof, 74-79, prof English, 79-86, J R Millikan Centennial Prof, 86-, Univ Tex, Austin Res Inst grant, 73-74, 80-81, 87-88, & 94-95; ed, Tex Studies Lit & Lang, 75-92; ed, Soc of Early Americanists Newsletter, 89-. **HONORS AND AWARDS** Pushcart Prize, 91. **RESEARCH** American literature; turn-of-the-century novel; theory of fiction. **SELECTED PUBLICATIONS** Auth, The Ethos of Romance at the Turn of the Century, Univ Tex, 94; Authority and Female Authorship in Colonial America, Kentucky Univ, 98; coauth, Paine, Scripture, and Authority: The Age of Reason as Religious and Political Idea, Lehigh Univ, 94; ed, The Critical Response to H G Wells, Greenwood, 95; Structures of Belief/Narrative Structures, Univ Texas, 95; Alice Maude Ewell's Atlantic Monthly Fiction 1892-1905, Scholars' Facsimilies, 97; Alice Maude Ewell's Peterson's Magazine Fiction 1883-1893, Scholars' Facsimilies, 98. **CONTACT ADDRESS** Dept of English, Univ Texas, Austin, Austin, TX, 78712-1164. **EMAIL** scheick@mail.utexas.edu

SCHEIDE, FRANK MILO
DISCIPLINE RHETORICAL AND MASS MEDIA CRITICISM **EDUCATION** Univ Wisc, BS, 71, MA, 72, PhD, 90. **CAREER** Lect, Univ Wisc, 73; Tchg asst, Univ Wisc, 73-75; Instr, Univ Wisc, 75-76; Asst prof, Ball State Univ, 76-77; Instr, Univ Ark, 77-83; 84-91; Asst prof, Univ Ark, 91-. **SELECTED PUBLICATIONS** Auth, Introductory Film Criticism: A Historical Perspective, Kendall/Hunt Publ Co, 94; Victorian South London, the English Music Hall, and the Early Films of Charlie Chaplin, Oxford Univ Press, Univ Ark Press,97. **CONTACT ADDRESS** Univ Ark, Fayetteville, AR, 72701.

SCHEINBERG, CYNTHIA
DISCIPLINE ENGLISH **EDUCATION** Harvard-Radcliffe Col, BA, 85; Rutgers Univ, PhD, 92. **CAREER** Asst prof; Mills Col, 92-. **RESEARCH** Victorian Literature, emphasis poetry; Anglo-Jewish literature and history; women's studies; religion and literature; feminist theory; genre studies; cinema studies; composition and pedagogy; community service/service learning curriculum development. **SELECTED PUBLICATIONS** Auth, Recasting Sympathy and Judgment: Amy Levy, Women Writers, and the Victorian Dramatic Monologue, Victorian Poetry, 97; Measure to yourself a prophet's place': Biblical Heroines, Jewish Difference, and Victorian Women's Poetry, in Women's Poetry late Romantic to late Victorian, Gender and Genre 1930-1900, London: Macmillan Press, 97 & Canonizing the Jew: Amy Levy's Challenge to Victorian Poetic Identity, Victorian Stud 39 2, 96; rev, The Complete Novels and Selected Poetry of Amy Levy, 1861-1889, Victorian Poetry, 95; Elizabeth Barrett Browning's Hebraic Conversions: Gender and Typology in Aurora Leigh, Victorian Lit and Cult, 95 & Rethinking Diversity, Creating Community: The Presence of Others' in the College Writing Classroom, Notes in the Margins, Stanford Univ, 95. **CONTACT ADDRESS** Dept of English, Mills Col, 5000 MacArthur Blvd, Oakland, CA, 94613-1301. **EMAIL** cyns@mills.edu

SCHELL, RICHARD
DISCIPLINE ENGLISH LITERATURE **EDUCATION** York Univ, PhD. **SELECTED PUBLICATIONS** Co-auth, Leonard Woolf, Yale Ed of Short Poems of Edmund Spenser, 90. **CONTACT ADDRESS** English Dept, Laurentian Univ, 935 Ramsey Lake Rd, Sudbury, ON, P3E 2C6.

SCHEPS, WALTER
PERSONAL Born 06/19/1939, New York, NY, m, 1963, 2 children **DISCIPLINE** ENGLISH **EDUCATION** City Col New York, BA, 63; Univ Ore, PhD(English), 66. **CAREER** Asst prof English, Case Western Reserve Univ, 66-69; from asst prof to assoc prof, Ohio State Univ, 69-75; ASSOC PROF ENGLISH, STATE UNIV NY STONY BROOK, 75-, Reader, Chaucer Rev, 72- **MEMBERSHIPS** MLA; Mediaeval Acad Am. **RESEARCH** Chaucer; 15th century literature; popular literature in the Middle Ages. **SELECTED PUBLICATIONS** Auth, Chaucer,Geoffrey The 'General Prologue' - Ruggiers,Pg, Ranson,Dj/, Anq-A Quart J Of Short Articles Notes And Rev, Vol 0008, 1995. **CONTACT ADDRESS** Dept of English, State Univ of NY, 100 Nicolls Rd, Stony Brook, NY, 11794-0002.

SCHEYE, THOMAS EDWARD
PERSONAL Born 07/02/1942, Savannah, GA, m, 1972 **DISCIPLINE** ENGLISH, DRAMA **EDUCATION** Georgetown Univ, AB, 63; Yale Univ, MA, 65; Univ Pa, PhD(English), 70. **CAREER** Asst prof, Essex Community Col, 65-67 & Towson State Univ, 65-70; assoc prof English & Acad vpres, Loyola Col, MD, 70-, theater critic, Baltimore News-Am, 65-77; host/writer, Survey of English Lit, Md Ctr Pub Broadcasting, 72-75. **HONORS AND AWARDS** Distinguished Teacher Award, Loyola Col, 74. **MEMBERSHIPS** MLA; SAtlantic Mod Lang Asn; Milton Soc Am. **RESEARCH** Shakespeare; modern drama; Renaissance. **SELECTED PUBLICATIONS** Auth, Two gentlemen of Milan, Shakespeare Studies, 75; The Glass Menagerie: It's no tragedy, Freckles, In: Tennessee Williams: A Tribute, 77. **CONTACT ADDRESS** Loyola Col, 4501 N Charles St, Baltimore, MD, 21210-2694. **EMAIL** scheye@loyola.edu

SCHIFF, FREDERICK
DISCIPLINE SOCIOLOGY AND COMMUNICATION **EDUCATION** Reed College, BA, 64; UCLA, MA, 65, PhD, 70. **CAREER** Assoc Prof comm, 89-, Univ Houston; Asst Prof, 86-89, Univ Dayton; Asst Prof, 70-75, Wash Univ. **HONORS AND AWARDS** NIMH; NSF. **MEMBERSHIPS** ASA; AEJMC; NSA; ICA; MESA. **RESEARCH** Media Corp; News Content; Ideology. **CONTACT ADDRESS** 701 Welch St, Houston, TX, 77006-1307. **EMAIL** fschiff@uh.edu

SCHIFFHORST, GERALD JOSEPH
PERSONAL Born 10/13/1940, St. Louis, MO **DISCIPLINE** ENGLISH, ART HISTORY **EDUCATION** St Louis Univ, BS, 62, MA, 63; Wash Univ, PhD(English), 73. **CAREER** Instr English, Univ Mo-St Louis, 66-67; asst prof to prof English, Univ Cent Fla, 70-, Nat Endowment for Humanities fel art hist, Southeastern Inst Medieval & Renaissance Studies, Duke Univ, 74; . **MEMBERSHIPS** MLA; Shakespeare Asn Am; Milton Soc Am; SAtlantic Mod Lang Asn. **RESEARCH** Milton; Renaissance iconography of patience; teaching English composition. **SELECTED PUBLICATIONS** Ed & coauth, The Triumph of Patience: Medieval and Renaissance Studies, Fla Univ, 78; coauth, Short English Handbook, Scott, 79, 2nd ed, 82, 3rd ed, 86; auth, Patience & the Humbly Exalted Heroism of Milton's Messiah (art), Milton Studies, XVI, 82; auth, John Milton, 90; Short Handbook for Writers, McGraw Hill, 91, 97; co-ed, The Witness of Times, Duquesne Univ Press, 93; assoc ed, Seventeenth-Century News, 96-99. **CONTACT ADDRESS** Dept of English, Univ Central Fla, PO Box 161346, Orlando, FL, 32816-1346. **EMAIL** gschiff@ucf1vm.cc.ucf.edu

SCHILLER, ANITA R.
PERSONAL Born 06/16/1926, New York, NY, m, 1946, 2 children **DISCIPLINE** LIBRARY SCIENCE **EDUCATION** NY Univ, BA, 49; Pratt Inst, MLS, 59. **CAREER** Res assoc, asst prof, 64-70, Univ Il; ref bibliog, 70-90, Univ Calif San Diego; Ralph R Shaw vis scholar, 78, Rutgers Univ; Librn Emeritus, 91-, Univ Calif San Diego. **HONORS AND AWARDS** Coun Libr Res Fel, 76-77; PEN Award for Magazine Writing, 82; Amer Libr Assoc Equality Award, 85. **MEMBERSHIPS** Amer Libr Assoc, Amer Soc for Infor Sci; Assoc of Col & Res Libr; Libr & Infor Tech assoc. **RESEARCH** Infor policy; intellectual property; women in librarianship. **SELECTED PUBLICATIONS** Auth, Women in Librarianship, in Advances in Librarianship, IV, Oryx Press, 79; art, Shifting Boundaries in Information, Libr J, 81; auth, Information as a Commodity: There's No Such Thing as a Free Hunch, Technicalities, 82; coauth, The Privatizing of Information: Who Can Own What America Knows?, Scarecrow Press, 83; auth, The Age of Information and the Year of the Reader, On Reading: In the Year of the Reader, Calif St Libr Found, 87. **CONTACT ADDRESS** 7109 Monte Vista, La Jolle, CA, 92037-5326. **EMAIL** aschiller@ucsd.edu

SCHIRMEISTER, PAMELA J.
DISCIPLINE ENGLISH **EDUCATION** Yale Univ, BA, 80; PhD, 88; Johns Hopkins Univ, MA, 81. **CAREER** ASST PROF, ENG, NY UNIV **MEMBERSHIPS** Am Antiquarian Soc **SELECTED PUBLICATIONS** Auth, The Consolations of Space: The Place of Romance in Hawthorne, Melville, and James, Stanford Univ Press, 90; ed and introd, Representative Man by Ralph Waldo Emerson, Marsilio, 96; auth, "Taking Precautions: Gender Identification as Masquerade in James Fenimore Cooper," Stud in Biog, vol 3, AMS Press, 97; coauth, biography of James Fenimore Cooper, Addison Wesley; coauth, "James Fenimore Cooper: Entrepreneur of the Self," Procs of the AAS. **CONTACT ADDRESS** 19 University Pl, No. 200, New York, NY, 10003.

SCHLACHTER, GAIL ANN
PERSONAL Born 04/07/1943, Detroit, MI, m, 1986, 2 children **DISCIPLINE** LIBRARY SCIENCE **EDUCATION** Univ Calif at Berkeley, BA, 64; Univ Wis, joint MA, 66; Univ Southern Calif, MPA, 76; Univ Minn, PhD, 71. **HONORS AND AWARDS** Title II-B Fel, Higher Ed Act, Univ Minn, 68-71; Beta Phi Mu, 71; Outstanding Libr Sci Prof, Univ Southern Calif, 73; Outstanding Reference Book, Choic, 78 & 97; Award for Lib Lit, Knowledge Industry Pub, 85; Best Professional Book, RQ, 86; Best of the Best Reference Book, Nat Ed and Infor Center, 88; Best Reference Book of the Year, School Libr J, 89; Best Reference Book, NY Public Libr, 89; Best Reference Book of the Year, Libr J, 90; Isador Gilbert Mudge Award, 92, Louis Shores-Oryx Press Award, Am Libr Asn, 97. **MEMBERSHIPS** Am Libr Asn; Calif Libr Asn. **SELECTED PUBLICATIONS** Coauth, RSP Funding for Nursing Students and Nurses, Reference Service Press, 98-; Financial Aid for African Americans, Reference Service Press, 97-; Financial Aid for Asian Americans, Reference Service Press, 97-; Financial Aid for Hispanic Americans, Reference Service Press, 97-; Financial Aid for Native Americans, Reference Service Press, 97-; The Back-to-School Money Book: A Financial Guide for Midlife and Older Women, 2nd Edition, Am Asn of Retired Persons, 96; Money for Graduate Students in the Humanities, Reference Service Press, 96-; Money for Graduate Students in the Sciences, Reference Service Press, 96-; Money of Graduate Students in the Social Sciences, Reference Service Press, 96-; College Student's Guide to Merit and Other No-Need Funding, Reference Service Press, 96; High School Senior's Guide to Merit and Other No-Need Funding, Reference Service Press, 96. **CONTACT ADDRESS** Reference Service Press, 5000 Windplay Dr, Ste 4, El Dorado Hills, CA, 95762. **EMAIL** findaid@aol.com

SCHLEINER, LOUISE
DISCIPLINE RENAISSANCE LITERATURE **EDUCATION** Brown, PhD. **CAREER** Prof & dir Grad Stud, Washington State Univ. **SELECTED PUBLICATIONS** Auth, The Living Lyre in English Verse, 84 & Tudor and Stuart Women Writers, 94. **CONTACT ADDRESS** Dept of English, Washington State Univ, 1 SE Stadium Way, PO Box 645020, Pullman, WA, 99164-5020. **EMAIL** jerrie@mail.wsu.edu

SCHLICK, YAEL
DISCIPLINE ENGLISH LITERATURE **EDUCATION** Duke Univ, PhD. **CAREER** Dept Eng, Queen's Univ **RESEARCH** Travel writing; autobiography; literary theory. **SELECTED PUBLICATIONS** Auth, pubs on colonial literature, nineteenth-century women writers, and French-Canadian Fiction. **CONTACT ADDRESS** English Dept, Queen's Univ, Kingston, ON, K7L 3N6. **EMAIL** ys2@post.queensu.ca

SCHLOBIN, ROGER CLARK
PERSONAL Born 06/22/1944, Brooklyn, NY, m, 1970 **DISCIPLINE** MEDIEVAL LITERATURE **EDUCATION** C W Post Col, BA, 66; Univ Wis-Madison, MA, 68; Ohio State Univ, PhD (English), 71. **CAREER** Teaching asst English & asst dir, Ctr Medieval & Renaissance Studies, Ohio State Univ, 69-71; asst prof, 71-78, assoc prof to prof English, Purdue Univ,

NCent Campus, 78-, instr English, Upward Bound Prog, Ohio Dominican Col, 68-71; consult, Michigan City Pub Libr, 72-; consult ed, Proceedings of the Int Conf on the Fantastic, 81. **MEMBERSHIPS** Int Arthurian Soc; Early English Text Soc; Midwest Mod Lang Asn; Sci Fiction Res Asn; Mediaeval Acad Am. **RESEARCH** Arthurian literature; Chaucer; fantasy. **SELECTED PUBLICATIONS** Co-ed, The Year's Scholarship in Science Fiction and Fantasy: 1974, Extrapolation, 12/76; coauth, The Research Guide to Science Fiction Studies, Garland, 77; auth, A Bibliography of the Works of Andre Norton, G K Hall; An Annotated Bibliography of Fantasy Fiction, CEA Critic, 1/78; co-ed, The Year's Scholarship in Science Fiction and Fantasy: 1975, Extrapolation, 5/78; The Year's Scholarship in Science Fiction and Fantasy: 1972-1975, Kent State Univ, 78; auth, Women Science Fiction Writers, In: Fantastic Females, Bowling Green Popular, 78; ed, Starment Reader's Guides to Contemporary Science Fiction and Fantasy Author, 79; The Aesthetics of Fantasy Literature and Art, 82; ed, J of the Fantastic in the Arts, 88-. **CONTACT ADDRESS** Dept of English, Purdue Univ, 1402 S U S Hwy 421, Westville, IN, 46391-9542. **EMAIL** rcs@purduenc.edu

SCHMEMANN, S.
PERSONAL Born 04/12/1945, Paris, France, m, 1970, 3 children **DISCIPLINE** ENGLISH **EDUCATION** Harvard, BA, 67; Columbia Univ, MA, 71. **CAREER** Reporter, 71-80, Associated Press; Bureau Chief, Moscow, 80-, 90-94, Bonn Germany, 86-90, Jerusalem, 95-98, NY Times. **HONORS AND AWARDS** 1991 Pulitzer Prize Intl Reporting; DLitt (HC) Middlebury Col, 92; Martha Albrand Awd, 98. **RESEARCH** Russian History **SELECTED PUBLICATIONS** Auth, Echoes of a Native Land Two Centuries of A Russian Village, Knopf, 97. **CONTACT ADDRESS** New York Times, 229 W 43 St, New York, NY, 10036. **EMAIL** schmemann@compuserve.com

SCHMIDT, BARBARA QUINN
PERSONAL Chicago, IL, m, 1966, 2 children **DISCIPLINE** VICTORIAN, BLACK AMERICAN LITERATURE, WOMEN'S STUDIES **EDUCATION** Univ Chicago, BA, 59; Creighton Univ, MA, 63; St Louis Univ, PhD(English), 80. **CAREER** Assoc prof English, Southern Ill Univ, 64-. **MEMBERSHIPS** Res Soc Victorian Periodicals (pres, 95-97). **RESEARCH** The Cornhill magazine; Smith Elder Publishers. **SELECTED PUBLICATIONS** Auth, Pearson's Magazine, British Lit Mag, 1890s Encyclopedia, Greenwood Press, Windsor Magazine, Coverbill Magazine. **CONTACT ADDRESS** English Dept, Southern Illinois Univ, 6 Hairpin Dr, Edwardsville, IL, 62026-0143. **EMAIL** rschmid@sive.edu

SCHMIDT, JACK
DISCIPLINE LIBERAL ARTS **EDUCATION** Wheaton Col, BA; DePaul Univ, MA; Northwestern Univ, PhD. **CAREER** Fac, Delaware Valley Col, Towson Univ, Northwestern Univ, Elgin Comm Col, present. **HONORS AND AWARDS** Conductor,Oregon Bach Festival, 96; coord cult affairs progs, Delaware Valley Col; band/chorale conductor, Delaware Valley Col. **RESEARCH** Musicology; Ger Baroque Music; Choral Music. **SELECTED PUBLICATIONS** Auth, articles about Ger baroque music for the Am Musicol Soc, Am Choral Dirs Asn; recs, Polygram and Liturgical Press. **CONTACT ADDRESS** Delaware Valley Col, 700 E Butler Ave, Doylestown, PA, 18901-2697. **EMAIL** SchmidtJ@devalcol.edu

SCHMIDT, PATRICIA LOIS
PERSONAL Born 11/08/1942, York, PA **DISCIPLINE** RHETORICAL THEORY & CRITICISM **EDUCATION** PA State Univ, BA, 64, MA, 68, PhD, 73. **CAREER** Instr debate & dir, Speech Commun, Univ DE, 68-71; asst prof behav studies, 73-76, assoc prof & chmn, 76-78, assoc prof Eng, 78-79, asst dean, Res Rhet Criticism, 79-80, Assoc Deam, Res Rhet Criticism, Univ FLA, 81-86, Assoc Vice Chancellor for Acad Prog, FL Board of Regents, 87-88; Actg Vice Chancellor for Acad Prog, FL Board of Regents, 88-89; PROF ENGL 89-; Referee, Quart J Speech, 78-; expert witness, Pub Doc Law, FL House Rep, 81; ed, Fla Patent Newslett, 82. **HONORS AND AWARDS** Sigma Tau Delta, 63; Delta Sigma Rho-Tau Kappa Alpha, 64; Phi Kappa Phi, 72; Sparks Diss Fel, PA State Univ, 72-73; Pres Scholar, Univ FL, 75-76; Speech Commun Asn of Am, 77; Winans-Wichelns Award nominee, Outstanding Article in Rhetorical Theory and Criticism; Golden Key Hon Fac Inductee, 78; Outstanding Young Women of Am, 79; Univ of FL, Col of Lib Arts & Sci Tchr of the Year Award, 95; Nat Press Club's Author's Night invitee, 96; Nominee, Joan Kelly Memorial Prize in Women's Hist, John H. Dunning Prize in US Hist, AHA, 97; MLA prize for First Book nominee, 97. **MEMBERSHIPS** Int Soc Hist Rhet; Eastern Forensic Asn; Speech Commun Asn Am; Nat Coun Univ Res Adminr; MLA; AHA; Southern Speech Commun Soc. **RESEARCH** The role of moral force in soc change; private morality and its rel to the public sphere; Brit public address. **SELECTED PUBLICATIONS** Auth, Lord Ashley: The role of moral force in social change, Quart J Speech, 2/77; The rhetoric of factory reform: The campaign for the ten hour bill, J President's Scholars, fall 80; The First Year Experience: A View from Florida, In: Proceedings of the Fourth Int Conf of the First Year Experience: An Int Phenomenon, Univ of Edinburgh, 89; A View from Mt. Olympus: Quality vs. Control, In: New Perspectives for the 1990's: The Role of the Graduate Dean, Proceedings of the Nineteenth Annual Meeting of Southern Graduate Schools, 90; Margaret Chase Smith: Beyond Convention, Univ of Maine Press, 96; Beyond Convention, and Epilogue, In: What Can I Do for You: People Remember Margaret Chase Smith, Central Maine Publ, 97; Rethinking Gender and Power at the Century's Mid-Point: Margaret Chase Smith and Her Times, In: A History of Women in Maine, Univ or Maine Press, 98. **CONTACT ADDRESS** Eng Dept, Univ of FL, PO Box 117310, Gainesville, FL, 32611-7310. **EMAIL** pats@english.ufl.edu

SCHMIDT, PETER JARRETT
PERSONAL Born 12/23/1951, IL **DISCIPLINE** AMERICAN LITERATURE **EDUCATION** Oberlin Col, AB, 75; Univ Va, PhD, 80. **CAREER** Asst prof Am lit, Swarthmore Col, 80, Nat Endowment for Hum grant, 82. **HONORS AND AWARDS** C Hugh Holman Award, 92. **MEMBERSHIPS** MLA **RESEARCH** Mod 20th century lit; contemp poetry. **SELECTED PUBLICATIONS** Auth, Some versions of modernist pastoral: William Carlos Williams and the precisionists, fall 80 & White: Charles Simic's thumbnail epic, fall 82, Contemp Lit; auth, The Heart of the Story: Eudora Weltys Short Fiction, 91; William Carlos Williams, The arts and Literary Traditions, 88. **CONTACT ADDRESS** Dept of Eng, Swarthmore Col, 500 College Ave, Swarthmore, PA, 19081-1306. **EMAIL** pschmid1@swarthmore.edu

SCHMIDT, ROGER
DISCIPLINE ENGLISH LITERATURE **EDUCATION** Univ Wash, PhD, 89. **CAREER** Assoc prof. **RESEARCH** Jacobitism in the Eighteenth Century. **SELECTED PUBLICATIONS** Auth, pubs in Eighteenth Century Studies, The Proceedings of the Northwest Society of Eighteenth Century Studies. **CONTACT ADDRESS** Dept of English and Philosophy, Idaho State Univ, Pocatello, ID, 83209. **EMAIL** schmroge@isu.edu

SCHMIDT, STEVEN J.
PERSONAL Born 04/01/1953, Indianapolis, IN, m, 1976, 3 children **DISCIPLINE** LIBRARY SCIENCE **EDUCATION** Butler Univ, BA, 75; IN Univ, MLS, 83. **CAREER** Team leader, IUPUI Univ Libr, 84-. **HONORS AND AWARDS** Outstanding Librarian, 92, IN Libray Fed; Pres, IN Libr Fed. **MEMBERSHIPS** ALA; ILF **RESEARCH** History of printing and bookmaking; librarian in the cinema. **SELECTED PUBLICATIONS** Auth, "Do Hoosiers Sell Best?," IN Libraries, 90; Indiana Telefax Directory, S Butler Press, 90; coauth, "Monitor Talk," Diabetes Forecast, 91; auth, "The Depiction of Libraries, Librarians and the Book Arts in Film and Television," IN Libraries, 96. **CONTACT ADDRESS** 755 W Michigan St, Indianapolis, IN, 46202.

SCHMIDTBERGER, LOREN F.
PERSONAL Born 10/10/1928, Victoria, KS, m, 1958, 6 children **DISCIPLINE** ENGLISH LITERATURE **EDUCATION** Ft Hays Ks State Col, AB, 51; Fordham Univ, MA, 57, PhD, 65. **CAREER** From instr to assoc prof, 55-76, chmn dept, 71-78, prof English, St Peters Col, 76-, chmn English dept, 81-. **MEMBERSHIPS** MLA; Col English Asn; AAUP; Asn Depts English. **RESEARCH** Medieval and American literature. **SELECTED PUBLICATIONS** Ed, Dreiser's An American Tragedy, 66 & Faulkner's Absalom, Absalom, 66, Simon & Schuster. **CONTACT ADDRESS** Dept English, St Peters Col, 2641 Kennedy Blvd, Jersey City, NJ, 07306-5997. **EMAIL** lorenfs@juno.com

SCHMITZ-BURGARD, SYLVIA
DISCIPLINE 19TH-CENTURY LITERATURE **EDUCATION** Univ Cologne & Univ Va, MA & PhD, 91-97. **CAREER** Past asst prof, Princeton Univ. **RESEARCH** 18th to 20th century German and Austrian literature; French and English lieterature of the 18th century. **SELECTED PUBLICATIONS** Auth, Das Schreiben des anderen Geschlechts: Richardson, Rousseau und Goethe, 98; essays include stud of, Wolf, Jelinek, Laplanche, Freud, Droste-Hnlshoff & exam of the aesthetics and politics of gender in Ger lit. **CONTACT ADDRESS** Dept of Germanic Languages and Literature, Harvard Univ, 8 Garden St, Cambridge, MA, 02138. **EMAIL** schmitz@fas.harvard.edu

SCHNEIDAU, HERBERT N.
PERSONAL Born 08/26/1935, New Orleans, LA, m, 1961, 2 children **DISCIPLINE** ENGLISH **EDUCATION** Dartmouth Col, BA, 57; Princeton Univ, MA, 60, PhD(English), 63. **CAREER** Instr English, Duke Univ, 61-63; from asst prof to assoc prof, State Univ NY Buffalo, 63-70; assoc prof English, Univ Calif, Santa Barbara, 70-75, prof, 75-80; prof English, Univ Ariz, 80-, Andrew Mellon vis prof, Rice Univ, 78. **RESEARCH** Modern literature; Bible and literature. **SELECTED PUBLICATIONS** Auth, Ezra Pound: The Image and the Real, La State Univ, 69; Sacred Discontent, La State Univ & Univ Calif, 76; Ezra Pound/Letters/John Theobald, ed with D Pearce, Black Swan, 84; Waking Giants, Oxford, 91. **CONTACT ADDRESS** Dept of English, Univ of Arizona, 1 University of Az, Tucson, AZ, 85721-0001.

SCHNEIDER, DUANE
PERSONAL Born 11/15/1937, South Bend, IN, m, 4 children **DISCIPLINE** ENGLISH **EDUCATION** Miami Univ, BA, 58; Kent State Univ, MA, 60; Univ Colo, PhD(English lit), 65. **CAREER** Instr English in engineering, Univ Colo, 60-65; from asst prof to assoc prof, 65-75, PROF ENGLISH, OHIO UNIV, 75- **MEMBERSHIPS** MLA; Charles Lamb Soc; Soc Study Southern Lit. **RESEARCH** Romantic movement in English literature; Thomas Wolfe; Anais Nin. **SELECTED PUBLICATIONS** Auth, Thomas Wolfe and the quest for language, Ohio Univ Rev, 69; The art of Anais Nin, Southern Rev, spring 70; The Lucas edition of Lamb's letters: Corrections and notes, Notes & Queries, 5/74; Thomas Wolfe 1900-1938, In: First Printings of American Authors, Gale Res Co, 77; Anais Nin in the Diary: The creation and development of a persona, Mosaic, winter 78; coauth, Anais Nin: An Introduction, Ohio Univ, 79. **CONTACT ADDRESS** Dept of English, Ohio Univ, Athens, OH, 45701-2979.

SCHNEIDER, KAREN
PERSONAL Chicago, IL **DISCIPLINE** WOMEN'S FICTION, MODERN BRITISH LITERATURE, WOMEN'S STUDIES. **EDUCATION** Univ Tex, BA; Colo State Univ, Ma; Ind Univ, PhD. **CAREER** Prof, Western Ky Univ. **RESEARCH** Film and contemporary women's fiction; With Violence if Necessary: Reaffirmation of the Traditional Family in the Contemporary Action thriller.. **SELECTED PUBLICATIONS** Auth, Loving Arms: British Women Writing the Second World War. **CONTACT ADDRESS** Western Kentucky Univ, 1526 Big Red Way Street, Bowling Green, KY, 42101.

SCHNEIDER, MATTHEW T.
DISCIPLINE ENGLISH AND COMPARATIVE LITERATURE **EDUCATION** Univ CA, Berkeley, BA, 80; Univ Chicago, MA, 82; UCLA, PhD, 91. **CAREER** Lect, Conspiracy Cult Conf, King Alfred's Col, Engl, Jl 98; Interdisciplinary 19th-century Stud Ann Conf, New Orleans, La, Apr 98; UCLA Ctr Stud Rel, Los Angeles, CA, Apr 97; Int Conf on Representations Despair and Desire, Atlanta, GA, Oct 96; Chapman Univy Fac Develop Workshop, Mar 96; Northeast Mod Lang Asn Ann Conv, Boston, MA, Apr 95; Chapman Univ Engl Grad Colloquium, Mar 95; referee, PMLA, Mosaic; ed bd, Anthropoetics. **HONORS AND AWARDS** Fac excellence, Chapman Univ Awd, 97; fac Summer res grant, Chapman Univ, 94; Valerie Scudder Awd, Chapman Univ, 94; fac Summer res grant, Chapman Univ; 93; best essay awd, UCLA grad stud asn, 91; HT Swedenberg dissertation fel, UCLA, 90; grad high Hon & distinction, Univ CA, Berkeley, 80. **MEMBERSHIPS** Colloquium on Violence and Rel; MLA; NAm Soc for the Stud Romanticism; Pac Ancient & Mod Lang Asn; Wordsworth-Coleridge Asn. **SELECTED PUBLICATIONS** Auth, The Sign, The Thing, and Titanic, Chronicles of Love and Resentment 132, Apr, 98; Violent Delights and Violent Ends: Abjection in Oliver Twist, J Asn Interdisciplinary Stud of the Arts 3:1, 97; Writing in the Dust: Irony and Lynch-Law in the Gospel of John, Anthropoetics III,97; Wrung by sweet enforcement: Druid Stones and the Problem of Sacrifice in British Romanticism, Anthropoetics II, 97; Mimetic Polemicism: Rene Girard and Harold Bloom contra the School of Resentment, Anthropoetics II, 96; Romantic Bards and English Composers: The Case of Keats and Holst, Europ Romantic Rev 6, 95; Original Ambivalence: Violence and Autobiography in Thomas De Quincey, Peter Lang Publ, Inc, 95; Sacred Ambivalence: Mimetology in Aristotle, Horace, and Longinus, Anthropoetics I, 95. **CONTACT ADDRESS** Dept of Eng and Comp Lit, Chapman Univ, Orange, CA, 92866. **EMAIL** schneide@chapman.edu

SCHNEIDER, ROBERT J.
PERSONAL Born 02/28/1939, Saginaw, MI, m, 1997 **DISCIPLINE** GENERAL STUDIES-HUMANITIES; MEDIEVAL STUDIES. **EDUCATION** Univ of the South, BA, 61; Univ of Notre Dame, MSM, 63, DSM, 65. **CAREER** Asst prof, 65-68, Univ of Southern CA; asst prof, 68, assoc 72, prof, 81, distinguished prof of general studies, 98, Berea Col. **HONORS AND AWARDS** Seabury Award for Excellence in Teaching, 89; Acorn Award for excellence in teaching and scholarship, 93; Templeton Found Sci and Relig Course Prize, 97. **MEMBERSHIPS** Medieval Acad of Amer; Soc for Values in Higher Education; Episcopal Church Working Group on Science, Technology, and Faith. **RESEARCH** Issues in science and religion. **SELECTED PUBLICATIONS** Auth, Vincent of Beauvais' Opus universale de statu principis: A Reconstruction of Its History and Contents, in Vincent de Beauvais: intentions et receptions d'une oeuvre encyclopedique au moyen-age, 91; coauth, The Medieval Circulation of the De morali principis institutione of Vincent of Beauvais, Viator, 91; auth, Vincentii belvacensis De morali principis institutione, 95; auth, Vincent of Beauvais, Dominican Author: From Compilatio to Tractatus, in Lector et compilator, Vincent de Beauvais, Frere Precheur: un intellectuel et son milieu au XIIIe siecle, 97. **CONTACT ADDRESS** Dept of Foreign Lang, Berea Col, CPO 1860, Berea, KY, 40404. **EMAIL** robert_schneider@berea.edu

SCHNEIDER, VALERIE LOIS
PERSONAL Born 02/12/1941, Chicago, IL **DISCIPLINE** SPEECH & COMMUNICATION **EDUCATION** Carrol l Col, BA, 63; Univ WI, Madison, MA, 66; Univ FL, PhD(speech),

69; Appalachian State Univ, cert, 81. **CAREER** Interim asst prof speech, Univ FL, 69-70; asst prof, Edinboro State Col, 70-71; assoc prof, 71-75, prof speech, 75-97, prof emeritus, speech & commun, E TN State Univ, 98-; Danforth assoc, 77. **HONORS AND AWARDS** Best Article Award, Relig Speech Commun Asn, 76; Finalist, Money Magazine Best Personal Finance Manager in America contest, 94. **MEMBERSHIPS** Speech Commun Asn; Southern Speech Commun Asn; Relig Speech Commun Asn. **RESEARCH** Persuasion; rhetorical criticism; study skills. **SELECTED PUBLICATIONS** Auth, Informal Persuasion Analysis, Speech Teacher, 1/71; Hugh Blair's Theories of Style and Taste, NC J Speech, 12/71; Role-playing and your Local Newspaper, Speech Teacher, 9/71; Parker's Assessment of Webster: Argumentative Synthesis through the Tragic Metaphor, Quart J Speech, 10/78; Mainlining the Handicapped: An Analysis of Butterflies are Free, J Humanics, 12/78; A Process for Self-mastery for Study Habits, J Develop & Remedial Educ, winter 79; Experimental Course Formats, Nat Asn Pub Continuing & Adult Educ Exchange, winter 80; Two Courses for the Price of One: A Study Skills Component for a Speech Communications Course, J Develop & Remedial Educ, spring 82; and various other articles in Speech Communication Teacher, 88-94; writer of Video Visions column, Kingsport Times-News, 84-86; ed, ETSY Evening and Off-Campus newsletter, 86-93. **CONTACT ADDRESS** East Tennesee State Univ, PO Box 23098, Johnson City, TN, 37614-0001.

SCHNELL, JAMES A.
PERSONAL Born 08/03/1955, Gahanna, OH, m, 1995 **DISCIPLINE** COMMUNICATION STUDIES **EDUCATION** Capital Univ, BA, 77; State Univ of NY/Plattsburgh, MA, 79; Ohio Univ, PhD, 82. **CAREER** Instr, Ohio Univ, 82-83; visiting asst prof, Miami Univ, 83-84; asst prof, Univ of Cincinnati, 84-89; ASSOC PROF, OHIO DOMINICAN COL, 89-. **HONORS AND AWARDS** Listed in Who's Who in Media Commun. **MEMBERSHIPS** Nat Commun Asn; Asn for Chinese Commun Studies. **RESEARCH** Cross-cultural communication; U. S.-China interaction. **SELECTED PUBLICATIONS** Three books and 35 published articles on interpersonal commun, cross-cultural commun, and China. **CONTACT ADDRESS** Dept of Commun Studies, Ohio Dominican Col, Columbus, OH, 43219. **EMAIL** schnellj@odc.edu

SCHNELLER, BEVERLY
DISCIPLINE PROFESSIONAL WRITING, COMPOSITION, 18TH AND 19TH CENTURY BRITISH LITERATURE **EDUCATION** Cath Univ Am, PhD, 87. **CAREER** Tenured assoc prof; Millersville Univ, 89-; postdr, Univ Va, 95 & Amer Antiquarian Soc, 95; Ch, Univ Promotion and Tenure comt 97-98; Enrollment Mgt Taskforce co-ch 96-97 Acad Theme; sec, Fac Sen;ch, Evaluation Comt; ch, Comp Comt; ch, Search Comt; ch, ad hoc Senate Policies Rev Comt; auth/creator, Admissions, Advisement, Stud Aff Comt, EC-ASECS 22nd Annual Meeting, ch; ch, Women's Film Evening; asst dir, Marist Col Writing Prog, 85-89. **HONORS AND AWARDS** NEH Summer Sem, 93; Folger Inst, 92; Folger Weekend Workshop,92 & NEH Summer Inst, 90. **MEMBERSHIPS** MLA; ASECS; Mod Poetry Assn.; Vergilian Soc Amer; BSA; SHARP; NASSR; NAmer Conf Bri Stud; Oxford Bibliog Soc. **RESEARCH** 18th and 19th Century Irish Literature; Textual Criticism; Canadian Literature; 18th Century British Book Trade. **SELECTED PUBLICATIONS** Auth, Writing About Business and Industry, Oxford UP, 95; Writing About Science, Oxford UP, 91; contrib, Shakespeare and Irish Nationalism, Macmillan, 97; The New DNB, Oxford at Clarendon, 96; Feminist Literary Theory, A Dictionary, Garland, 96; Masterplots, Salem Press, 96; Cyclopedia of World Auth, rev ed, Salem Press, 96; Writers, Books, and Trade, An 18th-century Miscellany for William B. Todd, AMS, 94; Teaching Composition from Literature, Harper Collins, 94; Magazines of the British Isles, Greenwood, 93; British Romantic Novelists, Gale, 92; British Literary Publishing Houses, 2 vols, Gale, 92; Encyclopedia of Romanticism, Greenwood, 92; British Women Writers, Critical Reference Guide, Continuum, 87. **CONTACT ADDRESS** Dept of English, Millersville Univ, Pennsylvania, PO Box 1002, Millersville, PA, 17551-0302. **EMAIL** bschnell@marauder.millersv.edu

SCHNITZER, DEBORAH
PERSONAL Sault Ste. Marie, ON, Canada **DISCIPLINE** ENGLISH **EDUCATION** Univ Western Ont, BA, 72; Univ Calgary, MA, 73; Univ Man, PhD, 86. **CAREER** Tchr, Dept Northern Affairs, Koostatak, Man, 75-77; lectr, Eng, Univ Man, 77-79, 84-86; dir, Writing Ctr, 88-91, asst prof, 91-94, ASSOC PROF ENGLISH, UNIV WINNIPEG, 94-. **HONORS AND AWARDS** Gold Medal English & Philos, Univ Western Ont, 72; Univ Man Grad Fel, 77-81; SSHRC Doctoral Fel, 83-84; Merit Award, Univ Winnipeg, 90; Red River Valley Educ Award, 91; Clifford J. Robson Award Excellence Tchg, 93. **MEMBERSHIPS** Asn Can Col & Univ Tchrs; Man Tchrs Eng; Hadassah Wizo Bk Club. **SELECTED PUBLICATIONS** Auth, The Pictorial in Modernist Fiction from Stephen Crane to Earnest Hemingway, 88; auth, English 300: A Community-Based University Entrance Curriculum, 89; auth, Tricks: Artful Photographs and Letters in Carol Shields' Stone Diaries and Anita Brookner's Hotel du Lac, in Prairie Fire, 95. **CONTACT ADDRESS** Dept of English, Univ Winnipeg, Winnipeg, ON, R3M 2E9. **EMAIL** schnitzer@uwpg02uwinnipeg.ca

SCHOENBAUM, SAMUEL
PERSONAL Born 03/06/1927, New York, NY, m, 1946 **DISCIPLINE** ENGLISH **EDUCATION** Brooklyn Col, AB, 47; Columbia Univ, AM, 49, PhD(English), 53. **CAREER** From lectr to instr English, Brooklyn Col, 48-53; from instr to prof English lit, Northwestern Univ, Evanston, 53-71, Snyder prof, 71-75; Distinguished prof English, Queens Col & Grad Ctr of City Univ NY, 75-76; DISTINGUISHED PROF RENAISSANCE STUDIES, UNIV MD, 76-, Guggenheim fels, 53-56 & 69-70; vis prof, King's Col, Univ London, 61; vis prof Shakespeare & Elizabethan drama, Univ Chicago, 65; Nat Endowment for Humanities sr fel, 73-74; mem adv comt, Int Shakespeare Conf, exec bd, Shakespeare Quart & Variorum Shakespeare Comt; trustee, Folger Shakespeare Libr, 74- **HONORS AND AWARDS** Non-Fiction Prize, Friends of Lit, 71; Distinguished Service Award, Soc Midland Auth, 76. **MEMBERSHIPS** MLA; AAUP **RESEARCH** Elizabethan drama; Shakespeare. **SELECTED PUBLICATIONS** Auth, Shakespeare In The Stratford-Records - Bearman,R/, Shakespeare Quart, Vol 0046, 1995. **CONTACT ADDRESS** Univ of Md, College Park, MD, 20742.

SCHOENECKE, MICHAEL KEITH
PERSONAL Born 03/17/1949, Oklahoma City, OK, m, 1971, 2 children **DISCIPLINE** FILM, AMERICAN LITERATURE **EDUCATION** Cent State Univ, Okla, BA, 71, MA, 74; Okla State Univ, PhD(Am studies), 79. **CAREER** Teacher hist, Edinburg Consolidated Sch Dist, 71-73; asst prof film & lit, Bellevue Col, 79-81; assoc prof film, Tex Tech Univ, 81- **MEMBERSHIPS** Popular Cult Asn; Am Cult Asn; SCent Mod Lang Asn; Univ Film Asn. **RESEARCH** American studies. **SELECTED PUBLICATIONS** Ed, Proceedings of the First Texas Southwest Popular Culture Association, Okla Hist Soc, 79; auth, Jack London's beauty ranch: A world view, J Regional Cult, 81. **CONTACT ADDRESS** English Dept, Texas Tech Univ, Lubbock, TX, 79409-0001. **EMAIL** cbmks@ttacs.ttu.edu

SCHOENFIELD, MARK
DISCIPLINE BRITISH ROMANTICISM **EDUCATION** Univ Southern Calif, PhD. **CAREER** Instr, Vanderbilt Univ. **RESEARCH** The relation of law, economics, and disciplinarity to literary studies. **SELECTED PUBLICATIONS** Auth, Voices Together: Lamb, Hazlitt, and the London, SIR; Professional Wordsworth: Law, Labor and the Poet's Contract, 96. **CONTACT ADDRESS** Vanderbilt Univ, Nashville, TN, 37203-1727.

SCHOLES, ROBERT
PERSONAL Born 05/19/1929, Brooklyn, NY **DISCIPLINE** ENGLISH, COMPARATIVE LITERATURE **EDUCATION** Yale Univ, AB, 50; Cornell Univ, MA, 56, PhD, 59. **CAREER** From instr to asst prof English, Univ Va, 59-63; from assoc prof to prof, Univ Iowa, 64-70; PROF ENGLISH, BROWN UNIV, 70-; Jr fel, Inst Res Humanities, Univ Wis, 63-64; Guggenheim Found fel, 77-78. **HONORS AND AWARDS** Am Acad Arts & Sci, 98. **MEMBERSHIPS** MLA; NCTE; PEN; Acad Lit Studies; Science Fiction Res Asn. **RESEARCH** Semiotics; composition; modern literature. **SELECTED PUBLICATIONS** Coauth, The Nature of Narrative, 66 & auth, The Fabulators, 67, Oxford Univ; auth, Structuralism in Literature, Yale Univ, 74; coauth, Science Fiction: History, Science, Vision, 77 & Elements of Literature, 78, Oxford Univ; auth, Fabulation and Metafiction, Univ Ill, 79; coauth, The Practice of Writing, St Martin's, 81; auth, Semiotics and Interpretation, Yale Univ, 82; auth, Textual Power, Yale Univ, 85; auth, Protocols of Reading, Yale Univ, 89; co-auth, Hemingway's Genders, Yale Univ, 94; auth, The Rise and Fall of English, Yale Univ, 98. **CONTACT ADDRESS** ENGLISH, Brown Univ, MCM Box 1957, Providence, RI, 02912-9127. **EMAIL** Robert_Scholes@brown.edu

SCHOLNICK, ROBERT JAMES
PERSONAL Born 06/22/1941, Boston, MA, m, 1964, 1 child **DISCIPLINE** AMERICAN LITERATURE & STUDIES **EDUCATION** Univ Pa, AB, 62; Brandeis Univ, MA, 64, PhD(English & Am lit), 69. **CAREER** Asst prof, 67-72, assoc prof, 73-80, PROF ENGLISH, COL WILLIAM & MARY, 80- **MEMBERSHIPS** MLA **RESEARCH** American literature; American poetry; Walt Whitman. **SELECTED PUBLICATIONS** Auth, The Original Eye, Whitman, Schelling And The Return To Origins/, Walt Whitman Quart Rev, Vol 0011, 1994; Cult Or Democracy - Whitman, Benson,Eugene, And The Galaxy/, Walt Whitman Quart Rev, Vol 0013, 1996. **CONTACT ADDRESS** Dept of English, Col of William and Mary, Williamsburg, VA, 23185.

SCHONHORN, MANUEL
PERSONAL Born 01/29/1930, Brooklyn, NY, m, 1958, 2 children **DISCIPLINE** ENGLISH **EDUCATION** Brooklyn Col, BA, 55; Univ Pa, MA, 59, PhD(English), 63. **CAREER** From instr to asst prof English, Univ Kans, 62-66; asst prof, State Univ NY, Binghamton, 66-68; assoc prof, 68-73, PROF ENGLISH, SOUTHERN ILL UNIV, 73-, Newberry Libr fel, 74, exchange fel, Brit Acad, 76-77. **MEMBERSHIPS** MLA; Am Soc 18th Century Studies. **RESEARCH** Daniel Defoe and Alexander Pope; 18th century history of ideas; literature and politics. **SELECTED PUBLICATIONS** Auth, Sterne 'Tristram Shandy' - New,M/, Scriblerian And The Kit-Cats, Vol 0027, 1995; 'Tristram Shandy' - A Book For Free Spirits - New,M/, Scriblerian And The Kit-Cats, Vol 0027, 1995. **CONTACT ADDRESS** Dept of English, Southern Ill Univ, Carbondale, IL, 62901.

SCHOR, ESTHER
DISCIPLINE BRITISH ROMANTICISM **EDUCATION** St John's College, BA, 83; Yale Univ, MA, 90, MPhil, 92, PhD, 95, **CAREER** Tchg asst, Yale Univ, 90; Instr, ELI, 90-93; Instr, Yale Univ, 92-95; Lect, Princeton Univ, 95-. **RESEARCH** Poetry; theory and criticism; British Romanticism. **SELECTED PUBLICATIONS** Co-ed, The Other Mary Shelley: Beyond Frankenstein; Women's Voices: Visions and Perspectives. **CONTACT ADDRESS** Princeton Univ, 1 Nassau Hall, Princeton, NJ, 08544.

SCHOR, HILARY
DISCIPLINE ENGLISH **EDUCATION** Stanford Univ, PhD. **CAREER** Assoc prof, Univ Southern Calif.. **RESEARCH** Contemporary fiction; feminist theory and representations of women in Victorian literature. **SELECTED PUBLICATIONS** Auth, Scheherezade in the Marketplace: Elizabeth Gaskell & the Victorian Novel, 92. **CONTACT ADDRESS** Col Letters, Arts & Sciences, Univ Southern Calif, University Park Campus, Los Angeles, CA, 90089.

SCHOTCH, PETER K.
PERSONAL Born 07/26/1946 **DISCIPLINE** PHILOSOPHY IN LITERATURE, INTERMEDIATE LOGIC, STOICISM. **EDUCATION** Waterloo Univ, PhD, 73. **CAREER** Prof, 84-. **RESEARCH** Formal logic and its applications, philosophy of Descartes, the early Stoa. **SELECTED PUBLICATIONS** Auth, Paraconsistent Logic: The View from the Right, PSA 92; Remarks on Copenhagen Semantics, Essays in Honour of R.E. Jennings, Simon Fraser Univ, 93; Hyperdeontic Logic: An Overview, Social Rules, Westview Press, Boulder, 96; co-auth, Logic on the Track of Social Change, Oxford, Clarenden, 95. **CONTACT ADDRESS** Dept of Philos, Dalhousie Univ, Halifax, NS, B3H 3J5. **EMAIL** peter.schotch@dal.ca

SCHRADER, RICHARD JAMES
PERSONAL Born 08/24/1941, Canton, OH **DISCIPLINE** MEDIEVAL ENGLISH LITERATURE; BIBLIOGRAPHY AND TEXTUAL CRITICISM **EDUCATION** Univ Notre Dame, BA, 63; Ohio State Univ, MA, 65, PhD(English), 68. **CAREER** From instr to asst prof English, Princeton Univ, 68-75, John Witherspoon Bicentennial Preceptor, 72-75; asst prof to assoc prof, 75-84, prof English, Boston Col, 84-. **HONORS AND AWARDS** Mellon Grants; NEH Summer Stipend. **MEMBERSHIPS** MLA; Medieval Acad Am; Mencken Soc; SABR; ALSC; New Chaucer Soc. **RESEARCH** Medieval English Literature; Bibliography and Textual Criticism. **SELECTED PUBLICATIONS** Auth, The Reminiscences of Alexander Dyce, Ohio State Univ, 72; Gaedmn and the Monks, the Beowulf-Poet and Literary Continuity in the early Middle Ages, Am Benedictive Revm 80; God's Handiwork: Images of Women in Early Germanic Lit, Greenwood Press, 83; Arator's On the Acts of the Apostles (De Actibus Apostolorum), Scholars Press, 87; Old English Poetry and the Geneology of Events, Colleagues Press, 93; H. L. Mencken: A Descriptive Bibliography, Univ Pittsburgh Press, 98. **CONTACT ADDRESS** Dept of English, Boston Col, Chestnut Hill, MA, 02167-3806.

SCHRAIBMAN, JOSEPH
PERSONAL Born 09/29/1935, Havana, Cuba, m, 1963 **DISCIPLINE** FOREIGN LANGUAGES & LITERATURES **EDUCATION** Brooklyn Col, BA, 55; Univ Ill, MA, 56, PhD, 59. **CAREER** From instr to asst prof Romance lang, Princeton Univ, 59-65, bicentennial preceptor, 63-65; assoc prof Span & Port, Ind Univ, Bloomington, 65-69; chmn dept, 72-78, Prof Romance Lang, Wash Univ, 69-, Am Coun Learned Soc grant-in-aid, 62-63; Fulbright res grant, Spain 62-63; consult, Educ Testing Serv Advan Placement Exam; chmn, Comt Advan Placement & consult cd, Xerox Publ Co, 65-; Danforth teaching assoc, 68; mem exec comt, Bks Abroad, 71-74; Mellon fel, Univ Pittsburgh-, 75- **MEMBERSHIPS** MLA; Am Asn Teachers Span & Port; Am Asn Teachers Fr. **RESEARCH** Stylistics; Galdos; Clarin. **SELECTED PUBLICATIONS** Auth, Sephardim, The Jews Of Spain - Diazmas,P/, Revista De Estudios Hispanicos, Vol 0028, 1994; 'Match Ball' - Skarmeta,A/, Revista Iberoamericana, Vol 0060, 1994; The Origins And Sociology Of The So-Called Celestinesco Theme - Spa - Marquezvillanueva,F/, Revista De Estudios Hispanicos, Vol 0029, 1995; Life Of The Hyphen, The Cuban-American Way - Perezfirmat,G/, Revista De Estudios Hispanicos, Vol 0030, 1996; Creation In Sephardic Language - Spa - Romero,E/, Revista De Estudios Hispanicos, Vol 0030, 1996; Popular Sephardic Cancionero And Spa Tradition - Spa - Jimenezbenitez,Ae/, Revista De Estudios Hispanicos, Vol 0030, 1996. **CONTACT ADDRESS** 10 Pricewoods Lane, St Louis, MO, 63132.

SCHUCHARD, W. RONALD
DISCIPLINE ENGLISH LANGUAGE AND LITERATURE **EDUCATION** Univ Tex Austin, PhD, 69. **CAREER** Fac, 69;

dir Emory Univ Brit Studies Prog Univ Col, Oxford Univ, present; Goodrich C. White Prof, concurrent. **RESEARCH** Modern British and Irish literature; T. S. Eliot and W. B. Yeats. **SELECTED PUBLICATIONS** Ed, T. S. Eliot's Clark and Turnbull Lectures, The Varieties of Metaphysical Poetry, Faber, 93; rptd Harcourt, 94; rptd Harvest, 96; co-ed, The Collected Letters of W. B. Yeats (v 3), Oxford UP, 94. **CONTACT ADDRESS** English Dept, Emory Univ, 1380 Oxford Rd NE, Atlanta, GA, 30322-1950. **EMAIL** engrs@emory.edu

SCHUHL, MARK
PERSONAL Born 12/05/1967, Camden, NJ **DISCIPLINE** LITERATURE **EDUCATION** BA, 90, MA, 93, PhD, 99, Univ Penn **CAREER** Visting Asst Prof, 96-97, Asst Prof 97-, Fort Hays S.U. **HONORS AND AWARDS** Andrew W. Mellon Dissertation Fel, Univ Penn, 95-96; Univ Fel, Univ Penn, 94-95; Andre W. Mellon Summer Award, Univ Penn, 99. **MEMBERSHIPS** MLA; AATSP **RESEARCH** 19th and 20th Century Latin American Literature **CONTACT ADDRESS** 601 Oak, Hays, KS, 67601. **EMAIL** mschuhl@fhsu.edu

SCHULER, ROBERT M.
DISCIPLINE RENAISSANCE LITERATURE **EDUCATION** Bellarmine Col, BA; Univ Colo, MA, PhD. **CAREER** Prof. **HONORS AND AWARDS** Ed, Eng Lit Stud Monogr Series. **RESEARCH** Shakespeare; relations between literature and science; textual criticism. **SELECTED PUBLICATIONS** Auth, Three Renaissance Scientific Poems, 78; English Magical and Scientific Poetry to 1700: An Annotated Bibliography, 79; Francis Bacon and Scientific Poetry, 92; Alchemical Poetry 1575-1700, 95. **CONTACT ADDRESS** Dept of English, Victoria Univ, PO Box 3070, Victoria, BC, V8W 3W1.

SCHULTE, RAINER
DISCIPLINE LITERATURE STUDIES **EDUCATION** Univ Mich, PhD, 65. **CAREER** Prof. **HONORS AND AWARDS** Dir, Center Translation Studies; ed, Translation Rev. **RESEARCH** Translation studies; 20th century Latin American and European literature; literature and the arts; poetry writing. **SELECTED PUBLICATIONS** Auth, The Craft of Translation, Univ Chicago, 89; Theories of Translation: From Dryden to Derrida, Univ Chicago, 91; Giant Talk: An Anthology of Third World Writing, Random House, 75; Contemporary Short Stories: The Modern Tradition, W.W. Norton, 68; Suicide at the Piano, book of poems, 70; The Other Side of the Word, 78. **CONTACT ADDRESS** Dept of Literature, Richardson, TX, 75083-0688. **EMAIL** schulte@utdallas.edu

SCHULTZ, HEIDI M.
DISCIPLINE ENGLISH **EDUCATION** Lenoir-Rhyne Coll, BA, 80; Univ N Carol at Charlotte, MA, 89; Univ of N Carol at Chapel Hill, PhD, 97. **CAREER** Adj asst prof, Kenena Flagler Sch Bus, Univ NC Chapel Hill **MEMBERSHIPS** Am Antiquarian Soc **SELECTED PUBLICATIONS** Auth, "Edgar Allan Poe Submits The Bells": Resources for American Literary Study, Nov 96; "The Editor's Desk at Sartain's Magazine," Am Per vol 6, 96. **CONTACT ADDRESS** Kenan-Flagler Business Sch, Univ of N Carol at Chapel Hill, Carroll Hall, CB 3490, Chapel Hill, NC, 27599-3490. **EMAIL** hschultz@email.unc.edu

SCHULTZ, R.
PERSONAL Born 09/20/1951, Fort Dodge, IA, m, 1975, 2 children **DISCIPLINE** ENGLISH; AMERICAN LITERATURE **EDUCATION** Luther Col, BA 74; Cornell Univ, MFA 76, MA 78, PhD 81. **CAREER** Luther Col, asst prof, prof, 85 to 97-; Univ Virginia, vis prof, 93-94, lect 82-85; Cornell Univ, lectr 79-81. **HONORS AND AWARDS** NEA fel; Lorson Bishop Poetry Prize; Emily Clark Balch Prize; Danforth fel; VFH and Pub Pol Res fel; Yale Younger Poets Prize Finalist; Walt Whitman Awd Finalist. **RESEARCH** Contemporary Lit; Literary Modernism; Ezra Pound; Film. **SELECTED PUBLICATIONS** Auth, The Madhouse Nudes, Simon & Schuster, 97; Winter in Eden, Loess Hills Books, 97; Vein Along the Fault, The Laueroc Press, 79; Numerous essays, poems, short stories reviews. **CONTACT ADDRESS** Dept of English, Luther Col, 201 East Pearl St, Decorah, IA, 52101. **EMAIL** schultz@luther.edu

SCHULTZ, WILLIAM J.
PERSONAL Born 10/05/1936, Dodge City, KS, m, 1960, 4 children **DISCIPLINE** AMERICAN LITERATURE **EDUCATION** Hastings Col, BA, 58; Univ Ark, Fayetteville, MA, 64; Kans State Univ, PhD(English), 68. **CAREER** Instr English, Sterling Col, 61-64; ASST PROF ENGLISH, MUSKINGUM COL, 68- **MEMBERSHIPS** AAUP; MLA **RESEARCH** William Faulkner; American literature before 1860. **SELECTED PUBLICATIONS** Auth, Moran,Thomas And The Surveying Of The American-W - Kinsey,Jl/, J Of The W, Vol 0033, 1994. **CONTACT ADDRESS** Dept of English, Muskingum Col, New Concord, OH, 43762.

SCHULTZE, QUENTIN J.
DISCIPLINE COMMUNICATION **EDUCATION** Univ of Ill, BS, 74, MS, 76, PhD, 78. **CAREER** Prof of mass commun, Drake Univ, 78-82; prof of commun, Calvin Col, 82-. **RESEARCH** Commun and culture, espec religion. **SELECTED PUBLICATIONS** Redeeming Television; American Evangelicals and the Mass Media; Televangelism and American Culture; Dancing in the Dark: Youth, Popular Culture and the Electronic Media. **CONTACT ADDRESS** Dept of Commun Arts and Sciences, Calvin Col, 3201 Burton St SE, Grand Rapids, MI, 49546. **EMAIL** schul@calvin.edu

SCHURLKNIGHT, DONALD E.
DISCIPLINE ROMANCE LANGUAGES; LITERATURE **EDUCATION** Duke Univ, BA, 69; Univ Pa, MA, 71, PhD, 75. **CAREER** Lectr, Rosemont Col, 72-76; assoc prof, Wayne St Univ, 76- . **HONORS AND AWARDS** Fulbright Fel, Coun for Int Exchange of Scholars; Amer Philos Soc Grant. **MEMBERSHIPS** AATSP; MLA. **RESEARCH** Spanish romanticism; Spanish eighteenth & nineteenth centuries lit. **SELECTED PUBLICATIONS** Auth, Some Forgotten Poetry by Larra, Romance Notes, 89; Romantic Literary Theory as Seen Through Post-Fernandine Periodicals: El Correo de las Damas, Rivista de Estudios Hispanicos, 91; Spanish Romanticism and Mannerism: Pedro de Madrazo, Critica Hispanica, 92; La conjuracion de Venecia , Revista de Estudios Hispanicos, 98; Spanish romanticism in Context: Of Subversion, Contradiction and Politics, Univ Press Amer, 98. **CONTACT ADDRESS** Dept of Romance Lang & Lit, Wayne St Univ, 487 Manoogian Hall, Detroit, MI, 48202. **EMAIL** D.Schurlknight@wayne.edu

SCHURMAN, LYDIA CUSHMAN
DISCIPLINE ENGLISH **EDUCATION** Cornell Univ, BA, 50; Harvard, MAT, 54; George Mason Coll, MA, 76; Univ of Maryland, PhD, 84. **CAREER** Prof, to PROF EMER, ENG, N VIRGINIA COMM COLL **MEMBERSHIPS** Am Antiquarian Soc **SELECTED PUBLICATIONS** Auth, "The Sensational Stories and Dime Novel Writing Days of Louisa May Alcott, Horatio Alger, Theodore Dreiser, and Upton Sinclair," Dime Novel Round-Up, Dec 88; auth, "Anthony Comstock's Lifelong Crusade Against 'Vampire Literature,'" Dime Novel Round-Up, Dec 89; auth, "Those Famous American Periodicals The Bible, The Odyssey and Paradise Lost-Or, The Great Second-Class Mail Swindle," Publ Hist XL, 96; co-ed, Pioneers, Passionate Ladies, and Private Eyes: Dime Novels, Service Books, and Paperbacks, 97. **CONTACT ADDRESS** 3215 N 22nd St, Arlington, VA, 22201. **EMAIL** nuschul@nv.cc.va.us

SCHWARTZ, DONA B.
DISCIPLINE MASS COMMUNICATION STUDIES **EDUCATION** Univ Pa, MA, PhD. **CAREER** Assoc prof **SELECTED PUBLICATIONS** Auth, Picturing Rural Change: Community Life in Waucoma Iowa, 92; Visual Ethnography: Using Photography in Qualitative Research, Qualitative Sociology, 89. **CONTACT ADDRESS** Mass Communication Dept, Univ of Minnesota, Twin Cities, 111 Murphy Hall, 206 Church St SE, Minneapolis, MN, 55455. **EMAIL** dona@tc.umn.edu

SCHWARTZ, HENRY J.
DISCIPLINE ENGLISH LITERATURE **EDUCATION** McGill Univ, BA; Rutgers Univ, MA; Duke Univ, PhD. **CAREER** Eng Dept, Georgetown Univ **RESEARCH** Literary theory and cultural studies; theory of history; South Asian literature; film. **SELECTED PUBLICATIONS** Auth, Writing Cultural History in Colonial and Postcolonial India, 97; Reading the Shape of the World: Toward an International Cultural Studies, Westview, 96. **CONTACT ADDRESS** English Dept, Georgetown Univ, 37th and O St, Washington, DC, 20057.

SCHWARTZ, HOWARD
DISCIPLINE ENGLISH LITERATURE **CAREER** Prof, Univ Mo, St Louis. **HONORS AND AWARDS** 1st Place Award, Acad of Am Poets poetry contest, Wash Univ, 69; Poetry fel, St Louis Arts and Hum Comn, 81; Am Bk Award, Before Columbus Found, 84; Sydney Taylor Bk Award, 92; Hon Doctorate, Spertus Inst Jewish Stud, 96; Nat Jewish Bk Award, Hebrew Un Col, NY, 96; Aesop Prize, Am Folklore Soc, 97. **SELECTED PUBLICATIONS** Auth, The Four Who Entered Paradise, Northvale, Jason Aronson, 95; Next Year in Jerusalem: 3000 Years of Jewish Stories, Viking Children's Bks, 96; The Wonder Child & Other Jewish Fairy Tales, Harper Collins, 96; ed, Elijah's Violin & Other Jewish Fairy Tales, Oxford UP, 94; Tales of Modern Wisdom, 3rd ed, Random House, 96; First Harvest: Jewish Writing in St. Louis: 1991-1996, St Louis: Brodsky Libr Press, 97. **CONTACT ADDRESS** Univ Mo, St Louis, 8001 Natural Bridge Rd, St Louis, MO, 63121. **EMAIL** sheschw@umslvma.umsl.edu

SCHWARTZ, JEFF L.
PERSONAL Born 02/18/1968, Culver City, CA **DISCIPLINE** LITERATURE **EDUCATION** Univ Calif Santa Cruz, BA, 90; Bowling Green St Univ, MA, 92; Univ Tx Austin, MLIS, 99. **CAREER** Teaching Fel, Bowling Green St Univ. **HONORS AND AWARDS** Amer Stud Prog Essay Prize, Bowling Green St Univ, 97; Acad Competitive Scholar, Univ Tx Austin, 98-99. **MEMBERSHIPS** MLA; ASA; ALA; ACRL. **RESEARCH** Jazz & popular musics; critical theory; polit & avant-garde art; library svc to interdisciplinary prog. **SELECTED PUBLICATIONS** Auth, Postmodernity, History, and the Assassination of JFK, Bowling Green St Univ, 92; Writing Jimi: rock Guitar Pedagogy as Postmodern Folkloric Practice, Popular Music, 93; Sister Ray: Some Pleasures of a Musical Text, in The Velvet Underground Companion, Schirmer, 97; It's Only rock and Roll?, review of The Sex Revolts: Gender, New Black Music: Amiri Baraka and Archie Shepp, dissertation, Bowling Green St Univ, forthcoming. **CONTACT ADDRESS** 1200 W 40th St, No 134, Austin, TX, 78756. **EMAIL** jeffs@gslis.utexas.edu

SCHWARTZ, LLOYD
PERSONAL Born 11/29/1941, Brooklyn, NY **DISCIPLINE** ENGLISH **EDUCATION** Harvard Univ, PhD, 76. **CAREER** University Mass Boston. **HONORS AND AWARDS** Pulitzer Prize for criticism; NEA Creative Writing Grant for poetry; 3 ASCAP Deems Taylor Awards for Music Criticism. **MEMBERSHIPS** PEN. **RESEARCH** Elizabeth Bishop. **SELECTED PUBLICATIONS** Auth, These People, 81; Goodnight, Gracie, 92; ed, Elizabeth Bishop and Her Art, 83. **CONTACT ADDRESS** Dept of English, Univ of Mass, Boston, MA, 02125. **EMAIL** schwartzll@umbsky.cc.umb.edu

SCHWARTZ, REGINA
DISCIPLINE ENGLISH **EDUCATION** Univ Va, PhD. **CAREER** Prof, Northwestern Univ. **HONORS AND AWARDS** Milton Society prize. **RESEARCH** 17th century literature, psychoanalytic and postmodern theory. **SELECTED PUBLICATIONS** Auth, Remembering and Repeating: Biblical Creation in Paradise Lost,88; The Book and the Text: The Bible and Literary Theory, 90; Desire in the Renaissance: Psychoanalysis and Literature, 94; The Postmodern Bible, 95; The Curse of Cain: The Violent Legacy of Monotheism; An interview with Regina M. Schwartz, Univ Chicago Press; Remembering and Repeating: Biblical Creation in Paradise Lost. **CONTACT ADDRESS** Dept of English, Northwestern Univ, 1801 Hinman, Evanston, IL, 60208.

SCHWARTZ, RICHARD B.
DISCIPLINE ENGLISH LITERATURE **EDUCATION** Univ Notre Dame, BA; Univ Ill, MA, PhD. **CAREER** Eng Dept, Georgetown Univ **RESEARCH** Eighteenth century intellectual and social history; contemporary American fiction and culture; creative writing. **SELECTED PUBLICATIONS** Auth, Samuel Johnson and the New Science, 71; Samuel Johnson and the Problem of Evil, 75; Boswell's Johnson: A Preface to the LIFE, 78; Daily Life in Johnson's London, 83; After the Death of Literature, 97; Frozen Stare, 89; ed, The Plays of Arthur Murphy, 79; Theory and Tradition in Eighteenth Century Studies, 90. **CONTACT ADDRESS** English Dept, Georgetown Univ, 37th and O St, Washington, DC, 20057.

SCHWARTZ, ROBERT BARNETT
PERSONAL Born 03/20/1950, New York, NY **DISCIPLINE** RENAISSANCE LITERATURE **EDUCATION** Tulane Univ, BA, 72; Univ Va, PhD, 78. **CAREER** Instr English, Univ Va, 74-78; from Asst Prof to Assoc Prof, 78-91, Prof English, Ore State Univ, 91-, Chair of English, 94-. **MEMBERSHIPS** Philol Asn Pacific Coast; Rocky Mt Mod Lang Asn. **RESEARCH** Shakespeare; Renaissance; folklore. **SELECTED PUBLICATIONS** Ed, Shakespeare and the Popular Tradition in the Theater, Johns Hopkins Univ Press, 78; auth, Birons Wortspielerisches'Spiel Aus Kinderzeit', Shakespeare Jahrbuch, 78; The social character of May games, Zeitschrift fur Anglistik und Amerikanistik, 79; Speaking the unspeakable: The meaning of form in Christabel, Lang Quart, 80; Approaching the sonnets: Shakespeare's Parted Eye, Wascana Rev, 82; Coming apart at the Seems: More on the complexity of Hamlet, Pac Coast Philol, 82; Shakespeare's Parted Eye: Perception, Knowledge and Meaning in the Sonnets and Plays, Peter Lang, 90. **CONTACT ADDRESS** Dept of English, Oregon State Univ, 238 Moreland Hall, Corvallis, OR, 97331-5302. **EMAIL** rschwartz@orst.edu

SCHWARZ, DANIEL ROGER
PERSONAL Born 05/12/1941, Rockville Centre, NY, m, 1963, 2 children **DISCIPLINE** ENGLISH **EDUCATION** Union Col, NY, BA, 63; Brown Univ, MA, 65, PhD(English), 68. **CAREER** Asst prof, 68-74, assoc prof, 74-80, dir undergrad educ, dept English, 77-80, PROF ENGLISH, CORNELL UNIV, 80- . Am Philos Soc grant, 81. **MEMBERSHIPS** MLA **RESEARCH** The British novel, especially Hardy, Conrad, Lawrence and Joyce; theory of the novel; 20th century British poetry. **SELECTED PUBLICATIONS** Auth, Herself Beheld - The Lit Of The Looking-Glass - Labelle,J/, D H Lawrence Rev, Vol 0023, 1991; Macropolitics Of 19th-Century Lit - Nationalism, Exoticism, Imperialism - Arac,J, Ritvo,H/, Albion, Vol 0024, 1992; The Fr Fate Of Conrad,Joseph - Hervouet,Y/, Nineteenth-Century Lit, Vol 0047, 1993l Classics And Contemporaries - Aldridge,Jw/, Michigan Quart Rev, Vol 0032, 1993; Conrad,Joseph And The Modern Temper - Erdinastvulcan,D/, Studies In The Novel, Vol 0025, 1993; Talents And Technicians - Literary Chic And The New Assembly-Line Fiction - Aldridge,Jw/, Michigan Quart Rev, Vol 0032, 1993; Sources Of The Modern Imagination .2. A Review-Essay/, English Lit In Transition 1880-1920, Vol 0037, 1994; Approaches To Teaching Joyce 'Ulysses' - Mccormick,K, Steinberg,Er/, Studies In The Novel, Vol 0028, 1996; The Humanistic And Pluralistic

Quest, Theory As Biog And Testament/, Biog-An Interdisciplinary Quart, Vol 0019, 1996; Performative Saying And The Ethics Of Reading - Newton,Adam,Zachary 'Narrative Ethics'/, Narrative, Vol 0005, 1997; Conrad Quarrel With Politics In 'Nostromo'/, Coll English, Vol 0059, 1997; Manet, James The 'Turn Of The Screw' And The Voyeuristic Imagination/, Henry James Rev, Vol 0018, 1997. **CONTACT ADDRESS** Dept of English, Cornell Univ, Ithaca, NY, 14850.

SCHWARZ, KATHRYN

DISCIPLINE RENAISSANCE LITERATURE AND CULTURE, SHAKESPEARE **EDUCATION** Harvard Univ, PhD. **CAREER** Instr, Vanderbilt Univ. **RESEARCH** Renaissance representations of gender, violence, and the body. **SELECTED PUBLICATIONS** Auth, Amazon Encounters in the Jacobean Queen's Masque; Missing the Breast. **CONTACT ADDRESS** Vanderbilt Univ, Nashville, TN, 37203-1727.

SCHWARZ, MARC LEWIS

PERSONAL Born 02/19/1938, Cambridge, MA, m, 1963 **DISCIPLINE** ENGLISH HISTORY **EDUCATION** Bates Col, AB, 59; Harvard Univ, MAT, 60; Univ Calif, Los Angeles, PhD(hist), 65. **CAREER** Asst prof hist, Univ Mass, Amherst, 65-67; asst prof, 67-72, ASSOC PROF HIST, UNIV NH, 72- **MEMBERSHIPS** Conf Brit Studies. **RESEARCH** Tudor-Stuart English history; English religious history. **SELECTED PUBLICATIONS** Auth, Forms Of Nationhood - The Elizabethan Writing Of Eng - Helgerson,R/, Historian, Vol 0056, 1994. **CONTACT ADDRESS** Dept of Hist, Univ of NH, 125 Technology Dr, Durham, NH, 03824-4724.

SCHWARZBACH, FREDRIC S.

PERSONAL New York, NY **DISCIPLINE** ENGLISH LITERATURE, URBAN STUDIES **EDUCATION** Columbia Univ, AB, 71, MA, 72; London Univ, PhD(English), 76. **CAREER** Res asst English, Univ Col London, 74-77; ASST PROF ENGLISH, WASH UNIV, ST LOUIS, 77-, Am Coun Learned Soc fel, 80. **MEMBERSHIPS** MLA **RESEARCH** Nineteenth century literature; social context of literature; literature and the city. **SELECTED PUBLICATIONS** Auth, Dickens And The 1830s - Chittick,K/, Victorian Studies, Vol 0036, 1992. **CONTACT ADDRESS** Dept of English, Wash Univ, St Louis, MO, 63130.

SCHWARZLOSE, RICHARD A.

DISCIPLINE JOURNALISM **EDUCATION** Univ Ill, BA, 59, MA, 60, PhD, 65. **CAREER** Assoc prof to PROF, JOUR, NORTHWESTERN UNIV **MEMBERSHIPS** Am Antiquarian Soc **SELECTED PUBLICATIONS** Auth, American Wire Services: A Study of Their Development as a Social Institution, 79; auth, Newspapers: A Reference Guide, Greenwood Press, 87; auth, The Nation's Newsbrokers: Vol 1: The Formative Years, from Pretelegraph to 1865, Northwestern, 88; auth, The Nation's Newsbrokers, Vol 2: The Rush to Institution, from 1865 to 1920, Northwestern, 89. **CONTACT ADDRESS** Medill School of Jour, Northwestern Univ, 1845 Sheridan Rd, Evanston, IL, 60208. **EMAIL** r-schwarzlose@nwu.edu

SCHWEDA, DONALD NORMAN

PERSONAL Born 04/18/1937, Chicago, IL, m, 1957, 1 child **DISCIPLINE** AMERICAN & ENGLISH LITERATURE **EDUCATION** Ill Inst Technol, BS, 62; Univ Fla, AM, 63; Loyola Univ Chicago, PhD(English), 73. **CAREER** Teacher English, Kelvyn Park High Sch, Chicago, 62 & Mount Prospect High Sch, 64; instr, 64-66, assoc prof, 68-76, prof English, Quincy Col, 76-, chemn dept, 68-96, Evaluator, Clearing House Reading & Commun Skills, Educ Resources Info Ctr, 74- **HONORS AND AWARDS** NEH Summer Seminars, CUNY, 77; CUNY, 81; Yale, 89; Yale, 94. **MEMBERSHIPS** NCTE; Midwest Mod Lang Asn. **RESEARCH** American poetry; 19th century American literature; Robert Frost. **SELECTED PUBLICATIONS** Auth, Emersonian ideas and Whitman's Song of Myself, J Loyola Hist Soc, fall 67; A History of Newness (A Review), rivernord, 78; Poetry, riverrun, 86, 83, 81; Arts Quincy, 85; consulting advisor, Norton Anthology of African American Literature, 97. **CONTACT ADDRESS** Dept of English, Quincy Col, 1800 College Ave, Quincy, IL, 62301-2670. **EMAIL** schweda@quincy.edu

SCHWEICKART, PATROCINIO PAGADUAN

PERSONAL Born 08/07/1942, Manilla, Philippines, m, 1966, 2 children **DISCIPLINE** CRITICISM & LITERARY THEORY **EDUCATION** Univ Philippines, BChem Eng, 63; Univ Va, MChE, 65, MA, 69; Ohio State Univ, PhD(English), 80. **CAREER** Lectr math, Loyola Univ, Chicago, 76-77, lectr English, 77-78; ASST PROF ENGLISH, UNIV NH, 79-, Consult, NH Coun for Humanities, 81-82; ed, New Eng Women's Studies Newslett, 81-; scholar, Sch Criticism & Theory, Northwestern Univ, 81- **MEMBERSHIPS** MLA; Nat Women's Studies Asn. **RESEARCH** Women's studies; science and literature; literary criticism and theory. **SELECTED PUBLICATIONS** Auth, Reading Feminisms/, College English, Vol 0059, 1997. **CONTACT ADDRESS** English Dept, Univ of NH, 125 Technology Dr, Durham, NH, 03824-4724.

SCHWEIK, ROBERT CHARLES

PERSONAL Born 08/05/1927, Chicago, IL, m, 1954, 2 children **DISCIPLINE** ENGLISH **EDUCATION** Loyola Univ, Ill, BA, 51; Univ Notre Dame, PhD, 58. **CAREER** Instr English, Marquette Univ, 53-58, from asst prof to assoc prof, 59-69; prof, 69-80, DISTINGUISHED TEACHING PROF, STATE UNIV NY COL FREDONIA, 80-, Mem Victorian bibliog comt, MLA, 68-72; vis prof, Univ Trier, Ger, 72-73. **MEMBERSHIPS** MLA; Int Asn Univ Prof English; Thomas Hardy Soc. **RESEARCH** Victorian novel; bibliography; nineteenth-century prose non-fiction. **SELECTED PUBLICATIONS** Auth, Hardy,Thomas - 'Tess Of The Durbervilles' - Kramer,D, Ed/, English Lit In Transition 1880-1920, Vol 0036, 1993; 'Jude The Obscure' - A Paradise Of Despair - Adelman,G/, English Lit In Transition 1880-1920, Vol 0036, 1993. **CONTACT ADDRESS** Dept of English, State Univ of NY Col, Fredonia, NY, 14063.

SCHWEITZER, IVY

DISCIPLINE ENGLISH LITERATURE **EDUCATION** Brandeis Univ, PhD, 83. **CAREER** Assoc prof, Dartmouth Col. **RESEARCH** Am lit and poetics; women's studies. **SELECTED PUBLICATIONS** Auth, The Work of Self-Representation: Lyric Poetry in Colonial New England, Univ NC P, 91; Maternal Discourse and the Romance of Self-Possession in Kate Chopin's The Awakening, boundary, 90, rptd in Revisionary Interventions into the Americanist Canon, Duke UP, 94. **CONTACT ADDRESS** Dartmouth Col, 3529 N Main St, #207, Hanover, NH, 03755.

SCHWENINGER, LEE

DISCIPLINE LITERATURE **EDUCATION** Univ of NC, PhD, 84; Univ of CT, MA, 80; Univ of CO, BA, 76 **CAREER** Prof, Univ of NC **HONORS AND AWARDS** Resig interdisc minor in Native Am studies **MEMBERSHIPS** Asn for the study of lit and the environ **RESEARCH** Early Am lit **SELECTED PUBLICATIONS** Auth, The Writings of Celia parker Woolley (1848-1918), Literary Activist, Lewiston: Edwin Mellen Press, 98; John Winthrop, Boston: Twayne Pub, 90 **CONTACT ADDRESS** Dept of English, Univ of Mo Carolina, Wilmington, Wilmington, NC, 28403. **EMAIL** schweningerl@uncwil.edu

SCOBIE, STEPHEN A.C.

PERSONAL Born 12/31/1943, Carnoustie, Scotland **DISCIPLINE** ENGLISH **EDUCATION** Univ St Andrews, MA, 65; Univ BC, PhD, 69. **CAREER** Fac mem, 69-81, prof, Eng, Univ Alta, 80-81; PROF ENGLISH, UNIV VICTORIA, 81-; guest prof, Christian-Albrechts-Universitat, Ger, 90. **HONORS AND AWARDS** Gov Gen Award Poetry, 80; fel, Royal Soc Can, 95. **MEMBERSHIPS** League Can Poets (vice pres, 72-74, 86-88); Victoria Lit Arts Festival Soc, 92-96. **RESEARCH** Canadian literature. **SELECTED PUBLICATIONS** Auth, Leonrad Cohen, 78; auth, Nichol: What History Teaches, 84; auth, Signature Event Cantext, 89; auth, Alias Bob Dylan, 91; auth, Earthquakes and Explorations: Language and Painting from Cubism to Concrete Poetry, 97; coauth, The Pirates of Pen's Chance, 81; co-ed, The Maple Laugh Forever: An Anthology of Canadian Comic Poetry, 81. **CONTACT ADDRESS** English Dept, Univ Victoria, Victoria, BC, V8W 3W1. **EMAIL** sscobie@uvic.ca

SCOTT, BONNIE KIME

PERSONAL Born 12/28/1944, Philadelphia, PA, m, 1967, 3 children **DISCIPLINE** ENGLISH, WOMEN'S STUDIES **EDUCATION** Wellesley Col, BA, 67; Univ NC, Chapel Hill, MA, 69, PhD(Eng), 73. **CAREER** Asst prof, 75-80, assoc, 80-86, prof Eng, Univ DE, 86-; dir grad stud in Eng; Fac res grants Eng, Univ DE, 76, 81, 87, 95. **HONORS AND AWARDS** DE Outstanding young woman, Outstanding Young Women Am, 77. **MEMBERSHIPS** MLA; Am Comt Irish Studies; James Joyce Found; VA Wolf Soc; Soc for the Study of Narrative Lit. **RESEARCH** James Joyce; Irish lit; women's studies; modernism. **SELECTED PUBLICATIONS** Auth, Joyce and Feminism. Indiana, 84; auth, James Joyce, Humanities, 87; ed and contribur, New Alliances in Joyce Studies: "Whan it's Aped to Foul a Delfian," Delaware, 88; ed and contribur, The Gender of Modernism, Indiana, 90; auth, Refiguring Modernism, 2v, Indiana, 95; co-ed, Images of Joyce: Papers of the 12th International James Joyce Symposium, 2v, Colin Smyth, 98; ed and contribur, The Selected Letters of Rebecca West, Yale, 99. **CONTACT ADDRESS** Dept of English, Univ of DE, Newark, DE, 19716. **EMAIL** bscott@udel.edu

SCOTT, JAMES F.

DISCIPLINE VICTORIAN LITERATURE **EDUCATION** Univ KS, PhD. **CAREER** Eng Dept, St. Edward's Univ **SELECTED PUBLICATIONS** Auth, Beat Literature and the American Teen Cult, American Quart, 62; Thomas Hardy's Use of the Gothic, Nineteenth Century Fiction, 63; Spectacle and Symbol in Thomas Hardy's Fiction, Philol Quart,65; The Achievement of Ingmar Bergman, Jour Aesthetics & Art Criticism, 65; Bergman in the 1950s, Film Focus: The Seventh Seal, Prentice Hall; 72; Blow-Up: Antonioni and the Mod World, Focus on Blow-up, 72; Comte, Positivism, and the Social Vision of Middlemarch, Victorian Studies, 72; The Emasculation of Lady Chatterley's Lover, Film/Lit, 73; D.H. Lawrence's Germania: Ethnic Psychology and Cultural Crisis in the Shorter Fiction, D.H. Lawrence Rev, 77; Thimble into Ladybird: Nietzsche, Frobenius, and Bachofen in the Later Works of D.H. Lawrence, Arcadia, 78; 'Continental': The Germanic Dimension of Women in Love, Literatur in Wissenschaft und Unterricht, 79; New Terms for Order: Network Style and Individual Experiment in American Documentary Film, In Ideas of Order in Literature and Film, Fla State Univ Press, 81; Cleansing the Valleys: John Knoepfle's Vision of the American Heartland, IATE: Ill Engl Bull, 97. **CONTACT ADDRESS** St Edward's Univ, 3001 S Congress Ave, Austin, TX, 78704-6489.

SCOTT, JAMES FRAZIER

PERSONAL Born 07/09/1934, Atchison, KS, m, 1961, 2 children **DISCIPLINE** ENGLISH, CINEMA, TELEVISION **EDUCATION** Rockhurst Col, BS, 55; Univ Kans, MA, 57, PhD(English), 60. **CAREER** Instr English, Univ Ky, 60-62; from asst prof to assoc prof, 62-72, prof English, St Louis Univ, 72-. **MEMBERSHIPS** MLA. **RESEARCH** Nineteenth century fiction; the aesthetics of cinema. **SELECTED PUBLICATIONS** Auth, The Gothic element in Thomas Hardy's fiction, Nineteenth-Century Fiction, 63; The achievement of Ingmar Bergman, J Aesthet, 65; George Eliot, positivism, and the social vision of Middlemarch, Victorian Studies, 72; Film: The Medium and the Maker, Holt, 75; D H Lawrence's Germania, D H Lawrence Rev, 77. **CONTACT ADDRESS** Dept of English, St. Louis Univ, 221 N Grand Blvd, St. Louis, MO, 63103-2097. **EMAIL** scotJF@slu.edu

SCOTT, MARY JANE W.

PERSONAL Born 05/18/1949, Washington, DC, m, 1973, 2 children **DISCIPLINE** SCOTTISH & ENGLISH LITERATURE **EDUCATION** Emory Univ, BA, 71; Univ Edinburgh, 72, PhD, 79; Midlands Tech Col, criminol just, 98. **CAREER** Tutor Scottish lit, 75-76, Univ Edinburgh; instr Eng, 78, Col Gen Studies, Univ SC; asst prof, 79-80, res & writing, 81-, reader & consult, studies Scottish Lit, 76- Columbia Col; adj instr, writing tutor, 85-90, 95-98, Midlands Tech Col; campus min, 90-91, St Thomas More Ctr, Univ SC; hum svcs, 92-95, Cetral SC Habitat for Hum; victim advoc, 98-, Forest Acres, SC Police Dept. **MEMBERSHIPS** Assn Scottish Lit Studies; Soc Antiquaries (Scotland). **RESEARCH** The poetry of James Thomson 1700-1748; 18th-20th century Anglo-Scottish poetry; the poetry of Norman MacCaig. **SELECTED PUBLICATIONS** Art, Neoclassical MacCaig, Studies Scottish Lit, 1/73; art, Robert Ayton: Scottish metaphysical, Scottish Lit J, 75; The Identity of MisJohn: A Footnote to James Thomson, The Bibl, Vol 8, 76; art, Alexander Smith: Poet of Victorian Scotland, Studies Scottish Lit, Vol XIV, 76; art, Hugh Blair on Campus in America, Univ Edinburgh J, Vol XXIX, 80; auth, Scottish Language in the Poetry of James Thomson, Neuphilol Mitt, Vol LXXXII, No 4; coauth, The Manuscript of James Thomson's Scot's Elegy, Studies Scottish Lit, Vol XVII; auth, James Thomson, Anglo-Scot, Univ Georgia Press, 88; auth, James Thomson and the Anglo-Scots, Hist of Scottish Lit, Hook, 87. **CONTACT ADDRESS** 1703 Belmont Dr, Columbia, SC, 29206.

SCOTT, NATHAN A., JR.

PERSONAL Born 04/24/1925, Cleveland, Ohio, m, 1946 **DISCIPLINE** HUMANITIES **EDUCATION** Univ of MI, BA 1944; Union Theol Sem, MDiv 1946; Columbia Univ, PhD 1949. **CAREER** VA Union Univ, dean of the chapel 1946-47; Howard Univ, assoc prof of humanities 1948-55; Univ of Chicago, prof of theology and literature 1955-76; Univ of VA, Wm R Kenan prof emeritus of religious studies, prof emeritus of English 1976-90; Priest of the Episcopal Church. **HONORS AND AWARDS** LittD, Ripon Coll, 1965; LHD, Wittenberg Univ, 1965; DD, Philadelphia Divinity School, 1967; STD, Gen Theological Seminary, 1968; LittD, St Mary's Coll Notre Dame, 1969; LHD, Univ of DC, 1976; LittD, Denison Univ, 1976; LittD, Brown Univ, 1981; LittD, Northwestern Univ, 1982; DD, Virginia Theological Seminary, 1985; HumD, Univ of Michigan, 1988; LittD, Elizabethtown Coll, 1989; LittD, Wesleyan Univ, 1989; DD, Bates College, 1990; STD, University of the South, 1992; DD, Kenyon Coll, 1993; DD, Wabash Coll, 1996; fellow, Amer Acad of Arts and Sciences, 1979; author, 25 books; contributor, 42 books; Amer Acad of Religion vice pres 1984, pres-elect 1985, pres 1986. **MEMBERSHIPS** Amer Philosophical Assn; Amer Acad of Religion; Modern Language Assn; Soc for Values in Higher Educ; advisory editor, Callalloo; mem of bd of consultants The Journal of Religion; mem advisory bd, Religion & Literature, Religion and Intellectual Life, The Journal of Literature and Theology. **CONTACT ADDRESS** Prof Religious Studies & English, Univ of Virginia, Charlottesville, VA, 22903.

SCOTT, PETER DALE

PERSONAL Born 01/11/1929, Montreal, PQ, Canada, m, 1956, 3 children **DISCIPLINE** ENGLISH, POLITICAL SCIENCE **EDUCATION** McGill Univ, BA, 49, PhD(polit sci), 55. **CAREER** Lectr polit sci, McGill Univ, 55-56; foreign serv off, Can Foreign Serv, 56-61; lectr speech, 61-62, acting asst prof, 62-63, asst prof, 63-66, asst prof, 66-68, assoc prof, 68-80, PROF ENGLISH, UNIV CALIF, BERKELEY, 80-, Humanities res fel, Univ Calif, Berkeley, 68; Guggenheim fel, 69-70. **RESEARCH** Covert Politics; medieval Latin poetry; literature and politics. **SELECTED PUBLICATIONS** Auth, Mcnamara

And Vietnam - Reply/, New York Rev Of Books, Vol 0042, 1995. **CONTACT ADDRESS** 2823 Ashby Ave, Berkeley, CA, 94705.

SCOTT, ROBERT LEE
PERSONAL Born 04/19/1928, Fairbury, NE, m, 1947, 3 children **DISCIPLINE** SPEECH **EDUCATION** Univ Colo, BA, 50; Univ Nebr, MA, 51; Univ Ill, PhD(speech), 55. **CAREER** Asst prof speech, Univ Houston, 53-57; from asst prof to assoc prof, 57-64, prof speech, Univ Minn, Minneapolis, 64-, ed, Quart J Speech, 72-74. **HONORS AND AWARDS** Winans Research Award, National Communication Asn, 69; Woolisert Research Award, NCA, 81; Distinguished Teaching Award, College of Liberal Arts, Univ of Mn, 81; Ehninger Research Award, NCA, 89; Distinguished Scholar of the Asn, NCA, 92. **MEMBERSHIPS** Speech Commun Asn; NCTE. **RESEARCH** Criticism of contemporary public address; contemporary rhetorical theory. **SELECTED PUBLICATIONS** Coauth, Thinking and Speaking: A Guide to Intelligent Oral Communication, Macmillan, 62, 68, 73 & 78; auth, On Viewing Rhetoric as Epistemic, Cent States Speech J, 2/67; coauth, The Rhetoric of Black Power, Harper, 69; Moments in the Rhetoric of the Cold War, Random, 72; auth, On not defining rhetoric, Philos & Rhet, spring 73; The Conservative Voice in Radical Rhetoric, Speech Monogr, 6/73. **CONTACT ADDRESS** Dept of Speech Commun, Univ of Minn, 9 Pleasant St S E, Minneapolis, MN, 55455-0194. **EMAIL** Scott033@maroon.tc.umn.edu

SCOTT, WILLIAM O.
DISCIPLINE ENGLISH **EDUCATION** Univ Chicago, BA, 52; Univ Mich, BA, 54; Duke Univ, MA, 55; Princeton Univ, PHD, 59. **CAREER** Instr, 58-61, asst prof, 61-65, assoc prof, 65-79, PROF, ENG, UNIV KANS, 79-. **CONTACT ADDRESS** English Dept, Univ of Kansas, Wescoe Hall, Lawrence, KS, 66045-2115. **EMAIL** wscott@ukans.edu

SCRIVENER, MICHAEL HENRY
PERSONAL Born 10/30/1948, Washington, DC, m, 1976, 2 children **DISCIPLINE** ENGLISH **EDUCATION** State Univ NY, Binghamton, MA, 72; State Univ NY, Buffalo, PhD, 76. **CAREER** Prof eng, Wayne State Univ, 76. **MEMBERSHIPS** MLA; AAUP. **RESEARCH** Romantic poetry; 19th century Brit lit; sociological criticism. **SELECTED PUBLICATIONS** Auth, Radical Shelley, Princeton, 82; Poetry and Reform, Wayne State, 92. **CONTACT ADDRESS** Dept of Eng, Wayne State Univ, 51 West Warren, Detroit, MI, 48202-1308. **EMAIL** aa1973@wayne.edu

SEABURY, MARCIA
DISCIPLINE ENGLISH LITERATURE **EDUCATION** Wooster Col, BA; Univ Ill, MA; PhD. **CAREER** Assoc prof, Hartford Univ. **SELECTED PUBLICATIONS** Auth, Interdisciplinary General Education in Action: Developing Integrative Skills; pubs on utopian fiction of Marge Percy. **CONTACT ADDRESS** English Dept, Univ of Hartford, 200 Bloomfield Ave, West Hartford, CT, 06117.

SEAMAN, JOHN
DISCIPLINE ENGLISH LITERATURE **EDUCATION** Princeton Univ, BA, 54; Stanford Univ, MA, 59, PhD, 62. **CAREER** Prof, Univ Pacific. **HONORS AND AWARDS** Lit Awd Jury. **SELECTED PUBLICATIONS** Auth, The Moral Paradox of Paradise Lost, Mouton, 71; pubs on Shakespeare, Milton, and lang and style. **CONTACT ADDRESS** Eng Dept, Univ Pacific, Pacific Ave, PO Box 3601, Stockton, CA, 95211.

SEAMON, ROGER
PERSONAL Born 05/29/1937, Perth Amboy, NJ, m, 1958, 2 children **DISCIPLINE** ENGLISH **EDUCATION** Univ Calif, Berkeley, BA, 59; Claremont Grad Sch, MA, 61, PhD(English), 66. **CAREER** Instr English, Whitman Col, 62-64; instr, 64-66, ASST PROF ENGLISH, UNIV BC, 6-, Can Coun res grant, 69-70. **MEMBERSHIPS** Assoc Can Univ Teachers English; Can Asn Am Studies. **RESEARCH** Naturalist fiction; critical theory; aesthetics. **SELECTED PUBLICATIONS** Auth, Machiavelli Intentions/, Pmla-Publications Of The Modern Lang Assoc Of Am, Vol 0108, 1993; Guided Rapid Unconscious Reconfiguration In Poetry And Art/, Philos And Lit, Vol 0020, 1996; Cultural Transactions - Nature, Self, Society - Hernadi,P/, Philos And Lit, Vol 0020, 1996; Theocratism - The Religious Rhetoric Of Academic Interpretation/, Philos And Lit, Vol 0021, 1997. **CONTACT ADDRESS** Dept of English, Univ of BC, Vancouver, BC, V6T 1W5.

SEARL, STANFORD J.
DISCIPLINE ENGLISH LITERATURE **EDUCATION** Syracuse Univ, BA; PhD; State Univ NY Buffalo, MA. **CAREER** Prof. **SELECTED PUBLICATIONS** Auth, Portraits in Black and White: Photographic Essay about Mental Retardation Institutions, 85; Education Reporter, 83; co-auth, The Disabled in America, 87; Achieving the Complete School, 85. **CONTACT ADDRESS** English Dept, Union Inst, 440 E McMillan St, Cincinnati, OH, 45206-1925.

SEARS, PRISCILLA F.
DISCIPLINE ENGLISH LITERATURE **EDUCATION** Tufts Univ, PhD, 75. **CAREER** Sr Lctr Eng and Women's Studies. **RESEARCH** Lit, compos, women's studies. **SELECTED PUBLICATIONS** Auth, All Purpose Valentine, Am Stage Festival, 92; Sasquatch, Plymouth Rec, 91;'Suspended in Language:' Revisioning Knowledge and the Cirrculum; Feminist Perspectives, Mich State Univ, 90. **CONTACT ADDRESS** Dartmouth Col, 3529 N Main St, #207, Hanover, NH, 03755.

SEAVER, PAUL SIDDALL
PERSONAL Born 03/19/1932, Philadelphia, PA, m, 1956, 2 children **DISCIPLINE** ENGLISH HISTORY **EDUCATION** Haverford Col, BA, 55; Harvard Univ, MA, 56, PhD(hist), 65. **CAREER** Instr hist, Reed Col. 62-64; asst prof, 64-70, ASSOC PROF HIST, STANFORD UNIV, 70-, John Simon Guggenheim Mem Found fel, 70-71. **MEMBERSHIPS** AHA; Hist Asn, Eng; Am Soc Church Hist; Royal Hist Soc. **RESEARCH** Sixteenth and 17th century English Puritanism. **SELECTED PUBLICATIONS** Auth, Profits In The Wilderness - Entrepreneurship And The Founding Of New-Eng Towns In The 17th-Century - Martin,Jf/, J Of Interdisciplinary Hist, Vol 0024, 1993; Bunyan,John And English Nonconformity - Greaves,R/, Church Hist, Vol 0063, 1994; The Early Stuart Church, 1603-1642 - Fincham,K, Ed/, Cath Hist Rev, Vol 0080, 1994; The Workplace Before The Factory - Artisans And Proletarians, 1500-1800 - Safley,Tm, Rosenband,Ln, Editors/, Sixteenth Century J, Vol 0025, 1994; Spenser Secret Career - Rambuss,R/, Historian, Vol 0056, 1994; The Huguenots In Eng - Immigration And Settlement C.1550-1700 - Cottret,B/, Church Hist, Vol 0064, 1995; Lit And Cult In Early-Modern London - Manley,L/, Renaissance And Reformation, Vol 0020, 1996; London - A Soc-Hist - Porters,R/, J Of Modern Hist, Vol 0069, 1997. **CONTACT ADDRESS** Dept of Hist, Stanford Univ, Stanford, CA, 94305-1926.

SEBOUHIAN, GEORGE
PERSONAL Born 11/29/1931, New York, NY **DISCIPLINE** LITERATURE **EDUCATION** OH State Univ, PhD, 73. **CAREER** Tchr Eng, Pub Schs, FL & OH, 60-65; instr, Miami Univ, 65-68; asst prof, 72-80, assoc prof eng, State Univ NY Col Fredonia, 80, prof, 87, Fulbright-Hays lectr, Poland, 76-77; japan, 92-93. **HONORS AND AWARDS** Woodrow Wilson fel, 59-60. **MEMBERSHIPS** MLA **RESEARCH** Am Puritans; Am transcendentalists; Ralph Waldo Emerson; jaoanese aestetics. **SELECTED PUBLICATIONS** Auth, Emerson's experience: An approach to content and method, Emerson Soc Quart, 67; The transcendental imagination to Merton Densher, Mod Lang Studies, 75; Thomas A Kempis and Emerson's first crisis, Am Transcendental Quart, 76; Henry James's transcendental imagination, Essays Lit, 76; The marginalia in James Pierrepont Greaves in Emerson's library, Papers Bibliog Soc Am, 78. **CONTACT ADDRESS** Dept of Eng, State Univ of NY Col, Fredonia, NY, 14063-1143. **EMAIL** sebouhian@ait.fredonia.edu

SECOR, ROBERT ARNOLD
PERSONAL Born 06/29/1938, Brooklyn, NY, m, 1965, 2 children **DISCIPLINE** ENGLISH & AMERICAN LITERATURE **EDUCATION** Syracuse Univ, BA, 60; Brown Univ, MA, 63, PhD(English), 69. **CAREER** Instr English, Northwestern Univ, 66-69; asst prof, 69-72, assoc prof English, Pa State Univ, 72-86; prof English, 86; dept head, 90-95; Vice Provost for Academic Affairs, 95-, dir, Grad Studies English, 78-. **MEMBERSHIPS** MLA **RESEARCH** Nineteenth century English and American literature, especially Ruskin; the Pre-Raphaelites; Henry James. **SELECTED PUBLICATIONS** Auth, The Rhetoric of Shifting Perspectives: Conrad's Victory, Pa State Univ, 71; American Literature I (Colonial Period to 1890), Simon & Schuster, 71; Christopher Newman: How Innocent is James's American?, Studies Am Fiction, autumn 73; ed, Pennsylvania 1776, Pa State Univ, 75; coauth, Violet Hunt's Tales of the Uneasy, Women & Lit, spring 78; Pre-Raphaelites and Aesthetes: Oscar Wilde and the Sweetest Violet in England, Tex Studies Lit & Lang, fall 79; Robert Browning and the Hunts of South Kensington, Browning Institute Studies: An Annual in Victorian Literary and Cultural History, Vol 7, 79; John Ruskin and Alfred Hunt: New Letters and the Record of a Friendship, Univ of Victoria, 82. **CONTACT ADDRESS** Office of the President, Pennsylvania State Univ, 201 Old Main, University Park, PA, 16802. **EMAIL** ry52@psu.edu

SECREAST, DONALD
DISCIPLINE CREATIVE FICTION WRITING AND MODERN BRITISH LITERATURE **EDUCATION** Univ IA, PhD. **CAREER** Prof, Radford Univ. **SELECTED PUBLICATIONS** Auth, The Rat Becomes Light, 90; White Trash, Red Velvet, 93; coauth, Adventuring in the Andes, 85. **CONTACT ADDRESS** Radford Univ, Radford, VA, 24142. **EMAIL** dsecreas@runet.edu

SEELIG, SHARON CADMAN
PERSONAL Born 01/08/1941, Mountain Lake, MN, m, 1967 **DISCIPLINE** ENGLISH LITERATURE **EDUCATION** Carleton Col, BA, 62; Columbia Univ, MA, 64, PhD(English, comp lit), 69. **CAREER** Instr English, Wellesley Col, 67-69; instr, Northfield Sch, 69-70; from lectr to asst prof, Mt Holyoke Col, 70-78, assoc prof, 78-80; LECTR ENGLISH, SMITH COL, 80-, Regional assoc, Am Lit Manuscripts Census, 70-74. **MEMBERSHIPS** MLA; AAUP **RESEARCH** Seventeenth-century English literature; Shakespeare. **SELECTED PUBLICATIONS** Auth, Loyal Fathers And Treacherous Sons - Familial Politics In 'Richard Ii'/, J Of English And Ger Philol, Vol 0094, 1995; Forms Of Reflection - Genre And Cult In Meditational Writing - Radcliffe,Dh/, J Of English And Ger Philol, Vol 0096, 1997. **CONTACT ADDRESS** Dept of English, Smith Col, Northampton, MA, 01060.

SEIDEL, MICHAEL ALAN
PERSONAL Born 08/24/1943, New York, NY, 4 children **DISCIPLINE** ENGLISH LITERATURE **EDUCATION** Univ Calif, Los Angeles, BA, 66, PhD(English), 70. **CAREER** From asst prof to assoc prof English, Yale Univ, 70-77; assoc prof, 77-80, prof English, Columbia Univ, 80-, Nat Endowment for Humanities jr fel, 74-75. **MEMBERSHIPS** MLA; Am Soc 18th Century Studies. **RESEARCH** Satire; 17th and 18th century English literature and 18th century narrative; 20th century British literature. **SELECTED PUBLICATIONS** Auth, Epic Geography: James Joyce's Ulysses, Princeton Univ, 76; Homer to Brecht, Yale Univ, 77; Satiric Plots of Gravity's Rainbow, In: Twentieth-Century Views, Englewood Cliffs, 77; Satiric Inheritance, Rabeluis to Sterne, Princeton Univ, 79; Crusoe's Exile, Publ Mod Lang Asn Am, 81; Exile and the Narrative Imagination, 86; Streak: Joe DiMaggio and the Summer of 9141, Ted Williams: A Baseball Life, 90; Robinson Crusoe: Island Myths and the Novel, 90; The Works of David Defoe, 98. **CONTACT ADDRESS** Dept of English, Columbia Univ, 2960 Broadway, New York, NY, 10027-6900. **EMAIL** mas8@columbia.edu

SEIDEN, MORTON IRVING
PERSONAL Born 07/29/1921, New York, NY **DISCIPLINE** ENGLISH, COMPARATIVE LITERATURE **EDUCATION** NY Univ, BS, 43; Columbia Univ, MA, 44, PhD, 52. **CAREER** Instr English, City Col New York, 45-46, NY Univ, 46-49, Smith Col, 49-52 & Queens Col, NY, 52-53; from instr to assoc prof, 53-70, PROF ENGLISH, BROOKLYN COL, 70-; Lectr, Columbia Univ Grad Sch, 48-49. **HONORS AND AWARDS** Brooklyn Col Excellence in Teaching Award, 67. **MEMBERSHIPS** MLA; Mod Humanities Res Asn; English Inst. **RESEARCH** Nineteenth and Twentieth Century English literature; English, Irish Renaissance; Comparative Literature. **SELECTED PUBLICATIONS** Auth, A psychoanalytical essay on William Butler Yeats, Accent, spring 46; Myth in the Poetry of William Butler Yeats, Am Imago, 12/48; W B Yeats as a playwright, Western Humanities Rev, winter 49; William Butler Yeats: The Poet as a Mythmaker-- 1865-19339, Mich State Univ, 62; The Paradox of Hate: A Study in Ritual Murder, Yoseloff, 68; coauth, Ivan Goncharov's Oblomov: A study of the anti-Faust as a Christian saint, Can Slavic Studies, spring 69. **CONTACT ADDRESS** Dept of English, Brooklyn Col, CUNY, 2901 Bedford Ave, Brooklyn, NY, 11210-2813.

SEIDMAN, STEVEN A.
DISCIPLINE COMMUNICATION STUDIES **EDUCATION** Univ Ind, PhD. **CAREER** Assoc prof. **SELECTED PUBLICATIONS** Auth, pubs on sex-role stereotyping, burnout in the workplace, media utilization, music soundtracks, and instructional development. **CONTACT ADDRESS** Dept of Communication, Ithaca Col, 100 Job Hall, Ithaca, NY, 14850.

SEILER, WILLIAM JOHN
PERSONAL Born 10/17/1942, Milwaukee, WI, m, 1966, 1 child **DISCIPLINE** SPEECH COMMUNICATION **EDUCATION** Univ Wis, Whitewater, BEd, 65; Kans State Univ, MA, 67; Purdue Univ, West Lafayette, PhD(speech), 71. **CAREER** Asst prof speech, Purdue Univ, Calumet Campus, 70-72; assoc prof speech commun, Univ Nebr, Lincoln, 75-83, prof, 84-, dept chmn, 90-, dir undergrad studies, 82-86, Courtesy Appt-Teachers College 3/10/80. **HONORS AND AWARDS** Outstanding Young Alumni, Univ of Wisc-Whitewater, 74; Outstanding Young Col Teacher, Nebr Speech Commun Asn, 75; Outstanding Educators of America, 76; International Who's Who in Education, 77; Distinguished Alumni Award, Univ of Wisc-Whitewater, 89; UNL Parent's Recognition Award, 90. **MEMBERSHIPS** Am Educ Res Asn; Nat Commun Asn; Int Commun Asn; Cent States Commun Asn. **RESEARCH** Classroom communication; organizational communication; communication apprehension. **SELECTED PUBLICATIONS** Auth, Audiovisual Materials in Classroom Instruction: A Theoretical Approach, 72 & coauth, Performance-Based Teacher Education Program in Speech and Drama, 75, Speech Teacher; The Effects of Talking Apprehension on Student Academic Achievement: Three Empirical Investigations in Communication-Restricted and Traditional Laboratory Classes in the Life Sciences, Int Commun Yearbk I, 77; Communication Apprehension and Teaching Assistants, J Chem Educ, 78; Effects of Communication Apprehension on Student Learning in College Science Classes, J Col Sci Teaching, 78; Learners Cognitive Style and Levels of Learning in TV & Print Instruction for Use in Open Learning: An Exploratory Study, Int & Nat J Instr Media, 81; Communications in Business & Professional Organizations, Addison-Wesley, 82; auth, PSI: An Attractive Alternative for the Basic Speech Communication Course, Commun Educ, Jan

83; Developing the Personalized System of Instruction for the Basic Speech Communication Course, with Marilyn Fuss-Reincki, Commm Ed, April 86; The Temporal Organization of Classrooms as an Interactional Accomplishment, with Drew McGukin, Journal of Thought, winter 87; The Comparative Effectiveness of Systematic Desensitation and Visualization Therapy Treatments in Treating Public Speaking Anxiety, with Ana Rossi, Imagination, Cognition, and Personality, 89; What We Know About the Basic Course: What has the Research Told Us?, with Drew McGukin, Basic Course Annual, 89; An Investigation Into the Communication Needs and Concerns of asian Students in Speech Performance Classes, with Ester Yook, Basic Course Annual, 90; The Nebraska Department of Communication Story: There are Happy Endings that Go Beyond Football and a Good Crop Year. JACA, 95; Learning Style Preferences and Academic Achievement within the Basic Communication Course, with Chuck Lubbers, Basic Course Annual, 98; and many publications, textbooks, and other materials. **CONTACT ADDRESS** Dept of Commun Studies, Univ of Nebr, PO Box 880329, Lincoln, NE, 68588-0329. **EMAIL** bseiler@unl.edu

SEITZ, JAMES E.
PERSONAL Born 09/20/1958, Oahu, HI, m, 1991, 1 child **DISCIPLINE** ENGLISH **EDUCATION** Univ Calif, Santa Barbara, BA, 80; Univ N Mex, MA, 85; NY Univ, PhD, 90. **CAREER** Asst prof, 88-92, dir of writing, 91-92, Long Island Univ; asst prof, 92-, Univ Pittsburgh **RESEARCH** Writing, rhetoric, metaphor, tchng, curriculum reform. **CONTACT ADDRESS** Dept of English, Univ of Pittsburgh, Pittsburgh, PA, 15260.

SELF, CHARLES C.
PERSONAL m, 4 children **DISCIPLINE** JOURNALISM **EDUCATION** Andrews Univ, BA, 66; Univ Mo, MA, 71; Univ Iowa, PhD, 74. **HONORS AND AWARDS** Phi Beta Delta Honor Soc for Int Scholars, 93; UA Dept Jour Outstanding Leadership Awd, 90; Omnichron Delta Kappa Leadership Hon, 87; Kappa Tau Alpha Commitment to Tchg Awd, 86. **RESEARCH** Alliances between practitioner organizations and journalism and mass communication schools and departments. **SELECTED PUBLICATIONS** Auth, News editing text: On Line Editing, Vision Press, 94. **CONTACT ADDRESS** Dept of Journalism, Texas A&M Univ, College Station, TX, 77843-4111. **EMAIL** c-self6@tamu.edu

SELF, ROBERT THOMAS
PERSONAL Born 03/01/1941, Portsmouth, VA, m, 1969 **DISCIPLINE** AMERICAN LITERATURE **EDUCATION** FL State Univ, BA, 63; Univ Chicago, MA, 65; Univ NC, PhD, 70. **CAREER** Tchg asst Eng, Univ NC, 65-68; instr, Duke Univ, 68-69; asst prof, 69-74, assoc prof eng, Northern IL Univ, 74. **MEMBERSHIPS** MLA; Midwest Mod Lang Asn; Am Fedn Tchr(s); Am Film Inst. **RESEARCH** Am lit hist; lit and film; film theory and criticism. **SELECTED PUBLICATIONS** Auth, The correspondence of Amy Lowell and Barrett Wendell, 1915-1919, New Eng Quart, 3/74; Barrett Wendell, Twayne, 75; Robert Richardson: Literature and film, Style, spring 75; Invention and death: Commodities of media in Robert Altman's Nashville, J Popular Film, winter 76; ed, Literature, Society and Politics: Selected Essays of Barrett Wendell, Colet, St Paul, 77; Systems of ambiguity in the art cinema, Film Criticism, 79; Ritual patterns in Western fiction and film, Narative Stategies in Fiction & Film, 81; Robert Altman and the art cinema, Velet Light Trap, 82. **CONTACT ADDRESS** Dept of Eng, No Illinois Univ, 1425 W Lincoln Hwy, De Kalb, IL, 60115-2825. **EMAIL** jpowers@holycross.edu

SELFE, RICHARD J.
PERSONAL Born 04/22/1951, Des Moines, IA, m **DISCIPLINE** RHETORIC AND TECHNICAL COMMUNICATION **EDUCATION** Mich Tech Univ, PhD, 1997 **CAREER** Mich Tech Univ, Tech Comm Spec, 75-87, ADJUNCT PROF RHETORIC & TECH COMMUN, 97-. **HONORS AND AWARDS** Ellen Nold Award, Best Article in Comput and Compos Studies, 95. **MEMBERSHIPS** AAHE, NCTE **RESEARCH** Critical and tech literacy studies. **SELECTED PUBLICATIONS** Co-ed, Electronic Commununication Across the Cirrculum, 98, NCTE; "What are we Doing to and for Ourselves?" in New Words, New Worlds: Exploring Pathways for Writing about and in Electronic Environments, J. Barber & D. Grigar, eds, forthcoming, MIT Press; Coauth, "Examining the Relevance of Technology Use in English Studies: Using Technology-Rich Communication Facilities as Sites of Teaching, Learning, Action, and Response" in The Relevance of English, R. P. Yagelski & S. A. Leonard, eds, forthcoming; Coauth "Traveling the Virtual Terrain: Practical Strategies for Survival in the Electronic Classroom," in The On-line Writing Classroom, R. Rickly, S. Harrington, & M. Day, eds, forthcoming, Hampton Press; Coauth, "Forces of Conservatism and Change in Computer- Supported Communication Facilities: Programmatic and Institutional Responses to Change," in Computers and Technical Communication: Pedagogical and Programmatic Perspectives, Stuart Selber, ed, 97, Ablex; Coauth, "Writing as Democratic Social Action in a Technological World: Politicizing and Inhabiting Virtual Landscapes," in Multidisciplinary Research in Nonacademic Writing, A. Duin and C. Hansen, eds, 96, Lawrence Erlbaum Asoc. **CONTACT ADDRESS** 1400 Townsend Dr, Houghton, MI, 49930. **EMAIL** rselfe@mtu.edu

SELFRIDGE-FIELD, ELEANOR
DISCIPLINE MUSIC; JOURNALISM; MUSIC HISTORY **EDUCATION** Magna cum laude, Drew Univ, 62; MSc, Columbia Univ, 63; DPHIl, Oxford Univ, 69. **CAREER** Consulting prof, Stanford Univ, admin, Center for Computer Asst Research in the Hum; lectr, writer, tchr and music technologist. **HONORS AND AWARDS** Research Grants: Am Council of Learned Soc; Ford Found, Gladys Krieble Delmas Found. **MEMBERSHIPS** IMS, AMS,SMT, IEEE CS. **RESEARCH** Tech for class music research; Vivaldi; Venetian music; hist of instrumental music; melodic similarity. **SELECTED PUBLICATIONS** The Handbook of Musical Codes, 97, ed The Works of Benedetto and Alessandro Marcello, 90, Writings on Music in Venetian Soc, 85-Venetian Instrumental Music form Gabrieli to Vivaldi, var ed, articles program and liner notes. **CONTACT ADDRESS** Stanford Univ, Stanford, CT, 94305-3076.

SELIG, ROBERT L.
PERSONAL Born 06/24/1932, New York, NY **DISCIPLINE** ENGLISH **EDUCATION** Univ NC, BA, 54; Columbia Univ, MA, 58, PhD(English), 65. **CAREER** Instr English, Queens Col, NY, 61-67; asst prof, 67-71, assoc prof, 71-81, PROF ENGLISH, PURDUE UNIV, CALUMET, 81- **MEMBERSHIPS** MLA **SELECTED PUBLICATIONS** Auth, The Collected Letters Of Gissing,George, Vol 2, 1881-1885 - Mattheisen,Pf, Young,Ac, Coustillas,P, Eds/, Nineteenth Century Prose, Vol 0020, 1993; Vol 0022, 1995. **CONTACT ADDRESS** Dept of English, Purdue Univ, Calumet, 2233 171st St, Hammond, IN, 46323-2094.

SELLERY, J'NAN MORSE
PERSONAL Oakland, CA, m, 4 children **DISCIPLINE** 20TH CENTURY BRITISH & AMERICAN LITERATURE **EDUCATION** Univ Calif, Riverside, BA, 65 (English Lit), MA, 67, PhD(Twentieth Century Brit and Am Lit), 70. **CAREER** Asst prof, 70-74, assoc prof, 74-80, PROF ENGLISH, HARVEY MUDD COL, 80-, Dir of Rhetoric, Freshman Div, 78-84, Reappointment, Promotion and Tenure Comt, 85-91, Chair, Dept of Humanities & Soc Services, 93, Executive Comt, 82-84, 92-98; Senior Ed, Psychol Perspectives, 69-95; Vis assoc prof English, Univ Calif, Riverside, 77-78; ed, W Coast Women Schol Newsletter of PAPC, 85-88; served on a number of other panels and committees. **HONORS AND AWARDS** NDEA Fel, Univ Calif, Riverside, 67-70; Shell Asst Fund, Harvey Mudd Col, 73; NEH Fel, Yale Univ, Summer 79; Louisa and Robert Miller Prof of Humanities, Harvey Mudd Col, 89-; Vis Res Fel, the Calgary Inst for the Humanities, Univ Calgary, Fall 92, 98-99; recipient numerous other grants and awards. **MEMBERSHIPS** MLA; Am Asn Univ Women; Asn for Can Studies in the U.S.; Am Film Studies Asn. **RESEARCH** Twentieth century comparative fiction in England. **SELECTED PUBLICATIONS** Auth, Fictive modes in Charles Williams' All Hallows Eve, Genre, 10/68; co-ed, Goethe's Faust Part I: Essays in Criticism, Wadsworth, 69; auth, Checklist of Elizabeth Bowen, Bull NY Pub Libr, 4/70; Language and moral intelligence in the Enlightenment: Fielding's plays and Pope's Dunciad, Enlightenment Essays, spring & summer 70; coauth, The Scapegoat, Some Literary Permutations, Houghton, 72; Bibliography of Elizabeth Bowen, Humanities Res Ctr, Tex, 80; coauth, Elizabeth Bowen: A Bibliography, Humanities Res Ctr, 81; ed, Women's Voices, Psychol Perspectives (special issue), Spring 86; ed, Gender, Psychol Perspectives (special issue), Fall 90; author of numerous other journal articles, review essays, poetry, lectures, conference presentations, and contributor to a number of other books. **CONTACT ADDRESS** Dept of Humanities, Harvey Mudd Col, 255 Parsons, Claremont, CA, 91711-5990. **EMAIL** Jnan_Sellery@hmc.edu

SELLIN, PAUL R.
PERSONAL Born 11/14/1930, Everett, WA, m, 1957, 3 children **DISCIPLINE** ENGLISH LITERATURE **EDUCATION** Washington State Univ, Pullman, BA, 52; Univ Chicago, MA, 55, PhD, 63. **CAREER** From instr to asst prof & asst to the Dean for Honors, Roosevelt Univ, 58-66; from asst to full prof, prof emeritus, Univ Calif, Los Angeles, 66- ; Prof Ordinarius English Lit after 1500, Free Univ of Amsterdam, Netherlands, 81-87; Eng Dept, Univ Stockholm, Sweden, 93-94. **HONORS AND AWARDS** Van Loon fel, Netherlands, 59-60; Roosevelt Univ fel, 63-64; Grants-in-aid, Am Philos Soc; NEH grants; ACLS grants., Adv Bd, Am Asn for Netherlandic Stud; vchemn, chemn, Netherlandic Stud Prog, 76-93; chemn, Dept English, Free Univ of Amsterdam, 84-86. **MEMBERSHIPS** MLA; John Donne Soc of Am; Milton Soc of Am; Int Asn for Neo-Latin Stud; Am Asn for Netherlandic Stud; Am Asn of Neo-Latin Stud. **RESEARCH** Renaissance criticism; Donne; Milton; Neo-Latin criticism; Anglo-Dutch relations; Sixteenth and Seventeenth centuries; Swedish-Anglo-Dutch relations. **SELECTED PUBLICATIONS** Auth, Daniel Heinsius and Stuart England, Oxford, 68; auth, John Donne and Calvinist Views of Grace, Amsterdam, 83; auth, So Doth, So Is Religion: John Donne and Diplomatic Contexts in The Reformed Netherlands, 1619-1620, Columbia, 88; auth, John Milton's Paradise Lost and De doctrina christiana on Predestination, Milton Stud, 96; auth, The Reference to John Milton's Tetrachordon in De doctrina christiana, Stud in Eng Lit, 97; auth, Michel Le Blon and England, 1632-1649: With Observations on Van Dyck, Donne, and Vondel, Dutch Crossing, 98. **CONTACT ADDRESS** Dept of English, Univ of California, Los Angeles, Los Angeles, CA, 90095-1980. **EMAIL** psellin@ucla.edu

SELMON, MICHAEL
DISCIPLINE RHETORIC, DRAMA AND BRITISH LITERATURE **EDUCATION** Univ Md, PhD. **CAREER** Assoc prof, Alma Col. **RESEARCH** The way literature and drama reflect broader cultural concerns. **SELECTED PUBLICATIONS** Published articles in Mod Drama, Ling and Old Northwest, exploring works by Eugene O'Neill, T. S. Eliot and Caryl Churchill, as well as broader topics like language theory and theatre history. **CONTACT ADDRESS** Alma Col, Alma, MI, 48801.

SEMINARA, GLORIA
DISCIPLINE SPEECH **EDUCATION** Brooklyn Col, BA, MA; Columbia Univ, MPhil, PhD. **CAREER** Asst prof, St John's Col, St John's Univ; ASSOC PROF & CHAIR, HUM, NOTRE DAME COL, ST JOHN'S UNIV. **CONTACT ADDRESS** 281 Benedict Rd, Staten Island, NY, 10304. **EMAIL** Seminarg@stjohns.edu

SENA, JOHN F.
PERSONAL Born 06/26/1940, Summit, NJ, m, 1966, 2 children **DISCIPLINE** ENGLISH LITERATURE **EDUCATION** Seton Hall Univ, BA, 62; Princeton Univ, MA, 65, PhD(English), 67. **CAREER** Asst prof, 67-71, ASSOC PROF ENGLISH, OHIO STATE UNIV, 71-, Am Philos Soc grant, 68; Ohio State Univ grant, 69. **MEMBERSHIPS** MLA; Am Soc 18th Century Sudies; Am Soc Hist Med. **RESEARCH** Eighteenth century English literature; history of medicine; satiric theory. **SELECTED PUBLICATIONS** Auth, Designs On Truth - The Poetics Of The Augustan Mock-Epic - Colomb,Gc/, Scriblerian And The Kit-Cats, Vol 0026, 1993. **CONTACT ADDRESS** Dept of English, Ohio State Univ, Columbus, OH, 43210.

SENDRY, JOSEPH M.
PERSONAL Born 10/22/1935, Cleveland, OH **DISCIPLINE** ENGLISH **EDUCATION** Cath Univ Am, BA, 57; Univ MI, MA, 58; Harvard Univ, PhD, 63. **CAREER** Asst prof, 63-66, Assoc Prof Eng, Cath Univ Am, 66-90, Chmn Dept, 78-93, prof eng, Cath Univ Am, 90-, Vis fel, St Edmund's Col, Cambridge Univ, 71, 83-84. **MEMBERSHIPS** MLA; ALSC; Victorians Inst; Amer Conf for Irish Stud; Am Conf on Christianity & Lit. **RESEARCH** Victorian poetry; Tennyson; mod Irish lit; Joyce. **SELECTED PUBLICATIONS** Auth, The In Memoriam manuscripts: Some solutions to the problems, 4/73 & In Memoriam: The minor manuscripts, 1/79, Harvard Lib Bull; Guide to the year's work in Victorian poetry: Tennyson, Victorian Poetry, fall 76-90; The Wreck of the Deutschland: the elegy as heroic poem, Thought, 12/90; The poet as interpreter: Richard Murphy's The Mirror Wall, In: Snow Path: Track 10, 94; In Memoriam as Apocalypse, In: Sense and Transcendence, 95. **CONTACT ADDRESS** Dept of Eng, Catholic Univ of America, 620 Michigan Ave NE, Washington, DC, 20064-0002.

SENSIBAR, JUDITH L.
DISCIPLINE LITERATURE **EDUCATION** Vassar Col, BA, 63; Univ Chicago, MA, 72, PhD, 82. **CAREER** Asst Teacher, The Bruno Bettelheim Orthogenic Sch, Univ Chicago, 72; Lectr, Chicago Inst Psychoanalysis, Fall 82; Lectr, Univ Chicago Extension Prog, 82, 84; Vis Asst Prof, Univ Ill - Chicago, 84; Asst Prof, 85-88, Assoc Prof, Ariz State Univ, 88-. **HONORS AND AWARDS** Jane Addams Fel, Am Asn Univ Women, 80-81; Departmental Late Awards Grant, Univ Chicago, 81-82; ACLS Fel for Recent Recipients of the PhD, 83-84; Summer Grant-in-Aid Fel, ASU, 86; Computer/Word Processor Award, ASU, 86; Women's Studies Fel, ASU, 87; Fac Grant-in-Aid Fel, ASU, 88; Col Mini-Grant, ASU, 88, 89; Am Coun Learned Soc Fel, 87-88; FIGA and Women's Studies Fel, ASU, 89; Departmental RA Award, ASU, 90; Women's Studies Fel - WS Fac Development Prog, 91; Rockefeller Regional Schol Fel, 92; NEH Travel Grant, 92; Va Found Humanities and Public Policy Fel, 93; NEH Sr. Fel Univ Teachers, 93-94; ASU Grad Students of English Asn Award for Outstanding Mentor to Grad Students in English, 98. **MEMBERSHIPS** Edith Wharton Soc; MLA; SMLA; MLA Women's Caucus; Faulkner & Wharton Soc; AAUW; ALA; ASA; NE-MLA; SSSL. **RESEARCH** Faulkner; modernism; cultural studies; American studies; feminist and psychoanalytic theory. **SELECTED PUBLICATIONS** Ed, Vision in Spring, Univ Tex Press, 84; auth, The Origins of Faulkner's Art, Univ Tex Press, 84; Faulkner's Poetry: A Bibliographical Guide to Texts and Criticism, Univ Mich Res Press, 88; author of numerous articles, chapters, and reviews. **CONTACT ADDRESS** English Dept, Arizona State Univ, Tempe, Tempe, AR, 85287-0302.

SERIO, JOHN NICHOLAS
PERSONAL Born 10/08/1943, Buffalo, NY, m, 1972, 2 children **DISCIPLINE** LITERATURE **EDUCATION** State Univ NY Col Buffalo, BS, 65; Northwestern Univ, MA, 66; Univ Notre Dame, PhD, 74. **CAREER** Instr, Valparaiso Univ, 66-70;

asst prof, 74-80, assoc prof lit, Clarkson Col, 80-88, prof lit, 89; Assoc ed, Wallace Stevens J, 80-, guest ed, 81. **HONORS AND AWARDS** Senior Fulbright lec award, 93, 98; NEH Summer Stipend, 91; Pheonix award for Significant Ed Ach, 90; Outstanding Journal Article Award, 89. **MEMBERSHIPS** MLA; Wallace Stevens Soc; Col Eng Asn; Northeast Mod Lang Asn. **RESEARCH** Mod Am poetry; Am lit; Eng lit. **SELECTED PUBLICATIONS** Auth, The comedian as the idea of order in Harmonium, Papers Lang & Lit, 76; Stevens' affair of places, Wallace Stevens J, 78; Stevens as a connoisseur of chaos, Notes Mod Am Lit, 78; Coleridge and the function of nature in romantic poetry, Ball State Univ Forum, 78; Stevens, Shakespeare, and Peter Quince, Mod Lang Studies, 79; The ultimate music is abstract: Charles Ives and Wallace Stevens, Bucknell Rev, 79; A hard rain in Hartford: The climate of Stevens' Poetics, Res Studies, 79; Landscape and voice in T S Eliot's poetry, Centennial Rev, 82; Wallace Stevens: AN Annotated Secondary Bibliography, Univ Pitts Press, 94; Teaching Wallace Stevens: Practical Essays, TN Studies in Lit, v 35, Univ TN Press, 94; ed in chief, The Wallace Stevens Journal, 84. **CONTACT ADDRESS** Clarkson Col, 1 Clarkson Ave, Potsdam, NY, 13699-5750. **EMAIL** serio@polaris.clarkson.edu

SERUM, ROBERT W.
PERSONAL Born 09/06/1941, Grand Rapids, Mich, m, 1967, 2 children **DISCIPLINE** ENGLISH LANGUAGE & LITERATURE **EDUCATION** Hope Col, AB, 63; Univ Ala, MA, 72, PhD(English), 74. **CAREER** Teacher, Hudsonville Mich Publ High Schs, 63-69; grad teaching asst English, Univ Ala, 69-72; asst prof, 74-75, assoc prof & head dept English, 75-80, assoc dir, Univ Col, 75-80, acad dean, 80-891 dean, Univ Col, 89-; dean, grad stu, 91-; VP of Acad and dean of int prgm, 93-. **MEMBERSHIPS** Soc Advan Scand Studies; NCTE; MLA; AAUP; Int Soc Gen Semantics. **RESEARCH** Ibsen; poetry (English & American); semantics. **CONTACT ADDRESS** 3225 Cook Rd, Midland, MI, 48640-2398. **EMAIL** serum@northwood.edu

SESSIONS, WILLIAM ALFRED
PERSONAL Born 08/04/1938, Conway, SC, m, 1961, 2 children **DISCIPLINE** ENGLISH **EDUCATION** Univ NC, Chapel Hill, AB, 57; Columbia Univ, MA, 59, PhD(English, Comp Lit), 66. **CAREER** Asst prof English, State Univ W Ga, 59-60; asst prof, Spring Hill Col, 60-62; asst prof, St John's Univ, 62-66; assoc prof, 66-72, dir grad sch, dept English, 69-75, prof, 72-93, REGENTS' PROF ENGLISH, GA STATE UNIV, 93-. **HONORS AND AWARDS** Nikos Kazantzakis Medal, Greece, 78. **MEMBERSHIPS** MLA; Renaissance Soc Am; Southeastern Renaissance Soc; Medieval Inst; Am Lit Asn; Inst Hist Res. **RESEARCH** Early Modern English; Henry Howard, the Poet Earl of Surrey; Francis Bacon; Spenser; Milton: Flannery O'Connor; Walker Percy; modern poetic theory. **SELECTED PUBLICATIONS** Auth, Henry Howard, the POet Earl of Surrey, A Life: Enough Survives, Oxford Univ Press, 99; auth, Francis Bacon Revisited, Twayne English Authors series, Simon and Schuster, 96; auth, Francis Bacon's Legacy of Texts: The Art of Discovery Grows with Discovery, AMS Press, 90; auth, Henry Howard, The Poet Early of Surrey 1517-1547, G. K. Hall & Co, 86; auth, How to Ready Flannery O'Connor: Passing by the Dragon, in Flannery O'Connor and the Christian Mystery, Literature and Belief 17, 97; auth, Surrey's Waytt: The New Poet in Autumn 1542, in Rethinking the Henrician Age, Univ Ill Press, 94; auth, Milton and the Dance, in Milton and the Fine Arts, Pa State Univ Press, 89; auth, Where Does a Poet Come From? The Southern Review 34:1, Winter 98; auth, Teaching Where Three Interstates Meet, Profession 93, 12; Jan 94. **CONTACT ADDRESS** Dept of Eng, Georgia State Univ, Rm 974, Gen Classroom Bldg, Atlanta, GA, 30303. **EMAIL** wsessions@gsu.edu

SETTLE, PETER
DISCIPLINE ORGANIZATIONAL AND INTERPERSONAL COMMUNICATION **EDUCATION** Marquette Univ, MA; Bowling Green Univ, PhD. **CAREER** Law, Caroll Col. **HONORS AND AWARDS** Andrew T. Weaver Award; Alumnus Award -- Wisconsin Gamma of Pi Kappa Delta. **SELECTED PUBLICATIONS** Articles, Asn Comm Administration Jour, Wis Comm Asn Jour. **CONTACT ADDRESS** Carroll Col, Wisconsin, 100 N East Ave, Waukesha, WI, 53186.

SEYMOUR, VICTOR
PERSONAL Born 05/17/1929, Brooklyn, NY, m, 1965, 1 child **DISCIPLINE** SPEECH, THEATRE **EDUCATION** Univ Utah, BS, 54; Columbia Univ, MA, 58; Univ Wis, PhD(-Theatre), 65. **CAREER** Instr speech, Bates Col, 58-60; lectr, Hunter Col in the Bronx, 62-65; asst prof Speech & Theatre, NY Inst Technol, 65-68; from asst prof to assoc prof, 68-77, prof speech & theatre, Queensborough Community Col, NY, 77-, Off observer, Actors Studio Dir Univ, NYC, 60-; dir theatre, NY Inst Technol, 65-68. **MEMBERSHIPS** Speech Commun Asn. **SELECTED PUBLICATIONS** Auth, Director's workshop: Six years' activity of the Actors Studio Directors Unit, 3/66 & Theatre Keeps pace in secondary education, 10/68, Educ Theatre J. **CONTACT ADDRESS** Dept of Speech & Drama, Queensborough Comm Col, CUNY, 22205 56th Ave, Flushing, NY, 11364-1432.

SHADDOCK, JENNIFER
DISCIPLINE ENGLISH LITERATURE **EDUCATION** Univ Colo Boulder, PhD. **CAREER** Fac, 93-. **RESEARCH** 19th and 20th Century British literature; cultural studies and criticism; composition. **SELECTED PUBLICATIONS** Auth, Narrative Enactments: Surviving Oppression through Story in Tracks and Ceremony in Feminist Nightmares: Women at Odds; Cultural Studies and Classroom Practice: An Introduction, Wis Eng Jour. **CONTACT ADDRESS** Dept of English, Univ of Wisconsin, Eau Claire, Hibbard Hall 618, PO Box 4004, Eau Claire, WI, 54702-4004. **EMAIL** shaddoj@uwec.edu

SHAFER, GREGORY
PERSONAL Born 11/16/1959, Muskegon, MI, m, 1992 **DISCIPLINE** ENGLISH **EDUCATION** Mich State Univ, BA, 82, MS, 84; Univ Mich, PhD, 92. **CAREER** Teach asst, Univ Mich, 89-92; Inst, Kellog Community Col, 93-97; INSTR ENG, MOTT COMMUNITY COL, 97-. **HONORS AND AWARDS** Kellogg Fdn Exc in Educ Award, 94, 95, 96, 96; Phi Kappa Phi; Golden Key; Kappa Delta Pi. **MEMBERSHIPS** Nat Counc Teachers Eng; Mich Counc Teachers Eng' Mich Reading Asn. **RESEARCH** Composition; reading; Eng educ; literacy stud; postmodernism. **SELECTED PUBLICATIONS** Auth, On the Importance of Writing with Students, Lang Arts J Mich, Fall 96; auth, School Reform and the High School Proficiency Test, Eng J, Sep 97; auth, Reader Response Makes History, Eng J, Nov 97; auth, Revision, Reflection, and Conferencing: An Alternative to Traditional Grading, Ariz Eng Bull, Fall 97; auth, Nostalgia and Back to Basics, bull J, Sep 97; auth, Conferences, Compassion, and Composition: A Modest Proposal for Inspiring the Alienated Student, lang Arts J Mich, Spring 97; auth, Facilitating Meaningful Parent/Teacher Conferences, Sec Educ Today, Fall 97; auth, From Prescriptive Grammar to Problem Psing; An Alternative to Traditional Grammar Instruction, Calif Eng, Spring 98; auth, Whole Language: Origins and Practice, Lang Arts J Mich, Spring 98; Some Basic Truths about Back to Basics, The Humanist, Nov/Dec 98; auth, The Myth of Competition and the Case Against School Choice, The Humanist, March/April 99; auth, What I Learned from Reading the Everglades, Mich Reading Teach, Spring 99; auth, Watching Three Sovereigns for Sarah, Eng J, forthcoming; auth, The Importance of Voice and Audience in the Writing Center, Teach Eng in the Two Year Coll, forthcoming. **CONTACT ADDRESS** 974 Touraine Ave, East Lansing, MI, 48823. **EMAIL** gshafer@email.mcc.edu

SHAFER, RONALD G.
PERSONAL Born 01/30/1946, Kittanning, PA, m, 1968, 2 children **DISCIPLINE** ENGLISH & AMERICAN LITERATURE **EDUCATION** Indiana Univ, Pa, BS, 68, MA, 70; Duquesne Univ, PhD(English), 75. **CAREER** Teacher, Ford City High Sch, 68-70; from asst prof to assoc prof, 70-76, PROF ENGLISH, INDIANA UNIV, PA, 76-, Asst ed, Shakespeare Newslett, 77-78; Fulbright-Hays vis prof, 78-79; dir, Int Milton Symposia, 81 & 83. **HONORS AND AWARDS** Indiana Univ, Pa, Excellence in Teaching Award, 77. **MEMBERSHIPS** Friends of Milton's Cottage (pres, 77-); MLA; Friends of Bemerton. **RESEARCH** Drama of William Shakespeare; poetry of George Herbert; poetry of John Donne. **SELECTED PUBLICATIONS** Auth, Updike,John Talks About Writing, His Life, And His Works + Discussions From The Writing Workshop Held At Indiana-Univ-Of-Penn On March-30,1992 .2./, Cea Critic, Vol 0057, 1995; Vol 0057, 1995. **CONTACT ADDRESS** Indiana Univ of Pennsylvania, 602 N Mckean St, Kittanning, PA, 16201-1265.

SHAFFER, BRIAN W.
DISCIPLINE ENGLISH **EDUCATION** Wash Univ, AB, 83; Univ Iowa, PhD, 89. **CAREER** Postdoc fel, Ctr Critical Inquiry Lib Arts, NEH, Col Arts & Scis, Univ NC, 89-90; tutor, Oxford Univ, 97; asst prof, 90-96, ASSOC PROF ENG, 96-, RHODES COL. **CONTACT ADDRESS** Dept of English, Rhodes Col, Memphis, TN, 38112.

SHAHEEN, NASEEB
PERSONAL Born 06/24/1931, Chicago, IL **DISCIPLINE** RENAISSANCE ENGLISH LITERATURE **EDUCATION** Am Univ Beirut, BA, 62; Univ Calif, Los Angeles, MA, 66, PhD(English), 69. **CAREER** Asst prof English lit, 69-77, assoc prof, 77-82, prof 83-, English,Univ of Memphis **MEMBERSHIPS** MLA **RESEARCH** Artistic use of the Bible in English literature; Shakespeare. **SELECTED PUBLICATIONS** Auth, The use of scripture in Cymbeline, Shakespeare Studies, 68; The 1590 and 1596 texts of The Faerie Queene, Papers Bibliog Soc Am, 74; Biblical References in The Faerie Queene, Memphis State Univ, 76; The Siloam end of Hezekiah's tunnel, Palestine Explor Quart, London, 77; Like the base Judean, Shakespeare Quart, 80; auth, Biblical References in Shakespeare's Tragedies, Univ Del, 87; auth, Biblical References in Shakespeare's History Plays, Univ Del, 93; auth, Biblical References in Shakespeare's Comedies, Univ Del, 99; auth, Ramallah: Its History and Its Genealogies, Birzeit Univ, 82; auth, A Pictoral History of Ramallah, Arab Inst for Res, 92; auth, The Use od Scripture in Cymbeline, Shakespeare Stu 4, 294-315, 68; auth, Of Oreb, or of Sinai, English Language Notes 9, 25-28, 71; auth, Spenser and the New Testament, American Notes and Queries 10, 4-5, 71. **CONTACT ADDRESS** Dept of English, Univ of Memphis, 3706 Alumni St, Memphis, TN, 38152-0001.

SHAHID, IRFAN ARIF
PERSONAL Nazareth, Palestine, m **DISCIPLINE** HISTORY, LITERATURE **EDUCATION** Oxford Univ, BA, 51; Princeton Univ, PhD, 54. **CAREER** Jr fel Arab-Byzantine rel, Ctr Byzantine Studies, 59-60; assoc prof, Ind Univ, Bloomington, 60-62; assoc prof, 62-66, prof Arabic, Georgetown Univ, 66-, Fulbright-Hays fel Arabic-Am lit, US Off Educ, 68-69; vis fel, Inst Advan Studies, Princeton, 76; Sultanate of Oman prof Arabic & Islamic lit, Georgetow Univ, 81- **HONORS AND AWARDS** Andrew W Mellon Fund Distinguished Lectureship in Lang & Ling, Sch Lang & Ling, Georgetown Univ, 77-79; Life mem, Clare Hall, Cambridge Univ, Engl, 89. **MEMBERSHIPS** Am Orient Soc; Mediaeval Acad Am; Mid East Studies Asn NAm; Mid East Inst; Am Asn Tchr(s) Arabic. **RESEARCH** Arab hist; Arab-Byzantine rel; Arabic lit. **SELECTED PUBLICATIONS** Auth, The martyrs of Najran: new documents, In: Subsidia Hagiographica, 71; Epistula de re publica genereda, In: Themistii Orationes, Vol III, Teubner Class Ser, 74; Rome and the Arabs, 84, Byzantium and the Arabs in the Fourth Century, 84, Byzantium and the Arabs in the Fifth Century, 89, Byzantium and the Arabs in the Sixth Century, 95, Dumbarton Oaks. **CONTACT ADDRESS** Dept of Arab Lang, Lit & Ling, Georgetown Univ, Washington, DC, 20057-1046. **EMAIL** arabic@guvax.georgetown.edu

SHAILOR, JONATHAN G.
DISCIPLINE COMMUNICATION **EDUCATION** Univ MA-Amherst, BA, MA, PhD. **CAREER** Assoc prof; dir, Prog in Conflict Analysis and Resolution; coordr, Dispute Resolution Ctr Theatre of Empowerment. **RESEARCH** Conflict resolution; narrative commun; intercultural commun; Asian Am commun; theatre of empowerment. **SELECTED PUBLICATIONS** Auth, Empowerment in Dispute Mediation: A Critical Analysis of Communication, Praeger, 94. **CONTACT ADDRESS** Commun Dept, Univ of Wisconsin, Parkside, 900 Wood Rd, CART 210, PO Box 2000, Kenosha, WI, 53141-2000. **EMAIL** jonathan.shailor@uwp.edu

SHAKINOVSKY, LYNN
DISCIPLINE 19TH- AND 20TH-CENTURY AMERICAN; BRITISH WOMEN WRITERS **EDUCATION** Witwatersrand, BA; Toronto, MA, PhD. **CAREER** Assoc Prof **SELECTED PUBLICATIONS** Auth, The Return of the Repressed: Illiteracy and the Death of the Narrative in Hawthorne's The Birthmark; No Frame of Reference: The Absence of Context in Emily Dickinson's Poems; Hidden Listeners: Dialogism in the Poetry of Emily Dickinson; Emily Dickinson's Poem 293. **CONTACT ADDRESS** Dept of English, Wilfrid Laurier Univ, 75 University Ave W, Waterloo, ON, N2L 3C5. **EMAIL** lshakino@mach1.wlu.ca

SHALE, RICK
DISCIPLINE FILM STUDY; POPULAR CULTURE **EDUCATION** Ohio esleyan Univ, BA, 69; Univ Mich, MA, 72, PhD, 76. **CAREER** Fac member, Youngstown State Univ, 76-. **HONORS AND AWARDS** Phi Beta Kappa; Phi Kappa Phi. **MEMBERSHIPS** Univ Film & Video Assoc; Popular Culture Asn; Col Eng Asn. **RESEARCH** Film study; screwball comedy; Hitchcock; screenwriting. **SELECTED PUBLICATIONS** Auth, Academy Awards: The Complete Categorical and Chronological Record, Greenwood Press, 93. **CONTACT ADDRESS** Dept of English, Youngstown State Univ, Youngstown, OH, 44555-3415.

SHANER, JAYE L.
DISCIPLINE COMMUNICATION **EDUCATION** Miami Univ (Ohio), BA, 90; Univ of Kans, MA, 93, PhD, 96. **CAREER** Asst prof, Ga State Univ, 96-. **MEMBERSHIPS** Nat Commun Assoc; Gerontological Soc of Am; Int Commun Assoc; Ga Alzheimer's Res Consortium. **RESEARCH** Intergenerational commun; commun & sterotypes of older adults; mass media messages about aging. **SELECTED PUBLICATIONS** Co-auth, Patronizaing speech to the elderly as a function of stereotyping, Communication Studies, vol 45, 145-158, 95; co-auth, Steroetypes of the elderly held by young, middle-aged, and elderly adults, Journal of Gerontology: Psychological Sciences, vol 49, 240-249, 94; co-auth, Judgements about sterotypes of the elderly: Attitudes, age associations, and typicality ratings of young, middle-aged and elderly adults, Research on Aging, vol 17, 168-189, 95; co-auth, Beliefs about language performance: Adults' perceptions about self and elderly targets, Journal of Language and Social Psychology, vol 14, 235-259, 95; co-auth, Cognitive processes affecting communication with older adults, Handbook of communication and aging research, Lawrence Erlbaum Associates, 105-131, 95; co-auth, Sterotyping of older adults, Psychology and Aging, vol 12, 107-114, 97; co-auth, Social skills of older people: Conversations in same and mixed age dyads, Discourse Processes, (in press); co-auth, Communication with older adults: The influence of age sterotypes, context, and communicator age, Human Communication Research, (in press). **CONTACT ADDRESS** Dept of Commun, Georgia State Univ, 1 Park Pl S, Atlanta, GA, 30303-2911. **EMAIL** joujls@panther.gsu.edu

SHANKS, HERSHEL
PERSONAL Born 03/08/1930, Sharon, PA, m, 1966, 2 children **DISCIPLINE** ENGLISH LITERATURE; SOCIOLOGY;

LAW **EDUCATION** Haverford Col, BA, 52; Colombia Univ, MA, 56; Harvard Law Sch, LLB, 56. **CAREER** Ed, Biblical Archaeology Review, Bible Review, Archaeology Odyssey, and Moment. **MEMBERSHIPS** ASOR; SBL; AOS; NEAS; ABA. **RESEARCH** Archaeol; Bible; Judaism. **SELECTED PUBLICATIONS** Ed, Understanding the Dead Sea Scrolls, Random Hse, 92; co-auth, The Rise of Ancient Israel, Biblical Archaeol Soc, 92; ed, Christianity and Rabbinic Judaism: A Parallel History of Their Origins and Early Development, Biblical Archaeol Soc, 92; auth, Jerusalem: An Archaeological Biography, Random Hse, 95; auth, The Mystery and Meaning of the Dead Sea Scrolls, Random Hse, 98. **CONTACT ADDRESS** 5208 38th St, NW, Washington, DC, 20015. **EMAIL** shanks@clark.net

SHANNON, LAURIE
DISCIPLINE ENGLISH LITERATURE **EDUCATION** Harvard Univ, JD, 89; Chicago Univ, PhD, 96. **CAREER** Assoc prof, Duke Univ. **RESEARCH** Sixteenth and early seventeenth century Eng lit. **SELECTED PUBLICATIONS** Auth, publ(s) on rhet of friendship; gender; soc hierarchy in Renaissance imaginings of commonwealth. **CONTACT ADDRESS** Eng Dept, Duke Univ, Durham, NC, 27706.

SHAPIRO, BARBARA JUNE
PERSONAL Born 08/07/1934, Chicago, IL, m, 1955, 1 child **DISCIPLINE** ENGLISH HISTORY **EDUCATION** Univ Calif, Los Angeles, BA, 56; Radcliffe Col, MA, 58; Harvard Univ, PhD(Hist), 66. **CAREER** Asst prof Hist, Occidental Col, 65-66; from asst prof to assoc prof, Pitzer Col, 66-70; lectr, Univ Calif, Berkeley, 70-71; prof & dean fac, Wheaton Col, 71-73; assoc prof, Univ Calif, San Diego, 73-76; prof Rhectoric, Univ Calif, Berkeley, 77-, vis assoc Hist, Wellesley Col, 69-70. **MEMBERSHIPS** Conf Brit Studies; Am Soc Legal Hist. **RESEARCH** English intellectual history 1500-1700; European intellectual history 1400-1700. **SELECTED PUBLICATIONS** Auth, Latitudinarianism and science in 17th century England, Past & Present, 68; John Wilkins: An Intellectual Biography, Univ Calif Press, 69; Law and science in 17th century England, Stanford Law Rev, 69; Law reform in 17th century England, 78 & Bacon & law reform, 81, Am J Legal Hist; History and Natural History in 17th Century England, Univ Calif Press, 81; Probability and Certainty in 17th century England: The Relationships between Science, Religion, History, Law and Literature, Princeton Univ Press, 83; Beyond Reasonable Doubt and Probable Cause Studies in the Anglo-American Law of Culture, Univ of California Press, 91; The Culture of Fact in Early Modern England (in progress). **CONTACT ADDRESS** Dept of Rhetoric, Univ of California, Berkeley, 2125 Dwinelle Hall, Berkeley, CA, 94720-2671. **EMAIL** bshapiro@socrates.berkeley.edu

SHAPIRO, JAMES S.
DISCIPLINE ENGLISH **EDUCATION** Columbia Univ, BA, 77; Univ Chicago, Phd, 82. **CAREER** Prof. **HONORS AND AWARDS** Bainton Prize, best bk on sixteenth-century lit; awards, NEH; Huntington Library; Memorial Found for Jewish Cult., Co-ed, Columbia Anthology of Brit Poetry; assoc ed, Columbia Hist Brit Poetry; Fulbright lectr, Bar Ilan and Tel Aviv Univ; columnist, The Chronicle for Higher Edu. **SELECTED PUBLICATIONS** Auth, Rival Playwrights: Marlowe, Jonson, Shakespeare, 91; Shakespeare and the Jews, 95. **CONTACT ADDRESS** Dept of Eng, Columbia Col, New York, 2960 Broadway, New York, NY, 10027-6902.

SHAPIRO, MICHAEL
PERSONAL Born 03/31/1938, Rochester, NY, m, 1961, 4 children **DISCIPLINE** ENGLISH **EDUCATION** Univ Rochester, BA, 59; Columbia Univ, MA, 60, PhD, 67. **CAREER** Lectr, City Col NY, 61-65; instr, NY Inst Technol, 66-67; from Asst Prof to Assoc Prof, 67-93, prof eng, Univ IL, Urbana, 93, Dir, Drobny Prog in Jewish Cult and Soc, 98-; Lectr Eng, Pace Col, 61-62; vis assoc prof, Cornell Univ, 75 & Reading Univ, Engl, 78-79; vis prof, Tamkaug Univ, Taiwan, 93. **MEMBERSHIPS** MLA; Renaissance Soc Am; Shakespeare Asn Am. **RESEARCH** Elizabethan drama; Renaissance lit; Am-Jewish writers. **SELECTED PUBLICATIONS** Auth, Children of the Revels: The Boy Companies of Shakespeare's Time and Their Plays, Columbia Univ, 77; Gender in Play on the Shakespeare Stage, Univ MI Press, 94. **CONTACT ADDRESS** Dept of Eng, Univ of Illinois, 608 S Wright St, Urbana, IL, 61801-3613. **EMAIL** mshapir@uiuc.edu

SHAPIRO, RAMI
DISCIPLINE COMMUNICATION **EDUCATION** SUNY at Binghamton, BA; Univ PA, MA, PhD. **CAREER** Dept Eng, Univ Wisc-Parkside **RESEARCH** Lang and soc interaction; ethnography of commun; childhood soc; intercultural commun; semiotics; commun theory. **SELECTED PUBLICATIONS** Auth, Communication in Everyday Life, Ablex, 89; Semiotics and Communication, Lawrence Erlbaum, 93; Social Approaches to the Study of Communication, Guilford, 95. **CONTACT ADDRESS** Commun Dept, Univ of Wisconsin, Parkside, 900 Wood Rd, CART 245, PO Box 2000, Kenosha, WI, 53141-2000. **EMAIL** wendy.leeds-hurwitz@uwp.edu

SHAPIRO, SUSAN
DISCIPLINE ENGLISH LITERATURE **EDUCATION** Bryn Mawr Univ, PhD. **CAREER** Fac, Fairleigh Dickinson Univ. **RESEARCH** Shakespeare; drama; ESL. **SELECTED PUBLICATIONS** Auth, essays in Rev Eng Studies, CEA Critic, Atlantis, 17th-Century News, Hist Today. **CONTACT ADDRESS** Fairleigh Dickinson Univ, 1000 River Rd, Teaneck, NJ, 07666.

SHARF, BARBARA F.
DISCIPLINE HEALTH COMMUNICATION, RHETORICAL ANALYSIS **EDUCATION** Univ Minn, PhD. **CAREER** Prof, Texas A&M Univ. **CONTACT ADDRESS** Dept of Speech Communication, Texas A&M Univ, College Station, TX, 77843-4234.

SHARMA, GOVIND NARAIN
PERSONAL Born 03/11/1927, Jaipur, India, m, 1947, 3 children **DISCIPLINE** ENGLISH **EDUCATION** Agra Univ, BA, 46; Rajasthan Univ, MA, 49; Univ Toronto, PhD(English), 63. **CAREER** Lectr English, Delhi Col, Univ Delhi, 49-54; lectr, Maharaja's Col, Jaipur, 54-56; lectr, Hindu Col, Univ Delhi, 56-64, sr lectr, Hastinapur Col, 64-66, reader, Dept English, 66-68; assoc prof, 68-73, PROF ENGLISH, ACADIA UNIV, 73- **MEMBERSHIPS** Asn Can Univ Teachers English; African Lit Asn. **RESEARCH** Victorian literature; Commonwealth literature; history of ideas. **SELECTED PUBLICATIONS** Auth, The Christian Dynamic In The Fictional World Of Achebe,Chinua/, Ariel-A Rev Of Int English Lit, Vol 0024, 1993. **CONTACT ADDRESS** Dept of English, Acadia Univ, Box 257, Wolfville, NS, B0P 1X0.

SHARP, RONALD ALAN
PERSONAL Born 10/19/1945, Cleveland, OH, m, 1968, 1 child **DISCIPLINE** ENGLISH **EDUCATION** Kalamazoo Col, BA, 67; Univ Mich, MA, 68; Univ Va, PhD, 74. **CAREER** Instr English, Western Mich Univ, 68-70; instr, 70-72, asst prof, 74-78, assoc prof, Eng, Kenyon Col, 78-, co-ed, Kenyon Rev, 78-. **HONORS AND AWARDS** Nat Endowment for Humanities fel, 81-82; Nat Humanities Ctr fel, 81-82. **MEMBERSHIPS** MLA; Wordsworth-Coleridge Assn; Keats-Shelley Assn. **RESEARCH** Romanticism; contemporary poetry; the epic. **SELECTED PUBLICATIONS** Auth, Reading George Steiner, John Hopkins Univ, 94; art, Friendship: Fast & Fleeting, Philadelphia Inquirer, 96, Washington Times, 96. **CONTACT ADDRESS** Kenyon Col, 105 College Park St, Gambier, OH, 43022-9623. **EMAIL** sharp@kenyon.edu

SHARPES, DONALD KENNETH
DISCIPLINE EDUCATIONAL PSYCHOLOGY **EDUCATION** Gonzaga Univ, AB, 58, MA, 61; Stanford Univ, MA, 67; AZ State, PhD, 68. **CAREER** Technical Div Dir, US Dept of Education, Washington, DC, 68-73; assoc prof and dir, Ed progs VPI and SU, 73-78; prof of Graduate Education, Weber State Univ, 78-. **HONORS AND AWARDS** Hinckley Award, Weber State, 96; UT Academy of Sciences, Arts and Letters (Best Paper), 97; **MEMBERSHIPS** Am Psychol Asn; Am Ed Res Asn; UT Academy of Sciences, Arts and Letters. **RESEARCH** Ed psychol; ed foundations; curriculum and instruction; ed policy. **SELECTED PUBLICATIONS** Auth, Special issue ed, Int Ed, Teacher Education Quart, winter 95; Preparing Youth for the Changing Work World, J of Pedagogics, 15 (2), 95; Higher Education Faces Deeper Cuts, Salt Lake Tribune, 9/28/95; Princess Pocahontas, Rebecca Rolfe (1595-1617), Am Indian Culture and Res J, 19 (4); review, Sexuality Education, a Guide for Educators, Canadian and Int Ed, 24 (1), 95; Defining a Multicultural Curriculum: The Anthropological Perspective, in The Dynamic Concept of Curriculum, Sharpes with A-L Leino, eds, Univ Helsinki Press, 95; The Dynamic Concept of Curriculum, Sharpes with A-L Leino, eds, Univ Helsinki Press, 95; Postmodern Philosophies and Educational Values, Proceedings, Mofet Inst, Ministry of Education, Culture & Sport, Israel, eds N Ephraty & R Lidor, 96; Skewed SAT Scores Give False Sense of Education, Salt Lake Tribune, 06/16/1996; The Manufactured Crisis, Educational Leadership, 53 (7), April 96; Educational Qualifications for Teachers in Former Soviet Republics, in W Bunder & K Rebel, eds, Teacher Education--Theoretical Requirements and Professsional Reality, Inst of Science Education, 97; Hong Kong Tentatively Steps Toward Chinese Control, Standard Examiner, 6/15/1997; Lindisfarne, Holy Island, Standard Examiner, 5/1/1997; China May Buy More Utah Goods, Salt Lake Tribune, 7/8/1997; China Looks at Taiwan as the Ultimate Prize, Salt Lake Tribune, 6/22/1997; There's More to See in Macao Than Gaming Tables, Standard Examiner, 1/11/1998; A Study of Adolescent Self-Concept Among Han, Mongolian and Korean Chinese, with Xinbing Wang, Adolescence, 32, 98; Covering Hong Kong's Handover, Junction, serialized in V-II, nos 7, 8, 9, 98; Advanced Psychology for Teachers, McGraw Hill, forthcoming fall 98; numerous other publications, several works in progress. **CONTACT ADDRESS** College of Education, Weber State Univ, 1300 Univ Circle, Ogden, UT, 84408.

SHARY, TIMOTHY
PERSONAL Born 08/17/1967, Cheverly, MD, s **DISCIPLINE** FILM HISTORY **EDUCATION** Hampshire Col, BA, 91; Ohio Univ, MA, 92; Univ of Mass, PhD, 98. **CAREER** VIS LECTR, CLARK UNIV, 97-. **HONORS AND AWARDS** Phi Kappa Phi. **MEMBERSHIPS** Soc for Cinema Studies; Univ Film & Video Asn. **RESEARCH** Film hist, theory, and criticism; media studies; media production. **SELECTED PUBLICATIONS** Auth, Reification and Loss in Postmodern Puberty: The Cultural Logic of Fredric Jameson and Young Adult Movies, Postmodernism in the Cinema, Berghahn Books, 98; The Teen Film and its Methods of Study, J of Popular Film and Television, 97; The Only Place To Go Is Inside: Confusions of Sexuality and Class in Clueless and Kids, Pictures of a Generation on Hold: Youth in Film and Television of the 90s, Media Studies Working Group, 96; Exotica: Atom Egoyan's Neurotic Thriller, Point of View, 95; Video as Accessible Artifact and Artificial Access: The Early Films of Atom Egoyan, Film Criticism, 95; Viewing Experience: Structures of Subjectivity in East and West European Films, Echoes and Mirrors, 94; Present Personal Truths: The Alternative Phenomenology of Video in I've Heard the Mermaids Singing, Wide Angle, 93. **CONTACT ADDRESS** Dept of Commun, Univ of Massachusetts, Machmer Hall, Amherst, MA, 01003. **EMAIL** shary@comm.umass.edu

SHATSKY, JOEL
PERSONAL Born 11/30/1943, Vancouver, WA, m, 1967, 2 children **DISCIPLINE** ENGLISH **EDUCATION** Queens Col, CUNY, 64; Univ Chigago, MA, 65; NYU, PhD, 70. **CAREER** Prof, SUNY Cortland, 68- **HONORS AND AWARDS** Phi Kappa Phi; Phi Eta Sigma, Faculty Exchange Scholar, 84-85; Coordinator, Honor's Prog, 90-95. **RESEARCH** Jewish-American lit; modern drama. **SELECTED PUBLICATIONS** Ed, Theresienstadt: Hitler's Gift to the Jews, Univ NC Chapel Hill, 91; coed, Contemporary Jewish-American Novelists; A Bio-bibliographical Sourcebook, Greenwood Press, 97; Contemporary Jewish-American Dramatists and Poets: A Bio-bibliographical Sourceboo **CONTACT ADDRESS** Dept of English, SUNY Cortland, Box 2000, Cortland, NY, 13045. **EMAIL** shatzky@snycorva.cortland.edu

SHAW, DONALD LEWIS
PERSONAL Born 10/27/1936, Raleigh, NC, m, 1960, 4 children **DISCIPLINE** MASS COMMUNICATIONS HISTORY **EDUCATION** Univ NC, Chapel Hill, AB, 59, MA, 60; Univ Wis, PhD(mass commun), 66. **CAREER** From asst prof to assoc prof, 66-76, prof jour, 76- ,KENAN PROF, 92- , UNIV NC, CHAPEL HILL. **MEMBERSHIPS** Asn Educ in Jour; AJHA; AAPOR; WAPOR. **RESEARCH** Relationship among technology, mass communication and culture. **SELECTED PUBLICATIONS** Coauth, The Agenda-Selling Function of Mass Media, Publ Opinion Quart, summer 72; coauth (with McCombs), The Emergence of American Political Issues: The Agenda-Setting Function of the Press, West Pub Co, 77; coauth, Communication and Democracy. **CONTACT ADDRESS** Sch of Journalism, Univ North Carolina, Chapel Hill, NC, 27514.

SHAW, HARRY EDMUND
PERSONAL Born 05/01/1946, Norristown, PA, m, 1982, 2 children **DISCIPLINE** ENGLISH LITERATURE **EDUCATION** Harvard Col, AB, 69; Univ Calif, Berkeley, MA, 74, PhD, 78. **CAREER** Prof English, Cornell Univ, 78-. **RESEARCH** 18th and 19th century British novel; Historical fiction. **SELECTED PUBLICATIONS** Auth, The Forms of Historical Fiction: Scott and his Successors, Cornell Univ Press, 83; Narratives of Reality: Austen, Scott, Eliot, Cornell Univ Press, in prep. **CONTACT ADDRESS** Dept of English, Cornell Univ, Rockefeller Ha, Ithaca, NY, 14853-0001. **EMAIL** HES3@Cornell.edu

SHAW, PATRICK W.
DISCIPLINE AMERICAN LITERATURE **EDUCATION** La State Univ, PhD, 71. **CAREER** Prof, TX Tech Univ. **RESEARCH** The mod Am novel. **SELECTED PUBLICATIONS** Auth, Willa Cather and the Art of Conflict: Re-Visioning Her Creative Imagination; his essays have been reproduced in such collections as Major Literary Characters: Antonia, The Viking Critical Edition of John Steinbeck's The Grapes of Wrath, and A New Study Guide to Steinbeck's Major Works. **CONTACT ADDRESS** Texas Tech Univ, Lubbock, TX, 79409-5015. **EMAIL** ditps@ttacs.ttu.edu

SHAW, W. DAVID
PERSONAL Born 07/02/1937, Ottawa, ON, Canada, m, 1969, 4 children **DISCIPLINE** ENGLISH **EDUCATION** Univ Toronto, BA, 59; Harvard Univ, AM, 60, PhD(English), 63. **CAREER** Tutor English, Harvard Univ, 62-63; asst prof, Cornell Univ, 63-69; assoc prof, 69-75, PROF ENGLISH, VICTORIA COL, UNIV TORONTO, 75-, Vis assoc prof, Univ Calif, Riverside, 68-69. **MEMBERSHIPS** MLA **RESEARCH** Victorian literature; literary theory. **SELECTED PUBLICATIONS** Auth, Impact And Tremor In Tennyson Elegies - The Power Of Genre/, Victorian Poetry, Vol 0031, 1993; Death And The Future Life In Victorian Lit And Theol - Wheeler,M/, Modern Philol, Vol 0091, 1993; Tennyson And The Text - Joseph,G/, Criticism-A Quart For Lit And The Arts, Vol 0035, 1993; Elegy And Theory, Is Historical And Critical Knowledge Possible/, Modern Lang Quart, Vol 0055, 1994; Arthurian Ghosts + Morris,William - The Phantom Art Of The 'Defence Of Guinevere'/, Victorian Poetry, Vol 0034, 1996; Burnejones,Edward

And Pre-Raphaelite Melancholy/, Univ Of Toronto Quart, Vol 0066, 1997. **CONTACT ADDRESS** Dept English, Univ of Toronto, Toronto, ON, M5M 2H5.

SHAWCROSS, JOHN THOMAS
PERSONAL Born 02/10/1924, Hillside, NJ **DISCIPLINE** ENGLISH **EDUCATION** NJ State Col, Montclair, AB, 48; NY Univ, AM, 50, PhD, 58. **CAREER** From instr to prof English, Newark Col Eng, 48-63; prof English, Douglass Col, Rutgers Univ, 63-67; prof, Univ Wis, Madison, 67-70; distinguished prof, Col Staten Island & Grad Ctr, City Univ New York, 70-79; PROF ENGLISH, UNIV KY, 79-, Lectr, City Col New York, 58-63; vis prof, NY Univ, 62 & 65, C W Post Col, Long Island Univ, 63, Univ Del, 65-66 & State Univ NY, Stony Brook, 74. **HONORS AND AWARDS** LittD, Montclair State Col, NJ, 75. **MEMBERSHIPS** Milton Soc (treas, 62-72, vpres, 73, pres, 74-75); Col English Asn; Renaissance Soc Am; Bibliog Soc Am; MLA. **RESEARCH** Milton; 17th century; modern poetry. **SELECTED PUBLICATIONS** Auth, Introduction + Issue On Cross-Gender Writing/, Cea Critic, Vol 0056, 1993; The Political And Liturgical Subtext Of Milton 'On The Death Of A Fair Infant Dying Of A Cough'/, Anq-A Quart J Of Short Articles Notes And Revs, Vol 0007, 1994; Catalog Of The Kohler Collection Of 550 Different Editions Of The Writings Of Milton,John Published Between 1641 And 1914 - Milton,J/, Anq-A Quart J Of Short Articles Notes And Revs, Vol 0008, 1995; The New-Eng Milton, Literary Reception And Cult Authority In The Early Republic - Vananglen,Kp/, Anq-A Quart J Of Short Articles Notes And Revs, Vol 0008, 1995; A Note On 'Paradise Lost' Book-2, Milton Quart, Vol 0029, 1995; The Christ-Figure In Some Literary-Texts - Images And Theme, Cithara-Essays In The Judeo-Christian Tradition, Vol 0035, 1996; Soc Visions - Wilding,M/, Anq-A Quart J Of Short Articles Notes And Revs, Vol 0009, 1996. **CONTACT ADDRESS** Dept of English, Univ of Ky, Lexington, KY, 40506.

SHEA, ANN MARIE
PERSONAL Born 12/17/1939, Worcester, MA **DISCIPLINE** PERFORMING ARTS **EDUCATION** Anna Maria Col, BA, 61; The Catholic Univ of Am, MA, 64; New York Univ, PhD, 84. **CAREER** Instr of Theatre, Col Misericordia, 66-68; PROF OF THEATRE, WORCESTER STATE COL, 68-. **HONORS AND AWARDS** Moss Hart Memorial Awd, New England Theatre Conf, 90; Zonta Club Scholar, 61; Anna Maria Col Scholar, 57-61. **MEMBERSHIPS** New England Theatre Conf; Asn for Theatre in Higher Ed; Kennedy Center/Am Col Theatre Festival. **SELECTED PUBLICATIONS** Auth, Mythic Realities in Miller's All My Sons, Worcester Forum Theatre, 92; St. Genesius, The New Catholic Encycl, 64; Winter Glory, Worcester Children's Theatre, 79; coauth, The Powwow of the Thunderbird American Indian Dancers, The Drama Rev, 82. **CONTACT ADDRESS** Dept of Visual and Performing Arts, Worcester State Col, 486 Chandler St, Worcester, MA, 06102. **EMAIL** ashed@worc.mass.edu

SHEA, DANIEL B.
PERSONAL Born 10/29/1936, Minneapolis, MN, m, 1978, 5 children **DISCIPLINE** EARLY AMERICAN LITERATURE **EDUCATION** Univ of St. Thomas, BA (summa cum laude), 58; Stanford Univ, MA, 62, PhD, 66. **CAREER** INST TO PROF, 62-, DEPT CHAIR, WASH UNIV, 78-84 & 95-98; fulbright lectr, Univ of Caen, 68-69; vis fel, Clare Hall, Cambirdge, 84-85. **HONORS AND AWARDS** Richard Beale Davis Prize, MLA, 88; tchg awds, Wash Univ, 89 & 90; Woodrow Wilson Fel, 58; Fulbright-Hays Sr Lectureship, 68; NEH Summber Grant, 61; distinguished fac awd, Washington Univ, 85; Phi Beta Kappa. **MEMBERSHIPS** MLA; AFTRA; Equity. **RESEARCH** Early American Lit; American women's fiction to 1900. **SELECTED PUBLICATIONS** Auth, Spiritual Autobiography in Early America, Wisconsin, 88; section ed, Columbia Literary History of the United States, Columbia, 88; ed, Some Account of the Fore Part of the Life of Elizabeth Ashbridge, Wisconsin, 90. **CONTACT ADDRESS** Dept of English, Washington Univ, St. Louis, MO, 63130. **EMAIL** dbshea@artsci.wustl.edu

SHEA, JOHN STEPHEN
PERSONAL Born 07/18/1933, New York, NY, m, 3 children **DISCIPLINE** ENGLISH **EDUCATION** Iona Col, AB, 54; Marquette Univ, AM, 56; Univ MN, PhD, 67. **CAREER** From instr to asst prof Eng, WA Univ, 64-69, chmn freshman Eng, 65-68; asst prof, 69-72, asst chmn dept, 73-76, assoc prof eng, Loyola Univ Chicago, 72-, chmn dept, 76-84, Director, Writing Across the Curriculum, 86-96, Prof Emeritus, 98-; Reader advan placement exam, Col Entrance Exam Bd, 68-73; ed, Restoration & 17th Century Theatre Res, 72-79; Mellon res grant, Mellon Found & Loyola Univ, 75. **MEMBERSHIPS** MLA; Am Soc 18th Century Studies. **RESEARCH** Restoration and 18th century Eng lit; literary criticism. **SELECTED PUBLICATIONS** Coauth, Themes and Exercises, Dept Eng, Univ MN, 60, 61 & 62; ed, Mandeville's Aesop Dress'd, Augustan Reprint Soc, 66; co-ed, Studies in Criticism and Aesthetics, 1660-1800, Univ MN, 67. **CONTACT ADDRESS** Dept Eng, Loyola Univ, 6525 N Sheridan Rd, Chicago, IL, 60626-5385.

SHEARON, FORREST BEDFORD
PERSONAL Born 09/07/1934, Bolivar, TN, m, 1981, 2 children **DISCIPLINE** BRITISH LITERATURE, INTERDISCIPLINARY HUMANITIES **EDUCATION** Union Univ, Tenn, AB, 56; Univ Louisville, MA, 65, PhD, 73. **CAREER** Teacher English, Halls High Sch, Tenn, 56-58, Pleasure Ridge Park High Sch, Ky, 58-65; asst prof English, Ky Southern Col, Louisville, 65-68; asst prof, Univ Louisville, 69-73; from asst prof to prof Humanites, 73-98, Prof Emeritus, Eastern Ky Univ, 98-. **HONORS AND AWARDS** Outstanding Graduating Senior, Union Univ, Summer 56; Phi Kappa Phi, Univ Louisville, 66; Outstanding Graduating Senior, Grad Sch, Univ Louisville, 74; John Hay Fel in the humanities, Northwestern Univ, 62-63; NEH Summer Seminar, Univ Va, 79; Fulbright/Hayes Fel travel/study tour of India, Summer 87. **MEMBERSHIPS** MLA; Southern Humanities Coun; SAtlantic Mod Lang Asn; Ky Philol Asn. **RESEARCH** Ethics, evolution, and the arts. **SELECTED PUBLICATIONS** Auth, The South from a distance, Tri-Quart, spring 63; The prince introduces Imlac to general semantics, Etc: A Review of General Semantics 30, 3/73; Visual Imagery and Internal Awareness in Pirsig's Zen and the Art of Motorcycle Maintenance, KPA Bull, 84; Report in Guidebook to Zen and the Art of Motorcycle Maintenance, William Morrow, 90; Taxi Ride from Jaipur to Delhi, Int Mag 9, Eastern Ky Univ, 88; Random Reflections on Teaching Humanities, Accent Marks 2, Eastern Ky Univ, Spring 88. **CONTACT ADDRESS** Humanities/Case Annex 368, Eastern Kentucky Univ, Richmond, KY, 40475-3140. **EMAIL** HumShear@acs.eku.edu

SHEATS, PAUL DOUGLAS
PERSONAL Born 06/17/1932, Albany, NY, m, 1964, 2 children **DISCIPLINE** ENGLISH **EDUCATION** Harvard Univ, BA, 54, MA, 63, PhD(English), 66; Oxford Univ, AB, 57. **CAREER** Instr English, Haverford Col, 58-60; teaching fel, Harvard Univ, 63-66; from asst prof to assoc prof, 66-78, vchmn dept, 76-78, PROF ENGLISH & CHMN DEPT, UNIV CALIF, LOS ANGELES, 78- **MEMBERSHIPS** MLA **RESEARCH** Wordsworth; Romantic poetry. **SELECTED PUBLICATIONS** Auth, Romanticism Revisions - Brinkley,R, Hanley,K/, Studies In Romanticism, Vol 0035, 1996; The Passion Of Meter - A Study Of Wordsworth Metrical Art - Odonnell,B/, Wordsworth Circle, Vol 0027, 1996; Center And Circumference - Essays In English Romanticism - Assoc-English-Romanticism-Japan/, Keats-Shelley J, Vol 0046, 1997; A Comparison Of Keats 'Hyperion' And The 'Fall Of Hyperion' - Ando,Y/, Keats-Shelley J, Vol 0046, 1997. **CONTACT ADDRESS** Univ of Calif, 2225 Humanities Bldg, Los Angeles, CA, 90024.

SHEDLETSKY, LEONARD JERALD
DISCIPLINE COMMUNICATION STUDIES **EDUCATION** Brooklyn Col, BA, 65; San Francisco State Col, MA, 68; Univ Ill, PhD, 74. **CAREER** Asst prof, Univ Conn, 74-79; asst prof, 79-84; assoc prof, 84-91; prof, 91-. **HONORS AND AWARDS** Asst ed, Nat Commun Asn. **MEMBERSHIPS** Speech Commun Asn; Int Commun Asn; Eastern Commun Asn; Western States Commun Asn; Int Listening Asn; Northeastern Edu Res Asn. **SELECTED PUBLICATIONS** Auth, A lot of teachers who can, don't, 97; Communication technology: Using e-mail and the World Wide Webin the communication course, 97; Teaching as experiential learning, 96; Teaching with computer-mediated communication, 95; Where do we locate intrapersonal communication within the cognitive domain?, 95; coauth, Intrapersonal Communication Processes, 95. **CONTACT ADDRESS** Dept of Communication, 37 Col Ave, Gorham, MN, 04038-1083. **EMAIL** Lenny@Portland.Maine.Edu

SHEEHAN, DONALD
DISCIPLINE ENGLISH LITERATURE **EDUCATION** Univ WI, PhD, 69. **CAREER** Sr Lctr Eng and Classics. **RESEARCH** Lit and compos. **SELECTED PUBLICATIONS** Auth, The Seeds of Iconography: Notes on Beginning the Practice, Orthodox New England, 88; Mary de Rachewiltz in Ital Transl of Pound's Cantos I-XXX: A Prosodic Note, Paideuma, 83. **CONTACT ADDRESS** Dartmouth Col, 3529 N Main St, #207, Hanover, NH, 03755.

SHEFFEY, RUTHE G.
PERSONAL Essex County, Virginia, m **DISCIPLINE** ENGLISH **EDUCATION** Morgan State Univ, BA 1947; Howard Univ, MA 1949; Univ of PA, PhD 1959. **CAREER** Howard Univ, graduate asst in English, 1947-48; Claflin Coll, instructor, English, French, 1948-49; Morgan State Coll, asst prof, 1959-64, assoc prof, 1964-70; chairperson, English dept, 1970-74, prof, dept of English, 1975-. **HONORS AND AWARDS** Coll Language Assn Creative Achievement Award, 1974; United Fund Award for Community Serv, 1975; Community Serv Award, Jack & Jill of Amer, 1979; Distinguished Alumni Citation, Natl Assn for Equal Opportunity, 1980; Faculty Rsch Grants for studies in Shakespearean Production, 1983; Achievement Award for Preservation of Higher Educ Standards & Contributions to African-American History & Culture, 1984; Morgan State Univ Women Award, 1985; Citations for Outstanding Service to Scholarly and Literary Communities, 1985-93; Maryland Assn for Higher Education, Faculty Member of the Year Award, 1994; Howard Univ, Baltimore Chapter, Alumna of the Year, 1987; Towson State Univ, Distinguished Black Woman of America, 1984; numerous other citations and awards; Morgan State Univ, Hall of Fame, 1998. **MEMBERSHIPS** Coll English Assn; Coll Language Assn; Modern Language Assn; Natl Cncl of the Teachers of English; Eighteenth Century Studies Assn; Middle Atlantic Writers Assn; vice pres, Langston Hughes Soc; founder, pres, Zora Neale Hurston Soc; editor, Zora Neale Hurston Forum; Assn for the Study of Afro-American Life & Culture; Kings Kids Mentor, Heritage United Church of Christ; Mayor's Cncl on Women's Rights; delegate, White House Conf on Women as Economic Equals; Morgan State, Howard Univ, & the Univ of PA Alumni Assns; communications comm, United Fund of MD, 1972-74; commnr & vice chair, Baltimore Co Human Relations Commn; MD state delegate, Paula Hollinger's Scholarship Award Panel; Maryland Council for the Humanities, 1990-96. **SELECTED PUBLICATIONS** Author of numerous books, articles, and reviews. **CONTACT ADDRESS** Professor of English, Morgan State Univ, Coldspring & Hillen Rds, Baltimore, MD, 21239.

SHELDON, TED P.
PERSONAL Oak Park, IL, m, 1965, 2 children **DISCIPLINE** LIBRARY **EDUCATION** Elmhurst Col, BA, 64; Ind Univ, MA, 65, PhD, 76; Univ Ill, Champaign-Urbana, MALS, 77. **CAREER** Instr, 66-68, Elmhurst Col; asst prof, 70-76, Millikin Univ; ref libr/hist bibl, 77-79, head, collect develop, 78-80, Univ Kansas Libraries; ass dir of libr, 80-83, SUNY, Binghamton; assoc dir of libr, 83-85, adj prof, hist, 88-, dir of libr, 85-, Univ Missouri-Kansas City; adj prof libr sci, 89-94, Univ Missouri-Columbia, **RESEARCH** Management of special collections and archives; audio archiving; standards for audio preservation; management issues in libraries. **CONTACT ADDRESS** Miller Nichols Library, 5100 Rockhill Rd, Kansas City, MO, 64110-2499. **EMAIL** sheldont@umkc.edu

SHELL, MARC
DISCIPLINE ENGLISH **EDUCATION** Stanford Univ, BA, 68; Trinity Coll, Cambridge, BA, 70; Yale Univ, MA, 72, PhD, 75. **CAREER** Assoc, prof, Eng, State Univ NY Buffalo; HARVARD UNIV. **MEMBERSHIPS** Am Antiquarian Soc **SELECTED PUBLICATIONS** Auth, Money, Language, and Thought: Literary and Philosophical Economies from the Medieval to the Modern Era, Univ Calif Press, 82; auth, The End of Kinship: "Measure for Measure," Incest, and the Idea of Universal Siblinghood, Stanford Univ Press, 88; auth, "Babel in America; or, The Politics of Language Diversity in the United States," Critical Inquiry 20, 93. **CONTACT ADDRESS** Dept of Eng and Am Lit and Language, Harvard Univ, 11 Prescott St, Cambridge, MA, 02138.

SHELTON, RICHARD WILLIAM
PERSONAL Born 06/24/1933, Boise, ID, m, 1956, 1 child **DISCIPLINE** ENGLISH, CREATIVE WRITING **EDUCATION** Abilene Christian Col, BA, 58; Univ Ariz, MA, 61. **CAREER** Asst prof, 70-74, assoc prof, 74-78, dir, Creative Writing prog, 79-81, prof English, Univ Az, 78-, dir, Univ Ariz Poetry Ctr, 64-65; consult, Ariz Comn Arts & Humanities, 74-; dir, Writer's Workshop, Ariz State Prison, 74-; Regents prof, 91-. **HONORS AND AWARDS** US Award, Int Poetry Forum, 70; Az Governor's Award, 91; Western States Award for Creative Nonfiction, 92; 2 NEA Writer's Fellowships. **MEMBERSHIPS** Pen Club; Poetry Soc Am. **RESEARCH** Surrealism, post-symbolist French poetry; translation of contemporary Mexican poets; contemporary American poetry. **SELECTED PUBLICATIONS** Auth, Journal of Return, Kayak, 69; The Tattooed Desert, Univ Pittsburgh, 71; Calendar, Baleen, 72; Of All the Dirty Words, Univ Pittsburgh, 72; Among the Stones, Monument Press, 73; You Can't Have Everything, Univ Pittsburgh, 75; Chosen Plance, Best Cellar Press, 75; The Bus to Veracruz, 78 & Selected Poems: 1969-81, 82, Univ Pittsburgh; A Kind of Glory, Copper Canyon Press, 82; Hohokam, Confluence Press, 86; Going Back to Bisbee, Univ of Az Press, 92. **CONTACT ADDRESS** Dept of English, Univ Ariz, 1 University of Az, Tucson, AZ, 85721-0001. **EMAIL** rshelton@u.arizona.edu

SHEN, FUYUAN
DISCIPLINE ADVERTISING **EDUCATION** Univ NC-Chapel Hill, PhD. **CAREER** Asst prof; fac, Univ SD, 97-. **MEMBERSHIPS** Am Acad Advert; Asn Educ in Jour & Mass Commun; Am Marketing Asn: Newspaper Asn Am. **SELECTED PUBLICATIONS** Auth, Characteristics of online consumers: A diffusion of innovation approach, Southern Asn of Public Opinion Res Annual Conf, Raleigh, 95; coauth, Assessment of television's anti-violence messages, In Nat TV Violence Study, Vol 1, Thousand Oaks, Sage Publ, 97; Audience reaction to commercial advertising in China in the 1980s, Int J of Advert, 14, 95; Position of TV advertisement in a natural pod, A preliminary analysis of concepts, measurements and effects, Proceedings of the 95 Annual Conf Amer Acad Advert, 95; Exploratory analysis of the effectiveness of television industry ¤s antiviolence public service announcements, Asn Educ Jour and Mass Commun Annual Conf, Anaheim, 96. **CONTACT ADDRESS** Dept of Mass Commun, Univ SD, 414 E Clark St, Vermillion, SD, 57069. **EMAIL** fshen@usd.edu

SHEPARD, ALAN
DISCIPLINE ENGLISH **EDUCATION** St. Olaf Col, BA, 83; Univ Va, PhD, 90. **CAREER** Writing Ctr Tutor, St. Olaf Col, 81-83; Tutor, 84-90, Instr, 87-89, Grad Instr, Univ Va, 86-90; Asst Prof, 90-96, Assoc Prof , Tex Christian Univ, 96-. **HONORS AND AWARDS** George Weida Spohn Prize, St. Olaf Col, 82; Phi Beta Kappa; recipient of numerous grants from The Folger Libr, Tex Christian Univ, and others; recipient of numerous fellowships. **MEMBERSHIPS** Mod Lang Asn; Renaissance Soc Am; Group for Early Mod Cult Studies; Soc Lit & Sci; Renaissance Early Text Soc. **SELECTED PUBLICATIONS** Auth, Endless Sacks: Soldiers' Desire in Tamburlaine, Renaissance Quart, 93; The Literature of a Medical Hoax: The Case of Mary Toft, The Pretended Rabbet-Breeder, Eighteenth-Century Life 2, 95; Aborted Rage in Beth Henley's Women, repr, States of Rage: Emotional Eruption, Violence, and Social Change, NY Univ Press, 96; Thou art no soldier; Thou art a merchant: The Mentality of War in Malta, In: Marlowe, History, and Sexuality: New Critical Essays on Christopher Marlowe, AMS Press, 98; co-ed, Coming to Class: Pedagogy and the Social Class of Teachers, Heinemann Boynton/Cook, 98; author of numerous other articles and publications. **CONTACT ADDRESS** English Dept, Tex Christian Univ, Box 297270, Fort Worth, TX, 76129. **EMAIL** a.shepard@tcu.edu

SHERMAN, SANDRA
DISCIPLINE RESTORATION AND EIGHTEENTH-CENTURY LITERATURE **EDUCATION** Univ Pa, PhD. **CAREER** English and Lit, Univ Ark. **SELECTED PUBLICATIONS** Auth, Printing the Mind: The Economics of Authorship in Areopagitica, ELH, 93; Trembling Texts: Margaret Cavendish and the Dialectic of Authorship, eng Literary Renaissance, 94; Servants and Semiotics: Reversible Signs, Capital Instability, and Defoe's Logic of the Market, ELH, 95; Instructing the 'Empire of Beauty': Lady Mary Wortley Montagu and the Politics of Female Rationality, S Atlantic Rev, 95; Promises, Promises: Credit as a Contested Metaphor in Early Capitalist Discourse, Modern Philol, 96; Finance and Fictionality in the Early Eighteenth Century, Cambridge, 96.s **CONTACT ADDRESS** Univ Ark, Fayetteville, AR, 72701.

SHERMAN, STUART
DISCIPLINE RESTORATION AND EIGHTEENTH-CENTURY LITERATURE **EDUCATION** Columbia Univ, PhD. **CAREER** Art, Washington Univ. **SELECTED PUBLICATIONS** Ed, Johnsonian News Letter. **CONTACT ADDRESS** Washington Univ, 1 Brookings Dr, St. Louis, MO, 63130.

SHERMAN, WILLIAM H.
DISCIPLINE ENGLISH **EDUCATION** Cambridge Univ, PhD 92, Mpil 89; Columbia Univ, BA 88. **CAREER** Univ Maryland Col Pk, asst prof 93-, dir 98-; Univ London Queen Mary and Westfield Coll, vis prof 95-96. **HONORS AND AWARDS** Brit Acad Hunt Lib Res Gnt; 2 Mellon fel; Jr Caird fel; Amer Friends Of Cambridge Sch; Euretta J. Kellet fel; Phi Beta Kappa. **RESEARCH** English renaissance lit and cult; History of the book. **SELECTED PUBLICATIONS** Auth, The Tempest and its Travels, coed, Reaktion Books, forthcoming; John Dee: The Politics of Reading and Writing in the English Renaissance, Amherst, U of MA Press, 95, pbk 97; Renaissance Commonplace Books from the Huntington Library, ed, Marlborough, Adam Matthew Microfilm Pub, 95; Anatomizing the Commonwealth: Language Politics and the Elizabethan Social Order, in: Elizabeth Fowler and Roland Greene, eds, The Project of Prose in Early Modern Europe and the New World, Cambridge, CUP, 97; The Place of Reading in the English Renaissance: John Dee Revisited, in: James Raven Naomi Tadmor Helen Small, eds, The Practice and Representation of Reading in England, Cambridge, CUP, 96. **CONTACT ADDRESS** Dept of English, Univ of Maryland, College Park, MD, 20742. **EMAIL** ws76@umail.umd.edu

SHERRILL, CATHERINE ANNE
PERSONAL Born 02/26/1938, Houston, TX **DISCIPLINE** ENGLISH **EDUCATION** Univ Texas, Austin, BA, 60, MA, 69; Univ Iowa, PhD, 81. **CAREER** Instr, 60-66, Houston Independent Schl Dist; tchr, 69-78, Col of Mainland; instr, prof English, E Tenn St Univ. **RESEARCH** Young people's literature **CONTACT ADDRESS** Dept of English, East Tennesee State Univ, Johnson City, TN, 37614.

SHERWOOD, TERRY G.
DISCIPLINE RENAISSANCE LITERATURE **EDUCATION** Univ Oregon, BA; Univ Calif, Berkeley, MA, PhD. **CAREER** Ch, 988-92; assoc VP Acad, 96; prof. **HONORS AND AWARDS** Post dr fel(s), Univ Toronto, Univ Victoria. **RESEARCH** Religion and literature; Spenser, Shakespeare; Donne, Jonson; Herbert, Milton. **SELECTED PUBLICATIONS** Auth, Fulfilling the Circle: A Study of John Donne's Thought, U of Toronto P, 84; Herbert's Prayerful Art, U of Toronto P, 89. **CONTACT ADDRESS** Dept of English, Victoria Univ, PO Box 3070, Victoria, BC, V8W 3W1. **EMAIL** sherwood@uvvm.uvic.ca

SHESGREEN, SEAN NICHOLAS
PERSONAL Born 12/05/1939, Derry City, Ireland, d, 1 child **DISCIPLINE** ENGLISH LITERATURE, ART HISTORY **EDUCATION** Loyola Univ Chicago, BA, 62, MA, 66; Northwestern Univ, PhD(English), 70. **CAREER** Teaching asst English, Northwestern Univ, 68-69; asst prof, 69-74, assoc prof, 74-82, PROF ENGLISH, NORTHERN IL UNIV, 82-, Presidential Res Prof, 90-95; Vis fac mem, Univ CA, Riverside, 74-75; Am Philos Soc grant-in-aid, 76; exchange prof English, Xian Foreign Lang Inst, People's Repub China, 81-82. **HONORS AND AWARDS** Huntington Library Summer fel, 98; Yale Univ Center for Art fel, 90; Ball Brothers Found fel, Lilly Library , IN Univ, Bloomington; NEH Newberry Library Sr fel, 98-99. **MEMBERSHIPS** MLA; Am Soc 18th Century Studies. **RESEARCH** Eighteenth century novel with emphasis on Henry Fielding; 18th century graphic art with emphasis on William Hogarth; criers of London. **SELECTED PUBLICATIONS** Auth, Literary Portraits in the Novels of Henry Fielding, Northern Ill Univ, 72; ed, Engravings by Hogarth, Dover, 73; auth, A Harlot's Progress and the Question of Hogarth's Didacticisms, 18th Century Life, 75; Hogarth's Industry and Idleness, 18th Century Studies, 76; Hogarth and the Times-of-the-Day Tradition, Cornell Univ Press, 82; Marcellus Laroon's Cryer of the City of London, Studies Bibliog, 82; The Crier and Hawkers of London, Stanford Univ Press, 90. **CONTACT ADDRESS** No Illinois Univ, 1425 W Lincoln Hwy, De Kalb, IL, 60115-2825. **EMAIL** shesgreen@niu.edu

SHIELDS, BRUCE E.
PERSONAL Born 08/09/1937, PA, m, 1957, 3 children **DISCIPLINE** NEW TESTAMENT AND HOMILETICS **EDUCATION** Milligan Col, BA, 59; Princeton Theol Sem, BD, 65; Eberhard-Karls Universiteit zu Tubingen, D Theol, 81. **CAREER** Prof, 77-83, Lincoln Christian Sem; prof , 83-, Emmanuel Sch Relig. **HONORS AND AWARDS** NEH sum grant, 91. **MEMBERSHIPS** Soc of Bibl Lit; Acad of Homiletics; Societas Homiletica. **RESEARCH** Preaching in the early church. **SELECTED PUBLICATIONS** Auth, Romans, Cincinnati: Standard Pub Co, 88; auth, Campbell on Language and Revelation and Modern Approaches to Language, Building Up the Church: Scripture, Hist, & Growth, A Festschrift in Honor of Henry E. Webb, Milligan Col, 93, TN; rev, Dale B. Martin, Slavery as Salvation: The Metaphor of Slavery in Pauline Christianity, Yale Univ Press, 90, Restor Quart vol 35, 93; rev, Sidney Greidanus, The Modern Preacher and the Ancient Text: Interpreting and Preaching Biblical Literature, Eerdmans Pub Co, 88, J for Christian Stud, 93; auth, The Areopagus Sermon as a Model for Apologetic Preaching, Faith in Pract: Stud in Bk of Acts, A Festschrift in Honor of Earl and Ottie Mearl Stuckenbruck, European Evangel Soc, 95; auth, John Henry Jowett, Concise Encycl of Preaching, Westminster/John Knox Press, 95; rev, Jeffrey T. Myers, Unfinished Errand into the Wilderness: Tendenzen und Schwerpunkte der Homilitic in den USA 1960-1985, doct diss, Johannes Gutenburg Univ, Mainz, Germany, in Homiletic, XXI/1, 96; rev, H. David Schuringa, Hearing the Word in a Visual Age in Encounter, 97; auth, Integrating Ministry and Theology: One Seminary's Story, Theological Ed, vol 33, no 2, 97; auth, Preaching and Culture, Homiletic vol XXII no 2, 97; auth, Readers Guide: Literary Resources for Worship, Leaven vol 6, no 1, 98. **CONTACT ADDRESS** Emmanuel Sch of Religion, One Walker Dr, Johnson City, TN, 37601-9989. **EMAIL** shieldsb@esr.edu

SHIELDS, CAROL
PERSONAL Oak Park, IL **DISCIPLINE** ENGLISH **EDUCATION** Univ Exeter, Eng, exchange student, 55-56; Hanover Col, Ind, 57; Univ Ottawa, MA, 75. **CAREER** Author, PROF UNIV MANITOBA, 80-. **HONORS AND AWARDS** Best Novel, Can Authors' Asn, 76; First Prize, CBC Drama Award, 83; First Prize, Nat Mag Award, 85; Arthur Ellis Award best Can crime novel, 87; Marian Engle Award, 90; Gov Gen Award, 93; Can Booksellers Award, 94; Nat Critics Circle Award, US, 95; Pulitzer Prize Lit, 95. **MEMBERSHIPS** TWUC; PUC; PEN; Can Coun. **SELECTED PUBLICATIONS** Auth, Small Ceremonies, 76; auth, The Box Garden, 77; auth, Happenstance, 80; auth, Swan, 87; auth, The Republic of Love, 92; auth, The Stone Diaries, 93. **CONTACT ADDRESS** Chancellor, Univ Winnipeg, Fletcher Avenue Building, Winnipeg, MB, R3T 5V5. **EMAIL** carolshields@uwinnipeg.ca

SHIELDS, DAVID S.
DISCIPLINE ENGLISH **EDUCATION** Coll Wm & Mary, BA, 73; Univ Chicago, MA, 75, PhD, 82. **CAREER** ASST PROF, ENG, CITADEL **MEMBERSHIPS** Am Antiquarian Soc **SELECTED PUBLICATIONS** Auth, "The Wits and Poets of Pennsylvania," Penn Mag of Hist & Biog, 85; auth, "The Religious Sublime and New England Poets of the 1720s," Early Am Lit 19, 85; auth, "Clio Mocks the Masons: Joseph Green's Anti-Masonic Satires," in Deism, Masonry and the Enlightenment, 86; auth, "Then Shall Religion to America Flee: Herbert and Colonial American Poetry," in Like Season'd Timber: New Essays on George Herbert, Peter Lang, 87; "Nathaniel Gardner, Jr. and the Literary Culture of Boston in the 1750s," Early Am Lit 24, 89; auth, Oracles of Empire: Poetry, Politics, and Commerce in British America, 1690-1750, Univ Chicago Press, 90; auth, "Belles Lettres in British America," in The Cambridge History of American Literature, Cambridge Univ Press, 92. **CONTACT ADDRESS** 49 South Hampton, Charleston, SC, 29407.

SHIELDS, DONALD C.
DISCIPLINE COMMUNICATION STUDIES **EDUCATION** Univ Mo Kans City, BA, MA; Univ Minn, PhD. **SELECTED PUBLICATIONS** Co-auth, Understanding Communication Theory: The Communicative Forces for Human Action, 98; An Expansion of the Rhetorical Vision Component of the Symbolic Convergence Theory: The Cold War Paradigm Case, Commun Monographs, 96; Symbolic Theories in Applied Communication Research: Bormann, Burke, and Fischer, Hampton, 95. **CONTACT ADDRESS** Communication Dept, Univ of Missouri, St. Louis, 590 Lucas Hall, St. Louis, MO, 63121. **EMAIL** sdcshie@umslvma.umsl.edu

SHIELDS, DONALD J.
PERSONAL Born 10/28/1937, Paris, IL, m, 1962, 2 children **DISCIPLINE** COMMUNICATION, POLITICAL SCIENCE **EDUCATION** Eastern IL Univ, BS, 59; Purdue Univ, MS, 61, PhD, 64. **CAREER** Staff asst speech, IN State Democratic Comt, 62; asst prof, Cornell Univ, 64-65; asst prof, 65-71, assoc prof, 71-79, prof speech, IN State Univ, Terre Haute, 79. **MEMBERSHIPS** Speech Commun Asn; Nat Soc Studies Commun; Am Forensic Asn; Am Asn Univ Prof. **RESEARCH** Polit persuasion and commun networks. **CONTACT ADDRESS** Dept of Speech, Indiana State Univ, 210 N 7th St, Terre Haute, IN, 47809-0002. **EMAIL** cmshield@ruby.indstate.edu

SHIELDS, JOHN CHARLES
PERSONAL Born 10/29/1944, Phoenix, AZ **DISCIPLINE** AMERICAN & CLASSICAL LITERATURES **EDUCATION** Univ Tenn, Knoxville, BA, 67, MACT, 79, PhD(English), 78; George Peabody Col Teachers, EdS, 75. **CAREER** Teacher English & art hist, Sevier County High Sch, Sevierville, Tenn, 67-68; head dept English & teacher Latin, Battle Ground Acad, Franklin, Tenn, 67-68; dir acad, Brentwood Acad, Tenn, 71-73; Instr English, Columbia State Community Col, 75-76; ASST PROF ENGLISH, ILL STATE UNIV, 80-, Instr English & dir writing lab, Univ Tenn, Nashville, 71-74; fac res grant, Ill State Univ, summers 80 & 81. **MEMBERSHIPS** MLA; Medieval Acad Am; Soc Cinema Studies. **SELECTED PUBLICATIONS** Auth, Wheatley,Phillis Subversion Of Classical Stylistics/, Style, Vol 0027, 1993; African-Am Poetics - Introd/, Style, Vol 0027, 1993; Wheatley,Phillis Subversive Pastoral/, Eighteenth-Century Studies, Vol 0027, 1994. **CONTACT ADDRESS** English Dept, Illinois State Univ, Normal, IL, 61761.

SHIELDS, KENNETH
DISCIPLINE ENGLISH **EDUCATION** Penn State Univ, BA, MA, PhD. **CAREER** Prof & dept ch, Millersville Univ Penn **RESEARCH** Historical Indo-European linguistics; language change; dialects of American English. **SELECTED PUBLICATIONS** Auth, A History of Indo-European Verb Morphology, Amsterdam: John Benjamin's, 92; Indo-European Noun Inflection: A Developmental History, Univ Park: Penn State Press, 82; Comments about IE oi-'1', J Indo-Europ Stud 22, 94; Germanic Locative Adverbs in on-, Amer J Ger Ling and Lit 7, 95; Gothic 1st Pl Pret -um, Historische Sprachforschung 107, 94; On the Origin of Hittite Accusative Plural Suffix - us, Hethitica 12, 94; Rattleband(ing)'Shivaree': Another Pennsylvania Variant, Amer Speech 68, 93; The Indo-European Genitive Marker *-r: Evidence from Germanic and other Dialects, Nowele 25, 95; The Origin of the IE r-/n-Stems: An Alternative Proposal, Folia Ling Historica 15, 94; The Role of Deictic Particles in the Indo-European Personal Pronoun System, Word 45, 94; Typological Inconsistencies in the Indo-European Color Lexicon: A Cosmic Connection, Indoger Forschungen 101, 96; A Proposal Regarding the Etymology of the Word God, Leuvense Bijdragen 85, 96. **CONTACT ADDRESS** Dept of English, Millersville Univ, Pennsylvania, PO Box 1002, Millersville, PA, 17551-0302. **EMAIL** kshields@marauder.millersv.edu

SHIFLETT, ORVIN LEE
PERSONAL Born 08/01/1947, Melbourne, FL, m, 1990, 2 children **DISCIPLINE** LIBRARY INFORMATION **EDUCATION** Univ FL, Bae 69; Rutgers Univ MLS 71; FL State Univ, PhD 79. **CAREER** LA State Univ, prof 94, assoc prof 83-94, asst prof 79-83. **MEMBERSHIPS** ALA; Assn Lib Info Sci Edu. **RESEARCH** Hist of the libr and hist of the bk. **SELECTED PUBLICATIONS** Louis Shores: Defining Educational Librarianship, Scarecrow Press, 96; Origins of American Academic Librarianship, Ablex Press, 81; Hampton, Fisk, and Atlanta: The Foundations, The American Library Association, and Library Education for Blacks, 1925-1941, with Robert Sydney Martin, Libs And Culture, 96; the American Library Association's Quest for a Black Library School, Jour Of Edu for Lib Info Sci, 94. **CONTACT ADDRESS** Sch of Libr and Info Sci, Louisiana State Univ, Baton Rouge, LA, 70803. **EMAIL** lsshif@lsuvm.sncc.lsc.edu

SHILLER, DANA
DISCIPLINE VICTORIAN LITERATURE **EDUCATION** Univ Wash, PhD. **CAREER** Prof; dir, Wrtg; Women's Stud Prog. . **SELECTED PUBLICATIONS** Auth, article on uses

of the past in contemporary historical fiction, in Studies in the Novel. **CONTACT ADDRESS** Dept of Eng, Univ Evansville, 1800 Lincoln Ave, Evansville, IN, 47714. **EMAIL** ds2@evansville.edu.

SHILLINGSBURG, PETER LEROY

PERSONAL Born 03/24/1943, Colombia, m, 1967, 5 children **DISCIPLINE** ENGLISH LITERATURE **EDUCATION** Univ SC, BA, 66, MA, 67, PhD, 70. **CAREER** Archivist, SC Archives Dept, 68-69; asst prof, 70-73, assoc prof, 73-78, prof English, Ms State Univ, 78-97; coordr CSE, MLA, 76-77; assoc dir grad stud, Lamar Univ, 97-; Guggenheim fel, 82. **HONORS AND AWARDS** Robert W Harrigan, III, Distinguished Fac Mem, 96; Wm L Giles, Distinguished Prof, 97. **MEMBERSHIPS** MLA; SCent MLA; SAtlantic MLA. **RESEARCH** Nineteenth century English literature; bibliography; editing. **SELECTED PUBLICATIONS** Auth, The first edition of Thackeray's Pendennis, Papers Bibliog Soc Am, 72; Thackeray texts: a guide to inexpensive editions, Costerus, 74; Thackeray's Pendennis: a rejected page of manuscript, Huntington Libr Quart, 75; Critical editing and the Center for Scholarly Editions, Scholarly Pub, 77; articles in Editing Nineteenth Century Fiction, 78, Review, 80, The Book Collector, 80, Etudes Anglaise, 81, Studies in the Novel, 81, Studies in Bibliography, 81, Institute Studies, 81; Pegasus in Harness, UP Va, 92; Scholarly Editing in the Computer Age, Univ Mi, 96; Resisting Texts, Univ Mi, 98. **CONTACT ADDRESS** Grad Studies & Res, Lamar Univ, Box 10078, Beaumont, TX, 77710. **EMAIL** SHILLINGPL@Hal.Lamar.edu

SHILSTONE, FREDERICK WILLIAM

DISCIPLINE ENGLISH LITERATURE **EDUCATION** Ind Univ, PhD, 74. **CAREER** Dept Eng, Clemson Univ **RESEARCH** British Romantic literature. **SELECTED PUBLICATIONS** Ed, MLA Approaches to Teaching Byron's Poetry. **CONTACT ADDRESS** Clemson Univ, 807 Strode, Clemson, SC, 29634. **EMAIL** sfreder@clemson.edu

SHINAGEL, MICHAEL

PERSONAL Born 04/21/1934, Vienna, Austria, m, 2 children **DISCIPLINE** ENGLISH LITERATURE **EDUCATION** Oberlin Col, AB, 57; Harvard Univ, MA, 59, PhD, 64. **CAREER** Tutor English, Harvard Univ, 58-64; from instr to asst prof, Cornell Univ, 64-67; from assoc prof to prof, Union Col, NY, 67-75, chmn dept, 67-73; DEAN CONTINUING EDUC & DIR UNIV EXTEN, HARVARD UNIV, 75-, SENIOR LECTURER ON ENGLISH, 83-; Mem regional selection comt, Woodrow Wilson Nat Fel Found, 66-68; NEH grant, 66-67. **HONORS AND AWARDS** Phi Beta Kappa. **MEMBERSHIPS** The Johnsonians, Mass Hist Soc, Saturday Club. **RESEARCH** English literature of the 18th century; satire; novel. **SELECTED PUBLICATIONS** Coauth, Handbook on Summer Institutes in English, Col Bd, 65; auth, The maternal theme in Moll Flanders: Craft and character, Cornell Libr J, winter 68; Daniel Defoe and Middle-Class Gentility, Harvard Univ, 68; Concordance to Poems of Jonathan Swift, Cornell Univ, 72; Memoirs of a woman of pleasure: Pornography and the mid-18th century English novel, In: Studies in Change and Revolution, Scholar, 72; Robinson Crusoe, Norton, 75, rev 93; co-ed, Harvard Scholars in English (1890-1990), 91. **CONTACT ADDRESS** Harvard Univ, 51 Brattle St, Cambridge, MA, 02138-3701. **EMAIL** shinagel@hudce.harvard.edu

SHINE, THEODIS

PERSONAL Born 04/26/1931, Baton Rouge, Louisiana, s **DISCIPLINE** DRAMA, ENGLISH **EDUCATION** Howard University, Washington, DC, BA, 1953; University of Iowa, 1958; University of California, Santa Barbara, CA, PhD, 1973. **CAREER** Dillard University, New Orleans, LA, instructor in drama and English, 1960-61; Howard University, Washington, DC, assistant professor of drama, 1961-67; Prairie View A & M University, Prairie View, TX, professor and head of department of drama, 1967-. **HONORS AND AWARDS** Brooks-Hines Award for Playwriting, Howard University. **MEMBERSHIPS** National Theatre Conference, National Conference of African American Theatres; Southwest Theatre Conference; Texas Educational Theatre Association; Texas Non-Profit Theatres, board member. **SELECTED PUBLICATIONS** Author of "Plantation," contribution, "The Woman Who Was Tampered with in Youth," "Shoes", " Three Fat Batchelors"; Delta Sigma Theta Award-teacher; Beanie Award-Teaching; author of over sixty television scripts for series "Our Street." **CONTACT ADDRESS** P O Box 2082, Prairie View, TX, 77446-0519.

SHINN, THELMA J.

PERSONAL Born 09/10/1942, Flint, MI, 5 children **DISCIPLINE** AMERICAN LITERATURE, WOMEN'S STUDIES **EDUCATION** Cent Conn State Col, BA, 65; Purdue Univ, MA, 67, PhD(English), 72. **CAREER** Instr English, Col of Our Lady of the Elms, 71-73; asst prof, Westfield State Col, 73-75; vis lectr, 75-76, dir women's studies, 77-80, ASSOC PROF ENGLISH, ARIZ STATE UNIV, 76- **MEMBERSHIPS** MLA; AAUP; Am Asn Univ Women; Women's Caucus Mod Lang. **RESEARCH** Nineteenth and twentieth century American women writers: especially Joyce Carol Oates, Harriet Prescott Spofford and Shirley Ann Grau. **SELECTED PUBLICATIONS** Auth, Whats In A Word, Possessing Byatt,A.S. Meronymic Novel/, Papers On Lang And Lit, Vol 0031, 1995. **CONTACT ADDRESS** Dept of English, Arizona State Univ, Tempe, Tempe, AZ, 85287.

SHIPPEY, T.A.

DISCIPLINE MEDIEVAL LITERATURE **EDUCATION** Cambridge Univ, PhD. **CAREER** Eng Dept, St. Edward's Univ **HONORS AND AWARDS** Ch, Hum dept . **SELECTED PUBLICATIONS** Auth, Poems of Wisdom and Learning in Old English, D.S. Brewer, 76, 77; The Road to Middle-earth, Allen & Unwin, 82, 92, 93; Beowulf, Chelseas House, 88; Old English Verse, Hutchinson's, 72; Coed, Poets and Prophets: Selected Medieval Essays of G. T. Shepherd, Boydell & Brewer, 91; Ed, Fictional Space: Essays on Contemporary Science Fiction, Blackwell, 91; The Oxford Book of Science Fiction Stories, Oxford Univ Press, 92; Coed, Fiction 2000: Cyberpunk and the Future of Narrative, Univ Ga Press, 93; Ed, The Oxford Book of Fantasy Stories, Oxford Univ Press, 94; Consult ed, Magills Guide to Science Fiction and Fantasy Literature, Salem Press, 96. **CONTACT ADDRESS** St Edward's Univ, 3001 S Congress Ave, Austin, TX, 78704-6489.

SHIPPS, ANTHONY WIMBERLY

PERSONAL Born 08/26/1926, Tryon, NC, m, 1949, 1 child **DISCIPLINE** ENGLISH, LIBRARY SCIENCE **EDUCATION** Mercer Univ, AB, 49; Northwestern Univ, MA, 51, PhD(English), 59; Univ Mich, AMLS, 60. **CAREER** Instr English, Wayne State Univ, 54-59; asst librn, Utah State Univ, 60-61; circulation librn, Univ Colo Libr, 61-62, humanities librn, 62-64, head ref dept, 64-67; LIBRN ENGLISH, IND UNIV LIBR, BLOOMINGTON, 67- **MEMBERSHIPS** MLA; Am Libr Asn. **RESEARCH** Literary quotations; English Renaissance. **SELECTED PUBLICATIONS** Auth, Webster,Daniel - Reply/, Notes And Queries, Vol 0040, 1993; Quotations And References In Hardy - Reply/, Notes And Queries, Vol 0040, 1993; Epigraph Of 'Blindness And Insight' - Reply/, Notes And Queries, Vol 0041, 1994; Poem Of World-War-Ii - Reply/, Notes And Queries, Vol 0041, 1994; Sources Wanted - Reply/, Notes And Queries, Vol 0042, 1995. **CONTACT ADDRESS** 2500 E 8th St, Bloomington, IN, 47401.

SHIRES, LINDA MARGUERITE

PERSONAL Born 07/29/1950, Providence, RI, m, 1988, 4 children **DISCIPLINE** ENGLISH LITERATURE **EDUCATION** Wheaton Coll, BA, 72; Brown Univ, MA, 73; Oxford Univ, BA, Post Grad Eng, 77; Princeton Univ, PhD, Eng, 81. **CAREER** Asst prof, ENG, Syracuse Univ, 81-88; assoc prof, Syracuse Univ, 88-96; vis prof, Princeton Univ, 90-92; vis prof, New York Univ, 97-98; PROF, ENG, SYRACUSE UNIV, 96-. **RESEARCH** 19th Century Literature & Culture; Criticism & Social Theory; narration & Film theory; Gender studies **SELECTED PUBLICATIONS** British Poetry of the Second World War, St. Martin's Press; 85; Rewriting the Victorians: History, Theory and the Politics of Gender, Routledge Press, 92; coauth, Telling Stories: A Theoretical Analysis of Narrative Fiction, Routledge, 96; edr, The Trumpet-Major, Penguin Press, 98. **CONTACT ADDRESS** Hall of Languages, Rm 401, Syracuse Univ, Syracuse, NY, 13210. **EMAIL** lmshires@aol.com

SHIRINIAN, LORNE

DISCIPLINE ARMENIAN-NORTH AMERICAN LITERATURE **EDUCATION** Univ of Montreal, PhD. **RESEARCH** Armenian-North American Lit; multiculturism; film noir, hard-boiled fiction, cinema and the cinematic adaptation of literary works. **SELECTED PUBLICATIONS** Auth, In a Dark Light: David Goodis and Film Noir; auth, Writing Memory: The Search for Home in Armenian Diaspora Literature and Film; auth, Survivor Memoirs and Photographs of the Armenian's Genocide. **CONTACT ADDRESS** Dept of English, Royal Military Col Canada, 323 Massey Bldg., PO Box 17000, Kingston, ON, K7K 7B4. **EMAIL** shirinian-l@rmc.ca

SHOAF, RICHARD A.

PERSONAL Born 03/25/1948, m, 2 children **DISCIPLINE** ENGLISH LITERATURE **EDUCATION** Wake Forest Univ, BA, 70; University E Anglia, BA, 72; Cornell Univ, MA, 75; Cornell Univ, PhD, 77. **HONORS AND AWARDS** Tchg incentive prog award, 94; spec Summer stipend, 95; selected distinguished tchr in the region, SAADE, 96; winner of an inaugural professional excellence program, 96; **MEMBERSHIPS** Mem, The South Atlantic MLA; Medieval Acad Am; Dante Soc Am; The John Gower Soc; Milton Soc Am; Amer Assn Italian Stud; Omicron Delta Kappa; Phi Beta Kappa. **RESEARCH** Medieval and Renaissance poetry. **SELECTED PUBLICATIONS** Auth, Dante, Chaucer, and the Currency of the Word: Money, Images, and Reference in Late Medieval Poetry, Pilgrim Bk(s), 83; The Poem as Green Girdle: Commercium in Sir Gawain and the Green Knight, Humanities Monographs Series, Fla Univ Press, 84; Milton, Poet of Duality: A Study of Semiosis in the Poetry and the Prose, Yale Univ Press, 85; All Information is Already in Formation: The Internet and Learned Journals, The Politics and Processes of Scholarship, Greenwood Press, 95; Allegory and Realism, Dante Encycl, Garland, 97; Business Life, Chaucer Encycl, Variorum Chaucer, 97; Critical Approaches to Middle English Literature, Medieval England: An Encyclopedia, Garland, 98; rev(s), Richard Kay, Dante's Christian Astrology, Choice, 94; Steven Botterill, Dante and the Mystical Tradition: Bernard of Clairvaux in the Commedia, Choice 95; James Paxson, The Poetics of Personification, Style, 95; Margo Swiss and David A. Kent, Heirs of Fame: Milton and Writers of the English Renaissance, Choice, 95; Lana Cable, Carnal Rhetoric: Milton's Iconoclasm and the Poetics of Desire, Choice, 95; Prue Shaw, Dante Monarchia, Bryn Mawr Medieval Rev, 96; Monica Brzezinski Potkay and Regula Meyer Evitt, Minding the Body: Women and Literature in the Middle Ages, Choice, 97; Chaucer: Life and Times (CD-ROM), Primary Source Media 95, Choice, 97; Amilcare Iannucci, Dante: Contemporary Perspectives, Choice, 97. **CONTACT ADDRESS** Dept of Eng, Univ Fla, 226 Tigert Hall, Gainesville, FL, 32611. **EMAIL** rashoaf@english.ufl.edu

SHOEMAKER, MELVIN H.

PERSONAL Born 02/11/1940, Jay County, IN, m, 1961, 3 children **DISCIPLINE** NEW TESTAMENT BIBLICAL LITERATURE; BIBLICAL THEOLOGY **EDUCATION** Indiana Wesleyan University, AB, 62; Hewbrew Seminar in Israel, Univ of Wisconsin, Graduate Studies, 66; Asbury Theological Seminary, MDiv, 67; Drew Univ, MPhil, 88; Fuller theological seminary, Pasadena, CA, D Min, 97. **CAREER** Instr, 66-67, Indiana Wesleyan Univ; prof, 79-84, Barlesville Wesleyan Col; prof, 86- , CP Haggard Sch of Theology, Dir, 95- , Azusa Pacific Univ. **HONORS AND AWARDS** Biographical listings in Dictionary of International Biography, 79; Who's Who in Religion, 92; Alphi Chi Teacher of the Year at Azusa Pacific Univ, 93; Who's Who in the West, 97; Who's Who in America, 99. **MEMBERSHIPS** Wesleyan Theological Soc, 80-82, 91-present; APU Honors Program Task Force/Council, 91-present; APU Eucation Council, 94-present; Soc of Biblical Lit, 87-present; International Soc of Theta Phi; Advisory Council for the Oxford Honors Semester of the Coalition for Christian Colleges & Universities, 97-2000; International Education Committee of the National Collegiate Honors Council 97-2000; Small College Honors Programs Committee of the National Collegiate Honors Council, 97-2000 **RESEARCH** NT Biblical Literature and theology; gospels. **SELECTED PUBLICATIONS** Auth, Good News to the Poor in Luke's Gospel, Connection, 94; King, Christ as, Lamb, Lamb of God, Life, Priest, Christ as, Baker BookHouse, 96; Discipling Generation X, Fuller Theological Seminary, 97; Jesus Used Headline News in His Preaching, Decision, Nov 98. **CONTACT ADDRESS** Azusa Pacific Univ, 901 E Alosta, Azusa, CA, 91702-7000. **EMAIL** mshoemaker@apu.edu

SHOEMAKER, PAMELA J.

PERSONAL Born 10/25/1950, Chillicothe, OH, d, 1 child **DISCIPLINE** MASS COMMUNICATIONS **EDUCATION** Ohio Univ, BS, 72, MS, 72; Univ of Wis-Madison, PhD, 82. **CAREER** Dept grad adviser, dept of journalism, 84-87, asst prof, 82-87, assoc prof 87-91, Univ of Tex at Austin; prof & dir of journalism, school of journalism, Ohio State Univ, 91-94; JOHN BEN SNOW PROF, SINEWHOUSE SCHOOL OF PUBLIC COMMUN, SYRACUSE UNIV, 94-. **HONORS AND AWARDS** Fel to the John A. Beul Centennial Prof in Commun, summer 84, fel to the Amon G. Carter Jr. Centennial Prof in Commmun, Univ of Tex, Austin, 86-87; Krieghbaum Under-40 Award, Assoc for Ed in Journalism and Mass Commun, 90. **MEMBERSHIPS** Coun of Commun Asns; Coun of Presidents of Nat Journalism Orgs; ICC; SCA; AAPOR; IAMGR; APSA; Midwest Asn for Public Opinion Res. **RESEARCH** Mass Communications; gatekeeping; media sociology; political communications; media public opinion. **SELECTED PUBLICATIONS** Coauth, Korean-language edition of Mediating the Message: Theories of Influences on Mass Media Content, NANAM Pub House, 97; coauth, Mediating the Message: Theories of Influences on Mass Media Content, Longman, 91 & 96; coauth, La Mediatizacion del Mensaje: Teorias de Las Influencias en el Contenido de los Medios de Comunicacion, Editorial Diana, 94; auth, Hard-wired for News: Using Biological and Cultural Evolution to Explain the News, J of Commun, 96; coauth, Communication in Crisis: Theory, Curricula and Power, J of Commun, 93; auth, Critical Thinking for Mass Communication Students, Critical Studies in Mass Commun, 93; auth, Reconsidering the Role of Scholarship, ASJMC Insights, 93. **CONTACT ADDRESS** Newhouse School of Public Commun, Syracuse Univ, Syracuse, NY, 13244-2100. **EMAIL** snowshoe@syr.edu

SHOKOFF, JAMES

PERSONAL Born 08/18/1935, Teaneck, NJ, m, 1962, 2 children **DISCIPLINE** ENGLISH LITERATURE, FILM **EDUCATION** Rutgers Univ, BA, 60; Columbia Univ, MA, 65; Univ Ill, Urbana PhD(English), 70. **CAREER** Teacher English, Benjamin Franklin High Sch, New York, 62-66; teaching asst, Univ Ill, Urbana, 66-68, instr, 68-70; asst prof, 70-73, ASSOC PROF ENGLISH, STATE UNIV NY COL FREDONIA, 73-, Managing ed, Drama & Theatre, 71-75. **RESEARCH** English Romantic literature; film study; comedy. **SELECTED PUBLICATIONS** Auth, Wordsworth Duty As A Poet In 'We Are Seven' And 'Surprised By Joy'/, J Of English And Ger Philol, Vol 0093, 1994. **CONTACT ADDRESS** Dept of English, State Univ of NY Col, 1 Suny at Fredonia, Fredonia, NY, 14063-1143.

SHORES, DAVID LEE
PERSONAL Born 01/28/1933, Tangier, VA, m, 1956, 2 children **DISCIPLINE** ENGLISH, LINGUISTICS **EDUCATION** Randolph-Macon Col, BA, 55; George Peabody Col, MA, 56, EdS, 64, PhD(English), 66. **CAREER** Instr English & Ger, Richard Bland Col, Col William & Mary, 61-62; from asst prof to assoc prof, 66-70, dir freshman English, 70-73, grad prog dir English, 73-75, chmn dept, 75-80, PROF ENGLISH, OLD DOMINION UNIV, 70-, Instr & assoc dir, US Off Educ Inst Col English Instr Black Cols, 70-73; consult, Nat Teachers Exam, Educ Testing Serv, 72-73. **MEMBERSHIPS** MLA; SAtlantic Mod Lang Asn; NCTE; Am Dialect Soc; Southeast Conf Ling. **RESEARCH** Old and Middle English language and literature; Chaucer; English linguistics. **SELECTED PUBLICATIONS** Auth, More On Porchmouth + Va Tidewater Pronunciation/, Am Speech, Vol 0069, 1994. **CONTACT ADDRESS** Dept of English, Old Dominion Univ, Norfolk, VA, 23508.

SHORTER, ROBERT NEWLAND
PERSONAL Born 05/11/1931, Canton, OH, m, 1957, 1 child **DISCIPLINE** ENGLISH **EDUCATION** Union Col, NY, AB; Duke Univ, MA, 58, PhD, 64. **CAREER** From instr to assoc prof, 58-77, prof English, 77-, chemn English dept, 75-, assoc dean grad sch, 95, Wake Forest Univ, 77-. **MEMBERSHIPS** MLA **RESEARCH** Chaucer; medieval drama. **SELECTED PUBLICATIONS** Auth, Becket as Job: T S Eliot's Murder in the Cathedral, SAtlantic Quart, fall 68. **CONTACT ADDRESS** Dept English, Wake Forest Univ, PO Box 7387, Winston Salem, NC, 27109-7387. **EMAIL** shorterr@wfu.edu

SHOUT, JOHN
DISCIPLINE ENGLISH **EDUCATION** Oberlin Col, BA; Univ MI, MA; PhD, 74. **CAREER** Eng Dept, Plattsburgh State Univ **RESEARCH** Drama and theater hist; musical theater. **SELECTED PUBLICATIONS** Auth, publ(s) about drama and theater hist. **CONTACT ADDRESS** SUNY, Plattsburgh, 101 Broad St, Plattsburgh, NY, 12901-2681.

SHOWALTER, ELAINE
DISCIPLINE 19TH AND 20TH CENTURY FICTION **EDUCATION** UC Davis, PhD, 70. **CAREER** Author **RESEARCH** Feminist criticism; history of psychiatry; popular history. **SELECTED PUBLICATIONS** Auth, A Literature of Their Own: British Women; Novelists from Bronte to Lessing; The Female Malady: Women Madness, and Society 1830-1980; Sexual Anarchy; Sister's Choice: Tradition and Change in American Women's Writing. **CONTACT ADDRESS** 45 Mc Cosh Hall, Princeton, NJ, 08544.

SHUCARD, ALAN ROBERT
PERSONAL Born 12/02/1935, Brooklyn, NY, m, 1962, 1 child **DISCIPLINE** AMERICAN & ENGLISH LITERATURE **EDUCATION** Union Col, NY, AB, 57; Univ Conn, MA, 63; Univ Ariz, PhD, 71. **CAREER** Instr II English, Univ BC, 65-70; from Asst Prof to Assoc Prof, 70-86, prof English, Univ of Wis Parkside, 86-. **HONORS AND AWARDS** Wis Alumni Res Found grant, 72; Fulbright Fel, 80-81; SE Wis Educ Hall of Fame, 98. **MEMBERSHIPS** MLA; Soc Values Higher Educ; Am Studies Asn. **RESEARCH** Modern poetry; Afro-American literature; American literature. **SELECTED PUBLICATIONS** Auth, The Gorgon Bag, 70 & The Louse on the Head of a Yawning Lord, 72, Ladysmith, Que; Mari Evans, Kenneth Leslie & Stanley Moss, in Contemporary Poets, 2nd ed, St James, London, 74; Tantalus, Sysyphus, and Kafka, Chronicle Higher Educ, 12/76; A J Cronin & Alec Waugh, in Contemp Novelists, 77; The contribution of faculty development to the humanities, Lib Educ, 12/77; Gwendolyn Brooks, Walter Van Tilburg Clark & Paul Laurence Dunbar, in Writers in English, 78; Countee Cullen, 84; American Poetry Puritans Through Walt Whitman, 90; Modern American Poetry, 1865-1950, 89. **CONTACT ADDRESS** Div of Humanities, Univ of Wis Parkside, Box 2000, Kenosha, WI, 53141-2000. **EMAIL** shucard@uwp.edu

SHUFFELTON, FRANK
DISCIPLINE ENGLISH **EDUCATION** Stanford Univ, PhD. **CAREER** Prof; taught at, Stanford Univ. **HONORS AND AWARDS** Mellon Fac fel& NEH sr fel. **MEMBERSHIPS** Pres, Northeast Am Soc for 18th-century Stud, 94-95; served on ed bd(s), Early Am Lit & Stud 18th-century Cult; exec bd, MLA Div Am Lit to 1800, 94-99. **RESEARCH** Am lit; hist; cult from the Puritans through the writers of the Am Renaissance and later. **SELECTED PUBLICATIONS** Auth, Thomas Hooker, 1586-1647; Thomas Jefferson: A Comprehensive, Annotated Bibliography; Thomas Jefferson, 1981-1990: An Annotated Bibliography; ed, A Mixed Race: Ethnicity in Early America; The American Enlightenment; aricles on, early and 19th-century Amer lit, Anne Bradstreet's Contemplations, character and narrative in early Amer hist writing, writing Jefferson biog & 18th-century travelers' recognition of an African Amer cult presence. **CONTACT ADDRESS** Dept of Eng, Univ of Rochester, 601 Elmwood Ave, Ste. 656, Rochester, NY, 14642. **EMAIL** fcsh@troi.cc.rochester.edu

SHUGER, DEBORA
PERSONAL Born 12/15/1953, New York, NY, m, 1973, 1 child **DISCIPLINE** ENGLISH LITERATURE **EDUCATION** Vanderbilt Univ, BA, 75, MA, 78, MAT, 78; Stanford Univ, PhD, 83. **CAREER** Asst prof, Univ Mich, 82-88; assoc prof, Univ Arkansas, 88-89; prof, Univ Calif, Los Angeles, 89- . **HONORS AND AWARDS** Rocekfeller Fel, Natl Hum Ctr, 87-88; Guggenheim fel, 91-92; UCLA Pres Fel, 91-92; NEH fel 97-98. **MEMBERSHIPS** MLA; RSA. **RESEARCH** Tudor-Stuart literature and culture; early modern religion, politics, and law. **SELECTED PUBLICATIONS** Auth, The Renaissance Bible: Scholarship, Subjectivity, and Sacrifice, California, 94; auth, Subversive Fathers and Suffering Subjects: Shakespeare and Christianity, in Strier, ed, Religion, Literature, and Politics in Post-Reformation England, 1540-1688, Cambridge, 95; co-ed and contribur, Religion and Culture in Early Modern England, Cambridge, 97; auth, Irishmen, Aristocrats, and Other White Barbarians, Renaissance Q, 97; auth, Castigating Livy: The Rape of Lucretia and the Old Arcadia, Renaissance Q, 98; auth, Civility and Censorship in Early Modern England, in Post, ed, Censorship and Silencing, Getty Research Inst, 98; auth, Gums of Glutinous Heat and the Stream of Consciousness: The Theology of Milton's Maske, Representations, 98. **CONTACT ADDRESS** Dept of English, Univ of California, Los Angeles, 405 Hilgard Ave, Los Angeles, CA, 90095-1530. **EMAIL** shuger@humnet.ucla.edu

SHULMAN, JEFFREY
DISCIPLINE ENGLISH LITERATURE **EDUCATION** Univ Md, BA; Univ Wis, MA, PhD. **CAREER** Eng Dept, Georgetown Univ **RESEARCH** Renaissance literature; Elizabethan and Jacobean drama; Restoration comedy. **SELECTED PUBLICATIONS** Auth, pubs in English Lit Hist; Studies English Lit; Classical Jour. **CONTACT ADDRESS** English Dept, Georgetown Univ, 37th and O St, Washington, DC, 20057.

SHUMAN, R. BAIRD
PERSONAL Born 06/20/1929, Paterson, NJ **DISCIPLINE** ENGLISH, EDUCATION **EDUCATION** Lehigh Univ, AB, 51; Temple Univ, EdM, 53; Univ Vienna, cert, 54; Univ Pa, PhD, 61. **CAREER** Asst instr English, Univ Pa, 55-57; instr humanities, Drexel Inst Technol, 57-59: asst prof English, San Jose State Col, 59-62; from asst prof to prof educ, Duke Univ, 62-77; PROF ENGLISH & DIR ENGLISH EDUC, UNIV ILL, URBANA-CHAMPAIGN, 77-, DIR FRESHMAN RHETORIC, 79-, Lectr Am lit, Linz Sem Austrian Teachers, Austria, 53; univ scholar, Univ Pa, 56; vis lectr English, Moore Inst Art, 58; vis prof humanities, Philadelphia Conserv Music, 58-59, King Faisal Univ, Saudi Arabia, 78, 81, East Tenn State Univ, 80, Bread Loaf Sch English, Middlebury Col, 80; consult, Am Col Testing Prog & NC Dept Pub Instr, 75-, Kans State Col, Pittsburg, 80, Univ Ark, Little Rock, 80, Nat Univ Singapore, 81; exec ed, The Clearing House, 75-; contribr ed, Reading Horizons, 75-80; consult ed, Poet Lore, 76-, Cygnus, 78-, J Aethetic Ed, 78-82; ed, Speaking out column, The Clearing House, 76- **MEMBERSHIPS** MLA; NCTE; Int Asn Univ Prof English; Conf English Educ; Conf Col Comp & Commun. **RESEARCH** The teaching of writing and the teaching of reading; humanities education; educational drama. **SELECTED PUBLICATIONS** Auth, Signifying As A Scaffold For Literary Interpretation - The Pedagogical Implications Of An African-Am Discourse Genre - Lee,Cd/, African Am Rev, Vol 0029, 1995. **CONTACT ADDRESS** Box 1687, Champaign, IL, 61820.

SHUMWAY, DAVID R.
DISCIPLINE LITERATURE **EDUCATION** Univ Pittsburgh, PhD. **CAREER** Lit, Carnegie Mellon Univ. **SELECTED PUBLICATIONS** Area: Victorian literature. **CONTACT ADDRESS** Carnegie Mellon Univ, 5000 Forbes Ave, Pittsburgh, PA, 15213.

SHUMWAY, ERIC BRANDON
PERSONAL Born 11/08/1939, Holbrook, AZ, m, 1963, 7 children **DISCIPLINE** ENGLISH LITERATURE & POLYNESIAN LANGUAGES **EDUCATION** Brigham Young Univ, BA, 64, MA, 66; Univ VA, PhD, 73. **CAREER** From instr to assoc prof, 66-78, prof eng, Brigham Young Univ, HI, 78. **RESEARCH** Browning's love poetry; love in 19th century lit; the Tongan oral tradition. **SELECTED PUBLICATIONS** Auth, Intensive Course in Tongan, Univ HI, 71, rev, Inst of Polynesian Studies, with tapes, 88; Coe Ta'ane: A Royal Marriage (video doc), fall 76 & The Punake of Tonga (video doc), fall 77, Brigham Young Univ-HI; The eulogistic function of the Tongan poet, Pac Studies, fall 77; Tonga Saints: Legacy of Fartl, Inst for Polynesian Studies, 91; Koe Fakapangai: In the Circle of the Sovereign, 93 (video doc). **CONTACT ADDRESS** 55-220 Kulanui St, Laie, HI, 96762-1294. **EMAIL** shumwaye@byuh.edu

SHURR, WILLIAM HOWARD
PERSONAL Born 08/29/1932, Evanstan, IL, m, 1968, 1 child **DISCIPLINE** AMERICAN LITERATURE **EDUCATION** Loyola Univ Chicago, AB, 55, PhL, 58, MA, 59, STL, 64; Univ NC, Chapel Hill, PhD(English), 68. **CAREER** Asst prof English, Univ Tenn, 68-72; assoc prof, Wash State Univ, 72-75, prof, 75-81; PROF ENGLISH, UNIV TENN, KNOXVILLE, 81-, Reader, Publ Mod Lang Asn Am, 71- **HONORS AND AWARDS** SAtlantic Mod Lang Asn Prize Manuscript, 72. **MEMBERSHIPS** MLA; Melville Soc; Hopkins Soc; Am Studies Asn (regional pres, 79-81). **RESEARCH** American literature; general world literature; history of theology. **SELECTED PUBLICATIONS** Auth, Irving And Whitman - Re-Historicizing The Figure Of Columbus In 19th-Century Am/, Am Transcendental Quart, Vol 0006, 1992; Bending The Rules - What Am Priests Tell Am-Catholics - Bowman,J/, Soundings, Vol 0078, 1995. **CONTACT ADDRESS** Dept of English, Univ of Tenn, Knoxville, TN, 37916.

SHUSTERMAN, RICHARD
DISCIPLINE LIBERAL STUDIES **EDUCATION** Oxford Univ, PhD, 79. **CAREER** Fac, Pierre Bourdieu and Col Internationale de Philosophie, present; prof pholos, Temple Univ, present; vis sr lctr liberal sutdies, Eugene Lang Col. **RESEARCH** Am and French philos. **SELECTED PUBLICATIONS** Auth, Pragmatic Aesthetics; Practicing Philosophy; essays and books include studies of T.S. Eliot's poems and of the analytic philosophy of art. **CONTACT ADDRESS** Eugene Lang Col, New Sch for Social Research, 66 West 12th St, New York, NY, 10011.

SHUTER, BILL
DISCIPLINE THE ROMANTIC REBELLION IN BRITAIN **EDUCATION** PhD. **CAREER** E Mich Univ **SELECTED PUBLICATIONS** Auth, Rereading Walter Pater, Cambridge Univ Press. **CONTACT ADDRESS** Eastern Michigan Univ, Ypsilanti, MI, 48197. **EMAIL** ENG_Shuter@online.emich.edu

SHUTTLEWORTH, JACK M.
PERSONAL Born 10/24/1935, Covington, OH, m, 1956, 3 children **DISCIPLINE** ENGLISH LITERATURE; AMERICAN LITERATURE **EDUCATION** Ohio Wesleyan Univ, BA, 57; Stanford Univ, MA, 64; Univ Denver, PhD(English lit), 68. **CAREER** Instr English, Prep Sch, 64-65, from asst prof to assoc prof, 67-77, PROF ENGLISH & HEAD DEPT, US AIR FORCE ACAD, 77-, Chmn, Humanities Div, 96-; Lectr English, Univ Colo, Colorado Springs, 68-71; contrib ed, Ann Bibliog English Lang & Lit, Mod Humanities Res Asn, 68-. **MEMBERSHIPS** Mod Humanities Res Asn; Shakespeare Oxford Soc. **RESEARCH** Seventeenth century drama; Herbert of Cherbury; 20th century novel; Shakespeare authorship question. **SELECTED PUBLICATIONS** Co-ed, Satire: Aesop to Buchwald, Odyssey, 71; ed, The Life of Lord Herbert of Cherbury, Oxford Univ, 74; coauth, Practical College Writing, 78 & Writing Research Papers, 80, Holt. **CONTACT ADDRESS** Dept of English, USAF Academy, CO, 80840. **EMAIL** shuttleworthjm.offeng@usafa.edu

SICHERMAN, CAROL MARKS
PERSONAL Born 05/08/1937, Boston, MA, m, 1969, 2 children **DISCIPLINE** ENGLISH LITERATURE **EDUCATION** Barnard Col, BA, 58; Univ WI, MA, 59, PhD, 64; Oxford Univ, BLitt, 62. **CAREER** From instr to asst prof Eng, Cornell Univ, 63-69; asst prof, 69-75, Assoc prof Eng, Lehman Col, 75; prof , Chmn Doctoral prog, Comp Lit, Columbia Univ. **HONORS AND AWARDS** Fel, Ctr Adv Studies in Behavioral Sci, Stanford, 75-76; Guggenheim Fel; Soc Sci Council Fel; Sr Fel, Natl Endowment Hum, 81. **MEMBERSHIPS** MLA; Renaissance Soc Am; AAUP. **RESEARCH** Shakespeare; 17th century poetry; metrics. **SELECTED PUBLICATIONS** Auth, Thomas Traherne and Christian Platonism, PMLA, 66; coed, Christian Ethicks, Cornell Univ, 68; auth, Donne's Discoveries, Studies English Lit, 71; Coriolanus: The Failure of Words, ELH, 72; Bellow's Seize the Day: Reverberations and Hollow Sounds, Studies Twentieth Century, 75; contribr, Donne's Timeless Anniversaries, In: Essential Articles for the Study of John Donne's Poetry, Archon, 75; King Hal: The integrity of Shakespeare's portrait, Texas Studies in Lit & Lang, 79; Meter and meaning in Shakespeare, Lang & Style, 82; After the Last Sky, Pantheon, 86; Blaming the Victims: Spurious Scholarship and the Palestinian Question, Verso Methuen, 87; Culture and Imperialism, Alfred A. Knopf, 93; The Pen and the Sword: Conversations with David Barasamin, Common Courage Press, 94; Peace and Its Discontents: Essays on Palestine in the Middle East Peace Process, Vintage, 95; Not Quite Right: A Memoir, Alfred Knopf, 98-99. **CONTACT ADDRESS** Dept of Eng, Lehman Col, CUNY, 250 Bedford Park W, Bronx, NY, 10468-1527.

SICKER, PHILIP
DISCIPLINE 20TH CENTURY BRITISH AND EUROPEAN FICTION **EDUCATION** Univ VA, PhD. **CAREER** Dir, grad stud; assoc prof, Fordham Univ. **SELECTED PUBLICATIONS** Auth, Pale Fire and Lyrical Ballads: The Dynamics of Collaboration, Papers on Language and Literature 28, 92; Lawrence's Auto da Fe: The Grand Inquisition in The Plumed Serpent, Comp Lit Stud 29, 92. **CONTACT ADDRESS** Dept of Eng Lang and Lit, Fordham Univ, 113 W 60th St, New York, NY, 10023.

SIDER, JOHN W.
DISCIPLINE ENGLISH **EDUCATION** Univ Notre Dame, PhD, 71. **CAREER** Adj prof, Santa Barbara City Col, 73-74; adj prof, Jesuit Novitate, 78; asst prof, Bethel Col, 66-68, 70-72; prof, 72-. **HONORS AND AWARDS** Fac res award, 85. **RE-**

SEARCH Brit & Am lit. SELECTED PUBLICATIONS Auth, Interpreting the Parables: A Hermeneutical Guide to Their Meaning, Zondervan, 95; One Man in His Time Plays Many Parts, Authorial Theatrics of Doubling in Early Renaissance Drama, Stud in Philol, 95; The Parables, The Complete Literary Guide to the Bible, Zondervan, 93. CONTACT ADDRESS Dept of Eng, Westmont Col, 955 La Paz Rd, Santa Barbara, CA, 93108-1099.

SIDNELL, MICHAEL JOHN
PERSONAL Born 09/29/1935, London, England, m, 1958, 4 children **DISCIPLINE** ENGLISH LITERATURE, DRAMA **EDUCATION** Univ London, BA, 56, MA, 61, PhD, 67. **CAREER** From lectr to asst prof English, Mt Allison Univ, 58-64; from asst prof to assoc prof English lit, Trent Univ, 64-69; assoc prof English, Trinity Col, 69-75, dir drama, Grad Ctr for Study Drama, 77-81, PROF ENGLISH, UNIV TORONTO, 75-, Marjorie Young Bell fel, 63; Can Coun res grants, 67, 68, 75, 76, 77, & sr fel, 71-72; vis prof, Grad Sch, York Univ, 68-69; vis scholar, Corpus Christi Col, Cambridge, 79-80; mem, Univs Comn, Int Fedn Theatre Res. **MEMBERSHIPS** Can Asn for Irish Studies; Int Fedn Theatre Res. **RESEARCH** Anglo-Irish literature; theatre; modern poetry and drama. **SELECTED PUBLICATIONS** Auth, Approaching Theater - Helbo,A, Johansen,Jd, Pavis,P, Ubersfeld,A/, Essays In Theatre-Etudes Theatrales, Vol 0011, 1993; Reading Plays, Interpretation And Reception - Scolnicov,H, Holland,P/, Essays In Theatre-Etudes Theatrales, Vol 0011, 1993; Theories Of The Theater - A Hist And Critical Survey, From The Greeks To The Present - Carlson,M/, Essays In Theatre-Etudes Theatrales, Vol 0013, 1994; Performing Writing - Inscribing Theater/, Modern Drama, Vol 0039, 1996; Selected Plays Of Macneice,Louis - Heuser,A, Mcdonald,P/, English Studies In Can, Vol 0022, 1996. **CONTACT ADDRESS** Dept of English, Trinity Col, Univ of Toronto, Toronto, ON, M5S 1H8.

SIEBENSCHUH, WILLIAM R.
PERSONAL Born 08/27/1942, Chicago, IL, m, 1965, 2 children **DISCIPLINE** ENGLISH LITERATURE, COMPOSITION **EDUCATION** Grinnell Col, BA, 64; Univ Calif, MA, 66; PhD, 70. **CAREER** Asst prof English, Fordham Univ, 71-78; asst prof, 78-80, prof Eng, Case Western Reserve Univ, 80-, dir compos & writing ctr, 80-. **RESEARCH** Biography-autobiography; Johnson and Boswell; the novel. **SELECTED PUBLICATIONS** Coauth, The Struggle for Modern Tibert: The Autobiography of Tasli Tsering, M.E. Sharpe, 97. **CONTACT ADDRESS** Case Western Reserve Univ, 10900 Euclid Ave, Cleveland, OH, 44106-4901. **EMAIL** wrs2@p.o.cwru.edu.

SIEBERT, HILARY
DISCIPLINE TEACHING WRITING, TEACHER TRAINING, THE SHORT STORY, AND AMERICAN LITERATUR **EDUCATION** Univ IA, BA, PhD; Middlebury Col, MA. **CAREER** Prof, Radford Univ. **SELECTED PUBLICATIONS** Publ articles on tchg writing and lit and on the short story, partic the stories of Raymond Carver. **CONTACT ADDRESS** Radford Univ, Radford, VA, 24142. **EMAIL** hsiebert@runet.edu

SIEGEL, ADRIENNE
PERSONAL Born 06/10/1936, New York, NY, m, 1972 **DISCIPLINE** AMERICAN HISTORY, POPULAR LITERATURE **EDUCATION** Univ Pa, BS, 57; Columbia Univ, MA, 59; New York Univ, PhD(hist), 73. **CAREER** Teacher, James Madison High Sch, 62-82; asst prof hist, Long Island Univ, 77-93: Fel, New York Univ, 71-72; assoc, Danforth Found, 72-82; Fulbright fel India, 78; fel, Inst Res in Hist, 81-82; ASST PROF, CITY UNIV NY, COL STATEN ISLAND, 93-. **HONORS AND AWARDS** Phi Delta Kappa Scholarship, 90; Phi Delta Kappa Chapter Editor & Fdn Rep, 88-93; Phi Delta Kappa Cert Rec, 89; NY Univ Alumnae Award, 74; Bronx Educ Endowment Fund Board 84-93. **MEMBERSHIPS** Orgn Am Historians; Popular Cult Asn. **RESEARCH** History of the American city. **SELECTED PUBLICATIONS** Auth, When cities were fun, J Popular Cult, 75; Philadelphia: A Chronological and Documentary History, Oceana, 75; Brothels, bets and bars, NDak Quart, 76; The Image of the American City in Popular Literature, Kennikat, 81; auth, The Marshall Court, Associated Faculty Press, 87; auth, Visions for the Reconstruction of the NYC School System, in Urban Education, Jan 86; auth, Incubator of Dreams: Directing College Guidance at America's Most Elite Minority High School, Education, Winter 89; auth, A Case for Colaboratives: Turning Around Bronx Public Schools, Urban Review, 88; auth, Mission Possible: The Rescue of Bronx Public Schools, Phi Delta Kappa Fastback, 88; auth, Don't Wait, Communicate: Helping Teachers to Talk Shop, The Effective School Report, 87; auth, Collective Dreams or Urban Realities: Psychohistory, Persons & Communities, 83; auth, The Myth of Mobility in the Media of Another Century, in The Many Faces of Psychohistory, Intl. Psychohistorical Assn, 84. **CONTACT ADDRESS** 330 W Jersey St, Elizabeth, NJ, 07202. **EMAIL** Siegel@postbox.CSI.CUNY.edu

SIEGEL, CAROL
DISCIPLINE MODERN BRITISH AND VICTORIAN LITERATURE **EDUCATION** Univ Calif at Berkeley, PhD. **CAREER** Assoc prof, Washington State Univ. **RESEARCH** Modern British and Victorian Literature, women writers, and feminist theory **SELECTED PUBLICATIONS** Auth, D. H. Lawrence Among the Women: Wavering Boundaries in Women's Literary Traditions, 91 & Male Masochism: Modern Revisions of the Story of Love, 95; co-ed, spec issues of Genders: Eroticism and Containment and Forming and Reforming Identity. **CONTACT ADDRESS** Dept of English, Washington State Univ, 1 SE Stadium Way, PO Box 645020, Pullman, WA, 99164-5020. **EMAIL** siegel@mail.wsu.edu

SIEGEL, GERALD
DISCIPLINE LITERATURE **EDUCATION** Western Md Col, BA; George Washington Univ, PhD. **HONORS AND AWARDS** Fulbright lect, Macedonia, Belguim; **RESEARCH** Middle-Eurean tales of terror. **CONTACT ADDRESS** York Col, Pennsylvania, 441 Country Club Road, York, PA, 17403.

SIEGEL, JOEL E.
DISCIPLINE ENGLISH LITERATURE **EDUCATION** Cornell Univ, BA; Northwestern Univ, Mam PhD. **CAREER** Eng Dept, Georgetown Univ **HONORS AND AWARDS** Fiction Award, 63; Washington Dateline Awd, 89; Grammy Awd, 93. **MEMBERSHIPS** Am Soc Composers; Artists and Publishers; Nat Soc Recording Arts and Sci. **SELECTED PUBLICATIONS** Auth, Val Lewton: The Reality of Terror, Viking, 73; pubs in City Paper, Film Heritage, December, American Film Institute Magazine, Premiere, Bright Lights, Washingtonian Magazine. **CONTACT ADDRESS** English Dept, Georgetown Univ, 37th and O St, Washington, DC, 20057.

SIEGEL, PAUL N.
PERSONAL Born 06/24/1916, Paterson, NJ, m, 1948, 1 child **DISCIPLINE** ENGLISH LITERATURE **EDUCATION** City Col NY, BS, 36; Harvard Univ, AM, 39, PhD, 41. **CAREER** Instr, Univ Conn, 46; instr, City Col NY, 46-49; from assoc prof to prof English, Ripon Col, 49-56; chmn dept, 56-71, prof, 56-78, EMER PROF ENGLISH, LONG ISLAND UNIV, 78-, Ford Found Fund Advan Educ fel, 52-53; ed consult, PMLA, 63-; consult mem, World Ctr Shakespeare Studies, London, 72; mem adv bd, World Ctr Shakespeare Studies, US, 72-; Columbia Univ Sem in the Renaissance. **MEMBERSHIPS** MLA **RESEARCH** Shakespeare; Marxist literary criticism; 20th century novel. **SELECTED PUBLICATIONS** Auth, Shakespearean Tragedy and the Elizabethan Compromise, NY Univ, 57; ed, His Infinite Variety, Lippincott, 63; contribr, Reader's Encycl of Shakespeare, Crowell, 66; auth, Shakespeare in His Time and Ours, Univ Notre Dame, 68; contribr, The Achievement of Isaac Bashevis Singer, Southern Ill Univ, 69; ed, Leon Trotsky on Literature and Art, 70 & Revolution and the 20th-Century Novel, 79, Pathfinder; contribr, Shakespearean Comedy, NY Lit Forum, 80; auth, Shakespeare's English and Roman History Plays, Fairleigh Dickinson Univ, 86; reprinted as The Gathering Storm, Redwords, 92; auth, The Meek and the Militant: Religion and Power Across the World, Zed, 86; auth, The Great Reversal: Politics and Art in Solzhenitsyn, Walnut, 91. **CONTACT ADDRESS** 101 W 85th St, New York, NY, 10024.

SIEMON, JAMES RALPH
PERSONAL Born 11/14/1948, St. Louis, MO, m, 1972, 4 children **DISCIPLINE** ENGLISH LITERATURE **EDUCATION** Washington Univ, AB, 70; State Univ NY Buffalo, MA, 76, PhD(English), 77. **CAREER** Asst prof English, Boston Univ, 77-94, prof English, 95-, vis asst prof, Harvard Univ, 81. **MEMBERSHIPS** Shakespeare Asn Am; Int Shakespeare Asn; MLA. **RESEARCH** Shakespeare; Bakhtin, Literary Theory. **SELECTED PUBLICATIONS** Auth, Poetic Contradiction in Resolution and Independence, In: On Contradiction, 74 & Turn our Impressed Lances in Our Eyes: Iconoclasm in King Lear, In: Literature and Iconoclasm: Shakespeare, 76, State Univ NY Press; Shakespearean Iconoclasm, Berkely: Univ of California Press, 85; Nay, that's not next: Othello, V.ii. in Performance, 1760-1900, Shakespeare Quart 37, 86; Dialogial Formalism: Word, Action, and Object in The Spanish Tragedy, Medieval and Renaissance Drama 5, 90; Subjected thus: Utterance, Character, and Richard II, Shakespeare Jahrbuch (DDR) 126, 90; Landlord Not King: Agrarian Change and Inarticulation, in Richard Burt and John Michael Archer, eds, Enclosure Acts: Discourses of Sexuality, Property, and Culture in Early Modern England, Ithaca: Cornell UP, 94; The Word Itself Against the Word: Close Reading After Voloshinov, in Russ McDonald, ed, Shakespeare Reread, Ithaca: Cornell UP, 94; Sporting Kyd, English Literary Renaissance 24, 94; Perplexed beyond Self-explication: Cymbeline and Early Modern/Post-modern Europe, in Derek Roper and Michael Hattaway, eds, Shakespeare in the New Europe, Sheffield: Sheffield UP, 94; ed, Christopher Marlowe, The Jew of Malta, London: A & C Black, 94; auth, Sign, Cause or General Habit: Toward an 'Historicist Ontology' of Character on the Early Modern Stage, in Hugo Keiper, ed, Nominalism and Literary Discourse: New Perspectives, Rodopi Press, 98. **CONTACT ADDRESS** Dept of English, Boston Univ, 236 Bay State Rd, Boston, MA, 02215-1403. **EMAIL** jsiemon@bu.edu

SIGMAN, STUART J.
PERSONAL Born 01/29/1955, Brooklyn, NY **DISCIPLINE** COMMUNICATION **EDUCATION** Univ PA, PhD, 82. **CAREER** Dean, School of Communication, Management and Public Policy, Emerson Col, 98-. **HONORS AND AWARDS** Development grant, State Ed Dept, New York State, 93-94; Eastern Commun Asn Scholar, 93-94; res grant, The Union Inst, Cincinnati, OH, 98-99. **MEMBERSHIPS** Int Commun Asn; Nat Commun Asn. **RESEARCH** Sociolinguitics; ethnography; social theory. **SELECTED PUBLICATIONS** Auth, A Perspective on Social Communication, Lexington Books, 87(Chapter 1 excerpted and reprinted as Social Communication, in John Corner and Jeremy Hawthorne, eds, Communication Studies: An Introductory Reader, 3rd ed, Edward Arnold, 89); toward an Intergration of Diverse Communication Contexts: Commentary on the Chapter by Fry, Alexander, and Fry, in James A Anderson, ed, Communication Yearbook 13, Sage, 90; Descriptive Respnsibility and Cultural Critique, m, Res on Lang and Social Interaction, vol 23, 90; Handling the Discontinuous Aspects of Continuous Social Relationships: Toward Research on the Persistance of Social Forms, Commun Theory, vol 1, no 2, 91; Do Social Approaches To Interpersonal Communication Constitute a Contribution to Communication Theory?, Commun Theory, vol 2, no 4, 92; Regles de Communication, in Lucien Sfez, ed, Dictionnaire Critique de la Communication, vol 2, Presses Universitaires de France, 93; Question: Evidence of What? Answer: Communication, Western J of Commun, 95; Order and Continuity in Human Relationships: A Social Communication Approach to Defining 'Relationship,' in Wendy Leeds-Hurwitz, ed, Social Approaches to Communication, Guilford Press, 95; The Consequentiality of Communication, Lawrence Erlbaum Assocs, 95; with Adam Kendon, Ray L Birdwhistell (1918-1994), Semiotica, vol 112, nos 1-2, 96. **CONTACT ADDRESS** School of Commun, Mgmt, Pub Policy, Emerson Col, 100 Beacon St, Boston, MA, 02116. **EMAIL** ssigman@emerson.edu

SIGNORIELLI, NANCY
PERSONAL Born 07/29/1943, New York, NY, m, 1980, 2 children **DISCIPLINE** COMMUNICATION **EDUCATION** Wilson Col, BA, 65; Queens Col, MA, 67; Univ Pa, PhD, 75. **CAREER** Res Adminr, Annenberg School for Commun, Univ of Pa, 75-87; assoc prof, 87-89, PROF, UNIV DELAWARE, 89-. **MEMBERSHIPS** Int Commun Asn; Nat Commun Asn; Broadcast Ed Asn; Asn for Ed in Journalism & Mass Commun. **RESEARCH** Television images and relationship to people's conceptions about social reality. **SELECTED PUBLICATIONS** Auth, Women in Communication: A Bibliographic Sourcebook, Greenwood Press, 96; Mass Media Images and Impact on Health, Greenwood Press, 93; Health Images on Television, Commun in Medical Ethics, Greenwood Press, 98; coauth, Television and Children's Conceptions of Nutrition, Health Commun, 97; Cultivation Analysis-Research and Practice, An Integrated Approach to Commun Theory and Res, 96; Violence on Television: The Cultural Indicators Project, J of Broadcasting & Electronic Media, 94; Gender Stereotypes in MTV Commercials: The Beat Goes On, J of Broadcasting & Electronic Media, 94; Growing Up With Television: The Cultivation Perspective, Media Effects: Advances in Theory and Res, 94. **CONTACT ADDRESS** Commun Dept, Univ Delaware, Newark, DE, 19716.

SIL, NARASINGHA P.
PERSONAL Born 12/11/1937, Calcutta, m, 1965, 1 child **DISCIPLINE** ENGLISH HISTORY **EDUCATION** Univ Calcutta, MA, 61; Univ Ore, MA, 73; M Ed, 74; PhD, 78. **CAREER** Asst prof, Univ Ore, 78-80; assoc prof, Univ Benin, Nigeria, 80-86; prof, W Ore Univ, 87-. **HONORS AND AWARDS** Dir of Pub Instr Scholarship, 2nd rank BA hist honors exam, Calcutta Univ, 58-59; facul honors award for tchg & scholar, W Ore Univ, 92. **MEMBERSHIPS** Amer Hist Asn; N Amer Conf on Brit Studies; Amer Acad of Relig; Brahmo Samaj of India, Calcutta. **RESEARCH** Administrative/political history of Tudor England; Hindu religious leaders of 19th and early 20th centuries. **SELECTED PUBLICATIONS** Monographs, Ramakrishna Revisited: A New Biography, Lanham, Univ Press of Amer, 98; Swami Vivekananda: A Reassessment, Selinsgrove, Susquehanna Univ Press, Cranbury, Assoc Univ Press, 97; William Lord Herbert of Pembroke (c. 1507-70): Politique and Patriot, 88, 2nd ed, Lewiston, Edwin Mellon Press, 92; Prophet Disarmed: Vivekananda and Nivedita, Monash Asia Inst Working Paper 2, Clayton, Ctr for South Asian Studies, Monash Univ, Australia, 97; articles, Muammar al-Qaddafi, Dict of World Bio: 20th Cent, Pasadena & London, Salem Press & Fitzroy Dearborn Pres, 98; Saradamani's Holy Motherhood: A Reappraisal, Asian Jour of Women's Studies, Ewha Womans Univ, Seoul, Korea, IV, 1, 98; Is Ramakrishna a Vedantin, a Tantrika, or a Vaishnava: An Examination, Asian Studies Rev, Clayton, Victoria, Australia, XXI, 2-3, nov, 97; Asceticism and Misogyny: Vivekananda's Concept of Woman, Asian Culture Quart, Asian-Pacific Cultural Ctr, Taipei, Taiwan, XXV, 2, summer, 97; 1991-1992 Civil War Rages in Yugoslavia, Fall of Granada, Founding of the Jesuits, Revolt of the Catalans, Wat Tyler Leads Peasants' Revolt, Enactment of the Provision of Oxford, King Alfred Defeats the Danes at Edington, Matteo Ricci Travels to Peking as Jesuit Missionary, Great Events from Hist : Europ Series, Rev Ed, Pasadena, Salem Press Inc, 97; Swami Vivekananda in the West: The Legend Reinterpreted, South Asia, Univ of New South Wales, XVIII, 1, jun 95. **CONTACT ADDRESS** Dept. of History, Western Oregon Univ, Monmouth, OR, 97361. **EMAIL** siln@wou.edu

SILCOX, MARY
DISCIPLINE ENGLISH LITERATURE **EDUCATION** Univ Western Ontario, BA; Queen's Univ, MA, PhD. **RESEARCH** 16th and 17th century lit; emblem studies. **SELECTED PUBLICATIONS** Auth, English Emblem Tradition II, 93; co-auth, The Modern Critical Reception of the English Emblem, 91; co-auth, The English Emblem: Bibliography of Secondary Literature, 90. **CONTACT ADDRESS** English Dept, McMaster Univ, 1280 Main St W, Hamilton, ON, L8S 4L9.

SILET, CHARLES LORING PROVINE
PERSONAL Born 04/25/1942, Chicago, IL, m, 1976, 4 children **DISCIPLINE** AMERICAN STUDIES, LITERATURE **EDUCATION** Butler Univ, BA, 66; Ind Univ, MA, 68, PhD(English & Am studies), 73. **CAREER** Instr, 73-74, asst prof, 74-79 PROF ENGLISH, IOWA STATE UNIV, 79-, Dir Grad Studies, Dept English, Iowa State Univ, 81- **MEMBERSHIPS** MLA; Am Studies Asn; Midcontinent Am Studies Asn. **RESEARCH** American culture and literature 1880-1930; contemporary cinema; bibliography. **SELECTED PUBLICATIONS** Auth, Fuller,Henry,Blake - Further Additions And Corrections/, Resources For Am Literary Study, Vol 0019, 1993; Hitchcock Rereleased Films - From 'Rope' To 'Vertigo' - Raubicheck,W, Srebnick,W/, Film Criticism, Vol 0018, 1993; Matthews,Brander, Roosevelt,Theodore And The Politics Of Am Lit, 1880-1920 - Oliver,Lj/, J Of Am Hist, Vol 0080, 1993; The Hunt For Willie-Boy - Indian-Hating And Popular-Cult - Sandos,Ja, Burgess,Le/, J Of Am Hist, Vol 0082, 1995. **CONTACT ADDRESS** Dept of English, Iowa State Univ, Ames, IA, 50011-0002.

SILL, GEOFFREY M.
PERSONAL Born 10/05/1944, Cleveland, OH **DISCIPLINE** ENGLISH LITERATURE **EDUCATION** Pa State Univ, PhD, 74. **CAREER** Assoc prof, Rutgers Univ, 74- . **MEMBERSHIPS** Am Soc for 18th Century Studies **RESEARCH** 18th century Brit novel; Daniel Defoe; Med and lit. **SELECTED PUBLICATIONS** Auth, Defoe and the Idea of Fiction, 83; The Authorship of An Impartial History of Michael Servetus, PBSA 87, 93; Crusoe in the Cave: Defoe and the Semiotics of Desire, Eighteenth-Century Fiction 6, 94; Swift's As Sure as God's in Gloc'ster and the Assurance of the Moderns, Notes and Queries 240, 95; Neurology and the Novel: Alexander Monro, Robinson Crusoe, and the Problem of Sensibility, Literatue and Medicine 16, 97; The Source of Robinson Crusoe's Sudden Joys, Notes and Queries 243, 98; coed, Walt Whitman and the Visual Arts, 92; The Witlings and The Woman-Hater, 97; ed, Walt Whitman of Mickle Street: A Centennnial Collection, 94. **CONTACT ADDRESS** Dept of English, Rutgers Univ, 311 N 5th St., Camden, NJ, 08102. **EMAIL** sill@camden.rutgers.edu

SILLARS, MALCOLM O.
PERSONAL Born 02/12/1928, Union City, NJ, m, 1948, 3 children **DISCIPLINE** SPEECH **EDUCATION** Univ Redlands, BA, 48, MA, 49; State Univ IA, PhD, 55. **CAREER** Instr speech, IA State Univ, 49-54; instr, Los Angeles State Col, 54-56; from asst prof to assoc prof speech, San Fernando Valley State Col, 56-61, prof, 62-71, chmn dept, 56-63 & 66-68, assoc dean sch lett & sci, 63-66, actg dean, 69-70, actg pres, 69; prof commun, Univ Mass, Amherst, 71-74; dean, Col Humanities, 74-81, prof commun, Univ UT, 74-98, Res assoc, Univ IL, 61-62; assoc ed, Quart J Speech, 63-66; chmn educ policies bd, Speech Commun Asn, 70-71, chmn awards comt, 72, mem finance bd, 74-76, vis prof, Univ UT, 71. **MEMBERSHIPS** Speech Commun Asn (pres, 79-80); Am Forensic Asn (secytreas, 55-57); Western Speech Commun Asn, pres, 90-91. **RESEARCH** Am public address; contemp rhetorical theory. **SELECTED PUBLICATIONS** Auth, Robert Penn Warren's All the Kings Men, a study in populism, Am Quart, 56; The 1960 Democratic Convention, Quart J Speech, 60; The rhetoric of the petition in Boots, Speech Monogr, 6/72; coauth, Argumentation and the Decision-Making Process, Longman, 97; Speech: Content and Communication, Waveland, 91; Messages Meaning and Culture, Harper Collins, 91. **CONTACT ADDRESS** 3508 E Oaks Dr, Salt Lake City, UT, 84124.

SILVER, BRENDA R.
DISCIPLINE ENGLISH LITERATURE **EDUCATION** Harvard Univ, PhD, 73. **CAREER** Prof, Dartmouth Col. **RESEARCH** Brit, postmodern, and feminist lit; Virginia Woolf. **SELECTED PUBLICATIONS** Auth, Periphrasis, Power, and Rape in A Passage to India in E. M. Forster, St Martin's, 95; Virginia Woolf's Reading Notebooks, Princeton UP, 83; Misfits: The Monstrous Union of Virginia Woolf and Marilyn Monroe, Discourse,93; Textual Criticism as Feminist Practice: Or, Who's Afraid of Virginia Woolf Part II in Representing Modernist Texts: Editing as Interpretation, U of Michigan P, 91; co-ed, Rape and Representation, Columbia UP, 91. **CONTACT ADDRESS** Dartmouth Col, 3529 N Main St, #207, Hanover, NH, 03755.

SILVER, CAROLE GRETA
PERSONAL Born 06/06/1937, New York, NY, m, 1991 **DISCIPLINE** VICTORIAN LITERATURE **EDUCATION** Alfred Univ, BA, 58; Univ Mich, MA, 59; Columbia Univ, PhD(English, comp lit), 67 **CAREER** Instr English, Vassar Col, 66 & Hunter Col, 67-68; asst prof, 68-74, assoc prof, 74-88, PROF ENGLISH, STERN COL, YESHIVA UNIV, 88-, CHAIR, HUMANITITIES DIV, 93-. **MEMBERSHIPS** Northeast Victorian Studies Asn (vpres, 77); NAm William Morris Soc; MLA **RESEARCH** William Morris; pre-Raphaelite poetry and art; myth and folklore in Victorian literature. **SELECTED PUBLICATIONS** Auth, The defense of Guenevere: A further interpretation, Studies in English Lit, 69; The earthly paradise: Lost, Victorian Poetry, 75; co-ed, Studies in the Late Romances of William Morris, 76 & auth, Myth and ritual in the last romances of William Morris, 76, William Morris Soc; The Romance of William Morris, 82; co-auth, Kind Words: A Thesaurus of Euphemism, 83, 90, 95; co-ed, Socialism...and William Morris, 91; auth, Strange and Secret People: Fairies and Victorian Consciousness, 98. **CONTACT ADDRESS** Stern Col for Women Yeshiva Univ, 245 Lexington Ave, New York, NY, 10016-4699. **EMAIL** csilver@ymail.yu.edu

SIMMONS, DONALD B.
DISCIPLINE PUBLIC ADDRESS; COMMUNICATION. **EDUCATION** Ohio Univ, PhD, 81. **CAREER** Prof Commun Asbury Col, 81-. **HONORS AND AWARDS** Mem Advisory Coun Documentary Channel, 98. **MEMBERSHIPS** Nat Commun Asn. **RESEARCH** Public speaking; speech criticism. **SELECTED PUBLICATIONS** Auth, The Golden Rule Philosophy of Samuel M. Jones, Proceedings of the Ky Commun Asn, 9/98. **CONTACT ADDRESS** Communication Arts Dept, Asbury Col, 1 Macklem Dr., Wilmore, KY, 40390. **EMAIL** don.simmons@asbury.edu

SIMMONS, JOSEPH LARRY
PERSONAL Born 12/09/1935, Tylertown, MS, m, 1964, 3 children **DISCIPLINE** ENGLISH **EDUCATION** Fla State Univ, BMus, 56; NY Univ, BA, 62; Univ Va, PhD(English), 67. **CAREER** Instr English, NTex State Univ, 62-64; from asst prof to assoc prof, 67-74, chmn dept, 77-80, PROF ENGLISH, TULANE UNIV, 74-, Nat Endowment for Humanities Younger Humanists fel, 73-74; Am Coun Learned Soc grant-in-aid, 76-77. **MEMBERSHIPS** MLA; Shakespeare Asn Am. **RESEARCH** Shakespearean and Renaissance drama; 17th century poetry. **SELECTED PUBLICATIONS** Auth, Coming Out In Shakespeare The 'Two Gentlemen Of Verona'/, Elh-English Lit Hist, Vol 0060, 1993; Masculine Negotiations In Shakespeare History-Plays - Hal, Hotspur, And The-Foolish-Mortimer/, Shakespeare Quart, Vol 0044, 1993. **CONTACT ADDRESS** Dept of English, Tulane Univ, 6823 St Charles Ave, New Orleans, LA, 70118-5698.

SIMONSON, HAROLD PETER
PERSONAL Born 12/27/1926, Tacoma, WA, m, 1951, 3 children **DISCIPLINE** ENGLISH & AMERICAN LITERATURE **EDUCATION** Univ Puget Sound, BA, 50, BEd, 51; Northwestern Univ, MA, 51, PhD, 58; Univ St Andrews, BPhil, 72. **CAREER** Instr English, Thessalonika Agr & Indust Inst, Greece, 53-54; from instr to prof Am lit, Univ Puget Sound, 55-68; PROF AM LIT, UNIV WASH, 68-, Fulbright grant, 53. **MEMBERSHIPS** MLA Am Studies Asn; Melville Soc Am. **RESEARCH** American Middle West realism; Frederick Jackson Turner's frontier thesis; literature and theology. **SELECTED PUBLICATIONS** Auth, W Of Everything - The Inner Life Of Westerns - Tompkins,J/, Pac Northwest Quart, Vol 0084, 1993; Tragedy And Beyond - Maclean,Norman 'Young Men And Fire'/, Montana-The Mag Of Western Hist, Vol 0043, 1993; Frontier Gothic, Terror And Wonder At The Frontier In Am Lit - Mogen,D, Sanders,Sp, Karpinski,Jb/, Western Am Lit, Vol 0028, 1993. **CONTACT ADDRESS** Dept of English, Univ of Wash, Seattle, WA, 98195.

SIMPSON, HASSELL ALGERNON
PERSONAL Born 05/08/1930, Barksdale, SC, m, 1953, 3 children **DISCIPLINE** ENGLISH & AMERICAN LITERATURE **EDUCATION** Clemson Univ, BS, 52; Fla State Univ, MA, 57, PhD(English), 62. **CAREER** Instr English, Fla State Univ, 58-59; instr, Auburn Univ, 59-62; assoc prof, 62-65, chm dept, 68-76, chm div humanities, 70-73, prof English, 65-95, PROF EMER, 95- , HAMPDEN-SYDNEY COL. **RESEARCH** Modern fiction; American literature; Shakespeare. **SELECTED PUBLICATIONS** Auth, Rumer Godden, Twayne, 73. **CONTACT ADDRESS** Dept of English, Hampden-Sydney Col, Hampden-Sydney, VA, 23943.

SIMS, JAMES HYLBERT
PERSONAL Born 10/29/1924, Orlando, FL, m, 1944, 5 children **DISCIPLINE** ENGLISH LITERATURE **EDUCATION** Univ Fla, BA, 49, MA, 50, PhD, 59 **CAREER** Asst, 49-50, Univ Fla; instr, 50-51, Tenn Temple Col; Tri-St Baptist Col, 51-54, & Univ Fla, 55-59; prof, chmn dept, 59-61, Tift Col; prof, chmn dept, 61-66, Austin Peay St Univ; prof, 66-76, Univ Okla; prof, dean, col of lib arts, 76-82, Univ S Miss; vice pres, Acad Affairs, 82-89; dist prof, 89-95; consult, choice, 64-; fel, 65 & 66, Southeastern Inst Medieval & Renaissance Stud; assoc ed, 68-, 17th Century News; Huntington Libr fel, 73; Natl Endowment for Humanities fel, 78-79, Huntington Libr & Art Gallery; dir, 79-81, pres, 88-90, Conf Christianity & Lit. **MEMBERSHIPS** S Cent Renaissance Conf; Milton Soc Am; MLA; Southeastern Renaissance Conf; Conf Christianity & Lit. **RESEARCH** Biblical lit; Renaissance lit, esp Milton. **SELECTED PUBLICATIONS** Auth, The Bible in Milton's Epics, Univ Fla, 62; auth, Dramatic Use of Biblical Allusions in Marlowe and Shakespeare, Univ Fla, 66; auth, Paradise Lost: Aria Document of Christian Poem? Etudes Anglaises, 67; auth, Christened Classicism in Paradise Lost and the Lusiads, Comp Lit, 72; auth, The Fortunate Fall of Sir Gawayne in Sir Gawayne and the Grene Knight, Orbis Literarum, 75; auth, The Narrator's Mortal Voice in Camoes and Milton, Rev Lit Comp 77; auth, Milton and the Bible as Literature and Literature as a Bible, Milton Tercentenary Essays, Univ Wisc, 78; contrib, Milton Encycl Bucknell, 78; auth, The Major Literary Prophecy of the Old Testament, Dalhousie Rev, 82; auth, Milton and Scriptural Tradition, Univ Mo, 84; auth, Comparative Literary Study of Daniel and Revelation, Mellen 95; auth, Essays in Milton Studies, 95; Comparative Literature, 97. **CONTACT ADDRESS** Dept of English, Univ of So Mississippi, PO Box 5037, Hattiesburg, MS, 39401. **EMAIL** j.sims@usm.edu

SINEATH, TIMOTHY W.
PERSONAL Born 05/21/1940, Jacksonville, FL, m, 1962, 2 children **DISCIPLINE** LIBRARY SCIENCE **EDUCATION** Florida State Univ, BS, 62, MS, 63; Univ Illinois, PhD, 70. **CAREER** Dean and Prof, School of Library and Infor Sci, Univ of Kentucky. **HONORS AND AWARDS** NEA federal fel, Lib and Infor Sci, Univ Ill; service award, Asn for Lib and Infor Sci Educ. **MEMBERSHIPS** ASIS; Asn for Lib and Infor Sci Educ; ALA. **RESEARCH** Management of nonprofits; organizational development; planning. **SELECTED PUBLICATIONS** Auth, Library Personnel and Training, Encyclopedia Americana, Grolier, 93; ed, Library and Information Science Education Statistical Report 1993, ALISE, 93; auth, Faculty, in, Library and Information Science Education Statistical Report 1998, ALISE, 98; auth, Managing the Information Organization: Creating and Maintaining a Learning Organization, ABLEX, 99. **CONTACT ADDRESS** School of Library and Information Science, Univ of Kentucky, 502 M.I. King South, Lexington, KY, 40506-0039. **EMAIL** tsineath@pop.uky.edu

SINGLEY, CAROL J.
DISCIPLINE ENGLISH **EDUCATION** Penn State Univ, BA, 72, MA, 75; Brown Univ, PhD, 86. **CAREER** ASSOC PROF, ENG, RUTGERS UNIV **MEMBERSHIPS** Am Antiquarian Soc **SELECTED PUBLICATIONS** Co-ed, Anxious Power: Reading, Writing, and Ambivalence in Narrative by Women, State Univ of NY Press, 93; auth, Edith Wharton: Matters of Mind and Spirit, Cambridge Univ Press, 95. **CONTACT ADDRESS** Dept of Eng, Rutgers Univ, Camden, NJ, 08102.

SIPAHIGIL, TEOMAN
PERSONAL Born 02/13/1939, Istanbul, Turkey **DISCIPLINE** ENGLISH LITERATURE, RHETORIC **EDUCATION** Earlham Col, BA, 61; Miami Univ, MA, 63; Univ Calif, Los Angeles, PhD(English), 70. **CAREER** Asst prof, 70-75, ASSOC PROF ENGLISH, UNIV IDAHO, 75- **MEMBERSHIPS** NCTE **RESEARCH** Shakespeare. **SELECTED PUBLICATIONS** Auth, Ovid And The Tempest In 'Othello' + Affinities Between Shakespeare And The Roman Poet/, Shakespeare Quart, Vol 0044, 1993. **CONTACT ADDRESS** Dept of English, Univ of Idaho, Moscow, ID, 83843.

SIPORIN, STEVE
DISCIPLINE ENGLISH; HISTORY **EDUCATION** Stanford Univ, BA, 69; Univ Ore, MA, 74; Ind Univ, PhD, 82. **CAREER** Lectr, Ind Univ, 76; folklore consult to Iowa Arts Coun, 77-78; folk arts coordr, Ore Arts Comn, 80-81; folk arts coordr, Idaho Comn on the Arts, 82-86; from asst prof to assoc prof, Utah State Univ, 90-. **HONORS AND AWARDS** Fulbright Lectureship, Portugal, 92-93; Hon. Mention, Giuseppe Pitre Internat Folklore Prize. **MEMBERSHIPS** Int Soc for Folk Narrative Res; Am Folklore Soc; Folklore Soc Utah; Int Conf Group on Portugal. **SELECTED PUBLICATIONS** Auth, We Came To Where We Were Supposed To Be: Folk Art of Idaho, 84; Our Way of Life Was Very Clear, Northwest Folklore 8, 90; The Fruit Jobber's Tales, Int Folklore Rev 7, 90; Immigrant and Ethnic Family Folklore, Western States Jewish Hist 22, 90; A Jew Among Mormons, Dialogue: A J of Mormon Thought 24, 91; Public Folklore: A Bibliographic Introduction, Public Folklore, Wash., D.C.: Smithsonian Inst. Press, 92; Folklife and Survival: The Italian- Americans of Carbon County, Utah, Old Ties, New Attachments: Italian-American Folklife in the West, Wash., D.C.: Libr. Of Congress, 92; American Folk Masters: The National Heritage Fellows, 92; The Sephardim: Field Report From Portugal, Jewish Folklore and Ethnology Review 15, 93; Memories of Jewish Life, New Horizons in Sephardic Studies, Albany: State Univ of NY Press, 93; From Kashrut to Cucina Ebraica: The Recasting of Italian Jewish Foodways, Jour of Am Folklore 107, 94; Halloween Pranks: Just a Little Inconvenience, Halloween and Other Festivals of Death and Life, Knoxville: Univ of Tenn. Press, 94; National Heritage Fellows, Am Folklore: An Encyclopedia, New York: Garland, 96. **CONTACT ADDRESS** Dept of English, Utah State Univ, Logan, UT, 84322-3200. **EMAIL** siporin@cc.usu.edu

SIRLUCK, ERNEST
PERSONAL Born 04/25/1918, Winkler, MB, Canada **DISCIPLINE** ENGLISH **EDUCATION** Univ Man, BA, 40; Univ Toronto, MA, 41, PhD, 48. **CAREER** Lectr, Univ Toronto, 46; asst prof, 47-53, assoc prof, 53-58, prof Eng, Univ Chicago, 58-

62; prof Eng & assoc dean grad stud, 62-64, dean, 64-68, vice pres & grad dean, Univ Toronto, 68-70; pres, Univ Man, 70-76 (RETIRED). **HONORS AND AWARDS** Guggenheim fel, 53-54; fel, Am Coun Learned Soc, 58-59; Churchill Col overseas fel, Cambridge Univ, 66. **SELECTED PUBLICATIONS** Auth, Complete Prose Works of John Milton, vol II, 59; auth, Paradise Lost: A Deliberate Epic, 67; auth, First Generation: An Autobiography, 96; co-ed, Patterns of Literary Criticism, 65-74. **CONTACT ADDRESS** 153 Strathallan Blvd, Toronto, ON, M5N 1S9.

SIROIS, ANTOINE
PERSONAL Born 09/29/1925, Sherbrooke, PQ, Canada **DISCIPLINE** LITERATURE **EDUCATION** Seminaire Sherbrooke, BA, 45; Grand seminaire Sherbrooke, dipl theo, 49; Univ Sherbrooke, BPed, 60; Univ Montreal, LL, 60; Univ Paris, DL, 67. **CAREER** Prof & prin, Ext classique Lac-Megantic, 52-58; secy gen, 60-65, prof lettres sci hum, 67-94, head Fre dept, 68-74, vice dean, 75-83, PROF EMER, UNIV SHERBROOKE, 94-. **HONORS AND AWARDS** Prix Gabrielle-Roy, 86; Prix Juge-Lemay, 88; Certificat de merite de l'ACS/AEC, 90; Prix d'excellence de la Ville de Sherbrooke, 91. **MEMBERSHIPS** Royal Soc Can; Can Comp Lit Asn; Can & Que Lit Asns; Asn Can Stud; Int Comp Lit Asn. **RESEARCH** Canadian and Quebec literature **SELECTED PUBLICATIONS** Auth, Montreal dans le roman canadien, 68; auth, Mythes et symboles dans le roman quebecois, 92; coauth, Un homme et son peche, 86; coauth & co-ed, A l'ombre de DesRochers, 85; coauth & co-ed, L'Essor culturel des Cantons de l'Est depuis 1950, 85; coauth & co-ed, Bibliography of Studies in Comparative Canadian Literature (1930-1987), 89. **CONTACT ADDRESS** 2497 Laurentie, Sherbrooke, PQ, J1J 1L3.

SITKO, BARBARA
DISCIPLINE CONTEMPORARY RHETORICAL THEORY **EDUCATION** Carnegie Mellon, PhD. **CAREER** Assoc prof, Washington State Univ. **RESEARCH** Studies of audience adaptation, instructional uses of computers, culturally sensitive writing instruction. **CONTACT ADDRESS** Dept of English, Washington State Univ, 1 SE Stadium Way, PO Box 645020, Pullman, WA, 99164-5020. **EMAIL** sitko@wsu.edu

SITTER, JOHN
DISCIPLINE ENGLISH LANGUAGE AND LITERATURE **EDUCATION** Harvard Univ, BA, 66; Univ Minn, PhD, 69. **CAREER** Fac, Univ Mass Amherst; fac, Univ Kent Canterbury; fac, Emory Univ, 80-; Charles Howard Candler Prof, present. **RESEARCH** 18th-century literature; satire and poetry; literary criticism; Restoration literature; contemporary poetry. **SELECTED PUBLICATIONS** Auth, The Poetry of Pope's "Dunciad"; Literary Loneliness in Mid-Eighteenth-Century England; Arguments of Augustan Wit; and articles on Restoration and 18th-century literature and on contemporary poetry. **CONTACT ADDRESS** English Dept, Emory Univ, 1380 Oxford Rd NE, Atlanta, GA, 30322-1950. **EMAIL** engjs@emory.edu

SITTERSON, JOSEPH
DISCIPLINE ENGLISH LITERATURE **EDUCATION** Univ NC, BA, PhD. **CAREER** Eng Dept, Georgetown Univ **RESEARCH** British Romantic literature; literary theory; epic; biblical interpretation. **SELECTED PUBLICATIONS** Auth, pubs on Wordsworth, Coleridge, Keats, psychoanalytic and literary theory, Ariosto, and biblical interpretation. **CONTACT ADDRESS** English Dept, Georgetown Univ, 37th and O St, Washington, DC, 20057.

SIVELL, JOHN
DISCIPLINE ENGLISH LITERATURE **EDUCATION** Univ Toronto, BA; Univ Cambridge, dipl; Univ Wales Inst Sci and Tech, Med; Univ East Anglia, Eng, PhD. **CAREER** Instr, 83; prof; dean. **RESEARCH** Celestin Freinet. **SELECTED PUBLICATIONS** Auth, classroom ESL Reading textbooks, From Near and Far, Full Blast Productions, 92; Jigsaw Activities for Reading and Writing, Full Blast Productions, 93; Canada from Eh to Zed: People, 95; pub(s), ELT Jour; The Mod Eng Tchr; TESL Can Jour; McGill Jour Edu; Eng Tchg Forum. **CONTACT ADDRESS** Humanities, Brock Univ, 500 Glenridge Ave, St Catharines, ON, L2S 3A1. **EMAIL** jsivell@spartan.ac.BrockU.CA

SIVIER, EVELYN M.
PERSONAL Born 05/15/1916, Milwaukee, WI, w, 1959, 1 child **DISCIPLINE** THEATRE **EDUCATION** San Jose St Univ, BA, 51; Stanford Univ, MA, 52; Wayne St Univ, PhD, 61. **CAREER** Instr, Stanford Univ, 51-52; instr, Wayne State Univ 52-57; asst prof, Humboldt State Univ, 57-59; assoc prof, Wayne State Univ, 63-81, assoc prof emer, 81- . **HONORS AND AWARDS** AAUW Honors Awd; Woman Student of the Year; first PhD candidate chosen (speech), Wayne St Univ. **MEMBERSHIPS** Nat Speech Asn; Am Assoc Univ Women. **RESEARCH** Change and professionalism; teaching of speech; concern over present day performance standards. **SELECTED PUBLICATIONS** Auth, English Poets, Teachers, and Festivals in a Golden Age of Poetry Speaking, 1920-1950,in Perfromance of Literature in Historical Perspectives, Univ Pr of Am, 83; auth, Penny Readings: Popular Elocution in Late Nineteenth Century England, in Performance of Literature in Historical Perspectives, Univ Pr of Am, 83. **CONTACT ADDRESS** 4185 Nature Trl Dr SE, Apt #11, Kentwood, MI, 49512.

SIZEMORE, CHRISTINE WICK
PERSONAL Born 11/17/1945, Washington, DC, m, 1968, 2 children **DISCIPLINE** ENGLISH RENAISSANCE & 20TH CENTURY LITERATURE **EDUCATION** Carnegie Inst Technol, BA, 67; Univ PA, MA, 68, PhD(English), 72. **CAREER** Asst prof, GA State Univ, 72-78; asst prof, 78-84, assoc prof, 84-92, PROF ENGLISH, SPELMAN COL, 92-. **MEMBERSHIPS** Southeastern Renaissance Soc; MLA; SAtlantic Mod Lang Asn. **RESEARCH** Contemporary British and post-Colonial novel; urban literature. **SELECTED PUBLICATIONS** Auth, The Author of the Mystery of Rhetoric Unveiled, Papers of the Bibliog Soc Am, winter 75; Seventeenth Century Advice Books: The Female Viewpoint, SAtlantic Bull, 1/76; Anxiety in Kafka: A Function of Cognitive Dissonance, J Mod Lit, fall 77; The Small Cardboard Box: A Symbol of the City and Winnie Verlac in Conrad's Secret Agent, Mod Fiction Studies, spring 78; Structural Repetition in John Bunyan's Holy War, Tenn Studies Lit, 79; Cognitive Dissonance and the Anxiety Response to Kafka's The Castle, Comparatist, 80; Attitudes to Ward the Education and Roles of Women: Sixteenth-century Humanista and Seventeenth Century Advice Books, Univ Dayton Rev, spring 81; Ridgway's Militant Weekly and the Serial Version of Conrad's Secret Agent, Anal & Enumerative Bibilog, spring 82; Reading the City as Palimpseat: The Experiential Perception of the City in Doris Lessing's Four-Gaited City, Women Writers and the City, ed Susan Squier, Univ TN Press, 84; A Female Vision of the City: London in the Novels of Five British Women, Univ TN Press, 89; Masculine and Feminine Cities: Marge Piercy's Going Down Fast and Fly Away Home, Frontiers: a Journal of Women Studies, 13.1, spring 92; The Outsider Within: Virginia Woolf and Doris Lessing as Urban Novelists, Woolf and Lessing: Breaking the Mold, eds Ruth Saxton and Jean Tobin, St Martin's Press, 94; The London Novels of Buchi Emecheta, Emerging Perspectives on Buchi Emecheta, ed Marie Umek, African World Press, 96; Virginia Woolf as Modernist Foremother in Maureen Duffey's A Nightingale in Bloomsberry Square, Unmanning Modernism: Gendered Rereadings, eds E. J. Harrison and Shirley Peterson, Univ TN Press, 97; Negotiating between Ideologies: the Search for Identity in Tsitsi Dangarembga's Nrevous Conditions and Margaret Atwood's Cat's Eye, Teaching African Literature, a Special Edition, eds, Tuzyline Allan and Florence Howe, Women's Studies Quart, 25, nos 3 & 4, fall/winter 97; Doris Lessing, Postcolonial African Writers: a Bio-Bibliographical Critical Sourcebook, eds Pushpa N. Parekh and Siga F. Jagne, Greenwood Press, 98. **CONTACT ADDRESS** Spelman Col, Box 273, Atlanta, GA, 30314.

SIZEMORE RIDDLE, RITA
PERSONAL Coeburn, VA **DISCIPLINE** SHAKESPEARE, THE ESSAY, AND POETRY **EDUCATION** Hiwassee Col, AA, 62; E TN State Univ, BS, 63, MA, 63; Univ TN, Knoxville, PhD, 71. **CAREER** Grad tchg asst, E TN State Univ, 65-66; grad tchg asst, Univ TN, 68-71; prof, Radford Univ, 71-. **HONORS AND AWARDS** Irene Leach Mem Award, 92; fac prof develop grant, Ctr for Acad Excellence, 95; James Still Award for Poetry, Appalachian Writers Asn, 95; prof leave, Radford Univ, 97; **SELECTED PUBLICATIONS** Auth, Chicken Hymns from Pipestem, Newsl of the Ctr for Acad Excellence, Vol IV, No 2, 94; Soot and Sunshine, Radford Univ Arts and Sci Occas Publ Comt, 94; Early Ripes, Story Stitches Vol II, No 1, 94; Pieces for Emma, Radford Univ Arts and Sci Occas Publ Comt, 94; Communication, Gingerbread Man, Asheville Poetry Rev, 95; Creation, Asheville Poetry Rev, 95; Aluminum Balloons and Other Poems, Pocahontas Press, 96; Still Lives, Asheville Poetry Rev, 97. **CONTACT ADDRESS** Radford Univ, Radford, VA, 24142. **EMAIL** rriddle@runet.edu

SKAGGS, MERRILL MAGUIRE
PERSONAL Born 10/01/1937, Florala, AL, m, 1960, 2 children **DISCIPLINE** AMERICAN LITERATURE **EDUCATION** Stetson Univ, BA, 58; Duke Univ, MA, 60, PhD, 65; Stetson Univ, PhD, 88. **CAREER** Tutor English, Duke Univ, 61-62; vis instr, Fairleigh Dickinson Univ, 62-63; lectr, Brooklyn Col, 65; assoc ed sch dept, Macmillan Co, 66-67; instr lit & lang, Columbia Teachers Col, 70-75; from Adj Assoc Prof to Assoc Prof Am Lit, 76-82, Dean, Grad Sch, 86-92, Baldwin Prof of the Humanities, Drew Univ, 92-; consult lit, Norton Anthology Am Lit, 81; grant consult, Am Coun Learned Soc, 82. **HONORS AND AWARDS** Ed Winfield Parks Award, Soc Study Southern Lit, 73; Bks of the Year Award, Am J Nursing, 75; Alumni Initiate, Phi Beta Kappa, 88. **MEMBERSHIPS** MLA; Soc Study Southern Lit. **RESEARCH** Nineteenth century American literature; Southern literature; early American literature. **SELECTED PUBLICATIONS** Auth, The Folk of Southern Fiction, Univ Ga, 72; coauth, The Mother Person, Bobbs Merrill, 75; After the World Broke in Two: The Later Novels of Willa Cather, Univ Press Va, 90; author of numerous articles on Willa Cather and southern writers. **CONTACT ADDRESS** Drew Univ, 36 Madison Ave, Madison, NJ, 07940-1493. **EMAIL** mskaggs@drew.edu

SKARBARNICKI, ANNE
DISCIPLINE BRITISH LITERATURE **EDUCATION** Toronto, BA, 71; Yale, Mphil, 73, PhD, 75. **CAREER** Yale Univ; Bucknell Univ; Lafayette Col; Prof, Royal Milit Col. **HONORS AND AWARDS** Assoc ed, Carlyle Newsl. **RESEARCH** Anglo-saxon and medieval language and literature. **SELECTED PUBLICATIONS** Ed, Jane Welsh Carlyle; Carlyle Encyclopedia. **CONTACT ADDRESS** Royal Military Col Canada, 315 Massey Bldg, PO Box 17000, Kingston, ON, K7K 7B4. **EMAIL** skarbarnicki-a@rmc.ca

SKARDA, PATRICIA LYN
PERSONAL Born 03/31/1946, Clovis, NM **DISCIPLINE** BRITISH LITERATURE **EDUCATION** Sweet Briar Col, 68; Tex Tech Univ, BA, 69; Univ Tex, Austin, PhD, 73. **CAREER** Teaching asst, Univ Tex, Austin, 69-70, 72-73; asst prof, 73-88, ASSOC PROF ENGLISH, SMITH COL, 88-; Dir, NMex Girls State, 73; govt suprv, Girls Nation, 73; secy fac, Smith Col, 76-78, Danforth assoc, 77-83; fel, Am Coun Educ, 78-79. **HONORS AND AWARDS** Phi Beta Kappa, 67; Sr fac teaching award, 86. **MEMBERSHIPS** MLA; NASSR **RESEARCH** Romantic and Victorian literature; Gerard Manley Hopkins; Gothic fiction. **SELECTED PUBLICATIONS** Auth, Smith writers, Smith Alumnae Quart, fall 75; Juvenilia of the family of Gerard Manley Hopkins, Hopkins Quart, summer 77; Expressions of form and formlessness, Smith Alumnae Quart, summer 77; The Evil Image: Two Centuries of Gothic Short Fiction & Poetry, New Am Libr, 81; Teaching Essays on Tintern Abbey, Christobel and Kubla Khan, in approaches to Teaching Wordsworth and Coleridge, 85 & 90; Vampirism and plaigarism: Byron's influence and Polidori's practice, Studies in Romanticism, summer 89; Samuel Rogers, in Dictionary of Literary Biography: Romantic Poets, 1st series, 89; Smith Voices: Selected Works by Smith College Women, 90; Thomas Moore, in Dictionary of Literary Biography: Romantic Poets, 2nd series, 90; William Hazlitt, in Dictionary of Liteary Biography: Romantic Prose, 91; For Yearbooks of Dictionary of Literary Biography, Robert Ludlum, 83, Alfred Coppel, 84, Peter Straub, 85, Susan Alba Toth, 86. **CONTACT ADDRESS** Dept of English, Smith Col, 98 Green St, Northampton, MA, 01063-0001. **EMAIL** pskarda@sophia.smith.edu

SKAU, MICHAEL WALTER
PERSONAL Born 01/06/1944, Chicago, IL **DISCIPLINE** LITERATURE **EDUCATION** Univ of Ill, Urbana-Champaign, BA, 65, MA, 67, PhD(English), 73. **CAREER** Asst prof to prof English, Univ Nebr, Omaha, 73-. **HONORS AND AWARDS** Jefferis Chair in English, 97-. **MEMBERSHIPS** MLA **RESEARCH** Modern and contemporary British and American literature. **SELECTED PUBLICATIONS** Auth, Flimnap, Lilliput's Acrobatic Treasurer, Am Notes & Queries, 70; coauth, Joyce's Araby, Explicator, 76; auth, Jack Kerouac--Visions of America, Periodical Art Nebr, 77; Toward Underivative Creation: Lawrence Ferlinghetti's Her, Critique, 78; Toward a Third Stream Theatre: Lawrence Ferlinghetti's Plays, Mod Drama, 79; American ethos: Richard Brautigan's Trout Fishing in America, Portland Rev, 81; The Central Verbal System: The prose of William S Burroughs, Style (in prep); coauth, A modern bestiary: Jerzy Kosinski's The Painted Bird, Polish Rev, 82; auth, The Poetas Poem: Ferlinghetti's Songs of Myself, Concerning Poetry, 87; Constantly Risking Absurdity: The Writings of Lawrence Ferlinghetti, Whitston, 89; To Dream, Perchance To Be: Gregory Corso and Imagination, Univ Daytona Rev, 89; The Comedy Gone Mad: Gregory Corso's Surrealism and Humor, McNeese Rev, 89. **CONTACT ADDRESS** Dept of English, Univ of Nebr, 6001 Dodge St, Omaha, NE, 68182-0002. **EMAIL** mskau@cwis.unomaha.edu

SKELLINGS, EDMUND
DISCIPLINE POETRY **EDUCATION** Univ of Mass, BA, 57; Univ of Iowa, PhD, 62. **CAREER** Dir & prof, State Univ Sywtem of Fla, 68-98. **HONORS AND AWARDS** Honorary doctor of fine arts, Int Col of Fine Arts; Poet Laureate of Fla. **MEMBERSHIPS** Acad of Am Poets. **RESEARCH** Poetry and supercomputing animation. **SELECTED PUBLICATIONS** Auth, Collected Poems, 1958-1998, Univ Press of Fla; Selected Poems: Compact Disk, Univ Press of Fla. **CONTACT ADDRESS** 600 NE Second Pl., Dania, FL, 33004. **EMAIL** poet1@laureate.cec.fau.edu

SKERPAN-WHEELER, ELIZABETH P.
PERSONAL Born 10/11/1955, Ravenna, OH, m, 1997 **DISCIPLINE** ENGLISH LITERATURE **EDUCATION** Miami Univ, AB, 76; Univ Wisc-Madison, MA, 77, PhD, 83. **CAREER** Asst Prof, 83-89, Assoc Prof, 89-97, Prof of English, 97-, SW Tex State Univ. **HONORS AND AWARDS** Short-term Res Fellow, William Clark Memorial Library, 94; Phi Beta Kappa; Phi Kappa Phi. **MEMBERSHIPS** Modern Lang Asn; Nat Coun of Tchrs of English; Renaissance Soc of Am; Milton Soc of Am; Tex Fac Asn. **RESEARCH** Milton; 17th century poetry & prose; history of rhetoric. **SELECTED PUBLICATIONS** Auth, The Rhetoric of Politics in the English Revolution, 1642-1660, Univ Mo Press, 92; auth, Sir John Denham, Dictionary of Leterary Biography, vol 126 2nd series, Bruccoli Clark Layman, 97-108, 93; auth, The Eikon Basilike, Dictionary of Literary Biography, vol 151, 143-48, 95; auth, Eikon Basilike and the Rhetoric of Self-Representation, The Royal Image: Representations of Charles I, Cambridge Univ Press, in press; auth, Sir Francis Bacon, Dictionary of Literary Biography, in press. **CONTACT ADDRESS** Dept of English, SW Tex State Univ, 601 Univ Dr, San Marcos, TX, 78666. **EMAIL** es10@swt.edu

SKINNER, EWART C.
PERSONAL Born 01/02/1949, s **DISCIPLINE** COMMUNICATIONS **EDUCATION** Univ of Hartford, Hartford, CT, 1967-69; Tarkio Coll, Tarkio, MO, BA, 1971; American Univ in Cairo, Cairo, Egypt, MA, 1974; MI State Univ, East Lansing, MI, PhD, 1984. **CAREER** Self-employed media consultant, Trinidad and Tobago, 1975-79; UNESCO, Trinidad and Tobago, West Indies, 1987; MI State Univ, East Lansing, MI, instructor, 1983-84; Purdue Univ, West Lafayette, IN, asst prof, 1984-. **HONORS AND AWARDS** Specialist in Caribbean Mass Media Systems and Intl Media; Poet. **MEMBERSHIPS** Intl Assn for Mass Communications Research; Intl Communication Assn; Intl Peace Research Assn; Semiotics Society of America; Assn for Education in Journalism ans Mass Communication; Caribbean Studies Assn. **CONTACT ADDRESS** Department of Communication, Purdue Univ, 1366 Heavilon Hall 304, West Lafayette, IN, 47907-1366.

SKINNER, KNUTE R
PERSONAL Born 04/25/1929, St. Louis, MO, m, 1954, 3 children **DISCIPLINE** ENGLISH **EDUCATION** Univ NColo, BA, 51; Middlebury Col, MA, 54; Univ of Iowa, PhD, 58. **CAREER** Teacher English, Boise Sr High Sch, 51-54; instr, State Univ Iowa, 54-55, 56-57, 60-61; asst prof, Okla Col Women, 61-62; asst prof, 62-63, lectr, 64-71, assoc prof, 71-73, PROF ENGLISH, WESTERN WASH UNIV, 73-97, PROF EMER, 97-; Fel creative writing, Nat Endowment for Arts, 75; co-ed & publ, Bellingham Rev, 77-95. **MEMBERSHIPS** Wash Poets Asn; Am Comt Irish Studies. **RESEARCH** Poetry; creative writing. **SELECTED PUBLICATIONS** Auth, Stranger With A Watch, Golden Quill, 65; A Close Sky Over Killaspuglonane, Dolmen, 68, 2nd ed, Burton Int, 75; In Dinosaur Country, Pierian, 69; The Sorcerers: A Laotian Tale, Goliards, 72; Six poems, in New Generations: Poetry Anthology, Ann Arbor Rev Bks, 71; Three Poems, in A Geography of Poets, Bantam, 79; Hearing of the Hard Times, Northwoods Press, 81; The Flame Room, Folley Press, 83; Selected Poems, Aquila Press, 85; Learning to Spell Zucchini, Salmon Publ, 88; the Bears and Other Poems, Salmon Publ, 91; The Cold Irish Earth, Trask House, 93; What Trudy Knows and Other Poems, Salmon Publ, 94; The Cold Irish Earth: Selected Poems of Ireland, 1965-95, Salmon Publ, 96; An Afternoon Quiet and Other Poems, Pudding House, 98 **CONTACT ADDRESS** M/S 9055, Bellingham, WA, 98225-5996.

SKINNER, ROBERT EARLE
PERSONAL Born 06/25/1948, Alexandria, VA **DISCIPLINE** AMERICAN LITERATURE **EDUCATION** Old Dominion Univ, Norfolk, Va, BA, 70; Ind Univ Bloomington, MA, 77; Univ New Orleans, MFA cand, 91-93. **CAREER** Asst prof, La St Univ, 79-84; sr consult, Robert L. Siegel & Assoc, 85-87; librn, Xavier Univ La, New Orleans, 87- . **HONORS AND AWARDS** Who's Who, 93-94, 99; Anthony Boucher Award nominee, 98. **MEMBERSHIPS** Mystery Writer of Amer; Amer Libr Assoc. **RESEARCH** Mystery & suspense lit; career of Chester Himes; western novelists. **SELECTED PUBLICATIONS** Auth, Chester Himes: An Annotated Primary and Secondary Bibliography, Greenwood Press, 92; coed, Plan B Univ Press Ms, 93; Conversations with Chester Himes, Univ Press Ms, 95; auth, The New Hard-Boiled Dicks: Heroes for a New Urban Mythology, Borgo Press, 95; coauth; Elmore Leonard, in Mystery and Suspense Writers: The Literature of Crime, Detections, and Espionage, Charles Scriber's Sons, 98. **CONTACT ADDRESS** 6823 Milne Blvd, New Orleans, LA, 70124-2313. **EMAIL** rskinner@mail.xula.edu

SKLOOT, ROBERT
PERSONAL Born 07/27/1942, Brooklyn, NY **DISCIPLINE** THEATRE, DRAMA, JEWISH STUDIES **EDUCATION** Union Col, NY, AB, 63; Cornell Univ, MA, 65; Univ Minn, Minneapolis, PhD, 68. **CAREER** Prof theatre & drama & Jewish studies, Univ of Wis-Madison, 68-, Assoc Vice-Chancellor Acad Affairs, 96-, Dir Ctr Jewish Studies, 99-; Fulbright prof theatre, Hebrew Univ, Jerusalem, Israel, 80-81, Univ Austria, Vienna, 88, Cath Univ Valparaiso, Chile, 96. **RESEARCH** Holocaust drama; British, classical and American drama; directing. **SELECTED PUBLICATIONS** Ed, The Theatre of the Holocaust: Four Plays, Univ Wis Press, 82, vol 2, 99; auth, The Darkness We Carry: The Drama of the Holocaust, Univ Wis Press, 88. **CONTACT ADDRESS** Dept of Theatre & Drama, Univ of Wis, 821 University Ave, Madison, WI, 53706-1497. **EMAIL** skloot@mall.wisc.edu

SKURA, MEREDITH ANNE
PERSONAL Born 05/11/1944, Brooklyn, NY, m, 1981, 1 child **DISCIPLINE** RENAISSANCE LITERATURE **EDUCATION** Swarthmore Col, BA, 65; Yale Univ, PhD(English), 71. **CAREER** Instr, Univ Bridgeport, 68-71, asst prof, 71-73; asst prof, Yale Univ, 73-78; asst prof, 78-80, ASSOC PROF ENGLISH, RICE UNIV, 80-, Fel, Am Coun Learned Soc, 81 & Guggenheim, 82. **MEMBERSHIPS** MLA; Coun Advan Psychoanal Educ; Shakespeare Asn Am; Medieval & Renaissance Drama Soc. **RESEARCH** Shakespeare's sources; Renaissance drama; cultural contexts for Renaissance literature. **SELECTED PUBLICATIONS** Auth, Understanding The Living And Talking To The Dead, The Historicity Of Psychoanalysis/, Modern Lang Quart, Vol 0054, 1993; The Undiscoverd-Country, New Essays On Psychoanalysis And Shakespeare - Sokol,Bj/, Shakespeare Quart, Vol 0046, 1995. **CONTACT ADDRESS** English Dept, Rice Univ, Houston, TX, 77251.

SLABEY, ROBERT M.
PERSONAL Born 08/21/1931, Hamden, CT **DISCIPLINE** AMERICAN LITERATURE **EDUCATION** Fairfield Univ, BSS, 53; Univ Notre Dame, MA, 55, PhD(English), 61. **CAREER** Teaching fel, Univ Notre Dame, 54-57, instr English, 57-58; instr, Pa State Univ, 58-60; asst prof, Villanova Univ, 60-63; Andrew Mellon fel, Univ Pittsburgh, 63-64; asst prof, 64-67, assoc prof English, Univ Notre Dame, 67-96, prof emer, 96-; Fulbright prof, Univ Oslo, 68-69. **HONORS AND AWARDS** Skaggs Found, 92-93; Indiana Humanities Council, 93. **MEMBERSHIPS** Am Studies Asn; MLA. **RESEARCH** Modern American fiction; Southern literary tradition; Literature and films of the Vietnam war. **SELECTED PUBLICATIONS** Auth, Henry James and The Most Impressive Convention in All History, Am Lit, 58; Myth and Ritual in Light in August, Tex Studies Lit & Lang, 60; The Structure of Hemingway's In Our Time, Moderna Sprak, 66; The Swimming of Amica, Crit Essays on John Cheever, ed R.G. Collins, G.K. Hall, 83; The United States and Vietnam: From War to Peace, McFarland, 96. **CONTACT ADDRESS** Dept of English, Univ of Notre Dame, 356 O'Shaugnessy Hall, Notre Dame, IN, 46556.

SLADE, CAROLE
PERSONAL CA **DISCIPLINE** COMPARATIVE LITERATURE, ENGLISH **EDUCATION** Pomona Col, BA, 65; Univ Wis, MA, 66; New York Univ, PhD(comp lit), 73. **CAREER** Lectr English, Bronx Community Col, City Univ New York, 71-74, asst prof, 74-78; asst prof, Baylor Univ, 78-80; Asst Prof English & Comp Lit, Columbia Univ, 80- **MEMBERSHIPS** MLA; Northeast Mod Lang Asn; Am Comp Lit Asn; Dante Soc Am; NCTE. **SELECTED PUBLICATIONS** Auth, Body And Soul - Essays On Medieval Women And Mysticism - Petroff,Ea/, Rel & Lit, Vol 0027, 1995; Kempe,Margery Dissenting Fictions - Staley,L/, Rel & Lit, Vol 0027, 1995; Julian-Of-Norwich 'Showings' - From Vision To Book - Baker,Dn/, Rel & Lit, Vol 0027, 1995; From Madrid To Purgatory - The Art And Craft Of Dying In 16th-Century Spain - Eire,Cmn/, J Of Rel, Vol 0077, 1997. **CONTACT ADDRESS** Dept of English, Columbia Univ, New York, NY, 10027.

SLAKEY, ROGER L.
DISCIPLINE ENGLISH LITERATURE **EDUCATION** Univ Ca, BA; Univ Mich, MA; Johns Hopkins Univ, PhD. **CAREER** Eng Dept, Georgetown Univ **RESEARCH** Victorian history; poetry; rhetoric; relations between religion and ethics and literature. **SELECTED PUBLICATIONS** Auth, pubs on Milton, Wordsworth, Frost and diverse Victorian writers. **CONTACT ADDRESS** English Dept, Georgetown Univ, 37th and O St, Washington, DC, 20057.

SLANE, ANDREA
DISCIPLINE FILM HISTORY **EDUCATION** Rutgers Univ, BA; Univ Calif, PhD. **CAREER** Engl, Old Dominion Univ. **RESEARCH** Video and Multimedia. **SELECTED PUBLICATIONS** Area: Kinks in the System: Six Shorts About People Left to their own Devices; Six short videos on the human processing of information received by machines; Irresistible Impulse (feature length video); Research on images of fascism. **CONTACT ADDRESS** Old Dominion Univ, 4100 Powhatan Ave, Norfolk, VA, 23058. **EMAIL** ASlane@odu.edu

SLATE, JOSEPH EVANS
PERSONAL Born 12/31/1927, Lubbock, TX, m, 1972, 3 children **DISCIPLINE** ENGLISH **EDUCATION** Univ Ok, BA, 49, MA, 52; Univ Wi, PhD, 57. **CAREER** Instr English, McMicken Col, Univ Cincinnati, 54-57; assoc prof, Austin Col, 57-59; instr, 59-62, asst prof, 62-66, assoc prof English, Univ Tx, Austin, 66-, Dir, Inst Advan Studies English, 66-68; guest prof Am lit & film, Univ Vienna, 72-73; Montpellier III, 92-93. **RESEARCH** Social history of authorship, reading, & publishing; film & literature **SELECTED PUBLICATIONS** Auth, W C Williams and the modern short story, Southern Rev, summer 68; Dahlberg's moral book of erotic beasts, Edward Dahlberg, American Ishmael, 68; Kora in opacity: Williams' improvisation, J Mod Lit, 5/71; Keaton and What No Beer, New Orleans Rev, spring 81. **CONTACT ADDRESS** Dept English, Univ Texas, Austin, TX, 78712-1026. **EMAIL** jeslate@mail.utexas.edu

SLATER, THOMAS J.
PERSONAL Born 12/16/1955, Kalamazoo, MI, m, 1981, 2 children **DISCIPLINE** ENGLISH **EDUCATION** Mich St Univ, BA, 78; Univ Maryland, MA, 81; Okla State Univ, PhD, 85. **CAREER** Lectr, NW Missouri State Univ, 85-86; lectr Missouri W State Col/Univ Missouri-KC, 86-87; asst prof, Ill State Univ, 87-90; asst prof to ASSOC PROF, INDIANA UNIV OF PENN, 90-. **HONORS AND AWARDS** Contemp Am Auth Gale Res, 93. **MEMBERSHIPS** Soc Cinema Stud; Univ Film Video Asn; NE Mod Lang Asn. **RESEARCH** Women screenwriters and directors in American silent film. **SELECTED PUBLICATIONS** auth Milos Forman: A Bio-Bibliography, Greenwood Press, 87; Teaching Vietnam: The Politics of Documentary, Inventing Vietnam: The War in Film and Television, Temple Univ Press, 91; A Handbook of Soviet and East European Film and Filmmakers, Greenwood Press, 91; June Mathis: A Woman Who Spoke Through Silents, Griffithiana: A Journal of Film History, 95; Olivier, Godard, and the Violence of Creation: Considering the Relationship of Theater and Film in a (Post-) Apocalypitic Age, Interdisciplinary Humanities, 97. **CONTACT ADDRESS** Dept of English, Indiana Univ of Pennsylvania, 110 Leonard Hall, Indiana, PA, 15705-1094. **EMAIL** tslater@grove.iup.edu

SLETHAUG, GORDON EMMETT
PERSONAL Born 09/22/1940, Kalispell, MT, m, 1964, 3 children **DISCIPLINE** ENGLISH **EDUCATION** Pac Lutheran Univ, BA, 62; Univ Nebr, MA, 64, PhD(English), 68. **CAREER** Instr English, Univ Nebr, 65-68; asst prof, 68-74, ASSOC PROF ENGLISH & DIR GRAD AFFAIRS, UNIV WATERLOO, 74- **MEMBERSHIPS** Can Asn Univ Teachers; MLA. **RESEARCH** Puritanism; transcendentalism; existential fiction. **SELECTED PUBLICATIONS** Auth, The Discourse Of Arrogance, Popular Power, And Anarchy - The Ist 'Chronicles Of Thomas Covent The Unbeliever'/, Extrapolation, Vol 0034, 1993. **CONTACT ADDRESS** Dept of English, Univ of Waterloo, Waterloo, ON, N2L 3G1.

SLEVIN, JAMES
DISCIPLINE ENGLISH LITERATURE **EDUCATION** Providence Col, BA; Univ Va, MA, PhD. **CAREER** Eng Dept, Georgetown Univ **RESEARCH** Rhetoric and composition; rhetorical theory; literary theory; theories of literacy; 18th century literature. **SELECTED PUBLICATIONS** Auth, Critical Theory and the Teaching of Literature: Politics, Curriculum, Pedagogy, 95; Making Faculty Work Visible: Reinterpreting Professional Service, Teaching, and Research in the Fields of Language and Literature, 96; The Next Generation: Preparing Graduate Students for the Professional Responsibilities of College Teachers, 93; co-ed, The Future of Doctoral Studies in English, 89; The Right to Literacy, 90. **CONTACT ADDRESS** English Dept, Georgetown Univ, 37th and O St, Washington, DC, 20057.

SLOANE, DAVID EDWARD EDISON
PERSONAL Born 01/19/1943, West Orange, NJ, 3 children **DISCIPLINE** AMERICAN LITERATURE **EDUCATION** Wesleyan Univ, BA, 64; Duke Univ, MA, 66, PhD, 70. **CAREER** Instr, Lafayette Col, 68-70, asst prof, 70-74; dir, Writing Ctr, Livingston Col, Rutgers Univ, 73-74; instr writing, Fashion Inst Technol, 74-75; asst chmn div acad develop, Medgar Evers Col, 75-76; assoc prof, 76-82, prof English, Univ New Haven, 82-. **HONORS AND AWARDS** Winchester Fel for Grad Study, Wesleyan Univ, 64; Yale-Mellon Vis Conn Fac Fel, 80-81; USIA lectr on American humor to the Asn Brazillian Prof of English annual convention, 88; First Henry Nash Smith Fel, Ctr for Mark Twain Studies, 89; Keynote Speaker, "Interpreting Edison," Edison Nat Hist Site, Edison Sesquicentennial Conf, 6/97. **MEMBERSHIPS** MLA; Am Humor Studies Asn (pres 89); ALA; Mark Twain Circle (pres 92-94); NEMLA. **RESEARCH** American literature, 1860-1910, remedial writing. **SELECTED PUBLICATIONS** Auth, Mark Twain as a Literary Comedian, La State Univ Press, 79, 82; The Literary Humor of the Urban Northeast, 1830-1890, La State Univ Press, 83; American Humor Magazines and Comic Periodicals, Greenwood, 87; Writing for Tax Professionals, KPMG-Peat Marwick, Rptd, 88; Adventures of Huckleberry Finn: American Comic Vision, G.K. Hall-Twayne, 88; Sister Carrie: Theodore Dreiser's Sociological Tragedy, Macmillan, 92; Mark Twain's Humor: Critical Essays, Garland Publ, 93; American Humor: New Studies, New Directions, Univ Ala Press, 98; author of numerous journal articles. **CONTACT ADDRESS** 300 Orange Ave, West Haven, CT, 06516-1999.

SLOANE, THOMAS O.
PERSONAL Born 07/12/1929, West Frankfort, IL, m, 1952, 3 children **DISCIPLINE** RHETORIC **EDUCATION** Southern Ill Univ, BA, 51, MA, 52; Northwestern Univ, PhD, 60. **CAREER** Lectr speech, Southern Ill Univ, 56; asst interpretation, Northwestern Univ, 57-58; instr English Washington & Lee Univ, 58-60; asst prof speech, Univ Ill, Urbana, 60-65, assoc prof, 65-70, fac fel, 64, instr develop award, 65, asst dean lib arts & sci, 66-67, assoc head dept speech, 67-68; vis assoc prof, 68-69, chmn dept, 72-76, PROF RHET, UNIV CALIF, BERKELEY, 70-, Guggenheim fel, 81-82. **HONORS AND AWARDS** Huntington Libr Res Award, 67; Humanities Res Award, Univ Calif Berkeley, 74. **MEMBERSHIPS** MLA; Renaissance Soc Am. **RESEARCH** Rhetoric and poetry in the English Renaissance; interpretation of literature. **SELECTED PUBLICATIONS** Auth, The Rhet Of Politics In The English-Revolution 1642-1660 - Skerpan,E/, Rhetorica-A J Of The Hist Of Rhet, Vol 0011, 1993. **CONTACT ADDRESS** Dept of Rhet, Univ of Calif, Berkeley, CA, 94720.

SLONIOWSKI, JEANNETTE
DISCIPLINE COMMUNICATIONS **EDUCATION** Univ Toronto, BA, PhD; Brock Univ, BA; State Univ NY, MA. **CAREER** Prof, Brock Univ. **HONORS AND AWARDS** Ed bd, Can Jour Commun. **RESEARCH** Television, docudrama, documentary, the grotesque, theories of transgression; ideology.

SELECTED PUBLICATIONS Co-auth, Documenting the Documentary, Wayne State UP, 96; auth, It Was an Atrocious Film: George Franju's Le Sang des betes, Documenting the Documentary, 96; The Boys of St. Vincent and The Valour and the Horror, Encycl of TV, 96. CONTACT ADDRESS Dept of Film Stud, Dramatic and Visual Arts, Brock Univ, 500 Glenridge Ave, St. Catharines, ON, L2S 3A1. EMAIL jeanette@spartan.ac.BrockU.CA

SLOTKIN, ALAN ROBERT
PERSONAL Born 11/07/1943, Brooklyn, NY DISCIPLINE ENGLISH LINGUISTICS, AMERICAN LITERATURE EDUCATION Univ Miami, AB, 65; Univ SC, MA, 70, PhD(English), 71. CAREER Asst prof, 70-80, Assoc Prof English, Tenn Technol Univ, 80-, Ed, Tenn Ling. MEMBERSHIPS Am Dialect Soc; Ling Soc Am; Southeastern Conf Ling; SAtlantic Mod Lang Asn. RESEARCH American dialects; American dialect literature; modern drama. SELECTED PUBLICATIONS Auth, A Back-To-The-Future-Formation Plus Back-Formation And The Etymology Of Contraption/, Am Speech, Vol 0068, 1993; Improvography + Dance Terminology - A Contradiction In Terms/, Am Speech, Vol 0068, 1993; 2 New Obscenities, The Acceptability Of Taboo Words In The Media/, Am Speech, Vol 0069, 1994. CONTACT ADDRESS Dept English, Tenn Technol Univ, Cookville, TN, 38501.

SLOUFFMAN, JAMES W.
PERSONAL Born 04/01/1950, Dayton, OH, m, 1981 DISCIPLINE PERFORMING ARTS EDUCATION Wright State Univ, BFA, 72; Univ Cincinnati, MFA, 76. CAREER Dir, dept chemn, 1979-; Antonelli Col. HONORS AND AWARDS Catholic Kolping Society Service Award., 1996 Tchr Year Award; 20 Years Tenure MEMBERSHIPS IGIA; Alpha Beta Kappa Nat Honor Society. RESEARCH The operas of Richard Wagner. CONTACT ADDRESS 124 E 7th St, Cincinnati, OH, 45202. EMAIL jimslouffman@antonellic.com

SMALL, RAY
PERSONAL Born 08/02/1915, Winters, TX, m, 1938, 2 children DISCIPLINE ENGLISH EDUCATION West Tex State Univ, BA, 37; Univ Tex, Austin, MA, 41, PhD(English), 58. CAREER From instr to prof English, Amarillo Col, 46-61; asst to pres, 61-63, dean arts & sci, 63-67, dean col lib arts, 67-79, prof English, Univ Tex, El Paso, 61-, emer dean Col Lib Arts, 80-, emer prof English, 84-, emer prof Communication, 93-. RESEARCH William Butler Yeats; Cardinal Newman and the Oxford movement. CONTACT ADDRESS Dept of English, Univ Texas, El Paso, 500 W University Ave, El Paso, TX, 79968-0001.

SMALLENBURG, HARRY RUSSELL
PERSONAL Born 07/17/1942, Burbank, Calif, 2 children DISCIPLINE ENGLISH LITERATURE EDUCATION Univ Calif, Santa Barbara, BA, 65; Univ Calif, Berkeley, MA, 66, PhD (English), 70; Cranbrook Art Acad, MFA, 78. CAREER Asst prof, Wayne State Univ, 70-; Chmn Dept Gen Studies, Ctr Creative Stu, 77-86; assoc prof, Pasadena City Col, 89-. MEMBERSHIPS MLA; Milton Soc Am. RESEARCH Milton; English Renaissance literature; creative writing; 20th century literature, humanities, music/composition SELECTED PUBLICATIONS Milton's cosmic sentences, Lang & Style, 72; Government of the spirit: Style, structure and theme in Treatise of civil power, In: Achievements of the Left Hand: Essays on the Prose of John Milton, Univ Mass, 74. CONTACT ADDRESS Dept of Eng and For Lang, Pasadena City Col, 1570 E Colorado Blvd, Pasadena, CA, 91106. EMAIL hrsmallenburg@paccd.cc.ca.us

SMART, PATRICIA
PERSONAL Born 02/03/1940, Toronto, ON, Canada DISCIPLINE LITERATURE EDUCATION Univ Toronto, BA, 61; Laval Univ, MA, 63; Queen's Univ, PhD, 77. CAREER Fac mem, 71-86, PROF FRENCH, CARLETON UNIV, 86-, Marston Lafrance Leave Fel, 86-87, dir, Inst Can Stud, 87-88. HONORS AND AWARDS Gov Gen Award Non-fiction (Fr lang); Gabrielle Roy Award. MEMBERSHIPS Royal Soc Can; Asn Can & Que Lit; Asn Can Stud. SELECTED PUBLICATIONS Auth, Hubert Aquin, Agent Double, 73; auth, Ecrire dans la maison du Pere: l'emergence du feminin dans la tradition litteraire du Quebec, 88; auth & transl, Writing in the Father's House: the Emergence of the Feminine in the Quebec Literary Tradition, 91; ed & transl, The Diary of Andre Laurendeau 1964-67, 91. CONTACT ADDRESS French Dept, Carleton Univ, 1125 Colonel By Dr, Ottawa, ON, K1S 5B6. EMAIL psmart@ccs.carleton.ca

SMEDICK, LOIS KATHERINE
DISCIPLINE ENGLISH LANGUAGE; LITERATURE EDUCATION Wilson, BA; Toronto, MSL; Bryn Mawr, PhD,-63. CAREER Prof RESEARCH Chaucer and his contemporaries; chivalric romance; and Middle English prose style. SELECTED PUBLICATIONS Pub (s), medieval devotional prose; Form of Living of Richard Rolle; Latin stylistic device, the cursus. CONTACT ADDRESS Dept of English Language and Literature, Univ of Windsor, 401 Sunset Ave, Windsor, ON, N9B 3P4. EMAIL smedick@uwindsor.ca

SMITH, BARBARA
DISCIPLINE WRITING, GENDER STUDIES EDUCATION Southern CT State Col, BS; SUNY, MA, 86, PhD, 92. CAREER Engl, Col Mt. St. Vincent HONORS AND AWARDS Adv, Fonthill Dial; Hum rep Undergrad Comt. SELECTED PUBLICATIONS Auth, A Case Study of Myself as a Writer. A Community of Writers: A Workshop Course in Writing, Random House, 89; The Women of Ben Jonson's Poetry: Female Representations in the Non-Dramatic Verse, Aldershot: Scolar Press, 95; Adapting Writing Pedagogies to Discipline- Specific Classrooms, Garland Press In. CONTACT ADDRESS Col of Mount Saint Vincent, 6301 Riverdale Ave, Riverdale, NY, 10471. EMAIL barbsmith9@aol.com

SMITH, BRUCE
PERSONAL Born 03/21/1946, Jackson, MS DISCIPLINE ENGLISH EDUCATION Tulane Univ, BA, 68; Rochester Univ, MA, 71; Rochester Univ, PhD, 73. CAREER Prof, eng, Georgetown Univ, 87-; assoc prof, eng, Georgetown Univ, 78-87; asst prof, eng, Georgetown Univ, 72-78; fac, Middlebury Col, Bread Loaf Sch of Eng, 94-. HONORS AND AWARDS Intl globe fel, 97; Mellon res fel, Huntington Libr, 96; Va Foundation for the Humanities fel, 89; NEH fel, Foljer Libr, 87-88; ACLS fel, 79-80. MEMBERSHIPS Shakespeare Asn of Amer; Renaissance Soc of Amer; Mod Lang Asn; Southeastern Renaissance Conf; Medieval and Renaissance Drama Soc; Comt for Gay and Lesbian Hist; Amer Hist Asn. RESEARCH Shakespeare; early modern culture; acoustic ecology; gay and lesbian history. SELECTED PUBLICATIONS Auth, Roasting the Swan of Avon: Shakespeare's Redoubtable Enemies and Dubious Friends, Washington, DC, Folger Shakespeare Libr, Seattle, Univ Wash Press, 94; Homosexual Desire in Shakespeare's England: A Cultural Poetics, Chicago, Univ Chicago Press, 91, paperback, 94; Ancient Scripts and Modern Experience on the English Stage, 1500-1700, Princeton, Princton Univ Press, 88; I, You, He, She, and We: On the Sexual Politics of Shakespeare's Sonnets, Shakespeare's Sonnets: Critical Essays, ed James Schiffer, Garland Ref Libr of the Humanities, NY, Garland, Dec, 98; William Shakespeare, Encycl of Homosexuality, 2nd ed, vol 2, ed George E. Haggerty, NY, Garland, 98; A Night of Errors and the Dawn of Empire: Male Enterprise in The Comedy of Errors, Shakespeare's Sweet Thunder, ed Michael Collins, Newark, Univ Del Press, 97; Circling the Subject in Early Modern Drama, Medieval Continuities in Shakespearean Drama, ed Wayne Neary, Detroit, Wayne State Univ Press, 97; Locating the Sexual Subject, Alternative Shakespeares, vol 2, ed Terry Hawkes, London, Routledge, 96; Rape, Rap, Rupture, Rapture: R-Rated Futures On the Global Market, Textual Practice 9, 421-444, 95. CONTACT ADDRESS English Dept, Georgetown Univ, Washington, DC, 20057-1131. EMAIL smithb@gunet.georgetown.edu

SMITH, BRUCE RAY
PERSONAL Born 03/21/1946, Jackson, MS DISCIPLINE ENGLISH LITERATURE EDUCATION Tulane Univ, BA, 68; Univ Rochester, MA, 71, PhD(English), 73. CAREER Asst prof, 72-78, assoc prof English, Georgetown Univ, 78-87, prof English, 87-, Folger Inst fel English, 78; Am Coun Learned Soc fel, 78-79; NEH fel, Folger Lib, 87-88; Virginia Foundation for Humanities fel, 89; Mellon fel, Huntington Lib, 96; Folger Institute fel, 96; Int Globe Fellowship, Shakespeare's Globe, London, 97; dir, grad program in English, Georgetown Univ, 87-91; dir, undergrad studies in English, 92-95. MEMBERSHIPS Southeastern Renaissance Conf; Medieval & Renaissance Drama Soc; Shakespeare Asn Am; Modern Language Asn of Am; Committee for Gay and Lesbian History; Renaissance Soc Am. RESEARCH Renaissance drama; Shakespeare; 17th century literature. SELECTED PUBLICATIONS Auth, Ben Jonson's Epigrammes: Portrait-Gallery, Theater, Commonwealth, Studies English Lit, 74; Sir Amorous Knight and the Indecorous Romans: Plautus and Terence Play Court in the Renaissance, 75, Landscape with Figures: The Three Realms of Queen Elizabeth's Country House Revels, 78 & Towards the Rediscovery of Tragedy: Seneca's Plays on the English Renaissance Stage, 79, Renaissance Drama; The Contest of Apollo and Marsyas: Ideas About Music in the Middle Ages, In: By Things Seen: Reference and Recognition in Medieval Thought, 79; On Reading the Shepheardes Calender, Spenser Studies, 80; Pageant's into Play: Shakespeare's Three Perspectives on Idea and Image, in David m. Bergeron, ed, Pageantry in the Shakespearean Theater, Athens: Univ of Ga Press, 85; Sermons in Stones: Shakespeare and Renaissance Sculpture, Shakespeare Studies 17, 85; Ancient Scripts and Modern Experience on the English Stage, 1500-1700, Princeton Univ Press, 88; Parolles' Recitations: Oral and Literate Structures in Shakespeare's Plays, Renaissance Papers 1989, Southeastern Renaissance Conference, 89; Homosexual Desire in Shakespeare's England: A Cultural Poetics, Univ of Chicago Press, 91, paperback, 94; Reading Lists of Plays in Early Modern England, Shakespeare Quart 42, 91; Makimg a Difference: Male/Male Desire in Tragedy, Comedy, and Tragi/Comedy, in Erotic Politics: The Dynamics of Desire on the English Renaissance Stage, ed Susan Zimmerman. London: Routledge, 92; Roasting the Swan of Avon: Shakespeare's Redoubtable Enemies and Dubious Friends Washington, D.C.: Folger Shakespeare Lib, and Seattle: Univ of Washington Press, 94; Prickly Characters, in Reading and Writing in Shakespeare, ed David M. Bergeron, Newark: Univ of Delaware Press, 96; Rape, Rap, Rupture, Rapture: R-Rated Futures On the Global Market, Textual Practice 9, 95; Locating the Sexual Subject, in Alternative Shakespeares, vol 2, ed Terry Hawkes, London: Routledge, 96; Circling the Subject in Early Modern Drama, commissioned essay for Medieval Continuities in Shakespearean Drama, ed Wayne Neary, Detroit: Wayne State Univ Press, 97; A Night of Errors and the Dawn of Empire: Male Enterprise in the Comedy of Errors, commissioned essay for Shakespeare's Sweet Thunder, ed Michael Collins, Newark: Univ of Delaware Press, 97; I, You, He, She, and We: On the Sexual Politics of Shakespeare's Sonnets, commissioned essay for Shakespeare's Sonnets: Critical Essays, ed James Schiffer, Garland Reference Lib of the Humanities, New York: Garland, forthcoming Dec 98; The Acoustic World of Early Modern England, Chicago: Univ of Chicago Press, forthcoming spring 99. CONTACT ADDRESS Dept of English, Georgetown Univ, P O Box 571131, Washington, DC, 20057-1131. EMAIL smithb@gunet.georgetown.edu

SMITH, CARL
DISCIPLINE ENGLISH EDUCATION Yale Univ, PhD. CAREER Cur, Chicago Historical Society exhibition, The Great Chicago Fire & Web of Memory. HONORS AND AWARDS CAS outstanding tchg awd; McCormick tchg professorship; awd(s), Best Book in North Am Urban History; Soc of Midland Authors' first prize for non-fiction, 94. SELECTED PUBLICATIONS Auth,Chicago and the American Literary Imagination, 1880-1920 ,84; Urban Disorder and the Shape of Belief: The Great Chicago Fire, the Haymarket Bomb, and the Model Town of Pullman, 94. CONTACT ADDRESS Dept of English, Northwestern Univ, 1801 Hinman, Evanston, IL, 60208.

SMITH, CAROL HERTZIG
PERSONAL Born 08/17/1929, Pittsburgh, PA, m, 1953, 1 child DISCIPLINE ENGLISH EDUCATION OH Wesleyan Univ, BA, 52; Univ MI, MA, 55, PhD, 62. CAREER From instr to assoc prof English, 59-70, PROF ENGLISH, RUTGERS UNIV, 70-, chmn dept, 80-86, DIR OF GRADUATE STUDIES, 98-. MEMBERSHIPS MLA RESEARCH Modern literature, especially drama, novel and poetry; women writers of modernism. SELECTED PUBLICATIONS Auth, T S Eliot's Dramatic Theory and Practice: From Sweeney Agonistes to The Elder Statesman, Princeton, 63, T S Eliot: The Poet as Playwright, Nation, 10/66; other critical articles on modernism. CONTACT ADDRESS Dept of English, Rutgers Univ, 510 George St, New Brunswick, NJ, 08903-1167. EMAIL chs@rci.rutgers.edu

SMITH, DAVE
DISCIPLINE POETRY (19TH, MODERN, CONTEMPORARY AMERICAN), 20TH CENTURY BRITISH AND AMER EDUCATION Ohio Univ, PhD, 76. CAREER Prof, La State Univ; coed, Southern Rev; poetry ed, Univ Utah Press, 77-87; Bd mem, 80-83, vpres, Assoc Writing Prog, 82; ed, Southern Messenger Signature Poets of La State UP, 95-. HONORS AND AWARDS Fel, Lyndhurst Found; John Simon Guggenheim Found; Nat Endowments for the Arts (2); Award of Excellence, Am Acad and Inst for Arts and Letters; Prarie Schooner Reader's Award, 95. MEMBERSHIPS The Fel of Southern Writers. RESEARCH Southern poetry; poetic form and theory. SELECTED PUBLICATIONS Auth, The Pure Clear Word: Essays on the Poetry of James Wright, 82; Local Essays: On Contemporary American Poetry, 85; The Essential Poe, 91; coed, The Morrow Anthology of Contemporary American Poetry, 85. CONTACT ADDRESS Dept of Eng, Louisiana State Univ, 43 Allen Hall, Baton Rouge, LA, 70803. EMAIL davesm@unix1.sncc.lsu.edu

SMITH, DAVID LEE
PERSONAL Born 06/29/1944, Portsmouth, VA, m, 1968, 4 children DISCIPLINE ENGLISH EDUCATION Old Dominion Univ, BA, 66, MA, 70; Univ NC, Chapel Hill, PhD(English), 75. CAREER Instr English, Univ NC, Chapel Hill, 75-76; asst prof to prof English, Cent Mo State Univ, 76-; chair, dept English and Philos, 93-. MEMBERSHIPS MLA RESEARCH Victorian literature; prose fiction. CONTACT ADDRESS Dept of English and Philosophy, Central Missouri State Univ, Warrensburg, MO, 64093-8888. EMAIL dls4426@cmsu2.cmsu.edu

SMITH, DAVID QUINTIN
PERSONAL Born 11/30/1938, Tiffin, OH, m, 1960, 2 children DISCIPLINE ENGLISH LITERATURE EDUCATION Columbia Univ, AB, 60; NY Univ, MA, 63; Univ Ill, Urbana, PhD(English), 68. CAREER Asst prof, 67-73, ASSOC PROF ENGLISH, UNIV TOLEDO, 73- MEMBERSHIPS MLA; AAUP RESEARCH English Romanticism; Wordsworth; Blake. SELECTED PUBLICATIONS Auth, Opera In London, Views Of The Press 1785-1830 - Fenner,T/, Wordsworth Circle, Vol 0026, 1995; Hunt,Leigh And The Poetry Of Fancy - Edgecombe,Rs/, Wordsworth Circle, Vol 0026, 1995. CONTACT ADDRESS Dept of English, Univ of Toledo, 2801 W Bancroft St, Toledo, OH, 43606-3390.

SMITH, DIANE M.
PERSONAL Born 03/22/1953, Lawrence, MA, m, 1995 **DISCIPLINE** EDUCATION/ENGLISH **EDUCATION** Univ of MA, MA, 98; Univ of So CA, BA, 81 **CAREER** Pub Svc libr, 93-, Bunker Hill Cmnty Col Lib; **MEMBERSHIPS** ALA; ACRL **RESEARCH** Infor Literacy **CONTACT ADDRESS** Library, Bunker Hill Comm Col, Boston, MA, 02129-2925. **EMAIL** smith@noblenet.org

SMITH, DUANE
DISCIPLINE SEVENTEENTH AND 18TH CENTURY BRITISH LITERATURE **EDUCATION** Auburn Univ, PhD. **CAREER** Eng Dept, St. Edward's Univ **SELECTED PUBLICATIONS** Auth, England, My England as Fragmentary Novel, D.H. Lawrence Rev, 92; Repetitive Patterns in Samuel Johnson's Rasselas, Studies Eng Lit, 96. **CONTACT ADDRESS** St Edward's Univ, 3001 S Congress Ave, Austin, TX, 78704-6489.

SMITH, F. LESLIE
PERSONAL Born 01/19/1939, Orlando, FL, m, 1961, 1 child **DISCIPLINE** MASS COMMUNICATIONS **EDUCATION** Univ FL, BS, 61; OH Univ, MA, 64; FL State Univ, PhD, 72. **CAREER** Instr radio-TV, St Petersburg Jr Col, 64-67; asst prof commun arts, Univ WFL, 67-70; asst prof radio-TV-film, NTX State Univ, 72-75, prof, 75-82; PROF Telecommunications, Univ FL, 82, Ch Telecommunication, Univ Fla 96-, Danforth assoc, 81. **HONORS AND AWARDS** Broadcast Preceptor Award, San Francisco State Univ, 81. **MEMBERSHIPS** Asn for Educ in Journalism & Mass Comm; Am Journalism Historians Asn; Broadcast Educ Asn. **RESEARCH** Hist of radio and TV; station management and programming; broadcast law and regulation. **SELECTED PUBLICATIONS** Auth, Education for broadcasting: 1929-1963, J Broadcasting, 11/64; The selling of the Pentagon: Case study of a controversy, In: Mass News, Prentice-Hall, 73; coauth, Perceived ethicality of some TV new production techniques by a sample of Florida legislators, Speech Monogr, 11/73; auth, Hunger in America controversy: Another view, J Broadcasting, winter 74; coauth, The cigarette commercial ban: A pattern for change, Quart J Speech, 12/74; auth, Selling of the Pentagon and the First Amendment, Jounalism Hist, spring 75; The Charlie Walker case, J Broadcasting, spring 79; Quelling radio's quacks: the FCC's first programming campaign, Jour Quart, autumn 94; Electronic media and government: regulation of wireless and wired communication, Longman, 95; Perspectives on Radio and Television: An Introduction to Telecommunication in the United States, 4th ed, Laurence Erlbaum Assoc, 98. **CONTACT ADDRESS** Univ FL, PO Box 118400, Gainesville, FL, 32611-8400. **EMAIL** lesmith@ufl.edu

SMITH, FRANCIS J.
PERSONAL Born 05/22/1920, Lorain, OH **DISCIPLINE** LITERARY CRITICISM **EDUCATION** Xavier Univ, Ohio, Litt B, 42; Loyola Univ, Ill, MA, 46; WBaden Col, STL, 53; Oxford Univ, AM, 60. **CAREER** Instr English & Latin, High Sch, Univ Detroit, 46-49; instr English, Univ, 58-60; asst prof, Colombiere Col, 60-63; from asst prof to assoc prof, 63-72, prof Eng, John Carroll Univ, 72-. **MEMBERSHIPS** MLA; Col English Assn. **RESEARCH** T S Eliot; Chaucer; modern fiction. **SELECTED PUBLICATIONS** Auth, First Prelude, Loyola Univ Press, winter 81; auth, All Is A Prize, The Pterodactyl Press, 89; auth, Haiku Yearbook, The Cobham & Hatherton Press, 91. **CONTACT ADDRESS** Dept of English, John Carroll Univ, 20700 N Park Blvd, Cleveland, OH, 44118-4581.

SMITH, GAIL K.
DISCIPLINE ENGLISH **EDUCATION** Yale Univ, BA, 85; Univ Virginia, PhD, 93. **CAREER** ASST PROF, ENG, MARQUETTE UNIV **MEMBERSHIPS** Am Antiquarian Soc **SELECTED PUBLICATIONS** Auth, "Reading with the Other: Hermeneutics and the Politics of Difference in Stowe's Dred," Am Lit, June 97; auth, "From the Seminary to the Parlor: The Popularization of Hermeneutics in The Gates Ajar," Ariz Quart, 98. **CONTACT ADDRESS** Dept of Eng, Marquette Univ, Coughlin Hall, Milwaukee, WI, 53233. **EMAIL** smithg@vms.csd.mu.edu

SMITH, GAYLE LEPPIN
PERSONAL Born 07/05/1946, New York, NY **DISCIPLINE** AMERICAN LITERATURE, STYLISTICS **EDUCATION** Univ Denver, BA, 68; Univ Mass, MA, 72, PhD(English), 77. **CAREER** Teaching asst compos, Univ Mass, 68-70, instr Am lit, 72 & 73; instr lang & lit, Holyoke Community Col, 75; ASST PROF ENGLISH, PA STATE UNIV, 77- **MEMBERSHIPS** MLA; NCTE; Conf Col Compos & Commun; Northeast Mod Lang Asn. **RESEARCH** Emerson studies; style studies; composition and rhetoric. **SELECTED PUBLICATIONS** Auth, Transformational theory and developmental compositon, Exercise Exchange, spring 80; When students grade themselves: What we teach and what we learn, Pa Coun Teachers English Bull, 5/81; Style and vision in Emerson's experience, ESQ: J Am Renaissance, spring 81; The language of transcendence in S O Jewett's A White Heron, Colby Libr Quart (in prep); From graveyard to classroom: Thinking about data, Teaching English Two-Yr Col; contribr, Revising: New Essays for Writing Teachers, NCTE; Reading Song Of Myself--Assuming What Whitman Assumes, Am Transcendental Quart, Vol 06, 92. **CONTACT ADDRESS** Dept of English, Pennsylvania State Univ, 120 Ridgeview Dr, Dunmore, PA, 18512-1602.

SMITH, GRANT WILLIAM
PERSONAL Born 07/26/1937, Bellingham, WA, m, 1961, 2 children **DISCIPLINE** ENGLISH **EDUCATION** Reed Col, BA, 64; Univ Nev, Reno, MA, 67; Univ Del, PhD(English lit), 75. **CAREER** Fac Pres, 76-77, asst prof, 68-72, assoc prof, 72-81, Prof English, Eastern Wash Univ, 81-, Chm Dept, 78-84; Coordr Humanities, 84-. **MEMBERSHIPS** Spokane Area Coun English Teachers; Am Asn Univ Prof; Am Dialect Soc (reg secy, 81-98); Archaeol Inst Am; Am Name Soc; Am Soc Geolinguistics; Brit Studies Asn; Can Soc for the Study of Names; Int Coun on Onomastic Sci; Mod Lang Asn; NW Conf on Brit Studies; Philol Asn of the Pacific Coast; Rocky Mountain Mod Lang Asn (prog ch, 87-95); Societe Internationale de Dialectologie et Geolinguistique; Western States Conf on Geographic Names. **RESEARCH** Onomastics; Shakespeare. **SELECTED PUBLICATIONS** Auth, Density Variations in Indian Placenames: A Comparison Between British Columbia & Washington State, Onomastica Canadiana, 71.4, 89; coauth, Computer Fields & the Classification of Toponymic Data, 90; auth, Shakespeare's Use of Feminine Names, Georgetown Univ, 90; Plans for the U.S. Survey of Geographic Names, Proceedings of the XVIIth Intl. Congress of Onomastic Sciences, Univ Helsinki Press, 91; A Comparison of Hispanic Names in Washington State and British Columbia, Onomastica Canadiana, 12/94; Amerindian Place Names: A Typology Based on Meaning and Form, Onomastica Canadiana, 12/96 (this article has been adopted as the basis for a national study of Amerindian Place Names to be published by Univ of Okla Press and involving leading specialists in all Amerindian language groups); What We Can Know About Onomastics, commissioned for an anthology edited by Wallace McMullen (forthcoming); author numerous other articles for NAMES and other journals. **CONTACT ADDRESS** Dept of English, Eastern Washington Univ, M/S 25, Cheney, WA, 99004-2496. **EMAIL** gsmith@ewu.edu

SMITH, JEFFREY A.
PERSONAL Born 01/25/1958, Valparaiso, IN **DISCIPLINE** ENGLISH/AMERICAN STUDIES **EDUCATION** Valparaiso Univ, BA, English/Humanities, 80; Univ Chicago, MA, English, 81; Univ Calif, Los Angeles, MFA, film/theater/television, 93. **CAREER** Lecturer, English, Univ Illinois-Chicago, 81-82; instructor, Dept of Popular Culture, Bowling Green State Univ, 86-87; lecturer, writing programs, Univ Calif-Los Angeles, 87-. **HONORS AND AWARDS** Fulbright Fellowship to Great Britain, 84-86; honorable mention, Danforth Graduate Fellowship, 80. **MEMBERSHIPS** Natl Coun of Teachers of English, Conf on Coll Composition and Commun; Modern Language Assn. **RESEARCH** Writing; commun and pedagogy; Amer culture; politics; popular arts and media. **SELECTED PUBLICATIONS** Auth, "Students' Goals, Gatekeeping, and Some Questions of Ethics," College English, Mar 97; "The L.A. Riots: A Case Study of Debate Across the Political Spectrum," in Writing and Reading Across the Curriculum, 97; "Why College," College English, Mar 96; "Against 'Illegeracy': Toward a New Pedagogy of Civic Understanding," College Composition and Commun, May 94; coauth, "In Search of Lost Pedagogical Synthesis," College English, Nov 93. **CONTACT ADDRESS** 8533 Cashio St., 5, Los Angeles, CA, 90035-3650. **EMAIL** smith@humnet.ucla.edu

SMITH, JOHN KARES
PERSONAL Born 06/29/1942, Oak Park, IL, m, 1968, 2 children **DISCIPLINE** COMMUNICATION STUDIES **EDUCATION** Northwestern Univ, BS, 64, MA, 65; Oxford Univ, postgraduate study, 71; Northwestern Univ, PhD, 74. **CAREER** Instr, speech, Benedictine Univ, 65-66, asst prof, 67-69; asst prof, 74-76, assoc prof, 77-85, prof, Communication Studies, State Univ of New York-Oswego, 86-. **HONORS AND AWARDS** IL State Scholar, 60-64; Oxford Univ, Univ College Scholar, 71; Northwestern Univ Graduate Assistantships, 69-71; Northwestern Univ fel, 71-72; Distinguished Humanities Scholar: A Learning Odyssey, NY Conference on Library Programming for Young Adults, 89; State of New York and United Univ Professions Excellence Award for Professional Service, 91; Chancellor's Award for Excellence in Teaching, SUNY, 93. **MEMBERSHIPS** Nat Commun Asn; Eastern Commun Asn; New York State Commun Asn; Oswego Opera Theatre, Inc. **RESEARCH** Presidential and political rhetoric; social movements theory; application of Internet resources in commun classrooms; infusing a Languages Across the Curriculum program into commun study, sponsored by the Languages Across the Curriculum Project. **SELECTED PUBLICATIONS** Auth, Upton Sinclair and the Celestial Crown: the Rhetoric of The Dead Hand Series, dissertation, Univ Microfilms, 74; Scarred Hopes Outworn: Unton Sinclair and the Decline of the Muckraking Movement, in Dieter Herms ed, Upton Sinclair: Literature and Social Reform, Peter Lang, 90; Why Shouldn't We Believe That? We Are Americans: Rhetorical Myths and Fantasies in the Reagan Inaugurals, in Ronald Reagan's America, vol II, ed by Eric Schmertz, Natalie Datlof and Alexej Ugrinsky, Greenwood Press, 97; Interdependence, Interaction and Influence: LAC in Communication 240: Group Interaction and Discussion, in Using Languages Across the Curriculum, ed by Virginia M Fichera and H Stephen Straight, Center for Research in Translation of State Univ of New York at Binghamton, 97; Once More Unto the Breach, Dear Friends: War in the Persian Gulf as a Rhetorical System, in George Bush, the Forty-First President, ed by William F Levantrosser and Rosanna Perotti, Greenwood Pub Co, 2000. **CONTACT ADDRESS** SUNY, Oswego, 3 Lanigan Hall, Oswego, NY, 13126. **EMAIL** smith@oswego.edu

SMITH, JULIAN
PERSONAL Born 12/14/1937, New Orleans, LA, m, 1964, 3 children **DISCIPLINE** FILM STUDIES, AMERICAN LITERATURE **EDUCATION** Tulane Univ, BA, 59, MA, 62. **CAREER** Instr Eng, Spring Hill Col, 62-63; instr, Georgetown Univ, 63-65; instr Univ NH, 65-69; asst prof, Ithaca Col, 69-73; hon fel, Univ NH, 73-75; vis fac, San Diego State Univ, 75-76; Assoc Prof, 77-85, prof film studies, Univ FL, 85. **HONORS AND AWARDS** Res grants, Nat Endowment for Hum, 70 & Am Coun Learned Soc, 79. **RESEARCH** Am film. **SELECTED PUBLICATIONS** Auth, Coming of age in America: Young Ben Franklin and Robin Molineux, Am Quart, 65; Hawthorne's Legends of the Province House, 19th Century Fiction, 69; Hemingway and the thing left out, J Mod Lit, 70; Looking Away: Hollywood and Vietnam, Scribner's, 75; Nevil Shute, In: Twayne English Authors Series, 76; The automobile in the American film, Mich Quart Rev, 80-81; Chaplin, Twayne Filmmakers Series, 84. **CONTACT ADDRESS** Dept of Eng, Univ of FL, PO Box 117310, Gainesville, FL, 32611-7310. **EMAIL** smithj@english.ufl.edu

SMITH, KAREN A.
PERSONAL Born 11/30/1965, Brooklyn, NY, s **DISCIPLINE** SPEECH COMMUNICATION **EDUCATION** CUNY, BA, 89; SUNY, MA, 92; S IL Univ, Carbondale, Speech Commun, 96 **CAREER** Lect, 96-97, SIU-Carbondale; Asst Prof, 97-, Col of St Rose **MEMBERSHIPS** Nat Commun Asn **RESEARCH** Methods, Critical Pedagogy **CONTACT ADDRESS** Col of Saint Rose, Albany, NY, 12203. **EMAIL** ksmith@rosnet.strose.edu

SMITH, LARRY D.
DISCIPLINE DEPARTMENT OF COMMUNICATIONS **EDUCATION** Ohio State Univ, PhD, 86. **CAREER** Assoc prof, Purdue Univ. **RESEARCH** Presidential nominating conventions; television advertising; popular media. **SELECTED PUBLICATIONS** Auth, Reagan's Strategic Defense Initiative as Political Innovation, Polit Commun Rev, 90; Party Platforms as Institutional Discourse, Presidential Stud Quart, 92; coauth, Cordial Concurrence: Orchestrating National Party Conventions in the Telepolitical Age, Praeger, 91. **CONTACT ADDRESS** Dept of Commun, Purdue Univ, 1080 Schleman Hall, West Lafayette, IN, 47907-1080.

SMITH, LORRIE
DISCIPLINE AMERICAN POETRY **EDUCATION** Brown Univ, PhD. **CAREER** Eng, St. Michaels Col. **SELECTED PUBLICATIONS** Area: Vietnam War. **CONTACT ADDRESS** St. Michael's Col, Winooski Park, Colchester, VT, 05439. **EMAIL** lsmith@smcvt.edu

SMITH, MARY ELIZABETH
PERSONAL Bridgetown, NS, Canada, m, 2 children **DISCIPLINE** ENGLISH **EDUCATION** Univ King's Col, BA, 58, Dalhousie Univ, MA, 60, Univ Exeter, PhD(English), 69. **CAREER** Teacher English & hist, Schs in NS & NB, 60-66; asst prof English, 70-75, assoc prof, 75-81, PROF ENGLISH, UNIV NB, 81-, CHMN DIV HUMANITIES & LANG, 81-, Univ NB res grants, 73, 76 & 77; Can Coun res grant, 76; Soc Sci & Humanities Res Coun Can grants, 78 & 79. **MEMBERSHIPS** MLA; Humanities Asn Can; Can Soc Renaissance Studies; Asn Can Theatre Hist; Malone Soc; Am Soc Theatre Res. **RESEARCH** Elizabethan drama; Canadian drama and theatre history. **SELECTED PUBLICATIONS** Auth, Too Soon the Curtain Fell: A History of Theatre in Saint John 1789-1900, Brunswick Press, 81; Responses to Theatre in Nineteenth Century Saint John, Theatre Hist Can, 81; On The Margins, Eastern Canadian Theater As Post-Colonialist Discourse, Theatre Res Int, Vol 21, 96; People, Place And Performance--Early Years Of The Halifax-Academy-Of-Music, Dalhousie Rev, Vol 75, 96. **CONTACT ADDRESS** Div of Humanities & Lang, Univ of NB, St John, NB, E2L 4L5.

SMITH, PATRICK J.
PERSONAL Born 09/07/1931, Menominee, MI, m, 1954, 7 children **DISCIPLINE** ENGLISH, FILM **EDUCATION** Marquette Univ, BS, 53, MA, 59; Univ Calif, Davis, PhD(English), 66. **CAREER** Assoc, Univ Calif, Davis, 62-64, assoc English, 64-66; PROF ENGLISH, UNIV SAN FRANCISCO, 66-, CHMN 78-, Publ, Pancake Press, 75-; assoc ed, Contemp Quart, 76; exec ed, San Francisco Rev Bks, 76-80. **RESEARCH** Modern English and American literature; film study and filmmaking; linguistics. **SELECTED PUBLICATIONS** Auth, Prelude for a Titan (film), released by AC Spark Plug Div, Gen Motors, 61; auth poem, In: Mark in Time, 71; ed, Smells like dead fish (film), Ichan Prod, 73; When Do the Cherries Ripen (poems), 75, Xmas Sutra (poems), 76; Photo Fiends (poems), 77 & Zen

Mover (poems), 77, Pancake Press; coauth, Eastwood,Clint--A Cultural Production, Sight And Sound, Vol 3, 93; Don-Juan And The Point Of Honor, Seduction, Patriarchal Society, And Literary Tradition, Mln-Modern Lang Notes, Vol 109, 94; Screening The Male--Exploring Masculinities In Hollywood Cinema, Sight And Sound, Vol 3, 93; An Introduction To Film Studies, Sight And Sound, Vol 06, 96; auth, And-I-Wondered-If-She-Might-Kiss-Me--Lesbian Panic As Narrative Strategy In British Womens Fictions, Modern Fiction Studies, Vol 41, 95; 'Zero Patience'--Greyson,J/, Sight And Sound, Vol 4, 94; Blue And The Outer-Limits + Aids, Homosexuality, And Questions Of Visibility On Film In 'Blue' By Jarman,Derek, Sight And Sound, Vol 3, 93. **CONTACT ADDRESS** Dept of English, Univ of San Francisco, San Francisco, CA, 94117.

SMITH, PAUL
DISCIPLINE VISUAL ARTS **EDUCATION** Kent Univ, PhD. **CAREER** Assoc prof. **RESEARCH** Cultural theory and criticism; film and visual studies; gender studies; Marxism. **SELECTED PUBLICATIONS** Auth, Clint Eastwood: A Cultural Production, 93; Madonnarama: On Sex and Popular Culture, 93; Discerning the Subject, 88. **CONTACT ADDRESS** Dept of Film and Media Studies, George Mason Univ, 4400 University Dr, Fairfax, VA, 22030.

SMITH, RALPH R.
DISCIPLINE PUBLIC RELATIONS **EDUCATION** Univ Southern CA, PhD, 73. **CAREER** Southwest Tex State Univ **SELECTED PUBLICATIONS** Area: movement rhetoric. **CONTACT ADDRESS** Southwest MS State Univ, 901 S. National, Ste. 50, Springfield, MO, 65804-0094.

SMITH, RILEY BLAKE
PERSONAL Born 07/07/1930, Mexico, MO **DISCIPLINE** ENGLISH, LINGUISTICS **EDUCATION** Univ Tex, Austin, BA, 58, PhD, 73. **CAREER** Asst prof English, Tex A&M Univ, 68-70; actg asst prof, Univ Calif, Los Angeles, 70-72; lectr Anglistics, Univ Duisburg, Ger, 74-76 & Univ Wuppertal, Ger, 76-77; asst prof, 77-81, Assoc Prof English, Bloomsburg Univ, 81-; Fulbright lectr, Leningrad Polytech Inst, USSR, 81. **HONORS AND AWARDS** Nat Endowment for Humanities fel, summer sem, Univ Pa, 80; Fulbright Grantee, USSR, 81. **MEMBERSHIPS** Ling Soc Am; Am Dialect Soc; Teachers English to Speakers Other Lang; Ling Asn Can & US; Int Sociol Asn. **RESEARCH** American dialects; language attitudes; language policy. **SELECTED PUBLICATIONS** Auth, Interrelatedness of certain deviant grammatical structures of Negro nonstandard dialects, 3/69 & Hyperformation and basilect reconstruction, 3/74, J English Ling; Black English: Books for English education, English educ, 4-5/75; Research perspectives on American Black English: A brief historical sketch, Am Speech, 76; Interference in phonological research in nonstandard dialects: its implication for teaching, In: Soziolinguistik, Hochschulverlag, Stuttgart, 78; coauth, Standard and disparate varieties of English in the United States: Educational and sociopolitical implications, Int J Sociol Lang, 79. **CONTACT ADDRESS** Dept of English, Bloomsburg Univ of Pennsylvania, 400 E 2nd St, Bloomsburg, PA, 17815-1399.

SMITH, ROBERT E.
DISCIPLINE LITERATURE AND COMMUNICATIONS **EDUCATION** Univ Mo, PhD, 69. **CAREER** Assoc prof; dir, basic crse, Purdue Univ. **RESEARCH** Writing of literature; performance of literature. **SELECTED PUBLICATIONS** Auth, Fundamentals of Oral Interpretation, 78; Principles of Human Communication, Kendall-Hunt, 91; The Outstanding Senior Award: A Realistic Small Group Decision-Making Exercise, The Speech Commun Tchr, 93. **CONTACT ADDRESS** Dept of Commun, Purdue Univ, 1080 Schleman Hall, West Lafayette, IN, 47907-1080. **EMAIL** resmith@sla.purdue.edu

SMITH, RONALD E.
DISCIPLINE COMPOSITION, DEVELOPMENTAL WRITING, TECHNICAL WRITING **EDUCATION** Mich State Univ, BA, 76, MA, 77; Ind Univ Pa, PhD, 88. **CAREER** Instr, Lansing Commun Col, 77-79; instr, Mary Holmes Col, 79-80; assoc prof Eng, Univ N Ala, 80-. **MEMBERSHIPS** NCTE, 77; Conf on Col Compos and Commun, 77; Asn of Tchr of Tech Writing, 90; Asn of Col Eng Tchr of Ala, 94. **SELECTED PUBLICATIONS** Auth, War Stories, N Am Rev, Jl/Aug, 92; Secretaries as Producers of Text, Bull of Asn for Bus Commun, Dec, 92; Yasunari Kawabata, Magill's Surv of World Lit, 93; Community and Self in First Year Composition, ERIC Clearinghouse on Reading, Writing and Commun, Mar 95. **CONTACT ADDRESS** Univ N Ala, Florence, AL, 35632-0001. **EMAIL** rsmith@unaalpha.una.edu

SMITH, ROWLAND
DISCIPLINE 20TH-CENTURY BRITISH LITERATURE **EDUCATION** Natal, BA; Oxon, MA; Natal, PhD. **CAREER** Prof **SELECTED PUBLICATIONS** Ed, Critical Essays on Nadine Gordimer, G.K. Hall, 90; Exile and Traditions: Studies in African and Caribbean Literature, Longman, 76; Black and White in Grey: Irony and Judgement in Gordimer's Fiction; Lyric and Polemic: The Literary Personality of Roy Campbell; McGill-Queen's Univ Press, 72. **CONTACT ADDRESS** Dept of English, Wilfrid Laurier Univ, 75 University Ave W, Waterloo, ON, N2L 3C5. **EMAIL** rsmith@mach2.wlu.ca

SMITH, SARAH
PERSONAL Born 12/09/1947, Boston, MA, m, 1979, 2 children **DISCIPLINE** ENGLISH **EDUCATION** Radcliffe Col, Harvard Univ, BA, 68; Slade Film School, London, 68-69; Harvard Grad School of Arts and Sciences, PhD, 75. **CAREER** Asst Prof, 76-82, Northeastern Univ, Tufts Univ & Boston Univ; Dept Mgr, 82-90, Computer Firms; Novelist, Consultant, 90-. **HONORS AND AWARDS** NY Times Notable Book of The Year-The Knowledge of Water, 96, The Vanished Child, 92; Woman of the Year Col Club of Boston, 97; Mellon Fel, Tufts Univ, 77; Bowdoin Prize, Harvard Univ, 75; Frank Know Fellow, Harvard, 72-73; Harvard Grad Prize Fel, 69-74; Fulbright Fel, 68-69; Phi Beta Kappa., Member of Contracts Com; Science Ficton and Fantasy Writers of Amer; Reg Bd Mem; Website Dev; Mystery Writers of Amer, 92. **MEMBERSHIPS** Science Fiction and Fantasy Writers of Amer, 88; Mystery Writers of Amer, 92; Sisters in Crime, 92; Cambridge Speculative Fiction Workshop, 86, Signet Soc, 74, Amnesty Intl, PEN/New England. **RESEARCH** 1890-1920, esp Feminism, socialism, the origins of WWI; hypermedia and non-paper based media. **SELECTED PUBLICATIONS** Auth, Christmas at the Edge, Christmas Forever, Tor Books, 93; CoAuth Future Boston, Tor Books, 93; auth, Touched by the Bomb, Fantasy & Science Fict, 93; auth, When the Red Storm Comes or the History of a Young Womans Awakening to her Nature, in: Shudder Again, 93; auth, The Knowledge of Water, Ballantine Books, 97; auth, Doll Street, Tribune Media Svcs, 96; auth, Riders, Tribune Media Svcs, 97, auth, Fearful, Crime Through Time II, Berkley, 98. **CONTACT ADDRESS** 32 Bowker St, Brookline, MA, 02445-6955. **EMAIL** swrs@world.std.com

SMITH, SHAWN M.
DISCIPLINE AMERICAN LITERATURE **EDUCATION** Univ Calif San Diego, PhD **CAREER** Asst prof, Washington State Univ. **RESEARCH** American cultural studies,visual culture. **CONTACT ADDRESS** Dept of English, Washington State Univ, 1 SE Stadium Way, PO Box 645020, Pullman, WA, 99164-5020. **EMAIL** smsmith@wsu.edu

SMITH, STEPHANIE A.
DISCIPLINE ENGLISH LITERATURE **EDUCATION** Boston Univ, BA, 81; Univ Calif, PhD, 90. **CAREER** Asst ed, W Imprints, 82-85; tchg asst, Univ Calif, 87-89; tchg assoc, Univ Calif, 89; asst prof, 90-95; assoc prof, 95-. **HONORS AND AWARDS** Phi Beta Kappa, Boston Univ, 79; Draper fel, Boston Univ, 81; outstanding tchg asst award, Univ Calif, 90; tchg improvement award excellence in tchg, 95-96; summer res grant, 91, 92, 97. **SELECTED PUBLICATIONS** Auth, Morphing, Materialism and the Marketing of Xenogenesis, Genders, 93; The Tender of Memory: Restructuring Value in Harriet Jacobs's Incidents in the Life of a Slave Girl, Harriet Jacobs and Incidents in the Life of a Slave Girl: New Critical Essays, Cambridge Univ Press, 95; Other Nature, St Martin's/TOR, 95; rev, Of The Culture of Sentiment, Women's Rev of Bk(s), Oxford, 93. **CONTACT ADDRESS** Dept of Eng, Univ Fla, 226 Tigert Hall, Gainesville, FL, 32611. **EMAIL** ssmith@english.ufl.edu

SMITH, STEPHEN A.
DISCIPLINE METHODOLOGY OF COMMUNICATION RESEARCH **EDUCATION** Northwestern Univ, PhD. **CAREER** Comm Stu, Univ Ark. **HONORS AND AWARDS** Vis fel,Univ Wisc's La Follette Inst Public Affairs; Vis fel, Princeton Univ; Vis Scholar, Stanford Law Sch; Andrew Mellon fel, Univ Pa; Vis Fel Wolfson Coll, Fac Law, Univ Cambridge; Vis Scholar, St. Benet's Hall; Vis Fel Manchester Col, Univ Oxford, Vis Prof, Univ Va. **SELECTED PUBLICATIONS** Auth, Myth, Media and the Southern Mind, 85; Clinton on Stump, State and Stage: The Rhetorical Road to the White House, 94; Prelude to the Presidency: The Speeches of Bill Clinton, 1974-1992, 96. **CONTACT ADDRESS** Univ Ark, Fayetteville, AR, 72701.

SMITH, VONCILE MARSHALL
PERSONAL Born 03/17/1931, Ft Myers, FL, m, 1951, 5 children **DISCIPLINE** SPEECH COMMUNICATION, COMMUNICATION THEORY **EDUCATION** Univ Fla, BAEd, 60, MA, 64, PhD(speech), 66. **CAREER** Asst prof speech, 60-70, assoc prof, 70-78, prof Commun, Fla Atlantic Univ, 78-, Chm Dept Commun, 73-82, 94-98, ed, Fla Speech Commun J, 78-81; ed, J Int Listening Asn, 86-88. **HONORS AND AWARDS** Phi Kappa Phi. **MEMBERSHIPS** Nat Commun Asn; Southern States Commun Asn; Asn for Commun Admin; Fla Commun Asn. **RESEARCH** Studies in listening; interpersonal communication; communication theory. **SELECTED PUBLICATIONS** Coauth, Communication for Health Professionals, Lippincott, 79. **CONTACT ADDRESS** Dept of Commun, Col of Arts and Letters, Florida Atlantic Univ, PO Box 3091, Boca Raton, FL, 33431-0991. **EMAIL** vsmith@acc.fau.edu

SMITH MCKOY, SHEILA
DISCIPLINE AMERICAN LITERATURE, AFRICAN LITERATURE, AFRICAN-AMERICAN LITERATURE, AFRO-**EDUCATION** Duke Univ, PhD. **CAREER** Instr, Vanderbilt Univ. **RESEARCH** South African literature and culture; diaspora oral traditions. **SELECTED PUBLICATIONS** Contribu, Oxford Companion to Women's Writing in the United States. **CONTACT ADDRESS** Vanderbilt Univ, Nashville, TN, 37203-1727.

SMITHEY, ROBERT ARTHUR
PERSONAL Born 12/18/1925, Norfolk, Virginia, s **DISCIPLINE** ENGLISH **EDUCATION** De Pauw Univ Greencastle IN, AB 1950; Univ of WI Madison, AM 1953; Univ of WI, PhD 1968. **CAREER** Talladega Coll Talladega AL, chmn lower div 1960-64; Univ of MO Kansas City, asst prof English 1968-70; Univ of Houston, assoc prof English 1970-72; Norfolk State Univ VA, prof English & communications 1972-95. **HONORS AND AWARDS** IBM Fellow Univ of WI 1964-68; Vilas Fellow Univ of WI 1965-68; Univ Fellow Univ of WI 1966-68; Ford Fellow Univ of WI 1967-68. **MEMBERSHIPS** Exec comm Conf on Coll Composition & Comm 1964-67; dir Natl Council of Teachers of English 1968-70; reader Coll Bd of Exams 1970-72; lay reader St James Episcopal Church Houston 1970-72; editorial bd Four C's 1972-76; lay reader, chalicer, Grace Episcopal Church Norfolk 1972-; pres, Natl Youth Conf; NAACP, 1944-45. **SELECTED PUBLICATIONS** Co-editor "Variations on Humankind," an anthology of world literature, Kendall How Publishers, 1995, revised 1996.

SNARE, GERALD
DISCIPLINE RENAISSANCE LITERATURE **EDUCATION** Univ CA at Santa Barbara, BA, 63; UCLA, PhD, 68. **CAREER** Instr, 88, Tulane Univ. **SELECTED PUBLICATIONS** Auth, The Countess of Pembroke's Ivychurch, Calif State UP, 75; The Mystification of George Chapman, Duke UP, 90; Grammatical Heresy and the Hermeneutics of Martin Luther, Renaissance Papers, 94; Glossing in Late Antiquity and the Renaissance, SP, 95. **CONTACT ADDRESS** Dept of Eng, Tulane Univ, 6823 St Charles Ave, New Orleans, LA, 70118.

SNOW, HELENA
DISCIPLINE ENGLISH LITERATURE **EDUCATION** Univ Birmingham, Eng, graduated; Shakespearean Inst, PhD. **CAREER** Sr mem, Brit fac, Harlaxton Col; vis prof, 97. **RESEARCH** Shakespeare, particularly on the roles of his fools. **SELECTED PUBLICATIONS** Asst ed, Shakespeare Survey. **CONTACT ADDRESS** Dept of Eng, Univ Evansville, 1800 Lincoln Ave, Evansville, IN, 47714. **EMAIL** hsnow@harlaxton.edu.

SNOW, VERNON F.
PERSONAL Born 11/25/1924, Milwaukee, WI, m, 1949 **DISCIPLINE** ENGLISH HISTORY **EDUCATION** Wheaton Col, BA, 48; Univ Chicago, MA, 49; Univ Wis, PhD, 53. **CAREER** Instr western civilization, Univ Ore, 53-56; vis lectr English hist, Univ Wis, 56-57; asst prof western civilization, Univ Ore, 57-60; from asst prof to assoc prof English hist, Mont State Univ, 60-66; prof hist, Univ Nebr, Lincoln, 66-74, chmn dept, 70-71; PROF HIST, SYRACUSE UNIV, 74-, Am Philos Soc grant, 58; vpres, Snow Found, 69-74, pres, 74- **MEMBERSHIPS** AHA; Conf Brit Studies; Int Comn Hist Rep & Parliamentary Insts; Midwest Conf Brit Studies(vpres, 72-); fel Royal Hist Soc. **RESEARCH** English constitutional history, Stuart period; English legal history. **SELECTED PUBLICATIONS** Auth, The grand tour diary of Robert C Johnson, Proc Am Philos Soc, 58; Parliamentary reapportionment proposals in the Puritan Revolution, English Hist Rev, 60; The concept of revolution in seventeenth century England, Hist J, 62; Essex the Rebel, Univ Nebr, 70; J B S: The Biography of John Ben Snow, NY Univ, 74; ed, Holinshead's Chronicles, AMS Press, 76; auth, Parliament in Elizabethan England, Yale Univ, 77; Private Member Journals of the Long Parliament, Yale, 82; ; The Teenage Diary Of Snow,Charles 1850, Ny Hist, Vol 74, 93. **CONTACT ADDRESS** Dept of Hist, Syracuse Univ, Syracuse, NY, 13210.

SNYDER, STEPHEN W.
DISCIPLINE ENGLISH LITERATURE **EDUCATION** Univ Idaho, BA; MA; Univ Fla, PhD. **CAREER** Assoc prof **RESEARCH** Italian cinema; contemporary literary criticism; 19th century American Literature; modern painting; cinematography. **SELECTED PUBLICATIONS** Auth, pub(s) on Vittorio De Sica. **CONTACT ADDRESS** Dept of English, Manitoba Univ, Winnipeg, MB, R3T 2N2.

SNYDER, SUSAN BROOKE
PERSONAL Born 07/12/1934, Yonkers, NY **DISCIPLINE** ENGLISH **EDUCATION** Hunter Col, AB, 55; Columbia Univ, MA, 58, PhD(Eng), 63. **CAREER** Lectr Eng, Queens Col, NY, 61-63; from instr to assoc prof, 63-75, chmn dept Eng, 75-80, Prof Eng, Swarthmore Col, 75-93, Eugene M. Lang res prof, 82-86; Gil and Frank Mustin Prof, 90-93; Nat Endowment for Hum fel, 67-68; Folger Shakespeare Libr sr fel, 72-73; Guggenheim fel, 80-81 Emer prof, 93-. **MEMBERSHIPS** Renaissance Soc Am, Council 79-81; Shakespeare Asn Am, Trustee 80-83; Ed Bd, Skaespeare Quarterly, 73-. **RESEARCH** Shakespeare; Spenser; Renaissance poetry. **SELECTED PUBLICATIONS** Ed, Sylvester's DuBartas, Oxford Univ, 79; The Comic Matrix of Shakespeare's Tragedies, Princeton Univ, 79; Othello: Critical Essays, Garland, 88; ed, All's Well That Ends Well, Oxford, 93; Pastoral Process, Stanford Univ, 98. **CONTACT ADDRESS** Folger Shakespeare Libr, 201 E Capitol St SE, Washington, DC, 20008. **EMAIL** sbsnyder@worldnet.att.net

SODERLIND, SYLVIA
DISCIPLINE ENGLISH LITERATURE **EDUCATION** Univ Toronto, PhD. **CAREER** Dept Eng, Queen's Univ **RESEARCH** Comparative postmodern fiction; modern Canadian and American literature; semiotics and literary theory; post-colonial literature. **SELECTED PUBLICATIONS** Auth, Margin/Alias: Language and Colonization in Canadian and Quebecois Fiction; pubs on postmodernism, Canadian, Quebecois and American fiction. **CONTACT ADDRESS** English Dept, Queen's Univ, Kingston, ON, K7L 3N6.

SODERLUND, JEAN R.
DISCIPLINE 17TH AND 18TH CENTURY BRITISH AMERICA **EDUCATION** PhD, Temple Univ. **CAREER** Prof, Lehigh Univ. **RESEARCH** History of ethnicity, gender, religion and class in the Delaware Valley. **SELECTED PUBLICATIONS** Au, Quakers and Slavery: a divided spirit; co-au, Freedom by Degrees: Emancipation in Pennsylvania and Its Aftermath. **CONTACT ADDRESS** Lehigh Univ, Bethlehem, PA, 18015.

SOENS JR., A.L.
DISCIPLINE LITERATURE **EDUCATION** Harvard Univ, PhD. **CAREER** Instr, Univ Notre Dame. **RESEARCH** The history of fencing and arms. **SELECTED PUBLICATIONS** Wrote on Shakespeare and other dramatists and edited Sidney's Defense of Poetry. **CONTACT ADDRESS** Univ Notre Dame, Notre Dame, IN, 46556.

SOLDATI, JOSEPH ARTHUR
PERSONAL Born 09/27/1939, Rochester, NH **DISCIPLINE** AMERICAN & EUROPEAN LITERATURE **EDUCATION** Oglethorpe Univ, BA, 61; Univ Calif, Santa Barbara, MA, 68; Wash State Univ, PhD(English), 72. **CAREER** Teaching asst, Wash State Univ, 68-71, asst prof, 71-72; asst prof English, 72-76, assoc prof, 76-80, PROF HUMANITIES, WESTERN ORE UNIV, 80-. **HONORS AND AWARDS** NEH Summiner Seminar, 79 & 82; Fulbright fel, Mansoura Univ, Egypt, 83-84, Cote d'Ivoire, West Africa, 89-90; Salzburg fel, Salzburg, Austria, 10/84; Teacher of the Year, Western Ore Univ, 93-94. **MEMBERSHIPS** Phi Kappa Phi; Asn Literary Scholars & Critics; Ore Int Counc; Mountian Writers (Portland, Ore). **RESEARCH** American Romantic Movement; Afro-American poetry. **SELECTED PUBLICATIONS** Auth, Notes on the American wasteland: A white man's way toward understanding, In: Man and the Land Convocation, II, Ore Col Educ, 73; The Americanization of Faust: A study of Brockden Brown's Wieland, Emerson Soc Quart, 1/74; Cosmic instability and modern man, Kronos: J Interdisciplinary Synthesis, summer 75; Functions of color in poetry, Essays in Lit, spring 77; Looking at the river: A literary view, In: The Columbia River Primer, Inst Rockies, spring 78; Configurations of Faust: Three Studies in the Gothic 1798-1820, Arno Press, 80; Talking like gods: New voices of authority, In: Pagan and Christian Anxiety: A Response to E R Dodds, Univ Press Am, 84; Making My Name (poems), Mellen Poetry Press, 92; co-auth, O Poetry! Oh Poesia! Poems of Oregon and Peru, Western Ore Univ & Cuardernos Trimestrales de Poesia, Trujillo, Peru, 97. **CONTACT ADDRESS** Dept of Humanities, Western Oregon Univ, 345 N Monmouth Ave, Monmouth, OR, 97361-1314. **EMAIL** joesol@aol.com

SOLEY, LAWRENCE C.
PERSONAL Born 11/01/1949, Minneapolis, MN, m, 1984, 3 children **DISCIPLINE** COMMUNICATIONS **EDUCATION** Mich State Univ, PhD, 81. **CAREER** Asst, Assoc Prof, Baruch Col, CUNY, 83-87; Prof & Assoc Prof, Univ Minn, 87-92; Colnik Prof of Commun, Marquette Univ, 92-98. **HONORS AND AWARDS** Soc of Pro Journalists Sigma Delta Chi Award, 91; Am Acad of Advertising, J of Advertising Best Article Award, 93; Project Censored Reporting Award, 98. **MEMBERSHIPS** Investigative Reporters & Eds; Soc of Pro Journalists. **RESEARCH** Media; propaganda, corporate power. **SELECTED PUBLICATIONS** Auth, Leasing the Ivory Tower, S End, 95; auth, Free Radio, Westview, 99. **CONTACT ADDRESS** Col of Commun, Marquette Univ, Milwaukee, WI, 53233. **EMAIL** soleyl@vms.csd.mu.edu

SOLLORS, WERNER
DISCIPLINE ENGLISH; AMERICAN STUDIES **EDUCATION** Freie Universitaet Berlin, Germany, PhD, 75. **CAREER** Asst prof, Berlin, 75-78; Columbia Univ, 78-82; assoc prof, Columbia Univ, 82-83; prof, Harvard Univ, 83- . **HONORS AND AWARDS** Guggenheim fel; Andrew W. Mellon fel; Constance Rouske Prize. **MEMBERSHIPS** MLA; ASA; OAH; ACLA. **RESEARCH** Am Studies; Comp Lit. **SELECTED PUBLICATIONS** Auth, Beyond Ethnicity: Consent and Descent in American Culture, 86; The Return of Thematic Criticism, 93; Theories of Ethnicity: A Classical Reader, 96; Neither Black Nor White Yet Both: Thematic Explorations of Interracial Literature, 97; Multilingual America: Transnationalism, Ethnicity, and the Languages of American Literature, 98. **CONTACT ADDRESS** Barker Center, Harvard Univ, 12 Quincy Ave, Cambridge, MA, 02138. **EMAIL** amcir@fas.harvard.edu

SOLOMON, ANDREW JOSEPH
PERSONAL Born 11/15/1944, New York, NY, d, 1 child **DISCIPLINE** ENGLISH LITERATURE, CREATIVE WRITING **EDUCATION** Univ Pittsburgh, BA, 66, MA, 70, PhD, 74. **CAREER** Asst prof, 75-80, dir creative writing prog, 75-, assoc prof to prof, Eng, Univ Tampa, 80-92. **MEMBERSHIPS** MLA; Shakespeare Assn Am; Natl Book Critics Circle **RESEARCH** The writing of fiction; Shakespeare. **SELECTED PUBLICATIONS** Art, Jim and Huck: Magnificent misfits, Mark Twain J, winter 72; auth, A reading of The Tempest, In: Shakespeare's Late Plays, Ohio Univ, 75; art, Oh His Kindness (poetry), Atlantic Monthly, 12/77; art, Use of Progress Intensive journal in creative writing courses, Fla English J, 4/82. **CONTACT ADDRESS** Dept of English, Univ of Tampa, 401 W Kennedy Blvd, Tampa, FL, 33606-1490.

SOLOMON, H. ERIC
PERSONAL Born 10/08/1928, Boston, MA, m, 1954, 2 children **DISCIPLINE** ENGLISH **EDUCATION** Harvard Univ, BA, 50, MA, 52, PhD, 58. **CAREER** Teaching fel English, Harvard Univ, 51-53 & 55-58; from instr to asst prof, OH State Univ, 58-64; assoc prof, 64-68, PROF ENGLISH, SAN FRANCISCO STATE UNIV, 68-; Am Philos Soc travel grant, 61-62. **MEMBERSHIPS** Am Studies Asn; MLA. **RESEARCH** Am literature; 19th century fiction. **SELECTED PUBLICATIONS** Auth, The Faded Banners: An Anthology of 19th Century Civil War Fiction, Yoseloff, 58; The incest theme in Wuthering Heights, 19th Century Fiction, 6/59; Huckleberry Finn once more, 12/60 & Jane Eyre: Fire and water, 12/63, Col English; Stephen Crane in England, Ohio State Univ, 64; Stephen Crane: From Parody to Realism, Harvard Univ, 66. **CONTACT ADDRESS** Dept of English, San Francisco State Univ, 1600 Holloway Ave, San Francisco, CA, 94132-1740.

SOLOMON, STANLEY J.
PERSONAL Born 01/03/1937, New York, NY, m, 1958, 2 children **DISCIPLINE** ENGLISH **EDUCATION** Brooklyn Col, BA, 57; Univ Kans, MA, 60; Temple Univ, PhD, 68. **CAREER** Instr, Doane Col, 60-62 & Chatham Col, 62-64; asst prof, Temple Univ, 67-68; from instr to assoc prof, 68-72, chmn, Dept English, 71-74, Dir Film Stud, 71-72, Dir Mass Commun, 73-76; PROF ENGLISH, IONA COL, 72-, Chmn, New Rochelle Coun Arts, 76; Dir, Multi-Image Ctr, 79-90. **MEMBERSHIPS** MLA; AAUP. **RESEARCH** Samuel Johnson; Film studies; Multi-media production. **SELECTED PUBLICATIONS** Auth, The Film Idea, 72 & ed, The Classic Cinema, 73, Harcourt; Beyond Formula: American Film Genres, Harcourt, 76; Film Genres, Writing and Film Genres, 82; Aristotle in twilight, Studies in the Literary Imagination, 83; Subverting propriety, Literature Criticism from 1400-1800, 85; Detective as moralist, A Short Guide to Writing about Literature, 85; They Know Where I Live, Alfred Hitchcock Mystery Mag, 92; Gift Givers, Alfred Hitchcock, Mystery Mag,93; Barterers, Raconteur Mag, 96; Columnist, Casino Mag, 94-96; Corresponding effects, artless writing in the age of e-mail, Mod Age, 98. **CONTACT ADDRESS** English Dept, Iona Col, 715 North Ave, New Rochelle, NY, 10801-1890. **EMAIL** ssolomon@iona.edu

SOLOSKI, JOHN
PERSONAL Born 11/18/1952, New York, NY, m, 1974, 2 children **DISCIPLINE** JOURNALISM & MASS COMMUNICATION **EDUCATION** Boston Col, AB, 74; Univ Iowa, MA, 76, PhD(Mass Commun), 78. **CAREER** From instr to assoc prof, 77-92, prof jour & mass commun, Univ Iowa, 92-, dir, Sch Jour & Mass Commun, 96-, head, grad studies, 85-95; vis fac mem, Univ Technology, Sydney, Australia. **HONORS AND AWARDS** Fel, Open Soc Inst; Distinguished Service Award for Research About Journalism, for Libel and the Press (book), Soc Professional Jour, Sigma Delta Chi, 87. **MEMBERSHIPS** Asn Educ Jour & Mass Commun; Int Commun Asn. **RESEARCH** Media law; media economics. **SELECTED PUBLICATIONS** Coauth, Libel and the Press: Myth and Reality, The Free Press, 87; co-ed, Reforming Libel Law, Guilford Publ, 92; coauth, On Defining the Nature of Graduate Education, Jour Educ, Summer 94; coauth, Sullivan's Paradox: The Emergence of Judicial Standards for Journalism, NC Law Rev 73, 94; auth, The United States Libel System, Medialine, Summer 96/97; coauth, The New Media Lords: Why Institutional Investors Call the Shots, Columbia Jour Rev, Sept-Oct/96. **CONTACT ADDRESS** Sch Jour & Mass Commun, Univ Iowa, Iowa City, IA, 52242. **EMAIL** john-soloski@uiowa.edu

SOLT, LEO F
PERSONAL Born 10/12/1921, Waterloo, IA, m, 1946, 2 children **DISCIPLINE** ENGLISH HISTORY **EDUCATION** Univ Northern Iowa, BA, 43; Univ Iowa, MA, 48; Columbia Univ, PhD, 55. **CAREER** Instr English hist, Univ Mass, 52-55; from asst prof to assoc prof, 55-64, chmn dept hist, 65-70, PROF ENGLISH HIST, IND UNIV, BLOOMINGTON, 64-, DEAN GRAD SCH, 78-, Am Philos Soc grant, 58; Soc Sci Res Coun grant, 59; Guggenheim fel, 61-62. **MEMBERSHIPS** AHA; Am Soc Church Hist; Conf Brit Studies; Midwest Conf Brit Studies (pres, 68-70). **RESEARCH** Stuart England; English Puritanism. **SELECTED PUBLICATIONS** Auth, The Widening Gate--Bristol And The Atlantic Economy, 1450-1700, Church Hist, Vol 62, 93; The Widening Gate--Bristol And The Atlantic Economy, 1450-1700, Church Hist, Vol 62, 93; The New Model Army In England, Ireland And Scotland, 1645-1653, Am Hist Rev, Vol 98, 93. **CONTACT ADDRESS** Dept of Hist, Indiana Univ, Bloomington, Bloomington, IN, 47401.

SOMMER, DORIS
PERSONAL Born 01/15/1947, Germany, m, 1975, 2 children **DISCIPLINE** LITERATURE **EDUCATION** Douglass Col, BA, 68; Hebrew Univ Jerusalem, MA, 70; Rutgers Univ, PhD, 77. **CAREER** Asst prof, Rutgers Univ, 77-80; prof, Amherst Col, 80-91; prof, Harvard Univ, 91- . **HONORS AND AWARDS** NEH Fel, 83-84; Guggenheim Fel, ACLS Fel, 93-94. **MEMBERSHIPS** LASA; MLA. **RESEARCH** Ethnic literature of the Americas; national and gender constructions in literature. **SELECTED PUBLICATIONS** Auth, Foundational Fictions: The National Romances of Latin America, Univ of Cal Pr, 93; auth, Proceed with Caution when Engaged by Minority Literatures of the Americas, Harvard Univ Pr, 99. **CONTACT ADDRESS** 50 S School St, Portsmouth, NH, 03801. **EMAIL** dsommer@fas.harvard.edu

SORKIN, ADAM J.
PERSONAL Born 08/09/1943, New York, NY, m, 1964, 2 children **DISCIPLINE** AMERICAN LITERATURE PROSE FICTION, TRANSLATION OF CONTEMPORARY ROMANIAN LIT **EDUCATION** Cornell Univ, AB, 64, MA, 65; Univ NC, PhD, 72. **CAREER** Instr Eng, Univ IL, Chicago Circle, 65-66; instr Eng & Am lit, Univ NC, Chapel Hill, 70-71; instr, Stockton State Col, 71-73; instr, Drexel Univ & Community Col Philadelphia, 73; asst prof Eng & Am lit, Bluefield State Col, 74-78; from Asst Prof to Prof Eng, PA State Univ, 78-; Fulbright lectr, Univ Bucharest, Romania, 80-81. **HONORS AND AWARDS** NEH Summer Seminar, 75; IREX Fel, 91; Rockefeller Found Residency, Study and Conf Ctr, Italy, 95; Recommended Transl, Poetry Bk Soc, for The Sky Behind the Forest, 96-97; Crossing Boundaries Translation Award, Int Quart, for The Europ Mechanism, Fall 97; Story Short Short Competition winner, 14th place, for The Telephone, 97. **MEMBERSHIPS** MLA; SAtlantic Mod Lang Asn; Northeast Mod Lang Asn; Am Lit Translr(s) Asn. **RESEARCH** Am lit; prose fiction; mod lit. **SELECTED PUBLICATIONS** Ed, Politics and the Muse: Studies in the Politics of Recent American Literature, Bowling Green State Univ Popular Press, 89; Conversations with Joseph Heller, Literary Conversations Series, Univ Press MS, 93; auth, Marin Sorescu: Comedian of Antiheroic Resistance, Romanian Civilization, Summer 92; Half in Flight Half in Chains: The Paradoxical Vision of Iona Ieronim's Poetry, Conn Rev, Fall 95; Petre Stoica's Tiananmen Square II: Anger, Protest, and an Angel with a Crow's Wings, Romanian Civilization, Winter 95-96; Liliana Ursu's Poetry, Delos: A J Transl & World Lit 18, 96; The Forbidden World and Hidden Words: Steadfast Illumination in Marin Sorescu's Poems Selected by Censorship, Romanian Civilization, Fall 96; Postmodernism in Romanian Poetry: The Abnormally Normal, Romania & Western Civilization / Romania si civilizatia occidentala, Iasi: The Ctr for Romanian Studies, 97; On The Circle by Martin Sorescu, Two Lines: A J of Transl, Spring 97; I Was of Three Minds: Some Notes on Translating, Metamorphoses, April 98; author and translator of numerous other articles, poems, and short stories. **CONTACT ADDRESS** Eng Dept, Pennsylvania State Univ, 25 Yearsley Mill Rd, Media, PA, 19063-5596. **EMAIL** ajs2@psu.edu

SOSNOSKI, JAMES JOSEPH
PERSONAL Born 06/18/1938, Dickson City, PA, m, 1965, 1 child **DISCIPLINE** ENGLISH **EDUCATION** Loyola Univ, Ill, AB, 60, MA, 65; Pa State Univ, PhD(English), 67. **CAREER** Asst prof, 67-72, ASSOC PROF ENGLISH, MIAMI UNIV, 72- **MEMBERSHIPS** MLA; Col English Asn; Mediaeval Acad Am; Early English Text Soc. **RESEARCH** Literary criticism; Medieval literature. **SELECTED PUBLICATIONS** Auth, Craft and intention in James Agee's A Death in the Family, J Gen Educ, 68; The Case For Hyper-Gradesheets, Col English, Vol 55, 93. **CONTACT ADDRESS** Dept of English, Miami Univ, Oxford, OH, 45056.

SOSSAMAN, STEPHEN
DISCIPLINE CREATIVE WRITING, WORLD LITERATURE, MODERN AMERICAN LITERATURE **EDUCATION** Columbia Univ, BA; State Univ NY, MA; NYU, PhD. **CAREER** Bus wrtg consult. **SELECTED PUBLICATIONS** Publ, Paris Rev, Centennial Rev, Southern Hum Rev. **CONTACT ADDRESS** Dept of Engl, Westfield State Col, 577 Western Ave., Westfield, MA, 01085.

SOULE, GEORGE
PERSONAL Born 03/03/1930, Fargo, ND, m, 1961, 1 child **DISCIPLINE** ENGLISH LITERATURE **EDUCATION** Carleton Col, BA, 51; Yale Univ, MA, 56, PhD, 60. **CAREER** Instr English, Oberlin Col, 58-60; asst prof, Univ Wis, 60-62; from asst prof to assoc prof, 62-71, chmn English dept, 78, PROF ENGLISH, CARLETON COL, 71-, CHMN ENGLISH DEPT, 80-, Consult, US Dept Health, Educ & Welfare, 65-66; dir centennial celebration, Carleton Col, 65-67 & NDEA Summer English Inst, 65; dir, Carleton London prog, 74 & 79 & dir, Carleton summer writing prog, 80- **MEMBERSHIPS** Johnson Soc Lichfield; Boswell Soc Auchinleck; MLA. **RESEARCH**

Shakespeare; Boswell and Johnson; British studies. **SELECTED PUBLICATIONS** Ed, The Theatre of The Mind, Prentice-Hall, 75; True And False Princesses In The Excursion, Wordsworth Circle, Vol 26, 95. **CONTACT ADDRESS** Dept of English, Carleton Col, Northfield, MN, 55057.

SOURIAN, PETER
PERSONAL Born 04/07/1933, Boston, MA, m, 1971, 2 children **DISCIPLINE** ENGLISH, MEDIA **EDUCATION** Harvard Univ, BA, 55. **CAREER** From instr to assoc prof, 65-75, PROF ENGLISH, BARD COL, 75-, TV critic, The Nation Mag, 75-80. **MEMBERSHIPS** MLA; AAUP; Nat Bk Critics Circle; Pen. **RESEARCH** The novel; television. **SELECTED PUBLICATIONS** Auth, Miri, Pantheon, 57; The Best & Worst of Times, Doubleday, 61; The Gate, Harcourt, 65; Open admissions: A Pilgrim's Progress, Nation, 4/73; Eric Rohmer, Transatlantic Rev, winter 73-74; Television, Nation, 11/79; At the French Embassy In Sofia, 92. **CONTACT ADDRESS** Dept of Eng, Bard Col, PO Box 5000, Annandale, NY, 12504-5000.

SOVEN, MARGOT
PERSONAL Born 10/18/1940, New York, NY, m, 1961, 3 children **DISCIPLINE** ENGLISH EDUCATION **EDUCATION** Univ Penn, PhD, 80. **CAREER** Prof, English dept, 81-, LaSalle Univ. **HONORS AND AWARDS** Instl Summer Grants; NEH Summer Seminar Grant **MEMBERSHIPS** MLA; NCTE **RESEARCH** The teaching of writing; Amer lit. **SELECTED PUBLICATIONS** Coauth, Writings from the Workplace Documents Models Cases, 96; auth, Write to Learn: A Guide to Writing Across the Curriculum, 96; auth, The Teaching of Writing in Middle & Secondary Schools, 98. **CONTACT ADDRESS** La Salle Univ, 1900 W Olney Ave, Philadelphia, PA, 19141. **EMAIL** Soven@lasalle.edu

SPANCER, JANET
DISCIPLINE ENGLISH LITERATURE **EDUCATION** University of Texas-San Antonio, B.A., M.A.University of Pennsylvania, Ph.D **CAREER** Ch; assoc prof. **HONORS AND AWARDS** Fel, NEH. **RESEARCH** Renaissance literature, Shakespeare's historical plays. **SELECTED PUBLICATIONS** Auth, articles on Shakespeare's plays. **CONTACT ADDRESS** Dept of Eng, Wingate Univ, Campus Box 3059, Wingate, NC, 28174. **EMAIL** jspencer@wingate.edu

SPANOS, WILLIAM
PERSONAL Born 01/01/1925, Newport, NH, m, 1954, 3 children **DISCIPLINE** ENGLISH, EXISTENTIAL PHILOSOPHY **EDUCATION** Wesleyan Univ, BA, 50; Columbia Univ, MA, 54; Univ Wis, PhD (Eng), 64. **CAREER** Master Eng, Mt Hermon Sch, 51-53; asst ed, Encycl Americana, Grolier, 54-56; instr Eng, Univ KY, 60-62; asst prof, Knox Col, 62-66; Asst Prof Eng & Comp Lit, State Univ NY Binghamton, 66-, Fulbright prof Am lit, Nat Univ Athens, 69-70; founder & ed, boundary 2, 72-. **MEMBERSHIPS** MLA; Col Eng Asn; Mod Greek Studies Asn. **RESEARCH** Mod Brit and Am poetry; mod drama; redefining modernism in lit. **SELECTED PUBLICATIONS** Ed, A Casebook on Existentialism, Crowell, 66; auth, The Christian Tradition in Modern British Verse Drama: The Poetic of Sacramental Time, Rutgers Univ, 67; Modern drama and the Aristotelian tradition: The formal imperatives of absurd time, Contemp Lit, summer 71; The detective and the boundary: Some notes on the postmodern literary imagination, fall 72, Heidegger, Kierkegaard and the Hermenentic circle: Toward a postmodern theory of interpretation as dis-closure, winter 76 & Breaking the circle: Hermenentics as dis-closure, winter 77, boundary 2; ed, Existentialism 2, Random House, 77; Repititions: the Postmodern Occasion in Literature and Culture, Louisiana State Univ Press, 87; Heidegger and Criticism: Retrieving The Politics of Destruction, Univ of MN Press, 93, The End of Education, Univ of MN Press, 93; The Errant Art of Moby Dick: The Canon, the Cold War and the Struggle for American Studies, Duke Univ, 95 Philosophy and Imperialism, Thinking the Specter of Postmodernity, Univ of MN Press, forthcoming. **CONTACT ADDRESS** Dept of English, SUNY, Harpur Col, Binghamton, NY, 13901. **EMAIL** wspanose@binghampton.edu

SPARKS, ELISA
DISCIPLINE ENGLISH LITERATURE **EDUCATION** Ind Univ, PhD, 79. **CAREER** Dept Eng, Clemson Univ **RESEARCH** Literary criticism; women's studies. **SELECTED PUBLICATIONS** Auth, Virginia O'Keeffe has an exhibit of drawings at 291: Paradoxes of Feminist Pin-Ups in Re: Reading, Re: Writing, Re: Teaching Virginia Woolf: Selected Papers from the Fourth Annual Conference on Virginia Woolf, Pace Univ Press, 95; Marge Piercy, Great Lives from History: American Women, Salem, 95; Woman on the Edge of Time by Marge Piercy, Masterplots II: Women's Literature Series, Salem, 95; A Match Burning in a Crocus: Modernism, Feminism, and Feminine Experience in Virginia Woolf and Georgia O'Keeffe in Virginia Woolf: Themes and Variations: Selected Papers from the Third Annual Conference on Virginia Woolf, Pace Univ Press, 94; Exhibition of ten prints--silkscreen, photointaglio, and computer generated--on Virginia Woolf and Georgia O'Keeffe at the Seventh Annual Conference on Virginia Woolf, 97. **CONTACT ADDRESS** Clemson Univ, Clemson, SC, 29634. **EMAIL** sparks@clemson.edu

SPARKS, GLENN G.
DISCIPLINE MEDIA EFFECTS **EDUCATION** Wheaton Col, BA, 75; Northern Ill Univ, MA, 76; Univ Wis, Madison, PhD, 83. **CAREER** Asst prof, Cleveland State Univ, 83-86; asst prof, 86-90, assoc prof, 90-95, prof, Purdue Univ, 95-. **HONORS AND AWARDS** Seven Top Paper Awards, Int Competition Serv., Interviewed or quoted on media effects research by AP Press, NBC-TV, CNN Radio, CBS-TV, National Public Radio, Newsweek Magazine, Time Magazine, The Cleveland Plain Dealer, The Boston Globe, The Washington Post, The Chicago Tribune, The Indianapolis Star, The London Daily Telegraph, The Atlanta Constitution, Psychology Today Magazine. **RESEARCH** Cognitive and emotional responses to various types of content, including frightening programs and movies, violence, and depictions of paranormal events. **SELECTED PUBLICATIONS** Auth, The Role of Preferred Coping Style and Emotional Forewarning in Predicting Emotional Reactions to a Suspenseful Film, Commun Rpt, 94; Media Impact on Fright Reactions and Belief in UFOs: The Potential Role of Mental Imagery, Commun Res, 95; The Relationship Between Exposure to Televised Messages About Paranormal Phenomena and Paranormal Beliefs, J of Broadcasting & Electronic Media, 97. **CONTACT ADDRESS** Dept of Commun, Purdue Univ, 1080 Schleman Hall, West Lafayette, IN, 47907-1080. **EMAIL** gsparks@purdue.edu

SPEAREY, SUSAN
DISCIPLINE EARLY VICTORIAN LITERATURE **EDUCATION** Leeds Univ, PhD, 93. **CAREER** Assoc prof **RESEARCH** Mmigrant/diaspora literature from Southeast Asia, literature of the British Empire. **SELECTED PUBLICATIONS** Auth, Mapping and Masking: The Migrant Experience in Michael Ondaatje's In the Skin of a Lion, Borderblur: Poetry and Poetics, Contemp Can Lit, Quadriga, 96, Jour of Commonwealth Lit, 94; "Cultural Crossings: The Shifting Subjectivities And Stylistics of Michael Ondaatje's Running In The Family and In The Skin Of A Lion," Brit Jour Can Stud, 96; rev(s), Canadian Canons: Essays in Literary Value, Univ Toronto Press, 91; Canadian Storytellers, Red Kite Press, 91; Can Lit, 93; Fawzia Afzal-Khan, Cultural Imperialism and the Indo-English Novel: Genre and Ideology, Univ Pa Press, 93, The Yearbook of Eng Stud 26, 96. **CONTACT ADDRESS** Department of English, Brock Univ, 500 Glenridge Ave, St Catharines, ON, L2S 3A1. **EMAIL** sspearey@spartan.ac.brocku.ca

SPEARS, LEE A.
DISCIPLINE TECHNICAL ND BUSINESS WRITING **EDUCATION** Western Ky Univ, Ma; Univ Ky, PhD. **CAREER** Prof, Western Ky Univ. **RESEARCH** Professional writing with a particular focus on pedagogy. **SELECTED PUBLICATIONS** Articles, Writing Inst; Bull Asn Bus Comm. **CONTACT ADDRESS** Western Kentucky Univ, 1526 Big Red Way Street, Bowling Green, KY, 42101. **EMAIL** lee.spears@wku.edu

SPEIRS, LOGAN
DISCIPLINE ENGLISH LITEREATURE **EDUCATION** Cambridge Univ, PhD, 65. **CAREER** ASSOC PROF, ENG, UNIV CALIF, SANTA BARBARA. **RESEARCH** Poetry and drama. **SELECTED PUBLICATIONS** Auth, Tolstoy and Chekhov, Cambridge, 71. **CONTACT ADDRESS** Dept of Eng, Univ Calif, Santa Barbara, CA, 93106-7150. **EMAIL** lspeirs@humanitas.ucsb.edu

SPENCER, GREGORY H.
DISCIPLINE RHETORIC AND COMMUNICATION **EDUCATION** Univ Oregon, PhD, 85. **CAREER** Instr, McKenzie Stud Ctr, 80-87; sem instr, Antioch Univ, 92, 94; assoc prof, Westmont Col, 87-. **HONORS AND AWARDS** Tchr yr, 90. **RESEARCH** Media ethics; rhetorical theory criticism. **SELECTED PUBLICATIONS** Auth, The Rhetoric of Malcolm Muggeridge's Gradual Christian Conversion, Jour Commun and Rel, 95; A Heart For Truth: Taking Your Faith to College, Baker Bk House, 92; Unethical Ethos? Flannery O'Connor's 'Wise Blood' in Word and Image, Rhetoric of Film, Kendall/Hunt, 94; Response to John E Phelan, Jr's Theology and Life: Expressing Our Faith Today, Covenant Comp, 92. **CONTACT ADDRESS** Dept of Commun, Westmont Col, 955 La Paz Rd, Santa Barbara, CA, 93108-1099.

SPENGEMANN, WILLIAM C.
DISCIPLINE ENGLISH LITERATURE **EDUCATION** Stanford Univ, PhD, 61. **CAREER** Patricia F. and William B. Hale '44 Prof Arts and Sci and Prof Eng. **RESEARCH** Am fiction and poetry. **SELECTED PUBLICATIONS** Auth, A New World of Words: Redefining Early American Literature, Yale UP, 94; ed, Herman Melville's Pierre or The Ambiguities, Penguin, 96; Herman Melville: Pierre, Penguin, 95; co-ed, 19th-century American Poetry, Penguin, 96. **CONTACT ADDRESS** Dartmouth Col, 3529 N Main St, #207, Hanover, NH, 03755.

SPERRY, STUART M.
PERSONAL Born 02/22/1929, New York, NY **DISCIPLINE** ENGLISH **EDUCATION** Princeton Univ, AB, 51; Harvard Univ, AM, 55, PhD, 59. **CAREER** Lectr, 58-59, from instr to assoc prof, 59-70, PROF ENGLISH, IND UNIV, BLOOMINGTON, 70-, Vis assoc prof, Univ Calif, Riverside, 68-69. **HONORS AND AWARDS** Wordsworth Bicentenary Colloquium Competition Prize Essay, The Wordsworth Circle & Dept English, Temple Univ, 70. **MEMBERSHIPS** MLA **RESEARCH** Romantic period. **SELECTED PUBLICATIONS** Auth, Richard Woodhouse's interleaved and annotated copy of Keats's Poems (1817), Lit Monogr, 67; Keats the Poet, Princeton Univ, 73; Toward a definition of romantic irony in English literature, In: Romantic and Modern: Revaluations of Literary Tradition, Univ Pittsburgh, 77; Necessity and the role of the hero in Shelley's Prometheus Unbound, Publ Mod Lang Asn Am, 81; Oracles And Hierophants--Constructions Of Romantic Authority, J Of English And Germanic Philology, Vol 92, 93. **CONTACT ADDRESS** Dept of English, Indiana Univ, Bloomington, Bloomington, IN, 47401.

SPEVACK, MARVIN
PERSONAL Born 12/17/1927, New York, NY, m, 1962, 1 child **DISCIPLINE** ENGLISH **EDUCATION** City Col New York, AB, 48; Harvard Univ, AM, 50, PhD(English), 53. **CAREER** Instr, City Col New York, 55-61, asst prof, 61-63; PROF ENGLISH, UNIV MsNSTER, WEST GER, 63-, DIR, INSTITUTUM ERASMIANUM, 74-, Fulbright lectr, 61-62; vis prof, Univ Munich, 62-63, NY Univ, summer, 66, Harvard Univ, summer, 73; sr fel, Folger Shakespeare Libr, 70; Guggenheim fel, 73-74; hon res fel, Univ Col, London, 80-81. **MEMBERSHIPS** Int Asn Univ Professors English; Int Shakespeare Asn; MLA; Shakespeare Asn Am; Asn Lit & Ling Comput. **RESEARCH** Shakespeare; Elizabethan literature; drama. **SELECTED PUBLICATIONS** Auth, James Halliwell ,Orchard + Early Shakespeare Editions--Outlines Of A Life, Anglia-Zeitschrift Fur Englische Philologie, Vol 114, 96; Beyond Individualism--Names And Namelessness In Shakespeare/ Huntington Libr Quart, Vol 56, 93; 'Jasper' + Identity Of Title In Alexander Dyce Letter--Query/, Notes And Queries, Vol 42, 95; gen ed, Renaissance Latin Drama in England, Georg Olms Hildesheim, 81-. **CONTACT ADDRESS** Englisches Sem, Univ Muenster, Munster, ..

SPIEGELMAN, WILLARD LESTER
PERSONAL Born 12/29/1944, St. Joseph, MO **DISCIPLINE** ENGLISH LITERATURE **EDUCATION** Williams Col, AB, 66; Harvard Univ, AM, 67, PhD, 71. **CAREER** Asst prof, 71-77, assoc prof, 77-86, prof eng, Southern Methodist Univ, 86, chmn, 91-94, Hughes Prof Engl, 93-; Vis prof, Williams Col, 87-88; Ed, Southwest Rev, 84-, Columnist, Wall Street Jour, 88. **HONORS AND AWARDS** Perrine Prize, Phi Beta Kappa, 81., NEH Summer Grant, 83 & 89, and year long stipend, 90-91; Rockefeller Found, Scholar-in-Residence, Poetry Center, 85-86; Guggenheim Fel, 94-95. **MEMBERSHIPS** MLA; Wordsworth-Coleridge Soc; Asn Literary Scholars & Critics. **RESEARCH** Eng romantic poetry; contemp poetry; class. **SELECTED PUBLICATIONS** Auth, Wordsworth's Aeneid, Comp Lit, 74; Landscape and knowledge: The poetry of Elizabeth Bishop, Mod Poetry Studies, 75; Ben Belitt's places, Mod Poetry Studies, 76; Elizabeth Bishop's Natural Heroism, Centennial Rev, 78; The Rake's Progress: An operatic version of pastoral, Southwest Rev, 78; The rituals of perception, Parnassus, 78; Alphabeting the void, Salmagundi, 78; Breaking the mirror: Interruption in the trilogy, In: James Merrill: Essays in Criticism, Cornell Univ Press, 82; Some Lucretian Elements in Wordsworth, Compartative Lit, 84; Wordsworth's Heroes, Univ Calif Press, 85; Peter Grimes: The development of a hero, Studies in Romanticism, 85; The Didactic Muse: Scenes of Instruction in Contemporary American Poetry, Princeton Univ Press, 89; Majestic Indolence: English Romantic Poetry and the Work of Art, Oxford Univ Press, 95. **CONTACT ADDRESS** Dept of Eng, Southern Methodist Univ, PO Box 750001, Dallas, TX, 75275-0001. **EMAIL** wspiegel@mail.smu.edu

SPILKA, MARK
PERSONAL Born 08/06/1925, Cleveland, OH, m, 7 children **DISCIPLINE** ENGLISH, COMPARATIVE LITERATURE **EDUCATION** Brown Univ, BA, 49; Ind Univ, MA, 53, PhD(-comp lit), 56. **CAREER** Ed asst, Am Mercury, 49-51; instr English lit, Univ Mich, 54-58, asst prof, English, 58-63; assoc prof, 63-67, chmn, Dept English, 68-73, PROF ENGLISH LIT, BROWN UNIV, 67-, Fel, Ind Sch Lett, 61; managing ed, Novel: A Forum on Fiction, Brown Univ, 67-77, ed, 78-; Guggenheim fel, 67-68; Nat Endowment for Humanitites fel independent study & res, 78-79; vis prof, Ind Univ, summer, 76. **MEMBERSHIPS** MLA **RESEARCH** English and American novel, especially 19th and 20th centuries; comparative literature; modern literary criticism. **SELECTED PUBLICATIONS** Auth, Love Ethic of D H Lawrence, 55 & Dickens and Kafka: A Mutual Interpretation, 63, Ind Univ; ed, D H Lawrence: A Collection of Critical Essays, Prentice-Hall, 63; Towards a Poetics of Fiction, Ind Univ, 77; auth, Virginia Woolf's Quarrel with Grieving, Univ Nebr Press, 80; auth, Renewing the Normative D. H. Lawrence: A Personal Progress, Missouri, 92; auth, Eight Lessons in Love: A Domestic Violence Reader, Missouri, 97. **CONTACT ADDRESS** 294 Doyle Ave, Providence, RI, 02906. **EMAIL** mark.spilka@brown.edu

SPINELLI, DONALD C.
PERSONAL Born 12/09/1942, Rochester, NY, m, 1971, 1 child **DISCIPLINE** LITERATURE **EDUCATION** SUNY, BA, 65, MA, 66; Ohio State Univ, PhD, 71. **CAREER** From asst prof to prof to assoc dean, 72-, Wayne State Univ. **HONORS AND AWARDS** NEH editor's grant, 92-94; Florence Gould Found Grant, 92-94. **MEMBERSHIPS** AATF; MLA. **RESEARCH** 18TH century French literature. **SELECTED PUBLICATIONS** Coauth, Beaumarchais. Correspondance, 78; auth, art, A Concordance to Marivaux's Comedies in Prose, 79; coauth, Beaumarchais: A Bibliography, 88; coauth, French Language and Literature: An Annotated Bibligraphy, 89; auth, art, L'Inventaire apres deces de Beaumarchais, 97. **CONTACT ADDRESS** Wayne State Univ, 2226 FAB, Detroit, MI, 48202. **EMAIL** d.c.spinelli@wayne.edu

SPIRES, JEFFREY
DISCIPLINE NINETEENTH-CENTURY FRENCH LITERATURE, FRENCH CULTURAL STUDIES **EDUCATION** Univ KS, BA, 86; Princeton Univ, MA, 91; PhD, 97. **CAREER** Engl, Colgate Univ. **HONORS AND AWARDS** Fulbright tchg asst, France, 86-1988; Armstrong fel, Princeton Univ, 88-92; McMahon grant, Princeton Univ, 90, 91. **SELECTED PUBLICATIONS** Auth, Revolutionary Grimace: Carnival in Victor Hugo's Notre-Dame de Paris, Nineteenth-Century Fr Stud, 97. **CONTACT ADDRESS** Dept of Romance Lang, Colgate Univ, 13 Oak Drive, Hamilton, NY, 13346.

SPITZBERG, BRIAN H.
DISCIPLINE COMMUNICATION **EDUCATION** Univ TX, BA, 78; Univ S CA, MA, PhD, 81. **CAREER** Vis asst prof, Univ WI-Madison; assoc prof, Univ N TX; prof-, Fordham Univ. **HONORS AND AWARDS** Grad dir, Interaction Stud, Intl and Intercult Stud and Applied Commun Stud. **RESEARCH** Conflict management, courtship violence, sexual commun. **SELECTED PUBLICATIONS** Auth, co-auth, over 45 scholarly articles and chapters, three scholarly bk(s); co-auth, The Dark Side of Interpersonal Communication. **CONTACT ADDRESS** Dept of Commun, San Diego State Univ, 5500 Campanile Dr, San Diego, CA, 92182. **EMAIL** spitz@mail.sdsu.edu

SPIVEY, TED RAY
PERSONAL Born 07/01/1927, Ft. Pierce, FL, m, 1962, 2 children **DISCIPLINE** ENGLISH LITERATURE **EDUCATION** Emory Univ, AB, 49; Univ Minn, MA, 51, PhD(English), 54. **CAREER** Instr, Emory Univ, 54-56; from asst prof to assoc prof English, 56-64, PROF ENGLISH, GA STATE UNIV, 64-, PROF URBAN LIFE, 70- **HONORS AND AWARDS** GSU Alumni distinguished prof; listed, Who's Who in America. **MEMBERSHIPS** SAtlantic Mod Lang Asn; MLA; AAUP. **RESEARCH** Modern poetry and modern British fiction; Southern literature. **SELECTED PUBLICATIONS** Auth, Revival: Southern Writers in the Modern City, Univ Press Fla, 86; auth, The Writer as Shaman: The Pilgrimages of Conrad Aiken and Walker Percy, Mercer Univ, 86; auth, Beyond Modernism: Toward A New Myth Criticism, Univ Press of America, 88; auth, Conrad Aiken: A Priest of Consciousness, AMS, 89; auth, Flannery O'Connor: The Woman, The Thinker, The Visionary, Mercer, 95; auth, Time's Stop in Savannah: Conrad Aiken's Inner Journey, Mercer, 97. **CONTACT ADDRESS** Dept of English, Georgia State Univ, University Plaza, Atlanta, GA, 30303.

SPOLSKY, ELLEN
PERSONAL Born 04/07/1943, New York, NY, m, 1962, 2 children **DISCIPLINE** ENGLISH LITERATURE **EDUCATION** McGill Univ, AB, 64; Ind Univ, Bloomington, AM, 68, PhD(English), 69. **CAREER** Asst prof English, Univ NMex, 68-74, assoc, 74-80; SR LECTR, BAR-ILAN UNIV, 80- **MEMBERSHIPS** MLA; Medieval Acad Am; Asn Comput Mach. **RESEARCH** Old and Middle English literature; semantics; literary theory. **SELECTED PUBLICATIONS** Auth, Computer-assisted semantic analysis of poetry, Comput Studies Humanities & Verbal Behav, 10/70; The semantic structure of the Wanderer, J Lit Semantics, 74; Old English kinship terms and Beowulf, Neuphilol Mitt, 77; coauth, The consolation of Alison: The speech acts of the wife of Bath, Centrum, 77; (with Ellen Schauber), Conversational noncooperation: The case of Chaucer's pardoner, Lang & Style; Stalking a generative poetics, NLH, spring 81; The Competence of the Experienced Reader: Preference Rules in Literary Theory, Ind Univ Press; A Theater Of Envy, William Shakespeare, Shakespeare Quarterly, Vol 44, 93. **CONTACT ADDRESS** Dept of English, Bar-Ilan Univ, Ramat Gan, ..

SPONBERG, ARVID FREDERIC
PERSONAL Born 11/08/1944, Minneapolis, MN, m, 1972, 2 children **DISCIPLINE** AMERICAN DRAMA **EDUCATION** Augustana Col, BA, 66; Univ Chicago, MA, 67; Univ Mich, PhD(English), 73. **CAREER** Instr, Henry Ford Community Col, 70-71; asst prof, 72-78, ASSOC PROF ENGLISH, VALPARAISO UNIV, 78-, Actg ed, The Cresset, 75-76; reader, Advan Placement Exams, Educ Test Serv, 77, 80 & 82; dir, Cambridge Overseas Study Ctr, Valparaiso Univ, 77-79 & chmn English Dept, 80-83. **MEMBERSHIPS** Int Asn Study Anglo-Irish Lit; Midwest Mod Lang Asn; NCTE. **RESEARCH** The history of American drama, especially the influence of economics on artistic decisions; Irish drama, especially the lives of the early Abbey actors; rhetoric, especially the structure of argument and metaphor in literature and science. **SELECTED PUBLICATIONS** Auth, The drama business, Times Lit Supplement, 78; Four theatres in five books, Cresset, 82; The Actor Speaks--Actors Discuss Their Experiences And Careers, Theatre Res Int, Vol 21, 96. **CONTACT ADDRESS** English Dept, Valparaiso Univ, 651 College Ave, Valparaiso, IN, 46383-6493.

SPRETNAK, CHARLENE M.
PERSONAL Pittsburgh, PA **DISCIPLINE** ENGLISH; AMERICAN LITERATURE **EDUCATION** St. Louis Univ (Jesuit), BA, 68; Univ Calif Berkeley, MA, 81. **CAREER** Adjunct prof, philos and relig, Calif Inst of Integral Studies, San Francisco, 92-. **HONORS AND AWARDS** Phi Beta Kappa; Ohio Women's Hall of Fame. **MEMBERSHIPS** Amer Acad of Relig. **RESEARCH** Ecological thought; Ecological/feminist spirituality; Ecological postmodernism; The spiritual dimension of modern art; Cultural history. **SELECTED PUBLICATIONS** Auth, The Resurgence of the Real: Body, Nature, and Place in a Hypermodern World, Addison-Wesley, 97; auth, States of Grace: The Recovery of Meaning in the Postmodern Age, Harper Collins, 91; auth, The Spiritual Dimension of Green Politics, Bear & Co, 86; co-auth, Green Politics: The Global Promise, Dutton, 84; auth, The Politics of Women's Spirituality: Essays on the Rise of Spiritual Power within the Feminist Movement, Anchor/Doubleday, 82; auth, Lost Goddesses of Early Greece: A Collection of Pre-Hellenic Myths, Beacon Press, 81. **CONTACT ADDRESS** PO Box 860, Moss Beach, CA, 94038.

SPRICH, C. ROBERT
PERSONAL St. Louis, MO, m, 1961, 2 children **DISCIPLINE** ENGLISH LITERATURE **EDUCATION** Mass Inst Technol, BS, 61; Brandeis Univ, MA, 63; Tufts Univ, PhD, 71. **CAREER** From asst prof to assoc prof, 66-77, PROF ENGLISH BENTLEY COL, 77-, Lectr, Grad Div Northeastern Univ, 66-68; lectr English, Exp Col, Tufts Univ, 69-71. **HONORS AND AWARDS** Fel, Ctr for Psychol Study Arts, State Univ NY, Buffalo, spring, 76; vis scholar, Univ Va Film Festival, 94. **MEMBERSHIPS** Popular Culture Asn; Am Film Inst. **RESEARCH** Late Victorian literature; the modern novel; applications of psychoanalysis to literary criticism. **SELECTED PUBLICATIONS** Coauth, Hell, Encycl Britannica, 64; auth, Theme and structure in T S Eliot's The Hippopotamus, CEA Critic, 4/69; Pressed flowers, fresh flowers: New directions in psychoanalytic criticism, Colby Libr Quart, 3/77; co-ed, The Whispered Meanings, Univ Mass, 77; auth, The appeal of Star Wars, Am Imago, summer 81; Essays on William Faulkner and Katherine Anne Porter, Literature and Psychoanalysis, Lisbon, 97. **CONTACT ADDRESS** Dept of English, Bentley Col, 175 Forest St, Waltham, MA, 02154-4705. **EMAIL** rsprich@bentley.edu

SPRINGER, HASKELL SAUL
PERSONAL Born 11/18/1939, New York, NY, m, 1993, 2 children **DISCIPLINE** AMERICAN LITERATURE & STUDIES **EDUCATION** Queens Col, NY, BA, 61; Ind Univ, MA, 65, PhD, 68. **CAREER** Instr, Univ Va, 66-68; from asst prof to assoc prof, 68-78, prof Eng, 78-, Univ Kans; Fulbright prof Am lit, Universidade Catolica & Universidade Fed, Rio de Janeiro, Brazil, 75-76; vis prof, amer lit, Sorbonne, Paris, 85-86. **MEMBERSHIPS** MLA; AAUP; Melville Soc; Amer Cult Assn. **RESEARCH** Classic American literature; American sea narrative; textual scholarship. **SELECTED PUBLICATIONS** Ed, America and the Sea: A Literary History, University of Georgia, 95; auth, The Captain's Wife at Sea, Iron Man, Wooden Women: Gender and Seafaring in the Atlantic World, 1700-1920, Johns Hopkins, 96. **CONTACT ADDRESS** Dept of English, Univ of Kansas, Lawrence, KS, 66045-0001. **EMAIL** springer@ukans.edu

SPRINKER, MICHAEL
PERSONAL Born 02/08/1950, m **DISCIPLINE** ENGLISH AND COMPARATIVE LITERATURE **EDUCATION** Northwestern Univ, BA, 72; Princeton Univ, MA, 74; PhD, 75. **CAREER** Prof, 88-. **SELECTED PUBLICATIONS** Auth, Counterpoint of Dissonance: The Aesthetics and Poetry of Gerard Manley Hopkins, Johns Hopkins Univ, 80; Imaginary Relations: Aesthetics and Ideology in the Theory of Historical Materialism, 87; History and Ideology in Proust: 'A la recherche du temps perdu' and the Third French Republic, Cambridge, 94; The Mughal Empire (rev), Radical History Rev, 94; co-ed, Late Imperial Culture, 95. **CONTACT ADDRESS** English Dept, SUNY Stony Brook, Stony Brook, NY, 11794. **EMAIL** mbishop@notes.cc.sunysb.edu

SPROW, RICHARD
DISCIPLINE ENGLISH **EDUCATION** Purdue University, PhD. **CAREER** Prof; dept ch. **HONORS AND AWARDS** NEH fel. **RESEARCH** Shakespeare; modern drama; modern lit; film; interdisciplinary studies; popular culture. **SELECTED PUBLICATIONS** Co-auth, Write This Way. **CONTACT ADDRESS** Dept of Eng, Westminister Col, New Wilmington, PA, 16172-0001.

SPRUNGER, DAVID A.
DISCIPLINE ENGLISH LITERATURE **EDUCATION** Bethel Col, BA, 82; Univ Kans, MA, 85; Univ Ill Urbana-Champaign, PhD, 92. **CAREER** Asst prof, 92-98, assoc prof, Concordia Col, 98-. **MEMBERSHIPS** Am Folklore Soc; Int Arthurian Asn; Medieval Acad Am; Medieval Asn Midwest; MLA. **SELECTED PUBLICATIONS** Auth, Parodic Animal Physicians from the Margins of Medieval Manuscripts, Garland, 96. **CONTACT ADDRESS** English Dept, Concordia Col, Minnesota, 901 8th St S, Moorhead, MN, 56562. **EMAIL** sprunger@cord.edu

SPURLOCK, JOHN HOWARD
PERSONAL Born 10/22/1939, Huntington, WV, m, 1962, 1 child **DISCIPLINE** LINGUISTICS, AMERICAN LITERATURE **EDUCATION** WVa Univ, BA, 62; Univ Louisville, MA, 64, PhD, 86. **CAREER** Instr English, Western Ky Univ, 64-69 & Louisville Country Day Sch, 69-70; assoc prof, 71-86, prof English, Western Ky Univ, 86-. **HONORS AND AWARDS** Award for Editorial Excellence, Jesse Stuart Found, 96. **MEMBERSHIPS** Appalachian Writers Asn; Jesse Stuart Found (ed and mem bd dir); Ky Speakers' Bureau. **RESEARCH** Sociolinguistics; Appalachian literature; Kentucky literature. **SELECTED PUBLICATIONS** Auth, He Sings For Us--A Sociolinguistic Analysis of the Appalachian Subculture and of Jesse Stuart as a Major American Author, Univ Press of Am, 80 & 82; Appalachian--Appalachia/strange man--strange land, In: Speechways of American Subcultures, Univ Press of Ky, 82; ed, Jesse Stuart's Daughter of the Legend, Jesse Stuart Found, 94; Jesse Stuart's Beyond Dark Hills, Jesse Stuart Found, 96. **CONTACT ADDRESS** 1 Big Red Way St, Box 495, Bowling Green, KY, 42101-3576.

ST. CLAIR, GLORIANA
PERSONAL Born 12/13/1939, Tonkawa, OK **DISCIPLINE** MANAGEMENT; LITERATURE **EDUCATION** Univ Okla, BA, 62, PhD, 70; Univ Calif, Berkeley, MLS, 63; Univ Tex, San Antonio, MBA, 80. **CAREER** Res asst, 62-63, asst librn, 63-65, Univ Calif, Berkely; cat, Univ Okla, 65-68; asst prof, Western Carolina Univ, 69-71; asst prof, Col Charleston, 71-76; vis lectr, Medical Univ, SC, 75; adj full prof, Walsh Col, 76-77; tchg assoc, Univ Tex, San Antonio, 79-81; sup librn, San Antonio Public Libr, 80-84; div head, 84-87, bibliogr, 85, Tex A&M Univ Libry; asst dir, Ore State Univ, 87-90; from int assoc dean to int dean, 96-97, assoc dean, 97-98, Pattee Libry, Pa State Univ; librn, Carnegie Mellon Univ, 98-. **HONORS AND AWARDS** Tex Libry Asn Resolution of Thanks, 86; Charles W. Plum Dist Service Award, 86; Partnership for Excellence, 93, Pa State Univ, Pa Quality Leadership Awards Examiner Training, 94; Pa Quality Leadership Found, 94; Who's Who Am Women, 97-98; Who's Who World, 97-98; The World Who's Who Women, 97-98. **MEMBERSHIPS** Ore Chapter Asn Col Res Librys; OR Libry Asn; Tex Libry Asn; Ore State Univ Fac Women's Network; Mythopoeic Soc; Libry Res Round Table; Libry, Information Technol Asn; Asn Col Res Librys; Nat Digital Libry Fed Board; Asn Res Librys, Inst Representative. **RESEARCH** Copyright law; digital libraries **SELECTED PUBLICATIONS** Auth, art, Steps Toward Writing a Sure Thing, 97; auth, art, Third-Party Payer System Explored, 97; coauth, art, Changing Copyright Legislation: Two Views, 97; coauth, art, Active and Collaborative Learning in Online Courses: Penn State's Project Vision, 97; auth, art, Assessment: How & Why, 99. **CONTACT ADDRESS** Univ Libraries, Carnegie Mellon Univ, 4909 Frew St, Pittsburgh, PA, 15213. **EMAIL** gstclair@andrew.cmu.edu

ST. OMER, GARTH
DISCIPLINE AMERICAN AND CARIBBEAN LITERATURE **EDUCATION** Princeton Univ, PhD, 75. **CAREER** PROF, ENG, UNIV CALIF, SANTA BARBARA. **RESEARCH** Fiction; creat writing. **SELECTED PUBLICATIONS** Auth, A Room on the Hill, Faber and Faber, 68; Shades of Grey, Faber and Faber, 68; Nor Any Country, Faber and Faber, 69; Black Bam and the Masqueraders, Faber and Faber, 72. **CONTACT ADDRESS** Dept of Eng, Univ Calif, Santa Barbara, CA, 93106-7150.

STAAL, ARIE
PERSONAL Born 09/27/1933, Grand Rapids, MI, m, 1963, 2 children **DISCIPLINE** AMERICAN & NETHERLANDIC LITERATURE **EDUCATION** Calvin Col, BA, 63; Univ Mich, MA, 64, PhD(English), 70. **CAREER** Instr, Calvin Col, 64-65 & Eastern Mich Univ, 68-70; lectr, Univ Helsinki, 70-71; asst prof, 71-76, assoc prof, 76-82, PROF ENGLISH, EASTERN MICH UNIV, 82-, Lectr, Bur of Sch Serv, Univ Mich, 68-70; Fulbright lectr, US Govt, 70. **MEMBERSHIPS** Can Asn Advan Netherlandic Studies; AAUP; Fine Arts Soc; Conf Christianity & Lit. **RESEARCH** Narrative techiques in traditional American fiction; narrative techniques in twentieth-century Netherlandic fiction; experimentation in twentieth-century Netherlandic poetry. **SELECTED PUBLICATIONS** Auth, Het Hotel, World Lit Today, Vol 69, 95; Cellojaren, World Lit Today, Vol 70, 96; The Following Story, World Lit Today, Vol 70, 96; Een Goede Zaak, World Lit Today, Vol 70, 96; De Zoektocht, World Lit Today, Vol 67, 93; Omhelzingen, World Lit Today, Vol 68, 94; Poems 1948-1993, World Lit Today, Vol 69, 95; Jazz, World Lit Today, Vol 67, 93; Okokas

Wonderpark, World Lit Today, Vol 69, 95; Eclips, World Lit Today, Vol 68, 94; De Vriendschap, World Lit Today, Vol 70, 96; Het Woeden Der Gehele Wereld, World Lit Today, Vol 69, 95; Groenten Uit Balen, World Lit Today, Vol 68, 94; Respyt, World Lit Today, Vol 68, 94; Ontroeringen, World Lit Today, Vol 66, 92. **CONTACT ADDRESS** English Dept, Eastern Michigan Univ, 612 Pray Harrold, Ypsilanti, MI, 48197-2201.

STACK, RICHARD
DISCIPLINE PUBLIC RELATIONS **EDUCATION** Ind Univ, BA; Univ Mo, JD. **CAREER** Asst prof, Am Univ. **HONORS AND AWARDS** Founder & pres, RAS Consulting. **RESEARCH** Legal communication and public service/public relations. **SELECTED PUBLICATIONS** Coauth, Litigation in Public Relations; contribur, Wash Post, LA Times, St. Louis Dispatch, WCA Agenda, Comm & Law, The Champion, Jour Mo bar. **CONTACT ADDRESS** American Univ, 4400 Massachusetts Ave, Washington, DC, 20016.

STADE, GEORGE
PERSONAL Born 11/25/1933, New York, NY, m, 1956, 4 children **DISCIPLINE** ENGLISH **EDUCATION** St Lawrence Univ, BA, 55; Columbia Univ, MA, 58, PhD, 65. **CAREER** Instr Eng, Rutgers Univ, 60-61; asst prof, 62-69, PROF ENGLISH, COLUMBIA UNIV, 69-, Coun Res Hum grant, 67-68; ed-in-chief, Columbia Essays on Mod Writers; ed-in-chief, Europ Writers, Scribner's. **MEMBERSHIPS** PEN Club; Nat Bk Critics Circle. **RESEARCH** Mod lit; popular fiction; theory of lit. **SELECTED PUBLICATIONS** Auth, Robert Graves, Columbia Univ, 67; coauth, Selected Letters of E E Commings, Harcourt, 68; contribr, A Closer Look at Ariel, Harper's Mag Press, 72; ed, Six Modern British Novelists, 74 & Six Contemporary British Novelists, 76, Columbia Univ; Confessions of a Lady-Killer, Norton, 79; over 150 reviews, articles and introductions. **CONTACT ADDRESS** Columbia Univ, 2960 Broadway, New York, NY, 10027-6900. **EMAIL** ggs3@columbia.edu

STADLER, EVA MARIA
PERSONAL Born 03/28/1931, Prague, Czechoslovakia, m, 1957 **DISCIPLINE** COMPARATIVE LITERATURE, FILM STUDIES **EDUCATION** Barnard Col, AB, 52; Columbia Univ, PhD(French), 67. **CAREER** Lectr French, Columbia Univ, 53-57; instr French & Ger, Wash Col, 57-58; instr French, Douglass Col, Rutgers Univ, 58-64; asst prof French & Ger, 65-67, assoc prof, Manhattan Community Col, 67-68; assoc prof Comp Lit, French & Film Studies, 68-95, chair Humanities div, 73-79, dir Media Studies, 88-95, ASSOC PROF ENGLISH COMMUN & MEDIA STUDIES, FORDHAM UNIV, LINCOLN CENTER, 95-. **MEMBERSHIPS** MLA; ACLA; Soc 18th Century Studies; ACLA Nat Cmt on Undergraduate prog, 71-75 & 78-82; Colloquium fel in Comp Lit, NYU, 72-92; Juror, Am Film Festival 80 & 81 **RESEARCH** History and theory of the novel; fiction and film; French film and film theory; 18th Century literature. **SELECTED PUBLICATIONS** Coauth, Premiers textes litteraires, Blaisdell, 66, Wiley, 75; auth, Rameau's Nephew by Diderot: Un film de Michael Snow, In: Interpeter Diderot Au-jourd'hui, Le Sycomore, 84; Espace acoustique et cinema moderne: l'exemple de Rovert Bresson, In: Bulletin de la SPFFA, 86-87; The Red Dress of Oriane de Guermantes, In: Reading Proust Now, Lang, 90; Diderot et le cinema: Les paradoxes de l'adaptation, Francographies, 92; Defining the Female Body within Social Space; The Function of Clothes in Some 18th Century Novels, Proceedings of the XIIth Congress of the ICLA, 90; Francophonie et cinema: l'exemple de deux cineastes senegalais, Francographies, 93; Addressing Social Boundaries: Dressing the Female Body in Early Realist Fiction, In: Reconfigured Spheres: Feminist Explorations of Literary Space, Univ Mass Press, 94; Une femme douce de Robert Bresson: Le cinema et ses pre-textes, Francographies, 95 **CONTACT ADDRESS** Dept of English, Fordham Univ, 113 W 60th St, New York, NY, 10023. **EMAIL** evastadler@aol.com

STAGG, LOUIS CHARLES
PERSONAL Born 01/03/1933, New Orleans, LA, m, 1959, 2 children **DISCIPLINE** ENGLISH **EDUCATION** La Col, BA, 55; Univ Ark, MA, 57, PhD, 63. **CAREER** Asst English, Univ Ark, 55-59; asst prof, William Jewell Col, 59-60; instr, Stephen F Austin State Col, 60-62; from asst prof to prof, 62-88, EMERITUS PROF ENGLISH, UNIV MEMPHIS, 88-, DIR ENGLISH DRAMA PLAYERS, 68-88, Memphis State Univ fac res grants, 69-71; consult, State Based Progs, Nat Endowment for Humanities, 75-78; circulation mgr, Interpretations, 76-80; assoc ed, SCent Bull, SCent Mod Lang Asn, 82-84. **HONORS AND AWARDS** Phi Beta Kappa, 57; Pres, Memphis Alumni Asn, Phi Beta Kappa, 85-88. **MEMBERSHIPS** MLA; Southern Humanities Coun (secy-treas, 74-76, Council Chair, 93-94); SCent Mod Lang Asn; SCent Renaissance Conf; Acad Exchange Quart Advisory Board, 97-; Shakespeare Asn Am; Renaissance Soc of Am; Col English Asn; Eugene O'Neill Soc; Soc for the Study of Harold Pinter (treas & mem Exec Comt, 94-98; Am Asn of Univ Prof; The Stratford Festival; Conf on Christianity and Lit; Int Shakespeare Asn; Am Asn for Theatre Res; Int Soc for Theatre Res; Marlowe Soc of Am (Reviewer of Books, 83-93); Samuel Beckett Soc; originator of the Alliance for Creative Theatre, Educ, and Res at the Univ Memphis in 1986 (Chair of Schedules and mem Steering Comt, 86, 89, 90, 92, 94, 96, and consultant, 98); Int Conf on Patristic, Medieval, and Renaissance Studies; Am Theatre Asn. **RESEARCH** Renaissance drama; development of English drama from the medieval beginnings through the Renaissance and on to existentialism and modern rock opera; world drama, tragedy. **SELECTED PUBLICATIONS** Coauth, An Index to Poe's Critical Vocabulary, Transcendental Bks, 66; auth, Figurative imagery in revenge tragedies by three seventeenth century contemporaries of Shakespeare, SCent Bull, winter 66; coauth, Special collections on Southern culture in college and university libraries, Humanities in the south, spring 67; auth, An index to the figurative language of John Webster's, Ben Jonson's, Thomas Heywood's, George Chapman's, John Marston's, Cyril Tourneur's, and Thomas Middleton's tragedies, Bibliog Soc, Univ Va, 67-70; Characterization through nature imagery in the tragedies of George Chapman, Ball State Univ Forum, winter 68; George Bernard Shaw and the existentialist-absurdist theatre, Tenn Philol Bull, 7/77; Index to the Figurative Language of the Tragedies of Shakespeare's Chief 17th Century Contemporaries: Chapman, Heywood, Jonson, Marston, Webster, Tourneur, Middleton, Memphis State Univ, 77, 3rd ed, Garland Publ Inc, 82; Critical essays on Thomas Heywood, Nicholas Rowe, William H Gillette, Lord Dunsany and Christopher Fry, In: Major Writers of the English Language, Vol III, St Martin's Press, 79 & Macmillan, UK, 79; Index to the Tragedies of Shakespeare's Chief 16th Century Contemporaries, Garland Publ, 84; Essays on William Gillette, Death of a Salesman, and Long Day's Journey Into Night, In: Reference Guide to American Literature, St. James Press, 2nd ed, 87. **CONTACT ADDRESS** 5219 Mason Rd, Memphis, TN, 38117-2104.

STALEY, LYNN
DISCIPLINE CHAUCER, MEDIEVAL LITERATURE AND CULTURE, SPENSER, EARLY RENAISSANCE LITERA **EDUCATION** Univ KY, AB, 69; Princeton Univ, MA, PhD, 73. **CAREER** Harrington and Shirley Drake, prof, 74. **RESEARCH** Medieval women writers. **SELECTED PUBLICATIONS** Co-auth, The Powers of the Holy. Religion, Politics, and Gender in Late Medieval English Culture, Univ Park: Pa, 96; auth, The Book of Margery Kempe Medieval Inst Publ, 96; The Voice of the Gawain-Poet, 84; The Shepheardes Calender: An Introduction, 90; Margery Kempe's Dissenting Fictions, 94; The Pearl Dreamer and the Eleventh Hour, Text and Matter, a New Critical Perspective of the Pearl-Poet, 91; rev(s), Am Notes and Queries, Mediaevalia et Humanistica, Renaissance Quart, Spenser Newsletter, Speculum. **CONTACT ADDRESS** Dept of Eng, Colgate Univ, 13 Oak Drive, Hamilton, NY, 13346.

STALEY, THOMAS F.
DISCIPLINE BRITISH LITERATURE **CAREER** Teaching fel, Univ of Pittsburgh, 58-60; asst prof, Rollins Col, 61-62; from asst prof to prof, Univ of Tulsa, 62-88; dean, Grad Sch, Univ of Tulsa, 69-76; vpres for acad affairs, Univ of Tulsa, 77; chemn, Grad Fac of Modern Letters, Univ of Tulsa, 79-81; dean, Col of Arts and Scis, Univ of Tulsa, 81-83; provost and vpres for acad affairs, Univ of Tulsa, 83-88; Chancellor's Coun Centennial prof in the Book Arts, Univ of Tex, 88-92; dir, Harry Ransom Hums Res Ctr and prof, Univ of Tex, 88-. **HONORS AND AWARDS** Fulbright Res Prof, Trieste, Italy, 66-67, 71; Am Coun of Learned Socs Grant, 69, ACLS Grant-in-Aid, 80, 82. **MEMBERSHIPS** Soc for Textual Scholar; MLA; Int Asn for the Study of Anglo-Irish Lit; Am Comt for Irish Studies; James Joyce Found; English Inst; Int Asn for Univ Profs of English; English Speaking Union; Philos Soc of Tex. **SELECTED PUBLICATIONS** Auth, James Joyce's Portrait of the Artist, 68; Dorothy Richardson, 76; Jean Rhys: A Critical Study, 79; An Annotated Critical Bibliography of James Joyce, 89; The Marginality of the Humanities, in The Center for the Book, 90; Literary Canons, Literary Studies and Library Collections: A Retrospective on Collecting Twentieth Century Writers, in Rare Books and Manuscripts Librarianship, 90; Selections from the Paris Diary of Stuart Gilbert, in Joyce Studies Annual I, 90; Religious Elements and Thomistic Encounters: Noon on Joyce andAquinas, in Re-Viewing Classics of Joyce Criticism, 91; On the Selling of Literary Archives, in The Author, vol. CIV, no 1, 93; Perspectives on the Rare Book Library at the End of the Century, in Rare Book and Manuscript Libraries at the End of the Century, 93; ed, James Joyce Today: Essays on the Major Works, 66; Italo Svevo: Essays on His Work, 69; Ulysses: Fifty Years, 74; Twentieth Century Women Novelists, 83; Joyce Studies: An Annual, 89-; Studies in Modernism, book series, 90-; James Joyce Quarterly; coed, Literature and Theology, 69; Dubliners: A Critical Handbook, 69; The Shapeless God: Essays on the Modern Novel, 68; Approaches to Ulysses: Ten Essays, 70; Approaches to Joyce's Portrait: Ten Essays, 76; Reflections on James Joyce, 93; Writing the Lives of Writers, 98. **CONTACT ADDRESS** Harry Ransom Humanities Research Center, Univ of Texas, Austin, PO Drawer 7219, Austin, TX, 78713-7219. **EMAIL** tfs@mail.utexas.edu

STAMBOVSKY, PHILLIP
PERSONAL Born 09/02/1952, Springfield, MA, m, 1978, 1 child **DISCIPLINE** ENGLISH **EDUCATION** Univ Mass, AMherst, BA, 77, MA, 79, PhD, 87. **CAREER** Prof, 87-88, dept chair, 88-98, Albertus Magnus Coll; independent scholar, 99-. **HONORS AND AWARDS** NEH vis scholar, Emory Univ, 93; NEH vis scholar, Univ Mo, 98; Univ Mass grad sch fel, 86-87; Yale Mellow vis fac fel, 90- 91. **MEMBERSHIPS** Asn Lit Scholars, Critics **RESEARCH** Emily Dickinson; myth theory; metaphor theory; philos approaches to lit. **SELECTED PUBLICATIONS** Auth, Louis, National Poetry Competition Winners, Chester H. Jones Fdn, 95, auth, Myth and the Limits of Reason, Rodopi, 96; auth, Poetic Work of Emily Dickinson: A Readers' Text, 96; auth, The Psychosocial Construction of Character in The Ambassadors, in Henry James ou le fluide sacre de la fiction, L'Harmattan, 98; auth, Hortense Calisher, George P Elliott, John O'Hara, and Delmore Schwartz in The Columbia Companion to the 20th Century American Short Story, Columbia Univ Press, forthcoming; auth, Vision and Discourse in Narrative Memory: Three Narratives of Therapeutic Remembering, Routledge, forthcoming. **CONTACT ADDRESS** 9 Birch Dr, New Haven, CT, 06515.

STANBACK, THURMAN W.
PERSONAL Born 03/20/1920, Washington, District of Columbia **DISCIPLINE** DRAMA **EDUCATION** VA Union U, BA 1941; Columbia U, MA 1947; Cornell U, PhD 1953-. **CAREER** FL Atlantic U, retired prof of theatre 1986; Bethune-Cookman Coll 1953-73 & 1953-70, artist-in-residence, 1991; Storer Coll, 1947-49; Glassboro State College, guest director, 1990. **HONORS AND AWARDS** Teacher of Yr Bethune Cookman Coll 1969; Distinguished Alumni in the Arts, Virginia Union University 1986; Distinguished Alumnus, National Assn for Equal Opportunity in Higher Education 1989. **MEMBERSHIPS** Mem Am Theatre Assn 1953-75; Speech Assn of Am 1953-75; Alpha Phi Alpha 1955-75; Nat Assn of & Dramatic & Speech Arts 1953-70.

STANFORD, DONALD ELWIN
PERSONAL Born 02/07/1913, Amherst, MA, m, 1953 **DISCIPLINE** ENGLISH **EDUCATION** Stanford Univ, BA, 33, PhD, 53; Harvard Univ, MA, 34. **CAREER** Instr English, Colo State Col, 35-37, Dartmouth Col, 37-41 & Univ Nebr, 41-42; from instr to assoc prof, 49-59, prof, 59-80, ALUMNI PROF ENGLISH, LA STATE UNIV, BATON ROUGE, 80-, CO-ED, SOUTHERN REV, 63-, Guggenheim fel, 59-60; vis assoc prof, Duke Univ, 61-62; ed, Humanities Ser, Univ Press, La State Univ, Baton Rouge, 62-68; La State Univ Found distinguished fac fel, 73-74. **MEMBERSHIPS** MLA; SCent Mod Lang Asn; PEN Club; SAtlantic Mod Lang Asn. **RESEARCH** The poetry of Edward Taylor; 17th century New England theology and literature; contemporary British and American poetry. **SELECTED PUBLICATIONS** Auth, New England Earth (poems), Colt, 41; The Traveler (poems), Cummington, 55; ed, The Poems of Edward Taylor, Yale Univ, 60; auth, Edward Taylor, Univ Minn, 62; ed, Edward Taylor's Metrical History of Christianity, Xerox, 62; Selected Poems of S Foster Damon, Abattoir Ed, 74; Selected Poems of Robert Bridges, Carcanet, 74; auth, In the Classic Mode: The Achievement of Robert Bridges, Univ Del, 78; As Far As Light Remains, Sewanee Rev, Vol 104, 96; Elizabeth Bishop--Life And The Memory Of It, Sewanee Rev, Vol 102, 94. **CONTACT ADDRESS** Dept of English, Louisiana State Univ, Baton Rouge, LA, 70803.

STANLEY, DONALD
DISCIPLINE ENGLISH LITERATURE **EDUCATION** Univ British Columbia, BA; PhD; NY State Univ, MA. **CAREER** Senior tutor. **SELECTED PUBLICATIONS** Auth, pubs on English literature. **CONTACT ADDRESS** English Dept, Open Learning Agency, 4355 Mathissi Place, Burnaby, BC, V5G 4S8. **EMAIL** ouocweb@ola.bc.ca

STANTON, DON
DISCIPLINE POLITICAL COMMUNICATION **EDUCATION** OH State Univ, PhD, 72. **CAREER** Southwest Tex State Univ **SELECTED PUBLICATIONS** Area: hist of polit commun. **CONTACT ADDRESS** Southwest MS State Univ, 901 S. National, Ste. 50, Springfield, MO, 65804-0094.

STANWOOD, PAUL GRANT
PERSONAL Born 04/25/1933, IA, m, 1964, 2 children **DISCIPLINE** ENGLISH LITERATURE **EDUCATION** Iowa State Teachers Col, BA, 54; Univ Mich, MA, 56, PhD, 61. **CAREER** Teaching fel, Univ Mich, 56-58 & 59-61; from instr to asst prof, Tufts Univ, 61-65; from asst prof to assoc prof, 65-75, PROF ENGLISH, UNIV BC, 75-, Can Coun fel, 68-69 & 74-75 & 79-80; vis prof, Peterhouse, Cambridge, 68-69 & 74-75; Folger Shakespeare Libr sr fel, 72. **MEMBERSHIPS** Renaissance Soc Am; Renaissance English Text Soc; MLA; Milton Soc Am; Bibliog Soc. **RESEARCH** Textual bibliography; Renaissance and 17th century English literature; devotional poetry and prose. **SELECTED PUBLICATIONS** Auth, St Teresa and Joseph Beaumont's Psyche, J English & Ger Philol, 7/63; ed, John Cosin, A Collection of Private Devotions, Oxford Univ, 67; Contemporary and patristic borrowing in the Caroline divines, Renaissance Quart, winter 70; Essential Joye in Donne's Anniversaries, Tex Studies in Lit & Lang, summer 71; John Donne's sermon notes, Rev English Studies, 8/78; ed, William Law, A Serious Call and Spirit of Love, Paulist, 78; auth, Time and Liturgy in Donne, Crashaw & T S Eliot, Nosaie, winter 79; Richard Hooker, Of the Laws of Ecclesiastical Polity, Books VI-VIII (Folger Libr Ed, vol 3), Harvard Univ, Belknap, 81; Lancelot Andrewes The Preacher: 1555-1626, The Origins Of The Mys-

tical Theology Of The Church-Of-England, J Of English And Germanic Philology, Vol 93, 94; Esteem Enlivened By Desire--The Couple From Homer To Shakespeare, J Of The Am Acad Of Religion, Vol 64, 96. **CONTACT ADDRESS** Dept of English, Univ of BC, Vancouver, BC, V6T 1W5.

STARGARDT, UTE
DISCIPLINE RHETORIC, ENGLISH AND AMERICAN LITERATURE, CHAUCER **EDUCATION** Univ Tenn,PhD. **CAREER** Prof, Alma Col. **RESEARCH** Medieval literatures and languages. **SELECTED PUBLICATIONS** Her articles have appeared in the US, Argentina and Germany. **CONTACT ADDRESS** Alma Col, Alma, MI, 48801.

STAROSTA, WILLIAM J.
PERSONAL Born 05/23/1946, Oconomowoc, WI, m, 1967, 1 child **DISCIPLINE** INTERCULTURAL COMMUNICATION **EDUCATION** Indiana Univ, AM, 70, PhD, 73. **CAREER** Univ of Va, asst prof, 72-78; Howard Univ, grad prof, 78-. **HONORS AND AWARDS** Fulbright diss. fel; Am Inst of Indian Studies fel; Wis-Berkeley Year-in-India scholar., Held professional office in regional and national socs. **MEMBERSHIPS** Nat Commun Asn; Eastern Commun Asn; World Commun Asn; Intl. Commun Asn. **RESEARCH** Ethnic conflict; Third Culture; Multiculturalism; Interethnic and intercultural communication; Culture and rhetoric. **SELECTED PUBLICATIONS** Coauth, Foundations of Intercultural Communication; ed, The Howard Jour of Communs. **CONTACT ADDRESS** Dept of Human Communication Studies, Howard Univ, 3015 Rosemoor Ln., Fairfax, VA, 22031. **EMAIL** wstarosta@fac.howard.edu

STATHOPOULOS, E.T.
DISCIPLINE COMMUNICATION **EDUCATION** Indiana Univ, PhD 80; Univ Wisconsin Mad, MS 73; Univ Wisconsin Milw, BSc 71. **CAREER** SUNY Buff, prof 79-; Univ Colorado, vis sen res 95-96; Univ Arizona, vis res sc 88-89; Indiana Univ, assoc inst 76-79. **HONORS AND AWARDS** ASHA PSI; Yng Res Awd; SUNY Res fel. **MEMBERSHIPS** ASLHA; ASA; NYS SLHA **RESEARCH** Normal speech production; development and aging of the speech system. **SELECTED PUBLICATIONS** Auth, Effects of a circumferentially-vented pneumotachograph mask on respiratory kinematic and volumetric measures, coauth, in: Jour of SLH Res, 98; Approximations of open and speech quotient from glottal airflow and electroglottographic waveforms: Effects of measurement criteria and sound pressure level, coauth, in: Jour of Voice, 98; Effects of varied intensity on ventilatory responses, coath, in: Jour SLH Res, 98; Expiratory muscle conditioning in hypotonic children with low vocal intensity levels, coauth, in: Jour of Med SL Pathology, 97; Developmental changes in laryngeal and respiratory function with variations in sound pressure level, coauth, in: Jour of SH Res, 97; Speech breathing during reading in women with vocal nodules, coauth, in: Jour of Voice, 97; Speech tasks effects on acoustic and aerodynamic measures of women with vocal nodules, coauth, in: Jour of Voice, 95; Glottal airflow - what can it tell us about a voice disorder? Coauth, In: Topicos em Fonoaudiologia, 96. **CONTACT ADDRESS** Dept of Commun Sci and Disorders, SUNY Buffalo, North Campus, Buffalo, NY, 14260. **EMAIL** stathop@acsu.buffalo.edu

STAUFFER, HELEN WINTER
PERSONAL Born 01/04/1922, Mitchell, SD, m, 1944, 4 children **DISCIPLINE** ENGLISH **EDUCATION** Kearney State Col, BA, 64, MA, 68; Univ Nebr, PhD(English), 74. **CAREER** Teacher English, Giltner High Sch, 64, Grand Island High Sch, 64-67; from instr to assoc prof, 68-75, PROF ENGLISH, KEARNEY STATE COL, 75- **MEMBERSHIPS** MLA; Western Lit Asn (pres, 80); Soc Study Midwestern Lit; Willa Cather Found; NEA. **RESEARCH** American literature; modern Western regional literature. **SELECTED PUBLICATIONS** Auth, Mari Sandoz and Western Biography, In: Women, Women Writers and the West, Whitston, 80; Two authors and a hero: Neihardt, Sandoz and Crazy Horse, Great Plains Quart, 1/81; Mari Sandoz and the university, Prairie Schooner, spring 81; Mari Sandoz, Story Catcher of the Plains, Univ Nebr Press, 82; co-ed (with Susan J Rosowski), Women in Western American Literature, Whitston, 82; auth, Mari Sandoz, In: Fifty Western American Writers, Greenwood, 82; Mari Sandoz, Boise State Univ; Neihardt's The River and I: The Beginning of an Epic, Neihardt Centennial Commemorative Collection; Mari Sandoz, Portrait Of An Artists Youth, Great Plains Quart, Vol 16, 96; Robert Henri Nebraska Years, Great Plains Quart, Vol 16, 96. **CONTACT ADDRESS** Dept of English, Kearney State Col, Kearney, NE, 68847.

STAVES, SUSAN
PERSONAL Born 10/05/1942, New York, NY **DISCIPLINE** ENGLISH **EDUCATION** Univ Chicago, AB, 63; Univ Va, MA, 64, PhD(English), 67. **CAREER** Woodrow Wilson Intern English, Bennett Col, Greensboro, NC, 66-67; vis assoc prof English, Univ Md, Baltimore, 74-75; asst prof, 64-76, ASSOC PROF ENGLISH, BRANDEIS UNIV, 76- **MEMBERSHIPS** MLA; Am Soc Eighteenth Century Studies; English Inst; AAUP; fel Am Coun Learned Soc. **RESEARCH** Restoration and 18th century British literature; legal history; social history. **SELECTED PUBLICATIONS** Auth, The Mansfield Manuscripts And The Growth Of English Law In The 18th-Century, Eighteenth-Century Studies, Vol 28, 94; Recent Studies In The Restoration And 18th-Century, Studies In English Lit 1500-1900, Vol 33, 93; Plots And Counterplots, Sexual Politics And The Body-Politic In English Literature, 1660-1730, Modern Lang Quart, Vol 56, 95. **CONTACT ADDRESS** Dept of English, Brandeis Univ, 415 South St, Waltham, MA, 02154-2700.

STECKLINE, C. TURNER
PERSONAL Born 12/28/1954, Sanborn, NY **DISCIPLINE** SPEECH COMMUNICATION, DRAMTIC ARTS, PERFORMANCE STUDIES **EDUCATION** Univ of Northern Colo, BA, 75; Univ of Iowa, MA, 78; Southern Ill Univ at Carbondale, PhD, 97. **CAREER** Chair, dept of speech commun, Univ of Dubuque, 79-82; asst prof of speech commun, Loras Col, 82-87; instr/asst dir of forensics, Iowa State Univ, 88-89; dir of forensics, 89-91, asst prof, 91-95, Univ of Wis-Platteville; ASST PROF OF SPEECH COMMUN AND THEATRE ARTS, NORTHEAST LA UNIV, 97-. **HONORS AND AWARDS** Marion Kleinau Theatre Award, Southern Ill Univ, 95; Kleinau Theatre Production Assistantship, 95 & 96; Graduate Teaching Assistantship, Southern Ill Unive, 92-95, 97; initiating honors sequence: Vision, Language & Reality, Univ of Wis-Platteville, 91-92; adjunct fac appointment, 80-82, teaching Excellence, Loras Col, 86; grad teaching asst, The Rhetoric Prog, Univ of Iowa, 76-79. **MEMBERSHIPS** Nat Commun Asn; Southern States Commun Asn; La Commun Asn; Nat Coun for Teachers of English; Nat Women's Studies Asn; Nat Storytelling Asn. **RESEARCH** Whistleblowing/ethical resistances; diffusion; response theory & bearing witness; disability and family communication; performance of ethnography/ethnography of performance. **SELECTED PUBLICATIONS** Auth, Ideas and Images of Performed Witnessing: A Cross-Genre Analysis, Southern Ill Univ at Carbondale, 97; auth, Books in Review: Ecological Feminism, Ecological Literary Criticism: Romantic Imagining and the Biology of the Mind, Text and Performance Quarterly, 96. **CONTACT ADDRESS** Dept of Speech Commun & Theatre, Northeast Louisiana Univ, Monroe, LA, 71203. **EMAIL** coyote@hc3.com

STEEN, SARA JAYNE
PERSONAL Born 12/09/1949, Toledo, OH, 3 children **DISCIPLINE** ENGLISH RENAISSANCE STUDIES **EDUCATION** Bowling Green State Univ, BS, 70, PhD(English), 78; Ohio State Univ, MA, 74. **CAREER** Prof English, Mont State Univ, 78-. **MEMBERSHIPS** MLA; Renaissance Soc Am. **RESEARCH** Shakespeare; women writers. **SELECTED PUBLICATIONS** Auth, The Letters of Lady Arbella Stuart. Women Writers in English 1350-1850; Oxford Univ Press, 94; Ambrosia in an Earthern Vessel: Three Centuries of Audience and Reader Response to the Works of Thomas Middleton, AMS Press, 93; contribur, Thomas Middleton: A Reference Guide, G K Hall, 84; coauth, Intersections: The Elements of Fiction in Science Fiction, The Popular Press, 78; guest co-ed, Shakespear Quarterly, 47, 4, 96. **CONTACT ADDRESS** Dept of English, Montana State Univ, Bozeman, MT, 59717-2300. **EMAIL** steen@english.montana.edu

STEENSMA, ROBERT CHARLES
PERSONAL Born 11/24/1930, Sioux Falls, SD **DISCIPLINE** ENGLISH LANGUAGE & LITERATURE **EDUCATION** Augustana Col, SDak, BA, 52; Univ SDak, MA, 55; Univ Ky, PhD, 61. **CAREER** Instr English, Augustana Col, SDak, 55-57; asst prof, Univ SDak, 59-62 & Utah State Univ, 62-66; assoc prof & asst chmn, 66-70, dir advan placement, 68-76, PROF ENGLISH, UNIV UTAH, 70-, Res grant, Utah State Univ, 63-64; Fulbright lectr, Finland, 72-73; David Gardner fac res fel, Univ Utah, 79. **MEMBERSHIPS** Naval Hist Found; Us Naval Inst; Oceanic Soc; Am Soc 18th Century Studies; Western Soc 18th Century Studies. **RESEARCH** Jonathan Swift; 18th century English literature; Graham Greene & Jane Austen. **SELECTED PUBLICATIONS** Auth, Our comings and goings: Herbert Krause's Wind Without Rain, In: Where the West Begins, Augustana Col, 78; Dr John Arbuthnot, Twayne, 79; Yanktonai Sioux Watercolors--Cultural Remembrances Of John Saul--Brokenleg, Western Amn Literature, Vol 29, 95; The Nature Of The Place--A Study Of Great-Plains Fiction, Western Am Lit, Vol 31, 97; Drop Him Till He Dies, The Twisted Tragedy Of Immigrant Homesteader Thomas Egan, Western Am Lit, Vol 30, 95. **CONTACT ADDRESS** Dept of English, Univ of Utah, Orson Spencer Hall, Salt Lake City, UT, 84112-8916.

STEER, HELEN V.
PERSONAL Born 05/20/1926, Manchester, England **DISCIPLINE** SPEECH/THEATRE **EDUCATION** LSU, BA, 54, MA, 58, PhD, 67. **CAREER** Theatre dir & spch asst, Howard Col, 56-59; Teaching asst, LSU, 60-63; Assoc prof, East Carolina Univ, 63-88; Dialect coach, The Lost Colony, 88. **HONORS AND AWARDS** Pres, NC Speech & Drama Assoc, 71. **MEMBERSHIPS** Nat Commun Assoc; Southern Speech Commun Assoc; Phi Kappa Phi. **RESEARCH** Dialects, especially stage use. **SELECTED PUBLICATIONS** Ed, co-auth, Your Speech, 3rd ed, 96. **CONTACT ADDRESS** 2306 E 3rd St, Greenville, NC, 27858.

STEIG, MICHAEL
PERSONAL Born 02/19/1936, New York, NY, m, 1956, 2 children **DISCIPLINE** ENGLISH LITERATURE **EDUCATION** Reed Col, BA, 58; Univ Wash, MA, 60, PhD(English), 63. **CAREER** Actg instr English, Univ Wash, 62-63; asst prof, Mich State Univ, 63-66; from asst prof to assoc prof, 66-71, PROF ENGLISH, SIMON FRASER UNIV, 71-, Can Coun leave fel, 68-69 & 77-78; Am Coun Learned Soc fel, 71-72. **MEMBERSHIPS** MLA; Asn Can Univ Teachers English; Children's Lit Asn; Dickens Soc. **RESEARCH** The English novel; 19th century English literature; literature and psychology. **SELECTED PUBLICATIONS** Auth, Dickens' Excremental Vision, Victorian Studies, 70; Anality in The Mill on the Floss, Novel, 71; George Cruikshank and the grotesque, Princeton Univ Libr Chronicle, 73; The intentional phallus, J Aesthet & Art Criticism, 77; Dickens and Phiz, Ind Univ, 78; At the Back of the Wind in the Willows, Victorian Studies, 81; George Cruikshank: Life, Times, And Art, Vol 1, 1792-1835, Dickens Quart, Vol 11, 94; George Cruikshank--A Revaluation, Dickens Quart, Vol 11, 94; Abuse And The Comic-Grotesque In The Old Curiosity Shop--Problems Of Response/, Dickens Quart, Vol 11, 94. **CONTACT ADDRESS** Dept of English, Simon Fraser Univ, Burnaby, BC, V5A 1S6.

STEIN, ARNOLD
PERSONAL Born 04/27/1915, Brockton, MA, m, 1942, 2 children **DISCIPLINE** ENGLISH LITERATURE **EDUCATION** Yale Univ, AB, 36; Harvard Univ, AM, 38, PhD, 42. **CAREER** Instr, Univ Minn, 40-46; asst prof, Ohio State Univ, 46-48; from assoc prof to prof English lit, Univ Wash, 48-71; prof English, Johns Hopkins Univ, 71-74, Sir William Osler prof, 74-80; PROF ENGLISH, UNIV ILL, URBANA, 80-, Ford Found Advan Educ fel, 53-54; Guggenheim fel, 59-60; sr ed, J English Lit Hist, 74-80. **MEMBERSHIPS** Renaissance Soc Am; MLA; Milton Soc Am; Acad Lit Studies. **RESEARCH** Criticism; 17th century and contemporary literature. **SELECTED PUBLICATIONS** Auth, Answerable Style 53, Heroic Knowledge, 57 & John Donne's Lyrics: The Eloquence of Action, 62, Univ Minn; ed, Theodore Roethke: Essays on the Poetry, Univ Wash, 65; auth, George Herbert's Lyrics, Johns Hopkins Univ, 68; ed, On Milton's Poetry, Fawcett, 69; auth, The Art of Presence, Univ Calif, 77; Imagining Death, The Ways Of Milton, Milton Studies, Vol 29, 92. **CONTACT ADDRESS** Dept of English, Univ Ill, Urbana, IL, 61801.

STEIN, ROBERT DAVID
PERSONAL Born 10/09/1937, Chicago, IL, m, 1960, 3 children **DISCIPLINE** ENGLISH **EDUCATION** Brown Univ, AB, 59; Northwestern Univ, MA, 61, PhD(English), 68. **CAREER** Lectr, Northwestern Univ, 64-65; from instr to asst prof, Univ Chicago, 65-73; prof English & chmn dept, Washburn Univ, Topeka, 73-; dean, Univ Honors Prog, 82-. **MEMBERSHIPS** MLA; Am Bus Commun Asn. **RESEARCH** Literature, science and religion in the 19th century; critical theory; the arts of Victorian prose. **CONTACT ADDRESS** Dept of English, Washburn Univ, 1700 SW College Ave, Topeka, KS, 66621-0001. **EMAIL** zzstei@washburn.edu

STEINBERG, ERWIN RAY
PERSONAL Born 11/15/1920, New Rochelle, NY, m, 1954, 2 children **DISCIPLINE** ENGLISH **EDUCATION** State Univ NY Albany, BS, 41, MS, 42; NY Univ, PhD, 56. **CAREER** From instr to assoc prof, 46-61, head dept gen studies, 56-60, dean, Margaret Morrison Carnegie Col, 60-73, dean div humanities & soc sci, 65-68, dean, Col Humanities & Soc Sci, 68-75; Prof English, 61-75, Prof, 75-80, Thomas S. Baker Prof English & Interdisciplinary Studies, 81-92, Prof English & Rhetoric, Carnegie-Mellon Univ, 93-, Vice-Provost for Educ, 91-96; Commun consult; coordr, Prof English, US Off Educ, 63-64; vis scholar, Ctr Advan Studies Behav Sci, 70-71; mem comn scholars, Bd Higher Educ, State Ill, 74-. **HONORS AND AWARDS** Carnegie Teaching Award, 56; Distinguished Alumnus, State Univ NY-Albany, 69; Alumnus of the Year, State Univ of NY Col-Plattsburgh, 71; Phi Beta Kappa; Phi Kappa Phi; Phi Delta Kappa; Kappa Delta Pi; Robert Doherty Prize for substantial and sustained contributions to excellence in education, 90. **MEMBERSHIPS** NCTE; MLA. **RESEARCH** The modern novel; myth in modern literature; communication in business and industry. **SELECTED PUBLICATIONS** Coauth, Communication in Business and Industry, Holt, 60; auth, Needed Research in the Teaching of English, US Govt Printing Off, 63; gen ed, Insight Series (14 vols), 68-73 & co-ed, English Education Today, 70, Noble; English Then and Now, Random, 70; auth, The Stream of Consciousness and Beyond in Joyce's Ulysses, Univ Pittsburgh, 73; ed, The Stream-of-Consciousness Technique in the Modern Novel, Kennikat, 79; co-ed, Approaches to Teaching Joyce's Ulysses, Mod Lang Asn, 92. **CONTACT ADDRESS** Col of Humanities & Soc Sci, Carnegie Mellon Univ, 5000 Forbes Ave, Pittsburgh, PA, 15213-3890. **EMAIL** es2t@andrew.cmu.edu

STEINBERG, THEODORE LOUIS
PERSONAL Born 01/08/1947, Baltimore, MD, m, 3 children **DISCIPLINE** MEDIEVAL ENGLISH; JEWISH LITERATURE **EDUCATION** Johns Hopkins Univ, BA, 68; Univ Ill, AM, 69, PhD(English), 71. **CAREER** Asst prof, 71-75, assoc prof, 75-79, prof English, State Univ NY Col Fredonia, 79-

HONORS AND AWARDS Chancellor's Award for Excellence in Teaching, 96; **MEMBERSHIPS** Medieval Acad Am; Am Asn Prof Yiddish; Spenser Soc. **RESEARCH** Medieval and Renaissance literature; Jewish literature. **SELECTED PUBLICATIONS** Auth, Spenser's Shepherdes Calender and EK's, Mod Lang Studies, winter 73; The schoolmaster: Teaching sixteenth century literature, English Rec, 73; I B Singer: Responses to catastrophe, Yiddish, 75; The anatomy of Euphues, Studies English Lit, 77; Mendele Mocher Seforim, G K Hall, 77; The humanities and the Holocaust, Humanist Educators, 80; Poetry and the perpendicular style, J Aesthet & Art Criticism, 81; Piers Plowman and Prophecy, Garland, 91. **CONTACT ADDRESS** Dept of English, SUNY, Fredonia, Fredonia, NY, 14063-1143. **EMAIL** steinberg@fredonia.edu

STEINBRINK, JEFFREY
PERSONAL Born 08/29/1945, Erie, PA **DISCIPLINE** ENGLISH **EDUCATION** Allegheny Col, BA, 67; Univ NC, Chapel Hill, MA, 68, PhD(English), 74. **CAREER** Instr English, Behrend Campus, Pa State Univ, 68-71; instr, Univ NC, Chapel Hill, 74-75; vis asst prof, 75-77, asst prof, 77-80, assoc prof, 80-91, prof English, 91- , chemn, 89-92, Franklin & Marshall Col. **HONORS AND AWARDS** NEH summer stipend, 76, 83; fel, Penn-Lilly Prog, 79; USIS AmPart lectr, Republic of Philippines, 85; NEH fel, 85-86; Natl Adv Bc, Elmira Col Ctr for mark Twain Stud, 86- . **MEMBERSHIPS** AAUP; MLA; Northeast Mod Lang Asn; Popular Cult Asn. **RESEARCH** Relationship between history and American literature; the American novel; Mark Twain. **SELECTED PUBLICATIONS** Auth, Why the Innocents Went Abroad: Mark Twain and American Tourism in the Late Nineteenth Century, Am Lit Realism, 83; auth, mark Twain and Hunter Thompson: Continuity and Change in American Outlaw Journalism, Stud in Am Humor, 83-84; auth, Who Wrote Huckleberry Finn: mark Twain's Control of the Early Manuscript, in Sattelmeyer, ed, One Hundred Years of Huckleberry Finn: The Boy, His Book, and American Culture, Missouri, 84; auth, Getting To Be Mark Twain,Univ Calif, 91. **CONTACT ADDRESS** Dept of English, Franklin and Marshall Col, PO Box 3003, Lancaster, PA, 17604-3003. **EMAIL** j_steinbrink@acad.fandm.edu

STEINER, JOAN ELIZABETH
PERSONAL Born 02/16/1933, Oberlin, OH **DISCIPLINE** ENGLISH & AMERICAN LITERATURE **EDUCATION** Oberlin Col, AB, 55; Univ Mich, Ann Arbor, MA, 56, PhD, 71. **CAREER** Teacher English, Grosse Pointe Pub Schs, Mich, 56-59; staff mem, Second Cong Dist Off, US House Rep, 65-67; from instr to asst prof, 68-76, assoc prof, 76-83, PROF ENGLISH, DREW UNIV, 83-98, PROF EMER, 98-, chmn, English dept, 86-90. **HONORS AND AWARDS** Phi Beta Kappa, Phi Kappa Phi. **MEMBERSHIPS** MLA; AAUP. **RESEARCH** Twentieth century British and American fiction; history of the novel; Afro-American literature. **SELECTED PUBLICATIONS** Auth, Conrad's The Secret Sharer; Complexities of the doubling relationship, Conradiana, Vol 12, 80; Modern pharisees and false apostles: Ironic New Testament parallels in Conrad's Heart of Darkness, 19th Century Fiction, Vol 37, 82. **CONTACT ADDRESS** Dept of English, Drew Univ, 36 Madison Ave, Madison, NJ, 07940-1493. **EMAIL** jsteiner@drew.edu

STEINER, THOMAS ROBERT
PERSONAL Born 08/18/1934, Budapest, Hungary, m, 1966, 2 children **DISCIPLINE** ENGLISH, COMPARATIVE LITERATURE **EDUCATION** Cornell Univ, BA, 55; Columbia Univ, MA, 60 PhD(English), 67. **CAREER** Lectr, Hunter Col, 61-64 & Brooklyn Col, 64-66; asst prof, 66-74, ASSOC PROF ENGLISH, UNIV CALIF, SANTA BARBARA, 74-, Fel, Calif Humanities Inst, 69-70; consult-reader, PMLA, 71; consult, Harcourt Brace Jovanovich, Inc, 72; vis assoc prof English, Univ Ill, Urbana-Champaign, 74-75; reader, J English & Ger Philol, 74; consult, Calif Coun for Humanities Pub Policy, 77-79. **HONORS AND AWARDS** Nathanael West Essay Contest Prize, Southern Rev, 70. **RESEARCH** Eighteenth century English literature; literary theory; detective fiction. **SELECTED PUBLICATIONS** Auth, Precursors to Dryden, Comp Lit Studies, 3/70; West's Lemuel and the American dream, Southern Rev, 10/71; English Translation Theory, 1650-1800, Van Gorcum, 75; The heroic ape: Teaching pope, Eighteenth Century Life, spring 79; The Origin Of Raymond Chandler: Mean-Streets, Anq-A Quart J Of Short Articles Notes And Reviews, Vol 7, 94. **CONTACT ADDRESS** Dept of English, Univ of Calif, Santa Barbara, CA, 93106.

STEINER, WENDY LOIS
PERSONAL Born 03/20/1949, Winnipeg, MB, Canada, 2 children **DISCIPLINE** ENGLISH LITERATURE **EDUCATION** McGill Univ, BA, 70; Yale Univ, MPhil, 72, PhD(English), 74. **CAREER** Asst prof English, Yale Univ, 74-76; asst prof, Univ Mich, Ann Arbor, 76-79; from Asst Prof to Prof, 79-93, Richard L. Fisher Prof English, Univ Pa, 93-. **HONORS AND AWARDS** Nat Endowment for Humanities summer grant, 80; Guggenheim fel, 82-83. **MEMBERSHIPS** MLA; Semiotic Soc Am. **RESEARCH** Modern literature; modern critical theory; relation of painting to literature. **SELECTED PUBLICATIONS** Auth, The relational axes of poetic language, In: On Poetic Language, Peter de Ridder Press, 76; Language as process: Sergej Karcevskij's semiotics of language, Sound, Sign & Meaning, 76; Exact Resemblance to Exact Resemblance: The Literary Portraiture of Gertrude Stein, Yale Univ, 78; American semiotics since 1945, In: Le Champ Semiotique, Le Creuset, 78; Structures and phenomena, PTL, 3/78; The case for unclear thinking: The new critics versus Charles Morris, Critical Inquiry, 6/79; Res Poetica: The problematics of the concrete program, New Lit Hist, 12/81; The Colors of Rhetoric: Problems in the Relation between Modern Painting and Literature, Chicago Univ, 82; Pictures of Romance, Chicago Univ, 88; The Scandal of Pleasure, Chicago Univ, 95. **CONTACT ADDRESS** Dept of English, Univ of Pennsylvania, 3340 Walnut St, Philadelphia, PA, 19104-6203. **EMAIL** wsteiner@english.upenn.edu

STEINMAN, LISA M.
PERSONAL Born 04/08/1950, Willimantic, CT, m, 1984 **DISCIPLINE** ENGLISH **EDUCATION** Cornell Univ, BA,71, MFA, 73, PhD, 76 **CAREER** Teaching asst, Cornell Univ, 70-76; asst prof to assoc prof to prof to Kenan Prof, Reed Col, 76- , dir NEH Summer Seminar for School Teachers, 86, 88, 90, 92, 99. **HONORS AND AWARDS** Burlington Northern Award, 87; Pablo Neruda Award, 87; elect to PEN, 89; Vollum Award, 90; Oregon Book Award, 93; Nat Endow for Humanities Fel, 96. **MEMBERSHIPS** AWP; ASA; MLA; ALA. **RESEARCH** Poetry **SELECTED PUBLICATIONS** Auth, Made In America: Science, Technology, and American Modernist Poets, Yale Univ Press, 87, 89; All that Comes to Light, Arrowood Books Inc, 89; A Book of Other Days, Arrowood Books Inc, 93; Ordinary Songs 26 books, 96; Masters of Repetition: Poetry, Culture, and Work, St. Martin's Press, 98. **CONTACT ADDRESS** Dept of English, Reed Col, 3203 SE Woodstock Blvd, Portland, OR, 97202. **EMAIL** lisa.steinman@reed.edu

STELZIG, EUGENE LOUIS
PERSONAL Born 08/18/1943, Bischofshofen, Austria, m, 1968 **DISCIPLINE** ENGLISH & AMERICAN LITERATURE **EDUCATION** Univ Pa, BA, 66; Cambridge Univ, BA, 68, MA, 72; Harvard Univ, MA, 69, PhD(English), 72. **CAREER** Asst prof, 72-79, assoc prof English, State Univ NY Col Genesco, 78-79, Nat Endowment for Humanities fel, 78-79; prof, 84-90; SUNY disting teaching prof, 96-. **HONORS AND AWARDS** NEH Fel, 85-86; SUNY Chancellor's Award for Excellence in Teaching, 85. **MEMBERSHIPS** MLA **RESEARCH** British and American and European romanticism; autobiography and confession. **SELECTED PUBLICATIONS** Auth, All Shades of Consciousness: Wordsworth's Poetry and the Self in Time, Mouton, 75; Herman Hesse's Fictions of the Self: Autobiography and the Confessional Imagination, Princeton UP, 1988. **CONTACT ADDRESS** Dept of English, SUNY, Geneseo, 1 College Cir, Geneseo, NY, 14454-1401. **EMAIL** stelzig@uno.cc.geneseo.edu

STEN, CHRISTOPHER WESSEL
PERSONAL Born 01/03/1944, Minneapolis, MN, m, 1969, 2 children **DISCIPLINE** AMERICAN LITERATURE **EDUCATION** Carleton col, BA, 66; Ind Univ, Bloomington, MA, 68, PhD(Am lit), 71. **CAREER** Asst prof, 70-78, assoc prof, 78-88, PROF AM LIT, GEORGE WASHINGTON UNIV, 88-, CHAIR 87-91, 94-98; Regional assoc, Am Lit Manuscripts, 72-74; Fulbrightr sr lectr Am lit, Institut fur Englische Philologie, Universitat Wurzburg, 75-76. **MEMBERSHIPS** MLA; Melville Soc, sec 97-. **RESEARCH** Herman Melville; 19th century American literature; American novel. **SELECTED PUBLICATIONS** Auth, Sounding the Whale: Moby-Dick as Epic Novel, Kent, OH: Kent State Univ Press, 66; Bartleby the Transcendentalist: Melville's Dead Letter to Emerson, Mod Lang Quart, 3/74; The Dialogue of Crisis in The Confidence-Man: Melville's New Novel, Studies Novel, 9/74; Vere's Use of the Forms: Means and Ends in Billy Budd, Am Lit, 3/75; Melville's Gentleman Forger: The Struggle for Identity in Redburn, Tex Studies Lit & Lang, fall 79; When the Candle Went Out: The Nighttime World of Huck Finn, Studies Am Fiction, spring 81; ed, Savage Eye: Melville and the Visual Arts, Kent, OH: Kent State Univ Press, 92; auth, The Weaver-God, He Weaves: Melville and the Poetics of the Novel, Kent, OH: Kent State Univ Press, 96. **CONTACT ADDRESS** Dept of English, George Washington Univ, 801 22nd St NW, Washington, DC, 20052-0001. **EMAIL** cstern@gwu.edu

STEPHENS, CHARLES RALPH
PERSONAL Born 01/14/1943, Nashville, TN, m, 1986, 3 children **DISCIPLINE** ENGLISH; AMERICAN LETERATURE **EDUCATION** Univ Md, PhD, 85. **CAREER** PROF ENGLISH & CHR HUMANITIES & ARTS, ESSEX COMMUN COL. **MEMBERSHIPS** Col Eng Assoc; Soc Study S Lit; MLA; SMLA **RESEARCH** South American literature. **SELECTED PUBLICATIONS** auth The Craft of Peter Taylor, Univ Alabama Press; The Fiction of Anne Tyler, The Correspondence of Flannery O'Connor and the Brainard Chaneys, Univ Press Miss. **CONTACT ADDRESS** Humanities & Arts, Essex Comm Col, Baltimore, MD, 21237. **EMAIL** crstephens@aol.com

STEPHENS, MARTHA THOMAS
PERSONAL GA, m, 3 children **DISCIPLINE** ENGLISH **EDUCATION** Indiana Univ, PhD. **CAREER** Univ Cincinnati, prof english. **RESEARCH** Literature of the South; Lit and Society; Lit and Medicine. **SELECTED PUBLICATIONS** Auth, Children of the World, SMU Press, 99; Cast a Wistful Eye, Macmillan, 77, condensed in Redbook; The Question of Flannery, O'Connor, LSU Press, 73. **CONTACT ADDRESS** Dept of English, Univ of Cincinnati, 4514 Bristol Lane, Cincinnati, OH, 45229. **EMAIL** stephem@email.uc.edu

STEPHENS, ROBERT OREN
PERSONAL Born 10/02/1928, Corpus Christi, TX, m, 1956, 3 children **DISCIPLINE** ENGLISH **EDUCATION** TX Col Arts & Indust, BA, 49; Univ TX, MA, 51, PhD(Eng), 58. **CAREER** Tchr high sch, Shiner, TX, 49-50; spec instr, Univ TX, 57-58, instr, 58-61; from asst prof to assoc prof, 61-66, dir grad studies Eng, 67-81, Prof Eng, Univ NC, Greensboro, 68-94, Head Dept Eng, 81-88; Duke Univ-Univ NC coop prog in hum fel, 65-66; Danforth assoc, 67. **MEMBERSHIPS** MLA; Am Studies Asn; S Atlantic Mod Lang Asn; NCTE. **RESEARCH** Contemp Am lit; Southern Am lit; Am Renaissance. **SELECTED PUBLICATIONS** Auth, Hemingway's Nonfiction: The Public Voice, Univ NC, 68; Language magic and reality in For Whom the Bell Tolls, Criticism, 72; Hemingway and Stendhal: The Matrix of A Farewell to Arms, PMLA, 73; Ernest Hemingway: The Critical Reception, Burt Franklin, 77; Cable's The Grandissimes and the Comedy of Manners, Am Lit, 80; The Family Saga in the South, La State Univ, 95. **CONTACT ADDRESS** 1706 Sylvan Rd, Greensboro, NC, 27403. **EMAIL** vjstep@aol.com

STEPTO, ROBERT BURNS
PERSONAL Born 10/28/1945, Chicago, Illinois, m, 1967 **DISCIPLINE** ENGLISH **EDUCATION** Trinity College, Hartford CT, BA (cum laude), English, 1966; Stanford University, Stanford, CA, MA, 1968, PhD, 1974. **CAREER** Williams College, Williamstown, MA, assistant professor, 1971-74; Yale University, New Haven, CT, assistant professor, 1974-79, associate professor, 1979-84, professor, 1984-. **HONORS AND AWARDS** Woodrow Wilson Fellowship, Woodrow Wilson Foundation, 1966-67; Morse Fellowship, Yale University, 1977-78. **MEMBERSHIPS** Chair, MLA Commn on the Literatures & Languages of America, 1977-78; Connecticut Humanities Council, 1980-82; trustee, Trinity College, 1982-92; associate editor, Callaloo, 1984-88; advisor, Yale-New Haven Teachers Institute, 1985-, Anson Phelps Stokes Institute, 1985-; board of editors, American Literature, 1987-88; advisor, Southern Connecticut Library Council, 1987; advisory editor, Callaloo, 1988-. **SELECTED PUBLICATIONS** From Behind the Veil: A Study of Afro-Amer Narrative, 1979; Edited with M Harper, Chant of Saints: Afro-Amer Literature, Art, Scholarship, 1979; Edited with D Fisher, D Fisher, Afro-Amer Literature: The Reconstruction of Instinction, 1979; Senior Fellowship, National Endowment for the Humanities, 1981-82; Alumni Medal, Trinity College, 1986; Editor, The Selected Poems of Jay Wright, 1987; Contributor to the Columbia Literary History of the United States, 1987; Robert Frost Professor, Brad Loaf School of English, 1995; Co-Editor of The Harpet American Literature since 1992. **CONTACT ADDRESS** Professor, English American Studies, African-American Studies, Yale Univ, PO Box 203388, New Haven, CT, 06520-3388.

STERN, JULIA
DISCIPLINE ENGLISH **EDUCATION** Columbia Univ, PhD. **CAREER** Prof, Northwestern Univ. **RESEARCH** Life on the Food Chain: Appetite and Identity in American Women's Narratives, 1850-1880. **SELECTED PUBLICATIONS** Auth, The Plight of Feeling: Sympathy and Dissent in the Early American Novel, 97. **CONTACT ADDRESS** Dept of English, Northwestern Univ, 1801 Hinman, Evanston, IL, 60208.

STERN, MILTON R.
PERSONAL Born 08/22/1928, Boston, MA, m, 1949, 2 children **DISCIPLINE** ENGLISH **EDUCATION** Northeastern Univ, AB, 49; Univ Conn, MA, 51; Mich State Univ, PhD(English), 55. **CAREER** Instr, Univ Conn, 49-51; from instr to asst prof, Univ Ill, 54-58; from asst prof to assoc prof, 58-63, PROF ENGLISH, UNIV CONN, 63-, Am Coun Learned Soc grant, 62; vis prof, Coe Inst Am Studies, Univ Wyo, 64; Fulbright prof Am lit, Univ Warsaw, 64-65; Guggenheim fel, 71-72; Nat Humanities Inst fel, Yale Univ, 77-78. **MEMBERSHIPS** MLA; Melville Soc. **RESEARCH** American literature; the politics of American literature; Hawthorne. **SELECTED PUBLICATIONS** Auth, Discussions of Moby Dick, Heath, 60; coauth, The Viking Portable American Literature Survey (4 vols), Viking, 62, 68 & 75; auth, Herman Melville, In: Patterns of Commitment in American Literature, Univ Toronto, 67; Millennium, Moby Dick and politics, Emerson Soc Quart, fall 68; The Golden Moment: Novels of F S Fitzgerald, Univ Ill, 70; ed, Billy Budd, Bobbs-Merrill, 74; auth, American Values and Romantic Fiction in American Fiction, Northeastern Univ & Twayne, 77; ed, House of the Seven Gables, Penguin, 81; F. Scott Fitzgerald--A Biography, Am Lit, Vol 67, 95. **CONTACT ADDRESS** Dept of English, Univ of Conn, Storrs, CT, 06268.

STERN, RICHARD G.
PERSONAL Born 02/25/1928, New York, NY, m, 1985, 4 children **DISCIPLINE** ENGLISH **EDUCATION** Univ NC, BA, 47; Harvard Univ, MA, 49; State Univ Iowa, PhD, 54. **CAREER** Fulbright asst, Jules Ferry Col, Versailles, France, 49-50; asst, Univ Heidelberg, 50-51; part-time instr English, Coe Col, 52-53; instr, State Univ Iowa, 53-54; instr, Conn Col, 54-55; from instr to assoc prof, 55-65, prof Eng, Univ Chigao, 65-; vis lectr, Univ Venice, 62-63; vis prof, State Univ NY Buffalo, 67; prof, Harvard, 69; prof, Nice, 71; prof, Urbine, 73; Guggenheim fel, 73-74; prof, Helen A Regenstein prof, 90. **HONORS AND AWARDS** Longwood Award, 61; Friends of Lit Award, 63; Rockefeller Award, 65; Nat Found Arts & Sci Award, 67-68; Nat Instr Arts & Lett Award, 68; Sandbury Award, 78; Medal of Merit for the Novel, American Academy of Arts & Sciences, 85; Heartland Award, Best Work of Non-Fiction, 85; Sun-Times Award, Best Fiction, 90. **MEMBERSHIPS** Am Acad of Arts & Sci; Quadrangle Club. **RESEARCH** Prose fiction. **SELECTED PUBLICATIONS** Auth, Noble Rot, Stories 1949-88, Grove, 90; auth, Shares and Other Fictions, Delphinium, 92; auth, One Person and Another, On Writers and Writing, Baskerville, 93; auth, A Sistermony, Donald I. Fine, 95. **CONTACT ADDRESS** 5845 Ellis Ave, Chicago, IL, 60637-1476. **EMAIL** rstern@midway.uchicago.edu

STERNBERG, JOEL
DISCIPLINE MASS COMMUNICATIONS **EDUCATION** Northwestern Univ, PhD. **CAREER** St Xavier Univ **SELECTED PUBLICATIONS** Chapters and biog essays, Dictionary Litery Biography, Encyclopedia Television, Encyclopedia Historic Chicago Women; Articles: Res Strategies, Nine, Chicago Hist, Screen, Chicago Film & Video; Sound & Commun. **CONTACT ADDRESS** Saint Xavier Univ, 3700 W 103rd Street, Chicago, IL, 60655.

STETZ, MARGARET
DISCIPLINE ENGLISH LITERATURE **EDUCATION** Queens Col, BA; Sussex Univ, MA; Harvard Univ, PhD. **CAREER** Eng Dept, Georgetown Univ **RESEARCH** Women's studies; comedy; Victorian fiction; modernism; women's war literature. **SELECTED PUBLICATIONS** Auth, England in the 1890s: Literary Publishing at the Bodley Head, 90; England in the 1880s: Old Guard and Avant-Garde, 89; pubs on Victorian history, poetry of E. Nesbit, and female authorship in the 1890s. **CONTACT ADDRESS** English Dept, Georgetown Univ, 37th and O St, Washington, DC, 20057.

STEVEN, LAURENCE
DISCIPLINE ENGLISH LITERATURE **EDUCATION** McMaster Univ, PhD. **RESEARCH** Mod lit in English; rhetoric composition. **SELECTED PUBLICATIONS** Auth, The Grain of Sand in the Oyster: Competency Testing as a Catalyst for Attitude Change at the University, 91; art, From Thimble to Ladybird: D. H. Lawrence's Widening Vision?, D. H. Lawrence Rev, 86; auth, Dissociation and Wholeness in Patrick White's Fiction, 89; co-auth, From Reading to Writing, 89; co-ed, Contextual Literacy: Writing Across the Curriculum, 94. **CONTACT ADDRESS** English Dept, Laurentian Univ, 935 Ramsey Lake Rd, Sudbury, ON, P3E 2C6.

STEVENS, EARL EUGENE
PERSONAL Born 04/06/1925, Chicago, IL, m, 1952 **DISCIPLINE** ENGLISH **EDUCATION** Ind Univ, AB, 49; Univ Mich, MA, 51; Univ NC, PhD, 63. **CAREER** Instr, Univ NC, 52-55 & 57-58; assoc prof English, WTex State Col, 56-57; asst prof, Pfeiffer Col, 58-63, chmn, Div Fine Arts, 61-62; assoc prof English, Trinity Univ, 63-64; from assoc prof to prof, Wis State Univ, Stevens Point, 64-68; PROF ENGLISH, RI COL, 68- **MEMBERSHIPS** MLA **RESEARCH** Victorian literature; the novel; criticism. **SELECTED PUBLICATIONS** Auth, The Tyrian trader in Mathew Arnold's The Scholar Gypsy, Victorian Newslett, 63; contribr, Joseph Conrad: An Annotated Secondary Bibliography, Northern Ill Univ, 71; auth, John Galsworthy, In: British Winners of the Nobel Literary Prize, Univ Okla, 73; co-ed, Annotated Secondary Bibliography of the Writings of John Galsworthy, Northern Ill Univ, 78; Pound, Thayer, Watson And The Dial--A Story In Letters, English Lit In Transition 1880-1920, Vol 39, 96; Waking Giants--The Presence Of The Past In Modernism, English Lit In Transition 1880-1920, Vol 36, 93. **CONTACT ADDRESS** Dept of English, Rhode Island Col, Providence, RI, 02908.

STEVENS, GEORGE E.
DISCIPLINE LEGAL DIMENSIONS OF COMMUNICATION **EDUCATION** Univ Minn, PhD, 68. **CAREER** Prof, asst dept hd, Purdue Univ. **SELECTED PUBLICATIONS** Auth, Freedom of Speech in Private Employment: Overcoming the State Action Problem, Am Bus Law J, 82; Legal Protection for a Magazine Article Idea, Jour Quart, 84; Names, Newsworthiness, and the Right to Privacy, Commun and the Law, 91. **CONTACT ADDRESS** Dept of Commun, Purdue Univ, 1080 Schleman Hall, West Lafayette, IN, 47907-1080. **EMAIL** gstevens@sla.purdue.edu

STEVENS, MARK
PERSONAL 2 children **DISCIPLINE** COMMUNICATION STUDIES **EDUCATION** FL State Univ, PhD. **CAREER** Tchr lit, Southern Polytech State Univ. **SELECTED PUBLICATIONS** Auth, publ(s) on compos; Brit lit; music appreciation. **CONTACT ADDRESS** Hum and Tech Commun Dept, Southern Polytech State Univ, S Marietta Pkwy, PO Box 1100, Marietta, GA, 30060.

STEVENS, PAUL
DISCIPLINE ENGLISH LITERATURE **EDUCATION** Univ Toronto, PhD. **CAREER** Dept Eng, Queen's Univ **HONORS AND AWARDS** Milton Soc Am Hanford Awd., Pres, Can Asn Chairs English, 98-99. **RESEARCH** Milton and Renaissance literature; the rhetoric of early modern colonialism; literary theory and history. **SELECTED PUBLICATIONS** Auth, Imagination and the Presence of Shakespeare in "Paradise Lost", Univ Wis, 85. **CONTACT ADDRESS** English Dept, Queen's Univ, Kingston, ON, K7L 3N6.

STEVENS, PETER S.
PERSONAL Born 11/17/1927, Manchester, England **DISCIPLINE** LITERATURE **EDUCATION** Univ Nottingham, BA, Cert Educ, 51; McMaster Univ, MA, 63; Univ Sask, PhD, 68. **CAREER** Tchr, Eng schs, 51-57; tchr, Hillfield-Strathallan Col (Hamilton, Ont), 57-64, head Eng, 61-64; lectr, McMaster Univ, 61-64; lectr to asst prof, Univ Sask, 64-69; assoc prof, 69, prof, 76, PROF EMER, UNIV WINDSOR. **RESEARCH** Poetry **SELECTED PUBLICATIONS** Auth, Modern English-Canadian Poetry, 78; auth, Coming Back, 81; auth, Revenge of the Mistresses, 82; auth, Out of the Willow Trees, 86; auth, Swimming in the Afternoon: New & Selected Poems, 92; auth, Dorothy Livesay: Patterns in a Poetic Life, 92; auth, Rip Rap: Yorkshire Ripper Poems, 95; auth, Thinking into the Dark, 97; auth, Attending to this World, 98; ed, The McGill Movement, 69; poetry ed, Can Forum, 68-73; poetry ed, Lit Rev Can, 94-. **CONTACT ADDRESS** 2055 Richmond St, Windsor, ON, N8Y 1L3.

STEVENSON, CATHERINE BARNES
PERSONAL Born 05/23/1947, Chicago, IL, m, 1970 **DISCIPLINE** VICTORIAN LITERATURE, WOMEN'S STUDIES **EDUCATION** Manhattanville Col, BA, 68; NY Univ, MA, 69, PhD(English), 73. **CAREER** Asst prof, Bryant Col, 75-77; ASST PROF ENGLISH, UNIV HARTFORD, 78-, Ed, Victorian Studies Bull, 78- **MEMBERSHIPS** Northeast Victorian Studies Asn; MLA; Tennyson Soc. **RESEARCH** Victorian poetry; women's travel writing; 19th century novel. **SELECTED PUBLICATIONS** Auth, The aesthetic function of the weird seizures in Tennyson's The Princess, Victorian Newsletter, 74; Tennyson's mutability canto: Time, memory, and art in The Princess, Victorian Poetry, 75; Druids, Bards, and Tennyson's Merlin, Victorian Newsletter, 79; Tennyson's Dying Swan: Mythology and the definition of the poet's role, Studies in English Lit, 80; Swinburne and Tennyson's Tristram, Victorian Poetry, 81; How it struck a contemporary: Tennyson's Lancelot and Elaine and Pre-Raphaelite art, Victorian Newsletter, 81; The shade of Homer exorcises the ghost of De Quincey: Tennyson's The Lotos-Eaters, Browning Inst Studies, 82; Victorian Women Travellers to Africa, G K Hall, 82; *Pub What Must Not Be Said, North And South And The Problem Of Womens Work, Victorian Lit And Culture, Vol 19, 91. **CONTACT ADDRESS** 380 W Mountain Rd, West Simsbury, CT, 06092.

STEVENSON, JOHN A.
PERSONAL Born 11/06/1952, Clinton, SC, m **DISCIPLINE** ENGLISH AND HISTORY **EDUCATION** Duke Univ, BA, 75; Univ Va, PhD, 83. **CAREER** Asst prof, 82-90, assoc prof, 90-, chair, 96-, eng, Univ Colo. **HONORS AND AWARDS** Nat Merit Scholar; AB Duke Scholar; Phi Beta Kappa; Boulder Facul Teaching Award, 90. **MEMBERSHIPS** MLA. **RESEARCH** 18th century British literature. **SELECTED PUBLICATIONS** Auth, Tom Jones and the Stuck, ELH, 94; auth, The British Nonl, Defoe to Austen, 90; auth, A Vampire in the Mirror, PMLA, 88; auth, Clarissa and the Harlowes Once More, ELH, 81. **CONTACT ADDRESS** Dept. of English, Univ of Colorado, Box 226, Boulder, CO, 80309. **EMAIL** john.stevenson@colorado.edu

STEVENSON, JOHN WEAMER
PERSONAL Born 07/24/1918, Pittsburgh, PA, m, 1941, 1 child **DISCIPLINE** ENGLISH **EDUCATION** Wofford Col, AB, 48; Vanderbilt Univ, MA, 49, PhD(English), 54. **CAREER** From instr to assoc prof, Presby Col, SC, 50-57; prof & chmn dept, 58-62; assoc prof, Millsaps Col, 57-58; prof, 62-75, chmn dept, 62-80, CHARLES A DANA PROF ENGLISH, CONVERSE COL, 75-, HEAD DIV LANG & LIT, 71-, Coop Prog in Humanities fel, Duke Univ & Univ NC, 66-67; assoc ed, Humanities in South, 71-82; Lilly vis scholar, Duke Univ, 78-79. **MEMBERSHIPS** SAtlantic Mod Lang Asn; SAtlantic Asn Dept Eng (pres, 73-74). **RESEARCH** Nineteenth century; modern poetry. **SELECTED PUBLICATIONS** Auth, The pastoral setting in the poetry of A E Housman, SAtlantic Quart; Arcadia re-settled: Pastoral poetry and romantic theory, Studies English Lit, fall 67; The ceremony of Housman's style, Victorian Poetry, spring 72; Wordsworth's Modern Vision, Va Quart Rev, winter 77; Walker Percy: The novelist as poet, Southern Rev, winter 81; Poetry As Prescription For The Worlds Body, Va Quart Rev, Vol 69, 93. **CONTACT ADDRESS** Dept of English, Converse Col, Spartanburg, SC, 29301.

STEWART, CHARLES J.
DISCIPLINE COMMUNICATION **EDUCATION** Univ Ill, PhD, 63. **CAREER** Prof, dept hd, Purdue Univ. **SELECTED PUBLICATIONS** Auth, Explorations in Rhetorical Criticism, Pa State Univ, 73; Persuasion and Social Movements, Waveland, 94; Interviewing: Principles and Practices, Wm C Brown, 97. **CONTACT ADDRESS** Dept of Commun, Purdue Univ, 1080 Schleman Hall, West Lafayette, IN, 47907-1080. **EMAIL** cstewart@sla.purdue.edu

STEWART, E. KATE
DISCIPLINE ENGLISH **EDUCATION** Univ Miss, BA, MA, PhD. **CAREER** Univ Miss, 75-82; Worcester Polytechnic Inst, 84-87; Univ Ark, Assoc Prof, 88-. **HONORS AND AWARDS** Alpha Chi Tchr Year, 91; Sigma Tau Delta Service Award, 97. **SELECTED PUBLICATIONS** Auth, Arthur Sherburne Hardy: Man of American Letters, Scripta Humanistica, 86; auth, 'The Raven' and 'The Bracelets': Another Source for Poe's Poem, Edgar Allan Poe Soc, 90; auth, Essays on Russell Baker and Sarah Kemble Knight in Encyclopedia of American Humorists, Garland, 88; auth, Essays on Cincinnati Mirror and Baltimore Mounument in American Humor Magazines and Comic Newspapers, Greenwood, 86. **CONTACT ADDRESS** Univ Ark- Monticello, BOX 3458, Monticello, AR, 71656.

STEWART, HENRY R., JR.
PERSONAL Born 04/16/1949, Wilmington, DE, m, 1 child **DISCIPLINE** LIBRARY SCIENCE **EDUCATION** Cornell Col, BA, 66; Univ Denver, MA, 67; Ind Univ, PhD, 72. **CAREER** Ref Libr, 67-69, Cornell Col; assoc prof, 72-77, Univ Alabama; assoc dir, manage & pub svc, 77-84, Old Dominion Univ; dir, libr svcs, 84-96, Emporia St Univ; dean, libr svc, 96-, Troy St Univ. **RESEARCH** Library management; distance education. **CONTACT ADDRESS** 405 Wilson Dr., Troy, AL, 36079. **EMAIL** hstewart@trojan.troyst.edu

STEWART, JACK F
PERSONAL Born 04/13/1935, Aberdeen, Scotland, m, 1962, 2 children **DISCIPLINE** ENGLISH **EDUCATION** Univ Edinburgh, MA, 57, dipl educ, 58; Univ Southern Calif, PhD(-English), 67. **CAREER** Instr English commun, Univ Southern Calif, 63-67; asst prof, 67-71, ASSOC PROF ENGLISH, UNIV BC, 71-, Can Coun leave fel, 77-78. **MEMBERSHIPS** Philol Asn Pac Coast; MLA. **RESEARCH** Literature and modern art; techniques of modern fiction, especially Lawrence and Woolf; theories of fiction. **SELECTED PUBLICATIONS** Auth, Apotheosis and apocalypse in Faulkner's Wash, Studies Short Fiction, fall 69; Sterne's Absurd Comedy, Univ Windsor Rev, spring 70; Existence and symbol in The Waves, Mod Fiction Studies, fall 72; Historical impressionism in Orlando, Studies in Novel, spring 73; Light in To the Lighthouse, Twentieth Century Lit, 10/77; The Myth Of The Fall In Women In Love, Philological Quart, Vol 74, 95; D.H. Lawrence, Aesthetics And Ideology, Modern Philology, Vol 93, 96; Metaphor And Metonymy, Color And Space, In Lawrence Sea And Sardinia, Twentieth Cent Lit, Vol 41, 95. **CONTACT ADDRESS** Dept of English, Univ of BC, Vancouver, BC, V6T 1W5.

STEWART, JOHN OTHNEIL
PERSONAL Born 01/24/1933, m **DISCIPLINE** ENGLISH **EDUCATION** CA State Univ, Los Angeles, CA, BA, 1960; Stanford Univ, MA 1965; Univ of IA, MFA 1966; Univ of CA LA, PhD 1973. **CAREER** Univ of IA, English instr; CA State Univ, prof of Engl; Univ of IL, prof of anthrop/writer; OH State Univ, prof English 1984-91; UC Davis, prof of African Studies, currently. **HONORS AND AWARDS** Fellow, Amer Anthropology Assn; Winifred Holtby Prize for Novel Royal Soc of Lit London 1972. **MEMBERSHIPS** Mem Inst for Advanced Study Princeton 1979-80. **CONTACT ADDRESS** African American & African Studies, UC Davis, 2143 Hart Hall, Davis, CA, 95616.

STEWART, LARRY
DISCIPLINE ENGLISH LITERATURE **EDUCATION** Simpson Col, BA, 63; Case W Reserve, MA, 64, PhD, 71. **CAREER** Prof. **SELECTED PUBLICATIONS** Auth, A Guide To Literary Criticism and Research. **CONTACT ADDRESS** Dept of Eng, Col of Wooster, Wooster, OH, 44691.

STEWART, MAAJA AGUR
PERSONAL Born 06/27/1938, Estonia, m, 1959, 1 child **DISCIPLINE** ENGLISH **EDUCATION** Oberlin Col, AB, 60; Univ Mich, MA, 61, PhD(English), 66. **CAREER** ASST PROF ENGLISH, NEWCOMB COL, TULANE UNIV, 65- **MEMBERSHIPS** MLA **RESEARCH** Theory of Comedy; English novel; 18th century English literature. **SELECTED PUBLICATIONS** Inexhaustible Generosity, The Fictions Of 18th-Century British Imperialism In Richard Cumberland: The West Indian, Eighteenth Century Theory And Interpretation, Vol 37, 96. **CONTACT ADDRESS** Dept of English, Tulane Univ, 6823 St Charles Ave, New Orleans, LA, 70118-5698.

STEWART, STANLEY N.
DISCIPLINE ENGLISH LITERATURE EDUCATION UCLA, BA, MA, PhD. CAREER PROF, UNIV CALIF, RIVERSIDE. HONORS AND AWARDS Fel(s), Mallon; Guggenheim. RESEARCH Wittgenstein and Renaissance criticism. SELECTED PUBLICATIONS Auth, The Enclosed Garden: The Tradition and the Image, 17th-Century Poetry, Univ Wis Press, 66; The Expanded Voice: The Art of Thomas Traherne, Huntington Lib, 70; George Herbert, G.K. Hall, 76; 'Renaissance' Talk: Ordinary Language and the Mystique of Critical Problems, Duquesne, 97; co-auth, Nietzsche's Case: Philosophy as/and Literature, Routledge, 92; Evidence and Historical Criticism, Duquesne Univ Press, 95; co-ed, The Ben Jonson Journal: Literary Contexts in the Age of Elizabeth, James, and Charles, Univ Nev Press. CONTACT ADDRESS Dept of Eng, Univ Calif, 1156 Hinderaker Hall, Riverside, CA, 92521-0209.

STIEB, JAMES
PERSONAL Born 09/10/1970, Denver, CO, s DISCIPLINE LIBERAL ARTS EDUCATION Temple Univ, MA, 96; Univ of CO, BA, 93; St. Johns Col, BA, 94 CAREER Adj Asst Prof, 98-pres, Chaney Univ MEMBERSHIPS Am Philos Assoc; Soc for the Discussion of Realism and Antirealism RESEARCH Logic and Critical Reason; Realism/Antirealism; Metaphysics; Philosophy of Language of Mind; Applied Ethics & Social Philosophy SELECTED PUBLICATIONS Auth, "Philosophy Reflections on the Analytic Continental Divide," Sch, 98 CONTACT ADDRESS Temple Univ, 1300 W Cecil B Moor #31, Philadelphia, PA, 19122. EMAIL jsteib@nimbus.ocis.temple.edu

STILLINGER, JACK
PERSONAL Born 02/16/1931, Chicago, IL, m, 1952, 4 children DISCIPLINE ENGLISH EDUCATION Univ Tex, BA, 53; Northwestern Univ, MA, 54; Harvard Univ, PhD, 58. CAREER From asst prof to assoc prof, 58-64, prof English, Univ Ill, Urbana, 64-, ed, J English & Ger Philol, 61-73; Guggenheim Mem Found fel, 64-65; permanent mem, Univ Ill Ctr Advan Study. HONORS AND AWARDS Natl Woodrow wilson fel, 53-54; Guggenheim Mem Found fel, 64-65; Keats-Shelley Asn Dist Scholar award, 86; fel Am Acad Arts & Sciences, 93. MEMBERSHIPS MLA; Keats-Shelley Asn Am; Wordsworth-Coleridge Asn; Byron Soc; Natl Council of Teachers of English; Soc for Textual Scholarship. RESEARCH English romantic movement; textual and literary thoery. SELECTED PUBLICATIONS Ed, The Early Draft of John Stuart Mill's Autobiography, Univ Ill, 61; Anthony Munday's Zelauto: The Fountaine of Fame, Southern Ill Univ, 63; Wordsworth: Selected Poems and Prefaces, Houghton, 65; The Letters of Charles Armitage Brown, Harvard Univ, 66; Twentieth Century Interpretations of Keats's Odes, Prentice-Hall, 68; John Stewart Mill: Autobiography and Other writings, Houghton, 69. Auth, The Hoodwinking of Madeline and Other Essays on Keats's Poems, Univ Ill, 71; The Texts of Keats's Poems, 74 & ed, The Poems of John Keats, 78, Harvard Univ. Ed, Collected Works of John Stuart Mill, vol 1, Univ Toronto, 81; John Keats: Complete Poems, Harvard Univ, 82; The Norton Anthology of English Literature, Norton, 86, 93; John Keats: Poetry Manuscripts at Harvard, Harvard Univ, 90. Auth, Multiple Authorship and the Myth of solitary genius, Oxford Univ, 91; Coleridge and Textual Instability: The Multiple Versions of the Major Poems, Oxford Univ, 94; Reading The Eve of St Agnes: The Multiples of Complex Literary Transaction, Oxford Univ, 99. CONTACT ADDRESS Univ of Ill, 608 S Wright St, Urbana, IL, 61801-3613. EMAIL jstill@uiuc.edu

STIMPSON, CATHARINE R.
PERSONAL Born 06/04/1936, Bellingham, WA DISCIPLINE CONTEMPORARY LITERATURE, WOMEN'S STUDIES EDUCATION Bryn Mawr Col, AB, 58; Cambridge Univ, BA, 60, MA, 65; Columbia Univ, PhD(English), 67. CAREER From instr to asst prof, 63-73, assoc prof, Columbia Univ, 73-80; prof English, Rutgers Univ, 80-, mem, Nat Emergency Civil Liberties Comt; ed, SIGNS: J Women in Cult & Soc, 74-80; Nat Humanities Inst fel, 75-76; consult, Nat Inst Educ, 78-80; dir, Rutgers Inst for Res Women; chemn, Mass Bd Scholarship, Res & Educ. MEMBERSHIPS MLA; PEN. RESEARCH Post-modern literature; women and literature; relationship of revolution to literature. SELECTED PUBLICATIONS Auth, J R R Tolkien, Columbia Univ, 69; ed, Women and the Equal Rights Amendment, 72 & Discrimination Against Women, 73, Bowker; Class Notes, Times Bks, 78 & Avon, 79. CONTACT ADDRESS GSAS Dean's Office, New York Univ, 6 Washington Square N, Rm 12, New York, NY, 10003-6668. EMAIL catharine.stimpson@nyu.edu

STINSON, JOHN JEROME
PERSONAL Born 09/30/1940, Brooklyn, NY, m, 1969, 2 children DISCIPLINE MODERN BRITISH LITERATURE EDUCATION St John's Univ, NY, BA, 62, MA, 63; NY Univ, PhD, 71. CAREER From instr to asst prof, 65-74, assoc prof, 74-78, prof English, State Univ NY Col Fredonia 78-, Res award, 73. MEMBERSHIPS MLA RESEARCH Modern American literature; popular culture. SELECTED PUBLICATIONS Auth, The Christian symbolism in After the Fall, Mod Drama, 12/67; Trying to exorcise the beast: The grotesque in the fiction of William Golding, Cithara, 11/71; Anthony Bur-

gess: Novelist on the margin, J Pop Cult, summer 73; Graham Greene's The Destructors: Fable for a world far east of Eden, Am Benedictine Rev, 12/73; The Manichee world of Anthony Burgess, Renascence, Autumn, 73; Nothing Like the Sun: The faces in Bella Cohen's mirror, J Mod Lit, 2/76; Dualism and paradox in the Puritan Plays of David Storey, Mod Drama, 6/77; Better to be hot or cold: 1985 and the dynamic of the manichean duoverse, Mod Fiction Studies, autumn, 81; Anthony Burgess Revisited, Twayne Publ, 91; V.S. Pritchett: A Study of the Short Fiction, Twayne-Macmillan, 92. CONTACT ADDRESS Dept of English, State Univ NY Col, 1 Suny at Fredonia, Fredonia, NY, 14063-1143. EMAIL stinson@ait.fredonia.edu

STITT, J. MICHAEL
DISCIPLINE FOLKLORE, MEDIEVAL LITERATURE EDUCATION Pa State Univ, BA, 73; Ind Univ, MA, 75, cert, 78, PhD, 81. CAREER Instr, Ind Univ-Purdue Univ, 79-81; asst prof, 81-91, assoc prof, 91-, interim dir, freshman compos, 91-92, Univ Nev, Las Vegas; sr Fulbright lectr, Univ Sofia, 97; ed bd, J Medieval Folklore. HONORS AND AWARDS Grant, Nevada Humanities Council, 82; University Research council grant, 83, 86, 88. MEMBERSHIPS Alternate rep, Nev State Bd Geog Names, 85-. RESEARCH Bulgarian folk music and dance. SELECTED PUBLICATIONS Auth, Conversational Genres at a Las Vegas '21' Table, Western Folklore 45, 86; Beowulf and The Bear's Son. Epic, Saga, and Fairytale in the Northern Germanic Area, Albert B Lord Monogr Ser, Garland, 92; coauth, A Type and Motif Index of Early American Almanac Narrative, Greenwood, 91. CONTACT ADDRESS Dept of Eng, Univ Nev, Las Vegas, 4505 Maryland Pky, PO Box 455011, Las Vegas, NV, 89154-5011. EMAIL stitt@nevada.edu

STITZEL, JUDITH GOLD
PERSONAL Born 03/23/1941, New York, NY, m, 1961, 1 child DISCIPLINE ENGLISH, WOMEN'S STUDIES EDUCATION Columbia Univ, BA, 61; Univ WI, MA, 62; Univ MN, PhD, 68. CAREER Asst prof, 68-72, assoc prof, 72-79, coor and dir Center for Women's Stud 80-92, prof eng and women's studies, WVA Univ, 92-98, Assoc, Danforth Found, 75-82; WVA deleg NCent Women's Studies Asn, 79. MEMBERSHIPS Nat Women's Studies Asn. RESEARCH Lit criticism; pedag; women's studies. SELECTED PUBLICATIONS Auth, The uses of humor, Doris Lessing Newslett, 77; Morning cycle, Colo Quart, autumn, 79; Humor and survival in the works of Doris Lessing, Regionalism and the Female Imagination, 4: 61-69; Reading Doris Lessing, Col English, 40: 498-504; Toward the new year, Trellis, summer 79; Challenging curricular assumptions: Teaching, learning women's literature from a regional perspective, Toward the Second Decade: The Impact of the Women's Movement on American Institutions, Greeenwood Press, summer 81; She who laughs firt, Stepping Off the Pedetal-Academic Women in the South, MLA, 82. CONTACT ADDRESS Dept of Eng, West Virginia Univ, 449 Devon Rd, Morgantown, WV, 26505. EMAIL jstitzel@wvu.edu

STIVALE, CHARLES J.
PERSONAL Born 12/13/1949, Glen Ridge, NJ, m, 1981 DISCIPLINE ROMANCE LANGUAGES; LITERATURE EDUCATION Knox Col, BA, 71; Sorbonne Paris-IV, MA, 73, Maitrise, 74; Univ Il Urbana-Champaign, PhD, 81. CAREER Inst, W Mich Univ, 80-81; res dir, Univ of Haute Bretagne, Rennes, France, 81-82; asst prof, Franklin & Marshall Col, 82-86; asst prof, Tulane Univ, 86-90; assoc prof to prof & chair, Wayne St Univ, 90-. MEMBERSHIPS Modern Lang Assoc; Midwest Modern Lang Assoc, Amer Assoc of Teachers of French; Alliance Francaise. RESEARCH Nineteenth-century French lit; twentieth-century critical theory; French cultural stud; cybercriticism; deleuze & Guattari. SELECTED PUBLICATIONS Auth, The Art of Rupture, Narrative Desire and Duplicity in the Tales of Guy de Maupassant, Univ Mich Press, 94; Comments on a Meeting With Gilles Deleuze, Nth Dimension, 96; 'help manners', Cyber-democracy and Its Vicissitudes, Enculturation, 97; On Cultural Lessons, French and Other, Contemporary French Stud, 97; The Two-Fold Thought of Deleuze and Guattari: Intersections and Animations. Guilford Publ, 98. CONTACT ADDRESS Dept of Romance Lang & Lit, Wayne St Univ, 487 Manoogian Hall, Detroit, MI, 48202. EMAIL C_Stivale@wayne.edu

STOCK, ROBERT DOUGLAS
PERSONAL Born 12/02/1941, Akron, OH, m, 1 child DISCIPLINE ENGLISH EDUCATION Kent State Univ, BA, 63; Princeton Univ, MA, 65, PhD(English), 67. CAREER From asst prof to assoc prof, 67-77, PROF ENGLISH, UNIV NEBR-LINCOLN, 77- HONORS AND AWARDS BA summa cum laude, 63; Wilson Fel and Dissertation Fel, 63, 66; Phi Beta Kappa, 95; teaching awards, 93, 94, 96, 98. MEMBERSHIPS Soc 18th Century Studies; Asn Lit Scholars & Critics; Nat Scholars Asn. RESEARCH Eighteenth-century literature; literary expression of religious experience; silent film. SELECTED PUBLICATIONS Auth, Samuel Johnson and Neoclassical Dramatic Theory, 73 & Samuel Johnson's Literary Criticism, 74, Univ Nebr; Prosser Hall Frye: Conservative humanist, Mod Age, 75; Agents of evil and justice in the novels of Sayers, In: As Her Whimsy Took Her, Kent State, 79; The New Humanists

in Nebraska, Univ Nebr, 79; The Tao and the objective room: A pattern in C S Lewis's novels, Christian Scholar's Rev, 80; The Holy and the Daemonic from Sir Thomas Browne to William Blake, Princeton Univ, 82; The Flutes of Dionysus: Daemonic Enthrallment in Literature, Univ Nebr, 89; Salem Witchcraft and Spiritual Evil, Christianity and Lit, 92. CONTACT ADDRESS Dept of English, Univ of Nebr, PO Box 880333, Lincoln, NE, 68588-0333. EMAIL rstock@unlinfo.unl.edu

STODOLA, ZABELLE
DISCIPLINE EARLY AMERICAN LITERATURE EDUCATION Univ Tex, PhD. CAREER English and Lit, Univ Ark SELECTED PUBLICATIONS Coauth, The Indian Captivity Narrative; Ed, Early American Literature and Culture, Jour & Occasional Writings of Sarah Wister; Auth, Puritan Orthodoxy and the 'Survivor Syndrome' in Mary Rowlandson's Indian Captivity Narrative; The Indian Captivity Narratives of Mary Rowlandson and Olive Oatman. CONTACT ADDRESS Univ Ark Little Rock, 2801 S University Ave., Little Rock, AR, 72204-1099. EMAIL kzstodola@ualr.edu

STOHL, CYNTHIA B.
DISCIPLINE ORGANIZATIONAL COMMUNICATION, SOCIAL NETWORKS EDUCATION Univ Purdue, PhD, 82. CAREER Prof, Purdue Univ. RESEARCH Participatory processes in multicultural/international organizations. SELECTED PUBLICATIONS Auth, European Managers Interpretations of Participation: a semantic network analysis, Human Commun Res, 93; Participating and Participation, Commun Monogr, 93; Organizational Communication: Connectedness in Action, Sage, 95; Paradoxes of Participation, Orgn and Commun, 95. CONTACT ADDRESS Dept of Commun, Purdue Univ, 1080 Schleman Hall, West Lafayette, IN, 47907-1080. EMAIL cstohl@purdue.edu

STOKES, JAMES
PERSONAL Born 09/09/1943, Conrad, MT, m, 1967, 2 children DISCIPLINE ENGLISH LITERATURE EDUCATION San Francisco State Univ, BA, 68, MA, 69; Wash State Univ, PhD, 79. CAREER Prof of English, 81-, Univ Wisconsin Stevens Point. HONORS AND AWARDS Disting Achiev Awd, 3 IRH Fels, H F Guggenheim Found Grant. MEMBERSHIPS MLA, M&RDS, Somersetshire Arch & Nat Hist Soc, Intl Soc for Stud Medieval Theatre. RESEARCH English drama, music, custom and ceremony 1100-1642. CONTACT ADDRESS Dept of English, Univ of Wis Stevens Point, Stevens Point, WI, 54481. EMAIL jstokes@uwsp.edu

STONE, DONALD DAVID
PERSONAL Born 01/17/1942, Los Angeles, CA DISCIPLINE ENGLISH LITERATURE EDUCATION Univ Calif, Berkeley, BA, 63; Harvard Univ, MA, 64, PhD(English), 68. CAREER Dexter traveling fel, 68; asst prof, 68-72, assoc prof, 72-80, PROF ENGLISH, QUEENS COL, NY, 80- HONORS AND AWARDS Howard Mumford Jones Prize, 68. MEMBERSHIPS MLA RESEARCH Victorian literature; history of the novel. SELECTED PUBLICATIONS Auth, The Brontes, Nineteenth-Century Lit, Vol 51, 96; The Art Of The Brontes, Nineteenth-Century Lit, Vol 51, 96; The Letters of Charlotte Bronte, With A Selection Of Letters By Family And Friends, Vol 1, 1829-1847, Nineteenth-Century Lit, Vol 52, 97; The Letters Of Arnold,Matthew, Vol 1, 1829-1859, Nineteenth-Century Lit, Vol 52, 97; An Edition Of The Early Writings Of Charlotte Bronte, Vol 2, The Rise Of Angria, 1833-1835, Nineteenth-Century Lit, Vol 47, 92. CONTACT ADDRESS Dept of English, Queens Col, CUNY, 6530 Kissena Blvd, Flushing, NY, 11367.

STONE, GREGORY
DISCIPLINE MEDIEVAL AND RENAISSANCE LITERATURE, LITERARY THEORY AND CRITICISM EDUCATION Yale Univ, PhD, 89. CAREER Assoc prof, dir, grad stud, La State Univ. SELECTED PUBLICATIONS Auth, The Death of the Troubadour, 94; Dante's Averoistic Hermeneutics, in Dante Stud, 94; The Philosophical Beast: On Boccaccio's Tale of Cimone, Animal Acts, 96. CONTACT ADDRESS Dept of Fr Grad Stud, Louisiana State Univ, Baton Rouge, LA, 70803.

STONE-BLACKBURN, SUSAN
PERSONAL WI DISCIPLINE ENGLISH EDUCATION Lawrence Col, BA, 63; Univ Colorado, MA, 67, PhD, 70. CAREER Asst prof, 73-79, assoc prof, 79-86, assoc dean hum, 85-89, PROF, UNIV CALGARY, 86-. MEMBERSHIPS Sci Fiction Res Asn; Asn Can Theatre Res; Maenad Theatre Prods. SELECTED PUBLICATIONS Auth, Robertson Davies, Playwright: A Search for the Self on the Canadian Stage, 85; auth, Consciousness Evolution and Early Telepathic Tales, in Sci Fiction Studs, 20, 2, 93; auth, Feminist Nurturers and Psychic Healers, in Imaginative Futures, 95. CONTACT ADDRESS Dept of English, Univ of Calgary, Calgary, AB, T2N 1N4. EMAIL sstonebl@acs.ucalgary.ca

STONUM, GARY LEE
PERSONAL Born 07/10/1947, Sacramento, CA, m, 1970 **DISCIPLINE** ENGLISH **EDUCATION** Reed Col, BA, 69; Johns Hopkins Univ, MA, 71, PhD(English), 73. **CAREER** Asst prof, 73-80, assoc prof English, Case Westerm Reserve Univ, 80-90; vis asst prof Criticism & Theory, Univ Calif, Irvine, 76-77. **MEMBERSHIPS** English Inst; MLA; Int Asn Philos & Lit; Am Studies Asn. **RESEARCH** Emily Dickinson Int Soc; literary theory; the novel. **SELECTED PUBLICATIONS** Auth, A prophet of desire, Diacritics, 77; For a cybernetics of reading, MLN, 77; Faulkner's Career, Cornell Univ, 78; The Dickenson Sublime, U of Wisconsin, 90. **CONTACT ADDRESS** Dept of English, Case Western Reserve Univ, 10900 Euclid Ave, Cleveland, OH, 44106-4901. **EMAIL** gxs11@po.cwtu.edu

STORY, KENNETH ERVIN
PERSONAL Born 07/09/1941, Albemarle, NC **DISCIPLINE** ENGLISH, NINETEENTH CENTURY BRITISH LITERATURE **EDUCATION** Pfeiffer Col, AB, 63; Univ Tenn, MA, 65, PhD, 67. **CAREER** Asst prof English, Va Polytech Inst, 67-69; asst prof, Ohio Wesleyan Univ, 69-72; prof Eng, 72-, Chmn Dept, 80-83, 95-98, Head Humanities Area, 81-, Hendrix Col. **HONORS AND AWARDS** Nat Endowment for Humanities fel, Princeton Univ, summer, 77. **MEMBERSHIPS** MLA; Mod Lang Assn; S Atlantic Mod Lang Assn. **RESEARCH** Fiction of Flannery O'Connor; poetry of Tennyson. **SELECTED PUBLICATIONS** Auth, Theme and image in The Princess, Tenn Studies Lit, 75; coauth, Browning's Soliloquy of the Spanish Cloister, Explicator, spring 80; auth, Throwing a Spotlight on the Past: Narrative Method in Ann Beatties's Jacklighting, Studies in Short Fiction, 92. **CONTACT ADDRESS** Dept of English, Hendrix Col, 1600 Washington Ave, Conway, AR, 72032-3080.

STORY, PATRICK LEE
PERSONAL Born 05/09/1940, St. Louis, MO, m, 2 children **DISCIPLINE** ENGLISH & AMERICAN LITERATURE **EDUCATION** Univ Mo-Columbia, BA, 62; Northwestern Univ, MA, 63, PhD, 68. **CAREER** Actg asst prof, Univ Calif, Los Angeles, 66-68, asst prof English, 68-74; lectr comp cult, Univ Calif, Irvine, 74-75; instr humanities, Univ Calif, Los Angeles, Exten, 75-76; asst prof, 76-79, ASSOC PROF ENGLISH, GEORGE MASON UNIV, 79-. **MEMBERSHIPS** MLA; Keats-Shelley Asn; Wordsworth-Coleridge Asn. **RESEARCH** British romanticism; literary criticism; composition. **SELECTED PUBLICATIONS** Auth, Byron's Death and Hazlitt's Spirit of the Age, English Lang Notes, 9/69; A contemporary continuation of Hazlitt's Spirit of the Age, Wordsworth Circle, spring 70; Pope, pageantry, and Shelley's Triumph of Life, Keats-Shelley J, 12/73; Hazlitt's definition of the Spirit of the Age, spring 75 & Emblems of infirmity: The contemporary portrait in Hazlitt's the Spirit of the Age, 79, Wordsworth Circle; A neglected cockney school parody of Hazlitt and Hunt, Keats-Shelley J, 80. **CONTACT ADDRESS** Dept of English, George Mason Univ, 4400 University Dr, Fairfax, VA, 22030-4444. **EMAIL** pstory@gmu.edu

STOTT, WILLIAM MERRELL
PERSONAL Born 06/02/1940, New York, NY, m, 1962, 2 children **DISCIPLINE** AMERICAN STUDIES, ENGLISH **EDUCATION** Yale Univ, AB, 62, MPh, 70, PhD(Am studies), 72. **CAREER** Foreign serv officer, US Info Agency, 64-68; asst prof, 71-74, assoc dean, Div Gen & Comp Studies, 75-77, assoc prof, 74-80, prof Am Studies & English, Univ Tex, Austin, 80-, dir, Am Studies Prog, 81-84, Guggenheim Mem Found Fel, 78; Fulbright lectr, Polytechnic of Cent London, 80-81; Univ of London, 86-87. **MEMBERSHIPS** Am Studies Asn. **RESEARCH** Journalism; mass culture; autobiography. **SELECTED PUBLICATIONS** Auth, Documentary Expression and Thirties America, Oxford Univ, 73, Chicago UP, 86; coauth, On Broadway, Univ Tex, 78; Write to the Point, Columbia UP, 90; Facing the Fire: Experiencing and Expressing Anger Appropriately, Doubleday, 93. **CONTACT ADDRESS** Dept of Am Studies, Univ of Texas, Austin, TX, 78712-1026. **EMAIL** wstott@mail.utexas.edu

STRAIN, ELLEN
DISCIPLINE MULTIMEDIA DESIGN AND VIDEO PRODUCTION **EDUCATION** Univ Southern Calif, PhD, 96. **CAREER** Asst prof, Ga Inst of Technol. **RESEARCH** The theorization of cross-cultural spectatorship in popular culture. **SELECTED PUBLICATIONS** Published articles on stereoscopic depictions of the building of the Panama Canal, the development of popular anthropology in the late 19th century, and the implications of cross-cultural filmic depictions for the Greek political situation. **CONTACT ADDRESS** Sch of Lit, Commun, & Cult, Georgia Inst of Tech, Skiles Cla, Atlanta, GA, 30332. **EMAIL** ellen.strain@lcc.gatech.edu

STRAITON, T. HARMON, JR.
DISCIPLINE LIBRARY SCIENCE **EDUCATION** Auburn Univ, BS, 63; Univ Alabama, MLS, 79. **CAREER** Head, Mathematics and science dept, Tallassee (Ala) City Schools, 66-79; Head, microforms and documents dept, 80-98, Asst Dean for Information Services, 98-, Auburn Univ. **CONTACT ADDRESS** PO Box 132, Auburn, AL, 36831. **EMAIL** straith@mail.edu

STRAND, DANA
DISCIPLINE LITERATURE **EDUCATION** Vanderbilt Univ, PhD. **CAREER** Literature, Carleton Col. **HONORS AND AWARDS** Chair, Romance Lang & Lit. **SELECTED PUBLICATIONS** Auth, Colette: A Study of the Short Fiction, Macmillan. **CONTACT ADDRESS** Carleton Col, 100 S College St., Northfield, MN, 55057-4016.

STRANDBERG, VICTOR
DISCIPLINE ENGLISH LITERATURE **EDUCATION** Brown Col, PhD, 62. **CAREER** Prof, Duke Univ. **SELECTED PUBLICATIONS** Auth, Religious Psychology in American Literature: The Relevance of William James, Studia Humanitas, 81; A Faulkner Overview: Six Perspectives, Kennikat, 81; Greek Mind Jewish Soul: The Conflicted Art of Cynthia Ozick, Univ Wis, 94. **CONTACT ADDRESS** Eng Dept, Duke Univ, Durham, NC, 27706.

STRATER, HENRY A.
PERSONAL Born 10/28/1934, Cleveland, OH, m, 3 children **DISCIPLINE** ENGLISH, CLASSICAL LANGUAGES **EDUCATION** John Carroll Univ, AB, 56, MA; Case Western Univ, MA, 59; Ohio State Univ, PhD, 71. **CAREER** Tchr, Shaker Heights Sch, Ohio, 56-84; holder of Waldron ch in Classics, Univ Sch, 84- . **HONORS AND AWARDS** Good tchr awd, Class Asn Mid W and S; Seelbach awd for excel in tchg. **MEMBERSHIPS** Amer Class League; Ohio Class Conf; Amer Philol Asn; Class Asn Mid W and S. **RESEARCH** Vergil; Methods of teaching Classical Languages. **SELECTED PUBLICATIONS** Auth, Greek to Me: An Introduction to Classical Greek. **CONTACT ADDRESS** Univ Sch, 1131 Blanchester Rd, Lyndhurst, OH, 44124. **EMAIL** hastrater@aol.com

STRATTON, CHARLES R.
DISCIPLINE ENGLISH LITERATURE **EDUCATION** Carroll Col, BS, 60; Rensselaer Polytech Inst, MA, 68; Univ Wis Madison, PhD, 71. **CAREER** Prof. Hartford Univ. **SELECTED PUBLICATIONS** Auth, Technical Writing: Process and Product, Holt, Rinehart and Winston, 84; Operation and Maintenance Manual, Rupert, 80. **CONTACT ADDRESS** English Dept, Univ Idaho, 415 W 6th St, Moscow, ID, 83844.

STRATTON, SUSAN B.
PERSONAL Born 10/06/1941 **DISCIPLINE** ENGLISH **EDUCATION** Lawrence Univ, BA, 63; Univ Colo, MA, 67, PhD 70. **CAREER** Asst to assoc prof, 73-86, assoc dean hum, 85-89, PROF ENGLISH, UNIV CALGARY, 86-, assoc dean grad stud, 93-98; bd dir, Maenad Theatre Prod, 91-93. **MEMBERSHIPS** Sci Fiction Res Asn; Soc Utopian Stud; Asn Stud Lit Environ; Asn Can Col Univ Tchrs Eng. **RESEARCH** Canadian theatre. **SELECTED PUBLICATIONS** Auth, Robertson Davies, Playwright: A Search for the Self on the Canadian Stage, 85. **CONTACT ADDRESS** Dept of English, Univ Calgary, Calgary, AB, T2N 1N4. **EMAIL** stratton@acs.ucalgary.ca

STRAUB, KRISTINA
DISCIPLINE EIGHTEENTH-CENTURY BRITISH LITERATURE **EDUCATION** Emory Univ, PhD. **CAREER** Lit, Carnegie Mellon Univ. **SELECTED PUBLICATIONS** Area: eighteenth century & feminist theory. **CONTACT ADDRESS** Carnegie Mellon Univ, 5000 Forbes Ave, Pittsburgh, PA, 15213.

STRAUS, BARRIE RUTH
DISCIPLINE ENGLISH LANGUAGE; LITERATURE **EDUCATION** Oregon Univ, BA; Iowa Univ, MA, PhD, 90. **CAREER** Prof **RESEARCH** Medieval literature; contemporary critical theory; women's studies; modern narrative. **SELECTED PUBLICATIONS** Auth, Catholic Church & Skirting the Texts. **CONTACT ADDRESS** Dept of English Language and Literature, Univ of Windsor, 401 Sunset Ave, Windsor, ON, N9B 3P4.

STRAUSS, ALBRECHT BENNO
PERSONAL Born 05/17/1921, Berlin, Germany, m, 1978, 3 children **DISCIPLINE** ENGLISH **EDUCATION** Oberlin Col, BA, 42; Tulane Univ, MA, 48; Harvard Univ, PhD(English), 56. **CAREER** Instr English, Tulane Univ, 48-49; instr, Brandeis Univ, 51-52; instr, Yale Univ, 55-59; asst prof, Univ Okla, 59-60; from asst prof to assoc prof, 60-70, dir grad studies, 67-68, PROF ENGLISH, UNIV NC, CHAPEL HILL, 70-, Ed, Studies Philol, 74-80. **MEMBERSHIPS** MLA; SAtlantic Mod Lang Asn; Am Soc 18th Century Studies; Col English Asn; Southeastern Am Soc 18th Century Studies (pres, 80-81). **RESEARCH** Eighteenth century English literature; English novel; stylistics. **SELECTED PUBLICATIONS** Auth, On Smollett's Language, In: English Institute Essays, 1958, Columbia Univ, 59; The dull duty of an editor: On editing the text of Johnson's Rambler, Bookmark, 6/65; co-ed, Essays in English Literature of the Classical Period Presented to Dougald MacMillan, Univ NC, 67; The Rambler, Vols III, IV & V, In: The Yale Edition of the Works of Samuel Johnson, Yale Univ, 69; You-Cant-Go-Home-Again, Thomas Wolfe And I, Southern Lit J, Vol 27, 95. **CONTACT ADDRESS** Dept English, Univ NC, Chapel Hill, NC, 27514.

STRAW, WILLIAM O.
DISCIPLINE COMMUNICATION STUDIES **EDUCATION** Carleton Univ, BA; McGill Univ, MA, PhD. **CAREER** Assoc prof. **SELECTED PUBLICATIONS** Auth, Montreal Confidential: Notes on an Imagined City, 92; auth, Systems of Articulation, Logics of Change: Scenes and Communities in Popular Music, 91; Esquivel, Y-Y and Me, 96; auth, Post-Referendary Positions: A Dossier, 96; Does the Cinema have a Future?, 94. **CONTACT ADDRESS** Dept Communications, McGill Univ, 845 Sherbrooke St, Montreal, PQ, H3A 2T5.

STRAZNICKY, MARTA
DISCIPLINE ENGLISH LITERATURE **EDUCATION** Univ Ottawa, PhD. **CAREER** Dept Eng, Queen's Univ **RESEARCH** Early modern women writers; theatre history; Renaissance drama; feminist and reception theory. **SELECTED PUBLICATIONS** Auth, pubs on Renaissance comedy and seventeenth-century women dramatists. **CONTACT ADDRESS** English Dept, Queen's Univ, Kingston, ON, K7L 3N6. **EMAIL** straznic@qsilver.queensu.ca

STREET, RICHARD L., JR.
DISCIPLINE HEALTH COMMUNICATION **EDUCATION** Univ Tex, PhD. **CAREER** Prof, Texas A&M Univ; res prof, Col Med, Texas A&M Univ & assoc dir, Inst for Health Care Evaluation. **HONORS AND AWARDS** Col Liberal Arts Distinguished Tchg Awd, Former Students Asn Texas A&M Univ. **SELECTED PUBLICATIONS** Co-ed, Health Promotion and Interactive Technology; contribur, Talk of the Clinic: Explorations in the Analysis of Medical and Therapeutic Discourse; Communication and Health Outcomes; Handbook of Interpersonal Communication; Applied CommunicationTheory and Research. **CONTACT ADDRESS** Dept of Speech Communication, Texas A&M Univ, College Station, TX, 77843-4234.

STREETER, DONALD
PERSONAL Born 04/24/1911, Huron, SD, d, 2 children **DISCIPLINE** ENGLISH, SPEECH **EDUCATION** Univ of Minn, BEd, 33; Univ of Iowa, MA, 38, PhD, 48. **CAREER** High school instr, 33-38; teaching fel, Univ of Iowa, 38-41 & 46-48; prof & chair, Univ of Memphis, 48-57; prof & chair emeritus, Univ of Houston, 57-76; adjunct, Tx A&M, Alvin Col, & Galveston Col, 76-96. **HONORS AND AWARDS** Outstanding Achievement, Galveston Col, 96; Educator of the Year, Rotary Int, 97. **MEMBERSHIPS** Tx Speech Commun; Speech Asn of Am. **SELECTED PUBLICATIONS** Auth, 50 Years of the Texas Speech Association; major public addreses of LQC Lamar, autobiography. **CONTACT ADDRESS** 6210 Sea Isle, Galveston, TX, 77554-9600.

STREIGHT, IRWIN
DISCIPLINE ENGLISH LITERATURE **EDUCATION** Queen's Univ, PhD. **CAREER** Dept Eng, Queen's Univ **RESEARCH** Christianity and literature; semiotic theory; post-modernity; sociolinguistics. **SELECTED PUBLICATIONS** Auth, A Good Hypogram is Not Hard to Find, Lit Belief, 97; Is There a Text in this Man?: A Semiotic Reading of 'Parker's Back', Flannery O'Connor Bull, 94. **CONTACT ADDRESS** English Dept, Queen's Univ, Kingston, ON, K7L 3N6. **EMAIL** ihs@post.queensu.ca

STRICKLAND, JOHNYE
DISCIPLINE WOMEN WRITERS **EDUCATION** Univ Ark, PhD. **CAREER** English and Lit, Univ Ark **SELECTED PUBLICATIONS** Auth, Vietnamese Refugees in America: Expectations and Realities, SW Asian Soc Newsl; Huy Luc and Phan Tung Mai: Prize Winning Vietnamese Writers, S Central Mod Lang Asn Bull; Oral History in the College Classroom, Oral Hist Rev; The Position of Women--Teachers and Students, Col Comm & Composition; Two Hundred Years of Law and Liberty, Ark Lawyer. **CONTACT ADDRESS** Univ Ark Little Rock, 2801 S University Ave., Little Rock, AR, 72204-1099. **EMAIL** jestrickland@ualr.edu

STRIPLING, MAHALA YATES
PERSONAL Born 06/04/1944, Eau Claire, WI, m, 1979, 2 children **DISCIPLINE** ENGLISH/RHETORIC **EDUCATION** Texas Christian Univ, BA, 75, MLA, 86, MA, 93, PhD, 97. **CAREER** Schl, Lectr, 98-, Yale Med Sch; Univ Texas Med Br; Texas Wesleyan Univ, et al; Asst editor, writing consul, 96-97, WM L Adams Writing Cen. **HONORS AND AWARDS** TCU creative writing Awds; Best Grad Essay, Poetry, News Story; Pres Vol Action Awd nom; Governor's Awd Outstanding Vol. **MEMBERSHIPS** NCIS; SHHV; MLAA; SCMLA; RRAA; et al. **RESEARCH** Rhetorical engendering of violence against women; Doctor-Patient Relationship; Richard Selzer, biography, literary criticism, and bibliography. **SELECTED PUBLICATIONS** Auth, Searching for Father, Med Humanities Rev, 98; Richard Selzer: Poet of the Body, Yale Med Sch's Humanities J, 98; Reclaiming Rhetorica: A Class Action, JAC, A J Composition Theory, 97; auth, The Tending Act-An Interview with Richard Slezer, J Med Humanities and Comp Studies, 96; A Dialogic/Rhetorical Analysis of Richard Selzer's, Smoking from Mortal Lessons, Readerly/Writerly, Texts, 96; The Ultimate Case History: A Doctor Describes His Own Coma, and Death, Med Humanities Rev, 94; Richard Slezer b 1928: A Checklist, Bulletin of Bibliography, 90. **CONTACT ADDRESS** 3301 Rogers Ave, Fort Worth, TX, 76109. **EMAIL** DrRhetoric@aol.com

STROHMAIER, MAHLA
DISCIPLINE COMMUNICATION **EDUCATION** Purdue Univ, PhD, 97. **CAREER** Lectr, Speech Commun, 89, instr of Commun, Univ Alaska, Fairbanks, 89-95; ADJUNCT FAC, TANANA VALLEY CAMPUS, UNIV ALASKA, 95-. **HONORS AND AWARDS** Cavett Robert Scholar, Nat Speakers Asn, 97; Alan H. Monroe Scholar, Purdue Univ, 97. **MEMBERSHIPS** Nat Commun Asn. **RESEARCH** Cross-cultural Commun; human-computer interaction; distance education. **SELECTED PUBLICATIONS** Coauth, Ethical Information Security in a Cross-cultural Environment, Infor Security-the Next Decade, 95; End-user Perception and Software Quality Assessment, J of Int Infor Management, 97; Implementing Speaking Across the Curriculum: A Case Study, 92; Faculty Development and Distance Education Proceedings of the International ED-MEDIA/ED-Telecom '98 Conference, in press; The Global Community and Cultural Diversity, Proceedings of the Soc for Infor Tech and Teacher Ed 8th Int Conf, 97; Ethical Accountability in the Cyberspace, Proceedings of the ACM Ethics in the Computer Age Conference, 94. **CONTACT ADDRESS** PO Box 80484, Fairbanks, AK, 99708-0484.

STROM, WILLIAM O.
PERSONAL Born 06/12/1958, Baton Rouge, LA, m, 1988, 3 children **DISCIPLINE** COMMUNICATION **EDUCATION** Wheaton Col, BA, 80; Northern Ill Univ, MA, 83; Univ of Iowa, PhD, 88. **CAREER** ASST TO ASSOC PROF OF COMMUN, CHEMN OF COMMUN DEPT, TRINITY WESTERN UNIV, 87-. **HONORS AND AWARDS** Paul K. Crawford Award for Outstanding Grad Study, Commun Studies Dept, Northern Ill Univ, 83. **MEMBERSHIPS** Nat Commun Asn; Religious Commun Asn. **RESEARCH** Religion and Communication; interpersonal communication; intercultural communication. **SELECTED PUBLICATIONS** Auth, Personal and cultural identity in cross-cultural relationships on the university campus, Mass Journal of Commun, 92; auth, The Effects of a Conversational Partners Program on ESL and University Students, The Howard Journal of Commun, 93; auth, More Than Talk: Communication Studies and the Christian Faith, Kendall/Hunt Pub Company, 98. **CONTACT ADDRESS** Dept of Communication, Trinity Western Univ, 7600 Glover Rd, Langley, BC, V2Y 1Y1. **EMAIL** strom@twu.ca

STROUD, THEODORE ALBERT
PERSONAL Born 01/25/1914, Marcella, AR, m, 1939 **DISCIPLINE** ENGLISH **EDUCATION** Ark Col, AB, 32; Univ Ark, AM, 37; Univ Chicago, PhD, 47. **CAREER** Instr, Univ Ark, 37-38; instr, Univ Chicago, 43-46; asst prof, Univ Fla, 46-47; assoc prof, 47-51, interim chmn dept, 57-58, PROF ENGLISH, DRAKE UNIV, 51-, Ford fel, 54-55. **MEMBERSHIPS** MLA; Mid West Mod Lang Asn; NCTE. **RESEARCH** Middle English; the Fi manuscript of Chaucer's Canterbury Tales. **SELECTED PUBLICATIONS** Co-ed, The Literature of Comedy, Ginn, 68; Lucio And The Balanced Structure Of Measure For Measure, English Studies, Vol 74, 93. **CONTACT ADDRESS** Dept of English, Drake Univ, Des Moines, IA, 50311.

STRYCHACZ, THOMAS
DISCIPLINE ENGLISH **EDUCATION** Warwick Univ, England, BA, 81; Princeton Univ,MA, 83 PhD, 86. **CAREER** Assoc prof; Mills Col, 88-. **RESEARCH** American literature; mass culture; political and cultural approaches to literature; science fiction. **SELECTED PUBLICATIONS** Auth, Modernism, Mass Culture, and Professionalism. Cambridge UP, 93; American Sports Writers and 'Unruly Rooters': The Significance of Orderly Spectating, J Amer Stud, 94; coauth, Beyond Mainstream: An Interdisciplinary Study of Music and the Written Word, J Lang and Learning Across the Disciplines, 96; contrib with, Soccer and Rock Climbing/Sport Climbing, in the Encycl US Popular Cult, 95. **CONTACT ADDRESS** Dept of English, Mills Col, 5000 MacArthur Blvd, Oakland, CA, 94613-1301. **EMAIL** toms@mills.edu

STUART, DABNEY
PERSONAL Born 11/04/1937, Richmond, VA, 3 children **DISCIPLINE** MODERN FICTION, POETRY **EDUCATION** Davidson Col, AB, 60; Harvard Univ, AM, 62. **CAREER** Instr English, Col William & Mary, 61-65; from instr to assoc prof, 65-71, prof English, Washington & Lee Univ, 72-, Poetry ed, Shenandoah, 66-76, editor-in-chief, 88-95; vis asst prof English, Middlebury Col, 68-69; poet-in-schs, Richmond Intercult Ctr for Humanities, Va, 71-72, 77 & 81 & Albemarle County Dept Educ, Va, 72-73; NEA creative writing fel, 75 & 82; Guggenheim fel in poetry, 87-88; Individual Artist fel, 96; adv ed, Poets in South, 76; poet-in-residence, Trinity Col, Hartford, spring, 78; lectr in writing, Univ Va, fall, 81; poet-in-residence, Univ Va, 82-83. **HONORS AND AWARDS** First Governor's Award for the Arts, Va, 79; S Blount Mason Jr Prof, 98. **MEMBERSHIPS** Auth Guild. **RESEARCH** Fiction of Vladimir Nabokov; modern and contemp poetry. **SELECTED PUBLICATIONS** Auth, The Diving Bell, 66 & A Particular Place, 69, Knopf; The Other Hand, La State Univ Press, 74; Friends of Yours, Friends of Mine, Rainmaker, 74; Round and Round, 77 & Nabokov: The Dimensions of Parody, 78, La State Univ Press; Rockbridge Poems, Iron Mountain, 81; Common Ground, La State Univ Press, 82; Don't Look Back, La State Univ Press, 87; Narcissus Dreaming, La State Univ Press, 90; Sweet Lucy Wine, La State Univ Press, 92; Light Years: New and Selected Poems, La State Univ Press, 94; Long Gone, La State Univ Press, 96; Second Sight: Poems for Paintings By Carroll Cloar, Univ of Mo Press, 96; The Way to Cobbs Creek, Univ Mo Press, 97. **CONTACT ADDRESS** Dept of English, Washington & Lee Univ, Lexington, VA, 24450-2504.

STUBER, FLORIAN
PERSONAL Born 03/01/1947, Buffalo, NY **DISCIPLINE** ENGLISH LITERATURE, THE NOVEL **EDUCATION** Columbia Univ, BA, 68, MA, 69, PhD(English), 80. **CAREER** Preceptor English, Columbia Col, Columbia Univ, 70-72, instr, 72-75; LECTR ENGLISH, BARNARD COL, COLUMBIA UNIV, 79-, Admin coordr, Conf Humanities & Pub Policy Issues, Columbia Univ, 74-76; consult, King-Hitzig Prod, 77; adj instr English, Fashion Inst Tech, 77-; consult, Citibank, New York City, 81 & Collectors Guild & Am Express, 82. **MEMBERSHIPS** MLA; Northeast Am Soc 18th Century Studies. **RESEARCH** Samuel Richardson; Charles Dickens; James Joyce. **SELECTED PUBLICATIONS** Co-ed & contribr, Small Comforts for Hard Times: Humanists on Public Policy, Columbia Univ Press, 77; Los humanistas y la politica, Fondo Cult Econ, Mexico City, 81; Clarissa, A Religious Novel, Studies In The Literary Imagination, Vol 28, 95. **CONTACT ADDRESS** 134 W 93rd St 3B, New York, NY, 10025.

STUMP, DONALD
DISCIPLINE RENAISSANCE LITERATURE **EDUCATION** Cornell Univ, PhD. **CAREER** Eng Dept, St. Edward's Univ **SELECTED PUBLICATIONS** Auth, Ed-in-Chief, 'Hamartia': The Concept of Error in the Western Tradition. Essays in Honor of John M. Crossett, Edwin Mellen Press, 83; Prim auth, of Sir Philip Sidney: An Annotated Bibliography of Texts and Criticism (1554-1984), G.K. Hall/Macmillan, 94. **CONTACT ADDRESS** St Edward's Univ, 3001 S Congress Ave, Austin, TX, 78704-6489.

STURM-MADDOX, SARA
PERSONAL Born 12/22/1938, Nashville, TN, m, 2 children **DISCIPLINE** ROMANCE LANGUAGES; MEDIEVAL LITERATURE **EDUCATION** Univ MN, BA, 63, MA, 65; Univ NC, PhD(Romance philol), 67. **CAREER** Asst prof French, Queens Col, NC, 66-67; asst prof Ital, Univ KY, 67-69; Prof French & Ital, Univ MA, Amherst, 75-, Am Coun Learned Soc. **HONORS AND AWARDS** Foundation Camargo, NEH **MEMBERSHIPS** MLA, Dante Soc Am; Int Arthurian Soc; Soc Rencesvals; Am Asn Tchrs; Int Courtly Lit Soc. **RESEARCH** Medieval French romance, epic and lyric; Dante; Renaissance Italian. **SELECTED PUBLICATIONS** Auth, The Lay of Guingamor: A Study, Univ NC, 68; Lorenzo de'Medici, Twayne, 74; Petrarch's Metamorphoses, Univ MO, 85; Petrarch's Laurels, Penn State Univ, 92; co-ed, Literary Aspects of Courtly Culture, Boydell & Brewer, 94; Transtextualities, MRTS, 96; Melusine of Lusignan, Univ of GA, 96; Froissart Across the Genres, Univ of FL, 98. **CONTACT ADDRESS** Dept of French & Ital, Univ of MA, Amherst, MA, 01003. **EMAIL** smadox@frital.umass.edu

STYAN, JOHN LOUIS
PERSONAL Born 07/06/1923, London, England, m, 1945, 4 children **DISCIPLINE** ENGLISH, DRAMA **EDUCATION** Cambridge Univ, MA, 47. **CAREER** Asst master grammar sch, Eng, 48-50; staff tutor lit & drama, Dept Adult Educ, Univ Hull, 50-62, sr staff tutor, 62-65; prof English, Univ Mich, Ann Arbor, 65-74, chmn dept, 73-74; Andrew W Mellon prof English, Univ Pittsburgh, 74-77; FRANKLYN BLISS SNYDER PROF ENGLISH LIT, NORTHWESTERN UNIV, 77-, Mem, Univs Coun Adult Educ Broadcasting Subcomt, Gt Brit, 62-65, adult educ liaison comt, Brit Broadcasting Corp, 62-65, adult educ adv comt, Independent TV Authority, 62-65 & adv bd, World Ctr Shakespeare Studies, 72-; Nat Endowment for Humanities fel, 78-79; chmn, Int Shakespeare Globe Theatre Ctr Acad Adv Coun NAm, 81- **MEMBERSHIPS** MLA; Guild Drama Adjudicators, Gt Brit; Brit Drama League; Shakespeare Asn Am,. **RESEARCH** Contemporary drama; Shakespeare; dramatic theory. **SELECTED PUBLICATIONS** Auth, The Elements of Drama, 60, The Dark Comedy, 62, The Dramatic Experience, 65, Shakespeare's Stagecraft, 67 & Chekhov in Performance, 71, Cambridge Univ; ed, The Challenge of the Theatre, Dickenson, 72; auth, Drama, Stage and Audience, 75, The Shakespeare Revolution: Criticism and Performance in the Twentieth Century, 77 & Modern Drama in Theory and Practice (3 Vols), 81. Cambridge Univ; The Play Of Personality In The Restoration Theater, Albion, Vol 25, 93. **CONTACT ADDRESS** Dept of English, Northwestern Univ, Evanston, IL, 60201.

SUBRAMANIAN, JANE M.
PERSONAL Born 03/07/1950, Schenectady, NY, m, 1973, 2 children **DISCIPLINE** LIBRARY SCIENCE **EDUCATION** SUNY Potsdam, BM, 72, MS, 74; Univ at Albany, MLS, 95. **CAREER** Lib tech asst, 74-87, staff assoc, 87-98, assoc librn, 98- , SUNY Potsdam. **MEMBERSHIPS** ALA; Asn for Lib Collections and Tech Serv; ACRL; SUNY Librns Asn; Eastern NY chap, ACRL; Music Lib Asn; NY/Ontario chap Music Lib Asn; Nat Flute Asn; Soc of Am Archivists; Mid Atlantic Regional Archives Conf; New England Archivists. **RESEARCH** American women's history; history of local musical community groups; reference service. **SELECTED PUBLICATIONS** Auth, Laura Ingalls Wilder: An Annotated Bibliography of Critical, Biographical, and Teaching Studies, Greenwood, 97; auth, Patron Attitudes Toward Computerized and Print Resources: Discussion and Considerations for Reference Service, Reference Librn, 98. **CONTACT ADDRESS** 63 Bay St, Potsdam, NY, 13676. **EMAIL** subramjm@potsdam.edu

SUBRYAN, CARMEN
PERSONAL Born 12/30/1944, Linden, Guyana, d **DISCIPLINE** ENGLISH **EDUCATION** Howard University, Washingtn DC, BA, 1971, MA, 1973, PhD, 1983. **CAREER** University of the District of Columbia, Washington DC, academic support, 1973-74; Howard University, Washington DC, instructor, program coordinator, 1974-. **HONORS AND AWARDS** Phi Beta Kappa, Howard University, 1971; Magna Cum Laude, Howard University, 1971; Reprise, a book of poetry, 1984. **MEMBERSHIPS** National Council of Teachers of English, 1980-84, College Language Association, 1981-86, National Association of Developmental Education, 1985-87, GUYAID, 1985-. **SELECTED PUBLICATIONS** "Walter Dean Myers," article in Dictionary of Literary Biography, 1984; "A B Spellman," article in Dictionary of Literary Biography, 1985; Woman's Survival, booklet, 1989; Black-Water Women, a novel, 1997. **CONTACT ADDRESS** Howard Univ, 2400 6th St, NW, Washington, VT, 20059.

SUCHY, PATRICIA
DISCIPLINE PERFORMANCE STUDIES **EDUCATION** Northwestern Univ, MFA, PhD. **CAREER** Asst prof, La State Univ. **RESEARCH** The narrative and cultural theory of Mikhall Bakhtin; 19th century Russion literature; post-war American fiction; contemporary experimental theatre and performance art. **SELECTED PUBLICATIONS** Writes about the nature of authorship in performance contexts. **CONTACT ADDRESS** Dept of Speech Commun, Louisiana State Univ, Baton Rouge, LA, 70803.

SUDOL, RONALD A.
PERSONAL Born 06/16/1943, New London, CT, m, 1973 **DISCIPLINE** RHETORIC **EDUCATION** St Michael's Col, BA, 65; Brown Univ, MA, 67; SUNY, Stony Brook, PhD, 76. **CAREER** Asst prof, 77-83, assoc prof, 83-91, prof of Rhetoric, Oakland Univ, 91-. **HONORS AND AWARDS** NEH summer seminar, 78; NEH summer stipend, 81; Danforth Found Assoc, 81-86; Oakland Univ Res Fel, 90. **MEMBERSHIPS** NCTE; CCCC. **RESEARCH** Writing and rhetoric; television criticism; rhetoric and public address. **SELECTED PUBLICATIONS** Auth, Textfiles: A Rhetoric for Word Processing, Harcourt Brace Jovanovich, 87; The Accumulative Rhetoric of Word Processing, College English, Dec 91; Writers, Computers, and Personality, Most Excellent Differences: Essays on Using Type Theory in the English Classroom, ed Thomas Thompson, Consulting Psychologists Press, 96; Self-Represention and Personality Type in Letter From Birmingham Jail, Understanding Literacy: Personality Preference in Rhetorical and Psycholinguistic Contexts, Hampton Press, 96; ed with Alice Horning, Understanding Literacy: Personality Preference in Rhetorical and Psycholinguistic Contexts, Hampton Press, 96; ed with Alice Horning, The Literary Connection, Hampton Press, 98. **CONTACT ADDRESS** Rhet, Commun & Journalism Dept, Oakland Univ, Rochester, MI, 48309. **EMAIL** sudol@oakland.edu

SUGANO, DOUGLAS
PERSONAL m, 2 children **DISCIPLINE** ENGLISH LITERATURE **EDUCATION** UC Berkeley, BA; UCLA, MA, PhD. **CAREER** Assoc prof, 88-. **RESEARCH** Early British literature, Shakespeare. **SELECTED PUBLICATIONS** Publ, articles on medieval English drama. **CONTACT ADDRESS** Dept of Eng, Whitworth Col, 300 West Hawthorne Rd, Spokane, WA, 99251. **EMAIL** dsugano@whitworth.edu

SUGG, RICHARD PETER
PERSONAL St. Louis, MO, 1 child **DISCIPLINE** AMERICAN LITERATURE FILM **EDUCATION** Univ Notre Dame, BA, 63; Univ Fla, MA, 67, PhD(Am Lit), 69. **CAREER** Asst prof Humanities, Univ Fla, 69-70; asst prof English, Ark State Univ, 71-73; asst prof, Univ Ky, 73-77; dir Humanities, 77-79, from assoc prof to prof English, Fla Int Univ, 79-85, Fulbright sr lectr, Czechoslovakia, 79-80. **HONORS AND AWARDS** Dir, NEH Summer Seminar, Fl U, 96; Teacher Incentive Award, FIU, 96. **MEMBERSHIPS** MLA; Am Film Inst. **RESEARCH** Modern American literature; film. **SELECTED PUBLICATIONS** Auth, Appreciating Poetry, Houghton, 75; The Bridge: A Description of its Life, Univ Ala, 76; Jungian Literary Criticism, Northwestern, 92. **CONTACT ADDRESS** Dept of Humanities, Florida Intl Univ, 3000 NE 151 St, Miami, FL, 33181-3612.

SUGIMOTO, NAOMI
PERSONAL Tokyo, Japan, s **DISCIPLINE** SPEECH COMMUNICATION **EDUCATION** Int Christian Univ, Japan, BA, 88; Univ Ill at Urbana-Champaign, MA, 90m, PhD, 95. **CAREER** Grad teaching/res asst, Univ Ill at Urbana-Champaign,

88-94; lecturer, Kanda Univ of Int Studs, Japan, 95-96; lecturer, Ferris Univ Japan, 96-98; asst prof, 98-. **HONORS AND AWARDS** Univ Fellowship, Univ Ill at Urbana-Champaign, 93; Rotary Int Scholar, 87-88; ICU Scholar, Int Christian Univ, 84-85. **MEMBERSHIPS** Nat Commun Assoc; Int Commun Assoc; Commun Assoc Japan; Soc for Int Educ, Training, Res, Japan; Int Assoc of Cross-Cultural Psychology; Pac Commun Assoc; Int Assoc for Intercultural Commun Studs; The Japan Soc for Corp Commun Studs. **RESEARCH** Intercultural communication; apology; comunication education; comunication research methods. **SELECTED PUBLICATIONS** Auth, Impromptu Fortune-telling exercise, Speech Commun Teacher, 8(1), 5, 93; A Comparison of conceptualizations of apology in English and Japanese, Intercultural Commun Studs, vol 8, 143-167, 96; auth, A Japan-US, comparison of apology styles, Commun Res, 24 (4), 349-269, 97; auth, Apology Research: Past, present, and a future-a case of Japan and the US, Ferris Studs, vol 33, 27-43, 98. **CONTACT ADDRESS** 3-6-8 Kugenuma-Kaigan, Fujisawa, Kanagawa, ., 251-0037. **EMAIL** naomi.@ city.fujisawa.kanagawa.jp

SUGNET, CHARLES JOSEPH
PERSONAL Born 06/20/1944, Port Huron, MI, 3 children **DISCIPLINE** ENGLISH & AMERICAN LITERATURE **EDUCATION** Boston Col, BA, 66; Univ Va, MA, 67, PhD(English), 70. **CAREER** Assoc prof, Univ Minn, 70- ; dir Program in Creative and Professional Writing, 86-89, 94; dir College in the Schools Literature Program, 84-94. **HONORS AND AWARDS** Loft Creative Nonfiction Award, 88; Bush Found grant, 90-91; Fulbright lectr and res fel, Senegal, 95-96; Morse-Alumni Award, 95; CLA Distinguished Teaching Award, 98. **MEMBERSHIPS** MLA; Midwest Mod Lang Asn. **RESEARCH** Postcolonial literature, especially fiction and film of the African diaspora; creative nonfiction writing; the contemporary novel; multi-cultural instruction in the high schools. **SELECTED PUBLICATIONS** Coauth, The Imagination on Trial: A Study of the Working Methods of Eleven Contemporary British and American Novelists, Schocken, 81; auth, Vile Bodies, Vile Places; Travel Writing and Neocolonialism in Granta, Transition, 91; auth, Nervous Conditions: Tsitsi Dangarembga's Feminist Reinvention of Fanon, in Nnaemeka, ed, Politics of Mothering: Epistemology, Ontology, and the Problematic of Womanhood in African Literature, Routledge, 96; **CONTACT ADDRESS** Dept of English, Univ of Minnesota, Minneapolis, MN, 55455-0156. **EMAIL** sugne001@tc.umn. edu

SUKENICK, RONALD
PERSONAL Born 07/14/1932, Brooklyn, NY, m **DISCIPLINE** ENGLISH & AMERICAN LIT **EDUCATION** Cornell Univ, BA, 55; Brandeis Univ, PhD, 62. **CAREER** Sarah Lawrence, Cornell Univ, Univ Cal, Irvine, Writer in Res; Univ Colorado, Boulder, Full Prof since, 75. **HONORS AND AWARDS** Guggenheim fel; Nat Endow Arts; Fulbright fel; Univ Colorado Faculty fel. **MEMBERSHIPS** Authors Guild; PEN; MLA; Nat Book Critics Circ. **RESEARCH** Contemp Am; writers theory; creative writing. **SELECTED PUBLICATIONS** Down & In; Doggy Bag; 98.6; Mosaic Man; Narralogues. **CONTACT ADDRESS** Univ Colorado, Dept Eng, Box 226, Boulder, CO, 80309.

SULLIVAN, CHARLES WILLIAM
PERSONAL Born 06/07/1944, Kingsport, TN, m, 1966, 2 children **DISCIPLINE** ENGLISH **EDUCATION** State Univ of NY at Albany, BA, 66, MA, 69; Univ of Ore, DA, 75; PhD, 76. **CAREER** Instr, State Univ of NY at Albany, 68-71; grad teaching asst, 72-76, instr, Univ of Ore, 76-77; **ASST PROF TO PROF, EAST CAROLINA UNIV**, 77-; visiting prof, Fife Folklore Conf, Utah State Univ, 94 & 95; visiting prof, Summer Inst in Children's Lit, Hollins Col, 94 & 97. **HONORS AND AWARDS** Centennial Award from the Am Folklore Soc, 89; full membership in the Welsh Acad, 95; membership in Phi Beta Delta, 97; Res Award from the Ambassador of Ireland, 98; Res Award, Col of Arts and Sci, East Carolina Univ, 97-98; Res Award, English Dept, East Carolina Univ, 96-97; **MEMBERSHIPS** Int Asn for the Fantastic in the Arts Round Table Member; Am Folklore Soc; Celtic Studies Asn of North Am; Children's Folklore Section; Children's Lit Asn; Int Asn for the Fantastic in the Arts; Irish Am Cultural Inst; MLA; North Carolina Folklore Soc, Ore Folklore Soc; Science Fiction Res Asn; South Atlantic MLA; Welsh Nat Centre for Children't Lit; Yr Academi Gymreig (The Welsh Acad). **RESEARCH** Mythology in literature; Welsh Celtic mythology and legend; the fantastic in literature. **SELECTED PUBLICATIONS** Ed, The Mabinogi: A Book of Essays, Garland, 96; ed, The Dark Fantastic: Selected Essays from the Ninth In Confr on the Fantastic in the Arts, Greenwood, 97; ed, Science Fiction for Young Readers, Greenwood, 93; refereed articles, Jumping the Broom: A Further Consideration of the Origins of an African American Wedding Custom, J of Am Folklore, 97; J.R.R. Tolkien and the Telling of a Traditional Narrative, J of the Fantastic in the Arts, 96; Cultural Worldview: Marginalizing the Fantastic in the Seventeenth Century, Para*doxa, 95; Children's Songs and Poems, Children's Folklore, Garland, 95; Place as Theme: Wales in Away, Away in China and A Roman Spring, An Open World: Essays on Leslie Norris, Camden House, 94. **CONTACT ADDRESS** English Dept, East Carolina Univ, Greenville, NC, 27858-4353. **EMAIL** sullivanc@mail.ecu.edu

SULLIVAN, DALE L.
PERSONAL Born 01/16/1951, Holyoke, CO, m, 1971, 4 children **DISCIPLINE** RHETORIC & COMMUNICATION **EDUCATION** Rensselaer Polytechnic Inst, PhD, 88. **CAREER** Teaching asst, Wichita State Univ, 77-79; asst prof, Kansas Tech Inst, 80-85; teaching asst, Rensselaer Polytechnic Inst, 85-87; dir of writing, Gordon Col, 87-88; asst prof of Rhetoric, Mich Tech Univ, 88-91; asst prof to assoc prof, Univ of Neb at Kearney, 91-94; assoc prof of English, Northern Ill Univ, 94-97; **ASSOC PROF OF RHETORIC & TECH COMMUN, MICH TECH UNIV**, 97-. **MEMBERSHIPS** Nat Commun Asn; Am Soc for the Hist of Rhetoric; Conf on Col Composition & Commun. **RESEARCH** Rhetoric of science; rhetoric of religion. **SELECTED PUBLICATIONS** Auth, Two-Year College Programs, Ed in Sci and Tech Commun: Acad Progs the Work, Soc for Tech Commun, 97; auth, Displaying Disciplinarity, Written Commun, 96; auth, Migrating Across Disciplinary Boundaries: The Case of David Raup's and John Sepkoski's Periodicity Paper, Social Epistemology, 95, Sci & Tech Commun, 97; auth, Galileo's Apparent Orthodoxy in The Letter to the Grand Duchess Christina, Rhetorica, 94; auth, Exclusionary Epideictic: NOVA's Narrative Excommunication of Fleischmann and Pons, Sci Tech & Human Values, 94; auth, A Closer Look at Education as Epideictic Rhetoric, Rhetoric Soc Quarterly, 93; auth, The Ethos of Epideictic Encounter, Philos and Rhetoric, 93; auth, The Epideictic Character of Rhetorical Criticism, Rhetoric Review, 93. **CONTACT ADDRESS** Humanities Dept, Michigan Tech Univ, Houghton, MI, 49931. **EMAIL** dsulliva@mtu.edu

SULLIVAN, MARY C.
PERSONAL Born 06/15/1931, Rochester, NY **DISCIPLINE** LITERATURE, RELIGION **EDUCATION** Nazareth Col Rochester, BA, 54; Univ Notre Dame, MA, 61, PhD(English), 64; Univ London, MTh, 88. **CAREER** Asst prof English, Catherine McAuley Col, 63-65, pres, 65-68; asst prof, Marymount Col, NY, 67-69; assoc prof lang & lit, 69-81, PROF LANG & LIT, ROCHESTER INST TECHNOL, 81-, dean col liberal arts, 77-87, chair, acad senate, 96-99; Consult & evaluator, Comn Higher Educ, Mid States Asn, 68-90. **MEMBERSHIPS** MLA; Mercy Higher Ed Colloquium **RESEARCH** Nineteenth and 20th century English and American literature; religion and literature; biography. **SELECTED PUBLICATIONS** Auth, The function of setting in Howells' The Landlord at Lion's Head, Am Lit, 63; Catherine of Dublin, Pageant, 65; Moby Dick, CXXIX: the cabin, Nineteenth Century Fiction, 65; Caroline Gordon: A Reference Guide, G K Hall, 77; Conrad's Paralipsis in the narration of Lord Jim, Conradiana, 78; Catherine McAuley and the Tradition of Mercy, Univ Notre Dame Press, 95; numerous articles in Jour Mercy Asn in Scripture & Theol (MAST). **CONTACT ADDRESS** Col of Lib Arts, Rochester Inst Technol, 1 Lomb Memorial Dr, Rochester, NY, 14623-5603. **EMAIL** mxsgsl@rit.edu

SULLIVAN, ROSEMARY
PERSONAL Montreal, PQ, Canada **DISCIPLINE** ENGLISH **EDUCATION** McGill Univ, BA, 68; Univ Conn, MA, 69; Univ Sussex, PhD, 72. **CAREER** Asst-associe, Univ Dijon, 72; asst associe, Univ Bordeaux, 73; asst prof, Univ Victoria, 74-77; asst prof, 77-80, assoc prof, 80-90, PROF, UNIV TORONTO, 90-. **HONORS AND AWARDS** Gerald Lampert Prize Poetry, League Can Poets, 86; Silver Medal Nat Mag Awards, 86; Guggenheim Fel, 92; Gov Gen Award Non-Fiction, 95; Can Authors Award Non-Fiction, 95; Medal Biog, Univ BC, 95. **MEMBERSHIPS** Writers' Union Can; Can PEN. **SELECTED PUBLICATIONS** Auth, The Garden Master: Style and Identity in the Poetry of Theodore Roethke, 75; auth, The Space A Name Makes, 86; auth, Blue Panic, 91; auth, By Heart: Elizabeth Smart/A Life, 91; auth, Shadow Maker: The Life of Gwendolyn MacEwen, 95. **CONTACT ADDRESS** Dept of English, Univ Toronto, Toronto, ON, M5S 1A1. **EMAIL** rsulliva@ credit.erin.utoronto.ca

SULLIVAN, SALLY A.
DISCIPLINE ENGLISH ROMANTICISM, NORTH CAROLINA LITERATURE, CREATIVE WRITING **EDUCATION** Univ NC, Greensboro, BA, MA, PhD. **CAREER** Assoc prof, Univ NC, Wilmington. **RESEARCH** English romanticism; North Carolina literature. **SELECTED PUBLICATIONS** Author of three books, the most recent two a composition text and a book of essays by fiction writers and poets on their writing. **CONTACT ADDRESS** Univ N. Carolina, Wilmington, Morton Hall, Wilmington, NC, 28403-3297. **EMAIL** sullivans@ uncwil.edu

SULLIVAN, SHEILA J.
PERSONAL Born 09/21/1952, Wells, MN, m, 1977, 2 children **DISCIPLINE** COMMUNICATION **EDUCATION** SUNY at Geneseo, BA (Comparative lit & English, magna cum laude), 75; SUNY at Buffalo, MA (Communication), 85, PhD (Commun), 90. **CAREER** Instr, Army Corps of Engineers, Buffalo, NY, June 86; instr, Fulbright Three-week Pre-Academic Orientation Prog, SUNY at Buffalo, summer 86; instr, Millard Fillmore Col at SUNY at Buffalo, 85-87, teaching asst, Dept of Commun, 83-87, co-dir, Com 101-Interpersonal Communication, 84-87; vis lect, Div of Humanities & Social Sciences, Penn State/Behrend Col, 88-89; asst prof of Commun, Dept of Com-

mun, MS State Univ, 89-90; lect, Dept of Commun, SUNY at Buffalo, 93; asst prof of Commun, Communication Studies, Canisius Col, 93-94; asst prof of Commun, Dept of Commun, MS State Univ, 96-. **HONORS AND AWARDS** Special Merit Assistantships at SUNY at Buffalo, 84-85, 85-86, & 86-87; Honorable Mention: Excellence in Teaching Award, SUNY at Buffalo, 86, 87. **RESEARCH** Communication theory; family relationships. **SELECTED PUBLICATIONS** Co-auth, with S J Sigman and M Wendell, Coversation Data Aquisition and Analysis in C Tardy, ed, Methods and Instruments of Communication Research: A Handbook for the Study of Human Interaction, Ablex, 87; auth, Why Do Women Do Such Womenly Things?: The Genre and Socio-Historical Analogs of Basket Parties, in Women's Studies in Communication, 91; Why Do Women Do Such Womenly Things?: The Genre and Socio-Historical Analogs of Home Parties, in S J Sigman, ed, Introduction to Communication: Behavior, Codes and Social Action, Ginn Press, 92; co-auth with W Leeds-Hurwitz and S J Sigman, Social Communication Theory: Communication Structures and Performed Innovations: A Revision of Scheflen's Notion of Programs, in S J Sigman, ed, The Consequentiality of Communication, A Volume in LEAS Communication Series, 95. **CONTACT ADDRESS** Dept of Communication, Mississippi State Univ, MS, 39762.

SULLIVAN, SHERRY A.
DISCIPLINE ENGLISH EDUCATION Univ Oregon, Ba, 68; Saskatchewan, MA, 71; Univ Toronto, PhD, 79. **CAREER** ASST PROF, ENG, UNIV ALA, BIRMINGHAM **MEMBERSHIPS** Am Antiquarian Soc **SELECTED PUBLICATIONS** Auth, "The Literary Debate over the Indians in the 19th Century," Am Indian Cult and Res Jour, 85; auth, "Indians in American Fiction: An Ethnohistorical Perspective, 1820-50," Clio, 86; auth, "The Indianization of Heroes and Heroines in 19th-Century American Fiction," JMMLA, 87. **CONTACT ADDRESS** 1459 Milner Crescent, Birmingham, AL, 35205.

SULLIVAN, WALTER L.
PERSONAL Born 01/04/1924, Nashville, TN, m, 1947, 3 children **DISCIPLINE** ENGLISH EDUCATION Vanderbilt Univ, BA, MFA, 49. **CAREER** From instr to assoc prof, 49-63, PROF ENGLISH, VANDERBILT UNIV, 63-, Ford Found fel, 51-52; Sewanee Rev fel, 55; lectr, WDCN-TV, Nashville, Tenn, 72-73. **HONORS AND AWARDS** O Henry Award, 80; founding member, Fellowship of Southern Writers, 87; elected alumni member, Phi Beta Kappa, 90; Literary achievement award from Southern Heritage Soc, 96; Vice Chancellor, Fel of Southern Writers, 97., LittD, Episcopal Theol Sem, Ky, 73. **MEMBERSHIPS** SAtlantic Mod Lang Asn; MLA. **RESEARCH** Fiction writing; contemporary British and American theological themes in modern literature. **SELECTED PUBLICATIONS** Auth, Sojourn of a Stranger, 57 & The Long, Long Love, 59, Henry Holt; Death by Melancoly, La State Univ, 72; A Requiem for the Renascence, Univ Ga, 76; ed, A Band of Prophets, La State Univ, 82; Writing from the Inside, W W Norton, 83; In Praise of Blood Sports, LSU Press, 90; A Time to Dance, LSU Press, 95; The War the Women Lived, J.S. Sanders & Co, 96. **CONTACT ADDRESS** Dept of English, Vanderbilt Univ, 2201 W End Ave, Nashville, TN, 37240-0001. **EMAIL** sullivwl@ctrvax.vanderbilt.edu

SULLIVAN, ZOHREH TAWAKULI
PERSONAL Born 12/18/1941, Tehran, Iran, m, 1969, 2 children **DISCIPLINE** ENGLISH LITERATURE **EDUCATION** Western Col, BA, 62; Univ IL, Urbana, MA & PhD, 71. **CAREER** Instr Eng lit, Webster Col, 69-70; prof, Damavand Col, Teheran, Iran, 70-72; assoc prof eng lit, Univ IL, Urbana-Champaign, 78. **HONORS AND AWARDS** Sch Hum Tchg Excellence Award, 78; Prog Study of Cult Values & Ethics Fel, 92-93; All Campus Luckman Award in Undergraduate Tchg, 84; Hum Award in Undergrad Tchg, 94. **MEMBERSHIPS** MLA. **RESEARCH** Mod novel; psychoanalytic criticism of fiction; the woman novelist in Engl. **SELECTED PUBLICATIONS** Auth, Narratives of Empire: the Fictions of Rudyard Kipling, Cambridge Univ Press, 93; Exiled Memories: Recovering Stories of Iranian Diaspora, forthcoming; numerous articles in Mod Fict Studies, Jour Narrative Techniques, Col English, Ariz Quart, Centennial Rev; Approaches to Teaching Achebe's Thnis Fall Apart, MLA, 91; Servants and Gender in Talat Abbasi's Fiction, Commonwealth and American Women's Discourse, Sterling, 96; Eluding the Feminist, Overthrowing the Modern: Transformations in 20th Century Iran, Remaking Women: Feminism and Modernity in the Middle-East, Princeton Univ Press, 98. **CONTACT ADDRESS** Dept of Eng, Univ of Illinois, 608 S Wright St, Urbana, IL, 61801-3613. **EMAIL** zsulliva@uiuc.edu

SULLOWAY, ALISON G.
PERSONAL Born 07/31/1917, New York, NY, w, 3 children **DISCIPLINE** ENGLISH EDUCATION Columbia Univ, MA, 58, PhD(English lit), 68. **CAREER** Lectr English, Columbia Univ, 58-59 & Barnard Col, 65-68; asst prof, Cedar Crest Col, 68-75, assoc prof, 72-75; **ASSOC PROF ENGLISH, VA POLYTECH INST & STATE UNIV**, 75-, sr fel, Nat Endowment for Humanites, 70-80. **HONORS AND AWARDS** Ansley Publ Award, Columbia Univ, 68. **MEMBERSHIPS** MLA; Int Hopkins Asn. **RE**-

SEARCH Hopkins' poetry; Jane Austen's novels; Victorian literature. **SELECTED PUBLICATIONS** Auth, Gerald Manley Hopkins and the Victorian Temper, Columbia Univ, 72 & Routledge & Kegan Paul, 72; St Ignatius Loyola and the Victorian Temper: Hopkins Windhover as diabolic gravity, Hopkins Quart, 74; Intimations of myth and tragedy in The Wreck of the Deutschland, Readings of The Wreck, Loyola Univ, 76; Emma Woodhouse and A Vindication of The Rights of Woman, Wordsworth Circle, 76; Hopkinsian biography and the grounds of our being: A study of representative biographical materials, priorities and techniques, Hopkins Quart, 77; Jane Austen--Real And Imaginary Worlds, Wordsworth Circle, Vol 25, 94; Jane Austen Sense And Sensibility, Wordsworth Circle, Vol 25, 94; Jane Austen Novels--The Art Of Clarity, Wordsworth Circle, Vol 25, 94. **CONTACT ADDRESS** Dept of English, Va Polytech Inst & State Univ, Blacksburg, VA, 24061.

SUMMERS, CLAUDE JOSEPH
PERSONAL Born 12/06/1944, Galvez, LA **DISCIPLINE** ENGLISH LITERATURE **EDUCATION** La State Univ, BA, 66; Univ Chicago, MA, 67, PhD, 70. **CAREER** From Asst Prof to Prof Eng, 70-89, William E. Stirton Professor in the Hum, Unic MI-Dearborn 89; Assoc ed, Seventeenth Century News, 73. **HONORS AND AWARDS** Crompton-Noll Award, 82; Fac Res Award, 86; Outstanding Acad Bk Award for "Gay Fictions...", Choice, 91-92; Donne Soc Publ Award, 92; Distinguished Tchg Award, 95; Lambda Literary Award, 96; Distinguished Fac Award, MI Asn Governing Bds, 97. **MEMBERSHIPS** MLA; Milton Soc Am; Renaissance Soc Am; John Donne Soc. **RESEARCH** Seventeenth century poetry; Renaissance drama; mod lit; gay studies. **SELECTED PUBLICATIONS** Auth, Gay Fictions / Wilde to Stonewall: Studies in a Male Homosexual Literary Tradition, Continuum, 90; E.M. Foster: A Guide to Research, Garland, 91; co-ed, On the Celebrated and Neglected Poems of Andrew Marvell, Univ Mo Press, 92; ed, Homosexuality in Renaissance and Enlightenment England: Literary Representations in Historical Context, special double issue of J Homosexuality, Haworth Press, 92; co-ed, Renaissance Discourses of Desire, Univ Mo Press, 93; The Wit of Seventeenth-Century Poetry, Univ Mo Press, 95; Selected Poems of Ben Jonson, Pegasus Books, Medieval and Renaissance Texts and Studies, 95; ed, The Gay and Lesbian Literary Heritage: A Companion to the Writers and Their Works from Antiquity to the Present, Henry Holt, 95; co-ed, Representing Women in Renaissance England, Univ MO Press, 97; author and editor of numerous other publ. **CONTACT ADDRESS** Dept of Hum, Univ of MI, 4901 Evergreen Rd, Dearborn, MI, 48128-1491. **EMAIL** csummers@umich.edu

SUPER, ROBERT HENRY
PERSONAL Born 06/13/1914, Wilkes-Barre, PA, m, 1953, 2 children **DISCIPLINE** ENGLISH LITERATURE **EDUCATION** Princeton Univ, AB, 35, PhD, 41; Oxford Univ, BLitt, 37. **CAREER** Instr English, Princeton Univ, 38-42; asst prof, Mich State Norm Col, 42-47; lectr, 47, from asst prof to assoc prof, 47-60, PROF ENGLISH, UNIV MICH, ANN ARBOR, 60-, Fulbright res grant, UK, 49-50; Am Coun Learned Socs fel, 59-60; Guggenheim fels, 62-63 & 70-71; vis prof, Rice Univ, 65-66; Nat Endowment for Humanities fel, 78-79. **MEMBERSHIPS** MLA **RESEARCH** English literature of the 19th century; Matthew Arnold; Anthony Trollope. **SELECTED PUBLICATIONS** Auth, Publication of Landor's Works, Bibliog Soc, London, 54; Walter Savage Landor: A Biography, NY Univ, 54; ed, Matthew Arnold's Complete Prose Works, 11 vols, 60-77, auth, The Time-Spirit of Matthew Arnold, 70, Trollope in the Post Office, 81 & ed, Anthony Trollope's Marion Fay, 82, Univ Mich; Truth And Fiction In Trollope Autobiography, Nineteenth-Century Lit, Vol 48, 93. **CONTACT ADDRESS** 1221 Baldwin Ave, Ann Arbor, MI, 48104.

SURRIDGE, LISA A.
DISCIPLINE ENGLISH LITERATURE **EDUCATION** Queen's Univ, BA, 86; Univ Toronto, MA, 87, PhD, 92. **CAREER** Asst prof **RESEARCH** Victorian fiction; sensation fiction; domestic violence in 19th century literature; 19th century women novelists. **SELECTED PUBLICATIONS** Auth, Dogs' /Bodies, Women's Bodies: Wives as Pets in Mid-Nineteenth-Century Narratives of Domestic Violence, Victorian Rev 20, 94; Representing the Latent Vashti: Theatricality in Charlotte Bronte's Villette, Victorian Newsletter 87, 95; Madame de Stael Meets Mrs Ellis: Geraldine Jewsbury's The Half Sisters, Carlyle Stud Annual 15, 95; Unspeakable Histories: Hester Dethridge and the Narration of Domestic Violence in Man and Wife, Victorian Rev 22, 96; Braddon, Mary Elizabeth, Aurora Floyd, Broadview Press, 98; Domestic Violence, Female Self-Mutilation, and the Healing of the Male in Dombey and Son, Victorians Inst Jour 25, 97. **CONTACT ADDRESS** Dept of English, Victoria Univ, PO Box 3070, Victoria, BC, V8W 3W1. **EMAIL** lsurridg@uvic.ca

SUSSMAN, HERBERT
PERSONAL Born 01/20/1937, New York, NY, m, 1960, 2 children **DISCIPLINE** ENGLISH **EDUCATION** Princeton Univ, BA, 58; Harvard Univ, MA, 59, PhD, 63. **CAREER** Asst prof English, Univ Berkeley, 63-71; assoc prof, 71-80, PROF ENGLISH, NORTHEASTERN UNIV, 80-. **RESEARCH** Victorian literature. **SELECTED PUBLICATIONS** Auth, Victorians and the Machine, Harvard Univ, 68; Fact into Figure, Ohio State, 81. **CONTACT ADDRESS** Dept of English, Northeastern Univ, 360 Huntington Ave, Boston, MA, 02115-5000.

SUTHERLAND, WILLIAM OWEN SHEPPARD
PERSONAL Born 01/19/1921, Wilmington, NC, m, 1947, 4 children **DISCIPLINE** ENGLISH LITERATURE **EDUCATION** Univ NC, AB, 42, AM, 47, PhD, 50. **CAREER** Part-time instr English, Univ NC, 46-50, instr, 50-51; instr, Northwestern Univ, 51-54; from asst prof to assoc prof, 54-65; prof English, Univ Tx, Austin, 65-, assoc Dean of the Graduate School, 70-73; dir Program in Humanities, 80-83; chair of the Dept of English, 83-89; R.A. Law and Thos. L.Law Centennial Professor of Humanities, 86-; consultant to Office of Education, 62-72; member then chair College Board AP Committee, 65-68; consultant to Educational Testing Service; consultant and panel member NEH; served on executive committee and other committees of NCTE, CCCC, SCMLA. **HONORS AND AWARDS** Scarborough Excellence in Teaching Award, 59; President's Associates Award for Excellence in Teaching, 82; Liberal Arts Pro Bene Meritis Award, 96. **MEMBERSHIPS** MLA; SCent Mod Lang Asn; NCTE; Conf Col Compos & Commun. **RESEARCH** Elizabethan drama; 18th century English literature, especially periodicals and drama; 18th century novel; website history of ghost town Buena Vista, MN, wwwv-ms.utexas.edu/üwos/index.html. **SELECTED PUBLICATIONS** Auth, Popular imagery in The Medal, Univ Tex Studies English, 56; Essay forms in Aaron Hill's Prompter, In: Studies in the Early English Periodical, Univ NC, 57; Art of the Satirist, Univ Tex, 65. **CONTACT ADDRESS** Dept of English, Univ of Tex, Univ of Texas, Austin, TX, 78712-1026. **EMAIL** woss@utxvms.cc.utexas.edu

SUTTON, MAX KEITH
PERSONAL Born 06/03/1937, Huntsville, AK, m, 1960, 3 children **DISCIPLINE** ENGLISH **EDUCATION** Univ AR, BA, 59; Duke Univ, MA, 60, PhD, 64. **CAREER** From asst prof to assoc prof, 64-76, prof eng, Univ KS, 76. **RESEARCH** Victorian literature; R D Blackmore; William Barnes; T E Brown, sabine Baring-Gould. **SELECTED PUBLICATIONS** Auth, Inverse sublimity in Victorian humor, Victorian Studies, 12/66; The mythic appeal of Lorna Doone, Nineteenth-Century Fiction, 74; W S Gilbert, G K Hall, 75; Blackmore's letters to Blackwood, English Lit in Transition, 77; R D Blackmore, G K Hall, 79; Truth and the pastor's vision, In: Survivals of Pastoral, Lawrence, 79; The Drama of StoryTelling, in T E Browns, Max Yarms, univ DE Press, 91. **CONTACT ADDRESS** Dept of Eng, Univ of Kansas, Lawrence, KS, 66045-0001. **EMAIL** msutton@eagle.cc.ukans.edu

SUTTON, SHARYN
DISCIPLINE PUBLIC RELATIONS **EDUCATION** Univ Toledo, BS; Univ Md, MS, PhD. **CAREER** Asst prof, Am Univ. **HONORS AND AWARDS** Golden Screen Award, Blue Pencil Award, Communication Excellence for Black Audiences award., Dir, nutrition, mkt & educ, U.S. Dept Agriculture; branch chief, Infor proj , Natl Inst Health. **SELECTED PUBLICATIONS** Auth, Strategic Questions forConsumer Based Health Communications. **CONTACT ADDRESS** American Univ, 4400 Massachusetts Ave, Washington, DC, 20016.

SUZUKI, MIHOKO
PERSONAL Born 12/16/1953, Kobe, Japan, m, 1990 **DISCIPLINE** ENGLISH **EDUCATION** Cornell Univ, AB, 75; Yale Univ, M Phil, 78, PhD, 82. **CAREER** Vis asst prof, 83-89, Dartmouth Col; asst prof, 92-94 assoc prof, 89,, Univ Miami. **RESEARCH** Renaissance lit and culture women's studies. **CONTACT ADDRESS** Dept of English, Univ of Miami, Coral Gables, FL, 33124. **EMAIL** msuzuki@miami.edu

SWAIM, KATHLEEN MACKENZIE
PERSONAL Born 01/23/1936, Carlisle, PA **DISCIPLINE** ENGLISH **EDUCATION** Gettysburg Col, BA, 57; Pa State Univ, MA, 58; Middlebury Col, MA, 63; Univ Pa, PhD(English), 66. **CAREER** Instr, Dickinson Col, 58-60; from instr to asst prof, Univ Pa, 64-67; from asst prof to assoc prof, 67-76, actg assoc head dept English, 73, dir grad studies English, 76-78, PROF ENGLISH, UNIV MASS, AMHERST, 76-, Vis prof, Brown Univ, 78; managing ed, Lit Renaissance, 78-79. **MEMBERSHIPS** MLA; NCTE; Milton Soc Am. **RESEARCH** Milton; Swift; allegory. **SELECTED PUBLICATIONS** Coauth, A Concordance to Milton's English Poetry, Clarendon, Oxford, 72; auth, A Reading of Gulliver's Travels, Mouton, The Hague, 72; The art of the maze in Book IX of Paradise Lost, Studies English Lit, 72; Lycidas and the Dolphins of Apollo, J English & Ger Philol, 73; Cycle and circle: Time and structure in L'Allegro and Il Penseroso, Tex Studies Lang & Lit, 76; Structural Parallelism in Paradise Lost, Milton Studies, 77; Hercules, Anaaeus, and Prometheus: A study of the climactic epic similes in Paradise Regained, Studies English Lit, 78; Allegorical Poetry in Milton's Ludlow Mark, Milton Studies, Vol XVI, 83; The Tudor And Stuart Monarchs And Monarchical Transition In The English Renaissance--Preface, English Literary Renaissance, Vol 26, 96. **CONTACT ADDRESS** Dept of English, Univ of Mass, Amherst, MA, 01002.

SWAN, WALLACE JOHN
PERSONAL Born 06/07/1938, Brooklyn, NY, m, 1991, 3 children **DISCIPLINE** ENGLISH **EDUCATION** Univ FL, AB, 63, PhD(English), 67. **CAREER** Asst prof, 67-68, assoc prof to PROF EMERITUS, Murray State Univ, 68-97, RETIRED. **HONORS AND AWARDS** Phi Beta Kappa; Phi Kappa Phi. **RESEARCH** Old English; Middle English literature; historical linguistics. **EMAIL** wjswan@ldd.net

SWANN, BRIAN
PERSONAL Born 08/13/1940, Wallsend **DISCIPLINE** ENGLISH **EDUCATION** Queens Col, BA, 62; Cambridge Univ, MA, 64; Princeton Univ, PhD(English), 70. **CAREER** Instr English, Princeton Univ, 65-66 & Rutgers Univ, 66-67; asst prof, Princeton Univ, 70-72; asst prof, 72-75, assoc prof, 75-80, PROF ENGLISH, COOPER UNION, 80-, Nat Endowment for Arts creative writing fel, 78. **HONORS AND AWARDS** John Florio Prize, 77. **MEMBERSHIPS** MLA; Asn Study Am Indian Lit. **RESEARCH** Nineteenth century English novel; modern-contemporary, British-American poetry; 20th century Italian poetry. **SELECTED PUBLICATIONS** Auth, Middlemarch: Realism and symbolic form, J English Lit Hist, 6/72; co-ed & co-transl, The Collected Poems of Lucio Piccolo, Princeton Univ, 73; The Mill on the Floss and tragedy, English Miscellany, spring 74; Daniel Deronda: Jewishness, Ecumenicism and the novel, Novel, spring 74; co-ed & co-transl, Selected Poetry of Andrea Zanzotto, 75 & Selected Poems of Tudor Arghezi, 76, Princeton Univ; ed, Smoothing the Ground: Essays on Native American Oral Literature, Am Indian Studies Ctr, Univ Calif, Los Angeles, 82; The Myth Of The Cave, Col English, Vol 57, 95; This House, Shenandoah, Vol 44, 94; The Method Of Liberation, Col English, Vol 57, 95; Stars Stars Stars, Col English, Vol 57, 95; Desert Sky, Sewanee Rev, Vol 105, 97; The Garden, Sewanee Rev, Vol 105, 97; The Lost Boy, Partisan Rev, Vol 64, 97; Ordinary, North Amn Rev, Vol 282, 97. **CONTACT ADDRESS** Dept of Humanities, Cooper Union for the Advancement of Science and Art, 41 Cooper Square, New York, NY, 10003-7136.

SWANSON, DONALD ROLAND
PERSONAL Born 11/20/1927, Pittsburgh, PA, m **DISCIPLINE** ENGLISH **EDUCATION** Washington & Jefferson Col, BA, 53, Univ CT, MA, 55; Rutgers Univ, PhD, 65. **CAREER** From instr to assoc prof, Upsala Col, 55-71; prof eng, Wright State Univ, 71-98, Coordr, Orange Opportunity Corp, 66; Upsala Col fac res fel, 69; dir, Col Eng Asn, 74-77; ed, Univ Monogr, 77-82; dir, grad studies in Eng, 92-98; prof Emeritus, 98. **MEMBERSHIPS** MLA; Eng Inst; Col Eng Asn (treas, 71-73). **RESEARCH** Mod Brit lit. **SELECTED PUBLICATIONS** Auth, Three Conquerers, Mouton, 69; Far and fair within: a walk to Wachusett, ESQ, 3rd quarter 69; The exercise of irony in Benito Cereno, Am Transcendental Quart, summer 70; The growth of a poem: Coleridge's Dejection, BSU Forum, fall 71; The uses of tradition: King Arthur in the Modern World, CEA Critic, 3/74; The observer observed: Notes on the narrator of Under Western Eyes, Renaissance & Mod, 76; The Transmutations of To One in Paradise, CEA Forum, 7/76; W.S Gilbert and Evelyn Waugh in Encyclopedia of British Humorists, NY Garland pub, 96; D.H Lawrence in British Travel Writers, 1910-1939, Detroit, Glae Research, 98. **CONTACT ADDRESS** 1550 Benson Dr, Dayton, OH, 45406-4514.

SWARDSON, HAROLD ROLAND
PERSONAL Born 09/16/1925, Chicago, IL, m, 1949, 3 children **DISCIPLINE** ENGLISH **EDUCATION** Tulane Univ, BA, 47, MA, 48; Univ Minn, PhD, 56. **CAREER** Instr English, Univ Cincinnati, 48-49; from instr to assoc prof, 54-69, PROF ENGLISH, OHIO UNIV, 69- **RESEARCH** Literary criticism; seventeenth century literature; philosophy. **SELECTED PUBLICATIONS** Auth, Poetry and the Fountain of Light, Allen & Unwin, London, 62; On the poetical, Ohio Univ Rev, 65; Sentimentality and the academic tradition, Col English, 4/76; The heritage of the New Criticism, Col English, 12/79; College teaching: The worst possible case, Philos Forum, summer 81; Teachers And Philosophers, Col English, Vol 56, 94; The Accessibility Of Derrida, PMLA-Publications of the MLA Of Am, Vol 108, 93. **CONTACT ADDRESS** 50 Sunnyside Dr, Athens, OH, 45701.

SWEENEY, MICHAEL S.
PERSONAL m, 1 child **DISCIPLINE** COMMUNICATION STUDIES **EDUCATION** Univ Nebr, BA, 80; Univ N Tex, MJ, 91; Univ Ohio, 96. **CAREER** Asst prof. **HONORS AND AWARDS** Pulitzer Prize, 86. **MEMBERSHIPS** Nebr Press Asn; Asn Edu Jour and Mass Commun. **RESEARCH** News writing; public affairs reporting and copy editing; mass media history. **SELECTED PUBLICATIONS** Auth, The Sound Historian; pubs on Ernie Pyle's most famous column, and death of Capt. Henry T. Waskow in World War II. **CONTACT ADDRESS** Dept of Communication, Utah State Univ, 3580 S Highway 91, Logan, UT, 84321. **EMAIL** msweeney@wpo.hass.usu.edu

SWEET, NAN
DISCIPLINE BRITISH ROMANTICISM **EDUCATION** Univ Mich, AB; Univ Mo, MA; Univ Mich, PhD, 93. **CAREER** Instr, Univ Mo, Columbia, 66-68; instr, Webster Groves

High Sch, St Louis, 76-81; sr lectr, Univ Mo, St Louis, 81-. **HONORS AND AWARDS** Jinx Walker Prize, Acad of Am Poets & Wash Univ, 81; Crse develop grant, Univ Mo-St Louis, 86; Rackham non-traditional fel, Univ Mich, 87-88; Rackham predoctoral fel, Univ Mich, 91-92; Heberle Award, Dissertation 2nd Prize, Univ Mich; Lectr of Yr, Col of Arts and Sci, Univ Mo, Columbia. **MEMBERSHIPS** MLA; Nat Women's Stud Asn; North Am Soc for Stud of Romanticism; Col Eng Asn; Midwest MLA; Byron Soc; Keats-Shelley Asn. **RESEARCH** British history and culture. **SELECTED PUBLICATIONS** Auth, Classics for Ninth Graders: Solace and Status, Eng J 72.3, Mar 83; Thirty-One Ways to Avoid Book Reports, Eng J 73.4. Apr 84; History, Imperialism, and the Aesthetics of the Beautiful:Hemans and the Post-Napoleonic Moment, in At the Limits of Romanticism: Essays in Cultural, Feminist, and Materialist Criticism, eds, Mary A Favret and Nicola J Watson, Ind UP, 93. **CONTACT ADDRESS** Univ Mo, St Louis, St Louis, MO, 63121. **EMAIL** snlswee@umslvma.umsl.edu

SWEETSER, WESLEY DUAINE
PERSONAL Born 05/25/1919, National City, CA, m, 1942, 4 children **DISCIPLINE** ENGLISH **EDUCATION** Univ Colo, BA, 38, MA, 46, PhD(English lit), 58. **CAREER** Instr English, Univ Colo, 45-48; asst prof, Peru State Teachers Col, 48-50; assoc prof, US Air Force Acad, 58-63; asst prof air sci, Univ Nebr, 63-66; vis prof English, Nebr Wesleyan Univ, 66-67; assoc prof, State Univ NY Col Oswego, 67-69, prof, 69-82; RES & WRITING, 82- **MEMBERSHIPS** MLA; Arthur Machen Soc. **RESEARCH** Arthur Machen; Ralph Hodgson; colonial backgrounds in 19th century British literature (Australasia). **SELECTED PUBLICATIONS** Auth, Machen: A biographical study, Aylesford Rev, winter 59-60; Arthur Machen: Surface realities or essence of spirit, ELT, 64; Arthur Machen, Twayne, 64; coauth, A Bibiography of Arthur Machen, Univ Tex, 65; auth, Arthur Machen: A bibliography of writings about him, English Lit in Transition, 68; contribr, Thomas Hardy: An Annotated Biliography of Writings About Him, Northern Ill Univ, 73; Ralph Hodgson: A Bibliography, privately publ, 74 & rev & annotated, Garland, 80. **CONTACT ADDRESS** 52 Ridgeway Sites Ave, Oswego, NY, 13126-6520.

SWERDLOW, DAVID G.
DISCIPLINE ENGLISH **EDUCATION** Ohio Univ, PhD **CAREER** Assoc prof. **HONORS AND AWARDS** Fel, Pa Coun Arts, 96., Fulbright prof, Am Lit in Peru; fel, Va Ctr for the Creative Arts; Penn coun for the arts fel, poetry. **SELECTED PUBLICATIONS** Auth, The Last Hill and the Wild Trees, Ohio Rev; Self and Duende, Am Letters and Commentary. **CONTACT ADDRESS** Dept of Eng, Westminister Col, New Wilmington, PA, 16172-0001.

SWETNAM, FORD
DISCIPLINE ENGLISH LITERATURE **EDUCATION** Cornell Univ, PhD, 67. **CAREER** Prof. **SELECTED PUBLICATIONS** Auth, Another Tough Hop and 301; co-ed, High Sky Over All: Idaho Fiction at the Centennial. **CONTACT ADDRESS** Dept of English and Philosophy, Idaho State Univ, Pocatello, ID, 83209. **EMAIL** swetford@isu.edu

SWETNAM, SUSAN
DISCIPLINE ENGLISH LITERATURE **EDUCATION** Univ Mich, PhD, 79. **CAREER** Prof. **SELECTED PUBLICATIONS** Auth, Lives of the Saints in Southeast Idaho: An Introduction to Mormon Pioneer Life Story Writing; pubs in Tough Paradise, Idaho and the American West, Journal of the West, Frontiers: A Journal of Women Studies, and Northwest Folklore. **CONTACT ADDRESS** Dept of English and Philosophy, Idaho State Univ, Pocatello, ID, 83209. **EMAIL** swetsusa@isu.edu

SWIFT, CAROLYN RUTH
PERSONAL Born 11/10/1928, East Orange, NJ, 2 children **DISCIPLINE** DRAMA, RENAISSANCE & REFORMATION **EDUCATION** Univ Chicago, PbB, 48; Columbia Univ, MA, 50; Brown Univ, PhD(English), 73. **CAREER** Teacher English, Rosemary Hall, 50-52; teacher English & hist, Prospect Hill Sch, 52-53; teacher English, Joseph Case High Sch, 53-54 & Cranston High Sch, 54-56; from instr to asst prof, 65-73, ASSOC PROF ENGLISH, RI COL, 73-, Fac res grants, RI Col, 74-80; Nat Endow for Humanites summer stipend, 81. **MEMBERSHIPS** MLA; Northeast Mod Lang Asn; Women's Caucus Mod Lang; Shakespeare Asn. **RESEARCH** Shakespeare; John Lyly; intellectual history. **SELECTED PUBLICATIONS** Auth, The Shakespearean Wild, Geography, Genus, and Gender, Shakespeare Quart, Vol 44, 93. **CONTACT ADDRESS** Rhode Island Col, 50 Armstrong Ave, Providence, RI, 02903.

SWINGLE, LARRY J.
PERSONAL Born 08/24/1940, Columbus, OH, m, 1962 **DISCIPLINE** ENGLISH **EDUCATION** Ohio State Univ, BA, 62; Univ Wis, MA, 63, PhD(English), 67. **CAREER** Asst prof English Univ Wash, 66-73; asst prof, 73-76, ASSOC PROF ENGLISH, UNIV KY, 76- **MEMBERSHIPS** MLA **RESEARCH** Nineteenth century English literature. **SELECTED PUBLICATIONS** Auth, The 'Lucy Poems'--A Case-Study in Literary Knowledge, Wordsworth Circle, Vol 27, 96; Keats, Narrative and Audience--The Posthumous Life of Writing, J English Germanic Philol, Vol 94, 95; Ecological Literary-Criticism, Romantic Imagining and the Biology of Mind, Wordsworth Circle, Vol 26, 95; The Oxford Pamphlets, Leaflets, and Circulars of Lutwidge Charles Dodgson, ANQ, Vol 7, 94; Romanticism and Trollope,Anthony--Reply To George Levine (rev), Wordsworth Circle, Vol 23, 92. **CONTACT ADDRESS** Dept of English, Univ of Ky, Lexington, KY.

SWINSON, WARD
DISCIPLINE ENGLISH LITERATURE **EDUCATION** Northwestern Univ, BA; Univ Ill, MA, PhD. **CAREER** Assoc prof. **RESEARCH** 20th century American literature. **SELECTED PUBLICATIONS** Auth, pubs on James Joyce, coauth, monograph on Ezra Pound's China Adams Cantos. **CONTACT ADDRESS** Dept of English, Colorado State Univ, Fort Collins, CO, 80523. **EMAIL** wswinson@vines.colostate.edu

SWIONTKOWSKI, GALE
DISCIPLINE MODERN ANGLO-IRISH LITERATURE **EDUCATION** Univ Bryn Mawr, PhD. **CAREER** Assoc prof, Fordham Univ. **RESEARCH** Psychological and feminist approaches to lit, mod and contemp poetry. **SELECTED PUBLICATIONS** Auth, The Psychic Struggle of the Narrative Ego in the Conclusion of Troylus and Creseyde, Philol Quart 72, 93; Rondo to Jazz: the Poetry of Michael O'Siadhail, Eire-Ireland 29, 94. **CONTACT ADDRESS** Dept of Eng Lang and Lit, Fordham Univ, 113 W 60th St, New York, NY, 10023.

SWITZER, LES
PERSONAL m, 5 children **DISCIPLINE** COMMUNICATION **EDUCATION** Univ CA, Berkeley, BA, MA, 59; Univ Natal (Pietermaritzburg, South Africa), PhD, 72. **CAREER** Dept of Journalism & Broadcasting, CA State Univ, Los Angeles, 71-73, chair, 72-73; Dept of Journalism & Media Studies, Rhodes Univ, Grahamstown, South Africa, 73-82, chair, 79-82; SCHOOL OF COMMUNICATION, UNIV HOUSTON, 83-, assoc dir, Telecommunications Res Inst, 85-86, dir grad studies, 92-93, head of Journalism Prog, 93-97; Herald Examiner, Los Angeles, 68-72; Natal Witness and World, Pietermaritzburg and Johannesburg, South Africa, 64-68; freelance journalist for British publications (London), 68, 81. **HONORS AND AWARDS** More than 30 individual grants and awards from Britain, South Africa and the United States for teaching and research activities. These include the NEH, Am Philos Soc, Am Coun of Learned Socs, South African Human Sciences Res Coun, and British Coun. Recipient of a Fulbright Senior Scholar Award and a Distinguished Faculty Recognition Award from the Houston City Council., Joint appointments with Communication and the African Am Studies Prog, 83-86, and Communication and Hist, 86-91, Univ Houston. Co-founder and codirector, Center for Critical Cultural Studies, Univ Houston, 90-96. Am Press Inst, 96 (Journalism Educators Seminar). **MEMBERSHIPS** African Studies Asn; Asn for Journalism and Mass Communication. **RESEARCH** Journalism and media studies, development studies, cultural studies, southern African studies. **SELECTED PUBLICATIONS** Auth, The Black Press in South Africa and Lesotho: A Descriptive Bibliographic Guide 1836-1976, 79; Media and Dependency in South Africa, 85, 87; Power and Resistance in an African Society: The Ciskei Xhosa and the Making of South Africa, 93; South Africa's Alternative Press: Voices of Protest and Resistance, 1880-1960, 97; two other books or monographs, 22 book chapters, articles and essays in scholarly journals, and an edited conference proceeding. **CONTACT ADDRESS** School of Communication, Univ of Houston, Houston, TX, 77204-3786. **EMAIL** lswitzer@uh.edu

SYLVESTRE, JEAN-GUY
PERSONAL Born 05/17/1918, Sorel, PQ, Canada **DISCIPLINE** LITERATURE **EDUCATION** Univ Ottawa, BA, 39, LPh, 40, MA, 41. **CAREER** Bk reviewer, Le Droit, Ottawa, 39-48; Wartime Info Bd, 44-45; Pvt secy Louis St. Laurent, 45-50; assoc librn, Libr Parliament, 56-68; Nat Librn Can, 68-83; pres, Can Inst Hist Microrepros, 83-86. **HONORS AND AWARDS** Fel, Royal Soc Can; DLS(hon), Univ Ottawa; DLitt(hon), Mt Allison Univ; LLD(hon), Univ Toronto; LLD(hon) Univ PEI; LLD(hon) Memorial Univ Nfld; LLD(hon) Concordia Univ; off, Order Can; comdr, Ordre internat du Bien public; Ordre du merite de Pologne; IFLA Medal; Outstanding Public Serv Award. **MEMBERSHIPS** Can Libr Asn; Asn Sci Tech Doc; Ont Libr Asn; Can Asn Info Sci; past comt chmn, Gov Gen Lit Awards; past chmn, Can Writers Found; Academie Canadienne-francaise, 65-92; pres, World Poetry Conf, 67. **RESEARCH** Canadian literature/poetry **SELECTED PUBLICATIONS** Auth, Louis Francoeur, journaliste, 41; auth, Situation de la poesie canadienne, 42; auth, Anthologie de la poesie d'expression francaise, 43; auth, Poetes catholiques de la France contemporaine, 44; auth, Jules Laforge, 45; auth, Sondages, 45; Impressions de theatre, 50; auth, Panorama des lettres canadiennes francaises, 64; auth, Canadian Writers/Ecrivains canadiens, 64; auth, Un siecle de litterature canadienne, 67; auth, Guidelines for national libraries, 87. **CONTACT ADDRESS** 2286 Bowman Rd, Ottawa, ON, K1H 6V6.

SYLVIE, GEORGE
PERSONAL Born 02/24/1954, Shreveport, LA, m, 1985, 2 children **DISCIPLINE** JOURNALISM **EDUCATION** La St Univ, BA, 76; Univ Missouri-Columbia, MA, 78; Univ Texas, PhD, 88. **CAREER** Assoc prof, Univ Tx, 92-; asst prof, Kent State Univ, 90-92; asst prof, La State Univ Shreveport, 87-90; Soc Sci Res assoc, Univ Tx, 87; Tchg asst & asst instr, Univ Tx, 84-86 **HONORS AND AWARDS** Outstanding Service Award, Assoc for Educ in Journalism & Mass Communication, 97; Who's Who in Amer Educ, 92-93; Who's Who in Amer, 91; La St Univ, Shreveport Jour Fac Grant, 88-90; Univ Tx Fel, 83-85, 86-87; Ntl School Board Assoc Certificate of Merit, 81; News Media Award, La Assoc of Educ, 79, 80. **RESEARCH** Technology and the Future **SELECTED PUBLICATIONS** Coauth, Real-Time Journalism: Instantaneous Change for Newswriting, Newspaper Res Jour, 96; auth, Departmental Influences on Interdepartmental Cooperation in Daily Newspapers, Journalism and Mass Communication Quarterly, 96; coauth, Pagination Impact on Newspaper Design, Southwestern Mass Communication Jourl, 96. **CONTACT ADDRESS** Dept of Journalism, Austin, TX, 78712. **EMAIL** g.sylvie@mail.utexas.edu

SYPHER, FRANCIS JACQUES
PERSONAL Born 11/04/1941, Hackensack, NJ, d, 1 child **DISCIPLINE** ENGLISH, COMPARATIVE LITERATURE **EDUCATION** Columbia Univ, AB, 63, MA, 64, PhD, 68. **CAREER** Precep, Eng, 65-68, Columbia Univ; asst prof, Eng, 68-75, SUNY, Albany; ed consul, 75-81, R.R. Bowker, NYU Press, & other publ; Fulbright Sr lectr, Amer lit, 81-83, Univ du Benin, W Africa; asst to pres, 83-85, NY Schl of Inter Design, concurrent, adj prof, Eng, NY Univ; dir, 85-86, Amer Eng Lang Prog, Amer Cult Ctr, US Info Svc, Dakar Senegal, W Africa; Fulbright Sr Lectr, 86-88, Amer Lit, Univ Omar Bongo, Libreville Gabon C Africa; writer, ed consul, 88-, NY. **HONORS AND AWARDS** NY St Regents Fel, 63-65; SUNY Res Found Award, 74; Fulbright Sr Lectr, 81-83, 86-88; Pres Bronze Medal, 93, St Nicholas Soc NY. **MEMBERSHIPS** Art Stud League of NY; NY Genealogical and Biographical Soc; Friends of the Columbia Univ Lib. **RESEARCH** English & comparative lit; life and works of Letitia Elizabeth Landon, 1802-1838; NY history & biography. **SELECTED PUBLICATIONS** Auth, Ethel Churchill, 92; auth, Critical Writings, 96; auth, The Vow of the Peacock, 97; auth, Romance and Reality, 98; coauth, ed, The Saint Nicholas Society, A 150 Year Record, 93; ed & trans, The Iskenius Letters from Germany to New York 1726-1737, 94; ed, The Image of Irelande, Derricke, 98; art, Victorian Poetry; art, Harvard Lib Bull; art, Quart Jour of the Lib of Cong; art, NY Genealogical & Biographical Record; art, Proceedings of Amer Antiquarian Soc; art, Annales de l'Universite du Benin, Colloque sur les Etudes Americaines 5-8, avril 83, Univ de Dakar; art, New Orleans Rev; art, NY History; art, Columbia Lib Col; art, Annals of Scholar; art, Connotations; art, Furn Hist; art, Trinity per Saecula; art, Review; art, Amer Natl Biography. **CONTACT ADDRESS** FDR Station, PO Box 1125, New York, NY, 10150-1125.

SZANTO, GEORGE
DISCIPLINE COMMUNICATION STUDIES **EDUCATION** Darmouth Col, BA; Harvard Univ, PhD. **CAREER** Prof. **RESEARCH** Cultural studies; artefactual analysis; Marxist cultural theory; propaganda theory; popular culture and intertextuality; Latin American culture; urbanization in Canada and America; Canadian cultural institutions; narratology; dramaturgy. **SELECTED PUBLICATIONS** Auth, Inside the Statues of Saints, 96; auth, Friends & Marriages, 94; auth, The Underside of Stones, Harper and Row, 90; auth, Narrative Taste and Social Perspective: The Matter of Quality, 87. **CONTACT ADDRESS** Dept Communications, McGill Univ, 845 Sherbrooke St, Montreal, PQ, H3A 2T5.

SZARMACH, PAUL E.
DISCIPLINE ENGLISH & MEDIEVAL STUDIES **EDUCATION** Canisius Col, AB, 63; Harvard Univ, AM 64; PhD, 68. **CAREER** Tchg fel, Harvard Univ, 66;Instr, US Military Acad, 68-70; Asst prof, 70-75, assoc prof, 75-83; prof, SUNY, 83-84; Prof, Western Mich Univ, 94-. **RESEARCH** Malory and the Arthurian Tradition. **SELECTED PUBLICATIONS** Co-ed, ACTA 4: The Fourteenth Century, CEMERS, 77; ed, Aspects of Jewish Culture in the Middle Ages, SUNY Press, 78; The Old English Homily and Its Backgrounds, SUNY Press, 78; Vercelli Homilies IX-XXIII, Toronto Univ Press, 81; The Alliterative Tradition in the Fourteenth Century, Kent State Univ Press, 81; co-ed, Mediaevalia 6, Festschrift for Bernard F. Hupp, 80; An Introduction to the Mediaeval Mystics of Europe; SUNY Press, 84; Studies in Earlier Old English Prose, SUNY Press, 86; Sources of Anglo-Saxon Culture, Studies in Medieval Culture, 20, The Medieval Inst, 86; Sources of Anglo-Saxon Literary Culture: A Trial Version, Medieval and Renaissance Texts and Studies 74; Suffolk: Boydell and Brewer; 94; Holy Men and Holy Women: Old English Prose Saints' Lives and Their Contexts, SUNY Press, 96; gen ed, Medieval England: An Encyclopedia, Garland Publ, 98. **CONTACT ADDRESS** Kalamazoo, MI, 49008.

SZEGEDY-MASZAK, ANDREW
PERSONAL Born 07/10/1948 **DISCIPLINE** DRAMA **EDUCATION** Univ Mich, BA, 70, Profinceton Univ, MA, 72, PhD, 76. **CAREER** Instr, Wesleyan Univ, 73-77; Asst Prof, Wesleyan Univ, 77-80; Assoc Prof, Wesleyan Univ, 80-88; Prof, Wesleyan Univ, 88-; Jane A. Seney Prof, Wesleyan Univ, 92-; Vis Assoc Prof, UCLA, 85-87; Vis Assoc Prof, Dartmouth Col, 87; Vis prof, 89, 90, 91; Contribut ed, Archaeology Mag, 88-; Consultant-lect, NEH-sponsored proj, Cabrini Col, 89; Vis Prof, Yale Sch Drama, 96, 98. **HONORS AND AWARDS** Woodrow Wilson Fel, 70; Summer Inst, Am Socy Papyrologists, 70; NDEA/Profinceton Univ fels, 70-73; NEH Summer Sem SUNY-Buffalo, 76; Wesleyan Ctr Hum, fac fel, 78; Wesleyan Profoj Grant, 79; NEH Summer Sem, 81; NEH Transl Grant, 85; Guest Scholar, J. Paul Getty Mus, 85; Am Philol Asn Award Excellence Tchng Clas, 86; Wesleyan Profoj Grant, 91; Wesleyan Univ Tchng Excellence Award, 97; 250th Anniversary Vis Prof Distinguished Tchng, Profinceton Univ, 98-99. **SELECTED PUBLICATIONS** Auth, The Nomo Theophrastus, NY, 81. **CONTACT ADDRESS** Wesleyan Univ, Middletown, CT, 06459.

SZITTYA, PENN
DISCIPLINE ENGLISH LITERATURE **EDUCATION** Univ NC, BA; Cornell Univ, PhD. **CAREER** Eng Dept, Georgetown Univ **RESEARCH** Medieval literature; Old and Middle English literature; Arthurian literature; medieval literary theory; medieval apocalyptic literature; medieval Icelandic literature; medieval Latin; patristic literature. **SELECTED PUBLICATIONS** Auth, Domesday Bokes: The Apocalypse in Medieval English Literary Culture, 91; The Trinity in Langland and Abelard, 89; The Antifraternal Tradition in Medieval Literature, 86; Metafiction: The Double Narration in Under Western Eyes, 81; The Living Stone and the Patriarchs: Typological Imagery in Andreas, 73; The Green Yeoman as Loathly Lady: The Friar's Parody of the Wife of Bath's Tale, 75. **CONTACT ADDRESS** English Dept, Georgetown Univ, 37th and O St, Washington, DC, 20057.

SZUCHEWYCZ, BOHDAN G.
DISCIPLINE COMMUNICATIONS **EDUCATION** Univ Regina, BA, 80; Univ Toronto, MA, 81, PhD, 87, MLS, 89. **CAREER** Prof, Brock Univ. **RESEARCH** Ethnography of communication and discourse analysis. **SELECTED PUBLICATIONS** Auth, Evidentiality in ritual discourse: the social construction of religious meaning, Lang in Soc, 94; Where are you getting your God from? Conflicting Sources of Authority in Religious Discourse, Discours social/Soc Discourse 7, 95; Silence in ritual communication, Silence: Interdisciplinary Perspectives, Mouton de Gruyter, 97; co-auth, Discourses of exclusion: The Irish press and the Travelling People, 97. **CONTACT ADDRESS** Dept of Communications Studies, Brock Univ, 500 Glenridge Ave, St. Catharines, ON, L2S 3A1. **EMAIL** bszuchew@spartan.ac.brocku.ca

T

TADIE, ANDREW A.
DISCIPLINE ENGLISH **EDUCATION** John Carroll Univ, BA, 66; Bradley Univ, MA, 67; St Louis Univ, PhD, 72. **CAREER** Eng, Seattle Univ. **SELECTED PUBLICATIONS** Auth, The Popularization of English Deism: Lord Herbert of Cherbury's De Veritate and Sir William Davenant's The Siege of Rhodes, Acta Conventus Neo-Latini Bononesis, Paris: J Vrin, 85; coauth, A Problem of Audience: A Semiotical Approach to the Deistic Elements in The Siege of Rhodes, Semiotic Themes, Univ Kansas Press, 81; ed, Hakluyt's and Purchas Use of the Latin Version of Mandeville's Travels, Acta Conventus Neo-Latini Turonensis, Paris: J Vrin, 80; co-ed, Permanent Things, Ferdmans, 95; The Riddle of Joy, Eerdmans, 89, 2nd ed, 90; rev(s), William McFadden's Discovering the Comic: Studies in American Humor, 83-84; Castiglione: The Ideal and the Real in Renaissance Culture, The Hist, 85; introd to, Personal Recollections of Joan of Arc, Ignatius Press, 89. **CONTACT ADDRESS** Dept of Eng, Seattle Univ, 900 Broadway, Seattle, WA, 98122-4460.

TALIAFERRO, CHARLES
PERSONAL Born 02/25/1952, New York, NY, m, 1987 **DISCIPLINE** PHILOSOPHY & LITERATURE **EDUCATION** Univ Rhode Island, MA; Harvard Univ, MTS; Brown, MA & PhD, 94. **CAREER** Instr, Univ Mass, 82-84; instr, Univ Notre Dame, 84-85; vis scholar, Univ Oxford, 91-92; vis fel, Princeton Univ, 98-99; prof, philos, St. Olaf Col, 85-. **HONORS AND AWARDS** NEH fel, 91. **MEMBERSHIPS** Amer Philos Asn. **RESEARCH** Philosophy of mind; Philosophy of religion; Ethics. **SELECTED PUBLICATIONS** Auth, Praying with C. S. Lewis, St. Mary's Press, 98; auth, Contemporary Philosophy of Religion, Blackwell, 98; co-ed, A Companion to Philosophy of Religion, Blackwell, 97; auth, Consciousness and the Mind of God, Cambridge Univ Press, 94. **CONTACT ADDRESS** Dept. of Philosophy, St. Olaf Col, Northfield, MN, 55057. **EMAIL** taliafer@stolaf.edu

TAMBURR, KARL
DISCIPLINE ENGLISH **EDUCATION** Princeton Univ, AB; VA Univ, MA; PhD. **CAREER** Prof, Sweet Briar Col. **HONORS AND AWARDS** Stu Govt Assn Excellence Tchg Awd, Sweet Briar Col, 93. **RESEARCH** Medieval lit; theology and iconography. **SELECTED PUBLICATIONS** Auth, articles on medieval drama and mysticism. **CONTACT ADDRESS** Sweet Briar Col, Sweet Briar, VA, 24595.

TANDBERG, GERILYN
DISCIPLINE DEPARTMENT OF THEATRE **EDUCATION** Minot State, BS; Univ Minn, MA, PhD. **CAREER** Assoc prof, fac mem, Women's and Gender Stud dept, adj prof, Sch of Human Ecology, La State Univ. **SELECTED PUBLICATIONS** Published on the field of costume history in several journals. **CONTACT ADDRESS** Dept of Theatre, Louisiana State Univ, Baton Rouge, LA, 70803.

TANKARD, JAMES WILLIAM
PERSONAL Born 06/20/1941, Newport News, VA, m, 1973, 3 children **DISCIPLINE** JOURNALISM **EDUCATION** VA Polytech Inst, BS 63; Univ NC, MA 65; Stanford Univ, PhD 70. **CAREER** Univ TX, Austin, bis prof 70; Univ WI, Madison, vis asst prof 70-71; Temple Univ, asst prof 71-72; Univ TX, Austin, asst prof 72-76, assoc prof 76-82, prof dept journalism 82-, Jesse H Jones Prof In Journalism, 89. **MEMBERSHIPS** Assn Edu in Jour Mass Commun; ICA; AAUP; **RESEARCH** Online journalism, inform graphics, sci reporting **SELECTED PUBLICATIONS** Samuel L Morison and the Government Crackdown on the Leaking of Classified Information, Journ Hist, 98; Propaganda Tests, in: Robert Cole, ed, The Ency of Propaganda, Sharpe Ref, 98; Expanding the News Frame: The Systems Theory Perspective, with Laura J Hendrickson, Jour Mass Comm Educator, 97; Communication Theories: Origins, Methods, Uses, with Werner J Severin, NT Longham, 97; Specificity and Imagery in Writing: Testing the Effects of Show, Don't tell, with Laura Hendrickson, Newspaper Res Journ, 96; Dorothy Thompson, in: Nancy Sigorelli, ed, Women in Communication; Westport Ct, Greenwood Press, 96. **CONTACT ADDRESS** Dept of Journalism, Univ of Texas, Austin, TX, 78712. **EMAIL** tankard@mail.utexas.edu

TANNER, JIM
DISCIPLINE ENGLISH LITERATURE **EDUCATION** Davidson Col, BA; Univ NC, MA, PhD. **CAREER** Assoc prof. **SELECTED PUBLICATIONS** Auth, pubs on rhetorical theory; stylistic analysis; composition pedagogy. **CONTACT ADDRESS** Dept of English, Colorado State Univ, Fort Collins, CO, 80523. **EMAIL** jtanner@vines.colostate.edu

TANNER, JOHN SEARS
PERSONAL Born 07/27/1950, Salt Lake City, UT, m, 1974, 5 children **DISCIPLINE** RENAISSANCE LITERATURE **EDUCATION** Brigham Young Univ, BA, 74; Univ Calif, Berkeley, PhD(English), 80. **CAREER** Teaching assoc Compos, Univ Calif, Berkeley, 78-80; asst prof Renaissance Lit & Rhet, Fla State Univ, 80-82; asst prof Renaissance Lit, Brigham Young Univ, 82-, vis instr, LDS Inst Relig, Univ Calif, Berkeley, 77-79; from assoc prof to prof 87-92; Brigham Young Univ; from assoc prof to prof, 93. **HONORS AND AWARDS** James Holly Hanford Award, 92: from the Milton Society of American for the most distinguished book on John Milton published in 92; honors prof of the year, Bringham Young Univ, disting lec, Phi Kappa Phi, Bringham Young Univ; C A Christensen Lecturer, Col of Humanities, Bringham Young Univ, 92-98; Fulbright Scholar to Brazil, 91. **MEMBERSHIPS** Milton Soc Am; Friends of Milton's Cottage; MLA; SAtlantic Mod Lang Asn; Col English Asn. **RESEARCH** Milton; Renaissance literature; religious literature and studies. **SELECTED PUBLICATIONS** Auth, The real world, Col English, 10/81; Lingering, Ensign, 2/82; Milton among the Mormons, Festschrift, Ind Univ Pa Press, fall 82. **CONTACT ADDRESS** English Dept, Brigham Young Univ, 3146 Jkhb, Provo, UT, 84602-0002.

TANNER, STEPHEN LOWELL
PERSONAL Born 04/18/1938, Ogden, UT, m, 1961, 3 children **DISCIPLINE** AMERICAN LITERATURE, LITERARY CRITICISM **EDUCATION** Univ Utah, BA, 62, MA, 64; Univ Wis, PhD (English), 69. **CAREER** From asst prof to assoc prof English, Univ Idaho, 69-74; sr Fulbright lectr Am lit, Fed Univ Minas Gerais, Brazil, 74-76; assoc prof English, Univ Idaho, 76-78; assoc prof, 78-80, PROF ENGLISH, BRIGHAM YOUNG UNIV, 80-, Sr Fulbright lectr Am lit, Brazil, 74-76. **RESEARCH** American literature; literary criticism. **SELECTED PUBLICATIONS** Auth, Kesey 'Cuckoos Nest' and the Varieties of American Humor--Ken Kesey and His 1962 Novel 'One Flew Over The Cuckoos Nest', Thalia-Studies Lit Humor, Vol 13, 93; Old-Testament Women in Western Literature, ANQ, Vol 6, 93. **CONTACT ADDRESS** Dept of English, Brigham Young Univ, Provo, UT, 84601.

TANNER, WILLIAM EDWARD
PERSONAL Born 12/27/1937, Youngsport, TX **DISCIPLINE** BRITISH LITERATURE, RHETORIC **EDUCATION** Univ Tx, Austin, BA, 64; ETx State Univ, MA, 67; Univ Tulsa, PhD, 72. **CAREER** Instr French & English, Grayson County Col, 65-69; grad fel English & French, Univ Tulsa, 69-71; asst prof Humanities, Hendrix Col, 71-72; assoc prof English & chmn dept, Tex Col, 72-73; asst prof, 73-79, assoc prof English, prof English, 79-85, Tx Woman's Univ, 79-; Instr French, ETex State Univ, 68; writing consult Rhetoric, Commun Skills Ctr Col Teachers English, Augusta, Ga, 73 & Tex Col, 77-80; consult ed, English Tex, 80-. **HONORS AND AWARDS** Col English Asn Prof Achievement Award, 94; Joe D Thomas Scholar Tchr, 94; Appreciation Award Serv & Ldr Higher Educ, 94. **MEMBERSHIPS** NCTE; MLA; SCent Mod Lang Asn; Conf Col Compos & Commun; Milton Soc Am. **RESEARCH** Twentieth century rhetoric; bibliography; seventeenth-century British literature. **SELECTED PUBLICATIONS** Auth, The Arthurian Myth of Quest and Magic, ed Dallas: Caxton's Mod Arts Press, 93; Rhetorical Designs: A Teacher's Guide, ed Dallas: Caxton's Mod Arts Press, 94; Nonfiction Prose: A Special Issue of the CEA CRitic, ed Youngstown, OH:CEA, 98; Rhetoric and Technology in the Next Millennium, ed with Suzanne Webb, Caxton's Mod Arts Press, 98. **CONTACT ADDRESS** Dept of English & Speech, Texas Woman's Univ, PO Box 425829, Denton, TX, 76204-5829. **EMAIL** wtanner@twu.edu

TANSELLE, GEORGE THOMAS
PERSONAL Born 01/29/1934, Lebanon, IN **DISCIPLINE** ENGLISH **EDUCATION** Yale Univ, BA, 55; Northwestern Univ, MA, 56, PhD, 59. **CAREER** Instr, 58-60, Chicago City Jr Col, Wright Br; from asst prof to prof, 60-78, Univ Wis-Madison; v pres, John Simon Guggenheim Mem Found, 78-; mem, Planning Inst Comn Eng, Col Entrance Exam Bd, 61; fels, Guggenheim, 69-70, Am Coun Learned Soc, 73-74 & NEH, 77-78; mem adv comt, 70-73, Ctr Eds Am Authors; mem adv comt for drama for Bicentennial, 75-75, Kennedy Ctr; comt mem, 76-, Ctr for Scholarly Ed; mem, 76, Soviet-Am Symp Ed, Ind Univ; adv, 77-, Ctr for the Bk, Libr Cong; mem, 78-, North Am Comt for 18th Century Short Title Catalog; mem, 78-79, Comt on Standards Rare Bk Cataloging in Machine Readable Form, Independent Res Libr Assn; bd dir & chmn, 79-, Ed Standards Comt, corp sec, 89-, Lit Classics US, Inc; mem adv comn, 80-92, N Am Imprints Prog; Hanes Lect, 81, Univ NC; mem adv coun, 80-, Rosenbach Mus & Lib; mem adv coun, 83-, Ind Univ Inst Adv Stud; mem fac, 84-, Sum Rare Bk Schl, mem adv bd, 85-94, Ctr for Amer Culture Stud, Columbia Univ; mem adv coun, 87-, Am Trust for the Brit Lib; lectr, 87, Rosenbach, Univ Pa; mem adv coun, 88-, Am Literary Manuscripts Proj; bd dir, 88-, 18th Century Short Title Catalogue/N Am Inc: chmn, 94-, Mark Twain Ed Proj, 91-, mem vis com, 88-92, Lilly Lib; mem adv bd, 90-, Ctr for Renaissance and Baroque Stud, Univ Md; mem adv com, 90-, Writings of J F Cooper. **HONORS AND AWARDS** Kiekhofer Tchng Award, Univ Wisc, 63; Jenkins Award in Bibliog, 73; Guggenheim fel, 69-70; Am Coun Learned Soc, fel, 73-74, NEH fel, 77-78; Laureate award, Am Printing Hist Assn, 87 . **MEMBERSHIPS** MLA; Bibliog Soc Am; Am Antiqn Soc; Mod Humanities Res Assn; London Bibliog Soc; Bibliog Soc Austrailia; Bibliog Soc Amer; Bibliog Soc Univ VA, Soc for Bibliog of Natural Hist; Amer Antiquarian Soc; Am Coun Learned Socs; Melville Soc; Renaissance Soc Amer; Soc History of Authorship, Reading and Publishing; Phi Beta Kappa. **RESEARCH** American literature; analytical bibliography; publishing history. **SELECTED PUBLICATIONS** Auth, Textual Criticism and Scholarly Editing, 90; auth, The Life and Work of Fredson Bowers, 93; auth, Literature and Artifacts, Univ Va Bib Svc, 98. **CONTACT ADDRESS** John Simon Guggenheim Mem Found, 90 Park Ave, New York, NY, 10016.

TARANOW, GERDA
PERSONAL New York, NY **DISCIPLINE** THEATRE HISTORY & ENGLISH **EDUCATION** NY Univ, BA, 52, MA, 55; Yale Univ, PhD, 61. **CAREER** From instr to asst prof, Univ KY, 63-66; asst prof, Syracuse Univ, 66-67; from asst prof to assoc prof, 67-76, prof English, Conn Col, 76-; fel, Yale Univ, 62-63; NEH fel, 80-81, referee, 72-. **MEMBERSHIPS** MLA; Am Soc Theatre Res; Int Fed Theatre Res; Asn Recorded Sound Collections; Societe d'histoire du Theatre (France); Soc for Theatre Res (England). **RESEARCH** Shakespeare; drama. **SELECTED PUBLICATIONS** Auth, Sarah Bernhardt: The Art Within the Legend, Princeton Univ, 72; The Bernhardt Hamlet: Culture and Context, Peter Lang, 97. **CONTACT ADDRESS** Dept English, Connecticut Col, 270 Mohegan Ave, Box 5567, New London, CT, 06320-4125. **EMAIL** gtar.@conncoll.edu

TARR, RODGER LEROY
PERSONAL Born 09/11/1941, Mercer, PA, m, 1962, 2 children **DISCIPLINE** NINETEENTH CENTURY ENGLISH LITERATURE **EDUCATION** Fla Southern Col, BA, 63; Kent State Univ, MA, 65; Univ SC, PhD(English), 68. **CAREER** Asst prof, 68-71, assoc prof, 71-78, PROF ENGLISH, ILL STATE UNIV, 78-, Res fel, Univ Edinburgh & Am Philos Soc res grant, 68-69; Fulbright sr res scholar, Great Britain, 81; Nat Endowment for Humanities sr res fel, 82. **MEMBERSHIPS** MLA **RESEARCH** Victorian novel and prose; bibliography. **SELECTED PUBLICATIONS** Auth, The Study of Modern Manuscripts--Public, Confidential, and Private, Nineteenth-Century Lit, Vol 49, 94. **CONTACT ADDRESS** Dept of English, Illinois State Univ, Normal, IL, 61761.

TASCH, PETER ANTHONY
PERSONAL Born 11/28/1933, Brooklyn, NY, m, 1961, 3 children **DISCIPLINE** ENGLISH **EDUCATION** Bucknell Univ, AB, 54; Columbia Univ, MA, 59; Univ Edinburgh, dipl English studies, 60. **CAREER** Instr English, Western Md Col, 58-59 & Brooklyn Col, 60-61; from instr to asst prof, 64-72, ASSOC PROF ENGLISH, TEMPLE UNIV, 72-, Jr fel, Harvard Univ, 61-64, ed, Scriblerian & Kit-Cats, 68-; Danforth assoc, 81- **MEMBERSHIPS** MLA; Am Soc 18th Century Studies. **RESEARCH** Restoration and 18th century drama; Kit-Cat and Scriblers Club members; 18th century novel. **SELECTED PUBLICATIONS** Motives of Woe--Shakespeare and Female Complaint, Scriblerian Kit-Cats, Vol 26, 93; 17th-Century Praise and Restoration Satire (Rev), Scriblerian Kit-Cats, Vol 26, 93; The Great Good Place--The Country House and English Literature, Scriblerian The Kit-Cats, Vol 27, 94; Selected Poems, Scriblerian Kit-Cats, Vol 27, 94; 'Clarissa'--or, The History of a Young Lady--Comprehending the Most Important Concerns of Private Life, Scriblerian Kit-Cats, Vol 27, 94. **CONTACT ADDRESS** Dept of English, Temple Univ, 1114 W Berks St, Philadelphia, PA, 19122-6029.

TASSI, MARGUERITE
DISCIPLINE ENGLISH RENAISSANCE DRAMA **EDUCATION** Columbia Univ, BA; Univ Va, MA, Claremont Grad Sch, PhD. **CAREER** Instr, Middlebury Col; asst prof, Univ Nebr, Kearney. **RESEARCH** Views of painting in English Renaissance drama. **SELECTED PUBLICATIONS** Published articles on the theaters of Shakespeare and Beckett and on 19th-century English views of Florence. **CONTACT ADDRESS** Univ Nebr, Kearney, Kearney, NE, 68849.

TATE, GEORGE SHELDON
PERSONAL Born 09/07/1944, Santa Monica, CA, w, 1969, 5 children **DISCIPLINE** MEDIEVAL LITERATURE **EDUCATION** Brigham Young Univ, BA, 69; MA, 70; Cornell Univ, PhD(Medieval studies), 74. **CAREER** Asst prof, 79-85, Assoc Prof Comp Lit, Brigham Young Univ, 86-, Chmn dept, Humanities, Class & Comp Lit, 81-85, 96-; assoc dean Gen Ed & Honors, 86-90. **HONORS AND AWARDS** Fulbright Fel Ireland, 71-72; Marshall Fel Denmark, 73; P A Christensen Lecturship, 85-86; Karl G Maeser Gen Ed professorship, 93-96; Alcuin Fellowship, 98-01. **MEMBERSHIPS** Mediaeval Acad Am; Soc Advan Scand Studies; Int Soc for the Classical Tradition; Classical Assn of Middle West and South. **RESEARCH** Old Norse literature, 12th-Century Renaissance **SELECTED PUBLICATIONS** Ed, Liknarbraut: A Skaldic Drapa on the Cross, Univ Microfilms, 74; auth, Good Friday Liturgy and the Structure of Liknarbraut, Scand Studies, 78; Chiasmus as Metaphor: The Figura Crucis Tradition and The Dream of the Rood, Neuphilologische Mitteilungen, 78; The Cross as Ladder: Geisli 15-16 and Liknarbraut 34, Mediaeval Scand, 78; Halldor Laxness, the Mormons, and the Promised Land, Dialogue, 78; Fertility, ergi, and Violence in Laxdoela saga, Allegonca, 89; Undifferentiation and Violence: Girard and the Sagas, Epic and Epoch, ed Oberhelman, 94; The Rest After the Desert: Ending Confessions, JRMMRA, 95-96. **CONTACT ADDRESS** Dept of Comp Lit, Brigham Young Univ, 3010 Jhkb, Provo, UT, 84602-0002. **EMAIL** george_tate@byu.edu

TATUM, NANCY R.
PERSONAL Born 08/14/1930, Pittsburg, KS **DISCIPLINE** ENGLISH LITERATURE & HISTORY **EDUCATION** Univ Ark, BA, 52; Bryn Mawr Col, MA, 54, PhD, 60. **CAREER** Instr English & asst to dean, Lake Erie Col, 58-59; from instr to assoc prof, 60-69, PROF ENGLISH, WASHINGTON COL, 69-, Ernest A Howard Prof, 79-. **MEMBERSHIPS** MLA; Shakespeare Asn Am. **RESEARCH** Restoration drama; Shakespearean stage technique; seventeenth century English social and economic history. **CONTACT ADDRESS** Dept of English, Washington Col, 300 Washington Ave, Chestertown, MD, 21620-1197.

TAVE, STUART MALCOLM
PERSONAL Born 04/10/1923, New York, NY, m, 1948, 4 children **DISCIPLINE** ENGLISH **EDUCATION** Columbia Univ, BA, 43; Harvard Univ, MA, 47; Oxford, DPhil(English), 50. **CAREER** Lectr English, Columbia Univ, 50-51; from instr to prof, 51-71, chemn dept, 72-78, master col div humanities & assoc dean col, 66-70, dean of humanities, 84-89,William Rainey Harper Prof English, 71-92, prof emer, Univ Chicago, 93-; Guggenheim fel, 59-60; vis assoc prof, Univ WI, 62 & Stanford Univ, 63; vis prof, Univ WA, 66; vis prof, WA Univ, 80 (Hurst prof); vis prof, Hawaii, 83 (Citizens prof); Am Coun Learned Soc fel, 70-71; Nat Endowment for Humanities fel, 78-79; Hurst prof, WA Univ, 80. **HONORS AND AWARDS** Quantrell Award, Univ Chicago, 58; Laing Prize, Univ Chicago Press, 74; Hon D H L Rifron Col, 86; Ryerson lect, 91; Stuart Tove fel, 93-; Rockefeller Bellagio Residency, 98. **MEMBERSHIPS** MLA. **RESEARCH** 18th and 19th century English literature. **SELECTED PUBLICATIONS** Auth, Amiable Humorist, Univ Chicago, 60; New Essays by De Quincey, Princeton Univ, 66; Some Words of Jane Austen, Univ Chicago, 73; ed, Bage's Hermsprong, PN State Univ, 82; Lovers, Clowns, and Fairies, Univ Chicago, 93. **CONTACT ADDRESS** Dept English, Univ Chicago, 5845 Ellis Av, Chicago, IL, 60637-1476.

TAYLER, EDWARD W.
DISCIPLINE ENGLISH POETRY OF THE SIXTEENTH AND SEVENTEENTH CENTURIES **EDUCATION** Amherst Col, BA, 54; Stanford, PhD, 60. **CAREER** English and Lit, Columbia Univ **HONORS AND AWARDS** Guggenheim Fel; two NEH-Huntington Grants, President's Award Tchg; Mark Van Doren Award. **MEMBERSHIPS** Renaissance Soc; Milton Soc; Spenser Soc, Acad Lit Studies; MLA. **SELECTED PUBLICATIONS** Auth, Nature and Art in Renaissance Literature, 64; Literary Criticism of Seventeenth-Century England, 67; Milton's Poetry, 79; Donne's Idea of a Woman, 91. **CONTACT ADDRESS** Columbia Univ, 2960 Broadway, New York, NY, 10027-6902.

TAYLOR, BRYAN C.
DISCIPLINE COMMUNCATION STUDIES **EDUCATION** Univ Mass, BA, 83; Univ Utah, MA, 87, PhD, 91. **CAREER** Assoc prof. **MEMBERSHIPS** Speech Commun Asn, 87-; Western States Commun Asn, 85-. **RESEARCH** Organizational communication; interpretive research methods; critical theory; cultural studies. **SELECTED PUBLICATIONS** Auth, Make Bomb, Save World: Reflections on Dialogic Nuclear Ethnography, Jour Contemp Ethnography, 96; Revis(it)ing Nuclear History: Narrative Conflict at the Bradbury Science Museum, 96; Home Zero: Images of Home and Field in Nuclear-Cultural Studies, Western Jour Commun, 96; The Bomb in Pop Culture, 95; Visions of the Past: The challenge of film to our idea of hisfory (rev), 96. **CONTACT ADDRESS** Dept of Communication, Univ Colo Boulder, Boulder, CO, 80309. **EMAIL** taylorbc@stripe.colorado.edu

TAYLOR, CINDY
DISCIPLINE AMERICAN LITERATURE, WOMEN IN LITERATURE, SOUTHWESTERN LITERATURE **EDUCATION** Univ ID, BA, 77, MA, 79; Univ MN, PhD, 93. **CAREER** Asst prof, Univ of Southern Co. **RESEARCH** 20th century Am lit; women in lit; western lit; native Am lit; lit; environment. **SELECTED PUBLICATIONS** Auth, Claiming Female Space: Mary Austin's Western Landscapes in The Big Empty: Essays on the Land as Narrative, Alburquerque, Univ NMex Press; rev, Dancing on the Rim of the World: An Anthology of Northwestern Native American Writers, Calapooya Collage, 91; Linda Hogan, Savings, Studies in American Indian Literature, 89; Josephine Miles, Collected Poems, l920-l983, J Amer Lit, 85; Nancy Westerfield, Welded Women, J Western Amer Lit, 85. **CONTACT ADDRESS** Dept of Eng, Univ of Southern Colorado, 2200 Bonforte Blvd, Pueblo, CO, 81001-4901. **EMAIL** Ctaylor@meteor.uscolo.edu

TAYLOR, DONALD STEWART
PERSONAL Born 08/08/1924, Portland, OR, m, 1952, 3 children **DISCIPLINE** ENGLISH **EDUCATION** Univ CA, AB, 47, MA, 48, PhD, 50. **CAREER** Instr Eng, Northwestern Univ, 50-54; from instr to assoc prof, Univ WA, 54-68; prof eng, Univ OR, 68, actg head classics, 75-78. **HONORS AND AWARDS** Guggenheim fel, 72-73. **RESEARCH** Textual criticism; 18th century Eng lit; theory of lit hist. **SELECTED PUBLICATIONS** Auth, Catalytic rhetoric: Henry Green's theory of the modern novel, Criticism, 65; Complete Works of Chatterton, Clarendon, 71; R G Collingwood: art, craft and history, 6/73 & Literary criticism and historical inference, 76, Clio; Thomas Chatterton's Art: Experiments in Imagined History, Princeton Univ, 78; Johnson on the Metaphysicals, Eighteenth Century Life, 86. **CONTACT ADDRESS** Dept of Eng, Univ of OR, Eugene, OR, 97403-1205. **EMAIL** dstaylor@oregon.uoregon.edu

TAYLOR, ESTELLE WORMLEY
PERSONAL Born 01/12/1924, Washington, DC, m, 1953 **DISCIPLINE** ENGLISH **EDUCATION** Miner Teachers College, Washington, DC, BS, 1945; Howard University, Washington, DC, MA, 1947; Catholic University, Washington, DC, PhD, 1969. **CAREER** Howard University, Washington, DC, instructor in English and Humanities, 1947-52; Langley Junior High, Washington, DC, English teacher, 1952-55; Eastern Senior High, Washington, DC, English teacher, 1955-63; District of Columbia Teachers College, Washington, DC, English instructor, professor, 1963-76; Federal City College, Washington, DC, associate provost, 1974-75; District of Columbia Teachers College, Washington, DC, acting academic dean, 1975-76; Howard University, Washington, DC, English professor, chairman of department, 1976-85, associate dean of College of Liberal Arts, 1985-86, director of Graduate Expository Writing, 1988-91. **HONORS AND AWARDS** Rockefeller/Aspen Institute fellowship, 1978-79; Outstanding Teacher in College of Liberal Arts, Howard University, 1980; Outstanding Contribution to Higher Education award, University of the District of Columbia, College of Human Ecology, 1988; Middle State Association Service Award, 1989; Outstanding Contributions to Historically Black Colleges Award, 1995; Howard University, Alumni Award for Distinguished Achievement in the Fields of Education and Literature, 1997. **MEMBERSHIPS** Member, National Council of Teachers of English, 1955-80; member, Modern Language Association of America, 1963-; member, College Language Association, life member, 1963-; member, Shakespeare Association of America, 1965; member, 1979-, vice president, 1979-81, corresponding secretary, 1989-91, recording sect, 1991-92, Capital City Links, Inc, Washington, DC; member, 1979-83, vice chairman, 1983, University of the District of Columbia board of trustees, Washington, DC; member of executive committee, Folger Institute, 1982-91; public member, US Department of State Foreign Service Selection Board, 1983; member, Commission on Higher Education, 1984-91; public member of Senior Threshold Foreign Service Appointments and Selections Board, Agency for InternationalDevelopment, 1984; member of research board of advis, American Bibliographical Institute, Inc, 1985-; member, Women's National Democratic Club, 1987-90; member, Malone Society, 1987-90; life member, National Council of Negro Women; member, District of Columbia Urban League; life member, NAACP; life mem, Assn for the Study of Afro-American Life and History; associate editor, Journal of the Afro-American and Genealogical Society, 1990-93; Delta Sigma Theta Sorority. **SELECTED PUBLICATIONS** Author of Survival or Surrender: The Dilemma of Higher Education, 1975; author of The Ironic Equation in Shakespeare's Othello: Appearances Equal Reality, 1977; author of The Masking in Othello and the Unmasking of Othello Criticism, 1984.

TAYLOR, GORDON OVERTON
PERSONAL Born 10/01/1938, Los Angeles, CA, m, 1964, 1 child **DISCIPLINE** ENGLISH, AMERICAN LITERATURE **EDUCATION** Harvard Univ, AB, 60; Univ Calif, Berkeley, MA, 62, PhD(Am Lit), 67. **CAREER** From instr English to lectr, Harvard Univ, 66-69; asst prof, Univ Calif, Berkeley, 69-76; assoc prof, 76-81, chmn, 81, prof English, grad fac Mod Lett, Univ Tulsa, 81-, chmn fac English Language & Literature, 82-, John Simon Guggenheim Mem Found fel, 80-81; vis assoc prof English, Harvard Univ, Summer 81. **MEMBERSHIPS** MLA; AAUP; S Cent Mod Lang Asn. **RESEARCH** Nineteenth and 20th century American literature; American cultural history. **SELECTED PUBLICATIONS** Auth, The Passages of Thought: Psychological Representation in the American Novel, 1870-1900, Oxford Univ, 69; Of Adams and Aquarius, Am Lit, 3/74; American personal narrative of the war in Vietnam, Am Lit, 5/80; Voices from the veil: Black American autobiography, Georgia Rev, Summer 81; The Country I Had Thought Was My Home: David Mura's Turning Japanese and Japanese American Narrative since World War II, Connotations, 6/97. **CONTACT ADDRESS** Fac English Lang & Lit, Univ of Tulsa, 600 S College, Tulsa, OK, 74104-3189.

TAYLOR, HENRY
PERSONAL Born 06/21/1942, Loudoun City, VA **DISCIPLINE** ENGLISH LITERATURE **EDUCATION** Univ VA, BA 65; Hollins Col, MA 66. **CAREER** Roanoke Col, instr, 66-68; Univ Utah, asst prof, 68-71; The Amer Univ, assoc prof, prof, 71 to 76-; Univ Utah Writers Conf, dir 69-71; Hollins College, writer in res, 78; The Amer Univ MFA creative writ, co-dir, 82-; Amer Univ, ASP dir, 83-85; Wichita State Univ, dist poet in res, 94; Randolph-Macon Womens College, poet in res, 97. **HONORS AND AWARDS** Acad Amer Poets Prize; Rinetti Mem IT Essay Awd; Ralph W Collins Fel; NEH Fel; Witter Bynner Prize; NEA Fel; Pulitzer Prize In poetry 86; Doc Human Letters Shen College Con; Golden Crane Awd; ME Fest Poetry Slam Winner, 96, 98; Dict Lit Biog Awd of Merit; Sm Press Bk Awd finalist; Who's Who In: Amer, S & SE, East, US Writers Editors and Poets, Emerging Leaders of Amer, the World., Directory Listings In: Contemp Auth, Dictionary Lit Biog, Contemp Lit Criticism, Contemp Auth Autobiog Series, Oxford Companion to Twentieth-Cent Poetry, Oxford Comp to Amer Lit, Contemporary Poets. **SELECTED PUBLICATIONS** Auth, Understanding Fiction: Poems 1986-1996, Baton Rouge, Louisiana State Univ Press, 96; auth, Leaves From the Dry Tree, by Vladimir Levchev, trans, NY, Cross Cult Comm, 96; auth, Compulsory Figures: Essays on Recent American Poets, BR, Louisiana State U Press, 92; The Horse Show At Midnight and an Afternoon of Pocket Billiards, BR, Louisiana State U Press, 92. **CONTACT ADDRESS** Dept of Literature, The American Univ, Washington, DC, 20016.

TAYLOR, JACQUELINE S.
PERSONAL Born 04/04/1951, Owensboro, KY, 2 children **DISCIPLINE** COMMUNICATION **EDUCATION** Georgtown Col, BA, 73; Univ TX, MA, 77, PhD, 80. **CAREER** Asst prof, 80-87, assoc prof, 87-92, full prof of Commun, DePaul Univ, 92-; assoc dean, Liberal Arts and Sciences, 95-98. **HONORS AND AWARDS** NEH summer grant, 88; hon fel, Women's Studies Res Center, Univ WI, Madison, July-Dec 93. **MEMBERSHIPS** Nat Commun Asn; Coun of Graduate Schools. **RESEARCH** Performing autobiography. **SELECTED PUBLICATIONS** Auth, Grace Paley: Illuminating the Dark Lives, Univ TX Press, 90; Performing the (Lesbian) Self: Teacher as Text, in Queer Words, Queer Images: Communication and the Construction of Homosexuality, R Jeffrey Ringer, ed, NY Univ Press, 94; Is There a Lesbian in this Text?: Sarton, Performance and Multicultural Pedagogy, Text and Performance Quart 15, Oct 95; with Lynn Miller, Editor's Introduction, special issue on Performing Autobiography, Text and Performance Quart, 17, Oct 97; Performing Commitment, in Readings in Cultural Contexts, Judith Martin, Tom Nakayama, and Lisa Flores, eds, Mayfield Pub Co, 98; Response to Strine's Essay, in Future of Performance Studies: The Next Millenium, ed Sheron Dailey, forthcoming; several other publications. **CONTACT ADDRESS** Col of Liberal Arts and Sciences, De-

Paul Univ, 2320 N Kenmore, Chicago, IL, 60614. **EMAIL** jtaylor@condor.depaul.edu

TAYLOR, JAMES R.
PERSONAL Born 12/13/1928, NB, Canada, m, 1966, 2 children **DISCIPLINE** COMMUNICATION **EDUCATION** Univ Penn, PhD 77; Mt Allison Univ, Sackville NB Canada, BA, MA. **CAREER** CBC, radio/tv producer, regional suprv pub affs productions, 56-66; Univ Penn, PhD stud, hd of Tv Lab, 66-70; Univ Montreal Canada, prof comm, 71-98. **HONORS AND AWARDS** Beaverbrook Overseas Sch. **MEMBERSHIPS** ICA; NCA; CCA; ACM. **RESEARCH** Communication theory; organization and communication; computerization of work. **SELECTED PUBLICATIONS** Auth, The computerization of work: Organization communication and change, coauth, Thousand Oaks CA, Sage, in press; the emergent organization: Communication as its site and surface, coauth, Mahwah NJ, Law Erlbaum Assoc, in press; Applying the socio-semiotic approach to the organization of environmental controversies: the Great Whale case, in: Connections and Directions: Technical Communication, deliberative rhetoric and environmental discourse, eds N. W. Coppola W. Karis, Norwood NJ, Ablex, in press; What is organizational communication?: Communications as a dialogic of text and conversation, Communication Rev, in press; The institutional and rhetorical modes of the organizing dimension of communication: Discursive analysis of a Parliamentary Commission, co auth, Comm Rev, in press; The Limits of Rationality: Asemiotic Reinterpretation of the Concept of speech Act, Stockholm Swed, 98; Modeling the Organization as a system of communication activity: A dialogue about the language; action perspective, coauth, Mgmt Comm Quart, 98. **CONTACT ADDRESS** Dept of Communication, Univ of Montreal, 3051 Cedar Ave, Montreal, PQ, H3Y 1Y8. **EMAIL** taylor@com.umontreal.ca

TAYLOR, JAMES SHEPPARD
PERSONAL Born 12/15/1943, Montgomery, AL, m, 1972, 2 children **DISCIPLINE** SPEECH **EDUCATION** Auburn Univ, BA, 65, MA, 66; Fla State Univ, PhD(speech), 68. **CAREER** Asst prof speech, NC State Univ, 68-69; asst prof, Auburn Univ, 69-73; assoc prof, 73-77, prof speech, Houston Baptist Univ, 77-, chmn dept, 73-98, dean, Arts & Humanities, 98-. **HONORS AND AWARDS** Teaching Excellence Award, 76-77, 88-89; Sears Found Teaching Excellence and Campus Leadership Award, 89-90; Piper Nominee, 88-89, 89-90. **MEMBERSHIPS** AAUP; Nat Commun Asn. **RESEARCH** Experimental persuasion; American public address; group dynamics. **SELECTED PUBLICATIONS** Coauth, William Huskisson and free trade, NC J Speech, 72; Loyalist propaganda in the sermons of Charles Inglis, 1770-1780, Western Speech, 73; Charles T Walker: The black spurgeon, Ga Speech J, 73. **CONTACT ADDRESS** Col of Arts and Humanities, Houston Baptist Univ, 7502 Fondren Rd, Houston, TX, 77074-3298. **EMAIL** jtaylor@hbu.edu

TAYLOR, MARK
PERSONAL Born 03/13/1939, White Plains, NY, m, 2 children **DISCIPLINE** ENGISH LITERATURE **EDUCATION** Yale Univ, AB, 61; City Univ New York, MA, 65, PhD(English), 69. **CAREER** Asst prof, 69-75, chmn dept, 78-82, assoc prof to prof English, Manhatten Col, 75-82, Poetry ed, Commonweal Mag, 72. **MEMBERSHIPS** MLA. **RESEARCH** Shakespeare; the Renaissance; modern fiction. **SELECTED PUBLICATIONS** Auth, Baseball as myth, 5/72, History, humanism and Simone Weil, 8/73 & W H Auden's vision of Eros, 10/73, Commonweal; The Soul in Paraphrase: George Herbert's Poetics, Mouton, 74; War novels, 9/77, Words and idioms, 1/78 & On biography, 1/80, Commonwealth; Shakespeare's Darker Purpose, AMS Press, 82; Farther Privileges: Conflict and Change in Measure for Measure, Philological Quarterly, 73, 94. **CONTACT ADDRESS** Dept of English, Manhattan Col, 4513 Manhattan Coll, Bronx, NY, 10471-4004. **EMAIL** mtaylor@manhatten.edu

TAYLOR, ORLANDO L.
PERSONAL Born 08/09/1936, Chattanooga, TN, m, 1957 **DISCIPLINE** COMMUNICATIONS **EDUCATION** Hampton Institute, Hampton VA, BS, 1957; Indiana Univ, Bloomington IN, MA, 1960; Univ of Michigan, Ann Arbor MI, PhD, 1966. **CAREER** Indiana Univ, Bloomington IN, asst prof, 1964-69; Center for Applied Linguistics, Washington DC, senior research fellow, 1969-75; University of District of Columbia, Washington DC, prof, 1970-73; HOWARD UNIV, WASHINGTON DC, PROF, 1973-; DEAN OF COMMUNICATIONS, 1985-. **HONORS AND AWARDS** Distinguished scholar award, Howard Univ, 1984; Award of Appreciation, American Speech-Language-Hearing Association, 1990. **CONTACT ADDRESS** Sch of Communications, Howard Univ, Washington, DC, 20059.

TAYLOR, SUSAN L.
DISCIPLINE WOMEN'S STUDIES, COMPOSITION **EDUCATION** Univ S Fla, BA, magna cum laude, 86; Fla State Univ, MA, 90, PhD, 94. **CAREER** Grad tchg asst, 87-93, vis instr, Fla State Univ, 93-94; lectr, 94-95, dir, Writing Ctr, 94-95, asst dir, freshman compos, 94-97, asst prof, 95-, dir, compos, Univ Nev, Las Vegas, 97-. **HONORS AND AWARDS** Eng Dept Excellence in Tchg Award, 92, Univ Excellence in Tchg Award, Fla State Univ, 93; State of Nev award for Distance Lrng, 96, 97. **MEMBERSHIPS** NCTE. **RESEARCH** Textbook selection. **SELECTED PUBLICATIONS** Auth, Time and Timelessness in Frank Waters' People of the Valley and Isak Dinesen's "The Blank Page," Stud in Frank Waters, 95; For a Good Time Type http://www.geekgirl.com.au/, Electronic Bk Rev, 96; Babes, BluBlockers, and Broncos, geekgirl, 96. **CONTACT ADDRESS** Dept of Eng, Univ Nev, Las Vegas, 4505 Maryland Pky, PO Box 455011, Las Vegas, NV, 89154-5018. **EMAIL** taylors@nevada.edu

TAYLOR, VELANDE P.
PERSONAL Born 09/10/1923, New York, NY, m, 1961 **DISCIPLINE** LITERATURE, PHILOSOPHY **EDUCATION** Hunter Col, BA, 44; Columbia Univ, MA, 45, PhD, 47. **CAREER** Instr, Paul Smiths Col, 46-47; asst prof, East Carolina Univ, 47-59; prof, head hum dept, Colorado Women's Col, 59-66; vis prof. St Mary's Univ, 66-69; prof, Middle Georgia Col, 69-72; prof, writer in residence and ed, Acad J, 74-84, Hong Kong Baptist Col; section ed, URAM J of Int Stud in the Philos of Understanding, 84-89; WordCraft by Lan, 93- ; ed, publ WordCraft Books, 96- . **HONORS AND AWARDS** Int Mark Twain Soc, 47; Freedom Found Order of the Dannebrog, 51, Bronze Medal, 52, Gold Medal, 52. **MEMBERSHIPS** APA; Acad of Am Poets; Int soc of Authors and Artists. **SELECTED PUBLICATIONS** Auth, Homilies in the Marketplace: Parables for Our Rimes, 96; Copper Flowers, 96; Walking Songs, 97; ZBYX: Tokens, 97; Tales from the Archetypal World, 98; Flowing Water, Singing Sand: The Metaphysics of Change, 99; Beside the Still Water, 99; Mode & Muse: Companions on the Journey, forthcoming. **CONTACT ADDRESS** 910 Marion St, #1008, Seattle, WA, 98104-1273.

TAYLOR, WELFORD DUNAWAY
PERSONAL Born 01/03/1938, Caroline Co, VA, m, 1960 **DISCIPLINE** ENGLISH **EDUCATION** Univ Richmond, BA, 59, MA, 61; Univ MD, PhD, 66. **CAREER** Instr Eng, Richmond Prof Inst, 61-63; from instr to assoc prof, 64-73, prof eng, Univ Richmond, 73 chmn dept, 78-, James A Bostwick Ch Eng, 91. **RESEARCH** Amelie Rives; Sherwood Anderson; Am lit 1890 to the present. **SELECTED PUBLICATIONS** Ed, The Buck Fever Papers, Univ VA, 71; Virginia Authors Past and Present, VA Asn Tchr(s) Eng, 72; auth, Amelie Rives (Princess Troubetzkoy), Twayne, 73; ed, The Winesburg Eagle, Sherwood Anderson Soc, 75-86; Sherwood Anderson, Frederick Ungar, 77; Sherwood Anderson, J J Lankes and the Illustration of Perhaps Women, Waves, 81; ed, Our American Cousin, The Play that Changed History, Beacham, 90; The Newsprint Mask, Iowa State, 91; Robert Frost and J J Lakes: Riders on Pegasus, Dartmouth, 96; co-ed (with Charles E Modlin), Southern Odyssey: Selected Writings by Sherwood Anderson, Georgia, 97. **CONTACT ADDRESS** Dept of Eng, Univ of Richmond, Richmond, VA, 23173-0002. **EMAIL** wtaylor@richmond.edu

TAYLOR-THOMPSON, BETTY E.
PERSONAL Born 02/06/1943, Houston, TX, m, 1985 **DISCIPLINE** ENGLISH **EDUCATION** Fisk Univ, Nashville TN, BA, 1963; Atlanta Univ, Atlanta GA, MLS, 1964; Howard Univ, Washington DC, MA, 1972, PhD, 1979. **CAREER** Washington DC Public Library, technology librarian, 1969-72; Texas Southern Univ, Houston TX, instructor in English, 1974-75; Houston Independent Schools, Houston TX, English teacher/librarian, 1965-68, 1982-84; TEXAS SOUTHERN UNIV, HOUSTON TX, assoc prof of English, 1984-89, chair, Dept of English and Foreign Language, 1989-91, associate professor of English, 1991, PROF OF ENGLISH, currently. **HONORS AND AWARDS** National Endowment for the Humanities; University of Illinois at Urbanna, Institute for African Studies for the General Curriculum, Fellow; Director, Masterworks Seminar on the Harlem Reniassance; Phi Beta Kappa; National Endowment for the Humanities (NEH) Director; Masterwork Project on the Harlem Renaissance; Masterwork Project on African American Autobiographies; Study Grant on African and African American Women Writers; Director Focus Grant on Literature, Art and Music of the Harlem Renaissance; Participant, Literature and Modern Experience Institute, Accra Ghana; Tanzania, Study & Research, Fulbright Award, summer 1997; Univ of Dar Es Saalam, Africa, Institute for Arts in Education, Humanities Scholar, summer 1997. **MEMBERSHIPS** Mem, College Language Assn, co-chair, Black Studies Comm; mem, National Council of Teachers of English; mem, Southern Conf of Modern Language Assn, sec of Afro-Amer Section; pres, Southern Conf of Afro-Amer Studies, 1990-92; Conference of College Teachers of English; American Literature Assn; Southern Conference of Afro-American Studies (past president); Natl College of Teachers of English; American Assn of University Women; Multi Ethnic Literature of the United States. **SELECTED PUBLICATIONS** Publications: Oxford Campanion to African American Literature, 1997; Essays: Grant and Proposal Writing Hand Book, 1997. **CONTACT ADDRESS** Dept of English and Foreign Language, Texas So Univ, 3100 Cleburne St, Houston, TX, 77004.

TCHUDI, STEPHEN
PERSONAL m, 4 children **DISCIPLINE** ENGLISH LANGUAGE AND LITERATURE **EDUCATION** Hamilton Col, BA, 63; Northwestern Univ, MAT, 64, PhD, 67. **CAREER** Instr, Mich State Univ; prof, 90-, ch, dept Eng, Univ Nev, Reno; ed, Eng J; ed, Silver Sage. **HONORS AND AWARDS** Distinguished Fac Award, Mich State Univ, 90; Mousel-Felter Award, Univ Nev, Reno, 97. **MEMBERSHIPS** Past pres, NCTE; past pres, Nev State Coun of Tchr of Eng. **SELECTED PUBLICATIONS** Auth, Lock & Key: The Secrets of Locking Things Up, In, and Out, Scribner's, 93; The Interdisciplinary Teachers' Handbook with Stephen Lafer, Heinemann/Boynton Cook, 96; Science, Technology, and the American West, Halcyon, 97; coauth, The New Literacy, Jossey Bass, 96. **CONTACT ADDRESS** Dept of Eng, Univ Nev, Reno, Reno, NV, 89557. **EMAIL** stuchu@powernet.net

TEAGUE, FRANCES NICOL
PERSONAL Born 01/16/1949, Toronto, ON, Canada, m, 1968 **DISCIPLINE** ENGLISH **EDUCATION** Rice Univ, BA, 70; Univ Tex, PhD(English), 75. **CAREER** Instr English, Univ Tex, 75-77; asst prof, 77-84, assoc prof, 84-91, PROF ENGLISH, UNIV GA, 91-, Am Coun Learned Soc grant-in-aid, 81. **HONORS AND AWARDS** Canada Counc doctoral fel, 74-75; Am Counc Learned Soc, grant-in-aid, summer 81; NEH fel, Folger Shakespeare Inst, summer 82; Assoc Col Res Libr travel grant, spring 85; Canadian Consulate fac res grant, 89-90; Sr fac teaching fel, Univ Ga, 95-96; Kappa Delta Epsilon Teaching Award, 96-97. **MEMBERSHIPS** MLA; Shakespeare Asn Am; Southeastern Renaissance Conf **RESEARCH** Renaissance drama; theater history; women writers before 1700. **SELECTED PUBLICATIONS** Auth, The Curious History of Bartholomew Fair, Bucknell, 85; co-ed, One Touch of Shakespeare, The Letters of Joseph Crosby, Folger, 86; auth, Shakespeare's Speaking Properties, Bucknell, 91; ed, Acting Funny, Fairleigh Dickinson, 93; auth, Bathsua Makin, Woman of Learning, Bucknell, 98. **CONTACT ADDRESS** Dept of English, Univ of Ga, Athens, GA, 30602-0001. **EMAIL** fteague@arches.uga.edu

TEBBETTS, TERRELL L.
DISCIPLINE ENGLISH **EDUCATION** Hendrix Col, BA; Univ AR, MA, PhD. **CAREER** WC Brown Jr prof; fac, Lyon Col, 70-. **HONORS AND AWARDS** Ark Prof Yr awd, Coun Advan and Support of Educ & Carnegie Found, 92. **RESEARCH** Fiction of Faulkner; plays of Shakespeare. **SELECTED PUBLICATIONS** Auth, Giving Jung a Crack at the Compsons. **CONTACT ADDRESS** Dept of Eng, Lyon Col, 300 Highland Rd, PO Box 2317, Batesville, AR, 72503.

TEDARDS, DOUGLAS MANNING
PERSONAL Born 02/12/1944, Greenville, SC, 4 children **DISCIPLINE** COMPOSITION, AMERICAN POETRY **EDUCATION** Vanderbilt Univ, BA, 66; Univ Fla, MA, 68; Univ Pac, DA(English), 76. **CAREER** Instr, Paine Col, 70-72; lectr, Univ Calif, Santa Barbara, 78-81; assoc prof English, Univ Pac, 82-. **HONORS AND AWARDS** NEH Summer Fel. **MEMBERSHIPS** NCTE. **RESEARCH** The teaching of writing; modern American poetry. **SELECTED PUBLICATIONS** Auth, Hush Puppies (poem), Fla Quart, fall 69; Agrarian poet, Appalachian J, spring 78; Mothers of Fruition (poem), Ga Rev, spring 79; chapter, In: When Writing Teachers Teach Literature, Boynton/Cook, 95. **CONTACT ADDRESS** Dept of English, Univ of Pac, 3601 Pacific Ave, Stockton, CA, 95211-0197. **EMAIL** dtedards@cs.uop.edu

TEDFORD, BARBARA WILKIE
PERSONAL Born 01/21/1936, Marshall, NC, m, 1958 **DISCIPLINE** ENGLISH **EDUCATION** Maryville Col, BA, 57; Univ TN, MA, 60; Univ Pittsburgh, PhD(English), 70. **CAREER** From instr to asst prof English, Davis & Elkins Col, 60-69; asst prof humanities, Robert Morris Col, 70-74; assoc prof to prof English, Glenville State Col, 75-98, RETIRED. **HONORS AND AWARDS** Phi Kappa Phi. **MEMBERSHIPS** SAtlantic MLA; Col English Asn; Henry James Soc. **RESEARCH** Nineteenth and twentieth century English, Am, Russian, and Canadian lit. **SELECTED PUBLICATIONS** Auth, A Recipe for Satire and Civilization, Costerus Essays Eng & Am Lang & Lit, 72; Of Libraries and Salmon-colored Volumes: James's Reading of Turgenev through 1873, Resources Am Lit Study, 79; The Attitudes of Henry James and Ivan Turgenev toward the Russo-Turkish War, The Henry James Rev, 80; Flannery O'Connor and the Social Classes, Southern Lit J, 81; West Virginia Touches in Eudora Welty's Fiction, Southern Lit J, 86; Solving Crimes and Teaching English: Kate Fansler, Bull WV Asn Col English Teachers, 87; Confronting the Other in the Fiction of Julia Davis, Bull WV Asn Col Eng Teachers, 89; Ghostlier Demarcations, Keener Sounds: Elusiveness in Wallace Stevens' The Idea of Order at Key West, Bull WV Asn Col Eng Teachers, 90; Robertson Davis the Manipulator of the Salterton Trilogy, ERIC 91; ed Julia Davis, The Embassy Girls, WVUP, 92; Facade: An Enduring Icon of Modernism, Bull WV Asn Col Eng Teachers, 97. **CONTACT ADDRESS** PO Box 1121, Elkins, WV, 26241. **EMAIL** btedford@neumedia.com

TELLER, STEPHEN J.
DISCIPLINE ENGLISH LITERATURE **EDUCATION** Roosevelt Univ, BA; Univ Ill, MA, PhD. **CAREER** Prof. **RESEARCH** Chaucer, mythology, science fiction, film, world literature. **SELECTED PUBLICATIONS** Publ, articles on

Shakespeare; bk rev(s). **CONTACT ADDRESS** Dept of Eng, Pittsburg State Univ, 1701 S Broadway St, Pittsburg, KS, 66762. **EMAIL** steller@pittstate.edu

TEMPLE, KATHRYN
DISCIPLINE ENGLISH LITERATURE **EDUCATION** Ga State Univ, BA; Emory Univ, MA, PhD. **CAREER** Eng Dept, Georgetown Univ **RESEARCH** 18th century British literature; 18th century popular culture; interactions between literature and law; history of intellectual property; feminist jurisprudence. **SELECTED PUBLICATIONS** Auth, pubs on eighteenth century authorship and "crimes of writing," the gothic, legal literature for women, recent developments in critical legal studies and critical race theory. **CONTACT ADDRESS** English Dept, Georgetown Univ, 37th and O St, Washington, DC, 20057.

TENGER, ZEYNEP
DISCIPLINE LITERATURE **EDUCATION** Bosphorus Univ, BA, 80; Univ Minn, MA, 85; NY Univ, PhD, 90. **CAREER** Teaching Asst, Univ Minn, 81-82; Instr, NY Univ, 86-90; Asst Prof, 90-96, Assoc Prof, Berry Col, 97-, Dir Honors Prog, 98-. **HONORS AND AWARDS** Univ Minn Res Fel, 80-81; Univ Minn Tuition Schol, 80-81; NY Univ Tuition Schol, 82-84; NY Univ Penfield Dissertation Fel, 89; Berry Col Travel Grants, 91-96; Berry Col Su Summer Stipend for Res, 92; Berry Col Fac Development Grant, 97; Berry Col Vulcan Teaching Excellence Award, 97. **MEMBERSHIPS** Mod Lang Asn; Am Comp Lit Asn; Am Soc Eighteenth-Century Studies; SAtlantic Mod Lang Asn; SCentral Soc Eighteenth-Century Studies; NEastern Soc Eighteenth-Century Studies; Int Asn Philos & Lit. **SELECTED PUBLICATIONS** Coauth, Genius versus Capital: Mid-Eighteenth-Century Theories of Genius and Adam Smith's The Wealth of Nations, Mod Lang Quart, 6/94; Impartial Critic or Muses Handmaid: The Politics of Critical Practice in the Early Eighteenth Century, Essays in Lit, Spring 94; Politics of the Enlightenment: The Reaction to the French Revolution and Changes in Editorial Policies of the English Literary Periodical, Studies in Eighteenth-Century Cult 24, 95; Criticism Against Itself: Subverting Critical Authority in Late-Seventeenth Century England, Philol Quart 75, 96. **CONTACT ADDRESS** English Dept, Berry Col, Mount Berry, GA, 30149.

TENNYSON, GEORG BERNHARD
PERSONAL Born 07/13/1930, Washington, DC, m, 1953, 2 children **DISCIPLINE** ENGLISH **EDUCATION** George Washington Univ, AB, 53, MA, 59; Princeton Univ, MA, 61, PhD(English), 63. **CAREER** Instr English, Univ NC, Chapel Hill, 62-64; from asst prof to assoc prof, 64-71, PROF ENGLISH, UNIV CALIF, LOS ANGELES, 71-, John Simon Guggenheim Mem Found fel, 70-71; ed, Nineteenth-Century Fiction, 71-74. **MEMBERSHIPS** MLA; Philol Asn Pac Coast; Carlyle Soc; Res Soc Victorian Periodicals; Int Asn Univ Prof English. **RESEARCH** Victorian literature, Anglo-German literary relations, romantic to modern; religion and literature. **SELECTED PUBLICATIONS** Auth, Prose in the Age of Poets--Romanticism and Biographical Narrative from Johnson to Dequincey, Modern Lang Rev, Vol 88, 93; 19th-Century-Literature, 50-Years, Nineteenth-Century Lit, Vol 50, 95. **CONTACT ADDRESS** Dept of English, Univ of Calif, Los Angeles, CA, 90024.

TERMINI, ROSEANN B.
DISCIPLINE LEGAL WRITING AND APPELLATE ADVOCACY **EDUCATION** Drexel Univ, BS, 75; Temple Univ, Med, 79; Temple Univ Sch Law, JD, 85. **CAREER** Instr, Villanova Univ; clerked, Honorable Donald E. Wieand, Superior Ct Pa; past regulatory aff atty, Pa Power and Light; past sr dep atty gen, Off Atty Gen, Commonwealth Pa; taught at, Dickinson Law Sch; past adj prof, Widener Univ Sch Law; **SELECTED PUBLICATIONS** Publ on, consumer contract law, the envt, food pharmaceutical and med device law. **CONTACT ADDRESS** Law School, Villanova Univ, 800 Lancaster Ave, Villanova, PA, 19085-1692. **EMAIL** termini@law.vill.edu

TERRELL, ROBERT L.
PERSONAL Born 07/19/1943, m **DISCIPLINE** JOURNALISM **EDUCATION** Morehouse Coll Atlanta, BA 1969; Univ CA Berkeley, MA 1971; Univ of CA Berkeley, PhD 1970. **CAREER** Publ poems short stories books 1967-; NY Post, reporter 1967-68; So Reg Council Atlanta, rsch writer 1968-69; Newsweek Mag, stringer 1968-69; Univ of CA,teaching asst 1969-70; Golden Gate Coll, instr 1969-71; San Francisco Chronicle, copy ed 1970; CA Jrnl Teacher Ed, asst prof 1971-76, ed 1972-73; OffRsch & Plnng, coord 1974-75; St Mary's Coll Morage CA, office experimental progs 1975-76; Stanford Univ, asst prof 1976; Univ of MO, assoc prof jrnlsm 1976-; School of Jrnlsm Univ of CA Berkeley, vstg prof 1979; Beijing Review Mag Beijing China, copy ed 1981-82; NY Univ Dept of Jrnlsm & Mass Commun, vstg prof 1985-86; Univ Nairobi School of Jrnlsm, fulbright prof 1984-85. **HONORS AND AWARDS** Fellowship CA State 1969-72, Grad Minority 1969-72, Fund for Peace 1970-71, NDEA 1971-74; Deans Fellowship Univ of CA 1974-75. **MEMBERSHIPS** Mem Amer Assoc Colls Teacher Ed, Amer Assoc Higher Ed, Amer Ed Rsch Assoc; bd dir CA Council Teacher Ed, Soc Coll & Univ; managing ed CA Jrnl Teacher Ed 1973; ed referee CA Jrnl Teacher Ed 1974-; adv screening comm commun Council for Intl Exchange of Scholars Fulbright Prog 1980-83. **CONTACT ADDRESS** Prof of News/Editing, Univ of MO, 16 Walter Williams, Columbia, MO, 65211.

TERRY, JAMES L.
PERSONAL Born 09/12/1949, Terre Haute, IN **DISCIPLINE** LIBRARY SCIENCE; SOCIOLOGY **EDUCATION** Long Island Univ, MLS, 90; Purdue Univ, PhD, 88. **CAREER** Libr, Assoc Curator, New York Univ, 90-. **HONORS AND AWARDS** Louis Schneider Memorial Award for Outstanding Dissertation, 88. **MEMBERSHIPS** Amer Libr Assoc; Amer Sociological Assoc. **RESEARCH** Political economy of information technology; information literacy; sociology of work and labor **SELECTED PUBLICATIONS** Auth, Authorship in College and Research Libraries revisited: Gender, Institutional Affiliation, Collaboration, College and Research Libraries, 96; auth, Automated Library Systems: A History of Constraints and Opportunities, Advances in Librarianship, 98. **CONTACT ADDRESS** Bobst Library, New York Univ, 70 Washington Sq S, New York, NY, 10012. **EMAIL** terryj@elmer4.bobst.nyu.edu

TERRY, REGINALD CHARLES
PERSONAL Born 11/02/1932, Buckinghamshire, England, m, 1960, 2 children **DISCIPLINE** ENGLISH LITERATURE **EDUCATION** Univ Leicester, BA, 59; Bristol Univ, MA, 64; Univ London, PhD(English), 70. **CAREER** Prin, Folk House Adult Educ Ctr, Bristol 60-65; asst prof English 65-77, ASSOC PROF ENGLISH, UNIV VICTORIA, BC, 77- **RESEARCH** Novels of Anthony Trollope. **SELECTED PUBLICATIONS** Auth, Trollope--A Biography, Victorian Studies, Vol 36, 92; Alan Ayckbourn, Theatre Res Int, Vol 18, 93. **CONTACT ADDRESS** Dept of English, Univ of Victoria, Victoria, BC, V8W 2Y2.

TETEL, JULIE
DISCIPLINE ENGLISH LITERATURE **EDUCATION** UNC Chapel Hill, PhD, 80. **CAREER** Prof lit, Duke Univ. **RESEARCH** French, Ger, and Am theories of lang from the eighteenth through the twentieth centuries **SELECTED PUBLICATIONS** Auth, Linguistics in America 1769-1924: A Critical History, Routledge, 90; pubs on linguistic historiography. **CONTACT ADDRESS** Relig Dept, Duke Univ, Durham, NC, 27706.

TETREAULT, RONALD
PERSONAL Born 12/31/1947, m, 1971, 2 children **DISCIPLINE** ENGLISH LITERATURE **EDUCATION** Univ Brit Columbia, BA, 69; Cornell Univ, MA, 72, PhD, 74. **CAREER** Lectr, Cornell Univ, 73-74; bibliog asst, Cornell Univ Lib, 74-75; asst prof, 75-81; assoc prof, 81-90; prof, 90-; fac assoc, 95-96. **RESEARCH** 19th century working-class autobiography, technology in teaching and learning. **SELECTED PUBLICATIONS** Auth, The Poetry of Life: Shelley and Literary Form, Univ Toronto Press, 87; "Shelley at the Opera," ELH: Eng Lit Hist 48, 81; "Shelley among the Chartists," Eng Stud in Can 16, 90; Women and Words in Keats, The Mind in Creation: Essays in honour of Ross Woodman, McGill-Queens, 92; Editing Lyrical Ballads for the Electronic Environment, Romanticism on the Net 9, 98; rev(s), numerous reviews in Dalhousie Rev; Eng Stud in Can; Nineteenth-Century Lit; JEGP: Jour Eng and Ger Philol; Keats-Shelley Jour. **CONTACT ADDRESS** Dept of Eng, Dalhousie Univ, Halifax, NS, B3H 3J5. **EMAIL** tetro@is.dal.ca

TEUNISSEN, JOHN J.
DISCIPLINE ENGLISH LITERATURE **EDUCATION** Univ Saskatchewan, BA; Ma; Univ Rochester, PhD. **CAREER** Prof emer. **HONORS AND AWARDS** Ed, Can Rev Am Stud, 77-86. **MEMBERSHIPS** MLA; Asn Can Univ Tchr English. **RESEARCH** Myth criticism; treatment of myth in literature. **SELECTED PUBLICATIONS** Auth, pub(s) on Roger Williams, Poe, Lawrence and Hemingway; coauth, A Key into the Language of America and Henry Miller's The World of Lawrence: A Passionate Appreciation (rev); ed, Other Worlds: Fantasy; Science Fiction Since 1939; Contexts: The Interdisciplinary Study of Literature. **CONTACT ADDRESS** Dept of English, Manitoba Univ, Winnipeg, MB, R3T 2N2.

THALER, DANIELLE
DISCIPLINE NINETEENTH CENTURY NOVEL; THEATRE **EDUCATION** Univ Toronto, PhD. **RESEARCH** Evolution of ideological discourse; genetic criticism; semiotics of drama; children's literature. **SELECTED PUBLICATIONS** Auth, La clinique de l'amour selon les freres Goncourt: Peuple, femme, hysterie, Editions Naaman, 86; Etait-il une fois? Litterature de jeunesse: panorama de la critique France-Canada, Toronto, Paratexte, 89; Jean-Come Nogues et les rites initiatiques, Rev francophone de Louisiane 5, 91-92; Ginette Anfousse et le jeu intertextuel, Can Children's Lit 72, 94. **CONTACT ADDRESS** Dept of French, Victoria Univ, PO Box 3045 STN CSC, Victoria, BC, V8W 3P4. **EMAIL** dthaler@uvic.ca

THAMELING, CARL L.
DISCIPLINE SPEECH COMMUNICATION **EDUCATION** Univ Louisville, BA, 79; Ind Univ, Bloomington, MA, 84, PhD, 90. **CAREER** Asst prof, Univ Col Cape Breton, 88-91; asst prof, Miami Univ, Ohio, 91-98; ASST PROF, NORTHEAST LA UNIV, 88-. **CONTACT ADDRESS** 322 Woodale Dr, #59, Monroe, LA, 71203. **EMAIL** CNThameling@alpha.nlu.edu

THATCHER, DAVID S.
DISCIPLINE ENGLISH LITERATURE **EDUCATION** Cambridge Univ, BA; Univ McMaster, MA; Univ Alberta, PhD. **CAREER** Prof **RESEARCH** Shakespeare; 20th-century British poetry. **SELECTED PUBLICATIONS** Auth, Nietzsche in England, Univ Toronto, 70; Musical Settings of Early and Mid-Victorian Literature: A Catalogue, Garland, 79; Musical Settings of British Romantic Literature, Garland, 82; A Shakespeare Music Catalogue, Oxford, Clarendon Press, 91. **CONTACT ADDRESS** Dept of English, Univ Victoria, PO Box 3070, Victoria, BC, V8W 3W1.

THAYER, CALVIN G.
PERSONAL Born 06/19/1922, San Francisco, CA, m, 1944, 5 children **DISCIPLINE** ENGLISH RENAISSANCE **EDUCATION** Stanford Univ, BA, 43, Univ Calif, Berkeley, MA, 47, PhD(English), 51. **CAREER** Instr English, La State Univ, 50-51; from instr to prof, Univ Okla, 51-66; vis prof, 66-67, PROF ENGLISH, OHIO UNIV, 67-, Assoc ed, Bucknell Rev, 67-; ed consult, The Milton Quart, 67-; ed, Ohio Rev, 72. **RESEARCH** Medieval and Renaissance drama; 16th century nondramatic literature. **SELECTED PUBLICATIONS** Auth, Shakespeare and the Goddess of Complete Being, English Lang Notes, Vol 33, 95. **CONTACT ADDRESS** Dept of English, Ohio Univ, Athens, OH, 45701.

THEALL, DONALD F.
PERSONAL Born 10/13/1928, Mt Vernon, NY, m, 1950, 6 children **DISCIPLINE** ENGLISH, COMMUNICATIONS **EDUCATION** Yale Univ, BA, 50; Univ Toronto, MA, 51, PhD(English), 54. **CAREER** Asst instr English, Univ Toronto, 52-53, lectr, 53-56, from asst prof to prof & chmn joint depts, 56-65; prof & chmn dept English & commun, York Univ, Ont, 65-66; chmn dept English, McGill Univ, 66-74, prof English, 66-79, Molson prof, 72-79, dir grad prog commun, 76-79; PRES, TRENT UNIV, 80-, Secy, Ford Found cult & commun sem, Univ Toronto, 53-54; Dept of Citizenship & Immigration res grant, 56-59; mem English sub-comt, Univ Toronto-Toronto Bd Educ Curric Studies & Publ Design for Learning, 60-61; Can govt & indust res grant, Studies AB Effects of Expo 67, 67-; cult exchange prof, Can & People's Repub of China, Govt Can, 74; Can Coun leave fel, 75-76; expert-coun commun, Conf Rector & Prin, Univ Quebec, 77; consult, Dept Commun, Quebec Delta Proj, 77-79. **HONORS AND AWARDS** Educ TV Award, Ohio State Univ, 62. **MEMBERSHIPS** Philol Soc Gt Brit; Int Commun Asn; Can Commun Asn (founding pres, 79-81); Asn Can Univ Teachers English; Int Inst Commun. **RESEARCH** Communications; esthetics; semiotics. **SELECTED PUBLICATIONS** Auth, Technology, Pessimism, and Postmodernism, SF Studies, Vol 24, 97. **CONTACT ADDRESS** Off of Pres, Trent Univ, Peterborough, ON, K9J 7B8.

THESING, WILLIAM BARNEY
PERSONAL Born 12/30/1947, St. Louis, MO, m, 1976 **DISCIPLINE** ENGLISH LITERATURE **EDUCATION** Univ Mo-St Louis, BA, 69; Ind Univ, Bloomington, MA, 70, PhD(English), 77. **CAREER** Counter intel agent, US Army, Stuttgart, Ger, 70-73; assoc instr, Ind Univ, Bloomington, 75-77; instr, 77-79, ASST PROF ENGLISH, UNIV SC, COLUMBIA, 79- **HONORS AND AWARDS** SAtlantic Mod Lang Asn Studies Award, 80. **MEMBERSHIPS** MLA; NCTE; Col English Asn; Asn Scottish Lit Studies; Tennyson Soc. **RESEARCH** Victorian literature, especially poetry and criticism; city in literature; teaching of composition and English studies. **SELECTED PUBLICATIONS** Auth, Hopkins--A Literary Biography, Victorian Studies, Vol 37, 94; A New Realism for a New Era--19th-Century Realism in Literature and Art, Studies Lit Imagination, Vol 29, 96; The Random-Grim-Forge--A Study of Social Ideas in the Work of Gerard Manley Hopkins, Victorian Studies, Vol 37, 94; Apprehending the Criminal, the Production of Deviance in 19th-Century Discourse, Nineteenth Century Prose, Vol 22, 95. **CONTACT ADDRESS** Dept of English, Univ of SC, Columbia, SC, 29208.

THIEM, JON
DISCIPLINE ENGLISH LITERATURE **EDUCATION** Dickinson Col, BA; Ind Univ, MA, PhD. **CAREER** Prof. **RESEARCH** History of ideas; postmodernist literature and theory. **SELECTED PUBLICATIONS** Auth, Selected Poems and Prose, Pa State Univ, 91; co-auth, Real Life: Ten Stories of Aging, Univ Colo, 94. **CONTACT ADDRESS** Dept of English, Colorado State Univ, Fort Collins, CO, 80523. **EMAIL** jthiem@vines.colostate.edu

THOMAS, AMY M.
DISCIPLINE ENGLISH **EDUCATION** Randolph-Macon, BA, 81; Univ Md, MA, 85; Duke, PhD, 91. **CAREER** Asst prof English, Mont State. **RESEARCH** Literature in Print; Litera-

ture in the Antebellum South. **SELECTED PUBLICATIONS** Fel Publ, Literature in Newsprint: Antebellum Family Newspapers and the uses of Reading, In: Reading Books: Essays on the Material Text and Literature, Univ Mass, 96. **CONTACT ADDRESS** Dept of English, Montana State Univ, Bozeman, MT, 59717. **EMAIL** thomas@english.montana.edu

THOMAS, CLARA M.
PERSONAL Born 05/22/1919, Strathroy, ON, Canada **DISCIPLINE** ENGLISH EDUCATION Univ Western Ont, BA, 41, MA, 44; Univ Toronto, PhD, 62; York Univ, DLitt, 86; Trent Univ, Dlitt, 91; Brock Univ, LLD, 92. **CAREER** Lectr, 61, prof, 69, Can Res fel, York Univ Libr, 84-, PROF EMER ENGLISH, YORK UNIV 84-. **HONORS AND AWARDS** Northern Telecom Int Can Stud Prize, 89; Univ Western Ont Alumni Award Merit, 95. **MEMBERSHIPS** Charter Secy, Drama Guild Can. **SELECTED PUBLICATIONS** Auth, Canadian Novelists 1920-45; auth, Love and Work Enough: The Life of Anna Jameson; auth, Margaret Laurence; auth, All My Sisters: Essays on Canadian Women Writers. **CONTACT ADDRESS** 15 Lewes Cres, Toronto, ON, M4N 3J1.

THOMAS, DEBORAH ALLEN
PERSONAL Born 09/01/1943, Biddeford, ME, m, 1966, 1 child **DISCIPLINE** ENGLISH LITERATURE **EDUCATION** Brown Univ, AB, 65; Duke Univ, MA, 66; Univ Rochester, PhD(English), 72. **CAREER** Adj asst prof English, Fairleigh Dickinson Univ, Florham-Madison, 73-76; co adj asst prof, Rutgers Univ, Newark & New Brunswick, 76-80; asst prof English, Villanova Univ 80-84; from assoc prof to prof, 84-91. **HONORS AND AWARDS** National Merit Scholarship, 61-65; Phi Beta Kappa, 65; NEH Fel, 85-86; vis scholar, Harvard Univ, 85-86; fac research grants, Villanova Univ, summer 84, 87, 92. **MEMBERSHIPS** MLA; Northeast Victorian Studies Assn; Dickens Soc. **RESEARCH** Nineteenth century British literature; the novel; the short story. **SELECTED PUBLICATIONS** Auth, contribr, to the Christmas numbers of Household words and All the year round, 1850-1867 (2 parts), Dickensin, 9/73 & 1/74; The equivocal explanation of Dickens' George Silverman, In: Vol III, Dickens Studies Annual, Southern Ill Univ, 74; The chord of the Christmas season: Playing house at the Holly-Tree Inn, Dickens Studies Newslett, 12/75; ed, Dickens, Selected Short Fiction, Penguin, 76; auth, Dickens' Mrs Lirriper and the evolution of a feminine stereotype, In: Vol VI, Dickens Studies Annual, 77; Thackeray and Slavery, Ohio Univ Press, 93; Hard Times: A Fable of Fragmentation and Wholeness, Twayne-Simon & Schuster Macmillan, 97. **CONTACT ADDRESS** Dept of English, Villanova Univ, 800 Lancaster Ave, Villanova, PA, 19085-1699. **EMAIL** dthomas@email.vill.edu

THOMAS, STAFFORD H.
PERSONAL Born 08/09/1929, Lynchburg, VA, m, 1964, 2 children **DISCIPLINE** SPEECH EDUCATION Univ Colo, BA, 51; Univ Wyo, MA, 57; Univ Wash, PhD(Speech), 64. **CAREER** Asst prof, 64-77, assoc head dept, 67-70, assoc prof Speech, Univ Ill, Urbana, 77-. **HONORS AND AWARDS** Chancellors' Summer Instr Develop Award, 65. **MEMBERSHIPS** Speech Commun Asn; Cent States Speech Commun Asn. **RESEARCH** Voice science; rhetoric and communication theory; speech and drama history. **SELECTED PUBLICATIONS** Auth, Effects of monotonous delivery on intelligibility, 6/69 & A terrorist's rhetoric: Citizen Lequinio's De L'eloquence, 3/72, Speech Monogr; Teaching segmental audience structure, Speech Teacher, 11/73; Parliamentary weakness in the French National Assemblies, 1789-1792, Southern Speech Commun J, fall 74; Teaching stagecraft through models, Commun Educ, 3/78. **CONTACT ADDRESS** Dept of Speech Commun, Univ of Illinois, Urbana-Champaign, 702 S Wright, Urbana, IL, 61801-3631. **EMAIL** shthomas@uiuc.edu

THOMASON, WALLACE RAY
DISCIPLINE COMMUNICATION STUDIES **EDUCATION** Lamar Univ, BS, 85; Univ Tex, MA, 89, PhD, 92. **CAREER** Asst prof. **SELECTED PUBLICATIONS** Co-auth, Pauses, transition relevance and speaker change, Human Commun Res; Requests for demographic information in telephone calls to the cancer information service, Southern Jour Commun, Employment Interviewing and Post Bureaucracy, Jour Bus Tech Commun. **CONTACT ADDRESS** Dept of Communication, East Tennessee State Univ, PO Box 70717, Johnson City, TN, 37614-0717. **EMAIL** saucemaf@etsu.edu

THOMPSON, GARY
PERSONAL Born 08/18/1950, Oklahoma City, OK, m, 1971, 2 children **DISCIPLINE** AMERICAN & ENGLISH LITERATURE EDUCATION Rice Univ, BA, 73, MA, 75, PhD, 79. **CAREER** Asst Prof Eng, Saginaw Valley State Col, 79-82; Fulbright Prof, Marie Curie-Sklodowska Univ, Lublin, Poland, 82-84; Assoc Prof, 84-87, 88-89, Prof Eng, Saginaw Valley State Univ, 89-; Fulbright Prof, Univ Gdansk, Gdansk, Poland, 87-88; Asst ed, Green River Rev, 79-82, 84-86, ed, Polish Lit issue, 86. **HONORS AND AWARDS** MI Asn Governing Bds, 85. **MEMBERSHIPS** MLA; NCTE; CCCC. **RESEARCH** Nineteenth and twentieth century Am fiction; rhetoric and compos; media studies. **SELECTED PUBLICATIONS** Auth, Barth's letters and Hawke's passion, Mich Quart Rev, spring,

80; Doubles, Doppelgangers, and Twins in Mark Twain's Work, In: Mark Twain: Ritual Clown, Siena Col, 90; An Interview with Tadeusz Konwicki, Fiction Int, Spring 87; ed, Rhetoric through Media, Allyn & Bacon, 97. **CONTACT ADDRESS** Dept of Eng, Saginaw Valley State Univ, 7400 Bay Rd, Univ Center, MI, 48710-0001. **EMAIL** glt@tardis.svsu.edu

THOMPSON, GARY RICHARD
PERSONAL Born 12/11/1937, Los Angeles, CA, 4 children **DISCIPLINE** ENGLISH & AMERICAN LITERATURE EDUCATION San Fernando Valley State Col, BA, 59; Univ Southern Calif, MA, 60, PhD(English), 67. **CAREER** Teaching asst English, Univ Southern Calif, 62; instr, Ohio State Univ, 62-63; instr Univ Calif, Los Angeles, 64-66; from instr to asst prof, Wash State Univ, 66-70, assoc prof, 71-75, chmn prog lit studies, 70-72; PROF ENGLISH, PURDUE UNIV, 75-, Ed, Poe Studies, 68-79; ESQ: J Am Renaissance, 71-78; exchange prof, Universitat Hamburg, Germany, 84-85. **HONORS AND AWARDS** NDEA fel, 59-62; NEH fel, 73; Emerson Soc Prize, 89. **MEMBERSHIPS** MLA; Melville Soc Am; Hawthorne Soc; Poe Studies Asn, hon life mem; Am Lit Asn; Int Gothic Asn; Baltimore Poe Soc, life mem **RESEARCH** American romantic movement; Gothic tradition in literature; 19th century literature; Romance tradition; Narrative theory. **SELECTED PUBLICATIONS** Auth, Poe's readings of Pelham, Am Lit, 5/69; Unity, death & nothingness--Poe's romantic skepticism, PMLA, 3/70; ed, Great Short Works of Edgar Allan Poe, Harper & Row, 70, rev 74, HarperCollins, 90; auth, Themes, topics criticism, In: American Literary Scholarship: An Annual, Duke Univ, 71-73; co-ed, Ritual, Realism & Revolt: Major Traditions in the Drama, Scribner, 72; auth, Poe's Fiction: Romantic Irony in the Gothic Tales, Univ Wis, 73; ed, The Gothic Imagination: Essays in Dark Romanticism, Wash State Univ, 74; Edgar Allan Poe, In: Dictionary of Literary Biography, Gale, 79; ed, Romantic Gothic Tales, 1790-1840, Harper & Row, 79; co-ed, Ruined Eden of the present: Hawthorne, Melville, Poe, Critical Essays in Honor of Darrel Abel, Purdue Univ, 81; ed, Essays and Reviews of Edgar Allan Poe, Libr Am, 84; auth, Circumscribed Eden of Dreams: Dreamvision and Nightmare in Poe's Early Poetry, Enoch Pratt Libr & Baltimore Poe Soc, 84; auth, Edgar Allan Poe and the Writers of the Old South, In: Columbia Literary History of the U S, Columbia Univ, 88; auth, Development of Romantic Irony in the U S, Budapest Akademiai Kiado, 88; Romantic Arabesque, Contemporary Theory and Postmodernism, ESQ, 89; The Art of Authorial Presence: Hawthorne's Provincial Tales, Duke Univ, 93; Literary Politics and the Legitimate Sphere: Poe, Hawthorne, and the Tale Proper, Nineteenth-Century Literature, 94; co-auth, Neutral Ground: New Traditionalism and the American Romance Controversy, LSU, 98. **CONTACT ADDRESS** Dept of English, Purdue Univ, West Lafayette, IN, 47907-1968.

THOMPSON, HILARY
DISCIPLINE ENGLISH LITERATURE **EDUCATION** Univ Alberta, PhD, 72. **CAREER** Children's Lit Asn. **RESEARCH** Art; literature; illustrated children's books; drama in education. **SELECTED PUBLICATIONS** Auth, Perspectives on Practice, Univ Victoria, 95; Children's Voices in Atlantic Literature and Culture, Guelph, 95; Warm is a Circle, Hantsport, 79; Fredericton, 82. **CONTACT ADDRESS** English Dept, Acadia Univ, Wolfville, NS, B0P 1XO.

THOMPSON, RAY
DISCIPLINE ENGLISH LITERATURE **EDUCATION** Queen's Univ, BA; Univ Mich, MA; Univ Alberta, PhD. **CAREER** Prof. **SELECTED PUBLICATIONS** Auth, pubs on Arthurian Legend. **CONTACT ADDRESS** English Dept, Acadia Univ, Wolfville, NS, B0P 1XO.

THOMSON, GEORGE HENRY
PERSONAL Born 07/22/1924, Bluevale, ON, Canada, m, 1956 **DISCIPLINE** ENGLISH EDUCATION Univ Western Ont, BA, 47; Univ Toronto, PhD(English), 52. **CAREER** Teaching fel, Univ Toronto, 48-51; lectr English, Mt Allison Univ, 53-55, from asst prof to assoc prof, 55-66; vis prof, Wayne State Univ, 66-67; Can Coun sr fel, 67-68; PROF ENGLISH, UNIV OTTAWA, 69- **MEMBERSHIPS** MLA; Asn Can Univ Teachers English; English Asn, Gt Brit; Virginia Woolf Soc. **RESEARCH** The Bloomsbury group; narrative theory; modern British fiction. **SELECTED PUBLICATIONS** Auth, Trumpet-major Chronicle, 19th Century Fiction, 62; The Lord of the Rings: The Novel as Traditional Romance, Wis Studies Contemp Lit, winter 67; The Fiction of E M Forster, Wayne State Univ, 67; A Forster miscellany, In: Aspects of E M Forster, Harcourt, NY, 69; Conrad's Later Fiction, English Lit Transition, Vol XII, 69; auth, The Four Story Forms: Drama, Film, Comic Strip and Narrative, Col English, 11/75; (with Oliver Stallybrass), E M Forester's The Life to Come: Description of the Manuscripts and Type-scripts at King's College, Cambridge, Papers of the Bibliog Soc Am, 10/78; Foreword To 'Pilgrimage,' 20th Century Lit, Vol 0042, 96; ed, Albergo Empedocle and Other Writings by E M Forster, Liveright, 71;. **CONTACT ADDRESS** 655 Echo Dr, Ottawa, ON, K1S 1P2.

THORN, ARLINE ROUSH
PERSONAL Born 11/22/1946, New Haven, WV, d, 1 child **DISCIPLINE** COMPARATIVE & ENGLISH LITERATURE

EDUCATION Marshall Univ, AB, 67; Univ IL, Urbana, MA, 68, PhD, 71. **CAREER** From Instr to Assoc Prof, 71-79, prof eng, WVA State Col, 79-, Ch, Dept Eng, 86-94; Adj prof Eng, Marshall Univ Grad Col, 75-; mem, State Col System Bd Dir, 94-97. **HONORS AND AWARDS** Woodrow Wilson Inst on Interpreting Hum, 86; Citation as Outstanding Fac Mem, WVA Legislature, 89; Fulbright Seminar in Brazil, 93; First Prize, WVA Writers statewide competition, poetry, 96, 98. **MEMBERSHIPS** Am Comp Lit Asn; MLA; Asn for Integrative Studies. **RESEARCH** Women's studies; hist and theory of the novel; Holocaust Studies. **SELECTED PUBLICATIONS** Coauth, The veluminous word: McLuhan-D H Lawrence, Midwest Monogr, 71; The pivotal character in Dickens' novels, Papers WV a Asn Col Eng Tchr(s), spring 72; Shelley's Cenci as Tragedy, Costerus: Essays Eng Lit & Lang, 12/73; Harriette Arnow's mountain women, Bull WVA Asn Col Eng Tchr(s), 77; Feminine time in Dorothy Richardson's Pilgrimage, Int J Women's Studies, 78; How I became a historian, Kanawha Rev, 80; A mighty maze: Ulysses, Perspectives Contemp Lit, 80; co-ed, Origins: Texts for an Inquiry, Tapestry Press, 91; author of poems in Pikeville Rev, Southern Humanities Rev, and various anthologies. **CONTACT ADDRESS** Dept of Eng, West Virginia State Col, PO Box 1000, Institute, WV, 25112-1000. **EMAIL** athorn@wvsvax.wvnet.edu

THORN, J. DALE
DISCIPLINE MASS COMMUNICATION **EDUCATION** Fla State Univ, PhD, 84. **CAREER** Prof in Residence, La State Univ; press secy to the Governor of La; assoc comnr, La Bd of Regents; area hd, PR, 93-97. **HONORS AND AWARDS** Ford Foundation/American Political Science Association award, 68; grant, Freedom Forum J prof publ prog, LSU coun on res; Bart Swanson Endowed Mem Professorship, 96-97. **RESEARCH** Media coverage and public relations impact on higher education desegregation litigation. **SELECTED PUBLICATIONS** Auth, Litigation Public Relations in the Civil Trial Setting, in Bus Res Yearbk, Vol. IV, UP of Am, 97; Media Mediocrity: A Perspective on Higher Education Desegregation News Coverage in the Second Reconstruction, in Kofi Lomotey and Charles Teddlie, eds, Readings on Equal Education, Vol 14, Forty Years After the Brown Decision: Social and Cultural Effects of School Desegregation, AMS Press, 97. **CONTACT ADDRESS** The Manship Sch of Mass Commun, Louisiana State Univ, Baton Rouge, LA, 70803.

THORPE, JAMES
PERSONAL Born 08/17/1915, Aiken, SC, m, 1941, 3 children **DISCIPLINE** ENGLISH & AMERICAN LITERATURE **EDUCATION** The Citadel, AB, 36; Univ of NC, MA, 37; Harvard Univ, PhD, 41. **CAREER** Colonel, US Air Force, 41-46; instr to prof, Princeton Univ, Master of Grad Col, 46-66; sr res assoc dir, Huntington Libr & Art Gallery, 66-83, Huntington Libr & Art Gallery, 66-. **HONORS AND AWARDS** Litt D, Occidental Col, 68; LHD, Claremont Grad Sch, 68; LLD, The Citadel, 71; HHD, Univ Toledo, 77. **MEMBERSHIPS** Mod Lang Asn; Soc for Textual Scholar; Amer Acad of Arts & Sci; Amer Philos Soc. **RESEARCH** 17th century English literature; Contemporary American literature; History of Huntington Library. **SELECTED PUBLICATIONS** Auth, Proverbs for Thinkers, Huntington Libr Press, 98; auth, Proverbs for Friends, Huntington Libr Press, 97; auth, A Pleasure of Proverbs, Huntington Libr Press, 96; auth, H. E. Huntington: A Short Biography, Huntington Libr Press, 96; auth, Henry Edwards Huntington: A Biography, Univ Calif Press, 94. **CONTACT ADDRESS** Huntington Library, San Marino, CA, 91108.

THORPE, JUDITH M.
PERSONAL Born 03/19/1941, Fort Wayne, IN, m, 1998 **DISCIPLINE** COMMUNICATION, MASS MEDIA **EDUCATION** Ohio State Univ, PhD, 86. **CAREER** Asst prof, Univ of Tenn at Knoxville, 86-87; PROF, UNIV OF WIS AT OSHKOSH, 87-. **HONORS AND AWARDS** Listed in Who's Who in Am, Who's Who in Media & Infor, and Who's Who in Entertainment; Maybelline's Revitalizing Award, 94; UWO Off-Campus Travel Award, 90 & 94; AAUW Named Gift Scholar, 93; Outstanding Scholarly Contribution, Commun Reports, 92; UWO Fac Development Grant, 87 & 91; AAUW Nat Partnership Grant, 91; C-Span fel, 90. **MEMBERSHIPS** NCA; BEA; AAUW. **RESEARCH** Corporate Media. **SELECTED PUBLICATIONS** Coauth, Media Criticism: Journeys in Interpretations, 92; coauth, Why Corporate Media Centers Implement Computer Applications, 92; coauth, End Users' Perceptions Concerning Computer Applications Implemented in Broadcast Stations, 93; auth, Corporate Media: Communicating for an Organization, in progress; auth, Inside Corporate media: Using Electronic Media to Communicate with Internal and External Audiences; auth, The Contributions of Marshall McLuhan to the Speech Communication Discipline When the Media is Not the Message, Canada Week Papers, 94; auth, How to Manage Corporate Crisis More Effectively by Using Electronic Media: Examples and Suggestions for Public Relations Practioneers and Communications Specialists, J of Commun Studies, 98. **CONTACT ADDRESS** Dept of Commun, Univ of Wis, Oshkosh, WI, 54901. **EMAIL** thorpe@uwosh.edu

THORSON, CONNIE C.
PERSONAL Born 07/25/1940, Dallas, TX, m, 1970 **DISCIPLINE** ENGLISH LITERATURE OF THE RESTORATION AND EIGHTEENTH CENTURY; LIBRARY SCIENCE **EDUCATION** Univ AR, Fayetteville, BA, 62, MA, 64; Univ NM, Albuquerque, PhD (English), 70; Univ IL, Urbana, MS (Library Science), 77. **CAREER** Asst to Assoc prof, Head of Acquisitions, 79-90, Prof and Head of Reference and Aquisitions, 90-95, PROF EMERITA, UNIV NM, 95-; DIR OF THE LIBRARY AND PROF, ALLEGHENY COL, MEADVILLE, PA, 95-. **HONORS AND AWARDS** Phi Phi Kappa Phi; Beta Phi Mu; Lifetime Achievement Award, South Central Soc for 18th-Century Studies, 94. **MEMBERSHIPS** Am Library Asn; Modern Lang Asn; Am Soc for 18th-Century Studies; SCSECS; MMLA; AAUP. **RESEARCH** Anti-Roman Catholic lit of the Restoration and eighteenth century; novel and drama, English and American; faculty status for Librarians. **SELECTED PUBLICATIONS** Auth, A Million Stars, 80; A Pocket Companion for Oxford, (1756), 89; The RFP Process: Effective Management of the Acquisition of Library Materials, 98. **CONTACT ADDRESS** 451 Hartz Ave., Meadville, PA, 16335-1326. **EMAIL** cthorson@alleg.edu

THORSON, JAMES LLEWELLYN
PERSONAL Born 01/07/1934, Yankton, SD, m, 1970 **DISCIPLINE** ENGLISH AND AMERICAN LITERATURE **EDUCATION** Univ Nebr, BS, 56, MA, 61; Cornell Univ, PhD(English), 66. **CAREER** Instr English, Univ Nebr, 61-62; asst prof, 65-70, dir grad studies English, 69-71, ASSOC PROF ENGLISH, UNIV N MEX, 70-, Greater univ fund grant, Univ NMex, 67; sr Fulbright lectr English, Univ Macedonia, Yugoslavia, 71-72; vis tutor, English, Jesus Col, Oxford, 73, vis sr res fel, 76-77 and 80. **MEMBERSHIPS** AAUP; MLA; Friends of Bodleian Libr; Am Soc Eighteenth Century Studies. **RESEARCH** Restoration and 18th century English literature; bibliography; American literature. **SELECTED PUBLICATIONS** Auth, The Publication of Hudibras, Papers Bibliog Soc Am, 66; Samuel Butler, 1612-1680: A Bibliography, Bull Bibliog, 1/73; A Broadside by Samuel Butler, Bodleian Libr Rec, 2/74; Authorial Duplicity: A Warning to Editors, Anal Enumerative Bibliog, 3/79; The Expedition of Humphry Clinker, Oxford Mag, 5/82; Prior, Matthew An 'Epitaph,' Explicator, Vol 0051, 93; coauth, Academic Fredom: University of Texas of the Permian Basin, AAUP Bull, 6/79; ed, Yugoslav Perspectives on American Literature: An Anthology, Ardis, 80; The Expedition of Humphry Clinker, Norton, 82. **CONTACT ADDRESS** Dept of English, Univ of NMex, 1 University Campus, Albuquerque, NM, 87131-0001.

THRALL, TREVOR
DISCIPLINE COMMUNICATION PROCESSES AND TECHNOLOGIES **EDUCATION** Univ MI, BA, 89; Mass Inst Technol, PhD, 96. **CAREER** Vis asst prof, Univ MI, 95-98. **SELECTED PUBLICATIONS** Auth, Public Perception of Interest Groups: How Journalistic Labeling Affects Interest Group Credibility, 1997 Annual Meeting Midwest Asn Public Opinion Res; Look Who's Talking: Elite Interest Group Dominance of the News, Am Polit Sci Asn, Mass Media Coverage of Interest Groups: Implications for Public Opinion, Annual Meeting Am Asn Public Opinion Res, Going Negative in '96, Wolverine Caucus; Competing Images of the Press, , Am Polit Sci Asn; The First Amendment and the Persian Gulf War, Gerald R. Ford Inst for Public Service; War and the Fourth Estate: Public Affairs from Vietnam to the Gulf, Am Polit Sci Asn; Return to Censorship? Government Control of the Press from Grenada to the Gulf, Annual Meeting, New Eng Pol Sci Asn. **CONTACT ADDRESS** Univ MI, 515 E. Jefferson St, Ann Arbor, MI, 48109-1316. **EMAIL** atthrall@umich.edu

THRONE, BARRY
DISCIPLINE ENGLISH LITERATURE **EDUCATION** Univ Wis, PhD. **CAREER** Dept Eng, Queen's Univ **RESEARCH** Theatre history; Renaissance drama; feminist and reception theory. **SELECTED PUBLICATIONS** Auth, pubs on Shakespeare and the modern Canadian novel. **CONTACT ADDRESS** English Dept, Queen's Univ, Kingston, ON, K7L 3N6.

THUENTE, MARY HELEN
PERSONAL Born 03/21/1946, Chicago, IL, m, 1967, 2 children **DISCIPLINE** ENGLISH, IRISH LIT **EDUCATION** Clarke Col, BA, 67; Univ Kans, MA, 69, PhD, 73. **CAREER** Asst prof, 75-80, assoc prof to prof Eng, 80-, Ind Univ/Purdue Univ. **MEMBERSHIPS** MLA; Am Comt Irish Studies; Can Assn Irish Studies; Int Assn Study Irish Lit. **RESEARCH** Irish literature, hist. **SELECTED PUBLICATIONS** Auth, The Harp Re-Strung, 94. **CONTACT ADDRESS** Dept of English, Indiana Univ-Purdue Univ, Fort Wayne, 2101 Coliseum Blvd E, Ft. Wayne, IN, 46805-1445. **EMAIL** thuentem@ipfw.edu

THUNDY, ZACHARIAS PONTIAN
PERSONAL Born 09/28/1936, Changanacherry, India **DISCIPLINE** ENGLISH, LINGUISTICS **EDUCATION** Pontif Atheneaum, India, BPh, 58, LPh, 59, BTh, 61, STL, 63; DePaul Univ, MA, 66; Univ Notre Dame, PhD(English), 69. **CAREER** Instr philos, Dharmaram Col, Bangalore, India, 63-64; from asst prof to assoc prof, 68-77, prof English, Northern Mich Univ, 77-, Am Inst Indian Studies sr fel, 74-75. **HONORS AND AWARDS** Citation & Medal, Mich Acad Sci, Arts & Lett, 77. **MEMBERSHIPS** MLA; Int Arthurian Soc; Midwest Mod Lang Asn; Ling Soc Am; AAUP. **RESEARCH** Anthropological linguistics; American dialect survey; feminism in the Middle Ages. **SELECTED PUBLICATIONS** Auth, Circumstance, circumference, and center, Hartford Studies Lit, 71; Oaths in Germanic folklore, Folklore, 71; Covenant in Anglo-Saxon Thought, Macmillan, 72; co-ed, Language and Culture, Northern Mich Univ, 73; auth, Beowulf and Jus diaboli, Christian Scholar's Rev, 73; co-ed, Chaucerian Problems and Perspectives, Univ Notre Dame, 78. **CONTACT ADDRESS** Dept of English, No Michigan Univ, 1401 Presque Isle Ave, Marquette, MI, 49855-5301. **EMAIL** zthundy@nmu.edu

THURIN, SUSAN MOLLY SCHOENBAUER
PERSONAL Born 01/24/1942, Jordan, MN, m, 1969 **DISCIPLINE** ENGLISH LITERATURE **EDUCATION** Col St Benedict, BA, 63; IN Univ, Bloomington, MA, 66; Univ WI-Milwaukee, PhD, 79. **CAREER** Teacher, Peace Corps, Liberia, W AFR, 63-65, teacher English, Marshall High Sch, Milwaukee, 66-67; teacher forms I & II, St Peter's Preparatory Sch, England, 67-68; instructor to assoc prof English, 68-85, PROF ENGLISH, UNIV WI-STOUT, 86-; fac exchange, Beijing Institute of Light Industry, CNA, 86-87; lecturer, English dept, Univ Gothenburg, SWE, 89-90. **HONORS AND AWARDS** Thomas Hardy Summer School, Weymouth, England, 82; Univ WI System Faculty Col, 85, 94; NEH Summer Seminar: The Novel of Dickens, Univ of Rochester, NY, George H. Ford, 84; Ed Testing Service: Reader, AP test, Princeton, NJ, 86; NEH Summer Seminar: Culture and Soc in England, 1800-1900, Brown Univ, Roger Henkle and Perry Curtis, 89; Dahlgren Prof, 96-98. **MEMBERSHIPS** MLA; Midwest MLA; Nat Council of Teachers of English; TESOL; MVSA. **RESEARCH** Eighteenth and 19th century British novel; women in literature; travel literature. **SELECTED PUBLICATIONS** Auth, The Relationship between Dora and Agnes, Dickens Studies Newslett, 81; To Be Brought Up By Hand, Victorian Newslett, fall 83; The Accomplished Lady in the English Novel, Trans WI Acad of Sciences, Arts, and Letters, 84; The Madonna and the Child Wife in Romola, Tulsa Studies in Women's Lit, spring 85; The Seven Deadly Sins in Great Expectations, Dickens Studies Annual 15, ed Michael Timko, Fred Kaplan, and Edward Guiliano, NY: AMS Press, 86; Pickwick and Podsnap Abroad: Dicken's Pictures From Italy, Dickensian 83, summer 87; Travel and Tourism, Victorian Britain: An Encyclopedia, ed Sally Mitchell. NY: Garland Press, 88; China in Dickens, Dickens Quart, Sept 91; Virginia Woolf: Writing Through Manic-Depression, Kaleidoscope 24, winter/spring 92; Zhang Jie's Love Must Not Be Forgotten, Masterplots II: Women's Literature, Pasadena: Salem Press, 95; Annotated Bibliography of Great Expectations, Masterplots, Pasadena: Salem Press, 95; Michael Cotsell's Creditable Warriors, Carlyle Studies Annual 15, 95; Alison Blunt, Mary Kingsley and Maria Frawley, A Wider Range, Nineteenth Century Prose 23, spring 96; Constance Gordon Cumming, British Travel Writers, vol II, Dictionary of Literary Biography, ed, Barbara Brothers and Julia Gergits, Gale Research, 97; Victorian Travelers and the Opening of China, 1842-1907, OH Univ Press, 98. **CONTACT ADDRESS** Univ Wisconsin-Stout, Menomonie, WI, 54751-0790. **EMAIL** thurins@uwstout.edu

THURSTON, BONNIE BOWMAN
PERSONAL Born 10/05/1952, Bluefield, WV, w, 1980 **DISCIPLINE** ENGLISH, PHILOSOPHY, RELIGION **EDUCATION** Bethany Col, BA, 74; Univ Va, MA, 75, PhD, 79. **CAREER** Grad inst, Eng, 76-79, asst dean, Col Arts and Sci, inst, Eng and Rel stud, 79-80, Univ Va; adj, Eng Theol, Wheeling Jesuit Univ, 80-81; asst prof, Eng, Human, Bethany Col, 81-83; tutor, inst stud Christian Origins, Tuebingen, Ger, 83-85; assoc prof Theol, dir, ch, dept Theol, Wheeling Jesuit Univ, 85-95; prof New Test, Pittsburgh Theol Sem. **HONORS AND AWARDS** Valedictorian, first hon lit, hon soc in Drama, Eng, Jour, Bethany Col , 74; Philip Francis du Pont fel, Univ Va, 76; Who's Who in Bibl studs and Archeol, 87; Who's Who in the World, 87; Who's Who in Rel, 91; schol-in-res, Wheeling Jesuit Univ, 92; Alpha Sigma Nu; Alum achiev awd in Rel. **MEMBERSHIPS** Amer Sch Oriental Res; Catholic Bibl Asn; Intl Thomas Merton Soc; Soc Bibl Lit; Soc Buddhist-Christian Stud. **RESEARCH** New Testament; Christian Origins; Christian Spirituality. **SELECTED PUBLICATIONS** Auth, The Conquered Self: Emptiness and God in Buddhist-Christian Dialogue, Japanese Jour Rel Studs, 12/4, 85; Matt 5:43-45: You, Therefore, must be perfect, Interpretation, 41/2, 87; The Gospel of John and Japanese Buddhism, Japanese Rel, 15/2, 88; Thomas Merton: Pioneer of Buddhist-Christian Dialogue, Cath World, May/June, 89; Wait Here and Watch: A Eucharistic Commentary on Matt 26-28, Chalice, 89; The Windows: A Women's Ministry in the Early Church, Fortress, 89; Language, Gender and Prayer, Lexington Theol Quart, 27/1, 92; Spiritual Life in the Early Church, Fortress, 93; Proclamation 5, Series C: Holy Week, Fortress, 94; Reading Colossians, Ephesians, and II Thessalonians, Crossroad, 95; Women in the New Testament, Crossroad, 98. **CONTACT ADDRESS** Dept of New Testament, Pittsburgh Theol Sem, 616 N Highland Ave, Pittsburgh, PA, 15206. **EMAIL** BThurston@pts.edu

TICHI, CECELIA
DISCIPLINE AMERICAN LITERATURE, WOMEN'S STUDIES **EDUCATION** UCLA, Davis, PhD. **CAREER** William R Kenan Jr Prof Eng, Vanderbilt Univ. **SELECTED PUBLICATIONS** Auth, New World, New Earth: Environmental Reform in American Literature from the Puritans through Whitman, 79; Shifting Gears: Technology, Literature, Culture in Modernist America; Electronic Hearth: Creating an American Television Culture, 91; High Lonesome: The American Culture of Country Music, 94. **CONTACT ADDRESS** Vanderbilt Univ, Nashville, TN, 37203-1727. **EMAIL** hickmald@ctrvax.vanderbilt.edu

TIDWELL, JOHN EDGAR
PERSONAL Born 12/13/1945, Independence, Kansas **DISCIPLINE** ENGLISH **EDUCATION** Washburn University, BA, English, 1969; Creighton University, MA, English, 1971; University of Minnesota, PhD, 1981; Yale University, visiting fellow, 1985-86. **CAREER** Atchison Neighborhood Center, Atchison, KS, director, 1969-70; Maur Hill Catholic College Preparatory School, Atchison, KS, instructor, 1969-70; Creighton University, instructor, 1970-71; University of Nebraska at Omaha, instructor, 1971-73, acting chairman of Black Studies Department, 1972-73; St Olaf College, director of American Minority Studies, 1973-74, instructor, 1973-75; University of Minnesota, teaching associate II, 1975-78; Carleton College, visiting instructor, Fall 1977, Spring 1979; University of Kentucky, assistant professor, 1981-87; Miami University, assistant professor, 1987-93, assoc prof, 1993-. **HONORS AND AWARDS** American Lutheran Church Future Faculty Fellowship, 1975-77; Putnam Dana McMillan Fellowship, University of Minnesota, 1979; National Fellowships Fund Award, 1978-81; NEH Fellowship for Independent Study and Research, 1985-86; several other fellowships and grants. **MEMBERSHIPS** Modern Language Association; Midwest Modern Language Association. **CONTACT ADDRESS** Department of English, Miami Univ, Oxford, OH, 45056.

TIEMENS, ROBERT K.
DISCIPLINE COMMUNICATION STUDIES **EDUCATION** Univ Iowa, PhD, 62. **CAREER** Prof. **MEMBERSHIPS** Nat Commun Asn; Western States Commun Asn. **RESEARCH** Visual communication; media production. **SELECTED PUBLICATIONS** Auth, A Visual Analysis of the 1976 Presidential Debates, 78; The Visual Context of Argument: An Analysis of the September 25, 1988 Presidential Debate, Nat Commun Asn, 89; coauth, Children's Perceptions of Changes in Size of Television Images, Human Commun Res, 81; Television's Coverage of Jesse Jackson's Speech to the 1984 Democratic National Convention, Jour Broadcasting Elec Media, 88. **CONTACT ADDRESS** Dept of Communication, Utah Univ, 100 S 1350 E, Salt Lake City, UT, 84112. **EMAIL** R.Tiemens@m.cc.utah.edu

TIERNEY, JAMES EDWARD
PERSONAL Born 01/23/1935, Newark, NJ, m, 1995 **DISCIPLINE** ENGLISH LITERATURE **EDUCATION** Seton Hall Univ, BA, 56; Fordham Univ, MA, 64; New York Univ, PhD(-English Lit), 69. **CAREER** From instr to asst prof English Lit, 68-75, from assoc prof to prof English, Univ MO-St Louis, 75-87; Nat Endowment for Humanities fel, 73-74: grants, Am Philos Soc, 76 & Am Coun Learned Soc, 77; Henry Huntington Libr fel, 76; bibliog ed, Eighteenth Century: A Current Bibliog, 78-; fel, inst res in Humanities, Univ Edinburgh, 82. **HONORS AND AWARDS** Univ of Missouri Research Board Grant, 93-94; UM-St Louis Research Office Grant, 94, 97; Fel Cen for Int Studies, UM-St Louis, 97. **MEMBERSHIPS** MLA; Am Soc 18th Century Studies; Johnson Soc; Bibliog Soc, London; Midwest Am Soc 18th Century Studies. **RESEARCH** Eighteenth century British periodical, novel and drama. **SELECTED PUBLICATIONS** Auth, Florio--an analogue of Tom Jones?, Yearbk English Studies, Spring 73; The Museum--the super-excellent magazine, Studies English Lit, Summer 73; Museum attributions in John Cooper's unpublished letters, Studies in Bibliog, Summer 74; Unpublished Garrick letters, Yearbk English Studies, 75; Four new Shenstone letters, Papers on Lang & Lit, 75; The study of the eighteenth century periodical: Problems and progress, Papers of Bibliog Soc Am, 75; Biblical allusion as character technique in Dryden's All for Love, English Studies, 77; Edmund Burke, John Hawkesworth, Annual Register, and Gentleman's Magazine, Huntington Libr Quart, 78; Book Advertisements in Mid-Eighteenth-Century Newspapers: The Example of Robert Didsley, in A Genious for Letters, eds Robin Myers and Michael Harris, Winchester, Eng: St Paul's Bibliographies, 95; Eighteenth-Century Authors and the Abuse of the Franking System, Studies in Bibliography, 95; Eighteenth-Century Dublin-London Publishing Relations: The Case of George Faulkner, in The Book Trade and Its Customers, 1450-1900, edited by Alison Shell, Arnold Hunt and Giles Mandelbrote, Winchester, Eng: St Paul's Bibliographies, 97. **CONTACT ADDRESS** Dept of English, Univ of Missouri, St. Louis, 8001 Natural Bridge, St. Louis, MO, 63121-4499. **EMAIL** c1953@umslvma.umsl.edu Batch 12 DAS Beth Babini

TIESSEN, PAUL
DISCIPLINE GENDER POLITICS IN FILM; BRITISH MODERNISM **EDUCATION** WLU, BA; Alberta, MA, PhD.

CAREER Prof **SELECTED PUBLICATIONS** Auth, and Apparently Incongruous Parts: The Worlds of Malcolm Lowry, Scarecrow Press, 90; The Letters of Malcolm Lowry and Gerald Noxon, 1940-1952 , UBC Press, 88; The Cinema of Malcolm Lowry: A Scholarly Edition of Lowry's Tender is the Night, UBC Press, 90; The 1940 Under the Volcano , MLR Editions Canada, 94; Co-ed, Joyce/Lowry: Critical Perspectives, UP of Kentucky, 97. **CONTACT ADDRESS** Dept of English, Wilfrid Laurier Univ, 75 University Ave W, Waterloo, ON, N2L 3C5. **EMAIL** ptiessen@mach1.wlu.ca

TIGER, VIRGINIA MARIE
PERSONAL Born 08/20/1940, Montreal, PQ, Canada, m, 1974, 1 child **DISCIPLINE** ENGLISH LITERATURE, WOMEN'S STUDIES **EDUCATION** Univ Toronto, BA, 63; Univ BC, MA, 65, PhD, 71. **CAREER** Exten lectr lit, Univ BC, 64-66; from instr to asst prof, 70-75, assoc prof, 75-, prof eng, Rutgers Univ, Newark, 76, DIR WOMEN'S STUDIES, 75-78, dir, Grad Eng, ch Eng Dept, Assoc dean fac, Dean Instruction; Broadcaster, Can Broadcasting Corp, 64-67; Drama critic, Toronto Daily Star, 60-63; Doc Res & partic sex roles, Can TV, Toronto, 77; bk critic, Wash Post, 74-76; bk critic, Soho News, 77-80. **MEMBERSHIPS** MLA; Nat Women's Studies Asn; AAUP; Doris Lessing Soc. **RESEARCH** Mod Brit lit; women's studies; hist of the novel. **SELECTED PUBLICATIONS** Auth, Advertisements for herself, Columbia Forum, spring 74; coauth, An Othello, Plays of the Open Space, Penguin, 74; auth, William Golding: The Dark Fields of Discovery, Calder & Boyars, 74; coauth, Everywoman, Random, 77; Inlaws/Outlaws: The language of women, In: Women's Language and Style, 78; Don's Lessing, G K Hall. **CONTACT ADDRESS** Dept of Eng, Rutgers Univ, 360 King Blvd, Newark, NJ, 07102-1897. **EMAIL** vtiger@andromida.rutgers.edu

TIMKO, MICHAEL
PERSONAL Born 08/16/1925, Garfield, NJ, m, 1947, 3 children **DISCIPLINE** ENGLISH LITERATURE **EDUCATION** Univ Mo, AB and BJ, 49, MA, 50; Univ Wis, PhD, 56. **CAREER** Instr English compos and lit, Univ Mo, 50-52; from instr to asst prof English lit, Univ Ill, 56-61; from asst prof to assoc prof English, 61-71, chmn dept, 72-78, PROF ENGLISH, QUEENS COL, NY, 71-; MEM GRAD FAC, GRAD CTR, CITY UNIV NEW YORK, 73-, DEP EXEC OFFICER, 78-, Mem bibliog comt and contrib ed, Victorian Studies, 63-66; chmn, Victorian comt, City Univ New York; ed, Dickens Studies Annual; fel, Inst Advan Studies, Edinburgh Univ, 82. **MEMBERSHIPS** MLA; Am Soc Theatre Res; English Inst; Browning Inst. **RESEARCH** Victorian literature; British and American drama; fiction. **SELECTED PUBLICATIONS** Auth, Ah, Did You Once See Browning Plain?, Studies English Lit, autumn 66; Innocent Victorian: The Satiric Poetry of A H Clough, Ohio Univ, 66; Thirty-Eight Short Stories: An Introductory Anthology, Knopf, 68; Wordsworth's Ode and Arnold's Dover Beach: Celestial light and Confused Alarms, Ciththara, 11/73; Arnold, Tennyson and the English Idyl: Ancient Criticism and Modern Poetry, Tex Studies Lit and Lang, spring 74; The Victorianism of Victorian literature, New Lit Hist, spring 75; The Central Wish: Human Passion and Cosmic Love in Tennyson's Idyls, Victorian Poetry, spring 78; Arthur Hugh Clough: Palpable Things and Celestial Fact in The Victorian Experience: The Poets, Ohio Univ P, 82; Literature in Context in Festschrift for Drescher, Horst W, Zeitschrift fur Anglistik und Amerikanistik, vol 0040, 92. **CONTACT ADDRESS** Dept of English, Queens Col, CUNY, 6530 Kissena Blvd, Flushing, NY, 11367-1597.

TIMS, ALBERT R.
DISCIPLINE MASS COMMUNICATION STUDIES **EDUCATION** Univ Wis Madison, PhD. **CAREER** Assoc prof **SELECTED PUBLICATIONS** Auth, The Cultivation of Consumer Confidence: A Longitudinal Analysis of News Media Influence on Consumer Sentiment, Advances Consumer Res, 89; The Impact of the News Media on Public Opinion: American Presidential Election 1987-88, Int J Public Opinion Res, 89. **CONTACT ADDRESS** Mass Communication Dept, Univ of Minnesota, Twin Cities, 111 Murphy Hall, 206 Church St SE, Minneapolis, MN, 55455. **EMAIL** timsx001@maroon.tc.umn.edu

TINKCOM, MATTHEW
DISCIPLINE ENGLISH LITERATURE **EDUCATION** Univ Ca, BA; Univ Tex, MA; Univ Pittsburgh, PhD. **CAREER** Eng Dept, Georgetown Univ **RESEARCH** Film, media and cultural studies; American studio film; avant-garde and experimental cinema. **SELECTED PUBLICATIONS** Auth, pubs in Cinema Jour, Film Quarterly. **CONTACT ADDRESS** English Dept, Georgetown Univ, 37th and O St, Washington, DC, 20057.

TIPPENS, DARRYL L.
DISCIPLINE ENGLISH **EDUCATION** Okla Christian Univ, BA, 68; La State Univ, MA, 71, PhD, 73. **CAREER** JAMES W. CULP DISTING PORF ENG, ABILENE CHRISTIAN UNIV, 96-, pres, S Central Renaissance Conf, 91-92; TREAS, CONF ON CHRISTIANITY AND LIT, 95-. **CONTACT ADDRESS** Dept of English, Abilene Christian Univ, ACU Station, Box 28252, Abilene, TX, 79699. **EMAIL** TippensD@nicanor.acu.edu

TISCHLER, NANCY MARIE
PERSONAL Born 03/20/1931, DeQueen, AR, m, 1958 **DISCIPLINE** LITERATURE **EDUCATION** Wilson Teachers Col, BS, 52; Univ Ark, MA, 54, PhD, 57. **CAREER** Asst, Univ Ark, 53-56; asst prof English, George Washington Univ, 56-62; assoc prof, Susquehanna Univ, 62-66; PROF HUMANITIES, PA STATE UNIV, CAPITOL CAMPUS, 66- **MEMBERSHIPS** MLA; Conf Christianity and Lit (pres, 70-72). **RESEARCH** Drama; modern novel; Southern literature. **SELECTED PUBLICATIONS** Auth, Tennessee Williams: Rebellious Puritan, Citadel, 61; Black Masks: Negro Characters in Modern Southern Fiction, Pa State Univ, 68; William Faulkner and the Southern Negro in Bear, Man and God, 2nd ed, 71; The Distorted Mirror, Tennessee Williams' Self-Portraits, Miss Quart, fall 72; Legacy of Eve, John Knox, 77; Dorothy L Sayers: A Pilgrim Soul, John Knox, 81; Williams, Tennessee Letters to Windham, Donald, 1940-1965, Miss Quart, Vol 0050, 97. **CONTACT ADDRESS** Dept of Humanities, Pennsylvania State Univ, Middletown, PA, 17057.

TISDALE, CELES
PERSONAL Born 07/31/1941, Salters, South Carolina, m **DISCIPLINE** ENGLISH **EDUCATION** State Univ Coll/ Buffalo, BS 1963, MS 1969, PhD 1991. **CAREER** PS 31 Buffalo, English teacher 1963-68; Woodlawn Jr High, English dept chmn 1968-69; WBEN TV, writer/producer 1969; WBFO-FM Radio, writer/announcer 1969-70; State Univ Coll Buffalo, English instructor 1969-72; WKBW TV, talk show host 1979-83; WKBW Radio, talk show host 1984-86; Erie Community Coll/ City, prof of English. **HONORS AND AWARDS** NY State Univ Chancellors Award for Teaching Excellence 1975; Man of Year, Business & Professional Women 1977; Media Award Sickle Cell Assn 1978. **MEMBERSHIPS** Assoc dir Buffalo Urban league 1966-92; bd of dirs Artpark 1981-84; dir Adolescent Vocational Exploration 1985-88; Young Audiences, Inc, 1975-; Career Educator for Buffalo Urban League 1987-91. **CONTACT ADDRESS** Professor of English, Erie Comm Col, City, 121 Ellicott St, Buffalo, NY, 14203.

TM, KING
PERSONAL Born 05/09/1929, Pittsburgh, PA, s **DISCIPLINE** RELIGIOUS STUDIES; THEOLOGY; ENGLISH **EDUCATION** Univ Pitts, BA, 51; Fordham Univ, MA, 59; Univ Strasbourg, DSR, 68. **CAREER** Asst prof, 68-74, assoc prof, 74-89, full prof, 89-, Georgetown Univ. **MEMBERSHIPS** Cosmos & Creation; Univ Fac for Life. **RESEARCH** Science and religion; Psychology and religion; History of spirituality. **SELECTED PUBLICATIONS** Auth, Sartre and the Sacred, Univ Chicago Press, 74; Teilhard's Mysticism of Knowing, Seabury, 81; Teilhard de Chardin, Glazier, 88; Enchantments, Religion and the Power of the Word, Sheed & Ward, 89; Merton: Mystic at the Center of America, Liturgical, 92; Jung's Four & Some Philosophers, Univ Notre Dame Press, 98; coed, Letters of Teilhard de Chardin and Lucile Swan, Georgetown Univ Press, 93. **CONTACT ADDRESS** Dept of Theology, Georgetown Univ, Washington, DC, 20057. **EMAIL** kingt@gunet.georgetown.edu

TOBIAS, MICHAEL CHARLES
DISCIPLINE WRITER, DIRECTOR, PRODUCER, EXEC PRODUCER **SELECTED PUBLICATIONS** Auth, A Naked Man, Asian Humanities Press, 94; A Vision of Nature-Traces of the Original World, Kent State Univ Press, 95; The Soul of Nature-Visions of a Living Earth, Continuum (hard cover), 95, Penguin-Dutton/Plume (soft cover), 96; World War III, Continuum Pubs, 2nd ed, rev, updated, with foreward by Jane Goodall, 98; World War III-Population and the Biosphere at the End of the Millennium, Bear, & Co, 94; A Parliment of Souls-In Search of Global Spirituality, KQED Books & Tapes, PBS, 95; India 24 Hours, Mapin Pub, India, 96; A Day in the Life of India, Harper Collins, 97; Kinship with Animals, Beyond Words Pub, 98; Ich Spurte Die Seele Der Tiere, Frankh-Kosmos Pub, 97; Nature's Keepers-On the Frontlines of the Fight to Save Wildlife in America, John Wiley & Sons Pub, 98; In Search of Reality-The Art of Documentary Filmmaking, Michael Wiese Pub, 98; Jan & Catharina, Smart Art Press, 98; numerous films; over 200 articles and essays published in numerous books, and in such magazines and journals as: The Kenyon Rev, The Athenian, Discovery Mag, Mother Earth news, Population & Environment, Bloomsbury Rev, The San Francisco Rev of Books, Parabola, Sciences, Greenpeace, The New Scientist, Psychology Today, Trilogy Mag, Lapis, and Terra Nova. **CONTACT ADDRESS** 2118 Wilshire Blvd #572, Santa Monica, CA, 90403. **EMAIL** mctobias@aol.com

TOBIN, DANIEL
DISCIPLINE 20TH CENTURY IRISH, BRITISH AND AMERICAN LITERATURE **EDUCATION** Iona Col, BA; Harvard Univ,MTS; Warren Wilson Col, MFA; Univ Va,PhD. **CAREER** English, Carthage Col. **HONORS AND AWARDS** fel, Univ Va; Commonwealth, Marchant, a du Pont, Rotary Int; The Nation. **SELECTED PUBLICATIONS** Auth, The Son's Book. **CONTACT ADDRESS** Carthage Col, 2001 Alford Dr., Kenosha, WI, 53140.

TOBIN, DANIEL
PERSONAL Born 01/13/1958, Brooklyn, NY, m **DISCIPLINE** LITERATURE **EDUCATION** Iona Col, BA, 80; Harvard Univ, MTS, 83; Warren Wilson Col, MFA, 90; Univ Virginia, PhD, 91. **CAREER** Assoc prof, 91- Carthage Col; assoc prof, 97-, Schl of the Art Inst of Chicago. **RESEARCH** Poetry, Irish poetry, relig and lit. **CONTACT ADDRESS** Dept of English, Carthage Col, 2001 Alford Dr, Kenosha, WI, 53140.

TOBIN, FRANK J.
DISCIPLINE MEDIEVAL LITERATURE AND PHILOSOPHY, GERMAN **EDUCATION** Stanford Univ, PhD. **CAREER** Prof Ger, Univ Nev, Reno; ed bd, Studia Mystica and Mystic Quart. **RESEARCH** Translation of Mechthild von Magdeburg. **SELECTED PUBLICATIONS** Published major books on Meister Eckhart and on Mechthild von Magdeburg, numerous articles on the German Middle Ages, and a coauthored two-volume anthology of German literature. **CONTACT ADDRESS** Univ Nev, Reno, Reno, NV, 89557. **EMAIL** tobinf@scs.unr.edu

TODD, DENNIS
DISCIPLINE ENGLISH LITERATURE **EDUCATION** Univ Ca, BA; Emory Univ, PhD. **CAREER** Eng Dept, Georgetown Univ **RESEARCH** Eighteenth century literature and culture; European encounters with New World cultures. **SELECTED PUBLICATIONS** Auth, Imagining Monsters, 95; pubs on Pope, Swift, Hogarth, Arbuthnot, and early science. **CONTACT ADDRESS** English Dept, Georgetown Univ, 37th and O St, Washington, DC, 20057.

TODD, WILLIAM B.
DISCIPLINE ENGLISH **EDUCATION** Lehigh, BA, 40, MA, 47; Univ Chicago, PhD, 49. **CAREER** Emer Prof English, Univ Tex, Austin. **HONORS AND AWARDS** LHD, Lehigh, 75. **RESEARCH** Sir Walter Scott. **SELECTED PUBLICATIONS** Coauth, Fel Publ, Scott's Commentary on The Journal of a Tour to the Hebrides with Samuel Johnson, Studies in Bibliog 48, 95; auth, A Bibliography of Edmund Burke, Rupert Harf-Davis, 64; A Directory of Printers and Others in London, London Print Hist Soc, 72; co-ed, The Writings and Speeches of Edmund Burke, Oxford, 61, 88. **CONTACT ADDRESS** Dept of English, Univ Texas, Austin, TX, 78712.

TOKARCZYK, MICHELLE M.
PERSONAL Born 01/02/1953, Bronx, NY, m, 1979 **DISCIPLINE** ENGLISH **EDUCATION** Herbert Lehman Col, BA, 75; SUNY Stony Brook, MA, 78, PhD, 85. **CAREER** Asst prof, 85-86, Hofstra Col; asst prof, Rutgers Univ, 86-87; asst prof, 89-95, ASST PROF, 95-, GOUCHER COL. **HONORS AND AWARDS** Susan Koppelman Award, 94. **MEMBERSHIPS** NEMCA, MCA, ASA, CCC **RESEARCH** Gender and class intersections; Contemporary literature; Composition and literature. **SELECTED PUBLICATIONS** auth Working-Class Women in the Academy: Laborers in the Knowledge Factory, Univ Mass Press, 93; Getting the Job: The Adjunct Game, Concerns: Publication of the Women's Caucus of the Mod Lang Asn, 94; "The City, The Waterworks, and Writing: An Interview with E L Doctorow," Kenyon Rev, 95; rev "Lifting a Ton of Feathers: A Woman's Guide to Surviving in the Academic World," Jour Higher Educ, 95; The Waterworks, Lit Rev, 96; Talk the Talk: Differences in Working-Class and Academic Vocabularies, Uncommon Threads, 96; The Illusions of Postmodernism, Theory & Event, 97. **CONTACT ADDRESS** Goucher Col, 1021 Dulaney Valley Rd, Baltimore, MD, 21204. **EMAIL** MTokarczyk@aol.com

TOLER, COLETTE
PERSONAL Pittsburgh, PA **DISCIPLINE** ENGLISH **EDUCATION** Seton Hill Col, BMus, 57; Univ Notre Dame, MA, 62, PhD, 65. **CAREER** From asst prof to assoc prof, 65-72, acad dean, 71-82, Prof English, Seton Hill Col, 73-, vis prof, Col Mt St Vincent, 68-69; mem task force higher educ Pa, Pa Dept Educ, 77-78; mem bd dirs, Southwestern Pa Higher Educ Coun, 77-; vis scholar, Cambridge Univ, 82- **MEMBERSHIPS** MLA **RESEARCH** Art and civilization in the fiction of Willa Cather; existential fiction; the American Twenties. **SELECTED PUBLICATIONS** Auth, Willa Cather's Vision of the Artist, in Personalist, autumn 64; Look On - Make No Sound, in Notre Dame English J, fall 64; Hemingway and Fitzgerald as Mirrors of the Twenties, in J Twenties, 72. **CONTACT ADDRESS** Dept of English, Seton Hill Col, 1 Seton Hill Dr, Greensburg, PA, 15601-1599.

TOLES, GEORGE E.
DISCIPLINE ENGLISH LITERATURE **EDUCATION** State Univ NY Buffalo, BA; Univ Virg, MA; PhD. **CAREER** Prof **HONORS AND AWARDS** Ed, Mosaic. **RESEARCH** American films; theatre; and 19th and 20th century European and American fiction. **SELECTED PUBLICATIONS** Auth, pub(s) on William Faulkner, Charles Brockden Brown, Mark Twain, Frank Capra, Alfred Hitchcock, Judith Thompson, F. Scott Fitzgerald, James Agee, Marilynne Robinson, Anne Tyler, Jean Renoir, Tennessee Williams, Vittorio De Sica, Greta Garbo, Jean-Claude Lauzon, movie humiliation scenes and movie sentiment. **CONTACT ADDRESS** Dept of English, Manitoba Univ, Winnipeg, MB, R3T 2N2.

TOLLERS, VINCENT LOUIS
PERSONAL Born 08/23/1939, Superior, WI, m, 1963, 2 children **DISCIPLINE** ENGLISH **EDUCATION** Univ Wis, Superior, BA, 61; Univ Colo, Boulder, MA, 65, PhD, 68. **CAREER** Asst prof English, Emporia State Univ, Emporia, 68-70; asst prof, 70-74, assoc prof, 74-80, PROF ENGLISH, STATE UNIV NY COL, BROCKPORT, 80-, Chmn, 80-83, PROJ DIR RONALD E MCNAIR POST-BACCALAUREATE ACHIEVEMENT PROG, 89- , & COL SCI & TECHNOL ENTRY PROG, 98- ; Compiler, Abstracts English Studies, 72-80; vis lectr English, Matlock Col Educ, Eng, 76-77; compiler, MLA Int Bibliog, 74-79; ed, Lit Res, 76-85. **MEMBERSHIPS** MLA; NCTE; CCCC; Nat Coun Educ Opportunity Asn; Am Asn Australian Lit Stud; Int Mentoring Asn; Nat Coun Undergrad Res. **RESEARCH** Victorian literature; bibliography; Bible studies. **SELECTED PUBLICATIONS** Ed, A Bibliography of Matthew Arnold, Pa State Univ, 74; auth, Eight New Arnold Letters, Arnoldian, 76; co-ed, The Bible in Its Literary Milieu: Contemporary Essays, W B Eerdmans, 79; Mapping of the Biblical Terrain, Bucknell Univ Press, 90; Guided Research in Freshman English, LRN, 81. **CONTACT ADDRESS** Dept of English, State Univ NY Col, 350 New Campus Dr, Brockport, NY, 14420-2914.

TOLOMEO, DIANE
DISCIPLINE ENGLISH LITERATURE **EDUCATION** Univ Rochester, BA; Princeton Univ, MA, Phd. **CAREER** Assoc prof **RESEARCH** Biblical and modern literature; Anglo-Irish literature. **SELECTED PUBLICATIONS** Rev(s), Joyce Carol Oates, Amer Writers, Scribners, 80; auth, Anglo Irish Research, MLA, 83; Mapping the Biblical Terrain, Bucknell, Dictionary of Literary Biography, Yeats. **CONTACT ADDRESS** Dept of English, Victoria Univ, PO Box 3070, Victoria, BC, V8W 3W1. **EMAIL** dtolomeo@uvic.ca

TOMASULO, FRANK P.
DISCIPLINE FILM AND TELEVISION STUDIES **EDUCATION** Brooklyn Col, BA, 67; NY Univ, MA, 73; UCLA, PhD, 86. **CAREER** Instr, NY Univ, UCLA, St Johns Univ, Ithaca Col, Cornell Univ, Univ Calif, Santa Cruz; assoc prof, ch, dept Commun, Ga State Univ, 91-94; ed, J of Film & Video. **HONORS AND AWARDS** NEH grant, Univ Calif, Berkeley; 1st prize, Scholarly Writing competition, Soc for Cinema Stud; Dana Award for Scholarly Res, Ithaca Col. **RESEARCH** Italian film director Michelangelo Antonioni. **SELECTED PUBLICATIONS** Published over 40 academic articles, book chapters, reviews, interviews, and translations on film and television topics. **CONTACT ADDRESS** Georgia State Univ, Atlanta, GA, 30303. **EMAIL** joufpt@panther.gsu.edu

TOMPKINS, JANE
DISCIPLINE ENGLISH LITERATURE **EDUCATION** Yale Univ, PhD, 66. **CAREER** Prof, Duke Univ. **RESEARCH** Am lit; popular cult; pedag. **SELECTED PUBLICATIONS** Auth, Sensational Designs: The Cultural Work of American Fiction, 1790-1860, Oxford, 85;), West of Everything, Oxford, 92; ed, Reader-Response Criticism: From Formalism to Post-Structuralism, Hopkins, 80. **CONTACT ADDRESS** Eng Dept, Duke Univ, Durham, NC, 27706.

TOMPKINS, PHILLIP K.
DISCIPLINE COMMUNCATION STUDIES **EDUCATION** Univ Northern Colo, BA, 56; Univ Nebr, MA; 57; Purdue Univ, PhD, 62. **CAREER** Prof. **RESEARCH** Organizational communication; rhetorical literary and social theory; communication and control. **SELECTED PUBLICATIONS** Auth, A Note on Burke, Goethe, and the Jews, Quarterly Jour Speech, 95; Identification in the Self-Managing Organization: Characteristics of Target and Tenure, 94; Principles of Rigor in 'Qualitative' Research in Communication, Western Jour Commun, 94. **CONTACT ADDRESS** Dept of Communication, Univ Colo Boulder, Boulder, CO, 80309. **EMAIL** Phillip.Tompkins@Colorado.edu

TONN, ANKE
PERSONAL Born 02/03/1944, Hamburg, Germany, d, 2 children **DISCIPLINE** LIBRARY SCIENCE **EDUCATION** BA; MILS **CAREER** Nova Scotia Tech Univ; Memorial Univ of New Foundland; Tulane Univ; Nichols State Univ, Thibodanx, LA. **MEMBERSHIPS** ALA; ACRL; Louisiana Library Assoc. **RESEARCH** German literature; art history **CONTACT ADDRESS** 512-B Parkside Dr, Thibodanx, LA, 70301. **EMAIL** el-at@nich.nsunet.nich.edu

TOOMBS, CHARLES PHILLIP
PERSONAL Born 12/02/1952, Indianapolis, IN, d **DISCIPLINE** LITERATURE **EDUCATION** Purdue University, West Lafayette, IN, BA, 1976, MA, 1978, MS, 1981, PhD, 1986. **CAREER** Purdue University, West Lafayette, Ind, graduate assistant, 1976-81, graduate instructor, 1982-85; Indiana University Northwest, Gary, IN, visiting instructor, 1985-86; California State University, Bakersfield, CA, assistant professor, 1986-88; UNIV OF GEORGIA, ATHENS, GA, ASST PROF, 1988-. **HONORS AND AWARDS** Lilly Fellowship, University of Georgia, 1989-90; Howard G McCall Award, Purdue U Black Cultural Center, 1978; First Place in Fiction and Poetry, Paul Robeson Literary Awards, 1976. **MEMBERSHIPS** Member, Modern Language Association, 1985-; member, Research Association of Minority Professors, 1986-; member, Southern Conference on Afro-American Studies, 1988-; member, National Council for Black Studies, currently. **SELECTED PUBLICATIONS** "Joyce Carol Thomas," Dictionary of Literary Biography, 1984; "Master Timothy," Indiana Experience, Indiana UP, 1978; "Seven Haiku," High/Coo, 1977. **CONTACT ADDRESS** English, Univ of Georgia, Park Hall, Athens, GA, 30602.

TOPPING BAZIN, NANCY
DISCIPLINE TWENTIETH-CENTURY WORLD LITERATURE **EDUCATION** Ohio Wesleyan Univ, BA; Middlebury Grad Sch French, MA; Stanford Univ, PhD. **CAREER** Engl, Old Dominion Univ. **RESEARCH** 20th century Brit lit; mod drama; Nadine gordimer; Athol Fugard; Doris Lessing; Virginia Woolf. **SELECTED PUBLICATIONS** Auth, Conversations with Nadine Gordimer, UP Miss, 90; Virginia Woolf and the Androgynous Vision, Rutgers UP, 73. **CONTACT ADDRESS** Old Dominion Univ, 4100 Powhatan Ave, Norfolk, VA, 23058. **EMAIL** NBazin@odu.edu

TORGOVNICK, MARIANNA
DISCIPLINE ENGLISH **EDUCATION** NY Univ, BA, 70; Columbia Univ, MA, 71, PhD, 75. **CAREER** Asst prof, Williams Col, 75-81; from asst prof to prof, Duke Univ, 81- ; ch of Engl Dept, 96- ; vis prof, Princeton Univ, 93. **HONORS AND AWARDS** Am Book Award Winner, for Crossing Ocean Parkway. **MEMBERSHIPS** MLA **RESEARCH** Prose fiction; Narrative theory; Lit and the Visual Arts; 19th and 20th century Brit Lit. **SELECTED PUBLICATIONS** Ed, Writing Cultural Criticism, SAQ spec issue, 92; Eloquent Obsessions: Writing Cultural Criticism, 94; auth, Closure in the Novel, 81; The Visual Arts, Pictorialism, and the Novel: James, Lawrence, and Woolf, 85; Gone Primitive: Savage Intellects, Modern Lives, 90; Crossing Ocean Parkway: Readings by an Italian American Daughter, 94; Discovering Jane Ellen Harrison, Seeing Double: Revisioning Edwardian and Modernist Literature, eds C. Kaplan and Anne B. Simpson, 96; A Passion for the Primitive: Dian Fossey Among the Animals, Yale Rev, 84:4, 96; Primitive Passions: Men, Women, and the Quest for Ecstasy, 97. **CONTACT ADDRESS** Dept of English, Duke Univ, 314 Allen Bldg, Durham, SC, 27706. **EMAIL** tor@acpub.duke.edu

TORRES, LOUIS
PERSONAL Born 01/22/1938, Orange, NJ, m, 1987 **DISCIPLINE** PSYCHOLOGY, ENGLISH **EDUCATION** Rutgers Univ, BA, 60; teachers Coll, Columbia Univ, 71. **CAREER** Teacher, Franklin School, NY City, 67-69; teacher, Indian Hills High School, NJ, 69-80; managing dir, William Carter Dance Ensemble, NY City, 80-82; teacher, Am Renaissance Schoolm NY, 81-84; founder, ed, publ, Aristos, 82-91; CO-ED, Publ, ARISTOS, 92-. **MEMBERSHIPS** Am Philos Asn; Am Soc for Aesthetics; Asn of Literary Scholars and Critics; Asn of Art Hist. **RESEARCH** Philosophy of Art. **SELECTED PUBLICATIONS** Auth, The New Dawn of Painting, ARISTOS, 86; The Child as Poet: An Insidious and Injurious Myth, Aristos, 88; Jack Schaefer, Teller of Tales, Aristos, 96; Jack Schaefer, Encycl of Frontier and Western Fiction, forthcoming; coauth, Ayn Rand's Philosophy of Art: A Critical Introduction, 91-92; What Art Is: The Esthetic Theory of Ayn Rand, forthcoming. **CONTACT ADDRESS** Aristos, Radio City Station, PO Box 1105, New York, NY, 10101. **EMAIL** aristos@aristos.org

TOSSA, WAJUPPA
PERSONAL Born 10/04/1950, Thatphanom, Thailand, s **DISCIPLINE** AMERICAN LITERATURE **EDUCATION** Drew Univ, PhD, 86. **CAREER** Asst prof, Humanities and Social Sci, Mahasavakham Univ, 78-98; vis prof, Center for Asian and Pacific Studies, Univ of Oregon, 98-99. **HONORS AND AWARDS** Witler Bynner Found for Poetry Award, 85, 92, & 94; Fulbright Sr Scholar Grant, 91 & 98. **MEMBERSHIPS** Nat Storytelling Asn; Am Higher Ed Asn. **RESEARCH** Language and cultural preservation; storytelling; translation. **SELECTED PUBLICATIONS** Auth, Phya Khankhaak, The Toad King, a Translation: Fertility Myth into English Verse, Bucknell Univ, Press, 96; Phadaeng Nang Ai, A Translation of a Thai/Isan Folk Epic into English Verse, Bucknell Univ Press, 90. **CONTACT ADDRESS** Center for Asian and Pacific Studies, Univ of Oregon, 110 Gerlinger Hall, Eugene, OR, 97403.

TOTH, BILL
DISCIPLINE ENGLISH AND AMERICAN LITERATURE **EDUCATION** BA, MA Calif State Univ, PhD The Union Institute **CAREER** Prof, 91-. **RESEARCH** Nature writing, literature of the American West, modern drama, film. . **SELECTED PUBLICATIONS** Rev, 80 bk reviews, bk(s) of the Southwest and Western American lit. **CONTACT ADDRESS** Dept of Eng, Western New Mexico Univ, 1000 West College Ave., Silver City, NM, 88061. **EMAIL** tothb@silver.wnmu.edu

TOTH, EMILY
DISCIPLINE LOUISIANA WRITERS **EDUCATION** Johns Hopkins Univ, PhD, 75. **CAREER** Prof, La State Univ; ed bd, Southern Stud; ed, Regionalism and the Female Imagination, 75-79. **HONORS AND AWARDS** Emily Toth Award, 86; LEH res and publ grants, 90, 93; Cert of Commendation, Am Asn for State and Local Hist, 93., Founder and ed, Regionalism and the Female Imagination, 75-79 (formerly the Kate Chopin Newsletter). **RESEARCH** Kate Chopin's papers; women's studies. **SELECTED PUBLICATIONS** Auth, Inside Peyton Place: The Life of Grace Metalious, 81; Daughters of New Orleans, 83; Women in Academia, The Acad's Handbk, 88; The Curse: A Cultural History of Menstruation, 88; Kate Chopin's New Orleans Years, New Orleans Rev, 88; A New Biographical Approach, in Approaches to Teaching Kate Chopin's "The Awakening", 88; Firing the Canon: The Fear That Literature is Fun, Earlhamite, 90; Kate Chopin: A Life of the Author of "The Awakening", 90; The Shadow of the First Biographer: The Case of Kate Chopin, Southern Rev, 90; Developing Political Savvy--Many Misadventures Later, Women's Stud Quart, 90; Kate Chopin on Divine Love and Suicide: Two Rediscovered Articles, Am Lit, 91; Ms. Mentor's Impeccable Advice for Women in Academica, 97; ed, Regionalism and Female Imagination, 85; A Vocation and a Voice by Kate Chopin, 91. **CONTACT ADDRESS** Dept of Eng, Louisiana State Univ, 236B Allen Hall, Baton Rouge, LA, 70803. **EMAIL** etoth@unix1.sncc.lsu.edu

TOULOUSE, TERESA
DISCIPLINE EARLY AMERICAN LITERATURE **EDUCATION** Oberlin Col, BA, 72; Harvard Univ, PhD, 80. **CAREER** Engl, Tulane Univ. **SELECTED PUBLICATIONS** Auth, The Art of Prophesying: New England Sermons and the Shaping of Belief, Univ Ga Press, 87; Mary Rowlandson's Narrative and the 'New' Theories of Early American Literature, Amerikastudien/Amer Stud 36, 92; Mine Own Credit': Strategies of (E)Valuation in Rowlandson's Captivity Narrative, Amer Lit 64, 92; Mary Rowlandson and the Rhetoric of Ambiguity, Stud Puritan Amer Spirituality III, 92; co-ed, The Sermons of Ralph Waldo Emerson, Univ Mo Press, 90. **CONTACT ADDRESS** Dept of Eng, Tulane Univ, 6823 St Charles Ave, New Orleans, LA, 70118. **EMAIL** toulouse@mailhost.tcs.tulane.edu

TOWNS, SANNA NIMTZ
PERSONAL Born 10/12/1943, Hawthorne, NV, d **DISCIPLINE** ENGLISH **EDUCATION** Southern Univ, BA 1964; Teachers Coll Columbia Univ, MA 1967; Univ of Southern MS, PhD 1985. **CAREER** Amer Language Prog Columbia Univ, English lang instructor 1969-71; Office of Urban Affairs SUNY at Buffalo, prog coord 1973-75; Kuwait Univ, instructor & admin 1975-79; English Dept Univ of New Orleans, lang coord & instructor 1980-82, 1985-86; DELGADO COMM COLL, asst prof, asst chair, 1986-87, chair, communication division, 1987-92, ASSOCIATE PROF OF ENGLISH, 1992-. **HONORS AND AWARDS** State of LA Bd of Regents Graduate Fellowship 1982-85; ; Black Achiever in Education, Dyrades YMCA, New Orleans, 1988-89; Fulbright-Hays Seminars Aboard Participant, American University in Cairo, 1988; Fulbright Scholar Award, Comenius Univ, Bratislava, Slovakia, Jan-June 1994. **MEMBERSHIPS** Mem Natl Council of Teachers of English 1980-, LA Assoc of Developmental Educ 1981-, Phi Delta Kappa 1984-, South Central Modern Language Assoc 1986-; speaker New Orleans Museum of Art Speakers Bureau 1987; member, Delta Sigma Theta Sorority, 1962-; member, Conference on College Composition & Communications, 1980-. **SELECTED PUBLICATIONS** Article "Integrating Reading & Writing Instruction" in ERIC 1984. **CONTACT ADDRESS** English, Communication Div, Delgado Comm Col, 615 City Park Ave, New Orleans, LA, 70119.

TOWNSEND, PATRICIA ANN
PERSONAL Born 05/25/1933, Lufkin, TX **DISCIPLINE** SPEECH **EDUCATION** Stephen F Austin State Col, BS, 53, MA, 56; Univ Wi, PhD, 59. **CAREER** Teaching asst, Stephen F Austin State Col, 53-54; teacher speech & English, Blocker Jr High Sch, Texas City, Tex, 54-56; res asst, Univ Wis, 56-57, teaching asst, 58-59; asst prof speech, Univ N Ia, 59-66; assoc prof, 66-68, prof speech, Univ Wi-Whitewater, 68-, ch dept communication, 88-93, assoc dean col arts & communication, 93-96, interim dean, 96-97, assoc dean, 97-98; Danforth Assoc, 78; ed, Wis Commun Asn J, 82-. **HONORS AND AWARDS** Wi Commun Asn Outstanding Col Educr, UWW Serv Award. **MEMBERSHIPS** Speech Commun Asn; Cent States Speech Commun Asn; AAUP; Rhetoric Soc Am; Nat Asn Parliamentarians. **RESEARCH** Speech writing; rhetoric. **SELECTED PUBLICATIONS** Auth, Using our heritage: Speeches as models, J Commun Asn Pac, fall 77; Asst ed & ed Wi Comm Asn J. **CONTACT ADDRESS** Col Arts & Communication, Univ Wi, 800 W Main, Whitewater, WI, 53190-1790. **EMAIL** ptownsen@idcnet.com

TOWNSEND, ROBERT CAMPBELL
PERSONAL Born 06/05/1935, New Rochelle, NY, m, 1957, 3 children **DISCIPLINE** ENGLISH LITERATURE **EDUCATION** Princeton Univ, BA, 57; Cambridge Univ, MA, 59; Harvard Univ, PhD, 62. **CAREER** Teaching fel gen educ, Harvard Univ, 60-62; from instr to assoc prof, 62-76, PROF ENGLISH, AMHERST COL, 76- **MEMBERSHIPS** MLA **RESEARCH** Romantic and literary criticism; American literature and culture. **SELECTED PUBLICATIONS** Auth, John Worksworth

and his brothers poetic development, PMLA, 3/66; W K Wimsatt's criticism, Mass Rev, winter 66; Cambridge English, Critical Surv, winter 67; Sherwood Andersen: A Biography, Houghton-Mifflin, 87; Manhood at Harvard: William James and Others, W.W. Norton, 96; author of numerous articles since 1967. **CONTACT ADDRESS** Dept of English, Amherst Col, Amherst, MA, 01002-5000.

TRACE, JACQUELINE BRUCH
PERSONAL Buffalo, NY, 2 children **DISCIPLINE** RENAISSANCE LITERATURE, HISTORY OF BUFFALO **EDUCATION** Bowling Green State Univ, BA, 57; OH Univ, MA, 59; Univ MA, PhD, 75. **CAREER** Prof lit, State Univ NY Fredonia, 78; dealer in bks. **MEMBERSHIPS** AAUW **RESEARCH** Historical influence on Shakespearean drama; the rhetoric of technical and business commun; parapsychological lit. **SELECTED PUBLICATIONS** Auth, The supernatural element in Barbour's Bruce, Mass Studies English, spring 68; Shakespeare's bastard Faulconbridge: An early Tudor hero, Shakespeare Studies Vol XIII, 80; Style and Strategy of the Business Letter, Prentice-Hall, 85; Dark Goddesses: Black Feminist Theology in Morrisons Beloved, Obsidian II, no 3, 91. **CONTACT ADDRESS** SUNY at Fredonia, Fredonia, NY, 14063-1143. **EMAIL** traceja@buffalostate.edu

TRACY, ANN B.
DISCIPLINE ENGLISH **EDUCATION** Colby Univ, BA; Brown Univ, MA; Univ Toronto, PhD. **CAREER** Eng Dept, Plattsburgh State Univ **HONORS AND AWARDS** Disting tchg prof, 74. **RESEARCH** 18th and 19th-century lit; Renaissance lit; Gothic novel. **SELECTED PUBLICATIONS** Auth, bk on Gothic romance; several novels and short story collections. **CONTACT ADDRESS** SUNY, Plattsburgh, 101 Broad St, Plattsburgh, NY, 12901-2681.

TRACY, KAREN
DISCIPLINE COMMUNCATION STUDIES **EDUCATION** Pa State Univ, BA, 72; Bowling Green State Univ, MA, 74; Univ Wis, PhD, 81. **CAREER** Prof. **RESEARCH** Discourse analysis; facework and identity processes; language and social interaction; institutional discourse; dilematic and multiple goal perspectives. **SELECTED PUBLICATIONS** Auth, Action-implicative discourse analysis, Jour Lang Soc Psychol, 95; coauth, Qualitative Contributions to the Empirical, 97. **CONTACT ADDRESS** Dept of Communication, Univ Colo Boulder, Boulder, CO, 80309. **EMAIL** Karen.Tracy@Colorado.edu

TRAUB, GEORGE WILLIAM
PERSONAL Born 01/30/1936, Chicago, IL **DISCIPLINE** THEOLOGY & LITERATURE, SPIRITUALITY **EDUCATION** Xavier Univ, BLitt, 58; West Baden Col, PhL, 61; Loyola Univ Chicago, MA, 68; Cornell Univ, PhD, 73. **CAREER** Instr English, Greek & Latin, Loyola Acad, Ill, 61-64; from Asst Prof to Assoc Prof English, 72-87, Jesuit Prof Theology & Dir Ignatian Programs, Xavier Univ, 87-; Dir Formation & Continuing Educ, Chicago Prov Soc of Jesus, 80-85. **MEMBERSHIPS** Coordrs for Mission & Identity, Assoc of Jesuit Cols and Univs. **RESEARCH** Ignatian sprituality; Jesuit history & education; theology and literature. **SELECTED PUBLICATIONS** Coauth, The Desert and the City: An Interpretation of the History of Christian Spirituality, Loyola Univ Press, 84; Do You Speak Ignatian? A Glossary of Terms Used in Ignatian & Jesuit Circles, 3rd ed, Xavier Univ, 98. **CONTACT ADDRESS** Xavier Univ, 3800 Victory Pky, Cincinnati, OH, 45207-5185. **EMAIL** kelleyc@xavier.xu.edu

TRAVIS, PETER W.
DISCIPLINE ENGLISH LITERATURE **EDUCATION** Univ Chicago, PhD, 72. **CAREER** Prof, Dartmouth Col. **RESEARCH** Lit theory; Brit lit; Brit Medieval lit. **SELECTED PUBLICATIONS** Auth, Deconstructing Chaucer's Retraction, Exemplaria, 91; The Social Body of the Dramatic Christ in Medieval England, ACTA, 87; Dramatic Design in the Chester Cycle, Univ Chicago P, 82. **CONTACT ADDRESS** Dartmouth Col, 3529 N Main St, #207, Hanover, NH, 03755.

TRAWICK, LEONARD MOSES
PERSONAL Born 07/04/1933, Decatur, AL, m, 2 children **DISCIPLINE** ENGLISH **EDUCATION** Univ of the South, BA, 55; Univ Chicago, MA, 57; Harvard Univ, PhD, 61. **CAREER** From instr to asst prof English, Columbia Univ, 61-69; assoc prof, 69-73, prof English, Cleveland State Univ, 73-98; prof Emeritus, 98; Ed, Gamut Jour, Cleveland State Univ, 80-92; Ed, Cleveland State Univ Poetry Centrer, 71-98. **HONORS AND AWARDS** James P Barry Ohioana Award for Editorial Excellence, 91; Ohioana Poetry Award for lifetime achievement in poetry, 94. **MEMBERSHIPS** MLA **RESEARCH** English romatic literature; American literature; poetics. **SELECTED PUBLICATIONS** Auth, Hazlitt, Reynolds and the ideal, Studies Romanticism, summer 65; Backgrounds of Romanticism, Ind Univ, 67; The present state of Blake studies, Studies Burke & His Time, winter 70-71; Beast Forms (poems), Cleveland State Univ, 71; Whittier's Snow-Bound: A poem about the imagination, Essays Lit, spring 74; Nature and art in Milton, Blake Newslett, winter 74; Blake's Empirical Occult, Wordsworth Circle, spring 77; Blake's German Connection, Colby

Libr Quart, 12/77; Beastmorfs, Cleveland State Univ Poetry Center, 94. **CONTACT ADDRESS** Dept of English, Cleveland State Univ, 1983 E 24th St, Cleveland, OH, 44115-2440. **EMAIL** l.trawick@csuohio.edu

TRAYLOR, ELEANOR W.
PERSONAL s **DISCIPLINE** ENGLISH **EDUCATION** Spelman College, BA; Atlanta University, MA; Catholic University, PhD. **CAREER** Department of Agriculture, Graduate School, English Department, chairperson, 1966-67; Howard University, College of Fine Arts, adjunct professor, drama, 1968-75; Hobart & William Smith Colleges, The Melvin Hill Professorship Chair, 1979; Cornell University, visiting professor, literature, 1979-80; Tougaloo College, visiting humanist, 1982; Montgomery College, professor, English, 1965-90; HOWARD UNIVERSITY, professor, English, Humanities Department, chair, 1990-93, CHAIR, DEPT OF ENGLISH, 1993-. **HONORS AND AWARDS** Midwest African-American Theatre Alliance, The Hazel Joan Bryant Recognition Award, 1987; Peoples Congregational Church, The Black History Achievement Award for contributions to the advancement & preservation of African-American Literature, 1989; Catholic University, The Alumni Achievement Award, Literary criticism, 1989; The Marcus Garvey Memorial Foundation, The Larry Neal-Georgia Douglas Johnson Award, literature and community service, 1989. **MEMBERSHIPS** The Larry Neal Cultural Series, designer, project director, 1984; Educators for the Advancement of American Literature in Public Schools, founder, 1984; College Language Association; Modern Language Association; Afro-American Museum Association, evaluator; The Smithsonian Institution, Program in Black American Culture, script writer; National Council of Teachers of English; National Endowment for the Humanities, panelist. **SELECTED PUBLICATIONS** Author, College Reading Skills, Random House, 1966; The Dream Awake: A Multi-Media Production, 1968; The Humanities and Afro-American Literature Tradition, 1988; Broad Sympathy: The Howard University Oral Tradition Reader, Simon and Schuster, 1996. **CONTACT ADDRESS** Department of English, Locke Hall, Rm 248, Howard Univ, Washington, DC, 20059.

TRELA, D.J.
PERSONAL Chicago, IL **DISCIPLINE** ENGLISH LITERATURE **EDUCATION** Univ Il Chicago, BA, 81; Univ Edinburgh, Scotland, PhD. **CAREER** Asst prof to assoc prof to prof, chair, asst dir to interim dir to dir, 89-, Roosevelt Univ. **HONORS AND AWARDS** Phi Beta Kappa; Phi Kappa Phi; Phi Eta Sigma; Univ Edinburgh Studentship, 81-84; NEH Travel to Collections Grant, 93; Roosevelt Univ res sabbatical, 93, 97; NEH Summer Stipend, 95; Univ Edinburgh Honorary Fel, 97; invited lectr, St. Joseph's Univ, Philadelphia, 97. **MEMBERSHIPS** Assoc of Governing Bds of Univ & Col; Amer Assoc of Univ Prof; Midwest Modern Lang Assoc; Modern Lang Assoc; Carlyle Soc; Midwest Victorian Stud Assoc; Res Soc for Victorian Per; Victorians Inst. **RESEARCH** British lit; Victorian prose & prose fiction; Victorian women writers espec Margaret Oliphant; Thomas Carlyle & Jane Welsh Carlyle: Victorian periodical lit & jour; race & lit; Scottish lit; bibliog & editing; literary criticism; gen educ courses; composition. **SELECTED PUBLICATIONS** Ed, Margaret Oliphant: Critical Essays on a Gentle Subversive, Assoc U Press, 95; coed, Victorian Urban Settings: The Nineteenth Century City and Its Contexts, Garland, 96; auth, Critical Response to Thomas Carlyle's Major Works, Greenwood Press, 97; auth, Margaret Oliphant: A Descriptive Bibliography, Locust Hill Press, 99; auth, Thomas Carlyle's Past and Present, Univ Calif Press, 00. **CONTACT ADDRESS** Sch of Liberal Stud, Roosevelt Univ, 430 S Michigan Ave, Chicago, IL, 60605-1394. **EMAIL** jtrela@roosevelt.edu

TREMBATH, PAUL
DISCIPLINE ENGLISH LITERATURE **EDUCATION** Univ Wis, BA, MA; Univ Va, PhD. **CAREER** Assoc prof. **RESEARCH** Contemporary critical theory and its historical backgrounds. **SELECTED PUBLICATIONS** Auth, pubs in The Journal of Aesthetics and Art Criticism, Postmodern Culture Philosophy and Literature. **CONTACT ADDRESS** Dept of English, Colorado State Univ, Fort Collins, CO, 80523. **EMAIL** ptrembath@vines.colostate.edu

TRENT, JIMMIE DOUGLAS
PERSONAL Born 11/17/1933, Lima, OK, m, 1969, 3 children **DISCIPLINE** SPEECH **EDUCATION** Emporia State Univ, BSEd, 55, MS, 59; Purdue Univ, PhD(speech), 66. **CAREER** Dir forensics, High Schs, Kans, 55-57; instr speech & dir forensics, Emporia State Univ, 57-60; instr speech, Purdue Univ, 60-62; asst prof, Eastern Ill Univ, 62-64; asst prof & dir masters degree prog, Wayne State Univ, 64-68; grad off & asst to dean col liberal arts, 68-69, assoc prof & chmn grad prog speech commun & theatre, 69-71; chmn dept, 71-82, prof commun & theatre Miami Univ, 71-, Ed, Winning Orations, Interstate Oratorical Asn, 65-70; vis scholar, Northwestern Univ, 82. **HONORS AND AWARDS** Distinguished Service Award, Speech Commun Asn Ohio, 80. **MEMBERSHIPS** Speech Commun Asn; Int Commun Asn; Interstate Oratorical Asn (exec secy, 64-70). **RESEARCH** Argumentation; leadership behavior; organizational communication. **SELECTED PUBLICATIONS**

Auth, Small group discussions, In: Introduction to the Field of Speech, Scott, 65; Toulmon's model of an argument: An examination and extension, Quart J Speech, 68; coauth, Concepts in Communication, Allyn & Bacon, 73; auth, The rhetoric of the challenger: George Stanley McGovern, Cent State Speech J, spring 74; Personnel evaluation: Developing institutional support for a department, Asn Dept & Adminr Speech Commun Asn Bull, 1/74; Public relations education: An opportunity for speech communication, Commun Educ, 11/76; auth, The Ideal Candidate: A Study of the Desired Attributes of the Public and the Media Across Two Presidential Campaigns. Am Behavioral Sci, 93; auth, The Ideal Candidate Revisited, Am Behavioral Sci, 97. **CONTACT ADDRESS** 101 County Club Ln, Oxford, OH, 45056-1602. **EMAIL** trentjd@muohio.edu

TRICOMI, ALBERT HENRY
PERSONAL Born 12/30/1942, New York, NY, m, 1968, 1 child **DISCIPLINE** ENGLISH, DRAMA **EDUCATION** Columbia Col, AB, 64; Northwestern Univ, MA, 65, PhD(English), 69. **CAREER** Asst prof English, NC Cent Univ, 68-69; asst prof, 69-75, ASSOC PROF ENGLISH, STATE UNIV NY BINGHAMTON, 75-, Fel, NC Cent Univ, 68-69. **MEMBERSHIPS** AAUP **RESEARCH** Shakespeare; Elizabethan-Jacobean drama and history; Renaissance literature. **SELECTED PUBLICATIONS** Auth, Fables of Power--Aesopian Writing and Political-History, Jour Eng and Ger Philol, Vol 0092, 93; Medicine and Shakespeare in the English Renaissance, Jour Eng and Ger Philol, Vol 0092, 93; The Stage and Social Struggle in Early-Modern England, Jour Eng and Ger Philol, Vol 0095, 96. **CONTACT ADDRESS** Dept of English, State Univ of NY, Binghamton, NY, 13901.

TRIECE, MARY E.
PERSONAL Born 02/27/1967, Lake Forest, IL **DISCIPLINE** RHETORICAL STUDIES **EDUCATION** Univ Tex, Austin, PhD, 97. **CAREER** Asst prof, Univ Akron. **MEMBERSHIPS** Nat Commun Assoc. **RESEARCH** Women's studies; labor history; cultural studies; social movements. **SELECTED PUBLICATIONS** Auth, The practical true woman: Reconciling women and work in popular mail-order magazines, 1900-1920, Critical Studs in Mass Commun, in press. **CONTACT ADDRESS** 772 Ardmore Ave, Akron, OH, 44302. **EMAIL** mtriece@uakron.edu

TRIMBLE, JOHN RALSTON
PERSONAL Born 11/25/1940, Niagara Falls, ON, Canada, m, 1963, 2 children **DISCIPLINE** ENGLISH **EDUCATION** Princeton Univ, AB, 62; Univ Calif, Berkeley, MA, 64, PhD(English), 71. **CAREER** Asst prof, 70-77, from assoc prof to prof English, Univ Tex, Austin, 77-95; disting teaching prof, English; 95. **HONORS AND AWARDS** Jean Holloway Award for Excellence in Teaching, Univ Tex, 75; Eyes of Texas Exc Award, Univ Tex, 93; Charter member, Academy of Disting Teachers, Univ Tex, 95. **MEMBERSHIPS** NCTE. **RESEARCH** Composition and rhetoric; 18th-century English literature. **SELECTED PUBLICATIONS** Auth, Clarissa's role in The Rape of the Lock, Tex Studies Lit & Lang, Winter 74; Writing with Style: Conversations on the Art of Writing, Prentice-Hall, 75. **CONTACT ADDRESS** Dept of English, Univ of Texas, Austin, TX, 78712-1026. **EMAIL** trimble@mailutexas.edu

TRIMMER, JOSEPH FRANCIS
PERSONAL Born 08/04/1941, Cortland, NY, m, 1966, 1 child **DISCIPLINE** AMERICAN LITERATURE & STUDIES **EDUCATION** Colgate Univ, BA, 63; Purdue Univ, MA, 66, PhD, 68. **CAREER** Tchg asst Eng, Purdue Univ, 65-68; asst prof, 68-72, assoc prof, 72-80, prof eng, Ball State Univ, 80, coordr gen educ eng,, 72, Adv ed, Alfred Publ Co, 78. **MEMBERSHIPS** MLA Conf Col Comp & Commun; Am Studies Asn. **RESEARCH** Am lit; Am studies; writing. **SELECTED PUBLICATIONS** Auth, Black American Notes on the Problem of Definition, Ball State Univ Monogr, 71; ed, A Casebook on Ralph Ellison's Invisible Man, Crowell, 72; auth, Ralph Ellison's Flying Home, Studies Short Fiction, spring 72; The Virginian: Novel and films, Ill Quart, 12/72; V K Ratliff: A portrait of the artist in motion, Mod Fiction Studies, winter 74; coauth, American Oblique: Writing About the American Experience, Houghton, 76; auth, Memoryscape: Jean Sheperd's midwest, Old Northwest, 12/76; ed, The National Book Award for Fiction: An Index to the First Twenty-Five Years, G K Hall, 78; Narration as Knowledge, Heinemann, 98; Fictions, Harcourt Brace, 98; Writing With a Purpose, Houghton Mifflin, 98. **CONTACT ADDRESS** Dept of Eng, Ball State Univ, 2000 W University, Muncie, IN, 47306-0002.

TRIPP, BERNELL E.
DISCIPLINE MASS COMMUNICATIONS **EDUCATION** Univ Ala, BA, 82, MA, 89, PhD cand. **CAREER** Mass Comm, Univ Ala. **RESEARCH** 19th century Black press. **SELECTED PUBLICATIONS** Auth, The Antebellum Press, 1827-1861: Effective Abolitionist or Reluctant Reformer?; The Black Media, 1865-Present: Liberal Crusaders or Defenders of Tradition? In: Perspectives on Mass Communication History. **CONTACT ADDRESS** Dept of Journalism, Univ Alabama, PO Box 870172, Tuscaloosa, AL, 34587-0172.

TROTTER, A.H., JR.
PERSONAL Born 10/10/1950, Meriville, TN, m, 1972, 3 children **DISCIPLINE** BIBLICAL STUDIES, FILM AND CULTURE **EDUCATION** Univ Virginia, BA, 72; Gordon-Conwell Theol Sem, MDiv, 75; Univ Cambridge, PhD, 87. **CAREER** Tchr, Westminster Schs, Atlanta, 75-78; exec dir, Elmbrook Christian Study Ctr, 81-87; exec dir, Center for Christian Study, 87- . **RESEARCH** Life of Jesus; Biblical interpretation, New Testament studies; systematic theology; film and culture. **SELECTED PUBLICATIONS** Auth, Interpreting the Epistle to the Hebrews, Baker Book House, 97. **CONTACT ADDRESS** Ctr for Christian Study, 128 Chancellor St, Charlottesville, VA, 22903. **EMAIL** drew@studycenter.net

TROTTER, MARY
DISCIPLINE ENGLISH LITERATURE **EDUCATION** Northwestern Univ, PhD. **CAREER** Asst prof, TX Tech Univ. **RESEARCH** Mod Europ and Am drama; Irish studies; Northern Irish women playwrights. **SELECTED PUBLICATIONS** Publ articles on polit theatre in early 20th century and contemp Ireland. **CONTACT ADDRESS** Texas Tech Univ, Lubbock, TX, 79409-5015. **EMAIL** M.Trotter@ttu.edu

TRUE, MICHAEL D.
PERSONAL Born 11/08/1933, Oklahoma City, OK, m, 1958, 6 children **DISCIPLINE** ENGLISH & AMERICAN LITERATURE **EDUCATION** Univ Okla, BA, 55; Univ Minn, MA, 57; Duke Univ, PhD, 64. **CAREER** Lectr English, Duke Univ, 60-61; lectr Eng, NC Col Durham, 61; from instr to asst prof, Ind State Univ, 61-65; from asst prof to assoc prof, 65-74, prof English, 74-97, Assumption Col; vis lectr English & educ, Clark Univ, 68-78; prof nonfiction, Upper Midwest Writers Conf, 73-80; NEH fel, 76-77; vis scholar Am lit, Columbia Univ, 76-77; consult, Nat Humanities Fac, 77-. **HONORS AND AWARDS** NEH fel, 76-77; Am Philos Soc grant, 79; F Andre Favat Award, Mass Counc Tchrs English, 80; Peace Teacher of the Year, Consortium on Peace Res, Educ and Dev, 96; Fulbright lectr, India, 97-98. **MEMBERSHIPS** Peace Stud Asn; IPRA; New England Col English Asn; MLA; NCTE; Am Studies Asn. **RESEARCH** American literature of World War I; American art and culture; contemporary poetry. **SELECTED PUBLICATIONS** Ed, Daniel Berrigan: Poetry, Drama, Prose, Orbis, 88; auth, Ordinary People: Family Life and Global Values, Orbis, 91; auth, To Construct Peace: 30 More Justice Seekers, Peacemakers, XXIII Publ, 92; auth, An Energy Field More Intense Than War: The Nonviolent Tradition and American Literature, Syracuse, 95; co-ed, The Frontiers of Nonviolence, IPRA, 98. **CONTACT ADDRESS** 4 Westland St, Worcester, MA, 01602. **EMAIL** mtrue@eve.assumption.edu

TRUJILLO, NICK L.
PERSONAL Born 12/14/1955, Pasadena, CA, m, 1985 **DISCIPLINE** COMMUNICATION **EDUCATION** Univ Utah, PhD 83. **CAREER** Purdue Univ, asst prof 82-84; Mich State Univ, vis asst prof, 84-85; S Methodist Univ, asst prof, 85-90; Calif State Univ Sacramento, prof 90-. **HONORS AND AWARDS** B Aubrey Fisher Awd; Quintus Wilson Alum Achv Awd. **MEMBERSHIPS** NCA; WSCA. **RESEARCH** Organizational Communication; Ethnography; Sport, Media and Society. **SELECTED PUBLICATIONS** Auth, The Meaning of Nolan Ryan, College Stn TX, TX A&M Univ Press, 94; auth, Shopping for Family, coauth, Qualitative Inq, forthcoming; In Search of Naunny's Grave, Text and Performance Quart, 98; Fragments of Self at the Postmodern Bar, coauth, Jour of Contemporary Ethnography, 97; auth, Machine Missiles and Men: Images of the Male Body on ABC's Monday Night Football, Sociology of Sport Jour, 95; auth, Emotionality in the Field and in the Stands: Expressing Self Through Baseball, Jour of Sport and Social Issues, 94; auth, Qualitative Research in Organizational Communication, coauth, New Handbook of Organizational Comm, eds Fred Jablin, Linda Putnam, Newberry Pk CA, Sage, forthcoming; From Wild Western Prodigy to the Ageless Wonder, The Mediated Revolution of Nolan Ryan, coauth, Heroes and Celebrities in American Culture, eds Robert Cathcart, Susan Drucker, Lanham MA, Hamilton, 94; auth, Five Reasons Why Nolan Ryan Should Not be Elected to the Hall of Fame, Elysian Fields Quart, 94; Remembering Nolan, A History of TX Baseball, 94. **CONTACT ADDRESS** Dept of Communication, California State Univ, Sacramento, 4125 Bruhn Ct, Sacramento, CA, 95821. **EMAIL** nickt@csus.edu

TRUMPENER, KATIE
PERSONAL Born 04/10/1961, San Francisco, CA, m **DISCIPLINE** ENGLISH **EDUCATION** Univ Alberta, BA (honours), English, 82; Harvard Univ, AM, English and Amer Lit, 83; Stanford Univ, PhD, comparative lit, 90. **CAREER** Visiting asst prof, commun, Univ Iowa, 88; asst prof, German, 90-95, assoc prof, Germanic studies, comparative lit, English, cinema and media studies, 95-, Univ Chicago; coeditor, Modern Philology , 98-. **HONORS AND AWARDS** Crawshay Prize, British Acad; ACLS Sr Scholarship; Mellon Postdoctoral Fellowship. **RESEARCH** 18th-20th century European Lit; 20th Germany; cinema. **SELECTED PUBLICATIONS** Auth, Bardic Nationalism: The Romantic Novel and the British Empire, 1997. **CONTACT ADDRESS** Dept. of Germanic Studies, Univ of Chicago, 1050 E. 59th St., Chicgao, IL, 60637. **EMAIL** ktrumpen@midway.uchicago.edu

TUCKER, CYNTHIA GRANT
PERSONAL Born 06/17/1941, New York, NY, m, 1966, 2 children **DISCIPLINE** COMPARATIVE LITERATURE, ENGLISH **EDUCATION** Denison Univ, BA, 63; Univ Iowa, PhD(comp lit), 67. **CAREER** Asst prof English, 67-75, dir prog Comp Lit, 72-75, assoc prof, 75-82, prof English, Univ Memphis, 82-, Nat Endowment for Humanities prog grants, 78-81 & fel col teachers, 82. **HONORS AND AWARDS** Disting Res Award nom, 80-87; Disting Teaching Award nom, 73, 96. **MEMBERSHIPS** MLA; Women's Caucus Mod Lang. **RESEARCH** Biography, Humor, Women's Studies, Women in Religion, Journals Diary Lit. **SELECTED PUBLICATIONS** Auth, Meredith's broken laurel: Modern Love and the Renaissance sonnet tradition, Victorian Poetry, 72; The Rilkean poet-lover and his laurel, Philol Quart, 74; Translation as resurrection: Rilke and Louise Labe, Mod Lang Notes, 74; Petrarchizing into the horrible: Baudelaire's Grotesque, Fr Rev, 75; Kate Freeman Clark: A Painter Rediscovered, Univ Press Miss, 81; Spirited Threads: The Writing and Art of Patricia Roberts Cline, Portland, OR, Sibyl Publications, Fall, 97. **CONTACT ADDRESS** Dept of English, Memphis State Univ, 3706 Alumni St, Memphis, TN, 38152-0001. **EMAIL** cgtucker@cc.memphis. edu

TUCKER, EDWARD LLEWELLYN
PERSONAL Born 11/19/1921, Crewe, VA **DISCIPLINE** ENGLISH **EDUCATION** Roanoke Col, BA, 46; Columbia Univ, MA, 47; Univ Ga, PhD, 57. **CAREER** Asst prof, 60-66, from assoc prof to prof English, VA Polytech Inst, 66-86. **RESEARCH** Southern literature. **SELECTED PUBLICATIONS** Auth, Richard Henry Wilde: Life and Selected Poems, Univ Ga, 66; Vocabulary Power, Bantam, 68; Faulkner's Drusilla and Ibsen's Hedda, Mod Drama, 9/73; ed, Philip Pendleton Cooke and the Southern Literary Messenger: Selected letters, Miss Quart, Winter 74; Jesse Stuart to Dayton Kohler: Selected letters, Regist Ky Hist Soc, 10/77; Joseph Hergesheimer to Mr Gordon, Studies Am Fiction, Fall 78; Two young brothers and their Orion, Southern Lit J, Fall 78; Longfellow's Bowdoin Dialogue, Studies Am Renaissance (in prep); References in Longfellow's Journals to Charles Dickens, Dickens Studies Annual, 95; Longfellow Manusacript Letters in the Fales Library, Resources for American Literary Study, Fall, 97. **CONTACT ADDRESS** Dept of English, Virginia Polytech Inst & State Univ, Blacksburg, VA, 24061. **EMAIL** edtucke2@vt.edu

TUCKER, MARTIN
PERSONAL Born 02/08/1928, Philadelphia, PA **DISCIPLINE** ENGLISH **EDUCATION** Wash Sq Col, NY Univ, BA, 49; Univ Ariz, MA, 54; NY Univ, PhD, 63. **CAREER** From asst prof to assoc prof, 58-69, PROF ENGLISH, LONG ISLAND UNIV, 69-, CHMN DEPT, 76-, Helene Wurlitzer Found grant, Taos, NMex, 56-57; grant, Long Island Univ, 64, ed, Confrontation Mag, 70; mem admis and scholar comt, British Univ summer sch prog, 65-; consult, col comprehensive test, Educ Testing Serv, 65-; co-moderator, Writers Alive, Brooklyn Acad Arts and Sci, 67-68; co-ed and consult, Belles-Lett English, Johnson Reprint Corp, 67-; fel creative writing, Ossabaw Island Proj, Ga, 68; ed, PEN Newslett, 73-78; MacDowell Colony residency grants, 77, 78 and 80. **HONORS AND AWARDS** Scholar Award, Bread Loaf Writing Ctr, 59; Merit Award, US Dept Health, Educ, Welfare, 72. **MEMBERSHIPS** MLA; African Studies Asn; PEN Club; Poetry Soc Am; Authors Guild. **RESEARCH** Contemporary British and American fiction; English and African literature; African prose fiction. **SELECTED PUBLICATIONS** Auth, Ellington,Duke Black Brown And Beige, Black Music Res Jour, Vol 0013, 93; Literary Magazine Editors on the State of the Story--Comparison With Masterpieces, Lit Rev, Vol 0037, 94. **CONTACT ADDRESS** Dept of English, Long Island Univ, Brooklyn, NY, 11201.

TUERK, RICHARD
PERSONAL Born 07/10/1941, Baltimore, MD, m, 1963, 2 children **DISCIPLINE** LITERATURE **EDUCATION** Columbia Col, AB, 63; Johns Hopkins Univ, MA, 64, PhD, 67. **CAREER** Asst prof, Univ Calif Riverside, 67-72; Assoc prof to prof, Tx A&M Univ, 72- . **HONORS AND AWARDS** Piper Prof, Minnie Stevens Piper Found, 91; Honors Prof of the Year, E Tx St Univ, 85; H. M. Lafferty Distinguished Faculty Award, Tx A&M Univ Commerce, 90. **MEMBERSHIPS** Amer Stud Assoc; Modern Lang Assoc; Popular Culture Assoc; MELUS; Amer Stud Assoc Tx; Tx Popular Culture Assoc. **RESEARCH** Amer lit; children's lit. **SELECTED PUBLICATIONS** Auth, What Side Was He On? Mike Gold During the Period of the Hitler-Stalin Pact, Modern Jewish Stud, 94; Michael Gold's Hoboken Blues: An Experiment that Failed, J of the Soc for the Study of Multi-Ethnic Lit of the US, 95; Dorothy's Adventures Underground, Baum Bugle, 96; Teaching Composition Via Distance Educ, 4th Annual Nat Distance Educ Conf 1997 Conf Proceedings, 97; Teaching Composition via Videoconferencing Using a Multi-Ethnic American Literature Reader, in Engines of Change: A Practical Guide for Using Technology to Teach American Culture, Amer Stud Assoc, 97. **CONTACT ADDRESS** Dept of Lit & Lang, Tx A&M Univ Commerce, Box 3011, Commerce, TX, 75429-3011. **EMAIL** Richard_Tuerk@ tamu-commerce.edu

TURCO, LEWIS
PERSONAL Born 05/02/1934, Buffalo, NY, m, 1956, 2 children **DISCIPLINE** ENGLISH **EDUCATION** Univ Conn, BA, 59; Univ Iowa, MA, 62. **CAREER** Grad asst and part-time instr English, Univ Conn, 59; instr English, Fenn Col (Cleveland State Univ), 60-64, founder and dir Cleveland Poetry Ctr, 61-64; asst prof, Hillsdale Col, 64-65; from asst prof to prof, 65-96, Poet-in-Residence, 95-, prof emeritus English, State Univ NY Col, Oswego, 96-, founder and dir Prog Writing Arts, 68-95; State Univ NY Res Found fac fels, 66, 67, 69, 71, 74 & 78; hon trustee, Theodore Roethke Mem Found, 68; vis prof, State Univ NY Col Potsdam, 68-69; State Univ NY Fac Exchange scholar, 76-; mem, Creative Writing Subcommittee Univ Awards Comt Res Found State Univ NY, 74-76, chm 76-77; Yaddo Found resident, 59 & 77; Bingham poet-in-residence, Univ Louisville, 82; writer-in-residence, Ashland Univ, 91. **HONORS AND AWARDS** Acad Am Poets Prize, Univ Iowa, 60; American Weave Chapbook Award, 62; Davidson Miscellany Fiction Prize, 69; Helen Bullis Prize, Poetry Northwest, 71; Nat Endowment for the Arts/PEN Syndicated Fiction Project Award, 83; Kans Quart/Kans Arts Comm First Poetry Award, 84-85; SUNY Col at Oswego President's Award for Schol and Creative Activity and Res, 85; Melville Cane Award in criticism of the Poetry Soc of Am, 86; Silverfish Rev Chapbook Award, 89; Cooper House Chapbook Award, 90; Distinguished Alumni Award, Alumni Asn of the Univ of Conn, 92; Meriden CT Hall of Fame, 93; Fac Enhancement Grant, SUNY Col at Oswego, 95; Bordighera Bilingual Poetry Prize, Bordighera, Inc, Purdue Univ, 97. **MEMBERSHIPS** Authors Guild; Poets & Writers; E.E. Cummings Soc. **RESEARCH** Writing arts; American and British poetry & poetics. **SELECTED PUBLICATIONS** Auth, First Poems, Golden Quill, 60; Awaken, Bells Falling: Poems 1959-1967, Univ Mo, 68; The Book of Forms: A Handbook of Poetics, Dutton, 68; Poetry: An Introduction Through Writing, Reston, 73; American Still Lifes (poems), Mathom, 81; The Compleat Melancholick, Bieler, 85; Emily Dickenson, Woman of Letters, Poems, and Centos from Lines in Emily Dickinson's Letters, Together with Essays, State Univ of NY, 93; auth, Bordello, poems, Grey Heron/Mathom, 96; Shaking the Family Tree, A Memoir, VIA Folios, 98; A Book of Fears, Bordighera, 98. **CONTACT ADDRESS** PO Box 161, Dresden, ME, 04342-0161.

TURNER, FREDERICK
PERSONAL Born 11/19/1943, East Haddon, England, m, 1966, 2 children **DISCIPLINE** ENGLISH **EDUCATION** Oxford Univ, BA, 65, MA, 67, PhD(English), 67. **CAREER** Asst prof English, Univ Calif, Santa Barbara, 67-72; ASSOC PROF ENGLISH, KENYON COL, 72-, Ed, Kenyon Rev. **MEMBERSHIPS** Fel Int Soc Study Time. **RESEARCH** Shakespeare; esthetics; philosophy in literature. **SELECTED PUBLICATIONS** Auth, Bix--Beiderbecke, Bix 1903-1931--The Story of a Young Man and His Horn, Smithsonian, Vol 0028, 97. **CONTACT ADDRESS** Dept of English, Kenyon Col, Gambier, OH, 43022.

TURNER, JEANINE W.
PERSONAL Louisville, KY, m, 1996 **DISCIPLINE** COMMUNICATION **EDUCATION** Univ of Dayton, BA, 87, MA, 93; Ohio State Univ, PhD, 96. **CAREER** Grad tchg assoc, Univ of Dayton, 92-93; Ohio State Univ, 93-96; adj res asst prof, Georgetown Univ Med Ctr, 97- ; asst prof, Georgetown Univ, 97- . **HONORS AND AWARDS** Outstanding Tchr Award, Univ of Dayton, 93; Phi Kappa Phi Honor Soc. **MEMBERSHIPS** Acad of Mgt.; Nat Commun Asn; Asn for Bus Communicators; Int Commun Asn; Am Telemedicine Asn. **RESEARCH** Telemedicine; Virtual orgs; Commun tech adaption. **SELECTED PUBLICATIONS** Coauth, Product, process, and practice: Telecompetence in Telemedicine, Teleconference Mag, 4(16), 97; The Effectiveness of Telemedicine in the Outpatient Pulmonary Clinic - Abstract, Am Jour of Respiratory and Critical Care Med, 153, 97; Patient Satisfaction with Telemedicine in a Prison Environment: A Matter of Context, Jour of Telemedicine and Telecare, forthcom.; The Effectiveness of Telemedicine in the Outpatient Pulmonary Clinic, Telemedicine Jour, forthcom.; Teaching Mass Communication and Telecommunication, Teaching Communication: Theory, Research, and Methods, eds Jour. Daly, G. Friedrich, A. Vangelisti, forthcom. **CONTACT ADDRESS** School of Business, Georgetown Univ, G-04 Old North, Washington, DC, 20057. **EMAIL** turnerjwegunet@georgetown.edu

TURNER, MYRON M.
DISCIPLINE ENGLISH LITERATURE **EDUCATION** Univ NY, BA; Rutgers Univ, MA; Univ Wash, PhD. **RESEARCH** Work of Philip Sidney; nature of poetic imagery and imagination in the 16th century. **SELECTED PUBLICATIONS** Auth, The River and the Window, 74; Things That Fly, 78; Rag Doll's Shadow, 80; pub(s) on Sidney, Spenser, Marlowe and American literature. **CONTACT ADDRESS** Dept of English, Manitoba Univ, Winnipeg, MB, R3T 2N2.

TURNER, RICHARD CHARLES
PERSONAL Born 08/01/1944, Boston, MA, m, 1966, 3 children **DISCIPLINE** ENGLISH LITERATURE **EDUCATION** Boston Col, AB, 66; Emory Univ, MA, 68, PhD(English), 72. **CAREER** Asst prof, 70-78, assoc prof English, Ind Univ-

Purdue Univ, Indianapolis, 78-85; prof, 85. **MEMBERSHIPS** MLA; Am Soc 18th Century Studies. **RESEARCH** Restoration and 18th century poetry and drama; literature and philanthropy. **SELECTED PUBLICATIONS** Auth, Ed, Taking Theoteeship Seriously, 95, Ken Folltee, 96. **CONTACT ADDRESS** Dept of English, Indiana Univ-Purdue Univ, Indianapolis, 1100 W Michigan St, Indianapolis, IN, 46202-2880. **EMAIL** rturner@iupui.edu

TURNER, ROBERT Y.
PERSONAL Born 02/19/1927, Marshalltown, IA **DISCIPLINE** ENGLISH **EDUCATION** Princeton Univ, AB, 49; Univ Chicago, AM, 51, PhD, 58. **CAREER** Instr, Dartmouth Col, 55-58; from instr to assoc prof, 58-74, grad chmn, 72-74 and 81-83, PROF ENGLISH, UNIV PA, 74-, Guggenheim Found fel, 74-75. **MEMBERSHIPS** Renaissance Soc Am; Shakespeare Asn Am; MLA. **RESEARCH** English Renaissance drama, including Shakespeare. **SELECTED PUBLICATIONS** Auth, Shakespeare Comic Changes--The Time-Lapse Metaphor as Plot Device, Shakespeare Quart, Vol 0043, 92; Shakespeare America, America Shakespeare, Shakespeare Quart, Vol 0045, 94. **CONTACT ADDRESS** Dept of English, Univ of Pa, 210 S 34th St, Philadelphia, PA, 19104.

TUROW, JOSEPH G.
PERSONAL Born 04/05/1950, New York, NY, m, 3 children **DISCIPLINE** COMMUNICATIONS **EDUCATION** Univ of Pa, BA, 71, MA, 73, PhD, 76. **CAREER** From asst prof to assoc prof, Purdue Univ, 76-86; vis asst prof, UCLA, 80, 85; from assoc prof to prof, Univ of Pa, 86- ; ed bd mem, Jour of Broadcasting, 85-94, 97- , Crit Studies in Mass Commun, 84-89, 98- , Sage Annual Revs of Commun Res, 86- , Encycl of Advert, Commun Educ, 78-82; adv ed, Jour of Commun, 81-91, 96- , Ablex Commun Book Series, 88-91. **HONORS AND AWARDS** Phi Beta Kappa, 71; Dean's List With Distinction; Univ fel, 74-75; Diss Res Schol, 75-76; Dept Best Tchg Award, 81, 83; Russel Nye Award, Popular Cult Asn, for best article in Jour of Popular Cult, 82-83; Book of the Month Award, Commun Booknotes, 84; Top Ten Mass Commun Div Paper, Int Commun Asn Confs, 81, 83, 84; Top Three Mass Commun Div Paper, Mass Commun and Speech Commun Asn Confs, 77, 84; Nat Endowment for the Hums Summer Stipend, Sen Div, 86, 94; App to the Nat Endowment for the Hums Summer Stipend Adv Comt, 87; Res grant, Pa Res Found, 88-89; App as a Commonwealth Speaker, Pa Hums Coun, 89, 91; Invited to teach a master's session' at the annual Int Commun Asn Conf, 91; Elected to ch the Mass Commun Div of the Int Commun Asn, 93-97; Appointed to the Nat Endowment for Children's Educ Televison of the U.S. Dept of Commerce, 95-97; Co-recip of a major grant, Ford Found for res, 96. **MEMBERSHIPS** Int Commun Asn; Speech Commun Asn. **RESEARCH** Mass Media Industries; Marketing and the media. **SELECTED PUBLICATIONS** Auth, Getting Books to Children: An Exploration of Publisher-Market Relations, 79; Entertainment, Education, and the Hard Sell: Three Decades of Network Children's Television, 81; Media Industries: The Production of News and Entertainment, 84; Playing Doctor: Television, Storytelling, and Medical Power, 89; The Challenge of Inference in Interinstitutional Research on Mass Communication, Commun Res, 18:2, 91; On Conceptualizing Mass Communication, Jour of Broadcasting & Electronic Media, spring, 92; The Organizational Underpinnings of Contemporary Media Conglomerates, Commun Res 19:6, 92; Media Systems in Society: Understanding Industries, Strategies, and Power, 92; Hidden Conflicts and Journalistic Norms: The Case of Self Coverage, Jour of Commun 44:2, 94; Television Entertainment and the US Health Care Debate, The Lancet 347: 9010, 96; Breaking Up America: Advertising and the New Media World, 97; Media Today: An Introduction to Mass Communication, 98; ed, Careers in Mass Media, 84. **CONTACT ADDRESS** Annenberg Commun Sch, Univ of Pennsylvania, 3620 Walnut St, Philadelphia, PA, 19104-6220. **EMAIL** jturow@pobox.asc.upenn.edu

TUROW, JUDITH G.
PERSONAL Born 04/05/1950, New York, NY, m **DISCIPLINE** COMMUNICATIONS **EDUCATION** Univ Penn, BA, 71; Univ Penn, MA, 73; Univ Penn, PhD, 76 **CAREER** Assoc prof, Univ Penn, 86-90; prof, Univ Penn, 90- **HONORS AND AWARDS** Ford foundation res grant, 96; Appointed to the Ntl Endowment for Children's Educational Television, US Dept Commerce, 95-97; Ntl Endowment Humanities Summer Stipend, 94; chair, Mass Comm Div of Intl Comm Assoc, 93-97 **SELECTED PUBLICATIONS** Auth, Media Today: An Introduction to Mass Communication, Houghton Mifflin, 98; auth, Breaking Up America: Advertising and the New Media World, Univ Chicago, 97; Media Systems in Society: Understanding Industries, Strategies, and Power, Longman, 92 **CONTACT ADDRESS** Annenberg School of Communication, Univ Penn, Philadelphia, PA, 19104.

TUTTLE, JON
PERSONAL Salt Lake City, UT, m, 1997, 1 child **DISCIPLINE** ENGLISH **EDUCATION** Univ Utah, BS, 82; Univ NM, MA, 84, PhD, 89. **CAREER** Honors dir, 95-96, Francis Marion Univ; playwright-in-res, 98-, Trustus Theatre. **HONORS AND AWARDS** SC Acad of Auth Fel, SC Arts Comm Fel; numerous playwriting awards, Phi Kappa Phi Honor Soc **MEMBERSHIPS** MLA; Dramatists Guild; Theatre Commun Group. **RESEARCH** Drama; playwriting. **SELECTED PUBLICATIONS** Auth, The Dramatic Climax and The Right Way to Write a Play, Carolina English Teacher, 95-96; auth, The Efficacy of Work: Arthur Miller and Camus' The Myth of Sisyphus, Amer Drama, 96; auth, Be What You Are: Identity and Morality in Edmond and Glengarry Glen Ross, Glengarry Glen Ross: Text and Performance, Garland Press, 96. **CONTACT ADDRESS** Dept of English, Francis Marion Univ, Florence, SC, 29501-0547. **EMAIL** jtuttle@fmarion.edu

TUTTLETON, JAMES WESLEY
PERSONAL Born 08/19/1934, St. Louis, MO **DISCIPLINE** ENGLISH **EDUCATION** Harding Col, BA, 55; Univ NC, MA, 57, PhD(English), 63. **CAREER** Instr English, Clemson Univ, 56-59; instr, Univ NC, 62-63; from instr to asst prof, Univ Wis-Madison, 63-68; assoc prof, 68-74, PROF ENGLISH and CHMN DEPT, NY UNIV, 74-, Univ Wis res coun grant, 64 and 65; Am Philos Soc res grant, 66; Nat Endowment for Humanities fel, 67-68; co-ed, The Gotham Libr NY Univ Press, 74-**MEMBERSHIPS** MLA; Am Studies Asn; Century Asn; Washington Irving Soc; Henry James Soc. **RESEARCH** American literature; English literature; American history. **SELECTED PUBLICATIONS** Auth, The Complete Short-Stories of London, Jack, Hudson Rev, Vol 0047, 94; Rehabilitating Victorian Values--Himmelfarb, Gertrude the De-Moralization of Society, Hudson Rev, Vol 0048, 95; No Gifts From Chance--A Biography of Wharton, Edith, Hudson Rev, Vol 0048, 95; Wharton, Edith--An Extraordinary Life, Hudson Rev, Vol 0048, 95; Wharton, Edith Inner Circle, Hudson Rev, Vol 0048, 95. **CONTACT ADDRESS** Dept of English, New York Univ, 19 University Pl, New York, NY, 10003-4556.

TWOMBLY, ROBERT GRAY
PERSONAL Born 05/16/1935, New York, NY, m, 1960, 4 children **DISCIPLINE** ENGLISH **EDUCATION** Amherst Col, BA, 57; Yale Univ, PhD(English), 65. **CAREER** From instr to asst prof, 63-69, ASSOC PROF ENGLISH, UNIV TEX, AUSTIN, 69-, Soc Relig Higher Educ fel, 69-70. **MEMBERSHIPS** MLA; Soc Higher Educ. **RESEARCH** John Donne; 16th century religious literature; Shakespeare. **SELECTED PUBLICATIONS** Auth, The Rhetoric of Death and Knowledge, Library Chronicle Univ Tex-Austin, Vol 0026, 96. **CONTACT ADDRESS** Dept of English, Univ of Tex, 0 Univ of Texas, Austin, TX, 78712-1026.

TWOMEY, MICHAEL W.
PERSONAL Born 12/23/1949, New York, NY, m, 1971, 2 children **DISCIPLINE** ENGLISH **EDUCATION** State Univ New York, BA, 72; Boston Col, AM, 74; Cornell Univ, PhD, 79. **CAREER** Instr, Cornell Univ, 79-80; from asst prof to assoc prof to prof to chemn, 80-, Ithaca Col. **HONORS AND AWARDS** Charles A. Dana Found, 84-85; Charles A. Dana Found Grant, 87-88; Phi Kappa Phi, 88, Sigma Tau Delta, 89, Ithaca Col; Fulbright Senior Lecturer, Institut fur Anglistik und Amerikanistik, 96-97. **MEMBERSHIPS** Medieval Acad Am; Int Arthurian Society; Int Society Anglo-Saxonist. **RESEARCH** Middle English literature; medieval encyclopedias; medieval apocalypticism. **SELECTED PUBLICATIONS** Coauth, art, Medieval Christian Literary Imagery: A Guide to Interpretation, 88; auth, art, Cleanness 1057-64 and the Roman de la Rose, 94; auth, art, Morgain la Fee in Sir Gawain and the Green Knight: From Toy to Camelot, 96; auth, art, Towards a Reception History of Western Mediaeval Encyclopedias in England Before 1500, 97; auth, art, Allegory and Related Symbolism, 98. **CONTACT ADDRESS** Dept of English, Ithaca Col, Ithaca, NY, 14850-7281. **EMAIL** twomey@ithaca.edu

TY, ELEANOR
DISCIPLINE FEMINIST LITERARY THEORY **EDUCATION** Toronto, BA; McMaster, MA, PhD. **CAREER** Assoc Prof **SELECTED PUBLICATIONS** Auth, Unsex'd Revolutionaries: Five Women Novelists of the 1790s, U of Toronto P, 93; Empowering the Feminine: The Narratives of Mary Robinson, Jane West, and Amelia Opie, 1796-1812, U of Toronto P, 98; Ed, The Victim of Prejudice by Mary Hays, Broadview Press. **CONTACT ADDRESS** Dept of English, Wilfrid Laurier Univ, 75 University Ave W, Waterloo, ON, N2L 3C5. **EMAIL** ety@mach1.wlu.ca

TYLER, CAROLE-ANNE
DISCIPLINE ENGLISH LITERATURE **EDUCATION** Williams Coll, BA; Brown Coll, MA, PhD, Eng. **HONORS AND AWARDS** Fel, Amer Coun Learned Soc, 91. **RESEARCH** Gender and sexuality, literary theory, cultural studies, 20th-Century fiction. **SELECTED PUBLICATIONS** Auth, "Boys Will Be Girls: The Politics of Gay Drag," Inside/Out: Lesbian Theories Gay Theories, 91; "Passing: Narcissism, Identity, and Difference," 94; "Death Masks," Rrose Is a Rrose Is a Rrose, cat, Guggenheim Museum exhib on gender performance in photography, 97. **CONTACT ADDRESS** Dept of Eng, Univ Calif, 1156 Hinderaker Hall, Riverside, CA, 92521-0209. **EMAIL** caroleanne.tyler@ucr.edu

TYLER, EDWARD W.
DISCIPLINE ENGLISH LITERATURE **EDUCATION** Amherst Col, BA, 54; Stanford Univ, PhD, 60. **CAREER** Ch, Comm on Logic and Rhet; Lionel Trilling prof, 60. **HONORS AND AWARDS** Guggenheim fel, 69; grants, NEH-Huntington, 75, 83; great tchr award, Soc Older Grad, 85; Mark Van Doren award, 86; hon scholar, Milton Soc, 89; pres award for tchg, 96., Exec bd, Eng Inst; ch, Seventeenth-Century div, MLA. **MEMBERSHIPS** Mem, Renaissance Soc; Milton Soc; Spenser Soc; Acad Lit Stud. **SELECTED PUBLICATIONS** Auth, Nature and Art, Renaissance Lit, 64, Literary Criticism of Seventeenth-Century England, 67; Milton's Poetry, 79; Donne's Idea of a Woman, 91. **CONTACT ADDRESS** Dept of Eng, Columbia Col, New York, 2960 Broadway, New York, NY, 10027-6902.

TYSON, NANCY J.
PERSONAL Born 02/25/1949, South Bend, IN **DISCIPLINE** ENGLISH **EDUCATION** Marshall Univ, BA, 71; Ohio State Univ, MA, 73; PhD, 81. **CAREER** Lectr, Ohio State Univ, 78-81; asst prof, Univ Richmond, 81-84; asst prof, 84-90, assoc prof 90- , Univ S Fla, 84- . **HONORS AND AWARDS** USF Alumni Prof Award, 86; USF Sr Class Outstanding prof award, 89; USF Outstanding Undergraduate Tchg Award, 96. ALA "Choice" award for academic books, 83. **MEMBERSHIPS** Browning Inst; Mod Lang Asn; S Atlantic Mod Lang Asn; Res Soc Victorian Per; 19th Century Studies Asn; William Morris Soc; Popular Cult Asso. **RESEARCH** Victorian literature; bibliography and research methods for English studies; popular culture. **SELECTED PUBLICATIONS** Auth, Art and Society in the Late Prose Narratives of William Morris, Pre-Raphaelite Rev, 78; Eugene Aram: Literary History and Typology of the Scholar-Criminal, Shoe String Press, 83; Thackeray and Bulwer: Between the Lines in Barry Lyndon, English Lang Notes, 89; Altars to Attics: The State of Matrimony in Brontes Jane Eyre, Mistreated Mates: Family Violence in Life and Literature, Plenum, 91; Caliban in a Glass: Autoscopic Vision in The Picture of Dorian Gray, The Haunted Mind: The Supernatural in Victorian Literature, Univ Press Am, 98. **CONTACT ADDRESS** English Dept, Univ S Fla, 4202 E Fowler Ave., CPR 107, Tampa, FL, 33620-5550. **EMAIL** tyson@chuma.cas.usf.edu

TYTELL, JOHN
PERSONAL Born 05/17/1939, Antwerp, Belgium, m, 1967 **DISCIPLINE** LITERATURE **EDUCATION** City Col New York, BA, 61; NY Univ, MA, PhD(English), 68. **CAREER** Lectr, 63-68, from asst prof to assoc prof, 68-77, prof English, Queens Col, 77-, Nat Endowment for Humanities fel, 74; US Info Agency lectr, Asia, 75; U.S.I.A. lecturer in Asia, 75; vis prof Rutgers, spring 80, and Univ of Paris, 83. **HONORS AND AWARDS** PBK; Oscar Lloyd Meyerson Award; Queens Col Presidential Research Award, spring 92. **RESEARCH** Modern and contemporary American literature. **SELECTED PUBLICATIONS** Co-ed, The American Experience: A Radical Reader, Harper & Row, 70; Affinities: An Anthology of Stories, Crowell, 70; auth, Sexual Imagery in the Sacred and Secular Poems of Richard Crashaw, Lit & Psychol, 71; Frederick Rolfe and His Age, Studies Twentieth Century, fall 72; The Jamesian Legacy in The Good Soldier, Studies in Novel, 72; The Beat Generation and the Continuing American Revolution, Am Scholar, spring 73; Naked Angels: The Lives and Literature of the Beat Generation (also editions in Japanese & Ger), McGraw, 76 & 77; Epiphany in Chaos: Fragmentation in Modernism, In: Fragments, NY Lit Forum, 81; Ezra Pound: The Solitary Volcano, Doubleday, 87; Passionate Lives: D.H. Lawrence, F.Scott Fitzgerald, Henry Miller, Dylan Thomas, Sylvia Plath--In Love, Birch Lane Press, Carol Pub, 91; The Living Theatre: Art, Exile and Outrage, Grove press: NY, 95; and other articles and reviews. **CONTACT ADDRESS** Dept of English, Queens Col, CUNY, 6530 Kissena Blvd, Flushing, NY, 11367-1597.

U

UEDA, MAKOTO
PERSONAL Born 05/20/1931, Ono, Japan, m, 1962, 2 children **DISCIPLINE** LITERATURE, AESTHETICS **EDUCATION** Kobe Univ, BLitt, 54; Univ Nebr, MA, 56; Univ Wash, PhD(comp lit), 61. **CAREER** Lectr Japanese, Univ Toronto, 61-62, from asst prof to prof, 62-71; PROF JAPANESE, STANFORD UNIV, 71-. **RESEARCH** Japanese literature, including theatre; comparative literature, especially Japanese and Western; literary theory and criticism. **SELECTED PUBLICATIONS** Auth, Comparative Poetics--An Intercultural Essay on Theories of Literature, Comparative Lit, Vol 0045, 93. **CONTACT ADDRESS** Dept of Asian Languages, Stanford Univ, Stanford, CA, 94305-1926.

UFFELMAN, LARRY KENT
PERSONAL Born 12/25/1938, Burlington, IA, m, 1960, 2 children **DISCIPLINE** BIBLIOGRAPHY, VICTORIAN ENGLISH LITERATURE **EDUCATION** IL Wesleyan Univ, BA, 60; Univ IL, MA, 62; KS State Univ, PhD(English), 69. **CAREER** Instr English, Valparaiso Univ, 62-65; assoc prof, 69-76, prof English, Mansfield State Col, 76-; bibliogr, Res Soc

Victorian Periodicals, 79-. **HONORS AND AWARDS** Cert of Excellence in Teaching, 79; Commonwealth Teaching Fel, 79; Distinguished Teaching Chair, 79; Distinguished Mentoring Cert, spring 94, fall 94, fall 96; grants of PA State System of Higher Ed Professional Development Comm, 90, 92, 95. **MEMBERSHIPS** MLA; Res Soc Victorian Periodicals; Browning Inst. **RESEARCH** Victorian serial fiction; British poetry of World War I; Textual criticism and editing. **SELECTED PUBLICATIONS** Auth, Sutton Hoo: A Summary, Bull Kans Asn Teachers English, 69; Charles Hamilton Sorley: An Annotated Checklist, Serif, 73; Kingsley, the Poet, and the Press, Kans Quart, 75; coauth, Kingsley's Serial Novels: Yeast, Victorian Periodicals Newslett, 76; Charles Kingsley, G K Hall, 79; coauth, with Patrick Scott, Kingsley's Serial Novels II: The Water-Babies, Victorian Periodicals Rev, 19, 86; auth, Kingsley's Hypatia: Revisions in Context, Nineteenth-Century Lit 41, 86; Kingsley's Hereward the Wake: From Serial to Book, Victorian Inst J, 14, 86; Faust and Freshman Humanities, in Approaches to Teaching Goethe's Faust, ed Douglas J McMillan, NY: MLA, 87; Articles in Victorian Britain: An Encyclopedia, ed Sally Mitchell, NY: Garland, 88; contrib to Joseph Conrad: An Annotated Bibliography, ed Bruce Teets, NY: Garland, 90; ed, The Nineteenth-Century Periodical Press in Britain: A Bibliography of Modern Studies 1972-1987, Res Soc for Victorian Periodicals, 92; Victorian Periodicals: Research Opportunuites to Faculty-Undergraduate Research, Coun on Undergraduate Res Quart, June 95. **CONTACT ADDRESS** Dept English, Mansfield Univ, Belknap Hall, Mansfield, PA, 16933-1308. **EMAIL** luffelman@mnsfld.edu

ULANOV, BARRY
PERSONAL Born 04/10/1918, New York, NY, m, 1939, 4 children **DISCIPLINE** ENGLISH **EDUCATION** Columbia Univ, AB, 39, PhD(comp lit), 55. **CAREER** Instr English, Princeton Univ, 50-51; from instr to assoc prof, 51-66, chmn dept English, 67-72, chmn prof in the arts, 72-79, chmn dept relig, 73-74, PROF ENGLISH, BARNARD COL and ADJ PROF ENGLISH, COLUMBIA UNIV, 66-. Guggenheim fel, 62-63; Am Coun Learned Socs grant, 62-63. **HONORS AND AWARDS** Spiritual Life Award, 63; O'Brien Award for Distinguished Teaching, Newman Soc, 65., DLitt, Villanova Univ, 65. **MEMBERSHIPS** MLA; Mediaeval Acad Am; Cath Renaissance Soc (pres, 60-66); PEN Club; Asn Am Achievements. **RESEARCH** Relationship between literature and the arts; literature, theology and the drama; psychology and religion. **SELECTED PUBLICATIONS** Auth, Mapping the Territory, Jour Rel and Health, Vol 0033, 94; Truth and Method, Jour Rel and Health, Vol 0033, 94; Women in Jazz--Do they Belong, Down Beat, Vol 0061, 94; Spiritualism and the Foundations of Jung,C.G. Psychology, Jour Rel and Health, Vol 0033, 94; The Muse in the Machine--Computerizing the Poetry of Human Thought, Jour Rel and Health, Vol 0033, 94; Philosophical Issues in the Psychology of Jung,C.G., Jour Rel and Health, Vol 0033, 94; Seeing Straight with Crooked Lines, Jour Rel and Health, Vol 0033, 94; Nursing as Nourishment, Jour Rel and Health, Vol 0034, 95; Tough Minds and Open Hearts, Jour Rel and Health, Vol 0035, 96; co-ed, Jour Rel and Health, Vol 0034, 95; Composing the Soul--Reaches of Nietzsche Psychology, Jour Rel and Health, Vol 0034, 95; The Short-Circuit Syndrome, Jour Rel and Health, Vol 0034, 95; Nietzsche and Psychoanalysis, Jour Rel and Health, Vol 0034, 95; Culture, Anyone, Jour Rel and Health, Vol 0034, 95; The Nietzsche Legacy in Germany 1890-1990, Jour Rel and Health, Vol 0034, 95; Dumbing Down--Essays on the Strip-Mining of American Culture, Jour Rel and Health, Vol 0035, 96; Staying Awake--Consciousness and Conscience, Jour of Rel and Health, Vol 0035, 96; A Matter of Faith, Jour of Rel and Health, Vol 0035, 96; The Trinity--Augustine, Jour Rel and Health, Vol 0035, 96; Why Freud Was Wrong, Jour Rel and Health, Vol 0035, 96; Crucial Words, Crucial Attitudes, Jour Rel and Health, Vol 0035, 96; Childhood and Children--A Compendium of Customs, Superstitions, Theories, Profiles, and Facts, Jour Rel and Health, Vol 0036, 97; The Healing Syndrome, Jour Rel and Health, Vol 0036, 97; The Iconography of Job Through the Centuries--Artists as Biblical Interpreters, Jour Rel and Health, Vol 0036, 97; Surviving in a Drifting Culture, Jour Rel and Health, Vol 0036, 97; Spiritual Exercises, Jour Rel and Health, Vol 0036, 97. **CONTACT ADDRESS** Dept of English, Columbia Univ, 3061 Broadway, New York, NY, 10027-5710.

UMLAND, REBECCA A.
PERSONAL Born 09/11/1954, Iowa City, m, 1992, 1 child **DISCIPLINE** BRITISH LITERATURE **EDUCATION** Univ Iowa, BA, 1974, MA, 1982 PhD, 85. **CAREER** Instr, Iowa State Univ, 86-89; assoc prof, 89-, grad fel, Univ Nebr, Kearney; ed bd, Arthuriana. **HONORS AND AWARDS** Mortar Board Soc; Phi Eta Sigma **MEMBERSHIPS** Assoc of Lit Schol and Critics; Int Arthurian Soc; Midwest Victorian Soc. **RESEARCH** 19th Century British Lit; modern British and European Lit; Arthurian Literature and Film; Tristan Legend **SELECTED PUBLICATIONS** Coauth, The Use of Arthurian Legend in Hollywood Film: From Connecticut Yankees to Fisher Kings; published several articles, primarily on the Arthurian revival (e.g. the Arthurian works of Tennyson, Swinburne, Morris, and E.A. Robinson). **CONTACT ADDRESS** Dept of English, Univ Nebr, Kearney, Thomas Hall, Kearney, NE, 68849. **EMAIL** umlandr@platte.unk.edu

UMLAND, SAMUEL J.
PERSONAL Born 06/22/1954, Nebraska City, NE, m, 1992, 3 children **DISCIPLINE** ENGLISH AND FILM STUDIES **EDUCATION** Univ Neb Lincoln, BA, 79, MA, 81, PhD, 87. **CAREER** Assoc prof, Univ Neb Kearney, 92-97; prof, eng, Univ Neb, Kearney, 97-; assoc dean, Univ Neb, Kearney, 94-97; interim dean, fine arts and humanities, Univ Neb, Kearney, 97-98; dir, Mus of Neb Art, 98-. **HONORS AND AWARDS** Pres grad fel, Univ Neb, Lincoln, 86-87. **MEMBERSHIPS** Amer Asn of Mus; Intl Arthurian Soc. **RESEARCH** Film studies; Film theory; Philip K. Dick; Electronic literacy. **SELECTED PUBLICATIONS** Coauth, with Rebecca A. Umland, The Use of Arthurian Legend in Hollywood Film: From Connecticut Yankees to Fisher Kings, Greenwood Press, 96; ed, Philip K. Dick: Contemporary Critical Interpretations, Greenwood Press, 95; articles, coauth, with Rebecca A. Umland, The King and I: Features of the Arthurian Legend in Twin Peaks, Wrapped in Plastic, 31, Oct, 97; Though Inland Far We Be: The Poetic Exile of Don Welch, Platte Valley Rev, 25, 1, Spr, 97; auth, When the Unabomber Strikes: On Terror, the Uncanny, and the Peculiarity of Postmodern Paranoia, Perforations, 7, Terrorism, Demographics, Propaganda, On-line, Internet, URL: http://noel.pd.org/topos/perforations.html; The Shape and Space of David Lynch's Hotel Room, Wrapped in Plastic, 22, 7-10, Apr, 96; Richard Rubenstein's Correspondence with William Carlos Williams, The William Carlos Williams Rev, 20, 1, 65-68, Spr, 94; Word, Sound and Image: A Challenge to Formalist Film Criticisms, The Platte Valley Rev, 22, 2, 55-73, Spr, 94; American Cultural Symbol and Myth in Nicholas Roeg's, The Man Who Fell to Earth, The Platte Valley Rev, 21, 2, 20-30, Spr, 93. **CONTACT ADDRESS** Museum of Nebraska Art, 2401 Central Av., Kearney, NE, 68847. **EMAIL** umlands@unk.edu

UMPHLETT, WILEY LEE
PERSONAL Born 10/25/1931, Norfolk, VA, m, 1966, 3 children **DISCIPLINE** AMERICAN LIT **EDUCATION** Florida State Univ, PhD, Am Lit. **CAREER** Univ West Florida, admin, teacher, 30 years. **RESEARCH** Pop Culture; Social Aspects of Sports. **SELECTED PUBLICATIONS** Fantasizing the American Century: A Sociocultural History of the Popular Vision; in progress; Creating the Big Game: John Heisman and the Intervention of American Football, Greenwood Press, 92; The Achievement of American Sport Literature: A Critical Appraisal, Fairleigh Dickenson UP, 91; numerous articles. **CONTACT ADDRESS** Univ West Florida, Bldg 53, Pensacola, FL, 32514.

UNDERINER, TAMARA
DISCIPLINE THEATRE ARTS **EDUCATION** Univ Wash, PhD. **CAREER** Asst prof **SELECTED PUBLICATIONS** Auth, pubs on Latin American theatre, post-colonial theatre, 20th century American theatre, and dramatic literature. **CONTACT ADDRESS** Theatre Arts and Dance Dept, Univ of Minnesota, Twin Cities, 106 Norris Hall, 172 Pillsbury Dr SE, Minneapolis, MN, 55455. **EMAIL** under009@tc.umn.edu

UNDERWOOD, RICHARD
DISCIPLINE ENGLISH LITERATURE **EDUCATION** Univ Mich, PhD, 70. **CAREER** Dept Eng, Clemson Univ **RESEARCH** Shakespeare; Milton; 17th century literature. **SELECTED PUBLICATIONS** Auth, The Two Nobel Kinsman and Its Beginnings, Salzburg, 93. **CONTACT ADDRESS** Clemson Univ, Clemson, SC, 29634. **EMAIL** urichar@clemson.edu

UNDERWOOD, WILLARD A.
PERSONAL Born 08/04/1943, Fairmont, IL, m, 1975, 4 children **DISCIPLINE** SPEECH **EDUCATION** Ill State Univ, BS, 65, MS, 67; Bowling Green State Univ, PhD, 72. **CAREER** Asst prof, 75-76, assoc prof, Ariz State Univ, 76-81; lect, Univ NH, 84-85; asst prof, 85-88, assoc prof, Bethany Col, 88-91; prof, Okla Panhandle State Univ, 91-. **HONORS AND AWARDS** Outstanding Educators of Am; Pi Kappa Delta. **MEMBERSHIPS** Nat Commun Asn; Central States Commun Asn; Okla Speech, Theatre and Commun Asn; Nat Educ Debate Asn. **RESEARCH** Health communication; intercultural communication; persuasion and argumentation; and social movements. **SELECTED PUBLICATIONS** Auth, Perceived Class and Ascribed Status of the Physically Disabled: A Case Study, in The Image of Class, Univ Southern Colo, 98; auth, Status Determination of Physically Different Members of Groups: Class Assigned by Others, The Image of Class, Univ Southern Colo, 98. **CONTACT ADDRESS** Oklahoma Panhandle State Univ, PO Box 453, Grover, TX, 79040.

UPHAUS, ROBERT WALTER
PERSONAL Born 06/15/1942, East Orange, NJ, 3 children **DISCIPLINE** ENGLISH AND AMERICAN LITERATURE **EDUCATION** Calif State Col, Los Angeles, BA, 64; Univ Wash, MA, 66, PhD, 69. **CAREER** Instr English, Bellevue Community Col, 66-68; asst prof, 68-72, assoc prof, 72-79, prof English Mich State Univ, 79-, Vis lectr English, Univ Leeds, 71-72. **MEMBERSHIPS** MLA; Am Soc 18th Century Studies. **RESEARCH** Shakespeare; 18th century English literature. **SELECTED PUBLICATIONS** Ed, American Protest in Perspective, Harper, 71; The Impossible Observer, 79; Beyond Tragedy, 81; auth, William Hazlitt, Twayne, 85; ed, The Idea of the Novel in the Eighteenth Century, Colleagues Press, 88; The 'Other' Eighteenth Century, Colleagues Press, 91. **CONTACT ADDRESS** Dept of English, Michigan State Univ, 201 Morrill Hall, East Lansing, MI, 48824-1036. **EMAIL** uphaus@pilot.msu.edu

V

VAILAKIS, IVAN GORDON
PERSONAL Quito, Ecuador **DISCIPLINE** LATIN AMERICA LITERATURE **EDUCATION** Univ Calf Irvine, PhD, **CAREER** Prof, Univ Redlands. **RESEARCH** Contemporary Latin American Poetry. **SELECTED PUBLICATIONS** Auth, Colibries en el exilio, 97; Nuestrario, 87; pubs on Gabriela Mistral, Alicia Y nez Cossio, Sandra Cisneros, and Helen Maria Viramontes. **CONTACT ADDRESS** History Dept, Univ Redlands, 1200 E Colton Ave, Box 3090, Redlands, CA, 92373-0999.

VALASKAKIS, GAIL
PERSONAL Born 05/09/1939, Ashland, WI **DISCIPLINE** COMMUNICATIONS **EDUCATION** Univ Wis, BS, 61; Cornell Univ, MA, 64; McGill Univ, PhD, 79. **CAREER** Lectr, comm arts, Loyola Col, 69-71, coordr Can studies, Loyola campus, 78-79; asst to assoc prof, 71-89, PROF COMMUNICATION STUD, CONCORDIA UNIV, 89-, dir MA prog media stud, 82-84, ch, 83-85, dean arts & sci, 92-98. **MEMBERSHIPS** Can Commun Asn; Int Soc Intercultur Educ, Training & Res; Can Asn Suport Native Peoples; Native N Am Stud Inst (Montreal). **SELECTED PUBLICATIONS** Dir, Can J Commun, 86-89. **CONTACT ADDRESS** 3611 Marlowe Ave, Montreal, PQ, H4A 3L8.

VALENTI, PETER LOUIS
PERSONAL Born 01/12/1945, Springfield, MS, m, 1972, 2 children **DISCIPLINE** ENGLISH **EDUCATION** Westfield State Col, BA, 67; E Carolina Univ, MA, 70; Univ NC, Chapel Hill, PhD(English), 74. **CAREER** Instr English, Univ NC, Chapel Hill, 73-74; chmn, Dept English, Holmes High Sch, Edenton, NC, 74-75; asst prof, 75-81, assoc prof 82-88; prof, English, Fayetteville State Univ, 89-. **HONORS AND AWARDS** Dist Visit Prof, US Milit Acad, 91-92; Bd of Gov Awd for Excel In Teach, 96 **MEMBERSHIPS** MLA; SAtlantic Mod Lang Asn; Popular Cult Asn; Am Film Inst; Philol Asn Carolinas; CCCC; ASLE. **RESEARCH** Film; 17th-19th century English literature; 19th century American literature. **SELECTED PUBLICATIONS** Auth, Images of authority in Benito Cereno, CLA J, 3/78; The Film Blanc: Suggestions for a variety of fantasy, 1940-45, J Popular Film, 77-78; The ordering of God's providence: Law and landscape, In: The Pioneers, Studies Am Fiction, Vol VII, 78; The cultural hero in the World War II fantasy film, J Popular Film & TV, Vol VII, 79; Gatsby: Franklin and Hoppy, Notes Mod Am Lit, Vol 3, 79; The theological rhetoric of It's a Wonderful Life, Film Criticism, Vol V, 81; auth, Errol Flynn, Greenwood, 84; auth, The Treasure of the Sierra Madre: Spiritual Quest and Studio Patriarchy, Paulist, 92; auth, Visual Documentary in The Grapes of Wrath, Steinbeck and the Environment, Univ of Ala, 96; auth, Reading the Landscape: Writing a World, Harcourt Brace Col, 96. **CONTACT ADDRESS** Dept of English, Fayetteville State Univ, 1200 Murchison Rd, Fayetteville, NC, 28301-4298. **EMAIL** valenti@uncfsu.edu

VALENTIS, MARY ARENSBERG
PERSONAL Born 06/27/1945, Albany, NY, m, 1991, 1 child **DISCIPLINE** ENGLISH AND AMERICAN LITERATURE **EDUCATION** CT College, BA, 67; SUNY Albany, MA, 74, PhD, 79. **CAREER** Lectr, 77 to 98-, SUNY Albany. **MEMBERSHIPS** MLA; ALS; Wallace Stevens Soc; Authors Guild. **RESEARCH** Literary theory; Psychoanalysis. **SELECTED PUBLICATIONS** Auth, Donne Che Non Hanno Paura De l Fucco, Frassinelli Pub, 97; auth, Die WUT Der Frauen, Knauer Pub, 96; coauth, Female Rage: Unlocking its secrets claiming its power, CSB div of Crown Pub, 94, Japanese edition, 96; Female Rage: How women can unlock their rage, Platkus Pub, 95; auth, Outing Rage, New Women Mag, 94; auth, Wallace Stevens and the Mythology of Gender, in: Wallace Stevens and the Feminine, ed, Melita Schawn, U of AL Press, 94. **CONTACT ADDRESS** Dept of English, SUNY Albany, Albany, NY, 12222. **EMAIL** mbvbooks@aol.comvalentis@csc.albany.edu

VALERIE M., BABB
DISCIPLINE ENGLISH **EDUCATION** CUNY Queen's Col, BA; SUNY Buffalo, MA, PhD. **CAREER** Georgetown Univ, prof. **RESEARCH** American studies; women's studies; American literature. **SELECTED PUBLICATIONS** Auth, Whiteness Visible: The Meaning of Whiteness in American Literature and Culture, 98. **CONTACT ADDRESS** Dept of English, Georgetown Univ, PO Box 571131, Washington, DC, 20057-1131.

VALESIO, PAOLO
PERSONAL Born 10/14/1939, Bologna, Italy, m, 1963, 1 child **DISCIPLINE** RHETORICS, LITERARY THEORY; RELI-

GION AND LITERATURE. **EDUCATION** Univ Bologna, Dr Lett, 61, libero docente, 69. **CAREER** Asst, Inst Glottology, Univ Bologna, 61-62, 66-68; lectr Romance lang & lit, Harvard Univ, 68-70, assoc prof, 70-73; assoc prof Ital & dir prog, NY Univ, 73-74, prof, 74-76; Prof Ital, Yale Univ, 76-, Fel, Harvard Univ, 65-66. **HONORS AND AWARDS** Poetry Prize, Cizza gi San Vite al Tagliamento, 92; Guggenheim Fel, 94. **MEMBERSHIPS** Am Assn of Italian Studies; Dante Soc Am. **RESEARCH** Religion and literature. **SELECTED PUBLICATIONS** Auth, Tradimenti, with a Postace by Salvatore Jemma, Bologna: Quaderni del Masaorita, 94; Nightchant: Selected Poems, trans Graziella Sidoli and Vanna Tessier, Edmonton: Snowapple Press, 95; Sonetos Profanos y Sacros, trans Taller de Traduccion Literaria de la Universidad di La Laguna, La Laguna, Tenerife: Ediciones Canarias, 96. **CONTACT ADDRESS** Dept of Ital, Yale Univ, PO Box 208311, New Haven, CT, 06520-8311.

VALGEMAE, MARDI
PERSONAL Born 11/10/1935, Viljandi, Estonia, m, 1957, 2 children **DISCIPLINE** ENGLISH **EDUCATION** Rutgers Univ, BA, 57; Univ Calif, Los Angeles, MA, 62, PhD(English), 64. **CAREER** Asst prof English, Univ Calif, Los Angeles, 64-68; assoc prof, 68-75, prof English, Lehman Col, City Univ New York, 75-, Drama Ed, Mana, 64-; fac res grant, City Univ New York, 69-70; Am Coun Learned Soc Europ travel grant, 70, 81; dir The City and Humanities Program, 84-88; chmn Dept English, 88-97. **HONORS AND AWARDS** Criticism Prize, Estonian Writers' Union, 91; Visnapuu Prize, 96. **MEMBERSHIPS** MLA; Am Comp Lit Asn; Asn Advan Baltic Studies. **RESEARCH** Modern drama; Baltic studies. **SELECTED PUBLICATIONS** Auth, Albee's great god Alice, Mod Drama, Winter 67; Socialist allegory of the absurd, Comp Drama, Spring 71; Expressionism and the new American drama, 20th Century Lit, 10/71; Accelerated Grimace: Expressionism in the American Drama of the 1920's, Southern Ill Univ, 72; co-ed, Baltic literature and linguistics, Asn Advan Baltic Studies, 73; contribr, Expressionism as an International Literary Phenomenon, Didier, Paris, 73; A Case Study of a Soviet Republic, 78 & Baltic Drama: A Handbook and Bibliography, 81, Westview; Linn ja teater, The City and the Theater, Vagabund, Tallinn, Estonia, 95. **CONTACT ADDRESS** Dept of English, Lehman Col, CUNY, 250 Bedford Park W, Bronx, NY, 10468-1527. **EMAIL** val11370@webtv.net

VALLETTA, CLEMENT LAWRENCE
PERSONAL Born 07/31/1938, Easton, PA **DISCIPLINE** AMERICAN CIVILIZATION, ENGLISH **EDUCATION** Univ Scranton, BA, 61; Univ Pa, MA, 62, PhD(Am Civilization), 68. **CAREER** From instr to assoc prof, 64-77, chmn dept, 71-80, prof English, King's Col, PA, 77-. **MEMBERSHIPS** MLA; Am Studies Asn; Am Folklore Soc; Christianity and Literature. **RESEARCH** Americanization of ethnic groups; influence of relativity physics in non-scientific aspects; American civilization, folk, rhetorical, literary aspects. **SELECTED PUBLICATIONS** Auth, Friendship and games in Italian American life, Keystone Folklore Quart, 70; Einstein, Edison and the conquest of irony, Cithara, 72; contrib, The ethnic experience in Pennsylvania, Bucknell Univ, 73; Studies in Italian American social history, Rowman & Littlefield, 75; auth, A study of Americanization in Carneta, Arno, 75; ed, Ethnic Drama: Video-Text and Study Guide, ERIC, 81; Pennsylavania History, 92; with Robert Paoletti In-Determindcy in Science and Discourse, Technical Writing and Communication, 95; Caring and Christian Irony in Ann Tyler's Novels, Repis Collage Proceedings, 96; A Christian Dispersion in Don DeLillo's The Names, Christianity and Literature, 98. **CONTACT ADDRESS** Dept of English, King's Col, 133 N River St, Wilkes Barre, PA, 18711-0801. **EMAIL** clvallet@kings.edu

VALLEY, DAVID B.
PERSONAL Born 09/12/1944, Rock Island, IL, m, 1990, 3 children **DISCIPLINE** SPEECH COMMUNICATIONS **EDUCATION** Univ of IL, PhD; IL St Univ, MS; Blackhawk Cmnty Col, AS **CAREER** 82-, Prof, S IL Univ **HONORS AND AWARDS** Tch Recog awd, 93 **MEMBERSHIPS** Nat Commun Asn; Cent Sts Speech Asn **RESEARCH** Parent-child conversation **SELECTED PUBLICATIONS** Auth, A History and Analysis of Democratic Presidential Nomination Acceptance Speeches to 1968, Univ Press of America, 88 **CONTACT ADDRESS** Dept of Speech Commun, So Illinois Univ, Edwardsville, IL, 62026-1772. **EMAIL** dvalley@siue.edu

VAN, THOMAS A.
PERSONAL Born 05/22/1938, New York, NY, m, 1963 **DISCIPLINE** ENGLISH, LINGUISTICS **EDUCATION** City Col New York, BA, 60; Duke Univ, MA, 63, PhD(English), 66. **CAREER** Instr English, Univ NC, Chapel Hill, 65-66; asst prof, Univ Ky, 66-70; ASSOS PROF ENGLISH, UNIV LOUISVILLE, 70-, CHMN DEPT, 80-. **MEMBERSHIPS** MLA; NCTE; Mediaeval Acad Am; fel NDEA. **RESEARCH** Dante; Chaucer; Shakespeare. **SELECTED PUBLICATIONS** Auth, False Texts and Disappearing Women in the Wife of Baths Prologue and Tale--An Analysis of the Thematic Development of Contradiction and Anomaly Between Teller and Tale in the Canterbury Tales of Chaucer, Geoffrey, Chaucer Rev, Vol 0029, 94. **CONTACT ADDRESS** Dept of English, Univ of Louisville, Louisville, KY, 40208.

VAN DOVER, JAMES K.
PERSONAL Born 01/01/1950, St. Louis, MO, m, 1979, 2 children **DISCIPLINE** ENGLISH **EDUCATION** Lafayette Col, AB, 72; Bryn Mawr Col, MA, 74, PhD, 78. **CAREER** Prof, Lincoln Univ, 78-. **HONORS AND AWARDS** Whiting Fel; Fulbright Professorships: Tubingen, 80-81, Stuttgart, 88-89; Lindback Award for Tchg; Presidential Award for Res. **RESEARCH** Am Literature; popular literature. **SELECTED PUBLICATIONS** Coauth, Isn't Justice Always Unfair? The Detective in Southern Literature, 96; auth, Centurions, Knights, Choirboys and Other Cops: The Fiction of Joseph Wambaugh, 95; auth, The Critical Response to Raymond Chandler, 95; auth, You Know My Method: The Science of the Detective, 94; auth, Polemical Pulps: The Novels of Sjowall and Wahloo, 93. **CONTACT ADDRESS** 212 Wilshire Ln, Newark, DE, 19711. **EMAIL** vandover@lu.lincoln.edu

VAN PELT, TAMISE
DISCIPLINE ENGLISH LITERATURE **EDUCATION** Univ Ill, PhD, 94. **CAREER** Asst prof. **RESEARCH** Critical and interpretive theories; pedagogy of theory; cybersubjectivity; virtual identity. **SELECTED PUBLICATIONS** Auth, The other Side of Desire: Lacan's Theory of the Registers, SUNY. **CONTACT ADDRESS** Dept of English and Philosophy, Idaho State Univ, Pocatello, ID, 83209. **EMAIL** vantamis@isu.edu

VAN SLYKE TURK, JUDY
DISCIPLINE COMMUNICATION **EDUCATION** Northwestern Univ, BSJ; Northern IL Univ, MA; Syracuse Univ, PhD. **CAREER** Dean & prof, Univ of SC. **MEMBERSHIPS** Pres, Asn Educ Jour & Mass Commun, 94-95; Publ Rel Soc Am, Educ of the Yr, 92; former ch, Col Fellows, Publ Rel Soc Am. **RESEARCH** Agenda-setting theory applied to public rel(s); public rel(s) management. **SELECTED PUBLICATIONS** Coauth, leading introductory publ rel textbk; publ on, res interest. **CONTACT ADDRESS** Col of Journalism & Mass Commun, Univ of S. Carolina, Carolina Coliseum rm 4000, Columbia, SC, 29208. **EMAIL** judy-turk@sc.edu

VANAUKEN, SHELDON
DISCIPLINE HISTORY, ENGLISH **EDUCATION** Oxford Univ, BLitt, 57. **CAREER** From asst prof to assoc prof, 48-73, PROF HIST and ENGLISH, LYNCHBURG COL, 73- **RESEARCH** Nineteenth century England. **SELECTED PUBLICATIONS** Auth, Employment Law Survey, Denver Univ Law Rev, Vol 0072, 95. **CONTACT ADDRESS** 100 Breckenbridge, Lynchburg, VA, 24501.

VANCE, JOHN ANTHONY
PERSONAL Born 08/09/1947, Oceanside, NY, m, 1974, 2 children **DISCIPLINE** ENGLISH LITERATURE **EDUCATION** Fla State Univ, BA, 74, MA, 75, PhD(English), 79. **CAREER** Grad teaching asst, Fla State Univ, 76-79; from Asst Prof to Assoc Prof, 79-93, PROF ENGLISH, UNIV GA, 93-. **MEMBERSHIPS** MLA; SAtlantic Mod Lang Asn; Am Soc 18th Century Studies; Southeastern Am Soc 18th Century Studies. **RESEARCH** Samuel Johnson and his circle; Restoration and 18th century drama. **SELECTED PUBLICATIONS** Auth, Joseph and Thomas Warton, G.K. Hall, 83; Joseph and Thomas Warton: An Annotated Bibliography, Garland Publ, 83; Samuel Johnson and the Sense of History, Univ Ga Press, 84; Boswell's Life of Johnson: New Questions, New Answers, Univ Ga Press, 85; coauth, A Bibliography of Johnson Studies, Univ Victoria, 87. **CONTACT ADDRESS** Dept of English, Univ of Georgia, Athens, GA, 30602-0001. **EMAIL** jvance@arches.uga.edu

VANCE, WILLIAM LYNN
PERSONAL Born 04/19/1934, Dupree, SD **DISCIPLINE** ENGLISH & AMERICAN LITERATURE **EDUCATION** Oberlin Col, AB, 56; Univ Mich, MA, 57, PhD, 62. **CAREER** From assoc prof to prof, 62-73, assoc chmn dept, 72-73 & 81-83, chmn dept, 85-88, PROF ENGLISH, BOSTON UNIV, 73-, dir, Am Studies, 88-90. **HONORS AND AWARDS** Ralph Waldo Emerson Prize (Phi Beta Kappa), 90; Nat Book Critics Circle Award Nomination, 90; guggenheim fel, 90-91; Doctor of Letters and Lit (hon), Univ S Dak, 92; Metcalf Cup and Prize, Excellence in Teaching, 92; NEH Distinguished teaching prof, 97-99. **MEMBERSHIPS** AAUP; ALSC; Soc Classic Tradition **RESEARCH** American literature and art; Italian culture. **SELECTED PUBLICATIONS** Co-ed, American Literature, Little, 70; co-ed, Imaginari a confronto, Jarsilio, Venice, 92; co-ed, The Faber Book of america, Faber, 92; auth, America's rome, 2 vol, Yale, 89; Selected articles: The comic element in Hawthorne's sketches, Studies in Romanticism, 3/64; Implications of form in The Sun Also Rises, The Twenties: Poetry and Prose, 66; Romance in The Octopus, Genre, 70; Tragedy and the tragic power of laughter: The Scarlet Letter and The House of the Seven Gables, Nathaniel Hawthorne Jour, 71; Dreiserian tragedy, Studies Novel, spring 72; Man or beast: The meaning of Cooper's The Prairie, PMLA, 3/74; Whitman's lonely orbit: Salut au Monde, Walt Whitman Rev, 79; Redefining Bostonian, In: The Bostonians: Painters of an Elegant Age: 1860-1930, Boston, Mus Fine Arts, 86; Seeing Italy: The realistic rediscovery by Twain, Howells, and James, In: The Lure of Italy: American Artists and the Italian Experience: 1760-1914, Boston, Mus Fine Arts and Abrams, 92; Stereotipi, differenze, e verita nel romanzo e nel racconto Americano sull'Italia, In: Immaginari a confronto, Venise, Marsilio, 92; Edit Wharton's Italian Mask: The Valley of Decision, In: The Cambridge Companion to Edith Wharton, Cambridge, 95; Guarda che cosa hai fatto, Cristoforo!, In: La Virtu e la liberta, Torino, Agnelli, 95; What legacy and whose? Arion, Fall 95-Winter 96; What they're saying about Whitman, Raritan, spring 97. **CONTACT ADDRESS** Dept of English, Boston Univ, 236 Bay State Rd, Boston, MA, 02215-1403.

VANCIL, DAVID
DISCIPLINE COMMUNICATION STUDIES **EDUCATION** Wayne State Univ, BA, MA; Univ Ill, PhD. **CAREER** Prof. **RESEARCH** Classical rhetorical theory; argumentation and debate; persuasion. **SELECTED PUBLICATIONS** Auth, Rhetoric and Argumentation; The Evolution of Parliamentary Procedure in the Assembly of Ancient Athens, Parliamentary J, 96; Ethnic Conflict and the Limitations of Parliamentary Communication and Debate, Parliamentary J, 94; Managing Conflict with Parliamentary Procedure, Parliamentary J, 93; co-auth, The Myth of Viewer-Listener Disagreement in the First Kennedy-Nixon Debate, Central States Speech J, 89. **CONTACT ADDRESS** Speech Communication Dept, Colorado State Univ, Fort Collins, CO, 80523. **EMAIL** dvancil@vines.colostate.edu

VANDE BERG, LEAH R.
PERSONAL Born 00/00/1949, IA, m, 1985 **DISCIPLINE** COMMUNICATION STUDIES **EDUCATION** Univ Iowa, BA, 72, MA, 75, PhD, 81, **CAREER** Assoc Prof, Prof, 90 to 95-, Cal State Univ; Asst Prof, 85-90, S Meth Univ; Asst Prof, 81-85, NW Univ. **HONORS AND AWARDS** Phi Beta Kappa; B Aubrey Fisher Awd; **MEMBERSHIPS** NCA; WSCA; BEA; Org Res Women and Comm. **RESEARCH** Television, media, cultural values; Images of women and men in the media and arts. **SELECTED PUBLICATIONS** Coed, Critical approaches to Television, Boston, Houghton Mifflin, 98; auth, The Sports Hero Meets Mediated Celebrity, in, L A Wenner, ed, Mediasport, London Routledge, 98; auth, Liminality: Worf as Metonymic Signifier of Racial Cultural and National Differences, in: Enterprise Zones: Critical Positions on Star Trek, T Harrison ed, et al, Boulder CO, Westview Press, 96; Aaron Spelling Dramedy and Moonlighting, in: Encyc of Television, ed H Newcomb, Chicago IL, Fitzroy Dearborn, 97; Living Room Pilgrimages: Television's Cynical Commemoration of the Assassination Anniversary of John Forthcoming; Kennedy, Comm Mono. 95; On Making A Difference: Samuel L Becker's Media and Society Criticism, IA J Comm, 93. **CONTACT ADDRESS** Communication Studies Dept, California State Univ, Sacramento, Sacramento, CA, 95819-2605. **EMAIL** vandeberglr@csus.edu

VANDEN BOSSCHE, CHRIS R.
DISCIPLINE VICTORIAN LITERATURE, NONFICTION PROSE **EDUCATION** Univ Calif, Santa Cruz, PhD. **CAREER** Instr, Univ Notre Dame. **RESEARCH** The history of literature and authorship as a social institution in the 19th century. **SELECTED PUBLICATIONS** Auth, Carlyle and the Search for Authority. **CONTACT ADDRESS** Univ Notre Dame, Notre Dame, IN, 46556.

VANDER MAY, RANDALL J.
DISCIPLINE 18TH AND 19TH CENTURY BRITISH LITERATURE **EDUCATION** Univ Iowa, PhD, 87. **CAREER** Asst prof, Dordt Col, 83-87; adj asst prof, Iowa State Univ, 87-90; assoc prof, Westmont Col, 90-. **HONORS AND AWARDS** First prize in fiction, Evangel Press Assn Nat Wrtg Competition, 80, 82; second prize in fiction, 77; Hopwood Award in fiction, Univ Mich, 72., Contrib ed, consult, The Write Source, 87-. **SELECTED PUBLICATIONS** Auth, God Talk, InterVarsity Press, 93; Phrasing the Lord, New Man mag, 96; Talks With Hands, PostScrip, 93; A Strange Chorale, Reformed Jour, 82. **CONTACT ADDRESS** Dept of Eng, Westmont Col, 955 La Paz Rd, Santa Barbara, CA, 93108-1099.

VANDER PLOEG, SCOTT D.
DISCIPLINE ENGLISH LITERATURE **EDUCATION** Purdue Univ, BA, 79, MA, 82; Univ Ky, PhD, 84. **CAREER** ASSOC PROF HUM, MADISONVILLE COMMUNITY COL, UNIV KY, 88-. **CONTACT ADDRESS** Madisonville Comm Col, 2000 College Dr, Madisonville, KY, 42431. **EMAIL** svander@pop.uky.edu

VANDERSEE, CHARLES ANDREW
PERSONAL Born 03/25/1938, Gary, IN **DISCIPLINE** AMERICAN LITERATURE **EDUCATION** Valparaiso Univ, BA, 60; Univ Calif, Los Angeles, MA, 61, PhD(English), 64. **CAREER** Asst prof, 64-70, dean Echols Scholars Prog, 73-97; assoc prof English, Univ Va, 70-, Bruern fel, Univ Leeds, 68-69; Am Coun Learned Soc fel, 72-73; Nat Endowment Humanities Ed grant, 77-82. **HONORS AND AWARDS** Danforth grad fel, 60-64; Bruern fel, Univ Leeds, 68-69; Am Coun Learned Soc fel, 72-73; Nat Endowment Humanities res grat, 77-82; Phi Beta Kappa chapter award (with J.C. Levenson) for best fac scholar, Univ Va, 83; Coolidge Colloquium fel, 88. **MEMBERSHIPS** ASA; MLA; Soc Values Higher Educ. **RE-**

SEARCH American literature--19th century; Henry Adams; American identity. **SELECTED PUBLICATIONS** Auth, Contesting Meaning in the Late 19th Century, Word and Image Interactions II, 98; American Parapedagogy for 2000 and Beyond, Am Lit Hist, 94; The Great Literary Mystery of the Gilded Age, Am Lit Realism, 74; The Hamlet in Henry Adams, Shakespeare Surv, 71; ed, John Hay's The Breawinnners, Col & Univ, 73; auth, The great literary mystery of the gilded age, Am Lit Realism, 74; assoc ed, The Letter of Henry Adams, Harvard Univ, Vol I-III, 82. **CONTACT ADDRESS** Dept of English, Univ of Virginia, 219 Bryan Hall, Charlottesville, VA, 22903. **EMAIL** cav7w@virginia.edu

VANDERWERKEN, DAVID LEON
PERSONAL Born 10/29/1945, Canastota, NY, m, 1981, 3 children **DISCIPLINE** AMERICAN LITERATURE **EDUCATION** Colgate Univ, BA, 68; Rice Univ, MA, 73, PhD(English), 73. **CAREER** Assoc prof to prof English, Tex Christian Univ, 71-. **MEMBERSHIPS** MLA; SCent Mod Lang Asn; Col English Asn; Conf Col Teachers English; Popular Cult Asn. **RESEARCH** John Dos Passos; modern American fiction in general; sports-centered literature. **SELECTED PUBLICATIONS** Auth, Trout fishing in America and the American tradition, Critique, 74; Dos Passos' Streets of Night: A Reconsideration, Markham Rev, 10/74; English 4503: Sports in Modern American Literature, Col Lit, spring 76; Manhattan Transfer: Dos Passos' Babel story, Am Lit, 5/77; USA: Dos Passos and the Old Words, Twentieth Century Lit, 5/77; The Americanness of The Moviegoer, Notes Miss Writers, summer 79; From Tackle to Teacher: James Whitehead's Joiner, NDak Quart, autumn 79; Dos Passos' Civil Religion, Res Studies, 12/80; auth, Faulkner's Literary Children: Patterns of Development, Lang, 97. **CONTACT ADDRESS** Dept of English, Tex Christian Univ, Box 297270, Fort Worth, TX, 76129-0002. **EMAIL** Vanderwerken@tcu.edu

VANGELISTI, ANITA L.
DISCIPLINE COMMUNICATION **EDUCATION** Univ Wash, BA, 83; Univ Wash, MA, 85; Univ Tex, PhD, 89. **CAREER** Teaching asst, Univ Wash, 83-85; asst instr, Univ Tex, 85-89; distinguished lectr, San Diego State Univ, 91; asst prof, Univ Iowa, 89-91; asst prof, 91-96, assoc prof, 96-, Univ Tex. **HONORS AND AWARDS** Univ fel, Univ Tex Austin, 88-89; Outstanding grad scholar award, Univ Tex at Austin, 88, 89; scholarly publ award, Univ Tex Austin, 89; Phi Kappa Phi; Old Gold Summer fel, Univ Iowa, 90; Interdisciplinary res asst grant, Univ Iowa, 90; Univ Res Inst summer res award, Univ Tex, 92; James W. Vick Tex excellence award for acad adv, 94; Univ Res Inst summer res award, Univ Tex, 94; New Contrib Award, Intl Soc for the Study of Personal Relationships, 94; Col of Comm teaching excellence award, 95; Eyes of Tex excellence award, 96. **MEMBERSHIPS** Nat Comm Asn; Intl Comm Asn; Nat Coun of Family Relations; Amer Psychol Asn; Intl Soc for the Study of Personal Relationships; Intl Network on Personal Relationships; Western Speech Comm Asn. **RESEARCH** Interpersonal communication; Communication in personal relationships; Communication and emotion; Gender differences in communication. **SELECTED PUBLICATIONS** Co-ed, Teaching communication: A handbook of theory, research and methods, 2nd ed, Lawrence Erlbaum, 98; co-auth, Interpersonal communication and human relationships, 3rd ed, Allyn & Bacon, 96; co-ed, Explaining family interactions, Thousand Oaks, Calif, Sage, 95; article, Evaluating the process, Teaching communication: A handgook of theory, research and methods, 2nd ed, 409-423, Lawrence Erlbaum, 98; article, co-auth, Reactions to messages that hurt: The influence of relational contexts, Comm Monogr, 65, 173-196, 98; co-auth, Guilt and hurt: Similarities, distinctions, and conversational strategies, Handbook of communication and emotion, 123-154, Academic, 98; article, Gender differences, similarities, and interdependencies: Some problems with the different cultures perspective, Personal Relationships, 4, 243-253, 97; co-auth, Gender differences in standards for romantic relationships, Personal Relationships, 4, 203-219, 97; co-auth, Revealing family secrets: The influence of topic, function, and relationships, Jour of Soc and Personal Relationships, 14, 679-705, 97; co-auth, Expressed attributions for academic success and failure by adolescents and young adults, Western Jour of Comm, 60, 124-145, 96; co-auth, Perceptions of siblings of children with hearing impairment, Tejas, 20, 19-21, 95; co-auth, Speaking in a double-voice: Role-making as influence in preschoolers' fantasy play situations, Res on Lang and Soc Interaction, 28, 351-389; co-auth, How parenthood affects marriage, Explaining family interactions, 147-176, Thousand Oaks, Calif, Sage, 95. **CONTACT ADDRESS** College of Communication, Univ of Texas at Austin, Austin, TX, 78712. **EMAIL** a.vangelisti@mail.utexas.edu

VANN, JERRY DON
PERSONAL Born 01/17/1938, Weatherford, TX, m, 1958, 2 children **DISCIPLINE** ENGLISH **EDUCATION** Tex Christian Univ, BA, 59, MA, 60; Tex Technol Col, PhD(English), 67. **CAREER** From instr to asst prof, 64-71, assoc prof, 71-78, PROF ENGLISH, N TEX STATE UNIV, 78-, Bibliogr, Studies in Novel, 68-; contribr ed, MHRA Annual Bibliog, 68-; bibliogr, Res Soc Victorian Periodicals, 69-; Am Philos Soc fel, 77. **RESEARCH** Serialization of Dickens' novels; Victorian poetry; the English novel. **SELECTED PUBLICATIONS** Auth, Eliot, George Serial Fiction, Nineteenth-Century Lit, Vol 0050, 95; Dickens Journalism, Vol 1, Sketches by Boz and Other Early Papers, 1833-1839, Albion, Vol 0027, 95. **CONTACT ADDRESS** 811 W Oak, Denton, TX, 76201.

VANNATTA, DENNIS
DISCIPLINE CONTEMPORARY LITERATURE **EDUCATION** Univ Miss, PhD. **CAREER** English and Lit, Univ Ark **SELECTED PUBLICATIONS** Auth, E.H. Bates; The English Short Story, 1945-1980; Tennessee Williams; This Time, This Place; Prayers for the Dead. **CONTACT ADDRESS** Univ Ark Little Rock, 2801 S University Ave., Little Rock, AR, 72204-1099. **EMAIL** dpvannatta@ualr.edu

VARADHARAJAN, ASHA
DISCIPLINE ENGLISH LITERATURE **EDUCATION** Univ Saskatchewan, PhD. **CAREER** Dept Eng, Queen's Univ **RESEARCH** Post-colonial and minority literatures; literary theory; cultural studies; race and gender theory; the Frankfurt School; theories of pedagogy and the politics of the institution. **SELECTED PUBLICATIONS** Auth, Exotic Parodies: Subjectivity in Adorno, Said, Spivak, Univ Minn, 95; Theory and Critical Practice, Univ Toronto, 94; Dissensus, Dissolution, and the Possibility of Community, Univ Toronto Quarterly, 97. **CONTACT ADDRESS** English Dept, Queen's Univ, Kingston, ON, K7L 3N6.

VARONA, FEDERICO
PERSONAL Born 01/06/1946, Spain, m, 1984, 2 children **DISCIPLINE** COMMUNICATIONS STUDIES **EDUCATION** Univ Kansas, PhD, 91. **CAREER** Chemn and prof, Univ Sandriar, Guatemala, 81-86; assoc prof, San Jose State Univ, 91- . **HONORS AND AWARDS** Vis grant, USIA, 84; Fulbright Scholar, 86-90. **MEMBERSHIPS** Natl Commun Asn; Int Commun Asn; ADELIN (Spain); Western States Commun Asn. **RESEARCH** Organizational communications; intracultural communications. **SELECTED PUBLICATIONS** Auth, Pedagogia y Educacion de la Fe, Bogota, Indo-American Press, 79; auth, Communication and Organizational Commitment, Commun Int Informes, 95; auth, The Impact of New Communication Technologies on Organizational Culture and Communication, Commun Int Informes, 95; auth, Relationship between Communication Satisfaction and Organizational Commitment in Three Guatemalan Organizations, J of Bus Commun, 96. **CONTACT ADDRESS** 2774 White Acres Dr, San Jose, CA, 95148. **EMAIL** fvarona@email.sjsu.edu

VARTABEDIAN, ROBERT A.
PERSONAL Born 08/27/1952, Fresno, CA, m, 1978, 2 children **DISCIPLINE** SPEECH COMMUNICATION **EDUCATION** CA State Univ, Fresno, BA (speech commun, magna cum laude), 74, CA Teaching Credential, 75; Wichita State Univ, MA (speech commun), 80; Univ OK, PhD (Commun), 81. **CAREER** Graduate asst, part-time instr, CA State Univ, Fresno, 74-75, 77; res asst, Wichita State Univ, 77-78; grad asst, Univ OK, 78-80; asst prof, East Central OK State Univ, 80-81; Dir of forensics, 81-86, head, div of rhetoric and commun, 85-88, coord, grad studies in commun, 86-87, asst dean of graduate studies, Wichita State Univ, 87-88; head, dept of Art, Commun, & Theatre, 88-93, assoc prof, 88-92, prof, West TX A&M Univ, 92-. **HONORS AND AWARDS** Outstanding Teaching award, Univ OK, 80; Outstanding Dir of Forensics Award, Univ UT, 83; President's Award, Nat Intercollegiate Cross Examination Debate Asn, 86; Mortar Board Teaching Award, Wichita State Univ, 88; Dean's nominee for Outstanding Graduate Fac Award, WTAMU, 91, 93; Carnegie Found Prof of the Year, WTAMU, 94; Greek Council, Outstanding Fac Member Award, WTAMU, 96; Univ Teaching Excellence Award, WTAMU, 96; Univ Piper Professorship, WTAMU, 97. **MEMBERSHIPS** Am Forensic Asn; Central States Commun Asn; Cross Examination Debate Asn; Int Commun Asn; TX Speech Commun Asn; Nat Forensic Asn; Nat Commun Asn; West TX Speech Commun Asn. **RESEARCH** Presidential rhetoric; political communication; rhetorical criticism. **SELECTED PUBLICATIONS** Co-auth, with L K Vartabedian, Humor in the Workplace: A Communication Challenge, in Resources in Ed, 93; auth, Recruitment and Retention of Graduate Faculty at the Non-Doctoral Graduate Program, in Resources in Ed, 93; with J M Burger, Self-Disclosure and Decreased Persuasiveness of Political Speakers, in Resources in Ed, 94; auth, the Loud, Clear, and Transporting Voice of Oral Interpretation, in Resources in Ed, 95; with J M Burger, Self-Disclosure and Decreased Persuasiveness of Political Speakers, Speech Commun Annual, 10, 96; auth, Scholarly vs Non-Scholarly Print Sources, in L W Hugenberg and B S Moyer, eds, Teaching Ideas for the Basic Communication Course, in press; Audience Analysis, in L W Hugenberg and B S Moyer, eds, Teaching Ideas for the Basic Communication Course, in press; with R A Knight, Jones v. Clinton and the Apologetic Imperative, Speaker and Gavel, in press; numerous other publications. **CONTACT ADDRESS** 95 Jynteewood Dr, Canyon, TX, 79015. **EMAIL** robert.vartabedian@wtamu.edu

VASTA, EDWARD
DISCIPLINE MEDIEVAL LITERATURE **EDUCATION** Stanford Univ, PhD. **CAREER** Instr, Univ Notre Dame. **RESEARCH** Bakhtinian approaches to medieval literature. **SELECTED PUBLICATIONS** Auth, The Spiritual Basis of Piers Plowman; ed, Interpretations of Piers Plowman and Chaucerian Problems and Perspectives. **CONTACT ADDRESS** Univ Notre Dame, Notre Dame, IN, 46556.

VATZ, RICHARD E.
PERSONAL Born 12/21/1946, Pittsburgh, PA, m, 1977, 2 children **DISCIPLINE** RHETORIC & COMMUNICATION **EDUCATION** Univ Pittsburgh, BA, 69, MA, 70, PhD, 76. **CAREER** Inst, Pa State, 69-73; inst, NC State Univ, 73-74; Asst prof, Towson Univ, 74-81; assoc prof, 81-89; present prof, 89-. **HONORS AND AWARDS** Thomas Szaz Award for Contributions to the Cause of Civil Liberties; 4 Outstanding Univ Teaching Awards; 4 Univ Merit Awards., Honors Col Fac. **MEMBERSHIPS** Nat Commun Assoc; Eastern Commun Assoc. **RESEARCH** Political rhetoric; rhetoric and psych; media criticism. **SELECTED PUBLICATIONS** Co-ed, Thomas Szaz: Primary Values and Major Contentions, Prometheus Press, 83; co-auth, TV on the Couch, Forbes Media Critic, 94; co-auth, The Rhetorical Paradigm in Psychiatric History: Thomas Szaz and the Myth of Mental Illness, Discovering the History of Psychiatry, Oxford Univ Press, 94; auth, Should we Destigmatize Mental Ilness?, USA Today Mag, 5/96; co-auth, Critiques of Szaszian Criticism of Psychiatry, Review of Existential Psychology and Psychiatry, 97-98; co-auth, Rhetorical Issues in Drug Legalization, How to Legalize Drugs, (in press). **CONTACT ADDRESS** Mass Commun/Commun Studs, Towson Univ, Van Bokkelen Hall, Towson, MD, 21252. **EMAIL** rvatz@towson.edu

VAUSE, DEBORAH
DISCIPLINE LITERATURE **EDUCATION** NC State Univ, BA; Univ NC, PhD. **SELECTED PUBLICATIONS** Area: the medieval monster; writer Stephen King. **CONTACT ADDRESS** York Col, Pennsylvania, 441 Country Club Road, York, PA, 17403.

VAUSE, L. MIKEL
PERSONAL m, 4 children **DISCIPLINE** ENGLISH **EDUCATION** Bowling Green Univ, PhD. **CAREER** Vis scholar, University of Leeds, 96; Prof, Weber State Univ. **HONORS AND AWARDS** Crystal Crest Master Award; The George & Beth Lowe Teaching Award; The Continuing Ed Prof of the Yr Award; Honors Cortez Prof Award., Dir, Weber State Univ Honors Prog. **MEMBERSHIPS** Weber Pathways; The Great West Trail Asn; Nat Undergrad Lit Conf (co-dir & founder); N Am Interdisciplinary Wilderness Conf, (co-dir & founder); Nat Advisory Bd for ASLE; MESA Advisory Bd. **SELECTED PUBLICATIONS** Auth, On Mountains and Mountaineers, Mountain n' Airs Books, 90; auth, Wilderness Tapestry, Univ of Nev Press, 92; auth, The Peregrine Reader, Gibbs M Smith, 97. **CONTACT ADDRESS** Dept of English, Weber State Univ, 2904 Univ Cir, Odgen, UT, 84408-2904.

VEANER, ALLEN B.
PERSONAL Born 03/17/1929, Harrisburg, PA, m, 1983, 2 children **DISCIPLINE** LIBRARY/INFORMATION SCIENCE **EDUCATION** Gettysburg Col, BA, 49; Hebrew Un Col, BHL, 52; Simmons Col, MLS, 60; Hebrew Un Col, MA, 69; Harvard Univ, 57 **CAREER** Chaplain, 54-58, US Army; Cataloger, 57-59, Widener Lib, Harvard Univ; Spec, 59-64, Harvard; Asst Head of Acquisit, 64-67, Stanford; Asst Dir, 67-77, Stanford; Libr, 77-83, Univ of CA, Santa Barbara; Principal, 83-91, Allen B. Veaner Assoc; Adj Asst Prof, 95-, Univ of AZ **HONORS AND AWARDS** Phi Beta kappa **MEMBERSHIPS** Am Lib Asn; Am Soc of Indexers **RESEARCH** Indexing **SELECTED PUBLICATIONS** Auth, Academic Librarianship in a Transformational Age: Program, Politics, and Personnel, Boston: G.K. Hall, 90 **CONTACT ADDRESS** PO Box 30786, Tucson, AZ, 85751-0786. **EMAIL** veaner@worldnet.att.net

VELEN, RICHARD
DISCIPLINE AMERICAN LITERATURE **EDUCATION** Wittenberg Univ, AB; Harvard Univ, MA; Ohio State Univ, PhD. **HONORS AND AWARDS** Woodrow Wilson fel, Harvard; Distinguished Tchng Award; Co Chairperson, Engl dept; Pres, Col Eng Asn Ohio, Vis Prof, England. **RESEARCH** Mark Twain, Edgar Allen Poe, **SELECTED PUBLICATIONS** Area:Poe **CONTACT ADDRESS** Wittenberg Univ, Springfield, OH, 45501-0720.

VELIE, ALAN R.
PERSONAL Born 11/16/1937, New York, NY, m, 1962, 2 children **DISCIPLINE** ENGLISH **EDUCATION** Harvard Univ, BA, 59; Stanford Univ, MA, 66, PhD, 69. **CAREER** From instr to prof, 67-94, David Ross Boyd Prof English, Okla Univ, 94-, chmn dept, 78-82. **HONORS AND AWARDS** NEH fel, 73; Amoco Award for Outstanding Teaching, 72; Baldwin Award for Excellence in Classroom Instruction, 86; Mortarboard Honor Soc Outstanding Fac Mem, 88-89; Summer Fac Instructional Award, 90. **MEMBERSHIPS** MLA; Am Folklore Soc. **RESEARCH** American Indian literature; Shakespeare; folklore. **SELECTED PUBLICATIONS** Co-ed, Blood and Knavery, Fairleigh Dickinson Univ Press, 73; auth, Shakespeare's Repentence Plays, The Search for an Adequate Form, Fairleigh Dickinson Univ Press, 73; co-ed, Appleseeds and

Beercans, Goodyear, 74; auth, Shakespeare's use of folklore in The Merchant of Venice, Fabula, 76; Aztekisches Erzahlgut, in Enzyklopadie des Marchens, 76; The Dragon Killer, The Wild Man, and Hal, Fabula, 77; ed, American Indian Literature, Okla Univ Press, 79, rev ed, 91; Four American Indian Literary Masters, Okla Univ, 82; co-transl, Structural Semantics, Univ Nebr Press, 83; auth, The Lightning Within, Univ Nebr Press, 91; Native American Perspectives on Literature and History, Univ Okla Press, 95; author of numerous journal articles and book chapters. **CONTACT ADDRESS** Dept of English, Univ of Okla, 760 Van Vleet Oval, Norman, OK, 73019-2020. **EMAIL** alanvelie@ou.edu

VERDERBER, RUDOLPH FRANCIS
PERSONAL Born 08/07/1933, Cleveland, OH, m, 1973, 3 children **DISCIPLINE** SPEECH **EDUCATION** Bowling Green State Univ, BS, 55, MA, 56; Univ MO, Columbia, PhD, 62. **CAREER** From instr to assoc prof, 59-71, Prof Speech, Univ Cincinnati, 71. **MEMBERSHIPS** Nat Commun Asn; Cent States Speech Asn. **RESEARCH** Rhetoric and public address; argumentation and debate; interpersonal commun. **SELECTED PUBLICATIONS** Auth, An Invitation to Debate, Krieg, 71; The Challenge of Effective Speaking, 70, 73, 76, 79, 82, 85, 88, 91, 94, 97; Communicate!, 75, 78, 81, 84, 87, 90, 93, 96, 99; Inter-Act, 77, 80, 83, 86, 89, 92, 95, 98, Wadsworth. **CONTACT ADDRESS** Dept of Commun, Univ of Cincinnati, PO Box 210184, Cincinnati, OH, 45221-0184. **EMAIL** rudolph.verderber@uc.edu

VERSLUIS, ARTHUR
DISCIPLINE LITERATURE **EDUCATION** Univ Mich, PhD, 90. **CAREER** Prof, Washburn Univ, 90-94; Fulbright scholar, Univ Duesseldorf, 94-95; prof, Mich State Univ, 95-. **HONORS AND AWARDS** Hopwood Award Lit. **MEMBERSHIPS** Am Acad Relig. **RESEARCH** American literature; American transcendentalism and Asian religions; Western esoteric traditions. **SELECTED PUBLICATIONS** Auth, Wisdom's Children: A Christian Esoteric Tradition, 99; auth, The Hermetic Book of Nature: An American Revolution in Consciousness, 97; auth, Gnosis and Literature, 96; auth, Theosophia: Hidden Dimensions of Christianity, 94; auth, Native American Traditions, 94; auth, American Transcendentalism and Asian Religions, 93. **CONTACT ADDRESS** Dept of Literature, Michigan State Univ, ATL Dept 235 Bessey Hall, East Lansing, MI, 48824. **EMAIL** versluis@pilot.msu.edu

VEST, DAVID
DISCIPLINE COMMUNICATION STUDIES **EDUCATION** Monteith Col, PhB, Wayne State Univ, MSA; Central Mich Univ, PhD. **CAREER** Prof. **RESEARCH** Film theory and criticism; video production; quantitative methods. **SELECTED PUBLICATIONS** Auth, Prime-Time Pilots: A Content Analysis of Changes in Gender Representation, J Broadcasting Electronic Media, 94; co-auth, Electrical Engineers; Perceptions of Communication Training and Their Recommendations for Curricular Change: Results of a National Survey, 96; Enhancing Engineering Students' Communication Skills through Multimedia Instruction, J Engineering Edu, 95; Developing Online Writing Aids for Electrical Engineering Majors-a Progress Report, 95; Relating Communication Training to Workplace Requirements: The Perspective of New Engineers, 95. **CONTACT ADDRESS** Speech Communication Dept, Colorado State Univ, Fort Collins, CO, 80523. **EMAIL** dvest@vines.colostate.edu

VESTERMAN, WILLIAM
PERSONAL Born 02/08/1942, East Orange, NJ, m, 1964, 3 children **DISCIPLINE** ENGLISH **EDUCATION** Amherst Col, BA, 64; Rutgers Univ, PhD(English), 71. **CAREER** From instr to asst prof, 69-75, ASSOC PROF ENGLISH, LIVINGSTON COL, RUTGERS UNIV, 75-, Consult writing, Bell Lab, 75- **MEMBERSHIPS** Am Soc 18th Century Studies; Asn Teachers Tech Writing. **RESEARCH** Modernism; Vladimir Nabokov; eighteenth century. **SELECTED PUBLICATIONS** Auth, Mastering the Free Spirit, Status and Contract in Some Fictional Polities, Eighteenth-Century Life, Vol 0016, 92. **CONTACT ADDRESS** Rutgers Univ, New Brunswick, NJ, 08903.

VIATOR, TIMOTHY
DISCIPLINE LATE RENAISSANCE BRITISH LITERATURE, CONTEMPORARY DRAMA **EDUCATION** Univ La, Lafayette, MA, BA; Auburn Univ, PhD. **CAREER** Instr, Rowan Col of NJ. **RESEARCH** Plays of Colley Cibber. **SELECTED PUBLICATIONS** Articles in drama, theater history, comedy, and bibliography. **CONTACT ADDRESS** Rowan Col of NJ, Glassboro, NJ, 08028-1701. **EMAIL** viator@jupiter.rowan.edu

VICKERY, JOHN B.
PERSONAL Born 08/20/1925, Toronto, ON, Canada, m, 1950, 1 child **DISCIPLINE** ENGLISH **EDUCATION** Univ Toronto, BA, 47; Colgate Univ, MA, 49; Univ Wis, PhD, 55. **CAREER** Instr English, Univ Tenn, 54-56 and Northwestern Univ, 56-59; from asst prof to assoc prof, Purdue Univ, 59-65; vis prof, Calif State Col, Los Angeles, 65-66; assoc prof, 66-72, PROF ENGLISH, UNIV CALIF, RIVERSIDE, 72-. **MEMBERSHIPS** MLA **RESEARCH** Modern literature. **SELECTED PUBLICATIONS** Auth, The Functions of Myth in Barth, John Chimera, Mod Fiction Stud, Vol 0038, 92; Ekphrasis, the Illusion of the Natural Sign, Mod Fiction Stud, Vol 0039, 93. **CONTACT ADDRESS** Dept of English, Univ of Calif, Riverside, CA, 92502.

VIERECK, PETER
PERSONAL Born 08/05/1916, New York, NY, m, 1972, 2 children **DISCIPLINE** POETRY, HISTORY **EDUCATION** Harvard Univ, BS, 37, AM, 39, PhD, 42. **CAREER** Instr hist and lit, Harvard Univ, 46-47; asst prof hist, Smith Col, 47-48; assoc prof, 48-49, assoc prof Europ and Russ hist, 49-55, alumni found prof Europ and Russ hist, 55-80, WILLIAM R KENAN JR PROF HIST, MT HOLYOKE COL, 80-; Vis lectr, Smith Col, 48-49; Guggenheim fels, 49 and 55; vis lectr, Poet's Conf, Harvard Univ, 53 and Univ Calif, Berkeley, 57 and 64; Whittal lectr poetry, Libr Cong, 54 and 63; Fulbright prof Am poetry, Univ Florence, 55; Elliston poetry lectr, Univ Cincinnati, 56; US Dept State cult exchange poet, USSR, 61; Twentieth Century Fund travel and poetry res grant, Russia, 62; lectr poetry, City Col New York and New Sch Social Res, 64; dir poetry workshop, NY Writer's Conf, 65-67. **HONORS AND AWARDS** Garrison Prize for Poetry, Phi Beta Kappa, 36; Harvard Bowdoin Medal for Prose, 39; Tietjens Prize for Poetry, 48; Pulitzer Prize for Poetry, 49., DHL, Olivet Col, 59. **MEMBERSHIPS** AHA **RESEARCH** Modern European and Russian history; Anglo-American poetry; modern Russian culture. **SELECTED PUBLICATIONS** Auth, Anti Form or Neo and Essay in a Curse on Both Houses, Parnassus Poetry Rev, Vol 18, 93; Dumped, Parnassus Poetry Rev, Vol 18, 93; Anyhow, Parnassus Poetry Rev, Vol 18, 93; Sinew, Parnassus Poetry Rev, Vol 18, 93; Where Find Us, Parnassus Poetry Rev, Vol 18, 93; Metrics, Not Hour Hand, Parnassus Poetry In Rev, Vol 18, 93; My Seventy-Seventh Birthday, Parnassus Poetry Rev, Vol 18, 93; Slack A While, Parnassus Poetry Rev, Vol 18, 93; ... and Sometimes Not, Parnassus Poetry Rev, Vol 18, 93; Invocation, Parnassus Poetry Rev, Vol 18, 93; Threnody Reversals, Parnassus Poetry Rev, Vol 18, 93; Moon Ode, Parnassus Poetry Rev, Vol 18, 93; Second Moon Ode, Parnassus Poetry Rev, Vol 18, 93; Topsy Turvy, Parnassus Poetry Rev, Vol 18, 93; Why I Sometimes Believe in God, Parnassus Poetry Rev, Vol 18, 93. **CONTACT ADDRESS** Dept of Hist, Mount Holyoke Col, South Hadley, MA, 01075.

VILLANUEVA, VICTOR
PERSONAL Born 12/19/1948, Brooklyn, Ny, m, 1971, 5 children **DISCIPLINE** ENGLISH **EDUCATION** Univ Wash, BA, 79, MA, 82, PhD, 86. **CAREER** Instr, 80, Big Bend Com Col; pre-dr assoc, 81-83, dir, ed opportunity prog, Engl, 84-85; Univ Wash; asst prof, 85-87, dir, greater Kansas City writing proj, 87, Univ Missouri; asst prof, 87-92, assoc prof, 92-95, N Arizona Univ; dir, composition, 95-, assoc prof, 95-, Wash St Univ. **RESEARCH** Literay **CONTACT ADDRESS** Dept of English, Washington State Univ, Pullman, WA, 99164-5020. **EMAIL** villav@mail.wsu.edu

VINCE, RONALD WINSTON
PERSONAL Simcoe, ON, Canada, m, 1967 **DISCIPLINE** ENGLISH LITERATURE, DRAMA **EDUCATION** McMaster Univ, BA, 60; Rice Univ, MA, 62; Northwestern Univ, PhD (English), 68. **CAREER** From lectr to asst prof, English, 66-72, asst dean humanities studies, 71-74, chmn dramatic arts, 73-74 and 75-76, ASSOC PROF ENGLISH, McMASTER UNIV, 72-. **MEMBERSHIPS** Can Asn Univ Teachers; Soc Theatre Res; Am Soc Theatre Res. **RESEARCH** Theatre history; comparative drama; critical theory. **SELECTED PUBLICATIONS** Auth, Staging the Renaissance, Reinterpretations of Elizabethan and Jacobean Drama, Theatre Surv, Vol 34, 93. **CONTACT ADDRESS** Dept of English, McMaster Univ, 1280 Main St W, Hamilton, ON, L8S 4L9.

VINCENT, THOMAS BREWER
PERSONAL Born 01/27/1943, Fredericton, NB, Canada, m, 1966, 2 children **DISCIPLINE** CANADIAN AND AMERICAN LITERATURE **EDUCATION** Dalhousie Univ, BA, 65; Queen's Univ, MA, 67, PhD (English), 72. **CAREER** ASSOC PROF ENGLISH, ROYAL MILITARY COL CAN, 69-; Ed and publ, Loyal Colonies Press, 78-. **MEMBERSHIPS** MLA; Asn Can Univ Teachers English; Asn Can and Que Lit; Humanities Asn Can; Am Soc 18th Century Studies. **RESEARCH** Colonial Canadian poetry; colonial American Poetry. **SELECTED PUBLICATIONS** Auth, the Mephisbosheth Stepsure Letters, Davies,G, Can Hist Rev, Vol 73, 92 **CONTACT ADDRESS** Dept of English, Royal Military Col, Kingston, ON, K7L 2W3.

VISER, VICTOR J.
DISCIPLINE COMMUNICATIONS **EDUCATION** Temple Univ, PhD. **MEMBERSHIPS** Int Comm Asn; Speech Comm Asn. **SELECTED PUBLICATIONS** Area: communication research. **CONTACT ADDRESS** York Col, Pennsylvania, 441 Country Club Road, York, PA, 17403.

VISOR, JULIA N.
PERSONAL New Albany, Mississippi **DISCIPLINE** ENGLISH **EDUCATION** Illinois State University, Normal, IL, BS, 1971; Ohio University, Athens, OH, MA, 1975; Illinois State University, Normal, IL, DA, 1987. **CAREER** Cornell University, Ithaca, NY, residential area coordinator, 1973-76; Illinois State University, Normal, IL, assistant director of residential life, 1976-79, instructor of English, 1979-80, 1981-86, director, student support svcs, 1980-81, assistant director, Univ Ctr for Learning Assistance, 1986-90, assistant prof of English, 1988-; Univ Ctr for Learning Assistance, associate director, 1990-97, coordinator, 1997-. **HONORS AND AWARDS** MAEOPP Distinguished Service Award, MAEOPP, 1982; Outstanding Svc Award, ISU Alumni Board of Directors, 1982; President's Award, ILAEOPP, 1984; Ada Belle Clark Welsh Scholarship, ISU, 1985; Outstanding Svc Award as co-editor, MAEOPP, 1989; David A Strand Diversity Achievement Award, Illinois State University, 1995-96. **MEMBERSHIPS** President, Mid-America Assn of Educational Opportunity Program Personnel (MAEOPP), 1991-92; Mid-America Assn of Educational Opportunity Program Personnel, 1980-; Illinois Assn for Learning Assistance Professionals, 1986-; National Council of Teachers of English, 1979-; Illinois Assn of Educational Opportunity Program Personnel (ILAEOPP), 1980-; Natl Assn for Developmental Education, 1990-; Illinois Assn of Teachers of English: Modern Language Assn, 1997-. **CONTACT ADDRESS** Coordinator, Univ Ctr for Learning Assistance, 4070 Illinois State University, Normal, IL, 61761-4070.

VISWANATHAN, GAURI
DISCIPLINE ENGLISH LITERATURE **EDUCATION** Univ Delhi, BA, 71, MA, 73; Columbia Univ, PhD, 85. **CAREER** Prof. **HONORS AND AWARDS** Grants, fel Guggenheim; NEH; Mellon; Amer Inst Indian Stud., Ed bd, Interventions; Jouvert; S Asia Res; sr fel, Intl Inst, Amsterdam, 98; lect, Hum Res Ctr, Australian Nat Univ. **RESEARCH** Indian literature. **SELECTED PUBLICATIONS** Auth, Outside the Fold: Conversion, Modernity, and Belief, Princeton UP, 98; Masks of Conquest: Literary Study and British Rule in India, Columbia UP: Faber, 89; Oxford UP, 98; auth, articles in Oxford Lit Rev; Yale Jour of Criticism; Comp Stud Soc and Hist; Stanford Hum Rev; Mod Lang Quart. **CONTACT ADDRESS** Dept of Eng, Columbia Col, New York, 2960 Broadway, New York, NY, 10027-6902.

VITTO, CINDY
DISCIPLINE BRITISH LITERATURE TO ROMANTICISM, AMERICAN ENGLISH GRAMMAR, CHAUCER **EDUCATION** Susquehanna Univ, BA; Duke Univ, MA; Rice Univ, PhD. **CAREER** Instr, Rowan Col of NJ. **RESEARCH** Medieval literature. **SELECTED PUBLICATIONS** Auth, The Virtuous Pagan in Middle English Literature; coed, The Rusted Hauberk: Feudal Ideals of Order and Their Declines. **CONTACT ADDRESS** Rowan Col of NJ, Glassboro, NJ, 08028-1701.

VOGEL, DAN
PERSONAL Born 02/12/1927, Brooklyn, NY, m, 1950, 3 children **DISCIPLINE** ENGLISH **EDUCATION** Brooklyn Col, BA, 48; Rutgers Univ, MA, 49; NY Univ, PhD (Am lit), 56. **CAREER** From instr to asst prof English, Yeshiva Univ, 49-62, prof, 62-76, asst registr, 51-55, actg resistr, Stern Col Women, 55-58, dean, 58-67; PROF ENGLISH, JERUSALEM COL WOMEN, 76-. **MEMBERSHIPS** MLA **RESEARCH** Herman Melville; Ralph Waldo Emerson; Nathanial Hawthorne. **SELECTED PUBLICATIONS** Auth, the Perversity of Peretz, Yitzhok, Lieb Vi Azoy Di Vald-Yeshive Is Botl Gevorn or How the Yeshiva in the Forest Ceased to Exist and Yiddish Literature, Yiddish, Vol 9, 94; Inside Hitler Greece in the Experience of Occupation 1941-1944, Militargeschichtliche Mitteilungen, Vol 53, 94; Battle by Job America, Midwest Quart J Contemp Thought, Vol 35, 94; A Source of Inspiration in 2 Poems by Lazarus, Emma Endowed Newport, Rhode Island Touro Synagogue and the Statue of Liberty with a Shared Theme and a Shared Symbolism, Am Hist, Vol 31, 96. **CONTACT ADDRESS** Dept of English, Jerusalem Col for Women, Jerusalem, ..

VOGEL, NANCY
PERSONAL Lawrence, KS **DISCIPLINE** ENGLISH **EDUCATION** Univ Kans, BA & BS, 63, MA, 65, PhD, 71. **CAREER** Asst prof, 71-74, assoc prof, 74-77, prof Engish, Ft Hays State Univ, 78-. **HONORS AND AWARDS** President's Distinguished Scholar Award, 95; Interdisciplinary Fell, Merringer, 88. **MEMBERSHIPS** NCTE; ALAN; Kansas Humanities Council, Board, 88-92; Natl Adv Board, Gales' Authors and Artists for Young Adults. **RESEARCH** The pastoral tradition; the initiation theme; the arts. **SELECTED PUBLICATIONS** Auth, Exitus, the videotape that went to Boston: A momentary stay against confusion, Kans English, 12/72; Set theory: A paradigm pertinent to English education, English Educ, Winter 73; Robert Frost, Teacher, Phi Delta Kappa, 74; A post mortem on the death of the hired man, In: Frost: Centennial Essays, Univ Miss, 74; Academic travel, In: Improving Instruction, Ft Hayes State Univ, 79; Poetry--Something Like a Star, ERIC; Felisa Rincon de Gautier: The Mayor of San Juan, Masterplots II: Juvenile and Young Adult Biography Series; Salem Press, 93;

Maureen Daly, Writers for Young Adults, Scribner's 97. **CONTACT ADDRESS** Dept of English, Fort Hays State Univ, 600 Park St, Hays, KS, 67601-4009. **EMAIL** ennv@fhsu.edu

VOGELER, MARTHA SALMON
PERSONAL New York, NY, m, 1962 **DISCIPLINE** ENGLISH LITERATURE, INTELLECTUAL HISTORY **EDUCATION** Jersey City State Col, BA, 46; Columbia Univ, MA, 52, PhD (English), 59. **CAREER** Lectr French Columbia Univ, 55-60; lectr, NY Univ, 56-59; instr, Vassar Col, 59-62; asst prof, Long Island Univ, 62-66; assoc prof, 69-73, PROF ENGLISH, CALIF STATE UNIV, FULLERTON, 73-; Am Coun Learned Soc grant, 67; Am Philos Soc grants, 67 and 70. **MEMBERSHIPS** MLA; AAUP; Tennyson Soc; Res Soc Victorian Periodicals; Pac Coast Conf British Studies. **RESEARCH** Victorian biography, aesthetics and religious thought. **SELECTED PUBLICATIONS** Auth, Gissing, George in Lost Stories from America, Eng Lit Transition, Vol 36, 93; Bridges, Robert in a Biography, Eng Lit Transition, Vol 36, 93; The Collected Letters of Gissing, George, Vol 4, 1889-1891,, Eng Lit Transition, Vol 37, 94; The Collected Letters of Gissing,George, Vol 5, 1892-1895, Eng Lit Transition, Vol 38, 95; The Collected Letters of Gissing, George, Vol 6, 1895-1897, Eng Lit Transition, Vol 38, 95; The Collected Letters of Gissing, George, Vol 7, 1897-1899, Eng Lit Transition, Vol 39, 96; Thomas,Edward in Selected Letters, Eng Lit Transition, Vol 40, 97; The Collected Letters of Gissing, George, Vol 8, 1900-1902, Eng Lit Transition, Vol 40, 97. **CONTACT ADDRESS** Dept of English, California State Univ, Fullerton, Fullerton, CA, 92831.

VOGELEY, NANCY JEANNE
PERSONAL Born 06/19/1937, San Pedro, CA **DISCIPLINE** LATIN AMERICAN AND SPANISH LITERATURE **EDUCATION** Pa State Univ, BA, 58, MA, 62; Univ Madrid, dipl Span, 60; Stanford Univ, PhD(Span), 80. **CAREER** Instr Span, Allegheny Col, 62-63, Ithaca Col, 63-64 & Col San Mateo, 65-66; instr, 66-70, asst prof, 70-81, Assoc Prof Span, 81-86, prof Span, Univ San Francisco, 86-. Instr Span, Univ San Francisco, Valencia, Spain, summer, 69. **MEMBERSHIPS** Am Asn Teachers Span & Port; MLA; Philol Asn Pac Coast; Am Soc 18th Century Studies; Latin Am Studies Asn. **RESEARCH** Jose Joaquin Fernandez de Lizardi and the period of Mexican Independence; Alfonso Sastre and contemporary Spanish theater. **SELECTED PUBLICATIONS** Auth, Jose Joaquin Fernandez Lizardi and the Inquisition, Dieciocho, fall 80; Alfonso Sastre on Alfonso Sastre (interview), Hispania, 9/81; Blacks in Peru: The poetry of Nicomedes Santa Cruz, Phylon 43, No 1, 82; The figure of the Black Payador in Martin Fierro, CLA Jour 26, 34-48, 9/82; Mexican Newspaper Culture on the Eve of Mexican Independence, Ideologies and Literature, 4 Second Cycle, 358-377, 9-10/82; The Concept of the People in El Periquillo Sarnieto, Hispania 70, 457-467, 9/87; Defining the Colonial Reader: El Periquillo Sarniento, PMLA 102, 784-800, 10/87, reprinted in Nineteenth-Century Literature Criticism, NCLC 30, Gale Res, 79-88, 91; Updating the Picaresque Tradition: Alfonso Sastre's Lumpen Marginacion U Herigonca, Ideologies and Literature 2 New Series, 25-42, 87, reprinted in Alfonso Sastre, Murcia: Universidad de Murcia, 65-80, 93; Questioning Authority: Lizardi's Noches tristes y dia alegre, Dispositio 15, 53-70, 90; Testamento de Napoleon Bonaparte-A Manuscript by Jose Joaquin Fernandez de Lizardi?, Dieciocho 13, 84-89, 90; Intertextuality and Nineteenth-Century Nationalism: Perucho: Nieto de Periquillo, Bul of Hispanic Stu 71, 485-497, 94; Colonial Discourse in a Post-Colonial Latin American Review 2, 189-212, 93; Formacion cultural despues de la independencia: Una revista mexicana de literatura, 1826, Estudios (Caracas) 5, 79-90, 95; El Amor Republicano: una novela del Mexico poscolonial, Revista Iberoamericana 61. 663-374, 95; Italian Opera in Early National Mexico, Modern Language Quarterly 57, 279-288, 96; Turks and Indians: Orientalist Discourse in Post-Colonial Mexico, Diacrtitcs, 25, 3-20, 95; China and the American Indies: A Sixteenth-Century History, Colonial Latin Am Rev 6, 165-184, 97; Eva Forest, Women Writers of Spain, Greenwood, 114-115, 86; Bernice Zamora, Chicano Writers First Series, Dictionary of Literary Biography, Gale Res, 289-294, 89; Jose Joaquin Fernandez de Lizardi, Latin American Writers, Vol 1, Scribners, 119-128, 89; The Discoure of Colonial Loyalty: Mexico, 1808m Nacropolitics of Nineteenth-Century Liturature: Nationalism, Exoticism, Imperialism, Univ of Penn, 37-55, 91, reprinted, Duke Univ, 95; Discurso colonial en un contexto post-colonial: Mesico, Siglo XIX, Critica y descolonizacion: El sujeto colonial en la cultura latinoamericana, Academia Nacional del al Historia, 607-624, 92; Heredia y el escribir de la historia, La imaginacion historica en el siglo XIX, UNR Editora, 39-56, 96; La figuracion de la mujer: Mexico en el momento de la Independencia, Mujer en la Colonia hispanoamericana, Biblioteca de America, instituto Internacional de Literatira Ieroamericana, 307-326, 96; Death and its Challenge to Decolonization: Jose Joaquin Fernandez de Lizardi's Last Will and Testament, Pos-Colonialismo e Identiadade, Edicoes Univ Fernando, 98. **CONTACT ADDRESS** Dept of Modern Lang, Univ of San Francisco, 2130 Fulton St, San Francisco, CA, 94117-1050. **EMAIL** vogeleyn@usfca.edu

VOIGT, JOHN F.
PERSONAL Born 06/26/1939, Boston, MA, m, 1990, 2 children **DISCIPLINE** LIBRARY SCIENCE; EDUCATION; ENGLISH **EDUCATION** State Col at Boston, AB, 68; Simmons Col, MLS, 72. **CAREER** Libr dir, Berklee Col, 70-. **MEMBERSHIPS** ALA; MLA. **RESEARCH** Jazz music bibliography; free jazz. **SELECTED PUBLICATIONS** Coed, The New Grove Dictionary of Jazz, 88; auth, art, Printed Jazz Music: A Selected Bibliography, 91; coed, Dictionary of American Biography, 94; coed, Dictionary of American Biography, Suppl 9, 94, Suppl 10, 95; auth, art, Jazz Music: A Selective Bibliography, 96. **CONTACT ADDRESS** Berklee Col of Music, 150 Massachusetts Ave, Boston, MA, 02115-2697. **EMAIL** jvoigt@berklee.edu

VOLOSHIN, BEVERLY R
PERSONAL New Haven, CT, 1 child **DISCIPLINE** AMERICAN AND ENGLISH LITERATURE **EDUCATION** Univ Calif, Los Angeles, BA, 71; Univ Calif, Berkeley, MA, 73, PhD (English), 79. **CAREER** Teaching asst, Univ Calif, Berkeley, 72-74 and teaching assoc, 75-76; instr, 77-79, ASST PROF ENGLISH, UNIV ROCHESTER, 79-. **MEMBERSHIPS** MLA; Am Studies Asn. **RESEARCH** The empiricist mode in american fiction; Melville; women novelists. **SELECTED PUBLICATIONS** Auth, Beulah, Legacy, Vol 11, 94; Macaria or Altars of Sacrifice, Legacy, Vol 11, 94. **CONTACT ADDRESS** Dept English, Univ Rochester, Rochester, NY, 14627.

VON DASSANOWSKY, ROBERT
PERSONAL New York, NY **DISCIPLINE** GERMANIC STUDIES; POLITICAL SCIENCE; FILM **EDUCATION** Am Acad of Dramatic Arts, 78; AFI Conservatory Prog, 81; Univ Calif, LA, BA, 85, MA, 88, PhD, 92. **CAREER** Vis Asst Prof German, UCLA, 92-93; Asst Prof of German & Fil Stud, Univ Colo, 93-; Head of German Prog, 93-; Dir, Film Studies, 97-. **HONORS AND AWARDS** Residency Award, Michael Karolyi Mem Fnd, France, 79; Julie Harris/BHTG Playwriting Award, 84; Accademico Honoris Causa, Italy, 89; LA Cultural Aff Off Grant, 90-92; Univ Colo CRCW Grant, 94, 95, 97; Univ Colo Pres Fund for the Hum Grant, 96; Outstanding Fac Award, Univ Colo, 98. **MEMBERSHIPS** Found pres, PEN Colo Chapt; Bd Member, PEN USA/W Ctr, LA; VP, Austrian Am Film Asn; VP, Int Alexander Lernet-Holenia Soc; Women's Issues Leadership Council; Proeuropa; MLA; Soc for Cinema Stud; Screen Actors Guild; AATG; Dramatists Guild; Authors League; Ed Bd Member for various publications. **RESEARCH** 19th/20th century Austrian & Germanic literature & culture; fin-de-siecle & interwar European artistic movements; fascism; Anglo/American, Central European, & Italian film; popular culture of the 1960s; feminist & women's literature & film; postmodernism. **SELECTED PUBLICATIONS** auth, The Southern Journey: Candy and The Magic Christian as Cinematic Picaresques, Stud in Popular Culture, XV:1, 93; auth, Finding the Words: Literary-Historical Revisionism in Christine Bruckner's Wenn du geredet hattest, Desdemona, Seminar: A J of Germanic Stud, 9/95; auth, Phantom Empires: The Novels of Alexander Lernet-Holenia and the Question of Postempirial Austrian Identity, Ariadne, 96; Verses of a Marriage: translation of Strophen einer Ehe by Hans Raimund, Event Horizon, 96; co-ed, Filmkunst, no 54, 97; Telegrams from the Metropole: Selected Poetry 1980-97, Univ Salzburg Press, 99; auth, Mars in Aries: translation of Mars im Widder by Alexander Lernet-Holenia, Sun & Moon, 99. **CONTACT ADDRESS** Dept of Lang & Cultures, Univ Colo, Colorado Springs, CO, 80933.

VON FLOTOW, LUISE
PERSONAL Born 12/18/1951, St. Thomas, ON, Canada **DISCIPLINE** LITERATURE **EDUCATION** Univ London, BA, 74; Univ Windsor, MA, 85; Univ Mich, PhD, 91. **CAREER** Tchr, Univ Windsor, Univ Mich, 82-91; Res & tchg, Univ Marburg, Univ Freiburg, 87, 91; ASST PROF TRANSLATION STUDIES, UNIV OTTAWA, 96-. **HONORS AND AWARDS** SSHRC doctoral fel, 86-89; post-doctoral fel, 94-96. **RESEARCH** Quebec literature; East German literature; translation. **SELECTED PUBLICATIONS** Auth, Gender & Translation: Translation in the "Era of Feminism", 97; anthologist & transl, Ink & Strawberries: Quebec Women's Writing, 88; anthologist & transl, Three by Three, 92; transl, The Sandwoman, 90; transl, The Man Who Painted Stalin, 91; transl, Deathly Delights, 91; transl, The Cracks, 92; transl, Das Fremde: Essays on Being Foreign, 95; transl, Maude, 97. **CONTACT ADDRESS** Sch Translation & Interpretation, Univ Ottawa, Ottawa, ON, K1N 6N5.

VON FRANK, ALBERT J.
DISCIPLINE ENGLISH **EDUCATION** Amherst, AB, 67; Univ Wisc, MA, 68; Univ Mo, PhD, 76. **CAREER** Prof English, American Studies, Wash State, Pullman. **RESEARCH** American studies, Ralph Waldo Emerson **SELECTED PUBLICATIONS** Fel Publ, Anthony Burns and the Revolution of 1854, Harvard Univ, 98; auth, The Sacred Game: Provincialism and Frontier Consciousness in American Literature, Cambridge Univ, 85; The Complete Sermons of Ralph Waldo Emerson, Univ Mo, 4 vols, 88-91; The Poetry Notebooks of Ralph Waldo Emerson, Univ Mo, 86; An Emerson Chronology, G.K. Hall/Macmillan, 95. **CONTACT ADDRESS** Dept of English, Washington State Univ, SW 900 Alcora Dr., Pullman, WA, 99164-5020. **EMAIL** vonfrank@mail.wsu.edu

VONALT, LARRY
PERSONAL Born 01/10/1937, Angola, IN, m, 1976, 1 child **DISCIPLINE** ENGLISH AND AMERICAN LITERATURE **EDUCATION** Univ Denver, BA, 59; Univ Fla, MA, 61, PhD (English), 68. **CAREER** Instr English, Murray State Col, 61-63; interim instr, Univ Fla, 63-68; asst prof, Wesleyan Univ, 68-74; asst prof, 75-78, ASSOC PROF ENGLISH, UNIV MO-ROLLA, 78-. **MEMBERSHIPS** MLA **RESEARCH** Contemporary literature and eighteenth century English literature. **SELECTED PUBLICATIONS** Auth, An Interview with Harington, Donald, Chicago Rev, Vol 38, 93. **CONTACT ADDRESS** Humanities Dept, Univ of Mo, Rolla, MO, 65401.

VOS, ALVIN
DISCIPLINE ENGLISH **EDUCATION** Calvin Col, BA, 65; Univ Chicago, MA, 66; PhD, 71. **CAREER** Asst prof, 70-77, assoc prof, 77-, dir undergrad prog, 83-98, fac, master, Hinman Col, 98-, Binghamton Univ (SUNY). **HONORS AND AWARDS** Chancellors award for excellence in teaching. **MEMBERSHIPS** MLA; Amer Acad Relig. **RESEARCH** English Renaissance. **SELECTED PUBLICATIONS** Trans and ed, Letters of Roger Ascham, New York and Berne, Peter Lang, 89; ed, Place and Displacement in the Renaissance, Binghamton, Medieval and Renaissance Texts and Studies, 95; auth, De copia and Classical Rhetoric, Class and Mod Lit, 7, pp 285-94, 87; Christopher Fry's Christian Dialectic in A Phoenix Too Frequent, Renaissance, 36, pp 230-42, 84; Good Matter and Good Utterance, The Character of English Ciceroianism, Studies in Eng Lit 1500-1900, 19, pp 3-18, 79; An Addition to the Biography of Janus Lascaris, Romance Notes, 19, pp 74-77, 78; Models and Methodologies in Renaissance Prose Stylistics, Studies in the Literary Imagination, 10, pp 1-15, 77; The Vita Longolii: Some Additional Considerations about Reginald Pole's Authorship, Renaissance Quart, 30, pp 324-333, 77; Form and Function in Roger Ascham's Prose, Philol Quart, 55, pp 305-322, 76; Humanistic Standards of Diction in the Inkhorn Controversy, Studies in Philol, 73, pp 376-396, 76. **CONTACT ADDRESS** English Dept., SUNY, Binghamton, Binghamton, NY, 13902. **EMAIL** avos@binghamton.edu

VOS, NELVIN LEROY
PERSONAL Born 07/11/1932, Edgerton, MN, m, 1958, 3 children **DISCIPLINE** ENGLISH, THEOLOGY **EDUCATION** Calvin Col, AB, 54; Univ Chicago, AM, 55 PhD(theol & lit), 64. **CAREER** Instr English, Univ Chicago, AM, Unity Christian High Sch, 55-57 & Calvin Col, 57-59; asst prof, Trinity Christian Col, 63-65; assoc prof, 65-70, prof Eng, 70- Head Dept 76-87, VP and Dean, 87-93, Muhlenberg Col. **MEMBERSHIPS** MLA; Conf Christianity & Lit (secy, 65-67, pres, 68-70); Phi Beta Kap; Soc for Arts, Religion, and Contemp Culture. **RESEARCH** Comic theory; contemporary drama; theology and culture. **SELECTED PUBLICATIONS** Auth, The drama of Comedy: Victim and Victor, 66 & For God's Sake Laugh, 67, John Knox; Versions of the Absurd Theater: Ionesco and Albee, Eerdmans, 68; The process of dying in the plays of Edward Albee, Educ Theatre J, 3/73; Monday's Ministries, Fortress, 79; The Great Pendulum of Becoming: Images in Modern drama, Eerdmans, 80. **CONTACT ADDRESS** Dept of English, Muhlenberg Col, 2400 W Chew St, Allentown, PA, 18104-5586. **EMAIL** vos@muhlenberg.edu

VRETTOS, ATHENA
DISCIPLINE 19TH-CENTURY ENGLISH LITERATURE **EDUCATION** Vassar, BA; Univ Pa, MA, PhD. **CAREER** English, Case Western Reserve Univ. **SELECTED PUBLICATIONS** Auth or ed, Somatic Fictions: Imagining Illness in Victorian Culture. **CONTACT ADDRESS** Case Western Reserve Univ, 10900 Euclid Ave, Cleveland, OH, 44106.

W

WABUDA, SUSAN
DISCIPLINE ENGLISH HISTORY **EDUCATION** Cambridge Univ, PhD. **CAREER** Asst prof, Fordham Univ. **SELECTED PUBLICATIONS** Auth, Shunamites and Nurses of the English Reformation: the Activities of Mary Glover, Niece of Hugh Latimer, Women in the Church, vol 27 Stud in Church Hist, 90. **CONTACT ADDRESS** Dept of Hist, Fordham Univ, 113 W 60th St, New York, NY, 10023.

WACHOLDER, BEN ZION
PERSONAL Born 09/21/1924, Dzarow, Poland, m, 1993, 4 children **DISCIPLINE** ENGLISH LITERATURE; CLASSICS; HISTORY **EDUCATION** Yeshiva Univ, BA, 51; UCLA, PhD, 60. **CAREER** Prof, Hebrew Union Col, 56-98. **HONORS AND AWARDS** Pursuing the Text: Studies in Honor of Ben Zion Wacholder on the Occasion of his Seventieth Birthday **MEMBERSHIPS** Soc of Bibl Lit; Asoc of Jewish Studies **RESEARCH** Judaism during the second temple period; Hellenistic Judaism; Dead Sea Scrolls; Talmudic Studies; ancient historiography, ancient calendars **SELECTED PUBLICATIONS** auth, Nicolaus of Damascus, 62; auth, Eupolemus, 74; Essays in Jewish Chronology and Chronography, 84; The Dawn of Qumran, 84; A Preliminary Edition of the Unpublished Dead Sea Scrolls, 96. **CONTACT ADDRESS** 7648 Greenland Pl., Cincinnati, OH, 45237. **EMAIL** ben648@aol.com

WACHSMUTH, WAYNE R.
PERSONAL Born 06/08/1958, WI, m, 1990, 4 children **DISCIPLINE** ENGLISH GRAMMER; BIBLICAL STUDY **EDUCATION** Bethany Bible Col, BS, 81; Trinity Evangelical Div School, MA, 90. **CAREER** Academic dean, Trinity Col, 96-99 **HONORS AND AWARDS** Joseph Gerhardt Scholar, Registr, dir, student svc **MEMBERSHIPS** Dietrich Bonheoffer Soc **RESEARCH** Contemporary theol **CONTACT ADDRESS** 301 N Emerson, Mt. Prospect, IL, 60056. **EMAIL** WWachs@concentric.net

WACKMAN, DANIEL B.
DISCIPLINE MASS COMMUNICATION STUDIES **EDUCATION** Univ Wis Madison, PhD. **CAREER** Prof **SELECTED PUBLICATIONS** Co-auth, 'To Thine Own Self Be True': Values, Framing, and Voter Decision Making Strategies, Commun Res, 96; Increasing Public Understanding of Heart Disease: An Analysis of Data from the Minnesota Heart Health Program, Health Commun, 93; Managing Media Organizations: Effective Leadership of the Media, 88; Effect of Chain Ownership on Newspaper Management Goals, Newspaper Res J, 88. **CONTACT ADDRESS** Mass Communication Dept, Univ of Minnesota, Twin Cities, 111 Murphy Hall, 206 Church St SE, Minneapolis, MN, 55455. **EMAIL** wackm001@maroon.tc.umn.edu

WADDINGTON, MIRIAM
PERSONAL Winnipeg, MB, Canada **DISCIPLINE** ENGLISH **EDUCATION** Univ Toronto, BA, 39, MA, 68; Univ Pa, MSW, 45. **CAREER** Lectr & res advisor, McGill Sch Social Work, 45-48; case worker, Montreal, 48-60; supervisor, Family Svcs Agency, North York, 60-63; PROF ENGLISH, YORK UNIV, 64-90, prof emer, 83-. **HONORS AND AWARDS** J.I. Segal prize, 72, 86. **SELECTED PUBLICATIONS** Auth, Green World, 45; auth, The Season's Lovers, 58; auth, The Price of Gold, 76; auth, The Last Landscape, 92. **CONTACT ADDRESS** Dept of English, York Univ, North York, ON, M3J 1P3.

WADDINGTON, RAYMOND BRUCE.
PERSONAL Born 09/27/1935, Santa Barbara, CA, m, 1985, 2 children **DISCIPLINE** ENGLISH LITERATURE **EDUCATION** Stanford Univ, BA, 57; Rice Univ, PhD, 63. **CAREER** Instr, 61-62, Univ Houston; Instr, Asst Prof, 62-65, Univ Kansas; Asst Prof, Assoc Prof, Prof, 66-82, Univ Wisconsin Madison; Prof, 82-, Univ Cal Davis. **HONORS AND AWARDS** JHU Postdoc Fel; Huntington Lib Fel; IRH Fel; Guggenheim fel; NEH Fel Newberry Lib; NEH Sr Fel. **MEMBERSHIPS** RSA; MSA; SCSC; ANS; BAMS. **RESEARCH** Renaissance Literature, art and culture; Iconography, rhetoric. **SELECTED PUBLICATIONS** Auth, The Mind's Empire, 74; coed, The Rhetoric of Renaissance Poetry, 74; coed, The Age of Milton, 80; coed, The Expulsion of the Jews: 1492 and After, 94. **CONTACT ADDRESS** English Dept, Univ Calif Davis, Davis, CA, 95616. **EMAIL** rbwaddington@ucdavis.edu

WADE, SETH
PERSONAL Born 11/12/1928, Decatur, KY, m, 1962, 3 children **DISCIPLINE** ENGLISH **EDUCATION** Univ Ky, AB, 52; La State Univ, MA, 54. **CAREER** Asst English, La State Univ, 52-53; asst, Univ Fla, 53-54; instr, Univ Ky, Northern Ctr, 54-55; teaching asst, Ohio State Univ, 57-59, asst instr, 59-60; mem fac, Western Ky State Col, 61-62; ASST PROF ENGLISH, PAN AM UNIV, 62-. **MEMBERSHIPS** NCTE **RESEARCH** Creative writing and modern poetry. **SELECTED PUBLICATIONS** Auth, Byzantium, New Eng Rev Middlebury Series, Vol 17, 95; Barn, New Eng Rev Middlebury Series, Vol 17, 95; The Conduit and Banjo Picker, Brown, Fleming, J Country Mus, Vol 17, 95; Turkish Bath, Poetry, Vol 168, 96; For my Mother, Am t The Poetry of Hamburger, Michael, Agenda, Vol 35, 97. **CONTACT ADDRESS** 1100 W Samano, Edinburg, TX, 78539.

WADE-GAYLES, GLORIA JEAN
PERSONAL Memphis, TN, m, 1967 **DISCIPLINE** ENGLISH **EDUCATION** LeMoyne Coll, AB (Cum Laude with Distinction) 1959; Boston Univ Woodrow Wilson Fellow, AM 1962; George Washington Univ, doctoral work 1966-67; Emory Univ NEH Fellow, 1975; Emory Univ, PhD 1981. **CAREER** Spelman Coll, instructor of English 1963-64; Howard Univ, instr of English 1965-67; Morehouse Coll, asst prof 1970-75; Emory Univ, graduate teaching fellow 1975-77; Talladega Coll, asst prof 1977-78; Spelman Coll, asst prof 1984-90, prof, beginning 1992; Dillard Univ, prof, currently. **HONORS AND AWARDS** Woodrow Wilson Fellowship 1959-62; Merrill Travel Grant to Europe The Charles Merril Found 1973; Danforth Fellow 1974; Faculty Award of the Year Morehouse Coll 1975; mem Alpha Kappa Mu Natl Honor Soc; editor CLA-NOTES 1975-; poems published in, Essence, Black World, The Black Scholar, First World; articles published in, Callaloo, Liberator, The Atlantic Monthly; wrote the preface to " Sturdy Black Bridges" Doubleday 1979; author of "No Crystal Stair, Visions of Race and Sec in Black Women's Fiction 1946-1976" Pilgrim Press 1984 (won 1983 manuscript award); UNCF Mellon Rsch Grant 1987-88, Liaison with Natl Humanities Faculty; Presidential Award for Scholarship, Spelman Coll, 1991; Named CASE Natl Prof of the Year, 1991; Dana Mentor, Spelmaoll, 1989-. **MEMBERSHIPS** Teacher COFO Freedom School/Valley View MS 1964; mem bd dir WETV 30 -WABE-FM 1976-77; sec Guardians for Quality Educ 1976-78; mem editorial bd of Callaloo 1977-80; exec bd Coll Language Assn 1977-80; mem NAACP, ASNLC, CORE; mem Alpha Kappa Alpha Sorority Inc; partner in Jon-Mon Consultants Inc; speech writer. **SELECTED PUBLICATIONS** Pushed Back to Strength, Beacon Press, 1993; My Soul Is a Witness, Beacon Press, Rooted Against the Wind, Beacon Press, 1996; Father Songs: Testimonies by African-American Sons and Daughters, Beacon Press, 1997; Author, Anointed to Fly, Harlem River, 1991. **CONTACT ADDRESS** Dillard Univ, 2601 Gentilly Blvd., New Orleans, LA, 70122.

WADLINGTON, WARWICK PAUL
PERSONAL Born 05/02/1938, New Orleans, LA, m, 1963, 3 children **DISCIPLINE** ENGLISH **EDUCATION** US Mil Acad, BS, 61; Tulane Univ, MA, 66, PhD(English), 67. **CAREER** From asst prof to assoc prof, 67-78, prof English, Univ TX, Austin, 78-. **HONORS AND AWARDS** Bromberg Excellence in Teaching, Univ TX, Austin, 70; Kelleher Centennial Prof, 87-; Who's Who in America, 87-; President's Associates Teaching Excellence Award, 86; Outstanding Graduate Teaching Award, 96. **MEMBERSHIPS** MLA; Soc Study Southern Lit. **RESEARCH** American literature; modern literature. **SELECTED PUBLICATIONS** Auth, Pathos and Dreiser, Southern Rev, 71; Ishmael's Godly Gamesomeness, English Lit Hist, 72; contribr, Nathanael West: The Cheaters and the Cheated, Everett/Edwards, 73; auth, The Confidence Game in American Literature, Princeton Univ, 75; Deep Within the Reader's Eye, Wallace Stevens J, 78; The Sound and the Fury: A Logic of Tragedy, Am Lit, 81; Reading Faulknerian Tragedy, Cornell Univ Press, 87; As I Lay Dying: Stories Out of Stories, Simon & Schuster/Twayne, 92; Doing What Comes Culturally: Collective Action and the Discourse of Belief in Faulkner and Nathaniel West, in Faulkner, His Contemporaries, and His Posterity, Franke, 92; The Guns of Light in August: War and Peace in the Second Thirty Years War, in Faulkner in Cultural Context, Univ Press MS, 97. **CONTACT ADDRESS** Dept English, Univ Texas, Austin, TX, 78712-1026. **EMAIL** wadl@uts.cc.utexas.edu

WAGES, JACK D.
DISCIPLINE AMERICAN LITERATURE **EDUCATION** Univ TN, PhD, 68. **CAREER** Prof, TX Tech Univ, 68-. **SELECTED PUBLICATIONS** Auth, Seventy-Five Writers of the Colonial South. **CONTACT ADDRESS** Texas Tech Univ, Lubbock, TX, 79409-5015. **EMAIL** J.Wages@ttu.edu

WAGNER, M. JOHN
PERSONAL Born 08/27/1917, Chicago, IL, m, 1954, 2 children **DISCIPLINE** ENGLISH **EDUCATION** Univ Chicago, BA, 39, MA, 40; Northwestern Univ, PhD (English), 56. **CAREER** Instr English, Northwestern Univ, 45-47, Ill Inst Technol, 51-52 and 55-56, Lake Forest Col, 52-55; asst prof, Humboldt State Col, 56-59, Univ Puget Sound, 59-62, Calif State Polytech Col Pomona, 62-64, from asst prof to assoc prof, 64-67, prof, 67-80, EMER PROF ENGLISH and CHMN DEPT, CALIF STATE UNIV, FULLERTON, 80-. **RESEARCH** Eighteenth century English; fiction writing. **SELECTED PUBLICATIONS** Auth, Eminence Choices in 3 Musical Genres and Music Media Preferences, J Res Mus Educ, Vol 43, 95. **CONTACT ADDRESS** Dept of English, California State Univ, Fullerton, Fullerton, CA, 92631.

WAGNER, VERN
PERSONAL Broadview, MT, m, 1941, 3 children **DISCIPLINE** ENGLISH, AMERICAN LITERATURE **EDUCATION** Univ Wash, BA, 46, MA, 48, PhD (English), 50. **CAREER** Instr, Univ Wash, 50; prof and chmn dept lang, Nebr State Teachers Col, Chadron, 50-52; From asst prof to assoc prof, 52-71, PROF ENGLISH, WAYNE STATE UNIV, 71-; Mem comt teacher training and qualification, NCTE, 57-; Fulbright prof, Univ Helsinki, 59-60; prof and dir, Am Studies Res Ctr, Hyderabad, India, 74-76; prof Am studies, Univ Indonesia, 80-81. **RESEARCH** Nineteenth and twentieth century American literature. **SELECTED PUBLICATIONS** Auth, Germs and Utopia and an Approach To 'Unveiling A Parallel', A Late Th-Century Feminist Utopian Novel By Jones, Alice, Ilgenfritz and Merchant, Ella, Genre Forms Discourse Cult, Vol 28, 95; Submachine Guns and Electronic Schoolmarms in a True Crime Western, Mod Fiction Studies, Vol 41, 95. **CONTACT ADDRESS** Dept of English, Wayne State Univ, Detroit, MI, 48202.

WAHLSTROM, BILLIE J.
DISCIPLINE RHETORIC STUDIES **EDUCATION** Univ Mich, MA, PhD. **CAREER** Prof **RESEARCH** Design of distance learning materials; effects of new and emerging technologies; gender, ethics, and technology interactions. **SELECTED PUBLICATIONS** Auth, Designing a Research Program in Sientific and Technical Communication, 96; co-auth, The Rhetoric of Midwifery: Conflicts and Conversations in the Minnesota Home Birth Community in the 1990s, Quarterly J Speech, 96; Designing and Managing Virtual Learning Communities, 96. **CONTACT ADDRESS** Rhetoric Dept, Univ of Minnesota, Twin Cities, 64 Classroom Office Bldg, 1994 Buford Ave, St. Paul, MN, 55108. **EMAIL** bwahlstr@mailbox.mail.umn.edu

WAINER, ALEX
DISCIPLINE COMMUNICATIONS **EDUCATION** Valdasta State Univ, BFA, 88; Regent Univ, MA, 90, PhD, 96. **CAREER** Prof. **SELECTED PUBLICATIONS** Auth, Batman as Mythic Evocation Through Comics Technique, scholarly paper presented at the Popular Cult Asn Convention, Las Vegas, 96 & Willing Suspension of Belief: Faith and Unbelief in Classic Horror Films, Scheduled, presented at Speech Commun Asn convention in New Orleans, 94. **CONTACT ADDRESS** Dept of Communications, Milligan Col, PO Box 9, Milligan Col, TN, 37682. **EMAIL** awainer@milligan.edu

WAINGROW, MARSHALL
PERSONAL Born 03/26/1923, Bridgeport, CT, m, 1950, 3 children **DISCIPLINE** ENGLISH **EDUCATION** Harvard Univ, BS, 44; Univ Rochester, MA, 46; Yale Univ, PhD, 51. **CAREER** Instr English, Pa State Univ, 48-49; From instr to asst prof, Yale Univ, 52-59; PROF ENGLISH, CLAREMONT GRAD SCH, 59-; Morse fel, Yale Univ, 56-57; Am Coun Learned Soc grant-in-aid, 63; Guggenheim fel, 70-71; Am Philos Soc grant, 72-73; vis prof, Univ Calif, Riverside, 73-74 and Univ Calif, Berkeley, 78. **MEMBERSHIPS** MLA; Am Soc 18th Century Studies. **RESEARCH** Eighteenth century literature; Boswell and Johnson. **SELECTED PUBLICATIONS** Auth, Source of Quotations Sought and Boswell, James and Cust, Francis, Cockayne, Query, Notes, Queries, Vol 41, 94. **CONTACT ADDRESS** Dept of English and Am Lit, Claremont Graduate Sch, Claremont, CA, 91711.

WAINWRIGHT, JOHN A.
PERSONAL Born 05/12/1946, Toronto, ON, Canada **DISCIPLINE** ENGLISH **EDUCATION** Univ Toronto, BA, 69; Dalhousie Univ, MA, 73, PhD, 78. **CAREER** PROF ENGLISH, DALHOUSIE UNIV, 79- **MEMBERSHIPS** Writers' Fedn NS; Writers' Union Can; PEN Can; Asn Can Univ Tchrs English. **SELECTED PUBLICATIONS** Auth, Moving Outward, 70; auth, The Requiem Journals, 76; auth, After the War, 81; auth, Flight of the Falcon: Scott's Journey to the South Pole 1910-12, 87; auth, World Enough and Time: Charles Bruce, A Literary Biography, 88; auth, Landscape and Desire: Poems Selected and New, 92; auth, A Deathful Ridge: A Novel of Everest, 97; ed, Notes for a Native Land, 69; ed, A Very Large Soul: Selected Letters from Margaret Lawrence to Canadian Writers, 95. **CONTACT ADDRESS** Dept of English, Dalhousie Univ, Halifax, NS, B3H 3J5.

WAITH, EUGENE MERSEREAU
PERSONAL Born 12/29/1912, Buffalo, NY, m, 1939 **DISCIPLINE** ENGLISH LITERATURE **EDUCATION** Yale Univ, AB, 35, PhD (English), 39. **CAREER** From instr to assoc prof, 39-63, PROF ENGLISH, YALE UNIV, 63-; Secy, English Inst, 53-58, chmn, 62-63; mem exec comt, Am Soc Theatre Res, 78-81. **MEMBERSHIPS** MLA; Shakespeare Asn Am; Am Soc Theatre Res; English Inst. **RESEARCH** Shakespeare; 17th century drama; modern drama. **SELECTED PUBLICATIONS** Auth, Ozymandias, Keats Shelley J, Vol 44, 95; Literature and Degree in Renaissance England in Nashe, Bourgeois Tragedy, Shakespeare, Shakespeare Quart, Vol 47, 96. **CONTACT ADDRESS** Dept of English, Yale Univ, New Haven, CT, 06520.

WAKEFIELD, ROBERT
DISCIPLINE COMMUNICATION **EDUCATION** Univ WY, BS, 67; Univ CO, MA, 71, PhD 76. **CAREER** Asst prof; fac adv, vox populi, stud video mag, TV/film Ad Club & TX High Sch Video Festival. **SELECTED PUBLICATIONS** Auth, Trail of the Jackasses, N Plains Press, 68; Schwiering And The West, N Plains Press, 73. **CONTACT ADDRESS** Dept of Commun, Univ of Texas-Pan Am, 1201 W. University Dr, Edinburg, TX, 78539. **EMAIL** Wakefield@PanAm.Edu

WAKS, LEAH
DISCIPLINE COMMUNICATION **EDUCATION** Univ MI, PhD, 91. **CAREER** Lectr, Univ MD. **RESEARCH** Commun behavior. **SELECTED PUBLICATIONS** Co-auth, The Social Construction of Attitudes Toward the Roles of Women and African Americans, Howard Jour Commun 2, 91. **CONTACT ADDRESS** Dept of Commun, Univ MD, 4229 Art-Sociology Building, College Park, MD, 20742-1335. **EMAIL** leahwaks@wam.umd.edu

WALD, ALAN MAYNARD
PERSONAL Born 06/01/1946, Washington, DC, w, 1975, 2 children **DISCIPLINE** AMERICAN STUDIES, ENGLISH LITERATURE **EDUCATION** Antioch Col, BA, 69; Univ Calif, Berkeley, MA, 71, PhD(English), 74. **CAREER** Lectr English, San Jose State Univ, 74; teaching assoc, Univ Calif, Berkeley, 75; asst prof English Lit & Am Cult, Univ Mich, Ann Arbor, 75-, from assoc prof to prof, 81-86; Am Coun Learned Soc grant-in-aid, 75-76; Rackham Fac Res grant, 76-77. **HONORS AND AWARDS** ACLS Natl Fel, 83-84; Beinecke llow, Yale, 89; Michigan Humanities fell, 85; Excellence in Research Award from UM, 96; A Bartlett Giamatti Faculty fel at UM Instit for Humanities, 97-98. **MEMBERSHIPS** MLA. **RESEARCH** American literary radicalism; Marxist aesthetics; the New York intellectuals. **SELECTED PUBLICATIONS** Auth,

James T Arrell: The Revolutionary Socialist Years, 78; The Responsibility of Intellectuals, 92; Writing From the Left, 94. **CONTACT ADDRESS** Dept of English, Univ of Michigan, 317 Angell Hall, Ann Arbor, MI, 48109-10003.

WALDAUER, JOSEPH
DISCIPLINE 18TH-CENTURY FRENCH LITERATURE **EDUCATION** Columbia Univ, PhD. **CAREER** Instr, Univ Minn, Twin Cities. **SELECTED PUBLICATIONS** Published on Diderot, Rousseau, and Stendhal. **CONTACT ADDRESS** Univ Minn, Twin Cities, Minneapolis, MN, 55455.

WALDELAND, LYNNE M.
PERSONAL Born 06/13/1941, St. Paul, MN **DISCIPLINE** AMERICAN LITERATURE, FILM **EDUCATION** St Olaf Col, BA, 63; Purdue Univ, MA, 66, PhD, 70. **CAREER** Asst prof English, Albion Col, 69-70; assoc prof Am lit, 70-, asst prof for acad planning & develop, 86-, Northern Ill Univ. **MEMBERSHIPS** MLA; Midwest Mod Lang Assn; Am Assoc of Higher Ed; Soc for Coll & Univ Planning. **RESEARCH** Contemporary American writers; film adaptations of novels and stories; literature and photography. **SELECTED PUBLICATIONS** Auth, The Deep Sleep: The fifties in the novels of Wright Morris, Silhouettes on the Shade: Images of the Fifties Reexamined, Ball State Univ Press, 73; auth, John Cheever, G K Hall, 79; auth, Wright Morris: Bibliographical essay, Bibliography of Midwestern Literature, Univ Iowa Press, 81; auth, Plains Song: Women's voices in the fiction of Wright Morris, Critique, 82; auth, John Cheever's Bullet Park: A key to his thought and art, John Cheever: Critical Essays, G K Hall, 82. **CONTACT ADDRESS** Dept of English, No Illinois Univ, 1425 W Lincoln Hwy, De Kalb, IL, 60115-2825. **EMAIL** lwaldeland@niu.edu

WALDOFF, LEON
PERSONAL Born 02/16/1935, Hattiesburg, MS, m, 1960, 1 child **DISCIPLINE** ENGLISH **EDUCATION** Northwestern Univ, BA, 57; Univ Mich, MA, 63, PhD (English), 67. **CAREER** Instr English, Univ Mich, 66-67; dir intro courses English, 71-73, asst prof, 67-73, ASSOC PROF ENGLISH, UNIV ILL, URBANA, 73-; ASSOC HEAD DEPT, 77-; Vis lectr, Univ Reading, Eng, 75-76. **MEMBERSHIPS** MLA; Keats-Shelley Asn Am. **RESEARCH** Romantic poetry; psychoanalytic criticism. **SELECTED PUBLICATIONS** Auth, the Romantic Dream in Wordsworth and the Poetics of the Unconscious, Wordsworth Circle, Vol 25, 94; Keats, Narrative and Audience in The Posthumous Life of Writing, Studies Romanticism, Vol 34, 95; Wordsworth, William and the Mind of Man in The Poet as Thinker, J Eng Ger Philol, Vol 94, 95. **CONTACT ADDRESS** Univ of Ill, 608 S Wright St, Urbana, IL, 61801-3613.

WALKER, ALBERT LYELL
PERSONAL Born 01/20/1907, Okla City, OK **DISCIPLINE** ENGLISH LITERATURE **EDUCATION** Park Col, AB, 29; State Univ Iowa, AM, 30, PhD, 36. **CAREER** Instr English, Univ Ark, 30-32; From instr to prof, 35-77, dir freshman English and chmn curric comt div sci and humanities, 42-59, chmn dept speech, 59-69, chmn dept English, 59-72, EMER PROF ENGLISH, IOWA STATE UNIV, 77-; Gen Educ Bd and Rockefeller fel, Univ Chicago, 40-41. **MEMBERSHIPS** NCTE; MLA **RESEARCH** Shakespeare, conventions of writing as modified and changed as plays increased and developments in his language and metaphor; modern American fiction, especially work and techniques of William Faulkner; theory of literature. **SELECTED PUBLICATIONS** Auth, Dialogue as a Strategy for Transformative Education, Relig Educ, Vol 91, 96. **CONTACT ADDRESS** Iowa State Univ, Ames, IA, 50010.

WALKER, CHARLOTTE ZOE
PERSONAL Born 07/13/1935, New Orleans, LA, m, 3 children **DISCIPLINE** LITERATURE **EDUCATION** San Diego St Univ, BA, 57; Syracuse Univ, MA, 66, PhD, 72. **CAREER** Prof, eng & women's stud, 70-, SUNY; founder & co-ed, Phoebe: an Interdisciplinary Jour of Feminist Scholar, Theory & Aesthetics, SUNY Oneonta, 88-92. **HONORS AND AWARDS** Cornelia C Ward Fel, Syracuse Univ, 67; NDEA fel in lit, Syracuse Univ, 68-70; SUNY Chancellor's Award for Excel in Tchng, 75; SUNY Fac Res Grants in Fine Arts, 75, 78; Walter B Ford Grants; Natl Endow for the Arts Creative Writing Fel, 87; NEH Sum Seminars; O.Henry Award, 91; Fac Award, 3rd Ann Undergraduate Women's Conf, 96. **MEMBERSHIPS** Natl Writers Union; Poets & Writers; Asn for Stud of Lit & Environ. **RESEARCH** Environmental writing & nature writing; women writers; fiction writing. **SELECTED PUBLICATIONS** Auth, Condor and Hummingbird, Women's Press, 87; auth, Loon Voice: Lying Words and Speaking World in Atwood's Surfacing, Margaret Atwood: Reflection and Reality, Pan Amer Univ Press, 87; art, That Vermeer Sky, N Amer Rev, 90; art, The Very Pineapple, Prize Stories 1991: The O. Henry Awards, Doubleday, 91; art, The Poetry of Rita Dove, Masterpieces of African Amer Lit, Salem Press, 92; art, Creative Breakthrough: Sequence and the Blade of Consciousness in Virginia Woolf's The Waves, Virginia Woolf: Critical Assessments, Vol IV, Helm Info, 94; art, The Virgin of the Rocks, Storming Heaven's Gate, Plume, 97; art, John Burroughs, Encycl of the Essay, Fitzroy & Dearborn, 97; art, Goat's Milk, Intimate Nature: The Bond Between Women and Animals, Fawcett, 98. **CONTACT ADDRESS** PO Box 14, Gilbertsville, NY, 13776. **EMAIL** walkercz@oneonta.edu

WALKER, CHERYL
PERSONAL Born 11/07/1947, Evanston, IL, m, 1989, 2 children **DISCIPLINE** BRITISH; AMERICAN LITERATURE **EDUCATION** Wellesley Coll, BA, 69; Brandeis Univ, MA, 70; PhD, 73. **CAREER** Robert Bentley Publishing Co, 68, 70; poetry ed, 71-72, Modern Occasions; reader, 72, Wellesley Coll; managing ed, 72-73, Modern Occasions; assoc dir, 73-74, Federation of Organization for Professional Women, 73-74; teaching fell, summer 89, Telluride Summer Program; 78-79, 87, 90-93, chair, intercollegiat amer studies program, 84-85, chair, english dept, 85-86 dir, interdisciplinary program for freshman, chair, chair, 88-89, humanities programScripps Coll. **HONORS AND AWARDS** Resident Scholar, Rockefeller Villa Serbelloni, Bellagio, Italy, Jan 31-Mar 1, 1994; Mary W. Johnson Faculty Recognition Award for Scholarly Achievement, 1995; dir, Scripps College Humanities Institute, 96-99; Mary W. Johnson Faculty Recognition Award For Teaching, 98. **MEMBERSHIPS** MLA; ALA; Emily Dickinson Soc; Elizabeth Bishop Soc. **RESEARCH** Amer Women Poets; 19th century Native Amer writers. **SELECTED PUBLICATIONS** Auth, Indian Nation: Native American Literature and Nineteenth-Century Nationalisms, 97; The Whip Signature: Violence, Feminism, and Women Poets, in Gender and Genre: Essays on Women's Poetry, Late Romantics to Late Victorians 1830-1900, 98; Helen Hunt Jackson and Maria White Lowell in The Encyclopedia of American Poetry: The Nineteeth Century, 98; Nineteeth-Century American Women Poets Revisited, in Nineteeth-Century American Women Writers: A Critical Anthology, 98. **CONTACT ADDRESS** English Dept, Scripps Coll, Balch 60, Claremont, CA, 91711. **EMAIL** cwalker@scrippscol.edu

WALKER, DAVID
DISCIPLINE BRITISH AND AMERICAN LITERATURE **EDUCATION** Oberlin Col, BA, 72; Cornell Univ, MA, 76, PhD, 79. **CAREER** Prof, Oberlin Coll, 77-; Dept Ch. **RESEARCH** Modern literature, poetry writing, playwriting. **SELECTED PUBLICATIONS** Au, Transparent Lyric: a Study of Wallace Stevens and William Carlos Williams; co-ed, FIELD Poetry magazine, Oberlin Col Press; rev ed, FIELD Guide to Contemporary Poetry and Poetics. **CONTACT ADDRESS** Dept of Eng, Oberlin Col, Oberlin, OH, 44074. **EMAIL** david.walker@oberlin.edu

WALKER, DAVID LEWIS
PERSONAL Born 09/14/1950, Richmond, VA **DISCIPLINE** MODERN LITERATURE **EDUCATION** Oberlin Col, BA, 72; Cornell Univ, MA, 76, PhD (English), 79. **CAREER** ASST PROF ENGLISH, OBERLIN COL, 77-; Assoc ed, Field: Contemporary Poetry and Poetics, 77-. **MEMBERSHIPS** MLA **RESEARCH** Modern and contemporary poetry and fiction. **SELECTED PUBLICATIONS** Auth, Chisholm, Jesse in Texas Trail Blazer and Houston, Sam Troubleshooter Southwestern Histl Quart, Vol 97, 93; Desert Lawmen, the High Sheriffs of New-Mexico and Arizona, 1846-1912, Western Histl Quart, Vol 24, 93. **CONTACT ADDRESS** English Dept, Oberlin Col, Oberlin, OH, 44074.

WALKER, ETHEL PITTS
PERSONAL Born 02/04/1943, Tulsa, OK, m, 1977 **DISCIPLINE** DRAMA **EDUCATION** Lincoln Univ MO, BS Ed 1964; Univ of CO, MA Speech & Drama 1965; Univ of MO Columbia, PhD Theatre 1975. **CAREER** Southern Univ Baton Rouge LA, instr 1965-68; Lincoln Univ Jefferson City MO, asst prof 1968-77; Univ of IL Urbana, asst prof 1977-79; Laney Coll Oakland CA, instr 1979-80; African Amer Drama Co San Francisco, exec dir 1980-; Univ of CA Berkeley, asst prof 1988; Wayne State Univ, visiting asst prof 1988-89; San Jose State University, San Jose, CA, professor, theatre arts dept, 1989-. **HONORS AND AWARDS** Ira Aldridge Scholarship 1963; Outstanding Ed 1974; Outstanding Instr Sr Class Lincoln Univ 1977; Best Actress Awd Lincoln Univ Stagecrafters 1963, Mother of the Year, Representative Teola Hunter of Michigan, 1989; "The Amer Negro Theatre" Black Amers in the Theatre; study, toured with Phelps/Stokes West African Heritage Seminar 1975; article "The Diction in Ed Bullins" In New Eng Winter, Encore 1977; Krigwa Players: A Theatre For, By, and About Black People in Theatre Journal 1989; directed, When the Jumbie Bird Calls at Bonstelle Theatre, Detroit MI 1989; director, To Be Young, Gifted And Black, 1991; "Incorporating African-American Theatre Into A Basic Theatre Course," Theatre Topic, Sept 1992; honorary lifetime membership, Black Theatre Network; Inducted into the Consortium of Doctors, 1993. **MEMBERSHIPS** Mem 1984-85, chmn 1985- Amer Theatre Assoc, Natl Assoc of Dramatic & Speech Arts, Theta Alpha Phi Dramatic Frat, Speech Commun of Amer, Zeta Phi Beta; Third Baptist Church (San Fransisco), parents alliance, public relations dir; Children's Performance Center, pres of advisory council; Black Theatre Network, past pres 1985-88; member, Association for Theatre in Higher Education; past pres, California Educational Theatre Assn; pres, Legislative Action Coalition for Arts Education. **CONTACT ADDRESS** San Jose State Univ, 1 Washington Square, San Jose, CA, 95192-0098.

WALKER, JAMES
DISCIPLINE MASS COMMUNICATIONS **EDUCATION** Univ IA, PhD. **CAREER** St Xavier Univ **SELECTED PUBLICATIONS** Couth, The Remote Control in the New Media Environment, Praeger, 93; Television and the Remote Control: Grazing on a Vast Wasteland, Guilford, 96; The Broadcast Television Industry, Allyn & Bacon, 98. **CONTACT ADDRESS** Saint Xavier Univ, 3700 W 103rd Street, Chicago, IL, 60655.

WALKER, JEANNE MURRAY
PERSONAL Born 05/27/1944, Parkers Prairie, MN, m, 1966, 1 child **DISCIPLINE** ENGLISH LITERATURE **EDUCATION** Wheaton Col, BA, 66; Loyola Univ Chicago, MA, 69; Univ Pa, PhD(English), 74. **CAREER** Lectr english, Harverford Col, 74-77; PROF ENGLISH, UNIV DEL, 80-. **HONORS AND AWARDS** NEA fel; Penn State Council on the Arts fel; Lewis Prize for drama, twice; Ctr for Advanced Res grant; Stage Time Award for Theater; Pew fel in the Arts; AWP award for poetry; Virginia Duvall Mann award for theatre. **MEMBERSHIPS** MLA; Northeast Mod Lang Asn; Poetry Soc Am; Soc Children's Bk Authors. **RESEARCH** Poet and playwright. **SELECTED PUBLICATIONS** Auth, Nailing Up the Home Sweet Home, Cleveland, 80; auth, Fugitive Angels, Dragon Gate Press, 85; auth, Coming Into History, Cleveland, 90; auth, Stranger than Fiction, Q Rev of Lit, 92; auth, Gaining Time, Copper Beech, 97. **CONTACT ADDRESS** Univ Del, Memorial Hall, Newark, DE, 19711.

WALKER, JEFFREY
DISCIPLINE COLONIAL AND EARLY 19TH CENTURY AMERICAN LITERATURE **EDUCATION** Pa State Univ, PhD, 77. **CAREER** Head, dept Engl, Okla State Univ. **SELECTED PUBLICATIONS** Areas: poetry of Benjamin Church; James Fenimore Cooper; early American poets and poetry; the American short story; and Edmund Wilson. **CONTACT ADDRESS** Oklahoma State Univ, 101 Whitehurst Hall, Stillwater, OK, 74078.

WALKER, JEFFREY
DISCIPLINE ENGLISH **EDUCATION** Shippenburg, BA, 68; Middlebury, MA, 71; Penn State, PhD, 77. **CAREER** Assoc prof English, Okla State. **RESEARCH** Collegiate literary culture in 18th century America. **CONTACT ADDRESS** RR 1, PO Box 476, Stillwater, OK, 44074.

WALKER, KIM
DISCIPLINE MEDIA RESEARCH, TELEVISION PRODUCTION **EDUCATION** S Ill Univ, PhD. **CAREER** Telecommun consult, Ill Off Edu; McLuhan Prog Cult Tech, Univ Toronto; Amer Assn of Retired Persons; prof-. **HONORS AND AWARDS** TV award winning. Journey Into Literacy, 93; grants, Nat Assn Broadcasters; Intl Commun Assn., Produced and directed, number of instructional and public aff prog(s). **SELECTED PUBLICATIONS** Publ, Commun Res Rpt; Commun Edu; Commun Monogr; Pub Pers Mgt; Jour Commun; Media Arts; Intl Jour Edu Telecommun. **CONTACT ADDRESS** Dept of Commun, Univ Colo, PO Box 7150, Colorado Springs, CO, 80933-7150.

WALKER, NANCY
DISCIPLINE AMERICAN LITERATURE, WOMEN'S STUDIES **EDUCATION** Kent State Univ, PhD. **CAREER** Instr, Vanderbilt Univ. **RESEARCH** 19th- and 20th-century American women writers; women's humor. **SELECTED PUBLICATIONS** Auth, A Very Serious Thing: Women's Humor and American Culture, 88; Feminist Alternatives: Irony and Fantasy in the Contemporary Novel by Women, 90; Fanny Fern, 92; Bedford Books edition of The Awakening, 92; The Disobedient Writer: Women and Narrative Tradition, Tex. **CONTACT ADDRESS** Vanderbilt Univ, Nashville, TN, 37203-1727.

WALKER, PIERRE (PETER)
DISCIPLINE ENGLISH **EDUCATION** Univ Massachusetts, BA, 78; MA, 83, PhD, 89, Columbia Univ. **CAREER** Asst Prof, 89-93, Univ Minnesota (Duluth); Asst Prof, 93-97, Western Michigan Univ; Asst Prof, 97-98, Assoc Prof, 98-, Salem State Col. **CONTACT ADDRESS** English Dept, Salem State Col, Salem, MA, 01970. **EMAIL** pwalker@salem.mass.edu

WALKER, ROBERT JEFFERSON
PERSONAL Born 04/22/1922, Gooding, ID, m, 1946, 2 children **DISCIPLINE** SPEECH, COMMUNICATION **EDUCATION** Univ Ill, BSEd, 46; Northwestern Univ, MA, 48; Wayne State Univ, PhD (mass commun), 66. **CAREER** Instr English and Speech, Kennedy-King Col, 46-48; asst prof speech and theatre, Chicago Teachers Col, 50-61; PROF SPEECH, NORTHEASTERN ILL UNIV, 61-. **MEMBERSHIPS** Int Commun Asn; Speech Commun Asn; Int Listening Asn. **RESEARCH** Interpersonal communication; mass media; organizational communication. **SELECTED PUBLICATIONS** Auth, A Contest of Faiths in Missionary Women and Pluralism in the American Southwest, Church Hist, Vol 65, 96; Presbyterian Missions and Cultural Interaction in The Far Southwest

1850-1950, Church Hist, Vol 65, 96; Winning the West for Christ in Jackson, Sheldon and Presbyterianism on the Rocky-Mountain Frontier, 1869-1880, NMex Histl Rev, Vol 72, 97. **CONTACT ADDRESS** Dept of Speech and Performing Arts, Northeastern Illinois Univ, Chicago, IL, 60625.

WALKER, RONALD GARY
PERSONAL Born 09/12/1945, Southgate, CA, m, 1967, 2 children **DISCIPLINE** ENGLISH AND AMERICAN LITERATURE **EDUCATION** Univ Redlands, BA, 67; Univ Calif, Los Angeles, MA, 68; Univ Md, College Park, PhD (English), 74. **CAREER** Instr, Barber-Scotia Col, 68-69; From instr to asst prof, 69-78, ASSOC PROF ENGLISH, UNIV HOUSTON, VICTORIA CAMPUS. 78-; CHAIR DIV ARTS and SCI, 81-. **HONORS AND AWARDS** Fulbright lectr Am lit and mod lett, Univ Nacional Autonoma de Mexico, 80-81. **MEMBERSHIPS** MLA; Col English Asn; SCent Mod Lang Asn; Am Asn for Advanc of Humanities. **RESEARCH** The modern novel; theory of fiction; interdisciplinary studies (myth, ritual, art, film and literature). **SELECTED PUBLICATIONS** Auth, Lawrence,D.H., A Study of the Short-Fiction, Eng Lit Transition 1880-20, Vol 38, 95; Lady Chatterleys Lover, Loss and Hope, Eng Lit Transition 1880-20, Vol 38, 95; Twilight in Italy and Other Essays, Eng Lit Transition 1880-20, Vol 39, 96; Kangaroo, Eng Lit Transition 1880-20, Vol 40, 97. **CONTACT ADDRESS** Dept of English, Univ of Houston, Victoria, TX, 77901.

WALKIEWICZ, EDWARD P.
DISCIPLINE 20TH CENTURY LITERATURE **EDUCATION** NMex, PhD, 80. **CAREER** Engl, Okla St Univ. **SELECTED PUBLICATIONS** Areas: Barth, Cheever, Joyce, Pound, and W. C. Williams. **CONTACT ADDRESS** Oklahoma State Univ, 101 Whitehurst Hall, Stillwater, OK, 74078.

WALKOM, THOMAS L.
PERSONAL Born 08/17/1950, Kirkland Lake, ON, Canada **DISCIPLINE** COMMUNICATIONS **EDUCATION** Univ Toronto, BA, 73, MA, 74, PhD, 83. **CAREER** Lectr econ, Univ Guelph, 78-79; Globe & Mail, 81-89; WRITER, TORONTO STAR 89-. **HONORS AND AWARDS** Winner, Nat News Awards (foreign reporting, 87, column-writing, 96). **SELECTED PUBLICATIONS** Auth, Rae Days: The Rise and Follies of the NDP, 94. **CONTACT ADDRESS** Toronto Star, 1 Yonge St, Toronto, ON, M5E 1ES.

WALL, EAMONN
PERSONAL Enniscorthy, Ireland **DISCIPLINE** CREATIVE WRITING AND IRISH LITERATURE **EDUCATION** Univ Col, Dublin, BA; Univ WI-Milwaukee, MA; CUNY Grad Sch, MPhil & PhD. **CAREER** Dir, Creighton Irish Summer Sch, Trinity Col, Dublin. **SELECTED PUBLICATIONS** Auth, Iron Mountain Road, Salmon, 97; Dyckman-200th Street, Galway, Ireland, Salmon Publ, 94; The Tamed Goose, NY, Hale Press, 91; poems in, Eire-Ireland, Nebraska Rev, Cuirt J, Crab Orchard Rev, HMB & stories in Ireland in Exile and The Sunday Tribune; publ on, Patrick Kavanagh, Aidan Higgins, Michael Stephens, James Joyce, John Montague, and Derek Mahon,in Colby Quart, Forkroads, New Essays on James Joyce, Eire-Ireland; rev(s) in, Wash Post, Chicago Tribune & Rev Contemp Fiction. **CONTACT ADDRESS** Dept of Eng, Creighton Univ, 2500 CA Plaza, CA 304C, Omaha, NE, 68178. **EMAIL** ewall@creighton.edu

WALL, WENDY
DISCIPLINE ENGLISH **EDUCATION** Univ Pa, PhD. **CAREER** Prof, Northwestern Univ. **RESEARCH** Renaissance poetry and drama. **SELECTED PUBLICATIONS** Auth, The Imprint of Gender: Authorship and Publication in the English Renaissance, 93; articles on, voyeurism and female authorship. **CONTACT ADDRESS** Dept of English, Northwestern Univ, 1801 Hinman, Evanston, IL, 60208.

WALL, WILLIAM G.
PERSONAL Born 01/18/1950, Cortland, NY, m, 1997, 4 children **DISCIPLINE** ENGLISH **EDUCATION** Univ MA, PhD, 96. **CAREER** PROF LIT & THEOL, INST FOR VALSNAUA STUDIES (GRADUATE THEOLOOGICAL UNION), 96-. **MEMBERSHIPS** AAR; ASECS; MLA; NSECS; Phi Kappa Phi; WSECS. **RESEARCH** Valsnaua lit; 17th century radical Christian lit; Hindutheology; 18th century poetry; Milton; Shakespeare; art of teaching. **SELECTED PUBLICATIONS** Auth, Proof Without Pain, Back to Godhead, 24:9-10, 89; The Dicken's Checklist, Dicken's Quart, 90-93; The Importance of Being Osric: Death, Fate and Foppery in Shakespeare's Hamlet, The Shakespearean Newsletter 42, winter 92; Mrs. Affery Flintwinch's Dreams: Reading and Remembering in Little Dorrit, Dickens Quart 10, 93; ISKCON's Response to Child Abuse: 1990-1998, ICJ 6, 98; Qualified Teachers, ICJ, forthcoming. **CONTACT ADDRESS** PO Box 1156, Alachua, FL, 32616. **EMAIL** wwall@ivs.edu

WALLACE, JOHN MALCOLM
PERSONAL Born 02/28/1928, London, England **DISCIPLINE** ENGLISH LITERATURE **EDUCATION** Cambridge Univ, BA, 50, MA, 55; Johns Hopkins Univ, PhD, 60. **CAREER** Instr high sch, London, Eng, 52-54; instr English, Cornell Univ, 60-63; asst prof, Johns Hopkins Univ, 63-66, assoc prof, 66-67; PROF ENGLISH, UNIV CHICAGO, 67-; Fel, Guggenheim Found, 69-70; overseas fel, Churchill Col, Cambridge, 69-70; chmn, Renaissance Sem, Univ Chicago, 76-79; sr fel, Nat Endowment for Humanities, 80-81; sr res fel, William Andrews Clark Libr, Univ Calif, Los Angeles; vis prof lit and hist, Washington Univ, St Louis, fall, 81; William Andrews Clark Libr prof, Univ Calif Los Angeles, 81-82. **RESEARCH** Seventeenth century English literature and history. **SELECTED PUBLICATIONS** Auth, the Senecan Context of Coriolanus, Mod Philol, Vol 90, 93. **CONTACT ADDRESS** Dept of English, Univ of Chicago, 1050 E 59th St, Chicago, IL, 60637.

WALLACE, ROBERT K.
PERSONAL Born 08/02/1944, Seattle, WA, m, 1979 **DISCIPLINE** ENGLISH AND AMERICAN LITERATURE **EDUCATION** Whitman Col, BA, 66; Columbia Univ, MA, 67, PhD (English and Am lit), 72. **CAREER** Asst prof humanities, 72-76, ASSOC PROF HUMANITIES, NORTHERN KY UNIV, 77-; Fulbright lectr Am Lit, Univ Deusto, Bilbao, Spain, 76-77. **MEMBERSHIPS** MLA; Am Comp Lit Asn. **RESEARCH** Nineteenth century fiction; music and literature; British novel. **SELECTED PUBLICATIONS** Auth, Melville Prints in The Reese Collection, Harvard Libr Bul, Vol 4, 93; Melville Prints, the Ambrose Group, Harvard Libr Bul, Vol 6,95. **CONTACT ADDRESS** Dept of Lit and Lang, No Kentucky Univ, Highland Heights, KY, 41076.

WALLACE, RONALD WILLIAM
PERSONAL Born 02/18/1945, Cedar Rapids, IA, m, 1968, 2 children **DISCIPLINE** MODERN LITERATURE **EDUCATION** Col Wooster, BA, 67; Univ Mich, MA, 68, PhD, 71. **CAREER** Assoc prof, 72-80, prof English & Dir Creative Writing, Univ of Wis-Madison, 80-; Am Coun Learned Soc fel comic novel, 75-76; Am Coun Learned Soc fel humor in poetry, 81. **HONORS AND AWARDS** Hopwood Award for poetry, Univ Mich, 70; Scholarly Book Award, Coun Wis Writers, 80. **MEMBERSHIPS** MLA; Poets & Writers; Acad Am Poets. **RESEARCH** Modern comic novel; contemporary poetry; humor. **SELECTED PUBLICATIONS** Auth, Henry James and the Comic Form, Univ Mich, 75; Installing the Bees (poems), Chowder, 77; Cucumbers (poems), Pendle Hill, 77; Never mind that the nag's a pile of bones: The modern comic novel and the comic tradition, Tex Studies Lit & Lang, 77; The Last Laugh: Form and Affirmation in the Contemporary American Comic Novel, 79; Plums, Stones, Kisses & Hooks (poems), 81; Babble and Doodle: Introducing Students to Poetry, Col English, 81; Tunes for Bears to Dance to (poems), Univ Pittsburgh Press, 83; God Be With the Clown: Humor in American Poetry, Univ Mo Press, 84; People and Day in the Sun (poems), Univ Pittsburgh Press, 87; The Makings of Happiness (poems), Univ Pittsburgh Press, 91; Time's Fancy (poems), Univ Pittsburgh Press, 94; The Uses of Adversity (poems), Univ Pittsburgh Press, 98. **CONTACT ADDRESS** Dept of English, Univ of Wis, 600 North Park St, Madison, WI, 53706-1403. **EMAIL** rwallace@facstaff.wisc.edu

WALLEN, MARTIN
DISCIPLINE BRITISH ROMANTICISM **EDUCATION** Vanderbilt, PhD, 85. **CAREER** Engl, Okla St Univ. **RESEARCH** British Romantic Poetry; continental philos - Schelling, Heidegger. **SELECTED PUBLICATIONS** Auth, Coleridge's Ancient Mariner: Texts and Revisions, 1798-1828, Station Hill Press, 93. **CONTACT ADDRESS** Oklahoma State Univ, 101 Whitehurst Hall, Stillwater, OK, 74078.

WALLENSTEIN, BARRY JAY
PERSONAL Born 02/13/1940, New York, NY, m, 1978, 2 children **DISCIPLINE** CONTEMPORARY LITERATURE, MODERN POETRY **EDUCATION** NY Univ, BA, 62, MA, 64, PhD (lit), 72. **CAREER** Lectr English, Stern Col, Yeshiva Univ, 63-64; prof English, 65-, dir, Poetry Outreach Center, City Col New York; Res Found grant, City Univ New York, 72-75, 81-82, & 94-95. **HONORS AND AWARDS** Macdowell Colony Fel, 95. **MEMBERSHIPS** Academy of American Poets; Poet's House. **RESEARCH** Poetry, especially contemporary and critical theory. **SELECTED PUBLICATIONS** Coauth, Years of Protest (Collection of Writings from the 1930's), Pegasus, 67; auth, Visions and Revisions: An Approach to Poetry, Crowell, 71; contribr, American Literary Naturalism, Carl Winter Univ, Heidelberg, 75; auth, Beast is a Wolf with Brown Fire (poetry), BOA Ed, 77; Roller Coaster Kid (poetry), Crowell, 82; Love and Crush, Persea Books, 91; The Short Life of the Five Minute Dancer, Ridgeway Press, 93. **CONTACT ADDRESS** Dept of English, City Col, CUNY, 138th St at Convent Ave, New York, NY, 10031-9198.

WALLING, WILLIAM
PERSONAL Born 12/19/1932, New York, NY, m, 1957, 2 children **DISCIPLINE** ROMANTICISM, AMERICAN LITERATURE **EDUCATION** Brooklyn Col, BA, 55; NY Univ, MA, 62, PhD(English), 66. **CAREER** Lectr English, City Col New York, Uptown, 62-63; from instr to assoc prof, 65-74, chmn dept, 72-77, chmn dept Humanities, 75-77, prof English, Univ Col, Rutgers Univ, New Brunswick, 74-, Chief reader, Educ Testing Serv, 78-; Fulbright-Hays sr lectureship, 69-70. **MEMBERSHIPS** MLA; AAUP; Wordsworth Circle. **RESEARCH** Literature; art; film. **SELECTED PUBLICATIONS** Auth, Mary Shelley, Twayne, 72; Tradition and Revolution: Byron's vision of judgment, Wordsworth Circle, Autumn 72; Ralph Ellison's Invisible Man, Phylon, 3 & 6/73; Hegel, helas, Partisan Rev, 75; The glorious anxiety of motion: Jane Austen's Persuasion, Wordsworth Circle, Autumn 76; contribr, Candy in Context, NJ Lit Forum, Spring 78; contribr & translr, Jean Starobinski, Andre Chenier, In: Images of Romanticism, Yale Univ, 78; co-ed & contribr, Images of Romanticism, Yale Univ, 78. **CONTACT ADDRESS** Dept of English, Rutgers Univ, 510 George St, New Brunswick, NJ, 08901-1167.

WALLIS, CARRIE G.
PERSONAL Clarksdale, MS, m, 1998 **DISCIPLINE** LIBRARY & INFORMATION SCIENCE **EDUCATION** Belhaven Col, BA, 98. **MEMBERSHIPS** Am Libr Asn; Special Libr Asn. **CONTACT ADDRESS** 307 Cedar Crest Sq, Apt. C, Tuscaloosa, AL, 35401. **EMAIL** cokeefe3@slis.ua.edu

WALLWORK, ERNEST
PERSONAL Born 10/06/1937, Orange, NJ, m, 1973, 2 children **DISCIPLINE** HUMANITIES **EDUCATION** Harvard Univ, PhD 71; Yale Univ, Mdiv 64; Harvard Business Sch, MBA 61; Bucknell Univ, BS 59. **CAREER** Syracuse Univ, prof 83 to 99-; National Inst Health, bioethicist 87-89; SUNY Health Sci Cen, adj prof, 84-99; Yale Univ, assoc prof, 74-79. **HONORS AND AWARDS** Woodrow Wilson Fel; Who's Who in the World; D R Sharpe lectr; Phi Beta Kappa; NEH; Major Figure for SSR. **MEMBERSHIPS** APA; APA; AAR; SCE; WPS. **RESEARCH** Psychoanalysis and Ethics; ethical theory and confidentiality. **SELECTED PUBLICATIONS** Auth, Psychoanalysis and Ethics, Yale Univ Press, 91; Critical Issues in Modern Religion, coauth, 2nd ed, Prentice Hall 90; Durkheim: Morality and Milieu, Harvard Press, 72. **CONTACT ADDRESS** Dept of religion, Syracuse Univ, 3021 Davenport St N W, Washington, DC, 20008. **EMAIL** eewallwork@juno.com

WALMSLEY, PETER
DISCIPLINE ENGLISH LITERATURE **EDUCATION** Univ Toronto, BA, MA; Cambridge Univ, PhD. **RESEARCH** British literature 1660-1800; histories of philosophy and science; 17th and 18th century philosophical writing. **SELECTED PUBLICATIONS** Auth, The Rhetoric of Berkeley's Philosophy and Thought, 90. **CONTACT ADDRESS** English Dept, McMaster Univ, 1280 Main St W, Hamilton, ON, L8S 4L9.

WALSER, RICHARD
PERSONAL Born 10/23/1908, Lexington, NC **DISCIPLINE** AMERICAN LITERATURE **EDUCATION** Univ NC, AB, 29, AM, 33. **CAREER** Teacher high schs, 30-42; instr English, Univ NC, 46; From instr to prof, 46-70, EMER PROF ENGLISH, NC STATE UNIV, 70-; Guggenheim fel, 57-58. **HONORS AND AWARDS** Gold Medallion Award, State of NC, 76. **MEMBERSHIPS** MLA **RESEARCH** Folklore; American humor; Thomas Wolf. **SELECTED PUBLICATIONS** Auth, Headbangers in The Worldwide Megabook of Heavy Metal Bands, Notes, Vol 50, 93; Out of Notes, Signification, Interpretation, and the Problem of Davis, Miles, Musical Quart, Vol 77, 93; Heavy Metal in a Cultural Sociology, Notes, Vol 49, 93; Disciplining Music in Musicology and Its Canons, Mus Letters, Vol 74, 93; A Passion for Polka in Old Time Ethnic Music in america, Am Music, Vol 12, 94; Theorizing the Body in african American Music, Black Mus Res J, Vol 14, 94; Rock and Popular Music in Politics, Policies, Institutions, Notes, Vol 51, 95; Heavy Metal Music and Response to Bjornberg, Alf Rev of Running with the Devil, Mus Letters, Vol 76, 95; Rhythm, Rhyme, and Rhetoric in The Music of Public Enemy, Ethnomusicology, Vol 39, 95; Its Not about a Salary in Rap, Race, and Resistance in Los Angeles, Ethnomusicology, Vol 39, 95; Kleist in Paris, AkzenteinZeitschrift Lit, Vol 43, 96; Adolescents and Their Music in If Its Too Loud, Youre Too Old, Notes, Vol 53, 96; Der Schriftsteller, AkzenteinZeitschrift Lit, Vol 43, 96; The Sex Revolts in Gender, Rebellion, and Rock NinRoll S, Notes, Vol 53, 97. **CONTACT ADDRESS** 3929 Arrow Drive, Raleigh, NC, 27612.

WALSH, CHAD
PERSONAL Born 05/10/1914, South Boston, VA, m, 1938, 4 children **DISCIPLINE** ENGLISH **EDUCATION** Univ Va, AB, 38; Univ Mich, AM, 39, PhD, 43. **CAREER** Res analyst, US War Dept, 43-45; From asst prof to prof English, Beloit Col, 45-77, chmn dept, 62-70, writer-in-residence, 71-77; RETIRED. Asst priest, St Pauls Episcopal Church, Beloit, Wis, 48-77; vis distinguished prof English and religion, Juniata Col, 77-78. **HONORS AND AWARDS** DLitt, Rockford Col, 63 and St Norbert Col, 72. **RESEARCH** The preposition at the end of a clause in early Middle English; utopian and dystopian literature; relation between religion and the arts. **SELECTED PUBLICATIONS** Auth, Realist Fiction and The Strolling Spectator, Notes Queries, Vol 40, 93; The Voices in Karshish in a Bakhtinian Reading of Browning, Robert Epistle, Victorian Poetry, Vol 31, 93; Nabokov, Vladimir, Notes Queries, Vol 40, 93;

Lawrence,D.H, Notes Queries, Vol 40, 93; Keneally, Thomas, Notes Queries, Vol 40, 93; Writers on Writing in an Anthology, Notes Queries, Vol 41, 94; Narrative Innovation and Incoherence in Ideology, Notes Queries, Vol 41, 94; The Incarnation and The Christian Socialist Conscience In The Victorian Church of England, J Brit Studies, Vol 34, 95; Stardom is Born in The Religion and Economy of Publicity, Am Lit Realism 1870in10, Vol 29, 97. **CONTACT ADDRESS** 745 Church St, Beloit, WI, 53511.

WALSH, DENNIS
DISCIPLINE ENGLISH LITERATURE **EDUCATION** Univ Notre Dame, PhD, 73. **CAREER** Prof. **SELECTED PUBLICATIONS** Auth, pubs in Studies in Short Fiction, The Journal of Technical Writing and Communication, and The American Indian Journal of Culture and Research; co-ed, The Idaho Stories and Far West Illustrations of Mary Hallock Foote. **CONTACT ADDRESS** Dept of English and Philosophy, Idaho State Univ, Pocatello, ID, 83209. **EMAIL** walsdenn@isu.edu

WALSH, ELIZABETH
PERSONAL Born 05/30/1933, Cumberland, MD **DISCIPLINE** ENGLISH LITERATURE, MEDIEVAL STUDIES **EDUCATION** Manhattanville Col, BA, 55, MA, 63; Harvard Univ, PhD (English and Am lit), 73. **CAREER** Sec sch teacher English and related subjects, Acad of the Sacred Heart, Conn, 59-63 and Albany, NY, 64-67; dean freshman class, Manhattanville Col, 67; teaching fel English, Harvard Univ, 70-72, resident tutor, 72-73, instr, 73-74; asst prof, La State Univ, Baton Rouge, 74-75; asst prof, 75-78, ASSOC PROF ENGLISH, UNIV SAN DIEGO, 78-; Am Coun Learned Soc travel grant, 78. **MEMBERSHIPS** MLA; Medieval Acad Am; Asn Scottish Lit Studies; Dante Soc Am; Medieval Asn Pac. **RESEARCH** The concept of the hero in epic and romance; cultural influences on fifteenth and sixteenth century Scottish literature. **SELECTED PUBLICATIONS** Auth, 3 Middle English Charlemagne Romances in The Sultan of Babylon, the Siege of Milan, and The Tale of Ralph the Collier,J Medieval Studies, Vol 68, 93. **CONTACT ADDRESS** Dept of English, Univ of San Diego, 5998 Alcala Park, San Diego, CA, 92110-2492.

WALSH, GRACE
PERSONAL Born 06/18/1910, St. Paul, MN **DISCIPLINE** SPEECH **EDUCATION** Wis State Col, BE, 32; Univ Wis, PhM, 39. **CAREER** Teacher, high sch, Wis, 32-42, 43-44 and Iowa, 42-43; prof, 45-80, EMER PROF SPEECH AND DIR FORENSICS, UNIV WIS-EAU CLAIRE, 80-. **MEMBERSHIPS** Speech Commun Asn; Cent States Speech Asn; NEA; Am Forensic Asn. **RESEARCH** Intercollegiate discussion, debate and oratory. **SELECTED PUBLICATIONS** Auth, A Bibliography of African Language Texts in the Collections of the School of Oriental and African Studies University of London, Int J African Hist Stud, Vol 28, 95. **CONTACT ADDRESS** Dept of Speech, Univ of Wis, Eau Claire, WI, 54701.

WALSH, JONATHAN D.
DISCIPLINE 17TH AND 18TH CENTURY FRENCH THEATER AND PROSE **EDUCATION** Univ Calif, Santa Barbara, PhD. **CAREER** Fr, Wheaton Col. **RESEARCH** Psychoanalysis and literature; jealousy and symbolic exchange in the French novel; French moralists and philosophes. **SELECTED PUBLICATIONS** Publ, on Abbo Provost, Marcel Proust and Enlightenment authors appear in Romance Quart and Esprit Createur. **CONTACT ADDRESS** Dept of Fr, Wheaton Col, 26 East Main St, Norton, MA, 02766.

WALSH, MARY ELLEN
DISCIPLINE ENGLISH LITERATURE **EDUCATION** Univ Ariz, PhD, 71. **CAREER** Prof. **RESEARCH** Feminism; Western women's writing; institutional issues of race and gender. **SELECTED PUBLICATIONS** Auth, A Vast Landscape: Time in the Novels of Thornton Wilder; Angle of Repose and the Writing of Mary Hallock Foote: a Source Study; co-ed, The Idaho Stories and Far West Illustrations of Mary Hallock Foote. **CONTACT ADDRESS** Dept of English and Philosophy, Idaho State Univ, Pocatello, ID, 83209. **EMAIL** walsmary@isu.edu

WALSH, PATRICK F.
PERSONAL North Adams, MA **DISCIPLINE** ENGLISH LITERATURE **EDUCATION** St. Francis Xavier Univ, BA, 58; Boston Col, MA, 67; Nat Univ Ireland, PhD, 73. **CAREER** Dept Eng, Xavier Univ **HONORS AND AWARDS** Univ Outreach Awd. **MEMBERSHIPS** Playwrights' Union Can. **RESEARCH** Modern drama; film; creative writing. **SELECTED PUBLICATIONS** Auth, The History of Antigonish; pubs about Ireland. **CONTACT ADDRESS** English Dept, St Francis Xavier Univ, Antigonish, NS, B2G 2W5. **EMAIL** pwalsh@stfx.ca

WALSH, THOMAS M.
DISCIPLINE RENAISSANCE LITERATURE **EDUCATION** Saint Louis Univ, PhD. **CAREER** Eng Dept, St. Edward's Univ **SELECTED PUBLICATIONS** Coauth, The Praise of Folly in Context: The Commentary of Gerardus Listrius, Renaissance Quart, 71; Mark Twain and the Art of Memory, Am Lit, 81. **CONTACT ADDRESS** St Edward's Univ, 3001 S Congress Ave, Austin, TX, 78704-6489.

WALTON, JAMES EDWARD
PERSONAL Born 09/13/1944, Bessemer, Alabama, m **DISCIPLINE** ENGLISH **EDUCATION** Andrews Univ, 1962-64; Kent State Univ, BS 1964-66; University of Akron, MA 1970-73, PhD 1973-78. **CAREER** Canton McKinley HS, english teacher 1967-70; Mount Union College, assoc prof of english 1970-. **MEMBERSHIPS** Dir Freedom House Project 1975; member Jaycees 1975; yearbook advisor Mount Union College 1975-83; board member Stark County Fair Housing Comm 1978-; board member Assoc for Better Community Development 1984-; member Alliance City Planning Commission 1984-. **SELECTED PUBLICATIONS** Poetry, essays Black Arts Society, Ohio State Univ 1971; essay English Language Arts Bulletin 1980; article Natl Council of Teachers of English 1980; essayModern Language Association 1985. **CONTACT ADDRESS** Mount Union Col, 1972 Clark Ave, Alliance, OH, 44601.

WALTON, JAMES H.
DISCIPLINE 18TH-CENTURY BRITISH LITERATURE **EDUCATION** Northwestern Univ, PhD. **CAREER** Instr, Univ Notre Dame. **RESEARCH** The child in English literature. **SELECTED PUBLICATIONS** Auth, The Romance of Gentility: Defoe's Heroes and Heroines; Margaret's Book. **CONTACT ADDRESS** Univ Notre Dame, Notre Dame, IN, 46556.

WALZ, EUGENE P.
DISCIPLINE ENGLISH LITERATURE **EDUCATION** St. John Fisher Univ, BA; Univ Ind, MA; Univ Mass, PhD. **CAREER** Assoc prof **HONORS AND AWARDS** Pres, Film Studies Asn Can. **RESEARCH** Canadian films; film genres; screenwriting; American films of the 30s and 60s; cultural studies. **SELECTED PUBLICATIONS** Auth, pub(s) on Francois Truffaut, crime films, Canadian films, Manitoba films and filmmakers. **CONTACT ADDRESS** Dept of English, Manitoba Univ, Winnipeg, MB, R3T 2N2.

WALZER, ARTHUR E.
DISCIPLINE RHETORIC STUDIES **EDUCATION** Univ Minn, MA, PhD. **CAREER** Assoc prof **RESEARCH** Rhetorical theory and criticism; 18th-century rhetorical theory; Aristotle's rhetoric; ethics and technical communication. **SELECTED PUBLICATIONS** Auth, The Meanings of 'Purpose', Rhet Rev, 91; Aristotle's Rhetoric, Dialogism, and Contemorary Research in Composition, Rhet Rev, 97; Rhetoric and Gender in Jane Austen's Persuasion, Col English, 95; Positivists, Postmodernists, Aristotelians, and the Challenger Disaster, Col English, 94; co-auth, The Challenger Disaster and the Revival of Rhetoric in Organizational Communication, Argumentation, 97. **CONTACT ADDRESS** Rhetoric Dept, Univ of Minnesota, Twin Cities, 64 Classroom Office Bldg, 1994 Buford Ave, St. Paul, MN, 55108. **EMAIL** awalzer@maroon.tc.umn.edu

WANCA-THIBAULT, MARYANNE
DISCIPLINE COMMUNICATIONS **EDUCATION** Univ Colo, BS, MA, PhD. **CAREER** Asst prof. **RESEARCH** Feminist issues as they affect organizations. **SELECTED PUBLICATIONS** Co-auth, Commun Interaction: A Practical Guide for Effective Skills, Observation, Analysis Presentation; Interactions Skills and Analysis: Workbook. **CONTACT ADDRESS** Commun Dept, Univ Colo, PO Box 7150, Colorado Springs, CO, 80933-7150.

WANG, BAN
DISCIPLINE ENGLISH AND COMPARATIVE LITERATURE **EDUCATION** Beijing Foreign Studies Univ, BA, 82, MA, 85; Univ Iowa, PhD, 90; Univ Ca, PhD, 93. **CAREER** Asst prof, 93-. **SELECTED PUBLICATIONS** Auth, The Sublime Figure of History: Aesthetics and Politics in Twentieth-Century China, Stanford, 97; Personal Reminiscences on Cultural Mix in East Asian Studies, 96. **CONTACT ADDRESS** English Dept, SUNY Stony Brook, Stony Brook, NY, 11794. **EMAIL** banwang@ccmail.sunysb.edu

WANG, JOAN PARSONS
PERSONAL Born 10/21/1925, Cincinnait, OH, w, 2 children **DISCIPLINE** ENGLISH, COMPARATIVE LITERATURE **EDUCATION** Radcliffe Col, AB, 47; Brown Univ, MA, 49; Ind Univ, PhD (comp lit), 64. **CAREER** Asst prof, 66-80, ASSOC PROF ENGLISH, INDEPENDENT STUDIES DIV, SCH CONTINUING STUDIES, IND UNIV, BLOOMINGTON, 80-. **HONORS AND AWARDS** Cert Merit, Nat Univ Exten Asn, 71 and 81. **MEMBERSHIPS** Nat Univ Exten Asn. **RESEARCH** Writing syllabi for indePENdent study courses in English and world literature; modern European drama; women's studies. **SELECTED PUBLICATIONS** Auth, the Muslim Protest in China and An Analysis of the Marxist in Islamic Confrontations, Temenos, Vol 32, 96. **CONTACT ADDRESS** Dept of English, Indiana Univ, Bloomington, Bloomington, IN, 47401.

WANG, MASON YU-HENG
PERSONAL Born 05/07/1936, China, m, 1963, 3 children **DISCIPLINE** SHAKESPEARE, COMPARATIVE LITERATURE **EDUCATION** Nat Taiwan Univ, BA, 59; IN Univ, MA, 65, PhD(English), 72. **CAREER** Instr English, Cent MO State Col, 65-68; from instr to asst prof, 69-76, chmn dept, 74-78, assoc prof, 76-83, PROF ENGLISH SAGINAW VALLEY STATE UNIV, 83-. **MEMBERSHIPS** Shakespeare Asn Am. **RESEARCH** Shakespeare; comparative literature; Chinese literature. **SELECTED PUBLICATIONS** Auth, Burlesque and Irony in The Two Gentlemen of Verona, Shakespeare Newslett, 9/72; Review of Ten Poems and Lyrics by Mao Tse-tung, Green River Rev, 76; ed, Perspectives in Contemporary Chinese Literature, Green River Press, 83; tr & ed, Zhang Siyang, Hamlet's Melancholy, and Zhang Xiaoyang, Shakespeare and the Idea of Nature in the Renaissance, Shakespeare and the Triple Play, ed Sidney Homan, Bucknell Univ Press, 88; contrib & ed, Meng Xianqiang. A Historical .Survey of Shakespeare in China, Shakespeare Res Center of NE Normal Univ, 96. **CONTACT ADDRESS** Dept of English, Saginaw Valley State Univ, 7400 Bay Rd, University Center, MI, 48710-0001. **EMAIL** mywang@tardis.svsu.edu

WANIEK, MARILYN NELSON
PERSONAL Born 04/26/1946, Cleveland, OH, m, 1979, 1 child **DISCIPLINE** AMERICAN LITERATURE **EDUCATION** Univ Calif, Davis, BA, 64; Univ Pa, MA, 70; Univ Minn, PhD (English), 79. **CAREER** Instr English, Lane Community Col, 70-72 and St Olaf Col, 74-79; ASST PROF ENGLISH, UNIV CONN, 79-; Vis asst prof, Reed Col, 71-72; vis lectr, Nv Nissum Seminarium, Denmark, 72-73; prof, Univ Hamburg, Ger, 77. **MEMBERSHIPS** MLA; Northeast Mod Lang Asn; Soc Study Multi-Ethnic Lit US. **RESEARCH** American ethnic literature; modern and contemporary Afro-American poetry; modern American poetry. **SELECTED PUBLICATIONS** Auth, Blessing the Boats, Am Poet Rev, Vol 23, 94; Post Prandial Conversation, Kenyon Rev, Vol 17, 95; Abba Jacob in the Well, Kenyon Rev, Vol 17, 95. **CONTACT ADDRESS** Dept of English, Univ of Conn, Storrs, CT, 06268.

WARD, AILEEN
PERSONAL Newark, NJ **DISCIPLINE** ENGLISH LITERATURE **EDUCATION** Smith Col, BA, 40; Radcliffe Col, MA, 42, PhD, 53. **CAREER** Teaching fel and tutor, Radcliffe Col, 43-45; instr English, Wellesley Col, 46-47 and Barnard Col, 47-49; assoc, Inst Int Educ, 52-53 and Found Advan Educ, 53; asst prof English, Vassar Col, 54-58; mem fac, Sarah Lawrence Col, 60-64; prof English, Brandeis Univ, 64-75, chmn dept, 73-74; prof, NY Univ, 75-78; prof English, 78-80, SCHWEITZER PROF HUMANITIES, BRANDEIS UNIV, 80-; Writing fel, Yaddo, 54-55, 66-67 and 71; Am Asn Univ Women Shirley Farr fel, 58-59; Guggenheim fel, 66-67; Radcliffe Inst fel, Cambridge, 70-71; chmn, English Inst, 76; mem bd, Keats-Shelley ASn, 77-; AM CTR, PEN, 77-; NEW YORK INST HUMANITIES FEL, 78-. **HONORS AND AWARDS** LittD, Skidmore Col, 73. **RESEARCH** The life of William Blake. **SELECTED PUBLICATIONS** Auth, Historical Claims Under the Treaty of Waitangi in avenue of Reconciliation or Source of New Divisions, J Pac Hist, Vol 28, 93; Which Side Are You on in the Rebellion Causes Pride and Pain for One Observer Who is Half Asian, Half Black, Amerasia J, Vol , 93; Blind Justice or Blinkered Vision, Meanjin, Vol 52, 93; Singer in a Songless Land in a Life of Tregear, Edward 1846-1931, Australian Hist Stud, Vol 25, 93; In Defense of Cbto, Opera, Vol 44, 93; Private and Public, Individuals, Households, and Body Politic in Locke and Hutcheson, Albion, Vol 26, 94; Seattle for the Wary Traveler, Am Heritage, Vol 45, 94; Seattle, Am Heritage, Vol 45, 94; Who Was Blake, Robert, Blake an Illustrated Quart, Vol 28, 95; Traveling the High Way Home in Stanley, Ralph and the World of Traditional Bluegrass Music, Folk Music J, Vol 7, 95; Hollywood History, American Heritage, Vol 46, 95; Dangerous Liaisons in Essays in Honor of Dening, Greg, J Pac Hist, Vol 31, 96; Oleary, Johnny of Sliabh Luachra in Dance Music from the Cork Kerry Border, Folk Music J, Vol 7, 96; Pacific Islands in Journeys and Transformations, J of Pac Hist, Vol 31, 96; New Wagnerism, Opera, Vol 47, 96; Psychoanalysis and its Critics and a Discussion with Michels, Robert Followed by a Question and Answer Session with the Audience, Partisan Rev, Vol 64, 97; Make a Better Offer in the Politics of Mabo, Meanjin, Vol 54, 95; Dimensioni Del Viaggio, No.8, Forum Italicum, Vol 31, 97; A Tribute to Sorrenson, Keith, New Zealand J of Hist, Vol 31, 97;. **CONTACT ADDRESS** Waltham, MA.

WARD, CAROL
DISCIPLINE ENGLISH LITERATURE **EDUCATION** Univ Tenn, PhD, 81. **CAREER** Dept Eng, Clemson Univ **RESEARCH** Film studies; women's literature. **SELECTED PUBLICATIONS** Auth, Rita Mae Brown, Twayne, 93; Rita Mae Brown, Reference Guide to American Literature, 94; Southern Landscape in Contemporary Film, Beyond the Stars: Locales in American Popular Film, 93. **CONTACT ADDRESS** Clemson Univ, 707 Strode, Clemson, SC, 29634. **EMAIL** wardc@clemson.edu

WARD, CAROLE GENEVA
PERSONAL Born 01/14/1943, Phoenix City, Alabama **DISCIPLINE** ENGLISH, FILM **EDUCATION** CA State Univ at San Jose, BA 1965; MA 1973; Univ of CA, Grad Studies 1970; Intl Comm Coll, PhD; Univ of Ile-Ife Nigeria, 1970; Univ of Sci & Tech, 1970; Kumasi Ghana Forah Bay Coll Sierra Leone, 1970; Sorbonne, 1963. **CAREER** Ethnic Studies Laney Coll,

chrwmn; Goddard Coll, mentor consult teacher for masters degree stud 1973-74; Laney Coll, 1970-; CA Coll of Arts Cabrillo Coll, 1970; Andrew Hill HS, 1965-69; airline stewardess, 1966-68. **HONORS AND AWARDS** Recip purchase award 27th Annual SF Art Festival 1973; alpha phi alpha award outstanding black woman for achvmnt & serv 1974; selec com chmn for Black Filmmakers Hall of Fame Paramount Theatre of the Arts; publ Images of Awareness Pan Africanist Mag 1973; Afro-Am Artists Bio-Biographical Dir Theres Dickason 1973; black artist on Art Vol 2 by Samella Lewis Ruth Waddy 1970. **MEMBERSHIPS** Mem Bay Area Black Artists 1972-; Nat Conf of Artists 1973-74. **CONTACT ADDRESS** Laney Coll, 900 Fallon St, Oakland, CA, 94607.

WARD, HERMAN M.
PERSONAL Born 03/11/1914, Jersey City, NJ, m, 1943, 4 children **DISCIPLINE** ENGLISH **EDUCATION** Montclair State Col, AB, 35; Princeton Univ, AM, 37, PhD, 40. **CAREER** Asst prof English, Jersey City State Col, 46-47; prof, 46-77, EMER PROF ENGLISH, TRENTON STATE COL, 77-; Fulbright fel, Anatolia Col, Greece, 52-53, Univ Iceland, 62-63; consult English, Princeton High Sch, 61-62; exchange prof, Univ Frankfurt, 66-67. **MEMBERSHIPS** NCTE **RESEARCH** Teaching of high school English; Irish and Greek literature; creative writing. **SELECTED PUBLICATIONS** Auth, Yankee Sailors in British Jails, Prisoners of War at Forton and Mill, 1777-1783, William Mary Quart, Vol 53, 96; Lincoln, Benjamin and the American Revolution, Va Quart Rev, Vol 72, 96; Escape in america, the British Convention Prisoners, 1777-1783, William Mary Quart, Vol 53, 96. **CONTACT ADDRESS** RD No 2, Belle Mead, NJ, 08502.

WARD, JEAN M.
PERSONAL Born 01/14/1938, Eugene, OR, m, 1960, 2 children **DISCIPLINE** SPEECH **EDUCATION** Univ OR, BS, 60, MS, 64, PhD, 89. **CAREER** Teacher high sch, Fern Ridge Sch Dist, OR, 62-64; instr speech commun, 64-67, asst prof, 67-72, assoc prof, 72-79, prof commmun, Lewis & Clark Col, 80-, chp dept commun, 74-. **MEMBERSHIPS** Nat Speech Commun Asn; Nat Women's Studies Asn; Western Speech Asn. **RESEARCH** Women in American public address; protest rhetoric; American Studies. **SELECTED PUBLICATIONS** Ed, Dollars for Education, 72, co-ed, Democratic Alternatives, 74 & In Short Supply, 75, Nat Textbk; Pacific Northwest Women, 1815-1925, Cosu Press, 95. **CONTACT ADDRESS** Dept Commun, Lewis & Clark Col, 0615 SW Palatine Hill Rd, Portland, OR, 97219-7879. **EMAIL** jean@lclark.edu

WARD, JERRY WASHINGTON, JR.
PERSONAL Born 07/31/1943, Washington, District of Columbia, s **DISCIPLINE** ENGLISH **EDUCATION** Tougaloo College, Tougaloo, MS, BS, 1964; Illinois Institute of Technology, Chicago, IL, MS, 1966; University of Virginia, Charlottesville, VA, PhD, 1978. **CAREER** SUNY at Albany, Albany, NY, teaching fellow, 1966-68; Tougaloo College, Tougaloo, MS, professor of English, 1970-; National Endowment for the Humanities, Washington, DC, program officer, 1985; Commonwealth Center, University of Virginia, Charlottesville, VA, program director/professor, 1990-91. **HONORS AND AWARDS** Kent Fellowship, 1975-77; Tougaloo College, Outstanding Teaching Award, 1978-80, 1992; UNCF Distinguished Scholar Award, 1981-82; UNCF Distinguished Scholar-in-Residence, 1987-88; Moss Professor, Univ of Memphis, 1996. **MEMBERSHIPS** Member, Alpha Phi Alpha Fraternity, Inc, 1961-; member, Black Studies Committee, College Language Assn, 1977-91; chair, Division of Black American Literature, Modern Language Assn, 1986-87; member, Mississippi Advisory Committee, US Civil Rights Commission, 1988-98; member, The Authors Guild, 1988-. **CONTACT ADDRESS** Professor, Dept of English, 500 W County Line Road, Tougaloo, MS, 39174.

WARD, JOHN C.
DISCIPLINE ENGLISH LITERATURE **EDUCATION** Amherst Col, BA; Univ Va, MA, PhD. **CAREER** Fac, Kenyon Col, 70; vice pres, dean acad affairs, prof Eng, Centre Col, 90-. **HONORS AND AWARDS** Asst ed, Kenyon Rev; rdr, Jour Midwest MLA. **MEMBERSHIPS** Midwest MLA. **SELECTED PUBLICATIONS** Auth, poetry, literary biography, and literary criticism. **CONTACT ADDRESS** Centre Col, 600 W Walnut St, Danville, KY, 40422. **EMAIL** wardj@centre.edu

WARD, ROBERT ERNEST
PERSONAL Born 04/17/1927, Utica, NY, m, 1969 **DISCIPLINE** EIGHTEENTH CENTURY ENGLISH LITERATURE **EDUCATION** Syracuse Univ, AB, 53; State Univ NY Albany, MA, 54; Univ Iowa, PhD, 69. **CAREER** Teacher English, Bainbridge Cent Sch, NY, 54-55 & Utica Free Acad, 55-65; asst prof, 69-73, assoc prof, 73-77, prof English, PROF EMER, WESTERN KY UNIV, 77- **MEMBERSHIPS** Can Asn Irish Stud. **RESEARCH** Anglo-Irish culture. **SELECTED PUBLICATIONS** Auth, Prince of Dublin Printers: The Letters of George Faulkner, Univ Ky, 72; coauth, Checklist and Census of 400 Imprints of G Faulkner, 1725-1775, Ragnarok, 73; auth, Literary reactions to the penal laws: Jonathan Swift and Charles O'Conor of Belanagare, In: Conflict in Ireland, Renaissance Publ Co, 77; coauth (with Catherine Coogan Ward), The ordeal of O'Conor of Belanagare, Eire-Ireland, summer 79; The Catholic pamphlets of Charles O'Conor of Belanagare, Studies, Irish Quart, winter 79; co-ed (with Catherine Coogan Ward), The Letters of Charles O'Conor of Belanagare, Vol I & Vol II, Univ Microfilms Int, 80; rev ed The Letters of Charles O'Conor of Belanagare, Cath Univ Am Press, 88; An Encyclopedia of Irish Schools 1500-1800, Edwin Mellen Press, 95. **EMAIL** wardre@wku.edu

WARE, TRACY
DISCIPLINE ENGLISH LITERATURE **EDUCATION** Univ Western Ontario, PhD. **CAREER** Dept Eng, Queen's Univ **HONORS AND AWARDS** W.J. Barnes Tchg Awd, 97. **RESEARCH** Canadian poetry; Canadian and Australian literary history; Romanticism past and present. **SELECTED PUBLICATIONS** Auth, pubs on the Canadian canon, writing of Canadian literary history, and Confederation poets; ed, Levi Adams, Jean Baptiste, Can Poetry, 96. **CONTACT ADDRESS** English Dept, Queen's Univ, Kingston, ON, K7L 3N6.

WARKENTIN, GERMAINE
PERSONAL Toronto, ON, Canada **DISCIPLINE** ENGLISH **EDUCATION** Univ Toronto, BA, 55, PhD, 72; Univ Man, MA, 62. **CAREER** Freelance film critic, 53-64; ed, Canadian Newsreel, 54-57; lectr, United Col, Winnipeg, 58-59; lectr, Victoria Col, 70-72, asst prof, 72-76, assoc prof, 76-90, PROF ENGLISH, UNIV TORONTO, 90-, dir, Ctr Reformation & Renaissance Studs, 85-90. **MEMBERSHIPS** Renaissance English Text Soc; Spencer Soc. **SELECTED PUBLICATIONS** Auth, James Reaney, Poems, 72; auth, Canadian Exploration Writing, in English: An Anthology, 93; auth, Ins and Outs of the Sidney family Library, in Times Lit Suppl, 85. **CONTACT ADDRESS** Dept of English, Victoria Col, Univ of Toronto, Toronto, ON, M5S 1K9. **EMAIL** warkent@chass.utoronto.ca

WARNER, JOHN M.
PERSONAL Born 04/30/1935, Haydenville, MA **DISCIPLINE** ENGLISH LITERATURE **EDUCATION** Univ Mass, BA, 56; Harvard Univ, MA, 60, PhD(English) lit), 64. **CAREER** From instr to asst prof, 62-71, assoc prof, 71-78, PROF ENGLISH LIT, DREW UNIV, 78-. **MEMBERSHIPS** MLA. **RESEARCH** Eighteenth century novel; 20th century British literature; religion and literature. **SELECTED PUBLICATIONS** Auth, Smollet's development as a novelist, Novel, Vol V, 148-61; An epistemological view of the funtion of the interpolated stories in the fiction of Fielding and Smollett, Studies in Novel, Vol V, 271-83; The religious dimension of James's The Ambassadors, Essay Lit, Vol IV, 78-94; Belief and imagination in The Windhover, Hopkins Quart, Vol V, 127-135; Joyce's Grandfathers: Myth and History in Defoe, Smollett, Sterne, and Joyce, Univ Ga Press, 93. **CONTACT ADDRESS** Dept of English, Drew Univ, 36 Madison Ave., Madison, NJ, 07940-1493.

WARNER, MICHAEL D.
DISCIPLINE ENGLISH **CAREER** Asst prof English, Rutgers. **RESEARCH** English literature. **SELECTED PUBLICATIONS** Fel Publ, Textuality and Legitimacy in the Printed Constitution, Procs of AAS 97, 87; auth, Professionalization and the Rewards of Literature, 1875-1900, 85; Value, Agency, and Stephen Crane's 'The Monster,' Nineteenth-Century Fiction , 85; The Letters of the Republic: Publication and the Public Sphere in Eighteenth-Century America, Harvard Univ, 90; ed, Fear of a Queer Planet: Queer Politics and Social Theory, 93; co-ed, The Origins of Literary Studies in America, Routledge, 89; co-ed, The English Literatures of America, 1500-1800, Routledge, 97. **CONTACT ADDRESS** Dept of English, Rutgers Univ, New Brunswick, NJ, 08903. **EMAIL** mwarner@interport.net.

WARNER, NICHOLAS OLIVER
PERSONAL Born 02/11/1950, San Francisco, CA, m, 3 children **DISCIPLINE** COMPARATIVE ; ENGLISH & AMERICAN LITERATURE **EDUCATION** Stanford Univ, BA, 72; Univ Calif, Berkeley, PhD, 77. **CAREER** Vis asst prof Eng, Oberlin Col, 78-80; asst prof Lit, Claremont McKenna Col, 80-86; assoc prof, Claremont McKenna Col, 86-94; full prof, Claremont McKenna Col, 94-. **HONORS AND AWARDS** Huntton Award for Superior Tchg, 83, 84, 88, 90; Graves fel in the Humanities. **MEMBERSHIPS** MLA; Am Asn Advan Slavic Studies; Am Studies Assoc. **RESEARCH** Literature and visual arts; 19th century British, Am & Russ lit. **SELECTED PUBLICATIONS** Auth, Blakes Moon-Ark symbolism, Blake Quart, fall 80; Spirits of America: Intoxication in 19th Century American Literature, Univ Oklahoma, 97; The theme of travel in Russian and English Romanticism, Russian Lit Triquart (in press); In search of literary science! The Russian formalist tradition, Pac Coast Philol (in press). **CONTACT ADDRESS** Dept of Literature, Claremont McKenna Col, 500 E 9th St, Claremont, CA, 91711-6400. **EMAIL** nwarner@mckenna.edu

WARNER, WILLIAM BEATTY
PERSONAL Born 02/03/1947, Montpelier, VT, m, 1971 **DISCIPLINE** ENGLISH LITERATURE, CRITICAL THEORY **EDUCATION** Univ Pa, BA, 68; Johns Hopkins Univ, MA, 74, PhD (English lit), 77. **CAREER** Asst prof, 77-79, ASSOC PROF ENGLISH LIT, STATE UNIV NY BUFFALO, 79-. **MEMBERSHIPS** MLA **SELECTED PUBLICATIONS** Auth, the Profession of 18th Century Literature, Reflections on an Institution, Eighteenth Century Stud, Vol 27, 94; The Beautiful, Novel, and Strange in aesthetics and Heterodoxy, Mln-Mod Lang Notes, Vol 111, 96. **CONTACT ADDRESS** State Univ NY at Buffalo, P O Box 604610, Buffalo, NY, 14260-4610.

WARREN, CLAY
PERSONAL Born 08/11/1946, Lexington Park, MD, m, 1985, 2 children **DISCIPLINE** COMMUNICATIONS **EDUCATION** Univ of CO, PhD, 76, MA, 73; US Naval Acad, BS, 68 **CAREER** Prof, 91-, Visit Assoc Prof, 90-91, Geo Wash Univ; Assoc Prof, 84-90, Univ col of Cape Breton; Sen Laerer, 82-84; Int People's Col; Asst Prof, 79-82, Univ of HI; Asst Prof, 78-79, Shepherd Col; Visit Asst Prof, 78, univ Col of Cape Breton; Asst Prof, 77, Inst for Shipboard Educ; Inst, 73-76, Univ of CO **HONORS AND AWARDS** DMEF Fel, 96 **MEMBERSHIPS** Am Asn of Univ Profs; Nat Commun Asn **SELECTED PUBLICATIONS** Auth, Coming Around, Budapest: Mora, 86; Beds of Strange, 90 **CONTACT ADDRESS** Commun Prog, George Washington Univ, Washington, DC, 20052. **EMAIL** claywar@gwn.edu

WARREN, JAMES PERRIN
DISCIPLINE ENGLISH **EDUCATION** Auburn Univ, BA, 76; Yale Univ, MA, 80, MPhil, 81, PhD, 82. **CAREER** Teaching fel to instr, Yale Univ, 80-82; asst, Universite de Geneve, Switzerland, 82-84; asst prof to assoc prof to prof to chair, Washington & Lee Univ, 84-. **SELECTED PUBLICATIONS** Auth, Reconstructing Language in Democratic Vistas, Walt Whitman: The Centennial Essays, Univ Iowa Press, 94; art, Reading Whitman's Post-War Poetry, Utopia in the Present Tense: Walt Whitman and the Language of the New World, Rome, 94; art, Reading Whitman's Post-War Poetry, Cambridge Companion to Walt Whitman, Cambridge Univ Press, 95; auth, Style and Techniques, Walt Whitman: An Encyclopedia, Garland, 98. **CONTACT ADDRESS** 448 Hollow Lane, Lexington, VA, 24450. **EMAIL** warrenj@wlu.edu

WARREN, JOSEPH W.
PERSONAL Born 07/02/1949, Rocky Mount, North Carolina, m, 1972 **DISCIPLINE** ENGLISH **EDUCATION** Oakwood Coll, BA (summa cum laude), 1971; Ohio State Univ, MA, 1973, PhD, 1982. **CAREER** Ohio State Univ, grad asst, 1973-76; Lake Michigan Coll, adjunct professor, 1978-80; Andrews Univ, assoc professor of English, 1976-. **HONORS AND AWARDS** United Negro Coll Fund Fellowship, 1971; PhD, Fellowship, Ohio State Univ, 1971; Research Grant, Andrews Univ, 1984, 1992. **MEMBERSHIPS** Founder, Mid-Amer Network Marketing, Inc, 1984-; Inst for Christian Educ and Youth Devel, 1985-; co-founder, Scholastic Study Lab, Andrews Univ, 1984; founder, owner, Mid-Amer Premiere Brokerage, 1986-; founder, director, The Center for Building Self-Esteem in African-American Youth, 1990-. **CONTACT ADDRESS** Andrews Univ, Berrien Springs, MI, 49103.

WARREN, LELAND EDDIE
PERSONAL Born 04/22/1944, Dublin, GA, m, 1967 **DISCIPLINE** ENGLISH LITERATURE **EDUCATION** Emory Univ, BA, 66; Univ Ga, MA, 68; Univ Ill, PhD(English), 76. **CAREER** Instr English, Col William & Mary, 69-72; asst prof, 76-81, from assoc prof to prof English, 81-87, Kansas State Univ; ed, The Eighteenth Century: A Current Bibliog, 76-; co ed, Eighteenth Century Life, 81-95. **MEMBERSHIPS** MLA; Am Soc 18th Century Studies. **RESEARCH** Narrative theory; 18th century culture; satire. **SELECTED PUBLICATIONS** Auth, Wordsworth's conception of man: A study in apocalyptic vision, Southern Humanities Rev, 70; A sudden vision of life: DeQuincey's The English Mail Coach, Studies in Humanities, 72; The constant speaker: Aspects of conversation in Tristram Shandy, Univ Toronto Quart, 76; Fielding's problem and ours: Allworthy and authority in Tom Jones, Essays Lit, 78; History-As-Literature and the Narrative Stance of Henry Fielding, Clio, 79; Of the conversation of women: The female Quixote and the dream of perfection, Studies Eighteenth-Century Cult, 81. **CONTACT ADDRESS** Dept of English, Kansas State Univ, 106 Denison Hall, Manhattan, KS, 66506-0701. **EMAIL** lwarren@ksu.edu

WARREN, THOMAS
DISCIPLINE TECHNICAL WRITING **EDUCATION** Univ Kans, PhD, 74. **CAREER** Engl, Okla St Univ. **HONORS AND AWARDS** Inst Scientific & Technical Communicators; Soc Technical Comm., Pres, Erik J. Visser Fund Found; Ed, Proceedings Okla Acad Sci; Past-pres, INTECOM; fel, Asn Tchs Technical Writing; Soc Technical Comm. **RESEARCH** Cross-cultural communication; Communication theory; Document design, and graphics. **SELECTED PUBLICATIONS** Areas: cross-cultural communication, communication theory, document design, and graphics. **CONTACT ADDRESS** Oklahoma State Univ, 101 Whitehurst Hall, Stillwater, OK, 74078.

WARTELLA, ELLEN A.
PERSONAL Born 10/16/1949, Kingston, PA, m, 1976, 2 children **DISCIPLINE** MASS COMMUNICATION **EDUCATION** Univ Pittsburgh, BA, 71; Univ Minn, MA, 74, PhD, 77. **CAREER** Instr, Univ Minn, 74, 75, 76; Asst Prof, Ohio State Univ, 76-79; Res Asst Prof, 79-83, Res Assoc Prof, 83-89, Univ Schol & Res Prof, Inst Commun Res, Univ Ill at Urbana-Champaign, 89-93; Vis Prof, Univ Calif - Santa Barbara, 92-93; Prof, Univ Tex-Austin, 93-. **HONORS AND AWARDS** NDEA Title IV Fel, Univ Minn, 71-74; Arnold O. Beckman Res Award, Univ Ill, 83-84; Krieghbaum Under 40 Award, Asn Educ Journalism & Mass Commun, 84; Res Award, Ctr Population Options, 86-87; Fel, Int Commun Asn; Leadership Tex Class 1997; Educr of the Year, The Ad Soc, Austin Advertising Federation, 98. **MEMBERSHIPS** Int Commun Asn; Asn Educ Journalism & Mass Commun; Nat Commun Asn; Broadcast Educ Asn; Am Asn Public Opinion Res; Kappa Tau Alpha. **RESEARCH** Children and mass media. **SELECTED PUBLICATIONS** Co-ed, American Communication Research: The Remembered History, Lawrence Erlbaum, 96; The Audience and Its Landscape, Westview Press, 96; coauth, MediaMaking, Sage Publ, 98; author of numerous other books, book chapters, articles, and conference presentations. **CONTACT ADDRESS** College of Communication, Univ Texas Austin, Austin, TX, 78712-1094.

WASERMAN, MANFRED
PERSONAL Born 03/21/1933, Free City of Danzig, Poland, 1 child **DISCIPLINE** AMERICAN HISTORY, LIBRARY SCIENCE **EDUCATION** Univ Md, BA, 59, MA, 61; Cath Univ Am, MS, 63, PhD (hist), 82. **CAREER** Teacher hist, Prince Geofe's County, Md, Pub Sch, 60-62; librn, Library, Yale Univ, 63-65; CURATOR, MOD MANUSCRIPTS, NAT LIBR MED, 65-. **MEMBERSHIPS** Am Asn Hist Med; AHA; Am Libr Asn; Oral Hist Asn. **RESEARCH** History of medicine and public health; history of child health care; primitive medicine and ethnology. **SELECTED PUBLICATIONS** Auth, Montefiore, Moses, A Hebrew Prayer Book, and Medicine in the Holy Land, Judaism, Vol 45, 96. **CONTACT ADDRESS** Hist Med Div, National Libr of Med, Bethesda, MD, 20209.

WASHINGTON, DURTHY A.
PERSONAL Born 02/20/1948, Nuremberg, Germany, d, 1 child **DISCIPLINE** CONTEMPORARY AMERICAN LITERATURE; TECHNICAL WRITING **EDUCATION** San Diego State Univ, BA, 73; Univ Southern Calif, MS, 79; San Jose State Univ, MA, 86 **CAREER** Writer/Seminar Leader, Self-Employed, 93-; owner, Springs Seminarz; instr, Pikes Peak Comm Col, 98; instr, Col Univ, 92-96; instr, Univ Calif Santa Cruz, 93; instr, Univ Texas, 81-83 **HONORS AND AWARDS** Profiled in the Gazette, Colorado Springs major newspaper, 98; Best Feature Award, Urban Spectrum News; 96; Award for Excellence in Tech Writing, Soc Tech Comm, 91 **MEMBERSHIPS** Amer Libr Assoc; Colorado Libr Assoc; Colorado Lang Arts Soc; MELUS; Modern Lang Assoc; Ntl Coalition Independent Scholars; Phi Kappa Phi Ntl Honor Soc; Toni Morriosn Soc **RESEARCH** Technical Communication; American Ethnic Literature **SELECTED PUBLICATIONS** Auth, "Womanist of Feminist?: Black Women and the Women's Movement," African Amer Voice, 98; auth, "Swing Low: Black Men Writing," Bloomsbury Rev, 97; auth, "Bone Black: Memoirs of Girlhood," Bloomsbury Rev, 97 **CONTACT ADDRESS** 4581 Castlepoint Dr, Colorado Springs, CO, 80917-1366. **EMAIL** durthy@aol.com

WASHINGTON, MARY HELEN
PERSONAL Born 01/21/1941, Cleveland, OH, s **DISCIPLINE** ENGLISH **EDUCATION** Notre Dame College, BA, 1962; University of Detroit, MA, 1966, PhD, 1976. **CAREER** High school teacher of English in Cleveland OH public schools, 1962-64; St. John College, Cleveland, instructor in English, 1966-68; University of Detroit, Detroit MI, assistant professor of English, 1972-75, director of Center for Black Studies, beginning 1975; currently ASSOCIATE PROFESSOR OF ENGLISH, BOSTON HARBOR COLLEGE, UNIVERSITY OF MASSACHUSETTS, BOSTON. **MEMBERSHIPS** National Council of Teachers of English, College Language Association, Michigan Black Studies Association. **SELECTED PUBLICATIONS** Richard Wright Award for Literary Criticism from Black World, 1974; anthologist, Memory of Kin: Stories About Family by Black Writers. **CONTACT ADDRESS** Dept of English, Univ of Massachusetts, Boston, Boston, MA, 02125.

WASHINGTON, SARAH M.
PERSONAL Born 08/10/1942, Holly Hill, South Carolina, d, 1967 **DISCIPLINE** ENGLISH **EDUCATION** Tuskegee Inst, Tuskegee AL, BS 1964; Univ of Illinois, Urbana IL, MS 1970, PhD 1980. **CAREER** Spartanburg District, Inman SC, English teacher, 1964-65; Anderson Public Schools, Anderson SC, Eng teacher, 1965-67; Sumter Schools, Sumter SC, social studies teacher, 1967-68; AL State Univ, Montgomery AL, English instructor, 1971-74; Univ of IL, Urbana IL, teaching asst, 1974-80; SC State Coll, Orangeburg SC, English prof, 1979-. **HONORS AND AWARDS** Sigma Tau Delta Natl Eng Honor Soc, 1981; field coordinator, Assessment Performance in Teaching, 1988-90; Scholar, Let's Talk About It, a national reading program. **MEMBERSHIPS** Pres, Orangeburg Branch, Assn of the Study of Afro-Amer Life & History, 1980-85; pres elect, 1991, chaplain, 1982-89, Phi Delta Kappa; mem, SC State Dept Writing Advisory Bd, 1983-89; mem, Amer Assn of Univ Women; reader, Natl Teachers Examination, 1989; Natl Council of Teachers of English; Natl Black Child Development Institute. **SELECTED PUBLICATIONS** Author of literary biog of Frank Horne, 1985; **CONTACT ADDRESS** Professor, English, South Carolina State Col, PO Box 2034, Orangeburg, SC, 29117.

WASHINGTON, VON HUGO, SR.
PERSONAL Born 03/09/1943, Albion, Michigan, m, 1974 **DISCIPLINE** DRAMA **EDUCATION** Western Michigan Univ, Kalamazoo, MI, BS, 1974, MA, 1975; Wayne State Univ, Detroit, MI, PhD, 1979. **CAREER** Univ of Michigan, Ann Arbor, MI, dir, black theatre, 1975-77; Wayne State Univ, Detroit, MI, dir, black theatre, 1979-88; Western Michigan Univ, Kalamazoo, MI, dir, multicultural & performance area, theatre, 1988-, professor, currently. **HONORS AND AWARDS** Achievement Award, Michigan Foundation for the Arts, 1984; Career Development Chair, Wayne State Univ, 1983; Carter G Woodson Education Award, Wayne State Univ, 1984; Alumni Faculty Service Award, Wayne State Univ, 1988; Best Actor, Detroit News, 1990. **MEMBERSHIPS** Black Theatre Network, 1986-96; artistic dir/co-founder; Afro-American Studio Theatre, Detroit, 1983-86; president/co-founder, Washington Prod Inc, 1992-. **CONTACT ADDRESS** Professor, Western Michigan Univ, PO Box 3253, Kalamazoo, MI, 49003.

WASSER, HENRY
PERSONAL Pittsburgh, PA, m, 1942, 2 children **DISCIPLINE** ENGLISH **EDUCATION** Ohio State Univ, BA and MA, 40; Columbia Univ, PhD (English and comp lit), 52. **CAREER** Teaching fel English, George Washington Univ, 40-43; instr, Univ Akron, 43-44, Ny Univ, 45-46; tutor, City Col New York, 46-52, from instr to assoc prof, 52-66; prof English and dean fac, Richmond Col, NY 66-73; prof English and acad vpres, Calif State Univ, Sacramento, 73-74; prof, Col Staten Island, 74-78; PROF ENGLISH, CITY UNIV NEW YORK, 78-; Fulbright prof, Univ Salonika, 55-56 and Univ Oslo, 62-64; dir, Am Inst Univ Oslo, 63-64; sem assoc, univ sem in am studies, Columbia Univ, 61-69, SEM HIGHER EDUC, 69-; Am-Scand Found Thord-Gray award, 71 and 72; 2nd vpres, An Upper Level Cols and Univs, 71-72; vis prof Am studies Univ Sussex, spring 72; Ger Acad Exchange Serv award, 73; CO-CHMN, SEM HIGHER EDUC PUBL, COLUMBIA UNIV, 78-. **MEMBERSHIPS** Melville Soc Am; MLA; Am Studies Asn. **RESEARCH** Henry Adams and the Adams family; post-Civil War American literature and thought; higher education. **SELECTED PUBLICATIONS** Auth, the Al Gray Musical Merit Scholarship Award, Down Beat, Vol 61, 94. **CONTACT ADDRESS** New York, NY.

WASSERMAN, JULIAN
PERSONAL Born 06/08/1948, Lubbock, TX **DISCIPLINE** MEDIEVAL LITERATURE **EDUCATION** Vanderbilt Univ, BA, 70; Southern Methodist Univ, MA, 72; Rice Univ, PhD (English), 75. **CAREER** From asst to assoc prof English, Univ Ark, Little Rock, 75-79; ASSOC PROF ENGLISH, UNIV ST THOMAS, 79-. **SELECTED PUBLICATIONS** Auth, Daddys Girls, Father Daughter Incest and Canadian Plays by Women, Essays in Theatre Etudes Theatrales, Vol 14, 95. **CONTACT ADDRESS** Dept of English, Univ of St Thomas, Houston, TX, 77006.

WATERHOUSE, CAROLE
DISCIPLINE CREATIVE WRITING, JOURNALISM, 20TH CENTURY LITERATURE **EDUCATION** Univ Pittsburgh, MFA; OH Univ, PhD. **CAREER** Instr, CA State Univ PA; vol instr, State Correctional Inst, Pittsburgh. **RESEARCH** International film and lit. **SELECTED PUBLICATIONS** Auth, Without Wings; publ short stories in Mass Rev, Artful Dodge, Ball State Univ Forum, Ceilidh, Bassettown Rev, and Eureka Lit Mag. **CONTACT ADDRESS** California Univ of Pennsylvania, California, PA, 15419. **EMAIL** waterhouse@cup.edu

WATERMEIER, DANIEL J.
DISCIPLINE THEATRE ARTS **EDUCATION** Univ IL, PhD, 68. **CAREER** Prof, Univ Toledo. **RESEARCH** Theatre hist; dramatic lit and criticism. **SELECTED PUBLICATIONS** Auth, Edwin Booth in Performance: The Mary Isabella Stone Commentaries, 90; Shakespeare Companies and Festivals: An International Guide, 95. **CONTACT ADDRESS** Dept of Theatre, Film and Dance, Univ Toledo, Toledo, OH, 43606. **EMAIL** danielwatermeier@pop3.utoledo.edu

WATERS, MICHAEL
PERSONAL Born 11/23/1949, New York, NY, d, 1 child **DISCIPLINE** AMERICAN LITERATURE **EDUCATION** SUNY-Brockport, BA, 71; MA, 72; Ohio Univ, PhD, 77. **CAREER** Prof, Univ Salisbury State Col, 78- ; vis prof, Univ of Athens, Greece, 81-82; writer-in Residence, Sweet Briar Col, 87-89; vis prof, Univ of Maryland, 95- . **HONORS AND AWARDS** Fel, Nat Endowment for the Arts, 84; Individual Artist Awards, Maryland State Arts Coun, 90, 92, 97; Pushcart Prizes, 84, 90; Towson State Univ Prizes for Lit, 85, 90; Lit Work-in-Progress Grants, Maryland State Arts Coun, 83, 85, 88, 89; Yaddo fels, 78, 80, 83, 84, 87, 92, 95; VA Ctr for Creative Arts Fels, 90, 91, 92, 94, 95, 97; MacDowell Colony Fels, 92, 94; Tyrone Guthrie Ctr Fel, 93; The Anderson Ctr for Interdisciplinary Studies Fel, 96. **SELECTED PUBLICATIONS** Auth, Fish Light, 75; Not Just Any Death, 79; Anniversary of the Air, 85; The Burden Lifters, 89; Bountiful, 92; Green Ash, Red Maple, Black Gum, 97; ed, Dissolve to Island: On the Poetry of John Logan, 84. **CONTACT ADDRESS** Dept of English, Salisbury State Col, Salisbury, MD, 21801. **EMAIL** mgwaters@ssu.edu

WATERS, RICHARD L.
PERSONAL Born 10/07/1937, Golden City, MO, m, 1988, 5 children **DISCIPLINE** LIBRARY SCIENCE **EDUCATION** Univ Wash, MLIS, 66. **CAREER** Principal consultant Providence Associates, 79-. **MEMBERSHIPS** ALA; Texas Library Assoc. **RESEARCH** Public library service **SELECTED PUBLICATIONS** Editor, Public Library Quarterly **CONTACT ADDRESS** Providence Association, Box 425979, Denton, TX, 76204-5979. **EMAIL** rwaters@twu.edu

WATERSTON, ELIZABETH H.
PERSONAL Born 04/18/1922, Montreal, PQ, Canada **DISCIPLINE** ENGLISH **EDUCATION** Univ Toronto, BA, 44, PhD, 50; Bryn Mawr Col, MA, 45. **CAREER** Asst prof, 45-47, assoc prof, Sir George Williams Col, 50-58, dept chair, 56-58; assoc prof, Univ W Ont, 58-67; assoc prof, 67-71, prof, 71-87, dept chair, 74-77, PROF EMER ENGLISH UNIV GUELPH 89-. **MEMBERSHIPS** Founding mem, Asn Can Univ Tchrs English; Asn Can & Que Lit; founding & life mem, Asn Can Stud; edit bd mem, Scottish Tradition, English Stud Can; founder & ed Can Children's Lit; Nat pres, Humanities Asn Can, 77-79. **SELECTED PUBLICATIONS** Auth, Brush up Your Basics, 1981; auth, The Travelers: Canada to 1900, 89; auth, Gilbert Parker, 89; auth, Children's Literature in Canada, 92; auth, Kindling Spirit, 94; coauth, John Galt, 85; coauth, Silenced Sextet, 93; coauth, Writing a Life, 95; ed, Seats of the Mighty, 68; ed, Bogle Corbet, 76; ed, Some Scots, 82; co-ed, Selected Journals of L.M. Montgomery vol 1 85, vol 2 87, vol 3 92. **CONTACT ADDRESS** 535 Colborne St, London, ON, N6B 217.

WATKINS, FLOYD C.
PERSONAL Born 04/19/1920, Cherokee Co, GA, m, 1942, 3 children **DISCIPLINE** ENGLISH **EDUCATION** Ga Southern Col, BS, 46; Emory Univ, AM, 47; Vanderbilt Univ, PhD, 52. **CAREER** Tchng fel, 47-49, Vanderbilt Univ; from instr to assoc prof, 49-61, prof, 61-, Emory Univ; Guggenheim fel, 62-63; vis prof, 80, Tex A&M. **MEMBERSHIPS** MLA; S Atlantic Mod Lang Assn; Soc Studies Southern Lit. **RESEARCH** Southern and modern literature; cultural origins. **SELECTED PUBLICATIONS** Auth, Thomas Wolfe's Characters, Univ Okla, 57; coauth, Old Times in the Faulkner Country, Univ NC, 61; coauth, Yesterday in the Hills, Quadrangle, 63; auth, The Death of Art, Univ Ga, 70; auth, The Flesh and the Word, Vanderbilt Univ, 71; auth, In Time and Place, Univ Ga, 77; co-ed, Robert Penn Warren Talking, Random House, 80; co-ed, Then and Now: The Personal Past in the Poetry of Robert Penn Warren, Univ Ky, 82. **CONTACT ADDRESS** 519 Durand Dr NE, Atlanta, GA, 30307. **EMAIL** fwatkins@college.emory.edu

WATSON, CRESAP SHAW
PERSONAL Ft Worth, TX, m, 1948, 3 children **DISCIPLINE** ENGLISH **EDUCATION** Brown Univ, BA, 49; Univ Dublin, Ireland, PhD (English), 53. **CAREER** From instr to asst prof English, La State Univ, 52-60; assoc prof and chmn dept English and speech, 60-72, PROF ENGLISH AND SPEECH, UNIV NEW ORLEANS, 72-; ED, LA ENGLISH J, 60-. **MEMBERSHIPS** NCTE; Col English Asn; SCent Mod Lang Asn. **RESEARCH** Anglo-Irish literature; modern fiction and drama; the novel. **SELECTED PUBLICATIONS** Auth, You Can Go Home Again, the Focus on Family in the Works of Foote, Horton, Mod Drama, Vol 39, 96. **CONTACT ADDRESS** Dept of English, Univ of New Orleans, New Orleans, LA, 70122.

WATSON, JAMES GRAY
PERSONAL Born 06/16/1939, Balitmore, MD, m, 1963, 2 children **DISCIPLINE** AMERICAN & MODERN LITERATURE **EDUCATION** Bowdoin Col, AB, 61; Univ Pittsburgh, MA, 63, PhD(English), 68. **CAREER** Asst dean arts & sci, Univ Pittsburgh, 68-69; asst prof to prof English, Tulsa Univ, 69-. **MEMBERSHIPS** MLA; SCent Mod Lang Asn; Soc Study Southern Lit. **RESEARCH** William Faulkner; modern American literature; modernism. **SELECTED PUBLICATIONS** Auth, The Snopes Dilemma: Faulkner's Trilogy, Univ Miami, 70; William Faulkner, Letters and Fiction, Univ Texas, 87; ed, Thinjing of Home: William Faulkner's Letters to His Mother and Father, 1918-1925, WW Norton, 92; auth, essays on American literature in: Am Lit; Ariz Quart; Faulkner J; Falkner Stud; Miss Quart; Mod Fiction Studies; Mosaic; Southern Quart; Fifty Years of Yoknapatawpha, 79; New Directions in Faulkner Studies, 82; The Artist and His Masks: William Faulkner's Metafiction, 89; Faulkner, His Contemporaries and His Posterity, 92. **CONTACT ADDRESS** Fac of English, Tulsa Univ, 600 S College, Tulsa, OK, 74104-3126. **EMAIL** watsonjg@centum.utulsa.edu

WATSON, JEAN LOUISE
PERSONAL Born 06/20/1943, Albuquerque, NM, 2 children DISCIPLINE BRITISH AND CHILDREN'S LITERATURE EDUCATION Baylor Univ, BA, 65; Midwestern Univ, MA, 67; Ohio Univ, PhD (English), 75. CAREER Instr, Univ Nebr, 66-68; asst prof, Stonehill Col, 68-72, Gustavus Adolphus Col, 76-81; ASST PROF ENGLISH, MARSHALL UNIV, 81-; Fel, Summer Inst Women Higher Educ Admin, Bryn Mawr Col, summer, 79; vis scholar, Columbia Univ, 80-81. MEMBERSHIPS MLA; SAtlantic Mod Lang Asn; Midwest Victorian Studies Asn; Children's Lit Asn; Carolinas Symp Brit Studies. RESEARCH Coleridge's poetry and prose; th century British poetry and literature. SELECTED PUBLICATIONS Auth, Gospel of Disunion in Religion and Separatism in the Antebellum South, J Church State, Vol 37, 95. CONTACT ADDRESS Dept of English, Marshall Univ, Huntington, WV, 25701.

WATSON, JOHN CLIFTON
PERSONAL Born 01/22/1954, Jersey City, NJ, m, 1994 DISCIPLINE JOURNALISM EDUCATION Rutgers Coll, BA, 1975; Rutgers Univ, School of Law, JD, 1980. CAREER Jersey City State Coll, writing instructor, 1992-94; RUTGERS COLL NEWARK, JOURNALISM INSTRUCTOR, 1992-; THE JERSEY JOURNAL, NEWS EDITOR, REPORTER, 1975-. HONORS AND AWARDS North Jersey Press Assn, 1st Place Spot News Reporting Award, 1983; NJ Press Assn, 1st Place Spot News Reporting Award, 1983; Hudson County Newspaper Guild, Sports Writing Award, 1983. MEMBERSHIPS Garden State Assn of Black Journalists, 1992-. CONTACT ADDRESS The Jersey Journal Newspaper, 30 Journal Sq, 3rd Fl Newsroom, Jersey City, NJ, 07306.

WATSON, ROBERT WINTHROP
PERSONAL Born 12/26/1925, Passaic, NJ, m, 1952, 2 children DISCIPLINE ENGLISH EDUCATION Williams Col, BA, 46; Johns Hopkins Univ, MA, 50, PhD(English), 55. CAREER Instr English, Williams Col, 46, 47-48, 52-53 & Johns Hopkins Univ, 50-52; from instr to assoc prof, 53-63, PROF ENGLISH, UNIV NC, GREENSBORO, 63-, Dir, Assoc Writing Prog, 67-72; vis prof, Calif State Univ, Northridge, 68-69. HONORS AND AWARDS Award in Lit, Am Acad & Inst Arts & Lett, 77; Nat Endow Arts, 78. MEMBERSHIPS MLA RESEARCH Modern poetry and literature; poetics; the novel. SELECTED PUBLICATIONS Auth, A Paper Horse and Other Poems, 62 & Advantages of Dark(poems), 66, Atheneum; Three Sides of the Mirror, Putnam, 66; Christmas at Las Vegas(poems), 71 & Selected Poems, 74, Atheneum; Lily Lang, St Martin's, 77, Island of Bones(poetry), Unicorn, 77; Night Blooming Cactus (poems), Atheneum, 80; auth, The Pendulum: New and Selected Poems, LSU Press, 95. CONTACT ADDRESS 9-D Fountain Manor Dr, Greensboro, NC, 27405.

WATT, WILLIS M.
PERSONAL Born 12/20/1950, Ottawa, KS, m, 1970, 1 child DISCIPLINE COMMUNICATION EDUCATION Manhattan Christian Col, BS, 76; Ks St Univ, BS, 76, MA, 78, PhD, 80. CAREER Grad TA to asst prof, Ks St Univ, 76-80; asst prof, Iowa St Univ, 80-84; dir to chair, Ft Hays St Univ, 80-97; vice pres, Manhattan Christian Col, Manhattan Ks, 97-. HONORS AND AWARDS Member, Mid-Amer Educ Hall of Fame, Ks City Comm Col; Ks Speech Comm Assoc Col Teacher of the Year, 96; Marquis' Who's Who in World, 97-99; Who's Who in Amer, 97-00; Who's Who in Educ, 97; Order of Highest Distinction, Pi Kappa Delta, Nat Debate/Speech Frat, 95; Ks Leadership Forum., Editor, Ks Speech J; Adv Coun for Acad Aff, Center for Policy in Higher Educ, Washington, DC; Adv Coun, Leadership Inst, Ks St Univ Ed Bd, Privacy on Campus, CPHE, Washington DC; Adjudicator, Region V, Kennedy Center-Amer Col Theatre Festival; Theta Alpha Phi, Nat Drama Frat, Ks St Univ; Alpha Psi Omega, Nat Theatre Frat, Ft Hays St Univ; Pi Delta Kappa, Int Educr Frat, Ks St Univ. RESEARCH Leadership; intercultural commun; conflict mgt; orgn commun; relig drama and art. SELECTED PUBLICATIONS Coauth, Fundamentals of Oral Communication, McGraw-Hill, 97; auth, Three-Phase Process For Documenting And Evaluating Faculty Performance For Pay Increases, Promotion, and Tenure, The Department Chair: A Newsletter For Academic Administration, Anker Press, 96; auth, Leadership Ministries, Leadership Education: A Source Book Of Courses And Programs, Center For Creative Leadership, Greensboro, NC, 98; art, Using Mock Debates As Structured Learning Experiences To Teach Argument, The Forensic Educator, 98; art, Organizational Communication And Leadership: A Collaborative Philosophy Toward Teaching Leadership With Syllabus, The J of Leadership Stud, 97. CONTACT ADDRESS Manhattan Christian Col, 1415 Anderson Ave, Manhattan, KS, 66502-4081. EMAIL wmwatt@mccks.edu

WATTERS, DAVID HARPER
PERSONAL Born 12/28/1950, Hartford, CT, m, 1980 DISCIPLINE AMERICAN LITERATURE EDUCATION Dartmouth Col, AB, 72; Brown Univ, PhD(English), 79. CAREER Asst Prof English, Univ Nh, 78-, Panelist, NH Comn for the Arts Folk Arts Panel, 80- MEMBERSHIPS Asn Gravestone Studies. RESEARCH Early American literature and material culture; gravestones. SELECTED PUBLICATIONS Auth, Emerson, Dickenson and the atomic self, Emily Dickenson Bull, 77; co-ed, Increase Mather's New Jerusalem: Millennialism in late seventeenth century New England, Proceedings of the Am Antiquarian Soc, 77; auth, The Park and Whiting family stones revisited: The iconography of the church covenant, The Can Rev of Am Studies, 78; A priest to the temple, Puritan Gravestone Studies II, 79; Gravestones and historical archeology: A review essay, Markers: Asn for Gravestone Studies, 79-80; With Bodilie Eyes: Eschatological Themes in Puritan Literature and Gravestone Art, Univ Microfilm Int Res Press, 81; A Reading Of Taylor,Edward - Davis,Tm, William And Mary Quarterly, Vol 0052, 1995. CONTACT ADDRESS Dept of English, Univ of NH, 125 Technology Dr, Durham, NH, 03824-4724.

WATTS, ANN CHALMERS
PERSONAL Born 04/14/1938, Evanston, IL, m, 1962, 2 children DISCIPLINE ENGLISH EDUCATION Radcliffe Col, BA, 59; Yale Univ, PhD, 65. CAREER Asst prof English, Tufts Univ, 64-71; ASSOC PROF ENGLISH, RUTGERS UNIV, NEWARK, 71-. MEMBERSHIPS MLA; Mediaeval Acad Am. RESEARCH Old English literature; Middle English literature 19th century English and American literature. SELECTED PUBLICATIONS Auth, The Lyre and the Harp, Yale Univ, 69; Chaucerian selves, Chaucer Rev, 70; Amor Gloriae in Chaucer's House of Fame, J Medieval & Renaissance Studies, 73. CONTACT ADDRESS Dept of English, Rutgers Univ, 360 Martin Luther King Jr Blvd, Newark, NJ, 07102-1897.

WAUGH, BUTLER HUGGINS
PERSONAL Born 05/09/1934, Pittsburgh, PA, m, 1953, 6 children DISCIPLINE FOLKLORE, ENGLISH EDUCATION Washington & Jefferson Col, AB, 55; IN Univ, PhD, 59. CAREER Instr Eng, Univ KS, 59-61; from asst prof to assoc prof, Univ FL, 61-70; exec asst to pres, 69-70, dean col arts & sci, 70-76, prof eng, FL Int Univ, 70, Coordr hum & fine arts, State Univ Syst FL, 68-69. MEMBERSHIPS Am Folklore Soc; MLA; S Atlantic Mod Lang Asn. RESEARCH Mod Brit and Am poetry; comp folktale study; structural analysis of traditional lit. SELECTED PUBLICATIONS Auth, Negro tales of John Kendry, Midwest Folklore, 58; The child and the snake in North America, Norveg, 60; Deep and surface structure, SAtlantic Bull, 68. CONTACT ADDRESS Col Arts & Sci, Florida Intl Univ, 1 F I U South Campus, Miami, FL, 33199-0001. EMAIL waugh@fiu.edu

WAUGH, CHARLES G.
PERSONAL Born 07/18/1943, Philadelphia, PA, m, 1968, 2 children DISCIPLINE COMMUNICATIONS EDUCATION Syracuse Univ, BS, 65, MA, 69; Kent State Univ, PhD, 82. CAREER Asst debate coach, teaching asst, Syracuse Univ, 65-66; instr, Ithaca Col, 67-69; teaching fel, Kent State Univ, 69-71; asst prof, Univ Maine at Augusta, 71-78; Chemn, Div of Soc Sci, Univ Maine at Augusta, 74-76; pres faculty assembly, Univ Maine at Augusta, 77-78; assoc prof, Univ Maine at Augusta, 78-81; prof, Univ Maine at Augusta, 81-; vp faculty assembly, Univ Maine at Augusta, 97-98. HONORS AND AWARDS Unit citation, USCG, 66. RESEARCH Social interaction and influences; popular culture; mass media; Maine studies. SELECTED PUBLICATIONS Co-ed, Alternative Histories, Garland Press, 86; co-ed, The Best Maine Stories, Lance Tapley, 86; coauth, Science Fiction and Fantasy Series and Sequels: Vol. 1, Garland Press, 86; coauth, Western Series and Sequels: A Reference Guide, Garland Press, 86; co-ed, Science Fiction: The Science Fiction Research Association Anthology, Harper & Row, 88; co-ed, The Best New England Stories, Lance Tapley, 90; coauth, Women Writers: From Page to Screen: A Guide to the Literary Sources of British and American Feature Films, Garland Press, 90; co-ed, Wife or Spinster: Stories by Nineteenth Century Women, Yankee Books, 91. CONTACT ADDRESS 5 Morrill St, Winthrop, ME, 04364.

WAWRZYCKA, JOLANTA
DISCIPLINE MODERN BRITISH AND IRISH LITERATURE; ANCIENT AND MODERN LITERARY THEORY AND EDUCATION Univ Wroclaw, Poland, MA, 80; Southern IL Univ, Carbondale, PhD, 87. CAREER Transl-interp, Univ Wroclaw, Poland;79-80; transl, Int Comput Med Ctr, Poland, 80-81; res fel, Southern IL Univ, Carbondale;81; writing tutor, Southern IL Univ, Carbondale, 82-84; vis scholar, World Inst of Phenomenol, Boston, 84; res asst, 83-84, tchg asst, 82-85, lectr, Southern IL Univ, Carbondale, 85-87; assoc prof, Radford Univ, 87-; Russ instr, Radva Corp, Radford, Va, 90. HONORS AND AWARDS Dissertation res award, Southern IL Univ, 85; fel, Northwestern Univ, 88; RU Found grant; Italy, 90; NEH, Univ CA, Santa Cruz, 89; RU fac develop grant, Switz, 92; RU grad sch summer res grant, Switz, 93, 94; RU fac prof develop leave, 96. MEMBERSHIPS Mod Lang Asn, 84-; Midwest Mod Lang Asn, 85-90; ch, Slavic Div of Midwest MLA, 87-88; Int Zurich James Joyce Found, 87-; Am Lit Transl Asn, 89-92; Soc of Phenomenol and Lit, 89-; Am Conf for Irish Stud, 91-; Friends of the Zurich James Joyce Found, 92-. RESEARCH Philos; philos of lang; hist; semiotics. SELECTED PUBLICATIONS Auth, Rev of Czeslaw Milosz and the Insufficiency of Lyric by Donald Davie; J of Mod Lit, Vol 15, no 3; Rev of Conversations with Czeslaw Milosz by Ewa Czarnecka and Aleksander Fiut, J of Mod Lit, Vol 15, no 3; Rev of Joyce, Modernity and its Mediation, Christine van Boheemen, ed, James Joyce Quart, Vol 28, no 4; Transcultural Criticism: 'jingish janglage' Joyce in Polish, in Festschrift Fritz Senn, Liliput Press, 97; Photomorpheme: Semiotisizing in Camera Lucida, in Writing the Image After Roland Barthes, ed Jean-Michel Rabate, Univ Pa Press, 97; coed, Gender in Joyce. UP of Fla, 97; transl, Our Art: Our Passports, Jonesfilm Gp, Inc, 96; On Translations by Roman Ingarden Analecta Husserliana, Vol XXXIII; On Responsibility, Analecta Husserliana, Vol XXVII; cotransl, International Bibliography of Works by Roman Ingarden, Analecta Husserliana, Vol XXX. CONTACT ADDRESS Radford Univ, Radford, VA, 24142. EMAIL jolanta@runet.edu

WAYNE, VALERIE
PERSONAL Born 08/02/1945, Chicago, IL, m, 1998, 1 child DISCIPLINE ENGLISH EDUCATION DePauw Univ, BA, philos, 66; Univ Chicago, MA, eng, 72, PhD, eng, 78. CAREER Teaching asst, philos, DePauw Univ, 64-65; teaching asst, humanities, Univ Chicago, 73-74; lectr, compos, Chicago State Univ, 74; lectr, compos, Univ Ill, 76-78; visiting lectr, Univ Liverpool, Jan-may, 88; visiting scholar, Alice F. Holmes Inst, Univ Kans, 97; visiting asst prof, 78-79, asst prof, eng, 79-86, dir, undergrad honors eng prog, 88-91, assoc prof, eng, 86-93, prof, eng, 93-, dir, eng grad prog, 94-97, dir, UH London Abroad Prog, spring, 98, Univ Hawaii Manoa. HONORS AND AWARDS Nat Endow for the Humanities, summer stipend, 92; Folger Inst Ctr for Shakespeare Studies, grant-in-aid, 88; Huntington Libr fel, 82; Woodrow Wilson Res grant for dissertation candidates in Women's Studies, 76; Phi Beta Kappa, 66; Alpha Lambda Delta, 66. MEMBERSHIPS Shakespeare Asn of Amer; Soc for the Study of Early Mod Women; Mod Lang Asn; Renaissance Eng Text Soc; The Malone Soc. RESEARCH Shakespeare; Early modern women; Renaissance literature; Feminist theory; Textual editing. SELECTED PUBLICATIONS Article, Shakespeare Wallah and Colonial Specularity, Shakespeare, the Movie, London, Routledge, 97; article, Advice for Women from Mothers and Patriarchs, Women and Literature in Britain, 1500-1700, Cambridge Univ Press, 56-79, 96; article, A Denaturalized Performance: Gender and Body Construction in Thailand's As You Like It, Gender and Culture in Literature and Film, East and West: Issues of Perception and Interpretation, Lit Studies East and West, vol 9, Div of Lang, Ling and Lit and the East-West Ctr, 197-204, 94; article, Debased, Defamed and Decomposed, The Office of Women's Research Working Paper Series, vol 2, Univ Hawaii Manoa, 36-46, 93-94; ed, The Flower of Friendship: A Renaissance Dialogue Contesting Marriage, Cornell Univ Press, 92; auth, The Matter of Difference: Materialist Feminist Criticism of Shakespeare, Harvester Wheatsheaf, Cornell Univ Press, 91. CONTACT ADDRESS Dept. of English, Univ of Hawaii at Manoa, 1733 Donaghho Rd., Honolulu, HI, 96822. EMAIL vwayne@hawaii.edu

WAZNAK, ROBERT P.
PERSONAL Born 02/05/1938, Scranton, PA, s DISCIPLINE RHETORIC EDUCATION Mt St Mary's Col, BA, 60, MA, 64; Temple Univ, PhD, 74. CAREER Asst prof Homiletics, St Mary's Sem & Univ, 68-69 & 80-84; vis prof Homiletics, Princeton Theol Sem, 77-78; Instr Homiletics, Cath Univ Am, 72-80; PROF HOMILETICS, WASHINGTON THEOL UNION, 80- ; CO-ED NEW THEOL REV, 97- . HONORS AND AWARDS Univ Doctoral fel, Temple Univ, 70. MEMBERSHIPS Am Acad Homiletics; Cath Asn Tchrs Homiletics, Cath Theol Soc Am; Soc Homiletica. RESEARCH Homiletics; Media; Narrative theological; Biblical hermeneutics. SELECTED PUBLICATIONS Auth, Like Fresh Bread: Sunday Homilies in the Parish, Paulist Press, 93; The Catechism and the Sunday Homily, America, 94; Jean-Baptiste Massillon, The Concise Encyclo of Preaching, John Knox Press, 95; Heralds of Hope, Liturgy 90, 96; Preaching the Gospel in a Video Culture, Religious Rhetoric in a Video Culture, Sheed & Ward, 96; The Media as Saint-Maker and Devil's Advocate, America, 97; The Church and the Scientist in the New Millennium, New Theol Rev, 98; Anatomy of a Homily, New Theol Rev, 98; An Introduction to the Homily, The Liturgical Press, 98. CONTACT ADDRESS Washington Theol Union, 6896 Laurel Street, NW, Washington, DC, 20012. EMAIL waznak@wtu.edu

WEALES, GERALD
PERSONAL Born 06/12/1925, Connersville, IN DISCIPLINE ENGLISH LITERATURE EDUCATION Columbia Col, AB, 49; Columbia Univ, AM, 50, PhD, 58. CAREER Instr English, GA Inst Technol, 51-53, Newark Col Engineering, 53-55 & Wayne State Univ, 55-56; asst prof, Brown Univ, 57-58; from asst prof to assoc prof, 58-67, Prof English, Univ PA, 67-, Lectr, Eng Inst, 59 & 63; Fulbright lectr, Sri Lanka, 79; Rockefeller Found, Residence Bellagio Study Ctr, 80; vis prof, Univ Hawaii, 81; Guggenheim fel, 81-82. HONORS AND AWARDS George Jean Nathan Award, 64-65. RESEARCH Modern American and English drama. SELECTED PUBLICATIONS Auth, Religion in Modern English Drama, Univ Pa, 61; American Drama Since World War II, Harcourt, 62; ed, Edwardian Plays, Hill & Wang, 62; A Play and its Parts, Basic Bks, 64; The Complete Plays of William Wycherley, Doubleday Anchor, 66 & NY Univ, 67; auth, American Drama in the 1960's, Macmillian, 69; Clifford Odets, Playwright, Bobbs, 71; Fugard Masters The Code + How He Has Succeeded In Making The The External Specifics Of A Story Run Parallel To A Need

To Make A Personal Statement/, Twentieth Century Literature, Vol 0039, 1993; The American Stage - Social And Economic-Issues From The Colonial Period To The Present - Engle,R, Miller,Tl/, Sewanee Review, Vol 0102, 1994; The Voice Of Davis,Elmer/, Virginia Quarterly Review, Vol 0071, 1995; American Theater Watch, 1994-1995/, Georgia Review, Vol 0049, 1995; A Call To The Colors + Thomas,Dana 'Lease On Liberty' And 'American Passport'/, Georgia Review, Vol 0049, 1995; Dumbocracy In America - Studies In The Theater Of Guilt, 1987-1994 - Brustein,R/, Sewanee Review, Vol 0104, 1996; Southern Playwrights - Plays From Actors-Theater-Of-Louisville - Dixon,Mb, Volansky,M/, Georgia Review, Vol 0050, 1996; American Theater Watch, 1995-1996, Georgia Review, Vol 0050, 1996; 'Shaw', Vol 14, Shaw And The Last 100 Years - Dukore,Bf, Sewanee Review, Vol 0105, 1997; Irving,Henry 'Waterloo' - King,Wd, Sewanee Review, Vol 0105, 1997. **CONTACT ADDRESS** Dept of English, Univ of PA, Philadelphia, PA, 19174.

WEARING, J.P.
PERSONAL Birmingham, England **DISCIPLINE** ENGLISH LITERATURE, THEATRE HISTORY **EDUCATION** Univ Wales, Swansea, BA, 67, PhD(English), 71; Univ Sask, MA, 68. **CAREER** Lectr English, Univ Alta, 71-74; asst prof, 74-77, assoc prof English, Univ Ariz, 77-84, Killam fel English, Univ Alta, 71-73; ed, Nineteenth Century Theatre Res, 72-; Guggenheim fel Theatre Hist, 78-79; prof English, Univ Ariz, 84-. **HONORS AND AWARDS** NEH Research Grant 87-91. **MEMBERSHIPS** Nineteenth Century Theatre Res; English Lit Transition. **RESEARCH** English theatre history; 19th and 20th century English drama; Shakespeare. **SELECTED PUBLICATIONS** Auth, Two early absurd plays in England, Mod Drama, 73; ed, The Collected Letters of Sir Arthur Pinero, Univ Minn, 74; auth, The London Stage 1890-1899: A Calendar of Plays and Players, Scarecrow, 76; The West End London Stage in the 1890's, Educ Theatre J, 77; coauth, English Drama and Theatre, 1800-1900, Gale Res, 78; auth, American and British Theatrical Biography: A Directory, Scarecrow, 78; Henry Arthur Jones: An Annotated Bibliography of Writings about Him, English Lit in Transition, 79; The London Stage 1900-1909: A Calendar of Plays and Players, Scarecrow, 81; The London Stage 1950-1959: A Calendar of Plays and Players, 2 vols, Metuchen, NJ & London: the Scarecrow Press, 93. **CONTACT ADDRESS** Dept of English, Univ of Arizona, 1 University of Arizona, Tucson, AZ, 85721-0001. **EMAIL** jpwearing@aol.com

WEASMER, JERIE
DISCIPLINE ENGLISH COMPOSITION AND LANGUAGE **EDUCATION** Upper IA Col, BA, 71; Univ IA, MA, 88, Purdue Univ, PhD, 96. **CAREER** Eng Dept, Eastern Ill Univ **MEMBERSHIPS** Nat Coun Tchrs Engl; Ill Asn Tchrs Eng IL; Asn Tchr Educators; IL Philol Asn. **SELECTED PUBLICATIONS** Coauth, A.M. Formative Assessment in Teacher Preparation, Clearing House, 97; Teaching is a Team Sport: Enhancing Collegial Roles, Kappa Delta Pi Record, 97. **CONTACT ADDRESS** Eastern Illinois Univ, 600 Lincoln Ave, Charleston, IL, 61920-3099.

WEATHERBY JR, HAROLD L.
DISCIPLINE RENAISSANCE AND VICTORIAN LITERATURE **EDUCATION** Yale Univ, PhD. **CAREER** Instr, Vanderbilt Univ. **SELECTED PUBLICATIONS** Auth, Cardinal Newman in His Age; The Keen Delight: The Christian Poet in the Modern World; Mirrors of Celestial Grace: Patristic Theology in Spenser's Allegory, 94. **CONTACT ADDRESS** Vanderbilt Univ, Nashville, TN, 37203-1727.

WEATHERS, WINSTON
PERSONAL Born 12/25/1926, Pawhuska, OK **DISCIPLINE** ENGLISH, RHETORIC **EDUCATION** Univ Okla, BA, 50, MA, 51, PhD(English), 64. **CAREER** Asst prof English, Cottey Col, 51-54; from instr to prof English, 58-76, chairperson fac lett, 74-76, Grad Prof Mod Lett, Univ Tulsa, 76-. **RESEARCH** Rhetoric and style; poetics; William Blake. **SELECTED PUBLICATIONS** Auth, The Archetype and the Psyche, Univ Tulsa, 68; Messages From the Asylum, Joseph Nichols, 70; The Lonesome Game, David Lewis, 70; Indian and White: Sixteen Eclogues, Univ Nebr, 70; coauth, The New Strategy of Style, McGraw, 78; auth, An Alternate Style, Boynton/Cook, 80; Mezzo Cammin: Poems from the Middle of My Life, Joseph Nichols, 81; The Broken Word: Communication Pathos in Modern Literature, Gordon & Breach, 81; A 'Sacrament', Poetry, Vol 0162, 1993; 'On Entering The Hospice', Poetry, Vol 0162, 1993. **CONTACT ADDRESS** Grad Fac of Mod Lett, Univ of Tulsa, Tulsa, OK, 74104.

WEAVER, GARY
DISCIPLINE INTERCULTURAL COMMUNICATION, ADAPTATION AND CONFLICT **EDUCATION** Am Univ, BA, MA, PhD. **CAREER** Prof, Am Univ; lect, Acad Educ Develop (AED), The Inst Int Educ (IIE); Ctr For Journalists. **HONORS AND AWARDS** Dir, Seminar Managing a Multicultural Workforce; Dir, The Fulbright Pre-Acad Prog, Dir, Community Studies Prog, Am Univ. **RESEARCH** Cross-cultural communications, contemporary social and political movements. **SELECTED PUBLICATIONS** Auth, The University and Revolution, Prentice-Hall, 69; Readings in Cross-Cultural Communication, Ginn Custom Publ, 87; Culture, Communication, and Conflict,Ginn Press, 94. **CONTACT ADDRESS** American Univ, 4400 Massachusetts Ave, Washington, DC, 20016.

WEAVER, JACK WAYNE
PERSONAL Born 04/07/1932, Damascus, VA, m, 1957, 3 children **DISCIPLINE** ENGLISH LITERATURE **EDUCATION** Berea Col, BA, 54; Univ NC, Chapel Hill, MA, 59, PhD(English), 66. **CAREER** From asst prof to assoc prof English, Greensboro Col, 59-67; assoc prof, 67-72, coordr freshman English, 68-73, Prof English, Winthrop Col, 72-, Piedmont Univ Ctr res grant, 65-66; Greensboro Col res grant, 66-67; Winthrop Col res grant, 68 & 73. **MEMBERSHIPS** MLA; Southern Mod Lang Asn; AAUP Am Comt Irish Studies. **RESEARCH** Modern Irish literature; Romantic English poetry and criticism; English novel. **SELECTED PUBLICATIONS** Auth, Stage-management in the Irish theatre, English Lit Transition, 66; An exile's return, Eire, 68; Moore's name for Gogarty in Hail & Farewell, English Lit Transition, 71; AE's use of Blake in Irish Homestead, 76, J Irish Lit; Romanticism as source in Joyces's Portrait, S Atlantic Bull, 77; Moore's Use of Celtic Materials: What & How, English Lit Transition, 79; William Trevor, In: Dictionary of Irish Literature, 79; ed, Selected proceedings of the Scotch-Irish heritage festival at Winthrop College, 81; Parnell In Perspective - Boyce,Dg, Oday,A, Victorian Studies, Vol 0036, 1993; Long,Walter, Ireland, And The Union, 1905-1920 - Kendle,J, English Literature In Transition 1880-1920, Vol 0037, 1994; Picking Up Airs - Hearing The Music In Joyce Text - Bauerle,Rh, English Literature In Transition 1880-1920, Vol 0037, 1994; Bloom Old Sweet Song, Essays On Joyce And Music - Bowen,Z, English Literature In Transition 1880-1920, Vol 0038, 1995; Modern Irish Literature, Sources And Founders - Mercier,V, English Literature In Transition 1880-1920, Vol 0038, 1995' The Prose Literature Of The Gaelic Revival, 1881-1921 - Oleary,P, English Literature In Transition 1880-1920, Vol 0039, 1996. **CONTACT ADDRESS** 144 Brookwood Lane, Rock Hill, SC, 29730.

WEBB, LYNNE M.
PERSONAL Born 03/20/1951, Shamokin, PA, m, 1984, 3 children **DISCIPLINE** COMMUNICATION AND COMMUNITY DEVELOPMENT **EDUCATION** Pa State Univ, BS, 72; Univ Ore, MS, 75, PhD, 80. **CAREER** Instr, Berea Col, 78-80; vis assoc prof, Univ Hawaii, 90; assoc prof, Univ Fla, 80-91; assoc prof, Univ Memphis, 91-. **HONORS AND AWARDS** Who's Who of Amer Women; Who's Who in the South and Southwest; Who's Who in the Media and Commun; Who's Who in Amer Educ; Outreach award, Southern States Commun Asn, 97; top res paper award, 98, 90, 86; teaching award, Col of Liberal Arts & Sci, 89-90, 85-86, 83-84; teaching award, Alpha Lambda Delta, 86-87. **MEMBERSHIPS** Intl Commun Asn; Nat Commun Asn; Southern States Commun Asn; Tenn Commun Asn. **RESEARCH** Commun theory; Interpersonal commun; Family commun; Commun and aging. **SELECTED PUBLICATIONS** Auth, Convention financing: Theft or misunderstanding, Connections, 97; co-auth, Socially constructing the aging experience: A review essay on the Handbook of Communication and Aging Research, Health Comm, 96; auth, Proactive collegiality: Stalking the demon where he lives, Spectra, 96; co-auth, Applied family commun res: Casting light upon the demon, Jour of Applied Commun Res, 95; co-auth, Maintaining effective interaction skills, Communication in Later Life, Butterworth-Heinemann, 95; auth, A proactive stance, Connections, 95. **CONTACT ADDRESS** Dept. of Communication, 143 TC Bldg., Memphis, TN, 38152. **EMAIL** lynne_webb@compuserve.com

WEBB JR, RALPH
DISCIPLINE INTERPERSONAL COMMUNICATION **EDUCATION** Univ Wis, PhD, 65. **CAREER** Prof, Purdue Univ. **RESEARCH** Language; gender; intercultural communication; communication theory. **SELECTED PUBLICATIONS** Auth, Interpersonal Speech Communication: Principles and Practices, 75; Graduate Education in Speech Communication: Current Status and Future Directions, Commun Educ, 79. **CONTACT ADDRESS** Dept of Commun, Purdue Univ, 1080 Schleman Hall, West Lafayette, IN, 47907-1080.

WEBER, BURTON JASPER
PERSONAL Born 01/30/1934, St. Louis, MO, m, 1959, 2 children **DISCIPLINE** ENGLISH LITERATURE **EDUCATION** Washington Univ, AB, 55; Univ Minn, MA, 58, PhD, 65. **CAREER** Asst prof, 65-70, assoc prof, 70-79, Prof English, Univ Regina, 80-. **RESEARCH** Milton; Shakespeare; 17th century English poetry. **SELECTED PUBLICATIONS** Auth, Construction of Paradise Lost, 71; Wedges and Wings, Southern Ill Univ, 74; The ordering of the tempest, Wascana Rev, spring 75; The nonnarrative approaches to Paradise Lost: A gentle remonstrance, Milton Studies, 76; The interlocking triads of the 1st Book Of The 'Faerie Queene' + Spenser,E., Studies in philology, vol 0090, 1993 **CONTACT ADDRESS** 2030 McTavish, Regina, SK, S4S 0A2.

WEBER, DONALD
PERSONAL Born 02/09/1951, Bronx, NY, m, 1973, 2 children **DISCIPLINE** AMERICAN LITERATURE **EDUCATION** State Univ NY, BA, 72; Columbia Univ, MA, 73, PhD(English), 78. **CAREER** Adj lectr English, Lehman Col, City Univ New York, 73-78; asst prof, Univ Calif, Los Angeles, 78-81; Asst Prof English, Mt Holyoke Col, Mass, 81-. **RESEARCH** Puritanism in American literature; Jonathan Edwards; American religion and culture. **SELECTED PUBLICATIONS** Auth, Perry Miller and the recovery of Jonathan Edwards, introduction to Perry Miller, Jonathan Edwards, Univ Mass Press, 81; The question of the New England mind, New England Quart, 82; Hawthorne in His Own Time, Nathaniel Hawthorne J, 78 & 82; Outsiders And Greenhorns, Christopher-Newman In The Old-World, David-Levinsky In The New + James,Henry The 'American', And Cahan,Abraham The 'Rise Of David Levinsky', American Literature, Vol 0067, 1995; From Limen To Border, A Meditation On The Legacy Of Turner,Victor For American Cultural-Studies, American Quarterly, Vol 0047, 1995; Edwards,Jonathan, Religious Tradition, And American Culture - Conforti,Ja, Early American Literature, Vol 0031, 1996; No Secrets Were Safe From Me - Situating Kureishi,Hanif, Massachusetts Review, Vol 0038, 1997. **CONTACT ADDRESS** Dept of English, Mount Holyoke Col, 50 College St, South Hadley, MA, 01075-1461.

WEDBERG, LLOYD W.
DISCIPLINE MODERN GERMAN AND ENGLISH WRITING **EDUCATION** Univ Mich, BA, MA, PhD. **CAREER** Prof, 61-. **HONORS AND AWARDS** Grant, Exxon Edu Found. **SELECTED PUBLICATIONS** Pub(s), 19th Century German Novelle; connections between the German Narrenschiff and Katherine Anne Porter's Ship of Fools. **CONTACT ADDRESS** Dept of Eng, Univ Detroit Mercy, 4001 W McNichols Rd, PO BOX 19900, Detroit, MI, 48219-0900.

WEE, DAVID LUTHER
PERSONAL Born 01/20/1939, Madison, WI, m, 1961, 3 children **DISCIPLINE** ENGLISH **EDUCATION** St Olaf Col, BA, 61; Stanford Univ, MA, 65, PhD(English), 67. **CAREER** Asst prof, 65-71, sr fel & sr tutor, Paracollege, 71-72, ASSOC PROF ENGLISH, ST OLAF COL, 71-, Sr Tutor, Paracollege, 76-, Danforth assoc, St Olaf Col, 69-; sr commons room visitor, Mansfield Col, England, 73; adj prof English, Macalester Col, 78. **MEMBERSHIPS** AAUP **RESEARCH** Victorian literature. **SELECTED PUBLICATIONS** Auth, Studying the humanities: Heaven on earth?, Minn English J, 4/68; Athletics as a human experience, Event, 10/71; The temptation of Christ and the motif of divine duplicity in the Corpus Christi cycle drama, Mod Philol, 8/74; October 1964 - Halberstam,D, Journal Of American History, Vol 0082, 1995. **CONTACT ADDRESS** Dept of English, St Olaf Col, 1520 St Olaf Ave, Northfield, MN, 55057-1099.

WEES, WILLIAM CHARLES
PERSONAL Born 06/20/1935, Joplin, MO, m, 1958, 3 children **DISCIPLINE** ENGLISH **EDUCATION** Northwestern Univ, BA, 57, PhD(English), 64; Univ Rochester, MA, 58. **CAREER** Asst prof English, Colby Col, 61-69; Assoc Prof English, Mcgill Univ, 69-. **MEMBERSHIPS** MLA; Asn Can Univ Teachers English; Film Studies Asn Can. **RESEARCH** Literature and film. **SELECTED PUBLICATIONS** Auth, Ezra Pound as a vorticist, Wis Studies Contemp Lit, 65; England's avant-garde: The vorticist-futurist phase, Western Humanities Rev, 68; Vorticism and the English Avant- Garde, Univ Toronto, 72; Dickens, Griffith and Eisenstein, Humanities Asn Rev, fall 73; The Cinematic Image as a Visualization of Sight, Wide Angle, 81; Back And Forth - Early Cinema And The Avant-Garde - Testa,B, University Of Toronto Quarterly, Vol 0063, 1993; To Free To Cinema - Mekas,Jonas And The New-York Underground - James,De, Film Quarterly, Vol 0046, 1993; Avant-Garde Film Motion Studies - Macdonald,S, Film Quarterly, Vol 0047, 1994; Direct Theory - Experimental Film/Video As Major Genre - Small,Es, Film Quarterly, Vol 0050, 1996. **CONTACT ADDRESS** Dept of English, McGill Univ, Montreal, PQ, H3A 2T6.

WEIDHORN, MANFRED
PERSONAL Born 10/10/1931, Vienna, Austria, 2 children **DISCIPLINE** ENGLISH **EDUCATION** Columbia Univ, BA, 54, PhD(English), 63; Univ Wis, MA, 57. **CAREER** Instr English, Univ Ala, 57-58, Brooklyn Col, 60-63; from asst prof to assoc prof, 63-73, prof English, Yeshiva Col, 73-, Danforth Assoc; prof English, Guterman, 88-. **RESEARCH** Sir Winston Churchill; Shakespeare; politics and literature. **SELECTED PUBLICATIONS** Auth, Dreams in 17th Century English Literature, Mouton, The Hague, 70; Richard Lovelace, Twayne, 70; Sword and Pen: A Survey of the Writings of Sir Winston Churchill, Univ NMex, 74; Turn Your Life Around, Prentice-Hall, 78; Sir Winston Churchill, Twayne, 79; auth, Napoleon, Atheneum, 86; auth, Churchill's Rhetoric and Political Dilemma, Univ Press of Am, 87; auth, Robert E. Lee, Atheneum, 88; auth, A Harmony of Interests, Fairleigh Dickinson, 92; auth, Jackie Robinson, Atheneum, 93. **CONTACT ADDRESS** Dept of English, Yeshiva Univ, 500 W 185th St, New York, NY, 10033-3299.

WEIGL, BRUCE
DISCIPLINE LITERATURE **EDUCATION** Univ Utah, PhD 79; Univ New Hampshire, MA 75; Oberlin Col, BA 74. **CAREER** Penn State Univ, prof, dir undergrad, dir MFA prog, 86-; Old Dominion Univ, prof, dir creat write, dir grad stud, 81-86; Univ Arkansas, prof, dir creat write, 79-81; Lorain Cnty Comm Col, inst, 76-77; Univ Utah, tchg fel, 77-79. **HONORS AND AWARDS** YADDO Found Fel; Acad Amer Poets Prize; Pushcart Prize; Breadloaf Fel; Tu Do Chien Kien Awd by Viet Vets of Amer; NEA Fel; Pulitzer Prize Nomin for SONG of NAPALM; Best Amer Poetry Prize., Prof Weigl's poetry has been translated into nine different languages. **RESEARCH** 20th Century Brit & Amer Poetry **SELECTED PUBLICATIONS** Auth, After the Others, TriQtly Books, Northwestern Univ Press, forthcoming; Wrestling Sharon: A Memoir, NY Grove, Atlantic Press, forthcoming; The Archeology of the Circle: New and Selected Poems, NY, Grove, Atlantic Press, 98; Angel Riding a Beast: Poems for America, translated with author, Liliana Ursu, Evanston, NUP, 98; Mountain River: Poetry from the Vietnam Wars: 1945-1995, coed, co-translated, Univ of Mass, 98; Between the Lines: Writings on War and its Social Consequences, coed, Boston Amherst, U of Mass Press, 96; Charles Simic: Essays on the Poetry, ed, Ann Arbor, U of Mich Press, 96; Poems from Captured Documents, co-trans, Amherst MA, U of Mass Press, 94. **CONTACT ADDRESS** Dept of English, Pennsylvania State Univ, 1251 South Garner St, State College, PA, 16801.

WEIHE, EDWIN
DISCIPLINE ENGLISH **EDUCATION** Brown Univ, BA, 63; Univ IA, MA, 65, MFA, 66, PhD, 72. **CAREER** Eng, Seattle Univ. **RESEARCH** Am lit; Modism; fiction writing. **SELECTED PUBLICATIONS** Auth, I Can See a Man, poetry, Orphic Lute, 93; Merleau-Ponty's Doubt: The Wild of Nothing, Int Symp, Leuven, Belgium, 91, publ in Phenomelogia, 93; Her Birthday Suit, fiction, Arterial, 91; Her Dress, poem, Arterial, 91; Flannery O'Connor's Misfits, Inst forum, RWTH-Aachen, 93; Mystery of Flannery O'Connor, Amer Stud Prog, Katholieke Univ, Nijmegen, 93; Persephone, fiction, Fragments, 74; American Artificial Limb Co, fiction, Fragments, 73. **CONTACT ADDRESS** Dept of Eng, Seattle Univ, 900 Broadway, Seattle, WA, 98122-4460. **EMAIL** eweihe@seattleu.edu

WEIL, HERBERT S.
DISCIPLINE ENGLISH LITERATURE **EDUCATION** Tulane Univ, BA; Stanford Univ, MA; PhD. **CAREER** Prof **RESEARCH** Psychology of audience and reader response; character; relations of performance to text; comparative literature; literature and art; film; modern fiction. **SELECTED PUBLICATIONS** Auth, pub(s) on Shakespeare's plays, Sophocles, modern drama, Alice Munro and Carol Shields. **CONTACT ADDRESS** Dept of English, Manitoba Univ, Winnipeg, MB, R3T 2N2.

WEIL, JUDITH R.
DISCIPLINE ENGLISH LITERATURE **EDUCATION** Univ Middlebury, BA; Stanford Univ, MA; PhD. **CAREER** Assoc prof **RESEARCH** Social contexts of Renaissance literature; women's studies; traditions of literary criticism. **SELECTED PUBLICATIONS** Auth, pub(s) on Peele, Marlowe, Shakespeare, Webster, and critical theory. **CONTACT ADDRESS** Dept of English, Manitoba Univ, Winnipeg, MB, R3T 2N2.

WEIMER, JOAN MYERS
PERSONAL Born 03/12/1936, Cambridge, MA, m, 1971, 3 children **DISCIPLINE** AMERICAN LITERATURE, WOMEN'S STUDIES, NON-FICTION WRITING **EDUCATION** Tufts Univ, AB, 57; Rutgers Univ, New Brunswick, MA, 64, PhD, 70. **CAREER** From instr to assoc prof, 68-82, prof eng, Drew Univ, 82, Vis scholar, Ctr Res Women, Stanford Univ, 78, 87; Vis scholar, Univ AZ, 96; Consulting ed, Legacy; Proj dir, State of NJ grant, 84-86; Producer/moderator, Women in the Center and Why They Belong There, 13-part television series, 83-84. **HONORS AND AWARDS** Phi Beta Kappa, 56; John H McGinnis Award, Southwest Rev, 77; Semi-finalist, Nat Play Award Competition of Nat Repertory Theater, 80; Res and travel grants, Drew Univ, 90-98. **MEMBERSHIPS** NJ Project on Curriculum Integration (mem, Advisory board); Central NJ/Masaya, Nicaragua Friendship City Project (corrdinating comt, 85; leader of delegation to Nicaragua, 1/87); Madison Area Chap Amnesty Int (co-founder, secy), 76-82; Westfield Area Comt for Hum Rights 63-66. **RESEARCH** Memoir; feminist criticism of lit; relationship between roles of mothers and polit repression and torture; machismo. **SELECTED PUBLICATIONS** Co-ed (with David R Weimer), Literature of America, America, 7 vol, McDougal, Littell, 73; The Belly Dancer and the Virgin: Mythic Women in Modern Egypt, Southwest Rev, winter 76; Magic in Brazil, North Am Rev, winter 76; The Mother, the Macho, and the State, Int Jour Women's Studies, 1/78; Co-auth (with David Weimer), Ready About, orig play, 78; Co-auth (with David Weimer), Pyramid, orig play, 79; The Story Tellers, orig play, 80; Mythic Parables of Female Power: Inanna, Demeter and Persephone and the Sleeping Beauty, Anima, fall 86; Women, Artists as Exiles in the Stories of Constance Fenimore Woolson, Legacy, fall 86; Individuation and Intimacy: Eleusis and the Sleeping Beauty, Anima, fall 88; Ed, Women Artists: Women Exiles: Miss Grief and Other Stories by Constance Fenimore Woolson, Rutgers Univ Press, 88; The Admiring Aunt and the Proud Salmon of the Pond: Constance Fenimore Woolson's Struggle with Henry James, In: Critical Essays on Constance Fenimore Woolson (Cheryl Torsney, ed), G K Hall, 92; But I'm Not Writing Fiction! And Other Autobiographical Fictions, Soundings, fall 93; Back Talk: Teaching Lost Selves to Speak, Random House, 94 and Univ Chicago Press, 95; Co-auth (with Phyllis Paullette), Back Talk, orig play, 95; Intimate Knowing: A Tale of a Haunted Biographer, Belles Lettres, summer 95; Life Stand Still Here, In: The Writer's Journal (Sheila Bender, ed), Dell 96. **CONTACT ADDRESS** Dept of Eng, Drew Univ, 36 Madison Ave, Madison, NJ, 07940-1493. **EMAIL** jweimer@drew.edu

WEINBROT, HOWARD D.
PERSONAL Born 05/14/1936, New York, NY **DISCIPLINE** ENGLISH **EDUCATION** Antioch Col, BA, 58; Univ Chicago, MA, 59, PhD, 63. **CAREER** Instr English lit, Yale Univ, 63-66; from asst prof to assoc prof, Univ Calif, Riverside, 66-69; from Assoc Prof to Prof, 69-84, Ricardo Quintana Prof English, Univ Wis-Madison, 84-, William F. Vilas Res Prof, 87-. **HONORS AND AWARDS** NEH Sr Fel, 75-76; Huntington Libr Fel, 77; Newberry-Brit Acad Fel, 77-78; Huntington-NEH Fel, 83; Huntington-Brit Acad Fel, 84; Newberry-NEH Fel, 86; ACLS Travel Fel, 86; Humanities Inst Fel, Univ Wis, 87; Guggenheim Fel, 88-89; Mellon Prof, Inst Advanced Study, 93-94. **MEMBERSHIPS** Johnsonians; Am Soc 18th Century Studies (pres, midwest chap, 79-80; exec bd, 96-99) Johnson Soc Cent Region (secy-treas, 70-95); Midwest ASECS; Scottish Studies Soc. **RESEARCH** Eighteenth century theory and practice of imitation and satire;18th century Anglo-classical and Anglo-French relations; Pope; Johnson; intellectual and literary history. **SELECTED PUBLICATIONS** Auth, The Formal Strain, Chicago, 69; ed, New Aspects of Lexicography, Southern Ill Univ, 72; co-ed, The Eighteenth-Century: A Current Bibliography, Philol Quart, 75; auth, Augustus Caesar in Augustan England, Princeton Univ, 78; Alexander Pope and the Traditions of Formal Verse Satire, Princeton Univ, 82; co-ed, Oxford Anthology of Poetry in English, 87; auth, Eighteenth Century Satire, Cambridge, 88; ed, Northrup Frye and 18th-Century Literature, Eighteenth-Century Studies, 91; auth, Britannia's Issue, Cambridge, 93; author numerous articles and reviews. **CONTACT ADDRESS** Dept of English, Univ of Wis, 600 North Park St, Madison, WI, 53706-1403. **EMAIL** weinbrot@facstaff.wisc.edu

WEINER, ANDREW DAVID
PERSONAL Born 06/29/1943, New York, NY, m, 1964, 3 children **DISCIPLINE** ENGLISH LITERATURE **EDUCATION** City Col NY, AB, 66; Princeton Univ, PhD, 69. **CAREER** Asst prof, 69-74, assoc prof, 74-82, prof, 82, Univ Wis-Madison. **HONORS AND AWARDS** Nat Endowment for Univ of Wisc Grad School Summer Support, 70, 72, 73, 76, 77, 79, 80, 82, 86, 87; NEH younger scholar, 73-74. **MEMBERSHIPS** MLA; Spenser Soc. **RESEARCH** Art history; Elizabethan literature; history of ideas. **SELECTED PUBLICATIONS** Auth, Graven Images 1, 94; co-ed and contrib, Graven Images 2: The Body, 95; co-ed and contrib, Madness, Melancholy and the Limits of the Self: Studies in Culture, Law, and the Sacred, Graven Images Vol 3, Madison: University of Wisconsin Law School, 96; co-ed and contrib, Burdens of Guilty Minds: Rape and Suicide in Shakespeare's Lucrece, Graven Images 2, 95; auth, Madness and the Limits of the Self in Shakespeare's King Lear, Madness, Melancholy and the Limits of the Self: Studies in Culture, Law, and the Sacred, Graven Images Volume 3, UW Law School, 96; coauth, Erasmus and Tyndale, Major Tudor Authors: A Bio-Critical Sourcebook, Greenwood Publishing, 97. **CONTACT ADDRESS** Dept of English, Univ Wisconsin, Madison, 600 North Park St, Madison, WI, 53706-1403. **EMAIL** adweiner@facstaff.wisc.edu

WEINGAND, DARLENE E.
PERSONAL Born 08/13/1937, Oak Park, IL, m **DISCIPLINE** LIBRARY; INFORMATION STUDIES **EDUCATION** Univ Minnesota, PhD 80; Dominican Univ, MA 73; Elmhurst Col, BA 72. **CAREER** Univ Wisconsin Madison, asst, assoc, prof, 81 to 98-, fac dir, 81-, SLIS asst dir, 90-94, 97-; Curtin Univ W Aus, vis fel, 90. **HONORS AND AWARDS** Dist Alum of the Yr, Dom U; ALISE res Gnt; Outstanding Achie Audio Apps; Fulbright lectshp; Contemporary Auth; Phi Delta Kappa; Beta Phi Mu. **MEMBERSHIPS** ALA; IFLA; ALISE; WLA; WAACE **RESEARCH** Cont EDU ; Mktg; Planning; Pub Lib; Library Futures; Tech Innovations; Dist EDU MBTI. **SELECTED PUBLICATIONS** Auth, Future Driven Library Marketing, ALA, 98; Customer Service Excellence: A Concise guide for Librarians, ALA, 97; Managing Today's Public Library, Lib Unlimited, 94. **CONTACT ADDRESS** Dept of Information Studies, Univ of Wisconsin, Madison, Madison, WI, 53706. **EMAIL** weingand@facstaff.wisc.edu

WEINSTEIN, MARK A.
DISCIPLINE 19TH CENTURY BRITISH LITERATURE **EDUCATION** Cornell Univ, BA, 59; Yale Univ, MA, 60, PhD, 62. **CAREER** Lt, US Army, 62-64; instr, Bronx Community Col, 64-65; instr, 65-68, asst prof, Brooklyn Col, 68-70; assoc prof, 70-74, prof, Univ Nev, Las Vegas, 74-. **SELECTED PUBLICATIONS** Auth, Scott, Walter, Saint Ronan's Well, Vol 16 of The Edinburgh Ed of the Waverley Novels, ed, Mark A. Weinstein, 30 vols, Edinburgh UP and Columbia UP, 93-2003; The Manuscript of The Pirate, Princeton Univ Libr Chronicle, 58, 97. **CONTACT ADDRESS** Univ Nev, Las Vegas, Las Vegas, NV, 89154. **EMAIL** weinstei@nevada.edu

WEINSTEIN, PHILIP MEYER
PERSONAL Born 07/08/1940, Memphis, TN, m, 1963, 2 children **DISCIPLINE** ENGLISH & AMERICAN LITERATURE **EDUCATION** Princeton Univ, AB, 62; Harvard Univ, MA, 66, PhD(English), 68. **CAREER** From instr to asst prof English, Harvard Univ, 68-71; asst prof, 71-74, assoc prof, 74-81, Prof English, Swarthmore Col, 81-, Chmn Dept, 80-. **MEMBERSHIPS** AAUP; MLA **RESEARCH** British fiction, Dickens through Joyce; American fiction, Hawthorne through Faulkner. **SELECTED PUBLICATIONS** Auth, Structure and collapse: A study of Bleak House, Dickens Studies, 68; The exploitative and protective imagination: Unreliable narration in The Sacred Fount, Harvard English Studies, 70; An interpretation of pastoral in The Winter's Tale, Shakespeare Quart, 71; Henry James and the Requirements of the Imagination, Harvard Univ, 71; Caddy Disparue: Exploring an episode common to Proust and Faulkner, Comp Lit Studies, 3/77; Precarious sanctuaries: Protection and exposure in Falkner's fiction, Studies Am Fiction, spring 79; Choosing between the Quick and the Dead: Three versions of Lady Chatterley's Lover, Mod Lang Quart, 82; Faulkner And Psychology - Faulkner And Yoknapatawpha, 1991 - Kartinger,Dm, Abadie,Aj, Mississippi Quarterly, Vol 0048, 1995. **CONTACT ADDRESS** Dept of English Lit, Swarthmore Col, 500 College Ave, Swarthmore, PA, 19081-1306.

WEINSTOCK, DONALD JAY
PERSONAL Born 09/02/1934, Chicago, IL, m, 1955 **DISCIPLINE** ENGLISH LITERATURE **EDUCATION** Univ Calif, Los Angeles, AB, 56, MA, 60, PhD(English), 68. **CAREER** Actg asst prof English, Univ Calif, Riverside, 65-68; lectr, Univ Calif, Los Angeles, 68-69; asst prof, 69-74, assoc prof, 74-80, prof English, Calif State Univ, Long Beach, 80-. **MEMBERSHIPS** MLA; Assn Poetry Ther. **RESEARCH** Victorian literature; psychological applications of poetry; contemporary African writing in English. **SELECTED PUBLICATIONS** Auth, The two swarms of locusts: Judgment by indirection, In: Things Fall Apart, Studies in Black Lit, Spring 71; The two Boer wars and the Jameson Raid: A checklist of novels in Dutch and Afrikaans, Spring 71 & The two Boer wars and the Jameson Raid: A checklist of novels in English, Spring 72; Poetry and the self, 78 & Poetry therapy: A bibliography, 79, ERIC; Jaggers in the country, NDak Quart, Summer 79; rev article Arthur Lerner, Poetry in the therapeutic experience, Maelstrom Rev, 80; Say not we are on a darkling plain: Clough's rejoinder to Dover Beach, Victorian Poetry, Spring 81. **CONTACT ADDRESS** Dept of English, California State Univ, Long Beach, 1250 N Bellflower, Long Beach, CA, 90840-0001.

WEINTRAUB, STANLEY
PERSONAL Born 04/17/1929, Philadelphia, PA, m, 1954, 3 children **DISCIPLINE** ENGLISH LITERATURE **EDUCATION** Pa State Col, West Chester, BS, 49; Temple Univ, MA, 51; PA State Univ, PhD(English), 56. **CAREER** From instr to prof English, 53-70, Res Prof, Pa State Univ, 70-, Dir Inst Arts & Humanistic Studies, 70-, Ed, Shaw Rev, 56-; Guggenheim fel, 68-69. **MEMBERSHIPS** Auth Guild; Int Asn Study Anglo-Irish Lit; MLA. **RESEARCH** George Bernard Shaw; biographical writing; English literature since 1880. **SELECTED PUBLICATIONS** Auth, Journey to Heartbreak: Bernard Shaw 1914-1918, Weybright & Talley, 71 & Routledge & Kegan Paul, 73: co-ed, Saint Joan: Fifty Years After 1923-24/1973-74, La State Univ, 73; auth, Whistler, a Biography, Collins, London & Weybright & Talley, 74; coauth, Lawrence of Arabia: The Literary Impulse, La State Univ, 75; auth, Four Rossettis: A Victorian Biography, Weybright & Talley (McKay), 77; ed, The Portable Bernard Shaw, Viking/Penguin, 77; auth, The London Yankees: Portraits of American Writers and Artists in London, 1894-1914, Harcourt Brace Jovanovich, 79; The Medievalism In Lawrence-Of-Arabia - Allen,Md, Comparative Literature Studies, Vol 0030, 1993; A Comparative-Study Of James,Henry And Major Japanese Writers - Akiyama,M, Comparative Literature Studies, Vol 0030, 1993; London In The 1890s - A Cultural History - Beckson,K, English Literature In Transition 1880-1920, Vol 0036, 1993; The Profession Of The Playwright, British Theater 1800-1900 - Stephens,Jr, Nineteenth-Century Literature, Vol 0048, 1993; The Laurel And The Ivy, The Story Of Parnell,Charles,Stewart And Irish Nationalism - Kee,R, English Literature In Transition 1880-1920, Vol 0038, 1995; Shaw And Joyce, The Last Word In Stolentelling - Black,Mf, English Literature In Transition 1880-1920, Vol 0038, 1995; Beardsley,Aubrey, Dandy Of The Grotesque - Snodgrass,C, English Literature In Transition 1880-1920, Vol 0039, 1996; Curtains Speech, A New Source For 'Heartbreak House', English Literature In Transition 1880-1920, Vol 0038, 1995; Victoria,Queen Secrets - Munich,A, Historian, Vol 0059, 1997. **CONTACT ADDRESS** Dept of Lit, Pennsylvania State Univ, 117 Burrowes Bldg, University Park, PA, 16802-6200.

WEISE, JUDITH ANDERSON
PERSONAL Born 11/04/1942, 1 child **DISCIPLINE** ENGLISH **EDUCATION** William Smith Col, BA, 63; Univ NC, Chapel Hill, MA, 66; State Univ NY Binghamton, PhD, 71. **CAREER** Ed asst, Hearthside Press, New York, 64; asst prof English, State Unive NY Col Potsdam, 69-. **HONORS AND AWARDS** Fulbright Sr Scholar, 86; Phi Kappa Phi Hon Soc, 97; SUNY Distinguished Teaching Prof, 98. **MEMBERSHIPS** MLA; Old English Sect Mod Lang; Women's Caucus Mod Lang; United Univ Prof; Int Soc Anglo-Saxonists. **RESEARCH** Dream visions; Chaucer; Old English poetry. **SELECTED PUBLICATIONS** Ambuguity in Old English Poetry, Neophilologus, Vol 60, 79; Romancing Seyart Cecylie: Chaucer's Tell-Tale Lexicon, Style, in print. **CONTACT ADDRESS** Dept English, State Univ NY, 44 Pierrepont Ave, Potsdam, NY, 13676-2299. **EMAIL** Weiseja@potsdam.edu

WEISL, ANGELA JANE
DISCIPLINE MEDIEVAL LITERATURE, WOMEN'S STUDIES, ENGLISH LITERATURE **EDUCATION** Middlebury Col, BA; Columbia Univ, PhD. **CAREER** Instr, Seton Hall Univ. **RESEARCH** Medieval women; narrative theory. **SELECTED PUBLICATIONS** Auth, Conquering the Reign of Femeny: Gender and Genre in Chaucer's Romance, DS Brewer, 95. **CONTACT ADDRESS** Seton Hall Univ, South Orange, NJ. **EMAIL** weislang@shu.edu

WEISS, ALEXANDER
PERSONAL 2 children **DISCIPLINE** ENGLISH **EDUCATION** Univ Md, College Park, BA, 64, MA, 66; Univ Calif, Berkeley, PhD(English), 73. **CAREER** Asst dir col sem prog, Univ Calif, Berkeley, 74-76; from Asst Prof to Assoc Prof, 76-85, PROF ENGLISH, RADFORD UNIV, 86-. **MEMBERSHIPS** SAtlantic Mod Lang Asn; Southeastern Medieval Asn; New Chaucer Soc; Nat Asn Schol; Va Org Schol; Asn Lit Schol and Critics. **RESEARCH** Middle English language and literature; Chaucer; Old English language and literature. **SELECTED PUBLICATIONS** Auth, Chaucer's early translations from French: The art of creative transformation, Proc Southeastern Medieval Convention, 81; Chaucer's Native Heritage, Peter Lang Publ, 85. **CONTACT ADDRESS** Dept of English, Radford Univ, PO Box 6935, Radford, VA, 24142-6935. **EMAIL** aweiss@runet.edu

WEISS, VICTORIA LOUISE
PERSONAL Born 07/21/1949, Cleveland, OH **DISCIPLINE** ENGLISH **EDUCATION** St Norbert Col, BA, 71; Lehigh Univ, MA, 74, PhD(English), 77. **CAREER** Asst Prof English, Oglethorpe Univ, 77-, Fac develop grant, Shell Oil Corp, 78. **MEMBERSHIPS** MLA **RESEARCH** Middle English literature, especially the relationship between history and literature; contemporary literature, especially experimental fiction. **SELECTED PUBLICATIONS** Auth, Form and meaning in Marguerite Duras' Moderato Cantabile, Critique, 74; Gawain's first failure: The beheading scene in Sir Gawain and the Green Knight, 76 & The Medieval knighting ceremony in Sir Gawain and the Green Knight, 11/78, Chaucer Rev; The Play World And The Real-World, Chivalry In 'Sir Gawain And The Green Knight', Philological Quarterly, Vol 0072, 1993; The Play World And The Real-World, Chivalry In 'Sir Gawain And The Green Knight', Philological Quarterly, Vol 0072, 1993; Grail Knight Or Boon Companion - The Inconsistent Sir-Bors Of Malory 'Morte Darthur', Studies In Philology, Vol 0094, 1997; Grail Knight Or Boon Companion - The Inconsistent Sir-Bors Of Malory 'Morte Darthur', Studies In Philology, Vol 0094, 1997. **CONTACT ADDRESS** Dept of English, Oglethorpe Univ, 4484 Peach Tree Rd, Atlanta, GA, 30319-2797.

WEITZMAN, ARTHUR JOSHUA
PERSONAL Born 09/13/1933, Newark, NJ, m, 1960, 2 children **DISCIPLINE** ENGLISH **EDUCATION** Univ Chicago, AB, 56, MA, 57; NY Univ, PhD(English), 64. **CAREER** Lectr English, Brooklyn Col, 60-63; instr Temple Univ, 63-64; asst prof, 64-69; assoc prof, 69-72, prof English, Northeastern Univ, 72-; co-ed & founder, The Scriblerian, 68-; Nat Endowment for Humanities, fel, 72-73; Mellon fel, Clark Libr, 76; 17th and 18th century field ed, G K Hall Publ Col, 77-. **MEMBERSHIPS** MLA; Am Soc 18th Century Studies; Conf of Eds of Learned Journals. **RESEARCH** Neo-classical English literature; bibiography and literature; urban studies. **SELECTED PUBLICATIONS** Ed, The Turkish Spy, Routledge & Kegan Paul, Columbia Univ & Temple Univ, 70; A Spider's Poison: Wit in Swift's Letter of Advice to a Young Poet, Ariel, 73; Addendum to Teerink and Scouten: Another Edition of Swift's poems, Papers Bibliog Soc Am, 73; Eighteenth century London: Urban Paradise or fallen city?, J Hist Ideas, 75; auth, Dr Johnson's er's Funeral, 16th Century Studies, 84; Luther and Lives of Saints, Harvard Library Bull, 85; German Humanist Lives of Saints, J Medieval and Renaissance Studies, 85. **CONTACT ADDRESS** Dept Theol, Boston Col, Chestnut Hill, MA, 02167-3800. **EMAIL** james.weiss@bc.edu

WEIXLMANN, JOSEPH NORMAN
PERSONAL Born 12/16/1946, Buffalo, NY, m, 1982, 3 children **DISCIPLINE** ENGLISH **EDUCATION** Kansas State Univ, PhD, Eng, 73, MA, 70; Canisius Col, AB, 68. **CAREER** Dean, Col Arts and Sciences, Indiana State Univ, 92-; Assoc Dean, CAS, ISU, 87-92; Prof Eng, ISU, 83; Assoc Prof Eng, ISU, 79-83; Asst Prof, 76-79; Asst Prof, Eng, Texas Tech Univ, 74-76; Inst Eng, Univ Oklahoma, 73-74. **HONORS AND AWARDS** NEH Fellow, 80-81; NEA Grants, 88-95; Lila Wallace, Readers Digest Fund Grants, 91, 92, 95; Am Lit Mag Awards, Ed Merit, 94-95; Intl Man of the Year Award, Intl Biographical Cen, 93. **MEMBERSHIPS** Modern Language Asn; Col Lang Asn; Council of Editors of Learned Journals; Soc for Scholarly Pub; Soc for the Study of Multi-Ethnic Literature in the USA; Council of Col Arts and Sciences. **RESEARCH** African Am Lit and Culture; Contem Am Fic. **SELECTED PUBLICATIONS** Editor-in Chief, African Am Review, 76-; (Prin Ed with Houston A Baker Jr) Black Feminist Literature and Literary Theory, Greenwood, Penkevill, 88; (Prin Ed with Chester J Fontenot) Belief Versus Theory in Black America Literary Criticism, Greenwood, Penevill, pp270, 86; (Prin Ed with Chester J Fontenot) Black America Prose Theory, Greenwood, Penkevill, 84. **CONTACT ADDRESS** Indiana State Univ, Stalker Hall 213, Terre Haute, IN, 47809. **EMAIL** ascweix@amber.indstate.edu

WELBURN, RONALD GARFIELD
PERSONAL Born 04/30/1944, Berwyn, PA, m, 1988 **DISCIPLINE** ENGLISH **EDUCATION** Lincoln University, PA, BA, 1968; University of Arizona, MA, 1970; New York University, PhD, 1983. **CAREER** Syracuse University, Syracuse NY, assistant professor of Afro-American studies, 1970-75; Rutgers University, New Brunswick NJ, formerly affiliated with Institute for Jazz Studies, assistant professor of English, 1983; WESTERN CONNECTICUT STATE UNIVERSITY, DANBURY, CT, ASSISTANT PROF OF ENGLISH, 1987-. **HONORS AND AWARDS** Silvera Award for poetry, Lincoln University, 1967 and 1968; fellow, Smithsonian Institute and Music Critics Association, 1975; Langston Hughes Legacy Certificate, Lincoln University, 1981. **MEMBERSHIPS** Board member, Eagle Wing Press, 1989-. **SELECTED PUBLICATIONS** Author of Peripheries: Selected Poems, 1966-1968, Greenfield Review Press, 1972; author of Heartland: Selected Poems, Lotus Press, 1981; author, Council Decisions: Poems, American Native Press Archives, 1991. **CONTACT ADDRESS** English Dept, Western Connecticut State Univ, 181 White St, Danbury, CT, 06810.

WELCH, DENNIS MARTIN
PERSONAL Born 09/23/1944, Artesia, CA, m, 1966, 2 children **DISCIPLINE** ENGLISH & AMERICAN LITERATURE **EDUCATION** Loyola Univ, Los Angeles, BA, 67; Univ Southern Calif, MA, 69, PhD(English), 72. **CAREER** From instr to asst prof English, Gonzaga Univ, 71-74; assoc prof humanities, Clarkson Col Technol, 74-81; Assoc Prof English & Humanities, VA Polytechnic Inst, 81-. **MEMBERSHIPS** MLA; Northeast Mod Lang Asn. **RESEARCH** English Renaissance and Romantic Age; 20th century American. **SELECTED PUBLICATIONS** Auth, America and Atlantis: Blake's ambivalent millennialism, Blake Newslett, 72; The meaning of nothingness in Donne's Nocturnall upon St Lucies Day, Bucknell Rev, 76; Center, circumference, and vegetation imagery in the writings of Blake, Studies Philol, 78; In the throes of Eros: Blakes's early career, Mosaic, 78; Hickey as satanic force in The Iceman Cometh, Ariz Quart, 78; Reading Blake,William - Behrendt,Sc, Blake-An Illustrated Quarterly, Vol 0027, 1994; Blake's response to Wollstonecraft's original stories, Blake Quart, Vol 13; Distance and progress in In Memoriam, Victorian Poetry, Vol 18; Blake 'Songs Of Experience', The Word Lost And Found, English Studies, Vol 0076, 1995; Blake 'Songs Of Experience', The Word Lost And Found, English Studies, Vol 0076, 1995; 'Christabel', 'King Lear' And The Cinderella Folktale, Papers On Language And Literature, Vol 0032, 1996; Expressive theory and Blake's audience, PMLA, Vol 96; Blake Illuminated Books, Vol 3, The Early Illuminated Books - Eaves,M, Essick,Rn, Viscomi,J, English Studies, Vol 0078, 1997; Blake Illuminated Books, Vol 5, Milton, A Poem And The Final Illuminated Books - Essick,Rn, Viscomi,J, English Studies, Vol 0078, 1997; Blake Illuminated Books, Vol 5, Milton, A Poem And The Final Illuminated Books - Essick,Rn, Viscomi,J, English Studies, Vol 0078, 1997; Blake Illuminated Books, Vol 1, Jerusalem - Paley,Md, English Studies, Vol 0078, 1997. **CONTACT ADDRESS** Dept of English & Humanities, VA Polytech Inst & State Univ, 100 Virginia Tech, Blacksburg, VA, 24061-0002.

WELCH, DONOVAN LEROY
PERSONAL Born 06/03/1932, Hastings, NE, m, 1953, 6 children **DISCIPLINE** ENGLISH **EDUCATION** Univ NE-Lincoln, PhD, 65. **CAREER** PROF ENGLISH & REYNOLDS DISTINGUISHED PROF POETRY, UNIV NE AT KEARNEY, 60- **HONORS AND AWARDS** Pablo Neruela Award Poetry; Best Prof: NE State Board Trustees, 90; Pratt-Heins Award Distinguished Tchg, 89. **RESEARCH** Contemporary American poetry. **SELECTED PUBLICATIONS** Carved by Obadiah Verity, Press Col Col, 93; A Brief History of Feathers, A Slow Tempo Press, 96; Fire's Tongue in the Cavelle's End, Univ NE-Kearney, 96. **CONTACT ADDRESS** Donovan LeRoy Welch, 611 W 27, Kearney, NE, 68847. **EMAIL** dlwelch@digitalis.net

WELCH, OLGA MICHELE
PERSONAL Born 12/30/1948, Salisbury, NC, m **DISCIPLINE** COMMUNICATIONS **EDUCATION** Howard Univ, BA (Salutatorian), history/English/educ 1971; Univ of TN, MS deaf educ 1972, EdD educ admin & super 1977. **CAREER** The Model Secondary Sch for the Deaf, instructor 1972-73, The TN Sch for the Deaf, instructor 1973-75, supervising principal 1977-78; UNIV OF TN DEPT OF SPEC EDUC & REHAB, ASSOC PROF & DIR 1978-, DIR DEAF EDUC PROG, REHABILITATION & DEAFNESS UNIT, PROFESSOR, currently. **HONORS AND AWARDS** Phi Beta Kappa; Phi Delta Kappa; Phi Kappa Phi; Phi Alpha Theta; Dept Awd "Most Creative Dissertation Topic" Univ TN; appointment to the Natl Educ Adv Bd 1983; E C Merrill Distinguished Research Award, 1990, 1992; Univ of TN, Chancellor's Award, 1998. **MEMBERSHIPS** Council of Exceptional Children; Alexander Graham Bell Assn; Convention of Amer Instructors of the Deaf; Natl Educ Assn; Assn for Supervision & Curriculum Develop; Project HELP tutorial prog for disadvantaged students 1983; vice pres, Knoxville Chap Natl Black Women's Hook-Up 1980-81; Girl Scout neighborhood chmn "NightHawks" Neighborhood 1977-; Interdenominational Concert Choir 1975-; American Educational Research Assn; Co-dir, Project Excel. **CONTACT ADDRESS** Deaf Education Prog, Univ of Tennessee, Claxton Addition Rm 129, Knoxville, TN, 37996.

WELLS, CORRI ELIZABETH
DISCIPLINE RHETORIC AND COMPOSITION **EDUCATION** Brigham Young Univ, BA, 77; Univ Houston, MA, 90; Univ TX at Arlington, PhD, 97. **CAREER** Adj fac, assoc dir, 1st Yr Composition, 95-97, grad tchg asst, 93-95 & instr, Univ TX at Arlington; adj fac, N Lake Col, Dallas Co Commun Col Dist 93-95; writing ctr asst, Northwest Campus, 92-93 & instr, Northeast Campus, 91-92, Tarrant Co Jr Col Dist; Instr, Extension Ctr, Salt Lake City & Tooele, 80 & grad tchg asst, Main Campus, Provo, 77-78, Brigham Young Univ. **MEMBERSHIPS** Nat Coun Tchrs Eng; Rhetoric Soc Am; MLA; Gorgias Soc. **SELECTED PUBLICATIONS** Auth, A Teacher's Guide to First Year English: Critical Reading, Thinking and Writing at the University of Texas at Arlington, 4th ed, Arlington, UTA Dept Engl, 96; Teaching Argument in the Computer Classroom, Instructor's Manual for Perspectives on Argument, By Nancy V. Wood, Englewood Cliffs, Prentice Hall, 95; Rev, Teaching Argument in the Computer Classroom & Teaching Students to Conduct Research Using Traditional and Online Sources, Instructor's Manual, 2nd ed Perspectives on Argument, 97; Toward a Poetics for Collecting Poetry by Women, Collection Building in Alternative Libr Lit, 6th ed, Jefferson, McFarland, 93. **CONTACT ADDRESS** Dept of Eng, Univ of Texas at Arlington, 203 Carlisle Hall, PO Box 19035, Arlington, TX, 76019-0595.

WELLS, DANIEL ARTHUR
PERSONAL Born 10/16/1943, Adams, MA, m, 1966, 2 children **DISCIPLINE** AMERICAN LITERATURE **EDUCATION** Union Col, NY, AB, 65; Duke Univ, MA, 68, PhD(English), 72. **CAREER** From asst prof to assoc prof, 70-81, prof English, Univ South FL, St Petersburg, 81-. **MEMBERSHIPS** The Melville Soc; The Poe Soc. **RESEARCH** Nineteenth century American literature. **SELECTED PUBLICATIONS** Auth, Engraved Within the Hills: Further Perspectives on the Ending of Pym, Poe Studies, Vol 10, 6/77; An Index of American Writers and Selected British Writers in Duyckinck's Literary World, Studies Am Renaissance, 78; The Literary Index to American Magazines, 1815-65, Scarecrow Pre ss, 80; An Annotated Checklist of Twain Allusions in Harpers's Monthly, 1850-1900, Am Lit Realism, spring 84; Whitman Allusions in Harper's Monthly t o 1900, Walt Whitman Quart Rev, summer 86; Thoreau's Reputation in the Major Magazines, 1862-1900, Am Periodicals, vol 4, 94; The Literary Index to American Magazines, 1850-1900, Greenwood Press, 96; Mark Twain Allusions in the Boston Literary World, 1870-1904, Resources for Am Literary Study, summer 98. **CONTACT ADDRESS** Dept English, Univ South FL, 140 7th Ave S, Saint Petersburg, FL, 33701-5016.

WELLS, WILLIAM D.
DISCIPLINE MASS COMMUNICATION STUDIES **EDUCATION** Stanford Univ, MA, PhD. **CAREER** Prof **SELECTED PUBLICATIONS** Auth, Planning for R.O.I.: Effective Advertising Strategy, 88; co-auth, Consumer Behavior, 96; Advertising: Principles and Practices, 94; Consumer Behavior, 77; ed, Lifestyle and Psychographics, 72; co-ed, Measuring Advertising Effectiveness, 96; Attitude Research at Bay, 76. **CONTACT ADDRESS** Mass Communication Dept, Univ of Minnesota, Twin Cities, 111 Murphy Hall, 206 Church St SE, Minneapolis, MN, 55455. **EMAIL** wells004@maroon.tc.umn.edu

WELSH, ALEXANDER
PERSONAL Born 04/29/1933, Albany, NY, d, 3 children **DISCIPLINE** ENGLISH **EDUCATION** Harvard Univ, AB, 54, MA, 57, PhD, 61. **CAREER** Instr, assoc prof, 60-67, Emily Sanford prof, engl, 91-, Yale Univ; prof, 67-72, Univ Pitts; prof, 72-91, Univ Calif, LA. **RESEARCH** Novel; 19th century stud; Shakespeare **CONTACT ADDRESS** English Dept, Yale Univ, New Haven, CT, 06520-8302.

WELSH, ANDREW
PERSONAL Born 11/20/1937, Pittsburgh, PA, m, 1971, 2 children **DISCIPLINE** ENGLISH LITERATURE **EDUCATION** Univ Pittsburgh, BS, 59, MA, 61, PhD(English), 70. **CAREER** Asst prof, 71-77, ASSOC PROF ENGLISH, RUTGERS UNIV, 77-, Mellon fel, Univ Pittsburgh, 74-75; Nat Endowment for Humanities fel, Univ Calif, Irvine, 77. **HONORS AND AWARDS** Melville Cane Award, Poetry Soc Am, 78; James Russell Lowell Prize, Mod lang Asn, 78. **MEMBERSHIPS** MLA; Mediaeval Acad Am; AAUP; CSNA; IAS/NAB. **RESEARCH** Medieval literature; folklore. **SELECTED PUBLICATIONS** Auth, Roots of Lyric, Princeton Univ, 78. **CONTACT ADDRESS** Dept of English, Rutgers Univ, 510 George St, New Brunswick, NJ, 08901-1167. **EMAIL** awelsh@rci.rutgers.edu

WELSH, JAMES MICHAEL
PERSONAL Born 07/15/1938, Logansport, IN, m, 1960, 2 children **DISCIPLINE** LITERATURE **EDUCATION** Ind Univ, BA, 63; Univ Kans, MA, 65, PhD, 96. **CAREER** From Instr to Assoc Prof, 71-97, PROF ENGLISH, SALISBURY STATE UNIV, 97-; Co-founding ed, Lit/Film Quart, 72; assoc ed, Washington Rev of Arts, 76-77; East Coast ed, Am Classic Screen, 77-84. **MEMBERSHIPS** MLA; Brit Film Inst; Am Film Inst; Soc Cinema Studies; Nat Film Soc. **RESEARCH** Film history and theory; literature and film. **SELECTED PUBLICATIONS** Auth, The sound of silents: An early Shrew, English J, 73; coauth, Ben Jonson: A Quadricentennial Bibliography, Scarecrow, 74; auth, To see it feelingly: King Lear through Russian eyes, Lit/Film Quart, 76; coauth, Peter Watkins: Therapeutic cinema and the repressive mind, Film & Hist, 77; auth, Beyond melodrama: Art, politics and State of Siege, Film Criticism, 77; The cinema of intimacy: Peter Watkins' Portrait of the Artist as a Young Munch, 1977 Film Studies Ann, Part 1, 77; coauth, His Majesty the American: The Cinema of Douglas Fairbanks, Sr, A S Barnes, 77; Able Gance, Twayne, 78; auth, Peter Watkins: A Guide to References and Resources, G.K. Hall, 86; coauth, The Encyclopedia of Novels into Film, Facts on File, 98; The Cinema of Tony Richardson: Essays and Interviews, SUNY Press, 98. **CONTACT ADDRESS** Dept of English, Salisbury State Univ, 1101 Camden Ave, Salisbury, MD, 21801-6800. **EMAIL** jxwelsh@ssu.edu

WELTMAN, SHARON
DISCIPLINE VICTORIAN POETRY AND PROSE **EDUCATION** Rutgers Univ, PhD, 92. **CAREER** Asst prof, La State Univ; ed asst, Praxis, 87; ed asst, Raritan Rev, 87-89. **HONORS AND AWARDS** Catherine Cantalupo Prize, 87; Catherine Moynahan Prize, 87; Marion Johnson fel, 88-89; Folger Libr Jr fel, 88; LSU summer grant, 93, 94; WGS Summer Inst grant, 95; LSU Arts and Sci res grant, 96. **RESEARCH** John Ruskin and gender; mythology and Victorian prose. **SELECTED PUBLICATIONS** Auth, The Least of It: Metaphor, Metamorphosis, and Synecdoche in Frost's 'The Subverted Flower,' The SC Rev, 89; Gender and the Architectonics of Metaphor in Ruskin's The Ethics of the Dust, Prose Stud, 93. **CONTACT ADDRESS** Dept of Eng, Louisiana State Univ, 212R Allen Hall, Baton Rouge, LA, 70803. **EMAIL** enwelt@unix1.sncc.lsu.edu

WENDLAND, ERNST R.
PERSONAL Born 10/14/1944, Washington, IA, m, 1971, 4 children **DISCIPLINE** AFRICAN LANGUAGES AND LITERATURE **EDUCATION** NW Col, BA, 68; Univ Wisc, MA, 75, PhD, 79. **CAREER** Instr, Lutheran Sem (Lusaka, Zambia), 68-; Lang coordr publ, Lutheran Church Cent Africa, 71-; transl adv, 75-96, transl consult, united bible soc, 96-. **MEMBERSHIPS** New Testament Soc S Africa; Old Testament Soc S Africa **RESEARCH** Discourse, stylistic, and rhetorical analysis of Biblical and Bantu language texts, especially poetry, prophecy, and preaching. **SELECTED PUBLICATIONS** Ed, Discourse Perspectives on Hebrew Poetry in the Scriptures, United Bible Soc, 94; auth, The Discourse Analysis of Hebrew Prophetic Literature, Mellen Bibl Press, 95; Buku Loyera: An Introduction to the New Chichewa Bible Translation, Kachere Books, 98; Analyzing the Psalms, Summer Inst Ling, 98. **CONTACT ADDRESS** American Embassy Lusaka, DOS, Washington, DC, 20521-2310. **EMAIL** wendland@zamnet.zm

WENDLING, RONALD CHARLES
PERSONAL Born 03/31/1939, Buffalo, NY, m, 1966, 2 children **DISCIPLINE** ENGLISH LITERATURE **EDUCATION** Fordham Univ, BA, 62, MA, 65; Case Western Reserve Univ, PhD(English), 70. **CAREER** Instr English, Canisius Col, 63-65 & St Joseph's Col, Pa, 65-66; from instr to asst prof, Hamilton Col, 69-72; asst prof, 72-81, from assoc prof to prof English, St Joseph's Univ, PA, 81-95. **HONORS AND AWARDS** Fac Merit Award for Teaching, 96. **MEMBERSHIPS** MLA; AAUP; Wordsworth Coleridge Assoc; Friends of Coleridge; North Am Soc for the Study of Romanticism, NASSR. **RESEARCH** Nineteenth century English literature; romantic poetry; Coleridge. **SELECTED PUBLICATIONS** Auth, Coleridge and the consistency of The Eolian Harp, Studies Romanticism, Fall 68; Dramatic reconciliation in Coleridge's conversation poems, Papers Lang & Lit, Spring 73; The undergraduate curriculum: What did we do to it?, AAUP Bull, Winter 73; Progress To Christianity: Experience and Authority in Religious Faith, Bucknell Univeristy Press, 95. **CONTACT ADDRESS** Dept of English, St. Joseph's Univ, 5600 City Ave, Philadelphia, PA, 19131-1395. **EMAIL** rwendlin@sju.edu

WENZEL, JOSEPH WILFRED
PERSONAL Born 11/30/1933, Elkhart, IN, m, 1959, 2 children **DISCIPLINE** SPEECH; COMMUNICATION **EDUCATION** Univ Ill, BS, 57, PhD(speech), 63; Northwestern Univ, MA, 58. **CAREER** Lectr speech, Hunter Col, City Univ NY, 60-63; from Asst Prof to Assoc Prof, 63-93, PROF SPEECH COMM, UNIV ILL, URBANA, 94-. **HONORS AND AWARDS** Am Forensic Asn Res Award. **MEMBERSHIPS** Nat Commun Asn; Am Forensic Asn; Int Soc Hist Rhetoric; Int Soc Study of Argumentation. **RESEARCH** Argumentation; rhetorical theory. **CONTACT ADDRESS** Dept of Speech Commun, Univ of Illinois, Urbana-Champaign, 702 S Wright, #244, Urbana, IL, 61801-3631. **EMAIL** jwengel@uiuc.edu

WENZEL, SIEGFRIED
PERSONAL Born 08/20/1928, Bernsdorf, Germany, m, 1958, 4 children **DISCIPLINE** ENGLISH, MEDIEVAL LITERATURE **EDUCATION** Univ Parana, BA, 52; Ohio Univ, MA, 56; Ohio State Univ, PhD(English), 60. **CAREER** Instr English, Ohio State Univ, 59-60; from instr to prof English & comp lit, Univ NC, Chapel Hill, 60-75; Prof English, Univ PA, 75-, Am Coun Learned Soc fel, 64-65; Guggenheim fel, 68-69; Nat Endowment for Humanities fel, 75-76. **MEMBERSHIPS** MLA; fel Medieval Acad Am; Early English Text Soc; fel, Mediaeval Acad Am. **RESEARCH** Medieval literature; Middle English and Chaucer; medieval Latin sermons. **SELECTED PUBLICATIONS** Auth, The Sin of Sloth, Univ NC, 67; Robert Grosseteste's Treatise on Confession, Deus est, Franciscan Studies, 70; The Source for the Remedia of the Parson's Tale, Traditio, 71; The Pilgrimage of Life as a Late Medieval Genre, Mediaeval Studies, 73; The Source of Chaucer's Seven Deadly Sins, Traditio, 74; Chaucer and the Language of Contemporary Preaching, Studies in Philos, 76; Verses in Sermons, Mediaeval Acad Am, 78; The Joyous Art of Preaching, Auglia, 79; Chaucer And Medieval Preaching - Rhetoric For Listeners In Sermons And Poetry - Volkbirke,S, Speculum-A Journal Of Medieval Studies, Vol 0068, 1993; Academic Sermons At Oxford In The Early-15th-Century + With Edition Of Latin Sermon-W-22 From Worcester-Cathedral-Ms-F10, Speculum-A Journal Of Medieval Studies, Vol 0070, 1995; Inventory Of Medieval Artes-Dictandi, Vol 1 - From The Beginning To Ad1200 - German - Worstbrock,Fj, Klaes,M, Lutten,J, Speculum-A Journal Of Medieval Studies, Vol 0069, 1994; Medieval exempla - introduction to research with reference to the critical tables of the so-called index-exemplorum of Tubach,Frederic,C. - french - Berlioz,J, Polodebeaulieu,Ma, editors, speculum-a Journal Of Medieval Studies, vol 0069, 1994; A Sermon In Praise Of Philosophy + Scholastic And Content Structuring Of A 15th-Century Latin Text In Praise Of Non-Theological Disciplines, Traditio-Studies In Ancient And Medieval History Thought And Religion, Vol 0050, 1995; Academic Sermons At Oxford In The Early-15th-Century + With Edition Of Latin Sermon-W-22 From Worcester-Cathedral-Ms-F10, Speculum-A Journal Of Medieval Studies, Vol 0070, 1995; Homelitic And Hagiographic Literature Of The City-Archive-Of-Cologne, Vol 1 - Manuscripts From The Gymnasialbibliothek - German - Vennebusch,J, Speculum-A Journal Of Medieval Studies, Vol 0071, 1996; Another Analog To The 'Pardoners Tale', Notes And Queries, Vol 0043, 1996. **CONTACT ADDRESS** Dept of English, Univ of PA, Philadelphia, PA, 19104.

WERGE, THOMAS
DISCIPLINE LITERATURE **EDUCATION** Cornell Univ, PhD. **CAREER** Instr, Univ Notre Dame; coed, Relig and Lit. **HONORS AND AWARDS** Sheedy Award for Excellence in Tchg. **RESEARCH** The opposition and tension between gnostic and sacramental visions of experience. **SELECTED PUBLICATIONS** Wrote on Thomas Shepard, essays on Dante, Melville and Twain, and introductions to the writings of several Puritan writers, including William Bradford, Thomas Hooker and Shepard. **CONTACT ADDRESS** Univ Notre Dame, Notre Dame, IN, 46556.

WERTHEIM, ALBERT
PERSONAL Born 07/03/1940, New York, NY, m, 1968, 2 children **DISCIPLINE** ENGLISH **EDUCATION** Columbia Univ, AB, 61; Yale Univ, MA, 63, PhD(English), 65. **CAREER** From instr English to asst prof, Princeton Univ, 65-69; vis asst prof, 69-70, asst prof, 70-71, dir, overseas study prog, Hamburg, Ger, 74-75, assoc prof, 71-79, Prof English, Ind Univ, Bloomington, 79-, Folger Shakespeare Libr fel, 66; mem selection comt, George Jean Nathan drama critic award, 66-68; vis prof, Univ Hamburg, 77; Deutscher Akademischer Austauschdienst fel, 77; The Newberry Libr fel, 78; grant-in-aid, Am Philos Soc, 77; asst to dir, Berkeley Repertory Theatre, 82-83; Eli Lilly Found fac open fel, 82-83. **HONORS AND AWARDS** Frederic J Lieber Distinguished Teaching Award, 81; Outstanding Teacher Award, Ind Univ Student Alumni Asn, 81. **MEMBERSHIPS** Am Soc Theatre Res; MLA; Renaissance Soc Am; Am Theatre Asn; Eugene O'Neill Soc (pres, 82-84). **RESEARCH** Seventeenth century drama; Shakespeare; Modern British and American drama. **SELECTED PUBLICATIONS** Auth, Courtship and games in James Shirley's Hyde Park, Anglia, 72; The presentation of sin in Friar Bacon and Friar Bungay, Criticism, 74; Things climb upward to what they were before: The reteaching and regreening of Macbeth, In: Teaching Shakespeare, Princeton Univ, 77; James Shirley, In: A Survey and Bibliography of Recent Studies in English Renaissance Drama, Univ Nebr, 78; The unrestrained and the unconventional: Etherege's The Man of Mode, Lit, 80; Trevor Griffiths: Playwriting and politics, In: Essays on Contemporary British Drama, 81 & Arthur Miller: After the fall and after, In: Essays on Contemporary American Drama, 81, Max Hueber; The McCarthy era and the American theatre, Theatre J, 82; Euripides In South-Africa 'Medea' And 'Demea', Comparative Drama, Vol 0029, 1995. **CONTACT ADDRESS** Dept of English, Indiana Univ, Bloomington, 1 Indiana University, Bloomington, IN, 47405.

WERTHEIM, STANLEY
DISCIPLINE ENGLISH **EDUCATION** BA, 53, MA, 54, PhD, 63, New York Univ. **CAREER** Asst Prof, 62-69, Farleigh Dickinson Univ; Assoc Prof, 70-78, Prof, 78-, William Patterson Univ. **CONTACT ADDRESS** 180 Cabrini Blvd, New York, NY, 10033. **EMAIL** warburg@earthlink.net

WERTHEIM, STANLEY CLAUDE
PERSONAL Born 11/11/1930, Warburg, Germany, m, 1963 **DISCIPLINE** ENGLISH **EDUCATION** NY Univ, BA, 53, MA, 54, PhD(English), 63. **CAREER** Instr English, NY Univ, 55-61; from instr to asst prof, Fairleigh Dickinson Univ, 62-70; assoc prof, 70-78, chmn dept, 70-72, PROF ENGLISH, WILLIAM PATERSON UNIV, 78-, Assoc ed, Lit & Psychol, 68-75. **RESEARCH** Modern & late 19th cent Am lit; Stephen Crane. **SELECTED PUBLICATIONS** Ed, Studies in Maggie and George's Mother, Merrill, 70; coauth, Hawthorne, Melville, Stephen Crane: A Critical Bibliography, Free Press, 71; co-ed, The Correspondence of Stepehn Crane, Columbia Univ Press, 88; co-auth, The Crane Log: A Documentary Life of Stephen Crane, Macmillan, 94; contr, A Stephen Crane Encyclopedia, Greenwood Press, 97; numerous essays and reviews on 19th and 20th cent Am authors; ed, Stephen Crane: A Photograph and a Letter, Black Sun Bks, 73; Stephen Crane remembered, Studies Am Fiction, Vol 4: 45-64, 76; H G Wells to Cora Crane: Some Letters and Corrections, Resources for Am Lit Study, fall 79; Libraries as Conserving Institutions, Manuscripts, spring 80; The Arthur Conan Dyle Mystery, Am Bk Collector, 1: 38-42. **CONTACT ADDRESS** Dept of Eng, William Paterson Col, 300 Pompton Rd, Wayne, NJ, 07470-2152. **EMAIL** warburg@earthlink.net

WESLING, DONALD TRUMAN
PERSONAL Born 05/06/1939, Buffalo, NY, m, 1961, 3 children **DISCIPLINE** ENGLISH LITERATURE **EDUCATION** Harvard Univ, AB, 60, PhD, 65; Cambridge Univ, AB, 62, MA, 68. **CAREER** Tchng asst, 62-65, Harvard Univ; asst prof, 65-67, Univ Calif, San Diego; lectr, 67-70, Univ Essex; assoc prof, 70-80, prof, 80-, Univ Calif, San Diego; NEH younger humanist fel, 73-74. **HONORS AND AWARDS** Otto Salgo Prof, Budapest, 97-98 **MEMBERSHIPS** MLA; Amnesty Intl. **RESEARCH** Wordsworth & English Romanticism; modern English and American poetry; English prosody; Bakhtin studies. **SELECTED PUBLICATIONS** Auth, Wordsworth and the Adequacy of Landscape, Routledge, 70; auth, The Chances of Rhyme: Device and Modernity, Univ Calif Press, 80; auth, John Muir: To Yosemite and Beyond, Univ Wis Press, 80; auth, American Sentences: The History of West Seneca, New York, Black Mesa Press, 81; coauth, Literary Voice: The Calling of Jonah, SUNY Press, 95; auth, The Scissors of Meter, Univ Mich Press, 96. **CONTACT ADDRESS** Dept of Literature, Univ of California, La Jolla, 9500 Gilman Dr, La Jolla, CA, 92093. **EMAIL** dwesling@ucsd.edu

WESS, ROBERT
DISCIPLINE 18TH CENTURY BRITISH LITERATURE **EDUCATION** Univ Chicago, BA, 63, MA, 66; PhD, 70. **CAREER** Engl, Oregon St Univ. **RESEARCH** Rhetoric. **SELECTED PUBLICATIONS** Auth, Utopian Rhetoric in The Man of Mode, The Eighteenth Century: Theory and Interpretation, 86; Narrative as a Socially Symbolic Act: The Example of Clarissa, Papers in Comparative Studies 5, 87; 1670's Comedy and the Problem of Periodization, Restoration: Studies in English Literary Culture, 87; Kenneth Burke's 'Dialectic of Constitutions, 91; The Question of Truth Rhetorically Considered, 91; Kenneth Burke: Rhetoric, Subjectivity, Postmodernism, Cambridge UP, 96. **CONTACT ADDRESS** Oregon State Univ, Corvallis, OR, 97331-4501. **EMAIL** rwess@orst.edu

WEST, JAMES L.W.
PERSONAL Born 11/15/1946, Roanoke, VA, d, 4 children **DISCIPLINE** ENGLISH **EDUCATION** Univ of SC, BA, 68, PhD, 71. **CAREER** Instr to prof, Virginia Tech, 71-86; prof, Penn State Univ, 86-. **HONORS AND AWARDS** Nat Hum. Ctr., 81-82; Guggenheim fel, 85-86; NEH fels, 94-95, 98-99; Fulbright Grants, 85-86, 89-90., Distinguished prof Eng; Fel Inst Arts & Humanistic Studies. **MEMBERSHIPS** Soc for the Hist of Authorship, Reading and Publishing, Int Dreiser Soc; Bibliog Soc Am. **RESEARCH** Am literature; Lit biography; Scholarly editing; Hist of the book. **SELECTED PUBLICATIONS** Auth, The Making of This Side of Paradise, 83; Ameri-

can Authors and the Literary Marketplace since 1900, 88; William Styron, A Life, 98; ed, Theodore Dreiser, Jennie Gerhardt, Univ of Penn Press, 92; F. Scott Fitzgerald, This Side of Paradise, Cambridge Univ Press, 95. **CONTACT ADDRESS** Dept of English, Pennsylvania State Univ, University Park, PA, 16802. **EMAIL** jlw14@psu.edu

WEST, JOHN OLIVER
PERSONAL Born 01/01/1925, El Paso, TX, m, 1970, 1 child **DISCIPLINE** ENGLISH **EDUCATION** Miss Col, BA, 48; Tex Tech Col, MA, 51; Univ Tex, PhD(Am lit & folklore), 64. **CAREER** Teacher English & jour, Cent High Sch, Jackson, Miss, 48-50; hist & jour, Gardiner High Sch, Laurel, 51-52; asst prof English & jour & publicity dir, Miss Col, 52-53, assoc prof, 53-54; asst prof English, W Tex State Col, 56-57; instr English, Odessa Col, 57-59 & 60-63, dir pub relat, 59-60; assoc prof English & folklore, 63-65, head dept, 65-71, prof English, Univ Tex, El Paso, 65-. **MEMBERSHIPS** Am Folklore Soc. **RESEARCH** American folklore; southwestern United States history and literature. **SELECTED PUBLICATIONS** Auth, The Historian, the Folklorist, and Juan Diego, Southwest Folklore, winter 80; Cowboy Folk Humor, August House, 90; Cowboys Do the Damnedest Things, The Catch Pen, The Ranching Heritage Center, 91; Grutas in the Spanish Southwest, Hecho in Tex: Tex-Mex Folk Arts and Crafts, Tex Folklore Soc Pub, 91; Jose cisneros: An Artist's Journey, Tex Western Press, 93; Ned Buntline, Nineteenth Cent Western Am Writers: Dictionary of Lit Biog, Vol. 186; Gale Research, 97; ed, The American Folklore Newsletter, 70-78. **CONTACT ADDRESS** Dept of English, Univ Texas, El Paso, 500 W University Ave, El Paso, TX, 79968-0001. **EMAIL** jwest@utep.edu

WEST, LARRY E.
PERSONAL Born 05/09/1942, Canada, KY, m, 1963, 2 children **DISCIPLINE** LANGUAGE; LITERATURE **EDUCATION** Berea Col, BA 64; Vanderbilt Univ, PhD, 69. **CAREER** Asst Prof, West Georgia Col, 67-69; Asst Prof, Assoc Prof, Prof, 69-, Wake Forest Univ. **HONORS AND AWARDS** Fullbright Grant for Study at Goethe Inst, 70; Amer Phil Soc Grant for Research, 80; Lower Division Advising Award, Wake Forest Univ, 95. **RESEARCH** Medieval German literature; The German Passion Play of Late Middle Ages **SELECTED PUBLICATIONS** Auth, The Alsfield Passion Play (Translated with an Introduction, 97. **CONTACT ADDRESS** Dept of German and Russian, Wake Forest Univ, Winston-Salem, NC, 27109. **EMAIL** westle@wfu.edu

WEST, MICHAEL DAVIDSON
PERSONAL Born 04/13/1937, Morristown, NJ, m, 1961, 1 child **DISCIPLINE** ENGLISH **EDUCATION** Harvard Univ, AB, 59, AM, 61, PhD, 65. **CAREER** Teaching fel English & humanities, Harvard Univ, 61-64; from instr English to asst prof, Wesleyan Univ, 64-72, res assoc 72-73; assoc prof English, 73-76, prof English, Univ of Pittsburgh, 76-. **HONORS AND AWARDS** First Prize, Cornell Classical Transl Contest, 71; cert excellence in teaching, Asn Depts English & MLA, 72; Sr fel, Wesleyan Ctr Humanities, 70; fel, Am Coun Learned Soc, 78-79; Fel, Newberry Libr, 85-86; NEH Fel, Huntington Libr, 85-86; Kate B. & Hall James Peterson Fel, Am Antiq Soc, 85; Hughes Award & Thomas Award (second), World Order of Narrative Poets, 86; DeGolyer Prize Essay, DeGolyer Inst for Am Studies, Southern Methodist Univ, 87; Hon Fel, Inst for Advanced Studies in the Humanities, Univ Edinburgh, 87. **MEMBERSHIPS** MLA; Northeast Mod Lang Asn; Renaissance Soc Am. **RESEARCH** Renaissance English literature, especially Spenser, Shakespeare, and Dryden; comparative literature, especially influence of the classics on European heroic conventions; American literature, especially Thoreau and 19th century theories of language. **SELECTED PUBLICATIONS** Auth, Dryden's ambivalence as a translator of heroic themes, Huntington Libr Quart, 73; Scatology and eschatology: The heroic dimensions of Thoreau's wordplay, PMLA, 74; The internal dialogue of Shakespeare's Sonnet 146, Shakespeare Quart, 74; Prothalamia in Propertius and Spenser, Comp Lit, 74; The genesis and significance of Joyce's irony in A Painful Case, ELH, 77; Evaluating periodicals in English studies, Col English, 80; Reflection on Star Wars and Scholarly Reviewing, Lit Rev, 87; Spenser's Art of War: Chivalric Allegory, Military Technology, and the Elizabethan Mock-Heroic Sensibility, Ren Quart, 88. **CONTACT ADDRESS** Dept of English, Univ of Pittsburgh, 526 Cathedral/Learn, Pittsburgh, PA, 15260-2504. **EMAIL** mikewest@pitt.edu

WESTBROOK, ELLEN E.
DISCIPLINE ENGLISH **EDUCATION** Simmons, BA, 77; Univ Mich, MA, 79, PhD, 87. **CAREER** Asst prof English, Southern Miss Univ. **RESEARCH** Euro-Amer-Indian literature. **CONTACT ADDRESS** HC74, Box 622, Stafford, NH, 03844-9269.

WESTBROOK, MAX ROGER
PERSONAL Born 04/06/1927, Malvern, AR, m, 1953, 3 children **DISCIPLINE** ENGLISH **EDUCATION** Baylor Univ, BA, 49; Univ OK, MA, 53; Univ TX, PhD, 60. **CAREER** From instr to asst prof Am lit, Univ KY, 60-62; from asst prof to assoc prof, 62-72, asst dean, 71-73, assoc dean col hum, 73-76, prof eng & Am lit, Univ TX, Austin, 72. **MEMBERSHIPS** Western Lit Asn (pres, 73-74). **RESEARCH** Am fiction and studies; Stephen Crane. **SELECTED PUBLICATIONS** Auth, Stephen Crane's social ethic, Am Quart, 12/62; Conservative, liberal and western: Three modes of American realism, SDak Rev, summer 66; The stewardship of Ernest Hemingway, Tex Quart, winter 66; ed, The Modern American Novel: Essays in Criticism, Random, 66; auth, Walter van Tilburg Clark, Twayne, 69. **CONTACT ADDRESS** Dept of Eng, Univ of Texas, Austin, TX, 78712-1026.

WESTFAHL, GARY
PERSONAL Born 05/07/1951, Washington, DC, m, 1983, 2 children **DISCIPLINE** ENGLISH LITERATURE **EDUCATION** Carleton Col, BA, 73; Claremont Grad Univ, MA, 75, PhD, 86. **CAREER** Lectr, English Dept, Calif State Polytechnic Univ, 80-85; lectr, English Dept, UC Riverside, 81-87; instr, English, Claremont Grad, 86-87; adj prof, Educ Progs in Corrections, Univ of LaVerne, 86- ; reading spec, Learning Ctr, UC Riverside, 87- . **HONORS AND AWARDS** Nominee, Pioneer Awd for best critical essay on science fiction, 95, 97. **MEMBERSHIPS** Sci Fic Res Asn. **RESEARCH** Science fiction; fantasy. **SELECTED PUBLICATIONS** Auth, Cosmic Engineers: A Study of Hard Science Fiction, Greenwood, 96; co-ed, Foods of the Gods: Eating and the Eaten in Fantasy and Science Fiction, Univ Georgia, 96; auth, Immortal Engines: Life Extension and Immortality in Science Fiction, Univ Georgia, 96; auth, Islands in the Sky: The Space Station Theme in Science Fiction Literature, Borgo, 96; co-ed, Science Fiction and Market Realities, Univ Georgia, 96; consult ed, Encyclopedia of Fantasy, St Martin's, 97; auth, Mechanics of Wonder: The Creation of the Idea of Science Fiction, Syracuse Univ Pr, 98; ed, Nursery Realms: Children in the Worlds of Science Fiction, Fantasy, and Horror, Univ Georgia Pr, 99; auth, Other Side of the Sky: An Annotated Bibliography of Space Stations in Science Fiction, 1869-1993, Borgo, forthcoming; auth, Science Fiction, Children's Literature, and Popular Culture: Coming of Age in Fantasyland, Greenwood, forthcoming; auth, Science Fiction Manifesto and Other Essays on Criticism, Borgo, forthcoming; ed, Space and Beyond: The Frontier Theme in Science Fiction, Greenwood, forthcoming; auth numerous articles and essays. **CONTACT ADDRESS** The Learning Ctr 052, Univ of California, Riverside, CA, 92521. **EMAIL** westfahl@pop.ucr.edu

WESTLING, LOUISE HUTCHINGS
PERSONAL Born 02/02/1942, Jacksonville, FL, m, 1975 **DISCIPLINE** ENGLISH, AMERICAN LITERATURE **EDUCATION** Randolph-Macon Woman's Col, BA, 64; Univ of Iowa, MA, 65; Univ of Ore, PhD, 74. **CAREER** Instr, Centre Col of Ky, 65-67; instr, Ore State Unive, 74-77; visiting asst prof, Honors Col, Univ of Ore, 78-81; INSTR, 81-84, ASST PROF, 85-88, ASSOC PROF, 88-94, PROF OF ENGLISH, 94-, DEPT HEAD, 94-97, UNIV OF ORE. **HONORS AND AWARDS** Clark Libr Fel, UCLA, 75; NEH Summer Inst, Univ of Tx at Austin, 90, Univ of Ore, 91; Fulbright Sr Lectureship, Univ of Heidelberg, Germany, 96. **MEMBERSHIPS** MLA; ALA; Asn for Study of Lit and Soc; PEN. **RESEARCH** 20th Century American Literature; Ecocriticism. **SELECTED PUBLICATIONS** Chair, Board of Eds, World Introduction to Literature, Prentic-Hall Pubs, 99; ed, Witness to Injustice, Univ Press of Miss, 95; ed, He Included Me: The Autobiography of Sarah Webb Rice, Univ of Ga Press, 89; auth, The Green Breast of the New World: Landscape, Gender, and American Fiction, Univ of Ga Press, 96; auth, Sacred Groves and Ravaged Gardens: The Fiction of Eudora Welty, Carson McCullers, and Flannery O'Connor, Univ of Ga Press, 85; auth, The Evolution of Michael Drayton's Idea, Institut fur Englische Sprache und Literatur, 74. **CONTACT ADDRESS** Dept of English, Univ of Oregon, Eugene, OR, 97403. **EMAIL** lhwest@oregon.uoregon.edu

WESTWATER, MARTHA
PERSONAL Boston, MA **DISCIPLINE** VICTORIAN & ENGLISH LITERATURE **EDUCATION** St John's Univ, BS, 57, MA, 62; Dalhousie Univ, PhD(English lit), 74. **CAREER** ASSOC PROF ENGLISH LIT, Mt St Vincent Univ, 73-. **MEMBERSHIPS** MLA; Asn Can Univ Teachers English; Res Soc Victorian Periodicals; Victorian Studies. **RESEARCH** Walter Bagehot; biography. **SELECTED PUBLICATIONS** Auth, Nothing on Earth, Bruce, 67; Walter Bagehot: A reassessment, Antioch Rev, Vol 35, No 1; The conservative argument from evolution, Humanities Asn Rev, Vol 28, No 2; Surrender to subservience, Int J Women's Studies, Vol 1, No 5; Some unidentified Victorian reviewers, Notes & Queries, Vol 28, No 5; The Journal and Diaries of Eliza Wilson Bagehot: An Introduction, Oxford Microfilm Publ, 80; Six Victorian Women: A Biographical Study of the Wilson Sisters, Ohio Univ Press (in prep); Tennyson Language - Hair,Ds, Dalhousie Review, Vol 0073, 1993. **CONTACT ADDRESS** 51 Marlwood Ave, Halifax, NS, B3M 3H4.

WEXLER, JOYCE
PERSONAL Born 02/26/1947, Chicago, IL, m, 1969, 2 children **DISCIPLINE** ENGLISH **EDUCATION** Univ Michigan, BA 68; Northwestern Univ, PhD 74. **CAREER** Loyola Univ, asst prof, assoc prof, assoc dean, prof, 80 to 98-, dir hon prog 86-; Barat College, lect 78-80. **HONORS AND AWARDS** Phi Beta Kappa; NDEA schshp; Woodrow Wilson Fel; Woodrow Wilson Diss Fel; IL Art Coun Essay Awd. **MEMBERSHIPS** MLA **RESEARCH** Modernism; cultural studies; psychoanalytic criticism; feminist criticism. **SELECTED PUBLICATIONS** Auth, Who Paid for Modernism? Art Money and the Fiction of Conrad, Joyce and Lawrence, Fayett, Univ Ark Press, 97; D. H. Lawrence Through a Postmodernist Lens, D. H. Law Rev, 97,98; Speaking Out: Dialogue and Over-determined Meaning, Style, 97; The Uncommon Language of Modernist Women Writers, Women's Studies, 96; Selling Sex as Art, in: Marketing Modernisms: Self Promotion, Canonization, Rereading, eds, J. H. Kevin, Dettmar and Steven Watt, Ann Arbor, Univ Mich Press, 96; Finnegans Wake: Breakthrough or Breakdown, Studies in Psychoanalytic Theory, 94; Requiem for Biography: The Case of Joseph Conrad, Conradiana, 94. **CONTACT ADDRESS** English Dept, Loyola Univ, 6525 N Sheridan Rd, Chicago, IL, 60626. **EMAIL** jwexler@luc.edu

WEXMAN, VIRGINIA WRIGHT
PERSONAL Born 04/02/1941, Winnipeg, MB, Canada, m, 1960, 2 children **DISCIPLINE** ENGLISH, FILM **EDUCATION** Univ Chicago, BA, 70, MA, 71, PhD(English), 76. **CAREER** Lectr, 73-77, Asst Prof English, Univ Ill, Chicago Circle, 77-. **MEMBERSHIPS** MLA; Soc Cinema Studies. **RESEARCH** American film; American popular culture; the American novel. **SELECTED PUBLICATIONS** Auth, The role of structure in Tom Sawyer and Huckleberry Finn, Am Literary Realism: 2870-1910, spring 73; The Maltese Falcon from fiction to film, Libr Quart, 1/75; Macbeth and Polanski's theme of regression, Univ Dayton Rev, fall 78; coauth, A Reference Guide to Roman Polanski, 78 & A Reference Guide to Robert Altman, 79, Hall; auth, Roman Polanski: A Critical Guide, Twayne, 79; Stardom - Industry Of Desire - Gledhill,C, Film Quarterly, Vol 0046, 1992; Film As Art And Filmmakers As Artists - A Century Of Progress, Arachne, Vol 0002, 1995. **CONTACT ADDRESS** 1143 Judson Ave, Evanston, IL, 60202.

WEYLER, KAREN A.
DISCIPLINE ENGLISH **EDUCATION** Center, BA, 88; Univ NC, MA, 90, PhD, 96. **CAREER** Vis asst prof English, Wake Forest. **RESEARCH** Early American fiction. **SELECTED PUBLICATIONS** Fel Publ, 'A Speculating Spirit': Trade, Speculation, and Gambling in Early American Fiction, Early Amer Lit 31.3, 96; auth, Melville's 'The Paradise of Bachelors and the Tartarus of Maids': A Dialogue About Experience, Understanding, and Truth, Studies in Short Fiction 31.3, 94); 'The Fruit of Unlawful Embraces': Sexual Transgression and Madness in Early American Sentimental Fiction, In: Sex and Sexuality in Early America, NYU, 97; Creating a Community of Readers: Mary Mebane's Exploitation of Difference in Mary and Mary, Wayfarer, South Quart vol 35.3, 97. **CONTACT ADDRESS** Dept of English, Box 7387, Wake Forest, Reynolda Station, Winston-Salem, NC, 27109-7387. **EMAIL** weylerKA@wfu.edu.

WHARTON, LAWRENCE
DISCIPLINE FICTION WRITING **EDUCATION** Univ of UT, PhD, 75. **CAREER** Univ Ala **SELECTED PUBLICATIONS** Auth, There Could Be No More to It, Tex A&M, 83. **CONTACT ADDRESS** Univ AL, 1400 University Blvd, Birmingham, AL, 35294-1150.

WHARTON BOYD, LINDA F.
PERSONAL Born 04/21/1961, Baltimore, MD **DISCIPLINE** COMMUNICATION **EDUCATION** Univ of Pgh, BA 1972, MA 1975, PhD 1979. **CAREER** Howard Univ, asst prof 1979-85; Washington DC Office of the Mayor, communications specialist 1984-86; DC Department of Administrative Services, dir of public affairs 1986-88; DC Department of Recreation, director of communications, 1988-92; The WHARTON GROUP, PRES, 1990-; Alcohol and Drug Abuse Services Administration, chief of criminal justice, 1992-95; DC DEPT OF HUMAN SVCS, SR AAST, DIR OF POLICY AND COMMUNICATION, currently. **HONORS AND AWARDS** Outstanding Black Women's Awd Communication Arts Creative Enterprises 1974; Doctoral Honor's Seminar Prog Howard Univ Speech Comm 1977; Bethune Legacy Award, Natl Council of Negro Women 1986; Natl Public Radio Documentary Award 1985. **MEMBERSHIPS** Delta Sigma Theta Sor 1971-; exec treas Natl Speech Comm Assn Black Caucus 1975-; honorary bd mem, Pgh Black Theatre Dance Ensemble 1978-; bd mem, Natl Arts Prog Natl Council of Negro Women 1979-; consultant, NAACP Labor & Indus Sub-com on Comm; chairperson, Joint Chapter Event, Natl Coalition of 100 Black Women Inc. **SELECTED PUBLICATIONS** Auth, "Black Dance, It's Origin and Continuity," Minority Voices, 1977; advisor: "Stuff," children's program, NBC-TV, Washington, DC. **CONTACT ADDRESS** DC Dept of Health, 800 9th St SE, Washington, DC, 20024.

WHATLEY, ERIC GORDON
PERSONAL Born 07/16/1944, Blackburn, England, m, 1980, 2 children **DISCIPLINE** ENGLISH LITERATURE, LANGUAGE **EDUCATION** Oxford Univ, BA, 66; Harvard Univ, PhD(English), 73. **CAREER** Asst prof English, Lake Forest Col, 72-78, asst dean fac, 76-79; asst prof English, 80-84, assoc

prof, 85-92, prof, Queens Col, NY, 93-; CUNY Grad Center, 89-. **HONORS AND AWARDS** Dir & fac fel, Newberry Libr Humanities Prog, Assoc Cols Midwest, 75-76; Nat Endowment for Humanities independent study fel, 79-80; Am Phil S oc grants, 75, 83; Nat Endowment for Humanities Res Tools grant (dir Paul Szarmach), 90-92; PSC-CUNY Res awards, 82-83, 85-87, 93, 97-98. **MEMBERSHIPS** Mediaeval Acad Am; Int Soc Anglo-Saxonists; Hagiography Soc N Am; Friends of the Saints. **RESEARCH** Old and Middle English hagiography; Medieval Latin hagiography. **SELECTED PUBLICATIONS** Auth, Cynewulf and Troy: A note on Cynewulf's Elene, Notes & Queries, 73; Bread and stone: Cynewulf's Elene 611-618, Neuphilol Mitteilungen, 75; Old English monastics and narrative art: Elene 1062, Mod Philol, 75; The Figure of Constantine the Great in Cynewulf's Elene, Traditio 37; The Middle English St Erkenwald in its liturgical context, Mediaevalia, 82; Opus dei, opus mundi: Patterns of Conflict in a Twelfth-century Miracle Collection, in Michael Sargent, ed, De cello in seculum, 89; The Saint of London: the Life and Miracles of St Erkenwald, 89; Acta Sanctorum, in Sources of Anglo-Saxon Literary Culture: A Trial Version, ed F Biggs et al, 90; Hagiography in Anglo-Saxon England: A Preliminary View from SASLC, Old English Newsletter, 90; with Jo Ann McNamara & John E Halborg, Sainted Women of the Dark Ages, 92; An Early Literary Quotation from the Inventio S. Crucis: a Note on Baudonivia's Vita S. Radegundis (BHL 7049), Analecta Bollandiana, 93; Late Old English Hagiography, ca 950-1150, in Hagiographies, ed Guy Philippart, 96; A Introduction to the Study of Old English Prose Hagiography: Sources and Resources, in Holy Men and Holy Women: Old English Prose Saints' Lives and Their Contexts, ed Paul E Szarmach, 96; Lost in Translation: Some Episodes in Old English Prose Saints' Lives, Anglo-Saxon England, 97. **CONTACT ADDRESS** Dept of English, Queens Col, CUNY, 6530 Kissena Blvd, Flushing, NY, 11367-1597.

WHEELER, ARTHUR M.
PERSONAL Born 11/20/1928, Toledo, OH, d, 3 children **DISCIPLINE** PHILOSOPHY; ENGLISH **EDUCATION** Bowling Green State Univ, BA, 51; Univ Chicago, MA, 53; Univ WI, Madison, PhD, 58. **CAREER** Instr, 58-62, asst prof, 62-66, assoc prof, 66-70, prof, 70-91, Kent State Univ, Ohio; RETIRED. **HONORS AND AWARDS** Summer res grants, 66, 79; Sigma Tau Delta (English). **MEMBERSHIPS** AAUP; Amer Philos Assoc; Ohio Philos Assoc; Tri-State Philos Assoc; Soc for the Philos Study of Relig; Southern Soc for Philos and Psychol; Ohio Academy of Relig. **RESEARCH** Ethics; philos of relig; free will. **SELECTED PUBLICATIONS** Auth, On Lewis' Imperatives of Right, Phil Studies, 61; God and Myth, Hibbert Journal, 64; Are Theological Utterances Assertions?, Sophia, 69; Bliks as Assertions and as Attackable, Phil Studies, 74; Prima Facie and Actual Duty, Analysis, 77; On Moral Nose, Phil Quart, 77; Fiat Justitia, ruat Caelum, Ethics, 86. **CONTACT ADDRESS** 7686 Diagonal Rd., Kent, OH, 44240.

WHEELER, RICHARD PAUL
PERSONAL Born 09/09/1943, Newton, IA, m, 1998, 3 children **DISCIPLINE** ENGLISH LITERATURE **EDUCATION** Cornell Col, BA, 65; State Univ NY, Buffalo, MA, 67, PhD(English lit), 70. **CAREER** Asst prof, 69-75, assoc prof English Lit, Univ Ill, Urbana, 75-87, prof 87-. **MEMBERSHIPS** MLA; Shakespeare Asn Am. **RESEARCH** Modern British literature; Shakespeare; psychoanalytic criticism. **SELECTED PUBLICATIONS** Auth, The King and the Physician's Daughter, Comp Drama, winter 74; Poetry and Fantasy in Shakespeare's Sonnets 88-96, Lit & Psychol, 72; Marriage and Manhood in All's Well That Ends Well, Bucknell Rev, spring 74; Yeats's Second Coming: What Rough Beast?, Am Imago, fall 74; Intimacy and Irony in The Blind Man, summer 76 & Give and take in Tickets Please, fall 77, D H Lawrence Rev; Since First We Were Dissevered, In: Representing Shakespeare, Johns Hopkins Univ Press, 80; Shakespeare's Development and the Problem Comedies, Univ Calif Press, Berkeley, 81; Fantasy and History in The Tempest, in The Tempest, ed Nigel Wood, Buckingham: Open Univ Press, Theory and Practice Series, 95; coauth, The Whole Journey: Shakespeare's Power of Development, Univ of Calif press, 86; Ed, Creating Elizabethan Tragedy: The Theater of Marlowe and Kyd, Univ of Chicago press, 88. **CONTACT ADDRESS** Dept of English, Univ Ill, 608 S Wright St, Urbana, IL, 61801-3613. **EMAIL** rpw@uiuc.edu

WHEELER, WAYNE R.
PERSONAL Born 03/17/1961, Tucson, AZ **DISCIPLINE** LIBRARY SCIENCE **EDUCATION** Northern Ariz Univ, BFA, 86; Univ Ariz, MLS, 89. **CAREER** Librn, Santa Cruz County Libr, 91-93; system librn, Luzern County Commun Col, 95-97; asst dir, Keystone Col, 97-. **MEMBERSHIPS** ALA; ACRL; SRRT; PALA; CRL; LIRT; NEPBC; CCAIT. **CONTACT ADDRESS** Miller Library, Keystone Col, One College Green, LaPlume, PA, 18440-0200. **EMAIL** wrwheeler@rocketmail.com

WHELCHEL, MARIANNE
DISCIPLINE AMERICAN LITERATURE AND WOMEN'S STUDIES **EDUCATION** LaGrange Col, BA; Purdue Univ, MA; Univ CT, PhD. **CAREER** Prof, Antioch Col. **HONORS AND AWARDS** NEH grant, 82-83. **RESEARCH** Alice Carr. **SELECTED PUBLICATIONS** Wrote on letters, jour(s), and oral testimony; publ on Adrienne Rich, and Alice Carr, a 1904 Antioch graduate who nursed in World War I and became internationally known for public health work in Greece during the 1920s. and 1930s. **CONTACT ADDRESS** Antioch Col, Yellow Springs, OH, 45387.

WHIDDEN, MARY BESS
DISCIPLINE ELIZABETHAN LITERATURE **EDUCATION** Univ Tex, PhD, 65. **CAREER** Instr, Univ NMex, 63-. **SELECTED PUBLICATIONS** Auth, Provincial Matters, 85. **CONTACT ADDRESS** Univ NMex, Albuquerque, NM, 87131.

WHIPPLE, ROBERT DALE, JR.
PERSONAL TX, m **DISCIPLINE** RHETORIC AND COMPOSITION **EDUCATION** TX Tech Univ, Lubbock, BA, 79; Univ TX at Austin, MA, 83; Miami Univ, Oxford, PhD, 90. **CAREER** Assoc prof 95; asst prof 90; assoc ch dept Eng 98- & dir, Compos 90-98, Creighton Univ; asst dir, Freshman Eng Col Compos, Miami Univ, 87-88; co-ed, NE Eng J, Creighton Univ, 91-95; adj prof, Birmingham-Southern Col, 89-90; lectr, Univ AL, 88-89; tchg fel, Miami Univ, 85-88; lectr, TX Tech Univ, 83-85; asst instr, Univ TX at Austin, 82-83; tchg asst, TX Tech Univ, 81. **HONORS AND AWARDS** Outstanding Advr Awd, Creighton Col Arts & Sci, 98; Nominee, Tchr for Tomorrow Awd, 97; US W Acad Technol & Develop fel, 95; Phi Kappa Phi Honor Soc, Miami Univ, 87; Sinclair fel, Miami Univ, 85., Ed bd(s), Engl J, 93-97, Writing Ctr J, 93-97 & H-Rhetor Discussion list and bk rev proj, 94-98; contrib bibliog, Longmans Bibliog of Rhet & Compos, 86, 87 & 88. **MEMBERSHIPS** Sec 92-93, ch 93-94 & Treas 94-95, Midwest Writing Ctr(s) Asn; Nat Coun Tchr(s) Eng; Nat Writing Ctr(s) Asn; Writing & Comput Asn, UK. **SELECTED PUBLICATIONS** Auth, Socratic Method and Writing Instruction, Lanham, UP Am, 97; Essays on the Literature of John P Marquand, Edwin Mellen Press, 98; Larry McMurtry, The Last Picture Show, Lonesome Dove, & Comanche Moon, Encycl Popular Fiction, Beacham Press, 98; The World-Wide Web and Composition Theory, Theorizing Composition: A Critical Sourcebook of Theory and Scholarship in Contemporary Composition Studies, Westport,Greenwood Press, 98; Bravo! Brava!, Nebraska Life, 98; Goya's Blanket, poem, Shadows, 97; Review of The Press of Ideas: Readings for Writers on Print Culture and the Information Age by Julie Bates Dock, Kairos: A J Tchr(s) of Writing in Webbed Environments 2 1, 97; Nevil Shute & On The Beach, Encycl Popular Fiction, Beacham Press, 96; Colleen McCullough, The Thorn Birds & Fortune's Favorites, Encycl Popular Fiction, Beacham Press, 96; WEB Griffin, The Aviators, Men In Blue, & Semper Fi, Encycl Popular Fiction, Beacham Press, 96; Glory Road by Robert A Heinlein, Magill's Guide to Sci Fiction and Fantasy Lit, Salem Press, 96; Florence Home, poem, Shadows 31 1: 8.; ed, Native Heritage: American Indian Literature, Urbana, Nat Coun Tch(s) Engl, 94; Cather in the Classroom, Urbana, Nat Coun Tch(s) Engl, 92; rev, A History of Professional Writing Instruction in American Colleges: Years of Acceptance, Growth, and Doubt by Katherine H Adams, J Bus & Tech Commun 9 1, 95. **CONTACT ADDRESS** Dept of Eng, Creighton Univ, 2500 CA Plaza, Omaha, NE, 68178.

WHITAKER, ELAINE E.
PERSONAL Born 11/23/1942, Oklahoma City, OK, m, 1964, 3 children **DISCIPLINE** ENGLISH, LATE MEDIEVAL MANUSCRIPTS **EDUCATION** NY Univ, PhD, 71. **CAREER** Adj to asst prof of Humanities, Rhodes Col, 78-85; asst to assoc prof, english, Univ Alabama, 85-. **HONORS AND AWARDS** Univ Ala Tchr of Year, 97-98. **MEMBERSHIPS** Early Book Soc; Early English Text Soc; Medieval Acad Am; Mod Lang Asn Amer; Soc Textual Scholar; PCTE; CCCC. **RESEARCH** 15th Century British books; Composition/Rhetoric; Pedagogy. **SELECTED PUBLICATIONS** Auth, The Awakening Conscience in Brideshead Revisited, Evelyn Waugh Newsletter and Studies, 93; A Pedagogy to Address Plagiarism, Col Compos & Commun, 93; Reading the Paston Letters Medically, English Lang Notes, 93; auth, A Collaboration of Readers: Categorization of the Annotations in Copies of Caxtons Royal Book, Univ Mich Press, 94; John of Arderne and Chaucers Physician, ANO: A Quart Jour of Short Articles, Notes, and Rev, 95; Traces of a Program of Illustration Specific to a Late Medieval Somme/Mirror Manuscripta, 95. **CONTACT ADDRESS** Dept of English, Univ Ala, Birmingham, AL, 35294-1260. **EMAIL** eew@uab.edu

WHITAKER, FAYE PAULI
PERSONAL Born 08/19/1941, Belleville, WI, m, 1970, 2 children **DISCIPLINE** ENGLISH LITERATURE **EDUCATION** Lakeland Col, AB, 63; Western Mich Univ, MA, 65; Northwestern Univ, PhD(English), 74. **CAREER** Instr English, Western Mich Univ, 64-67; instr, 70-74, asst prof English, Iowa State Univ, 74-91; assoc prof, 91; asst provost, 94. **MEMBERSHIPS** MLA; **RESEARCH** Seventeenth century English poets; American Puritan poets; Renaissance drama; Biblical Lit. **CONTACT ADDRESS** Dept of English, Iowa State Univ, Ames, IA, 50011-0002. **EMAIL** fwhitake@iastate.edu

WHITAKER, ROSEMARY
DISCIPLINE ENGLISH LITERATURE **EDUCATION** Univ Okla, BM; Univ Tulsa, MA; Univ Okla, PhD. **CAREER** Prof. **RESEARCH** American women writers. **SELECTED PUBLICATIONS** Auth, pubs on Mari Sandoz and Helen Hunt Jackson. **CONTACT ADDRESS** Dept of English, Colorado State Univ, Fort Collins, CO, 80523. **EMAIL** services@colostate.edu

WHITAKER, THOMAS RUSSELL
PERSONAL Born 08/07/1925, Marquette, MI, m, 1950, 4 children **DISCIPLINE** ENGLISH **EDUCATION** Oberlin Col, AB, 49; Yale Univ, AM, 50, PhD(English), 53. **CAREER** From instr to prof, Oberlin Col, 52-64; teacher lit, Goddard Col, 64-66; prof English, Univ Iowa, 66-75; PROF ENGLISH, YALE UNIV, 75-, CHMN DEPT ENGLISH, 79-, Haskell fel, Oberlin Col, 58-59; Am Coun Learned Soc fel, 69-70; ed, Iowa Review, 74-77; Huntington fel Nat Endowment for Humanities, 81. **HONORS AND AWARDS** Harbison Award, Danforth Found, 72. **MEMBERSHIPS** MLA **RESEARCH** Twentieth century English and American literature; modern drama, continental, English and American. **SELECTED PUBLICATIONS** Auth, Swan and Shadow: Yeats's Dialogue with History, Univ NC, 64; William Carlos Williams, Twayne, 68; ed, Twentieth Century Interpretations of the Playboy of the Western World, Prentice-Hall, 69; auth, On speaking humanly, In: The Philosopher-Critic, Univ Tulsa, 70; Voices in the open: Wordsworth, Eliot and Stevens, Iowa Rev, 71; Since we have been a conversation, Clio, 76; Fields of Play in Modern Drama, Princeton Univ, 77; Sight Unseen - Beckett, Pinter, Stoppard, And Other Contemporary Dramatists On Radio - Guralnick,Es, English Language Notes, Vol 0035, 1997. **CONTACT ADDRESS** Dept of English, Yale Univ, New Haven, CT, 06520.

WHITE, CECIL R.
PERSONAL Born 10/15/1937, Hammond, IN, d, 2 children **DISCIPLINE** LIBRARY AND INFORMATION SCIENCE **EDUCATION** Southern IL Univ, BS in Ed, 59; Southwestern Baptist Theol Sem, M Div, 69; Univ North TX, MLS, 70, PhD, 83. **CAREER** Asst Dir of the Library, Southwestern Baptist Sem, 69-80; Dir of Libraries, Golden Gate Baptist Theol Sem, 80-87; Dir of the Library, West Oahu Col, 88-89; Special Projects Dir, North State Cooperative Library Asn, 89-90; DIR OF THE LIBRARY, ST. PATRICK'S SEMINARY, 90-. **HONORS AND AWARDS** Who's Who in the West; Who's Who in Religion; Who's Who in America; Who's Who in the World; Lilly Found grantee, Am Theol Lib Asn; Beta Phi Mu Library Honorary Soc. **MEMBERSHIPS** Am Library Asn; Asn of Col and Res Librarians; Catholic Library Asn; Am Theol Library Asn. **RESEARCH** Theology; religion and social issues; ecumenism. **CONTACT ADDRESS** Dir, McKeon Memorial Library, Saint Patrick's Sem, 320 Middlefield Rd., Menlo Park, CA, 94025-3596. **EMAIL** cecilrwhite@juno.com

WHITE, CINDY H.
DISCIPLINE COMMUNCATION STUDIES **EDUCATION** Tex Tech Univ, BA, MA; Univ Ariz, PhD. **CAREER** Asst prof. **RESEARCH** Interpersonal communication. **SELECTED PUBLICATIONS** Co-auth, Research on nonverbal message production, 97; Interpersonal deception: XI. Relationship of suspicion to communication behaviors and perceptions, 96; Interpersonal deception: VII. Behavioral profiles of falsification, concealment, and equivocation, Jour Lang Soc Psychol, 96. **CONTACT ADDRESS** Dept of Communication, Univ Colo Boulder, Boulder, CO, 80309. **EMAIL** Cindy.White@Colorado.edu

WHITE, DEBORAH
DISCIPLINE ROMANTICISM AND CONTEMPORARY LITERARY THEORY **EDUCATION** Yale Univ, BA, 82, MPhil, 87, PhD, 93. **CAREER** Assoc prof. **RESEARCH** Romantic theories of imagination. **SELECTED PUBLICATIONS** Pubs on Shelley, DeMan, and Freud. **CONTACT ADDRESS** Dept of Eng, Columbia Col, New York, 2960 Broadway, New York, NY, 10027-6902.

WHITE, DONALD JERRY
PERSONAL Born 06/05/1946, Anderson, IN, m, 1967, 1 child **DISCIPLINE** RENAISSANCE & MEDIEVAL LITERATURE **EDUCATION** Barton Col, AB, 68; Univ Ill, Urbana, AM, 72, PhD(English), 77. **CAREER** Asst prof, Albertson Col Idaho, 75-78; asst prof, Eureka Col, 78-80; asst prof, assoc prof, prof English, Cent Mo State Univ, 80-. **HONORS AND AWARDS** Hon Woodrow Wilson Fellow, 68; Phi Kappa Phi National Honor Soc, 73; Phi Beta Delta Honor Soc for International Scholars, 94. **MEMBERSHIPS** MLA; Shakespeare Asn Am; Renaissance Soc Am; Medieval Acad Am. **RESEARCH** Renaissance drama; Shakespeare; Medieval drama. **SELECTED PUBLICATIONS** Auth, Irony and the three temptations in Philaster, Thoth, spring 75; Richard Edwards' Damon and Pithias: A Critical, Old Spelling Edition, Garland Press, 80; contribr, William Blake, John Bunyan, Dante, Holy Grail, C S Lewis, and John Milton, In: Abingdon Dictionary of Living Religions, Abingdon, 81; Early English Drama: Everyman to 1580, G. K. Hall, 86; Richard Edwards, in Elizabethen Dramatists, ed Fredson Bowers, Dictionary of Literary Biography 62, Bruccoli, 87; Contrib, World Shakespeare Bibliography (1988-present). **CONTACT ADDRESS** Dept of English, Central Missouri State Univ, Warrensburg, MO, 64093-5046. **EMAIL** jwhite@cmsu1.cmsu.edu

WHITE, DONNA
DISCIPLINE ENGLISH LITERATURE **EDUCATION** Univ Minn, PhD, 91. **CAREER** Dept Eng, Clemson Univ **RESEARCH** Children's literature. **SELECTED PUBLICATIONS** Auth, The Crimes of Lady Charlotte Guest, Proceedings 15th Harvard Celtic Colloquium, 97; The Game Plan of the Hunting of the Snark, Proceedings 2nd Int Lewis Carroll Conf, 95; Labyrinth: Jim Henson's Game of Children's Literature and Film, The Antic Art: Enhancing Children's Literary Experience Through Film and Video, Highsmith, 93. **CONTACT ADDRESS** Clemson Univ, 315 Strode, Clemson, SC, 29634. **EMAIL** donna@clemson.edu

WHITE, DOUGLAS HOWARTH
PERSONAL Born 08/26/1929, Omaha, NE, m, 1964 **DISCIPLINE** ENGLISH **EDUCATION** Univ Omaha, BA, 51; Univ Nebr, MA, 54; Univ Chicago, PhD, 63. **CAREER** Instr English, Coe Col, 57-59; from instr to asst prof, Ill Inst Technol, 60-67; from asst prof to assoc prof, 67-78, Prof English, Loyola Univ, Chicago, 78-, Nat Endowment for Humanities fel, 67-68; Newberry Libr-Brit Acad fel, 76. **MEMBERSHIPS** MLA; Am Soc 18th Cent Studies. **RESEARCH** Eighteenth century literature; intellectual history of 18th century England. **SELECTED PUBLICATIONS** Auth, Pope and the Context of Controversy The Manipulation of Ideas in an Essay on Man, Univ Chicago, 70; Swift and the definition of man, Mod Philol, Vol 73, No 4, 5/76; Sources Of Dramatic Theory, Vol 2, Voltaire To Hugo - Sidnell,Mj, University Of Toronto Quarterly, Vol 0066, 1996. **CONTACT ADDRESS** Dept of English, Loyola Univ, Chicago, 6525 N Sheridan Rd, Chicago, IL, 60626-5385.

WHITE, EDWARD MICHAEL
PERSONAL Born 08/16/1933, Brooklyn, NY, m, 1976, 2 children **DISCIPLINE** ENGLISH **EDUCATION** NY Univ, BA, 55; Harvard Univ, MA, 56, PhD, 60. **CAREER** From instr Eng to asst prof, Wellesley Col, 60-65; assoc prof, 65-69, chmn freshman compos, 65-66, chmn dept Eng, 66-76, prof Eng, 69-98, prof emer eng, CA State Univ, San Bernardino, 98-; sr lectr Eng, Univ AZ, 98; Pres, CA State Univ & Col Eng Coun, 73-75; consult, Eng testing & measurement writing ability to many schs and col, 73-; coordr, Eng testing prog & consult, credit by evaluation, CA State Univ & Cols, 76-80; dir, CA State Univ & Cols freshman Eng equivalency exam, 73-; dir, Nat Inst Educ res in effective tchg. **MEMBERSHIPS** MLA; NCTE; Soc for Values Higher Educ; Conf Col Compos & Commun; AAUP. **RESEARCH** Eng and Am fiction; compos; Eng testing, particularly direct measurement of writing ability. **SELECTED PUBLICATIONS** Auth, Thackeray's contribution to Fraser's magazine, Studies Bibliog, 66; A critical theory of Mansfield Park, Studies English Lit, fall 67; The Writer's Control of Tone, 70 & The Pop Culture Tradition, 72, Norton; Equivalency testing in freshman English, Bull Asn Dept English, 3/73; Freedom is restraint: The pedagogical problem of Jane Austen, San Jose Studies, 2/76; Racial minorities and writing skills assessment in the California State University and Colleges, Col English, 3/81; Teaching and Assessing Writing, Jossey-Bass, 85, 2nd ed, 94; Developing Successful College Writing Programs, Jossey-Bass, 89; Assigning, Responding, Evaluating: A Writing Teacher's Guide, 3rd ed, St Martins, 95; Inquiry: A Cross Cultural Reader, Prentice-Hall, 93; Composition in the 21st Century: Crisis and Change, Southern Ill Univ Press, 96; Writing Assessment: Politics, Policies, Practices, MLA, 96. **CONTACT ADDRESS** Dept of Eng, California State Univ, San Bernardino, 5500 University Pky, San Bernardino, CA, 92407-7500. **EMAIL** ewhite@wiley.csusb.edu

WHITE, FRED D.
PERSONAL Born 08/06/1943, Los Angeles, CA, 2 children **DISCIPLINE** COMPOSITION **EDUCATION** Univ Minn, BA, 67, MA, 74; Univ Iowa, PhD, 80. **CAREER** Assoc prof English, Santa Clara Univ, 80-; Instr English, Lakewood Community Col, 74-75 & Anoka-Ramsey Community Col, 76-77. **HONORS AND AWARDS** Brutocao Award for Teaching Excellence, 97. **MEMBERSHIPS** MLA; Conf Col Compos & Commun. **RESEARCH** Composition theory and pedagogy; interrelationships of the literary and scientific imagination. **SELECTED PUBLICATIONS** Auth, Whitman's cosmic spider, Walt Whitman Rev, 77; Robert Sheckley, in Twentieth Century Science-Fiction Writers, St Martin's, 81; Releasing the self: Teaching journal writing to freshmen, Writing Instr, summer 82; Albee's hunger artist: The Zoo Story as a parable of the writer vs society, Ariz Quart, 83; Science, Discourse, & Authorial Responsibility, San Jose Studies, 84; The Writer's Art, Wadsworth, 86; Poetic Responses to Einstein, San Jose Studies, 89; Science and the Human Spirit, Wadsworth, 89; Science in the Poetry of Emily Dickinson, Col Lit, 92; Rachel Carson: Encounters with the Primal Mother, NDak Quart, 91; Communicating Technology, Harper Collins, 96. **CONTACT ADDRESS** Dept of English, Santa Clara Univ, 500 El Camino Real, Santa Clara, CA, 95053-0001.

WHITE, PETER
DISCIPLINE AMERICAN LITERATURE **EDUCATION** Pa State Univ, PhD, 76. **CAREER** Instr, 76-, dir, grad stud Eng, 93-95, assoc dean, Col Arts and Sci, Univ NMex. **SELECTED PUBLICATIONS** Auth, The Lore of New Mexico, 88. **CONTACT ADDRESS** Univ NMex, Albuquerque, NM, 87131.

WHITE, ROBERTA
DISCIPLINE BRITISH LITERATURE **EDUCATION** Albion Col, BA; Univ Chicago, MA; Stanford Univ, PhD. **CAREER** Fac, 67; Charles J. Luellen Prof and chr Dept Eng; chr, Hum Div. **HONORS AND AWARDS** Dir, writer-in-res prog, Centre Col. **RESEARCH** Modern British literature, Irish literature, Virginia Woolf, John Milton, and 17th-century poetry. **SELECTED PUBLICATIONS** Auth, articles on modern contemporary writers including John Berryman, Margaret Atwood; contrib, Mother Puzzles, Greenwood Press. **CONTACT ADDRESS** Centre Co!, 600 W Walnut St, Danville, KY, 40422. **EMAIL** whiter@centre.edu

WHITEMAN, D. BRUCE
PERSONAL Born 06/18/1952, Toronto, ON, Canada, m, 1973, 2 children **DISCIPLINE** ENGLISH LITERATURE & LIBRARIANSHIP **EDUCATION** Trent Univ, BA, 75; Univ Toronto, MA, 77, PhD, 79. **CAREER** Librn, 79-88, McMaster Univ; dept head, 88-96, McGill Univ; head librn, 96-, William Andrews Clark Mem Libr, UCLA. **MEMBERSHIPS** Amer Libr Assoc; Bibliog Soc Amer; Bibliog Soc Canada; SHARP. **RESEARCH** Canadian literary hist; descriptive bibliog; hist of the book; forgery. **SELECTED PUBLICATIONS** Coauth, A Bibliography of Macmillan of Canada Imprints, 1906-1980, Dundern Press, 85; auth, The Letters of John Sutherland, ECW Press, 92; auth, Scholarly Publishing in Canada and Canadian Bibliography: Selected Papers on Two Themes, Assoc for Canadian Stud, 93; auth, Lasting Impressions: A Short History of English Publishing in Quebec, Vehicule Press, 94; auth, J.E.H. MacDonald, Quarry Press, 95. **CONTACT ADDRESS** William Andrews Clark Mem Lib, UCLA, 2520 Cimarron St, Los Angeles, CA, 90018-2019. **EMAIL** whiteman@humnet.UCLA.edu

WHITLARK, JAMES S.
DISCIPLINE WORLD LITERATURE **EDUCATION** Univ Chicago, PhD, 76. **CAREER** Prof, TX Tech Univ. **RESEARCH** Relig in lit. **SELECTED PUBLICATIONS** Auth, Illuminated Fantasy: From Blake's Visions to Recent Graphic Fiction, Assoc UP, 88; Behind the Great Wall: A Post-Jungian Approach to Kafkaesque Literature, Assoc UP, 91; coed, The Literature of Emigration and Exile, TX Tech, 92. **CONTACT ADDRESS** Texas Tech Univ, Lubbock, TX, 79409-5015. **EMAIL** ditjw@ttacs.ttu.edu

WHITNEY, CHARLES C.
DISCIPLINE EARLY MODERN DRAMA, SEVENTEENTH CENTURY, SIXTEENTH CENTURY, LITERARY THEORY **EDUCATION** San Francisco State Col, BA, 69; CUNY, PhD, 77. **CAREER** Adj lectr, Mercy Col, 77-78, 79; adj lectr, CUNY, 75-81; asst prof, Penn State Univ, 81-87; vis assoc prof, St Bonaventure Univ, 87-88; assoc prof, Univ Nev, Las Vegas, 88-. **HONORS AND AWARDS** A W Mellon fel in the Hum, CUNY, 78-79; NEH summer sem, Yale Univ, 79; NEH summer sem, Huntington Libr, 83; Penn State res grants, 86-87, 86, 84, 81-82; NEH summer inst, Newberry Libr, 86; sem fel, Folger Inst, 86; Choice Mag Outstanding Acad Bk Sel, 87; vis fac mem, NEH summer inst, Univ Fla, 90; URGF grant, Huntington Libr, 94-95; Am Philos Soc grant, Guildhall Libr, London, 97. **RESEARCH** Theater audiences of Shakespeare and his contemporary dramatists. **SELECTED PUBLICATIONS** Auth, Festivity and Topicality in the Coventry Scene of 1 Henry IV, Eng Lit Renaissance 24:2, May 94; Charmian's Laughter: Women, Gypsies, and Festive Ambivalence in The Tragedy of Antony and Cleopatra, The Upstart Crow: A Shakespeare J XIV, 94; 'Like Richard the 3d's Ghost': Dorothy Osborne and the Uses of Shakespeare, Eng Lang Notes 34:2, Dec 96. **CONTACT ADDRESS** Dept of Eng, Univ Nev, Las Vegas, 4505 Maryland Pky, PO Box 455011, Las Vegas, NV, 89154-5011. **EMAIL** whitney@nevada.edu

WICK, AUDREY
DISCIPLINE RHETORIC AND COMPOSITION, MINORITY LITERATURE, FEMINIST LITERARY CRITICISM **EDUCATION** OH State Univ, BA, 75; Univ TX at Arlington, MA, 90, PhD, 96. **CAREER** Dir, 1st-Yr Eng & asoc dir, 91-94, Univ TX at Arlington; ch, Freshman Eng Comt & Grad Tchg Asn Comt, 92-96; mem, Curric Task Force, 92-96, Dept Goals Comt, 94-96, Travel Comt, 94-96, Rhetoric Curric Comt, 93-96, Freshman Eng Comt, 88-91 & Comt for Curric Design Prog in Freshman & Sophomore Eng, 85-87; co ch, Freshman Eng Comt, 91; res asst to dir Freshman Eng, 88-89. **MEMBERSHIPS** Pres, Gorgias Soc, 87; Univ TX at Arlington Current: Mod Lang Soc; Writing Prog Admin; Rhetoric Soc Am; Nat Coun Tchrs Engl; Gorgias Soc. **SELECTED PUBLICATIONS** Auth, Rhetoric: Concepts, Definitions, Boundaries, an anthology, The Feminist Sophistic Enterprise: From Euripides to the Vietnam War, 95; Rhetoric Society Quarterly, The Feminist Sophistic Enterprise: From Euripides to the Vietnam War, 92; Tulsa Studies in Women's Lit, Book Rev(s), 91. **CONTACT ADDRESS** Dept of Eng, Univ of Texas at Arlington, 203 Carlisle Hall, PO Box 19035, Arlington, TX, 76019-0595.

WICK, ROBERT L.
PERSONAL Born 12/06/1938, Sioux City, IA, m, 1964, 3 children **DISCIPLINE** FINE ARTS; ENGLISH; LIBRARY SCIENCE **EDUCATION** Univ SD, BFA, 61, MA, 64; Univ Denver, MALS, 71. **CAREER** Band dir, Gregory High Sch, 61-63; prof, Sioux Falls Col, 64-69; libr, Metropolitan St Col, Denver Co, 71-78; Bibliogr, Univ Co Denver, 78- . **HONORS AND AWARDS** Excellence in Teaching Award, Univ Co Denver, 88; Excellence in Svc Award, Univ Co Denver, 93; Excellence in Res Award, Univ of Co, 97. **MEMBERSHIPS** Modern Lang Soc; Modern Libr Assoc. **RESEARCH** Biography; electronic music bibliogr; music ref bibliogr. **SELECTED PUBLICATIONS** Auth, A Library/Media Marriage That Works, Medium, 76; Denver's Dining Delights: A Midwinter Guide to Mile-High Eating, Amer Libr, 93; The Literature of electronic and computer Music: A Basic Library Collection, Choice, 93; Electronic and Computer Music: An Annotated Bibliography, Greenwood Press, 97; ed, ARBA - Guide to Biographical Resources, Libr Unlimited Press, 98. **CONTACT ADDRESS** Univ Co Denver, 3398 S Oneida Way, Denver, CO, 80224-2832. **EMAIL** bwick@castle.cudenver.edu

WICKERT, MAX ALBRECHT
PERSONAL Born 05/26/1938, Augsburg, Germany, d, 1 child **DISCIPLINE** ENGLISH & AMERICAN LITERATURE **EDUCATION** St Bonaventure Univ, BA, 58; Yale Univ, MA, 59, PhD, 65. **CAREER** From instr English to asst prof, Nazareth Col Rochester, 61-66; asst prof, 66-70, ASSOC PROF ENGLISH, STATE UNIV NY BUFFALO, 70-; Dir, Outriders Poetry Prog, Buffalo, NY, 71-. **HONORS AND AWARDS** New Poets Rev Prize, 80. **RESEARCH** Anglo-German literary relations; 19th century aesthetics; history and criticism of opera; translation of Italian verse. **SELECTED PUBLICATIONS** Auth, Structure and ceremony in Spenser's Epithalamion, ELH, 6/68; various poems in Poetry, Choice, Works & Mich Quart Rev, 69-82; transl various poems by Georg Trakl in Chicago Rev, Choice, Extensions & Malahat Rev, 69-; co-transl, 1001 Ways to Live Without Working, Er"ffnungen, Vienna, 71; auth, All the Weight of the Still Midnight (poems), Outriders, 72; Dismemberment of Orpheus: Operatic myth goes underground, Salmagundi, 5/77; Myth and meaning in early opera, Opera J, 4/78; Pat Sonnets, Street Press, 98. **CONTACT ADDRESS** Dept of English, State Univ of NY, P O Box 604610, Buffalo, NY, 14260-4610. **EMAIL** wickert@acsu.buffalo.edu

WICKES, GEORGE
PERSONAL Born 01/06/1923, Antwerp, Belgium, m, 1975, 4 children **DISCIPLINE** ENGLISH **EDUCATION** Univ Toronto, BA, 44; Columbia Univ, MA, 49; Univ Calif, PhD, 54. **CAREER** Asst secy, Belgian-Am Educ Found, 47-49; exec officer, US Educ Found, Belgium, 52-54; instr English, Duke Univ, 54-57; from asst prof to prof, Harvey Mudd Col & Claremont Grad Sch, 57-70; dir, Comp Lit Prog, 74-77, Prof English & Comp Lit, Univ Ore, 70-93, Prof Emeritus, 93-, Head Dept English, 76-83; Fulbright lectr, France, 62-63 & 78; US Info Serv lectr, Europe, 69 & Africa, 78 & 79; vis prof, Univ Rouen, 70, Univ Tubingen, 81, Univ Heidelberg, 96; adv ed, Northwest Rev. **HONORS AND AWARDS** Am Philos Soc grant, 71; sr fel, Ctr Twentieth Century Studies, Univ Wis-Milwaukee, 71; Am Coun Learned Soc grant, 72; Camango Fel, 72-93; Nat Endowment for Arts creative writing fel, 73. **MEMBERSHIPS** MLA; PEN. **RESEARCH** Renaissance poetry; modern literature; comparative literature. **SELECTED PUBLICATIONS** Ed, Durrell-Miller Correspondence, Dutton, 63; Masters of Modern British Fiction, Macmillan, 63; Henry Miller and the Critics, Southern Ill Univ, 63; Aldous Huxley at UCLA: A Catalogue of the Manuscripts in the Aldous Huxley Collection, Univ Calif Libr, 64; Henry Miller, Univ Minn, 66; Americans in Paris, Doubleday, 69; The Amazon of Letters, Putnam, 76; transl, The Memoirs of Frederic Mistral, New Directions, 86; ed, Henry Miller, Letters to Emil, New Directions, 89; auth, Henry Miller and James Laughlin, Selected Letters, Norton, 95. **CONTACT ADDRESS** Dept of English, Univ of Oregon, Eugene, OR, 97403-1205.

WICKHAM CROWLEY, KELLEY M.
DISCIPLINE ENGLISH LITERATURE **EDUCATION** Georgetown Univ, BA; Univ Durham, MA; Cornell Univ, MA, PhD. **CAREER** Eng Dept, Georgetown Univ **RESEARCH** Old English and Early Middle English literature; intersections of physical and intellectual culture; archaeology of the British Isles; feminist gender theory; Anglo-Saxon architecture. **SELECTED PUBLICATIONS** Auth, La3amon's Narrative Innovations and Bakhtin's Theories, 94; pubs on archaeology for Year's Work in Old English. **CONTACT ADDRESS** English Dept, Georgetown Univ, 37th and O St, Washington, DC, 20057.

WIDDICOMBE, RICHARD TOBY
PERSONAL Born 04/12/1955, Salisbury, England, m, 1979 **DISCIPLINE** ENGLISH AND AMERICAN LITERATURE **EDUCATION** Cambridge Univ, BA, 77, MA, 81; Univ CA, Irvine, MA, 79, PhD, 84. **CAREER** Vis lect, Univ CA, Santa Barbara, 84-86, lect, 86-89; asst prof, NY Inst of Technology, 89-92; asst prof, 92-95, assoc prof, Univ AK, Anchorage, 95-, chair, dept English, 95-97. **HONORS AND AWARDS** Arthur E Lewis Award, 89; AAUP Award, 92; Several fac research and travel awards, 92-; Who's Who Among America's Teachers, 96, 98. **MEMBERSHIPS** Modern Lang of Am; Soc for Utopian Studies. **RESEARCH** 19th and 20th century Am lit; bibliographical and textual studies. **SELECTED PUBLICATIONS**

Auth, Edward Bellamy: An Annotated Bibliography of Secondary Criticism, Garland Pub, 88; Utopia at the Movies & Scholarship: 1992-February 1993, in Utopus Discovered ns 1, spring, 93; A Few Soiled Flowers': Nathanael West and Greek Tragedy, English Lang Notes 30-3, March 93; Scholarship: January-August 1993, Notes and Queries (on Looking Backward), & Booktalk (on Today Then and Dinotopia), in Utopus Discovered ns 2, fall 93; Scholarship: Sept 1993 to Feb 1994, in Utopus Discovered ns 3, spring 94; Utopia and Popular Culture, Scholarship: Mar-Oct 1994, & Internet as Cyber-Utopia, in Utopus Discovered ns 4, winter 94; America and Americans: A Long Journey into Publishing, Marginalia 1-2, April 95; Scholarship: Nov 1994-June 1995, in Utopus Discovered ns 5, summer 95; America and the Americans in 1833-1834, Fordham Univ Press, 95; Reply to Neil Easterbrook, Extrapolation, forthcoming; four entries on Edward Bellamy in Le Dictionnaire de l'Utopie, Slatkine, forthcoming 99; A Reader's Guide to Raymond Chandler, Greenwood Press, forthcoming 99. **CONTACT ADDRESS** Dept of English, Univ of Alaska, Anchorage, Anchorage, AK, 99508. **EMAIL** afrtw@uaa.alaska.edu

WIEBE, MEL
DISCIPLINE ENGLISH LITERATURE **EDUCATION** Univ Manitoba, PhD. **CAREER** Dept Eng, Queen's Univ **HONORS AND AWARDS** Ed, Disraeli Project, 83-. **RESEARCH** Victorian age; scholarly editing. **SELECTED PUBLICATIONS** Auth, pubs on Tennyson, Hardy and Disraeli; ed, Benjamin Disraeli Letters, Univ Toronto. **CONTACT ADDRESS** English Dept, Queen's Univ, Kingston, ON, K7L 3N6.

WIEGENSTEIN, STEVE
DISCIPLINE ENGLISH **EDUCATION** Univ Mo-Columbia, BJ, 76, MA, 81, PhD, 87. **CAREER** Assoc prof & adv stud newspaper, Culver-Stockton Col, 96- & asst prof, 92-96, granted tenure, 96; asst prof, Drury Col, Springfield, 88-92; stud newspaper adv, 88-92; yearbk adv, 89-92; actg adv, radio station, 90-91; instr, Engl & Jour, Centenary Col La, Shreveport, 85-88; news ed, Wayne Co Jo Banner, Piedmont, 76-79. **HONORS AND AWARDS** MO Governor's Awd Excellence Tchg, 96; Huggins Grad Scholar, Univ MO, 82-85; Univ MO Dept Engl Awd Excellence Tchg, 81; DR Francis fel, Univ MO, 79-80., Who's Who in the Midwest, Who's Who in Am Educ. **MEMBERSHIPS** Col Media Advisers, MO Col Media Asn, elected liaison to MO Press Asn, 96; Soc Prof Jour; Nat Icarian Heritage Soc; AAUP, Local Chap Sec/Treas 89-90 & pres, 90-91; bd dir, Lit Vol(s) Am, Shreveport Chap, 87-88. **SELECTED PUBLICATIONS** Auth, The Academic Novel and the Academic Ideal: John Williams' Stoner, McNeese Rev 33, 94; The Image of Nature in Annie Dillard's The Living, in The Image of Nature: Selected Papers, Univ Southern CO, 93; Naturalism, Literary History, and The Story of a Country Town, Univ MS Stud in Eng, NS 7, 89; The Media and/in Politics, address to Quincy, Ill, Rotary Club, 96; Signs and Wonders, short story, NE Rev 22 2, 94; Jailer's Experiences Become 'Prison Rhymes,' Ozarks Mountaineer, 91; Commemorating the Trail of Tears, Ozarks Mountaineer, 89; The Trouble with Women, short story, Oxford Mag, 89; The End of the World, short story, Kans Quart 20:3, 88; Why Miss Elizabeth Never Joined the Shakespeare Club, short story, La Lit, 87; Bill Burkens and Peter Krull, short story, Beloit Fiction J, 86; ed & wrote critical preface to 2 previously unpubl plays by Tennessee Williams, "Beauty is the Word" and "Hot Milk at Three in the Morning," MO Review 7:3, Summer 1984. **CONTACT ADDRESS** Dept of Eng, Culver-Stockton Col, 1 College Hill, Canton, MO, 63435-1299. **EMAIL** swiegenstein@culver.edu

WIEMANN, JOHN M.
PERSONAL Born 07/11/1947, New Orleans, LA, m, 1969, 2 children **DISCIPLINE** INTERPERSONAL COMMUNICATION **EDUCATION** Loyola Univ (La), AB, 69; Purdue Univ, MS, 73, PhD(commun), 75. **CAREER** Employee rels specialist, Int Bus Machines Corp, 69-71; grad instr commun, Purdue Univ, 71-75; asst prof human commun, Rutgers Univ, 75-77; Asst Prof Commun Studies, Univ Calif, Santa Barbara, 77-, Res Assoc, Instrnl Develop, Measurement & Res Ctr, Purdue Univ, 73-74; vis scholar, Col Commun, Univ Tex, Austin, fall 80; W K Kellogg Found nat fel, 80-83. **HONORS AND AWARDS** Industry Award Outstanding Applied Res, Orgn Commun Div, Int Commun Asn, 74; Outstanding Res Report, Interpersonal Commun Div, Int Commun Asn, 76. **MEMBERSHIPS** Int Commun Asn; Speech Commun Asn; AAAS; Am Educ Res Asn; Am Psychol Asn. **RESEARCH** Effective interpersonal communication; nonverbal communication; organizational communication & development. **SELECTED PUBLICATIONS** Coauth, Turn-taking in conversations, J Commun, 75; auth, Explication & test of a model of communicative competence, Human Commun Res, 77; Needed research & training in speaking & listening literacy, Commun Educ, 78; coauth, Nonverbal communication: Issues and appraisal, Human Commun Res, 78; Current theory & research in Communicative competence, Rev Educ Res, 80; Pragmatics of Interpersonal Competence, Rigor & Imagination, Praeger Press, 81; auth, Effects of laboratory videotaping procedures on selected conversation behaviors, Human Commun Rec, 81; co-ed, Nonverbal Communication, Sage, 83; The Dark Side Of Interpersonal-Communication - Cupach,Wr, Spitzberg,Bh, Journal Of Language And Social Psychology, Vol 0013, 1994. **CONTACT ADDRESS** Commun Studies Prog, Univ of Calif, 552 University Rd, Santa Barbara, CA, 93106-0001.

WIENER, HARVEY SHELBY
PERSONAL Born 04/07/1940, Brooklyn, NY, m, 1965, 3 children **DISCIPLINE** ENGLISH/AMERICAN LITERATURE **EDUCATION** Brooklyn Col, BS, 61, MA, 68; Fordham Univ, PhD, English, 71. **CAREER** Asst, 70, Fordham Univ; Instr, 70-71, prof, English, 71-, Queensborough Comm Col, CUNY; prof, English, LaGuardia, CUNY, 71-; adj asst prof, 70-72, Brooklyn Col; NEH Fel, 72-73; vis asst prof, 74-, SUNY, Stony Brook; vis Assoc prof, Eng, 76-77, PA St Univ; Dean, AC AF CUNY; Vice Provost, Adelphi Univ, Vis Pres, 97-, Marymount-Manhattan Col. **HONORS AND AWARDS** Phi Beta Kappa **MEMBERSHIPS** MLA; NCTE; Conf Col Compos & Comm. **RESEARCH** 17th cent non-dramatic lit; Shakespeare; 20th cent Amer novel. **SELECTED PUBLICATIONS** Auth, Science or providence: Towards knowledge in the New Atlantis, Enlightenment Essays, 72; auth, Creating Compositions, McGraw-Hill, 6th ed; auth, Media Compositions: Preludes to Writing, Col English, 2/74; auth, Bacon and Poetry: A View of the New Atlantis, Anglia, 76; auth, Any Child Can Write, McGraw-Hill, 78; auth, The Writing Room, Oxford, 81; auth, The Short Prose Reader, McGraw-Hill, 8th ed, 97. **CONTACT ADDRESS** 309 Clearview Lane, Massapequa, NY, 11758. **EMAIL** Hswien@aol.com

WIESENFARTH, JOSEPH JOHN
PERSONAL Born 08/20/1933, Brooklyn, NY, m, 1971 **DISCIPLINE** ENGLISH & AMERICAN LITERATURE **EDUCATION** Cath Univ Am, BA, 56, PhD, 62; Univ Detroit, MA, 59. **CAREER** Asst prof Eng, La Salle Col, 62-64; from asst prof to assoc prof, Manhattan Col, 64-70; assoc prof, 70-76, prof eng, Univ WI, Madison, 76-, Sally Mead Hands-Bascom, prof, 92-, Nat Endowment for Hum, fel, 67-68; Inst Res Hum, fel, 74-75, fulbright fel, 82-83; chair eng dept, 83-86, 89-92; assoc dean, grd sch, 95-96; assoc dean, letters & sci, 97. **HONORS AND AWARDS** Chancellors award disting tch, 79; cath univ Am award for outstand ach field of resear scholar, 96. **MEMBERSHIPS** MLA; English Inst. **RESEARCH** The Eng novel; George Eliot; Henry James; Ford Madox Ford; Katherine Ann Porter; lit theory. **SELECTED PUBLICATIONS** Auth, Henry James and the Dramatic Analogy, Fordham Univ, 63; Criticism and the semiosis of The Good Soldier, Mod Fiction Studies, spring 63; The Errand of Form: An Essay of Jane Austen's Art; George Eliot's Mythmaking, Carl Winter, Heidelberg, W Ger, 77; ed, george Eliot: A Writers Notebook 1854-1879; For Madox Ford and the Arts, Contemp Liter 89. **CONTACT ADDRESS** Dept of Eng, Univ of Wisconsin, 600 North Park St, Madison, WI, 53706-1403. **EMAIL** jjwiesen@facstaff.wisc.edu

WIESENTHAL, CHRISTINE
DISCIPLINE ENGLISH LITERATURE **EDUCATION** Univ Manitoba, BA; MA; Univ Alberta, PhD. **CAREER** Asst prof **RESEARCH** Victorian literature; nineteenth century British and American fiction and poetry; critical theory; contemporary poetry. **SELECTED PUBLICATIONS** Auth, Figuring Madness in Nineteenth Century Fiction, Macmillan; pub(s) on Victorian poetry and Pat Lowther. **CONTACT ADDRESS** Dept of English, Manitoba Univ, Winnipeg, MB, R3T 2N2.

WIGAL, GRACE J.
DISCIPLINE LEGAL RESEARCH AND WRITING **EDUCATION** Marshall Univ, BA, 72, MA, 76; W Va Univ Col Law, JD, 89. **CAREER** Instr, Col Law, 90; dir, Legal Res and Wrtg Prog, 92; dir, Acad Support Prog, 93; dir, Appellate Advocacy Prog; act dir, -. **HONORS AND AWARDS** W Va Law Rev Lit award, 89. **MEMBERSHIPS** Order of the Coif. **SELECTED PUBLICATIONS** Ed, W V Law Rev; Auth, bk(s), articles, on legal issues that arise in the medical and construction settings. **CONTACT ADDRESS** Law Sch, W Va Univ, PO Box 6009, Morgantown, WV, 26506-6009.

WIKANDER, MATTHEW H.
PERSONAL Born 03/21/1950, Philadelphia, PA, m, 1980 **DISCIPLINE** ENGLISH **EDUCATION** Williams Coll, BA, 70; Cambridge Univ - UK, BA, 72, MA, 79; Univ Mich, PhD, 75. **CAREER** Lectr, Univ Mich, Drama, 74-78; asst prof, Eng, Columbia Univ, 78-87; assoc prof, Eng, Univ Toledo, 87-90; PROF, ENG, UNIV TOLEDO, 90-. **MEMBERSHIPS** Shakespeare Asn Am; Am Soc Theatre Res; Midwest Lang Asn; Phi Beta Kappa **RESEARCH** 17th & 18th Cent English & French drama; Shakespeare; Modern drama. **SELECTED PUBLICATIONS** Princes to Act: Royal Audience and Royal Performance, 1578-1792, Johns Hopkins Univ Press, 93; "Reinventing the History Play," Cambridge Companion ot Shaw, Cambridge Univ Press, 98; "Eugene O'Neill and the Cult of Sincerity," Cambridge Companion to O'Neill, cambridge Univ Press, 98. **CONTACT ADDRESS** Dept Eng, Univ Toledo, Toledo, OH, 43606. **EMAIL** mwikand@uoft02.utoledo.edu

WILCOX, DEAN
PERSONAL Born 04/20/1964, Mt. Kisco, NY, m, 1987, 1 child **DISCIPLINE** THEATRE HISTORY, THEORY, AND CRITICISM **EDUCATION** Glasboro State College (now Rowan Univ), NJ, BA (Theatre Arts), 86; Univ SC, MFA (Lighting Design), 89; Univ WA School of Drama, Seattle, PhD (Theatre Hist, Theory, and Criticism), 94. **CAREER** Teaching asst, Dept of Drama, Univ WA, 91-94; lect, Theatre Hist, Univ CA, San Diego, spring 95; vis asst prof, Dartmouth Col, June-Aug 98; ASST PROF, THEATRE HISTORY, THEORY, AND CRITICISM, TX TECH UNIV, 96-. **HONORS AND AWARDS** Univ WA Fowler Graduate travel grant, 93; Univ WA Grad School Dissertation Fel, 93; Mellon Postdoctoral Fel at Cornell Univ, 95-96; accepted to Teaching Academy at TX Tech Univ, April 98. **MEMBERSHIPS** Asn of Theatre in Higher Ed; Int Federation for Theatre Res; Am Soc for Theatre Res; Am Soc for Aesthetics. **RESEARCH** Performance studies; postmodernism; semiotics; deconstruction; design hist and theory; chaos theory; performance art. **SELECTED PUBLICATIONS** Auth, book review of Phillip B. Zarilli's Acting (Re)Considered and Mariellen R. Sanford's Happenings and Other Acts, Theatre Survey, Vol 37, no 2, Nov 96; Political Allegory or Multimedia Extravaganza? A Historical Reconstruction of the Opera Company of Boston's Intolleranza, Theatre Survey, Vol 37, no 2, Nov 96; What Does Chaos Theory Have to Do with Art?, Modern Drama, Vol XXXIX, no 4, winter 96; book review of Alma Law and Mel Gordon's Meyerhold, Eisenstein and Biomechanics, Theatre Res Int, Vol 22, no 2, Autumn 97; book review of Marvin Carlson's Performance: A Critical Introduction and Richard Schechner's The Future of Ritual, Theatre Survey, Vol 38, no 2, Nov 97; Karen Finley's Hymen, Theatre Res Int, Vol 22, no 1, spring 97; A Complex Tapestry of Text and Imagery: Karen Finley, The American Chestnut, Cornell University, May 10, 1996, The Jour of Dramatic Theory and Criticism, Vol XII, no 1, fall 97; book review of Colin Counsell's Signs of Performance and Walter Gropius' The Theatre of the Bauhaus, Theatre Jour, Vol 50, no 3, Oct 98; book review of William Demastes' Theatre of Chaos: Beyond Absurdism, Into Orderly Disorder, Theatre Survey, Vol 39, no 2, Nov 98; book review of Arthur Holmberg's The Theatre of Robert Wilson, Theatre Res Int, Vol 23, no 3, Autumn 98; book review of Jonathan Kalb's The Theatre of Heiner Muller, Theatre Res Int, forthcoming; The Historical Nature of Time: Dramatic Criticism and New Historicism, Theatre Insight, forthcoming. **CONTACT ADDRESS** Dept of Theatre and Dance, Texas Tech Univ, Box 42061, Lubbock, TX, 79409-2061. **EMAIL** thdea@ttu.edu

WILCOX, DENNIS LEE
PERSONAL Born 03/31/1941, Rapid City, SD, m, 1969 **DISCIPLINE** MASS COMMUNICATIONS, AFRICAN AFFAIRS **EDUCATION** Univ Denver, BA, 63; Univ IA, MA, 66; Univ MO, PhD, 74. **CAREER** Reporter, Daily Sentinel, Grand Junction, CO, 63-64; ed, OH State Univ Publ, 66-68; reporter, Congwer Legis News Serv, Columbus, 67-68; dir pub rel, Ketchum Inc, Pittsburgh, 68-71; public rel officer, Chapman Col Semester at Sea, 71-72; Public rel prof, San Jose State Univ, 74. **HONORS AND AWARDS** Rex Harlow Award, 82; PRSA outstanding educator, 84; East-West Center fel, 86; vis prof, Rhodes Univ, South Africa, 86; vis prof, Chulalongkorn Univ, Thailand, 87; vis prof, Queensland Univ, Australia, 89; Fulbright scholar, Univ Botswana, 94-95. **MEMBERSHIPS** Asn Educ Jour; Pub Rel Soc Am; Int Pub Rel Asn; Intl Asn Bus Comm; Arthur Page Soc; SF Round Table. **RESEARCH** Public rel, organizational commun, nat media policy. **SELECTED PUBLICATIONS** Auth, English Language Dailies Abroad, Gale, 67; Mass Media in Black Africa, Praeger, 75; Effective Public Relations Writing, John Wiley, 82; Public Relations Writing & Media Techniques, 3rd ed, Longman, 97; Public Relations Strategies & Tactics, 5th ed, Longman, 98. **CONTACT ADDRESS** Sch of Jour, San Jose State Univ, 1 Washington Sq, San Jose, CA, 95192-0055. **EMAIL** wilcox@jmc.sjsu.edu

WILDE, ALAN
PERSONAL Born 05/26/1929, New York, NY **DISCIPLINE** ENGLISH, AMERICAN LITERATURE **EDUCATION** NY Univ, BA, 50, MA, 51; Harvard Univ, PhD, 58. **CAREER** From instr English to asst prof, Williams Col, 58-64; assoc prof, 64-67, Prof English, Temple Univ, 67-, Grad Chmn, 75-, Scholar, NY Univ, 50-51 & Harvard Univ, 51-52, teaching fel, 54-58; Fulbright fel, Univ Paris, 52-53. **HONORS AND AWARDS** Lindback Found Award for Distinguished Teaching, 75. **MEMBERSHIPS** MLA; AAUP **RESEARCH** Modern novel; British literature between the wars; contemporary American fiction. **SELECTED PUBLICATIONS** Auth, Art and Order: A Study of E M Forster, NY Univ, 64; The illusion of St Mawr: Technique and vision in D H Lawrence's novel, PMLA, 3/64; Christopher Isherwood, Twayne, 71; Language and surface: Isherwood and the thirties, Contemp Lit, autumn 75; Barthelme unfair to Kierkegaard: Some thoughts on modern and postmodern irony, boundary 2, fall 76; Desire and consciousness: The anironic Forster, Novel, winter 76; Modernism and the Aesthetics of Crisis, Contemporary Lit, winter 79; Horizons of Assent: Modernism, Postmodernism, and the Ironic Imagination, Johns Hopkins Univ, 81; The Once And Future Novel - Letters To Iwp-L-Muri@Ucsbuxa.Bitnet, Anq-A Quarterly Journal Of Short Articles Notes And Reviews, Vol 0005, 1992; The Vanishing Subject, Early Psychology And Literary Modernism - Ryan,J, Modern Fiction Studies, Vol 0039, 1993. **CONTACT ADDRESS** Dept of English, Temple Univ, Philadelphia, PA, 19122.

WILKENS, KENNETH G.
PERSONAL Born 01/17/1921, MN, m, 1981, 3 children **DISCIPLINE** RHETORIC, PUBLIC ADDRESS **EDUCATION** Northwestern Univ, PhD, 54. **CAREER** Asst Prof, St Olaf Coll,

47-56; prof, Univ Tex, 56-58; prof, Speech, St. Olaf Coll, 58-86. **HONORS AND AWARDS** Melvin Jones Fellow, Internatl Assoc of Lions. **MEMBERSHIPS** Speech Commun Asn; Speech Asn Minn. **RESEARCH** Rhetoric/Public address. **CONTACT ADDRESS** 1111 W 2nd St, Northfield, MN, 55057.

WILKERSON, MARGARET BUFORD
PERSONAL Born 04/03/1938, Los Angeles, California, m **DISCIPLINE** ENGLISH **EDUCATION** Univ of Redlands, BA History (magna cum laude) 1959; UCLA, Teachers Cred 1960-61; Univ Of CA Berkeley, MA Dramatic Art 1967, PhD Dramatic Art 1972. **CAREER** YWCA Youngstown OH, adlt pgm dir 1959-60; YWCA Los Angeles, adlt pgm dir 1960-62; Jordan HS LA CA, drama/engl tchr 1962-66; English Dept Dramatic Art Dept, lctr 1968-74; Dept Afro-Am Studies UC Berkeley, lctr 1976-83; Ctr for Study Ed & Adv of Women, dir 1975-83; Univ of CA Berkeley African American Studies Dept, prof and chair, 1988-94; The Ford Foundation, program officer (gender, Ethnicity & Identity in Higher Education), 1998-; Univ of CA Berkeley, chair/dir, Dramatic Art Dept Ctr for Theater Arts, 1995-98. **HONORS AND AWARDS** Hon dr/Humane Letters Univ of Redlands 1980; humanities flwshp Rockefeller Fndtn 1982-83; sr postdoctoral flwshp Natl Rsrch Cncl/Ford Found 1983-84; Ford Flwshp/Dissertation Ford Fndtn 1970; otstndng black alumna Univ of CA Berkeley Black Alumni Club 1976; Kellogg Lecturer Am Cncl on Ed 1980; co-editor Black Scholar theatre issue & other publs; author of "9 Plays by Black Women" New Amer Library 1986; Honoree, Equal Rights Advocates, 1989; College of Fellows of the American Theatre/JF Kennedy Ctr for Performing Arts, 1990; Award for Exemplary Educational Leadersip/Black Caucus of American Assn of Higher Education, 1990; Profile of Excellence, KGO-TV, San Francisco, 1990; Association of American Theatre, Career Achievement Award for Outstanding Educator, 1996; Black Theatre Network Lifetime Membership Award. **MEMBERSHIPS** V pres/adm Am Theatre Asso 1983-85; chair Black Theatre Prog/Am Theatre Asso 1979-83; adv bd Bus & Prof Womens Fndtn 1983-; consult Am Cncl on Ed Natl Identification Prog for Womdn Adms 1980-; panelist Natl Rsrch Cncl/ Lhumanitgies Doct Comm 1983-; consult CA Arts Cncl 1984-; mem Natl Cncl of Negro Women; mem Univ of CA Berkeley Black Alumni Club; mem NAACP; founder/dir Kumoja Players 1971-75; bd of trustees, San Francisco Theological Seminary, 1987-97; Assoc of Theatre in Higher Education, chair, Awards Comm, 1996-98. **CONTACT ADDRESS** Program Officer, EMAC Division, The Ford Foundation, 320 E 43rd St, New York, NY, 10017.

WILKIE, BRIAN
DISCIPLINE ROMANTIC POETRY **EDUCATION** Univ Wisc, PhD. **CAREER** English and Lit, Univ Ark. **SELECTED PUBLICATIONS** Auth, Romantic Poets and Epic Tradition, Wisc, 65; Blake's 'Four Zoas': The Design of a Dream, Harvard, 78; Blake's Thel and Oothoon, Engl Lit Studies, 90; Structural Layering in Jane Austen's Problem Novels, Nineteenth-Century Lit, 92; Jane Austen: Amor and Amoralism, JEGP, 92; Literature of the Western World, Macmillan, 96. **CONTACT ADDRESS** Univ Ark, Fayetteville, AR, 72701.

WILL, BARBARA E.
DISCIPLINE ENGLISH LITERATURE **EDUCATION** Duke Univ, PhD, 93. **CAREER** Asst prof, Dartmouth Col. **RESEARCH** Contemp Am lit; women writers. **SELECTED PUBLICATIONS** Auth, 1990 Rencontres Gertrude Stein (film), Univ Geneva; Pound's Feminine Other: A Reading of Canto XXIX, Paideuma, 90. **CONTACT ADDRESS** Dartmouth Col, 3529 N Main St, #207, Hanover, NH, 03755.

WILLARD, BARB
DISCIPLINE COMMUNICATION STUDIES **EDUCATION** Fla State Univ, BS; MS; Univ Iowa, PhD. **CAREER** Prof. **RESEARCH** Oral reading; rhetoric of social movements, women and communication. **SELECTED PUBLICATIONS** Auth, Performing Nature: The Bioregional Enactment of the Biotic Community, J NW Commun Asn, 97; Theory and Practice in the Speaking Lab: Speech Assignments and Rhetorical Assumptions, Iowa J Commun, 95. **CONTACT ADDRESS** Speech Communication Dept, Colorado State Univ, Fort Collins, CO, 80523. **EMAIL** bwillard@vines.colostate.edu

WILLARD, CHARLES A.
DISCIPLINE COMMUNICATIONS **EDUCATION** KS State Tchr Col, BA, 67; Univ IL, MA, 68, PhD, 72. **CAREER** Prof; ch, Univ KS. **RESEARCH** Argumentation, persuasion and soc knowledge. **SELECTED PUBLICATIONS** Auth, Argumentation and the Social Grounds of Knowledge; Theory of Argumentation; Liberalism and the Problem of Knowledge: A New Rhetoric for Modern Democracy. **CONTACT ADDRESS** Dept of Commun, Univ Louisville, 2301 S 3rd St, Louisville, KY, 40292. **EMAIL** cawill01@ulkyvm.louisville.edu

WILLARD, THOMAS SPAULDING
PERSONAL Born 11/25/1944, Richmond, VA, m, 1976, 2 children **DISCIPLINE** ENGLISH **EDUCATION** George Washington Univ, BA, 67, MA, 70; Univ Toronto, PhD(English), 78. **CAREER** Asst, 78-87, ASSOC PROF ENGLISH, UNIV ARIZ, 87-, Rev ed, Cauda Pavonis, 82- **MEMBERSHIPS** MLA **RESEARCH** Renaissance magic; 17th century prose; rhetorical theory. **SELECTED PUBLICATIONS** Auth, The publisher of Olor Iscanus, Papers Bibliog Soc Am, 81; Alchemy and the Bible, in Centre and Labyrinth: Essays to Honour Northrop Frye, Univ Toronto Press, 82; ed, Visionary Poetics: Essays on Northrop Trye's Criticism, Peter Lang, 91; ed, Jean Espagnet's The Summary of Physics Restored, Garland Publishing, 99. **CONTACT ADDRESS** Dept of Eng, Univ of Ariz, 1 University of Az, Tucson, AZ, 85721-0001. **EMAIL** willard@u.arizona.edu

WILLBANKS, RAY
DISCIPLINE AUSTRALIAN, BRITISH, COMMONWEALTH & AMERICAN LITERATURE **EDUCATION** TX State Univ, PhD. **CAREER** Lit, Univ Neb. **SELECTED PUBLICATIONS** Areas: sub-spec Australian lit and nationally in the sub-spec Southern Am Lit. **CONTACT ADDRESS** Univ NE, NE.

WILLEN, DIANE
PERSONAL Born 05/19/1943, Hartford, CT, 1 child **DISCIPLINE** ENGLISH HISTORY **EDUCATION** Conn Col, BA, 65; Harvard Univ, MA, 66; Tufts Univ, PhD(hist), 72. **CAREER** Asst prof hist, Kalamazoo Col, 72; from asst prof to assoc prof, 72-91, PROF HIST, GA STATE UNIV, 91-, Chair, Hist Dept, 98-; vis prof, Oxford Univ, Summer 91. **HONORS AND AWARDS** Phi Beta Kappa, 64; Winthrop Schol, 64; Conn Col Hist Prize and Honors in Hist, 65; Rosemary Park Fel, 65; Omicron Delta Kappa, 75; Dale Somers Memorial Award, 82, 89; Ga State Univ Res Grants, 84, 89, 95; Am Hist Asn, Bernadotte E. Scmitt Grant for Res, 88; Am Philos Soc Res Grant, 89. **MEMBERSHIPS** AHA; Conf Brit Studies; Southern Asn Women Historians. **RESEARCH** Tudor-Stuart England, especially political, social and religious history; women's history, especially the pre-industrial period. **SELECTED PUBLICATIONS** Auth, Lord Russell and the Western Countries, J Brit Studies, autumn 75; Robert Browne and the Dilemma of Religious Dissent, J United Reformed Church Hist Soc, 10/80; John Russell, First Earl of Bedford. One of the King's Men, Royal Hist Soc, 81; Godly Women in Early Modern England: Puritanism and Gender, J of Ecclesiastical Hist, 10/92; Communion of the Saints: Spritual Reciprocity and the Godly Comunity in Early Modern England, Albion, Spring 95; author of numerous other journal articles and book reviews. **CONTACT ADDRESS** Dept Hist, Georgia State Univ, 33 Gilmer St SE, Atlanta, GA, 30303-3080. **EMAIL** hisddw@panther.gsu.edu

WILLERTON, CHRISTIAN WILLIAM
PERSONAL Born 08/16/1947, Borger, TX, m, 1969, 3 children **DISCIPLINE** VICTORIAN & MODERN LITERATURE **EDUCATION** TX Christian Univ, BA, 69; Univ NC, Chapel Hill, MA, 70, PhD, 79. **CAREER** Instr, 70-73, asst prof, 76-81, assoc prof, 81-85, Prof Eng, Abilene Christian Univ, 85. **MEMBERSHIPS** Nat Coun Tchr(s) Eng; Conf Christianity & Lit; Pater Soc. **RESEARCH** Walter Pater; hypertext. **SELECTED PUBLICATIONS** Auth, John Payne, In: Dict of Literary Biography, #35; Reginald Gibbons, In: Dict of Literary Biograhpy, #120. **CONTACT ADDRESS** Dept of Eng, Abilene Christian Univ, Box 28242, Abilene, TX, 79699-8242. **EMAIL** willerto@nicanor.acu.edu

WILLEY, EDWARD
DISCIPLINE ENGLISH LITERATURE **EDUCATION** Univ NC, PhD, 68. **CAREER** Dept Eng, Clemson Univ **RESEARCH** 17th and 18th century literature. **SELECTED PUBLICATIONS** Auth, Matriarchs, Re: Arts & Letters, 95; Neoclassic, Re: Arts & Letters, 95; 1940s Southern Circus, Crossroads: Jour Southern Cult. **CONTACT ADDRESS** Clemson Univ, 605 Strode, Clemson, SC, 29634. **EMAIL** wedward@clemson.edu

WILLIAMS, DANIEL E.
DISCIPLINE ENGLISH **EDUCATION** Univ Wash, BA, 73; Univ Denver, MA, 76, 84, PhD, 80. **CAREER** Assoc prof English, Univ Miss. **RESEARCH** The theft of authorship. **CONTACT ADDRESS** Dept of English, Univ Mississippi, University, MS, 38677.

WILLIAMS, DAVID
PERSONAL Born 06/22/1945, Souris, MB, Canada **DISCIPLINE** ENGLISH **EDUCATION** Univ Sask, BA, 68; Univ Mass, MA, 70, PhD, 73. **CAREER** Lectr, 72-73, asst prof, 73-77, assoc prof, 77-83, PROF ENGLISH, ST PAUL'S COL, UNIV MANITOBA, 83-; guest prof, MS Univ Baroda, India, 92; guest prof, SNDT Univ, Bombay, 94, 96. **HONORS AND AWARDS** Woodrow Wilson fel, 68-69; Can Coun fel, 69-73, grants, 77-78, 81-82; Univ Man Tchg Awards, 86-87, 89-90; Rh Inst Award res hum, 87; Olive Beatrice Stanton Award Excellence Tchg, 92. **SELECTED PUBLICATIONS** Auth, Faulkner's Women: The Myth and the Muse, 77; auth, Confessional Fictions: A Portrait of the Artist in the Canadian Novel, 91; ed, To Run With Longboat: Twelve Stories of Indian Athletes in Canada, 88. **CONTACT ADDRESS** St. Paul's Col, Univ of Manitoba, Winnipeg, MB, R3T 2M6.

WILLIAMS, DAVID E.
PERSONAL Born 09/14/1963, Heath, OH, m, 1990, 1 child **DISCIPLINE** RHETORIC **EDUCATION** Ohio Univ, 90. **CAREER** Visiting asst prof, Kent State, 90-91; ASST/ASSOC PROF, TX TECH, 91-. **MEMBERSHIPS** Nat Commun Asn. **RESEARCH** American temperance movement; crisis communication. **SELECTED PUBLICATIONS** Auth, The Question of Audience in Forensic Education, The Sourthern J of Forensics, 98; auth, Over-quantification in Public Address Events, The Southern J of Forensics, 97; auth, Impromptu Speaking, Understanding Forensics: Direction, Coaching and Performing Competitive Individual Events, Ally & Bacon, in press; auth, Educational Criteria in Forensics: An Argument for Lincoln-Douglas Debate, Nat Forensic J, 96; auth, The Drive for Prohibition: A Transition from Social Reform to Legislative Reform, The Southern Commun J, 96; coauth, Teaching Honors Public Speaking, Basic Commun Course Annual, 98; Introducing Parliamentary Debate in the Public Speaking Course, Teaching the Public Speaking Course, Kendall/Hunt, 97; coauth, Introducing Parliamentary Debate in the Argumentation and Debate Course, The Forensic, 96; coauth, Judging the Space/Time Case in Parliamentary Debate, Southern Forensic J, 96; coauth, Burkian Counternature and the Vigilant Response: An Anticipatory model of Crisis Management and Technology, Commun in Crisis: Theory and Application, in press; coauth, Able-bodied Instructors Communication With Students With Disabilities: A Relationship Handicapped by Communication, Commun Educ, 95; coauth, Communication Distortion: An Intercultural Lesson From the Visa Application Process, Commun Quarterly, 95. **CONTACT ADDRESS** Dept of Commun Studies, Texas Tech Univ, Lubbock, TX, 79409. **EMAIL** modav@ttacs.edu

WILLIAMS, GARY J.
DISCIPLINE ENGLISH **EDUCATION** Univ Wash, AB, 69; Cornell, MA, PhD, 73. **CAREER** Prof English, Univ Idaho. **RESEARCH** James Fenimore Cooper. **SELECTED PUBLICATIONS** Fel Publ, Edition of Cooper's Notions of the Americans, SUNY, 91. **CONTACT ADDRESS** Dept of English, Univ of Idaho, Moscow, ID, 83844-1102. **EMAIL** jwg@uidaho.edu.

WILLIAMS, HAZEL BROWNE
PERSONAL Kansas City, Missouri, w **DISCIPLINE** ENGLISH **EDUCATION** Univ of KS, AB 1927; Univ of KS, MA 1929; Columbia Univ, MA 1943; Pi Lambda Theta; NY Univ, PhD 1953; Univ of Berlin, Kappa Delta Pi foreign study 1930; Alpha Kappa Alpha Foreign fellowship. **CAREER** Univ of MO KC, prof emeritus english educ; Southern Univ, visiting lectr 1967; Atlanta Univ, 1946-47; Vienna Austria, fulbright exchange teacher 1956-57; TN A&I State Univ, prof 1953-56; NY Univ, instr 1948-51; Louisville Muni Coll, asst prof 1932-42; KC MO Public Schools, english teacher 1927-32. **MEMBERSHIPS** Life mem NCTE; Internatl Soc of Gen Semantics; inst for Gen Semantics; MLA, AAUP; Phi Beat Kappa; Gr Assn of Chappers; MO State Tchrs Assn Golden Heritage; mem NAACP; mem KC NAACP Exec Bd; YWCA; life mem Univ of MO KC Friends of the Library; Univ of KS Alumni Assn. **CONTACT ADDRESS** School of Education, Univ of Missouri, Kansas City, MO, 64110.

WILLIAMS, HELEN ELIZABETH
PERSONAL Born 12/13/1933, Timmonsville, South Carolina **DISCIPLINE** LIBRARY SCIENCE **EDUCATION** Morris College, BA 1954; Phoenix College, Certificate 1959; Atlanta Univ, MSLS 1960; Queens College, Certificate 1966; Univ of IL-Urbana, CAS 1969; Univ of WI-Madison, PhD 1983. **CAREER** Williams Memorial High School, St George, SC, teacher/librarian 1955-57; Carver High School, Spindale, NC, teacher/librarian 1957-58; Percy Julian Elem Sch, librarian 1959-60; Brooklyn Public Library, librarian 1960-62; Mt Vernon Public Library, librarian 1963-64; Jenkins Hill High School,librarian/ teacher 1964-66; Westchester Co Library System, librarian 1966; White Plains City Public Schools, librarian 1966-68, 1969-73; Bro-Dart Inc, library consultant 1976-81; Univ of MD, College Park, MD, lecturer 1981-83, professor 1983-. **HONORS AND AWARDS** Beta Phi Mu Intl Library Sci Honor Frat 1960-; Fellow Higher Education Act 1966; Fellow Natl Defense Educ Act 1967-68; Fellow Comm on Institutional Cooperation 1973-76; Book Reviewer School Library Journal 1981-; Disting Alumnus Awd Morris Coll 1985; Disting Alumni of the Year Citation Natl Assoc for Equal Oppor in Higher Educ 1986; Fulbright Professorship, University of the South Pacific, Suva, FIJI 1988-89; editor "The High/Low Consensus," Bro-Dart Publishing Co 1980; editor "Independent Reading, K-3" Bro-Dart Publishing Co 1980; editor Books By African American Authros and Illustrators for Children and Young Adults, American Library Assn. **MEMBERSHIPS** Mem Library Adminis and Managerial Assoc 1977-80; mem Black Caucus of the Amer Library Assoc 1977-; mem MD Educ Media Organization 1981-; mem Amer Library Assoc 1977-; mem Amer Assoc of School Librarians; mem Young Adults Serv Div; mem Assoc of Library Services to Children; member National Council of Negro Women, Inc 1990-. **CONTACT ADDRESS** Professor of Librarianship, Univ of Maryland, Hornbake Bldg Rm 4105, College Park, MD, 20742.

WILLIAMS, JOHN ALFRED
PERSONAL Born 12/05/1925, Jackson, Mississippi, m, 1955 **DISCIPLINE** AFRICAN-AMERICAN LITERATURE **EDUCATION** Syracuse Univ, BA 1950, Grad Sch, 1950-51. **CAREER** Coll of the Virgin Islands, lecturer black lit 1968; CUNY, lecturer creative writing 1968-69; Sarah Lawrence Coll, guest writer 1972-73; Univ of CA Santa Barbara, regents lecturer 1973; CUNY LaGuardia Comm Coll, disting prof 1973-78; Univ of HI, vstg prof 1974; Boston Univ, vstg prof 1978-79; Exxon vstg prf New York Univ 1986-87; Rutgers Univ, prof of Engl 1979-93, Paul Robeson Prof of English, 1990-93; Bard Ctr, fellow, 1994-95. **HONORS AND AWARDS** Syracuse Univ, DLih, 1995; Univ Mass, Dartmouth, DLih, 1978; Natl Inst of Arts and Letters, 1962; Syracuse Univ, Centenial Medal, Outstanding Achievement, 1970; Natl Endowment for the Arts, 1977; US Observer, 23rd Premio Casa Awd, 1985, Disting Writer Awd, Middle Atlantic Writers, 1987; NJ Lit Hall of Fame, Michael Awd, 1987; Africa, Her History, Lands & People, 1963; Drama: Last Flight from Ambo Ber, 1981; August Forty-Five, 1991: Vangui (libreto), 1999; Safari West, 1998, American Book Award, 1983, 1998. **MEMBERSHIPS** Columnist, stringer, spec assignment, staff The Natl Leader, Progressive Herald, Assoc Negro Press, The Age, The Defender, Post-Standard, The Tribune, The Courier; Holiday Magazine Europe 1965-66; corresp Newsweek Africa 1964-65; dir of info Amer Comm on Africa 1957, spec events WOV NY 1957; corresp Ebony-Jet Spain 1958-59; WNET-TV writer, narrator on location Nigeria, Spain, 1964-65; bd of dir Coord Council Literary Mags 1983-85; bd of dir Jrnl of African Civilizations 1980-;contrib ed Politicks 1977, Amer Jnrl 1972-74; ed bd Audience Mag 1970-72; contrib ed Herald-Tribune Book Week 1963-65; asst to publ Abelard Schuman 1957-58; editor & publ Negro Mkt Newsletter 1956-57. **SELECTED PUBLICATIONS** Novels: The Berhama Account, 1985; Mothersill and the Foxes, 1975; The Man Who Cried I Am, 1967; Click Song, 1982; Junior Bachelor Soc, 1975; Jacob's Ladder, 1987; non-fiction books incl: If I Shop I'll Die: The Comedy and Tragedy of Richard Pryor, 1991; The McGraw-Hill Intro to Lit, 1st ed, 1984, 2nd ed, 1994; Flashbacks: A 20-Year Diary of Article Writing, 1973; The King God Didn't Save: Martin Luther King, Jr, 1970; The Most Native of Sons: Richard Wright, 1970; Amistad 1, 1970, Amistad 2, 1971; This is My Country, Too, 1965. **CONTACT ADDRESS** Barbara Hogenson Agency, 165 West End Ave, New York, NY, 10024.

WILLIAMS, JOHN S.
DISCIPLINE ENGLISH LITERATURE **EDUCATION** Cornell Col, BA, 58; Univ Chicago, MA, 61, PhD, 69. **CAREER** Prof, Univ Pacific . **SELECTED PUBLICATIONS** Auth, publ(s) on Faulkner, Sartre, Dostoevsky, and Jerzy Kosinski. **CONTACT ADDRESS** Eng Dept, Univ Pacific, Pacific Ave, PO Box 3601, Stockton, CA, 95211.

WILLIAMS, JOSEPH M.
PERSONAL Born 08/18/1933, Cleveland, OH, m, 1960, 2 children **DISCIPLINE** ENGLISH, LINGUISTICS **EDUCATION** Miami Univ, BA, 55, MA, 60; Univ Wis, PhD(English), 66. **CAREER** Instr English, Miami Univ, 59-60; from instr to assoc prof, 65-76, Prof English, Univ Chicago, 76-, Consult med writing, Am Med Asn, 66. **MEMBERSHIPS** MLA; Lang Soc Am; Col English Asn. **RESEARCH** Stylistics; rhetoric; generative grammars. **SELECTED PUBLICATIONS** Auth, the source of Spenser's Labryde, Mod Lang Notes, 61; Caliban and Ariel meet Trager & Smith, Col English, 62. **CONTACT ADDRESS** Dept of English, Univ of Chicago, 5845 Ellis Av, Chicago, IL, 60637-1476.

WILLIAMS, KENNY J.
DISCIPLINE ENGLISH LITERATURE **EDUCATION** PA Univ, PhD, 61. **CAREER** Prof, Duke Univ. **SELECTED PUBLICATIONS** Auth, Prairie Voices: A Literary History of Chicago from the Frontier to 1893, Townsend, 80; A Storyteller for a City: Sherwood Anderson s Chicago, Northern Ill, 88; co-ed, Chicago s Public Wits, LSU, 83. **CONTACT ADDRESS** Eng Dept, Duke Univ, Durham, NC, 27706.

WILLIAMS, MELVIN GILBERT
PERSONAL Born 11/07/1937, Collingswood, NJ, m, 1958, 3 children **DISCIPLINE** ENGLISH **EDUCATION** Univ PA, AB, 60, MA, 61; Univ MA, PhD, 73, dr minis, Hartford seminary. **CAREER** From instr to asst prof, 61-73, assoc prof eng, Am Int Col, 73-, interim pastor, United Church of Christ in MA, CT; prof ch, dept Eng commun, 89. **HONORS AND AWARDS** Ordained Minister, United Church of Christ, certified spec in edu United Church of Christ. **MEMBERSHIPS** MLA; New Eng MLA; Col English Asn; Conf Christianity & Lit. **RESEARCH** Bible as lit; relig and lit; African Am Lit. **SELECTED PUBLICATIONS** Auth, Martin Luther: Portraits in prose, Christian Century, 10/67; Samuel Johnson and the concrete universal, 3-4/72 & Black literature: A stereophonic experience for monophonic students, 3/77, CEA Critic; The Psalms as literature, Christianity & Lit, summer 73; The Last Word, Boston, 73; The Gospel according to Simple, spring 77 & Black literature vs Black studies: Three lynchings, fall 77, Black Am Lit Forum. **CONTACT ADDRESS** Dept of Eng, American Intl Col, 1000 State St, Springfield, MA, 01109-3151. **EMAIL** revdrmel@aol.com

WILLIAMS, PENNY
PERSONAL m, 1 child **DISCIPLINE** JOURNALISM **EDUCATION** CA State Univ Northridge, BA, 80; SUNY Buffalo, MS, 91; PhD, 98. **CAREER** Co-anchor/reporter, KCSN-FM, 77-79; anchor/reporter/producer/assignment ed/shooter, KNAZ-TV, 80; gen assignment reporter and anchor, WAVY-TV, 80-82; gen assignment/med reporter and anchor, WGRZ-TV,.82-87; weekend anchor/reporter, WBEN-AM, 87-88; asst prof, Buffalo State Col, 88-95; publ affairs host and prod, WUTV, 91-93; asst prof, St Bonaventure Univ, 95-. **HONORS AND AWARDS** NY AP Broadcasters' Awd., TV journalist; fac adviser, WSBU-FM; Internship Coord for the Sch of Journalism and MA Commun. **MEMBERSHIPS** Buffalo Broadcasters' Assn, Radio-Television News Dirs Assoc; Soc Prof Journalists. **RESEARCH** Broadcast media, commun, and journalism. **SELECTED PUBLICATIONS** Auth, articles on broadcast journalism for Communicator, and an article on electronic database reporting for SPJ's Quill. **CONTACT ADDRESS** St Bonaventure Univ, St Bonaventure, NY, 14778. **EMAIL** pwilliam@sbu.edu

WILLIAMS, SUSAN
DISCIPLINE ENGLISH **EDUCATION** Yale Univ, BA, 85, MA, 89, PhD, 91. **CAREER** Asst prof English, Ohio State. **RESEARCH** Female authorship and print culture. **CONTACT ADDRESS** Dept of English, Ohio State Univ, 164 W 17th Ave., Columbus, OH, 43210-1370.

WILLIAMS, TONY
PERSONAL Born 01/11/1946, Swansea, Wales, m, 1991 **DISCIPLINE** CINEMA STUDIES **EDUCATION** Manchester Univ, 67-73; Warwick Univ, PhD, theology, 76-77, MA, film studies. **CAREER** Southern IL Univ, assoc prof, eng, 84-. **HONORS AND AWARDS** Jack London Found Man of the Year, 89. **MEMBERSHIPS** Soc for Cinema Studies. **RESEARCH** Am Film Genres; Hong Kong Cin; Brit Cin; Lit Naturalism; Jack London; James Jones. **SELECTED PUBLICATIONS** Jack London: The Movies, Los Angeles, 92; Vietnam War films: over 600, feature made for TV, pilot and short movies, 1939-1992, Tony Williams, Jean-Jacques Malo, eds, Jefferson NC, McFarland & Co Inc, 94; Hearths of Darkness: The Family in the American Horror Film, Cranbury NJ, Farleigh Dickinson Univ Press, 96; Larry Cohen: The Radical Allegories of an Independent Filmmaker, Jefferson NC, McFarland &co, 97; Jack London's Sea Wolf, screen play by Robert Rossen, ed by Rocco Fumento and Tony Williams, Carbobale IL, SO Univ IL Press, 98; numerous articles. **CONTACT ADDRESS** Dept English, Southern Illinois Univ, Carbondale, IL, 62901. **EMAIL** tonyw@siucvmb.edu

WILLIAMS, TREVOR LLOYD
PERSONAL Born 01/12/1942, Llangollen, Wales, m, 1965, 4 children **DISCIPLINE** MODERN BRITISH LITERATURE **EDUCATION** Univ Manchester, BA, 64, MA, 67; Univ Wales, PhD(English), 70. **CAREER** Instr, 65-70, asst prof 70-77, ASSOC PROF ENGLISH, UNIV VICTORIA, BC, 78-, Pres fac asn, Confederation Fac Asn BC, 77-78; pres, Univ Victoria Fac Asn, 80-81. **MEMBERSHIPS** James Joyce Found. **RESEARCH** Twentieth century British literature; interaction of literature, politics and modern history; Marxist theory & practice. **SELECTED PUBLICATIONS** Auth, Hungry Man is an Angry Man, a Marxist Reading of Consumption in Joyce 'Ulysses', Mosaic-J Interdisciplinary Study Lit, Vol 0026, 93; 'Ulysses', 'Wandering Rocks', and the Reader--Multiple Pleasures in Reading, James Joyce Quart, Vol 0030, 93; Brothers of the Great White Lodge--Joyce and the Critique of Imperialism, James Joyce Quart, Vol 0033, 96. **CONTACT ADDRESS** Dept of English, Univ Victoria, Victoria, BC, V8W 2Y2.

WILLIAMS, WILLIAM PROCTOR
PERSONAL Born 09/01/1939, Glade, KS, m, 1984, 2 children **DISCIPLINE** ENGLISH **EDUCATION** Kans State Univ, BA, 61, MA, 64, PhD(English), 68. **CAREER** Instr freshman rhet, Kans State Univ, 66-67; from asst prof to assoc prof, 67-78, PROF ENGLISH, NORTHERN ILL UNIV, 78-, Am Philos Soc fel, 72-73; Newberry Libr fel, 74; Am Coun Learned Soc grant, 75 & 79; Nat Endowment for Humanities res grant, 78; dir, Grad Studies English, Northern Ill Univ, 78-81, actg assoc dean res, Grad Sch, 82. **MEMBERSHIPS** Bibliog Soc England; Malone Soc **RESEARCH** Bibliography and textual studies; Renaissance English literature; Shakespeare **SELECTED PUBLICATIONS** Auth, The Stationers-Company Archives--An Account of the Records, 1554-1984, 18th Century Stud, Vol 0027, 93; The Reception of Shakespeare in the 18th Century France and Germany, 18th Century Stud, Vol 0026, 93; Shakespeare Domesticated--The 18th Century Editions, 18th Century Stud, Vol 0026, 93; Early Cambridge Theaters, Notes and Queries, Vol 0042, 95; The Cambridge Illustrated History of British Theater, Notes and Queries, Vol 0043, 96; The Elizabethan Theater XIII, Notes and Queries, Vol 0043, 96; Winter Fruit--English Drama 1642-1660, Notes and Queries, Vol 0044, 97. **CONTACT ADDRESS** Dept of English, No Illinois Univ, 1425 W Lincoln Hwy, De Kalb, IL, 60115. **EMAIL** wwilliam@niu.edu

WILLIAMS ELLIOTT, DORICE
PERSONAL Born 01/19/1951, Boone, IA, m, 1975, 3 children **DISCIPLINE** ENGLISH **EDUCATION** Brigham Young Univ, BA, 73; Univ Utah, MA, 86; Johns Hopkins Univ, MA, 89, PhD, 94. **CAREER** Tchr, Eisenhower Jr High, 73-80; instr, Brigham Young Univ, 84-87; grad tchg asst, John Hopkins Univ, 88-94; instr, York Col, 95-96; asst prof, Univ Kans, 96-. **HONORS AND AWARDS** Deans Tchg Fel, Nat Merit Scholar, 69; US Presidential Scholar, 69; Phi Kappa Phi, 72, 85; Johns Hopkins Univ Fel, 87-91. **MEMBERSHIPS** MLA; Australasian Victorian Stud Asn; British Women Writers Asn; AAUP; AAUW. **RESEARCH** Victorian literature & culture; historical criticism & literary theory; womens studies; Australian literature; 18th-century novel. **SELECTED PUBLICATIONS** Auth, Hearing the Darkness: The Narrative Chain in Conrad's Heart of Darkness, 85; auth, The Marriage of Classes in Gaskell's North and South, 94; auth, Sarah Scott's Millenium Hall and Female Philanthropy, 95; auth, The Care of the Poor Is Her Profession: Hannah More and Women's Philanthropic Work, 95; auth, Feminist Criticism of Narrative and The Victorian Novel of Social Criticism. **CONTACT ADDRESS** Dept of English, Univ of Kansas, Lawrence, KS, 66045. **EMAIL** delliott@eagle.cc.ukans.edu

WILLIAMS-HACKETT, LAMARA
PERSONAL Born 01/17/1967, Inkster, MI, m, 1997 **DISCIPLINE** JOURNALISM; LIBRARY SCIENCE **EDUCATION** Alcorn State Univ, BA, 96; La State Univ, MLIS, 97. **CAREER** Librn, Univ Iowa Libr, 98-. **HONORS AND AWARDS** ACRL, 99; Nat Conference Scholar Recipient. **MEMBERSHIPS** Am Libr Asn; Asn Col & Res Libr; New Members Roundtable. **RESEARCH** Current events; African Am hist; women's hist; African American women's hist. **CONTACT ADDRESS** 425 D 6th Ave, Coralville, IA, 52241. **EMAIL** lamara-williams-hackett@uiowa.edu

WILLIAMSON, J.W.
PERSONAL Born 03/17/1944, Dallas, TX, m, 1985 **DISCIPLINE** ENGLISH LITERATURE **EDUCATION** Wayland College, BA, 66; Univ Utah, MA, 68, PhD, 70. **CAREER** Appalachian State Univ, 70 to present, Prof 78-. **HONORS AND AWARDS** Thomas Wolfe Literary Awd. **MEMBERSHIPS** ASA **RESEARCH** Appalachian Literature; Appalachian Imagery in Amer Popular Culture. **SELECTED PUBLICATIONS** Auth, Southern Mountaineers in Silent Films, McFarland, 94; Hillbillyland: What the Movies Did to the Mountains and the Mountains Did to the Movies, Univ NC Press, 95; coed, Interviewing Appalachia: The Appalachian J Interviews, Univ Tenn Press, 94. **CONTACT ADDRESS** 2737 Hwy 421 S, Boone, NC, 28607. **EMAIL** williamsonjw@appstate.edu

WILLIAMSON, JANE LOUISE
PERSONAL St. Louis, MO **DISCIPLINE** ENGLISH LITERATURE **EDUCATION** WA Univ, AB, 58; Bryn Mawr Col, MA, 60, PhD, 63. **CAREER** Instr Eng, Univ WI, Madison, 63-64; asst prof, Univ MO, St Louis, 64-66; asst prof, Univ CA, Santa Barbara, 66-67; asst prof, 67-69, assoc prof eng, Univ MO, St Louis, 69, chmn dept, 72-75, 94, Chmn Univ Senate, 76-77. **HONORS AND AWARDS** Amoco Award for Outstanding Tchr in the Hum, Univ MO, 74; Outstanding Academic Bks List, Am Libr Asn, for Charles Kemble. **MEMBERSHIPS** MLA; Am Soc Theatre Res; Soc Theatre Res, Eng; Shakespeare Asn Am; AAUP. **RESEARCH** Shakespeare and Elizabethan drama; theatre hist. **SELECTED PUBLICATIONS** Auth, Charles Kemble, Man of the Theatre, Univ Nebr, 70; The Duke and Isabella on the mod stage, In: The Triple Bond, PA State Univ, 75. **CONTACT ADDRESS** Dept of Eng, Univ of MO, 8001 Natural Bridge, Saint Louis, MO, 63121-4499.

WILLIAMSON, JANICE
PERSONAL Brandon, MB, Canada **DISCIPLINE** ENGLISH **EDUCATION** Carleton Univ, BA, 75; York Univ, MA, 81, PhD, 87. **CAREER** Asst prof, 87-91, ASSOC PROF, UNIV ALBERTA, 91-. **HONORS AND AWARDS** The Pushcart Prize, 89; bp nichol Chapbook Award, 96. **MEMBERSHIPS** Acad Women's Asn, Univ Alta; Writers' Union Can. **SELECTED PUBLICATIONS** Auth, Tell Tale Signs: Fictions, 91; auth, Sounding Differences: Conversations with Seventeen Canadian Women Writers, 93; auth, A Family Holiday in Sunny Puerto Plata, in Am Voice, 16, 89; co-ed, Up and Doing: Canadian Women and Peace, 89. **CONTACT ADDRESS** Dept of English, Univ of Alberta, Edmonton, AB, T6G 2E5. **EMAIL** jwilliam@gpu.srv.ualberta.ca

WILLIAMSON, JOHN STEWART
PERSONAL Born 04/29/1908, Bisbee, AZ, m, 1947, 2 children **DISCIPLINE** ENGLISH LITERATURE **EDUCATION** Eastern NMex Univ, BA & MA, 57; Univ Colo, PhD, 64. **CAREER** Instr, 57-59, NMex Mil Inst; from asst prof to prof, 60-77, Eastern NMex Univ, dir,77-80, Inst for Lib & Fine Arts;. **HONORS AND AWARDS** Grand Master Award, Sci Fiction Writers of Am, 76., LHD, Eastern NMex Univ, Portales. **MEMBERSHIPS** Sci Fiction Writers of Am (pres, 78-79); Am Assn for Adv of Sci; Sci Fiction Res Assn. **RESEARCH** Science fiction; H G Wells. **SELECTED PUBLICATIONS** Auth, Mazewau, 90; coauth, The Singers of Time, 91; auth, Beach-

head, 92; auth, Demon Moon, 94; auth, The Black Sun, 96; auth, The Silicon Dagger, 99. **CONTACT ADDRESS** Box 761, Portales, NM, 88130-0761. **EMAIL** jack.williamson@enmu.edu

WILLIAMSON, KEITH
DISCIPLINE INTERPERSONAL COMMUNICATION, COMMUNICATION THEORY **EDUCATION** Temple Univ, PhD. **CAREER** Asst prof, Director of the Basic Course. Chair Depart Speech Commun,Wichita State Univ. **SELECTED PUBLICATIONS** Publ, Communication Education; co-auth, Leading Interpersonal Communication Textbook. **CONTACT ADDRESS** Wichita State Univ, 1845 Fairmont, Wichita, KS, 67260-0062. **EMAIL** williamson@elliott.es.twsu.edu

WILLIAMSON, MARILYN LAMMERT
PERSONAL Born 09/06/1927, Chicago, IL, m, 1950, 1 child **DISCIPLINE** ENGLISH **EDUCATION** Vassar Col, BA, 49; Univ Wis, MA, 50; Duke Univ, PhD(English), 56. **CAREER** Instr English, Duke Univ, 55-56 & 59; instr, NC State Univ, 57-58 & 61-62; from asst prof to assoc prof, Oakland Univ, 65-72; chmn dept English, 72-74, assoc dean Col Lib Arts, 74-79, PROF ENGLISH, WAYNE STATE UNIV, 72-, DIR WOMEN'S STUDIES, 76-, CHMN DEPT, 81-, Fel, Radcliffe Inst, Harvard Univ, 69-70. **MEMBERSHIPS** MLA; Asn Depts of English (pres, 76); Renaissance Soc Am; Shakespeare Asn. **RESEARCH** Shakespeare; Renaissance drama; women's studies. **SELECTED PUBLICATIONS** Auth, The Imprint of Gender, Authorship and Publication in the English Renaissance, Criticism-Quart For Lit and the Arts, Vol 0037, 95; Shakespeare Studies, Col Engl, Vol 0058, 96. **CONTACT ADDRESS** Women's Studies, Wayne State Univ, 431 State Hall, Detroit, MI, 48202-1308.

WILLIAMSON DAMERON, GEORGE
DISCIPLINE ENGLISH **EDUCATION** Duke Univ, BA, 75; Harvard Univ,AM, 79, PhD, 83. **CAREER** Asst prof, 83-87, 87-; Assoc prof, 91-, Prof, 97-,St. Michael's Col. **HONORS AND AWARDS** Sch & Artistic Achievement Award, Numerous Saint Michael's Col Fac Develop Grants; Am Philos Soc; Nat Endowment Hum, Fel, Harvard Ctr Italian Renaissance Studies; Harvard Lehman Fund Grad Sch Fel. **SELECTED PUBLICATIONS** Auth, Episcopal Power and Florentine Society, 1000-1320, Harvard Univ Press, 91. **CONTACT ADDRESS** St. Michael's Col, Winooski Park, Colchester, VT, 05439. **EMAIL** gdameron@smcvt.edu

WILLIAMSON-IGE, DOROTHY KAY
PERSONAL Born 04/18/1950, Parma, Missouri, m **DISCIPLINE** SPEECH, DRAMA **EDUCATION** Southeast Missouri State Univ, BS, Speech, 1971; Central Missouri State Univ, MA, Speech Comm, 1973; Ohio State Univ, PhD, Speech, 1980. **CAREER** Webster Grove Schools, speech & drama teacher, 1971-77; DOD Dependents Schools, drama teacher, 1977-78; Bowling Green State Univ, faculty & field exper coord, 1980-84; Indiana Univ NW, faculty, 1985-. **HONORS AND AWARDS** Academic Scholarship Certificate Southeast Missouri State Univ, 1970; (Civilian) Intl Talent Search Judge, US Military, Ramstein, Germany, Air Force Base, 1978; TV, radio, newspaper interviews and keynote speeches, papers, consultantships in Midwest US, Africa, Caribbean & Europe, 1978-; published over 20 articles & book chapters on communication education for minorities, the handicapped and women, 1981-87; Third World Peoples Award, Bowling Green State Univ, 1984; Department Head, Community WPA; Acting Department Head, Minority Studies. **MEMBERSHIPS** Public adv bd, Bowling Green State Univ, 1980-83; assoc, Ohio State Univ Black Alumni, 1980-; Phi Delta Kappa, 1980-; speech comm, assoc black caucus pres, legislative council, Black Oppor Task Force, 1981-87; State of Ohio Bd Redesign of Educ Programs, 1982; pres, Women Investing Together & program chairperson, Human Relations Comm, Bowling Green State Univ, 1984; TV radio newspaper interviews, keynote speeches, papers & consultantships in Midwest USA, Africa, Caribbean & Europe. **CONTACT ADDRESS** Communications Dept, Indiana Univ, Northwest, 3400 Broadway, Gary, IN, 46408.

WILLIS, DEBORAH
DISCIPLINE ENGLISH LITERATURE **EDUCATION** Univ Calif-Berkeley, BA, MA, PhD. **CAREER** PROF, UNIV CALIF, RIVERSIDE. **RESEARCH** Shakespeare; Renaissance drama; Cultural studies. **SELECTED PUBLICATIONS** Auth, "The Tempest and Colonial Discourse," Stud Eng Lit 1500-1900, 89; Malevolent Nurture: Witch-hunting and Maternal Power in Early Modern England, Cornell Univ Press, 95. **CONTACT ADDRESS** Dept of Eng, Univ Calif, 1156 Hinderaker Hall, Riverside, CA, 92521-0209.

WILLIS, GLADYS JANUARY
PERSONAL Born 02/29/1944, Jackson, Mississippi, m **DISCIPLINE** ENGLISH **EDUCATION** Jackson State Univ, BA 1965; Bryn Mawr Coll, Independent Study 1966; Michigan State Univ, MA 1967; Princeton Univ, PhD 1973; Lutheran Theological Seminary, Philadelphia PA, MDiv 1996. **CAREER** Cheyney State Univ, instructor, English, 1967-68; Rider Coll, instructor, English, 1968-70; City University of New York, asst prof, English 1973-76; Pennsylvania Human Relations Commn, educ representative 1976-77; Lincoln Univ, assoc prof, chair 1977-84, prof, dept chair 1977-; First Redemption Evangelical Church, asst pastor, 1992-. **HONORS AND AWARDS** Woodrow Wilson Natl Fellowship, Woodrow Wilson Natl Fellowship Found 1966-67; Princeton Univ Fellow, Princeton Univ 1970-73; author, The Penalty of Eve; John Milton and Divorce New York, Peter Lang 1984; Ordained Chaplain 1988; Outstanding Young Women of America, 1978; Lindback Distinguished Teachers Award, Lincoln Univ, 1984; Service Award, Lincoln Univ, 1992. **MEMBERSHIPS** Founder, dir Coll Preparatory Tutorial 1974; mem, bd of dir Philadelphia Christian Academy 1977-, Natl Council of Teachers of English; reviewer Middle States Assn. **CONTACT ADDRESS** English Dept, Lincoln Univ, Lincoln University, PA, 19352.

WILLIS, PAUL J.
DISCIPLINE ENGLISH **EDUCATION** Wash State Univ, PhD, 85. **CAREER** Instr, Sierra Treks, 74-; asst prof, Houghton Col, 85-88; adj instr, Whitwhort Col, 82-85; assoc prof, Westmont Col, 85-. **HONORS AND AWARDS** Individual artist award for poetry, The Arts Fund of Santa Barbara, 96; choice award for The Stolen River, Christianity Today Critics',92. **RESEARCH** Lit and the environ; renaissance lit; Shakespeare; Milton. **SELECTED PUBLICATIONS** Auth, The Stolen River, Crossway Bk(s), 92; No Clock in the Forest: An Alpine Tale, Crossway Bk(s), 91; The Trouble with Fiction, Other Side, 94; The Next Generation, Summit, 94. **CONTACT ADDRESS** Dept of Eng, Westmont Col, 955 La Paz Rd, Santa Barbara, CA, 93108-1099.

WILLIS, RESA
DISCIPLINE ENGLISH LITERATURE **EDUCATION** SW MO State Univ, BA; Univ AR, MA, Univ Tulsa, PhD. **CAREER** Prof lit, 80, Drury Col. **RESEARCH** Biog. **SELECTED PUBLICATIONS** Auth, Mark and Livy: The Love Story of Mark Twain and the Woman Who Almost Tamed Him, Atheneum, 92. **CONTACT ADDRESS** Eng Dept, Drury Col, N Benton, PO Box 900, Springfield, MO, 65802. **EMAIL** rwillis@lib.drury.edu

WILLIS, SUSAN
DISCIPLINE ENGLISH LITERATURE **EDUCATION** Univ CA San Diego, PhD, 77. **CAREER** Prof, Duke Univ. **SELECTED PUBLICATIONS** Auth, Specifying: Black Women Writing the American Experience, Univ Wis, 87; A Primer For Daily Life, Routledge, 90; co-auth, Inside the Mouse: Work and Play at Walt Disney World, Duke, 95. **CONTACT ADDRESS** Eng Dept, Duke Univ, Durham, NC, 27706.

WILLIS, SUSAN
PERSONAL Born 08/23/1947, Nashville, TN **DISCIPLINE** ENGLISH **EDUCATION** Emory Univ, BA (with honors), 69; Univ of Va, MA, 70, PhD, 74. **CAREER** Tchg asst to adjunct instr, Univ of Va, 70-74; asst prof Eng, Univ of Minn, 74-78; PROF ENG, AUBRUN UNIV AT MONTGOMERY, 78-; DRAMATURG, ALABAMA SHAKESPEARE FESTIVAL, 85-. **HONORS AND AWARDS** Phi Beta Kappa; Mortar Board; Phi Kappa Phi. **MEMBERSHIPS** MLA; VAMLA; Shakespeare Asn of Am; Lit Managers & Dramaturgs of the Americas. **RESEARCH** Shakespeare in production. **SELECTED PUBLICATIONS** Auth, The BBC Shakespeare Plays: Making the Televised Canon, Univ of NC Press, 91; numerous articles on Shakespeare in production, W.H. Auden, fantasy lit, and dramaturgy; extensive writing for the Ala Shakespeare Festival. **CONTACT ADDRESS** 621 Felder Ave, Montgomery, AL, 36106. **EMAIL** swillis@edla.aum.edu

WILLMOTT, GLENN
DISCIPLINE ENGLISH LITERATURE **EDUCATION** Duke Univ, PhD. **CAREER** Dept Eng, Queen's Univ **RESEARCH** Canadian fiction; modernity theory; critical theory. **SELECTED PUBLICATIONS** Auth, McLuhan, or Modernism in Reverse, Univ Toronto; pubs on modernity and Canadian literature. **CONTACT ADDRESS** English Dept, Queen's Univ, Kingston, ON, K7L 3N6.

WILLS, DAVID
DISCIPLINE CINEMA AND FILM THEORY, LITERARY THEORY, 20TH CENTURY LITERATURE **EDUCATION** Univ Sorbonne, Nouvelle-Paris III, Doctorat, 79. **CAREER** Prof, La State Univ. **SELECTED PUBLICATIONS** Auth, Screen/Play: Derrida and Film Theory, 89; Writing Pynchon: Strategies in Fictional Analysis, 90; Deconstruction and the Visual Arts, 94; Prosthesis, 95. **CONTACT ADDRESS** Dept of Fr Grad Stud, Louisiana State Univ, Baton Rouge, LA, 70803.

WILLS, JACK CHARLES
PERSONAL Born 12/10/1936, Beaver, WV, m, 1958, 2 children **DISCIPLINE** ENGLISH **EDUCATION** WVa Univ, BSF, 60; Univ Del, MA, 63, PhD(English), 66. **CAREER** Asst prof English, Va Polytech Inst, 66-67 & Westhampton Col, Univ Richmond, 67-71; assoc prof, 71-74, PROF ENGLISH, FAIRMONT STATE COL, 74-, Nat Endowment for Humanities summer sem, 79. **HONORS AND AWARDS** William A Borma Award, Teaching Excellence, 97-98. **MEMBERSHIPS** Bronte Soc; MLA; S Atlantic Mod Lang Asn; Byron Soc; Soc Study Social Lit **RESEARCH** Eighteenth and 19th century novel, especially Charlotte Bronte; romantic period, 18th century; Southern literature. **SELECTED PUBLICATIONS** Auth, The shrine of truth: An approach to the works of Charlotte Bronte, Bronte Soc Trans, 70; The Deserted Village, Ecclesiastes, and the enlightenment, Enlightenment Essays, fall-winter, 73; The narrator of the Deserted Village: A reconsideration, WVa Univ Philol Papers, 12/75; The enchanted rocks at Uncle Billy Basham's, 75 & An unnamed Ballad, 77, WVA Folklore J; Lord Byron and 'Poor Dear Sherry', Richard Brinsley Sheridan, In: Lord Byron and His Contemporaries: Essays from the Sixth International Byron Seminar, Univ Delaware Press, 82; The theme of education and communication in Journey to the Western Islands of Scotland, Bull West Va Asn Col English Teachers, fall, 89; Villette and The Marble Faun, Studies in the Novel, fall, 93. **CONTACT ADDRESS** Dept of English, Fairmont State Col, 1201 Locust Ave, Fairmont, WV, 26554-2470. **EMAIL** jcw@fscvax.wvnet.edu

WILLUMSON, GLENN GARDNER
PERSONAL Born 06/22/1949, Glendale, CA, m, 1970, 2 children **DISCIPLINE** ART HISTORY; ENGLISH **EDUCATION** St. Mary's Col, BA, 71; Univ Calif Davis, MA, 84; Univ Calif Santa Barbara, PhD, 88. **CAREER** Teacher, Calif Secondary Sch, 71-81; cur, Amer Art and Photog, Getty Res Inst, 88-92; affil prof, Dept of Art Hist, Pa State, 93-; cur, Palmer Mus of Art, Pa State, 92-. **HONORS AND AWARDS** Nat Endow for the Humanities fel, 97-98; Haynes fel, Huntington Libr, fac res grant, 94; J. Paul Getty Publ grant, 91; Annette Baxter prize, Amer studies, 87; Kress found fel, 87; Nat Writing Proj fel, 87; teaching resources grant, 84. **MEMBERSHIPS** Col Art Asn; Amer Studies Asn; Asn of Hist of Amer Art; Asn of Univ Mus and Galleries. **RESEARCH** History of photography; American art. **SELECTED PUBLICATIONS** Auth, The Getty Research Institute: Materials for a New Photo-History, Hist of Photog, XXII, 1, 31-39, Spring, 98; auth, Clement Greenberg, Encycl of World Bio, Jan, 95; auth, A Family Album: Portraits by John Sloan, Amer Art Rev, 116-117, June-July, 94; auth, Collecting with a Passion: Selections from the Pincus Collection of Contemporary Art, Univ Pk, Palmer Mus of Art, 93; auth, Silver Salts and Blueprints, London Times Lit Suppl, 19 Mar, 93; auth, W. Eugene Smith and the Photographic Essay, NY, Cambridge Univ Press, 92; essays, Van Dyck's Iconographie, Mus Plantin-Moretus, Stedelijk Prenteenkabinet, 376-387, 91; auth, Alfred Hart: Photographer of the Transcontinental Railroad, Hist of Photog, XII, 1, 61-75, Jan-Mar, 88. **CONTACT ADDRESS** Palmer Museum of Art, Pennsylvania State Univ, University Park, PA, 16802-2507. **EMAIL** ggw2@psu.edu

WILMETH, DON B.
PERSONAL Born 12/15/1939, Houston, TX, m, 1963, 1 child **DISCIPLINE** THEATRE HISTORY, POPULAR CULTURE **EDUCATION** Abilene Christian Col, BA, 61; Univ AR, MA, 62; Univ IL, PhD, 64. **CAREER** Asst prof theatre, Eastern NM Univ, 64-65, head dept drama, 65-67; from Asst Prof to Prof, 67-98, The Asa Messer Prof of Theatre & English, Brown Univ, 98-, actg chmn theatre arts prog, 72-73, exec officer, Theatre Arts Dept, 73-, Chmn Dept, 79-87, Coordr, Grad Prog in Theatre Studies, 87-, Honorary Curator, H. Adrian Smith Collection of Conjuring Books & Magiciana (In Brown Special Collections); consult, Asn Col & Res Libr, 70-; theatre ed, Intellect Mag, 74-; bk rev ed, The Theatre J, 78-80; assoc ed, Mod Lang Studies, 80; consult, Libr Congress Am theatre project, 92-94; Vis Schol, Osaka Univ and Japan Found, Summer 93; Selection Comt, Robert Lewis Medal for Lifetime Achievement in Theater Res, 94-99; O.R. and Eva Mitchell Distinguished Vis Prof, Trinity Univ, 95; Dean, Col Fels Am Theatre, 96-98; Corresponding Schol, Shaw Festival, Ontario, 98. **HONORS AND AWARDS** Eastern NM Univ res grants, 66-68; George Freedley Theatre Bk Award, Theatre Libr Asn, 71-72; Guggenheim fel, 82., MA, Brown Univ, 70. **MEMBERSHIPS** Theatre Libr Asn (vpres, 81); Am Theatre Asn; Am Soc Theatre Res (pres 91-94, secy 95-01); Int Fedn Theatre Res (exec comt 94-97); New Engl Theatre Conf; Am Theatre & Drama Soc (exec bd 95-99). **RESEARCH** Popular entertainment; life and art of the 19th century actor, G F Cooke; Am theatre of the 19th century. **SELECTED PUBLICATIONS** Contribr, Drama/theatre, In: Books for College Libraries, 2nd ed, Am Libr Asn, 74; auth, The American Stage to World War I, 78 & American and English Popular Entertainment, 80, Gale Res Co; The Language of American Popular Entertainment, 81 & Variety Entertainment and Outdoor Amusements, 82, Greenwood Press; co-ed, Plays by William Hooker Gillette, Cambridge Univ Press, 83; auth, Mud Show: American Tent Circus Life, Univ NMex Press, 88; co-ed and contribr, Cambridge Guide to World Theatre, Cambridge Univ Press, 88; contribr, Theatre in the Colonies and United States, 1750-1915: A Documentary History, Cambridge Univ Press, 96; co-ed, The Cambridge Guide to the American Theatre, Cambridge Univ Press, 93; auth, Staging the Nation: Plays from the American Theatre, 1787-1909, Bedford Bks, 98; co-ed, The Cambridge History of American Theatre, Beginnings to 1870, Cambridge Univ Press, 98. **CONTACT ADDRESS** Dept of Theatre Arts, Brown Univ, 1 Prospect St, Providence, RI, 02912-9127. **EMAIL** donwilmeth@brown.edu

WILSON, DOUGLAS LAWSON
PERSONAL Born 11/10/1935, St. James, MN, m, 1957, 2 children DISCIPLINE ENGLISH EDUCATION Doane Col, AB, 57; Univ Pa, AM, 59, PhD(English), 64. CAREER Asst instr English, Univ Pa, 59-61; from instr to asst prof, 61-69, assoc prof, 69-79, PROF ENGLISH, KNOX COL, ILL, 79-, DIR LIBR, 72-. RESEARCH Thomas Jefferson; agrarian tradition in America. SELECTED PUBLICATIONS Auth, Jefferson, Thomas Library and the Skipwith List, Harvard Libr Bull, Vol 0003, 92; Jefferson, Thomas Library and the French Connection, 18th Century Stud, Vol 0026, 93; Dating Jefferson Early Architectural Drawings, Va Mag Hist and Biog, Vol 0101, 93; A Most Abandoned Hypocrite + Cartwright, Peter and the Early Political Writings of Lincoln, Abraham, Amer Heritage, Vol 0045, 94; The Percentage of Consonants Correct PCC Metric--Extensions and Reliability Data, J Speech Lang and Hearing Res, Vol 0040, 97; The Speech Disorders Classification System Sdcs--Extensions and Life Span Reference Data, J Speech Lang and Hearing Res, Vol 0040, 97. CONTACT ADDRESS Col Libr, Knox Col, Galesburg, IL, 61401.

WILSON, JOHN FLETCHER
PERSONAL Born 06/01/1923, Keyser, WV DISCIPLINE SPEECH EDUCATION Wayne Univ, BA, 47, MA, 48; Univ Wis, PhD(speech), 55. CAREER Instr speech, Monmouth Col, 48-50; from instr to assoc prof speech & drama, Cornell Univ, 53-67; assoc prof, 67-71, PROF SPEECH & THEATRE, LEHMAN COL, 71-, CHMN, 79-, Spec instr, exten div, col indust & labor relat, Cornell Univ, 55-56. MEMBERSHIPS Am Forensic Asn; Speech Commun Asn. RESEARCH Rhetoric and public address; speech criticism; argumentation. SELECTED PUBLICATIONS Auth, Rhetorical echoes of a (Woodrow) Wilsonian idea, Quart J Speech, 12/57; Fifty years of rhetorical criticism by laymen, In: Reestablishing the Speech Profession: The First Fifty Years, Speech Asn Eastern States, 59; coauth, Public Speaking as a Liberal Art, 64, rev eds, 68, 74 & 78 & Dimensions of Public Communication, 76, Allyn & Bacon; auth, Six rhetorics for perennial study, Today's Speech, winter 71. CONTACT ADDRESS Number 3k 201 E 21st St, New York, NY, 10010.

WILSON, JOHN H.
PERSONAL Born 06/20/1936, Binghamton, NY DISCIPLINE ENGLISH EDUCATION Col Holy Cross, AB, 58; Yale Univ, MA, 60, PhD(English), 66. CAREER From instr to asst prof, 61-72, ASSOC PROF ENGLISH, COL HOLY CROSS, 72-. RESEARCH Middle English literature; 18th century literature. SELECTED PUBLICATIONS Auth, Nell Gwyn: Royal Mistress, McCosh Bkstore, 52; ed, Six Restoration Plays, HM Publ, 59; co-ed, City Politiques, Univ Nebr, 67; auth, Ordeal of Mr Pepys's Cler, Ohio State Univ, 72; All the King's Ladies: Actresses of the Resoration, Univ Chicago, 74; Court Satires of the Restoration, Ohio State Univ, 76. CONTACT ADDRESS 142 Wheelock Ave, Millbury, MA, 01527.

WILSON, JOHN HAROLD
PERSONAL Born 02/11/1900, Springfield, OH DISCIPLINE ENGLISH EDUCATION Oberlin Col, AB, 22; Syracuse Univ, AM, 24; Ohio State Univ, PhD, 27. CAREER Instr English, Syracuse Univ, 22-24; from instr to prof, 24-68, EMER PROF ENGLISH, OHIO STATE UNIV, 68-, Vis prof, Univ Tenn, 36 & 38; Guggenheim fel, 50- MEMBERSHIPS MLA RESEARCH The influence of Beaumont and Fletcher on restoration drama; court wits of the restoration; early 17th century plays. SELECTED PUBLICATIONS Auth, All the King's Ladies, Chicago Univ, 58; Private Life of Mr Pepys, Farrar, Straus, 59; Mr Goodman the Player, Univ Pittsburgh, 64; A Preface to Restoration Drama, Houghton, 65; ed, Crowne's City Politiques, Univ Nebr, 67; auth, Mr Pepys' Clerk, 72 & Restoration Court Satires, 76, Ohio State Univ. CONTACT ADDRESS Dept of English, Ohio State Univ, Columbus, OH, 43210.

WILSON, KEITH G.
PERSONAL Born 12/15/1945, London, England DISCIPLINE ENGLISH EDUCATION Magdalene Col, Cambridge Univ, BA, 67, MA, 70; Queen's Univ, MA, 69, PhD, 73. CAREER Lectr, Royal Univ Malta, 72-74; instr, Carleton Univ, 74-76; asst prof, 76-82, assoc prof, 82-90, dir grad stud Eng, 85-87, PROF ENGLISH, UNIV OTTAWA, 90-, CHMN DEPT, 96-. HONORS AND AWARDS Ont grad fel, 69-70; Can Coun doctoral fel, 70-72; SSHRCC & Univ Ottawa res grants, 80, 81, 86, 88, 93, 94. MEMBERSHIPS Asn Can Univ Tchrs Eng; Thomas Hardy Soc; Victorian Stud Asn; Soc Theatre Res; Cambridge Soc; vice pres(Can), Thomas Hardy Soc N Am, 97-. RESEARCH 19th & 20th century literature; Thomas Hardy. SELECTED PUBLICATIONS Auth, Thomas Hardy on Stage, 95; ed, The Mayor of Casterbridge (Thomas Hardy), 97; ed adv bd, Eng Lit Transition, 90-; ed adv bd, Eng Stud Can, 93-. CONTACT ADDRESS English Dept, Univ Ottawa, 70 Laurier Ave E, Ottawa, ON, K1N 6N5.

WILSON, L. AUSTIN
DISCIPLINE ENGLISH EDUCATION Univ SC, PhD. CAREER Dept Eng, Millsaps Col SELECTED PUBLICATIONS Contribur, Mississippi Writers: Reflections of Childhood and Youth, vol 1 & 2. CONTACT ADDRESS Dept of English, Millsaps Col, 1701 N State St, Jackson, MS, 39210.

WILSON, LAURIE J.
PERSONAL Born 08/05/1952 DISCIPLINE COMMUNICATIONS, PUBLIC RELATIONS EDUCATION Brigham Young Univ, BA, 79, MA, 82; American Univ, PhD, 88. CAREER Adj prof, Int Commun, American Univ, 82-89; program mgr and marketing consult, 83-89; prof, chemn dept, 94-97, Brigham Young Univ, 89- . HONORS AND AWARDS Outstanding Scholarship, 89; Outstanding Fac Adv, Public Rel Stud Soc of Am, 90; Int Media Stud Grant, 93; Student Award for Excellence in Tchg, 94-95, 95-96, 96-97; Hall of Fame, Public Rel Stud Soc of Am, 95; IABC First Place Award, 97; forum participant, Am Asn for Higher Educ; Mem, Col of Fel, Public Rel Soc of Am, 98. MEMBERSHIPS Pub Rel Soc of Am; Asn for Educ in Journalism and Mass Commun; Int Commun Asn; Int Acad of Business Disciplines; Asn of Latter-day Saint Pub Rel Professionals; Radio and Television News Director Asn; Broadcast Educ Asn. SELECTED PUBLICATIONS Auth, The Return to Gemeinschaft; Toward a Theory of Public Relations and Corporate Community Relations as Relationship-Building, Business Research Yearbook: Global Business Perspectives, v.1, 94; auth, Excellent Companies and Coalition-Building among the Fortune 500: A Value- and Relationship-Based Theory, Public Relations Rev, 94; auth, Communication and Russia: Evolving Media in a Changing Society, The Social Science Journal, 95; coauth, Public Relations Program Management, Kendall/Hunt, 96; auth, Strategic Program Planning for Effective Public Relations Campaigns, 2d ed, Kendall/Hunt, 97. CONTACT ADDRESS Dept of Communication, 509 HFAC, Brigham Young Univ, Provo, UT, 84602. EMAIL laurie_wilson@byu.edu

WILSON, NORMA CLARK
PERSONAL Born 01/30/1946, Clarksville, TN, m, 1973, 2 children DISCIPLINE AMERICAN & BRITISH LITERATURE EDUCATION TN Technol Univ, BA, 68; Austin Peay State Univ, MA, 70; Univ OK, PhD, 78. CAREER Instr commun, comp & lit, Western OK State Univ, 77-78; prof eng, Univ SD, 78. HONORS AND AWARDS Ch, SD Hum Coun, 97-99. MEMBERSHIPS SD Peace and Justice Ctr; NOW; SD Resources Coalition. RESEARCH Contemp Am Indian lit; contemp Am poetry; contemp lit. SELECTED PUBLICATIONS Auth, Wild Iris, Point Riders Press, 78; Old ones have passed here: The poetry of Lance Henson, A: J Contemp Lit Contemp Lit, Vol 4, No 2; Turtles and learning to be a human: An interview with Linda Hogan, English Notes, Vol 26, No 1; Lost in a Dream, Dakota Woman, & Splendid Woman (poems), NDak Quart, Vol 48, No 4; Heartbeat: Within the Visionary Tradition, Walt Whitman of Mickle Street, Univ Tenn Press, 94; Outlook for survival, Denver Quart, Vol 14, No 4; Joy Harjo, Linda Henderson Hogan, Wendy Rose, Roberta Hill Whiteman, entries in: Handbook of Native American Literature, Garland, 96; Nesting in the Ruins, In: English Postcoloniality: Literatures from Around the World, Greenwood Press, 96; Ceremony: from Alienation to Reciprocity, In: Teaching American Ethnic Literatures, Univ NMex Press, 96. CONTACT ADDRESS Dept of Eng, Univ SD, 414 E Clark St, Vermillion, SD, 57069-2390. EMAIL nwilson@usd.edu

WILSON, REBECCA A.
PERSONAL Born 06/18/1944, St. Petersburg, FL, 2 children DISCIPLINE LIBRARY SCIENCE/BRITISH LITERATURE EDUCATION PA St Univ, Ded, 97; FL St Univ, MSLS, 67, BA, 66 CAREER Assoc Dir, 95-, Asst Dir, 87-95, Act Dir, 93-94, Susquehanna Univ; Site Librn, 85-87, PA St Univ; Ref Librn, 83-84, St Col of Arts and Sci; Ref Librn, 82-83, St Lawrence Univ; Map Librn, 80-81, Micronesian Area Res Ctr; Ref Librn, 70-75, St Clair County Commun Col; Ref Librn, 69-70, Univ of S FL HONORS AND AWARDS Res, Inst Tech Grants, 94, 95; ELCA admin study grants, 91-92 MEMBERSHIPS Am lib Assoc; PA Lib Assoc SELECTED PUBLICATIONS Auth, Students' Use of the Internet for Course-Related Research: Factors Which Account for Use or Non-use, PA St Univ, 97; Index to the Readex Microfilm Collection of Early American Newspapers, Readex Corp, 91 CONTACT ADDRESS Selinsgrove, PA, 17870-1611. EMAIL wilsonb@susqu.edu

WILSON, ROBERT H.
PERSONAL Born 01/21/1928, Des Moines, IA, m, 1963 DISCIPLINE AMERICAN LITERATURE EDUCATION State Univ Iowa, BA, 48, MA, 50. CAREER From instr to asst prof, 54-73, dir grad asst & exten courses English, 67, chmn tenured fac, 74-75, ASSOC PROF ENGLISH, NORTHERN ILL UNIV, 73-, DIR UNDERGRAD STUDIES, 76-, Consult, Price-Waterhouse, 70; consult writing, Farm Credit Admin, Washington, DC, 77- MEMBERSHIPS MLA; Midwest Mod Lang Asn. RESEARCH American fiction; American drama since 1920. CONTACT ADDRESS Dept of English, No Illinois Univ, De Kalb, IL, 60115.

WILSON, STEVEN R.
PERSONAL Born 10/26/1960, Lincoln, IL, m, 1992, 6 children DISCIPLINE COMMUNICATION EDUCATION Western IL Univ, BA 82; Indiana Univ, MA 84; Purdue Univ, PhD 89. CAREER Northwestern Univ, assoc, 98-; Northern IL, assoc, 94-98; Michigan State Univ, asst, asst, assoc prof, 88-94. MEMBERSHIPS NCA; ICA; APA; INPR; ISSPR RESEARCH Persuasion; family violence; conflict and negotiation; social cognition and communication. SELECTED PUBLICATIONS Auth, Identity implications of influence goals: A revised analysis of face-threatening acts and applications to seeking compliance with same sex friends, coauth, Hum Comm Res, 98; Regulative communication strategies within mother-child interactions: Implications for the study of reflection-enhancing parental communication, coauth, Res on Lang and Soc Interaction, 97; Attribution complexity and actor observer bias, coauth, Jour of Soc Behavior and Personality; 97; Developing theories of persuasive message production: The Next generation, in: J. O. Greene, ed, Message Production: Advances in communication theory, Hillsdale NJ, Law Erlbaum, 97; Communication discipline and physical child abuse, in: Parents Children Communication: Frontiers of Theory and Research, eds, T. J. Socha G. H. Stamp, Mahwah NJ, Law Erlbaum, 95. CONTACT ADDRESS Dept of Communication Studies, Northwestern Univ, 1881 Sheridan Rd, Evanston, IL, 60208. EMAIL s-wilson2@nwu.edu

WILSON JR., CHARLES E.
DISCIPLINE AFRICAN AMERICAN LITERATURE EDUCATION W Ga Univ, BA; N Ca State Univ, MA; Univ Ga, PhD. CAREER Engl, Old Dominion Univ. SELECTED PUBLICATIONS Area: Black Manhood; Race, Class, and Gender in Southern Fiction; Intersection of Past and Present in the South. CONTACT ADDRESS Old Dominion Univ, 4100 Powhatan Ave, Norfolk, VA, 23058. EMAIL CWilson@odu.edu

WILT, DAVID E.
PERSONAL Born 11/05/1955, Washington, DC DISCIPLINE RADIO, TV, FILM. EDUCATION Univ MD, BA 77, MA 80, MLS 85, PhD 91. CAREER Univ MD, Circulation Librarian, 86-. RESEARCH Pop culture and society; cinema and hist. SELECTED PUBLICATIONS Poster Art from the Golden Age of Mexican Cinema, contr, Agrasanchez Film Archive-IMCINE-Univ of Guadalajara, 97; Mondo Macabro, Titan books, UK, 97; Encyclopedia of Physical Sciences and Engineering Information Sources, 2d, Co ed, Gale Research, 96; Hollywood War Films, 1937-1945, with Michael Shull, McFarland 7 Co, 96; Mexican Fantasy Films, Cinefantastique, 96; The Baron of Terror: Abel Salazar, Filmfax, 96; Los Vampiros, Imagi-Movies, 94. CONTACT ADDRESS 4812B College Park Av # 12, College Park, MD, 20740. EMAIL dw45@umail.umd.edu

WILT, JUDITH
PERSONAL Born 09/17/1941, Pittsburgh, PA DISCIPLINE ENGLISH LITERATURE EDUCATION Duquesne Univ, BA, 67; Ind Univ, PhD(English), 72. CAREER Asst prof English, Princeton Univ, 72-78; assoc prof, 78-82, PROF ENGLISH, BOSTON COL, 82- HONORS AND AWARDS AAUW fel, 78-79; NEH summer seminar, 91. MEMBERSHIPS MLA RESEARCH British fiction; women's studies SELECTED PUBLICATIONS Auth, The Readable People of George Meredith, Princeton Univ, 75; Ghosts of the Gothic: Austen, Eliot and Lawrence, Princeton Univ, 80; Secret Leaves: The Novels of Walter Scott, Univ Chicago, 85; Abortion, Choice and Contemporary Fiction: The Armageddon of the Maternal Instinct, Univ Chicago, 91. CONTACT ADDRESS Dept of English, Boston Col, 140 Commonwealth Ave, Chestnut Hill, MA, 02167-3800. EMAIL judith.wilt@bc.edu

WIMSATT, JAMES I.
PERSONAL Born 09/25/1927, Detroit, MI, m, 1960, 2 children DISCIPLINE ENGLISH EDUCATION Univ Mich, BA, 50; Wayne State Univ, MA, 59; Duke Univ, PhD(English), 64. CAREER Instr, Univ Tenn, 63-64; asst prof, Tex Christian Univ, 64-66; from asst prof to prof, Univ NC, Greensboro, 66-77; PROF ENGLISH, UNIV TEX, AUSTIN, 77-, Fels, Duke Univ & Univ NC Coop Prog in Humanities, 70-71; Am Coun Learned Soc fel, 74-75; Guggenheim fel, 81-82. MEMBERSHIPS MLA; Mediaeval Acad Am; New Chaucer Soc; Mod Humanities Res Asn. RESEARCH Chaucer; Middle English literature; Old French literature. SELECTED PUBLICATIONS Auth, Rhyme-Reason, Chaucer-Pope, Icon-Symbol, Mod Lang Quart, Vol 0055, 94; Duns-Scotus, John, Peirce, Charles, Sanders, and Chaucer, Geoffrey Portrayal of the Canterbury Pilgrims + Exploring Philosophical Realism and the Image of Society in Medieval and Contemporary Literature, Speculum-J Medieval Stud, Vol 0071, 96; Rhyme, the Icons of Sound, and the Middle English 'Pearl', Style, Vol 0030, 96; The French Tradition and the Literature of Medieval England, Speculum-J Medieval Stud, Vol 0071, 96. CONTACT ADDRESS Dept of English, Univ of Tex, Austin, TX, 78712.

WINANS, ROBERT B.
DISCIPLINE ENGLISH EDUCATION Cornell, BA, 64; Univ NY, MA, 65, PhD, 72. CAREER Asst prof English, Gettysburg. RESEARCH Folklore, minstrel shows. SELECTED PUBLICATIONS Fel Publ, A Descriptive Checklist of Book Catalogues Separately Printed in America, 1639-1800, AAS, 81; auth, The Folk, the Stage, and the Five-String Banjo in Nineteenth-Century America, Jour of Amer Folklore 89, 76; 'Sadday Night and Sunday Too': The Uses of Slave Songs in the WPA Ex-Slave Narratives for Historical Study, NJ Folklore

7, 82; Bibliography and the Cultural Historian: Notes on the Eighteenth-Century Novel, Printing and Society in Early America, 83; Early Minstrel Show Music, In: Musical Theater in America: Papers and Proceedings of the Conference on Musical Theater in America, 84; The Early Minstrel Show, New World Records, NW 338, 85. **CONTACT ADDRESS** Dept of English, Gettysburg Col, Gettysburg, PA, 17325.

WINCHATZ, MICHAELA R.
PERSONAL Born 01/04/1967, Summit, NJ, m, 1992 **DISCIPLINE** SPEECH COMMUNICATION AND PSYCHOLINGUISTICS **EDUCATION** Rutgers Col, BA, 88; Ludwig-Maximilians Univ, Germany, MA, 92; Univ of Washington, PhD, 97. **CAREER** Asst Prof, 97-, Southern Illinois University-Carbondale. **HONORS AND AWARDS** Alice Schlimmbach Alumnae Soc Scholar stud in Germany, Rutgers Univ, 86; Class of 1920 Merit Scholar, Rutgers Univ, 88; Fulbright Full Grant, 90-91, renewal grant, 91-92; DAAD Annual Grant to Germany, 95-96; Humanities Dissertation Fel, Univ of Washington, 96; Joint Womens Stud and Univ Womens Prof Advancement Juried Comp Res Awd, 97., Ed Asst, Quarterly Jour of Speech, 97. **MEMBERSHIPS** NCA, WSCA **RESEARCH** Ethnography of communication; intercultural communication; interpersonal communication; conversations analysis. **SELECTED PUBLICATIONS** CoAuth, Reading Ella CaraDelorias Waterlily for Cultured Speech, Iowa Jour of Comm, 97; CoAuth, Acting Out Our Minds Incorporating Behavior into Models of Stereotype Based Expectancies for Cross Cultural Interactions, Comm Mono, 97. **CONTACT ADDRESS** Southern Illinois Univ, Dept of Speech Communication, Mailcode 6605, Carbondale, IL, 62901-6605. **EMAIL** winchatz@siu.edu

WINCHELL, DONNA
DISCIPLINE ENGLISH LITERATURE **EDUCATION** Tex Christian Univ, PhD, 83. **CAREER** Dept Eng, Clemson Univ **RESEARCH** Rhetoric and composition. **SELECTED PUBLICATIONS** Auth, Cries of Outrage: Three Novelists' Use of History, Miss Quart, 96; Alice Walker, Dictionary of Literary Biography, 94; Tracing the Motherlines, Miss Quart, 93; Alice Walker: Biographical and Bibliographic Beginning, Notes on Tchg Eng, 93; The Wound and the Fiddle Bow, SC Rev, 93. **CONTACT ADDRESS** Clemson Univ, Clemson, SC, 29634. **EMAIL** winched@clemson.edu

WINCHELL, MARK
DISCIPLINE ENGLISH LITERATURE **EDUCATION** Vanderbilt Univ, PhD, 78. **CAREER** Dept Eng, Clemson Univ **RESEARCH** American literature and literary criticism. **SELECTED PUBLICATIONS** Auth, The Myth is the Message, or, Why Streetcar Keeps Running, Confronting Streetcar, Greenwood, 92; Rod Serling's Requiem for a Heavyweight: A Drama for Its Time, Studies Am Drama, 1945-The Present, 93; South of Boston, Sewanee Rev, 95; Come Back to the Locker Room Ag'in, Brick Honey, Miss Quart, 93. **CONTACT ADDRESS** Clemson Univ, 307 Strode, Clemson, SC, 29634. **EMAIL** ixtlan@clemson.edu

WINDERL, CARL A.
DISCIPLINE ENGLISH **EDUCATION** Trevecca Nazarene Col, BA; Univ Chicago, MA; NY Univ, PhD. **CAREER** Eng Dept, Eastern Nazarene Col **RESEARCH** Gerard Manley Hopkins. **SELECTED PUBLICATIONS** Area: poems. **CONTACT ADDRESS** Eastern Nazarene Col, 23 East Elm Ave, Quincy, MA, 02170-2999.

WINDHAUSER, JOHN W.
DISCIPLINE MASS COMMUNICATION **EDUCATION** Ohio Univ, PhD, 75. **CAREER** Ed, Col Press Rev; ed bd, Jour Quart, Newspaper Res J; prof, mem, grad fac, area hd, polit commun, La State Univ. **RESEARCH** Health and political communications. **SELECTED PUBLICATIONS** Auth, How the Metropolitan Press Covered the 1970 General Election Campaigns in Ohio, in Jour Quart, 75; coauth, Reliability of Six Techniques for the Content Analysis of Local Coverage, in Jour Quart, 79; The Media in the 1984 and 1988 Presidential Campaign; the Editorial Process; Coverage by the Prestige Press of the 1988 Presidential Campaign, in Jour Quart, 89; What Children Saw in 16 Years: A Nutrient Analysis of Foods in Television Advertisements, in FASEB J, 94. **CONTACT ADDRESS** The Manship Sch of Mass Commun, Louisiana State Univ, Baton Rouge, LA, 70803.

WINEAPPLE, BRENDA
PERSONAL Born 02/05/1949, Boston, MA, m **DISCIPLINE** ENGLISH AND AMERICAN LITERATURE **EDUCATION** Brandeis Univ, BA; Univ of Wis at Madison, PhD. **CAREER** Vis prof, NYU, 97; co-dir, biography seminar, NYU; Washington Irving Prof of Modern Literary and Hist Studies, Union Col, 94-. **HONORS AND AWARDS** Am Coun of Learned Societies Fel, 97-98; Guggenheim Fel, 91; Donald C. Gallop Fel, Yale Univ, 91; Nat Endowment of the Humanities Fel, 87. **MEMBERSHIPS** MLA; Am Studies Asn; Columbia Univ Seminar in Am Civilization. **RESEARCH** Biography; American literature; women's studies. **SELECTED PUBLICATIONS** Auth, Sister, Brother: Gertrude and Leo Stein, Johns Hopkins Univ Press, 97; Jenet: A biography of Janet Hannes, Univ of Nebr Press, 91; The Conqueror's Hat: Poetry and Biography, Pennanus, 98; Gertrude Stein and the Lost Ark: A Woman's a Woman IS, Am Scholar, 98; Mourning Becomes Biography, Am Image, 97/98; Gertrude Stein Reads JAMA, J of the Am Medical Asn, 96. **CONTACT ADDRESS** English Dept, Union Col, Schenechtady, NY, 12308. **EMAIL** wineappb@union.edu

WING, NATHANIEL
DISCIPLINE 19TH AND 20TH CENTURY LITERATURE, LITERARY THEORY **EDUCATION** Columbia Univ, PhD, 68. **CAREER** Prof, assoc dir, Ctr of Fr and Francophone Stud, La State Univ. **SELECTED PUBLICATIONS** Auth, Present Appearance: Aspects of Poetic Structure in Rimbaud's Illuminations, 74; The Limits of Narrative, 86; Reading Simplicity: Flaubert's 'Un Coeur simple,' in 19th Century Fr Stud, 93. **CONTACT ADDRESS** Dept of Fr Grad Stud, Louisiana State Univ, Baton Rouge, LA, 70803.

WINKLER, CAROL
DISCIPLINE SPEECH COMMUNICATION **EDUCATION** Univ Md, PhD, 87. **CAREER** Assoc prof, ch, dept Commun, Ga State Univ, 94-. **HONORS AND AWARDS** Mortarboard Distinguished Prof Award. **MEMBERSHIPS** Exec Comt, Southern Speech Commun Asn; Legis Coun, Speech Commun Asn. **RESEARCH** Visual communication. **SELECTED PUBLICATIONS** Wrote three books and published more than forty articles in political debates, visual communication, and presidential foreign policy rhetoric. **CONTACT ADDRESS** Georgia State Univ, Atlanta, GA, 30303. **EMAIL** cwinkler@gsu.edu

WINNER, ANTHONY
PERSONAL Born 08/17/1931, New York, NY, m, 1964, 1 child **DISCIPLINE** ENGLISH, COMPARATIVE LITERATURE **EDUCATION** Harvard Univ, AB, 53, PhD, 62; Columbia Univ, MA, 54. **CAREER** Instr English, Univ Pa, 61-63 & Hunter Col, 63-65; asst prof, 65-68, ASSOC PROF ENGLISH, UNIV VA, 68-. **MEMBERSHIPS** MLA **RESEARCH** The novel; realism; character in fiction. **SELECTED PUBLICATIONS** Auth, Malouf, David 'Childs Play', Narrative Traditions in a Postmodern Game, Southerly, Vol 0054, 94; Disorders of Reading Short Novels and Perplexities, Kenyon Rev, Vol 0018, 96; Imagining Argentina, Kenyon Rev, Vol 0019, 97; On the Valuing of Narratives + Excerpt from a Set of Studies to be Entitled the 'Borderlines of Narrative', Va Quart Rev, Vol 0073, 97; One Hundred Years of Solitude, Kenyon Rev, Vol 0019, 97; See Under, Love, Kenyon Rev, Vol 0019, 97; Midnights Children, Kenyon Rev, Vol 0019, 97. **CONTACT ADDRESS** Dept of English, Univ of Va, 219 Bryan Hall, Charlottesville, VA, 22903.

WINNER, VIOLA HOPKINS
PERSONAL Born 03/13/1928, Cleveland, OH, m, 1964, 1 child **DISCIPLINE** AMERICAN LITERATURE **EDUCATION** Oberlin Col, BA, 49; NY Univ, MA, 53, PhD, 60. **CAREER** Instr, 54-57, Adelphi Univ; instr, Hunter Col, 60-64; asst prof, 65-72, Univ Va; prof, 73-76, Sweet Briar Col; ed assoc, 77-, Letters Henry Adams, Univ Va; NEH sr fel, 72-73. **MEMBERSHIPS** Am Studies Assn; MLA. **RESEARCH** Henry James; American fiction; literature and the visual arts. **SELECTED PUBLICATIONS** Auth, On Faulkner's The Hamlet: A Study in Meaning and Form, Accent, 55; auth, Gloriani and the Tides of Taste, 19th Century Fiction, 63; auth, Henry James and the Visual Arts, Univ Va, 70; ed, Edith Wharton's Fast and Loose, Univ Press of Va, 77; contribr, American Fiction: Historical and Critical Essays, Northeastern Univ, 77; auth, Thackeray and Richard Doyle, the Wayward Artist of the Newcomes, Harvard Libr Bull, 4/78. **CONTACT ADDRESS** 950 Locust Ave, Charlottesville, VA, 22901.

WINSECK, DWAYNE
DISCIPLINE POLITICAL ECONOMY OF COMMUNICATION, MEDIA HISTORY **EDUCATION** Univ Oregon, PhD. **CAREER** Instr, universities in the People's Rep of China; US; Turkish Rep of N Cyprus; UK; assoc prof. **RESEARCH** Communication policy, theories of democracy and global communication. **SELECTED PUBLICATIONS** Co-ed, Democratizing Communication?: Comparative Perspectives on Information and Power, Hampton Press, 97; Media in Global Context, Edward Arnold, 97; Reconvergence: A Political Economy of Telecommunications in Canada, Hampton Press, 98; pub(s), several articles in the Can Jour of Commun; Gazette; Media, Cult and Soc; Information Soc; Europ Jour Commun. **CONTACT ADDRESS** Dept of Commun, Carleton Univ, 1125 Colonel By Dr, Ottawa, ON, K1S 5B6.

WINSHIP, MICHAEL B.
DISCIPLINE ENGLISH **EDUCATION** Harvard, AB, 71; Simmons, MS, 82; Oxford, DPhilos, 89. **CAREER** Asst prof English, Univ Tex, Austin; ed, Bibliog of Amer Lit. **RESEARCH** Literary publishing. **SELECTED PUBLICATIONS** Auth, Bibliography of American Literature vols 7-9,Yale Univ, 83-91; American Literary Publishing in the Mid-Nineteenth Century: The Business of Ticknor and Fields, Cambridge Univ, 85; Publishing in America, Procs of the AAS 96, 86; Hermann Ernst Ludewig, Columbia Univ, 86; Ticknor and Fields: The Business of American Literary Publishing in the 19th Century, Hanes Fdn. and Univ NC Libr, 92; Epitome and Selective Index, North Amer Press, 95. **CONTACT ADDRESS** Dept of English, Univ of Texas, Austin, TX, 78712-1164.

WINSHIP, PETER
PERSONAL Pensacola, FL, m, 1966, 2 children **DISCIPLINE** HISTORY; LITERATURE (18TH -20TH CENTURIES-EUROPE) **EDUCATION** Harvard, AB, 64, LLB, 68; London Univ, London Sch of Economics and political sci, LLM, 73. **CAREER** Lectr, 70-72, Addis Ababa Univ; 74-present, Southern Methodist Univ **MEMBERSHIPS** American Law Inst. **RESEARCH** Legal history; Comparative law; International law **SELECTED PUBLICATIONS** Auth, The U.N. Sales Convention and the Emerging Caselaw, in EMPTIO-VENDITIO INTER NATIONES: IN ANERKENNUNG FUR LEHRTATIGKEIT KARL HEINZ NEUMAYER, 97; auth, Selected Security Interests in the United States, Emerging Financial Markets and Secured Transactions, Kluwer, 98; auth, Karl Llewellyn in Rome, 98. **CONTACT ADDRESS** Dallas, TX, 75275-0116. **EMAIL** pwinship@mail.smu.edu

WINTER, DARIA PORTRAY
PERSONAL Born 09/07/1949, Washington, DC **DISCIPLINE** ENGLISH **EDUCATION** Hampton Inst, BS, English educ, 1972; Univ of Virginia, MA, English, 1973; George Washington Univ, PhD program, 1988-89. **CAREER** DC Office of Bicentennial Programs, asst to exec dir 1975-76; UDC Coop Extension Program, education specialist 1976-77; UNIV OF THE DISTRICT OF COLUMBIA, instructor of English 1977-97, ASST PROF OF ENGLISH, 1995-; Mayor of District of Columbia, general assistant, 1992-95; Southeastern Univ, asst prof of English; Univ of District of Columbia Lorton Coll Prison Program, faculty, 1998. **HONORS AND AWARDS** Appreciation Award, University of District of Columbia Student NEA, 1984; Appreciation Award in Support of Public Education, from superintendent, Floretta McKenzie, 1983; Outstanding Service Award; Distinguished Public Service Award, 1994; Univ of the District of Columbia, College of Liberal and Fine Arts, Image Award, 1996; Steering Committee of DC, Reclaim Our Youth Award, 1996. **MEMBERSHIPS** Alternate natl committeewoman DC Dem State Comm 1980-92; NEA Standing Comm on Higher Educ 1981-87; vice chair DC Democratic State Comm 1984-92; Democratic Natl Comm 1984-92; delegate to Democratic Convention 1984, 1988, 1992; Modern Language Assn, Coll Language Assn; NCTE; editor, Newsletter Natl Educ Assn Black Caucus 1987-89; Public Defender Service Bd of Trustees, 1988-92, commissioner, 1987-; District Statehood Commn, 1979-92; vice chair, DNC Eastern Region Caucus, 1988-92; bd mem, DC Juvenile Justice Advisory Group; bd mem, United Planning Organization; mem appointed by Pres Wm Clinton, Presidential Rank Commssion, 1994; chairperson, Univ of the District of Columbia Advocacy Committee, 1996; chairperson, DC Juvenile Justice Advisory Group, 1998. **CONTACT ADDRESS** Univ of the District of Columbia, 4200 Connecticut Ave NW, Bldg 52, Rm 409, Washington, DC, 20008.

WINTER, KARI J.
PERSONAL Born 10/18/1960, Minneapolis, MN, m, 1 child **DISCIPLINE** ENGLISH **EDUCATION** Ind Univ, BA, 81; Univ Minn, PhD, 90. **CAREER** Tchng asst, 84-90, Univ Minn; asst prof, 90-92, Fisk Univ; asst prof, 92-97, assoc prof, 97-, Univ Vt. **HONORS AND AWARDS** Tchng Award Fel, 87-88, Univ Minn; Doct Diss Fel, Univ Minn, 88; Choice Outstanding Acad Book; Univ Vt Comm on Res & Scholars Sum Grant, 93; Tchng Award, Golden Key Natl Honor Soc, 95; Univ Vt Instruct Incentive Grants, 93-94, 96-97. **MEMBERSHIPS** Modern Lang Assn; Amer Stud Assn; New Eng Amer Stud Assn. **RESEARCH** Amer Indian Lit; African-Amer Lit; feminist theory. **SELECTED PUBLICATIONS** Auth, Subjects of Slavery, Agents of Change: Women and Power in Gothic Novels and Slave Narratives, 1790-1865, Univ Ga Press, 92. **CONTACT ADDRESS** Dept of English, Univ of Vermont, Burlington, VT, 05405. **EMAIL** Kwinter@200.uvm.edu

WINTON, CALHOUN
PERSONAL Born 01/21/1927, Ft Benning, GA, m, 1948, 2 children **DISCIPLINE** ENGLISH **EDUCATION** Univ of the South, BA, 48; Vanderbilt Univ, MA, 50; Princeton Univ, MA, 54, PhD(English), 55. **CAREER** Ford Found teaching fel, Dartmouth Col, 54-55, instr English, 55-57; asst prof, Univ Va, 57-60; Winterthur asst prof, Univ Del, 60-64, assoc prof, 64-67, coordr Winterthur Grad Prog Early Am Cult, 61-67; prof English, Univ SC, 67-75, chmn dept, 70-75, dir grad studies, 68-70; actg chmn dept, 76-77, dir Grad Studies, 76-79, PROF ENGLISH, UNIV MD, 75-, Am Philos Soc grant, 60; Am Coun Learned grant, 63; Guggenheim fel, 65-66; Fulbright lectureship, Turkey, 79-80. **MEMBERSHIPS** MLA; Conf Brit Studies; Am Studies Asn; Am Soc 18th Century Studies; S Atlantic Mod Lang Asn. **RESEARCH** Colonial American literature; 18th century literature. **SELECTED PUBLICATIONS** Auth, Genre and Generic--Change in English Comedy, 1660-1710, Scriblerian and the Kit-Cats, Vol 0027, 94. **CONTACT ADDRESS** Dept of English, Univ of Md, College Park, MD, 20742-0001.

WION, PHILIP KENNEDY
PERSONAL Born 09/06/1941, Bellefonte, PA, m, 1967, 2 children **DISCIPLINE** ENGLISH LITERATURE **EDUCATION** Swarthmore Col, BA, 63; Yale Univ, MA, 64, PhD(English), 67. **CAREER** Asst prof, 67-72, assoc prof English, Univ Pittsburgh, 72-. **MEMBERSHIPS** NCTE; AAUP; Am Fedn Teachers. **RESEARCH** Sixteenth century English literature; psychoanalytic criticism. **SELECTED PUBLICATIONS** Auth, Marlowe's Doctor Faustus, the Oedipus Complex, and the Denial of Death, Colby Libr Quart, XVI: 190-204; The Absent Mother in Emily Bronte's Wuthering Heights, American Image, XLII, No 2, pp 143-64. **CONTACT ADDRESS** Dept of English, Univ of Pittsburgh, 526 Cathedral/Learn, Pittsburgh, PA, 15260-2504. **EMAIL** pwion@pitt.edu

WISEMAN, CHRISTOPHER S.
PERSONAL Born 05/31/1936, Hull, England **DISCIPLINE** ENGLISH **EDUCATION** Trinity Hall, Cambridge Univ, BA, 59, MA, 62; Univ Strathclyde, PhD, 71. **CAREER** R.A.F., 54-56; Univ Iowa Poetry Workshop, 59-62; tchg asst, 60-62, lectr & founder mem, Eng stud, Univ Strathclyde, 63-69; asst to assoc prof, 69-80, PROF ENGLISH, UNIV CALGARY, 80-. **HONORS AND AWARDS** Alta Achievement Award, 88; Tchg Excellence Award, Univ Calgary, 88; Writers Guild Alta Poetry Award, 88. **MEMBERSHIPS** Hum Asn; Writers Guild Alta. **SELECTED PUBLICATIONS** Auth, Waiting for the Barbarians, 71; auth, The Barbarian File, 74; auth, Beyond the Labyrinth, 78; auth, The Upper Hand, 81; auth, An Ocean of Whispers, 82; auth, Closings, 86; auth, Postcards Home, 88; auth, Missing Persons, 89; auth, Remembering Mr. Fox, 89; poetry ed, Ariel, 72-87; poetry ed, Dandelion, 88-91. **CONTACT ADDRESS** English Dept, Univ of Calgary, Calgary, AB, T2N 1N4.

WISHART, LYNN
DISCIPLINE LEGAL RESEARCH **EDUCATION** W Va Univ, BA, 69; Univ Mich, AMLS, 71; Wash Univ, JD, 77. **CAREER** Assoc dir, law libraries, Georgetown Univ, 81-84, Washington Univ, 78-81, Lee Univ, 78-81; Prof, Yeshiva Univ; Dir Law Library, Yeshiva Univ. **HONORS AND AWARDS** West Excellence Acad Law Librarianship Award, 96. **MEMBERSHIPS** Am Library Asn; Am Asn Law Libraries. **SELECTED PUBLICATIONS** Area: library literature. **CONTACT ADDRESS** Yeshiva Univ, 55 Fifth Ave, NY, NY, 10003-4301. **EMAIL** wishart@ymail.yu.edu

WITEMEYER, HUGH
DISCIPLINE VICTORIAN AND MODERN BRITISH AND AMERICAN LITERATURE **EDUCATION** Princeton Univ, PhD, 66. **CAREER** Instr, Univ NMex, 73-. **SELECTED PUBLICATIONS** Auth, Pound/Williams: Selected Letters of Ezra Pound and William Carlos Williams, 96; coed, Ezra Pound and Senator Bronson Cutting: A Political Correspondence 1930-1935, 95. **CONTACT ADDRESS** Univ NMex, Albuquerque, NM, 87131.

WITMER, DIANE F.
PERSONAL Born 01/20/0000, Pasadena, CA, d, 1 child **DISCIPLINE** COMMUNICATION ARTS & SCIENCES **EDUCATION** Univ of La Verne, BS, 80; Univ S Cal, MS, 89, MA, 93, PhD, 94. **CAREER** Instr, 90, Univ of La Verne; Instr, 90-91 & 92-94, dept of comm, Cal State Univ, Fullerton; researcher, 92, Nat Acad of Sci, Wash DC; Asst Lectr, 91-94, Univ S Cal, LA; Asst Prof, Communication, 94-97, Purdue Univ, IN; Assoc Prof, 97-, Cal State Univ, Fullerton. **HONORS AND AWARDS** Dept Honors 4.0/4.0 gpa, Univ La Verne, 2 Protos Awds, Top Four Paper Awd, Who's Who in; of Amer Women, in America, in the West & in the Midwest. **MEMBERSHIPS** CIOR, ICA, NCA, PRSA, WSCA. **RESEARCH** Computer-mediated communications, organizational communications & public relations. **SELECTED PUBLICATIONS** Auth, Understanding the Human Communication Process, Study Guide, Englewood CO, Jones Intl Ltd, 98; Public Relations, Study Guide, Englewood CO, Jones Intl Ltd, 97; Human Communications, Study Guide, Englewood CO, Jones Intl Ltd, 97; co-auth, From Paper-and-Pencil to Screen-and-Keyboard, Toward a Methodology for Survey Research on the Internet, in: Doing Internet Research, ed, S Jones, forthcoming; Practicing Safe Computing, Why People engage in Risky Computer-mediated Communication, in: Network and Netplay, Virtual Groups on the Internet, eds, F Sudweeks, M L McLaughlin & S Rafaeli, Menlo Park CA, AAAI/MIT Press, 98; Risky Business, Do People Feel Safe in Sexually Explicit Online Communication? in: J of Computer-Mediated Communication, 97. **CONTACT ADDRESS** Dept of Communications, California State Univ, Fullerton, Box 6846, Fullerton, CA, 92834-6846. **EMAIL** dwitmer@fullerton.edu

WITT, ROBERT WAYNE
PERSONAL Born 03/26/1937, Scottsville, KY **DISCIPLINE** SEVENTEETH CENTURY LITERATURE **EDUCATION** Georgetown Col, BA, 59; Univ Miss, MA, 61, PhD(English), 70. **CAREER** Instr English, Univ Miss, 65-70; asst prof, 70-75, assoc prof, 75-80, prof English, Eastern KY Univ, 80-. **MEMBERSHIPS** MLA; Southern Atlantic Mod Lang Asn. **RESEARCH** Dramatic literature and non-dramatic poetry of the 17th century. **SELECTED PUBLICATIONS** Auth, Building a pillar of fame, Univ Miss Studies in English, 72; Kipling as representative of the counter-aesthetes Kipling J, 70; Yeats, Plato, and the editors, T S Eliot Newslett, 74; Caliban upon Plato, Victorian Poetry, 75; Mirror Within A Mirror: Ben Jonson and the Play-Within, 75 & Of Comfort and Despair: Shakespeare's Sonnet Sequence, 79, Salzburg: Institut fur Englische Sprache und Literatur; Reason is not enough: Hamlet's recognition, Hamlet Studies, 81; On Faulkner and Verbena, Southern Literary Journal, 94; Montague or Capulet, Utstart Crow, 95. **CONTACT ADDRESS** Dept of English, Eastern Kentucky Univ, 521 Lancaster Ave, Richmond, KY, 40475. **EMAIL** engwitt@acs.eku.edu

WITTEBOLS, JAMES H.
PERSONAL Born 08/22/1955, Mt. Clemens, MI **DISCIPLINE** COMMUNICATION **EDUCATION** Cent Mich Univ, BA, 77; Wa St Univ, MA, 79, PhD, 83. **CAREER** Educ res, Washington DC, 85-87; asst prof to chair to assoc prof to prof, 87-. **MEMBERSHIPS** AEJMC; ICA. **RESEARCH** Political communication; politics of popular culture. **SELECTED PUBLICATIONS** Auth, Words and Worlds of Terror: Context and Meaning of a Media Buzzword, Etc: A Review of General Semantics, 91; art, Media and the Institutional Perspective: U. S. and Canadian Coverage of Terrorism, Polit Commun & Persuasion, 92; art, News and the Institutional Perspective: Sources in Terror Stories, Canadian J of Commun, 95; art, News from the Noninstitutional World: US and Canadian Coverage of Social Protest, Polit Commun, 96; auth, Watching M*A*S*H, Watching America: A Critical Analysis and Episode Guide, McFarland Publ, 98. **CONTACT ADDRESS** 64 Greenfield St, Buffalo, NY, 14214. **EMAIL** jhw@niagara.edu

WITTIG, JOSEPH SYLVESTER
PERSONAL Born 08/18/1939, Pittsburgh, PA, m, 1969 **DISCIPLINE** ENGLISH, MEDIEVAL STUDIES **EDUCATION** Wheeling Col, BA, 63; Univ Scranton, MA, 65; Cornell Univ, PhD(English, medieval studies), 69. **CAREER** Asst prof, 69-76, ASSOC PROF ENGLISH, UNIV NC, CHAPEL HILL, 76-. **MEMBERSHIPS** MLA; Mediaeval Acad Am; New Chaucer Soc; AAUP; Southern Atlantic Mod Lang Asn. **RESEARCH** Middle English literature; Old English literature; medieval studies. **SELECTED PUBLICATIONS** Auth, The Yearbook of Langland Studies, Vol 3, Anglia-Zeitschrift fur Engl Philol, Vol 0110, 92; A Glossarial Concordance to the Riverside Chaucer, 2 Vols, Speculum-J Medieval Stud, Vol 0070, 95. **CONTACT ADDRESS** Dept of English, Univ of NC, Chapel Hill, NC, 27514.

WITTLIN, CURT
PERSONAL Born 04/13/1941, Basel, Switzerland **DISCIPLINE** MEDIEVAL LITERATURE **EDUCATION** Humanistisches Gymnasium Basel, BA, 60; Univ Basel, MA, PhD, 65. **CAREER** Prof, Union Col, Ky, 65-66; fac mem, 66-76, PROF FRENCH, UNIV SASKATCHEWAN, 76-, dept head, 85-91. **HONORS AND AWARDS** Swiss Nat Fund res grant; SSHRC res grant. **MEMBERSHIPS** Can Asn Hispanists (dir, 76-81); N Am Catalan Soc (dir, 82-95). **SELECTED PUBLICATIONS** Over 100 scholarly publs: medieval Catalan lit, lang & civilization; medieval Fr & Span lit; Romance philol **CONTACT ADDRESS** Dept of French, Univ of Saskatchewan, Saskatoon, SK, S7N 5A5.

WOJCIK, DANIEL
PERSONAL Born 12/21/1955, Detroit, MI **DISCIPLINE** ENGLISH; FOLKLORE **EDUCATION** BA, anthrop, Univ Calif Santa Barbara, 78; MA, folklore and myth, Univ Calif Los Angeles, 86; PhD, folklore and myth, Univ Calif Los Angeles, 92. **CAREER** Asst prof, 91-97, assoc prof, 97-, dept of eng, Univ Ore. **HONORS AND AWARDS** Amer Acad of Relig individual res grant, 96; summer res award, Office of Res and Sponsored Prog, Univ Ore, 95; Arnold Rubin award, Fowler Mus of Cultural Hist, Univ Calif Los Angeles, 90. **MEMBERSHIPS** Amer Acad of Relig; Amer Culture Asn; Amer Folklore Soc; Amer Studies Asn; Calif Folklore Soc; Intl Soc for Contemp Legend Res; Popular Culture Asn. **RESEARCH** Millennialist movements and apocalyptic beliefs; Contemporary American folklore; Popular culture; Subcultures and youth cultures; Body art; Popular religion. **SELECTED PUBLICATIONS** Auth, The End of the World As We Know It: Faith, Fatalism, and Apocalypse in America, NY Univ Press, 97; article, Embracing Doomsday: Faith, Fatalism, and Apocalyptic Beliefs in the Nuclear Age, Western Folklore, 55, no 4, 297-330, 96; article, Polaroids from Heaven: Photography, Folk Religion, and the Miraculous Image Tradition at a Marian Apparition Site, Jour of Amer Folklore, 109, no 432, 129-148, 96; auth, Punk and Neo-Tribal Body Art, Folk Art and Artists Series, Univ Press of Miss, 95. **CONTACT ADDRESS** English and Folklore Studies, Univ of Oregon, 1286 University of Oregon, Eugene, OR, 97403-1286. **EMAIL** dwojcik@oregon.uoregon.edu

WOLAK, WILLIAM J.
DISCIPLINE THEATRE ARTS **EDUCATION** CT State Col, BA; St Louis Univ, MA; Tulane Univ, PhD. **CAREER** Prof, Univ Pacific. **HONORS AND AWARDS** UOP. **SELECTED PUBLICATIONS** Auth, The Inspector General (rev); The Servant of Two Masters (rev). **CONTACT ADDRESS** Dept of Theatre Arts, Univ Pacific, Pacific Ave, PO Box 3601, Stockton, CA, 95211.

WOLF, DONALD
PERSONAL Born 04/12/1924, Sandpoint, ID, m, 1955, 1 child **DISCIPLINE** ENGLISH **EDUCATION** Lehigh Univ, BS, 48, MA, 52; Columbia Univ, PhD, 60. **CAREER** Instr English, Lehigh Univ, 50-52; from instr to asst prof, 53-70, PROF ENGLISH, ADELPHI UNIV, 70-, CHMN DEPT, 75-. **RESEARCH** Romantic and Victorian English literature. **SELECTED PUBLICATIONS** Auth, 'Law and Order' Creator-Executive Producer Wolf, Dick + An Interview--Its the Writing, Stupid, Television Quart, Vol 0028, 97. **CONTACT ADDRESS** Dept of English, Adelphi Univ, Garden City, NY, 11530.

WOLFE, GARY KENT
PERSONAL Born 03/24/1946, Sedalia, MO, m, 1966 **DISCIPLINE** LITERATURE **EDUCATION** Univ Kans, BA, 68; Univ Chicago, MA, 69, PhD(English), 71. **CAREER** Danforth tutor humanities, Univ Chicago, 70-71; asst prof, 71-77, ASSOC PROF HUMANITIES, ROOSEVELT UNIV, 77-, DEAN COL CONTINUING EDUC, 82-, Ed, Science Fiction Res Asn Annual Vol, 81-82. **HONORS AND AWARDS** Eaton Award, 81. **MEMBERSHIPS** Sci Fiction Res Asn; Popular Cult Asn; Coun Advan Experiential Learning; Int Conf on Fantastic. **RESEARCH** Science fiction and fantastic literature; film and television; adult continuing education. **SELECTED PUBLICATIONS** Auth, Vonnegut, Kurt, Sci-Fiction Stud, Vol 0020, 93; The Dark Descent, Sci-Fiction Stud, Vol 0020, 93; On Some Recent Scholarship, Sci-Fiction Stud, Vol 0021, 94. **CONTACT ADDRESS** Roosevelt Univ, 430 S Michigan Ave, Chicago, IL, 60605.

WOLFE, RALPH HAVEN
PERSONAL Born 06/23/1931, Weston, OH **DISCIPLINE** ENGLISH **EDUCATION** Bowling Green State Univ, BS, 51, MA, 56; Ind Univ, PhD(English), 60. **CAREER** Instr English, Bowling Green State Univ, 60-61; asst prof, Monmouth Col, Ill, 61-62; assoc prof, Ind State Univ, Terre Haute, 62-69; asst chmn dept, 69-76, PROF ENGLISH, BOWLING GREEN STATE UNIV, 69-, Vis assoc prof, Bowling Green State Univ, 67-69. **MEMBERSHIPS** MLA **RESEARCH** English and American literature; drama. **SELECTED PUBLICATIONS** Coauth, The Ohio Roots of Gish, Dorothy and Gish, Lillian, J Popular Film and Television, Vol 0022, 94. **CONTACT ADDRESS** Dept of English, Bowling Green State Univ, Bowling Green, OH, 43403.

WOLFF, CYNTHIA GRIFFIN
DISCIPLINE ENGLISH AND AMERICAN LITERATURE **EDUCATION** Radcliffe Col, BA, 58; Harvard Univ, PhD(English), 65. **CAREER** Instr English, Boston Univ, 63-64; instr, Queens Col, NY, 65-68; asst prof, Manhattanville Col, 68-71; assoc prof, Univ Mass, Amherst, 71-76, dir honors prog, 72-74, prof, 76-80; PROF LIT, MASS INST TECHNOL, 80-. **MEMBERSHIPS** MLA; Am Studies Asn. **RESEARCH** English and American fiction; 19th and early 20th century American literature; psychology and literature. **SELECTED PUBLICATIONS** Auth, Lily Bart and the Drama of Feminity + Wharton, Edith 'House of Mirth', Amer Lit Hist, Vol 0006, 94; Masculinity in 'Uncle Toms Cabin' + Stowe, Harriet, Beecher, American Literature, American Quart, Vol 0047, 95; Passing Beyond the Middle Passage, Brown, Henry, Box Translations of Slavery, Mass Rev, Vol 0037, 96; Un Utterable Longing + Chopin, Kate--The Discourse of Feminine Sexuality in the 'Awakening', Stud in Amer Fiction, Vol 0024, 96. **CONTACT ADDRESS** Dept of English, Massachusetts Inst of Tech, 77 Massachusetts Ave, Cambridge, MA, 02139.

WOLFF, FLORENCE I.
PERSONAL Pittsburgh, PA, 7 children **DISCIPLINE** SPEECH COMMUNICATION **EDUCATION** Temple Univ, BS, 41; Duquesne Univ, MA, 67; Univ Pittsburgh, PhD, 69. **CAREER** Sec tchr bus educ & Eng, Charleroi Sr High Sch, 41-46, Pub & Pvt High Schs, 56-60 & Cent Dist Cath High Sch, 61-69; from Instr to Prof Speech Commun, 70-89, Prof Emeritus Commun, Univ Dayton, 89; Dir, Wolff Innovative Training System - conducts management training seminars for corporations, the military, and law enforcement. **HONORS AND AWARDS** Inductee, Int Listening Asn Hall of Fame. **MEMBERSHIPS** Relig Speech Commun Asn (exec secy, 78-81, 2nd vpres, 82, 1st vpres, 83); Int Listening Asn; Speech Commun Asn; hon mem Nat Forensic League. **RESEARCH** Listening; oral interpretation; public address. **SELECTED PUBLICATIONS** Auth, A survey of evaluative criteria for faculty promotion in college and university speech departments, Speech Teacher, 11/71; A teacher oriented eclectic review of recent interpersonal and small group communication research, Speech Asn Minn J, 5/75; Student evaluation of college and university speech communication courses and faculty: A survey, Speech Teacher, 9/75; A 1977 Survey: General insights into the status of listening course offerings in selected colleges and universities, NC J Speech Commun, winter 79; A lector's nightmare: Professional tips for proclaiming the word, Today's Parish, 9/80; A unique synthesized motivational evaluation strategy for assessing high school students' speech performance: An instructional unit, Ohio Speech J, 80; Re-creative bible reading, Relig Commun Today, 9/80; Perceptive Listening, Holt, Rinehart & Winston, 2nd ed, 93. **CONTACT ADDRESS** Dept of Commun, Univ of Dayton, 300 College Park, Dayton, OH, 45469-0000.

WOLGAST, ELIZ H.
PERSONAL Born 02/27/1929, NJ, m, 1949, 2 children **DISCIPLINE** ENGLISH; PHILOSOPHY **EDUCATION** Cornell Univ, BA, 50, MA, 52; Univ Wash, PhD, 55. **CAREER** Univ Calif Davis, 66-67; Calif State Hayward, 68-97; visiting prof, Dartmouth Col, 75-76; Univ Wales, Lampeter, 95, 96. **HONORS AND AWARDS** NEH fel, 78, 88; Finnish Acad fel, 92; Rockefeller Bellagio fel, 88. **MEMBERSHIPS** APA. **RESEARCH** Wittgenstein; Ethics; Epistemology. **SELECTED PUBLICATIONS** Auth, Democracy: The Message from Athens, Consequences of Modernity in Contemporary Legal Theory, Dunker & Humbolt, 98; auth, Mental Causes and the Will, Philos Investigations, Winter, 97; auth, Moral Paradigms, Philos, Spring, 95; auth, Individualism and Democratic Citizenship, Democrazia e Diritto, Summer, 94; auth, The Demands of Public Reason, Columbia Law Rev, Oct, 94; auth, Primitive Reactions, Philos Investigations, Oct, 94; auth, Ethics of an Artificial Person: Lost Responsibility in Professions and Organizations, Stanford Univ Press, 92; auth, La Grammatica della Giustizia, Riuniti, Italy, 91; auth, The Grammar of Justice, Cornell Univ Press, 87; auth, Equality and the Rights of Women, Cornell Univ Press, 80; auth, Paradoxes of Knowledge, Cornell Univ Press, 77. **CONTACT ADDRESS** 1536 Olympus Av., Berkeley, CA, 94708. **EMAIL** ewolgast@csuhayward.edu

WOLLAEGER, MARK A.
DISCIPLINE 20TH-CENTURY BRITISH LITERATURE **EDUCATION** Yale Univ, PhD. **CAREER** Instr, dir, col writing prog, Vanderbilt Univ. **RESEARCH** Modernism; postcolonial literature and theory; film; Conrad; Forster; Joyce; Woolf. **SELECTED PUBLICATIONS** Auth, Joseph Conrad and the Fictions of Skepticism, Stanford Univ Press, 90; co-ed Joyce and the Subject of History, Mich, 96. **CONTACT ADDRESS** Vanderbilt Univ, Nashville, TN, 37203-1727.

WOLPER, ROY S.
PERSONAL Born 07/07/1931, Pittsburgh, PA, m, 1957, 2 children **DISCIPLINE** ENGLISH **EDUCATION** Univ Pittsburgh, MA, 52, MA, 59, PhD, 65. **CAREER** Instr Eng lit, Carnegie Inst Technol, 61-64 & Univ Pittsburgh, 64-65; asst prof, Univ Sask, 65-67; from asst prof to assoc prof, 67-75, prof eng, lit, Temple Univ, 75, Co-ed, The Scriblerian; Nat Endowment for Arts fel, creative writing, 74-75. **HONORS AND AWARDS** Option Award, Doubleday & Co. **MEMBERSHIPS** MLA; Northeastern Mod Lang Asn; Am Soc 18th Century Studies. **RESEARCH** The Scriblerians; Voltaire; Jews in 18th century lit. **SELECTED PUBLICATIONS** Auth, Johnson's neglected muse: The drama, Studies in Eighteenth Century, 68; Candide, gull in the garden?, Eighteenth Century Studies, 69; The rhetoric of gunpowder and the idea of progress, J Hist Ideas, 70; Zadig, a grim comedy?, Romanic Rev, 74; The final foolishness of Babouc: The dark center of Le Monde comme il va, Mod Lang Rev, 75; The lustful Jew in the eighteenth century: A sympathetic stereotype?, Proc 6th World Congr Jewish Studies, 77; Voltaire's Contes: A reconsideration, Forum, 78; The toppling of Jeannot, Studies on Voltaire and the Eighteenth Century, 80. **CONTACT ADDRESS** Dept of Eng, Temple Univ, 1114 W Berks St, Philadelphia, PA, 19122-6029. **EMAIL** rwolpe00@nimbus.ocis.temple.edu

WOLVIN, ANDREW D.
DISCIPLINE ORGANIZATIONAL COMMUNICATION AND COMMUNICATION EDUCATION **EDUCATION** Purdue Univ, PhD, 68. **CAREER** Dir undergrad stud; prof, Univ MD. **RESEARCH** The study of listening behavior. **SELECTED PUBLICATIONS** Co-auth, Listening, 5th edn, Brown, 96; Communicating: A Social and Career Focus, 7th edn, Houghton-Mifflin, 98. **CONTACT ADDRESS** Dept of Commun, Univ MD, 4229 Art-Sociology Building, College Park, MD, 20742-1335. **EMAIL** aw30@umail.umd.edu

WOOD, BARBARA
DISCIPLINE COMMUNICATION STUDIES **EDUCATION** Univ WI, PhD. **CAREER** Prof, Univ Il at Chicago. **RESEARCH** Commun competence and lang; develop of functional commun of children and youth. **SELECTED PUBLICATIONS** Auth, pubs on communication behaviors; communication training. **CONTACT ADDRESS** Dept of Commun, Univ Illinois Chicago, S Halsted St, PO Box 705, Chicago, IL, 60607. **EMAIL** bwood@uic.edu

WOOD, GERALD CARL
PERSONAL Born 03/22/1944, Valparaiso, IN, d, 2 children **DISCIPLINE** BRITISH LITERATURE, FILM STUDY **EDUCATION** Wabash Col, AB, 66; Univ Fla, PhD, 71. **CAREER** Prof English, Carson-Newman Col, 71-, Vis scholar, Univ Iowa, 79-80; vis assoc prof English, Univ Tn-Knoxville, 82. **MEMBERSHIPS** MLA; S Atlantic Mod Lang Asn; Byron Soc. **RESEARCH** Writings of Lord Byron; film studies; theories of comedy. **SELECTED PUBLICATIONS** Auth, Nature and narrative in Byron's Prisoner of Chillon, Keats-Shelley J, 75; Lord Byron, the metaphor of the climates and Don Juan, Byron J, 78; Francois Truffaut's Day for Night and the life of art in contemporary film, Interpretations: Studies Lang & Lit, 78; And Now...who knows: The Nature or Mystery in Horton Foote's The Young Man From Atlanta, S Atlantic Mod Lang Asn, Atlanta, Ga, 95; Old Beginnings and Roads to Home: Horton Foote and Mythic Realism, Christianity and Lit, 96; Horton Foote's Politics of Intimacy, J Am Drama and Theatre, 97; Ed, Horton Foote: A Casebook, Garland, 98; Horton Foote and the Theatre of Intimacy, La State Univ, 98. **CONTACT ADDRESS** Dept English, Carson-Newman Col, 1634 Russell Ave, Jefferson City, TN, 37760-2204. **EMAIL** woody@cncacc.cn.edu

WOOD, JULIA T.
DISCIPLINE COMMUNICATIONS **EDUCATION** Pa State Univ, PhD, 75. **CAREER** PROF, UNIV NC, CHAPEL HILL, 75-. **CONTACT ADDRESS** Univ of No Carolina, Chapel Hill, CB 3285, Chapel Hill, NC, 27599. **EMAIL** jwoods@email.unc.edu

WOOD, NANCY
DISCIPLINE ENGLISH **EDUCATION** Univ OR, Eugene, BA, 56; Cornell Univ, MA, 63; Rutgers Univ, PhD, 72. **CAREER** Prof, 96-, prof & ch, 94-96, assoc prof & ch, 93-94, assoc prof, ch & dir freshman Eng, 92-93, assoc prof, actg ch, & dir freshman Eng, 91 & assoc prof and dir freshman Eng, 89-90, Univ TX at Arlington; vis scholar, Cambridge Univ, 97; founder & dir, Study Skills and Tutorial Serv, 73-89; dir, Study Skills and Tutorial Services, 80-81, Study Skills Couns in Freshman Serv Off, 72-73 & instr, 68-72, Univ TX at El Paso; mem Ed Staff, Partisan Rev Magazine, Rutgers Univ, 63-64; instr, 59, 60 & 61 and tchg asst, 58-62, Cornell Univ; Judging, most outstanding article in the 92 vol, J Develop Educ, 93; sec & mem, Exec Bd, Nat Asn Develop Educ, 90-92; pres, TX Asn Develop Educ, 88-89; pres-elect & prog ch, Annual Conf Acad Support Prog, El Paso, 88; mem, Adv Coun, Nat Asn Develop Educ, 88-89; reg rep, TX Asn Develop Educ, 86-87; mem ch, TADE, 86-87; coordr, Chp(s) Nat Conf Col Reading and Learning Asn, 85; mentor, 2 CRLA conf, 85 & 87. **HONORS AND AWARDS** Hon mem, Sigma Tau Delta, Engl Honor Soc, 89, Certificate of Appreciation, 96; hon mem, Golden Key Nat Honor Soc, 89; Certificate Merit for Adv, Am Coun Testing/Nat Acad Adv Asn, 86; Distinguished Achievement Awd, UT El Paso, 84; 1st annual Mortar Bd Achievement Awd, 74. **MEMBERSHIPS** Asn Dep Eng; MLA; Coun Writing Prog Admin; Conf Col Tchrs Eng TX; Nat Coun Tchrs Eng; Int Reading Asn; Nat Reading Conf; Nat Asn Develop Educ; TX Asn Develop Educ; Col Reading and Learning Asn; Nat Acad Adv Asn, hon mem. **SELECTED PUBLICATIONS** Auth, Perspectives on Argument with Instructor's Manual, NJ, Prentice Hall, 95. 2nd ed, 97; Strategies for College Reading and Thinking with Instructor's Manual, NY, McGraw Hill, 91; Improving Reading with Instructor's Manual, NY, Holt, Rinehart, & Winston, 84; College Reading and Study Skills: A Guide to Improving Academic Communication, NY, Holt, Rinehart, & Winston, 78, 2nd ed, with Instructor's Manual, 82, 3rd ed with Instructor's Manual, 86, 4th ed with Instructor's Manual, 91, 5th ed College Reading and Study Skills: Learning, Thinking, Making Connections with Instructor1/4s Manual, 96; College Reading Instruction as Reflected by Current Reading Textbooks, J Col Reading and Learning, 97; Codifying Literacy: Identifying and Measuring Reading Competencies in Statewide Basic Skills Assessment Programs, J Col Reading and Learning, Vol XXXII, 89; Reading Tests and Reading Assessment, J Develop Educ, Vol 13, 89; Standardized Reading Tests and the Postsecondary Reading Curriculum, J Reading, Vol XXXII, 88. **CONTACT ADDRESS** Dept of Eng, Univ of Texas at Arlington, 203 Carlisle Hall, PO Box 19035, Arlington, TX, 76019-0595.

WOOD, RUTH
DISCIPLINE ENGLISH LITERATURE **EDUCATION** Bowling Green State Univ, MA; Univ MN, PhD. **CAREER** Prof, Univ of WI. **RESEARCH** Portfolio assessment. **SELECTED PUBLICATIONS** Auth, Lolita in Peyton Place. **CONTACT ADDRESS** Eng Dept, Univ Wisconsin, S 3rd St, PO Box 410, River Falls, WI, 54022-5001.

WOOD, SUSAN H.
PERSONAL Born 12/20/1963, Columbus, OH, s **DISCIPLINE** ENGLISH **EDUCATION** Carleton Col, BA, 86; Wash Univ, St Louis, AM, 88; Univ Tenn, PhD, 94. **CAREER** Adj instr, 88-89, Tourism Chinese Culture U, Yangmingshan; grad tchng assoc, 89-94, Univ Tenn; lectr, eng, 94-97, UNLV; instr, eng, 97-, Louisiana St Univ. **RESEARCH** historical novel, 19th century women authors, Chinese & Japanese lit, 18th century lit, the novel, world/multicultural. **CONTACT ADDRESS** Dept of English, Louisiana State Univ, Baton Rouge, LA, 70803. **EMAIL** swood@unixl.sncc.lsu.edu

WOODBRIDGE, JOHN M.
PERSONAL Born 01/26/1929, New York, NY, m, 1975, 3 children **DISCIPLINE** ENGLISH AND ARCHITECTURE **EDUCATION** Amherst Col, AB, 51; Princeton Univ, MFA, archit, 56. **CAREER** Archit, Princeton Univ Archaeol expedition to Morgantina, Sicily, 56; Holden Egan Wilson & Corser, NY and Wash DC, 56-57; archit, John Funk, San Francisco, 57-58; John Lyon Reid and Partners, San Francisco, 57-58; assoc partner, Skidmore Owings & Merrill, 59-73; pres adv coun on Penn Ave, chief of design, 63-64, staff dir, 65-66, exec dir, 73-77; vpres, Braccia Joe & Woodbridge, 77-80; cons, Stoller Partners, Berkeley, 80-82; **HONORS AND AWARDS** Phi Beta Kappa, 50; AIA Student Medal, 56; fel, Amer Inst of Archit, 74; Fed Design Achievement Award, 88. **MEMBERSHIPS** AIA. **RESEARCH** Spanish colonial architectural history especially Mexico; Architectural history in Europe and U.S. **SELECTED PUBLICATIONS** Coauth,with Sally B. Woodbridge, San Francisco Architecture, San Francisco, Chronicle Books, 92; with Sally B. Woodbridge, Architecture San Francisco, San Francisco, 101 Prod, 82; with David Gebhard, Roger Montgomery, Robert Winter and Sally B. Woodbridge, A Guide to the Architecture of San Francisco and Northern California, Salt Lake City, Peregrine Smith, 73; with Sally B. Woodbridge and Philip Thiel, Buildings of the Bay Area, NY, Grove Press, 60; auth, The Bay Area Style, Casabella 232, Oct 59; For the Cathedral of St. John the Divine, Relig Bldgs for Today, NY, F. W. Dodge, 57. **CONTACT ADDRESS** 19772 - 8th St. E, Sonoma, CA, 95476.

WOODBRIDGE, LINDA
PERSONAL Born 03/23/1945, Chelsea, MA, m, 1994, 2 children **DISCIPLINE** LITERATURE **EDUCATION** Univ Calif, LA, PhD, 70. **CAREER** Asst prof, 70-76, assoc prof, 76-82, prof, 82-97, dept chmn, 86-89, Univ Alberta; prof, 94-, Penn St Univ. **RESEARCH** Women and the English Renaissance; magical thinking; poverty and vagrancy. **CONTACT ADDRESS** Dept of English, Pennsylvania State Univ, University Park, PA, 16803. **EMAIL** LXW18@psu.edu

WOODELL, HAROLD
DISCIPLINE ENGLISH LITERATURE **EDUCATION** Univ UC, PhD, 74. **CAREER** Dept Eng, Clemson Univ **RESEARCH** American literature; Southern literature. **SELECTED PUBLICATIONS** Auth, All the King's Men: The Search for a Usable Past, 93; Archibald Rutledge, A Literary Map of South Carolina. **CONTACT ADDRESS** Clemson Univ, 811 Strode, Clemson, SC, 29634. **EMAIL** wcharle@clemson.edu

WOODMANSEE, MARTHA
DISCIPLINE LITERARY THEORY **EDUCATION** Northwestern Univ, BA; Stanford Univ, MA, PhD. **CAREER** English, Case Western Reserve Univ. **SELECTED PUBLICATIONS** Auth or ed, The Author, Art and the Market: Rereading the History of Aesthetics; The Construction of Authorship: Textual Appropriation in Law and Literature; Erkennen und Deuten: Essays sur Literature und Literaturtheorie. **CONTACT ADDRESS** Case Western Reserve Univ, 10900 Euclid Ave, Cleveland, OH, 44106.

WOODRESS, JAMES
PERSONAL Born 07/07/1916, Webster Groves, MO, m, 1940 **DISCIPLINE** AMERICAN LITERATURE **EDUCATION** Amherst Col, AB, 38; NY Univ, AM, 43; Duke Univ, PhD, 50. **CAREER** Asst news ed, Sta KWK, St Louis, Mo, 38-40; radio writer, United Press Asn, NYC, 40-43; asst, Duke Univ, 47-49, vis lectr & res assoc, 54-55; instr English, Grinnell Col, 49-50; from asst prof to assoc prof, Butler Univ, 50-58; from assoc to prof, San Fernando Valley State Col, 58-66, chmn dept, 58-63, dean sch lett & sci, 63-65; chmn dept, 70-74, PROF ENGLISH, UNIV CALIF, DAVIS, 66-, Fund Advan Educ fel, 52-53; Guggenheim fel, 56-57; secy, Am lit group, MLA, 61-65; Fulbright lectr, France, 62-63, Italy, 65-66; vis prof, Univ Paris, 74-75 & 83. **MEMBERSHIPS** MLA; AAUP **RESEARCH** American civilization. **SELECTED PUBLICATIONS** Auth, Howells in the 1890s, Social Critic for All Seasons, Amer Lit Realism 1870-1910, Vol 0025, 93. **CONTACT ADDRESS** Dept of English, Univ of Calif, Davis, CA, 95616.

WOODRING, CARL
PERSONAL Born 08/29/1919, Terrell, TX, m, 1942 **DISCIPLINE** ENGLISH LITERATURE **EDUCATION** Rice Inst, AB, 40, AM, 42; Harvard Univ, AM, 47, PhD, 49. **CAREER** Asst, Rice Inst & Harvard Univ; from instr English to prof English lit, Univ Wis, 48-61; prof, 61-76, GEORGE EDWARD WOODBERRY PROF OF LIT, COLUMBIA UNIV, 76-, Fels, Fund Avan Educ & Guggenheim Found, 55, Am Coun Learned Soc, 65. **HONORS AND AWARDS** Christian Gauss Prize, Nat Phi Beta Kappa, 71; Vis Scholar, Phi Beta Kappa, 74-75. **MEMBERSHIPS** MLA; Int Asn Univ Prof English; Asn Depts English (pres, 71); Keats-Shelley Asn Am; Acad Lit Studies. **RESEARCH** Nineteenth century English literature. **SELECTED PUBLICATIONS** Auth, Cruikshank, George Life, Times, and Art, Vol 1, 1792-1835, Wordsworth Circle, Vol 0025, 94; The Planters of the English Landscape Garden, Amer Hist Rev, Vol 0100, 95; The English Garden, Amer Hist Rev, Vol 0100, 95; Radical Satire and Print Culture 1790-1822, Wordsworth Circle, Vol 0026, 95; Talking Coleridge, Wordsworth Circle, Vol 0027, 96; Shelley, Keats-Shelley J, Vol 0046, 97. **CONTACT ADDRESS** Dept of English & Comp Lit, Columbia Univ, New York, NY, 10027.

WOODS, ALAN LAMBERT
PERSONAL Born 11/23/1942, Philadelphia, PA, m, 1967, 1 child **DISCIPLINE** THEATRE HISTORY **EDUCATION** Columbia Univ, AB, 64; Univ Southern Calif, MA, 69, PhD(theatre), 72. **CAREER** Lectr drama, Univ Southern Calif, 68-71; instr theatre, Long Beach City Col, 71-72; asst prof to assoc prof Theatre, Ohio State Univ, 72-, Lectr theatre, Calif State Univ, Los Angeles, 70; ed, Theatre Studies, 72-77; coordr res

panel Comt Instnl Coop, 73-; lectr, Am Asn Health, Phys Educ & Recreation, 74; co-ed, Educ Theatre J, Univ Col Theatre Asn, 78-80; mem, res comn Am Theatre Asn, 78 & exec comt, Am Soc Theatre Res, 76-78, 89-92; visiting prof, Ind Univ, 78-79; dir, Lawrence and Lee Theatre Res Inst, 79-; pres, Ohio Theatre Alliance, 90-91. **HONORS AND AWARDS** Fel, Col of the Am Theatre, 96. **MEMBERSHIPS** Am Theatre Asn; Am Soc Theatre Res. **RESEARCH** Ancient theatre; 19th century popular theatre; theatre historiography. **SELECTED PUBLICATIONS** Coauth, A note on the symmetry of Delphi, Theatre Surv, 5/72; auth, Popular theatre in Los Angeles, Players, 5/73; A quantification approach to popular American theatre, Res in Educ, 1/74; James J Corbett, theatrical star, J Sports Hist, 76; Theatre historiography, Ohio Speech J, 76; Reconstructions of performances, Copenhagen, Royal Libr, 76; Frederick B Warde, tragedian, Educ Theatre J, 77; The Ohio Theatre, 80; Selected Plays of Jerome Lawrence and Robert E. Lee, Ohio State Univ Press, 95. **CONTACT ADDRESS** Dept of Theatre, Ohio State Univ, 1806 Cannon Dr, Columbus, OH, 43210-1230. **EMAIL** woods1@osu.edu

WOODS, DAVID L.
PERSONAL Born 07/23/1932, San Jose, CA, m, 1998, 5 children **DISCIPLINE** COMMUNICATION **CAREER** Marshall Univ, 97-98; Shepherd College, 94-95; Univ Virginia, 67-83; George Washington Univ, 65-82, 86-88; spec Asst Chf Naval Material, Dir Naval sci tech info, 65 to 93-, US Navy Civl; Univ Maryland, 59-67; Aerospace Elec Firms, 59-65, US Navy; Ohio State Univ, 56-59; Lehigh Univ, 55-56; 54-55, Stanford Univ; Also Current, K-12 Sub Teacher, Berkeley, Jefferson Cnty Pub Schls. **HONORS AND AWARDS** Navy Superior Civl Ser Medal; ROA Ntl Pres; United Way Honor TS E Dole., Republican Candidate for WV House of Delegates. **MEMBERSHIPS** NCA; AFCEA; VSNI; SHT; NAFE; NRA; NERA; APCWS. **RESEARCH** Military signals and signal systems; Mass media and society; Early broadcasting; Radio drama; Broadway musicals. **SELECTED PUBLICATIONS** Auth, A History of Tactical Communication Techniques, Arno Press; Signaling and Communications at Sea, Arno Press; The Development of Visual Signals on Land or Sea; US Navy Speakers Guide; Outstanding Navy Speeches; Quotable Navy Quotes. **CONTACT ADDRESS** RR #1, Box 161, Middleway, WV, 25430-9726. **EMAIL** dwoods7807@aol.com

WOODS, JEANNIE MARLIN
PERSONAL Born 10/06/1947, Shreveport, LA, m, 1973 **DISCIPLINE** THEATER **EDUCATION** Univ Idaho, BA, 70; Hunter College, MA, 87; CUNY, MPh, 88, PhD, 89. **CAREER** Artistic Dir, Asst Prof, Assoc Prof, 89 to 95-, Winthrop Univ. **HONORS AND AWARDS** Fulbright Sch; Outstanding Jr Prof; Diss Fel. **MEMBERSHIPS** ATHE; STA. **RESEARCH** The realist process of the stage dir; Connections between Asian and Western theater in performance. **SELECTED PUBLICATIONS** Auth, Theater to Change Men's Souls, the Artistry of Adrian Hall, Univ Delaware Press, 93; Maureen Stapleton: A Bio-Bibliography, Westport CT, Greenwood Press, 92; Sex Clothing Popularity Whatever!, Congreve's World for a Clueless Audience, Assoc Theater in Higher Edu, TX, 98; stage directing: The Fantasticks, Blowing Rock Stage Co, 98; The Way of the World, by Congreve, Winthrop U, 97; Fiddler on the Roof, Fort Mill SC Comm Theater, 97; On the Verge, by Eric Overmyer, charlotte NC, 97; The Complete Works of Wllm Shakespeare, abridged, by Adam Long, Daniel Singer, Jeff Borgeson, SCAC Tour, 97, 98; As You Like It, by Wm Shakespeare, Winthrop Univ, 96; The Sea, by Edward Bond, Winthrop Univ, 95. **CONTACT ADDRESS** Dept of Theater and Dance, Winthrop Univ, 115 Johnson Hall, Rock Hill, SC, 29733. **EMAIL** woodsj@winthrop.edu

WOODS, ROBIN
DISCIPLINE ROMANTIC LITERATURE, VICTORIAN LITERATURE, NARRATIVE, CRIME LITERATURE, COM **EDUCATION** Univ CA, Berkeley, BA, PhD. **CAREER** Assoc prof, Ripon Col. **RESEARCH** The lit of murder and crime. **SELECTED PUBLICATIONS** Auth, The Emergence of the Detective, in The Cunning Craft: Original Essays on Detective Fiction and Contemporary Literary Theory. **CONTACT ADDRESS** Ripon Col, Ripon, WI. **EMAIL** WoodsR@mac.ripon.edu

WOODS, WILLIAM FORRESTERE
PERSONAL Born 02/03/1942, Syracuse, NY, m, 1967, 2 children **DISCIPLINE** RHETORIC, COMPOSITION **EDUCATION** Dartmouth Col, BA, 64; Univ Chicago, MA, 67; Ind Univ, PhD(English), 75. **CAREER** Instr, Cleveland State Univ, 67-69; asst prof, 75-80, ASSOC PROF ENGLISH, WICHITA STATE UNIV, 80-. **MEMBERSHIPS** MLA; NCTE **RESEARCH** Medieval literature; 19th and 20th century history of composition teaching; Middle English narrative poetry. **SELECTED PUBLICATIONS** Auth, Private and Public Space in the 'Millers Tale' + Merging Metaphors of Personal, Domestic, and Societal Domains in the Concentric Narrative Movement of the 'Canterbury Tales' by Chaucer, Geoffrey, Chaucer Rev, Vol 0029, 94; The Logic of Deprivation in the 'Reeves Tale' + Chaucer, Geoffrey, Chaucer Review, Vol 0030, 95; Society and Nature in the 'Cooks Tale', Papers on Lang and Lit, Vol 0032, 96. **CONTACT ADDRESS** Dept English, Wichita State Univ, Wichita, KS, 67208.

WOODS, WILLIE G.
PERSONAL Yazoo City, MS, s **DISCIPLINE** ENGLISH **EDUCATION** Shaw Univ Raleigh NC, BA Ed 1965; Duke Univ Durham NC, MEd 1968; Temple Univ PA, PA State Univ, NY Univ, attended; Indiana University of Pennsylvania, Indiana, PA, PhD English, 1995. **CAREER** Berry O'Kelly School, language arts teacher 1965-67; Preston School, 5th grade teacher 1967-69, adult ed teacher 1968-69; HARRISBURG AREA COMM COLL, PROF ENGLISH/ed 1969-, dir acad found prog, 1983-87, asst dean of Academic Foundations and Basic Education Division, 1987-89, asst dean of Social Science, Public Services, and Basic Education Division, 1989-92. **HONORS AND AWARDS** Cert of Merit for Community Serv Harrisburg 1971; Meritorious Faculty Contrib Harrisburg 1977; Outstanding Serv Awd PA Black Conf on Higher Ed 1980; Central Reg Awd for Serv PA Black Conf on Higher Ed 1982; Alpha Kappa Alpha Sor Outstanding Comm Serv Awd Harrisburg 1983; YMCA Youth Urban Serv Volunteer of the Year Awd 1983; Alpha Kappa Alpha Sor Basileus' Awd for Excellence as Comm Chair 1985; Administrative Staff Merit Award, Harrisburg Area Comm College, 1986; Outstanding Service Award, Black StudentUnion at Harrisburg Area Comm College, 1989; tribute for outstanding contributions to Harrisburg Area Comm College and to comm-at-large, HACC Minority Caucus, 1989; Alpha Kappa Mu Natl Hon Soc; Brooks Dickens Mem Award in Education. **MEMBERSHIPS** Bd of mgrs Camp Curtin Branch of Harrisburg YMCA 1971-79; rep council 1972-, sec 1977-79, assoc ed 1981-, PA Black Conf on Higher Ed; exec bd 1978-, council chairperson 1981-82, Western Reg Act 101 Dir Council; bd of dir Alternative Rehab Comm Inc 1978-; bd of dir 1979-, charter mem sec 1981-82, treas 1982-83, PA Assoc of Devel Ed; bd of dir 1981-, sec 1984-85, Dauphin Residences Inc; bd of advisors 1981-, chairperson, acting chairperson, bd sec Youth Urban Serv Harrisburg YMCA; inst rep Natl Council on Black Amer Affairs of the Amer Assoc of Comm & Jr Coll 1983-. **CONTACT ADDRESS** Acting Vice President, Faculty and Instruction, Harrisburg Area Comm Col, One HACC Dr, Harrisburg, PA, 17110-2999.

WOODSON, THOMAS
PERSONAL Born 04/24/1931, Hartford, CT, m, 3 children **DISCIPLINE** ENGLISH, AMERICAN LITERATURE **EDUCATION** Yale Univ, BA, 53; MA, 56, PhD(English), 63. **CAREER** Instr English, Williams Col, 59-62; asst instr, Yale Univ, 62-63; from asst prof to assoc prof, 63-74, chmn comp lit, 74-78, PROF ENGLISH, OHIO STATE UNIV, 74-, Fulbright lectr, Univ Pau, France, 68-69; vis assoc prof English & Am studies, Yale Univ, 69-70. **MEMBERSHIPS** MLA; Hawthorne Soc; Thoreau Soc. **RESEARCH** American fiction and Renaissance; style and stylistics. **SELECTED PUBLICATIONS** Auth, In Respect to Egotism, Amer Lit, Vol 0064, 92; Beyond the Classroom, Cithara Essays in the Judeochristian Tradition, Vol 0036, 96. **CONTACT ADDRESS** Dept of English, Ohio State Univ, Columbus, OH, 43210.

WOODWARD, CAROLYN
DISCIPLINE THEORY, 18TH-CENTURY BRITISH LITERATURE, AND FEMINIST STUDIES **EDUCATION** Univ Wash, PhD, 87. **CAREER** Instr, Univ NMex, 87-. **RESEARCH** 18th-century cultural deviance and experimental fiction. **SELECTED PUBLICATIONS** Auth, 'My Heart S o Wrapt': Lesbian Disruptions in 18th-Century British Literature, Signs, 93; Who Wrote The Cry: a Fable for Our Times, 18th-Century Fiction, 96. **CONTACT ADDRESS** Univ NMex, Albuquerque, NM, 87131.

WOODWARD, PAULINE
DISCIPLINE ENGLISH LANGUAGE AND LITERATURE **EDUCATION** Boston Univ, AB; Univ Hartford, MA; Tufts Univ, PhD. **CAREER** Eng Dept, Endicott Col **RESEARCH** 20th century traditions in Am Lit, concentrating on the works of Asian Am, Native Am, black Am, and Chicanos. **SELECTED PUBLICATIONS** Auth, study of Louise Erdich's fiction in American Writers: Supplement IV, Scribner's/Macmillan. **CONTACT ADDRESS** Endicott Col, 376 Hale St, Beverly, MA, 01915.

WOOLF, LEONARD
PERSONAL Born 03/27/1916, Baltimore, MD, m, 1944, 1 child **DISCIPLINE** ENGLISH **EDUCATION** Johns Hopkins Univ, BS, 52; Univ Md, MEd, 51, DEd, 59. **CAREER** Chmn dept English, Jr High Sch, Md, 50-54; teacher, Baltimore Polytech Inst, 54-56; English specialist, Baltimore City Pub Schs, 56-63; supvr English, Anne Arundel County Publ Schs, 63-66; assoc prof sec educ & coordr English Educ, 66-73, prof English, 73-80, EMER PROF SEC EDUC, UNIV MD, COLLEGE PARK, 80-, Consult, English for foreign internes, Church Home & Hosp, 60-61; consult, US Off Educ, 65- **HONORS AND AWARDS** Distinguished Service Award, Phi Delta Kappa, 72 & Md Coun Teachers English, 73. **RESEARCH** Secondary education; reading, especially literature for slow learner. **SELECTED PUBLICATIONS** Auth, Conrad, Joseph Vision + From the Monks House Papers of Woolf, Leonard, Engl Lit in Transition 1880-1920, Vol 0036, 93; Alive or Dead, Hunting the Highbrow, Cambridge Quart, Vol 0024, 95. **CONTACT ADDRESS** Col of Educ, Univ of Md, College Park, MD, 20742.

WOOLLEY, JAMES
PERSONAL Born 07/19/1944, Shelbyville, KY, m, 1970 **DISCIPLINE** ENGLISH **EDUCATION** Wake Forest Univ, BA, 66; Univ Chicago, MA, 67, PhD, 72. **CAREER** From instr to asst prof English, Marquette Univ, 71-74; asst prof English, Univ Pa, 74-80; from asst prof English to Frank Lee and Edna M Smith prof English, 80-; head, dept English, 93-97, clerk of fac, 97-, Lafayette Col; Am Coun Learned Socs res fel, 77. **HONORS AND AWARDS** Summer fac fel, 75; sum res fel, 83; Jones Fac lectr, 90; Jones Award for Tchg and Scholarship, 91; Student Government Award for Superior Tchg, 94; Lindback Found Award for Distinguished Tchg, 95. **MEMBERSHIPS** MLA; Am Soc 18th Century Studies; Bibliog Soc; AAUP; Asn for Computers and the Hum; Asn for Documentary Ed; Br Soc for Eighteenth Century Stud; Eighteenth-Century Ireland Soc; Soc for Textual Scholarship; Soc for the Hist of Authorship, reading, and Publ. **RESEARCH** Eighteenth-century British and Irish literature and social history; bibliography; satire. **SELECTED PUBLICATIONS** Co-ed and contribur, Swift and His Contexts, AMS, 89; ed, The Intelligencer by Jonathan Swift and Thomas Sheridan, Oxford, 92; auth, "The Canon of Swift's Poems: The Case of An Apology to the Lady Carteret," in Reading Swift, Wilhelm Fink, 93; auth, Annotation: Some Guiding Considerations, East-Central Intelligencer, 94; coauth, The Full Text of Swift's On Poetry: A Rapsody, Swift Stud, 94; auth, "Sarah Harding as Swift's Printer," in Walking Naboth's Vineyard: New Studies of Swift, Notre Dame, 95; auth, "Writing Libels on the Germans: Swift's Wicked Treasonable Libel," in Swift: The Enigmatic Dean, Stauffenburg, 98. **CONTACT ADDRESS** Dept of English, Lafayette Col, Easton, PA, 18042-1781. **EMAIL** woolleyj@lafayette.edu

WORK, JAMES
DISCIPLINE ENGLISH LITERATURE **EDUCATION** Colo State Univ, BA, MA; Univ NMex, PhD. **CAREER** Prof. **HONORS AND AWARDS** Excellence Tchg Awd, 92. **MEMBERSHIPS** Western Lit Asn; MLA. **RESEARCH** Western American literature. **SELECTED PUBLICATIONS** Auth, Following Where the River Begins; ed, Prose and Poetry of the American West. **CONTACT ADDRESS** Dept of English, Colorado State Univ, Fort Collins, CO, 80523. **EMAIL** services@colostate.edu

WORTH, FABIENNE ANDRE
PERSONAL Born 05/24/1944, Lyon, France, m, 1967, 2 children **DISCIPLINE** FRENCH LITERATURE, CINEMA **EDUCATION** Univ NC, Chapel Hill, BA, 70, MA, 73, PhD(comp lit), 79. **CAREER** Vis lectr, 78-79, VIS LECTR FRENCH LIT, DUKE UNIV, 80-, Instr, French Cinema Arts Sch, Carrboro, NC, 80. **MEMBERSHIPS** MLA; Am Asn Teachers Fr; Am Comp Lit Asn. **RESEARCH** History and the novel; authorship in the cinema. **SELECTED PUBLICATIONS** Auth, Le Sacre Et Le Sida--Representations of Sexuality and Their Contradictions in France, 1971-1996, a Perspective from Across the Atlantic, Temps Modernes, Vol 0052, 97. **CONTACT ADDRESS** 209 Pritchard Ave, Chapel Hill, NC, 27514.

WORTH, GEORGE JOHN
PERSONAL Born 06/11/1929, Vienna, Austria, m, 1951, 2 children **DISCIPLINE** ENGLISH **EDUCATION** Univ Chicago, AB, 48, AM, 51; Univ Ill, PhD(English), 54. **CAREER** Instr English, Univ Ill, 54-55; from instr to assoc prof, 55-65, from asst chmn dept to assoc chmn dept, 61-63, chmn dept, 63-79, PROF ENGLISH, UNIV KANS, 65-, Am Philos Soc grant, 62. **MEMBERSHIPS** Midwest Mod Lang Asn: MLA; Int Asn Univ Prof English; Dickens Soc. **RESEARCH** Victorian fiction. **SELECTED PUBLICATIONS** Auth, Dickens on Literature, Dickens Quart, Vol 0009, 92; The Dickens Aesthetic, Dickens Quart, Vol 0009, 92; The Companion to 'Oliver Twist', Dickens Quart, Vol 0010, 93; Dickens, Charles and the Image of Woman, Dickens Quart, Vol 0011, 94; Life as History, J Engl and Ger Philol, Vol 0094, 95; Stephen, Leslie Life in Letters, a Bibliographical Study, 19th Century Prose, Vol 0022, 95; Muscular Christianity, Embodying the Victorian Age, 19th Century Prose, Vol 0023, 96; Oliphant, Margaret, J Engl and Ger Philol, Vol 0096, 97; Dickens, Charles, Dickens Quart, Vol 0014, 97, **CONTACT ADDRESS** Dept of English, Univ Kans, Lawrence, KS, 66045.

WORTHAM, THOMAS
PERSONAL Born 12/05/1943, Liberal, KS **DISCIPLINE** ENGLISH **EDUCATION** Marquette Univ, AB, 65; IN Univ, PhD (English), 70. **CAREER** Asst prof, 70-76, assoc prof, 76-82, PROF ENGLISH, UNIV CA, LOS ANGELES, 82-, vice chair, dir of Undergrad Studies, 92-97, CHAIR, 97-; Fulbright lect, Univ Warsaw, Poland, 76-77; Ed, Nineteenth-Century Lit, 83-; member, ed bd, The Collected Works of Ralph Waldo Emerson, Harvard Univ Press, 96-. **HONORS AND AWARDS** Regent's Faculty Fel in the Humanities, Univ CA, 71; Grants-in-Aid of Res, Am Philos Soc, 76, 81; Sr fel, Am Coun of Learned Socs, 83-84; travel grants, NEH, 85-86, 88-89. **MEMBERSHIPS** MLA; Asn for Documentary Editing; Soc for Textual Scholarship; Int Asn of Univ Profs of English. **RESEARCH** 19th-Centrury Am lit and culture; textual scholarship and criticism. **SELECTED PUBLICATIONS** Auth, Co-compiler, Am Literary Manuscripts, 2nd ed, Univ GA Press, 77; James Russell Lowell's The Bigelow Papers (first series): A

Critical Edition, Northern IL Univ Press, 77; Letters of W. D. Howells: 1892-1901, Twayne, 81; The Early Prose Writings of William Dean Howells, OH Univ Press, 90; ed, My Mark Twain by W. D. Howells, Dover, 97; ed, Mark Twain's Some Chapters from My Autobiography, Dover, 99; ed, The Poems of Ralph Waldo Emerson, Harvard Univ Press, forthcoming. **CONTACT ADDRESS** Dept of English, Univ of California, Los Angeles, Box 951530, Los Angeles, CA, 90095-1530. **EMAIL** wortham@humnet.ucla.edu

WORTMAN, WILLIAM A.
PERSONAL Born 09/19/1940, Council Bluffs, IA, m, 1966, 2 children **DISCIPLINE** ENGLISH **EDUCATION** Wesleyan Univ, BA, 62; Univ Neb, MA, 65; Case West Res Univ, PhD, 72; Columbia Univ, MS, 75. **CAREER** Hum librn, Miami Univ, 75-. **HONORS AND AWARDS** Beta Phi Mu. **MEMBERSHIPS** Prof Lib Asn; Mod Lib Asn; Soc for the Hist of Authorship, Reading, and Publishing. **RESEARCH** Hist of printing and publishing, lib collections and info services. **SELECTED PUBLICATIONS** Auth, Collection Management: Background and Principles, 89; auth, Collection Management, 93; auth, A Guide to Serial Bibliographies for the Modern Literatures, 95. **CONTACT ADDRESS** 4879 Somerville Rd, Oxford, OH, 45056. **EMAIL** wortmawa@muohio.edu

WRIGHT, DEBORAH KEMPF
PERSONAL Born 03/10/1949, South Bend, IN, m, 1975 **DISCIPLINE** ENGLISH LITERATURE **EDUCATION** Univ Evansville, BA, 71; Miami Univ, MA, 73, PhD(English), 80. **CAREER** Grad asst res, 71-72, grad asst English, 72-teaching fel, 73-76, diss fel, 76-77, instr, 77, ASST PROF ENGLISH, MIAMI UNIV, 80-, Fel, William Andrews Clark Mem Libr, Univ Calif, Los Angeles, 82. **MEMBERSHIPS** Col English Asn; Johnson Soc Cent Region; Midwest Branch Am Soc 18th Century Studies; Midwest Mod Lang Asn; MLA. **RESEARCH** Matthew Prior, 18th century English poet and diplomatist; Robert Sidney, Earl of Leicester, English Renaissance poet. **SELECTED PUBLICATIONS** Auth, An Autobiographical Ballad by Prior, Matthew, Brit Libr J, Vol 0018, 92. **CONTACT ADDRESS** 1033 Cedar Dr, Oxford, OH, 45056.

WRIGHT, GEORGE THADDEUS
PERSONAL Born 12/17/1925, Staten Island, NY, m, 1955 **DISCIPLINE** ENGLISH **EDUCATION** Columbia Univ, AB, 46, MA, 47; Univ Calif, Berkeley, PhD, 57. **CAREER** Lectr English, Univ Calif, Berkeley, 56-67; vis asst prof, NMex Highlands Univ, summer 57; instr, Univ Ky, 57-59, asst prof, 59-60; asst prof, San Francisco State Col, 60-61; assoc prof, Univ Tenn, 61-68; chmn dept, 74-77, prof English, Univ Minn, Minneapolis, 68-89, Regents prof, 89-93, EMERITUS 93-. **HONORS AND AWARDS** Fulbright lectr Am lit, Univ Aix-Marseille, 64-66, Univ Thessaloniki, Greece, 77-78; ed, Univ Minn pamphlets on Am writers, 68-; NEH grant, summer 81; NEH fel, 84-85; Guggenheim fel, 82, William Riley Parker Prize, MLA, 74 & 81. **MEMBERSHIPS** MLA; Shakespeare Asn **RESEARCH** English and American poetry; modernist lit; Shakespeare. **SELECTED PUBLICATIONS** Auth, Sustained Stages and States: T S Eliot's Peculiar Personae in: T S Eliot Annual, 90; Voices that Figure in Four Quartets, in the Placing of T S Eliot, Univ Missouri, 91; An Almost Oral Art: Shakespeare's Language on Stage and Page, Shakespeare Quart, 92; Blank Verse in the Jacobean Theater: Language that Vanishes, Language that Keeps, in: The Elizabethan Theatre XII, 93; cont, New Princeton Encyclopedia of Poetry and Poetics, 93; Troubles of a Professional Meter Reader, in: Shakespeare Rered, Cornell Univ, 94; Hearing the Measures, Style, 97. **CONTACT ADDRESS** 2617 West Crown King Dr, Tucson, AZ, 85741. **EMAIL** twright@u.arizona.edu

WRIGHT, H. BUNKER
PERSONAL Born 03/26/1907, Woodstock, IL, m, 1931, 1 child **DISCIPLINE** ENGLISH LITERATURE **EDUCATION** Northwestern Univ, BS, 30; AM, 31, PhD, 37. **CAREER** Asst English, Northwestern Univ, 31-35, instr, 35-38; from instr to prof, 38-74, chmn dept, 56-59, dean grad sch, 59-69, EMER PROF ENGLISH, MIAMI UNIV, 74-, Lectr, Univ Cincinnati, 39-55; chmn Midwest Conf Grad Studies & Res, 65-66; ed, Prior Proj, 74-; fel, Huntington Libr, 82. **MEMBERSHIPS** MLA; Midwest Mod Lang Asn; Am Soc 18th Century Studies; Midwest Am Soc 18th Century Studies; Johnson Soc Cent Region. **RESEARCH** English literature and history of the 17th and 18th centuries; unpublished correspondence, literary and diplomatic; Matthew Prior. **SELECTED PUBLICATIONS** Auth, An Autobiographical Ballad by Prior,Matthew, Brit Lib Jour, Vol 0018, 92. **CONTACT ADDRESS** 1033 Cedar Dr, Oxford, OH, 45056.

WRIGHT, ROOSEVELT R., JR.
PERSONAL Born 07/24/1943, Elizabeth City, North Carolina, s **DISCIPLINE** COMMUNICATIONS **EDUCATION** Elizabeth City State Univ, BS 1964; North Carolina Central Univ, MA 1969; Virginia State University, CGS, 1970; Syracuse Univ, PhD 1992. **CAREER** SI Newhouse School of Comm, assoc prof, radio/TV, 1975-; NBC Radio Div WRC/WKYS Washington, acc exec 1974-75; Howard Univ Washington, DC, adj prof radio TV 1974-75; WTNJ Radio Trenton, NJ, gen manager 1973-74; North Carolina Central Univ, asst prof ed media 1972-73; WDNC-AM/FM Durham, NC, announcer radio engr 1972-73; Elizabeth City State Univ, asso dir ed media 1968-69; DC State Coll Dover, dir ed media 1969-70; WNDR Radio Syracuse, announcer radio engr 1970-72; WLLE Radio Raleigh, NC, program dir 1973-74; WOLF Radio Syracuse, NY, chief engineer 1980-84. **HONORS AND AWARDS** Soldier of the Quarter 32AADC AUS 1967; Doctoral Flwsp Syracuse Univ 1970-72; Men's Day Awd Mt Lebanon AMEZ Ch Eliz City 1974, 1997; Upward Bound Prog Awd LeMoyne Coll Syracuse 1977; Ed Media & Speaker Awd NC Ed Media Assn 1977; Natl Council of Negro Women Communications Awd 1984, 1994; Syracuse Univ Pan Hellenic Council Awd 1986, 1987, 1989, 1990; Outstanding Mass Media Teacher Awd 1987-91; Naval Achievement Medal 1987, 1997; Keynote Speaker Awd, NAACP Jefferson Co Chapter, Watertown, NY 1989; Comm Serv Awd, Syracuse Univ 1988; consulting editor, "Cobblestone Magazine, History of Radio", 1988; Naval Commendation Medal, 1992, 1993, 1995; US Navy Campus Liaison Officer of the Year, 1992. **MEMBERSHIPS** Historian Chi Pi Chap Omega Psi Phi Frat 1975-95; radio com mem Natl Assn of Educ Broadcasters 1976-80; adv Natl Acad of TV Arts & Scis Syracuse Chpt 1976-80; public affairs officer natl naval Officers Assoc 1983-85; chmn communications comm Amer Heart Assoc New York 1985-87; CEO WJPZ-FM Syracuse NY; US naval liaison officer, Syracuse Univ, 1981-; steward AME Zion Church; public affairs officer, US Navy, Great Lakes Cruise 1985-; mem communications comm, United Way of Onondaga County 1988-; bd mem Hiawatha Council Boy Scout of America, 1992-. **CONTACT ADDRESS** Schl of Publ Comms, Syracuse Univ, Syracuse, NY, 13244-0003. **EMAIL** rrwright@mailbox.syr.edu

WRIGHT, STEPHEN CALDWELL
PERSONAL Born 11/11/1946, Sanford, Florida, s **DISCIPLINE** ENGLISH **EDUCATION** St Petersbury Jr Coll, AA, 1967; FL Atlantic Univ, BA, 1969; Atlanta Univ, MA, 1972; Indiana Univ of Pennslyvania, PhD, 1983. **CAREER** Seminole County School Bd, teacher, 1969-70; Seminole Comm Coll, professor, 1972-. **HONORS AND AWARDS** Morgan State Univ, Distinguished Authors Series Award, 1998; Illinois Poet Laureate, Illinois Salutes Award, 1992; Gwendolyn Brooks Poetry Prize, 1984; Univ of South FL, First Superior Poet Award, 1969. **MEMBERSHIPS** Zora Festival of Arts & Humanities, national planning comm, 1989-99; Boys & Girls Club, chair, advisory council, 1993-96; Gwendolyn Brooks Writers Assn of FL, founder & pres, 1987-; Revelry Poetry Journal, editor, 1987-; Florida Div of Cultural Affairs Literary Organizations Panel, panelist, 1996-98. **SELECTED PUBLICATIONS** First Statement, poetry collection, 1983; Poems In Movement, poetry collection, 1984; Making Symphony: New & Selected Poems, 1987; "Pearl," New Visions: Fiction by Florida Writers, 1989; Inheritance, poetry collection, 1992; Editor "On Gwendolyn Brooks: Reliant Contemplation," 1995. **CONTACT ADDRESS** Prof, English Dept, Seminole Community Coll, 100 Weldon Blvd, Sanford, FL, 32773.

WRIGHT, TERRENCE C.
DISCIPLINE PHENOMENOLOGY AND CONTEMPORARY PHILOSOPHIES OF LITERATURE AND AESTHETICS **EDUCATION** St Vincent Col, BA; Villanova Univ, MA; Bryn Mawr Col, PhD. **CAREER** Fac, Mt Saint Mary's Col, 89-. **RESEARCH** Theories of interpretation in art and literature and the nature of poetic expression. **SELECTED PUBLICATIONS** Publ on, relationship between poetry and philos. **CONTACT ADDRESS** Dept of Philosophy, Mount Saint Mary's Col, 16300 Old Emmitsburg Rd, Emmitsburg, MD, 21727-7799. **EMAIL** wright@msmary.edu

WRIGHT, THOMAS L.
PERSONAL Born 12/19/1925, Hattiesburg, MS **DISCIPLINE** MEDIEVAL LITERATURE **EDUCATION** Tulane Univ, BA, 49, MA, 51, PhD, 60. **CAREER** Asst prof English, Auburn Univ, 60-61; assoc prof, Tex Christian Univ, 62-64; assoc prof, 64-75, PROF ENGLISH, AUBURN UNIV, 64-. **MEMBERSHIPS** Mediaeval Acad Am; MLA; Int Arthurian Soc. **RESEARCH** Arthurian romance; Chaucer. **SELECTED PUBLICATIONS** Auth, The Life of Chaucer,Geoffrey--A Critical Biography, So Hum Rev, Vol 0028, 94; Chaucer,Geoffrey, So Hum Rev, Vol 0028, 94. **CONTACT ADDRESS** Dept of English, Auburn Univ, Auburn, AL, 36830.

WROBEL, ARTHUR
PERSONAL Born 07/14/1940, Jamaica, NY, 1 child **DISCIPLINE** AMERICAN AND ENGLISH LITERATURE **EDUCATION** Queens Col, NY, AB, 62; Univ NC, MA, 64, PhD(English), 68. **CAREER** Grad asst freshman compos, Univ NC, 64-68; asst prof, 68-75, ASSOC PROF AM LIT, UNIV KY, 75-, Ed, Am Notes & Queries. **MEMBERSHIPS** Am Lit Group; MLA; Popular Cult Asn. **RESEARCH** Nineteenth century American poetry and fiction. **SELECTED PUBLICATIONS** Auth, The Great Gatsby and Modern Times, Anq-Quart Jour of Short Articles Notes and Rev(s), Vol 0008, 95. **CONTACT ADDRESS** Dept of English, Univ Ky, 500 S Limestone St, Lexington, KY, 40506-0003.

WULFF, DONALD H.
PERSONAL Born 08/05/1944, Billings, MT, d, 2 children **DISCIPLINE** SPEECH COMMUNICATION **EDUCATION** Univ Mont, MA, 75; Univ Wash, PhD, 85. **CAREER** Instruct Develop Specialist, 85-88; asst dir, 99-92, assoc dir, Center for Instruct Develop and Res, Univ Wash Seattle, 92-. **HONORS AND AWARDS** Distinguished tchg Award, Univ Wash, 84; Univ Wash Tchg Acad, 98-. **MEMBERSHIPS** Nat Commun Asn; Prof Orgn Develop network; Am Asn for Higher Educ; Am Educ Res Asn. **RESEARCH** Teaching Effectiveness/Student Learning; The evelopment of graduate teaching assistants as Future professors. **SELECTED PUBLICATIONS** Auth, The Case of worrisome workload, Learning from students: Early term student feedback in higher education, 94; coauth, Working Effectively with Graduate Assistants, 96; Professional development for consultants at the University Washington's Center for Instructional Development and Research, Practically speaking: A sourcebook for instructional consultants in higher education, 97; Engaging students in learning in the communication classroom, forthcoming. **CONTACT ADDRESS** Center for Instructional Development and Research, Univ of Wash, Box 351725, Seattle, WA, 98195-1725. **EMAIL** wulff@cidr.washington.edu

WYATT, DAVID M.
PERSONAL Born 10/07/1948, Lynwood, CA, m, 1991, 3 children **DISCIPLINE** ENGLISH **EDUCATION** Yale Univ, BA 70; Univ Calif Berkeley, PhD 75. **CAREER** Univ Maryland, prof 89-, assoc prof 87-89; VA Found for Hum and Pub Policy, prog assoc, 82-87; Princeton Univ, vis prof, 84-85; Univ Virginia, asst prof, 75-82. **HONORS AND AWARDS** Outstanding SchTchr UMD. **RESEARCH** American West; 19th and 20th Century American Literature. **SELECTED PUBLICATIONS** Auth, Five Fires: Race and the Making of California, Addison-Wesley, 97; auth, Bret Harte, Oxford World's Classics, Oxford Univ Press, 95; auth, Out of the Sixties: Storytelling and the Vietnam Generation, Cambridge Univ Press, 93; East of Eden, PTCCS, Introduction Bibliography and Notes, 92; auth, New essays On Steinbeck's, The Grapes of Wrath, Cambridge Univ Press, 90. **CONTACT ADDRESS** Dept of English, Univ of Maryland, College Park, MD, 20742.

WYCZYNSKI, PAUL
PERSONAL Born 06/29/1921, Zelgoszcz, Poland **DISCIPLINE** LITERATURE **EDUCATION** Univ Lille, LL, 49, DES, 50; Univ Ottawa, PhD, 57. **CAREER** Dir-fondateur, Centre de recherche en litterature canadienne-francaise, 58-73, prof agrege 60-64, prof titulaire, 64-70, PROF TITULAIRE DE RECHERCHE, UNIV OTTAWA, 70-. **HONORS AND AWARDS** Prof de l'annee, Univ Ottawa, 68; DLitt(hon), Univ Laurentienne, 78; Killam res fel, 84; Prix Champlain, 86; DLitt(hon), Univ Guelph, 89; Ordre des francophones d'Amerique, 88; DL(hon), Univ Laval, 89; Chevalier de l'ordre des arts et des lettres de France, 90; off, Order Can, 93; DL(hon), Univ Kulv (Poland), 96. **MEMBERSHIPS** Royal Soc Can; Asn de litterature comparee; Soc des ecrivains canadiens-francais; Soc francaise d'histoire d'outre-mer; Inst polonias des arts et des sciences en Amerique du Nord; Asn Can Profs. **RESEARCH** French Canadian literature; Emile Nelligan; Francois-Xavier Garneau. **SELECTED PUBLICATIONS** Auth, Emile Nelligan: Sources et Originalite de son oeuvre, 60; auth, Poesie et Symbole, 65; auth, Francois-Xavier Garneau: Aspects litteraires de son oeuvre, 66; auth, Emile Nelligan, 67; auth, Francois-Xavier Garneau: Voyage en Angleterre et en France..., 68; auth, Nelligan et la Musique, 71; auth, Albert Laberge-Charles Gill, 71; auth, Bibliographie descriptive et critique d'Emile Nelligan, 73; auth, Francois-Xavier Garneau 1809-1866, 77; auth, 'La Scouine' d'Albert Laberge, 86; auth, Nelligan, biographie, 87; Ostatnie Dni Bohatera w Powstaniu Warszawskim, 96; Semper fidelis, 97; coauth, Dictionnaire pratique des auteurs quebecois, 76; coauth, Textes poetiques du Canada francais, 9 vols, 87-96; coauth, Poesies completes d'Emile Nelligan, 91; coauth; A Search for Knowledge and Freedom - A la recherche du savoir et de la liberte, 95. **CONTACT ADDRESS** Univ Ottawa, Ottawa, ON, K1N 6N5.

WYKE, CLEMENT HORATIO
PERSONAL Born 12/22/1934, Port-of-Spain, Trinidad, m, 1964, 2 children **DISCIPLINE** ENGLISH **EDUCATION** Univ Man, BA Hons, 63, MA & cert educ, 65; Univ Toronto, PhD(English), 70. **CAREER** Lectr English, Med Hat Col, Univ Calgary, 65-67; teaching asst, Univ Toronto, 68-70; sr instr lang & commun, Cambrian Col, 70-71; asst prof English 71-76, ASSOC PROF ENGLISH, UNIV WINNIPEG, 77-, Teaching fel, Govt Ont, Univ Toronto, 68-69 & 69-70. **MEMBERSHIPS** Asn Can Teachers English; Can Asn Commonwealth Lit & Lang Studies. **RESEARCH** Seventeenth century literature; Donne, Bunyan and Milton. **SELECTED PUBLICATIONS** Auth, Voice and Identity in Selvon,Sam Late Short-Fiction, Ariel-Rev Intl Eng Lit, Vol 0027, 96. **CONTACT ADDRESS** Univ of Winnipeg, 515 Portage Ave, Winnipeg, MB, R3B 2E9.

WYKES, DAVID
DISCIPLINE ENGLISH LITERATURE **EDUCATION** Univ VA, PhD, 72. **CAREER** Prof, Dartmouth Col. **RESEARCH** Brit lit. **SELECTED PUBLICATIONS** Auth, Cortazar's 'The Night Face Up' and the War of the Flower, Studies in Short Fic,

88; The Barbinade and the She-Tragedy: On John Banks's The Unhappy Favourite in Essays in Honor of Irvin Ehrenpreis, Univ Del P, 85; Orwell in the Trenches,Va Quart Rev, 83. **CONTACT ADDRESS** Dartmouth Col, 3529 N Main St, #207, Hanover, NH, 03755.

WYLDER, DELBERT E.
PERSONAL Born 10/05/1923, Jerseyville, IL, m, 1965, 2 children **DISCIPLINE** ENGLISH **EDUCATION** Univ Iowa, BA, 48, MFA, 50, PhD(English), 68. **CAREER** Asst prof English, Bemidji State Col, 68-69; prof lit, Southwest Minn State Univ, 69-77; PROF ENGLISH & CHMN DEPT, MURRAY STATE UNIV, 77-. **MEMBERSHIPS** MLA; AAUP; Western Lit Asn (pres, 67); Am Studies Asn; Asn Dept English. **RESEARCH** Ernest Hemingway; Western American literature; modern American literature. **SELECTED PUBLICATIONS** Auth, The Meadow, West Amer Lit, Vol 0028, 93; First Horses--Stories of the New West, West Amer Lit, Vol 0028, 94; End of a War, S Dakota Rev, Vol 0033, 95; Prologue to End of a War, S Dakota Rev, Vol 0033, 95; Angels and Others, West Amer Lit, Vol 0028, 93. **CONTACT ADDRESS** Dept of English, Murray State Univ, Murray, KY, 42071.

WYMAN, LINDA LEE
PERSONAL Born 04/01/1937, Rockford, IL **DISCIPLINE** ENGLISH LITERATURE **EDUCATION** Southern Methodist Univ, AB, 58; Univ MoColumbia, MA, 60; George Peabody Col, PhD(English), 71. **CAREER** Instr English, Western Ky Univ, 60-65; assoc prof, Motlow State Community Col, 71-74; assoc prof, 75-80, prof English, Lincoln Univ, 80-. **HONORS AND AWARDS** CASE Missouri Prof of the Year, 90; Governor's Award for Excellence in Teaching, 96; Dean's Award for Excellence in Teaching, 97. **MEMBERSHIPS** MLA; NCTE; Missouri Assoc of Teachers of English MATE, pres, 90; T S Eliot Soc, pres 98. **RESEARCH** T S Eliot's plays; modern poetry; the teaching of English. **SELECTED PUBLICATIONS** Auth, Concerning the relevance of Falconers (poem), 3/71, Anthologizing (poem), 5/73 & How plot and sub-plot unite in Marlowe's Faustus, 11/74, CEA Critic; CEA Forum; Murder in the Cathedral: The plot of diction, Mod Drama, 6/76; Poetry for those who need it and can't read it, Notes on Teaching English, 5/78; Common Liberation: The idea of salvation in T S Eliot's plays, Christianity & Lit, Summer 80; On Teaching Murder in the Cathedral, in Approaches to Teaching Eliot's Poetry and Plays, ed J Brooker, MLA, 88; Language as Plot in The Family Reunion, in The Placing of T S Eliot, ed, J Brooker, UMissouri P, 91. **CONTACT ADDRESS** Dept of English, Lincoln Univ, 820 Chestnut St, Jefferson City, MO, 65101-3500. **EMAIL** wymanl@lincolnu.edu

Y

YAHNKE, ROBERT EUGENE
PERSONAL Born 09/11/1947, Green Bay, WI, m, 1975 **DISCIPLINE** FILM, HUMANITIES, AND THE ARTS **EDUCATION** Univ WI-Madison, BA, 69, MA, 71, PhD, 75. **CAREER** Asst prof, 76-90, prof film, hum & arts, Gen Col, Univ MN, 90. **MEMBERSHIPS** Gerontological Soc Am; MN Gerontological Soc; Am Soc Aging. **RESEARCH** Tchg film and the arts to developmental students; hum and aging. **SELECTED PUBLICATIONS** Ed, A Time of Humanities: An Oral History Recollections of David H Stevens as Director of the Division of the Humanities, Rockefeller Foundation, 1930-1950, Wis Acad Sci, Arts & Lett, 76; The Great Circle of Life: A Resource Guide to Films and Videos on Aging, Wilkins & Wilkins, 88; co-auth (with Richard M Eastman), co-auth (with Richard M Eastman), Aging in Literature, ALA, 90; Literature and Gerontology: A Research Guide, Greenwood, 95. **CONTACT ADDRESS** Univ MN Gen Col, 254 Appleby Hall, 128 Pleasa, Minneapolis, MN, 55455-0434. **EMAIL** yahnk001@maroon.tc.umn.edu

YANCY, KATHLEEN BLAKE
PERSONAL Born 07/05/1950, San Mateo, CA, m, 1973, 2 children **DISCIPLINE** ENGLISH: RHETORIC AND WRITING **EDUCATION** VA Tech, BA, 72, MA, 77, Purdue Univ, PhD, 83. **CAREER** Tchr in MD; TA, 77-83; Dir, Off Writing Rev, Purdue Univ, 87-90; Assoc Prof & Dir, Writing Project, Dept of English, UNC, Charlotte, 90-. **MEMBERSHIPS** NCTE, CCCC, WPA. **RESEARCH** Writing assessor; electronic writing (theory and practice). **SELECTED PUBLICATIONS** Ed, Portfolios in the Writing Classroom: An Introduction, NCTE, 92; Still Hopeful After All These Years: Teachers as Agents of Change, Lang Arts J of MI, 93; Ed, Voices on Voice: Perspectives, Definitions, Inquiry, NCTE, 94; Contrib, New directions in Portfolio Assessment: Reflective Practice, CriticalTheory, and Large-scale Scoring, Make Haste Slowly: Portfolios and New Teaching assistants, Heinemann, 94; Contr, When Writing Teachers Teach Literature, Portfolios, Literature, and Learning: Story as a Way of Constructing the World, Heinemann, 95; Contr, Portfolios in the Writing Classroom: Policy and Practice, Promise and Peril, Dialogue, Interplay, and Discovery, Erlbaum Assoc, 96; Reflecting on Reflection: Notes on Developing a Reflective Frame of Mind, Iowa Eng Bul, 96; Ed, Situating Portfolios: Four Perspectives, Utah St Univ Press, 97; Ed, Assessing Writing across the Curriculum: Diverse Methods and Practices, Ablex, 97; Auth, Reflection in the writing Classroom, Utah St Univ Press, 98; Contr, The Theory and Practice of Grading Writing, Construction, Deconstruction, and (Over) Determination: A Foucaultian Analysis of Grades, SUNY Press, 98. **CONTACT ADDRESS** UN. Carolina Charlotte, Dept of English, Charlotte, NC, 28223. **EMAIL** kbyancey@email.uncc.edu

YANCY, PRESTON MARTIN
PERSONAL Born 10/18/1938, Sylvester, Georgia, m **DISCIPLINE** COMMUNICATIONS **EDUCATION** Morehouse Coll, BA 1959; Univ of Richmond, MH 1968; Syracuse Univ, MSS 1974, PhD 1979. **CAREER** USAF, civilian supply clerk 1959-61; US Dept of Defense, civilian supply clerk 1961-69; VA Union Univ, professor 1969-, vice pres for academic affairs, 1994-97; Richmond Free Press, columnist 1992-94, 1997-. **HONORS AND AWARDS** Emory O Jackson Best Column Awards 1975-78, 1980; Doctoral Grants Ford Found 1973-75; Doctoral Grants United Negro Coll Fund 1978-79; Post Doctoral Grants United Negro Coll Fund 1981-84. **MEMBERSHIPS** Columnist, Richmond Afro-Amer Newspaper 1967-71, 1974-82; Assoc for the Study of Afro Amer Life and History; member, Langston Hughes Society 1981-91; treasurer, Urban League of Greater Richmond, 1996-. **SELECTED PUBLICATIONS** Auth, The Afro-Amer Short Story Greenwood Press 1986. **CONTACT ADDRESS** Professor, Communications, Virginia Union Univ, 1500 N Lombardy, Richmond, VA, 23220-1711.

YANG, HEEWAN
PERSONAL Born 11/27/1939, Seoul, Korea, m, 1970, 2 children **DISCIPLINE** RHETORIC, PUBLIC SPEAKING **EDUCATION** Univ WI-Madison, Dept of Communication Arts, PhD, 85. **CAREER** Full prof English, Composition, Korea Military Academy, 68-. **MEMBERSHIPS** Nat Commun Asn; Korean Am Studies Asn. **RESEARCH** Public speaking; movement; intercultural communication. **SELECTED PUBLICATIONS** Auth, Roots of Military Culture; Speeches of World Leaders (in the War Time); Korean War. **CONTACT ADDRESS** English Lang Dept, Korea Military Acad, Box 77, Seoul, ., 139-799.

YEAGER, ROBERT FREDERICK
PERSONAL Born 03/07/1948, San Jose, CA **DISCIPLINE** MEDIEVAL ENGLISH LITERATURE **EDUCATION** Stanford Univ, BA, 70; Oxford Univ, MA, 72; Yale Univ, MPhil & PhD(English lit), 76. **CAREER** Instr, Yale Univ, 74-76 & Wesleyan Univ, 75-76; ASST PROF ENGLISH, WARREN WILSON COL, 76-, Am Coun Learned Soc fel, 82-83; Mellon fac fel, Harvard Univ, 82-83; fel, Inst Advan Studies, Univ Edinburgh, 83. **MEMBERSHIPS** MLA; SAtlantic Mod Lang Asn; Mediaeval Acad Am; New Chaucer Soc; John Gower Soc. **RESEARCH** Old English language and literature; Middle English literature; John Gower's poetry. **SELECTED PUBLICATIONS** Auth, The Origins of Beowulf and the Pre-Viking Kingdom of East-Anglia, Medium Aevum, Vol 0064, 95; Studies in Troilus--Chaucer Text, Meter and Diction, Medium Aevum, Vol 0065, 96. **CONTACT ADDRESS** Dept of English, Warren Wilson Col, Swannanoa, NC, 28778.

YEANDLE, LAETITIA
PERSONAL Born 07/11/1930, Hong Kong, m, 1966 **DISCIPLINE** ENGLISH HISTORY **EDUCATION** Trinity Col, Dublin, BA, 53; Univ Col, London, dipl arch admin, 56. **CAREER** Asst archivist, Shropshire Rec Off, 55-57; manuscript cataloguer, 57-70, CUR MANUSCRIPTS, FOLGER SHAKESPEARE LIBR, 70-, Fel, Folger Libr-Brit Acad Exchange Prog, 75; Brit Acad Exchange Prog fel, Folger Libr, 75. **MEMBERSHIPS** Brit Rec Asn; Conf Brit Studies; Renaissance Soc Am; Soc Textual Scholar; Soc Am Archivists. **RESEARCH** Textual editing and criticism; Tudor and Stuart history. **SELECTED PUBLICATIONS** Auth, The 2nd Best Bed--Shakespeare Will in a New Light, Shakespeare Quart, Vol 0045, 94; Playhouse Wills, 1558-1642--An Edition of Wills by Shakespeare and His Contemporaries in the London Theater, Shakespeare Quart, Vol 0045, 94. **CONTACT ADDRESS** Folger Shakespeare Libr, 201 E Capitol St, Washington, DC, 20003.

YEAZELL, RUTH BERNARD
PERSONAL Born 04/04/1947, New York, NY, d **DISCIPLINE** ENGLISH **EDUCATION** Swarthmore Col, BA, 67; Yale Univ, MPhil, 70, PhD, 71. **CAREER** Asst prof, 71-75, Boston Univ; asst prof, 75-77, assoc prof, 77-80, prof, 80-91, UCLA; prof, 91-, Chace Family prof, 95-, Yale Univ; dir, 96- Lewis Walpile Lib. **RESEARCH** British & Amer novel; hist of gender & sexuality; lit & visual arts. **CONTACT ADDRESS** Dept of English, Yale Univ, PO Box 208302, New Haven, CT, 06520-8302. **EMAIL** ruth.yeazell@yale.edu

YELLIN, JEAN FAGAN
PERSONAL Born 09/19/1930, Lansing, MI, m, 1948, 3 children **DISCIPLINE** AMERICAN LITERATURE AND STUDIES **EDUCATION** Roosevelt Univ, BA, 51; Univ Ill, Urbana, MA, 63, PhD(English), 69. **CAREER** Asst prof, 68-74, assoc prof, 74-80, PROF ENGLISH & DIR, NEW YORK CITY HUMANITIES PROG, PACE UNIV, 80-, Nat Endowment for Humanities younger humanist fel, 74-75; guest lectr, Univ Heidelberg, Sorbonne Nouvelle, Univ East Anglia, Univ Sussex, 75, 76; Nat Humanities Inst, Yale Univ, fel, 76-77; fels, Nat Endowment for Humanities, 78, Smithsonian Inst, Nat Collection of Fine Arts, 78-79 & Am Asn Univ Women, 81-82; proj dir, Nat Endowmnet for Humanities demonstration grant, Pace Univ, 79-81. **MEMBERSHIPS** MLA; Am Studies Asn; Asn Studies Afro-Am Life & Hist; Nat Women's Studies Asn. **RESEARCH** American literature and culture; women's studies; radical literature. **SELECTED PUBLICATIONS** Auth, Jacobs, Harriet Family History, Amer Lit, Vol 0066, 94; Written By Herself--Literary Production by African-American Women, 1746-1892, African Amer Rev, Vol 0030, 96. **CONTACT ADDRESS** 38 Lakeside Dr, New Rochelle, NY, 10801.

YERKES, DAVID
DISCIPLINE ANGLO-SAXON LANGUAGE AND LITERATURE **EDUCATION** Yale Univ, 71; Oxford Univ, BA, 73 Dphil, 76. **CAREER** Prof, 77-. **MEMBERSHIPS** Mem, London Medieval Soc; Medieval Acad; Soc Text Scholar. **SELECTED PUBLICATIONS** Auth, An Old English Thesaurus; Syntax and Style in Old English; The Old English Life of Machutus. **CONTACT ADDRESS** Dept of Eng, Columbia Col, New York, 2960 Broadway, New York, NY, 10027-6902.

YETMAN, MICHAEL G
PERSONAL Born 08/16/1939, New York, NY, m, 1963, 3 children **DISCIPLINE** ROMANTIC AND VICTORIAN LITERATURE **EDUCATION** St Peter's Col, NJ, BS, 61; Univ Notre Dame, MA, 62, PhD(English), 67. **CAREER** Instr English, St Mary's Col, Ind, 65-68; asst prof, 68-73, ASSOC PROF ENGLISH, PURDUE UNIV, WEST LAFAYETTE, 73-. **MEMBERSHIPS** MLA **RESEARCH** Modern literature. **SELECTED PUBLICATIONS** Auth, In Xanadu, Mass Rev, Vol 0035, 94. **CONTACT ADDRESS** Dept of English, Purdue Univ, West Lafayette, IN, 47907-1968.

YETUNDE FAELARIN SCHLEICHER, ANTONIA
DISCIPLINE AFRICAN LITERATURE **EDUCATION** Univ Kans, PhD. **CAREER** Dept African Lang, Wisc Univ **MEMBERSHIPS** African Lang Tchr Asn. **RESEARCH** Interface between phonology and morphology; experimental phonetics; foreign language learning and teaching; Yoruba culture. **SELECTED PUBLICATIONS** Auth, Je K'A Sae Yoruba, Yale, 93. **CONTACT ADDRESS** Dept of African Languages and Literature, Univ of Wisconsin, Madison, 500 Lincoln Drive, Madison, WI, 53706. **EMAIL** ayschlei@facstaff.wisc.edu

YINGLING, JULIE
PERSONAL Born 02/19/1948, Washington, DC **DISCIPLINE** SPEECH COMMUNICATION **EDUCATION** Univ Denver, PhD, 81. **CAREER** Asst prof, Univ WI, 81-85; assoc prof, Univ Northern CO, 85-88; vis assoc prof, Univ IA, 93-94; prof, Humboldt State Univ, 88-98. **MEMBERSHIPS** Int Network on Personal Relationships; Nat Commun Asn; Western States Commun Asn. **RESEARCH** Commun development in children; relational commun. **SELECTED PUBLICATIONS** Auth, Does That Mean No? Negotiating Protoconversations in Infany-Caregiver Pairs, Res on Lang and Social Interaction, vol 24, 91; Childhood: Talking the Mind Into Existence, in D R Vocate, ed, Intrapersonal Communication: Different Voice, Different Minds, Lawrence Erlbaum Assocs, 94; Constituting Friendship in Talk and Metatalk, J of Social and Personal Relationships, 11 (3), 94; Development as the Context of Student Assessment, in S Morreale & M Brooks, eds, 1994 SCA summer conference: Proceedings and prepared remarks, The Speech Commun Asn, 94; The First Relationship: Infant-Parent Communication, in T J Socha & G H Stamp, eds, Parents, Children and Communication: Frontiers of Theory and Research, Lawrence Erlbaum Assocs, 95; Resource review of Children Communication: The First 5 Years, by B B Haslett & W Samter, and Normal Conversation Aquisition: An Animated Database of Behaviors, Version 1-0 for Macintosh and Windows by K S Retherford, in Communication Education, in press. **CONTACT ADDRESS** 1850 Lime Ave, McKinleyville, CA, 95519. **EMAIL** jmy2@axe.humboldt.edu

YOCOM, MARGARET ROSE
PERSONAL Born 01/23/1948, Pottstown, PA **DISCIPLINE** FOLKLORE, ENGLISH LITERATURE **EDUCATION** Univ PA, BA, 70; Univ MA, Amherst, MA, 73, PhD, 80. **CAREER** Asst prof eng & folklore, George Mason Univ, 77-, Consult folklife, Festival Am Folklife, Smithsonian Inst, 75. **MEMBERSHIPS** Am Folklore Soc; Oral Hist Asn; Mid Atlantic Folklife Asn (treas, 81-83); Northeast Folklore Asn. **RESEARCH** Family folklore and fieldwork; material cult; folk narrative; women's studies. **SELECTED PUBLICATIONS** Folklore and the Tchg of Composition, Jour Am Folklore, 75; Women's Oral Hist, Folklore Feminists Commun, fall 75; Coauth, Family Folklore: Interviewing Guide and Questionnaire, Smithsonian Inst, 77; Ellis Island and American Immigration and The Dunham School Exhibit, Festival of American Folklife Program Book, Smithsonian Inst, 78; Teaching a Folksong and Literature Course, Folklore Women's Commun, 80; Folklore and Literature: A Bibliography, Folklore Women's Commun,

81; Blessing the Ties that Bind: Storytelling at Family Celebrations and How to Collect Your Own Family Folklore, In: Celebration of American Family Folklore: Tales and Traditions from the Smithsonian Collection, Pantheon, 82; Family Folklore and Oral History Interviews: Strategies for Introducing a Project to One's Own Relatives, Western Folklore, 82; Transferring Words from Tape to Print: The Story of Elmer and the Bull and Regionalism, Negative Definitions, and the Suburbs, Folklife in Northern Virginia, Folklore and Folklife in Va, 84; A Past Created for the Present: Selectivity and the Fold Paintings of Jessie Rhoads, Ky Folklore Record, 84; Woman to Woman: Fieldwork and the Private Sphere, In: Women's Folklore, Women's Culture, Univ Penn Press, 85; Asst ed, Ugiuvangmiut Quliapyuit: King Island Tales, Univ Alaska Press, 88; Fieldwork, Gender, and Transformation: The Second Way of Knowing, Southern Folklore, 90; Wave-walking, Friends Jour, 90; Awful Real: Dolls and Development in Rangeley, Main, In: Feminist Messages, Univ Ill Press, 93; Waking Up the Dead: Old Texts and New Critical Directions, In: Feminist Theory and the Study of Folklore, Univ Ill Press, 93; Producer, ed, auth, Logging in the Main Woods: The Paintings of Alden Grant, Rangeley lakes Region Logging Museum, 94, reprint 95; Cut my teeth on a spud!, Rodney Richard, Mad Whittler from Rangeley, Maine, Chip Chats, 1-2/94; What is Culture? and Ethics from a Folklorist's Perspective, In: Cultural Reporter: Reporter's Handbook, Tom Snyder Prod and Smithsonian Inst, 95; Marie Campbell, In: American Folklore: An Encyclopedia, Garland Publ, 96, and In: Notable American Women Folklorists, Am Folklore Soc, 97; Woodcarving, In: American Folklore: An Encyclopedia, Garland Publ, 96; The Yellow Ribboning of the USA: Contested Meanings in theConstruction of a Political Symbol, Western Folklore, 96; Family Folklore, In: Folklore: An Encyclopedia of Beliefs, Customs, Tales, Music, and Art, ABC-CLIO, 97; Women's Folklife, In: Encyclopedia of New England Culture, Yale Univ Press, forthcoming; If we don't joke with each other, we won't have no fun, will we? Storytelling in the Richard Family of Rangeley, Maine, In: Traditional Storytelling Today, forthcoming; Exuberance in Control: Dialogic Discourse in the Repertoire of Wood Carver and Storyteller William Richard, Northeast Folklore. **CONTACT ADDRESS** Dept of Eng, George Mason Univ, 4400 University Dr, MSN 3E4, Fairfax, VA, 22030-4444. **EMAIL** myocom@osf1.gmu.edu

YODER, DON
PERSONAL Mediapolis, IA **DISCIPLINE** ORGANIZATIONAL COMMUNICATION **EDUCATION** Iowa State Univ, BA, 73; Univ Nebr, MA, 75; Ohio State Univ, PhD, 82. **CAREER** Instr, Iowa State Univ; asst, assoc prof, Creighton Univ; assoc prof, chp, Univ Dayton, 89. **RESEARCH** Motivation in communications; conflict management; commununication education. **SELECTED PUBLICATIONS** Co-author, Creating Competent Communication. **CONTACT ADDRESS** Dept of Commun, Univ Dayton, 300 Col Park, Dayton, OH, 75062. **EMAIL** Yoder@udayton.edu

YODER, R. PAUL
DISCIPLINE LITERARY HISTORY FROM MILTON TO KEATS **EDUCATION** Duke Univ, PhD. **CAREER** English and Lit, Univ Ark **SELECTED PUBLICATIONS** Auth, Milton's The Passion, Milton Studies; William Blake, Hanoverian Britain, 1714-1834; Coed, Critical Essays on Alexander Pope; Approaches to Teaching Alexander Pope; Wordsworth Reimagines Thomas Gray, Criticism. **CONTACT ADDRESS** Univ Ark Little Rock, 2801 S University Ave., Little Rock, AR, 72204-1099. **EMAIL** rpyoder@ualr.edu

YORDON, JUDY E.
PERSONAL Born 11/06/1946, Chicago, IL, s **DISCIPLINE** PERFORMANCE STUDIES **EDUCATION** Southern Ill Univ, PhD, 77. **CAREER** Dist prof, Ball State Univ, 76-. **HONORS AND AWARDS** Creative Endeavor Award, 89; Dean's Teaching Award, 95; Distinguished Professorship, 96. **MEMBERSHIPS** Nat Commun Assoc; Cent States Commun Assoc. **RESEARCH** Experimental Theatre, Waveland Press, 97; auth, Shakespeare in performance; adapting non-dramatic lit for the stage. **SELECTED PUBLICATIONS** Roles in Interpretation, McGraw Hill, 4th ed, 99. **CONTACT ADDRESS** Dept of Theatre/Dance, Ball State Univ, Muncie, IN, 47306. **EMAIL** 00jeyordon@bsuvc.bsu.edu

YORK, LORRAINE
PERSONAL London, ON, Canada **DISCIPLINE** ENGLISH **EDUCATION** McMaster Univ, BA, 81, MA, 82, PhD, 85. **CAREER** Asst prof, McGill Univ, 85-88; asst prof, 88-91, ASSOC PROF, McMASTER UNIV, 91-. **HONORS AND AWARDS** Tchr Award Hum, McMaster Students Union. **MEMBERSHIPS** MLA; Asn Can Col Univs Tchrs Eng; Asn Can Stud US. **RESEARCH** Canadian literature. **SELECTED PUBLICATIONS** Auth, The Other Side of Dailiness: Photography in the Works of Alice Munroe, Timothy Findley, Michael Ondaatji and Margaret Laurence; auth, Front Lines: The Fiction of Timothy Findley; auth, Various Atwoods: Essays on the Later Poems, Short Fiction and Novels, 95. **CONTACT ADDRESS** Dept of English, McMaster Univ, Hamilton, ON, L8S 4L5. **EMAIL** york@mcmaster.ca

YOUM, K.H.
PERSONAL Born 09/06/1952, South Korea, m, 1980, 2 children **DISCIPLINE** JOURNALISM AND LAW **EDUCATION** Southern Ill Univ, PhD, 85; Yale Law Sch, MSL, 98. **CAREER** Prof, Ariz State Univ, 96- . **HONORS AND AWARDS** Most Productive Scholar in J and Mass Commun in U.S. **MEMBERSHIPS** EAJMC; ICA. **RESEARCH** Media law; press freedom; international journalism. **SELECTED PUBLICATIONS** Press Freedom and Judicial Review in South Korea, Stanford J Int Law, 94; Suing U.S. Media in Foreign Countries, Hastings Comm/ENT Law J, 94; Media Countersuits in Libel Law, Hastings Comm/ENT Law J, 95 Press Law in South Korea, 96; Neutral Repartage Doctrine, Commun Law and Policy, 98. **CONTACT ADDRESS** Cronkite School of Journalism and Telecom., Arizona State Univ, Tempe, Tempe, AZ, 85287-1305.

YOUNG, ARLENE
DISCIPLINE ENGLISH LITERATURE **EDUCATION** Univ Manitoba, BA; MA; Cornell Univ, PhD. **CAREER** Asst prof **RESEARCH** Victorian literature and culture; representations of class and gender; writing by and about women and members of the lower middle class. **SELECTED PUBLICATIONS** Auth, pub(s) on nineteenth century British and American novels. **CONTACT ADDRESS** Dept of English, Manitoba Univ, Winnipeg, MB, R3T 2N2.

YOUNG, ARTHUR Y.
DISCIPLINE ENGLISH LITERATURE **EDUCATION** Miami Univ, PhD, 71. **CAREER** Dept Eng, Clemson Univ **RESEARCH** Professional communication; composition. **SELECTED PUBLICATIONS** Auth, Monograph: Writing Across the Curriculum, Blair Resources for Teaching Writing, Prentice Hall, 94; Writing Across the Curriculum, Skriving ved Universitetet (Writing at the University), Univ Tromso Press, 94; The Wonder of Writing Across the Curriculum, Lang Lrng Across Disciplines, 94; Recalling James Britton, Eng Int, 95; coauth, Portfolios in the Disciplines: Sharing Knowledge in the Contact Zone, New Directions in Portfolio Assessment, Heinemann Boynton/Cook, 94; Resisting Writing/Resisting Writing Teachers, The Subject is Writing, Boynton/Cook Heinemann, 93; ed, Programs and Practices: Writing Across the Secondary Curriculum, Boynton/Cook Heinemann, 94; When Writing Teachers Teach Literature: Bringing Writing to Reading, Boynton,Cook Heinemann, 95; Critical Theory and the Teaching of Literature: Politics, Curriculum, Pedagogy, Nat Coun Tchrs Eng, 96. **CONTACT ADDRESS** Clemson Univ, 416 Strode, Clemson, SC, 29634. **EMAIL** apyoung@clemson.edu 1

YOUNG, DAVID
DISCIPLINE LITERATURE **EDUCATION** Carleton Col, BA, 58; Yale Univ, MA, 59, PhD, 65. **CAREER** Ch, Oberlin's Danenburg Oberlin-in-London Prog; Longman prof, 61. **RESEARCH** Modern poets, creative writing, renaissance drama. **SELECTED PUBLICATIONS** Au, Night Thoughts and Henry Vaughan (poetry); trans, The Book of Fresh Beginnings: Selected Poems of Rainer Maria Rilke; The Action to the Word: Structure and Style in Shakespearean Tragedy (criticism); co-ed, FIELD, Oberlin Col Press; Models of the Universe (an anthology of prose poems). **CONTACT ADDRESS** Dept of Eng, Oberlin Col, Rice 30, Oberlin, OH, 44074. **EMAIL** David_Young@qmgate.cc.oberlin.edu

YOUNG, ELIZABETH BELL
PERSONAL Born 07/02/1929, Durham, NC, m **DISCIPLINE** SPEECH **EDUCATION** NC Central U, BA 1948, MA 1950; OH St U, PhD 1959. **CAREER** Catholic Univ, graduate school prof 1966-79; Barber Scotia Coll NC; Talladega Coll AL; VA State Coll; OH State Univ; FL A&M Univ; Fayetteville State Univ NC; Howard Univ Wash DC; Univ of MD, Eastern Shore; Princess Anne, MD; Univ of the DC, Dept Speech Science (communications) & English, univ prof & chmn 1949-84; NATL & INTL ORGANIZATIONS & UNIVERSITIES, CONSULTANT & LECTURER, 1981-; Congressional Staff Aide, 1980, 1987-91, Staff aide US House of Reps (Office of Congressman Walter E Fauntroy) 1980, 1987-91; Lecturer & Consultant US Govt (Office of Ed) 1981-87; FIELD READER & TEAM REVIEWER, US ST DEPT PROMOTION PANELIST 1980-. **HONORS AND AWARDS** Flw Am Speech, Lang, Hearing Asso 1980; Otstndng Alumni Awd OH St Univ 1976; publ Journal Articles in Field of Communications & Made Over 450 Speeches in US; Pioneer in field of speech Pathology & Audiology; 1st African-American to receive PhD in Speech Science; 1st African-American to obtain dual certification in Speech Pathology and Audiology; 1st African-American to obtain PhD from Ohio State Univ in communications and speech science, and started 1st certified speech & learning clinics in historically black colleges and universities. **MEMBERSHIPS** Mem of Bd (Public Mem Asso) 1979-; mem bd of dir Washington Ctr Music Thrpy Clinic; mem adv bd United Negro Clg Fund 1979-82; mem Congressional Adv B D on Educ 1979-82; mem Alpha Kappa Alpha Sor 1946-; bd mem Clinical Cert Am Speech-L & H Assn 1979-83; bd dir Handicapped Intervention Prog for High Risk Infants Wash DC 1978-87. **CONTACT ADDRESS** Natl & Intrl Organ & Univ, 8104 W Beach Dr NW, Washington, DC, 20012.

YOUNG, ELIZABETH V.
PERSONAL Born 09/27/1962, Ithaca, NY **DISCIPLINE** ENGLISH **EDUCATION** Cornell Univ, BA, 84; Univ MI, PhD, 89. **CAREER** Assoc prof, CSULB. **HONORS AND AWARDS** Phi Beta Kappa, Cornell, 84. **MEMBERSHIPS** MLA; ASECS; AAUW; NEA. **RESEARCH** Restoration and 18th-century poetry; women writers in England and America. **SELECTED PUBLICATIONS** Auth, Engendering Response: Staging in Introductory Shakespeare Courses, with Mimi Hotchkiss, Proceedings of the CA State Univ Shakespeare Conference, 91; Aphra Behn, Gender, and Pastoral, Studies in English Lit, 33-3, 93; Images of Women in Early Modern England and America, with Patricia Cleary, Am Soc for Eighteenth-Century Studies Teaching Competition: Three Courses, 95; Aphra Behn's Elegies, Genre, 28 1-2, 95; Eve (poem), Phoebe, 7 1-2, 95; Pleasure(poem), Amaranth, 2, 96; Fireflies and Containment(poems), Folio, summer 96; Tabula Rasa and Saguaro-(poems), Frontiers, 17-3, 96; Some Current Publications, Restoration, 96; Aphra Behn and Anne Bradstreet (entries in reference work), Feminist Writers, St James Press, 96; The Farming of a Verse': Storytelling in the Classroom, Reflections, 3 1, 98; Aphra Behn's Horace, Restoration, forthcoming. **CONTACT ADDRESS** Dept of English, California State Univ, Long Beach, Long Beach, CA, 90840. **EMAIL** evyoung@csulb.edu

YOUNG, KAY
DISCIPLINE ENGLISH LITERATURE **EDUCATION** Harvard Univ, PhD, 92. **CAREER** ASST PROF, ENG, UNIV CALIF, SANTA BARBARA. **RESEARCH** Victorian fiction; Hollywood films of the '30s and '40s; Relationship of narrative to architect, philos, music, and dance. **SELECTED PUBLICATIONS** Auth, "Hollywood, 1934: 'Inventing' Romantic Comedy," Look Who's Laughing: Studies in Gender and Comedy, 94; "'Everyday a Little Death': Stephen Sondheim's Unmusicaling of Marriage," Ars Lyrica, 94. **CONTACT ADDRESS** Dept of Eng, Univ Calif, Santa Barbara, CA, 93106-7150. **EMAIL** kayyoung@humanitas.ucsb.edu

YOUNG, RICHARD E.
PERSONAL Born 07/12/1932, Owosso, MI, m, 1983, 5 children **DISCIPLINE** ENGLISH LITERATURE, RHETORIC **EDUCATION** Univ MI, BA, 54 PhD, 64; Univ CT, MA, 56. **CAREER** From instr to prof Eng, Col Engineering, Univ MI, Ann Arbor, 58-78, chmn dept hum, 71-76; prof eng & rhetoric, chmn dept, Carnegie Mellon Univ, 78, Mem staff, Ctr Res Lang & Lang Behavior, 64-68; consult, NDEA Inst, 65-68; Educ prof Develop Act Inst, 68-70; Nat Endowment for Humanities grant, 71-72; Nat Adv Comt, Formative Evaluation Res Assoc, 77-78; dir fels in residence, Nat Endowment for Humanities, 78; Nat Endowment for the Humanities Summer Sem grants, 77, 79 & 81. **HONORS AND AWARDS** Distinguished Serv Award, Col Engineering, Univ MI, Ann Arbor, 68; LHD, St Edwards Univ, 80; E D Smith Distinguished Tchg Award, 93; Thomas S. Becker Ch, Eng, 93; prof Emeritus, 98., LHD, St Edward's Univ, 80. **MEMBERSHIPS** NCTE; Conf Col Compos & Commun; Speech Commun Asn; Mod Lang Asn; Rhetoric Soc Am. **RESEARCH** Rhetoric; lit; linguistics. **SELECTED PUBLICATIONS** Auth, Toward a modern theory of rhetoric: A tagmemic contribution, Harvard Educ Rev, fall 65; The psychological reality of the paragraph, J Verbal Learning & Verbal Behavior, 69; coauth, Rhetoric: Discovery and Change, Harcourt, 70; contribr, Invention: A Topographical Survey, Teaching Composition, Tex Christian Univ, 76; contribr, Paradigms and problems: Needed research in rhetorical invention, research on composing, NCTE, 78; auth, Arts, crafts, gifts, and knacks: Some disharmonics in the New Rhetoric, Visible Lang, 80. **CONTACT ADDRESS** Dept of Eng, Carnegie Mellon Univ, 5000 Forbes Ave, Pittsburgh, PA, 15213-3890.

YOUNG, ROBERT VAUGHAN
PERSONAL Born 06/20/1947, Marianna, FL, m, 1968, 5 children **DISCIPLINE** RENAISSANCE ENGLISH, COMPARATIVE LITERATURE **EDUCATION** Rollins Col, BA, 68; Yale Univ, 71, PhD(English), 72. **CAREER** Asst prof, 72-79, ASSOC PROF ENGLISH, NC STATE UNIV, 80-, Fel, Southestern Inst Medieval & Renaissance Studies, summer, 78; prof English & social theory, Kairos Inst, El Escorial Spain, summer, 79; vis prof & actg chmn English, Christendom Col, 79-80; Fulbright res fel, Cath Univ Louvain & Free Univ Brussels, winter, 83. **MEMBERSHIPS** MLA; SAtlantic Mod Lang Asn; Soc Christian Cult; Fel Cath Scholars. **RESEARCH** Comparative literature of Baroque Age, especially English, Latin and Spanish; neo-Latin rhetorical studies, especially Justus Lipsius; contemporary moral & social issues. **SELECTED PUBLICATIONS** Auth, The Wit of 17th-Century Poetry, Renaissance and Reformation, Vol 0020, 96; Herbert and the Real Presence, Renascence-Essays on Values in Lit, Vol 0045, 93; Donne, John, Pseudo-Martyr, Renaissance Quart, Vol 0049, 96. **CONTACT ADDRESS** Dept of English, No Carolina State Univ, Raleigh, NC, 27650.

YOUNG, THOMAS DANIEL
PERSONAL Born 10/22/1919, Louisville, MS, m, 1941, 3 children **DISCIPLINE** ENGLISH **EDUCATION** Miss Southern Col, BS, 41; Univ Miss, MA, 48; Vanderbilt Univ, PhD, 50. **CAREER** Instr English, Univ Miss, 46-48; asst prof, Miss

Southern Col, 50-51, prof & chmn dept, 51-57, acting dean, Basic Col, 54-55; prof & dean, Delta State Col, 57-61; lectr English & dean admis, Undergrad Col, 61-67, prof & chmn dept English, 67-73, GERTRUDE VANDERBILT PROF ENGLISH, VANDERBILT UNIV, 73-, Vis prof Am lit, Univ Leeds, 73-74. **HONORS AND AWARDS** Jules Landra Award, LSU, 76. **MEMBERSHIPS** Gen Educ Conf; SCent Mod Lang Asn; Am Studies Asn; SAtlantic Mod Lang Asn Lower Miss, (pres, 55-57). **RESEARCH** Jack London; William Faulkner; modern Southern poetry. **SELECTED PUBLICATIONS** Auth, The Kenyon-Review, 1939-1970--A Critical History, Res American Lit Stud, Vol 0020, 94. **CONTACT ADDRESS** Vanderbilt Univ, Sta B, Box 1509, Nashville, TN, 37235.

YOWELL, ROBERT L.
PERSONAL Born 07/16/1941, St. Louis, MO, m, 1966, 2 children **DISCIPLINE** SPEECH AND THEATRE **EDUCATION** Southeast Mo State Univ; AB, St Louis Univ, MA, 68; Bowling Green State Univ PhD, 72. **CAREER** Chair, theatre and dance, Univ Ark Little Rock, 73-81; chair, theatre and dance, Univ Birmingham, 81-88; chair, theatre, Calif State Univ, San Bernadino, 88-93; prof, theatre, Northern Ariz Univ, 93-. **HONORS AND AWARDS** ACTF, Kennedy Ctr, nat finalist; Oblesik award, Birmingham, Ala. **MEMBERSHIPS** Nat Comm Asn; Amer Col Theatre Festival. **RESEARCH** New play development; Drama as a learning medium. **SELECTED PUBLICATIONS** Interview, with playwright Octavio Solis, Eric Montana Love Story, Nancy & Charlie Russell, Pancakes are forbidden, new play develop. **CONTACT ADDRESS** School of Performing Arts, No Arizona Univ, Box 6040, Flagstaff, AZ, 86011-6040. **EMAIL** robert.yowell@nau.edu

Z

ZACHARIAS, GREG
DISCIPLINE 19TH-CENTURY AMERICAN LITERATURE AND WRITING **EDUCATION** NY Univ, BA, MA, PhD. **CAREER** Ch & co-dir, MA prog Liberal Stud, 96; dir, Ctr Henry James Stud, Creighton & co-gen ed, Complete Letters of Henry James, 96; taught at, Hofstra Univ, Cooper Union NY City & NY Univ. **SELECTED PUBLICATIONS** Publ on, Milton, Mark Twain, Henry James. **CONTACT ADDRESS** Dept of Eng, Creighton Univ, 2500 CA Plaza, CA 304D, Omaha, NE, 68178. **EMAIL** gwzach@creighton.edu

ZACHER, CHRISTIAN KEELER
PERSONAL Born 03/06/1941, St. Louis, MO, m, 1967, 2 children **DISCIPLINE** ENGLISH LITERATURE, MEDIEVAL STUDIES **EDUCATION** Col of the Holy Cross, BA, 63; Univ Calif, Riverside, MA, 65, PhD(English), 69. **CAREER** Teaching asst English, Univ Calif, Riverside, 64-67; asst prof, 68-74, ASSOC PROF ENGLISH, OHIO STATE UNIV, 74-. **MEMBERSHIPS** MLA; Mediaeval Acad Am; Soc Hist Discoveries; AAUP. **RESEARCH** Medieval English and Latin literature; medieval and Renaissance travel literature. **SELECTED PUBLICATIONS** Auth, Framing the Canterbury Tales--Chaucer,Geoffrey and the Medieval Frame-Narrative-Tradition, Speculum-Jour Medieval Stud, Vol 0069, 94. **CONTACT ADDRESS** Dept of English, Ohio State Univ, 164 W 17th Ave, Columbus, OH, 43210-1326.

ZAFREN, HERBERT C.
PERSONAL Born 08/25/1925, Baltimore, MD, m, 1951, 2 children **DISCIPLINE** LIBRARY SCIENCE **EDUCATION** Johns Hopkins Univ, BA, 44; Baltimore Hebrew Col, diploma, 44; Univ Mich, AMLS, 50; **CAREER** Librn, 50-91, dir of libr, 66-94, dir emeritus, 94- , prof Jewish Bibl, 68-95, prof emeritus, 95- , Hebrew Union Col Jewish Inst Relig; exec dir, 56-80, co-dir, 80-96, dir, 96- , Am Jewish Periodical Ctr. **HONORS AND AWARDS** Phi Beta Kappa; Beta Phi Mu. **MEMBERSHIPS** ALA; Asn of Jewish Libr; Coun of Archives and Res Libr in Jewish Stud; Am Hist Asn; World Union of Jewish Stud. **RESEARCH** Library science; history of Hebrew. **SELECTED PUBLICATIONS** Auth, Was Gutenberg Jewish? And Other Conundrums: Exploring the Margins of Jewish Bibliography, Council of Archives and Research Libraries in Jewish Studies, 97; coauth, Vilnius Judaica: Still Portrait - Dynamic Reality: Report of the CARLJS Delegation on Its Survey of Judaica in Vilnius, 97; auth, Hebrew Printing by and for Frankfurt Jews -- to 1800, in, Grozinger, ed, Judische Kultur in Frankfurt am Main von den Anfangen bis zur Gegenwart, Harrassowitz, 97. **CONTACT ADDRESS** 3863 Middleton, Cincinnati, OH, 45220-1126. **EMAIL** hzafren@huc.edu

ZAGANO, PHYLLIS
DISCIPLINE RELIGION; LITERATURE **EDUCATION** Marymount Col, BA, 69; Boston Univ, MS, 70; C.W. Post Center of Long Island Univ, MA, 72; St. John's Univ, MA, 90; State Univ New York Stony Brook, PhD **CAREER** Boston Univ, 88- **MEMBERSHIPS** Amer Acad Rel; Amer Cath Philos Assoc; Amer Jour Historians Assoc; Col Theol Soc; Soc Study Christian Spirituality; Spiritual Directors Int **SELECTED PUBLICATIONS** Co-ed, Twentieth Century Apostles, Liturgical, 99; co-ed, The Exercise of the Primacy: Continuing the Dialogue, Crossroad/Herder, 98; auth, "The Language of Prayer," Handbook of Spirituality for Ministers, Vol.2, Paulist Press, 99 **CONTACT ADDRESS** 250 E 63rd St, New York, NY, 10021. **EMAIL** pzagano@su.edu

ZAHAROPOULOS, THIMIOS
DISCIPLINE BROADCASTING, MASS MEDIA THEORY **EDUCATION** S Ill Univ-Carbondale, BS, MA, PhD. **CAREER** Assoc prof, 85-86, 88. **SELECTED PUBLICATIONS** Publ, Mass Media in Greece, articles on intl news flow and intercultural commun. **CONTACT ADDRESS** Dept of Commun, Pittsburg State Univ, 1701 S Broadway St, Pittsburg, KS, 66762.

ZAHORSKI, KENNETH
PERSONAL Born 10/23/1939, Cedarville, IN, m, 1962, 2 children **DISCIPLINE** ENGLISH, SPEECH **EDUCATION** Univ Wis-River Falls, BS, 61; Ariz State Univ, MA, 63; Univ Wis, PhD(English), 67. **CAREER** Asst prof English, Univ Wis-Eau Claire, 67-69; asst prof, 69-71, asoc prof, 71-80, prof English, St Norbert Col, 80-, consult, Choice, 72-; sr assoc, CIC, 94-. **HONORS AND AWARDS** Outstanding Teacher of the Year Award, St Norbert Col, 74; Outstanding Alumnus Award, Univ Wis-River Falls, 75; Distinguished Scholar Award, St Norbert Col, 87; Sears Roebuck Found, Teaching Excellence and Campus Leadership Award, 91. **MEMBERSHIPS** MLA; NCTE; AAUP; Col English Asn. **RESEARCH** Renaissance Drama; modern drama; Fantasy literature. **SELECTED PUBLICATIONS** Co-ed, Visions of Wonder: An Anthology of Christian Fantasy, Avon Bks, 81; Fantasists on Fantasy, Avon, 84; Visions and Imaginings, Acad Chicago Pubs, 92; auth, Peter S Beagle, Starmont Press, 88; The Sabbatical Mentor, Anker Pub Co, 94. **CONTACT ADDRESS** Dept of English, St. Norbert Col, 100 Grant St, De Pere, WI, 54115-2099. **EMAIL** zahokj@sncac.snc.edu

ZALACAIN, DANIEL
PERSONAL Born 12/15/1948, Havana, Cuba, m, 1976, 1 child **DISCIPLINE** LATIN AMERICAN LITERATURE & THEATRE **EDUCATION** Wake Forrest Univ, BA, 71; Univ NC, Chapel Hill, MA, 72, PhD, 76. **CAREER** Asst prof Span lang & lit & bus Span, Northern IL Univ, 77-80; Asst Prof Span Lang & Lit & Bus Span, Seton Hall Univ, 80. **MEMBERSHIPS** Am Asn Tchr(s) Span & Port; MLA. **RESEARCH** Latin Am theatre of the absurd; Span for business careers; Latin Am myths. **SELECTED PUBLICATIONS** Auth, Rene Marques, del absurdo a la realidad, Latin Am Theatre Rev, fall 78; El arte dramatico en Cuculcan, Explicacion textos lit, 78; Calabar: O elogio da traicao, Chasqui: Rev Lit Latinoam, 2/79; Falsa alarma: Vanguardia del absurdo, Romance Notes, 80; El tiempo, tema fundamental en la obra de Rene Marques, Ky Romance Quart, 80; El personae fuera del juego en el teatro de Griselda Gambaro, Rev Estudios Hispanicos, 5/80; Los recursos dramaticos en Soluna, Latin Am Theatre Rev, spring 81; La Antigona de Sanchez: Recreacion puertorriquena del mito, Explicacion Textos Lit, 81. **CONTACT ADDRESS** Dept of Mod Lang, Seton Hall Univ, 400 S Orange Ave, South Orange, NJ, 07079-2697.

ZATLIN, LINDA GERTNER
PERSONAL Born 11/28/1938, New York, NY, m, 1960, 2 children **DISCIPLINE** VICTORIAN LITERATURE, LITERATURE AND SOCIETY **EDUCATION** Univ Md, BA, 60; Emory Univ, MA, 64, PhD(English), 74. **CAREER** Instr English, Ga Inst Technol, 67; instr, 67-70, asst prof, 74-78, ASSOC PROF ENGLISH, MOREHOUSE COL, 78-, LECTR HUMAN VALUES IN MED, 80-, Vis asst prof, Emory Univ, 74; Fulbright fel, 81; United Negro Col Fund-Mellon Found Grant, 82; consult, Atlanta Bur Jewish Educ, 80- & Dept Educ Curric Serv, State Ga, 81- **MEMBERSHIPS** MLA; Southeastern Nineteenth-Century Studies Asn (sec-treas, 80-82, vpres, 82-84); SAtlantic Mod Lang Asn; AAUP; Soc Study Multi Ethnic Lit. **RESEARCH** Literature and society; the Victorian novel. **SELECTED PUBLICATIONS** Auth, The Victorian Novel, Eng Lang Notes, Vol 0031, 93; The Complete Novels and Selected-Writings of Levy, Amy, 1861-1889, Stud Short Fiction, Vol 0031, 94; The Invention of Pornography--Obscenity and the Origins of Modernity, 1500-1800, Jour Mod Hist, Vol 0067, 95; Beardsley, Aubrey, Dandy of the Grotesque, Criticism-Quarterly Lit and Arts, Vol 0038, 96; Figures of Conversion--The Jewish Question and English National Identity, Anq-Quart Jour Short Articles Notes and Rev(s), Vol 0009, 96. **CONTACT ADDRESS** 2525 Northside Dr NW, Atlanta, GA, 30305.

ZAVARZADEH, MAS'UD
PERSONAL Born 05/17/1938, Tehran, Iran **DISCIPLINE** CONTEMPORARY AMERICAN LITERATURE AND LITERARY THEORY **EDUCATION** Tehran Univ, BA, 63; Univ Nottingham, dipl English studies, 64; Univ Birmingham, MA, 66; Ind Univ, Bloomington, PhD, 73. **CAREER** From asst prof to assoc prof Am lit, Univ Ore, Eugene, 71-77; ASSOC PROF ENGLISH, SYRACUSE UNIV, 78-, Nat Endowment Humanities res fel, 77-78; Nat Humanities Ctr fel, 81-82. **MEMBERSHIPS** MLA; Semiotic Soc Am; NCTE; Can Semiotic Res Asn. **RESEARCH** Narratology; Postmodern American literature; Innovative fiction. **SELECTED PUBLICATIONS** Auth, The Stupidity that Consumption is Just as Productive as Production, In the Shopping-Mall of the Post-Al Left, Col Lit, Vol 0021, 94; The Pedagogy of Pleasure 2. the Me-In-Crisis, Col Lit, Vol 0021, 94; The Pedagogy of Pleasure 2. the Me-In-Crisis--Reading My Readers, Col Lit, Vol 0021, 94. **CONTACT ADDRESS** Dept of English, Syracuse Univ, Syracuse, NY, 13210.

ZEBOUNI, SELMA
DISCIPLINE 17TH CENTURY LITERATURE **EDUCATION** La State Univ, PhD, 63. **CAREER** Assoc prof, La State Univ. **SELECTED PUBLICATIONS** Auth, Dyrden, A Study in Heroic Characterization, 65; Pr?sentation, repr?sentation: Le Classicisme au carrefour, in l'Esprit Createur, 93; Mim?sis et sublime: Boileau, Kant, Derrida, in Cahiers du dix-septieme, 94. **CONTACT ADDRESS** Dept of Fr Grad Stud, Louisiana State Univ, Baton Rouge, LA, 70803.

ZEGURA, ELIZABETH CHESNEY
PERSONAL Born 09/07/1949, Knoxville, TN, m, 1983, 1 child **DISCIPLINE** RENAISSANCE LITERATURE, FRENCH, ITALIAN **EDUCATION** Bryn Mawr Col, AB, 71; Duke Univ, MA, 74, PhD, 76. **CAREER** Instr, Davidson Col, 75-76; asst prof, DePauw Univ, 81-82; VISTING ASST PROF, 78-80, LECTR, 85, 87-88, 89-, UNIV OF ARIZ. **HONORS AND AWARDS** AB (magna cum laude), Bryn Mawr, 71; NDEA Fel, Duke Univ. **MEMBERSHIPS** Renaissance Soc of Am. **RESEARCH** Renaissance Literature: Rabelais, Ariosto, Marguerite de Navarre. **SELECTED PUBLICATIONS** Auth, The Countervoyage of Rabelais and Ariosto: A Comparative Reading of Two Renaissance Mock Epics, Duke Univ Press, 82; coauth, Rabelais Revisited, MacMillan/Twayne, 93. **CONTACT ADDRESS** Dept of French and Italian, Univ of Ariz, Tucson, AZ, 85721. **EMAIL** zeguras@u.arizona.edu

ZEIGER, MELISSA F.
DISCIPLINE ENGLISH LITERATURE **EDUCATION** Cornell Univ, PhD, 86. **CAREER** Assoc prof, Dartmouth Col. **RESEARCH** Am and Brit lit, women's lit. **SELECTED PUBLICATIONS** Auth, Beyond Consolation: Death, Sexuality, and the Changing Shapes of Elegy, Cornell UP, 96; 'A Muse Funereal': The Critique of Elegy in Swinburne's 'Ave atque Vale,' Victorian Poetry, 86. **CONTACT ADDRESS** Dartmouth Col, 3529 N Main St, #207, Hanover, NH, 03755.

ZENDER, KARL FRANCIS
PERSONAL Born 09/10/1937, Portsmouth, OH, m, 1968, 2 children **DISCIPLINE** ENGLISH **EDUCATION** Case Inst Technol, BS, 59; Western Reserve Univ, MA, 62; Univ Iowa, PhD, 70. **CAREER** Instr English, Univ Iowa, 65-66; from instr to asst prof, Wash Univ, St Louis, 66-73; from Lectr to Assoc Prof, 73-89, prof English, Univ Calif, Davis, 89-; from Actg Chair to Chair, Dept English, 93-98. **MEMBERSHIPS** MLA **RESEARCH** Faulkner and Southern literature; Renaissance drama; 20th century American literature. **SELECTED PUBLICATIONS** Auth, A hand of poker: Game and ritual in Faulkner's Was, Studies Short Fiction, 74; The death of Young Siward: Providential order and tragic loss in Macbeth, Tex Studies Lang & Lit, 75; The function of Propertius in Jonson's Poetaster, Papers Lang & Lit, 75; contribr, William Faulkner, In: American Literary Scholarship, Duke Univ, annual, 74, 75, 80, 81; auth, The unveiling of the Goddess in Cynthia's Revels, J English & Ger Philol, 78; Reading in The Bear, Faulkner Studies, 80; Faulkner at forty: The artist at home, Southern Rev, 81; Faulkner and the Power of Sound, PMLA, 84; The Coming of the Days: William Faulkner, the South, and the Modern World, Rutgers, 89; author of numerous other essays and reviews. **CONTACT ADDRESS** Dept of English, Univ of Calif, Davis, CA, 95616-5200. **EMAIL** kfzender@ucdavis.edu

ZEVELECHI WELLS, MARIA XENIA
DISCIPLINE FRENCH; ITALIAN **EDUCATION** Univ of Pisa, Italy, PhD, 59. **CAREER** Teacher, Am High Sch, Pisa, Italy and asst prof, Univ of Pisa, Italy, 57-62; lectr, Univ of Tex, 62-72; cur of Ital Collections, H. Ransom Hums Res Ctr, Univ or Tex, 73-97; adj prof, H. Ransom Ctr, Univ of Tex, 97-. **HONORS AND AWARDS** Fulbright Scholar, 54-55; Inst of Am Studies in Rome Scholar, 56; App to the Libr Servs and Construct Act Adv Coun, 86, 89; App to attend the Conv of Ital Lang and Cult in Rome, Italy, Ital Ministry of Foreign Affairs, 87; J.R. Dougherty Jr. Found Grant, 87; Ital Private Found Grant, 89; Fulbright Res Grant, 91; App to the Fulbright Campus Screening Comt, 92; App mem fo the Am Comt for the Medici Arch Proj Inc. Florence and NY, 96 TIL Coun, the Soerette Diehl Fraser Transl Award Adv Coun, 97. **MEMBERSHIPS** Am Asn for Ital Studies; Associazione Internazionale di Studi di Lingua e Letteratura Italiana; Am Translators Asn; Fulbright Asn; Minerva Hist Asn; Nat Fulbright Alumni Asn; Soc for Ital Hist Studies; Nat Ital Am Found. **RESEARCH** Carlo Levi **SELECTED PUBLICATIONS** Auth, The Ranuzzi Manuscripts, in exhibit catalog, H. Ransom Hums Res Ctr Publs, 80; Annibale Ranuzzi e La Repubblica del Texas, 1842, in Il Carrobbio 10, 84; Una Biblioteca Italiana nel Texas, in Biblioteche Oggi, vol VII-n.1, 89; Libraries and Cultures, issue on the history of Italian libraries, twelve essays, vol 25/no. 3, 90; Italian Post-1600 Manuscripts and Family Archives in North American Li-

braries, 92; The Italian Collections Across the Centuries: Literature, Art, and Theatre, exhibit catalog as double issue of The Libr Chronicle, vol 21, nos. 2/3, 93; Fuochi d'Artificio: manoscritto del 1500, in FMR aprile, 95; I Paladini di Sicilia, in FMR dicembre, 95; Il manoscritto di Cristo si e' fermato a Eboli, lettura su piano storico e critico, in Stanford French and Ital Studies, 97; Memoriale di Paolo Volponi: L'uomo e la Fabbrica, esame delle varianti nel manoscritto, in selected procs of the Conf: Letteratura e Industria, AISILLI, 94; Aldine Press Books at the Harry Ransom Humanities Research Center: A descriptive catalogue, in H. Ransom Spec Publs, September, 98. **CONTACT ADDRESS** Harry Ransom Humanities Research Center, Univ of Texas, Austin, Austin, TX, 78713-7219. **EMAIL** mxwells@nora.hrc.utexas.edu

ZIAREK, EWA

DISCIPLINE LITERATURE **EDUCATION** SUNY, Buffalo, PhD. **CAREER** Instr, Univ Notre Dame. **RESEARCH** Modernism; comparative fiction. **SELECTED PUBLICATIONS** Auth, The Rhetoric of Failure: Deconstruction of Skepticism, Reinvention of Modernism. **CONTACT ADDRESS** Univ Notre Dame, Notre Dame, IN, 46556.

ZIAREK, KRZYSZTOF

DISCIPLINE LITERATURE **EDUCATION** SUNY, Buffalo, PhD. **CAREER** Instr, Univ Notre Dame. **HONORS AND AWARDS** NEH fel; ACLS fel. **RESEARCH** The interrelations between literature and philosophy. **SELECTED PUBLICATIONS** Auth, Inflected Language: Toward a Hermeneutics of Nearness. Heidegger, Levinas, Stevens, Celan. **CONTACT ADDRESS** Univ Notre Dame, Notre Dame, IN, 46556.

ZIEGELMUELLER, GEORGE WILLIAM

PERSONAL Born 07/28/1930, Indianapolis, IN, 1 child **DISCIPLINE** SPEECH **EDUCATION** DePauw Univ, BA, 52; Southern Ill Univ, MA, 54; Northwestern Univ, PhD, 62. **CAREER** Asst, Northwestern Univ, 54-57; from instr to assoc prof, 57-68, dir forensics, 62-, PROF SPEECH, WAYNE STATE UNIV, 68-, COMMUN STUDIES, 70-, DISTINGUISHED UNIV PROF, 97; Ed jour, Am Forensic Asn, 73-77. **MEMBERSHIPS** Commun Speech Asn; Am Forensic Asn, (secy-treas, 61-63; vpres, 63-65; pres, 65-68); Cent State Speech Asn. **SELECTED PUBLICATIONS** Coauth, An audience debate tournament, Speech Teacher, 64; auth, The role of the coach & forensic tournaments, in Coaching Debate and Other Forensic Activities, Int Textbk, 68; coauth, Argumentation: Inquiry and Advocacy, Prentice-Hall, 74. **CONTACT ADDRESS** Dept of Commun, Wayne State Univ, 530 Manoogian Hall, Detroit, MI, 48202-3919.

ZIEGLER, DHYANA

PERSONAL Born 05/05/1949, New York, New York, s **DISCIPLINE** ENGLISH **EDUCATION** Baruch Coll CUNY BA Program, BS (Cum Laude) 1981; Southern IL Univ-Carbondale, MA 1983, PhD 1985. **CAREER** Essence Magazine, market researcher 1972-75; Rosenfeld Sirowitz & Lawson, copywriter & radio producer 1974-75; Patten and Guest Productions NY, regional mgr 1976-79; WNEW TV, internship desk asst & production asst; Seton Hall Univ, counselor for high school students 1979-81; Baruch Coll CUNY, English tutor & instructor for writing workshops 1979-81; Westside Newspaper, reporter 1980-; CBS TV Network, production intern 1980-81; Southern IL Univ Dept of Radio & Television, lab instructor 1981-83; Jackson State Univ Dept of Mass Comm, asst prof 1984-85; Univ of TN-Knoxville Dept of Broadcasting, asst prof of broadcasting 1985-90, assoc professor, 1990-. **HONORS AND AWARDS** Seek Scholarship Awards for Academic & Service 1979-81 Baruch Coll; Rita Leeds Service Award 1981 Baruch Coll; Sheldon Memorial Award Baruch Coll 1981; Scrippt-Howard Award Baruch Coll 1981; United Press Intl Outstanding Achievement Radio Documentary 1982; Dept of Radio and TV SIUC Outstanding Radio Production Award 1982-83; Grad Dean's Doctoral Fellowship 1983-84; Paul Robinson's Roby Scholar Award Black Affairs Council 1984; Certificate of Merit Award Southern IL Univ Broadcasting Serv 1984; Ebony Bachelorette 1985; Seek Alumni Award Baruch Coll 1985; numerous publications and other professional works; Outstanding Faculty Member of the Year, Coll of Communications, UTK, 1987-88; Chancellor's Citation for Service, Univ of TN Knoxville, 1988; Faculty Research Award, 1992; Chancellor Citation for Extraordinary Service, 1992; State of Tennessee Governor's Award for Outstanding Achievement, 1991; Consortium of Doctors Award, 1991. **MEMBERSHIPS** Natl Political Congress of Black Women; Delta Sigma Theta Sor Inc; Phi Delta Kappa; grad fellow Post Doctoral Acad of Higher Educ; Speech Comm Assn; pres & founder Blacks in Communications Alliance; Natl Cncl of Negro Women Inc; legislative council Southern IL Univ Alumni Assn; panelist Metro Black Media Coalition Conference 1984, Southern IL Univ/Blacks in Communications Alliance 1985, Natl Black Media Coalition Conf 1985; speaker/consultant US Armed Forces Azores Portugal 1986; chmn/public relations, Kiwanis Club of Knoxville, 1988-; Southern Regional Devel Educ Project Coord, Delta Sigma Theta, 1988-; Women in Communications, Inc, vice pres of develop, pres-elect 1989, pres 1990-91;Society of Professional Journalists, 1988-. **SELECTED PUBLICATIONS** Coauthor, Thunder and Silence: The Mass Media in Africa; several book chapters and journal articles, MaxRobinson, Jr, Turbulent Life of a Media phet, Journal of Black Studies, 1989, Challenging Racism in the Classrom: Paving the Road to the Future/ Thoughts and Action-The Journal of the Natl Educ Assn, 1989; articles, "Women and Minorities on Network Television News," Journal of Broadcasting, Spring 1990, "Teaching Television News: A Classroom Newsroom Model," Feedback, Spring 1990. **CONTACT ADDRESS** Univ of Tennessee, 295 Communications Bldg, Knoxville, TN, 37996.

ZIFF, LARZER

PERSONAL Born 10/02/1927, Holyoke, MA, m, 1952, 4 children **DISCIPLINE** AMERICAN LITERATURE **EDUCATION** Univ Chicago, MA, 50, PhD, 55; Oxford Univ, MA, 72. **CAREER** Test constructor English, Educ Testing Serv, 51-52; lectr humanities, Univ Chicago, 52-53, dir spec prog, 53-56; from asst prof to prof English, Univ Calif, Berkeley, 56-72; lectr Am lit, Oxford Univ, 72-78; prof English, Univ Pa, 78-81; CAROLINE DONOVAN PROF ENGLISH, JOHNS HOPKINS UNIV, 81-, Huntington Libr fel, 57; Univ Calif pres fel, 58; Fulbright lectr, Univ Copenhagen, 59-60; Am Coun Learned Soc fel, 63-64; Nat Coun Teachers English distinguished lectr, 66-67; mem comt, Am Studies Int Exchange Persons, 66-; Nat Endowment for Humanities sr fel, 67-68; univ lectr Am lit & fel, Exeter Col, Oxford, 73-78; Guggenheim fel, 77-78. **HONORS AND AWARDS** Christian Gauss Award, 67; Ford Found lectr, Univs of Poland, 60; Fulbright lectr, Univ Sussex, 64. **MEMBERSHIPS** MLA; Am Studies Asn; Am Antiquarian Society; Soc Am Historians. **RESEARCH** Colonial American culture; modern American literature; 19th century culture. **SELECTED PUBLICATIONS** Auth, The Genteel Tradition and the Sacred Rage--High Culture Versus Democracy in Adams, James, and Santayana, Amer Lit, Vol 0064, 92; Franklin, Benjamin, Edwards, Jonathan, and the Representation of American Culture, Jour Amer Hist, Vol 0081, 94; The Cambridge History of American Literature, Vol 1, 1590-1820, Mod Lang Quart, Vol 0056, 95; Conquest and Recovery in Early Writings from America, Amer Lit, Vol 0068, 96; Memoirs--Editorship of Chicago Review--1940s, Chicago Rev, Vol 0042, 96; Voicing America--Language, Literary Farm, and the Origins of the United-States, William and Mary Quart, Vol 0054, 97. **CONTACT ADDRESS** Dept of English, Univ of Pa, Philadelphia, PA, 19174.

ZIMBARDO, ROSE A.

PERSONAL Born 05/29/1932, m, 1957, 1 child **DISCIPLINE** ENGLISH **EDUCATION** Brooklyn Col, AB, 56; Yale Univ, MA, 57, PhD, 60. **CAREER** From instr to assoc prof English, City Col NY, 60-72, grant, 62; ASSOC PROF ENGLISH, STATE UNIV NY, STONY BROOK, 72- **MEMBERSHIPS** English Inst; MLA. **RESEARCH** Restoration literature; Shakespeare; modern drama. **SELECTED PUBLICATIONS** Auth, At Zero-Point, Discourse, Politics, and Satire in Restoration England, Elh-Eng Lit Hist, Vol 0059, 92; African-American Culture in 18th-Century, Eighteenth-Century Stud, Vol 0027, 94. **CONTACT ADDRESS** Dept of English, State Univ of NY, Stony Brook, NY, 11790.

ZIMMERMAN, EVERTETT

DISCIPLINE EIGHTEENTH-CENTURY BRITISH LITERATURE **EDUCATION** Temple Univ, PhD, 66. **CAREER** PROF, ENG, UNIV CALIF, SANTA BARBARA. **RESEARCH** The sentimental novel, satire. **SELECTED PUBLICATIONS** Auth, Defoe and the Novel, Univ Calif, 75; Swift's Narrative Satires, Cornell, 83; Historical Faith: British Fiction and Historiography in the Eighteenth Century, Cornell, 96. **CONTACT ADDRESS** Dept of Eng, Univ Calif, Santa Barbara, CA, 93106-7150. **EMAIL** ezimmer@humanitas.ucsb.edu

ZIMMERMAN, MICHAEL

PERSONAL Born 07/29/1937, North Adams, MA, 4 children **DISCIPLINE** JOYCE, AMERICAN LITERATURE **EDUCATION** Columbia Univ, Ba, 59, MA, 60, PhD(English), 63. **CAREER** Lectr English, Columbia Col, Columbia Univ, 61-62, preceptor, Sch Gen Studies, 62-63; from actg instr to asst prof, Univ Calif, Berkeley, 63-68; from lectr to assoc prof, 68-69, prof English, San Francisco State Univ, 74-, Fulbright lectr, Japan, 67-68; ed, Dialogue: J Psychoanal Perspectives, 78-. **MEMBERSHIPS** Philol Asn Pac Coast. **RESEARCH** Nineteenth and 20th century American literature; James Joyce. **SELECTED PUBLICATIONS** Auth, Literary Revivalism in America, Am Quart, spring 68; Sociological Criticism, of the 1930's, Harper, 73; Stephen's Mothers in Ulysses, Pac Coast Philol, 4/75; James Joyce's Mothers, Dialogue, spring, 78. **CONTACT ADDRESS** Dept of English, San Francisco State Univ, 1600 Holloway Ave, San Francisco, CA, 94132-1740. **EMAIL** mzimman@sfsu.edu

ZIOLKOWSKI, ERIC JOZEF

PERSONAL Born 12/28/1958 **DISCIPLINE** RELIGION; LITERATURE **EDUCATION** Dartmouth Col, BA, 80; Univ Chicago, MA, 81; Univ Chicago, PhD, 87 **CAREER** Asst prof Comparative Literature, Univ Wisconsin Madison, 87-88; asst prof Religion, Lafayette Col, 88-94; assoc prof Religion, Lafayette Col, 94- **HONORS AND AWARDS** Fel, Soc Arts Relig Cult, 97-; Thomas Roy and Lura Forrest Jones Award for Superior Teaching, 98 **MEMBERSHIPS** Amer Acad Relig; Amer Assoc Univ Prof; Amnesty Int **RESEARCH** Religion and Literature, History of Religion, Philosophy of Religion **SELECTED PUBLICATIONS** A Museum of Faiths: Histories and Legacies of the 1893 World's Parliament of Religions, Scholars Press, 93; The Sanctification of Don Quixote: From Hidalgo to Priest, Penn St Univ, 91; "Religion and Literature and the History of Religions: Grounds for Alliance." Jour Lit Theol, 98; "Sancho Panza and Nemi's Priest: Reflections on Myth and Literature." Myth and Method, 96 **CONTACT ADDRESS** Dept Relig, Lafayette Col, Easton, PA, 18042. **EMAIL** ziolkowski@lafayette.edu

ZLOGAR, LAURA

DISCIPLINE ENGLISH LITERATURE **EDUCATION** Marquette Univ, MA, PhD. **CAREER** Prof, Univ of WI. **RESEARCH** 19th century Brit lit; African-Am lit; ethnic Am women writers. **SELECTED PUBLICATIONS** Auth, pubs on Amiri Baraka, Toni Morrison, Amy Tan, Charles Chesnutt, and Paule Marshall. **CONTACT ADDRESS** Eng Dept, Univ Wisconsin, S 3rd St, PO Box 410, River Falls, WI, 54022-5001.

ZLOTNICK, JOAN C.

PERSONAL Born 07/14/1942, New York, NY, m, 1963, 2 children **DISCIPLINE** AMERICAN & URBAN LITERATURE **EDUCATION** Brooklyn Col, BA, 63; Hunter Col, MA, 65; New York Univ, PhD, 69. **CAREER** From lectr to asst prof, 64-77, assoc prof English, 77-84, prof English, Brooklyn Col, City Univ New York, 77- **HONORS AND AWARDS** Founders Day Award, New York Univ, 70. **RESEARCH** Jewish literature; women's literature; New York literature. **SELECTED PUBLICATIONS** Auth, The medium is the message, or is it: A study of Nathanael West's comic strip novel, J Popular Cult, 8/71; Abraham Cohen: A Neglected Realist in Am Jewish Arch, 71; The Damnation of Thereon Ware, with a Backward Glance at Hawthorne, Markham Rev, 71; Day of the locust, a night at the movies: Nathanael West's Hollywood novel, Film Libr Quart, winter 73; Nathanael West and the pictorial imagination, Western Am Lit, 11/74; Influence or coincidence: A comparative study of The Beast in the Jungle and A Painful Case, Colby Libr Quart, 6/75; Dubliners in Winesburg, Ohio: A note on Joyce's The Sisters and Anderson's The Philosopher, Studies in Short Fiction, fall 75; Malamud's The Assistant: Of Frank, Morris, and St Francis, Studies in Am-Jewish Lit, winter, 75; The inflation of the negative: A study of Nathanael West's use (and abuse) of literary sources, Descant, winter 76; Of Dubliners and Ohioans: A Comparative Study of Joyce's Debliners and Anderson's Winesburg Ohio, Ball State Univ Forum, 76; The Day of the Locust: Comparing John Schlessinger's Film and Nathanial West's Novel, Filmograph, 76; Portrait of an American City: The Novelists' New York, Kennikat Press, 82; Msings from the Brooklyn Bridge: The Brooklyn Bridge as Literary Inspiration, New Brooklyn Quart, 83; The Chosen Borough: Chaim Potok's Brooklyn, Studies in American Jewish Literature, 84; A Woman's Will: Kate Chopin on Selfhood, Wifehood, and Motherhood, Markham Rev, 88. **CONTACT ADDRESS** Dept English, Brooklyn Col, CUNY, 2901 Bedford Ave, Brooklyn, NY, 11210-2813.

ZOCH, LYNN M.

PERSONAL NY **DISCIPLINE** COMMUNICATION **EDUCATION** St Lawrence Univ, BA; Syracuse Univ, MS, PhD. **CAREER** Asst prof, Univ SC, 93-; taught at, Univ W FL & Syracuse Univ. **RESEARCH** Organizational boundary spanning and organizational crisis management. **SELECTED PUBLICATIONS** Publ in, Publ Rel Quart, Jour Educ & Small Gp Res; chap in, Beyond the Velvet Ghetto, which focuses on women in publ rel. **CONTACT ADDRESS** Col of Journalism & Mass Commun, Univ of S. Carolina, Carolina Coliseum rm 4005E, Columbia, SC, 29208. **EMAIL** lynn_zoch@jour.sc.edu

ZOLBROD, PAUL GEYER

PERSONAL Born 12/10/1932, Pittsburgh, PA, m, 1967, 2 children **DISCIPLINE** LITERARY CRITICISM, LINGUISTICS **EDUCATION** Univ Pittsburgh, BA, 58, MA, 62, PhD(English), 67. **CAREER** Instr English, Univ Pittsburgh, Titusville, 63-64; from instr to assoc prof 64-77, PROF ENGLISH, ALLEGHENY COL, MEADVILLE, 77-, Fel, Univ NMex, 71-72; consult, Public Broadcasting Northwest Pa, 76-78; Res fel, Nat Endowment Humanities, 78-79. **MEMBERSHIPS** MLA; AAUP; NCTE; Northwest Mod Lang Asn; Soc Am Indian Studies. **RESEARCH** Renaissance literature; ethnopoetics; linguistics. **SELECTED PUBLICATIONS** Auth, The Wind in a Jar, Amer Indian Cult and Res Jour, Vol 0018, 94; Saanii-Dahataal--The Women Are Singing, Amer Indian Cult and Res Jour, Vol 0018, 94. **CONTACT ADDRESS** Dept of English, Allegheny Col, Park Ave, Meadville, PA, 16335.

ZOMPETTI, JOSEPH P.

PERSONAL Born 10/27/1970, Indianapolis, IN, s **DISCIPLINE** COMMUNICATION **EDUCATION** Wayne State Univ, PhD, 98. **CAREER** Asst prof, Mercer Univ, 98- . **HONORS AND AWARDS** Fulbright scholar. **MEMBERSHIPS** Nat Commun Asoc; Speech Pedag. **RESEARCH** Labor rhetoric; postcolonialism; speech pedagogy. **SELECTED PUBLICATIONS** Auth, Developing a Critical Speech Pedagogy, Mich Asoc of Speech Commun J, 96; auth, Toward a Gramscian Critical Rhetoric, Western J Commun, 97; auth, Reading

Postcolonial Identity: The Rhetoric of Devolution from Sri Lanka's President, Chandrika Kumaratunga, Howard J Commun, 97; co-auth with S.J. Berkowitz and S. Aonuma, Transforming the Quest for Meaning: A Case Study in Public Argument, 1997 Proceedings of the SCA/AFA Conference on Argumentation, 98. **CONTACT ADDRESS** Communications Dept, Mercer Univ, 1400 Coleman Ave, Macon, GA, 31207-0001. **EMAIL** zompetti_jp@mercer.edu

ZUCKER, DAVID HARD
PERSONAL Born 05/27/1938, Cleveland, OH **DISCIPLINE** ENGLISH & AMERICAN LITERATURE **EDUCATION** Oberlin Col, BA, 60; Syracuse Univ, MA, 64, PhD(English), 68. **CAREER** Asst ed, Columbia Encycl, 60-62; asst prof English, Washington & Lee Univ, 68-71; from asst prof to assoc prof, 71-78, prof English, Quinnipiac Col, 78-. **MEMBERSHIPS** Asn of Literary Scholars & Critics. **RESEARCH** Elizabethan drama; autobiography; modern poetry. **SELECTED PUBLICATIONS** Co-ed, Selected Essays of Delmore Schwartz, Univ Chicago, 70; auth, Stage and Image in the Plays of Christopher Marlowe, Univ Salzburg, 72; An American Elegist: The Poetry of Horace Gregory, 73, Mod Poetry Studies; Self and History in Delmore Schwartz, Iowa Rev, 78. **CONTACT ADDRESS** Dept of English, Quinnipiac Col, 275 Mt Carmel Ave, Hamden, CT, 06518-1908. **EMAIL** dzucker@quinnipiac.edu

ZUKER, JOEL
DISCIPLINE FILM STUDIES **EDUCATION** NY Univ, MA, PhD. **CAREER** Taught crse(s) in film, NYU, Saint Peters Col, Rutgers & Hunter; instr, Hunter Univ, 72-; have lect or presented papers at colleges, Utah, Fla, Mont, NH, Vermont & Ohio. **HONORS AND AWARDS** PSC-CUNY grants. **RESEARCH** Films of Mel Brooks. **SELECTED PUBLICATIONS** Auth, on Ralph Steiner: Filmmaker and Photographer, Arno Press; bk(s) on, Arthur Penn, G.K Hall & Francis Coppola, G.K. Hall. **CONTACT ADDRESS** Dept of Education, Hunter Col, CUNY, 695 Park Ave, New York, NY, 10021.

ZURAKOWSKI, MICHELE M.
PERSONAL Born 03/06/1960, Bay City, MI, m, 1982, 1 child **DISCIPLINE** SPEECH COMMUNICATION **EDUCATION** Univ Minn, PhD, 92. **CAREER** Asst Prof Speech Commun, Col St. Catherine, 94-, Dept Chair, 94-. **MEMBERSHIPS** NCA; CSCA; CTAM. **RESEARCH** Women and public address; birth control rhetoric. **SELECTED PUBLICATIONS** Auth, "Interiors" as Interdisciplinary Text: A Case Analysis Using Film to Integrate Classroom Discussion of Interpersonal and Mass Mediated Meanings, Mich Asn Speech Commun J, 94; From Doctors and Lawyers to Wives and Mothers: Enacting "Feminine Style" and Changing Abortion Rights Arguments, Women's Studies in Communication, Spring 94; Ti-Grace Atkinson, Women Public Speakers in the United States, 1925-1993: A Bio-Critical Sourcebook, Greenwood Press, 94; Modeling Rhetorical Criticism, The Speech Commun Teacher 11, 97. **CONTACT ADDRESS** Speech Communication Dept, Col of St. Catherine, 2004 Randolph Ave., St. Paul, MN, 55105. **EMAIL** mmzurakowski@stkate.edu

ZWEIG, ELLEN
PERSONAL Born 01/27/1947, Chicago, IL **DISCIPLINE** CONTEMPORARY POETRY AND POETICS **EDUCATION** Columbia Univ, MFA, 70; Univ Mich, BA, 67, PhD(English), 80. **CAREER** LECTR INTERDISCIPLINARY ART, SAN FRANCISCO UNIV, 80-, Res fel poetics & ling, Mass Inst Technol, summer 81; writer-in-residence, Griffith Univ, Australia, summer 82. **MEMBERSHIPS** MLA **RESEARCH** Contemporary poetry; performance art; history of interdisciplinary art. **SELECTED PUBLICATIONS** Auth, Presence and Resistance--Postmodernism and Cultural Politics in Contemporary American Performance, Amer Bk Rev, Vol 0016, 94; Acting-Out--Feminist Performances, Amer Bk Rev, Vol 0016, 94; Mendicant Erotics Sydney, a Performance for Radio, Tdr-Drama Rev-Jour Performance Stud, Vol 0040, 96. **CONTACT ADDRESS** 201 Ridgeway #2, Oakland, CA, 94611.

ZWERDLING, ALEX
PERSONAL Born 06/21/1932, Breslau, Germany **DISCIPLINE** ENGLISH **EDUCATION** Cornell Univ, BA, 53; Princeton Univ, MA, 56, PhD(English), 60. **CAREER** Instr English, Swarthmore Col, 57-61; from asst prof to assoc prof, 61-73, PROF ENGLISH, UNIV CALIF, BERKELEY, 73-, Am Coun Learned Soc study fel, 64-65; Ctr Advanced Studies Behav Sci fel, 64-65; Nat Endowment for Humanities fel, 73-74; vis prof English, Northwestern Univ, 77; Guggenheim fel, 77-78; consult fel panel, Nat Endowment Humanities, 77-. **MEMBERSHIPS** MLA **RESEARCH** Modern literature; contemporary literature; literature and politics. **SELECTED PUBLICATIONS** Auth, American Salons--Encounters with European Modernism, 1885-1917, Comparative Lit Stud, Vol 0032, 95. **CONTACT ADDRESS** Dept of English, Univ of Calif, Berkeley, CA, 94720.

ZWICKER, STEVEN NATHAN
PERSONAL Born 06/04/1943, San Diego, CA, m, 1965, 4 children **DISCIPLINE** SEVENTEENTH CENTURY LITERATURE **EDUCATION** Univ Calif, Los Angeles, BA, 65; Brown Univ, PhD(English), 69. **CAREER** ASSOC PROF ENGLISH, WASH UNIV, 69-, Taft fel, Univ Cincinnati, 70-71. **MEMBERSHIPS** MLA **RESEARCH** Seventeenth century political poetry; typology; political history. **SELECTED PUBLICATIONS** Auth, Marvell,Andrew and Waller, Edmund--17th-Century Praise and Restoration Satire, Renaissance Quart, Vol 0047, 94; Dryden, John--A Literary-Life, Mod Philol, Vol 0092, 94; The Paradoxes of Tender Conscience--Dryden Hind and the Panther, Elh-Eng Lit Hist, Vol 0063, 96. **CONTACT ADDRESS** Dept of English, Wash Univ, 1 Brookings Dr, Saint Louis, MO, 63130-4899.

ZYTARUK, GEORGE J.
DISCIPLINE ENGLISH **EDUCATION** BA, Univ Alberta; BEd, MA, PhD, Dlitt. **CAREER** Prof Nipissing Univ, 67-92; Prof Emer, 92-. **HONORS AND AWARDS** Founding pres, Nipissing Univ, 1967, **RESEARCH** D.H. Lawrence; **SELECTED PUBLICATIONS** Ed, D.H. Lawrence's letters; ed, Correspondence of Jessie Chambers. **CONTACT ADDRESS** Dept of English, Nipissing Univ, 100 College Dr, Box 5002, North Bay, ON, P1B 8L7.

Geographic Index

ALABAMA

Athens
Laubenthal, Penne J.

Auburn
Backscheider, Paula R.
Straiton, T. Harmon, Jr.
Wright, Thomas L.

Birmingham
Bach, Rebecca Ann
Baker, Tracey
Boden, Jean
Bodon, Jean
Chapman, David W.
Frost, Linda Anne
Grimes, Kyle
Haarbauer, Don Ward
Haddin, Theodore
Hickson, Mark
Hutchings, William
Jeffreys, Mark
Kemp, Theresa D.
Kurata, Marilyn J.
Long, Ada
Neiva, Eduardo
Person, Leland S.
Quinlan, Kieran
Sullivan, Sherry A.
Wharton, Lawrence
Whitaker, Elaine E.

Florence
Smith, Ronald E.

Jacksonville
Freier, Mary P.

Maxwell AFB
Kline, John A.

Mobile
Dendinger, Lloyd N.

Montgomery
Bibb, T. Clifford
Bryson, Ralph J.
Ely, Robert Eugene
Little, Anne Colclough
Michael, Marion C.
Moore, Nathan
Willis, Susan

Troy
Lee, Hsiao-Hung
Stewart, Henry R., Jr.

Tuscaloosa
Burke, John J.
Galli, Barbara E.
Harris, Thomas E.
Johnson, Rhoda E.
Tripp, Bernell E.
Wallis, Carrie G.

Tuskegee
Robinson, Ella S.

University
Johnson, Claudia Durst
Latimer, Dan Raymond
Salem, James Morris

ALASKA

Anchorage
Babb, Genie
Crosman, Robert
Kline, Daniel
Linton, Patricia
Moore, Judith
Patterson, Becky
Widdicombe, Richard Toby

Fairbanks
Strohmaier, Mahla

ARIZONA

Flagstaff
Yowell, Robert L.

Phoenix
Pritchard, Susan V.

Searcy
Elliott, Gary D.

Tempe
Alisky, Marvin Howard
Allen, Craig Mitchell
Brink, Jeanie Renee
Chambers, Anthony Hood
Harris, Mark
Horan, Elizabeth R.
Kehl, Delmar George
Lightfoot, Marjorie Jean
Luey, Beth Edelmann
Ney, James Walter
Shinn, Thelma J.
Youm, K.H.

Tucson
Aiken, Susan Hardy
Bowen, Roger
Canfield, John Douglas
Clark, L.D.
Dahood, Roger
Dinnerstein, Myra
Dryden, Edgar A.
Eisner, Sigmund
Hogle, Jerrold Edwin
Langendoen, Donald Terence
Mcelroy, John Harmon
Medine, Peter Ernest
Mills, John Arvin
Schneidau, Herbert N.
Shelton, Richard William
Veaner, Allen B.
Wearing, J.P.
Willard, Thomas Spaulding
Wright, George Thaddeus
Zegura, Elizabeth Chesney

ARKANSAS

Arkadelphia
Halaby, Raouf J.

Batesville
Counts, Michael L.
Lankford, George E.
Robbins, Helen W.
Tebbetts, Terrell L.

Conway
Story, Kenneth Ervin

Fayetteville
Adams, Charles H.
Allen, Myria
Amason, Patricia
Arenberg, Nancy
Bennett, James Richard
Bolsterli, Margaret Jones
Booker, M. Keith
Brady, Robert M.
Burris, Sidney
Candido, Joseph
Frentz, Thomas S.
Guilds, John C.
Hassel, Jon
Heffernan, Michael
Jimoh, A. Yemisi
Juhl, M.E.
Kinnamon, Keneth
Macrae, Suzanne H.
Marren, Susan M.
Montgomery, Lyna Lee
Quinn, William A.
Rogers, Jimmie N.
Rosteck, H. Thomas
Rushing, Janice H.
Scheide, Frank Milo
Sherman, Sandra
Smith, Stephen A.
Wilkie, Brian

Little Rock
Anderson, Steve
Garnett, Mary Anne
Gibbens, E. Byrd
Jauss, David
Knutson, Roslyn L.
Kwasny, Andrea
Levernier, James
Littlefield, Dan F.
Moore, Patrick
Murphy, Russell E.
Parins, James
Parins, Marylyn
Ramsey, C. Earl
Stodola, Zabelle
Strickland, Johnye
Vannatta, Dennis
Yoder, R. Paul

Monticello
Adams, Tyrone L.
Stewart, E. Kate

State University
Bayless, Ovid Lyndal

Tempe
Sensibar, Judith L.

CALIFORNIA

Alpine
Butler, Gerald Joseph

Arcata
Hahn, Laura K.

Azusa
Shoemaker, Melvin H.

Bakersfield
Flachmann, Michael C.

Balboa Island
Leedom, Tim C.

Belmont
Gavin, Rosemarie Julie

Berkeley
Adelman, Janet Ann
Bagdikian, Ben Haig
Bloom, Robert
Booth, Stephen
Butler, J.
Christ, Carol Tecla
Christian, Barbara T.
Clader, Linda
Coolidge, John Stanhope
Crews, Frederick
Duggan, Joseph John
Friedman, Donald M.
Lesser, Wendy
Littlejohn, David
Marcus, Sharon
Melia, Daniel Frederick
Michaels, Leonard
Middleton, Anne Louise
Miles, Josephine
Ogden, Dunbar Hunt
Richardson, Anne
Richmond, Hugh M.
Richmond, Velma B.
Rosenberg, Marvin
Scott, Peter Dale
Shapiro, Barbara June
Sloane, Thomas O.
Wolgast, Eliz H.
Zwerdling, Alex

Campbell
Nichols, Patricia Causey

Canoga Park
Levy, William Turner

Carson
Geller, Lila Belle

Chico
Downes, David Anthony

Chula Vista
Bekendorf, Ray R.

Claremont
Barnes, Richard G.
Elsbree, Langdon
Greene, Gayle Jacoba
Groves, Jeffrey D.
Lohrli, Anne
Mezey, Robert
Redfield, Marc
Sellery, J'nan Morse
Waingrow, Marshall
Walker, Cheryl
Warner, Nicholas Oliver

Cupertino
Bogus, Diane Adamz

Davis
Carter, Everett
Gilbert, Sandra Mortola
Hays, Peter L.
Hoffman, Michael Jerome
Landau, Norma Beatrice
Levin, Richard A.
Major, Clarence
Sarlos, Robert Karoly
Stewart, John Othneil
Waddington, Raymond Bruce.
Woodress, James
Zender, Karl Francis

Dominguez Hills
Ravitz, Abe C.

El Dorado Hills
Schlachter, Gail Ann

Encinitas
Fisher, Edith Maureen

Fresno
Adams, Katherine L.
Bloom, Melanie
Bluestein, Gene
Bochin, Hal William
Faderman, Lillian
Fraleigh, Douglas
Levine, Philip
Rosenthal, Judith Ann

Fullerton
Axelrad, Arthur Marvin
Cummings, Sherwood
Jaskoski, Helen
Myers, Mitzi
Vogeler, Martha Salmon
Wagner, M. John
Witmer, Diane F.

Glendora
Salwak, Dale F.

Hayward
Fuchs, Jacob

Irvine
Barney, Stephen Allen
Folkenflik, Robert
Rieckman, Jens

La Jolla
Cancel, Robert
Cole, Mike
Cox, Stephen D.
Davis, Susan
Dijkstra, Bram
Engestrom, Yrjo
Fitch, Noel Riley
Foster, Frances Smith
Gaffney, Floyd
Hallin, Daniel C.
Hartouni, Valerie
Horwitz, Robert
Keyssar, Helene
Mukerji, Chandra
Padden, Carol
Rafael, Vicente
Wesling, Donald Truman

La Jolle
Schiller, Anita R.

La Mirada
Lewis, Todd Vernon

Laguna Beach
Krieger, Murray

Loma Linda
Baker, Delbert Wayne

Long Beach
Aspiz, Harold
Cargile, Aaron C.
Locklin, Gerald Ivan
May, Charles Edward
Weinstock, Donald Jay
Young, Elizabeth V.

Los Angeles
Allmendinger, Blake
Band, Arnold J.
Banet-Weiser, Sarah
Banta, Martha
Behdad, Ali
Beniger, James R.
Berst, Charles A.
Borsch, Frederick Houk
Braudy, Leo
Braunmuller, A.P.
Brier, Peter A.
Colley, Nathaniel S.
Cooper, Marilyn Marie
Cope, Jackson Irving
Dane, Joseph A.
Dutton, William H.
Fisher, Walter R.
Free, Katherine B.
Friedman, Philip Allan
Fulk, Janet
Grassian, Esther
Green, Lawrence Donald
Kelly, Henry Ansgar
Klob, Gwin Jack
Kolb, Jack
Komar, Kathleen Lenore
Ladefoged, Peter
Laird, David
Lanham, Richard Alan
Lazar, Moshe
Lewis, Jane Elizabeth
Lincoln, Kenneth
Maniquis, Robert Manuel
Manning, Peter J.
Martines, Lauro
Mellor, Anne Kostelanetz
Noble, Douglas
Novak, Maximillian E.
Nussbaum, Felicity
Orenstein, Gloria Feman
Pecora, Vincent P.
Perez-Torres, Rafael
Post, Jonathan F.S.
Quintero, Ruben
Roper, Alan
Rosenthal, Margaret F.
Rowe, Karen E.
Schor, Hilary
Sellin, Paul R.
Sheats, Paul Douglas
Shuger, Debora
Smith, Jeffrey A.
Tennyson, Georg Bernhard

Whiteman, D. Bruce
Wortham, Thomas

Malibu
Buchanan, Raymond W.
Casey, Michael W.
Casmir, Fred L.
Clegg, Cyndia Susan
Holmes, David
Lowry, David

McKinleyville
Yingling, Julie

Menlo Park
White, Cecil R.

Merced
Cabezut-Ortiz, Delores J.

Mission Viejo
Heffernan, William A.

Moraga
Beran, Carol L.

Moss Beach
Spretnak, Charlene M.

Northridge
Bjork, Robert Eric
Clendenning, John
Goss, James
Johnson, Dewayne Burton
Klotz, Marvin
Marlane, Judith

Oakland
Abinader, Elmaz
Adisa, Opal Palmer
Bloch, Chana
Kahn, Madeleine
Milowicki, Edward John
Potter, Elizabeth
Ratcliffe, Stephen
Scheinberg, Cynthia
Strychacz, Thomas
Ward, Carole Geneva
Zweig, Ellen

Orange
Schneider, Matthew T.

Palo Alto
Ginsberg, Lesley

Pasadena
Clark, Justus Kent
Smallenburg, Harry Russell

Playa del Rey
Mahoney, John Francis

Pomona
Bellman, Samuel Irving
Morsberger, Robert E.

Redlands
Musmann, Klaus
Vailakis, Ivan Gordon

Riverside
Axelrod, Steven Gould
Bredbeck, Gregory W.
Briggs, John C.
Childers, Joseph W.
Devlin, Kimberly J.
Dunn, Robert P.
Dunn, Robert P.
Eigner, Edwin Moss
Elliott, Emory B.
Essick, Robert N.
Fabricant, Carole
Fagundo, Ana Maria
Ganim, John Michael
Haggerty, George E.
Kinney, Katherine
Kronenfeld, Judy
Lopez, Tiffany Ana
Mileur, Jean-Pierre
Morton, Carlos
Roy, Parama
Stewart, Stanley N.
Tyler, Carole-Anne
Vickery, John B.
Westfahl, Gary
Willis, Deborah

Rohnert Park
Abernethy, Cecil Emory
Haslam, Gerald William
Raskin, Jonah

Sacramento
Bankowsky, Richard James
Trujillo, Nick L.
Vande Berg, Leah R.

San Bernardino
Barnes, Ronald Edgar
Blackey, Robert Alan
Golden, Bruce
Jandt, Fred E.
White, Edward Michael

San Diego
Adams, Elsie B.
Benson, Jackson J.
Brown, Ruth Christiani
Dionisopoulos, George N.
Farber, Gerald Howard
Foster, Frances Smith
Fussell, Edwin
Geist, Patricia
Griswold, Jerome Joseph
Jackson, James Harvey
Keller, Karl
Lauzen, Martha M.
Lustig, Myron W.
Martin, Donald R.
McGowan, Joseph P.
Neumeyer, Peter F.
Nyce, Benjamin M.
Real, Michael
Savvas, Minas
Spitzberg, Brian H.
Walsh, Elizabeth

San Francisco
Bassan, Maurice
Berger, Arthur A.
Browning, Judith
Burneko, Guy
Busby, Rudolph E.
Dickey, William
Feinstein, Herbert Charles
    Verschleisser
Gottesman, Les
Gregory, Michael Strietmann
Harrison, Randall Paul
Hill, Patricia Liggins
Jewell, James Earl
MacKinnon, Patricia L.
Middlebrook, Jonathan
Schechter, Joel
Smith, Patrick J.
Solomon, H. Eric
Vogeley, Nancy Jeanne
Zimmerman, Michael

San Jose
Blouin, Lenora
Mengxiong, Liu
Varona, Federico
Walker, Ethel Pitts
Wilcox, Dennis Lee

San Luis Obispo
Gish, Robert F.

San Marino
Thorpe, James

Santa Barbara
Abbott, H. Porter
Allaback, Steve
Bazerman, Charles
Blau, Sheridan
Bliss, Lee
Boscagli, Maurizia
Bowers, Edgar
Braun Pasternack, Carol
Butler-Evans, Eliot
Carlson, Julie
Cook, Stephan H.
Delaney, Paul
Duffy, Andrew Enda
Erickson, Robert A.
Fradenburg, Louise
Fumerton, Patricia
Geok-lin Lim, Shirley
Giuliano, Michael J.
Gunn, Giles
Guss, Donald Leroy
Gutierezz-Jones, Carl
Harrison, Victoria

Heckendorn Cook, Elizabeth
Helgerson, Richard
Heller, Lee Ellen
Liu, Alan
Maslan, Mark
McCarthy, Patric J.
McConnell, Frank
Miko, Stephen
Newfield, Cristopher
Potter, Robert Alonzo
Ridland, John
Sider, John W.
Speirs, Logan
Spencer, Gregory H.
St. Omer, Garth
Steiner, Thomas Robert
Vander May, Randall J.
Wiemann, John M.
Willis, Paul J.
Young, Kay
Zimmerman, Everett

Santa Clara
Burnham, Michelle
Dreher, Diane Elizabeth
Osberg, Richard H.
White, Fred D.

Santa Cruz
Halverson, John
Hull, Akasha
Moglen, Helene

Santa Monica
Tobias, Michael Charles

Sonoma
Woodbridge, John M.

Stanford
Bar, Francois
Breitrose, Henry S.
Brown, George Hardin
Carnochan, Walter Bliss
Castle, Terry
Chaffee, Steven H.
Evans, John Martin
Felstiner, John
Fliegelman, Jay
Franco, Jean
Glasser, Theodore L.
Gumbrecht, Hans Ulrich
Leets, Laura
Nass, Clifford I.
Perloff, Marjorie Gabrielle
Polhemus, Robert M.
Reeves, Byron
Risser, James V.
Roberts, Donald F.
Ryan, Lawrence Vincent
Seaver, Paul Siddall
Ueda, Makoto

Stockton
Borden, Diane M.
Camfield, Gregg
Cox, Robert
Kahn, Sy M.
Knighton, Robert Tolman
Lutz, Reinhart
McCullen, Maurice
Mueller, Roger
Norton, Camille
Schedler, Gilbert W.
Seaman, John
Tedards, Douglas Manning
Williams, John S.
Wolak, William J.

Turlock
Mcdermott, Douglas

COLORADO

Boulder
Allen, Brenda J.
Anthes, Susan H.
Baker, Donald C.
Craig, Robert T.
Deetz, Stanley A.
Ellsworth, Ralph E.
Guralnick, Elissa Schagrin
Hauser, Gerard A.
Jackson, Michele
Jones, Stanley E.
Kawin, Bruce Frederick

Laffoon, Elizabeth Anne
LeBaron, Curtis D.
Mcintosh, Marjorie Keniston
Stevenson, John A.
Sukenick, Ronald
Taylor, Bryan C.
Tompkins, Phillip K.
Tracy, Karen
White, Cindy H.

Colorado Springs
Blackburn, Alexander
Butte, George
Hackman, Michael
von Dassanowsky, Robert
Walker, Kim
Wanca-Thibault, Maryanne
Washington, Durthy A.

Denver
Aubrey, James R.
Barbour, Alton Bradford
Barbuor, Alton
Clark, Patricia
Fleck, Richard F.
Furness, Edna Lue
Howard, W. Scott
Jones, John F.
Kiteley, Brian
Nice, J.A.
Olsen, Alexandra H.
Salzberg, Joel
Wick, Robert L.

Durango
Greenwood, Tina Evans

Fort Collins
Aoki, Eric
Ben Zvi, Linda
Bucco, Martin
Burgchardt, Carl
Campbell, SueEllen
Cantrell, Carol
Cowell, Pattie Lee
Delahunty, Gerald
Flahive, Doug
Gill, Ann
Gravlee, Jack
Griffin, Cindy
Irvine, James Richard
Kiefer, Kate
Krahnke, Karl
Lakin, Barbara
Matott, Glenn
McBride, William
Mogen, David Lee
Ott, Brian L.
Palmquist, Mike
Pendell, Sue
Petrie, Neil
Phillips, Denny
Pratt, John
Reid, Louann
Reid, Stephen
Ronda, Bruce
Schamberger, Ed
Swinson, Ward
Tanner, Jim
Thiem, Jon
Trembath, Paul
Vancil, David
Vest, David
Whitaker, Rosemary
Willard, Barb
Work, James

Greeley
Arneson, Pat
Ferguson, Sherilyn
Karre, Idahlynn
Keaten, James A.

Littleton
Schaefer, Josephine O'Brien

Pueblo
Barber, Margaret
Griffen, John R.
Griffin, John R.
Hochman, Will
Taylor, Cindy

USAF Academy
Shuttleworth, Jack M.

CONNECTICUT

Burlington
Leeds, Barry Howard

Cheshire
Ellison, Jerome

Danbury
Briggs, John
Briggs, John P.
Welburn, Ronald Garfield

Deep River
Hieatt, Constance B.

Fairfield
Campos, Javier F.
Dykeman, Therese B.

Guilford
Deresiewicz, William

Hamden
Brown, Pearl Leblanc
Zucker, David Hard

Hartford
Benton, Richard Paul
Cohn, Henry S.
Hunter, Dianne McKinley
Kuyk, Dirk Adriaan, Jr.
Lang, Robert

Haven
Martz, Louis Lohr

Killingworth
Sampson, Edward C.

Mashantucket
Newport, William H.A.

Middletown
Rose, Phyllis Davidoff
Szegedy-Maszak, Andrew

New Britain
Gigliotti, Gilbert L.

New Haven
Bloom, Harold
Brisman, Leslie
Bromwich, David
Eder, Doris Leonora
Ferguson, Margaret Williams
Franklin, Ralph William
Garvey, Sheila Hickey
Hollander, John
Holley, Sandra Cavanaugh
Krasner, David
Lawler, Traugott
Metlitzki, Dorothee
Parks, Stephen Robert
Peterson, Linda H.
Stambovsky, Phillip
Stepto, Robert Burns
Valesio, Paolo
Waith, Eugene Mersereau
Welsh, Alexander
Whitaker, Thomas Russell
Yeazell, Ruth Bernard

New London
Bleeth, Kenneth Alan
Evans, Robley Jo
Hartman, Charles O.
Taranow, Gerda

North Haven
Culler, Arthur Dwight

Stamford
Selfridge-Field, Eleanor

Storrs
Bloom, Lynn Z.
Carlson, Eric Walter
Charters, Ann D.
Chow, Karen
Gatta, John, Jr.
Hamilton, Mark A.
Higonnet, Margaret Randolph
Hollenberg, Donna Krolik
Jacobus, Lee Andre
Molette, Carlton Woodard, II

Peterson, Richard S.
Roberts, Thomas J.
Stern, Milton R.
Waniek, Marilyn Nelson

West Hartford
Arthur, Gwen
Ellis, Donald
Ghnassia, Jill Dix
Katz, Sandra
Roderick, John M.
Seabury, Marcia

West Haven
Emma, Ronald David
Marx, Paul
Sloane, David Edward Edison

West Simsbury
Stevenson, Catherine Barnes

Willimantic
Catlett Anderson, Celia
Jacobik, Gray
Mama, Raouf
Molette, Barbara J.
Phillips McGowan, Marcia

Woodbridge
Kimnach, Wilson H.

DELAWARE

Dover
Nielsen, Michael

Newark
Afifi, Walid A.
Beasley, Jerry Carr
Brock, Dewey Heyward
Calhoun, Thomas O.
Courtright, John A.
Cox, Roger Lindsay
Dee, Juliet L.
Detenber, Benjamin H.
Gates, Barbara Timm
Goodman, Susan
Halio, Jay Leon
Haslett, Betty J.
Hogan, Robert
Lemay, Joseph Alberic Leo
Martin, Ronald Edward
Mcleod, Douglas M.
Mell, Donald Charles
Merrill, Thomas F.
Pauly, Thomas Harry
Pavitt, Charles
Perse, Elizabeth M.
Pifer, Ellen
Safer, Elaine Berkman
Samter, Wendy
Scott, Bonnie Kime
Signorielli, Nancy
Van Dover, James K.
Walker, Jeanne Murray

Wilmington
Jian-Zhong, Zhou

DISTRICT OF COLUMBIA

Washington
Arnez, Nancy L.
Aufderheide, Patricia
Austin, Bobby William
Babb, Valerie M.
Bennett, Betty T.
Betz, Paul F.
Boswell, Jackson Campbell
Boykin, Keith
Brady, Leo
Broderick, John Caruthers
Brown, Theressa Wilson
Captain, Yvonne
Cardaci, Paul F.
Cima, Gay Gibson
Claydon, Margaret
Cole, John Y., Jr.
Collins, Michael J.
Comor, Edward
Corrigan, Maureen
Crane, Milton

Dunn, Ellen Catherine
Farr, Judith Banzer
Fernandes, James
Fisher, Leona
Fort, Keith
Fox, Pamela
Gewanter, David
Glavin, John
Gopalan, Lalitha
Hall, Kim
Hammer, Mitchell R.
Hendrix, Jerry
Hirch, John C.
Hirsh, John Campion
Holmer, Joan Ozark
Ingebretsen, Edward J.
Irvine, Martin
Jackson, Mary E.
Jamme, Albert W.F.
Jorgens, Jack J.
Kadlec, David
Kaplan, Lindsay
Kent, Carol Fleisher
Lanoette, William John
Leche, Emma Jean
Loesberg, Jonathan
Maddox, Lucy
Mahony, Robert E.P.
Malek, Abbas
Mann, Thomas J.
Matabane, Paula W.
Mcaleavey, David Willard
McCann, Richard
Miller, Jeanne-Marie A.
Mitchell, Angelyn
Mowlana, Hamid
Moyer, Kermit W.
Niles, Lyndrey Arnaud
Noble, Marianne K.
O'Brien, George
O'Connor, Patricia E.
Parry-Giles, Trevor
Pfordresher, John P.
Pike, David
Pope, Rebecca A.
Ragussis, Michael
Reilly, John Marsden
Ribeiro, Alvaro
Robinson, Amy
Rosenblatt, Jason Philip
Rubenstein, Roberta
Schwartz, Henry J.
Schwartz, Richard B.
Sendry, Joseph M.
Shahid, Irfan Arif
Shanks, Hershel
Shulman, Jeffrey
Siegel, Joel E.
Sitterson, Joseph
Slakey, Roger L.
Slevin, James
Smith, Bruce
Smith, Bruce Ray
Snyder, Susan Brooke
Stack, Richard
Sten, Christopher Wessel
Stetz, Margaret
Sutton, Sharyn
Szittya, Penn
Taylor, Henry
Taylor, Orlando L.
Temple, Kathryn
Tinkcom, Matthew
Tm, King
Todd, Dennis
Traylor, Eleanor W.
Turner, Jeanine W.
Valerie M., Babb
Wallwork, Ernest
Warren, Clay
Waznak, Robert P.
Weaver, Gary
Wendland, Ernst R.
Wharton Boyd, Linda F.
Wickham Crowley, Kelley M.
Winter, Daria Portray
Yeandle, Laetitia
Young, Elizabeth Bell

FLORIDA

Alachua
Wall, William G.

Boca Raton
Smith, Voncile Marshall

Coral Gables
Benstock, Shari
Foreman, Kathryn S.
Guttenberg, Barnett
Kelleghan, Fiona
McCarthy, Patrick A.
Palmeri, Frank
Russo, John Paul
Suzuki, Mihoko

Dania
Skellings, Edmund

DeLand
Kaivola, Karen
McCoy, Ken
McCoy, Ken W.
Pearson, John H.

Destin
Beavers, Myrtle B.

Fort Myers
Golian, Linda Marie

Gainesville
Cailler, Bernadette Anne
Carnell, Corbin Scott
Derrick, Clarence
Duckworth, Alistair Mckay
Gordon, Andrew
Hill-Lubin, Mildred Anderson
Holland, Norman N.
Kershner, R. Brandon
New, Melvyn
Paris, Bernard J.
Schmidt, Patricia Lois
Shoaf, Richard A.
Smith, F. Leslie
Smith, Julian
Smith, Stephanie A.

Hollywood
Samra, Rise J.

Lakeland
Lott, Raymond

Melbourne
Matar, Nabil

Miami
Johnson, Kenneth E.
Sugg, Richard Peter
Waugh, Butler Huggins

Orlando
Adicks, Richard R.
Schiffhorst, Gerald Joseph

Pensacola
Auter, Philip J.
Umphlett, Wiley Lee

Plantation
Ferrari, Roberto

Sanford
Wright, Stephen Caldwell

St. Petersburg
Dunlap, Karen F. Brown
Meinke, Peter
Wells, Daniel Arthur

Tallahassee
Baker, Stuart Eddy
Barbour, Paula Louise
Berry, Ralph M.
Blazek, Ronald David
Braendlin, Bonnie Hoover
Cunningham, Karen
Fallon, Richard Gordon
Hawkins, Hunt
Irvine, Carolyn Lenette
Kirby, David
Lhamon, W.T.
McElrath, Joseph R.
Morris, Harry
Pratt, Louis Hill
Rowe, Anne Ervin

Tampa
Moss, S.
Runge, Laura
Solomon, Andrew Joseph
Tyson, Nancy J.

Winter Park
Cohen, Edward H.
Flick, Robert Gene

GEORGIA

Albany
Hill, James Lee
Hill, James Lee

Athens
Adams, Michael F.
Algeo, John T.
Brooks, Dwight E.
Colvert, James B.
Craige, Betty Jean
Dickie, M.
Doyle, Charles Clay
Franklin, Rosemary F.
Free, William Joseph
Freer, Coburn
Gordon, Walter Martin
Gruner, Charles R.
Hellerstein, Nina Salant
Kibler, James Everett, Jr.
Klein, Jared S.
Kraft, Elizabeth
Kretschmar, William A., Jr.
McAlexander, Hubert Horton
Mcalexander, Patricia Jewell
Miller, Ronald Baxter
Moore, Rayburn Sabatzky
Moran, Mary H.
Moran, Michael G.
Ower, John
Ruppersburg, Hugh
Teague, Frances Nicol
Toombs, Charles Phillip
Vance, John Anthony

Atlanta
Abraham, Julie L.
Arnold Twining, Mary
Askew, Timothy
Austin, Gayle M.
Balsamo, Anne
Bauerlein, Mark
Bean, Bobby Gene
Beaty, Jerome
Bell, Linda A.
Bernstein, Matthew H.
Black, Daniel
Brownley, Martine Watson
Bugge, John Michael
Campbell, C. Jean
Caruth, Cathy
Cavanagh, Sheila T.
Chace, William M.
Christopher, Georgia B.
Dillingham, William B.
Dowell, Peter W.
Duncan, Charles
Elliott, Michael
Ervin, Hazel A.
Fine, Laura
Foote, Bud
Gallant, Christine
Gruber, William E.
Grusin, R.
Guy-Sheftall, Beverly
Harpold, Terry
Hesla, David H.
Higgins, Elizabeth J.
Hirsch, James
Hirsh, James
Hollahan, Eugene
Jin, Xuefei
Johnston, John
Kalaidjian, Walter
Keenan, Hugh Thomas
Kramer, Victor Anthony
Kropf, Carl R.
Ladd, Barbara
Lane, Christopher
Levenduski, Cristine
Liddell, Janice Lee
Lisby, Gregory C.
Long, Richard Alexander
Ma, Qian
Manley, Frank
Mcclure, Charlotte Swain
McGuire, Peter
Mchaney, Thomas Lafayette
Metzger, Lore
Meyers, Marian J.
Morey, James
Nickerson, Catherine Ross

Osinubi, Olumide
Pederson, Lee
Petraglia-Bahri, Deepika
Petraglia-Bahri, Joseph
Pickens, Ernestine W. McCoy
Pickens, William Garfield
Rambuss, Richard
Ramsey, Mary K.
Reed, Walter
Sanders, Mark
Schaller, Kristi
Schuchard, W. Ronald
Sessions, William Alfred
Shaner, Jaye L.
Sitter, John
Sizemore, Christine Wick
Spivey, Ted Ray
Strain, Ellen
Tomasulo, Frank P.
Watkins, Floyd C.
Weiss, Victoria Louise
Willen, Diane
Winkler, Carol
Zatlin, Linda Gertner

Augusta
Rice, Louise Allen

Avondale Estates
Bulger, Peggy A.

Carrollton
Doxey, William S.
Earnest, Steve
Goodson, Carol F.
Hynes, Thomas J., Jr.

Columbus
Ross, Daniel W.

Dahlonega
Daigle, Lennet

Decatur
De Ortego Y Gasca, Felipe
Pinka, Patricia G.

Demorest
Greene, David Louis

Fort Valley
Jenkins, Joyce O.

La Grange
Freeman, Bernice

Macon
Cass, Michael Mcconnell
Zompetti, Joseph P.

Marietta
Barnum, Carol
Haimes Korn, Kim
Kelly, Rebecca
Pfeiffer, Sandy W.
Rainey, Kenneth T.
Stevens, Mark

Milledgeville
Glowka, Arthur Wayne
Jenkins, Ronald Bradford

Mount Berry
Tenger, Zeynep

Savannah
Baker, Christopher P.
Fisher, James Randolph
Milledge, Luetta Upshur
Nordquist, Richard

Statesboro
Humma, John Ballard

Valdosta
Campbell, Lee
Marks, Patricia

HAWAII

Hilo
Doudna, Martin Kirk

Honolulu
Brandon, James R.
Carroll, William Dennis
Creed, Walter Gentry
Levy, Alfred J.
Marshall, W. Gerald
McCutcheon, Elizabeth North
Menikoff, Barry
Morse, Jonathan
Quirk, Ruthmarie
Wayne, Valerie

Kaneohe
Jackson, Miles Merrill

Laie
Shumway, Eric Brandon

IDAHO

Boise
Boyer, Dale Kenneth
Jones, Daryl
Lauterbach, Charles Everett
Maguire, James Henry
Sahni, Chaman Lall

Caldwell
Attebery, Louie Wayne

Moscow
McFarland, Ronald E.
Meldrum, Barbara H.
Sipahigil, Teoman
Stratton, Charles R.
Williams, Gary J.

Pocatello
Attebery, Brian
Attebery, Jennifer
Goldbeck, Janne
Hamlin, William
Hellwig, Hal
Jones, Christopher
Kijinski, John
King, Kathleen
Langstraat, Lisa
Levenson, Carl
Mullin, Anne
Prineas, Matthew
Schmidt, Roger
Swetnam, Ford
Swetnam, Susan
Van Pelt, Tamise
Walsh, Dennis
Walsh, Mary Ellen

ILLINOIS

Bloomington
Brown, Jared
Plath, James

Carbondale
Bennett, Paula
Collins, K.K.
Cox, Shelly
Fanning, Charles F.
Howell, John M.
Hoyt, Charles Alva
Mcleod, Archibald
Moss, Sidney Phil
Paddon, Anna R.
Schonhorn, Manuel
Williams, Tony
Winchatz, Michaela R.

Champaign
Christians, Clifford G.
Dussinger, John Andrew
Marder, Herbert
Neely, Carol Thomas
Nerone, John
Shuman, R. Baird

Charleston
Calendrillo, Linda T.
Ibelema, Minabere
Moore, John David
Oseguera, Anthony
Weasmer, Jerie

Chicago
Barushok, James William
Bevington, David M.
Biester, James
Bledstein, Adrien
Booth, Wayne Clayson
Bouson, J. Brooks
Brande, David
Brommel, Bernard
Carrig, Maria
Castiglia, Christopher
Caughie, Pamela L.
Chinitz, David
Clarke, Micael
Coogan, David
Fennell, Francis L.
Fields, Beverly
Foster, Teree E.
Foster, Verna A.
Fox Good, Jacquelyn
Frantzen, Allen J.
Friedrich, Paul
Fromm, Gloria Glikin
Gardiner, Judith Kegan
Gossett, Suzanne
Greeley, Andrew Moran
Guenther, Barbara J.
Hardy, John Edward
Howard, C. Jeriel
Hulse, Clark
Janangelo, Joseph
Jay, Paul
Jones, Steven
Kaminski, Thomas
Kendrick, Christopher
Kolb, Gwin Jackson
Koptak, Paul E.
Leer, Norman Robert
Leighton, Lauren Gray
Lightfoot, Jean Harvey
Livatino, Melvin W.
Lochrie, Karma
Lucas, James L.
Lukacher, Ned
Marshall, Donald G.
Messbarger, Paul Robert
Messenger, Christian Karl
Mitchell, W.J. Thomas
Nabholtz, John R.
Nims, John Frederick
O'Donnell, Thomas G.
Oliker, Michael A.
Pavel, Thomas
Phillips, Gene D.
Ranes, Barbara
Rinehart, Lucy
Robinson, Edward A.
Rocks, James E.
Sachdeva Mann, Harveen
Shea, John Stephen
Stern, Richard G.
Sternberg, Joel
Tave, Stuart Malcolm
Taylor, Jacqueline S.
Trela, D.J.
Trumpener, Katie
Walker, James
Walker, Robert Jefferson
Wallace, John Malcolm
Wexler, Joyce
White, Douglas Howarth
Williams, Joseph M.
Wolfe, Gary Kent
Wood, Barbara

Da Kalb
Darsey, James

De Kalb
Abbott, Craig Stephens
Berkowitz, Gerald Martin
Burwell, Rose Marie
Court, Franklin Edward
Dust, Philip Clarence
Giles, James Richard
Johannesen, Richard Lee
Kipperman, Mark
Mellard, James Milton
Self, Robert Thomas
Shesgreen, Sean Nicholas
Waldeland, Lynne M.
Williams, William Proctor
Wilson, Robert H.

Decatur
Rozema, Hazel J.

Deerfield
Graddy, William E.

Edwardsville
Bukalski, Peter J.
Haas, James M.
Meyering, Sheryl L.
Murphy, Patrick D.
Richardson, Betty
Schmidt, Barbara Quinn
Valley, David B.

Eureka
Logsdon, Loren

Evanston
Achinstein, Sharon
Appel, Alfred, Jr.
Avins, Carol Joan
Breslin, Paul
Brkkila, Betsy
Cheah, Pheng
Cirillo, Albert
Dubey, Madhu
Evans, Lawrence
Froula, Christine
Gibbons, Reginald
Goodnight, G. Thomas
Griswold, Wendy
Herbert, Christopher
Kinzie, Mary
Law, Jules
Lipking, Lawrence
Manning, Susan
Marshall, David
Mulcaire, Terry
Newman, Barbara
Rumold, Raiuer
Schwartz, Regina
Schwarzlose, Richard A.
Smith, Carl
Stern, Julia
Styan, John Louis
Wall, Wendy
Wexman, Virginia Wright
Wilson, Steven R.

Galesburg
Hord, Frederick Lee
Wilson, Douglas Lawson

Jacksonville
Decker, Philip H.
Metcalf, Allan Albert

Lake Forest
Greenfield, Robert Morse

Lebanon
Brailow, David Gregory

Lisle
Komechak, Michael E.

Macomb
Chu, Felix T.
Colvin, Daniel Lester
Conger, Syndy Mcmillen
Dunlap, Isaac H.
Frazer, June
Hallwas, John Edward
Harrison Leland, Bruce
Helm, Thomas Eugene
Mann, John Stuart
Mann, Karen Berg

Mount Prospect
Wachsmuth, Wayne R.

Naperville
Kanwar, Anju

Normal
Baldwin, John R.
Carr, Robin
Dammers, Richard Herman
Harris, Charles Burt
Kagle, Steven Earl
Nourie, Alan Raymond
Poole, John R.
Reitz Mullenix, Elizabeth
Shields, John Charles
Tarr, Rodger Leroy
Visor, Julia N.

Oglesby
Lynch, Rose Marie

Payson
House, Kay S.

Peoria
Claussen, Ernest Neal

Quincy
Schweda, Donald Norman

River Forest
McGinty, Carolyn

Rock Island
Huse, Nancy Lyman

Rockford
Hesselgrave, David J.

Skokie
Lu, Xing L.

Springfield
Jackson, Jacqueline Dougan

University Park
Rank, Hugh Duke

Urbana
Baron, Dennis
Baym, Nina
Berube, Michael
Brockman, William
Campbell, Jackson Justice
Carringer, Robert L.
Cole, Howard Chandler
Douglas, George Halsey
Fontenot, Chester J.
Friedman, John Block
Garrett, Peter K.
Garrett, Peter Kornhauser
Guibbory, Achsah
Hendrick, George
Hibbard, Caroline Marsh
Hurt, James Riggins
Kay, W. David
Klein, Joan Larsen
Kramer, Dale Vernon
Lieberman, Laurence
Michelson, Bruce Frederic
Mullin, Michael
Nelson, Cary Robert
Shapiro, Michael
Stein, Arnold
Stillinger, Jack
Sullivan, Zohreh Tawakuli
Thomas, Stafford H.
Waldoff, Leon
Wenzel, Joseph Wilfred
Wheeler, Richard Paul

Western
Hawkinson, Kenneth S.

Wheaton
Hein, Rolland Neal
Ryken, Leland

Wilmette
Avram, Wesley D.

INDIANA

Anderson
Chapman, Virginia

Bloomington
Anderson, Judith Helena
Beaty, Frederick L.
Curtin, Michael
David, Alfred
Eakin, Paul John
Fletcher, Winona Lee
Forker, Charles Rush
Gray, Donald
Johnston, Kenneth R.
Justus, James Huff
Klotman, Phyllis Rauch
Nord, David P.
Nordloh, David Joseph
Shipps, Anthony Wimberly
Solt, Leo F
Sperry, Stuart M.
Wang, Joan Parsons
Wertheim, Albert

Crawfordsville
Baker, Donald Whitelaw
Fisher, James

Windhauser, John W.
Wing, Nathaniel
Wood, Susan H.
Zebouni, Selma

Lafayette
Fackler, Herbert Vern
Patterson-Iskander, Sylvia W.
Raffel, Burton

Monroe
Kauffman, Bette J.
Steckline, C. Turner
Thameling, Carl L.

Natchitoches
Dillard, Joey L.
Jerred, Ada D.

New Orleans
Abel Travis, Molly
Ahearn, Barry
Bonner, Thomas
Cohen, Joseph
Cooley, Peter John
Cotton, William Theodore
Engel, Kirsten H.
Finneran, Richard John
Harpham, Geoffrey Galt
Holditch, William Kenneth
Koritz, Amy
Liuzza, Roy
Mark, Rebecca
Mosier, John
Pizer, Donald
Simmons, Joseph Larry
Skinner, Robert Earle
Snare, Gerald
Stewart, Maaja Agur
Toulouse, Teresa
Towns, Sanna Nimtz
Wade-Gayles, Gloria Jean
Watson, Cresap Shaw

Ruston
Robbins, Kenneth

Shreveport
Guerin, Wilfred Louis
Leitz, Robert C.

Thibodanx
Tonn, Anke

Thibodaux
Fletcher, Marie

MAINE

Bar Harbor
Carpenter, William Morton

Dresden
Turco, Lewis

Farmington
Franson, John Karl

Hebron
Kuritz, Paul

Machias
Huggins, Cynthia

Orono
Donovan, Josephine
Hatlen, Burton Norval
Ives, Edward Dawson
Langellier, Kristin M.
Peterson, Eric E.

Portland
Gish, Nancy K.

Presque Isle
Petress, Kenneth C.

South Berwick
Olbricht, Thomas H.

Standish
Reilly, Edward J.

Waterville
Bassett, Charles Walker
Lepley, Doug

Winthrop
Waugh, Charles G.

MARYLAND

Annapolis
Jason, Philip Kenneth

Baltimore
Bowman, Leonard Joseph
Cameron, Sharon
Carruthers, Virginia
Daley, Guilbert Alfred
Fleishman, Avrom
Gibson, Stephanie
Hawthorne, Lucia Shelia
Irwin, John Thomas
Kaplan, Nancy
Kelley, Delores G.
Kleinman, Neil
Korenman, Joan Smolin
Macksey, Richard Alan
Matanle, Stephen
Morgan, Leslie Zurker
Moulthrop, Stuart
Oden, Gloria
Scheye, Thomas Edward
Sheffey, Ruthe G.
Stephens, Charles Ralph
Tokarczyk, Michelle M.

Bethesda
Linton, Calvin Darlington
Waserman, Manfred

Catonsville
Hostetter, Edwin C.

Chestertown
Deprospo, Richard Chris
Tatum, Nancy R.

Chevy Chase
Larson, Charles Raymond

College Park
Auerbach, Jonathon
Barry, Jackson Granville
Bode, Carl
Cai, Deborah A.
Caramello, Charles
Davis, Johnetta Garner
Fink, Edward L.
Fraistat, Neil Richard
Freedman, Morris
Freimuth, Vicki S.
Gaines, Robert N.
Gaines, Robert N.
Gillespie, Patti P.
Hiebert, Ray Eldon
Holton, William Milne
Isaacs, Neil D.
Kelly, R. Gordon
Klumpp, James F.
Kolodny, Annette
Lawson, Lewis Allen
Leonardi, Susan J.
McCaleb, Joseph L.
Mintz, Lawrence E.
Parks, Sheri L.
Rao, Nagesh
Rutherford, Charles Shepard
Schoenbaum, Samuel
Sherman, William H.
Waks, Leah
Williams, Helen Elizabeth
Wilt, David E.
Winton, Calhoun
Wolvin, Andrew D.
Woolf, Leonard
Wyatt, David M.

Emmitsburg
Craft, William
Dorsey, Peter
Ducharme, Robert
Gandal, Keith
Hamel, Mary
Heath, William
Malone, M.J.
Wright, Terrence C.

Frederick
Caminals-Heath, Roser

Frostburgh
Lutz, Mary Anne

La Plata
Klink, William

Lanham
Kari, Daven M.

Princess Anne
Hedgepeth, Chester Melvin, Jr.
Keenan, Richard Charles

Salisbury
Waters, Michael
Welsh, James Michael

Silver Spring
Graham, Maryemma
Moore, Robert Henry
Null, Elisabeth M.

Takoma Park
Loizeaux, Elizabeth Bergmann

Towson
Bergman, David L.
Chen, Ni
Faller, Greg
Flippen, Charles
Gissendanner, John M.
Hahn, H. George
Hedges, William Leonard
Kim, Soon Jin
Lev, Peter
McElreath, Mark
McGrain, John W.
Vatz, Richard E.

MASSACHUSETTS

Amherst
Berlin, Normand
Cameron, John
Carlson, Melvin, Jr.
Chametzky, Jules
Chang, Briankle G.
Cheney, Donald
Clayton, John J.
Cody, Richard John
Collins, Dan Stead
Cooks, Leda M.
Craig, George Armour
Edwards, Lee R.
Erdman, Harley M.
Frank, Joseph
French, Roberts Walker
Heath, William Webster
Keefe, Robert
Kinney, Arthur F.
Koehler, G. Stanley
Lowance, Mason Ira
Mariani, Paul L.
Moran, Charles
O'Connell, Barry
Pritchard, William H.
Russo, Mary
Sanchez-Eppler, Karen
Shary, Timothy
Sturm-Maddox, Sara
Swaim, Kathleen Mackenzie
Townsend, Robert Campbell

Babson Park
Bruner, M. Lane

Belmont
Fairley, Irene R.

Beverly
Woodward, Pauline

Boston
Amato, Philip P.
Bellow, Saul
Blanch, Robert James
Blessington, Francis Charles
Brown, Julia Prewitt
Clark, Edward
Collins, Martha
Crossley, Robert Thomas
Fine, Marlene G.

Frederick (second column top)
Franklin, Wayne S.
Friedman, Sidney Joseph
Harbert, Earl
Hernon, Peter
Horton, Susan R.
Knight, Charles Anthony
Korom, Frank J.
Levine, Robert
Mcalpine, Monica Ellen
Payne, J. Gregory
Peterfreund, Stuart S.
Petronella, Vincent F.
Pinsky, Robert
Reno, J. David
Riely, John C.
Schwartz, Lloyd
Siemon, James Ralph
Sigman, Stuart J.
Smith, Diane M.
Sussman, Herbert
Vance, William Lynn
Voigt, John F.
Washington, Mary Helen

Bridgewater
Curley, Thomas Michael

Brookline
Smith, Sarah

Cambridge
Bate, Walter Jackson
Benson, Larry Dean
Berthoff, Warner Bement
Brustein, Robert
Bryson, Norman
Buckley, Jerome Hamilton
Damrosch, Leo
Donaldson, Peter Samuel
Elliott, Clark Albert
Evans, Gwynne Blakemore
Fanger, Donald Lee
Fisher, Philip
Gates, Henry Louis, Jr.
Harris, Joseph
HennessyVendler, Helen
Kaplan, Justin
Lee, Helen Elaine
Lewalski, Barbara Kiefer
McJannet, Linda
Pearsall, Derek A.
Perkins, David
Ritvo, Harriet
Sawyer-Laucanno, Christopher
Schmitz-Burgard, Sylvia
Shell, Marc
Shinagel, Michael
Sollors, Werner
Wolff, Cynthia Griffin

Chestnut Hill
Appleyard, Joseph A.
Blake, Richard
Haskin, Dayton
Lamparska, Rena A.
Mccarthy, John F.
Michalczyk, John Joseph
Picklesimer, Dorman
Sarkodie-Mensah, Kwasi
Schrader, Richard James
Weitzman, Arthur Joshua
Wilt, Judith

Concord
Berthoff, Ann Evans

Deerfield
Junkins, Donald A.

Framingham
Heineman, Helen
Nolletti, Arthur E., Jr.

Gloucester
Ronan, John J.

Harvard
Finkelpearl, Philip J.

Leverett
King, Roger

Lexington
Mahoney, John L.

Lowell
Holladay, Hilary
Kramer, Mary Duhamel

Marblehead
Keyes, Claire J.

Mashpee
Carpenter, Delores Bird

Medford
Buzzard, Karen S.
Mccabe, Bernard

Millbury
Wilson, John H.

Newton
Saunders, William

North Dartmouth
Dace, Tish
Ingraham, Vernon Leland
Marlow, James Elliott
Sandstroem, Yvonne Luttropp

Northampton
Banerjee, Maria Nemcova
Berkman, Leonard
Chinoy, Helen Krich
Davis, Charles Roger
Ellis, Frank Hale
Flower, Dean Scott
Moulton, Janice
Patey, Douglas L.
Sajdak, Bruce T.
Seelig, Sharon Cadman
Skarda, Patricia Lyn

Northfield
Reid, Ronald F.

Norton
Drout, Michael D.C.
Lyon Clark, Beverly
Pearce, Richard
Walsh, Jonathan D.

Quincy
Cameron Munro, Ruth A.
Rice Winderl, Ronda
Winderl, Carl A.

Salem
Brown, Robert E.
Carter, Steven Ray
Damon-Bach, Lucinda
Elia, Richard Leonard
Flibbert, Joseph Thomas
Kessler, Rod
La Moy, William T.
Parker, Patricia L.
Walker, Pierre (Peter)

South Hadley
Collette, Carolyn Penney
Farnham, Anthony Edward
Hill, Eugene David
Kesterson, David Bert
Viereck, Peter
Weber, Donald

Springfield
Rempel, Gerhard
Williams, Melvin Gilbert

Waltham
Engelberg, Edward
Gillan, Jeniffer
Hale, Jane Alison
Herzberg, Bruce
Sprich, C. Robert
Staves, Susan
Ward, Aileen

Watertown
Goodheart, Eugene

Wayland
Clogan, Paul Maurice

Wellesley
Edelstein, Arthur
Lynch, Kathryn
Rosenwald, Lawrence A.

West Newton
Langer, Lawrence L.

St. Louis
Cargas, Harry James
Carkeet, David Corydon
Dunne, Joseph Fallon
Early, Gerald
Jung, Donald J.
Kizer, Elizabeth J.
Knipp, Thomas Richard
McPhail, Thomas Lawrence
Milder, Robert
Miller, Clarence Harvey
Morris, John Nelson
Murray, Michael D.
Nolan, Barbara
Rozbicki, Michael J.
Ruland, Richard
Schraibman, Joseph
Schwartz, Howard
Schwarzbach, Fredric S.
Scott, James Frazier
Shea, Daniel B.
Sherman, Stuart
Shields, Donald C.
Sweet, Nan
Tierney, James Edward
Williamson, Jane Louise
Zwicker, Steven Nathan

Warrensburg
Cox, E. Sam
Phillips, Kendall R.
Smith, David Lee
White, Donald Jerry

MONTANA

Billings
Gross, Daniel D.

Bozeman
Brown, Alanna Kathleen
O'Donnell, Victoria
Poster, Carol
Steen, Sara Jayne
Thomas, Amy M.

Missoula
Bier, Jesse
Harrington, Henry R.
Kittredge, William Alfred

NEBRASKA

Crete
Haller, Evelyn
Price, David C.

Kearney
George, Susanne K.
Luscher, Robert M.
Petruzzi, Anthony
Stauffer, Helen Winter
Tassi, Marguerite
Umland, Rebecca A.
Umland, Samuel J.
Welch, Donovan LeRoy

Lincoln
Behrendt, Stephen C.
Braithwaite, Dawn O.
Crompton, Louis
Dixon, Wheeler Winston
Ford, James Eric
Hilliard, Stephen Shortis
Kaye, Frances Weller
Lee, Ronald E.
Link, Frederick M.
Marcus, Mordecai
Mignon, Charles William
Miller, Tice Lewis
Norland, Howard Bernett
Owomoyela, Oyekan
Pratt, Linda Ray
Rosowski, Susan Jean
Seiler, William John
Stock, Robert Douglas

Omaha
Allen, Chris
Andrus, Kay L.
Bauer, Otto Frank
Brown, Marion Marsh
Churchill, Robert J.
Dornsife, Rob

Glaser, Hollis F.
Hilt, Michael
Lipschultz, Jeremy Harris
Newkirk, Glen A.
O'Neill, Megan
Okhamafe, Imafedia
Paterson, Douglas L.
Skau, Michael Walter
Wall, Eamonn
Whipple, Robert Dale, Jr.
Zacharias, Greg

NEVADA

Las Vegas
Bowers, John M.
Campbell, Felicia F.
Coburn, William Leon
Crawford, Jerry L.
Dodge, Robert Kendall
Engberg, Norma J.
Erwin, D. Timothy
Gajowski, Evelyn J.
Hazen, James F.
Hudgins, Christopher Chapman
Irsfeld, John Henry
Lockette, Agnes Louise
Ma, Ming-Qian
McCullough, Joseph B.
Mcdonough, Ann
Mullen, Lawrence J.
Rosenberg, Beth C.
Stitt, J. Michael
Taylor, Susan L.
Weinstein, Mark A.
Whitney, Charles C.

Reno
Boardman, Kathy
Howard, Anne Bail
Key, Wilson B.
Ronald, Ann
Tchudi, Stephen
Tobin, Frank J.

NEW HAMPSHIRE

Dublin
Germain, Edward B.

Durham
Deporte, Michael Vital
Hageman, Elizabeth H.
Marshall, Grover Edwin
Schwarz, Marc Lewis
Schweickart, Patrocinio Pagaduan
Watters, David Harper

Hanover
Bien, Peter Adolph
Boose, Lynda E.
Chay, Deborah
Cosgrove, Peter
Crewe, Jonathan V.
Desjardins, Mary
Eberhart, Richard
Favor, J. Martin
Gaylord, Alan T.
Halasz, Alexandra W.
Heffernan, James Anthony Walsh
Jahner, Elaine A.
Kuypers, Jim A.
LaValley, Al
Luxon, Thomas H.
Mansell, Darrel
McKee, Patricia
Ortiz, Ricardo L.
Otter, Monika
Pease, Donald E.
Rege, Josna E.
Renza, Louis A.
Rowlinson, Matthew C.
Saccio, Peter
Schweitzer, Ivy
Sears, Priscilla F.
Sheehan, Donald
Silver, Brenda R.
Spengemann, William C.
Travis, Peter W.
Will, Barbara E.
Wykes, David
Zeiger, Melissa F.

Keene
Grayson, Janet

Manchester
Begiebing, Robert J.
Klenotic, Jeffrey F.

Nashua
Malachuk, Daniel S.

New London
Freeburg, Ernest

Plymouth
Dubino, Jeanne

Portsmouth
Sommer, Doris

Rindge
Cervo, Nathan Anthony

Stafford
Westbrook, Ellen E.

NEW JERSEY

Belle Mead
Ward, Herman M.

Caldwell
Kramer, Jennifer

Camden
Sill, Geoffrey M.
Singley, Carol J.

Chester
Pizzo, Joseph S.

Dover
Castellitto, George P.

Edison
Manogue, Ralph Anthony

Elizabeth
Siegel, Adrienne

Glassboro
Doskow, Minna
Grupenhoff, Richard
Haba, James
Kaleta, Kenneth C.
Patrick, Barbara
Viator, Timothy
Vitto, Cindy

Jersey City
Kharpertian, Theodore
Lynch, Thomas Patrick
Mintz, Kenneth A.
Schmidtberger, Loren F.
Watson, John Clifton

Lawrenceville
Mcleod, Alan L.

Madison
Bicknell, John W.
Cummins, Walter M.
Green, Martin
Keyishian, Harry
Marchione, Margherita Frances
Skaggs, Merrill Maguire
Steiner, Joan Elizabeth
Warner, John M.
Weimer, Joan Myers

Mahwah
Alaya, Flavia M.

Montclair
Newman, Geoffrey W.

Morris Plains
Padovano, Anthony T.

Morristown
Marlin, John
Sand, R.H.

New Brunswick
Adams, Kimberly V.
Attridge, Derek
Belton, John
Blumenthal, Eileen
Bowden, Betsy
Chandler, Daniel Ross
Charney, Maurice Myron
Cornelia, Marie E.
Crane, Susan
Crozier, Alice Cooper
Davidson, Harriet
DeKoven, Marianne
Diamond, Elin
Dowling, William C.
Fitter, Chris
Flitterman-Lewis, Sandy
Galperin, William
George, Kearns
Gibson, Donald B.
Gibson, Donald Bernard
Gossy, Mary S.
Guetti, James L.
Habib, M.A. Rafey
Harris, Daniel A.
Hoffman, Tyler B.
Jehlin, Myra
Levine, George L.
Lutz, William
Lyons, Bridget G.
Maman, Marie
Martin, Timothy
Matro, Thomas G.
McClure, John
Mccolley, Diane K.
McKeon, Michael
Mull, Donald L.
Ostriker, Alicia
Poirier, Richard
Qualls, Barry V.
Roberts, Brian
Ruben, Brent David
Ryan, Robert M.
Smith, Carol Hertzig
Vesterman, William
Walling, William
Warner, Michael D.
Welsh, Andrew

Newark
Crew, Louie
Foley, Barbara
Franklin, H. Bruce
Hadas, Rachel
Lyngstad, Sverre
Miller, Gabriel
O'Connor, John E.
Tiger, Virginia Marie
Watts, Ann Chalmers

Newton
Carducci, Eleanor

Piscataway
Ellis, Katherine
Gliserman, Martin

Princeton
Aarsleff, Hans
Bartow, Charles L.
Crain, Patricia
Drewry, Cecelia Hodges
Dubrovsky, Gertrude
Fagles, Robert
Hollander, Robert
Kay, James F.
Knoepflmacher, U.C.
Litz, Arthur Walton
Ludwig, Richard Milton
Rampersad, Arnold
Rigolot, Francois
Schor, Esther
Showalter, Elaine

South Orange
Carpentier, Martha C.
Gray, Jeffrey
MacPhee, Laurence Edward
Weisl, Angela Jane
Zalacain, Daniel

Teaneck
Baker, J. Robert
Becker, John
Goodman, Michael B.
Gordon, Lois G.
Hussey, John
Kime, Wayne R.

Rye, Marilyn
Salem Manganaro, Elise
Shapiro, Susan

Trenton
Halpern, Sheldon

Upper Montclair
Brewton, Butler E.
Gencarelli, Thomas F.

Wayne
Hand, Sally Nixon
Radford, Gary P.
Wertheim, Stanley Claude

West Long Branch
Dell, Chad E.

NEW MEXICO

Albuquerque
Bartlett, Lee
Beene, LynnDianne
Block, Steven
Clark Smith, Pat
Damico, Helen
Fischer, Michael
Fleming, Robert
Fresch, Cheryl
Gaines, Barry
Goodman, Russell B.
Harrison, Gary
Johnson-Sheehan, Richard
Lindskold, Jane M.
Mares, E.A.
Marquez, Antonio
Martin, Wanda
Martinez, Nancy Conrad
McPherson, David
Melada, Ivan
Power, Mary
Sanders, Scott P.
Thorson, James Llewellyn
Whidden, Mary Bess
White, Peter
Witemeyer, Hugh
Woodward, Carolyn

Gallup
Dye, Gloria

Las Cruces
Allen, Orphia Jane
Crabtree, Robin D.

Portales
Berne, Stanley
Williamson, John Stewart

Silver City
Gutierrez, Donald
Toth, Bill

NEW YORK

Albany
Barlow, Judith Ellen
Burian, Jarka Marsano
Edwards, Janis
Fetterley, Judith
Kendall, Kathleen E.
Lawrence, Samuel G.
Maclean, Hugh Norman
Noller, David K.
Salomon, Herman Prins
Sanders, Robert E.
Smith, Karen A.
Valentis, Mary Arensberg

Amherst
Daly, Robert
Lahood, Marvin John
Morace, Robert Anthony

Annandale
Sourian, Peter

Ballston Spa
Barba, Harry

Old Westbury
Reynolds, David S.

Oneonta
Beattie, Thomas Charles
Devlin, James E.
Lilly, Paul R., Jr.

Oswego
Hill, David
Loe, Thomas
Loe, Thomas Benjamin
Loveridge-Sanbonmatsu, Joan
O'Shea, Edward
Schaber, Bennet
Smith, John Kares
Sweetser, Wesley Duaine

Pittsford
Albright, Daniel

Plains
Larson, Richard Leslie

Plattsburgh
Burde, Edgar J.
Butterfield, Bruce A.
Corodimas, Peter
Davis, Ron
Groth, Janet
Johnston, Paul
Kiefer, Lauren
Kutzer, M. Daphne
Levitin, Alexis
Morrissey, Thomas J.
Shout, John
Tracy, Ann B.

Port Washington
Muller, Gilbert Henry

Potsdam
Brady, Owen E.
Coleman, Mark
Ratliff, Gerald Lee
Serio, John Nicholas
Subramanian, Jane M.
Weise, Judith Anderson

Poughkeepsie
DeMaria, Robert
Foster, Donald W.
Imbrie, Ann Elizabeth

Purchase
Grebstein, Sheldon Norman
Lemire, Elise V.

Quaker Street
Black, Steve

Riverdale
Brennan, Anne Denise
Noone, Pat
Smith, Barbara

Rochester
Baldo, Jonathan
Bleich, David
Cartwright, Lisa
Cherchi-Usai, Paolo
Eaves, Morris
Gollin, Richard M.
Grella, George
Gross, Kenneth
Hahn, Thomas George O'Hara
Higley, Sarah
Howard, Hubert Wendell
Johnson, James William
Kegl, Rosemary
Levy, Anita
Lipscomb, Drema Richelle
London, Bette
Longenbach, James
Lupack, Alan
Madigan, Mark J.
Marvin, Elizabeth W.
Michael, John
Middleton, Joyce Irene
Peck, Russell A.
Ramsey, Jarold
Rodowick, David N.
Shuffelton, Frank
Sullivan, Mary C.
Voloshin, Beverly R

Rushville
Kane, Peter

Saratoga Springs
Ciancio, Ralph Armando
Lee, Patricia-Ann
Lewis, Thomas Spottswood Wellford
Roth, Phyllis Ann

Schenectady
Wineapple, Brenda

Selden
Becker, Lloyd George

Southampton
Garcia-Gomez, Jorge
Haynes, Jonathon

St. Bonas
Martine, James John

St. Bonaventure
Williams, Penny

Staten Island
Seminara, Gloria

Stony Brook
Brennan, Timothy Andres
Burner, David B.
Gardaphe, Fred L.
Goldenberg, Robert
Huffman, Clifford Chalmers
Levine, Richard Allan
Scheps, Walter
Sprinker, Michael
Wang, Ban
Zimbardo, Rose A.

Suffern
Bay, Libby

Syracuse
Booth, Philip
Comstock, George Adolphe
Crowley, John W.
Echeruo, Michael
Leuthold, Steven M.
MacKillop, James John
McClure, Charles R.
Shires, Linda Marguerite
Shoemaker, Pamela J.
Snow, Vernon F.
Wright, Roosevelt R., Jr.
Zavarzadeh, Mas'ud

Troy
Halloran, Stephen Michael

Utica
Bergmann, Frank
Gifford, James J.
Labuz, Ronald
Nassar, Eugene Paul

Valhalla
Costanzo, William Vincent
Courage, Richard A.

Vestal
Jackson, Allan Stuart

Wayne
Rosen, Robert Charles

West Point
Hartle, Anthony E.

NORTH CAROLINA

Asheville
Moseley, Merritt

Boiling Springs
Brown, Joyce Compton

Boone
Dorgan, Howard
Rupp, Richard Henry
Williamson, J.W.

Cary
Hammerback, John C.

Chapel Hill
Breen, Marcus
Dessen, Alan Charles
Eaton, Charles Edward
Flora, Joseph Martin
Grossberg, Lawrence
Gura, Philip F.
Harris, Trudier
Hobson, Fred Colby, Jr.
Jackson, Blyden
McGowan, John
Moran, Barbara B.
Rust, Richard Dilworth
Sasson, Jack Murad
Schultz, Heidi M.
Shaw, Donald Lewis
Strauss, Albrecht Benno
Wittig, Joseph Sylvester
Wood, Julia T.
Worth, Fabienne Andre

Charlotte
Crane, Jon
Doerfel, Marya L.
Govan, Sandra Yvonne
Huffman, John L.
Knoblauch, Cyril H.
Leeman, Richard W.
Pizzato, Mark
Yancy, Kathleen Blake

Cullowhee
Loeffler, Donald Lee
Nicholl, James Robert

Davidson
Abbott, Anthony S.
Lewis, Cynthia
McIntosh, Anne
Nelson, Randy Franklin

Durham
Aers, David
Applewhite, James W.
Baucom, Ian
Beckwith, Sarah
Brett, Sally A.
Budd, Louis John
Butters, Ronald R.
Clarke, George E.
Clarke, George Elliott
Clum, John M.
Davidson, Arnold E.
DeNeef, Leigh A.
Ferguson, Oliver Watkins
Ferraro, Thomas J.
Fish, Stanley E.
Gaines, Jane M.
Gleckner, Robert F.
Gopen, George D.
Herrnstein Smith, Barbara
Herzog, Kristin
Hillard, Van E.
Holloway, Karla F.C.
Jackson, Wallace
Jones, Buford
Kellogg, David
Kennedy, Christopher
Malouf, Melissa
Mellown, Elgin Wendell
Moses, Michael Valdez
Nelson, Dana D.
O'Barr, William M.
Perry, Patsy Brewington
Pfau, Thomas
Pope, Deborah
Porter, Joseph A.
Radway, Janice
Randall, Dale B.J.
Riddell, Richard
Ruderman, Judith
Ryals, Clyde De L.
Sasson, Sarah Diane Hyde
Shannon, Laurie
Strandberg, Victor
Tetel, Julie
Tompkins, Jane
Williams, Kenny J.
Willis, Susan

Elon College
Angyal, Andrew J.
Blake, Robert Grady

Fayetteville
Valenti, Peter Louis

Greensboro
Alexander, Sandra Carlton
Baker, Denise Nowakowski
Beale, Walter Henry
Brown, Linda Beatrice
Chappell, Fred Davis
Deagon, Ann Fleming
Edwards, Emily D.
Evans, James Edward
Goodall, H. L. (Bud), Jr.
Hansen, Bob
Kellett, Pete
Kelly, Robert Leroy
Linder, Laura R.
Natalle, Elizabeth
Reeder, Heidi M.
Stephens, Robert Oren
Watson, Robert Winthrop

Greenville
Steer, Helen V.
Sullivan, Charles William

High Point
Moehlmann, John Frederick

Laurinburg
Bennett, Carl D.

Mars Hill
Kinnamon, Noel James

Murfreesboro
Gay, Richard R.

Raleigh
Champion, Larry Stephen
Clark, Edward Depriest, Sr.
Harrison, Antony Howard
Hester, Marvin Thomas
Mackethan, Lucinda Hardwick
Meyers, Walter Earl
Miller, Carolyn R.
Pettis, Joyce
Richmond, Maureen
Walser, Richard
Young, Robert Vaughan

Salisbury
Mccartney, Jesse Franklin

Swannanoa
Yeager, Robert Frederick

Wilmington
Atwill, William D.
Berliner, Todd
Ellerby, Janet Mason
Furia, Philip
Furia, Philip George
Kamenish, Paula K.
Richardson, Granetta L.
Richardson, Stephanie A.
Schweninger, Lee
Sullivan, Sally A.

Wingate
Cannon, Keith
Doak, Robert
Spancer, Janet

Winston-Salem
Angelou, Maya
Hans, James Stuart
Milner, Joseph O'Beirne
Shorter, Robert Newland
West, Larry E.
Weyler, Karen A.

NORTH DAKOTA

Fargo
Burnett, Ann K.

Grand Forks
Dixon, Kathleen
Fiordo, Richard A.
Lewis, Robert William

Mayville
Brunsdale, Mitzi Mallarian

OHIO

Akron
Anderson, Carolyn M.
Birdsall, Eric
Egan, James J.
Harpine, William
Triece, Mary E.

Alliance
Walton, James Edward

Ashland
Fleming, Deborah Diane
Gaines, Elliot I.

Athens
Atlas, Marilyn Judith
Crowl, Samuel
Dodd, Wayne Donald
Fitch, Raymond E.
Flannagan, Roy C.
Knies, Earl Allen
Rauschenberg, Roy A.
Schneider, Duane
Swardson, Harold Roland
Thayer, Calvin G.

Berea
Allman, William Arthur
Kennelly, Laura B.
Martin, Terry J.

Bexley
Esposito, Steven

Bowling Green
Browne, Ray B.
Dixon, Lynda D.
Mccord, Howard
Myers, Norman J.
Myers, Norman Jerald
Patraka, Vivian
Wolfe, Ralph Haven

Canal Fulton
Higgins, Mary Anne

Canton
Bittle, William George

Cedarville
Robey, David H.

Cincinnati
Arcana, Judith
Arner, Robert David
Atkinson, Michael
Bahk, C.M.
Bodo, Murray
Bruce Pratt, Minnie
Daniel, Hershey
Elder, Arlene Adams
Finkelstein, Norman Mark
Godshalk, William Leigh
Huang, Shaorong
Meeker, Joseph W.
Natov, Roni
Patterson, Ward L.
Pratt, Minnie Bruce
Rubenstein, Jill
Searl, Stanford J.
Slouffman, James W.
Stephens, Martha Thomas
Traub, George William
Verderber, Rudolph Francis
Wacholder, Ben Zion
Zafren, Herbert C.

Cleveland
Abelman, Robert
Allen, M. Austin
Atkin, David J.
Bassett, John E.
Beatie, Bruce A.
Beatty, Michael
Benseler, David P.
Berry, Margaret
Bishop, Thomas G.
Evett, David Hal
Ferguson, Suzanne
Friedman, Barton Robert
Gerlach, John Charles
Giannetti, Louis Daniel
Goist, Park Dixon
Jeffres, Leo
Kogler Hill, Susan E.

Kolker, Delphine
Kraus, Sidney
Larson, David Mitchell
Lee, Jae-Won
Lin, Carolyn
Marling, William H.
Neuendorf, Kimberly A.
Oster, Judith
Perloff, Richard M.
Pettey, Gary R.
Ray, Eileen Berlin
Ray, Georgr B.
Rudd, Jill
Saha, Prosanta Kumar
Salomon, Roger B.
Samuels, Marilyn S.
Siebenschuh, William R.
Smith, Francis J.
Stonum, Gary Lee
Trawick, Leonard Moses
Vrettos, Athena
Woodmansee, Martha

Cleveland Heights
Milic, Louis Tonko

Columbus
Barnes, Daniel Ramon
Battersby, James L.
Beja, Morris
Bracken, James K.
Bruning, Stephen D.
Burkman, Katherine H.
Cegala, Donald Joseph
Cooley, Thomas Winfield
Davidson, John E.
Donovan, Maureen H.
Erickson, Darlene E. Williams
Frantz, David Oswin
Harms, Paul W.F.
Kiser, Lisa J.
Lunsford, Andrea Abernethy
Makau, Josina M.
Mancini, Albert Nicholas
Markels, Julian
Maurer, A.E. Wallace
Phelan, James Pius X.
Rice, Grantland S.
Schnell, James A.
Sena, John F.
Williams, Susan
Wilson, John Harold
Woods, Alan Lambert
Woodson, Thomas
Zacher, Christian Keeler

Dayton
August, Eugene R.
Blatt, Stephen J.
Cary, Cecile Williamson
Guthrie, James Robert
Howard, Lillie Pearl
Lain, Laurence B.
Martin, Herbert Woodward
Robinson, James D.
Sammons, Martha Cragoe
Swanson, Donald Roland
Wolff, Florence I.
Yoder, Don

Delaware
Lewes, Ulle Erika

Gambier
Finke, L.A.
Klein, William Francis
Sharp, Ronald Alan
Turner, Frederick

Granville
Baker, David Anthony

Hamilton
Friedenberg, Robert Victor
Inness, Sherrie A.

Hudson
Dyer, Joyce

Huron
Currie, William W.

Kent
Andrews, Larry Ray
Apseloff, Marilyn Fain
Beer, Barrett L.
Davis, Thomas M.
Fried, Lewis Fredrick

Hakutani, Yoshinobu
Krause, Sydney Joseph
Larson, Orville K
Marovitz, Sanford E.
Rubin, Rebecca B.
Wheeler, Arthur M.

Lima
Anspaugh, Kelly C.

Lyndhurst
Strater, Henry A.

Marietta
O'Donnell, Mabry Miller

Medina
Madden, Deidre

Mentor
Johnston, Stanley Howard

New Concord
Fisk, William Lyons
Schultz, William J.

Newark
Loucks, James F.

Oberlin
Ganzel, Dewey Alvin
Gorfain, Phyllis
Goulding, Daniel J.
Jones, Nicholas
Koch, Christian Herbert
Walker, David
Walker, David Lewis
Young, David

Oxford
Branch, Edgar Marquess
Brock, James W.
Clark, James Drummond
Coakley, Jean Alexander
Dolan, Frances E.
Erlich, Richard Dee
Fox, Alice
Fritz, Donald Wayen
Fryer, Judith
Harwood, Britton James
Mann, David Douglas
Sosnoski, James Joseph
Tidwell, John Edgar
Trent, Jimmie Douglas
Wortman, William A.
Wright, Deborah Kempf
Wright, H. Bunker

Pepper Pike
Glavac, Cynthia
Podis, Joanne

Springfield
Davis, Robert Leigh
Dixon, Mimi S.
Faber, J. Arthur
Inboden, Robin L.
Jones, Mary E.
Otten, Terry Ralph
Velen, Richard

Toledo
Barden, Thomas E.
Dessner, Lawrence Jay
Gregory, Elmer Richard
Kopfman, Jenifer E.
Kydd, Elspeth
Manheim, Michael
Many, Paul
Riebling, Barbara
Rudolph, Robert Samuel
Russell, Charles G.
Smith, David Quintin
Watermeier, Daniel J.
Wikander, Matthew H.

Wilberforce
Fleissner, Robert F.

Wooster
Bostdorff, Denise M.
Christianson, Paul
Clareson, Thomas Dean
Frye, Joanne S.
Grace, Nancy
Herring, Henry
Hilty, Deborah Pacini

Stewart, Larry

Yellow Springs
Filemyr, Ann
Whelchel, Marianne

Youngstown
Attardo, Salvatore
Harrison, W. Dale
Shale, Rick

OKLAHOMA

Bethany
Brackell, Pamela
Bracken, Pamela
Jennings, Lawrence Charles

Edmond
Lehman, Paul Robert
Lewis, Gladys Sherman

Enid
Bowers, Paul

Lawton
Ostrowski, Carl

Norman
Diehl, Huston
Friedrich, Gustav William
Gross, David Stuart
Velie, Alan R.

Shawnee
Hall, Larry Joe

Stillwater
Anderson, Eric Gary
Austin, Linda
Batteiger, Richard P.
Berkeley, David Shelley
Broadhead, Glenn J.
Decker, William
Evenson, Brian
Grubgeld, Elizabeth
Leff, Leonard J.
Lewis, Lisa
Mayer, Robert
Rollins, Peter
Walker, Jeffrey
Walker, Jeffrey
Walkiewicz, Edward P.
Wallen, Martin
Warren, Thomas

Tulsa
Belasco, Susan
Taylor, Gordon Overton
Watson, James Gray
Weathers, Winston

Weatherford
Jones, Robin A.

OREGON

Corvallis
Ahearn, Kerry
Anderson, Chris
Barbour, Richmond
Campbell, Elizabeth
Copek, Peter Joseph
Daniels, Richard
Daugherty, Tracy
Davison, Neil
Dean Moore, Kathleen
Ede, Lisa
Frank, Robert
Helle, Anita
Johnson, Simon
Leeson, Ted
Lewis, Jon
Oriard, Michael
Robinson, David
Schwartz, Robert Barnett
Wess, Robert

Eugene
Boren, James Lewis
Brown, James Dale
Coleman, Edwin Leon, II
Frank, David A.

Grudin, Robert
Love, Glen A.
Taylor, Donald Stewart
Tossa, Wajuppa
Westling, Louise Hutchings
Wickes, George
Wojcik, Daniel

McMinnville
Konick, Steve

Medford
Barret, Harold
Dunaway, David King

Monmouth
Baker, Robert Samuel
Sil, Narasingha P.
Soldati, Joseph Arthur

Portland
Brown, John E.
Callahan, John Francis
Carafiol, Peter
Cooper, John Rex
Fortier, Jan M.
Giarelli, Andrew
Gradin, Sherrie L.
Hunt, Steven B.
Knapp, Robert Stanley
Sawaya, Francesca
Steinman, Lisa M.
Ward, Jean M.

Salem
Eddings, Dennis Wayne

PENNSYLVANIA

Allentown
McCracken Fletcher, LuAnn
Pychinka, C.A. Prettiman
Vos, Nelvin Leroy

Ambler
Morse, Josiah Mitchell

Bethlehem
Beidler, Peter Grant
Fifer, Elizabeth
Jitendra, Asha
Soderlund, Jean R.

Bloomsburg
Baillie, William Mayan
Bertelsen, Dale A.
Fuller, Lawrence Benedict
Smith, Riley Blake

Bryn Athyn
Gladish, Robert Willis

Bryn Mawr
Bernstein, Carol L.
Burlin, Robert B.
Dean, Susan Day
Kramer, Joseph Elliot

California
Korcheck, Robert
Murdick, William
Pagen, Michele A.
Waterhouse, Carole

Carlisle
Johnston, Carol Ann
Nichols, Ashton
Rosen, Kenneth Mark

Charlottesville
Cushman, Stephen B.

Chester
Clark, Michael
Danford, Robert E.
LeStourgeon, Diana E.

Collegeville
Decatur, Louis Aubrey

Dallas
Blanchard, Scott
Johnson, Jeffrey

Doylestown
Corbett, Janice
Dimond, Roberta R.
Kuehl, Linda Kandel
Schmidt, Jack

Dunmore
Smith, Gayle Leppin

East Stroudsburg
Meyers, Ronald J.

Easton
Lusardi, James P.
Woolley, James
Ziolkowski, Eric Jozef

Erie
Baldwin, Dean
Minot, Walter S.

Gettysburg
Fredrickson, Robert Stewart
Winans, Robert B.

Glenside
Bracy, William

Greensburg
Toler, Colette

Grove City
Arnold, Edwin P.
Kring, Hilda Adam

Gwynedd Valley
Duclow, Donald F.

Hanover
Capps, Jack L.

Harrisburg
Woods, Willie G.

Hazelton
Price, Alan

Huntingdon
Doyle, Esther M.

Indiana
Ault, C. Thomas
Slater, Thomas J.

Kittanning
Shafer, Ronald G.

Kutztown
Nigro, August John

La Plume
Wheeler, Wayne R.

Lancaster
Grushow, Ira
Pinsker, Sanford
Steinbrink, Jeffrey

Lewisburg
Baumwoll, Dennis
Holzberger, William George
Payne, Michael

Lincoln University
Willis, Gladys January

Lock Haven
Coltrane, Robert
Hybels, Saundra
Jenkins, Charles M.

Lumberville
Fallon, Robert Thomas

Mansfield
Gertzman, Jay Albert
Hindman, Kathleen Behrenbruch
Uffelman, Larry Kent

Meadville
Nesset, Kirk
Thorson, Connie C.
Zolbrod, Paul Geyer

Media
McMullen, Wayne J.
Sorkin, Adam J.

Middletown
Graham, Theodora Rapp
Tischler, Nancy Marie

Millersville
Duncan, Bonnie I.
Hopkins, Leroy Taft, Jr.
Schneller, Beverly
Shields, Kenneth

New Wilmington
Macky, Nancy
McTaggart, William
Perkins, James Ashbrook
Sprow, Richard
Swerdlow, David G.

Newtown
Bursk, Christopher

Philadelphia
Baker, C. Edwin
Baker, Houston A.
Beckman, Richard
Bentman, Raymond
Butler, James Albert
Cappella, Joseph N.
Cohen, Eileen Z.
Curran, Stuart Alan
DeLaura, David Joseph
Feeney, Joseph John
Frye, Roland Mushat
Fusco, Richard
Gaull, Marilyn
Gilman, Owen W.
Harty, Kevin John
Hoffman, Daniel
Hughes, Robert G.
Hunt, John Dixon
Jackson, Arlene M.
Karcher, Carolyn Lury
Korshin, Paul J.
Lebofsky, Dennis Stanley
Lent, John Anthony
Letzring, Monica
Levitt, Morton Paul
Lucid, Robert Francis
Lyons, Timothy James
Mellen, Joan
Morris, Francis J.
Norberg, Peter
Paglia, Camille
Parker, Jo Alyson
Soven, Margot
Steiner, Wendy Lois
Stieb, James
Tasch, Peter Anthony
Turner, Robert Y.
Turow, Joseph G.
Turow, Judith G.
Weales, Gerald
Wendling, Ronald Charles
Wenzel, Siegfried
Wilde, Alan
Wolper, Roy S.
Ziff, Larzer

Pittsburgh
Brockmann, Stephen
Carr, Stephen Leo
Downing, David
Edwards, Clark
Flower, Linda S.
Gounaridou, Kiki
Groch, John R.
Hart, John Augustine
Hart, John Augustine
Hayes, Ann Louise
Helfand, Michael S.
Hopper, Paul
Jones, Granville Hicks
Kaufer, David S.
Knapp, James Franklin
Knapp, Peggy Ann
Labriola, Albert C.
Landy, Marcia
Liu, Yameng
Seitz, James E.
Shumway, David R.
St. Clair, Gloriana
Steinberg, Erwin Ray
Straub, Kristina
Thurston, Bonnie Bowman
West, Michael Davidson

Wion, Philip Kennedy
Young, Richard E.

Pittsburgh.
Lenz, William Ernest

Reading
Peemoeller, Helen C.

Scranton
Casey, Ellen Miller
DeRitter, Jones
Friedman, Michael D.
Gougeon, Len Girard
Gougeon, Leonard

Selinsgrove
Mura, Karen E.
Wilson, Rebecca A.

Slippery Rock
Bass, Eben E.
Curry, Elizabeth Reichenbach
Egan, Mary Joan
Lasarenko, Jane
McIlvaine, Robert Morton

St. Davids
Bittenbender, J. Christopher
Cherry, Caroline Lockett
Morgan, Betsy

State College
Bell, Bernard W.
Pfaff, Daniel W.
Weigl, Bruce

Swarthmore
Blackburn, Thomas
Devin, Lee
Schmidt, Peter Jarrett
Weinstein, Philip Meyer

Uniontown
Hovanec, Evelyn Ann

University Park
Astroff, Roberta J.
Begnal, Michael Henry
Benson, Thomas W.
Bialostosky, Don
Buckalew, Ronald Eugene
Cheney, Patrick
Clausen, Christopher
Ebbitt, Wilma Robb
Eckhardt, Caroline Davis
Fearnow, Mark
Gentry, F.G.
Hale, Thomas Albert
Hogan, J. Michael
Holmes, Charlotte A.
Hume, Kathryn
Hume, Robert David
Kiernan, Michael Terence
Lankewish, Vincent A.
Lougy, Robert E.
Meserole, Harrison Talbot
Morrisson, Mark S.
Mulford, Carla
Secor, Robert Arnold
Weintraub, Stanley
West, James L.W.
Willumson, Glenn Gardner
Woodbridge, Linda

Verona
Matthews, Jack

Villanova
Cherry, Charles L.
Edelman, Diane Penneys
Flannery, Michael T.
Greene, Thomas R.
James, William
Magid, Laurie
Prince, John R.
Termini, Roseann B.
Thomas, Deborah Allen

West Chester
Lavasseur, David G.

Wexford
Arnett, Ronald C.

Wilkes-Barre
Amos, Mark A.
Bedford, Bonnie C.
Fields, Darin E.
Napieralski, Edmund Anthony
Valletta, Clement Lawrence

Wynnewood
Lammers Gross, Nancy

York
Abudu, Gabriel
Barr, Jeanine R.
Jones, Edward T.
McGjee, James
Siegel, Gerald
Vause, Deborah
Viser, Victor J.

RHODE ISLAND

Adamsville
Lawrence, Elizabeth Atwood

Greenville
Kozikowski, Stanley John

Kingston
Gullason, Thomas Arthur
Jacobs, Dorothy Hieronymus
Ketrow, Sandra M.
Kunz, Don
Maclaine, Allan Hugh

Providence
Barbour, Brian Michael
Blasing, Mutlu Konuk
Chaika, Elaine
Curran, Sonia Terrie
Delasanta, Rodney
Denniston, Dorothy L.
Hennedy, John Francis
Hirsch, David Harry
Honig, Edwin
Kahn, Coppelia
Landow, George Paul
Reddy, Maureen T.
Robinson, William Henry
Rosenberg, Bruce
Scanlan, J.T.
Schapiro, Barbara
Scholes, Robert
Spilka, Mark
Stevens, Earl Eugene
Swift, Carolyn Ruth
Wilmeth, Don B.

Wakefield
Coffin, Tristram Potter

SOUTH CAROLINA

Aiken
Mack, S. Thomas
Roy, Emil L.

Central
Marrus, Francine E.

Charleston
Holbein, Woodrow Lee
Hutchisson, James M.
Leon, Philip Wheeler
Leonard, James S.
Shields, David S.

Clemson
Andreas, James
Barfield, Rayford
Bell, Kimberly
Bennett, Alma
Bzdyl, Donald
Calhoun, Richard James
Chapman, Wayne
Charney, Mark
Collier, Cheryl A.
Daniell, Beth
Dettmar, Kevin
Hilligoss, Susan
Howard, Tharon
Jacobi, Martin

Koon, G.W.
Longo, Bernadette
Lovitt, Carl
Morrissey, Lee
Palmer, Barton
Rollin, Lucy
Shilstone, Frederick William
Sparks, Elisa
Underwood, Richard
Ward, Carol
White, Donna
Willey, Edward
Winchell, Donna
Winchell, Mark
Woodell, Harold
Young, Arthur Y.

Columbia
Bruccoli, Matthew J.
Davis, Marianna White
Dickey, James
Dillon, Bert
Farrar, Ronald
Feldman, Paula R.
Franklin, Benjamin
Grant, August E.
Greiner, Donald James
Hark, Ina Rae
Layman, Richard
Myerson, Joel Arthur
Nolan, Edward Francis
Quirk, William J.
Roy, George Ross
Scott, Mary Jane W.
Thesing, William Barney
Van Slyke Turk, Judy
Zoch, Lynn M.

Due West
Erickson, Nancy Lou

Durham
Davidson, Cathy N.
Torgovnick, Marianna

Florence
Tuttle, Jon

Greenville
Allen, Gilbert Bruce
Hill, Philip George
Horton, Ronald A.
Lawson, Darren P.

Greenwood
Bethel, Elizabeth Rauh

Holly Hill
Morant, Mack Bernard

Orangeburg
Harris, Gil W.
Johnson, Alex C.
Washington, Sarah M.

Rock Hill
Weaver, Jack Wayne
Woods, Jeannie Marlin

Spartanburg
Bullard, John Moore
Carson, Warren Jason, Jr.
Crosland, Andrew Tate
Stevenson, John Weamer

SOUTH DAKOTA

Brookings
Bareiss, Warren J.
Evans, David Allan
Marken, Jack Walter

Madison
Johnson, Eric

Vermillion
Cunningham, Frank Robert
Moyer, Ronald L.
Shen, Fuyuan
Wilson, Norma Clark

Yankton
Neville, Mary Eileen

TENNESSEE

Athens
Folks, Jeffrey J

Chattanooga
McClary, Ben Harris
Sachsman, David B.

Clarksville
Joyce, Donald Franklin

Cleveland
Kailing, Joel

Collegedale
Dick, Donald
McClarty, Wilma King- Doering

Cookeville
Bode, Robert Francis
Deese, Helen R.
Slotkin, Alan Robert

Dyersburg
Griffin, Larry D.

Franklin
Harrington, E. Michael

Henderson
Fulkerson, Raymond Gerald

Hermitage
Moser, Harold Dean

Jefferson City
Wood, Gerald Carl

Johnson City
Bonnyman-Stanley, Isabel
Brown, Dan
Harris, William Styron, Jr.
Hilliard, Jerry
Hines, Randy
Kirkwood, William
Mooney, Jack
Ralston, Steven
Roberts, Charles
Schneider, Valerie Lois
Sherrill, Catherine Anne
Shields, Bruce E.
Thomason, Wallace Ray

Knoxville
Adams, Percy Guy
Ashdown, Paul George
Bates, Benjamin J.
Cox, Don Richard
Drake, Robert Y., Jr.
Evelev, John
Fisher, John Hurt
Hunt, Barbara Ann
Leggett, B. J.
Shurr, William Howard
Welch, Olga Michele
Ziegler, Dhyana

Memphis
Bensman, Marvin Robert
Carlson, Thomas Clark
Dameron, John Lasley
Entzminger, Robert L.
Kriegel, Abraham David
Lasslo, Andrew
Ranta, Richard R.
Shaffer, Brian W.
Shaheen, Naseeb
Stagg, Louis Charles
Tucker, Cynthia Grant
Webb, Lynne M.

Milligan College
Wainer, Alex

Murfreesboro
Clark, Bertha Smith
Felton, Sharon

Nashville
Allen, Harriette Louise
Bell, Vereen M.
Church, Dan M.
Clayton, Jay
Davis, Thadious
Doody, Margaret A.
Elledge, Paul

Buena Vista
Cluff, Randall

Charlottesville
Barolsky, Paul
Battestin, Martin Carey
Blackwell, Marilyn Johns
Blotner, Joseph Leo
Cantor, Paul Arthur
Casey, John Dudley
Connolly, Julian Welch
Lang, Cecil Y.
Langbaum, Robert
Levenson, Jacob Clavner
Malone, Dumas
Nohrnberg, James Carson
Picker, John
Ramazani, Jahan
Scott, Nathan A., Jr.
Trotter, A.H., Jr.
Vandersee, Charles Andrew
Winner, Anthony
Winner, Viola Hopkins

Emory
Reid, Robert L.

Fairfax
Brown, Lorraine Anne
Brown, Stephen Jeffry
Brunette, Peter
Fuchs, Cynthia
Irvine, Lorna Marie
Jann, Rosemary
Kelley, Michael Robert
Smith, Paul
Starosta, William J.
Story, Patrick Lee
Yocom, Margaret Rose

Falls Church
Moore, Robert Hamilton
Pearson, Judy C.

Hampden-Sydney
Simpson, Hassell Algernon

Hampton
Brown, Jessie Lemon
Porter, Michael LeRoy

Harrisonburg
Arthur, Thomas H.
Cohen, Ralph Alan
Gabbin, Joanne Veal
Hawthorne, Mark D.
Nickels, Cameron C.

Lexington
Craun, Edwin David
Emmitt, Helen
Gentry, Thomas Blythe
Hodges, Louis Wendell
Stuart, Dabney
Warren, James Perrin

Lynchburg
Hanenkrat, Frank Thomas
Vanauken, Sheldon

Norfolk
Altegoer, Diana B.
Aycock, Roy E.
Bing, Janet
Card, James Van Dyck
Carroll, William
Comfort, Juanita R.
Cooper, Virginia W.
Dandridge, Rita Bernice
Davis, Katie Campbell
Edgerton, Gary R.
Greene, Douglas G.
Habib, Imtiaz
Hassencahl, Frances J.
Heller, Dana
Hoffmann, Joyce
Jackson, Kathy Merlock
Jacobs, Edward
Metzger, David
Moorti, Sujata
Mourao, Manuela
Neff, Joyce
Pearson, Michael
Raisor, Philip
Richards, Jeffrey H.
Shores, David Lee
Slane, Andrea
Topping Bazin, Nancy

Wilson, Charles E., Jr.

Radford
Baker, Moira
Christianson, Scott
Edwards, Grace Toney
Gainer, Kim
Gallo, Louis
Graham, Joyce
Guruswamy, Rosemary
Kovarik, Bill
Kranidis, Rita
Lanier, Parks
Murphy, Richard
Poe, Elizabeth
Poland, Tim
Samson, Donald
Saperstein, Jeff
Secreast, Donald
Siebert, Hilary
Sizemore Riddle, Rita
Wawrzycka, Jolanta
Weiss, Alexander

Richmond
Berry, Boyd Mcculloch
Coppedge, Walter Raleigh
Dance, Daryl Cumber
Engel, Arthur Jason
Griffin, Claudius Williams
Hilliard, Raymond Francis
Jones, Suzanne W.
Kinney, James Joseph
Longest, George Calvin
Mcmurtry, Josephine
Meeker, Michael W.
Morse, Charlotte Cook
Taylor, Welford Dunaway
Yancy, Preston Martin

Roanoke
Fallon, Jean

Staunton
Reich, Robert D.

Sweet Briar
Aiken, Ralph
Dabney, Ross H.
Mares, Cheryl
Piepho, Lee
Tamburr, Karl

Williamsburg
Catron, Louis E.
Donaldson, Scott
Meyers, Terry L.
Nettels, Elsa
Pinson, Hermine Dolorez
Scholnick, Robert James

Winchester
Jacobs, John T.

Wise
Benke, Robin Paul

Wytheville
Jones, Dan Curtis

WASHINGTON

Bellingham
Brown, Robert D.
McDonald, Kelly M.
Skinner, Knute R

Cheney
Lester, Mark
Smith, Grant William

College Place
Dickinson, Loren

Ellensburg
Benton, Robert Milton
Olson, Steven

Kirkland
Inslee, Forrest
MacDonald, Margaret R.

Pullman
Burbick, Joan
Condon, William

Ehrstine, John
Faulkner, Thomas Corwin
Fulton, Richard Delbert
Gillespie, Diane F.
Hammond, Alexander
Harris, Laurilyn J.
Hellegers, Desiree
Hunt, Timothy
Hyde, Virginia Crosswhite
Hyde, Virginia M.
Jankowski, Theodora
Kennedy, George E.
Kiessling, Nicolas
Law, Richard G.
Linden, Stanton J.
McLeod, Susan
Oliver, Eileen
Orr, Leonard
Roman, Camille
Schleiner, Louise
Siegel, Carol
Sitko, Barbara
Smith, Shawn M.
Villanueva, Victor
Von Frank, Albert J.

Seattle
Adelman, Mara
Bosmajian, Hamida
Bullon-Fernandez, Maria
Ceccarelli, Leah M.
Cobb, Jerry
Cumberland, Sharon L.
Dunn, Richard John
Fearn-Banks, Kathleen
Gastil, John Webster
Griffith, Malcolm A.
Heilman, Robert Bechtold
Iyer, Nalini
Kaplan, Sydney Janet
Korg, Jacob
Leigh, David
Mccracken, David
McElroy, Colleen J.
Philpott, Jeffrey S.
Post, Robert M.
Rowan, Stephen C.
Simonson, Harold Peter
Tadie, Andrew A.
Taylor, Velande P.
Weihe, Edwin
Wullf, Donald H.

Sequim
Clark, David Ridgley

Spokane
Hazel, Harry Charles
Hunt, Linda
Jackson, Gordon
Sugano, Douglas

Tacoma
Curley, Michael Joseph
Garratt, Robert Francis
Johnson, Lucille Marguerite
Ostrom, Hans
Proehl, Geoffrey

Walla Walla
Davidson, Roberta
Desmond, John F.
DiPasquale, Theresa M.
Foster, Edward E.
Hashimoto, I.Y.
Maxfield, James F.
Mesteller, Jean C.

WEST VIRGINIA

Buckhannon
Baldwin, Arminta Tucker

Elkins
Tedford, Barbara Wilkie

Fairmont
Wills, Jack Charles

Huntington
McKernan, John Joseph
Watson, Jean Louise

Institute
Thorn, Arline Roush

Middleway
Woods, David L.

Morgantown
Adams, Timothy D.
Blaydes, Sophia Boyatzies
French, William Wirt
Ginsberg, Elaine Kaner
Johnston, John H.
Stitzel, Judith Gold
Wigal, Grace J.

Salem
Runyan, William Ronald

Shepherdstown
Austin, Michael

WISCONSIN

Appleton
Fritzell, Peter Algren
Goldgar, Bertrand Alvin

Baraboo
Cole, David William

Beloit
Walsh, Chad

De Pere
Zahorski, Kenneth

Eau Claire
Bushnell, Jack
Dale, Helen
Duyfhuizen, Bernard
Fairbanks, Carol
Harder, Sarah
Jerz, Dennis G.
Kelly, Erna
Knoeller, Christian
Meiser, Mary
Onwueme, Tess
Shaddock, Jennifer
Walsh, Grace

Green Bay
Bennett, John

Kenosha
Canary, Robert Hughes
Chell, Samuel L.
Dean, Dennis Richard
Dean, James S.
DuPriest, Travis Talmadge, Jr.
Krause, David H.
Kummings, Donald D.
Leeds-Hurwitz, Wendy
Lindner, Carl Martin
Mclean, Andrew Miller
Shailor, Jonathan G.
Shapiro, Rami
Shucard, Alan Robert
Tobin, Daniel
Tobin, Daniel

La Crosse
Hyde, William James
Niedzwiecki, Charissa K.

Madison
Baker, Robert Samuel
Bender, Todd K.
Bush, Sargent, Jr.
Cassidy, Frederic Gomes
Coutenay, Lynn
Doane, Alger Nicolaus
Doran, Madeleine
Draine, Betsy
Eccles, Mark
Filipowicz, Halina
Hall, Joan H.
Hayman, David
Hinden, Michael Charles
Hunter, Linda
Ingwersen, Niels
Knowles, Richard Alan John
Lucas, Stephen E.
Naess, Harald S.
Nelson, James Graham
Pfau, Michael
Skloot, Robert
Wallace, Ronald William
Weinbrot, Howard D.

Weiner, Andrew David
Weingand, Darlene E.
Wiesenfarth, Joseph John
Yetunde Faelarin Schleicher,
 Antonia

Menomonie
Levy, Michael Marc
Thurin, Susan Molly Schoenbauer

Middleton
Black, Edwin

Milwaukee
Baron, F. Xavier
Bates, Milton James
Bieganowski, Ronald
Blau, Herbert
Chang, Joseph S.
Friedman, Melvin Jack
Gillespie, Michael Patrick
Goldzwig, Steven R.
Guerinot, Joseph Vincent
Jay, Gregory S.
Kuist, James Marquis
Smith, Gail K.
Soley, Lawrence C.

Oshkosh
Burt, Susan Meredith
Herzing, Thomas Wayne
Nuernberg, Susan M.
Thorpe, Judith M.

Ripon
Martz, William J.
Northrop, Douglas A.
Peterson, Brent O.
Woods, Robin

River Falls
Brantley, Jennifer
Brown, Terry
Gerster, Carole
Karolides, Nicholas J.
Luebke, Steve
Wood, Ruth
Zlogar, Laura

Stevens Point
Meisel, Martin
Missey, James L.
Stokes, James

Stoughton
Knapp, John Victor

Waukesha
Dailey, Joseph
Hemmer, Joseph
Jones, Sidney C.
Settle, Peter

Whitewater
Adams, George Roy
Haven, Richard P.
Ostermeier, Terry H.
Townsend, Patricia Ann

WYOMING

Cody
Bender, Nathan E.

Laramie
Durer, Christopher
Harris, Duncan Seely
Harris, Janice Hubbard
Kalbfleisch, Pamela J.
Reverand, Cedric D.

Powell
Carlson, Kay

PUERTO RICO

San Juan
Guerro, Maria C.M. de
Hurley, Andrew
Morales Degarin, Maria A.

Fogel, Stan
Froese Tiessen, Hildi
Harris, Randy Allen
Hinchcliffe, Peter
Jewinski, Edwin
Macnaughton, William Robert
Martin, W.R.
McCormack, Eric
McGee, Christopher Edward
Moore, Michael
Russell, Anne
Shakinovsky, Lynn
Slethaug, Gordon Emmett
Smith, Rowland
Tiessen, Paul
Ty, Eleanor

West Hill
Brown, Russell Morton

Windsor
Atkinson, Colin B.
Bebout, Linda J.
de Villers, Jean-Pierre
Dilworth, Thomas
Ditsky, John M.
Harder, Bernhard D.
Herendeen, Wyman H.
Janzen, Henry David
Mackendrick, Louis King
MacLeod, Alistair
Quinsey, Katherine M.
Ruggles, Myles A.
Smedick, Lois Katherine
Stevens, Peter S.
Straus, Barrie Ruth

Winnipeg
Schnitzer, Deborah

PRINCE EDWARD ISLAND

Charlottetown
Bourne, Lesley-Anne
Epperly, Elizabeth Rollins

QUEBEC

Lennoxville
Grogan, Claire
McLean, Ken
Norman, Joanne S.

Montreal
Brennan, Kit
Brennan Watters, Kathleen
Crowley, David
Dorsinville, Max
Gillett, Margaret
Ginter, Donald Eugene
Gravel, Pierre
Groening, Laura S.
Haines, Victor Yelverton
Joch Robinson, Gertrude
Joos, Ernest

Levin, Charles
Picot, Jocelyne
Richard, Ron
Robert, Lucie
Roth, Lorna
Straw, William O.
Szanto, George
Taylor, James R.
Valaskakis, Gail
Wees, William Charles

Sherbrooke
Bonenfant, Joseph
Jones, Douglas Gordon

Ste. Anne de Bellevue
Leith, Linda J.

Ste. Foy
Demers, Francois
Greenstein, Michael
Lemire, Maurice
Sirois, Antoine

SASKATCHEWAN

Regina
Blackstone, Mary A.
Cowasjee, Saros
Givner, Joan
Howard, William J.
Mitchell, Kenneth R.
Weber, Burton Jasper

Saskatoon
Berry, Herbert
Calder, Robert L.
Findlay, Leonard Murray
Henderson, Judith Rice
Wittlin, Curt

OTHER COUNTRIES

AUSTRALIA
Breen, Myles P.
Lemire, Eugene D.

BAHAMAS
Grow, Lynn Merle

BELGIUM
Kuczynski, Peter

ENGLAND
Madsen, Deborah
Junker, Kirk W.
Robertson, Fiona

FRANCE
Lucas, Alec

GERMANY
Spevack, Marvin

HONG KONG
Ling, Chen
Powers, John H.

ISRAEL
Budick, Sanford
Vogel, Dan
Spolsky, Ellen

ITALY
Alexander, Doris M.

JAPAN
Chikage, Imai
Sugimoto, Naomi
Rothfork, John G.

NEW ZEALAND
Boyd, Brian David

NIGERIA
Nnolim, Charles E.

SINGAPORE
Cave, Roderick George

SOUTH KOREA
Yang, Heewan

TAIWAN
Chen, Shih-Shin